Index

Preface

Humanity marches on at a rapidly advancing rhythm, and reference works intended to serve it, such as this dictionary, should keep in step with progress if they are to provide satisfactorily the information sought. That is why the *Velázquez Dictionary,* recognized throughout the world as the highest authority in bilingual Spanish-English dictionaries, needs to keep pace with all the new terms which the prodigious progress of our times is introducing in the fields of science, inventions and discoveries, as well as with those terms which constantly evolving customs and events introduce into both languages.

Thus the NEW REVISED VELÁZQUEZ DICTIONARY, without sacrificing any of the traditional characteristics which have made predecessor editions the pattern for dictionaries of this type, is without doubt the most modern and complete edition of the work ever published. Included in the main alphabetical word lists are thousands of new terms and idiomatic expressions of general use, replacing expressions no longer in common usage which consequently have no place in a book as eminently practical as this one.

This latest revision of the text has been exhaustive. The aim has been to have the *Velázquez Dictionary* respond more efficiently each day to the needs of those consulting it as a practical medium to solve their translation problems in the fields of business, of current events, of technology, of science in general, of literature, etc. At the same time particular attention has been paid to the terms and idioms commonly used in Spanish America and in the United States, since commercial and friendly relations between these two great regions of the modern world are daily becoming more frequent and important.

The equivalents of geographical names and adjectives which are not written identically in Spanish and English have been meticulously revised. The lists making up the present edition include all the changes which such names have undergone through recent historical events.

A similar study has been made of the lists of proper names appearing in the supplements of the book, as well as those of weights and measures. The list of abbreviations has been brought up-to-date so that it may also respond to the fundamentally practical nature of the book.

Through such innovations the usefulness of this dictionary has been tremendously enhanced, and its editors and publishers dare to hope that it may prove even more valuable than earlier editions to its users, whether they be students in process of learning a second tongue, scholars engaged in literary research in either or both languages, or professional and commercial translators—in fact anyone and everyone who has need of authoritative guidance over the difficult road of English-Spanish or Spanish-English translation.

A Synopsis of the

Spanish or Castilian Language.

THE PARTS OF SPEECH are: the *Article*, the *Noun* (substantive and adjective), the *Pronoun*, the *Verb*, the *Participle*, the *Adverb*, the *Preposition*, the *Conjunction*, and the *Interjection*.

THE ARTICLE

The article has the function of:

a) Pointing out the gender and the number of the grammatical elements before which it is placed, as it agrees with them in gender and number.

b) Pointing out the substantive character of these elements.

1. The articles are always placed before the noun, never behind. They admit another word between them and the name they determine.

- **Los** inquietos niños. - **El** ya famoso futbolista.

2. The masculine article e̲l̲ may indicate also the feminine when the word which determines starts by accented a̲.

-**El** agua, **el** alma, **el** hacha, **el** águila, **el** hambre, **el** ama.

There are also other exceptions:

- **El** turista, **el** problema, **el** esquema, **el** tema.

- **La** radio, **la** foto, **la** moto.

3. The article is used:

a) Before rivers, mountains and seas.

- **El** río Duero - **Los** Pirineos - **El** Mar Mediterráneo.

b) Before some countries:

- **La** Argentina, **El** Brasil, **El** Canadá, **La** China, **El** Ecuador, **Los** Estados Unidos.

Anyway, if there is any doubt, the article can be omitted.

- **La** China es un país enorme. - Voy a China.

c) Before the name of some regions and some cities:

- **La** Rioja, **La** Mancha, **La** Coruña, **La** Plata, **El** Cairo.

d) Before time expressions:

- Son **las** cinco. - Llegaré **el** sábado.

e) Before the parts of the body and garments:

- **El** niño tiene **la** cara sucia. - Se puso **el** abrigo.

f) With formulas of treatment, except before "Don".

- **El** señor Rodriguez. -**El** señor Presidente. - **La** señorita Carmen.

g) With abstract nouns or used in a generative way.

- **La** belleza. - **Los** profesores. **El** mar.

h) With percentages:

- **El** diez por ciento. - **El** quince por ciento.

i) With titles:

-**El** conde de Montecristo - **El** Marqués de Villaverde

THE INDEFINITE ARTICLE OR INDETERMINATE

1. The indeterminate article is used preceding the substantive to which is refered.

- Es **un** genio. - Tenía **una** mirada profunda. - Fue **una** reacción unánime.

2. The indeterminate article is used to emphasize.

- Era **un** valiente. - Sois **unos** cobardes. - Eres **un** idiota.

The indefinite article can be emphasized with the word **todo**.

- Era todo **un** valiente. - Es todo **un** héroe.

3. The feminine singular form **una** is transformed to **un** before the words which starts by accented **a** or **ha**, although these words are feminine.

- **un** alma. - **un** hacha. - **un** ala. - **un** aro. - **un** arco.

- Tengo **un** hambre feroz. - Hay **un** águila en el árbol.

Exceptions:

- Esta palabra tiene **una** hache. - Vimos **una** árabe.

The words which haven't got the accented **a**, don't change.

- **una** alumna. - **una** antena. - **una** alubia.

4. The indefinite article is sometimes used in an approximate sense:

- Había **unas** cien personas. - Tardaré **unas** dos horas.

5. Behind the impersonal "HAY" it is also used the indefinite article:

- Hay **un** árbol en la plaza. - En mi casa siempre hay **una** botella de vino.

However, with countless or plural things no article is used.

- Hay árboles - Hay café - Hay mucho tiempo.

6. The indefinite article is used to indicate that an object is included in a more general group or kind, at the same time it is individualized in that group.

- Eso es **un** castillo medieval. - Esto es **un** hotel de lujo.

7. It is used with some exlamations:

- ¡Hace **un** frío glacial! - ¡Hacía **un** calor tórrido!

- ¡Había **una** cantidad de gente terrible!

8. The indefinite article will be used before an abstract noun followed by a qualificative adjective.

- Había **una** quietud extraña. - Reinaba **un** caos terrible.

THE OMISSION OF THE ARTICLE

- Vendemos libros - Viajaron en avión

- Mi padre es profesor - Esa chica es artista.

In all these examples we want to specify that it´s referred to a kind of objects or realities instead of an object or individual reality. So an article in not used.

1. The article is also omitted when a partitive sense is indicated, when the quantity is not specified.

- En las comidas bebemos agua.

- Yo no como pan.

If we want to specify we´ll say:

- En las comidas bebo **un** poco de vino.

2. When we address to a person in a formal way:

- Buenos días, señor Presidente.

- Adiós, señor Pérez.

- Hasta el lunes, señor director.

3. The article is omitted with:

a) Names of people.

- Vi a Juan en el cine. - Estuvimos con Pedro en el parque.

b) With some words when verbs of movement are used (casa, caza, misa, palacio, paseo, presidio)

- Fue llevado a presidio. - Los domingos vamos a misa.

c) Before the names which indicate titles.

- Don Francisco. - Su Alteza Real Felipe.

d) With **medio** and **otro** the definite article can be used, but the indefinite cannot be used.

- Quiero **el** medio kilo de uva que le encargué.

- Prefiero **el** otro.

e) When an exact number in measures and distances is used.

- La aldea estaba a diez kilómetros.

- Tardarán tres horas en llegar.

f) With degrees (University).

- Mi hija estudia medicina.

g) Between the name of a king or pope and the number.

- Felipe IV Felipe Cuarto.

CONTRACTIONS

When "EL" goes after "A" or after "DE", both forms are contracted by "AL" or "DEL", respectively.

However, the contraction is not placed before proper names built with an article . (Although in spoken language this contraction exists).

- Ésta es una nueva edición de **El Quijote**.

- Ésta es la historia de **El Algarrobo**.

- Nos dirigimos a **El Ferrol**.

THE ARTICLE "LO"

The article "LO" never goes with substantives, because in Spanish neutral nouns don´t exist. It normally goes with other elements with noun function:

a) It goes before adjectives, corresponding to them the singular masculine.

- Lo difícil es saber lo que va a hacer.

- Lo bueno es que tenemos mucho tiempo.

- Lo interesante sería llegar antes que ellos.

b) It is placed before adjectives, showing an intensity aspect. It must be noted that the substantive corresponds to the adjective.

- Ya sé **lo difícil** que es este problema.

- Comentaron **lo interesante** que fue la película.

c) With the same intensifying function it is placed before the adverbs.

- Verás **lo bien** que lo pasamos.

- Da pena **lo mal** que lo está pasando esa chica.

- Es increíble **lo temprano** que te levantas.

d) **Lo que** has a relative usage.

- Eso es **lo que** quería.

   - **Lo que** me dices es mentira.

e) "Lo" is normally used when we refer to something wich is not specified.

   - Es increíble **lo de** tu madre.

   - **Lo del** otro día fue vergonzoso.

   - **Lo de ese** chico no tiene sentido.

THE NOUN - GENDER

The **masculine** and the **feminine** are the only existing genres in Spanish.

   La casa.

   El profesor.

   La canción.

   El piano es grande.

   La casa es pequeña.

   La mesa es bonita.

   Los libros son difíciles.

   Las canciones son preciosas.

   He vendido **el** coche.

---

1. Diferences in the gender.

a) The masculine and the femenine normally alternate **O/A**.

   chico / chica, niño / niña, perro / perra, hijo / hija

b) Sometimes the masculine ends with the following consonants: **L, N, R, S, Z.**

   chaval / chavala, patrón / patrona, pastor / pastora, francés / francesa, rapaz / rapaza.

c) There are also words in which the feminine is very different from the masculine.

   padre / madre, hombre / mujer, toro / vaca, carnero / oveja, macho / hembra, caballo / yegua, yerno / nuera.

d) Some words are written the same in both genders.

   El debutante / **La** debutante. **El** estudiante / **La** estudiante

   El periodista / **La** periodista. **El** cantante / **La** cantante

   El principiante / **La** principiante. **El** artista / **La** artista

However, some words change the meaning completely when the gender changes.

   El cólera / **La** cólera. **El** cura / **La** cura. **El** radio / **La** radio

   El orden / **La** orden. **El** corte / **La** corte. **El** guía / **La** guía

e) Some terminations are specific for the femenine:

   Actor / Actriz. Emperador / Emperatriz. Poeta / Poetisa. Sacerdote / Sacerdotisa

   Abad / Abadesa. Alcalde / Alcaldesa

f) Animals normally have one form; the sex is specified adding **macho** or **hembra**.

   Elefante macho / Elefante hembra. Rana macho / Rana hembra. Araña macho / Araña hembra. Serpiente macho / Serpiente hembra.

2. The tipical masculine terminations are:

a) **aje, ambre, an, ma, o, or**.

   Poema, fonema, hambre, sabotaje, color, cielo, pan.

Although there are a lot of exceptions: **la** moto, **la** radio, **la** mano, **la** foto.

Others are tipically feminine:

b) **a, dad, cia, ción, eza, nza, ncia, sión, tud, umbre**.

   Mesa, casa, piedad, licencia, pronunciación, esperanza, presión, quietud, lumbre.

THE ADJECTIVE.

In Spanish the *Adjective* must agree with its noun, in *Gender* and *Number*; as, "un hombre *rico*" (a *rich* man), "**una mujer rica**" (a *rich* woman); "**hombres ricos**" (rich men), "**mujeres ricas**" (rich women).

PRONOUNS.

Personal Pronouns.

I, yo.	*We,* nosotros, nosotras.
Me, me	*Us,* nos, nos.
Me, mí.	*Us,* nosotros, nosotras.
With me, conmigo.	*With us,* con nosotros, as.
You, tú.	*You,* vosotros, vosotras.
You, te,	*You,* os, os.
You, ti.	*You,* vosotros, vosotras.
With you, contigo.	*With you,* con vosotros, as.

You, in familiar polite style, is translated *usted* for both genders, and the verb agrees with it in the singular or plural, according to the sense. *Usted* and its plural are always written in abbreviation, thus: *V.* or *Vd.* for the first, and *Vds.* for the latter.

You, usted, (V.).	*You,* ustedes, (Vds.)
You **a** usted, le, la, se.	*You,* **a** Vds. los, las, se.

You, **a** V. le, se; **a** él, ella, sí.

With you, con Vds.

He or *it,* él.

Him or *it,* le, se; él, sí.

Him or *it,* le, se; él, sí.

With him, it, con él, consigo.

She or *it,* ella.

Her or *it,* la, se; ella sí.

Her or *it,* le, se; ella sí.

With her, it, con ella, consigo.

You, **a** Vds. les, se; **a** ellos ellas, sí.

They, ellos.

Them, los, se; ellos, sí.

Them, les, se; ellos, sí.

With them, con ellos, consigo.

They, ellas

Them, las, se; ellas, sí.

Them, les, se; elles, sí.

With them, con ellas, consigo

Mí, ti, sí, are always preceded by prepositions.

Me, te, se, le, los, la, las, les, are never placed after prepositions.

Possessive Adjectives.

My, mi, mis.   *His,* su, sus.   *Its,* su, sus.

Your, tu, tus.   *Her,* su, sus.   *Their,* su, sus.

Your, with reference to *Usted* or *Ustedes,* su, sus.

These adjectives agree in number with the noun that follows them; as, he sold *his horses* (él vendió *sus caballos*); they fulfilled *their* promise *(ellos cumplieron **su promesa**).*

Possessive Pronouns.

Mine, mío, míos.   *His,* suyo, suyos.   *Its,* suyo, suyos.
mía, mías.   suya, suyas.   suya, suyas.

Your, tuyo,.   *Hers,* suyo,   *Theirs,* suyo,
tuyos   suyos.   suyos.suya,

tuya, tuyas.   suya, suyas.   suyas.

Our, nuestro,   *Your,* vuestro,   *Your,* de Usted.
nuestros.nuestra,   vuestros.   de Ustedes.

nuestras.   vuestra, vuestras.

Your, with reference to *Usted,* is also translated suyo, suyos, suya, suyas, or su, sus . . . de. V. or Vds.

Relative and Interrogative Pronouns.

Who, which,   que, quien, quienes.

What, that,   que.

Which, what,   cual, cuales;

also,   el cual, los cuales, la cual, las cuales.

Whose,   cuyo, cuyos, cuya, cuyas;

also,   de quien, de cual, etc.

Demonstrative Pronouns

This, éste.   *These,* éstos.   *That,* aquél.

Those, aquéllos.

« ésta. « estas. « aquélla. « aquéllas.

That, ése,   *Those,* ésos.   *This,* esto.

That, aquello.

« ésa. « ésas. *That,* eso.

Indefinite Pronouns

One, uno.   *Such,* tal.

Each, cada.   *Something,* algo.

Nobody, { nadie, ninguno.   *Nothing,* nada.
    Each one, cada cual.

Somebody,
Anybody, } alguien.   *Each other,* uno y otro.

VERBS

All Spanish verbs are classed into there conjugations. Verbs ending in *ar* belong to the first; those in *er,* to the second; and those in *ir,* to the third.

A TABLE

OF THE TERMINATIONS OF ALL THE REGULAR VERBS.

The numbers in the margin refer to the conjugation, those at the head of the columns, to the Persons.

Infinitive Mode.

1. Present, *ar.* Gerund, *ando.* Past or Passive Part. *ado.*
2.   "   *er.*   "   *iendo.* "   "   "   *ido.*
3.   "   *ir.*   "   *iendo.* "   "   "   *ido.*

Indicative Mode

Present

1. amo,	as,	a:	amos,	áis,	an.
2. temo,	es,	e:	*emos,*	éis,	en.
3. subo,	es,	e:	imos,	ís,	en.

Imperfect.

1. amaba,	abas,	aba:	ábamos,	abais,	aban.
2. temía,	ías,	ía:	íamos	íais,	ían.
3. subía,	ías,	ía:	íamos,	íais,	ían.

Preterite or Perfect.

1. amé,	aste,	ó:	amos,	asteis,	aron.
2. temí,	iste,	ió:	imos,	isteis,	ieron.
3 subí,	iste,	ió:	imos,	isteis,	ieron.

Future.

1. amaré,	arás,	ará:	aremos,	aréis,	arán.
2. temeré,	erás,	erá:	eremos	eréis,	erán.
3. subiré,	irás,	irá:	iremos	iréis,	irán.

Imperative Mode.

1.	ama,	e:	emos,	ad,	en.
2.	teme,	a:	amos,	ed,	an.
3	sube,	a:	amos,	id,	an.

Subjunctive Mode

Present.

1.	ame,	es,	e:	emos,	éis,	en.
2.	tema,	as,	a:	amos ,	áis,	an.
3.	suba,	as,	a:	amos,	áis,	an.

Imperfect.—(First Termination.)

1. amara, aras, ara: áramos, arais, aran.
2. temiera, ieras, iera: iéramos, ierais, ieran.
3. subiera, ieras, iera: iéramos, ierais, ieran.

Conditional.

1. amaría, arías, aría: aríamos, aríais, arían.
2. temería, erías, ería: eríamos, eríais, erían
3. subiría, irías, iría: iríamos, iríais, irían

Imperfect.-(Second Termination.)

1. amase, ases, ase: asemos, áseis, asen.
2. temiese, ieses, iese: iésemos, iéseis iesen.
3. subiese, ieses, iese: iésemos, iéseis, iesen.

COMPOUND TENSES.

These tenses are formed by placing after the verb *haber* (to have), the participle past of the verb that is conjugated; as (I *have* loved), "yo *he* armado."

CONJUGATION OF THE AUXILIARY VERBS.

Infinitive Mode.

Present.

Haber. Tener. *To have.*   Ser. Estar. *To be.*

Gerund.

Habiendo. Teniendo. *Having.*   Siendo. Estando. *Being.*

Past Participle.

Habido. Tenido. *Had.*   Sido. Estado. *Been.*

Indicative Mode.

Present.

I have   I am

1. He.	Tengo.	Soy	Estoy
2. Has.	Tienes.	Eres.	Estás
3. Ha.	Tiene.	Es.	Está

1. Hemos.	Tenemos.	Somos.	Estamos.
2. Habéis.	Tenéis.	Sois.	Estáis.
3. Han.	Tienen.	Son.	Están.

Imperfect

I had.   I was

1. Había.	Tenía.	Era.	Estaba.
2. Habías.	Tenías.	Eras.	Estabas.
3. Había.	Tenía.	Era.	Estaba.
1. Habíamos.	Teníamos.	Éramos.	Estábamos.
2. Habíais.	Teníais.	Erais.	Estabais.
3. Habían	Tenían.	Eran.	Estaban.

Preterite

I had.   I was

1. Hube.	Tuve.	Fui.	Estuve.
2. Hubiste.	Tuviste.	Fuiste	Estuviste.
3. Hubo.	Tuvo.	Fue.	Estuvo.
1. Hubimos.	Tuvimos.	Fuimos.	Estuvimos.
2. Hubisteis.	Tuvisteis.	Fuisteis	Estuvisteis.
3. Hubieron	Tuvieron.	Fueron.	Estuvieron.

Future

I will have-   I will be

1. Habré.	Tendré.	Seré.	Estaré.
2. Habrás.	Tendrás.	Serás	Estarás.
3. Habrá.	Tendrá.	Será.	Estará.
1. Habremos.	Tendremos.	Seremos.	Estaremos.
2. Habréis.	Tendréis.	Seréis	Estaréis.
3. Habrán	Tendrán.	Serán.	Estarán.

Imperative Mode

Let me have.   Let me be

1.	Ten tú.	Sé.	Está.
2.	Tenga él.	Sea.	Esté.
3.	Tenga V.	Sea V.	Esté V.
1.	Tengamos.	Seamos.	Estemos.
2.	Tened.	Sed.	Estad.
3.	Tengan.	Sean.	Estén.
4.	Tengan Vds.	Sean Vds.	Estén Vds.

Subjuntive Mode

Present.

I may have.   I may be.

1 Haya	Tenga	Sea	Esté.
2. Hayas.	Tengas.	Seas	Estés.
3. Haya.	Tenga.	Sea.	Esté.
1. Hayamos.	Tengamos.	Seamos.	Estemos.
2. Hayáis.	Tengás.	Seáis.	Estéis.
3. Hayan	Tengan.	Sean.	Estén.

Imperfect-(First Termination.)

I would have. I would be

1. Hubiera.	Tuviera.	Fuera.	Estuviera.
2. Hubieras.	Tuvieras.	Fueras	Estuvieras.
3. Hubiera.	Tuviera.	Fuera.	Estuviera.
1. Hubiéramos.	Tuviéramos.	Fuéramos.	Estuviéramos.
2. Hubierais.	Tuvierais.	Fuerais	Estuvierais.
3. Hubieran.	Tuvieran.	Fueran.	Estuvieran.

Conditional.

I would have. I would be

1. Habría.	Tendría.	Sería.	Estaría.
2. Habrías.	Tendrías.	Serías.	Estarías.
3. Habría.	Tendría.	Sería.	Estaría.
1. Habríamos.	Tendríamos.	Seríamos.	Estaríamos.
2. Habríais.	Tendríais.	Seríais	Estaríais.
3. Habrían.	Tendrían.	Serían.	Estarían.

Imperfect-(Second Termination.)

I should have. I should be

1. Hubiese.	Tuviese.	Fuese.	Estuviese.
2. Hubieses.	Tuvieses.	Fueses	Estuvieses.
3. Hubiese.	Tuviese.	Fuese.	Estuviese.
1. Hubiésemos.	Tuviésemos.	Fuésemos.	Estuviésemos.
2. Hubieseis.	Tuvieseis.	Fueseis	Estuvieseis.
3. Hubiesen.	Tuviesen.	Fuesen.	Estuviesen.

Passive Verbs

Passive verbs are formed from active transitive verbs by adding their *participle past* to the auxiliary verb *ser* (to be), through all its changes, as in English, thus, from the active verb *amar* (to love), is formed the passsive verb *ser amado* (to be loved).

The participle must agree in gender and number with the nominative it refers to; thus, he is loved *(él es amado); she is loved (ella es amada); they are loved (ellos, son amados).*

Pronominal or Reflexive Verbs.

A *pronominal* or *reflexive verb* is conjugated by prefixing the pronouns *me, te, se, V. se; nos, os, se, Vds. se* to the verb according to its person and number; as, he arms himself, *él se arma.*

In the infinitive and imperative modes the pronouns are placed after the verb, and in one word with it; the pronoun, therefore, must be suppressed, in order to find out the conjugation: thus, to approach; acercarse, (se) acercar, first conjugation.

Remarks On The Use Of The Subjunctive Mode.

Three are the terminations of the imperfect tense subjunctive mode; *ra, ría, se.*—The termination *ra,* or *se,* is used when the verb is governed by a conditional conjunction, and the verb that completes the sense of the phrase is placed in the termination *ría; If* he *had* money, he *would buy* the house, *si él tuviera dinero,* compraría *la casa:*—If the verb begins without a conditional conjunction, the termination *ría* may be used, placing the verb that completes the sense in the termination *se;* as, It would be proper that you should write to him, *sería bueno que V. le escribiese.*

Verbs signifying *command, wish, supplication,* etc., being in the present indicative, require the governed verb in the present subjunctive; and if they are in any of the past tenses of the indicative, the governed verb must he in the termination *ra* or *se,* of the subjunctive.

The Gerund.

The *gerund* is that part of the verb that terminates in *ando* in verbs of the first conjugation, and in *iendo* in those of the second and third, as *publicando* (publishing), from *publicar; prometiendo* (promising), from *prometer; asistiendo* (assisting), from asistir. It admits no change for gender or number.

It is translated by the English present participle, and conjugated with the verb *estar* (to be), as, Ana is reading, and Mary is playing on the piano *(**Ana está leyendo, y María está tocando el piano**).*

PARTICIPLE.

The passive or past participle terminates in *ado* in the first conjugation, and in *ido* in the second and third. It changes its termination according to the number and gender of the person it refers to; except when it follows immediately after the verb *haber,* in which case it does not admit of any change.

All passive participles that do not terminate in *ado* or *ido* are called irregular; such are the following from the verbs:

To open, **abrir, abierto.**   To die, **morir, muerto.**

To cover, **cubrir, cubierto.** To resolve, **resolver,**

To say, **decir, dicho.**   **resuelto.**

To write, **escribir, escrito.**To see, **ver, visto.**

To try, **freír, frito.**   To put, **poner, puesto.**

To do, **hacer, hecho.**   To turn, **volver, vuelto.**

To print, **imprimir, impreso**.

Their compounds have the same irregularity.

Verbs That Have Two Participles.

There are some verbs that have two passive participles, the one regular and the other irregular. They are eighty-three in number. Such are: To bless, *bendecir,* bendecido, *bendito;* to compel, *compeler,* compelido, *compulso,* to convert, convertir, convertido, *converso;* to awake, *despertar,* despertado, *despierto,* to elect, *elegir,* elegido, *electo;* to express, *expresar,* expresado, *expreso*; to fix, *fijar*, fijado, *fijo;* to satiate, hartar, hartado, *harto*; to include, *incluir*, incluido, *incluso;* to join, *juntar*, juntado, junto; to arrest, *prender*, prendido, *preso;* to provide, *proveer*, proveído, *provisto;* to loosen, *soltar*, soltado, *suelto;* to suspend, *suspender*, suspendido, *suspenso,* etc.

The *regular* participles of these verbs are used to form the compound tenses with *haber;* as, he has awaked early (**él ha despertado temprano***).*

The irregular participles are used as verbal adjectives, and with the verbs ser, etc., and do not form compound tenses with *haber;* excepting *preso, prescrito, provisto, roto, injerto, proscrito,* and *supreso,* which have both uses; as, he is early awaked (**él está despierto temprano**); They have provided *(***ellos han provisto or proveído),**

THE PLURAL

In Spanish the plural is formed adding **s** or **es** to the singular.

rosa	-	rosas.
edificio	-	edificios.
café	-	cafés.
piano	-	pianos.
mesa	-	mesas.
canción	-	canciones.
cárcel	-	cárceles.
árbol	-	árboles.
rubí	-	rubíes.
rey	-	reyes.

If we observe we´ll see an **s** when the substantives finish with a non-accented vowel or with **é.**

But we add **es** to the substantives that finish with a consonant and with an accented vocal which is not **é.** - **Y** is considered a consonant in this case.

There are some exceptions: papá - papás, mamá - mamás, sofá - sofás, dominó - dominós.

1. The nouns which in singular finish with **s,** don´t change in plural.

    * el martes - los martes; el paraguas - los paraguas; el parabrisas - los parabrisas.

But there are some exceptions.

    * interés - intere**s**es, tos - tos**es**.

The grave or esdrújulos substantives that finish with x or z don´t have a plural.

    * clímax, mantis, tórax, Pérez.

2. Other words only are used in plural:

alicates, tijeras, gafas, pantalones, tenazas, pinzas, nupcias, comestibles, víveres, tinieblas, esponsales, cosquillas, bragas, calzoncillos.

Changes in pronunciation and writing

    a) Pronunciation:

    El car**á**cter - Los caract**e**res. El r**é**gimen - Los reg**í**menes.

    b) Writing:

The final **z** is changed to **c** in the plural form **es.**

    capaz - capa**ces,** capataz - capata**ces,** rapaz - rapa**ces,** voraz - vora**ces,** lápiz - lápi**ces.**

Some words accented in the last sillable are:

    canción - cancion**es,** francés - frances**es**

    varón - varon**es,** balón - balon**es.**

Sometimes the meaning of the word changes when it´s put into plural.

    * Está **bien** hecho. No tengo **bienes**

    * Tiene una **esposa** francesa. Le pusieron las **esposas.**

The Personal Pronoun

The 1° and the 2° persons.

a) With the prepositions **según** and **entre** the forms **yo/tú** are used.

    * **Según tú** eso no es verdad.

    * **Entre tú y yo,** creo que se casará con él.

b) With the other prepositions we use the forms **mí/ti**:

    * Este vaso es **para ti**.

    * Están hablando **de mí**.

c) The preposition **con** originates the forms **conmigo** y **contigo**:

    * Ven **conmigo** a Madrid.

    * Ella no quiere ir **contigo.**

La 3ª persona.

It uses the forms subject, going before the following preposition:

    *Tu madre está hablando **con él.**

    * Esta carta es **para ella.**

The non-accented forms which correspond to the direct and indirect object, are placed before the verb.

    * **Me** pidió que viniera.

    * **Te** dije que fueras a la estación.

The forms **le, les** placed in front of **lo, la, los** or **las** acquire the form **se.**

    * Yo **le** di dinero * Yo **se** lo di (**le** changes to **se,** and money changes to **lo**).

    * Yo **le** compré los libros (a él). Yo **se** los compré (**le** changes to **se,** and the books change to **los**).

    * Yo **les** di pan - yo **se** lo di (**les** changes to **se,** and pan changes to **lo**).

    * He entregado un paquete al cartero = **Le** (to the postman) he entregado un paquete = **Se** lo he entregado (**Le** changes to **se,** and packet changes to **lo**).

The form **se** will always go before when it is combined with **te** or **me.**

    * **Se** me ocurre. * **Se** te advirtió.

LA LE LO

When only a pronoun-complement appears:

1. If the sentence is refered to objects, the forms **lo(s)** or **la(s)** are used for the masculine and feminine respectively:

* Visitaron el museo .... **Lo** visitaron.

* Vieron la foto .... **La** vieron.

With verbs of <u>adding, accumulation...</u> or their contraries, <u>add, put, to take away etc.,</u> the sentences are formed with the preposition **A**, and the pronoun will **LE(s).**

* **A este coche le** falta velocidad.

* **A este motor le** añadieron más potencia.

* **A esta casa le** pusieron el tejado ayer.

2. If it is personal:

a) When it is an indirect complement, the form **le(s)** is always used.

* Yo compré un libro a Pedro/María - Le compró un libro (to Pedro or to María).

* Yo vendí el coche a los vecinos/las vecinas. - **Les** vendí el coche.

b) When it is a direct complement:

i) If it is feminine it is used the form **la(s).**

* Juan vio a Luisa. - Juan **la** vio.

* Enrique besó a su madre. - Enrique **la** besó.

* Culparon a las mujeres del asesinato. - **Las** culparon.

* Mató a la niña. - **La** mató.

ii) If it is masculine **lo(s) o le(s)** can be used.

* María vio a Pedro. - María **le/lo** vio.

* Ella contempló al niño. - Ella **le/lo** contempló

* Ellos asesinaron al anciano. - Ellos **le/lo** asesinaron.

* Pedro esperó a los niños. - Él **les/los** esperó.

iii) If the pronoun refers to usted(es), it is normally used the form **le(s).**

* Tenía muchas ganas de conocer**le** (a usted).

* Teníamos muchas ganas de conocer**les** (a ustedes).

GENERAL IRREGULARITIES OF SPANISH VERBS.

EUPHONIC CHANGES.

Verbs That Require A Change In Their Radical Letters.

1 Verbs ending in CAR change the **c** into **qu** when the first letter of the termination is E.

2. Verbs ending in CER change the c into z }

3. " CIR c " z } When the first letter

4. " GER G " J } of the termination

5. " GIR G " J } is O *or* A

6. " QUIR QU " C }

7. " GUIR drop U " }

8. " GAR add U " } When the first letter of

9. " ZAR change z " c } the termination is E.

THE IRREGULAR VERBS.

Irregular verbs suffer some changes either in their radical letters or in the termination of the conjugations to which they belong, or in both cases. The total number of such verbs in the Spanish language is about eight hundred and seventy-six. Of these, however, four hundred and sixty-one are compound forms. But this apparently very long list may be reduced to six classes, as follows:

I. To the first class belong certain verbs like **acertar, ascender, sentir,** which have the vowel e in the penultimate syllable of the infinitive, and change this e when it bears the tonic accent, or is in the singular or the third person plural of the present tense (indicative, subjunctive, imperative), into **ie.** As a general rule, and with very rare exceptions, if in the kindred noun there is the diphthong *ie,* the verb is irregular of this class. Verbs of the third conjugation belonging to this class have the further peculiarity that the vowel *e* of the stem changes into *i* when unaccented and followed by a strong termination (that is, containing a strong vowel, viz., *a* or *o*), and in the preterite before a diphthong. To this class belong also the verbs **adquirir, concernir** (defective), **and discernir.**

II. To the second class belong certain verbs like**, mover,** and **dormir,** which have the vowel **o** in the penultimate syllable of the infinitive, and change this **o** into **u** when it bears the tonic accent or is in the singular and the third person plural of the present tense (indicative, subjunctive, and imperative). If the kindred noun has the diphthong *ue,* the verb generally belongs to this class. *Dormir* and *morir* (3d conj.) have *ue* in the same positions where *sentir* (class I) has *i.* The gerund in this class belongs uniformly to the *aorist* (or preterite) system.

III. To the third class belong verbs of the second and third conjugations ending in **cer** or **cir** preceded by a vowel, the irregularity consisting in their taking a **z** before the **c** when the terminations begin with *a* or *o.* This occurs in the first person singular of the present indicative, in all persons of the present subjunctive, and in those of the imperative which are formed from the subjunctive. About two hundred and eight verbs belong to this class, the forms in **ecer** being very numerous.

IV. This class is composed wholly of verbs of the third conjugation with the stem vowel **e** (like **pedir**), and change this **e** for **i** in the gerund in the third person (singular and plural) of the present indicative, the whole of the present subjunctive, and the imperative formed therefrom, the third persons of the past definite, and all those of the imperfect subjunctive.

NOTE: -The verbs which end in **eír** and **ñir,** like **reír, ceñir,** lose the **i** of their endings when it is not accented (gerund, third person past definite, and imperfect and future subjunctive), and thus is avoided the double sound of *i* which results; thus:

*Riendo, Rieron, Riera, Riese, etc.

V. To this class belong those verbs ending in **uir** in which both vowels are sounded, like **argüir** (excluding therefore those in *guir, quir*). Their irregularity consists in adding **y** to the stem when this is accented or followed by a strong vowel.

The preterite (florist) stem is regular, but the initial *i* of the diphthongal terminations *ie, io,* is changed to *y,* since it comes between two vowels. The gerund in this class belongs always to the *aorist* system.

VI. To this class are assigned all the remaining irregular verbs, among which there is, however, no common principle of classification. A portion of these have *florist* (preterite) systems resembling more or less closely the Latin, while the remainder are irregular in the strictest sense. These verbs are therefore given individually.

Examples:

1. *Acrecentar,* Acreciento, acrecientas, etc.: acreciente, acrecienta, etc.; acreciente, acrecientes, etc.

Attender, Atiendo, atiendes, etc.; atienda, atiende, etc.; atienda, atiendas, etc.

Asentir, Asiento, asientes, etc.; asienta, asiente, etc., asienta, asientas, etc.

Asintió, asintieron; asintiera: asintiese;

2. *Acordar* Acuerdo, acuerdas, etc.; acuerde, acuerda, etc.; acuerde, acuerdes, etc.

Mover Muevo, mueves, etc.; mueva, mueve, etc.; mueva, muevas, etc.

Dormir, Duermo, duermes, etc.; duerma, duerme, etc.; duerma, duermas, etc.

3. *Conocer* Conozco, conozca. *Obedecer,* obedezco, obedezca. *Lucir,* luzco, luzca.

Conducir Conduzco; conduzca, conduzcas, conduzcamos, etc.

Conduje, condujiste, condujo, V. condujo; condujimos, condujisteis, condujeron, VV. condujeron.—*Subj. Imperf. 1st term.* Condujera. etc.—*2d term.* Conduciría., etc.—*3d term.* Condujese, etc.—*Fut.* Condujere, etc.

4. *Poseer,* Poseyendo; poseyó, poseyera, etc.; poseyese, etc.; poseyere, etc.

Pedir, Pido, pides, etc.; pida, pide, etc.; pida, pidas, etc.

Pidió, pidieron, pidiera, etc. pidiese, etc.; pidiere, etc.

5. *Instruir,* Instruyendo, instruyo, instruyeron, instruyera, etc. instruyese, etc., instruyere, etc.

Instruyo, instruyes, etc.; instruya, instruye, etc.; instruya, instruyas, etc.

6. The auxiliary verbs *Ser, Estar, Haber; Tener; Dar, Caber,* etc.,are given individually just below.

Verbs Whose Irregularity Is Confined To Them And Their Compounds.

N. B. The tenses not conjugated in the following verbs are regular. Thus in *Andar,* for instance, the present of the indicative mood is: 1 *ando,* 2 *andas,* 3 *anda,* etc. The imperfect tense: 1 *andaba,* 2 *andabas,* etc. The tenses or persons printed in *italics* are also regular.

ADQUIRIR, to *acquire.* Cl. I.

Indic. Pres. 1 Adquiero, 2 adquieres, 3 él/Vd adquiere: 1 *adquirimos,* 2 *adquirís,* 3 ellos/Vds adquieren.

Imperative. 2 adquiere, 3 adquiera, adquiera Vd., 2 no adquieras: 1 *adquiramos,* 2 *adquirid.,* 2 *no adquiráis.*

Subj. Pres. 1 Adquiera, 2 adquieras, 3 él/Vd. adquiera: 1 *adquiramos,* 2 *adquiráis,* 3 ellos/Vds. adquieran.

ANDAR, *to walk.* Cl. VI.

Indic. Preterit. 1 Anduve, 2 anduviste, 3 él/Vd. anduvo: 1 anduvimos, 2 anduvisteis, 3 ellos/Vds. anduvieron.

Subj. Imperf. 1st term. 1 Anduviera, 2 anduvieras, 3 él/Vd. anduviera: 1 anduviéramos, 2 anduvierais, 3 ellos/Vds. anduvieran.

Conditional. 1 *andaría,* etc. 1 anduviese, 2 anduvieses, etc.

BENDECIR, *to bless.* Cl. VI.

Is conjugated like *Decir,* except in the tenses and persons following, which are regular.

Past participle. —— | Bendito. / Bendecido.

Indic. Future. 1. Bendeciré, 2 bendecirás, 3 él/Vd. bendecirá: 1 bendeciremos, 2 bendeciréis, 3 ellos/Vds. bendecirán. —*Conditional.* 1 Bendeciría, 2 bendecirías, 3 él/Vd. bendeciría: 1 bendeciríamos, 2 bendeciríais, 3 ellos/Vds. bendecirían.—*Imperative.* 2 Bendice tú: 2 Bendecid.

CABER, *to be contained.* Cl. VI.

Indic. Pres. 1 Quepo, 2 *cabes,* 3 *él/Vd. cabe:* 1 cabemos, 2 *cabéis,* 3 *ellos/Vds.* caben.—*Perf.* 1 Cupe, 2 cupiste, 3 cupo, Vd. cupo: 1 cupimos, 2 cupisteis, 3 cupieron, Vds. cupieron.

Fut. 1 Cabré, 2 cabrás, 3 él/Vd. cabrá: 1 cabremos, 2 cabréis, 3 ellos/Vds. cabrán.—*Imperative.* 2 *cabe,* 3 quepa él/Vd., 2 no quepas, 1 quepamos, 2 *cabed,* 3 quepan ellos/Vds., 2 no quepáis.

Subj. Pres. 1 Quepa, 2 quepas, 3 ellos/Vds. quepa: 1 quepamos, 2 quepáis, 3 ellos/Vds. quepan.— *Imperf. 1st term.* 1 Cupiera, 2 cupieras, 3 él/Vd. cupiera: 1 cupieramos, 2 cupierais, 3 ellos/Vds. cupieran.—*2d term.* 1 Cabría, 2 cabrías, 3 él/Vd. cabría: 1 cabríamos, 2 cabríais, 3 ellos/Vds. cabrían.—*3d term* 1 Cupiese, 2 cupieses, 3 cupiese, Vd. cupiese: 1 cupiésemos, 2 cupieseis, 3 cupiesen, Vds. cupiesen.

CAER, *to fall.* Cl. VI.

Gerund. Cayendo. *Past participle.* Caído.

Indic. Pres. 1 Caigo, 2 caes, 3 *él/vd.* cae:

1 *caemos,* 2 caéis, 3 ellos/Vds. caen.—*Prest.* 1 Caí, 2 *caíste,* 3 él/Vd. cayó: 1 *caímos,* 2 *caísteis,* 3 ellos/Vds. cayeron.

Imper. 2 cae. 3 *caiga* el, caiga él/Vd., 2 no caigas: 1 caigamos, 2 *caed,* 3 caigan ellos/Vds.. 2 no caigáis.—*Subj. Pres.* 1 Caiga, 2 caigas. 3 él/Vd caiga: 1 caigamos, 2 caigáis, 3 *ellos/Vds.* caigan.— *Imperf. 1st term.* 1 Cayera, 2 cayeras, 3 él/Vd cayera: 1 cayéramos, 2 cayerais, 3 ellos/Vds. cayeran.—*Conditional.* 1 *Caería,* etc., 1 *caeríamos,* etc.—*3d term.* 1 Cayese, 2 cayeses, 3 él/Vd cayese: 1. cayésemos, 2 cayeseis, 3 ellos/Vds. cayesen.— *Fut.* 1 Cayere, 2 cayeres, 3 cayere, él/Vd cayere: 1 cayéremos, 2 cayereis, 3 ellos/Vds. cayeren.

COCER, *to boil.* Cl. II.

Indic. Pres. 1 Cuezo, 2 cueces, 3 él/Vd cuece 1 cocemos, 2 *cocéis,* 3 ellos/Vds. cuecen.—*Subj. Pres.* 1 Cueza, 2 cuezas, 3 él/Vd cueza: 1 cozamos, 2 cozáis, 3 ellos/Vds. cuezan.—*Imper.* 2 cuece, 3 cueza él/Vd, 2 no cuezas: 1 cozamos, 2 *coced,* 3 cuezan ellos/Vds., 2 no cozáis.—*Subj. Pres.* 1. Cueza, 2 cuezas, etc.

DAR, *to give.* Cl. VI.

Indic. Pres. 1 Doy, 2 *das,* 3 *él/Vd da:* 1 *damos,* 2 *dáis,* 3 *ellos/Vds.* dan.—*Imperf.* 1 *Daba,* etc. 1 *Dábamos, etc.*—*Perf.* 1 *Dí,* 2 diste, 3 él/Vd dio: 1 dimos, 2 disteis, 3 ellos/Vds. dieron.

Fut. 1 *Daré,* etc. 1 *Daremos.*—*Imper.* 2 *Da tú,* etc. 1 *Demos,* etc.—*Subj. Pres.* 1 *Dé,* etc.: 1 *Demos,* etc. —*Imperf. 1st term.* 1 Diera, 2 dieras, 3 él/Vd diera: 1 diéramos, 2 dierais, 3 ellos/Vds. dieran.— *2d term.* 1 *Daría,* etc.: 1 *daríamos,* etc.—*3d term.* 1 Diese, 2 dieses, 3 él/Vd diese: 1 diésemos, 2 dieseis, 3 ellos/Vds. diesen.

DECIR, *to say.* Cl. VI.

Gerund, Diciendo. *Past participle.* Dicho.

Indic. Pres. 1 Digo, 2 dices, 3 él/Vd dice: 1 *decimos,* 2 *decís,* 3 ellos/Vds. dicen.—*Imperf.* 1

Decía, etc. —*Pret.* 1 Dije, 2 dijiste, 3 él/Vd dijo: 1 dijimos, 2 dijisteis, 3 ellos/Vds. dijeron.

Fut. 1 Diré, 2 dirás, 3 él/Vd dirá: 1 diremos, 2 diréis, 3 ellos/Vds. dirán.—*Imper.* 2 di tú, 3 diga él/Vd, 2 no digas :1 digamos, 2 *decid,* 3 digan ellos/ Vds., 2 no digáis.—*Subj. Pres.* 1 diga, 2 digas, 3 él/Vd diga: 1 digamos, 2 digáis, 3 ellos/Vds. digan.—*Imperf. 1st term.* 1 dijera, 2 dijeras, 3 dijera, él/Vd dijera: 1 dijéramos, 2 dijerais, 3 ellos/ Vds. dijeran.—*Conditional.* 1 diría, 2 dirías, 3 él/ Vd diría: 1 diríamos, 2 diríais, 3 ellos/Vds. dirían.—*3d term.* 1 Dijese, 2 dijeses, 3 él/Vd dijese: 1 dijésemos, 2 dijeseis, 3 ellos/Vds. dijesen.

Contradecir, *to contradict;* Desdecirse, *to retract;* Predecir, *to predict.* These three verbs are conjugated like *decir,* except in the second person singular of the imperative, which is *contradice, predice, desdícete.*

DORMIR, *to sleep.* Cl. II.

Gerund. Durmiendo. *Past participle.* Dormido.

Indic. Pres. 1 Duermo, 2 duermes, 3 duerme: 1 *dormimos,* 2 *dormís,* 3 duermen.

Pret. 1 *Dormí,* 2 *dormiste,* 3 durmió: 1 *dormimos,* 2 *dormisteis,* 3 durmieron.—*Imper.* 2 duerme, 3 duerma él/Vd., 2 no duermas: 1 durmamos, 2 *dormid,* 3 duerman *ellos/Vds.,* 2 no durmáis.—*Subj. Pres.* 1 Duerma, 2 duermas, 3 duerma: 1 durmamos, 2 durmáis, 3 duerman.—*Imperf. 1st term.* 1 Durmiera, 2 durmieras, 3 durmiera: 1 durmiéramos, 2 durmierais, 3 durmieran.—*Conditional.* 1 *Dormiría,* etc.—*3d term.* 1 Durmiese, 2 durmieses, 3 durmiese: 1 durmiésemos, 2 durmieseis, 3 durmiesen.

MORIR, *to die.* Cl. II.

Past participle. Muerto.

The rest is conjugated like *Dormir.*

ESTAR, *to be.* Cl. VI.

HABER, *to have.* Cl. VI.

As an auxiliary verb.

HABER, when signifying *there to be,* is conjugated only in the third person singular of each tense, whether the nominative be singular or plural; thus:

There to be, *Haber.* There being, *Habiendo.*

There is *hay*	There had been *había habido*
There are *hay*	There will have been *habrá*
There *was había*	*habido*
There were *hubo*	There may have been *haya*
There will be *habrá*	*habido*
Let there be *haya*	
There may be *haya*	
There has been *ha habido*	
There have been *ha habido*	

HACER, *to make.* C1. VI.

Gerund. Haciendo. *Past Participle.* Hecho.

Indic. Pres: 1 Hago, 2 haces, etc.—*Imperf.* 1. *Hacía,* etc.—*Pret.* 1 Hice, 2 hiciste, 3 hizo: 1 hicimos 2 hicisteis, 3 hicieron.—*Fut.* 1 Haré, 2 harás, 3 hará: 1 haremos, 2 haréis, 3 harán.—*Imper.* 2 haz, 3 haga: 1 hagamos, 2 *haced,* 3 hagan.—*Subj. Pres.* 1 Haga, 2 hagas, etc.—*Imperf. 1st term.* 1 Hiciera, 2 hicierais, 3 hiciera: 1 hiciéramos, 2 hicieras, 3 hicieran.—*Conditional.* 1 Haría, 2 harías, 3 haría: 1 haríamos, 2 haríais, 3 harían.—*2d term.* 1 Hiciese, 2 hicieses, 3 hiciese: 1 hiciésemos, 2 hicieseis, 3 hiciesen.

IR, *to go.* Cl. VI.

Gerund. Yendo. *Past participle.* Ido.

Indic. Pres. 1 Voy, 2 vas, 3 va: 1 vamos, 2 vais, 3 van.—*Imperf.* 1 Iba, 2 ibas, 3 iba: 1 Íbamos, 2 ibais, 3 iban.—*Pret.* 1 Fui, 2 fuiste, 3 fue: 1 fuimos, 2 fuisteis, 3 fueron.—*Fut.* 1 Iré, 2 irás, 3 iré: 1 iremos, 2 iréis, 3 irán.—*Imper.* 1 Vaya, 2 ve, 3 vaya: 1 vayamos, 2 *id,* 3 vayan.—*Subj. Pres.* 1 Vaya, 2 vayas, 3 vaya: 1 vayamos, 2 vayáis, 3 vayan.— *imperf. 1st. term.* 1 Fuera, 2 fueras, 3 fuera: 1 fuéramos, 2 fuerais, 3 fueran.—*Conditional.* 1 Iría, 2 irías, 3 iría: 1 iríamos, 2 iríais, 3 irían.—*2d term.* 1 Fuese, 2 fueses, 3 fuese: 1 fuésemos, 2 fueseis, 3 fuesen.

JUGAR, *to play.* C1. II.

Gerund. Jugando. *Past participle.* Jugado.

Indic. Pres. 1 juego, 2 juegas, 3 juega: 1 *jugamos,* 2 *jugáis,* 3 juegan.—*Imperf.* 1 *jugaba,* etc.—*Pret.* 1 jugué, 2 *jugaste,* etc.—*Fut.* 1 *jugaré,* etc.— *Imperf.* 2 juega, 3 juegue: 1 juguemos, 2 *jugad,* 3 jueguen.—*Subj. Pres.* 1 juegue, 2 juegues, 3 juegue: 1 juguemos, 2 juguéis, 3 jueguen.—*Imperf. 1st term.* 1 *jugara,* etc.—*Conditional.* 1 *jugaría,* etc.—*3d term.* 1 *jugase,* etc.—*Fut.* 1 *jugaré,* etc.

OIR, *to hear.* Cl. VI.

Gerund. Oyendo. *Past participle.* Oído.

Indic. Pres. 1 Oigo, 2 oyes, 3 oye: 1 *oímos,* 2 *oís,* 3 oyen.—*Imperf.* 1 *Oía,* etc.—*Pret.* 1 Oí, 2 oíste, 3 oyó: 1 oímos, 3 oyeron.—Fut. 1 Oiré etc.—*Imper.* 2 oye, 3 oiga: 1 oigamos, 2 *oíd,* 3 oigan.—*Subj. Pres.* 1 Oiga, 2 oigas, 3 oiga: 1 oigamos, 2 oigáis, 3 oigan.—*Imperf. 1st term.* 1 Oyera, 2 oyeras, oyera: 1 oyéramos, 2 oyerais, 3 oyeran.—*Conditional.* 1 Oiría, etc.—*2d term.* 1 Oyese, 2 oyeses, 3 oyese: 1 oyésemos, 2 oyeseis, 3 oyesen.

OLER, *to smell.* C1. II.

Gerund. Oliendo. *Past participle.* Olido.

Indic. Pres. 1 Huelo, 2 hueles, 3 huele: 1 olemos, 2 *oléis,* 3 huelen.—*Imperf.* 1 Olía, etc.—*Pret.* 1 Olí. etc.—*Fut.* 1 Oleré, etc.—*Imper.* 2 huele, 3 huela: 1 olamos, 2 *oled,* 3 huelan.—*Subj. Pres.* 1 Huela, 2 huelas, 3 huela: 1 *olamos,* 2 *oláis,* 3 huelan.—

Imperf. 1st term. 1 Oliera, etc.—*Conditional.* 1 Olería, etc.—*2d term.* 1 Oliese, etc.

PODER, *to be able.* Cl. VI.

Gerund. Pudiendo. *Past participle.* Podido.

Indic. Pres. 1 Puedo, 2 puedes, 3 puede: 1 *podemos,* 2 *podéis,* 3 pueden.—*Imperf.* 1 Podía, etc.—*Pret.* 1 Pude, 2 pudiste, 3 pudo: 1 pudimos, 2 pudisteis, 3 pudieron.—*Fut.* 1 Podré, 2 podrás, 3 podrá: 1 podremos, 2 podréis, 3 podrán.—It has no *Imperative.*—*Subj. Pres.* 1 Pueda, 2 puedas, 3 pueda: 1 *podamos,* 2 *podáis,* 3 puedan.—*Imperf. 1st term.* 1 Pudiera, 2 pudieras, 3 pudiera: 1 pudiéramos, 2 pudierais, 3 pudieran.—*Conditional.* 1 Podría. 2 podrías, 3 podría. 1 podríamos, 2 podríais, 3 podrían.—*2d term.* 1 Pudiese, 2 pudieses, 3 pudiese: 1 pudiésemos, 2 pudieseis, 3 pudiesen.

PODRIR or PUDRIR, *to rot.* Cl. VI.

Gerund. Pudriendo. *Past Participle.* Podrido.

Indic. Pres. 1 Pudro, 2 pudres, 3 pudre: 1 *podrimos,* 2 *podrís,* 3 pudren. —*Imperf.* 1 *Pudría* or *podría,* etc.—*Pret.* 1 *Podrí,* 2 *podriste,* 3 pudrió: 1 *podrimos,* 2 *podristeis,* 3 pudrieron.—*Fut.* 1 *podriré,* etc.—*Imper.* 2 pudre, 3 pudra: 1 pudramos, 2 *podrid,* 3 pudran.—*Subj. Pres.* 1 Pudra, 2 pudras, 3 pudra, etc.—*Imperf. 1st term.* 1 pudriera, 2 pudrieras, 3 pudriera: 1 pudriéramos, 2 pudrierais, 3 pudrieran.—*Conditional.* 1 *pudriría, podriría,* etc.—*2d term.* 1 pudriese, 2 pudrieses, 3 pudriese: 1 pudriésemos, 2 pudrieseis, 3 pudriesen.

PONER, *to put.* Cl. VI.

Gerund. Poniendo. *Past participle.* Puesto.

Indic. Pres. 1 pongo, 2 *pones,* etc.—*Imperf.* 1 ponía, etc.—*Pret.* 1 puse, 2 pusiste, 3 puso: 1 pusimos, 2 pusisteis, 3 pusieron.—*Fut.* 1 pondré, 2 pondrás, 3 pondrá: 1 pondremos, 2 pondréis, 3 pondrán.—*Imper.* 2 pon, 3 ponga: 1 pongamos, 2 poned, 3 pongan.—*Subj. Pres.* 1 ponga, 2 pongas, 3 ponga: 1 pongamos, 2 pongáis 3 pongan.— *Imperf. 1st term.* 1 pusiera, 2 pusieras, 3 pusiera: 1 pusiéramos, 2 pusierais, 3 pusieran.—*Conditional.* 1 pondría, 2 pondrías, 3 pondría: 1 pondríamos, 2 pondríais, 3 pondrían.—*2d term.* 1 pusiese, 2 pusieses, 3 pusiese: 1 pusiésemos, 2 pusieseis, 3 pusiesen.

QUERER, *to want.* Cl. VI.

Gerund. Queriendo. *Past Participle.* Querido.

Indic. Pres. 1 quiero, 2 quieres, 3 quiere: 1 *queremos,* 2 *queréis,* 3 quieren.—*Imperf.* 1 *quería,* etc.—*Pret.* 1 quise, 2 quisiste, 3 quiso: 1 quisimos, 2 quisisteis, 3 quisieron.—*Fut.* 1. querré, 2 querrás, 3 querrá: 1 querremos, 2 querréis, 3 querrán.—*Subj. Pres.* 1 quiera, 2 quieras, 3 quiera: 1 *queramos,* 2 *queráis,* 3 quieran.—*Inperf. 1st term.* 1 quisiera, 2 quisieras, 3 quisiera: 1 quisiéramos, 2 quisierais, 3 quisieran.—*Conditional.* 1. querría, 2 querrías, 3 querría: 1 querríamos, 2 querríais, 3 querrían.—*2d*

Imperf. 1st term. 1 Oliera, etc.—*Conditional.* 1 Olería, etc.—*2d term.* 1 Oliese, etc.

term. 1 quisiese, 2 quisieses, 3 quisiese: 1 quisiésemos, 2 quisieseis. 3 quisiesen.

REÍR, *to laugh.* Cl. IV.

Gerund. Riendo. *Past participle.* Reído.

Indic. Pres. 1 río, 2 ríes, 3 ríe: 1 *reímos,* 2 *reís,* 3 ríen.—*Imperf.* 1 *Reía, etc.*—*Pret.* 1 *Reí.* 2 *reíste,* 3 rió: 1 *reímos,* 2 *reísteis,* 3 rieron.—*Fut.* 1 *reiré, etc.*—*Imper.* 2 ríe, 3 ría: 1 riamos, 2 *reíd.* 3 rían. —*Subj Pres.* 1 ría, 2 rías, 3 ría: 1 riamos. 2 riáis, 3 rían.—*Imperf. 1st* term. 1 riera, 2 rieras, 3 riera, *etc.*—*Conditional.* 1 *reiría, etc.*—*2d term* 1 riese, 2 rieses, 3 riese: 1 riésemos, 2 rieseis, 3 riesen, etc.

Freír, *to fry. Past participle.* **Frito.**

SABER, *to know.* C1. VI.

Gerund. Sabiendo. *Past participle.* Sabido.

Indic. *Pres.* 1 sé, 2 *sabes, etc.*—*Imperf.* 1 *sabía, etc.*—*Pret.* 1 supe, 2 supiste, 3 supo: 1 supimos, 2 supisteis, 3 supieron.—*Fut.* 1 sabré, 2 sabrás, 3 sabrá: 1 sabremos, 2 sabréis, 3 sabrán.—*Imper.* 2 *sabe,* 3 sepa: 1 sepamos, 2 *sabed,* 3 sepan.— *Subj. Pres.* 1 sepa, 2 sepas. 3 sepa: 1 sepamos, 2 sepáis, 3 sepan.—*Imperf. 1st term.* 1 supiera, 2 supieras, 3 supiera: 1 supiéramos, 2 supierais, 3 supieran.— *Conditional.* 1 sabría, 2 sabrías, 3 sabría: 1 sabríamos, 2 sabríais, 3 sabrían.—*2d term.* 1 supiese, 2 supieses, 3 supiese, etc.

SALIR, to go out. Cl. VI.

Gerund. Saliendo. *Past participle.* Salido.

Indic. Pres. 1 salgo, 2 sales, *etc.*—*Imperf. salía, etc.* —*Pret.* 1 *salí, etc.*—*Fut.* 1 saldré, 2 saldrás, 3 saldrá: 1 saldremos, 2 saldréis, 3 saldrán.—*Imper.* 2 sal, 3 salga: 1 salgamos, 2 *salid,* 3 salgan.—*Subj. Pres.* 1 salga, 2 salgas, 3 salga: 1 salgamos, 2 salgáis, 3 salgan.—*Imperf. 1st term.* 1 *saliera* etc.— *Conditional.* 1 saldría, 2 saldrías, 3 saldría: 1 saldríamos, 2 saldríais, 3 saldrían,—*3d term.* 1 saliese, etc.

SATISFACER, *to satisfy.* Cl. VI.

SATISFACER is a verb compounded of *satis* and *hacer,* and is conjugated like *hacer,* changing the *h* into *f;* thus, *satisfago, satisfaces, etc.,* satisfacía, *etc., satisfice, satisficiste, satisfizo, etc.* Except the imperative, the second person singular of which is, *satisface,* or *satisfaz.*

TRAER, *to* bring. Cl. VI.

Gerund. Trayendo. *Past participle.* Traído.

Indic. Pres. 1 traigo, 2 *traes, etc.*—*Imperf.* 1 traía, *etc.*—*Pret.* 1 traje, 2. trajiste, 3 traje: 1 trajimos, 2 trajisteis, 3 trajeron.—*Fut.* 1 traeré, *etc.*—*Imper.* 2 *trae,* 3 traiga, traiga V., 2 no traigas: 1 traigamos, 2 *traed,* 3 traigan., 2 no traigais.—*Subj, Pres.* 1 traiga, 2 traigas, 3 traiga, *etc.*—*Imperf. 1st term.* 1 trajera, 2 trajeras. 3 trajera: 1 trajéramos, 2 trajerais,

3 trajeran.—*Conditional.* 1 *traería, etc.*—*2d term.* 1 trajese, 2 trajeses, 3 trajese, *etc.*—*Fut.* 1 trajere, 2 trajeres, 3 trajere: 1 trajéremos, 2 trajereis, 3 trajeron.

VALER, *to be worth.* Cl. VI.

I ndic. Pres. 1 valgo, 2 *vales,* etc.: 1 *valemos,* etc.— *Fut.* 1 valdré, 2 valdrás, 3 valdrá: 1 valdremos. 2 valdréis, 3 valdrán.—*Imper.* 2 *vale,* 3 valga, 2 no valgas, etc., 2 no valgáis.—*Subj. pres.* 1 valga, 2 valgas, 3 valga: 1 valgamos, 2 valgáis, 3 valgan.— *Imperf. 1st term.* 1 *valiera, etc.*—*Conditional.* 1 valdría, 2 valdrías, 3 valdría: 1 valdríamos, 2 valdríais 3 valdrían.—*3d term.* 1 *valiese- ,* 2 valieses etc.

VENIR, *to come.* Cl. VI.

Gerund. Viniendo. *Past participle.* Venido.

Indic. Pres. 1 vengo, 2 vienes, 3 viene, V. viene. 1 *venimos,* 2 *venís,* 3 vienen.—*Pret.* 1 vine, 2 *viniste,* 3 vino: 1 *vinimos, 2 vinisteis,* 3 vinieron.—*Fut.* 1 vendré, 2 vendrás, 3 vendrá: 1 vendremos, 2 vendréis, 3 vendrán.—*Imper.* 2 ven tú, 3 venga él, 2 no vengas: 1 vengamos, 2 *venid,* 3 vengan, 2 no vengais.—*Sub. Pres.* 1 venga, 2 vengas, 3 venga: 1 vengamos, 2 vengáis, 3 vengan.—*Imperf. 1st term.* 1 viniera, 2 vinieras, 3 viniera: 1 viniéramos, 2 vinierais, 3 vinieran.—*Conditional.* 1 vendría, 2 vendrías. 3 vendría, V. vendría: 1 vendríamos, 2 vendríais, 3 vendrían.—*2d term.* 1 viniese, 2 vinieses, 3 viniese V. viniese: 1 viniésemos, 2 vinieseis, 3 viniesen.

VER, *to see.* C1. VI.

Gerund. Viendo. *Past participle.* Visto.

Indic. Pres. 1 Veo, 2 ves 3 ve: 1 *vemos,* 2 *veis,* 3 ven.—*Imperf.* 1 veía, 2 veías, 3 veía: 1 veíamos, 2 veíais, 3 veían.—*Pret.* 1 *Vi,* 2 viste, 3 vió: 1 *vimos,* 2 *visteis,* 3 vieron.—*Fut.* 1 veré, 2 verás, 3 verá, *etc.*—*Imper.* 2 ve tú, 3 vea él., 2 no veas: 1 veamos, 2 *ved,* 3 vean, 2 no veáis.—*Subj. Pres.* 1 vea, 2 veas, 3 vea, V. vea: 1 veamos, 2 veáis, 3 vean.— *Imperf. 1d term.* 1 viera, 2 vieras, etc.—*Conditional.* 1 vería, 2 verías, etc.—*2d term.* 1 viese, 2 vieses, etc.

Impersonal Verbs.

Impersonal verbs are those which are conjugated in the third person singular of each tense only, without expressing the nominative, as:

GRANIZAR, *to hail.*

-It hails *graniza* -It has hailed *ha granizado*

-It had hailed *había granizado*

-It hailed *granizaba, granizó*

-It will have hailed *habrá granizado*

-It will hail *granizará* -It may have hailed *quizá haya granizado*

-Let it hail *granice*

-It may hail *quizá granice*

-If it hailed, *granizara* -If it had hailed *hubiera granizado*

-If it would hail *granizaría* -It would have hailed *habría granizado*

The following are some of the impersonal verbs:

-To freeze *helar,* irr. -To lighten *relampaguear*

-To frost *escarchar* -To thunder *tronar, irr.*

-To thaw *deshelar* -To rain *llover*

-To drizzle *lloviznar* -To happen *suceder, acaecer, acontecer.*

-To snow *nevar* -To dawn *amanecer*

-To be cold *hacer frío* -To become night *anochecer*

Defective Verbs.

SOLER, *to accustom.* Cl. II.

This verb is used only in the two following tenses:

Indic. Pres. 1 suelo, 2 sueles, 3 suele, 2 Vd. suele: 1 *solemos;* 2 *soléis,* 3 suelen.—*Imperf.* 1 *solía,* 2 *solías,* 3 *solía:* 1 *solíamos,* 2 *solíais,* 3 *solían.*

PLACER, *to please.* Cl. III.

This verb is used only in the third person singular or plural, in the moods and tenses as follows: it is always accompanied by a personal pronoun in the objective case.

Indic. Pres. 1 me place, 2 *te* place, 3 *le* place, 2 *le* place a Vd.: 1 *nos* place, 2 *os* place, 3 *les* place. 2 *les* place a Vds.; *or* 1 me placen, 2 *te* placen, etc.— *Imperf.* 1 me *placía, or placían,* 2 *te* placía, *or* placían, etc.—*Pret.* 1 me plugo, 2 *te* plugo, etc.: 1 *me* pluguieron. 2 te pluguieron, etc.—*Subj. Pres.* 1 me plegue, etc.—*Imperf. 1st there.* me pluguiera, etc.—*2d term. Me* pluguiese. etc.

ROER, *to gnaw.* Cl. VI.

Indic. Pres. 1 roo, roigo, royo, 2 roes, 3 roe: 1 roemos, 2 roéis, 3 roen.—*Subj. Pres.* 1 roa, roiga, roya, 2 roes, roigas, royas, 3 roe, roiga, roya: 1 roamos, roigamos, royamos, 2 roáis, roigáis, royáis, 3 roan, roigan, royan.

Remark.—Corroer, to *corrode,* makes corroe, corroen, in the present indicative, and corroa, corroan, in the subjunctive.

A LIST OF ALL THE IRREGULAR VERBS.

Obs. 1. The compound verbs are not inserted, when they have the same irregularity as the simple ones from which they are derived: as, *componer, contraponer,* etc., which are conjugated like *poner.*

For the convenience of the learner the strictness of this principle has been departed from in the two cases following: 1st. When the simple is no longer used by itself. To this list belong these nine: *cluir* (Cl. V), *cordar* (Cl. I), *ducir* (Cl. III), *manecer* (Cl. III), *stituir* (Cl. V), *tribuir* (Cl. V), *vertir* (Cl. I), *blandecer, bravecer* (Cl. III). 2d. Some compounds of *ad* (reduce to *a*) have been included, such as *asonar, atender,* and *asentir.*

On the other hand, compounds from nominal roots, as *enflaquecer, florecer,* have been inserted.

Obs. 2. The most general irregularities of the Spanish verbs consist in their taking *i, j,* y, or *ue,* or *i,* instead of *o,* or *e.* To find the infinitive mode of such verbs, separate the regular termination, and omit the letter or letters that do not belong to the radicals of such verbs: as in *comienzo, muestras, sintió, condujeron, trajeran, construyesen,* the terminations are *o, as, ió, eron, eran, esen.* The remaining letters are, *comienz, muestr, sint, conduj, tray, construy.* Add to these the regular terminations of the infinitive mode, and they will read *comienzar, muestrar, sintir, condujir, trajer, construyir.* Take off the *i, j,* and *y,* change *ue* into *o,* and the *i* into *e;* add a *c* before the termination to those in *ij* or *uj;* and they will be *comenzar, mostrar, sentir, conducir, traer, construir.*

Obs. 3. The irregular participles are set in italics after their verbs.

The verbs of the first column are conjugated like those of the second, which must be consulted in their respective places.

Cl.	Aferrar, I
Abastecer, III	Afluir, V
Aborrecer III	Aforar, II
Abrir, reg.	Agradecer, III
Abierto.	Alborecer, III
Abstenerse, VI	Alentar, I
(Abs)traer. VI	Aliquebrar, I
Abstracto and	Almorzar, II
Abstraído.	Amarillecer, III
Acaecer, III	Amoblar, II
Acertar, I	Amolar, II
Acollar, II	Andar, VI
Acontecer, III	Anochecer, III
Acordar, II	Apacentar, I
Acostar, II	Aparecer, III
Acrecentar, I	Apernar, I
Acrecer, III	Apetecer, III
(Ad)herir, I	Apostar, II
Adolecer, III	Apretar, I
Adormecer, III	Aprobar, II
Adquirir, I	Arrecirse, IV
Advertir, I	Arrendar, I
Aducir, III	Arrepentirse, I

Ascender, I

Asentar, I

Asentir, I

Aserrar, I

Asir, VI

Asolar, II

Asoldar, II

Asonar, II

Asosegar, I

Atender, I

Atento and

Atendido.

(A)tentar, I

Aterirse, I

Atestar,(relle-

nar) I

(A)traer, VI

Atravesar, I

Atribuir, V

(A)tronar, II

Avanecerse, III

(A)venir, VI

Aventar(se), I

Avergonzar, II

Azolar, II

Bendecir, VI

Bendito and

Bendecido.

Bienquerer, VI

Blanquecer, III

Caber, VI

Caer, VI

Calentar, I

Canecer, III

Carecer, III

Cegar, I

Ceñir, IV

Cerrar, I

Cimentar, I

Clarecer, III

Clocar, II

Cocer, II

Colar, II

Colgar, II

Comedirse, IV

Comenzar, Y

Competir, IV

Complacer, III

Concebir, IV

Concernir, I

Concertar, I

Concluir, V

Concluso and

Concluído.

Concordar, II

Condescender, I

Condolerse, II

Conducir, III

Conferir, I

Confesar, I

Confluir, V

Conocer, III

Conseguir, IV

Consentir, I

Consolar, II

Constituir, V

Construir, V

Contar, II

(Con)tener, VI

Contribuir, V

Controvertir, I

Convalecer, III

Convertir, I

Converso and

Convertido.

Corregir, IV

Correcto and

Corregido.

Costar II

Crecer III

Cubrir, reg.

Cubierto.

Dar, VI

Decentar, I

Decir, VI

Dicho.

Deducir, III

Defender, I

Deferir, I

Degollar, II

Demoler, II

Demostrar, II

Denegar, I

Denostar, II

Dentar, I

Derrengar, I

Derretir, IV

Derrocar, II

Derruir, V

Desbastecer, III

Desbravecer, III

Descaecer, III

Descender, I

Descollar, II

Descordar, II

Descornar, II

Describir, reg.

Descrito, or *des-*

cripto.

Desertar, I

Desflocar, II

Desherbar, I

Deshombre- ü III

cerse

Desleír, IV

Desmembrar, I

Desolar, II

Desollar, II

Desosar, II

Desovar, II

Despernar, I

Despertar, I

Despierto and

Despertado.

Desterrar, I

Destruir, V

Desvergon

zarse, II

Diferir, I

Digerir, I

Diluir, V

Discernir, I

Discordar, II

Disminuir, V

Disolver, II

Dispertar, I

Dispierto and

Dispertado.

Distribuir, V

Divertir, I

Cl.

Doler, II

Dormir, II

Educir, III

Elegir, IV

Electo and Ele-

gido.

Embarbecer, III

Embebecer(se), III

Embellecer, III

Embermejecer, III

Embestir, IV

Emblandecer, III

Embobecer, III

Embosquecer, III

Embravecer, III

Embrutecer, III

Emparentar, I

Empecer, III

Empederne- III

cerse

Empedernir, IV

Empedrar, I

Empellar, I

Empequeñecer, III

Empezar, I

Emplastecer, III

Emplumecer, III

Empobrecer, III

Empodrecer, III

Emporcar, II

Enaltecer, III

Enardecer, III

Encabellecerse, III

Encalvecer, III

Encallecer, III

Encandecer, III

Encarecer, III

Encender, I

Encentar I

Encerrar I

Enloquecer, III

Encomendar, I

Encontrar, II

Encorar II

Encordar, II

Encorecer, III

Encornar, II

Encovar, II

Encrudecer, III

Encruele- III

cer(se),

Encubertar, I	Entontecer III	Guarecer(se), III	Languidecer, III
Endentecer, III	Eutorpecer III	Guarnecer, III	Leer, IV
Endurecer, III	Entortar, II	Haber (see	Liquefacer, *V*. VI
Enfierecer(se), III	Entristecer, III	auxiliary VI	Lobreguecer, III
Enflaquecer, III	Entullecer, III	verbs),	Lucir, III
Enfranquecer, III	Entumecer III	Hacendar, I	Luir, V
Enfurecer, III	Envanecer III	Hacer, VI	Llover, II
Engorar, II	Envejecer, III	*Hecho.*	(Mal)decir, VI
Engrandecer, III	(En)verdecer III	Heder, I	*Maldito* and
Engreírse, IV	Envestir, IV	Helar, I	Maldecido.
Engrosar, II	Envilecer, III	Henchir, IV	Manifestar, I
Engrumecer- III	Erguir, I or IV	Hender, I	*Manifiesto* and
(se),	Errar, I	Heñir, IV	Manifestado.
Enloquecer, III	Escandecer, III	Herbar, I	(Man)tener, VI
Enmarecer, III	Escarmentar, I	Herbecer, III	Mecer, III
Enmarillecer- III	Escarnecer, III	Herir, I	Medir(se), IV
(se),	Esclarecer, III	Herrar, I	Melar, I
Enmelar, I	Escocer II	Hervir, I	Mentar, I
Enmendar, I	Escribir, reg.	Holgar II	Mentir, I
(En)mohecer, III	*Escrito.*	Hollar II	Merecer, III
Enmollecer III	Esforzar, II	Huir, V	Merendar, I
Enmudecer III	Establecer, III	Humedecer, III	Mohecer, III
Ennoblecer, III	*Estar* (see the	Imbuir, V	Moler, II
Ennudecer, III	auxiliary VI	Imprimir, reg.	Morder, II
Enorgullecer- III	verbs),	*Impreso.*	Morir, II
(se),	Estremecer(se), III	Incensar, I	*Muerto.*
Enrarecer. III	Estreñir, IV	Incluir, V	Mostrar, II
Enriquecer, III	Excluir, V	*Incluso* and In-	Mover, II
Enrobustecer, III	*Excluso* and Ex-	cluído.	Nacer, III
Enrodar, II	cluído.	Inducir, III	*Nato* and Nacido.
Enrojecer, III	Expedir, IV	Inferir, I	Negar, I
Enronquecer, III	Extender, I	Infernar, I	Negrecer, III
Enroñecer, III	*Extreso* and Ex-	Ingerir, I	Nevar, I
Enrudecer, III	tendido.	*Ingerto* and In-	Obedecer, III
Enruinecerse, III	Fallecer, III	gerido.	Obscurecer, III
Ensalmorar II	Favorecer, III	Ingerir(se), I	Obstruir, V
Ensandecer III	Ferrar, I	Cl.	Ofrecer, III
Ensangrentar, I	Florecer, III	Inquirir, I	Oír, VI
Ensarnecer, III	Fluir, V	Instituir, V	Oler, II
Ensoberbecer, III	Follar, II	Instruir, V	Oponer, VI
Cl.	Fortalecer, III	Introducir, III	Oscurecer, III
Ensordecer, III	Forzar II	Invernar, I	Pacer, III
Entallecer, III	Fregar I	Invertir, I	Padecer, III
Entender, I	Freír, IV	*Inverso* and In-	Palidecer, III
Entenebrecer, III	*Frito*	vertido.	Parecer(se), III
Enternecer(se), III	Frutecer, III	Investir, IV	Pedir, IV
Enterrar, I	Gemir, IV	Ir, irse, VI	Pensar, I
Entesar, I	Gobernar, I	Jugar, II	Perder, I

Perecer, III
Permanecer, III
Pertenecer, III
Pervertir, I
Pimpollecer, III
Placer (def.), III
Plastecer, III
Plegar, I
Poblar, II
Poder, VI
Podrecer, III
Podrir, VI
Poner, VI
Puesto.
Poseer, IV
Poseso and Po-
seído.
Preferir, I
Prescribir, reg.
Prescripto.
Prevalecer, III
Probar, II
Producir, III
Proferir, I
Proscribir, reg.
Proscripto.
Prostituir, V
Proveer, IV
Provisto and
Proveído.
Quebrar, I
Querer, VI
Raer (def.), VI
Reblandecer, III
Recordar, II
Recostar, II
Recrudecer, III
Reducir, III
Referir, I
Regar, I
Regimentar, I
Regir IV
Regoldar, I
Reír, IV
Rejuvenecer, III
Relentecer, III
Remanecer , III
Remendar, I

Rendir, IV
Renovar, II
Reñir, IV
Repetir, IV
Requebrar, I
Requerir, I
Rescontrar, II
Resollar. II
Resplandecer, III
Restablecer, III
Restituir, V
Restregar, I
Retentar, I
Retoñecer, III
Retribuir, V
Revejecer, III
Reventar, I
Reverdecer, III
Revolcar, II
Robustecer, III
Rodar II
Roer (def.), VI
Rogar, II
Saber, VI
Salir VI
Salpimentar, I
Sarmentar, I
Satisfacer, V
Seducir, V
Segar, I
Seguir, IV
Sembrar, I
Sementar, I
Sentar(se), I
Sentir(se), I
Ser (see aux-
iliary verbs) VI
Serrar, I
Servir(se), IV
Sofreír, V. REIR IV
Sofrito
Solar, II
Soldar, II
Soler (ref.) II
Soltar, II
Suelto and Soltado.
Solver, II
Suelto

Sonar, II
Soñar, II
Sonreír, *V.* REÍR IV
Sosegar, I
Sugerir, I
Tallecer, III
Temblar I
Tender, I
Tener, VI
Tentar, I
Teñir, IV
Tinto and Teñido
Torcer, II
Tuerto and torcido
Tostar, II
Traducir, III
Traer, VI
Trascender, I
Trascordarse, II
Trasegar, I

Travesar, I
Trocar, II
Tronar, II
Tropezar, I
Tumefacerse, VI
Tumefacto.
Valer(se), VI
Venir, VI
Ventar, I
Ver, VI
Visto.
Verdecer, III
Vertir, I
Vestir, IV
Volar, II
Volcar, II
Volver, II
Vuelto.
Yacer, III
Zaherir, Y

THE REFLEXIVE PRONOUNS

Subject After a preposition Reflexive
   yo conmigo me
   tú contigo te
   él consigo se
   ella consigo se
   ello ello se
   nosotros, nosotros, nos
   vosotros, vosotros, os
   ellos, ellas ellos, ellas se

We talk about reflexive pronouns when the action of the verb is referred to the subject. The position of the reflexives is the same as those of the complements.

   * **Me** he comprado un coche.
   * La mujer **se** puso el sombrero.
   * Los niños **se** compraron helados.

Placing of the reflexive pronoun:

a) With the INFINITIVE, the GERUND, and the afirmative IMPERATIVE they always go after and together.

   * Cálla**te** y no hables.
   * Lo mejor es callar**nos**.
   * Estaban bañándo**se** en la playa.

b) With nos and os in the first person and the second person of the imperative plural, the verb loses its final **s** and **d** respectively before the pronouns.

* sentémos - sentémonos.

* sentad - sentaos.

If **me** or **te** come together with **se**, the last is always placed in the first place.

* Se **me** ha caído el libro.

* Se **te** ha roto el vestido.

2. It also expresses an idea of reciprocity:

* Mis padres **se** quieren. (each other)

* Ella y yo **nos** encontramos a la puerta del cine.

* Vosotros **os** odiáis.

3. The impersonal **se**:

* Se han hecho muchas averiguaciones.

* Se obtienen buenos resultados.

b) It is also called " the impersonal voice". **Se** + verb in the 3ª person in singular.

* Se cree que no vendrá.

* Se habla mucho de él.

* Se trabaja poco en esta empresa.

* Se espera que venga pronto.

PRONOUNS AND DEMONSTRATIVE ADJECTIVES

1. The demonstrative adjective accompanies the noun and agrees with the gender and the person (it has not accent).

* **Este** hombre. * **Esa** mujer. * **Esos** niños.

2. The demonstratives point out the relation of proximity between the object which is referred and the different participants of the dialogue.

It can be about the different kinds of proximity.

a) **Este, esta, esto, estos, estas** serve to express the proximity of the object which is referred.

* **Este** vaso que tengo en la mano.

* **Estos** periódicos que estoy leyendo.

b) Ese, esa, eso, esos, esas express a medium grade between proximity and distance according to the person who speaks.

* **Esa** revista que estás leyendo.

* **Esas** casas de enfrente.

c) **Aquel, aquella, aquello, aquellos, aquellas** indicate a certain distance according to the person who speaks.

* **Aquellos** árboles en la colina.

* **Aquellas** casas al otro lado del río.

3. There can be proximity or distance in the time:

* **Aquellas** vacaciones fueron más divertidas que **éstas**.

* **Aquel** año fue más seco que **éste**.

It can also be referred to the order of the sentence.

* Tuvieron dos hijos y una hija: **ésta** se casó, **aquéllos** trabajaron con su padre.

* Tenemos dos perros y un gato. **Éste** es muy independiente, **aquellos** son my cariñosos.

THE RELATIVE PRONOUN

The relative pronoun which:

Is invariable for masculine and feminine, singular and plural. It can be subject and direct complement.

Subject direct complement

Tengo un amigo **que** vive en París **que** no conoces todavía.

Jon tenía una hermana **que** estudiaba **que** tú no conocías.

Tengo un libro **que** es divertido **que** tú no has leído.

Vi una película **que** era aburrida **que** tú no has visto todavía.

Ella rompió un jarrón **que** era carísimo **que** yo todavía no había pagado.

Tengo un primo **que** vive en Nueva York **que** tú no has visto nunca.

The relative pronoun QUIEN/ QUE as circumstantial complement (with preposition).

Persons Things

La chica **con la que** comparto la habitación es estudiante.

con quien

El chico **con el que** salgo es muy simpático.

con quien

La gente **para la que** trabajo es muy honrada.

para quien

El hombre **del que** te hablé está aquí.

de quien

Cosas

El edificio **en el que** vivimos es muy viejo.

La pluma **con la que** te escribo es un regalo tuyo.

La playa **desde la que** te mando la postal es muy bonita.

El examen **para el que** me estoy preparando es muy difícil.

El lugar **en el que** nos encontramos es maravilloso.

The antecedent

The antecedent is the word to which the relative is referred.

It can be:

A substantive:

* Ganó **el atleta que** estaba mejor preparado.

A pronoun:

* ¿ Y te preocupas por **ella, que** tanto daño te ha hecho?

An adjective:

* Es alto como un pino.

An adverb:

* Vete **ahora que** no hay nadie.

A whole sentence:

* **Era muy desdichada**, por lo **que** pensaba suicidarse.

SER

Present

Yo soy

Tú eres

Él /Ella / Usted es

Nos. somos

Vos. sois

Ellos /Ustedes son

a) In Spanish there is an obvious difference between the verbs **ser** and **estar.** Many students of the language find this difference dificult to see.

La mesa **es** redonda.

La habitación **es** grande.

Nuestra casa **es** vieja, pero **es** muy grande.

Estos chicos **son** muy simpáticos.

Mis zapatos **son** negros.

Pedro **es** alto, pero su hermana **es** baja.

If you see all these sentences, all of them show how the objects are. There is a description. A quality is pointed out.

---

b) The verb **ser** shows origin.

- Yo **soy** de España.

- Mi amigo **es** de Suiza.

- Este mármol **es** de Italia.

- Esa porcelana **es** de China.

c) When we talk about time we always use the verb **ser**.

- Hoy **es** lunes, 5 de marzo.

- Todavía **es** verano.

- ¿ Qué hora **es**? **Son** las dos.

- " ¡**Es** muy tarde!" " ¡No, todavía **es** pronto!

d) The verb **ser** always shows possession.

- Ese coche **es** de mi hermano.

- Esa **es** la casa de mi tío.

- Esos **son** los libros de mi amigo.

e) The professions and jobs are used with the verb **ser**.

- Mi padre **es** médico.

- Este hombre **es** carpintero.

- Nosotros **somos** estudiantes.

- Esos hombres **son** jugadores de fútbol.

ESTAR

Present

Yo estoy	Nos. estamos
Tú estás	Vos. estáis
Él / Ella / Usted está	Ellos / Ustedes están

a) Situation and place.

Learn the following sentences:

Madrid **está** en el centro de España.

Los vasos **están** en la mesa.

El árbol **está** en el jardin.

Los niños **están** en el parque.

Tus zapatos **están** debajo de la cama.

All these sentences show a **situation or place** in which something or someone is. All of them answer the question **¿dónde? ¿Dónde está Madrid? ¿Dónde están los vasos? etc**.

---

b) Physical State

The verb **estar** denotes a physical state or a mind state.

Have a look at these examples.

- Mi madre **está** enfadada.

- Mi hermano siempre **está** alegre.

- La habitación **está** desordenada.

- La mesa **está** sucia.

- Pedro **está** enfermo.

- Hoy **estoy** muy nervioso.

All these sentences would answer the question **¿cómo está? ¿cómo se siente?**

c) Tense (estar a, estar en)

We normally use **estar a** with dates and days of the week. **Estar en** is also used with months and seasons.

- Todavía **estamos en** Febrero.

- **Estamos a** 5 de abril de 1999.

- Ya **estamos en** invierno.

- Hoy **estamos a** viernes, 10 de junio.

If the sentence is negative we put the negative but **not** before the verb.

- La taza **no está** en la mesa.

- Burdeos **no está** en España.

If the sentence is interrogative the order is changed subject-verb, verb-subject.

- Juanita está en el parque. - ¿Está Juanita en el parque?

THE ADJECTIVE

a) In Spanish the adjective is changeable; it agrees in gender and number with the noun.

- mesa **blanca.** - muro **pequeño.**

- puerta **pequeña.** - pasillo **largo.**

The adjective is normally placed after the substantive to which qualifies. It is called then qualifying adjective and it is used to describe the substantive.

- Es un hombre **alto.** - Es una mujer **alta.**

- Son unos hombres **altos.** - Son unas mujeres **altas.**

- Es un chico **listo.** - Es una chica **lista.**

b) However, the adjectives which don´t describe but limit they are normally placed **before** the substantive. This category includes the ordinal numbers (once jugadores), quantity adjectives such as mucho, poco, demasiado, tanto, varios, cuanto, cada, demás, otro, tal; and the demonstrative and possessive adjectives.

- Esto es **demasiado** caro.

- Eso es **poco** educativo.

- Dame **otro** helado.

- **Cada** persona es un mundo.

c) The **predicative** adjectives change the substantive in an indirect way, so they go together by means of a verb.

- La casa es **grande.** - Ese libro parece **interesante.**

- Esos chicos son **listos.** - Esas chicas son **altas.**

d) A few adjectives don´t change the gender, but they change the number.

- Ese chico es **inteligente.** - Esa chica es **inteligente.**

- Un hombre **hipócrita.** - Una mujer **hipócrita.**

- Esos chicos son **inteligentes.**

- Esos hombres son **hipócritas.**

Other similar adjectives are: grande, indígena, cosmopolita, probable, independiente, árabe, veloz, verde, azul, gris, peor, fenomenal, espectacular, etc.

To know if they are masculine or singular we must refer to the noun or to the article which goes with it.

- Un caballo veloz. - Una yegua veloz.

- Un lío fenomenal. - Una actuación fenomenal.

- El cielo gris. - La nube gris.

e) The following adjectives normally go before the noun: bueno, malo, joven, viejo, pequeño, hermoso, although this not a fixed rule. In general, if the adjective goes before the substantive, the emphasis goes in the substantive.

Some adjectives, when they go before, they apocopate in the singular masculine, it gets shorter (bueno - buen; malo - mal; alguno - algún; ninguno - ningún; primero - primer; tercero - tercer; cualquiera - cualquier).

- Un buen **libro.** - Una buena **revista.**

If the adjective is placed after the substantive is given more emphasis to the adjective.

- Un comienzo **bueno.** - Un libro **malo.**

Generally we give more emphasis with the word **muy**.

- Es un libro **muy bueno.** - Es una revista **muy mala.**

A Key to the Pronunciation as Represented in This Dictionary.

SPANISH ALPHABET.

Give to the vowel the sound that the syllable that follow it in *italics* has in English; and sound also, as in English, each of the syllables that represent said sound throughout all the dictionary.

VOWELS.

Pronounce a, *ah;* e, *ay;* i, *ee;* o, *oh,* u, *u* (in *bull*); y, *ee.*

The vowels have invariably the same sound, and must be fully and distinctly pronounced. The *u* is silent in the syllables *gue, gui, que, qui,* which are pronounced *gay, gee, kay, kee:* when the *u* is to be sounded, it is marked thus, *ü,* as in *argüir* (ar-goo-eer).

CONSONANTS.

b, bay,	f, *ai´fay,*	l, *ai´lay,*	ñ, *ai´nyay,*	s, *es´say,*	y griega *or* ye, *jay,*
c, *thay,*	g, *hay,* ll,	*ai´lyay,*	p, *pay,*	t, *tay,*	z, *thai tah.*
ch, *tchay,*	h, *ah´tchay,*	m, *ai´may,*	q, *coo,*	v, *vay,*	
d, *day,*	j, *hoe´tah,*	n, *ai´nay,*	r, *eráy, er´ray,*	x, *ay´kiss,*	

N. B. The *z* and the *c* (when the latter precedes *e* and *i*) are marked in this Dictionary to be pronounced as the English *th* in *thought,* which is the Castilian pronunciation. However, throughout Latin America they have the regular sound of *s.*

EXPLANATION OF THE ABBREVIATIONS.

a. .... article.
Acad. .... Academy.
adv. .... adverb.
Aer. .... Aerial.
Agr. .... Agriculture.
Am. .... Ante Meridian.
Amer. .... America.
Anat. .... Anatomy.
And. .... Andes.
Andal. .... Andalucía.
Ant. .... Antique.
Arab. .... Arab.
Arch. .... Architecture.
Argen. .... Argentina.
Arith. .... Arithmetic.
Art. .... Art.
Astro. .... Astronomy.
Aug. .... August.
aug. .... augmentative.
Aut. .... Automate.
Biol. .... Biology.
Bol. .... Bolivia.
Bot. .... Botany.
Calif. .... California.
CAm. .... Central America.
Carib. .... Caribbean.
Cf. .... Confer.
Col. .... Colombia.
Coll. .... Colloquial.
Com. .... Commerce.
Comput. .... Computer.
conj. .... conjunction
Culin. .... Culinary.
Chem. .... Chemistry.
defect. .... defective.

Dim. .... Diminutive.
Divin. .... Divinity.
Ec. .... Ecuador.
Elec. .... Electricity.
Ent. .... Entomology.
Esp. .... Especially
etc. .... etcetera.
f. .... feminine.
Fig. .... Figurative.
Geog. .... Geography.
Geol. .... Geology.
Geom. .... Geometry.
gr. .... gram.
Gram. .... Grammar.
Her. .... Heraldy.
imp. .... imperfect; imperative
impers. .... impersonal.
Inc. .... Inclusive.
int. .... interrogative.
Ir. ....Ireland.
irr. .... irregular.
LAm. .... Latin America.
Lat. .... Latin.
Log. .... Logarithm.
lux. .... luxury.
m. .... masculine.
Math. .... Mathematics.
Mech. .... Mechanic.
Med. .... Medical.
Met. .... Metaphorical.
Mex. .... Mexico.
Mil. .... Military.
Min. .... Minerology.
Miner. .... Mineral.
Mus. .... Music.

Myth. .... Mythology.
n. .... neuter.
Naut. .... Nautical.
Neol. .... Neologism.
Obs. .... Obsolete.
Opt. .... Optics.
Orn. .... Ormithology.
pa. .... present participle.
Per. .... Persia.
Phil. .... Philosophy.
Phy. .... Physics.
pl. .... plural.
Poet. .... Poetry.
Pol. .... Poland.
poss. .... possessive.
pp. .... past participle.
prep. .... preposition.
Print. .... Printing.
pron. .... pronoun.
Prov. .... Province; Provincial.
Rhet. .... Rhetoric.
sing. .... singular.
sup. .... superlative.
Surg. .... Surgery.
Theol. .... Theology.
Typ. .... Typography.
Univ. .... Universe.
V. .... Verbe.
va. .... verb active (transitive).
Vet. .... Veterinary.
vn. .... verb neuter.
vr. .... verb reflexive.
Vulg. .... Vulgarism.
Zool. .... Zoology.

A

a [ah], First letter of the Spanish alphabet. It is pronounced as the **a** in **alarm**.

a, *prep.* **to, in, at,** according to, on, by, for, and of; as **voy a Madrid,** I am going to Madrid. **A la inglesa,** the English way. **A oriente,** to the east. **Jugar a los naipes,** to play cards. **A las ocho,** at eight o'clock. **Vino a pie,** he came on foot. **Quien a hierro mata a hierro muere,** he who lives by the sword, dies by the sword. **Dos a dos,** two by two. **¿A cómo sale el kilo? A diez pesos,** how much a kilo? Ten pesos. **Este vaso huele a vino,** this glass smells of wine. *V.* REAL. -A coalesces with the masculine article **el,** forming **al: Al rey,** to the king. **Al papa,** to the pope. This masculine article is also used before the infinitive form of verbs taken substantively: **Al amanecer,** at the break of day. **Al ir yo allá,** when I was going there. -A is equivalent to the limit or end of any place or time. **Pagaré a su debido tiempo,** I will pay in due course. **Desde aquí a San Juan,** from here to St. John. **Me llegaba el agua a la cintura,** the water was up to my waist. -A sometimes signifies the motive or reason: **A instancia de la ciudad,** at the request of the city. **¿A qué propósito?,** to what purpose? -It also serves to express distributive numbers: **A perdiz por barba,** a partridge a head. -Before the infinitive form, and at the beginning of a sentence, it sometimes has a conditional sense: **A decir verdad,** to tell the truth. -This preposition governs almost all parts of speech, whether nouns, adjectives, pronouns, or verbs: **A los hombres,** to men. **De mal en peor,** from bad to worse. **A mí, a ti, a vosotros,** to me, to you. **A jugar,** to play. **Vamos a pasear,** let's go for a walk. -It points out the person in whom the action of the verb terminates, and then is placed before the accusative or objective case, as **Amo a Pedro,** I love Peter. -A is still used in some phrases instead of **por, en, sin, para,** and **la;** and in obsolete writings for **con** and **de.** -In composition it serves to convert substantives and adjectives into verbs, as **abocar** from **boca, ablandar** from **blando.** Formerly it was prefixed to many words, as **abajar, amatar, etc.;** but being redundant, these words are now written **bajar, matar, etc.** -A is frequently used adverbially, as **A deshora,** unseasonably. **A diferencia de esto,** contrary to this. **A consecuencia de eso,** in consequence to that. **A decir verdad,** to tell the truth. **Al menos,** at least. **A sabiendas,** knowingly. **A veces,** sometimes. **A ojos vistas,** plainly, publicly; barefacedly. **A cuestas,** on the shoulders. **A escondidas,** privately, in a secret manner. **A prueba de bomba,** bomb-proof. -A denotes the number, price, rate, manner of action, instrument, height, depth, etc., as, **El gasto asciende a cien pesos,** the expense amounts to a hundred pesos. **Se hizo el seguro a tres por ciento,** the insurance was taken out at three per cent. **El azúcar se vende a tres pesos la libra,** sugar is sold at three pesos a pound. **Él se viste a la española,** he dresses after the Spanish fashion. **Pasaron el río con el agua a la cintura,** they crossed the river up to their waists in water. **No le llega el vestido a la rodilla,** her dress does not reach her knees. **A fe de hombre de bien,** on the faith of an honest man.

AA [ah-ah], contraction for *Aerolíneas Argentinas.*

aba [ah'-bah], *m.* 1. A woollen fabric, manufactured in the East. 2. Patriarch of Alexandria in older times.

ababa [ah-bah'-bah], *f.* Red poppy. *V.* AMAPOLA.

abacá [ah-bah-cah'], *m.* Abaca, Manila, hemp, inner fiber of a plant of the banana family, a native of the Philippine Islands.

abacería [ah-bah-thay-ree'-ah], *f.* A shop where oil, vinegar, etc., are sold. Grocery.

abacero, ra [ah-bah-thay'-ro, rah], *m. & f.* A retailer of provisions, oil, vinegar, etc. Grocer.

abacial [ah-bah-the-ahl'], *a.* Belonging to an abbot.

abaco [ah'-bah-co], *m.* 1. *(Arch.)* Abacus, highest moulding on the capital of a column. 2. Abacus, a calculating frame. 3. *(Miner.)* A washing-trough.

abad [ah-bahd'], *m.* 1. An abbot. 2. In some provinces the rector of a parish. Abbot having almost episcopal jurisdiction.

abada [ah-bah'-dah], *f.* The female rhinoceros.

abadejo [ah-bah-day'-ho], *m.* 1. A codfish, pollack, cod (bacalao). 2. Yellow crested wren (ave). 3. *(Ant.)* Spanish fly, cantharides (insecto).

abandengo, ga [ah-bah-den'-go, gah], *a.* Abbatial, belonging to an abbot. 2. *m.* Abbacy

abadesa [ah-bah-day'-sah], *f.* An abbess.

abadía [ah-bah-dee'-ah], *f.* 1. An abbey (convento). 2. Abbacy (rango). 3. Parsonage, vicarage (vicaría).

abadiado [ah-bah-de-ah'-do], *m. (Obs.)* Abbey-lands.

abadir [ah-bah-deer'], *m.* A stone from which ancient man made idols, and to which they attributed marvelous virtues.

abajadero [ah-bah-hah-de rho'], *m.* 1. Slope, incline.

abajamiento [ah-bah-hah-me-en'-to], *m. (Obs.)* 1. Dejection, casting down. 2. Abatement.

abajarse [ah-bah-har'-say], *vr.* To abase oneself, to be humbled.

abajeño, ña [ah-bah-hay'-nyo, nyah], *a. (Amer.)* A lowlander, coastal dweller. *(Mex.)* (costeño).

abajero [ah-bah-hay'ro], *m.* Cliff, precipice.

abajo [ah-bah'-ho], *adv.* Under, underneath, below. **Venirse abajo,** to fall, to tumble downstairs, (en casa). **¡Abajo el gobierno!,** down with the government! **Aquí abajo,** down here. **Cuesta abajo,** downhill. **Desde abajo,** from below. **El abajo firmante,** the undersigned. **Más abajo,** further down. **Río abajo,** downstream. - *prep.* below, under.

abalado, da [ah-bah-lah'-do, dah], *a. (Obs.)* Spongy, soft.

abalanzar [ah-bah-lan-thar'], *va.* 1. To balance. 2. To weigh, to compare. 3. To dart, to impel. *-vr.* 1. To rush on with impetuosity. **Se abalanzaron sobre el enemigo,** they rushed at the enemy 2. To venture. 3. To swoop. **El águila se abalanzó sobre el conejo,** the eagle swooped on the rabbit.

abalaustrado, da [ah-bah-lah-oos-trah'-do, dah], *a.* Balustered. *V.* BALAUSTRADO

abaldonar [ah-bal-d-nar'], *va. (Obs.)* 1. To debase, to revile, to undervalue, to reproach. 2 To abandon.

abalear [ah-bah-lay-ar'], *va.* To fan or winnow corn.

abalizar [ah-bah-le-thar'], *va. (Naut.)* To lay down buoys.

aballar [ah-bal-lvar'], *va, (Obs,)* 1. To strike down. 2. To carry off. 3. To move. 4. *(Ict.) V.* REBAJAR

aballestar [ah-bah-lyes-tar'], *m.* 1. A standard-bearer.

abalone [ah-bah-lo'-nay] *m.* A large Californian mollusk.

abalorio [ah-bah-lo'-re-o], *m. pl.* Bugle, glass bead. **No vale un abalorio,** it's worthless.

abaluartar [ah-bah-loo-ahr-tahr'] *va.* To fortify with bastions.

abanderado [ah-bahn-day-rah'-do] *m. (Mil.)* Standard-bearer. *(fig.)* Champion (defensor de una causa)

abanderizador, ra [ah-ban-day-re-thah- dor', rah], *m. & f.* A factious person; a ringleader, agitator.

abanderizar [ah-ban-day-re-thar'], *va.* To cabal; to stir up disturbances, to incite to revolution.

abandonado, da [ah-ban-do-nah'-do, dah], *a.* 1. Abandoned, helpless, forlorn; despondent. 2. Abandoned, profligate, graceless. *-pp.* of ABANDONAR.

abandonamiento [ah-ban-do-nah-me- en'-to], *m.* 1. The act of abandoning. 2. Lewdness, debauchery. 3. Forlornness.

abandonar [ah-ban-do-nar'], *va.* 1. To abandon, to leave, to desert, to fling up. **Abandonar la casa de los padres,** to leave home. **Abandonar a los hijos,** to abandon one's children. To forego, to fall from; to fail. 2. To give away, to relinquish. *-vr.* To despond, to despair; to flinch; to give oneself up to. **Abandonarse a la tentación,** to give way to temptation. **Abandonarse al alcohol,** to give oneself over to alcohol.

abandonismo [ah-ban-do-nes-mo] Defeatism.

abandono [ah-ban-do'-no], *m. V.* ABANDONAMIENTO. Abandon.

abanicar [ah-bah-ne-car'], *va.* To fan. *vr.* To fan oneself.

abanico [ah-bah-nee'-co], *m.* 1. A fan. 2. A spritsail. **En abanico,** fan-shaped, like a fan. 3. *(Mil.)* Defensive parapet of wood. 4. *(Naut.)* Derrick, sheers, a machine used for setting up and taking out masts; crane, outrigger, spritsail. 5. *(Phot.)* Screen. 6. *(Arch.)* Winding stairs; semicircular window. 7. *(Miner.)* Ventilator.

abaniquear [ah-bah-ne-kay-ahr] *va.* To fan (dar aire). *-vr.* To fan oneself (darse aire).

abaniquero [ah-bah-ne-kay'-ro], *m.* A fan-maker.

abanto [ah-bahn'-to], *m.* A bird of the vulture species.

abaratar [ah-bah-rah-tar'], *va.* To cheapen, to abate. *-vn.* To fall in price.

abarbetar [ah-bar-bay-tar'], *va. (Naut.)* To rack, to seize; to span, to lash, to jam, to mouse.

abarca [ah-bar'-cah], *f.* Sandal (worn by peasants).

abarcado, da [ah-bar-cah'-do, dah], *a.* Wearing peasant sandals on the feet. *-pp.* of ABARCAR. Embraced, contained.

abarcador, ra [ah-bar-cah-dor', rah], *m. & f.* 1. Embracer, clasper. 2. Monopolist.

abarcar [ah-bar-car'], *va.* 1. To clasp, to embrace, to take in (incluir). 2. To contain, to comprise (contener); to undertake many things at once. 3. To expand (extenderse a). 4. To monopolize goods, to corner (the market in), (monopolizar). **Este capítulo abarca un siglo,** this chapter covers one century. **Quien mucho abarca poco aprieta,** to bite off more than you can chew.

abarquillar [ah-bar-keel-lyar'], *va.* 1. To give a thing the form of a boat, also of a tube. 2. To warp. *vr.* To curl up, to roll up, (arrollarse).

abarrado, da [ah-bar-rah'-do, dah], *a. (Obs.)* Striped, clouded. *V.* BARRADO.

abarraganamiento [ah-bar-rah-gah-nah -me-en'-to]. *m. V.* AMANCEBAMIENTO.

abarraganarse [ah-bar-rah-gah-nar'-say], *vr.* To live in concubinage.

abarrajado, da [ah-bar-rah-hah'-do, dah], *a. (Amer.)* Libertine.

abarrajar [ah-bah-rrah-har], *vn.* To run away, to flee. 1. *-vr.* To fall flat on one's face. 2. To prostitute, to become corrupt (prostituirse).

abarrajo [ah-bah-rrah-ho] *m.* fall, stumble.

abarrancadero [ah-bar-ran-cah-day'-ro], *m.* 1. A deep, heavy road. 2. A precipice, rocky ledge. 3. *(Met.)* Difficult business.

abarrancamiento [ah-bar-ran-cah-me -en'-to], *m.* Act of making or falling into holes or pits; embarrassment.

abarrancar [ah-bar-ran-car'], *va.* To break up a road; to dig holes. *-vr.* 1. To fall into a pit. 2. To become embarrassed. 3. To get stopped up (atascarse).

abarrar [ah-bar-rar'], *va. (Obs.) V.* ACIBARRAR.

abarrisco [ah-bar-rees'-co], *adv. (Obs.)* Indiscriminately, promiscuously.

abarrotar [ah-bar-rotar'], *va.* 1. To put bars on (barrotes). 2. *(Naut.)* To stow the cargo (la carga). 3. To overstock, to cram, to overload (atestar). *(LAm.)* To buy up (acaparar). 4. To be over-plentiful (superabundar).

abarrote [ah-bar-ro'-tay], *m. (Naut.)* Fill-in package. *-pl. (Amer.)* 1. Groceries, provisions (artículos). 2. Grocery store (tienda). 3. Ironmongery (ferretería).

abarrotería [ah-bar-ro-tay-ree'-ah], *f. (Amer.)* Grocery store, general store.

abarrotero, ra [ah-bar-ro-tay'-ro, rah] *m. & f. (Amer.)* Grocer.

abastardarse [ah-bas-tar-dar'-say], *vr.* To degenerate, to vitiate.

abastecedor, ra [ah-bas-tay-thay-dor', rah], *m. & f.* A caterer, provider, purveyor, supplier. *(Amer.)* Butcher (carnicero). *a.* Providing, supplying.

abastecer [ah-bas-tay-therr'], *va.* 1. To provide necessities, to purvey. 2. To supply; **Abastecer un ejército de víveres,** to supply an army with provisions. (*Yo abastezco, abastezca,* from *Abastecer. V.* verbs in *ecer.*)

abastecido, da [ah-bas-tay-the'-do, dah] Supplied, provisioned. **Una ciudad bien abastecida,** a well-stocked city. 2. Stocked; **Un supermercado bien abastecido,** a well-stocked supermarket.

abastecimiento [ah-bas-tay-the-me-en'- to], *m.* 1. Provisioning, supplying (avituallamiento), the act and the effect of providing. 2. Provisions. 3. Supply; **abastecimiento de aguas,** the supply of water.

abastionar [ah-bas-te-o-nar'], *va.* To bastion, to construct bastions.

abasto [ah-bas'-to], *m.* 1. Provisioning, supplying (abastecimiento), the supply of a town with provisions, grist. 2. Abundance, great amount. Small embroideries. *(Amer.)* Slaughterhouse, abattoir. 3. *adv.* Copiously, abundantly.

abatanado, da [ah-bah-tah-nah'-do, dah] *a.* Fulled (paño).

abatanador [ah-bah-tah-nah-dor] *m.* Fuller.

abatanar [ah-bah-tah-nar'], *va.* To beat or full (el paño). 2. *(fig.)* To beat (golpear).

abatatar [ah-bah-tah-tahr] *va. (Amer.) (fam.)* To intimidate, to frighten (asustar).

abate [ah-bah'-tay], *m. (Rel.)* Father. **El abate Pierre,** Father Pierre.

abatí [ah-bah-te] *(Amer.)* Corn; drink distilled from corn (bebida).

abatidamente [ah-bah-tee-dah-men'-tay], *adv.* Dejectedly, heavily; basely.

abatidísimo [ah-bah-te-dee'-se-mo], *a.* sup. Very low-spirited, very dejected.

abatido, da [ah-bah-tee'-do, dah], *a.* 1. Downcast, dejected, spiritless, flat, low, faint, disheartened (desanimado). **Estaba muy abatido por la muerte de su esposa,** he was very depressed by the death of his wife. 2. Abject, mean, base. 3. Drooping. **Párpados abatidos,** drooping eyelids. *-pp.* of ABATIR.

abatimiento [ah-bah-te-me-en'-to], *m.* 1. Discouragement, lowness of spirits, heaviness, faintness, flatness. 2. Humbleness, obscure condition. Abatimiento del rumbo, *(Naut.)* The leeway of a ship.

abatir [ah-bah-teer'], *va.* 1. To throw down, to overthrow, to cut down, to flatten, to fall, to demolish (destruir). **Abatir un edificio,** demolish a building; to fell, to cut down (árbol). **Abatí la tienda de campaña,** I took down the tent; to bring down, to shoot down (pájaro, avión). 2. To humble, to debase, to overwhelm, to lower, to discourage. 3. *(Mech.)* To depress, lower. *-vn.* To descend, to stoop. *-vr.* 1. To be disheartened, to be dismayed; to crouch. 2. *(Naut.)* To have leeway.

abayado [ah-bah-ya-do, da] *a. (Bot.)* Berry-shaped.

abdicación [ab-de-cah-the-on'], *f.* Abdication.

abdicar [ab-de-car'], *va.* 1. To abdicate. **Abdicar de algo,** to renounce something. **Abdicar en uno,** to abdicate in favor of somebody. 2. To revoke, to annul. **Abdicar la corona,** give up the crown.

abdomen [ab-doh'-men], *m.* Abdomen, belly.

abdominal [ab-doh-me-nahl'], *a.* Abdominal.

abducción [ab-dooc-the-on'], *f. (Anat.)* Abduction.

abductor [ab-dooc-tor'], *m. (Anat.)* Abductor, the muscles which draw back several members.

abecé [ah-bay-thay'], *m.* The alphabet. *(fig.)* Rudiments, basic elements.

abecedario [ah-bay-thay-dah'-re-o], *m.* 1. The alphabet. 2. A spelling-book. 3. A table of contents.

abedul [ah-bay-dool'], *m.* The common birch-tree. **Abedul plateado,** silver birch.

abeja [ah-bay'-hah], *f.* A bee. **Abeja reina,** queen-bee. **Abeja machiega,** breeding-bee. **Abeja albañila,** mason-bee. **Abeja obrera,** worker-bee. *(fig.)* Hard worker (hormiguita).

abejar [ah-bay-har'], *m.* A bee-hive. *V.* COLMENAR.

abejar [ah-bay-har'], *m.* **Uva abejar**, a grape of which bees are very fond.

abejarrón, abejorro [ah-bay-har-rone', or ah-bay-hor'-ro], *m.* 1. Bumblebee. *(Acad.)* 2. A large fly.

abejaruco, abejeruco [ah-bay-ha-roo'-co], [ah-bay-hay-roo'-co], *m.* 1. The bee-eater, a bird. 2. *(Met.)* A mean, despicable fellow.

abejera [ah-bay-hay'-rah], *f.* Apiary (colmenar).

abejero [ah-bay-hay'-ro], *m.* 1. A keeper of bee-hives. 2. V. ABEJARUCO.

abejica, illa, ita, juela [ah-bay-hee'-cah] *f. dim.* A little bee.

abejón [ah-bay-hone'], *m.* 1. A drone; a hornet; bumble-bee. **Jugar al abejón con uno**, *(coll.)* to make light of one, to mock him. 2. A rustic game of buzzing in and striking the ear. *(CAm.)* to whisper (cuchichear).

abejonazo [ah-bay-ho-nah'-tho], *m.* A large wild bee.

abejoncillo [ah-bay-hon-theel'-lyoh], *m. dim.* A small wild bee, a small drone.

abejonear [ah-bay-ho-nay-ahr'], *(And., Carib.)* 1. *vr.* *(fig.)* To whisper. 2. *va. (Carib.)* To mumble, to whisper (susurrar).

abejorro [ah-bay-hor'ro], *m.* V. ABEJARRÓN.

abejuno, na [ah-bay-hoo'-no, nah], *a.* Belonging to bees; bee.

abellacado, da [ah-bel-lyah-cah'-do, dah], *a.* Mean-spirited, accustomed to meanness. *-pp.* of ABELLACARSE.

abellacarse [ah-bel-lyah-car'say], *vr.* To become mean; to degrade oneself.

abellar [ah-bel-lyar'], *m.* V. ABEJAR

abellotado [ah-bel-lyo-tah'-do], *a.* Made in the form of acorns.

abenuz [ah-bay-nooth'], *m. (Obs.)* The ebony-tree. V. ÉBANO.

aberengenado, da [ah-bay-ren-hay-nah' -do, dah], *a.* 1. Having the color or form of an eggplant, lilac. 2. Cut slantwise (carpintería).

aberración [ah-ber-rah-the-on'], *f.* 1. *(Astr.)* Aberration. **Es una aberración bañarse cinco veces al día**, it´s crazy to have a bath five times a day. 2. *(Med.)* Hallucination, aberration. 3. *(Opt.)* Aberration, divergence of light-rays.

aberrante [ah-bay-rrahn-tay], *a.* Aberrant; (disparatado) crazy, ridiculous.

aberrar [ah-bay-rrahr], *vn.* To be mistaken, to err.

aberrear [ah-bay-rrahr], *vn.* To anger, to annoy.

aberrugado, da [ah-ber-roo-gah'-do, dah], *a.* Full of warts, warty.

abertura [ah-ber-too'-rah], *f.* 1. Aperture. 2. Outset, beginning. 3. An opening, chink, crevice, fissure, gap, loophole, a hole, a passage: *(Opt.)* stop. 4. Openness of mind; plain dealing. 5. A leak. 6. *(Mus.)* Overture.

abestiar [ah-bes-te-ar'], *va.* To stupefy.

abetal [ah-bay-tahl'], *m.* A spot covered with silver firs, fir wood.

abete [ah-bay'-tay], *m.* Hook for holding cloth while shearing it. V. ABETO.

abeterno [ab-ay-ter'-no] From all eternity.

abetinote, or **abietino** [ah-bay-te-no'-tay, ah-be-ay-te'-no], *m.* Resin which distills from the fir-tree. V. ACEITE.

abeto [ah-bay'-to], *m.* Fir, fir tree; the yew-leave fir. **Abeto blanco**, silver fir.

abetunado, da [ah-bay-too-nah'-do, dah], *a.* Resembling bitumen, bituminous; dark skinned (persona).

abetunar [ah-bay-too-nar'], *va.* To bituminize; to do over with bitumen. To polish, to clean.

abiertamente [ah-be-er-tah-men'-tay], *adv.* Frankly, openly, fairly, plainly.

abierto, ta [ah-be-er'-to, tah], *a.* 1. Open, free, clear. 2. Sincere, candid, open-hearted, generous. 3. Full-blown. *-pp. irr.* of ABRIR. **La puerta está abierta**, the door is open. **Abierta de par en par**, wide open. **Dejar un grifo abierto**, to leave a tap running.

abigarrado, da [ah-be-gar-rah'-do, dah], *a.* Variegated, motley, of many colors, vivid, colorful. *-pp.* of ABIGARRAR.

abigarrar [ah-be-gar-rar'], *va.* To paint with a diversity of colors, without order or union; to fleck.

abigarramiento [ah-be-gah-rrah-me- ayn'-to], *m.* Variegation; many colors; motley coloring, vividness, colorfulness.

abigeato [ah-be-hay-ah'-to], *m. (Law.)* Theft of cattle. Rustling.

abigeo [ah-be-hay'-go], *m. (Law.)* A thief of cattle, rustler.

abigotado, da [ah-be-go-tah'-do, dah], *a.* A person wearing long mustaches.

abihares [ah-be-ah'-res], *m.* 1. Narcissus or daffodil. 2. A Precious stone of the color of the daffodil.

abiltar [a-beel-tar'], *vn.* To depress, to humiliate, to depreciate.

abinicio [ab-e-nee'-the-o] From the beginning.

abintestato [ab-in-tes-tah'-to], *m.* Process of a judge in cases where there is no will.

abiosa [ah-be-oh'-sah], *f.* The boa snake. The boa constrictor.

abiselar [ah-be-say-lar'], *va.* To bevel.

abisinio, a [ah-be-see'-ne-o, ah], *a.* Abyssinian.

abismado, da [ah-bis-mah'-do, dah], *a.* 1. Cast down, dejected, depressed. 2. Absorbed in profound meditation.

abismal [ah-bis-mahl'], *a.* Belonging to an abyss.

abismal [ah-bis-mahl'], *m.* Clasp nail, shingle nail.

abismar [ah-bis-mar'], *va.* To depress, to humble, to destroy. **Abismar a uno en la tristeza**, to plunge somebody into sadness. *-vr.* To be astonished, to be shocked or astounded.

abismo [ah-bees'-mo], *m.* 1. Abyss; gulf. 2. That which is immense, or incomprehensible. 3. Hell. **Desde los abismos de la Edad Media**, from the dark depths of the Middle Ages. **Estar al borde del abismo**, to be on the brink of ruin.

abitadura [ah-be-ta-doo'-rah], *f. (Naut.)* A turn of the cable around the bitts.

abitaque [ah-be-tah'-kay], *m.* A rafter or joist, the fourth part of a girder.

abitar [ah-be-tar'], *va.* To bitt (barcos).

abitas [ah-bee'-tas], *m. pl. (Naut.)* Bitts. **Abitas del molinete**, Carrickbitts.

abitones [ah-be-to-nes], *m. pl.* Topsail sheet, bitts.

abizcochado, da [ah-beth-co-chah'-do, dah], *a.* In the form of a biscuit. Spongy.

abjuración [ab-hoo-rah-the-on'], *f.* Abjuration, recantation.

abjurar [ab-hoo-rar'], *va.* To abjure, to recant upon oath. 2. *vn.* **Adjurar de**, to adjure.

ablación [ah-blah-the-on'], *f.* The removal of an organ or portion of the body by surgical means; ablation.

ablandador [ah-blahn-dah-dor'], *m.* **Ablandador de agua**, water-softener. Mollifier.

ablandabrevas [ah-blan-dah-bray-bahs], *m. & f.* A useless person, good-for-nothing.

ablandamiento [ah-blan-dah-me-en'-to], *m.* Softening.

ablandar [ah-blan-dar'], *va. & n.* 1. To soften, to mellow, to relent. 2. To loosen. 3. To assuage, to mitigate, to melt, to soothe. 4. To grow mild or temperate; to give. *-vr.* To soften, to soften up, to get soft (persona); to become less severe (frío).

ablande [ah-blan-day], *m. (LAm.)* Running-in.

ablano [ah-blah'-no], *m. (Prov. Ast.)* The hazel-tree.

ablativo [ah-blah-tee'-voh], *m.* Ablative. **Ablativo absoluto**, ablative absolute.

ablución [ah-bloo-the-on'], *f.* Ablution, (lavatorio).

abnegación [ab-nay-gah-the-on'], *f.* Abnegation, self-denial.

abnegadamente [ab-nay-gah-dah-men'- tay], *adv.* With abnegation.

abnegado [ab-nay-gah-do], *a.* Self-denying, self-sacrificing; unselfish.

abnegar [ab-nay-gar'], *va.* To renounce, to deny oneself anything. (*Yo abniego, abniegue,* from *Abnegar.* V. ACRECENTAR). -*vr.* To deny oneself, to go without, to act unselfishly.

abobado, da [ah-bo-bah'-do, dah], *a.* Stultified, simple, silly. **Mirar abobado,** to look bewildered. -*pp.* of ABOBAR.

abobamiento [ah-bo-bah-me-en'-to], *m.* Stupefaction, stupidity.

abobar [ah-bo-bar'], *va.* 1. To stupefy. 2. V. EMBOBAR. -*vr.* To grow stupid.

abocado [ah-bo-cah'-do], *a.* Mild, agreeable (vino). -*pp.* of ABOCAR.

abocamiento [ah-bo-cah-me-en'-to], *m.* A meeting, an interview.

abocar [ah-bo-car'], *va.* To take or catch with the mouth. **Abocar la artillería,** to bring the guns to bear. **Abocar un estrecho,** to enter the mouth of a channel or strait. -*vr.* To meet by agreement.

abocarse [ah-bo-cahr-say], *vr.* To approach (aproximarse). **Abocarse con uno,** to meet somebody, to have an interview with someone.

abocardado, da [ah-bo-car-dah'-do, dah], *a.* Wide-mouthed, like a trumpet.

abocardar [ah-bo-car-dar'], *va.* To countersink, to widen the mouth.

abocardo [ah-bo-car'-do], *m. (Miner.)* Countersinking drill.

abocastro [ah-bo-cahs-tro], *m. (And. Cono Sur)* Ugly devil.

abocetar [ah-bo-thay-tahr], *va.* Sketch.

abochornado, da [ah-bo-chor-nah'-do, dah], *a.* Out of countenance, flushed. -*pp.* of ABOCHORNAR. **Quedar abochornado,** to feel mortified.

abochornar [ah-bo-chor-nar'], *va.* 1. To swelter, to overheat. 2. To provoke by abusive language. -*vr.* To blush, to feel mortified.

abochornarse [ah-bo-chor-nahr-say], *vr.* To get flushed, to get overheated. *(Bot.)* to wilt. **Abochornarse de,** to feel ashamed at, to get embarrassed about.

abocinado [ah-bo-the-nah'-do], *a.* Bent: applied to an elliptic arch, the two faces of which are nearly the same. -*pp.* of ABOCINAR.

abocinar [ah-bo-the-nar'], *vn. (Low.)* To fall upon the face. *va.* To raise, to broaden an arch upon one side. *vt.* To shape like a trumpet.

abocinarse [ah-bo-the-nahr-say], *vr.* To fall flat on one's face.

abodocarse [ah-bo-do-cahr-say], *vr. (CAm.)* To go lumpy (líquido); *(Mex.) (Med.)* To break out in boils.

abofado, *a. (Carib. Mex.)* Swollen.

abofarse [ah-bo-fahr-say], *vr. (Mex.)* To stuff oneself (tragar).

abofellar [ah-bo-fel-lyar'], *vn.* To puff, to pant.

abofeteador, ra [ah-bo-fay-tay-ah-dor', rah**],** *m. & f.* One who slaps, one who insults.

abofetear [ah-bo-fay-tay-ar'], *va.* 1. To slap one's face. 2. To insult.

abogacía [ah-bo-gah-thee'-ah]. *f.* Profession of a lawyer or advocate.

abogada [ah-bo-gah'-dah] *f.* 1. Mediatrix. 2. A counsellor's wife.

abogadear [ah-bo-gah-day-ar'], *vn.* To play the advocate: used in contempt.

abogaderas [ah-bo-gah-day-rahs], *f pl.* **Abogaderías.** 1. *(LAm.)* Specious (or false) arguments.

abogadillo [ah-bo-gah-deel'-lyo], *m.* dim. of ABOGADO. Ignorant or poor lawyer.

abogado [ah-bo-gah'-do] *m.* 1. Advocate, counsellor. 2. Mediator. 3. **Abogado criminalista,** criminal lawyer. **Abogado del diablo,** devil's advocate. **Abogado picapleito,** pettifogging lawyer. **Ejercer de abogado,** to practise law, be a lawyer. -*pp.* of ABOGAR.

abogar [ah-bo-gar'], *vn.* 1. To advocate, to plead the cause of another. 2. To intercede on behalf of another. (**Yo abogué,** from **Abogar.** V. verbs. in *gar.*)

abohetado, da [ah-bo-ay-tah'-do, dah], *a.* Inflated, swollen.

abolengo [ah-bo-len'-go], *m.* 1. Ancestry. 2. Inheritance coming from ancestors.

abolición [ah-bo-le-the-on'], *f.* Abolition, abrogation, extinction.

abolicionista [ah-bo-le-the-o-nees'-tah], *m.* Abolitionist.

abolir [ah-bo-leer'], *va.* To abolish, to annul, to revoke, to repeat.

abollado [ah-bol-lyah'-do], *a. & m.* V. ALECHUGADO. -*pp.* of ABOLLAR.

abolladura [ah-bo-lya-doo'-rah], *f.* 1. Inequality. 2. Embossed work, relief. 3. Bruise. 4. Dent.

abollar [ah-bo-lyar'], *va.* 1. To emboss. 2. To annoy with an unpleasant discourse. 3. To stun and confound. 4. To bruise. 5. To dent. *6. (Mex.)* To blunt (filo).

abollarse [ah-bo-lyahr-say], *vr.* To get dented, to get bruised.

abollón [ah-bol-lyon'], *m. (Prov.)* A bud, in particular of the vine.

abollonar [ah-bol-lyo-nar'], *va.* To emboss. -*vn. (Prov.)* To bud, applied in particular to the vine.

abolorio [ah-bo-lo'-re-o], *m.* Ancestry. V. ABOLENGO.

abolsado, da [ah-bol-sah'-do, dah], *a.* Puckered, folded in the form of a purse.

abolsarse [ah-bol-sahr-say], *vr.* To form pockets, to be baggy.

abomaso [ah-bo-mah'-so], *m.* Abomasum, the fourth stomach of ruminating animals.

abombachado [ah-bom-bah-cha-do], *a.* Baggy (pantalón).

abombado [ah-.bom-baha-do], *a. (gen.)* Convex; domed. **Estar abombado** *(LAm. fig.),* to be bewildered (aturdido); to be silly (tonto); to be tight (or tipsy) (borracho). *(LAm.)* rotten (comida); **estar abombado,** to stink, to smell foul.

abombarse [ah-bom-bahr-say], *vr. (LAm.)* To rot, to decompose, to smell bad (pudrirse). To get tight; to get drunk. To go mad, lose one's head (enloquecer). To go soft (in the head) (atontarse).

abominablemente [ah-bo-me-nah-blay -men'-tay], *adv.* Abominably, detestably, execrably.

abominable [ah-bo-me-nah'-blay**],** *a.* Detestable, abominable, execrable, odious, heinous, cursed.

abominación [ah-bo-me-nah-the-on']. *f.* Abomination, detestation, execration, cursedness.

abominar [ah-bo-me-nar'], *va.* To detest, to abhor, to execrate, abominate.

abonable [ah-bo-nah-blay], *a.* Payable (pagadero). *(Agri.)* improvable.

abonado, da [ah-bo-nah'-do, dah], *m. & f.* A subscriber to a telephone company or any other thing. Holder of a season-ticket.

abonado, da [ah-bo-nah'-do, dah], *a.* 1. Creditable, rich. 2. Fit and disposed for anything: commonly understood in an ill sense. 3. Manured land. **Testigo abonado,** an irrefragable witness. -*pp.* of ABONAR.

abonamiento [ah-bo-nah-me-en'-to], *m.* V. ABONO. Bail, security.

abonanzar [ah-bo-nan-thar'], *vn.* To grow calm (tormentas). To clear up (tiempo).

abonar [ah-bo-nar'], *va.* 1. To bail, to insure. 2. To improve or ameliorate. 3. To make good an assertion. 4. To manure lands, to compost. 5. To give one credit; to allow. *(Com.)* To indemnify, to compensate. -*vr.* To subscribe to any work; to buy a season-ticket (for a theater, etc.); to pay in advance for anything. -*vn.* V. ABONANZAR.

abonaré [Ah-bo-na-ray'], *m.* Promissory note: a security for payment of a sum. V. PAGARÉ.

abonero [ah-bo-nay-ro], *m.* Street vendor, door-to-door salesman. *(Mex.)* (vendedor).

abono [ah-bo'-no], *m.* 1. Season ticket. 2. Part payment. **Pagar por abonos**, pay by instalments 3. Dung, manure. **Abono verde**, green manure. 4. Subscription (revista). 5. *(Mex.)* Receipt (recibo).

aboquillado [ah-bo-que-lyah-do], *a.* **Cigarrillo aboquillado**, tipped cigarette, filter-tipped.

abordable [ah-bor-dah'-blay], *a.* Accessible, of easy access, approachable, that can be tackled.

abordador [ah-bor-dah-dor'], *m.* 1. He that boards a ship. 2. An intruder, who accosts a person with an air of impudence.

abordaje [ah-bor-dah'-hay], *m. (Naut.)* Boarding (barco). Accosting, approach (en la calle).

abordar [ah-bor-dar'], *va.* 1. To board a ship, to fall aboard. 2. To run foul of a ship. 3. To put into a port. 4. *va. (Mex.) (Naut.)* To dock.

abordo [ah-bor'-do], *m.* 1. *(Met.)* Address, attack, shock or force in execution. 2. *(Obs.)* V. ABORDAJE.

aborigen [ah-bo-ree'-hen], *a.* Aboriginal, indigenous.

aborígenes [ah-bo-ree'-hay-nes], *m. pl.* Aborigines, the earliest inhabitants of a country.

aborrachado, da [ah-bor-rah-chah'-do, dah], *a.* 1. High-colored. 2. Inflamed, fiery, flushed.

aborrascarse [ah-bor-ras-car'-say], *vr.* To be tempestuous or stormy.

aborrecedor, ra [ah-bor-ray-thay-dor', rah], *m. & f.* A detester, a hater.

aborrecer [ah-bor-ray-therr'], *va.* 1. To hate, to abhor. 2. To relinquish, to desert: in the last sense it is chiefly applied to birds, which desert their eggs or young ones. 3. To spend money.

aborrecible [ah-bor-ray-thee'-blay], *a.* Hateful, detestable, loathsome, cursed, damned, forbidding.

aborreciblemente [ah-bor-ray-thee-blay -men'-tay], *adv.* With abhorrence, hatefully.

aborrecimiento [ah-bor-ray-thee-me -en'-to], *m.* Abhorrence, detestation, dislike, hate, grudge.

aborregado [ah-bo-rray-gah-do], *a.* **Cielo aborregado**, mackerel sky.

aborregarse [ah-bor-ray-gar'-say], *vr.* To be covered with light, fleecy clouds (firmamento).

aborrer, aborrescer [ah-bor-rerr', ah-bor-res-therr'], *va. (Obs.)* V. ABORRRECER. (Aborrezco. V. ABORRECER.)

abortamiento [ah-bor-tah-me-en'-to], *m.* Abortion.

abortar [ah-bor-tar'], *va.* 1. To miscarry. **Hacerse abortar**, to abort. 2. To fail. 3. *(Med.)* To have a miscarriage (por accidente), To abort (con intención). **Hacer abortar a una mujer**, to procure an abortion for a woman.

abortista, [ah-bor-tes-tah] 1. *m. & f.* 1. Abortionist (criminal). 2. (partidario) abortion campaigner, person seeking to legalize abortion. 2. *f.* Woman who has had an abortion.

abortivamente [ah-bor-tee'-vah-men'-tay], *adv.* Abortively, untimely.

abortivo, va [ah-bor-tee'-vo, vah], *a.* Abortive; producing abortion.

aborto [ah-bor'-to], *m.* 1. A miscarriage, abortion. 2. A monster. 3. A failure 4. Ugly man, ugly woman (persona).

abortón [ah-bor-tone'], *m.* 1. The abortion of a quadruped. 2. The skin of a lamb born before its time.

aborujar [ah-bo-roo-har'], *va.* To make parcels. *vr.* To be muffed or wrapped up.

abotagamiento [ah-bo-tah-gah-me-ayn-to], *m.* Swelling.

abotagarse [ah-bo-tah-gar'-say], *vr.* 1. To be swollen, to be inflated. 2. *(Met.)* To grow foolish, or stupid.

abotinado, da [ah-bo-te-nah'-do, dah], *a.* Made in the form of half-gaiters (bluchers), closing at the instep.

abotonador [ah-bo-to-nah-dor'], *m.* An instrument used for buttoning gaiters; button-hook.

abotonar [ah-bo-to-nar'], *va.* 1. To button, to fasten with buttons. 2. *(Naut.)* To lash, to rack, to seize. *-vn.* 1. To bud, to germinate. 2. To form a button: applied to eggs boiled with the white obtruding.

abovedado, da [ah-bo-vay-dah'-do, dah], *a.* Arched, vaulted. *-pp.* of ABOVEDAR.

abovedar [ah-bo-vay-dar'], *va.* To arch, to vault, to shape as a vault.

aboyado, da [ah-bo-yah'-do, dah], *a.* A farm rented, with the necessary stock of oxen for ploughing the ground. *-pp.* of ABOYAR.

aboyar [ah-bo-yar'], *va. (Naut.)* To lay down buoys, mark with buoys. *(Mex.)* To float (flotar).

abozalar [ah-bo-tha-lar'], *va.* To muzzle.

abra [ah'-brah], *f.* 1. Bay, haven; cover or creek. 2. A dale or valley. 3. A fissure in mountains; gorge.

abracadabra [ah-brah-cah-dah-brah], *f* Abracadabra.

abracadabrante [ah-brah-cah-da-brahn-tay], *a.* Spectacular (aparatoso); enchanting (atractivo), captivating; magic-seeming (mágico).

abracar [ah-brah-cahr], *va. (Mex.) V.* ABRAZAR.

abracijo [ah-brah-thee'-ho], *m. (coll.)* An embrace, a hug.

Abraham [ah-brah-ahm], *m.* Abraham.

abrahonar [ah-brah-o-nar'], *va. (coll.)* To hold one fast by the garment.

abrasadamente [ah-brah-sah-dah-men'-tay], *adv.* Ardently, eagerly.

abrasado [ah-brah-sah-do], *a.* Burnt, burnt up. **Estar abrasado**, to burn with shame. **Estar abrasado en cólera**, to be in a raging temper.

abrasador, ra [a-brah-sah-dor', rah], *a.* Very hot, burning, steaming. **Un sol abrasador**, a steaming, burning sun. **Una llama abrasadora**, an ardent flame.

abrasamiento [ah-brah-sah-me-en'-to], *m.* 1. The act of burning. 2. Inflammation. 3. The excess of passion. 4. Flagrancy.

abrasar [ah-brah-sar'], *va.* 1. To burn; to fire; to parch the ground. 2. To dissipate, to squander. 3. To provoke. *-vr.* To be agitated by any violent passion, to glow. **Abrasarse vivo**, to be burnt alive; to feel extremely hot. **Abrasarse en deseos**, to be aflame with desire.

abrasilado, da [ah-brah-se-lah'-do, dah], *a.* Of the color of Brazil-wood.

abrasión [ah-brah-se-on], *f.* Graze, abrasion.

abrasivo [ah-brah-se-vo], 1. *a.* Abrasive. 2. *m.* Abrasive.

abrazadera [ah-brah-thah-day'-rah], *f.* 1. Ferule, clasp. 2. A ring put around a thing as a band. 3. A cleat. 4. A piece of timber which fastens the plough-tail to the plough. 5. (Printing) A brace or bracket {.-*a. V.* SIERRA ABRAZADERA.

abrazador, ra [ah-brah-tha-dor'-rah], *m. & f.* 1. One that embraces.

abrazamiento [ah-brah-thah-me-en'-to], *m.* Embracing.

abrazar [ah-brah-thar'], *va.* 1. To embrace, to hug, to caress; to clasp, to clip, to lock in, to fathom, to compress. 2. To surround. 3. To embrace the opinion of another; to go into. 4. To take one's charge. 5. To comprise.

abrazarse [ah-brah-thahr-say], *vr.* To embrace (each other).

abrazo [ah-brah'-tho], 1. *m.* A hug, an embrace. 2. **Un fuerte abrazo** (cartas), with best wishes, with kind regards, yours.

abreboca [ah-bray-bo-cah] *(LAm.)* 1. *a.* Absent-minded. 2. *m.* Appetizer.

abrecartas [ah-bray-cahr-tahs] *m.* Letter opener, paperknife.

abrego [ah'-bray-go], *m.* A south west wind.

abrelatas [ah-bray-lah'-tahs], *m.* Can opener, tin-opener.

abrepuño [ah-bray-poo'-nyo] *m. (Bot.)* Milk-thistle. *V.* CARDO LECHERO.

abrevadero [ah-bray-vah-day'-ro], *m.* Watering-place for cattle.

abrevado [ah-bray-vah'-do], *a.* Softened in water (pieles). *-pp.* of ABREVAR.

abrevador [ah-bray-vah-dor'], *m.* 1. He who waters cattle. 2. Waterer. 3. Watering-place.

abrevar [ah-bray-var'], *va.* To water cattle, to give a drink to, to irrigate.

abrevarse [ah-bray-bahr-say], *vr.* 1. To drink, to quench its thirst (animal). 2. **Abrevarse en sangre**, to wallow in blood.

abreviación [ah-bray-vee-ah-the-on'], *f.* Abbreviation, abridgment, shortening, reduction.

abreviadamente [ah-bray-vee-ah-dah-men'-tay], *adv.* In few words, concisely.

abreviado [ah-bray-be-ah-do], *a.* Brief, short, shortened (breve). **Abreviador, ra** [ah-bray-vee-ah-dor', rah], *m. & f.* 1. An abridger one who abridges writings.

abreviar [ah-bray-vee-ar'], *va.* To abridge, to cut short.

abreviatura [ah-bray-vee-ah-too'-rah], *f.* 1. Abbreviation, contraction. 2. Shorthand. **En abreviatura**, in an abbreviated form, briefly; expeditiously.

abreviaturía [ah-bray-vee-ah-too-ree'-ah], *f.* Office of abreviator.

abribonarse [ah-bre-bo-nar'-say], *vr.* 1. To grow abject, to degenerate. 2. To act the scoundrel, to stroll about.

abridero [ah-bre-day'-ro] *m.* A sort of peach, which, when ripe, opens easily and drops the stone; freestone.

abridero, ra [ah-bre-day'-ro, rah], *a.* Of an aperitif nature; easily opened; freestone.

abridor [ah-bre-dor¡] *m.* 1. *(Bot.)* Nectarine, a species of the peach-tree. 2. Opener, the person who opens or unlocks. **Abridor de láminas**, an engraver. **Abridor en hueco**, a die or punch sinker. 3. Iron used for opening ruffs or plaits. 4. *(Agri.)* Grafting-knife. 5. **Abridor de guantes**, glove-stretcher. 6. **Abridor de heno**, hay-spreader, tedder. 7. **Abridor de latas**, can-opener.

abrigada [ah-bre-gah-dah], *f* Shelter, windbreak.

abrigadamente [ah-bre-gah-dah-men'-tay], *adv.* Warmly, well protected.

abrigadero [ah-bre-gah-day'-ro], *m.* Sheltered place. **Abrigadero de ladrones**, *(Mex.)* den of thieves.

abrigado [ah-bre-gah'-do], *m. V.* ABRIGADERO. *-pp.* of ABRIGAR.

abrigador [ah-bre-gah-dor], 1. *a. (And. Mex.)* Warm (que abriga). 2. Person who covers up for another.

abrigaña [ah-bre-gah'-nyah], *f. (Hort.)* Canvas screen, awning.

abrigaño [ah-bre-gah'-nyoh], *m.* A shelter for cattle.

abrigar [ah-bre-gar'], *va.* To shelter, to protect, to patronize; to over-shadow, to cover; to warm, to lodge. **Abríguese Vd. con ello**, *(coll.)* defend yourself with it.

abrigarse [ah-bre-gahr-say] *vr.* To take shelter, to cover up. **¡Abrígate bien!**, keep yourself warm!

abrigo [ah-bree'-go], *m.* 1. Coat, overcoat, topcoat, wrap. **Abrigo de pieles**, fur coat. 2. Shelter, protection, cover. 3. *(Naut.)* Harbor, haven.

abril [ah-breel'], *m.* April, the fourth month of the year. **Estar hecho un abril o parecer un abril**, to be young, florid, handsome. **Abril, aguas mil**, april showers bring May flowers. **Abril y Mayo, llaves de todo el año**, on the weather of these two months depends the goodness of the crops.

abrileño [ah-bre-lay-nyoh], *a.* Of Abril.

abrillantador [ah-brel-lyan-tah-dor'] *m.* Diamond-cutter; lapidary.

abrillantar [ah-brel-lyan-tar'], *va.* 1. To cut a diamond into angles; to make any precious stone sparkle by polishing it. 2. To impart brilliancy; to glaze, to polish.

abrimiento [ah-bre-me-en'-to], *m.* 1. The act of opening. 2. An opening.

abrir [ah-breer'], *va.* 1. To open, to begin, to inaugurate, to unlock. **Abrir una puerta con llave**, to unlock a door. **En un abrir y cerrar de ojos**, in the twinkling of an eye. 2. To remove obstacles. 3. To engrave. To expand, as flowers; to distend. **Abrir a chasco**, *(coll.)* To jest, to mock. **Abrir el día**, to dawn. **Abrir el ojo**, to be alert. **Abrir la mano**, to accept bribes; to be generous. **Abrir los ojos a uno**, to undeceive; to enlighten. *-vr.* 1. To be

open, to tear. 2. To extend itself. 3. To chink, to cleave, to yawn. 4. *(Met.)* To communicate, to disclose a secret. **Abrirse con alguno**, to disclose one's secret, or to reveal it to a friend. **Abrirse o abrir una entrada al agua**, *(Naut.)* to spring a leak. 5. **Abrir registro** (barcos), to begin to take a cargo.

abrirse [ah-brer-say] *vr.* To open, to open out, to unfold, to spread out, to expand.

abrochador [ah-bro-chah-dor'], *m.* An instrument used by tailors to button on clothes; button-hook. *V.* ABOTONADOR.

abrochadura, *f.* **abrochamiento**, *m.* [ah-bro-chah-doo'-rah], [ah-bro-chah-me'en'-to]. The act of lacing or buttoning on.

abrochar [ah-bro-char'], *va.* To clasp, to buckle; to button on, to fasten with hooks and eyes, to do up. *(Mex.)* To tie up (atar).

abrocharse [ah-bro-chahr-say], *vr. (LAm.)* To struggle, to wrestle (luchar).

abrogable [ah-bro-gah'-blay], *a.* Repealable, abrogable.

abrogación [ah-bro-gah-the-on'], *f.* Abrogation, repeal, the act of repealing a law.

abrogar [ah-bro-gar'], *va.* To abrogate, to annul, to repeal. *(yo abrogué, from Abrogar. V.* Verbs in *gar.)*

abrojal [ah-bro-hal'], *m.* A place covered with thistles.

abrojo [ah-bro'-ho], *m.* 1. *(Bot.)* Caltrops. Thistle, thorn, prickle. 2. *(Mil.)* A thistle; a crowfoot. 3. Thistle fixed on a whip, and used by the flagellants to flog the shoulders. 4. A crab whose carapace has eight spines. *-pl.* Hidden rocks in the sea.

abromado, da [ah-bro-mah'-do, dah], *a.* (nauto.) 1. Dark, hazy, foggy. 2. Worm-eaten. *-pp.* of ABROMARSE.

abromarse [ah-bro-mar'-say], *vr. (Naut.)* To be worm-eaten.

abroncar [ah-bron-car'], *va. (coll.)* To tease, to vex, to make angry, to make ashamed.

abroncarse [ah-bron-cahr-say], *vr.* To get angry.

abroquelado, da [ah-bro-kay-lah'-do, dah], *a. (Bot.)* Shield-shaped.

abroquelar [ah-bro-kay-lar'], *va. (Naut.)* To boxhaul. *vr.* 1. To cover oneself with a shield. 2. To use means of defence in support of one's character or opinion.

abroquelarse [ah-bro-kay-lahr-say], *vr.* **Abroquelarse con, abroquelarse de**, to shield oneself with, to defend oneself with.

abrótano [ah-bro'-tah-no], *m. (Bot.)* Southernwood, allied to wormwood.

abrumado, da [ah-broo-mah'-do, dah], *a.* Wary. *-pp.* of ABRUMAR.

abrumador [ah-broo-mah-dor], *a.* Crushing, burdensome, tiresome, overwhelming. **El trabajo es abrumador**, the work is killing.

abrumadoramente [ah-broo-mah-do-rah-mayn-tay], *a.* Crushingly, vastly, overwhelmingly.

abrumar [ah-broo-mar'], *va.* 1. To crush, to overwhelm, to oppress. 2. To cause great pain or trouble.

abrumarse [ah-broo-mahr-say], *vr.* To get foggy, to get misty.

abrupto, ta [ah-broop'-to, tah], *a.* Craggy, rugged, abrupt. **Pendiente**, steep.

abrutado, da [ah-broo-tah'-do, dah], *a.* Brutish, ungovernable in manners and habits.

absceso [abs-thay'-so], *m.* 1. An abscess; collection of pus. 2. A blemish.

abscisa [abs-thee'-sah], *f. (Geom.)* Abscisse.

abscisión [abs-the-se-on'], *f. (Med.)* 1. Ulcer. 2. Incision.

absenta [ahb-sayn-tah], *f.* Absinth (e).

absentista [ab-sen-tees'-tah], *a.* Absentee. *-m. & f.* Absentee landowner.

abside [ab'-se-day], *m. & f.* 1. The central arch of a temple. 2. *V.* APSIDE.

absintio [ab-seen'-te-o], *m. V.* AJENJO.

absolución [ab-so-loo-the-on'], *f.* 1. The act of pardoning. 2. Absolution. 3. Acquittal.

absoluta [ab-so-loo'-tah], 1. *f.* Dogma, universal proposition. 2. Discharge. **Tomar la absoluta,** to take one´s discharge.

absolutamente [ab-so-loo-tah-men'-tay], *adv.* Absolutely, without limits or restrictions, definitely. **Absolutamente nada,** nothing at all.

absolutismo [ah-so-loo-tees'-mo], *m.* Absolutism, unrestrained, despotism.

absolutista [ab-so-loo-tes-tah], 1. *a.* Absolutist, absolute. 2. *f.* Absolutist.

absolutizar [ab-so-loo-te-thahr], *va.* To pin down, be precise about.

absoluto, ta [ab-so-loo'-to, tah], *a.* 1. Absolute; unconditional, without condition or stipulation. 2. Imperious, domineering. 3. (en sentido negativo) **en absoluto,** nothing at all, by no means. **No sabía nada en absoluto de eso,** I knew nothing at all about it.

absolutorio, a [ab-so-loo-to'-re-o, ah], *a.* Absolutory, absolving, verdict of not guilty.

absolvederas [ab-sol-vay-day'-ras], *f. pl.* The facility of giving absolution.

absolver [ab-sol-verr'], *va.* 1. To absolve. 2. To acquit. *(Yo absuelvo, yo absuelva, from Absolver, V.* MOVER).

absorbencia [ab-sor-ben'-the-ah], *f.* The act of absorbing.

absorbente [ab-sor-ben'-tay], *m. (Med.)* Absorbent, demanding. *-pa.* of ABSORBER.

absorber [ab-sor-berr'], *va.* 1. To absorb, to imbibe. *V.* EMPAPAR. 2. *(Met.)* To attract, to charm. **Absorber la atención,** to captivate the attention. 3. To take up (energías).

absorberse [ab-sol-bayr-say], *vr.* **Absorberse en,** to become absorbed in, to become engrossed in.

absorbible [ab-sor-be-blay], *a.* Absorbable.

absorbido [ab-sor-bee'-do], *a. (Med.)* Absorbed. *-pp.* of ABORSBER.

absorción [ab-sor-the-on'], *va. (Med.)* Absorption.

absortar [ab-sor-tar'], *va. (Obs.)* To strike with amazement.

absorto, ta [ab-sor'-to, tah], *a.* Amazed, absorbed in thought. *-pp. irr.* of ABSORBER and of ABSORTAR.

abstemio, mia [abs-tay'-me-o, me-ah], *a.* Abstemious. teetotal. *s.* Teetotaler.

abstención [abs-ten-the-on'], *f.* Forbearance, self-denial, not participation.

abstencionismo [abs-tayn-the-o-nes-mo], *m.* Non-participation, refusal to take part.

abstencionista [abs-tayn-the-o-nes-tah], *f.* Non-participant, person who opts out.

abstenerse [abs-tay-ner-say], *vr.* To abstain, to forbear. **En la duda, abstente,** when in doubt, don´t.

abstergente, abstersivo, va [abs-ter-hen'-tay, abs-ter-see'-vo, vah], *a.* Detergent, cleansing, abstergent.

absterger [abs-ter-herr'], *va.* To cleanse; to dispel purulent matter.

abstersión [abs-ter-se-on'], *f.* Abstersion, purification.

abstinencia [abs-te-nen'-the-ah], *f.* Forbearance, abstinence. **Día la abstinencia,** a day of abstinence, a fast-day. Abstinence, withdrawal (de drogas).

abstinente [abs-te-nen'-tay], *a.* Abstinent, abstemious.

abstracción [abs-trac-the-on'], *f.* 1. Abstraction, the act of abstracting and state of being abstracted. 2. Retirement from the world. 3. In art, pure abstraction, an abstract composition.

abstraccionismo [abs-trac-the-o-nee's-mo], *m.* Abstractionism.

abstractivo, va [abs-trac-tee'-vo, vah], *a.* Abstractive.

abstracto, ta [abs-trac'-to, tah], *a.* Abstract. *-pp. irr.* of ABSTRAER.

abstraer [abs-trah-err'], *va.* 1. To abstract, to separate ideas. 2. To pass over in silence. 3. To refrain from. 4. To differ in opinion. *-vr.* To withdraw the intellect from sensible objects, in order to employ it in contemplation.

abstraerse [abs-trah-ayr-say], *vr.* To be absorbed, to be lost in thought.

abstraído, da [abs-trah-ee'-do, dah], *a.* Retired. *-pp.* of ABSTRAER. *(Yo abstraigo, yo abstraje, yo abstraiga, from Abstraer. V.* TRAER)

abstruso, sa [abs-troo'-so, sah], *a.* Abstruse, difficult, recondite, absent-minded.

absuelto, ta [ab-soo-el'-to, tah], *a.* Free. *-pp. irr.* of ABSOLVER. *(Yo absuelvo, yo absuelva, from Absolver, V.* MOVER)

absurdamente [ab-soor-dah-mayn-tay], *adv.* Absurdly.

absurdidad [ab-soor-de-dahd], *f.* Absurdity.

absurdo, da [ab-soor'-do, dah], *a.* Nonsensical, absurd. **Es absurdo que...,** it´s absurd that....

abubilla [ah-boo-beel'-lyah], *f. (Orn.)* The hoopoe, or hoopoo, a bird with a beautiful crest.

abucate [ah-boo-cah'-tay], *m.* The runner of a velvet loom.

abuchear [ah-boo-chay-ahr], *va.* To boo, hoot at. **Ser abucheado,** to be hissed at.

abucheo [ah-boo-chay-o], *m.* Booing, hooting.

abuela [ah-boo-ay'-la], *f.* Grandmother; *(fig.)* old woman, old lady. **No tiene abuela,** he´s full of himself. **Éramos pocos y parió la abuela,** and that was the last straw.

abuelado [ah-boo-ay-lah-do], *adj (Cono Sur)* Spoiled by one´s grandparents.

abuelita [ah-boo-ay-le-tah], *f.* Grandma, granny, grandmother.

abuelito [ah-boo-ay-le-to], *m.* Granddad, grandpa, grandfather.

abuelo [ah-boo-ay-lo], *m.* Grandfather, ancestor. *(fig.)* Old man, forbear. **Abuelos,** grandparents. **Está hecho un abuelo,** he looks like an old man.

abulia [ah-boo-le-ah], *f.* Lack of willpower, spinelessness, apathy.

abúlico [ah-boo-le-co], *a.* Lacking in willpower, weak-willed, spineless.

abultado, da [ah-bool-tah'do, dah], *a.* 1. Increased. 2. Bulky, massive, exaggerated. *-pp.* of ABULTAR.

abultamiento [ah-bool-tah-me-ayn-to], *m.* Bulkiness, (large) size, swelling, increase, exaggeration.

abultar [ah-bool-tar'], 1. *va.* To increase, to enlarge. *-vn.* To be bulky or large. 2. *vn.* To be bulky, to be big, to take up a lot of room.

abundamiento [ah-boon-tah-me-ayn-to], *m.* Abundance, plenty

abundancia [ah-boon-dan'-the-ah], *f.* Abundance, fruitfulness, fertility, opulence, plenty. **Nadar en la abundancia,** to be rolling in money.

abundante [ah-boon-dahn'-tay], *a.* Abundant, plentiful. **Abundante en,** abounding in.

abundantemente [ah-boon-dan-tay-men'-tay], *adv.* Abundantly, plentifully, luxuriantly.

abundar [ah-boon-dar'], *vn.* To abound, to have plenty. *(Met.)* Followed by **en,** to hold identical opinions. **Abundar en dinero,** to be well supplied with money.

abuñuelar [ah-boo-nyoo-aylar'], *va.* To make something in the shape of a fritter.

aburar [ah-boo-rar'], *va. (Prov.)* To burn, to scorch.

aburelado, da [ah-boo-ray-lah'-do, dah], *a.* Of a dark red color.

aburguesado [ah-boor-gay-sah-do], *a.* **Un hombre aburguesado,** a man who has become burgeois, a man who has adopted middle class ways.

aburguesamiento [ah-boor-gay-sah-me-ayn-to], *m.* Process of becoming bourgeois.

aburguesarse [ah-boor-gay-sar'-say], *vr.* To turn bourgeois, to become middle class.

aburrición [a-boor-ree-the-on'], *f. V.* ABURRIMIENTO.

aburridamente [ah-boor-re-dah-men'-tay], *adv.* Wearily, in a boring manner.

aburrido, da [ah-boor-ree'-do, dah], *a.* Boring, tedious, dull. Weary. *-pp.* of ABURRIR.

aburridón, [ah-boo-rre-don], *a. (And)* Rather boring.

aburrimiento [ah-boor-re-me-en'-to], *m.* Uneasiness of mind, despondency, tediousness; weariness, heaviness, tiresomeness, disquiet, sorrow.

aburrir [ah-boor-reer'], *va.* 1. To vex, to perplex, to weary; to be tedious, tired dull; to grow impatient; to bore. 2. To venture, to hazard. 3. To relinquish.

aburrirse [ah-boo-rrer-say], *vr.* To be bored, to get bored.

aburujado, da [ah-boo-roo-hah'-do, dah], *a.* 1. Pressed together. 2. Perplexed, entangled in difficulties. *-pp.* of ABURUJAR.

aburujonarse [ah-boo-roo-ho-nar'-say] *vr.* To clot, to curdle.

abusado- [ah-boo-sah-do], *(Mex.)* 1. *interj.* Look out!, careful! 2. *a.* Watchful, wary.

abusador [ah-boo-sah-dor], *a. (Cono Sur)* Abusive.

abusar [ah-boo-sar], *va.* To abuse or misapply a thing; to impose upon, to go too far, to exceed one's rights. **Abusar del tabaco,** to smoke too much.

abusión [ah-boo-se-on], *f.* Abuse, superstition.

abusivamente [ah-boo-se-vah-men'-tay], *adv.* Abusively, improperly.

abusivo, va [ah-boo-see'-vo, vah], *a.* Abusive, improper.

abuso [ah-boo'-so], *m.* Misusage, the abuse or ill use of a thing, imposition, demand, betrayal. **Abuso del tabaco,** excessive smoking. **Abuso de confianza,** betrayal of trust.

abusón- [ah-boo-son], *a.* Selfish (egoísta), big-headed (engreído).

abyección [ab-yee-the-on'], *f.* Abjection, abjectness, degradation.

abyecto, ta [ab-yee'-to, tah] *a.* Abyect, dejected, degraded.

A.C. *abr.* after Christ.

a/c. *abr.* a cuenta (on account).

acá [ah-cah'], *adv.* Here, hither, this way, this side. **Acá no se estila,** that's not the custom here. **Ven acá,** come along. **Acá y allá,** here and there. **Acá,** hey, (used in calling). **Está muy acá,** it's right here.

acabable [ah-cah-bah'-blay], *a.* What may be finished, achievable.

acabadamente [ah-cah-bah-dah-men'-tay], *adv.* 1. Perfectly. 2. Imperfectly, badly.

acabadero [ah-cah-bah-day-ro*], m. (Mex.)* the limit, the last straw.

acabado, da [ah-cah-bah'-do, dah], *a.* 1. Perfect, complete, faultless. 2. Old; ill-dressed; dejected. **Está muy acabado,** he's looking very old. *-pp.* of ACABAR.

acabador, ra [ah-cah-bah-dor', rah], *m. & f.* Finisher, completer.

acabalar [ah-cah-bah-lar'], *va.* To complete, to finish.

acaballadero [ah-cah-bal-lyah-day'-ro], *m.* The time and place when horses cover mares; stud farm.

acaballado, da [ah-cah-bal-lyah-do, dah], *a.* Like a horse. *-pp.* of ACABALLAR, Covered.

acaballar [ah-cah-bal-lyar'], *va.* To cover a mare.

acaballerado, da [ah-cah-bal-lyay-rah-do, dah], *a.* Gentleman-like. *-pp.* of ACABALLERAR.

acaballerar [ah-cah-bal-lyay-rar'], *va.* 1. To render genteel. 2. To make a person behave as a gentleman.

acabamiento [ah-cah-bah-me-en'-to], *m.* End, completion, death, consummation.

acabar [ah-cah-bar'], *va. & vn.* 1. To finish, to conclude, to complete, to make up; to compass; to archieve; to grow toward an end. **Acaba ya,** determine, resolve. 2. To harass. 3. To obtain. 4. To terminate in anything, as a sword which ends in a point. 6. To die; to consume; to extinguish; to fail, to destroy. **Esto acabará conmigo,** this will be the end of me. **Acabar con el negocio,** to make an end of the affair. **Acaba de salir,** it is just fresh from. *-vr.* To grow feeble. **La vela se está acabando,** the candle is flickering. **Es cosa de nunca acabarse,** it is an endless affair. **Acaba de llegar,** he has just arrived, **acabar de,** to have just. **Acabóse,** *(coll.)* No more to be said; that's the end of it.

acabarse [ah-cah-bahr-say], *vr.* To finish, to stop, to come to an end (terminar); to die (morir), to run out. **¡Se acabó!,** it's all over!.

acabestrillar [ah-cah-bes-trill-lyar'], *vn.* To stalk, or to fowl with a stalking-horse or ox that approaches the game and shelters the fowler.

acabildar [ah-cah-bil-dar'], *va.* To unite many persons by dint of persuasion to do something. 2. To put to vote.

acabóse [ah-cah-bo-say], *m.* The end, the limit. **La fiesta fue el acabóse,** it was the best party ever.

acachetear [ah-cah-chay-tay-ar'], *va.* To tap, to pat, to strike, to slap.

acachihuite [ah-cah-che-ooe-tay], *m. (Mex.)* Straw, hay (paja); straw basket (cesto).

acacia [ah-cah'-the-ah], *f.* 1. Acacia, a shrub of the thorn kind. 2. Acacia, the concentrated juice of acacia.

acacito [ah-cah-the-to], *adv. (LAm.)* V. Acá.

academia [ah-cah-day'-me-ah], *f.* 1. Academy; university; literary society, school. **Academia de baile,** dance school. **Academia de comercio,** business school. **Academia de conductores,** driving school. **Academia de idiomas,** language school. **Academia militar,** military academy. **Academia de música,** music school. In particular, the Spanish Academy, officially charged with the pureness of the language. It was founded in Madrid early in the eighteenth century. 2. A naked figure designed from nature.

académico [ah-cah-day'-me-co], *m.* An academician, member of an academy.

académico, ca [ah-cah-day'-me-co, cah], *a.* Academical, belonging to a university, etc.

acaecedero, ra [ah-cah-ay-thay-day'-ro, rah], *a.* Incidental.

acaecer [ah-cah-ay-therr'], *vn.* To happen, to come to pass, to take place.

acaecimiento [ah-cah-ay-the-me-en'-to], *m.* Event, incident, occurrence.

acahul [ah-cah-ool], *m. (Mex.)* Sunflower (girasol); tall grass (hierba).

acáis [Ah-cah-es], *mpl.* Peepers, eyes.

acal [ah-cahl'], *m.* Canoe used by Mexicans.

acalambrado, da [ah-cah-lam-brah'-do, dah], *a.* Cramped.

acalambrarse [ah-cah-lahm-brahr-say], *vr.* To get cramped.

acalaminado [ah-cah-lah-me-nah-do], *a. (Cono Sur)* Rough, uneven, bumpy (camino).

acalefos [ah-ca-lay'-fos], *m. pl.* Acalephs, a group of radiates, incluing jelly-fishes and hydroids.

acalenturarse [ah-cah-len-too-rar'-say], *vr.* To be feverish.

acalia [ah-cah'-leah], *f.* V. MALVAVISCO. Marsh-mallow.

acalicino, na [ah-cah-le-thee'-no, nah], *a.* Wanting a calyx.

acaloradamente [ah-cah-lo-rah-dah-men'-tay], *adv.* Warmly, with vehemency.

acalorado [ah-cah-lo-rah-do], *a.* Heated, hot; tired; *(fig.)* heated, excited (discusión). Agitated (agitado).

acaloramiento [ah-cah-lo-rah-me-en'-to], *m.* Ardor, heat; agitation.

acalorar [ah-cah-lo-rar'], *va.* 1. To warm. 2. To inflame, to overheat. 3. To urge on. 4. To forward, to promote. *-vr.* To grow warm in debate.

acalorarse [ah-cah-lo-rahr-say], *vr.* To get hot, to become overheated; *(fig.)* (persona) to get excited, get worked up, to get angry.

acaloro [ah-cah-lo-ro], *m.* Anger.

acalote [ah-cah-lo-tay], *m. (Mex.)* Channel.

acallamiento [ah-cah-lyah-me-ayn-to], *m.* Silencing, quietening; pacification.

acallar [ah-cal-lyar'], *va.* 1. To quiet, to silence, to hush. 2. To mitigate, to soften, to assuage.

acamado, da [ah-cah-mah'-do, dah], *a.* Laid flat. **Mieses acamadas,** crops laid by heavy storms.

acamar [ah-cah-mahr], *va.* To beat down, to lay (cosecha).

acamastronarse [ah-cah-mas-tro-nahr-say], *vr.* To get crafty, to become artful.

acambrayado, da [ah-cam-brah-yah'-do, dah], *a.* Cambrie-like.

acampada [ah-cahm-pah-dah], *f.* Camp.

acampamento [ah-cam-pah-men'-to], *m.* *(Mil.)* Encampment, camp.

acampanado [ah-cahm-pah-nah-do], *a.* Bell-shaped.

acampar [ah-cam-par'], *va.* To encamp.

acampo [ah-cahm'-po], *m.* Portion of common given to graziers or herds for pasture, pasture.

acamuzado, da [ah-cah-moo-thah'-do, dah], *a.* Chamois-colored. *v.* AGAMUZADO.

acana [ah'-cah-nah], *f.* A hard reddish wood, which grows in the island of Cuba, used in ship-building.

acanalado, da [ah-cah-nah-lah'-do, dah], *a.* 1. What passes through a narrow passage or channel. 2. Striated, fluted. *-pp.* of ACANALAR.

acanalador [ah-cah-nah-lah-dor'], *m.* An instrument to cut grooves in timber; chamfering-plane, grooving-plane.

acanalados [ah-cah-nah-lah'-dos], *m. pl.* The ridge of a horse's back.

acanaladura [ah-cah-nah-lah-doo-rah], *f.* Groove, furrow; striation.

acanalar [ah-cah-nah-lar'], *va.* 1. To make a canal or channel. 2. To flute, to groove, to chamfer, to corrugate.

acanallado [ah-cah-nah-lah-do], *a.* Disreputable, low; worthless; degenerate.

acandilado, da [ah-can-de-lah'-do, dah], *a.* **Sombrero acandilado**, a hat cocked with sharp points.

acanelado, da [ah-cah-nay-lah'-do, dah], *a.* Of a cinnamon color.

acangrenarse [ah-can-gray-nar-say], *vr.* To mortify.

acanillado, da [ah-cah-nil-lyah'-do, dah], *a.* Ribbed, applied to any sort of cloth which forms furrows from the unevenness of its threads.

acantalear [ah-can-tah-lay-ar'], *vn.* *(coll.)* To hail large hail-stones.

acantarar [ah-can-tah-rar'], *va.* To measure by **cántaras** or four-gallon vessels.

acantilado, da [ah-can-te-lah'-do, dah], *a.* Bold, steep. **Costa acantilada**, accessible coast.

acantio [ah-cahn'-te-oh], *m.* *V.* TOBA

acanto [ah-cahn'-to], *m.* *(Bot.)* 1. Prickly thistle. 2. *(Arch.)* Acanthus leaf.

acantonamiento [ah-can-to-nah-me-en'-to], *m.* Cantonment.

acantonar [ah-can-to-nar'], *va.* To canton, to quarter troops, to billet.

acañaverear [ah-cah-nyah-vay-ray-ar'], *va.* To wound the flesh with sharp-pointed canes.

acañonear [ah-cah-nyo-nay-ar'], *va.* To cannonade.

acap [ah-cahp'], *m.* A Mexican wood suitable for cabinet-work.

acaparador [ah-cah-pah-rah-dor'] 1. *a.* Acquisitive. **Tendencia acaparadora**, monopolizing tendency.

acaparamiento [aha-cah-pah-rah-me-ayn-to], *m.* Monopolizing; covering the market.

acaparar [ah-cah-pah-rar'], *va.* To monopolize, engross. **Ella acapara la atención**, she captures everyone's attention. *V.* ACOPIAR.

acapararse [ah-cah-par-rar'-say], *vr.* 1. To take refuge under another's cloak. 2. To resort to the protection of someone else; to take sides with.

acaparrosado, da [ah-cah-par-ro-sah'-do, dah], *a.* Of a copper color.

acapetate [ah-cah-pe-tah-tay], *m.* *(Mex.)* Straw mat.

acapillar [ah-cah-pe-lyahr], *va.* To grab.

acaponado, da [ah-cah-po-nah'-do, dah], *a.* Capon-like; eunuch.

acapullado, da [ah-cah-poo-lyah-do], *a.* In bud. (flores)

Acapulco [ah-cah-pool-co], *m.* Acapulco.

acapulqueño [ah-cah-pool-kay-nyo], *f.* From Acapulco.

acaracolado [ah-cah-rah-co-lah-do], *a.* Spiral, winding.

acaramelado [ah-cah-rah-may-lah-do], *a.* Toffee-flavored (sabor).

acaramelar [a-cah-rah-may-lar'], *va.* To reduce sugar to caramel.

acarar [ah-cah-rar'], *va.* *V.* CAREAR.

acardenalar [ah-car-day-nah-lar'], *va.* To make livid, to beat black and blue, to pinch, to bruise. *-vr.* To be covered with livid spots.

acardenalarse [ah-cahr-day-nah-lahr-say], *vr.* To get bruised.

acareamiento [ah-cah-ray-ah-me-en'-to], *m.* Comparing, confronting.

acariciador, ra [ah-cah-re-the-ah-dor', rah], *m.* & *f.* One who fondles and caresses.

acariciar [ah-ca-re-the-ahr'], *va.* To fondle, to caress, to hug.

acaricida [ah-cah-re-the-ah], *f.* *(Cono Sur)* Insecticide.

ácaro [ah'-ca-ro], *m.* Mite. **Ácaro de queso**, cheese-mite.

acarraladura [ah-cah-rrah-lah-doo-ra], *f.* *(And. Cono Sur)* Run, ladder (in stocking).

acarrarse [ah-car-rar'-say], *vr.* To shelter oneself from the heat of the sun: applied to sheep.

acarreadizo, za [ah-car-ray-ah-dee'-tho, thah], *a.* Portable.

acarreador, ra [ah-car-ray-ah-dor', rah], *m.* & *f.* A carrier; a porter.

acarrear [ah-car-ray-ar'], *va.* 1. To carry something in a cart or other carriage; to convey, to forward. 2. *(Met.)* To occasion, to cause. **Ello le acarreó muchos disgustos**, it brought him lots of trouble. 3. *vr.* To bring upon oneself.

acarreo [ah-car-ray'-oh], *m.* Carriage, the act of carrying, conveyance, cartage. *-pl.* Supplies. **Cosas de acarreo**, Goods forwarded.

acarreto [ah-cah-rray-to], *m.* *(Carb, Mex.)* *V.* ACARREO.

acartonado [ah-car-to-nah'-do], *a.* Resembling pasteboard, wizened.

acartonarse [ah-cahr-to-nahr-say], *vr.* To get like cardboard.

acaso [ah-cah'-so], *m.* Chance.

acaso [ah-cah'-so], *adv.* By chance, by accident; may be, maybe, perhaps. **¿Acaso?** How? how now? **Por si acaso**, just in case. **Por si acaso viene**, if by any chance he comes.

acastañado [ah-cahs-tah-nyah-do], *a.* Hazel (color).

acastillaje [ah-cas-til-lyah'-hay], *m.* *(Obs. Naut.)* The upper works of a ship.

acastorado, da [ah-cas-to-rah'-do, dah], *a.* Beavered; resembling the texture of beaver.

acatable [ah-cah-tha'-blay], *a.* Venerable.

acataléctico [ah-cah-tah-lec'-te-co], *a.* Verse which has the complete number of syllables; acatalectic.

acatamiento [ah-cah-tah-me-en'-to], *m.* 1. Esteem, veneration, respect, reverence, obeisance. 2. Acknowledgment. 3. Presence, view.

acatar [ah-cah-tar'], *va.* To respect, to revere, to venerate.

acatarrarse [ah-cah-tar-rar'-say], *vr.* To catch a cold.

acato [ah-cah'-to], *m.* *V.* ACATAMIENTO.

acatólico [ah-cah-to-le-co], *a.* Non-catholic.

acaudalado, da [ah-cah-oo-dah-lah'-do, dah], *a.* Rich, wealthy, opulent, affluent, well-off. *-pp.* of ACAUDALAR.

acaudalar [ah-cah-oo-dah-lar'], *va.* 1. To hoard up riches. 2. To acquire a reputation.

acaudillador [ah-cah-oo-dil-lyah-dor'], *m.* Commander of troops.

acaudillar [ah-cah-oo-de-lyahr], *va.* To lead, to command, to head.

acaule [ah-cah'-oo-lay], *a.* *(Bot.)* Acaulous: wanting a stem.

accedente [ac-thay-den'-tay], *va.* Acceding; he who accedes.

acceder [ac-thay-derr'], *vn.* To accede, to become accessory to a treaty or agreement concluded by others; to fall in or into an agreement. **Acceder a una base de datos**, to have access to a data base. **Acceder al trono**, to succeed to the throne.

accesibilidad [ac-thay-se-be-le-dahd], *f.* Accessibility.

accesible [ac-thay-see'-blay], *a*. 1. Accesible. 2. Attainable. 3. Of easy access, approachable.

accesión [ac-thay-se-on'], *f*. 1. Accession, the act of acceding. 2. Access or paroxysm of a fever.

accésit [ac-thay-set], *m*. Consolation prize, second prize.

acceso [ac-thay'-so]. 1. Access. **Prohibido el acceso**, no admittance. **De fácil acceso**, of easy access. 2. Sexual intercourse. 3. Approach. **Acceso dirigido desde tierra**, Ground-control approach. 4. *(Med.)* Attack, fit (tos). **Acceso protegido** *(Comp.)*, protected access.

accesoria [ac-thay-so'-re-ah], *f*. 1. Outbuilding. 2. *(Andal.)* A room in the lower story of a house with the door opening to the street.

accesoriamente [ac-thay-so-re-ah-men'-tay], *adv*. Accessorily.

accesorio, a [ac-thay-so'-re-o, ah], *a*. Accessory, additional. **Obras accesorias**, *(Mil.)* The outworks of a fortress. **Accesorio del escritorio** *(Comp.)*, desk accessory.

accidentado, da [ac-the-den-tah'-do, dah], *a*. 1. Eventful (viaje); turbulent (history); troubled (vida); rough, rugged (terreno); broken (costa); 2. Hurt, injured (persona). *s*. Injured. **Llevaron a los accidentados al hospital**, the injured were taken to hospital. *-pp.* of ACCIDENTARSE.

accidental [ac-the-den-tahl'], *a*. Accidental, casual, fortuitous, contingent.

accidentalmente, accidentariamente [ac-the-den-tal-men'-tay, ac-the-den-tah-re-ah-men'-tay], *adv*. Accidentally, casually, fortuitously.

accidentarse [ac-the-den-tar'say], *vr*. To have an accident.

accidente [ac-the-den'-tay], *m*. 1. Accident, an unessential quality of something. 2. Chance, that which happens unforeseen, accident. 3. Privation of sensation. 4. Mode, integral part. 5. Accidental (música).

acción [ac-the-on'], *f*. 1. Action: feat. **Acción de gracias**, act of thanking, thanksgiving. 2. Faculty of doing something. 3. Lawsuit. 4. Gesticulation, gesture. 5. Battle. 6. Action, in the series of events represented in a fable, and the manner of representing them. 7. *(Art.)* Posture. 8. *(Com.)* Stock, capital in a company; share. 9. *(Poetic.)* The principal subject of a poem. *m*. Acción industrial (Com. e.g. de ferrocarril), Share (e.g. railway share).

accionamiento [ac-the-o-nah-me-en'-to], *m*. Drive, propulsion, operation.

accionar [ac-the-o-nar'], *vn*. to gesticulate. *-va*. 1. To sue, to bring suit. 2. To activate, to drive, to propel

accionista [ac-the-o-nees'-tah], *m*. Shareholder in a company's stock, actionary, stockholder.

acebadar [ah-thay-bah-dar'], *va*. V. ENCEBADAR.

acebedo [ah-thay-bay-do], *m*. A plantation of holly-trees.

acebo [ah-thay'-bo], *m*. *(Bot.)* Holly-tree.

acebolladura [ah-thay-bol-lyah-doo'-rah], *f*. Damage to a tree from splitting of the woody layers.

acebuchal [ah-thay-boo-chahl'], *m*. A plantation of wild olive-trees.

acebuche [ah-thay-boo'-chay], *m*. *(Bot.)* The wild olive-tree. Olea.

acebucheno, na [ah-thay-boo-chay'-no, nah], *a*. Belonging to the wild olive.

acebuchina [ah-thay-boo-chee'-nah], *f*. Fruit of the wild olive-tree.

acechador, ra [ah-thay-chah-dor', rah], *m*. & *f*. 1. A thief lying in ambush. 2. An intruder who pries into other people's affairs, watcher.

acechar [ah-thay-char'], *va*. 1. To waylay, to lie in ambush, to lurk, to spy on, to watch. 2. To pry into other people's affairs.

aceche [ah-thay'chay], *m*. V. CAPARROSA

acecho [ah-thay'-cho], *m*. The act of waylaying, or laying in ambush, spying, watching. **Al acecho, en acecho**, *a*. in wait, in ambush.

acechón, na [ah-thay-chone', nah], *m*. & *f*. *(coll.)* V. ACECHADOR. **Hacer la acechona**, to scrutinize, to inquire with care, to be inquisitive.

acecinar [ah-thay-the-nar'], *va*. To salt meat and dry it in the air or smoke. *-vr*. To grow old, dry, and withered.

acedar [ah-thay-dar'], *va*. 1. To sour, to make sour, to make bitter. 2. To displease, to vex.

acedera [ah-thay-day'-rah], *f*. *(Bot.)* Sorrel. **Acedera de Indias**, *(Bot.)* Indian sorrel.

acederilla [ah-thay-day-reel'-lyah], *f*. *(Bot.)* Wood-sorrel.

acedia [ah-thay-dee'-ah], *f*. 1. Acidity, sourness. 2. Squeamishness, roughness. 3. Asperity of address. 4. A flounder.

acedo, da [ah-thay'-do, dha], *a*. 1. Acid, sour. 2. Harsh, unpleasant.

acefalia [ah-thay-fah-lee'-ah], *f*. Deprivation of a head; headlessness.

acéfalo, la [ah-thay'-fah-lo, lah], *a*. Headless, acephalous.

aceitada [ah-thay-e-tha'-dah], *f*. *(coll.)* 1. Oil spilled. 2. Cake kneaded with oil.

aceitar [ah-thay-e-tar'], *va*. To oil, to rub with oil

aceite [ah-thay'-e-tay], *m*. (a)1. Oil; any unctuous liquor drawn from olives, almonds, nuts, fish, etc. 2. Resin which distils from the fir-tree. **Aceite de oliva**, olive oil. **Aceite de girasol**, sunflower oil. **Aceite de bergamota**, essence of bergamot. **Aceite de espliego**, spike oil, **aceite de trementina**, turpentine oil. **Aceite de pescado**, train oil. **Aceite de bacalao**, cod oil. **Aceite de linaza**, linseed oil. **Aceite de ricino**, castor oil. **Aceite de hígado de bacalao**, cod-liver oil. **Aceite de carbón, o aceite mineral**, coal-oil, petroleum. **Aceite lubricante**, *(Mech.)* Lube.

aceitera [ah-thay-e-tay'-rah], *f*. Oil jar, oil cruet, oil horn, **aceiteras**, vials for oil and vinegar.

aceitería [ah-thay-e-tay-ree'-ah], *f*. Oil-shop.

aceitero, ra [ah-thay-e-tay'-ro, rah], *m*. & *f*. 1. Oil merchant, oil-seller. 2. Any vessel for holding oil.

aceitoso, sa [ah-thay-e-toh'-so, sha], *a*. Oily, containing oil.

aceituna [ah-thay-e-too'-nah], *f*. Olive, the fruit of the olive-tree. **Aceituna rellena**, stuffed olive.

aceitunada [ah-thay-e-too-nah'-dah], *f*. The season for gathering olives.

aceitunado, da [ah-thay-e-too-nah'-do, dah], *a*. Of an olive color.

aceitunero [ah-thay-e-too-nay'-ro], *m*. A person who gathers, carries, or sells olives.

aceituno [ah-thay-e-too'-no], *m*. *(Bot.)* Olive-tree. V. OLIVO.

aceleración [ah-thay-lay-rah-the-on'], *f*. Acceleration, hastening.

acelerada [ah-thay-lay-rah-dah], *f*. Acceleration, speed-up.

aceleradamente [ah-thay-lay-rah-dah-men'-tay], *adv*. Speedily, swiftly, hastily.

acelerado [ah-thay-lay-rah-do], *a*. Jumpy, nervous (nervioso).

acelerador [ah-thay-lay-rah-dor'], *m*. Accelerator.

aceleramiento [ah-thay-lay-rah-me-en'-to], *m*. V. ACELERACIÓN

acelerar [ah-thay-lay-rar'], *va*. To accelerate, to hasten, to hurry, to forward, to expedite.

acelerarse [ah-thay-lay-rhar-say], *vr*. To hurry up, hasten.

aceleratriz [ah-thay-lay-rah-treeth'], *a*. Accelerative.

acelerómetro [ah-thay-lay-ro'-may-tro], *m*. *(Aer.)* Accelerometer.

acelerón [ah-thay-lay-ron], *m*. Sudden acceleration, leap forward.

acelga]ah-thel'-gah], *f*. *(Bot.)* Beet.

acémila [ah-thay'-me-la], *f*. 1. A mule, a beast of burden.

acemilar [ah-thay-me-lar'], *a*. Belonging to mules and muleteers.

acemilería [ah-thay-me-lay-ree'-ah], *f*. The stable or place where mules are kept.

acemilero, ra [ah-thay-me-lay'-ro, rah], *a.* Belonging to mules. *-m.* A muleteer.

acemita [ah-thay-mee'-tah], *f.* Bread made of fine bran. Graham bread.

acemite [ah-thay-mee'-tay], *m.* Fine bran, middlings.

acendrado, da [ah-then-drah'-do, dah], *a.* 1. Purified. 2. Refined. *-pp.* of ACENDRAR.

acendrar [ah-then-drar'], *va.* 1. To purify or refine metals. 2. To free from stain or blemish.

acensuar [ah-then-soo-ar'], *va.* To lease out for a certain rent; impose a tax.

acento [ah-then'-to], *m.* 1. Accent, a modulation of the voice. 2. Accent, a character placed over a syllable, to mark the modulation of the voice, to stress, emphasis. **Acento ortográfico**, written accent. **Acento agudo**, acute accent. **Con fuerte acento Andaluz**, with a strong Andalusian accent. **Poner acento en algo**, to emphasize something.

acentor [ah-thayn-tor], *m.* Acentor común, hedgesparrow, dunnock.

acentuación [ah-then-too-ah-the-on'], *f.* Accent, accentuation.

acentuamiento [ah-thayn_too-ah-me-en-to], *m. (Cono Sur)* Accent, emphasis.

acentuar [ah-then-too-ar'], *va.* 1. To accent, to stress. 2. To put a written accent on. 3. *(Met.)* To accentuate, to stress.

acentuarse [ah-thayn-too-ahr-say], *vr.* To become more noticeable, be accentuated. **Se acentúa la tendencia a la baja en la Bolsa**, the slide on the Stock Exchange is accelerating.

aceña [ah-thay'-nyah], *f.* Water mill (for grinding flour).

aceñero [ah-thay-nyay-ro], *m.* Miller.

acepar [ah-thay-par'], *vn.* To take root, to become rooted.

acepción [ah-thep-the-on'], *f.* Meaning, acceptation. **Acepción de personas**, Partiality, prejudice.

acepilladora [ah-thay-pil-lyah-do'-rah], *f.* Planer, planing machine.

acepilladura [ah-thay-pil-lyah-doo'-rah, *f.* 1. The act of planing. 2. Timber shavings.

acepillar [ah-thay-pil-lyar'], *va.* 1. To plane. 2. To brush clothes. 3. To polish one's manners.

aceptabilidad [ah-thep-tah-be-le-dad'], *f.* Acceptability.

aceptable [ah-thep-tah'-blay], *a.* Worthy of acceptance, acceptable.

aceptablemente [ah-thep-tah'-blay-men'-tay], *adv.* Acceptably.

aceptación [ah-thep-tah-the-on'], *f.* 1. Acceptation. 2. Approbation. 3. Acceptance of a bill of exchange. **Aceptación de herencia**, acceptance of an inheritance. **Aceptación de personas.** *V.* ACEPCION.

aceptador, ra [ah-thep-tah-dor', rah], *m. & f.* Acceptor.

aceptante [ah-thep-tahn'-tay], *pa.* He who accepts.

aceptar [ah-thep-tar'], *va.* To accept. **Aceptar personas**, to favor particular persons. **Aceptar una letra**, to accept or to honor a bill. *-vr.* To be pleased.

acepto, ta [ah-thep'-to, tah], *a.* Acceptable, agreeable.

acequia [ah-thay'-ke-ah], *f.* Canal, trench, or drain. *(Arab.)*

acequiado, da [ah-thay-ke-ah'-do, dah], *a.* Intersected by canals. *-pp.* of ACEQUIAR.

acequiador [ah-thay-ke-ah-dor'], *m.* Canal-maker.

acequiar [ah-thay-ke-ar'], *va.* To construct canals or drains.

acequiero [ah-tahy-ke-ay'-ro], *m.* Person appointed to construct canals, a dike reeve.

acera [ah-thay'-rah], *f.* 1. Sidewalk, pavement. 2. The stones which form the face of a wall. **Ser de la cera de enfrente**, to be gay.

acerado, da [ah-thay-rah'-do, dah], *a.* 1. Steeled, made of steel. 2. Strong. *-pp.* of ACERAR.

acerar [ah-thay-rar'], *va.* 1. To steel, to point or edge with steel. 2. To impregnate liquors with steel. 3. To strengthen, to harden, to toughen.

acerarse [ah-thay-rahr-say], *vr.* To toughen.

acerbamente [ah-ther-bah-men'-tay], *adv.* Harshly, rudely.

acerbidad [ah-ther-be-dad'], *f.* 1. Acerbity, asperity. 2. Rigor, cruelty.

acerbo, ba [ah-ther'-bo, bah], *a.* 1. Rough to the taste, as unripe fruit. 2. Severe, cruel.

acerca [ah-ther'-cah], *prep.* About, relating to, bringing near. **Acerca de lo que hemos hablado**, in regard to what we have said.

acercar [ah-ther-car'], *va.* To approach, to place a person or thing close to another. *-vr.* To accost, to come near to, or up to.

acercarse [ah-thayr-cahr-say], *vr.* 1. To approach, to come near, draw near, to come close to. 2. To be reconciled (amantes). 3. **Acercarse a** *(Comp.)*, to close in on.

ácere [ah-thay-ray], *m.* Maple.

acería [ah-thay-ree'-ah], *f.* Steel mill.

acerico, acerillo [ah-thay-ree'-co, ah-thay-reel'-lyo], *m.* 1. Pin-cushion. 2. A small pillow.

acerino, na [ah-thay-ree'-no, nah], *a. (Poetic.)* Made of, or belonging to steel.

acerista [ah-thay-rees'-tah], *m.* Steel manufacturer.

acernadar [ah-ther-nah-dar'], *va.* To cover with ashes.

acero [ah-thay'-ro], *m.* 1. Steel. **Acero colado**, cast steel. **Acero inoxidable**, stainless steel. 2. Edged or pointed small arms. **Espada de buenos aceros**, sword of well-tempered steel. Aceros, *(fig.)* Spirit, courage. **Tener buenos aceros**, to have guts.

acerola [ah-thay-ro'-lah], *f.* Azarole, the fruit of the parsley-leaved hawthorn.

acerolo [ah-thay-ro'-lo], *m. (Bot.)* The parsley-leaved hawthorn.

acerrar [ah-ther-rar'], *va. (Low.)* To seize, to grasp.

acérrimamente [ah-ther'-re-mah-men-tay], *adv.* Strenuously.

acérrimo, ma [ah-ther'-re-mo, mah], *a. sup.* Very vigorous and strong.

acerrojar [ah-thay-rro-hahr], *va.* To lock, bolt.

acertadamente [ah-ther-tah-dah-men'-tay], *adv.* Opportunely, fitly.

acertado, da [ah-ther-tah'-do, dah], *a.* Fit, proper. **Su conducta fue acertada**, he conducted himself with propriety. **Me parece muy acertado**, that seems right to me. *-pp.* of ACERTAR.

acertante [ah-thayr-tahn-tay], 1. *a.* **Tarjeta acertante**, winning card. 2. *m. & f.* Solver, winner. **Hubo acertantes**, there were winners.

acertar [ah-ther-tar'], *va.* 1. To hit the mark. 2. To hit by chance; to meet or find, to succeed. **A ver si acertamos esta vez**, let's see if we can get it right this time. **No aciertas el modo de hacerlo**, you don't manage to find the proper way to do it. 3. To conjecture right. *vn.* 1. To happen unexpectedly, to be right, to hit the mark, to manage it. 2. To take root, as plants.

acertijo [ah-ther-tee'-ho], *m.* A riddle.

aceruelo [ah-thay-roo-ay'-lo], *m.* A sort of small pack-saddle used for riding.

acervo [Ah-ther'-vo], *m.* 1. A heap, common property. **Acervo Comunitario**, community. **Acervo Cultural**, cultural tradition. 2. The totality of titles, or of an inheritance.

acescencia [ah-thes-then'-the-ah], *f.* Acidosis.

acetato [ah-thay-tah'-to], *m.* Acetate.

acético, ca [ah-thay'-te-co, cah], *a.* Acetic; pertaining to vinegar.

acetificar [ah-thay-te-fe-car'], *va.* To acetify, convert into vinegar.

acetilénico [ah-thay-te-lay-ne-co], *a.* Acetylene.

acetileno [ah-thay-te-lay'-no], *m. (Chem.)* Acetylene.

acetímetro [ah-thay-tee'-may'-tro], *m.* Acetimeter.

acetona [ah-thay-to'-nah], *f.* Acetone; pyroacetic spirit.

acetosa [ah-thay-to'-sah], *f. (Bot.)* Sorrel. *V.* ACEDERA.

acetosilla [ah-thay-to-seel'-lyah], *f. (Bot.)* Wood-sorrel.

acetoso, sa [ah-thay-to'-so, sha], *a.* 1. Acetous. 2. *(Obs.)* Acid.

acezar [ah-thay-thahr], *vn.* To puff, to pant.

achacable [ah-chah-cah-blay], *a.* Attributable to.

achacar [ah-chah-car'], *va.* 1. To impute; to father. To put something down. **Achacar la culpa a uno,** to lay the blame on someone. 2. To frame an excuse.

achacarse [ah-chah-cahr-say], *vr.* To ascribe a thing or action to oneself.

achacosamente [ah-chah-co-sah-men'-tay], *adv.* Sickly.

achacoso, sa [ah-chah-co'-so, sah], *a.* Sickly, unhealthy.

achaflanar [ah-chah-flah-nar'], *va.* To lower one end of a table, plank, or board; to chamfer, bevel.

achahuistlarse [ah-chah-oo-es-tlahr-say], *vr.* To become depressed (entristecerse).

achampañado [ah-chahm-pah-nyah-do], *a.* Champagne-flavored.

achamparse [ah-chahm-pahr-say], *vr.* *(Cono Sur)* **Achamparse algo,** to keep something which does not belong to one.

achancharse [ah-chan-char'-say], *vr.* 1. (Peru) To become lazy like a hog. 2. *(Cono Sur)* To get fat (engordar). 3. To become embarrassed (encontrarse violento).

achantado [ah-chahn-tah-do], *a.* *(CAm.)* Bashful, shy.

achantar [ah-chahn-tahr], 1. *va.* To close. 2. *vn.* To be quiet, to shut up.

achantarse [ah-chahn-tahr-say], *vr.* 1. To hide away. 2. *(fig.)* To give in, comply. **Achantarse por las buenas,** to be easily intimidated.

achaparrado, da [ah-chah-par-rah'-do, dah], *a.* Of the size of a shrub. **Hombre achaparrado,** a short and lusty man.

achaparrarse [ah-chah-par-rahr'-say], *vr.* To grow stunded.

achapinarse [ah-chah-pe-nahr-say], *vr.* *(CAm.)* To adopt the local customs.

achaque [ah-chah'-kay], *m.* 1. Habitual indisposition. 2. Monthly courses. 3. Excuse, pretext. **Con achaque de,** under the pretext of. 4. A failing. 5. *(Law.)* Mulet, penalty.

achaquiento, ta [ah-chah-kee-en'-to, tah], *a.* V. ACHACOSO.

achaquillo, ito [ah-chah-keel'-lyo, kee'-to], *m.* dim. A slight complaint.

achara [ah-chah-rah], *interj:* ¡Achara! *(CAm.)* What a pity! (lástima)

achares [ah-cah-rays], *m. pl.* Jealously; **dar achares a uno,** to make someone jealous.

achalorado [ah-chah-lo-rah-do], *a.* Patent leather.

acharolar [ah-chah-ro-lar'], *va.* To paint in imitation of varnish.

achatamiento [ah-chah-tah-me-ayn-to], *m.* 1. Flattening (allanamiento). 2. *(LAm.* Loss of morale (desmoralización). **Sufrieron un achatamiento,** they felt down.

achatar [ah-chah-tar'], *va.* To flatter.

achatarse [ah-chah-tahr-say], *vr.* 1. To get flat. 2. *(Cono Sur, Mex.)* To grow weak, decline (declinar). **Perder ánimo,** to lose heart; feel down. 3. *(Cono Sur, Mex.)* To be overcome with shame, be embarrassed (avergonzarse). 4. **Quedarse achatado,** *(Mex.)* to be put to shame.

achicado, da [ah-che-cah'-do, dah], *a.* Diminished. V. ANIÑADO, childish. *-pp.* of ACHICAR.

achicador, ra [ah-che-cah-dor', rah], *m. & f.* 1. Diminisher, reducer. 2. *(Naut.)* Scoop for baling boats. 3. He who bales a mine.

achicadura [ah-che-cah-doo'-rah], *f.* Diminution, reduction.

achicalado [ah-che-cah-lah-do], *a.* *(Mex.)* Sugared, honeyed.

achicalar [ah-che-cah-lahr], *va.* *(Mex.)* To cover in honey.

achicar [ah-che-car'], *va.* 1. To diminish, to lessen, to shorten, to take in. 2. To bale a boat or drain a mine. **Achicar un cabo,** to shorten a rope. **Achicar el agua del navío,** to free the ship. 3. *(fig.)* To humiliate; to intimidate. 4. To kill. 5. *(Carib.)* To fasten, hold down (sujetar).

achicarse [ah-che-cahr-say], *vr.* 1. To get smaller; to shrink. 2. *(fig.)* To humble, to eat humble pie. 3. *(LAm.)* To do oneself down, to belittle oneself (rebajarse).

achicharradero [ah-che-chah-rrah-day-ro], *m.* Place of oppressive heat.

achicharrante [ah-che-chah-rrahn-tay], *a.* Sweltering heat.

achicharrar [ah-che-char-rar'], *va.* To fry meat too much; to overheat, burn, scorch. **El sol achicharraba la ciudad,** the sun was roasting the city.

achicharrarse [ah-che-chah-rrahr-say], *vr.* To scorch, to get burnt.

achicharronar [ah-che-chah-rro-nahr], *va.* *(LAm.)* To flatten, crush.

achichiguar [ah-che-che-goo-ahr], *va.* *(Mex.)* *(fig.)* (Mimar), to cosset, spoil.

achichincle [ah-che-chen-clay], *m. & f.* *(Mex.)* Camp follower.

achiguado [ah-che-goo-ah-do], *a.* *(Mex.)* Spoiled.

achiguarse [ah-che-goo-ahr-say], *vr.* *(Cono Sur)* To grow a paunch.

achicopalado [ah-che-co-pah-lah-do], *a.* *(Mex.)* Down, depressed.

achichinque [ah-che-cheen'-kay], *m.* A miner whose business is to drain mines of water.

achicoria [ah-che-co'-re-ah], *f.* *(Bot.)* Succory, wild endive, chicory.

achilarse [ah-che-lahr-say], *vr.* *(Cono Sur)* To turn cowardly.

achimero [ah-che-may-ro], *m.* *(CAm.)* Peddler, hawker.

achimes [ah-che-mays], *mpl.* *(CAm.)* Cheap goods, trinkets.

achín [ah-chen], *m.* *(CAm.)* Peddler, hawker.

achinado [ah-che-nah-do], *a.* 1. *(Cono Sur)* **De aspecto indio,** with Indian features. 2. *(Carib.)* **De aspecto chino,** Chinese-like.

achinar [ah-che-nar'], *va.* *(coll.)* To intimidate, to terrify.

achinarse [ah-che-nahr-say], *vr.* *(Cono Sur)* To become coarse.

achinelado, da [ah-che-nay-lah'-do, dah], *a.* Slipper-shaped.

achique [ah-che-kay], *m.* Baling; pumping.

achiquillado [ah-che-ke-lyah-do], *a.* *(Mex.)* Childish.

achiquitar [ah-che-ke-tahr], *va.* *(LAm.)* To make smaller, to reduce in size.

achipolarse [ah-che-po-lahr-say], *vr.* *(Mex.)* To grow sad.

achirarse [ah-che-rahr-say], *vr.* **Nublarse,** to cloud over. **Oscurecerse,** to get dark.

achís [ah-ches*]*, *interj* Atishoo!

achispado, da [ah-chis-pah'-do, dah], *a.* Tipsy.

achispar [ah-ches-pahr], *va.* *(LAm.)* To cheer up, to liven up.

achisparse [ah-chis-par'-say], *vr.* *(coll.)* To get tipsy.

acho, acha [ah-cho, cha], **suf.** de *n.* y *a.* ej: **hombracho,** hulking great brute, **vivaracho.**

achocar [ah-cho-car'], *va.* 1. To throw one against the wall. 2. To knock asunder. 3. *(coll.)* To hoard money.

achocharse [ah-cho-chahr-say], *vr.* To get doddery, begin to dodder.

achocolatado [ah-cho-co-lah-tah-do], *a.* 1. *(LAm.)* Like chocolate. 2. *(LAm.)* Dark brown (color), chocolate-colored, tan. 3. **Estar achocolatado** (borracho), to be drunk.

acholado [ah-cho-lah-do], *a.* *(LAm.)* 1. Racially mixed (mestizo), part-indian. 2. Cowed (acobardado); abashed (avergonzado).

acholar [ah-cho-lahr], *va.* *(LAm.)* To embarrass (avergonzar); to intimidate.

acholarse [ah-cho-lahr-say], *vr.* To have half-breed ways (adoptar).

acholo [ah-cho-lo], *m.* *(LAm.)* Embarrassment.

-achón, -achona [ah-chon, na], **suf** de *n.* y *a.* = **-acho; bonachón** etc.

achoramiento [ah-cho-rah-me-ayn-to], *m.* *(Cono Sur)* Threat.

achorizado, da [ah-cho-re-thah'-do, dah], *a.* Slashed; made into sausages.

achubascarse [ah-choo-bas-car'-say], *vr. (Naut.)* To get squally and showery, to become threatening, to cloud over.

achuchado [ah-choo-chah-do], *a.* **Estar achuchado** *(Cono Sur)* To have malaria (paludismo); To catch a chill (tener escalofríos); To be feverish (tener fiebre); *(fig.)* to be scared.

achuchar, achuchurrar [ah-choo-char', ah-choo-choor-rar'], *va. (coll.)* 1. To crush with a blow. 2. To shove, jostle (empujar); to harass, pester (acosar). 3. To urge on. **Achuchar un perro contra uno**, to set a dog on someone.

achucharse [ah-choo-char-say], *vr. (Cono Sur)* To catch malaria (paludismo); to catch a chill (acatarrarse); to get feverish (tener fiebre).

achuchón [ah-choo-chone'], *m.* 1. *(coll.)* A push, a squeeze. 2. **Tener un achuchón**, to fall ill; to have a relapse.

achucutado [ah-choo-coo-tah-do], *a. (LAm.)* Down (deprimido); overwhelmed (agobiado).

achucutarse [ah-choo-coo-tahr-say], *vr. (LAm.)* To be dismayed (estar afligido); to be down (deprimido); to wilt (marchitarse).

achucuyarse [ah-choo-coo-yahr-say], *vr. (CAm.)* V. ACUCHUTARSE.

achuicarse [ah-choo-e-cahr-say], *vr (Cono Sur)* To be embarrassed, to feel small (avergonzarse).

achulado, da [ah-choo-lah'-doo, dah], *a.* Waggish, frolicsome, cocky.

achumado [ah-choo-mah-do], *a. (LAm.)* Drunk.

achumarse [ah-choo-mahr-say], *vr. (LAm.)* To get drunk.

achunchar [ah-choon-chahr], *(LAm.) va.* 1. To shame, cause to blush (avergonzar). 2. To get scared (intimidar).

achuncharse [ah-choon-char-say], *vr.* To feel ashamed, blush (avergonzarse).

achuntar [ah-choon-chahr], *va. (Cono Sur)* To do properly, to get right, to do at the right time.

achuñuscar [ah-choo-nyoos-cahr], *va. (Cono Sur)* To squeeze.

achupalla [ah-choo-pah-lyah], *f. (LAm.)* Pineapple.

achura [ah-choo-rah], *f. (LAm.)* Offal.

achurar [ah-choo-rahr], 1. *va. (LAm.)* To gut (animal); to stab to death (persona), cut to pieces. 2. *vn. (LAm.)* To benefit from a share-out, to get something free.

achurrucarse [ah-choo-roo-cahr-say], *vr. (CAm.)* To wilt (marchitarse).

achurruscado [ah-choo-roos-cah-do], *a.* Rumpled, crumpled up.

achurruscar [ah-choo-rroos-cahr-say], *va.* To rumple, to crumple up.

aciago, ga [ah-the-ah'-go, gah], *a.* Unfortunate, melancholy, sad, fateful.

acial, aciar [ah-the-ahl', ah-the-ar'], *m.* Barnacle, twitch, an instrument put upon the nose of a horse to make him stand quiet.

aciano [ah-the-ah'-no], *m.* Corn-flower. V. ESTRELLAMAR.

acíbar [ah-thee'-bar], *m.* 1. The juice pressed from the aloes. 2. Aloes-plant. **Acíbar caballuno**, Horse aloes; Barbadoes aloes. *(Met.)* Harshness, bitterness, displeasure.

acibarar [ah-the-bah-rar'], *va.* 1. To put the juice of aloes into anything; to make bitter. 2. *(Met.)* To bitter, to cause displeasure.

acicalado [ah-the-cah-lah-do], *a.* Metal polished, bright and clean; smart, neat, spruce (persona).

acicalador, ra [ah-the-cah-lah-dor'-rah], *m. & f.* 1. A polisher, burnisher, furbisher. 2. A tool used for burnishing.

acicaladura, *f.* **acicalamiento,** *m.* [ah-the-cah-lah-doo'-rah, ah-the-cah-lah-me-en'-to]. The act and effect of burnishing.

acicalar [ah-the-cah-lar'], *vn.* To polish, to burnish. *-vr. (Met.)* To dress in style, to set oneself off to advantage; to prink.

acicalarse [ah-the-cah-lahr-say], *vr.* To smarten up, to get dressed up.

acicate [ah-the-cah'-tay], *m.* Long necked Moorish spur with a rowel at the end of it.

aciche [ah-thee'-chay], *m.* Tow-edged tool used by tilers for cutting and adjusting tiles.

acicula [ah-the-coo-lah], *f. (Bot.)* Needle.

acidez]ah-the-deth'], *f.* 1. *(Med.)* Acidosis. 2. Acidity.

acidia [ah-thee'-de-ah], *f. (Obs.)* V. PEREZA. Laziness, indolence, sloth.

acidificación [ah-the-de-fe-cah-the-on'}, *f. (Chem.)* Acidification.

acidificar [ah-the-de-fe-car'], *va.* To acidify.

acidificarse [ah-the-de-cahr-say], *vr.* To acidity.

acidímetro [ah-the-dee'-may-tro], *m.* Acidimeter.

acidismo [ah-the-dees'-mo], *m.* Acidosis.

ácido [ah'-the-do], *m. (Chem.)* Acid. **Ácido acético**, acetic acid. **Ácido deoxiribonucleico**, deoxyribonucleic acid. **Ácido nítrico**, nitric acid. **Ácido sulfúrico**, sulphuric acid.

ácido, da [ah'-the-do, dah], *a.* Acid, sour.

acidular [ah-the-doo-lar'], *va.* To acidulate, to make sour.

acídulo, la [ah-thee'-doo-lo, lah], *a. (Chem.)* Acidulous, disagreeable.

acierto [ah-the-er'-to], *m.* 1. The act and effect of hitting; a good hit. **Con acierto**, with effect. 2. Prudence, dexterity. 3. Chance, casualty. *(Yo acierto, yo acierte.* V. ACERTAR)

aciguatado, da [ah-the-goo-ah-tah'-do, dah], *a.* Jaundiced, silly, stupid. *-pp.* of ACIGUATARSE.

aciguatarse [ah-the-goo-ah-tahr-say], *vr. (Carib. Mex.)* To grow stupid; to go crazy, lose one´s head.

acijado, da [ah-the-hah'-do, dah], *a.* Copperas-colored; of the color of acije.

acimboga [ah-thim-bo'-gah], *f.* The citron-tree. Citrus medica.

ación [ah-the-on'], *f.* Stirrup-leather.

acionero [ah-thi-o-nay'-ro], *m.* Maker of stirrup-leathers.

acipado, da [ah-the-pah'-do, dah], *a.* Well-milled; applied to broadcloth and other woollens.

acirate [ah-the-rah'-tay], *m.* Landmark which shows the limits and boundaries of fields.

actara [ah-the-tah'-rah], *f.* Thin wall, a partition wall; the rail of a bridge.

acitrón [ah-the-tron'], *m.* 1. Lemon dried and made into sweetmeat; candied lemon. 2. *(LAm.) (Bot.)* Bishop´s weed, goutweed.

aclamación [ah-clah-mah-the-on'], *f.* Acclamation, the act of shouting with joy. **Elegir por aclamación**, to elect by acclamation.

aclamador, ra [ah-clah-mah-dor', rah], *m. & f.* Applauder.

aclamar [ah-clah-mar'], *va.* 1. To shout with joy, to applaud. **Aclamar a uno por jefe**, to claim somebody

aclamideo, a [ah-clah-mee'-day-o, ah], *a.* Having no floral envelopes; naked.

aclaración [ah-clah-rah-the-on'], 1. *f.* Illustration, explanation. 2. Rinse, rinsing (ropa).

aclarado [ah-clah-rah-do], *m.* Rinse.

aclarador, ra [ah-clah-rah-dor', rah], *a.* Explanatory, illustrative. *-m.* A kind of comb in looms for making silk fringes.

aclarar [ah-clah-rar'], *va.* 1. To rinse (ropa) 2. To clear from obscurity, to make bright. 3. To illustrate, to explain. **No me aclaro,** I can´t work it out. 4. To widen, to clarify, to resolve. *-vn.* To clear into, to recover brightness.

aclaratorio [ah-clah-rah-to-reo], *a.* Explanatory, illuminating.

aclayos [ah-clah-yos], *mpl. (Mex.)* Eyes.

aclimatación [ah-cle-mah-tah-the-on'], *f.* Acclimation; acclimatization.

aclimatar [ah-cle mah tar'], *va.* To acclimatize, to habituate to a strange climate.

aclimatarse [ah-cle-mah-tahr-say], *vr.* To acclimatize oneself, to get acclimatized, acclimate (US). **Aclimatarse a algo**, to get used to something.

aclocado, da [ah-cloh-cah'-do, dah], *a.* Stretched at a fire, table, etc. *-pp.* of ACLOCARSE.

aclocarse [ah-cloh-car'say], *vr.* 1. To brood, to hatch eggs. 2. To stretch oneself on the ground, bench, etc.

acné [ac'-nay], *f.* Acne, a skin condition.

ACNUR [ac-noor], *m. abr.* de **Alto Comisario de las Naciones Unidas para los Refugiados** (United Nations High Commision for Refugees, UNHCR).

acobardar [ah-co-bar-dar'], *va.* To daunt, to intimidate, to terrify.

acobardarse [ah-co-bahr-dahr-say], *vr.* To be frightened, to get frightened; to flinch, to shrink back.

acobe [ah-co-bay], *m. (Carib.)* Iron.

acobrado [ahco-brah-do], *a.* Copper-colored, coppery.

acocear [ah-co-thay-ar'], *va.* To kick, to wince, to flinch. *(fig.)* **Maltratar,** to ill-treat, trample on. **Insultar,** to insult.

acocil [ah-co-thel], *m. (Mex.)* **Camarón,** freshwater shrimp.

acochambrar [ah-co-chahm-brahr], *vt. (Mex.)* To make filthy.

acocharse [ah-co-char'-say], *vr.* To squat, to stoop down.

acochinar [ah-co-che-nar'], *va.* 1. To murder, to assassinate. 2. *(Met.)* To prevent or obstruct the regular course of a suit at law; to hush up. 3. To humble.

acocotar [ah-co-co-tar'], *va.* To kill by a blow upon the neck.

acocote [ah-co-coh'-tay], *m.* A long gourd pointed at both ends, used in Mexico for extracting the nectar of the maguey.

acodado [ah-co-dah-do], *a.* Bent, elbowed.

acodadura [ah-co-dah-doo'-rah], *f.* 1. The act of bending the elbow. 2. *(Agri.)* Layering.

acodalar [ah-co-dah-lar'], *va. (Arch.)* To put lintels or transoms in a wall to support a window or niche, to shore up, to prop up.

acodar [ah-co-dar], *va.* 1. *(Obs.)* To lean the elbow upon. 2. To lay cuttings of vines or other plants in the ground, that they may take root. 3. To square timber.

acoderarse [ah-co-day-rar'-say], *vr.* 1. To put a spring on a cable. 2. *(Naut.)* To bring the broadside to bear. 3. To lean on. **Acodarse en,** leaning on.

acodiciar [ah-co-de-the-ar'], *va. (Obs.)* To urge on; to urgently long for, covet, something. *-vr.* To be provoked, to be inflamed with passion.

acodiciarse [ah-co-de-the-ahr-say], *vr.* **Acodiciarse a,** to covet.

acodillar [ah-co-dil-lyar'], *va.* 1. To bend something to an elbow or angle. 2. To sink down under a burden. **Acodillarse con la carga,** *(Met.)* not to be able to fulfil one's engagements.

acodo [ah-co'-do], *m.* A shoot or knot of a layer; a scion.

acogedizo, za [ah-co-hay-dee'-tho, thah], *a.* Collected or gathered easily.

acogedor, ra [ah-co-hay-do', rah], *m. & f.* Harborer, protector. *a.* Welcoming, friendly, hospitable, warm.

acoger [ah-co-herr'], *va.* 1. To admit one into our house or company; to receive. 2. *(Met.)* To protect, to give asylum. *-vr.* 1. To take refuge, to resort to. 2. *(Obs.)* To embrace the opinion of another. 3. To make use of a pretext for dissimulation.

acogerse [ah-co-hayr-say], *vr.* To take refuge. **Acogerse a la ley,** to have recourse to the law.

acogible [ah-co-he-blay], *a. (Cono Sur)* Acceptable.

acogida [ah-co-hee'-dah], *f.* 1. Reception. 2. The concurrence of a multitude of things in the same place; confluence; asylum. **Dar acogida a una letra,** *(Com.)* to honor or protect a bill. **Reservar buena acogida a,** to meet prompt attention.

acogido [ah-co-hee'-do], *m.* 1. Collection of breeding mares given to the owner of the principal steed, to keep them at a certain price. 2. Temporary admission of flocks into pasture-ground. *-pp.* of ACOGER.

acogimiento [ah-co-he-me-en'-to], *m.* V. ACOGIDA.

acogollar [ah-co-gol-lyar'], *va.* To cover delicate plants with straw to provide shelter.

acogolladura [ah-co-gol-lyah-doo'-rah], *f.* Earthing up of plants.

acogombradura [ah-co-gom-brah-doo'-rah], *f.* Digging up of the ground about plants.

acogombrar [ah-co-gom-brar'], *va.* To dig up the ground about plants; to cover plants with earth.

acogotar [ah-co-go-tar'], *va.* To kill by a blow on the neck, to knock down. *(coll.)* To overcome a person.

acohombrar [ah-co-om-brahr], *va. (Agri.)* To earth up.

acojinar [ah-co-he-nahr], *va. (Tec.)* To cushion.

acojonador [ah-co-ho-nah-dhor], *a. V.* ACOJONANTE.

acojonar [ah-co-ho-nahr], *m. (Esp.)* 1. *va.* 1. To put the wind up (atemorizar), intimidate. 2. To impress (impresionar); to amaze (asombrar), overwhelm.

acojonarse [ah-co-ho-nahr-say], *vr* To back down (acobardarse); To be amazed (asombrarse), be overwhelmed.

acojono [ah-co-ho-no], *m. (Esp.)* funk, fear.

acolada [ah-co-lah'-da], *f.* Accolade, a ceremony which consisted of an embrace and a touch with the flat of the sword on each shoulder of one who was receiving knighthood.

acolar [ah-co-lar'], *va. (Her.)* To arrange or unite two coats of arms under the same crown, shield, etc.

acolchado [ah-col-chah-do], *a.* Quilted, padded.

acolchar [ah-col-char'], *va.* To quilt, pad.

acólito [ah-co'-le-to], *m.* 1. Acolyte, assistant to a priest at mass. 2. An assistant.

acolladores [ah-col-lyah-do'-res], *m. pl. (Naut.)* Lanyards. **Acolladores de los obenques,** The lanyards of the shrouds.

acollarado, da [ah-col-lyah-rah'-do, dah], *a.* **Pájaros acollarados,** birds having about their necks a ring of feathers of a different color.

acollarar [ah-col-lyah-rar'], *va.* 1. To yoke or harness horses, oxen, etc. 2. To couple hounds. 3. *(Agri.)* To earth up. 4. *(Naut.)* To caulk.

acollerar [ah-co-lyahr], *va.* To gather, herd together.

acombar [ah-com-bar'], *va.* To bend, to crook.

acomedido [ah-co-may-te-do], *a. (LAm.)* Helpful, obliging (generoso); concerned, solicitous (solícito).

acomedirse [ah-co-may-der-say], *vr. (LAm.)* To offer to help. **Acomedirse a hacer algo,** to do something willingly.

acomendador [ah-co-men-dah-dor'], *m. (Obs.)* Protector, aider.

acometedor, ra [ah-co-may-tay-dor', rah], *m. & f.* An aggressor, energetic, enterprising.

acometer [ah-co-may-terr'], *va.* 1. To attack, to assault. 2. To undertake. 3. To tempt. **Acometerse mutuamente,** to jostle.

acometida, *f.* **acometimiento,** *m.* [ah-co-may-tee'-dah, ah-co-may-te-me-en'-to]. Attack, assault. **Acometimiento de calentura,** a fit or accesss of fever.

acometividad [ah-co-may-te-be-dahd], *f.* 1. Energy, enterprise (energía). 2. Aggressiveness (agresividad).

acomodable [ah-co-mo-dah'-blay], *a.* Accommodable, suitable.

acomodación [ah-co-mo-dah-the-on'], *f.* Accommodation, adaptation.

acomodadamente [ah-co-mo-dah-dah-men'-tay], *adv.* Commodiously, suitably.

acomodado, da [ah-co-mo-dah'-do, dah], *a.* 1. Convenient, fit. 2. Rich, wealthy. 3. Fond of comfort. 4. Moderate. *pp.* of ACOMODAR.

acomodador, ra [ah-o-mo-dah-dor', rah], *m. & f.* 1. The person that accommodates; box-keeper in the theater. 2. Usher.

acomodamiento [ah-co-mo-dah-me-en'-to], *m.* Accommodation, the act an effect of accommodating, convenience.

acomodar [ah-co-mo-dar'], *va.* 1. To accommodate. 2. To put in a convenient place. 3. To reconcile; to compound. 4. To furnish. *-vn.* To fit, to suit. *-vr.* To condescend, to conform oneself, to comply.

acomodarse [ah-co-mo-dahr-say], *vr.* 1. To comply, conform. 2. To install, settle down. **¡Acomódese a su gusto!,** make yourself at home! 3. *(Cono Sur)* To fix oneself up (with a job) (colocarse), to pull strings; *(fig.)* to marry into money. 4. To reconcile oneself (acomodarse con); to come to an agreement.

acomodaticio, cia [ah-co-mo-dah-tee'-the-o, ah], *a.* 1. Accommodating, compliant. 2. *(Ant.)* Figurative, metaphorical.

acomodo [ah-co-mo'-do], *m.* 1. Employment, place, situation; lodgings. Agreement, understanding. 2. Post, job (puesto); *(LAm.)* soft (pluma), job. 3. *(LAm.)* bribe (soborno); *(Mex.)* deal (arreglo).

acompañado, da [ah-com-pah-nyah'-do, dah], *a.* 1. Accompanied. 2. Busy, frequented (lugar). 3. **Con falda acompañada**, with skirt to match, with a skirt of the same color. 4. **Estar acompañado**, *(Carib.)* to be drunk. 2. *m.* An asssistant judge, surgeon, physician, etc. *-pp.* of ACOMPAÑAR.

acompañador, ra [ah-com-pah-nyah-dor', rah], *m. & f.* 1. A chaperon, an attendant; companion. 2. *(Mus.)* Accompanyist.

acompañamiento [ah-com-pah-nyah-me-en'-to], *m.* 1. Attendance. 2. Retinue. 3. *(Mus.)* Accompaniment. 4. Supernumeraries at a theater. 5. *(Her.)* The ornament which is constantly placed at the side of the escutcheon. 6. Escort (persona).

acompañanta [ah-com-pah-nyan-tah], *f.* Female companion, chaperon. *(Mus.)* accompanist.

acompañante [ah-compah-nyan-tay], *m.* Companion, escort, *(Mus.)* accompanist.

acompañar [ah-com-pah-nyar'], *va.* 1. To accompany, to attend, to conduct, to follow, to lead along. **Prefiero que no me acompañen**, I prefer to go alone. **¿Quieres que te acompañe?**, do you want me to come with you? **Acompañar a uno a la puerta**, to see somebody to the door. 2. To join, or unite. 3. *(Mus.)* To sing or play in concert with others. 4. *(Mus.)* Accompany (a, con). 5. To enclose, attach (carta). 6. **Acompañar a uno en**, to join somebody in. 7. **Acompañar a la flaca,** *(Mex.)* to kick the bucket. *-vr.* To hold a consultation.

acompaño [ah-com-pah-nyo], *m. (CAm. Mex.)* Meeting, group, crowd.

acompasado, da [ah-com-pah-sah'-do, dah], *a.* 1. Measured by the metronome. 2. *(coll.)* Monotonous and slow in tone. 3. Of fixed, regular habits.

acompasar [ah-com-paha-sahr], *va.* 1. *(Mat.)* To measure with a metronome. *(Mus.)* To mark the rhythm of.

acomplejado [ah-com-play-hah-do], *a.* Full of complexes.

acomplejante [ah-com-play-hahn-tay], *a. (Cono Sur)* Inhibiting, embarrassing.

acomplejar [ah-com-play-hahr], *va.* To cause complexes in, to give a complex to.

acomplejarse [ah-com-play-hahr-say], *vr.* To get a complex.

acompletadores [ah-com-play-tah-do-rays], *mpl. (Mex.)* Beans.

acomplexionado, da [ah-com-plex-e-o-nah'-do, dah], *a.* Of a good or bad complexion or constitution.

acomunarse [ah-co-moo-nahr-say], *vr.* To join forces.

Aconcagua [Ah-con-cah-goo-ah], *m.* **El monte Aconcagua**, *(Arg.)* (Mount) Aconcagua.

aconchabarse [ah-con-chah-bar'-say], *vr.* To gang up. *(coll.)* V. ACOMODARSE.

aconchado [ah-con-chah-do], *m. (Mex.)* Sponger, scrounger.

aconchar [ah-con-char'], *va.* 1. *(Naut.)* To fit out or repair a ship. 2. To drive ashore. 3. To put safety. 4. *(Mex.)* To tell off (reprender).

aconcharse [ah-con-chahr-say], *vr.* 1. *(Naut.)* To keel over; to run aground. 2. *(Cono Sur)* To settle, clarify (líquido). 3. **Vivir de otro**, to sponge, to live off somebody else.

aconcia [ah-con'-the-ah], *f. (Astr.)* Generic name of comets with a thick nebulosity and delicate tail.

acondicionado, da [ah-con-de-the'-o-nah'-do, dah], *a.* Of a good or bad condition. **Hombre bien o mal acondicionado**, a man of a good or bad disposition. **Géneros bien o mal acondicionados**, goods in a good or bad condition. *-pp.* of ACONDICIONAR.

acondicionador [ah-con-de-the-o-nah-dor'], *m.* **Acondicionador de aire**, air conditioner.

acondicionamiento del aire [ah-con-de-the-o-nah-me-en'-to del ah'-e-ray], *m.* or **clima artificial** [clee'-mah ar-te-fe-the-ahl'], *m.* Air conditioning.

acondicionar [ah-con-de-the-o-nar'], *va.* 1. To prepare, to arrange, to dispose, to fit. 2. To affect. 3. To constitute. *-vr.* To acquire a determined quality or condition. **Acondicionar para uso invernal**, to winterize.

acongojado [ah-con-go-hah-do], *a.* Distressed, anguished.

acongojar [ah-con-go-har'], *va.* To vex, to oppress, to afflict.

acongojarse [ah-con-go-hahr-say], *vr.* To become distressed, to get upset. **¡No te acongojes!,** don´t get upset.

acónito [ah-co'-ne-to], *m. (Bot.)* Aconite, wolf's bane.

aconsejable [ah-con-say-hah'-blay], *a.* Advisable, sensible, politic. **Nada aconsejable**; **poco aconsejable**, inadvisable.

aconsejado [ah-con-say-hah-do], *a.* Bien aconsejado, well advised.

aconsejador, ra [ah-con-say-hah-dor'- rah], *m. & f.* An adviser, counsellor.

aconsejar [ah-con-say-har'], *va.* To advise, to counsel. *-vr.* To take advice, to be advised.

aconsejarse [ah-con-say-hahr-say], *vr.* To seek advice, to take advice. **Aconsejarse con; aconsejarse de**, to consult.

aconsonantar [ah-con-so-nan-tar'], *va.* 1. To observe a complete rhyme at the end of each verse. 2. To use in prose rhymes suitable to poetry only.

acontecedero, ra [ah-con-tay-thay-day'-ro, rah], *a.* That which may happen.

acontecer [ah-con-tay-therr'], *v. impers.* To happen, to come about, to fare. **Acontecimiento** [ah-con-tay-the-me-en'-to], *m.* Event, incident, casualty, occurrence. **Fue realmente un acontecimiento**, it was an event of some importance.

acopado, da [ah-coh-pah'-do, dah], *a.* Having the form of a cup or vase. *-pp.* of ACOPAR.

acopar [ah-coh-par'], *vn.* To form a round head in the shape of a cup: applied to trees and plants.

acopiador [ah-co-pe-ah-dor'], *m. (Com.)* One who buys up goods to keep them off the market.

acopiamiento [ah-co-pe-ah-me-en'-to], *m.* The act and effect of gathering.

acopiar [ah-co-pe-ar'], *va.* To gather, to store up, to forestall.

acopio [ah-co'-pe-o], *m.* Gathering, storing. **Acopio usuario**, illicit or unfair buying up of goods; «rigging the market». **Hacer acopio**, to stock up, to lay in stocks.

acoplado, da [ah-co-plah'-do, dah],1. *a.* Fitted, adjusted. 2. *m. (LAm.)* trailer. 3. *(Cono Sur)* hanger-on, sponger (parásito). *-pp.* of ACOPLAR.

acoplador [ah-co-plah-dor], *m.* **Acoplador acústico**, acoustic coupler.

acopladura [ah-co-plah-doo'-rah], *f. (Carp.)* Coupling, junction.

acoplamiento [ah-co-plah-me-ayn-to], *m. (Mech.)* Coupling, joint. *(Elec.)* Connection, hookup. **Acoplamiento en serie,** series connection. **Acoplamiento Universal**, universal joint.

acoplar [ah-co-plar'], *va.* 1. To accouple, to join. 2. To frame timber. 3. To settle differences. *-vr.* To make up matters, to be agreed.

acoplo [ah-co-plo], *m. (Elec.)* Feedback.

acoquinamiento [ah-co-ke-nah-me-ayn-to], *m.* Intimidation.

acoquinar [ah-co-ke-nahr], *va.* To scare, to intimidate, to cow.

acoquinarse [ah-ko-kee-nahr'-say], *vr.* To become terrified.

acorar [ah-ko-rar'], *va.* To grieve, to distress, to afflict, to upset.

acorazado [ah-ko-rah-thah'-do], *m.* Battleship, battlewagon.

acorazar [ah-ko-rah-thar'], *va.* To armor, to cover with armor plate. *-vr.* To steel oneself.

acorazonado, da [ah-co-rah-tho-nah'-do, dah] *a.* Heart-shaped.

acorchar [ah-cor-chahr], *va.* To cover with cork.

acorcharse [ah-cor-char'-say], *vr.* 1. To shrivel: applied to the fruits (from *corcho*, cork.) 2. To become torpid.

acordación [ah-cor-dah-the-on'], *f. (Obs.)* Remembrance.

acordada [ah-cor-dah'-dah], *f.* Resolution, decision.

acordadamente [ah-cor-dah-dah-men'-tay], *adv.* By common consent, jointly; with mature deliberation.

acordado, da [ah-cor-dah'-do, dah], *a.* 1. Agreed. 2. Done with mature deliberation. **Lo acordado**, decree of a tribunal enforcing the observance of prior proceedings. -*pp.* of ACORDAR.

acordar [ah-cor-dar'], *va.* 1. To resolve by common consent, to concert. 2. To remind. 3. To tune musical instruments; to dispose figures in a picture. -*vn.* To agree, to level. -*vr.* 1. (ponerse de acuerdo) to agree. To remember. **Si mal no recuerdo,** if my memory serves me right. **Acordarse de algo,** to remember something, to recollect. 2. To come to an agreement. **Te acordarás de mí,** you will remember me. **Acordarse o estar de acuerdo con uno,** to agree with one. (Yo acuerdo, yo acuerde. *V.* ACORDAR).

acorde [ah-cor'-day], *a.* 1. Conformable, correspondent. 2. Coinciding in opinion. -*m.* 1. Consonance. 2. Harmony of sounds or colors.

acordelar [ah-cor-day-lar'], *va.* To measure with a cord; to draw a right line by a wall or street, in order to make it straight.

acordemente [ah-cor-day-men'-tay], *adv.* By common consent.

acordeón [ah-cor-day-on'], *m.* Accordion, musical instrument.

acordeonista [ah-cor-day-o-nes-tah], *f.* Accordionist.

acordeón-piano [ah-cor-day-on], *m.* Piano-accordion.

acordonado, da [ah-cor-do-nah'-do, dah], *a.* 1. Surrounded, ribbed, cordoned off. 2. Made in the form of a cord. -*pp.* of ACORDONAR.

acordonamiento [ah-cor-do-nah-me-ayn-to], *m.* Ribbing, cordoning off; milling.

acordonar [ah-cor-do-nar'], *va.* 1. To make in the form of a cord or rope, to tie up. 2. To surround. 3. To mill (moneda). 4. *(LAm.)* To prepare (terreno).

acores [ah-co'-res], *m. pl. (Med.)* Achor, a species of herpes.

acornear [ah-cor-nay-ar'], *va.* To fight or strike with the horns, to butt.

acoro [ah'-cor-ro], *m. (Bot.)* Sweetsmelling lag, sweet cane, sweet grass.

acorralamiento [ah-co-rrah-lah-me-ayn-to*]*, *m.* Enclosing, cornering, trapping.

acorralar [ah-co-rrah-lar'], *va.* 1. To shut up cattle or sheep in pens; to corral. 2. To intimidate. 3. To silence.

acorrer [ah-cor-rrer'], *va.* 1. To help. 2. To run to. 3. To shame.

acortamiento [ah-cor-tah-me-en'-to], *m.* 1. Shortening. 2. *(Astr.)* Difference in the distance from the center of the globe to the ecliptic and center of a planet in its orbit. 3. Restraint.

acortar [ah-cor-tar'], *va.* 1. To shorten, to lessen. 2. To obstruct. **Acortar la vela,** *(Naut.)* To shorten sail. -*vr.* 1. To shrivel, to be contracted. 2. To be bashful; to fall back.

acorullar [ah-cor-rro-lyar'], *va. (Naut.)* To bridle or hold up the cars.

acorvar [ah-cor-var'], *va.* To double, to bend. *V.* ENCORVAR.

acosador, ra [ah-co-sah-dor', rah], *m. & f.* A pursuer, persecutor.

acosamiento [ah-co-sah-me-en'-to], *m.* Persecution, molestation.

acosar [ah-co-sar'], *va.* 1. To pursue closely. 2. To vex, to molest, to harass. **Acosar a uno a preguntas,** to pester somebody with questions.

acosijar [ah-co-se-hahr*]*, *va. (Mex.)* Acosar.

acoso [ah-co-so], *m.* Relentless pursuit; hounding, harassing; relentless questioning. **Acoso sexual,** sexual harassment.

acostado, da [ah-cos-tah'-do, dah], *a.* 1. Stretched, laid down. 2. *(Obs.)* Salaried. 3. *(Her.)* Accosted. -*pp.* of ACOSTAR.

acostamiento [ah-cos-tah-me-en'-to], *m.* 1. The act of stretching or laying down. 2. *(Obs.)* A certain pay, a salary.

acostar [ah-cos-tar'], *va.* To lay down, to put one in bed.

acostarse [ah-cos-tahr-say], *vr.* To incline to one side; to lie down. To give birth. **Estar acostado,** to be lying down.

2. To approach. 3. *(Naut.)* To stand inshore. 4. *(Naut.)* To lie along; to have a list. **Acostarse con,** to sleep with.

acostumbradamente [ah-cos-toom-brah-dah-men'-tay], *adv.* Customarily, according to custom.

acostumbrado [ah-cos-toom-brah-do], *a.* Usual, customary, habitual.

acostumbrar [ah-cos-toom-brar'], *va.* To accustom, to use. **Acostumbrar a uno a hacer algo,** to accustom somebody to do something. -*vn.* To be accustomed, to habituate. **Los sábados acostumbra a ir al cine,** on Saturdays he usually goes to the movies.

acostumbrarse [ah-cos-toom-brahr-say], *vr.* 1. **Acostumbrarse a algo,** to accustom oneself to something, to get accustomed to something. 2. *(LAm.)* **No se acostumbra aquí,** it isn´t usual here.

acotación [ah-co-tah-the-on'], *f.* 1. The act and the effect of setting bounds; limit. 2. Annotation or quotation in the margin.

acotado [ah-co-tah-do], *a.* Enclosed, fenced.

acotamiento [ah-co-tah-me-en'-to], *m.* Limitation.

acotar [ah-co-tar'], *va.* 1. To limit, to set bounds. **Acótome a Dios,** let God fix my end; used at sports to express confidence in the actual safety of the place. 2. To fix, to mark. 3. To quote, to make annotations in the margin. 4. To accept for a certain price. 5. To witness.

acotiledóneo, a [ah-co-te-lay-do'-nay-o, ah], *a.* Not provided with seed-leaves.

acotillo [ah-co-teel'-lyo], *m.* A large hammer used by smiths. Sledge-hammer.

acoyundar [ah-co-yoon-dar'], *va.* To yoke oxen to a load.

acr., *abr.* de **acreedor** (creditor, Cr.)

acracia [ah-crah-the-ah], *f.* Anarchy.

ácrata [ah-crah-tah], 1. *a.* Non-conformist, hippy, free-and-easy, unconventional, loose living. 2. *m. & f.* Non-conformist, hippy, drop out, unconventional.

acrático [ah-crah-te-co], *a. V.* ÁCRATA

acre [ah'-cray], *a.* 1. Sour, acrimonious, hot. 2. Mordant, keen. 3. Rough, rude.

acre [ah-cray], *m.* Acre (medida).

acrebite [ah-cray-bee'-tay], *m. & f.* Sulphur. *V.* ALCREBITE. *(Arab.).*

acrecencia, *f.* **acrecentamiento,** *m.* [ah-cray-then'-the-ah, ah cray-then-tah-me-en'-to], Increase, augmentation, growth.

acrecentador, ra [ah-cray-then-tah-dor', rah], *m. & f.* One that increases.

acrecentar, acrecer [ah-cray-then-tar', ah-cray-therr'], *va.* To increase. **Derecho de acrecer,** The right of accretion in cathedral chapters, where a distribution is made according to the present residence of the prebendaries. *(Yo acreciento, yo acreciente,* from *Acrecentar. V.* ACERTAR).

acrecentarse [ah-cray-thayn-tahr-say], *vr.* To increase, to grow.

acrecer [ah-cray-thayr], *va.* To increase.

acrecimiento [ah-cray-the-me-ayn-to], *m.* Increase, growth.

acreditación [ah-cray-de-tah-the-on], *f.* Accreditation.

acreditado, da [ah-cray-de-tah'-do, dah], *a.* Accredited, distinguished. Marca acreditada, reputable make. -*pp.* of ACREDITAR.

acreditar [ah-cray-de-tar'], *va.* 1. To assure, to affirm a thing for certain. 2. To credit, to procure credit. 3. To prove.

acreditarse [ah-cray-de-tahr-say], *vr.* To justify, to prove one´s worth. **Acreditarse en,** to get a reputation in.

acreditivo [ah-cray-de-tah-te-bo], *a.* **Documentos acreditivos,** supporting documents.

acreedor [ah-cray-ay-dor'], *m.* 1. A creditor. **Acreedor hipotecario,** mortgagee. 2. *(Met.)* A meritorious person. 3. *a.* **Acreedor a,** worthy of.

acreedora [ah-cray-ay-do'-rah], *f.* Creditrix, creditress.

acreencia [ah-cray-en'-the-ah], *f. (Com.)* Claim, credit balance, debt.

acremente [ah-cray-men'tay], *adv.* Sourly, with acrimony.

acribadura [ah-cre-bah-doo'-rah], *f.* Sifting. *-pl.* Siftings, the remains of grain which has been sifted.

acribar [ah-cre-bar'], *va.* 1. To sift. 2. *(Met.)* To pierce like a sieve.

acribillado [ah-cre-be-lyah-do], *a.* Pitted, pockmarked. **Acribillado de,** filled with. **Acribillado de picaduras,** covered with stings.

acribillar [ah-cre-bil-lyar'], *va.* 1. To pierce like a sieve. 2. *(Met.)* To molest, to torment. **Acribillar a uno a preguntas,** to pester somebody with questions.

acridia [ah-cree'-de-ah], *f.* Acridia, a genus of locusts.

acridófago [ah-cre-do'-fah-go], *a.* Living on locusts.

acrílico, ca [ah-cree'-le-co, cah], *a.* Acrylic.

acriminación [ah-cre-me-nah-the-on'], *f.* Incrimination, the act of accusing or impeaching.

acriminador, ra [ah-cre-me-nah-dor', rah], *m. & f.* Accuser, informer.

acriminar [ah-cre-me-nar'], *va.* 1. To exaggerate a crime or fault. 2. To accuse, to impeach. 3. *(Law.)* To aggravate.

acrimonia [ah-cre-mo'-ne-ah], *f.* 1. Acrimony, sharpness, sourness. 2. *(Met.)* Asperity of expression, keenness, sharpness of temper. 3. *(Met.)* Vehemence in talking.

acrimonioso [ah-cre-mo-ne-o-so], *a.* Acrimonious.

acriollarse [ah-cre-o-lyah-say], *vr (LAm.)* To take on local habits (or the habits of the country).

acrisolado [ah-cre-so-lah-do], *a.* Pure; tried, tested; unquestionable. **El patriotismo más acrisolado,** the noblest kind of patriotism.

acrisolar [ah-cre-so-lar'], *va.* 1. To refine, to purify gold or other metals, to cleanse. 2. *(Met.)* To clear up a thing by means of witnesses.

acristalado [ah-cre-so-lah-do], *a.* Glazed.

acristalamiento [ah-cres-tah-lah-me-ayn-to], *m.* Glazing. **Los acristalamientos,** windows. **Doble acristalamiento,** double glazing.

acristianar [ah-cris-te-ah-nar'], *va. (coll.)* To baptize, to christen.

acritud [ah-cree-tood'], *f.* V. ACRIMONIA.

acrobacia [ah-cro-bah'-the-ah], *f.* Acrobatics; **Acrobacia aérea,** stunt flying.

acróbata [ah-cro'-ba-tah], *m. & f.* Rope-dancer, acrobat.

acrobático, ca [ah-cro-bah'-te-co, cah], *a.* Acrobatic.

acrobatismo [ah-cro-bah-tes-mo], *m.* Acrobatics.

acromático, ca [ah-cro-mah'-te-co, cah], *a. (Opt.)* Achromatic.

acromatismo [ah-cro-mah-tees'-mo], *m.* Achromatism, freedom from spherical aberration.

acromatizar [ah-cro-mah-tee-thar'], *va.* To render achromatic; to achromatize.

acrónicamente [ah-cro'-ne-cah-men'-tay], *adv. (Astr.)* Acronycally.

acrónico, ca [ah-cro'-ne-co, cah], *a.* Acronycal, applied to the rising of a star when the sun sets, or its setting when the sun rises.

acrópolis [ah-cro-po-les], *f.* Acropolis.

acróstico, ca [ah-cros'-te-co, cah], *a.* **Versos acrósticos,** acrostic verses.

acrotera, acroteria [ah-cro-tay-ra, ah-cro-tay'-re-a], *f.* 1. A small pedestal placed at the extremities of pediments, and serving also to support figures, etc. 2. The highest part of columns or buildings.

acroterio [ah-cro-tay'-re-o], *m.* The superior of the three parts of which the frontispiece of a building is composed.

acta [ahc'-tah], *f.* Act or record of proceedings. *-pl.* 1. The acts or records of communities, chapters, councils. Papers, file, etc. **Acta de defunción,** death certificate. **Acta constitutiva,** charter. **Acta de nacimiento,** birth certificate. *(Com.)* 2. **Actas de los santos,** the lives of the saints.

actimo [ac-tee'-mo], *m.* The twelfth part of a measure called **punto;** there are 1,728 actimos in a geometric foot.

actina [ac-tee'-nah], *m.* Actin.

actinia [ac-tee'-ne-ah], *f.* Actinia, sea anemone.

actínico [ac-te-ne-co], *a.* Actinic.

actinio [ac-te-ne-o], *m.* Actininium.

actitud [ac-te-tood'], 1. *f.* Attitude, position, posture. 2. *(fig.)* Attitude, position, outlook, policy. **La postura del gobierno,** the government's attitude. **Adoptar una actitud firme,** to take a firm stand.

activación [ac-te-va-the-on], *f.* Activation, expediting, speeding-up, stimulation.

activador [ac-te-vah-dor'], *m. (Chem.)* Activator.

activamente [ac-te-vah-men'-tay], *adv.* Actively.

activar [ac-te-var'], *va.* 1.To push, to make brisk, to hasten. 2. *(Comp.)* To switch on.

activas, *f. pl.* **activo,** *m.* [ac-tee'-vahs, ac-tee'-vo], *(Com.)* Assets, outstanding claims.

actividad [ac-te-ve-dad'], *f.* 1. Activity. 2. Quickness in performing; liveliness, nimbleness. **Estar en plena actividad,** to be in full swing.

activismo [ac-te-ves-mo], *m. (LAm.)* Political activity.

activista [ac-te-ves-tah], *m. & f.* Activist, political activist.

activo, va [ac-tee'-vo, vah],1. *a.* Active, diligent, forward, fiery, lively, energetic. **Voz activa,** suffrage. 2. *m.* Assets. **Activo neto,** net worth. **Activo y pasivo,** assets and liabilities. 3. **Oficial en activo,** *(Mil.)* serving officer, to be on active service.

acto [ahc'-to], *m.* 1. Act or action. **Actos de los apóstoles,** acts (of the apostles) 2. Act of a play. 3. Thesis defended in universities. **Acto inaugural,** opening ceremony. 4. Carnal communication. **Actos *(Obs.)*** 1. *V.* AUTOS. 2. Document, papers.

actor [ac-tor'], *m.* 1. Performer, player, actor. 2. *(Obs.)* Author. 3. Plaintiff, claimant. 4. Proctor, attorney.

actora [ac-to'-rah], *f.* Plaintiff, she who seeks justice.

actriz [ac-treeth'], *f.* Actress. **Primera actriz,** leading lady.

actuación [ac-too-ah-the-on'], *f.* 1. Actuation, moving, acting. **Su actuación fue importante,** his role was an important one. 2. **Actuaciones** *(Jur.)* legal proceedings. 3. **Actuación pericial,** expert valuation.

actuado, da [ac-too-ah'-do, dah], *a.* 1. Actuated. 2. Skilled, experienced. *-pp.* of ACTUAR.

actual [ac-too-ahl'], *a.* Actual, present, fashionable. **El 6 del actual,** the 6th day of this month. **El rey actual,** the present king.

actualidad [ac-too-ah-le-dad'], *f.* 1. The actual or present state of things. **En la actualidad,** at present. 2. Present importance, current importance. **Ser de gran actualidad,** to be current. 3. **Actualidades,** current events.

actualización [ac-too-ah-le-thah-the-on], *f.* Modernization, bringing up to date; refresher course, course of retraining (curso); update, updating; discounting (contabilidad).

actualizador [ac-too-ah-le-thah-dor], *va.* Modernizing (influencia).

actualizado [ac-too-ah-le-thah-do], *a. (Comp.)* Refreshed.

actualizar [ac-too-ah-le-thar'], *va. (Prov.)* To realize. To modernize, bring up to date. To discount (contabilidad).

actualmente [ac-too-al-men'-tay], *adv.* At present, at the moment. **Actualmente está fuera,** he's away at the moment.

actuante [ac-too-an'-tay], *pa.* Defender of a thesis in colleges.

actuar [ac-too-ar'], *va.* 1. To work, to actuate, to operate . 2. *(Met.)* To consider, to weigh maturely. 3. To perform judicial acts. 4. To instruct; to support a thesis. *-vn.* to work, actuate, function; to act, perform (persona); **actuar de,** to act as. **Actúa de manera rara,** he's acting strangely

actuarial [ac-too-ah-re-ahl], *a.* Actuarial.

actuario [ac-too-ah'-re-o], *m.* The clerk of a court of justice (who is always a notary public.)

acuache [ah-coo-ah-chay], *m. (Mex.)* Mate, pal.

acuadrillar [ah-coo-ah-dril-lyar'], *va.* To collect or head a band of armed men; to conduct a squadron of soldiers; to form or to head parties.

acuadrillarse [ah-coo-ah-dre-lyahr-say], *vr.* To band together, to gang up.

acuafortista [ah-coo-ah-for-tees'-tah, *m.* Etcher.
acuanauta [ah-coo-ah-nah'-oo-tah], *m.* Aquanaut.
acuaplano [ah-coo-ah-plah-no], *m.* Surfboarding.
acuarela [ah-coo-ah-ray-lah], *f.* Watercolor.
acuarelista [ah-coo-ah-ray-lees'-tah], *m.* Watercolorist.
acuarelístico, ca [ah-coo-ah-ray-lees'-te-co, cah], *a.* Watercolor.
acuario [ah-coo-ah-re-o], *m.* (Zodíaco) Aquarius.
acuartelado, da [ah-coo-ar-tay-lah'-do, dah], *a.* Divided into quarters. *-pp.* of ACUARTELAR.
acuartelamiento [ah-coo-ar-tay-lah-me-en'-to], *m.* 1. The act of quartering the troops. 2. Quarters.
acuartelar [ah-coo-ar-tay-lar'], *va.* To quarter troops. **Acuartelar las velas** (*Naut.*) To flat in the sails.
acuartelarse [ah-coo-ahr-tay-lahr-say], *vr.* To withdraw to barracks.
acuartillar [ah-coo-ar-til-lyar'], *vn.* To bend in the quarters under a heavy load; applied to beasts of burden.
acuático, ca [ah-coo-ah'-te-co, cah], *a.* V. ACUATIL.
acuátil [ah-coo-ah'teel], *a.* Aquatic, living or growing in water.
acuatinta [ah-coo-ah-ten-tah], *f.* Aquatint.
acuatizaje [ah-coo-ah-te-tha-hay], *m.* (*Aer.*) Touchdown (or landing) on the sea.
acuatizar [ah-coo-ah-te-thahr], *vn.* (*Aer.*) To come down on the water, to land on the sea.
acuchamado [ah-coo-chah-mah-do], *a.* (*Carib.*) Sad, depressed (triste).
acuchamarse [ah-coo-chah-mahr-say], *vr.* (*Carib.*) To get depressed.
acucharado, da [ah-coo-chah-rah'-do, dah], *a.* Spoon-like.
acuchillado, da [ah-coo-chee-lyah'-do, dah], *a.* 1. Slashed, stabbed. 2. (*Met.*) Experienced, skilful by long practice. 3. Slashed or cut in oblong pieces: applied to garments. *-pp.* of ACUCHILLAR.
acuchillador, ra [ah-coo-cheel-lyah-dor', rah], *m.* & *f.* 1. A quarrelsome person, a bully. 2. Gladiator.
acuchillar [ah-coo-cheel-lyar'], *va.* 1. To cut or hack, to give cuts with a knife. 2. (*Obs.*) To murder. 3. (*Tec.*) To plane down.
acuchillarse [ah-coo-che-lyahr-say], *vr.* To fight with knives or swords. **Se acuchillaron**, they fought with knives.
acuchucar [ah-coo-choo-cahr], *va.* (*Cono Sur*) To crush, to flatten; to crumple.
acucia [ah-coo-the-ah], *f.* Zeal, diligence, haste.
acuciadamente [ah-coo-the-ah-me-ayn-to], *a.* Diligently, keenly; hastily; longingly.
acuciador [ah-coo-the-ah-dor], *a.* **Acuciante** *a.* Pressing, urgent.
acuciar [ah-coo-the-ahr], *va.* To urge on, to goad, to prod (instar); to hasten (dar prisa); to harass (acosar); to mob.
acucioso, sa [ah-coo-the-o'-so, sah], *a.* Zealous, hasty, diligent.
acuclillado, da [ah-coo-cleel-lyah'-do, dah], *a.* Cowering, squatting (fr. *Cuclillas*).
acuclillarse [ah-coo-cleel-lyar'-say], *vr.* To crouch, squat.
acudimiento [ah-coo-de-me-en'-to], *m.* Aid, assistance.
acudir [ah-coo-deer'], *vn.* 1. To come (venir); to succour, to support; to run to, to repair to. **Asistir a la puerta**, to come to the door. 2. To produce; to be docile. 3. To have recourse. **A casa quemada acudir con el agua**, to come with the water when the house is burnt down. 4. To come to the rescue, to go to help (en auxilio).
acueducto [ah-coo-ay-dooc'-to], *m.* 1. Aqueduct. 2. Eustachian tube.
acueo, a [ah-coo-ay-oh, ah], *a.* Watery, aqueous.
acuerdado, da [ah-coo-er-dah'-do, dah], *a.* Constructed by line or rule.
acuerdo [ah-coo-er'-do], *m.* 1. Agreement, understanding 2. Body of the members of a tribunal assembled in the form of

a court. 3. Opinion, advice. 4. Concurrence, accord. 5. Reflection, prudence. 6. Memory. 7. (*Art.*) Harmony of colors. **El acuerdo de dos colores**, the harmony of two colors. **De acuerdo**, Unanimously, by common consent. **Ponerse** or **estar de acuerdo**, To agree unanimously, to come to an understanding. (*Yo acuerdo, yo acuerde*, from *Acordar.* V. ACORDAR). (*Yo me acuerdo, yo me acuerde*, from *Acordarse.* V. ACORDAR).
acuicultura [ah-coo-e-cool-too-rah], *f.* Development of water resources, aquaculture.
acuidad [ah-coo-e-dahd], *f.* Acuity.
acuífero [ah-coo-e-fay-ro], *m.* Aquifer.
acuilmarse [ah-coo-el-mahr-say], *vr.* (*CAm.*) To get depressed; to cower, shrink away.
acuitadamente [ah-coo-e-tah-dah-mayn-tay], *a.* Sorrowfully, with regret.
acuitar [ah-coo-e-tar'], *va.* To afflict, to oppress.
acuitarse [ah-coo-e-tahr-say], *vr.* To grieve.
acular [ah-coo-lar'], *1. va.* (*coll.*) To force one into a corner; to oblige one to retreat. 2. *vn.* To back away.
aculebrinado, da [ah-coo-lay-bree-nah'-do, dah], *a.* Made in the form of a culverin: applied to a cannon which resembles a culverin.
acúleo, a [ah-coo'-lay-o, ah], *a.* Aculeate, possessing a string. *-m.* A section of hymenoptera. (*Bot.*) Aculeate, having prickles.
acullá [ah-cool'lyah'], *adv.* On the other side, yonder; opposite. **Aquí y acullá**, here and there.
acullicar [ah-coo-lyahr], *vn.* (*And. Cono Sur*) To chew coca (leaves).
aculturación [ah-cool-too-rah-the-on], *f.* Acculturation.
aculturar [ah-cool-too-rahr], *va.* To acculturate.
acúmetro [ah-coo'-may-tro], *m.* An acoumeter, a device for testing the hearing.
acumíneo, ea [ah-coo-me'-nay-o, ah], *a.* Acuminate, ending in a point.
acumuchar [ah-coo-moo-chahr], *va.* (*Cono Sur*) To pile up, to accumulate.
acumulación [ah-coo-moo-lah-the-on'], *f.* 1. Accumulation, gathering. 2. Act of filing records.
acumulador, ra [ah-coo-moo-lah-dor', rah], *a.* Accumulating *-m.* & *f.* Accumulator. *m.* Storage battery.
acumular [ah-coo-moo-lar'], *va.* 1. To accumulate, to heap together, to treasure up, to hoard, to lay up. **Acumular vapor**, to get steamed up. 2. To impute, to upbraid with a fault. 3. To file records.
acumularse [ah-coo-moo-lahr-say], *vr.* To accumulate, gather, collect.
acumulativamente [ah-coo-moo-lah-te-vah-men'-tay], *adv.* (*Law.*) 1. By way of prevention; by way of precaution. 2. Jointly, accumulatively.
acumulativo, va [ah-coo-moo-lah-te'-vo, vah], *a.* 1. Precautionary. 2. Accumulative.
acunar [ah-coo-nahr] *va.* To rock (to sleep).
acuñación [ah-coo-nyah-the-on'], *f.* Coining, milling.
acuñador, ra [ah-coo-nyah-dor, rah], *m.* & *f.* Coiner.
acuñar [ah-coo-nyar'], *va.* 1. To coin. 2. To wedge, or fasten with wedges. **Acuñar dinero**, (*Met.*) to hoard up money. **Hermano ayuda y cuñado acuña**, brothers and sisters-in-law are always at variance.
acuñarse [ah-coo-nyahr-say], *vr.* (*CAm.*) To hit, to sustain a blow.
acuosidad [ah-coo-o-se-dad'], *f.* Wateriness.
acuoso, sa [ah-coo-o'-so, sah], *a.* Watery, aqueous.
acupuntura [ah-coo-poon-too'-rah], *f.* Acupuncture, a surgical mode of counter-irritation by needle thrusts.
acurrado [ah-coo-rrah-do], *a.* 1. (*Mex.*) Handsome (guapo). 2. (*CAm.*) Squat, chubby (rechoncho).
acurrucarse [ah-coor-roo-car'-say], *vr.* To muffle oneself up, to squat, crouch; to huddle up (frío), to curl up.
acurrullar [ah-coor-rool-lyar'], *va.* (*Naut.*) To take down the sails of a galley.

acusable [ah-coo-sah'-blay], *a.* Accusable, indictable.

acusación [ah-coo-sah-the-on'], *f.* Accusation, impeachment, charge, expostulation. **Negar la acusación,** to deny the charge, to plead not guilty.

acusado, da [ah-coo-sah-do, dah], 1. *a.* 1. *(Jur.)* Accused. 2. Marked, pronounced (fuerte). 3. *m. & f* Accused, defendant.

acusador, ra [ah-coo-sah-dor', rah], *m. & f.* Accuser, informer.

acusar [ah-coo-sar'], *va.* 1. To accuse, to incriminate, to lay against, to indict. **Acusar a uno de haber hecho algo,** to accuse someone of having done something. 2. To acknowledge the receipt of. 3. To take charge of. 4. to show, reveal (revelar). **Su silencio acusa cierta cobardía,** his silence betrays a certain cowardice.

acusarse [ah-coo-sahr-say] *vr.* 1. To acknowledge sins to a confessor. **Acusarse de haber hecho algo,** to confess to having done it. 2. To become more marked, get stronger. **Esta tendencia se acusa cada vez más,** this tendency is becoming ever more marked, this tendency gets stronger all the time.

acusativo [ah-coo-sah-tee'-vo], *m.* Accusative, the fourth case in the declension of the Latin nouns.

acusatorio, ria [ah-coo-sah-to'-re-o, ah], *a.* Accusatory, belonging to an accusation.

acuse [ah-coo'-say], *m.* At cards, a certain number estimated to win so much. **Acuse de recibo,** acknowledgement of receipt.

acusetas [ah-coo-say-tahs], *m. & f. (And. Cono Sur)* Telltale, sneak.

acusica [ah-coo-se-cah] *m. & f.* Acusique, tell-tale, sneak.

acusón, na [ah-coo-son, na], *a.* Telltale, sneaking.

acústica [ah-coos'-te-cah], *f.* Acoustics, the doctrine or theory of sounds.

acústico, ca [ah-coos'-te-co, cah], *1. a.* Acoustic. 2. *m.* Hearing aid.

acutángulo [ah-coo-tahn'-goo-lo], *a. (Geom.)* Acute-angled.

ada [ah'-dah], *f.* 1. Small apple of the pippin kind. 2. A very poisonous snake. 3. *(Comp.)* Ada (Programming language).

adad [ah-dahd'], *m.* Name of the Creator among the Syrians; the dragon, a noted idol among the Philistines.

adagio [ah-dah'-he-o], *m.* 1. Proverb. 2. *(Mus.)* Adagio, a term used by musicians to mark a slow time. 3. A piece of music in adagio time.

adaguar [ah-dah-goo-ar'], *va. (Obs.) V.* ABREVAR.

adala [ah-dah'-lah], *f. (Naut.)* Pumpdeal.

adalid [ah-dah-leed'], *m.* A chief, a commander, a leader, a champion.

adamado, da [ah-dah-mah'-do, dah], *a.* Lady-like: applied to vulgar women.

adamantino, na [ah-dah-man-tee'-no, nah], *a.* Adamantine.

adamar [ah-dah-mar'], *va.* To love violently. *-vr.* To become as delicate in the face, or in manners, as a lady: to degenerate.

adamascado, da [ah-dah-mas-cah'-do, dah], *a.* Damask-like. *-pp.* of ADAMASCAR.

adamascar [ah-dah-mahs-cahr'], *va.* To damask.

adamita [ah-dah-mee'-tah], *m.* Adamite.

Adán [ah-dan'], *m.* 1. Adam. 2. Slovenly fellow (sucio); Lazy guy (vago); **estar hecho un Adán,** to go about in rags.

adaptabilidad [ah-dap-tah-be-le-dahd'], *f.* Adaptability, adjustment to environmental conditions.

adaptable [ah dap tah' blay], *a.* Capable of being adapted.

adaptación [ah-dap-tah-the-on'], *f.* The act of fitting one thing to another accommodation, adaptation.

adaptadamente [ah-dap-tah-dah-men'-tay], *adv.* In a fit manner.

adaptador [ah-dap-tah-dor], *m. (Elec.)* Adapter.

adaptar [ah-dap-tar'], *va.* To adapt, to fit, to apply one thing to another, to fashion.

adaptarse [ah-dap-tahr-say], *vr.* To cohere, to adapt. **Saber adaptarse a las circunstancias,** to be able to cope.

adaraja [ah-dah-rah'-hah], *f. (Arch.)* Projecting stones left to continue a wall. Toothing.

adarce [ah-dar'-thay], *m.* 1. Salt froth of the sea dried on canes. 2. *pl.* Carbonate of lime which certain mineral waters deposit.

adarga [ah-dar'-gah], *f.* A shield of an oval form made of leather.

adargar [ah-dar-gar'], *va.* To shield.

adarguero [ah-dar-gay'-ro], *m. (Obs.)* One who used a shield.

adarguilla [ah-dar-geel'-lyah], *f.* A small shield.

adarme [ah-dar'-may], *m.*1. Half a drachm, the sixteenth part of an ounce. 2. Whit, jot. **Ni un adarme,** not a whit. **No me importa un adarme,** I couldn't care less.

adarvar [ah-dar-var'], *va. (Obs.)* To astonish, to astound.

adarve [ah-dar'-vay], *m.* The flat top of a wall.

adatar [ah-dah-tar'], *va.* To open an account; to credit. 2. To annotate, to comment.

adatoda [ah-dah-to'-dah], *f. (Bot.)* The willow-leaved Malabar nut-tree.

adaza [ah-dah'-thah], *f. (Bot.)* Common panic-grass. *V.* PANIZO.

A. de C. *m. abr.* de año de Cristo.

adecenamiento [ah-day-thay-nah-me-en'-to], *m.* Act of forming by ten and ten.

adecentar [ah-day-then-tar'], *va.* To render decent, to tidy up, clean up.

adecentarse [ah-day-thayn-tahr-say], *va.* To tidy oneself up.

adecuación [ah-day-coo-ah-the-on'], *f.* Fitness.

adecuadamente [ah-day-coo-ah-dah-men'-tay], *adv.* Fitly, properly, to the purpose.

adecuado, da [ah-day-coo-ah'-do, dah], *a.* Adequate, fit, competent. **Los documentos adecuados,** the appropriate documents. *-pp.* of ADECUAR.

adecuar [ah-day-coo-ar'], *va.* To fit, to accommodate.

adefesiero [Ah-day-fay-se-ay-ro], *a. (And. Cono Sur)* Comic, ridiculous (ridículo).

adefesio [ah-day-fay'-se-o], *m. (coll.)* Extravagance, folly; something not to the purpose. Ridiculous attire. **Ella está hecha un adefesio,** she looks a fright.

adefesioso [ah-day-fay-se-o-so], *a.* Nonsensical, ridiculous.

adehala [ah-day-ah'-lah], *f.* Gratuity, perquisite.

adehesado [ah-day-ay-sah'-do], *m.* Place converted into pasture. *-pp.* of ADEHESAR.

adehesamiento [ah-day-ay-sah-me-en'-to], *m.* Turning land to pasture, pasturage.

adehesar [ah-day-ay-sar'], *va.* To convert land into pasture.

A. de J.C. *abr.* de **antes de Cristo,** before Christ, B.C.

adela [ah-day-lah], *f. (CAm.)* Bittersweet.

adelaida [ah-day-lah-e-dah], *f. (Mex.)* Fuchsia.

adelantadamente [ah-day-lan-tah-dah-men-tay], *adv.* Beforehand.

adelantadillo [ah-day-lan-tah-deel'-lyo] *a. (Ant.)* Red wine made of the first ripe grapes.

adelantado [ah-day-lan-tah'-do], *m.* An appellation formerly given to the governor of a province.

adelantado, da [ah-day-lan-tah'-do, dah], *a.* 1. Anticipated, advanced, forehand, onward, bold, forward. 2. Early, when applied to fruit or plants. *-pp.* of ADELANTAR.

adelantador, ra [ah-day-lan-tah-dor', rah], *m. & f.* One that advances, extends, or amplifies.

adelantamiento [ah-day-lan-tah-me-en'-to], *m.* 1. Progress, improvement, increase, growth, furtherance; cultivation, good. 2. Anticipation. 3. The dignity of the governor formerly called **adelantado,** and the district of his jurisdiction.

adelantar [ah-day-lan-tar'], *va.* 1. To advance, to accelerate, to forward; to graduate; to grow, to keep on. **Adelantar los acontecimiento,** to anticipate events. 2. To advance, to pay beforehand. 3. *(Met.)* To improve. 4. *(Obs.)* To push forward. 5. To get ahead. **Estamos a punto de que se nos adelanten,** we are about to be overtaken. *-vr.* 1. To take the lead, to overrun, to come forward. 2. *(Met.)* To excel, to outdo.

adelantarse [ah-day-lahn-tahr-say], *vr.* 1. To go forward, to go ahead (tomar la delantera; to improve, to progress). 2. **Adelantarse a uno**, to get ahead of someone, to outstrip somebody, to pass someone. 3. **Adelantarse a algo,** to anticipate something. **Anticiparse a los deseos de uno**, to anticipate somebody's wishes.

adelante [ah-day-lahn'-tay], *adv.* 1. Farther off; higher up; forward, onward. **En adelante**, henceforth, in future, or for the future. **Quien adelante no mira, atrás se queda**, look before you leap, **adelante**, go on; or, I understand. 2. (cantidad) **De 100 ptas en adelante**, from 100 pesetas up. 3. (tiempo) **De aquí en adelante; de hoy en adelante**, in the future.

adelanto [ah-day-lahn'-to], *m. (Com.)* Advance, progress. **Con los adelantos modernos**, with all the modern improvements. Advance payment.

adelfa [ah-del'-fah], *f. (Bot.)* Oleander. Rosebay.

adelfal [ah-del-fahl'], *m.* Plantation of rose-bay trees.

adelfilla [ah-del-feel'-lyah], *f.* The flowering osier, a shrub.

adelfo, fa [ah-del'-fo, fah], *a. (Bot.)* Adelphous, having stamens united by their filaments; chiefly used in composition.

adelgazado, da [ah-del-gah-tha'-do, dah], *a.* Made slender or thin. *-pp.* of ADELGAZAR.

adelgazador, ra [ah-del-gah-thah-dor', rah], *m. & f.* One that makes thin or slender.

adelgazamiento [ah-del-gah-tha-me-en'-to] *m.* Act of making slender.

adelgazante [ah-dayl-gah-than-tay], *a.* Slimming.

adelgazar [ah-dayl-gah-thar'], *va.* 1. To attenuate, to make thin (madera), to slender (persona). 2. To lessen. 3. To refine. 4. To taper (una punta). *Vr.* To get thin, to lose weight (persona), to slim. **He adelgazado mucho**, I have slimmed a lot.

adelgazarse [ah-dayl-gah-thahr-say], *vr.* To become slender, to slim.

adelógeno, na [ah-day-lo'-hay-no, nah], *a.* Adelogenous (rocas).

adema [ah-day'-mah], *f.* **ademe** [ah-day'-may], *m. (Miner.)* The timber with which the sides of mines are secured. Shore, strut.

ademador [ah-day-mah-dor'], *m. (Miner.)* A workman employed in lining the sides of mines with boards.

ademán [ah-day-mahn'], *m.* 1. A gesture, by which approbation or dislike is expressed; look, manner. 2. *(Art.)* Attitude. **En ademán**, in the attitude or posture of performing something.

ademar [ah-day-mar'], *va. (Miner.)* To secure the sides of mines with planks or timber; to shore.

además [ah-day-mahs'], *adv.* Moreover, likewise, further; short of this; besides. **Y además le pegó**, and he also beat her.

adementar [ah-day-men-tar'], *va.* To disturb the reason, to addle.

Adén [ah-dayn], *m.* Aden.

ADENA [ah-day-nah], *f. (Esp.) abr.* de **Asociación para la Defensa de la Naturaleza.**

adenitis [ah-day-nee'-tis], *f.* Adenitis, inflammation of a gland.

adenografía [ah-day-no-grah-fee'-ah], *f.* A treatise on the glands.

adenoideo [ah-day-no-e-do], *a.* Adenoidal.

adenología [ah-day-no-lo-hee'-ah], *f. (Anat.)* Description of the glands.

adenoso, sa [ah-day-no'-so, sah], *a.* Glandular.

adentellar [ah-den-tel-lyar'], *va.* To bite, to catch with the teeth. **Adentellar una pared**, To leave toothing-stones or bricks to continue a wall.

adentrarse [ah-dayn-trahr-say], *vr.* **Adentrarse en**, to go into; get into; get inside. **Adentrarse en la selva**, to go deep(er) into the forest.

adentro [ah-den'-tro], *adv.* Inside, within. **De botones adentro**, in my heart. **Ser muy de adentro**, to be intimate in a house. **Tierra adentro**, inland. **Mar adentro**, out to sea. **Reírse para sus adentros**, to laugh inwardly. *Interj.* ¡**Adentro!** Come in!

adepto [ah-dep'-to], *m.* Adept, supporter, follower. *a.* In favor, supporting, who supports.

aderezado [ah-day-ray-thah-do], *a.* Favorable, suitable.

aderezar [ah-day-ray-thar'], *va.* 1. To dress, to adorn. 2. *(Obs.)* To prepare. 3. To clean, to repair. **Aderezar la comida,** to dress victuals.

aderezarse [ah-day-ray-thahr-say], *vr.* To dress up, to get ready.

aderezo [ah-day-ray'-tho}, *m.* 1. Dressing and adorning; finery. 2. Gum, starch, and other ingredients, used to stiffen cloth with. **Aderezo de mesa**, a service for the table; applied to oil vinegar, and salt. **Aderezo de comida**, condiment. **Aderezo de diamantes**, a set of diamonds. **Aderezo de caballo**, trappings or caparisons of a saddle-horse. **Aderezo de casa**, furniture. **Aderezo de espada**, hilt, hook, and other appendages of a sword.

aderra [ah-der'-rah], *f.* A rope, made of rush, used for pressing the husks of grapes.

adestrado, da [ah-des-trah'-do, dah], *a.* 1. Broken in. 2. *(Her.)* On the dexter side of the escutcheon; it is also applied to the principal figure in an escutcheon, on the right of which is another. *-pp.* of ADESTRAR.

adestrador, ra [ah-des-trah-dor', rah] *m. & f.* 1. Teacher. 2. Censor, critic.

adestrar [ah-des-trar'], *va.* 1. To guide, to lead. 2. To teach. 3. To train. *-vr.* To exercise oneself.

adeudado, da [ah-day-oo-dah'-do, dah], *a.* 1. Indebted. 2. *(Obs.)* Obliged. *-pp.* of ADEUDAR.

adeudar [ah-day-oo-dar'], *va.* 1. To pay duty. 2. *(Com.)* To charge debit. 3. *vn.* To become related by marriage.

adeudarse [ah-day-oo-dahr-say], *vr.* To be indebted, to incur debt.

adeudo [ah-day-oo-do], *m.* Debit, indebtedness (deuda).

adeveras [ah-day-vay-rahs], *(LAm.)* **de adeveras= de veras**.

adherencia [ad-ay-ren'-the-ah], *f.* 1. Alliance, adherence to a sect or party. 2. Relationship, friendship. 3. Adhesion. *-pl. (Surg.)* Adhesions.

adherente [ad-ay-ren'-tay], *a.* Adherent. *-m.* Follower. *-pl.* Ingredientes.

adherido, da [ah-day-ree-do], *m. & f.* Adherent, follower.

adherir [ad-ay-reer'], *vn.* To adhere to a sect or party; to espouse an opinion, to cleave to.

adherirse [ah-day-rer-say], *vr.* To hold. To glue.

adhesión [ah-ay-se-on'], *f.* Adhesion; cohesion, attachment.

adhesividad [ah-day-de-ve-dahd], *f.* Adhesiveness.

adhesivo, va [ad-ay-see'-vo, vah], *a.* Adhesive, capable of adhering. **(Yo adhiero, yo adhiera; él adhirió, él adhiriera, from Adherir.** *V.* ASENTIR.

adiado [ah-de-ah'-do]. *-pp.* ADIAR.

adiamantado, da [ah-de-ah-man-tah'-do, dah], *a.* Adamantine.

adiar [ah-de-ahr'], *va. (Obs.)* To appoint, to set a day.

adición [ah-de-the-on'], *f.* 1. Addition. 2. Remark or note put to accounts. **Adición de la herencia**, acceptance of an inheritance. 3. Addition, the first rule of arithmetic. 4. Advance (of salary).

adicionador, ra [ah-de-the-o-nah-dor', rah], *m. & f.* One that makes additions.

adicional [ah-de-the-o-nahl'], *a.* Supplementary.

adicionalmente [ah-de-the-o-nal-men'-tay], *adv.* Additionally.

adicionar [ah-de-the-o-nar'], *va.* To make additions, to add.

adictivo [ah-dec-te-vo*], a. (Cono Sur)* Addictive.

adicto, ta [ah-deec'-to, tah], *1. a.* Addicted, attached.

adicto, *m.* Addict.

adieso [ah-de-ay'-so], *adv. (Obs.)* At the moment, instantly.

adiestrado [ah-de-ays-trah-do], *a.* Trained.

adiestramiento [ah-de-ays-trah-me-ayn-to], *m.* Training; drilling; practice.

adiestrar [ah-de-es-trar'], *va.* V. ADESTRAR. (**Yo adiestro, yo adiestre,** from *Adestrar.* V. ACERTAR). To train, to teach, to coach; to drill; to guide, to lead.

adiestrarse [ah-de-ays-trahr-say], *vr.* To practise, to train.

adietar [ah-de-ay-tar'], *va.* To diet.

adifés [ah-de-fays] *a.* 1. With difficulty. 2. *(Carib.)* On purpose (a propósito), deliberately.

adinamia [ah-de-nah'-me-ah], *f.* Adynamia, debility, great weakness.

adinámico, ca [ah-de-nah'-me-co, cah], *a.* Adynamic, lacking force.

adinas [ah-dee'-nas], *f. pl.* V. ADIVAS.

adinerado, da [ah-de-nay-rah'-do, dah], *a.* Rich, wealthy.

adintelado, da [ah-din-tay-lah'-do, dah], *a.*falling from an arch gradually into a straight line.

adiós [a-de-os'], *int.* Goodbye, bye-bye. **Ir a decir adiós a uno,** to go to say good-bye to somebody.

adiosito [ah-de-o-see-to], *int. (LAm.)* Bye-bye!, cheerio!

adipocira [ah-de-po-thee'-rah], *f.* Adipocere.

adiposidad [ah-de-po-see-dahd], *f.* V. ADIPOSIS

adiposo, sa [ah-de-po'-so, sah], *a. (Med.)* Fat, adipose, V. SEBOSO.

adir [ah-deer'], *va.* To accept, to receive an inheritance.

aditamento [ah-de-tah-men'-to], *m.* Addition.

aditivo [ah-de-te-vo], *m.* Additive.

adivina, *f.* V. ADIVINANZA.

adivinable [ah-de-ve-nah'-blay], *a.* Capable of conjecture, or foretelling.

adivinación [ah-de-ve-nah-the-on'], *f.* Divination, guessing, solving. **Adivinación de pensamientos,** thought-reading.

adivinador, ra [ah-de-ve-nah-dor', rah], *m. & f.* A diviner, a soothsayer.

adivinamiento [ah-de-ve-nah-me-en'-to], *m.* V. ADIVINACION.

adivinanza [ah-de-ve-nan'-thah], *f. (coll.)* 1. Prophesy, prediction. 2. Enigma, riddle, conundrum. 3. Guess. 4. V. ADIVINACION.

adivinar [ah-de-ve-nar'], *va.* 1. To foretell future events, to soothsay. 2. To conjecture, anticipate, or divine, to give a guess. **Adivina quién lo hizo,** it´s anyone´s guess who did it. 3. To unriddle an enigma or difficult problem; to find out.

adivino, na [ah-de-vee'-no, nah], *m. & f.* 1. Soothsayer. 2. Foreboder, fortuneteller.

a. abr. de **adjunto** (enclosed).

adjetivación [ad-hay-te-vah-the-on'], *f.* Act of uniting one thing to another.

adjetivar [ad-hay-te-var'], *va. (coll.)* To unite.

adjetivo [ad-hay-tee'-vo], *1. m. (Gram.)* Adjective. 2. *a.* Adjectival.

adjudicación [ad-hoo-de-cah-the-on'], *f.* Act of adjudging. *a.* **Pública subasta,** auction-sale; «knocking-down» at auction-**al mejor postor,** to the highest bidder.

adjudicar [ad-hoo-de-car'], *va.* To adjudge, to sell at auction. **Adjudicar algo a uno en 500 dólares,** to knock something down to someone for $ 500.

adjudicarse [ad-hoo-de-cahr-say], *vr.* To appropriate to oneself. **Adjudicarse el premio,** to win the prize.

adjudicativo, va [ad-hoo-de-cah-tee'-vo, vah], *a.* Adjudicating.

adjudicatario, ria [ad-hoo-de-cah-tah'-re-o, ah], *m. & f.* One to whom something is adjudged, grantee.

adjunta [ad-hoon'-tah], *f.* Letter enclosed in another.

adjuntar [ad-hoon-tahr], *va.* To append, attach, to enclose. **Adjuntamos factura,** we enclose our bill.

adjunto, ta [ad-hoo'-to, tah], *a.* 1. Joined, annexed, inclosed. Adjunct. 2. Assistant, profesor (persona).

adjurar [ad-hoo-rar'], *va. (Obs.)* to conjure, exorcise; supplicate.

adjutor, ra [ad-hoo-tor'-rah], *a. & n.* Adjuvant; helper.

adlátere [ad-lah-tay-ray], *m.* Companion; associate.

adminicular [ad-me-ne-coo-lar'], *va. (Law.)* To increase the power and efficacy of a thing by adding collateral aids.

adminículo [ad-me-nee'-coo-lo], *m.* Prop, support, aid, accessory.

administración [ad-me-nis-trah-the-on'], *1. f.* 1. Administration, managerement. 2. Office of an administrator. **En administración,** in trust: applied to places in which the occupant has no property. **Administración de Correos,** General Post Office. 3. Government administration. 4. Headquarters, central office.

administrador, ra [ad-me-nis-trah-dor', rah], *m. & f.* Administrator, management; steward, director, trustee. **Administrador de correos,** postmaster. **Administrador de fincas,** land agent.**Administrador de archivos de datos** *(Comp.),* data file manager. **Administrador de bases de datos** *(Comp.),* data base manager. **Administrador de operaciones informáticas** *(Comp.),* computer operations manager. **Administrador de redes informáticas** *(Comp.),* computer network manager. **Administrador de sistemas** *(Comp.),* system manager.

administrar [ad-me-nis-trar'], *va.* 1. To administer, to govern. 2. To serve an office.

administrarse [ad-me-nes-trahr-say], *vr.* To manage one´s own affairs. to organize one´s life.

administrativo, va [ad-me-nis-trah-tee'-vo, vah], *a.* Administrative, the one who administers.

administratorio, ria [ad-me-nis-trah-to'-re-o, ah], *a. (Law.)* Belonging to an administration or administrator.

admirable [ad-me-rah'-blay], *a.* Admirable, excellent.

admirablemente [ad-me-rah-blay-men'-tay], *adv.* Admirably, marvelously.

admiración [ad-me-rah-the-on'], *f.* 1. Wonder; sudden surprise. **Esto llenó a todos de admiración,** this filled everyone with wonder. 2. Point of exclamation. ¡! 3. Prodigy. **Es una admiración,** it is a thing worthy of admiration.

admirador, ra [ad-me-rah-dor', rah], *m. & f.* Admirer.

admirar [ad-me-rar'], *va.* To cause admiration; to marvel, to contemplate. **Esto admiró a todos,** this astonished everyone.

admirarse [ad-me-rahr-say], *vr.* To be seized with admiration; to make a wonder, to be surprised.

admirativo, va [ad-me-rah-tee'-vo, vah], *a.* Admiring, wondering.

admisibilidad [ad-me-se-be-le-dahd], *f.* Admissibility.

admisible [ad-me-see'-blay], *a.* Admissible; acceptable, credible, legitimate. **Eso no es admisible,** that cannot be allowed.

admisión [ad-me-se-on'], *f.* Admission, acceptance.

admitir [ad-me-teer'], *va.* 1. To receive, to give entrance. **La sala admite 500 personas,** the hall holds 500 people. 2. To concede; to accept. **No admite otra explicación,** it allows no other explication. 3. To admit; to permit; to find. **Bien admitido,** well received. **El asunto no admite dilación,** the affair admits no delay.

admón *f. abr.* de **administración.**

admonición [ad-mo-ne-the-on'], *f.* Warning, counsel, advice.

admonitor [ad-mo-ne-tor'], *m.* Monitor, in some religious communities.

admonitorio [ad-mo-ne-to-reo], *a.* Señal, voz of warning. **ADN** *abr.* de **ácido desoxirribonucléico.**

adnado, da [ad-nah'-do, dah], *m. & f.* Step-son, stepdaughter.

adnata [ad-nah'-tah], *f. (Anat.)* Adnata, the external white membrane of the eye.

adnato, ta [ad-nah'-to, tah], *a. (Bot.)* Adnate, adherent.

adobado, da [ah-do-bah'-do, dah], *a.* Marinated, pickled; curried, dressed. *-pp.* of ADOBAR.

adobado [ah-do-bah'-do], *m.* 1. Pickled pork. 2. Any sort of dressed meat.

adobador, ra [ah-do-bah-dor', rah], *m. & f.* Dresser, preparer.

adobamiento, *m.* A kind of stew.

adobar [ah-do-bar'], *va*. 1. To dress or make something up. 2. To pickle pork or other meat. 3. To cook. 4. To tan hides. 5. *(Obs.)* To contract, to stipulate.

adobasillas [ah-do-bah-seel'-lyas], *m*. One that makes or repairs straw bottoms for chairs.

adobe [ah-do'-bay], *m*. 1. Brick not yet burnt, baked in the sun. 2. *(Cono Sur)* Big foot, plate of meat. 3. Descansar haciendo adobes *(Mex.)* to moonlight, to do work on the side.

adobera [ah-do-bay'-rah], *f*. 1. Mould for making bricks. 2. *(Cono Sur, Mex.)* (queso) Brick-shaped cheese, (molde) cheese mould. 3. *(Cono Sur)* Big foot.

adobería [ah-do-bay'-re-ah], *f*. Brickyard. 2. *V*. TENERIA.

adobo [ah-do'-bo], *m*. 1. Repairing, mending. 2. Pickle-sauce. 3. Ingredients for dressing leather or cloth. 4. Pomade, cosmetic.

adocenado, da [ah-do-thay-nah'-do, dah], *a*. Common, ordinary, vulgar. *-pp*. ADOCENAR.

adocenar [ah-do-thay-nar'], *va*. 1. To count or sell by dozens. 2. To despise.

adocenarse [ah-do-thay-nahr-say], *vr*. 1. To become commonplace. 2. To become mediocre; to remain stagnant.

adoctrinador [ah-doc-tre-nah-do], *a*. Indoctrinating, indoctrinatory.

adoctrinamiento [ah-doc-tre-nah-me-ayn-to], *m*. Indoctrination.

adoctrinar [ah-doc-tree-nar'], *va*. To instruct, to teach. *V*. DOCTRINAR.

adolecer [ah-do-lay-therr'], *vn*. 1. To be seized with illness. 2. To labor under disease or affliction. *-va*. *(Obs.)* To produce pain or disease.

adolescencia [ah-do-les-then'-the-ah], *f*. Adolescence.

adolescente [ah-do-les-then-tay], *a*. Adolescent, young. *-m*. & *f*. Adolescent, teenager. (Yo adolezco, from Adolecer, *V*. ABORRECER.)

Adolfo [ah-dol-pho], *m*. Adolphus, Adolph, Adolf.

adolorado, adolorido, *a*. *V*. DOLORIDO.

adomiciliarse [ah-do-me-the-le-ar'-say], *va*. *V*. DOMICILIARSE.

adonado, da [ah-do-nah'-do, dah], *a*. *(Obs.)* 1. Endowed by Nature; gifted. 2. Witty.

adonde [ah-don'-day], *adv*. Where, whither. El lugar adonde voy, the place I am going to. -Observ. In an interrogative sentence, *adonde* has a written accent: ¿adónde vas?, where are you going?

adondequiera *adv*. Wherever, wheresoever (movimiento). Adondequiera que vayas, wherever you go.

adonis [ah-do'-nis], *m*. Adonis, handsome youth.

adopción [ah-dop-the-on'], *f*. 1. Adoption taking another woman's child for one's own. 2. Madrileño de adopción, a citizen of Madrid by adoption.

adoptable [ah-dop-tah'-blay], *a*. Adoptable, suitable for adopting.

adoptado, da [ah-dop-tah-do], *m*. & *f*. *(Mex.)* Adopted child.

adoptador, ra [ah-dop-tah-dor, rah], *m*. & *f*. Adopter.

adoptar [ah-dop-tar], *va*. 1. To adopt, to father. 2. To embrace an opinion. 3. *(Obs.)* To graft.

adoptivo, va [ah-dop-tee'-vo, vah], *a*. Adoptive.

adoquier, adoquiera [ah-do-ke-err', ah-do-ke-ay'-rah], *adv*. *(Obs.)* Where you please.

adoquín [ah-do-keen'], *m*.1. Paving-stone, binding-stone of a pavement. 2. Fool, dope (tonto).

adoquinado [ah-do-ke-nah-do], *m*. Paving.

adoquinar [ah-do-ke-nar'], *va*. To pave.

ador [ah-dor'], *m*. The time for watering land, where the water is distributed.

adorable [ah-do-rah'-blay], *a*. Adorable, worshipful.

adoración [ah-do-rah-the-on'], *f*. Adoration, worship. Una mirada llena de adoración, an adoring look.

adorador, ra [ah-do-rah-dor'-rah], *m*. & *f*. One that adores, worshipper.

adorar [ah-do-rar'], *va*. 1. To adore, to reverence with religious worship, to idolatrize. 2. To love excessively.

adoratorio [ah-do-rah-to'-re-o], *m*. A name given by the Spaniards to the temples of idols in America; teocalli.

adormecedor, ra [ah-dor-may-thay-dor', rah], *a*. Soporiferous, soporific.

adormecer [ah-dor-may-therr'], *vr*. 1. To cause drowsiness or sleep; to lull asleep. 2. To calm, to lull.

adormecerse [ah-dor-may-thayr-say], *vr*. 1. To fall asleep. 2. To grow benumbed or torpid. 3. *(Met.)* To grow or persist in vice.

adormecido, da [ah-dor-may-thee'-do, dah], *a*. Mopish; sleepy, drowsy. *-pp*. of ADORMECER.

adormecimiento [ah-dor-may-the-me-en'-to], *m*. Drowsiness, slumber, sleepiness, numbness, mopishness. (Yo adormezco, from Adormecer. *V*. ABORRECER)

adormidera [ah-dor-me-day'-rah], *f*. *(Bot.)* Poppy, sleeping pill.

adormilarse [ah-dor-me-lahr-say], *vr*. To doze, to drowse.

adormir [ah-dor-meer'], *vn*. 1. To fall asleep. 2. *(Obs.)* To sound softly (said of a musical instrument).

adormitarse [ah-dor-me-tar'-say], *vr*. *V*. DORMITAR.

adornador, ra [a-dor-nah-dor', rah], *m*. & *f*. Adorner.

adornar [ah-dor-nar'], *va*. 1. To beautify, to embellish, to grace, to ornament. 2. To furnish: to garnish. 3. To accomplish; to adorn with talents.

adornista [ah-dor-nees'-tah], *f*. Decorator.

adorno [ah-dor'-no], *m*. 1. Adorning, accomplishment. 2. Ornament, finery, decoration, habiliment. 3. Garniture. 4. Adorno de una casa, Furniture.

adosado [ah-do-sah-do], 1. *a*. Casa adosada, Semi-detached house.

adosar [ah-do-sahr], *va*. 1. Adosar algo a una pared, to lean something against a wall. 2. *(LAm.)* To join firmly, to attach (juntar).

adquirido [ad-ke-re-do], *a*. mal adquirido, ill-gotten.

adquiridor, ra [ad-ke-re-dor', rah], *m*. & *f*. Acquirer. A buen adquiridor buen expendedor, after a gatherer comes a scatterer.

adquirir [ad-ke-reer'], *va*. To acquire, to obtain, to get. (Yo adquiero, yo adquiera; él adquirió, él adquiriera. *V*. ADQUIRIR.

adquisición [ad-ke-se-the-on'], *f*. 1. Acquisition; attainment; accomplishment. 2. Goods obtained by purchase or gift, not inherited. Poder de adquisición, Purchasing power.

adquisidor, ra [ad-ke-se-dor', rah], *m*. & *f*. Purchaser, acquirer.

adquisitivo, va [ad-ke-se-tee'-vo, vah], *a*. *(For.)* Acquisitive.

adquisitorio, ria [ad-ke-se-to'-re-o, re-ah], *a*. Purchasing, purchase.

adquisividad [ad-ke-se-ve-dahd], *f*. Acquisitiveness.

adra [ah'-drah], *f*. 1. Turn. 2. Section of town, neighborhood.

adral [ah-drahl], *m*. Rail, sideboard (carreta).

adragantina [ah-drah-gahn-tee'-nah], *f*. Tragacanthin.

adraganto [ah-drah-gahn'-to], *m*. Tragacanth.

adral [ah-drahl'], *m*. Sideboard (camión).

adrede, adredemente [ah-dray'-day, ah-dray-day-men'-tay], *adv*. Purposely, on purpose, knowingly.

adrenalina [ah-dray-nah-lee'-nah], *f*. Adrenaline, type of heart stimulant.

Adriano [ah-dre-ah-no], *m*. Hadrian.

Adriático, ca [ah-dree-ah'-te-co, cah], *a*. Adriatic.

adrizar [ah-dree-thar'], *va*. *(Naut.)* To right. Adrizar un navío, to right a ship.

adrolla [ah-drol'-lya], *f*. *(Obs.)* Deceit in trade.

adscribir [ads-cre-beer'], *va*. To appoint a person to a place or employment. Estuvo adscrito al servicio de..., he was attached to ....., he was in the service of....

adscripción [ads-crip-the-on'], *f*. Nomination, appointment.

aduana [ah-doo-ah'-nah], *f.* A custom-house. **Pasar por todas las aduanas**, to undergo a close examination. **En la aduana**, *(Com.)* in bond.

aduanar [ah-doo-ah-nar'], *va.* 1. To enter goods at the custom-house. 2. To pay duty, to put in bond.

aduanero [ah-doo-ah-any'-ro], *m.* Custom-house officer, customs officer.

aduar [ah-doo-ar'], *m.* 1. Horde, a migratory crew. 2. Village of Arabs.

adúcar [ah-doo'-car], *m.* A coarse sort of silk stuff, silk refuse, ferret silk.

aducir [ah-doo-therr'], *va.* 1. To adduce, to cite. 2. To guide, to bring.

aductor [ah-dooc-tor'], *m. (Anat.)* Adductor (muscle).

aduendado, da [ah-doo-en-dah'-do, dah], *a.* Ghost-like, walking about like a ghost.

adueñarse [ah-doo-ay-nyar'-say], *vr.* To take possession of, to seize.

adufa [ah-doo'-fah], *f.* A half-door.

adufaso [ah-doo-fah'-so], *m.* Blow with a timbrel or tambourine.

adufe [ah-doo'-fay], *m.* Timbrel or tambourine. *V.* PANDERO.

adufero, ra [ah-doo-fay'-ro, rah], *m. & f.* Timbrel or tambourine player.

adujadas, adujas [ah-doo-hah'-das, ah-doo'-has], *f. pl. (Naut.)* Coil or a colled cable.

adujar [ah-doo-har'], *va. (Naut.)* To coil a cable.

adula [ah-doo'-lah], *f.* 1. *(Prov.)* A piece of ground for which there is no particular manner of irrigation.

adulación [ah-doo-lah-the-on'], *f.* Flattery, fawning, coaxing, cogging, soothing.

adulada [ah-doo-lah-dah], *f. (Mex.)* Flattery.

adulador, ra [ah-doo-lah-dor', rah], *m. & f.* Flatterer, fawner, soother.

adular [ah-doo-lar'], *va.* 1. To flatter, to soothe, to coax, to court, to compliment. 2. To fawn, to creep, to crouch.

adulate [ah-doo-lah-tay], *a, m. (LAm.)* . ADULON

adulonería [ah-doo-lo-nay-re-ah], *f. (LAm.)* 1. Flattering, fawning. 2. Fawning nature, soapiness.

adulatorio, ria [ah-doo-lah-to'-re-o, ah], *a.* Flattering, honey-mouthed; parasitical.

adulear [ah-doo-lay-ar'], *vn.* To bawl, to cry out.

adulero [ah-doo lay' ro], *m.* Driver of horses or mules.

adulón, na [ah-doo-lone', nah], *m. & f. (coll. Amer.)* Flatterer.

adúltera [ah-dool'-tay-rah], *f.* Adulteress.

adulteración [ah-dool-tay-rah-the-on'], *f.* Adulteration, falsification (of goods, etc.)

adulterado, da [ah-dool-tay-rah'-do, dah], *a.* Sophisticated. *-pp.* of ADULTERAR.

adulterador, ra [ah-dool-tay-rah-dor', rah], *m. & f.* One who adulterates; falsifier.

adulterar [ah-dool-tay-rar'], *va.* To adulterate, to falsify. *-vn.* to commit adultery.

adulterinamente [ah-dool-tay-re-nah-men'-tay], *adv.* In an adulterous manner.

adulterino, na [ah-dool-tay-ree'-no, nah], *a.* 1. Adulterous; begotten in adultery. 2. Adulterated, falsified, forged.

adulterio [ah-dool'-tay-re-o], *m.* Adultery.

adúltero, ra [ah-dool'-tay-ro, rah], *m. & f.* Adulterer.

adultez [ah-dool-tayth], *f. (Cono Sur)* Adulthood.

adulto, ta [ah-dool'-to, tah], *a.* Adult, grown up.

adulzar [ah-dool-thar'], *va. (Obs.)* 1. To sweeten. 2. To soften. **Adulzar los metales**, To render metals more ductile.

adunación [ah-doo-nah-the-on'], *f. (Obs.)* The act of uniting, and the union itself.

adunar [ah-doo-nar'], *va.* To unite, to join; to unify.

adunco, ca [ah-doon'-co, cah], *a.* Aduncous, curved.

adustez [ah-doos-teth'], *f.* Disdain, aversion, asperity, austerity, severity.

adustamente [ah-doos-tha-men'-tay], *adv.* Austerely, severely.

adustión [ah-doos-te-on'], *f. (Med.)* Burning up or drying as by fire; cauterization.

adustivo, va [ah-doos-tee'-vo, vah], *a.* That which has the power of burning up.

adusto, ta [aah-doos'-to, tah], *a.* Gloomy, **austero**, intractable, sullen.

adútero [ah-doo'-tay-ro], *m. (Anat.)* The Fallopian tube.

advenedizo, za [ad-vay-nay-dee'-tho, thah], *a.* 1. Foreign. 2. Applied to a foreign immigrant.

advenimiento [ad-vay-ne-me-en'-to], *m.* Arrival; advents.

adventicio, cia [ad-ven-tee'-the-o, ah], *a.* 1. Adventitious; accidental. 2. *(Law.)* Acquired by industry or inheritance, independent of a paternal fortune.

adverar [ad-vay-rar'], *va. (Obs.)* To aver, affirm.

adverbial [ad-ver-be-ahl'], *a.* Belonging to an adverb.

adverbialmente [ad-ver-be-al-men'-tay], *adv.* Adverbially.

adverbio [ad-ver'-be-o], *m.* Adverb, one of the parts of speech.

adversamente [ad-ver-sah-men'-tay], *adv.* Adversely.

adversario [ad-ver-sah'-re-o], *m.* Opponent; antagonist, foe. *-pl.* Notes in a common-place book; a common-place book.

adversativo, va [ad-ver-sah-tee'-vo, vah], *a. (Gram.)* A particle which expresses some difference and opposition between that which precedes and follows.

adversidad [ad-ver-se-dad'], *f.* Calamity, misfortune, affliction, adversity.

adverso, sa [ad-ver'-so, sah], *a.* 1. Adverse, calamitous, afflictive. 2. Opposite, averse. 3. Favorless. 4. Facing, in front of.

advertencia [ad-ver-ten'-the-ah], *f.* 1. Attention to; regard to. 2. Advice. 3. Advertisement to the reader, remark. 4. Admonition, counsel.

advertidamente [ad-ver-te-dah-men'-tay], *adv.* Advisedly, deliberately.

advertido, da [ad-ver-tee'-do, dah], *a.* 1. Noticed. 2. Skillful, intelligent; acting with deliberation, sagacious, clever, prudent. *-pp.* of ADVERTIR.

advertimiento [ad-ver-te-me-en'-to], *m. V.* ADVERTENCIA.

advertir [ad-ver-teer'], *va.* 1. To take notice of, to observe. 2. To instruct, to advise, to give notice or warning. 3. To acquaint. 4. To mark, to note. **Se lo advierto a usted**, I warn you. **El señor Norton no dejó de advertir esta observación**, this remark was not lost upon Mr. Norton. *(Yo advierto, yo advierta; él advirtió, él advirtiera;* from **Advertir.** *V.* ASENTIR.)

Adviento [ad-ve-en'-to], *m.* Advent, the four weeks before Christmas.

advocación [ad-vo-cah-the-on'], *f.* 1. Appellation given to a church, chapel or altar, dedicated to the holy Virgin or a saint. 2. *(Obs.)* Profession of a lawyer. *V.* ABOGACION. Patronage, protection.

advocar [ad-vo-cahr], *va. (LAm.)* To advocate.

advocatorio, ria [ad-vo-cah-to'-re-o, ah], *a.* **Carta advocatoria or convocatoria**, a letter of convocation calling an assembly.

adyacencia [ad-yah-thayn-the-ah], *f. (Cono Sur)* Nearness, proximity; (en las adyacencias) in the vicinity.

adyacente [ad-yah-then'-tay], *a.* Adjacent; contiguous.

adyuntivo, va [ad-yoon-tee'-vo, vah], *a.* Conjunctive; joining.

AECE *f. abr.* de **Asociación Española de Cooperación Europea.**

aechadero [ah-ay-chah-day'-ro], *m.* The place where grain is winnowed from the chaff; winnowing-floor.

aechador, ra [ah-ay-chah-dor', rah], *m. & f.* Winnower.

aechaduras [ah-ay-chah-doo'-ras], *f. pl.* The refuse of grain, chaff.

aechar [ah-ay-char'], *va.* To winnow, to sift grain from chaff.

aecho [ah-ay'-cho], *m.* Winnowing, cleansing.

aeración [ah-ay-rah'-the-on'], *f.* 1. Aeration, charging with gas. 2. Ventilation of air. (*Acad.*).

aéreo [ah-ay'-ray-o, ah], *a.* 1. Aerial. 2. (*Met.*) Airy, fantastic.

aerífero, a [ah-ay-ree'-fay-ro, rah], *a.* Air-conducting.

aeriforme [ah-ay-re-for'-may], *a.* (*Chem.*) Aeriform, gaseous.

aero [ah-ay-ro], *pref.* Aereo.

aerobic [ah-ay-ro-bek], *m.* **aeróbica**, *f.* Aerobics.

aeróbico [ah-ay-ro-be-co], *a.* Aerobic.

aerobismo [ah-ay-ro-bes-mo], *m.* (*Cono Sur*) Aerobics.

aerobús [ah-ay-ro-boos], *m.* (*Aer.*) Airbus.

aerocar [ah-ay-ro-cahr], *m.* Airbus.

aeroclub [ah-ay-ro-cloob] *m.* Airclub.

aerochati [ah-ay-ro-chah-te], *f.* Air hostess.

aerodeslizador [ah-ay-ro-days-le-thah-dor], *m.* **aerodeslizante**, *m.* Hovercraft.

aerodinámica [ah-ay-ro-de-nah'-me-cah], *f.* Aerodynamics.

aerodinámico, ca [ah-ay-ro-de-nah'-me-co, cah], *a.* 1. Aerodynamic. 2. Streamlined.

aerodinamismo [ah-ay-ro-de-nah-mes-mo], *m.* Streamlining.

aerodinamizar [ah-ay-ro-de-nah-me-thahr], *va.* To streamline.

aeródromo [ah-ay-ro'-dro-mo], *m.* Airdrome.

aeroembolismo [ah-ay-ro-em-bo-lees'-mo], *m.* (*Med.*) Aeroembolism.

aeroenviar [ah-ay-ro-ayn-ve-ahr], *va.* To send by air.

aeroespacial [ah-ay-ro-ays-pa-the-ahl], *a.* Aerospace (*Aer.*).

aerofaro [ah-ay-ro-phah-ro], *m.* (*Aer.*) Beacon.

aerofoto [ah-ay-ro-pho-to], *f.* Aerial photograph.

aerofumigación [ah-ay-ro-foo-me-gah-the-on], *f.* Crop-dusting.

aerografía [ah-ay-ro-grah-fee'-ah], *f.* Aerography.

aerógrafo [ah-ay-ro'-grah-fo], *m.* Air brush.

aerograma [ah-ay-ro-grah'-mah], *m.* Wireless message.

aerolínea [ah-ay-ro-lee'-nay-ah], *f.* Airline.

aerolito [ah-ay-ro-lee'-to], *m.* Aerolite.

aerología [ah-ay-ro-lo-hee'-ah], *f.* Aerology.

aerolito [ah-ay-ro-lee'-to], *m.* Aerolite.

aerología [ah-ay-ro-lo-hee'-ah], *f.* Aerology.

aeromancia [ah-ay-ro-mahn'-the-ah], *f.* Aeromancy.

aeromedicina [ah-ay-ro-may-de-thee'-nah], *f.* Aeromedicine.

aerómetro [ah-ay-ro'-may-tro], *m.* (*Chem.*) Aerometer.

aeromodelismo [ah-ay-ro-mo-day-les-mo], *m.* Aeromodelling, making model aeroplanes.

aeromodelo [ah-ay-ro-mo-day-lo], *m.* Model aeroplane.

aeromotor [ah-ay-ro-mo-tor], *m.* Aero-engine.

aeromoza [ah-ay-ro-mo'-thah], *f.* Airline hostess, stewardess.

aeronauta [ah-ay-ro-nah'-oo-tah], *m.* Aeronaut.

aeronáutica [ah-ay-ro-nah'-oo-te-cah], *f.* Aeronautics.

aeronáutico, ca [ah-ay-ro-nah'-oo-te-co, cah], *a.* Aeronautical.

aeronaval [ah-ay-ro-nah-val], *a.* Air-sea; **base**, air-sea base.

aeronave [ah-ay-ro-nah'-vay], *f.* Airship.

aeronavegabilidad [ah-ay-ro-nah-vay-gah-be-le-dahd], *f.* Airworthiness.

aeronavegable [ah-ay-ro-nah-vay-gah-blay], *a.* Airworthy.

aeroplano [ah-ay-ro-plah'-no], *m.* Airplane. **Aeroplano de combate**, fighter plane.

aeroportuario [ah-ay-ro-por-too-ah-reo], *a.* Airport.

aeroposta [ah-ay-ro-pos-tah], *f.* (*LAm.*) Airmail.

aeropostal [ah-ay-ro-pos-tahl'], *a.* Airmail.

aeropuerto [ah-ay-ro-poo-err'-to], *m.* Airport. **Aeropuerto para helicópteros**, Heliport.

aerosol [ah-ay-ro-sol'], *m.* Aerosol.

aerospacio [ah-ay'ro-spah'-the-o], *m.* Aerospace.

aerostático, ca [ah-ay-ros-tah'-te-co, cah], *a.* Aerostatic.

aeróstato [ah-ay-ros-tah-to], *m.* Balloon, aerostat.

aerotermodinámica [ah-ay-ro-ter-mo-de-nah'-me-cah], *f.* Aerothermodynamics.

aeroterrestre [ah-ay-ro-tay-rrays-tray], *a.* Air-ground.

aerotransportado, da [ah-ay-ro-trans-por-tah'-do, dah], *f.* Airlifted, airborne.

aerovía [ah-ay-ro-vee'-ah], *f.* Airway.

AES *m. abr.* de **acuerdo económico social** (wages pact).

a/f *abr.* de **a favor** (in favor).

afabilidad [ah-fah-be-le-dad'], *f.* Affability, graciousness, courteousness.

afable [ah-fah'-blay], *a.* Affable, complacent, kind; agreeable, familiar.

afablemente [ah-fah-blay-men'-tay], *adv.* Affably, good-naturedly.

afamado, da [ah-fah-mah'-do, dah], *a.* 1. Celebrated, noted. 2. (*Obs.*) Hungry.

afamar [ah-fah-mahr], *va.* To make famous.

afamarse [ah-fah-mahr-say], *vr.* To become famous, to make a reputation.

afán [ah-fahn'], *m.* 1. Anxiety, solicitude, eagerness, laboriousness in pursuit of worldly affairs. **El afán de**, the desire of. 2. (*Obs.*) Toil, fatigue.

afanadamente, afanosamente [ah-fa-nah-dah-men'-tay, ah-fah-no-sah-men'-tay], *adv.* Anxiously, laboriously.

afanador, ra [ah-fah-nah-dor', rah], *m. & f.* One eager for riches: painstaker.

afanar [ah-fah-nar'], *vn. & vr.* 1. To toil, to labor; to be over-solicitous. 2. (*Obs.*) To be engaged in corporeal labor. **Afanar, afanar y nunca medrar**, Much toil and little profit.

afanarse [ah-fah-nahr-say], *vr.* 1. To toil too much. (*coll.*) **Afanarse por nada**, to fidget. 2. To get angry (enfadarse).

afaneso [ah-fah-nay'-so], *m.* Arsenite of copper; Scheele's green.

afanoso, sa [ah-fah-no'-so, sah], *a.* Solicitous; laborious, painstaking.

afantasmado [ah-fahn-tahs-mah-do], *a.* Conceited.

afarolado [ah-fah-ro-lah-do], *a.* (*LAm.*) Excited, worked up.

afarolarse [ah-fah-ro-lahr-say], *vr.* (*LAm.*) To get excited, make a fuss, get worked up.

afasia [ah-fah'-see-a], *f.* Aphasia.

afásico [ah-fah-se-co], *a.* (*Med.*) Aphasic, suffering from aphasia.

afeador, ra [ah-fay-ah-dor, rah], *m. & f.* One that deforms or makes ugly.

afeamiento [ah-fay-ah-me-ayn-to], *m.* 1. Defacing, disfigurement (físicamente). 2. (*fig.*) Condemnation, censure.

afear [ah-fay-ar'], *va.* 1. To deform, to deface, to misshape. 2. (*Met.*) To decry, to censure, to condemn.

afeblecerse [ah-fay-blay-ther'-say], *vr.* To grow feeble, or delicate.

afección [ah-fec-the-on'], *f.* 1. Affection, inclination, fondness. **Afecciones del alma**, emotions. 2. Affection, the state of being affected by any cause or agent. 3. (*Phil.*) Quality, property. 4. Right of bestowing a benefice.

afeccionarse [ah-fayc-the-o-nahr-say], *vr.* **Afeccionarse a** (*Cono Sur*) To take a liking to, become fond of.

afectación [ah-fec-tah-the-on'], *f.* 1. Affectation, artificial appearance; daintiness, finicalness. 2. Presumption, pride.

afectadamente [ah-fec-tah-dah-men'-tay], *adv.* Affectedly, formally, hypocritically.

afectado, da [ah-fec-tah'-do, dah], *a.* 1. Affected, formal, conceited, finical, foppish. 2. (*Med.*) **Estar afectado del corazón**, to have heart trouble. *-pp.* of AFECTAR.

afectante [ah-fayc-tahn-tay], *a.* (*Cono Sur*) Disturbing, distressing.

afectar [ah-fec-tar'], *va.* 1. To make a show of something, to feign. 2. To affect, to act upon, to produce effect in any other thing; to affect, assume a manner. **Nos afecta gravemente**, it seriously affects us. 3. To unite benefices or livings. 4. (*Jur.*) To tie up, encumber. 5. (*LAm.*) To hurt, harm, damage (dañar). 6. (*LAm.*) To take on (forma), assume.

afectarse [ah-fayc-tahr-say], *vr.* To wound, to sadden.

afectísimo, ma [ah-fec-tee'-se-mo, mah], *a.* Yours sincerely, yours faithfully, yours truly (ending of a letter).

afectividad [ah-fayc-te-ve-dahd], *f.* Emotional nature, emotion; sensitivity.

afectivo, va [ah-fec-tee'-vo, vah], *a.* Affective, proceeding from affection.

afecto [ah-fec'-to], *m.* 1. Affection, love, kindness, fancy; concern. 2. Passion, sensation. 3. Pain, disease. 4. *(Art.)* Lively representation. **Afectos desordenados**, inordinate desires. 5. *(Med.)* **Afecto de**, afflicted with. 6. *(Jur.)* subjected to, liable for.

afecto, ta [ah-fec'-to, tah], *a.* 1. Affectionate, loving. 2. Inclined. 3. Subject to some charge or obligation for lands, rents. 3. Dear. **Un amigo afecto**, a dear friend.

afectuosamente [ah-fayc-too-o-sah-mayn-tay], *adv.* Affectionately.

afectuosidad [ah-fec-too-o-se-dad'], *f.* Tenderness, benevolence, kindness. affection.

afectuoso, sa [ah-fec-too-o'-so, sah], *a.* Kind, gracious, loving, tender, affectionate.

afeitada [ah-fay-e-tah'-dah], *f.* Shave.

afeitadora [ah-fay-e-tah-do'-rah], *f.* Razor, shaver.

afeitar [ah-fay-e-tar'], *va.* 1. To shave. 2. To clip the box, walltrees, etc, in a garden. 3. To trim (crines, colas). 4. To make up (mujer). 5. To brush.

afeitarse [ah-fay-e-tahr-say], *vr.* 1. To shave, have a shave (hombre). 2. (Mujer) to make up, put one´s make-up on.

afeite [ah-fay'-e-tay], *m.* Paint, rouge, cosmetic.

afelio [ah-fay'-le-o], *m. (Astr.)* Aphelion, that part of a planet's orbit which is most remote from the sun.

afelpado, da [ah-fel-pah'-do, dah], *a.* Shaggy, villous, like plush or velvet.

afelpar [ah-fel-par'], *va.* To make a nap, to shag or velvet.

afeminación [ah-fay-me-nah-the-on'], *f.* Effemination; emasculation.

afeminadamente [ah-fay-me-nah-dah-men'-tay], *adv.* Womanly.

afeminado, da [ah-fay-me-nah'-do, dah], *a.* Effeminate. -*pp.* of AFEMINAR.

afeminamiento [ah-fay-me-nah-me-en'-to], *m. V.* AFEMINACION.

afeminar [ah-fay-me-nar'], *va.* 1. To effeminate, to unman. 2. To debilitate, to enervate, to melt into weakness.

afeminarse [ah-fay-me-nahr-say]. *vr.* To become effeminate, feeble, lose courage.

aferente [ah-fay-ren'-tay], *a.* Afferent, conducting inward to a part or organ.

aféresis [ah-fay'-ray-sis], *f.* Apheresis, a figure in grammar that takes away a letter or syllable from the beginning of a word, as **Norabuena** for **Enhorabuena**.

aferrado, da [ah-fer-rah'-do, dah], *a.* Headstrong, obstinate; **seguir obstinado a**, to remain firm in. -*pp.* of AFERRAR.

aferramiento [ah-fer-rah-me-en'-to], *m.* 1. Grasping, grappling; seizing or binding. **Aferramiento de las velas**, *(Naut.)* The furling of the sails. 2. Headstrongness.

aferrar [ah-fer-rar'], *va.* 1. To grapple, to grasp, to seize. 2. *(Naut.)* To furl. 3. *(Naut.)* To moor.

aferrarse [ah-fay-rrahr-say], *vr.* 1. *(Naut.)* To grasp one another strongly. 2. *(Met.)* To persist obstinately in an opinion. **Aferrarse a una esperanza**, to clutch at a hope.

afestonado [ah-fays-to-nah-do] *a.* Festooned.

afgán, na [af-gahn', gah'-nah], *a.* Afghan, of Afghanistan.

Afganistán [af-gah-nes-tahn], *m.* Afghanistan.

afianzado, da [ah-fe-ahn-thah-do], *m. & f. (LAm.)* fiancé(e).

afianzamiento [ah-fe-an-thah-me-en'-to], *m.* 1. Security, guarantee, bail. 2. Prop, support.

afianzar [ah-fe-an-thar'], *va.* 1. To become bail or security, to guarantee. 2. To prop, to secure with stays, ropes, etc.: buttress. 3. To obligate, to make fast, to clinch.

afianzarse [ah-fe-ahn-thahr-say], *vr.* To steady oneself; to become strong, become established.

afición [ah-fe-the-on'], *f.* 1. Affection, inclination for a person or thing; mind. **Tener afición a**, to like. 2. Hobby, pastime, interest. **¿Qué aficiones tiene?**, what are his interests? 3. **La afición**, the experts; the fans; the supporters.

aficionado, da [ah-fe-the-o-nah'-do, dah], *a.* Fond of, enthusiastic about. **Es muy aficionado**, he´s very keen. *m. & f.* 1. Fan, admirer, enthusiast. 2. Amateur. -*pp.* of AFICIONAR.

aficionar [ah-fe-the-o-nar'], *va.* To affect, to cause or inspire affection. **Aficionarse con exceso a**, to fancy, to give one's mind to.

aficionarse [ah-fe-the-o-nahr-say], *vr.* Aficionarse a algo, to get fond of something.

afidos [ah'-fe-dohs], *m. pl. (Ent.)* Aphids, aphidians.

afiche [ah-fe-chay], *m.* Poster (cartel); *(Cono Sur)* illustration, picture (dibujo).

aficávit [ah-fe-cah-vet], *m.* Affidavit, sworn statement.

áfido [ah-fe-do], *m.* Aphid.

afiebrado [ah-fe-ay-brah-do], *a.* Feverish.

afijo, ja [ah-fee'-ho, hah], *a. (Gram.)* Affix, united to the end of a word.

afiladera [ah-fe-lah-day'-rah], *f.* Whetstone.

afilado [ah-fe-lah'-do], *pp.* of AFILAR.-*a.* Sharp, keen.

afiladora [ah-fe-lah-do'-rah], *f. (Cono Sur)* Flirt, coquette.

afiladura [ah-fe-lah-doo'-rah], *f.* Sharpening, whetting.

afilalápices [ah-fe-lah-lah-pe-thays], *m.* Pencil sharpener.

afilamiento [ah-fe-lah-me-en'-to], *m.* 1. The slenderness of the face or nose. 2. *V.* AFILADURA.

afilar [ah-fe-lar'], *va.* 1. To whet, to grind. 2. To render keen. **Afilar las uñas**, to make an extraordinary effort of genius or skill. 3. *(Cono Sur)* To court, to flirt with.

afilarse [ah-fe-lahr-say], *vr.* To grow thin and meagre.

afiliación [ah-fe-le-ah-the-on'], *f.* Affiliation.

afiliado [ah-fe-le-ah'-do], *pp. & a.* Affiliated, adopted. **Los países afiliados**, the member countries.

afiliar [ah-fe-le-ar'], *va.* To adopt; to affiliate; to connect with a central body or society.

afiliarse [ah-fe-le-ahr-say], *vr.* To affiliate, to join.

afiligranado, da [ah-fe-le-grah-nah'-do, dah], *a.* 1. Resembling filigree. 2. *(Met.)* Applied to persons who are slender, and small-featured.

afilo, la [ah-fee'-lo, lah], *a. (Bot.)* Aphyllous, destitute of leaves.

afilón [ah-fe-lone'], *m.* 1. Whetstone. 2. An instrument made of steel for whetting any edged tool. 3. Leather strap, or strop (for razors, etc.)

afilorar [ah-fe-lo-rahr], *va. (Carib.)* To adorn.

afilosofado, da [ah-fe-lo-so-fah'-do, dah], *a.* 1. Eccentric. 2. Applied to the person who plays the philosopher.

afín [ah-feen'], *a.* Close by, contiguous, adjacent. -*m.* Relation by affinity.

afinación [ah-fe-nah-the-on'], *f.* 1. Completion; the act of finishing. 2. Refining. 3. Tuning of instruments.

afinadamente [ah-fe-nah-dah-men'-tay], *adv.* Completely, perfectly.

afinado, da [ah-fe-nah'-do, dah], *a.* Well-finished, perfect, complete. -*pp.* of AFINAR.

afinador, ra [ah-fe-nah-dor', rah], *m. & f.* 1. Finisher. 2. Key with which stringed instruments are tuned, as harp, piano, etc.

afinamiento [ah-fe-nah-me-en'-to], *m.* 1. *V.* AFINACION. 2. Refinement. *V.* FINURA.

afinar [ah-fe-nar'], *va.* 1. To complete, to polish. 2. To tune musical instruments. **Afinar los metales**, To refine metals. **Afinar la voz**, to tune the voice.

afinarse [ah-fe-nahr-say],*vr.* To become polished, civilized.

afincado [ah-fen-cah-do], *m. (Cono Sur)* Farmer.

afincarse [ah-fen-cahr-say], *vr.* To establish, to settle.

afincamiento [ah-fin-cah-me-en'-to], *m. (Obs.)* 1. Eagerness. 2. Anxiety polished, civilized.

afincar [ah-fin-car'], *va.* To buy up real estate; to acquire real property.

afine [ah-fee'-nay], *a.* Related, affinal.

afinidad [ah-fe-ne-dad'], *f.* 1. Affinity, relation by marriage. 2. *(Met.)* Analogy. 3. Relation to, connection with. 4. Friendship.

afirmación [ah-feer-mah-the-on'], *f.* Affirming, declaring; assertion.

afirmadamente [ah-feer-mah-dah-men'-tay], *adv.* Firmly.

afirmado [ah-fer-mah-do], *m.* (*Cono Sur*) Paving, paved surface (acera).

afirmador, ra [ah-feer-mah-dor', rah], *m. & f.* One who affirms.

afirmante [ah-feer-man'-tay], *pa.* The person who affirms.

afirmar [ah-feer-mar'], *va.* 1. To make fast, to secure, to clinch. 2. To affirm, to assure for certain; to contend. **Afirmar una carta**, at cards, to give one card a fixed value. *-vn.* To inhabit, to reside.

afirmarse [ah-fer-marh-say], *vr.* 1. To fix oneself in the saddle or stirrup. 2. To maintain firmly; to advance steadily.

afirmativa [ah-feer-mah-tee'-vah], *f. V.* AFIRMACION.

afirmativamente [ah-feer-mah-te-vah-men'-tay], *adv.* Affirmatively; positively. **Contestar afirmativamente**, to answer in the affirmative.

afirmativo, va [ah-fer-mah-tee'-vo, vah], *a.* Affirmative; opposed to negative.

afistolar [ah-fis-to-lar'], *va.* To render fistulous; applied to a wound.

aflautado [ah-flah-oo-tah-do], *a.* High, fluty (voz).

aflechada [ah-flay-chah'-dah], *a.* Arrow-shaped: used of leaves.

aflicción [ah-flic-the-on'], *f.* 1. Affliction, sorrow, grief, painfulness, mournfulness. 2. Heaviness, anguish of mind.

aflictivo, va [ah-flic-tee'-vo, vah], *a.* Afflictive, distressing; causing pain and grief. **Pena aflictiva**, Corporeal punishment.

aflicto, ta [ah-flic'-to, tah], *pp. irr.* of AFLIGIR.

afligente [ah-fle-hayn-tay], *a.* (*CAm. Mex.*) Distressing, upsetting.

afligidamente [ah-fle-he-dah-men'-tay], *adv.* Grievously.

afligido [ah-fle-he-do], *a.* Grieving, sorrowing, heartbroken. **Los afligidos padres**, the bereaved parents.

afligimiento [ah-fle-he-me-en'-to], *m. V.* AFLICCION.

afligir [ah-fle-heer'], *va.* To afflict, to put to pain, to grieve, to torment, to curse, to mortify.

afligirse [ah-fle-her-say], *vr.* To make one miserable, to lament, to languish, to repine. **No te aflijas**, don´t grieve over it.

aflojadura [ah-flo-hah-doo'-rah], *f.* **aflojamiento** [ah-flo-hah-me-en'-to], *n.* 1. Relaxation, loosening or slackening. 2. Looseness. 3. Cooling.

aflojar [ah-flo-har'], *va.* 1. To loosen, to slacken, to relax, to let loose; to relent; to debilitate. 2. (*Pict.*) To soften the color in shading. 3. (*Naut.*) **Aflojar los obenques**. 4. To fork out (dinero). To ease the shrouds.

aflojarse [ah-flo-hahr-say], *vr.* 1. To grow weak; to abate. 2. To grow cool in fervor or zeal; to lose courage, to languish.

afloración [ah-flo-rah-the-on], *f.* Outcrop.

aflorado [ah-flo-rah'-do], *a. V.* FLOREADO.

afloramiento [ah-flo-rah-me-ayn-to], *m. V.* AFLORACION.

aflorar [ah-flo-rahr], *vn.* (*Geol.*) To crop out, To outcrop; to appear on the surface.

afluencia [ah-floo-en'-the-ah], *f.* 1. Plenty, abundance. 2. Fluency, volubility, crowd. **La afluencia de turistas**, the influx of tourists.

afluente [ah-floo-en'-tay], *a.* 1. Affluent, copious, abundant. 2. Loquacious. *-m.* Affluent, a tributary river.

afluir [ah-floo-eer'], *vn.* 1. To congregate, assemble. 2. To discharge into, or join another stream.

aflujo [ah-floo-ho] *m.* (*Med.*) Afflux, congestion.

aflús [ah-floos], *a.* (*LAm.*) Broke, skint.

afluxionarse [ah-flooc-se-o-nahr-say], *vr.* (*LAm.*) To catch a cold.

afma., afmo. *abr.* de **afectísima, afectísimo** (yours).

afocador, ra [ah-fo-cah-dor', rah], *a.* Focusing; as, **Cremallera afocadora**, Focusing-rack.

afocar [ah-fo-car'], *va.* To focus (optical instruments).

afoetear [ah-fo-ay-tay-ahr], *vt.* (*And. Carib.*) To whip, to beat.

afogarar [ah-fo-gah-rar'], *va.* 1. To scorch a sowed field through excessive heat. 2. To scorch a stew, by lack of juices or water. 3. (*Met.*) To be irritated or distressed.

afollado, da [ah-fol-lyah'-do, dah], *a.* Wearing large or wide trousers. *-pp.* of AFOLLAR.

afondar [ah-fon-dar'], *va.* 1. To put under water. 2. (*Naut.*) To sink. *-vn.* (*Naut.*) To founder.

afonía [ah-fo-nee'-ah], *f.* (*Med.*) Loss of voice, from disease of larynx, as distinguished from aphasia, loss of power to speak, due to brain-disease.

afónico, ca [ah-fo'-ne-co, cah], *a.* 1. Aphonic, not able to use or control the voice. 2. Silent; used of letters, as *h* in *hacer*.

afono [ah-fo-no] *V.* AFÓNICO.

aforado [ah-fo-rah'-do], *a.* Privileged person. *-pp.* of AFORAR.

aforador [ah-fo-rah-dor], *m.* Gauger, appraiser.

aforamiento [ah-fo-rah-me-en'-to], *m.* 1. Gauging. 2. Duty on foreign goods.

aforar [ah-fo-rar'], *va.* 1. To gauge, to measure vessels or quantities. 2. To examine goods for determining the duty. 3. To take to a court of justice. To give or take lands or tenements under the tenure of meliorating. 4. To give privileges. 5. To appraise.

aforisma [ah-fo-rees'-mah], *f.* A swelling in the arteries of beasts: aneurisin.

aforismo [ah-fo-rees'-mo], *m.* Aphorism, brief sentence, maxim.

aforístico, ca [ah-fo-rees'-te-co, cah], *a.* Aphoristica.

aforjudo [ah-for-hoo-do], *a.* (*Cono Sur*) Silly, stupid.

aforo [ah-fo'-ro], *m. 1.* Gauging, examination and appraisal of wine and other commodities for the duties; appraisement. 2. Capacity (teatro); **el teatro tiene un aforo de 2.000**, the theater has a capacity of 2,000, the theater can seat 2,000.

aforrador, ra [ah-for-rah-dor'- rah] *m. & f.* One who lines the inside of clothes.

aforrar [ah-for-rar'], *va.* 1. To line, to cover the inside of clothes; to face. **Aforrar una casa**, to ceil a house. 2. (*Naut.*) to sheathe. 4. (*Naut.*) **Aforrar un cabo**, to serve a cable.

aforrarse [ah-fo-rrahr-say], *vr.* 1. To wrap up warm (arropar). 2. To stuff (atiborrarse).

aforro [ah-for'-ro], *m.* 1. Lining. 2. (*Naut.*) Sheathing. 3. (*Naut.*) Waist of a ship.

afortunadamente [ah-for-too-nah-dah-men'-tay], *adv.* Luckily, fortunately.

afortunado, da [ah-for-too-nah'-do, dah], *a.* Fortunate, happy, lucky. **¡Qué afortunado eres!** How lucky you are! **Tiempo afortunado**, (*Obs.*) blowing weather. **Hombre afortunado en amores**, a man who is lucky in love. *-pp.* of AFORTUNAR.

afortunar [ah-for-too-nar'], *va.* To make happy.

afosarse [ah-fo-sar'-say], *vr.* (*Mil.*) To defend oneself by making a ditch.

afrailado [ah-frah-ee-lah-do], *a.* (*LAm.*) Churchy.

afrailar [ah-frah-e-lar'], *va.* (*Prov.*) To rim trees.

afrancesada, da [ah-fran-thay-sah'-do, dah], *a.* Frenchified, French-like. *-pp.* of AFRANCESAR.

afrancesamiento [ah-fran-thay-sah-me-ayn-to], *m.* Francophilism, pro-French feeling.

afrancesar [ah-fran-thay-sahr'], *va.* To Gallicize, to give a French termination to words.

afrancesarse [ah-fran-thay-sahr-say], *vr.* 1. To imitate the French. 2. To be naturalized in France.

afrechillo [ah-fray-che-lyo], *m.* (*Cono Sur*) (*Agri.*) Bran.

afrecho [ah-fray'-cho], *m.* (*Prov.*) Bran, the husks of grain ground.

afrenillar [ah-fray-nil-lyar'], *vn.* (*Naut.*) To bridle the oars.

afrenta [ah-fren'-tah], *f.* 1. Affront, dishonor, or reproach: outrage; an insult offered to the face; abuse. 2. Infamy resulting from the sentence passed upon a criminal. 3. Stigma.

afrentar [ah-fren-tar'], *va.* To affront; to insult to the face.

afrentarse [ah-fren-tahr-say], *vr.* To be affronted; to blush.

afrentosamente [ah-fren-to-sah-men'-tay], *adv.* Ignominiously; disgracefully.

afrentoso, sa [ah-fren-to'-so, sah], *a.* Ignominious; insulting.

afretar [ah-fray-tar'], *va.* To scrub and clean the bottom of a vessel.

África [ah-fre-cah], *f.* Africa; **África del Norte**, North Africa. **África del Sur**, South Africa.

africaans [ah-free-cah-ahns], *m.* Afrikaans.

africado [ah-fre-cah-do], *a. (Ling.)* Affricate.

africánder [ah-fre-cahn-dayr], *m.* Afrikander.

africanista [ah-fre-cah-nes-tah], *m. & f.* Person interested in Africa.

africanizar [ah-fre-cah-ne-thar'], *va.* To Africanize.

africano, na or **Afro** [ah-fre-cah'-no, nah], *a.* African.

Áfrico [ah'-fre-co], *m.* The south-west wind. *V.* ABREGO.

afrijolar [ah-fre-ho-lahr], *va.* To bother, to annoy.

afrisonado, da [ah-fre-so-nah'-do, dah], *a.* Resembling a Friesland draughthorse.

afro [ah-fro], *a.* Afro. **Peinado Afro**, afro hairstyle.

afroamericano, na [ah-fro-ah-may-re-cah'-no, nah], *a.* Afro-American.

afroasiático [ah-fro-ah-see-ah-te-co], *a.* Afro-Asian.

afrocubano, na [ah-fro-coo-bah'-no, nah], *a.* Afro-Cuban.

afrodisíaco [ah-fro-de-see'-ah-co], *a.* Aphrodisiac; exciting sexual appetite.

Afrodita [ah-fro-de-tah], *f.* Aphrodite.

afrontar [ah-fron-tar'], *va.* 1. To confront. 2. To reproach one with a crime to his face. *-vn.* To face.

afrutado, da [ah-froo-tah-do], 1. *a.* **Vino**, fruity. 2. *m.* Fruity flavor.

afta [af-tah], *f. (Med.)* sore.

aftoso, sa [af-to'-so, sah], *a.* Aphthous. **Fiebre aftosa**, *(Vet.)* Hoof-and-mouth disease.

afuera [ah-foo-ay'-ra], *adv.* 1. Abroad, out of the house, outward. 2. In public. 3. Besides, moreover. **¡Afuera! ¡Afuera!** Stand out of the way! clear the way!

afueras [ah-foo-ay'-ras], *f. pl.* Environs of a place.

afuereño [ah-foo-ay-ray-nyo], *a. (LAm.)* Foreign, strange.

afuerino, a [ah-foo-ay-re-no], *m. & f.* Itinerant worker.

afuetear [ah-foo-ay-tay-ahr], *va. (LAm.)* To whip, beat.

afufa [ah-foo'-fah], *f. (coll.)* Flight. **Estar sobre las afufas,** *(coll.)* preparing for flight; looking for «a soft place.»

afufar, afufarse [ah-foo-far', ah-foo-far'-say], *vn. & vr. (coll.)* To run away, to escape. **No pudo afufarlas,** he could not escape.

afufón [ah-foo-fon], *m.* Flight, escape.

afusilar [ah-foo-se-lahr], *va. (LAm.)* To shoot.

afusión [ah-foo-se-on'], *f.* Affusion, dashing on water.

afuste [ah-foos'-tay], *m.* A gun-carriage. **Afuste de mortero.** A mortar-bed.

afutrarse [ah-foo-trahr-say], *vr. (Cono Sur)* To dress up.

agabachado, da [ah-gah-bah-chah'-do, dah], *a.* Frenchified.

agachada [ah-gah-chah'-dah], *f. (coll.)* Stratagem, artifice.

agachadiza [ah-gah-chah-dee'-thah], *f. (Zool.)* A snipe. **Hacer la agachadiza.** *(coll.)* to stoop down, to conceal oneself.

agachar [ah-fah-chahr], *va.* To bend, to bow (cabeza).

agacharse [ah-gah-char'-say], *vr.* 1. To stoop, to squat, to crouch, to cower. **Agachar las orejas,** *(coll.)* To be humble; also, to be dejected, dispirited, chopfallen. 2. *(fig.)* to go into hiding, lie low. 3. *(LAm.)* (rendirse) to give in. 4. *(LAm.)* (prepararse) to get ready. 5. **Agacharse algo,** *(Mex.)* to keep quiet about something. 6. **Agacharse con algo** *(And. Mex.)* to make off with something.

agache [ah-gah-chay] *m. (And)* Fib, tale.

agachón [ah-gah-chon], *a. (LAm.)* Weakwilled, submissive.

agafar [ah-gah-fahr], *va.* To pinch.

agalbanado, da [ah-gal-bah-nah'-do, dah], *a.* Lazy. *V.* GALBANERO.

agalerar [ah-gah-lay-rar'], *va. (Naut.)* To tip an awning so as to shed rain.

agalla [ah-gal'-lyah], *f. (Bot.)* Gallnut. **Agalla de ciprés,** cypress gall. **Quedarse de la agalla,** or **colgado de la agalla,** to be deceived in his hopes. *-pl.* 1. Glands on the inside of the throat. 2. Fish gills . 3. Distemper of the glands under the cheeks or in the tensils. 4. Wind-galls of a horse. 5 Beaks of a shuttle. 6. The side of the head of birds corresponding to the temple. 7. Forced courage. **Es hombre de agallas,** he's got guts.

agallón [ah-gal-lyone'], *m.* A large gall-nut. **agallones,** *pl.* 1. Strings of large silver beads hollowed like gallnuts. 2. Wooden beads put to rosaries.

agalludo, da [ah-gah-lyoo-do], *a. (LAm.)* Daring, bold (atrevido).

agalluela [ah-gal-lyoo-ay'-lah], *f. dim.* A small gall-nut.

agamitar [ah-gah-me-tar'], *va.* To imitate the voice of a fawn.

agamo, ma [ah'-gah-mo, mah], *a.* Agamous, deprived of sexual organs: said of mollusks, and of such plants as fungi and algae.

agamuzado, da [ah-gah-moo-thah'-do, dah], *a.* Chamois-colored.

agangrenarse [ah-gan-gray-nar'-say], *vr.* To become gangrenous.

agapas [ah-gah'-pas], *f. pl.* Agapae, love-feast.

ágape [ah'-gah-pay], *m.* Banquet, testimonial dinner.

agarbado, da [ah-gar-bah'-do, dah], *a. V.* GARBOSO. *-pp.* of AGARBARSE.

agarbanzar [ah-gar-ban-thar'], *vn. (Prov.)* To bud.

agarbarse [ah-gar-bar'-say], *vr.* To hide away, to hide oneself.

agarbillar [ah-gar-beel-lyar'], *v.* AGAVILLAR.

agarbizonarse [ah-gar-be-tho-nar'say], *vr.* To make up into sheaves.

agareno, na [ah-gah-ray'-no, nah], *a.* A descendant of Agar; a Mohammedan.

agárico [ah-gah'-re-co], *m. (Bot.)* Agaric, a fungous excrescence on the trunks of larch-trees.

agarrada [ah-gar-rah-day'-ro], *f. (coll.)* Altercation, wordy quarrel.

agarradero, a [ah-gar-rah-day'-ro], *m.* 1. *(Naut.)* Anchoring-ground. 2. *(coll.)* Hold, haft.

agarrado, da [ah-gar-rah'-do, dah], *a.* Miserable, stingy, close fisted. *pp.* of AGARRAR

agarrador, ra [ah-gar-rah-dor', rah], *m. & f.* 1. One that grasps or seizes. 2. Catch-pole, bailiff. 3. Holder, utensil to grasp plates when hot. 4. *(And. Cono Sur)* strong liquor.

agarrafar [ah-gahr-rah-fahr], *va.* To grab hold of.

agarrama [ah-gar-rah'-mah], *f. V.* GARRAMA.

agarrar [ah-gar-rar'], *va.* 1. To grasp, to seize, to lay hold of, to compass. 2. To obtain, to come upon. 3. *(LAm.)* (coger) **Agarrar un autobús,** to catch a bus. 4. **Agarrarla,** to get plastered, get drunk. 5. *(Cono Sur)* **Agarrar el vuelo,** to take off. **Agarrar un resfriado,** to catch a cold. **Agarrar el brazo,** to take by the arm.

agarrarse [ah-gahr-rahr-say], *vr.* 1. To clinch, to grapple. **Agarrarse de un pelo,** to grasp at a hair to support an opinion or furnish an excuse. 2. To fight. **Se agarraron a puñetazos,** they fought it out with fists. 3. **Se le agarró la fiebre,** the fever took hold of him.

agarre [ah-gahr-ray], *m.* 1. *(LAm.)* Hold. 2. Handle. 3. Tener **agarre,** to have pull.

agarrete [ah-gahr-ray-tay], *a. (And)* Mean, stingy.

agarro [ah-gar'-ro], *m.* Grasp.

agarrochador [ah-gar-ro-chah-dor'], *m.* Pricker, goader.

agarrochar, agarrochear [ah-gar-rochar', ah-gar-ro-chay-ar'], *va.* To prick with a pike or spear; to goad.

agarrón [ah-gahr-ron], *m. (LAm.)* Jerk, pull, tug (tirón).

agarroso [ah-gahr-ro-so], *a. (CAm.)* Sharp, acrid, bitter.

agarrotamiento [ah-gahr-ro-tah-me-ayn-to], *m.* Tightening; strangling.

agarrotar [ah-gar-ro-tar'], *va.* To compress bales with ropes and cords. **Esta corbata me agarrota,** this tie is strangling me.

agarrotarse [ah-gahr-ro-tahr-say], *vr. (Med.)* To stiffen, to become numb.

agasajado, a [ah-gah-sah-hah-do], *m. & f.* Chief guest, guest of honor.

agasajador, ra [ah-gah-sah-hah-dor', rah], *m. & f.* Officious, kind, obliging person.

agasajar [ah-gah-sah-har'], *va.* 1. To receive and treat kindly; to fondle. 2. *(coll.)* To regale.

agasajo [ah-gah-sah'-ho], *m.* 1. Graceful and affectionate reception. 2. Kindness. 3. A friendly present. 4. Refreshment or collation served up in the evening.

ágata [ah'-gah-tah], *f.* Agate, a precious stone.

agatas [ah-gah-tahs], *adv. (Cono Sur)* 1. With great difficulty. 2. Hardly, scarcely.

agauchado [ah-gah-oo-chah-do], *a. (Cono Sur)* Like a gaucho.

agaucharse [ah-gah-oo-chahr-say], *vr. (Cono Sur)* to imitate.

agavanzo [ah-gah-vahn'-tho], *m.* or **Agavanza** [ah-gah-vahn'-thah], *f. (Bot.)* Hip-tree, dog-rose, Rosa canina. *V.* ESCARAMUJO.

agave [ah-gah'-vay], *m. V.* PITA.

agavillar [ah-gah-veel-lyar'], . To bind or tie in sheaves.

agavillarse [ah-gah-ve-lyahr-say], *vr. (Met.)* To associate with, to form groups.

agazapar [ah-gah-thah-par], *va. (coll.)* To nab a person.

agazaparse [ah-gah-thah-pahr-say], *vr.*To nab a person. *-vr.* To hide oneself.

agencia [ah-hen'-the-ah], *f.* 1. Agency: ministration, commission. **Agencia de colocaciones,** employment agency. **Agencia de viajes,** travel agency. 2. Diligence, activity.

agenciar [ah-hen-the-ar'], *va.* To solicit.

agenciarse [ah-hen-the-ahr-say], *vr.* To manage, to get along. **Agenciarse algo,** to get hold of something.

agenciero [ah-hen-the-ay-ro], *m. (Cono Sur)* Lottery agent; representative.

agencioso, sa [ah-hen-the-oh'-so, sah], *a.* 1. Diligent, active. 2. Officious.

agenda [ah-hen'-dah], *f.* Note-book: memorandum.

agenesia [ah-hay-nay'-se-ah], *f. (Med.)* Impotence.

agente [ah-hen'-tay], *m.* 1. Agent, actor, minister. 2. Solicitor, attorney. **Agente de cambios,** bill broker. **Agente publicitario,** adman. **Agente inmobiliario,** estate agent. **Agente de policía,** policeman.

agerasia [ah-hay-rah'-se-ah], *f.* Old age free from indispositions.

agerato [ah-hay-rah'-to], *m. (Bot.)* Sweet milfoil or maudin.

agible [ah-hee'-blay], *a.* Feasible.

agigantado, da [ah-he-gan-tah'-do, dah], *a.* Gigantic; extraordinary, out of the general rules.

agigantar [ah-he-gan-tahr'], 1. *va.* To enlarge, to increase greatly. 2. **Agigantar algo,** to make something seem huge.

agigantarse [ah-he-gan-tahr-say], *vr.* To become huge.

ágil [ah'-heel], *a.* Nimble, ready, fast, light, agile.

agilidad [ah-he-le-dad'], *f.* Agility, nimbleness, activity, lightness, liveliness, sprightliness.

agilipollarse [ah-he-le-po-lyahr-say], *vr.* 1. To become all confused, act like an idiot. 2. To get very stuck up (engreírse).

agilitar [ah-he-le-tar'], *va.* To render nimble, to make active.

agilitarse [ah-he-le-tahr-say], *vr.* To limber up.

agilización [ah-he-le-thah-the-on], *f.* Speeding-up.

agilizar [ah-he-le-thahr], *va.* To speed up.

agilizarse [ah-hge-le-thar-say], *vr.* To speed up.

ágilmente [ah'-hell-men-tay], *adv.* Nimbly, actively.

agio, agiotaje [ah'-he-oh, ah-he-o-tah'-hay], *m.* 1. Usury, high rate of interest on loans. 2. Premium on exchange of drafts, foreign money, etc.

agiógrafo [ah-he-oh'-grah-fo], *m.* Hagiographer, a holy writer.

agiógrafos [ah-he-oh'-grah-fos], *m. pl.* Hagiographa, holy writings, a name given to part of the books of Scripture.

agiotador [ah-he-oh-tah-dor'], *m.* Bill-broker, stock-broker.

agiotaje [ah-he-o-tah'-hay], *m.* Jobbing: «fing» in America.

agiotista [ah-he-oh-tees'-tah], *m.* Money-changer, bill-broker.

agitable [ah-he-tah'-blay], *a.* Agitable, capable of agitation.

agitación [ah-he-tah-the-on'], *f.* 1. Agitation, flurry, flutter, jactitation, fluctuation; fidget. 2. Fretting.

agitado [ah-he-tah-do], *a.* 1. Rough, choppy (agua); Jumpy (vuelo). 2. *(fig.)* agitated; upset, anxious (persona).

agitador, ra [ah-he-tah-dor', rah], *m. & f.* Fretter, agitator, shaker.

agitanado, da [ah-he-tah-nah'-do, dah], *a.* 1. Gipsy-like. 2. Bewitching.

agitar [ah-he-tar'], *va.* 1. To agitate, to ruffle, to fret, to irritate. 2. To stir, to discuss.

agitarse [ah-he-tahr-say],*vr.* To flutter, to palpitate.

aglomeración [ah-glo-may-rah-the-on'], *f.* Agglomeration, heaping up. **Aglomeración de tráfico,** traffic jam.

aglomerado [ah-glo-may-rah-do], *a.* Massed together, in a mass.

aglomerar [ah-glo-may-rar'], *va.* To heap upon, crowd together.

aglomerarse [ah-glo-may-rahr-say], *vr.* To agglomerate, form a mass.

aglutinación [ah-gloo-te-nah-the-on'], *f.* Agglutination.

aglutinante [ah-gloo-te-nan'-tay], *a.* Agglutinating. *-pa.* of AGLUTINAR. *- f. (Med.)* Sticking-plaster.

aglutinar [ah-gloo-te-nar'], *va.* To glue together, to agglutinate.

aglutinarse [ah-gloo-te-nahr-say], *vr.* To agglutinate; *(fig.)* to come together.

aglutinativo, va [ah-gloo-te-nah-tee'-vo, vah], *a.* agglutinative.

agnación [agnah-the-on'], *f. (Law.)* Relation by blood on the father's side.

agnado, da [agnah'-do, dah], *a. (Law.)* Related to a descendant of the same paternal line.C.f COGNADO, a relative on the mother's side.

agnaticio, cia [agnah-tee'-the-o, ah], *a.* Belonging to the *aguado.*

agnición [ag-ne-the-on'[, *f.* Recognition of a person on the stage.

agnocasto [ag-no-cahs'-to], *m. (Bot.)* Agnus castus or chaste-tree. *V.* SAUZGATILLO.

agnomento [ag-no-men'-to], *m. (Obs.) V.* COGNOMENTO and SOBRENOMBRE.

agnominación [agn-no-me-na-the-on'], *f. (Rhet.)* Paronomasia.

agnosticismo [agn-nos-te-thees'-mo], *m.* Agnosticism.

agnóstico, ca [ag-nos'-te-co, cah], *a. & m. & f.* Agnostic.

agobiador [ah-go-be-ah-dor], *a.* **agobiante.** Oppresive, unbearable.

agobiar [ah-go-be-ar'], *va.* 1. To bend the body down. 2. *(Met.)* To oppress, to grind. **Sentirse agobiado por,** to be overwhelmed by.

agobiarse [ah-go-be-ahr-say], *vr.* To bow, to couch. **Agobiarse con,** to be weighed down with.

agobio [ah-go-be-o], *m.* Burden, weight, oppression.

agolar [ah-go-lar'], *va. (Naut.)* To furl the sails. *V.* AMAINAR.

agolpamiento [ah-gol-pah-me-ayn-to], *m.* Throng, crush, rush, crowd.

agolparse [ah-gol-par'-say], *vr.* To crowd, to rush.

agonía [ah-go-nee'-ah], *f.* 1. Agony, the pangs of death. 2. Violent pain of body or mind. 3. An anxious or vehement desire.

agónico [ah-go-ne-co], *a.* Dying; *(fig.)* agonizing.

agonioso [ah-go-ne-o-so], *a. (LAm.)* Selfish; bothersome; **es tan agonioso**, he´s such a pest.

agonista [ah-go-nees'-tah], *m. (Obs.)* A dying person.

agonizante [ah-go-ne-thahn'-tay], *pa.* 1. One that assists a dying person. 2. A monk of the order of St. Camillus. 3. A dying person. 4. In some universities, he who assists students in their examinations.

agonizar [ah-go-ne-thar'], *va.* 1. To be dying, to be moribund. 2. *(Obs.)* To desire anxiously. 3. *(Met.)* To annoy, to importune intolerably. **Estar agonizando**, To be in the agony of death.

agonizos [ah-go-ne-thos], *mpl (Mex.)* Worries, troubles.

agono [ah-go'-no], *a.* Without angles.

agora [ah-go'-rah], *adv. (Obs.)* AHORA.

agorar [ah-go-rar'], *va.* To divine to prognosticate.

agorería [ah-go-ray-ree'-ah], *f.* Divination.

agorero, ra [ah-go-ray'-ro, rah] *m. & f.* Diviner.

agorgojarse [ah-gor-go-har'-say], *vr.* To be destroyed by grabs; applied to corn.

agostadero [ah-gos-tah-day'-ro], *m.* Summer, pasture.

agostar [ah-gos-tar'], *va.* 1. To be parched. 2. *(Prov.)* To plough the land in August. *-vn.* To pasture cattle on stubbles in summer.

agostarse [ah-gos-tahr-say], *vr.* To dry up, shrivel; *(fig.)* to die.

agosteño [ah-gos-tay-nyo], *a.* August.

agostero [ah-gos-tay-ro], *m.* 1. A laborer in the harvest.

agostizo, za [ah-gos-tee'-tho, thah], *a.* A person born in August; a colt foaled in that month; weak.

agosto [ah-gos'-to], *m.* 1. August. 2. Harvest-time. 3. Harvest.

agotable [ah-go-tah'-baly], *a.* Exhaustible.

agotado [ah-go-tah-do], *a.* **Estar agotado**, to be exhausted, be worn out.

agotador [ah-go-tah-dor], *a.* Exhausting.

agotamiento [ah-go-tah-me-en'-to], *m.* Exhaustion.

agotar [ah-go-tar'], *va.* 1. To drain off waters. 2. *(Met.)* to beat out one's brains. 3. To run through a fortune; to misspend it. 4. To exhaust. **Agotar la paciencia**, To tire one's patience.

agotarse [ah-go-tahr-say], *vr.* to become exhausted; to be finished.

agracejo [ah-grah-thay'-ho], *m.* 1. A grape remaining small and failing to ripen. 2. *(Prov.)* An olive which falls before it is ripe. 3. A kind of shrub. *V.* MAROJO.

agraceño, ña [ah-grah-thay'-nyo, nyah], *a.* Resembling verjuice, tart, sour.

agracera [ah-grah-thay'-rah], *f.* Vessel to hold verjuice. *-a.* Applied to vines when their fruit never ripen.

agraciado, da [ah-grah-the-ah'-do, dah], *a.* Graceful, genteel, handsome. *-pp.* of AGRACIAR. *-m.* A grantee.

agraciar [ah-grah-the-ar'], *va.* 1. To adorn or embellish. 2. To grant a favor. 3. To communicate divine grace. 4. To give employment.

agracillo [ah-grah-theel'-lyo], *m. V.* AGRACEJO,

agradable [ah-grah-dah'-blay], *a.* 1. Agreeable, pleasing. 2. Merry, lovely, glad, gracious. 3. Luscious, grateful. **Ser agradable**, *(Com.)* To accommodate.

agradablemente [ah-grah-dah-blay-men'-tay], *adv.* Merrily, graciously.

agradar [ah-grah-dar'], *va.* To please, to gratify, to render acceptable; to humor, to like. **Esto no me agrada**, I don´t like this. *vn.* To please; **su presencia siempre agrada**, it´s always pleasant to have you with us.

agradarse [ah-grah-dahr-say], *vr.* To be pleased.

agradecer [ah-grah-day-therr'], *va.* 1. To acknowledge a favor, to show gratitude in any way. 2. To reward, to recompense. **Agradezco tu ayuda**, I am grateful for your help. **Se lo agradezco**, I am grateful to you.

agradecerse [ah-grah-day-thayr-say], *vr.* ¡Se agradece!, much obliged! **Una copita de jerez siempre se agradece**, a glass of sherry is always welcome.

agradecidamente [ah-grah-day-the-dah-men'-tay], *adv.* Gratefully.

agradecido, da [ah-grah-day-thee'-do, dah], *a.* 1. Acknowledged. 2. Grateful, thankful. **Estamos muy agradecidos**, we are very grateful. *-pp.* of AGRADECER.

agradecimiento [ah-grah-day-the-me-en'-to], *m.* Gratefulness; act of acknowledging a favor conferred. (**Yo agradezco**, from **Agradecer**. *V.* ABORRECER).

agrado [ah-grah'-do], *m.* 1. Affability, agreeableness, the quality of pleasing, courteousness, grace; favorableness. 2. Comfortableness, gratefulness. 3. Pleasure, liking. **Esto no es de mi agrado**, that does not please me, I do not like that.

agramadera [ah-grah-mah-day'-rah], *f.* Brake, an instrument for dressing flax or hemp; scutcher.

agramar [ah-grah-mar'], *va.* To dress flax or hemp with a brake.

agramilar [ah-grah-me-lar'], *va.* To point and color a brick wall; to make even, adjust, the bricks.

agramiza [ah-grah-mee'-taht], *f.* 1. The stalk of hemp. 2. Refuse of dressed hemp.

agrandamiento [ah-gran-dah-me-en'-to], *m.* Enlargement.

agrandar [ah-gran-dar'], *va.* To increase, to greaten, to make larger.

agrandarse [ah-gran-dahr-say], *vr.* To get bigger.

agranijado [ah-grah-ne-hah-do], *a.* Pimply.

agranujado, da [ah-grah-noo-hah'-do, dah], *a.* 1. Filled or covered with grain. 2. Grain-shaped.

agrario, ria [ah-grah'-re-o, ah+, *a.* Agrarian, rustic. **Ley agraria**, agrarian law.

agrarismo [ah-grah-res-mo], *m. (Mex.)* Agrarian reform movement.

agrarista [ah-grah-res-tah], *m. & f. (Mex.)* Supporter (advocate) of land reform.

agravación [ah-grah-vah-the-on'], *f.* Aggravation.

agravador, ra [ah-grah-vah-dor' rah], *m. & f.* Oppressor.

agravamiento [ah-grah-vah-me-en'-to], *m.* The act of aggravating.

agravante [ah-grah-vahn'-tay], *a.* Aggravating, irritating, trying. **Circunstancia agravante**, (for.) Aggravating circumstance.

agravar [ah-gra-var'], *va.* 1. To oppres with taxes and public burdens; to aggrieve. 2. To render more intolerable. 3. To exaggerate, to complicate, to aggravate. 4. To ponder.

agravarse [ah-grah-vahr-say], *vr.* To worsen, get worse.

agravatorio, ria [ah-grah-vah-to'-re-o, ah], *a. (Law.)* Compulsory, aggravating.

agraviadamente [ah-grah-ve-ah-dah-men'-tay], *adv. (Obs.)* 1. Injuriusly, insultingly. 2. Efficaciously, strongly.

agraviador, ra [ah-grah-ve-ah-dor', rah], *m. & f.* One that gives offence or injuries.

agraviar [ah-grah-ve-ar'], *va.* To wrong, to offend, to grieve, to harm.

agraviarse [ah-grah-ve-ahr-say], *vr.* To be aggrieved; to be piqued; to be offended.

agravio [ah-grah'-ve-o], *m.* 1. Offence, harm, grievance, mischief; insult; injury, affront. 2. *(Obs.)* Appeal.

agravión [ah-grah-ve-on], *a. (Cono Sur)* Touchy, quick to take offence.

agravioso [ah-gra-ve-o-so], *a.* Offensive, insulting.

agraz [ah-grath'], *m.* 1. Verjuice, the juice expressed from unripe grapes. 2. An unripe grape. 3. Displeasure, disgust. **En agraz**, *adv.* Unseasonably; unsuitably.

agrazar [ah-grah-thar'], *vn.* To have a sour taste. *-va.* To disgust, to vex.

agrazón [ah-grah-thone'], *m.* 1. Wild grape, grapes which do not ripen. 2. *(Bot.)* Gooseberry-bush. 3. Displeasure, resentment, disgust.

agredir [ah-gray-deer'], *va.* To assume the aggressive, assault, attack.

agregación [ah-gray-gah-the-on'], *f.* Aggregation, collecting into one mass.

agregado, da [ah-gray-gah'-do], *m.* 1. Aggregate. 2. Congregation. 3. An assistant, a supernumerary. 4. *(Tech.)* Concrete block (bloque). 5. **Agregada**, attaché. **Agregada cultural**, cultural attaché. 6. *(LAm.)* person newly added to a group.

agregar [ah-gray-gar'], *va.* 1. To aggregate, to collect and unite, to heap together. 2. To collate, to nominate.

agremiación [ah-gray-me-ah-theon']. *f.* 1. Unionization. 2. Labor union.

agremiar [ah-gray'-me-ar], *va. & vr.* To form a guild or society.

agremiarse [ah-gre-me-ahr-say], *vr.* To form a union.

agresión [ah-gray-se-on'], *f.* Aggression, attack, assault.

agresivamente [ah-gray-se-vah-men'-tay], *adv.* Aggressively.

agresividad [ah-gray-se-ve-dahd'], *f.* Aggressiveness.

agresivo, va [ah-gray-see'-vo, vah], *a.* Aggressive, provoking.

agresor, ra [ah-gray-sor', rah] *m. & f.* Aggressor, assaulter.

agreste [ah-gres'-tay], *a.* 1. Rustic, clownish, illiterate, churlish, homebred. 2. Wild.

agrete [ah-gray'-tay], *m.* Sourness with a mixture of sweet.

agriado [ah-gre-ah-do], *a. (Cono Sur)* 1. Sour, sharp. 2. *(fig.)* Sour, resentful (resentido).

agriamente [ah'-gre-ah-men-tay], *adv.* Sourly; with asperity or harshness.

agriar [ah-gre-ar'], *va.* 1. To make sour or tart. 2. *(Met.)* To make peevish, to irritate, to exasperate.

agriarse [ah-gre-ahr-say], *vr.*1. To sour, turn acid. 2. *(fig.)* to get cross.

agrícola [ah-gree'-co-lah], *a. & n.* Agricultural; agriculturist.

agricultor [ah-gre-cool-tor'], *m.* Husbandman, farmer. 2. A writer upon agriculture.

agricultora [ah-gre-cool-to'-rah], *f.* The woman who tills the ground.

agricultura [ah-gre-cool-too'-rah], *f.* Agriculture, farming.

agricultural [ah-gre-cool-too-rahl'], *a. (LAm.)* Agricultural, farming.

agridulce [ah-gre-dool'-thay], *a.* Between sweet and sour, sub-sour.

agriera [ah-gre-ay-rah], *f. (LAm. Med.)* heartburn.

agrietado, da [ah-gre-ay-tah'-do, dah], *a.* Flawy, defective.

agrietar [ah-gre-ay-tahr], *va.* To crack, to crack open.

agrietarse [ah-gre-ay-tar'-say], *vr.* To be filled with cracks.

agrifolio [ah-gre-fo'-le-o], *m. (Bot.)* Holly-tree.

agrillado, da [ah-greel-lyah'-do, dah], *a.* Chained, put in irons. -*pp.* of AGRILLARSE.

agrillarse [ah-greel-lyar'-say], *vr. V.* GRILLARSE.

agrillo, lla [ah-greel'-lyo, lyah], *a. dim.* Sourish, tartish.

agrimensor,a [ah-gre-men-sor'], *m. & f.* Land surveyor.

agrimensura [ah-gre-men-soo'-rah], *f.* Art of surveying land.

agrimonia [ah-gre-mo'-ne-ah], *f. (Bot.)* Agrimony, liverwort. Agrimonia.

agringado [ah-gren-gah-do], *a. (LAm.)* Like (imitating) a foreigner.

agringarse [ah-gren-gahr-say], *vr.* To act like a foreigner.

agrio, ria [ah'-gre-o, ah], *a.* 1. Sour, acrid. 2. *(Met.)* Rough, applied to a road full of stones. 3. *(Met.)* Sharp, rude, unpleasant. **Una respuesta agria**, a smart reply. 4. Brittle, apt to break, unmalleable; applied to metals. 5. *(Art.)* Of bad taste in coloring or drawing.

agrio [ah'-gre-o], *m.* The acidity of some fruits, sour. **Agrios**, Sour fruit trees.

agrión [ah-gre-on'], *m. (Vet.)* Callosity in the joint of a horse's knee.

agripado [ah-gre-pah-do], *a. (LAm.)* **Estar agripado**, to have the flu.

agrisetado, da [àh-gre-say-tah'-do, dah], *a.* 1. Flowered like silks. 2. Gray-colored.

agriura [ah-gre-oo-rah], *f. (LAm.)* Sourness, tartness.

agro [ah-gro], *m.* Farming, agriculture.

agrobiología [ah-gro-be-o-lo-hee'-ah], *f.* Agrobiology.

agroindustria [ah-gro-en-doos-tre-ah], *f. (Cono Sur Econ.)* Agroindustry.

agronomía [ah-gro-no-mee'-ah], *f.* Theory of agriculture.

agronómico, ca [ah-gro-no'-me-co, cah], *a.* Agronomical.

agrónomo, ma [ah-gro'-no-mo, mah], *a.* Agronomous. -*m.* Agronomist.

agropecuario [ah-gro-pay-coo-ah-re-o], *a.* Farming, stockbreeding. **Política agropecuaria**, farming policy.

agrumarse [ah-groo-mar'-say], *vr.* To curdle, as in making cheese.

agrupación [ah-groo-pah-the-on], *f.* 1. Association, group. 2. Crowding, crowd.

agrupar [ah-groo-par'], *va.* To group, to cluster.

agruparse [ah-groo-pahr-say], *vr.* To form a group; to gather, to come together, to cluster.

agrura [ah-groo'-rah], *f.* 1. Acidity; acerbity. 2. *(Obs.)* A group of trees which yield fruit of sourish taste.

agua [ah'-goo-ah], *f.* 1. Water. 2. *(Chem.)* Liquor distilled from herbs, flowers, or fruit. 3. Lustre of diamonds. 4. *(Naut.)* Leak. **Agua de azahar**, orange-flower water. **Agua de olor**, scented water. **Agua rica**, a name given indifferently to all kinds of scented water in several provinces of Peru. **Agua llovediza**, rain-water. **Agua fuerte**, agua fortis. **Agua bendita**, holy water. **¡Agua va!** a notice to passers-by that water will be thrown. **Nunca digas de este agua no beberé**, don´t be too sure. **Cambiar el agua al canario**, *(Esp.)* to take a leak. **Echarse al agua**, to dive in. **Estar con el agua al cuello**, to be over a barrel. **Agua viva**, running water. -*pl.* 1. Mineral waters in general. 2. Clouds in silk and other stuffs. 3. Urine. 4. Tide. **Aguas muertas**, neap-tides. **Aguas vivas**, spring tides. **Entre dos aguas**, between wind and water; in doubt, perplexed. **Agua abajo**, *adv.* down the stream. **Agua arriba**, *adv.* 1. Against the stream. 2. *(Met.)* With great difficulty. **Agua de Colonia**, Cologne-water. **Agua dulce**, fresh water. **Agua oxigenada**, hydrogen peroxide. **Agua potable**, drinking-water. **Agua del timón**, wake of a ship. **Agua de cepas**, *(coll.)* Wine. (Comparaciones), **como agua**, like water. **Venir como agua de mayo**, to be a godsend, be very welcome. **Aguas**, waters. **Aguas residuales**, sewage. **Aguas territoriales**, territorial waters.

aguacate, or **agualate** [ah-goo-ah-cah'-tay, or ah-goo-ah-lah-tay], *m.* 1. (In Peru, **Palta**). A tree of this name and its fruit, resembling a large pear, miscalled alligator-pear. (From Mexican **ahuacatl**.) The fruit of Persea gratissima. 2. Shaped as a pear. 3. *(CAm.)* Idiot, fool.

aguacatero [ah-goo-ah-kah-tay-ro], *m. (Mex.)* Avocado pear tree.

aguacero [ah-goo-ah-thay'-ro], *m.* A heavy shower of rain.

aguacibera [ah-goo-ah-the-bay'-rah], *f. (Prov.)* A piece of ground sowed when dry and afterward irrigated.

aguacil [àh-goo-ah-thell'], *m.* A constable. *V.* ALGUACIL. *(Cono Sur)* dragonfly.

aguachirle [ah-goo-ah-cheer'-lay], *f.* 1. Inferior wine. 2. Slipslop; any bad liquor.

aguacola [ah-goo-ah-co-lah], *f. (Mex.)* Fish glue.

aguachacha [ah-goo-ah-cha-cha], *f. (CAm.)* Weak, stagnant water.

aguachado [ah-goo-ah-cha-do], *a. (Cono Sur)* tame.

aguachento [ah-goo-ah-chayn-to], *a. (And. Cono Sur)* Watery, very juicy.

aguachinado [ah-goo-ah-che-nah-do], *a. (Carib.)* Watery (acuoso); Soft (blando).

aguachinarse [ah-goo-ah-che-nahr-say], *vr. (Mex. Agri.)* To be flooded.

aguachirle [ah-goo-ah-cher-lay], *f.* 1. Weak drink, nasty drink. 2. Trifle.

aguada [ah-goo-ah'-dah], *f.* 1. *(Naut.)* Water on board a ship. **Hacer aguada**, to water. 2. *(Art.)* Sketch, outline. 3. Flood, flooding.

aguadero [ah-goo-ah-day'-ro], *m.* 1. Watering-place for cattle. 2. *(Naut.)* watering-port for ships.

aguadija [ah-goo-ah-dee'-hah], *f.* Humor in pimples or sores.

aguado, da [ah-goo-ah'-do, dah], *a.* 1. Watered. 2. Abstemious, like a teetotaller. -*pp.* of AGUAR.

aguador, ra [ah-goo-ah-dor', rah], *m. & f.* 1. Water-carrier. 2. *(Mil.)* **Aguador del real,** Sutler. 3. Bucket of a water-wheel.

aguaducho [ah-goo-ah-doo'-cho], *m.* 1. Water-course. 2. Stall for selling water. 3. *(Prov.)* Place where earthen vessels with drinking water are kept.

agua dulce [ah'-goo-ah- dool'-thay], *f.* 1. Fresh water. 2. Sweet water.

aguafiestas [ah-goo-ah-fee-ess'-tahs], *m. & f.* Wet blanket, kill-joy.

aguafuerte [ah-goo-ah-foo-err'-tay], *m.* or *f.* Etching.

aguafuertista [ah-goo-ah-foo-err-tees'-tah], *m. & f.* Etcher.

aguagma [ah-goo-ah-go'-mah] *f.* Gum-water, used in the preparation of paints.

aguaitador, ra [ah-goo-ah-e-tah-dor', rah], *m. & f.* *(Obs.)* A spy.

aguaitar [ah-goo-ah-e-tar'], *va.* 1. *(Low.)* To discover by close examination. To spy on. 2. *(And. Carib.)* To wait for (esperar). 3. *(Cono Sur)* To look, to see (ver).

aguajaque [ah-goo-ah-hah'-kay], *m.* A sort of ammoniac gum.

aguajas [ah-goo-ah'-has], *f. pl.* Ulcers above the hoofs of a horse.

aguaje [ah-goo-ah'-hay], *m.* 1. A running spring. 2. *(Naut.)* A current in the sea, persistent or periodical; e.g. The Gulf Stream. 3. Place where ships go for water. 4. *(And. CAm.)* rainstorm. 5. *(CAm.)* Dressing-down (regañina).

aguajirado [ah-goo-ah-he-rah-do], *a.* *(Carib.)* Withdrawn, timid.

aguajirarse [ah-goo-ah-he-rahr-say], *vr.* *(Carib.)* To become countrified, acquire peasant's habits.

agualotal [ah-goo-ah-lo-tahl], *m.* *(CAm.)* Swamp, marsh.

aguamala [ah-goo-ah-mah-lah], *f.* *(And.)* Jellyfish.

aguamanil [ah-goo-ah-mah-neel'], *m.* 1. Water-jug. 2. A wash-stand.

aguamar [ah-goo-ah-mahr], *m.* Jellyfish.

aguamarina [ah-goo-ah-mah-ree'-nah], *f.* Aqua marina, a precious stone, pale green; a variety of bery.

aguamarse [ah-goo-ah-mahr-say], *vr.* *(And)* to get scared, be intimidated.

aguamelado, da [ah-goo-ah-may-lah'-do, dah], *a.* Washed or rubbed over with water and honey.

aguamiel [ah-goo-ah-me-el'], *f.* 1. Hydromel, honey and water, mead, metheglin. 2. The unfermented juice of the Mexican agave or **maguey.**

aguamuerta [ah-goo-ah-moo-ayr-tah], *f.* *(Cono Sur)* Jellyfish.

aguana [ah-goo-ah'-nah], *f.* A wood used in canoe-making in South America.

aguanafa [ah-goo-ah-nah'-fah], *f.* *(Prov.)* Orange-flower water.

aguanieve [ah-goo-ah-ne-ay'-vay], *f.* 1. Bird of the family of magpies. 2. Sleet, snow.

aguano [ah-goo-ah-no], *m.* *(And)* Mahogany.

aguanosidad [ah-goo-ah-no-se-dad'], *f.* Serous humors in the body.

aguanoso, sa [ah-goo-ah-no'-so, sah], *a.* Aqueous; extremely moist.

aguantable [ah-goo-ahn-tah-blay], *a.* Bearable, tolerable.

aguantaderas [ah-goo-ahn-tah-day-rahs], *f. & pl.* *(LAm.)* **Tener aguantaderas,** to be tolerant.

aguantadero [ah-goo-ahn-tah-day-ro], *m.* *(Cono Sur)* Hide-out.

aguantador [ah-goo-ahn-tah-dor], *a.* *(LAm.)* V. AGUANTÓN.

aguantar [ah-goo-an-tar'], *va.* 1. To sustain, to suffer, to bear, to endure; to abide. 2. To maintain. 3. *(Naut.)* To carry a stiff sail.

aguantarse [ah-goo-ahn-tahr-say], *vr.* 1. To restrain oneself, hold oneself, back, sit tight. 2. *(LAm.)* To keep one's mouth shut. **Tendrá que aguantarse,** he'll just have to put up with it.

aguante [ah-goo-ahn'-tay], *m.* 1. Fortitude, firmness; vigor in bearing labor and fatigue. 2. Patience. 3. *(Naut.)* **Navío de aguante,** a ship that carries a stiff sail.

aguantón [ah-goo-ahn-ton], 1. *a.* *(Carib. Mex.)* Long-suffering, extremely patient. 2. *m.* *(Carib.)* **Te darás un aguantón,** you'll have a long wait.

aguapié [ah-goo-ah-pe-ay], *m.* Weak wine, plonk.

aguañón [ah-goo-ah-nyon'], *m.* Constructor of hydraulic machines.

aguapa [ah-goo-ah'-ah], *f.* The white water-lily.

aguapié [ah-goo-ah-pe-ay'], *m.* Small wine. V. AGUACHIRLE.

aguar [ah-goo-ar'], *va.* 1. To mix water with wine, vinegar, or other liquor. 2. *(Met.)* To disturb or interrupt pleasure. 3. *(Naut.)* To disturb or interrupt pleasure.

aguarse [ah-goo-ahr-say], *vr.* To be filled with water.

aguardada [ah-goo-ahr-dah-dah], *f.* Wait, waiting.

aguardadero [ah-goo-ahr-dah-day-ro], *m.* Hide (caza).

aguardar [ah-goo-ar-dar'], *va.* 1. To expect, to wait. 2. To grant time, e.g. to a debtor.

aguardentería [ah-goo-ar-den-tay-ree'-ah], *f.* Liquor-shop.

aguardentero, ra [ah-goo-ar-den-tay-ro, rah], *m. & f.* Retailer of liquors.

aguardentoso [ah-goo-ahr-den-to-so], *a.* Alcoholic.

aguardiente [ah-goo-ar-de-en'-tay], *m.* 1. Brandy. 2. Whisky. **Aguardiente de cabeza,** the first and strongest spirits drawn from the still.

aguardientoso [ah-goo-ahr-de-ayn-to-so], *a.* *(LAm.)* V. AGUARDENTOSO.

aguardo [ah-goo-ar'-do], *m.* Place where a sportsman waits to fire at the game.

aguarrás [ah-goo-ar-rahs'], *m.* Oil of turpentine.

aguarse [ah-goo-ar'-say], *vr.* 1. To be inundated. 2. To get stiff after much fatigue (caballos, mulas).

aguate [ah-goo-ah-tay], *m.* *(Mex.)* Prickle, thorn.

aguatero [ah-goo-ah-tay'-ro], *m.* Water carrier.

aguatocha [ah-goo-ah-to'-chah], *f.* Pump.

aguatocho [ah-goo-ah-to'-cho], *m.* *(Prov.)* Small quagmire.

aguatoso [ah-goo-ah-to-so], *a.* *(Mex.)* Prickle.

aguaturma [ah-goo-a-toor'-mah], *f.* *(Bot.)* Jerusalem artichoke.

aguavientos [ah-goo-ah-ve-en' tos], *m.* *(Bot.)* Yellow sage-tree.

aguaviva [ah-goo-ah-ve-vah], *f.* *(Cono Sur)* Jellyfish.

aguayo [ah-goo-ah-yo], *m.* *(And)* Multicolored woolen cloth.

aguaza [ah-goo-ah'-thah], *f.* 1. Aqueous humor. 2. Juice extracted from trees by incision.

aguazal [ah-goo-ah-thahl'], *m.* Marsh, fen. V. PANTANO.

aguazar [ah-goo-ah-thahr], *va.* To flood, to waterlog.

aguazo [ah-goo-ah'-tho] (Pintura de). Painting drawn with gum-water of a dull, cloudy color.

aguazoso, sa [ah-goo-ah-tho'-so, sah], *a.* Aqueous.

agudamente [ah-goo-dah-men'-tay], *adv.* 1. Sharply, lively, keenly. 2. Ingeniously, finely; clearly.

agudeza [ah-goo-day'-thah], *f.* 1. Sharpness of instruments. 2. Acuteness, force of intellect, subtlety, fineness. 3. Witty saying, repartee. 4. Acidity of fruits and plants. 5. Smartness.

agudización [ah-goo-de-thah-the-on], *f.* Sharpening; worsening.

agudizar [ah-goo-de-thahr], *va.* To sharpen, to make more acute.

agudo, da [ah-goo'-do, dah], *a.* 1. Sharp-pointed, keen-edged; smart. 2. *(Met.)* Acute, witty. 3. Dangerous. 4. Brisk, ready, active. 5. *(Med.)* Acute, of rapid development.

agué [ah-goo-ay], *interj.* *(CAm.)* hello!

agüela [ah-goo-ay'-lah], *m. & f.* *(Obs.)* Grandfather, grandmother.

agüero [ah-goo-ay'-ro], *m.* Augury, prognostication, omen. *(Yo agüero, yo agüere, from Agorar.* V. ACORDAR).

agüeitar [ah-goo-ay-tahr], *(LAm.) V.* AGUAITAR.

aguerrido, da [ah-ger-ree'-do, dah], *a.* Hardened, veteran. *-pp.* of AGUERRIR.

aguerrir [ah-ger-reer'], *va.* To accustom to war.

agüevar [ah-goo-ay-vahr] *va. (CAm. Mex.)* To put down, to shame.

agüevarse [ah-goo-ay-vahr-say], *vr.* To cower, to shrink.

aguijada [ah-ge-hah'-dah], *f.* 1. Spur, goad. 2. Stimulant, pungency.

aguijador, ra [ah-ge-hah-dor, rah], *m. & f.* One that goads or stimulates.

aguijadura [ah-ge-hah-doo'-rah], *f.* Spurring; the act of exciting.

aguijar [ah-ge-har'], *va.* 1. To prick, to spur, to goad. 2. To incite, to stimulate. *-vn.* To march fast.

aguijón [ah-ge-hone'], *m.* 1. Sting of a bee, wasp, etc. 2. Power of exciting motion or sensation. 3. Prick, spur, goad. **Dar o tirar coces contra el aguijón,** to kick against the spur or goad.

aguijonazo [ah-ge-ho-nah'-tho], *m.* Thrust with a goad.

aguijoncillo [ah-ge-hon-theel'-lyo], *m. dim.* Petty exciter.

aguijoneador, ra [ah-ge-ho-nay-ah-dor', rah], *m. & f.* One who pricks or goads.

aguijonear [ah-ge-ho-nay-ar'], *va.* 1. To thrust. *V.* AGUIJAR. 2. To incite.

águila [ah'-ge-lah], *f.* 1. Eagle. **Ve más que un águila,** he is more sharpsighted than an eagle. 2. A gold coin with an eagle of the reign of Charles *V.*

aguileño, ña [ah-ge-lay'-nyo, nyah], *a.* Aquiline; hooked, hawk-nosed.

aguilera [ah-ge-lay-rah], *f.* Eagle´s nest, eyrie.

aguililla [ah-ge-leel'-lyah], *f. dim.* A little eagle, an eaglet. *V.* CABALLO AGUILILLA.

aguilón [ah-ge-lone'], *m.* 1. The boom of the instrument called a crane, used for lifting heavy weights. 2. *aug.* of AGUILA.

aguilucho [ah-ge-loo'-cho], *m.* 1. A young eagle. 2. Hobby.

aguinaldo [ah-ge-nahl'-do], *m.* New Year's gift, Christmas box.

aguisado [ah-gee-sah'-do], *a. & n. (Obs.)* Just, reasonable, prudent.

aguisar [ah-ge-sar'], *va. (Obs.)* 1. To dress, to arrange. 2. To cook or provide provisions.

agüita [ah-goo-ee'-tah], *f. dim.* A little rain or mist.

agüitado [ah-goo-ee-tah-do], *a. (Mex.)* depressed, down.

aguja [ah-goo'-hah], *f.* 1. Needle (de coser). 2. Spire (obelisco), steeple. 3. Needle-fish, horn-fish. 4. Needle-shell. 5. Hand (reloj). 6. Switch-rail (r. w.). 7. Spindle. 8. Pin (in typography and in artillery); a brad. 9. Graft. **Aguja de marear,** *(Naut.)* A mariner's compass. **Aguja de cámara,** *(Naut.)* a hanging compass. **Aguja capotera,** *(Naut.)* sailing needle. **Aguja de relinga,** *(Naut.)* boltrope-needle. **Aguja de hacer media,** knitting-needle. **Aguja de pastor,** *(Bot.)* shepherd's needle. **Aguja de mechar,** skewer. **Aguja imantada,** magnetic needle. **Aguja de gancho,** crochet hook. *pl.* 1. Ribs of the fore quarter of an animal. 2. Distemper of horses, affecting the legs, neck, and throat.

agujazo [ah-goo-hah'-tho], *m.* A prick with a needle.

agujerar [ah-goo-hay-rar'], *va.* To pierce. *V.* AGUJEREAR.

agujereado [ah-goo-hay-ray-ah-do], *a.* Full of holes, pierced with holes.

agujerear [ah-goo-hay-ray-ar'], *va.* To pierce, to bore, to make holes.

agujerico, illo, uelo [ah-goo-hay-ree'-co, reel'-lyo, oo-ay'-lo], *m. dim.* A small hole.

agujero [ah-goo-hay'-ro], *m.* 1. Hole in clothes, walls, etc. 2. Needle-maker, needle-seller. 3. *(Obs.)* Pin-case; needle-case. 4. *(Naut.)* Port, mouth of a river, or any opening in the coast. 5. A dug-out.

agujeta [ah-goo-hay'-tah], *f.* String or strap of leather. *-pl.* 1. Pains felt from fatigue. **Estar lleno de agujetas,** to be stiff all over.

agujetería [ah-goo-hay-tay-ree'-ah], *f.* Shop where leather straps, or girths, called **agujetas,** are made or sold.

agujetero, ra [ah-goo-hay-tay'-ro, rah], *m. & f.* Maker or seller of **agujetas** or laces.

agujón [ah-goo-hone'], *m. aug.* A large needle.

aguosidad [ah-goo-o-se-dad], *f.* Lymph, a transparent, colorless liquid in the human body.

aguoso, sa [ah-goo-o'-so, sah], *a.* Aqueous.

agur [ah-goor'], *adv. (coll.)* Adieu, farewell. Goodbye.

agusanado [ah-goo-sah-nah-do], *a.* Maggoty, wormy.

agusanarse [ah-goo-sah-nar'-say], *vr.* To be worm eaten, to be rotten.

Agustín [ah-goos-teen], *m.* Augustine.

agustiniano, na [ah-goos-te-ne-ah'-no, nah], *m. & f.* 1. *V.* AGUSTINO. 2. Belonging to the order of St. Augustine.

agustino, na [ah-goos-tee'-no, nah], *m. & f.* Monk or nun of the order of St. Augustine.

agutí [ah-goo-tee'], *m.* Agouti, a rodent of tropical America.

aguzadera [ah-goo-thah-day'-rah], *f.* Whetstone.

aguzadero [ah-goo-thah-day'-ro], *m.* Haunt of wild boars, where they whet their tusks.

aguzado, da [ah-goo-thah'-do, dah], *a.* Sharp, pointed, keen.

aguzadura [ah-goo-thah-doo'-rah], *f.* Whetting or sharpening a tool or weapon.

aguzamiento [ah-goo-thah-me-ayn-to], *m.* Sharpening.

aguzanieve [ah-goo-thah-ne-ay'-vay], *f.* Wagtail, a small bird.

aguzar [ah-goo-thar'], *va.* 1. To whet or sharpen. 2. *(Met.)* To stimulate, to excite. **Aguzar el ingenio,** to sharpen the wit. **Aguzar las orejas,** to cock up the ears, to listen quickly. **Aguzar la vista,** to sharpen the sight.

aguzonazo [ah-goo-tho-nah'-tho], *m. V.* HURGONZAO.

¡ah! [ah], *interj.* Ah! *V.* ¡AY!.

ahebrado, da [ah-ay-brah'-do, dah], *a.* Thread-like, fibrous.

ahechaduras [ah-ay-chah-doo-rahs], *f. & pl.* Chaff.

ahechar [ah-ay-chahr], *va.* To sift; to winnow.

ahelear [ah-ay-lay-ar'], *va.* To give gall to drink, to make bitter. *-vn.* To taste very bitter.

ahembrado, da [ah-em-brah'-do, dah], *a. (Obs.)* Effeminate. *V.* AFEMINADO.

aherrojamiento [ah-er-ro-hah-me-en'-to], *m.* Putting in irons.

aherrojar [ah-er-ro-har'], *va.* To chain, to put in irons.

aherrumbrarse [ah-er-room-brar'-say], *vr.* 1. To have the taste and color of iron or copper, to be ferruginous: applied especially to water which has percolated through an iron-bearing stratum. 2. To be full of scoria.

ahervorarse [ah-er-vo-rar'-say], *vr.* To be heated by fermentation: applied to piled-up grain.

ahí [ah-ee'], *adv.* There, in that place; over there; yonder. **De por ahí,** about that, indicating a common trifling thing. **Está por ahí,** it´s around here. **¡Hasta ahí podíamos llegar!,** it has come to this! **¡Ahí es nada!,** fancy that! **¡Ahí va!,** there it is! **Por ahí,** that way. **¡Vete por ahí!,** get away!

ahidalgado, da [ah-e-dal-gah'-do, dah], *a.* Gentlemanly.

ahijada [ah-e-hah'-dah], *f.* 1. Godchild, goddaughter. 2. *V.* AHIJADO. 3. A paddle-staff. *-pp.* of AHIJAR.

ahijado [ah-e-hah'-do], *m.* 1. Godchild. 2. Client, one protected or peculiarly favored.

ahijar [ah-e-har'], *va.* 1. To adopt. 2. (Among shepherds) To put every lamb with its dam. 3. *(Met.)*. To impute. *-vn.* 2. To bring forth young: applied only to cattle. 2. To bud, to shoot out.

ahijuna [ah-e-hoo-nah], *interj. (Cono Sur)* Son of a bitch.

ahilado [ah-e-lah'-do], *a.* Withered (of plants and trees). *Cf.* AHILARSE. 4.

ahilar [ah-e-lahr] 1. *va.* To line up. 2. *vn.* To go in single file.

ahilarse [ah-e-lar'-say], *vr.* 1. To be faint for want of nourishment. 2. To grow sour, applied to leaven and bread. 3. To grow thin. 4. To be weak, applied to plants. *-vn.* To go single file. **Ahilarse el vino,** to turn ropy.

ahilo [ah-ee'-lo], *m.* Faintness, weakness for want of food.

ahincadamente [ah-en-cah-dah-mayn-tay], *adv.* hard, earnestly.

ahinco [ah-een'-co], *m.* Earnestness, eagerness, ardor.

ahitar [ah-e-tar'], *va.* To surfeit; to overload the stomach, to cloy, to satiate.^*vr.* To be surfeited.

ahitera [ah-e-tay'-rah], *f. (coll.)* Violent or continued indigestion.

ahito, ta [ah-ee'-to, tah], *a.* 1. One that labors under an indigestion. 2. *(Met.)* Disgusted, tired of a person or thing. -*irr.* of AHITAR.

ahito [ah-ee'-to], *m.* Indigestion; surfeit; repletion.

AHN *abr.* de **Archivo Historico Nacional.**

¡aho! [ah-o] *int. (Obs.)* Hallo!

ahobachonado, da [ah-o-bah-cho-nah'-do, dah], *a. (coll.)* Dull, slovenly, lazy; cowardly.

ahocicar [ah-o-the-car'], *vn. (Naut.)* To pitch or plunge.

ahocinarse [ah-o-the-nar'-say], *vr.* To run precipitately (riachuelo).

ahogadero [ah-o-gah-day'-ro], *m.* 1. Hangman's rope. 2. Place difficult to breathe in. 3. Throat-band, a part of the head-stall of a bridle or halter.

ahogadizo, za [ah-o-gah-dee'-tho, thah], *a.* Harsh, unpalatable. **Carne ahogadiza,** Flesh of animals suffocated or drowned.

ahogado, da [ah-o-gah'-do, dah], *a.* Suffocated; close, unventilated. **Carnero ahogado,** Stewed mutton. **Dar mate ahogado,** to pin up the king at the game of chess. *(Met.)* To insist upon things being done without delay. **Estar ahogado or verse ahogado,** to be overwhelmed with business or trouble. -*pp.* of AHOGAR.

ahogador, ra [ah-o-gah-dor', rah], *m. & f.* One who suffocates another, hangman.

ahogamiento [ah-o-gah-me-en'-to], *m.* 1. Suffocation. 2. *V.* AHOGO. **Ahogamiento de la madre,** Hysterics, an hysteric fit.

ahogar [ah-o-gar'], *va.* 1. To choke, to throttle, to kill by stopping the breath, to smother. 2. To drown. 3. *(Met.)* To oppress. 4. *(Met.)* To quench, to extinguish. 5. To water plants to excess. 6. *(Naut.)* To founder. -*vr.* 1. To be suffocated. 2. To drown oneself, be drowned.

ahogo [ah-o'-go], *m.* Oppression, anguish, pain, severe affliction. (Fin) financial difficulty.

ahoguido [ah-o-gee'-do], *m. V.* AHOGUIO.

ahojar [ah-o-har'], *vn. (Prov.)* To eat the leaves of trees (ganado).

ahombrado, da [ah om brah do, dah], *a. (coll.)* Masculine, applied to a woman. *V.* HOMBRUNO.

ahondar [ah-on-dar'], *va.* To sink. -*vn.* 1. To penetrate into a thing: to hollow out; to dip, as of the ground. 2. *(Met.)* To advance in the knowledge of things; to investigate. -*vr.* To go in more deeply.

ahonde [ah-on'-day], *m.* 1. Act and effect of sinking. 2. The depth to which a mine ought to reach in some countries of America to acquire title of ownership (7 varas).

ahora [ah-o'-rah], *adv.* Now, at present, **ahora mismo,** Just now. **Ahora mismo ha empezado la reunión,** the meeting began this moment. **Por ahora,** for the present. **Ahora bien,** well, granted, nevertheless. **Hasta ahora,** hitherto. **No puedo ir ahora,** I can't go just now. **Ahora o nunca,** it's now or never. **De ahora en adelante,** from now on. *conj.* Now, now then. **Lo hemos discutido, ahora, ¿qué hacemos?,** we've talked about it, now, what shall we do? **Ahora bien, si quieres te lo regalo,** I don't like it, but if you insist, I'll buy it for you.

ahorcado [ah-or-cah'-do], *m.* Hanged man. -*pp.* of AHORCAR.

ahorcadura [ah-or-cah-doo'-rah], *f.* The act of hanging.

ahorcajarse [ah-or-cah-har'-say], *vr.* To sit astride.

ahorcar [ah-or-car'], *va.* To kill by hanging. **Ahorcar los hábitos,** To abandon the ecclesiastical garb for another

profession. **Que me ahorquen si lo hago,** hang me if I do. -*vr.* To be vexed, to be very angry.

ahorita [ah-o-ree'-tah], *adv. (coll.)* Just now; this minute.

ahormar [ah-or-mar'], *va.* 1. To fit or adjust. 2. To wear clothes or shoes until they fit easy. 3. *(Met.)* To bring one to a sense of his duty.

ahornagarse [ah-or-nah-gar'-say], *vr.* To get scorched or burned: said of young leaves or shoots of plants.

ahornar [ah-or-nar'], *va.* To put in an oven. -*vr.* To be scorched or burnt in the oven without being baked inwardly: applied to bread.

ahorquillado, da [ah-or-kel-lyah'-do, dah], *a.* Forked. -*pp* of AHORQUILLAR.

ahorquillar [ah-or-keel-lyar'], *va.* To stay, to prop up with forks. -*vr.* To become forked.

ahorrado, da [ah-or-rah'-do, dah], *a.* Saved. -*pp.* of AHORRAR.

ahorrador, ra [ah-or-rah'-dor, rah], *m. & f.* Thrifty person.

ahorramiento [ah-or-rah-me-en'-to], *m.* Saving, enfranchisement.

ahorrar [ah-or-rar'], *va.* 1. To save, to economize, to spare. **Hemos ahorrado para irnos de vacaciones,** we have saved to go on vacation. 2. To enfranchise, to emancipate. 3. To shun labor, danger, or difficulties. -*vr.* **Ahorrarse molestias,** to save oneself troubles. **Ahorrarse trabajo, tiempo,** to save work, time.

ahorrativa [ah-or-rah-tee'-vah], *f. (coll.) V.* AHORRO.

ahorrativo, va [ah-or-rah-tee'-vo, vah], *a.* Frugal, thrifty, saving. **Andar or ir a la ahorrativa,** to go frugally to work.

ahorro [ah-or'-ro], *m.* 1. Parsimony, frugality, husbandry. 2. Saving, sparingness. **Banco de ahorros,** Savings-bank.

ahoyador [ah-o-yah-dor'], *m.* 1. *(Prov.)* One that makes holes for the pupose of planting. 2. *(Met.)* Gravedigger.

ahoyadura [ah-o-yah-doo'-rah], *f.* Making holes in the ground.

ahoyar [ah-o-yar'], *va.* To dig holes for trees.

ahuchador, ra [ah-o-chah-dor'-rah], *m. & f.* One who hoards; a miser.

ahuchar [ah-oo-char'], *va.* To hoard up.

ahuecamiento [ah-oo-ay-cah-me-en'-to], *m.* Excavation.

ahuecar [ah-oo-ay-car'], *va.* 1. To excavate, to scoop out. 2. To loosen a thing which was close pressed or matted. -*vr.* To grow haughty, proud, or elated.

ahuehué, or **ahuehuete** [ah oo ay oo ay'], *(Bot.)* Tree like a cypress.

ahuizote [ah-oo-e-tho-tay], *m. (CAm. Mex.)* 1. Bore, drag (persona). 2. Evil spell, curse (maleficio).

ahulado [ah-oo-lah-do], *m. (CAm. Mex.)* Oilskin; **ahulados,** rubber shoes.

ahumada [ah-oo-mah'-dah], *f.* 1. Signal given with smoke, from the coast, watch-towers, or high places. 2. Sea-fish.

ahumar [ah-oo-mar'], *va.* To smoke, to cure in smoke. -*vn.* To fume. -*vr.* To acquire a a burnt taste (comida).

ahur [ah-oor']. *V.* AGUR.

ahusado, da [ah-oo-sah'-do, dah] *a.* Spindle-shaped. -*pp.* of AHUSAR.

ahusar [ah-oo-sar'], *va.* To make slender as a spindle. -*vr.* To taper.

ahuyentador, ra [ah-oo-yen-tah-dor', rah], *m. & f.* A scarecrow.

ahuyentar [ah-oo-yen-tar'], *va.* 1. To drive away, to put to flight. **Ahuyentar los pajaros, o las moscas,** To scare away birds or flies. 2. *(Met.)* To overcome a passion; to banish care. -*vr.* To run away; *(Mex.)* to stay away.

AI *f. abr.* de **Amnistia Internacional** , Amnesty International.

AIH *abr.* de **Asociación Internacional de Hispanistas.**

aijada [ah-e-hah'-dah], *f.* Goad. *V.* AGUIJADA.

aína [ah-e-nah], *adv.* Speedily.

aindíado [ah-en-de-ah-do], *a. (LAm.)* Like Indians.

AINS *f. (Esp.) abr.* de **Administración Institucional Nacional de Sanidad.**

aiófilo, la [ah-e-ó-fe-lo, lah], *a.* Evergreen, whose leaves last more than a year.

airadamente [ah-e-rah-dah-men'-tay], *adv.* Angrily; in an angry manner, hastily.

airado, da [ah-e-rah'-do, dah], *a.* Angry, wrathful. *(Met.)* Furious, vexed.

airar [ah-e-rar'], *va.* To anger, to irritate. *-vr.* To grow angry.

airazo [ah-e-rah'-tho], *m. aug.* A violent gust of wind.

aire [ah'-e-ray], *m.* 1. Air. 2. Briskness, of the motion of a horse. 3. *(Met.)* Gracefulness of manners and gait; air, carriage, demeanor, sprightliness. 4. Aspect, countenance, look. 5. Musical composition. 6. Frivolity. 7. The veil which covers the chalice and paten in the Greek rite. **Aires naturales**, the native air. **Beber los aires** or **los vientos**, to desire anxiously. **Creerse del aire**, to be credulous. **Hablar al aire**, to talk idly. **¿Qué aires le traen a Vd. por acá?** what good wind brings you here? **Tomar el aire**, to take a walk. **En aire**, in a good mood. **De buen o mal aire**, in a pleasing or peevish manner. **En el aire**, in a moment. *(fig.)* air, appearance; **darse aires**, to give oneself airs. **Darse aires de**, to boast of being. *(fig.)* resemblance; **aires de familia**, family likeness. **Darse un aire a**, to resemble. *(fig.)* elegance. *(Mus.)* tune, air. *(Med. Cono Sur)* stiff neck; paralysis.

aireación [ah-e-ray-ah-the-on], *f.* Ventilation.

airear [ah-e-ray-ar'], *va.* 1. To give air, to ventilate. 2. To aerate, charge with gas. *-vr.* 1. To take the air. 2. To cool oneself, to obstruct perspiration.

airecico, llo, to [ah-e-ray-thee'-co, thell'-lyo, thee'-to], *m. dim.* A gentle breeze.

aireo [ah-e-ray-o], *m.* Ventilation.

airón [ah-e-ron'], *m. aug.* 1. Violent gale. 2. Ornament of plumes; crest of hats or caps, or feminine headgear. 3. The crested heron, egret. 4. A deep Moorish well.

airosamente [ah-e-ro-sah-men'-tay], *adv.* Gracefully, lightly.

airosidad [ah-e-ro-se-dad'], *f.* Gracefulness, elegance, grace.

airoso, sa [ah-e-ro'-so, sah], *a.* 1. Airy, windy. 2. Graceful, genteel, lively. 3. Successful.

aislable [ah-is-lah'-blay], *a.* Insoluble; capable of being obtained pure.

aislación [ah-es-lah-the-on], *f.* Insulation; **aislación de sonido**, soundproofing.

aislacionismo [ah-is-lah-the-o-nees'-mo], *m.* Isolation, keeping aloof from other countries.

aislacionista [ah-is-lah-the-o-nees'-tah], *m. & f.* Isolationist, advocate of isolationism in international relations.

aisladamente âh-is-lah-dah-men'-tay], *adv.* Isolately; one by one.

aislado, da [ah-is-lah'-do, dah], *a.* Isolated, embarrassed. *-pp.* of AISLAR.

aislador, ra [ah-is-lah-dor', rah], *a.* Isolating, insulating.

aislamiento [ah-is-lah-me-en'-to], *m.* Isolation.

aislante [ah-is-lahn'-tay], *a.* Insulating. **Material aislante** or *aislador*, *(Elec.)* Insulating material.

aislar [ah-is-lar'], *va.* 1. To surround with water. 2. To insulate. *-vr.* To isolate; to live in isolation.

AITA *f. abr.* de **Asociación Internacional de Transporte Aéreo** (International Air Transport Association, IATA)

ajá [ah-hah'], *int.* Aha! Also *¡Ajajá!*

ajada [ah-hah'-dah], *f.* A sauce made of bread steeped in water, garlic, and salt.

ajado, da [ah-hah'-do, dah], *a.* Garlicky. *-pp.* of AJAR.

ajamiento [ah-hah-me-en'-to], *m.* Disfiguration; deformity.

ajamonarse [ah-hah-mo-nahr-say], *vr.* To get plump.

ajar [ah-har'], *m.* Garlic-field.

ajar [ah-har'], *va.* 1. To spoil, to mar, to tarnish, to fade. 2. To abuse. **Ajar la vanidad a alguno**, to pull down one's pride. *-vr.* To get crumpled, get messed up.

ajardinar [ah-hahr-de-nahr], *va.* To landscape.

ajay [ah-hah-e], *interj.* *(LAm:* risa) ha!

ajazo [ah-hah'-tho], *m.* A large head of garlic.

aje [ah'-hay], *m.* 1. A chronic complaint. 2. *(Bot.)* A tuber from the Antilles, like a yam, or sweet potato. 3. *(Met.)* Humiliation, disrespect.

ajea [ah-hay'-ah], *f.* A sort of brushwood used for firing in the environs of Toledo.

ajear [ah-hay-ar'], *va.* To cry like a partridge closely pursued.

ajedrea [ah-hay-dray-ah], *v. (Bot.)* savory.

ajedrecista [ah-hay-dray-thees'-tah], *m. & f.* Chess player.

ajedrez [ah-hay-dreth'], *m.* 1. Chess, a game. 2. *(Naut.)* Netting, grating.

ajedrezado, da [ah-hay-dray-thah'-do, dah], *a.* Checkered.

ajenabe [ah-hay-nah'-blay], *m. (Bot.)* Wild mustard.

ajenable [ah-hay-nah'-blay], *a.* Alienable.

ajengibre [ah-hen-hee'-bray], *m. V.* JENGIBRE.

ajenjo [ah-hen'-ho], *m.* 1. *(Bot.)* Wormwood. 2. Sagebrush.

ajeno, na [ah-hay-no, nah], *a.* 1. Another's. 2. Foreign, strange. 3. Abhorrent, contrary to, remote. 4. Ignorant. 5. *(Met.)* Improper. **Ajeno de verdad**, void of truth. **Estar ajeno de sí**, to be unselfish, without self-love. **Estar ajeno de una cosa**, not to have heard a rumor.

ajenuz [ah-hay-nooth'], *m. (Bot.)* Field fennnelflower.

ajeo [ah-hay-oh], *m. Perro de ajeo*, Setter-dog.

ajete [ah-hay'-tay], *m.* 1. Young or tender garlic. 2. Sauce made with garlic.

ajetreado [ah-hay-dray-ah-do], *a.* Busy, tiring (vida).

ajetrearse [ah-hay-tray-ar'-say], *vr.* To become bodily fatigued, to fidget.

ajetreo [ah-hay-tray-o], *m.* Bustle; fuss; drudgery.

ají [ah-hee'], *m.* 1. The red Indian dwarf pepper. *V.* CHILE. Capsicum. 2. A sort of sauce made in America of the aji-pepper.

ajiaceite [ah-he-ah-thay'-e-tay], *m.* Mixture of garlic and oil.

ajiaco [ah-he-ah'-co], *m.* 1. A dish made of boiled meat and vegetables. 2. A sort of sauce made with the *ají* for certain dishes in America.

ajibararse [ah-he-bah-rahr-say], *vr. (Carib.)* V. AGUAJIRARSE.

ajicola [ah-he-co'-lah], *f.* Glue made of cuttings of leather boiled with garlic.

ajigolones [ah-he-go-lo-nays], *m. & pl. (CAm. Mex.)* Troubles, difficulties.

ajilar [ah-he-lahr], *vn. (CAm. Mex.)* To set out for a place.

ajilimoje, or **ajilimójili** [ah-he-le-mo'-hay, ah-he-le-mo'-he-lee], *m.* Sauce of pepper and garlic.

ajillo [ah-heel'-lyo], *m.* Tender young garlic.

ajimez [ah-he-meth'], *m.* An arched window with a pillar in the centre to support it.

ajipuerro [ah-he-poo-er'-ro], *m.* Leek, *V.* PUERRO.

ajiseco [ah-he-say-co], *m. (And)* Mild red pepper.

ajises [ah-he-says], *m. & pl. (LAm.)* de ají.

ajizarse [ah-he-thahr-say], *vr. (Cono Sur)* To lose one´s temper, to get mad.

ajo [aj'-ho], *m.* 1. *(Bot.)* Garlic. 2. Garlic-sauce for meat. 3. *(Met.)* Paint for ladies. 4. *(Met.)* Affair discussed by many. **Revolver el ajo** or **el ruido**, to stir up new disturbances. **Ajo blanco**, dish made of bruised garlic, bread, oil, an water. **Echar ajos y cebollas**, to insult one vilely. **Se fué echando ajos y cebollas**, *(coll.)* he went off uttering oaths and imprecations. **En el ajo**, to be mixed in it.

ajoaceite [ah-ho-ah-thay-e-tay], *m.* Sauce of garlic and oil.

ajoarriero [ah-ho-ahr-re-ay-ro], *m.* Dish of cod with oil, garlic and peppers.

ajobar [ah-ho-bar'], *va. (coll.)* To carry upon one's back heavy loads.

ajobo [ah-ho'-bo], *m.* 1. *(Obs.)* Carrying heavy loads. 2. A heavy load.

ajofaina [ah-ho-fah'-e-nah], *f. V.* ALJOFAINA.

ajolio [ah-ho-le-o], *m. (Prov.)* Sauce made of oil and garlic.

ajolote. [ah-ho-lo'-tay], *m.* An amphibian of the Lake of Mexico; the axolotl.

ajomate [ah-ho-mah'-tay], *m. (Bot.)* A delicate aquatic plant.

ajonjeo [ah-hon-hay-o], *m.* Ajonjo birdlime.

ajonjera [ah-hon-hay'-rah], *f.* **ajonjero** [ah-hon-hay'-ro], *m.* *(Bot.)* The low carline thistle, yielding ajonje.

ajonjolí, aljonjolí [ah-hon-ho-lee', al-hon-ho-lee'], *m.* *(Bot.)* Benne, sesame, an oily grain. Sesamum orientale.

ajoqueso [ah-ho-kay'-so], *m.* Dish made of garlic and cheese.

ajorca [ah-hor'-cah], *f.* Rings worn by the Moorish women about the wrists or ankles.

ajordar [ah-hor-dar'], *va.* *(Prov.)* To bawl, to cry out.

ajornalar [ah-hor-nah-lahr], *va.* To employ by the day.

ajoto [ah-ho-to], *m.* *(Carib.)* rebuff.

ajuagas [ah-hoo-ah'-gas], *f. pl.* Malanders, a disease in horses; or ulcera over the hoofs. V. ESPARAVAN.

ajuar [ah-hoo-ar'], *m.* 1. Apparel and furniture which a bride brings to her husband. 2. Household furniture. **Ajuar de novia,** trousseau.

ajuarar [ah-hoo-ah-rahr*]*, *m.* To furnish.

ajudiado, da [ah-hoo-de-ah-do, dah], *a.* Jewish; Jew-like.

ajuiciado, da [ah-hoo-e-the-ah'-do, dah], *a.* Judicious, prudent. *-pp.* AJUICIAR.

ajuiciar [ah-hoo-e-the-ar'], *va.* To acquire judgment; to become prudent.

ajumado [ah-hoo-mah-do], 1. *a.* Tight. 2. *m.* drunk. *-vr.* To get tight.

ajuntarse [ah-hoon-tahr-say], *vr.* To live together.

ajurídico [ah-hoo-re-de-co], *a.* *(Cono Sur)* Illegal.

ajustadamente [ah-hoos-tah-dah-men'-tay], *adv.* Justly, rightly.

ajustado, da [ah-hoos-tah'-do, dah], *a.* Exact, right; stingy. **Es un hombre ajustado,** he is a man of strict morals. *-pp.* of AJUSTAR.

ajustador [ah-hoos-tah-dor'], *m.* 1. Close waistcoat, jacket. 2. Waist, jacket. 3. The person in a printing-office who arranges the form; justifier. 4. *(Mech.)* Adapter, coupler, adjusting tool.

ajustamiento [ah-hoos-tah-me-en'-to], *m.* 1. Agreement. 2. Settling of accounts. 3. Receipts.

ajustar [ah-hoos-tar'], *va.* 1. To regulate, to adjust, to accord, to compose, to guide, to measure, to justify type. 2. To concert, to make an agreement, to bargain. 3. To reconcile, to heal. 4. To examine accounts. 5. To settle a balance. 6. To press close, to oppress. 7. To fit; to fashion; to accommodate. *-vr.* 1. To settle matters. 2. To conform; to combine. **Ajustarse a las reglas,** to abide by the rules. 3. To approach. 4. To engage. **Ajustarse el cinturón,** to tighten the belt. **Ajustarse a razones,** to yield to reason.

ajuste [ah-hoos-tay], *m.* 1. Proportion of the constituent parts of a thing. 2. Agreement, contract, covenant, accommodation; engagement; settlement. *-pl.* Couplings.

ajusticiar [ah-hoos-te-the-ar'], *va.* To execute, to put to death.

ajustón [ah-hoos-ton], *m.* *(And)* Punishment (castigo); Ill-treatment (mal trato).

al [al], *art.* 1. Article formed by a syncope of the preposition *a* and the article *el*, and placed before nouns, etc.; e.g. **El juez debe castigar al delincuente,** the judge ought to punish the delinquent. 2. An Arabic article corresponding to the Spanish articles *el* and *la* in compound words; e.g. **Al árabe,** the Arab. 3. Used with the infinitive of various verbs; e.g. **Al amanecer,** at the dawn of day. **Traduce al inglés,** translate into English. **Dar la vuelta al mundo,** to go round the world.

al [al], *pron. indef.* *(Obs.)* Other, contrary, all other things. V. DEMÁS and OTRO. *Por al,* V. POR TANTO.

ala [ah'-lah], *f.* 1. Wing (ave, insecto, avión, edificio, ejército); aisle (iglesia). 2. Row or file. 3. *(Mil.)* Flank, wing (ejército). 4. Brim (sombrero). 5. Auricle (oreja). **Alas del corazón** *(Anat.)*, auricles of the heart. 6. Fin of a fish. 7. Leaf of a hinge; of a door, of a table. **Ala de mesana,** *(Naut.)* a driver. *-pl.* *(Naut.)* upper studding-sails. **Alas de gavia,** main-top studding-sails. **Alas de velacho,** fore studding-sails. **Alas de sobremesa,** mizzen-top studding-sails. **Alas de proa,** head of the ship. **Alas,** protection. Boldness. **Cortar las**

alas, to take one down a peg. *(Poetic.)* Velocity. *(Pol.)* **El ala izquierdo del partido,** the left wing of the party. (Frases) **ahuecar el ala,** to beat it. **Andar con el ala caída,** to be downcast.

alabado [ah-lah-bah'-do], *m.* 1. *(Cono Sur)* at dawn. 2. *(Mex.)* at nightfall.

alá [ah-lah'], *m.* Allah, an Arabic word for God.

alabado [ah-lah-bah'-do], *a.* Praised. **¡Alabado sea Dios!** God be praised! LAm. Down call. **Al alabado,** at dawn. *-pp.* of ALABAR.

alabador, ra [ah-lah-bah-dor', rah], *m. & f.* Applauder, commender.

alabacioso, sa [ah-lah-bah-the-oh'-so, sah], *a.* *(coll.)* Boastful, ostentatious.

alabamiento [ah-lah-bah-me-ayn-to], *m.* Praise.

alabancioso [ah-lah-ban-the-o-so], *a.* Boastful.

alabandina [ah-lah-ban-dee'-nah], *f.* 1. Manganese sulphide. 2. Alabandine, spinel ruby.

alabanza [ah-lah-bahn'-thah], *f.* Praise, commendation; glory. **Cantar las alabanzas a uno,** to sing someone's praises.

alabar [ah-lah-bar'], *va.* To praise, to extol, to glorify, to magnify, to commend, to cry up. *-vr.* To praise oneself.

alabarda [ah-lah-bar'-dah], *f.* 1. Halberd, a kind of battle-axe and pike at the end of a long staff. 2. *(Obs.)* Sergeant's place, from a halberd having formerly been borne by sergeants.

alabardazo [ah-lah-bar-dah'-tho], *m.* A blow with a halberd.

alabardero [ah-lah-bar-day'-ro], *m.* 1. Halberdier, armed with a halberd. 2. Claqueur, clapper, hired to applaud in a theatre. (Recent.)

alabastrado, da [ah-lah-bas-trah'-do, dah], *a.* Resembling alabaster.

alabastrina [ah-lah-bas-tree'-nah], *f.* A thin sheet of alabaster.

alabastrino, na [ah-lah-bas-tree'-no, nah], *a.* *(Poetic.)* 1. Made of alabaster. 2. Like alabaster.

alabastro [ah-lah-as'-tro], *m.* Alabaster.

álabe [ah'-lah-bay], *m.* 1. Drooping branch of an olive or other tree. 2. Bucket, flier of a water-wheel, float-board, which serves to set it in motion. 3. Mat used in carts. 4. Cam. 5. Tile of the caves.

alabear [ah-lah-bay-ahr], 1. *va.* To warp. 2. *vr.* To warp, to grow bent or crooked.

alabega [ah-lah-bay'-gah], *f.* *(Bot.)* Sweet basil. V. ALBAHACA.

alabeo [ah-lah-bay' o], *m.* Warping, the state of being warped.

alabiado, da [ah-lah-be-ah'-do, dah], *a.* Lipped or ragged; applied to uneven coined money.

alacalufe [ah-lah-cah-loo-fay], *m. & f.* *(Cono Sur)* Indian inhabitant of Tierra del Fuego.

alacena [ah-lah-thay'-na], *f.* 1. Sideboard, buffet, a cupboard, small pantry in the wall. 2. *(Naut.)* Locker, a small box in the cabin and sides of a ship.

alaciar [ah-lah-the-ar'], *vn* V. ENLACIAR.

alacrán [ah-lah-crahn'], *m.* 1. A scorpion, a small poisonous animal. 2. Ring of the bit of a bridle. 3. Stop or hook fixed to the rocker of organbellows. 4. Chain or link of a sleevebutton. 5. Swivel.

alacranado, da [ah-lah-crah-nah'-do, dah], *a.* 1. Bit by a scorpion. 2. *(Met.)* Infected with some vice.

alacranear [ah-lah-crah-nay-ahr], *vn.* *(Cono Sur)* To gossip, to scandal monger.

alacraneo [ah-lah-crah-nay-o], *m.* *(Cono Sur)* Gossip, scandal.

alacranera [ah-lah-crah-nay'-rah], *f.* *(Bot.)* Mouse-ear, scorpion-grass.

alacridad [ah-lah-cre-dad'], *f.* Alacrity.

alada [ah-lah'-dah], *f.* Fluttering of the wings.

aladares [ah-lah-dah'-res], *m. pl.* Locks of hair over the temples; forelocks.

ALADI *f. abr.* de **Asociación Latinoamericana de Integración.**

aladierna [ah-lah-de-er'-nah], V. ALATERNO.

Aladino [ah-lah-de-no], *m.* Aladdin.

alado, da [ah-lah'-do, dah], *a.* Winged, feathered.

aladrada [ah-lah-drah'-dah], *f. (Prov.)* A furrow.

aladrar [ah-lah-drar'], *va. (Prov.)* To plough the ground.

aladro [ah-lah'-dro], *m.* 1. Plough. 2. Ploughed land.

aladroque [ah-lah-dro'-kay], *m. (Prov.)* An unsalted anchovy.

alafia [ah-lah'-fe-ah], *f. (coll.)* **Pedir alafia,** to implore mercy and pardon.

alafre [ah-lah-fray], *(Carib.)* 1. *a.* Wretched, miserable. 2. *m* Wretch.

alaga [ah'-lah-gah], *f.* A species of yellow wheat.

alagartado, da [ah-lah-gar-tah'-do, dah], *a.* Variegated; motley.

alaica [ah-lah'-ee-cah], *f.* Winged ant or emmet.

alajor [ah-lah-hor'], *m.* Ground-rent.

alajú [ah-lah-hoo'], *m.* Paste made of almonds, walnuts, honey, etc.

alama [ah-lah'-mah], *f. (Prov.)* Gold or silver cloth.

alamar [ah-lah-mar'], *m.* Loop of silken twist, or cord, used for buton-holes or trimming.

alambicado, da [ah-lam-be-cah-do, dah], *a.* 1. Distilled. 2. Euphuistic, pedantic (of diction). 3. *(Met.)* Given with a sparing hand. *-pp.* of ALAMBICAR.

alambicamiento [ah-lam-be-cah-me-en'-to], *m.* 1. Distillation. 2. Subtlety, euphuism of language.

alambicar [ah-lam-be-car'], *va.* 1. To distil. 2. To investigate closely. **Alambicar los sesos,** to cudgel one's wits. 3. To minimize, to reduce to a minimum.

alambique [ah-lam-bee'-kay], *m.* Alembic, still. **Por alambique,** sparingly, in a penurious manner.

alambiquería [ah-lam-be-kay-re-ah], *f. (Carib.)* Distillery.

alambiquero [ah-lam-be-ke-ro], *m. (Carib.)* Distiller.

alambor [ah-lam-bor'], *m. (Obs. Mil.)* Inside slope of a ditch. *V.* ESCARPA.

alambrada, do [ah-lam-brah-dah], *f.* Wire netting; Wire fence (cerca).

alambre [ah-lam'-bray], *m.* 1. Wire of any metal. 2. In olden times copper, or an alloy of copper; bronze. **alambre de latón,** brass wire. 3. Bells belonging to sheep, or to beasts of burden. 4. File for papers.

alambre de tierra [ah-lam'-bray day te-er'-rah], *m. (Elec.)* Ground wire.

alambrera [ah-lam-bray'-rah], *f.* 1. Wire netting. 2. *(Agri.)* Wire trellis. 3. Car basket (ferrocarril).

alambrista [ah-lam-bres-tah], *m. & f.* Tightrope walker.

alambrito [ah-lam-bre-to], *m. (LAm.)* Tall, thin person.

alameda [ah-lah-may'-dah], *f.* 1. A grove of poplar-trees. 2. Public walk, mall.

alamín [ah-lah-meen'], *m.* 1. *(Obs.)* Clerk of the market appointed to inspect weights and measures. 2. *(Prov.)* Architect, surveyor of buildings. 3. *(Prov.)* Farmer appointed to superinted irrigation or distribution of water.

alamirré [ah-lah-mir-ray'], *m.* Musical sign.

álamo [ah'-lah-mo], *m. (Bot.)* Poplar. **Álamo blanco,** white poplar. **Álamo temblón,** aspen-tree, trembling poplar-tree. **Álamo negro,** black poplar-tree.

alampar, va. alamparse [ah-lam-par'say], *vr. (coll.)* To long for, to crave.

alamud [ah-lah-mood'], *m.* A square bolt for a door.

alanceador [ah-lah-thay-ah-dor'], *m.* One who throws a lance, lancer.

alancear [ah-lan-thay-ar'], *va.* To dart, to spear.

alandrearse [ah-lan-dray-ar'-say], *vr.* To become dry, stiff, and blanched (gusanos de seda).

alanés [ah-lah-ness'], *m.* A kind of stag in New Mexico (*Cervus alces*).

alano [ah-lah'-no], *m.* Mastiff of a large kind.

alano, na [ah-lah'-no, nah], *a.* Belonging to the *Alans* or Vandals of the fifth century.

alanquía [ah-lan-kee'-ah], *f.* Cardass, waste-card used in silk-weaving.

alantoides [ah-lan-to'-e-des], *f. & a.* Allantois, the foetal urinary vesicle.

alanzada [ah-lan-thah'-dah], *f. (Obs.)* *V.* ARANZADA.

alanzar [ah-lan-thar'], *va.* To throw lances.

alaqueca [ah-lah-kay'-cah], *f.* Blood-stone.

alaqueques [ah-lah-kay'-kes], *m. pl. V.* ALAQUECA.

alar [ah-lar'], *va. (Naut.)* To haul (cuerda). Overhanging roof, eaves (tejado). *(LAm.)* acera, pavement. *V.* HALAR.

alara [ah-lah'-rah] *(Obs.)* An egg without a shell.

alárabe [ah-lah'-rah-bay], **alarbe** [ah-lar'-bay], *m.* 1. Arabian. 2. An unmannerly person.

alarde [ah-lar'-day], *m.* 1. Review of soldiers, muster, parade. 2. Ostentation, boasting, vanity. **Hacer alarde,** *(Met.)* To boast or brag of something. 3. Manifestation.

alardeado [ah-lahr-day-ah-do], *a.* Vaunted, much boasted-of.

alardear [ah-lar-day-ar'], *vn.* 1. To brag. 2. *(Obs.)* To review.

alardeo [ah-lahr-day-o], *m.* Boasting, bragging.

alargadera [ah-lar-gah-day'-rah], *f. (Chem.)* Nozzle, adapter; lengthening tube.

alargado [ah-lahr-gah-do], *a.* Long, extended.

alargador, ra [ah-lar-gah-dor', rah], *m. & f.* One who delays, or lengthens out a thing.

alargamiento [ah-lar-gah-me-en'-to], *m.* The act of lengthening out.

alargar [ah-lar-gar'], *va.* 1. To lengthen, to expand, to extend. 2. *(Met.)* To protract, to dwell upon. 3. To increase a marked number or quantity. 4. To reach or hand a thing to another. 5. To resign: yet in this sense *largar* is more used. 6. To send before; to hold out. **Alargar la conversación,** to spin out a conversation. **Alargar el salario,** to increase or augment the pay. **Alargar el cabo,** *(Naut.)* to pay out the cable. *-vr.* 1. To be prolonged. **Se alargan los días,** the days grow longer. 2. To launch; to withdraw from a place. 3. To expatiate or enlarge on an argument, to go beyond, to exceed. 4. *(Naut.)* To sheer off.

alarguez [ah-lar-geth'], *m. (Bot.)* Dogrose.

alargo [ah-lahr-go], *m. (Elec.)* Extension, lead.

alaria [ah-lah'-re-ah], *f.* A flat iron instrument used by potters to finish and polish their work; chisel.

alarida [ah-lah-ree'-dah], *f.* Hue and cry.

alarido [ah-lah-ree'-do], *m.* Outcry, shout, howl.

alarifazgo [ah-lah-re-fath'-go], *m.* Office of an architect and surveyor.

alarife [ah-lah-ree'-fay], *m.* Architect, builder.

alarijes [ah-lah-ree'-hes], *f. pl.* A large sort of grapes. *V.* ARIJE.

alarma [ah-lar'-mah], *m.* 1. *(Mil.)* Alarm. **Falsa alarma,** false alarm. **Alarma de incendios,** fire alarm. 2. Notice of any sudden danger.

alarmante [ah-lar-mahn'-tay], *a.* Alarming, dangerous.

alarmar [ah-lar-mar'], *va.* To alarm, to call to arms. *-vr.* To get alarmed, be alarmed; to get fright.

alarmismo [ah-lahr-mes-mo], *m.* Alarmism.

alarmista [ah-lar-mees'-tah], *m.* An alarmist.

alasálet [ah-lah-sah'-let], *m.* Sal ammoniac.

alastrar [ah-las-trar'], *va.* 1. To throw back the ears. *V.* AMUSGAR. 2. *(Naut.)* To ballast. **Alastrar un navío,** to ballast a ship. *-vr.* To squat close: applied to game.

alaterno [ah-lah-ter'-no], *m. (Bot.)* Mock-privet.

alatón [ah-lah-tone'], *m.* 1. *(Obs.)* Latten, brass. *V.* LATON. 2. *(Bot. Prov.)* The fruit of the lote-tree.

alatonero [ah-lah-to-nay'-ro], *m. (Bot. Prov.)* Nettle or lote-tree.

alatrón [ah-lah-trone'], *m.* Froth of saltpetre. Afronitro.

alavanco [ah-lah-vahn'-co], *m. V.* LAVANCO.

alazán, na [ah-lah-thahn', nah], *a.* Sorrel-colored.

alazo [ah-lah'-tho], *m.* A stroke with the wings.

alazor [ah-lah-thor'], *m. (Bot.)* Bastard saffron.

alba [ahl'-bah], *f.* 1. Dawn of day, day-spring. **Al rayar el alba,** at dawn. **Misa del alba,** early morning mass. 2. Alb, the white gown worn by priests.

albacea [al-bah-thay'-ah], *m.* Testamentary executor. *-f.* Executrix. *V.* TESTAMENTARIO.

albaceazgo [al-bah-thay-ahth'-go], *m.* Executorship.

albacora [al-bah-co'-rah], *f.* 1. Seafish much resembling a tunny, albicore. 2. An early fig of the largest kind. *V.* BREVA.

albada [al-bah'-dah], *f. (Prov.)* Matinade, music which young men in the country give their sweethearts at the break of day. *V.* ALBORADA. *(Mex.)* An attack at day break.

albahaca [al-bah-ah'-cah], *f. (Bot.)* Sweet basil. **Albahaca acuática,** a sort of winter thistle. **Albahaca salvaje or silvestre,** stone or wild thistle.

albahaquero [a-bah-ah-kay'-ro], *m.* 1. A flower-pot. 2. A vender of sweet basil.

albahaquilla (DE RIO) [al-ah-ah-keel'-lyah], *f. V.* PARIETARIA.

albaida [al-bah'-e-dah], *f. (Bot.)* The shrubby gypsophila.

albalá [al-bah-lah'], *m. & f.* 1. *(Obs.)* Royal letters patent. 2. A quittance given by the custom-house. **Albalá de guía,** a passport.

albanega [al-bah-nay'-gah], *f.* Net for catching partridges or rabbits.

albanés, esa [al-bah-ness', sah], *a.* Albanian. **Albania** [ahl-bah-ne-ah], *f.* Albania.

albano [ahl-bah-no] *V.* ALBANÉS.

albañal, albañar [al-bah-nyah', al-bah-nyar'], *m.* Common sewer, gully-hole.

albañil [al-bah-nyeel'], *m.* Mason, bricklayer.

albañilería [al-bah-nye-lay-ree'-ah], *f.* Masonry.

albaquía [al-ban-kee'-ah], *f.* 1. *(Obs.)* Remnant. 2. In collecting titles, an odd portion which does not admit of division. *(Arab.)*

albar [al-bar'], *a.* White. This adjective is confined to a few botanical terms only.

albarán [al-bah'-rahn'], *m.* 1. Placard of apartments to let. 2. Delivery note, invoice (mercancías).

albarás [al-bah-rahs'], *m. V.* ALBARAZO.

albarazada [al-bah-rah-thah'-dah], *f.* A marble-colored grape, common in Andalucía.

albarazado, da [al-bah-rah-thah'-do, dah], *a.* 1. Affected with white leprosy. 2. Pale, pallid.

albarazo [al-bah-rah'-tho], *m.* White leprosy.

albarca [al-bar'-cah], *f. V.* ABARCA.

albarcoquero [al-bar-co-kay'-ro], *m. (Prov.)* Apricot-tree.

albarda [al-bar'-dah], *f.* Pack-saddle. **Bestia de albarda,** beast of burden. **Albarda sobre albarda,** verbiage, useless repetition.

albardado, da [al-bar-dah'-do, dah], *a.* Applied to animals having a different colored skin at the loins. *-pp.* of ALBARDAR.

albardán [al-bar-dahn'], *m. (Obs.)* Jester, buffoon.

albardar [al-bar-dar'], *va.* 1. To put on a pack-saddle. 2. To cover fowls which are to be roasted with large slices of bacon. 3. *(Met.)* To put upon one, take advantage of another's patience. **No se deja poner la albarda,** Not to allow oneself to be maltreated.

albardear [ahl-bahr-de-ahr], *va. (CAm.)* To bother, vex.

albardela [al-bar-day'-lah], *f.* Small saddle.

albardería [al-bar-day-ree'-ah], *f.* 1. Place where packsaddles are made and sold. 2. The trade of a packsaddle maker.

albardero [al-bar-day'-ro], *m.* Pack saddle maker.

albardilla [al-bar-deel'-lyah], *f.* 1. Small packsaddle. 2. Coping of a wall. 3. Border of a garden-bed. 4. Small saddle made use of to tame colts. 5. Wood on the back of sheep or lambs. 6. Earth which sticks to a ploughshare. 7. Batter, with which hogs' tongues and feet are covered. *-pl.* Ridges of earth on the sides of deep foot-paths.

albardín [al-bar-deen'], *m. (Bot.)* Matweed.

albardón [al-bar-done'], *m.* Pannel, a pack-saddle.

albardoncillo [al-bar-don-theel'-lyo], *m. dim.* A small pack-saddle.

albarejo, albarigo [al-ah-ray'-ho, al-bah-ree'-go], *m. (Prov.)* A species of wheat. *V.* CANDEAL.

albarela [al-bah-ray'-lah], *f. (Bot.)* A species of edible fungus which grows upon the chestnut and polar.

albareque [al-bah-ray-kay], *m.* Sardine net.

albaricoque [al-bah-re-co'-kay], *m. (Bot.).* Apricot.

albaricoquero [al-bah-re-co-kay'-ro], *m.* Apricot-tree.

albarillo [a-bah-reel'-lyo], *m.* 1. A tune played on the guitar, for country dances. 2. A small kind of apricot.

albarino [al-bah-ree'-no], *m.* A white paint formerly used by women.

albarrada [al-bar-rah'-dah], *f.* 1. A dry wall, inclosure. 2. Ditch for defence in war.

albarradón [al-bar-rah-done'], *m.* A mound to hinder inundation.

albarrana [al-bar-rah'-nah], *f. (Bot.)* **Cebolla albarrana,** squill. **Torre albarrana,** a sort of watch-tower.

albarranilla [al-bar-rah-neel'-lya], *f.* A blue-flowered variety of onion.

albarraz [al-bar-rath'], *m. (Bot.)* 1. *V.* ALBARAZO. 2. Lousewort.

albatoza [al-bah-to'-thah], *f.* A small covered boat.

albatros [al-bah'-tros], *m.* The albatross.

albayaldado, da [al-bah-yal-dah'-do, dah], *a.* Covered with white-lead.

albayalde [al-bah-yahl'-day], *m.* White-lead, ceruse, lead carbonate.

albazano, na [al-bah-thah'-no, nah], *a.* Of a dark chestnut color.

albazo [al-bah'-tho], *m. (Obs.)* A military term implying an assault at day-break.

albeador [ahl-bay-ah-dor], *m. (Cono Sur)* Early riser.

albear [al-bay-ar'], *va.* To whiten. *V.* BLANQUEAR.

albedrío [al-bay-drec'-o], *m.* 1. Freedom of will. 2. Free will directed by caprice, and not by reason. **Libre albedrío,** liberty.

albéitar [al-bay'-e-tar], *m.* A farrier-veterinary surgeon.

albeitería [al-bay-e-tay-ree'-ah], *f.* Farriery; veterinary surgery.

albenda [al-ben'-dah], *f.* Hangings of white linen.

albendera [al-ben-day'-rah], *f.* 1. Woman who makes hangings. 2. A gadding idle woman.

albéntola [al-ben'-to-lah], *f.* A slight net, made of a very fine thread.

alberca [al-ber'-cah], *f.* 1. A pond or pool. 2. Reservoir, tank, mill-pond. 3. Vat (of tannery).

albercón [al-ber-cone'], *m. aug.* A large pool or pond.

albérchiga, or Albérchigo [al-ber'-che-gah, or al-ber'-che-go], *m. & f. (Bot.)* Peach, strictly a clingstone peach.

alberengena [al-bay-ren-hay'-nah], *f. (Bot.)* Eggplant. Solanum melongena. *V.* BERENGENA.

albergador, ra [a-ber-gah-dor', rah], *m. & f.* A hotel-keeper.

albergar [al-ber-gar], *va.* 1. To lodge, to harbor. 2. To keep a lodging-house. *-vr.* To take a lodging.

albergue [al-ber'-gay], *m.* 1. Lodging or lodging-house. 2. Den for wild beasts. 3. Hospital for orphans. 4. Place, space, shelter. **Albergue para jóvenes,** youth hostel.

alberguería [al-ber-gay-ree'-ah], *f. (Obs.)* 1. Inn. 2. Hospital for poor travelers. *V.* POSADA.

alberguero [al-ber-gay'-ro], *m. (Obs.)* Innkeeper.

alberguista [ahl-bayr-ges-tah], *m. & f.* Youth-hosteller.

albercoque [al-bay-re-co'-kay], *V.* ALBARICOQUE.

albero [al-bay'-ro], *m.* 1. Whitish earth. 2. A cloth for cleaning plates and dishes.

alberquero [al-ber-kay'-ro], *m.* One who takes care of the pond where flax is steeped.

alberquilla [al-ber-keel'-lyah], *f. dim.* A little pool.

albicante [al-be-can'-tay] *a.* That which whitens or blanches.

albihar [al-be-ar'], *m. (Bot.)* Ox-eye. Buphthalmum.

albilla [al-beel'-lyah], *f.* **albillo** [al-beel'-lyo], *m.* An early white grape. Sweet water.

albillo [al-beel'-lyo], *a.* Applied to the wine of a white grape.

albin [al-been'], *m.* 1. Maltites or bloodstone, a sort of iron ore of a brown color. 2. Dark carmine pigment from this ore, used in fresco paintings.

albina [al-bee'-nah], *f.* A marshy piece of ground covered with nitre in the summer season.

albino, na [al-bee'-no, nah], *a.* 1. Albino. 2. *m.* A person having the skin and hair perfectly white, and the iris of the eye generally pink.

Albión [al-be-on'], *f.* Albion, the ancient name of England.

albis [ahl'-bis], *(Met.)* **Quedarse in albis**, to be frustrated in one's hopes, to be disappointed.

albitana [al-be-tah'-nah], *f.* 1. Fence used by gardeners to inclose plants. 2. *(Naut.)* An apron. **Albitana del codaste**, *(Naut.)* Inner post.

albo, ba [ahl'-bo, bah], *a.* Very white. *(Poetic.)*

alboaire [al-bo-ah'-ee-ray], *m.* Glazed tile work.

albogalla [al-bo-gahl'-lyah], *f.* A kind of gall-nut.

albogue [al-bo'-gay], *m.* 1. A pastoral flute much used in Biscay. 2. Martial music, played with two plates of brass resembling the *rotalum* of the ancients; a cymbal.

alboguero, ra [al-bo-gay'-ro, rah], *m. & f.* One who makes *albogues*, or pastoral flutes, or plays on them.

albohol [al-bo-ole'], *m. (Bot.)* A red poppy. *V.* AMAPOLA.

albóndiga [al-bon'-de-gah], *f.* A meatball, ball made of meat chopped fine with eggs and spice.

albondigón [ahl-bon-de-gon], *m.* Hamburger.

albondiguilla [al-bon-de-geel'-lyah], *f. dim.* A small ball of meat.

albor [al-bor'], *m. (Poetic.)* 1. Whiteness. 2. Dawn. **Los primeros albores del juicio**, the first dawnings of the mind.

alborada [al-bo-rah'-dah], *f.* 1. Twilight, the first dawn of day. 2. *(Mil.)* Action fought at the dawn of day. 3. Reveille, the first military call of the day. 4. Morning watch. *V.* ALBADA.

alborear [al-bo-ray-ar'], *vn.* To dawn.

alborga [al-bor'-gah], *f.* A sort of sandal made of mat-weed.

albornía [al-bor-nee'-ah], *f.* A large glazed jug.

alborno [al-bor'-no], *m. (Bot.)* Alburnum.

albornoz [al-bor-noth'], *m.* 1. Coarse woollen stuff, bathing wrap. 2. Cloak which forms part of the Moorish dress.

alboronía [al-bo-ro-nee'-ah], *f.* A dish made with eggplant, tomatoes, pumpkins, and pimento.

alboroque [al-bo-ro'-kay], *m.* Regalement given at the conclusion of a bargain: treat.

alborotadamente [al-bo-rotah-dah-men'-tay], *adv.* Noisily, confusedly.

alborotadizo, za [al-boro-tah-dee-tho', thah], *a. V.* ALBOROTADO.

alborotado, da [al-bo-rotah'-do, dah], *a.* Of a restless disposition, turbulent. *-pp.* of ALBOROTAR.

alborotador, ra [al-bo-ro-tah-dor', rah], *m. & f.* A violator of peace, rioter.

alborotapueblos [al-bo-ro-tah-poo-ay'-bos], *m.* 1. A mover of sedition. **alborotar** [al-bo-ro-tar'], *va.* To disturb, to vex , to excite, stir up. *-vr.* 1. To come over. 2. To fling out. 3. *(CAm.)* To become amorous (ponerse amoroso). 4. *(Cono Sur)* To rear up (caballos).

alboroto [al-bo-ro'-to], *m.* 1. Disturbance, tumult, riot, faction; convulsion. 2. Outcry, clatter, noisinness; fuss, hubbub.

alborotoso, sa [ahl-bo-ro-to-so], *(And. Carib.)* a. Troublesome, riotous.

alborozado [ahl-bo-ro-thah-do], *a.* Jubilant, overjoyed.

alborozador, ra [al-bo-ro-thah-dor', rah], *m. & f.* Promoter of mirth.

alborozar [al-bo-ro-thar'], *va.* To exhilarate, to promote mirth. *-vr.* To be overjoyed, rejoice.

alborozo [al-bo-ro'-tho], *m.* Merriment, exhilaration, gaiety.

albrán [al-brahn'], *m.* A duckling.

albricias [al-bree'-the-as], *f. pl.* Reward given for some good news. **Ganar las albricias**, to obtain a reward for some good news. *-int.* **¡Albricias, albricias!** Joy! Joy!

albudeca [al-boo-day'-cah], *f. (Bot.)* A watermelon. *V.* SANDIA.

albuérbola [al-boo-er'-bo-lah], *f.* Exhilaration, acclamation.

albufera [al-boo-fay'-rah], *f.* A large lake formed by the sea.

albugíneo, nea [al-boo-hee'-nay-o, nay-ah], *a.* Albugineous, entirely white, like the sclerotic. *(Anat.)* Albuminous.

albuginoso, sa [al-boo-he-no'-so, sah], *a. V.* ALBUGINEO.

albugo [al-boo'-go], *m.* Leucoma, a white opacity upon the cornea of the eye.

albuhera [al-boo-ay'-rah], *f.* A fresh-water lake. *V.* ALBUFERA.

álbum [ahl'-boom], *m.* Album. **Álbum de recortes**, scrapbook. **Álbum de sellos**, stamp album.

albumen [al-boo'-men], *m. (Bot.)* Albumen. Nourishing matter, not a part of the embryo, stored up in the seed.

albúmina [al-boo'-me-nah], *f. (Chem.)* Albumin, as represented in the white of an egg; a constituent of some animal fluids, and sparingly found likewise in some plants.

albuminoso, sa [al-boo-me-no'-so, sah], *a.* Albuminous.

albur [al-boor'], *m.* 1. Dace, a river fish. 2. A sort of game at cards. 3. Risk, contingency. **Correr un albur**, to venture, to chance.

albura [al-boo'-rah], *f.* 1. Whiteness. 2. *(Bot.)* *V.* ALBORNO. **Albura de huevo**, *(Obs.)* *V.* CLARA DE HUEVO.

alburear [ahl,-boo-ray-ahr], 1. *va. (CAm.)* To disturb, upset. 2. *vn.* To make money, get rich.

alburero [al-boo-ray'-ro], *m.* A player at the game *albures*.

albures [al-boo'-res], *m. pl.* A game at cards.

alburno [al-boor'-no], *m.* 1. *(Bot.)* *V.* ALBORNO.

alca [ahl'-cah], *f.* Razorbill, a bird.

alcabala [al-cah-bah'-lah], *f.* 1. Excise. **Alcabala del viento**, duty paid on goods sold by chance. **El caudal del fulano está en alcabala de viento**, he lives upon what he earns. 2. A net. *V.* JABEGA.

alcabalatorio [al-cah-bah-lah-to'-re-o] *m.* Book of rates of the *alcabala*.

alcabalero [al-cah-bah-lay'-ro], *m.* A tax-gatherer; revenue officer.

alcabiaz [al-cah-be-ath'], *m.* Aviary, a large cage for birds. *V.* ALCAHAZ.

alcabor [al-cah-bor'], *m. (Prov.)* Flue of a chimney.

alcabuz [al-cah-booth'], *m. (Obs.)* *V.* ARCABUZ.

alcacel, alcacer [al-cah-thel', al-cah-therr'], *m.* Green barley.

alcachofa [al-cah-cho'-fah], *f.* 1. *(Bot.)* Artichoke. 2. Instrument serving to stop a flux of blood. 3. Fluted mallets used by ropemakers.

alcachofado, da [al-cah-cho-fah'-do, dah], *a.* Resembling an artichoke.

alcachofado [al-cah-cho-fah'-do], *m.* Dish of artichokes.

alcachofal [al-cah-cho-fahl'], *m.* Ground where artichokes grow.

alcachofera [al-cah-cho-fay'-rah], *f.* An artichoke-plant.

alcahaz [al-cah-ahth'], *m.* A large cage for birds.

alcahazada [al-cah-ah-thah'-dah], *f.* A number of birds in a cage.

alcahazar [al-cah-ah-thar'], *va.* To shut up birds in the **alcahazar**.

alcaheta [al-cah-ay'-tah], *f.* Alcahest, a supposed universal solvent.

alcahué [ahl,-cah-oo-ay], *m. V.* CACAHUETE.

alcahuete, ta [al-cah-oo-tay'-tay, tah], *m. & f.* Pimp, procurer, bawd, whoremonger, gossip.

alcahuetear [al-cah-oo-ay-tay-ar'], *va.* To bawd, to pander, to procure women.

alcahuetería [al-cah-oo-ay-tay-ree'-ah], *f.* 1. Bawdry. 2. Hiding persons who want concealment.

alcahuetillo, lla [al-cah-oo-ay-teel'-lyo, lyah], *m. & f. dim.* A little pimp.

alcahuetón, na, alcahuetazo, za [al-cah-oo-ay-tone', nah, al-cah-oo-ay-tah'-tho, thah], *m. & f. aug.* A great pander, a great bawd.

alcaicería [al-cah-e-thay-ree'-ah], *f.* Market-place for raw silk.

alcaide [al-cah'-e-day], *m.* 1. Governor of a castle or fort. 2. Jailer, warden.

alcaidesa [al-cah-e-day'-sah], *f.* Wife of a governor or jailer.

alcaidía [al-cah-e-dee'-ah], *f.* 1. Office of a governor, and district of his jurisdiction; wardenship. 2. Office of a jailer. 3. Ancient duty paid for the passage of cattle.

alcaldable [ahl-cahl-dah-blay], *m. & f.* Candidate for mayor.

alcaldada [al-cal-dah'-dah], *f.* 1. An inconsiderate action of an *alcalde* or petty judge. 2. *(coll.)* Any word said, or action performed, with an air of mock authority. 3. A preposterous act or deed that causes a great noise.

alcalde [al-cahl'-day], *m.* 1. Justice of the peace. 2. Mayor of a city, or chairman of a council (of town government). 3. He who leads off a country dance. **Tener al padre alcalde.** To enjoy the protection of a judge or other man in power. 4. Game at cards. **Alcalde de barrio.** Justice of the peace of a ward. **Alcalde de primera elección,** The senior judge. *De segunda elección,* The junior judge. The **alcalde** acts as the *mayor* of the city council.

alcaldear [al-cal-day-ar'], *vn. (coll.)* To play the alcalde.

alcaldesa [al-cal-day'-sah], *f.* The wife of an alcalde.

alcaldía [al-cal-dee'-ah], *f.* Office and jurisdiction of an **alcalde**.

alcalescencia [al-cah-les-then'-the-ah], *f. (Chem.) V.* ALCALIZACION.

alcalescente [al-cah-les-then'-tay], *a. (Chem.)* Partaking of alkaline properties.

álcali [ahl'-cah-le], *m. (Chem.)* An alkali. **Álcali fijo,** fixed alkali.

alcalificable [al-cah-le-fe-cah'-baly], *a.* Changeable into an alkali.

alcalígeno, na [al-cah-lee'-hay-no, nah], *a.* Alkaligenous, producing alkali.

alcalímetro [al-cah-lee'-may-tro], *m.* Alkalimeter, an instrument for estimating percentage of fixed alkali.

alcalinidad [al-cah-le-ne-dad'], *f.* Alkalinity, state of being alkaline.

alcalino, na Alcalizado, da [al-cah-lee'-no, nah, al-cah-le-thah'-do, dah], *a.* Alkaline. *Alcalizado, da, pp.* of ALCALIZAR.

alcalización [al-cah-le-thah-the-on'], *f. (Chem.)* Alkalization.

alcalizar [al-cah-le-thar'], *va. (Chem.)* To render alkaline.

alcaloide [al-cah-lo'-e-day], *m.* Alkaloid, an organic base.

alcam [al-cahm'], *m. (Bot.)* Bitter apple.

alcamonias [al-cah-mo-nee'-as], *f. pl.* 1. Various aromatic seeds used in the kitchen, and other stimulants. 2. *m. V.* ALCAHUETE.

alcamonero [ahl-cah-mo-nay-ro], *a. (Carib.)* Interfering (entrometido).

alcaná [al-cah-nah'], *f.* 1. *(Obs.)* A place where shops are kept. 2. *(Bot.)* Alcanna, from which henna is obtained. Alkanet.

alcance [al-cahn'-thay], *m.* 1 Following and overtaking a person. 2. Balance of an account. 3. Arm's length. 4. Range of fire-arms. 5. Capacity, ability. 6. Fathom, compass. 7. The supplement of a newspaper; a postcript. 8. Portion of copy which a compositor takes for setting up. 9. Capacity, talent. **Ir a los alcances,** to be at one's heels. **No poderle dar alcance,** to be unable to get sight of one. **Estar al alcance de uno,** to be within one´s reach. 10. **El alcance del problema**, the extent of the problem. 11. Adverse balance, deficit. 12. **Buzón de alcance,** late collection postbox. 13. *(CAm.)* Calumnies (calumnias).

alcancia [al-can-thee'-ah], *f.* 1. Money-box. 2. *(Mil.)* Inflamed combustible balls.

alcancil [al-can-thel], *m. (Cono Sur)* Procurer, pimp.

alcándara [al-can'-dah-rah], *f.* Perch of a falcon.

alcandía [al-can-dee'-ah], *f. (Bot.)* Turkey millet. *V.* ZAHINA.

alcandial [al-can-de-ahl'], *m.* Ground sown with millet.

alcandora [al-can-do-rah], *f.* Beacon.

alcanfeno [al-can-fay'-no], *m.* Camphene.

alcanfor [al-can-fore'], *m.* 1. Camphor. 2. *(LAm.)* Procurer, pimp (alcahuete).

alcanforada [al-can-fo-rah'-dah], *f.* Camphor-tree.

alcanforado, da [al-can-fo-rah-do, dah], *a.* Impregnated with camphor.

alcanforar [al-can-fo-rahr], 1. *va.* To camphorate. 2. *-vr. (And. CAm, Carib.)* To disappear.

alcanforero [al-can-fo-ray'-ro], *m.* The camphor-tree.

alcantarilla [al-can-tah-reel'-lyah], *f.* 1. Sewer. 2. Small bridge. 3. Drain. 4. Culvert. 5. *(Carib. Mex.)* Public fountain.

alcantarillado [al-can-tah-reel-lyay'-ro], *m.* Sewerage system, drains.

alcantarillar [al-can-tah-re-lyahr], *va.* To lay sewers in.

alcantarillero *m.* Sewer man.

alcanzable [al-can-thah'-blay], *a.* Attainable.

alcanzadizo, za [al-can-thah-dee'-tho, thah], *a.* Within reach, easily reached. **Hacerse el alcanzadizo,** *(Met.)* to affect ignorance.

alcanzado, da [al-can-thah'-do, dah], *a.* 1. Needy, hard up, broke. 2. *(And)* Tired (fatigado). *-pp.* of ALCANZAR.

alcanzadera [al-can-thah-dor'-rah], *f. (Vet.)* 1. A tumor or wound in the pastern of a horse. 2. Wound or contusion arising from a horse's cutting the fore hoof with the hind shoe.

alcanzamiento [al-can-thah-me-en'-to], *m. (Obs.) V.* ALCANCE.

alcanzar [al-can-thar'], *va.* 1. To catch up with. 2. To overtake, to come up, to reach, to carry far. 3. To reach a thing, to extend the hand to take it. 4. To acquire, to obtain, to possess power of obtaining a thing desired. 5. To comprehend. 6. To be creditor of a balance. 7. To know a long while. **La bala le alcanzó en el pecho,** the bullet hit him in his chest. *-vn.* 1. To share. 2. To suffice. 3. To reach: applied to a ball. 4. **Alcanzar en días,** to survive. *-vr.* To overreach. **Alcanzársele poco a alguno,** to prevail upon any one. **Alcanzar a ver,** to descry. **No alcanzar con mucho,** to fall short.

alcanzativo [al-can-thah-te-vo], *a. (CAm.)* Suspicious.

alcaparras, *f.* **alcaparro,** *m.* [al-cah-pahr'-rah, al-cah-pahr'-roh], *(Bot.)* 1. Caper-bush. Capparris. 2. Caper, the bud of the caper-bush.

alcaparrado, da [al-cah-par-rah'-do, dah], *a.* Dressed with capers.

alcaparral [al-cah-par-rahl'], *m.* Ground planted with caper-bushes.

alcaparrón [al-cah-par-rone], *m. aug.* A large caper.

alcarrosa [al-cah-par-ro'-sah], *f. V.* CAPARROSA.

alcarahueya [al-cah-rah-oo-ay'-yah], *f. (Bot.)* Caraway-seed.

alcaraván [al-cah-rah-vahn'], *m. (Orn.)* Bittern.

alcaravea [al-ah-rah-vay'-ah], *f. (Bot.) V.* ALCARAHUEYA.

alcarón [al-cah-rone'], *m.* Alcaron, a species of scorpion found in Africa.

alcarracero, ra [al-car-rah-thay'-ro, rah], *m. & f.* 1. A potter. 2. Shelf on which earthenware is placed.

alcarraza [al-car-rah'-thah], *f* Pitcher or jug unglazed and porous.

alcartaz [al-cartath'], *m. V.* CUCURUCHO.

alcatifa [al-cah-tee'-fah], *f.* 1. A sort of fine carpet. 2. Layer of earth put under bricks in paving. 3. Roof of a house.

alcatife [al-cah-tee'-fay], *m.* Silk. *V.* SEDA.

alcatraz [al-cah-trath'], *m.* 1. Pelican. *V.* CUCURUCHO.

alcaucil [al-cah-oo-theel'], *m.* 1. *(Prov.)* Wild artichoke. 2. *(Cono Sur)* Informer. *V.* ALCACHOFA.

alcaudón [ahl-cah-oo-don], *m.* Shrike, butcher-bird (ave).

alcayata [al-cah-yah'-tah], *f.* 1. A hook. 2. Scarp of a fortification. 3. A kind of knot often used on board ship. *V.* ESCARPIA.

alcayota [al-cah-yo-tah], *f.* Squash, vegetable marrow.

alcazaba [al-cah-tha-bah], *f.* Castle.

alcázar [al-cah'-thar], *m.* 1. Castle. 2. Fortress. 3. *(Naut.)* Quarter-deck.

alcazuz [al-cah-thooth'], *m. V.* REGALIZA and OROZUZ. Licorice.

alce [ahl'-thay], *m.* 1. *(Zool.)* Elk or moose. *V.* ANTA. 2. The «cut», at cards.

alcea [al-tahy'-ah], *f. (Bot.)* Marshmallow.

alcedón [al-thay-done'], *m.* A king-fisher. *V.* MARTIN PESCADOR.

alcino [al-thee'-no], *m. (Bot.)* Wild basil.

alcista [al-thees'-tah], *f. (coll.)* Bull. **Tendencia alcista,** upward tendency (bolsa). *a.* Rising.

alcoba [al-co'-bah], *f.* 1. Alcove. 2. Bedroom. 3. Case in which the tongue of a balance moves to regulate the weight.

alcobilla, alcobita [al-co-beel'-lyah, bee'-tah], *f. dim.* A small alcove.

alcohol [al-co-ole'], *m.* Alcohol, **alcohol etílico,** ethyl alcohol, grain alcohol. **Alcohol de granos,** grain alcohol. **Alcohol metílico,** wood alcohol. **Alcohol de quemar,** methylated spirit.

alcoholado, da [al-co-o-lah'-do, dah], *a.* Being of a darker color around the eyes than the rest of the body; applied to cattle. *-pp.* of ALCOHOLAR.

alcoholar [al-co-o-lar'], *va.* 1. To alcoholize. 2. To make up with kohl (pintarse). 3. To clear up with alcohol. 4. To tar (barcos) *-vn. (Obs.)* To pass in a tilt the adverse party of combatants.

alcoholemia [alco-o-lay-me-ah], *f.* Blood-level of alcohol.

alcoholera [al-co-o-lay'-rah], *f.* Vessel for antomony or alcohol.

alcoholero [al-co-o-lay-ro], *a.* Alcohol .

alcohólico, ca [al-co-o'-le-co, cah], *a.* Alcoholic, containing alcohol or spirits of wine.

alcoholímetro [al-co-o-lee'-may-tro], *m.* Alcoholimeter, alcoholometer.

alcoholismo [al-co-o-lees'-mo], *m.* Alcoholism, a diseased state caused by continued abuse of alcoholic beverages.

alcoholista [al-co-o-les-tah], *m. & f. (Cono Sur)* Drunk.

alcoholización [al-co-o-le-thah-the-on'], *f. (Chem.)* Alcoholization.

alcoholizado, da [al-co-le-thah'-do, dah], *a.* 1. Containing alcohol. 2. Affected by alcoholism.

alcoholizar [al-co-o-le-thar'], *va.* To alcoholize. *-vr.* **To drink heavily,** to become an alcoholic. *V.* ALCOHOLAR.

alcor [al-cor'], *m. V.* CERRO.

alcorán [al-co-rahn'], *m.* The Koran, the sacred book of the Mohammedans.

alcoranista [al-co-rah-nees'-tah], *m.* One who expounds the law of Mohammed.

alcornocal [al-cor-no-cahl'], *m.* Plantation of cork-trees.

alcornoque [al-cor-no'-kay], *m.* 1. *(Bot.)* Cork-tree. 2. *(Met.)* A person of rude, uncouth manners.

alcornoqueño, ña [al-cor-nokay'-nyo, nyah], *a.* Belonging to the cork-tree.

alcorque [al-cor'-kay], *m.* 1. *(Bot.)* Cork-tree. 2. *(Met.)* A person of rude, uncouth manners.

alcorza [al-cor'-thah], *f.* 1. A paste for sweetmeats. 2. A piece of sweetmeat. **Parece hecho de alcorza,** he looks as if he were made of sweetmeat.

alcorzar [al-cor-thar'], *va.* To cover with iced sugar.

alcotán [al-co-tahn'], *m.* Lanner, a bird of prey. Hobby.

alcotana [al-co-tah'-nah], *f.* Pickaxe, gurlet.

alcotancillo [al-co-tan-theel'-lyo], *m. dim.* A young lanner.

alcrebite [al-cray-bee'-tay], *m.* Sulphur. *V.* AZUFRE.

alcribis [al-cree'-bis], *m.* A small tube at the back of a forge through which runs the pipe of the bellows; twyer, tuyere.

alcubilla [al-coo-beel'-lyah], *f. (Prov.)* Reservoir of an aqueduct; basin, millpond.

alcucero, ra [al-coo-thay'-ro], *a.* Belonging to an oil-bottle.

alcucilla [al-coo-theel'-lyah], *f. dim.* A small oil-bottle or can.

alcuña [al-coo'-nyah], *f. (Obs.) V.* ALCURNIA.

alcurnia [al-coor'-ne-ah], *f.* Family, lineage, race.

alcurniado [al-koor-ne-ah-do], *a.* Aristocratic, noble.

alcuza [al-coo'-thah], *f.* Oil-bottle or cruet; oilcan, oiler (aceitera).

alcuzada [al-coo-thah'-dah], *f.* The oil contained in a full cruet.

alcuzcuz [al-cooth-cooth'], *m.* Flour, water, and honey, made into balls, and esteemed by the Moors.

alcuzón [al-coo-thone'], *m. aug.* A large oil-bottle.

aldaba [al-dah'-bah], *f.* 1. Knocker, hammer on the door, clapper; door-handle, latch. 2. A cross-bar to secure doors and windows. **Caballo de aldaba,** a steed, a horse for state or war. 3. **Tener buenas aldabas,** to have influence. 4. Tits (pechos).

aldabada [al-dah-bah-dah], *f.* Knock (en puerta).

aldabazo, aldabonazo [al-dah-bah'-tho, al-dah-bo-nah'-tho], *m.* Knocking.

aldabear [al-da-bay-ar'], *vn.* To rap or knock at the door.

aldabia [al-dah-bee'-ah], *f.* Beam horizontally placed on two walls, to which is a hanging partition.

aldabilla [al-dah-beel'-yah], *f. dim.* A small knocker.

aldabón [al-dah-bone'], *m.* 1. *(aug.)* A large knocker. 2. An iron handle of trunks.

aldabonazo [al-dah-bo-nah-tho], *m.* Bang, loud knock (puerta); *(fig.)* Knock, blow.

aldea [al-day'-ah], *f.* Small village, hamlet, a large farm.

aldeana [al-day-ah'-nah], *f.* Villager, country woman, lass.

aldeanismo [al-day-ah-nes-mo], *m.* Provincialism.

aldeano [al-day-ah'-no], *m.* Villager, a countryman.

aldebarán [al-day-bah-rahn'], *m. (Astr.)* Aldebaran or Bull's-Eye, a fixed star of first magnitude in the constellation of Taurus.

aldehida [al-day-ee'-dah], *f.* Aldehyde, a volatile, colorless fluid obtained by the oxidation of alcohol.

aldehuela, aldeilla [al-day-oo-ay'-lah, al-day-eel'-lyah], *f. dim.* A little village.

aldeorrio [al-day-or'-re-o], *m.* 1. A small, unpleasant village. 2. A town whose inhabitants are rude.

alderredor [al-dayr-ray-dor], *adv. V.* ALREDEDOR.

aldiza [al-dee'-thah], *f.* A sort of small reed without knots.

aleación [al-lay-ah-the-on'], *f.* The art of alloying metals; alloy, compound metal.

aleador [al-lay-ah-dor'], *m.* Alloyer.

alear [ah-lay-ar'], *vn.* 1. To flutter. 2. *(Met.)* To move the arms quickly. 3. *(Met.)* To recover from sickness, to regain strength after fatigue. *-va.* To alloy.

aleatoriedad [ah-lay-ah-to-re-ay-dahd], *f.* Randomness.

aleatorio [ah-lay-ah-to-re-o], *a.* Accidental, fortuitous; uncertain.

aleatorizar [ah-lay-ah-to-re-thar'], *va.* To randomize.

alebrarse, alebrastrarse, alebrestarse [ah-lay-brar'-say, ah-lay-bras-trar'-say, ah-lay-brays-tar'-say], *vr.* 1. To squat close to the ground as hares do (agazaparse). 2. To cower.

alebestrarse [ah-lah-bays-trahr-say], *vr. (LAm.)* To become agitated.

alebronarse [ah-lay-bro-nar'-say], *vr.* To be dispirited.

aleccionador [ah-layc-the-o-nah-dor], *a.* Instructive, enlightening.

aleccionamiento [ah-layc-the-o-nah-me-ayn-to], *m.* Instruction, enlightenment; training.

aleccionar [ah-le-the-o-nar'], *va.* To teach, to instruct.

alece [ah-lay-thay], *m.* A ragout made of the livers of a large fish, called *mújo*, caught on the coast of Valencia.

alechado [ah-lay-chah-do], *a. (LAm.)* Milky, like milk.

alechigar [ah-lay-che-gar'], *va.* To soften. *-vr.* To turn milky.

alechugado, da [ah-lay-choo-gah'-do, dah], *a.* Curled like the leaf of lettuce. Fluted, plaited. *-pp.* of ALECHUGAR.

alechugar [ah-lay-choo-gar'], *va.* 1. To curl or contract like the leaf of lettuce. 2. To plait, to flute.

aleda [ah-lay'-dah], *f.* CERA ALEDA. Propolis, or bee-glue, used by bees in stopping cracks and cementing the comb to the hive.

aledaño [ah-lay-dah'-nyo], *m. & a.* Common boundary, border, limit.

alefanginas [ah-lay-fan-hee'-nas], *f. pl.* Purgative pills made of cinnamon, nutmeg, and the juice of aloes.

alefra [ah-lay-frah], *interj. (Carib.)* Touch wood!

alefris, alefruz [ah-lay-frees'], *m.* 1. Mortise, a hole cut into wood. 2. Rabbet.

alefrizar [ah-lay-fre-thar'], *va.* To rabbet.

alegación [ah-lay-gah-the-on'], *f.* Allegation; argument. **Alegación de inocencia,** *(Mex. Jur.)* Plea of not guilty.

alegador, ra [ah-lay-gah-dor], *a. (Cono Sur)* Argumentative.

alegal [ah-lay-gahl], *a. (Cono Sur Jur.)* Illegal.

alegar [ah-lay-gahr'], *va.* To allege, to affirm, to quote, to maintain, to adduce. *(LAm.)* (Disputar) To argue against, dispute.

alegata [ah-lay-gah-tah], *f. (LAm.)* Fight.

alegato [ah-lay-gah'-to], *m. (Law.)* Allegation, showing the ground of complaint by the plaintiff. Complaint, petition.

alegoría [ah-lay-go-ree'-ah], *f.* Allegory.

alegóricamente [ah-lay-go'-re-cah-men-tay], *adv.* Allegorically.

alegórico, ca [ah-lay-go'-re-co, cah], *a.* Allegorical, not literal.

alegorista [ah-lay-go-rees'-tah], *m.* Allegorist.

alegorizar [ah-lay-go-re-thar'], *va.* To turn into allegory.

alegrado, da [ah-lay-grah'-do, dah], *a.* Delighted. *-pp.* of ALEGRAR.

alegrador, ra [ah-lay-grah-dor', rah], *m. & f.* 1. *(Obs.)* One who produces merriment: a jester. 2. *(coll.)* Twisted slip of paper to shake the snuff of a candle. 3. *(Mech.)* Reamer, round broach; riming bit.

alegrar [ah-lay-grar'], *va.* 1. To make merry, to gladden, to comfort, to exhilarate. 2. *(Met.)* To enliven, to beautify. 3. *(Mech.)* To round, to make a bore; to ream, to widen. **Alegrar las luces,** to snuff the candles. *-vr.* 1. To rejoice, to congratulate, to exult. **Me alegro de saberlo,** I am glad to hear it. 2. To grow merry by drinking.

alegre [ah-lay'-gray], *a.* 1. Merry, joyful, content, light-hearted, full of gaiety, gleeful. 2. Lightsome, comic, ludicrous, facetious. 3. Gay, showy, fine: applied to inanimate things. **Un cielo alegre,** a clear, beautiful sky. 4. Brilliant, pleasing: applied to colors. 5. Lucky, fortunate, genial. 6. Bold, reckless (atrevido). 7. Fast, immoral (vida). 8. **Estar alegre,** to be merry, to be tight.

alegremente [ah-lay-gray-men'-tay], *adv.* 1. Merrily, gladly, gaily. 2. Facetiously, mirthfully, laughingly, good-humoredly.

alegría [ah-lay-gree'-ah], *f.* 1. Mirth, merriment, exhilaration, gaiety, glee, rejoicing. **Saltar de alegría,** to jump with joy. 2. Festivity. 3. Light-someness, 4. Ecstasy, pleasure. 5. *(Bot.)* Sesamum, oily grain. 6. Paste made of sesamum and honey. *-pl.* Rejoicings, public festivals.

alegrillo [ah-lay-greel'-lyo], *a.* Sprightly, gay.

alegro [ah-lay'-gro], *m.* 1. *(Mus.)* Allegro, a word denoting in music a sprightly motion. 2. A movement, or division of a sonata, in this time.

alegrón [ah-lay-grone'], *m. (coll.)* 1. Sudden, unexpected joy. 2. A flash.

alegrona [ah-lay-gro-nah], *f. (LAm.)* Prostitute.

alejado [ah-lay-hah-do], *a.* Distant, remote.

alejamiento [ah-lay-hah-me-en'-to], *m.* 1. Elongation, removal to a distance. 2. Distance. 3. Strangeness.

Alejandría [ah-lay-han-dre-ah], *n.* Alexandria.

alejandrino, na [ah-lay-han-dree'-no, nah], *a.* Alexandrine.

Alejandro [ah-lay-han-dro], *m.* Alexander.

alejar [ah-lay-har'], *va.* To remove to a greater distance, to separate. **Conviene alejar tales libros de los niños,** such books should be kept out of children's hands. *(fig.)* To cause a rift between, to separate, to estrange. *-vr.* To move away, to go away. **Alejémonos un poco más,** let's go a bit farther away.

alejijas [ah-lay-hee'-has], *f. pl.* Porridge made of barley, cleaned and roasted. **Tiene cara de alejijas,** he looks half-starved.

alelado [ah-lay-lah-do], *a.* Stupefied, bewildered.

alelamiento [ah-lay-lah-me-ayn-to], *m.* Bewilderment; stupidity.

alelar [ah-lay-lahr], *va.* To stupefy.

alelarse [ah-lay-lar'-say], *vr.* To become stupid.

alelí [ah-lay-lee'], *m. (Bot.)* The winter gilliflower of various colors: also a general name for violets.

aleluya [ah-lay-loo'-yah], *f.* 1. Allelujah. 2. Joy, merriment. 3. Easter time. **Al aleluya nos veremos,** we'll meet again at Easter. 4. *(Bot.)* Woodsorrel (planta). V. ACEDERILLA. So called because it flowers at Easter. 6. *pl. (coll.)* Dull, poor verses.

alema [ah-lay'-mah], *f.* The allotted quantity of water for irrigating a piece of ground.

alemán, na [ah-lay-mahn'- mah'-nah], *a. & m.* 1. German. 2. German language.

Alemania [ah-lay-mah-ne-ah], *f.* Germany.

alemanisco, ca [ah-lay-mah-nees'-co, cah], *a.* Germanic: cloth made in Germany; huckaback; damask tablelinen.

alenguamiento [ah-len-goo-ah-me-en'-to], *m.* An agreement relative to pasture.

alenguar [ah-len-goo-ar'], *va.* To agree respecting sheep-walks or pasturage.

alentada [ah-len-tah'-dah], *f. (Obs.)* Interval between two respirations, a continued respiration; a full, deep breath.

alentadamente [ah-len-tah-dah-men'-tay], *adv.* Bravely, gallantly.

alentado, da [ah-len-tah'-do, dah], *a.* 1. Spirited, courageous, valiant. 2. *(Obs.)* Bold. *-pp.* of ALENTAR.

alentador, ra [ah-len-ta-dor', rah], *m. & f.* One who inspires courage.*-a.* Encouraging, animating.

alentar [ah-len-tar'], *vn.* To breathe. *(fig.)* To burn, to glow. *-va.* 1. To animate, to encourage, to comfort. **Alentar a uno a hacer algo,** to encourage somebody to do something. 2. *(And)* To clap (aplaudir). *-vr.* 1. To take heart, to cheer up. 2. *(Med.)* To get well. 3. *(And. CAm.)* To give birth (dar a luz).

aleonarse [ah-lay-o-nahr-say], *vr. (Cono Sur)* To get excited, to get worked up.

aleoyota [ah-lay-o-yo-tah], *f. (Cono Sur Bot.)* Pumpkin.

alepantado [ah-lay-pahn-tah-do], *a. (And)* Absent-minded.

alepín [ah-lay-peen'], *m.* A kind of bombasin, or bombazine.

alerce [ah-ler'-thay], *m. (Bot.)* Larch-tree.

alérgeno [ah-lehr-hay'-no], *m.* Allergen.

alergia [ah-lehr'-he-ah], *f.* Allergy.

alérgico, ca [ah-lehr'-hee-co, cah], *a.* Allergic.

alero [ah-lay'-ro], *m.* 1. The projecting part of a roof; eaves, gable-end, corona hood moulding, water-table. 2. Splash-board of a carriage. *-pl.* Snares for partridges.

alerón [ah-lay-rone'], *m.* Aileron (avión).

alerta [ah-ler'-tah], *f. (Mil.)* Watchword.

alerta, alertamente [ah-ler'-tah, ah-ler-tah-men'-tay], *adv.* Vigilantly, carefully. **Estar alerta,** to be on the watch. **Alerta a la buena guardia a proa,** *(Naut.)* lookout well there afore.

alertar [ah-ler-tar'], *va.* To render vigilant, to put one on his guard.

alerto, ta [ah-ler'-to, tah], *a.* Vigilant, alert, guarded.

alesna [ah-lays'-nah], *f. (Obs.)* Awl, a pointed instrument. V. LESNA.

alesnado, da [ah-les-nah'-do, dah], *a.* Awl-shaped, pointed like an awl.

aleta [ah-lay'-tah] , *f.* 1. *(dim.)* A small wing. 2. Fin of fish. **Aletas,** *(Naut.)* Fashion pieces. 3. *(Arch.)* Aletta. 4. *(Mech.)* Leaf of a hinge, leaf of a pinion, teeth of a pinion. 5. *(Aer.)* Flap. **Aleta de la hélice,** 1. *(Aer.)* Propeller blade. 2. *(Naut.)* Screw blade.

aletada [ah-lay-tah'-dah], *f.* Motion of the wings.

aletargado, da [ah-lay-tar-gah'-do, dah], *a.* Lethargic. *-pp.* of ALETARGARSE.

aletargamiento [ah-lay-tahr-gah-me-ayn-to], *m.* Drowsiness, lethargy, numbness.

aletargar [ah-lay-tahr-gahr], *va.* To make drowsy, to make lethargic.

aletargarse [ah-lay-tar-gar'-say], *vr.* To fall into a state of lethargy.

aletazo [ah-lay-tah'-tho], *m.* 1. Stroke of the wing, flapping. 2. *(Cono Sur) (fig.)* Slap (bofetada). 3. *(CAm.)* Robbery (hurto).

aleteado, da [ah-lay-tay-ah'-do, dah], *a.* Finlike, finned. -*pp.* of ALETEAR.

aletear [ah-lay-tay-ar'], *vn.* To flutter, to take short flights, to flit.

aleteo [ah-lay-tay'-o], *m.* 1. Clapping of the wings. 2. *(Med.)* Palpitation.

aletón [ah-lay-tone'], *m. aug.* A large wing.

aletría [ah-lay-tree'-ah], *m. (Prov.)* Vermicelli. *V.* FIDEOS.

aleudar [ah-lay-oo-dahr], *va.* To leaven, to ferment with yeast.

aleudarse [ah-lay-oo-dar'-say], *vr. (Obs.)* To become fermented, (fermentarse) (masa).

aleve [ah-lay'-vay], *a.* Treacherous, perfidious, guileful.

alevilla [ah-le-veel-lya], *a.* A moth like that of the silkworm, but differing in having the wings entirely white.

alevín [ah-lay-veen], *m.* Young fish, fry; *(fig.)* beginner, novice.

alevino [ah-lay-vee-no], *m. (LAm.)* Young fish, alevin, fry.

alevosa [ah-lay-vo'-sah], *f. (Vet.)* A tumor under the tongue of cows and horses. *V.* RANULA.

alevosamente [ah-lay-vo-sah-men'-tay], *adv.* Treacherously, guilefuly.

alevosía [ah-lay-vo-see'-ah], *f.* Perfidy, breach of trust.

alevoso, sa [ah-lay-vo'-so, sah], *a.* Treacherous. *m.* Traitor.

alexifármaco, ca [ah-lex-e-far'-mah-co, cah], *a. (Med.)* Antidotal, possessing the power of destroying or expelling poison.

alfa [ahl'-fah], *f.* Alpha, the first letter of the Greek alphabet. *(Met.)* The beginning.

alfábega [al-fah'-bay-gah], *f. V.* ALBAHACA.

alfabéticamente [al-fah-bay-te-cah-men-tay], *adv.* Alphabetically.

alfabético, ca [al-fah-bay'-te-co, cah], *a.* Alphabetical.

alfabetismo [al-fah-bay-tees-mo], *m.* Literacy.

alfabetista [al-fah-bay-tees'-tah], *m.* One that studies the alphabet and orthography.

alfabetización [al-fah-bay-te-thah-the-on], *f.* Teaching literacy.

alfabetizado [al-fah-bay-te-thah-do], *a.* Literate, that can write and read.

alfabetizador [al-fah-bay-te-thah-dor], *m. & f.* Literacy tutor.

alfabetizar [al-fah-bay-te-thahr], *va.* 1. To alphabetize. 2. **Alfabetizar a uno**, to teach someone to read and write.

alfabeto [al-fah-bay'-to], *m.* Alphabet.

alfadía [al-fah-dee'-ah], *f. (Obs.)* Bribe.

alfahar, alfaharero [al-fah-ar', al-fah-ah-ray'-ro], *V.* ALFAR, aLFARERO.

alfaharería [àl-fah-ah-ray-ree'-ah], *V.* ALFAR, aLFARERIA.

alfajía [al-fah-hee'-ah], *f.* Wood for windows and doors.

alfajor [al-fah-hor'], *m. V.* ALAJU.

alfalfa, *f.* **alfalfe,** *m.* [al-fahl'-fah, al-fahl'-fay]. *(Bot.)* Lucerne, alfalfa.

alfalfal, alfalfar [al-fal-fahl', al-fal-far'], *m.* A piece of ground sown with lucerne.

alfana [al-fah'-nah], *f.* A strong and spirited horse.

alfandoque [al-fan-do'-kay], *m.* A hollow cane shaken for a musical instrument. *(Ec.)*. 2. *(CAm. Carib. Mex.)* A kind of sweet pastry (pasta). 3. *(Carib.)* Small honey cake.

alfaneque [al-fah-nay'-kay], *m.* 1. The white eagle. Falco albus. 2. Tent or booth.

alfanjazo [al-fan-hah'-tho], *m.* A wound with a cutlass.

alfanje [al-fahn'-hay], *m.* Hanger, cutlass.

alfanjete [al-fan-hay'-tay], *m. dim.* A small cutlass.

alfanjón [al-fan-hone'], *m. aug.* A large hanger or cutlass.

alfanjonazo [al-fan-ho-nah'-tho], *m.* A cut with a large hanger.

alfaque [al-fah'-kay], *m.* A shoal or bar.

alfaquí [al-fah-kee'], *m.* A doctor of, or wise in the law, among Moslems. *Cf.* FAKIR.

alfar [al-far'], *m.* 1. Pottery. 2. *V.* ARCILLA.-*a.* That raises the head too much: relating to horses.

alfar [al-far'], *vn.* To raise the forehead too much.

alfaraz [al-fah-rath'], *a.* Applied formerly to the horses on which the light cavalry of the Moors rode.

alfarda [al-far'-dah], *f.* 1. *(Prov.)* Duty paid for the irrigation of lands. 2. Thin beam.

alfardero [al-far-day'-ro], *m. (Prov.)* A collector of the duty for watering lands.

alfardilla [al-far-dell'-lyah], *f.* 1. Silk, now called galloon. 2. *(dim. Prov.)* A small duty for watering lands.

alfardón [al-far-done'], *m. (Prov.)* 1. Washer of a wheel. 2. Duty paid for watering lands.

alfarería [al-fah-ray-ree'-ah], *f.* 1. The art of a potter. 2. Pottery.

alfarero [al-fah-ray'-ro], *m.* Potter.

alfarje [al-far'-hay], *m.* 1. The lower stone of an oil-mill. 2. Ceiling of a room adorned with carved work. Wainscot.

alfarjía [al-far-hee'-ah], *f. V.* ALFAJIA.

alfayate [al-fah-yah'-tay], *m. (Obs.)* A tailor.

alféizar [al-fay'-e-thar], *m.* The aperture in a wall at the inside of a door or window; embrasure.

alfeñicado, da [al-fay-nye-cah'-do, dah], *a.* Weakly, delicate.

alfeñicar [al-fay-nye-car'], *va.* To ice with sugar.

alfeñicarse [al-fay-nye-car'-say], *vr. (coll.)* To affect peculiar delicacy.

alfeñique [al-fay-nyee'-kay], *m.* 1. A sugar-paste made with oil of sweet almonds. 2. *(Met.)* A person of a delicate constitution.

alferecía [al-fay-ray-thee'-ah], *f.* 1. Epilepsy, a nervous affection, in which the patient often falls. 2. *(Obs.)* An ensign's commission.

alférez [al-fay-reth], *m.* 1. Ensign. 2. **Alférez de navío**, ensign of the navy. 3. **Alférez real**, the chief ensign of the town.

alfil [al-feel'], *m.* Bishop in the game of chess.

alfiler [al-fe-lerr'], *m.* 1. A pin. 2. Jeweller's, broach. **Alfileres de gancho o de pelo**, hairpin. **Alfileres**, pin-money. **Con todos sus alfileres** *or* **de veinte y cinco alfileres**, in full dress, dressed in style. **No estar con todos sus alfileres**, not to be in good temper.

alfilerar [al-fe-lay-rahr], *va.* To pin together.

alfilerazo [al-fe-lay-rah'-tho], *m.* 1. Prick of a pin. 2. A large pin.

alfilerera [al-fe-lay-ray'-rah], *f.* (Alfilería) the seed of some of the geranium family; form its shape.

alfilerero [al-fe-lay-ray-ro], , *m.* A maker or seller of pins.

alfilerillo [al-fe-lay-re-lyo], *m. (And. Cono Sur)* 1. Fodder plant. 2. Cactus (pita).

alfilete, alfiletete [al-fe-lay'-tay, al-fe-lay-tay'-tay], *m.* Paste made of coarse wheat flour.

alfiletero [al-fe-lay-tay'-ro], *m.* Pincase, needle-case, pin-cushion.

alfolí [al-fo-lee'], *m.* 1. Granary. 2. Magazine of salt.

alfoliero, alfolinero [al-fo-le-ay'-ro, al-fo-le-nay'-ro], *m.* Keeper of a granary or magazine.

alfombra [al-fom'-brah], *f.* 1. Floor-carpet. 2. *(Poetic.)* Field adorned with flowers. 3. *(Med.)* Measles, an eruptive fever.

alfombrado [al-fom-brah-do], *m.* Carpeting.

alfombrar [al-fom-brar'], *va.* To cover with carpets.

alfombraza [al-fom-brah'-tha], *f. aug.* A large carpet.

alfombrero, ra [al-fom-bray-ro], *m. & f.* Carpet-maker.

alfombrilla [al-fom-breel'-lyah], *f.* 1. *(dim.)* A small carpet. 2. *(Med.)* Measles. 3. *V.* ALFOMBRA.

alfóncigo [al-fon'-the-go], *m.* 1. Pistachio, the fruit of the pistachio-tree. 2. Pistachio-tree.

alfonsearse [al-fon-say-ar'-say], *vr. (coll.)* To joke with each other, to ridicule each other.

alfonsí [al-fon-see'], *m. (Obs.) V.* ALFONSIN.

alfonsín, no, na [al-fon-seen', no, nah], *a.* Belonging to the Spanish kings called Alphonso.

alfonsina [al-fon-see'-nah], *f.* A solemn act held in the church of the Alphonsine college of Alcalá, where several questions, either theological or medical, are publicly discussed.

Alfonso [al-fon-so], *m.* Alphonso. **Alphonso el Sabio,** Alphonso The Wise.

alforfón [al-for-fon], *m.* Buckwheat.

alforja [al-for'-hah], *f.* 1. Saddle-bag, knapsack. **Hacerle a alguno la alforja.** to fill one's saddle-bag with provisions. 2. *(Cono Sur)* Go too far. **Para este viaje no se necesitan alforjas,** a fat lot of good that is.

alforjero [al-for-hay'-ro], *m.* 1. Maker or seller of saddle-bags. 2. One who carries the bag with provisions.

alforjilla, ita, uela [al-for-heel'-layh, hee'-tah, hoo-ay'-lah], *f. dim.* A small saddle-bag, a small wallet or knapsack.

alforjudo [al-for-hoo-do], *a. (Cono Sur)* Silly, stupid.

alforza [al-for'-thah], *f.* A plait in a skirt, a tuck. *(fig.)* Slash, scar.

alforzar [al-for-thahr], *va.* To plead, to tuck.

alfredo [al-fray-do], *m.* Alfred.

alfronito [al-fro-nee'-tro], *m. V.* ALATRON.

alga [ahl'-gah], *f. (Bot.)* Seaweed, alga; *pl. algae* o *algas.*

algadonera [al-gah-do-nay'-rah], *f. (Bot.)* Cudweed, graphalium.

algaida [al-gah'-e-dah], *f.* A ridge of shifting sand; sand-dune.

algaido, da [al-gah'-e-do, dah], *a. (Prov.)* Thatched, covered with straw. **Casas algaidas,** Thatched houses.

algalaba [al-gah-lah'-bah], *f. (Bot.)* White briony, wild hops.

algalia [al-gah'-le-ah], *f.* 1. Civet, a perfume. 2. Catheter, a hollow instrument used in surgery.

algaliar [al-gah-le-ar'], *va. (Obs.)* To perfume with civet.

algara [al-gah'-rah], *f.* 1. The thin integument which covers an egg, onion, etc. 2. *(Obs.)* A foraging party of cavalry.

algarabía [al-gah-rah-bee'-ah], *f.* 1. The Arabic language. 2. *(Met.)* Gabble, jargon. 3. *(Met.)* A confused noise of several people speaking or shouting at the same time. 4. *(Bot.)* Centaury, cornflower.

algarada [al-gah-rah'-dah], *f.* 1. A loud cry. 2. A sudden attack. 3. A sort of battering-ram of the ancients.

Algarbe [al-gahr-hay], *m.* **El algarbe,** the Algarve.

algarero, ra [al-gah-ray'-ro, rah], *a.* Prating, chattering, talkative. **La mujer algarera nunca hace larga tela,** a prating woman works but little.

algarero [al-gah-ray-ro], *m. (Obs.)* A horseman of the foraging party called **algara.**

algarrada [al-gar-rah'-dah], *f.* 1. Driving bulls into the pen for the bullfight. 2. *(Obs.)* Battering-ram.

algarroba [al-gar-ro'-bah], *f. (Bot.)* 1. Carob bean. 2. The honey-mesquite.

algarrobal [al-gar-ro-bahl'], *m.* Ground planted with carob-trees.

algarrobera, *f.* **algarrobo,** *m.* [al-gar-ro-bay'-rah, al-gar-ro'-bo], *(Bot.)* Carob-tree, or St. John's bread.

algazara [al-gah-thah'-rah], *f.* 1. Huzza. 2. The shout of a multitude.

algazul [al-gah-thool'], *m.* A seaweed, which when burned produces barilla, or impure soda.

algebra [ahl'-hay-brah], *f.* 1. Algebra, a branch of the higher mathematics. 2. *(Obs.)* Art of setting joints.

algebraico, ca [al-hay-brah'-e-co, cah], *a.* Algebraic.

algebrista [al-hay-brees'-tah], *m.* 1. Algebraist, a person that understands algebra. 2. *(Obs.)* One who understands setting dislocated members. Bone-setter.

algidez [al-he-deth'], *f. (Med.)* Icy coldness.

álgido, da [ahl'-he-do, dah], *a.* Icy.

algo [ahl'-go], *pron.* Somewhat, something, aught. **Habrá algo para ti,** there will be something for you. **Esto es algo**

nuevo, this is something new. **Más vale algo que nada,** something is better than nothing. **Tener un algo,** to have a certain charm.

algo [ahl'-go], *pron.* Something. **Aquí hay algo raro,** there is something strange here. Anything (cualquier cosa). **Daría algo por verla,** I'd give anything to see her. **Algo así,** something like that. **Más vale algo que nada,** something is better than nothing. **Algo es algo,** something is better than nothing. **Quiero algo original,** I want something original. **¿Tienes algo para mí?,** have you got anything for me? **Por algo será,** there must be a reason. *adv.* Somewhat, rather, quite, a little. **La medida es algo escasa,** the measure is somewhat short. **Algo o nada,** all or nothing. **Ser algo tímido,** to be a little timid. **Ando algo escaso de dinero,** I'm somewhat short of money. *m.* Snack, something to eat. **Tomó algo antes de salir,** he had something to eat before going out.

algodón [al-go-done'], *m.* 1. Cotton. 2. *(Bot.)* The cotton-plant. **Algodón de azúcar,** cotton plant. **Algodón dulce,** candy-floss. **Algodón en rama,** raw cotton. *Algodones, V.* CENDALES.

algodonado, da [al-go-do-nah'-do- dah], *a.* Filled with cotton.

algodonal [al-go-do-nahl'], *m.* A cotton-plantation.

algodonar [al-go-do-nar'], *va.* To cover or fill with cotton.

algodoncillo [al-go-don-thee-lyo], *m.* Milkweed.

algodonería [al-go-do-nay-ree'-ah], *f.* 1. Cotton-factory. 2. Cotton-trade.

algodonero [al-go-do-nay'-ro], *m.* The cotton-plant. 2. The cottonwood poplar.

algodonero, ra [al-go-do-nay'-ro, rah], *m. & f.* A cotton-broker.

algodonoso, sa [al-go-do-no'-so, sa], *a.* Cottony, covered with thick down; woolly, tasteless (fruta).

algol [al-gole'] *m.* Name of a variable star in the constellation Perseus.

algología [al-go-lo-hee'-ah], *f.* Algology, that branch of botany which treats of sea-weeds, marine or fresh-water.

algorín [al-go-reen'], *m. (Prov.)* A place in oil-mills for receiving the olives which are to be ground.

algoritmo [al-go-reet'-mo], *m.* Algorithm, an Arabic word signifying the science of numbers; arithmetic.

algoso,sa [al-go'-so, sah], *a.* Weedy, full of seaweeds.

alguacil [al-goo-ah-theel'], *m.* 1. Constable, a peace officer; a bum-bailiff. 2. The short-legged spider. 3. **Alguacil mayor,** high constable. **Alguacil de campo** or **del campo,** guard or watchman of corn-fields or vineyards.

alguacilazgo [ál-goo-ah-the-lath'-go], *m.* The place or office of an *alguacil.*

alguarín [al-goo-ah-reen'], *m. (Prov.)* 1. A small room, on the ground-floor in which anything is kept. 2. Bucket in which flour falls from the millstones.

alguaza [al-goo-ah'-thah], *f. (Prov.)* Hinge.

alguien [ahl'-gee-en], *pron.* Somebody, someone. **Si alguien viene,** if somebody comes. **Para alguien que conozca la materia,** for anyone who is familiar with the subject. **Alguien llama a la puerta,** somebody is knocking at the door. **¿Hay alguien en casa?,** is there anybody at home? **Si llama alguien...,** if anyone calls...

alguita [al-gees-tah], *f. (And)* Money.

alguito [al-gee-to], *(LAm.) V.* ALGO.

algún [al-goon'], *a.* Some, any *(V.* ALGUNO). **Algún pobre anciano,** some poor old man. **Algún tiempo,** some time. **En algún sitio,** somewhere. **Algún que otro libro,** the odd book.

alguno, na [al-goo'-nonah], *a.* Some, some or other, a, a certain. **¿Vino alguna niña?,** did a little girl come? **Quiero algunos libros,** I want some books. **¿Necesitáis alguna ayuda?,** do you need any help? **¿Ha venido alguno?,** has anyone come? **Alguna vez,** sometimes, now and then. *Pron.* **Alguno de ellos,** one of them. **Busco alguno que me ayude,** I'm looking for somebody to help me. **Alguna que otra**

vez, from time to time. **Algunas veces,** sometimes. **Sin prisa alguna,** without hurrying.

alhábega [al-ah'-bay-gah], *f. (Prov.) V.* ALBAHACA.

alhadida [al-ah-dee'-dah], *f.* 1. *(Chem.)* Burnt copper from which the saffron of copper is extracted. 2. *V.* MALAQUITA.

alhaja [al-ah'-hah], *f.* 1. Jewel, a thing of great value. 2. Showy furniture, gaudy ornament. **Él es una buena alhaja** (ironically), he is a good fellow: he is a good-for-nothing; beware of him. **Quien trabaja tiene alhaja,** he that labors spins gold.

alhajado [ah-lah-hah-do], *a. (LAm.)* Wealthy.

alhajar [al-ah-har'], *va.* 1. To adorn. 2. To furnish, to fit up.

alhajera [al-ha-hay-rah], *f. (Cono Sur)* Jewel box.

alhajuela [al-ah-hoo-ay-lah], *f. dim.* A little jewel.

alhamel [al-ah-mel'], *m. (Prov.)* 1. A beast of burden. 2. A porter. 3. Muleteer.

alhana [al-ah'-nah], *f.* Alhanna, Tripoli earth.

alhandal [al-an-dahl'], *m. (Pharm.)* Colocyth, bitter apple.

alharaca [al-ah-rah'-cah], *f.* Clamor, angry vociferation, complaint without sufficient reason.

alharaquiento,ta [al-ah-rah-ke-en'-to,ah], *a.* Noisy, clamorous, grumbling.

alhárgama, alharma [al-ar'-gah-mah,l-ar'-mah], *f. (Bot.)* Wild rue.

alhasa [al-ah'-sah], *f.* Hydroa, a vesicular disease of the skin.

alhehí [al-ay-lee']. *V.* ALELI.

alheña [al-ay'-nyah], *f.* 1. *(Bot.)* Privet. 2. Flower of privet; privet ground to powder. 3. *V.* AZUMBAR. 4. Laurentinus. 5. The blasting of corn. *V.* ROYA.

alheñar [al-ay-nyar'], *va.* To dye with the powder of privet. *-vr.* To be mildewed: applied to corn. *V.* ARROYARSE.

alhoja [al-o'-hah], *f.* A small bird resembling a lark.

alholva [al-ol'-vah], *f. (Bot.)* Fenugreek.

alhóndiga [al-on'-de-gah], *f.* A public granary. *V.* POSITO.

alhondiguero [al-on-de-gay'-ro], *m.* The keeper of a public granary.

alhorma [al-or'-mah], *f.* Moorish camp, or royal tent.

alhorre [al-or'-ray], *m.* 1. The first dark discharge from an infant's bowels. 2. Eruption in the skin of infants.

alhoz [al-oth'], *m.* Limit or lot of land.

alhucema [al-oo-thay'-mah], *f. (Bot.)* Lavender. *(Andal.) V.* ESPLIEGO.

alhumajo [al-oo-mah'-ho], *m.* Name applied to leaves of the pine-tree.

aliabierto, ta [al-le-ah-be-er'-to, tah], *a.* Open-winged: applied to birds that have the wings expanded.

aliacán [ah-le-ah-cahn'], *m.* Jaundice. *V.* ICTERICIA.

aliacanado, da [ah-le-ah-cah-nah'-do,dah], *a.* Jaundiced.

aliáceo, a [ah-le-ah'-thay-o,ah], *a.* Alliaceous: like onions or garlic.

aliado, da [al-le-ah'-do,dah], *a.* & *m.* 1. Ally. 2. Allied, confederate; leagued. 3. *(Cono Sur)* Toaste *-pp.* of ALIARSE.

aliaga [ah-le-ah'-gah], *f. (Bot.)* Furze, whin.

aliagar [ah-le-ah-gar'], *m.* Place covered with furze.

alianza [ah-le-ahn'-thah]. *f.* 1. Alliance, league, coalition, confederacy, consociation. **Alianza Atlántica,** the Atlantic Alliance. 2. Agreement, convention, covenant. 3. An alliance contracted by marriage.

aliar [ah-le-ahr], 1. *va.* To ally, to bring into alliance. 2. *-vr.* To become allied.

aliara [ah-le-ah'-rah], *f.* A goblet made of a cow's horn.

aliaria [ah-le-ah'-re-ah], *f. (Bot.)* Garlic hedge-mustard.

aliarse [ah-le-ar'-say], *vr.* To be allied, leagued, or coalesced.

alias [ah-le-as], *adv. (Lat.)* 1. Otherwise. 2. By another name.

alible [ah-lee'-blay], *a.* Nutritive.

alica [ah-lee'-cah], *f. dim.* A small wing.

alica [ah-le-cah], *f.* Pottage made or corn, wheat, and pulse.

alicaído, da [ah-le-cah-ee'-do, dah], *a.* 1. Drooping. 2. Weak, extenuated. **Sombrero alicaído,** an uncocked hat.

alicántara [ah-le-cahn'-ta-rah], *f.* A kind of viper whose bite is said to be mortal.

alicante [ah-le-cahn'-tay], *m.* A poisonous snake. *V.* ALICANTARA.

alicantina [ah-le-can-tee'-nah], *f. (coll.)* Artifice, stratagem, cunning. **Tiene muchas alicantinas,** he is full of stratagems.

alicantino, na [ah-le-can-tee'-no, nah], *a.* Of Alicante.

alicatado [ah-le-cah-tah'-do], *m.* Work inlaid with Dutch tiles.

alicatar [ah-le-cah-tahr], *va.* To cut, to shape (azulejo).

alicates [ah-le-cah'-tes], *m. pl.* Finepointed pincers; nippers.

Alicia [ah-le-the-ah], *f.* Alice; "Alicia en el país de las maravillas", "Alice in Wonderland".

aliciente [ah-le-the-en'-tay], *m.* Attraction, incitement, inducement.

alicón [ah-le-cone'], *m.* The name of the seventh heaven to which the angel Azrael carries the souls of the just [Mohammedan].

alicorarse [ah-le-co-rahr-say], *vr. (And)* To get boozed.

alicorear [ah-le-co-ray-ahr], *va. (CAm.)* To decorate, adorn (adornar).

alicrejo [ah-le-cray-ho], *m. (CAm.)* Spider-like.

alicuanta [ah-lee-coo-ahn'-tah], *a.* **Parte alicuanta,** aliquant number, or odd part of a number.

alícuota [ah-lee'-coo-oh-tah], *a.* **Parte alícuota,** aliquot number, or even part of a number.

alicurco [ah-le-coor-co], *a. (Cono Sur)* Sly, cunning.

alidada [ah-le-dah'-dah], *f.* Geometrical ruler, sight vane, transom; alidade.

alidona [ah-le-do'-nah], *f.* 1. Stone in the intestines of a swallow. 2. Chalk.

alienación [ah-le-ay-nah-the-on'], *f.* Alienation (mente).

alienado, da [ah-le-nay-ah-do], *a.* Insane, mentally ill.

alienante [ah-le-nay-ahn-tay], *a.* Inhuman, dehumanizing.

alienar [ah-le-ay-nar'], *va. (Obs.) V.* ENAJENAR.

alienígena [ah-le-ay-ne-hay-nah], 1. *a.* Foreign; alien; extraterrestrial. 2. *m.* & *f.* Foreigner; alien.

alienista [ah-le-ay-nees'-tah], *m.* Alienist, specialist in treating disorders of the mind.

aliento [ah-le-en'-to], *m.* 1. Breath. 2. Vigor of mind, spirit, manfulness, courageousness. **Yo fuí allá de un aliento,** I went thither in a whiff, without drawing breath. (**Yo me aliento,** from Alentarse. *V.* ACERTAR.)

alier [ah-le-err'], *m. (Naut.)* 1. A rower. 2. Marine stationed on board a ship.

alifafe [ah-le-fah'-fay], *m.* 1. A callous tumor growing on a horse's hock. 2. *(coll.)* Chronic complaint.

alifar [ah-le-far'], *va. (Prov.)* To polish, to burnish.

alifara [ah-le-fah'-rah], *f. (Prov.)* Colation, luncheon.

alifero, ra [ah-lee'-fay-ro, rah], *a.* Aliferous, bearing wings.

aliforme [ah-le-for'-may], *a.* Aliform, wing-shaped.

aligación [ah-le-gah-the-on'], *f.* Alligation, tying together, **Regla de aligación,** rule of alligation, in arithmetic.

aligador [ah-le-gah-dor'], *m.* Alligator.

aligamiento [ah-le-gah-me-en'-to], *m.* Alligation, the act of binding together.

aligar [ah-le-gar'], *va.* 1. To tie, to unite. 2. *(Met.)* To oblige, to lie down.

aligeramiento [ah-le-hay-rah-me-en'-to]. *m.* Alleviation; lightening.

aligerar [ah-le-hay-rar'], *va.* 1. To lighten. 2. *(Met.)* To alleviate, to ease. 3. To hasten. 4. To shorten. **Aligerar un caballo,** to make a horse move light and free. *-vr.* To get lighter. To put on lighter clothes.

aligero, ra [ah-lee'-hay-ro, rah], *a. (Poetic.)* Winged, quick, fast, fleet.

aligustre [ah-le-goos-tray], *m.* Privet (alheña).

alijador, ra [ah-le-hah-dor',dah], *m.* & *f.* 1. Smuggler. 2. *(Naut.)* One who lightens. **Lanchón alijador,** a lighter, used in unloading ships. 3. He who separates the seed from cotton wool.

alijar [ah-le'-har'], *va.* 1. *(Naut.)* To lighten, 2. To separate cotton from the seed by hand or with a gin. 3. To smuggle.

alijar [ah-le-har'], *m.* Waste, stony ground. To tile.

alijarar [ah-le-hah-rar'], *va.* To divide waste lands for cultivation.

alijarero [ah-le-hah-ray'-ro], *m.* One who takes waste lands to cultivate.

alijares [ah-le-hah'-res], *m. pl.* A royal pleasure resort of Granada.

alijariego, ga [ah-le-hah-re-ay'-go,gah], *a.* Relating to waste lands.

alijo [ah-lee'-ho], *m.* 1. (Naut.) Lightening of a ship. **Embarcación de alijo,** (Naut.) Lighter. 2. Alleviation. 3. Smuggled goods.

alilaya [ah-le-lah-yah], *f.* (And. Carib) excuse (excusa). 2. *m. & f.* Cunning person, sharp character.

alilla [ah-leel'-lyah], *f.* 1. (dim.) A small wing. 2. Fin of a fish.

alimaña [ah-le-mah'-nyah], *f.* Animal which destroys game, as the fox, etc.

alimañero [ah-le-mah-nyay-ro], *m.* Gamekeeper, vermin destroyer.

alimentación [ah-le-men-tah-the-on'], *f.* Act of nourishing. **El coste de la alimentación,** the cost of food. (fig.) Feed, supply; **bomba de alimentación,** feed pump. **Alimentación por arrastre** (Comp.), tractor feed. **Alimentación por fricción** (Comp.), friction feed.

alimentador [ah-le-mayn-tah-dor], *m.* (Tec.) Feed, feeder. **Alimentador de hojas sueltas** (Comp.), cut sheet feeder.

alimentar [ah-le-men-tar'], *va.* 1. To feed, to nourish, to nurse, to fatten. 2. To supply a person with the necessities of life. 3. (Tec.) To feed. **Alimentar una máquina de algo,** to feed something into a machine. -*vr.* To gorge, to feed.

alimentario, alimentista [ah-le-men-tah'-re-o, ah-le-men-tees'-tah], *m. & f.* One who enjoys a maintenance.

alimenticio, cia [ah-le-men-tee'-the-o, ah], *a.* Nutritious.

alimento [ah-le-men'-to], *m.* 1. Nourishment, food, nutriment. 2. (Met.) Encouragement, incentive. -*pl.* 1. Allowance given by the heir to his relatives; a pension, alimony, means of living.

alimentoso, sa [ah-le-men-to'-so, sah], *a.* Alimentary, nutritious.

alimón [ah-le-mon], *adv.* In collaboration.

alindado, da [ah-lin-dah-do, dah], *a.* Affectedly nice, or elegant. -*pp.* of ALINDAR.

alindar [ah-lin-dar'], *va.* 1. To mark limits. 2. To embellish, to adorn. **Alindar el ganado,** to drive the cattle to pasture as far as the limits extend. *V.* LINDAR.

alinde [ah-leen'-day], *m.* (Obs.) Quicksilver prepared for mirrors.

alinderar [ah-len-day-rahr], *va.* (CAm. Cono Sur) To mark out the boundaries of.

alineación [ah-le-nay-ah-the-on'], *m.* Laying out a line. **Estar fuera de alineación,** to be out of alignment.

alineado [ah-le-nay-do], *a.* **Está alineado con el partido,** he is in line with the party.

alineamiento [ah-le-nay-ah-me-ayn-to], *m.* Non-alignment.

alinear [ah-le-nay-ar'], *va.* To lay out by line. **Alinearse los soldados,** to fall in line. -*vr.* To line up.

aliñador, ra [ah-le-nyah-dor', ah], *m. & f.* 1. One who embellishes. 2. (Obs.) Executor, administrator.

aliñar [ah-le-nyar'], *va.* 1. To arrange, to adorn. 2. To dress or cook victuals.3. To season.

aliño [ah-lee'-nyo], *m.* 1. Dress, ornament, decoration, cleanliness. 2. Preparation for the performance of something. 3. (Culin.) Dressing, seasoning.

aliñoso, sa [ah-le-nyo'-so, sah], *a.* Dressed, decked out, decorated.

alioli [ah-le-o'-le], *m.* (Prov.) V. AJIACEITE.

alionar [ah-le-o-nahr], *va.* (Cono Sur) To stir up.

alionin [ah-le-o-neen'], *m.* The blue-feathered duck.

alipata [ah-le-pah'-tah], *m.* A tree of the Philippine Islands whose shade is harmful.

alipede [ah-lee'-pay-day], *a.* (Poetic.) One with winged feet, swift, nimble.

alipedo, da [ah-lee'-pay-do, dah], *a.* Cheiropterous, provided with a wing like membrane between the toes.

alípego [ah-le-pay-go], *m.* (CAm.) Extra, bonus.

aliquebrado, da [ah-le-kay-brah'-do, dah], *a.* 1. Broken-winged. 2. Dejected.

alisado [ah-le-sah-do], *a.* Smooth, polished.

alisador, ra [ah-le-sah-doo', rah], *m. & f.* 1. Polisher, planisher, smoothing-iron; silk stick. 2. An instrument used to make wax candles round and tapering.

alisadura [ah-le-sah-doo'-rah], *f.* Planing, smoothing, or polishing.

alisaduras [ah-le-sah-doo'-ras], *f. pl.* Shavings, cutting of any thing made smooth.

alisar [ah-le-sar'], *va.* To plane, to make smooth, to polish, to mangle.

alisar, *m.* **Aliseda,** *f.* [ah-le-sar', ah-le-say'-dah]. Plantation of alder-trees.

alisios [ah-lee'-se-os], *m. pl.* East winds, in particular those which blow in the tropics. Trade-winds.

alisma [ah-lees'-mah], *f.* (Bot.) Water-plantain.

aliso [ah-lee'-so], *m.* (Bot.) Alder-tree.

alistado, da [ah-lees-tah'-do, dah], *a.* 1. Enlisted, 2. Striped. -*pp.* of ALISTAR.

alistador [ah-lis-tah-dor'], *m.* 1. One who keeps accounts. 2. One who enlists.

alistamiento [ah-lis-tah-me-en'-to], *m.* Enrollment, conscription, levy.

alistar [ah-lis-tar'], *va.* 1. To enlist, to enrol, to recruit. 2. To get ready. 3. -*vr.* To enrol.

aliteración [ah-le-tay-rah-the-on'], *f.* V. PARONOMASIA.

aliterado [ah-le-tay-rah-do], *a.* Alliterative.

alitranca [ah-le-trahn-cah], *f.* (And. Cono Sur) Brake, braking device.

alitúrgico, ca [ah-le-toor'-he-co, cah], *a.* Said of days when there is no liturgy.

aliviadero [ah-le-ve-ah-day-ro], *m.* To overflow channel.

aliviador, ra [ah-le-ve-ah-dor', rah], *m. & f.* 1. An assistant. 2. A spindle that serves to raise or lower the running mill-stone. 3. Comforting.

alivianarse [ah-le-ve-ah-nahr-say], *vr.* (Mex.) To play it cool, to be cool.

aliviar [ah-le-ve-ar'], *va.* 1. To lighten, to help, to loose. 2. (Met.) To mitigate, grief, to relieve, to exonerate. 3. To hasten, to move with swiftness. 4. -*vr.* To become more bearable, to gain relief. **¡Que se alivie!,** get better soon!

alivio [ah-lee'-ve-o], *m.* 1. Alleviation, ease. 2. Mitigation of pain; comfort. 3. **De alivio,** awful; horrible.

alizace [ah-le-thah'-thay], *m.* A trench for the foundations of a building.

alizarina [ah-le-thah-ree'-nah], *f.* Alizarine.

aljaba [al-hah'-bah], *f.* 1. A quiver. 2. (Cono Sur) (Bot.) Fuchsia.

aljafana [al-hah-fah'-nah], *f.* V. ALJOFAINA.

aljama [al-hah'-mah], *f.* An assembly of Moors or Jews. A synagogue.

aljamía [al-hah-mee'-ah], *f.* (Obs.) 1. Corrupted Arabic spoken by the Moors. 2. Moorish name of Spanish language. 3. (Prov.) Synagogue.

aljamiado [al-hah-me-ah-do], *a.* Text of Spanish written in Arabic characters.

aljarfa, *f.* **aljarfe,** *m.* [al-har'-fah, al-har'-fay], a tarred net with small meshes.

aljecero, ra [al-hay-thay'-ro, rah], *m. & f.* (Prov.) Plasterer.

aljevena [al-hay-vay'-na], *f.* (Prov.) V. ALJOFAINA.

aljez [al-heth'], *m.* Gypsum in its crude state.

aljezar [al-hay-thar'], *m.* Pit of gypsum. V. YESAR.

aljezón [al-hay-thone'], *m.* Gypsum, plaster of Paris. V. YESON.

aljibe [al-hee'-bay], *m.* A cistern, a reservoir of water. *(Mar.)* A tank-boat for supplying vessels with water.

aljibero [al-hee-bay'-ro], *m.* One who takes care of cisterns.

aljimierado [al-he-me-ay'-rah-do], *a.* Shaved, trimmed.

aljofaina [al-ho-fah'-e-nah], *f.* 1. An earthen jug. 2. A wash-bowl.

aljófar [al-ho'-far], *m.* 1. A misshapen pearl. 2. *(Met. Poet.)* Drops of water or dew.

aljofarado, da [al-ho-fah-rah'-do, dah], *a. (Poetic.)* Full of little drops or pearls. -*pp.* of ALJOFARAR.

aljofarar [al-ho-fah-rar'], *va.* 1. To adorn with pearls. 2. To imitate pearls.

aljofifa [al-ho-fee'-fah], *f.* A mop for floors.

aljofifar [al-ho-fe-far'], *va.* To rub with a cloth, to mop.

aljonje [al-hon'-jay], *m.* V. AJONJE.

aljonjera [al-hon-hay'-rah], *f.* V. AJONJERA.

aljonjero [al-hon-hay'-ro], *a.* V. AJONJERO.

aljonjoli [al-hon-ho-lee'], *m.* V. ALEGRIA.

aljor [al-hor'], *m.* Gypsum in its crude state.

aljorozar [al-ho-ro-thar'], *va.* To level, render smooth; to plaster.

aljorra [al-hor'-rah], *m. (Cuba.)* A very small insect which, carried by the wind, destroys plantations.

allá [al-lyah'], *adv.* 1. There, in that place; thither, or to that place; anciently, in other times. **Allá va con Dios,** *(Naut.)* about ship. **Allá arriba,** up there. **Allá mismo,** right there. **No sabe contar más allá de diez,** she can´t count beyond 10. 2. **Allá en 1600,** back in 1600 (tiempo).

allacito [al-lyah-the-to] *adv. (LAm.)* V. ALLA.

allanador [al-lyah-nah-dor'], *m.* 1. Leveller. 2. Gold-beater's paper which contains the beaten gold-leaves. 3. Consent, agreement.

allanamiento [al-lyah-nah-me-en'-to], *m.* 1. Levelling, the act of making even. 2. Consent. 3. *(Met.)* Affability, suavity. 4. Removal (de obstáculos). 5. Pacification. 6. **Allanamiento de morada,** housebreaking.

allanar [al-lyah-nar'], *va.* 1. To level, to make even, to flatten, to reduce to a flat surface. 2. To remove or overcome difficulties. 3. To pacify, to subdue. **Allanar la casa,** to enter a house by force with a search-warrant. **Allanar el camino,** to pave the way for obtaining something. -*vr.* 2. To abide by a law or agreement, to acquiesce, to conform. 2. To fall to ruin.

allegadizo, da [al-lyay-gah-dee'-tho, thah], *a.* Collected without choice.

allegado, da [al-lyay-gah'-do, dah], *a.* Near, conjunct. **Según fuentes allegadas al ministro,** according to sources close to the minister. -*m.* Friend, ally. **Los más allegados y queridos,** those attached to..., those closest to..... -*pp.* of ALLEGAR.

allegador, ra [al-lyay-gah-dor', rah], *m. & f.* One who gathers or collects. **A padre allegador hijo expendedor,** after a gatherer comes a scatterer.

allegamiento [al-lyay-gah-me-en'-to], *m.* 1. Collecting, uniting. 2. Close friendship, union.

allegar [al-lyay-gar'], *va.* 1. To gather, to unite. 2. To draw near. 3. To solicit, to procure. -*vr.* To come near, to approach. **Allegarse a uno,** to go up to somebody. *(fig.)* **Allegarse a una opinión,** to adopt a view.

allende [al-lyen'-day], *adv. (Obs.)* On the other side. **Allende de** *v.* ÁDEMAS.

allí [al-lyee'], *adv.* 1. There, in that place. **Allí mismo,** in that very place. **De allí,** Thence, from that place. 2. At that moment.

allicito [ah-lye-the-to], *adv. (LAm.)* V. ALLI.

allo [ahl'-lyo], *m. (Amer.)* V. GUACAMAYO.

alloza [al-lyo'-thah], *f.* A green almond. *V.* ALMENDRUCO.

allozo [al-lyo'-tho], *m. (Bot.)* The wild almond-tree.

alludel [al-lyoo-del'], *m.* Earthen water-pipe. V. ALUDEL.

alma [ahl'-mah], *f.* 1. Soul, the spirit of man. 2. Human being. **No parece ni se ve un alma en la plaza,** there is not a soul in the market-place. 3. That which imparts spirit or vigor. **Un buen general es el alma de un ejército,** a good

general is the soul of an army. 4. The principal part of a thing. *(Mech.)* Attic ridge, scaffolding pole. *(Arm.)* Bore. Core (of rope, of a casting). **Vamos al alma del negocio,** let us come to the main point of the business. 5. *(Naut.)* Body of a mast. **En mi alma,** upon my soul. 6. Ghost. 7. The sounding-post in a fiddle, etc. **Alma mía, mi alma,** my dear, my love. **Alma de cántaro,** an ignorant, insignificant fellow. **El alma me da,** my heart tells me. **Dar el alma,** to expire. **Dar el alma al diablo,** to sacrifice everything to a caprice. **Alma de Dios,** he who is good-natured and simple. **Con el alma y la vida,** with all my heart. **Hablar al alma,** to speak plainly and fearlessly. **Írsele a uno el alma por** or **tras alguna cosa,** to be anxious. 8. (Comparaciones) **Estar como un alma perdida,** to be completely undecided. **Ir como alma que lleva el diablo,** to go like a bat out of hell. 9. *(And)* Corpse (cadáver). 10. *(Bot.)* Pitch.

almacén [al-mah-then'], *m.* 1. Warehouse. 2 Magazine. 3. Naval arsenal or dock-yard. 4. *(Naut.)* **Almacén de agua,** a water-cask. 5. *(Naut.)* **Almacén de una bomba de agua,** the clamber of a pump.

almacenado, da [al-mah-thay-nah'-do,ah], *a.* Warehoused, stored, bonded.

almacenador [al-mah-thay-nah-dor'], *m.* Warehouseman.

almacenaje [al-mah-thay-nah'-hay], *m.* Warehouse rent, storage.

almacenamiento [al-mah-thay-nah-me-ayn-to], *m. (Comp.)* Storage. **Almacenamiento intermedio** *(Comp.),* buffer.

almacenar [al-mah-thay-nar'], *va.* To lay up, to hoard; to warehouse. *(fig.)* To keep, to collect.

almacenero [al-mah-thay-nay-ro], *m.* Warehouse-keeper.

almacenista [al-mah-thay-nees'-tah], *m.* The person who sells goods in a warehouse.

almáciga [al-mah'-the-gah], *f.* 1. Mastic, a gum of the Pistacia lentiscus. 2. A nursery of trees or plants.

almacigado, da [al-mah-the-gah'-do] , *a.* Composed of or perfumed with mastic.

almacigar [al-mah-the-gar'], *va.* To perfume anything with mastic.

almácigo [al-mah'-the-go], *m.* 1. Collection of plants for transplanting. 2. Mastic-tree. *V.* LENTISCO.

almaciguero, ra [al-mah-the-gay'-ro, rah], *a.* Relating to mastic.

almadana, ena, ina [al-mah-dah'-nah, day'-nah,de'-nah], *f.* A large hammer.

almadén [al-mah-den'], *m. (Obs.)* Mine or mineral.

almadía [al-mah-dee'-ah], *f.* 1. Canoe used in India. 2. Raft.

almadiado, da [al-mah-de-ah'-do, dah], *a. (Obs.)* Fainting.

almadiarse [al-mah-de-ahr-say], *vr.* To be sick.

almadiero [al-mah-de-ay'-ro], *m.* A raft-pilot.

almadraba [al-mah-drah'-bah], *f.* 1. Tunny-fishery. 2. Net used in the tunny-fishery. 3. *(Obs.)* Brickyard.

almadrabero [al-mah-drah-bay'-ro], *m.* 1. Tunny-fisher. 2. *V.* TEJERO.

almadraque [al-mah-drah'-kay], *m. (Obs.)* 1. A quilted cushion. 2. A mattress.

almadreña [al-mah-dray'-nyah], *f.* Wooden shoes or sabots. *V.* ZUECO.

almagacén [al-ma-gah-then'], *m. (Obs.)* Magazine. *V.* ALMACEN.

almaganeta [al-mah-gah-nay'-tah], *f. V.* ALMADANA or ALMADENA.

almagesto [al-mah-hays'-to], *m.* Almagesta, work on astronomy written by Ptolemy.

almagra [al-mah'-grah], *f. V.* ALMAGRE.

almagral [al-mah-grahl'], *m.* Place abounding in ochre.

almagrar [al-mah-grar'], *va.* 1. To color with red ochre. 2. *(Low.)* To draw blood in a quarrel.

almagre [al-mah'-gray], *m.* Red ochre, red earth, Indian red.

almaizal, almaizar [al-mah-e-thahl', al-mah-e-thar'], *m.* 1. A gauze veil worn by Moors. 2. A belt or sash worn by priests and sub-deacons.

almajar [al-mah-hah'-rah], *f. (Prov.)* V. ALMACIGA and SEM-ILLERO. A forcing-bed, hotbed.

almajara [al-mah-hah-rah], *f. (Agri.)* Hotbed, forcing frame.

almajo [al-mah'-ho], *m.* A fucus or other seaweed yielding barilla

almaleque [al-mah-lay'-kay], *f. (Obs.)* A long robe resembling a surtout, worn by Moors.

alma mater [ahl'-mah mah'-ter], *f.* Alma mater, one's university or college.

almanac, almanaque [al-mah-nak', al-mah-nah'-kay], *m.* almanac. **Hacer almanques,** *(Met.)* To muse, to be pensive. *(Arab.)*

almanaquero [al-mah-nah-kay-ro], *m.* A maker and vender of almanacs.

almancebe [al-man-thay'-bay], *m. (Obs.)* A fishing-boat used on the river Guadalquivir near Seville.

almandina [al-man-dee'-nah], *f. (Miner.)* The common red variety of garnet; almandine.

almanguena [al-man-gay'-nah], *f.* V. ALMAGRE.

almanta [al-mahn'-tah], *f.* 1. Space between the rows of vines and olive-trees. 2. Ridge between two furrows. **Poner a almanta,** to plant vines irregularly.

almarada [al-mah-rah'-dah], *f.* A triangular poniard. 2. Iron poker with wooden handle. Shoemaker's needle.

almarcha [al-mar'-cha], *f.* A town situated on marshy ground.

almariarse [al-mah-re-ahr-say], *vr. (CAm. Cono Sur)* To be sick, vomit.

alamario [al-mah'-re-o], *m.* V. ARMARIO.

almarjal [al-mar-hahl'], *m.* 1. Plantation of glasswort. 2. Marshy ground where cattle graze.

almarjo [al-mar'-ho], *m. (Bot.)* Glasswort.

almaro [al-mah'-ro], *m. (Bot.)* Common clary.

almarraes [al-mar-rah'-ess], *m. pl.* Instrument (cotton-gin) with which cotton is separated from the seed.

almarraja, almarraza [al-mar-rah'-hah, al-mar-rah'-thah], *f.* A glass vial with holes formerly used in sprinkling water.

almártaga, almártega, almártiga [al-mar'-tah-gah, al-mar'-tay-gah, al-mar'-tee-gah], *f.* 1. Litharge. 2. A sort of halter. 3. Massicot or lead made up with linseed-oil for painting.

almástiga [al-mahs'-te-gah], *f.* V. ALMACIGA. Mastic.

almastigado, da [al-mas-te-gah'-do, dah], *a.* Containing mastic.

almatrero [al-mah-tray'-ro], *m.* One fishing with shad-nets.

almatriche [al-mah-tree'-chay], *m.* A canal for irrigating land. V. REGUERA.

almazara [al-mah-thah'-rah], *f. (Prov.)* Oil-mill.

almazarero [al-mah-thah-ray'-ro], *m.* Oil-miller.

almazarrón [al-mah-thar-rone'], *m.* V. ALMAGRE.

almea [al-may'-ah], *f.* 1. A woman who improvises verses among the orientals. 2. The bark of the storax-tree. 3. *(Bot.)* The star-headed water-plantain.

almear [al-may-ar'], *m.* A stack of hay, corn, or straw.

almeja [al-may'-hah], *f.* Mussel, a shell-fish.

almejía [al-me-hee'-ah], *f.* A small cloak used by poor Moors.

almelga [al-mel'-gah], *f. (Agri.)* V. AMELGA.

almena [al-may'-anh], *f.* Each of the merlons of a battlement.

almenado [al-may-nah'-do], *m.* V. ALMENAJE

almenado, da [al-may-nah'-do, dah], *a.* Embattled. *-pp.* of ALMENAR.

almenaje [al-may-nah'-hay], *m.* A series of merlons around a rampart; battlement.

almenar [al-may-nar'], *va.* To crown a rampart or castle with merlons.

almenara [al-may-nah'-rah], *f.* 1. A beacon-light. 2. *(Prov.)* A channel which conveys back the overplus water in irrigation.

almenas [al-may-nahs'], *f. & pl.* Battlements, crenellations.

almendra [al-men'-drah], *f.* 1. Kernel, the seed of pulpy fruits. 2. An almond. **Almendra amarga,** bitter almond. 3. (Among jewellers) A diamond of an almond-shape. 4. *(Prov.)*

A cocoon which contains but one worm. **almendras de garapiña,** *or* **garapiñadas,** sugar almonds.

almendrada [al-men-drah'-dah], *f.* 1. Almond milk, an emulsion made of almonds and sugar. 2. *(Met.)* **Dar una almendrada,** to say something pleasing or pretty.

almendrado, da [al-men-drah'-do, dah], *a.* Almond-like. **De ojos almendrados,** almond-eyed.

almendrado [al-men-drah'-do], *m.* Macaroon, a kind of sweet biscuit.

almendral [al-men-drahl'], *m.* 1. A plantation of almond-trees. 2. V. ALMENDRO.

almendrera [al-men-dray'-rah], *f.* **almendrero** [al-men-dray'-ro], *m.* V. ALMENDRO.

almendrero, ra [al-men-dray'-ro, rah], *a.* **Plato almendrero,** a dish in which almonds are served.

almendrica, illa, ita [al-men-dree'-cah, eel'-layh, ee'-tah], *f. dim.* A small almond.

almendrilla [al-men-dreel'-lyah], *f.* A locksmith's file in the shape of an almond. **Almendrillas,** almondshaped diamond ear-rings.

almendrillo [al-mayn-dre-lyo], *m. (LAm.)* Almond tree.

almendro [al-men'-dro], *m.* Almond-tree.

almendrón [al-men-drone'], *m.* An American (cherry) tree and its fruit.

almendruco [al-men-droo'-co], *m.* A green almond.

almenilla [al-may-neel'-lyah], *f.* 1. *(dim.)* A small merlon. 2. Ancient fringe for dresses.

almería [al-may-re-ah], *f.* Almería.

almeriense [al-may-re-ayn-say], *a.* Of Almería.

almete [al-may'-tay], *m.* 1. A helmet. 2. A soldier wearing a helmet.

almez, almezo [al-meth', al-may'-tho], *m.* The lote-tree, or Indian nettle-tree, hackberry.

almeza [al-may'-thah], *f. (Bot.)* The fruit of the lote-tree.

almiar [al-me-ar'], *m.* Haystack.

almíbar [al-mee-bar'], *m.* Simple syrup. **Almíbares.** Preserved fruit.

almibarado, da [al-me-bah-rah'-do, dah], *a.* 1. *(Met.)* Soft, endearing, applied to word. 2. Effeminate. *-pp.* of ALMIBARAR.

almibarar [al-me-bah-rar'], *va.* 1. To preserve fruit in sugar. 2. *(Met.)* To conciliate with soft words.

almicantáradas [al-me-can-tah'-rah-das], *f. pl. (Astr.)* Circles parallel to the horizon imagined to pass through all the degrees of the meridian, and indicating the altitude and depression of the stars.

almidón [al-me-done'], *m.* Starch; amylum, fecula.

almidonado, da [al-me-do-nah'-do, dah], *a.* 1. Starched. 2. *(Met.)* Dressed with affected nicety; spruce. *-pp.* of ALMIDONAR.

almidonar [al-me-do-nar'], *va.* To starch. **Los prefiero sin almidonar,** I prefer them unstarched.

almijara [al-me-hah'-rah], *f.* Oil-tank (minas, ferrocarril).

almijarero [al-me-hah-ray'-ro], *m.* Porter in the mines of almadén.

almilla [al-meel'-lyah], *f.* 1. An under waistcoat. 2. A short military jacket. 3. Tenon. 4. Pork-chop.

almimbar [al-meem-bar'], *m.* The pulpit of a mosque.

alminar [al-me-nar'], *m.* Minaret, turret of a mosque.

almiranta [al-me-rahn'-tah], *f. (Naut.)* 1. The vice-admiral's ship, the flagship. 2. The admiral's lady.

almirantazgo [al-me-ran-tath'-go], *m. (Naut.)* 1. Board of admiralty. 2. Admiralty court. 3. Admiral's dues. 4. Duty of an admiral.

almirante [al-me-rahn'-tay], *m.* 1. Admiral, a commander of a fleet. **Vicealmirante,** Vice-admiral. 2. *(Prov.)* Swimming-master. 3. A beautiful shell, belonging to the species of rhomb-shells.

almirez [al-me-reth'], *m.* 1. A brass mortar, for kitchen use. 2. A wood engraver's tool of tempered steel.

almirón [al-me-rone'], *m.* Wild chicory.

almizclar [al-mith-clar'], *va.* To perfume with musk.

almizcle [al-mith'-clay], m. Musk.

almizcleña [al-mith-clay'-nyah], f. (Bot.) Musk, grape-hyacinth.

almizcleño, ña [al-mith-clay'-nyo, ah], a. Musky.

almizclera [al-mith-clay'-rah], f. Muskrat.

almizclero, ra [al-mith-clay'-ro, rah], a. V. ALMIZCLEÑO. The musk-deer which yields musk.

almizteca [al-mith-tay'-cah], f. (Obs.) V. ALMACIDA.

almo, ma [ahl'-mo, mah], a. (Poetic.) 1. Any source of support or maintenance; creating vivifying. 2. (Poetic.) Venerable, holy.

almocadén [al-mo-cah-den'], m. The commander of a troop of militia.

almocafrar [al-mo-cah-frar'], va. To make holes with a dibble.

almocafre [al-mo-cah-fray], m. A gardener's hoe, dibble.

almoceda [al-mo-thay-dah], f. 1. Impost on water for irrigation. 2. Right of taking water for irrigation upon fixed days.

almocrate [al-mo-crha'-tay], m. Sal ammoniac.

almocri [al-mo-cree'], m. Reader of the Koran in a mosque.

almodí [al-mo-dee'], m. V. ALMUDI.

almodrote [al-mo-dro'-tay], m. 1. A sauce for the eggplant, composed of oil, garlic, cheese, etc. 2. Hodgepodge, a confused mixture of various ingredients.

almofar [al-mo-far'], m. A part of ancient armor reclining on the helmet.

almofía [al-mo-fee'-ah], f. V. ALJOFAINA.

almofré [al-mo-fray], m. (LAm.) Sleeping bag.

almogama [al-mo-gah'-mah], f. (Naut.) The stern-post of a ship. V. REDEL.

almogárabe, almogávar [al-mo-gah'-rah -bay, al-mo-gah'-var], m. An expert forager. Almogávares, a sort of light troops in the ancient militia of Spain chiefly employed to make frequent incursions into the Moorish dominions.

almohada [al-mo-ah'-dah], f. 1. Pillow or bolster, cushion, pillow-case. 2. (Naut.) A piece of timber on which the bowsprit rests. Consultar con la almohada, to think about something. Almohada para arrodillarse, a cushion to kneel upon.

almohadilla [al-mo-ah-deel'-lyah], f. 1. (dim.) A small bolster or pillow. 2. Working-case; sewing cushion; the pads of a harness. 3. Stone projecting out of a wall. 4. A callous excrescence on the backs of mules where the saddle is put.

almohadillado, da [al-mo-ah-deel-lyah'-do, dah], 1. a. In the form of a cushion. 2. m. Ashlar; dressed ashlar.

almohadón [al-mo-ah-done'], m. aug. A large cushion.

almohatre, almojatre [al-mo-ah'-tray, al-mo-hah'-tray], m. Sal ammoniac.

almohaza [al-mo-ah'-thah], f. Curry comb.

almohazado, da [al-mo-ah-thah'-do, dah], a. Curried. -pp. of ALMOHAZAR.

almohazador [al-mo-ah-thah-dor], m. A groom.

almohazar [al-mo-ah-thar'], va. To curry with a curry-comb.

almojaba [al-mo-hah'-bah], f. (Obs.) Smoked tunny-fish.

almojábana [al-mo-hah'-bah-nah], f. 1. Cake made of cheese and flour. 2. Hard sauce.

almojarifadgo, almojarifazgo [al-mo-hah-re-fad'-go, al-mo-hah-re-fath'-go], m. A duty on imports or exports.

almojarife [al-mo-ha-ree'-fay], m. 1. Tax-gatherer for the king. 2. Custom-house officer.

almojaya [al-mo-hah'-yah], f. Putlog, a cross-piece used in scaffolding.

almona [al-mo'-nah], f. 1. (Prov.) Soap manufactory. 2. (Obs.) Store-house. 3. Shad-fishery.

almóndiga, almondiguilla [al-mon'-de-gah, al-mon-de-geel'-lyah], f. va. ALBONDIGA an ALBONDIGUILLA

almoneda [al-mo-nay'-dah], f. An auction.

almonedear [al-mo-nay-day-ar'], va. To sell by auction.

almoradux [al-mo-rah-dooks'], m. 1. (Bot.) Sweet marjoram. 2. V. SANDALO.

almorávide [al-mo-rah-ve-day], a. Almoravid.

almorí, almurí [al-mo-ree', al-moo-ree'], m. A sweetmeat or cake.

almoronía [al-mo-ro-nee'-ah], f. V. ALBORONIA.

almorranas [al-mor-rah'-nas], f. pl. (Med.) Hemorrhoids or piles.

almorrefa [al-mor-ray'-fah], f. A mosaic floor; tiled floor.

almorta [al-mor-tah], f. (Bot.) Blue vetch.

almorzada [al-mor-thah´-dah], f. (Prov.) V. ALMUERZA.

almorzado, da [al-mor-thah'-do, dah], a. One who has breakfasted. -pp. of ALMORZAR.

almorzar [al-mor-tahr'], va. To have lunch.

almotacén [al-mo-tah-then'], m. 1. Inspector of weights and measures. 2. Clerk of the market.

almotazala [al-mo-tah-thah'-lah], f. (Ant.) Counterpane for a bed.

almozárabe [al-mo-thah'-rah-bay], m. A Christian who lived subject to the Moors.

almud [àl-mood'], m. A measure of grain and dry fruit, in some places the twelfth part of a fanega, and in some others half a fanega. Almud de tierra, (Prov.) about half an acre of ground.

almudada [al-moo-dah'-dah], f. A piece of ground which takes half a fanega of grain for sowing it.

almudí, almudín [al-moo-de', al-moo-deen'], m. 1. (Prov.) V. ALHONDIGA. 2. (Prov.) A measure containing six bushels.

almuecín [al-moo-ay-theen], m. Muezzin.

almuédano [al-moo-ay'-dah-no], m. Muezzin, one who calls to prayer from the minaret.

almuérdago [al-moo-er'-dah-go], m. Bird-lime. V. MUERDAGO.

almuerza [al-moo-er'-thah], f. A double-handful. (Yo almuerzo, yo almuerce, from Almorzar. V. ACORDAR).

almuerzo [al-moo-er'-tho], m. 1. Breakfast, lunch. 2. Set of dishes, etc, for breakfast; breakfast cover.

alnado, da [al-nah'-do, dah], m. & f. A step-child. V. HIJASTRO.

aló [ah-lo], interj. (LAm.) Hullo?

alobadado, da [ah-lo-bah-dah'-do, dah], a. 1. Bit by a wolf. 2. Laboring under morbid swellings.

alobunadillo, lla [ah-lo-boo-nah-deel'-lyo, lyah], a. Resembling a wolf somewhat.

alobunadado, da [ah-lo-boo-nah'-do, dah], a. Resembling a wolf in color.

alocadamente [ah-lo-cah-dah-men'-tay], adv. Rashly, inconsiderately.

alocado, da [ah-lo-cah'-do, dah], a. 1. Half-witted, foolish. 2. Wild.

alocar [ah-lo-cahr'], va. To drive crazy. -vr. To go crazy.

alocución [ah-lo-coo-the-on'], f. 1. Allocution. 2. Address, speech, harangue. 3. Address of the Pope to the cardinals.

alodial [ah-lo-de-ahl'], a. (Law.) Allodial, free, exempt.

alodio [ah-lo'-de-o], m. Allodium, a possession not held by tenure of a superior lord.

áloe [ah'-lo-ay], m. 1. (Bot.) Aloes-tree. 2. Aloes.

aloético, ca [ah-lo-ay'-te-co, cah], a. Aloetic, any drug containing aloes.

aloina [ah-lo-ee'-nah], f. Aloin, active principle of aloes.

aloja [ah-lo'-hah], f. A beverage made of water, honey, and spice; metheglin. In South America, a fermented liquor from carob-beans.

alojado, a [ah-lo-hah-do], m. & f. (LAm.) Guest, lodger.

alojamiento [ah-lo-hah-me-en'-to], m. 1. Lodging. 2. (Naut.) Steerage.

alojar [ah-lo-har'], va. 1. To lodge, to let lodgings. 2. To dwell, to reside. -vr. To station troops, to put up at. La bala se alojó en el pulmón, the bullet lodged in the lung.

alojería [ah-lo-hay-ree'-ah], f. A place where metheglin is prepared and sold.

alojero [ah-lo-hay'-ro], m. 1. One who prepares or sells metheglin.

alomado, da [ah-lo-mah'-do, dah], *a.* Having a curved back: applied to horses. *-pp.* of ALOMAR.

alomar [ah-lo-mar'], *va.* 1. To distribute equally the load on a horse. 2. To cover with a seed-plough. *-vr.* To grow strong and vigorous.

alón [ah-lone'], *m.* The plucked wing of any bird.

alondra [ah-lon'-drah],1. *f. (Orn.)* A lark (pájaro).

alongadero [ah-lon-gah-day'-ro], *a.* Dilatory. *V.* LARGA.

alongamiento [ah-lon-gah-me-en'-to], *m.* Delay.

alongar [ah-lon-gar'], *va.* To enlarge, to extend. *-vr.* To move away.

alónimo [ah-lo'-ne-mo], *m.* Allonymous, published under an assumed name.

alópata [ah-lo'-pah-tah], *m.* Allopath.

alopatía [ah-lo-pah-tee'-ah], *f.* Allopathy.

alopático, ca [ah-lo-pah'-te-co, cah], *a.* Allopathic.

alopecia [ah-lo-pay'-the-ah], *f. (Med.)* Alopecia, loss of the hair; baldness.

alopiado, da [ah-lo-pe-ah-do, dah], *a.* Composed of opium.

aloque [ah-l'o-kay], *a.* Applied to clear white wine, or a mixture of red and white.

aloquín [ah-lo-keen'], *m.* A stone wall of the inclosure where wax is bleached.

alosa [ah-lo'-sah], *f.* Shad.

alosna [ah-los'-nah], *f. (Bot. Prov.)* Wormwood.

alotar [ah-lo-tar'], *va. (Naut.) V.* ARRIZAR. **Alotar las anclas.** *(Naut.)* 1. To stow the anchors. 2. To sell fish by auction.

alpaca [al-pah'-cah], or **alpaga** [al-pah'-gah], *f.* 1. Alpaca and *Llama*, a ruminant of South America, esteemed for the fineness of its wool. 2. A fabric made from the wool of this animal. 3. An alloy of copper, zinc, and nickel, called white metal.

alpañata [al-pah-nyah'-tah], *f.* A piece of chamois-skin which potters use to smooth their work.

alpargata, *f.* **alpargate,** *m.* [al-pargah'-tah, al-par-gah'-tay], A sort of shoes or sandals made of hemp. **Compañía de la alpargata,** *(Prov.)* a set of ragamuffins.

alpargatado, da [al-par-gah-tah'-do, dah], *a.* Wearing hempen sandals. *-pp.* of ALPARGATAR.

alpargatar [al-par-gah-tar'], *va.* To make hempen sandals.

alpargatería [al-par-gah-tay-ree'-ah], *f.* A manufactory of hempen sandals, sandal shop.

alpargatero [al-par-gah-tay'-ro], *m.* A manufacturer of hempen sandals.

alpargatilla [al-par-gah-teel'-lyah], *f.* 1. *dim.* A small hempen sandal. 2. *(Met.)* A crafty, designing fellow.

alpechín [al-pay-cheen'], *m.* Water which oozes from a heap of olives.

alpende [al-pen'-day], *m.* Shed to keep mining implements in.

Alpes [al-pays], *m. & pl.* Alps.

alpestre, alpino, na [al-pes'-tray, al-pee'-no, nah], *a.* Alpine.

alpícola [al-pee'-co-lah], *a.* Growing in the Alps.

alpicoz [al-pe-coth'], *m. (Prov.) V.* ALFICOZ.

alpinismo [al-pe-nees'-mo], *m.* Alpinism, climbing the Alps.

alpinista [al-pe-nees'-tah], *m. & f.* Alpinist, climber.

alpino [al-pe-no], *a.* Alpine.

alpiste [al-pees'-tay], *m.* Canary-seed.

alpistela, alpistera [al-pis-tay'-lah, al-pis-tay'-rah], *f.* A cake made of flour, eggs, sesamum, and honey.

alpistero [al-pis-tay'-ro], *m.* A sieve for canary-seed.

alquequenje [al-kay-kane'-hay], *m.* Bardoes winter-cherry, used as diuretic.

alquería [al-kay-ree'-ah], *f.* A farm-house, generally a farm with a house at a distance from neighbors.

alquermes [al-ker'-mes], *m.* 1. A compound cordial, of exciting character, in which the kermes is a principal ingredient. 2. A celebrated confection.

alquerque [al-ker'-kay], *m.* Place in oil-mills for laying the bruised olives.

alquez [al-keth'], *m.* A wine measure containing 12 cántaras.

alquibla [al-kee'-blah], *f.* The point towards the Mecca, where Mohammedans direct their eyes when praying.

alquicel, alquicer [al-ke-thel', al-ke-theer'], *m.* 1. Moorish garment resembling a cloak. 2. Covers for benches, tables, etc.

alquifol [al-ke-fol'], *m. (Miner.)* Alquifou, or potter's ore: lead ore.

alquiladizo, za [al-ke-lah-de-tho, tha], *a.* For rent, for hire, that can be rented.

alquilado, a [al-ke-lah-do, dah], *m. & f. (Carib.)* Tenant.

alquilamiento [al-ke-lah-me-en'-to], *m.* The act of hiring or letting.

alquilar [al-ke-lar'], *va.* To let, to hire, to rent, to fee. *-vr.* To serve for wages. **¡Se alquila!**, to let; for rent.

alquiler [al-ke-lerr'], *m.* 1. Wages or hire. 2. The act of hiring or letting. **Alquiler de una casa,** house-rent.

alquilón, na [al-ke-lone', nah] *a.* That which can be let or hired.

alquilona [al-ke-lo'-nah], *f.* A woman hired occasionally for odd work.

alquimia [al-kee'-me-ah], *f.* Alchemy.

alquímico, ca [al-kee'-me-co, cah], *a.* Relating to alchemy.

alquimila [al-ke-mee'-lah], *f. (Bot.)* Ladies' mantle. Alchemilla.

alquimista [al-ke-mees'-tah], *m.* Alchemist.

alquinal [al-ke-nahl'], *m.* A veil or head-dress for women.

alquitara [al-ke-tah'-rah], *f. V.* ALAMBIQUE.

alquitarar [al-ke-tah-rar'], *va.* To distil, to let fall in drops.

alquitira [al-ke-tee'-rah], *f.* Tragacanth, a gum.

alquitrán [al-ke-trahn'], *m.* 1. Tar or liquid pitch. 2. *(Naut.)* Stuff for paying a ship's bottom, composed of pitch, grease, resin, and oil: it is also used as a combustible matter. *(Met.)* **Es un alquitrán,** he is a passionate man.

alquitranado [al-ke-trah-nah'-do], *m. (Naut.)* Tarpaulin, a tarred hempen cloth. **Cabos alquitranados,** *(Naut.)* black or tarred cordage. **Alquitrado, da,** *pp.* of ALQUITRANAR.

alquitranar [al-ke-trah-nar'], *va.* To tar.

alrededor [al-ray-day-dor'], 1. *adv.* Around. **Todo alrededor,** all around. 2. *prep.* **Alrededor de,** around; about. **Mirar alrededor de sí,** to look about one. 3. *(fig.)* About, in the region of.

alrededores [al-ray-day-do'-res], *m. pl.* Environs.

alrota [al-ro'-tah], *f.* A very coarse sort of tow. *V.* ARLOTA.

alsacia [al-sah-thee-ah], *f.* Alsace.

alsaciano, na [al-sah-the-ah'-no, nah], *a.* Alsatian: of Alsace or Elsass.

alt. *abr.* de **altura.**

alta [ahl'-tah], *f.* 1. *(Mil.)* Orders to active duty. 2. Discharge (de un hospital). 3. New member. **Dar de alta,** to discharge, to release. **Darse de alta,** to join, to become a member. **Ser alta,** *(Mil.)* to go on active duty. **Alta densidad** (Inform), high density.

altabaque [al-tah-bah'-kay], *m.* Wicker basket.

altabaquillo [al-tah-bah-keel'-lyo], *m. (Bot.)* Field bindweed.

alta fidelidad [ahl'-tah fe-day-le-dadh'], *f.* High fidelity.

altaico, ca [al-tah'-e-co, cah], *a.* Altaic.

altamente [al-tah-men'-tay], *adv.* Highly, extremely, exceedingly.

altamía [al-tah-mee'-ah], *f. (Obs.)* A deep plate.

altamisa [al-tah-mee'-sah], *f. V.* ARTEMISA.

altanería [al-tah-nay-ree'-ah], *f.* 1. *(Lit. us.)* The towering flight of some birds. 2. Hawking.3. *(Met.)* Haughtiness, loftiness, contemptuousness.

altanero, ra [al-tah-nay'-ro, rah], *a.* 1. Soaring, towering. 2. *(Met.)* Haughty, arrogant, proud.

altar [al-tar'], *m.* 1. Altar, the table in Christian churches where the mass is celebrated. **Altar mayor,** high altar. **Llevar a una mujer al altar,** to lead a woman to the altar. 2. *(Astr.)* A southern constellation. 3. **Poner a una en un altar,** to put someone on a pedestal.

altarero [al-tah-ray'-ro], *m.* One who adorns altars for great festivals.

altaricón [al-tah-re-con], *a.* Big-built, large.

altavoz [al-tah-voth'], *m.* Loudspeaker. **Altavoz para sonidos agudos**, tweeter. **Altavoz para sonidos graves**, woofer.

altea [al-tay'-ah], *f. (Bot.)* Common mallow, marsh-mallow.

altear [al-tay-ar'],1. *vn. (Naut.)* To rise above; said of a portion of a coast which rises beyond what adjoint it. 2. *va. (Cono Sur)* To order to stop.

al-tec *abr.* de **alta tecnología,** high technology.

alterabilidad [al-tay-rah-be-le-dahd'], *f.* Changeableness, mutability.

alterable [al-tay-rah-blay], *a.* That may be changed, alterable.

alteración [al-tay-rah-the-on'], *f.* 1. Alteration, mutation. 2. Unevenness of the pulse. **Alteración digestiva**, digestive upset. 3. Strong emotion of anger or other passion. 4. Disturbances, tumult, commotion. 5. Quarrel, dispute (disputa)

alterado, da [al-tay-rah'-do, dah], *a.* Alterative, agitated, disturbed; angry. **Caldo alterado**, medicated or alterative broth. *-pp.* of ALTERAR.

alterador, ra [al-tay-rah-dor, rah], *m. & f.* Alterer, one who alters.

alterante [al-tay-rahn'-tay], *pa. (Med.)* Alterative.

alterar [al-tay-rar], *va.* 1. To alter, to change. 2. To disturb, to stir up. **Alterar la moneda**, to raise or lower the value of coin. *-vr.* 1. To fling, alter, change. 2. To go bad, go off (comida). 3. To get upset, become agitated, become disturbed (enfadarse).

alterativo, va [al-tay-rah-tee'-vo, vah], *a.* Alterative.

altercación, *f.* **altercado,** *m.* [al-ter-cah-the-on', al-ter-cah'-do], a controversy; contest, strife, quarrel.

altercado [al-ter-cah'-do], *m.* Altercation, wrangle, quarrel.

altercador, ra [al-ter-cah-dor'- rah], *m. & f.* One who argues obstinately.

altercar [al-ter-car'], *va.* To contend, to dispute obstinately, to debate, to quarrel, to bicker, to expostulate.

alteridad [al-tay-re-dahd'], *f.* Otherness.

alternación [al-ter-nah-the-on'], *f.* Alternation, reciprocate succession.

alternadamente [al-ter-nah-dah-men'-tay], *adv.* Alternately. *V.* ALTERNATIVAMENTE.

alternado [al-tayr-nah-do], *a.* Alternate.

alternador [al-tayr-nah-dor], *m. (Elec.)* Alternador.

alternancia [al-tayr-nahn-the-ah], *f.* Alternation; *(Pol.)* **Alternancia en el poder**, taking turns in office.

alternante [al-tayr-nan-tay], *a.* Alternating.

alternar [al-ter-nar'], *va.* 1. To alternate, to perform by turns, to change one for another. **Alternar a los mandos**, to take turns at the controls. 2. To mix, take part in the social round, socialize (participar). **Participar con un grupo**, to mix with a group. *-vn.* To succeed reciprocally. **Los gustos y los pesares alternan**, pleasures and sorrows alternate.

alternativa [al-te-nah-tee'-vah], *f.* 1. Alternative, choice of two things. 2. The right of archbishops and bishops to dispose of prebends and benefices alternately with the Pope in their dioceses. 3. Alternation (Sucesión); shift work (trabajo). 4. Ceremony by which a novice becomes a fully-qualified bullfighter.

alternativamente [al-ter-nah-te-vah-men'-tay], *adv.* Alternatively.

alternativo, va [al-ter-nah-tee'-vo, vah], *a.* Alternate. *-m.* Rotation of crops.

alterne [al-tayr-nay], 1. *m.* Mixing, socializing. **Club de alterne**, singles club. 2. *f.* Hostess.

alterno, na [al-ter'-no, nah], *a. (Poetic.)* Alternate. *(Bot.)* Alternate.

alteza [al-tay'-thah], *f.* 1. Elevation sublimity. 2. Highness, a title given to the board of Castle, exchequer, etc. 3. *(Obs.)* Height.

altibajo [al-te-bah'-ho], *m.* 1. A downright blow in fencing. 2. *(Obs.)* A kind of lowered velvet. *-pl.* 1. Uneven ground. 2. *(Met.)* vicissitudes, the ups and downs in life.

altillo, lla [al-teel'-lyo, lyah], *a. dim.* Somewhat high.

altillo [al-teel'-lyo], *m. dim.* A hillock.

altilocuencia [al-te-lo-coo-en'-the-ah], *f.* Grandiloquence, high-sounding words.

altilocuente [al-te-lo-coo-en'-tay], *a. (Poetic.)* Pompous in language, grandiloquent.

altillo [al-te-lyo], *m.* 1. *(Geog.)* Small hill. 2. *(LAm.)* Attic (desván).

altimetría [al-te-may-tree'-ah], *f.* The art of taking or measuring altitudes or heights.

altímetro [al-tee'-may-tro], *m. (Naut., Aer.)* Altimeter.

altiplanicie [al-te-plah-nee'-the-ay], *f.* Highland.

altiplano [al-te-plah-no], *m.* High plateau; *(Geog. Bol.)* Altiplano.

altísimo, ma [al-tee'-se-mo, mah], *a. aug.* Extremely lofty.

altísimo [al-tee'-se-mo], *m.* The Most High, God.

altisonancia [al-te-so-nahn-the-ah], *f.* High-flown style; high-sounding nature.

altisonante, altísono, na [al-te-so-nahn'-tay, al-tee'-so-no, nah], *a.* highsounding.

altitonante [al-te-to-nahn'-tay], *a. (Poetic.)* Thundering.

altitud [al-te-tood'], *f. (Geog.)* V. ALTURA. Elevation or altitude above the level of the ocean. **Altitud absoluta,** *(Aer.)* absolute altitude.

altivamente [al-te-vah-men'-tay], *adv.* Highly, loftily, lordly.

altivarse [al-te-vahr-say], *vr.* To give oneself airs.

altivez [al-te-veth'], *f.* Haughtiness, arrogance, pride, lordliness.

altivo, va [al-tee'-vo, vah], *a.* 1. Haughty, proud, lofty, lord-like. 2. High, high-minded, consequential. 3. Overbearing.

alto, ta [ahl'-to, tah], *a.* 1. High, elevated; alto (cosa) **Es una montaña alta**, it is a high mountain. **Alta mar,** *(Naut.)* High seas. 2. Tall (persona). **Es un hombre alto,** he's a tall man. 3. *(Met.)* Arduous, difficult. 4. *(Met.)* Eminent. 5. Enormous. 6. Deep. 7. Late: applied to movable feasts. **Altas por abril son las pascuas,** Easter falls late in April.

alto [ahl'-to], *m.* 1. Height. 2. Story. **Casa de tres altos,** a house three stories high. 3. *(Naut.)* Depth or height of a ship. 4. High ground. 5. *(Mil.)* Halt; command to stop; and a place or time or fest. 6. *(Mus.)* Notes put over the bass. Contralto (voice). **Alto, or tenor violin;** viola. 7. **No hacer alto,** not to mind, not to observe. **Pasar por alto,** to overlook.

alto [ahl'-to], *int.* 1. **Alto ahí**, stop there. 2. **Alto de aquí,** move off.

alto [ahl'-to], *adv.* 1. Loud. 2. High. **De lo alto,** from above. 3. **Se me pasó por alto,** I forgot. 4. **Por alto,** by stealth; by particular favor. **Metió los géneros por alto,** he smuggled the goods.

altoparlante [al-to-par-lahn'-tay], *m.* Loudspeaker.

altorrelieve [al-to-ray-le-ay-vay], *m.* High relief.

altozanero [al-to-thah-nay-ro], *m. (And)* Porter.

altozano [al-to-thah'-no], *m.* 1. A height or hill. 2. *(And. Carib.)* Cathedral forecourt, church.

altramuz [al-trah-mooth'], *m. (Bot.)* Lupine, Lupinus. **Altramuces,** Lupines which are mixed with ivory beads, and used as black balls in giving votes in cathedral chapters, especially in Castle.

altruísmo [al-troo-ees'-mo], *m.* Altruism, unselfishness.

altura [al-too'-rah], *f.* 1. Height, loftiness. 2. One of the three dimensions of a solid body. 3. Summit of mountains. 4. Altitude, the elevation of the pole or of any of the heavenly bodies. *(Naut.)* the latitude. 5. *(Met.)* Exaltation of spirits. **Estar en grande altura,** to be raised to a high degree of dignity, favor, or fortune. **Alturas,** the heavens. **Dios de las alturas,** God, the Lord of the heavens. 6. *(fig.)* Sublimity, loftiness. **Ha sido un partido de gran altura,** it has been a match of real class.

ALU (Unidad Aritmética Lógica) [ah-loo], . *(Comp.)* ALU (Arithmetic Logical Unit). **ALU vectorial** *(Comp.)*, vectorial ALU.

aluar, or **tomar por la lúa**, *vn. (Naut.)* To bring under the lee.

alubia [ah loo' be ah], *f.* (Bot.) French bean. V. JUDIA.

aluciar [ah loo the ar'], *va.* To polish an article.

alucinación, *f.* **alucinamiento**, *m.* [ah loo the nab the on' ah loo the nah me en' to]. Hallucination.

alucinadamente [ah loo the nah dah men tay], *adv.* Erroneously.

alucinado [ah-loo-the-nah-do], *a.* Deluded, suffering hallucinations.

alucinador [ah-loo-the-nah-dor], *a.* Hallucination, delusion.

alucinante [ah-loo-the-nahn-tay], 1. *a. (Med.)* Hallucinatory. *(Esp. fig.)* Attractive, beguiling; mysterious. *(Esp.)* Absurd; fantastic (absurdo).

alucinar [ah loo the nar'], *va.* To deceive, to lend into error, to fascinate, to delude. *-vr.* To be hallucinated, be decluded.

alucinógeno [ah-loo-the-no-hay-no], *a.* Hallucinogenic (droga).

alucón [ah loo-cone'], *m.* The barn owl. Strix aluco.

alud [ah-lood'] *m.* Avalanche.

aluda [ah-loo'-dah], *f. (Ent.)* Winged ant or emmet. Formica.

aludel [ah-loo-del'], *m. (Chem.)* Subliming pots used in chemistry.

aludir [ah-loo-deer'], *vn.* To allude, to refer to.

aludo, da [ah-loo'-do, dah], *a.* Winged; large winged.

aluengar [ah-loo-en-gar'], *va.* V. ALONGAR.

aluego [ah-loo-ay-go], *adv.* Etc. *(LAm.)* = luego.

alueñe [ah-loo-ay'-nyay], *adv. (Obs.)* Far off.

alujado [ah-loo-hah-do], *a. (CAm. Mex.)* Bright, shining.

alumbrado, da [ah-loom-brah'-do,- dah], *a.* 1. Aluminous, relating to Alum. **Alumbrado eléctrico**, electring lighting. 2. *(coll.)* Flustered with wine. *-pp.* of ALUMBRAR.

alumbrado [ah-loom-brah'-do], *m.* Illumination. **Alumbrado fluorescente**, fluorescent lighting. **Luz fluorescente**, fluorescent light.

alumbrador, ra [ah-loom-brah-dor', rah], *m. & f.* One who gives light, link boy.

alumbramiento [ah loom brah me en'-to], *m.* 1. The act of supplying with light. 2. *(Obs.)* Illusion, deceit, false appearance. 3. *(Met.)* Child birth. V. PARTO. **Alumbramiento bueno, or feliz**, a happy child birth.

alumbrar [ah loom brar'], *va.* 1. To light, to supply with light. 2. *(Obs.)* To restore sight to the blind. 3. To enlighten, to instruct, to adorn with knowledge. 4. Among dycrs, to dip cloth into alum-water. 5. To dig about the roots of vines. 6. To bring forth. **Dios alumbre a Vd. con bien**, or **Dios dé a Vd. feliz parto**, God grant you a safe delivery. *-vr. (coll.)* To be intoxicated, to get drunk.

alumbre [ah loom' bray], *m.* Alum, a mineral salt. **Alumbre catino**, a kind of alkali drawn from the plant glass wort. **Alumbre de rasuras**, Salt of tartar. **Alumbre sucarino or zucarino**, alum and the white of an egg formed into a paste: alum-whey.

alumbrera [ah-loom-bray'-rahl], *f.* Alum mine. **Alumbrera artificial**, alum-works.

alúmina [ah-loo'-me-nah], *f. (Chem.)* Alumina or alumine.

aluminado, da [ah-loo-me-nah'-do, dah], *a. (Chem.)* Mixed with alum,

aluminio [ah-loo-mee'-ne-o], *m.* Aluminium or aluminum, one of the metallic elements.

aluminoso, sa [ah-loo-mi-no'-so, sah], *a.* Aluminous, consisting of alum.

alumnado [ah-loom-nah-do], *m.* Pupils (personas). *(Univ.)* Students.

alumno, na [ah-loom'-no, nahl, *m. & f.* Foster-child; disciple, pupil.

alunado, da [ah-loo-nah'-do, dah], *a.* 1. Insane, lunatic. 2. Spasmodic. 3. Spoiled, tainted.

alunarse [ah-loo-nahr-say], *vr. (CAm.)* To get saddlesore (horse).

alunita [ah-loo-nee'-tah], *f.* Alunite.

alunizaje [ah-loo-ne-thah' hay], *m.* Landing on the moon.

alunizar [ah-loo-ne-thar'], *vn.* To land on the moon.

alusión [ah-loo-se-on'], *f.* Allusion, reference.

alusivamente [ah-loo-se-vah-men'-tay,], *adv.* Allusively.

alusivo, va [ah-loo-see'-vo, vah], *a.* Allusive, hinting at.

alustrar [ah-loos-trar'l, *va.* To give lustre to anything.

alutación [ah-loo-tah-the on'], *f. (Miner.)* Stratum of grains of gold, found in some mines.

aluvial [ah-loo-ve-ahl'], *a.* Alluvial.

aluvión [ah-loo-ve-on'], *f.* Alluvion, wash. *(fig.)* Flood. **Aluvión de improperios**, shower of insults.

alveario [al-vay-ah'-re-o], *m. (Anat.)* The inward cavity of the ear.

álveo [ahl'-vay-o], *m.* 1. Bed of a river. 2. Source of a river.

alveolar [al-vay-o-lar'], *a.* Alveolar, relating to the alveolus. **Alvéolo** [al vay' o lo], *m.* 1. Alveolus or socket of the teeth. 2. *(Bot.)* Alveolus, the cavity in which the seeds of plants are lodged.

alveolo [al-vay-o-lo], *m. (Anat.)* alveolus; socket.

alverja, alerjana [al ver' hah, al ver hah' nah], *f. (Bot.)* Common vetch or tare.

alverjas [al-ver'-hahs], *f. pl. (Bot.) (Sp. Amer.)* Peas.

alverjilla [al-vayr-he-lya], *f.* Sweet pea.

alvidriar [al-ve-dree-ar'], *va. (Prov.)* To glaze earthenware.

alvino, na [al-vee'-no, nah], *a. (Med.)* Alvine, relating to the bowels.

alvitana [al-ve-tah'-nah], *f.* A wind break (hedge or fence).

alza [ahl'-thah], *f.* 1. A piece of leather put round the last to make a shoe wider. 2. An instrument used in rope walks to hold up the rope yarn in the act of spinning it. 3. Advance in the price of anything. 4. *(Typ.)* Overlay, frisket sheet. **Alza y baja**, or **caída de los fondos públicos**, the rise and fall of public stocks.

alzacuello [al-thah-coo-ayl'-lyo], *m.* A black collar bound with linen, which clergymen wear.

alzada [al-thah'-dah], *f.* 1. Height, stature; of horses. 2. A town, village, etc. situated on an eminence. 3. Appeal. **Juez de alzadas**, a judge in appeal causes.

alzadamente [al-thah-dah-men'-tay], *adv.* Wholesale.

alzado [al thah' do], *m.* 1. A plan of a building which shows its front and elevation. 2. A fraudulent bankrupt. *(LAm.)* Vain, stuck-up (soberbio). 3. **Estar alzado**, *(Cono Sur)* to be on heat. **Alzados**, spare stores. **Alzado, da**, *pp.* of ALZAR. *-a.* Fraudulent.

alzadura [al-thah-doo'-rah], *f.* Elevation.

alzamiento [at-thah-me-en'-to], *m.* 1. The act of lifting or raising up. 2. Bidding a higher price at an auction. 3. *(Pol.)* Rising, revolt.

alzapaño [al-thah-pah'-nyo], *m.* A hook to hold up a curtain.

alzapié [al-thah-pe-ay'l, *m.* A foot stool.

alzaprima [ah-thah-pree'-mah], *f.* 1. A lever. 2. *(Naut.)* Heaver. 3. *(Mech.)* Fulcrum. **Dar alzaprima**, *(Met.)* to deceive, to ruin by artifice.

alzaprimar [al-thah-pre-mar'], *va.* 1. To raise by means of a lever. 2. *(Naut.)* To move with handspikes. 3. To incite, spur on.

alzapuertas [al-thah-poo-er'-tas], *m.* A player who acts only the part of dumb servant.

alzar [al-thar'], *ra.* 1. To raise, to lift up, to heave, to erect, to construct. 2. To repeal a decree of excommunication; to recall from banishment. 3. To carry off. 4. To hide, to lock up. 5. To deal cards; to gather up and arrange in order the printed sheets for the binder. 6. To elevate the host, in mass. 7. *(Naut.)* To heave. **Alzar cabeza**, to recover from a calamity or disease. **Alzar de codo or el codo**, to drink much wine or liquor. **Alzar de obra**, to cease working. **Alzar de eras**, to finish the harvesting of grain in the farm-yards. **Alzar figura**, to assume an air of importance. **Alzar el dedo**, to raise the forefinger in asseveration or affirmation of anything. **Alzar**

la casa, to quit a house, to move out of it. **Alzar velas**, *(Naut.)* to set the sails. *(Met.)* To move off. *-vr.* 1. To rise in rebellion. 2. To rise from kneeling. 3. To make a fraudulent bankrupt. 4. To appeal. **Alzarse con el dinero**, to run away with the money. **Alzarse a mayores**, to be petulant. **Alzarse con algo.** 5. *(And.)* To get drunk (emborracharse). 6. *(LAm.)* To run away (animal). *V.* APROPIARSE.

alzatirantes [al-thah-te-rahn'-tes], *m. pl.* Straps attached to the harness of a horse to suspend the traces.

alzaválvulas [al-thah-val-voo-lahs], *m.* Invar *(Mech.)* tappet.

alzo [al-tho], *m. (CAm.)* Theft.

A.M. *abr.* de **amplitud.**

a.m. *(LAm.) abr.* de **ante meridiem.**

ama [ah'-mah], *f.* 1. A mistress of the house. **El ama de casa**, the lady or mistress of the house. **Ama de llaves** or **de gobierno**, house-keeper. **Ama de leche**, wet-nurse. 2. Foster mother (de niño).

amabilidad [ah-mah-be-le-dahd'], *f.* Amiability, affability, loveliness. **Tuvo la amabilidad de**, he was good enough to.

amable [ah-mah'-blay], *a.* Amiable, pleasing, lovely. **Muy amable**, thanks very much. **Si es tan amable**, if you would be so kind.

amablemente [ah-mah-blay-men'-tay], *adv.* Amiably, lovely.

amacena [ah-mah-thay'-nah], *f. (Bot.)* A damson plum.

amaceno, na [ah-mah-thay'-no, nah], *a.* Damascene.

amachambrarse [ah-mah-cham-brahr-say], *vr. (Cono Sur)* etc. *V.* AMACHINARSE.

amacharse [ah-mah-chahr-say], *vr. (LAm.)* To dig one´s heels in, to refuse to be moved.

amachinarse [ah-mah-che-nahr-say], *vr. (LAm.)* To live with somebody.

amacho [ah-mah-cho], *a. (CAm. Cono Sur)* Strong, vigorous (fuerte).

amacollarse [ah-mah-col-lyar'-say], *vr.* To throw out shoots.

amacrático, ca [ah-ma-crah'-te-co, cah], *a.* Amacratic, said of a photographic lens which brings all the chemical rays to one focus.

amadamado, da [ah-mah-dah-mah'-do, dah], *a.* Effeminate, womanish, frivolous.

amado, da [ah-mah-do, dah], *a.* Dear, beloved.

amador, ra [ah-mah-dor', rah], *m. & f.* A lover, a sweetheart, suitor.

amadriada [ah-mah-dree'-ah-dah], *f.* Hamadryad, a wood nymph.

amadrigar [ah-mah-dre-gar'], *va.* To receive well, especially one not deserving. *-vr.* 1. To burrow. 2. *(Met.)* to live retired, to decline all intercourse with the world.

amadrinar [ah-mah-dre-nar'], *va.* 1. To couple, to yoke together. 2. *(Naut.)* To join one thing to another. 3. To act as godmother or bridesmaid.

amadroñado, da [ah-mah-dro-nyah'-do, dah], *a.* Resembling **madroños**, the fruit of the madroño-tree. **Rosario amadroñado**, rosary, the beads of which resemble madroños.

amaestrado, da [ah-mah-es-trah'-do, dah], *a.* 1. Taught, tutored. **Caballo amaestrado**, horse completely broken in. 2. *(Obs.)* rightfully contrived. *-pp.* of AMAESTRAR.

amaestradura [ah-mah-es-trah-doo'-rah], *f.* 1. Artifice, cunning. 2. Awning before a window.

amaestramiento [ah-mah-ays-trah-me-ayn-to], *m.* Training; drill.

amaestrar [ah-mah-es-trar'], *va.* To instruct, to break in, to lead.

amagar [ah-mah-gar'], *va.* 1. To be in a threatening attitude. 2. To threaten. 3. To have some symptoms of a disease. 4. *(Met.)* To manifest a desire. *-vr. (Prov.)* To couch, to stoop.

amago [ah-mah'-go], *m.* Bitter stuff found in some bee-cells. *(Met.)* Nausea, loathing. Threat (amenaza). Sign, symptom. **Amago tormentoso**, outbreak of bad weather.

amainar [ah-mah-e-nar'], *va.* 1. *(Naut.)* To lower the sails. 2. To relax. *-vr.* To abate, to moderate (ira, viento etc.).

amaine [ah-mah-e-nay], *m.* Shortening, moderation, lessening.

amaitinar [ah-mah-e-te-nar'], *va.* To observe attentively, to watch closely.

amaizado [ah-mah-e-tha-do], *a. (And)* Rich.

amajadar [ah-mah-hah-dar'], *vn.* 1. To seek shelter in a sheep-fold. 2. To secure sheep.

amalaya [ah-mah-lah-lya], *interj. (LAm.) V.* OJALA.

amalayar [ah-mah-lah-yahr], *va. (And.* CAm, *Mex.)* To covet, to long for.

amalecita [ah-mah-lay-thee'-tah], *m.* Amalekite.

amalgama [ah-mal-gah'-mah], *f.* Amalgam.

amalgamación [ah-mal-gah-mah-the-on'], *f.* Amalgamation.

amalgamar [ah-mal-gah-mar'], *va.* To amalgamate, to unite metals with quicksilver.

amalo, la [ah-mah'-lo, lah], *a.* One of the most noted families of the Goths.

amamantar [ah-mah-man-tar'], *va.* To nurse, to suckle.

amamblucea [ah-mam-bloo-tahy-ah], *f.* A sort of cotton stuff.

amancebado, da [ah-man-tahy-bah'-do, dah], *a.* Attached, excessively devoted. *-pp.* of AMANCEBARSE.

amancebamiento [ah-man-thay-bah-me-en'-to], *m.* Concubinage.

amancebarse [ah-man-thay-bar'-say], *vr.* To live in concubinage.

amancillar [ah-man-theel-lyar'], *va.* 1. To stain, to pollute. 2. To offend, to injure. 3. *(Met.)* to tarnish one's reputation.

amanecer [ah-mah-nay-therr'], *vn.* 1. To dawn. 2. To arrive at break of day. **Al amanecer**, at the break of day. 3. *(Met.)* To begin to appear, or to show itself. 4. *(LAm.)* **Amaneció bailando**, he danced all night. 5. *(LAm.)* **¿Como amaneció?,** how are you?

amanecida [ah-mah-nay-the-dah], *f.* Dawn, daybreak.

amanerado, da [ah-mah-nay-rah'-do, dah], *a.* Applied to painters, mannerists, and to their works.

amaneramiento [ah-mah-nay-rah-me-ayn-to], *m.* Affectation; mannerism.

amanerarse [ah-mah-nay-rar'-say], *vr.* To adopt a mannerism, or affectation in style. Used of artists or writers.

amanezca [ah-mah-nayth-cah], *f. (Carib. Mex.)* Dawn; breakfast (desayuno).

amanezquera [ah-mah-nayz-kay-rah], *f. (Carib. Mex.)* Early morning, daybreak.

amanojar [ah-mah-no-har'], *va.* To gather by handfuls.

amansa [ah-mahn-sah], *f. (Cono Sur)* Taming; breaking in.

amansado [ah-mahn-sah-do], *a.* Tame.

amansador, ra [ah-man-sah-dor', rah], *m. & f.* 1. Tamer, subduer. 2. Soother, appeaser.

amansamiento [ah-man-sah-me-en'-to], *m.* The act of taming.

amansar [ah-man-sar'], *va.* 1. To tame to domesticate, to subdue. 2. *(Met.)* To soften, to pacify. *-vr.* To calm down (persona).

amanse [ah-mahn-say], *m. (And. Mex.)* Taming.

amantar [ah-man-tar'], *va. (coll.)* To cover with any loose garment.

amante [ah-mahn'-tay], *pa. & n.* Loving, lover, sweetheart, fond. *-pl. (Naut.)* ropes which form part of the running rigging of a ship.

amantillar [ah-man-teel-lyar'], *va. (Naut.)* To top the lifts, to hoist one end of the yard-arms higher than the other.

amantillo [ah-man-teel'-lyo], *m. (Naut.)* Lift.

amanuense [ah-mah-noo-en'-say], *m.* Amanuensis, clerk.

amañado [ah-mah-nya-do], *a.* 1. Skilful, clever. 2. Fake, faked (falso).

amañar [ah-mah-nyar'], *va.* To do a thing cleverly. To fake, to alter, tamper with. *-vr.* 1. To accustom oneself to do things with skill, to be handy. 2. *(Carib.)* To tell lies. **Amañarse con**, to get along with.

amaño [ah-mah'-nyo], *m.* Way or means of doing a thing, expertness, cleverness. **Tener amaño**, to have an aptitud for. *-pl.* 1. Tools or implements. 2. *(Met.)* Intrigue or machinations.

amapola ah-mah-po'-lah], *f. (Bot.)* Poppy. Papaver. **Amapola morada**, corn poppy, corn rose.

amar [ah-mar'], *va.* 1. To love, to like, to fancy. 2. *(Met.)* To have a tendency to: applied to inanimate things.

amaraje [ah-mah-rah-hay], *m. (Aer.)* Landing (on the sea); splashdown, touchdown.

amaracino [ah-mah-rah-thee'-no], *a.* **Ungüento amaracino**, a sort of ointment made of marjoram.

amáraco [ah-mah'-rah-co], Marjoram. *V.* MEJORANA.

amaranto [ah-mah-rahn'-to], *m. (Bot.)* Amaranth, flowering bush.

amarar [ah-mah-rahr], *vn. (Aer.)* To land (on the sea), to come down, to splash down.

amarchantarse [ah-mahr-chan-tahr-say], *vr.* Amarchantarse en *(LAm.)* To become a customer of.

amargado, da [ah-mar-gah'-do, dah], *a.* Embittered. *-pp.* of AMARGAR.

amargaleja [ah-mar-gah-lay'-hah], *f.* The bitter or wild plum. *V.* ENDRINA.

amargamente [ah-mar-gah-men'-tay], *adv.* Bitterly.

amargar [ah-mar-gar'], *va.* 1. To make bitter. 2. *(Met.)* To exasperate, to offend. *-vn.* To be bitter or acrid; to taste bitter. *-vr.* To get bitter.

amargo, ga [ah-mar'-go, gah], *a.* 1. Bitter, having a hot, acrid taste. 2. Painful. 3. *(Cono Sur)* Cowardly.

amargo [ah-mar'-go], *m.* 1. *V.* AMARGOR. 2. Sweetmeat made of bitter almonds. *-pl.* Bitters.

amargón [ah-mar-gone'], *m. (Bot.)* Dandelion.

amargor [ah-mar-gor'], *m.* 1. Bitterness. 2. Sorrow, vexation.

amargosamente [ah-mar-go-sah-men'-tay], *V.* AMARGAMENTE.

amargoso, sa [ah-mar-go'-so, sah], *a.* Bitter. *V.* AMARGO.

amarguillo, lla [ah-mar-geel'-lyo, lyah], *a. dim.* Somewhat bitter. It is also used as a substantive.

amargura [ah-mar-goo'-rah], *f.* Bitterness, acerbity, sorrow.

amaricado, da [ah-mah-re-cah'-do, dah], *a. (coll.)* Effeminate.

amarilis [ah-mah-ree'-lis], *f.* Amaryllis.

amarilla [ah-mah-reel-lyah], *f.* 1. Gold coin, especially the ounce. 2. A vat. 3. A liver disease of woolly flocks.

amarillazo, za [ah-mah-reel-lyah'-tho, thah], *a.* Of a pale yellow color.

amarillear [ah-mah-reel-lyay-ar'], *vn.* 1. To incline to yellow. 2. To be yellowish (tirar a amarillo). 3. To pale (palidecer).

amarillecer [ah-mah-reel-lyay-thayr], *vn.* To turn yellow.

amarillejo, ja [ah-mah-reel-lyay-ho, hah], *a. dim.* Yellowish.

amarillento, ta [ah-mah-reel-lyen'-to, tah], *a.* Inclining to yellow golden.

amarillez [ah-mah-reel-lyeth'], *f.* The yellow color of the body.

amarillismo [ah-mah-reel-lyes-mo], *m.* Sensationalist; paleness, sallowness.

amarillito, ta [ah-mah-reel-lyee'-to, tah], *a. dim. V.* AMARILLEJO.

amarillo, lla [ah-mah-reel'-lyo, lyah], *a.* 1. Yellow; gold color. 2. Gutter (prensa sensacionalista). 3. **Sindicato amarillo**, trade union which is in league with the bosses.

amarillo [ah-mah-reel'-lyo], *m.* 1. Jaundice. 2. A disease of the silkworm.

amarilloso [ah-mah-reel-lyo-so], *a. (Cono Sur)* Yellowish.

amarinar [ah-mah-re-nar'], *va. V.* MARINAR.

amariposado, da [ah-mah-re-po-sah'-do, dah], *a.* 1. *(Bot.)* Papilionaceous, applied to flowers. 2. Butterfly-like. 3. Effeminate.

amaro [ah-mah'-ro], *m. (Bot.)* Common clary.

amarra [ah-mar'-rah], *f.* 1. A cable. 2. A martingale. **Amarra**, *(Naut.)* A word of command, corresponding to the English

belay, lash, or fasten. **Amarras fijas**, moorings. **Amarras de popa**, stern-fasts. **Amarras de proa**, bow-fasts. **Amarras de través**, fasts amidships. **Tener buenas amarras**, *(Met.)* to have powerful friends or interest.

amarradera [ah-mahr-rah-day-rahs], *f. (And)* mooring (para barcos); *(Mex.)* Rope, line (cuerda).

amarradero [ah-mar-rah-day'-ro], *m.* 1. A post to which anything is made fast. 2. *(Naut.)* A berth, the place where a ship is moored.

amarrado [ah-mahr-rah-do], *a. (LAm.)* Mean, stingy.

amarradura [ah-mahr-rah-doo-rah], *f.* Mooring.

amarraje [ah-mahr-rah-hay], *m.* Mooring charges.

amarrar [ah-mar-rar'], *va.* To tie, to fasten, to lash. **Amarrar un cabo de labor**, to belay a running rope. **Amarrar un bajel entre viento y marea**, to moor a vessel between wind and tide. **Amarrar un bajel con codera sobre el cable**, to moor a ship with a spring on the cable. **Amarrar con reguera**, to moor by the stern. *-vr. (And.* CAm) To get drunk.

amarrazones [ah-mar-rah-tho'-nes], *pl. (Naut.)* Ground-tackle.

amarre [ah-mahr-ray], *m.* Fastening, tying; mooring.

amarrete [ah-mahr-ray-tay], *(LAm.)* 1. *a.* Mean, stingy.

amarrido, da [ah-mar-ree'-do, dah], *a.* Dejected, gloomy, melancholy.

amarro [ah-mahr-ro], *m. (And)* Knotted string, knotted rope (cuerda).

amarrocar [ah-mahr-ro-cahr], *va. (Cono Sur)* To scrimp and save.

amarroso [ah-mahr-ro-so], *a. (CAm.)* Acrid, sharp (fruta).

amartelado [ah-mahr-tay-lah-do], *a.* Lovesick; **andar amartelado con**, to be in love with.

amartelamiento [ah-mahr-tay-lah-mee-ayn-to], *m.* Lovesickness, infatuation.

amartelar [ah-mar-tay-lar'], *va.* 1. To court, to make love to a lady. 2. To love most devotedly.

amartillar [ah-mar-teel-lyar'], *va.* 1. To hammer, to knock in. 2. To cock a gun or pistol.

amasadera [ah-mah-sah-day-rah], *f.* A kneading-trough.

amasado [ah-mah-sah-do], *a. (Carib.)* Doughy (sustancia). Plump (persona).

amasador, ra [ah-mah-sah-dor', rah], *m. & f.* Kneader.

amasadura [ah-mah-sah-doo'-rah], *f.* Act of kneading.

amasamiento [ah-mah-sah-me-en'-to], *m.* 1. The act of uniting or joining. 2. *V.* AMASADURA.

amasandería [ah-mah-sahn-day-re-ah], *f. (And. Cono Sur)* Bakery, baker's shop.

amasandero, ra [ah-mah-sahn-day-ro], *m. & f. (And. Cono Sur)* Bakery worker.

amasar [ah-mah-sar'], *va.* 1. To kned. 2. To mould. 3. *(Met.)* To arrange matters well for the attainment of some purpose. 4. *(fig.)* To cook up, concoct. 5. To pile up, accumulate.

amasiato [ah-mah-se-ah'-to], *m. (Sp. Amer.)* Concubinage.

amasigado [ah-mah-se-gah-do], *a. (And)* Dark, swarthy.

amasijar [ah-mah-se-hahr], *va. (Cono Sur)* To do in (matar).

amasijo [ah-mah-see'-ho], *m.* 1. Dough. 2. The act of kneading, or the preparation for it. 3. A quantity of mortar or plaster. 4. *(Met.)* A medley. 5. A task. 6. A plotting agreement. 7. The place where the dough for bread is made.

amasio [ah-mah-se-o], *m. & f. (CAm. Mex.)* Lover, mistress (mujer).

amate [ah-mah'-tay], *m. (Mex.)* A fig-tree, the milky juice of which is used as a resolvent.

amateur [ah-mah-tayr], 1. *a.* Amateur.

amateurismo [ah-mah-te-oo-res-mo], *m.* Amateurism.

amatista [ah-mah-tees'-tah], *f. (Miner.)* Amethyst, a precious stone of purplish violet color.

amatorio, ría [ah-mah-to'-re-o, ah], *a.* Amatory.

amarufis [ah-mah-roo'-fis], *m.* A kind of Indian linen.

amaurosis [ah-mah-oo-ro'-sis], *f.* blindness from disease of the optic nerve.

amaurótico, ca [ah-mah-oo-ro'-te-co, cah], *a.* Amaurotic, affected by amaurosis.

amauta [ah-mah-oo-tah], *m.* (And Hist.) Inca elder.

amayorado [ah-mah-yo-rah-do], *a.* (And) Precious, forward (niño).

amayorazgado, da [ah-mah-yo-rath-gah'-do, dah], *a.* Entailed.

amazacotado [ah-mah-thah-co-tah-do], *a.* Heavy, clumsy, awkward; shapeless, formless.

amazona [ah-mah-tho'-nah], *f.* 1. An amazon; a masculine woman. 2. A large parrot of Brazil. 3. A long riding-skirt or habit.

Amazonas [ah-mah-tho-nahs], *m*: **el río Amazones**, the Amazon.

amazónico, ca [ah-mah-tho'-ne-co, cah], *a.* Amazonian.

ambages [am-bah'-hes], *m. pl.* 1. (Obs.) circuit. 2. (Met.) Circumlocution or multiplicity of words used to describe or explain a thing.

ambagioso [am-bah-he-o-so], *a.* Involved, circuitous, roundabout.

ámbar [ahm'-bar], *m.* Amber. Succinum. **ambar gris**, ambergris. **Es un ámbar**, it is excellent, it is very sweet: applied to liquors.

ambareado [am-bah-ray-ah-do], *a.* (And) Chestnut, auburn (pelo).

ambarilla [am-bah-reel'-lyah], *f.* (Bot.) Amber-seed or musk-seed.

ambarina [am-bah-ree'-nah], *f. V.* ALGALIA.

ambarino, na [am-bah-ree'-no, nah], *a.* Relating to amber.

ambición [am-be-the-on'], *f.* 1. Ambition, a desire of preferment or honour. 2. Covetousness.

ambicionar [am-be-the-o-nar'], *va.* To pursue with anxious desire, to covet. **Ambicionar ser algo**, to have an ambition to be somebody.

ambiciosamente [am-be-the-oh-sah-men'-tay], *adv.* Ambitiously; highly.

ambicioso, sa [am-be-the-oh'-so, sah], *a.* 1. Ambitious, aspiring. 2. covetous. 3. High-minded.

ambidextro, tra [am-be-decs'-tro, trah], *a.* Ambidextrous.

ambientación [am-be-ayn-tah-the-on], *f.* 1. Orientation. 2. Sound-effects (cine).

ambientado [am-be-ayn-tah-do], *a.* (LAm.) Air-conditioned; **Estar ambientado**, to be settled in (persona).

ambientador, ra [am-be-ayn-tah-dor], *m. & f.* Dresser (TV.)

ambiental [a-be-en-tahl'], *a.* Environmental. **Música ambiental**, piped music.

ambientalismo [am-be-ayn-tah-les-mo], *m.* Environmentalism.

ambientalista [am-be-ayn-tah-les-tah], *a.* Environmentalist.

ambientar [am-be-en-tar'], *va.* 1. To provide with a suitable environment. **Ambienta el escenario con bailes folklóricos**, he enlivens the scene with folk dances. 2. To set; **la novela está ambientada en una sociedad de...**, the novel is set in a society of.... 3. To orientate, direct. *-vr.* To orientate oneself, get a sense of direction.

ambiente [am-be-en'-tay], *m.* Environment. (fig.) Atmosphere; climate; environment. **No me gusta el ambiente**, I don´t like the atmosphere. **Se crió un ambiente de violencia**, he grew up in an atmosphere of violence. (And) Room; **ambiente artificial**, air-conditioning.

ambigú [am-be-goo'], *m.* Ambigu, a French word signifying a meal, ussually served in the evening at entertainments or receptions, and composed of cold and warm dishes, set all at once on the table.

ambiguamente [am-be-goo-ah-men'-tay], *adv.* Ambiguously.

ambigüedad [am-be-goo-ay-dahd'], *f.* Ambiguity, doubt, uncertainty, double meaning.

ambiguo, gua [am-be'-goo-o, ah], *a.* Ambiguous, doubtful.

ambilado [am-be-lah-do], *a.* (Carib.) **Estar ambilado**, to be left open-mouthed.

ámbito [am'-be-to], *m.* Circuit, circumference, compass. **Dentro del ámbito**, within the limits of; **en el ámbito nacional**, on a nationwide basis.

ambivalencia [am-be-va-layn-the-ah], *f.* Ambivalence.

ambivalente [am-be-vah-layn-tay], *a.* Ambivalent.

ambivertido [am-be-ver-tee'-do], *m.* Ambivert.

ambladura [am-blah-doo-rah], *f.* **A paso de ambladura**, at an amble.

amblar [am-blar'], *va.* (Obs.) To amble: to pace.

ambleo [am-blay-o], *m.* A short, thick wax-candle.

ambligonio [am-ble-go'-neo], *m.* Obtuse-angled. *V.* TRIANGULO.

ambliopía [am-ble-o-pee'-ah], *f.* Weakness of sight, without any opacity of the cornea.

ambo [ahm'-bo], *m.* Combination of two numbers in the lottery. (Cono Sur) two-piece suit.

ambón [am-bone'], *m.* A pulpit on each side of the high altar.

ambos, bas [ahm-bos, bas], *a.* Both. **Ambos or Ambas a dos**, both, or both together.

ambrosía [am-bro-see'-ah], *f.* 1. Ambrosia. 2. (fig.) Any delicious viand or liquor. 3. (Bot.) Ragweed.

ambucía [am-boo-thee-ah], *f.* (Cono Sur) greed, greediness.

ambuciento [am-boo-thee-ayn-to], *a.* (Cono Sur) greedy; voracious.

ambulancia [am-boo-lahn'-the-ah], *f.* Ambulance, a field hospital; also the conveyance.

ambulante [am-boo-lahn'-tay], *a.* Ambulatory, walking; roving; itinerant; traveling, etc.

ambulativo, va [am-boo-lah'-tee'-vo, vah], *a.* Of a roving turn (personas).

ambulatorio, a [am-boo-lah-to'-re-o, ah], *a.* Ambulatory, used for walking or progressing. (Zool.). State-health-service hospital.

ameba [ah-may-bah], *f.* Amoeba.

amebeo, bea [ah-may-bay'-o, ah], *a.* Amebean, a kind of dialogue in verse.

amedrentador, ra [ah-may-dren-tah-dor', rah], *m. & f.* Threatener, discourager. *-a.* Terrifying, frightening.

amedrentar [ah-may-dren-tar'], *va.* to frighten, to deter, to discourage, to fear; to intimidate;: vulgarly, to cow. *-vr.* To get scared.

amejoramiento [ah-may-ho-rah-me-ayn-to], *m.* (LAm.) V. MEJORAMIENTO.

amejorar [ah-may-ho-rahr], *va.* (LAm.) V. MEJORAR.

amelcocharse [ah-mayl-co-char-say], *vr.* (Carib.) To fall in love; (Mex.) To harden.

amelga [ah-mel'-gah], *f.* A ridge between two furrows thrown up by the plough.

amelgado [ah-mel-gah'-do], *m.* (Prov.) A little hillock to mark the boundaries of a field. **Amelgado, da, pp.** of AMELGAR.

amelgar [ah-mel-gar'], *va.* 1. To open furrows. 2. (Prov.) To throw up earth to mark boundaries.

amelo [a-may'-lo], *m.* (Bot.) Golden star-wort.

amelonado, da [ah-may-lo-nah'-do, dah], *a.* Shaped liked a melon.

amén [ah-men'], *m.* Amen, so be it. **Voto de amén**, a partial vote, given without the least previous discussion or inquiry. **Sacristán de amén**, one who blindly adheres to the opinion of another. **amén de,** (coll.) besides: except; over and above.

amenaza [ah-may-nah'-thah], *f.* A threat, a menace.

amenazador, ra [ah-may-nah-thah-dor', rah], *m. & f.* One who threatens. *-a.* Threatening.

amenazante [a-may-nah-thahn'-tay], *pa.* Minacious, threatening.

amenazar [ah-may-nah-thar'], *va.* To threaten, to menace. **Amenazar a uno a muerte**, to threaten somebody with death. **Una especie amenazada de extinción**, a species threatened with extinction. *-vn.* To threaten; to loom.

amencia [ah-men'-the-ah], *f.* (Ant. and Amer.) Dementia; insanity.

amenguar [ah-men-goo-ar'], *va.* 1. To diminish. 2. To defame.

amenidad [ah-may-ne-dahd'] *f.* 1. Amenity, agreeableness. 2. (Met.) A pleasant strain of language.

amenizar [ah-may-nee-thar'], *va.* 1. To render pleasant or agreeable. 2. *(Met.)* To adorn a speech with pleasing sentiments.

ameno, na [ah-may'-no, nah], *a.* 1. Pleasant, delicious. 2. Delightful, elegant: applied to the language of a work. 3. Pleasant, readable (libro). **Prefiero una lectura más amena**, I prefer lighter reading.

amentáceo, cea [ah-men-tah'-tahy-o, ah], *a. (Bot.)* Amentaceous, resembling a thong.

amento [ah-men'-to], *m. (Bot.)* Ament, amentum, eatkin.

ameos. *V.* AMI.

amerar [ah-may-rar'], *va.* To mix wine or liquor with water. *-vr.* To soak or enter gradually, as water.

amerengado, da [ah-may-ren-gah'-do, dah], *a.* 1. Like, or having, meringue. 2. *(coll.)* Nice, prudish.

América [ah-may-re-cah], *f.* America (depending on context, may mean the whole continent, the United States, or Latin America); **América Central**, Central America. **América del Norte**, North America. **América del Sur**, South America. **Hacerse las Américas**, to make a fortune.

americana [ah-may-re-cah'-nah], *f.* Sackcoat, jacket.

americanada [ah-may-re-cah-nah-dah], *f.* Typically American thing (to do).

americanismo [ah-may-re-cah-nees'-mo], *m.* 1. Americanism, feeling for Spanish-American culture. 2. Spanish-American expression.

americanista [ah-may-re-cah-nes-tah], *m. & f.* Americanist, specialist in indigenous American culture; specialist in American culture; specialist in American literature.

americanización [ah-may-re-cah-ne-thah-the-on'], *f.* Americanization.

americanizar [ah-may-re-cah-ne-thar'], *va.* To Americanize, to make Spanish-American, to make North American. *-vr.* To be Americanized.

americano, na [ah-may-ree-cah'-no, nah], *a. & m. & f.* American.

americio [ah-may-ree-thee-o], *m.* (Quim.) Americium.

amerindio, a [ah-may-reen-dee-o], *a., m. & f.* American, American Indian.

ameritado [ah-may-ree-tah-do], *a. (LAm.)* Worthy.

ameritar [ah-may-ree-tahr], *va. (LAm.)* To win credit, do well.

amerizaje [ah-may-ree-thah-hay], *m.* Landing (on the sea); splashdown.

amerizar [ah-may-ree-thahr], *vn (Aer.)* To land (on the sea).

amestizado [ah-mays-tee-thah-do], *a.* Like a half-breed.

ametalado, da [ah-may-tah-lah'-do, dah], *a.* Having the color of brass.

ametista, *f.* **ametisto**, *m.* [ah-may-tees'-tah, ah-me-tees'-to], *V.* AMATISTA.

ametrallador [ah-may-trahl-lyah-dor], *m.* Machine gunner.

ametralladora [ah-may-trahl-lyah-do'-rah], *f.* Machine gun.

ametrallar [ah-may-trahl-lyar'], *va.* To machine gun.

amia [ah'-me-ah], *f.* Lamia, the white shark.

amianto, *m.* **amianta,** *f.* [ah-me-ahn'-to, ah-me-ahn'-tah]. *(Miner.)* Amiarchus a filamentous fossil: asbestos.

amiba [ah-mee'-bah], *f.* Amoeba, a rhizopod; a type of the simplest animal life.

amiento [ah-mee-ayn'-to], *m.* A leather strap, with which a helmet is tied on.

amiga [ah-mee'-gah], *f.* 1. *(Prov.)* A school for girls; Friend; lover (amante); girlfriend (de chico). 2. *(Obs.)* V. BARRAGANA. Mistress.

amigable [ah-me-gah'-blay], *a.* 1. Friendly. 2. *(Met.)* Fit, suitable.

amigablemente [ah-me-gah'-baly-men'-tay], *adv.* Amicably.

amigacho [ah-me-gah-cho], *m.* Mate, buddy (esp. US), bachelor friend.

amigarse [ah-me-gahr-say], *vr.* To get friendly; to set up house together (amantes).

amigazo [ah-me-gah-tho], *m. (Cono Sur)* pal, buddy (esp. US).

amígdala [ah-meeg'-dah-lah], *f.* A tonsil.

amigdalitis [ah-meeg-dah-lee'-tis], *f. (Med.)* Tonsilitis.

amigo, ga [ah-mee'-go, gah'], *m. & f.* 1. A friend: comrade. 2. Lover. **Un amigo íntimo**, a familiar, an intimate. **Es amigo de ganar la vida**, he is fond of gain; he is eager to do any thing to procure a livelihood. **Amiga del alma**, intimate friend. **Amigo por correspondencia**, penfriend.

amigo, ga [ah-mee'-go, gah], *a. V.* AMISTOSO an AMIGABLE.

amigote [ah-me-go'-tay], *m. aug. (coll.)* A great friend, an intimate. *(Cono Sur)* sidekick, crony.

amiguero [ah-me-gay-ro], *a. (LAm.)* Friendly.

amiguete [ah-me-gay-tay], *m.* Buddy, mate; influential friend.

amiguismo [ah-me-gees-mo], *m.* Old buddy (esp. US); *(Cono Sur)* sidekick.

amiguita [ah-me-gee-tah], *f.* Girlfriend; lover.

amiguito [ah-me-gee-to], *m.* boyfriend; lover.

amiláceo [ah-me-lah'-thay-o], *a.* Amylaceous, starchy.

amilanamiento [ah-me-lah-nah-me-en'-to], *m.* Spiritlessness.

amilanar [ah-me-lah-nar'] *va.* To frighten, to terrify, to crush. *-vr.* To flag, to get scared.

amillaramiento [ah-meel-lyah-rah-me-en'-to], *m.* Assessment of a tax.

amillarar [ah-meel-layh-rar'], *va.* To assess a tax.

amillonado, da [ah-meel-lyo-nah'-do, dah], *a.* 1. Liable to pay a tax called millones, which is levied on wine, vinegar, etc. 2. Very rich *-m.* A millionaire.

aminoácido [ah-mee-no-ah'-thee-do], *m.* Amino acid.

aminorar [ah-me-no-rar'], *va.* To lessen, to enfeeble.

amir [ah-meer'], *m.* Ameer, one of the Mohammedan nobility of Afghanistan and Seinde.

amistad [ah-mis-tahd'], *f.* 1. Amity, friendship; commerce. 2. A connection founded upon a carnal intercourse. 3. Gallantry. 4. Civility, favor. 5. *(Obs.)* inclination, desire. **hacer las amistades**, to make up. **Invitar a las amistades**, to invite one´s friends.

amistar [ah-mis-tar'], *va. & vr.* To reconcile, to bring together, make friends (hacer amigos). To bring about a reconciliation. *-vr.* To become friends, establish a friendship.

amistosamente [ah-mis-to-sah-men'-tay], *adv.* In a friendly manner, familiarly.

amistoso, sa [ah-mis-toh'-so, sah], *a.* Friendly, amicable, cordial.

amito [ah-mee'-to], *m.* Amice, a square piece of linen with a cross in the middle, which forms the undermost part of a priest's garment when he officiates at the mass.

amnesia [am-nay'-se-ah], *f.* Amnesia; loss of memory.

amnios [ahm'-ne-os], *f.* Amnion, a foetal envelope.

amnistia [am-nis-tee'-ah], *f.* An amnesty.

amnistiar [am-nis-te-ar'], *va.* To grant a pardon, to amnesty. *-vr.* To receive amnesty.

amo [ah'-mo], *m.* 1. Master of a house. 2. Proprietor. 3. Foster-father. 4. Overseer. 5. (Vulg.) Good-man. 6. Lord. **Amo de casa**, a householder. *V.* AMA. **Amo de buque**, a shipowner.

amoblado [ah-mo-blah-do], 1. *a.* Furnished. 2. *m. (CAm.)* Furniture.

amoblar [ah-mo-blar'], *va.* To furnish. *V.* MOBLAR = AMUEBLAR.

amodita [ah-mo-dee'-tah], *f.* A sort of horned serpent. *V.* ALICANTE.

amodorrado, da [ah-mo-dor-rah'-do, dah], *a.* Heavy with sleep. *-pp.* of AMODORRARSE.

amodorramiento [ah-mo-dor-rah-me-ayn-to], *m.* Sleepiness, drowsiness.

amodorrarse [ah-mo-dor-rar'-say], *vr.* To be drowsy, to grow heavy with sleep.

amodorrido, da [ah-mo-dor-ree'-do, dah], *a. V.* AMODORRADO.

amogotado, da [ah-mo-go-tah'-do, dah], *a.* Steep with a flat crown: applied to a mountain descried at sea.

amochecerse [ah-mo-chay-therr'-say], *vr.* To grow mouldy or rusty. *V.* ENMOHECERSE.

amohinar [ah-mo-e-nar'], *va.* To irritate. *-vr.* To get annoyed.

amohosado [ah-mo-o-sah-do], *a. (Cono Sur)* Rusty.

amojonador [ah-mo-ho-nah-dor'], *m.* One who sets landmarks.

amojonamiento [ah-mo-ho-nah-me-en'-to], *m.* The act of setting landmarks.

amojonar [ah-mo-ho-nar'], *va.* To set landmarks, to mark roads.

amojosado [ah-mo-ho-sah-do], *a. (Cono Sur)* Rusty.

amoladera [ah-mo-lah-day'-rah], *f.* Whetstone, grindstone.

amolado [ah-mo-lah-do], *a.* 1. *(Cono Sur)* Bothered, irritated (fastidiado). 2. *(And. Mex.)* Offended (ofendido).

amolador [ah-mo-lah-dor'], *m.* 1. Grinder, whetter. 2. *(coll.)* Unskillful couchman. 3. An unskillful artist.

amoladura [ah-mo-lah-doo'-rah], *f.* The act of whetting or grinding. **Amoladruas**, the small sand which falls from the whetstone at the time of whetting.

amolar [ah-mo-lar'], *va.* To whet, grind, or sharpen an edged tool by attrition. To upset, to annoy, to pester, to damage, ruin. *-vr. (Cono Sur, Mex.)* To get cross (enfadarse).

amoldador, ra [ah-mol-dah-dor, rah], *m. & f.* A moulder: one who moulds.

amoldar [ahmol-dar'], *va.* 1. To cast in a mould, to fashion, to figure. **Amoldar las agujas**, to polish needles. 2. *(Met.)* To adjust according to reason, to bring one to his duty. 3. *(Obs.)* To brand or mark cattle. *-vr.* To adapt oneself.

amole [ah-mo'-lay], *m.* Soap-root. *(Mex.)* Chlorogalum.

amollar [ah-mol-lyar'], *va.* 1. *(Naut.)* To ease off. 2. To play an inferior card to a winning one.

amolletado, da [ah-mol-lyay-tah'-do, dah], *a.* Having the shape of a loaf of bread.

amomo [ah-mo'-mo], *m. (Bot.)* Grain of paradise.

amonarse [ah-mo-nahr-say], *vr.* To get tight.

amondongado, da [ah-mon-don-gah'-do, dah], *a. (coll.)* Sallow, coarse, stout. **Mujer amondongada**, a coarse-featured stout woman.

amonedación [ah-mo-nay-dah-the-on], *f.* Coining, minting.

amonedar [ah-mo-nay-dar'], *va.* To coin.

amonestación [ah-mo-nes-tah-the-on'], *f.* 1. Advice, admonition, warning. 2. Publication of marriage banns. **Correr las amonestaciones**, to publish the banns of marriage.

amonestador, ra [ah-mo-nes-tah-dor'-rah], *m. & f.* A monitor, an admonisher.

amonestar [ah-mo-nes-tar'], *va.* 1. To advise, to admonish; to correct. 2. To publish banns of marriage, or of ordination.

amoniacal [ah-mo-ne-ah-cahl'], *a.* Ammoniacal.

amoníaco [ah-mo-nee'-ah-co], *m.* 1. Ammonia, NH3. 2. Ammoniac, a gumresin.

amonio [ah-mo'-ne-o], *m. (Chem.)* Ammonium.

amonita [ah-mo-nee'-tah], *f.* 1. Ammonite, a fossil mollusk. 2. *m.* Ammonite, tribe.

amontarse [ah-mon-tar'-say], *vr.* To flee or take to the mountains.

amontillado [ah-mon-teel-lyah-do], *m.* (pale dry sherry).

amontonador, ra [ah-mon-to-nah-dor', rah], *m. & f.* Heaper, accumulator.

amontonadamente [ah-mon-to-nah-dah-mayn-tay], *adv.* In heaps.

amontonado [ah-mon-to-naah-do], *a.* heaped, piled up; **Viven amontonados**, they live on top of each other.

amontonamiento [ah-mon-to-nah-me-en'-to], *m.* The act of heaping, accumulating, hoarding, gathering; lodgment.

amontonar [ah-mon-to-nar'], *va.* 1. To heap or throw things together without order or choice; to accumulate, to gather, to hoard, to lay up. **Vive amontonando fichas**, he´s been collecting data in large quantities. 2. *(Pict.)* To group a crowd of figures in a painting. *-vr. (coll.)* To fly into a passion; to grow angry or vexed, and not listen to reason, to pile up, to accumulate. To go up in smoke. *(And)* To revert to scrub

(terreno). **La gente se amontonó en la salida**, people crowded into the exit.

amor [ah-mor'], *m.* 1. Tenderness, affection, love, fancy. 2. The object of love. 3. A word of endearment, **amor mío or mis amores**, my love. **Por amor de Dios**, for God's sake. **Amor de hortelano**, *(Bot.)* goose-grass. **Al amor de la lumbre**, close to the fire. **Amor propio**, self-love; conceitedness. *-m. & f. pl.* 1. gallantry. 2. Amours. **De mil amores**, *adv.* with all my heart.

amoral [ah-mo-ral'], *a.* Amoral, without a sense of moral responsibility.

amoralidad [ah-mo-rah-le-dahd], *f.* Amorality.

amoratado, da [ah-mo-rah-tah'-do, dah], *a.* Livid, purple, purplish. **Ojo amoratado**, black eye.

amoratarse [ah-mo-rah-tahr-say], *vr. (LAm.)* To turn purple.

amorcillo [ah-mor-theel'-lyo], *m. dim.* Slight love, kindness.

amordazar [ah-mor-dah-thar'], *va.* 1. To gag. *(Naut.)* to fasten with bitts. 2. *(Met.)* To deprive of the liberty of speaking or writing.

amores, or **Amores mil** [ah-mo'-res], *m. (Bot.)* Red valerian.

amorfo, fa [ah-mor'-fo, fah], *a.* Amorphous, without definite shape.

amorgado, da [ah-mor-gah'-do, dah], *a.* Stupefied from eating the husks of pressed olives.

amoricones [ah-mo-re-co'-nes], *m. pl. (coll.)* Looks, gestures, and actions, expressive of love and fondness.

amorío [ah-mo-ree'-o], *m. (coll.)* Friendship, love affair, romance. *V.* ENAMORAMIENTO.

amoriscado, da [ah-mo-ris-cah'-do, dah], *a.* Resembling the Moors.

amormado, da [ah-mor-mah'-do, dah], *a.* Applied to horses having the glanders.

amorochado [ah-mo-ro-chah-do], *a. (LAm.) V.* MOROCHO.

amorosamente [ah-mo-ro-sah-men'-tay], *adv.* Lovingly.

amoroso, sa [ah-mo-ro'-so, sah], *a.* 1. Affectionate, kind, loving. **En tono amoroso**, in an affectionate tone. 2. Pleasing. 3. Gentle, mild, serene. **La tarde está amorosa**, it is a charming evening. 4. Tractable, easy.

amorrar [ah-mor-rar'], *vn. (coll.)* 1. To hold down the head; to muse. 2. To remain silent with downcast looks. 3. *(Naut.)* To pitch.

amortajar [ah-mor-tah-har'], *va.* To shroud a corpse.

amortecer [ah-mor-tay-therr'], *va. V.* AMORTIGUAR. *-vr.* To faint, to be in a swoon.

amortecimiento [ah-mor-tay-the-me-en'-to], *m.* Swoon, fainting. **(Yo me amortezco**, from **Amortecerse.** *V.* ABORRECER)

amortiguación, *f.* **amortiguamiento**, *m.* [ah-mor-te-goo-ah-the-on', ah-mor-te-goo-ah-me-en'-to] 1. Deadening, absorption. 2. Softening, toning down.

amortiguador, ra [ah-mor-te-goo-ah-dor', rah], *a.* Cushioning, absorbing. *-m.* Bumper. **Amortiguador de golpes**, Shock absorber. **Amortiguador de luz**, Dimmer. **Amortiguador de sonido**, Muffler, silencer.

amortiguamiento [ah-mor-te-goo-ah-me-ayn-to], *m.* Deadening; muffling, cushioning.

amortiguar [ah-mor-te-goo-ar'], *va.* 1. To cushion, to deaden, to absorb. 2. To tone down, to lessen. 3. To soften. *-vr. (Cono Sur) (Bot.)* To wither.

amortizable [ah-mor-te-thah'-blay], *a.* Amortizable.

amortización [ah-mor-te-thah-the-on'], *f.* Amortization, paying off.

amortizar [ah-mor-te-thar'], *va.* 1. To amortize, to pay back. 2. To write off, to depreciate. 3. To recuperate, to regain. *-vn.* To depreciate, to decrease in value.

amoscar [ah-mos-car'], *va.* To flap flies. *-vr.* 1. To shake off the flies. 2. To become irritated.

amosquilado, da [ah-mos-ke-lah'-do, dah], *a.* Applied to cattle when tormented with flies.

amostachado [ah-mos-tah-cha'-do], *a.* Wearing mustaches.

amostazar [ah-mostah-thar'], *va. (coll.)* To exasperate, to provoke. *-vr.* to fly into a violent passion; to be vexed.

amotinadamente [ah-mo-te-nah-dah-men'-tay], *adv.* Mutinouly.

amotinado, da [ah-mo-te-nah'-do, dah], *a.* Mutinous, rebellious. *-pp.* of AMOTINAR.

amotinador, ra [ah-mo-te-nah-dor', rah], *m. & f.* Mutineer.

amotinamiento [ah-mo-te-nah-me-en'-to], *m.* The act of stirring up a sedition: mutiny.

amotinar [ah-mo-te-nar'], *va.* 1. To excite rebellion. 2. *(Met.)* To disorder the mind. *-vr.* To rise against authority.

amover [ah-mo-verr'], *va.* To remove, to dismiss from employment.

amovibilidad [ah-mo-ve-be-le-dahd'], *f.* The possibility of being removed, or revoked.

amovible [ah-mo-vee'-blay], *a.* Removable: a term applied to ecclesiastical livings.

ampac [am-pahk'], *m. (Bot.)* Champak, a tree of the East Indies, possessing an odor like styrax.

ampara [am-pah'-rah], *f.* 1. *(Law.)* Seizure of chattels or movable property. 2. *(Obs.)* V. AMPARO.

amparada [am-pah-rah'-dah], V. MINA.

amparador, ra [am-pah-rah-dor', rah], *m.* Protector; shelter.

amparar [am-pah-rar'], *va.* 1. To shelter, to protect, to help, to support, to assist. **Amparar a los pobres,** to help the poor. 2. *(Law. Prov.)* To make a seizure of chattels or movable property; to sequestrate. **Amparar en la posesión,** *(Law.)* to maintain in possession. *-vr.* 1. To claim or enjoy protection. 2. To preserve; to recover. 3. To avail oneself of. **Ampararse de,** to seek the protection of.

amparo [am-pah'-ro], *m.* 1. Favor, aid, protection, sanction, support, countenance. 2. Guardship, refuge, asylum. 3. *(Obs.)* Brenstwork, parapet.

ampáyar [am-pah-yahr], *m. (LAm.)* Referee, umpire.

ampe [am-pay], *interj. (And)* please!

ampelita [am-pay-lee'-tah], *f.* Cannelcoal.

ampelografía [am-pay-lo-grah-fee'-ah], *f. (Agri.)* Ampelography, a description of the wine.

amperaje [am-pay-rah'-hay], *m. (Elec.)* Amperage.

amperímetro [am-pay-ree'-may-tro], *m. (Elec.)* Ammeter.

amperio [am-pay-re-o], *m.* Ampère, amp.

amplectivo, va [am-plec-tee'-vo, vah], *a.* Amplective, embracing other organs (of plants.).

ampliable [am-ple-ah-blay], *a.* Expandable *(Comp.).*

ampliación [am-ple-ah-teh-on'], *f.* enlargement; the act of enlarging.

ampliado [am-ple-ah-do], *m.* (LAm Pol) General meeting.

ampliador, ra [am-ple-ah-dor', rah], *m. & f.* Amplifier.

ampliamente [am-ple-ah-men'-tay], *adv.* Largely, copiously, fully.

ampliar [am-ple-ar'], *va.* To amplify, to enlarge.

ampliativo, va [am-ple-ah-tee'-vo, vah], *a.* Amplifying, having the power of enlarging.

amplificación [am-ple-fe-cah-the-on'], *f.* 1. Enlargement. 2. *(Rhet.)* Amplification.

amplificador [am-ple-fe-cah-dor'], *m.* Amplifier, loudspeaker.

amplificar [am-ple-fe-car'], *va.* 1. To amplify, to enlarge, to extend. 2. To use the figure of speech termed **amplification.**

amplio, ia [ahm'-ple-o, ah], *a.* Ample, extensive; large; handsome; absolute.

amplitud [am-ple-tood'], *f.* 1. Extend, greatness, largeness. 2. *(Naut.)* **Amplitud magnética,** magnetic amplitude. 3. *(Astr.)* Amplitude, an arch of the horizon intercepted between the true east and west point thereof, and the centre of the sun or star at their rising or setting. 4. Absoluteness.

amplo, la [ahm'-plo, plah], *(Obs.)* V. AMPLIO.

ampo [am-po], *m.* Whiteness. **Blanco como el ampo de la nieve,** white as the driven snow. V. LAMPO.

ampolla [am-pol'-lyah], *f.* 1. A blister on the skin. 2. Avial, a cruet. 3. A small bubble of water.

ampollar [am-pol-lyar'], *va.* 1. To blister. 2. To make hollow, to excavate. *-vr.* To rise in bubbles by the force of the wind.

ampolleta [am-pol-lyay'-tah], *f. dim.* 1. A small vial: a cruet. 2. An hourglass. 3. *(Naut.)* Watch-glass.

ampón [am-pon], *a.* Bulky.

amprar [am-prar'], *vn. (Prov.)* To borrow.

ampulosamente [am-poo-lo-sah-mayn-tay], *adv.* bombastically, pompously.

ampulosidad [am-poo-lo-see-dahd], *f.* bombast.

ampuloso, sa [am-poo-lo'-so, sah], *a.* Pompous, bombastic.

amputación [am-poo-tah-the-on'], *f.* Amputation.

amputar [am-poo-tar'], *va.* To amputate, or to cut off a limb.

amuchachado, da [ah-moo-chah-chah'-do, dah], *a.* Boyish, childish.

amuchar [ah-moo-chahr], *va. (And. Cono Sur)* To increase.

amuchigar [ah-moo-chee-goo-ar'], *vn. (Obs.)* To augment, to multiply.

amueblado, da [ah-moo-ay-blah-do], *a & f.* Furnished, hotel.

amueblar [ah-moo-ay-blar'], *va.* To furnish. **(Yo amueblo, amueble,** *etc.,* from **Amoblar.** *v.* ACORDAR).

amuermar [ah-moo-ayr-mahr], *va.* To bore. *-vr.* To feel sleepy. To vegetate, rot.

amugamiento [ah-moo-gah-me-en'-to], *m.* V. AMOJONAMIENTO.

amugronador, ra [ah-moo-gro-nah-dor', rah], *m. & f.* One who trains vine-shoots.

amugronar [ah-moo-gro-nar'], *va.* To lay the shoot of a vine under the earth in order that it may take root.

amuinar [ah-moo-e-nahr] *(Mex.)* 1. *va.* To annoy, irritate. 2. *-vr.* To get cross.

amujerado, da [ah-moo-hay-rah'-do, dah], *a.* Effeminate.

amujeramiento [ah-moo-hay-rah-me-en'-to], *m.* V. AFEMINACION.

amularse [ah-moo-lar'-say], *vr.* To become sterile (yeguas). *(Mex.)* To get stubborn (persona).

amulatado, da [ah-moo-lah-tah'-do, dah], *a.* Of a tawny complexion, resembling a mulatto.

amuleto [ah-moo-lay'-to], *m.* An amulet.

amunicionar [ah-moo-ne-the-o-nar'], *va.* To supply with ammunition.

amuñecado, da [ah-moo-nyay-cah'-do, dah], *a.* Puppet-like.

amura [ah-moo'-rah], *f.* 1. *(Naut.)* Tack of a sail. **Amura mayor, amura de trinquete,** the foretack. 2. *(Naut.)* A word of command. **Amura a babor,** aboard board tacks. **Amura a estribor,** aboard starboard-tacks. **Cambiar la amura,** to stand on the other tack.

amuradas [ah-moo-rah'-das], *f. pl. (Naut.)* The range of planks between the water-ways and the lower edge of the gun-ports of a ship of war.

amurallado [ah-moo-rahl-lyah-do], *a.* Walled city .

amurallar [ah-moo-rahl-lyar'], *va.* To wall. V. MURAR.

amurar [ah-moo-rar'], *va. (Naut.)* To haul the tack aboard.

amurcar [ah-moor-car'], *va.* To gore with the horns.

amurco [ah-moor'-co], *m.* Blow or stroke with the horns.

amurillar [ah-moo-reel-lyar'], *va. (Agri.)* To earth up.

amurrarse [ah-moor-rhar-say], *vr. (LAm.)* To get depressed, become sad.

amurriarse [ah-moo-rre-ahr-say], *vr. (Esp.)* To become sad.

amurruñarse [ah-moor-roo-nyahr-say] *vr. (Carib.)* To cuddle up.

amusco [ah-moos'-co], *a.* Brown.

amusgar [ah-moos-gar'], *va.* 1. To throw back the ears (caballos). **Amusgar las orejas,** *(Met. Obs.)* To listen. 2. To contract the eyes to see better. *-vr. (CAm.)* To feel ashamed.

Ana [ah'-nah], *f.* 1. An ell. 2. A kind of fox in the Indies. 3. An abbreviation used by medical men to signify equal parts. 4. Ann(e).

anabaina [ah-nah-bah'-e-nah], *f. (Bot.)* Euphorbiaceous plant of Brazil.

anabatista, anabaptista [ah-nah-bah-tees'-tah, ah-nah-bap-tees'-tah], *m.* Anabaptist.

anabás [ah-nah-bahs'], *m.* The climbing-fish. Anabas.

anabeno, na [ah-nah-bay'-no, nah], *a. (Zool.)* Tree-climbing.

anabólico [ah-nah-bo-le-co] *a*. Anabolic.

anacalifa [ah-nah-cah-lee'-fah], *m*. A poisonous animal of Madagascar.

anacalo, la [ah-nah-cah'-lo, lah], *m. & f. (Obs.)* A baker's servant.

anacarado, da [ah-nah-cah-rah'-do, dah], *a*. Of a pearly white color.

anacardel [ah-nah-car-del'], *m*. A kind of Madagascar serpent.

anacardina [ah-nah-car-dee'-nah], *f*. Confection made of anacardium or cashew-nut.

anacardo [ah-nah-car'-de-o], *m. (Bot.)* Cashew-tree.

anacatártico, ca [ah-nah-cah-tar'-te-co, cah], *a. & m. (Med.)* Emetic.

anaco [ah-nah'-co], *m*. Dress of Indian women in Peru and Bolivia; in Ecuador their hair-dressing.

anaconda [ah-nah-con'-dah], *f. (Zool.)* Anaconda.

anacoreta [ah-nah-co-ray-tah], *m*. An anchorite, a hermit.

anacorético, ca [ah-nah-co-ray'-te-co, cah], *a*. Anchoretical, belonging to a recluse.

anacosta [ah-nah-cos'-tah], *f*. A sort of woollen stuff.

anacreóntico, ca [ah-nah-cray-on'-te-co, cah], *a*. Anacreontic.

anacronía [ah-nah-cro-ne-ah], *f*. Timelessness.

anacrónico [ah-nah-cro-ne-co], *a*. Anachronistic, anachronic.

anacronismo [ah-nah-cro-nees'-mo], *m*. Anachronism, an error in computing time.

ánade [ah'-nah-day], *m. & f*. Duck.

anadear [ah-nah-day-ar'], *vn*. To waddle.

anadeja [ah-nah-day'-hah], *f. dim*. A duckling.

anadeo [ah-nah-day-o], *m*. Waddle, waddling.

anadeón [ah-nah-day-on], *m*. Duckling.

anadino, na [ah-nah-dee'-no, nah], *m. & f*. A young duck.

anadón [ah-nah-done'], *m*. Mallard.

anadoncillo [ah-nah-don-theel'-lyo], *m. dim*. A grown duckling.

anaerobio [ah-nah-ay-ro-be-o], *a*. Anaerobic.

anafalla, or **anafaya** [ah-nah-fahl'-lyah], *f*. A kind of thick corded silk.

anafe, or **anafre** [ah-nah'-fay], *m*. A portable furnace or stove.

anáfora [ah-nah'-fo-rah], *f*. Anaphora, a figure in rhetoric when several periods of a speech are begun with the same word.

anafrodisia [ah-nah-fro-dee'-se-ah], *f*. Anaphrodisia, loss of sexual appetite.

anáglifo [ah-nah'-glee-fo], *m*. Vase, vessel, or other work adorned with sculpture in basso relievo.

anagoge, *m*. **anagogía**, *f*. [ah-nah-go'-hay, ah-nah-go-hee'-ah]. Anagogices. the mystic sense of the Holy Scriptures.

anagógicamente [ah-nah-go'-he-cah-men-tay], *adv*. In an anagogical manner.

anagógico, ca [ah-nah-go'-he-co, cah], *a*. Anagogical.

anagrama [ah-nah-grah'-mah], *f*. An anagram, a transposition of the letters of a name.

anal, [ah-nahl] *a*. Anal, relating to the anus.

analcohólico [ah-nahl-co-le-co], *a*. Non-alcoholic, soft (bebida).

analéptico, ca [ah-nah-lep'-te-co, cah], *a. (Med.)* Analeptic, restorative, comforting.

analepsia [ah-nah-lep'-se-ah], *f. (Med.)* Analepsis.

anales [ah-nah'-les], *m. pl*. Annals or historical accounts related in order.

analfabeta [ah-nahl-fah-bay'-tah], *m. & f*. Illiterate person. -a. Illiterate, ignorant.

analfabetismo [ah-nahl-fah-bay-tees'-mo], *m*. Illiteracy.

analfabeto, ta [ah-nahl-fah-bay-to], *a*. illiterate.

analgesia [ah-nahl-hay-se-ah], *f*. Analgesia.

analgésico, ca [ah-nal-hay'-se-co, cah], *m. & a*. Analgesic.

análisis [ah-nah'-le-sis], *m. & f*. 1. Analysis. 2. *(Gram.)* Parsing. 3. *(Math.)* Algebraic solution. **Análisis de mercados**, marketing research, market research.

analista [ah-nah-lees'-tah], *m*. Annalist. **Analista de sistema**, systems analyst *(Comp.)*.**Analista programador** *(Comp.)*, programmer analyst.

analíticamente [ah-nah-lee'-te-cah-men-tay], *adv*. Analytically.

analítico, ca [ah-nah-lee'-te-co, cah], *a*. Analytical, method of resolving something into first principles.

analizable [ah-nah-le-thah'-blay], *a*. Capable of analysis, analyzable.

analizador [ah-nah-le-thah-dor'], *m*. Analyzer. **Analizador de instrucciones** *(Comp.)*, instruction analyser.

analizar [ah-nah-le-thar'], *va*. To analyze.

análogamente [ah-nah'-lo-gah-men-tay], *V*. ANALOGICAMENTE.

analogía [ah-nah-lo-hee'-ah], *f*. 1. Analogy, resemblance or relation which things bear to each other. 2. A part of grammar.

analógicamente [ah-nah-lo'-he-cah-men-tay], *adv*. Analogically.

analógico, ca, análogo, ga [ah-nah-lo'-he-co, cah, ah-nah'-lo-go, ah], *a*. Analogous.

analogismo [ah-nah-lo-hees'-mo], *m*. Analogism, an argument form the cause to the effect.

analogizar [ah-nah-lo-he-thar'], *va. (Lit. us.)* To explain by way of analogy.

análogo, ga [ah-nah'-lo-go, gah], *a*. Analogous, similar.

anama [ah-nah'-mah], *m*. A longicorn beetle of Java.

anamnesia [ah-nam-nay'-se-ah], *f*. Mnemonics, the art of remembering or acquiring memory.

anamorfosis [ah-nah-mor-fo'-sis], *f*. A deformed image drawn upon a curved or plane surface in such a way that when viewed from some particular point it appears perfectly regular and well-proportioned.

anana [ah-nah'-nah], *f*. or **Ananas** *(Bot.)* Ananas, pineapple. This is the European name; in America it is called *piña*.

anapelo [ah-nah-pay'-lo], *m. (Bot.)* Wolf's bane.

anaplastia [ah-nah-plas'-te-ah], *f*. Anaplasty, plastic surgery.

anaquel [ah-nah-kel'], *m*. Shelf or board on which any thing may be placed.

anaquelería [ah-nah-kay-lay-ree'-ah], *f*. Shelving, case of shelves.

anaranjado, da [ah-nah-ran-hah'-do, dah], *a*. Orange-colored.

anarca [ah-nahr-cah] *V*. ANARQUISTA.

anarcosindicalismo [ah-nahr-co-sen-de-cah-les-mo], *m*. Anarcho-syndicalism.

anarcosindicalista [ah-nahr-co-sen-de-cah-les-tah], *a. & m. & f*. Anarcho-syndical.

anarquía [ah-nar-kee'-ah], *f*. Anarchy.

anárquico, ca [ah-nar'-ke-co, cah], *a*. Anarchical, confused, without rule.

anarquismo [ah-nar-kes-mo], *m*. Anarchism.

anarquista [ah-nar-kees'-tah], *m*. Anarchist: enemy of organized government.

anarquizante [ah-nahr-ke-than-tay], *a*. Anarchic.

anarquizar [ah-nahr-ke-thahr], *va*. To produce anarchy in.

anasarca [ah-nah-sar'-cah], *f. (Med.)* Anasarca, general dropsy of the connective tissue.

anascote [ah-nas-co'-tay], *m*. A kind of woollen stuff like serge.

anastasia [ah-nas-tah'-se-ah], *f. V*. ARTEMISA.

anastomosis [ah-nas-to-mo'-sis], *f. (Anat.)* Anastomosis, the inosculation of blood-vessels. *(Bot.)* Junction of branches which should be separate.

anástrofe [ah-nahs'-tro-fay], *m. (Rhet.)* Anastrophe, an inversion of words.

anata [ah-nah'-tah], *f*. Annates, the first fruits or emoluments which a benefice or employ produces. **Media anata**. The annats of the half year.

anatema [ah-nah-tay'-mah], *m. & f.* 1. Anathema, excommunication. 2. *(Obs.)* A person anathematized or excommunicated.

anatematismo [ah-nah-tay-mah-tees'-mo], *m.* V. EXCOMUNION.

anatematizar [ah-nah-tay-mah-te-thar'], *va.* 1. To anathematize, to excommunicate. 2. To curse.

anatista [ah-nah-tees'-tah], *m.* Officer for the half-year annates.

anatomía [ah-nah-to-mee'-ah], *f.* 1. Anatomy. 2. *(Pict.)* Skeleton by which painters and sculptors study the structure of the human frame.

anatómicamente [ah-nah-to'-me-cah-men-tay], *adv.* Anatomically.

anatómico, ca [ah-nah-to'-me-co, cah], *a.* Anatomical.

anatomista [ah-nah-to-mees'-tah], *m.* Anatomist.

anatomizar [ah-nah-to-me-thar'], *va.* 1. To anatomize or dissect. 2. *(Pict.)* To draw, with the utmost exactness, the bones and muscles in statues and figures.

anca [ahn'-cah], *f.* The croup of a horse, haunch. **A ancas or a las ancas,** Behind. **A ancas or a las ancas de fulano,** with the assistance of somebody. *(fig.)* **No sufre ancas,** he can´t take a joke.

ancado [ah-cah'-do], *m. (Vet.)* A distemper, consisting in a painful contraction of the muscles.

ancestral [an-thays-trahl], *a.* Ancestral; *(fig.)* Ancient.

ancestro [an-thays-tro], *m. (LAm.)* 1. Ancestor. 2. Ancestry.

ancharguantes [an-chah-goo-ahn'-tes], *m.* A glove-stretcher.

anchamente [an-chah-men'-tay], *adv.* Widely, largely.

ancharia [an-chah'-re-ah], *f. (Obs.)* Among merchants and traders, the width of cloth.

ancheta [an-chay'-tah], *f.* 1. Venture. 2. Gain, profit; *(Mex.)* Bargain; profitable deal. 3. *(And Cono Sur)* Prattle, babble (panadería). 4. *(Carib.)* Joke.

anchicorto, ta [an-che-cor'-to, tah], *a.* That which is wider than it is long.

ancho, cha [ahn'-cho, chah], *a.* 1. Broad, large. **Ponerse muy ancho,** *(Met.)* to look big; to be elated with pride. **Vida ancha,** a loose life. **Recorrer un país a lo ancho y a lo largo,** to cross and recross a country. 2. *(fig.)* Liberal, broad-minded; fast (vida); **ancho de conciencia,** not overscrupulous. **Quedarse tan ancho,** to go on as if nothing had happened. 3. **Estar a sus anchas,** to be at one´s ease, to be comfortable.

ancho, anchor [ahn'-cho, an-chor'], *m.* V. ANCHURA.

anchoa, anchova [an-cho'-ah, an-cho'-vah], *f.* Anchovy.

anchoas [an-cho'-ahs], *f. pl. (Mex.)* Pin curls (in hair curling).

anchoveta [an-cho-vay-tah], *f. (And.)* Anchory (for fishermeal).

anchuelo, la [an-choo'-lo, lah], *a. dim.* Somewhat wide.

anchura [an-choo'-rah], *f.* 1. Width, largeness, extensiveness; latitude. 2. Laxity. **A mis anchuras,** or **a sus anchuras,** at large, at full liberty. **Vivo a mis anchuras,** I live just as I choose.

anchuroso, sa [an-choo-ro'-so, sah], *a.* Large, spacious, extensive, broad.

anchusa [an-choo'-sah], *f. (Bot.)* Alkanet. Anchusa.

ancianar [ah-the-ah-nar'], *vn. (Poetic.)* V. ENVEJECER.

ancianidad [an-the-ah-ne-dahd'], *f.* 1. Old age. 2. Antiquity.

anciano, na [an-the-ah'-no, nah], *a.* Old, elderly.

ancilar [an-the-lahr'], *a.* Ancillary.

ancla [an'-clah], *f.* Anchor. **Echar ancla,** to cast anchor, to anchor. **Levar ancla,** to weigh anchor. **Zafar el ancla para dar fondo,** to clear the anchor for coming to. **El ancla viene al bajel,** the anchor comes home. **El ancla ha soltado el fondo,** the anchor is a-trip. **Pescar un ancla,** to drag for an anchor. **Alotar las anclas,** to stow the anchors. **Arganeo de ancla,** an anchoring. **Caña del ancla,** the shank of the anchor. **Cepa del ancla,** the anchor-stock. **Cruz del ancla,** the crown of the anchor. **Orejas del ancla.** the flukes of the anchor. **Uñas del ancla,** the anchor arms. **Pico del ancla,** the bill of the anchor. **Al ancla or anclado,** at anchor. **Ancla de**

esperanza, sheet-anchor. **Ancla del ajuste** or *de uso,* the best bower-anchor. **Ancla sencilla** or the leva, the small bower-anchor. **Ancla del creciente,** the flood-anchor. **Ancla del menguante,** the ebb-anchor. **Ancla de la mar hacia fuera,** sea-anchor. **Ancla de la tierra or playa,** shore-anchor. **Anclas de servidumbre.** bower-anchors.

ancladero [an-clah-day'-ro], *m. (Naut.)* Anchorage, anchoring-place.

anclaje [an-clah'-hay], *m.* 1. The act of casting anchor. 2. Anchoring-ground. **Derecho de anclaje,** anchorage.

anclar [an-clar'], *vn.* To anchor.

anclote [an-clo'-tay], *m.* Stream-anchor, grapple, kedge.

anclotillo [an-clo-teel'-lyo], *m.* Kedge anchor.

ancón, *m.* anconada, *f.* [an-cone', an-co-nah'-dah]. An open road, a bay. *(And. Mex.)* Corner.

áncora [ahn'-co-rah], *V.* ANCLA.

ancoraje [an-co-rah'-hay], *m.* V. ANCLAJE.

ancorar [an-co-rar'], *V.* ANCLAR.

ancorca [an-cor'-cah], *f.* A yellow ochre.

ancorel [an-co-rel'], *m.* A large stone used by fishermen to secure their nets.

ancorería [an-co-ray-ree'-ah], *f.* Anchor-forge.

ancorero [an-co-ray'-ro], *m.* Anchor-smith.

ancusa [an-coo'-sah], *f. (Bot.)* V. ANCHUSA. **Ancusa oficinal,** common alkanet. **Lengua de buey.**

¡anda! [an-dar'], *int.* Well, never mind. **¡Anda!** Get off the way. **¡Anda, hijo!** Come along, child!

andada [an-dah'-dah], *f.* 1. Track, trail, pathway. 2. A thin, hard-baked cake. **Andadas,** the traces of game on the ground. **Volver a las andadas,** to relapse back into some vice or bad habit.

andaderas [an-dah-day'-ras], *f. pl.* Gocarts, baby-walker.

andadero, ra [an-dah-day'-ro, rah], *a.* Of easy access: applied to the ground.

andado [an-dah'-do], *m.* Stepchild. V. ALNADO.

andado, da [an-dah'-do, dah], *a.* 1. Beaten: applied to a path. 2. Worse for use, threadbare. 3. Customary. *-pp.* of ANDAR.

andador, ra [an-dah-dor', rah], *m. & f.* 1. A good walker. **Es andador,** he´s a good walker. 2. Messenger of a court. 3. Wanderer (andarín). 5. Alley or small walk in a garden (senda). 6. *(Mex.)* Prostitute, streetwalker.

andadura [an-dah-doo'-rah], *f.* 1. Gait; pacing. 2. Amble. 3. Advance; **comenzar nuevas andaduras,** to start again.

andalia [an-dah'-le-ah], *f. (Obs.)* Sandal. V. SANDALIA.

andalón [an-dah-lon], *a. (Mex.)* Well-paced, long-striding (caballo).

andaluz, za [an-da-looth', thah], *a.* Andalusian.

andaluzada [an-dah-loo-thah'-dah], *f.* 1. Bullying, boasting, rodomontade. 2. Exaggeration.

andamiada [an-dah-me-ah'-dah], *f.* Scaffolding.

andamiaje [an-dah-me-ah'-hay], *m.* Scaffolding.

andamio [an-dah'-me-o], *m.* 1. Scaffold. 2. *(Obs.)* Platform of a rampart. 3. *(Naut.)* Gang Board.

andana [an-dah'-nah], *f.* 1. Row, line. 2. *(Naut.)* **Andana de los cañones de un costado,** a tier of guns. 3. *(Naut.)* **Andana de rizos,** the reefs in the sails of ships. 4. **Andana de cuartos,** a suite of apartments. 5. A tier. **Llamarse andana,** not to fulfil a promise.

andanada [an-dah-nah'-dah], *f.* 1. Barrage. 2. Broadside. 3. Tirade, severe reprimand. **Andanada verbal,** verbal broadside. 4. Layer, row (de ladrillos etc.).

andaniño [an-dah-nee'-nyo], *m.* A kind of go-cart in which children learn to walk. V. POLLERA.

andante [an-dahn'-tay], *m. (Mus.)* Andante.

andantesco, ca [an-dan-tes'-co, cah], *a.* Belonging to knighthood, or knight-errants.

andantino [an-dan-tee'-no], *m. (Mus.)* Andantino.

andanza [an-dahn'-thah], *f. (Obs.)* Occurrence, event, fortune. **Buena or mala andanza,** good or bad fortune.

andar [an-dar'], *va.* 1. To walk, to come, or to move along. 2. To act, to behave, to transact. 3. To elapse. 4. To act:

applied to machine. 5. To be. **Andar en cuerpo,** to go out without a coat. **Andar por decir** or **por hacer una cosa,** to be determined to say or do a thing. **Andar a caza de gangas,** to waste one's time in fruitless pursuits. **Andar en carnes or en cueros,** to go stark naked. **Andar de Ceca en Meca,** to be roving and wandering about. **Todo se andará,** everything will be looked into. **Es preciso andar con el tiempo,** it is necessary to conform to the times. **Andar en dares y tomares** or **en dimes y diretes,** to dispute and quarrel. **Andar a sombra de tejado,** to hide, to skulk. **Andar a trompis.** to come to blows. **Andar en buena vela.** *(Naut.)* To keep the sails full. **Andar todo,** *(Naut.)* to put up the helm. **A mejor andar,** at best, at most. **A peor andar,** at worst. **A más andar,** in full speed. **Andar el mundo al revés,** to reverse the order of nature, to do something contrary to the manner it ought to be. **No andar en contemplaciones,** not to spare a person; to have recourse to hard measures. **El poco andar del barco,** *(Naut.)* the slow way of the vessel. **Andando el tiempo,** in the lapse of time. **Anden y ténganse,** fast and loose. **Andar de nones,** to be idle. **Andar con mosca,** to fly into a passion. **Mal me andarán las manos,** if nothing prevents me, I will do it. **Andar a derechas,** to act honestly. **Andársele a uno la cabeza,** to have vertigo, to become dizzy. **Andarse en flores,** to decline entering into a debate.

andar [an-dahr] *m.* To walk.

andaraje [an-dah-rah'-hay], *m.* The wheel of a well.

andaribel [an-dah-re-bel'], *m.* *(Naut.)* A light rope improvised to lower or lift some object; a gantline.

andarica [an-dah-re-cah], *f.* Crab *(Prov.).*

andariego, ga [an-da-re-ay'-go, gah], *a.* Restless, of a roving disposition.

andarilla [an-dah-rel-lya], *f. (And. Mus.)* Type of flute.

andarín [an-dah-reen'], *m. (coll.)* A fast walker. **Andarines,** an Italian paste.

andario [an-dah-ree'-o], *m. (Orn.)* The white wagtail.

andarivel [an-dah-re-vayl], *m.* 1. *(Tec.)* Cableway, cable ferry; *(Cono Sur)* Rope, barrier. 2. *(And)* Adornments, trinkets (adornos).

andas [ahn'-das], *f. pl.* 1. A frame on which a person or most commonly an image is carried; a stretcher. 2. A bier with shafts, to be carried on men's shoulders.

ándele [an-day-lay], *interj. (Mex.)* Come on! (¡siga!); See what I mean! (¡ya ves!).

andén [an-den'], *m.* 1. A shelf. *V.* ANAQUEL. 2. A path for the horse round the draw-well or in a mill. 3. The sidewalk by a road or on a dock. 4. The platform of a railway station.

andero [an-day'-ro], *m.* One who carries the shafts of a bier on his shoulders.

Andes [an-days], *m. & pl.* Andes.

andilú [an-de-loo'], *m.* A burnishing stick used by shoemakers.

andinismo [an-de-nes-mo], *m. (LAm.)* Mountaineering, mountain climbing; **hacer andinismo,** to go mountaineering.

andinista [an-de-nes-tah], *m. & f. (LAm.)* Mountaineer, climber.

andino [an-de-no], *a.* Andean, of the Andes.

andito [an'-de-to], *m.* A gallery which surrounds the whole or a part of a building.

andoba [an-do-bah], *m.* Guy, bloke.

andola [an-do'-lah], *f.* An meaningless jocular expletive.

andolina, andorina, andarina [an-do-lee'-nah, an-do-ree'-nah, an-dah-ree'-nah], *f.* **Swallow.** *V.* GOLONDRINA.

andón [an-don], *a. (LAm.) V.* ANDADOR.

andonear [an-do-nay-ahr], *va. (Carib.)* To amble (persona).

andorga [an-dor'-gah], *f. (coll.)* Belly. **Llenar la andorga,** To eat much.

andorina [an-do-ree'-nah], *f. (Naut.)* A truss, swallow.

Andorra [an-dor'-rah], *f.* Andorra.

andorrear [an-dor-ray-ar'], *vn.* To go about.

andorrera [an-dor-ray'-rah], *f.* Street-walker.

andorrero [an-dor-ray'-ro], *m.* A person of a roving disposition; tramp.

andosco, ca [an-dos'-co, cah], *a.* Two years old; applied to sheep.

andrajo [an-drah'-ho], *m.* 1. Rag, tatter. **Estar hecho un andrajo,** to be in rags. 2. *(Met.)* A despicable person. **Hacer andrajos,** to tear to rags.

andrajosamente [an-drah-ho-sah-men'-tay], *adv.* Raggedly.

andrajoso, sa [an-drah-ho'-so, sah], *a.* Ragged, dressed in tatters.

andriana [an-dree-ah'-nah], *f.* A kind of gown formerly worn by women.

andrina [an-dree'-nah], *f.* A sloe. *V.* ENDRINA.

andrino [an-dree'-no], *m. (Bot.)* Sloetree, blackthorn.

andrógeno [an-dro'-hay-no], *m.* Androgen.

andrógino [an-dro'-he-no], *m.* Hermaphrodite, androgynus, androgyne.

androide [an-dro-e-day], *m.* Android.

andrómina [an-dro'-me-nah], *f. (coll.)* Trick, fraud, artifice.

androsemo [an-dro-say'-mo], *m. (Bot.)* Parkleaves. *V.* TODABUENA.

androtomia [an-dro-to-mee'-ah], *f.* Dissection of human bodies.

andularios [an-doo-lah'-re-os], *m. pl. (coll.)* A long and wide gown.

andullo [an-dool'-lyo], *m.* A long. rolled leaf of tobacco *(Cuban).*

andurriales [an-door-re-ah'-les], *m. pl.* By-roads, retired places.

aneaje [ah-nay-ah'-hay], *m.* Alnage, ell measure.

anear [ah-nay-ar'], *va.* 1. To measure by ells. 2. *(Prov. Sant.)* To rock in a cradle.

aneblar [ah-nay-blar'], *va.* To cloud, to darken, to obscure. -*vr.* To get misty, get cloudy.

anécdota [ah-nee'-do-tah], *f.* Anecdote.

anecdotario [ah-nayc-do-tah-re-o], *m.* Collection of stories.

anecdótico [ah-nayc-do-te-co], *a.* Anecdotal; **contenido anecdótico,** story content.

anega [ah-nay-gah], *f. (Cono Sur) V.* FANEGA.

anegación [ah-nay-gah-the-on'], *f.* Overflowing, inundation.

anegadizo, za [ah-nay-gah-dee'-tho, thah], *a.* Liable to be overflowed.

anegado, da [ah-nay-gah'-do, dah], *a.* Overflowed. **Navío anegado,** *(Naut.)* A water-logged ship. -*pp.* of ANEGAR.

anegadizo [ah-nay-gah-de-tho], *a.* Subject to flooding, frequently flooded (tierra).

anegamiento [ah-nay-gah-me-en'-to], *m. (Obs.) V.* ANEGACION.

anegar [ah-nay-gar'], *va.* To inundate, to submerge. *(fig.)* Destroy. -*vr.* To be inundated. **Anegarse en llanto,** to dissolve into tears.

anegociado, da [ah-nay-go-the-ah'-do, dah], *a. (Obs.)* Overwhelmed with business.

anejo, ja [ah-nay'-ho, hah], *a.* Annexed, joined. *V.* ANEXO, XA.

anejo [ah-nay'-ho], *m.* A benefice or church depending on another as its principal or head.

anélido [ah-nay'-le-do], *m. (Zool.)* Annelid, a many-jointed worm.

anemia [ah-nay'-me-ah], *f. (Med.)* Anaemia, diminution of red corpuscles in the blood.

anémico, ca [ah-nay'-me-co, cah], *a.* Anaemic, affected with anaemia.

anemografía [ah-nay-mo-grah-fee'-ah], *f.* Anemography, the description of the winds.

anemometría [ah-nay-mo-may-tree'-ah], *f.* Anemometry, measuring the force of the winds.

anemómetro [ah-nay-mo'-may-tro], *m.* Anemometer, an instrument to measure the force of the wind.

anémona or **Anémone** [ah-nay'-mo-nay], *f. (Bot.)* Anemone or windflower. Anemone.

anemoscopio [ah-nay-mos-co'-pe-o], *m.* Anemoscope, a machine to show the changes of the wind.

anepígrafo, fa [ah-nay-pee'-grah-fo, fah], *a.* Without title or inscription. *V.* MEDALLA.

anequín (A), or **de anequín** [ah-nay-keen'], *adv.* So much a head: applied to the shearing of sheep.

aneroide [ah-nay-ro'-e-day], *a. & m.* Aneroid, without fluid; barometer in clock-form.

anestesia [ah-nes-tay'-se-ah], *f.* Anaesthesia.

anestesiar [ah-nes-tay-se-ar'], *va.* To anaesthetize.

anestésico, ca [ah-nes-tay'-se-co, cah], *a.* Anesthetic, producing insensibility. *-m.* Anesthetic.

anestesista [ah-nays-tay-ses-tah], *f. & m.* Anaesthetic.

aneurisma [ah-nay-oo-rees'-mah], *m. & f. (Med.)* Aneurism, a disease of the arteries and of the heart.

anexar [ah-nees-sar'], *va.* To annex, to join, to unite.

anexidades [ah-nees-se-dah'-des], *f.* . Annexes, belongings.

anexión [ah-necs-se-on'], *f.* Annexion, union; annexation.

anexionar [ah-nec-se-o-nahr], *va.* To annex.

anexionista [an-nec-se-o-nees'-tah], *m.* Annexationist.

anexo, xa [ah-nec-so, sah], *a. m. (Arquit.)* Annexe, outbuilding. *V.* ANEJO, JA.

anfeta [an-fay-tah], *f. V.* ANFETAMINAS.

anfetaminas [an--fay-tah-me-nahs], *f. & pl.* Amphetamines.

anfibio, bia [an-fee'-be-o, ah], *a.* Amphibious.

anfibología [an-fe-bo-lo-hee'-ah], *f.* Amphibology, words or sentences of a double or doubtful meaning.

anfibológicamente [an-fe-bo-lo'-he-cah-men-tay], *adv.* Amphibologically.

anfibológico, ca [an-fe-bo-lo'-he-co, cah], *a.* Amphibological, doubtful.

anfisbena, anfisibena [an-fis-bay'-nah, an-fe-se-bay'-nah], *f.* Amphisb+na, an amphibious serpent of America.

anfiscios [an-fees'-the-os], *m. pl.* Amphiscii, people of the torrid zone, whose shadows at different times fall north and south.

anfiteatro [an-fe-tay-ah'-tro], *m.* Amphitheater, arena. *(Theat.)* Dress circle.

anfitrión [an-fe-tre-on'], *m. (Met.)* Host, he who does the honors at the table before invited company.

anfitriota [an-fe-tree-o-tah], *f.* Hostess.

anfitrite [an-fe-tree'-tay], *f.* Amphitrite. *(Poet. and Zool.)*

ánfora [ahn'-fo-rah], *f.* 1. Amphora, ancient vase. 2. *(pl.)* Jars or cruets of silver to preserve consecrated oils. 3. Ancient name of the sign Aquarius. 4. The lower valve of certain fruits which opens on ripening. 5. Ancient Greek and Roman measure for liquids equivalent to about eight gallons.

anfractuosidad [an-frac-too-o-se-dahd'], *f.* Crookedness. *-f. pl. (Ant.)* Anfractuosities, convolutions of the brain or cerebrum.

anfractuoso, sa [an-frac-too-oh'-so, sah], *a.* Anfractuous, sinuous, unequal, rough, uneven.

angaria [an-gah'-re-ah], *f.* 1. Ancient servitude. 2. Forced delay in the sailing of a ship, for employ in public service.

angarillas [an-gah-reel'-lyas], *f. pl.* 1. Handbarrow. 2. Panniers. 3. Cruet stands. *V.* AGUADERAR.

angarillón [an-gah-reel-lyon'], *m.* A large wicker basket; a large handbarrow.

angaripola [an-gah-re-po'-lah], *f.* Calico. **Angaripolas,** Gaudy ornaments on clothes.

ángaro [ahn'-gah-ro], *m.* Fire or smoke, used as a signal.

angarrio [an-gahr-re-o], *a. (And. Carib.)* Terribly thin.

angas [an-gahs], **por angas o por mangas,** like it or not *(And.)*.

ángel [ahn'-hel], *m.* 1. Angel, a spiritual being. 2. A sort of fish much resembling a ray. **Manga de ángel,** sleeve of a coat ruffled or plaited. **Ángel custodio,** or **de la guarda,** guardian angel. **Ángel de guarda,** protector. **Ángel patudo,** nickname of a person rather malicious.

Ángeles [an-hay-lays], *m. & pl.* Los Angeles.

angélica [an-hay'-le-cah], *f. (Bot.)* Garden angelica. Angelica archangelica. **Angélica carlina,** *(Bot.)* Carline thistles. **Angélica palustre,** Wild angelica.

angelical, angélico, ca [an-hay-le-cal', an-hay'-le-co, cah], *a.* Angelical or angelic, heaven born.

angelicalmente [an-hay-le-cal-me-tay], *adv.* Angelically.

angelico, ito [an-hay-lee'-co, an-hay-lee'-to], *m. dim.* A little angel.

angelino, na [an-hay-le-no, nah], *a.* Of **Los Angeles. Los Angelinos,** the people of Los Angeles.

angelito [an-hay-le-to], *m.* Little angel; *(LAm.)* Dead child; *(Cono Sur)* Don´t play the innocent!; **¡no seas angelito!** *(Cono Sur)* Don't be silly!

angelón, angelonazo [an-hay-lone', an-hay-lo-nah'-tho], *m. aug.* Great angel. **Angelón de retablo,** nickname given to a person, commonly a child, disproportionately corpulent.

angelopolitano, na [an-hay-lo-po-le-tah-no, nah], *m. & f. (Mex.)* Of Puebla.

angelote [an-hay-lo'-tay], *m. aug.* 1. A large figure of an angel placed on altars. 2. A fat, good-natured child.

Ángelus [ahn'-hay-loos], *m.* The angelus, a midday prayer in the Roman Catholic Church.

angeo [an-hay'-o], *m.* A coarse sort of linen: upholsterer's canvas.

angina [an-hee'-nah], *f.* Tonsilitis, sore throat. **Angina de pecho,** angina Pectoris.

angiografía [an-he-o-grah-fee'-ah], *f.* Angiography, a description of vessels in the human body.

angiología [an-he-o-lo-he'-ah], *f.* Angiology, the doctrine of the vessels of the human body.

angiosperma [an-he-os-per'-mah], *a. (Bot.)* Angiospermous.

anglicanismo [an-gle-cah-nees'-mo], *m.* Anglicanism, the church religion in England.

anglicano, na [an-gle-cah'-no, nah], *a.* Anglican, belonging to England. **La Iglesia Anglicana,** the Anglican Church.

anglicismo [an-gle-thees'-mo], *m.* Anglicism.

anglicista [an-gle-thes-tah], 1. *a.* **Tendencia anglicista,** anglicising tendency. 2. *m. & f.* Anglicist.

angliparla [an-gle-pahr-lah], *f.* Spanglish *(hum.)*.

anglo, gla [ahn'-glo, ah], *a.* Anglian, English-speaking. *-m. & f.* English-map.

angloamericano, na [an-glo-ah-may-re-cah'-no, nah], *a.* Anglo-american.

anglófobo [an-glo-to-bo], 1. *a.* Anglophobe, anglophobic. 2. Anglophobe.

anglófono [an-glo-fo-no], *a , m& f.* English-speaking.

anglohablante, angloparlante [an-glo-ah-blahn-tay], *a., m. & f.* English-speaking.

anglomanía [an-glo-mah-nee'-ah], *f.* Anglomania, excessive enthusiasm for the English people and their belongings.

anglómano [an-glo'-mah-no], *m.* Anglomaniac, servile imitator of the English.

anglosajón, na [an-glo-sah-hone', nah], *a. & m.* Anglo-Saxon.

angora [an-go'-rah], *a.* The Angora cat or goat: long-haired creatures.

angorina [an-go-re-nah], *f.* Artificial angora.

angostamente [an-gos-tah-men'-tay], *adv.* Narrowly.

angostar [an-gos-tar'], *va.* To narrow, to contract. *-vr.* To narrow, to get narrow.

angosto, ta [an-gos'-to, tah], *a.* Narrow, close. **Venir angosto,** to fall short of one's expectations, ambition, or merit.

angostura [an-gos-too'-rah], *f.* 1. Narrowness. 2. A narrow pass.

angra [ahn'-grah], *f.* A small bay, a cove.

anguarina [an-goo-ah-ree'-nah], *f.* A loose coat hanging down to the knees.

anguila [an-gee'-lah], *f. (Zool.)* Eel. **Anguila de cabo,** *(Naut.)* a port rope with which the sailors were flogged on board the galleys. **Anguilas**, ways on which a ship slides when launching.

anguilazo [an-ge-lah'-tho], *m.* A stroke with a port-rope.

anguilero, ra [an-ge-lay'-ro, rah], *m. & f.* Basket or pannier for eels.

anguina [an-gee'-nah], *f. (Vet.)* The vein of the groins.

angula [an-goo'-lah], *f.* The brood of eels, elver, baby eel.

angulado, da [an-goo-lah'-do, dah], *a.* Having angles.

angular [an-goo-lar'], *a.* Angular. **Piedra angular**, the corner-stone.

angularmente [an-goo-lar-men'-tay], *adv.* With angles; in the form of an angle.

angulema [an-goo-lay'-mah], *f.* A sort of coarse linen manufactured at Angouleme of hemp or tow. *-pl. (coll.) V.* ZALAMERIAS.

ángulo [ahn'-goo-lo], *m.* Angle, corner; nook. **ángulo óptico**, the visual angle. **Ángulos de un picadero**, the corners of a riding-house. **ángulo recto**, right angle. **En ángulo**, at an angle. **Formar ángulo con**, to be at an angle to.

anguloso, sa [an-goo-lo'-so, sah], *a.* Angular, cornered.

angurria [an-goor-re-ah], *f. (And. Cono Sur)* Voracious hunger, greed, meanness, stinginess.

angurrimiento [an-goor-re-me-ayn-to], *a. (And. Cono Sur)* Greedy, mean.

angustia [an-goos'-te-ah], *f.* Anguish, affliction, pang; heartache, heaviness.

angustiadamente [an-goos-te-ah-dah-men'-tay], *adv.* Painfully.

angustiado, da [an-goos-te-ah'-do, dah], *a.* 1. Painful. 2. *(Met.)* Narrow-minded, miserable. *-pp.* of ANGUSTIAR.

angustiar [an-goos-te-ar'], *va.* To cause anguish, to afflict. *-vr.* To be distressed, to grieve.

angustiosamente [an-goos-te-o-sah-mayn-tay], *a.* In an anguished tone.

angustioso [an-goos-te-o-so], *a.* 1. Distressed, anguished; anxious. 2. Distressing, agonizing; heartbreaking.

angustura [an-goos-too'-rah], *f. (Bot.)* Angustura bark.

anha [ah-nah], *interj. (Cono Sur) V.* ANJÁ.

anhelación [an-ay-lah-the-on'], *f.* 1. Panting, difficulty of breathing. 2. *(fig.)* Longing, yearning.

anhelante [an-ay-lahn'-tay], *a.* Eager, avid, keenly desirous.

anhelar [an-ay-lar'], *vn.* 1. To breathe with difficulty. 2. To desire anxiously, to long, to covet. 3. To gape, to gasp. **Anhelar honores**, to aspire at honors.

anhélito [an-ay'-le-to], *m.* Difficult respiration.

anhelo [an-ay'-lo], *m.* A vehement desire; anxiousness, eagerness. **Anhelo de superación**, urge to do better.

anheloso, sa [an-ay-lo'-so, sah], *a.* Anxious, desirous. *(Med.)* Gasping, panting.

anhídrico, ca [an-ee'-dre-co, cah], *a. V.* ANHIDRO.

anhidrita [an-e-dree'-tah], *f.* Anhydrite, a rock, the base of which is sulphate of lime.

anhidro, dra [an-ee'-dro, drah], *a.* Anhydrous, lacking water.

anhinga [an-een'-gah], *f. (Orn.)* An aquatic bird of prey in Brazil, called the darter.

ani [ah-nee'], *m.* A pretty creeping bird indigenous to South America.

anidar [an-ee-dar'], *vn.* 1. To nestle, to make a nest. 2. *(Met.)* To dwell, to reside. 3. To cherish, to shelter. **andar anidando**, to prepare for lying in.

anieblar [ah-ne-ay-blar'], *va.* To darken, to obscure, to mystify.

aniego [ah-ne-ay-go], *m. (And. Cono Sur)*, *m. (Mex.)* Flood.

anilina [ah-ne-lee'-nah], *f. (Chem.)* Aniline.

anilla [ah-ne-lyah], *f.* Curtain ring (de cortina); small ring (anillito); cigar band (de puro).

anillado, da [ah-neel-lyah'-do, dah], *a.* Annulated, ringed. *-pl.* Annelids, worms whose bodies are a series of ringed segments.

anillar [ah-neel-lyar'], *va.* To form rings circles in work; used by cutlers.

anillejo, anillete [ah-neel-lyay'-ho, ah-neel-lyay'-tay], *m. dim.* A small ring.

anillo [ah-neel'-lyo], *m.* 1. A finger ring; circlet. **Anillo de compromiso**, engagement ring. 2. *(Naut.)* Hank or grommet. **Venir como anillo al dedo**, to come in the very nick of time. 3. *(Arch.)* Astragal.

ánima [ah'-ne-mah], *f.* 1. Soul. *V.* ALMA. 2. *(Mech.)* The bore of a gun. **Ánimas**, ringing of bells at sunset, in the old days. **A las ánimas me volví a casa**, at sunset I returned home.

animable [ah-ne-mah'-blay], *a.* Susceptible of animation.

animación [ah-ne-mah-the-on'], *f.* Animation, liveliness. **Campaña de animación social**, campaign of social awakening. **Había poca animación**, there wasn´t much life about it.

animadamente [ah-ne-mah-dah-mayn-tay], *adv.* In lively fashion, gaily; animatedly.

animado, da [ah-ne-mah'-do, dah], *a.* Manful, lively, gay; bustling, busy, animated; merry, in high spirits. *-pp.* of ANIMAR.

animador, ra [ah-ne-mah-dor', rah], *m. & f.* 1. One who animates or cheers. 2. Entertainer (cabaret); compère (presentador); hostess (presentadora).

animadversión [ah-ne-mad-ver-se-on'], *f.* Animadversion, remark, stricture.

animal [ah-ne-mal'], *m.* 1. Animal. 2. Animal; used in contempt. **El animal de Juan**, that beast of John.

animal [ah-ne-mah'], *a.* Animal, relating to an animal.

animalada [ah-ne-mah-lah-dah], *f.* 1. *(LAm.)* group of animals. 2. *(fig.)* Foolishness, stupidity (cualidad). **Hacer una animalada**, to do something silly.

animalaje [ah-ne-mah-lah-hay], *m. (Cono Sur)* Animals; herd of animals.

animalejo [ah-ne-mah-lay-ho], *m.* Odd-looking creature.

animalidad [ah-ne-mah-le-dahd], *f.* Animality; sensuality.

animalización [ah-ne-mah-le-thah-the-on'], *f.* Animalization; effect of making an animal.

animalizar [ah-ne-mah-le-thar'], *va.* To animalize. *-vr.* To grow brutish.

animalazo [ah-ne-mah-lah'-tho], *m. aug.* A large or big animal.

animalejo, ico, illo [ah-ne-mah-lay'-ho, lee'-co, leel'-lyo], *m. dim.* A small animal, animalcule.

animalón, animalote [ah-ne-mah-lone', ah-ne-mah-lo'-tay], *m. aug.* A large or big animal.

animalucho [ah-ne-mah-loo'-cho], *m.* An ugly, hideous animal.

animar [ah-ne-mar'], *va.* 1. To animate, to enliven, to comfort, to revive. **Animar a uno a hacer algo**, to encourage somebody to do something. 2. To incite, to excite. 3. To give power or vigor to inanimate things. *-vr.* To become more lively; to brighten up. **A ver si se animan**, we´ll wait and see if they do anything about it. **No me animo a hacerlo**, I can´t bring myself to do it.

anime, or **Goma Anime** [ah-nee'-may], *1. f.* A resin resembling myrrh. 2. *m. (Carib.)* Polyethylene.

animero [ah-ne-may'-ro], *m.* One who used to ask for charity for the souls in purgatory.

anímico [ah-ne-me-co], *a.* Mental, of mind; **Estado anímico**, state of mind.

anímita [ah-ne-me-tah], *f. (Cono Sur)* Roadside shrine.

ánimo [ah'-ne-mo], *m.* 1. Spirit. **Apaciguar los ánimos**, to calm people down. 2. Courage, valor, fortitude, manfulness; hardiness. **Dar ánimos a**, to encourage. 3. Mind, intention, meaning, will. **Con ánimos de**, with the intention of. **Tener ánimos para algo**, to be in the mood for something. 4. Thought, attention. **Hacer buen ánimo**, to bear up under adversities. *-int.* Come on!

animosamente [ah-ne-mo-sah-men'-tay], *adv.* In a spirited manner, courageously.

animosidad [ah-ne-mo-se-dahd'], *f.* Animosity, valor, courage; boldness.

animoso, sa [ah-ne-mo'-so, sah], *a.* Brave, spirited, courageous, gallant.

aniñadamente [ah-nee-nyah-dah-men'-tay], *adv.* In a childish, puerile manner.

aniñado, da [ah-nee-nyah'-do, dah], *a.* 1. Childish. 2. *(Cono Sur)* Spirited, lively. 3. *(Cono Sur)* Handsome (guapo).

aniñarse [ah-nee-nyar'-say], *vr.* To grow childish.

aniquilable [ah-ne-ke-lah-blay], *a.* Annihilable, destructible.

aniquilación [ah-ne-ke-lah-the-on'], *f.* Annihilation, extinction.

aniquilador, ra [ah-ne-ke-lah-dor'- rah], *m. & f.* A destroyer.

aniquilar [ah-ne-ke-lar'], *va.* To annihilate, to destroy, to overthow. *-vr.* To decline, to decay; to humble; to consume.

anís [ah-nees'], *m. (Bot.)* Anise. **Anises**, anise-seeds preserved in sugar. **Llegar a los anises**, to come the day after the feast. **Estar hecho un anis**, to be elegantly dressed.

anisado, da [ah-ne-sah'-do, dah], *a.* Applied to spirits tinctured with anise. *-pp* of ANISAR.

anisar [ah-ne-sar'], *va.* To tincture with anise.

aniseros [ah-ne-say-ros], *m. & pl. (And.)* **Entregar los aniseros**, to kick the bucket.

anisete [ah-ne-say'-tay], *m.* Anisette.

anisófilo, la [ah-ne-so'-fe-lo, lah], *a.* Anisophyllous, having unequal leaves.

anisol [ah-ne-sole'], *m.* A liquid substance isomeric with creasote.

anisómero, ra [ah-ne-so'-may-ro, rah], *a.* An isomeric, composed of unequal parts.

anivelar [ah-ne-vay-lahr], *va.* V. NIVELAR.

aniversaria, ria [ah-ne-ver-sah'-re-o, ah], *a.* Annual, yearly.

aniversario [ah-ne-ver-sah'-re-o], *m.* 1. Anniversary. **Aniversario de boda,** wedding anniversary.

¡anjá! [an-hah'], *int.* (Cuba) Well! bravo!

anjeo [an-hay-o], *m.* Anjou.

Ankara [an-kah-rah], *f.* Ankara.

ano [ah'-no], *m.* The anus.

anoche [ah-no'-chay], *adv.* Last night.

anochecedor, ra [ah-no-chay-thay-dor], *m. & f.* Late bird, person who keeps late hours.

anochecer [ah-no-chay-therr'], *vn.* To grow dark. **Anochecerle a uno en alguna parte**, to be benighted somewhere. **Al anochecer**, at nightfall. *-vr. (Poetic.)* to grow dark. **Yo amanecí en Veracruz, y anochecí en Acapulco, I** was in Vera0cruz at dawn, and in Acapulco at dusk.

anochecida [ah-no-chay-thee'-dah], *f.* Dusk, nightfall.

anodinar [ah-no-de-nar'], *va.* To administer anodyne medicines.

anodino, na [ah-no-dee'-no, nah], `a. (Med.)` Anodyne, allaying pain.

anodizar [ah-no-de-thar'], *va.* To anodize.

ánodo [ah'-no-do], *m. (Elec.)* Anode.

anomalía [ah-no-mah-lee'-ah], *f.* 1. Anomaly, deviation from rules. 2. *(Astr.)* Distance of a planet at its aphelion.

anómalo, la [ah-no'-mah-lo, lah], *a. (Gram.)* Anomalous.

anón [ah-none'], *m. (Bot.)* The custard apple-tree. Annona.

anona [ah-no'-nah], *f.* 1. Annona or custard-apple. In some parts it is called guanara. 2. Store of provisions. *V.* CHIRIMOYA.

anonadación [ah-no-nah-dah-the-on'], *f.* **Anonadamiento,** *m.* 1. Annihilation. 2. Self-contempt.

anonadar [ah-no-nah-dar'], *va.* 1. To annihilate. 2. *(Met.)* To diminish or lessen in a considerable degree. *vn.* To humble oneself to a low degree.

anónimamente [ah-no'-ne-mah-men-tay], *ad.* Anonymously.

anonimato [ah-no'-ne-mah-to], *m.* Anonimity. **Mantenerse en el anonimato**, to remain anonymous.

anónimo, ma [ah-no'-ne-mo, mah], *a.* Anonymous; nameless. **Guardar el anónimo**, to preserve one´s anonymity. Anonymous person, unknown person.

anorac [ah-no-rak], *m.* V. ANORAK.

anorexia [ah-no-ree'-se-ah], *f. (Med.)* Anorexia, loss of appetite.

anormal [ah-nor-mahl'], *a.* Abnormal; irregular, unusual. Mentally handicapped.

anormalidad [ah-nor-mah-le-dahd], *f.* Abnormality; irregularity; unusual nature.

anormalmente [ah-nor-mal-mayn-tay], *adv.* Abnormality.

anotación [ah-no-tah-the-on'], *f.* Annotation, note, notation.

anotador, ra [ah-no-tah-dor', rah], *m. & f.* 1.Commentator. 2. *m. (LAm.)* Scorecard.

anotar [ah-no-tar'], *va.* To write notes, to comment.

anoxia [ah-noe'-ce-ah], *f. (Med.)* Anoxia.

anquera [an-kay'-rah], *f. (Mex.)* A round covering for the hind quarter of a horse; semi-lunar tail-piece of a saddle.

anqueta [an-kay'-tah], **Estar de media anqueta**. to be incommodiously seated.

anquiboyuno, na [an-ke-bo-yoo'-no, nah], *a.* Having a croup like an ox; applied to horses and mules.

anquilosado [an-ke-lo-sah-do], *a. (fig.)* Stagnant; paralyzed.

anquilosamiento [an-ke-lo-sah-me-ayn-to], *m. (fig.)* Stagnation; paralysis.

anquilosar [an-ke-lo-sahr], 1. *va.* To paralyze. 2. *vn. (Aut. Mec.)* To seize up. 3. *-vr.* To decline; to become eroded.

anquilosis [an-ke-lo'-sis], *f. (Anat.)* Anchylosis, a stiff joint.

anquilostoma [an-ke-los-to-mah], *m.* Hookworm.

anquiseco, ca [an-ke-say'-co, cah], *a.* Lean crouped.

ansa [ahn'-sah], *f.* Commercial bond among the free cities of Germany.

ánsar [ahn'-sar], *m.* A goose. **Ánsar macho**, gander.

ansarería [an-sah-ray-ree'-ah], *f.* The place where geese are reared.

ansarero [an-sah-ray'-ro], *m.* A gooseherd.

ansarino, na [an-sah-ree'-no, nah], *a. (Poetic.)* Belonging to geese.

ansi [an-see'], *(Obs.) V.* Así.

ansia [ahn'-see-ah], *f.* Anxiety anguish, eagerness, ardent desire; longing, hankering; greediness.

ansiadamente [an-se-ah-dah-men'-tay], *adv.* Anxiously, earnestly.

ansiado [an-se-ah-do], *a.* Longed-for; **el momento tan ansiado**, the moment which we had so much longed for.

ansiar [an-se-ar'], *va.* To desire anxiously, to long, to hanker. **Ansiar por uno**, to be madly in love with somebody.

ansiedad [an-se-ay-dahd'], *f.* A state of anxiety. *V.* ANSIA.

ansina [an-see'-nah], *(Obs.) V.* Así.

ansiosamente [an-se-o-sah-men'-tay], *adv.* Anxiously, earnestly, ardently, eagerly, fervently; heartily.

ansiolítico [an-se-o-le-te-co], *a.* Sedative, tranquillizer.

ansioso, sa [an-se-oh'-so, sah], *a.* 1. Anxious, eager, greedy; hot. **Esperamos ansiosos**, we waited anxiously. 2. Attended with great uneasiness.

anta [ahn'-tah], *f.* An elk. *-pl. (Arch.)* Antes, pillars of a building.

antaceo [an-tah'-thay-o], *m. (Zool.)* A large fish of the family of sturgeons.

antagallas [an-tah-gahl'-lyas], *f. pl. (Naut.)* Spritsail, reef-bands.

antagónico, ca [an-tah-go'-ne-co, cah], *a.* Antagonistic; in opposition.

antagonismo [an-tah-go-nees'-mo], *m.* Antagonism, antipathy.

antagonista [an-tah-go-nees'-tah], *m.* 1. Antagonist, an opponent; competitor. 2. Opposer, foe, foeman.

antana [an-tah'-nah], **Llamarse antana**, to contradict, to retract.

antañazo [an-tah-nyah'-tho], *adv.* A long time since.

antaño [an-tah'-nyo], *adv.* 1. Last year. **En los nidos de antaño no hay pájaros hogaño,** time must be seized by the forelock. *(Lit.)* There are no birds in last year's nest. 2. Long ago.

antañón [an-ta-nye-on], *a.* Ancient, very old.

antañoso [an-tah-nyo-so], *a. (LAm.)* Ancient, very old.

antara [an-tah-rah], *f. (And.)* Pan pipes.
antártico, ca [an-tar'-te-co, cah], *a.* Antarctic.
Antártida [an-tahr-te-dah], *f.* Antartica.
ante [ahn'-tay], *m.* 1. Buckskin, a dressed buck or buffalo skin. 2. An elk. **Piel de ante,** suede. **Guantes de ante,** suede gloves.
ante [ahn'-tay], *prep.* Before. **Ante mí,** before me, in my presence. **Ante todas cosas or ante todo,** before all things, above all.
ante [an-tay], *pref.* Ante.
anteado, da [an-tay-ah'-do, dah], *a.* Buff-colored, of a pale-yellow color.
anteanoche [an-tay-ah-no'-chay], *adv.* The night before last.
anteanteanoche [an-tay-an-tay-ah-no'-chay], *adv.* Three nights ago.
anteanteayer [an-tay-an-tay-ah-yerr'], *adv.* Three days ago.
anteantier [an-tay-an-te-err'], *adv. (Obs.) V.* ANTEANTEAYER.
anteayer [an-tay-ah-yerr'], *adv.* The day before yesterday.
antebrazo [an-tay-brah'-tho], *m.* The fore-arm.
antecama [an-tay-cah'-mah], *f.* A carpet laid in front of a bed.
antecámara [an-tay-cah'-mah-rah], *f.* 1. Antechamber. 2. Lobby; hall. 3. *(Naut.)* The steerage.
antecamarilla [an-tay-cah-mah-reel'-lyah], *f.* A room leading to the king's antechamber.
antecapilla [an-tay-cah-peel'-lyah], *f.* The porch.
antecedente [an-tay-thay-den'-tay], *m.* Antecedent, previous, preceding. **Visto lo antecedente,** in view of the foregoing. **Antecedentes;** record, history, background; **¿cuáles son sus antecedentes?,** what´s his history? **Antecedentes delictivos,** criminal record. **Tener buenos antecedentes,** to have a good record.
antecedentemente [an-tay-thay-den-tay-men'-tay], *adv.* Antecedently, previously, beforehand.
anteceder [an-tay-thay-derr'], *va.* To precede, to forege.
antecesor, ra [an-tay-thay-sor', rah], *m. & f.* Predecessor, forefather. **Antecesores,** ancestors.
antechinos [an-tay-chee'-nos], *m. pl. (Arch.)* Fluted mouldings.
anteco, a [an-tay'-co, cah], *a.* Antoeci, or inhabitants of the same meridian.
antecoger [an-tay-co-herr'], *va.* 1. To bring any person or thing before one. 2. To gather in fruit before the due time.
antecolumna [an-tay-co-loom'-nah], *f. (Arch.)* A column of a portico.
antecomedor [an-tay-co-may-dor], *m. (LAm.)* Room adjoining the dining room.
antecocina [an-tay-co-the-nah], *f.* Scullery.
antecoro [an-tay-co'-ro], *m.* The entrance which leads to the choir.
Antecristo [an-tay-crees'-to], *m.* Antichrist.
antedata [an-tay-dah'-tah], *f.* Antedate.
antedatar [an-tay-dah-tar'], *va.* To antedate.
antedecir [an-tay-day-theer'], *va.* To predict, to foretell.
antedicho, cha [an-tay-dee'-cho, chah], *a.* Foresaid.
ante diem [an-tay-dee'-em]. *(Lat.)* The preceding day.
antediluviano, na [an-tay-de-loo-ve-ah'-no, nah], *a.* Antediluvian.
antefechar [an-tay-fay-char'], *va.* To anticipate the date of. *V.* ANTEDATAR.
antefirma [an-tay-feer'-mah], *f.* The style of address which is put before the signature in any communication.
anteiglesia [an-tay-e-glay'-se-ah], *f. (Obs.)* The porch of a church.
antejuela [an-tay-hoo-ay-lah], *f. (CAm.) V.* LENTEJUELA.
antelación [an-tay-lah-the-on'], *f.* Precedence in order of time. **Con mucha antelación,** long in advance.
antelina [an-tay-le-nah], *f.* Suede, artificial buckskin.
antellevar [an-tay-lyay-vahr'], *va. (Mex. Aut.)* To run down.
antellevón [an-tay-lyay-von], *m. (Mex. Aut.)* Accident.

antemano [an-tay-mah'-no], *adv.* **De antemano,** beforehand.
antememoria [an-tay-may-mo-re-ah], *(Comp.)* Cache memory. **Antememoria de Video** *(Comp.),* Video buffer.
antemeridiano, na [an-tay-may-re-de-ah'-no, nah], *a.* In the forenoon.
antemural [an-tay-moo-ral'], *m.* 1. A fort, rock, or mountain, which serves for the defence of a fortress. 2. *(Met.)* A safeguard.
antemuralla [an-tay-moo-rahl'-lyah], *f.* or **Antemuro** [an-te-moo'-ro], *m. V.* ANTEMURAL.
antena [an-tay'-nah], *f.* 1. (Radio) Aerial. 2. Antenna or feeler of insects. *(fig.)* **Tener antena para,** to have a feeling for. 3. *(Naut.)* Lateen yard.
antenallas [an-tay-nahl'-lyas], *f. pl.* Pincers.
antenatal [an-tay-nah-tahl], *a.* Antenatal, prenatal.
antenoche [an-tay-no'-chay], *adv.* 1. The night before last. 2. *(Obs.)* Before nightfall.
antenombre [an-tay-nom'-bray], *m.* Title (Sir, Saint, etc., en inglés; (Don, San, etc. en español).
anténula [an-tay'-noo-lah], *f.* Antennule: applied to the smaller pair of antennas or feelers of crustacea.
antenupcial [an-te-noop-the-ahl'], *a.* Antenuptial, before marriage.
anteojera [an-tay-o-hay'-rah], *f.* 1. Spectacle-case. 2. Eye-flap.
anteojero [an-tay-o-hay'-ro], *m.* Spectacle-maker.
anteojo [an-tay-o'-ho], *m.* A spy-glass; an eye-glass. **Anteojo de larga vista,** a telescope. **Anteojo de puño,** or **de teatro,** opera-glass. *-pl.* 1. Spectacles. **Anteojos de camino,** goggles. 2. Pieces of felt or leather put before the eyes of vicious horses.
antepagar [an-tay-pah-gar'], *va.* To pay beforehand.
antepasado, da [an-tay-pah-sah'-do, dah], *a.* Passed, elapsed, previous, before last. *m.* Ancestor.
antepasados [an-tay-pah-sah'-dos], *m. pl.* Ancestors, predecessors.
antepecho [an-tay-pay'-cho], *m.* 1. Balcony, bridge-rail; sill of a window. 2. Breastwork, parapet, battlement. 3. Footstep of a coach. 4. Harness for the breast of a draught-horse; poitrel. 5. Breast roller of a loom. 6. The part of a ribbon frame or loom, which passes from the right to the left, to the point in which the weaver's strap is placed. **Antepechos,** *(Naut.)* The iron horse of the head.
antepenúltimo, ma [an-tay-pay-nool'-te-mo, mah], *a.* Antepenult, last but two.
anteponer [an-tay-po-nerr'], *va.* 1. To prefer. 2. *(Obs.)* To place before. **(Yo antepongo,** from **Anteponer.** *V.* PONER). *-vr.* To be in front.
anteportada [an-te-por-tah'-dah], *f.* A fly-leaf bearing the title only of a book.
anteportal, or **antepórtico** [an-tay-por'-te-co], *m.* Vestibule or porch.
anteprotecto [an-tay-pro-tayc-to], *m.* Preliminary sketch, preliminary plan.
antepuerta [an-tay-poo-er'-tah], *f.* 1. A curtain placed before a door. 2. Anteport.
antepuerto *m. (Naut.)* Anteport.
antepuesto [an-tay-poo-ays-to], *a.* Preceding, coming before.
antequino [an-tay-kee'-no], *m. (Arch.) V.* ESGUCIO.
antera [an-tay'-rah], *f. (Bot.)* Anther, the part of the stamen which contains the pollen of flowers.
anterior [an-tay-re-or'], *a.* Anterior, former. **Cada uno es mejor que el anterior,** each one is better than the last. **Se había olvidado de todo lo anterior,** he had forgotten all that had happened previously. Front, fore. **En la parte anterior del coche,** on the front part of the car.
anterioridad [an-tay-re-o-re-dahd'], *f.* Priority (prioridad); preference; anteriority (tiempo). **Con anterioridad,** previously.
anteriormente [an-tay-re-or-men'-tay], *adv.* Previously, before.

anteroversión [an-tay-ro-ver-se-on'], *f. (Med.)* Anteversion of an organ.

antes [ahn'-tes], *adv.* 1. Before. **Tres días antes,** three days before. **Antes que llegues,** before you arrive. 2. Beforehand, in advance (con antelación). **Su hijo había ido anteriormente a preparar la entrevista,** his son had gone beforehand to prepare the meeting. **La última bocacalle antes de los semáforos,** the last turning before the traffic lights. **Antes que nada,** above all. **Mucho antes,** a long time before. **Lo antes posible, cuanto antes,** as soon as possible. *conj.* On the contrary (más bien). **No temo la muerte, antes la deseo,** I don't fear death, on the contrary, I long for it. *a.* Before, previous. **La semana antes,** the week before, the previous week.

antesacristía [an-tay-sah-cris-tee'-ah], *f.* An apartment which leads to the sacristy.

antesala [an-tay-sah'-lah], *f.* Antechamber. **Hacer antesala,** to attend in an antechamber.

antesalazo [an-tay-sah-lah-tho], *m. (Mex.)* Long wait.

antestatura [an-tes-tah-too'-rah], *f. (Mil.)* A small intrenchment of palisadoes and sandbags.

antetemplo [an-tay-tem'-plo], *m.* Portico.

anteúltimo [an-tay-ool-te-mo], *a. (Cono Sur)* Penultimate.

antever [an-tay-verr'], *va.* To foresee. **(Yo anteveo,** from **Antever.** *V.* VER.)

antevíspera [an-tay-vees'-pay-rah], *f.* The day before yesterday.

anti [ahn'-te], *pref.* Anti [indicating «against» or «opposite»].

antiácido, da [an-te-ah'-the-do, dah], *a.* Antacid.

antiadherente [an-te-ah-day-rayn-tay], *a.* Non-stick.

antiaéreo, rea [an-te-ah-ay'-ray-o, ray-ah], *a.* Antiaircraft.

antiafrodisíaco, ca [an-te-ah-fro-de-se-ah'-co, cah], *a.* Anaphrodisiac.

antialcohólico, ca [an-te-al-co-o-le-co], *a.* Teetotal. *m. & f.* Teetotaller.

antialcoholismo [an-te-al-co-o-lees'-mo], *m.* Antialcoholism.

antiamericano [an-te-ah-may-re-cah-no], *a.* Anti-American.

antiartrítico, ca [an-te-ar-tree'-te-co, cah], *a.* Arthritis-combatting.

antiatómico [an-te-ah-to-me-co], *a.* **Refugio antiatómico,** nuclear fallout shelter.

antibalas [an-te-bah-lahs], *a.* Bullet proof.

antibelicista [an-te-bay-le-thees-tah], *a. m. & f.* Anti-war; pacifist.

antibiótico, ca [an-te-be-o'-te-co, cah], *a. & m.* Antibiotic.

anticanceroso, sa [an-te-can-the-ro'-so, sah], *a.* Cancer-fighting.

anticarro [an-te-car'-ro], *a.* Antitank.

anticatarral [an-te-ca-tar-rahl'], *a.* Cold-fighting, cold-curing.

anticiclón [an-te-the-clon'], *m.* Anticyclone.

anticiclonal [an-te-the-clo-nahl], *a.* Anticiclonic.

anticipación [an-te-the-pah-the-on'], *f.* 1. Anticipation. 2. Expectation. **Hacer algo con anticipación,** to do something well beforehand. **Reservar con anticipación,** to book in advance.

anticipada [an-te-the-pah'-dah], *f.* Catching one's opponent off guard.

anticipadamente [an-te-the-pah-da-men'-tay], *adv.* In advance, with plenty of time.

anticipado [an-te-the-pah-do], *a.* Future, prospective; in advance.

anticipar [an-te-the-par'], *va.* 1. To anticipate. 2. To move up (a date), to move up the date of. **Anticiparon las vacaciones,** they took their holiday early. -*vr.* 1. To get ahead. 2. To come early, to occur early. **Anticiparse a hacer algo,** to do something ahead of time.

anticipo [an-te-thee'-po], *m.* 1. Anticipation. 2. Advance payment. **Esto es sólo un anticipo,** this is just a foretaste.

anticlerical [an-te-clay-re-cahl'], *a.* Anticlerical.

anticlericalismo [an-te-clay-re-cah-lees-mo], *m.* Anticlericalism.

anticlinal [an-te-cle-nal], *m. (LAm.)* Watershed.

anticoagulante [an-te-co-a-goo-lahn'-tay], *m. & a.* Anticoagulant.

anticoba [an-te-co-bah], *f.* Brutal frankness.

anticolonialismo [an-te-co-lo-ne-a-lees'-mo], *m.* Anticolonialism.

anticomunismo [an-te-co-moo-nees'-mo], *m.* Anticommunism.

anticomunista [an-te-co-moo-nees'-tah], *m. com.* Anticommunist.

anticoncepcional [an-te-con-thep-the-o-nahl'], *m. & a.* Contraceptive, birth control.

anticoncepcionismo [an-te-con-thep-the-o-nees'-mo], *m.* Birth control, use of contraceptives.

anticonceptivo [an-te-con-thep-te-vo], *a.* Birth control, family-planning. **Métodos anticonceptivos,** birth control methods.

anticonformismo [an-te-con-for-mees'-mo], *m.* Nonconformity.

anticogelante [an-te-con-hay-lahn'-tay], *m. & a.* Antifreeze.

anticonstitucional [an-te-cons-te-too-the-o-nahl'], *a.* Unconstitutional.

anticontaminante [an-te-con-tah-me-nahn-tay], *a. (Cono Sur)* Anti-pollution.

anticorrosivo [an-te-cor-ro-se-vo], *a.* Anticorrosive, antirust.

anticonstitucional [an-te-cons-te-too-the-o-nahl], *a.* Unconstitutional.

anticresis [an-te-cray'-sis], *f.* A contract between debtor and creditor by which the former yields to the latter the fruits of a farm until the debt is paid.

anticresista [an-te-cre-sees'-tah], *m.* The creditor in anticresis.

anticristiano, na [an-te-cris-te-ah'-no, nah], *a. & m. & f.* Antichristian.

anticrítico [an-te-cree'-te-co], *m.* Anticritic, an opponent to a critic.

anticristo [an-te-crees-to], *m.* Antichrist.

anticuado, da [an-te-coo-ah'-do, dah], *a.* Antiquated; obsolete, out of use (machine). Old fashioned (person). Out-of-date (película). -*pp.* of ANTICUAR.

anticuar [an-te-coo-ar'], *va.* To antiquate, to outdate.

anticuario [an-te-coo-ah'-re-o], *m.* Antiquary, antiquarian.

anticuarse [an-te-coo-ahr-say], *vr.* To become antiquated, to get out of date.

antieucho [an-te-coo-cho], *m. (And. Culin.)* Kebab.

anticuerpo [an-te-coo-err'-po], *m. (Chem.)* Antibody.

antidemocrático, ca [an-te-day-mo-crah'-te-co, cah], *a.* Nondemocratic.

antideportividad [an-te-por-te-ve-dahd], *f.* Unsporting attitude.

antideportivo [an-te-day-por-te-vo], *a.* Unsporting.

antidepresivo [an-te-day-pray-se-vo], *a.m.* Antidepressant, antidepressing.

antideslizante [an-te-des-le-thahn'-tay], *a.* Nonskid.

antideslumbrante [an-te-days-loom-brahn-tay], *a.* Anti-dazzle.

antidetonante [an-te-day-to-nahn'-tay], *a.* Antiknock.

antidiabético, ca [an-te-de-ah-bay'-te-co, cah], *a.* To control diabetes.

antidisturbios [an-te-des-toor-be-os], *a.:* **Policía antidisturbios,** riot police.

antídoto [an-tee'-do-tol, *m.* 1. Antidote, counterpoison 2. *(Met.)* A preventive or preservative against vice or error.

antidroga [an-te-dro-gah], *a.* **Brigada antidroga,** drug squad.

antidumping [an-te-doom-pin], *a.* **Medidas antidumping,** antidumping measures.

antieconómico [an-te-ay-co-no-me-co], *a.* Uneconomic; wasteful.

antiemético, ca [an-te-ay-may'-te-co, cah], *a. (Med.)* Antemetic.

antiepiléptico, ca [an-te-ay-pe-lep'-te-co, cah], *a. (Med.)* Antiepileptic.

antiescorbútico, ca [an-te-es-cor-boo'-te-co, cah], *a. (Med.)* Antiscorbutic.

antier [an-te-err'], *adv. (coll.)* The day before yesterday; a contraction of **antes de ayer.**

antiespamódico, ca [an-te-es-pas-mo'-de-co,cah], *a. (Med.)* Antispasmodic.

antifanático, ca [an-te-fah-nah'-te-co, cah], *a.* Antifanatic.

antifascismo [an-te-fahs-thes-mo], *m.* Antifascism.

antifascista [an-te-fahs-thes-tah], *a. m. & f.* Antifascist.

antifatiga [an-te-fah-te-gah], *a.* **Píldora antifatiga,** antifatigue pill.

antifaz [an-te-fath'], *m.* A veil which covers the face. A mask.

antifebril [an-te-fay-breel'], *a. (Med.)* Antifebrile.

antifeminismo [an-te-fay-me-nes-mo], *m.* Antifeminism.

antifeminista [an-te-fay-me-nes-tah], *a. m. & f.* Antifeminist.

antiflogístico, ca [an-te-flo-hees'-te-co, cah], *a. & m. (Med.)* Antiphlogistic. **antífona** [an-tee'-fo-nah], *f.* Antiphony, an anthem.

antifonal, antifonario [an-te-fo-nahl', an-te-fo-nah'-re-o], *m.* Antiphonal, a book of anthems.

antifrasis [an-tee'-frah-sis], *f.* Antiphrasis.

antifricción [an-te-free-the-on'], *f.* Antifriction alloy.

antifriccional [an-te-frac-the-o-nahl], *a.* Antifriction.

antifrís [an-te-fres], *m. (LAm.)* Antifreeze.

antigás [an-te-gahs], *a.* **Careta antigás,** gasmask.

antígeno [an-tee'-hay-no], *m.* Antigen.

antigolpes [an-te-gol-pay], *a.* Shockproof.

antígona [an-te-go-nah], *f.* Antigone.

antigravedad [an-te-grah-vay-dhad'], *f.* Weightlessness.

antigripal [an-te-gre-pahl], *a.* **Vacuna antigripal,** flu vaccine.

antigualla [an-te-goo-ahl'-lyah], *f.* 1. A monument of antiquity; antique. 2. Antiquity. 3. Ancient custom out of use.

antiguamente [an-te-goo-ah-men'-tay], *adv.* Anciently, formerly.

antiguar [an-te-goo-ar'], *vn.* To obtain seniority, as member of a tribunal, college, etc. *-va. (Obs.)* 1. To make obsolete. 2. To abolish the ancient use of a thing.

antigüedad [an-te-goo-ay-dahd'], *f.* 1. Antiquity, oldness. 2. Ancient times, the days of yore. **La fábrica tiene una antigüedad de 200 años,** the factory is 200 years old. 3. The ancients. 4. Antique.

antiguerra [an-te-gay-rrah], *a.* Anti-war.

antiguo, gua [an-tee'-goo-o, goo-ah], *a.* Antique, stricken in years, old; having long held an employment or place. **Un antiguo alumno mío,** an old pupil of mine.

antiguo [an-tee'-goo-o], *m.* 1. An antique of Greece or Rome. 2. An aged member of a college or community; senior of a college. **Antiguos,** The ancients; the illustrious men of antiquity.

antihelmíntico, ca [an-te-el-meen'-te-co, cah], *a. (Med.)* Anthelminthic.

antihéroe [an-te-ay-ro-ay], *m.* Antihero.

antihigiénico, ca [an-te-he-ay'-ne-co, cah], *a.* Unsanitary, unhygienic.

antihistamina [an-tees-tah-me'-nah], *f.* Antihistamine.

antihistamínico [an-te-es-tah-me-ne-co], *a. m.* Antihistamine.

antiflacionista [an-te-en-flah-the-o-nes-tah], *a.* Antiinflationary.

antilogaritmo [an-te-lo-gah-reet'-mo], *m.* Antilogarithm.

antilogía [an-te-lo-hee'-ah], *f.* An apparent contradiction between two sentences or passages of an author.

antilógico, ca [an-te-lo'-he-co, cah], *a.* Illogical, contrary to logic.

antílope [an-tee'-lo-pay], *m.* Antelope.

antillanismo [an-te-lyah-nes-mo], *m.* Word or phrase peculiar to the Antilles.

antillano, na [an-teel-lyah'-no, nah], *a.* Native or relating to the Antilles.

antillas [an-te-lyahs], *f. & pl.* Antilles, West Indian, of the Antilles.

antimacasar [an-te-mah-cah-sahr], *m.* Antimacasar.

antimateria [an-te-mah-tay'-re-ah], *f.* Antimatter.

antimisil [an-te-me-seel], *a.* Antimissile: **misil antimisil,** antimissile missile.

antimonárquico, ca [an-te-mo-nar'-ke-co, cah], *a.* Antimonarchic, antimonarchical.

antimonial [an-te-mo-ne-ahl'], *a.* Antimonial, belonging to antimony.

antimonio [an-te-mo'-ne-o], *m.* Antimony.

antimonopolio [an-te-mo-no-po'-le-o], *a.* Antitrust, antimonopoly.

antinacional [an-te-nah-the-o-nahl'], *a.* Against one's national interests.

antinatural [an-te-nah-too-rahl'], *a.* Unnatural.

antineutrón [an-te-ne-oo-tron'], *m.* Antineutron.

antimoral [an-te-mo-rahl'], *a.* Contrary to morality.

antinomía [an-te-no'-me-ah], *f. (Law.)* A conflict between laws or parts of a law.

antioquía [an-te-o-ke-ah], *f.* Antioch.

antioxidante [an-te-oc-se-dahn-tay], *a.* Antirust.

antipalúdico [an-te-pah-loo-de-co], *a.* Antimalarial.

antipapa [an-te-pah'-pah], *m.* Antipope, a pope who is not canonically elected.

antipapado [an-te-pah-pah'-do], *m.* The unlawful dignity of antipope.

antipapal [an-te-pah-pahl'], *a.* Antipapal.

antipara [an-te-pah'-rah], *f.* 1. A screen, or anything which serves as a screen.

antiparabólico [an-te-pah-rah-bo-le-co], *a. (Carib.)* Wild.

antiparásito, antiparasitario [an-te-pah-rah'-se-to, an-te-pah-rah-se-tah'-re-o], *a.* Preventing or reducing static or interference. *-m.* Static suppressor, interference filter.

antiparras [an-te-pahr'-ras], *f. pl. (coll.)* Specs, glasses.

antipartícula [an-te-par-tee'-coo-lah], *f.* Antiparticle.

antipatía [an-te-pah-tee'-ah], *f.* Antipathy.

antipático, ca [an-te-pah'-te-co, cah], *a.* Having a natural aversion for anything. Disagreeable, unpleasant. **Es un tipo antipático,** he´s a disagreeable sort.

antipatizar [an-te-pah-te-thar'], *vn. (Amer.)* To dislike, to have a feeling against.

antipatriótico [an-te-pah-tre-o-te-co], *a.* Unpatriotic.

antiperístasis [an-te-pay-rees'-tah-sis], *f.* Antiperistasis, the action of two contrary qualities.

antiperistáltico, ca [an-te-pay-ris-tahl'-te-co, cah], *a.* Antiperistaltic, a reverse movement of the intestines; also, quieting the natural peristalsis.

antiperras [an-te-pay-rrahs], *f. & pl. (And.)* Half-moon glasses.

antípodas [an-tee'-po-das], *m. pl.* 1. Antipodes. 2. *(Met.)* Persons of contrary dispositions, sentiments or manners.

antipolilla [an-te-po-le-lyah], *a.* Mothproof.

antiprotón [an-te-pro-ton'], *m.* Antiproton.

antiproyectil [an-te-pro-yayc-teel], *a.* Antimissile.

antipútrido, da [an-te-poo'-tre-do, dah], *a.* Antiseptic.

antiquísimo, ma [an-te-kee'-se-mo, mah], *a. sup.* Very ancient.

antiquista [an-te-kes-tah], *(Mex.) a & m.* Antiquarian.

antirrábico [an-ter-rah-be-co], *a.* **Vacuna antirrábica,** antirabies vaccine.

antirradar [an-teer-rah-dar'], *a.* Antiradar.

antirreligioso, sa [an-te-ray-le-he-oh'-so, sah], *a.* Antireligious.

antirresbaladizo [an-ter-res-ba-lah-de-tho], *a. (Aut.)* Non-skid.

antirrevolucionario, ria [an-tee-ray-vo-loo-the-onah'-re-o, ah], *a.* Antirevolutionary.

antirrino [an-te-rre-no], *m.* Antirrhinum.

antirrobo [an-te-rro-bo], *a.* **Sistema antirrobo,** anti-theft system.

antisemita [an-te-say-mee'-tah], *a.* Anti-Semitic. *-m. & f.* Anti-Semite.
antisemítico, ca [an-te-say-mee'-te-co, cah], *a.* Anti-Semitic.
antisemitismo [an-te-say-me-tees'-mo], *m.* Anti-Semitism.
antiséptico, ca [an-te-sep'-te-co, cah], *a.* Antiseptic, counteracting existing sepsis, and thus contrasted with aseptic.
antisifilítico, ca [ah-te-se-fe-lee'-te-co, cah], *a.* Antisyphilitic.
antisociable [an-te-so-the-ah'-blay], *a.* Antisocial.
antisocial [an-te-so-the-ahl'], *a.* Antisocial.
antisodural [an-te-so-doo-rahl], *(LAm.) a & m.* Deodorant.
antisubmarino, na [an-te-soob-mah-ree'-no, nah], *a.* Antisubmarine.
antisuero [an-te-soo-ay'-ro], *m.* Antiserum.
antitanque [an-te-tahn-ke], *a.* Antitank.
antiterrorista [an-te-tayr-ro-res-tah], *a.* **Medidas antiterroristas**, measures against terrorism.
antítesis [an-tee'-tay-sis], *f.* 1. *(Gram.)* Antithesis. 2. *(Rhet.)* A contrast or opposition in the words of a discourse.
antitético, ca [an-te-tay'-te-co, cah], *a.* Antithetical.
antitipo [an-te-tee'-po], *m.* Antitype, figure, image, symbol.
antitoxina [an-te-toc-see'-nah], *f.* Antitoxin.
antivirus [an-te-vee'-roos], *m.* Antivirus.
antiviviseccionista [an-te-ve-ve-sayc-the-o-nes-tah], *m. & f.* Antivivisectionist.
Antofagasta [an-to-fo-gahs-tah], *f.* Antofagasta.
antofagastino [an-to-fah-gahs-te-no], *(Cono Sur). a.* Of Antofagasta.
antófago, ga [an-to'-fah-go, gah], *a.* Living on flowers.
antojadizo, za [an-to-ha-dee'-tho, thah], *a.* Capricious, whimsical, fickle.
antojado, da [an-to-hah'-do, dah], *a.* Anxious, longing. *-pp.* of ANTOJARSE.
antojarse [an-to-har'-say], *vr.* To long, to desire earnestly. **Antojársele a uno alguna cosa**, to desire or judge without reflection. **No se le antoja ir**, he doesn't feel like going.
antojera [an-to-hay'-rah], *f.* 1. A spectacle-case. 2. An eye-flap for horses; blinder, blinker.
antojitos [an-to-he-tos], *m. & pl. (Cono Sur)* Sweets, candy.
antojo [an-to'-ho], *m.* 1. Whim; a vehement desire, a longing, a hankering; fancy. **Hacer a su antojo**, to do as one pleases. **Tener antojos**, to have cravings.2. A surmise.
antología [an-to-lo-hee'-ah], *f.* Anthology.
antológica [an-to-lo-he-cah], *f.* (Arte) Selective exhibition.
antológico [an-to-lo-he-co], *a* **Exposición antológica,** selective exhibition (arte).
antónimo [an-to'-ne-mo], *m.* Antonym.
antonomasia [an-to-no-mah' se ah], *f. (Rhet.)* antonomasia, a figure by which a title is put for a proper name; as, The Orator, for Cicero.
antor [an-tor'], *m. (Law. Prov.)* Vendor of stolen goods, bought in good faith.
antorcha [an-tor'-chah], *f.* 1. Torch, flambeau, taper. 2. A cresset.
antorchero [an-tor-chay'-ro], *m. (Obs.)* A candlestick for tapers, etc.
antoría [an-to-ree'-ah], *f.* 1. *(Law. Prov.)* The action of discovering the first seller of stolen goods. 2. Right of reclaiming against the seller of stolen goods.
antracita [an-trah-thee'-tah], *f.* Anthracit coal; hard coal.
antrax [ahn-trahx], *m. (Med.)* Carbuncle; also anthrax or splenic fever.
antro [ahn'-tro], *m.* 1. *(Poetic.)* Cavern, den, grotto. 2. *(Med.)* Antrum, a cavity in bone.
antropofagia [an-tro-po-fah-hee'-ah], *f.* Anthropophagy.
antropófago [an-tro-po'-fah-go], *m.* A cannibal. *-pl.* Anthropophagi. In English it has no singular.
antropografía [an-tro-po-grah-fee'-ah], *f.* Anthropography, descriptive anatomy of man.
antropoide [an-tro-poy'-day], *m. & f.* Anthropoid.
antropoideo [an-tro-poy'-day-oh], *a.* Anthropoid. **Mono antropoideo**, anthropoid, ape.

antropología [an-tro-po-lo-hee'-ah], *f.* Anthropology, the science of the human structure.
antropológico, ca [an-tro-po-lo'-he-co, cah], *a.* Anthropological.
antropólogo [an-tro-po'-lo-go], *m.* Anthropologist.
antropomorfismo [an-tro-po-mor-fees'-mo], *m.* The attribution to God of a human body.
antropomorfo, fa [an-tro-po-mor'-fo, fah], *a.* Anthropomorphous, said of apes.
antroposofía [an-tro-po-so-fee'-ah], *f.* Anthroposophy, the knowledge of the nature of man.
antruejar [an-troo-ay-har'], *va. (Prov.)* To wet with water, or play some trick.
antruejo [an-troo-ay'-ho], *m.* The three days of the carnival.
antruido [an-troo-ee'-do], *m. (Obs.)* V. ANTRUEJO.
antucá [an-too-cah], *m. (Cono Sur)* Sunshade, parasol.
antuviada [an-too-ve-ah-dah], *f.* Sudden blow, bump.
antuvión [an-too-ve-on'], *m. (coll.)* A sudden, unexpected stroke or attack. **De antuvión**, unexpectedly. **Fulano vino de antuvión**, so and so came unexpectedly.
anual [ah-noo-ahl'], *a.* Annual. **Plantas anuales**, *(Bot.)* annual plants.
anualidad [ah-noo-ah-le-dahd'], *f.* 1. State or quality of being annual. 2. Pensions paid by the state. 3. Annuity. *(Com.)*
anualmente [ah-noo-al-men'-tay], *adv.* Annually.
anuario [ah-noo-ah'-re-o], *m.* A year book of information. **Anuario telefónico**, telephone directory.
anúbada [ah-noo'-bah-dah], *f.* 1. *(Obs.)* An ancient tax paid in Spain. 2. A call to arms.
anubarrado, da [ah-noo-bar-rah'-do, dah], *a.* Clouded.
anubarse [ah-noo-bar'-say], *vr.* To vanish.
anubladamente [ah-noo-blah-dah-men'-tay], *adv.* Mistily.
anublado, da [ah-noo-blah'-do, dah], *a.* 1. Overcast, clouded, dim, mistful. 2. (Speaking of colors), somewhat more obscure than the rest. *-pp.* of ANUBLAR.
anublar [ah-noo-blar'], *va.* 1. To cloud, to darken the light of the sun. 2. To overcast. 3. *(Met.)* To cloud or obscure merit. *-vr.* 1. To be blasted, withered, or mildewed: applied to corn and plants. 2. *(Met.)* To miscarry, to be disconcerted: speaking of plans.
anudar [ah-noo-dar'], *va.* 1. To knot. 2. To join, to unite. *-vn.* To wither, to fade, to pine away. **Anudarse la voz,** *(Met.)* to throb from passion or grief; not to be able to speak.
anuencia [ah noo-en'-thc-ah], *f.* Compliance, consent.
anuente [ah-noo-en'-tay], *a.* Condescending, courteous.
anulable [ah-noo-lah'-blay], *a.* That which can be annulled.
anulación [ah-noo-lah-the-on'], *f.* 1. Cessation, abrogation. 2. Abscission.
anulador, ra [ah-no-lah-dor', rah], *m. & f.* A repealer.
anular [ah-noo-lar'], *va.* 1. To annul, to make void, to frustrate. 2. To cancel, rescind. *(For.)* To irritate. *-vr.* To lose one's identity; to renounce to everything.
anular [ah-noo-lar'], *a.* Annular, ring-shaped. **Dedo anular**, the ring-finger, or fourth finger.
anulativo, va [ah-noo-lah-tee'vo, vah], *a.* Having the power of making void.
anuloso, sa [ah-noo-lo'-so, sah], annular, composed of many rings.
anunciación [ah-noon-the-ah-the-on'], *f.* Annunciation; the angel's salutation to the blessed Virgin.
anunciada [ah-noon-the-ah'-dah], *f.* 1. An order of monks. 2. A religious order for women. 3. An order of knights, instituted by Amadeus VI., Duke of Savoy.
anunciador, ra [ah-noo-the-ah-dor', rah], *m. & f.* Announcer, one who announces.
anunciante [ah-noon-the-ahn'-tay], *m. & f. (Com.)* Advertiser.
anunciar [ah-noon-the-ar'], *va.* 1. To announce, to proclaim, to declare. **No nos anuncia nada nuevo**, it augurs ill for us. 2. To advertise, to publicize. 3. To forbode, to portend. *-vr.* **El festival se anuncia animado,** the festival lools like it'll be lively.

anuncio [ah-noon'-the-o], *m.* 1. Omen, forerunner. 2. Advertisement. **Anuncios económicos, anuncios por palabras,** classified advertisements, small advertisements. 3. *(Com.)* Statement, advice.

anuo, ua [ah'-noo-o, ah], *a. V.* ANUAL.

anúteba [ah-noo'-tay-bah], *f.* 1. *V.* ANUBADA. 2. Call to war.

anverso [ah-verr'-so], *m.* Obverse: applied to the head side in coins and medals.

anvir [ahn'-veer], *m.* (South Amer.) A red liquor expressed from the fermented leaves of tobacco.

anzolero [an-tho-lay'-ro], *m. (Prov.)* One whose trade it is to make fish-hooks.

anzuelo [an-thoo-ay-lo], *m.* 1. Fish-hook. 2. *(Met.)* Allurement, incitement. 3. A kind of fritters made in the shape of a hook. **Caer en el anzuelo,** to be tricked or defrauded. **Roer el anzuelo,** to escape a danger. **Tragar el anzuelo,** to swallow the bait.

aña [ah'-nyah], *f.* Hyena.

añada [ah-nyah'-dah], *f.* 1. The good or bad season in a year. 2. Piece of arable land.

añadido [ah-nyah-dee'-do], *m.* False hair.

añadidura [ah-nyah-de-doo'-rah], *f.* Addition, extra, thing added. **Dar algo de añadidura,** to give something extra.

añadimiento [ah-nyah-de-me-en'-to], *m.* Addition. **Añadidura a los pesos en la venta de cosas,** over-weight allowed in the sale of goods.

añadir [ah-nyah-deer'], *va.* 1. To add. 2. To exaggerate.

añafea [ah-nyah-fay'-ah], *f.* **Papel de añafea,** brown paper.

añafil [ah-nyah-feel'], *m.* A musical pipe used by the Moors.

añafilero [ah-nyah-fe-lay'-ro], *m.* A player on the *añafil.*

añagaza [ah-nyah-gah'-thah], *f.* 1. A call, lure, or decoy, for catching birds. 2. *(Met.)* Allurement, enticement to mischief.

añal [ah-nyahl'], *a.* Annual. **Cordero añal,** a yearling lamb.

añal [ah-nyahl'], *m.* 1. An annual offering on the tomb of a person deceased. 2. *(Obs.)* Anniversary.

añalejo [ah-nyah-lay'-ho], *m.* An ecclesiastical almanac, pointing out the regulations of the divine service.

añangá [ah-nyahn-gah], *m. (Cono Sur)* The devil.

añañay [ah-nyah-nyah-e], *interj. (Cono Sur)* Great.

añapar [ah-nyah-pahr], *va. (LAm.)* To smash to bits.

añascar [ah -nyas-car'], *va.* 1. *(Col.)* To collect by degrees small things of little value. 2. *(Obs.)* To entangle.

añaz [ah-nyath], *m. (And.)* Shrunk.

añeja [ah-nyay-hah], *f. (Carib.)* Old lady.

añejar [ah-nyay-har'], *va.* To make old. *-vr.* To grow old, to become stale.

añejo, ja àh-nyay'-ho, hah], *a.* Old. stale, musty.

añicos [ah-nyee'-cos], *m. pl.* Bits or small pieces of something. **Hacer añicos,** to break into small bits. **Hacerse añicos,** to take too much exercise, to overheat oneself.

añil [ah-nyell'], *m.* 1. *(Bot.)* The indigo plant. 2. Indigo, a mass extracted from the indigo plant: the best quality is called **añil flor,** or **tisate;** the middling sort, (sobresaliente); and the common kind, (corte).

añilar [ah-nye-lar'], *va.* To treat the clothes with bluing, in laundry-work.

añinero [ah-ny-nay'-ro], *m.* A dealer in lambskins.

añinos [ah-nyee'-nos], *m. pl.* The fleecy skins of yearling lambs.

año [ah'-nyo], *m.* Year. **Año bisiesto,** leap-year. **Tener diez años,** to be ten years old. **El año de gracia,** the year of our Lord. **Año luz,** light year. **¡Feliz Año Nuevo!** Happy New Year! **Hace años,** years ago. **No pasan los años para él,** he doesn't seem to get any older. **Una vez al año,** once a year. **Estar de buen año,** to be in good health.

añojal [ah-nyo-hahl'], *m.* Fallow land.

añojo, ja [ah-nyo'-ho, hah], *m. & f.* A yearling calf.

año luz [ah'-nyo-looth], *m. (Astr.)* Light year.

añorante [ah-nyo-rahn-tay], *a.* Yearning, longing; nostalgic; affectionate.

añoranza [ah-nyo-rahn-tha], *f.* Longing, yearning, sense of loss.

añorar [ah-nyo-rahr], 1. *va.* To long for, yearn for, pine for. 2. *vn.* To yearn, pine, grieve.

añoso, sa [ah-nyo'-so, sah], *a.* Very old, ancient.

añublado, da [ah-nyoo-blah'-do, dah], *a.* Blindfolded. *-pp.* of AÑUBLAR.

añublar, se [ah-nyoo-blahr], *V.* ANUBLAR.

añublo [ah-nyoo'-blo], *m.* Mildew. *V.* TIZON.

añudador, ra [ah-nyoo-dah-dor, rah], *m. & f.* One who knots or ties.

añudar [ah-nyoo-dar'], *va.* 1. *v.* ANUDAR. 2. To make fast, to unite, to tie close. **Añudar los labios,** to impose silence.

aojado, da [ah-o-hah'-do, dah], *a.* Bewitched. *-pp.* of OJAR.

aojador, ra [ah-o-hah-dor', rah], *m. & f.* A conjurer.

aojadura [ah-o-hah-doo'-rah], *f.* **Aojamiento** [ah-o-hah-me-en'-to], *m.* Witchcraft, fascination.

aojar [ah-o-har'], *va.* To fascinate, to charm to bewitch.

aojo [ah-o-ho], *m.* Evil eye, hoodoo.

aoristo [ah-o-res-to], *m. (Ling.)* Aorist.

aorta [ah-or'-tah], *f. (Anat.)* Aorta, the great artery.

aorteurismo [ah-or-tay-oo-rees'-mo], *m.* Aneurism of the aorta.

aórtico, ca [ah-or'-te-co, cah], *a.* Aortic: relating to the aorta.

aovado, da [ah-o-vah'-do, dah], *a.* Oviform, in the shape of an egg. *-pp.* of AOVAR.

aovar [ah-o-var'], *va.* To lay eggs.

aovillarse [ah-o-veel-lyar'-say], *vr.* To grow or be contracted into the shape of a clew.

a.p. *abr.* de **apartado de correos** (Post Office Box, P.O.B.).

APA *abr.* de **Asociación de Padres de Alumnos** (Parent-Teacher Association).

apa [ah-pah], *interj. (Mex.)* Good God! Cheer up!, get up!

apabilar [ah-pah-be-lar'], *va.* To prepare the wick of a wax-candle for being lighted. *-vr.* 1. *(Obs.)* To die away (luz). 2. *(Met.)* To sink under the hand of death.

apabullante [ah-pah-boo-lyahn-tay], *a.* Shattering, crushing.

apabullar [ah-pah-bool-lyar'], *va.* Coll.) to flatten, squeeze, crush.

apacentadero [ah-pah-then-tah-day'-ro], *m.* Pasture; feeding-place for cattle.

apacentador [ah-pah-then-tah-dor'], *m.* A herdsman.

apacentamiento [ah-pah-then-ta-me-en'-to], *m.* 1. The act of tending grazing cattle. 2. Pasturage.

apacentar [ah-pah-then-tar'], *va.* 1. To tend grazing cattle. 2. To graze, to feed cattle. 3. *(Met.)*. To teach, to instruct spiritually. 4. *(Met.)* to inflame the passions. *-vr.* 1. *(Agri.)* To graze, feed. 2. *(fig.)* To feed. *(Yo apaciento, yo apaciente,* from *Apacentar. V.* ACERTAR.

apacibilidad [ah-pah-the-be-le-dahd'], *f.* Affability, mildness of manners, meekness of temper.

apacible [ah-pah-thee'-blay[, *a.* 1. Affable, meek, gentle, inoffensive. 2. Placid, still, quiet. 3. Pleasant, calm. moderate. **Tiempo apacible,** *(Naut.)* moderate weather. **Semblante apacible,** a serene countenance. **Sitio apacible,** a pleasant place.

apaciblemente [ah-pah-the-blay-men'-tay], *adv.* Mildly, gently, agreeably.

apaciguador, ra [ah-pah-the-goo-ah-dor', rah], *m. & f.* Pacificator, peace-maker.

apaciguamiento [ah-pa-the-goo-ah-me-en'-to], *m.* Pacification.

apaciguar [ah-pah-the-goo-ar'], *va.* To appease, to pacify, to calm, to compose. *-vn. (Naut.)* To grow moderate (viento, mar). *-vr.* To calm down, quieten down.

apache [ah-pah'-chay], *m.* Apache (Indian); *(Esp. Fig.)* Apache, street ruffian, thug.

apacheta [ah-pah-chay-tah], *f. (Amer.)* A heap of stones on hills. *(Met.)* **Hacer la apacheta,** to accomplish the most difficult part of a task. **Hacer su apacheta**, to have made a fortune: to make one's «pile».

apachico [ah-pah-che-co], *m.* *(LAm.)* Bundle.

apachurrar [ah-pah-choor-rar'], *va.* *(Amer.)* To crush, to squeeze, to flatten. **Morir a apachurrones**, To be squeezed to death. *V.* DESPACHURRAR.

apadrinador, ra [ah-pah-dre-nah-dor', rah], *m. & f.* 1. Patron, defender, protector. 2. Second, in a duel.

apadrinamiento [ah-pah-dre-nah-me-ayn-to], *m.* Sponsorship; patronage.

apadrinar [ah-pah-dre-nar'], *va.* 1. To support, to favor, to patronize, to protect. 2. To sponsor. 3. To serve as godfather. 4. To act as second in a duel.

apadronarse [ah-pah-dro-nahr-say], *vr.* To register (as a resident).

apagadizo [ah-pah-gah-de-tho], *a.* Slow to burn, difficult to ignite.

apagado, da [ah-pah-gah'-do, dah], *a.* Humble-minded, submissive, pusillanimous. *-pp.* of APAGAR.

apagador [ah-pah-gah-dor'], *m.* 1. One who extinguishes. 2. Damper, extinguisher, a hollow cone. 3. A small bit of cloth to deaden the echo of the strings; damper.

apagaincendios [ah-pah-gah-in-then'-de-os], *m.* A fire-engine.

apagamiento [ah-pah-gah-me-en'-to], *m.* The act of quenching.

apagapenoles [ah-pah-gah-pay-no'-les], *m. pl. (Naut.)* Leech-ropes, leech-lines.

apagar [ah-pah-gar'], *va.* 1. To quench (sed), to extinguish, to put out (fire). 2. *(Met.)* To efface, to destroy. 3. *(Art.)* To glaring colors which are too bright or garling. 4. To switch off, to turn off (luz). 5. *(Mech.)* To dead, deaden. **Apagar la cal**, to slake lime. **Apagar la sed**, to quench the thirst. **Apagar la voz**, to put a mute on the bridge of stringed musical instruments for the purpose of softening the sound. **Apagarse la lumbre, la luz o el fuego**, to go out.

apagavelas [ah-pah-gah-vay-lahs], *m.* Canddle snuffer.

apagógico, ca [ah-pah-go'-he-co, cah], *a.* Apagogical, that shows the absurdity which arises from denying a thing.

apagón [ah-pah-gone'], *a. (Mex.)* Blackout.

apagoso [ah-pah-go-so], *a.* *(LAm.)* *V.* APAGADIZO.

apainelado, da [ah-pah-e-nay-lah'-do, dah], *a. (Arch.)* In imitation of half an ellipsis (arcos).

apaisado, da [ah-pah-e-sah'-do, dah], *a.* Resembling a landscape: applied to a painting broader than it is high. Squat, flattened.

apajarado [ah-pah-hah-rah-do], *a.* *(Cono Sur)* Daft, scatterbrained.

apalabrar [ah-pah-lah-brahr], *va.* To agree to; **estar apalabrado**, to be committed, have given one's word. *-vr.* To come to a verbal agreement.

apalabrear [ah-pah-lah-bray-ahr], *(LAm.)* *V.* APALABRAR.

Apalaches [ah-pah-lah-chays], *m. & pl.* **Montes Apalaches**, Appalachians.

apalambrar [ah-pah-lam-brar'], *va. (Obs.)* To set on fire. **Apalambrarse de sed**, to be parched with thirst.

apalancamiento [ah-pah-lahn-cah-me-ayn-to], *m.* Leverage.

apalancar [ah-pah-lan-car'], *va.* To move with a lever. *(fig.)* To support; *(Cono Sur)* **apalancar a uno**, to wangle a job for somebody. *-vn.* To hide; to settle down.

apalé [ah-pah-lay], *interj. (Mex.)* Goodness me!, look out!, watch it!.

apaleada [ah-pah-lay-ah-dah], *f.* *(Cono Sur, Mex.) (Agri.)* Winnowing.

apaleador, ra [ah-pah-lay-ah-dor' rah], *m. & f.* One who uses cudgels, cudgeller.

apaleamiento [ah-pah-lay-ah-me-en'-to], *m.* Drubbing; beating.

apalear [ah-pah-lay-ar'], *va.* 1. To cane, to drub, to cudgel, to maul. 2. To beat out the dust, to horsewhip. 3. To move grain to prevent its being spoiled. **Apalear el dinero**, to heap up money with shovels, to be excessively rich.

apaleo [ah-pah-lay'-o], *m.* Act of moving or shovelling grain.

apalmada [ah-pal-mah'-dah], *a.* (her.) Palm of the hand stretched out in a coat of arms.

apallar [ah-pah-lyahr], *va.* *(LAm.)* To harvest.

apamparse [ah-pahm-pahr-say], *vr.* *(Cono Sur)* to become bewildered, to lose one's grip.

apanado [ah-pah-nah-do], 1. *a.* *(LAm.)* Breaded, cooked in breadcrumbs. 2. *m.* *(And)* Beating.

apanaje [ah-pah-nah'-hay], *m.* Appanage, yearly income.

apanalado, da [ah-pah-nah-lah'-do, dah], *a.* Like honeycomb; deeply pitted.

apanar [ah-pah-nahr], *va.* *(LAm. Culin.)* To cover in breadcrumbs.

apancle [ah-pahn-clay], *m.* *(Mex.)* Irrigation ditch.

apancora [ah-pan-co'-rah], *f.* The seahedgehog: echinus.

apandar [ah-pan-dar'], *va.* *(coll.)* To pilfer, to steal.

apandillar [ah-pan-deel-lyar], *va.* To form a league, a party, or a faction. *vr.* To be united to form a party or a faction: it is taken generally in a bad sense.

apandorgarse [ah-pan-dor-gar'-say], *vr.* To grow fat (used of women).

apanicar [ah-pah-ne-cahr], *va.* *(Cono Sur)* To cause panic.

apani(a)guarse [ah-pah-ne-ah-goo-ahr-say], *vr.* *(And. Carib.)* To gang up.

apanojado, da [ah-pah-no-hah'-do, dah], *a.* *(Bot.)* Paniculate, bearded like seeds.

apantallado [ah-pahn-tah-lyah-do], *a.* *(Mex.)* Impressed, overwhelmed; crushed; **quedar apantallado**, to be left open-mouthed.

apantallar [ah-pahn-tah-lyahr], *va.* *(Mex.)* To impress; to fill with wonder.

apantanar [ah-pan-tah-nar'], *va.* 1. To fill a piece of ground with water; to make a pool of water.

apantuflado, da [ah-pan-too-flah'-do, dah], *a.* Wearing slippers.

apañado, da [ah-pah-nyah-do, dah], *a.* 1. Resembling woollen cloth in body. *(coll.)* 2. Suitable, fit (for), apposite. 3. Dexterous, skillful. *-pp.* of APAÑAR.

apañador, ra [ah-pah-nyah-dor', rah], *m. & f.* 1. One who grasps or seizes. 2. A pilferer.

apañadura [ah-pah-nyah-doo'-rah], *f.* The act of seizing, snatching, or grasping away.

apañamiento [ah-pah-nyah-me-en'-to], *m.* *V.* APAÑO.

apañar [ah-pah-nyar'], *va.* 1. To grasp or seize. 2. *(Met.)* To carry away. 3. To pilfer. 4. To dress, to clothe. 5. To patch, to mend. *-vr.* *(coll.)* To submit to, to reconcile oneself to a thing. To be skillful, to be clever, to manage, to get along without help, to find a way. **Apañaos como podáis**, manage as best you can. *(Cono Sur)* **apañarse algo**, to get one's hands on something.

apaño [ah-pah'-nyo], *m.* 1. The act of seizing or grasping. 2. Cleverness or ability to do a thing. 3. *(Prov.)* A patch or other way of mending a thing. **Esto no tiene apaño**, there's no answer to this one.

apañuscar [ah-pah-nyoos-car'], *va.* *(coll.)* To rumple, to crush.

apapachar [ah-pah-pah-chahr], *va.* *(Carib.)* To cuddle.

apapagayado, da [ah-pah-pah-gah-yah'-do, dah], *a.* Parrot-like; very often applied to the nose.

aparador [ah-pah-rah-dor'], *m.* 1. Sideboard; dresser. 2. Side-table in churches for the service of the altar. 3. Workshop of an artisan. 4. Plate rack. **Estar de aparador**, *(coll.)* to be decked out or dressed in style.

aparadorista [ah-pah-rah-do-res-tah], *m. & f.* *(Mex.)* Window dresser.

aparadura [ah-pah-rah-doo'-rah], *f.* *(Naut.)* Garboard, garboard plank, garboard strake.

aparar [ah-pah-rar'], *va.* 1. To stretch out the hands or skirts for catching any thing. 2. To heap the earth round plants. 3. Among shoemakers, to close the quarters of a shoe. 4. To dress with an adze, dub. **Aparar un navío**, *(Naut.)* to dub a ship.

aparasolado, da [ah-pah-rah-so-lah'-do, dah], *a. (Bot.)* Umbelliferous.

aparatarse [ah-pah-rah-tahr-say], *vr. (And. Cono Sur)* Se **aparata,** it's brewing up for a storm.

aparato [ah-pah-rah'-to], *m.* 1. Apparatus, preparation, disposition. **Aparato auditivo,** hearing aid. **Aparato fotográfico,** camera. **Aparato de fax,** facsimile machine (fax). **"Aparato de datos preparado" (DSR)** *(Comp.),* "data set ready" (DSR). 2. Pomp, ostentation, show. 3. Circumstance or token which precedes or accompanies something. 4. Appliance, engine, machine. 5. Collection of instruments for a surgical operation.

aparatosamente [ah-pah-rah-to-sah-mayn-tay], *adv.* Showily, ostentatiously; pretentiously.

aparatosidad [ah-pah-rah-to-see-dahd], *f.* Showiness, ostentation; pretentiousness.

aparatoso, sa [ah-pah-rah-to'-so, sah], *a. (Ant.)* Pompous, showy, ushered in with great preparations.

aparcadero [ah-par-cah-day-ro], *m.* Parking lot.

aparcamiento [ah-par-ca-me-en'-to], *m.* 1. Parking. 2. Parking lot. **Aparcamiento subterráneo,** underground parking.

aparcar [ah-par-car'], *va.* To park.

aparcería [ah-par-thay-ree'-ah], *f.* Partnership.

aparcero [ah-par-thay'-ro], *m.* 1. Partner in a farm. 2. An associate in general.

aparear [ah-pah-ray-ar'], *va.* To match, to mate, to suit one thing to another. *-vr.* To be coupled in pairs.

aparecer [ah-pah-ray-therr'], *vn. & vr.* To appear unexpectedly, to go forth, to come up. **Apareció borracho,** he turned up drunk. **No ha aparecido ese libro,** that book still hasn´t turned up.

aparecido [ah-pah-ray-thee'-do], *m.* Ghost. **Aparecido,** *da, pp.* of APARECER.

aparecimiento [ah-pah-ray-the-me-en'-to], *m.* An apparition, appearing.

aparejado, da [ah-pah-ray-hah'-do, dah], *a.* Prepared, fit, ready. *-pp.* of APAREJAR.

aparejador, ra [ah-pah-ray-hah-dor', rah], *m. & f.* 1. One who prepares or gets ready. 2. Overseer of a building. 3. *(Naut.)* Rigger.

aparejar [ah-pah-ray-har'], *va.* 1. To get ready. 2. To saddle or harness horses. 3. *(Naut.)* To rig a ship, to furnish. 4. To prepare the work which is to be painted or gilded. 5. To prepare the timber and stones for a building. *-vr.* To get ready, to equip.

aparejo [ah-pah-ray'-ho], *m.* 1. Preparation, disposition. 2. Harness, gear. 3. *(Pict.)* Sizing of a piece of linen or board. 4. *(Naut.)* Tackle and rigging on a ship, furniture. **Aparejo de amante y estrella,** runner and tackle. **Aparejo de amura,** tacktackle. **Aparejo de bolinear,** bowline tackle. **Aparejo de combés,** luff-tackle. **Aparejo de estrelleras de combés,** winding-tackle. **Aparejo de estrique,** garnet, a tackle with which goods are hoisted in and out of the hold. **Aparejo de peñol,** yard-tackle. **Aparejo de pescante,** fish-tackle. **Aparejo de polea,** burton, a small tackle used in hoisting things in and out of a ship. **Aparejo real,** main-tackle. **Aparejo de virador,** Top-tackle. **Aparejo de rolín,** rolling-tackle. **Aparejo del tercio de las vergas mayores,** quarter-tackle. 5. Pack-saddle. *V.* ALBARDA. *-pl.* 1. The apparatus, tools, or instruments necessary for a trade. 2. *(Art.)* The materials necessary for priming, burnishing, and gilding.

aparejuelo [ah-pah-ray-hoo-ay'-lo], *m. dim.* A small apparatus. **Aparejuelos,** *(Naut.)* Small-tackle. **aparejuelos de portas,** port-tackle.

aparencial [ah-pah-ren-the-ahl], *a.* Apparent.

aparentado, da [ah-pah-ren-tah'-do, dah], *a. (Obs.)* Related, allied, *-pp.* of APARENTAR.

aparentar [ah-pah-ren-tar'], *va.* To affect, to pretend, to make a false show. **El rico aparenta pobreza y el vicioso virtud,** the rich man affects poverty, and the vicious virtue. *-vn.* To show off.

aparente [ah-pah-ren'-tay], *a.* 1. Apparent, not real, flashy. 2. Convenient, seasonable, fit, suited. 3. Conspicuous, evident.

aparentemente [ah-pah-ren-tay-men'-tay], *adv.* Apparently, outwardly.

aparición [ah-pah-re-the-on'],*f.* Apparition, act of appearing. **Un libro de próxima aparición,** a book soon to be published.

apariencia [ah-pah-re-en'-the-ah], *f.* 1. Appearance, outside. **Las aparencias engañan,** appearances are deceptive. 2. Face, likeness, resemblance. 3. Vestige. 4. Pageant. 5. *(Obs.)* Probability, conjecture. **Caballo de apariencia,** a stately horse. *-pl.* 1. Phenomena discovered by astonomical observations. 2. Decorations of the stage.

aparrado, da [ah-par-rah'-do, dah], *a.* Crooked, or like vines, shrubby: applied to trees and plants.

aparragado [ah-pah-rrah-gah-do], *(Cono Sur) a. m.* Dwarfish.

aparragarse [ah-pah-rrah-gahr-say], *vr.* 1. *(CAm.)* To roll up, to curl up. 2. *(Cono Sur)* To squad, to crouch down. 3. *(CAm. Cono Sur, Mex.)* To remain stunted, to stay small. 4. *(CAm. Cono Sur)* To shrink, to grow small.

aparroquiado, da [ah-par-ro-ke-ah'-do, dah], *a.* Belonging to a parish, parishioner. *-pp.* of APARROQUIAR.

aparroquiar [ah-par-ro-ke-ar'], *va.* To bring or attract customers.

apartación [ah-par-tah-the-on'], *f. (Chem.)* Separation of some one or more of the component parts of a body.

apartadamente, *adv.* Privately, apart.

apartadero [ah-par-tah-day'-ro], *m.* 1. Parting-place, crossroads, cross way, side-track, siding, railroad switch; shunting. 2. A turn-out; widened space, in canals. 3. A sorting-room for wool or other materials.

apartadijo [ah-par-tah-dee'-ho], *m.* A small part, share or portion. **Hacer apartadijos,** to divide a whole into shares.

apartadizo [ah-par-tah-dee'-tho], *m.* A small room, separated or taken from another apartment.

apartado, da [ah-par-tah'-do, dah], *a.* 1. Separated. 2. Distant, retired. 3. Distinct, different. *-pp.* of APARTAR.

apartado [ah-par-tah'-do], *m.* 1. Post-office box. 2. A room separate from the rest of the house. 3. A smelting house. 4. (Metal) Extraction.

apartador, ra [ah-par-tah-dor', rah], *m. & f.* 1. One who divides or separates. 2. A sorter in paper-mills. **Apartador de ganado,** one who steals sheep or cattle. **Apartador de metales,** smelter, one who smelts ores.

apartamiento [ah-par-tah-me-en'-to], *m.* 1. Apartment. **Apartamiento amueblado,** furnished apartment. 2. Separation, withdrawal.

apartar [ah-par-tar'], *va.* 1. To part, to separate, to divide. 2. To dissuade one. **Apartar a uno de un propósito,** to dissuade somebody from an intention. 3. To remove a thing. **Apartó el plato con la mano,** he pushed his plate aside. 4. To sort letters. *-vr.* 1. To withdraw from a place, to hold off. **Apartarse de un camino,** to turn off a road. 2. To be divorced. 3. To desist from a claim, action, or plea. 4. *va. & vr.* **Apartar,** or **apartarse del derecho,** to cancel any claim or right.

aparte [ah-par'-tay], *m.* 1. Break in a line, space marking a paragraph. 2. *(Theat.)* An aside. 3. Apart, aside; separately; **eso aparte,** we shall to consider that separately. 3. *prep.* **Aparte de,** apart from that.

apartidismo [ah-par-te-des-mo], *m.* Non-political nature, non-party character.

apartidista [ah-par-te-des-tah], *a.* Apolitical.

aparvar [ah-par-var'], *va.* 1. To arrange the corn for being thrashed. 2. To heap, to throw together.

apasionadamente [ah-pah-se-o-nah-dah-men'-tay], *adv.* Passionately, intensely, fervently.

apasionado, da [ah-pah-se-o-nah'-do, dah], *a.* 1. Passionate. 2. Affected with pain. 3. Devoted to a person or thing. *-pp.* of APASIONAR. *-m.* Admirer.

apasionamiento [ah-pah-se-o-nah-mee-en'-to], *m.* Passion, intense emotion, vehemence.

apasionante [ah-pah-se-o-nahn'-tay], *a.* Exciting. **Una novela apasionante,** a thrilling, exciting novel.

apasionar [ah-pah-se-o-nar'], *va.* To inspire a passion. **Me apasionan las gambas,** I adore prawns. **Es una lectura que apasiona,** it´s stirring stuff to read. *-vr.* To be taken with a person or thing to excess **Apasionarse de,** to dote upon.

apaste [ah-pas-tay], *m.* Apaxte *(CAm.)* Clay to pot.

apasturar [ah-pas-too-rar'], *va.* To pasture, to forage.

apatía [ah-pah-tee'-ah], *f.* Apathy.

apático, ca [ah-pah'-te-co, cah], *a.* Apathetic, indifferent.

apátrida [ah-pah-tre-dah], *a. m. & f.* Stateless, unpatriotic.

apatronarse [ah-pah-tro-nahr-say], *vr. (And. Cono Sur)* To find a protector in somebody; to seek a domestic post with somebody.

apatusco [ah-pah-toos'-co], *m.* 1. *(coll.)* Ornament, dress. 2. A thing done with precipitation and confusion.

apazote [ah-pah-tho'-tay], *m. (Mex. Epasote) (Bot.)* American basil.

apdo. *abr.* de **Apartado de correos** (post office box).

apea [ah-pay'-ah], *f.* A roe with which the fore feet of horses are fettered.

apeadero [ah-pay-ah-day'-ro], *m.* An alighting-place, halt (ferrocarriles). **La línea cuenta con 10 estaciones y dos apeaderos,** the line has 10 stations and 2 halts. Horse block (apoyo). Small flat (casa).

apeador [ah-pay-ah-dor'], *m.* A land surveyor.

apeamiento [ah-pay-ah-me-en'-to], *m.* V. APEO.

apear [ah-pay-ar'], *va.* 1. To alight from a horse, or carriage. 2. To measure lands, tenements, or buildings; to set landmarks. 3. To block or scotch a wheel. 4. To prop a building. 5. *(Arch.)* To take a thing down from its place; to prop, stay, or shore a building, while alterations are in progress. 6. *(Met.)* To dissuade. 7. *(Met.)* To remove difficulties. **Apear el río,** to wade or ford a river. **Apear una caballería,** to shackle a horse or mule. 8. **Apear a uno de su opinión,** to make somebody give up his view, to persuade somebody that his opinion is wrong. 9. **Apear el tratamiento a uno,** to drop somebody´s title, address somebody without formality. 9. To dismiss, to sack. 10. *(And.)* To kill. *-vr.* 1. To alight. **Apearse por la cola or por las orejas,** to give some absurd answer. 2. To get out, to dismount. 3. **Apearse de algo,** to get rid of something.

apechugar [ah-pay-choo-gar'], *va.* 1. To push with the breast. 2. *(Met.)* To undertake a thing with spirit and boldness, without consideration. *-vr.* **Apechugarse algo,** *(CAm.)* To snatch something.

apedazar [ah-pay-dah-thar'], *va.* 1. To patch, to mend, to repair. 2. V. DESPEDAZAR.

apedernalado, da [ah-pay-der-anh-lah'-do, dah], *a.* Flinty.

apedrar [ah-pay-drar'], *va. (Obs.)* V. APEDREAR.

apedreadero [ah-pay-dray-ah-day'-ro], *m.* A place where boys assemble to throw stones at each other.

apedreado, da [ah-pay-dray-ah'-do, dah], *a.* 1. Stoned, pelted. 2. **Cara apedreada,** a face pitted with the small pox. *-pp.* of APEDREAR.

apedreador [ah-pay-dray-ah-dor'], *m.* One who throws stones.

apedreamiento [ah-pay-dray-ah-me-en'-to], *m.* Lapidation.

apedrear [ah-pay-dray-ar'], *va.* 1. To stone; to kill with stones. *-vn.* 1. To hail. 2. *(Met.)* To talk in a rude manner. *-vr.* To be injured by hail.

apedreo [ah-pay-dray'-o], *m.* A stoning. *(Met.)* Hail; damage by hail.

apegadamente [ah-pay-gah-dah-men'-tay], *adv.* Studiously, devotedly.

apegado [ah-pay-gah-do], *a.* Apegado a, attached to.

apegamiento [ah-pay-gah-me-en'-to], *m. (Obs.)* 1. Adhesion. 2. V. APEGO.

apegarse [ah-pay-gar'-say], *vr.* 1. To abide by. 2. To become attached (to).

apego [ah-pay'-go], *m.* Attachment, fondness.

apelable [ah-pay-lah'-blay], *a.* Appealable, subject to appeal.

apelación [ah-pay-lah-the-on'], *f.* Appeal from an inferior to a superior court. **Médico de apelación,** consultant doctor. **Recurso de apelación,** appeal. **Tribunal de apelación,** court of appeal. **Sin apelación,** hopeless. **No haber or no tener apelación,** to be despaired.

apelado, da [ah-pay-lah'-do, dah], *a.* Of the same coat or color: applied to mules or horses. *-pp.* of APELAR.

apelambrar [ah-pay-lam-brar'], *va.* To steep skins or hides in vats filled with lime-water.

apelante [ah-pay-lahn'-tay], *pa.* Appellant.

apelar [ah-pay-lar'], *vn.* 1. To appeal, to transfer a cause from an inferior to a superior court. **Apelar a,** to resort to, to recourse to. 2. To have recourse to, to seek remedy. 3. To be of the same color. **Apelar una sentencia,** to appeal against a sentence. **Apelar el enfermo,** to escape from the jaws of death in a fit of sickness.

apelativo [ah-pay-lah-tee'-vo], *a. (Gram.)* Appellative. **Nombre apelativo,** an appellative name.

apeldar [ah-pel-dar'], *vn. (coll.)* To flee, to set off, to run away, used generally with *las. va.* **Apeldarlas,** to beat it.

apelde [ah-pel'-day], *m. (coll.)* 1. Flight, escape. 2. The first ringing of a bell before daybreak in convents.

apellar [ah-pel-lyar'], *va.* To dress leather; to prepare for receiving any color.

apellidado, da [ah-pel-lye-dah'-do, dah], *a* Named. *-pp.* of APELLIDAR.

apellidamiento [ah-pel-lye-dah-me-en'-to], *m.* The act of giving a name.

apellidar [ah-pel-lye-dar'], *va.* 1. To call one by his name. 2. To proclaim, to raise shouts. 3. *(Obs.)* To convene; to assemble troops.

apellido [ah-pel-lyee'-do], *m.* 1. Surname. 2. A peculiar name given to things. 3. A nickname; epithet. 4. *(Obs.)* The assembling of troops.

apelmazado [ah-payl-mah-thah-do], *a.* Compact, compressed, solid.

apelmazar [ah-pel-mah-thar'], *va.* 1. To compress, to render less spongy. 2. *(Amer.)* To be lazy, sluggish.

apelotonar [ah-pay-lo-to-nar'], *va. & r.* 1. To form balls, to mass. 2. To crowd together.

apellidar [ah-pay-lyc-dahr], *va.* To name, to surname, to call. *vr.* To be called. **¿Cómo se apellida usted?,** what's your family name?

apellido [ah-pay-lye-do], *m.* Name; surname, family name.

apenado [ah-pay-nah-do], *a. (LAm.)* Ashamed, embarrassed.

apenar [ah-pay-nar'], *va. & vr.* 1. To grieve. 2. To become embarrassed. **Apenarse por algo,** to grieve about something.

apenas [ah-pay'-nas], *adv.* 1. Scarcely, hardly; with a deal of trouble. **Apenas si pude levantarme,** I could hardly get up. 2. No sooner than, as soon as. **Apenas hube llegado cuando....,** no sooner had I arrived than...

apencar [ah-pen-car'], *vn.* To accept with repugnance.

apendectomía [ah-pen-dayc-to-me-ah], *f.* Appendectomy.

apendejarse [ah-pen-day-hahr-say], *vr. (Carib.)* To get silly.

apéndice [ah-pen'-de-thay], *m.* Appendix, supplement.

apendicitis [ah-pen-de-thee'-tis], *f. (Med.)* Appendicitis.

Apenino, na [ah-pay-nee'-no, nah], *a.* Apennine.

apenitas [ah-pay-ne-tahs], *adv. (And. Cono Sur)* V. APENAS.

apensionado [ah-pen-se-o-nah-do], *a. (And. Cono Sur, Mex.)* Depressed, sad; grieved.

apensionar [ah-pen-se-o-nahr], *(And. Cono Sur, Mex.)* To sadden, to grieve. *-vr.* To become sad.

apeñuscarse [ah-pay-nyoos-car-say], *vr. (Cono Sur)* To crowd together.

apeo [ah-pay'-o], *m.* 1. Survey, mensuration of lands or buildings. 2. Props, stays, etc., put under the upper parts of a building, while the lower are repaired.

apeonar [ah-pay-o-nar'], *va.* To walk or run swiftly: used of birds.

apeorar [ah-pay-o-rahr], *vn.* To get worse.

apepsia [ah-pep'-se-ah], *f. (Med.)* Apepsy, indigestion.

aperado [ah-pay-rah-do], *a. (Cono Sur)* Well-equipped.

aperador [ah-pay-rah-dor'], *m.* 1. A farmer. 2. A wheelwright.

aperar [ah-pay-rar'], *va.* To carry on the trade of a wheelwright. -*vr.* **Aperarse de algo,** *(Cono Sur)* To equip oneself.

apercibimiento [ah-per-the-be-me-en'-to], *m.* 1. The act of providing or getting ready. 2. Arrangement. 3. Order, advice, warning. 4. Summons.

apercibir [ah-per-the-beer'], *va.* 1. To provide, to get ready. 2. To warm, to advise. 3. *(Law.)* To summon. **(Yo apercibo, yo apercibí,** from **Apercibir,** *V.* PEDIR). 4. *(LAm.)* To notice. -*vr.* To prepare oneself, To get ready.

aperción [ah-per-the-on'], *f.* Act of opening. *V.* ABERTURA.

apercollar [ah-per-col-lyar'], *va.* 1. *(coll.)* To seize one by the collar. 2. *(Met.)* To snatch away (arrebatar). 3. *(coll.)* To assassinate (asesinar).

aperchar [ah-payr-chahr], *va. (CAm. Cono Sur)* To pile up, to stack up.

aperdigado, da [ah-per-de-gah'-do, dah], *a.* 1. Broiled, toasted. 2. Condemned and burned by the Inquisition. -*pp.* of APERDIGAR.

aperdigar [ah-per-de-gar'], *va. V.* PERDIGAR.

apergaminado, da [ah-per-gah-me-nah'-do, dah], *a.* Dry and yellow like parchment.

apergaminarse [ah-payr-gah-me-nahr-say], *vr.* To get like parchment; to dry up, to get yellow and wrinkled.

apergollar [ah-payr-go-lyahr], *va. (LAm.)* To grab by the throat.

aperital [ah-pay-re-tahl], *m. (Cono Sur) V.* APERITIVO.

aperitivo, va [ah-pay-re-tee'-vo, vah], *a.* 1. Aperitive. 2. Appetizer (bebida).

apero [ah-pay'-ro], *m.* 1. The implements used on a farm. 2. The tools necessary for a trade. 3. Gear (utensilio).

aperreado, da [ah-per-ray-ah'-do, dah], *a.* Harassed. **Andar aperreado,** to be harassed or fatigued. -*pp.* of APERREAR.

aperredor, ra [ah-per-ray-ah-dor', rah], *m. & f. (coll.)* One that is importunate, an intruder.

aperrear [ah-per-ray-ar'], *va.* To throw one to the dogs. -*vr.* To toil and beat about; to overwork oneself.

aperreo [ah-pay-rray-o], *m.* Harassment, worry; toil, overwork. *(LAm.)* Nuisance.

apersogar [ah-payr-so-gahr], *va.* To tether, tie up. *(Carib.)* To string together.

apersonado [ah-payr-so-nah-do], *a.* **Bien apersonado,** presentable, nice looking.

apersonarse [ah-per-so-nar'-say], *vr.* 1. *(Law.) V.* COMPADECER. 2. *(Obs.)* To appear genteel.

apertura [ah-per-too'-rah], *f. V.* ABERTURA. The calling to order of assemblies, corporations, etc.

aperturismo [ah-payr-too-res-mo], *m.* Liberalization; relaxation, loosening-up.

aperturista [ah-payr-too-res-tah], *a.* Liberalizing.

apesadumbrado, da [ah-pay-sah-doom-brah'-do, dah], *a.* Anxious, vexed, mournful. -*pp.* of APESADUMBRAR.

apesadumbrar[ah-pay-sah-doom-brar'], *va.* To vex, to cause affliction. -*vr.* To grieve.

apesaradamente [ah-pay-sah-rah-dah-men'-tay], *adv.* Mournfully, grievously.

apesarar [ah-pay-sah-rar'], *va. V.* APESADUMBRAR.

apescollar [ah-pays-co-lyahr], *va. (Cono Sur)* To seize by the neck.

apesgamiento [ah-pes-gah-me-en'-to], *m.* The act of sinking under a burden.

apesgar [ah-pes-gar'], *va.* To overload, to sink under a load. -*vr.* To grow dull; to be aggrieved.

apestado, da [ah-pes-tah'-do, dah], *a.* 1. Pestered, annoyed. 2. Full. **Estar apestado de alguna cosa,** to have plenty of a thing, even to loathing and satiety. **La plaza está apestada de verduras,** the market-place is full of greens. -*pp.* of APESTAR.

apestar [ah-pes-tar'], *va.* 1. To infect with the plague. 2. To cause an offensive smell. In this sense it is commonly used as a neuter verb in the third person; e.g. **aquí apesta,** there is here an offensive smell. 3. *(Met.)* To corrupt, to turn putrid. 4. To pester, to cause displeasure, to nauseate. **Fulano me apesta con su afectación,** he sickens me with his affectation. -*vr. (Med.)* To catch the plague. *(LAm.* Bot.) To be blighted. *(And.)* To catch a cold.

apestillar [ah-pays-te-lyahr], *va.* 1. *(Cono Sur)* To catch, to grab, to hold of. 2. To tell off.

apestoso, sa [ah-pes-to'-so, sah], *a.* Foul-smelling, sickening, nauseating.

apétalo, la [ah-pay-tah-lo, ah], *a. (Bot.)* Apetalous, without flower-leaves.

apetecedor, ra [ah-pay'-tah-lo, lah], *m. & f.* One who longs for a thing.

apetecer [ah-pay-tay-therr'], *va.* To long for a thing, to crave. **Me apetece un helado,** I feel like an ice-cream.

apetecible [ah-pay-tay-thee'-blay], *a.* Desirable, worthy of being wished for.

apetencia [ah-pay-ten'-the-ah], *f.* 1. Appetite, hunger. 2. Natural desire of something. **(Yo apetezco,** from **apetecer,** *V.* ABORRECER).

apetite [ah-pay-tee'-tay], *vn.* Sauce. *m.* Appetizer; *(fig.)* incentive.

apetitivo, va [ah-pay-te-tee'-vo, vah], *a.* Appetitive, having a strong wish or urge.

apetito [ah-pay-tee'-to], *m.* 1. Appetite, the natural desire for food. 2. Hunger. 3. Desire, liking, willingness

apetitoso, sa [ah-pay-te-to'-so, sah], *a.* 1. Pleasing to the taste, tempting the appetite. 2. *(Obs.)* Pursuing sensual pleasures.

apezuñar [ah-pay-thoo-nyar'], *vn.* To tread firm on the hoof.

API *m. & f.* Abr de **Agente de la propiedad immobiliaria** (Real estate agent).

apí [ah-pe'], *m. & f.* A non- alcoholic maize drink. *(And. Cono Sur)* **El vaso se hizo apí,** the glass was smashed to pieces.

apiadar [ah-pe-ah-dahr'], *va.* To move to pity.

apiadarse [ah-pe-ah-dar'-say], *vr.* To pity, to treat with compassion.

apiado [ah-pe-ah-do], *m. (Cono Sur)* Celery liquor.

apiaradero [ah-pe-ah-ra-day-ro], *m.* A shepherd's account of the number of sheep which compose his flock.

apiario, ria [ah-pe-ah'-re-o, ah], *a.* Resembling or relating to the honey-bee.

apicarado, da [ah-pe-cah-rah'-do, dah], *a.* Roguish, knavish, impudent.

apicararse [ah-pe-cah-rar'-say], *vr.* To acquire the manners of a rogue.

ápice [ah'-pe-thay], *m.* 1. Apex, summit, utmost height. 2. The upper part of a thing. 3. *(Met.)* The most intricate or most arduous point of a question. **Ápices,** anthers of flowers. **Estar en los ápices,** to have a complete and minute knowledge of a thing.

apichicarse [ah-pe-che-car-say], *vr. (Cono Sur)* To squat, to crouch.

apiculado, da [ah-pe-coo-lah'-do, dah], *a.* Apiculate; sharp-pointed.

apículo [ah-pee'-coo-lo], *m.* A small, keen point.

apicultor, ra [ah-pe-cool-tor'], *m. & f.* Beekeeper, apiculture.

apicultura [ah-pe-cool-too'-rah], *f.* Apiculture, raising of bees.

apilador [ah-pe-lah-dor'], *m.* One who piles the wool up at the sheep-shearing time.

apilar [ah-pe-lar'], *va.* To heap up, to put one thing upon another.

apilonar [ah-pe-lo-nahr'], *va. (LAm.) V.* APILAR.

apimplado [ah-pem-plah-do], *a. (LAm.)* Tight, tipsy.

apimpollarse [ah-pim-pol-lyar'-say], *vr.* To germinate.

apiñado, da [ah-pe-nyah-do'-dah], *a.* Pyramidal, pine-shaped. Crowded, packed, congested. *-pp.* of APIÑAR.

apiñadura [ah-pe-nyah-doo'-rah], *f.* Crowding, congestion.

apiñamiento [ah-pe-nyah-me-en'-to], *m.* The act of pressing together.

apiñar [ah-pe-nyar'], *va.* To press together, to join, to unite. *-vr.* To clog, to crowd. **La multitud se apiñaba alrededor de él,** the crowd pressed round him.

apio [ah'-pe-o], *m. (Bot.)* Celery. **Apio montano or levístico,** *(Bot.)* Common lovage. **Apio de risa,** *(Bot.)* Crow-foot.

apiolar [ah-pe-o-lar'], *va.* 1. To gyve a hawk. 2. To tie game together by the leg. 3. *(Met. Coll.)* To seize, to apprehend. 4. *(coll.)* To kill, to murder.

apio-nabo [ah-pe-o-nah-bo], *m.* Celeriac.

apiparse [ah-pe-pahr-say], *vr.* To stuff oneself.

apir(i) [ah-pe-re], *m. (LAm.)* Mineworker.

apirético, ca [ah-pe-ray'-te-co, cah], *a.* Apyretic, free from the access of fever.

apirularse [ah-pe-roo-lahr-say], *vr. (Cono Sur)* To get dressed up to the nines.

apisonadora [ah-pe-so-nah-do'-rah], *f.* Steam roller.

apisonar [ah-pe-so-nar', *va.* 1. To roll. 2. To tamp, to drive down.

apitiquarse [ah-pe-te-car-say], *vr. (Cono Sur)* To get depressed.

apitonamiento [ah-pe-to-nah-me-en'-to], *m.* 1. Putting forth the tenderlings. 2. Passion, anger.

apitonar [ah-pe-to-nar'], *vn.* 1. To put forth the tenderlings; applied to horned animals. 2. To bud, to germ. *-va,* To pick as chickens in the eggshell. *-vr.* To treat with abusive language. To get into a huff.

apizarrado, da [ah-pe-thar-rah'-do, dah], *a.* Slate-colored.

APL *(Comp.)* APL (A Programming Language).

aplacable [ah-plah-cah'-blay], *a.* Placable, easy to be appeased, meek, gentle.

aplacación [ah-plah-cah-the-on'], *f.*

aplacamiento [ah-plah-cah-me-en'-to], *m.* Appeasableness. *-m.* Stay of execution.

aplacador, ra [ah-plah-cah-dor', rah], *m. & f.* One who appeases.

aplacar [ah-plah-car'], *va.* To appease, to pacify, to mitigate.

aplacer [ah-plah-therr'], *va.* To please. *V.* AGRADAR.

aplacerado, da [ah-plah-thay-rah'-do, dah], *a.* 1. *(Naut.)* Level and not very deep: said of the bottom of the sea. 2. *(Amer.)* Open, cleared of trees. **Sitio aplacerado,** a clearing.

aplacible [ah-plah-thee'-blay], *a.* Pleasant.

aplaciente [ah-plah-the-en'-tay], *pa.* Appeasive.

aplanacalles [ah-plah-nah-cah-llays], *m. (LAm.)* Idler, layabout.

aplanadera [ah-plah-nah-day'-rah], *f.* 1. A roller for levelling the ground. 2. Beetle, rammer.

aplanador [ah-plah-nah-dor'], *m.* 1. A leveller. 2. *(Mech.)* Battledoor, brusher, riveter; ingot hammer; cylinder roller. 3. *(Typ.)* Planer, planishing mallet.

aplanamiento [ah-plah-nah-me-en'-to], *m.* Levelling, the act of making level.

aplanar [ah-plah-nar'], *va.* 1. To level, to make even, to flatten (terreno). 2. To terrify, or astonish by some unexpected novelty. *-vr.* 1. To tumble down (edificio). 2. To lose animation or vigor (persona).

aplanático, ca [ah-plah-nah'-te-co, cah], *a.* Aplanatic, free of spherical aberration.

aplanchado [ah-plan-chah'-do], *m.* 1. Linen which is to be, or has been ironed. 2. Act of smoothing or ironing linen.

aplanchadora [ah-plan-chah-do'-rah], *f.* A woman whose trade is to iron linen.

aplanchar [ah-plan-char'], *va.* To iron linen.

aplantillar [ah-plan-teel-lyar'], *va.* To adjust or fit stones, timber, or boards, according to the model.

aplastado, da [ah-plas-tah'-do, dah], *a.* Caked; dispirited. *-pp.* of APLASTAR.

aplastante [ah-plas-tahn-tay], *a.* Overwhelming, crushing.

aplastar [ah-plas-tar'], *va.* 1. To cake, to flatten, or crush a thing, to smash. 2. To confound an opponent. *-vr.* To become flat. **Se aplastó contra la pared,** he fattened himself against the wall. 3. *(Arquit.)* To collapse. 4. *(Cono Sur)* To get discouraged. 5. *(Cono Sur)* To be drained (exhausto).

aplatanado [ah-plah-tah-nah-do], *a.* **Está aplatanado,** *(Carib.)* he has gone native. *(fig.)* Lumpish, lacking all ambition.

aplatanarse [ah-plah-tah-nahr'-say], *vr.* To become lethargic, sink into lethargy.

aplatarse [ah-plah-tahr'-say], *vr. (Carib.)* To get rich.

aplaudir [ah-plah-oo-deer'], *va.* To applaud, to extol with shouts. *vr.* To boast of, to be elated by.

aplauso [ah-plah'-oo-so], *m.* Applause, approbation, praise.

aplayar [ah-plah-yar'], *vr.* To overflow the banks.

aplazamiento [ah-plah-thah-me-en'-to], *m.* 1. Convocation, citation. 2. Deferring, postponement.

aplazar [ah-plah-thar'], *va.* 1. To convene. 2. To invest. 3. To concert, to regulate, to summon. 4. To defer, to adjourn (asunto); to treat something later. To postpone. **Se ha aplazado decisión por tiempo indefinido,** the decision has been postponed indefinitely.

aplebeyado [ah-play-bay-lyah-do], *a.* Coarse, coarsened.

aplebeyar [ah-play-bay-yar'], *va. (Obs.)* To render vile or servile. To degrade, to coarsen. *-vr.* To become coarse.

aplegar [ah-play-gar'], *va. (Prov.)* To join, to unite.

aplicabilidad [ah-plah-cah-be-le-dahd], *f.* Applicability.

aplicable [ah-plc-cah'-blay], *a.* Applicable.

aplicación [ah-ple-cah-the-on'], *f.* 1. Application. 2. Assiduity, laboriousness, close study. **Aplicación de bienes or hacienda,** the act of adjudging estates or other property. **Aplicaciones de gestión,** management applications.

aplicado, da [ah-ple-cah'-do, dah], *a.* 1. Studious, intent on a thing. 2. Industrious, laborious, painful. *-pp.* of APLICAR.

aplicar [ah-ple-car'], *va.* 1. To apply, to put one thing to another; to clap. 2. *(Met.)* to consider a subject under discussion. 3. *(Met.)* To attribute or impute. 4. *(Law.)* To adjudge. *vr.* 1. To study or devote oneself to a thing. 2. To earn a living.

aplique [ah-ple-kay], *m.* Wall lamp, *(Theat.)* Piece of stage decor.

aplomado, da [ah-plo-mah'-do, dah], *a.* 1. Of the color of lead. 2. Leaden. 3. *(Met.)* Heavy, dull, lazy. 4. Self-confident. *-pp.* of APLOMAR.

aplomar [ah-plo-mar'], *va. (Obs.)* To overload, to crush. *-vn.* To use a plummet and line to see if a wall has been perpendicularly raised. *-vr.* To tumble, to fall to the ground: applied to buildings. *(fig.)* To gain confidence. *(Cono Sur)* To get embarrassed.

aplomo [ah-plo'-mo], *m.* 1. Tact, prudence, management, self-possession. 2. Plumb-line, plummet. 3. *(Mus.)* Exactness in time. 4. Due proportion among the figures of a picture. *-a.* Plumb, perpendicular. *V. (á)* PLOMO.

apnea [ap-nay'-ah], *f.* Apnea, temporary inability to breathe.

apoca [ah'-po-cah], *f. (Law. Prov.)* Receipt, acquittance, discharge.

apocado, da [ah-po-cah'-do, dah], *a.* 1. Pusillanimous, mean-spirited, cowardly. 2. Narrow-hoofed. 3. Of mean, low extraction. *-pp.* of APOCAR.

apocador, ra [ah-po-cah-dor', rah], *m. & f.* One who lessens or diminishes.

apocalipsi, apocalipsis [ah-po-cah-leep'-se, sis], *m.* Apocalypse, the Relation of St. John.

apocalíptico, ca [ah-po-cah-lep'-te-co, cah], *a.* Apocalyptical.

apocamiento [ah-po-cah-me-en'-to], *m.* Abjectness of mind, meanness of spirit, littleness.

apocar [ah-po-car'], *va.* 1. To lessen. 2. *(Met.)* To cramp, to contract. *-vr.* To humble oneself, to undervalue oneself.

apócema, apócima [ah-po'-thay-mah, ah-po'-the-mah], *f. (Med.)* Apozem, a decoction.

apocopar [ah-po-co-par'], *va.* To take away the last letter or syllable of a word. To apocopate.

apócope [ah-po'-co-pay], *f. (Poetic.)* A figure, where the last letter or syllable of a word is taken away.

apócrifamente [ah-po'-cre-fah-men-tay], *adv.* Apocryphally, uncertainly, on a false foundation.

apócrifo, fa [ah-po'-cre-fo, fah], *a.* Apocryphal, fabulous, of doubtful authority.

apocrisiario [ah-po-cre-se-ah'-re-o], *m.* A Greek ambassador.

apochongarse [ah-po-chon-gahr-say], *vr. (Cono Sur)* To get scared.

apodador [ah-po-dah-dor'], *m.* A wag, one who ridicules or scoffs.

apodar [ah-po-dar'], *va.* To give nicknames, to ridicule.

apodencado, da [ah-po-den-cah'-do, dah], *a.* Pointer-like.

apoderado, da [ah-po-day-rah'-do, dah], *a.* 1. Empowered, authorized. 2. *(Obs.)* Powerful. *-pp.* of APODERAR.

apoderado [ah-po-day-rah'-do], *m.* Proxy, attorney, agent.

apoderar [ah-po-day-rar'], *va.* To empower; to grant a power of attorney. *-vr.* To possess oneself of a thing. 2. *(Obs.)* To become powerful or strong.

apodíctico, ca [ah-po-deec'-te-co, cah], *a.* Apodictical, demonstrative.

apodo [ah-po'-do], *m.* A nickname.

ápodo, da [ah'-po-do, dah], *a. (Zool.)* Apodous, without feet.

apódosis [ah-po'-do-sis], *f.* Apodosis, the conclusion of a conditional sentence; correlative to protasis.

apófise, apófisis [ah-po'-fe-say, ah-po'-fe-sis], *f. (Med.)* The prominent part of some bones, the same as process.

apoflegmático, ca [ah-po-fleg-mah'-te-co, cah], *a.* Apophlegmatic, drawing away phlegm.

apogeo [ah-po-hay'-o], *m.* 1. *(Astr.)* Apogee. 2. Culmination, apex. **En todo su apogeo,** in all its glory, at is peak.

apógrafo [ah-po'-grah-fo], *m.* Apograph, transcript, or copy of some book or writing.

apolillado, da [ah-po-leel-lyah'-do, dah], *a.* Moth-eaten, worm-eaten. *-pp.* of APOLILLAR.

apolilladura [ah-po-leel-layh-doo'-rah], *a.* A hole eaten by moths in clothes and other things made of wool.

apolillar [ah-po-le-lyar'], *va.* To gnaw or eat clothes, or other things. *(Cono Sur)* **Estar apolillado,** to be snoozing. *-vr.* To be moth-eaten.

apolinar, apolíneo, nea [ah-po-le-nar', ah-po-lee'-nay-o, ah], *a. (Poetic.)* Belonging to Apollo.

apolinarista [ah-po-le-nah-rees'-tah], *m.* Apollinarian, name given to the followers of a sect of Christians in the fourth century.

apolismar [ah-po-les-mah], *va. (LAm.)* To ruin, destroy. *-vr. (LAm.)* To grow weak, weaken.

apolítico [ah-po-le'-te-co], *a.* Apolitical, non-political.

apoliyar [ah-po-le-yahr], *va. V.* APOLILLAR.

Apolo [ah-po-lo], *m.* Apollo.

apologético, ca [ah-po-lo-hay'-te-co, cah], *a.* 1. Apologetic, excusatory. 2. Belonging to an apologue or fable. 3. Applied to the writers of apologues.

apología [ah-po-lo-hee'-ah], *f.* Apology, defence, excuse. **Una apología del terrorismo,** a statement in support of terrorism.

apológico, ca [ah-po-lo'-he-co, cah], *a.* That which relates to an apologue.

apologista [ah-po-lo-hees'-tah], *m.* An apologist.

apólogo [ah-po'-l-go], *m.* Apologue, a fable or story, to convey moral truth.

apoltronado [ah-pol-tro-nah-do], *a.* Lazy.

apoltronarse [ah-pol-tro-nar'-say], *vr.* To grow lazy, to loiter.

apolvillarse [ah-pol-ve-lyahr-say], *vr. (Cono Sur Agri.)* To be blighted.

apomazar [ah-po-mah-thar'], *va.* 1. To glaze printed linens with pumice-stone for the purpose of painting on them. 2. To burnish a surface with pumice-stone.

apomeli [ah-po-may'-le], *f.* A decoction prepared of honeycomb dissolved in vinegar and water.

aponeurosis [ah-po-nay-oo-ro'-sis], *f.* Aponeurosis, fascia.

aponeurótico, ca [ah-po-nay-oo-ro'-te-co, cah], *a.* Aponeurotic, fascia-like.

apoplejía [ah-po-play-hee'-ah], *f.* Apoplexy.

apoplético, ca [ah-po-play'-te-co, cah], *a.* Apoplectic.

apoquinar [ah-po-ke-nahr], *va.* To fork out, to pay up.

aporcadura [ah-por-cah-doo'-rah], *f.* The act of raising earth around plants; earthing up.

aporcar [ah-por-car'], *va.* To cover garden-plants with earth for the purpose of whitening them and making them tender; to hill.

aporisma [ah-po-rees'-mah], *m.* Ecchymosis, an extravasation of blood between the flesh and skin.

aporismarse [ah-po-ris-mar'-say], *vr.* To become an ecchymosis.

aporracear [ah-por-rah-thay-ar'], *va. (Prov.)* To pommel, to give repeated blows.

aporrar [ah-por-rar'], *vn. (coll.)* To stand mute, to get stuck for words. *-vr. (coll.)* To become a bore.

aporreado, da [ah-por-ray-ah'-do, dah] *a.* 1. Cudgelled. 2. Dragged along. *-pp.* of APORREAR.

aporreamiento [ah-por-ray-ah-me-en'-to], *m.* The act of beating or pommelling.

aporreante [ah-por-ray-ahn'-tay], *pa. (coll.)* Cudgeller, applied to bad fencers.

aporrear [ah-por-ray-ar'], *va.* 1. To beat or cudgel, to knock, to maul. **Aporrear el piano,** to thumb the piano. 2. *(fig.)* To bother, pester. 4. To bang away at, to thump. *-vr,* To slave away, slog. To study with intense application.

aporreo [ah-por-ray'-o], *m.* The act of beating, pommelling, or cudgelling.

aporrillarse [ah-por-reel-lyar'-say], *vr.* to get swellings in the joints; a term applied to horses.

aporrillo [ah-por-reel'-lyo], *adv. (coll.)* Plentifully.

aportación [ah-por-tah-the-on'], *f.* Contribution.

aportadero [ah-por-tah-day'-ro], *m.* A place where a ship or person may stop.

aportar [ah-por-tar'], *vn.* 1. To make a port, to arrive at a port. 2. To reach an unexpected place when one is benighted. 3. *-va.* To bring, contribute, to bring forward.

aporte [ah-por-tay], *m.* Contribution.

aportellado [ah-por-tel-lyah'-do], *m. (Obs.)* Formerly an officer of justice, a member of the council of large towns, that administered justice to the people of the neighboring villages.

aportillar [ah-por-teel-lyar'], *va.* 1. To make a breach in a rampart. 2. To break down, to break open. *-vr.* To tumble down, to fall into ruins.

aposentador, ra [ah-po-sen-tah-dor', rah], *m.& f.* 1. One who lets lodgings. 2. Usher in a theater (acomodador).

aposentamiento [ah-po-sen-tah-me-en'-to], *m.* The act of lodging or affording a temporary habitation.

aposentar [ag-po-sen-tar'], *va.* To lodge. *-vr.* To take a lodging; to tarry at night.

aposentillo [ah-po-sen-teel'-lyo], *m. dim.* A small room, a bedroom.

aposento [ah-po-sen'-to], *m.* 1. A room or apartment. 2. A temporary habitation; an inn. 3. A box or seat in the theater.

aposesionar [ah-po-say-se-o-nar'], *va.* To give possession. -*vr.* To take possession; to possess oneself of a thing.

aposición [ah-po-se-the-on'], *f. (Gram.)* Apposition a grammatical term.

aposiopesis [ah-po-se-o-pay'-sis], *f. (Rhet.)* A figure of speech, in which the speaker breaks off suddenly, as if unable or unwilling to declare his mind.

apósito [ah-po'-se-to], *m.* Any external medicinal application.

apospelo [ah-pos-pay'-lo], *adv. (Obs.)* 1. Against the grain. 2. Contrary to the natural order.

aposta, apostadamente [ah-pos'-tah, ah-pos-tah-dah-men'-tay], *adv.* Designedly, on purpose. *V.* ADREDE.

apostadero [ah-pos-tah-day'-ro], *m.* 1. A place where soldiers or other persons are stationed. 2. *(Naut.)* A naval station.

apostador, ra [ah-po-tah-dor'], *m. & f.* Better, one that wagers or bets.

apostal [ah-pos-tahl'], *m. (Prov.)* A convenient fishing-place in a river.

apostáleos [ah-pos-tah'-lay-os], *m. pl. (Naut.)* Thick planks for gun platforms.

apostar [ah-pos-tar'], *va.* 1 To bet, to hold a wager, to lay a bet. 2. To place relays. 3. To post soldiers or other persons in a place. **Apostarlas or apostárselas,** to contend, to defy. *-vr.* To emulate, to rival, to stand in competition. **Apostar carreras,** to run races.

apostasia [ah-pos-tah-see'-ah], *f.* 1. Apostasy. 2. *(Bot.)* A plant of the orchid family.

apostasis [ah-pos-tah'-sis], *f. (Med.)* 1. A purulent deposit at a distance from the seat of inflammation; metastatic abscess. 2. A splinter of bone.

apóstata [ah-pos'-tah-tah], *m.* Apostate; forsaker, fugitive.

apostatar [h-pos-tah-tar'], *vn.* To apostatize, to fall away.

apostema [ah-pos-tay'-mah], *f.* An aposteme, abscess.

apostemación [ag-pos-tay-mah-the-on'], *f. (Med.)* Forming an abscess, apostemation.

apostemar [ah-pos-tay-mar'], *va.* To form an abscess. *-vr.* To get an abscess; to be troubled with a purulent humor.

apostemero [ah-pos-tay-may'-ro], *m.* Bistoury, an instrument for opening abscesses.

apostemilla [ah-pos-tay-meel'-lyah], *f.dim.* 1. A small abscess or pimple. 2. Gum-boil.

apostemoso, sa [ah-pos-tay-mo'-so, sah], *a.* Relating to abscesses.

apostlllla [ah-pos-teel'-lyah], *f.* A marginal note put to a book or writing; annotation, remark; gloss.

apostillar [ah-pos-teel'-lyar], *va.* To put marginal notes to a book or writing. *-vr.* To break out in pimples or pustules.

apóstol [ah-pos'-tol], *m.* Apostle, missionary. **Apóstoles,** *(Naut.)* Hawsepieces.

apostolado [ah-pos-to-lah'-do], *m.* 1. Apostleship. 2. The congregation of the apostles. 3. The images or pictures of the twelve apostles.

apostólicamente [ah-pos-to'-le-cah-men-tay], *adv.* Apostolically.

apostólico, ca [ah-pos-to'-le-co, cah], *a.* 1. Apostolical. 2. Apostolic; that which belongs to the Pope, or derives from him apostolical authority.

apóstolos [ah-pos'-to-los], *m. pl. (Law. Obs.)* Dimissory apostolical letters.

apostrofar [ah-pos-tro-far'], *va.* To apostrophize, to address one by apostrophe; to insult.

apóstrofe [ah-pos'-tro-fay], *f. (Rhet.)* Apostrophe; insult, reprimand.

apóstrofo [ah-pos'-tro-fo], *m.* Apostrophe, a typographical sign.

apostura [ah-pos-too'-rah], *f.* 1. Gentleness, neatness in person. 2. Good order and disposition of things; high breeding.

apoteca [ah-po-tay'-cah], *f. V.* BOTICA.

apotecario [ah-o-tay-cah'-re-o], *m. (Prov.) V.* BOTICARIO

apotegma [ah-po-teg'-mah], *m.* Apothegm; maxim.

apoteósico [ah-po-tay-o'-se-co], *a. (fig.)* Huge, tremendous.

apoteosis [ah-po-tay-oh'-sis], *f.* Apotheosis, deification.

apotome [ah-po-to'-may], *m.* (Alg.) The remainder or difference of two incommensurable qualities.

apotrerar [ah-po-tray-rar'], *va.* To turn horses out to pasture.

apotrosis [ah-po-tro'-sis], *f. (Surg.)* 1. A fracture of the skull, with splinters. 2. Extraction of a splinter of bone.

apoyabrazos [ah-po-yah-brah-thos], *m.* Armrest.

apoyadero [ah-po-yah-day-ro], *m.* Prop, support.

apoyador [ah-po-yah-dor], *m.* Support, bracket.

apoyadura [ah-po-yah-doo'-rah], *f.* A flow of the milk when nurses give the bottle to babies.

apoyar [ah-po-yar'], *va.* 1. To favor, to protect, to patronize, to countenance, to further. 2. To bear upon the bit; spoken of horses which hang down their heads. **Apoyar las espuelas,** to spur. 3. To confirm, to prove, to corroborate, to hold up; to ground, to found. **Apoya esta sentencia con un texto de la Escritura,** he confirms this sentence by a text of Scripture. **Apoyar una proposición or propuesta,** to second a motion. *-vn.* To rest on; to lie. **La columna apoya sobre el pedestal,** the column rests on the pedestal. *-vr.* To lean upon a person or thing. **Apoyarse en los estribos,** to bear upon the stirrups. To rest on, be supported by. **Apoyarse contra una pared,** to lean against a wall.

apoyatura [ah-po-yah-too'-rah], *f. (Mus.)* Appoggiatura, leaning or leading note, used to prepare the ear for, or guide it to, the note it precedes.

apoyo [ah-po'-yo], *m.* 1. Prop, stay, support, fulcrum. 2. *(Met.)* Protection, patronage, help, countenance, muniment, maintenance.

apozarse [ah-po-thahr-say], *va. (And. Cono Sur)* To form a pool.

apreciable [ah-pray-teh-ah'-blay], *a.* 1. Valuable, respectable, worthy of esteem, creditable. **Los apreciables esposos,** the esteemed couple. 2. That which can fetch a price; marketable. **Una cantidad apreciable,** an appreciable quantity.

apreciación [ah-pray-teh-ah-the-on'], *f.* Estimation, valuation, appreciation. **Según nuestra apreciación,** according to our estimation.

apreciadamente [ah-pray-the-ah-dah-men'-tay], *adv.* In a valuable, respectable manner.

apreciador, ra [ah-pray-the-ah-dor', rah], *m. & f.* Estimator, appraiser, a person appointed to set a price upon a thing.

apreciar [ah-pray-the-ar'], *va.* 1. To appreciate, to appraise, to estimate, to value. 2. *(fig.)* To esteem, value. **Aprecia mucho a los niños,** she´s very fond of children. 3. *(Art., mus.* etc.) To appreciate. 4. To see, notice, observe. 4. *(LAm.)* To add value to enhance, improve. 5. *(LAm.)* To be grateful for, appreciate; **lo aprecio mucho,** I much appreciate it.

apreciativo, va [ah-pray-the-ah-tee'-vo, vah], *a.* Relating to the value set upon a thing. **Una mirada apreciativa,** an appraising look.

aprecio [ah-pray'-the-o], *m.* 1. Appraisement, appreciation, the value set upon a thing; account. **No hacer aprecio de algo,** to pay no attention to something. 2. Esteem, approbation, regard. **Tener a uno en gran aprecio,** to hold somebody in high regard.

aprehender [ah-pray-en-derr'], *va.* 1. To apprehend, to seize. 2. To fancy, to conceive, to form an idea of a thing. **Aprehender la posesión,** to take possession. **Aprehender los bienes,** to seize or distrain goods.

aprehensible [ah-prayn-se-blay], *a.* Understandable, conceivable; **una idea difícilmente aprehensible,** an idea which is difficult to pin down.

aprehensión [ah-pray-en-se-on'], *f.* 1. The act of seizing, apprehending, or taking up a criminal. 2. Apprehension, perception, acuteness; a ready and witty saying. 3. Apprehension, fear. 4. Misapprehension.

aprehensivo, va [ah-pray-en-see'-vo, vah], *a.* Apprehensive, quick to understand, fearful; sensitive; perceptive.

aprehensor, ra [ah-pray-en-sor', rah], *m. & f.* One who apprehends.

aprehensorio, ria [ah-pray-en-so'-re-o, rah], *m. & f.* Apprehending, seizing.

apremiador, ra [ah-pray-me-ah-dor', rah], *m. & f.* Compeller, one who compels to do a thing.

apremiante [ah-pray-me-ahn'-tay], *a.* Urgent, pressing. *-pa.* of APREMIAR.

apremiar [ah-pray-me-ar'], *va.* 1. To press, to urge. 2. To compel, to oblige by a judicial order. **Apremiar a uno a hacer algo,** to press somebody to do something. 3. To hurry. 4. To oppress, to harass. 5. *-vn.* To press, to be urgent. **El tiempo apremia,** time presses.

apremio [ah-pray'-me-o], *m.* 1. Pressure, constriction; constrain, force, urgency. **Por apremio de tiempo,** because time is pressing. **Por apremio de trabajo,** because of pressure of work. 2. Judicial compulsion.

aprendedor, ra [ah-pren-day-dor', rah], *a.* Learning; apt to learn.

aprender [ah-pren-der'], *va.* 1. To learn; to acquire knowledge. 2. To retain in the memory. **Aprender a hacer algo,** to learn to do something.

aprendiz, za [ah-pren-deeth', thah], *m. & f.* Apprentice or prentice; learner. **Aprendiz de todo, oficial de nada,** Jack of all trades. **Estar de aprendiz con uno,** to be apprenticed to somebody.

aprendizaje [ah-pren-de-tha'-hay], *m.* 1. Apprenticeship. 2. *(Comp.)* Training.

aprensador [ah-pren-sah-dor'], *m.* A presser or calenderer.

aprensar [ah-pren-sar'], *va.* 1. To dress cloth in a press, to calender. 2. To vex, to crush, to oppress. 3. *(Naut.)* To stow wool, cotton, etc., on board a ship.

aprensión [ah-pren-se-on'], *f.* 1. Apprehension. 2. False concept, and unfounded fear. 3. Mistrust, suspicion; particularly of one believing himself sick.

aprensivo, va [ah-pren-see'-vo, vah], *a.* Apprehensive, hypochondriac, fearful of being ill; squeamish.

apresador, ra [ah-pray-sah-dor', rah], *m. & f.* 1. Privateer, cruiser. 2. Captor.

apresamiento [ah-pray-sah-me-en'-to], *m.* Capture; clutch, hold.

apresar [ah-pray-sar'], *va.* 1. To seize, to grasp. 2. *(Naut.)* To take or capture an enemy's ship.

aprestado [ah-prays-tah-do], *a.* Ready; **estar aprestado para** , to be ready to.

aprestar [ah-pres-tar'], *va.* 1. To prepare, to make ready. 2. *-vr.* To prepare, get ready. **Aprestarse para,** to get ready to.

apresto [ah-press'-to], *m.* Preparation (preparación). Sizing (acción).

apresuración [ah-pray-soo-rah-the-on'], *f.* Acceleration, the act of quickening motion, or making haste.

apresuradamente [ah-pray-soo-rah-dah-men'-tay], *adv.* Hastily, quickly.

apresurado, da [ah-pray-soo-rah'-do, dah], *a.* 1. Brief, hasty. 2. Acting with precipitation. *-pp.* of APRESURAR.

apresuramiento [ah-pray-soo-rah-meen'-to], *m.* Eagerness, readiness to act, forwardness. *V.* APRESURACIÓN.

apresurar [ah-pray-soo-rar'], *va.* To accelerate, to hasten, to hurry, to cut off delay, to rush. *-vr.* To accelerate, to hurry, make haste. **Me apresuré a sugerir que**..., I hastened to suggest that...

apretadamente [ah-pray-tah-dah-men'-tay], *adv.* Tightly, closely; nearly; close, fast.

apretadera [ah-pray-tah-day'-rah], *f.* A strap (correa).

apretadero [ah-pray-tah-day'-ro], *m.* Truss or bandage by which ruptures are restrained from relapsing. *V.* BRAGUERO.

apretadillo, lla [ah-pray-tah-deel'-lyo, lyah], *a.dim.* Somewhat constrained, rather hard put to it. **Apretadillo está el enfermo,** The patient is in great danger.

apretadizo, za [ah-pray-tah-dee'-tho, thah], *a.* Easily compressible.

apretado, da [ah-pray-tah'-do, dah], *a.* 1. Mean, miserable, narrow-minded, illiberal; close, close-fisted; costive. 2. Hard, difficult, dangerous. **Estar apretado de dinero,** to be short of money. **En un caso apretado,** it´s a tricky business. *-pp.* of APRETAR.

apretador [ah-pray-tah-dor'], *m.* 1. One who presses or beats down. 2. A sort of doublet without sleeves. 3. A sort of corset for chidren. 4. A broad bandage put upon infants. 5. A net for tying up the hair. 6. An instrument which serves for tightening; a rammer.

apretadura [ah-pray-tah-doo'-rah], *f.* Compression.

apretamiento [ah-pray-tah-me-en'-o], *m.* 1. Crowd, great concourse of people. 2. Conflict. 3. *(Obs.)* Avarice, closeness; contractedness.

apretar [ah-pray-tar'], *va.* 1. To compress, to tighten, to press down, to crowd, to constrict, to contract, to hug. **Apretar a uno entre los brazos,** to hug somebody in one´s arms. **Apretar a uno contra la pared,** to pin somebody against the wall. 2. To constrain, to clutch. 3. To distress, to afflict with calamities. 4. To act with more vigor than usual. 5. To urge earnestly. 6. To darken that part of a painting which is too bright and glaring. **Apretar de soletas,** to run away. **Apretar con uno,** To attack a person. **Apretar la mano,** to correct with a heavy hand, to punish severely. 7. To get worse; **cuando el calor aprieta,** when the heat becomes oppresive.

apretón [ah-pray-tone'], *m.* 1. Pressure. **Apretón financiero,** financial squeeze. 2. Struggle, conflict. 3. A short but rapid race. 4. The act of throwing a thicker shade on one part of a piece of painting. 5. Press, crush, jam; **el apretón en el metro,** the crush in the subway.

apretujar [ah-pray-too-har'], *va. (coll.)* To squeeze, to crowd in a crowd of persons. **Estar apretujado entre dos personas,** to be crushed between two people.

apretujón [ah-pray-too-hon], *m.* 1. Hard squeeze; big hug. 2. Press, crush, jam.

apretura [ah-pray-too'-rah], *f.* 1. A crowd, a multitude crowding. 2. Distress, conflict, anguish. 3. A narrow, confined place; narrowness.

apriesa [ah-pre-ay'-sah], *adv.* In haste, in a hurry.

aprieto [ah-pre-ay'-to], *m.* Difficulty, pinch, pressure, stress. **Estar en un aprieto,** To be in a jam, to be in a tight position, under stress.

apriorismo [ah-pre-o-res-mo], *m.* Tendency to resolve matters hastily.

apriorístico [ah-pre-o-res-te-co], *a.* 1. A priori, deductive (deductivo). 2. Hasty, premature (precipitado).

aprisa [ah-pree'-sah], *adv.* Swiftly, promptly; fast; in a hurry.

aprisar [ah-pre-sar'], *va. (Obs.)* To hasten, to hurry, to push forward.

apriscadero [ah-pris-cah-day'-ro], *m. (Obs.) V.* APRISCO.

apriscar [ah-pris-car'], *va.* To carry to the sheep-fold, to a sure spot.

aprisco [ah-prees'-co], *m.* Sheep-fold.

aprisionar [ah-pre-se-o-nar'], *va.* 1. To confine, to imprison. 2. To bind, to subject.

aproar [ah-pro-ar'], *vn. (Naut.)* To turn the head of a ship toward any part; to trim by the head.

aprobación [ah-pro-bah-the-on'], *f.* Approbation, concurrence; consent, liking; run. **Dar su aprobación,** to give one´s consent, approve.

aprobado, da [ah-pro-bah'-do, dah], *a.* 1. Approved. 2. Passed (in an examination). *-m.* Passing mark.

aprobador, ra [ah-pro-bah-dor', rah], *m. & f.* Approver, one who approves.

aprobante [ah-pro-bahn'-tay], *pa.* 1. Approver. 2. One who proves the qualifications of a person for being a member of some corporations.

aprobar [ah-pro-bar'], *va.* To approve; to like, to be pleased with; to find. *-vn. (Univ.)* To pass. **Aprobé en francés,** I passed in French.

aprobatorio, ria [ah-pro-bah-to'-re-o, re-ah], *a.* Approbative, approving. **Una mirada aprobatoria,** an approving look.

aproches [ah-pro'-ches], *m.pl. (Mil.)* approaches, the several works made by besiegers for advancing and getting nearer to a fortress. **Contraaproches,** Counter-approaches. **Las trincheras se llaman líneas de aproches,** the trenches are called lines of approach.

aprón [ah-prone'], *m. (Zool.)* A small fresh-water fish resembling a gudgeon.

aprontamiento [ah-pron-tah-me-ayn-to], *m.* Quick delivery, rapid service.

aprontar [ah-pron-tar'], *va.* To prepare hastily, to get ready with despatch.

apronte [ah-pron-tay], *m. (Cono Sur)* 1. Heat, preliminary race. 2. **Aprontes,** preparations; **irse en los aprontes,** to waste one´s energy on unnecessary preliminaries.

apronto [ah-pron'-to], *m.* A speedy preparation.

apropiación [ah-pro-pe-ah-the-on'], *f.* Appropriation, assumption, the act of appropriating or assuming a thing. **Apropiación ilícita,** illegal seizure, misappropriation.

apropiadamente [ah-pro-pe-ah-dah-men'-tay], *adv.* Conveniently, fitly, properly.

apropiado, da [ah-pro pe-ah'-do, dah], *a.* Appropriate, fit; official. *-pp.* of APROPIAR.

apropiador [ah-pro-pe-ah-dor'], *m.* Appropriator.

apropiar [ah-pro-pe-ar', *va.* 1. To appropriate, to assume. 2. To bring to a resemblance. 3. To accommodate, to apply. *-vr.* To appropriate any thing to oneself, to encroach. **Apropiarse de algo,** to appropriate something.

apropincuación [ah-pro-pin-coo-ah-the-on'], *f.* Approach.

aprovechable [ah-proh-vay-chah'-blay], *a.* Profitable, useful, or serviceable.

aprovechadamente [ah-pro-vay-chah-dah-mayn-tay], *adv.* Profitably

aprovechado, da [ah-pro-vay-chah-do, dah], *a.* 1. Improved; taken advantage of. 2. Sparing, parsimonious. 3. Hard working, diligent. 4. Thrifty, economical. 4. Well spent (tiempo). *-pp.* of APROVECHAR.

aprovechamiento [ah-pro-vay-chah-me-en'-to], *m.* 1. Profit, utility, advantage. 2. Progress made in an art or science; growth. 3. Lands, commons, houses, etc., belonging to a town or city. *V.* PROPIOS.

aprovechar [ah-pro-bay-char'], *vn.* To make progress, to become useful, to come forward, to get forward. **Eso aprovecha poco,** that is of little use. **No aprovechar para nada,** to be completely useless. *-va.* 1. To profit by a thing, to employ it usefully. 2. *(Obs.)* To protect, to favor. 3. *(Obs.)* To meliorate. *-vr.* To avail oneself of a thing.

aprovechón [ah-pro-vay-chon'], *a.* Opportunistic, having an eye to the main chance.

aprovisionamiento [ah-pro-ve-se-o-nah-me-ayn-to], *m.* Supply, supplying.

aprovisionar [ah-pro-ve-se-o-nahr'], *va.* To supply.

aproximación [ah-proc-se-mah-the-on'], *f.* Approximation, closeness, nearness, approach.

aproximadamente [ah-proc-se-mah-dah-men'-tay], *adv.* Nearly, about.

aproximado [ah-proc-se-mah'-do], *a.* Approximate.

aproximar [ah-proc-se-mar'], *va.* To approximate, to approach, to bring near, to bring up. *-vr.* To come near, come closer, approach; **el tren se aproxima a su destino,** the train was nearing its destination.

aproximativo, va [ah-proc-se-mah-tee'-vo, vah], *a.* Approximate, rough (aproximado).

apside [ahp'-se-day], *m. (Astr.)* The extremities of the major axis of the orbit of a star. Mostly used in plural.

aptamente [ap-tah-men'-tay], *adv.* Conveniently, fitly, commodiously, expediently.

aptero, ra [ahp'-tay-ro, rah], *a. (Ent.)* Apterous: applied to insects.

aptitud [ap-te-tood'], *f.* 1. Aptitude or fitness for an employment; ability. **Desmostrar tener aptitudes,** to show ability. **Carece de aptitud,** he hasn´t got the talent. 2. Expediency; aptness.

apto, ta [ahp'-to, tah], *a.* Apt, fit; competent, clever, congruous; good, convenient. **Ser apto para aprender,** to be quick to learn. **No es apto para conducir,** he´s not fit to drive.

apto [ap'-to], *abr.* de **apartamento**.

apuesta [ah-poo-ess'-tah], *f.* A bet, a wager. **Apuestas mutuas,** pari-mutuel.

apuesto, ta [ah-poo-ess'-to, tah], *a.* 1. Elegant, smart (elegante), handsome, good-looking (guapo). 2. *(Obs.)* Opportune, fit. **(Yo apuesto, yo apueste,** from **Apostar.** *V.* ACORDAR.)

apulgarar [ah-pool-gah-rar'], *va.* To force with the thumb. *-vr. (coll.)* To contract black spots (ropa blanca).

apunarse [ah-poo-nahr'-say], *vr. (And. Cono Sur)* To get mountain sickness.

apunchar [ah-poon-char'], *va.* Among comb-makers, to cut out the teeth of a comb.

apuntación [ah-poon-tah-the-on'], *f.* 1. Annotation, the act of noting down; memorial 2. The act of marking musical notes with exactness.

apuntado, da [ah-poon-tah'-do, dah], *a.* 1. Pointed, marked. 2. **El cañón está apuntado muy bajo,** the gun dips. *-pp.* of APUNTAR.

apuntador [ah-poon-tah-dor'], *m.* 1. Observer, one who notes or marks. 2. *(Naut.)* Gunner, who points the guns. **Apuntador de comedias,** a prompter to the players. **Apuntador electrónico,** teleprompter. 3. *(Mex. Dep.)* Scorer.

apuntalamiento [ah-poon-tah-lah-me-en'-to], *m.* Propping, pinning. **Apuntalamiento por la base,** Underpinning.

apuntalar [ah-poon-tah-lar'], *va.* 1. To prop, to support with props. 2. *(Naut.)* To shore a vessel. 3. *-vr.* To have a snack.

apuntamiento [ah-poon-tah-me-en'-to], *m.* 1. Remark. 2. Abstract, summary, a judicial report.

apuntar [ah-poon-tar'], *va.* 1. To aim; to level, to make after. **Apuntar a un blanco,** to aim at a target. 2. To point out, to mark, to hint. 3. To put down in writing; to note. 4. To touch lightly upon a point. 5. To fix or fasten provisionally a board or any other thing; (sew) to stitch. 6. To begin to appear or show itself. **Apunta el día,** the day peeps or begins to appear. 7. To sharpen edged tools. 8. To prompt or help actors by suggesting the word to them. 9. To offer. **Apuntar y no dar,** to promise readily and not perform. 10. *(LAm.)* To bet (apostar). *-vn.* To begin to show, appear. *-vr.* 1. To begin to turn: applied to wine. 2. *(Low.)* To be half-seas over, or half-drunk. **Apuntar los vegetales,** to grow up. 3. To get tight (emborracharse). 4. To sign on, to sign up. 5. To agree. 5. **¿Te apuntas a un café?,** how about a coffee?

apunte [ah-poon'-tay], *m.* 1. *V.* APUNTAMIENTO. 2. Annotation, memorandum. (Engin.) Rough sketch. **Sacar apuntes,** to take notes. 3. The words suggested by a prompter on the stage; in the act of prompting. 4. Stake in some games. **Apunte de cambios,** exchange-list. 5. *(Cono Sur)* Note of debts; **llevar el apunte,** to respond to somebody´s advances. 6. *(LAm.)* Bet (apuesta).

apuntillar [ah-poon-te-lyahr'], *va.* 1. To finish off (toro). 2. *(fig.)* To round off.

apuñadar [ah-poo-nyah-dar], *va. (Prov.)* To strike with the fist.

apuñadura [ah-poo-nyah-doo-rah], *f.* Knob, handle.

apuñalado, da [ah-poo-nyah-lah'-do, dah], *a.* Shaped like a dagger.

apuñalar [ah-poo-nyah-lar'], *va.* To thrust with a dagger. *(fig.)* **Apuñalar a uno por la espalda,** to stab somebody in the back. **Apuñalar a uno con la mirada,** to look daggers at somebody.

apuñar [ah-poo-nyar'], *va. (Obs.)* To seize with the fist.

apuñear [ah-poo-nyay-ar'], *va. (coll.)* To strike with the fist.
apuracabos [ah-poo-rah-cah-bos], *m.* A candle-safe; save-all.
apuración [ah-poo-rah-the-on'], *f.* 1. *(Obs.)* Investigation. 2. *V.* APURO. Trouble, misfortune.
apuradamente [ah-poo-rah-dah-men'-tay], *adv.* 1. In the nick of time. 2. Punctually, exactly. 3. *(Obs.)* Radically.
apuradero [ah-poo-rah-day'-ro], *m. (Obs.)* Inquiry, disquisition which ascertains the true nature of a thing.
apurado, da [ah-poo-rah'-do, dah], *a.* 1. Rushed, in a hurry. 2. Needy. **Estar apurado,** 1. To be in a hurry. 2. To be in need (of money). 3. Exhausted (agotado). 4. Precise, exact.
apurador [ah-poo-rah-dor'], *m.* 1. A refiner, purifier. 2. One who spends or consumes. 3. *(Prov.)* One who gleans and picks up olives left by the first reapers.
apuramiento [ah-poo-rah-me-en'-to], *m.* Research, inquiry, verification.
apurar [ah-poo-rar'], *va.* 1. To purify. 2. To clear up, to verify, to investigate minutely, to know a thing radically. 3. To consume, to drain, to exhaust. **Apurar a uno,** to tease and perplex one, to press. 4. To hurry, to press, urge on. *-vr.* 1. To grieve, to be afflicted. 2. To exert oneself. **Verse apurado,** to be hard up; to be put to. **¡ Apure Vd. que es tarde!** Hurry! it is late. 3. To make an effort, go hard at it. **Apurarse por hacer algo,** to strive to do something.
apurativo [ah-poo-rah-tee'-vo], *a.* Detersive.
apuro [ah-poo'-ro], *m.* 1. Want. 2. Anguish, pain, affliction. 3. Exigency; gripe. 4. Want, financial need. **Pasar apuros,** to suffer hardships; **verse en apuros,** to be in trouble. 5. *(LAm.)* Haste, hurry.
apurón [ah-poo-ron'], *m. (LAm.)* Great haste; *(Cono Sur)* **Andar a los apurones,** to do things in a rush.
apurruñar [ah-poo-roo-nyahr'], *va. (Carib.)* To maltreat, handle roughly.
aquejar [ah-kay-har'], *va.* 1. To complain, to lament, to grieve. 2. To fatigue, to afflict. **¿Qué le aqueja?,** what´s up with him? 3. *(Obs.)* To stimulate, to incite. 4. *(Obs.)* To pin up closely.
aquél, aquélla, llo [ah-kel', ah-kel'-lyah, ah-kel'-lyo], *pron. dem.* That one;. It denotes persons or objects at a distance from both the speaker and the person addressed. **Éste es más barato que aquél,** this one is cheaper than that one. **Aquéllos, aquéllas,** Those. **Éstos son más grandes que aquéllos,** these are bigger than those.
aquel, aquella, llo [ah-kel, ah-kel-lyah, ah-kel-lyo] *a. dem.* That *(pl.* those). **Aquel hombre,** that man. **Aquella casa,** that house. **Aquellos años,** those years. **Aquellas chicas,** those girls.
aquelarre [ah-kel-lar'-ray], *m.* Witches' Sabbath. Also applied to any motley and noisy meeting.
aquende [ah-ken'-day], *adv.* Hither, here.
aqueno [ah-kay'-no], *m.* Akene, a single, hard pericarp.
aquerenciado [ah-ke-rayn-the-ah-do], *a. (Cono Sur. Mex.)* In love, loving.
aquerenciarse [ah-kay-ren-the-ar'-say], *vr.* To be fond of a place: applied to cattle.
aqueridarse [ah-ke-re-dahr-say], *vr. (Carib.)* To set up house together, move in together.
aquese, sa, so [ah-kay'-say, sah,so], *pron. dem.* That. **Aquesos, aquesas,** Those. This pronoun is used mainly in speaking of persons or things not very distant. Hardly used except in poetry.
aqueste, ta, to [ah-kess'-tay, tah, to], *pron. dem.* This, that.
aquí [ah-kee'], *adv.* 1. Here, in this place. 2. To this place. 3. Now, at present. 4. Then, on that occasion. **De aquí en adelante,** Henceforth. **De aquí para allí,** to and fro, up and down. **De aquí,** from this, hence. **De aquí en adelante,** henceforth, henceforward. **Aquí alrededor,** hereabouts. **Aquí dentro,** here in, hereinto. **Fuera de aquí,** out of here. **Hasta aquí,** hitherto. **Aquí abajo,** down here. **Aquí está,** here it is. **¡Aquí fue Troya!,** that was when it started. **Aquí yace,**

here lies. **Hasta aquí,** as far as here. **Por aquí y por allí,** here and there.
aquiescencia [ah-ke-es-then'-the-ah], *f. (Law.)* Aquiescence, consent.
aquiesciente [ah-ke-ays-the-ayn-tay], *f.* Acquiescence.
aquietar [ah-ke-ay-tar'], *va.* 1. To quiet, to lull, to pacify; to hush; to allay. *-vr.* To grow calm, to be quiet.
aquila-alba [ah'-ke-lah-ahl'-bah], *f.* Corrosive sublimate mixed with fresh mercury.
aquilatar [ah-ke-lah-tar'], *va.* 1. To assay gold and silver. 2. To examine closely, to find out the truth of a thing. 3. *-vr. (Cono Sur)* To improve.
aquilea [ah-ke-lay'-ah], *f. (Bot.)* Milfoil, yarrow.
Aquiles [ah-ke'-lays], *m.* Achilles.
aquileña [ah-ke-lay'-nyah], *f. (Bot.)* Columbine.
aquilífero [ah-ke-lee'-fay-rao], *m.* Among the Romans, the standard-bearer, he who carried the Roman eagle.
aquilino, na [ah-ke-lee'-no, nah], *a.* Aquiline, hooked: applied commonly to the nose. *V.* AGUILEÑO.
aquilón [ah-ke-lone'], *m.* 1.Due north wind. 2. The north point.
aquilonal, aquilonar [ah-ke-lo-nahl', ah-ke-lo-nar'], *a.* Northern, northerly. **Tiempo aquilonal,** *(Met.)* the winter season.
aquillado, da [ah-keel-lyah'-do, dah], Keel-shaped.
aquísito [ah-ke'-se-to], *adv. (LAm.)* = aquí.
aquistar [ah-kes-tahr'], *va.* To win, gain, acquire.
Aquitania [ah-ke-tah-ne-ah], *f.* Aquitaine.
A.R. *abr.* de **Alteza Real** (Royal Highness, R. H.)
ara [ah'-rah], *f.* 1. An altar. 2. The consecrated stone, on which a consecrated linen cover is laid during the celebration of the mass. 3. Among plumbers, a cistern-head. 4. *m. (LAm.)* Parrot.
árabe, arábigo [ah'-rah-bay, ah-rah'-be-go],1. *m.* The Arabic language; Arabic. 2. *m. & f. (Mex.)* Hawker, street vendor. 3. *m. (Ling.)* Arabic.
arabesco [ah-rah-bess'-co], *m. (Pict.)* Arabesque, whimsical ornaments of foliage in painting; moresque-work.
arabias [ah-rah'-be-as], *f. pl.* Arabias, a kind of linen so called.
arábico, ca o go, ga [ah-rah-be-co, cah], *a.* Arabian. **Estar en arábico,** to be incomprehensible.
arabismo [ah-rah-bees'-mo], *m.* Arabism: idiom of the Arabic language transferred to some other.
arabista [ah-rah-bes'-tah], *m. & f.* Arabist.
arabizar [ah-rah-be-thar'], *va.* To Arabicize, to Arabize.
arable [ah-rah'-blay], *a. (LAm.)* Arable.
aracacha [ah-rah-cah'-chah], *f.* An umbelliferous plant of Colombia, having an edible farinaceous root, cultivated in large quantities.
arácnido, da [ah-rahc'-ne-do, dah], *a. (Zool.)* Arachnid, a class of arthropods; relating to the arachnoids.
aracnoides [ah-rac-no'-e-des], *f.* The archnoid membrane of the brain and spinal cord.
arada [ah-rah'-dah], *f. (Agri.)* 1. Ploughed ground, husbandry. 2. *V.* ARADURA. 3. Work in the fields.
arado [ah-rah'-do], *m.* A plough.
arador [ah-rah-dor'], *m.* 1. A ploughman. 2. A sarcoptic mite that causes itch or scabies. 3. Harvest-mite, or harvest-bug: Leptus.
aradro [ah-rah'-dro], *m. (Prov.) V.* ARADO.
aradura [ah-rah-doo'-rah], *f.* 1. The act or practice of ploughing. 2. *(Prov.)* Quantity of land which a yoke of oxen can conveniently plough in the course of a day.
araguato [ah-rah-goo-ah'-to], 1. *a. (Carib.)* Dark, tawny-colored. 2. *m. (And. Carib. Mex.)* Howler monkey.
arambel [ah-ram-bel'], *m. (Obs.)* 1. Drapery, furniture of a room or bed. 2. *(Met.)* Rag, or piece hanging from cloths.
arambre [ah-ran'-bray], *m. (Obs.) V.* ALAMBRE.
aramía [ah-rah-mee'-ah], *f. (Prov.)* A piece of ploughed ground fit for sowing.
arana [ah-rah'-nah], *f. (Obs.)* Imposition, trick, deception.

araná [ah-rah-nah'], *m. (Carib.)* Straw hat.

aranata [ah-rah-nah'-tah], *f.* An animal of the shape and size of a dog, a native of America.

arancel [ah-ran-thel'], *m.* 1. The regulations by which the rate and price of bread and other things are fixed. 2. The tariff of duties, fees, taxes, etc., of the custom-house, courts, etc.; the book of rates.

arancelario, ria [ah-ran-thay-lah'-re-o, re-ah], *a.* Pertaining or referring to the tariff. **Protección arancelaria,** tariff protection.

arándano [ah-rahn'-dah-no], *m.* Cranberry. **Arándano azul,** Blueberry.

arandela [ah-ran-day'-lah], *f.* 1. The pan of the socket of a candlestick. 2. A guard around the staff of a lance. 3. Nave-box of a gun-carriage. *(Mech.)* Washer, axle-guard; rivet-plate, collar-plate. 4. *(Naut.)* Halfports, square boards with a hole in the middle, to which a piece of canvas is nailed, to keep the water out when the cannon is in the port-hole. 5. A tin trough or funnel put around trees, with water, to prevent ants from climbing up. 6. A candelabrum, of glass, to be set upon a table.

arandillo [ah-ran-del-lyo] *m.* Marsh warbler (pájaro)

aranero, ra [ah-rah-nay'-ro, rah], *a.* Deceptive, tricky.

araniego [ah-rah-ne-ay'-go], *a.* Taken in a net, which is called *arañuelo:* applied to a young hawk.

aranzada [ah-ran-thah'-dah], *f.* A measure of land.

araña [ah-rah'-nyah], *f.* 1. *(Ent.)* Spider. 2. *(Zool.)* Common weaver, seaspider. 3. Chandelier, girandole, sconce. *(Bot.)* Crow foot. **Es una araña,** He is an industrious man. 4. *(Prov.) V.* ARREBATIÑA.

arañador, ra [ah-rah-nyah-dor', rah], *m. & f.* Scratcher, one who scratches.

arañamiento [ah-rah-nya-me-en'-to], *m.* The act of scratching.

arañar [ah-rah-nyar'], *va.* 1. To scratch, to claw, to scrabble. 2. To scrape, to gather by penurious diligence. **Arañar riquezas,** to gather riches with great eagerness. **Arañarse con los codos,** to rejoice in other people's misfortunes. **Arañar la cubierta,** to make great exertions; to get clear of danger.

arañazo [ah-rah-nayh-tho], *m. aug.* A long, deep scratch.

arañero, ra [ah-rah-nyay'-ro, rah], *a. V.* ZAHAREÑO.

araño [ah-rah'-nyo], *m.* A scratch, any slight wound; nipping.

arañón [ah-rah-nyon'], *m. (Prov.)* Sloe, the fruit of the backthorn.

arañuela [ah-rah-nyoo-ay'-lah], *f.dim.* 1. A small spider. 2. *V.*ARAÑUELO. 3. A plant.

arañuelo [ah-rah-nyoo-ay'-lo], *m.* 1. A small species of spider; grub or larva, web-spinning, which destroys plants. 2. *V.* CAPARILLA. 3. Foldnet, a very slight net for catching birds.

arao [ah-rah'-o], *m.* Guillemot.

arar [ah-rahr'], *va.* To plough; to till, to cultivate.

arapende [ah-rah-pen'-day], *m.* Ancient measure of 120 square feet.

arar [ah-rar'], *va.* 1. To plough, to labor. 2. *(Poetic.)* To run or pass through the surface of a liquid. **Arar con el ancla,** *(Naut.)* to drag the anchor. **No me lo harán creer cuántos aran y cavan,** no man shall ever make me believe it.

arar [ah-rar'], *m.* An African coniferous tree; its wood was employed in constructing the cathedrals of Seville and Córdoba.

arate [ah-rah-tay], *m.* Blood.

araucano, na [ah-rah-oo-cah'-no], *a. m. & f.* Araucanian.

araucaria [ah-rah-oo-cah'-re-ah], *f.* Araucaria, a tall conifer, of pine family, native of South America.

arbellón [ar-bel-lyone'], *m. (Prov.)* Gutter for drawing off the water from roads. *V.* ARBOLLON.

arbelo [ar-bay'-lo], *m. (Geom.)* A curvilinear figure composed of three segments of a circle and three acute angles.

arbitrable [r-be-trah'-blay], *a.* Arbitrable, depending upon the will.

arbitración [ar-be-trah-the-on'], *f.* Arbitration.

arbitrador [ar-be-trah-dor'], *m.* Arbitrator, umpire, referee.

arbitradora [ar-be-trah-do'-rah], *f.* Arbitress, a female arbitrator.

arbitraje, arbitramento, arbitramiento [ar-be-trah'-hay, ar-be-trah-men'-to, ar-be-trah-me-en'-to], *m.* Arbitration, the award of an arbitrator; arbitrament. **Arbitraje de bus,** bus arbitration.

arbitral [ar-be-trahl], *a.* Arbitral; of a referee. **Una decisión arbitral,** a referee´s ruling. *V.* ARBITRATORIO.

arbitrar [ar-be-trar'], *va.* 1. To adjudge, to award. 2. To judge after one's own feelings and sentiments. 3. To contrive means and expedients. 1. *-vn.* To arbitrate; *(Dep.)* To umpire, referee; **arbitrar en una disputa,** to arbitrate in a dispute. 2. To act freely, to judge freely. *-vr.* To get along, to manage.

arbitrariamente [ar-be-trah-re-ah-men'-tay], *adv.* Arbitrarily, in an arbitrary manner; without control.

arbitrariedad [ar-be-trah-re-ay-dahd'], *f.* Arbitrariness.

arbitrario, ria, arbitrativo, va [ar-be-trah'-re-o, ah, ar-be-trah-tee'-vo, vah], *a.* 1. Arbitrary, that which depends upon the will; absolute. 2. *(For.)* Relating to arbitrators.

arbitratorio, ria [ar-be-trah-to'-re-o, ah], *a.* That which belongs or relates to arbitrators.

arbitrio [ar-bee'-tre-o], *m.* 1. Free and uncontrolled will and pleasure; mercy. 2. Means, expedient. 3. Arbitration, bond, compromise. 4. **Arbitrio de juez,** the discretionary power of a judge in cases not clearly decided by law. 5. **Arbitrios,** duty or taxes imposed on provisions exposed for sale. **Propios y arbitrios,** ways and means. **No hay arbitrio,** there is no change.

arbitrista [ar-be-trees'-tah], *m.* Schemer, projector, contriver.

árbitro [ar'-be-tro], *m.* 1. Arbitrator. 2. Umpire.

árbol [ar'-bol], *m.* 1. *(Bot.)* A tree. 2. *(Naut.)* Mast. *V.* PALO. 3. In some machines, the upright post which serves to give them a circular motion. *(Mech.)* Arbor, upright shaft; wheel spindle. 4. A drill. 5. Body of a shirt without sleeves. 6. Crown post, upright post, around which winding stairs turn. **Árbol de amor,** *(Bot.)* Judas-tree. **Árbol de clavo,** clove-tree. **Árbol de fuego,** a wooden frame of fireworks. **Árbol del paraíso or árbol paraíso,** flowering-ash. **Árbol del pan,** bread-fruit-tree. **Árbol marino,** a radiate much ressembling the star-fish, but larger. **Árbol pagano,** a wild or uncultivated tree. **De árbol caído todos hacen leña,** overthrown pride inspires only contempt.

arbolado, da [ar-bo-lah'-do, dah], *a.* 1. Wooded, woodland; planted with trees. **Región arbolada,** wooded area. 2. Masted. **Arbolado en la hoya,** Masted hoy-fashion. *-pp.* of ARBOLAR.

arboladura [ar-bo-lah-doo'-rah], *f. (Naut.)* A general name for masts, yards, and all sorts of round timber. **Maestre de arboladura,** a master mast-maker.

arbolar [ar-bo-lar'], *va.* To hoist, to set upright. **Arbolar el navío,** *(Naut.)* To mast a ship. *-vr.* Arbolarse, to rear on the hind feet: applied to horses.

arbolario [ar-bo-lah'-re-o], *m.* 1. *V.* HERBOLARIO. 2. Madcap.

árbol de levas [ar'-bol day lay'-vash], *f.* Camshaft.

arbolecico, arbolecillo, arbolico, arbolito, arborcillo [ar-bo-lay-thee'-co, etc.], *m. dim.* Arboret, a small tree.

arboleda [ar-bo-lay'-dah], *f.* Grove, plantation of trees.

arboledo [ar-bo-lay'-do], *m.* Woodland.

arbolejo [ar-bo-lay'-ho], *m. dim.* A small tree.

arbolete [ar-bo-lay'-tay], *m.* Branch of a tree put on the ground, to which bird-catchers fasten their lime-twigs.

arbolillo [ar-bo-leel'-lyo], *m.* Side of a blast-furnace.

arbolista [ar-bo-lees'-tah], *m.* A dresser or planter of trees, arborist.

arbollón [ar-bol-lyone'], *m.* Flood-gate, sluice, conduit, channel.

arbóreo, rea [ar-bo'-ray-o, ah], *a.* Relating or belonging to trees.

arborescencia [ar-bo-res-then'-the-ah], *f.* Arborescence, tree-like growth or formation.

arborescente [ar-bo-res-then'-tay], *a.* Arborescent, having the form of a tree.

arboricultor [ar-bo-re-cool-tor'], *m. & f.* Forester.

arboricultura [ar-bo-re-cool-too'-rah], *f.* Arboriculture, cultivation of trees.

arborización [ar-bo-re-thah-the-on'], *f.* Replanting (of trees).

arborizado, da [ar-bo-re-thah'-do, dah], *a.* Arborescent, resembling trees and foliage: applied to dendrites or stones having the appearance of foliage.

arborizar [ar-bo-re-thahr'], *vn.* To plant trees, replant trees.

arbotante [ar-bo-tahn'-tay], *m.* Arch of stone or brick raised against a wall to support a vault. **Arbotante de pie de campana**, *(Naut.)* bell-crank, the place where the ship's bell is hung.

arbusto [ar-boos'-to], *m.* Shrub.

arbustillo [ar-boos-tell'-lyo], *m. dim.* Arbuscle, a small shrub.

arca [ar'-cah], *f.* 1. A chest. **Arcas**, Coffer, iron chest for money. **Hacer arcas**, to open the coffers or treasury chest. 2. In glass-houses, the tempering oven, in which glassware, just blown, is put to cool. 3. *(Met.)* A reserved person. **Arca de Noé**, *(Met.)* lumber-chest. **Arca de fuego**, *(Naut.)* fire-chest, a small box, filled with combustibles, used to annoy an enemy that attempted to board a ship. **Ser arca cerrada**, to be yet unknown (personas, cosas). **Sangrar a uno de la vena del arca**, to drain one of his money. **Arca de agua**, reservoir, cistern. **Arcas**, cavities of the body under the ribs.

arcabucear [ar-cah-boo-thay-ar'], *va.* 1. To shoot with the crossbow. 2. To shoot a criminal by way of punishment.

arcabucería [ar-cah-boo-thay-ree'-ah], *f.* 1. A troop of archers. 2. A number of cross-bows. 3. Manufactory of bows and arrows.

arcabucero [ar-cah-boo-thay'-ro], *m.* 1. Archer. 2. Gunsmith. 3. Manufacturer of bows and arrows.

arcabuco [ar-cah-boo'-co], *m. (Amer.)* A caggy spot full of brambles.

arcabuz [ar-cah-booth'], *m.* Arquebuse, a fire-arm, a hand-gun.

arcabuzazo [ar-cah-boo-thah'-tho], *m.* A shot from a gun and the wound it causes.

arcacil [ar-cah-theel'], *m. (Bot.)* A wild artichoke.

arcada [ar-cah'-dah], *f.* 1. Violent motion of the stomach, which excites vomiting. 2. Arcade or row of arches.

arcade [ar'-cah-day], *a.* Arcadian, belonging to the Roman academy of polite literature called *Arcades*.

arcadia [ar-cah-de-ah], *f.* Arcady.

arcadio, dia [ar-cah'-de-o, ah], *a.* Arcadian.

arcádico [ar-cah'-de-co], *a.* Arcadian.

arcaduz [ar-cah-dooth'], *m.* 1. Conduit or pipe for the conveyance of water. 2. Bucket for raising water out of a draw-well. 3. *(Met.)* Channel for enforcing a claim, obtaining a place, etc. **Llevar una cosa por sus arcaduces**, to conduct an affair through its proper channel.

arcaduzar [ar-cah-doo-thar'], *va. (Obs.)* To convey water through conduits.

arcáico, ca [ar-cah'-e-co, cah], *a.* Archaic, ancient.

arcaismo [ar-cah-ees'-mo], *m.* Archaism, the mixture of ancient or antiquated words with modern language.

arcaizante [ar-cah-e-than'-tay], *a.* Archaic.

arcaizar [ar-cah-e-thar'], *vr.* To use archaisms.

arcam [ar-cahm'], *m.* A very venomous serpent, spotted black and white, which is found in Turkestan.

arcángel [ar-cahn'-hel], *m.* Archangel.

arcangelical [ar-cahn-hay-le-cahl'], *a.* Archangelical.

arcanidad [ar-cah-ne-dahd'], *f. (Obs.)* A profound secret of great moment.

arcano [ar-cah'-no], *m.* Arcanum, a secret which is carefully kept. -*a.* Secret, recondite, reserved.

arcar [ar-car'], *va.* To beat the wool with a bow of one or two cords.

arcaza [ar-cah'-thah], *f. aug.* A large chest.

arcazón [ar-cah-thone'], *m.* 1. Arbuscle. 2. Osier, water-willow. 3. Willow-plot.

arce [ar'-thay], *m. (Bot.)* Maple-tree. Acer.

arcedianato [ar-thay-de-ah-nah'-to], *m.* Archdeaconship; archdeaconry.

arcediano [ar-thay-de-ah'-no], *m.* Archdeacon.

arcedo [ar-thay'-do], *m.* Maple-grove.

arcén [ar-then'], *m.* 1. *(Ant.)* Border, brim, edge. 2. *(Prov.)* Stone laid round the brim of a well.

arcilla [ar-theel'-lyah], *f.* Argil, white pure earth, alumina, clay. **Arcilla cocida**, baked clay.

arcilloso, sa [ar-theel-lyo'-so, sah], *a.* Clayey, argillaceous.

arciprestadgo, arciprestazgo [ar-the-pres-tad'-go, ar-the-pres-tath'-go], *m.* The dignity of an archpriest.

arcipreste [ar-the-pres'-tay], *m.* Archprelate, archpriest, the first or chief presbyter.

arco [ar'-co], *m.* 1. Arc, a segment of a circle. 2. Arch, arc, a part of a circle not more than the half. 3. Arch of a building, bridge, and other works. 4. Bow for throwing arrows. 5. Fiddle-bow. 6. Hoop, anything circular with which something else is bound, particularly casks and barrels. 7. *(Naut.)* Bow of a ship. **Arco Iris**, rainbow.

arcón [ar-cone'], *m. aug.* 1. A large chest, bin, bunker. 2. A great arch or arc.

arcontado [ar-con-tah'-do], *m.* Archonship.

arconte [ar-con'-tay], *m.* Archon, a magistrate of Athens.

ártico, ca [arc'-te-co, cah], *a. V.* ÁRTICO.

archera [ar-chay'-rah], *f.* Archeress.

archero [ar-chay'-ro], *m.* Archer.

archi Arch-. a prefix from the Greek, meaning pre-eminent. **Un niño archimalo**, a terribly naughty child.

archicofradía [ar-che-co-frah-dee'-ah], *f.* A privileged brotherhood or confraternity.

archiconocido [ar-che-co-no-the'-do], *a.* Extremely well-known.

archidiácono [ar-che-de-ah'-co-no], *m. V.* ARCEDIANO.

archidiócesis [ar-che-de-o'-thay-sees], *f.* Archdiocese.

archiducado [ar-che-doo-cah'-do], *m.* 1. Archdukedom, archduchy, the territory belonging to an archduke. 2. The dignity or an archduke.

archiducal [ar-che-doo-cahl'], *a.* Archducal, that which belongs or relates to an archduke or archduchy.

archiduque [ar-che-doo'-kay], *m.* Archduke.

archiduquesa [ar-che-doo-kay'-sah], *f.* Archduchess.

archienemigo [ar-che-ay-nay-me-go], *m.* Arch-enemy.

archilaúd [ar-che-lah-ood'], *m.* A musical instrument shaped and stringed as a lute, but of a larger size.

archimandrita [ar-che-man-dree'-tah], *m.* Name in the orient, of the abbot of a monastery.

archimillonario, ria [ar-che-meel-lyo-nah'-re-o, ah], *a.* Multimillionaire.

archipámpano [ar-che-pahm'-pah-no], *m. (coll.)* A word used to express an imaginary dignity or authority.

archipiélago [ar-che-pe-ay'-lah-go], *m.* Archipelago, a part of the sea crowded with islands.

archisabido [ar-che-sah-be-do], *a.* Extremely well-known; **Un hecho archisabido**, a perfectly well-known fact.

architonto [ar-che-ton-to], *a. m. & f.* Utterly silly.

architriclino [ar-che-tre-clee'-no], *m.* (Antiquities) He who ordered and directed banquets.

archivado [ar-che-vah-do], *a. (LAm.)* Out-of-date, old-fashioned.

archivador, ra [ar-che-vah-dor], *m. f.* Filing cabinet.

archivar [ar-che-var'], *va.* 1. To deposit a thing or writing in an archive. 2. To hide away (esconder). 3. *(LAm.)* To take away of circulation. 4. *(Cono Sur. Mex.)* To jail.

archivero, archivista [ar-che-vay'-ro, ar-che-vees'-tah], *m.* Keeper of the records.

archivo [ar-chee'-vo], *m.* 1. Archives, the place where public records are kept. **Archivo Nacional**, Public Record Office. 2. *(Met.)* A person who is intrusted with the most profound secrets, a confidant. 3. *(Cono Sur. Mex.)* Jail. **Archivo de tarjetas** *(Comp.)*, card file. **Archivos integrados** *(Comp.)*, integrated filestore.

arda [ar'-dah], *f.* Squirrel. *V.* ARDILLA.

ardalear [ar-dah-lay-ar'], *va.* To make thin or clear. *V.* RAL-EAR.

ardasa, ardases [ar-dah'-sas, ar-dah-ses], *f. pl.* The coarser sort of Persian silk.

ardasinas, ardazinas [ar-dah-see'-nas, ar-dah-thee'-nas], *f. pl.* The finer sort of Persian silk.

ardea [ar-day'-ah], *f.* Bittern. *V.* ALCARAVAN.

ardedor [ar-day-dor'], *m.* A species of serpent. *a.* (*Carib. Mex.*) Quick burning, easy to light.

ardentía [ar-den-tee'-ah], *f.* 1. Heat. 2. *(Naut.)* Phosphoric sparkling of the sea when it is agitated.

ardeola [ar-day-o'-lah], *f.* A small kind of heron.

arder [ar-derr'], *vn.* 1. To burn, to blaze, to glow. 2. To be agitated by the passions of love, hatred, anger, etc., to heat, to kindle. **Arderse en pleitos**, to be entangled in law-suits. **Arder de amor**, to burn with love. 3. To ferment. *-vr.* To burn away.

ardero, ra [ar-day'-ro, rah], *a.* Squirrel-hunter: applied to dogs.

ardid [ar-deed'], *m.* Stratagem, artifice, cunning.

ardido, da [ar-dee'-do, dah], *a.* 1. Heated: applied to grain, olives, tobacco, etc. 2. *(Obs.)* Bold, intrepid, valiant. 3. *(LAm.)* Cross, angry. *-pp* of ARDER.

ardiente [ar-de-en'-tay], *pa.* and *a.* 1. Ardent, flagrant, burning. **Calentura ardiente**, a burning fever. 2. Passionate, active, mettlesome, hot, fervent, fiery, fearless; feverish.

ardientemente [ar-de-en-tay-men'-tay], *adv.* Ardently, flagrantly, fervidly; fearlessly.

ardiloso [ar-de-lo'-so], *a.* (*And. Cono Sur*) Crafty, wily.

ardilla [ar-dee'-lyah], *f.* 1. Squirrel. 2. *(Mech.)* Granulating machine. 3. *(LAm.)* Clever businessman; businesswoman. *a.* Sharp, clever.

ardimiento [ar-de-me-en'-to], *m.* 1. *(Obs.)* Conflagration. 2. *(Met.)* Valor, intrepidity, undaunted courage.

ardínculo [ar-deen'-coo-lo], *m.* (*Vet.*) An inflamed swelling or ulcer on the back of animals.

ardita [ar-dee'-tah], *f.* A squirrel. *V.* ARDILLA.

ardite [ar-dee'-tay], *m.* An ancient coin of little value, formerly current in Spain. **No vale un ardite**, it is not worth a dime.

ardor [ar-dor'], *m.* 1. Great heat, hotness, flagrancy. 2. *(Met.)* Valor, vivacity, spirit, vigor, mettle. 3. Fieriness, fervency. 4. Life.

ardoroso, sa [ar-do-ro'-so, sah], *a.* Fiery, restless: applied to a horse. Hot, burning. **En lo más ardoroso del estío**, in the hottest part of the summer.

arduamente [ar-doo-ah-men'-tay], *adv.* Arduously, in a difficult, arduous manner.

arduidad [ar-doo-e-dahd'], *f.* Arduousness.

arduo, dua [ar'-doo-o, ah], *a.* Arduous, difficult; high.

área [ah'-ray-ah], *f.* 1. Area, the surface contained between any lines or boundaries. **Área de servicios,** service area. 2. Area of a building. 3. Halo, a bright circle which surrounds the sun, moon, or stars. 4. A square decametre: equivalent to about 143 square varas. **Área de la hoja de trabajo** *(Comp.)*, worksheet area. **Área de la ventana** *(Comp.)*, window area.

areca [ah-ray'-cah], *f.* A palm-tree of the Philippine Islands, used in building huts.

arefacción [ah-ray-fac-the-on'], *f.* Dryness, extenuation.

arel [ah-rel'], *m.* A kind of large sieve used to sift the corn.

arelar [ah-ray-lar'], *va.* To sift the corn with the kind of sieve called *arel.*

arena [ah-ray'-nah], *f.* 1. Sand, grit. **Arenas movedizas,** quicksands, shifting sands. 2. Arena, place where

wrestlers and gladiators fought. **Sembrar en arena**, to labor in vain. **Arena hoya**, pit-sand. **Arenas**, gravel formed in the kidneys.

arenáceo, ea [ah-ray-nah'-thay-o, ah], *a.* Arenaceous, gravelly.

arenal [ah-ray-nahl'], *m.* A sandy ground, a sandy beach.

arenalejo, arenalillo [ah-ray-nah-lay'-ho, ah-ray-nahleel'-lyo], *m. dim.* 1. A small sandy piece of ground. 2. Small, fine sand.

arenar [ah-ray-nar'], *va.* To cover with sand; to fill with sand.

arenaria [ah-ray-nah'-re-ah], *f.* (*Orn.*) Sandpiper.

arencar [ah-ren-car'], *va.* To salt and dry sardines, etc., like herrings.

arencón [ah-ren-cone'], *m. aug.* of ARENQUE.

arenero [ah-ray-nay'-ro], *m.* One who deals in sand; sand-box.

arenga [ah-ren'-gah], *f.* Harangue, speech, oration, address. *(Cono Sur)* Argument.

arengador [ah-ren-gah-dor'], *m.* A speech-maker.

arengar [ah-ren-gar'], *vn.* To harangue, to deliver a speech or oration; to hold forth.

arenguear [ah-ren-gay-ahr'], *vn.* *(Cono Sur)* To argue, quarrel.

arenícola [ah-ray-nee'-co-lah], *f.* *(Zool.)* An annelid, used by fishermen for bait; lugworm, or lobworm.

arenilla [ah-ray-neel'-yah], *f.* 1. Moulding sand, sand. 2. Powder to dry writing. *-pl.* In gunpowder-mills, saltpetre refined, and reduced to grains as small as sand. *(Med.)* Stones, gravel.

arenisca [ah-ray-nees'-cah], *f.* (*Miner.*) Sandstone.

arenisco, ca, arenoso, sa [ah-ray-nees'-co, cah, ah-ray-no'-so, sah], *a.* Sandly, abounding with sand; gravelly, gritty.

arenque [ah-ren'-kay], *m.* Herring. **Arenque ahumado,** smoked herring.

aréola [ah-ray'-oh-lah], *f.* 1. (*Anat.*) Areola, circle around the nipple. 2. The reddened area around a pustule.

areómetro [ah-ray-o'-may-tro], *m.* Areometer, an instrument for measuring the density and gravity of spirituous liquors.

areopagita [ah-ray-o-pah-hee'-tah], *m.* Areopagite, judge of the supreme court of judicature in Athens.

areópago [ah-ray-o'-pah-go], *m.* Areopagus, the supreme court of judicature in Athens.

areóstilo [ah-ray-os'-te-lo], *m.* Aræostyle, the distance from column to column of eight or more modules.

areotectónica [ah-ray-o-tec-to'-ne-cah], *f.* Areotectonics, a part of the science of fortification.

arepa [ah-ray'-pah], *f.* (*Amer.*) A griddle-cake made of soaked corn ground into a paste or dough. *V.* TORTILLA.

arepero [ah-ray-pay-ro], *m.* (*Carib.*) Poor wretch.

arequipa [ah-ray-ke-pah], *f.* (*And.*) Rice pudding. Arequipa.

arequipeño, ña [ah-ray-ke-pay'-nyo, nya], *a.* Of Arequipa.

aresta [ah-res'-tah], *f.* (*Obs.*) 1. Coarse tow. 2. *V.* ESPINA.

arestín [ah-res-teen'], *m.* (*Vet.*) Frush, a disease in the heel of horses.

arestinado, da [ah-res-te-nah'-do, dah], *a.* Afflicted with the disease called the frush.

arete [ah-ray'-tay], *m.* *V.* ZARCILLO, PENDIENTE. Ear-drop.

arfada [ar-fah'-dah], *f.* (*Naut.*) The pitching of a ship.

arfar [ar-far'], *va.* (*Naut.*) To pitch: applied to a ship.

arfil [ar-feel'], *m.* *V.* ALFIL.

argadijo, argadillo [ar-gah-dee'-ho, ar-gah-deel'-lyo], *m.* 1. Reel, bobbin, winder. *V.* DEVANADERA. 2. *(Met.)* A blustering, noisy, restless person. 3. *(Prov.)* Large basket made of twigs of osier.

argado [ar-gah'-do], *m.* Prank, trick, artifice.

argal [ar-gahl'], *m.* Argol, crude tartar.

argalia [ar-gah'-le-ah], *f.* *V.* ALGALIA.

argallera [ar-gal-lyay'-rah], *f.* A saw for cutting grooves; forkstaff plane, reed-plane.

argamandel [ar-gah-man-del'], *m.* Rag, tatter.

argamandijo [ar-gah-man-dee'-ho], *m.* 1. *(coll.)* Collection of trifling implements used in trade or business. **Dueño or señor del argamandijo**, powerful lord and master. 2. Set of tools.

argamasa [ar-gah-mah'-sah], *f.* Mortar, a cement for building.

argamasar[ar-gah-mah-sar'], *va.* 1. To make mortar. 2. To cement with mortar.

argamasón [ar-gah-mah-sone'], *m.* A large piece of mortar found among the ruins of a building.

argamula [ar-gah-moo'-lah], *f. (Bot. Prov.)* V. AMELO.

argana, *f.* **argano,** *m.* [ar'-gah-nah]. A machine resembling a crane, for raising stones and other weighty things. **Arganas,** 1. Baskets or wicker vessels in which things are carried on a horse. 2. Large nets in which forage is carried.

arganel [ar-gah-nel'], *m.* A small brass ring used in the composition of an astrolabe.

argano [ar-gah'-nay-o], *m. (Naut.)* Anchor-ring, a large ring in the anchor to which the cable is fastened.

Argel [ar-hek], Algiers.

argel [ar-hel'], *a.* 1. Horse whose right hind foot only is white. 2. *(Met.)* Unlucky, unfortunate.

argelino, na [ar-hay-lee'-no, nah], *a.* Algerine; of Algiers.

argema, argemón [ar-hay'-mah, ar-hay-mone'], *m. (Med.)* Argema or argemon, a small white ulcer of the globe of the eye.

argémone [ar-hay-mo-nay], *f. (Bot.)* Prickly or horned poppy. Argemone mexicana.

argén [ar-hen'], *m. (Her.)* White or silver color, argent.

argentado, da [ar-hen-tah'-do, dah], *a.* Silver plated, silvered (bañado en plata). 2. Silvery (color de plata). *-pp.* of ARGENTAR.

argentador [ar-hen-tah-dor'], *m.* One who silvers or covers superficially with silver.

argentar [ar-hen-tar'], *va.* 1. To plate or cover with silver. 2. To give a silver color (platear).

argénteo [ar-hayn'-tay-o], *a.* 1. *(Tec.)* Silver-plated. 2. *(Poetic)* Silver, silvery.

argentería [ar-he-tay-ree'-ah], *f.* 1. Embroidery in gold or silver. 2. *(Met.)* An expression more brilliant than solid.

argentífero, ra [ar-hen-tee'-fay-ro, rah], *a.* Argentiferous; silver-bearing.

argentifodina [ar-hen-te-fo-dee'-nah], *f.* Silver-mine.

Argentina [ar-hen-tee'-nah], *f.* Argentina. *(Bot.)* Satin cinquefoil.

argentino, na [ar-hen-tee'-no, nah], *a.* 1. Of silver, or like it; argentine. 2. *(Geog.)* Belonging to the River la Plata: Argentine Republic, southern-most country of South America.

argento [ar-hen'-to], *m.* 1. *(Poetic.)* Silver. 2. **Argento vivo sublimado,** Sublimate. V. SOLIMAN.

argilla [ar-heel'-lyah], *f.* V. ARCILLA.

argiritas [ar-he-ree'-tas], *m. pl.* Marcasites, which are found in silver-mines; white pyrites.

argo [ar'-go], *m.* The ship of Jason and the Argonauts. Argon.

argolla [ar-gol'-lyah], *f.* 1. Large iron ring; buckle, ring, collar; a staple. **Argollas de cureña,** draught-hooks of a gun-carriage. **Argollas de amarra,** lashing-rings. 2. Carcan, iron collar (castigo público). 3. *(LAm.)* Engagement ring. 4. Serviette ring. 5. Collar (adorno).

argollar [ar-go-lyahr'], *va. (And.)* To ring (cerdo); *(Mex.)* To hitch to a ring; **argollar a uno** *(Mex.)* To have a hold over somebody. *-vr. (And.)* To get engaged.

argolleta, ica, ita [ar-gol-lyay'-tah], *f. dim.* A small staple; a small iron ring.

argollón [ar-gol-lyone'], *m. aug.* A very large iron ring; a large staple.

argoma [ar'-go-mah], *f. (Bot.)* V. ALIAGA. Furze. V. AULAGA.

argomal [ar-go-mahl'], *m.* Ground covered with furze.

argomón [ar-go-mone'], *m. aug.* Large prickly broom.

Argón [ar-gon'], *m.* Argon.

argonauta [ar-go-nah'-oo-tah], *m.* 1. Argonaut, 2. *(Zool.)* The paper nautilus (molusco). 4. A group of diurnal butterflies.

Argos [ar'-gos], *m. (Myth.)* Argus, fabled to have a hundred eyes; watchful person. **Ser un argos** *or* **estar hecho un argos,** to be very vigilant, to be very solicitous.

argot [ar-got'], *m. pl.* Argots, slang.

argótico [ar-go'-te-co], *a.* Slang.

argoudán [ar-go-oo-dahn'], *m.* A kind of cotton, manufactured in India.

arguajaque [ar-goo-ah-hah'-kay], *m.* Gum-ammoniac.

argucia [ar-goo'-the-ah], *f.* Subtilty, which degenerates into sophistry.

argüe [ar'-goo-ay], *m.* 1. Machine for moving large weights; windlass, crane; whim. 2. Machine for drawing fine gold wire.

argüellarse [ar-goo-ayl-layr'-say], *vr. (Prov.)* To be emaciated; to be in bad health: applied to children.

argüello [ar-goo-el'-lyo], *m.* Faintness, want of health.

argüende [ar-goo-ayn'-day], *m. (LAm.)* Argument.

argueñas [ar-gay'-nyas], *f. pl.* V. ANGARILLAS.

arguerita [ar-gay-ree'-tah], *f. (Miner.)* Argyrite, or argentite.

argüir [ar-goo-eer'], *vn.* To argue, to dispute, to oppose. *-va.* To give signs, to make a show of something. **Argüirle a uno su conciencia,** to be pricked by one's conscience. To reproach, to accuse. **Me argüían con vehemencia,** they vehemently reproached me.

arguma [ar'-goo-mah], *f.* V. ALIAGA.

argumentación [ar-goo-men-tah-the-on'], *f.* Argumentation.

argumentador, ra [ar-goo-men-tah-dor', rah], *m.& f.* Arguer, a reasoner, a disputant.

argumentar [ar-goo-men-tar'], *vn.* To argue, to dispute; to conclude.

argumentativo, va [ar-goo-men-tah-tee'-vo, vah], *a.* Argumentative.

argumentillo [ar-goo-men-teel'-lyo], *m. dim.* A slight argument, an unreasonable objection.

argumento [ar-goo-men'-to], *m.* 1. Argument, a reason alleged for or against a thing. 2. Argument, the subject of a discourse or writing. 3. The person who argues or disputes (universidades). 4. Argument, summary of the points treated on in a work, or in a book or chapter of a poem. **Argumento de la obra,** summary of the plot. 5. Indication, sign, token.

arguyente [ar-goo-yen'-tay], *pa.* Arguer; opponent.

aria [ah'-re-ah], *f. (Mus.)* 1. Tune or air for a single voice. 2. Verses to be set to music.

aribar [ah-re-bar'], *va.* To reel yarn into skeins.

aribo [ah-ree'-bo], *m.* Reel for making skeins.

Arica [ah-re-cah], *f.* Arica.

aricar [ah-re-car'], *va.* To plough across the ground sown with corn (arar); to clear it of weeds. V. ARREJACAR.

aridecer [ah-re-day-thayr'], 1. *va.* To dry up. 2. *vn. & vr.* To dry up, become arid.

aridez [ah-re-deth'], *f.* Drought.

árido, da [ah'-re-do, dah], *a.* 1. Dry, wanting moisture. 2. *(Met.)* Dry, barren, jejune (conversación). **Terreno árido,** arid land.

Aries [ah'-re-es], *m.* Aries or ram, one of the signs of the zodiac.

arieta [ah-re-ay'-tah], *f. dim.* Arietta, a short air, song, or tune.

ariete [ah-re-ay'-tay], *m.* Battering ram (máquina de guerra). Center forward (fútbol).

arietino, na [ah-re-ay-tee'-no, nah], *a.* Resembling the head of a ram.

arigua [ah-re-goo-ah], *f. (Carib.)* Wild bee.

arigue [ah-ree'-gay], *m.* A Philippine timber.

arije [ah-ree'-hay], *m.* V. UVA ARIJE.

arijo, ja [ah-ree'-ho, hah], *a.* Light, easily tilled: applied to soil.

arillo [ah-reel'-lyo], *m. dim.* 1. A small hoop. 2. Ear-ring. -*pl.* Hoops for ear-rings.

arimez [ah-re-meth'], *m.* Part of a building which juts or stands out.

arindajo [ah-rin-dah'-ho], *m. (Orn.)* Jay. Corvus glandarius.

ario, ia [ah'-re-o, ah], *a.* Aryan, a primitive people and language of Central Asia.

arisaro [ah-re-sah'-ro] *m. (Bot.)* Wake-robin.

ariscar [ah-res-cahr'], *va. (CAm. Carib, Mex.)* To pacify, control (animal).

arisco, ca [ah-rees'-co, cah], *a.* 1. Fierce, rude, wild, untractable, stubborn (animales). 2. *(Met.)* Harsh, unpolished, churlish, shy (personas).

arismética [ah-ris-may'-te-cah], *f. (Obs.)* Arithmetic. *V.* ARITMETICA.

arismético [ah-ris-may'-te-co], *a. (Obs.) V.* ARITMETICO.

arisnegro, arisprieto [ah-ris-nay'-gro, ah-ris-pre-ay'-to], *a.* Trigo **arisnegro** or **arisprieto**, species of wheat with a blackish beard.

arisquillo, lla [ah-ris-keel'-lyo, lyah], *a. dim.* of ARISCO.

arista [ah-rees'-tah], *f.* 1. Beard or awn of cereal grains; chaff. 2. Edge of a rough piece of timber in naval architecture. 3. Cant, edge, groin, rib, arris. -*pl. (Mil.)* Salient angles.

aristado, da [ah-ris-tah'-do, dah], *a.* Awned, bearded.

aristarco [ah-ris-tar'-co], *m.* A severe censurer of another's writings.

aristino [ah-ris-tee'-no], *m. V.* ARESTIN.

aristocracia [ah-ris-to-crah'-the-ah], *f.* An aristocracy.

aristócrata [ah-ris-to'-rah-tah], *m.* Aristocrat, a favorer of aristocracy.

aristocrático, ca [ah-ris-to-crah'-te-co, cah], *a.* Aristocratical.

Aristófanes [ah-res-to'-fah-nays], *m.* Aristophanes.

aristoloquia [ah-ris-to-lo'-ke-ah], *f. (Bot.)* Birthwort.

aristón [ah-ris-ton'], *m. (Mus.)* Mechanical organ.

aristoso, sa [ah-ris-to'-so, sah], *a.* 1. Having many beards on the ear (grano).

Aristóteles [ah-res-to'-tay-lays], *m.* Aristotle.

aristotélico, ca [ah-ris-to-tay'-le-co, cah], *a.* Aristotelian, belonging to the doctrine of Aristotle.

aritmancia [ah-rit-mahn'-the-ah], *f.* Arithmancy, foretelling future events by numbers.

aritmética [ah-rit-may'-te-cah], *f.* Arithmetic.

aritméticamente [ah-rit-may'-te-cah-men-tay], *adv.* Arithmetically, in an arithmetical manner.

aritmético [ah-rit-may'-te-co], *m.* Arithmetician, accountant.

aritmético, ca [ah-rit-may'-te-co, cah], *a.* Arithmetical.

aritmo [ah-reet'-mo], *a.* Arrhythmic, irregular (pulso).

arlequín [ar-lay-keen'], *m.* Harlequin, a buffoon who plays tricks to amuse the populace. Neapolitan ice cream.

arlequinada [ar-lay-ke-nah'-dah], *f.* A harlequin's trick, or joke; a clownish action.

arlequinesco [ar-lay-ke-nays-co], *a. (fig.)* Grotesque, ridiculous.

Arlés [ar-lays], *f.* Arles.

arlo [ar'-lo], *m. (Bot.)* Barberry or piperidge bush.

arlota [ar-lo'-tah], *f.* Tow of flax or hemp.

arlote [ar-lo'-tay], *m. (Obs.)* Vagabond, idler.

arma [ar'-mah], *f.* 1. Weapon, instrument of offence, arm. **Armas portátiles,** small arms. **Arma de caballería,** cavalry arm. **Armas nucleares,** nuclear weapons. **Arma arrojadiza,** missile, projectile. **Arma blanca,** steel, cold steel. **Arma de fuego,** firearm. **Arma homicida,** murder weapon. **De armas tomar,** formidable (temible). **Descansar las armas,** to order arms. **Licencia de armas,** firearm licence. **Llegar a las armas,** to take up arms. **Medir las armas,** to cross swords. **Presentar armas,** to present arms. **Rendir las armas,** to surrender one's arms. **Tomar las armas,** to take up arms. **Velar las armas,** to carry out the vigil of arms. **Volver el arma contra alguien,** to turn the tables on someone. 2. -*pl.* 1. Troops, armies. 2. Armorial ensigns, coat of arms. 3. **Armas de agua,** *(Mex.)* skins attached to the pommel of the saddle to protect the thighs and legs from rain.

Armas y dineros buenas manos quieren, arms and money ought to be put into wise hands. **Hombre de armas,** a military man. **Maestro de armas,** fencing-master. **Pasar por las armas,** to be shot as a criminal. **Rendir las armas,** to lay down the arms. **No dejar las armas de la mano,** not to lay down the arms. **Estar sobre las armas,** to be under arms, and ready for action. **Un hecho de armas,** an achievement, exploit. 3. *(Met.)* Means, power, reason. **Hacerse a las armas,** to inure oneself to do or perform something.

armada [ar-mah'-dah], *f.* Navy; fleet, squadron, armada. **Armada de barlovento,** *(Naut.)* fleet stationed to the windward. *(Cono Sur)* Noose, lasso (lazo).

armadera [ar-mah-day'-rah], *f. (Naut.)* The principal timbers of a ship.

armadía [ar-mah-dee'-ah], *f.* Raft, a frame or float made by pieces of timber.

armadijo [ar-mah-dee'-ho], *m.* Trap or snare for catching game.

armadillo [ar-mah-deel'-lyo], *m.* Armadillo, a small four-footed animal, covered with hard scales like armor.

armado, da [ar-mah'-do, dah], *a.* 1. Armed (en armas). **Armado hasta los dientes,** armed to the teeth. 2. Loaded. **La pistola está armada,** the gun is loaded. 3. Gold or silver placed on other metal. 4. *(Mech.)* Assembled, mounted (montado). set. -*pp.* of ARMAR.

armado [ar-mah'-do], *m.* A man armed with a coat of mail.

armador [ar-mah-dor'], *m.* 1. One who fits out privateers. 2. Privateer, cruiser. 3. One who recruits sailors for the whale and cod fishery. 4. Outfitter, shipowner. 5. *(Mech.)* Framer, adjuster, fitter. 6. Jacket.

armadura [ar-mah-doo'-rah], *f.* 1. Armor. 2. The union of the integral parts of a thing; framework 3. *(Mech.)* Setting, fitting; truss; armature *(Elec.)* 4. Skeleton. 5. Frame of a roof. **Armadura del tejado,** The shell of a building. **Armadura de una mesa,** the frame of a table.

armaduría [ar-mah-doo-re'-ah], *f. (LAm.)* Car assembly plant.

armagedón [ar-mah-gay-don'], *m.* Armageddon.

armajara [ar-mah-hah'-rah], *f. (Prov.)* A plot of ground well dug and dunged for rearing garden plants.

armamentista [ar-mah-mayn-tes'-tah], *a.* Arms; carrera armamentista, arms race.

armamento [ar-mah-men'-to], *m.* Armament, warlike preparation.

armandijo [ar-man-dee'-ho], *m. (Obs.) V.* ARMADIJO.

armar [ar-mar'], *va.* 1. To arm, to furnish with arms; to man. 2. To furnish, to fit up. 3. To square with one's opinion. 4. To arm or to plate with anything that may add strength. 5. To set a snare. 6. To place one thing above another. 7. To set up a person in business. 8. *(Mech.)* To adjust, set, mount; truss, put together. **Armar a la cuenta,** to make up an account. **Armarla,** to cheat at cards. **Armarla con queso,** to decoy. **Armar navío or bajel,** to fit out a ship. **Armar pleito or ruido,** to stir up disturbances; to kick up a dust. **Armar un lazo,** to lay a snare. **Armar una cama,** to set up a bed-sted. **Armar una casa,** to frame the timber-work of the roof of a house. **Armar caballero,** to knight. -*vr.* 1. To prepare oneself for war. **Armarse de paciencia,** to prepare oneself to suffer. 2. To prepare, to get ready. 3. *(CAm. Carib, Mex.)* To become obstinate. 4. *(LAm.)* To be lucky. 5. **¡Te vas a armar!** *(Cono Sur)*, forget it!

armario [ar-mah'-re-o], *m.* Wardrobe (ropa), cupboard (cocina), cabinet, commode. **Armario botiquín,** first-aid chest. **Armario empotrado,** built-in wardrobe, fitted wardrobe.

armatoste [ar-mah-tos'-tay], *m.* 1. Hulk, monstrosity (cosa grande y fea). 2. A trap, a snare. *V.* ARMADIJO. 3. A great brute (persona corpulenta).

armazón [ar-mah-thone'], *f.* 1. Framework, skeleton, frame. 2. Hulk of a ship. -*m.* 3. Skeleton, of the animal body. **No tener más que la armazón,** to be skin and bones.

armelina [ar-may-lee'-nah], *f.* Ermine skin.

armella [ar-mayl'-lyah], *f.* Staple or ring made of iron or other metal; box staple, bushing, screw-eyes. **Armellas,** *(Naut.)* Pieces of iron doubled in shape of a **U.**

armelluela [ar-mayl-lyoo-ay'-lah], *f. dim.* A small staple or ring.

armenio, nia [ar-may'-ne-o, ne-ah], *a.* Armenian, relating to Armenia.

armería [ar-may-ree'-ah], *f.* 1. Armory, arsenal. 2. *(Obs.)* Trade of an armorer or gunsmith. 3. Heraldry.

armero [ar-may'-ro], *m.* 1. Armorer or gunsmith. 2. Keeper of arms or armor. 3. *(Mil.)* A rack or stand for fire-arms.

armígero, ra [ar-mee'-hay-ro, rah], *a. (Poetic.)* Warlike.

armilar [ar-me-lar'], *a.* **Esfera armilar,** armillary sphere.

armilla [ar-meel'-lyah], *f.* Principal part of the base of a column.

armiño [ar-mee'-nyo], *m.* 1. Ermine, a small animal furnishing a valuable fur. *a.* 2. The fur of the ermine. **Armiños** *(Her.)* Figures of a white field interspersed with black spots.

armipotente [ar-me-po-ten'-tay], *a. (Poetic.)* Mighty in war.

armisticio [ar-mis-tee'-the-o], *m.* Armistice, suspension of hostilities.

armoisín [ar-mo-e-seen'], *m.* A thin silk or taffeta.

armón [ar-mone'], *m.* The fore carriage of a piece of artillery.

armonía [ar-mo-nee'-ah], *f.* 1. Harmony, just proportion or concord of sound; harmoniousness, number. 2. Concord or correspondence of one thing with another. **Hacer or causar armonía,** to excite admiration, to produce novelty. 3. Friendship. **Correr con armonía,** to live in peace.

armónica [ar-mo'-ne-cah], *f.* Harmonica, mouth organ.

armónicamente [ar-mo'-ne-cah-mayn-tay], *adv.* Harmoniously; harmonically.

armónico, ca [ar-mo'-ne-co, cah], *a.* Harmonical, adapted to each other, musical, rhythmical.

armonio [ar-mo'-ne-o], *m.* Harmonium, or reed organ. Strictly, the harmonium has force-bellows and the cabinet organ suction-bellows.

armoniosamente [ar-mo-ne-osah-men'-tay], *adv.* Harmoniously.

armonioso, sa [ar-mo-ne-o'-so, sah], *a.* 1. Harmonious, sonorous, pleasing to the ear; consonous. 3. *(Met.)* Adapted to each other, having the parts proportioned to each other.

armonista [ar-mo-nees'-tah], *f.* Harmonist.

armonizable [ar-mo-ne-tha'-blay], *a. (fig.)* That can be reconciled.

armonización [ar-mo-ne-thah-the-on'], *f.* Harmonization; *(fig.)* Reconciliation; co-ordination. **Ley de cordinación,** coordinating law.

armonizador [ar-mo-ne-thah-dor'], *a.* **Ley armonizadora;** *V.* ARMONIZACIÓN.

armonizar [ar-mo-ne-thar'], *va.* To harmonize, to put in harmony: to produce harmony. *-vn.* To harmonize; *(fig.)* To harmonize, to blend with, to be in keeping with; **armonizar con,** to blend with, to tone in with (colores).

armuelle [ar-moo-el'-lyay], *m. (Bot.)* Orach. Atriplex.

arna [ar'-nah], *f. (Prov.)* Bee-hive.

arnacho [ar-nah'-cho], *m.* 1. *(Bot.)* Rest harrow. 2. Wild amaranth. 3. Orach.

arnaco [ar-nah'-co], *m. (And.)* Useless object, piece of lumber.

arnero [ar-nay-ro], *m. (LAm.)* Sieve.

arnés [ar-ness'], *m.* 1. Harness, coat of mail or steel network for defence; armor. 2. Store-room for the accoutrements of cavalry. **Arneses,** necessary tools, utensils, furniture used in a house, trade or kitchen. **Arnés de caballo,** gear, trapping, and furniture of a horse.

árnica [ar'-ne-cah], *f.* Arnica, a medicinal plant.

arnilla [ar-neel'-lyah], *f. dim. (Prov.)* A small bee-hive.

aro [ah'-ro], *m.* 1. Hoop of wood, iron, or other metals, iron staple; hoop poles. 2. *(Bot.) V.* YARO. **Meterle a uno por el aro or arillo,** to decoy somebody. 3. *(LAm.)* **Pasar a uno por el aro,** to play tricks on somebody.

aroca [ah-ro'-cah], *f.* A sort of linen.

aroma [ah-ro'-mah], *m.* Aroma, perfume, fragance. **El aroma del café,** the aroma of coffee. *f.* Flower of the aromatic myrrh-tree. *-m.* 1. *(Chem.)* The odorant principle, the volatile spirit of plants. 2. A general name given to all balsams, woods, and herbs of strong fragrance.

aromaticidad [ah-ro-mah-te-the-dahd'], *f.* An aromatic or fragrant quality, perfume.

aromático, ca [ah-ro-mah'-te-co, cah], *a.* Aromatic, fragrant.

aromatización [ah-ro-mah-te-thah-the-on'], *f.* Aromatization, the act of scenting with aromatics.

aromatizador [ah-ro-mah-te-thah-dor'], *m.* Aromatizer, spray.

aromatizar [ah-ro-mah-te-thar'], *va.* To aromatize, to perfume.

aromo [ah-ro'-mo], *m. (Bot.)* The aromatic myrrh-tree.

aroza [ah-ro'-thah], *m.* Foreman in iron-works or forges.

arpa [ar'-pah] *f.* 1. Harp, lyre. **Tocar el arpa,** to be a thief. 2. *(Astr.)* Harp, a constellation.

arpado [ar-pah'-do], *a.* Serrated, toothed. *-pp.* of ARPAR.

arpador [ar-pah-dor'], *m. (Obs.)* Harp player.

arpadura [ar-pah-doo'-rah], *f. V.* ARAÑO.

arpar [ar-par'], *va.* 1. To tear clothes to pieces, to rend to tatters. 2. To claw, to tear with nails or claws. 3. *(LAm.)* To pinch, nick.

arpegio [ar-pay'-he-o], *m. (Mus.)* Arpeggio.

arpella [ar-payl'-lyah], *f. (Orn.)* Harpy.

arpeo [ar-pay'-o], *m. (Naut.)* Grappling iron.

arpero [ar-pay'-ro], *m. & f. (Mex.)* Thief, burglar (ladrón).

arpía [ar-pee'-ah], *f.* 1. *(Poetic.)* Harpy, a bird of prey represented by poets. 2. Harpy, a ravenous woman; an ugly, scolding shrew.

arpicordio [ar-pe-cor'-de-o], *m.* Harpsichord.

arpillar [ar-pe-lyahr'], *va. (CAm.)* To pile up.

arpillera [ar-peel-lyay'-rah], *f.* Sackcloth, coarse linen made of tow, packcloth.

arpir [ar-peer'], *m. (And. Cono Sur)* Mineworker.

arpista [ar-pees'-tah], *m.* 1. Harper, player on the harp by profession, harpist. 2. *(Cono Sur)* Thief (ladrón).

arpón [ar-pone'], *m.* 1. Harpoon, a harping-iron. 2. *(Naut.)* Fish-gig.

arponado, da [ar-po-nah'-do, dah], *a.* Harpooned, like a harpoon.

arponar [ar-pon-nahr'], *va,* To harpoon; to gaff.

arponear [ar-po-nay-ar'], *va.* To throw the harpoon.

arponero [ar-po-nay'-ro], *m.* Harpooner, he who throws the harpoon.

arqueada [ar-kay-ah'-dah], *f.* Stroke with the fiddle-bow, whereby sounds are produced from the strings of a musical instrument. **Dar arqueadas,** *(coll.)* to show symptoms of nausea.

arqueador [ar-kay-ah-dor'], *m.* 1. Ship-gauger, an officer whose job is to measure the dimensions of ships. 2. One who forms arches. 3. Woolbeater.

arqueaje [ar-kay-ah'-hay], *m.* The gauging of a ship.

arqueamiento [ar-kay-ah-me-en'-to], *m. V.* ARQUEO.

arquear [ar-kay-ar'], *va.* 1. To arch, to form in the shape of an arch. 2. Among clothiers, to beat the dust out of the wool. 3. *(Naut.)* To gauge or measure the dimensions of ships. **Arquear las cejas,** to arch the eyebrows; to frown. **Arquear para vomitar,** to retch. 4. *(LAm.)* To check. *-vr.* To arch, to bend.

arqueo [ar-kay'-o], *m.* 1. The act of bending anything into the form of an arch. 2. *(Naut.)* The tonnage or burden of a ship. *V.* ARQUEAJE. 3. Verification of money and papers in a safe *(Com.)*.

arqueolítico [ar-ke-o-le'-te-co], *a.* Stone-Age.

arqueología [ar-kay-o-lo-hee'-ah], *f.* Archaeology, a discourse on antiquity.

arqueológico [ar-ke-o-lo'-he-co], *a.* Archaeological.

arqueólogo [ar-kay-o'-lo-go], *m.* Archaeologist.
arquería [ar-kay-ree'-ah], *f.* 1. Series of arches. 2. *(Mex.)* Aqueduct.
arquero [ar-kay'-ro], *m.* 1. One whose trade is to make bows for arrows. 2. Treasurer, cashier. 3. Bowman, archer.
arqueta [ar-kay'-tah], *f. dim.* A little chest, a small trunk.
arquetipo [ar-kay-tee'-po], *m.* Archetype.
arquetón [ar-kay-tone'], *m. aug.* A large trunk.
arquetoncillo [ar-kay-ton-theel'-lyo], *m. dim.* A trunk or chest of a middling size.
arquibanco [ar-kay-bahn'-co], *m.* A bench or seat with drawers.
arquiepiscopal [ar-ke-ay-pis-co-pahl'], *a.* Archiepiscopal. *V.* ARZOBISPAL.
arquifilósofo [ar-ke-fe-lo'-so-fo], *m.* Archphilosopher.
arquilla, ita [ar-keel'-lyah, kke'-tah], *f. dim.* A little chest.
arquillo [ar-keel'-lyo], *m. dim.* A small arch or bow.
arquimesa [ar-ke-may'-sah], *f. (Prov.)* Scrutoire, a case of drawers for writing, with a desk, escritoire.
Arquímides [ar-ke'-may-days], *m.* Archimedes.
arquimesa [ar-ke-may-sah], *f.* Desk, escritoire.
arquisinagogo[ar-ke-se-nah-go'-go], *m.* Principal in the synagogue.
arquitecto [ar-ke-tec'-to], *m.* An architect. **Arquitecto de sistemas de datos** *(Comp.)*, data systems architect.
arquitectónico, ca [ar-ke-tec-to'-ne-co, cah], *a.* Architectonic, architectural.
arquitectura [ar-ke-tee-too'-rah], *f.* Architecture. **Arquitectura de jardines**, landscape gardening, landscaping.
arquitrabe [ar-ke-trah'-bay], *m.* Architrave, that part of a column which lies immediately upon the capital, and is the lowest member of the entableture.
arrabal [ar-rah-bal'], *m.* Suburb. *pl.***Arrabales**, suburbs or outskirts of a large town.
arrabalero, ra [ah-rah-bah-lay'-ro, rah], *a.* 1. Belonging to the outskirts; illbred, churlish. 2. Coarse in dress or manners.
arrabio [ar-rah'-be-o], *m.* Cast iron.
arraca [ar-rah'-cah], *f. (Naut.)* Traveler, an iron traveler.
arracacha, cho [ar-rah-cah'-cha], *f. & m. (And.)* Idiocy, silliness.
arracada [ar-rah-cah'-dah], *f.* Earring.
arracimado, da [ar-rah-the-mah'-do, dah], *a.* Clustered *-pp* of ARRICIMARSE. Botryoid, botryoidal.
arracimarse [ar-rah-the-mar'-say], *vr.* To cluster, or to be clustered together like a bunch of grapes.
arraclán [ar-rah-clahn'], *m. V.* ALISO. Alder-tree.
arráez [ar-rah'-eth], *m.* Captain or master of a Moorish ship. Used also in the Philippine Archipelago.
arraigadamente [ar-rah-e-gah'-dah-mayn-tay], *adv.* Firmly, securely.
arraigadas [ar-rah-e-gah'-das], *f. pl. (Naut.)* Futtock-shrouds.
arraigado, da [ar-rah-e-gah'-do, dah], *a.* 1. Possessed of landed property, real estate. Well-rooted, deep-rooted. 2. Fixed, inveterate, speaking of evils.
arraigar [ar-rah-e-gar'], *vn.* 1. To root. 2. To give security in land. 3. *-va. (LAm. Jur.)* To put somebody under a restriction. *-vr.* 1. To establish oneself in a place. 2. To be of long continuance, as a custom, habit, etc. **La costumbre se arraigó en él**, the habit grew on him.
arraigo [ar-rah'-e-go], *m.* 1. Landed property. **Es hombre de arraigo**, he is a man of considerable landed property. 2. Rooting; **de fácil arraigo**, easily-rooted. 3. *(fig.)* Settling, establishment. 4. *(fig.)* Hold, influence; **Tener arraigos**, to have influence.
arralar [ar-rah'-lar¡], *vn.* To thin out (árboles). *V.* RALEAR.
arramblar [ar-ram-blar'], *va.* 1. To cover with sand and gravel (arroyos, torrentes). 2. To sweep away, to drag along. *-vn.* **Arramblar con**, to make off with (robar).
arranca-clavos [ar-rahn'-cah-clah'-vos], *m.* Nail-puller.

arrancada [ar-ran-cah'-dah], *f. (coll.)* Sudden departure, violent sally.
arrancadera [ar-ran-cah-day'-rah] *f.* Large bell worn by those animals which guide the rest of the flocks.
arrancadero [ar-ran-cah-day'-ro], *m.* 1. *(Prov.)* The thickest part of the barrel of a gun. 2. Starting-point, course, or route.
arrancado, da [ar-ran-cah'-do, dah], *a.* 1. *(coll.)* Poor, penniless. 2. *(Naut.)* **Boga arrancada**, with long strokes of the oars. 3. Uprooted (plantas, árboles) *-pp.* of ARRANCAR.
arrancador, ra [ah-rran-cah-dor', rah], *m. & f.* An extirpator, a destroyer. *(Aut.)* Starter.
arrancadura [ar-ran-cah-doo'-rah], *f. (Obs.)* **Arrancamiento** [ar-ran-cah-me-en'-to], *m.* Extirpation, the act of pulling up by the roots.
arrancapinos [ar-ran-cah-pee'-nos], *m.* Nickname for little persons.
arrancar [ar-ran-car'], *va.* 1. To pull up by the roots, to extirpate. **Una historia que arranca lágrimas**, a story to make one cry. 2. To force out, to wrest. **Le arrancó el bolso**, he snatched her handbag. 3. To pull out a nail, to draw out a tooth. 4. To carry off with violence. 5. To force up phlegm, bile, etc. 6. To start and pursue one's course. 7. To begin an arch or vault. 8. *(Naut.)* To get afloat, or set sail. **Arrancar de raíz**, to root out or up. **Arrancar la espada**, to unsheath the sword. **Arrancársele a uno el alma**, to die brokenhearted. *-vr. (And. Carib. Mex.)* To peg out, to kick the bucket; **arrancarse con los tarros**, *(Cono Sur)* to run off with the profits.
arrancasiega [ar-ran-cah-se-ay'-gah], *f.* 1. Poor corn, half mowed and half pulled up. 2. *(Prov.)* A quarrel or dispute, with injurious language.
arranciarse [ar-ran-the-ar'-say], *vr.* To grow rancid.
arranchar [ar-rahn-chahr'], *vt.* 1. To brace (velas). 2. To skirt, to sail close to (costa). 3. *(And.)* To snatch away. *-vr.* 1. To mess together. 2. *(Carib. Mex.)* To settle in, to make oneself comfortable.
arrancón [ar-rahn-con'], *m. (Mex.) V.* ARRANCADA.
arranque [ar-rahn'-kay], *m.* 1. Extirpation, act of pulling up by the roots. 2. Wrench. 3. Flight of the imagination, sudden, unexpected gesture. 4. Violent fit, impetuousness. 5. Initiative, daring. **Arranque del caballo**, sudden start of the horse. **Arranque automático**, self-starter. **Un hombre de mucho arranque**, a man of daring, a man of an enterprising nature. 6. *(Arquit.)* Starting point. 7. *(LAm.)* **Estar en el arranque**, to be completely broke. 8. *(fig.)* Sally, witty remark. 9. *(Comp.)* Starting up.
arranquera [ar-rahn-kay-rah], *f. V.* ARRANQUE.
arrapar [ar-rah-par'], *va.* To snatch away, to carry off. *V.* ARREBATAR.
arrapiezo, arrapo [ar-rah-pe-ay'-tho, ar-rah'-po], *m.* 1. Tatter or rag hanging from old clothes. 2. *(Met.)* A mean, worthless, despicable person.
arras [ar'-ras], *f. pl.* 1. Thirteen pieces of money, which the bridegroom gives to the bride, as a pledge, in the act of marriage. 2. Dowry. 3. Earnest-money, handsel. **Arras de la bodega**, *(Naut.)* Wings of the hold.
arrasado [ar-rah-sah'-do], *m.* A silk stuff, satin face; satin.
arrasador [ar-rah-sah-dor'], *a. V.* ARROLLADOR.
arrasadura [ar-rah-sah-doo'-rah], *f. V.* RASADURA.
arrasamiento [ar-rah-sah-me-en'-to], *m.* Demolition of a fortress or fortified place.
arrasar [ar-rah-sar'], *va.* 1. To level, to make even, to smooth the surface of a thing. 2. To destroy, to raze, to demolish. 3. To obliterate. **Arrasar un bajel**, *(Naut.)* to cut down a vesel, to cut away part of her dead works. *-vn. & vr.* 1. To clear up, to grow fine (tiempo). 2. To fill with tears (ojos). **Arrasarse los ojos de lágrimas**, to weep bitterly.
arrastracueros [ar-rahs-trah-coo-ay'-ros], *m. (Carib.)* Crook; rascal, rogue.

arrastradamente [ar-ras-trah-dah-men'-tay], *adv.* 1. Imperfectly. 2. Painfully, wretchedly.

arrastraderas [ar-ras-trah-day'-ras], *f. pl. (Naut.)* Lower studding-sails.

arrastradero [ar-ras-trah-day'-ro], *m. (Naut.)* 1. A place on the seacoast, gently sloping toward the sea, where ships are careened; a careening-place. 2. Road by which logs are dragged. 3. Spot whence dead bulls are taken off.

arrastradizo [ar-rahs-trah-de'-tho], *a.* Dangling, trailing.

arrastrado, da [ar-ras-trah'-do, dah], *a.* 1. Dragged along. 2. Rascally, knavish. 3. Living in abject poverty. *-f. (coll.)* A fallen woman, prostitute. **Andar arrastrado,** to live in the utmost misery and distress. *-pp.* of ARRASTRAR.

arrastramiento [ar-ras-trah-me-en'-to], *m.* The act of dragging along the ground.

arrastrante [ar-ras-trahn'-tay], *m.* Claimant of a degree in colleges.

arrastrar [ar-ras-trar'], *va. & vn.* 1. To creep, to crawl. 2. To drag along the ground. 3. To bring one over to our opinion. 4. To lead a trump at cards. **Arrastrar la causa, el pleito, los autos,** etc., to move a lawsuit into another court. **Hacer alguna cosa arrastrando,** to do a thing against one's will, to do it ill. 5. To carry away; **No te dejes arrastrar por esa idea,** don´t get carried away by that idea. 6. **Arrastrar a uno a hacer algo,** to lead somebody to do something. *-vr.* To crawl, creep; **Se arrastró hasta la puerta,** he dragged himself to the door. 2. To drag, to trail along the ground, to hang down. 3. To drag (tiempo). 4. To grovel, to fawn, to creep.

arrastre [ar-ras'-tray], *m.* 1. The act of leading a trump at cards. 2. The act of dragging; haulage, drayage. **Flota de arrastre,** trawling fleet. **Arrastre por correa,** belt-drive. 3. Slope of the wall of a shaft. 4. *(Amer.)* A mill where silver ores are pulverized. 5. *(Carib.)* Influence, pull. 6. *(Taur.)* Dragging away of the dead bull. 7. **Arrastre de dientes,** tractor. **Arrastre de papel por tracción,** tractor feed.

arrate [ar-rah'-tay], *m.* A pound of sixteen ounces.

arrayán [ar-rah-yahn'], *m. (Bot.)* Myrtle.

arrayanal [ar-rah-yah-nahl'], *m.* Plantation of myrtles.

arre [ar'-ray], Gee, get up; a word used by drivers to horses, mules, etc. **¡Arre aborrico!** Go on, ass!

¡Arre allá! Be off with you!

arreada [ar-ray-ah'-dah], *f. (Amer.)* 1. Act of herding the grazing flock. 2. Conscription for military service.

arreado [ar-ray-ah'-do], *a. (And. Cono Sur, Mex.)* Sluggish, ponderous.

arreador [ar-ray-ah-dor'], *m.* Muleteer.

arrear [ar-ray-ar'], *va.* 1. To drive horses, mules, etc. 2. To harness (caballo). 3. *(CAm. Cono Sur, Mex.)* To steal, rustle (ganado). *-vn.* To hurry along, get moving; *(fig.)* get away! *-vr. (Obs.)* To be a muleteer.

arrebañador, ra [ar-ray-bah-nyah-dor', rah], *m. & f.* Gleaner, gatherer.

arrebañadura [ar-ray-bah-nyah-doo'-rah], *f.* The act of gleaning, picking up, or scraping together.

arrebañar [ar-ray-bah-nyar'], *va.* To glean, to gather, to scrap together.

arrebatadamente [ar-ray-bah-tah-dah-men'-tay], *adv.* Precipitately, headlong.

arrebatadizo [ar-ray-bah-tah-dee'-tho], *a.* Excitable, hot-tempered.

arrebatado, da [ar-ray-bah-tah'-do, dah], *a.* 1. Rapid, violent. 2. Precipitate, rash, inconsiderate, impetuous. **Muerte arrebatada,** a sudden death. **Hombre arrebatado,** a rash, inconsiderate man. *-pp.* of ARREBATAR.

arrebatador, ra [ar-ray-bah-tah-dor', rah], *m. & f.* One who snatches away, or takes a thing by violence.

arrebatamiento [ar-ray-bah-tah-me-en'-to], *m.* 1. The act of carrying away by violence or precipitation. 2. Fury, rage, extreme passion. 3. Rapture, ecstasy, fit.

arrebatar [ar-ray-bah-tar'], *va.* 1. To carry off, to take away by violence. 2. To snatch and seize things with

precipitation. **Le arrebató el revólver,** he snatched the pistol from him. 3. To attract attention, notice, etc. 4. *(fig.)* To move deeply, to stir; to captivate, enrapture. 5. *(Agri.)* To parch. *-vr.* 1. To be led away by passion. **Arrebatarse de cólera,** to be overcome with anger. 2. To be gathered earlier than usual on account of hot weather (cosecha). 3. To get roasted or scorched. **Arrebatarse el caballo,** said of a horse which is overheated.

arrebatiña [ar-ray-bah-tee'-nyah], *f.* The act of carrying off a thing precipitately out of a crowd.

arrebato [ar-ray-bah'-to], *m.* Surprise, a sudden and unexpected attack upon an enemy; paroxysm, start. **Arrebato de cólera,** sudden burst of passion.

arrebiatarse [ar-ray-be-ah-tahr'-say], *vr. (CAm.)* To join up; *(Mex.)* To follow the crowd.

arrebol [ar-ray-bole'], *m.* 1. The red glow in the sky. 2. Rouge, red paint for ladies. **El sol poniente tiene arreboles magníficos,** the sun sets off a magnificent red glow at sunset.

arrebolada [ar-rah-bo-lah-dah], *f.* Red clouds (at sunrise or sunset).

arrebolar [ar-ray-bo-lar'], *va.* To paint red, to redden, to give a red glow. *-vr* To rouge or to lay on rouge. *(Carib.)* To dress up.

arrebolera [ar-ray-bo-lay'-rah], *f.* 1. *(Prov.)* A woman who sells rouge. 2. Alkanet, a plant of which vegetable rouge is made. 3. A small pot or saucer with red paint. 4. *(Bot.)* Marvel of Peru.

arrebozar [ah-rray-bo-thar'], *va.* To cover; to conceal. *(Culin.)* To cover, to coat. *-vr.* To cover one´s face; to muffle up.

arrebozo [ar-ray-bo'-tho], *m. V.* REBOZO.

arrebujadamente [ar-ray-boo-hah-dah-men'-tay], *adv.* Confusedly, with disorder.

arrebujar [ar-ray-boo-har'], *va.* To gather up without order; to throw together with confusion, to huddle. *-vr.* To cover and roll oneself in the bed-clothes.

arrecafe [ar-ray-cah'-fay], *m.* Cardoon.

arrechada [ah-rray-chah-dah], *f. (CAm. Mex.) V.* ARRECHERA.

arrechar [ah-rray-char'], *vn.* 1. *(CAm.)* To show energy, to begin to make an effort. 2. *(CAm. Mex.)* To feel randy. *-vr. (CAm. Mex.)* To get angry.

arrechera [ah-rray-chay-rah], *f.* 1. *(Cono Sur)* Heat, mating urge; *(Mex.)* Randiness, lust. 2. *(Mex.)* Whim, fancy.

arrecho [ah-rray-cho], 1. *a. (CAm. Mex.)* Vigorous, energetic. 2. *(CAm.)* Randy, lecherous; **estar arrecho,** to be on heat; to be in the mood (persona). 3. *(CAm. Mex.)* In heat. 4. *(CAm.)* **Es un arrecho,** he´s a bloody nuisance.

arrechucho [ah-rray-choo'-cho], 1. A fit of anger. 2. Sudden and passing indisposition.

arreciar [ar-ray-the-ar'], *vn.* To become intensified. **Arreció la lluvia,** it rained harder. To get worse. *-vr. (Med.)* To get stronger.

arrecife [ar-ray-thee'-fay], *m.* 1. Causeway, a road paved with stone; mole. 2. *(Naut.)* A reef, ridge of hiden rocks lying close under the surface of the water.

arrecil [ar-ray-theel'], *m. (Prov.)* A sudden flood.

arrecirse [ar-ray-theer'-say], *vr.* To be benumbed with excessive cold, to grow stiff with cold.

arredilar [ar-ray-de-lar'], *va.* To put into the sheep-fold.

arredo [ah-rray'-do], *adv. (CAm. Mex.)* **¡Arredo vaya!,** get lost!

arredomado, da [ar-ray-do-mah'-do, dah], *a. V.* REDOMADO.

arredondar, arredondear [ar-ray-don-dar', ar-ray-don-day-ar'], *va. (Obs.)* To round. *V.* REDONDEAR.

arredramiento [ar-ray-drah-me-en'-to], *m.* The act of removing to a greater distance.

arredrar [ar-ray-drar'], *va.* 1. To remove to a greater distance. 2. To terrify, to cause dread. *-vr. V.* ATEMORIZARSE.

arregazado, da [ar-ray-gah-thah'-do, dah], *a.* Having the point turned up. **Nariz arregazada** *or* **arremangada**, a cocked nose. *-pp.* of ARREGAZAR.

arregazar [ar-ray-gah-thar'], *va.* To truss, to tuck up the skirts of clothes.

arregionado, da [ah-rre-he-o-nah'-do], *a. (And. Mex.)* Ill-tempered, sharp; impulsive, cross.

arreglada [ah-rray-glah'-dah], *f. (Cono Sur)* **Arreglada de bigotes**, dirty deal, shady business.

arregladamente [ar-ray-glah'-dah-men-tay], *adv.* Regularly.

arreglado, da [ar-ray-glah'-do, dah], *a.* Regular, moderate. *-pp.* of ARREGLAR.

arreglador [ar-ray-gla-dor'], *m. (Com.)* Surveyor, valuer (of averages).

arreglamiento [ar-ray-glah-me-en'-to], *m. (Obs.)* Regulation, instruction in writing.

arreglar [ar-ray-glar'], *va.* 1. To regulate, to reduce to order, to guide, to moderate. 2. To compound; to frame. *(Com.)* To arrange, to settle; to adjust. **Yo lo arreglaré**, I´ll see to it. 3. To adjust the administration of provinces, and enact laws for them. 4. To tidy up, to smarten up, to do. **Voy a que me arreglen el pelo**, I´m going to have my hair done. *-vr.* 1. To conform to law. 2. To come to terms; **por fin se arreglaron**, eventually they reached an agreement. 3. **Arreglarse el pelo**, to have one´s hair done. 4. To work out, to solve. **Ya es hora de arreglarse**, it´s time to get ready.

arreglo [ar-ray'-glo], *m.* 1. Rule, order. **Vivir con arreglos**, to live an orderly life. 2. *(Com.)* Arrangement, settlement. **Con arreglo**, conformably, according to. 3. Agreement, understanding. **Llegar a un arreglo**, to reach a settlement. 4. Trim (pelo).

arregostarse [ar-ray-gos-tar'-say], *vr.* To relish or have a taste for a thing, to be attached to it.

arregosto [ah-rray-gos'-to], *m.* Fancy, taste.

arrejaca [ar-ray-hah'-cah], *f. V.* ARREJAQUE.

arrejacar [ar-ray-hah-car'], *va.* To plough across a piece of ground, to clear of weeds.

arrejaco [ar-ray-hah'-co], *m. (Orn.)* Swift, martin. *V.* VENCEJO.

arrejada [ar-ray-hah'-dah], *m.* Fork with three prongs bent at the point.

arrejarse [ah-rray-hahr'-say], *vr. (Cono Sur.)* To take a risk.

arrejuntarse [ah-rray-hoon-tahr'-say], *vr.* To move in together.

arrel, arrelde [ar-rel', ar-rel'-day], *m.* 1. Weight of four pounds. 2. A bird of a very small size.

arrellanarse [ar-rel-lyah-nar'-say], *vr.* 1. To sit at ease; to incline one's seat for greater ease. 2. *(Met.)* To make oneself comfortable. 3. To be satisfied with one's employment.

arremangado, da [ar-ray-man-gah'-do, dah], *a.* Lifted upward. **Ojos arremangados**, uplifted eyes. *-pp.* of ARRREMANGAR.

arremangar [ar-ray-man-gar'], *va.* To tuck up the sleeves or petticoats. *-vr.* To be fully resolved. To roll up one´s sleeves. To take a firm line (actitud).

arremango [ar-ray-mahn'-go], *m.* The act of tucking up the clothes.

arrematar [ah-rray-mah-tahr'], *va.* To finish, to complete.

arremedador, ra [ar-ray-may-dah-dor', rah], *m. & f. (Obs.)* A mimic, a ludicrous imitator.

arremetedor [ar-ray-may-tay-dor'], *m.* Assailant, aggressor.

arremeter [ar-ray-may-ter'], *va.* 1. To assail, to attack with impetuosity, to make at. 2. To seize briskly. 3. To shock or offend the sight. *-vn.* 1.To rush forth, to attack. **Arremeter a uno**, to rush at somebody. 2. *(fig.)* To offend good taste, to shock the eye.

arremetida [ar-ray-may-tee'-dah], *f.* 1. Attack, assault, invasion. 2. Start of horses from a barrier or other place.

arremolinado, da [ar-ray-mo-le-nah'-do, dah], *a.* Whirled, turned round; (trigo) blown down by a storm.

arremolinar [ar-ray-mo-le-nar'], *va. & vr.* 1. To eddy, to form eddies. 2. To gather together, to form a crowd.

arrempujar [ar-rem-poo-har'], *va. V.* REMPUJAR.

arremueco [ar-ray-moo-ay'-co], *vn.* 1. A Caress. 2. A movement of the lips expressive of contempt or scorn. *V.* ARRUMACO.

arrendable [ar-ren-dah'-blay], *a.* Rentable; farmable, tenantable.

arrendación [ar-ren-dah-the-on'], *f.* The act of renting, or taking at a certain rent.

arrendadero [ar-ren-dah-day'-ro], *m.* An iron ring fastened to the manger, to which horses are tied.

arrendado, da [ar-ren-dah'-do, dah], *a.* Obedient to the reins, applied to horses. *-pp.* of ARRENDAR.

arrendador [ar-ren-dah-dor'], *m.* 1. Landlord lessor, hirer, tenant, lessee, holder; farmer; copyholder. 2. *V.* ARRENDADERO. **Arrendador de plomo**, a very tiresome person.

arrendadorcillo [ar-ren-dah-dor-theel'-lyo],*m. dim.* A petty tenant.

arrendajo [ar-ren-dah'-ho], *m.* 1. *(Orn.)* The mocking-bird. 2. Mimic, buffoon.

arrendamiento [ar-ren-dah-me-en'-to], *m.* 1. The act of renting, letting, or hiring to a tenant; lease. 2. The house or lease-rent. 3. Contract, agreement.

arrendante [ar-ren-dahn'-tay], *m.* A tenant.

arrendar [ar-ren-dar'], *va.* 1. To rent (alquilar), to hold by paying rent, for rent, to lease, to hire. 2. To bridle a horse. 3. To tie a horse by the reins of a bridle. 4. To mimic, to imitate as a buffoon, to ridicule by a burlesque imitation. 5. To thin out plants. **Arrendar tierras**, to lease land. **No le arriendo la ganancia**, I wouldn't like to be in his shoes.

arrendatario, ria [ar-ren-dah-tah'-re-o, ah], *m. & f.* 1. One who rents, a lessor. 2. Lessee, 3. Farmer.

arrendero [ah-rrayn-day'ro], *m. (Cono Sur. Mex.) V.* ARRENDATARIO.

arrentado, da [ar-ren-tah'-do, dah], *a.* Enjoying a considerable income from landed property.

arreo [ar-ray'-o], *m.* Dress , ornament, decoration. *-pl.* 1. Appendages. 2. Trappings of a horse.

arreo [ar-ray'-o], *adv. (coll.)* Successively, uninterruptedly. **Llevar arreo**, to carry something on one's shoulders.

arrepápalo [ar-ray-pah'-pah-lo], *m.* A sort of fritters or buns.

arrepentida [ar-ray-pen-tee'-dah], *f.* A woman of previous evil life who repents and shuts herself within a convent.

arrepentidamente [ah-rray-payn-te'-dah-mayn-tay], *adv.* Regretfully, repentantly.

arrepentido, da [ar-ray-pen-tee'-do, dah], *a.* Repentant. *-pp.* of ARREPENTIRSE.

arrepentimiento [ar-ray-pen-te-me-en'-to], *m.* 1. Repentance, penitence, contriteness, compunction; conversion. 2. Emendation in composition and drawing (pintura).

arrepentirse [ar-ray-pen-teer'-say], *vr.* To repent, to express sorrow for having said or done something. **(Yo me arrepiento, yo me arrepienta; él se arrepintió, él se arrepintiera**; from **Arrepentirse.** *V.* ASENTIR).

arrepistar [ar-ray-pis-tar'], *va.* To grind or pound rags into a fine pulp (papeleras, fábricas de papel).

arrepisto [ar-ray-pees'-to], *m.* The act of grinding or pounding rags.

arrepticio, cia [ar-rep-tee'-the-o, ah], *a.* Possessed or influenced by the devil.

arrequesonarse [ar-ray-kay-so-nar'se], *vr.* To be curded or coagulated; to curdle.

arrequife [ar-ray-kee'-fay], *m.* Singeing-iron for burning or taking off the down which remains on cotton goods.

arrequín [ah-rray-ken'], *m.* 1. *(LAm.)* Helper, assistant. 2. *(LAm.) (Agri.)* Leading animal.

arrequives [ar-ray-kee'-ves], *vn. pl.* 1. Ornaments, adornments. 2. Circumstances of a case. 3. Requisites.

arrestado, da [ar-res-tah'-do, dah], *a*. Intrepid, bold, audacious. *-pp*. of ARRESTAR.

arrestar [ar-res-tar'], *va*. To arrest, to confine, to imprison. **Arrestar en el cuartel**, to confine to barracks. *-vr*. To be bold and enterprising, to engage with spirit in an enterprise or undertaking.

arresto [ar-res'-to], *m*. 1. Spirit, boldness in undertaking an enterprise. 2. Detention. *(Mil.)* Prison, arrest. **Estar bajo arresto**, to be under arrest.

arretín [ar-ray-teen'], *m*. V. FILIPICHIN.

arretranca [ar-ray-trahn'-cah], *f*. A broad crupper for mules.

arrevesado [ar-ray-vay-sah'-do], *a*. Queer, odd.

arrezafe [ar-ray-thah'-fay], *m*. A place full of thistles, brushwood, and brambles.

arria [ar'-re-ah], *f*. Drove of beasts.

arriada [ar-re-ah'-dah], *f*. *(Prov.)* Swell of waters, flood, overflowing.

arriado [ah-rre-ah'-do], *a*. *(LAm.)* V. ARREADO.

arrianismo [ar-re-ah-nees'-mo], *m*. Arianism.

arriano, na [ar-re-ah'-no, anh], *a*. Arian (hereje), adherent to the teachings of Arius.

arriar [ar-re-ar'], *va*. *(Naut.)* 1. To lower, to strike. **Arriar la bandera**, to strike the colors. **Arriar las vergas y los masteleros**, to strike the yards and top-masts. **Arriar un cabo**, to pay out the cable. **Arriar la gavía**, to let go the maintop-sail. 2. *vr*. To destroy by floods or a sudden fall of rain. **¡Arría!** Let go!

arriata [ar-re-ah'-tah], *f*. V. ARRIATE.

arriate [ar-re-ah'-tay], *m*. 1. A border in gardens where herbs, flowers, etc., are planted. 2. Trellis around beds or walks in a garden. 3. Causeway, a paved road.

arriaz, arrial [ar-re-ath'-, ar-re-ahl'], *m*. Hilt-bar of a sword.

arriba [ar-ree'-bah], *adv*. 1. Above, over, up, high, overhead, upstairs (en casa). 2. *(Naut.)* Aloft. 3. In writings, previously mentioned. **Lo escrito arriba**, what has been said above. 4. *(Met.)* A high post or station with respect to others. 5. In the hands of the king. **Está decretado de arriba**, it is decreed by high authority. **Arriba dicho**, above mentioned. **De arriba, abajo**, from top to bottom. **Arriba de seis varas**, *(coll.)* above six yards. **Ir aguas arriba**, *(Naut.)* to work up the river. **De arriba**, from heaven.

arribada [ar-re-bah'-dah], *m*. 1. Arrival. 2. Spot where a ship may approach.

arribaje [ah-rre-bah'-hay], *m*. *(Naut.)* Arrival, entry into harbor.

arribar [ar-re-bar'], *vn*. *(Naut.)* 1. To put into a harbor in distress. 2. To arrive by land at a stopping-place. 3. To fall off to leeward; to bear away. 4. *(Met.)* To recover from a disease or calamity; to convalesce. 5. *(coll.)* To accomplish one's desire. **Arribar todo**, to bear away before the wind. **Arribar a escote larga**, to bear away large. **Arribar sobre un bajel**, to bear down upon a ship.

arribazón [ah-rre-bah-thon'], *f*. Coastal abundance of fish, off-shore shoal.

arribeño [ah-rre-bay'-nyo], *m*. & *f*. *(LAm.)* Highlander, inlander. *(Cono Sur)* Stranger.

arribista [ah-rre-bes'-tah], *m*. & *f*. Go-getter, arriviste, social climber.

arribo [ar-ree'-bo], *m*. Arrival.

arricete [ar-re-thay'-tay], *m*. Shoal, sand-bank.

arricisces [ar-re-thee'-ses], *m. pl*. The saddle-straps to which the girths are fastened.

arriendo [ar-reen'-do], *m*. Ablocation, lease, rental. V. ARRENDAMIENTO. **(Yo arriendo, yo arriende,** from **arrendar**. V. ACERTAR.)

arriería [ar-re-ay-ree'-ah], *f*. The calling of a driver of mules.

arrierico, illo, ito [ar-re-ay-ree'-co, eel'-yo, ee'-to], *m. dim*. One who carries on mule-driving in a petty way.

arriero [ar-re-ay'-ro], *m*. Muleteer, he who used to drive mules, carrying goods from one place to another.

arriesgadamente [ar-re-es-gah-dah-men'-tay], *adv*. Dangerously, hazardously.

arriesgado, da [ar-re-es-gah'-do, dah], *a*. 1. Perilous, dangerous, hazardous. 2. Dangerous to be dealt with; daring. **Hombre arriesgado**, a dangerous man. *-pp*. of ARRIESGAR.

arriesgar [ar-re-es-gar'], *va*. To risk, to hazard, to expose to danger, to jeopard. *-vr*. To be exposed to danger; to dare. **Arriesgarse a hacer algo**, to dare to do something.

arrimadero [ar-re-mah-day'-ro], *m*. Scaffold, a stage; a stick or support to lean upon.

arrimadillo [ar-re-mah-deel'-lyo], *m*. A mat or wainscot upon a wall.

arrimadizo [ar-re-mah-dee'-tho], *a*. & *m*. 1. That which is designed to be applied to any thing. 2. *(Met.)* Parasite, sponger, one who meanly hangs upon another for subsistence. 3. *(Obs.)* Support, prop.

arrimado, da [ar-re-mah'-do, dah], *pp*. of ARRIMAR. **Tener arrimado or arrimados**, To be possessed by evil spirits.

arrimador [ar-re-mah-dor'], *m*. The back-log in a fire-place.

arrimadura [ar-re-mah-doo'-rah], *f*. The act of approaching.

arrimar [ar-re-mar'], *va*. 1. To approach, to draw near, to join one thing to another. **Lo arrimamos a la ventana,** we put it against the window. 2. *(Naut.)* To stow the cargo, to trim the hold. 3. To lay a thing aside, to put by; to reject. **El plan quedó arrimado,** the plan was shelved. 4. To lay down a command. 5. To displace, to dismiss. 6. **Arrimar el clavo,** to prick a horse at the time of shoeing him. **Arrimar el clavo a uno,** *(Met.)* to impose, to deceive. 7. *(Cono Sur)* **Arrimar la culpa a uno,** to lay the blame on somebody. *-vr*. 1. To lean upon a thing. 2. To join others for the purpose of forming a body with them. 3. *(Met.)* To come to the knowledge of a thing. **Arrimarse al punto de la dificultad,** to come to the point. **Arrimarse al parecer de otro**, to espouse another's opinion. 4. *(LAm.)* To sponge.

arrime [ar-ree'-may], *m*. In the game of bowls, the mark for the balls to arrive at.

arrimo [ah-ree'-mo], *m*. 1. The act of joining one thing to another. 2. Staff, stick, crutch. 3. *(Met.)* Protection or support of a powerful person; help. 4. Among builders, an insulated wall which has no weight to support; idle wall.

arrimón [ar-re-mone'], *m*. *(Hacer el) (coll.)* 1. To stagger along a wall, supported by it, in a state of intoxication. 2. **Estar de arrimón,** To stand watch over somebody.

arrinconado, da [ar-rin-co-nah'-do, dah], *a*. Out of favor, retired from the world, abandoned. *-pp*. of ARRINCONAR.

arrinconar [ar-rin-co-nar'], *va*. 1. To put a thing in a corner; to lay aside, to reject. 2. *(Met.)* To remove one from a trust, to withdraw one's favor or protection. *-vr*. To retire from the world.

arriñonado [ah-rre-nyo-nah'-do], *a*. Kidney-shaped; **estar arriñonado,** to be knackered.

arriscadamente [ar-ris-cah-dah-men'-tay], *adv*. Boldly, audaciously.

arriscado, da [ar-ris-cah'-do, dah], *a*. 1. Forward, bold, audacious, impudent. 2. Brisk, easy, free. **Caballo arriscado,** a high-mettled horse. 3. Broken or craggy ground. *-pp*. of ARRISCARSE.

arriscador [ar-ris-cah-dor'], *m*. *(Prov.)* A gleaner of olives.

arriscamiento [ah-rres-cah-me-ayn'-to], *m*. Boldness, resolution.

arriscar [ar-ris-car'], *va*. **To risk.** *-vr*. 1. To hold up one's head; to be proud, haughty, or arrogant. 2. To plunge over a cliff (rebaño ovejas). *(Acad.)* **Quien no arrisca, no aprisca,** nothing ventured, nothing gained.

arriscar [ah-rres-cahr'], 1. *va*. *(And. Cono Sur, Mex.)* To turn up (doblarse). 2. *vn*. To draw oneself up, to straighten up. 3. *-vr*. To get conceited. To dress up to the nines.

arriscocho [ah-rres-co'-cho], *a*. *(And.)* Restless; turbulent.

arristranco [ar-ris-trahn'-co], *m*. *(Cuba)* Useless furniture; lumber.

arrivista [ah-rre-ves'-tah], V. ARRIBISTA.

arrizar [ar-re-thar'], *va*. *(Naut.)* 1. To reef. 2. To stow the boat on deck. **Arrizar el ancla,** to stow the anchor. **Arrizar la**

artillería, to house the guns. 3. On board the galleys, to tie or lash one down.

arroba [ar-ro'-bah], *f.* 1. Spanish weight of twenty-five pounds; a quarter = 11.5 kilos. 2. A Spanish measure, containing thirty-two pints.; about four gallons. **Por arrobas,** wholesale. **Echar por arrobas,** *(Met.)* to exaggerate, to make hyperbolical amplifications.

arrobadizo, za [ar-ro-bah-dee'-tho, thah], *a. (coll.)* Feigning ecstasy and rapture.

arrobado [ar-ro-bah'-do], *pp.* of ARROBAR. *Por arrobado, (Obs.)* By wholesale.

arrobador, ra [ar-ro-bah-dor', rah], *a.* Enchanting, delightful, ecstatic.

arrobamiento [ar-ro-bah-me-en'-to], *m.* 1. Ecstatic rapture, or elevation of the mind to God. 2. Amazement, astonishment, high admiration. 3. Ecstasy, ravishment.

arrobar [ar-ro-bar'], *va. (Obs.)* To weigh or measure by arrobas. To entrance, enchant. -*vr.* To be in a state or rapturous amazement, to be out of one's senses.

arrobero, ra [ar-ro-bay'-ro, rah], *m. & f. (Prov.)* 1. About an *arroba* or quarter in weight. 2. Baker for a community.

arrobita [ar-ro-bee'-tah], *f. dim.* The weight of an *arroba* in a small compass.

arrobo [ar-ro'-bo], *m. V.* ARROBAMIENTO and EXTASIS.

arrocabe [ar-ro-cah'-bay], *m.* A wooden frieze.

arrocero [ar-ro-thay'-ro], *m.* A grower of or dealer in rice.

arrochelarse [ar-ro-chay-lahr'-say], *vr. (And.)* To take a liking to a place; to refuse to go out; to balk, to shy.

arrocinado, da [ar-ro-the-nah'-do, dah], *a.* 1. Dull, stupid, like a worn-out horse or *rocín.* 2. Hack-like (caballos). *-pp.* of ARROCINARSE.

arrocinar [ar-ro-the'-nar], *va.* To reduce, to brutish habits, to brutify. *-vr.* To become dull and stupid.

arrodajarse [ar-ro-dah-har'-say], *vr. (Costa Rica)* To sit upon the ground.

arrodelado, da [ar-ro-day-lah'-do, dah], *pp.* of ARRODELARSE. Bearing a target, shield, or buckler.

arrodelarse [ar-ro-day-lar'-say], *vr.* To be armed with a shield or buckler.

arrodeo [ar-ro-day'-o], *m. V.* RODEO.

arrodilladura [ar-ro-deel-lyah-doo'-rah], *f.* **Arrodillamiento** [ar-ro-deel-lyah-me-en'-to], *m.* The act of kneeling or bending the knee.

arrodillar [ar-ro-deel-lyar'], *vn.* To bend the knee down to the ground. *-vr.* To kneel to the ground.

arrodrigar, arrodrigonar [ar-ro-dre-gar', ar-ro-dre-go-nar'], *va. (Prov.)* To prop vines.

arrogación [ar-ro-gah-the-on'], *f.* 1. Arrogation, the act of claiming in a proud manner. 2. Adoption of a child which has no father or is independent of him.

arrogador [ar-ro-gah-dor'], *m.* One who claims in a proud manner.

arrogancia [ar-ro-gahn'-the-ah], *a.* 1. Arrogance, haughtiness, loftiness, conceit; confidence. 2. Stately carriage of a high-mettled horse.

arrogante [ar-ro-gahn'-tay], *a.* 1. Highminded, spirited. 2. Arrogant, haughty, proud, assuming; magisterial, masterly.

arrogantemente [ar-ro-ga-tay-men'-tay], *adv.* Arrogantly, haughtily, forwardly; highly; magisterially.

arrogar [ar-ro-gar'], *va.* 1. *(Law.)* To adopt. 2. To arrogate, to claim in a proud manner. *-vr.* To appropriate to oneself, to claim unjustly.

arrojadamente [ar-ro-hah-dah-men'-tay], *adv.* Audaciously, boldly.

arrojadillo [ar-ro-hah-deel'-lyo], *m. (Obs.)* Handkerchief, or other piece of silk or linen, which women used formerly to tie around the head to keep warm.

arrojadizo, za [ar-ro-hah-dee'-tho, thah], *a.* 1. That which can be easily cast, thrown, or darted; missile. 2. *(Obs.)* Spirited, bold, courageous.

arrojado, da [ar-ro-hah'-do, dah], *a.* 1. Rash, inconsiderate, forward, foolhardy, hasty, dashing. 2. Bold, intrepid, fearless. *-pp.* of ARROJAR.

arrojador [ar-ro-hah-dor'], *m.* A thrower, a flinger.

arrojallamas [ar-ro-hah-lyah'-mahs], *m. & pl.* Flamethrower.

arrojar [ar-ro-har'], *va.* 1. To dart, to launch, or to fling something, to hurl, to jerk, to dash, to belch out (lava), to drop (bombas), to give out (rayos). **Arrojar una piedra,** to throw a stone. **El volcán está arrojando lava,** the volcano is belching out lava. **Arrojar rayos,** to give off rays. 2. To shed a fragrance, to emit light. **Este estudio arroja alguna luz sobre el tema,** this study throws some light on the subject. 3. To shoot, to sprout, to grow up (plantas). 4. *(Naut.)* To drive or cast on rocks or shoals (viento). 5. To make red hot, as an oven. 6. To turn away or dismiss in an angry manner. -*vr.* 1. To launch, to throw oneself forward with impetuosity. **Arrojarse al agua,** to jump into the water. 2. *(Met.)* To venture upon an enterprise in an inconsiderate manner.

arroje [ar-ro'-hay], *m.* 1. The left side of the stage of a theater. 2. The person who throws himself from this spot, with a rope fastened, to raise the curtain.

arrojo [ar-ro'-ho], *m.* Boldness, intrepidity, fearlessness. **Arrojo al agua,** or **a la mar,** jettison, jetsam.

arrollado [ar-ro-lyah'-do], *m. (Cono Sur) (Culin.)* Rolled pork.

arrollador [ar-rol-lyah-dor'], *m.* 1. Roller, a kind of cylinder used for moving weighty things. 2. *(fig.)* Sweeping, overwhelming, crushing. **Por una mayoría arrolladora,** by an overwhelming majority. 3. *(Obs.) V.* ARRULLADOR.

arrollamiento [ar-roh-lyah-me-en'-to], *m.* 1. Winding, coiling. 2. Sweeping, carrying of.

arrollar [ar-rol-lyar'], *va.* 1. To roll up, to roll any thing round, to wrap or twist round. 2. To carry off, to sweep away (tormentas, torrente). To expel. 3. *(Met.)* To defeat, to rout an enemy. 4. *(Met.)* To confound an opponent. 5. **Arrollar a un niño,** *(Prov.)* to dandle a child. 6. *(Obs.)* To lull to rest.

arromadizarse [ar-ro-mah-de-thar'-say], *vr.* To catch cold.

arromanzar [ar-ro-man-thar'], *va. (Obs.)* To translate into the common or vernacular Spanish language.

arromar [ar-ro-mar'], *va.* To blunt, to dull the edge or point.

arromper [ar-rom-perr'], *va. (Obs.)* To break up the ground for sowing.

arrompido [ar-rom-pee'-do], *m.* A piece of ground newly froken.

arronzar [ar-ron-thar'], *va. (Naut.)* To haul a hawser, without the aid of the capstan, windlass, or tackle.

arropado, da [ar-ro-pah'-do, dah], *a.* Mixed with must (vino). *-pp.* of ARROPAR.

arropamiento [ar-ro-pah-me-en'-to], *m.* The act of clothing or dressing.

arropar [ar-ro-par'], *va.* 1. To cover the body with clothes, to dress. **Arrópate que sudas,** cover yourself, as you sweat: ironically addressed to a person who has done little and affects to be fatigued. 2. **Arropar el vino,** To mix wine, to give it a body. 3. **Arropar las viñas,** to cover the roots of vines with dung and earth. *-vr.* To wrap oneself up.

arrope [ar-ro'-pay], *m.* 1. Must or new wine boiled until it is as dense as a sirup. 2. A kind of decoction made in imitation of boiled honey. **Arrope de moras,** mulberry sirup.

arropea [ar-ro-pay'-ah], *f.* Irons, fetters; shackles for horses.

arropera [ar-ro-pay'-rah], *f.* Vessels for holding boiled must, sirup, etc.

arropia [ar-ro-pee'-ah], *f. (Prov.)* Cake made of flour, honey, and spice. *V.* MELCOCHA.

arropiero [ar-ro-pe-ay'-ro], *m. (Prov.)* Maker or seller of sweet cakes.

arrorró [ar-ro-rro'], *m. (LAm.)* Lullaby.

arrostrado [ah-rros-trah'-do], *a.* **Bien arrostrado,** nice-looking.

arrostrar [ar-ros-trar'], *va.* 1. To set about or perform a thing in a cheerful manner. 2. **Arrostrar los peligros, los trabajos, la muerte,** to encounter dangers, fatigues, death. *-vr.* To close with the enemy, to fight him face to face.

arroyada, *f.* **arroyadero,** *m.* [ar-ro-yah'-dah, ar-ro-yah-day'-ro], 1. The valley through which a rivulet runs. 2. The channel of a rivulet.

arroyar [ar-ro-yar'], *va.* To flood sown ground; to form gutters from heavy rain. -*vr.* To be affected with rust (trigo, grano).

arroyato [ar-ro-yah'-to], *m. (Obs.)* V. ARROYO.

arroyico, arroyuelo [ar-ro-yee'-co, ar-ro-yoo-ay'-lo], *m. dim.* A little river, a small brook, a rivulet.

arroyo [ar-ro'-yo], *m.* 1. Rivulet, a small river, current. 2. The watercourse of a street; *(Mex.)* **Estar en el arroyo,** to be on one´s uppers; **poner a uno en el arroyo,** to turn somebody out of the house.

arroyuelo [ar-ro-yoo-ay'-lo], *m.* Small stream, brook.

arroz [ar-roth'], *m.* Rice. **Arroz blanco,** boiled rice. **Arroz a la cubana,** rice with banana and fried egg. **Arroz integral,** brown rice. *a. (coll.)* **Arroz y gallo muerto,** a grand dinner, a banquet.

arrozal [ar-ro-thal'], *m.* Field sown with rice

arrozar [ar-ro-thar'] *va.* To ice a liquid, to freeze it a little.

arruar [ar-roo-ar'], *vn.* To grunt like a wild boar when it sniffs pursuers.

arrufado, da [ar-roo-fah'-do, dah], *pp.* of ARRUFAR. Sheered, curved. **Navío muy arrufado,** *(Naut.)* moon-sheered ship.

arrufadura [ar-roo-fah-doo'-rah], *f. (Naut.)* Sheer of a ship.

arrufar [ar-roo-far'], *va. (Naut.)* To incurvate, to form the sheer of a ship. -*vr.* To snarl, to show teeth (perro), to get angry.

arrufianado, da [ar-roo-fe-ah-nah'-do, dah], *a.* Ruffianly, impudent.

arrufo [ar-roo'-fo], *m.* V. ARRUFADURA.

arruga [ar-roo'-gah], *f.* 1. Wrinkle, corrugation. 2. Rumple, or rude plait in clothes, fold, crease. 3. *(And.)* Trick, swindle.

arrugación, *f.* **arrugamiento,** *m.* [ar-roo-gah-the-on', ar-roo-gah-me-en'-to], Corrugation, the act and effect of wrinkling.

arrugado [ar-roo-gah'-do], *a.* Wrinkled, lined (cara); creased (papel); rucked up, crumpled (vestido).

arrugar [ar-roo-gar'], *va.* 1. To wrinkle, to contract into wrinkles, to corrugate, to constrict, to crumple, to cockle. 2. To rumple, to fold, to gather, to crease, to pleat. **Arrugar la frente,** to knit the brow, to frown. -*vr.* To wrinkle, to get wrinkled, to crease, to get creased.

arrugia [ah-roo'-hee-ah], *f. (Obs. Miner.)* A hole dug in the ground to discover gold.

arrugón [ar-roo-gone'], *m.* Prominent decoration of carved work.

arrugue [ar-roo'-gay], *m. (Carib.)* V. ARRUGA.

arruinado [ar-roo-e-nah'-do], *a.* 1. Ruined. 2. *(Cono Sur. Mex.)* Sickly, stunted; *(Cono Sur)* wretched, down and out (miserable).

arruinador, ra [ar-roo-e-nah-dor', rah], *m. & f.* Ruiner, demolisher, a destroyer.

arruinamiento [ar-roo-en-nah-me-en'-to], *m.* Ruin, destruction, ruinousness.

arruinar [ar-roo-e-nar'], *va.* 1. To throw down, to demolish, to lay level. 2. To ruin, to confound, to crack; to crush. 3. *(Met.)* To destroy, to cause great mischief. -*vr.* To be ruined, to fall down.

arrullador, ra [ar-rool-lyah-dor', rah], *m. & f.* 1. A person who lulls babies to rest. 2. Flatterer, cajoler.

arrullar [ar-rool-lyar'], *va.* 1. To lull babes. 2. To court, to coo and bill. -*vr.* To bill and coo, to whisper endearments.

arrullo [ar-rool'-lyo], *m.* 1. The cooing and billing of doves. 2. Lullaby.

arrumaco [ar-roo-mah'-co], *m.* Caress, the act of endearment, profession of friendship.

arrumaje [ar-roo-mah'-hay], *m. (Naut.)* Stowage of a ship's cargo.

arrumar [ar-roo-mar'], *va. (Naut.)* To stow the cargo.

arrumazón [ar-roo-mah-thone'], *f.* 1. *(Naut.)* The act and effect of stowing. 2. Horizon overcast with clouds.

arrumbadas [ar-room-bah'-das], *f. pl. (Naut.)* Wales of a row-galley.

arrumbador, ra [ar-room-bah-dor', rah], *m. & f.* 1. One who heaps or piles. 2. *(Naut.)* Steersman.

arrumbamiento [ar-room-bah-me-en'-to], *m.* The direction of a thing as it moves, with respect to another.

arrumbar [ar-room-bar'], *va.* 1. *(Prov.)* To put something away in a lumber-room. 2. *(Met.)* To refute one in conversation. 3. To decant wine, to pour it off gently. -*vr. (Naut.)* To resume and steer the proper course. 2. To be seasick. 3. *(And. Cono Sur)* To rust; to turn sour.

arruncharse [ar-roon-chahr'-say], *vr. (And.)* To curl up, to roll up.

arrunflarse [ar-roon-flar'-say], *vr.* To have a flush of cards of the same suit.

arrurruz [ar-roo-rooth'], *m.* Arrowroot.

arrutanado [ar-roo-tah-nah'-do], *a. (And.)* Plump.

arsenal [ar-say-nahl'], *m.* 1. Shipyard, dockyard, navy-yard. 2. Arsenal (armas).

arsenalera [ar-say-nah-lay'-rah], *f. (Cono Sur) (Med.)* Surgeon´s assistant.

arseniato [ar-say-ne-ah'-to],*m. (Chem.)* Arseniate.

arsenical [ar-say-ne-cahl'], *a. (Chem.)* Arsenical, relating to arsenic.

arsénico [ar-say'-ne-co], *m. (Chem.)* Arsenic, a mineral substance, which facilitates the fusion of metals, and is a violent poison; ratsbane.

arsenioso [ar-say-ne-o'-so], *a.* Arsenious.

arsenito [ar-say-nee'-to], *m.* Arsenite.

arsolla [ar-sol'-lyah], *f.* V. ARZOLLA.

arta [ar'-tah], *f.* V. PLANTAIN *a.* Plantain, **arta de agua.** V. ZARAGATONA.

artal [ar-tahl'], *m.* A kind of pie.

artalete [ar-tah-lay'-tay], *m.* A sort of tart.

artanica, artanita [ar-tah-nee'-cah, ar-tah-nee'tah], *f. (Bot.)* Sow-bread.

arte [ar'-tay], *m. & f.* 1. Art. **Una obra de arte,** a work of art. **El arte culinario,** the art of cooking. 2. Art, the power of doing something not taught by nature and instinct. 3. Caution, skill, craft, cunning. 4. Artifice, machine. 5. Everything done by human industry. **No tener arte ni parte en alguna cosa.** to have neither art nor part in a thing, to have nothing to do with the business. **Arte tormentaria,** art of artillery or military enginery. **Artes,** *f. pl.* Intrigues, improper means. **Artes mecánicas,** mechanical arts, occupations, or handicrafts. **Artes liberales,** liberal arts. **Las bellas artes,** the fine arts. **Buen arte,** gracefulness of manners and gait. **Mal arte,** awkwardness of manners and gait. **Por amor al arte,** for the love of it. *pl.* **Artes.** The word *arte* is always feminine in plural. **Las artes gráficas,** the graphic arts.

artecillo, lla [ar-tay-theel'-lyo, lyah], *m. & f. dim.* Petty art or trade.

artefacto [ar-tay-fac'-to], *m.* 1. Device, contrivance. 2. Artifact. **Artefacto sideral,** space artifact.

artejo [ar-tay'-ho], *m.* Joint or knuckle of the fingers.

artemisa, artemisia [ar-tay-mee'-sah, ar-tay-mee'-se-ah], *f. (Bot.)* Mugwort, feverfew.

artena [ar-tay'-nah], *f.* An aquatic fowl of the size of a goose.

arteramente [ar-tay-rah-men'-tay], *adv.* Craftily, fraudulently.

arteria [ar-tay'-re-ah], *f. (Anat.)* Artery (vena). **Arterias de la madera,** veins formed in wood and timber by the various ramifications of the fibres. **Áspera arteria or traquiartería,** the wind-pipe.

artería [ar-tay-ree'-ah], *f.* Artifice, stratagem, cunning; sagacity.

arterial [ar-tay-re-ahl'], *a.* Arterial, belonging to the arteries.

arteriola [ar-tay-re-oh'-lah], *f. dim.* Small artery; arteriole.

arteriosclerosis [ar-tay-re-os-clay-ro'-sis], *f.* Arteriosclerosis, hardening of the arteries.

arterioso, sa [ar-tay-re-o'-so, sah], *a.* V. ARTERIAL.

arteriotomía [ar-tay-re-o-to-mee'-ah], *f. (Anat.)* Arteriotomy, the letting blood from an artery.

artero, ra [ar-tay'-ro, rah], *a.* Dexterous, cunning, artful.

artesa [ar-tay'-sah], *f.* 1. Trough in which dough of bread is worked. 2. Canoe. **Artesa de panaderos,** wooden bowl.

artesanal [ar-tay-sah-nahl'], *a.* Craft; **industria artesanal,** craft industry.

artesanía [ar-tay-sah-ne-ah'], *f.* Craftsmanship; handicraft, skill; **objeto de artesanía,** hand-made article.

artesano [ar-tay-sah'-no], *m.* Artisan, mechanic, artificer, handicraftsman.

artesiano, na [ar-tay-se-ah'-no, nah], *a.* Artesian. **Pozo artesiano,** artesian well.

artesilla [ar-tay-seel'-lyah], *f.* 1. (*dim.*) A small trough. 2. A sort of festive exercise on horseback. 3. A trough for water at a draw-well.

artesón [ar-tay-sone'], *m.* 1. A round kitchen trough for dishes, plates, etc. 2. Ceiling carved in the shape of a trough; ornamented vaulting; panelled ceiling. **Artesón de lavar,** washtub.

artesonado, da [ar-tay-so-nah'-do, dah], *a.* Panelling, trellis-work: applied to ceilings.

artesonar [ar-tay-so-nahr'], *va.* To coffer, to stucco, to mould.

artesoncillo [ar-tay-son-theel'-lyo], *m. dim.* A small trough.

artesuela [ar-tay-soo-ay'-lah], *f.* dim A small kneading-trough.

artético, ca [ar-tay-te-co, cah], *a.* 1. Afflicted with arthritis. 2. Arthritis.

ártico, ca [ar'-te-co, cah], *a.* (*Astr.*) Arctic, northern.

articulación [ar-te-coo-lah-the-on'], *f.* 1. Articulation, a joint. 2. Articulation, distinct pronunciation of words and syllables. **Articulación universal,** (*Mech.*) universal joint.

articuladamente [ar-te-coo-lah-dah-men'-tay], *adv.* Distinctly, articulately.

articulado, da [ar-te-coo-lah'-do, dah], *a.* Articulate, provided with a joint. (*Zool.*) Articulate, belonging to that large division of the animal kingdom, the articulate.

articular [ar-te-coo-lar'], *va.* 1. To articulate, to pronounce words clearly and distinctly. 2. To form the interrogatories which are put to witnesses examined in the course of law proceedings. 3. (*Poetic.*) To accent. 4. (*And. Cono Sur*) To tell off, to dress down. *-vn.* (*Cono Sur*) To quarrel.

articular, articulario, ria [ar-te-coo-lar', ar-te-coo-lah'-re-o, ah], *a.* Articular, belonging to the joints.

articulista [ar-te-coo-lees'-tah], *m. & f.* Newspaper or magazine feature writer.

artículo [ar-tee'-coo-lo], *m.* 1. Article, section; a word or term separately defined in a dictionary. **Artículos alimenticios,** food stuffs. 2. Plea put in before a court of justice. 3. Article, essay, in a periodical. **Un artículo de periódico,** a newspaper article. 4. (*Gram.*) Article, part of speech. **Artículo definido, indefinido,** definite, indefinite articles. 5. Clause, condition, stipulation. 6. (*Bot.*) Geniculation. 7. (*Anat.*) Joint of movable bones. **Varios artículos,** (*coll.*) sundry articles, things, knick-knacks. **Formar artículo,** to start an incidental question in the course of a lawsuit. **Artículo de la muerte,** point of death. 8. (*Comp.*) Item; **Artículo del equipo,** item of equipment.

artífice [ar-tee'-fe-thay], *m.* 1. Artificer, artisan, craftsman. 2. Inventor, contriver, maker.

artificial [ar-te-fe-the-ahl'], *a.* Artificial, made by art. **Fuegos artificiales,** fire works.

artificialidad [ar-te-fe-the-ah-le-dahd'], *f.* Artificiality.

artificializar [ar-te-fe-the-ah-le-thar], *va.* To make artificial.

artificialmente [ar-te-fe-the-al-men'-tay], *adv.* Artificially.

artificiero [ar-te-fe-the-ay'-ro], *m.* Explosives expert, bomb-disposal officer.

artificio [ar-te-fee'-the-o], *m.* 1. Art with which a thing is performed, workmanship, craft. 2. (*Met.*) Artifice, cunning, trick, guilefulness, contrivance, finesse, craft, fraud. 3. Machine which facilitates the exercise of some art.

artificiosamente [ar-te-fe-the-o-sah-men'-tay], *adv.* 1. Artificially. 2. Artful, craftily, fraudulently.

artificioso, sa [ar-te-fe-the-o'-so, sah], *a.* 1. Skilful, ingenious. 2. Artful, crafty, cunning, fraudulent.

artiga [ar-tee'-gah], *f.* Land newly broken up.

artigar [ar-te-ar'][, *va.* To break and level land before cultivation.

artillar [ar-teel-lyar'], *va.* To mount cannon.

artillería [ar-teel-lyah-ree'-dah], *f.* 1. Gunnery. 2. Artillery, cannon, piece or ordenance. 3. The division of the army assigned to this service. **Parque de artillería,** park of artillery. **Tren de artillería,** train of artillery. **Poner** *or* **asestar toda la artillería,** (*Met.*) to set all engines at work for obtaining something, to leave no stone unturned. **Artillería pesada,** heavy artillery. **Artillería antiaérea,** antiaircraft guns.

artillero [ar-teel-lyay'-ro], *m.* Gunner (aviones, barcos); artilleryman.

artimaña [ar-te-mah'-nyah], *f.* 1. Trap, snare, gin. 2. Device, stratagem, artifice, counterfeit, cunning.

artimón [ar-te-mone'], *m.* (*Naut.*) Mizzen-mast; sail of a galley.

artina [ar-tee'-nah], *f.* (*Prov.*) The fruit of the box-thorn.

artista [ar-tees'-tah], *m.* 1. Artist (pintor, escultor); artisan, tradesman, craftsmaster. **Artista de teatro,** artist, actor; actress (actriz). 2. He who studies logic, physics, or metaphysics.

artísticamente, *adv.* Artistically.

artístico, ca [ar-tees'-te-co, cah], *a.* Artistic, belonging to art.

artolas [ar-to'-las], *f. pl.* Pannier; a pack-saddle for two persons.

artólitos [ar-to'-le-tos], *m.* A concave stone of the nature of a sponge.

artos [ar'-tos], *m.* 1. Various species of thistles. 2. (*Prov.*) The box thorn. *V.* CAMBRONERA .

artrítico, ca [ar-tree'-te-co, cah], *a.* Arthritic, arthritical.

artritis [ar-tree'-tees], *f.* (*Med.*) Arthritis.

artrópodo [ar-tro'-po-do], *m. & a.* (*Zool.*) Arthropod.

artuña [ar-too'-nyah], *f.* A ewe whose lamb has perished.

Arturo [ar-too'-ro], *m.* 1. (*Astr.*) Arcturus, a fixed star of the first magnitude in the constellation Bootes. 2. Proper name, Arthur.

arugas [a-roo'-gas], *f.* (*Bot.*) *V.* MATRICARIA. Feverfew.

aruñar [ah-roo'-nyar], *va. V.* ARAÑAR.

aruñazo [ah-roo'-nyah'-tho], *m.* A large scratch. *V.* ARAÑAZO.

aruño [ah-roo'-nyo], *m. V.* ARAÑO.

aruñón [ah-roo-nyon'], *m.* 1. A scratcher. 2. Pickpocket.

arúspice [ah-roos'-pe-thay], *m.* Augurer, soothsayer.

aruspicina [ah-roos-pe-thee'-nah], *f.* Aruspicy, divining from the intestines of animals.

arveja [ar-vay'-hah], *f.* (*Bot.*) Vetch, tare.

arvejal, arvejar [ar-vay-hahl', ar-vay-har'], *m.* Field sown with vetches.

arvejo [ar-vay'-ho], *m.* (*Bot.*) Bastard chick-pea, or Spanish pea.

arvejón [ar-vay-hone'], *m.* (*Bot.*) Chickling-vetch.

arvejona [ar-vay-ho'-nah], *f.* (*Prov.*) 1. *V.* ARVEJA. 2. *V.* ALGARROBA.

arvela [ar-vay-lah], *f.* A blue-feathered bird, the kingfisher.

arvense [ar-ven'-say], *a.* (*Bot.*) A term applied to all plants which grow in sown fields.

arza [ar'-thah], *f.* (*Naut.*) Fall of a tackle.

arzobispado [ar-tho-bis-pah'-do], *ml.* Archbishopric (dignidad, territorio). Archiepiscopate (dignidad, duración).

arzobispal [ar-tho-bis-pahl'], *a.* Archiepiscopal.

arzobispo [ar-tho-bees'-po], *m.* Archbishop.

arzolla [ar-thol'-lyah], *f.* (*Prov.*) *V.* ALMENDRUCO. 1. Lesser brudock, 2. Milk thistle.

arzón [ar-thone'], *m.* Fore and hind bow of a saddle, saddle-tree.

as [ahs], *m.* 1. Ace. 2. Roman copper coin.

asa [ah'-sah], *f.* 1. Handle, haft. 2. Vault made in the form of the handle of a basket. 3. **Asa dulce,** gum benzoin, asa dulcis. 4. **Asafétida,** asafoetida, a gum resin. **Amigo del asa or ser muy del asa,** To afford or borrow a pretence. **En asas,** having the hands on the hips. **En asas,** a kimbo.

asacar [ah-sah-car'], *va.* 1. To impute, defame, vilify. 2. To invent, newly apply.

asadero, ra [ah-sah-day'-ro, rah], *a.* That which is fit for roasting. -*m.* *(Mex.)* A small, flat cheese made of the richest of the milk and by beating the curd while making it.

asado, da [ah-sah'-do, dah], *a.* Roasted; dressed. **Asado a la parrilla,** broiled; grilled. 2. *(LAm.)* Cross, angry. 3. *(Carib.)* To be broke. -*pp.* of ASAR.

asador [ah-sah-dor'], *m.* 1. A spit. 2. Jack, an engine which turns the spit. **Parece que come asadores,** he walks as stiffly as if he had swallowed a spit. 3. **Asador de bomba,** *(Naut.)* the pump-hook.

asadorazo [ah-sah-do-rah'-tho], *m.* Blow with a spit.

asadorcillo [ah-sah-dor-theel'-lyo], *m. dim.* Small spit.

asadura [ah-sah-doo'-rah], *f.* 1. Entrails of an animal, chitterlings. **Asadura de puerco,** hastet or harslet. 2. Laziness. **Tiene asaduras,** he´s terribly lazy. 3. Stolid person.

asaeteador [ah-sah-ay-tay-ah-dor'], *m.* Archer, bow-man.

asaetear [ah-sah-ay-tay-ar'], *va.* To attack, wound, or kill with arrows.

asaetinado, da [ah-sah-ay-te-nah'-do, dah], *a.* Like satin (ropa).

asafétida [ah-sah-fay'-te-dah], *f.* Asafoetida, a gum resin, of fetid odor.

asainetado, da [ah-sah-e-nay-tah'-do, dah], *a.* That which ought to be serious, but seems farcical.

asalariado, da [ah-sah-lah-re-ah'-do, dah], *a.* Paid; wage-earning.

asalariar [ah-sah-lah-re-ar'], *va.* To give a fixed salary or pay.

asalmonado, da [ah-sal-mo-nah'-do, dah], *a.* V. SALMONADO.

asaltabancos [ah-sal-tah-ban'-cos], *m. & f.* Bank robber.

asaltador [ah-sal-tah-dor'], *m.* 1.Assailant, assaulter. 2. Highwayman.

asaltar [ah-sal-tar'], *va.* 1. To form an assault, to storm a place. **Le asaltaron 4 bandidos,** he was held up by 4 bandits. 2. To assail, to surprise, to fall upon. 3. To occur suddenly. **Le asaltó una idea,** he was struck by an idea.

asalto [ah-sahl'-to], *m.* 1. Assault against a place. 2. Assault, the act of offering violence to a person. 3. *(Met.)* A sudden gust of passion.

asamblea [ah-sam-blay'-ah], *f.* 1. Assembly, meeting (reunión), congress (congreso), junta, congregation, convention, gathering. 2. In the order of Malta, a tribunal established in every grand priory of the order. 3. A beat of the drum directing the soldiers to join their companies, or to assemble in the alarmplace.

asambleario, ria [ah-sam-blay-ah'-re-o], *m. & f.* Member of an assembly.

asapán [ah-sah-pahn'], *m. (Mex.)* Flying squirrel.

asar [ah-sar'], *va.* 1. To roast. **Asar al horno,** to bake. 2. *(fig.)* To pester, plague. 3. To shoot, gun down. -*vr.* To be excessively hot. **Me aso de calor,** I´m roasting.

asáraca, asarabácara, [ah-sah'-rah-cah],[ah-sah-rah-bah'-cah-rah] *f. (Bot.)* Wild ginger or nard, common asarabacca.

asarero [ah-sah-ray'-ro], *m. (Bot.)* V. ENDRINO.

asargado, da [ah-sar-gah'-do, dah], *a.* Serge-like, made in imitation of serge; twilled.

asarina [ah-sah-ree'-nah], *f. (Bot.)* Bastard asarum.

asaro [ah'-sah-ro], *m.* V. ASARABACAR *a.*

asascuarse [ah-sahs-coo-ahr'-say], *vr. (Mex.)* To roll up into a ball.

asativo, va [ah-sah-tee'-vo, vah], *a. (Pharm.)* Dressed or boiled in its own juice, without any other fluid.

asaz [ah-sath'], *adv. (Obs. Poet.)* Enough, abundantly.

asbestino, na [as-bes-tee'-no, nah], *a.* Belonging to asbestos.

asbesto [as-bes'-to], *m.* 1. Asbestos, a mineral, incombustible. 2. A sort of incombustible cloth made of the filaments of asbestos.

ascalonia [as-cah-lo'-ne-ah], *f.* A seed onion.

ascárides [as-cah'-re-des], *f. pl.* Ascarides, thread-worms in the rectum.

ascendencia [as-then-den'-the-ah], *f.* A line of ancestors, as parents, grandparents, etc.; family-tree; origin, original.

ascendente [as-then-den'-tay], *m.* 1. An ascendant. 2. Horoscope, the configuration of the planets at the hour of birth. -*pa.* Ascending.

ascender [as-then-derr'], *vn.* 1. To ascend, to mount, to climb. 2. To be promoted. **Fue ascendido a teniente,** he was promoted to lieutenant. 3. **Ascender a,** *(Com.)* to amount to.

ascendiente [as-then-de-en'-tay], *m. & f.* 1. An ancestor, forefather. 2. *m.* Ascendency, influence, power.

ascensión [as-then-se-on'], *f.* 1. Ascension, the act of mounting or ascending. 2. Feast of the ascension of Christ. 3. Exaltation to the papal throne. 4. Rising point of the equator.

ascensional [as-then-se-o-nahl'], *a. (Astr.)* Ascensional, that which belongs to the ascension of the planets, right or oblique.

ascesionista [as-thayn'-se-o-nest], *m. & f.* Balloonist

ascenso [as-then'-so], *m.* Promotion.

ascensor [as-then-sor'], *m.* Elevator, lift, hoist.

ascensorista [as-thayn-so-res-tah], *m. & f.* Elevator operator, lift attendant.

ascesis [as-thay'-ses], *f.* Asceticism.

asceta [as-thay'-tah], *m.* Ascetic, hermit.

asceticismo [as-thay-te-thees-mo], *m.* Asceticism.

ascético, ca [as-thay'-te-co, cah], *a.* Ascetic, employed wholly in exercises of devotion and mortification.

ascetismo, *m.* V. ASCETICISMO.

ascidio [as-thee'-de-o], *m. (Zool.)* An ascidian.

ascios [as'-the-os], *m. pl.* Ascii, people of the torrid zone, who, at certain times of the year, have no shadow at noon.

asciro [as-thee'ro], *m. (Bot.)* St. John's wort. St. Andrew's cross.

ascitis [as-thee'-tis], *f.* Ascites, dropsy of the abdominal cavity.

ascítico, ca [as-thee'-te-co, cah], *a.* Belonging to the ascites, ascitic.

asclepiada [as-clay-pe-ah'-dah], *f. (Bot.)* Swallow-wort.

asclepias [as-clay'-pe-as], *f.* Asclepias, milkweed or silkweed; type genus of the Asclepiadae.

asco [ahs'-co], *m.* Nausea, loathsomeness, quality of raising disgust. **Es un asco,** it is a mean, despicable thing. **Hacer ascos,** to excite loathsomeness, to turn the stomach. **Coger asco a algo,** to get sick of something. **Me dan asco las aceitunas,** I loathe olives.

ascua [ahs'-coo-ah], *f.* Red-hot coal. **Estar como ascua de oro,** to be shining bright. **Arrimar el ascua a sus sardina,** to look after number one. V. BRASA. *pl.* **Ascuas. Estar en ascuas,** to be very uneasy; to be upon thorns. **Estar hecho un ascua or echar ascuas,** to be flushed in the face by agitation or anger. **Tener a uno sobre ascuas,** to keep somebody on tenterhooks.

aseadamente [ah-say-ah-dah-men'-tay], *adv.* Cleanly, elegantly, neatly.

aseado, da [ah-say-ah'-do, dah], *a.* Clean, elegant, neatly finished. -*pp.* of ASEAR.

asear [ah-say-ar'], *va.* To wash (lavar), to clean (limpiar), to decorate (adornar), to tidy up (arreglar), to set off, to adorn, to embellish; to polish. -*vr.* To tidy oneself up (lavarse).

asechador [ah-say-chah-dor'], *m.* Insnarer, waylayer; plotter.

asechamiento [ah-say-chah-me-en'-to], *m.* **Asechanza** [ah-say-chahn'-thah], *f.* 1. Waylaying. 2. Artifice, trick, stratagem; plot, intrigue.

asechar [ah-say-char'], *va.* To waylay, to watch insidiously, to lie in wait, to lie in ambush.

asechoso, sa [ah-say-cho'-so, sah], *a. (Obs.)* Inclined to insidious artifices, intriguing.

asedado, da [ah-say-dah'-do, dah], *a.* Silky, that which resembles silk in softness and smoothness. -*pp.* of ASEDAR.

asedar [ah-say-dar'], *va. (Prov.)* To work flax and hemp so as to make it feel like silk (suavizar). To hackle (el cáñamo).

asediador, ra [as-say-de-ah-dor', rah], *m. & f.* Besieger, one who besieges or blockades.

asediar [ah-say-de-ar'], *va.* 1. To besiege, to lay siege to a strong place or fortress; to blockade. 2. *(fig.)* To bother, to pester.

asedio [ah-say'-de-o], *m.* A siege, a blockade.

aseglararse [ah-say-glah-rar'-say], *vr.* To secularize oneself, or to make oneself worldly (sacerdotes, clérigos).

asegún [ah-say-goon'], *adv. prep. (LAm.)* V. SEGÚN.

asegundar [ah-say-goon-dar'], *va.* To repeat with little or no intermission of time.

asegurable [ah-say-goo-rah'-blay], *a.* Insurable.

aseguración [ah-say-goo-rah-the-on'], *f.* 1. *(Obs.)* Security, safety. 2. Insurance.

asegurado, da [ah-say-goo-rah'-do, dah], *a.* 1. Assured, guaranteed. 2. Decided, fixed; anchored. *-m.* The insured.

asegurador, ra [ah-say-goo-rah-dor'], *m. & f.* Insurer, underwriter.

aseguradora [ah-say-goo-rah-do'-rah], *f.* Insurance company.

aseguramiento [ah-say-goo-rah-me-en'-to], *m.* 1. The act of securing; security, safe conduct. 2. Insurance.

asegurar [ah-say-goo-rar'], *va.* 1. To secure, to insure; to fasten, to fix firm. 2. To preserve, to shelter from danger. 3. To bail, to give security. 4. To state, to assert. **Se lo aseguro,** I assure you. 5. *(Com.)* To insure against the dangers of the seas or fire, or other risk. 6. To secure, by mortgage, the fulfilment of an obligation. *-vr.* To escape danger. To be certain of a thing. **Asegurar las velas,** to secure the sails. **Asegurarse de la altura,** to ascertain the degree of latitude in which we find ourselves. **Asegurar la bandera,** to salute the flag when raising it.

aseidad [ah-say-e-dahd'], *f.* Self-existence, an attribute of God.

aselarse [ah-say-lar'-say], *vr. (Prov.)* To make ready for passing the night (aves).

asemejar [ah-say-may-har'], *va.* To assimilate, to bring to a likeness or resemblance, to favor. *-vr.* To resemble, to be like another person or thing.

asendereado, da [ah-sen-day-ray-ah'-do, dah], *a.* Beaten, frequented (caminos, carreteras). *-pp.* of ASENDEREAR. Deserted, afflicted.

asenderear [ah-sen-day-ray-ar'], *va.* 1. To persecute, to pursue with vengeance and enmity. 2. To open a path.

asengladura [ah-sen-glah-doo' rah], *f. (Naut.)* A day's run, the way a ship makes in twenty-four hours. V. SINGLADURA.

asenso [ah-sen'-so], *m.* Assent, consent, aquiescence, credence, credit.

asentada [ah-sen-tah'-dah], *f.* A stone ranged in its proper place. **De una asentada,** at once, at one sitting. A **asentadas,** V. A ASENTADILLAR.

asentaderas [ah-sen-tah-day'-ras], *f. pl. (coll.)* Buttocks, behind, bottom. V. NALGAS.

asentadillas (A) [ah-sen-tah-deel'-lyas], *adv.* Sitting on horseback, like a woman, with both legs on one side.

asentado, da [ah-sen-tah'-do, dah], *a. (Obs.)* 1. Seated, planted, situated (situado). 2. Clear, serene. **El hombre asentado ni capaz tendido, ni camisón curado,** idleness is the source of vice. *-pp.* of ASENTAR.

asentador [ah-sen-tah-dor'], *m.* 1. *(Obs.)* A stone-mason, stone-cutter. 2. Razor-strop. 3. Grinding slip; turning chisel.

asentadura [ah-sen-tah-doo'-rah], *f.*

asentamiento [ah-sen-tah-me-en'-to], *m.* 1. *(Law.)* Possession of goods given by a judge to the claimant or plaintiff for non-appearance of the defendant. 2. Establishment, settlement, residence. 3. *(Obs.)* Session. 4. *(Obs.)* Site.

asentar [ah-sen-tar'], *va.* 1. To place on a chair, or set; to cause to sit down. **Asentar el rancho,** to stop in any place or station to eat, to sleep, or to rest. 2. To suppose, to take for granted. 3. To affirm, to assure. 4. To adjust, to make an agreement. 5. To note, to take down in writing, to register. **Asentar al crédito de,** to place to one's credit. 6. To fix a thing in any particular place, to form, to adjust. 7. *(Law.)* To put a claimant or plaintiff in possession of the goods claimed for non-appearance of the respondent or defendant. 8. To assess. **Asentar bien su baza,** to establish one's character or credit. **Asentar casa,** to set up house for oneself. **Asentar con maestro,** to bind an apprentice to a master. **Asentar plaza,** to enlist in the army. *-vn.* 1. To fit (ropa). 2. To sit down. 3. To settle, to establish a residence (establecerse). *-vr.* 1. To subside (licores). 2. To perch or settle after flying (pájaros). 3. *(Arch.)* To sink, to give way under weight; to settle.

asentimiento [ah-sen-te-me-en'-to], *m.* Assent. V. ASENSO.

asentir [ah-sen-teer'], *vn.* To coincide in opinion with another; to acquiesce, to concede, to yield. **Asentir a la verdad de algo,** to recognize the truth of something.

asentista [ah-sen-tees'-tah], *m.* A contractor, one who contracts to supply the navy or army with provisions, ammunition, etc. **Asentista de construcción,** *(Naut.)* contractor for shipbuilding.

aseñorado [ah-say-nyo-rah-do], *a.* Lordly; dressed like a gentleman.

aseo [ah-say'-o], *m.* Cleanliness (limpieza), neatness (pulcritud). Bathroom, toilet (retrete, servicios). **Aseo personal,** personal toilet.

aséptico [ah-sayp'-te-co], *a.* Aseptic; germ-free.

asequible [ah-say-kee'-blay], *a.* Attainable, obtainable, that which may be acquired.

aserción [ah-ser-the-on'], *f.* Assertion, affirmation.

aserradero [ah-ser-rah-day'-ro], *m.* 1. A saw-pit. 2. Horse or wooden machine on which timber or other things are sawed.

aserradizo, za [ah-ser-rah-dee'-tho, thah], *a.* Proper to be sawed.

aserrado, da [ah-ser-rah'-do, dah], *a.* Serrate, serrated, dented, like a saw (plantas). *-pp.* of ASERRAR.

aserrador [ah-ser-rah-dor'], *m.* Sawer or sawyer.

aserradura [ah-ser-rah-doo'-rah], *f.* Sawing, the act of cutting timber with the saw; saw-cut, kerf. **Aserraduras,** Saw-dust.

aserrar [ah-ser-rar'], *va.* 1. To saw, to cut with a saw, to cut down. 2. *(Met. and coll.)* To saw, to play the violin badly. **Aserrar piedras en un molino,** to saw stones in a sawmill.

aserrido [ah-ser-ree'-do], *m.* Noisy, rasping respiration in diseases of the chest.

aserrín [ah-ser-reen'], *m.* Saw-dust.

asserruchar [ah-sayr-roo-chahr'], *va. (LAm.)* V. ASSERRAR.

asertivo, va [ah-ser-tee'-vo, vah], *a.* Assertive. V. AFIRMATIVO.

aserto [ah-ser'-to], *m.* V. ASERCION.

asertorio [ah-ser-to'-re-o], *a.* V. JURAMENTO. Affirmatory.

asesar [ah-say-sar'], *vn.* To become prudent, to acquire discretion.

asesina [ah-say-se'-nah], *f.* Murderess.

asesinado, da [ah-say-se-nah'-do,-dah], *m. & f.* Murder victim, murdered person.

asesinar [ah-say-se-nar'], *va.* 1. To assassinate, to kill treacherously. 2. To betray the confidence of another, to be guilty of a breach of trust.

asesinato [ah-say-se-nah'-to], *m.* 1. Assassination, murder. 2. Treachery, deceit, fraud.

asesino [ah-say-see'-no], *m.* 1. Assassin, murderer, cutthroat. 2. Impostor, cheat, one who practises fraud, and betrays the confidence of another. 3. Small spot of black silk which ladies put near the corner of the eye.

asesor, ra [ah-say-sor'-rah], *m. & f.* 1. A counseller, adviser, conciliator. **Asesor de imagen,** public-relations adviser. 2. Assessor. **Asesor jurídico,** legal adviser.

asesoramiento [ah-say-so-rah-me-ayn-to], *m.* Advice.

asesorar [ah-say-so-rahr'], *va.* To advise, to give legal advice to.

asesorarse [ah-say-so-rar'-say], *vr.* To take the assistance of counsel.

asesorato [ah-say-so-rah-to], *m. (LAm.)* 1. Advising. 2. Consultant´s office.

asesoría [ah-say-so-ree'-ah], *f.* 1. Consultant's office (oficina). 2. Consultant's fee, (estipendio, honorarios).

asestador [ah-ses-tah-dor'], *m.* Gunner, who points the cannon.

asestadura [ah-ses-tah-doo'-rah], *f.* Aim, pointing cannon, or taking aim.

asestar [ah-ses-tar'], *va.* 1. To aim, to point, to level, to make after. **Asestar una puñalada a uno,** to stab somebody. 2. *(Met.)* To try to do some mischief to others.

aseveración [ah-say-vay-rah-the-on'], *f.* Asseveration, solemn affirmation.

aseveradamente [ah-say-vay-rah-dah-men'-tay], *adv.* V. AFIRMATIVAMENTE.

aseverar [ah-say-vay-rar'], *va.* To asseverate; to affirm with great solemnity, as upon oath.

asexuado [ah-sayc-soo-ah-do], *a.* Sexless.

asexual [ah-sec-soo-ahl'], *a.* Asexual.

asfaltado [as-fahl-tah'-do], 1. *a.* Asphalt, asphalted. **Caretera asfaltada,** asphalted road. 2. *m.* Asphalting.

asfaltar [as-fal-tar'], *va.* To apply or cover with asphalt, to asphalt.

asfáltico, ca [as-fahl'-te-co, cah], *a.* Of asphaltum; bituminous.

asfalto [as-fahl'-to], *m.* Asphaltum, a kind of bitumen.

asfíctico, ca [as-fic'-te-co, cah], *a.* Asphyxial, or asphyctic.

asfixia [as-fic'-se-ah], *f. (Med.)* Asphyxia, a disease.

asfixiador [as-fic-se-ah-do], *a.* Suffocating.

asfixiante [as-fic-se-ahn'-tay], *a.* Asphyxiating. **Calor asfixiante,** suffocating heat.

asfixiar [as-fic-se-ar'], *va.* 1. To asphyxiate, suffocate. 2. **Estar asfixiado,** to be broke (dinero). *-vr.* To be asphyxiated, suffocated.

asfódelo [as-fo'-day-lo], *m.* Asphodel, day-lily. V. GAMON.

así [ah-see'], *adv.* 1. So, thus, in this manner. 2. Therefore, so that, also, equally. **Así bien,** as well, as much so, equally. **Así que,** so that, therefore. **Es así, o no es así,** thus it is, or it is not so. **Así fuera yo santo, como fulano es docto,** if I were as sure of being a saint, as he is learned. 3. Followed immediately by *como,* is equivalent to, in the same manner or proportion, as, **así como la modestia atrae, así se huye la disolución,** in the same proportion that modesty attracts, dissoluteness deters. But when the particle *como* is in the second part of the sentence, **así** is equal to so much. **Así, así,** So, so; middling. **Así que llegó la noticia,** as soon as the news arrived. **Así como así,** or **Así que así,** any way; it matters not. **Así que asá** or **asado,** any way; it makes no difference. **Así me estoy,** it is all the same to me. **Como así,** even so, just so, how so. **Así como así,** by all means. **Iremos si llueva a cántaros,** we'll go even if it pours down. **¿Cómo así?,** how's that? **Así sea,** let it be so.

Asia [ah'-se-ah], Asia.

asiano, na *a.* Asian.

asiático, ca [ah-se-ah'-te-co, cah], *a.* Asiatic.

asidero [ah-se-day'-ro], *m.* 1. Handle. 2. *(Met.)* Occasion, pretext. **Asideros,** *(Naut.)* Ropes with which vessels are hauled along the shore. 3. *(Cono Sur)* Basis, support.

asido, da [ah-see'-do, dah], *pp.* of ASIR. Seized, grasped, laid hold of. *a.* Fastened, tied, attached. **Fulano está asido a su propia opinión,** he is wedded to his own opinion. (*Yo asgo, tú ases; yo asga,* from ASIR).

asiduamente [ah-se'-doo-ah-mayn-tay], *adv.* Assiduously; frequently, regularly.

asiduidad [ah-se-doo-e-dahd'], *f.* Assiduity, assiduousness.

asiduo, dua [ah-see'-doo-o, ah], *a.* Assiduous, laborious. **Parroquiano asiduo,** regular customer. **Era un asiduo del café,** he was a regular customer of the coffee-shop.

asiento [ah-se-en'-to], *m.* 1. Chair. **Asiento trasero,** rear seat. 2. Seat in a tribunal or court of justice. 3. Spot on which a town or building is or was standing; site. 4. Solidity of a building resulting from the reciprocal pressure of the materials upon each other: settling. 5. Bottom of a vessel. 6. Sediment of liquors. 7. Treaty. 8. Contract for supplying an army, town, etc., with provisions, etc. 9. Entry, the act of registering or setting down in writing. 10. Judgment, prudence, discretion. 11. District of the mines in South America. 12. List, roll. 13. Sort of pearls, flat on one side and round on the other. 14. Surfeit, fit of indigestion. 15. The state and order which things ought to take. **Hombre de asiento,** a prudent man. **Asientos de popa,** *(Naut.)* stern seats in the cabin. **Asiento de molino,** bed or lowest stone in a mill. **Dar** or **tomar asiento en las cosas,** to let things take a regular course. (**Yo asiento, yo asienta,** from **Asentir.** V. **ASENTIR**). (**Yo asiento, yo asiente,** from **Asentar.** V. ACERTAR).

asignable [ah-sig-nah'-blay], *a.* Assignable.

asignación [ah-sig-nah-the-on'], *f.* 1. Assignation. 2. Distribution, partition. 3. Destination. **Asignación de bus,** bus allocation.

asignado [ah-sig-nah'-do], *m.* Assignat: paper money issued by France in 1790. *-pp.* of ASIGNAR.

asignar [ah-sig-nar'], *va.* To assign, to mark out, to determine, to ascribe, to attribute.

asignatario, ria [ah-seg-nah-ta'-re-o], *f. (LAm.)* Heir, legatee.

asignatura [ah-sig-nah-too'-rah], *f.* Subject (disciplina). **Aprobé cinco asignaturas y suspendí una,** I passed five subjects and failed one.

asigunas [ah-se-goo'-nahs], *f. & pl.* **Según asigunas** *(Carib.),* it all depends.

asilado, da [ah-se-lah-do, dah], *m. & f.* Inmate, refugee.

asilar [ah-se-lahr'], *va.* To take in, to give shelter. Put into a home. *-vr.* To take refuge, to seek political asylum. To enter a home.

asilo [ah-see'-lo], *m.* 1. Asylum, sanctuary, place of shelter and refuge. **Derecho de asilo,** right of sactuary. 2. Harborage. 3. *(Met.)* Protection, support, favor. 4. *(Ent.)* Asilus, a genus of large and voracious diptera; represented by the bee-killer and robber-fly.

asilla [ah-seel'-lyah], *f. dim.* 1. A small handle. 2. A slight pretext. *-pl.* 1. The collar-bones of the breast. 2. Small hooks or keys employed in the different parts of an organ.

asimesmo [ah-se-mes'-mo], *adv. (Obs.)* V. ASIMISMO.

asimetría [ah-se-may-tree'-ah], *f.* Lack of symmetry, asymmetry.

asimétrico, ca [ah-se-may'-tre-co, cah], *a.* Asymmetrical, out of proportion.

asimiento [ah-se-me-en'-to], *m.* 1. Grasp, the act of seizing or grasping. 2. Attachment, affection.

asimilable [ah-se-me-lah'-blay], *a.* Assimilable; capable of assimilation.

asimilación [ah-se-me-lah-the-on'], *f.* Assimilation.

asimilar [ah-se-me-lar'], *vn.* To resemble, to be like. *-va.* To assimilate; to convert into living tissue.

asimilativo, va [ah-se-me-lah-tee'-vo, vah], *a.* Assimilating, having the power of rendering one thing like another.

asimismo [ah-se-mees'-mo], *adv.* Exactly so, in the same manner, likewise (del mismo modo).

asimplado, da [ah-sim-plah'-do, dah], *a.* Like a simpleton, or silly person.

asín, asina [ah-seen', ah-see'-nah], *adv. (Low.)* V. ASI.

asinarias [ah-se-nah'-re-as], *f. pl.* Birds, in Brazil, which are very ugly, and whose voice resembles the braying of an ass.

asindeton [ah-seen'-day-tone], *m.* Asyndeton, a figure of speech in which conjunctions are supressed to give liveliness to the style.

asinino, na [ah-se-nee'-no, nah], *a.* Asinine, ass-like.

asíntota [ah-seen'-to-tah], *f. (Geom.)* Asymptote.

asir [ah-seer'], *va. & vn.* 1. To grasp or seize with the hand, to lay hold of. 2. To hold, to gripe, to come upon. 3. To strike or take root. *-vr.* To dispute, to contend, to rival. **Asirse de alguna cosa**, to avail oneself of an opportunity to do or say something.

asiriano, na or **asirio, ria** [ah-se-re-ah'-no, nah, ah-see'-re-o, ah], *a.* Assyrian.

asisia [as-see'-se-ah], *f. (Law. Arab.)* 1. Part of law proceedings containing the depositions of witnesses. 2. Court of assizes.

asisito [ah-se-se-to], *adv. (And. etc.) V.* ASÍ.

asísmico [ah-ses'-me-co], *a. (LAm.)* **Construcción asísmica,** earthquake-resistant building.

asisón [ah-se-sone'], *m. (Prov.)* Bird belonging to the family of *francolins.*

asistencia [ah-sis-ten'-the-ah], *f.* 1. Actual presence. 2. Reward gained by personal attendance. 3. Assistance, favor, aid, help, comfort, furtherance. **La asistencia es obligatoria,** assistance is compulsory. **Asistencias,** allowance made to any one for his maintenance and support; alimony. **Se alquila un cuarto amueblado, con asistencia o sin ella,** to rent a furnished room, with or without board. **Hónreme Vd. con su asistencia,** please, honor me with your company (presencia).

asistencia social [ah-sis-ten'-the-ah, so-thee-ahl'], *f.* Social work, social service.

asistenta [ah-sis-ten'-tah], *f.* 1. Charwoman, charlady, daily help (criada no permanente). Assistant (convento). Chambermaid (en un palacio). **Asistenta social,** welfare worker.

asistente [ah-sis-ten'-ta], *p a. & m.* 1. Assistant, helper, helpmate. 2. The chief officer of justice in Seville. 3. The soldier who attends an officer as a servant, an orderly.

asistido, da [ah-ses-te'-do, dah], *a. m. & f.* **Asistido por ordenador,** computer assisted.

asistir [ah-sis-teer'], *vn.* 1. To be present, to assist, to attend (clase). 2. To live in a house, or frequent it much. *-va.* 1. To accompany one in the execution of some public act. **No asistió a la clase,** he did not attend the class. 2. To minister, to further, to countenance. 3. To serve or act provisionally in the room of another. 4. To attend a sick person. **El médico que le asiste,** the doctor who attends him.

asma [ahs'-mah], *f.* Asthma.

asmático, ca [as-mah'-te-co, cah], *a.* Asthmatic, troubled with asthma.

asna [ahs'-nah], *f.* A she-ass, jenny. **Asnas,** rafters of a house.

asnacho [as-nah'-cho], *m. (Bot.) V.* GATUÑA.

asnada [as-nah'-dah], *f.* A foolish action.

asnado [as-nah'-do], *m.* Large piece of timber with which the sides and shafts in mines are secured.

asnal [as-nahl'], *a.* 1. Asinine. 2. Brutal.

asnales [as-nah'-les], *m. pl.* Stockings larger and stronger than the common sort.

asnalmente [as-nal-men'-tay], *adv.* 1. Foolishly. 2. Mounted on an ass.

asnallo [as-nahl'-lyo], *m. (Bot.) V.* GATUÑA.

asnaucho, cha [as-nah'-oo-cho], *m.* A sort of very sharp pepper of South America.

asnazo [as-nah'-tho], *m. aug.* 1. A large jackass. 2. *(Met.)* A brutish, ignorant fellow.

asnear [as-nay-ahr'], *vn. (LAm.)* To act the fool.

asnería [as-nay-ree'-ah], *f. (coll.)* Stud of asses. *V.* ASNADA.

asnerizo, asnero [as-nay-ree'-tho, as-nay'-ro], *m. (Obs.)* Asskeeper.

asnico, ca [as-nee'-co, cah], *m. & f.* 1. *(dim.)* A little ass. 2. *(Prov.)* Irons at the end of a fire-grate in which the spit turns.

asnilla [as-neel'-lyah], *f.* Stanchion or prop which supports a ruinous building.

asnillo, lla [as-neel'-lyo, layh], *m. & f. dim.* A little ass. *Asnillo,* field-cricket.

asnino, na [as-nee'-no, nah], *a. (coll.)* resembling an ass.

asno [ahs'-no], *m.* 1. An ass. 2. *(Met.)* A dull, stupid, heavy fellow. **Asno de muchos, lobos le comen,** everybody's business is nobody's business. **Cada asno con su tamaño,** birds of a feather flock together. **No se hizo la miel para la boca del asno,** it is not for asses to lick honey, we should not throw pearls before swine.

asobinarse [ah-so-be-nar'-say], *vr.* To fall down with a burden (bestias de carga).

asocarronado, da [ah-so-car-ro-nah'-do, dah], *a.* Crafty, cunning, waggish.

asociación, *f.* **asociamiento,** *m.* [ah-so-the-ah-the-on', ah-so-the-ah-me-en'-to], association; fellowship, copartnership; knot. Union.

asociado [ah-so-the-ah'-do], *m.* Associate; comrade. *(Com.)* Partner. *-pp.* of ASOCIAR.

asociar [ah-so-the-ar'], *va.* To associate, to unite with another as a confederate, to conjoin. *-vr.* To accompany, to consociate, to consort, to herd. **Asociarse con uno,** to team up with somebody.

asocio [ah-so'-the-o], *m. (LAm.)* **En asocio,** in association.

asolación, asoladura [ah-so-lah-the-on', ah-so-lah-doo'-rah], *f.* Desolation, devastation.

asolador, ra [ah-sol-lah-dor', rah], *m. & f.* A destroyer, desolater.

asolamiento [ah-so-lah-me-en'-to], *m.* Depopulation, destruction, havoc.

asolanar [ah-so-lah-nar'], *va.* To parch or dry up (vientos).

asolapar [ah-so-lah-par'], *V.* SOLAPAR.

asolar [ah-so-lar'], *va.* To level with the ground, to destroy, to waste, to harrow, to pillage, to devastate. *-vr.* To settle and get clear (licores).

asoldar, or **asoldadar** [ah-sol-dar'], *va.* To hire (mercenarios).

asoleado, da [ah-so-lay-ah'-do, dah], *a.* 1. Sunny. 2. Suntanned. Stupid (persona).

asolear [ah-so-lay-ar'], *va.* To sun, to expose to the sun. *-vr.* To be sunburnt. *(Cono Sur, Mex.)* To get sunstroke. *(CAm.)* To get stupid.

asoleo [ah-so'-lay-o], *m. (Mex.)* Sunstroke.

asolvamiento [ah-sol-vah-me-en'-to], *m.* Stoppage, the act of stopping.

asolvarse [ah-sol-var'-say], *vr.* To be stopped (tuberías, canales). *V.* AZOLVAR.

asomado, da [ah-so-mah'-do, dah], *a.* Fuddled. *-pp.* of ASOMAR.

asomadero [ah-so-mah-day'-ro], *m. (And.)* Viewing point.

asomar [ah-so-mar'], *vn.* 1. To begin to appear, to become visible. **Asoma el día,** the day begins to peep. 2. *(Naut.)* To loom. *-va.* To show a thing, to make it appear. **Asomé la cabeza a la ventana,** I poked my head out of the window. *-vr.* To be flustered with wine. To show, appear. Show up. **Ella estaba asomada a la ventana,** she was leaning out of the window.

asombradizo, za [ah-som-brah-dee'-tho, thah], *a.* Fearful, timid, easily frightened.

asombrador, ra [ah-som-brah-dor', rah], *m. & f.* Terrifier, one who frightens. Amazing.

asombramiento [ah-som-bra-me-en'-to], *m. V.* ASOMBRO.

asombrar [ah-som-brar'], *va.* 1. To shade, to darken, to obscure, to overshadow. 2. To frighten, to terrify. 3. To astonish, to cause admiration. **No deja de asombrarme,** it never ceases to amaze me. *vr.* To take fright. To be astonished. **Asombrarse de saber algo,** to be surprised to learn something.

asombro [ah-som'-bro], *m.* 1. Dread, fear, terror. 2. Amazement, astonishment, high admiration.

asombrosamente [ah-som-bro-sah-men'-tay], *adv.* Amazingly, wonderfully, marvellously.

asombroso, sa [ah-som-bro'so, sah], *a.* Wonderful, astonishing, marvellous.

asomo [ah-so'-mo], *m.* 1. Mark, token, sign. 2. Supposition, conjecture, surmise. **Ni por asomo,** not in the least, by no means.

asonada [ah-so-nah'-dah], *f.* Tumultuous hostility.

asonancia [ah-so-nahn'-the-ah], *f.* 1. Assonance, consonance. A peculiar kind of rhyme, in which the last accented vowel and those which follow it in one word correspond in sound with the vowels of another word, while the consonants differ: as *cálamo* and *plátano.* 2. Harmony or connection of one thing with another.

asonantar [ah-so-nan-tar'], *va. (Poetic.)* To mix assonant with consonant, verses in Spanish poetry, which is inadmissible in modern verse.

asonante [ah-so-nahn'-tay], *a.* Assonant, last word in a Spanish verse whose vowels are the same, beginning with that in which the accent is, as those of the other word, with which it must accord.

asonar [ah-so-nar'], *vn.* 1. To be assonant, to accord. 2. To unite in riots and tumultuous assemblies.

asordar [ah-sor-dar'], *va.* To deafen with noise.

asorocharse [a-so-ro-chahr-say], *vr. (And. Cono Sur)* To get mountain sickness.

asosegar, *va.* **Asosegarse,** *vr. V.* SOSEGAR.

asotanar [ah-so-tah-nar'], *va.* To vault, to make vaults or arched cellars.

aspa [ahs'-pah], *f.* 1. A cross. A reel, a turning frame. 3. Wings of a wind-mill. 4. Cross stud, diagonal stays. *(Naut.)* Cross gore, bentinck shrouds. Knitting-bar. **Aspa de cuenta,** a clock-reel. **Aspa de San Andrés,** colored cross on the yellow cloaks of penitents by the Inquisition.

aspadera [as-pah-day'-rah], *f. (Mech.)* A reel.

aspado, da [as-pah'-do, dah], *a.* 1. Having the arms extended in the form of a cross, by way of penance or mortification. 2. *(Met.)* Having one's arms confined, and their movements obstructed by tight clothes. *-pp.* of ASPAR.

aspador [as-pah-dor'], *m.* A reel.

aspador, ra [as-pah-dor', rah], *m. & f.* Reeler, one who reels yarn, thread, or silk.

aspalato [as-pah-lah'-to], *m. (Bot.)* Rosewood, aspalathus.

aspalto [as-pahl'-to], *m.* 1. Asphalt. 2. *V.* ESPALTO.

aspamentero [as-pah-mayn-tay'-ro], *a. (Cono Sur. Mex.) V.* ASPAVENTERO.

aspar [as-par'], *va.* 1. To reel, to gather yarn off the spindle, and form it into skeins. 2. To crucify. 3. *(Met.)* To vex or mortify. **Asparse a gritos,** to hoot, to cry out with vehemence. *-vr.* To writhe. *(fig.)* To do one's utmost.

aspaventero [as-pah-vayn-tay'-ro, rah], *a. m. & f.* Excitable, emotional; fussy.

aspaviento [as-pah-ve-en'-to], *m.* 1. Exaggerated dread, fear, consternation. 2. Astonishment, admiration, expressed in confused and indistinct words. **Aspavientos,** boasts, brags, bravadoes.

aspecto [as-pec'-to], *m.* 1. Sight, appearance; **un hombre de aspecto feroz,** a man with a fierce look, appearance. 2. Look, aspect, countenance. 3. *(Arch.)* Situation or position of a building with reference to the cardinal points; outlook. 4. *(Astr.)* Relative position of stars and planets. **A primer aspecto** or **al primer aspecto,** at first sight. **Tener buen o mal aspecto,** to have a good or bad aspect; to be in a good or bad state.

ásperamente [ash'-pay-rah-men-tay], *adv.* Rudely, in a harsh manner, grumly, crabbedly, abruptly, obdurately, gruffly.

asperear [as-pay-ray-ar'], *vn.* To be rough and acrid to the taste. *-va. (Obs.)* To exasperate, to irritate.

asperete [as-pay-ray'-tay], *m. V.* ASPERILLO.

aspereza, asperidad [as-pay-ray'-thah, as-pay-re-dahd'], *f.* 1. Asperity; acerbity, acrimony, gall, keenness. **Contestar con aspereza,** to answer with asperity. 2. Roughness, ruggedness, inequality or unevenness of the ground, craggedness, gruffness. 3. Austerity, sourness, gruffness, harshness of temper, snappishness, moroseness.

asperges [ahs-per-hess]. Sprinkling. **Quedarse asperges,** To be disappointed in one's expectations; not to understand a thing.

asperiego, ga [as-pay-re-ay'-go, gah], *a.* Applied to a sour apple of the pippin kind.

asperilla [as-pay-reel'-lyo], *m.* The sourish taste of unripe fruit and other things.

asperillo, lla [as-pay-reel'-lyo, lyah], *a. dim.* Tart, sourish.

asperjar [as-per-har'], *va.* To sprinkle.

áspero, ra [ahs'-pay-ro, rah], *a.* 1. Rough, rugged, cragged, grained, knotty; horrid. 2. *(Met.)* Harsh and unpleasing to the taste or ear; acerb; hard; crabbed. 3. *(Met.)* Severe, rigid, austere, gruff, crusty. **Áspera arteria.** *V.* TRAQUIARTERIA.

asperón [as-pay-rone'], *m.* Grindstone; flag-stone; holy-stone.

aspérrimo, ma [as-per'-re-mo, mah], *a.* Sup. of ASPERO.

aspersión [as-per-se-on'], *f.* Aspersion, the act of sprinkling. *(Agri.)* Spray; **riego por aspersión,** watering by spray.

aspersorio [as-per-so'-re-o], *m.* Water-sprinkler; instrument with which holy water is sprinkled in the church.

áspid, áspide [ahs'-pid, ahs'-pe-day], *m.* Asp, aspic, a small kind of serpent.

aspidistra [as-pe-des-trah], *f.* Aspidistra.

aspillera [as-pel-lyay'-rah], *f.* Loop-hole, embrasure, crenel.

aspiración [as-pe-rah-the-on'], *f.* 1. Aspiration. 2. Inspiration, the act of drawing in the breath. 3. Aspiration, pronunciation of a vowel with full breath. 4. *(Mus.)* A short pause which gives only time to breathe.

aspirada, do [as-pe-rah'-dah], *a & f.* Aspirate.

aspirador [as-pe-rah-dor'], 1. *a.* Suction; **bomba aspirador,** suction pump. 2. *m.* **Aspirador de polvo,** vacuum cleaner.

aspiradora [as-pe-rah-do'-rah], *f.* Vacuum cleaner.

aspirante [as-pe-rahn'-tay], *pa.* 1. Aspirant, neophyte. **Aspirante de marina,** naval cadet. 2. **Bomba aspirante,** suction pump.

aspirar [as-pe-rar'], *va.* 1. To inspire the air, to draw in the breath. 2. To aspire, to covet. 3. To pronounce a vowel with full breath. *-vn.* **Aspirar a algo,** to aspire to something. **El que no sepa eso que no aspire a aprobar,** whoever doesn't know that can have no hope of passing.

aspiratorio, ria [as-pe-ra-to'-re-o, ah], *a.* Proper to inspiration, or what produces it.

aspirina [as-pe-ree'-nah], *f.* Aspirin.

aspisera [as-pe-say'-rah], *f. V.* ALPISTERA.

aspudo [as-poo'-doh], *a. (Cono Sur)* Big-horned.

asquear [as-kay-ar'], *va.* To nauseate, to sicken, to turn the stomach. **Me asquean las ratas,** I loathe rats. *-vr.* To be nauseated, feel disgusted.

asquerosamente [as-kay-ro-sah-men'-tay], *adv.* Nastily, nauseously, foully, filthily.

asquerosidad [as-kay-ro-se-dahd'], *f.* Nastiness, filthiness, fulsomeness. Obscenity.

asqueroso, sa [as-kay-ro'-so, sah], *a.* 1. Nasty, filthy, nauseous, impure. 2. Loathsome, fastidious, disgusting, squeamish, fulsome. **Una comida asquerosa,** a revolting meal. **Tienes unas manos asquerosas,** your hands are filthy. 3. Dirty, squalid. 4. Disgusting (conductas). 5. Vile, loathesome (muy malo).

asquia [ahs'-ke-ah], *f. (Zool.)* A kind of grayling or umber, a delicate freshwater fish.

asquiento [as-ke-ayn'-to], *a.* 1. *(And.)* Fussy. 2. *V.* ASQUEROSO.

asta [ahs'-tah], *f.* 1. Lance. 2. Part of the deer's head which bears the antlers; horn. 3. Handle of a pencil, brush. 4. *(Naut.)* Staff or light pole erected in different parts of the ship, on which the colors are displayed. 5. *(Mas.)* Binder, curb-stone. Shank of a tool; shaft, spindle. **Asta de bandera de popa,** ensign-staff. **Asta de bandera de proa,** jack-staff. **Asta de tope,** flag-staff. **Asta de bomba,** pump-spear. **Astas,** horns of animals, as bulls, etc. **Darse de las astas,** to snap and carp at each other.

astabandera [as-tah-bahn-day'-rah], *f. (LAm.)* Flagstaff, flagpole.

ástaco [ahs'-tah-co], *m.* Lobster, crayfish, or crawfish.

astado, astero [as-tah'-do, as-tay-ro], *m*. Roman pikeman or lancer.

astático, ca [as-tah'-te-co, cah], *a*. Astatic, in equilibrium.

astear [as-tay-ahr'], *va*. *(Cono Sur)* To gore.

astenia [as-tay-ne-ah], *f*. Asthenia, physical debility.

asténico, ca [as-tay'-ne-co, cah], *a*. *(Med.)* Asthenic.

aster [as-ter'], *m*. *(Bot.)* Starwort.

asteria [as-tay'-re-ah], *f*. 1. Star-stone, a kind of precious stone. 2. Cat's eye, a sort of false opal.

asterisco [as-tay-rees'-co], *m*. 1. An asterisk, a mark in printing. **Señalar con un asterisco**, to asterisk. 2. *(Bot.)* Oxeye.

asteroide [as-tay-ro'-e-day], *m*. Asteroid, a telescopie planet, of a group between Mars and Jupiter.

astigmático [as-teg-mah'-te-co], *a*. Astigmatic.

astigmatismo [as-tig-mah-tees' mo], *m*. *(Med.)* Astigmatism.

astil [as-teel'],*m*. 1. Handle of an axe, hatchet, etc. 2. Shaft of an arrow. 3. Beam of a balance. 4. *(Obs.)* Anything which serves to support another.

astilejos [as-te-lay'-hos], *m. pl*. V. ASTILLEJOS.

astilico [as-te-lee'-co], *m. dim*. A small handle.

astilla [as-teel'-lyah], *f*. 1. Chip of wood, splinter of timber. **Hacer algo astillas**, to smash something into little pieces. 2. *(Obs.)* Reed or comb of a loom. 3. **Astilla muerta de un bajel**, *(Naut.)* the dead rising of the floor-timbers of a ship. **De tal palo, tal astilla**, or **astilla del mismo palo**, a chip of the same block. **Sacar astilla**, to profit by a thing.

astillar [as-teel-lyar'], *va*. To chip, to splinter. *-vr*. To splinter, to shatter.

astillazo [as-teel-lyah'-tho], *m*. 1. Crack, the noise produced by a splinter being torn from a block. 2. *(Met.)* The damage which results from an enteprise to those who have not been its principal authors and promoters.

astillejos [as-teel-lyay'-hos], *m. pl*. *(Astr.)* Castor and Pollux, two brilliant stars.

astillero [as-teel-lyay'-ro], *m*. 1. Rack on which lances, spears, pikes, etc., are placed. 2. Shipwright's yard, dockyard. **Poner en astillero**, *(Met.)* to place one in an honorable post.

astracán [as-trah-kahn'], *m*. Karakul.

astracanada [as-trah-cah-nah-dah], *f*. Silly thing; piece of buffoonery.

astrágalo [as-trah'-gah-lo], *m*. 1. *(Arch.)* Astragal, an ornament at the tops and bottoms of columns. 2. *(Mil.)* A kind of ring or moulding on a piece of ordenance. 3. *(Bot.)* Milkvetc. 4. *(Anat.)* Astragalus, the anklebone, articulating with the tibia. 5. Round moulding; beads.

astral [as-trahl'], *a*. Astral, that which bclongs to the stars.

astrancia [as-trahn'-the-ah], *f*. *(Bot.)* Master-wort.

astreñir [as-tray-nyr'], V. ASTRINGIR.

astricción, astringencia [as-tric-the-on', as-trin-hen'-the-ah], *f*. Astriction, compression.

astrictivo, va [as-tric-tee'-vo, vah], *a*. Astrictive, styptic.

astricto, ta [as-treec'-to, tah], *a*. 1. Contracted, compressed. 2. Determined, resolved. *-pp. irr.* of ASTRINGIR.

astrífero, ra [as-tree'-fay-ro, rah], *(Poetic.)* Starry, full of stars.

astrilla [as-tre'-lyah], *f*. *(Cono Sur)* V. ASTILLA.

astringencia [as-trin-hen'-the-ah], *f*. Astringency, constriction.

astringente [as-trin-hen'-tay], *a*. Astringent.

astringir [as-trin-heer'], *a*. To astringe, to contract, to com press; *(Med.)* To bind.

astro [ahs'-tro], *m*. 1. Luminous body of the heavens, such as the sun, moon and stars. 2. Illustrious persons of uncommon merit.

astrobiología [as-tro-be-o-lo-hee'-ah], *f*. Astrobiology.

astrofísica [as-tro-fee'-se-cah], *f*. Astrophysics.

astrofísico, ca [as-tro-fe'-se-co], *m. & f.* Astrophysicist.

astrografía [as-tro-grah-fee'-ah], *f*. Astrography, the science of describing the stars.

astroite [as-tro'-e-tay], *m*. Astroite, a radiated fossil.

astrolabio [as-tro-lah'-be-o], *m*. Astrolabe, an instrument chiefly used for taking the altitude of stars at sea, now disused. Sextant.

astrología [as-tro-lo-hee'-ah], *f*. Astrology.

astrológico, ca, astrólogo, ga [as-tro-lo'-he-co, cah, as-tro'-lo-go, gah], *a*. Astrological, that which belongs to astrology.

astrólogo [as-tro'-lo-go], *m*. Astrologer.

astronauta [as-tro-nah'-oo-tah], *m. & f.* Astronaut.

astronáutica [as-tro-nah'-oo-te-cah], *f*. Astronautics, space travel.

astronave [as-tro-nah'-vay], *f*. Spaceship.

astronavegación [as-tro-nah-vay-gah-the-on'], *f*. Astronavigation.

astronomía [as-tro-no-mee'-ah], *f*. Astronomy.

astronómicamente [as-tro-no'-me-cah-men-tay], *adv*. Astronomically.

astronómico, ca [as-tro-no'-me-co, cah], *a*. Astronomical, that which belongs to astronomy.

astrónomo, ma [as-tro'-no-mo], *m. & f.* Astronomer.

astroso [as-tro'-so], *a*. 1. Ill-fated, unfortunate. 2. Contemptible. 3. Dirty; untidy.

astucia [as-too'-the-ah], *f*. Cunning, craft, finesse, slyness. **Actuar con astucia**, to act cunningly.

asturión [as-too-re-on'], *m*. 1. A pony, a small horse. 2. *(Zool.)* V. SOLLO.

astutamente [as-too-tah-men'-tay], *adv*. Cunningly, craftily, feigningly, jesuitically.

astuto, ta [as-too'-to, tah], *a*. Astute, cunning, sly, crafty, fraudulent.

asueto [ah-soo-ay'-to], *m*. Holiday for schoolboy and students, vacation. **Día de asueto**, day off.

asumir [ah-soo-meer'], *va*. 1. To take to, or for oneself, to take for granted; assume. 2. To raise by election or acclamation to certain dignities. *-vr.* V. ARROGARSE.

asunceño, ña [ah-soon-thay'-nyo], *(Cono Sur)* *a. m. & f*. From Asunción.

Asunción [ah-soon-the-on'], *f*. 1. Assumption. 2. Elevation to a higher dignity. 3. Ascent of the Holy Virgin to heaven. 4. Assumption, the thing supposed, a postulate.

asunto [ah-soon'-to], *m*. Subject, the matter or thing treated upon; affair, business. **El asunto está concluido**, the matter is closed. **Asunto de honor**, affair of honor. 2. Study, attention. 3. *(Cono Sur)* **¿A asunto de qué lo hiciste?**, why did you do it? *-pl.* **Asuntos,** effects, business, stock.

asurar [ah-soo-rahr], *va*. *(Culin.* etc.) To burn; to burn up.

asuramiento [ah-soo-rah-me-en'-to], *m*. The act of burning, and the state of being burnt: applied only to ragouts, and to the corn before it is reaped.

asurarse [ah-soo-rar'-say], *vr.* 1. To be burnt in the pot or pan (carne). 2. To be parched with drought.

asurcano, na [ah-soor-cah'-no, nah], *a*. Neighboring: said of lands which adjoin, and their tillers.

asurcar [ah-soor-car'], *va*. To furrow sown land, in order to kill the weeds. V. SURCAR.

asuso [ah-soo'-so], *adv*. *(Obs.)* Upward, above.

asustadizo, za [ah-soos-tah-dee'-tho, thah], *a*. Applied to a person easily frightened.

asustar [ah-soos-tar'], *va*. To frighten, to terrify. *-vr.* To be frightened. **Asustarse de o por algo**, to be frightened at something, get alarmed about something. **¡No te asustes!,** don´t be alarmed.

asusto [ah-soos-to], *m*. *(And.)* V. SUSTO.

A. T. *abr.* de **Antiguo Testamento** (Old Testament).

atabaca [ah-tah-bah'-cah], *f*. *(Bot.)* Groundsel. V. OLIVARDA.

atabacado, da [ah-tah-bah-cah'-do, dah], *a*. Having the color of tobacco.

atabal [ah-tah-bahl'], *m*. 1. Kettledrum. 2. V. ATABALERO.

atabalear [ah-tah-bah-lay-ar'], *vn*. To imitate the noise of kettledrums (caballos).

atabalejo, atabalete, ataballillo [ah-tah-bah-lay'-ho, etc.], *m. dim.* A small kettle-drum.

atabalero

atabalero [ah-tah-bah-lay'-ro], *m.* Kettle-drummer.

atabanado, da [ah-tah-bah-nah'-do, dah], *a.* Spotted white (caballos).

atabardillado, da [ah-tah-bar-deel-lyah'-do, dah], *a.* Applied to diseases of the nature of spotted fevers.

atabe [ah-tah'-bay], *m.* A small vent or air-hole left in water-pipes.

atabernado, da [ah-tah-ber-nah'-do, dah], *a.* Retailed in taverns (licores).

atabillar [ah-tah-beel-lyar'], *va.* To fold a piece of cloth so that the selvages are open to view on both sides.

atabladera [ah-tah-blah-day'-rah], *f.* A kind of roller or levelling board to level land sown with corn.

atablar [ah-tah-blar'], *va.* To level land sown with corn by means of a levelling board.

atacable [ah-tah-cah'-blay], *a.* Attackable, assailable.

atacadera [ah-tah-cah-day'-rah], *f.* Rammer used in splitting stones with gunpowder.

atacado, da [ah-tah-cah'-do, dah], *a.* 1. *(Met.)* Irresolute, inconstant, undecided. 2. *(Met.)* Close, miserable, narrow-minded. **Calzas atacas**, breeches formerly worn in Spain. **Hombre de calzas atacadas**, a strict and rigid observer of old customs. *-pp.* of ATACAR.

atacador [ah-tah-cah-dor'], *m.* **1**. Aggressor, he that invades or attacks. 2. Ramrod or rammer for a gun.

atacadura, *f.* **atacamiento**, *m.* [ah-tah-cah-doo'-rah, ah-tah-cah-me-en'-to], Stricture, act and effect of tightening.

atacamita [ah-tah-cah-mee'-tah], *f.* *(Miner.)* Native oxychloride of copper.

atacante [ah-tah-chan'-tay], *m. & f.* Attacker, assailant.

atacar [ah-tah-car'], *va.* 1. To attack, to assault, to fall upon, to come upon. 2. To pin down an argument. **Atacar a un adversario**, to attack an adversary. To overcome (sueño). To corrode (ácido). To tackle (una dificultad, un problema). To begin, to start. **Atacaron el Everest**, they started to climb Everest. *-vr.* *(LAm.)* To scoff, stuff oneself.

atachar [ah-tah-chahr'], *va.* *(Mex. Elec.)* To plug in.

ataché [ah-tah-shay'], *m.* *(CAm. Carib.)* Paper clip.

atacir [ah-tah-theer'], *m.* *(Astrol.)* A division of the celestial arch into twelve parts by circles which pass through points north and south of the horizon.

atacola [ah-tah-co'-lah], *f.* A strap for a horse's tail.

ataderas [ah-tah-day'-rahs], *f. & pl.* Garters.

atadero [ah-tah-day'-ro], *m.* 1. Cord or rope, with which something may be tied. 2. The place where a thing is tied. **No tener atadero**, to have neither head nor tail: applied to a discourse without meaning, and to the person uttering it.

atadijo, ito [ah-tah-dee'-ho, dee'-to], *m. dim. (coll.)* An ill-shaped little bundle or parcel.

atadito, ita [ah-tah-dee'-to, tah], *a. dim.* Somewhat cramped or contracted: a little bundle.

atado [ah-tah'-do], *m.* Bundle, parcel. **Atado de cebollas**, a string of onions. Atado de cigarrillos, *(Cono Sur)* Packet of cigarettes.

atado, da [ah-tah'-do, dah], *a.* Pusillanimous, easily embarrassed, good for nothing. *-pp.* of ATAR.

atador, ra [ah-tah-dor'], *m. & f.* 1. The person who ties. 2. Binder, The person who binds sheaves of corn. 3. The sting of a child's bonnet or cap.

atadura [ah-tah-doo'-rah], *f.* 1. Alligation, the act of tying together. 2. Tie, fastening. 3. *(Met.)* Union, connection. **Atadura de galeotes y presos**, a number of prisoners tied together, to be conducted to the galleys.

atafagar [ah-tah-fah-gar'], *va.* 1. To stupefy, to deprive of the use of the senses, especially by strong odors, good or bad. 2. *(Met.)* To tease, to molest by incessant importunity.

atafetanado, da [ah-tah-fay-tah-nah'-do, dah], *a.* Taffeta-like, resembling taffeta.

ataguía [ah-tah-gee'-ah], *f.* Cofferdam.

ataharre [ah-tah-ar'-ray], *m.* The broad crupper of a pack-saddle.

atahona [ah-tah-o'-nah], *f. V.* TAHONA. A mill turned by horse-power.

atahorma [ah-tah-or'-mah], *f.* *(Orn.)* Osprey, a kind of sea-eagle.

ataifor, ataiforico [ah-tah-e-for', ah-tah-e-fo-ree'-co], *m.* 1. Soup plate or deep dish. 2. A round table formerly used by the Moors.

atairar [ah-tah-e-rar'], *va.* To cut mouldings in the panels and frames of doors and windows.

ataire [ah-tah'-e-ray], *m.* Moulding in the panels and frames of doors and windows.

atajadero [ah-tah-hah-day'-ro], *m.* A sluice-gate.

atajadizo [ah-tah-hah-dee'-tho], *m.* Partition of boards, linen, etc., by which a place or ground is divided into separate parts. **Atajadizo de la caja de agua**, *(Naut.)* the manger-board.

atajador [ah-tah-hah-dor'], *m.* 1. One that intercepts or stops a passage, or obstructs the progress of another. 2. *(Mil.)* Scout. 3. **Atajador de ganado**, a sheep-thief. 4. *(Miner.)* The lad who unloads the work-horses.

atajar [ah-tah-har'], *vn.* To go the shortest way; or cut off part of the road. *-va.* 1. To overtake flying beasts or men, by cutting off part of the road, and thus getting before them. 2. To divide or separate by partitions. 3. To intercept, stop, or obstruct the course of a thing. **Este mal hay que atajarlo**, we must put an end to this evil. 4. To mark with lines, in a play or writing, the parts to be omitted in acting or in reading. 5. **Atajar ganado**, to steal sheep. 6. **Atajar la tierra**, to reconnoitre the ground. *-vr.* To be confounded with shame, dread, or reverential fear. **Hay que atajar la delincuencia juvenil**, juvenile delinquency must be checked. **Atajar un incendio**, to stop a fire. **Atajar una enfermedad**, to check an illness.

atajasolaces [ah-tah-hah-so-lah'-thes], *m.* A disturber of a pleasant reunion.

atajea, atajía [ah-tah-hay'-ah, ah-tah-hee'-ah], *f. V.* ATARJEA.

atajo [ah-tah'-ho], *m.* 1. Cut by which a road or path is shortened; short cut. 2. Ward or guard made by a weapon in fencing. 3. *(Obs.)* Agreement, means taken to conclude any difference or dispute. 4. Net with frame. **No hay atajo sin trabajo**, no gains without pains. **Salir al atajo**, to interrupt another's speech, and anticipate in a few words what he was going to say in many. **Tirar por el atajo**, to take the easy way out.

atalajar [ah-tah-lah-har'], *va. (Obs.)* To stun, to stupefy. *-vn.* To agree, to accord; to be pleased.

atalaje [ah-tah-lah'-hay], *m. V.* ATELAJE.

atalaya [ah-tah-lah'-yah], *f.* 1. Watchtower, which overlooks the adjacent country and sea-coast. 2. Height, from where a considerable part of country may be seen. 3. *m.* Guard, placed in a watchtower to keep a watchful eye over the adjacent country and sea-coast.

atalayador, ra [ah-tah-lah-yah-dor', rah], *m. & f.* 1. Guard or sentry stationed in a watchtower. 2. *(Met.)* Observer, investigator.

atalayar [ah-tah-lah-yar'], *va.* 1. To overlook and observe the country and seacoast form a watchtower. 2. To spy or pry into the actions of others.

atamiento [ah-tah-me-en'-to], *m.* 1. *(coll.)* Pusillanimity, meanness of spirit, want of courage. 2. Embarrassment, perplexity.

atanasia [ah-tah-nah'-se-ah], *f.* 1. *(Bot.)* Costmary or alecost. 2. *(Print.)* A size of type named English (14-point).

atanor [ah-tah-nor'], *m.* *(Prov.)* A siphon or tube for conveying water.

atanquía [ah-tan-kee'-ah], *f.* 1. Depilatory, a sort of ointment, to take away hair; mixture of orpiment and lime. 2. Refuse of silk which cannot be spun. 3. *V.* CADARZO.

atañer [ah-tah-nyerr'], *v. imp.* To belong, to appertain. To concern, to have to do; **En lo que atañe a eso,** with regard to that. **Eso no te atañe,** that is not your business.

atapuzar [ah-tah-poo-thar'], *(Carib.)* 1. *va.* To fill, to stop up. 2. *vr.* To stuff oneself.

ataque [ah-tah'-kay], *m.* 1. Attack, onset. **Ataque fingido**, sham attack. 2. Fit of apoplexy. 3. Fit of anger. 4. *(Mil.)* Attack. **Ataque aéreo o incursión aérea**, air raid, air attack. 5. *(Med.)* Stroke. **Ataque cardíaco**, heart attack.

ataquiza [ah-tah-kee'-thah], *f.* The act of layering or laying a branch of a vine in the ground to take root.

ataquizar [ah-tah-ke-thar'], *va.* To layer or lay a branch of a vine in the ground to take root.

atar [ah-tar'], *va.* 1. To tie, to bind, to fasten, to knit; to lace. 2. *(Met.)* To deprive of motion, to stop. **Atar bien su dedo**, to take care of oneself, to be attentive to one's own interest. **Al atar de los trapos**, at the close of the accounts. **Loco de atar**, as mad as a hatter. **Atar cabos**, to put two and two together. **Este trabajo me ata mucho**, this work ties me down a lot. **Atar corto a uno**, to keep a tight rein over someone. **Atar de pies y manos**, to tie hand and foot. *-vr.* 1. To be embarrassed or perplexed, to be at a loss how to extricate oneself from some difficulties. **Atarse en una dificultad**, to get tied in a difficulty. 2. To confine oneself to some certain subject or matter. **Atarse a la letra**, to stick to the letter of the text. **Atarse las manos**, to tie oneself down by promise.

ataracea [ah-tah-rah-thay'-ah], *f.* Marquetry, checker, checker-work; inlaid work, veneer work.

ataracear [ah-tah-rah-thay-ar¡], *va.* To checker, to inlay or variegate.

atarantado, da [ah-tah-ran-tah'-do, dah], *a.* 1. Bitten by a tarantula. 2. Stunned, stupefied, dazed (aturdido). 3. Restless (bullicioso). 4. Frightened, terrified (espantado). 5. *(Met.)* Surprised, astonished, amazed.

atarantar [ah-tah-rahn-tahr'], *va.* To stun (aturdir), to daze; **quedó atarantado**, he was stunned. *(fig.)* To stun, to dumbfound. *-vr.* To be stunned. 2. *(And.)* To hurry, to dash. 3. *(Mex.)* To stuff oneself. 4. *(CAm. Mex.)* To get drunk.

ataranza [ah-tah-rahn'-tah], *f.* Dockyard.

atarazana [ah-tah-rah-thah'-na], *f.* 1. *(Obs.)* Arsenal, a public dockyard. 2. Shed in rope-walks, for the spinners to work under cover. 3. *(Prov.)* Cellar, where wine is kept in casks.

atarazar [ah-tah-rah-thar'], *va.* To bite or wound with the teeth.

atardecer [ah-tahr-day-thayr'], 1. *vn.* To get dark; **atardecía**, it was getting dark. 2. *m.* Late afternoon; dusk, evening.

atareado, da [ah-tah-ray-ah'-do, dah], *a.* Busied, occupied; intent. **Andar muy atareado**, to be very busy. *-pp.* of ATAREAR.

atarear [ah-tah-ray-ar'], *va.* To task, to impose a task, to exercise. *-vr.* To overdo oneself, to labor or work with great application. **Atarearse a hacer algo**, to be busy doing something

atarjea [ah-tar-hay'-ah], *f.* 1. A small vault over the pipes of an aqueduct, to prevent them from being damaged. 2. A small sewer or drain.

atarquinar [ah-tar-ke-nar'], *va.* To bemire, to cover with mire. *-vr.* To be bemired, to be covered with mire.

atarraga [ah-tar-rah'-gah], *f. (Bot.)* V. OLIVARDA.

atarragar [ah-tar-rah-gar'], *va.* To fit a shoe to a horse's foot. *-vr. (Carib. Mex.)* To stuff oneself, to overeat.

atarrajar [ah-tar-rah-har'], *va.* To form the thread of a screw. V ATERRAJAR

atarraya [ah-tar-rah'-yah], *f.* A castnet.

atarugado, da [ah-tah-rro-gah'-do, dah], *a. (coll.)* Abashed, ashamed. *-pp.* of ATARUGAR.

atarugar [ah-tah-roo-gar'], *va.* 1. To fasten or secure with wedges. 2. *(Mech.)* To plug, to bung; to cram. 3. *(Met.)* To silence and confound a person. *-vr.* 1. To swallow the wrong way, choke. 2. *(fig.)* To get confused, be in a daze. 3. To stuff oneself, to overeat.

atasajado, da [ah-tah-sah-hah'-do, dah], *a. (coll.)* Stretched across a horse. *-pp.* of ATASAJAR.

atasajar [ah-tah-sah-har'], *va.* To cut meat into small pieces, and dry it in the sun.

atascadero, atascamiento [ah-tas-cah-day'-ro, ah-tas-cah-me-en'-to], *m.* 1. Bog, mire, mudhole 2. *(Met.)* Obstruction, impediment (estorbo).

atascar [ah-tas-car'], *va.* 1. *(Naut.)* To stop a leak, to plug (agujero). 2. *(Met.)* To obstruct, to block [up], to choke, to clog (tubería) *-vr.* 1. To stick in a deep miry place. 2. To get stopped up: applied to drains, etc. 3. *(Met.)* To stop short in a discourse, unable to proceed.

atasco [ah-tahs'-co], *m.* 1. Barrier, obstruction, blockage (cosa que atasca). 2. Bogging down (de un coche). 3. Traffic jam (tráfico). 4. Jamming, sticking (mecanismo). 5. Stumbling block (obstáculo). 6. Muddle, tangle (discurso).

ataúd [ah-tah-ood'], *m.* 1. Casket in which dead bodies are put into the ground, coffin. 2. *(Obs.)* A measure for corn.

ataudado, da [ah-tah-oo-dah'-do, dah] *a.* Made in the shape of a coffin.

ataujía [ah-tah-oo-hee'-ah], *f.* Damaskeening, the art of adorning metals with inlaid work.

ataujiado, da [ah-tah-oo-he-ah'-do, dah], *a.* Damaskeened.

ataviado, da [ah-tah-ve-ah'-do, dah], *a.* Ornamented, ornated. *-pp.* of ATAVIAR.

ataviar [ah-tah-ve-ar'], *va.* To dress out, to trim, to adorn, to embellish, to accoutre. *(LAm.)* To adapt, to adjust. *-vr.* To dress up, to get oneself up.

atavío [ah-tah-vee'-o], *m.* The dress and ornament of a person, accoutrement, finery, gear.

atavismo [ah-tah-vees'-mo], *m.* Atavism, resemblance to ancestor; the tendency of hybrids to revert to the original type.

ataxia [ah-tac'-se-ah], *f.* 1. *(Med.)* Ataxia, ataxy. 2. A graminaceous plant of Java.

atáxico, ca [ah-tac'-se-co, cah], *a.* Ataxic, in disordered movement.

ate [ah'-tay], *f. (Bot.)* A rochidaccous plant, resembling habenaria. *(CAm. Mex.)* *(Culin.)* Jelly.

atediante [ah-tay-de-ayn'-tay], *a.* Boring, wearisome.

atediar [ah-tay-de-ar'], *va.* To disgust or displease, to consider with disgust. *-vr.* To be vexed, to be tired.

ateísmo [ah-tay-ees'-mo], *m.* Atheism; denial of God.

ateísta [ah-tay-ees'-tah], *m.* Atheist; infidel, unbeliever.

atejonarse [ah-tay-ho-nahr'-say], *vr. (Mex.)* 1. To curl up into a ball. 2. To become sharp.

atelaje *V.* ATALAJE. Also a team.

atembado [ah-taym-bah'-do], *a. (And.)* Silly, stupid; lacking in will-power.

atemorizar [ah-tay-mo-re-thar'], *va.* To terrify, to strike with terror, to daunt. *-vr.* To get scared.

atempa [ah-tem'-pah], *f.* (Asturian) Pasture in plains and open fields.

atempar [ah-taym-pahr'], *vn. (CAm.)* To wait, to hang around.

atemperación [ah-tem-pay-rah-the-on'], *f.* The act and effect of tempering.

atemperar [ah-tem-pay-rar'], *va.* 1. To temper, to form metals to a proper degree of hardness. 2. To soften, to mollify, to assuage; to cool. 3. To accommodate, to modify. **Atemperar los gastos a los ingresos**, to balance outgoings with income.

atemporado, da [ah-tem-po-rah'-do, dah], *a. (Obs.)* Alternate, serving by turns. Moderate, temperate.

atemporal [ah-taym-po-rahl'], *a.* Timeless.

atemporalidad [ah-taym-po-rah-le-dahd'], *f.* Timelessness.

atenacear, atenazar [ah-tay-na-thay-ar', ah-tay-na-thar'], *va.* To tear off flesh with pincers.

Atenas [ah-tay-nahs'], Athens.

atenazar [ah-tay-nah-thahr'], *va. (fig.)* 1. To torment, to beset; **El miedo me atenazaba**, I was gripped by fear. 2. To tear [the flesh] with red hot pincers (suplicio).

atención [ah-ten-the-on'], *f.* 1. Attention, the act of being attentive; heed, heedfulness, mindfulness. **¡Atención a los**

pies!, mind your feet! 2. Civility, kindness, complaisance, courteousness, observance, courtesy, politeness (cortesía). 3. In the wool-trade, a contract of sale, whereby the price is not determined. **En atención,** attending; in consideration. **Hacer un trabajo con mucha atención,** to do a job with great care. *-pl.* Affairs, business, occupation. **Atenciones,** affairs.

atencioso [ah-tayn-the-o'-so], *a. (LAm.)* V. ATENTO.

atender [ah-ten-derr'], *va.* 1. To attend or be attentive, to mind, or to fix the mind upon a subject. 2. To heed, to hearken. 3. To expect, to wait or stay for, to look at. 4. To meet an emergency with succour or money. 5. To look after. **Atiende a esta gente,** look after these people. 6. To comply with; **atender a un cliente,** to serve a customer. 7. To meet one´s obligations; **atender el teléfono,** to mind the telephone. 8. *(LAm.)* To attend, to be present at. *-vn.* To attend to, to pay attention to. **Atender a un caso urgente,** to see about an urgent matter.

atendible [ah-ten-dee'-blay], *a.* Meriting attention.

ateneo [ah-teay-nay'-o], *m.* Atheneum, in its various significations. Cultural association.

ateneo, a *a. (Poetic.)* or **ateniense** [ah-tay-ne-en'-say], athenian.

atener [ah-tay-nerr'], *vn. (Obs.)* 1. To walk at the same pace with another. 2. To guard, to observe. *-vr.* 1. To stick or adhere to one for greater security. **Atenerse a alguna cosa,** to abide. 2. To rely on. **No saber a qué atenerse,** not to know what to expect. **Atenerse a las consecuencias,** to bear the consequences in mind.

ateniense [ah-tay-ne-ayn'-say], *a. m. & f.* Athenian.

atentación [ah-ten-tah-the-on'], *f. (Law.)* procedure contrary to the order and form prescribed by the laws.

atentadamente [ah-ten-tah-dah-men'-tay], *adv.* 1. Attentively (con atención). Courteously, politely. V. ATENTAMENTE.

atentado, da [ah-ten-tah'-do, dah], *a.* 1. Discreet, prudent, moderate. 2. Done without noise, and with great circumspection. *-pp.* of ATENTAR.

atentado [ah-ten-tah'-do], *m.* 1. *(Law.)* Proceeding of a judge not warranted by the law. 2. Excess, transgression. Illegal act, offense; outrage, crime; assault, attack. **Atentado terrorista,** terrorist outrage.

atentamente [ah-ten-tah-men'-tay], *adv.* 1. Attentively, with attention, mindfully. 2. Civilly, politely, obligingly, observingly. **Suyo atentamente,** yours sincerely (cartas).

atentar [ah-ten-tar'], *va.* 1. To attempt, to commit a crime. 2. To try with great circumspection. *-vn.* **Atentar contra,** to commit an outrage against. *-vr. (Obs.)* To proceed with the utmost circumspection in the execution of an enterprise.

atentatorio, ria [ah-ten-tah-to'-re-o, ah], *a. (Law.)* Contrary to the order and form prescribed by the laws. Illegal, criminal.

atento, ta [ah-ten'-to, tah], *a.* 1. Attentive, bent upon a thing, listful, helpful; observing; mindful. **Estar atento a los peligros,** to be mindful of the dangers. 2. Polite, civil, courteous, mannerly, compliant, complaisant, considerate; notable. **Ser atento con uno,** to be kind to somebody. *-pp. irr.* of ATENDER, *adv.* **Atento,** in consideration.

atenuación [ah-tay-noo-ah-the-on'], *f.* 1. Attenuation, the act of making thin or slender. 2. Maceration. 3. The rhetorical figure litotes.

atenuante [ah-tay-noo-ahn'-tay], *a.* Attenuating, palliative. Extenuating (circumstancias), lessening fault.

atenuar [ah-tay-noo-ar'], *va.* To attenuate, to render thin and slender; to dimisnish, to lessen, to macerate, to mince. *-vr.* To weaken.

ateo [ah-tay'-o], *m.* **Atheist.** V. ATEISTA.

ateperetarse [ah-tay-pay-ray-tahr'-say], *vr. (CAm. Mex.)* To get confused.

atepocate [ah-tay-po-cah'-tay], *m. (Mex.)* Frog spawn.

atercianado, da [ah-ter-the-ah-nah'-do, dah], *a.* Afflicted with a tertian or intermittent fever.

aterciopelado, da [ah-ter-the-o-pay-lah-do, dah], *a.* Velvet-like, resembling velvet.

aterido, da [ah-tay-ree'-do, dah], *a.* Stiff with cold. *-pp.* of ATERIRSE.

aterimiento [ah-tay-re-me-en'-to], *m.* Act of growing stiff with cold.

aterino [ah-tay-ree'-no], *m.* Atherine, a sand-smelt, about 0.15 meter in length, and which presents the rare distinction of being translucent.

aterirse [ah-tay-reer'-say], *vr.* To grow stiff with cold.

aternerao, da [ah-ter-nay-rah'-do, dah], *a.* Calf-like.

ateroma [ah-tay-ro'-mah], *f.* Atheroma, fatty degeneration of an artery.

aterrada [ah-tay-rrah-dah], *f. (Naut.)* Landfall.

aterrador, ra [ah-ter-rah-dor', rah], *a.* Frightful, terrible, dreadful.

aterrajar [ah-ter-rah-har'], *va.* To cut the thread of a screw; to tap with the die.

aterraje [ah-tayr-rah'-hay], *m. (Aer.)* Landing; *(Naut.)* Landfall.

aterramiento [ah-ter-rah-me-en'-to], *m.* 1. Ruin, destruction. 2. Terror, communication of fear. 3. *(Naut.)* A landing-place.

aterrar [ah-ter-rar'], *va.* 1. To destroy, to pull or strike down; to prostrate. 2. To terrify, to appal, to cause terror or dismay. *-vr. (Naut.)* To stand inshore, to keep the land on board.

aterrizaje [ah-ter-re-thah'-hay], *m. (Aer.)* Landing. **Aterrizaje forzoso,** emergency landing.

aterrizar [ah-ter-re-thar'], *vn. (Aer.)* To land.

aterronar [ah-ter-ro-nar'], *va.* To clod, to gather into concretions, to coagulate. *-vr.* To get lumpy; to cake, harden.

aterrorizar [ah-ter-ro-re-thar'], *va.* To frighten, to terrify.

atesador [ah-tay-sah-dor'], *m. (Mech.)* Stretcher, line-tightener, tensor, take-up. Brace-pin.

atesar [ah-tay-sar'], *va.* 1. To brace, or stiffen a thing. 2. *(Naut.)* To haultaut.

atesorador [ah-tay-so-rah-dor'], *m.* A hoarder.

atesorar [ah-tay-so-rar'], *va.* 1. To treasure or hoard up riches, to lay in, to lay up. 2. To possess many amiable qualities.

atestación [ah-tes-tah-the-on'], *f.* Attestation, testimony, evidence.

atestado, da [ah-tes-tah'-do, dah], *a.* 1. Attested, witnessed. *-pp.* of ATESTAR.

atestado [ah-tays-tah'-do], *a.* Packed, cram-full; **atestado de,** packed with.

atestados [ah-tes-tah'-dos], *m. pl.* Certificates, testimonials.

atestadura [ah-tes-tah-doo'-rah], *f.* 1. The act of cramming or stuffing. 2. Must, poured into pipes and butts, to supply the leakage.

atestamiento [ah-tes-tah-me-en'-to], *m.* The act of cramming, stuffing or filling.

atestar [ah-tes-tar], *va.* 1. To cram, to stuff; to overstock, to clog. 2. To stuff, to crowd. 3. To fill up pipes or butts of wine. 4. To attest, to witness. **Una palabra no atestada,** an unattested word. 5. *(Prov.)* V. ATRACAR.

atestiguación, *f.* **atestiguamiento,** *m.* [ah-tes-te-goo-ah-the-on', ah-tes-te-goo-ah-me-en'-to]. Deposition upon oath.

atestiguar [ah-tes-te-goo-ar'], *va.* To depose, to witness, to attest, to affirm as a witness, to give evidence. **Atestiguar con alguno,** to cite or summon one as a witness.

atesto [ah-tes'-to], *m.* Certificate, paper. *(Com.)*

atetado, da [ah-tay-tah'-do, dah], *a.* Mammillated, mammiform. *-pp.* of ATETAR.

atetar [ah-tay-tar'], *va.* To suckle, to nurse.

atetillar [ah-tay-teel-lyar'], *va.* To dig a trench around the roots of trees.

atezado, da [ah-taay-thah'-do, dah], *a.* Black, tanned. *-pp.* of ATEZAR.

atezamiento [ah-tay-thah-me-en'-to], *m.* The act and effect of blackening.

atezar [ah-tay-thar'], *va.* To blacken, to make black, to tan. *-vr.* To grow black, to get tanned.

atiborrado [ah-te-bor-rah'-do], *a.* **Atiborrado de**, full of.

atiborrar [ah-te-bor-rar'], *va.* 1. To stuff or pack up close with locks of wool, tow, etc. **Atiborrar a un niño de dulces**, to stuff a child with sweets. 2. To cram with victuals. *-vr.* To stuff oneself.

aticismo [ah-te-thees'-mo], *m.* 1. Atticism, elegance and grace in language. 2. Nice, witty, and polite joke.

ático, ca [ah'-te-co, cah], *a.* 1. Attic, elegant, poignant: applied to wit and humor. 2. Superior to objection or confutation. **Testigo ático**, *an* irrefragable witness. *-m.* Upper part of a building, attic.

aticurga [ah-te-coor'-gah], *f.* Base of an attic column. *(Yo atiendo,* from *Atender. V.* ATENDER.) *(Yo atierro, yo atierre,* from *Aterrar. V.* ACERTAR.) *(Yo atiento,* from *Atentar. V.* ACERTAR.)

atierre [ah-te-err'-ray], *m.* Attle, heap of waste ore.

atiesar [ah-te-ay-sar'], *va.* To make hard or stiff. *-vr.* To get stiff, to stiffen.

atifle [ah-tee'-flay], *m.* An instrument in the shape of a trevet, which potters place between earthen vessels to prevent them from sticking to each other in the kiln or oven.

atigrado [ah-te-grah'-do], 1. *a.* Striped, marked like a tiger. 2. *m.* Tabby.

atigronarse [ah-te-gro-nahr'-say], *vr. (Carib.)* To get strong.

Atila [ah-te'-lah], *m.* Attila.

atildado, da [ah-teel-dah'-do, dah], *a.* Elegant, neat, fastidious. **Atildado caballero**, perfect gentleman.

atildadura [ah-teel-dah-doo'-rah], *f.* 1. Dress, attire, ornament. 2. Culture of the mind, good breeding. 3. Punctuation.

atildar [ah-teel-dar'], *va.* 1. To put a dash or stroke over a letter. 2. To censure the speeches and actions of others. 3. To deck, to dress, to adorn. *-vr.* To spruce oneself up.

atilincar [ah-te-len-cahr'], *(CAm.)* To tighten, to stretch.

atillo [ah-teel'-lyo], *m.* Bundle. *V.* HATILLO. **Hacer atillo**, To pack up.

atinadamente [ah-te-nah-dah-men'-tay], *adv.* 1. Cautiously, judiciously, prudently. 2. Pertinently, appositely, to the purpose. 3. Considerately, consideringly.

atinado [ah-te-nah'-do], *a.* Accurate, correct, wise, sensible, judicious; **unas observaciones atinadas**, some pertinent remarks.

atinar [ah-te-nr'], *vn.* 1. To hit the mark, to reach the point. 2. To hit upon a thing by conjecture, to guess. **Él siempre atina**, he always gets it right. 3. To find out. 4. **Atinar al blanco**, to hit the target. 5. **Atinar a hacer algo**, to succeed in doing something. *-va.* To hit upon, find.

atincar [ah-teen'-car], *m.* Tincal: when refined, it is the borax of commerce.

atinconar [ah-tin-co nar'], *va.* To secure temporarily the walls of an excavation.

atingencia [ah-ten-hayn'-the-ah], *f. (LAm.)* 1. Connection, bearing. 2. Obligation. 3. Qualification.

atingido [ah-ten-he'-do], *a. (And.* Cono Sur.) 1. Depressed, down-in-the-mouth; feeble, weak; timid. 2. *(And.)* Penniless

atingir [ah-ten-gerr'], *va.* 1. *(LAm.)* To concern, to bear on, to relate to. 2. *(And.)* To oppress.

atiparse [ah-te-pahr'-say], *vr.* To eat one´s fill.

atípico [ah-te'-pe-co], *a.* Atypical, untypical, exceptional.

atiplado [ah-te-plah'-do], *a.* Treble, high-pitched (voz).

atiplar [ah-te-plar'], *va.* To raise the sound of a musical instrument. *-vr.* To grow very sharp or acute (instrumento, voz).

atipujarse [ah-te-poo-hahr'-say], *vr. (CAm. Mex.)* To stuff oneself.

atirantar [ah-te-ran-tar'], *va. (Arch.)* To fix collar-beams in a building. To tighten, tauten; to stretch; **estar atirantado entre dos decisiones**, to be torn between two decisions. *-vr. (Mex.)* To peg out.

atisba [ah-tis'-bah], *m. (And.)* Watchman, look-out; spy.

atisbadero [ah-tis-bah-day'-ro], *m.* Peephole.

atisbador, ra [ah-tis-bah-dor', rah], *m. & f.* A person who pries into the business and actions of others.

atisbadura [ah-tis-bah-doo'-rah], *f.* The act of prying into the business and actions of others.

atisbar [ah-tis-bar'], *va.* 1. To scrutinize, to pry, to examine closely. 2. **Atisbar a uno a través de una grieta**, to peep at somebody through a crack. To watch, to waylay.

atisbo [ah-tis'-bo], *m.* 1. Spying; watching; look, peep. 2. *(fig.)* Inkling, slight sign.

atisuado, da [ah-te-soo-ah'-do, dah], *a.* Tissue-like. *-i. e.* like *tisú*, a silk stuff interwoven with gold and silver, presenting a flower pattern.

atizadero [ah-te-thah-day'-ro], *m.* 1. Pocker. 2. *(fig.)* Spark, stimulus.

atizador, ra [ah-te-thah-dor', rah], *m. & f.* 1. One who stirs up or incites others. 2. Poker, an instrument to stir the fire. 3. In oil-mills, the person who puts the olives under the mill-stone. 4. In glasshouses, he who supplies the furnace with wood or coals; feeder.

atizar [ah-te-thar'], *va.* 1. To stir the fire with a poker. 2. *(Met.)* To stir up or rouse and incite the passions. **Atizar la lámpara or el candil**, to raise the lamp wick, and fill it with oil. **Atizar la lámpara**, *(coll.)* to fill the glasses. **Pedro ¿por qué atiza? Por gozar de la ceniza**, Why does Peter sow? Because he expects to reap. 3. To give; **se atizó el vaso**, he knocked back a glassful. *-vn.* **¡Atiza!**, gosh! *-vr.* To smoke pot.

atizonar [ah-te-tho-nar'], *va.* To join bricks and stones close together, and fill up the chinks in a wall with mortar and brickbats. *-vr.* To be smutted: applied to grain.

atlante [at-lahn'-tay], *v.* He who bears the weight of government, in allusion to Atlas. **Atlantes**, *(Arch.)* Figures or half-figures of men, sometimes used instead of columns; atlantes or telamones. Cf. CARIATIDES.

Atlántico [at-lahn'-te-co], *a.* Atlantic.

Atlántida [at-lahn'-te-dah], *f.* Atlantis.

atlantista [at-lahn-tes'-tah], 1. *a.* Relating to the Atlantic Alliance. 2. *m. & f.* Supporter of the Atlantic Alliance.

Atlas [at'-las], *m.* 1. Atlas, a range of mountains, a collection of maps. 2. *(Naut.)* Atlas, the name of the first cervical vertebra. 3. *(Com.)* A kind of rich satin, manufactured in the East Indies.

atleta [at-lay'-tah], *m.* Athlete, wrestler, gymnast.

atlético, ca [at-lay'-te-ci, cah], *a.* Athletic, belonging to gymnastics; robust.

atletismo [at-lay-tis'-mo], *m.* Athletics.

atmósfera [ar-mos'-fay-rah], *f.* 1. Atmosphere, the air. 2. The space over which the influence of anything extends, or is exerted. 3. Measure of force founded upon the pressure exerted by the atmosphere.

atmosférico, ca [at-mos-fay'-re-co, cah], *a.* Atmospherical.

atoaje [ah-to-ah'-hay], *m.* Towage, warping.

atoar [ah-to-ar'], *va. (Naut.)* to tow a vessel with the help of a rope.

atoe [ah-toc'], *m. (And.)* Fox.

atocar [ah-to-cahr'], *va. (LAm.) V.* TOCAR.

atocinado, da [ah-to-the-nah'-do, dah], *a. (Low.)* Corpulent, fut, fleshy. *-pp.* of ATOCINAR.

atocinar [ah-to-the-nar'], *va.* 1. To cup up a pig, to make bacon. 2. *(Met.)* To assassinate or murder. *-vr.* 1. *(coll.)* To sell with anger and rage, to be exasperated. 2. To be violently enamoured.

atocle [ah-to'-clay], *m. (Mex.)* Sandy soil rich in humus.

atocha [ah-to'-chah], *f. (Bot.)* Tough feather-grass, bassweed, esparto.

atochal, atochar [ah-to-chahl', ah-to-char'], *m.* A field where bass-weed grows.

atochamiento [ah-to-chah-me-ayn-to], *m. (Cono Sur)* Traffic jam.

atochar [ah-to-chahr'], *m. V.* ATOCHAL.

atochón [ah-to-chone'], *m. (Bot.)* Name of the tender panicle of the tough feather-grass.

atolada [ah-to-lah'-dah], *m. (CAm.)* Party.

atole [ah-to'-lay], or **Atol,** *m. (Mex. and Cuba)* A gruel made by boiling Indian corn, or maize, pounded to flour, in water, and also in milk. In Peru called mazamorra.

atoleada [ah-to-lay-ah'-dah], *f. (CAm.)* Party.

atolería [ah-to-lay-re'-ah], *f. (LAm.)* Stall where atol is sold.

atolón [ah-to-lone'], *m.* Atoll, a coral island.

atolondrado [ah-tolon-drah'-do, dah], *a.* Harebrained, thoughtless, mad-brain, giddy, careless, heedless; harumscarum. *-pp.* of ATOLONDRAR.

atolondramiento [ah-to-lon-drah-me-en'-to], *m.* Stupefaction, the act and effect of stupefying, consternation.

atolondrar [ah-to-lon-drar'], *va.* To stun, to stupefy, to confound, to render stupid. *-vr.* To be stupefied, to grow dull or stupid.

atolladero [ah-tol-lyah-day'-ro], *m.* 1. A deep miry place. 2. *(Met.)* Obstacle, impediment, obstruction. **Estar en un atolladero,** to be in a jam.

atollar [ah-tol-lyar'], *vn.* To fall into the mire, to stick in the mud. *-vr. (Met.)* To be involved in great difficulties.

atomía [ah-to-me'-ah], *f. (LAm.)* 1. Evil deed, savage act. 2. **Decir atomías,** to shoot one´s mouth off.

atómico, ca [ah-to'-me-co, cah] *a.* Atomic. **Bomba atómica,** atomic bomb. **Era or edad atómica,** atomic age.

atomismo [ah-to-mees'-mo], *m.* Atomism, the atomical philosophy.

atomista [ah-to-mees'-tah], *m.* Atomist, one who holds the atomical philosophy, or the system of atoms.

atomístico, ca [ah-to-mees'-te-co, cah], *a.* Atomical, consisting of atoms.

atomizar [ah-to-me-thahr'], *va.* To atomize; to spray.

átomo [ah'-to-mo], *m.* 1. Atom, corpuscle, ace, mote. 2. Anything extremely small. **No exceder en un átomo,** to stick closely to one's orders and instructions. **Reparar en un átomo,** to remark the minutest actions. **atómos,** minute parts seen by a solar ray in any place.

atonal [ah-to-nahl'], *a.* Atonal.

atondar [ah-ton-dar'], *va.* To spur a horse.

atónito, ta [ah-to'-ne-to, tah], *a.* Astonished, amazed. **Me miró atónito,** he looked at me in amazement.

átono, na [ah'-to-no, nah], *a.* Unaccented; used of a syllable in prosody, atonic.

atontadamente [ah-ton-tah-dah-men'-tay], *adv.* Foolishly, stupidly.

atontado, da [ah-ton-tah'-do, dah], *a.* Mopish, foolish, stupid. *-pp.* of ATONTAR.

atontamiento [ah-ton-tah-me-en'-to], *m.* Stupefaction, the act of stupefying, and state of being stupefied.

atontar [ah-ton-tar'], *va.* To stun, to stupefy, to flatten, to confound. *-vr.* To be stupid, to grow stupid.

atontolinar [ah-ton-to-le-nhar'], *va.* To daze; to stun; **quedar atontolinado,** to be in a daze.

atora [ah-to'-rah], *f.* Law of Moses.

atorafo [ah-to-fo-rah'-do], *a. (Carib.)* Anxious.

atorar [ah-to-rahr'], *va.* To stop up, to choke, to obstruct. *(Carib. Mex.)* To block, impede. *-vr.* To choke, to swallow the wrong way; *(Mex.)* To get tongue-tied.

atorarse [ah-to-rar'-say], *vr.* 1. To stick in the mire. 2. To fit closely the bore of a cannon: applied to a ball. 3. To choke, to suffocate.

atormentadamente [ah-tor-men-tah-dah-men'-tay], *adv.* Anxiously, tormentingly.

atormentado, da [ah-tor-men-tah'-do, dah], *a.* Painful, full of pain, beset with affliction. *-pp.* of ATORMENTAR.

atormentador, ra [ah-tor-men-tah-dor', rah], *m. & f.* Tormentor.

atormentar [ah-tor-men-tar'], *va.* 1. To torment, to give pain. 2. *(Met.)* To cause affliction, pain, or vexation. 3. To rack or torment by the rack. *-vr.* To torment oneself.

atornillar, [ah-tor-neel-lyar'], *va.* To screw, to fasten with screws. *(LAm.)* To pester, harass.

atoro [ah-to'-ro], *m. (LAm.)* Destruction; *(fig.)* Tight spot, difficulty.

atorozonarse [ah-to-ro-tho-nar'-say], *vr.* To suffer gripes or colic, to be griped (caballos).

atorozarse [ah-to-ro-thar'-say], *vr. (CAm.)* To choke, to swallow the wrong way.

atorrante [ah-tor-rahn'-tay], *m. (Arg.)* Vagabond, idler, tramp.

atorrantear [ah-tor-rahn-tay-ahr'], *vn. (Cono Sur)* To live like a tramp, to be on the bum.

atortolado [ah-tor-to-lah'-do], *a.* **Están atortolados,** they are like two turtle-doves.

atortolar [ah-tor-to-lar'], *va. (coll.)* To confound, to intimidate. *-vr.* To be frightened or intimidated, like a turtle-dove.

atortorar [ah-tor-to-rar'], *va. (coll.)* To confound, to intimidate. *-vr.* To be frightened or intimidated, like a turtle-dove.

atortorar [ah-tor-to-rar'], *va. (Naut.)* to frap a ship, to strengthen the hull with ropes tied round it.

atortujar [ah-tor-too-har'], *va. (coll.)* To squeeze, to make flat. *-vr. (CAm.)* To be shattered.

atorunado [ah-to-roo-nah'-do], *a. (Cono Sur)* Stocky, bull-necked.

atosigador [ah-to-se-gah-dor'], *a.* 1. Poisonous. 2. *(fig.)* Pestering, harassing, harrying (que apremia).

atosigamiento [ah-to-se-gah-me-en'-to], *m.* The act of poisoning, and state of being poisoned.

atosigar [ah-to-se-gar'], *va.* 1. To poison. 2. *(Met.)* To harass, to oppress.

atoxicar [ah-too-se-car'], *va.* To poison.

atóxico, ca [ah-toc'-se-co,cah], *a.* Non-poisonous.

atrabancar [ah-trah-ban-car'], *va.* To huddle, to perform a thing in a hurry, and carelessly. *-vr.* To be in a fix, to get into a jam.

atrabanco [ah-trah-bahn'-co], *m.* The act of huddling, or doing a thing hurriedly.

atrabiliario [ah-trah-be-la'-re-o], *a.* Bad-tempered, difficult, moody.

atrabilis [ah-trah-bee'-lis], *f.* The state of being atrabilious; black bile. *(fig.)* Bad temper.

atracable [ah-trah-cah'-blay], *a.* Approachable.

atracadero [ah-trah-cah-day'-ro], *m. (Naut.)* A landing-place for small vessels.

atracado [ah-trah-cah'-do], *a. (CAm.)* Mean, stingy.

atracador [ah-trah-cah-dor'], *m.* Hold-up man, bandit.

atracar [ah-trah-car'], *va.* 1. *(Naut.)* To overtake another ship; to approach land; to come alongside. 2. To cram with food and drink, to glut, to pamper. 3. To hold up, to attack. *-vn. (Naut.)* To tie up, to moor, to bring alongside. *-vr.* 1. To be stuffed with eating and drinking, to fill. 2. *(Naut.)* **Atracarse al costado,** To come alongside of a ship.

atracción [ah-trac-the-on'], *f.* Attraction, the act or power of attracting. Appeal, charm. **Atracción sexual,** sexual attraction.

atraco [ah-trah'-co], *m.* Hold-up, robbery; hijack; **atraco a mano armada,** armed robbery.

atracón [ah-trah-cone'], *m.* Over-eating; gluttony.

atractivamente [ah-trac-tee'-vah-mayn-tay], *adv.* Attractively.

atractivo, va [ah-trac-tee'-vo, vah], *a.* 1. Attractive, having the power of attracting, magnetic, magnetical. 2. Engaging.

atractivo [ah-trac-tee'-vo], *m.* Charm, something fit to gain the affections; grace; cooing.

atractriz [ah-trac-treeth'], *a.* Powerful to attract.

atraer [ah-trah-err'], *va.* 1. To attract, to draw to something; to lead. **Dejarse atraer por,** to allow oneself to be drawn towards. 2. To allure, to lure, to invite, to make another submit to one's will and opinion, to conciliate. *-vr. (Obs.) V.* JUNTARSE and EXTENDERSE.

atrafagado, da [ah-trah-fah-gah'-do, dah], *a.* 1. Much occupied; laborious. *-pp.* of ATRAFAGAR. 2. Fidgety.

atrafagar [ah-trah-fah-gar'], *vn.* To toil, to exhaust oneself with fatigue. *-vr.* To fidget.

atragantarse [ah-trah-gan-tar'-say], *vr.* 1. To stick in the throat or windpipe. **Se me atragantó una miga,** a crumb went the wrong way. 2. *(Met.)* To be out short in conversation. 3. **Pepe se me ha atragantado,** *(fig.)* Pepe sticks in my throat.

atrague [ah-trah'-gay], *m.* **¡Que atrague!,** what an idiot!

atraible [ah-trah-ee'-blay], *a.* Attractable, subject to attraction.

atraidorado, da [ah-trah-e-do-rah'-do, dah], *a.* Treacherous, faithless, perfidious. *(Yo atraigo,* from *Atraer. V.* TRAER).

atraillar [ah-trah-eel-lyar'], *va.* 1. To leash, to bind with a string. 2. To follow game guided by a dog in leash.

atraimiento [ah-trah-e-me-en'-to], *m. (Obs.)* The act of attracting, and state of being attracted.

atramento [ah-trah-men'-to], *m.* Black color.

atramentoso, sa [ah-trah-men-to'-so, sah], *a. (Obs.)* That which has the power of dyeing black.

atramparse [ah-tram-par'-say], *vr.* 1. To be caught in a snare. 2. To be choked, to be stopped or blocked up. 3. To be involved in difficulties.

atramuz [ah-trah-mooth'], *m. (Bot.)* Lupine. *V.* ALTRAMUZ.

atrancar [ah-tran-car'], *va.* 1. To bar a door. 2. Coll.) To step out, to take long steps. 3. *(Met. Coll.)* To read hurriedly. *-vr.* 1. To get stuck, to get bogged down. 2. *(Cono Sur) (Med.)* To get constipated. 3. *(Mex.)* To dig one´s heels in.

atranco [ah-trahn'-co], *m.* 1. Mudhole. 2. Jam, difficulty, embarrassment.

atrapa-moscas [ah-trah'-pa-mos'-cas], *f. (Bot.)* The Venus's fly-trap.

atrapar [ah-trah-par'], *va.* 1. To catch, to trap, to lay hold of one who is running away. 2. To impose upon, to deceive.

atrás [ah-trahs'], *adv.* 1. Backward, toward the back. **Estar atrás,** to be behind. 2. Past, in time past. **Hacerse atrás,** to fall back. **Quedarse atrás,** to remain behind. **Volverse atrás,** *(Met.)* to retract, to unsay. **Hacia atrás,** *(coll.)* far from that, quite the contrary. **En las filas de atrás,** in the back rows. **Marcha atrás,** reverse. **Quedarse atrás,** to fall behind. **Echarse para atrás,** to change one's mind.

atrasado, da [ah-trah-sah'-do, dah], *pp.* of ATRASAR. 1. **Atrasado de medios,** short of means. **Atrasado de noticias,** *(coll.)* behind the times. **Estar atrasado en pagos,** to be behind in payments, to be in arrears. 2. Backward; underdeveloped; slow, backward. 3. *(Cono Sur)* ill. *m.* **Es un atrasado,** he´s behind the times. **Un número atrasado,** back number (revista). **Un atrasado mental,** a mentally retarded person.

atrasados [ah-trah-sah'-dos], *m. pl.* Arrears, sums remaining unpaid though due.

atrasar [ah-trah-sar'], *va.* 1. To put back, to set back; to retard, to slow down. **Atrasar un reloj,** to put a clock back. 2. To postpone the execution or performance of something. *vr.* 1. To remain behind. 2. To be in debt.

atraso [ah-trah'-so], *m.* 1. Backwardness, lateness, delay. **El tren lleva atraso,** the train is late. 2. Loss of fortune or wealth. 3. Arrears of money.

atravesado, da [ah-trah-vay-sah'-do, dah], *a.* 1. Squint-eyed, looking obliquely. 2. Oblique. 3. Cross-grained, perverse, troublesome. 4. Mongrel, of a mixed or cross breed. 5. Lying across. **Hay un árbol atravesado,** There is a tree lying across. *-pp.* of ATRAVESAR.

atravesador [ah-trah-vay-sah-dor'], *m.* Disturber, a violator of peace.

atravesaño [ah-trah-vay-sah'-nyo], *m.* Cross-timber, timber which crosses from one side to another. **Atravesaño firme**

de colchar, *(Naut.)* a cross-piece for belaying ropes. **Atravesaños de los propaos,** Cross-pieces of the breast-work. **Atravesaños de las latas,** Carlines or carlings, two pieces of timber lying fore and aft from one beam to another, directly over the keel.

atravesar [ah-trah-vay-sar'], *va.* 1. To lay , or put across (árbol, viga). 2. To run through with a sword, to pass through the body. **Atravesar a uno con una espada,** to run somebody through with a sword. 3. To cross, to cross over, to pass over, to get or go over, to go through, to overpass. 4. *(Low.)* to bewitch by a spell or charm. 5. To bet, to stake at a wager. 6. To lay a trump on a card which has been played. 7. *(Naut.)* to lie to. **Atravesar el corazón,** *(Met.)* To move to compassion. **Atravear los géneros,** to buy goods by wholesale in order to sell them by retail. **Atravesar todo el país,** to overrun or traverse the whole country. **No atravesar los umbrales,** not to darken one's door. *-vr.* 1. To be obstructed by something thrown in the way. 2. To interfere in other people's business or conversation. **Atravesarse en una conversación,** to butt into a conversation. 3. To have a dispute. 4. *(Naut.)* to cross the course of another vessel under her head or stern. **(Yo atravieso, yo atraviese,** from **Atravesar.** *V.* ACERTAR).

atrayente [ah-tra-yen'-tay], *a.* Attractive.

atrazar [ah-tra-thar'], *va.* To practise artifices, to scheme.

atrechar [ah-tray-chahr'], *vn. (Carib.)* To take a short cut.

atrecho [ah-tray'-cho], *m. (Carib.)* A short cut.

atreguado, da [ah-tray-goo-ah'-do, dah], *a.* Rash, foolish, precipitate, or deranged.

atreguar [ah-tray-goo-ahr'], *va.* To grant a truce to. *-vr.* To agree to a truce.

atrenzo [ah-trayn'-tho], *m. (LAm.)* Trouble, difficulty; **estar en un atrenzo,** to be in trouble.

atresia [ah-tray'-se-ah], *f.* Closure or absence of a natural passage or channel of the body; atresia.

atresnalar [ah-tres-nah-lar'], *va. (Prov.)* To collect sheaves of corn into heaps.

atreverse [ah-tray-verr'-say], *vr.* 1. To dare, to venture. **No me atrevo, no me atrevería,** I wouldn´t dare. **Atreverse a hacer algo,** to dare to do something. 2. To be insolent or disrespectful. 3. To manage. **¿Te atreves con un pastel?** Can you manage a cake?

atrevidamente [ah-tray-ve-dah-men'-tay], *adv.* Audaciously, daringly, boldly, confidently.

atrevidillo, lla [ah-tray-ve-deel'-lyo, lyah], *a. dim.* Somewhat audacious.

atrevidísimo, ma [ah-tray-ve-dee'-se-mo, mah], *a. sup.* Most audacious.

atrevido, da [ah-tray-vee'-do, dah], *a.* 1. Bold, audacious, daring, fearless, high-spirited, hardy. 2. Forward, free, confident, insolent. *-pp.* of ATREVERSE.

atrevido [ah-tray-vee'-do], *m.* A muscle on the shoulder-blade.

atrevimiento [ah-tray-ve-me-en'-to], *m.* 1. Boldness, audaciousness, daringness. 2. Confidence, face, front.

atrevismo [ah-tray-vcs'-mo], *m.* Ostentatious daring.

atrezzo [ah-tray'-tho], *m. (Theat.)* Properties.

atriaquero [ah-tre-ah-kay'-ro], *m.* A manufacturer and retailer of treacle.

atribución [ah-tre-boo-the-on'], *f.* 1. The act of attributing something to another. 2. Attribute.

atribuible [ah-tre-boo-e'-blay], *a.* Attributable. **Obras atribuibles a Góngora,** works which are attributed to Góngora.

atribuir [ah-tre-boo-eer'], *va.* To attribute, to ascribe as a quality, to impute as a cause, to count, to charge to. **Las funciones atribuidas a mi cargo,** the powers conferred on me by my post. *-vr.* To assume, to arrogate to oneself.

atribulación [ah-tre-boo-lah-the-on'], *f.* affliction, suffering, tribulation.

atribulado [ah-tre-boo-lah-do], 1. *a.* Afflicted, suffering. 2. *m.* **Los atribulados,** the afflicted.

atribular [ah-tre-boo-lar'], *va.* To vex, to afflict. *-vr.* To be vexed, to suffer tribulation.

atributar [ah-tre-boo-tar'], *va. (Obs.)* to impose tribute.

atributivo, va [ah-tre-boo-tee'-vo, vah], *a.* Attributive.

atributo [ah-tre-boo'-to], *m.* Attribute, the thing attributed to another; a quality adherent. *(Yo atribuyo, atribuya; atribuyó, atribuyeron,* from *Atribuir. V.* INSTRUIR).

atricapilla [ah-tre-cah-peel'-lyah], *f. (Orn.)* The Epicurean warbler.

atriceses [ah-tre-tahy'-ses], *m. pl.* The staples or iron rings to which the stirrup-straps are fastened.

atrición [ah-tre-the-on'], *f.* 1. Contrition, grief for sin arising from the fear of punishment. 2. *(Vet.)* Contraction of the principal nerve in a horse's fore leg. 3. Attrition, the wearing away of anything by rubbing, or friction.

atril [ah-treel'], *m.* 1. Reading-desk; stand for the missal. 2. A music-stand, or holder.

atrincar [ah-treen-cahr'], *va. (LAm.)* To tie up tightly. *-vr. (Mex.)* To be stubborn, dig one's heels in.

atrincheramiento [ah-trin-chay-rah-me-en'-to], *m.* Entrenchment, lodgment, mound. **Atrincheramientos de abordaje,** *(Naut.)* Close quarters, breast-works on board of merchant ships, from behind which the crew defend themselves when boarded by an enemy.

atrincherar [ah-trin-chay-rar'], *va.* To entrench, to fortify with a trench, to mound. *-vr.* To cover oneself from the enemy by means of trenches. **Están muy fuertemente atrincherados,** *(fig.)* They are very strongly entrenched.

atrio [ah'-tre-o], *m.* 1. Porch, a roof supported by pillars between the principal door of a palace and the staircase. 2. Portico, a covered walk before a church-door. 3. An interior, uncovered courtyard.

atrípedo, da [ah-tree'-pay-do, dah], *a. (Zool.)* Black-footed.

atrirrostro, tra [ah-trir-ros'-tro, trah], *a.* Black-beaked (pájaros).

atrito, ta [ah-tree'-to, tah], *a.* Contrite through fear.

atrochar [ah-tro-char'], *vn.* To go by cross paths; to make a short cut.

atrocidad [ah-tro-the-dahd'], *f.* 1. Atrocity or atrociousness, flagitiousness, foulness, outrage, grievousness; enormous wickedness. 2. Excess. **Es una atrocidad lo que come o lo que trabaja,** he eats or works to excess. 3. Silly remark; **decir atrocidades,** to say silly things.

atrofia [ah-tro'-fe-ah], *f.* Atrophy, a gradual wasting of the body.

atrofiar [ah-tro-fe-ahr'], *f.* Atrophy. *vr.* To waste away, to atrophy.

atrojarse [ah-tro-har'-say], *vr. (Mex. Coll.)* To be stumped, to find no way out of a difficulty.

atrompetado, da [ah-trom-pay-tah'-do, dah] *a.* Trumpet-like, having the shape of a trumpet. **Tiene narices atrompetadas,** his nostrils are as wide as the mouth of a trumpet.

atronadamente [ah-tro-nah-dah-men'-tay], *adv.* Precipitately, without prudence or reflection.

atronado [ah-tro-nah'-do], *m.* Blunderer, wild. *-a.* Acting in a precipitate, imprudent manner. *-pp.* of ATRONAR.

atronador, ra [ah-tro-nah-dor, rah], *m. & f.* Thunderer, one who makes a thundering noise.

atronadura [ah-tro-nah-doo'-rah], *f.* 1. Crack or split in wood, from periphery inward, following the medullary rays. 2. *V.* ALCANZADURA.

atronamiento [ah-tro-nah-me-en'-to], *m.* 1. The act of thundering. 2. Stupefaction caused by a blow. 3. Crepance or ulcer in the feet or legs of horses.

atronar [ah-tro-nar'], *va.* 1. To make a great noise in imitation of thunder. 2. To stun, to stupefy. 3. To stop the ears of horses, to prevent their fright at noises. *-vr.* 1. To be thunder-struck. 2. To die from effect of a thunder-storm, said of chickens in the egg and of silkworms in the cocoon.

atronerar [ah-tro-nay-rar'], *va.* To make embrasure in a wall.

atropado, da [ah-tro-pah'-do, dah], *a.* Grouped, clumped (árboles, plantas). *-pp.* of ATROPAR.

atropar [ah-tro-par'], *va.* To assemble in groups without order, to conglomerate, to clutter.

atropelladamente [ah-tro-pel-lyah-dah-men'-tay], *adv.* Tumultuously, confusedly, helter-skelter.

atropellado, da [ah-tro-pel-lyah'-do, dah], *a.* Hasty, precipitate, speaking or acting in a hasty, precipitate manner. *-pp.* of ATROPELLAR.

atropellador, ra [ah-tro-pel-lyah-dor', rah], *m. & f.* 1. Trampler, one who overturns or tramples underfoot. 2. Transgressor, violator. 3. Lout, hooligan.

atropellamiento [ah-tro-pel-lyah-me-en'-to], *m.* Trampling underfoot; confusedness.

atropellaplatos [ah-tro-pel-lyah-plah'-tos], *f.* Clumsy servant; clumsy sort.

atropellar [ah-tro-pel-lyar'], *va.* 1. To run over, to tread underfoot. 2. **Atropellar las leyes,** to act in defiance of the law. 3. To insult with abusive language. 4. To hurry, to confuse. **Atropellar al caballo,** to overwork a horse. 5. *(LAm.)* To make love to; to seduce, dishonor. *-vn. (fig.)* To disregard; **atropellar por todo,** not to respect anything. *-vr.* To hurry oneself too much.

atropello [ah-tro-payl'-lyo], *m.* 1. Upset, act of upsetting. 2. Abuse, insult, outrage. **Los atropellos del dictador,** the dictator's crimes.

atropina [ah-tro-pee'-nah], *f.* Atropine, an alkaloid extracted from (Atropa) belladonna: highly poisonous.

atropos [ah-tro'-pos], *f.* 1. One of the three Fates. 2. A species of African viper. 3. *m.* The death's-head moth.

atroz [ah-troth'], *a.* 1. Atrocious, enormous, heinous, fiend-like. 2. Cruel, dreadful, outrageous. 3. Huge, vast, immense. **Estatura atroz,** enormous stature.

atrozar [ah-tro-thar'], *va. (Naut.)* To truss a yard to the mast.

atrozmente [ah-troth'-men-tay], *adv.* 1. Atrociously, heinously. 2. Excessively, to excess. **Trabajar atrozmente,** to work to excess.

atruhanado, da [ah-troo-ah-nah'-do, dah], *a.* Scurrilous, acting the buffoon, using low jests. *(Yo atrueno, yo atruene,* from *Atronar. V.* ACORDAR).

A.T.S. *m. & f. abr.* de **ayudante técnico sanitario** (nursing assistant).

atta., atto. *abr.* de **atenta, atento** (in courtesy formula in letters).

attaché [ah-tah-shay'], *m.* Attaché case.

attrezzo [ah-tray'-tho], *m. (Theat.)* Properties.

atuendo [ah-too-enn'-do], *m.* Attire, garb. 2. Pomp, ostentation.

atufado [ah-too-fah'-do], *a. (Cono Sur)* Angry, mad. *(CAm. Carib.)* Proud, vain, stuck-up.

atufamiento [ah-too-fah-me-ayn'-to], *m. (fig.)* Irritation, vexation.

atufar [ah-too-far'], *va.* To vex, to plague; to inhale noxious vapors. To irritate. *-vr.* 1. To be on the fret (licores fermentados). 2. To be angry. 3. *(CAm. Carib.)* To be proud.

atufo [ah-too'-fo], *m.* Vexation, irritation.

atulipanado [ah-too-le-pah-nah-do], *a.* Tulip-shaped.

atún [ah-toon'], *m.* 1. Tunny, tunnyfish, tuna, tuna fish. **Pedazo de atún,** an ignorant, stupid fellow. **Por atún y ver al duque,** to kill two birds with one stone. 2. A shrub of the Moluccas.

atunara [ah-too-nah'-rah], *f.* A place where tunny-fishes are caught.

atunera [ah-too-nay'-rah], *f.* A fishing-hook used in the tunny-fishery.

atunero [ah-too-nay'-ro], *m.* A fisherman engaged in the tunny fishery; a fishmonger who deals in tunny-fish.

aturar [ah-too-rar'], *va.* 1. To endure; to bear toil. 2. To work with judgement or prudence. 3. To stop or close tightly, hermetically.

aturdidamente [ah-toor-dee'-dah-men-tay], *adv.* 1. Thoughtlessly, recklessly. 2. In a bewildered way.

aturdido, da [ah-toor-dee'-do, dah], *a.* Hare-brained, madbrain, giddy, wild, stupid. *-pp.* of ATURDIR.

aturdidura [ah-toor-de-doo'-rah], *f. (Cono Sur)* Stunned, dazed condition; bewilderement, confusion.

aturdimiento [ah-toor-de-me-en'-to], *m.* Perturbation of mind; dullness, drowsiness; consternation.

aturdir [ah-toor-deer'], *va.* 1. To perturb or perturbate, to confuse, to stun. 2. To stupefy with wonder or admiration. **La noticia nos aturdió**, the news stunned us. *-vr.* To be out of one's wits; to be perturbed or stupefied.

aturrullado [ah-too-roo-lyah'-do], *a.* Bewildered, perplexed; flustered.

aturrullar [ah-too-roo-lyar'], 1. *va.* To bewilder, perplex; to fluster. *-vr.* To get bewildered; to get flustered; **no te aturrulles cuando surja una dificultad**, don´t get flustered when something awkward comes up.

aturullar [ah-toor-rool-lyar'], *va. (coll.)* To confound, to reduce to silence. Cf. TURULATO.

atusador [ah-too-sah-dor'], *m.* 1. Hair-dresser. 2. One who trims plants in a garden.

atusar [ah-too-sar'], *va.* 1. To cut hair even, to comb it smooth and even. 2. To trim the plants in a garden. *-vr.* To dress oneself with too much care.

atutía [ah-too-tee'-ah], *f.* Tutty, a sublimate of calamine collected in a furnace; crude zinc oxide.

auca [ah'-oo-cah], *f.* A goose. *V.* OCA.

audacia [ah-oo-dah'-teh-ah], *f.* Audacity, boldness.

audaz [ah-oo-dath'], *a.* Bold, audacious, fearless.

audazmente [ah-oo-dath'-men-tay], *adv.* Boldly, audaciously.

audibilidad [ah-oo-de-be-le-dahd'], *f.* Audibility.

audible [ah-oo-dee'-blay], *a.* Audible, that may be heard.

audición [ah-oo-de-the-on'], *f.* Audition, hearing. 2. *(Theat. etc.)* Audition; **dar audición a uno**, to audition somebody. 3. *(Mus.)* Concert. 4. *(LAm.)* Audit.

audiencia [ah-oo-de-en'-the-ah], *f.* 1. Audience, a hearing given by men in power to those who have something to propose or represent. 2. Audience-chamber. 3. A court of oyer and terminer. 4. Law-officers appointed to institute some judicial inquiry. 5. **Audiencia pública**, public hearing. 6. **Audiencia pretorial en Indias**, a court of judicature in the West Indies.

audífono [ah oo dee' fo no], *m.* 1. Earphone, hearing aid. 2. Telephone receiver.

audiófilo, la [ah-oo-de-o'-fe-lo, lah], *m. & f.* Audiophile.

audiofrecuencia [ah-oo-de-o-fray-coo-en'-the-ah], *f.* Audiofrequency.

audiología [ah-o -de-o-lo-hee'-ah], *f.* Audiology.

audiómetro [ah-oo-de-o'-may-tro], *m.* Audiometer.

audión [ah-oo-de-on'], *m.* Audion, (used in long distance telephone calls and radio communication).

audioteleconferencia [ah-oo-de-o-tay-lay-con-fay-ren-the-ah], *f. (Comp.)* Audio teleconferencing

audiovisual [ah-oo-de-o-ve-soo-ahl'], *a.* Audio-visual.

auditar [ah-oo-de-tahr'], *va.* To audit.

auditivo, va [ah-oo-de-tee'-vo, vah], *a.* 1. Auditive, auditory, having the power of hearing. 2. Invested with the right of giving an audience.

audito [ah-oo-de'-to], *m.* Audit, auditing.

auditor [ah-oo-de-tor'], *m.* 1. Auditor, a hearer. 2. A judge advocate. **Auditor de la nunciatura**, a delegate of the Nuncio, appointed to hear and decide appeal causes respecting complaints against bishops. **Auditor de Rota**, one of the twelve prelates who compose the Rota at Rome, a court which inquires into and decides appeal causes in ecclesiastical matters. **Auditor de proceso electrónico de datos** *(Comp.)*, Electronic data processing auditor (o EDP auditor).

auditoría [ah-oo-de-to-ree'-ah], *f.* The place and office of an *auditor*.

auditorio [ah-oo-de-to'-re-o], *m.* Auditory, an audience; congregation.

auditorio, ría [ah-oo-de-to'-re-o, ah], *a.* Auditory, *V.* AUDITIVO.

auge [ah'-oo-hay], *m.* 1. Meridian, the highest point of glory, power, dignity or fortune. 2. *(Astr.)* Apogee of a planet or star.

augur [ah-oo-goor'], *m.* Augur, augurer, person who pretends to predict future events by the flight of birds.

auguración [ah-oo-goo-rah-the-on'], *f.* Auguration, the act or prognosticating by the flight of birds.

augurar [ah-oo-goo-rahr'], *va.* To augur, to foresee, to foretell, to predict (predecir).

augurual [ah-oo-goo-rahl'], *a.* Augurial, belonging to augury.

augurio [ah-oo-goo'-re-o], *m.* Augury; omen, portent; prediction; **consultar los augurios**, to take the auguries. *V.* AGÜERO.

augustal [ah-goos-tahl'], *a.* Augustan.

Augusto, ta [ah-goos'-to, tah], *a.* August, magnificent, majestic. *-m.* title of the Roman emperors after Octavious Cesar.

aula [ah'-oo-lah], *f.* 1. Hall where lectures are given. 2. The court or palace of a sovereign.

aulaga [ah-oo-lah'-gah], *f.* Furze, gorse.

aulario [ah-oo-lah'-re-o], *m. (Univ.)* Lecture room building, block of lecture rooms.

áulico [ah'-oo-le-co], 1. *a.* Court, palace. 2. *m.* Courtier.

aullador, ra [ah-ool-lyah-dor', rah], *m. & f.* Howler.

aullar [ah-ool-lyar'], *vn.* To howl, to yell, to cry: applied to wolves and dogs.

aullido, aúllo [ah-ool-lyee'-do, ah-ool'-lyo], *m.* Howl, the cry of a wolf or dog; a cry of horror or distress.

aumentación [ah-oo-men-tah-the-on'], *f.* 1. Augmentation, increase. 2. *(Rhet.)* Climax.

aumentado, da [ah-oo-men-tah-do, dah], *a.* Increased, augmented, onward. *-pp.* of AUMENTAR.

aumentador, ra [ah-oo-men-tah-dor', rah], *m. & f.* Enlarger, amplifying.

aumentar [ah-oo-men-tar'], *va.* To augment, to increase, to enlarge. **Aumento de población**, population increase. **Aumento de precio**, rise in price. **En aumento**, to increase. *-vr.* To gather, to grow larger.

aumentativo, va [ah-oo-men-tah-tee'-vo, vah], *a.* Increasing, enlarging.

aumento [ah-oo-men'-to], *m.* 1. Augmentation, increase, enlargement. 2. Access, accession; growth. **Aumento**, Promotion, advancement.

aun [ah-oon'], *adv.* 1. Even, nevertheless. **Te daría 100 dólares, y aun 200**, I'd give 100 dollars, even 200. **El libro es bueno aun con esas faltas**, the book is good even with those faults. 2. **Aun cuando**, even though.

aún [ah-oon'] *adv.* Still, yet. *V.* TODAVÍA and TAMBIÉN. **No ha llegado aún**, he hasn't arrived yet. **Aún está aquí**, he's still here.

aunar [ah-oo-nar'], *va.* 1. To unite, to assemble. 2. To incorporate, to mix. *-vr.* To be united or confederated for one end.

aunque [ah-oon-kay'], *adv.* Though, although, even if. **Aunque llueva vendremos**, we´ll come even if it rains. **Es guapa aunque algo bajita**, she´s pretty although rather short.

aúpa [ah-oo'-pah], *(coll.)* Up, up: a word used to animate children to get up. *-a.* **Una función de aúpa**, a slap-up do. **Una paliza de aúpa**, a thrashing and a half.

aupar [ah-oo-pahr'], *va.* To help up, get up (persona); *(fig.)* To boost, praise up; **aupar a uno al poder**, to raise somebody to power.

aura [ah'-oo-rah], *f.* 1. A vulture of Mexico and Cuba. 2. *(Poetic.)* A gentle breeze. **Aura popular**, *(Met.)* Popularity. 3. Aura, a peculiar premonitory symptom of epilepsy, a feeling as of a breath of air rising from below to the trunk and head.

auranciáceo [ah-oo-ran-the-ah'-thay-o], *a.* *(Bot.)* Citrus, citrous.

áureo, rea [ah'-oo-ray-o, ah], *a.* Golden, gilt, gold.

aureolar, auréola [ah-oo-ray-o'-lah], *f* Aureola, a circle of rays of light emblematic of glory.

aurícula [ah-oo-ree'-coo-lah], *f.* 1. Auricle, one of the two upper cavities of the heart. 2. *(Bot.)* The bear's-ear. 3. Auricle, the external ear.

auricular [ah-oo-re-coo-lar'], *a.* 1. Auricular, within the sense or reach of hearing. 2. Auricularis (dedo meñique).

auricular, *m.* 1. Headphone. 2. Earpiece or telephone receiver. **Auricular de casco**, headset.

aurífero, ra [ah-oo-ree'-fay-ro, rah], *a.* *(Poetic.)* Auriferous, containing or producing gold.

auriga [ah-oo-ree'-gah], *m.* 1. *(Poetic.)* A coachman. 2. *(Astr.)* Charioteer or Wagoner, one of the Northern constellations.

aurora [ah-oo-ro'-rah], *f.* 1. Dawn. 2. *(Poetic.)* The first appearance of a thing. 3. A beverage, simond-milk and cinnamon-water. 4. *(Naut.)* The morning watch-gun. 5. **Aurora boreal**, aurora borealis, or northern lights.

auscultación [ah-oos-cool-tah-the-on'], *f.* Sounding, auscultation.

auscultar [ah-oos-cool-tar'], *va.* To auscultate, to listen with ear or stethoscope as a means of diagnosis.

ausencia [ah-oo-sen'-the-ah], *f.* Absence. **Servir ausencias y enfermedades**, to perform the functions of absent or sick persons. **Tener alguno buenas o malas ausencia**, to be ill or well spoken of in one's absence. **En ausencia del gato se divierten los ratones**, when the cat´s away the mice will play.

ausentarse [ah-oo-sen-tar'-say], *vr.* To absent oneself.

ausente [ah-oo-sen'-tay], *a.* Absent, distant. **Estar ausente de**, to be absent from.

auspiciado [ah-oos-pe-the-ah'-do], *a.* *(LAm.)* Sponsored, backed.

auspiciar [ah-oos-pe-the-ar'], *va.* To promote, sponsor, foster.

auspicio [ah-oos-pee'-the-o], *m.* 1. Auspice, or presage drawn from birds. 2. *(Met.)* Prediction of future events. 3. Protection, favor, patronage. **Bajo los auspicios de Vd.**, under your protection or your guidance.

austeramente [ah-oos-tay-rah-men'-tay], *adv.* Austerely, frowningly.

austeridad [ah-oos-tay-re-dahd'], *f.* Austerity, severity, rigor. **Austeridad económica**, economic austerity.

austero, ra [ah-oos-tay'-ro, rah], *a.* 1. Harsh, astringent to the taste. 2. Retired, mortified, and penitent. 3. Severe, rigid, harsh, austere.

austral, austrino, na [ah-oos-trahl', ah-oos-tree'-no, nah], *a.* Austral, southern.

Australia [ah-oos-trah-le-ah] Australia.

australiano, na [ah-oos-trah-le-an'-no, nah], *a. & m. & f.* Australian.

austriaco, ca [ah-oos-tre-ah'-co, cah[, *a.* Austrian; of Austria.

austro [ah'-oos-tro], *m.* South wind; Notus.

autarquía [ah-oo-tar-kee'-ah], *f.* 1. Autarchy. Self government. 2. Autarky.

autazo [ah-oo-tah'-tho], *m.* *(LAm.)* Theft of a car.

auténtica [ah-oo-ten'-te-cah], *f.* Certificate, certification; authorized copy.

autenticación [ah-oo-ten-te-cah-the-on'], *f.* Authentication.

auténticamente [ah-oo-ten'-te-cah-men'-tay], *adv.* Authentically.

autenticar [ah-oo-ten-te-car'], *va.* To authenticate, to attest.

autenticidad [ah-oo-ten-te-the-dahd'], *f.* Authenticity.

auténtico, ca [ah-oo-ten'-te-co, cah], *a.* Authentic, genuine, veritable, indisputable, official. **Es un auténtico campeón**, he´s a real champion. **Días de auténtico calor**, days of real heat.

autentificar [ah-ten-te-fe-cahr'], *va.* To authenticate.

autería [ah-oo-tay-re'-ah], *f.* *(Cono Sur)* Evil omen, bad sign; witchcraft.

autero, ra [ah-tay'-ro], *m. & f.* *(LAm.)* Car thief.

autero, ra [ah-oo-tay'-ro], *m. & f.* *(Cono Sur)* Pessimistic, defeatist; jins, person who brings bad luck.

autillo [ah-oo-teel'-lyo], *m.* 1. *(dim.)* A particular act of decree of the Inquisition. 2. *(Orn.)* The barn-owl.

autismo [ah-oo-tes'-mo], *m.* Autism.

autista [ah-oo-tes'-tah], *a.* Autistic.

auto [ah'-oo-to], *m.* 1. A judicial decree or sentence. 2. A writ, warrant. 3. An edict, ordinance. **Auto de Fe**, the sentence given by the Inquisition. 4. *(Obs.)* Act, action. **Auto definitivo**, definitive act, which has the force of a sentence. **Auto sacramental**, an allegorical or dramatical piece of poetry on some religious subject, represented as a play. **Autos**, the pleadings and proceedings in a lawsuit. **Estar en autor or en los autos**, to know a thing profoundly. **Auto acordado**, a sentence or decision of a supreme court, to be observed as a precedent.

auto [ah'-oo-to], *m.* Auto, automobile, car.

autoabastecerse [ah-oo-to-ah-bas-tay-thayr'-say], *vr.* To supply oneself.

autoacusación [ah-oo-to-ah-coo-sah-the-on'], *f.* Self-accusation.

autoacusarse [ah-oo-to-ah-coo-sahr'-say], *vr.* To accuse oneself.

autoadhesivo [ah-oo-to-ah-day-se'-vo], *a.* Self-adhesive; self-sealing.

autoadulación [ah-oo-to-ah-doo-lah-the-on'], *f.* Self-pray.

autoaislarse [ah-oo-to-ah-es-lahr'-say], *vr.* To isolate oneself.

autoalimentación [ah-oo-to-ah-le-mayn-tah-the-on'], *f.* **Autoalimentación de hojas**, automatic paper feed.

autoanálisis [ah-oo-to-ah-nah'-le-ses], *m.* Self-analysis.

autoayuda [ah-to-ah-yoo'-dah], *f.* Self-help.

autobiografía [ah-oo-to-be-o-gra-fee'-ah], *f.* Autobiography.

autobiográfico, ca [ah-oo-to-be-o-grah'-fe-co, cah], *a.* Autobiographical.

autobombearse [ah-oo-to-bom-bay-ahr-say], *vr.* To blow one´s own trumpet, to shoot a line.

autobombo [ah-oo-to-bom'-bo], *m.* Self-praise.

autobús [ah-oo-to-boos'], *m.* Bus, motorbus. **Autobús de dos pisos**, double-decker bus.

autocamión [ah-oo-to-cah-me-on'], *m.* Motor truck.

autocar [ah-oo-to-car'], *m.* Coach, bus.

autocaravana [ah-oo-to-cah-rah-vah'-nah], *f.* Camper, camping vehicle.

autocarril [ah-oo-to-car-reel'], *m.* *(LAm.)* Railway car.

autocensura [ah-oo-to-thayn-soo-rah], *f.* Self-censorship.

autocine [ah-oo-to-the'-nay], *m.* Drive-in cinema.

autoclave [ah-oo-to-clah'-vay], *f.* Autoclave, sterilizer.

autoconfesado [ah-oo-to-con-fay-sah'-do], *a.* Self-confessed.

autoconfesarse [ah-oo-to-con-fay-sahr'-say], *vr.* To confess oneself.

autoconfesión [ah-oo-to-con-fay-se-on'], *f.* Self-confession.

autoconfianza [ah-oo-to-con-fe-ahn'-thah], *f.* Self-confidence.

autoconservación [ah-oo-to-con-ser-vah-the-on'], *f.* Self-preservation.

autoconvencerse [ah-oo-to-con-vayn-thayr'-say], *vr.* To convince oneself.

autocracia [ah-oo-to-crah'-the-ah], *f.* Autocracy, absolute sovereignty.

autócrata [ah-oo-to'-crah-tah], *m.* Autocrat.

autocrático, ca [ah-oo-to-crah'-te-co, cah], *a.* Autocratical.

autocremarse [ah-oo-to-cray-mahr'-say], *vr.* To set fire to oneself, to burn oneself.

autocrítica [ah-oo-to-cre'-te-cah], *f.* Self-criticism, self examination.

autocrítico [ah-oo-to-cre'-te-co], *a.* Self-critical.

autóctono, na [ah-oo-toc'-to-no, nah], *a.* Autochthonous, native of the country.

auto-choque [ah-oo-to-cho'-ke], *m.* Bumper car.
autodefensa [ah-to-day-fen'-sah], *f.* Self-defence.
autodegradación [ah-oo-to-day-grah-dah-the-on'], *f.* Self-abasement.
autodenominarse [ah-oo-to-day-no-me-nahr'-say], *vr.* To call oneself.
autodestructivo [ah-oo-to-days-trooc-te'-vo], *a.* Self-destructive.
autodestruirse [ah-oo-to-days-troo-eer'-say], *a.* To self-destruct.
autodeterminación [ah-oo-to-day-tayr-me-nah-the-on'], *f.* Self-determination.
autodidacta [ah-to-de-dac'-tah], *a. m. & f. V.* AUTODIDACTO.
autodidacto [ah-oo-to-de-dac'-to], 1. *a.* Self-educated, self-taught. 2. *m. & f.* Autodidact.
autodisciplina [ah-oo-to-dis-the-plee'-na], *f.* Self-discipline.
autodominio [ah-oo-to-do-me'-ne-o], *m.* Self-control.
autoengaño [ah-oo-to-ayn-gah'-nyo], *m.* Self-deception.
autoescuela [ah-oo-to-es-coo-ay'-lah], *f.* Driving school.
autoexpresión [ah-oo-to-ex-pray-se-on'], *f.* Self-expression.
autofinanciarse [ah-oo-to-fe-nahn-the-ahr'-say], *vr.* To finance oneself.
autógena [ah-oo-to'-hay-nah], *f.* Welding.
autogiro [ah-oo-to-hee'-ro], *m.* Autogiro.
autogobernarse [ah-oo-to-go-bayr-nahr'-say], *vr.* To govern itself.
autogobierno [ah-oo-to-go-be-ayr-no], *m.* Self-government.
autogol [ah-oo-to-gol'], *m.* Own goal.
autografía [ah-oo-to-grah-fee'-ah], *f.* The art of copying a writing or drawing by lithography.
autográfico, ca [ah-oo-to-grah'-fe-co, cah], *a.* Autographical.
autógrafo [ah-oo-toh'-grah-fo], *m.* Autograph.
autohotel [ah-oo-to-o'tel'], *m.* Motel.
autoimpuesto [ah-oo-to-em-poo-ays'-tao], *a.* Self-imposed.
autoinducción [ah-oo-to-in-dooc-the-on'], *f.* (*Elec.*) Self-induction.
autoinducido [ah-oo-to-en-doo-the'-do], *a.* Self-induced.
autoinflamación [ah-oo-to-en-flah-mah-the-on'], *f.* Spontaneous combustion.
autoinfligido [ah-oo-to-en-fle-he'-do], *a.* Self-inflicted.
autointoxicación [ah-oo-to-in-toc-se-cah-the-on'], *f.* Autointoxication, poisoning from toxic substances in the body.
autolesionarse [ah oo-to-lay-sc-o-nahr'-say], *vr.* To inflict injury on oneself.
autolimpiable [ah-oo-to-leem-pe-ah'-blay], *a.* Self-cleaning.
autollamarse [ah-oo-tol-lyah-mahr'-say], *vr.* To call oneself.
automación [ah-oo-to-mah-the-on'], *f.* Automation.
automarginado, da [ah-oo-to-mahr-he-nah-do], *a. m. & f.* Drop-out.
automarginarse [ah-oo-to-mahr-he-nahr'-say], *vr.* To drop out, to stay away from, to keep clear of.
autómata [ah-oo-toh'-mah-tah], *m.* 1. A machine containing in itself the power of motion. 2. Automaton, a machine imitating the actions of living animals.
automáticamente [ah-to-mah-te-cah-mayn-tay], *adv.* Automatically.
automático, ca [ah-oo-to-mah'-te-co, cah], *a.* Automatic.
automatismo [ah-oo-to-mah-tees'-mo], *m.* Automatism.
automatización [ah-oo-to-mah-tee-tha-the-on'], *f.* Automation. **Automatización de la oficina** (*Comp.*), office automation.
automatizar [ah-oo-to-mah-tee-thar'], *va.* To automate.
automedicarse [ah-oo-to-may-de-cahr'-say], *vr.* To treat oneself.
automedonte [ah-oo-to-may-don'-tay], *m.* (*LAm.*) Busdriver; driver.
automercado [ah-oo-to-mayr-cah'-do], *m.* (*Carib.*) Supermarket.
automoción [ah-oo-to-mo-the-on'], *f.* **La industria de la automoción**, the car industry.

automotor, ra [ah-oo-to-mo-tor', rah], *a.* Self-propelling.
automotriz [ah-oo-to-mo-treeth'], *a.* Automotive.
automóvil [ah-oo-to-mo'-veel], *m.* Automobile, car. **Automóvil acorazado**, armored car. **Automóvil de plaza**, taxi, taxicab. **Automóvil de segunda mano**, used car, second-hand car. **Automóvil de turismo**, touring car.
automovilismo [ah-oo-to-mo-ve-lees'-mo], *m.* Motoring; **automovilismo deportivo**, motor racing.
automovilista [ah-oo-to-mo-ve-lees'-tah], *m. & f.* Motorist, automobile rider.
automovilístico [ah-oo-to-mo-ve-lees'-te-co], *a.* Car; **accidente automovilístico**, car accident.
automutilación [ah-oo-to-moo-te-lah-the-on'], *f.* Self-mutilation.
automutilarse [ah-oo-to-moo-te-lahr'-say], *vr.* To mutilate oneself.
autonomía [ah-oo-to-no-mee'-ah], *f.* Autonomy, the condition of self-government, independence. 2. (*Náut. Aer.*) Range; **un avión de gran autonomía**, a long-range aircraft.
autonómico [ah-oo-to-no'-me-co], *a.* Relating to autonomy; **elecciones autonómicas**, elections for the autonomous regions.
autónomo, ma [ah-oo-to'-no-mo,mah], *a.* Autonomous, independent, free.
autopatrulla [ah-oo-to-pah-troo'-lyah], *m.* (*Mex.*) Patrol car.
autopegado [ah-oo-to-pay-gah-do], *a.* Self-sealing (sobre).
autopiano [ah-oo-to-pe-ah'-no], *m.* Player piano.
autopista [ah-oo-to-pees'-tah], *f.* Highway, freeway. **Autopista de acceso limitado**, freeway.
autoplastia [ah-oo-to-plahs'-te-ah], *f.* Anaplasty, plastic surgery.
autopolinización [ah-oo-to-po-le-ne-thah-the-on'], *f.* Self-pollination.
autoproclamado [ah-oo-to-pro-cla-mah-do], *a.* Self-proclaimed.
autoprofesor [ah-oo-to-pro-fay-sor'], *m.* Teaching machine.
autopropulsado [ah-oo-to-pro-pool-sah'-do], *a.* Self-propelled.
autopropulsión [ah-o-to-pro-pool-se-on'], *f.* Self-propulsion.
autoprotegerse [ah-oo-to-pro-tay-her'-say], *vr.* To protect oneself.
autopsia [ah-oo-top'-se-ah], *f.* Autopsy.
autopublicidad [ah-oo-to-poo-ble-the-dahd'], *f.* Self-advertisement.
autor [ah-oo-tor'], *m.* 1. Author, maker, composer. 2. Writer, one that composes a literary work. 3. Manager of a theater. 4. (*Law.*) Plaintiff or claimant. **Autor de nota**, a celebrated writer. 5. Speaking of watches, the maker. 6. The cause of anything. **Ser autor de**, to author.
autora [ah-oo-to'-rah], *f.* Authoress.
autoría [ah-oo-to-re'-ah], *f.* Authorship.
autoridad [ah-oo-to-ree-dahd'], *f.* 1. Authority or power derived from a public station, merit, or birth; credit. **Las autoridades**, the authorities. 2. Ostentation, display of grandeur. 3. Authority, words cited from a book or writing.
autoritario, ria [ah-oo-to-re-tah'-re-oh, ah], *m. & f. a.* Authoritarian.
autoritarismo [ah-oo-to-re-tah-res'-mo], *m.* Authoritarianism.
autoritativo, va [ah-oo-to-re-tah-tee'-vo, vah], *a.* Arrogant, assuming.
autorización [ah-oo-to-re-tha-the-on'], *f.* Authorization, permission, licence.
autorizadamente [ah-oo-to-re-thah-dah-men'-tay], *adv.* Authoritatively.
autorizado, da [ah-oo-to-re-thah'-do, dah, *a.* Respectable, commendable. *-pp.* of AUTORIZAR.
autorizador [ah-oo-to-re-thah-dor'], *m.* He who authorizes.
autorizar [ah-oo-to-re-thar'], *va.* 1. To authorize, to give power or authority to. **Autorizar a uno para**, to authorize somebody to. 2. To legalize, 3. To exalt.
autorradio [ah-oo-tor-rah'-de-o], *f.* Car radio.

autorretrato [ah-oo-to-ray-trah'-to], *m.* Self-portrait.

autorzuelo [ah-oo-tor-thoo-ay-lo], *m.* Scribbler, hack, penpusher.

autoservicio [ah-oo-to-ser-vee'-the-o], *m.* Self-service.

autosostenerse [ah-oo-to-sos-tay-nayr'-say], *vr.* To pay one´s own way, to be self-supporting.

auto-stop [ah-oo-to-stop'], *m.* Hitch-hiking. **Hacer autostop**, to hitch-hike.

autostopismo [ah-oo-to-ays-to-pes'-mo], *m.* Hitch-hiking.

autostopista [ah-oo-to-ays-to-pes'-tah], *m. & f.* Hitch-hiker.

autosuficiencia [ah-oo-to-soo-fe-the-en'-the-ah], *f.* Self-sufficiency.

autosuficiente [ ], *a.* Self-sufficient.

autosugestión [ah-oo-to-soo-hes-te-on'], *f.* Autosuggestion, self-suggestion.

autotitularse [ah-oo-to-tee-too-lahr'-say], *vr.* To title oneself.

autoventa [ah-oo-to-vayn'-tah], *atr.* **vendedor autoventa**, traveling salesman.

autovía [ah-oo-to-ve'-ah], *f.* Main road.

autovivienda [ah-oo-to-ve-ve-ayn'-dah], *f.* Caravan, trailer.

auvernia [ah-oo-ver'-ne-ah], *f.* Auvergne.

auxiliador, ra [ah-ook-se-le-ah-dor', rah], *m. & f.* Auxiliary, assistant.

auxiliar [ah-ook-se-le-ar'], *va.* 1. To aid, to help, to assist. 2. To attend a dying person.

auxiliar [ah-ook-se-le-ar'], *a.* Auxiliar, auxiliatory, helping, assistant. **Tropas auxiliares**, auxiliary troops. **Obispo auxiliar**, an assistant bishop. **Verbo auxiliar**, an auxiliary verb.

auxiliatorio, ria [ah-ook-se-le-ah-to'-re-o, ah], *a. (Law.)* Auxiliary.

auxilio [ah-ook-se'-lyo],*m.* Aid, help, assistance. **Auxilio social**, social work.

av. *abr.* de **Avenida** (avenue, av, ave.).

a/v. *(Com.) abr.* de **a vista** (at sight).

avacado, da [ah-vah-cah'-do, dah], *a.* Cow-like, resembling a cow: applied to a big-bellied horse.

avada [ah-vah'-dah], *m. (Carib.)* Queer.

avadarse [ah-vah-dar'-say], *vr.* 1. To become fordable. 2. *(Obs.)* To subside: applied to passion.

avahar [ah-vah-ar'], *va.* 1. To warm with the breath, or with steam and vapor. 2. To wither (plantas). *-vr.* To steam, to give off steam.

aval [ah-vahl'], *m.* Security, guarantee, indorsement (letras, cheques).

avalancha [ah-vah-lahn'-chah], *f.* Avalanche. *V.* ALUD.

avalar [ah-vah-lar'], *v. imp. (Prov.)* (The earth) trembles. *-va. (Com.)* To guarantee; *(fig.)* To support.

avalentado, da [ah-vah-len-tah'-do, dah], *a.* Bragging, boasting.

avalizar [ah-vah-le-thar'], *va.* To mark the dangerous spots in a channel with buoys.

avalo [ah-vah'-lo], *m. (Prov.)* 1. A slight movement. 2. An earthquake.

avalorar [ah-vah-lo-ar'], *va.* 1. To estimate, to value. 2. *(Met.)* To inspirit, to animate.

avaluación [ah-vah-loo-ah-the-on'], *f.* Valuation, rate, assessment.

avaluar [ah-vah-loo-ar'], *va.* To value, to appraise, to estimate.

avalúo [ah-vah-loo'-oh], *m.* Valuating, official appraisement.

avallar [ah-val-lyar'], *va.* To inclose a piece of ground with pales or hedges.

avambrazo [ah-vam-brah'-tho], *m.* Piece of ancient armor that served to cover the forearm.

avampiés [ah-vam-pe-ess'], *m. (Obs.)* Instep of boots, or spatterdashes.

avancarga [ah-van-car'-gah]: **cañon de avancarga**; muzzle loader.

avance [ah-van'-thay], *m.* 1. *(Mil.)* Advance, attack, assault. 2. Among merchants, an account of goods received and

sold. 3. A balance in one's favor. 4. *(Elec.)* Lead; *(Med.)* feed. 5. *(Cine)* Trailer; preview. **avance informativo**, advanced news, update. 6. *(CAm.)* Theft, looting.

avandicho [ah-van-dee'-cho], *(Obs.) V.* SOBREDICHO. Aforesaid.

avantal [ah-van-tahl'], *m. (Obs.)* Apron. *V.* DELANTAL.

avantalillo [ah-van-tah-leel'-lyo], *m. dim. (Obs.)* A small apron.

avante [ah-van'-tay], *adv.* 1. *(Naut.)* Ahead. **Hala avante**, pull ahead. 2. *(Obs.) V.* ADELANTE.

avantrén [ah-van-tren'], *m.* Limbers of a gun-carriage.

avanzada [ah-van-thah'-dah], *f. (Mil.)* Quitpost, reconnoitring body.

avanzado, da [ah-van-thah'-do, dah], *a.* Advanced; onward. **Avanzado de edad**, or **de edad avanzada**, advanced in years, stricken in years. *-pp.* of AVANZAR.

avanzar [ah-van-thar'], *vn.* 1. To advance, to attack, to engage, to come on. 2. To have a balance in one's favor. *-va.* 1. To advance, to push forward. 2. *(Carib.)* To vomit, to throw up. *-vr.* To advance, to move on, to push on. **No avanzo nada**, I'm not making any headway. **Avanzar a velocidad máxima** *(Comp.)*, to hurtle.

avanzo [ah-van'-tho], *m.* 1. Among merchants an account of goods received and sold. 2. A balance in one's favor.

avaramente [ah-vah-rah-men'-tay], *adv.* Avariciously, in a covetous manner, miserably.

avaricia [ah-vah-ree'-the-ah], *f.* Avarice, cupidity, covetousness.

avariciar [ah-va-ree-the-ar'], *va. & vn. (Obs.)* To covet, to desire anxiously.

avariciosamente [ah-vah-re-the-o-sah-men'-tay], *adv.* Greedily, covetously.

avaricioso, sa [ah-vah-re-the-o'-so, sah], *a.* 1. *V.* AVARIENTO. 2. Anxious to eat or drink.

avariento, ta [ah-vah-re-en'-to, tah], *a.* Avaricious, covetous, miserly, miserable, close, narrow.

avariosis [ah-v-ah-re-o'-sees], *f. (LAm.)* Syphillis.

avaro, ra [ah-vah'-ro, rah], *a.* Miserably, mean; **ser avaro de alabanzas**, to be sparing in one´s praise, to be mean with one´s praises. *V.* AVARIENTO.

avasallador [ah-vah-sah-lyah-dor'], *a.* Overwhelming; domineering.

avasallamiento [ah-vah-sah-lyah-me-ayn-to], *m.* Subjugation.

avasallar [ah-vah-sal-lyar'], *va.* To subdue, to subject, to enslave, to mancipate. *-vr.* To become subject, to become a vassal.

avatar [ah-vah-tahr'], *m.* Avatar, change, transformation; incarnation.

avda. *abr.* de **Avenida** (Avenue, av., ave.).

ave [ah'-vay], *f.* 1. Bird, a general name for the feathered kind. 2. Fowl. **Ave de rapiña**, a bird of prey. **Ave brava or silvestre**, a wild bird. **Ave fría**, lapwing, a kind of plover. Vanellus. **Todas las aves son sus pares,** birds of a feather flock together. **Es un ave**, he is very swift, active. **Ave nocturna**, *(Met.)* one who rambles about in the night-time. **Ave zonza**, a lazy, half-foolish person. **Ave de mal agüero**, bird of ill omen. **Ave de paso**, migratory bird, rolling stone (personas). **Ave zancuda**, Wader.

avecinar [ah-vay-the-nar'], *va.* 1. *(Obs.)* To bring near. 2. *V.* AVECINAR. *-vr.* To come near, to approach.

avecidamiento [ah-vay-thin-dah-me-en'-to], *m.* 1. Acquisiton of the rights of a citizen or freeman. 2. The act of residing in a place invested with the rights of a citizen.

avecindar [ah-vay-thin-dar'], *va.* To admit to the privilege of a denizen, to enrol in the number of the citizens of a place. *-vr.* 1. To acquire the rights and priviledges of a denizen or citizen. 2. To approach, to join.

avechucho [ah-vay-choo'-cho], *m.* 1. An ugly bird. 2. *(Orn.)* Sparrowhawk. 2. *(Met.)* Ragamuffin, a paltry mean fellow.

avechuco [ah-vay-choo'-co], *m.* Ugly bird (pájaro). Ragamuffin, pest (persona).

avefría [ah-vay-fre'-ah], *f.* Lapwing.
avejentado, da [ah-vay-hen-tah'-do, dah], *a.* Appearing old without being really so, oldish. *-pp.* of AVEJENTAR.
avejentar [ah-vay-hen-tar'], *va. & vr.* To look old, to appear older than one really is.
avejigar [ah-vay-he-gar'], *va.* To produce pimples or small blisters. *-vr.* To blister.
avelar [ah-vay-lar'], *vn. (Naut.)* To set sail.
avellana [ah-vel-lyah'-nah], *f.* Filbert, hazelnut. **Avellana índica** or **de la India**, or **nuez ungüentaria**, myrobalan, or Indian nut, used only in perfumes.
avellanado, da [ah-vel-lyah-nah'-do, dah], *a.* Nut-brown, of the color of nuts. *-pp.* of AVELLANARSE.
avellanador [ah-vel-lyah-na-dor'], *m.* Countersink bit, rose-bit; rimer.
avellanal [ah-vayl-lyah-nah], *m.* Hazel wood, hazel plantation.
avellanar [ah-vel-lyah-nar'], *m.* 1. A plantation of hazels or nut-trees. 2. *-va. (Tec.)* To countersink.
avellanarse [ah-vel-lyah-nar'-say], *vr.* To shrivel, to grow as dry as a nut.
avellanedo [ah-vay-lyah-nah'-do], *m.* Hazel wood, hazel plantation.
avellanera [ah-vel-lyah-nay'-rah], *f. V.* AVELLANO.
avellanero, ra [ah-vel-lyah-nay'-ro, rah], *m. & f.* A dealer in nuts and filberts.
avellanica [ah-vael-lyah-nee'-cah], *f. dim.* A small filbert.
avellano [ah-vel-lyah'-no], *m. (Bot.)* The common hazel-nut tree. Filbert-tree.
Avemaría [ah-vay-mah-ree'-ah], *f.* Ave Mary, the angel's salutation of the holy Virgin. **Al avemaría**, at the fall of night. **Es un avemaría**, in an instant. **Saber una cosa como el avemaría**, to know by heart, thoroughly. **¡Ave María!** Exclamation denoting surprise. **¡Ave María purísima!** God bless you!. **Un Avemaría**, a Hail Mary.
avena [ah-vay'-nah], *f. (Bot.)* 1. Oats. Avena, L. **Avena blanca**, Cultivated white oat. **Avena sativa alba. Avena negra**, cultivated black oat. **Avena sativa negra. Avena desnuda**, naked oat. (Avena nuda). **Avena estéril, cugua** or **cula**, bearded oat-grass. Avena esterilis. **Avena estrigosa**, or **afreitas** of the Gallicians, bristle-pointed oat. Avena estrigosa. **Avena pubescens**, downy oat-grass. Avena pubescens. **Avena flavescente**, narrow-leaved oat-grass. Avena pratensis. **Avena alpina**, great alpine oat-grass. Avena alpina. **Avena flavescente**, yellow oat-grass. Avena flavescens. **Avena loca** or **silvestre**, wild oat. **Avena común**, French oat. **Avena oriental**, tartarian oat. Avena orientalis. **Avena geórgica**, potato oat. 2. *(Poetic.)* A pastoral pipe, made of the stalks of corn, and used by shepherds.
avenáceo, cea [ah-vay-nah'-thay-o, ah], *a.* Oat-like.
avenado, da [ah-vay-nah'-do, dah], *a.* 1. *(Obs.)* Belonging or relating to oats. 2. Lunatic, liable to fits of madness, with lucid intervals. *-pp.* of AVENAR.
avenal [ah-vay-nahl'], *m.* A field sown with oats.
avenamiento [ah-vay-nah-me-en'-to], *m.* The act of draining off water.
avenar [ah-vay-nar'], *va.* To drain or draw off water.
avenate [ah-vay-nah'-tay], *m.* Water-gruel, oatmeal-gruel.
avenenar [ah-vay-nay-nar'], *va.* To poison. *V.* ENVENENAR.
avenencia [ah-vay-nen'-the-ah], *f.* 1. Agreement, compact, bargain. 2. Conformity, union, concord. **Más vale mala avenencia, que buena sentencia**, a bad compromise is better than a good lawsuit.
avenenteza, aveninteza [ah-vay-nen-tay'-thah, ah-vay-nin-tay'-thah], *f. (Obs.)* Occassion, opportunity. *(Yo avengo, yo avine,* from *Avenir. V.* VENIR). *(Yo me avengo, yo me avine,* from *Avenirse, V.* VENIR).
aveníceo, cea [ah-vay-nee'-tahy-o, ah], *a.* Oaten, belonging to or made of oats.
avenida [ah-vay-nee'-dah], *f.* 1. Avenue (calle). 2. Flood, inundation, freshet. 3. *(Met.)* A concurrence of several things.

4. Agreement, concord. **Avenidas**, 1. Avenues or roads meeting in a certain place. 2. *(Naut.)* Freshes.
avenido, da [ah-vay-nee'-do, dah], *a.* Agreed. **Bien or mal avenidos**, Living on good or bad terms. *-pp.* of AVENIR.
avenidor, ra [ah-vay-ne-dor'-rah], *m. & f. (Lit. us.)* Mediator, one that interferes between two parties to reconcile them.
avenimiento [ah-vay-ne-me-en'-to], *m.* Convention.
avenir [ah-vay-neer'], *va.* To reconcile parties at variance. *-vr.* 1. To settle differences on friendly terms. **No se avienen**, they don´t get on. 2. To join, to unite, to consent; be in harmony with. 3. To compound, to compromise.
aventadero [ah-ven-tah-day'-ro], *m. (Prov.)* A winnowing-place.
aventado, da [ah-ven-tah'-do, dah], *a.* **Escotas aventadas**, flowing sheets. *(CAm. Mex.)* Brave, daring. *-pp.* of AVENTAR.
aventador [ah-ven-tah-dor'], *m.* 1. Fanner, blower, blowing fan, ventilator. *(Arch.)* Scutcher. (Gas) Bat-wing. 2. Winnover, one who separates chaff from grain. 3. A wooden fork with three or four prongs, used for winnowing corn. 4. A fan used for blowing the fire.
aventadora [ah-vayn-tah-do'-rah], *f.* Winnowing machine.
aventadura [ah-ven-tah-doo'-rah], *f.* Wind-gall, a disease of horses, **aventadura de estopa**, *(Naut.)* A leak.
aventaja [ah-ven-tah'-hah], *f.* 1. Advantage, profit. 2. *(Law. Prov.)* Part of the personal estate or chattels of a person deceased, which his or her surviving consort takes before a division of the furniture is made.
aventajadamente [ah-ven-tah-hah-dah-men'-tay], *adv.* 1. Advantageously, conveniently, opportunely. 2. *(Prov.)* Exceedingly, well.
aventajado, da [ah-ven-tah-hah'-do, dah], *a.* 1. Advantageous, profitable, convenient. 2. Beautiful, excellent. 3. Having additional pay (soldados). *-pp.* of AVENTAJAR.
aventajar [ah-ven-tah-har'], *va.* 1. To acquire or enjoy advantages. 2. To ameliorate, to improve. 3. To surpass, to excel, to cut out. 4. To exceed, to excel.
aventar [ah-ven-tar'], *va.* 1. To move the air, to fan, to air. 2. To toss something in the wind, such as corn, to winnow it. 3. To expel, to drive away. 4. *(Naut.)* To work out the oakum (barcos). *-vr.* 1. To be inflated or puffed up. 2. To escape, to run away. 3. *(Prov.)* To be tainted (carne). 4. To beat it (largarse). 5. *(Mex.)* To decide. 5. *(LAm.)* To throw oneself, to take risks.
aventino [ah-ven-tee'-no], *m.* Aventine, one of the seven hills of Rome.
aventón [ah-vayn-ton], *m. (Mex.)* Throw; lift; **pedir aventón**, to hitch a lift.
aventura [ah-ven-too'-rah], *f.* 1. Adventure, event, incident. 2. Casualty, contingency, chance. 3. Adventure, an enterprise in which something must be left to hazard. 4. Hazar, risk. 5. Duty formerly paid to lords of the manor.
aventurado, da [ah-ven-too-rah'-do, dah], *a.* **Bienaventurado**, fortunate. **Malaventurado**, unfortunate. *-pp.* of AVENTURAR.
aventurar [ah-en-too-rar'], *va.* To venture to, to hazard, to risk, to endanger, to jump. *-vr.* To dare, take risks, take a chance.
aventurera [ah-vayn-too-ray'-rah], *f.* Adventuress.
aventurero [ah-ven-too-ray'-ro, rah], *a.* 1. Voluntary; undisciplined (reclutas, soldados). 2. Applied to a person who voluntarily goes to market to sell any articles. 3. *V.* ADVENEDIZO.
averamia [ah-vay-rah'-me-ah], *f.* A kind of duck.
averar [ah-vay-rar'], *va.* To aver, to certify, or affirm.
avergonzado, da [ah-ver-gon-thah'-do, dah], *a.* Ashamed, embarrassed, abashed.
avergonzar [ah-ver-gon-thar'], *va.* To shame, to abash, to confound, or to make ashamed, to put to the blush, to put out of countenance. *-vr.* To shame, or be ashamed, to blush for. **Avergonzarse por**, to be ashamed about. *(Yo avergüen-*

zo, yo avergüence, from *Avergonzar. V.* ACORDAR). (*Yo me avergüenzo, yo me avergüence,* from *Avergonzarse. V.* ACORDAR).

avería [ah-vay-ree'-ah], *f.* 1. Breakdown (coche). **Tuvieron una avería,** they had a breakdown. 2. Damage (mercancías). 3. Average. **Avería gruesa,** general average. **Avería particular,** particular average. **Avería ordinaria,** usual average. 4. In the India trade, a certain duty laid on merchants and merchandise. 5. A collection of birds; an aviary. **Hacer una avería,** to suffer an average. 6. (*Cono Sur*) Dangerous criminal, thug.

averiado, da [ah-vay-re-ah'-do, dah], *a.* Averaged, damaged. **Los faros están averiados,** the lights have failed. *-pp.* of AVERIARSE.

averiar [ah-vay-re-ahr'], *va.* To damage, spoil; (*Mech.*) To cause a breakdown.

averiarse [ah-vay-re-ar'-sa], *vr.* To make average, to sustain damage, to be damaged.

averiguable [ah-vay-re-goo-ah'-blay], *a.* Investigable, what may be verified or ascertained.

averiguación [ah-vay-re-goo-ah-the-on'], *f.* Investigation. **Averiguación judicial,** a judicial inquiry, an inquest.

averiguadamente [ah-vay-re-goo-ah-dah-men'-tay], *adv.* Certainly, surely.

averiguado [ah-vay-re-goo-dah'-do], *a.* Certain, established. **Es un hecho averiguado,** it is an established fact.

averiguador, ra [ah-vay-re-goo-ah-dor', rah], *m. & f.* A scarcher or examiner.

averiguar [ah-vay-re-goo-ar'], *va.* To inquire, to investigate, to find out. **Averiguarse con alguno,** to bring one to reason. **Averígüelo Vargas,** it is difficult to investigate. *-vn.* (*CAm. Mex.*) To quarrel, fight. *-vr.* **Averiguarse con uno,** to tie somebody down; to get along with somebody.

averiguata [ah-vay-re-goo-ah'-tah], *f.* (*Mex.*) Argument, fight.

averigüetas [ah-vay-re-goo-ay'-tahs], *m. & f.* Snooper, busybody.

averío [ah-vay-ree'-o], *m.* 1. (*Prov.*) Beast of burden. 2. Flock of birds. 3. Aviary.

averrugado, da [ah-ver-roo-gah'-do, dah], *a.* Having many pimples in the face. Warty.

averrugarse [ah-ver-roo-gar'-say], *vr.* (*Med.*) To show pimples or warts (piel).

aversión [ah-ver-se-on'], *f.* 1. Aversion, opposition, dislike. 2. Malevolence, abhorrence, loathing. 3. Fear, apprehension.

averso, sa [ah-ver'-so, sah], *a.* Averse, hostile; perverse.

avertir [ah-ver-teer'], *va. V.* APARTAR.

avestruz [ah-ves-trooth'], *m.* 1. (*Orn.*) Ostrich. 2. (*LAm.*) Idiot.

avetado, da [ah-vay-tah'-do, dah], *a.* Veined, scamed (minerales, madera).

avetarda, *f. V.* AVUTARDA.

avetoro [ah-vay-to'-ro], *m.* Bittern.

avezado [ah-vay-thah'-do], *a.* Accustomed; inured, experienced. **Los avezados en estos menesteres,** those experienced in such activities.

avezar [ah-vay-thar'], *va.* 1. To accustom, to habituate. 2. To train the hawk. *-vr.* To get used; to become accustomed. *V.* ACOSTUMBRAR.

aviación [ah-ve-ah-the-on'], *f.* Aviation, flying. **Aviación comercial,** commercial aviation or flying.

aviado [ah-ve-ah-do], *m.* (*Amer.*) One supplied with money and other articles to work a silver-mine. **Dejar a uno aviado,** to leave somebody in the lurch.

aviador [ah-ve-ah-dor'], *m.* 1. Aviator, flyer. 2. Supplier, provider. 3. (*And.* Carib, *Cono Sur*) (*Com.*) Mining speculator; moneylender.

aviadora [ah-ve-ah-do'-rah], *f.* Aviator, pilot.

aviar [ah-ve-ar'], *va.* 1. To provide articles for a journey. 2. To accoutre. To furnish one what is lacking for some object, especially money. 3. To hasten the execution of a thing. 4. **Aviar a uno,** to hurry somebody up. 5. (*LAm.*) (*Agri.*) To cas-

trate. *-vr.* To get ready, to prepare oneself. **Aviarse para hacer algo,** to get ready to do something.

aviatorio [ah-ve-ah-to-re-o], *a.* (*LAm.*) **Accidente aviatorio,** air crash, plane crash.

aviciar [ah-ve-the-ar'], *va.* 1. (*Obs.*) To render vicious. 2. To give a luxuriant bloom and verdure to plants and trees.

avícola [ah-ve'-co-lah], *a.* Chicken, poultry; **granja avícola,** chicken farm.

avicultor, ra [ah-ve-cool-tor'], *m. & f.* Chicken farmer, poultry farmer; bird fancier.

avicultura [ah-ve-cool-too'-rah], *f.* Aviculture, rearing of birds.

ávidamente [ah'-ve-dah-mayn-tay], *adv.* Avidly, eagerly; greedily.

avidez [ah-ve-deth'], *f.* Covetousness, greediness, avidity.

ávido, da [ah'-ve-do, dah], *a.* (*Poetic.*) Greedy, covetous; open-mouthed.

aviejarse [ah-ve-ay-har'-say], *vr.* To grow old. *V.* AVEJENTARSE.

aviento [ah-ve-en'-to], *m.* A winnowing fork with two or three prongs *V.* BIELDO. (*Yo aviento, yo aviente,* from *Aventar. V.* ACERTAR). (*Yo me aviento, yo me aviente,* from *Aventarse. V.* ACERTAR)

aviesamente [ah-ve-ay-sah-men'-tay], *adv.* Sinistrously, perversely.

avieso, sa [ah-ve-ay'-so, sah], *a.* 1. Fortuitous, irregular. 2. (*Met.*) Mischievous, perverse. 3. *m.* Abortion.

avigorar [ah-ve-go-rar'], *va.* To invigorate; to revive.

avilanado, da [ah-ve-lah-nah'-do, dah], *a.* (*Bot.*) Villous, downy (simiente de plantas). (*Zool.*) Hairy, feathery (insectos).

avilantarse [ah-ve-lan-tahr'-say], *vr.* To be insolent.

avilantez, avilanteza [ah-ve-lan-teth', ah-ve-lan-tay'-thah], *f.* Forwardness, boldness, audaciousness; shamelessness.

avillanado, da [ah-veel-lyah-nah'-do, dah], *a.* Having the manners of a peasant, clownish, mean. *-pp.* of AVILLANAR.

avillanar [ah-veel-lyah-nar'], *va.* To villanize, to debase. *-vr.* To grow mean or abject, to degenerate.

avinado, da [ah-ve-nah'-do, dah], *a.* Wine-colored; bibulous, hard-drinking (personas).

avinagrado, da [ah-ve-nah-grah'-do, dah], *a.* (*Met.*) Harsh of temper, crabbed, peevish. Sour, acid. *-pp.* of AVINAGRAR.

avinagrar [ah-ve-nah-grar'], *va.* To render sour, to make acid. *-vr.* To turn sour.

avío [ah-vee'-o], *m.* 1. Preparation, provision. 2. (*Amer.*) Money and other articles advanced for working silver-mines. 3. **Hacer su avío,** to make one´s pile. 4. **¡Al avío!,** get cracking!, get on with it! *-pl.* **Avíos de pescar,** fishing-tackle; the trimmings and other necessary articles for anything.

avión [ah-ve-on'], *m.* Airplane, aeroplane, plane. **Avión de bombardeo,** bomber. **Avión de reacción,** jet. **Avión de turbohélice,** turboprop. **Avión de turborreacción,** turbojet. **Avión supersónico,** supersonic plane. **Por avión,** By plane, by air mail. 2. (*Orn.*) Martin. 3. **Hacer el avión a uno,** to do somebody down, to cause harm to somebody.

avionazo [ah-ve-o-nah'-tho], *m.* Plane crash, accident to an aircraft.

avionero [ah-ve-o-nay'-ro], *m.* (*And. Cono Sur*) Airman, aircraftsman.

avioneta [ah-ve-o-nay'-tah], *f.* Light aircraft.

avisadamente [ah-ve-sah-dah-men'-tay], *adv.* Prudently.

avisado, da [ah-ve-sah'-do, dah], *a.* 1. Prudent, cautious. 2. Expert, sagacious, skilful, clever, clear-sighted. **Mal avisado,** Il-advised, injudicious. *-pp.* of AVISAR.

avisador [ah-ve-sah-dor'], *m.* Adviser; admonisher. (*Cine., Theat.*) Program seller.

avisar [ah-ve-sar'], *va.* 1. To inform, to give notice, to acquaint. **Avisar a uno con una semana de anticipación,** to let somebody know a week in advance, give somebody a week´s notice. 2. To advise, to counsel, to admonish. **Avisar**

con tiempo, avisar anticipadamente, to warn or to give warning.

aviso [ah-vee'-so], *m.* 1. Information, intelligence, notice, legal notice in the newspapers. 2. Prudence, care, attention; counsel. **Estar or andar sobre aviso**, to be on one's guard. 3. *(Naut.)* Advice-boat, a light vessel sent with despatches.

avispa [ah-vees'-pah], *f.* Wasp.

avispado, da [ah-vis-pah'-do, dah], *a.* Lively, brisk, vigorous. *(LAm.)* Jumpy, nervous. *-pp.* of AVISPAR.

avispar [ah-vis-par'], *va.* 1. To spur, to drive with the spur. 2. To investigate, to observe closely. *-vr.* To fret, to be peevish.

avispero [ah-vis-pay'-ro], *m.* 1. Nest made by wasps. 2. Cavities in which wasps lodge their eggs. 3. *(Med.)* Carbuncle: so named for the numerous perforations resembling the cells of a wasp-nest.

avispón [ah-vis-pone], *m.* Hornet, a large wasp.

avistar [ah-vis-tar'], *va.* To descry at a distance, to see far off. *-vr.* To have an interview, to transact business.

avitar [ah-ve-tar'], *va. (Naut.)* To bitt the cable.

avitelado [ah-ve-tay-lah'-do], *a.* Vellum-like.

avituallamiento [ah-ve-too-ah-lyah-me-ayn'-to], *m.* Victualling, provisioning, supplying.

avituallar [ah-ve-too-al-lyar'], *va. (Mil.)* To victual, to supply with provisions.

avivadamente [ah-ve-vah-dah-men'-tay], *adv.* In a lively manner, briskly.

avivado [ah-ve-vah'-do], *a. (Cono Sur)* Forewarned, alerted.

avivador, ra [ah-ve-vah-dor', rah], *m. & f.* 1. Enlivener; hastener. 2. Rabbet-plane; panel-plane. 3. *(Prov.)* Paper full of pin-holes laid over the eggs of silk-worms, that the young worms may creep through it. 4. *(Arch.)* Groin between mouldings; quirk.

avivar [ah-ve-var'], *va.* 1. To quicken, to enliven, to encourage, to hasten, **avivar el paso**, to hasten one's step. 2. To heat, to inflame. 3. To vivify the eggs of silk-worms; to revive. 4. To heighten colors. 5. *(Carp.)* To rabbet. *-vr.* To revive, to cheer up, to grow gay. **Avivar el ojo**, to be watchful.

avizor [ah-ve-thor'], *a.* **Estar ojo avizor**, to be on the alert.

avizorar [ah-ve-tho-rar'], *va.* To watch with attention, to spy, to search narrowly.

avo [ah'-vo], *m.* 1. One of the fractional parts into which a whole number is divided. Used as a suffix; as, *dozavo*, twelfth. 2. A tree from which Indians make paper.

avocable [ah-vo-cah'-blay], *a.* Transferable to a superior court.

avocación, *f.* **avocamiento,** *m.* [ah-vo-cah-thc-on', ah-vo-cah-me-en'-to], *(Law.)* The act of removing a lawsuit to a superior court.

avocado [ah-vo-cah'-do], *m.* The fruit of Persea gratissima, «alligator-pear». *V.* AGUACATE.

avocar [ah-vo-car'], *va. (Law.)* To remove a lawsuit to a superior court.

avocastro [ah-vo-cas'-tro], *m. (Cono Sur) V.* AVOCASTRO.

avoceta [ah-vo-thay'-tay], *f.* Avocet, a wading bird.

avogalla [ah-vo-gahl'-lyah], *f.* Gall-nut.

avolcanado, da [ah-vole-cah-nah'-do, dah], *a.* Volcanic.

avora [ah-vo'-rah], *f.* A kind of medicinal palm.

avorazado [ah-vo-rah-thah'-do], *a. (Mex.)* Greedy, grasping.

avucasta [ah-voo-dahs'-tah], *f.* Widgeon, a kind of wild duck.

avucastro [an-voo-cahs'-trol, *m.* Troubler or importunate person.

avugés *V.* AVUGUES.

avugo [ah-voo'-go], *m.* The fruit of the avuguero.

avuguero [ah-voo-gay'-ro], *m. (Bot.)* A kind of pear-tree.

avugués [ah-voo-gays'], *m. (Bot.) V.* GAYURA.

avulsión [ah-vool-se-on'], *f. (Surg.)* A forcible separation, tearing away.

avutarda [ah-voo-tar'-dah], *f.* Bustard, a wild turkey.

avutardado, da [ah-voo-tar-dah'-do, dah], *a.* Bustard-like.

axial [ac-see-ahl'], *a.* Axial.

axil [ac-seel'], *a. (Bot.)* Axial, relating to the axis. *(Zool.)* Axillary, relating to the base of the wing, or to the thoracic limb of some animals. *-m.* The axil of a plant.

axila [ac-see'-lah], *f.* 1. *(Anat.)* Axilla, armpit. 2. *(Bot.)* Axilla, upper end and inside of the base of leaves or branches.

axilar [ac-se-lar'], *a.* 1. Axillar, axillary, belonging to the armpit. 2. *(Bot.)* Axillary.

axioma [ac-se-oh'-mah], *m.* Axiom, maxim.

axiomático, ca [ac-se-o-mah'-te-co, cah], *a.* Axiomatic, self-evident.

axiómetro [ac-se-o'-may-tro], *m. (Naut.)* An instrument which marks the movements of the helm.

axis [ac'-sis], *m. (Anat.)* The second vertebra of the neck. 2. *(Zool.)* Indian deer.

¡ay! [i, or ah'-e], *int.* Alas! an exclamation of pain or grief. **¡Ay de mi!** Alas, poor me! Woe is me!. 2. Oh!, goodness! 3. Moan, groan; cry. **Un ay desgarrador**, a heartrending cry. *-m. V.* QUEJIDO and GEMIDO.

aya [ah'-yah], *f.* Governess, instructress. *V.* AYO.

ayanque [ah-yahn'-kay], *m. (Naut.)* The main halliard.

ayate [ah-yah'-tay], *m.* A kind of fabric manufactured of the thread of the agave, or *pita*.

ayatola [ah-yah-to-lah'], *m.* Ayatollah.

ayax [ah'-yacs], *m.* Ayax.

aye aye [ah'-yay-ah'-yay], *m. (Zool.)* The aye-aye, a nocturnal lemur of Madagascar.

ayer [ah-yerr'], *adv.* 1. Yesterday. **Ayer por la mañana**, yesterday morning. 2. Lately, not long ago, **De ayer acá**, from yesterday to this moment. 3. *m.* Yesterday, past; **el ayer madrileño**, Madrid in the past.

ayllu [ah-ee-lyoo'], *m. (And.) (Hist. Famil.)* Family, tribe, community.

aymará [ah-ee-mah'-rah], *(And.)* 1. *m. & f.* Aymara Indian. 2. *m. (Ling.)* Aymara, language of the Aymara Indians.

ayo [ah'-yo], *m.* Tutor or governor; a teacher.

ayocote [ah-yo-co'-tay], *(Mex.)* A kidney-bean larger than the common sort.

ayocuantoto [ah-yo-coo-an-to'-to], *m.* A mountain bird of Mexico.

ayote [ah-yo-tay], *m. (Mex.)* Small pumpkin; *(CAm.)* pumpkin, squash.

ayotoste [ah-yo-tos'-tay], *m.* Armadillo.

ayto. *abr.* de **Ayuntamiento**.

ayuda [ah-yoo'-dah], *f.* 1. Help, aid, assistance, comfort; support, succour, friendship. **Ayuda de parroquia**, chapel of ease. 2. An injection, enema, or clyster. 3. Syringe. 4. *(Naut.)* Preventer-rope. **Ayuda de costa**, a gratification paid over and above a salary, a gratuity. *-m.* 1. Deputy or assistant of one of the high officers at court. **Ayuda de cámara**, a valet-de-chambre, valet. **Ayuda de cámara del rey**, groom of the bed-chamber. 2. Helper, a supernumerary servant. **Dios y ayuda**, this cannot bc done but with the assistance of God. **Ayuda de oratorio**, clergyman in an oratory who performs the office of sacristan. **Ayuda de cocinero**, *(Naut.)* the cook's shifter. **Ayuda de dispensero**, *(Naut.)* the steward's mate. **Ayuda de virador**, *(Naut.)* a false preventer. **Prestar ayuda**, to give help. **Ayuda estatal**, state aid.

ayudado [ah-yoo-dah'-do], *m. (Taur.)* Two-handed pass with the cape (toros).

ayudador, ra [ah-yoo-dah-dor', rah], *m. & f.* Assistant, helper; a shepherd's assistant.

ayudante [ah-yoo-dahn'-tay], *m.* 1. *(Mil.)* Adjutant, aide-de-camp. 2. **Ayudante de cirujano**, a surgeon's assistant. 3. **Ayudante de dirección** *(Theat. etc.)*, production assistant.

ayudantía [ah-yoo-dahn-te'-ah], *f.* Assistantship; adjutancy; *(Tec.)* post of technician.

ayudar [ah-yoo-dar'], *va.* To aid, to help, to favor, to assist. **Ayudar a misa**, to serve the priest at mass. *-vr.* To adopt proper measures to obtain success.

ayudista [ah-yoo-des'-tah], *m. & f. (Cono Sur)* Supporter.

ayuga [ah-yoo'-gah], *f. (Bot.)* Groundpine. *V.* PINILLO.

ayunador, ra [ah-yoo-nah-dor', rah], *m. & f.* Faster, one who fasts.

ayunar [ah-yoo-nar'], *vn.* To fast; to keep the canonical fast. **Ayunar al traspaso**, to fast from holy Thursday to the following Saturday. **Ayunar después de harto**, to fast after a good repast.

ayunas (En) [ah-yoo'-nas], *adv.* 1. Fasting. 2. Without knowledge. **Quedar en ayunas**, to be ignorant of an affair. 3. **Salir en ayunas**, to go out without any breakfast.

ayuno [ah-yoo'-no], *m.* Fast, abstinence.

ayuno, na [ah-yoo'-no, nah], *a.* 1. Fasting, abstaining from food. **Estoy ayuno**, I have not yet broken my fast. 2. Abstaining from certain pleasures. 3. Ignorant of a subject of conversation.

ayunque [ah-yoon'-kay], *m.* Anvil. *V.* YUNQUE.

ayuntable [ah-yoon-tah'-blay], *a.* Capable of being joined.

ayuntador, ra [ah-yoon-tah-dor, rah], *m. & f.* One who unites, joins, or assembles.

ayuntamiento [ah-yoon-tah-me-en'-to], *m.* 1. City, town council (institución). City hall, Town hall (edificio). Meeting (reunión). **Ayuntamiento carnal**, sexual intercourse.

ayuntar [ah-yoon-tar'], *va.* 1. *(Naut.)* To splice. 2. *(Agri.)* To yoke. *(Obs.) V.* JUNTAR and AÑADIR.

ayustar [ah-yoos-tar'], *va. (Naut.)* To bend two ends of a cable or rope, to splice. **Ayustar con costura**, to bend with a splice.

ayuste [ah-yoos'-tay], *m. (Naut.)* Bending or splicing whereby two ends of a rope or cable are joined; scarf, scarfing.

ayuya [ah-yoo'-yah], *f. (Cono Sur)* Flat roll, scone.

azabachado, da [ah-thah-bah-chah'-do, dah], *a.* Jetty, black as jet.

azabache [ah-thah-bah'-chay], *m. (Miner.)* Jet, a black shining mineral. *pl.* **Azabaches**, trinkets of jet.

azábara [ah-thah'-bah-rah], *f. (Bot.)* Common aloe.

azacán [ah-thah-can'], *m. (Obs.)* 1. Water-carrier. 2. *V.* ODRE. **Estar or andar hecho un azacán**, To be very busy.

azacanarse [ah-thah-cah-nahr'-say], *vr.* To drudge, slave away.

azacaya [ah-thah-cah'-yah], *f. (Prov.)* Conduit of water, a water-pipe.

azache [ah-thah'-chay], *a.* Of an inferior quality (seda)**.**

azada [ah-thah'-dah], *f. (Agri.)* Spade, hoe.

azadada [ah-thah-dah'-dah], *f.* Blow with a spade.

azadica, ill, ita [ah-thah-dee'-cah, deel'-lyah, dee'-tah], *f. dim.* A small spade.

azadón [ah-thah-done'], *m.* Pickaxe, mattock, hoe. **Azadón de peto**. hand-spike, or lever armed with a kind of chisel.

azadonada [ah-thah-do-nah'-dah], *f.* Blow with a pickaxe. **A la primera azadonada dísteis en el agua**, to detect straightway that one is not worthy of the consideration in which he is held. **A la primera azadonada ¿queréis sacar agua?,** do you expect to accomplish a difficult task without effort? **A tres azadonadas sacar agua.** *(Met.)* To obtain easily the object of one's wishes.

azadonar [ah-thah-do-nar'], *va.* To dig with a spade or pickaxe.

azadonazo [ah-thah-do-nah'-tho], *m.* Stroke with a mattock.

azadoncillo [ah-thah-don-theel'-lyo], *m. dim.* A small pickaxe.

azadonero [ah-thah-do-nay'-ro], *m.* 1. Digger, one that opens the ground with a spade. 2. *(Mil. Obs.)* Pioneer.

azafata [ah-thah-fah'-tah], *f.* 1. Airline hostess, stewardess. 2. Queen's maid of the wardrobe.

azafate [ah-thah-fah'-tay], *m.* A low, flat-bottomed basket; a kind of waiter, a tray.

azafrán [ah-thah-frahn'], *m. (Bot.)* Saffron. **Azafrán bastaror** *o* **azafrán romí or romín,** *(Bot.)* bastard saffron, dyers' saffron. **Azafrán del timón,** *(Naut.)* after-piece of the rudder. **Azafrán del tajamar,** *(Naut.)* forepiece of the cut-water. **Azafrán de Venus,** *(Chem.)* crocus Veneris, the caix or

oxide of metals of a saffron color. **Azafrán de Marte**, crocus powder; copperas calcined to a reddish or purple color, for polishing *(Arab.)*.

azafranado, da [ah-thah-frah-nah'-do, dah], *a.* Saffron-like, croceous. *-pp.* of AZAFRANAR.

azafranal [ah-thah-frah-nahl'], *m.* A plantation of saffron.

azafranar [ah-thah-frah-nar'], *va.* To tinge or dye with saffron.

azafranero [ah-thah-frah-nay'-ro], *m.* Dealer in saffron.

azagador [ah-thah-gah-dor'], *m.* The path for cattle.

azagaya [ah-thah-gah'-yah], *f.* Javelin, a spear or half-pike.

azagayada [ah-thah-gah-yah'-dah], *f.* Cast of a javelin.

azahar [ah-thah-ar'], *m.* Orange or lemon flower. **Agua de azahar**, orange-flower water. **Azahar bravo**, arrow-leaved blue lupine. **azainadamente** [ah-thah-e-nah-dah-men'-tay], *adv.* Perfidiously, viciously.

azalá [ah-thah-lah'], *m.* Prayer, among the Mohammedans.

azalea [ah-thah-lay'-ah], *f.* Azalea.

azalón [ah-thah-lone'], *m. (Orn.)* A small bird.

azamboa [ah-tham-bo'-ah], *f. (Bot.)* The fruit of the zamboa-tree; a kind of sweet quince; citron. *V.* ZAMBOA.

azamboo, or **azamboero** [ah-tham-bo'-o, ah-tham-bo-ay'-ro], *m. (Bot.)* The zamboa-tree; citron.

azanca [ah-trahn'-cah], *f. (Miner.)* Subterranean spring.

azándar [ah-thahn'-dar], *m. (Prov.) V.* SANDALO.

azanoria [ah-thah-no'-re-ah], *f. (Bot.)* Carrot. *V.* ZANAHORIA.

azanoriate [ah-thah-no-re-ah'-tay], *m. (Prov.)* 1. Preserved carrots. 2. *(Prov.)* Fulsome, affected compliments.

azar [ah-thar'], *m.* 1. Unforeseen disaster, an unexpected accident, disappointment. 2. Unfortunate card or throw a dice. 3. Obstruction, impediment. 4. Hazard. **Los azares de la vida**, life´s ups and downs.

azarado, da [ah-thah-rah'-do, dah], *a. & pp.* of AZARAR. Confused, rattled; used especially of a player. A term much used in billiards.

azarar [ah-thah-rar'], *va.* To confuse, to bewilder, to rattle. *-vr.* To get rattled in a game. **Azararse una bola**, said of a ball which loses its direction or effect by striking against a pocket.

azarbe [ah-thar'-bay], *m. (Prov.)* Trench or drain for irrigation waters.

azarbeta [ah-thar-bay'0-tah], *dim.* Azarbe, small trench for irrigating.

azarcón [ah-thar-cone'], *m.* 1. Minium, red lead. 2. Orange color. 3. Earthen pot.

azarear [ah-thah-ray-ahr'], *va.* Azarearse, *vr. V.* AZORARSE.

azaría [ah-tha-ree'-ah], *f.* A kind of coral.

azarja [ah-thar'-hah], *f.* Instrument for winding raw silk.

azarnefe [ah-thar-nay'-fay], *m.* Orpiment. *V.* OROPIMENTE.

azarolla [ah-thah-rol'-lyah], *f. (Bot. Prov.)* The fruit of the true service-tree. *V.* ACEROLA.

azarollo [ah-thah-rol'-lyo], *(Bot. Prov.)* True service-tree.

azarosamente [ah-thah-ro-sah-men'-tay], *adv.* Unfortunately.

azaroso, sa [ah-thah-ro'-so, sah], *a.* Unlucky, unfortunate, ominous, risky.

azaya [ah-thah'-yah], *f.* 1. Instrument used for reeling silk. 2. *(Prov. Gal.) V.* CANTUESO. French lavender.

azazel [ah-thah'-thel], *m.* 1. In Islam, the angel nearest to Allah. 2. The scape-goat of the Mosaic dispensation.

azcón *m.* **azonca**, *f.* [ath-cone' ath-co'-nah], *(Obs.)* A dart.

azer [ah'-ther], *m.* 1. Name of the fire adored by the Magi. 2. A title of Zoroaster.

azimo, ma[ah'-the-mo, mah], *a.* Azymous, unleavened.

azimut [ah-themoot'], *m. (Astr.)* Azimuth.

azimutal [ah-the-moo-tahl'], *a.* Azymous, unleavened.

azimut [ah-the-moot'], *m. (Astr.)* Azimuth.

azimutal [ah-the-moo-tahl'], *a.* Relating to the azimuth.

aznacho, aznallo [ath-nah'-cho, ath-nahl'-lyo], *m. (Bot.)* 1. Scotch fir. 2. A species of the three-toothed rest-harrow.

azce [ah'-thay], *m. (Chem.)* Azote or nitrogen.

-azo, -aza sufijo de *n*. 1. **Librazo**, big book (aumentativo). 2. **Exitazo**, huge success. 3. **Actorazo**, top-flight actor. 3. **Cornetazo**, bugle call. 4. **Dar un frenazo**, to brake hard.

azocar [ ], *va. (Carib.)* To pack tightly.

azofaifa [ah-tho-fah'-e-fah], *f. V.* AZUFAIFA.

azófar [ah-tho'-far], *m.* Brass, latten. *V.* LATON.

azogadamente [ah-tho-gah-dah-men'-tay], *adv.* In a quick and restless manner.

azogado, da [ah-tho-gah'-do, dah], *a. (Amer.)* Restless, in perpetual movement; trembling.

azogamiento [ah-tho-gah-me-en'-to], *m.* 1. The act of overlaying with quicksilver. 2. Slaking lime. 3. State of restlessness.

azogar [ah-tho-gar'], *va.* To overlay with quicksilver, to coat a mirror. **Azogar la cal**, to slake lime. -*vr.* 1. To suffer from mercurialism. 2. To be in a state of agitation.

azogue [ah-tho'-gay], *m.* 1. *(Miner.)* Mercury, quicksilver. **Es un azogue**, he is as restless as quicksilver. **Azogues**, ships which carry quicksilver. 2. A market-place.

azoguejo [ah-tho-gay'-ho], *m.* A market-place.

azoguería [ah-tho-gay-ree'-ah], *f. (Amer.)* The place where quicksilver is incorporated with metals; amalgamating works.

azoguero [ah-tho-gay'-ro], *m.* 1. Dealer in quicksilver. 2. *(Amer.)* A workman who incorporates quicksilver, etc., with pounded silver ore, to extract the silver.

azoico, ca [ah-tho'-e-co, cah], *a.* 1. Nitric. 2. *(Geol.)* Azoic, antedatin life. **Era azoica**, azoic era.

azolar [ah-tho-lar'], *va.* To model timber.

azolvar [ah-thol-var'], *va.* To obstruct water-conduits.

azolve [ah-thol'-vay], *m. (Mex.)* Sediment, deposit.

azolvo [ah-thol'-vo], *m.* The blocking of pumps or water-pipes.

azomar [ah-tho-mar'], *va. (Obs.)* To incite animals to fight.

azonzado [ah-thon-tha'-do], *a. (Cono Sur)* Silly, stupid.

azor [ah-thor'], *m. (Orn.)* Goshawk.

azora [ah-tho-rah], *f. (LAm.) V.* AZORAMIENTO.

azorado [ah-tho-rah'-do], *a.* **Navío azorado**, a ship which sails heavily on account of her cargo being badly stowed. Alarmed, upset. Embarrassed, flustered. -*pp.* of AZORAR.

azoramiento [ah-tho-rah-me-en'-to], *m.* Trepidation, confusion. Alarm, embarrassment.

azorar [ah-tho-rar'], *va.* 1. To terrify; to confound. 2. To incite, to irritate. -*vr.* To be restless, to get upset, alarmed.

Azores [ah-tho'-rays], *f. & pl.* Azores.

azoro [ah-tho'-ro], *m.* 1. *(LAm.)* Azoramiento. 2. *(CAm.)* Ghost.

azorrado, da [ah-thor-rah'-do, dah], *a.* Drowsy, sleepy. -*pp.* of AZORRARSE. *(Naut.)* Water-logged.

azorramiento [ah-thor-rah-me-en'-to], *m.* Heaviness of the head.

azorrarse [ah-thor-rar'-say], *vr.* To be drowsy from heaviness.

azorrillarse [ah-thor-ree-lyar'-say], *vr. (Mex.)* To hide away, keep out of sight.

azotacalles [ah-tho-tah-cahl'-lyes], *m.* Street-lounger, idler.

azotado [ah-tho-tah'-do], *m.* 1. A criminal publicly whipped. 2. He who lashes himself by way of mortification. -*pp.* of AZOTAR.

azotador, ra [ah-tho-tha-dor', rah], *m. & f.* Whipper, one who inflicts lashes with a whip.

azotaina, azotina [ah-tho-tah'-e-nah, ah-tho-tee'-nah], *f. (coll.)* A drubbing, a sound flogging, beating.

azotalengua [ah-tho-ta-len'-goo-ah], *f. (Bot.)* Goose-grass, cleavers.

azotar [ah-tho-tar'], *va.* 1. To whip, to lash, to horsewhip, to flagellate. **Azotar las calles**, to lounge about the streets. 2. *(Met.)* **Azotar el aire**, to act to no purpose. 3. *(Naut.)* **Azotar con paleta**, to inflict the punishment called *cobbing* on board English ships. 4. *(Naut.)* **Azotar la ampolleta**, to flog the glass, when the steersman turns it before the sand has entirely run out. -*vr. (Mex.)* To put on airs.

azotazo [ah-tho-tah'-tho], *m. aug.* A severe lash or blow on the breech.

azote [ah-tho-tay], *m.* 1. Whip. 2. Lash given with a whip. 3. *(Met.)* Calamity, affliction. 4. The person who is the cause of a calamity. **Pena de azotes**, a public shipping. **Mano de azotes**, or **vuelta de azotes**, the number of lashes a criminal is to receive.

azotea [ah-tho-tay'-ah], *f.* The flat roof of a house, a platform. 2. **Estar mal de la azotea**, to be round the bend.

azotera [ah-tho-tay-rah], *f. (LAm.)* Beating, thrashing.

azótico [ah-tho'-te-co], *a.* **Gas azótico**, *(Chem.)* azotic gas.

azre [ath'-ray], *m. (Bot.)* Maple-tree.

azteca [ath-tay'-cah], *a. & m.* Aztec; belonging to the race, dynasty, or language of ancient Mexico.

azúa [ah-thoo'-ah], *f.* Beverage prepared by the Indians from Indian corn.

azúcar [ah-thoo'-car], *m.* Sugar. **Azúcar de pilón**, loaf-sugar. **Azúcar de lustre**, double loaves, fine powdered sugar. **Azúcar mascabado**, unclarified sugar. **Azúcar quebrado**, brown sugar. **Azúcar prieto** or **negro**, coarse brown sugar. **Azúcar piedra** or **cande**. sugar-candy. **Azúcar terciado** or **moreno**, brown sugar. **Azúcar pardo**, clayed sugar. **Azúcar de plomo**, calcined sugar of lead. **Azúcar y canela**, sorrel-gray: a color peculiar to horses.

azucarado, da [ah-thoo-car-rah'-do, dah], *a.* 1. Sugared. 2. Sugary, having the taste of sugar. 3. Sugar coated. 4. *(Met.)* Affable, pleasing. **Palabras azucaradas**, soothing, artful words -*pp.* of AZUCARAR.

azucarado [ah-thoo-car-rah'-do], *mm.* A kind of paint for ladies.

azucarar [ah-thoo-ca-rar'], *va.* 1. To sugar, to sweeten; to soften. 2. To ice with sugar, to coat with sugar.

azucarería [ah-thoo-cah-ray-re'-ah], *f.* Sugar refinery; *(Carib., Mex.)* Sugar shop.

azucarero [ah-thoo-ca-ray'-ro], *m.* 1. Sugar-dish, sugar-bowl. 2. *(Prov.)* Confectioner.

azucarillo [ah-thoo-ca-reel'-lyo], *m.* Sweetmeat of flour, sugar, and rosewater.

azucena [ah-thoo-thay'-nah], *f. (Bot.)* White lily. **Azucena amarilla**, yellow amaryllis. **Azucena anteada**, Copper-colored day-lily. **Azucena pajiza**, yellow day-lily. **Azucenas**, the military order of the lily, founded by Kind Ferdinand of Aragón.

azud [ah-thood'], *f.* A dam with a sluice or flood-gate.

azuda [ah-thoo'-dah], *f.* Persian wheel to raise water for irrigation. *cf.* NORIA.

azuela [ah-thoo-ay'-lah], *f.* Adze, a carpenter's tool; howell, a cooper's tool. **Azuela de construcción**, a ship-wright's adze. **Azuela curva**, a hollow adze.

azufaifa [ah-thoo-fah'-e-fah], *f.* Jujube or jujubes, the fruit of the jujube-tree.

azufaifo, azufeifo [ah-thoo-fah'-e-fo, ah-thoo-fay'-e-fo], *m.* Jujube-tree.

azufrado, da [ah-thoo-frah'-do, dah], *a.* 1. Whitened or fumigated with sulphur. 2. Sulphureous. 3. Greenish yellow. *pp.* of AZUFRAR.

azufrador [ah-thoo-frah-dor'], *m.* 1. Machine for drying linen. 2. Instrument for sulphuring vines.

azufrar [ah-thoo-frar'], *va.* To bleach, to fumigate with sulphur.

azufre [ah-thoo'-fray], *m.* Sulphur, brimstone. **Azufre vivo** native sulphur.

azufrón [ah-thoo-frone'], *m.* Pyrites in powder.

azufroso, sa [ah-thoo-fro'-so, sah], *a.* Sulphureous.

azul [ah-thool'], *a.* Blue. **Azul celeste**, sky-blue. **Azul oscuro**, dark blue. **Azul de Prusia**, Prussian blue. **Azul subido**, bright blue. **Azul turquí or turquizado**, Turkish or deep blue; indigo, sixth color of the spectrum. **Azul de esmalte**, smalt. **Azul verdemar** or **de costras**, sea-blue. **Darse un verde con dos azules**, to be highly entertained.

azul [ah-thool'], *m.* Lapis lazuli; a mineral.

azulado, da [ah-thoo-lah'-do, dah], *pp.* of AZULAR. **Azulado claro**, azure, azured; bluish.

azulaque [ah-thoo-lah'-kay], *m.* V. ZULAQUE.

azular [ah-thoo-lar'], *va.* To dye or color blue.

azulear [ah-thoo-lay-ar'], *vn.* To have a bluish cast.

azulejado, da [ah-thoo-lay-hah'-do, dah], *a. (Prov.)* Covered with bluish tiles.

azulejar [ah-thoo-lay-hahr'], *va.* To tile.

azulejeria [ah-thoo-lay-hay-re'-ah], *f.* Tiling. Tile industry.

azulejillo [ah-thoo-lay-heel'-lyo], *m.* Little bluebird.

azulejo [ah-thoo-lay'-ho], *m.* 1. Glazed tile painted with various colors, or plain white. 2. *(Bot.)* Blue-bottle, cornflower. -*a.* Applied in Spain to several kinds of wheat. 3. *(Orn.)* The blue jay.

azulenco, ca [ah-thoo-len'-co, cah], *a.* V. AZULADO.

azulete [ah-thoo-lay'-tay], *m.* Blue color given to stockings and other garments.

azulino, na [ah-thoo-lee'-no, nah], *a.* Bluish.

azuloso [ah-thoo-lo'-so], *a. (LAm.)* Bluish.

azumagarse [ah-thoo-mah-gahr'-say], *vr. (Cono Sur)* To rust, get rusty.

azumar [ah-thoo-mar'], *va.* To dye the hair.

azumbrado, da [ah-thoom-brah'-do, dah], *a.* Measured by *azumbres.*

azumbre [ah-thoom'-bray], *f.* A measure of liquids, containing about half an English gallon.

azur [ah-thoor'], *a. (Her.)* Azure.

azurita [ah-thoo-ree'-tah], *f* 1. Blue variety of copper carbonate, azurite. 2. Double phosphate aluminium and magnesium.

azurumbado [ah-thoo-room-bah'-do], *a. (CAm.)* Silly, stupid; drunk (borracho).

azutero [ah-thoo-tay'-ro], *m.* Sluice-master, he who has the care of dams, Sluices, etc.

azuzador, ra [ah-thoo-thah-dor', rah], *m. & f.* Instigator.

azuzar [ah-thoo-thar'], *va.* 1. To halloo, to set on dogs. 2. To irritate, to provoke.

azuzón [ah-thoo-thone'], *m.* Instigator, provoker of quarrels.

B

b [bay]. The second letter of the Spanish alphabet: it is pronounced in Spanish as in English.

baba [bah'-bah], *f.* Drivel, slaver, spittle, saliva, slobber; *(Bio.)* mucus; secretion. **Echar baba**, to drool, to slobber. **Se le cae la baba**, *(fig.)* he's thrilled to bits.

bababuí [bah-bah-boo-ee'], *m.* The mocking-bird V. ARRENDAJO.

babadero, babador [bah-bah-day'-ro, bah-bah-dor'], *m.* Bib, chin-cloth.

babasfrías [bah-bah-fre'-ahs], *m. (And. Méx.)* Fool.

babaza [bah-bah'-thah], *f.* 1. Frothy fluid from the mouth. Slime, mucus. 2. Aloe. 3. A viscous worm of the snail kind. Slug.

babazorro [bah-bah-thor'-ro], *m. (Prov.)* Clown, an ill-bred man.

babear [bah-bay-ar'], *vn.* 1. To drivel, to slaver. 2. *(Met. and coll.)* To be smitten with; to court, to woo. -*vr. (Cono Sur)* To feel flattered, to grow with satisfaction.

Babel [bah-bayl'], *m.* Babel. **Torre de Babel**, tower of Babel.

babel [bah-bayl'], *m.* of bedlam; confusion, mess.

babeo [bah-bay'-o], *m.* The act of drivelling or slavering.

babera [bah-bay'-ra], *f.* 1. Fore part of the helmet which covers the cheeks, mouth, and chin. 2. A silly fellow. 3. A bib.

babero [bah-bay'-ro], *m.* Bib. V. BABADOR.

baberol [bah-bay-role'], *m.* V. BABERA, as part of the helmet.

babia [bah'-bee-ah], *f.* **Estar en babia**, to be absent in mind, heedless, or inattentive.

babieca [bah-be-ay'-cah], *m.* **Es un babieca**, he is an ignorant, stupid fellow; an idiot.

babilla [bah-beel'-lyah], *f.* Thin skin about the flank of a horse .

Babilonia [bah-be-lo'-ne-h], *f.* **Es una babilonia**, there is such a crowd, it is all uproar and confusion. Babylon.

babilónico, ca, or **onio, nia** [bah-be-lo'-ne-co, cah, ne-o, ne-ah], *a.* Babylonian.

babilla [bah-bee'-lyah], *f. (Vet.)* Stifle.

babismo [bah-bees'-mo], *m.* Babism, Persian religious doctrine.

bable [bah'-blay], *m.* The Asturian dialect.

babor [bah-bor'], *m. (Naut.)* Port, the left-hand side of a ship, looking forward. **A babor del timón**, a-port the helm. **A babor todo**, head a-port. **De babor a estribor**, athwart ship.

babosa [bah-bo'-sah], *f.* 1. A slug. 2. Aloe. 3. An old onion transplanted. 4. A young onion.

babosada [bah-bo-sah'-dah], *f. (LAm.)* Stupid things; dead loss, useless thing. *(CAm. Méx.)* Stupid comment.

babosear [bah-bo-say-ar'], *va.* 1. To drivel, to slaver. 2. *(fig.)* To drool over; *(CAm.)* Insult; *(Mex.)* To manhandle; *(CAm. Méx.)* To take for a fool. **Muchos han baboseado este problema** *(Mex.)*, many have taken a superficial look at this problem. -*vn.* To drool.

baboseo [bah-bo-say'-o], *a.* Drooling, slobbering; slimy. *(fig.)* Infatuation, drooling.

babosilla [bah-bo-seel'-lyah], *f. dim.* Slug.

babosillo, illa; uelo, uela [bah-bo-seel'-lyo, lyah, oo-ay'-lo, lah], *a. dim.* Somewhat drivelling or slavering.

baboso, sa [bah-bo'-so, sah], *m. & f.* Idiot, simpleton.-*a.* Idiotic. *a.* Drooling, slobbering; slimy. *(fig.)* Sloppy (sobre mujeres). Foolishly sentimental; fawning, snivelling; dirty.

babucha [bah-boo'-chah], *f.* A kind of slipper. *(Carib.)* Child's bodice; *(LAm.)* Loose blouse, smock. **Babuchas** *(Carib.)* Rompers; *(Mex.)* High-heeled boot. **Llevar algo a babuchas** *(Cono Sur)*, to carry something on one's back.

babuino [bah-boo-e'-no], *m.* Baboon.

babuyal [bah-boo-yahl'], *m. (Carib.)* Witch, sorcerer.

baby [bah'-be], *m. & f.* 1. *(LAm.)* baby; *(Aut.)* Small car, mini. **Baby crece**, babygrow. **Baby fútbol**, table football. 2. Bib (babero).

baca [bah'-cah], *f.* 1. Berry. **Baca de laurel**, bay-berry. 2. Breach in a dike or dam. 3. *(Jew.)* A kind of pearl. 4. Leather cover of a car or stage-coach.-*m. & f. pl.* Quick tune on the guitar.

bacal [bah-cahl'], *m. (Mex.) (Agri.)* Corncob.

bacalada [bah-cah-lah'-dah], *f.* Sweetener, bribe.

bacalao [bah-cah-lah'-o], *m.* 1. Codfish. **Aceite de hígado de bacalao**, cod-liver oil. **Bacalao a la vizcaína**, Codfish stew made with olive oil, tomatoes, olives, capers, etc. 2. **¡Te conozco bacalao!**, I've rumbled you! 3. *(Cono Sur)* Miser. 4. *(Esp.)* Cunt (vajina).

bacán [bah-can'], *m. (Cono Sur)* Wealthy man; sugar daddy; playboy, dundy.

bacanal [bah-cah'-nah], *a.* Bacchanalian.

bacanalear [bah-cah-nah-lay-ahr'], *va. (CAm.)* To have a wild time.

bacanales [bah-cah-nah'-les], *f. pl.* Bacchanals, feasts of Bacchus.

bacane [bah-cah'-nay], *m. (Carib.) (Aut.)* Driving license, driver's licence (GB).

bacanería [bah-cah-nay-re'-ah], *f. (Cono Sur)* Sharp dressing, nattiness; vulgar, display.

bacante [bah-cahn'-tay], *f.* 1. Bacchante, bacchant, priestess of Bacchus. 2. Bacchante, a lewd drinking person.

bácara, bacaris [bah'-ca-rah, bah'-ca-ris], *f. (Bot.)* Great flea-bane. Baccharis.
bacelador [bah-thay-lah-dor'], *m. (Carib.)* Con man.
bacelar [bah-thay-lar'], *m.* Land newly planted with vines. *-va. (Carib.)* To con, to trick.
bacenica [bah-the-ne'-cah], *f. (LAm.) V.* BACINICA.
bacera [ba-thay'-rah], *f. (Coll.)* Obstruction in the milt, a swelling of the belly, in cattle.
bacía [ba-thee'-ah], *f.* 1. A metal basin; wash-pot. 2. Barber's basin; shaving-dish.
báciga [bah'-the-gah], *f.* A game played with three cards.
bacilar [bah-the-lahr'], *a.* Bacillary.
bacilarse [bah-the-lahr'-say], *vr. (And.)* To have a good time.
bacilo [bah-thee'-lo], *m.* Bacillus, a rodshaped bacterium.
bacilón [bah-thee-lon'], 1. *a.* Brilliant, great. 2. *m. (And.)* Fun, good time.
bacín [bah-theen'], *m.* 1. A large and very high vase, or basin, which serves as a close-stool. 2. A despicable man.
bacina [bah-thee'-nah], *f.* 1. *(Coll.)* Poor-box. 2. *V.* BACIA. 3. A small basin which serves as a close-stool.
bacinada [bah-tbe-nah'-dah], *f.* Filth thrown from a close-stool.
bacinejo [bah-the-nay'-ho], *m. dim.* A small close-stool.
bacineta [bah-the-nay'-tah], *f.* **Bacineta de arma de fuego,** the pan of a gun-lock.
bacinete [bah-the-nay'-tay], *m.* A head-piece formerly worn by soldiers, in the form of a helmet, basinet (de armadura).
bacinica [bah-the-nee'-cah], *f.* 1. A small earthen close-stool for children. 2. Chamber-pot.
bacinilla [bah-the-neel'-lyah], *f.* 1. A chamber-pot.
bacitracina [bah-the-trah-thee'-nah], *f. (Med.)* Bacitracin.
background [bac-go'-oon], *m. (Cono Sur)* Background.
baco [bah'-co], *m.* Bacchus. Wine.
bacon [bah-con'], *m.* Bacon.
bacteria [bac-tay'-re-ah], *f.* Bacteria, germ.
bacteriano [bac-tay-re-ah'-no], *a.* Bacterial.
bactericida [bac-tay-re-thee'-dah], *m.* Bactericide, bacteria killer.
bactérico [bac-tay'-re-co], *a.* Bacterial.
bacteriología [bac-tay-re-o-lo-ge'-ah], *f.* Bacteriology.
bacteriólogo, ga [bac-tay-re-o'-lo-go, gah], *m. & f.* Bacteriologist.
báculo [bah'-coo-lo], *m.* 1. Walking-stick, a staff. **Báculo de Jacob,** Jacob's staff, a mathematical instrument which serves to measure heights and distances. **Báculo de peregrino,** pilgrims staff. **Báculo pastoral,** bishop's crosier. 2. *(Met.)* Support, relief, consolation.
bacha [bah'-chah], *f. (Carib.)* Spree, merry outing.
bachata [bah-chah'-tah], *f. (Carib.)* Party, good time.
bachatear [bah-chah-tay-ahr'], *vn. (Carib.)* To go on a spree, to go out for a good time.
bachatero [bah-chah-tay'-ro], *m. (Carib.)* Reveller, carouser.
bache [bah'-chay], *m.* 1. A deep hole in a road. 2. A place where sheep are put to sweat, previous to their being shorn. *V.* SUDADERO. 3. Stick of a hatter for beating felt. 4. Economic depression. **Salir del bache,** to get out of the rut.
bachicha [bah-che'-chah], *m.* 1. *(Cono Sur)* Dago, wop. 2. Leftovers (restos); Cigarette end, cigar stub; dregs (de bebida). 3. *(Mex.) (Fin.)* Nest egg, secret hoard.
bachiche [bah-chee'-chay], *m. (And.) V.* BACHICHA.
bachiller [bah-cheel-lyerr'], *m.* 1. Bachelor, one who has obtained the first degree in sciences and liberal arts. 2. Babbler, prater.
bachiller [bah-cheel-lyerr'], *a.* Garrulous, loquacious.
bachillera [bah-cheel-lyay'-rah], *a.* Forward, loquacious woman.
bachillerato [bah.cheel-lyay-rah'-to], *m.* Bachelorship, the degree and function of a bachelor. **Bachillerato comercial,** certificate in business studies. **Bachillerato elemental,** lower examination.

bachillerear [bah-cheel-lyay-ray-ar'], *vn.* To babble, to prattle, to talk a lot.
bachillerejo [bah-cheel-lyay-ray'-ho], *m. dim.* A talkative little fellow.
bachillería [bah-cheel-lyay-ree'-ah], *f.* Babbling, prattling.
bada [bah'-dah], *f. V.* ABADA.
badajada [bah-dah-hah'-dah], *f.* 1. A stroke of the clapper against the bell. 2. Idle talk.
badajazo [bah-dah-bah'-tho], *m. aug.* A large clapper.
badajear [bah-dah-hay-ar'], *vn. (Obs.)* 1. To talk nonsense. 2. To swing to and fro.
badajo [bah-dah'-ho], *m.* 1. Clapper of a bell. 2. An idle talker.
badajuelo [bah-dah-hoo-ay'-lo], *m. dim.* A small clapper.
badal [bah-dahl'], *m.* 1. Muzzle. **Echar un badal a la boca,** to stop one's mouth. 2. *(Prov.)* Shoulder and ribs of butcher's meat. 3. *(Surg.)* Instrument for opening the mouth.
badana [bah-dah'-nah], *f.* A dressed sheep-skin. **Zurrar la badana,** to dress a sheep-skin; to give one a flogging.
badaza [bah-dah-tha], *f. (Carib.)* Strap (para pasajeros de pie).
badazas [bah-dah'-thas], *f. pl. (Naut.)* Keys of the bonnets, ropes with which the bonnets are laced to the sails. *V.* BARJULETA.
badea [bah-day'-ah], *f.* 1. Pompion or pumpkin. 2. *(Met.)* A dull, insipid being.
badén [bah-den'], *m.* 1. Channel made by a sudden fall of water. 2. Catchwater, conduit.
badiana [bah-de-ah'-nah], *f. (Bot.)* Indian aniseed, badiana.
badil, *m.* **badila,** *f.* [bah-deel', bah-dee'-lah]. Fire-shovel.
badilejo [bah-de-lay'-ho], *m. (And.)* Trowel (de constructor).
badina [bah-dee'-nah], *f. (Obs.)* Pool of water in the roads.
bádminton [bahd'-meen-ton], *m.* Badminton.
badomía [bah-do-mee'-ah], *f.* Nonsense, absurdity.
badulacada [bah-doo-lah-cah'-dah], *f. (Peru.) V.* CALAVERADA.
badulaque [bah-doo-lah'-kay], *m.* 1. Ragout of stewed-livers. 2. A stupid person. 3. A person not to be relied on.
badulaquear [bah-doo-lah-kay-ahr'], *vn.* To be an idiot, act like an idiot. 2. *(Cono Sur)* To be a rogue, to be dishonest, to act like a rogue.
bafetas [bah-fay'-tas], *f. pl.* Fabric, of white cotton from India.
baf(f)le [bah'-flay], *m. (Elec.)* Speaker, loudspeaker.
baga [bah'-gah], *f.* 1 *(Prov.)* A rope or cord with which the loads of beasts of burden are fastened. 2. A little head of flax with its seeds.
bagaje [bah-gah'-hay], *m.* 1. Beast of burden. 2. Baggage, the furniture of an army and the beasts of burden on which it is carried.
bagajero [bah-gah-hay'-ro], *m.* Driver, he who conducted the beasts which carried military baggage.
bagar [bah-gar'], *vn.* To yield the seed: applied to flax.
bagasa [bah-gah'-sah], *f.* A prostitute.
bagatela [bah-gah-tay'-lah], *f.* Bagatelle, trifle. **Son bagaletas,** those are trivialities.
bagayo [bah-gah'-yo], *m. (Cono Sur)* 1. Bundle, tramp's bundle; heavy (carga), loot. 2. *(fig.)* Useless lump, berk, old bag (mujer fea).
bagazo [bah-gah'-tho], *m.* 1. *(Prov.)* The remains of sugar-cane, grapes, olives, palms, etc., which have been pressed. 2. *(fig.)* Dead loss. 3. *(Carib.)* Down-and-out.
bagre [bah'-gray], *m.* 1. Catfish. 2. *m. & f. (LAm.)* Unpleasant person, sly sort; ugly mug. Old bag (mujer). 3. *(Cono Sur)* **Pica el bagre,** I'm starving. *-a.* 1. *(And.)* Vulgar, coarse, loud. 2. *(CAm.)* Clever, sharp.
bagrero [bah-gray'-ro], *a. (And.)* Fond of ugly women.
bagual [bah-goo-ahl'], 1. *a. (And. Cono Sur)* 1. Wild, untamed. 2. Rough, loutish, rude. 3. *m. (And. Cono Sur)* Wild horse. **Ganar los aguales,** *(Cono Sur) (Hist.)* to escape.

bagualada [bah-goo-ah-lah'-dah], *f.* *(Cono Sur)* 1. Herd of wild horses. 2. *(fig.)* Stupid thing (to do).

bagualón [bah-goo-ah-lon'], *a.* *(Cono Sur)* Half-tamed.

baguío [bah-gee'-o], *m.* A hurricane in the Philippine Islands.

¡bah! *int.* Bah! That´s nothing!

Bahama [bah-ah'-mah],*f. & pl.* **Las Bahamas**, the Bahamas.

baharí [bah-ah-ree'], *m.* *(Orn.)* Sparrow-hawk.

bahía [bah-ee'-ah], *f.* 1. Bay, an arm of the sea. 2. **Bahía**, a city of Brazil.

baho [bah'-o], *m.* *(CAm.)* *(Culin.)* Dish of meat and yucca.

bahorrina [bah-or-ree'-nah],*f.* 1. Collection of filthy things. 2. Rabble.

bahuno, na [bah-oo'-no, nah], *a.* Base, vile. *V.* BAJUNO.

baila [bah'-e-lah], *f.* 1. *(Obs.)* *V.* BAILE. 2. *(Zool.)* Sea-trout. **Ser dueño de la baila**, *(Prov.)* to be the principal of any business.

bailable [bah-e-lah'-blay], *a.* Danceable.-*m.* A pantomime with dancing. Ballet.

bailada [bah-e-lah'-dah], *f.* *(LAm.)* Dance, dancing.

bailadero [bah-e-lah-day'-ro], *m.* Dance hall, dance floor.

bailador, ra [bah-e-lah-dor', rah], *m. & f.* 1. Dancer. 2. *(Low.)* Thief.

bailaor(a) [bah-e-lah-or', rah], *m. & f.* Flamenco dancer.

bailar [bah-e-lar´], *vn.* 1. To dance. 2. To move by a short, brisk gallop (caballos). **Bailar el agua adelante**, to dance attendance. **Bailar sin son**, to dance without music; to be too eager for performing anything to require a stimulus. 3. *(fig.)* **Bailar al son que tocan**, to toe the line. **Le bailaban los ojos de alegría**, her eyes sparkled with happiness. **Le bailaron la casa**, *(LAm.)* they cheated her out of her house.

bailarín, na [bah-e-lah-reen', nah], *m. & f.* 1. Dancer, caperer. 2. A fiery, high-mettled horse.

baile [bah'-e-lay], *m.* 1. Dance. 2. Ball, rout. 3. *(Prov.)* Bailiff, a judge or justice. **Baile de disfraces**, *o* **trajes**, fancy ball. **Baile de San Vito**, St. Vitus´s dance, chorea.

bailecito(s) [bah-e-lay-the'-tos], *m. & pl.* *(LAm.)* Folk dance.

bailete [bah-e-lay'-tay], *m.* A short dance introduced into some dramatic works.

bailía, *f.* **bailiazgo**, *m.* [bah-e-lee'-ah, bah-e-le-ahth'-go]. 1. District of the jurisdiction of a *baile* or bailiff. 2. District of commandery in the order of the Knights of Malta.

bailiaje [bah-e-le-ah'-hay], *m.* A commandery or dignity in the order of Malta.

bailío [bah-e-lee'-o], *m.* The knight commander of the order of Malta.

bailón [bah-e-lon'], *a.* Fond of dancing.

bailongo [bah-e-lon'-go], *m.* *(LAm.)* Local dance.

bailotear [bah-e-lo-tay-ar'], *vn.* To skip and jump in dancing; to dance without grace.

bailoteo [bah-e-lo-tay'-o], *m.* A mean ball.

baivel [bah-e-vel'], *m.* In masonry and joinery, bevel, a kind of square, one leg of which is frequently crooked.

bajá [bah-hah'], *m.* Pasha, bashaw, a Turkish title.

baja [bah'-hah], *f.* 1. Fall or diminution of price. **Una baja de 5 por ciento**, a fall of 5%. 2. *(Obs.)* A dance. 3. *(Mil.)* Ticket of admission to a hospital. 4. *(Mil.)* List of casualties in a muster-roll. Places vacant in a company, or regiment. 5. Blackball, adverse vote. **Dar de baja**, to make a return of the casualties which have happened in a military corps. 6. Casualty. **Las bajas son grandes**, the casualties are heavy. 7. **Dar de baja a un empleado**, to give notice to an employee.

bajada [bah- hah´-dah], *f.* 1. Descent, the road or path by which a person descends. 2. Inclination of an arch

bajado, da [bah-hah'-do, dah], *a.* Descended, fallen down, lowered. **Bajado del cielo**, dropped from heaven, uncommonly excellent; unexpected. -*pp.* of BAJAR.

bajalato [bah-hah-lah'-to], *m.* The dignity and office of a pasha, and the territory belonging thereto.

bajamar [bah-hah-mar'],*f.* Low water, low tide.

bajamente [bah-hah-men'-tay], *adv.* Basely, meanly, abjectly, lowly.

bajante [bah-hahn'-tay], *m.* Drainpipe.

bajar [bah-har'], *vn.* 1. To descend, to come down, to fall. **La venta nunca ha bajado de mil**, sales have never been less than a thousand. 2. To lower, to lessen. -*va.* 1. To lower, to hang down, to let down. **Bajar el equipaje al taxi**, to take the luggage down to the taxi. 2. To reduce the price in selling. 3. To lessen the value of a thing; to narrow. 4. To humble, to bring down. 5. *(Carib.)* To pay up, to cough up. 6. *(And.)* To do in (matar). -*vr.* To crouch, to grovel, to lessen. **Bajar de punto**, to decay, to decline. **Bajar el punto**, to temper. **Bajar la cerviz**, to humble oneself. **Le bajaré los bríos**, I will pull down his courage. **Bajar los humos**, to become more humane. **Bajar los ojos**, to be ashamed. **Bajar la cabeza**, to obey without objection. **Bajar la tierra**, *(Naut.)* to lay the land. **Bajar por un río** *(Naut.)* to drop down a river. **Bajar las velas**, *(Naut.)* to lower the sails. To get off, to get out (vehículo). *(Comp.)* Downloading

bajareque [bah-hah-ray'-kay], *m.* 1. *(LAm.)* Mud wall; *(Carib.)* Hovel, shack. 2. *(CAm.)* Drizzle (llovizna).

bajativo [bah-hah-tee'-vo], *a.* *(Cono Sur)* Digestive.

bajel [bah-hel'], *m.* Vessel: a general name for water-craft. **Bajel desaparejado**, a ship laid up in ordinary. **Bajel boyante**, a light ship. **Bajel de bajo bordo**, a low-built ship. **Bajel marinero**, a good sea-boat. **Bajel velero**, a swift sailor.

bajelero [bah-hay-lay'-ro], *m.* Owner or master of a vessel.

bajero, ra [bah-hay'-ro, rah], *a.* *(Prov.)* That which is under. **Sábana bajera**, the under sheet. 1. Lower ground floor, basement. 2. *(And. CAm, Carib.)* Lower leaves of the tobacco plant; rough tobacco. 3. *(And. Cono Sur, Carib.)* *(fig.)* Insignificant person.

bajete [bah-hay'-tay], *m.* *dim.* 1. A person of low stature. 2. *(Mus.)* Voice between a tenor and a bass, barytone.

bajetón [bah-hay-ton'], *a.* *(And.)* Short, small.

bajeza [bah-hay'-thah], *f.* 1. Meanness, fawning, paltriness. 2. A mean act. 3. Abjectness, littleness. 4. Lowliness, lowness, mechanicalness. 5. *(Obs.)* A low, deep place. **Bajeza de ánimo**, weakness of mind, lowness of spirits. **Bajeza de nacimiento**, meanness of birth.

bajini(s) [bah-hee'-nee], *adv.* **Por lo bajini**, very quietly.

bajío [bah-hee'-o], *m.* 1. A shoal, sandbank, shallow, or flat. 2. Decline of fortune or favor. 3. *(Mex.)* Fertile plateau of northern Mexico.

bajista [bah-hees'-tah], *m.* 1. *(Com.)* Bear, a broker who speculates upon the fall of prices or stocks. 2. A double-bass viol, and one who plays it. Bass guitar player.

bajo, ja [bah'-ho, hah], *a.* 1. Low. 2. Abject, despicable, faint. 3. Common, ordinary; mechanical, humble. 4. Dull, faint (colores). 5. Mean, coarse, vulgar (lenguaje). 6. Bent downward. **Bajo de ley**, Of a base quality (metales). **Con los ojos bajos**, with downcast eyes.

bajo [bah'-ho], *adv.* 1. Under, underneath, below. *V.* ABAJO and DEBAJO. 2. Low, with depression of the voice. 3. Low, in a state of subjection. 4. In a humble, submissive manner. **Por lo bajo**, cautiously, in a prudent manner. **Bajo mano**, Underhand secretly.

bajo [bah'-ho], *m.* 1. Bass, the lowest part in music. **Bajo profundo**, basso profundo. 2. Player on the bassviol or bassoon. 3. Low situation or place. **Bajo relieve**, *(Sculp.)* Bassrelief. **Cuarto bajo**, Ground-floor. -*pl.* 1. Underpetticoats of women. 2. Hoofs or feet of horses.

bajoca [bah-ho'-cah],*f.* *(Prov.)* 1. Green kidney-beans. 2. A dead silk worm.

bajón [bah-hone'], *m.* 1. Bassoon. 2. A player on the bassoon. 3. Decline, fall. *(Fin.)* 4. Sharp fall in price; slump. 5. Slump in moral. **Dar un bajón**, to fall away sharply.

bajoncillo [bah-hon-theel'-lyo], *m.* Counter-bass.

bajonista [bah.ho-ness'-tah], *m.* Bassoon player.

bajorrelieve [bah-hor-ray-le-ay'-vay], *m.* Bas-relief.

bajovientre [bah-ho-ve-en'-tray], *m.* Hypogastrium.

bajuno, na [bah-hoo'-no, nah], *a.* Vile, low, contemptible (personas).

bajura [bah-hoo'-rah], *f.* 1. *a.* Lowness; shortness, smallness, small size. 2. *(Carib.) (Geog.)* Lowland. 3. **Pesca de bajura,** inshore fishing, coastal fishing.

bakelita [bah-kay-lee-tah], *f.* V. BAQUELITA.

bala [bah'-lah], *f.* 1. Bullet, shot. **Bala de metralla,** grapeshot. **Bala expansiva,** dumdum bullet. **Como una bala,** quick as a flash. 2. Bale (de papel, mercancías). 3. Small ball of wax to play tricks at carnival time. 4. *(Com.)* Bale. **Bala de algodón,** bale of cotton. 5. **Bala de entintar** *(Typ.)* inkball, inking ball.

balaca [bah-lah'-cah], *f.* *(LAm.)* Boast, piece of boasting, brag; *(And)* Show, pomp.

balacada [bah-lah-cah'-dah], *f.* *(Cono Sur)* V. BALACA.

balacear [bah-lah-thay-ar'], *va.* *(Mex.)* To shoot haphazardly, to shoot at random.

balacera [bah-lah-thay'-rah], *f.* *(Mex.)* Haphazard shooting, shooting at random.

balada [bah-lah'-dah], *f.* Ballad, a song.

baladí [bah-lah-dee'], *a.* Mean, despicable, worthless, trivial.

balador, ra [bah-lah-dor', rah], *m. & f.* Bleating animal.

baladrar [bah-lah-drar'], *vn.* To cry out, to shout.

baladre [bah-lah'-dray], *m.* *(Bot.)* Rose bay.

baladrero [bah-lah-dray'-ro], *a.* Loud, noisy.

baladro [bah-lah'-dro], *m.* Scream, howl; shout.

baladrón [bah-lah-drone'], *m.* Boaster bragger, bully.

baladronada [ba-lah-dro-nah'-dah], *f.* 1. Boast, brag, fanfaronade, bravado. 2. Rodomontade.

baladronear [bah-lah-dro-nay-ar'], *vn.* To boast, to brag, to hector.

balagar [bah-lah-gar'], *m.* *(Prov.)* Long straw or hay preserved for winter fodder.

bálago [bah'-lah-go], *m.* 1. V. BALAGAR. 2 Hayrick. 3. Thick spume of soap, of which wash-balls are made. **Sacudir or menear a uno el bálago,** to give a sound scrubbing.

balaguero [bah-lah-gay'-ro], *m.* Rick of straw.

balahú [bah-lah-oo'], *m.* A schooner.

balaj [bah-lah'], *m.* Balas or spinel ruby.

balance [bah-lahn'-thay], *m.* 1. Fluctuation, vibration. 2. Libration, swinging, see-saw. 3. Equilibrium or equipoise of a rider on horseback. 4. Balance of accounts, balance-sheet. **Balance de situación,** balance sheet. 5. *(Obs.)* Doubt. 6. Rolling of a ship. **Balance de comercio,** balance of trade.

balanceado [bah-lahn-thay-ah'-do], *m.* Swing.

balancear [bah-lan-thay-ar'], *va. & vn.* 1. To balance, to vibrate; to librate, to poise, to hold in equipoise. 2. *(Met.)* To waver, to be unsettled. 3. To weigh, to examine. 4. To settle accounts.

balanceo [bah-lan-thay'-o], *m.* Oscillation, rocking motion.

balancero, *m.* V. BALANZARIO.

balancín [bah-lan-theen'], *m.* 1. Splinter-bar of a carriage, swing-bar of a cart. Singletree, whiffletree. *(Mech.)* Walking-beam, balance-beam. 2. Iron beam for striking coins and medals; minting mill. 3. Poy, a rope-dancer's pole. 4. *(Amer.)* A sort of gig drawn by three horses abreast. **Balancines** *(Naut.)* lifts, ropes serving to raise or lower the yards. **Balancines de la brújula,** *(Naut.)* brass rings by which the compass is suspended in the binnacle.

balandra [bah-lahn'-drah], *f.* *(Naut.)* 1. Bilander, a small vessel carrying but one mast. 2. Sloop.

balandrán [bah-lahn-drahn'], *m.* A loose surtout worn by priests, cassock.

balandrista [bah-lahn-drees'-tah], *m. & f.* Yachtman, yachtswoman; sailing enthusiast.

balandro [bah-lahn'-dro], *m.* Yacht; *(Carib.)* Fishing vessel.

balano [bah-lahn'-tay], *m.* 1. Balanus, the glans penis. 2. Barnacle.

balante [bah-lahn'-tay], *pa.* *(Poet.)* Bleating.

balanza [bah-laan'-thah], *f.* 1. Scale. **Balanza de presión,** precision balance. 2. Balance, a pair of scales. 3. A kind of fishing-net. 4. *(Met.)* Comparative estimate, judgment. **Fiel de balanza de la romana,** needle of the balance. **Fiel de balanza,** (in the mints) the weigh-master. **Andar en balanza,** *(Met.)* to be in danger of losing one's property or place. 5. Gallows, in cant.

balanzar [bah-lan-thar'], *va.* *(Obs.)* V. BALANCEAR.

balanzario [bah-lan-thah'-re-o], *m.* Balancer, he who weighs and adjusts the coins in the mint.

balanzón [bah-lan-thone'], *m.* Copper pan used by silversmiths.

balaou [bah-lah'-o-oo], *m.* *(Zool.)* A kind of sprat.

balaquear [bah-lah-kay-ahr'], *vn.* To boast.

balar [bah-lar'], *vn.* To bleat. **Andar balando por alguna cosa,** to be gaping after something.

Balasor [bah-lah-sor'], *m.* Balassor.

balastar [bali-las-tar'], *va.* To ballast a railroad track.

balaste [bah-lahs'-tay], *m.* Ballast, a layer of gravel between the ties.

balasto [bah-lahs'-to], *m.* Ballast. Sleeper *(Ferro.)*.

balastro [bah-lahs'-to], *m.* V. BALASTO.

balate [bah-lah'-tay], *m.* 1. A boundary mark (heap of stones, etc.). 2. Border of a trench.

balaustrada, balaustrería [bah-lah-oos-trah'-dah, oos-tray-ree'-ah], *f.* Balustrade.

balaustrado, da [bah-lah-oos-trah'-do, dah], **Balaustral,** *a.* Balustered.

balaustre [bah-lah-oois'-tray], *m.* Baluster. **Balaustres de navío,** *(Naut.)* Balusters or head-rails of a ship.

balay [bah-lah'-ee], *m.* *(LAm.)* Wicker basket.

balazo [bah-lah'-tho], *m.* A shot; wound from a ball.

balboa [bal-bo-ah], *m.* Balboa, monetary unit of Panama.

balbucear [bal-boo-thay-ar'], *m.* To speak and pronounce indistinctly like little children; to stutter, to stammer.

balbucencia [hal-boo-then'-the-ah], *f.* Stuttering speech.

balbuceo [bal-boo-thay'-o], *m.* Stammering, stuttering.

balbuciente [bal-boo-the-en'-tay], *a.* Stammering, stuttering.

balbucir [bal-boo-theer'], *vn.* To lisp.

Balcanes [bahl-cah'-nays], *m. & pl.* The Balkans. **La Península de los Balcanes,** the Balkan Peninsula.

balcánico [bahl-cah'-nee-co], *a.* Balkan.

balcanización [bahl-cah-nee-thah-thee-on'], *f.* Balkanization.

balcarrias [bahl-cah'-rree-ahs], *f. & pl.* **Balcarrotas** *(And.)* Sideburns.

balcón [bal-cone'], *m.* Balcony; (mirador).

balconada [bahl-co-nah'-dah], *f.* Row of balconies.

balconaje [bal-co-nah'-hay], *m.* **balconería,** *f.* Range of balconies.

balconazo [bai-co-nah'-tho], *m. aug.* A large balcony.

balconcillo [bal-con-theel'-lyo], *m. dim.* A small balcony.

balconeador(a) [bahl-co-nay-ah-dor'], *m. & f.* Onlooker, observer.

balconear [bahl-co-nay-ahr'], 1. *va.* *(Cono Sur)* To watch closely. 2. *(CAm.)* To talk at the window.

balconero [bahl-co-nay'-ro], *m.* Cat burglar.

balda [bahl'-dah], *f.* Trifle, a thing of little value. **A la balda,** living in a heedless, imprudent manner. Shelf.

baldada [bahl-dah'-dah], *f.* *(Cono Sur)* Bucketful.

baldado [bahl-dah'-do], 1. *a.* Crippled, disabled. **Estar baldado,** to be knackered. 2. *m. f.* Cripple, disabled person.

baldaquín [bahl-dah-keen'], *m.* **baldaquino,** canopy, daldachin.

baldar [bal-dar], *va.* 1. To cripple. 2. *(Prov.)* To break a set of books, or other things. 3. To trump or win a trick in a game at cards. 4. To obstruct, or hinder.

balde [bahl'-day], *m.* Bucket, used on board ships.

balde (De), *adv.* (Gratis) free of cost. **En balde,** in vain, to no purpose.

baldear [bal-day-ar'], *vn.* *(Naut.)* To throw water on the deck and sides of a ship for the purpose of cleaning them.

baldeo [bal-day'-o], *m.* *(Naut.)* Washing the decks with bucketfuls of water.

baldés [bal-dess'], *m.* A piece of soft dressed skin for gloves, etc.

baldío, día [bal-dee'-o, ah], *a.* 1. Untilled, uncultivated (tierras). 2. Unappropriate. **Los baldíos,** the lay-land, the commons; waste or waste land. 3. *(Ibs.)* Idle, lazy. **Hombre baldío,** vagrant, vagabond.

baldón [bal-done'], *m.* Affront, reproach, insult, contumely.

baldonar, baldonear [Bal-do-nar', bal-do-nay-ar'], *va.* To insult with abusive language, to reproach, to stigmatize.

baldosa [bal-do'-sah], *f.* 1. A fine square tile. 2. Flat paving-stones.

baldosado [bahl-do-sah'do], *m.* Tiled floor, tiling; paving.

baldosar [bahl-do-sahr'], *va.* To tile; to pave.

balduque [bal-doo'-kay], *m.* Narrow red tape, for tying papers.

balear [bah-lay-ahr'], 1. *va. (LAm.)* To shoot, to shoot dead. 2. To cheat. -*vr. (LAm.)* To exchange shots.

baleárico, ca [bah-le-ah'-re-co, cah], **baleario, ia** [bah-le-ah'-re-o, ah], *a.* Balearic.

baleo [bah-lay'-o], *m.* 1. *(LAm.)* Shooting. 2. *(Mex.)* Fan.

balero [bah-lay'-ro], *m.* A ball-mould.

baleta [bah-lay'-tah], *f. dim.* A small bale of goods.

balí [ba-lee'], *m.* 1. A learned language of the Indo-Chinese. 2. One of the five Indian commandments, that of offering food to every animated being.

balido [bah-lee'-do], *m.* Bleating, bleat.

balija [bah-lee'-hah], *f.* 1. Portmanteau. 2. Mail, the postman's bag. 3. Post.

balijero [bah-le-hay'-ro], *m.* A post or post-boy who carries letters out of the post-road.

balijilla [bah- le-heel'-lyah], *f. dim.* A small bag.

balijón [bah-lee'-hone], *m. aug.* A large portmanteau.

balín [bah-leen'], *m.* Small bullet, pellet.

balinera [bah-lee-nay'-rah], *f. (And.)* Ball-bearing.

balines [bah-lee'-nes], *m. pl. (Amer.)* Mould-shot, buckshot.

balista [bah-lees'-tah], *f.* Ballista, engine used in ancient warfare for hurling heavy stones.

balística [bah-lees'-te-cah], *f.* Ballistics, science that deals with the impact, path, and velocity of projectiles.

balístico, ca [bah-lees'-te-co, cah], *a.* Ballistic. **Proyectil balístico,** ballistic missile.

balita [bah-lee'-tah], *f.* 1. Small bullet, pellet. 2. *(Cono Sur)* Marble.

baliza [bah-lee'-tha], *f. (Naut.)* Buoy, marker; *(Aer.)* Beacon, marker.

balizaje [bah-lee-thah'hay], *m.* **Balizaje de pista,** runway lighting.

ballena [bahl-lyay'-nah], *f.* 1. Whale (mamífero). 2. Train-oil. 3. Bone (de cuello). 4. *(Astr.)* One of the northern constellations. 5. **Parece una ballena,** she's as fat as a whale.

ballenato [bahl-lyay-nah'-to], *m.* Cub, the young of a whale.

ballener [bahl-lyay-ner'], *m. (Obs.)* A vessel in the shape of a whale.

ballenera [bahl-lyay-nay'-rah], *f.* Whaler, whaling ship.

ballenero [bahl-lyay-nay'-ro], 1. *a.* Whaling. **Industria ballenera,** whaling industry. 2. *m.* Whaler (persona). 3. Whaling ship.

ballesta [bal-lyes'-tah], *f.* Shot from a cross-bow, **A tiro de ballesta,** *(Met.)* at a great distance.

ballestazo [bal-lyes-tah-tho'], *m.* Blow given by or received from a cross-bow.

ballesteador [bal-lyes-tay-ah-dor'], *m.* Cross-bowman.

ballestear [bal-lyes-tay-ar'], *va.* To shoot with a cross-bow.

ballestera [bal-lyes-tay'-rah], *f.* Loopholes through which crossbows were discharged.

ballestería [bal-lyes-tay-ree'-ah], *f.* 1. Archery, the art of an archer. 2. Number of crossbows, or persons armed with crossbows. 3. Place where crossbows are kept, or arbalists quartered.

ballestero [bal-lyes-tay'-ro], *m.* 1. Archer, crossbowman. 2. Crossbow maker. 3. King's archer or armorer. **Ballestero**

de maza, mace-bearer. **Ballesteros de corte,** the King's porters and the portes of the privy council were formerly so called.

ballestilla [bal-lyes-teel'-lyah], *f.* 1. *(Dim.)* Small crossbow. 2. *(Obs.)* The instrument for bleeding cattle, at present called a *fleam.* 3. Cross-staff, an instrument for measuring heights, 4. *(Naut.)* Fore-staff, an instrument used for measuring the altitude of the sun, stars, etc.

ballestón [bal-lyes-tone'], *m. aug.* Large cross-bow, arbalet.

ballestrinque [bal-lyes-treen'-kay], *m. (Naut.)* Clove-hitch, by which one rope is fastened to another.

ballet [bah-lay'], *m.* Ballet.

ballico [bal-lyee'-co], *m. (Bot.)* Red or perennial darnal, rye-grass.

ballueca [bal-lyoo-ay'-cah], *f. (Bot. Prov.)* Wild oats.

balneario, *m.* Spa, bathing beach (con playa), bathing resort.

balneario, ria [bal-nay-ah'-re-o, ah], *a.* Of or pertaining to baths and bathing.

balompédico [bah-lon-pay'-dee-co], *a.* Football.

balompié [bah-lom-pe-ay'], *m.* Soccer.

balón [bah-lon'], *m.* 1. Soccer ball. 2. Glass ball. 3. Balloon. 4. Bale. **Balón medicinal,** Medicine ball. 5. *(And. Cono Sur)* Drum, canister.

baloncestista [bah-lon-thays-tees'-tah], *m. & f.* Basketball player.

baloncestístico [bah-lon-thays-tees'-tee-co], *a.* Basketball.

baloncesto [bah-lon-thes'-to], *m.* Basketball.

balonmanear [bah-lon-mah-nay-ahr'], *vn.* To handle, to handle the ball.

balonmano [bah-lon-mah'-no], *m.* Handball.

balonvolea [bah-lon-vo-lay'-ah], *m.* Volleyball.

balota [bah-lo'-tah], *f.* Ballot, a little ball used in voting.

balotada [bah-lo-tah'-dah], *f.* Balotade, leap of a horse, in which he shows the shoes of his hinder feet.

balotaje [bah-lo-tah-hay], *m. (Mex.)* Balloting, voting; continuing of votes.

balotar [bah-lo-tar'], *vn.* To ballot, to choose by ballot.

balsa [bahl'-sah], *f.* 1. Pool, lake. 2. *(Naut.)* Raft of float for conveying persons across a river. 3. *(Prov.)* Half a butt of wine. 4. In oil-mills, the room where the oil is kept. **Estar como una balsa de aceite,** to be as quiet as a pool of oil; spoken of a place or country, or of the sea.

balsadera [bahl-sah-day-rah], *f.* **Balsadero** *m.* Ferry (station).

balsámico, ca [bal-sah'-me-co, cah], *a.* Balsamic, balsamical, balmy.

balsamina [bal-sah-mee'-nah], *f. (Bot.)* Balsam-apple.

balsamita mayor [bal-sab-mee'-tah mah-yor']. *(Bot.)* V. ATANASIA. **Balsamita menor,** *(Bot.)* Maudlin, annual costmary, tansy.

bálsamo [bahl'-sah-mo], *m.* 1. Balsam balm. **Bálsamo de María,** gum of the calaba-tree. **Bálsamo de copaiba,** copaiba balsam. **Es un bálsamo,** it is a balsam (licores). 2. *(Med.)* The purest part of the blood. *(fig.)* Balm, comfort.

balsar [bal-sar'], *m.* A marshy piece of ground with brambles.

balsear [bal-say-ar'], *va.* To cross rivers on rafts.

balsero [bal-ay'-ro], *m.* Ferry-man.

balsón [bahl-son'], *m. (Mex.)* Swamp, bog; stagnant pool. *a. (And.)* Fat, flabby.

balsopeto [bal-so-pay'-to], *m. (Coll.)* 1.A large pouch carried near the breast. 2. Bosom, the inside of the breast.

balsoso [bahl-so'-so], *a. (And.)* Soft, spongy.

Baltasar [bal-tah-sar'], *m.* Belshazzar, the last King of Babylon.

Báltico [bahl'-te-co], *m.* The Baltic Sea.

bálteo [bahl'-tay-o], *m.* Officer's belt.

baluarte [bah-loo-ar'-tay], *m.* 1. *(Fort.)* Bastion, formerly bulwark, a mass of earth raised in the angles of a polygon. 2. *(Met.)* Bulwark, defence, support.

balumba [bah-loom'-bah], *f.* Bulk or quantity of things heaped together.

balumbo, balume [bah-loom'-bo, bah-loo'-may], *m.* A heap of things which take up a lot of room.

balumoso [bah-loo-mo'-so], *m. (And. Cam. Méx.)* Bulky.

baluquero [bah-loo-kay'-ro], *m. (Fin.)* Forger.

balurdo [bah-loor'-do], 1. *a. (LAm.)* Flashy. 2. *m. (Cono Sur)* Crooked deal.

balzo [bahl'-tho], *m. (Naut.)* A bend.

bamba [bam'-bah], *m. &f.* 1. *(Carib.)* Negro, negress. 2. *(And.) (Bot.)* Bole, swelling. & Fat, flabbiness.

bambalear, babanear [bam-bah-lay-ahr], *vn.* V. BAMBOLEAR.

bambalina [bam-bah-lee'-nah],*f.* The upper part of the scenes in theaters.

bambalúa [bam-bah-loo'-ah], *m. (LAm.)* Clumsy fellow, lout.

bambarria [bam-bar'-re-ah], *m.* 1. *(Low.)* A fool, an idiot. 2. An accidental but successful stroke at billiards

bambochada bam-bo-chah'-dah], *f.* **bamboche** [bam-bo'-chay], *m.* A landscape representing banquets or drunken feasts, with grotesque figures. **Es un bamboche,** or **parece un bamboche;** applied to a thick, short person with a red, bloated face.

bambolear, bambonear [bam-bo-lay-ar', bam-bo-nay-ar'], *vn.* To reel, to stagger, to totter. *-vr.* To swing, sway; to sway, roll, ree.

bamboleo, bamboneo [bam-bo-lay'-o, bam-bo-nay'-o], *m.* Reeling, staggering.

bambolla [bam-bol'-lyah],*f.* Ostentation, boast, vain show, froth.

bambollero [bam-bol-laye'-ro], *a.* Showy, flashy; sham, bogus.

bambú, or **bambuc** [bam-boo' or bam-book], *m.* Bamboo, the largest of the grass family.

bambuco [bam-boo'-co], *m.* Popular musical rhythm of Colombia.

bambudal [bam-boo-dahl], *m. (And.)* Bamboo grove.

ban [ban], *m.* A sort of fine Chinese muslin.

banal [bah-nahl], *a.* Banal, trivial, ordinary.

banalidad [bah-nah'-lee-tee], *f.* 1. Banality, triviality, ordinariness. 2. Banality, trivial thing. **Intercambiar banalidades con uno,** to exchange trivialities with somebody.

banana, *f.* V. PLÁTANO.

bananal [bah-nah-nahl'], *m. (LAm.)* Banana plantation.

bananero [bah-nah-nay'-ro], 1. *a. (LAm.)* Banana. **Compañía bananera,** banana company ? *m.* Banana plantation. Banana tree.

banano, *m. (Bot.)* V. PLÁTANO.

banas [bah'-nahs], *f. & pl. (Mex.)* Banns.

banasta [bah-nahs'-tah],*f.* A large basket made of twigs or laths. **Meterse en banasta;** to meddle with things which do not concern one.

banastero [bah-nas-tay'-ro], *m.* 1. Basket-maker or dealer. 2. *(Low.)* Jailer.

banasto [bah-nahs'-to], *m.* A large round basket.

banca [bahn'-cah],*f.* 1. Bench. 2. Banking. **Horas de banca,** banking hours. 3. Bank (juegos). **Hacer saltar la banca,** to break the bank. 4. *(Cono Sur)* Pull, influence. **Tener banca,** to have pull.

bancada [ban-cah'-dah],*f.* A sort of bench on which to spread cloth to be measured.

bancal [ban-cahl'], *m.* 1. An oblong plot of ground for raising, roots, and fruit-trees. 2. Terrace in a garden. 3. Cover placed over a bench by way of ornament.

bancar [bahn-cahr'], *va. (Cono Sur)* To pay for. *(fig.)* To put up with (aguantar). *-vr.* **Bancarse algo a uno,** to put up with something/somebody.

bancaria, [ban-cah'-ree-ah] *f.* V. FIANZA, BANCARIA.

bancario, ria [ban-cah'-re-o, ah], *a.* Bank, banking, **Cuenta bancaria,** bank account.

bancarrota [ban-car-ro'-tah],*f.* Bankruptcy, failure.

bancaza [ban-cah'-thah],*f.* **Bancazo** [ban-cah'-tho], *m. aug.* A large form or bench. *m. (Mex.)* Bank robbery.

banco [bahn'-co], *m.* 1. Form or bench without a back. 2. A strong bench for the use of carpenters. **Banco de acepillar,** a planing-bench. 3. A thwart, or bench for rowers. 4. A bank, a place where money is kept. 5. Company of persons concerned in managing a joint stock of money. 6. The cheeks of the bit of a bridle. 7. A pedestal on which any piece of architecture is raised. **Banco de ahorros,** savings-bank. **Banco de arena,** sand-bank. **Banco de hielo,** field of ice. **Banco de río,** sand-bank in a river. **Banco pinjado,** ancient warlike machine for battering. **Pasar Banco,** to flog the sailors on board a galley. **Razón de pie de banco,** an absurd reason, a groundless motive. **Banco de la paciencia,** *(Naut.)* bench on the quarter-deck. **Banco de piedra,** a vein or stratum of a single kind of stone.

banco de sangre [bahn'-co day sahn'-gray], *m.* Bloodbank.

banda [bahn'-dah] *f.* 1. Sash formerly worn by military officers when on duty. 2. Ribbon worn by the knights of the military orders. 3. Band or body of troops. 4. Scarf. 5. Party of persons; crew; military band; brass band: 6. Covey, a number of birds together. V. BANDADA. 7. Bank, border, edge: side of a ship. 8. Felloe, of wheel. 9. Cushion (billiards). **La banda del norte,** the north side. **La banda izquierda del río,** the left bank of the river. **A la banda,** *(Naut.)* heeled or hove down. **En banda,** *(Naut.)* amain. **Arriar en banda,** to let go amain. **Caer or estar en banda,** to be amain. **Dar a la banda,** to heel. **Bandas del tajamar,** *(Naut.)* the cheeks of the head. **No ir or tirar a ninguna banda,** not to make any odds. **De banda a banda,** from party to party, from one side to another. 10. **Coger a uno por banda,** to make somebody do the dirty work.

bandada [ban-dah'-dah], *f.* Covey: flock of birds.

bandarria [ban-dar'-re-ah], *f. (Naut.)* An iron maul.

bandazo [bahn-dah'-tho], *m.* Heavy fall; *(Naut.)* Heavy roll (de un barco). *(LAm.)* Air pocket, sudden drop.

bandear [Ban-day-ar'], *va.* 1. *(Obs.)* To traverse, to pass, to cross from one side to another; to band. 2. *(CAm.)* To pursue, to chase. 3. *(CAm.)* To wound severely, to hurt. *-vn.* To conduct oneself with prudence, to shift for oneself. **Saber bandeárselas,** to know how to look for himself. *-vr.* To move to and fro; *(Mex.)* To move to the other side of a boat. 2. *(Cono Sur)* To change parties. 3. *(Mex.)* To vacillate; to go one way and then another. 4. To manage, to get organized.

bandeja [ban-day'-hah],*f.* Tray, kind of metallic waiter. *(fig.)* **Servir algo a uno en bandeja,** to hand something to somebody on a plate.

bandera [ban-day'-rah], *f.* 1. Banner, standard. 2. Flag, ensign, a pair of colors of a regiment of infantry. 3. Infantry. 4. Flag or colors which distinguish the ships of the different nations. **Bandera de popa,** *(Naut.)* the ensign. **Bandera de proa** *(Naut.)*, the jack. **Bandera blanca or de paz,** the flag of truce. **Vuelo de la bandera,** the flag of the ensign. **Arriar la bandera,** to strike the colors **Salir con banderas desplegadas,** to get off with flying colors. **Asegurar la bandera,** to fire a cannon-shot with ball at the time of hoisting the colors. **Dar la bandera,** *(Met.)* to submit to the superior talents or merits of another. **Levantar banderas,** *(Met.)* to put oneself at the head of a party. **De banderas,** terrific, marvellous.

bandereta [ban-day-ray'-tah], *f. dim.* Banneret, bannerol, a small flag. **Baderetas,** *(Mil.)* Camp-colors.

bandería [bahn-day-ree'-ahs],*f.* Faction; *(fig.)* Bias, partiality.

baderica, illa [ban-day-raree'-cah, eel' lyah], *dim.* Banneret, a small flag.

banderilla [ban-day-reel'-lyah], *f.* 1. A small dart with a banderole, thrust into the nape of a bull. **Poner a uno una banderilla,** *(Met.)* to taunt, to ridicule to revile, to vex. 2. *(LAm.)* Swindle. 3. *(Culin.)* Savory appetizer (tapa en bar).

banderillear [ban-day-reel'-lyay-ar'], *va.* To put *banderillas* on bulls.

banderillero [ban-day-reel-lyay'-ro], *m.* He who sticks *banderrillas* in a bull's nape.

banderín [ban-day-reen´], *m.* 1. Camp colors. 2. Flag, railway signal. 3. Recruiting post.

banderita [bahn-day-ree'-tah], *f.* Little flag; flag sold for charity.

banderizar, *va.* V. ABANDERIZAR.

banderizo, za [ban-day-ree´-tho, thah], *a.* Factious, given to party.

banderola [ban-day-ro´-lah], *f.* 1. Banderol, camp colors. 2. Carabine belt. 3. Streamer, a pennant.

bandidaje [bahn-dee-dah-hay], *m.* Banditry.

bandido [ban-dee´-do], *m.* 1. Bandit, highwayman, outlaw, freebooter. 2. Fugitive pursued with judicial advertisements.

bandín [ban-deen´], *m. (Naut.)* Seat in a row-galley.

bandita [ban-dee´-tah], *f. dim.* A small band.

bando [bahn´-do], *m.* 1. Proclamation. A public declaration by government. 2. Edict or law solemnly published by superior authority. 3. Faction, party. **Echar bando,** to proclaim an edict. **Pasarse al otro bando,** to go over to the other side.

bandola, *f.* **bandolín,** *m.* [ban-do´-lah]. 1. Mandolin, a small musical instrument resembling a lute. 2. *(Naut.)* Jury-mast. 3. *(And.)* Bullfighter´s cape. 4. *(Carib.)* Knotted whip.

bandolera [ban-do-lay´-rah], *f.* 1. Bandoleer, carabine belt, cross belt. 2. Woman bandit.

bandolerismo [bahn-do-lay-rees'-mo], *m.* Brigandage, banditry.

bandolero [ban-do-lay´-ro], *m.* Highwayman (bandido), robber.

bandolina [ban-do-lee´-nah], *f.* Bandoline, viscous substance used as a hair fixative.

bandoneón [ban-do-lay-on'], *m. (LAm.)* Large accordion.

bandujo [ban-doo´-ho], *m. (Obs.)* Large sausage.

bandullo [ban-dool'-lyo], *m. (Vulg.)* Belly; the bowels.

bandurria [ban-door´-re-ah], *f.* Bandurria, a musical instrument resembling a fiddle.

bangaña [ban-gah´-nyah], *f.* Bangaño *m. (LAm.)* Calabash, gourd; vessel made from a gourd.

Bangladesh [ban-glah-desh'], *m.* Bangladesh.

banjo [bahn´-ho], *m. (Mus.)* Banjo.

bánova [bah'-no-vah], *f. (Prov.)* Bedquilt, bed-cover.

banquear [ban-kay-ahr'], *va. (And.)* To level, flatten out.

banqueo [ban-kay'-o], *m.* Terraces, terracing.

banquera [ban-kay'-rah], *f. (Prov.)* 1. Small open beehouse. 2. Frame, on which bee-hives are placed in a beehouse.

banquero, ra [ban-kay'-ro], **m, f.** Banker, exchanger. *V.* CAMBISTA.

banqueta [ban-kay'-tah], *f.* 1. A stool with three legs. 2. *(Mil.)* Banquette or footbank behind the parapet. 3. A sidewalk. **Banquetas de cureña,** *(Naut.)* Gun-carriage beds. **Banquetas de calafate,** *(Naut.)* calking-stools.

banquetazo [ban-kay-tah'-tho], *m.* Spread, blow out.

banquete [ban-kay'-tay], *m.* 1. Banquet, a splendid repast. **Banquete casero,** family feast. 2. Stool.

banquetear [ban-kay-tay-ar'], *vn.* To banquet, to feast.

banquillo [ban-keel'-lyo], *m. dim.* A little stool, bench. **Banquillo de los acusados,** prisoner´s seat.

banquisa [ban-kee'-sah], *f.* Ice field, ice floe.

banquito [ban-kee'-to], *m. dim.* (from BANCO). A stool, footstool.

bantam [ban'-tam] *f.* Bantam. *(LAm.) (fig.)* Small restless person.

bantú [ban-too'], 1. *a.* Bantu. 2. *m.* Bantu.

banyo [ban'-yo], *m. (LAm.)* Banjo.

banzo [bahn'-tho], *m.* Check or side of an embroidering or quilting-frame.

bañada [ban-nyah'dah], *f. (LAm.)* Bath, dip, swim.

bañadera [ba-nyah-day'-rah], *f.* 1. Bathtub, bath. 2. Tub, vat. 3. *(Naut.)* Skeet, a narrow oblong ladle or scoop for wetting the sails, decks, and sides of a ship, or for bailing a boat.

bañadero [ba-nyah-day´-ro], *m.* Puddle, in which wild beasts wallow; bathing-place.

bañado [bah-nyah'-do], *m. (And. Cono Sur)* Swamp, marsh-land; flash, rain pool.

bañador, ra [ba-nyah-dor´, rah], *m. & f.* Swimmer, bather (que se baña). 2. Swimming suit, swimsuit, bathing costume, bathing suit (de hombre y mujer), bathing trunks (de hombre).

bañar [bah-nyar'], *va.* 1. To bathe, to wash in water. 2. To water, to irrigate. **El río baña las murallas de la ciudad,** the river washes the walls of the town. 3. To candy biscuits, plums, etc., with sugar. 4. *(Art.)* To wash over a painting, with a second coat of transparent colors. 5. To overlay with something shining or pellucid. **Loza bañada or vidriada,** glazed earthenware. **Bañarse en agua de rosas,** to bathe in rose-water, to be highly pleased. 6. To extend or enlarge.

bañata [bah-nyah'-tah], *m. (Esp.)* Swimsuit, bathing costume.

bañera [bah-nyay'-rah], *f.* Bathtub.

bañero [bah-nyay'-ro], *m.* 1. Owner of baths. 2. Bath-keeper or attendant.

bañil [bah-nyeel'], *m.* A pool in which deer bathe.

bañista [bah-nyees'-tah], *m.* He who bathes in or drinks mineral waters.

baño [bah´-nyo], *m.* 1. Bath. **Tomar un baño,** to bath. 2. Bathing. **3.** Bath, bathtub. **Cuarto de baño,** bathroom. **Baño de María,** cooking in a double boiler. 4. Coat of paint put over another. 5. Basting (in cooking).

bañuelo [bah-nyoo-ay'-lo], *m. dim.* A little bath.

bao [bah'-oh], *m. (Naut.)* Beam, the main cross timber. **Baos de las cubiertas altas,** the beams of the upper deck. **Bao maestro,** the midship beam. **Baos del saltillo de proa,** the collar beams. **Baos de los palos,** trestle-trees. **Baos y crucetas de los palos,** cross and trestle trees.

baobal [bah-o-bahl'], *m. (Bot.)* Baobab; a great tree of Africa. (Native name).

baptismo, *m. (Obs.) V.* BAUTISMO.

baptista [bap-tees'-tah], *m. & f.* Baptist. **La iglesia Baptista,** the Baptist church.

baptisterio [bap-tis-tay'-re-o], *m.* Baptistery.

baque [bah'-kay], *m.* 1. The blow which a body gives in falling. 2. A water-trough in glasshouses.

baqueano [bah-kay-ah'-no], *m.* etc. *V.* Baquiano.

baquelita [bah-kay-lee'-tah], *f.* Bakelite. (A trade mark for a synthetic resin.)

baqueriza [bah-kay-ree'-thah], *f.* Stable, place to keep cow in winter.

baqueta [bah-kay'-tah], *f.* 1. Ramrod, gunstick. 2. Switch used in a riding-house, in breaking in young horses. **Mandar a baqueta, a la baqueta,** to command imperiously. **Tratar a baqueta,** to treat a person in a haughty manner. *-pl.* 1. Drumsticks. 2. Gantlet, gantlope, a military punishment. 3. *(Arch.)* Beads, reeds, a semicylindric moulding. 4. Rods of hollywood, used in beating wool.

baquetazo [bah-kay-tah'-tho], *m.* 1. Violent fall, great blow given by the body when falling. 2. A blow with the ramrod. **Tropecé y di un baquetazo,** I tripped and fell violently. 3. **Tratar a uno a baquetazo limpio,** to treat somebody harshly.

baqueteado, da [bah-kay-tay'-ah-do, dah], *a.* Inured, habituated.*-pp.* of BAQUETEAR.

baquetear [bah-kay-tay-ar'], *va.* 1. *(Obs.)* To inflict the punishment of the gantlet. 2. To annoy, vex. 3. To make someone toil heavily. **Baquetear la lana,** to beat wool.

baqueteo [bah-kay-tay'-o], *m.* Beating of wool. Annoyance, bother.

baquetón [bah-kay-tone'], *m.* Gunworm, wiper, cleaning-rod. *V.* SACATRAPOS.

baquetilla [bah-kay-teel'-lyah], *f. dim.* A little rod.

baquetudo [bah-kay-too'-do], *a. (Carib.)* Sluggish, slow.

baquía [bah-kee'-ah], *f.* 1. *(LAm.)* Intimate knowledge of a region, local expertise. 2. *(And. Cono Sur)* Expertise, dexterity, skill.

baquiano [bah-kee-ah'-no], *a. (LAm.)* 1. Familiar with a region. 2. *(And. Cono Sur)* Expert, skillful. **Para hacerse**

baquiano hay que perderse alguna vez, one learns the hard way. -*m.* (*LAm.*) Pathfinder, guide; local expert.

báquico, ca [bah'-ke-co, cah], *a.* Bacchanal, relating, to Bacchus. Drunken.

baquio [bah'-ke-o], *m.* (*Poet.*) A metrical foot consisting of a short and two long syllables.

baquira [bah-kee'-rah], *f.* (*Amer.*) A wild hog; peccary.

bar [bar], *m.* 1. Bar (taberna); café; snack bar. 2. Bar (unidad de presión atmosférica).

baracutey [bah-ra-coo-tay'-e], *a.* (*Amer. Cuba*) Morose, sad, retired, fond of solitude.

baradero [bah-rah-day'-ro], *m.* (*Naut.*) Skeed or skid. **Baradero de baja mar**, a muddy place in which vessels stick at low water.

baradura [bah-rah-doo'-rah], *f.* (*Naut.*) The grounding of a vessel.

baraha [ba-rah'ah], *f.* A burlesque song of Indians.

barahunda, *f.* V. BARAÚNDA. Uproar, hubbub, racket, din.

baraja [bah-rah'-hah], *f.* 1. A complete pack of cards. 2. (*Obs.*) A quarrel. **Meterse en barajas**, to seek a quarrel.

barajador, ra [ba-rah-ha-dor', rah], *m. & f.* One who shuffles or jumbles together.

barajadura [bah-rah-hah-doo'-rah], *f.* 1. Shuffling of cards. 2. Dispute, difference.

barajar [bah-rah-har'], *va.* 1. To shuffle the cards. 2. (*Met.*) To jumble things or persons together. **Barajar un negocio**, to entangle or confuse an affair. **Barajarle a alguno una pretensión**, to frustrate one's pretensions. **Barajar una proposición**, to reject a proposal. -*vn.* (*Obs.*) To wrangle, to contend. -*vr.* 1. (*Cono Sur*) To fight. 2. To get mixed up. 3. **Se baraja la posibilidad de que...**, they are juggling the possibility that...

barajo [bah-rah'-ho], 1. *interj.* (*LAm.*) V. CARAJO. 2. (*And.*) Pretext, excuse; loophole.

barajuste [bah-rah-hoos'-tay], *m.* (*Carib.*) Stampede, rush.

baranda [bah-rahn'-dah], *f.* Railing, handrail, banister (escalera). **Barandas de los corredores de popa de un navío**, sternrails. **Echar de baranda** (*Met.*) to exaggerate something, to boast. -*m.* Boss, chief.

barandado, daje [bah-ran-dah'-do, dah'-hay], *m.* Balustrade.

barandal [bah-ran-dahl'], *m.* 1. The upper and under-piece of a balustrade, in which the balusters are fixed. 2. A balustrade or railing.

barandilla [bah-ran-deel'-lyah], *f. dim.* A small balustrade, a small railing.

barangay [bah-ran-gah'-e], *m.* 1. An Indian vessel, worked with oars. 2. Each group of forty-five or fifty families of Indians, into which a Philipine village is divided.

barata [bah-rah'-tah], *f.* 1. (*Coll.*) Barter, exchange. 2. Low price of things exposed for sale. V. BARATURA. **A la barata**, confusedly, disorderly. **Mala barata**, (*Obs.*) profusion, prodigality. -*f.* (*Cono Sur*) Cockroach.

baratador [bah-rah-tah-dor'], *m.* 1. Barterer. 2. Impostor, deceiver.

baratar [bah-rah-tar'], *va.* 1. To barter, to traffic by exchanging commodities. 2. To make fraudulent barters, to deceive. 3. To give or receive a thing under its just value.

baratear [bah-rah-tay-ar'], *vn.* To sell under price, at a loss.

baratería [bah-rah-tay-ree'-ah], *f.* 1. Barratry. 2. Fraud, deception.

baratero [bah-rah-tay'-ro], *m.* 1. He who obtains money from fortunate gamesters. 2. One who provokes quarrels.

baratez [bah-rah-tayth'], *f.* (*Carib.*), **baratía** *f.* (*And.*) Cheapness.

baratijas [bah-rah-tee'-has], *f. pl.* Trifles, toys. Cheap novelty, inexpensive articles.

baratillero [bah-rah-teel-lyay'-ro], *m.* 1. A peddler. 2. A seller of second-hand goods or articles.

baratillo [bah-rah-teel'-lyo], *m.* 1. A place where new and second-hand furniture, clothing, jewellery, etc., are sold cheap. 2. A heap of trifling articles.

baratista [bah-rah-tees'-tah], *m.* Barterer, trafficker.

barato, ta [bah-rah'-to, tah], *a.* 1. Cheap, inexpensive, bought or sold for a low price. **De barato**, gratuitously. 2. (*Met.*) Easy.

barato [bah-rah'-to], *m.* Money given by the winners at a gaming-table to the bystanders. **Hacer barato**, to sell under value in order to get rid of goods, to sell things under cost price. **Dar de barato**, (*Met.*) to grant for argument's sake, to grant readily, without objection. **Lo barato es caro**, the cheapest goods are dearest. **Ni juega, ni da barato**, to act with indifference, without taking part with a faction. -*adv.* Cheaply.

baratón [bah-rah-ton'], *a.* (*And. CAm., Méx.*) 1. Weak, feeble (argumento). 2. Bargain.

báratro [bah'-rah-tro], *m.* (*Poet.*) Hell, abyss.

baratura [bah-rah-too'-rah], *f.* Cheapness, little value set upon things.

baraúnda [bah-rah-oon'-dah], *f.* Noise, hurly-burly, confusion, din, fluttering.

barauste, *m.* (*Obs.*) V. BALAUSTRE.

barba [bar'-bah'], *f.* 1. Chin. 2. Beard, the hair which grows on the chin. 3. The first swarm of bees which leaves the hive. **Barba cabruna**, (*Bot.*) yellow goat's-beard. **Barba de Aarón**, (*Bot.*) green dragon arum. **Barba de cabra or cabrón**, goat's-beard. **Amarrado a barba de gato**, (*Naut.*) moored by the head. **Temblar la barba**, to shake with fear. **Barba a barba**, face to face. **A barba regada**, in great plenty. **Barba cabosa**, noble, earnest fellow. **A la barba, en la barba**, to his face, in his presence. **Por barba**, a head, apiece. **A polla por barba**, every man his bird. -*m.* 1. Actor who acts the part of old men. 2. *pl.* The portion of rays opposite to the tail of a comet; the head. 3. (*Bot.*) Slender roots of trees or plants; fibres. **Barbas enredadas**, a full hawse. **Barbas de ballena**, whale bone. **Barbas de gallo**, wattle. **Barbas honradas**, A respectable or honorable man. **Cuales barbas, tales tobajas**, treat every one with due respect. **De tal barba, tal escama**, we must expect people to act in accordance with their condition and education. **Decir a uno en sus barbas alguna cosa**, to tell a man a thing to his face. **Echarlo a las barbas**, to reproach a man with something. **Hacer la barba**, 1. To shave, to take off beard. 2. To suck up to somebody. **Mentir por la barba**, to tell a barefaced lie. **Pelarse las barbas**, to fly into a violent passion. **Subirse a las barbas**, to fly in one's face. **Tener buenas barbas**, to have a graceful mien, applied to a fine woman. **Echar a la buena barba**, to induce one to pay for what he and his companions have eaten and drunk. **Andar, estar**, or **traer la barba sobre el hombro**, to wear one's face on one's shoulder, to be alert, to live watchful and careful. **Tener pocas barbas**, to be young or inexperienced. **Hacerse la barba**, to shave oneself. **Hacer la barba a alguno**, (*Amer.*) to flatter, to cajole.

barbacana [bar-bah-cah'-nah], *f.* 1. (*Mil.*) Barbican, an advanced work defending a castle or fortress, or loopholes in a fortification to fire missiles through. 2. A low wall around a church-yard.

barbacoa [bar-ba-co'-ah], *f.* (*Amer.*) 1. Barbecue, meat roasted in a pit in the earth. 2. A framework suspended from forked sticks. 3. (*And.*) Loft (desván). 4. (*And.*) Tap dance.

barbada [bar-bah'-dah], *f.* 1. Lower part of the lower jaw of a horse (where the bridle-curb rests). 2. Curb or iron chain, made fast to the upper part of the bridle, and running under the beard of the horse. 3. Dab, a small flat fish, related to the codfishes. **Agua de la Barbada**, Barbadoes water, a liquor distilled from sugar-cane.

barbadillo, illa [bar-bah-deel'-lyo, lyah], *a. dim.* 1. Having little beard. 2. Having slender filaments (plantas).

barbado, da [bar-bah'-do, dah], *a.* 1. Bearded. 2. Barbed, barbated. -*pp.* of BARBAR.

barbado [bar-bah'-do], *m.* 1. Full grown man. 2. Vine or tree transplanted. 3. Shoots issuing from the roots of trees.

Barbados [bar-bah'-dos], *m.* Barbados.

barbaja [bar-bah'-hah],*f. (Bot.)* Cut leaved viper's grass. *-pl. (Agri.)* The first roots of the plants.

barbar [bar-bar'], *vn.* 1. To get a beard. 2. Among bee-masters, to rear or keep bees. 3. To begin to strike root (plantas).

Bárbara [bar'-ba-rali], *f.* **Santabárbara**, *(Naut.)* Powder-room or magazine on board a warship.

bárbaramente [bar'-ba-rah-men-tay], *adv.* 1. Barbarously, savagely. 2. Rudely, without culture.

barbárico, ca [bar-bah'-re-co, cah], *a.* Barbarous, barbarian.

barbaridad [bar-bah-re-dahd'], *f.* 1. Barbarity, barbarism, cruelty. **Es capaz de hacer cualquier barbaridad,** he's capable of doing something terrible. 2. Rashness, temerity. 3. Rudeness, want of culture. 4. Barbarous expression or action. 4. *(fig.)* **¡Que barbaridad!,** how awful! 5. A huge amount, loads, tons. **Había una barbaridad de gente,** there were an awful lot of people. 6. **Una barbaridad,** a lot; lots. **Me quiere una barbaridad,** he's terribly fond of me.

barbarie [bar-bah'-re-ay], *f.* 1. Barbarousness, incivility of manners; rusticity. 2. Cruelty.

barbarismo [bar-boh-reea'-mo], *m.* 1. Barbarism, impurity of language; use of words foreign to the language in which they are employed. 2. *(Poet.)* Crowd of barbarians. 3. Barbarousness. *V.* BARBARIE.

barbarizar [bar-bah-re-thar'], *va.* To barbarize, to make barbarous, wild, or cruel.

bárbaro, ra [bar'-bah-ro, rah], *a.* 1. Barbarous, barbarian, fierce, cruel, heathenish, murderous. 2. Rash, bold, daring. 3. Rude, ignorant, unpolished. 4. Tremendous, terrific, smashing; **¡Que bárbaro!,** How marvellous! **Es un tío bárbaro,** he's a great guy. *Adv.* Marvellous; terrifically. **Lo pasamos bárbaro,** we had a tremendous time. *m. (fig.)* Rough sort, uncouth person. **Conduce como un bárbaro,** he drives like a madman.

barbarote [bar-bah-ro'-tay], *m. aug.* A great savage or barbarian.

barbasco [bar-bahs'-co], *m.* A poison from Jacquinia armillaris, an ever-green bush.

barbato,ta [bar-bah'-to, tah], *a.* Bearded: applied to a comet.

barbaza [bar-bah'-thah], *f. aug.* A long beard.

barbear [bar-bay-ar'], *vn.* 1. To reach with the beard or lips. 2. To reach one thing almost to the height of another. *-va.* 1. *(LAm.)* To shave. 2. *(CAm. Méx.)* To fawn on, suck up to. 3. *(LAm.)* To throw, fell. 4. To see, spot. 5. *(CAm.)* To tell off.

barbechar [bar-bay-char'], *va.* To prepare ground for sowing; to fallow.

barbechazón [bar-bay-chah-thone'], *f.* Among, farmers, the fallowing-time.

barbechera [bar-bay-chay'-rah], *f.* 1. Series of successive ploughings. 2. Fallowing season. 3. Act and effect of ploughing or fallowing.

barbecho [bar-bay'-cho], *m.* 1. First ploughing of the ground. 2. Fallow, ground ploughed in order to be sown. **Como en un barbecho or por un barbecho,** with too much confidence or assurance.

barbel [bar-bel'], *m.* A small barbo; barbel, a river fish.

barbélula [bar-bay-loo-lah], *f.* Spiny involucre of certain flowers.

barbera [bar-bay'-rah], *f.* 1. Chin-piece of a helmet.

barbería [bar-bay-ree'-ah],*f.* 1. Trade of a barber. 2. Barber's shop.

barbero [bar-bay'-ro], *m.* 1. Barber. 2. *(Zool.)* Mutton-fish. 3. Barber, hairdresser. 4. *(CAm. Méx.)* Flattered. 5. *a. (CAm. Méx.)* Groveling, cuddly, affectionate (niño).

barbeta [bar-bay'-tah], *f.* 1. *(Naut.)* Rackline, gasket. 2. *(Naut.)* Ring-rope, a rope occasionally tied to the ingbolts of the deck. **Batería a barbeta,** barbet-battery, having neither embrasures nor merlons. 4. *(Cono Sur)* Fool.

barbetear [bar-bay-tay-ahr'], *va. (Mex.)* To throw, to fell, to throw to the ground.

barbiblanco, ca [bar-be-blahn'-co, cah], *a.* Having a beard gray or white with age.

barbica, ita [bar-bee'-cah, ee'-tah], *f. dim.* A small beard.

barbicacho [bar-be-cah'-cho], *m. (Prov.)* Ribbon or band tied under the chin; guard ribbon.

barbicano, na [bar-be-cah'-no, nah], *a.* Graybeard, having, a gray beard.

barbiespeso, sa [bar-be-es-pay'-so, sah], *a.* One who has a thick beard.

barbihecho, cha [bar-be-ay'-cho, chah], *a.* Freshly shaved.

barbijo [bar-be'-ho], *m.* 1.*(And. Cono Sur)* Chinstrap; *(And. Carib. Cono Sur)* Headscarf. 2. *(And. Cono Sur)* Scar.

barbilampiño, ña [bar-be-larn-pee'-nyo,_nyah], *a.* Having a thin beard, or none. Inexperience. *m. (fig.)* Novice, greenhorn.

barbilindo, da [bar-be-leen'-do, dah], *a.* Well-shaved and trimmed; effeminate and pretty,

barbilucio, cia [bar-be-loo'-the-o, ah], *a.* Smooth-faced, pretty, genteel.

barbilla [bar-beel'-lyah], *f.* 1. Point of the chin. 2. Morbid tumor under the tongue of horses and cattle. 3. *(Dim.)* Small beard.

barbillera [bar-beel-lyay'-rah], *f.* 1. Tuft of tow, put between the staves of a cask or vat to prevent it from leaking. 2. Bandage put under the chin of a dead person.

barbinegro, gra [bar-be-nay'-gro, grah], *a.* Black-bearded.

barbiponiente [bar-be-po-ne-en'-tay], *a.* 1. *(Coll.)* Having the beard growing; applied to a boy or lad. 2. *(Met.)* Beginning to learn an art or profession.

barbiquejo [bar-be-kay'-ho], *m.* 1. Handkerchief, which females in some parts of America muffle the chin with, or put round their heads and tie under the chin. 2. A guard-ribbon for a hat. 3. *(Naut.)* Bobstay. 4. Curb-chain.

barbiquí or **barbiquejo** [bar-be-kee',bar-be-kay'-ho], *m.* A brace and bit.

barbirrubio, bia [bar-be-roo'-be-o, ah], *a.* Having a black and white beard.

barbital [bar-be-tahl], *m. (Chem.)* Barbital.

barbiteñido, da [bar-be-tay-nyee'-do, dah], *a.* Having a dyed beard.

barbiturato [bar-be-too-rah'-to], *m. V.* BARBITURICO.

barbitúrico [bar-be-too´-ree-co], *m. (Chem.)* Barbiturate.

barbo [bar'-bo], *m. (Zool.)* Barbel, a river fish.

barbón [bar-bone'], *m.* 1. An old man of a grave and austere aspect. 2. A man with a thick, strong beard. 3. A lay brother of the Carthusian order.

barboquejo [bar-bo-kay'-ho], *m.* 1. Chin-strap. 2. Bandage put under the chin of a dead person.

barbotar [bar-bo-tar'], *vn.* To mumble, to mutter.

barbote [bar-bo'-tay], *m.* Fore part of a helmet. *V.* BABERA.

barbotear [bar-bo-tay-ahr'], *vti.* Mutter, mumble.

barboteo [bar-bo-tay'-o], *m.* Mutter, muttering, mumbling.

barbudo,da [bar-boo'-do, dah], *a.* Having a long beard.

barbudo [bar-boo'-do], *m.* Vine transplanted with the roots.

barbulla [bar-bool'-lyah], *f.* Loud, confused noise, made by people talking all at the same time. Clamor.

barbullar [bar-bool-lyar'], *vn.* To talk loud and fast, with disorder and confusion.

barbullón, na [bar-bool-lyone', nah], *a.* Talking loud, fast, and confusedly.

barca [bar'-cah], *f. (Naut.)* Boat, barge, bark, barkentine. **Barca chata para pasar gente,** a ferry-boat. **Barca longa,** fishing-boat. **Conduce bien su barca,** he steers his course well.

barcada [bar-cah'-dah],*f.* 1. Passage across a river in a ferry-boat. 2. A boat full of persons or goods. **Barcada de lastre,** a boat-load of ballast.

barcaje [bar-cah'-hay], *m.* 1. Ferriage. 2. Ferry, passage-boat for carrying goods or persons. Toll.

barcal [bar-cahl'], *m. (Prov. Gal.)* A wooden vessel in which a caldron is put.

barcarola [bar-cah-ro'-lah], *f.* Barcarole, the song of an Italian boatman or gondolier.

barcaza [bar-cah'-thah], *f.* A privilege conceded in some ports of loading and unloading.

barcazo [bar-cah'-tho], *m.* A large barge.

Barcelona [bar-thay-lo-nah], Barcelona.

barceo [bar-thay'-o], *m.* Dry bass or sedge for making mats, ropes, etc.

barcia [bar'-thee-ah], *f.* Chaff.

barcina [bar-thee'-nah], *f.* (*Prov.*) 1. Net for carrying straw. 2. Large truss of straw.

barcinar [bar-thee-nar'], *va.* (*Prov.*) To load a cart or wagon with heaves of corn.

barcino, na [bar-thee'-no, nah], *a.* Ruddy, approaching to redness.

barco [bar'-co], *m.* Boat, ship, barge. A word comprising every floating craft, of whatever size, strength, or use. **Barco aguador**, a watering boat. **Barco chato**, A flat-bottomed boat. **Barco de pasajeros**, passenger-boat.

barcolongo, barcoluengo [bar-co-lon'-go, bar-co-loo-en'-go], *m.* An oblong boat with a round bow.

barco-madre [bar'-co-mah'-dray], *m, pl.* **Barcos madre**, mother ship.

barcón, barcote [bar-cone', bar-co'-tay], *m. aug.* A large boat.

barchilón, na [ ], *m. & f.* Nurse, hospital aide; quack doctor, quack surgeon.

barda [bar'-dah], *f.* 1. Bard, ancient armor of horses. 2. Straw, brush-wood, etc., laid on fences, etc., to preserve them. **Aún hay sol en bardas**, there are still hopes of attaining it.

bardado, da [bar-dah'-do, dah], *a.* Barbed, caparisoned with defensive armor (caballos).

bárdago [bar'-dah-go], *m.* (*Naut.*) Pendant; luff-tackle-rope.

bardaguera [bar-dah-gy'-rah], *f.* Chaste-tree; a willow.

bardal [bar-dahl'], *m.* Mud wall, covered at the top with straw or brush. **Saltabardales**, a nickname given to mischievous boys.

bardana [bar-dah'-nah], *f.* Common burdock, or cockle burr. Bardana menor, (*Bot.*) Lesser burdock.

bardanza [bar-dahn'-thah], *f.* **Andar de bardanza**, to go here and there.

bardar [bar-dar'], *va.* To cover the tops of fences or walls with straw or brushwood.

bardilla [bar-deel' lyah], *f. dim.* Small brushwood.

bardiota [bar-de-o'-tah], *a. & m.* Soldier of the Byzantine court.

bardo [bar'-do], *m.* Bard, poet.

bardoma [bar-do'-mah], *f.* (*Prov.*) Filth, mud.

bardomera [bar-do-may'-rah], *f.* (*Prov.*) Weeds or small wood carried off by currents.

baremo [bah-ray'-mo], *m.* Table; ready-reckoner; (*fig.*) Scale, schedule; yardstick, gauge, criterion.

bareo [bah-ray'-o], *m.* **Ir de bareo**, to go drinking, to go around the bars.

barfol [bar-fol'], *m.* A coarse stuff, from the coast of Gambia.

barga [bar'-gah], *f.* 1. The steepest part of a declivity. 2. (*Obs.*) Hut covered with straw or thatched.

barganal [bar'-gah-nahl], *m.* A fence of wooden stakes.

bárgano [bar'-gah-no], *m.* A stake, six or seven feet high, of split wood.

barí, or **baril** [bah-ree' or bah-reel'], *a.* (*Andal.*) Excellent.

bariga [bah-ree'-gah], *f.* A sort of silk from India.

barillero [bah-reel-lyah'-ro], *m.* (*Mex.*) Hawker, street vendor.

barillo [bah-reel'-lyo], *m.* An inferior sort of silk from the East Indies.

barimetría [bah-re-may-tree'-ah], *f.* A treatise on the measure and weight of bodies.

bario [bah'-re-o], *m.* (*Chem.*) Barium.

baripto [bah-reep'-to], *m.* A precious stone of a blackish color.

barita [bah-ree'-tah], *f.* (*Chem.*) Baryta, or barytes.

baritel [bah-re-tel'], *m.* A hoisting winch, or whim, used in mines.

barítico, ca [bah-ree'-te-co, cah], *a.* (*Chem.*) Barytic, belonging to baryta.

baritina [bah-re-tee'-nah], *f.* Barium sulphate, heavy spar.

barítono [bah-ree'-to-no], *m.* (*Mus.*) Voice of a low pitch, between a tenor and a bass; baritone.

barjuleta [bar-hoo-lay'-tah], *f.* Knapsack, haversack, tool-bag. **Ladroncillo de agujeta, después sube a barjuleta**, a young filcher becomes an old robber.

barloar [bar-lo-ar'], *vn.* (*Naut.*) To grapple for the purpose of boarding. *V.* ABARLOAR.

barloas [bar-lo'-as], *f. pl.* (*Naut.*) Relieving tackles, or relieving tackle pendants.

barloventear [bar-lo-ven-tay-ar'], *m.* (*Naut.*) To ply to windward, to about. 2. (*Met.*) To rove about.

barlovento [Bar-lo-ven'-to], *m.* (*Naut.*) Weather-gage, the point whence the wind blows. **Costa de barlovento**, the weather shore. **Costado de barlovento**, the weather side. **Ganar el barlovento**, to get to windward.

barman [bar'-man], *m, pl.* **Barmans, bármanes, barmen**. Barman, bartender.

barnabita [bar-nah-bee'-ah], *m.* Member of the religious community of St. Paul.

barnacle [bar-nah'-clay], *m.* Barnacle, a kind of shell-fish.

barniz [bar-neeth'], *m.* 1. Varnish; japan, lacquer, gloss. **Dar de barniz a**, to varnish. 2. Paint or colors laid on the face. 3. Gum of the juniper-tree. 4. Printer's ink.

barnizado [bar-nee-thah'-do], *m.* Varnish, varnishing.

barnizar [bar-ne-thar'], *va.* To varnish, to gloss, to lacquer.

barométrico, ca [bah-ro-may'-tre-co, cah], *a.* Barometrical.

barómetro [bah-ro'-may-tro], *m.* Barometer, weather-glass.

barón [bah-rone'], *m.* Baron, a degree of nobility. **Barones del timón**, (*Naut.*) Rudder pendants and chains. (*Carib.*) Pal, buddy.

baronesa [bah-ro-nay'-sah], *f.* Baroness, a baron's lady.

baronía [bah-ro-nee'-ah], *f.* 1. Barony, honor or lordship which gives title to a baron. 2. Baronage, the dignity of a baron, and the land which gives his title.

baronial [bah-ro-nee'-ah], *a.* Baronial.

barosánemo [bah-ro-sah'-nay-mo], *m.* Aerometer, an instrument for measuring the air.

barquear [bar-kay-ar'], *vn.* To cross in a boat.

barquero [bar-kay'-ro], *m.* Bargeman, waterman, boatman, ferryman.

barqueta [bar-kay'-tah], *f. dim.* A small boat.

barquía [bar-kee'-ah], *f.* Skiff, rowing boat.

barquichuelo [bar-ke-choo-ay'-lo], *m. dim.* Small bark or boat.

barquilla [bar-keel'-lyah], *f.* 1. (*Dim.*) A little boat. 2. **Barquilla de la corredera**, (*Naut.*) the log, a triangular piece of wood which serves to measure the ship's way. 3. Thin boat-formed of conical pastry cake. 4. (*Carib.*) Ice-cream cone.

barquillero [bar-keel-lyay'-ro], *m.* 1. One who makes or sells rolled cakes, and the iron mould for making them. 2. Waffle-iron.

barquillo [bar-keel'-lyo], *m.* 1. Cock-boat, a small boat used on rivers and near a sea-coast. 2. Cot or cott, a little boat. 3. Paste made to close letters. 4. A thin pastry cake rolled up in the form of a tube or cone. 5. A mould with holes, used by wax-chandlers.

barquín [bar-keen'], *m.* **barquinera** [bar-ke-nay'-rah], *f.* Large bellows for iron-works or furnaces.

barquinazo [bar-ke-nah'-tho], *m.* (*Coll.*) The blow which a body gives in falling

barquinero [bar-ke-nay'-ro], *m.* Bellows-maker.

barquino [bar-kee'-no], *m.* Wine-bag. *V.* ODRE.

barra [bar'-rah], *f.* 1. Iron crow or lever. 2. Bar or ingot of gold, silver, etc. 3. Bar, rock, or sand-bank at the mouth of a harbor. 4. List or gross-spun thread in cloth. 5. A mould for small (wax) candles. 6. *(Mech.)* Lever, rod, cross-bar, chase-bar. 7. The shaft of a carriage. 8. *(Her.)* The third part of a shield. 9. *(Naut.)* Spar. 10. *(Mus.)* Bar, or measure. 11. Bar, or railing in a court-room. **Estirar la barra** *(Met.)* to make the utmost exertions for attaining some purpose. **Tirar la barra** *(Met.)* to increase the price. **De barra a barra**, from one point to another. **Barras**, among pack-saddle makers, the arched trees of a pack-saddle. **Barras de cabrestante y molinete**, *(Naut.)* the bars of the capstan and windlass. **Barras de escotilla**, *(Naut.)* bars of the hatches. **Barras de portas**, *(Naut.)* gun-port bars. **Estar en barras**, *(Met.)* to be on the point of settling an affair. **Sin daño de barras**, *(Met.)* without injury or danger. **A barras derechas**, fairly. 12. *(LAm.)* Public, members of the public; *(Cono Sur)* Spectators, audience. 13. *(Carib. Cono Sur, Méx.)* River mouth, estuary.

Barrabás [bar-rah-bahs'], *m.* Barrabas. **Ser un Barrabás**, to be wicked.

barrabasada [bar-rah-bah-sah'-dah], *f. (Coll.)* Trick, plot, intrigue; a bold action.

barraca [bar-rah'-cah], *f.* 1. Barrack for soldiers; a cabin, a hut. 2. *(And.)* Booth, stall. **Barraca del tiro al blanco**, shooting gallery. 3. *(LAm.)* Large store shed. 4. **Creerse algo a la barraca**, to believe something implicitly.

barrachel [bar-rah-chel'], *m. (Obs.)* Head-constable, the principal *alguacil.*

barraco [bar-rah'-co], *m. (Prov.)* 1. A boar. 2. Spume thrown up by must when in a state of fermentation. 3. An ancient kind of ship guns. 4. *(Prov.)* Snag, a tooth which grows over another.

barracón [bar-rah-cone'], *m.* 1. Big hut; *(Carib.)* Farmworkers´ living quarter.

barracuda [bar-ra-coo'-dah], *f.* A Californian food fish.

barrado, da [bar-rah'-do, dah], *a.* 1. Among clothiers, corded or ribbed; striped. 2. *(Her.)* Barred. *-pp.* of BARRAR.

barragán [bar-rah-gahn'], *m.* 1. *(Obs.)* Companion. 2. Barracan, a strong kind of camlet.

barragana [bar-rah-gah'-nah], *f. (Obs.)* Concubine.

barraganería [bar-rah-gah-nay-ree'-ah], *f.* Concubinage.

barraganía [bar-rah-gah-nee'-ah], *f. (Obs.)* V. AMANCEBAMIENTO.

barraganete [bar-rah-gah-nay'-tay], *m. (Naut.)* Top-timber, timber-head, futtock.

barrajes [bar-rah'-hays], *m. & pl. (And.)* Shanty town.

barral [bar-rahl'], *m.* A large bottle containing an *arroba* or twenty-five pints.

barranca, *f.* **barrancal**, *m.* [bar-rahn'-cah, bar-ran-cahl']. 1. A deep break or hole made by heavy falls of rain. 2. Ravine. 3. A precipice.

barranco [bar-rahn'-co], *m.* 1. V. BARRANCA. 2. Dell, a narrow valley. 3. *(Met.)* Great difficulty which obstructs the attainment of a purpose.

barrancoso, sa [bar-ran-co'-so, sah], *a.* Broken, uneven, full of breaks and holes.

barranquera [bar-ran-kay'-rah], *f.* 1. V. BARRANCA. 2. Obstruction, embarrassment.

barraque [bar-rah'-kay], V. TRAQUE BARRAQUE.

barraquear [bar-rah-kay-ar'], *vn.* To grunt like a bear.

barraquilla [bar-rah-keel'-lyah], *f. dim* A little hut.

barraquillo [bar-rah-keel'-lyo], *m.* A short light field-piece.

barraquismo [bar-rah-kees'-mo], *m.* Phenomenon of shanty towns, shanty town problem.

barrar [bar-rar'], *va.* 1. To daub, to smear, to paint coarsely. 2. To bar, to barricade.

barrate [bar-rah'-tay], *m.* A little joist.

barreal [bar-ray-ahl'], *m. (Cono Sur)* Heavy clay land; *(CAm.)* Bog (pantano).

barrear [bar-ray-ar'], *va.* 1. To bar, to barricade, to fortify with timbers, stakes, etc. 2. *(Prov.)* To cancel a writing. 3. To secure or fasten a thing with a bar of iron. *-vn.* To graze a knight´s armor without piercing it: applied to a lance. *-vr.* 1.

V. ATRINCHERARSE. 2. *(Prov.)* To wallow, to roll in mire: applied to wild boars.

barreda [bar-ray'-dah], *f.* V. BARRERA.

barredera [bar-ray-day'-rah], *f.* Street sweeper; *(Aut.)* Street cleaning vehicle. **Barrera de alfombras**, carpet sweeper.

barrederas [bar-ray-day'-ras], *f. pl. (Naut.)* Studding-sails.

barredero [bar-ray-day'-ro], *m.* Mop; generally, the mop used for wiping an oven where bread is baked.

barredero, ra [bar-ray-day'-ro, rah], *a.* Sweeping along anything met with. **Red barredera**, drag-net.

barredura [bar-ray-doo'-rah], *f.* Act of sweeping. *-pl.* 1. Sweeping. 2. Remains, residue, that which is left.

barreminas [bar-ray-me'-nahs], *m.* Minesweeper.

barrena [bar-ray'-nah], *f.* 1. Boring bit, auger. **Barrena grande**, auger borer. **Barrena pequeña**, gimlet. **Barrena de gusano**, wimble. 2. A rock-drill for blasting. **Barrena de diminución**, a taper auger. **Barrena de guía**, a center-bit.

barrenado, da [bar-ray-nah'-do, dah], *a. (Met.)* **Barrenado de cascos**, crack brained, crazy.*-pp.* of BARRENAR.

barrenador [bar-ray-nah-dor'], *m. (Naut.)* Auger or borer.

barrenar [bar-ray-nar'], *va.* 1. To bore, to pierce, to make holes, to drill. **Barrenar un navío**, *(Naut.)* to scuttle or sink a ship. **Barrenar una roca or mina**, to blast a rock or a mine. 2. *(Met.)* To defeat one´s intentions, to frustrate one´s designs.

barrendero, ra [bar-ren-day'-ro, rah], *m. & f.* Sweeper, dustman.

barrenero [bar-ray-nay'-ro], *m.* Driller, borer.

barrenillo [bar-ray-neel'-lyo], *m.* 1. An insect which gnaws through the bark and attacks the sap-wood. 2. A disease produced by it in elms and other trees. 3. Borer. 4. *(Carib.)* Foolish; *(Cono Sur. Méx.)* Constant worry.

barreno [bar-ray'-no], *m.* 1. A large borer or auger. 2. Hole made with a borer, auger, or gimlet; blast-hole. 3. *(Met.)* Vanity, ostentation. **Dar barreno**, *(Naut.)* to bore and sink a ship. 4. *(Cono Sur. Méx.)* Constant worry.

barreño [bar-ray'-nyo], *m.* 1. Earthen pan. 2. A tub. 3. Washing-up basin.

barrer [bar-rerr'], *va.* 1. To sweep. 2. *(Met.)* To carry off the whole of what there was in a place. **Barrer un navío de popa a proa**, *(Naut.)* To rake a ship fore and aft. **Al barrer**, on an average. *(Com.)* 3. *(fig.)* To sweep aside; to sweep clean. **Los candidatos del partido barrieron a sus adversarios**, the party´s candidates swept aside their rivals. *-vn.* 1. **Comprar algo al barrer**, *(Cono Sur)* To buy something in a job lot. 2. **Barrer hacia dentro**, to look after number one. *-vr.* 1. *(Mex.)* To shy, to start. 2. *(Mex.)* To grovel.

barrera [bar-ray'-rah], *f.* 1. Clay-pit. 2. Barrier, circular paling within which bullfights are performed. 3. Mound or heap of earth from which saltpetre is extracted. 4. Cupboard with shelves where crockery is kept. 5. Barricade, barrier, parapet. 6. Barrier, a bar to mark the limits of a place. 7. Toll-gate, barrier, turnpike. **Barrera antiaérea**, flak. **Barrera sónica**, sonic barrier. **Salir a barrera**, *(Met.)* to expose oneself to public censure.

barrero [bar-ray'-ro], *m.* 1. Potter. 2. *(Prov.)* Height, eminence, a high ridge of hills. 3. Clay-pit

barreta [bar-ray'-tah], *f.* 1. *(Dim.)* Small bar. 2. Lining of a shoe. 3. Helmet, casque. **Barretas**, pieces of iron which hold the bows of a saddle together.

barretear [bar-my-tay-ar'], *va.* 1. To fasten a thing with bars. 2. To line the inside of a shoe.

barretero [bar-ray-tay'-ro], *m.* In mining, one who works with a crow, wedge, or pick.

barretina [bar-ray-tee'-nah], *f.* Catalan cap.

barretón [bar-ray-tone'], *m. aug.* Large bar.

barriada [bar-re-ah'-dah], *f.* Suburb, district or precinct of a city: applied frequently to a part of a suburb.

barrial [bar-re-ahl'], *m.* V. LODAZAL. A muddy spot.

barrica [bar-ree'-cah], *f.* A cask containing sixty gallons.

barricada [bar-re-cah'-dah], *f.* Barricade, a collection of barrels or beams to form a cover like a parapet.

barrida [bar-ree'-dah], *f.* *(LAm.)* 1. Sweep, sweeping; sweep raid. 2. Landslide.

barrido [bar-ree'-do], *m.* 1. Sweep, the act of sweeping. *-pp.* of BARRER. 2. **Barrido de televisión o barrido de trama** *(Comp.)*, raster scan.

barriga [bar-ree'-gah], *f.* 1. Abdomen, belly, stomach. 2. Pregnancy, state of being pregnant. 3. Middle part of a vessel where it swells out into a larger capacity. 4. *V.* COMBA. **Estar, hallarse, con la barriga a la boca**, to be near confinement. **Tener la barriga a la boca**, *(Coll.)* to be big with child. **Volverse la albarda a la barriga**, to be frustrated in one's wishes and expectations.

barrigón, na [bar-re-gone'], *a.m.f. aug.* Potbelly, a big belly.

barrigudo, da [bar-re-goo'-do, dah], *a.*Big-bellied, pot-bellied.

barriguera [bar-re-gay'-rah], *f.* Girth (de caballos).

barriguilla [bar-re-geel'-lyah], *f. dim.* A little belly.

barril [bar-reel'], *m.* 1. Barrel. **Cerveza de barril**, draft beer. 2. Jug. 3. *(Naut.)* Water-cask. 4. *(LAm.)* Hexagonal kite.

barilame, *m.* **barrilería**, *f.* [bar-re-lah'-may, bar-re-lay-ree'-ah]. A number of barrels collected in one place; stock of casks.

barrilejo [bar-re-lay'-ho], *m. dim.* Rundlet, a small barrel.

barrilería [bar-re-lay-ree'-ah], *f.* 1. Barrel store. 2. Cooper's shop. 3. *(Art.)* Cooperage.

barrilero [bar-re-lay'-ro], *m.* One who makes barrels, cooper.

barrilete [bar-re-lay'-tay], *m.* 1. Holdfast, dog, clamp. 2. *(Naut.)* Mouse. 3. *(Zool.)* A crab covered with prickles. **Barrilete de estay**, the mouse of a stay. **Barrilete de remo**, the mouse of an oar. **Barrilete de virador**, the mouse of a voyol. **Barrilete de banco**, hold-fast, a tool used by joiners, to keep their stuff steady. 4. *(Dim.)* Keg. 5. *(Prov.)* Kite. 6. Chamber. *-f. (Cono Sur)* Restless woman.

barrilico, illo, ito [bar-re-lee'-co, eel'-lyo, ee'-to], *m. dim.* Keg, rundlet, a small barrel, firkin.

barrilla [bar-reel'-lyah], l. *(Dim.)* A little bar. 2. A rod. 3. *(Bot.)* Saltwort, glass-wort, an herb. **Barrilla fina**, cultivated saltwort. **Barrilla borde**, prickly saltwort. **Barrilla salicor**, long fleshy-leaved saltwort. **Barrilla carambillo o caramillo**, small-leaved salt-wort. **Barrilla escobilla**, tamarisk-leaved salt-wort. 4. Impure soda, called in commerce barilla, a mineral alkali extracted from plants belonging to the genus Salicornia. **Barrilla de Alicante**, *(Com.)* Spanish or Alicante soda.

barrillar [bar-reel-lyar'], *m.* Barillapits, where the plants, from which the barilla is extracted, are burnt, and collected at the bottom in a stony mass. Called *rocheta;* it is the barilla ashes of commerce.

barrillo [bar-reel'-lyo], *m.* Blackhead, pimple.

barrio [bar'-re-o], *m.* 1. One of the districts or wards into which a large town or city is divided. **Barrio chino**, *(Esp.)* Red-light district. *(fig.)* **Irse al otro barrio**, to snuff it. 2. Suburb. **Andar de barrio or vestido de barrio**, to wear a plain, simple dress.

barriobajero [ ], *a.* Slum; *(fig.)* Vulgar, coarse, common.

barriquita [bar-re-kee'-tah], *f.* A cask. **Barrita** [bar-ree'-tah], *f. dim.* 1. A small bar. 2. A small keg.

barrisco [bar-rees'-co], *adv.* Jumbled together, in confusion; indiscriminately.

barritar [bar-ree-tahr'], *vn.* To trumpet (elefante).

barrito [bar-ree'to], *m.* Trumpeting.

barrizal [bar-ree-thahl], *m.* Clay-pit, a place full of clay and mud.

barro [bar'-ro], *m.* Clay, mud. 2. Earthenware. 3. Drinking-vessel of different shapes and colors, made of sweet-scented clay; sugar-clay. 4. Lock of wool put into the comb. **Dar or tener barro a mano**, to have money or the necessary means to do a thing.*-pl* 1. Red pustules or pimples in the faces of young persons. 2. Fleshy tumors growing on the skin of horses or mules.

barrocho, *m.* *V.* BIRLOCHO.

barroco [bar-ro'-co], 1. *a.* Baroque. 2. *m.* Baroque; baroque period.

barroquismo [bar-ro-kees'-mo], *m.* Baroque (stilo); baroque taste.

barroso, sa [bar-ro´-so, sah], *a.* 1. Muddy, full of mire. **Camino barroso**, muddy road. 2. Pimpled, full of pimples-called *barros*. 3.-Reddish (bueyes).

barrote [bar-ro'-tay], *m.* 1. Iron bar with which tables are made fast. 2. Ledge of timber laid across other timbers. **Barrotes**, *(Naut.)* battens, scantlings, or ledges of stuff, which serve many purposes on board ship. **Barrotes de las escotillas**, battens of the hatches.

barrotines [bar ro-tee'-ncs], *m. pl.* **Barrotines de los baos**, *(Naut.)* carlings or carlines. **Barrotines o baos de la toldilla** *(Naut.)*, carling knees, or the beams of the stern.

barrueco [bar-roo-ay'-co], *m.* Pear of irregular form.

barrumbada [bar-room-bah'-dah], *f.* 1. *(Coll.)* Great and ostentatious expense. 2. Boastful saying.

barruntador, ra [bar-roon-tah-dor', rah], *m. & f.* Conjecturer, one who guesses by signs and tokens.

barruntamiento [bar-roon-tah-me-en'-to], *m.* The act of conjecturing or guessing by signs and tokens.

barruntar [bar-roon-tar'], *va.* To foresee or conjecture (by signs or tokens); to guess, to have a presentiment. **Barruntar algo**, to sense something.

barrunte [bar-roon'-tay], *m.* Sign, indication. *V.* NOTICIA.

barrunto [bar-roon'-to], *m.* Conjecture, the act of conjecturing. *(Carib. Méx.)* North wind which brings rain.

bartola [bar-to'-lah], *f. (Coll.)* Belly. **A la bartola**, on the back, in lazy fashion, careless.

bartolear [bar-to-lay-ahr'], *vn. (Cono Sur)* To be lazy, to take it easy.

bartolillo [bar-to-leel'-lyo], *m.* A little meat pie, in triangular form.

bártulos [bar'-too-los], *m. pl. (Coll.)* Tools, affairs or business. **Liar los bártulos**, to pack up one's belongings.

baruca [bah-roo'-cah], *f.* Artífice, cunning, deceit.

barullento [bah-rool-lyayn'-do], *a. (Cono Sur)* Noisy, rowdy.

barullo [bah-rool'-lyo], *m.* 1. Confusion, disorder, tumult. 2. **A barullo**, in abundance.

barzón [bar-thone'], *m.* 1. *(Prov.)* Idle walk. 2. The strap with which oxen are yoked to the plough-beam.

barzonear [bar-tho-nay-ar'], *vn. (Prov.)* To loiter about without a certain design. To wander about.

basa [bah'-sah], *f.* 1. Basis or pedestal of a column or statue, base. 2. *(Met.)* Basis or foundation of a thing.

basácula [bah-sah´-coo-lah], *f.* Locker of the thumb-plate in a stocking frame.

basáltico, ca [bah-sahl'-te-co], *a.* Basaltic, of basalt.

basalto [bah-salil'-to], *m.* Basalt, basaltes, a kind of stone.

basamento [bah-sah-men'-to], *m. (Arch.)* Basement, base and pedestal.

basar [bah-sar'], *va.* 1. To fix, to establish; to secure upon a base. 2. To rest upon, to set up a theory. 3. To start from a fixed base-line. *-vr.* 1. **Basarse en**, to be based on, to rest on. 2. *(fig.)* To base oneself on, to rely on.

basca [bahs'-cah], *f.* 1. Squeamishness, inclination to vomit, nausea. **Dar bascas a uno**, to make somebody feel sick. 2. *(fig.)* Fit of rage, tantrum. 3. Group, set of people. **Toda la basca**, all of them, every one of them.

bascosidad [bas-co-se-dahd'], *f.* Uncleanliness, nastiness, filth.

bascoso [bas-co'-so], *a.* 1. Squeamish, easily upset. 2. *(And.)* Nauseating, sickening; obscene.

báscula [bahs'-coo-lah], *f.* 1. Lever, pole, staff. 2. Platform-scale.

basculable [bas-coo-lah'-blay], *a. (Aut.)* Directional, with swinging beam.

basculante [bas-coo-lahn'-tay], *m.* Dump truck, tip-up lorry.

báscula-puente [bas'-coo-lah-poo-ayn'-tay], *f.* Weighbridge.

bascular [bas-coo-lahr'], *vn.* To tilt, to tip up; to seesaw; to rock to and fro; to swing.

base [bah´-say], *f.* 1. Base, basis; ground, foot, footing; groundwork. 2. Chief or ground color, the principal color used in dyeing any stuff. **Base de distinción**, focus of glasses convex on both sides. 3. Baseline in surveying. 4. *(Mus.)* Bass or base. 5. *(Chem.)* In any combination, the most electro-positive element. 6. *(fig.)* Basis, foundation. **A base de**, on the basis of. **En base a que...**, in view of the fact that... 7. *(Inform. Mat.)* **Base de datos**, database. **Base de misiles**, missile base. 8. **Bases**, conditions; rules. *-a.* Basic, base. **Color base**, basic color.

baseballista [bah-say-bahl-lyees'-tah], *m. f.* Baseball player.

basebolero, ra [bah-say-bo-lay'-ro], *a. m. & f.* Baseball, baseball player.

basic [bah-seek], *(Comp.)* Basic (Beginner´s All-purpose Symbolic Instruction Code).

básico [bah´-see-co], *a.* Basic.

Basilea [bah-see-lay'-ah], *f.* Bastle, Basel, Bâle.

basílica [bah-see´-le-cah], *f.* 1. Royal or imperial palace. 2. Public hall where courts of justice hold their sittings. 3. *(Anat.)* Basilica. 4. Basilica, large and magnificent church.

basilicón [bah-see-le-cone´], *m. (Med.)* Basilicon, an ointment, resin salve.

basilio, lia [bah-see´-le-o, ah], *a.* Basilian, monk or nun of the order of St. Basil.

basilisco [bah-see-lees'-co], *m.* 1. Basilisk, cockatrice, a fabulous kind of serpent. 2. Basilisk, an ancient piece of artillery. **Estar hecho un basilisco**, to get angry.

basketbol [bas-ket-bol'], *m.* Basketball.

basquear [bas-kay-ar'], *vn.* To be squeamish, or inclined to vomit.

básquet [bas'-ket], *m,* , **básquetbol** *m. (CAm. Méx.)* Basketball.

basquetbolero, ra [bas-ket-bo-lay'-ro], *a. m. & f.* Basketball player.

basquetbolista [bas-ket-bo-lees'-tah], *m. & f. (LAm.)* Basketball player.

basquetbolístico [bas-ket-bo-lees'-tee-co], *a. (LAm.)* Basketball.

basquilla [bas-keel'-lyah], *f.* Disease in sheep.

baisquiña [bas-kee´-nyah], *f.* Upper petticoat that Spanish women used to wear.

basta [baha'-tah], *adv.* Enough; halt, stop.

basta [bahs´-tah], *f.* Stitch made by tailors to keep clothes even when basting. **Bastas**, Stitches put into a mattress at certain distances to form a quilt.

bastaje [bas-tah'-hay], *m.* Porter, carrier.

bastante [bas-tahn'-tay], *adv.* 1. Sufficient, enough, competent. 2. Not a little. 3. *(LAm.)* Too much, more than enough. **Estoy bastante cansado**, I´m really tired. **Bastante bueno**, fairly good.

bastar [bas-tar'], *vn.* To suffice, to be proportioned to something, to be enough. **¡Basta ya!**, that´s quite enough. **Eso me basta**, that´s enough for me. *-vr.* **Bastarse a sí mismo**, to be self-sufficient.

bastarda [bas-tar'-dah], *f.* 1. Bastard file. 2. Piece of ordnance. 3. *(Naut.)* Bastard, a lateen main-sail. 4. *(Print.)* Italic, a type. 5. *a.* A packsadle.

bastardear [bas-tar-day-ar'], *vn.* 1. To degenerate, to fall from its kind (animales, plantas). 2. *(Met.)* To fall from the virtues of our ancestors, or the nobleness of our birth. 3. To bastardize, or to bastard.

bastardelo [bas-tar-day'-lo], *m. (Prov.)* Draft-book of a notary, which contains the minutes or first drafts of acts, deeds, instruments, etc.; blotter. *V.* MINUTARIO.

bastardía [bas-tar-dee'-ah], Bastardy, state of being born out of wedlock. 2. *(Met.)* Speech or action unbecoming the birth or character of a gentleman; meanness.

bastardilla [bas-tar-deel'-lyah], *f.* 1. *(Obs.)*, A kind of flute. 2. *(Print.)* Italic, a type.

bastardo, da [Bas-tar´-do, dah], *a.* Bastard, spurious, degenerating from its kind and original qualities. 2. Bastard, illegitimate. 3. Bastard, a type having a face smaller or larger than proper for its body.

bastardo [bas-tar´-do], *m.* 1. Bastard, a son born out of wedlock. 2. Boa, a short, thick-bodied, and very poisonous snake. **Bastardo de un racamento**, *(Naut.)* Parrel rope.

baste [bahs'-tay], *m. (Prov.) V.* BASTO.

bastear [bas-tay-ar'], *va.* To baste, to stitch loosely, to sew slightly.

bastero [bas-tay'-ro], *m.* One who makes or retails packsaddles. *-ro,-ra m. f. (Mex.)* Pickpocket.

bastes [bas'-tays], *m. & pl. (Esp.)* Dabs, fingers.

bastez [bas-tayth'], *f.* Coarseness, vulgarity.

bastida [bas-tee´-dah], *f.* An ancient warlike engine for covering approaches.

bastidor [bas-tee-dor'], *m.* 1. Frame for stretching linen, silk, etc., which is to be painted, embroidered, or quilted. 2. Frame, sash, panel. 3. A frame through which passes the shaft of a screw propeller. 4. Linen stretched in frames: applied to the painted linen used on the sides of the stage to represent the scene. 5. *(Phot.)* Carrier, for films; plate-holder. **Bastidores**, *(Naut.)* Frames for canvas bulkheads, provisional cabins, and other temporary compartments. **Bastidos or bastidores**, (on the stage) Scenery.

bastilla [bas-teel'-lyah], *f.* Hem, the edge of cloth doubled and sewed.

bastillar [bas-teel-lyar'], *va.* To hem.

bastimentar [bas-te-men-tar'], *va.* To victual, to supply with provisions.

bastimento [bas-te-men´-to], *m.* 1. Supply of provisions for a city or army. 2. Building, structure 3. Thread with which a mattress is quilted. 4. *(Naut.)* Vessel. **Bastimentos**, first fruits, in the military order of *Santiago* or St. James.

bastión [bas-te-on'], *m.* Bastion. *V.* BALUARTE.

basto [bahs'-to], *m.* 1. Packsaddle for beasts of burden. 2. Pad. 3. Ace of clubs in several games of cards. **Bastos**, clubs, one of the four suits at cards.

basto, ta [bahs'-to, tah], *a.* 1. Coarse, rude, unpolished, unhewn, clumsy, gross, rugged; cyclopean; linsey-woolsey. 2. Home-spun, clownish. 3. Rude, uncouth.

bastón [bas-tone´], *m.* 1. Cane or stick with a head or knob to lean upon; gad. 2. Truncheon, a staff of command. 3. *(Met.)* Military command. **Empuñar el bastón**, to take command. 4. Among silk-weavers, the roller of a silk-frame which contains the stuff. 5. Carrot of snuff, weighing about three pounds. 6. *(Arch.)* Fluted moulding. **Dar bastón**, to stir must with a stick, to prevent its being ropy. **Bastones**, *(Her.)* Bars in a shield.

bastonada [bas-to-nah´-dah], *f.* **bastonazo** [bas-to-nah'-tho], *m.* Bastinado, stroke or blow given with a stick or cane.

bastoncillo [bas-ton-theel'-lyo], *m.* 1. *(Dim.)* Small cane or stick. 2. Narrow lace for trimming clothes.

bastonear [bas-to-nay-ar'], *va.* To stir must with a stick to prevent its becoming ropy.

bastonera [bas-to-nay'-rah], *f.* Umbrella stand.

bastonero [bas-to-nay'-ro], *m.* 1. Canemaker or seller. 2. Marshal or manager of a ball, steward of a feast. 3. Assistant jail-keeper. 4. *(Carib.)* Scoundrel, tough.

bastón-taburete [bas-tone'-tah-boo-ray-tay], *m.* Shooting stick.

basura [bah-soo'-rah], *f.* 1. Trash, garbage, sweepings, filth swept away, rubbish. 2. Dung, manure, ordure, excrement used to manure the ground; off-scouring. **Basura radioactiva**, radioactive waste. 3. *(fig.)* Trash, rubbish. **La novela es una basura**, the novel is rubbish.

basural [bah-soo'-rah], *m. (LAm.)* Rubbish dump.

basurear [bah-soo-ray-ar'], *va. (Cono Sur)* **Basurear a uno**, to push somebody along; to humiliate somebody; to be rude to somebody.

basurero [bah-soo-ray'-ro], *m.* 1. Dustman, he who carries dung to the field. 2. Dust-pan. 3. Dung-yard, dung-hill.

basuriento [bah-soo-ree-ayn'-to], *a. (And. Cono Sur)* Dirty, full of rubbish.

bata [bah'-tah], *f.* 1. Dressing-gown, wrapper, a loose gown. 2. Refuse of silk. 3. A lady's dress with a train. Laboratory coat. 4. Mother.

bata [bah'-tah], *m.* An Asiatic of minor age in the Philippine Islands.

batacazo [bah-tah-cah'-tho], *m.* Violent contusion from a fall. *(fig.)* Stroke of luck, fluke.

bataclán [bah-tah-clan'], *m. (LAm.)* Burlesque show, striptease show.

bataclana [bah-tah-clah'-nah], *f. (LAm.)* Striptease girl, stripper.

batahola [bah-tah-oh'-lah], *f* Hurley-burley, bustle, clamor, clutter, hubbub.

bataholear [bah-tah-o-lay-ar'], *vn.* To brawl, to be mischievous, to play pranks.

batalla [bah-tahl'-lyah], *f.* 1. Battle, the contest, conflict, or engagement of one army with another; fight, combat. 2. Center of an army, in contradistinction to the van and rear. 3. Fencing with foils. 4. *(Met.)* Struggle or agitation of the mind. **Batalla campal**, pitched battle. 5 *(Art.)* Battle-piece, a painting which represents a battle. 6. Joust, tournament. **Campo de batalla**, field of batttle. **Cuerpo de batalla de una escuadra**, the center division of a fleet. **En batalla**, *(Mil.)* with an extended front.

batallador, ra [bah-tal-lyah-dor', rah], *m. & f.* 1. Battler, combatant; warrior. 2. Fencer with foils.

batallar [bah-tal-lyar'], *vn.* 1. To battle, to fight, to be engaged in battle. 2. To fence with foils. 3. *(Met.)* To contend, to argue, to dispute.

batallita [bah-tahl-lyee'-tah], *f.* **Contar batallitas**, to shoot a line.

batallón [bah-tal-yone'], *m.* 1. Battalion, a division of infantry. 2. *(Cono Sur)* Dry cleaner's. 3. *(And.)* Thickness.

batán [bah-tahn'], *m.* Fulling-mill where cloth is fulled, or cleaned from oil and grease. **Batanes**, a boyish game of striking the soles of the feet, hands, etc.

batanar [bah-tah-nar'], *va.* To full cloth.

batanear [bah-tah-nay-ar'], *va. (Coll.)* To bang or beat, to handle roughly. **Batanero** [bah-tah-nay'-ro], *m.* Fuller, a clothier.

batanga [bah-tahn'-gah], *f.* An outrigger of bamboo applied to boats in the Philippine Islands.

bataola [bah-tah-o'-lah], *f. V.* BATAHOLA.

batata [bah-tah'-tah], *f* 1. *(Bot.)* Spanish potato, or sweet potato of Malaga, yam. 2. *(And. Carib.)* Calf. 3. *(Cono Sur)* Bashfulness, embarrassment. 4. *(Cono Sur)* Car. -a. 1. *(Cono Sur)* Bashful, shy. 2. *(Carib. Cono Sur)* Simple. 3. *(Carib.)* Chubby, plump.

batatar [bah-tah-tar'], *m. (LAm.)* Sweet potato field.

batatazo [bah-tah-tah'-tho], *m. (LAm.) V.* BATACAZO.

bátavo, va [bah'-tah-vo, vah], *a.* 1. Batavian, relating to ancient Batavia, or the Netherlands; now Holland. 2. Of Batavia, in Java.

batayola [bah-tah-yo'-lah], *f. (Naut.)* Rail. **Batayolas de los empalletados**, *(Naut.)* Quarter-netting rails. **Batayolas de las cofas**, *(Naut.)* Top-rails. **Batayolas del pasamano**, *(Naut.)* Gangway rails.

bate [bah'-tay], *m. (LAm.)* (baseball) Bat. *(CAm. Carib.)* **Estar al bate de algo**, to be in charge of something.

batea [bah-tay'-ah], *f.* 1. Painted tray or hamper of Japanned wood which comes from the East Indies. 2. Trough for bathing hands and feet. 3. Boat made in the form of a trough, punt. 4. Flat car.

bateador, ra [bah-tay-ah-dor', rah], *m. & f.* 1. *(Sports)* Batter, hitter. 2. *(Mech.)* Tamper.-*f.* Power tamper.

batear [bah-tay-ar'], *va. & vn. (Sports)* 1. To bat, to hit. 2. *(Mech.)* To tamp.

batei [bah-tay'-e], *m. (Cuba)* 1. A grass-plot. 2. *V.* BATEY.

batel [bah-tel'], *m.* Small vessel.

batelero [bah-tay-lay'-ro], *m.* Boatman.

batelón [bah-tay-lone'], *m. (And.)* Canoe.

bateo [bah-tay'-o], *m. V.* BAUTIZO.

batería [bah-tay-ree'-ah], *f.* 1. Battery, a number of pieces of ordnance arranged to play upon the enemy; also, the work in which they are placed. **Batería a barbeta**, a barbet battery. **Batería enterrada**, a sunk battery. **Batería a rebote**, a ricochet battery. **Batería cruzante**, cross battery. **Batería de cocina**, kitchen furniture. 2. *(Naut.)* Tier or range of guns on one side of a ship. **Batería entera de una banda**, *(Naut.)* a broadside. **Navío de batería florada**, *(Naut.)* a ship which carries her ports at a proper height out of the water. 3. Battery, the act and effect of battering. 4. *(Met.)* Anything which makes a strong impression on the mind. 5. *(And.)* Round of drinks. 6. *(LAm.)* Hit, stroke. 7. *(Mex.)* **Dar batería**, to keep at it. **Dar batería a**, to make trouble for. -*m. & f.* Drummer.

baterista [bah-tay-rees'-tah], *m. & f. (LAm.)* Drummer.

batero, ra [bah-tay'-ro, rah], *m. & f.* Mantua-maker, one whose trade is to make gowns.

batey [bah-tay'], *m.* 1. Machinery and appurtenances for sugar-making. 2. Premises surrounding a sugar mill in the West Indies. 3. *(Carib.)* Clearing in front of a country house, forecourt.

batiborrillo [bah-te-bor-reel'-ly], *m.* BATIBURRILLO.

batiburrillo [bah-te-boor-reel'-lyo], *m.* Hotchpotch.

baticola [bah-te-co´-lah], *f.* Crupper, *(And.)* Loincloth; *(Cono Sur)* Nappy.

batida [bah-tee'-dah], *f.* 1. A hunting party for chasing wild animals; battue. 2. Noise made by huntsmen to cheer the hounds and rouse the game. 3. *(Cono Sur)* Raid.

batidera [bah-te-day'-rah], *f.* 1. Beater, an instrument used by plasterers and bricklayers for beating and mixing mortar. 2. An instrument used by glass-makers for stirring the sand and ashes in melting-pots. 3. Batlet. 4. Batting arm, scutcher. 5. Flap of a churn. 6. Small instrument for cutting honey-combs from the hives.

batidero [bah-te-day'-ro], *m.* 1. Collision, the clashing of one thing against another. 2. Uneven ground, which renders the motion of carriages unpleasant. **Guardar los batideros**, to drive carefully on broken road. **Guardar batideros**, *(Met.)* to guard against inconveniences. 3. *(Naut.)* wash-board. **Batidero de una vela**, foot-tabling of a sail. **Batidero de proa**, war-board of the cut-water.

batido, da [bah-tee´-do, dah], *a.* 1. Changeable; shot, chatoyant (seda). 2. Beaten, as roads.-*pp.* of BATIR.

batido [bah-tee'-do], *m.* Batter of flour and water for making the host, wafers, or cookies.

batidor [bah-te-dor'], *m.* 1. Scout, one who is sent to explore the condition of the enemy, and the condition of the roads. 2. Ranger, one who rouses the game in the forest. 3. One of the life-guards, who rides before a royal coach 4. An out-rider. 5. Leather beater. 6. Stirring-rod. 7. *(Naut.)* Strengthening line. **Batidor de oro o plata**, a gold or silver beater. 8. *(CAm. Méx.)* Wooden bowl, mixing bowl. 9. Wide-toothed comb.

batidora [bah-tee-do'-rah], *f. (Culin.)* Beater, whisk, mixer; *(Tec.)* Beater; **batidora eléctrica**, electric mixer.

batiente [bah-te-en´-tay], *m.* 1. Jamb or post of a door. 2. Leaf of a folding-door. 3. Port-sill. 4. Hammer of a pianoforte. 5. Spot where the sea beats against the shore or a dike. **Batiente de la bandera**, *(Naut.)* Fly of an ensign. **Batiente de un dique**, apron of a dock.-*pa.* of BATIR.

batifondo [bah-tee-fone'-do], *m. (Cono Sur)* Uproar, din.

batifulla [bah-te-fool´-lya], *m. (Prov.) V.* BATIHOJA.

batihoja [bah-te-o'-hah], *m.* 1. Gold-beater. 2. Artisan who works iron and other metals into sheets. 3. Warp of cloth which crosses the woof.

batimiento [bah-te-me-en'-to], *m. (Obs.)* 1. The act and effect of beating. 2. The thing beaten.

batín [bah-teen'], *m.* A morning gown.

batintín [bah-tin-teen'], *m.* A gong used on Chinese junks.

bationdeo [bah-te-on-day'-o], *m.* The fluttering of a banner, or curtain, caused by the wind.

batiportar [bah-te-por-tar'], *va. (Naut.)* To house a gun on board a ship, to secure it by tackles and breechings.

batiportes [bah-te-por'-tes], *m. pl* Portsills.

batir [bah-teer'], *va.* 1. To beat, to dash, to strike two bodies together. 2. To clash , to clout, to clap. 3. To demolish, to raze, to throw down. 4. To move in a violent manner. 5. In paper-mills, to fit and adjust the reams of paper already made up. 6. To strike or fall on without injury: spoken of the sun or wind. **El cierzo bate a Madrid**, the north wind blows on Madrid. **Batir banderas**, to salute with the colors, *(Naut.)* to strike the colors. **Batir el campo**, *(Mil.)* to reconnoitre the enemy´s camp. **Batir moneda**, to coin money. **Batir las olas**, to ply the seas. **Batir las cataratas** *or* **nubes de los ojos**, to crouch. **Batir hoja**, to foliate, or to beat metals into leaves or plates. 7. *(And.)* To rinse (ropa). 8. *(Cono Sur)* To inform. *-vn.* 1. To lose courage, to decline in health or strength. 2. *(Med.)* To beat violently. *-V.*ABATIRSE. 1. *(Met.)* **Batirse el cobre**, to toil hard for useful purposes. 2. To fight, to have a fight.

batíscafo [bah-tees'-cah-fo], *m.* Bathyscaphe.

batista [bah-tees'-tah], *f.* Batiste, the finest cambric or lawn.

bato [bah'-to], *m.* 1. A rustic, simpleton. 2. Father.

batojar [bah-to-har'], *va. (Prov.)* To beat down the fruit of a tree.

batología [bah-to-to-hee'-ah], *f.* Needless repetition.

batonista [bah-to-nees'-tah], *f.* Drum majorette.

batracios [bah-trah'-the-ose], *m. pl.* Batrachians, aquatic amphibians like the frog.

batucar [bah-too-car'], *va.* To beat liquors and other things; to mix things by agitation.

batuque [bah-too'-kay], *m. (Cono Sur)* Rumpus, racket.

batuquear [bah-too-kay-ar'], *va. (CAm.)* To pester, annoy.

baturrillo [bah-toor-reel'-lyo], *m.* 1. Hodge-podge, hotchpotch, mash, salmagundi, a miscellany, potpourri. 2. *(Met.)* Mixture of unconnected and incongruous ideas.

batusino, -na [bah-too-se'-no], *m. & f.* Idiot, fool.

batuta [bah-too'-tah], *f. (It.)* A conductor´s wand; baton. **Llevar la batuta**, to be the boss.

baudio [bah-oo-de-o], *(Comp.)* Baud.

baúl [bah-ool'], *m.* 1. Trunk, a chest for clothes. 2. Belly. **Llenar el baúl**, *(Low.)* To fill the paunch. 3. *(Aut.)* Boot, trunk.

bauprés [bah-oo-press'], *m. (Naut.)* Bowsprit. **Botalón del bauprés**, the bowsprit boom.

bausa [bah'-oo-sah], *f. (And. Méx.)* Laziness, idleness.

bausán, na [bah-oo-sahn', nah], *m. & f.* 1. Manikin, effigy; image or likeness. 2. Fool, idiot. 3. *(Naut.)* Bowsprit. 4. Down, downy hair.

bausano [bah-oo-sah'-no], *m. (CAm.)* Idler, lazy person.

bauseador [bah-oo-say-ah-dor'], *m. (And.)* Idler, lazy person.

bautismal [bah-oo-tees-mahl'], *a.* Baptismal.

bautismo [bah-oo-tees'-mo], *m.* 1. Baptism. 2. *(Naut.)* Ducking.

bautista [bah-oo-tees'-tah], *m.* **El bautista, San Juan**, St. John the Baptist. *-a.* **Iglesia Bautista**, Baptist church.

bautisterio [bah-oo-tis-tay'-re-o], *m.* Baptistery.

bautizante [bah-oo-te-thahn'-tay], *pa.* Baptizing, christening.

bautizar [bah-oo-te-thar'], *va.* 1. To baptize, to christen. 2. *(Naut.)* To duck seamen in those seas where they have not been before. **Bautizar un bajel**, to give a name to a ship. **Bautizar el vino**, to add water to the wine. **Bautizo** [bah-oo-tee'-tho], *m.* 1. Baptism, christening. 2. Christening party.

bauxita [bah-ook-xe'-tah], *f.* Bauxite, a mineral.

bávaro, ra [bah'-vah-ro, rah], *a.* Bavarian.

baya [bah'-yah], *f.* 1. Berry. Any small fruit with seeds or stones. V. VAINA. 2. *(Prov.)* Pole used to separate horses in a stable.

bayajá [bah-yah-hah'], *m. (Carib.)* Headscarf.

bayal [bah-yahl], *a.* Not steeped or soaked: applied to flax.

bayal [ba -yahl'], *m.* Lever used in raising: mill-stones.

báyer [bah'-yah], *f. (Cono Sur)* Dope, pot.

bayeta [bah-yay'-tah], *f.* Baize, a sort of flannel. 2. Blanket in typography. **Bayeta de alconcher**, colchester baize. **Bayeta fajuela**, lancashire baize. **Bayeta miniquina**, long baize. **Bayeta del sur** or **de cien hilos**, white list baize. **Bayeta fina**, swanskin. **Arrastrar bayetas**, to claim a degree in superior colleges, the claimants being obliged to visit the college in wide loose gowns, with a train of baize. **Arrastrar bayetas**, *(Met.)* to enforce a claim with care and assiduity. 3. Diaper. *-pl.* 1. Pall, the covering of the dead. 2. In paper-mills, felts used in the manufacture of paper.

bayetón [bah-yay-tone´], *m.* 1. Coating. **Bayetón moteado**, spotted coating. **Bayetón de nubes**, clouded coating. **Bayetón rayado**, striped coating. **Bayetón común**, coarse baize. 2. *(And.)* Long poncho.

bayo, ya [bah´-yo, yah], *a.* Bay, inclining to a chestnut color: spoken of a horse.*-m.* Brown butterfly used in angling.

bayoco [bah-yo´-co], *m.* 1. Copper coin current in Rome and other parts of Italy. 2. *(Prov.)* Unripe or withered fig.

bayón [bah-yone´], *m.* Sack of matting for baling.

bayoneta [bah-yo-nay´-tah], *f.* Bayonet. **Bayoneta calada**, A fixed bayonet.

bayonetazo [bah-yo-nay-tah´-tho], *m.* Thrust with a bayonet.

bayonetear [bah-yo-nay-tay-ar'], *va. (LAm.)* To bayonet.

bayoya [bah-yo´-yah], *m. (Carib.)* Row, uproar. **Es un bayoya aquí**, it´s pandemonium here.

bayunca [bah-yoon´-cah], *f.* Tippling house; tavern. *(Coll.) (Naut.).*

bayunco [bah-yoon'-co], 1. *a. (CAm.)* Silly, stupid; shy; crude, vulgar. 2. *m.* **Bayunca** *f. (CAm.)* Uncouth peasant.

baza [bah´-thah], *f.* 1. Trick at cards. **No dejar meter baza**, not to allow anyone to put in a single word. **Tener bien asentada su baza**, to have one´s character well established. 2. *(Naut.)* Oozy ground. 3. **Meter baza**, to butt in. **No deja meter baza a nadie**, not to let somebody get a word in edgeways. **Tiene sentada la baza de discreto**, he has a reputation for good sense. *(fig.)*

bazar [bah-thar'], *m.* Bazaar, market-place, second-hand shop. *(Cono Sur)* Ironmonger´s.

bazo [bah'-tho], *m.* Spleen or milt.

bazo, za [bah'-tho, thah], *a.* Brown inclining to yellow. **Pan bazo**, brown bread.

bazofia [bah-tho´-fe-a], *f.* 1. Offal, waste meat. 2. Refuse, thing of no value, remnants. 3. Hogwash.

bazuca [bah-thoo-cah], *f.* Bazooka.

bazucar [bah-thoo-car'], *va.* 1. To stir liquids by shaking. 2. To dash.

bazuqueo [bah-thoo-kay'-o], *m.* The act of stirring liquids by shaking; jumble.

be [bay'], *m.* Baa, the cry of sheep.*-f.* The name of the second letter, B.

be [bay'], *m.* Baa.

bearnés, esa [bay-ar-ness', nay'-sah], *a.* Of Berne, in Switzerland, Bernese.

beata [bay-ah'-tah], *f.* 1. Woman who wears a religious habit, and is engaged in works of charity. 2. Female hypocrite.

beatería [bay-ah-tay-ree'-ah], *f.* Act of affected piety , bigotry.

beaterio [bay-ah-tay'-re-o], *m.* House inhabited by pious women.

beatico, ca [bay-ah-tee'-co, cah], *m. & dim.* Hypocrite.

beatificación [bay-ah-te-fe-cah-the-on'], *f.* Beatification.

beatificamente [bay-ah-tee'-fe-cah-men-tay], *adv.* Beatifically.

beatificar [bay-ah-te-fe-car'], *va.* 1. To beatify. 2. To render a thing respectable.

beatífico, ca [bay-ah-tee'-fe-co, cah], *a. (Theol.)* Beatific, beatifical.

beatilla [bay-ah-teel'-lyah], *f.* A sort of fine linen.

beatísimo, ma [bay-ah-tee'-se-mo, mah], *a. sup.* **Beatísimo padre**, Most holy father: applied to the Pope:

beatitud [bay-ah-te-tood'], *f.* 1. Beatitude, blessedness. 2. Holiness, a title given to the Pope.

beatnik [beat'-neek], *m, pl.* **beatniks**. Beatnik.

beato, ta [bay-ah'-to, tah], *a.* 1: Happy, blessed; beatified. 2. Wearing a religious habit without being a member of a religious community. 3. Devout.

beato, ta [bay-ah'-to, tah], *m. & f.* 1. A pious person abstaining from public diversions. 2. One who lives in pious retirement, and wears a religious dress.

beatón, na [bay-ah-tone', nah], *m.* Hypocrite, bigot.

bebé [bay-bay'], *m. & f.* Baby.

bebecina [bay-bay-thee'-nah], *f. (And.)* Drunkenness.

bebedero [bay-bay-day'-ro], *m.* Drinking vessel for birds and domestic animals; drawer of a bird-cage. 2. A drinking trough for beasts. 3. Place where birds drink. 4. Gate hole, jet. **Bebederos**, strips of cloth used by tailors for lining clothes, facing.

bebedero, ra, bebedizo, za [bay-bay-day'-ro, rah, bay-bay-dee'-tho, thah], *a.* Potable, drinkable. Given to drink.

bebedizo [bay-bay-dee'-tho], *m.* 1. Philter or love potion. 2. A physical potion, a drench.

bebedo, da [bay'-bay-do, dah], *a. (Prov.)* Drunk, intoxicated.

bebedor, ra [bay-bay-dor', rah], *m. & f.* Tippler, toper. Hard drinking.

bebendurria [bay-bayn-door'-ree-ah], *f.* 1. *(Cono Sur)* Drinking party. 2. *(And. Méx.)* Drunkenness.

bebé-probeta [bay-bay'-pro-bay-tah], *m. & f.* Test-tube baby.

beber [bay-berr'], *va.* 1. To drink. 2. To pledge, to toast. **Beber a la salud de alguno**, to drink to another's health. **Sin comerlo ni beberlo**, to suffer an injury without having had any part in the cause or motive of it. **Beber de codos**, to drink at leisure and luxuriously. **Beber las palabras, los acentos, los semblantes,** or **las acciones a otro**, to listen with the greatest care, to swallow or adopt the speech, accent, features, and actions of another. **Beber los pensamientos a alguno**, to anticipate one's thoughts. **Beber los vientos,** to solicit with much eagerness. **Le quisiera beber la sangre**, I would drink his heart's blood. **Beber como una cuba**, to drink as a fish. **Beber en las fuentes**, to obtain information at headquarters, or first hand. **Beber el pilón**, to believe current rumors. **Beber los sesos**, to bewitch. **Beber fresco,** to be tranquil.

beberaje [bay-bay-rah'-hay], *m. (Cono Sur)* Drink.

beberrón [bay-ber-rone'], *m. (Lit. us.)* Tippler, malt-worm, low drunkard.

bebestible [bay-bays-tee'-blay], *a.* 1. *(LAm.)* Drinkable. 2. *m.pl.* **Bebestibles**, drinks.

bebezón [bay-bay-thonc'], *f.* 1. *(Carib.)* Drink, booze. 2. *(Carib.)* Drunkenness; drinking spree.

bebible [bay-bee'-blay], *a.* Drinkable. **No bebible**, undrinkable.

bebida [bay-bee'-dah], *f.* 1. Drink, beverage, potion. **Bebida alcohólica**, alcoholic drink. 2. *(Prov.)* The time allowed to workmen to drink and refresh themselves in the interval of labor. 3. *(Cono Sur)* Bib.

bebido, da [bay-bee'-do, dah], *pp. of* BEBER.-*a.* Applied to an intoxicated person. **Bien bebido**, drunk.-*m. & f.* 1. Drench or physical potion for brutes. 2. *(Obs.)* V. BEBIDA.

bebistrajo [bay-bis-trah'-ho], *m. (Coll.)* An irregular and extravagant mixture of drinks.

beca [bay'-cah], *f.* 1. Grant, scholarship. 2. Part of a collegian's dress worn over the gown. 3. Fellowship, pension, an establishment in a college. 4. Fellow or member of a college, who shares the revenue. 5. Tippet worn formerly by the dignitaries of the church. **Beca de merced**, scholarship. **Becas**, strips of velvet, satin, etc., with which cloaks are faced.

becada [bay-cah'-dah], *f. (Orn.)* Wood-cock. V. CHOCHA.

becado [bay-cah-do], *a.* 1. *a.* Who holds scholarship; who holds an award. **Está aquí becado**, *(LAm.)* He's here on a grant. 2. *m.* **Becada** *f.* Scholarship holder; award holder.

becafigo [bay-cah-fee'-go], *m. (Orn.)* Fig-pecker, epicurean warbler. Motacilla ficedula, *Becafigo raro, (Orn.)* Great red-pole, or red-headed linnet. V. PAPAFIGO.

becardón [bay-car-done'], *m. (Prov.)* Snipe. V. AGACHADIZA.

becar [bay-car'], *va.* To award scholarship.

becario, ria [bay-cah'-ree-o], *m. & f.* Scholarship holder; award holder.

becerra [bay-the'-rah], *f.* 1. *(Bot.)* Snap-dragon. V. ANTIRRINO MAYOR, 2. Earth and stones swept down by mountain floods.

becerrada [bay-thayr-rah'-dah], *f. (Taur.)* Fight with young bulls.

becerril [be-ther-reel'], *a.* Bovine calf.

becerrillo, illa, ito, ita [bay-ther-ree'-lyo, lyah, ee'-to, ee'-tah], *m. & f. dim.* 1. Cal 2. Tanned and dressed calf-skin.

becerro, ra [be-ther'-ro, rah], *m. & f.* 1. A yearling calf, 2. Calf-skin tanned and dressed. **Becerros barnizados**, varnished calf-skins. **Becerros charolados**, patent leather calf-skins. 3. Registers in which are entered the privileges and appurtenances of cathedral churches and convents. 4. Manuscript bound in calf-skin, and found in the archives of Simancas, containing an account of the origin and titles of the Spanish nobility. **Becerro marino**, A sea-calf, the seal.

becoquín [bay-co-keen'], *m.* Cap tied under the chin.

becuadrado [bay-coo-ah-drah'-do], *m.* The first property in plain song, or Gregorian mode.

becuadro [bay-coo-ah'-dro], *m. (Mus.)* A natural; the sign.

bedel [bay-del'], *m.* 1. Beadle, an officer in universities, whose business it is to inspect the conduct of the students. 2. Warden. 3. Apparitor of a court of justice.

bedelía [bay-day-lee'-ah], *f.* Beadleship, wardenship.

bedelio [bay-day'-le-o], *m.* Bedellium, an aromatic gum.

bedoya [bay-do'-yah], *m. (And.)* Idiot.

beduino, na [bay-doo-ee'-no, nah], *a.* 1. Bedouin, Arab of the desert. 2. Harsh, uncivil.

befa [bay'-fah], *f.* 1. Derision, jeer, scoff, mock, taunt.

befabemí [bay-fah-bay-mee'], *m.* A musical sign.

befar [bay-far'], *va.* 1. To mock, to scoff, to ridicule, to jeer, to laugh at. 2. To move the lips, and endeavor to catch the chain of the bit (caballos).

befo, fa [bay'-fo, fah], *a.* 1. Blubber-lipped. 2. Bandy-legged.

befo [bay'-fo], *m.* 1. Lip of a horse or other animal. 2. A person with thick skin projecting under lip and bandy legs.

begardo, da [bay-gar-do, dah], *m. & f.* Beggardus, heretic of the 18th century.

begonia [bay-go'-ne-ah], *f. (Bot.)* Begonia.

beguino, na [bay-gee'-no, nah], *m. & f.* Beguin, heretic of the 14th century.

behetria [bay-ay-tree'-ah], *f.* 1. A town whose inhabitants were free from subjection to any lord. 2. Confusion, disorder. **Lugar de behetría**, a place where perfect equality prevails.

beige [baysh'], *a.* Beige.

béisbol [base'-ball], *m.* Baseball.

bejín [bay-heen'], *m.* 1. *(Bot.)* Puff, common puff-ball, fuzz-ball. 2. Whining, peevish child. 3. One who is angry over trifles.

bejinero [bay-he-nay'-ro], *m. (Prov.)* One who separates the lees or watery sediment from the oil.

bejucal [bay-hoo-cabl'], *m.* A place where reeds grow.

bejuco [bay-hoo'-co], *m.* 1. Thin or pliable reed or cane growing in India. 2. Filaments growing on some trees in America.

bejuquear [bay-hoo-kay-ar'], *va. (LAm.)* To beat, to thrash.

bejuquillo [bay-hoo-keel'-lyo], *m.* 1. A small gold chain of Chinese manufacture. 2. Root of a Brazilian plant called ipecacuanha. 3. A rattan.

belcho [bel'-cho], *m. (Bot.)* Great ephedra, or horsetail-tree.

beldad [ble-dahd'], *f.* Beauty: applied only to the beauty of women. **Una beldad**, fair, a beauty, elliptically for a fair woman.

beldar [bel-dahd'], *va.* To winnow (with a fork).

belduque [bel-doo'-kay], *m.* A large heavy knife *(Mex.)*.

beledín [bay-lay-deen'], *m.* Sort of cotton stuff.

belemnita [bay-lem-nee'-tah], *f.* Belemnites, arrow-head or finger-stone.

Belén [bay-len'], *m.* 1. Birth. 2. Confusion, bedlam. 3. Nativity scene.

beleño [bay-lay'-nyo], *m.* 1. *(Bot.)* Henbane. **Beleño negro,** Common henbane. 2. Poison.

belérico [bay-lay'-re-co], *m. (Bot.)* The fruit and the tree of a kind of myrobalan. *V.* MIRABOLANOS.

belfo, fa [bel'-fo, fah], *a.* Blob-lipped, or blubber-lippped. **Diente belfo,** snag tooth, a tooth which projects.

belfo [bel'-fo], *m.* Thick underlip of a horse.

belga [bel'-gah], *m. & f.* Belgian, a native of Belgium.

Bélgica [bel'-he-cah], Belgium.

belicista [bay-lee-thees'-tah], 1. *a.* Warmongering, militarism.

bélico, ca [bay'-le-co-, cah], *a.* Warlike, martial, military.

belicoso, sa [bay-le-co'-so, sah], *a.* 1. Warlike, martial, military, belligerent, belligerous, 2. Quarrelsome, irascible, easily irritated.

belicosidad [bay-le-co-se-dahd'], *f.* Warlike state.

belicoso [bay-lee-co'-se], *a.* Warlike; bellicose, aggressive; militant.

beligerancia [bay-lee-hay-rahn-the-ah], *f.* Belligerency; militancy, warlike spirit.

beligerante [bay-le-hay-rahn'-tay], *a.* Belligerent, militant, warlike.

belígero, ra [bay-lee'-hay-ro, rah], *a.* *(Poet.)* Warlike, belligerent.

belitre [bay-lee'-tray], *a.* *(Coll.)* Low, mean, vile, vulgar; roguish. *(And. CAm.)* Shrewd child; restless child.

bellacada [bel-lyah-cah'-dah], *f.* 1. A nest of rogues, a set of villains. 2. *(Low.)* Knavery, roguery.

bellacamente [bel-lyah-cah-men'-tay] *adv.* Knavishly, roguishly.

bellaco, ca [bel-lyah'-co, cah], *a.* 1. Artful, sly. 2. Cunning, roguish, deceitful.

bellaco [bel-lyah'-co], *m.* Rogue, a villain, a swindler, a knave.

bellacón, na, bellaconazo, za [bel-lyah-cone', nah], *m. & f. aug.* Great knave, an arrant rogue.

bellacuelo [bel-lyah-coo-ay'-lo], *m. dim.* Artful, cunning little fellow.

belladama, belladona [bel-lyah-dah'-mah], *f.* 1. *(Bot.)* Deadly nightshade, belladonna, dwale. 2. *(Zool.)* A butterfly whose caterpillar lives in thistles.

bellamente [bel-lyah-men'-tay], *adv.* Prettily, gracefully, fairly.

bellaquear [bel-lyah-kay-ar'], *vn.* To cheat, to swindle, to play knavish; roguish tricks. 2. *(fig.)* To be stubborn.

bellaquería [bel-lyah-kay-ree'-ah], *f.* Knavery, roguery, the act of swindling or deceiving; cunning, counterfeit.

belleza [bel-lyay'-thah], *f.* 1 Beauty fair, fairness, handsomeness, flourish. **Las bellezas de Mallorca,** the beauties of Majorca. 2. Decoration or ornament for the front of buildings. **Decir bellezas,** to say things wittily, or with grace.

bello, lla [bel'-lyo, lyah], *a.* Beautiful handsome, fair, fine; perfect. **Bella pedrería,** fine jewels. **Bello principio,** an excellent beginning. **Por su bella cara no se le concederá,** it will not be granted for his pretty face's sake, or without a good reason.

bellorio, ia [bel-lyo'-re-o, ah], *a.* Mouse-colored (caballos).

bellorita [bel-lyo-ree'-tah], *f.* *(Bot.)* Primrose, cowslip. **Bellorita primaveral,** common cowslip.

bellota [bel-lyo'-tah], *f.* 1. Acorn. 2. Balsam or perfume box, in the shape of an acorn. **Bellota marina,** centre shell, a shell in the shape of an acorn.

bellote [bel-lyo'-tay], *m.* Large round headed nail.

bellotear [bel-lyo-tay-ar'], *vn.* To feed upon acorns (cerdos).

bellotera [bel-lyo-tay'-rah], *f.* Season for gathering acorns, and feeding swine with them.

bellotero, ra [bel-lyo-tay'-ro, rah], *m. & f.* One who gathers or sells acorns.

bellotero [bel-lyo-tay'-ro], *m.* *(Obs.)* A tree which bears acorns.

bellotica, illa, ita [bel-lyo-tee'-cah, eel'-lyah, ee'-tah],*f. dim.* Small acorn.

belorta [bay-lor'-tah], *f.* The ring or screw with which the plough is fastened to the beam.

Beltrán [bel-trahn'], *m.* *(Pro. n.)* Bertram. **Quien bien quiere a Beltrán bien quiere a su can,** love me, love my dog.

belvedere [bel-vay-day'-ray], *m.* Arbor, belvedere.

bemol [bay-mole'], *m.* *(Mus.)* A flat; the sign. **Esto tiene muchos bemoles,** this is a tough one.

bemolado [bay-mo-lah'-do], *a.* Flat (ted), lowered a semitone.

bemolar [bay-mo-lar'], *va.* To flat.

ben, behén [ben', bay-en'], *m.* Fruit of the size of a filbert which yields a precious oil.

benarriza [bay-nar-ree'-thah], *f.* A savory bird of the family of ortolans.

benceno [ben-thay'-no], *m.* Benzene.

bencina [ben-thee'-nah], *f.* Benzine, a light hydrocarbon fluid.

bendecir [ben-day-theer'], *va.* 1. To devote to the service of the church; to consecrate. **Bendecir la bandera,** to consecrate the colors. 2. To bless, to praise, to exalt. **Dios te bendiga,** God bless you.

bendición [ben-de-the-on'], *f.* 1. Benediction. **Bendición de la mesa,** grace. 2. The marriage ceremony. **Echar la bendición,** to give one's blessing to somebody. **Es una bendición,** it is a blessing, it's a godsend. **Toca que es una bendición,** he plays marvellously. **Nos echaron las bendiciones,** the knot has been tied (matrimonio). **(Yo bendigo, yo bendiga, from Bendecir.)**

bendito, ta [ben-dee'-to, tah], *a.* 1. Sainted, blessed. 2. Simple, silly. **Es un bendito,** he is a simpleton. **El bendito,** a prayer which begins with this word. 3. Happy, lucky. 4. **¡Benditos los ojos que te ven!,** lucky eyes to be looking at you. -*m.* 1. Saint. 2. *(fig.)* Simple soul, good soul. **Es un bendito,** he's a good kind person. 3. *(Cono Sur)* Player. 4. *(Cono Sur)* Native hut (cabaña). -*pp. err.* of BENDECIR

benedicta [bay-nay-deec'-tah], *f.* Benedict. An electuary.

benedictino, na [bay-nay-dic-tee'-no, nah], *a.* Benedictine, of the order of St. Benet.

benefactor [bay-nay-fac-tor'], *m.* *(Ant. and Amer.)* Benefactor. -*a.* Salutary; beneficient. *V.* BIENHECHOR.

beneficencia [bay-nay-fe-then'-the-ah], *f.* 1. Beneficence, kindness, well-doing. 2. Charity; charitable organization.

beneficiación [bay-nay-fe-the-ah-the-on'], *f.* Benefaction.

beneficiado [bay-nay-fe-the-ah'-do], *m.* The incumbent of a benefice which is neither a curacy nor prebend; curate, beneficiary.

beneficiador, ra [bay-nay-fe-the-ah-dor', rah], *m. & f.* 1. Benefactor. 2. Improver. 3. A careful administrator.

beneficial [bay-nay-fe-the-ahl'], *a.* Relating to benefices or ecclesiastical livings.

beneficiar [bay-nay-fe-the-ar'], *va.* 1. To benefit. 2. To cultivate the ground. 3. To work and improve mines; to submit ores, etc., to metallurgical processes. 4. *(Prov.)* To confer an ecclesiastical benefice. 5. To purchase a place or employ. **Beneficiar los efectos, libranzas y otros créditos,** to resign and make over effects, credits, and other claims. -*vn.* To be of benefit. -*vr.* To benefit, profit. **Beneficiarse de,** to benefit from, to take advantage of.

beneficiario, ria [bay-nay-fe-the-ah'-re-o], *m. f.* Beneficiary.

beneficiencia [bay-nay-fe-then'-the-ah], *f.* *(Mex.)* Welfare.

beneficio [bay-nay-fee'-the-o], *m.* 1. Benefit, favor, kindness, benefaction. **A beneficio de,** for the benefit of. **En beneficio propio,** to one's own advantage. 2. The proceeds of a public entertainment given in favor of some person or charity. 3. Right belonging to one either by law or charter. 4. Labor and culture: applied to the ground, trees, mines. 5. Utility, profit. **Beneficio bruto,** gross profit. **Beneficio neto,** net profit. 6. Benefice, ecclesiastical living. **Beneficio curado,** benefice to which a curacy is annexed. 7. Purchase of public places, employs, or commissions in the army. 8. Act of resigning and making over credits and demands for sums not equal to their amount. **Beneficio de inventario**, benefit of inventory, the effect of which pay debts to a larger amount than that of the inheritance. **No tener oficio ni beneficio**, to have neither profession nor property (vagabundos). 9. (LAm.) Slaughter, slaughtering (matanza). 10. (LAm.) Slaughterhouse (matadero).

benefio marginal [bay-nay-fee'-the-o mar-he-nahl´], *m.* (Com.) Fringe benefit.

beneficioso, sa [bay-nay-fe-the-o'-so, sah], *a.* Beneficial, advantageous, profitable.

benéfico, ca [bay-nay'-fe-co, cah], *a.* 1. Beneficent, kind, charitable. 2. Charitable (trabajo, organismo etc.). **Obra benéfica**, charity.

benemérito, ta [bay-nay-may'-re-to, tah], *a.* 1. Meritorious, deserving of reward, worthy. **Benemérito de la patria**, well-deserving of the country. 2. **El benemérito hispanista**, the distinguished hispanist.

beneplácito [bay-nay-plah'-the-to], *m.* Goodwill, approbation, permission, consent.

benevolencia [bay-nay-vo-len'-the-ah], *f.* Benevolence, goodwill, kindness, humanity, good-nature, courteousness.

benevolente [bay-nay-bo-len'-tay], *a.* Benevolent, kind, kindly; genial. **Benevolente con**, well-disposed towards, kind to.

benévolo, la [bay-nay'-vo-lo, lah], *a.* Benevolent, kind, gentle, courteous, favorable, good, kind-hearted, good-natured, gracious.

bengala [ben-gah'-lah], *f.* 1. Bengal, a sort of thin slight stuff. 2. Cane from which walking-sticks are made.

bengalí [ben-gah-lee'], *m.* 1. Native of Bengal or belonging to it. 2. Language of the Bengalese people, Bengalee.

benignamente [be-nig-nah-men´-tay], *adv.* Kindly, benevolently, mercifully, favorably, graciously, humanely, clemently.

benignidad [bay-nig-ne-dahd´], *f.* 1. Benignity, graciousness, mercifulness, kindness, piety, courtesy, lenity. 2. Mildness of the air or weather.

benigno, na [bay-neeg'-no, nah], *a.* 1. Benign (tumor), merciful, gracious, pious, clement, humane. 2. Kind, courteous, favorable. 3. Mild (clima), temperate, gentle.

benito, ta [bay-nee'-to, tah], *m. & f. & a.* Benedictine friar or nun.

benjamín [ben-hah-meen'], *m.* Baby of the family, youngest child; favorite child.

benjuí [ben-hoo-ee'], *m.* Benzoin or benjamín, a gum-resin.

benzina [ben-thee'-nah], *f.* (Cono Sur) V. BENCINA.

beodo, da [bay-o'-do, dah], *a.* Drunk.

beorí [bay-o-ree'], *m.* American tapir.

beque [bay'-kayl, *m.* (Naut.) 1. Head of the ship. 2. Privies for sailors in the head gratings. -a. (CAm.) Stammering.

bequebo [bay-kay'-bo], *m.* (Orn.) Woodpecker.

berám [bay-rahm'], *f.* Coarse cotton stuff brought from the East Indies.

berberecho [ber-bay-ray'-cho], *m.* Cockle.

berberí, isco. or **bereber** [ber-bay-ree', rees'-co, bay-ray-berr'], *a.* Belonging to Barbary, Berber.

berberís [ber-bay-rees'], *m.* (Bot.) Barberry, berberry, piperidge-bush.

berbí [ber-bee'], *m.* A sort of woollens.

berbiquí [ber-be-kee'], *m.* A carpenter's brace. Wimble.

bercería [ber-thay-ree'-ah], *f.* Green-market, where vegetables are sold.

bercero, ra [ber-thay'-ro, rah], *m. & f.* Greengrocer.

berdel [ber-dayl'], *m.* Mackerel.

bereber, beréber [bay-ray-ber'], *a. m. & f.* Berber.

berenjena [bay-ren-hay'-nah], *f.* (Bot.) Aubergine, eggplant. 2. (Carib.) Nuisance, bother (fastidio).

berenjenado, da [bay-ren-hay-nah'-do, dah], *a.* (Obs.) Having the color of an egg-plant.

berenjenal [bay-ren-hay-nahl'], *m.* A bed of eggplants. **Meterse en un berenjenal**, to involve oneself in difficulties.

bergamota [ber-gah-mo'-tah], *f.* 1. Bergamot, a sort of pear. 2. Bergamot, snuff scented with the essence of bergamot.

bergamote, bergamoto [ber-gah-mo'-tayl, *m.* (Bot.) Bergamot-tree.

bergante [ber-gan'-tay], *m.* Brazenfaced villain, a ruffian, rascal.

bergantín [ber-gan-teen'], *m.* (Naut.) Brig or brigantine, a two-masted vessel with square sail.

bergantinejo [ber-gan-te-nay'-ho], *m. dim.* Small brig.

bergantón, na [ber-gan-tone', nah], *m. & f. aug.* Brazen-faced, impudent person.

bergantonazo [ber-gan-to-nah'-tho], *m. aug* Most impudent ruffian.

berilo [bay-ree'-lo], *m.* Beryl, a precious stone.

berkelio [ber-kay'-lee-o], *m.* Berkelium.

berlín [ber-leen'], *m.* 1. Berlin. 2. (Cono Sur) (Culin.) Doughnut, donut.

berlina [ber-lee'-nah], *f.* Landau or berlin, an open carriage.

berlinés, sa [ber-lee-nays', sah], *a.* Of Berlin, berliner.

berlinga [ber-leen'-gah], *f.* 1. (Prov.) Pole driven into the ground, at the top of which is fastened a rope, carried to another pole, which serves to hang clothes upon to be dried. 2. (Naut.) Round timber of six inches in diameter.

bermejear, bermejecer [ber-may-hay-ar', ber-may-hay-therr'], *vn.* To be of a reddish color.

bermejizo, za [ber-may-hee'-tho, thah], *a.* Reddish.

bermejo, ja [ber-may'-ho, hah], *a.* Of a bright reddish color; (Carib. Méx.) Light brown (vaca). 2. (Carib.) Matchless, unsurpassed (único).

bermejón, na [ber-may-hone, nah], *a.* 1. Reddish. 2. V. BERMEJO. 3. (Obs.) V. BERMELLÓN.

bermejuela [ber-may-hoo-ay'-lah], *f.* 1. (Zool.) Red gurnard, a small river fish. 2. (Bot.) Heather.

bermejuelo, la [ber-may-hoo-ay'-lo, lah], *a. dim.* A little reddish.

bermejura [ber-may-hoo'-rah], *f.* Reddishness, ruddy color.

bermellón, bermillón [ber-mel-lyone'], *m.* Vermilion.

Bermudas [ber-moo'-dahs], *m. & pl.* Bermuda shorts.

bermudiana [ber-moo-de-ah'-nah], *f.* (Bot.) Grass-flower, blue-eyed grass.

Berna [ber'-nah], *f.* Berne.

bernardina [ber-nar-dee'-nah], *f.* (Coll.) Fanfaronade, false boast, lie.

bernardo, da [ber-nar'-do, dah], *m. & f. & a.* Bernardine monk or nun.

bernegal [ber-nay-gahl'], *m.* Bowl, a vessel to hold liquids.

bernés, sa [ber-ness', sah], *a.* Bernese, relating to Berne.

bernia [ber'-ne-ah], *f.* 1. Rug, a coarse woollen cloth, of which coverlets are made. 2. Cloak made of rug. 3. (Coll.) A bore.

bernicla [ber-nee'-clah], *f.* Barnacle, a bird like a goose.

berra [ber´-rah], *f.* (Bot.) The strong, watercress plant.

berraza [ber-rah'-thah], *f.* Waterparsnip. **Berraza común** or **nodiflora**, procumbent water parsnip.

berrear [ber-ray-ar'], *vn.* 1. To cry like a calf, to bellow; to howl (niño); (Mus.) to bawl; to screech. 2. (fig.) To fly off the handle. -va. To squeal.

berrenchín [ber-ren-cheen'], *m.* 1. Foaming, grunting, and blowing of a wild boar. 2. Cry of wayward-children.

berrendearse [ber-ren-day-ar'-say], *vr.* 1. (Prov.) To grow yellow: applied to wheat nearly ripe. 2. To be stained or tinged with two colors.

berrendo, da [ber-ren'-do, dah], *a.* 1. Stained or tinged with two colors. 2. Ripe wheat which gets a yellow color. 3. (Prov.) Applied to a silkworm which has duskish brown color.

berrido [ber-ree'-do], *m.* The bellowing of a calf or other animal, howl (niño); (Mus.) Bawl, bawling; screech.

berrín [ber-reen'], *m.* Person in a violent passion. V. BEJIN.

berrinche [ber-reen'-chay], *m.* 1. Anger, passion, great petulance (niños); sulkiness. **Coger un berrinche,** to fly into a rage. 2. (*LAm.*) Pong, stink (hedor).

berrizal [ber-re-thahl'], *m.* Place full of watercresses.

berro [ber'-ro], *m.* (*Bot.*) Watercress, common watercress, fen-cress; (*Carib.*) Rage, anger (enojo).

berrocal [ber-ro-cahl'], *m.* A craggy or rocky place.

berroqueña [ber-ro-kay'-nyah], *a.* **Piedra berroqueña,** coarse-grained granitic stone.

berrueco [ber-roo-ay'-co], *m.* 1. Rock. 2. Pin, a small horny induration of the membranes of the eye.

berrusa [ber-roo'-sah], *f.* Sort of stuff manufactured at Lyons.

Berta [bayr'-tah], *f.* 1. Bertha, proper name. 2. A kind of cape called bertha.

berza [bayr'-thah], *f.* (*Bot.*) Cabbage. Brassica. **Berza or col común,** savoy cabbage. **Berza colinabo,** V. COLINABO. **Berza coliflor,** V. COLIFLOR. **Berza bróculi,** V. BRÓCULI. **Berza rizada or bretón,** V. BRETÓN. **Berza lombarda,** Red cabbage. **Berza repollo,** V. REPOLLO. **Berza de perro,** (*Bot.*) wild mercury dog´s cabagge.

berzal [ber'-thahl], *m.* (*Esp.*) Cabbage patch.

berzaza [ber-thah'-thah], *f. aug.* A large head of cabbage.

besamel [bay-sah-mayl'], *f.* (*Culin.*) White sauce, bechamel sauce.

besana [bay-sah'-nah], *f.* First furrow opened in the ground with a plough.

besar [bay-sar'], *va.* 1. To kiss. 2. To touch closely, applied to inanimate things. **A besar,** (*Naut.*) Home, or block on block. **Llegar y besar el santo,** no sooner said than done. **Besar la mano** or **los pies,** old expressions of courtesy and respect. -*vr.* 1. To strike heads or faces together accidentally. 2. To kiss, to kiss one another.

besico, sillo, sito [bay-see'-co, seel'-lyo, see´-to], *m. dim.* A little kiss. **Besicos de monja,** (*Bot.*) V. FAROLILLOS.

beso [bay'-so], *m.* 1. Kiss. **Beso de tornillo,** French kiss. **Echar un beso,** to blow a kiss. 2. Violent collision of persons or things. 3. Among bakers, kissing-crust, where one loaf-touches another. **Dar un beso al jarro,** (*Low.*) to toss about the pot, to drink freely.

bestezuela [bes-tay-thoo-ay'-lah], *f. dim.* A little beast.

bestia [bes'-te-ah], *f.* 1. Beast, a quadruped. **Bestia de carga,** beast of burden. **Bestia de tiro,** draught animal. **Bestia de silla,** a saddle mule. **Gran bestia,** an elk, an animal of the stag kind. 2. (*Met.*) Dunce, idiot, ill-bred fellow. **¡No seas bestia!,** don´t be an idiot! 3. Creature, an animal not human. 4. **¡Estás hecho un bestia!,** you are great! (admirativo). -*a.* Stupid. **Juan es muy bestia,** John is a bit stupid. **El muy bestia,** the great idiot.

bestiaje, bestiame [bes-te-ah'-hay, beste-ah'-may], *m.* An assembly of beasts of burden.

bestial [bes-te-ahl'], *a.* 1. Bestial, brutal. 2. Terrific (estupendo); tremendous, marvellous; smashing.

bestialidad [bes-te-ah-le-dahd'], *f.* 1. Beast-like nature, bestiality. 2. (*fig.*) Stupidity (estupidez); silly thing (disparate). 3. **Una bestialidad de gente,** lots and lots of people. V. BRUTALIDAD.

bestialmente [bes-te-al-men'-tay], *adv.* Bestially, brutally, marvellously. **Lo pasamos bestialmente,** we had a super time.

bestiaza [bes-te-ah'-thah], *m. aug.* 1. A great beast. 2. An idiot.

bestiecica, illa, ita, bestiezuela [bes-te-ay-thee'-cah, eel'-yah, ee'-tah, bes-te-ay-thoo-ay'-lah], *f. dim.* 1. A little beast. 2. An ignorant person.

béstola [bes'-to-lah], *f.* Paddle, or paddle-staff, for cleaning the coulter of the plough.

best-seller [best-say'-layr], *m. pl.* Best-sellers, best seller.

besucar [bay-soo-car'], *va.* To give many kisses, kiss repeatedly. V. BESUQUEAR.

besucón [bay-soo-cone'], *m.* (*Low.*) Hearty kiss, smack. -*a.* Fond of kissing.

besugada [bay-soo-gah'-dah], *f.* A luncheon or dinner of sea breams.

besugo [bay-soo'-go]. *m.* (*Zool.*). 1. Sea bream, or red gilthead. 2. **Ojo de besugo,** squint-eyed. 2. **Ya te veo, besugo,** 4. (*Met.*) I can anticipate your design. 5. Idiot (idiota).

besuguera [bay-soo-gay'-rah], *f.* 1. A pan for dressing besugos or breams.

besuguero [bay-soo-gay´-ro], *m.* 1. Fishmonger who sells breams. 2. (*Prov.*) Fishing-tackle for catching breams.

besuguete [bay-soo-gay'-tay], *m.* (*Zool.*) Red sea-bream.

besuquear [bay-soo-kay-ar'], *va.* To cover with kisses, keep on kissing. -*vr.* To kiss (each other) a lot; to pet.

besuqueo [bay-soo-kay'-o], *m.* Hearty and repeated kisses.

beta [bay'-tah], *f.* (*Prov.*) 1. A bit or line of thread (cuerda). 2. Beta, the second letter of the Greek alphabet. **Rayos beta,** beta rays. **Betas,** (*Naut.*) pieces of cordage, all sorts of tackle.

betabel [bay-tah-bell'], *m.* (*Bot.*) (*Mex.*) Sugar beet.

betarraga, betarrata [bay-tar-rah'-gah, bay-tai,-rah'-tah], *f.* (*Bot.*) V. REMOLACHA. Beet.

betarraga [bay-tar-rah'-gah], *f.* (*LAm.*), **betarrata** *f.* Beet, beetroot.

betatrón [bay-tah-tron'], *m.* Betatron.

betel [bay-tel'], *m.* Betel, an Indian shrub.

Bética [bay'-te-cah]. *f.* Ancient name of the province now *Andalucía.*

bético, ca [bay'-te-co, cah], *a.* Andalusian.

betlemita [bet-lay-mee'-tah], *m.* Bethlemite, a friar of a religious order established in America.

betón [be-tone'], *m.* Hydratilic cement.

betónica [bay-to'-ne-cah], *f.* (*Bot.*) Betony. Betonica.

betum, betume, betumen [bay-toon', bay-too'-may, bay-too'-men], *m.* V. BETÚN.

betún [bay-toon'], *m.* 1. Bitumen. 2. Cement made chiefly of lime and oil. 3. Shoe-blacking, shoe polish. **Dar de betún a,** to polish. 4. (*Naut.*) Substance with which the masts and bottoms of ships are treated. **Betún de colmena,** Coarse wax, found at the entrance of a bee-hive. **Betún judaico,** V. ASFALTO.

betunar [bay-too-nar'], *va.* To pay or cover a thing with pitch, tar, resin, etc.

beuna [bay-oo'-nah], *f.* (*Prov.*) A gold-colored wine, made of a grape of the same name.

beut [bay-oot'], *m.* A kind of sea-fish.

bevatrón [bay-vah-trone´], *m.* (*Phy.*) Bevatron.

bey [bay'-e], *m.* Bey, a Turkish governor.

bezante [bay-thahn'-tay], *m.* (*Her.*) Round figure on a shield.

bezo [bay'-tho], *m.* 1. Blubber-lip, a thick lip.

bezoar [bay-tho-ar'], *m.* Bezoar, a calculous concretion found in the intestines of certain ruminant animals, and once considered antidotal to poison.

bezoárico, ca [bay-tho-ah'-re-co, cah], *a.* 1. Bezoaric. 2. An ancient preparation of the oxide of antimony.

bezón [bay-thone'], *m.* (*Obs.*) Battering-ram.

bezote [bay-tho'-tay], *m.* A ring, which the Indians wear in their under lip.

bezudo, da [bay-thoo'-do,dah], *a.* Blubber-lipped or blob-lipped.

bi [be], *pref.* bi.

biambonas [be-am-bo'-nas], *f. pl.* A stuff made in China, of bark.

biangular [be-an-goo-lar'], *a.* Biangulated, biangulous.

bianual [be-ah-noo-al'], *a. m.* (*Bot.*) Biennial.

biasa [be-ah'-sah], *f.* A kind of coarse silk, from the Levant.

biazas [be-ah'-thas], *f. pl.* Saddle-bags. V. BIZAZA.

biberón [be-bay-rone'], *m.* A baby-bottle for infants.

Biblia [be'-ble-ah], *f.* 1. Bible. **La Santa Biblia,** the Holy Bible. 2. **Saber la biblia,** to know everything.

bíblico, ca [be'-ble-co, cah], *a.* Biblical.

bibliobús [be-ble-o-boos'], *m.* Traveling library, library van.

bibliofilia [be-ble-o-fe'-lee-ah], *f.* Bibliophily, love of books.

bibliófilo, a [be-ble-o'-fe-lo], *m. & f.* Booklover, bookworm, bibliophile.

bibliografía [be-ble-o-grah-fee'-ah], *f.* Bibliography.
bibliográfico, ca [be-ble-o-grah'-fe-co, cah], *a.* Bibliographical, bibliographic.
bibliógrafo, fa [be-ble-o'-grah-fo], *m. & f.* Bibliographer.
bibliomanía [be-ble-o-mah-nee'-ah], *f.* Bibliomania.
bibliómano, na [be-ble-o'-mah-no, nah], *m. & f.* Bibliomaniac.
biblioteca [be-ble-o-tay'-cah], *f.* 1. Library. **Biblioteca pública**, public library. **Biblioteca de consulta**, reference library. Catalog, catalogue, collection of authors. 2. Bookcase, bookshelves (estante).
bibliotecario, ria [be-ble-o-tay-cah'-re-o], *m. & f.* Librarian, bibliothecary. **Bibliotecario de sistemas** *(Comp.)*, systems librarian.
bibliotecnia, bibliotecnología, biblioteconomía [be-ble-o-tayc'-ne-ah], *f.* Librarianship.
blca [be-cah], *f.* 1. A sea-fish resembling a bream. 2. An unleavened cake of corn.
bicameral [be-cah'-may-rahl], *a. (Pol.)* Two-chambered, bicameral.
bicameralismo [be-cah-may-rah-lees'-mo], *m.* System of two-chamber government.
bicapsular [be-cap-soo-lar'], *a. (Bot.)* Bicapsular.
bicarbonato [be-car-bo-nah'-to], *m.* Bicarbonate. **Bicarbonato sódico, bicarbonato de sosa** bicarbonate of soda; *(culin.)* Baking soda.
bicentenario [be-then-tay-nah'-re-o], *m.* Bicentenary.
biceps [be-theps'], *m. (Anat.)* A muscle of two heads or points of origin.
bicerra [be-ther'-rah], *f.* A kind of wild or mountain goat.
bici [be'-the], *f.* Bike.
bicicleta [be-the-clay'-tah], *f.* Bicycle, cycle. **Bicicleta estática**, exercise bicycle. **Andar en bici**, to cycle.
bicloruro [be-clo-roo'-ro], *m. (Chem.)* Bichloride.
bicoca [be-co'-cah], *f.* 1. Sentrybox. 2. Thing of little esteem or value; trifle. 3. Bargain (ganga); plumb job. 4. *(And. Cono Sur)* Priest´s skull cap. 4. *(And. Cono Sur)* snap of the fingers (capirotazo); slap, smack (golpe).
bicolor [be-co-lor'], *a.* Of two colors, *(Aut.)* Two-tone.
bicóncavo, va [be-con'-cah-vo, vah], *a.* Biconcave.
biconvexo, a [be-con-vec'-so, sah], *a.* Double convex.
bicoquete [be-co-kay'-tay], *m.* A bonnet or head dress formerly worn.
bicoquín [be-co-keen'], *m.* Cap. *V.* BECOQUÍN and BIRRETE.
bicorpóreo, rea [be-cor-po'-ray-o, ah], *a.* Bicorporal.
bicos [bee'-cos], *m. pl.* Small gold points or lace, formerly put on velvet bonnets.
bicromato [be-cro-mah'-to], *m.* Bichromate or dichromate.
bicuadrática [be-coo-ah-drah'-te-cah], *a. (Alg.)* Biquadrate, biquadratic.
bicúspide [be-coos'-pe-day], *a.* Bicuspid.
bicha [bee-chah], *f.* 1. *(Naut.)* Trailboard. 2. *(Arch.)* Caryatid in form of a savage. 3. *(Ant.)* Strumpet, bitch. 4. Snake (serpiente); *(fig.)* Bogy. **Mentar la bicha**, to bring up an unpleasant subject. 5. *(CAm.)* Child, little girl. 6. *(And.)* Large cooking pot. 7. *(Obs.)* V. BICHO.
biche [be'-chay], 1. *a. (Cono Sur)* Weak (debil); of an unhealthy color; *(And.)* stunted, immature (no desarrollado); *(Mex.)* Soppy, empty-headed (foto). 2. *m. (And.)* Large cooking pot.
bicherío [be-chay-ree'-o], *m. (LAm.)* Insects, bugs, creepy-crawlies.
bichero [be-chay´-ro], *m. (Naut.)* Boathook. **Asta de bichero**, the shaft of boat-hook. **Gancho de bichero**, the hook of a boat-hook.
bicho [bee'-cho], *m.* 1. A general name for small grubs or insects; bug, creepy crawly; *(Carib. Cono Sur)* Maggot, brub (gusano); *(And.)* Snake (serpiente); *(LAm.)* Odd-looking creature (animal extraño). 2. *(Met.)* A little fellow of a ridiculous figure and appearance. **Mal bicho**, a mischievous urchin. 3. *(Taur.)* Bull. 4. Odd-looking person,

queer fish (persona), **bicho raro**, weirdo. **Mal bicho**, rogue, villain. 5. Brat (niño); *(Mil.)* Squaddle, recruit (niño); *(CAm.)* Child, little boy. 6. *(LAm.)* **De puro bicho**, out of sheer pig-headedness. **Matar el bicho**, to have a drink. 7. *(Carib.)* Thingummy (fulano). *-pl.* Vermin. (Hindu.)
BID *m.* abr de **Banco Internacional de Desarrollo.**
bidé, bidel, bidet, bidets [be-day'], *m.pl.* Bidet.
bidente [be-den'-tay], *m.* 1. *(Poet.)* Two-pronged spade. 2. Sheep. 3. *(Bot.)* A sort of hemp called waterhamp.
bidimensional [be-de-men-see-o-nal'], *a.* Two-dimensional, bidimentional.
bidireccional [be-de-rayc-the-o-nal'], *a. In* Duplex, bidirectional.
bidón [be-done'], *m.* Drum; can, tin.
biela [be-ay'-lah], *f.* 1. Brace-strut. 2. Axle-tree, connecting-rod.
bielda [be-el'-dah], *f.* Pitchfork with six or seven prongs, and a rack used in gathering and loading straw.
bieldar [be-el-dar'], *va.* To winnow corn by means of a wooden fork with two or three prongs.
bieldo, bielgo [be-el'-do, be-el'-go], *m.* Winnowing-fork.
bien [be-en], *m.* 1. Supreme goodness. 2. Object of esteem or love. 3. Good, utility, benefit. **El bien de la comunidad**, the public welfare. **Hombre de bien**, honest man. **En bien de**, for the good of. **Hacer bien**, to do good. **Bienes**, property, fortune, riches, land. **Bienes de fortuna**, worldly goods. **Bienes de consumo**, consumer goods. **Bienes de equipo**, capital goods. **Bienes inmuebles**, landed property. **Bienes públicos**, government property. **Bienes de la tierra**, produce. 4. **Mi bien**, my dear.
bien [be-en], *adv.*1. Well, right, properly. **Ha vivido bien**, he has lived uprightly. **Contestar bien**, to answer right. **No veo muy bien**, I can´t see all that well. **De bien en mejor**, better and better. **Ya está bien de quejas**, we´ve had enough complaints. 2. Happily, prosperously. **El enfermo va bien**, the patient is doing well. 3. Willingly, readily. 4. Heartily. **Comió bien**, he dined heartily. **Caminó bien**, he walked at a great rate. After a negative, it means, as soon as. **No bien la vio**, as soon as (just as) he saw her. It is used sometimes as a distributive conjunction: **bien . . . bien . . .**; whether . . . or. 5. Well, well: it is all well: often used in an ironical sense. 6. As well as, in the same manner as. 7. **Bien que**, although. 8. **Bien si**, but if. 9. **Ahora bien**, now this being so. **Bien está**; very well. 10. **Más bien**, rather. **Más bien bajo**, rather short. **Si bien me acuerdo**, to the best of my recollection. **Hay bien de eso**, there is plenty of that. **Un coche bien caro**, a very expensive car. **¿Y bien, y qué tenemos con eso?** Well, and what of that? Joined to adjectives or adverbs it is equivalent to **very**, as **bien rico**, very rich; and to verbs, *much*, as. **El bebió bien**, he drank much. **Tener a bien**, to be kind enough.
bienal [be-ay-nahl'], *a.* Biennial.
bienamado, da [be-en-ah-mah'-do, dah], *a.* Dearly, beloved.
bienandante [be-en-an-dahn'-tay]. *a.* Happy, successful, prosperous.
bienandanza [be-en-an-dahn'-thah], *f.* Felicity, prosperity, success.
bienaventuradamente [be-en-ah-ven-too-rah-dah-men'-tay], *adv.* Fortunately, happily.
bienaventurado, da [be-en-ah-ven-too-rah'-do, dah], *a.* 1. Blessed; happy. 2. Fortunate, successful, felicitous. 3. Simple; silly harmless.
bienaventuranza [be-en-ah-ven-too-rahn'-thah], *f.* 1. *(Ecl.)* Blessedness; bliss (eternal). **Las bienaventuranzas**, the beatitudes. 2. Happiness (felicidad); well-being, prosperity (bienestar).
bienestar [be-en-es-tar'], *m.* Well-being, welfare, comfort.
bienfortunado, da [be-en-for-too-nah'-do, dah]. *a.* Fortunate, successful.
bienhablado, da [be-en-ha-blah'-do, dah], *a.* Well and civilly spoken.

bienhadado, da [be-en-ah-dah'-do, dah], *a.* Lucky, fortunate, happy.

bienhecho, cha [be-en-ay'-cho, chah], *a.* Well shaped, well-performed.

bienhechor, ra [be-en-ay-char', rah], *m. & f.* Benefactor.

bienintencionado [be-en-een-ten-the-o-nah'-do], *a.* Well-meaning.

bienio [be-ay'-ne-o], *m.* Term or space of two years.

bienquerencia [be-en-kay-ren'-the-ah], *f.* Goodwill. *V.* BIENQUERER as noun.

bienquerer [be-en-kay-rerr'], *va.* To wish the good of another, to esteem.

bienquerer [be-en-kay-rerr'], *m.* Esteem, attachment.

bienquistar [be-en-kees-tar'], *va.* To reconcile, to bring together. *-vr.* To become reconciled. **Bienquistarse con uno**, to gain somebody´s esteem.

bienquisto, ta [be-en-kees'-to, tah], *a.* Generally esteemed and respected. *-pp.* of BIENQUISTAR.

bienvenida [be-en-vay-nee'-dah], *f.* WELCOME.

bienvenido, da [be-en-vay-nee'-do, dah], *a.* Welcome; greeting (saludo). **Dar la bienvenida a uno**, to welcome somebody, make somebody welcome.

bienventuranza [be-en-ah-ven-too-rahn-thah], *f.* 1. Beatitude. 2. Prosperity, human felicity. **Bienaventuranzas**, the eight beatitudes mentioned in the Scriptures.

bienvivir [be-en-vee-veer'], *vn.* To live in comfort; to live decently, lead a decent life.

bies [be-ays'], *m. (Cos.)* **Al bies**, cut on the cross.

bifásico [be-fah'-see-co], *a. (Elec.)* Two-phase.

bifocal [be-fo-cahl'], *a.* Bifocal. **Lentes bifocales**, bifocals, bifocal glasses.

biforme [be-for'-may], *a. (Poet.)* Biformed, biform.

bifronte [be-fron'-tay], *a. (Poet.)* Double-fronted or double-faced.

biftec [beef-tayc'], *m.* Steak, beefsteak.

bifurcación [be-foor-cah-the-on'], *f.* Branch, bifurcation, junction.

bifurcado, da [be-foor-cah'-do, dah], *a.* Forked, branched, bifurcated.

bifurcarse [be-foor-car'-say], *vr* To branch off, as a river or railway, to fork, to bifurcate.

bigamia [be-gah'-me-ah], *f.* 1. Bigamy. 2. *(Law.)* Bigamy, second marriage.

bígamo, ma [bee' -gah-mo], *m. & f.* 1. Bigamist. 2. *(Law.)* Person who has married a widow or widower 3. *(Law.)* A widower or widow who has married again.

bigardear [be-gar-day-ar'], *vn.* To live licentiously; to wander without an object.

bigardía [be-gar-dee'-ah], *f.* Jest, fiction, dissimulation.

bigardo [be-gar'-do], *m.* 1. An opprobrious appellation given to a friar of loose morals and irregular conduct; a lubber. 1. *a.* Lazy, idle; licentious. 2. *m.* Idler (vago); libertine (libertino).

bigarrado, da [be-gar-rah'-do, dah], *a. V.* ABIGARRADO.

bigarro [be-gar'-ro], *m. (Prov.)* A large sea-snail.

bignonia [be-no'-ne-ah], *f. (Bot.)* Trumpet-flower.

bigorneta [be-gor-nay-tah], *f. dim.* A small anvil.

bigornia [be-gor'-ne-ah], *f.* Anvil.

bigotazo [be-go-tah'-tho], *m. aug.* Large mustache.

bigote [be-go'-tay], *m.* 1. Mustachio, mustache; whiskers (de gato etc.). **De bigote**, terrific, marvellous. 2. Block. *(Typ.)* Dash rule. **Hombre de bigote**, *(Met.)* A man of spirit and vigor. *(Cono Sur)* **chuparse los bigotes**, to lick one´s lips.

bigotera [be-go-tay'-rah], *f.* 1. Leather cover for mustache, mustache protector. 2. *(Obs.)* Ornament of ribbons worn by women on the breast 3. Folding seat put in the front of a chariot. 4 Bow compass **Pegar una bigotera**. To play one a trick. **Bigoteras**, Face, mien. **Tener buenas bigoteras**, *(Coll.)* To have a pleasing face, or graceful mien (mujeres).

bigotería [be-go-tay-ree'-ah], *f.* Bigotry.

bigotudo [be-go-too'-do] *a.* Having a large mustache, full-whiskered.

bigudí [be-goo-dee'], *m.* Hair-curler.

bikini [be-kee'-nee], *m.* Bikini.

bilánder [be-lahn'-der], *m. (Naut.)* Bilander, a small merchant vessel.

bilateral [be-lah-tay'-rahl], *a.* Bilateral.

biliario, ria [be-le-ah'-re-o, ah], *a.* Biliary.

biliar [be-le-ar'], *a.* Bile, gall.

bilingüe [e-leen'-goo-ay], *a.* Bilingual. Double-tongued, deceitful.

bilingüismo [be-leen-goo-ees'-mo], *m.* Bilingualism.

bilioso, sa [be-le-oh'-so, sah], *a.* 1. *(gen.)* Bilious. 2. *(fig.)* Bilious, peevish (irritable).

bilis [bee'-lis], *f.* 1. *(Anat.)* Bile. 2. *(fig.)* Bile, spleen (cólera). **Se le exalta la bilis**, he gets very cross.

billa [beel'-lyah], *f.* In billiards; the pocketing of a ball after it has struck another.

billalda, or **billarda** [beel-larh'-dah], *f.* A kind of children's play.

billar [beel-lyar'], *m.* 1. Billiards (juego). **Billar americano**, pool. **Billar ruso**, snooker. **Billar automático**, pin table. 2. Billard room (sala).

billete [beel-lyeh'-tay], 1. *(Esp.)* Ticket *(ferro.)*. **Billete de abono**, season ticket. **Billete de ida y vuelta**, return ticket. **Billete sencillo**, single ticket. **Pagar el billete**, to pay one´s fare. **Sacar un billete**, to get a ticket. 2. *(Fin.)* Banknote; note, bill. **Billete de banco**, banknote. 3. Note, short letter (carta).

billetera, ro [beel-lay-tay'-rah], *f. & m.* Wallet, pocketbook.

billetero, ra [beel-lyeh-tay'-ro, rah] *m. & f.* Vendor of lottery tickets. *-f.* Billfold.

billón [beel-lyee-on'], *m.* **Un billón**, a trillion (GB billion).

billonario, ria [beel-lyo-nah'-re-o, ah], *m. & f.* Billionaire.

billonésimo, ma [beel-lyo-nay'-se-mo, mah], *m. & f. & a.* Billionth, one of a billion equal parts.

bilocarse [be-lo-car'-say], *vr.* To be in two different places at the same time.

bilongo [be-lon'-go], *m. (Carib.)* Evil influence, evil eye. **Echar bilongo en**, to put the evil eye on. **Tener bilongo**, to bristle with difficulties.

bilorta [be-lor'-tah], *m.* 1. Ring made of a twisted yellow twig. 2. Flying report 3. *(Naut.)* Burr, a kind of iron ring used for various purposes on board ships. 4. A sport among country people, resembling cricket.

bimano, na [be-mah'-no, nah], *m. & f. & a.* Bimanous: said only of mankind.

bimba [beem'-bah], *f. (Mex.)* 1. Drunkenness (embriaguez); drinking spree (juerga). 2. Top hat, topper. 3. Wallet.

bimbollo [beem-bol'-lyo], *m. (Mex.)* Bun.

bimensual [be-men-soo-al'], *a.* Twice-monthly.

bimensuario, ria [be-men-soo-ah'-ree-o], *a. m.* Twice-monthly, publication appearing twice-monthly.

bimestral [be-mes-trahl'], *a.* Bimonthly, once in two months. **Publicación bimestral**, bimonthly, bimonthly publication.

bimestre [be-mes'-tray], *a.* Of two months' duration. *-m.* Two months' leave of absence or furlough.

bimotor [be-mo-tor'], *m.* Two-engine plane.

binadera, dor [be-nah-day'-rah], *m. & f.* Weeding hoe.

binar [be-nar'], *va.* To dig or plough ground the second time.

binario, ria [be-nah-re-o], *a.* Binary; of two elements or units.

bincha [been'-chah], *f. (And. Cono Sur)* Hairband.

bingo [been'-go], *m.* Bingo (juego); bingo hall (sala).

binocular [be-no'-coo-lar], *a.* Binocular.

binóculo [be-no'-coo-lo], *m.* Binocle, a dioptric telescope; marine or field glasses.

binomial, binominal [be-no-me-ahl', be-no-me-nahl] *a.* Binomial. **Sistema binomial**, *(Math.)* Binomial system.

binomio [be-no'-me-o], *m.* 1. Binominal. 2. **El binomio pueblo**, *(fig.)* the people-army relationship.

binza [been'-thah], *f.* Pellicle, lining of the shell of an egg; any thin membrane.

bio .....*pref.* bio....
biodegradable [be-o-day-grah-dah'-blay], *a.* Biodegradable.
biodegradar [be-o-day-grah-dar'], 1. *va.* To biodegrade. 2. *-vr.* To biodegrade.
biodinámica [be-o-de-nah'-me-cah], *f.* Biodynamics, the doctrine of vital force or energy.
bioecología [be-o-ay-co-lo-hee'-ah], *f.* Bioecology.
biofísica [be-fee'-see-cah], *f.* Biophysics.
biofísico, ca [be-o-fee'-se-co, cah], *a.* Biophysical.
biografía [be-o-grah-fee'-ah], *f.* Biography, life.
biográfico, ca [be-o-grah'-fe-co, cah], *a.* Biographical.
biógrafo [be-o'-grah-fo], *m.* Biographer. *(Cono Sur)* Cinema.
biología [bi-o-lo-hee'-ah]. *f.* Biology. **Biología molecular,** molecular biology.
biológico, ca [be-o-lo'-he-co, cah] *a.* Biological.
biólogo, ga [be-o'-lo-go], *m&* **f.** Biologist.
biomasa [be-o-mah'-sah], *f.* Biomass.
biombo [be-om'-bo], *m.* Folding screen (Chinese word).
biometría [be-o-may-tree'-ah], *f.* Biometry, biometrics.
biónica [be-o'-ne-cah], *f. (Biol.)* Bionics.
biónico, ca [be-o'-ne-co], *a.* Bionic.
biopsia [be-op'-see-ah], *f.* Biopsy.
bioquímica [be-o-kee'-me-cah], *f.* Biochemistry.
bioquímico, ca [be-o-kee'-me-co, cah] *a.* Biochemical. *-m.* Biochemist. *-f.* Biochemistry.
biosfera [be-os-fay'-rah], *f.* Biosphere.
biotecnología [be-o-tayc-no-lo-hee'-ah], *f.* Biotechnology.
biótico [be-o'-tee-co], *a.* Biotic.
biotina [be-o-tee'-nah], *f.* Biotin.
bióxido [be-ok'-se-do], *m. (Chem.)* Dioxide. **Bióxido (or dióxido) de carbons,** carbon dioxide.
bipartido, da [bee-par-tee'-do, dah], *a. (Poet.)* Bipartite.
bipartidismo [be-par-tee-dees'-mo], *m.* Two-party system.
bipedal [be-pay-dahl'], *a.* Bipedal.
bipede, or bípedo [bee'-pay-day, do], *a.* Biped.
bipétalo, la [be-pay'-tah-lo, lah] *a. (Bot.)* Bipetalous.
biplano [be-plah'-no], *m.* Biplane.
biplaza [be-plah'-thah], *m. (Aer.)* Two-seater.
biricu [be-re-coo'], *vn.* Sword-belt.
birimbao [be-rim-bah'-o], *m. (Mus.)* A Jew's harp. (imitative word.)
birla, *f. (Prov.)* **birlo,** *vn.* [bee-lah, lo] Bowl for playing.
birlador [beer-lah-dor'], *m.* 1. One who knocks down with one blow; used in the game of nine-pins. 2. Pilferer.
birlar [beer-lar'], *va.* 1. At the game of nine-pins, to throw a bowl a second time from the same place. 2. To knock down with one blow, to kill with one shot. 3. To snatch away an employment which another was aiming at. 4. To rob, to pilfer. **Juan le birló la novia,** John pinched his girl. **Le birlaron el empleo,** he was done out of the job.
birlibirloque [beer-le-beer-lo'-kay], *m.* **Por arte de birlibirloque,** *(Coll.)* To do something by occult and extraordinary means.
birlocha [beer-lo'-chah], *f.* 1. Paper kite. 2. *(Mex.) (Aut.)* Old banger, old crock.
birlocho [beer-lo'-cho], *m.* High open carriage.
birlón [beer-lone'], *m. (Prov.)* Large middle pin in the game of nine-pins.
birlonga [beer-lon'-gah], *f.* Mode of playing in the game at cards called *ombre*. **A la birlonga,** in a negligent, careless manner.
Birmania [beer-mah'-nee-ah], *f.* Burma.
birmano, na [beer-mah'-no, nah], *a. m. & f.* Burmese.
birreactor [beer-ray-ac-tor'], *m. & f.* Twin-jet (plane).
birreme [beer-ray'-may], *a.* Two-oared (barco); bireme.
birreta [beer-ray'-tah], *f.* Cardinal's red cap.
birrete [beer-ray'-tay], *m.* Mortarboard, professional cap.
birria [ber'-ree-ah], f. 1. *(Esp.)* Monstrosity, ugly old thing (cosa fea); wretched piece of work (obra); trash (basura); useless object (cosa inútil). **La novela es una birria,** the novel is trash. **Entre tanta birria,** among so much trash. 2. *(Cono Sur. Méx.)* Tasteless drink; *(Mex.)* Stew (guiso). 3.

(And.) Set idea, mania; obstinacy (obsesión). 4. *(LAm.)* **Jugar de birria,** to play heartedly. 5. *(CAm.)* Beer (cerveza).
bis [bees], a Latin word meaning twice; used in composition.
bisabuela [be-sah-boo-ay'-lah], *f.* Great-grandmother.
bisabuelo [be-sah-boo-ay'-lo], *m.* Great-grandfather.
bisagra [be-sah'-grah], *f.* 1. Hinge. 2. Piece of boxwood, with which shoemakers polish soles of shoes. **Bisagras y pernos,** hooks and hinges. **Bisagras de la portería,** *(Naut.)* port hinges.
bisanuo, nua [be-sah'-noo-o, ah], *a. (Bot.)* Bisannual.
bisar [be-sar'], 1. *va.* To give an encore, to repeat. 2. *(Cono Sur)* To encore, demand as an encore. *-vn.* To give an encore.
bisbisar [bis-be-sar'], *va.* To mutter, to mumble; *(Cono Sur.)* to whisper (susurrar).
bisbiseo [bis-be-say'-o], *m.* Mutter, muttering, mumbling.
bisecar [be-say-car'], *va.* To bisect.
bisección [be-sec-the-on'], *f.* Bisection.
bisector, triz [be-sec-tor', treeth], *a. (Geom.)* Bisecting.
bisel [be-sel'], *m.* The bevel, bevel edge, chamfer. *(Coop.)* Sloping tool.
biselado [be-say-lah-do], *a.* Bevel, bevelled.
biselar [be-say-lar'], *va.* To bevel.
bisemanal [be-say-mah-nah], *a.* Semiweekly, twice a week.
bisemanario [be-say-mah-nah'-re-o], *m.* Semiweekly publication.
bisexual [be-sec-soo-ahl'], *a.* Bisexual.
bisexualidad [be-sec-soo-ah-lee-dahd'], *f.* Bisexuality.
bisiesto [be-se-es'-to], *a.* Bissextile; leap year (año).
bisílabo, ba [be-see'-lah-bo, bah], *a.* Consisting of two syllables.
bismuto [bis-moo'-to], *m.* Bismuth.
bisnieto, ta [bis-ne-ay'-to, tah], *m. & f.* V. BIZNIETO.
bisojo, ja [be-so'-ho, hah], *a.* Squint-eyed, cross eyed.
bisonte [be-son'-tay], *m.* Bison, buffalo.
bisoñada [be-so-nyah'-dah], *f.* Naïve remark, naïve thing to do.
bisoñé [be-so-nyay'], *m.* Wig, toupee.
bisoñería [be-so-nyay-ree'-ah], *f.* A rash and inconsiderate speech or action.
bisoñez [be-so-nyayth'], *f.* Inexperience; rawness.
bisoño, ña [be-so'-nyo, nyah], *a.* 1. Raw, undisciplined: applied to recruits or new-levied soldiers. 2. Novice, tyro. 3. Horse not yet broken.
bispón [bis-pone'], *m.* Roll of oil-cloth, a yard in length, used by sword cutlers.
bistec, bisté, bisteck, bisteque [bees-tec'], *m.* Beefsteak, steak. 2. Tongue (lengua). **Achatar el bisté,** to shut one's trap.
bisturí [bee-too-ree'], *m.* Scalpel, surgeon's knife.
bisulco, ca [be-sool'-co, cah], *a.* Bisulcate, cloven-footed.
bisulfato [be-sool-fah'-to], *m. (Chem.)* Bisulfate.
bisulfito [be-sool fee'-to], *m. (Chem.)* Bisulfite.
bisunto, to [be-soon'-to, tah], *a. (Obs.)* Dirty or greasy.
bisutería [be-soy-tay-ree'-ah], *f.* Imitation jewelery, trinkets.
bit [beet'], *m. pl. (Comp.)* Bit. **Bit de inicio,** start bit. **Bit de parada,** stop bit. **Bit de control,** check bit. **Bit de ejecución,** running bit. **Bit de orden inferior,** low order bit. **Bit de orden superior,** high order bit. **Bit de paridad par,** even parity bit.
bitácora [be-tah'-co-rah], *f. (Naut.)* Binnacle. **Lámpara de la bitácora,** binnacle-lamp.
bitadura [be-tah doo' rah], *f. (Naut.)* Cable-bitt, a turn of the cable round the bitts. **Bitadura entera de cable,** weather-bitt of a cable. **Tomar la bitadura con el cable,** to bitt the cable.
bitas [bee'-tas], *f. pl. (Naut.)* Bitts, large pieces of timber placed abaft the manger, to belay the cable, when the ship rides at anchor. **Forro de las bitas,** lining of the bits. **Contrabitas,** standards of the bitts. **Bita de molinete,** knight-head of the windlass.
bitensional [be-ten-see-o-nahl'], *a. (Elec.)* Equipped to work at two different voltages.

bitones [be-to´-nes], *m. pl.* (*Naut.*) Pins of the capstan.

bitoque [be-to´-kay], *m.* (*Prov.*) Bung, the wooden stopple of a cask. **Tener ojos de bitoque**, (*Cold.*) to squint.

bitor [be-tor´], *m.* (*Orn.*) Rail, a bird called the king of the quails.

bitumen [be-too´-men], *m. V.* BETÚN.

bituminoso, sa [be-too-me-no´-so, sah], *a.* Bituminous.

bivalvo, va [be-vahl´-vo, vah], *a.* (*Conch.*) Bivalve, bivalvular.

biverio [be-vay´-re-o], *m.* 1. *V.* BÍBARO 2. *V.* VIVERO.

bivio [be-vee-o], *m.* (*LAm.*) Road junction.

biza [bee´-thah], *f.* (*Zool.*) Fish belonging to the family of tunnies. *V.* BONITO.

Bizancio [be-than´-the-o], *n.* Byzantium.

bizantino [be-than-te´-no], *a.* 1. Byzantine. 2. (*fig.*) Decadent (decadente). 3. (*fig.*) Idle, pointless (discusión). *-m.* (Bizantina) *f.* Byzantine.

bizarramente [be-thar-rah-men´-tay], *adv.* Courageously (generosamente), gallantly (valientemente), with spirit.

bizarrear [be-thar-ray-ar´], *vn.* To act in a spirited and gallant manner.

bizarría [be-thar-ree´-ah], *f.* 1. Gallantry, valor, fortitude; mettle. 2. Liberality, generosity, splendor, gentility.

bizarro, rra [be-thah´-ro, rah], *a.* 1. Gallant, brave, high-spirited (valiente). 2. Generous, liberal, high-minded.

bizaza [be-thah´-thah], *f.* Saddlebag.

bizbirindo [beeth-be-reen-do], *a.* (*Mex.*) Lively, bright.

bizcacha [bith-cah´-chah], *f.* An animal with a long tail in Peru, the flesh of which resembles that of a rabbit.

bizcar [bith-car´], *vn.* To squint, to be cross-eyed. *-va.* To wink (ojo).

bizco, ca [beeth´-co, cah], *a.* Cross-eyed, squinting, cross-eyed look. **Dejar a uno bizco**, to impress somebody strongly. **Ponerse bizco**, to squint, to look cross-eyed. *-adv.* **Mirar bizco**, to squint, to look cross-eyed. *V.* BISOJO.

bizcochada [bith-co-chah´-dah], *f.* Soup made of cookies boiled in milk with sugar and cinnamon.

bizcochar [bith-co-char´], *va.* To make or bake cookies. To bake bread a second time.

bizcochero [bith-co-chay´-ro] *m.* 1. Cookies-cask. 2. One who makes or sells cookies.

bizcocho [bith-co´-cho], *m.* 1. (*Naut.*) Cookie, hard tack. **Embarcarse con poco bizcocho**, to set out unprepared. 2. Sponge, sponge cake; sponge finger; paste made of fine flour eggs and sugar. 3. Whiting made of the plaster of old walls.

bizcochuelo [bith-co-choo-ay´-lo], *m.* 1. Dim. of BIZCOCHO. 2. (*Amer.*) Sponge-cake.

bizma [beeth´-mah], *f.* Cataplasm, poultice.

bizmar [bith-mar´], *va.* To poultice, to apply a cataplasm.

bizna [beeth´-nah], *f.* Zest, membrane which quarters the kernel of a walnut.

biznaga [bith-nah´-gah], *f.* 1. (*Bot.*) Carrot-like ammi, the sprigs of which are used as toothpicks. Ammi visnaga. 2. (*Coll. and Amer.*) A useless, worthless thing.

biznieta [bith-ne-ay´-tah], *f.* Great-granddaughter.

biznieto [bith-ne-ay´-to], *m.* Great-grandson.

bizquear [bith-kay-ar´], *vn.* To squint.

bizquera [bith-kay´-rah], *f.* (*And.*) Squint.

blanca [blahn´-cah], *f.* 1. Copper coin of the value of half a maravedí; mite. **No tener blanca or estar sin blanca**, to be broke. 2. (*Orn.*) Magpie. 3. **Blanca morfea**, (*Vet.*) alphosis, a white scurf, tetter, or ring-worm. 3. White woman (mujer). 5. (*Mus.*) Minim. 6. Cocaine (cocaína); heroin (heroína).

blanca-espina [blahn´-cah-es-pee´-nah], *f.* Hawthorn, white thorn.

blancal [blan-cahl´], *a. & m.* White wheat.

blancazo, za [blan-cah´-tho, thah], *a.* 1. (*aug.*) Very white. 2. (*Coll.*) *V.* BLANQUECINO.

blanco, ca [blahn´-co, cah], *a.* 1. White, blank: hoar, hoary; fair. **La raza blanca**, the white race. **Más blanco que la nieve**, as white as snow. 2. Honored, respected (personas).

3. (*Naut.*) Untarred. 4. Blank (página). 5. Blank (verso). 6. Cowardly (cobarde). 7. **Estar blanco**, to have a clean record.

blanco [blahn´-co], *m.* 1. White star, or any other remarkable white spot in horses. 2. Target, blank, mark to shoot at. **Dar en el blanco**, to hit the mark. 3. Blank left in writing. **Con dos páginas en blanco**, with two blank pages. **Cheque en blanco**, blank cheque. **Botar en blanco**, to return a blank voting paper. 4. (*Met.*) Aim; object of our desire. 5. First white sheet pulled at a printing-press, after the form is got ready. 6. Interlude: speaking of plays. 7. Interval (intervalo). 8. White page. 9. (*Her.*) Argent. 10. Mixture of whiting, lime, etc., to size or lay the first coat for painting. **Blanco de estuco**, stucco whiting, made of lime and pounded marble. **Blanco de ballena**, Spermaceti. **Blanco de España**, Spanish white. **Blanco de perla**, pearl white. **Tela or ropa blanca**, linen. **Armas blancas**, side-arms. **De punta en blanco**, point-blank. **Dejar en blanco alguna cosa**, to pass over a thing in silence. **Quedarse en blanco**, to be frustrated in one's expectations, to be left in the lurch.

blancor [blan-cor´], *m.* **blancura** [bland-coo´-rah], *f.* Whiteness, freedom from color, hoariness. **Blancura del ojo**, (*Vet.*) A white spot or film on the eye.

blancuzco [blan-cooth´-co], *a.* Whitish.

blandamente [blahn´-dah-men-tay], *adv.* Softly, mildly, gently, sweetly, smoothly.

blandeador, ra [blan-day-ah-dor´, rah] *m. & f.* Softener.

blandear [blan-day-ar´], *va.* 1. To soften, to render mild. 2. To make one change his opinion. 3. To brandish, to flourish. *-vn.* 1. To slacken, to yield, to be softened, 2. To tread tenderly. 3. **Blandear con otro**, to fall in with another's opinion. *-vr.* To be unsteady, to move from one place to another; to give way. **Blandearse con uno**, to humor somebody.

blandengue [blan-den´-gay], *m.* 1. A soldier, armed with a lance, who defended the limits of the province of Buenos Aires. 2. Soft sort, softie. *-a.* Soft, weak.

blandeo [blan-day´-o], *m.* The good or bad quality of the soil of forests and pasture-lands.

blandicia [blan-dee´-the-ah], *f.* Flattery, adulation.

blandiente [blan-de-en´-tay], *a.* Having a tremulous motion from one side to another.

blandillo, illa [blan-deel´-lyo, -yah], *a. dim.* Somewhat soft.

blandimiento [blan-de-me-en´-to], *m.* Adulation, flattery.

blandir [blan-deer´], *va.* 1. To brandish a sword, pike, lance, etc. 2. To hurtle, to whirl round. 3. To flatter. *-vr.* To quiver, to move tremulously from one side to another.

blando, da [blahn´-do, dah], *a.* 1. Soft pliant, smooth to the touch; cottony; milky; flabby liquid. **Blando al tacto**, soft to the touch. 2. Lithe. 3. (*Met.*) Soft, mild, bland, gentle, grateful, pleasing. **Blando de corazón**, sentimental, tender-hearted. 4. Mild, moderate (tiempo). 5. Soft, effeminate, delicate, not bearing fatigue or labor. 6 Tractable, good-natured, kindly; fair. 7. Tender-mouthed (caballos). **Blando de boca**, tender-mouthed. 8. (*Met.*) Indiscreet, talkative. 9. (*Met.*) Soft. 10 (*Met.*) Fond of women, apt to fall in love. **Hombre blando**, a gentle, mild man.

blandón [blan-done´], *m.* 1. Wax taper with one wick. 2. A large church candlestick, in which wax tapers or flambeaux are placed. 3. Light of the stars.

blandoncillo [blan-don-theel´-lyo], *m. dim.* A small candlestick for wax tapers.

blanducho, cha, blandujo, ja [blan-doo´-cho, chah, blan-doo´-ho, hah], *a.* (*Low.*) Flabby, loose, soft, not firm; flabby, slack (carne).

blandujo [ban-doo´-ho], *a.* Softish.

blandura [blan-doo´-rah], *f.* 1. Softness, litheness. 2. Daintiness, delicacy. 3. (*Met.*) Gentleness of temper, sweetness of address; favor, lenity 4. Lenitive or emollient application 5. Soft, endearing language; blandishing. 6. White paint, used by women. 7. Mild temperature of the air.

blandurilla [blan-doo-reel´-yah], *f.* A sort of fine soft pomatum.

blanduzco [blan-dooth´-co], *a.* Softish.

blanqueación [blan-kay-ah-the-on'], *f.* Blanching, the act of blanching metal before it is coined.

blanqueador, ra [blan-kay-ah-dor', rah], *m. & f.* Blancher, whitener, bleacher.

blanqueadura [blan-kay-ah-doo'-rah], *f.* Whitening, bleaching.

blanqueamiento [blan-kay-ah-me-en'-to], *m. (Obs.) V.* BLANQUEADURA.

blanquear [blan-kay-ar'], *va.* 1. To bleach, to whiten, to blanch, to fleece, to clear. 2. To whitewash (tela). 3. To give coarse wax to bees in winter. **Blanquear cera**, To bleach wax; to launder (dinero). 4. *(Carib.)* To kill (matar); to beat (ganar). *vn.* To go white (volverse blanco); to show white (mostrarse blanco).

blanquecedor [blan-kay-thay-dor'], *m.* An officer employed in the mint to blanch, clean, and polish the coin.

blanquecer [blan-kay-therr'], *va.* To blanch coin, to give gold, silver, and other metals their due colors. *V.* BLANQUEAR.

blanquecimiento [blan-kay-the-me-en'-to], *m. (Obs.) V.* BLANQUEACIÓN.

blanquecino, na [blan-kay-thee'-no, nah], *a.* Whitish, hoary.

blanqueo [blan-kay'-o], *m.* 1. Whitening, making white or bleaching. 2 Whitewash. **El blanqueo del lienzo** the bleaching of linen.

blanquería [blan-kay-ree'-ah], *f.* 1. Bleaching-place, bleach-field.

blanquero [blan-kay'-ro], *m. (Prov.)* Tanner.

blanqueta [blan-kay'-tah], *f. (Obs.)* Coarse blanket.

blanquete [blan-kay'-tay], *m.* White wash.

blanquilla [blan-keel'-lyah], *f.* 1. Doit, a very small coin. 2. Sort of long yellowish plum. 3. White grape. 4. Blanket, a kind of pear.

blanquillo, lla [blan-keel'-lyo, lya], *a. dim.* Whitish, somewhat white. *-m.* A Californian fish.

blanquimiento [blan-ke-me-en'-to], *m.* Water mixed with salt of tartar and other things, to bleach wax, linen, etc.

blanquinegro [blan-kee-ne'-gro], *a.* White-and-black.

blanquita [blan-kee'tah], *f. (Carib.)* Cocaine.

blanquizal, or **blanquizar** [blan-ke-thahl], *m. (Agri.)* Whitish clay, pipeclay. *V.* GREDAL.

blanquizco, ca [blan-keeth'-co, cah], *a.* Whitish.

blao [blah'-o], *a. (Her.)* Azure, faint blue.

blasfemador, ra [blas-fay-mah-dor', rah], *m. & f.* Blasphemer.

blasfemar [blas-fay-mar'], *vn.* 1. To blaspheme. 2. To curse, to make use of imprecations.

blasfematorio, ria [blas-fay-mah-to'-re-o, ah], *a.* Blasphemous.

blasfemia [blas-fay'-me-ah], *f.* 1. Blasphemy. 2. Blaspheming. **Decir blasfemias**, to blaspheme.

blasfemo, ma [blas-fay'-mo, mah], *a.* Blasphemous. *-m. & f.* Blasphemer.

blasón [blah-sone'], *m.* 1. Heraldry, blazon, blazonry, drawing or explaining coats of arms. 2. Figures and devices which compose coats of arms or armorial ensigns. 3. Honor, glory. **Hacer blasón**, to blazon, to boast, to bray.

blasonador, ra [blah-so-nah-dor', rah] *m. & f.* Boaster, bragger.

blasonante [blah-so-nahn'-tay], *pa.* Vainglorious; boaster.

blasonar [blah-so-nar']. *va.* 1. To blazon, to draw or explain armorial ensigns. 2. To make a pompous display of one's own merits. **Blasonar del arnés**, to boast of achievements never performed.

blavo, va [blah'-vo, vah], *a.* Yellowish gray and reddish color.

blázer [blah'-thayr], *m.* Blazer.

bledo [blay'-do], *m. (Bot.)* Wild amaranth. **No me importa un bledo**, I don't care a straw. **No vale un bledo**, it is not worth a cent.

blefaritis [blay-fah-ree'-tis], Blepharitis, inflammation of the borders of the eyelids.

blenda [blen'dah], *f. (Miner.)* Blende.

bleno, blino [blay'no, blee'no], *(Zool.)* Hake, blenny.

blenorragia [blay-nor-rah'-heah], *f. (Med.)* Blennorrhagia, a disease.

blindado, da [blin-dah'-do, dah], *a. & m.* Iron-clad, armored; an armored war-vessel; armored-plated; *(Mech.)* Shielded, protected, encased. **Puertas blindadas**, reinforced doors.

blindaje [blin-dah'-hay], *m.* 1. *(Mil.)* Blind, a covering made by the besiegers of a strong place, to protect themselves from the enemy's fire. 2. Armor-plate; *(Tec.)* Shield, protective plating, casing.

blindar [blin-dar'], *va.* To apply plates of armor; to armor; *(Tec.)* to shield.

bloc [bloc'], *m, pl.* Pad, writing pad; calendar pad; note-book; *(Escol.)* Exercise book. **Block de dibujos**, sketching pad. **Block de notas**, pad for notes; (reporter's) notebook.

blocaje [blo-kah-hay], *m. (Dep.)* Tackle; stop; *(Mil.)* Blockade.

blocar [blo-kay-ar'], *va. (Dep.)* To tackle (jugador); to stop (balón), to trap, to catch.

blofear [blo-fay-ar'], *(LAm.) vn.* To boast, to brag.

blonda [blon'-dah], *f.* Broad lace made. of silk, blond lace. **Escofieta de blonda**, Headdress made of silk lace.

blondina [blon-dee'-nah], *f.* Narrow silk lace, narrow blonde lace.

blondo, da [blon'-do, dah], *a.* Flaxen, flaxy, light, having a fair complexion or flaxen hair. 2. *(LAm.)* Soft, smooth, silken (liso); *(CAm.)* Lank; *(Cono Sur. Méx.)* Curly (rizado).

bloque [blo'-kay], *m.* 1. Block (of stone). **Bloque de casas**, block of houses. **Bloque de hormigón**, block of concrete. 2. *(Mech.)* Cylinder block. **En bloque**, *(fig.)* As a whole, without distinction. 3. *(Pol.)* Bloc, group. **El bloque comunista**, the communist bloc. 4. **Bloque de datos** *(Comp.)*, data block.

bloquear [blo-kay-ar'], *va.* 1.*(Mil.)* To form a blockade, to obstruct; *(Dep.)* To tackle (jugador); to stop (pelota); *(Rad.)* To jam. **Bloquear una ley en el congreso**, to block a bill in the congress. **Los manifestantes bloquearon las calles**, the demonstrators blocked the streets. **Bloquear un puerto**, *(Naut.)* To blockade a port. 2. *(Mech.)* To block, jam. **El mecanismo está bloqueado**, the mechanism is jammed, the mechanism is stuck. 3. To cut off (aislar). **La inundación bloqueó el pueblo**, the flood cut off the village. 4. *(Aut.)* To brake, to pull up; to lock (volante). 5. *(Com.) (Fin.)* To freeze, block. **fondos bloqueados**, frozen assets. *-vr.* **Boquearse de** *(fig.)*, to shut oneself off from, to shield oneself from.

bloqueo [blo-kay-o] *m.* 1. *(Mil.)* Blockade. **Burlar el bloqueo**, to run the blockade. 2. *(Com.) (Fin.)* Freezing, blocking; squeeze. **Bloqueo de fondos**, freezing of assets. 3. **Bloqueo mental**, mental block.

bluff [bloof'], *m.* Bluff.

blusa [bloo'-sah], *f.* A blouse.

blusón [bloo-sone'], *m.* Smock; *(Mil.)* Jacket.

B.° *m.* 1. *(Fin.)* abr. de **banco** *(Bank.)* 2. *(Com.)* abr. de **beneficiario** (beneficiary).

boa [bo'-ah], *f.* 1. Boa, a large serpent. 2. Boa, tippet.

boaleje [bo-ah-lah'-hay], *m. (Prov.)* Pasturage of black cattle.

boato [bo-ah'-to], *m.* 1. Ostentation, pompous show. 2. Shout of acclamation.

bob [bob], *m.* Bobsleigh.

bobada [bo-bah'-dah], *f.* Silly thing, stupid thing. **Esto es una bobada**, this is nonsense. **Decir bobadas**, to say silly things, talk nonsense. *V.* BERÍA.

bobalías [bo-bah-lee'-as], *m. (Coll.)* A very stupid fellow, a dolt.

bobalicón, bobazo [bo-bah-le-cone', bo-bah'-tho], *m.* 1. *(aug.)* Great blockhead. 2. Stupid: used commonly in jest, particularly with children.

bobamente [bo-bah-men'-tay], *adv.* 1. Without trouble or care. 2. Foolishly, stupidly. **Está comiendo su renta bobamente**, he spends his income in a foolish manner.

bobarrón, na [bo-bar-rone', nah], *a. (Coll.)* Slightly foolish, a little stupid.

bobatel [bo-bah-tel'], *m. (Coll.)* V. BOBO.

bobático, ca [bo-bah'-te-co, cah], *a.* Silly, foolish, stupid.

bobazo, za [bo-bah'-tho, thah], *a. aug.* Very foolish: often used as an endearing expression.

bobear [bo-bay-ar'], *va.* 1. To act or talk in a foolish and stupid manner. 2. To dally, to fribble. 3. To waste one's time in trifles, to loiter about.

bobería [bo-bay-ree'-ah], *f.* Foolish speech or action; foolery, folly, foolishness. *-l.* Idle conceits.

bóbilis [bo'-be-lis], *adv.* **De bóbilis bóbilis**, *(Coll.)* Without pain or merit; without effort; free; for nothing.

bobillo, illa, ito, its [bo-bee'-lyo, lyah, ce'-to, ce'-tah], *m. & a; f. dim.* A little dolt or fool.

bobillo [bo-bee'-lyo], *m.* 1. Big-bellied jug with one handle. 2. Modesty piece, a frill or lace formerly worn by women around the tucker.

bobina [bo-bee'-nah], *f.* Bobbin, a large sort of spool used in ribbon looms and electrical machines; reel (de cinta); *(Aut. Elec.)* Coil. **Bobina de encendido**, ignition coil.

bobinado [bo-be-nah'-do], *m. (Elec.)* Winding.

bobinadora [bo-be-nah-do'-rah], *f.* Winder, winding machine.

bobinar [bo-be-nar'], *va.* To wind.

bobísimamente [bo-bee'-see-mah-men-tay], *adv.* Most foolishly.

bobo, ba [bo'-bo, bah], *m. & f* 1. Dunce, dolt, fool, mooncalf, silly, stupid; *(Theat.)* clown, funny man. **A los bobos se les aparece la madre de Dios**, fortune favors fools. **Entre bobos anda el juego**, they are well matched. 2. One who is easily cheated. 3. Sort of ruff formerly worn by women. 4. Stage buffoon. 5. *(Orn.)* Booby. **A bobas**, foolishly. *-a.* Ample, large.

bobón, na [bo-bone', nah], *m. & f. aug.* Big dolt, great fool.

boboncillo, lla [bo-bon-theel'-lyo, lyah], *m. & f. dim.* A little dolt.

bobote [bo-bo'-tay], *m. aug.* Great idiot or simpleton.

bobsleigh [bob'-es-lay-e], *m.* Bobsleigh.

boca [bo'-cah], *f.* 1. Mouth. 2. Entrance, opening, hole, nozzle. 3. Muzzle, the mouth of anything: vulgarly, chops. 4. Chops, the mouth of man, in contempt. 5. Bunghole. 6. Pincers with which cray-fish hold something. 7. Thin or cutting part of edge tools. 8. Taste, flavor, relish; one who eats. **Instrumento de boca**, wind-instrument. 9. *(Zool.)* Shrimp. **Boca de escorpión**, calumniator. **Boca de estómago**, pit of the stomach. **Boca de un arma de fuego**, the muzzle of a fire arm. **Boca de lobo**, wolf's mouth. 10. *(Met.)* Dark dungeon. 11. *(Naut.)*, mast-hole, lubbers' hole. **Boca de la escotilla**, hatchway. **Boca de río o de puerto**, mouth of a river or of a harbor. **Andar de boca en boca**, to be the talk of the town. **Cerrar or tapar a uno la boca**, to stop one's mouh. **Coserse la boca**, to shut one's mouth. **Boca de oro**, mellifluous tongue. **A boca de jarro**, 1. A hearty draught, drinking without glass or measure. 12. Very near. **Decir alguna cosa con la boca chica**, to offer a thing for mere ceremony's sake. **Andar con la boca abierta**, to go gaping about. **Irse de boca**, to speak much without reflection. **No decir esta boca es mía**, to keep a profound silence. **No tener boca para negar or decir no**, not dare to say no. **Tener buena o mala boca**, to talk well or ill of others. **A boca de invierno**, about the beginning of winter. **Boca arriba**, reversed, upside down, on one's back. **Boca abajo**, face downward. **Boca a boca**, *adv.* by word of mouth. **Boca con boca**, face to face. **A boca llena**, perspicuously, openly. **A pedir de boca**, according to one's desire. **De boca**, verbally; not really; used of boasting or threatening. **Andar en boca de la gente**, to be talked about. **Se me hace la boca agua**, my mouth is watering. **Meter a uno en la boca del lobo**, to put somebody on the spot. **Por la boca muerde el pez**, silence is gold. *-m* Screw, warder.

bocacalle [bo-cah-cahl'-lyay], *f.* Entry, end or opening of a street.

bocacaz [bo-cah-cath'], *m.* Opening left in the weir or dam of a river, sluice, or flood-gate.

bocací, bocacín [bo-cah-thee', bo-cah. theen'], *m.* Fine glazed buckram; crimson calico.

bocada [bo-cah'-dah], *f.* A mouthful.

bocadear [bo-cah-day-ar'], *va.* To divide into bits or morsels; to cut up for eating.

bocadico, illo, ito [bo-cah-dee'-co, eel'-lyo, ee'-to], *m. dim.* Small bit or morsel.

bocadillo [bo-cah-dee'-lyo], *m.* 1. Sandwich (emparedado); snack, bite to eat. **Un bocadillo de queso**, a cheese sandwich. 2. Thin, middling sort of linen. 3. Narrow ribbon or lace, tape, gimp.

bocado [bo-cah'-do], *m.* 1. Morsel, a mouthful of food. **Bocado exquisito**, titbit. 2. Gobbet, a mouthful, as much as can be swallowed at once. 3. Modicum, small portion. 4. Bite, a wound made with the teeth. 5. Part of a thing torn off with the teeth or pincers. 6. Poison given in eatables. 7. Bit of a bridle. 8. *(Art.)* Wad of a large cannon. 9. *(Naut.)* The hold of a ship. **Bocado sin hueso**, profitable employment without labor; a sinecure. **Con el bocado en la boca**, immediately after dinner or supper. **Contarle a uno los bocados**, to watch how another eats. **No tener para un bocado**, to be in extreme distress, to be completely broke. 10 Bit, briddle (freno). 11. *(And.)* Poison (veneno). *-pl.* 1. Slices of quinces, apples, pumpkins, etc., made up into conserves. 2. *(Naut.)* Wads of great guns, hawseplugs. **A bocados or bocaditos**, by piecemeals.

bocaina [bo-cah'-ee-nah], *f. (Naut.)* The mouth of a bar.

bocajarro [bo-cah-hah'-rro], *adv. (Mil.)* **A bocajarro**, at close range, point blank. **Decir algo a bocajarro**, to say something straight out.

bocal [bo-cahl'], *m.* 1. Pitcher. 2. Mouth-piece of a wind instrument 3. *(Naut.)* The narrows of a harbor.

bocamanga [bo-cah-mahn'-gah], *f.* 1. That part of a sleeve which is closest to the wrist, cuff, wristband (puño). 2. *(Mex.)* Hole for the head (agujero) (in a cape).

bocamina [bo-cah-me'-nah], *f.* Pithead, mine entrance.

bocana [bo-cah'-nah], *f.* (River) mouth.

bocanada [bo-cah-nah'-dah], *f.* 1. A mouthful of liquor. 2. Whiff, puff of smoke. **Bocanada de gente**, mob, a rout. **Bocanada de viento**, sudden blast of wind. **Echar bocanadas**, to boast of one's valor, noble birth, etc. **Echar bocanadas de sangre**, 1. To throw up mouthfuls of blood. 2. To vaunt of noble blood.

bocarán [bo-cah-rahn'], *m.* Fine sort of buckram.

bocarón [bo-cah-rone'], *m.* Wind chest of an organ; wind trunk.

bocarte [bo-car-tay], *m.* 1. Ore-crusher, stamp, stamp mill. 2. Small sardine.

bocata [bo-cah'-tah], *m. V.* BOCADILLO.

bocateja [bo-cah-tay'-hah], *f.* The last tile of each line on a tiling.

bocatijera [bo-ca-te-hay'-rah], *f.* Socket for the pole of a carriage.

bocaza [bo-cah'-thah], *f. aug. (Coll.)* A large, wide mouth.

bocel [bothel'], *m.* 1. Astragal; a fluted moulding, torus. 2. Fluting-plane, an instrument for fluting mouldings.

bocelar [bo-thay-lar'], *va.* To make fluted mouldings.

bocelete [bo-they-lay'-tay], *m. dim.* Small moulding-plane.

bocelón [bo-thay-lone'], *m. aug.* Large moulding-plane.

boceras [bo-thay'-rahs], *m. & f.* Idiot, fool; bigmouth.

boceto [bo-thay'-to], *m.* A sketch, delineation, cartoon.

bocezar [bo-thay-thar'], *va. (Vet.)* To move lips from one side to another, as horses and other animals do when they eat.

bocín [bo-theen'], *m.* 1. Round piece of bass mat put about the nave of a cart, as a cap of defence. 2. The iron, nozzle. 3. Hub of wheel.

bocina [bo-thee'-nah], *f.* 1. Large trumpet, bugle-horn. **Bocina de cazador**, a huntsman's horn. 2. Hearing trumpet. 3. Automobile horn. 4. *(Cono Sur)* Informer (soplón). 5. *(LAm.)* Ear-trumpet (trompetilla).

bocinada [bo-the-nah'-dah], *f.* Empty boast, rant.

bocinar [bo-the-nar'], *va.* To sound the trumpet, bugle-horn, or huntsman's horn.

bocinazo [bo-the-nah'-tho], *m. (Aut.)* Hoot, toot, blast (of the horn). **Dar el bocinazo**, to grass.

bocinero [bo-the-nay'-ro], *m. & f.* Trumpet or, horn-blower.

bocio [bo'-the-o], *m. (Med.)* Goitre.

bocón [bo-cone'], *m.* 1. *(aug.)* A wide-mouthed person. 2. Braggart, a talkative boaster. 3. *(Carib. Cono Sur)* loud-mouthed; backbiting (chismoso), gossipy; *(Mex.)* Indiscreet.

bocoy [bo-co'-e], *m.* Hogshead.-*pl.* **Bocoyes abatidos**, shooks of hogsheads.

bocudo, da [bo-coo'-do, dah], *a.* Large. mouthed.

bocha [bo'-chah], *f.* 1. Bowl, a wooden ball for playing at bowls. 2. *(Prov.)* Fold or double in clothes. **Juego de las bochas**, the game of bowls.

bochar [bo-char'], *va.* 1. To throw a ball so that it hits another, in the game of bowls. 2. *(Carib. Méx.)* To rebuff, reject. 3. *(Cono Sur)* to fail, to flunk.

bochazo [bo-chah'-tho], *m.* Stroke of one bowl against another.

boche [bo'-chay], *m.* 1. Cherry-pit or chuck-hole. *V.* BOTE. 2. *(Cono Sur)* Husks, chaff. 3. *(Carib.)* Telling off, dressing down. 4. *(Carib.)* Snub, slight. **Dar boche a uno**, to snub somebody. 5. *(And. Cono Sur)* uproar, din. 6. *(Carib.)* Muddle, mess.

bochinche [bo-cheen'-chay], *m.* 1. Uproar, disorder, tumult 2. *(Sp. Amer.)* Mess, quarrel, gossip. 3. *(And. Carib.)* Piece of gossip. 4. *(Mex.)* Rave up; wild party. 5. *(Mex.)* Seedy bar, dive; local stores. 6. *(Carib.)* Muddle, mess.

bochista [bo-chees'-tah], *m.* A good bowler or player at bowling.

bochorno [bo-chor'-no], *m.* 1. Hot, sultry weather, scorching heat. 2. Blush, flushing, the color of cheeks raised by shame or passion. 3. *(fig.)* Embarrassment, flush, shame; stigma (tacha), dishonor.

bochornoso, sa [bo-chor-no'so, sah], *a.* 1. Shameful, reproachful, causing shame or confusion. **Es un espectáculo bochornoso**, it's a degrading spectacle. 2. Sultry. 3. *(Met.)* Sultry, oppressive; thundery; stuffy.

boda [bo'-dah], *f.* Marriage, nuptials, match, the feast by which it is solemnized, a wedding. **Bodas de diamante**, diamond wedding. **Bodas de oro**, golden wedding. **Bodas de plata**, silver wedding.

bode [bo'-day], *m.* A he-goat.

bodega [bo-day'-gah], *f.* 1. Wine-vault, a cellar. 2. Abundant vintage or yield of wine. 3. Storeroom, warehouse, magazine. 4. A grocery. 5. *(Naut.)* Hold of a ship. **Bodega de popa**, after-hold. **Bodega de proa**, fore-hold.

bodegón [bo-day-gone'], *m.* 1. Eating-house, or cook's shop. 2. Sign of a cook's shop or eating-house. **¿En qué bodegón hemos comido juntos?** where have we ever eaten together? A rebuke for too much familiarity.

bodegoncillo [bo-day-gon-theel'-lyo], *m. dim.* Low chophouse.

bodegonear [bo-day-go-nay-ar'], *va.* To run from one tippling house to another, to frequent mean eating-houses.

bodegonero, ra [bo-day-go-nay'-ro, rah], *m. & f.* One who keeps a low chophouse or tippling-house.

bodegonista [bo-day-go-nees'-tah], *m. & f.* Still life painter.

bodeguero, ra [bo-day-gay'-ro, rah], *m. & f.* 1. Butler, one who has the care of a cellar. 2. *(Cuba)* Grocer. 3. *(Carib.)* Coarse, common. 2. Wine producer (productor); *(Com.)* owner of wine cellar.

bodeguilla [bo-day-geel'-lyah], *f. dim.* Small cellar or vault.

bodián [bo-de-ahn'], *m.* Sea-fish, resembling a tench.

bodigo [bo-dee'-go], *m.* A small loaf made of the finest flour and presented as an offering in the church.

bodijo [bo-dee'-ho], *m. (Coll.)* Unequal match, a hedge-marriage, performed with little ceremony or solemnity.

bodocal [bo-do-cahl'], *a. (Prov.)* Applied to a kind of black grapes.

bodocazo [bo-do-cah'-tho], *m.* Stroke of a pellet shot from a cross-bow.

bodollo [bo-dol'-lyo], *m. (Prov.)* Pruning-knife, pruning-hook.

bodoque [bo-do'-kay], *m.* 1. Pellet, a small ball of clay shot from a crossbow. 2. Dunce, idiot. **Hacer bodoques**, *(Coll.)* To be reduced to dust, to be dead. 3. *(Mex.)* Badly-made thing. 4. *(CAm. Méx.)* Lump, swelling; lump, ball (bolita).

bodoquera [bo-do-kay'-rah], *f.* 1. Mould in which pellets are formed. 2. Cradle, or that part of the stock of a cross-bow where the pellet is put. 3. Strings with which the cord of a cross-bow is tied.

bodoquero, ra [bo-do-kay'-ro, rah], *a. (Amer.)* Contraband, smuggling.

bodoquillo [bo-do-keel'-lyo], *m. dim.* Small pellet or bullet of clay.

bodrio [bo'-dre-o], *m.* 1. Soup, broken meat, and garden-stuff, given to the poor at the doors of convents. 2. A hash poorly prepared, a medley of broken meat. 3. Piece of trash. **Un bodrio de sitio**, an awful place.

B.O.E. *m. (Esp.)* abr de **Boletín Oficial del Estado**.

boezuelo [bo-ay-thoo-ay'-lo], *m.* Stalking-ox, which serves to screen fowlers engaged in the pursuit of birds.

bofada [bo-fah'-dah], *f.* Ragout or fricassee made of the livers and lungs of animals.

bofe [bo'-fay], *m.* Lung, lights. **Echar el bofe or los bofes**, to strain one´s lungs; to labor very closely; to be very anxious.

bofeta [bo-fay'-tah], *f.* **bofetán** [bo-fay. tahn'], *m.* A sort of thin, stiff linen.

bofetada [bo-fay-tah'-dah], *f.* Slap, buffet, box, a blow on the face with the hand. **Dar una bofetada, to hit somebody**. *(Met.)* to treat with the utmost contempt.

bofetón [bo-fay-tone'], *m.* 1. A cuff or violent blow with the hand upon the face. 2. Stage decorations representing folding-doors.

bofetoncillo [bo-fay-ton-theel'-lyo], *m. dim.* A slight box or slap, on the face.

bofia [bo'-fee-ah], 1. *f.* **La bofía**, the cops. 2. *m.* Cop, copper.

bofordo [bo-for'-do], *m. (Obs.)* A short lance or spear. *V.* BOHORDO.

boga [bo'-gah], *f.* 1. *(Zool.)* Ox-eyed cackerel, mendole. 2. Act of rowing. 3. *(Naut.)* Rower, one who rows: in this sense it is masculine. 4. *(Prov.)* Small knife in the shape of a poinard. 5. Vogue, fashion. *V.* VOGA. **Boga arrancada**, *(Naut.)* All hands rowing together with all their strength. **Boga larga**, a long stroke. **Dar la boga**, to give the stroke. **Estar en boga alguna cosa**, to be fashionable; to be commonly used.

bogada [bo-gah'-dah], *f.* 1. Rowing stroke. 2. Bucking of clothes with lye.

bogador, ra [bo-gah-dor'], *m. & f.* Rower, oarsman, oarswoman.

bogar [bo-gar'], *vn.* To row. **Bogar a cuarteles**, to row by divisions. **Bogar a sotavento**, to row to leeward. (**Yo bogué**, from *Bogar. V.* verbs in *gar.)*

bogavante [bo-gah-vahn'-tay], *m.* 1. *(Naut.)* Strokesman of a row galley. 2. Lobster of a large size.

Bogotá [bo-go-tah'], *m.* Bogotá.

bogotano, na [bo-go-tah'-no, nah], *a.* Of Bogotá.

bohemiano, na, or **bohemo, ma** [bo-ay-me-ah'-no, nah, bo-ay'-mo, mah], *a.* A Bohemian.

bohémico, ca [bo-ay'-me-co], *a.* Belonging to Bohemia or its people.

bohemio, mia [bo-ay'-me-o, ah], *a.* Bohemian, unconventional. *m. & f.* Bohemian, unconventional person.

bohena, boheña [bo-ay'-nah, bo-ay'-'nyah], *f.* 1. *V.* BOFES. 2. Pork sausages.

bohío [bo-ee'-o], *m.* Indian hut, a humble hut in the West Indies.

bohordo [bo-or'-do], *m.* 1. Blade of flag, a water-plant. 2. Wands, the hollow end of which is filled with sand, which tilters threw at each other in tournaments. 3. *(Bot.)* A scape: flower-peduncle.

boicot [bo-e-cot'], *m. pl.* **Boicots**, boycott.

boicotear [bo-e-co-tay-ahr'], *va.* To boycott.

boicoteo [bo-e-co-tay'-o], *m.* Boycott.

boíl [bo-eel'], *m.* Ox-stall, a stand for oxen. V. B0YERA.

boina [bo'-e-nah], *f.* Flat, round woollen cap; beret.

boite [bo'-e-tay], *m.* Discotheque, night club, ballroom.

boj [boh], *m.* 1. Box-tree, boxwood. 2. A boxwood tool, on which shoemakers close their work.

bojar [bo-har'], or **bojear**, *va.* 1. *(Naut.)* To sail round an island or cape and measure its circumference. 2. To scrape off the rough integuments; stains, and moisture of leather. -*vn.* To measure around, to contain.

bojedal [bo-hay-dahl'], *m.* Plantation of box-trees.

bojeta [bo-hay'-tah], *f. (Ichth. Prov.)* A kind of herring.

bol [bole], *m.* 1. Bowl. V. PONCHERA. 2. Bolo, by apocope. 3. Armenian bole, a red earth, used chiefly by gilders.

bola [bo'lah], *f.* 1 Ball, globe; marble, bolus. **Bola de billar**, billiard ball. **Bola de cristal**, crystal ball. **Bola de nieve**, snow ball. **Bola del mundo**, globe. 2. Game of throwing bullets or bowls. 3. *(Coll.)* Lie, falsehood, humbug, hoax, fib. 4. *(Naut.)* Truck, acorn; a round piece of wood at the end of the ensign staffs and vanes. 5. Blacking for shoes. 6. Basin of the glassgrinder. **Escurrir la bola**, to take French leave, to run away. **No da pie con bola**, he's always wrong. **Bola de jabón**, wash-ball. **Juego de bolas**, bowling-green, bowling-ground; playing marbles. 7. *(Carib.)* **Cambiar la bola,** to change one's mind. *(Cono Sur)* **Dar bola**; take notice. *(LAm.)* **Hacerse bolas**, to get oneself tied up in knots. 8. Slam, grand slam (naipes). 9. Fib, tale (cuento). 10. *(Mex.)* **Una bola de gente**, a crowd of people.

bolada [bo-lah'-dah], *f.* 1. Throw or cast of a ball or bowl. 2. *(Cono Sur)* **bolada de aficionado**, intervention. 3. *(LAm.)* Piece of luck (suerte). 3. *(LAm.)* Fib, lie; *(Mex.)* Joke, witty, comment (chiste). 4. *(Cono Sur)* Titbit, treat (golosina).

bolado [bo-lah'-do], *m. (Prov.)* 1. Cake of clarined sugar used in Spain to sweeten water for drinking. 2. *(CAm. Cono Sur, Méx.)* Deal; *(Mex.)* Love affair, flirtation (amorío). 3. *(CAm.)* Clever stroke (billar). 4. *(LAm.)* **¡Hazme un bolado!,** do me a favor!

bolantín [bo-lan-teen'], *m.* Fine sort of packthread.

bolarménico [bo-lar-may'-ne-co], *m.* V. BOL.

bolazo [bo-lah'-tho], *m.* 1. Violent blow with a bowl. 2. *(Cono Sur)* silly remark, piece of nonsense (disparate); false news; fib, lie; mistake, error. **Mandarse un bolazo**, to put one's foot in it. 3. *(LAm.)* **¡Hazme un bolazo!**, do me a favor!

bolchaca, *f.* **bolchaco,** *m.* [bol-chah'-cah, co]. *(Prov.)* Pocket, purse.

bolchevique [bol-chay-vee'kay], *m. & f. & a.* Bolshevik.

bolchevismo [bol-chay-vees'-mo], *m.* Bolshevism.

bolea [bo-lay'-ah], *f. (Dep.)* Volley.

boleadoras [bo-lay-ah-do'-rahs], *f. pl. (Cono Sur)* Lasso with balls.

bolear [bo-lay-ar'], *vn.* 1. To play billiards for mere amusement. 2. To throw wooden or iron balls for a wager. 3. *(Prov.)* To boast; to lie extravagantly.-*va.* 1. To launch. 2. *(LAm.)* To hunt (cazar); to catch with (atrapar bolas). 3. *(LAm.)* To reject, blackball (candidato); to sack, fire (obrero). -*vr.* 1. *(Cono Sur)* to rear and fall on its back (caballo); *(Aut.)* to overturn. 2. *(Cono Sur)* To get confused, to get bewildered.

boleo [bo-lay'-o], *m.* The road or place where balls are thrown.

bolera [bo-lay'-rah], *f.* Bowling alley.

bolero [bo-lay'-ro], *m.* 1. Bolero, a Spanish dance and musical rhythm. 2. Bolero, a lady's garment. 3. *(Mex.)* Bootblack. 4. *(CAm. Méx.)* Top hat (chistera). *a.* 1. Truant. 2. Fibbing, lying.

boleta [bo-lay'-tah], *f.* 1. Ticket giving the right of admission to a place. 2. Billet or ticket which directs soldiers where they are to lodge. 3. Voucher or warrant for receiving money or other things 4. *(Prov.)* Small paper with tobacco, sold at chandlers' shops. 4. *(Cono Sur)* **Hacer la bola a uno**, to murder somebody, to knock off somebody.

boletar [bo-lay-ar'], *va. (Prov.)* To roll up tobacco in small bits of paper for the purpose of selling them.

boletería [bo-lay-tay-ree'-ah], *f. (Amer.)* 1. Box office, ticket office. 2. Gate, takings (recaudación).

boletero [bo-le-tay'-ro], *m.* Ticket agent.

boletín [bo-lay-teen'], *m.* 1. Warrant given for the payment of money. 2. Ticket for the quartering of soldiers. 3. Ticket granting free admittance at a theater or other place of amusement. **Boletín de inscripción**, registration form. 4. Bulletin of news: official military or medical notice. **Boletín facultativo**, medical report. 5. *(Com.)* List, statement. **Boletín de precios**, price list. **Boletín de prensa**, press release.

boleto [bo-lay'-to], *m.* 1. Ticket. **Boleto de ida y vuelta** or **boleto redondo**, Roundtrip ticket. 2. Coupon (quiniela). **Boleto de apuestas**, betting slip.

bolichada [bo-le-chah'-dah], *f.* At one throw, at once. **De una bolichada**, by chance.

boliche [bo-lee'-chay], *m.* 1. Jack, a small bell which serves as a mark for bowl-players: block. 2. All the small fish caught at once in a drag-net near the shore, and the dragnet with which they are caught. **Juego de boliche**, pigeon-holes, a game played on a concave table with a ball; troll-madam. **Boliches**, *(Naut.)* Fore-top bowlines, and top-gallant bowlines. 3. A furnace for lead-smelting. 4. The toy called cup and ball. *(And. Cono Sur)* Small grocery shop (tienda); *(Cono Sur)* cheap snack bar; *(And.)* Low-class bakery; *(Cono Sur)* gambling den (garita). 5. *(LAm.)* Bolivian.

bolichero, ra [bo-le-chay'-ro, rah], *m. & f.* One who keeps a pigeon-hole; small shopkeeper.

bólido [bo'-le-do], *m.* 1. Meteorite, shooting-star. 2. *(Aut.)* Racing car, hot rod; *(hum.)* Car. **iba como un bólido**, he was really shifting.

bolígrafo [bo-lee'-grah-fo], *m.* Ballpoint pen.

bolillo [bo-leel'-lyo], *m.* 1. Dim. of BOLO. 2. Jack, a small ball. 3. Bobbin, a small pin of box or bone used in making bone-lace. 4. Mould or frame on which the cuffs of linen or gauze, worn on the sleeves of counsellors of state, are starched and made up. 5. Bone joined to skull of horses. 6. *(LAm.) (Mus.)* Drumstick. 7. *(Mex.) (Culin.)* Bread roll. *pl.* 1. Paste-nuts, small balls made of sweet paste.

bolín [bo-leen'], *m.* Jack, a small ball which serves as a mark for bowl-players. **De bolín, de bolán,** *(Coll.)* At random, inconsiderately, rashly, thoughtlessly.

bolina [bo-lee'-nah], *f.* 1. *(Coll.)* Noise and clamor of a scuffle or dispute. 2. *(Naut.)* Bowline, a rope fastened to the leech or edge of a square-sail, to make it stand close to the wind. 3. A kind of punishment on shipboard like baqueta, or the gantlet. **Bolina de barlovento**, weather bowline. **Bolina de sotavento o de revés**, lee bowline. **Bolina de trinquete,** forebowline. **Dar un salto a la bolina,** to ease or check the bowline. **Navegar de bolina**, to sail with bowlines hauled. **Ir a la bolina**, to sail with a side wind. **Navío buen bolinador**, a good player, a ship which makes great progress against the wind. **Echar de bolina**, *(Met.)* to make fanfaronades, or idle boasts.

bolinear [bo-le-nay-ar'], *va.* To haul up the bowline in light winds.

bolinete [bo-le-nay'-tay], *m. (Naut.)* A movable capstan on deck, in which the whipstaff moves.

bolisa [bo-lee'-sah], *f. (Prov.)* Embers, hot cinders.

bolita [bo-le'-tah], *f.* 1. Small ball; pellet; *(Cono Sur)* marble (canica). 2. *(Cono Sur)* ballot paper.

bolívar [bo-le'-vahr], *m.* Bolivar (Venezuelan unit of currency). **No verle la cara a Bolivar**, to be broke.

Bolivia [bo-le'-ve-ah], *f.* Bolivia.

boliviano, na [bo-le-ve-ah'-no], *a. m. & f.* Bolivian.

bolla [bol'-lyah], *f.* 1. Duty on woollens and silks retailed for home consumption formerly levied in Catalonia. 2. In South America, great richness of an ore.

bollar [bol-lyar'], *va.* 1. To put a leaden seal on clothes to indicate their place of manufacture. 2. To emboss, to raise figures.

bollería [bol-lyay-re'-ah], *f.* Baker's, bakery, pastry shop.

bollero, ra [bol-lyay-ro, rah], *m. & f.* Pastry-cook, seller of sweet cakes.

bollo [bol'-lyo], *m.* 1. Small loaf or roll made of fine flour. 2. Small cookie or cake made of sugar, flour, milk, and eggs. 3. Bruise made in metal or any similar matter. 4. Morbid swelling. 5. **Bollos**, ancient headdress of women, consisting of large buckles. 6. In Peru, bars of silver extracted from the ore by means of fire or quicksilver. **Bollos de relieve**, embossed or raised work. 7. *(fig.)* Confusion; mix-up. **meter a uno en el bollo**, to get somebody in trouble. 8. *(CAm. Cono Sur)* punch (puñetazo). 9. *(And.)* **Bollos**, troubles. 10. *(CAm. Carib.)* Cunt (vagina).

bollón [bol-yone'], *m.* 1. Brass-headed nail used in coaches and furniture. 2. *(Prov.)* Button which shoots from a plant, especially from a vine-stock. 3. Button earring.

bollonado, da [bol-lyo-nah'-do, dah], *a.* 1. Adorned with brass-headed nails. 2 Furnished with shoots, buds, or buttons.

bolo [bo'-lo], *m.* 1. One of the ninepins set up to be knocked down by a bowler. 2. *(Prov.)* Round or oblong cushion on which women make lace. 3. Large piece of timber, in which the shafts and rests of a winding staircase are fitted. 4. Idiot, stupid. 5. Bolus, a very large pill. 6. The game of ninepins or tenpins. 7. A large knife, like a machete, used in the Philippines. **Es un bolo**, he is an idiot, an ignorant, stupid fellow. **Juego de bolos**, a game of nine-pins. *(And.)* **Andar en bolos**, to be naked. *(Carib.)* **Ir en bolos**, to run off. **Echar a rodar los bolos**, *(fig.)* to create a disturbance. 8. *(Med.)* Large pill. 9. *(Carib. Méx.)* One-peso coin; *(Ven.)* one-bolívar coin. 10. Slam (cartas). 11. *(Mex.)* Christening present (regalo).

bolo [bo'-lo], *a. (CAm.)* Drunk, plastered (borracho).

bolonio [bo-lo'-ne-o], *m.* An ignorant rattle-brained fellow.

bolsa [bol'-sah], *f.* 1. Purse. 2. Pursenet made of silk or worsted, with strings to draw the mouth together. 3. Money. 4. Exchange, the place where merchants meet to negotiate their affairs. **Bolsa de trabajo**, labor exchange. **Precio en la bolsa**, price on the stock exchange. *V.* LONJA. 5. Pouch or net used by sportsmen to put game in. 6. Bag in which public papers and despatches are carried by ministers and secretaries of state. 7. Bag for the hair. 8. Bag lined with furs or skins to keep the feet warm. 9. In a gold-mine, the vein which contains the purest gold: a pocket. 10. *(Med.)* A morbid swelling full of matter. 11. *(Anat.)* Scrotum. **Bolsa de pastor**, *(Bot.)* shepherd's-purse. **Bolsa rota**, spendthrift. **Tener or llevar bien cerrada la bolsa**, to have the purse well lined; to have money. **Bolsa de agua caliente**, hot-water bottle. **Bolsa de compra**, shopping bag. **Bolsa de herramientas**, toolbag. **Bolsa de patatas fritas**, packet of potato chips. **Bolsa de té**, tea bag. 12. *(Cos.)* Bag. **Hacer bolsa**, to bag. 13. *(Mil.)* Pocket.

bolsear [bol-say-ar'], *vn. (Prov.)* To purse up, to pucker: applied to clothes, hangings, and other things.

bolsería [bol-say-ree'-ah], *f.* Manufacture of purses, and the place where they are sold.

bolsero [bol-say-ro], *m.* 1. *(Obs.)* Cashier, treasurer 2. Manufacturer of purses, one who makes purses.

bolsico [bol-see'-co], *m.* Pocket.

bolsillo [bol-see'-lyo], *m.* 1. Purse. 2. Pocket. 3. Money. 4. *Dim.* of BOLSO. **Guardar algo en el bolsillo**, to put something in one's pocket. **Meterse a uno en el bolsillo**, to win somebody over. **Rascarse el bolsillo**, to pay up, to fork out. 5. **De bolsillo**, pocket *(atr.)*, Pocket size. **Edición de bolsillo**, pocket edition.

bolsín [bol-seen'], *m.* Gathering of brokers out of the stock exchange and the hours observed there.

bolsista [bol-sees'-tah], *m.* Stookbroker, speculator.

bolso [bol'-so], *m.* Purse of money, a money-bag. **Bolso de mano, bolso de mujer**, handbag, purse. **Bolso de viaje**, traveling bag.

bolsón [bol-sone'], *m.* 1. *Aug.* of BOLSO Large purse. 2. Large bar of iron put in vaults or arches to secure the building. 3. In oilmills, large plank or board with which the oil-reservoir is lined. 4. Stone on which an arch or vault is sprung. 5. *(Mex.)* Lagoon (lago). 6. *(And.)* Fool. -a. 1. *(And.)* Silly, foolish. 2. *(Carib. Méx.)* Lazy (perezoso).

bomba [bom'bah], *f.* 1. Pump, pumping engine. 2. Bomb; shell, bomb shell. 3. Lamp chimney. 4. Earthen jar for skimming oil from water. **¡Bomba!** your attention, please. **Bomba atómica**, atomic bomb. **Bomba de alimentación**, feed pump. **Bomba de apagar incendios**, fire engine. **Bomba de cadena** or **de rosario**, chain pump. **Bomba de circulación**, circulating pump. **Bomba de cobalto**, cobalt pump. **Bomba de compresión, de impelente**, force pump. **Bomba de fragmentación**, fragmentation pump. **Bomba de fuego** or **de vaho**, steam engine. **Bomba de guimbalete**, *(Naut.)* common pump. **Bomba de hidrógeno**, hydrogen bomb. **Bomba de mano**, hand pump. **Bomba de proa**, head pump. **Bomba de profundidad**, depth charge. **Bomba de vacío**, vacuum pump. **Bomba de vapor**, steam engine. **Bomba incendiaria**, incendiary bomb. **Bomba inyectora**, injection pump. **Bomba or manga marina**, water spout. **Bomba neutrona**, neutron bomb. **Cargar la bomba**, to prime the pump. **Estar a prueba de bomba**, to be bomb-proof. **La bomba está atascada**, the pump is clogged. 5. *(fig.)* surprise; bombshell, surprising item of news; great success. **Es la bomba del año**, it's the surprise of the year. 6. Shade; glass, globe (de lámpara). 7. *(And.)* Soap bubble. 8. *(Carib.)* Big drum (tambor). 9. *(And. Carib.)* Balloon (globo); *(Carib. Cono Sur)* Round kite. 10. *(Carib. Méx.)* Top hat. 11. *(And. CAm, Cono Sur)* drinking spree; drunkenness (embriaguez). 12. *(LAm.)* False rumor; lie; *(Carib.)* Piece of news. 13. *(Carib. Cono Sur)* gas station. 14. *(Comp.)* **"Bomba lógica"**, "logic bomb". -a. 1. Sensational. **Noticia bomba**, shattering piece of news. 2. *(And.)* **Estar bomba**, to be clapped out. -adv. **Pasarlo bomba**, to have a grand time.

bombacho [bom-bah'-chos], 1. *a. (LAm.)* Baggy, loose-fitting. 2. *m. (Mex.)* Baggy trousers.

bombardear [bom-bar-day-ar'], *va.* To bombard, to discharge bombs; to shell.

bombardeo [bom-bar-day'-o], *m.* Bombardment, bombing, **bombardeo aéreo**, air raid, air bombing. **Bombardeo en picado**, dive bombing.

bombardero [bom-bar-day'-ro], *m.* 1. Bomber (plane). 2. Bombardier. -a. Bombing.

bombardino [bom-bar-dee'-no], *m.* Saxhorn.

bombasí [bom-bah'-see'], *m.* Bombazine, dimity, fustian.

bombazo [bom-bah'-tho], *m.* Report of a bursting bomb.

bombear [bom-bay-ar'], *va.* To shell. 2. To pump (líquido). 3. *(Cos.)* To pad. 4. *(fig.)* To praise up, inflate the reputation of. 5. *(Cono Sur)* To sabotage, wreck; *(Univ.)* to fail, flunk. 6. *(And.)* *(Hist.)* To spy on; to reconnoitre. 7. *(CAm.)* To steal. -*vn.* 1. *(CAm. Méx.)* To screw, to fuck (copularse). 2. *(Carib.)* To get drunk (emborracharse). -*vr. (Arquit.)* To camber; to wrap, to bulge. *V.* BOMBARDEAR.

bombeo [bom-bay'-o], *m.* 1. Pumping (bomba). 2. *(Arquit.)* Camber; warping; bulging; crown (of the road).

bombero [bom-bay'-ro], *m.* 1. Fireman. **Cuerpo de bomberos**, fire brigade. 2. Pumper.

bombilla [bom-beel'-lyah], *f.* 1. *(Amer.)* A small silver or gold perforated tube for drinking *Mate*. 2. *(Elec.)* Light bulb. **Bombilla de flash**, flash bulb. 3. *(Mex.)* Ladle (cuchara).

bombillo [bom-beel'-lyo], *m.* 1. Lamp chimney. 2. Water-closet trap. 3. Small pump. 4. Tube to draw off liquids. 5. *(Carib. And. CAm.)* light bulb.

bombín [bom-been'], *m.* 1. Bowler hat (sombrero). 2. *(Cono Sur)* pump, bicycle pump.

bombo [bom'-bo], *m.* 1. Large drum. **Hacer algo a bombo y platillos**, to make a great song and dance about something. **Tengo la cabeza hecha un platillo**, I've got a splitting headache. 2. Player on bass drum. 3. *(Naut.)* Barge or lighter. 4. Ballyhoo, excessive praise. **Darse el bombo mutuo**, to indulge in mutual backslapping. 5. *(Carib.)* Bowler hat (sombrero). 6. *(Cono Sur)* **irse al bombo**, to come to grief, to blow it. *(Cono Sur)* **mandar a uno al bombo**, to knock somebody off. 7. **Estar con bombo**, to be in the family way. *a.* 1. Astonished. 2. *(Cuba and Amer.)* Tepid. 3. *(Mex.)* Bad, off (carne).

bombón [bom-bon'], *m,* 1. Chocolate. 2. Beauty, gem (objeto); peach (chica), smasher. 3. Gift (chollo).

bombona [bom-bo'-nah], *f.* Carboy. **Bombona** (de gas), canister, cylinder.

bombonaje [bon-bo-nah'-hay], *m.* A screw-pine (sombreros de paja).

bombonera [bom-bo-nay'-rah], *f.* Sweet box (caja para dulces); sweet can (lata para dulces). 2. Cosy little place (lugar).

bombonería [bom-bo-nay-re'-ah], *f.* Sweetshop, confectioner's (shop).

bonachón, na [bo-nah-chone', nah], *m. &. f. & a.* Good-natured, easy person.

bonaerense [bo-nah-ay-ren-say], *m. & f.* Native or resident of Buenos Aires, Argentina.

bonancible [bo-nan-thee-blay], *a.* Moderate, calm, fair, serene: applied to the weather at sea.

bonanza [bo-nahn'-thah], *f.* 1. Fair weather at sea. **ir en bonanza**, *(Naut.)* to sail with fair wind and weather. 2. Prosperity, success. **ir en bonanza**, *(Met.)* To go on prosperously, to do well.

bonaso [bo-nah'-so], *m.* Bonasus, a kind of buffalo.

bonazo, za [bo-nah-tho, thah], *a. (Coll.)* Good-natured, kind.

bondad [bon-dahd'], *f.* 1. Goodness, either moral or physical; excellence, healthfulness. 2. Goodness, kindness, good-will, graciousness, clemency; frankness, courtesy, suavity, or madness of temper. **Tener la bondad de**, to be so kind as to. **Tenga la bondad de no fumar**, please do not smoke. 3. Liberality.

bondadoso, sa [bon-dah-do'-so, sah], *a.* Kind, generous, beautiful *V.* BENÉVOLO.

bonetas [bo-nay'-tas], *f. pl. (Naut.)* Bonnets, pieces of canvas laced to the sails to make more way in light winds.

bonete [bo-nay'-tay], *m.* 1. Bonnet or cap used by clergymen, collegians, and doctors or professors of the universities. 2. Secular clergyman who wears a bonnet, in contradistinction to a monk who wears a hood or cowl. 3. Bonnet, a kind of outworks of a fortress. **Tirarse los bonetes**, to pull caps. **Bravo or gran bonete** A great dunce. 4. *(Obs.)* Widemouthed vial for conserves. 5. Second stomach, reticulum, of ruminants. 6. *(CAm. Méx.)* Not on your life!, no way. **A tente bonete**, insistently.

bonetería [bo-nay-tay-ree'-ah], *f.* Shop where bonnets are made or sold.

bonetero, ra [bo-nay-tay'-ro, rah], *m. & f.* 1. Bonnet maker. 2. *(Bot.)* Prickwood, gatheridge, or common spindletree.

bonetillo [bo-nay-teel'-lyo], *m.* 1. *(Dim.)* Small cap or bonnet. 2. Ornament in the shape of a bonnet, which women wear over their headdress.

boniato (BUNIATO or MONIATO) [bo-ne-ah'-to], *m.* A sweet potato.

bonico, ca [bo-nee'-co, cah], *a.* Pretty good, passable. **Andar a las bonicas**, *(Met.)* To take things easily, to do them at ease, not to burden oneself with business. **Jugar a las bonicas**, to play at ball by passing it from one hand into another.

bonificación [bo-ne-fe-cah-the-on'], *f. (Com.)* Allowance, discount, bonus; allowance of points.

bonificar [bo-ne-fe-car'], *va.* 1. *(Obs.)* To credit, to place to one's credit. 2. To meliorate, to improve. *-vr.* To improve.

bonijo [bo-nee'-ho], *m.* The pit of the olive after having been crushed in the mill.

bonillo, illa [bo-neel'-lyo, lyah], *a. dim.* 1. Somewhat handsome. 2. Somewhat great, or big.

bonísimo, ma [be-nee'-se-mo, mah], *a. sup.* of BUENO.

bonitamente [bo-ne-tah-men'-tay], *adv.* Nicely, neatly, craftily. *(Coll.)* V. BONICAMENTE.

bonito [bo-nee'-to], *m.* Sea-fish, resembling a tuna. (Pacific Ocean) Striped tuna.

bonito, ta [bo-nee'-to, tah], *a.* 1. Dim of BUENO. Pretty good, passable. Nice-looking; handsome. **Bonito como un sol**, as pretty as a picture. **Una bonita cantidad**, a nice little sum. 2 Affecting elegance and neatness. 3 Pretty. 4. Graceful, minion. 5. Soft, effeminate. 6. *(Cono Sur)* Well, nicely. **Ella canta bonito**, she sings nicely. **Se te ve bonito**, it looks good on you.

bono [bo'-no], *m. (Com.)* Bond, certificate. **Bono alimenticio**, food stamp. **Bono del estado**, government bond.

bono-bus [bo-no-boos'], *m, pl. (Esp.)* Bus pass.

bonzo [bon'-tho], *m.* Bonze, a priest of Buddha in China, Japan, and other heathen nations.

boñiga [bo-nyee'-gah], *f.* Cow-dung, horse dung.

boom [boom], *m.* Boom. **Dar boom a un problema**, to exaggerate a problem.

boomerang [boo-may-rahn'], *m, pl.* **Boomerangs**, boomerang.

bootes [bo-o'-tes], *m.* Bootes, a northern constellation.

boqueada [bo-kay-ah'-dah], *f.* Act of opening the mouth, a gasp. **A la primera boqueada**, immediately, without delay. **La última boqueada**, the last gasp.

boquear [bo-kay-ar'], *vn.* 1. To gape, to gasp, to open the mouth wide. 2 To breathe one's last, to expire. 3. *(Met.)* To end to terminate.*-va.* To pronounce, to utter a word or expression.

boquera [bo-kay'-rah], *f.* 1. Sluice made in a canal for irrigating lands 2. *(Prov.)* Opening made in inclosures to let in cattle. 3. Lip sore, mouth ulcer. 4. Ulcer in the mouth of beasts. *-m.* Screw, warder.

boquerón [bo-kay-rone'], *m.* 1. Wide opening, a large hole. 2. *(Zool.)* Anchovy. 3. *(Naut.)* Mouth of a channel between shallow bottoms.

boquete [bo-kay'-tay], *m.* Gap, narrow entrance.

boquiabierto, ta [bo-ke-ah-be-err'-to, tah], *a. (Coll.)* Gaping, having the mouth open; walking about gaping. **Estar boquiabierto**, to stand open-mouthed.

boquiancho, cha [bo-ke-ahn-'cho, chah], *a.* Wide-mouthed.

boquiangosto, ta [bo-ke-an-gos'-to, tah], *a.* Narrow-mouthed.

boquiconejuno na [bo-ke-co-nay-hoo'-no, nah], *a.* Rabbit-mouthed; harelipped (caballos).

boquiduro, ra [bo-ke-doo'-ro, rah], *a.* Hard-mouthed (caballos).

boquifresco, ca [bo-ke-fres'-co, cah], *a* Fresh-mouthed: applied to horses which have a soft salivous mouth; outspoken; cheeky.

boquifruncido, da [bo-ke-froon-thee' do, dah], *a.* Having the mouth contracted.

boquihendido, da [bo-ke-en-dee'-do, dah], *a.* Large-mouthed, flewed.

boquihundido, da [bo-ke-oon-dee'-do, dah], *a.* Having the mouth sunk in, from age or toothlessness.

boquilla [bo-keel'-lyah], *f.* 1. *(Dim.)* Little mouth. 2. Opening of breeches at the knees. 3. Opening in a canal for irrigating lands. 4. Chisel for mortising. 5. Mouthpiece of a musical wind instrument. 6. Cigar holder. 7. *(Mas.)* Verge, course. 8. *(Mech.)* Bushing, bush. 9. Bomb-hole. 10. *(Cos.)* Trouser bottom. **Boquilla de filtro**, filter tip. **Hablar de boquilla**, to talk out of the side of one's mouth. 11. (And.) Rumor, piece of gossip. 12. **Promesa de boquilla**, insincere promise.

boquín [bo-keen'], m. Coarse sort of balize.

boquirroto, ta [bo-keer-ro'-to, tah], a. Loquacious, garrulous.

boquirrubio,bia [bo-keer-roo'-be-o, ah], a. Simple, artless, easily imposed upon. 2. Talkative (gárrulo); indiscreet, loose-tongued.

boquita [bo-kee'-tah], f. dim. Small mouth.

borácico, ca [bo-rah'-the-co, cah], a. Boracic. V. BÓRICO.

borato [bo-rah'-to], m. Borate.

bórax [bo'-rax], m. Borax; sodium biborate.

borbollar, borbollonear [bor-bol-lyar'], vn. To bubble out, to stream or to gush out, to flash.

borbollón, borbotón [bor-bol-lyone', bor-bo-tone'], m. 1. Bubbling, gushing up of water in large bubbles, flash 2. (Met.) Flow of language hastily and incorrectly uttered. **A borbollones**, in a bubbling or impetuous manner, in hurry and confusion. **Hirviendo a borbollones** or **a borbotones**, boiling hot.

borbónico, ca [bor-bo'-ne-co, cah], a. Bourbon.

borborigno [bor-bo-reeg'-mo], m. Rumbling in the bowels.

borbotar [bor-bo-tar'], vn. To gush out with violence; to boil over, to bubble (burbujas).

borceguí [bor-thay-gee'], m. 1. Buskin, a kind of half-boot. 2. Laced shoes.

borceguinería [bor-thay-gee-nay-ree'-ah], f. A shop where buskins are made or sold.

borceguinero, ra [bor-thay-gee-nay'-ro, rah], m. & f. Maker or retailer of buskins.

borcellar [bor-thel-lyar'], m. (Prov.) Brim of a vessel.

borda [bor'-dah], f. 1. (Prov.) Hut, cottage. 2. (Naut.) Gunwale of a ship. **Motor fuera de borda**, outboard motor. **Echar algo por la borda**, to throw something overboard. 3. (Naut.) Mainsail (vela).

bordada [bor-dah'-dah], f. (Naut.) Board, tack. **Dar una bordada**, to tack, to make a tack.

bordadillo[bor-dah-deel'-lyo],m. Double-flowered, taffeta.

bordado [bor-dah'-do], m. Embroidery. **Bordado de pasado**, plain embroidery, without light or shade.-pp of BORDAR.

bordador, ra [bor-dah-dor', rah], m. & f. Embroiderer.

bordadura [bor-dah-doo'-rah],f. 1. Embroidery; variegated needlework.

bordage [bor-dah'-hay], m (Naut.) Side planks of a ship.

bordar [bor-dar'], va. 1. To embroider. 2. To perform a thing according to art. **Baila que lo borda**, he dances charmingly. **Bordar a tambor**, to tambour, to embroider with a tambour needle.

borde [bor'-day], m. 1. Border, the outer edge. 2. Margin, the edge of a thing; verge, fringe. **Borde de la acera**, kerb. **Borde del camino, de la carretera**, roadside, verge. 3. Ledge, a rising or projecting ridge. 4. Hem of a garment. 5. Brim of a vessel. 6. Bastard child. 7. Shoot or bud of a vine. 8. Board the side of a ship. **A borde**, On the brink; on the eve. 9. (fig.) **Estar al borde de una crisis nerviosa**, to be on the verge of a nervous breakdown. **Estar en el mismo borde del desastre**, to be on the very brink of disaster. -a. Wild, savage, uncultivated: applied to trees not ingrafted or cultivated. -a. 1. Anti-social; difficult, bad tempered (persona). 2. Illegitimate (niño). 3. (Bot.) Wild.

bordear [bor-day-ar'], vn. 1. (Naut.) To ply to windward. 2. To skirt, to go along (seguir el borde de). 3. To border on; to flank; (fig.) To verge on. 4. (Cono Sur) **Bordear un asunto**, to skirt round (avoid) a subject. 5. (Cono Sur) to border, line. **Los árboles bordean el camino**, trees line the road.

bordo [bor'-do], m. 1. Border, the outer edge. 2. Ship or vessel. **Fue a bordo**, (Naut.) He was aboard ship. 3. Board the side of a ship. **Bordo con bordo**, board and board, side by side: when two ships are close to each other. **Bordo sobre bordo**, hank for hank: when two ships tack together, and ply to windward. **Bordo a la mar**, to stand off. 4. (Naut.)

Board, tack. **Bordo corto**, a short board. **Bordo largo**, a long board. **Buen bordo**, a good board. **Dar bordos**, (Naut.) 1. To tack. 2. (Met.) To go frequently to and fro. 5. (Cono Sur) raised furrow; (CAm.) Peak, summit.

bordón [bor-done'], m. 1. Jacob's staff, a pilgrim's staff. 2. Bass-string. 3. Bass of an organ. 4. Repetition of words in a discourse. 5. Refrain of a song. 6. (Met.) Staff, guide, or support of another. 7. **Bordones**, (Naut.) Shores, outriggers. 8. (And. CAm.) Youngest son.

bordoneado, da [bor-do-nay-ah'-do, dah], a. (Her.) Pommelled.-pp. of BORDONEAR.

bordonear [bor-do-nay-ar']; vn. 1. To try the ground with a staff or stick. 2. To strike with a staff or cudgel. 3. To rove or wander about, to avoid labor. 4. To play well on the thorough bass. 5. (Aer.) To buzz.

bordonería [bor-do-nay-ree'-ah], f. Vicious habit of wandering idly about, on pretence of devotion.

bordonero, ra [bor-do-nay'-ro, rah], m. & f. Vagrant, vagabond, tramp.

bordura [bor-doo'-rah], f. (Her.) V. BORDADURA.

Boreal [bo-ray-ahl'], a. Boreal, northern **Boreas** [bo'-ray-as], m. Boreas, the north wind.

Borgoña [bor-go'-nyah], f. Burgundy wine. Burgundy, the district.

borgoñota [bor-go-nyo'-tah], f. Sort of ancient helmet. **A la borgoñota**, in the Burgundy fashion.

bórico, ca [bo-re-co, cah], a. Boric.

borinqueño, ña [bo-ren-kay'-nyo, nyah], a. & m. & f. Puerto Rican.

borla [bor'-lah]. f. 1. Tassel, bunch of silk, gold, or silver lace. 2. Tuft, lock, flaunt. 3. In universities, doctor's bonnet decorated with a tassel. 4. Doctorship. 5. Powder staff (de empolvarse).

borlilla [bor-leel'-lyah], f. Anther.

borlón [bor-lone'], m. 1. (aug.) Large tassel. 2. Napped stuff, made of thread and cotton yarn.

borne [bor'nay], m. 1. The end of a lance. 2. Kind of oak tree. 3. (Elec.) Terminal.

borneadero [bor-nay-ah-day'-ro], m. (Naut.) Berth of a ship at anchor, swinging berth.

borneadizo, za [bor-nay-ah-dee'-tho, thah], a. Pliant, flexible.

bornear [bor-nay-ar'], va. 1. To bend, turn, or twist. 2. (Arch.) To model and cut pillars all round. **Bornear la verdad**, to comment, to explain or expound. **Bornear las palabras**, to turn words into different senses. 3.(Mex.) To spin, turn (pelota). -vn. 1. To edge, to sidle. 2. To warp, to turn. **El navío bornea**, (Naut.) The ship swings or turns round her anchor. -vr. To warp, bulge.

borneo [bor-nay'-o], m. 1. Act of turning or winding a thing. 2. (Naut.) Swinging round the anchor. 3. Twisting, bending (torcer).

bornera [bor-nay'-rah], a. Applied to a blackish sort of millstone.

bornero, ra [bor-nay'-ro, rah], a. Ground by a black millstone: applied to wheat.

borní [bor-nee'], m. (Orn.) Lanner, a kind of falcon.

boro [bo'-ro], m. Boron, one of the chemical elements.

borona [bo-ro'-nah], f. 1. A sort of grain resembling Indian corn. 2. Bread made from this grain. 3. (LAm.) Crumb (migaja).

boronía [bo-ro-nee'-ah], f Dish made of chopped apples, pumpkins, and green peppers. V. ALBORONÍA.

borra [bor'-rah], f. 1. Yearling ewe. 2. The thickest part of the wool. 3. Goat's hair. 4. Nap on the cloth; floss, burl. 5. Tax on sheep. 6. Lees sediment, waste. 7. Refined borax. **Borra de castor**, beaver's hair. **Borra de lana**, flock wool, waste wool. **Borra de seda**, floss silk, waste silk. 8. Empty talk (charla insustancial); trash, basura.

borracha [bor-rah'-chah], f. (Coll.) Leather bag or bottle for wine.

borrachear [bor-rah-chay-ar'], vn. To be drunk often.

borrachera, borrachería [bor-rah-chay'-rah, bor-rah-chay-ree'-ah], *f.* 1. Drunkenness, hard-drinking. **Quitarse la borrachera,** to sober up, get rid of one's hangover. 2. Revelry; drunken feast, wassail. 3. *(Met.)* Madness, great folly.

borrachero [bor-rah-chay'-ro], *m.* A shrub of South America: the seed ingested causes delirium.

borrachez [bor-rah-cheth'], *f.* 1. Intoxication, drunkenness. 2. Perturbation of the judgment or reason.

borrachín [bor-rah-cheen'], *m.* Drunkard, sot, toper.

borracho, cha [bor-rah'-cho, chah], *a.* 1. Drunk, intoxicated. **Estar más borracho que una cuba,** to be as drunk as a Lord. 2. *(Met.)* Inflamed by passion. 3. Applied to cookie baked with wine. 4. Applied to fruits and flowers of a violet color. 5. *(Esp.)* **Es un negocio borracho,** it's a real money-spinner, it's money for old rope.

borrachón, borrachonazo [bor-rah-chone', bor-rah-cho-nah'-tho], *m. aug.* Great drunkard, a tippler.

borrachuela [bor-rah-choo-ay'-lah], *f. (Bot.)* Ray-grass: its seeds, mixed with breadcorn, intoxicate.

borrador [bor-rah-dor'], *m.* 1. Rough draft of a writing in which corrections are made. 2. Waste-book of merchants, blotter. 3. Eraser (para borrar).

borraja [bor-rah'-hah], *f. (Bot.)* Borage.

borrajear [bor-rah-hay-ar'], *vn.* To scribble, to write carelessly on any subject.

borrajo [bor-rah'-ho], *m. (Prov.)* V. RESCOLDO .

borrar [bor-rar'], *va.* 1. To cross out, to strike out. 2. To blot with ink, to efface. 3. To blur, to erase, to rub out, obliterate. 4. To cause to vanish. 5. *(Met.)* To cloud, to darken, to obscure. **Borrar la plaza,** to abolish a place or employ. 6. To eliminate, dispose of. **Eliminar a uno de una lista,** to cross somebody off a list. *-vr.* To resign (from a club, etc.). *(Comp.)* To wipe out.

borrasca [bor-rahs'-cah], *f.* 1. Storm, tempest, violent squall of wind. 2. Barren rock. **Dar o caer en borrasca,** in the mines, a mine that yields nothing, unprofitable. 3. *(Met.)* Hazard, danger, obstruction. 4. Orgy, spree.

borrascoso, sa [bor-ras-co'-so , sah], *a.* Stormy, boisterous, gusty, tempestuous.

borregada [bor-ray-gah'-data], *f.* Large flock of sheep or lambs.

borrego, ga [bor-ray'-go, gah], *m. & f.* 1. Lamb not yet a year old. 2. *(Met.)* Simpleton, a soft, ignorant fellow. **No hay tales borregos,** *(Coll.)* there is no evidence of its truth, there is not such a thing. 3. *(Carib.)* Con, hoax (trampa); *(Mex.)* Lie, tall story (mentira). *-m.pl.* Fleecy clouds (nubes); white horses, foamy crests of waves.

borreguero [bor-ray-gay'-ro], *m.* Shepherd who tends lambs.

borreguito [bor-ray-gee'-to], *m. dim.* Little lamb.

borrén [bor-ren'], *m.* A saddlecloth; saddle; bolster, straw cushion.

borriba [bor-ree'-bah], *f.* Engine for raising water.

borrica [bor-ree'-cah], *f.* 1. A she-ass. 2. Stupid woman. *V.* BORRICO.

borricada [bor-re-cah'-dah], *f.* 1. Drove of asses. 2. Procession on asses. 3. *(Met.)* Silly or foolish word or action.

borrico [bor-ree'-co], *m.* 1. Ass, donkey. 2. Fool. 3. Trestle-horse of carpenters. **Es un borrico,** he can bear great labor and fatigue.

borricón, borricote [bor-re-cone', bor-re-có-tay], *m.* 1. *(aug.)* Large jackass. 2. *(Met.)* Plodder, dull, heavy, and laborious man. 3. Among sawyers, horse, a frame on which timber is sawed.

borrilla [bor-reel'-lyah], *f.* 1. The downy matter enveloping fruits. 2. Shearing or flue cut from clothes.

borriqueño, ña [bor-re-kay'-nyo, nyah], *a.* Asinine.

borriquero [bor-re-kay'-ro], *m.* One who keeps or tends asses.

borriquete de proa [bor-re-kay'-tay], *m. (Naut.)* Fore-topmast.

borriquillo, illa; ito, ita [bor-re-keel'-lyo, lyah, bor-re-kee'-to, tah], *m. & f dim.* A little ass.

borriquillos [bor-re-keel'-lyos], *m. pl.* Cross-bars of a table-frame.

borro [bor'-ro], *m.* 1. Wether not two years old. 2. *(Coll.)* Dolt, of slow understanding. 3. Duty laid on sheep.

borrón [bor-rone'], *m.* 1. Blot of ink on paper, blur. 2. Rough draft of a writing. 3. First sketch of a painting. **Estos borrones,** these humble jottings. 4. Blemish which tarnishes or defaces. 5. Stigma, slur. **Hacer borrón y cuenta nueva,** to wipe the slate clean (and start again).

borronear [bor-ro-nay-ar'], *va.* 1. To sketch. 2. To waste paper by scribbling on it.

borroso, sa [bor-ro'-so, sah], *a.* 1. Full of dregs and lees: turbid, thick, muddy. 2. Done in a bungling manner. **Letra borrosa,** letter badly written, and full of blots and corrections.

borroso [bor-ro'-so], *m. (Prov.)* Bungler, a petty mechanic.

borrufalla [bor-roo-fahl'-yah], *f. (Coll. Prov.)* Bombast, a pompous show of empty sounds or words.

borujo [bo-roo'-ho], *m.* Lump, pressed mass, packed mass. *V.* ORUJO.

borujón [bo-roo-hone'], *m.* Knob, protuberance; *(Med.)* Bump, lump.

borusca [bo-roos'-cah], *f.* Withered leaf. *V.* SEROJA.

bosar [bo-sar'], *va.* 1. To run over, to overflow. 2. To vomit. 3. *(Met.)* To utter lofty words.

boscaje [bos-cah'-hay], *m.* 1. Boscage, cluster of trees, grove. 2. *(Pict.)* Boscage, landscape.

boscoso [bos-co'-so], *a.* Wooded.

bósforo [bos'-fo-ro], *m.* Bosphorus, channel by which two seas communicate.

bosque [bos'-kay], *m.* Wood, tract of land planted with trees and brushwood: forest, grove; any woody place.

bosquecillo [bos-kay-theel'-lyo], *m. dim.* Small wood, a coppice, a knoll covered with trees.

bosquejar [bos-kay-har'], *va.* 1. To make a sketch of a painting. 2. To design or project a work without finishing it. 3. To explain a thought or idea in a rather obscure manner 4. To make a rough model of a figure; or *basso-relievo,* in clay, plaster, or any soft substance.

bosquejo [bos-kay'-ho], *m.* 1. Sketch of a painting. 2. Any unfinished work. 3. Unfinished writing or composition. **Estar en bosquejo,** to be in an unfinished state.

bosquete [bos-kay'-tay], *m.* An artificial grove, small wood.

bosquimano [bos-ke-mah'-no], *m.* Bosquimano, African bushman.

bosta [bos'-tah], *f.* Dung, droppings; manure.

bostar [bos-tar'], *m.* Ox-stall, or stand for oxen.

bostezar [bos-tay-thar'], *vn.* To yawn, to gape, to oscitate.

bostezo [bos-tay'-tho], *m.* Yawn, yawning, oscitation.

bota [bo'-tah], *f.* 1. Small leather wine-bag. 2. Butt or pipe, to contain wine or other liquids. 3. Boot. **Botas de campaña,** top boots. **Botas de esquí,** ski boots. **Botas de goma,** gumboots. **Botas de fútbol,** football boots. 4. *(Naut.)* Water-cask. **Bota fuerte;** jackboot, a wide, strong boot. **Morir con las botas puestas,** to die in harness. **Ponerse las botas,** to strike it rich (enriquecerse), to get a lot of something. **Cotes de botas,** Bootlegs.

botadero [bo-tah-day'-ro], *m. (And. Méx.)* Ford; *(LAm.)* Rubbish dump (vertedero).

botado [bo-tah'-do], *a.* 1. Cheeky (descarado). 2. *(CAm.)* Spendthrift (gastador). 3. *(And.)* Resigned, ready for anything. 4. *(CAm.)* Dirt cheap. 5. *(CAm. Méx.)* Blind drunk (borracho). *m.* **Botada** *f. (LAm.)* Abandoned child, foundling.

botador [bo-tah-dor'], *m.* 1. Driver, one who drives. 2. Punch, an instrument for driving out nails. 3. Nail set. 4. Crow's bill or pelican, used by dentists to draw teeth. 5. *(Naut.)* Starting-pole used to shove off a boat from the shore, boathook. 6. *(Mech.)* Furnace-bar, fire-iron; bolt-driver. 7. *(Med.)* Retractor. 8. *(LAm.)* Spendthrift.

botadura [bo-tah-doo'-rah], *f. (Naut.)* Launching. *(LAm.) V.* BOTADA.

botafuego [bo-tah-foo-ay'-go], *m.* 1 . Linstock, a staff with a match at the end of it, used by gunners in firing cannons. 2. An irritable, quick-tempered person.

botagueña [bo-tah-gay'-nyah], *f.* Sausage made of pigs' haslets.

botal [bo-tahl'], *a*.1. *(Anat.)* **Agujero botal or de botal,** foramen ovale, formerly called botale foramen, an opening between the two auricles of the heart of the foetus. 2. *(Arch.)* Arched buttress.

botalón [bo-tah-lone'], *m. (Naut.)* Boom, a pole used in setting up studding or stay-sails. **Botalón de foque,** Jib-boom. **Botalones,** fire-booms.

botana [bo-tah'-nah], *f.* 1. Plug or stopple used to stop up the holes made on the leather bags to carry wine. 2. *(Coll.)* Cataplasm or plaster put on a wound 3. *(Low.)* Scar remaining after a wound is healed.

botánica [bo-tah'-ne-cah], *f.* Botany, the science treating of plants.

botánico, ca [bo-tah'-ne-co, cah], *a.* Botanic, botanical.

botánico, botanista [bo-tah'-ne-co, bo-tah-nees'-tah], *m.* Botanist.

botanoancia [bo-tah-no-mahn'-the-ah], *f.* Botanomancy, superstitious divination by herbs.

botantes [bo-tahn'-tes], *m. pl. (Naut.)* Shores, outriggers.

botar [bo-tar'], *va.* 1. To cast, to throw, to fling, to launch. 2. To bound, to rebound. 3. To squander, to misspend. **Le botaron de su trabajo,** they sacked him from his job. 4. *(Naut.)* To shift the helm. **Botar al agua alguna embarcación,** *(Naut.)* to launch a ship. **Botar en vela,** to fill the sails. 5. *(LAm.)* To lose. -vn. 1. To bounce (pelota); *(Aut.)* To bump, to bounce, jolt; to buck, to rear (caballo). **Está que bota,** he´s hopping mad. 2. **Botar a babor** *(Naut.),* to put over to port. 3. *vr. (Cono Sur)* to change jobs.

botaratada [bo-tah-ra-tah'-dah], *f. A* blustering, thoughtless action; wild thing.

botarate [bo-ta-rah'-tay], *m.* 1. *(Coll.)* Madcap, thoughtless, blustering person. 2. *(LAm.)* Spendthrift.

botarel [bo-tah-rel], *m. (Arch.)* Buttress, a mass of stone which supports the spring of arches or vaults; abutment, spur, counter pillar.

botarga [bo-tar'-gah], *f.* 1. Sort of wide breeches formerly worn, gaskins. 2. Motley dress of a harlequin. 3. Harlequin, buffoon. 4. Kind of large sausages. 5. *(Prov.) V.* DOMINGILLO.

botavante [bo-tah-vahn'-tay], *m. (Naut.)* Pike used by seamen to defend themselves against an enemy who attempted to board.

botavara [bo-tah-vah'-rah], *f. (Naut.)* 1. A small boom or pole which crosses the sail of a boat in a diagonal direction, gaff, sprit. 2. Boat-hook. **Botavara de cangreja,** gaff-sail boom.

bote [bo'-tay], *m.* 1. Thrust with a pike, lance, or spear. 2. Rebound or bound of a ball on the ground. **De bote y boleo,** instantly. **Dar un bote,** to jump. **Darse el bote;** to beat it. 3. Gallipot, a small glazed earthen vessel. 4. Canister, a tin vessel for tea, coffee, etc. **Bote de tabaco,** snuff canister. **Bote de basura** *(Mex.),* dustbin. **Bote de humo,** smoke bomb. **Estar en el bote,** it´s in the bag. 5. *(Naut.)* Boat. **Bote de pasaje,** ferryboat. **Bote de remos,** rowing boat. **Bote patrullero,** patrol boat. **Bote salvavidas,** lifeboat. **Bote de pescar,** fishingboat. **Estar de bote en bote,** to be full of people. **De bote y voleo,** instantly. -*pl.* 1. In places where wool is washed, heaps of wool piled separately. 2. Frolicsome bounds of a horse.

botecico, illo, ito [bo-tay-thee'-co, eel'-yo, ee´-to], *m. dim.* 1. Small canister. 2. Skiff.

botella [bo-tel'-lyah], *f.* 1. Bottle, flask; also the liquor contained in a bottle. **Hemos bebido tres botellas,** we drank three bottles. **Cerveza de botella,** bottled beer. 2. *(Carib.)* Sinecure, soft job (in government.).

botellazo [bo-tayl-lye-ah'-tho], *m.* A blow with a bottle.

botellero [bo-tayl-lay'-ro], *m.* Wine rack.

botellín [bo-tayl-lyeen'], *m.* Small bottle, half bottle.

botellón [botel-lyone'], *m.* A demijohn.

botepronto [bo-tay-pron'-to], *m. (Dep.)* Half-volley.

botequín [bo-tay-keen'], *m. (Naut.)* Cog, a small boat.

botero [bo-tay'-ro], *m.* 1. One who makes leather bags and bottles for wine. 2. Boatman, wherryman.

botica [bo-tee'-cah], *f.* 1. Apothecary's shop; pharmacy, drugstore. 2. Potion given to a sick person. 3. Shop in general. 4. Furnished house or lodging.

boticario [bo-te-cah'-re-o], *m.* Pharmacist, druggist, apothecary.

botiguero [bo-te-cay'ro], *m. (Prov.)* Shopkeeper.

botija [bo-tee'-hah], *f.* 1. Earthen jug. **Botija para aceite,** an oil-jar. 2. Fat person. **Estar como una botija,** to be as fat as a sow. **Poner a uno como botija verde** *(LAm.),* to call somebody every name under the sun. 3. *(CAm. Carib.)* Buried treasure. *-m. & f. (Cono Sur)* baby, child.

botijero [bo-te-har'-ro], *m.* One who makes or sells jars.

botijo [bo-tee'-ho], *m.* 1. An earthen jar. 2. *(Met.)* A plump little child.

botijón [bo-te-hone'], *m.* 1. *(aug.)* A large earthen jar. 2. A plump little child. *-a. (Mex.)* Potbellied.

botillería [bo-teel-lyay-ree'-ah], *f.* 1. Ice-house, where iced creams, jellies, etc., are prepared or sold. 2. *(Naut.)* Steward's room and stores. 3. Ancient war tax.

botillero [bo-teel-lyar'-ro], *m.* 1. One who prepares or sells iced liquids and jellies. 2. *(Mex.)* Shoemaker, cobbler.

botillo [bo-teel'-lyo], *m. dim.* A small wine-bag, a leather bottle.

botín [bo-teen'], *m.* 1. Buskin, a half-boot formerly worn by stage-players. 2. Spatterdash; leggings. 3. Booty taken by soldiers; excoriation. 4. *(Naut.)* Lashing.

botina [bo-tee'-nah], *f.* A gaiter, high shoe.

botinero [bo-te-nar'-ro], *m.* 1. A soldier who takes care of and sells the booty. 2. One who makes and sells gaiters.

botinico, illo, ito [bo-te-nee'-co, eel'-lyo, ee'-to], *m. dim.* A little gaiter or spatterdash.

botiquería [bo-te-kar-ree´-ah], *f.* Perfumer's shop.

botiquín [bo-te-keen´], *m.* 1. First aid kit. 2. Medicine chest (in a bathroom, etc.) 3. *(Carib.)* Drinks, cupboard.

boto, ta [bo'-to, tah], *a.* 1. Blunt, round at the point. 2. *(Met.)* Dull of understanding.

botón [bo-one'], *m.* 1. Sprout, bud, or gem put forth by vines and trees in the spring. 2. Button, of wood or bone. **Botón de metal dorado or plateado,** a gilt or plated button. 3. *(Fen.)* Tip of a foil. 4. Button or knob of doors or windows. **Botón de cerradura,** the button of a lock. **Botón de contacto,** push-button. **Botón de arranque,** starter, starting switch. 5. Annulet of balusters, and also of keys, serving for ornament 6. Piece of wood which fastens a fowling-net. 7. Crank-pin. 8. Dowel. 9. Handle, knob (cerraduras). **Botón de fuego,** cautery in the form of a button. **Botón de oro,** *(Bot.)* Creeping double flowered crow-foot. **Botón del ratón** *(Comp.),* mouse button.

botonadura [bo-to-nah-doo´, rah], *f.* Set of buttons for a suit of clothes.

botonar [bo-to-nahr'], *(LAm.)* 1. *va.* To button. 2. *vn.* To bud, sprout.

botonazo [bo-to-nah'-tho], *m. (Fen.)* Thrust given with a foil.

botoncito [bo-ton-thee'-to], *m. dim.* A small button.

botonería [bo-to-nay-ree'-ah], *f* Button-maker's shop.

botonero, ra [bo-to-nay'-ro, rah], *m. & f.* Button-maker; button-seller.

botones [bo-to'-nees], *m. pl.* Bellboy.

bototo [bo-to'-to], *m.* Gourd or calabash to carry water. *(Amer.)*

botulismo [bo-too-lees´-mo], *m.* Botulism.

bou [bo'-oo], *m.* A joint casting of a net by two boats, which separate and bring up the haul.

boutique [boo-teek'], *f*, Boutique.

bóveda [bo´-vay-dah], *f*. 1. Arch or vault. 2. Vault, cave or cavern, a subterraneous habitation. **Bóveda de cañón**, barrel vault. 3. Vault for the dead in churches. **Bóveda de jardín**, Bower.

bovedar [bo-vey-dar'], *va*. *(Obs.)* To vault or cover with arches. *V*. ABOVEDAR.

bovedilla [bo-vay-deel'lyah], *f*. A small vault in the roof of a house. **Bovedillas**, *(Naut.)* Counters, arched part of a ship's poop. **Subirse a las bovedillas**, *(Met.)* To be nettled, to be in a passion; to go up the wall.

bovino, na [bo-vee'-no, nah], *a*. Belonging to cattle.

box [box]. *m*. **boxes** *pl*. Stall (de caballo); pit (en carreras de coches); *(CAm. Carib.)* Post office box. *(LAm.)* Boxing.

boxeador [boc-say-ah-dor], *m*. Boxer.

boxear [boc-say-ar'] *vn*. To box.

boxeo [boc-say'-o], *m*. Boxing.

boxer [boc'-sayr], *m*. Boxer (dog).

boxeril [boc-say-reel'], *a*. *(Cono Sur)*, **boxítisco** *a*. Boxing.

boya [bo-yah], *f*. 1. *(Naut.)* Float for a net or submerged rope; beacon, buoy. 2. Butcher. 3. Hangman, executioner. **Boya de barril**, nun-buoy. **Boya cónica**, canbuoy. **Boya de palo**, wooden buoy. **Boya de cable**, cable-buoy. **Echar afuera la boya a la mar**, to stream the buoy.

boyada [bo-yah'-dah], *f*. Drove of oxen.

boya [bo-yahl'], *a*. Relating to cattle: applied generally to pasture-grounds where cattle are kept.

boyante [bo-yahn'-tay], *pa*. Buoyant, floating. -*a*. 1. *(Naut.)* Light, sailing well (barcos). 2. *(Met.)* Fortunate, successful.

boyar [bo-yar'], *m*. *(Naut.)* To buoy, to be afloat (barcos).

boyazo [bo-yah'-tho], *m. aug*. 1. Large ox. 2. *(CAm. Cono Sur)* Punch.

boyé [bo-yay'], *m*. *(Cono Sur)* Snake.

boyera, boyeriza [bo-yay'-rah, bo-yay-ree'-thah], *f*. Ox-stall, ox-house, cowhouse, a stand for oxen.

boyero [bo-yay'-ro], *m*. Oxherd, cattle shed, oxdriver, cowherd.

boyezuelo [bo-yay-thoo-ay'-lo], *m. dim*. A young or small ox.

boyuno, na [bo-yoo'-no, nah], *a*. Belonging to cattle; bovine.

boza [bo-thah], *f*. *(Naut.)* One end of a rope made fast in a bolt-ring, till the other brings the tackle to its place. **Bozas**, *(Naut.)* Stoppers, short ends of cables used to suspend or keep something in its place. **Bozas de la uña del ancla**, shank-painter. **Bozas de cable or cubiertas**, cable-stoppers. **Bozas de combate or de las vergas**, the stoppers of the yards. **Bozas de los obenques**, the stoppers of the shrouds.

bozal [bo-thahl´], *m*. 1. Muzzle worn by horses, dogs, and calves. 2. A temporary headstall for a horse.

bozal [bo-thal'], *a*. 1. Novice, inexperienced in trade or business. 2. Stupid, foolish. 3. Wild, not broken in (caballos).

bozo [bo'-tho], *m*. 1. Down, which precedes the beard. 2. Head-stall of a horse. 3. Mouth, lips.

brabante [brah-bahn'-tay], *m*. Brabant or Flemish linen.

brabera [brah-bay'-rah], *f*. Airhole, ventilator.

bracamonte [Brah-cah-mon'-tay], *m*. *(And.)* Ghost.

braceada [brah-thay-ah-dah], *f*. Violent extension of the arms.

braceaje [brah-thay-ah'-hay], *m*. 1. Coinage, the art and act of coining money. 2. Act of beating the metal for coining in the mint. 3. *(Naut.)* Bracing of the yards. Depth of water 4. Brewing.

bracear [brah-thay-ar'], *vn*. To move or swing the arms. -*va*. 1. *(Naut.)* To brace. **Bracear las vergas**, to brace the yards. 2. To measure by fathoms. 3. To brew.

bracero [brah-thay'-ro], *m*. 1. Day-laborer. 2. A strong-armed man.

bracete [brah-thay'-tsy], *adv*. **De bracete**, arm in arm.

bracillo [brah-theel'-lyo], *m*. Branch of the mouth-bit of a horse's bridle.

Bracmán [brac-mahn'], *m*. Brahmin, a Hindu priest.

braco, ca [brah'-co, cah], *a*. 1. Pointing or setting: applied to a pointer. 2. Broken-nosed, flat-nosed. -*m. & f*. A pointer-dog.

bráctea [brahc'-tay-ah], *f*. *(Bot.)* Bract.

bractéola [brahc-tay'-o-lah], *f*. Bractlet.

bredipepsia [brah-de-pep'-se-ah], *f*. Bradypepsia, slow digestion.

brafonera [brah-fo-nay'-rah], *f*. 1. Piece of ancient armor for the arm. 2. In clothes, a roller which girded the upper part of the arms; a plaited sleeve.

braga [brah'-gah], *f*. *(Prov.)* 1. Child's diaper. 2. **Bragas**, gaskins, a kind of wide breeches; breeches in general; hose. 3. *(Mil.)* Breeching, lashing-rope. **Calzarse las bragas**; to wear the pants (mujeres). **Coger a uno en bragas**, to catch somebody with his pants down.

bragada [brah-gah´-dah], *f*. 1. The flat of the thigh in beasts. 2. Elbow, throat. **Bragada de una curva**, *(Naut.)* the throat of a knee. **Madera de bragada**, compass-timber.

bragado, da [brah-gah´-do, dah], *a*. 1. Having the flanks of a different color from the rest of the body (animales). 2. *(Met.)* Ill-disposed, of depraved sentiments. 3. Energetic, tough; wicked, vicious.

bragadura [brah-gah-doo'-rah], *f*. 1. Part of the human body where it begins to fork, crotch. 2. Fork of a pair of breeches. 3. Flat of the thigh in beasts, from the flank to the trough.

bragazas [brah-gah-thas], *f. pl*. 1. *(aug.)* Wide breeches. 2. *m*. *(Met.)* A person easily persuaded or ruled: generally applied to a hen-pecked husband .

braguero [brah-gay'-ro], *m*. 1. Truss, bandage for a rupture, brace. 2. **Braguero de cañón**, *(Naut.)* breeching of a gun, with which it is lashed to the ship's side. **Braguero de una vela**, bunt of a sail. 3. Piece put into clothes to make them stronger.

bragueta [brah-gay'-tah], *f*. Pants fly. **Estar como bragueta de fraile**, *(Cono Sur)* to be very solemn. **Ser hombre de bragueta**, to be a real man.

braguetazo [brah-gay-tah´-tho], *m. aug*. **Dar braguetazo**, *(Coll.)* to marry a rich woman.

braguetero [brah-gay-tay'-ro], *a*. 1. Lecherous, randy (lascivo). 2. *(LAm.)* Who marries for money. *m*. Lecher, womanizer.

braguillas [brah-geel'-lyas], *m*. 1. Boy wearing long pants for the first time. 2. *(Coll.)* Brat, little whippersnapper.

braguita(s) [brah-gee'-tahs], *f*. Panties.

Brahma [brah'mah], *f*. Brahma, a deity of the Hindus.

brahmán, or **brahmín** = BRACMAN.

brahminismo [brah-me-nees'-mo], *m*. Brahminism, the religious system of the Brahmins.

brahón [brah-on'], *m*. A fold which, in ancient apparel, surrounded the upper part of the arm.

brama [brah'-mah], *f*. Rut, the season of copulation of deer and other wild animals.

bramadera [brah-mah-day'-rah], *f*. 1. Rattle. 2. Call or horn used by shepherds to rally and conduct the flock. 3. Horn used by keepers of vineyards and olive plantations, to frighten away cattle.

bramadero [brah-mah-day'-ro], *m*. 1. Rutting-place of deer and other wild animals. 2. *(LAm.)* Tethering, post.

bramador, ra [brah-mah-dor', rah], *m. & f*. 1. Roarer, brawler, a noisy person. 2. *(Poet.)* Inanimate things, emitting a sound like roaring or groaning

bramante [brah-mahn'-tay], *m*. 1. Packthread, a strong thread made of hemp. 2. Bramant or brabant, a linen so called. **Bramante blanco**, white bramant. **Bramante crudo**, unbleached bramant. 3. Roaring. 4. Twine, string.

bramar [brah-mar'], *vn*. 1. To roar, to groan, to bellow. 2. *(Met.)* To roar, to storm, to bluster, to be boisterous (viento, mar). 3. *(Met.)* To fret, to be in a passion, to be sorely vexed, to cry.

bramido [brah-mee'-do], *m*. 1. Cry uttered by wild beasts. 2. Clamor of persons enraged. 3. Tempestuous roaring of the elements.

bramil [brah-meel´], *m.* Chalk-line used by sawyers to mark the place where timbers are to be cut.

bramín [brah-meen'], *m. V.* BRACMÁN.

bramo [brah'-mo], *m.* Shout, cry. *(Slang.)*

bramona [brah-mo´-nah], *f.* **Soltar la bramona,** to break out into injurious expressions, to use foul language: chiefly applied to gamblers.

branca [brahn'-cah], *f.* 1. Gland of the throat. 2. Point. *Brancas,* Claws, talons, etc.

brancada [bran-cah'-dah], *f.* Dragnet or sweep net, used at the mouth of rivers or in arms of the sea.

brancaursina [bran-cah-oor-see'-nah], *f. (Bot.)* Bear's breech, brank-ursine.

branchas [brahn´-chas], *f. pl.* Gills of a fish.

brandales [bran-dah'-les], *m. pl. (Naut.)* Backstays. **Brandales del mastelero de gavia,** the maintop backstays. **Brandales volantes,** shifting backstays.

brandís [bran-dees'], *m.* Great coat used formerly. **Brandises,** collars of ladies' nightgowns.

brando [brahn'-do], *m.* Tune adapted to a dance.

brano [brah´no], *m. V.* ESTAMENTO.

branquia [brahn'-kee-ab], *f.* The gill of a fish or other aquatic creature.

branquiado, da [bran-ke-ah'do, dah], *a.* Gillbreathing, branchiate.

branquial [bran-keahl'], *a.* Branchial, relating to gills.

branquifero, ra [bran-kee'-fay-ro, rah], *a.* Gillbearing

branza [brahn'-thah], *f.* Staple or ring to which the chains of galley slaves were fastened.

braña [brah'-nyah], *f. (Prov.)* 1. Summer pasture. 2. Dung, withered leaves, and other remains of fodder, found on summer pasture grounds.

braquial [brah-ke-ahl´], **a.** Brachial, belonging to the arm.

braquiceros [brah-ke-thay'-ros], *m. pl.* The brachycera, a suborder of the diptera, having short antennae.

braquigrafía [brah-ke-grah-fee'-ah], *f.* Brachygraphy, the art of writing in short-hand.

braguigrafo [brah-kee'-grah-fo], *m.* Brachygrapher, a shorthand writer.

braquillo, lla [brah-keel´-lyo, lyah], *m. & f. dim.* Small pointer.

braquiocefálico [brah-ke-o-thay-fah'-le-co], *a.* Brachycephalic, in relation with the arm and the head.

brasa [brah´-sah], *f.* Live coal; burning wood that has ceased to flame; redhot coal or wood. **Estar hecho a la brasa,** grilled. **Ir, correr or pasar como gato por brasas,** to run as light as a cat on burning coals. **Estar hecho unas brasas,** to be all in a blaze; redfaced.

braserito [brah-say-ree´-to], *m. dim.* A small pan to hold coals; a chafing-dish.

brasero [brah-say'-ro], *m.* 1. Brazier, a pan to hold coals. 2. Firepan. 3. Place where criminals were burnt. 4. Hearth, fireplace. *(Mex.)*

Brasil [brah-seel'], *m.* 1. *(Bot.)* Braziletto. 2. Brazilwood, used by dyers. 3. Rouge, a red paint used by ladies. 4. Brazil.

brasilado, da [brah-se-lah'-do, dah], *a.* Of a red or Brazilwood color; ruddy.

brasileño, ña [bra-se-lay'-nyo, nyah], *a.* Brazilian.

brasilete [bra-se-lay´-tay], *m.* Jamaica-wood, braziletto, an inferior sort of Brazilwood.

brasilina [bra-se-lee'nah], *f.* Brazilin, a red coloring matter from Brazilwood.

brasmología [bras-molo-he-ah], *f.* The science which treats of the flux and reflux of the sea.

braulis [bra-hoo'-lis], *f.* Cloth or stuff, with white and blue stripes, which comes from the coast of Barbary.

brava [brah'-vah], *f.* 1. *(Naut.)* Heavy swell of the sea. 2. *(Mex.)* Row, fight (disputa). 3. **A la brava tendrás que ir,** you´ll have to go whether you like it or not. 4. *(Carib.)* **Dar una brava a,** to intimidate.

bravada [brah-vah'-dah], *f. V.* BRAVATA.

bravamente [bra-vah-men'-tay], *adv.* 1. Bravely, gallantly. 2. Cruelly, inhumanly, barbarously. 3. Finely, extremely well. 4. Plentifully, copiously. **Hemos comido bravamente,** we have made a hearty dinner.

bravata [brah-vah'-tah], *f.* Bravado, boast, or brag, braggardism, an arrogant menace, impudent sally, intended to frighten and intimidate.

bravato, ta [brah-vah'-to, tah], *a.* Boasting, impudent.

braveador, ra [brah-vay-ah-dor', rah], *m. & f.* Bully, hector.

bravear [brah-vay-ar'], *vn.* 1. To bully, to hector, to menace in an arrogant manner. 2. To applaud, shout bravo.

bravera [brah-vay'-rah], *f.* Vent or chimney of ovens, wind. *V.* SUSPIRALES. 1. Bravery, valor. 2. Vigor. 3. Ferocity. 4. Fury of the elements.

bravero [brah-vay'-ro], *(Carib.)* 1. *a.* Bullying. 2. *m.* Bully.

braveza [brah-vay'-tha], *f.* 1. Ferocity, savageness; *(met.)* Fury, violence. 2. Bravery.

bravillo, illa [brah-veel'-lyo, lyah], *a. dim.* Rather wild, not yet tamed.

bravío, vía [brah-vee'-o, ah], *a.* 1. Ferocious, savage, wild, untamed. 2. Wild, propagated by nature, not cultivated (plantas). 3. Coarse, unpolished (modales).

bravío [brah-vee'-o], *m.* Fierceness or savageness of wild beasts.

bravo, va [brah´-vo, vah], *a.*1. Brave, valiant, strenuous, manful, hardy, fearless. 2. Bullying, hectoring. 3. Savage, wild, fierce (animales). 4. *(Met.)* Severe, untractable. 5. *(Met.)* Rude, unpolished, uncivilized, angry. **Ponerse bravo con uno,** to get angry with somebody. 6. Sumptuous, expensive. 7. Excellent, fine. **Brava cosa,** Very fine indeed! **Mar bravo,** swollen sea. **¡Bravo!** *int.* Bravo!. 8. *(LAm.)* Hot, strong (picante). *-m.* Thug.

bravonel [brah-vo-nel'], *m. (Obs.)* Brave, a hector.

bravosidad [brah-vo-se-dahd], *f. (Obs.) V.* GALLARDIA.

bravucón, na [bra-voo-cone´, nah], *a.* Boastful, braggart.

bravuconada [bra-voo-co-nah'-dah], *f.* 1. Bluster (cualidad), boastfulness. 2. Boast (acto); boasting, bragging.

bravura [brah-voo'-rah], *f.* 1. Ferocity, fierceness (animales). 2. Courage, manliness (personas). 3. Bravado, boast, brag.

braza [brah'-thah], *f.* 1. Fathom, a measure of six feet. 2. *(Naut.)* Brace which is tied to the yards. **Brazas,** *(Naut.)* Braces, ropes belonging to the yards of a ship. **Afirmar las brazas de barlovento,** to secure the weatherbraces. 3. **Braza de pecho,** breast stroke. **Braza de mariposa,** butterfly stroke (natación).

brazada [brah-thah'-dah], *f.* 1. Movement of the arms out and up. 2. Armful. **Brazada de pecho,** crawl stroke (natación). 3. Stroke (remo). 4. *(LAm.) (Naut.)* Fathom.

brazado [brah-thah'-do], *m.* An armful. **Un brazado de leña,** an armful of firewood. **Un brazado de heno,** a truss of hay.

brazaje [brah-thah'-hay], *m.* 1. *(Naut.)* Number of fathoms, depth of water. 2. *V.* BRACEAJE.

brazal [brah-thahl'], *m.* 1. Brachial muscle. 2. Bracer, ancient piece of armor for the arms. 3. Bracelet. 4. *(Prov.)* Ditch or channel from a river or canal, to irrigate lands. 5. Bracer, a wooden instrument for playing balloons. 6. *(Naut.)* Rail. **Brazales de proa,** headrails. **Brazal de medio de proa,** the middle rail of the head.

brazalete [brah-thah-lay'-tay], *m.* (Vul. BRACELETE) 1. Armlet, bracelet. *V.* MANILLA, PULSERA. 2. Bracelet, ancient iron piece of armor. **Brazaletes,** *(Naut.)* Brace pendants.

brazazo [brah-thah´-tho], *m. aug.* Large or long arm.

brazo [brah'-tho], *m.* 1. Arm, anatomically from the shoulder to the elbow. By extension, arm of a lever, of a balance beam; each half of a yard. etc. 2. The correlative limb in some of the inferior creatures. 3. *(Met.)* Bough of a tree. 4. *(Met.)* Valor, strength, power. 5. Each end of a beam or balance. **Brazo de dirección,** steering arm. **Brazo de gitano** *(Culin.),* Swiss roll. **Ir del brazo** *(LAm.),* to walk arm-in-arm. **Mover algo a brazo,** to move something by hand. **Brazo de**

una trompeta, branch of a trumpet. **Brazo de silla**, arm of a chair. **Con los brazos abiertos**, with open arms, cheerfully. **Cruzados los brazos**, with the arms folded, idle. **Ser el brazo derecho de alguno**, to be one's right hand, or confidant. 7. **Brazos** (fig.) Hands, workers (trabajadores).

brazolas [brah-tho'-las], f. pl. (Naut.) Coamings of the hatchways.

brazuelo [brah-thoo-ay'-lo], m. 1. (Dim.) Small arm. 2. Shoulder or forethigh of beasts. 3. Branch of the mouthbit of a bridle for a horse or mule.

brea [bray'-ah], f. 1. Pitch. 2. Tar, artificial bitumen composed of pitch, resin, and grease. 3. Coarse canvas for wrapping up wares, sackcloth.

brear [bray-ar'], f. va. 1. To pitch. 2. To tar, to vex, to plague, to thwart. 3 (Met.) To cast a joke upon one. 4. To abuse, to ill-treat. **Brear a uno a golpes**, to beat somebody up.

brebaje [bray-bah'hay], m. 1. Beverage, a drink made up of different ingredients harsh to the taste, medicine. 2. (Naut.) Grog.

breca [bray'-cah], f. Bleak or bray, a river fish. V. ALBUR.

brecina [bray-the'-nah], f. (Bot.) Heath.

brécol, m. **brecolera**, f. [bray-col, bray- colay'-rah]. (Bot.) Broccoli V. BRÓCULI.

brecha [bray'-chah], f. 1. Breach made in the ramparts of a fortress. 2. Opening made in a wall or building. **Abrir brecha en una muralla**, to breach a wall. 3. (Met.) Impression made upon the mind. 4. Ball of pebbles. **Batir en brecha**, 1. To batter a breach in a fortification. 2. (Met.) To persecute someone, and cause his destruction. 6. Wound. 7. **Estar en la brecha**, to be in the thick of things. **Seguir en la brecha**, to go on with one's work, keep at it.

brecho [bray'-cho], m. V. ESCARO.

bredo [bray'-cho], m. (Bot.) V. BLEDO.

brega [bray'-gah], f. 1. Strife, contest, affray. 2. (Met.) Pun, jest, or trick played upon one. **Dar brega**, to play a trick. 3. vn. Struggle, fight (luchar).

bregar [bray-gar'], vn. 1. To contend, to struggle. 2. (Met.) To struggle with troubles, difficulties, and dangers. 3. To quarrel, to scrap (reñir). 4. To slog away, to toil hard (trabajar). **Tendremos que hacerlo bregando**, we shall have to do it by sheer hard work. -va. To work up dough with a rolling-pin. (**Yo bregué**, from **Bregar**. V. verbs in gar.)

breguetear [bray-gay-tay-ahr'], vn. (And.) To argue.

brejetero [bray-hay-tay'-ro], a. (Carib.) Trouble-making, mischief-making. **bren** [brayn], m. Bran. V. SALVADO.

brenca [bren'-cah], f. 1. (Bot. Obs.) Maidenhair. Veneris, V. CULANTRILLO. 2. Sluicepost, one of the posts of a water or floodgate. 3. Filament, one of the three cristated anthers of saffron.

breña [bray'-nyah], f. Craggy, broken ground.

breñal, breñar [bray-nyahl', bray-nyar'], m. Place where the ground is craggy and broken, and full of briers and brambles.

breñoso, sa [bray -nyo'-so, sah], a. Craggy and brambled (terreno).

breque [bray'-kay], m. 1. Small river fish. 2. (LAm.) (Hist.) Break (vehículo). 3. (And. Cono Sur) Luggage van, baggage car. 4. (LAm.) (Mech.) Brake. V. BRECA. **Ojos de breque**, weak or bloodshot eyes.

brequear [bray-kay-ahr'], (LAm.) To brake.

brequero [bray-kay'-ro], m. (And. CAm, Méx.) Brakeman.

bresca [bres'-cah], f. (Prov.) Honey comb.

brescadillo [bres-cah-deel'-lyo], m. A small tube made of gold or silver.

brescado [bres-cah'-do], m. Embroidered with **brescadillo**.

bretador [bray-tah-dor'], m. Call, whistle, or pipe to call birds.

Bretaña [bray-tah'-nyah], f. Brittany.

brete [bray'-tay], m. 1. Fetters, shackles, irons for the feet. 2. Indigence; perplexity, difficulties. **Estar en un brete**, to be hard put to. 3. Kind of food in India. 4. (Carib.) Screw, lay.

breton [bray-tone'], m. 1. (Bot.) Bore-core, kale. 2. A native of Brittany.

breva [bray'-vah], f. 1. The early fruit of a variety of the common figtree. 2. Early large acorn. **Más blando que una breva**, more pliant than a glove; brought to reason. 3. Pure cigar, rather flat. 4. (Coll.) Any valuable thing or position easily obtained. **¡No caerá esa breva!**, (Esp.) No such luck! **Poner a uno como una breva**, to beat somebody black and blue.

breval [bray-vahl'], m. (Prov. Bot.) Early figtree.

breve [bray'-vay], m. 1. Apostolic brief, granted by the Pope or his legates. 2. Card of invitation, ticket, memorandum in a pocketbook. 3. f. Breve, the longest note in music, seldom used.

breve [bray'-vay], a. Brief, short, concise, laconic, compact, compendious, close. **En breve**, shortly, in a little time.

brevecico, illo, ito [bray-vay-thee'-co, eel´-lyo, ee'to], a. dim. Somewhat short or concise.

brevedad [bray-vay-dahd'], f. Brevity, briefness, shortness, conciseness, compendiousness. **Con la mayor brevedad**, as soon as possible. **Llamado por brevedad**, call for short.

brevemente [bray-vay-men´-tay], adv. Briefly, concisely.

brevería [bray-vay-ree'-ah], f. (Typ.) Note, short news item.

brevete [bray-vay'-tay], m. Note, memorandum; (LAm.) Driving licence. V. MEMBRETE.

breviario [bray-ve-ah'-re-o], m. 1. Breviary, which contains the daily service of the church of Rome. 2. Brevier, a small size of type between minion and bourgeois: of eight points. 3. Memorandum book. 4. Abridgment, epitome.

brezal [bray-thahl'], m. Heath, place planted with heaths.

brezar [bray-thar'], va. To rock, to lull (cuna).

brezo [bray'-tho], m. (Bot.) Heath, heather.

briaga [bre-ah'-gah], f. 1. Rope made of bass-weed, tied round the shaft or beam of a winepress. 2. (Mex.) Drunkenness.

briago [bre-ah-go], a. (Mex.) Drunk.

brial [bre-ahl'], m. 1. Rich silken skirt, formerly worn by ladies.

briba [bree'-bah], f. Truantship, idleness, neglect of business or duty. **A la briba**, in an idle and negligent manner.

bribia [bree'-be-ah], f. A beggar's tale to move compassion. **Echar la bribia**, to go begging.

bribón, na [bre-bone', nah], m. & f. & a. Vagrant, impostor; a knave, a scoundrel, rascal, lazy, idle (vago).

bribonada [bre-bo-nah'-dah], f. Knavery, petty villainy, mischievous trick or practice, beggar's trick, mean cunning.

bribonazo [bre-bo-nah'-tho], m. aug. Great cheat, impudent impostor.

briboncillo [bre-bon-theel' -lyo], m. dim. Little gull, young impostor.

bribonear [bre-bo-nay-ar'], vn. To rove and loiter about; to lead a vagabond's life.

bribonería [bre-bo-nay-ree´-ah], f. Life of a vagrant or vagabond, a beggar's trade.

bribonesco [bre-bo-nays'-co], a. Rascally, knavish.

bribonzuelo [bre-bon-thoo-ay'-lo], m. dim. V. BRIBONCILLO.

bricho [bree'-cho], m. Spangle, used in embroidery.

bricolage [bre-co-lah'-hay], m. Do-it-yourself.

bricolagista [bre-co-lah-hes'-tah], m. & f. Do-it-yourself expert.

bricolaje [bre-co-lah'-hay], m. V. BRICOLAGE.

brida [bree'-dah], f. 1. Bridle of a horse. 2. The reins of a bridle. **Ir a toda brida**, to go at top speed. **Tener a uno a brida corta**, to keep somebody on a tight rein. 3. Horsemanship; the art of managing a horse by means of a bridle. 4. (Met.) Curb, restraint, check. **A bridas**, riding a bur-saddle with long stirrups. 5. Rail-coupling, fish-plate 6. Flange. 7. Clamp, staple (watch-making).

bridar [bre-dar'], *va.* 1. To put a bridle to a horse, to bridle. 2. To curb, to check, to restrain.

bridge [breach], *m.* Bridge (cartas).

bridón [bre-done'], *m.* 1. Horseman riding a bur-saddle with long stirrups. 2. Horse accoutred with a bur-saddle and long stirrups. 3. Small bridle used instead of a larger one.

brigada [bre-gah'-dah], *f.* 1. Brigade, a certain number of battalions or squadrons. 2. A certain number of soldiers in some military bodies. 3. A certain number of beasts of burden to carry the baggage and provisions of an army. 4. Squad, gang (de obreros). 5. Squad (de policía, etc.). **Brigada antidisturbios**, riot squad. **Brigada antidrogas**, drug squad. **Brigada de bomberos**, bomb-disposal unit. **Brigada sanitaria**, sanation department. *-m. (Mil.)* Staff-sergeant, sergeant-mayor; warrant officer.

brigadier [bre-gah-de-err'], *m.* 1. Brigadier or general of brigade. 2. **Brigadier en la real armada**, officer of the navy, who commands a division of a fleet.

brigán [bre-gahn'], *m. (CAm. Carib.) (Hist.)* Brigand, bandit.

brigandaje [bre-gahn-dah'-hay], *m. (Carib.) (Hist.)* Brigandage, banditry.

brigola [bre-go'-lah], *f.* Ram, ancient machine for battering walls.

brillador, ra [bree'-lyah-dor', rah], *a.* Brilliant, sparkling, radiant.

brilladura [breel-lyah-doo'-rah], *f. (Obs.)* V. BRILLO.

brillante [breel-lyahn'-tay], *a.* 1. Brilliant, bright, shining, sparkling, radiant, glossy. 2. Resplendent, golden, lustrous, light, lucid. 3. Glittering, gaudy, gorgeous, gay, grand. 4. *(fig.)* Brilliant.

brillante [breel-lyahn'-tay], *m.* Brilliant, a diamond cut in triangular faces.

brillantemente [breel-lyan-tay-men'-tay], *adv.* Brilliantly, brightly, resplendently, splendidly.

brillantez [breel-lyan-teth'], *f.* 1. Brilliance, brightness (color); splendor. 2. *(fig.)* Brilliance. V. BRILLO.

brillantina [bril-lyan-tee'-nah], *f.* Brilliantine, hair oil.

brillar [breel-lyar'], *vn.* 1. To shine, to emit rays of light, to sparkle, to glisten, to glister, to glitter, to gleam. 2. To flare. 3. To glare, to glance. 4. *(Met.)* To outshine in talents, abilities, or merits. 4. *(fig.)* To shine; to be outstanding. **Brillar por su ausencia**, to be conspicuous by one's absence.

brillazón [brel-lyah-thone'], *f. (Cono Sur)* mirage.

brillo [breel'-lyo], *m.* 1. Brilliancy, brilliantness, brightness, luminousness 2. Lustre, splendor, glitter. **Sacar brillo a**, to polish, to shine. 3. Resplendence, resplendency, shining.

brilloso [breel-lye-o'-so], *a. (And. Carib. Cono Sur)* V. BRILLANTE.

brin [breen'], *m.* 1. *(Prov.)* Fragments of the stamens of saffron. 2. Sailcloth. **Brin ancho**, wide Russia sheeting. **Brin angosto**, raven duck.

brincador, ra [brin-cah-dor', rah], *m. & f.* Leaper, jumper.

brincar [brin-car'], *vn.* 1. To leap, to jump, to frisk. 2. To skip, to gambol, to hop, to bounce. 3. *(Met.)* To step over others in point of promotion. 4. *(Met.)* To omit something on purpose and pass to another. 5. *(Met.)* To fling, to flounder, to flounce, to fret, to fly into a passion. **Está que brinca**, he is in a great passion.

brincia [breen'-the-ah], *f.* Peel of an onion

brinco [breen'-co], *m.* 1. Leap, jump, frisk, hop, jerk, bounce, bound. **De un brinco**, in one bound. **De un brinco** *(LAm.)*, On the spot. **Dar brincos**, to hop, jump. **¿Para que son tantos brincos estando el suelo parejo?**, *(CAm. Méx.)* What's all the fuss about? 2. Small jewel fastened to a spring, formerly worn by ladies in their headdress.

brindar [brin-dar'], *vn.* 1. To drink one's health, to toast. **¡Brindemos por la unidad!**, let's drink to unity! 2. To offer cheerfully to invite. 3. To allure, to entice. *(Ger.)* *-va.* 1. To offer, present, afford. **Brindar a uno con algo**, to offer something to somebody. **Le brinda la ocasión**, it offers him the opportunity. 2. *(Taur.)* To dedicate. 3. **Brindar a uno a hacer algo**, to invite somebody to do something.

brindis [breen'-dis], *m.* Health or the act of drinking to the health of another; a toast. 2. *(And. Carib.)* Official reception; cocktail party.

bringabala [brin-gah-bah'-lah], *f. (Naut.)* Brake or handle of a pump. V. GUIMBALETE.

bringas [breen'-gas], *f. pl.* 1. The osiers which cross the ribs of baskets. 2. The fleshy part of lean meat.

brinquillo, brinquiño [brin-keel'-lyo, kee'-nyo], *m.* 1. Gewgaw, a small trinket. 2. Sweetmeat which comes from Portugal. **Estar or ir hecho un brinquiño**, to be as spruce and trim as a game-cock.

brinza [breen'-thah], *f.* 1 Blade, slip. 2. Sprig, shoot.

brío [bree'-o], *m.* 1. Strength, force, vigor, manliness. 2. *(Met.)* Spirit, resolution, courage, valor. **Es un hombre de bríos**, he is a man of spirit, he is a man of mettle. **Bajar los bríos a alguno**, to pull down one's spirits, to humble.

briol [bre-ol'], *m. (Naut.)* Buntline, line fastened to sails to draw them up to the yards.

briolín [bre-o-leen'], *m. (Naut.)* Slabline, fastened to the footrope of the mainsail and foresail, to draw them up a little.

brión [bre-on'], *m.* Bryum, wall-moss.

brionia [bre-oh'-ne-ah], *f. (Bot.)* Briony.

briosamente [bre-ho-sah-men'-tay], *adv.* Spiritedly, courageously, mettlesomely, vigorously, lively.

brioso, sa [bre-o'-so, sah], *a.* Vigorous, spirited, high-minded, mettlesome, courageous, lively.

briqueta [bre-kay-tah], *f.* Briquette.

brisa [bree'-sah], *f.* 1. Breeze from the northeast. 2. **Brisa carabinera**, a violent gale. 3. *(Prov.)* Skin of pressed grapes. V. ORUJO.

brisca [brees-cah], *f.* A game at cards.

briscado, da [bris-cah'-do, dah], *a.* Mixed with silk: applied to gold and silver twist.*-pp.* of BRISCAR.

briscar [bris-car'], *va.* To embroider with gold and silver twist mixed with silk.

brisera, ro [bre-say'-rah], *f. m. & f. (LAm.)* Windshield (for a lamp, etc.).

brisita [bre-se'-tah], *f.* **Tener una brisita**, to be hungry, to have an empty stomach.

británica [bre-tah'-ne-cah], *f. (Bos.)* Great water-dock.

británico, ca [bre-tah'-ne-co, cah], *a.* British, *m. & f.* Britisher.

britano, na [ ], *a. m. & f. (Hist.)* British, Briton.

brizar [bre-thar'], *va. (Obs.)* To rock the cradle.

brizna [breeth'-nah], *f.* 1. Fragment, splinter, chip. **No me queda ni una brizna**, I haven't a scrap left. 2. Nervure or filament in the pod of a bean *(Acad.).* 3. *(Carib.)* Drizzle (llovizna).

briznar [breth-nahr'], *vn. (Carib.)* To drizzle.

briznoso, sa [brith-no'-so, sah], *a.* Full of fragments or scraps.

brizo [bree'-tho], *m.* 1. Cradle which is rocked. 2. A species of sea-urchin.

broa [bro'-ah], *f. (Naut.)* A cove of shallow depth and dangerous. 2. Mouth of a river.

broca [bro'-cah], *f.* 1. Reel for twist, silk, or thread. 2. Drill for boring holes in iron. 3. Shoemaker's tack. 4. Button.

brocadel, brocatel [bro-cah-del', tel'], *m.* Brocade, a silk stuff.

brocadillo [bro-cah-deel'-lyo], *m.* Brocade with gold or silver flowers.

brocado [bro-cah'-do], *m.* Brocade; gold or silver brocade.

brocado, da [bro-cah'-do, dah], *a.* Embroidered, like brocade.

brocadura [bro-cah-doo-rah], *f.* Bite of a bear.

brocal [bro-cahl'], *m.* 1. Curbstone of a well. 2. Metal ring of the scabbard of a sword. **Brocal de bota**, mouthpiece of a leathern wine-bottle.

brocamantón [bro-cah-man-tone'], *m.* Crochet of diamonds worn by ladies.

brocatel [bro-cah-tel'], *m.* 1. Stuff made of hemp and silk. 2. Spanish marble with white veins.

brocato [bro-cah'-to], *m. (Prov.)* BROCADO.

brócula [bro'-coo-lah], *f.* Drill for piercing metals.

bróculi /bro'-coo-le], *m.* Broccoli, a sort of cabbage.

brocha [bro'-chah], *f.* 1. Painter's brush. **Brocha de afeitar,** shaving brush. **De brocha gorda,** poorly done (pintores, decoradores). 2. Cogged dice used by gamblers. 3. *(Cono Sur)* Skewer, spit. 4. *(CAm.)* Creep (zalamero). *-a. (CAm.)* meddling; creeping; servile. **Hacerse brocha** *(CAm.)*, to play the fool.

brochada [bro-chah'-dah], *f.* Each stroke of the brush made in painting;

brochado da [bro-chah'-do, dah], *a.* Relating to brocade.

brochadura [bro-chah-doo'-rah], *f.* Set of hooks and eyes.

broche [bro'-chay], *m.* Clasps; hooks and eyes; locket; hasp; brooch; *(LAm.)* Cufflink; *(And. Carib. Cono Sur)* paper clip (sujetapapeles); *(Cono Sur)* **broche para la ropa,** clothes peg.

brocheta [bro-chay'-tah], *f.* Skewer.

brochón [bro-chone'], *m.* 1. *(aug.)* Large brush. 2. Whitewash-brush. *-a. (Carib.)* Flattering.

brochura [bro-choo'-rah], *f.* The act of putting a book in boards.

bróder [bro'-dayr], *m. (CAm.)* Lad, fellow.

brodio [bro'-de-o], *m.* 1. *V.* BODRIO. 2. A mixture of things put together without order. 3. Hotchpotch.

broker [bro'-kayr], *m. (Cono Sur)* lad, fellow.

brollero [brol-lyay'-ro], *a. (Carib.)* Trouble-making, mischief-making.

broma [bro'-mah], *f.* 1. Joke, jest. **Broma pesada,** practical joke. **Dar broma,** to tease, to indulge in jokes applied to anyone present. **No es ninguna broma,** this is serious. **Fue una broma nada más,** it was just a joke. **No está para bromas,** he´s in no mood for jokes. **La broma me costó cara,** the affair cost me dearly. **Lo decía en bromas,** I was only joking. **En bromas,** in fun. **Ni en bromas,** never. 2. Clatter, confused noise. 3 Rubbish mixed with mortar formerly used to fill up chinks of foundations of walls. 4. *(Carib. Cono Sur)* disappointment, annoyance (molestía). 5. *(Zool.)* Shipworm.

bromado, da [bro-mah'-do, dah], *a.* Worm-eaten: applied to the bottom of a ship. *-pp.* of BROMAR.

bromar [bro-mar'], *va.* To gnaw, like the shipworm called woodborer.

bromato [bro-mah'-to], *m.* Bromate.

bromazo [bro-mah'-tho], *m.* Unpleasant joke, stupid practical joke.

brómico [bro´-me-co], *a.* Bromic.

bromear [bro-may-ar'], *vn.* To droll, to jest. **Estaban bromeando,** they were ragging each other, they were pulling each other´s leg. **Creía que bromeaba,** I thought he was joking.

bromista [bro-mees'-tah], *m.* A droll, comical, merry fellow, joker, leg-pulling. **Lo ha hecho algún bromista,** some joker did this. *-a.* Fond of joking, full of fun. **Es muy bromista,** he´s full of jokes, he´s a great one for jokes.

bromo [bro'-mo], *m.* 1. *(Bot.)* Brome grass. 2. Bromine, one of the elements.

bromuro [bro-moo'-ro], *m.* Bromide.

bronca [bron'-cah], *f.* 1. Row, scrap, set-to (follón). **Armar una bronca,** to kick up a row; make a great fuss. **Se armó una tremenda bronca,** there was an almighty row. 2. Ticking off (reprimenda). **Nos echó una bronca fenomenal,** he gave us a severe ticking-off. 3. *(Cono Sur)* anger, fury. *-a.* Boring, tedious.

broncamente [bron-ca-men'-tay], *adv.* Peevishly, morosely, crustily, rudely, roughly.

bronce [bron'-thay], *m.* 1. Bronze, brass. **Bronze dorado,** ormolu. **Bronze de cañon,** gunmetal. 2. *(Poet.)* Trumpet. 3. Anything strong and hard. **Ser un bronce,** to be indefatigable. **Ser de bronce or tener un corazón de bronce,** to have a heart as hard as steel. *(Per.)* 4. Copper coin (moneda).

bronceado [bron-thay-ah'-o], *m.* 1. Brassiness; the act and effect of bronzing. 2. Tan, suntan (de piel).

bronceado, da [bron-thay-ah'-do, dah], *a.* Brass-paved, brazen. *pp.* of BRONCEAR.

bronceador [bron-thay-ah-dor'], *m.* Suntan lotion.

bronceadura [bron-thay-ah-doo´-rah], *f. V.* BRONCEADO.

broncear [bron-thay-ar'], *va.* 1. To bronze, to give a bronze or brass color. 2. To adorn with pieces of brass, latten, or gilt copper. *-vr.* To brown, to get a suntan.

broncería [bron-thay-ree'-ah], *f.* 1. Collection of things made of bronze. 2. *(Cono Sur)* ironmonger´s (shop), ironmongery.

broncista [bron-thees´-tah], *m.* A worker in bronze.

bronco, ca [bron´-co, cah], *a.* 1. Rough, coarse, unpolished. 2. Crusty, sturdy, morose, crabbed. 3. Rude, unmannerly, clownish, hard, abrupt. 4. Hoarse (voz). 5. Applied to musical instruments of a harsh sound.

bronconeumonía [bron-co-nay-oo-mo-nee'-ah], *f. (Med.)* Bronchopneumonia.

broncotomía [bron-co-to-mee'-ah], *f. (Surg.)* Bronchotomy.

broncha [bron'-chah], *f.* 1. Kind of poniard. 2. Jewel. 3. Plasterer's washing-brush.

bronquedad [bron-kay-dahd'], *f.* 1. Harshness, roughness of sound. 2. Rudeness of manners. 3. Unmalleability (metales). 4. *V.* ASPEREZA.

bronquial [bron-ke-ahl'], *a. (Anat.)* Bronchial, belonging to the throat.

bronquina [bron-kee'-nah], *f. (Coll.)* Dispute, contention, quarrel.

bronquinoso [bron-ke-o'-so], *a. (Carib.)* Quarrelsome, brawling.

bronquio, *m.* **Bronquia,** *f.* [bron'-ke-o, ah]. Bronchia.

bronquitis [bron-kee'-tis], *f.* Bronchitis.

brontología [bron-to-lo'-he-ah], *f.* The study of storms and their causes.

broquel [bro-kel'], *m.* 1. Shield; buckler of wood, iron, etc. 2. *(Met.)* Support, protection. **Raja broqueles,** bully, bragger, boaster.

broquelarse [bro-kay-lar'-say], *vr.* To shield oneself.

broquelero [bro-kay-lay'-ro], *m.* 1. One who makes shields or bucklers. 2. He that wears shields or bucklers. 3. Wrangler, disputer.

broquelillo [bro-kay-leel'-lyo], *m.* 1. *(Dim.)* Small shield. 2. Small earrings worn by women.

broquero [bro-kay'-ro], *m. (Mex.)* Brace.

broqueta [bro-kay'-tah], *f.* Skewer. *V.* BROCHETA.

brota [bro'-tah], *f.* Bud, shoot. *V.* BROTE.

brotadura [bro-tah-doo'-rah], *f.* Budding, the act of shooting forth buds and germs.

brótano [bro'-tah-no], *m. (Bot.)* Southern-wood. *V.* ABRÓTANO.

brotar [bro-tar'], *vn.* 1. To bud, to germinate, to put forth shoots or germs: to come out. 2. To gush, to flow or rush out. 3. *(Med.)* To issue, to break out, to appear (granos, diviesos). 4. To appear, spring up. **Han brotado las manifestaciones,** demonstrations have occurred. **Como princesa brotada de un cuento de hadas,** like a princess out of a fairy tale. *-va.* To bring forth (tierra); to sprout (planta); *(fig.)* To sprout; to pur out.

brote, broto [bro'-tay, bro´-to], *m.* 1. Germ of vines, bud of trees. 2. *(Prov.)* Fragment, crumb, chip. 3. *(Med.)* To break out, appearance; rash, pimples (erupción cutánea). **Un brote de sarampión,** an outbreak of measles. 4. *(fig.)* Outbreak, rash (ola). 5. *(fig.)* Origin; earliest beginnings, first manifestation (comienzo).

brotón [bro-tone'], *m.* 1. Large clasp for a kind of wide coat called *sayo* 2. Shoot, tender-twig. 3. Sprout of cabbage.

broza [bro'-thah], *f.* 1. Dead leaves, bark of trees, and other rubbish. 2. Thicket, brushwood, on mountains. 8. Useless stuff spoken or written, a hotchpotch. 4. Printer's brush to brush off the ink from types. **Gente de toda broza,** people without trade or employment. **Servir de toda broza,** to do all sorts of work.

brozar [bro-thar'], *va.* Among printers, to brush the types.

brozoso, sa [bro-tho'-so, sah], *a.* Full of rubbish.

brucero [broo-thay'-ro], *m.* Brush-maker.

bruces [broo'-thes], *adv.* **A bruce's** or **de bruces;** with the face to the ground. **Caer** *or* **dar de bruces,** to fall headlong to the ground.

brugo [broo'-go], *m.* *(Prov.)* A sort of vine-grub, plantlouse.

bruja [broo'-ha], *f.* 1. Witch, hag, sorceress. **Parece una bruja,** she looks like a witch. 2. Hag, old witch, shrew. 3. *(Carib. Cono Sur)* spook, ghost (fantasma); whore (prostituta). *-a. (Mex. coll.)* Broke; out of funds.

brujear [broo-hay-ar'], *vn.* 1. To practise witchcraft 2. To rove about in the night-time. *-va. (Carib.) (fig.)* To stalk, to pursue.

brujería [broo-hay-ree'-ah], *f.* Witchcraft, hagship. 2. *(Carib.)* Poverty.

brujidor [broo-he-dor'], *m.* Glaziers' nippers used in paring glass.

brujidura [broo-he-doo'-rah], *f.* Bewitching, casting spells.

brujir [broo-heer'], *va.* To pare off the corners and edges of panes of glass.

brujo [broo'-ho], *m.* Sorcerer, conjurer, wizard, warlock, a male witch, *(LAm.)* Medicine man.

brújula [broo'-hoo-lah], *f.* 1. *(Naut.)* Sea-compass. **Brújula de bolsillo,** pocket compass. **Perder la brújula,** to lose one's bearings. 2. Sight, a small hole which serves as a direction to point a gun. **Mirar por brújula,** *(Met.)* To pry into other people's affairs.

brujulear [broo-hoo-lay-ar'], *va.* 1. At cards, to examine the cards for the purpose of knowing one's hand. 2. *(Met.)* To discover by conjectures the nature and issue of an event. *-vn.* 1. To manage, get along, keep going. 2. *(And. Carib.)* To go on the booze, to go on a bender.

brujuleo [broo-hoo-lay'-o], *m.* 1. Act of examining the cards held at a game, 2. Scrutation, close examination. 3. Guess, conjecture.

brulote [broo-lo'-tay], *m.* 1. *(Naut.)* Fire-ship, a vessel loaded with combustible matters. 2. Warlike machine of the ancients for throwing darts or fire-arrows. 3. *(And. Cono Sur)* obscene remark (comentario); *(Cono Sur)* Obscene letter (escrito).

bruma [broo'-mah], *f.* 1. Winter season. 2. Mist rising from the sea. 3. Haziness.

brumador, ra [broo-mah-dor', rah], *m. & f.* V. ABRUMADOR.

brumal [broo-mahl'], *a.* Brumal, belonging to winter.

brumamiento [broo-mah-me-en'-to], *m.* Weariness, lassitude.

brumar [broo-mar'], *va.* V. ABRUMAR.

brumazón [broo-mah-thone'], *m.* Thick fog or mist at sea.

brumo [broo'-mo], *m.* The whitest and finest wax, which wax-chandlers use to polish tapers and wax-candles.

brumoso, sa [broo-mo'-so, sah], *a.* Foggy, misty.

brunela [broo-nay'-lah], *f.* *(Bot.)* Common selfheal or hcal-all.

bruneta [broo-nay'-tah], *f.* 1. Sort of black cloth. 2. Unwrought silver.

brunete [broo-nay-tay], *m.* Coarse black cloth.

bruno, na [broo'-no, nah], *a.* Of a brown-dark; color; almost black.

bruno [broo'-no], *m.* *(Prov.)* 1. A little black plum. 2. Plum-tree.

bruñido [broo-nyee'-do], *m.* Polish, burnish. **Bruñido de zapato,** shoeshine. *-pp.* of BRUÑIR

bruñidor, ra [broo-nye-dor', rah], *m. & f.* Burnisher, polisher.

bruñidor [broo-nye-dor], *m.* 1. Burnisher, an instrument used in burnishing 2. Tool of boxwood, used in finishing leather breeches.

bruñimiento [broo-nye-me-en, to], *m.* 1. Act of polishing or burnishing. 2. Polish, the effect of burnishing or polishing.

bruñir [broo-nyeer'], *va.* 1. To burnish, to polish. 2. To put on rouge. 3. *(CAm.)* To harass, to pester. *-vr.* To make oneself up.

brusca [broos'-cah], *f.* 1. *(Naut.)* Bevel, sweep, or rounding of masts, yards, etc., on board a ship. 2. Brush wood, small wood.

bruscamente [broos-cah-men'-tay], *adv.* Abruptly, peevishly.

bruscate [broos-cah'-tay], *m.* A sort of hash made of milt, lambs' livers, chopped up with eggs, and stewed in a pan with almond-milk, herbs, and spice.

brusco [broos'-co], *m.* 1. *(Bot.)* Kneeholly, butcher's-broom or prickly pettigree. 2. Trifling remains of little value; as, loose grapes dropping at the vintage; fruit blown from the tree, etc. 3. Refuse of wool at shearing-time.

brusco, ca [broos'-co, cah], *a.* Rude, peevish, forward; sudden (ataque); Sharp (de temperatura); sudden, marked, violent (cambio).

brusela [broo-say'-lah], *f.* 1. *(Bot.)* Lesser periwinkle. 2. **Bruselas,** pincers used by silversmiths.

Bruselas [broo-say'-lahs], *f.* Brussels.

brusquedad [broos-kay-dahd], *f.* Brusqueness, rudeness, suddenness, sharpness. **Hablar con brusquedad,** to speak sharply.

brutal [broo-tahl], *a.* 1. Brutal, brutish, churlish, currish, savage, ferocious. 2. Terrific, tremendous (estupendo) 3. *(CAm.)* Incredible, extraordinary (asombroso). 4. *(LAm.)* Great, brilliant (estupendo). *m.* V. BRUTO.

brutalidad [broo-tah-le-dahd'], *f.* 1. Brutality, savageness, brutishness. 2. Brutal action. 3. Clownishness, hoggishness. 4. Stupidity. 5. **Me gusta una brutalidad,** I like it tremendously.

brutalizar [broo-tah-lee-thar'], *va.* To brutalize, to treat brutally; to rape (mujer). *-vr.* To become brutalized.

brutalmente [broo-tahl-men'-tay], *adv.* Brutally, currishly, churlishly, brutishly.

brutesco, ca [broo-tes'-co, cah], *a.* Grotesque.

brutez [broo-teth'], *f.* V. BRUTALIDAD.

bruteza [broo-tay'-thah], *f.* 1. Roughness, want of polish (piedras). 2. Brutality. 3. Coarseness, roughness.

bruto [broo'-to], *m.* 1. Brute. 2. *(Met.)* An ignorant, rude, and immoral person.

bruto, ta [broo'-to, tah], *a.* 1. Coarse, unpolished, in a rough state. **Diamante en bruto,** a rough diamond. **Madera en bruto,** rough timber. 2. Stupid. **Más bruto que un adoquín,** as dumb as an ox. **Pepe es muy bruto,** Joe is pretty rough. 3. Gross. **Peso bruto,** gross weight. 4. Brute, brutish; bestial (brutal). 5. *(Carib.)* **Pegar a uno en bruto,** to beat somebody mercilessly. 6. *(Cono Sur)* Poor-quality, inferior. 7. **Estar bruto,** to be randy. 8. *(LAm.)* Silly, foolish. *-m.* Brute, beast.

bruza [broo'-thah], 1. Round brush for cleaning horses and mules. **Bruzas,** brushes (fábricas textiles). **De bruzas,** *(Obs.)* V. DE BRUCES.

Bs.As. *abr.* de **Buenos Aires** (B.A.).

Rta, Bto *a. abr.* dc **Beata, Beato** (Beatus, Blessed, B.)

búa [boo'-ah], *f.* Pustule, a pimple containing pus.

buaro, buarillo [boo-ah'-ro, boo-ah-reel'-lyo], *m.* Buzzard, a bird of prey.

buba [boo'-bah], *f.* Pustule, small tumor. **Bubas,** buboes.

búbalo [boo'-bah-lo], *m.* *(Obs.)* BÚFALO.

bubático, ca [boo-bah'-te-co, cah], *a.* Having buboes or glandular tumors.

bubilla [boo-beel'-lyah], *f. dim.* Small pustule, a pimple.

bubón [boo-bone'], *m.* Morbid tumor, full of matter.

bubónico, ca [boo-bo'-ne-co, cah], *a.* Bubonic. **Peste bubónica,** bubonic plague.

buboso, sa [boo-bo'-so, sah], *a.* Afflicted with pustules or buboes.

bubute [boo-boo-tay], *m.* *(Carib.)* Beetle.

bucal [boo-cal'], *a.* Oral, of the mouth. **Por vía bucal,** through the mouth.

bucanero [boo-cah-nay'-ro], *m.* Buccaneer.

bucarán [boo-ca-rahn'], *m.* *(Prov.)* Fine glazed buckram.

bucare [boo-cah'-ray], *m.* A tree in Venezuela planted to shield plants of coffee and cocoa from the sun.

bucarito

bucarito [boo-ca-ree'-to], *m. dim.* Small earthen vessel of odoriferous earth.

búcaro [boo'-ca-ro], *m.* Vessel made of an odoriferous earth of the same name.

buccino [book-thee'-no], *m.* Buccinum, whelk, a gasteropod mollusk.

buceador, ra [boo-thay-ah-dor'], *m. & f.* Diver, underwater swimmer, skin-diver.

bucear [boo-thay-ar'], *vn.* 1. To dive, to go underwater in search of anything; to skin-dive; to work as a diver . 2. *(fig.)* To delve, to explore, to look below the surface.

bucéfalo [boo-thay'-fah-lo], *m.* 1. Bucephalus, horse of Alexander. 2. *(Met.)* A stupid, dull man.

buceo [boo-thay'-o], *m.* Diving, the act of going underwater in search of anything.

bucero [boo-thay'-ro], *a.* Black-nosed (perro rastreador).

bucle [boo'-clay], *m.* 1. Ringlet, curl, hair crisped and curled. 2. *(fig.)* Curve, bend, loop; *(Comp.)* Loop.

buco [boo'-co], *m.* 1. *(Naut.)* Ship, vessel. 2. Buck, a male goat. 3. Opening, aperture.

bucólica [boo-co'-le-cah], *f.* 1. Bucolic, a bucolical poem; Pastoral or rural poetry. 2. *(Coll.)* Food.

bucólico, ca [boo-co'-le-co, cah], *a.* Bucolic, bucolical, relating to pastoral poetry.

bucha [boo'-chah], *f.* Large chest or box. V. HUCHA. **Bucha pescadera,** *(Naut.)* Buss, a vessel employed in the herring-fishery.

buchaca [boo-chah'-cah], *f.* (CAm. Carib. Méx.) Bag; saddlebag (de caballo); pocket (billar).

buchada [boo-chah'-dah], *f.* Mouthful of liquid. V. BOCANADA.

buchante [boo-chahn'-tay], *m.* Shot.

buche [boo'-chay], *m.* 1. Craw or crop, of birds and fowls. 2. Maw or stomach of quadrupeds. 3. Mouthful of a fluid. 4. Young sucking ass, foal. 5. Purse, wrinkle, or pucker in clothes. **Hacer buche,** to be baggy, wrinkle up. 6. Breast, the place where secrets are pretended to be kept. 7. *(Coll.)* Human stomach. **Ha llenado bien el buche,** *(Coll.)* He has stuffed his belly well. **Hacer el buche,** *(Low.)* to eat. **Hacer el buche a otro,** to make one dine heartily. 8. *(Carib.)* Idiot, fool. 9. *(And.)* Top hat. 10. *(LAm.) (Med.)* Goitre, thyroid; mumps (paperas).

buché [boo-chay'], *m.* (CAm.) Rustic, peasant.

buchear [boo-chay-ar'], *va.* To jest, to mock.

buchecillo [boo-chay-theel'-lyo], *m. dim.* Little craw.

buchete [boo-chay'-tay], *m.* Cheek puffed with wind.

buchinche [boo-cheen'-chay], *m. (Carib.)* Hovel; pokey little shop (tienda).

Buda [boo'-dah], *m.* Buddha, founder of Buddhism.

búdico, ca [boo'-de-co, cah], *a.* Buddhic, Buddhistic.

budín [boo-deen'], *m.* Pudding; cake (pastel); trifle (postre). **Budín de pescado,** fish pie. **Esa chica es un budín,** that girl´s a smasher.

budión [boo-de-on'], *m.* *(Zool.)* Peacock fish.

budismo [boo-dees'-mo], *m.* Buddhism, the religion of the followers of Buddha.

budista [boo-dees'-tah], *m. & f.* Buddhist adherent of Buddhism.

buen [boo-en'], *a.* Apócope de **bueno.** Used only before a masculine noun. **Buen hombre,** good man, and before a substantive feminine beginning with accented *a,* as **buen alma,** a good soul.

buenamente [boo-ay-nah-men'-tay], *adv.* 1. Freely, spontaneously, conveniently. 2. Easily, commodiously, without much exertion.

buenamoza [boo-ay-nah-mo'-tha'], *f. (And.)* Jaundice.

buenaventura [boo-ay-nah-ven-too'-rah], *f.* 1. Fortune, good luck. 2. Prediction of fortune-tellers. **Decir la buenaventura a uno,** to tell somebody´s fortune.

buenazo [boo-ay-nah'-tho], *a.* Kindly, good-natured; long-suffering. 2. *m.* Good-natured person; ser un buenazo, to be kind-hearted, be easily imposed upon.

bueno, na [boo-ay'-no, nah], *a.* 1. Good, nice. **El bueno del cura,** *(Coll.)* the good curate. **La buena gente,** good people, decent people. **Lo bueno es que,** the best thing about it is that. 2. Simple, fair, plain, without cunning or craft. 3. Fit or proper for something. **En el momento bueno,** at the right moment. **Ser bueno para,** to be suitable for. **Bueno de comer,** good to eat. 4. Sociable, agreeable, pleasant, loving, gracious. **Tener buen día en buena compañía,** to spend a pleasant day in agreeable company. 5. Great, strong, violent. **Buena calentura,** a strong fever. **No estar bueno de la cabeza,** to be weak in the head. 6. Sound, healthy. 7. Useful, serviceable. 8. Strange, wonderful, notable. **Buenos días,** good morning, good-day: a familiar salute. **Buenas noches,** good-night. **Buenas tardes,** good afternoon or evening. **Las bellas artes y las buenas letras,** the fine arts and belles-lettres. **A buenas,** willingly. 9. **¿Adónde bueno?,** where are you off to? **¿De dónde bueno?,** ¿where do you come from? 10. *(Cono Sur)* **Estar en la buena,** to be in a good mood.

bueno [boo-ay'-no], *adv.* Enough, sufficiently. **Bueno** or **bueno está,** enough, no more.

buenón [boo-ay-non'], *a.* Nice-looking, good-looking.

buenparecer [boo-en-pah-ray-therr'], *m. (Coll.)* Pleasing aspect.

buenpasar [boo-en-pah-sar'], *m. (Prov.)* Independent situation, comfortable subsistence.

bueña [boo-ay'-nyah], *f. V.* MORCILLA.

buera [boo-ay'-rah], *f. (Prov.)* Pustule or pimple near the mouth.

buey [boo-ay'-e], *m.* 1. Ox, bullock. 2. **Buey marino,** sea-calf. 3. **Buey de cazo,** stalking-ox. **A paso de buey,** at a snail's gallop. **Buey de agua,** body of water issuing from a conduit or spring. *-pl.* Oxen. 4. *(LAm.)* *(fig.)* Cuckold (cornudo). 5. *(Carib.)* *(fig.)* Big sum of money. 6. *(fig.) (And. Cono Sur)* **Buey corneta,** busybody, nose-poker (entrometido). *(Carib.)* **Buey muerto,** bargain. **Como bueyes,** enormous bedbugs. **Es un buey para el trabajo,** he´s a tremendous worker. **Cuando vuelen los bueyes,** when pigs learn to fly.

bueyazo [boo-ay-yah'-tho], *m. aug.* Big ox.

bueyecillo, bueyzuelo [boo-ay-yay-theel'-lyo, thoo-ay'-lo], *m. dim.* Little ox.

bueyuno, na [boo-ay-yoo'-no, nah], *a.* Pertaining to cattle, bovine.

bufa [boo'-fah] *a. (Carib. Méx.)* Tight, drunk. 2. *f.* Joke, piece of clowning. 3. *(Carib. Méx.)* Drunkenness (embriaguez).

bufado, da [boo-fah'-do, dah], *a.* Bursting with a noise, blown: applied to glass drops blown extremely thin. *-pp.* of BUFAR.

bufalino, na [boo-fah-lee'-no, nah], *a.* Belonging to buffaloes.

búfalo [boo'-fah-lo], *m.* 1. Buffalo (animal). 2. Emery stick, buff-stick.

bufanda [boo-fahn'-dah], 1. Muffler, comforter.

bufar [boo-far'], *vn.* 1. To puff and blow with anger, to swell with indignation or pride. 2. To snort.

bufarrón [boo-fahr-ron'], *m. (Cono Sur)* pederast, child molester.

bufé [boo-fay'], *m. V.* BUFET.

bufeo [boo-fay'-o], *m. (CAm. Carib. Méx.)* Tunny (atún); dolphin (delfín).

bufet [boo-fayt'], *m. pl.* bufets. 1. Sideboard (mueble). 2. Buffet, supper. 3. Dining-room.

bufete [boo-fay'-tay], *m.* 1. Desk or writing-table. 2. An office designed for writing documents, as of a lawyer or notary. 3. Bureau, sideboard.

bufetillo [boo-fay-teel'-lyo], *m. dim.* Small desk or writing table.

bufí [boo-fee'], *m. (Prov.)* Kind of watered camlet.

bufido [boo-fee´-do], *m.* 1. Blowing of an animal, snorting of a horse. 2. Huff, swell of sudden anger or arrogance; expression of anger and passion.

bufo [boo´-fo], *m.* 1. Harlequin or buffoon on the stage, funny man. 2. *(Cono Sur)* Queer (homosexual).

bufo, fa [boo´-fo, fah], *a.* 1. **Ópera bufa**, comic opera. 2. *(Carib.)* Spongy.

bufón [boo-fone´], *m.* 1. Buffoon, harlequin, merry-andrew, mimic, masquerader. 2. Scoffer, jester, humorist.

bufón, na [boo-fone´, nah], *a.* Funny, comical.

bufonada [boo-fo-nah-dah], *f.* 1. Buffoonery, a low jest, waggery, scurrility. 2. Jesting, mimicry pleasantry. Raillery, sarcastic taunt, ridicule; repartee.

bufonazo [boo-fo-nah´-tho], *m. aug.* Great buffoon.

bufoncillo [boo-fon-theel´-lyo], *m. dim.* Little merry-andrew.

bufonear [boo-fo-nay-ar´], *vn. V.* BUFONEARSE.

bufonearse [boo-fo-nayar´-say], *vr.* To jest, to turn into ridicule.

bufonería [boo-fo-nay-ree´-ah], *f. V.* BUFONADA.

bufonesco [boo-fo-nays´-co], *a.* Funny, comical; clownish.

bufos [boo´-fos], *m. pl.* Ancient headdress of women.

buga [boo´-gah], *m.* Car.

bugaceta, bugaleta [boo-gahthay´-tah, lay´tah], *f. (Naut.)* A small vessel.

bugalla [boo-gahl´-lyah], *f.* Gallnut growing on oak leaves.

bugle [boo´-glay], *m.* Bugle.

buglosa [boo-glo´-sah], *f. (Bot.)* Alkanet; bugloss, oxtongue.

bugui-bugui [boo´-ge-boo´-ge], *m.* Boogie-woogie.

buharda [boo-ar´-dah], *f.* 1. Window in the roof, garret-window, dormer-window. 2. Skylight, a window placed horizontally in the ceiling of a room. 3. Garret, a room on the highest floor of a house

buhardilla [boo-ar-deel´-lyah], *f. dim.* Small garret.

buharro [boo-ar´-ro], *m. (Orn.)* Eagleowl.

buhedera [boo-ay-day´-rah], *f.* Embrasure, loophole. *V.* TRONERA.

buhedo [boo-ay´do], *m.* Marl, a kind of calcareous earth.

búho [boo´-o], *m.* Owl. **Es un búho**, he is an unsocial man, he shuns all intercourse with others.

buhonería [boo-o-nay-ree´-ah], *f.* 1. Peddler's box, in which his wares are carried and sold. 2. Peddlery, the hardware or other small commodities carried in the peddler´s box. 3. Peddling, hawking (acto).

buhonero [boo-o-nay´ro], *m.* Peddler or hawker.

buído da [boo-ee´do, dah], *u. (Met.)* 1. Thin, lean, slender. 2. Sharp-pointed (armas blancas.)

buir [boo-eer´], *va.* To polish, to burnish.

buitre [boo-ee´-tray], *m.* 1. Vulture. 2. Go-getter (ambicioso).

buitrear [boo-ee-tray-ar´], *va.* 1. *(LAm.)* To kill. 2. *(And. Cono Sur)* to throw up, vomit. -*vn. (And. Cono Sur)* To be sick.

buitrera [boo-ee-tray´rah], *f.* Place where fowlers put carrion to catch vultures. **Estar ya para buitrera**, spoken of a beast so lean as to be fit food for vultures.

buitrero [boo-ee-tray´-ro], *m.* Vulturefowler; one who feeds vultures.

buitrero, ra [boo-e-tray´-ro, rah], *a.* Vulturine, belonging to a vulture.

buitrón [boo-´e-trone´], *m.* 1. Osier basket to catch fish. 2. Partridge net. 3. Furnace where silver ores are smelted. 4. Snare for game.

buja [boo´-hah], *f.* Chuck (relojería).

bujano [boo´-hah-no], *m. V.* TARANTELA.

bujarra [boo-hahr´-rah], *f. m.* **Bujarrón**, *a.* Queer.

bujarrón [boo-hahr-rone´], *m. (Vul.) V.* SODOMITA.

buje [boo´-hay], *m.* Axlebox, bushbox, iron ring; pillow of a shaft.

bujeda, *f.* **bujedal, bujedo**, *m.* [boo-hay´-dah, dahl´, do]. Plantation of boxtrees.

bujería [boo-hay-ree´-ah], *f.* Gewgaw, bauble, toy, knickknack.

bujero [boo-hay´-ro], *m.* Hole.

bujeta [boo-hay´-tah], *f.* 1. Box made of boxwood. 2. Perfume box. 3. Box of any kind of wood.

bujeto [boo-hay´-to], *m.* Burnisher, a polishing stick used by shoemakers.

bujía [boo-hee´-ah], *f.* 1. Wax candle. 2. Candlestick for wax candle. 3. Spark plug. 4. Candle, candlepower.

bujiería [boo-he-ay-ree´-ah], *f.* Office at court where wax-candles are kept, and given out for the use of the palace.

bujo [boo´-ho], *m.* Wooden frame on which painters fix their canvas.

bul [bool´], *m.* Arse.

bula [boo´-lah], *f.* 1. Bull, an instrument despatched from the papal chancery, and sealed with lead. **Echar las bulas a uno**, *(Met.)* to impose a burden or troublesome duty. **No poder con la bula**, to have no strength left for anything. 2. Bubble on water.

bulario [boo-lah´-reo], *m.* Collection of papal bulls.

bulbo [bool´-bo], *m. (Bot.)* Bulb. **Bulbo costaño**, *(Bot.)* Great earthnut, pignut.

bulboso, sa [bool-bo´-so, sah], *a.* Bulbous.

bule [boo-lay], *m. (Mex.) (Bot.)* Gourd; water pitcher (jarro). **Llenarse hasta los bules**, to stuff oneself.

bulero [boo-lay´ro], *m.* One charged with distributing bulls of crusades, and collecting the alms contributed for them.

buleto [boo-lay´-to], *m.* Brief or apostolic letter granted by the Pope, or by his legate or nuncio.

bulevar [boo-lay-var], *m.* Boulevard.

Bulgaria [bool-gah´-ree-ah], *f.* Bulgaria.

búlgaro, ra [bool´-gah-ro, rah], *a.* Bulgarian; native of or belonging to Bulgaria.

bulimia [boo-lee´-me-ah], *f. (Med.)*, Bulimy or bulimia, voracious appetite.

bulímico, ca [boo-lee´-me-co, cah], *a.* Bulimic, relating to voracious appetite.

bulín [boo-leen´], *m. (Cono Sur)* 1. Bachelor flat (de soltero). 2. Room (especie de burdel).

bulla [bool´-lyah], *f.* 1. Noise, any sound made by one or more persons. **Armar bulla**, to make a row. 2. Clatter, shout, or loud cry. 3. Crowd, mob. **Meterlo a bulla**, to carry off the matter with a joke. 4. Crowd, mob. 5. *(Carib.)* **Ser el hombre de la bulla**, to be the man of the moment.

bullaje [bool-lyah´-hay], *m.* Crowd, a multitude confusedly pressed together.

bullanga [bool-lyahn´-gah], *f.* Tumult, riot.

bullanguero, ra [bool-lyan-gay´-ro, rah], *m. & f.* Rioter, a seditious, turbulent person.

bullar [bool-lyar´], *va.* To cut the wild boar's throat while the dogs hold him.

bullaranga [bool-lya-rahn´-gah], *f. (LAm.)* Noise, row; riot (disturbio).

bullarengue [bool´-lyah-rayn´-gay], *m.* Bottom (mujer).

bulldozer [bool-do´-thayr], *m. pl.* **Bulldozers**, bulldozer.

bullebulle [bool-lyay-bool´lyay], *m. (Coll.)* Busybody, bustler, a person of lively and restless disposition, vulgarly smart.

bullero [bool-lyay´ro], *a. (LAm.) V.* BULLICIOSO.

bullicio [bool-lyee´-the-o], *m.* 1. Bustle, noise, and clamor raised by a crowd. 2. Tumult, uproar, sedition heat.

bulliciosamente [bool-lye-the-oh-sah-men´-tay], *adv.* In a noisy, tumultuous manner, mutinously.

bullicioso, sa [bool´-lyo-tho-oh´-so, sah], *a.* 1. Lively, restless, noisy, clamorous, busy. 2. Seditious, turbulent. 3. *(Poet.)* Boisterous (mar).

bullidor, ra [bool-lye-dor´, rah], *a.* BULLICIOSO.

bullir [bool-lyeer´], *m.* 1. To boil, as water and other liquids. 2. *(Met.)* To bustle, to be lively or restless, to fluster. 3. *(Met.)* To be industrious and active in business. -*va.* To move a thing from place to place; to stir; to manage a business. **No bulló pie ni mano**, he did not lift a finger. -*vn.* 1. To boil (hervir); to bubble, bubble up. **El agua bullía ligeramente**, the water rippled slightly. 2. To swarm; to teem; (bullir de)

(fig.), To teem with, swarm with. **Bullía de indignación,** he was seething with indignation. *-vr.* To move, to stir, to budge.
bullón [bool-lyone'], *m.* 1. Kind of knife. 2. Dye bubbling up in a boiler. 3. A metallic ornament for large books. 4. Bouillon, a clear meat broth; particularly used in bacteriology. 5. Puff, in sewing.
bulo [boo'-lo], *m.* Hoax, false report.
bulón [boo-lon'], *m.* Bolt; spring pin.
bultito [bool-tee'-to], *m. dim.* Little lump or tumor.
bulto [bool'-to], *m.* 1. Bulk, any thing which appears bulky. **De gran bulto,** bulky. **De mucho bulto,** heavy. **De poco bulto,** small. **Agumentos de bulto,** arguments of substance. **Hacer bulto,** to swell the number. 2. Protuberance, tumor, swelling; massiness. 3. Bust, image of the human head and neck. 4. Pillowcase. **A bulto,** indistinctly, confusedly. **Comprar las cosas a bulto,** to buy wholesale, or by the lump. 5. *(Com.)* Package, parcel. 6. Shape, form (forma). **Estimación a bulto,** rough estimate. **Buscar el bulto a uno,** to provoke. **Calcular a bulto,** to calculate roughly. **Escurrir el bulto,** to dodge, duck out of it. 7. *(Mil.)* Squaddie, recruit.
bululú [boo-loo-loo'], *m.* 1. Strolling comedian, who formerly represented all the characters in a farce, by changing his voice. 2. *(Carib.)* Excitement, agitation.
bumerán, bumerang [boo-may-rahn'], *m.* Boomerang.
bunga [boon-gah], *f. (Carib.)* Lie.
bungalow [boon'-gah-lo], *m. pl.* **bungalows,** bungalow.
bungo [boon'-go], *m.* A Nicaraguan flatboat.
buniato [boo-neah'-to], *m. V.* BONIATO.
bunio [boo'-ne-o], *m.* Sort of earthnut or pignut.
bunjo [boon'-ho], *m.* **Hacer bunjo** *(Carib.),* To hit the jacket.
búnker [boon'-kayr], *m. pl.* **Bunkers.** 1. Bunker (golf, fortificación). 2. *(Pol.)* Reactionary clique, reactionary core.
buñolada [boo-nyo-lah'-dah], *f.* A large plate of buns.
buñolería [boo-nyo-lay-ree'-ah], *f.* A bunshop; place where fritters are made and sold.
buñolero, ra [boo-nyo-lay'-ro, rah], *m. & f* One that makes or sells buns.
buñuelo [boo-nyoo-ay'lo], *m.* 1. Fritter made of flour and eggs, and fried in oil; pancake. 2. *(Coll.)* Anything poorly done or spoiled; a failure.
B.U.P. [boop], *m. (Esp.) (Escol.) abr.* de **Bachillerato Unificado y Polivalente** (secondary school education, 14-17 age group, and leaving certificate).
bupréstidos [boo-pres'-te-dos], *m. pl.* Buprestidans, a family of beetles, destructive of wood in their larval state.
buque [boo'-kay], *m.* 1. Ship, vessel, boat. 2. Hull of a ship. **Buque de guerra,** war vessel. **Buque de vela,** sailboat. **Buque de abastecimiento,** supply ship. **Buque de carga,** freighter. **Buque hospital,** hospital ship. **Buque mercante,** merchant-man, merchant-ship. **Buque de pasajeros,** passenger ship. **Buque de vapor,** steamer. 3. Capacity, tonnage. 4. Hull (casco).
buqué [boo-kay'], *m.* Bouquet (of wine).
buquinista [boo-ke-nees´-tah], *m.* A collector of old books.
buraco [boo-rah'-co], *m. (Cono Sur)* hole.
burata [boo-rah'-tah], *f. (Carib.)* Cash, dough.
burato [boo-ran'-to], *m.* 1. Canton crape. 2. Cyprus, sort of woollen stuff much worn for mourning, and by clergymen. 3. Transparent veil of light silk, worn by women.
burbá [boor-bah], *f.* African coin of small value.
burbalur [boor-ba-loor'], *m.* Whale of a large kind.
burbuja [boor-boo'-hah], *f.* Bubble; bleb.
burbujeante [boor-boo-hay-ahn'-tay], *a.* Bubbly, fizzy; bubbling.
burbujear [boor-boo-hay-ar'], *vn.* To bubble.
burbujeo [boor-boo-hay'-o], *m.* bubbling.
burbujita [boor-boo-hee'-tah], *f. dim.* Small bubble.
burcho [boor'-cho], *m. (Naut.)* Large sloop or barge.
burda [boor'-dah], *f.* Door.
burdas [boor'-das], *f. pl. (Naut.)* Backstays.

burdégano [boor-day'-gah-no], *m.* Hinny, offspring of a stallion and a she-ass; mule.
burdel [boor-del'], *m.* Brothel, brothel-house. *-a.* Libidinous
burdelero, ra [boor-day-lay'-ro, rah], *m. & f. V.* ALCAHUE.
Burdeos [boor-day'-os], *m.* 1. Bordeaux. 2. Claret, Bordeaux (vino). *a.* Maroon, dark red.
burdinalla [boor-de-nahl'-lyah], *f. (Naut.)* Sprit-topsail stay.
burdo, da [boor'-do, dah], *a.* Coarse, common, ordinary.
burear [boo-ray-ar'], *(And.)* 1. *va.* To con, to trick. 2. *vn.* To go out on the town.
burel [boo-rel'], *m.* 1. *(Her.)* Bar, the ninth part of a shield. 2. *(Naut.)* Fid, marline-spike.
bureles [boo-ray'-les], *m. pl. (Naut.)* Pointed wooden rollers. **Bureles de hierro para engarzar motones,** splicing-fids. *V.* PASADOR.
burengue [boo-ren'-gay], *m. (Prov.)* Mulatto slave.
bureo [boo-ray'-o], *m.* 1. Court of justice, in which matters are tried relative to persons of the king's household. 2. Entertainment, amusement, diversion. **Entrar en bureo,** to meet for the purpose of inquiring into or discussing a subject. **Ir de bureo,** to have a good time. 3. Stroll (paseo).
bureta [boo-ray'-tah], *f.* Burette, drop measurer.
burga [boor'-gah], *f. (Prov.)* Hot spring of mineral waters used for bathing.
burgés [boor-ges'], *m.* Native or inhabitant of a village.
burgo [boor'-go], *m.* Borough.
burgomaestre [boor-go-mah-es-tray], *m.* Burgomaster, magistrate of a Dutch or German city.
burgués, sa [boor-gess´-sah], *a.* Burgess; a citizen of a town of the middle class.
burguesía [boor-gay-see'-ah], *f.* Burgesship; yeomanry; middle-class. **Alta burguesía,** upper middle class.
burí [boo-ree'], *m.* A palm growing in the Philippine Islands; the pith yields sago.
buriel [boo-re-el'], *a.* Reddish, dark red.
buriel [boo-re-el'], *m.* 1. Kersey, a coarse cloth. 2. Ropewalk, manufactory for cordage.
buril [boo-reel'], *m.* Burin, tool of an engraver. **Buril de punta,** sharp-pointed burin. **Buril chaple redondo,** curved burin.
burilada [boo-re-lah'-dah], *f.* 1. Line or stroke of a burin. 2. Silver taken by an assayer to be tested.
buriladura [boo-re-lah-doo'-rah], *f.* Act of engraving with a graver or burin.
burilar [boo-re-lar'], *va.* To engrave with a burin or graver.
burjaca [boor-hah'-cah], *f.* Leather bag carried by pilgrims or beggars.
burla [boor'lah], *f.* 1. Scoff, flout, mock mockery, fling, abuse, derision, sneer. 2. Jest, run, trick. 3. Jeer, jeering, flirt, gibe. 4. Hoax, low trick. **Burla pesada,** biting jest, bad trick. **Burlas,** falsities uttered in a jocular style. **Burlas aparte,** setting jokes aside. **Hablar de burlas,** to speak in jest. **Decir algunas cosas entre burlas y veras,** to say something between joke and earnest. **De burlas,** in jest. **Fue una broma cruel,** it was a cruel sort of joke. **Gastar bromas a uno,** to make fun of somebody.
burladero [boor-lah-day'-ro], *m.* A narrow doorway in the bullring, for protection of the fighter; *(Taur.)* Refuge, shelter.
burlador, ra [boor-lah-or', rah], *m. & f.* 1. Wag, jester, scoffer, mocker, jeerer. 2. Libertine, seducer. *(Acad.)* 3. Conjurer's cup, a vessel so contrived that the liquor runs out through hidden holes when it is put to the lips. 4. Concealed squirt, which throws out water on those who come near.
burlar [boor-lar'], *va.* 1. To ridicule, to mock, to scoff, to laugh, to burlesque. 2. To hoax, to gibe, to fetch over, to flout, to abuse, to play tricks, to deceive. 3. To destroy one's hopes. *-vr.* 1. To jest, to laugh at. 2. To fleer, to gibe, to flout. **Yo no me burlo,** I´m not joking. 3. **Burlarse de,** to mock, to ridicule.
burlería [boor-lay-ree'-ah], *f.* 1. Fun, pun, artifice; drolling. 2. Romantic tale. 3. Deceit, illusion. 4. Derision, reproach.

burlescamente [boor-les-ca-men'-tay], *adv.* Comically, ludicrously.

burlesco, ca [boor-les'-co, cah], *a.* Joker, jocular, ludicrous, comic, mock, funny.

burlesco [boor-les'-co], *m.* Burlesquer, wag, jester, scoffer; mimic.

burleta, illa, ita [boor-lay'-tah, eel-lyah, ee'-tah], *f. dim.* Little trick, fun, or joke.

burlete [boor-lay'-tay], *m.* Weather-strip; kersey.

burlisto [boor-lees'-to], *a. (Cono Sur, CAm, Méx.) V.* BURLON.

burlón, na [boor-lone', nah], *m. & f.* Great wag, jester, or scoffer.

buro [boo'-ro], *m. (Prov.)* Chalk, marl.

buró [boo-roh'], *m.* Bureau; a chest of drawers, with or without conveniences for writing.

burocracia [boo-ro-crah'-the-ah], *f.* Bureaucracy.

burócrata [boo-ro'-crah-tah], *m. & f.* Civil servant, administrative official, official of the public service.

burocrático [boo-ro-crah'-te-co]. *a.* Bureaucratic; civil service.

burra [boor'-rah], *f.* 1. A she-ass. **Caer de su burra**, to fall from one's hobbyhorse, to become sensible of one's errors. 2. A dirty, ignorant, and unteachable woman. *Cf.* BURRO, 2d def. *(Acad.)* 3. A laborious woman of much patience.

burrada [boor-rah'-dah], *f.* 1. Drove of asses. 2. Stupid or foolish action or saying. **Decir burradas**, to talk nonsense, to say silly things. 3. A play contrary to rule in the game of *burro*. 4. **Una burrada de cosas**, a whole heap of things, heaps of things. 5. *adv,* **Me gusta una burrada**, I like it a lot.

burrajo [boor-rah'-ho], *m.* Dry stable-dung to heat ovens. -*a. (Mex.)* Vulgar, rude.

burrazo, za [boor-rah'-tho, thah], *m. & f. aug.* Large or big ass.

burrear [boor-ray-ahr'], *va.* To rip off (robar); to con (engañar).

burrero [boor-ray'-ro], *m.* 1. Ass-keeper, who sells asses' milk for medicine. 2. Jackass-keeper. 3. *(CAm.)* A large herd of donkeys. 4. *(Carib.)* Coarse (malhablado). -*a. (Cono Sur)* horse loving; racegoing.

burricie [boor-re'-the-ay], *f.* Stupidity.

burrillo [boor-reel'-lyo], *m. (Coll.) V.* AÑALEJO.

burrito [boor-ree'-to], *m. dim.* A little ass.

burro [boor'-ro], *m.* 1. Ass, jument. 2. Ass, a stupid, ignorant being. **Burro cargado de letras**, pompous ass. 3. Jack or horse on which sawyer saw boards or timber. 4. Wheel which puts the machine in motion that twists and reels silk. 5. A game at cards. 6. Windlass, in mining. **Caer de su burro**, to fall from one's hobbyhorse. **Es un burro en el trabajo**, he works and drudges like an ass. **Poner a uno a caer de un burro**, to beat somebody black and blue. **No ver tres en un burro**, to be as blind as a bat. **Ver burros negros** *(Cono Sur)*, to see stars. 7. *(LAm.)* Step ladder. 8. *(And. Carib.)* Swing (columpio). -*a.* 1. Stupid. **El muy burro**, the great oaf. 2. **Estar burro**, to feel hot. **Poner burro a uno**, to make somebody feel hot (cachondo).

burrucho [boor-roo'-cho], *m.* Young or little ass.

burrumazo [boor-roo-mah'-tho], *m. (Carib.)* Blow, thump.

burrumbada [boor-room-bah'-dah], *f. V.* BARRUMBADA.

bursátil [boor-sah'-teel], *a.* Stock-exchange.

bursitis [boor-see'-tes], *f.* Bursitis.

burujaca [boo-roo-hah'-cah], *f. (LAm.)* Saddlebag.

burujo [boo-roo'-ho], *m.* 1. Dregs of pressed olives or grapes. 2. Lump of pressed wood or other matter. 3. Parcel, package.

burujón, burullón [boo-roo-hone', boo-rool-lyone',], *m.* 1. *(aug.)* Large knob or lump. 2. Protuberance in the head caused by a stroke.

burujoncillo [boo-roo-hon-theel'-lyo], *m. dim.* Little knob or protuberance.

burundanga [boo-roon-dahn-gah], *f. (Carib.)* 1. Worthless object; piece of junk. **De burundanga**, worthless. 2. Mess, mix-up (lío).

burusca [boo-roos-cah], *f. (CAm.)* Kindling.

bus [boos], *m.* 1. Bus, long-distance bus. 2. *(Comp.)* **Bus asíncrono**, asynchronous bus. **Bus Camac**, Camac bus. **Bus de control**, control bus. **Bus de datos**, data bus. **Bus de dirección**, address bus. **Bus EISA**, EISA bus. **Bus IBM PC**, IBM PC bus. **Bus múltiple**, multiple bus. **Bus PC / AT**, PC / AT bus. **Bus principal**, primary bus. **Bus privado**, private bus. **Bus S-100**, S-100 bus. **Bus SBI**, SBI bus. **Bus síncrono**, synchronous bus. **Bus VME**, VME bus.

busa [boo'-sah], *f.* **Tener busa** *(Esp.)*, To feel hungry.

busaca [boo-sah'-cah], *f. (And. Carib.)* Saddlebag; *(Carib.)* Satchel.

busardas [boo-sar'-das], *f pl. (Naut.)* Breast-hooks, compass-timbers, which serve to strengthen the stem.

busardo [boo-sar'-do], *m.* Buzzard, bird of prey.

busca [boos'-cah], *f.* 1. Search, the act of searching. 2. Pursuit. 3. Terrier or other dog which starts or springs game. 4. Troop of huntsmen, drivers, and terriers, that overrun a forest to rouse game.

buscabulla [boos-cah-bool'-lyah], *m. (Carib. Méx.)* Brawler, troublemaker.

buscabullas [boos-cah-bool'-lyahs], *a. (Mex.)* Troublemaker.

buscada [boos-cah'-dah], *f.* Search, research; inquiry, the act of searching.

buscador, ra [boos-cah-dor', rah], *m. & f.* Searcher, investigator. -*m.* Viewfinder (cámara, máquina fotográfica).

buscamiento [boos-cah-me-en'-to], *m. (Obs.)* Search, research, inquiry.

buscaniguas [boos-cah-ne'-goo-as], *m. (And. CAm.)* Squib, cracker.

buscapié [boos-cah-pe-ay'], *m. (Met.)* Hint, feeler.

buscapiés [boos-cah-pe-ess'], *m.* Squib running about between people's feet, serpent (pirotécnia).

buscar [boos-car'], *va.* 1. To seek, to search, to endeavor to find out. 2. To look, to look after, to look for, or to look out; to hunt or hunt after. **Buscar por todos lados**, to hunt up and down. **Buscar tres pies al gato**, to pick a quarrel. **Quien busca halla**, he that seeks will find. **Ven a buscarme a la oficina**, come and find me in the office. **Nadie nos buscará aquí**, nobody will look for us here. **El terrorista más buscado**, the most wanted terrorist. 3. *(LAm.)* To ask for (pedir). 4. *(Mex.)* To provoke (riña). 5. *(LAm.)* Perks, extras. -*vr.* To bring upon oneself. 2. **Se busca piso** *(Esp.)*, apartment wanted. 3. To manage, to get along; to be looking for trouble (buscar camorra). 4. **Buscarlas**, to fend for oneself.

buscarruidos [boos-car-roo-ee'-dos], *m.* Restless, quarrelsome fellow.

buscas [boos'-cas], *f. pl. (Carib. Mex. And.)* Perks, profits on the side.

buscavidas [boos-cah-vee'-das], *m.* 1. A person prying into the actions of others. 2. One diligent in finding subsistence for himself and his family. 3. Hustler (ambicioso); snooper (entrometido).

busco [boos'-co], *m.* Track of an animal.

buscón, na [boos-cone', nah], *m. & f.* 1. Searcher. 2. Cheat, pilferer, filcher, petty robber. 3. Whore.

busilis [boo-see'-lis], *m. (Coll.)* The point in question where the difficulty lies; a mystery, riddle. **Dar en el busilis**, to hit the mark.

buso [boo'-so], *m. (Obs.)* Hole. *V.* AGUJERO. *(Yo busqué, from Buscar. V.* verbs in *car.)*

búsqueda [boos'-kay-dah], *f.* Search, investigation. **Búsqueda de un modelo** *(Comp.)*, search and pattern matching. *V.* BUSCADA.

buten [boo'-tayn], **De buten**, terrific, tremendous.

busto [boos'-to], *m.* 1 Bust. 2. *(Obs.)* Tomb.

bustrófedon [boos-tro'-fay-done], *m.* Method of writing continuously from left to right, and vice versa. It receives its name from the trail of oxen ploughing.

butaca [boo-tah'-cah], *f.* 1. Armchair, easychair. 2. Seat in a theater.

butifarra [boo-te-far'-rah], *f.* 1. Sort of sausage made in Catalonia. 2. Gaskins, long wide breeches.

butiondo [boo-te-on'-do], *a.* Fetid, goatish, lustful.

butiráceo, cea [boo-te-rah'-thay-o, ah], *a.* Butyraceous, of a consistency like butter.

butírico, ca [boo-tee'-re-co, cah], *a.* Butyric, an acid found in butter, which gives it its odour.

butorio [boo-to'-re-o], *m. (Orn.)* Bittern.

butrino [boo-tree'-no], *m.* Fowling-net for catching birds.

butrón [boo-tro-ne'], *m.* Net for birds. Burglary. *V.* BUITRÓN.

butronero [boo-tro-nay-ro], *m.* Burglar.

butuco [boo-too'-co], *m.* A thick stumpy plantain.

buya [boo'-yah], *m. V.* CASTOR.

buyador [boo-yah-dor'], *m. (Prov.)* Brazier. *V.* LATONERO.

buyo [boo'-yo], *m.* 1. *(Prov.)* Hut shepherd's cottage. 2. Boa constrictor. 3. A compound of bonga-fruit, betel-leaves, and lime, for chewing.

buzamiento [boo-thah-me-ayn'-to], *m. (Geol.)* Dip.

búzano [boo'-thah-no], *m. (Obs.)* 1, Diver. 2. Kind of culverin.

buzar [boo-thar'], *va.* To dip downward, as a geological stratum.

buzardas [boo-thar'-das], *f. pl. (Naut.)* Breast-hooks, fore-hooks.

buzo [boo'-tho], *m.* 1. Diver, one that goes underwater in search of things dropped into the sea or rivers. 2. An ancient kind of ship.

buzón [boo-thone'], *m.* 1. *(Arch.)* Conduit, canal. 2. *(Prov.)* Hole through which letters are thrown into the post-office, letterbox, dropbox. **Cerrar el buzón,** to keep one´s trap shut. **Echar una carta al buzón,** to post a letter. **Vender un buzón a uno,** *(Cono Sur)* to sell somebody a dummy. 3. Lid or cover of cisterns, ponds, jars; etc. 4. In foundries, hooks to take off the lids of melting pots. 5. Sluice of a watercourse at a mill. 6. Ancient kind of battering-ram.

buzonero [boo-tho-nay'-ro], *m. (LAm.)* Postal employee.

buzonora [boo-tho-nay'-rah], *f.* A drain or gutter in a courtyard.

byte [bah'-eets], *m. (Comp.)* Byte. **Bytes por pulgada,** bytes per inch.

C

c [thay], is the third letter of the alphabet, and before *e* and *i* has generally the sound of the English *th* in *thick;* before *a, o, u, l,* and *r,* it sounds like *k.* **C** 1. *abr.* de **Centígrado** (Centigrade, C). 2. *abr.* de **Compañía** (Company, Co). 3. *(Inform.)* C (Portable assembly language).

C/ *abr.* de **Calle** (Street, st.).

c/ *abr.* de **cuenta** (account, a/c.) 2. *abr.* de **capítulo** *(Chapter.).*

¡ca! [cah], *int. (coll.)* Oh, no! No, indeed! *V.* ¡QUIÁ!

C.A. *abr.* de **corriente alterna,** (altering current, A.C.).

cabal [cah-bahl'], *a.* 1. Just, exact (pesos, medidas). 2. Perfect, complete, accomplished, faultless, consummate; clever. 3. Falling to one's share or dividend. **Por su cabal,** With all his might, most earnestly. **Por sus cabales,** exactly, perfectly, to the very point; according to rule and order: for its just price, according to what it is worth. **Estar en sus cabales,** to be in one´s right mind.

cábala [cah'-bah-lah], *f.* 1. Cabala, mystical knowledge of the celestial bodies. 2. Secret science of the Hebrew rabbis. 3. Cabal, intrigue, plot, conspiracy. 4. Confederation or confederacy; (junta).

cabalgada [cah-bal-gah'-dah], *f.* 1. Foray. 2. Cavalcade, a procession on horseback. 3. Booty or spoils taken by an incursion into an enemy's country.

cabalgadero [cah-bal-gah-day'-ro], *m.* Mounting block.

cabalgador [cah-bal-gah-dor'], *m.* 1. Rider. 2. Horseman who goes in procession. 3. Horse-block.

cabalgadura [cah-bal-gah-doo'-rah], *f.* A beast of burden, mount, horse.

cabalgar [cah-bal-gar'], *vn.* 1. To parade on horseback, to go in a cavalcade. 2. To get on horseback, to mount on horseback. *-va.* 1. To cover a mare (semental). 2. **Cabalgar la artillería,** to mount cannon on their carriages. 3. Harness.

cabalgata [cah-bal-gah'-tah], *f.* Cavalcade, procession. **Cabalgata de los Reyes Magos,** the procession of the Three Wise Men.

cabalista [cah-bah-lees'-tah], *m.* Cabalist, one skilled in the traditions of the Hebrews.2. Schemer, intriguer.

cabalístico, ca [cah-bah-lees'-te-co, cah], *a.* Cabalistic; *(fig.)* Occult, mysterious.

cabalmente [cah-bal-men'-tay], *adv.* Exactly, completely, perfectly, fairly.

caballa [cah-bahl'-lyah], *f.* Horsemackerel.

caballada [cah-bal-lyah'-dah], *f.* 1. *(Lit. us.)* Stud of horses or mares. 2. A number of horses. 3. *(Prov.)* Any game performed by horsemen at public festivals. 4. Gaffe, blunder (animalada). **Has hecho una caballada,** that was a stupid thing to do.

caballaje [cah-bal-lyah'-hay], *m.* 1. Place where mares and she-asses are covered by stallions or jackasses. 2. Money paid for that service. 3. Horsepower.

caballar [cah-bal-lyar'], *m.* Mackerel.

caballar [cah-bal-lyar'], *a.* Belonging to or resembling horses, equine.

caballazo [cah-bahl-lya-tho], *m. (LAm.)* Collision between two horsemen, accident involving a horse.

caballejo [cah-bal-lyar'-ho], *m.* 1 *(dim.)* Little horse, nag. 2. Wooden frame for shoeing unruly horses.

caballerango [cah-bahl-lyay-rahn'-go], *m. (Mex.)* Groom.

caballerato [cah-bal-lya-rah'-to], *m.* 1. Right of laymen to enjoy ecclesiastical benefices by virtue of the Pope's dispensation. 2. The benefice enjoyed by virtue of the said dispensation. 3. Privilege of a gentleman or esquire.

caballerescamente [cah-bal'-lya-res-cah-men'-tay], *adv.* Knightly, cavalierly, gentlemanly.

caballeresco, ca [cah-bal-lyar-res´-co, cah], *a.* 1. Knightly, befitting a knight; adventurous. **Literatura caballeresca,** chivalresque literature, books of chivalry. 2. Chivalrous. 3. Belonging to or having the appearance of a gentleman.

caballerete [cah-bal-lyay-ray'-tay], *m. dim.* Spruce young gentleman.

caballerete [cah-bahl-lyay-ray'-tay], *m.* Dandy, fop, dude.

caballería [cah-bal-lyay-ree'-ah], *f.* 1. A riding beast. **Caballería de carga,** beast of burden; **caballería menor,** ass. 2. Cavalry horse or horsetroops. **Caballería ligera,** light horse, light cavalry. 3. Art of managing and mounting a horse. 4. Chivalry, the order of knights, and particularly military order. **Caballería andante,** knight-errantry. 5. Knighthood; martialism, nobleness of mind. 6. Assembly of knights of military orders. 7. Chivalry, the institution and profession of knights 8. Body of nobility of a province or place. 9. Service rendered by knights and nobles. 10. Share of spoils given to a knight, according to his rank and merit. 11. A tract of land about thirty-three and one third acres, U. S. measure. 12. Preeminence and privileges of knights. **Libros de caballería,** books of knight errantry. **Andarse en caballerías,** *(Met.)* to make a fulsome show of superfluous compliments.

caballericero [cah-bahl-lyay-re-thay'-ro], *m. (CAm. Carib.)* Groom.

caballerito [cah-bal-lyay-ree'-to], *m. dim.* A young gentleman.

caballeriza [cah-bal-lyay-ree´-thah], *f.* 1. Stable. 2. Number of horses, mules, etc., standing in a stable. 3. Stud of horses. 4. The staff of grooms, coachmen, etc., in any establishment.

caballerizo [cah-bal-lyay-ree-tho], *m.* Head groom of a stable. **Caballerizo del rey**, equerry to the king. **Caballerizo mayor del rey**, master of the king´s horse.

caballero [cah-bal-lyay´-ro], *m.* 1 Knight. 2. Cavalier, knight. 3. A nobleman. 4. A gentleman. **Cosas indignas de un caballero**, things unworthy of a gentleman. **Es un mal caballero**, he´s no gentleman. 5. A rider. 6. Horseman, soldier on horseback. 7. Cavalier, a sort of fortification. 8. *(Orn.)* Redlegged horseman, gambet. 9. **Caballero andante**, knight errant. **Armar a uno caballero**, to knight, to make one a knight. **Caballero de industria**, a defrauder, a knave. **Meterse a caballero**, to assume the character of a gentleman or knight. **Ir caballero** or **caballera**, to go on horseback.

caballero, ra [cah-bal-lyay´-ro, rah], *a.* Applied to a person who goes on horseback. **Ir caballero en burro**, *(Coll.)* to ride on an ass.

caballerosamente [cah-ba'l-lyay-ro-sah-men'-tay], *adv.* 1. Generously, nobly, in a gentlemanlike manner. 2. Knightly.

caballerosidad [cah-bal-lyay-ro-se-dahd´], *f.* Gentlemanliness, behavior of a gentleman. **Caballerosidad deportiva**, good sportsmanship.

caballeroso, sa [cah-bal-lyay-ro´-so, sah] *a.* 1. Noble, generous, genteel. 2. Gentlemanlike.

caballerote [cah-bal-lyay-ro'tay], *m.* 1. A gentleman of an ancient family, and of an unblemished character. 2. *(Coll.)* Graceless, unpolished gentleman.

caballeta [cah-bal-lyay'-tah], *f.* Field cricket.

caballete [cah-bal-lyay'-tay], *m.* 1. *(Aruit.)* Ridge of a house forming an acute angle (**de techo**); bolster, ridge-piece, hip; carpenter's horse, trestle-horse, bench, *(Tec.)* Trestle. 2. Horse, an instrument of torture. 3. Brake, for dressing hemp and flax. 4. Ridge between furrows, raised by a ploughshare. 5. Cover over the funnel of a chimney in a pyramidal form. 6. Bridge (of the nose). 7. Gallows of a printing-press. 8. *(Arte)* easel. 9. *(Aer.)* Gantry tower. **Caballete de aserrar**, sawyer's trestle or horse. **Caballete de pintor**, painter's easel.

caballico, ito [cah-bal-lyee'-co, ee'to], *m.* 1. *(dim.)* Little horse, pony. 2. Hobby or hobby-horse, a rocking-horse; a stick or cane on which children ride.

caballista [cah-bah-lyees'-tah], *m.* Horse-man, expert in horses.

caballito [cah-bahl-lee to],*m.* Small horse, pony. **Caballito de niño**, hobby-horse. **Caballito del diablo**, dragonfly. **Caballito de mar**, sea horse.

caballitos [cah-bah-lyee'-tos], *m. pl.* 1. Small horses. 2. Merry-go-round, carrousel.

caballo [cah-bahl-lyo], *m.* 1. Horse. **Caballo padre**, a stallion, stone horse. **Caballo de montar** or **silla**, saddle horse. **Caballo de carga**, packhorse. **Caballo castrado** or **capado**, gelding. **Caballo de coche,** coachhorse. **Caballo de guerra**, charger. **Caballo de caza**, hunter. **Caballo de carrera** or **corredor**, racer, racehorse. **Caballo desorejado**, cropped horse. **Caballo de alquiler**, hack, hackney. **Caballo de tiro**, draught-horse. **Caballo de vaivén**, rocking horse. **Las cosas andan a caballo** *(Cono Sur)*, the price of things is sky-high. **Pararle el caballo a uno**, *(Mex.)* to be stupid; **caballo bayo dorado**, bright bay horse. **Caballo moro**, piebald horse. **Caballo pardo**, gray horse. **Caballo desbocado**, runaway horse. **Caballo de buena boca**, *(Met.)* A person who accommodates himself readily to circumstances. **Caballo de palo**, 1. *(Coll.)* Any vessel fit for sea. 2. *(Vulg.)* Rack for criminals. 3. (Tannery) Tanner's beam. **Caballo marino**, 2. Pipefish, seahorse. 3. Figure on horseback, equivalent to the queen, at cards. 4. Trestle, bench on which planks or boards are laid for masons and plasterers to work on. 5. Knight in the game of chess. **A caballo**, on horseback. **Caballos**, horses, cavalry, mounted soldiers. 6. Bubo, tumor in the groin. *V.* POTRO. 7. Thread which ravels others. 8. Barren rook in a vein (mining). **Huir a uña de caballo**, to have a

hairbreadth escape; to extricate oneself from difficulty by prudence and energy. **Echarle a uno el caballo de cara**, *(Coll.)* to upbraid roughly. **A caballo regalado no le mires el diente**, you must not look a gift horse in the mouth. **Una dosis de caballo**, a huge dose, a massive dose. 9. *(Mech.)* **Caballo de vapor**, a dynamic unit which represents the force necessary to raise seventy-five kilograms one meter in one second. **Caballo de fuerza**, horsepower. **Un motor de 18 caballos**, an 18 horsepower engine. **Caballo de Troya**, *(Inform.)* "Trojan Horse".

caballón [cah-bal-lyone'], *m.* 1. *(aug.)* Large, clumsy horse. 2. Ridge of ploughed land between two furrows.

caballuelo [cah-bal-lyoo-ay'-lo], *m. dim.* Little horse.

caballuno, na [cah-bal-lyoo'-no, nah], *a.* Belonging to a horse.

cabanga [cah-bahn-gah], *f. (CAm.)* Homesickness (nostalgia). **Estar de nostalgia**, to be homesick.

cabaña [cah-bah'-nya], *f.* 1. Shepherd's hut, cottage, cot, cabin. **Cabaña de madera**, log cabin. 2. Hole, hovel, mean habitation. 3. Flock of ewes or breeding sheep. 4. Drove of asses for carrying grain. 5. *(Prov.)* Weekly allowance of bread, oil vinegar, and salt, for shepherds. 6. Balk, a line drawn on a billiard table, limiting the players. 7. Landscape representing a shepherd's cottage, with fowls, and other domestic animals. 8. Cabana.

cabañal [cah-bah-nyahl'], *a.* Applied to the road for flocks of traveling sheep and droves of cattle.

cabañería [cah-bah-nyay-ree´-ah], *f.* Rations for a week, of bread, oil, vinegar, and salt, allowed to shepherds.

cabañero, ra [cah-bah-nyay'-ro, rah], *a.* Belonging to the drove of mules and asses which go with a flock of traveling sheep. -*m.* Herdsman.

cabañil [cah-bah-nyeel'], *a.* Applied to the mules which go with the flocks of traveling sheep *m.* Herd or keeper of mules and asses, kept for carrying corn.

cabañuela [cah-bah-nyoo-ay'-lah], *f. dim.* Small hut or cottage.

cabañuelas [cah-bah-nyoo-ay'-lahs], *f. pl. (LAm.)* Weather predictions; *(And.)* First summer rains; *(Mex.)* First twelve days of January (used to predict the weather).

cabaré [cah-bah-ray'], *m.* Cabaret.

cabaret [cah-bah-ret'], *m.* Cabaret, night club, floor show. **Cabaret de desnudo**, nude show, striptease show, strip club.

cabaretera [cah-bah-ray-tay'-rah], *f.* Cabaret dancer, cabaret entertainer; night club hostess, showgirl.

cabas [cah'-bahs], *m.* Schoolbag, satchel.

cabaza [cab-bah´-thah], *f. (Obs.)* Large or wide cloak with hood and sleeves.

cabe [cah'-bay], *m.* 1. Stroke given by balls, in the game of *argolla*, whereby the player gains a point. **Dar un cabe al bolsillo, a la hacienda**, *etc.* *(Met.)* to give a shake to one's purse, to hurt one in his business, fortune, etc. **Dar un cabe a**, to harm. 2. Header.

cabeceada [cah-bay-thay-ah'-dah], *f. (LAm.)* Nod, shake of the head.

cabecear [cah-bay-thay-ar'], *vn.* 1. To nod with sleep, to hang the head on one side. 2. To shake the head in disapprobation (negando). 3. To raise or lower head (caballos). 4. To incline to one side, to hang over (peso, carga). 5. *(Naut.)* To pitch. 6. *(Aut.)* To lurch: used of carriages. -*va.* 1. In writing, to give letters the necessary thick stroke or loop. 2. Among bookbinders, to put the headband to a book. 3. To garnish cloth with edgings of tape or lace. 4. To cauterize a vein. 5. To head new wine, by adding some old wine to give it strength. 5. To head (balón).

cabeceo [cah-bay-thay´-o], *m.* 1. Nod of the head (negativa); toss of the head (de caballo). 2. *(Naut.)* Pitching; *(Aut.)* Lurch, lurching, shifting; slipping.

cabecequia [cah-bay-thay'-ke-ah], *m. (Prov.)* Inspector of sluices, guardian of watercourses.

cabecera [cah-bay-thay'-rah], *f.* 1. The beginning or principal part of something. 2. Head or headboard of a bed; also a railing at the head of a bed to prevent pillows from falling. 3. Seat of honor. 4. Headwaters, source of a river. **Cabecera (de río)**, headwaters. 5. Capital of a province, district, or nation. 6. A fortified point of a bridge. 7. Headpiece or vignette at the beginning of a chapter. 8. Each extremity of the back of a book. 9. A pillow or bolster of a bed. 10. The summit of a hill or ridge. 11. **Cabecera del cartel**, *(Theat.)* top of the bill. **Médico de cabecera**, family doctor.

cabecero [cah-bay-thay'-ro], *m.* 1. Lintel, the upper part of a doorframe. 2. *(Obs.)* Head of a branch of a noble family. 3. Compress.

cabeciancho, cha [cah-bay-the-ahn'-cho, chah], *a.* Broad or flat headed (clavos).

cabeciduro [cah-bay-the-doo'-ro], *a. (And. Cono Sur)* Stubborn, pigheaded.

cabecil [cah-bay-theel'], *m.* A pad of cloth which women place on their head for carrying a pail or anything heavy.

cabecilla [cah-bay-theel'-lyah], *m.* 1. Wrongheaded person, full of levity, indiscretion, and whims. 2. Leader of rebels. 3. Ringleader.

cabellazo [cah-bel-lyah'-tho], *m. aug.* Large bush of hair.

cabellera [cah-bel-lyay'-rah], *f.* 1. Long hair spead over shoulders; (**soltarse las melenas**), to act or speak in a forthright way. 2. False hair. 3. Tail of a comet. Any other body which presents a tuftlike appearance, as the branches of willows, etc.

cabello [cah-bayl'-lyo], *m.* Hair of the head. **Cabello de Venus**, *(Bot.)* maidenhair. **Estar pendiente de un cabello**, to hang by a thread. **Estar en cabello**, to have one´s hair down. *-pl.* 1. Large sinews in mutton. 2. Fibres of plants; the silk of corn. **Cabellos de ángel**, conserve of fruit cut into small threads. **Estar colgado de los cabellos**, to be in anxious expectation of the issue of a critical affair. **Tomar la ocasión por los cabellos**, to take time by the forelock, *(Met.)* o profit by the occasion. **Traer alguna cosa por los cabellos**, *(Met.)* to appropriate a phrase, an authority, or a quotation, to a thing which has no relation with it. **Arrancarse los cabellos**, to pull or tear one's hair. **Arrastrar a uno por los cabellos**, to drag one away by the hair.

cabelludo, da [cah-bel-lyoo'-do, dah], *a.* Hairy. **Cuero cabelludo**, scalp.

caber [cah-berr'], *vn.* 1. To be able or capable to contain, or to be contained; to fit. 2. To have room, place, or right of admission. **No cabe el libro**, the book won´t go in. **Caben 3 más**, there´s room for three more. **En este depósito caben 20 litros**, this tank holds 20 litres. **Eso no cabe por esta puerta**, that won´t go through this door. 3. To be entitled to a thing. 4. To fall to one's share. **No caber de gozo**, to be overjoyed. **No caber de pies**, to have no room to stand. **No caber en el mundo**, to be elated with excessive pride, to be puffed up with vanity. **No caber en sí,** to be full of one's own merits; to be very uneasy. **Todo cabe**, it is all possible; it may well be so. **No cabe más**, nothing more to be desired: applied to something that has arrived at its ultimate point. **No cabe en él hacerlo**, it is not in him to do it. **Todo cabe en ese chico**, that lad is capable of any mischief. *-va.* To contain, to comprise, to include.

cabero [cah-bay'-ro], *m. (Prov.)* Maker of handles for tools.

cabestraje [cah-bes-trah-hay], *m.* 1. Halter, and other headtackling for beasts. 2. Money paid to a driver for conducting cattle to market.

cabestrante [cah-bes-trahn'-tay], *m.* V CABRESTANTE.

cabestrar [cah-bes-trar'], *va.* To halter, to bind with a halter. *-vn.* To fowl with a stalking-ox.

cabestrear [cah-bay-thahl'], *vn.* To follow one willingly who leads by a halter or collar (animales).

cabestrería [cah-bes-tray-ree'-ah], *f.* Shop where halters and collars are made and sold.

cabestrero [cah-bes-tray'-ro], *m.* One who makes or retails halters and collars.

cabestrero, ra [cah-bes-tray'-ro, rah], *a. (Prov.)* Being so tame as to be led by a halter.

cabestrillo [cah-bes-treel'-lyo], *m.* 1. Sling suspended from the neck, in which a sore arm or hand is carried. Kind of hoop which keeps the cheeks of a saw tight. **Con el brazo en cabestrillo**, with one´s arm in a sling 3. Gold or silver chain. **Buey de** *cabestrillo*, stalking-ox.

cabestro [cah-bes'-tro], *m.* 1. Halter. 2. Bellox, a tame bullock that leads the rest of a drove of black cattle. **Traer a alguno de cabestro**, to lead one by the nose. 3. *(Obs.)* Chain. *V.* CABESTRILLO. 4. Cuckold (cornudo).

cabeza [cah-bay'-thah], *f.* 1. Head. 2. Part of the head which comprehends the cranium and forehead. **Cabeza de chorlito**, scatterbrain. 3. Head, the whole person, and more generally the person as exposed to any danger or penalty. 4. Head, chief, principal person; leader. 5. Head, understanding, faculties of the mind, judgment, talents. 6. Beginning of a thing, e. g. of a book. 7. End or extremity of a thing, e. g. of a beam or bridge. 8. Head, the top of many things, as the head of a nail, of a pin, etc. **Cabeza sonora**, recording head. 9. Head, the upper part of many things. 10. The principal town of a province, district, etc. 11. Head of cattle. **Cabeza menor**, head of sheep, goats etc. 12. *(Naut.)* Head of a ship. 13. Diameter of a column. 14. **Cabeza de autos** or **proceso**, head of a process. **Cabeza de ajos**, bulb of garlic. **Cabeza de moro**, moorshead. **Cabeza de turco**, scapegoat. **Cabeza de perro**, *V.* ANTIRRINO MAYOR and BECERRA. **Cabezas**, principal parts of a vessel, an equestrian game. **Cabeza torcida**, wrongheaded fellow. **Cabeza hueca**, addled head. **Cabeza redonda**, *(Met.)* blockhead. **Dar de cabeza**, to fall into misfortunes, to decline in one's fortune, power, or authority. **Hablar de cabeza**, to speak without ground or foundation. **Levantar** or **alzar cabeza**, to take courage, to retrieve one's health or fortune. **No levantar** or **no alzar cabeza**, to continue to be ill, or unfortunate in business. **Andar de cabeza**, to be snowed under. **Meterse de cabeza en algo**, to plunge into something. **Calentarse la cabeza**, to get tired out. **Se me fue la cabeza**, I felt giddy. **Está que no levanta cabeza**, she´s totally engrossed in her work. **Mover la cabeza afirmativamente**, to nod (one´s head). **Sentar la cabeza**, to settle down. **Volver la cabeza**, to look round. **No tener pies ni cabeza alguna cosa**, to not make sense. **Otorgar de cabeza**, to give a nod of approbation. **Perder la cabeza**, to lose one's senses, to be at a loss how to act. **Sacar de su cabeza alguna cosa**, to strike out a thing. **No tener a quien volver la cabeza**, to have neither money nor friends. **Ser** or **tener mala cabeza**, to be a man of bad principles; to be weakminded, without judgment or reflection. **Volvérsele la cabeza a alguno**, to lose one's senses. **De cabeza**, 1. From memory. 2. Headlong. **Caer con la cabeza abajo** or **caer de cabeza,** to fall headlong. **Pagar a tanto por cabeza**, to pay so much a piece or so much a head. *-m. & f.* Head; chief, leader (persona). **Cabeza de familia**, head of the household. **Cabeza de lista**, person at the head of the list.

cabezada [cah-bay-thah'-dah], *f.* 1. Headshake, stroke or butt given with the head, or received upon it. 2. Halter collar. 3. Headstall of a bridle. 4. Pitching of a ship. **Dar cabezadas**, to pitch. 5. Among bookbinders, headband of a book. 6. Instep of a boot. 7. The part of a piece of ground more elevated than the rest. 8. Nod, of one asleep with the head unsupported. **Dar cabezadas** to nod, to fall asleep. **Darse de cabezadas**, to screw one's wits in the investigation of a thing without success.

cabezal [cah-bay-thahl'], *m.* 1. Headpiece in a powdermill. 2. Small square pillow. 3. Compress of folded linen used by surgeons. 4. Long round bolster which crosses a bed. 5. Post of a door. **Cabezales de coche**, standards of the fore and hind parts of a coach, to which the braces are fastened. 6. Mattress or piece of cloth on which peasants sleep on benches or stones at the fire. 7. Title page of a book.

cabezazo [cah-bay-tha-tho], *m.* Butt; header.

cabezo [cah-bay'-tho], *m.* 1. Summit of a hill. 2. Shirt-collar.

cabezón [cah-bay-thone'], *m.* 1. Register of the taxes paid to government, and of the names of the contributors 2. Collar of a shirt. 3. Opening of a garment for the head to pass through. 4. Cavesson or noseband, used in breaking in a horse. **Llevar por los cabezones**, to drag along by the collar. **Entra por la manga, y sale por el cabezón**, applied to favorites who assume authority and dominion, and originating in the ancient ceremony of adoption, by passing the person through the wide sleeve of a shift.

cabezorro [cah-bay-thor'-ro], *m. aug. (Coll.)* Large disproportioned head.

cabezota [cah-bay-thoh'-tah], *m. aug.* 1. Bigheaded. 2. Clubheaded, having a thick head.

cabezudo [cah-bay-thoo'-do], *m. (Zool.)* Chub, mullet. *V.* MÚJOL. *(Acad.)*

cabezudo, da [cah-bay-thoo'-do, dah], *a.* 1. *(fig.)* Big head. 2. *(fig.)* pigheaded. 3. Heady (vino). 4. Headstrong, obstinate, morose, stubborn.

cabezuela [cah-bay-thoo-ay´-lah], *f.* 1. *(dim.)* Small head. 2. Blockhead, dolt, simpleton. 3. Coarse flour. 4. Rosebud, from which rosewater is distilled. 5. Little glass tube in a velvet loom. 6. *(Bot.)* Eryngo. 7. *(Bot.)* Ragwort-leaved centaury.

cabezuelo [cah-bay-thoo-ay'-lo], *m. dim.* Little head or top of something.

cabida [cah-bee'-dah], *f.* 1.Content, space, or capacity of something. *(Coll.)* **Eso no tiene cabida**, that cannot be permitted or allowed. **Dar cabida a**, to make room for. **Tener cabida**, to have room for. 2. *(fig.)* Tener cabida en uno, to have influence with somebody.

cabido [cah-bee'-do], *m.* Knight of the order of Malta, who has the right to claim a commandery. -**Cabido, da**, *pp.* of CABER.

cabildada [cah-beel-dah'-dah], *f. (Coll.)* Hasty, ill-grounded proceeding of a chapter or other body.

cabildeo [cah-beelday'o], *m.* Lobbying, intriguings.

cabildero, ra [cah-beel-day'-ro], *a. m. & f. (Obs.)* Belonging to a chapter. 2. Lobbyist; member of a pressure group.

cabildo [cah-beel'-do], *m.* 1. Chapter of a cathedral or collegiate church. 2. Meeting of a chapter, and the place where the meeting is held. 3. *(Prov.)* The corporation of a town.

cabilla [cah-beel'-lyah], *f. (Naut.)* 1. Dowell, round iron bar for securing the knees of a vessel. 2. Treenail, belaying-pin. 2. **Dar cabilla a**, to fuck, to screw.

cabillo [cah-beel´-lyo], *m.* 1. *(Bot.)* Flowerstalk. 2. *(dim.)* Small end of a rope.

cabimiento [cah-be-me-en'to], *m.* 1. Right of claiming a commandery in the order of Malta. 2. *V.* CABIDA.

cabina [cah-bee'-nah], *f.* 1. Cabin. 2. Cockpit (of a plane). 3. Booth, encasing. **Cabina a presión**, pressurized cabin. **Cabina cerrada transparente**, *(Aer.)* Canopy. **Cabina telefónica**, telephone booth. **Cabina del conductor**, driver´s cap.

cabinera [cah-bee-nay-rah], **f.** *(And.)* Air hostess, stewardess.

cabío [cah-bee'-o], *m.* 1. Lintel of a door. 2. A kind of rafter used in building.

cabito [cah-bee'-to], *m. dim.* The small end of a candle. *V.* CABO, CABILLO; *cabitos, pl.* Small lines, ends of lines.

cabizbajo, ja [cah-bith-bah'-ho, hah], *a.* 1. Down in the mouth, crestfallen. 2. Thoughtful, pensive, melancholy. 3. *(Bot.)* Drooping.

cabiztuerto, ta [cah-bith-too-er'-to, tah], *m. & f.* Hypocritical, sly.

cabla [cah-blah], *f. (LAm.)* Trick.

cable [cah'-blay], *m.* 1. Cable; rope, hawser. **Cable sencillo** or **de leva**, small bower cable. **Cable de alambre**, wire cable. **Cable submarino**, submarine cable. **Cable telegrafico**, telegraphic cable. **Echar un cable a uno**, to give somebody a helping hand. 2. Cable's length, a measure of 120 fathoms.

cablear [cah-blay-ar'], *va.* To cable.

cablegrafiar [cah-blay-grah-fee-ar'], *vn.* To cable.

cablegráfico, ca [cah-blay-grah'-fe-co, cah], *a.* By cable; **dirección cablegráfico**, cable address; **mensaje cablegráfico**, cable message.

cablegrama [cah-blay-grah-mah], *m.* A cablegram, message sent by cable. **cablero** [cah-blay'-ro], *m.* Cable ship (barco).

cablista [cah-blees'-tah], *a. (LAm.)* Sly, cunning.

cabo [cah'-bo], *m.* 1. Extreme, extremity; end of a thing; tip. 2. Cape, headland, or promontory, foreland. 3. Handle, haft, hold. 4. The extremity of a thing remaining after the principal part has been consumed or destroyed. **Cabo de vela**, candle-end. **Cabo suelto**, loose end. **No dejar ningún cabo suelto**, to leave no loose ends. 5. Lowest card in the game called *revesino*. 6. *(Prov.)* Paragraph, article, head. 7. Chief, head, commander. 8. *(Naut.)* Any of the cords employed on a ship. 9. Thread. 10. Complement, perfection, completion. 11. At the custom-house a parcel or package smaller than a bale. 12. Place, position, site. **13**. End; termination, conclusion (de periodo, proceso). **Al cabo de 3 meses**, at the end of 3 months. **Estar al cabo de la calle**, *(fig.)* to know what´s going on; **llevar a cabo**, to carry out, to execute. 14. *(Geog.)* Cape, point; **Cabo de Buena Esperanza**, cape of Good Hope. **Islas de Cabo Verde**, Cape Verde Island. *-pl.* 1. The tail and mane of horses. 2. Loose pieces of apparel, as stockings, shoes, hat, etc. 3. Divisions of a discourse. **Cabo de año**, the religious office performed on the anniversary of a person's death. **Cabo de barras, chiselled dollar of Mexico**. Last payment or balance of an account. **Cabo de escuadra**, corporal. **Cabo de presa**, prizemaster. **Coger todos los cabos**, *(Met.)* To weigh all the circumstances of a case. **Atar cabos**, to collect and examine together various circumstances bearing on a case. **Cabos blancos**, *(Naut.)* Untarred cordage. **Car cabo**, *(Naut.)* To throw out a rope for another to take hold of. **Al cabo**, at last. **De cabo a rabo**, from head to tail. **Estar al cabo de algún negocio**, to be thoroughly acquainted with the nature of an affair. **No tener cabo ni cuenta una cosa**, to have neither head nor tail (negocios). **Por ningún cabo**, by no means.

cabotaje [cah-bo-tah'-hay] *m. (Naut.)* 1. Coasting trade. 2. Pilotage.

cabra [cah'-brah], *f.* 1. Goat. Capra. 2. Engine formerly used to throw stones. 3. **Cabra montés**, wild goat. **Estar como una cabra**, to be crazy. **La cabra siempre tira al monte**, what is bred in the bone will come out in the flesh: a man's acts show what he is. 4. *(And. Carib.)* Trick, swindle (trampa), loaded dice (dado). 5. Light carriage (carro). 6. *(Cono Sur)* little girl. *-pl.* 1. Red marks on the legs caused by fire. 2. Small white clouds floating in the air. **Piel de cabra**, goatskin.

cabrahigal, cabrahigar [cah-bra-he-gahl', cah-bra-he-gar'], *m.* Grove or plantation of wild fig-trees.

cabrahigar [cah-brah-e-gar'], *va.* To improve a fig-tree; that is, to string up some male figs, and hang them on the branches of the female fig-tree, to make it produce better fruit.

cabrahigo [cah-brah-ee'-go], *m.* The male wild fig-tree, or its fruit which does not ripen.

cabreante [cag-bray-ahn'-tay], *a.* Infuriating.

cabrear [cah-bay-ar'], *va.* To infuriate, make livid. *-vr.* 1. To get furious, to get livid (enojarse). 2. To get suspicious. 3. *(Cono Sur)* to get bored.

cabreía [cah-bray-ee'-ah], *f.* Wooden machine for throwing stones.

cabreo [cab-bray´o], *m.* 1. *(Prov.)* Register, especially of the privileges and charters of cathedral churches. 2. Fury, anger; fit of bad temper. **Coger un cabreo**, to get angry.

cabrería [cah-bray-ree'-ah], *f.* 1. Herd of goats. 2. The place where goat's milk is sold.

cabreriza [cah-bray-ree'-thah], *f.* A hut for goatherds, goat shed.

cabrerizo [cah-bray-ree'-tho], *m. V.* CABRERO. *-a.* Goatish.

cabrero, ra [cah-bray'-ro, rah], *m. & f.* 1. Goatherd. 2. *(Cono Sur)* bad-tempered.

cabrestante [cah-bres-tahn'-tay], *m. (Naut.)* Capstan.

cabria [cah'-bre-ah], *f.* 1. Axle-tree. 2. *(Naut.)* Sheers, a machine used for setting up and taking out masts. 3. Crane, wheel and *(atr.)*winch, windlass, hoist.

cabrial [cah-bre-ahl'], *m. (Obs.)* Beam. *V.* VIGA.

cabrilla [cah-breel'-lyah], *f.* 1. *(dim.)* Little goat. 2. *(Zool.)* Prawn. *-pl.* 1. *(Astr.)* Pleiades, a constellation. 2. Stones thrown obliquely on the water, called duck and drake. 3. Marks on the legs, produced by being continually too near the fire. 4. *(Naut.)* White caps on the water.

cabrilleo [cah-breel-lyay'-o], *m.* The lapping of the waves when the sea is not high.

cabrillo [cah-breel'-lyo], *m.* Cheese from goat's milk.

cabrina [cah-bree'-nah], *f.* Goatskin.

cabrio [cah'-bree-o], *m.* Rafter, beam, or other timber, used in building.

cabrío [cah-bree'-o], *a.* Belonging to goats, goatish. **Ganado cabrío**, goats.

cabriol [cah-bree'-ol], *m.* Rafter. *V.* CABRÍO.

cabriola [cah-bre-oh'-lah], *f.* 1. Caper movement made in dancing, gamble; hop, skip, prance. **Hacer cabriolas**, to caper about. 2. Nimble leap, hop, or jump, gambol, skip. **Dar cabriolas**, to leap for joy. 3. *(Carib.)* Prank, piece of mischief.

cabriolar, cabriolear [cah-bre-o-lar', cah-bre-o-lay-ar'], *vn.* To caper or cut capers, to jump, to curvet, to frisk.

cabriolé [cah-bre-o-lay'], *m.* 1. Kind of cloak used by ladies. 2. Narrow riding-coat without sleeves. 3. **Cabriolet**, a kind of open carriage.

cabriolear [cah-bree-o-lay-ar'], *vn. V.* CABRIOLAR.

cabrión [cah-bre-on'], *m.* 1. Block or wedge for checking the wheel of a carriage. 2. *(Naut.)* Quoin, wedge for fastening the wheels of cannon to the decks in a gale.

cabrita [cah-bree'-tah], *f.* 1. *(dim.)* Little she-kid up to one year of age. 2. Kidskin dressed. 3. Ancient engine for cast stones.

cabritada [cah-bre-tah'-dah], *f.* Dirty trick.

cabritero [cah-bre-tay'-ro], *m.* 1. Dealer in kids. 2. One who dresses or sells kidskins.

cabritilla [cah-bre-teel'l-yah], *f.* A dressed lamb or kidskin.

cabritillo [cah-bre-teel'-lyo], *m. dim.* Kid.

cabrito [cah-bree'-to], *m.* 1. Kid, kidling, up to one year of age. 2. Cuckold (cornudo); client (de prostituta). 3. *(Cono Sur)* Popcorn.

cabro [cah'-bro], *m.* 1. *(LAm.)* *(Zool.)* He-goat, billy goat. 2. *(Cono Sur)* small child; boy; lover, sweetheart; guy (sujeto).

cabrón [cah-brone'], *m.* 1. Buck, he-goat. 2. One who consents to the adultery of his wife. 3. **El muy cabrón le robó el coche**, the bastard stole his car (insulto). 4. *(LAm.)* Brothel keeper; *(And. Cono Sur)* pimp; *(CAm. Cono Sur)* traitor.

cabronada [cah-bro-nah'-dah], *f.* 1. *(Low.)* Infamous action which a man permits against his own honor. 2. Dirty trick. **Hacer una cabronada a uno**, to play a dirty trick on somebody. 3. Tough job, (faena).

cabronazo [cah-bro-nah'-tho], *m. aug.* 1. One who prostitutes his own wife. 2. Rotter, villain.

cabroncillo, cito, zuelo [cah-bron-theel-yo, thee'-to, thoo-ay'-lo], *m.* 1. *(dim.)* Easy husband. 2. Fetid herb resembling the Celtic spikenard.

cabronismo [cah-bro-nees'-mo], *m.* Cuckoldism by consent; the state of a husband who consents to the adultery of his wife.

cabruno, na [cah-broo'-no, nah], *a.* Goatish; goatlike.

cabu [cah'-boo], *m. (Prov.)* Barren ground.

cabujón [cah-boo-hone'], *m.* Rough, unpolished ruby.

cabula [cah-boo-lah], *f.* 1. *(And. Cono Sur)* amulet (amuleto). 2. *(Cono Sur)* cabal, intrigue (intriga). 3. *(And. Carib. CAm.)* Trick, stratagem.

cabulear [cah-boo-lay-ar'], *vn. (And. CAm. Carib.)* To scheme (intrigar).

cabulero [cah-boo-lay'-ro], *(And. CAm. Carib.)* 1. *a.* Tricky, cunning, scheme. 2. *m.* Trickster, schemer.

cabuya [cah-boo'-yah], *f.* 1. *(Bot.)* Common American agave, a sort of sedge or grass, of which cords are made. 2. *(Prov.)* Cord or rope made of the aloes-plant. 3. Sisal hemp. **Dar cabuya**, to tie. **Ponerse en la abuya**, to grasp the trend of a topic. **Verse a uno las cabuyas**, to see what somebody is up to, to see through somebody's scheme.

cabuyero [cah-boo-yay'-ro], *m. (Amer.)* Ship chandler.

cabuyería [cah-boo-yay-ree'-ah], *f. (Amer.)* Ship chandlery.

caca [cah'-cah], *f.* 1. Excrements, cack, muck (excremento, suciedad). **Eso es una caca**, that's junk, trash. **Tira eso, es una caca**, throw that away, it's dirty.

cacaguatal [cah-cah-goo-ah-tahl'], *m. (CAm.)* Cocoa field.

cacahual, cacaotal [cah-cah-oo-ahl', cah-cah-oh-tahl'], *m.* Plantation of chocolate-trees.

cacahuate, cacahuete [cah-cah-oo-ah'-tay, cah-cah-oo-ay'-tay],*m. (Bot.) V.* MANÍ. The peanut, or earthnut; called also goober and pindar.

cacalote [cah-cah-lo'-tay], *m.* 1. A sweet paste made in Cuba from corn toasted without being ground. 2. *(Prov.)* A very absurd blunder.

cacao [cah-cah'-o], *m.* 1. *(Bot.)* Smooth-leaved chocolate nut-tree. 2. Cocoa, the fruit of the chocolate-tree. **Manteca de cacao**, cocoa-butter, or butter of cacao. 3. **Ser gran cacao**, to have influence. **Tener un cacao en la cabeza**, to be all mixed up. **No vale un cacao** *(LAm.)*, to be worthless, to be insignificant.

cacaotal [cah-caho-tahr'], *m.* A cacao orchard, cacao plantation.

cacaraña [cah-cah-rah'-nyah], *f.* Pit; the mark made by smallpox.

cacarañado, da [cah-cah-rah-nyah'-do, dah] *m. & f. & a.* Pitted by smallpox.

cacarañar [cah-cah-rah-nyar'], *va. (Mex.)* To scratch, to pinch; to pit, to scar, to pockmark.

cacareador, ra [cah-cah-ray-ah-dor', rah], *m. & f.* 1. Cackler. 2. Cock that crows, a hen that cackles. 3. Cackler, boaster, braggart.

cacarear [cah-cah-ray-ar'], *vn.* 1. To crow, to cackle. 2. To exaggerate one's own actions, to brag, to boast. **Ese triunfo tan cacareado**, that triumph that was so much talked of. 3. To humbug.

cacareo [cah-cah-ray'-o], *m.* 1. Crowing of a cock, cackling of a hen. 2. Boast, brag, humbug.

cacarico [cah-cah-ree'-co], *a. (CAm.)* Numb.

cacarizo [cah-cah-ree'-tho], *a. (Mex.)* Pitted, pockmarked.

cacaste [cah-cahs-tay], *m.* A box or crate to carry fruit.

cacastle [cah-cahs'-tlay], *m. (CAm. Mex.)* Skeleton; large wicker basket (canasta); wicker carrying frame (armazón).

cacatoes, or **cacatue** [cah-cah-to'es, or cah-cah-too'-ay], *m. (Zool.)* Cockatoo, a bird of the parrot family.

cacatúa [cah-cah-too'-ah], *f.* 1. Cockatoo. 2. Old bat, old cow (bruja).

cacaxtle [cah-cax'-tlay], *m. (CAm. Mex.)* Skeleton; frame.

cacera [cah-thay'-rah], *f.* 1. Canal, channel, or conduit of water, employed in watering lands. 2. Sort of pignuts.

cacería [cah-thay-ree'-ah], *f.* 1. Hunting or fowling party. **Cacería de brujas**, witch-hunt. **Cacería de zorros**, fox hunt. **Organizar una cacería**, to organize a hunt. 2. *(Art.)* Landscape representing field sports. 3. Bag, total of animals (animales cazados).

cacerilla [cah-thay-reel'-lyah], *f. dim.* Small drain or canal.

cacerina [cah-thay-ree'-nah], *f.* Cartridge-box or pouch for carrying powder and ball.

cacerola [cah-thay-ro'-lah], *f.* Stewpan, saucepan.

caceta [cah-thay'-tah], *f. dim.* Small pan used by apothecaries.

cacha [cah'-chah], *f.* 1. Handle of a razor. **Hasta las cachas**, full to the brim. 2. *(Prov.)* Tardiness, inactivity. 3. *(And.)* Horn. 4. *(And.)* metal spur attached to the leg of a fighting cock (de gallo). 5. *(And.)* Large chest (arca). 6. **Cachas**, bottom (culo); legs (piernas). 7. *(Mex.)* **Estar a medias cachas**, to be tipsy (locuciones); *(CAm.)* **Hacer cachas**, to try hard. 8. *(LAm.)* Cheek (cachete). 9. *(CAm.)* Crooked deal (negocio). 10. *(CAm.)* Opportunity.

cachaciento [cah-chah-the-ayn'-do], *a. (CAm. Cono Sur) V.* CACHAZUDO.

cachaco [cah-chah'-co], *m.* 1. *(And. Carib.)* Fop, dandy. 2. *(And.)* Copper (policía). 3. *(Carib.)* Busybody, noseyparker (entrometido).

cachada [cah-chah'-dah], *f.* 1. Stroke of one top against another, when boys play at tops. 2. *(LAm.) (Taur.)* Butt, thrust; goring. 3. *(Cono Sur)* Joke, leg-pull.

cachador [cah-chah-dor'], *(Cono Sur)* 1. *a.* Fond of practical jokes. 2. *m.* Practical joker.

cachafaz [cah-cha-fath'], *a. (LAm.)* Rascally (pillo); crafty (taimado); cheeky (fresco).

cachalote [cah-chah-loh'-tay], *m.* The sperm whale. *V.* MARSOPLA.

cachancha [cah-chan'-cha], *f. (Carib.)* Patience. **Estar de cachancha con uno,** to grease up to somebody.

cachaña [cah-cha'-nya], *f. (Cono Sur)* 1. Small parrot. 2. Hoax, leg-pull (broma). 3. Arrogance (arrogancia). 4. Stupidity (estupidez). 5. Rush, scramble (arrebatiña).

cachañar [cah-cha-nyar'], *va. (Cono Sur) V.* CACHAR. **Cachañar a uno,** to pull somebody's leg.

cachapa [cah-chah'-pa], *f.* Cornbread with sugar, used in Venezuela.

cachar [cah-char'], *va.* 1. *(Prov.)* To break in pieces. 2. To divide a plank in two lengthwise by a saw or axe. 3. *(And. CAm.)* To butt, gore. 4. *(And. CAm. Cono Sur)* to scoff at, deride, ridicule (ridiculizar). 5. *(And. Cono Sur)* To screw. 6. *(Mex.)* To search (registrar).

cachar [cah-char'], *va.* 1. *(Cono Sur)* to catch (autobús). 2. *(CAm.)* To get, obtain (obtener); *(CAm. Cono Sur)* to steal (robar). 3. *(Cono Sur, Mex.)* To surprise, to catch in the act. 4. *(Cono Sur)* To penetrate. 5. *(And. CAm. Carib.)* To catch (pelota).

cacharado [cah-chah-rah'-do], *m.* Kind of linen.

cacharpas [cah-char'-pas], *f. pl. (LAm.)* Useless objects, lumber, junk; odds and ends.

cacharpaya [cah-char-pah'-ya], *f. (And. Cono Sur)* sendoff, farewell party; *(Cono Sur)* farewell; minor festivity.

cacharpearse [cah-chahr-pay-ar'-say], *vr. (LAm.)* To dress up.

cacharra [cah-chahr'-rah], *f.* Rod, pistol.

cacharrear [cah-chahr-ray-ar'], *va. (Cam, Carib.)* To throw into jail.

cacharrería [cah-chahr-ray-ree'-ah], *f.* 1. Crockery shop. 2. Crockery pots (cacharros). 3. *(And.)* Ironmongery.

cacharro [cah-char'-ro], *m.* 1. Coarse earthen pot; also a piece of it. 2. *(Met.)* Any useless, worthless thing. 3. Piece of pottery, postsherd. 4. *(CAm. Carib.)* Jail (cárcel). 5. Rod, pistol.

cachas [cáh-chas], *a.* **Estar cachas,** to be tough, to be well set-up. **Está cachas,** he's buff.

cachativa [cah-chah-tee-vah], *f.* **Tener cachativa** *(Cono Sur)*, to be quick on the uptake.

cachaza [cah-chah'-thah], *f. (Con.)* 1. Inactivity, tardiness: forbearance. 2. *(Amer.)* Rum. 3. First froth on canejuice when boiled to make sugar.

cachazo [cah-chah-tho], *m. (LAm.)* Butt, thrust (golpe); goring (herida).

cachazudamente, [cah-chah-thoo-dah-mayn'-tay] *adv.* Calmly

cachazudo, da [cah-chah-thoo'-do, dah], *a.* Cool, calm, phlegmatic, tranquil.

caché [cah-chay'], *m.* Cachet.

cachear [cah-chay-ar'], *va.* 1. *(LAm.) (Taur.)* To butt, gore. 2. *(LAm.)* To punch, slap. 3. To frisk (registrar), search (for weapons).

cachejo [cah-chay-ho], *m. (Esp.)* **Un cachejo de pan,** a little bit of bread.

cachemarín [cah-chay'-mah-reen'], *m.* A small two-masted craft used in Brittany and on the northern Spanish coast.

cachemir [cah-chay-meer'], *m.* Cashmere, a fine, soft, costly fabric.

cachemira [cah-che-mee'-rah], *f. V.* CACHEMIR.

cacheo [cah-chay-o], *m.* Searching, frisking (for weapons).

cachera [cah-chay'-rah], *f.* Coarse shagged cloth or baize.

cachería [cah-chay-ree-ah], *f.* 1. *(And. CAm.)* Small business, sideline. 2. *(Cono Sur)* bad taste; slovenliness (desaseo).

cachero [cah-chay'-ro], *a.* 1. *(CAm. Carib.)* Lying, deceitful. 2. *(CAm.)* Hard-working (trabajador). *-m. (LAm.)* Sodomite.

cachet [cah-chayt'], *m.* 1. Cachet (sello distintivo); character, temperament. 2. Appearance money, fee (de artista).

cachetada [cah-chay-tah'-dah], *f. (LAm.)* Slap, box on the ear; beating (paliza).

cachetas [cah-chay'-tas], *f. pl.* Teeth or wards in a lock.

cachetazo [cah-chay-tah'-tho], *m.* 1. *(LAm.)* Slap, punch (bofetada); *(fig.)* Snub. 2. *(LAm.)* Swig, slug (trago). 3. **¡Hazme un cachetazo!** *(CAm. Carib.)* Do me a favor.

cachete [cah-chay'-tay], *m.* 1. Cheek. 2. Fist, a blow given with the hand clenched. 3. A cuff on the ear. **Cachetes de un navío,** *(Naut.)* Bow of a ship.

cacheteada [cah-chay-tay-ah'-dah], *f. (Cono Sur)* Slap, box on the ear.

cachetear [cah-chay-tay-ar'], 1. *vr. (And. Cono Sur)* To slap on the face. 2. *vn. (Cono Sur)* to eat well.

cachetero [cah-chay-tay'-ro], *m.* Short and broad knife.

cachetina [cah-chay-tee'-nah], *f.* A hand to hand fight.

cachetón, ona [cah-chay-tone', nah], *a.* 1. Fatcheeked. 2. *(Mex.)* Impudent, barefaced (descarado); *(Cono Sur)* proud, haughty (orgulloso). 3. *(CAm.)* Attractive, congenial (atractivo).

cachetudo, da [cah-chay-too'-do, dah], *a.* Plumpcheeked, fleshy.

cachicamo [cah-che-cah'-mo], *m.* An armadillo. South American name.

cachicán [cah-che-cahn'], *m.* Overseer of a farm.

cachicuerno, na [cah-che-coo-er'-no, nah], *a.* Having a handle or haft of horn.

cachidiablo [cah-che-de-ah'-blo], *m.* 1. Hobgoblin. 2. Disguised in a devil's mask. 3. Having an odd and extravagant appearance

cachifa [cah-che'-fah], *f. (CAm. Carib.)* Girl, kid.

cachifo [cah-che'-fo], *m. (And. CAm. Carib.)* Lad, kid; young boy.

cachifollar [cah-che-fol-lyar'], *va.* 1. To puff or blow with the cheeks. 2. *(Prov.)* To play a trick.

cachigordete, eta, ito, ita [cah-che-gor-day'-tay, tah, dee'-to, tah], *a.* Squat, thick, and plump.

cachilla [cah-cheel'-lyah], *f. (Cono Sur)* jalop(p)y, old banger.

cachillada [cah-cheel-lyah'-dah], *f. (Coll.)* Litter, young brought forth by an animal.

cachimba [cah-cheem'-bah], *f.* 1. *(Cuba)* A smoking-pipe. 2. *(LAm.)* Empty cartridge (cartucho). 3. *(Carib.)* Tart, slut (puta). 4. **Fregar la cachimba,** to get on somebody's nerves. *-a.* Fantastic, terrific.

cachimbazo [cah-cheem-bah'-tho], *m. (CAm.)* 1. Thump, blow (golpe). 2. Shot, slug (trago).

cachimbo [cah-cheem'-bo], *m.* 1. A ladle with a long handle. (para hacer azúcar) 2. *(LAm.)* Pipe. 3. *(Carib.)* Small sugar mill. 3. *(Carib.)* Poor man (pobre). 4. Freshman. 4. *(CAm.)* Pile, heap (montón). 5. *(And.)* Soldier, squaddy.

cachimbón [cah-cheem-bon'], *a. (CAm.)* Smart, sharp.

cachipolla [cah-che-pol'-lyah], *f.* Dayfly, or mayfly: of very brief life, hence the name. One of the Ephemerids.

cachiporra, *f.* **cachiporro,** *m.* [cah-che-por'-rah]. 1. A stick with a big knob used by country people; a cudgel. 2. A fruiteating bat. 3. An Indian club.

cachiporra [cah-che-por'-rah], *int.* A vulgar exclamation. *-f.* Truncheon; club, big stick, cosh. 2. *(Cono Sur)* braggart.

cachiporrazo [cah-chee-por-rah'-tho], *m.* Blow with a truncheon (etc.).

cachiporrear [cah-chee-por-ray-ar'], 1. *va.* (*Mus.*) To bash, pound. 2. *vr.* (*Cono Sur*) to brag, boast.

cachiporro [cah-che-por'-roh], *m.* (*Prov. Coll.*) Chubface.

cachirulo [cah-che-roo´-lo], *m.* 1. Earthen, glass, or tin pot for preserving brandy or other liquors. 2. Bow or rosette worn on the head by women toward the end of the 18th century. 3. (*Mex.*) Lining of cloth or chamois placed in the seat and legs of trousers for riding.

cachirulo [cah-che-roo'-lo], *m.* Small three-masted vessel.

cachito [cah-chee'-to], *m.* 1. (*And.*) Dice game; dice cup (cubito). 2. (*LAm.*) **Espera un cachito,** just a minute, hang on.

cachivache [cah-che-vah'-chay], *m.* 1. Broken crockery, or other old trumpery, laid up in a corner. 2. (*Met.*) A despicable, useless, worthless fellow. 3. **Cachivaches,** pots, pants, kitchen utensils.

cacho [cah'-cho], *m.* 1. Slice, piece (fruta, pan). 2. Small horn. 3. Game of chance at cards. 4. (*Zool.*) Red surmullet. 5. (*And. Cono Sur*) dice, set of dice (dados); **Jugar al cacho,** to play dice. 6. (*Cono Sur*) Bunch of bananas (plátanos). 7. (*Cono Sur*) unsaleable goods. 8. (*LAm.*) Funny story, joke (chiste); prank (broma), practical joke. 9. (*Carib.*) Joint (marijuana). 10. (*Carib.*) Prick (pene) 11. **Echar cacho a uno** (*And.*), to do better than someone. **Estar fuera de cacho,** to be safe. **Raspar el cacho a uno** (*Cono Sur*), to tell somebody off.

cacho, cha [cah'-cho, chah], *a.* Bent, crooked, inflected. *V.* GACHO.

cachó [cah-cho'], *m.* Chub (pez de río); surmullet (de mar).

cacholas [cah-cho'-las], *f. pl.* (*Naut.*) Cheeks of the masts.

cachón [cah'-chone], *m.* 1. A breaker, wave. *V.* CACHONES. 2. A fall of water.

cachondear [cah-chon-day-ar'], (*CAm. Mex.*) 1. *vn.* To pet (acariciar); to snog (besarse). 2. *vr.* To take things as a joke. **Cachondearse de uno,** to take the mickey out of somebody; to make fun of somebody; (*LAm.*) To get turned on (calentarse sexualmente).

cachondeo [cah-chon-day'-o], *m.* 1. Joking; teasing; nagging; messing about (guasa). **Estar de guasa,** to be in a joking mood. **Tomar algo a cachondeo,** to take something as a joke, to live it up, have a good time. 2. Trouble, disturbance (jaleo). Farce, mess (farsa); poor show. **¡Esto es un cachondeo!,** what a mess!

cachondez [cah-chon-deth'], *f.* 1. (*Coll.*) Sexual appetite. 2. Heat, rut, readiness to mate.

cachondo, da [cah-chone'-do, dah], *a.* Ruled by sexual appetite; in heat (hembra). **Cachondas,** Slashed trousers formerly worn. **Estar cachondo,** to feel randy, be in the mood. **Cachondo mental,** crazy but likable.

cachones [cah-cho'-nes], *m. pl.* Breakers, waves broken by the shore, rocks, or sandbanks.

cachopo [cah-cho'-po], *m.* 1. (*Naut.*) Gulf of the sea between rocks. 2. (*Prov.*) Dry trunk or stump of a tree.

cachorrenas [cah-chor-ray'-nas], *f. pl.* (*Prov.*) Sort of soap, made of oil, orange, bread, and salt.

cachorrillo, ito [cah-chor-reel'-lyo, ree'-to], *m. dim.* 1. A little cub or whelp. 2. A young man (despectivo). 3. A little pistol.

cachorro, ra [cah-chor'-ro, rah], *m. & f.* 1. Grown whelp or puppy. 2. Cub, the young of a beast. 3. Pocket pistol. 4. A lizard.

cachucha [cah-choo'-chah], *f.* 1. A wellknown Spanish dance in triple measure. 2. Man´s cloth or fur cap. 3. A little boat used in rivers and ports of America. 4. (*And.*) Nick, prison.

cachucho [cah-choo'-cho], *m.* 1. Oil measure, containing the sixth part of a pound. 2. (*Obs.*) Cartridge. 3. (*Prov.*) Clumsy earthen pot. 4. Place for each arrow in a quiver. 5. Sea bream (pez). 6. Pin box (alfiletero). 7. (*And.*) Daily bread. **Ganarse el cachucho,** to make a living.

cachudo [cah-choo'-do], *a.* 1. (*And. Mex.*) Horned, with horns (con cuernos). 2. (*And.*) Wealthy (rico). 3. (*Cono Sur*) Suspicious, distrustful (receloso); cunning (taimado). 4.

(*Mex.*) Long-faced, miserable (triste). *-m.* **El cachudo, the devil,** the horned one.

cachuela [cah-choo-ay'-lah], *f.* 1. Fricassee made of the livers and lights of rabbits. 2. (*And.*) Rapids (remolinos).

cachuelo [cah-choo-ay'-lo], *m.* (*Zool.*) Small river fish resembling an anchovy.

cachulera [cah-choo-lay'-rah], *f.* (*Prov.*). Cavern or hiding place.

cachumbo [cah-choom'bo], *m.* Kind of hard cocoa-wood.

cachunde [cah-choon'-day], *f.* Paste made of musk and other aromatics, which the Chinese carry in their mouth to strengthen the stomach.

cachupín [cah-choo-peen'], *m.* A Spaniard who settles in Mexico or South America. *V.* GACHUPÍN. (*Port. cachopo,* child.).

cachureo [cah-choor-ray'-o], *m.* (*Cono Sur*) Bric-à-brac.

cachuzo [cah-choo'-do], *a.* (*Cono Sur*) Worn-out, old.

cacicada [cah-the-cah'-dah], *f.* Despotic act, high-handed; abuse of authority.

cacicazgo [cah-the-cath'-go]' *m.* The dignity of a chief or cacique and his territory.

cacillo, ito [cah-theel'-lyo, ee'-to], *m. dim.* Small saucepan.

cacimba [cah-theem-bah], *f.* 1. (*And. Carib. Cono Sur*) Well (pozo); (*Carib.*) Hollow of tree where rainwater is collected; (*And.*) Outdoor privy. 2. (*Carib. Mex.*) Hovel, slum (casucha).

cacique [cah-thee'-kay], *m.* 1. Cacique, a prince or nobleman among the Indians 2. Any leading inhabitant of a small town or village, party boss, local boss; (*fig.*) Petty tyrant, despot; (*Cono Sur*) person who lives idly in luxury (vago). 2. (*And. CAm. Mex.*) Oriole (ave).

caciquismo [cah-the-kees'-mo], *m.* (*Pol.*) (system of) dominance by the local boss; petty tyranny, despotism.

cacle [cah'-clay], *m.* (*Mex.*) A kind of sandals worn by friars, indians, and soldiers.

caco [cah'-co], *m.* 1. Pickpocket, burglar. 2. A coward.

cacófago, ga [cah-co'-fah-go, gah], *a.* Cacophagous, having a depraved appetite.

cacofonía [cah-co-fo-nee'-ah], *f.* Cacophony, a harsh or unharmonious sound.

cacofónico [cah-co'-fo-no], *a.* Cacophonous.

cacografía [cah-co-grah-fee'-ah], *f.* Bad spelling.

cacomite [cah-co-mee'-tay], *m.* A Mexican plant which produces handsome flowers.

cacoquimia [cah-co-kee'-meah], *f.* Abnormal metabolism.

cacoquímico, ca [cah-co-kee'-me-co. cah], *a.* Suffering from or related to abnormal metabolism.

cacoquimio [cah-co-kee'-me-o], *m.* Suffering from melancholy.

cácteo, ea [cahc'-tay-o, ah], *a.* Cactaceous, relating to cacti

cacto [cahc'-to], *m.* The cactus.

cacumen [cah-coo'-men], *m.* 1. The top, the height. 2. Insight, understanding; comprehension.

cada [cah'-dah], *pron.* Every, everyone, each. **Cada uno** or **cada cual,** every one, each. **Cada vez,** every time. **Cada día,** every day. **A cada palabra,** at every word. **Dar a cada uno,** to give to every one. **Cada vez que,** every time that. **Cada y cuando,** whenever, as soon as. **Cada cierto tiempo,** every so often.

cadalso [cah-dahl'-so], *m.* 1. Scaffold raised for the execution of malefactors. 2. Temporary gallery or stage, erected for shows or spectators. 3. Fortification or bulwark made of wood.

cadañal, cadañego, ga, cadañero, ra [cah-dah-nyahl', cah-dah-nyay'-go, gah, cah-dah-nyay'-ro, rah], *a.* Annual. **Mujer cadañera,** a woman who bears every year.

cadarzo [cah-dar'-tho], *m.* Coarse, entangled silk, which cannot be spun with a wheel

cadáver [cah-dah'-ver], *m.* Corpse, corse, cadaver. **Cadáver en el armario,** (*fig.*) skeleton in the cupboard. **¡Sobre mi cadáver!,** over my dead body! **Ingresó cadáver,** he was dead on arrival (at the hospital).

cadavérico, ca [cah-dah-vay'-re-co, cah], *a.* Cadaverous; death-like; ghastly, deathly.

caddie [cah'-dee], *n.* (Golf) caddle.

cadejo [cah-day'-ho], *m.* 1. Entangled skin of thread. 2. Entangled hair. 3. Threads put together to make tassels.

cadena [cah-day'-nah], *f.* 1. Chain. **Cadenas antideslizantes**, tire chains. 2. *(Met.)* Tie caused by passion or obligation. 3. Mortice, a hole cut into wood. 4. *(Met.)* Series of events. 5. Chain, link, any series linked together. 6. Number of malefactors chained together to be conducted to the galleys: punishment next after the death penalty. **Cadena perpetua**, life imprisonment. 7. Bar of iron with which a way is strengthened. 8. Frame of wood put round the hearth of a kitchen. 9. Treadle of a ribbon, weaver's loom. 10. Turning handle which moves a wheel. 11. **Cadena alimenticia**, food chain. **Cadena de hoteles**, chain of hotels. **Reacción en cadena**, chain reaction. 12. *(Jur.)* Chain-gang.

cadencia [cah-den'-the-ah], *f.* 1. Cadence, fall of the voice. 2. Cadence, number, measure, flow of verses or periods. 3. In dancing, the correspondence of the motion of the body with the music. **Hablar en cadencia**, to affect the harmonious flow of rhythm when speaking in prose.

cadencioso, sa [cah-den-the-o'-so, sah], *a.* Belonging to a cadence, numerous.

cadeneta [cah-day-nay'-tah], *f.* 1. Lace or needlework wrought in form of a chain; chain-stitch. 2. Work put upon the heads of books for security of the sewing.

cadenilla, ita [cah-day-neel'-lyah, ee'-tah], *f. dim.* Small chain. **Cadenilla y media cadenilla**, pearls distinguished by their size.

cadente [cah-den'-tay], *a.* 1. Decaying, declining, going to ruin. 2. Having a correct modulation in delivering prose or verse.

cadera [cah-day'-rah], *f.* Hip, the joint of the thigh.

caderamen [cah-day-rah'-men], *m.* Hips (de mujer).

cadereta [cah-day-ray'-tah], *f. (Mus.)* A kind of small organ, manipulated by a second keyboard, that imitates the great organ which contains it; echo organ.

caderillas [cah-day-reel'-lyas], *f. pl.* 1. Hoops worn by ladies to distend the skirts over the hips. 2. Bustle.

cadetada [cah-day-tah'-dah], *f.* Thoughtless action, irresponsible act.

cadete [cah-day'-tay], *m.* 1. Cadet, a volunteer in the army who serves in expectation of a commission. 2. A young man in a military school.

cadí [cah-dee'], *m.* Cadi, a magistrate among the Turks and Moors.

cadí [cah-dee'], *m.* (Golf) Caddie.

cadillar [cah-deel-lyar'], *m.* Place abounding with bur-parsley.

cadillero, ra [cah-dee-lyay'-ro, rah], *a. (Bot.)* Applied to plants bearing fruit covered with hooked bristles or prickles.

cadillo [cah-deel'-lyo], *m. (Bot.)* Bur-parsley.

cadmía [cad-mee'-ah], *f.* Calamine. *V.* CALAMINA. Tutty, impure oxide of zinc, collected from a furnace or a crucible.

cadmio [cahd'-me-o], *m.* Cadmium, a metal, in color like tin, associated with zinc.

cado [cah'-do], *m. (Prov.)* Ferret-hole. *V.* HURONERA.

cadoce [cah-do'-thay], *m. (Zool. Prov.)* Gudgeon.

caducamente [cah-doo-cah-men'-tey], *adv.* In a weak, doting manner.

caducante [cah-doo-cahn'-tay], *pa.* Doting, one who dotes.

caducar [cah-doo-car'], *vn.* 1. To dote, to have the intellect impaired by age. 2. To be worn out by service, to fall into disuse, to become superannuated. **El abono ha caducado**, the season ticket has expired. 3. To deteriorate.

caduceo [cah-doo-thay'-o], *m.* 1. Caduceus or caduce, the wand with which Mercury is depicted. 2. Herald's staff among the ancient Greeks.

caducidad [cah-doo-the-dahd'], *f. (Law.)* Caducity, decrepitude, the state or quality of being worn out by age or labor; lapsed, expiry. **Fecha de caducidad** (alimentos), sell-by date.

caduco, ca [cab-doo'-co, cah], *a.* 1. Worn out or broken with fatigue, senile, enfeebled by age, decrepit. 2. Perishable, frail. *3. (Bot.)* Deciduous. 4. Fleeting, perishable. 5. *(Com. Jur.)* Lapsed, expired, invalid. **Quedar caduco**, to lapse.

caduquez [cah-doo-keth'], *f.* Caducity, senility, last stage of life.

C.A.E., Abbreviation of **Cóbrese al entregar**, C.O.D., cash on delivery.

caedizo, za [cah-ay-dee'-tho, thah], *a.* 1. Ready to fall, being of short duration, or little consistence. **Hacer caediza una cosa**, to let a thing fall on purpose. **Peras caedizas**, pears dropping from the tree. 2. *(Bot.)* Deciduous.

caedura [cah ay doo'-rah], *f.* Among weavers, the loose threads dropping from the loom when weaving.

caer [cah-err'], *vn.* 1. To fall to the ground, to tumble down: to lighten. **El edificio se está cayendo**, the building is falling down. **Cayó un rayo en la torre**, the tower was struck by lighting. 2. To lose one's situation, fortune, or influence. 3. To fall into an error or danger. 4. *(Met.)* To deviate from the right road, or to take the wrong one. 5. *(Met.)* To fall due: as instalments or payments of debts. 6. To fall, to decrease, to decline, to come into any state of weakness, misery, etc. 7. To fall to one's lot. 8. To fall, to befall, to happen to, to come to pass. 9. To die. 10. *(Mil.)* To fall, to yield, to surrender. 11. To decline, to approach the end. **La luz cae**, the light declines. **El día cae**, the day is drawing to a close. 12. To be situated. **Caer a esta parte**, to be situated on this side. **Las ventanas caen al río**, the windows overlook the river; **caer a la mar**, *(Naut.)* To fall overboard. **Caer de espaldas**, to fall backward. **Caer en la cuenta**, to bethink oneself, to see the point, to correct one's habits. **No caer en las cosas**, not to comprehend a thing. **Caerse de sueño**, to fall asleep. **Caer bien alguna cosa**, to fit, to suit, to become. **Este color cae bien con este otro**, this color is well matched with the other. **Caer en cama**, to become sick. **Caer en alguna cosa**, to remember or obtain knowledge of a thing. **Caer en gracia**, to please, to be agreeable. **Caer la balanza**, to be partial. **Caerse a pedazos**, to be very fatigued, or very foolish. **Caerse de ánimo**, to be dejected. **Caerse de risa**, to shake with laughter. **Al caer de la hoja**, at the fall of the leaf, about the end of fall. **Dejar caer alguna cosa en la conversación**, to drop something, in the course of conversation. **Caer en ello**, to understand or comprehend a thing. **Estar a la que cae**, to be alert. **Ya caigo en ello**, now I have it. **Estar al caer**, to be arriving. **Caérsele a uno la cara de vergüenza**, to blush deeply with shame. 13. To fall, to lie, to be located. **Cae en el segundo tomo**, it comes in the second volume. 14. *(Com. fin.)* To fall due. 15. **Caer a** (herencia), to fall to, to come to. 15. **No me cae bien** (impresión), I don´t like him at all. 16. **Caer mal a** (comida), to disagree with. 17. *(Cono Sur)* To come by, to visit, to drop in. **Suele caer por aquí**, he often comes here.

caerse [cah-er'-say], *vr.* 1. All the meanings of the active form. 2. To be, afflicted, to be overwhelmed, to be disconsolate. **Dejarse caer**, to allow oneself to be down-hearted. **Caerse de su peso**, to be very true, or manifest.

cafa [cah'-fah], *f.* Cotton stuff of various colors and kinds.

café [cah-fay'], *m.* 1. Coffee tree. 2. Coffee, beverage prepared from the coffee bean. **Café americano**, large black coffee. **Café cortado**, coffee with a dash of milk. **Café soluble**, instant coffee. **Café molido**, ground coffee. **Café tostado**, roasted coffee. 3. **Estar de mal café**, to be in a bad mood.

café, *m.* Cafe, restaurant, coffee-house.

cafecito [cah-fay-thee'-to], *m.* (LAm.) Black coffee.

cafeína [cah-fay-ee'-nah], *f.* Caffein, an alkaloid extracted from coffee.

cafetal [cah-fay-tahl'], *m*. Plantation of coffee-trees.

cafetalero [cah-fay-tah-lay'-ro], *(LAm.)* 1. *a*. Coffee, coffee-growing. **Industria cafetalera**, coffee-growing industry. 2. *m*. **Cafetalera** *f*. Coffee grower.

cafetalista [cah-fay-tah-lees'-tah], *m. & f. (LAm.)* Coffee grower.

cafetán, caftán [cah-fay-tahn'], *m*. Caftan, embroidered garment worn by the chief Turkish or Persian officers.

cafetear [cah-fay-tay-ar'], *va. (Cono Sur)* to tick off, to tell off.

cafetera [cah-fay-tay'-rah], *f*. 1. Coffee-pot. **Cafetera automática**, electric ketle. **Cafetera filtradora**, percolator. 2. *(Aut.)* Old car, old crock. 3. Coffee-service.

cafetería [cah-fay-tay-ree'-ah], *f*. 1. Café, coffee-house. 2. Buffet, refreshment room (ferrocarril); *(And. Carib, Cono Sur)* coffee retailer.

cafetero [cah-fay-tay'-ro], *m*. 1. One who makes or sells coffee. 2. *(Bot.)* Coffee-tree. **Cafetero árabe**, Arabian coffee-tree. **Cafetero occidental** or **americano**, Jamaica or western coffee-tree.

cafetín [cah-fay-teen'], *m*. Low-class bar, small café.

cafeto [cah-fay-to], *m*. The coffee-tree.

cafetucho [cah-fay-too'-cho], *m*. Seedy little café.

caficultor [cah-fee-cool-tor'], *m. & f. (CAm.)* Coffee grower.

caficultura [cah-fee-cool-too'-rah], *f. (CAm.)* Coffee growing.

cafiche [cah-fee'-chay], *m*. Pimp.

cafila [cah'-fe-lah], *m*. 1. Multitude of people, animals, or other things. 2. Caravan. 3. Single file, one after another.

cafiolo [cah-fee-o'-lo], *m. (Cono Sur)* Pimp, ponce.

cafishear [cah-fee-shay-ar'], *vn. (Cono Sur)* to live off somebody else.

cafisho [cah-fee'-sho], *m. (Cono Sur)* Pimp, ponce.

cafre [cah'-fray], *a*. 1. Savage, inhuman. 2. Belonging or relating to the Caffres. 3. *(Prov.)* Clownish, rude, uncivil.

caftán [caf-tahn'], *m*. Caftan, kaftan.

cafúa [cah-foo-ah], *f. (Arg. Coll.)* Jail, arrest. **Ir a la cafúa**, to go to jail, to be arrested.

cagada [cah-gah'-dah], *f. (Coll.)* 1. Excrement. 2. Ridiculous action; unfortunate issue.

cagadero [cah-gah-day'-ro], *m*. Latrine.

cagadillo [cah-gah-deel'-lyo], *m. dim. (Low.)* A sorry little fellow.

cagado [cab-gah'-do], *a. (Low.)* A mean-spirited, chicken-hearted fellow, yellow, funky. *pp.* of CAGAR.

cagafierro [cah-gah-fe-er'-ro], *m*. Scoria, dross of iron.

cagajón [cah-gah-hone'], *m*. 1. Horsedung. 2. The dung of mules or asses.

cagalar [cah-gah-lar'], *m. V.* TRIPA. *(Anat.)* Caecum.

cagalera [cah-gah-lay-rah], *f*. Looseness of the body, diarrhoea.

cagamelos [cah-gah-may´-los], *m*. Kind of mushroom.

cagar [cah-gar'], *va*. 1. To defecate. 2. *(Low.)* To soil, stain, or defile a thing. 3. To shit, to crap. 4. To dirty, to soil (ropa). 5. *(fig.)* To cock up, to fuck up. **¡La cagamos!**, we blew it! - *vn.* To shift, to have a shift. -*vr.* **¡Me cago en la mar!**, well, I´m damned!, **¡me cago en el gobierno!**, to hell with the government! ...**y se caga la perra**... *(Esp.)*, and you never saw anything like it.

cagarrache [cah-gar-rah'-chay], *m*. 1. One who washes the olives in an oilmill. 2. Bird of the family of starlings.

cagarria [cah-gar'-re-ah], *f*. Kind of mushroom, called St. George's agaric.

cagarruta [cah-gar-roo'-tah], *f*. Dung of sheep, goats, and mice.

cagatinta [cah-gah-teen'-tah], *m*. 1. Pettifogger. 2. A nickname given in contempt to attorneys' clerks. 3. *(And.)* Miser.

cagón, na [cah-gone', nah], *m. & f.* 1. Person afflicted with diarrhoea. 2. Cowardly, timorous person.

cagueta [cah-gay-tah], *m. & f.* Coward.

caguitis [cah-gee'-tis], *f*. Fear. **Le entra caguitis**, he gets the wind up.

cahiz [cah-eeth'], *m*. Nominal measure, commonly of twelve fanegas, or about twelve English bushels.

cahizada [cah-e-thah'-dah], *f*. Tract of land which requires about one *cahiz* of grain in order to be properly sown.

cahué [cah-oo-ay'], *m*. Turkish name of coffee and a café.

cahuín [cah-boo-een'], *m. (Cono Sur)* 1. Drunkenness, drunken spree. 2. Rowdy gathering. 3. *(Cono Sur)* mess, cock up (lío).

caída [cah-ee'-dah], *f*. 1. Fall, falling; tumble. 2. Fall, the effect of falling. 3. Fall, downfall; lapse. 4. Fall, diminution, declination, declension. 5. Fall, declivity, descent. 6. Anything which hangs down, as a curtain or tapestry. 7. Fall, the violence suffered in falling. 8. *(Geol.)* A landslip. 9. An interior gallery in houses of Manila, with views upon the courtyard. (See CAER, 12th accept.) 10. *(Vulg.)* The earnings of a harlot. 11. Failure. **La caída del gobierno**, the fall of the government. **La caída del imperio**, the collapse of the empire. **La caída de los dientes**, the falling-out of the teeth. **Sufrir una caída**, to have a fall. **Caída de una vela**, depth or drop of a sail. **Caída de agua**, waterfall. **Caída incontrolada**, free fall. **Ir o andar de capa caída**, *(Met.)* to decline in fortune and credit. **A la caída de la tarde**, at nightfall. **A la caída del sol**, at sunset. 12. **Caída radiactiva**, radioactive fallout. -*pl.* 1. That part of a headdress which hangs loose. 2. Coarse wool cut off the skirts of fleece. 3. *(Tec.)* Low-grade wool. 4. Witty remarks. **¡Qué caídas tiene!**, isn´t he witty!

caído, da [cah-ee'-do, dah], *a*. 1. Languid: downfallen. **Estar de sueño caído**, to be dead tired. 2. *(fig.)* Crestfallen, dejected. 3. **Caído de color**, pale. -*m*. 1. **Los caídos**, the fallen. **Monumento a los caídos**, war memorial. 2. *(Mex.)* Backhander (soborno), graft. -*pp.* of CAER.

caídos [cah-ee'-dos], *m. pl* 1. Rents or annual payments become due and not paid. 2. Arrears of taxes. 3. Sloping lines to show the proper slant in writing. *(Yo caigo, yo caiga; yo caí, él cayó; yo cayera*, from *Caer. V.* CAER.)

caifán [cah-ee-fahn'], *m. (Mex.)* Pimp, ponce.

caigo [cah'-ee-go], etc. *V.* CAER.

caimacán [cah-ee-mah-can'], *m. (And.)* Important person, big shot; star, expert.

caimán [cah-e-mahn'], *m*. 1. Cayman, alligator, an American crocodile. 2. A cunning man. 3. *(LAm.)* Twister, swindler (estafador). 3. *(Mex.) (Mech.)* Chain wrench. 4. *(And.)* Lazy fellow (gandul).

caimanear [cah-ee-mah-nay-ar'], *(LAm.)*. 1. *va*. To swindle, cheat. 2. *vn*. To hunt alligators.

caimiento [cah-e-me-en'-to], *m*. 1. Lowness of spirits; languidness, want of bodily strength. 2. Fall, the act of falling.

Caín [cah-een'], *m*. Cain. **Pasar las de Caín**, to have a ghastly time.

caique [cah-ee'-kay], *m. (Naut.)* Caic, a kind of skiff or small boat.

cairel [cah-e-rel'], *m*. 1. False hair or wig worn by women to embellish their head-dress. 2. Furbelow, a wind of flounce with which women's dresses are trimmed. 3. Silk threads to which wig-makers fasten the hair of wigs.

caireIado, da [cah-e-ray-lah´-do, dah], *a*. Adorned with flounces. -*pp.* of CAIRELAR.

cairelar [cah-e-ray-lar'], *va*. To adorn with flounces.

cairelear [cah-e-ray-lay-ar'], *va*. To trim, fringe.

Cairo [cah'-e-ro], *m*. **El Cairo**, Cairo.

caita [cah-e'-tah], 1.*a (Cono Sur)* Wild, untamed; unsociable, withdrawn (huraño). 2. *m. (Cono Sur)* Migratory agricultural worker.

caite [cah-e'-tay], *m. (CAm.)* Rough rubber-soled sandal.

caitearse [cah-e-tay-ar'-say], *vr*. **Caitearselas**, *(CAm.)* To run away.

caja [cah'-hah], *f*. 1. Box, case. 2. Coffin. *V.* ATAÚD. 3. Chest in which money is kept; cash-box or safe. *(Com.)* Cash, funds; cashier's office. 4. A sheath. 5. Drum. 6. Printer's case. 7. Room in post-office where letters are sorted. 8. Portable writing-desk. 9. The well or cavity in which a staircase is raised. 10. Wooden case of an organ. **Caja alta, caja baja,** *(Typ.)* upper case, lower case. **Caja de polvo,** snuffbox. **Caja de brasero,** a wooden case where the brasier is placed in the room. **Caja de coche,** body of a coach. **Caja de balas,** shotlocker. **Caja de bombas,** *(Naut.)* Pump-well of a ship. **Caja de cartuchos,** *(Mil.)* cartridge-box. **Libro de caja,** among merchants, cash-book. **Estar en caja,** to equilibrate, to be in equipoise. **Caja de música,** music box. **Caja de herramientas,** toolbox. **Caja del tambor, del tímpano,** *(Anat.)* Eardrum. **Caja de seguridad,** safe-deposit. **Caja de engranajes,** gear-box. **Caja de empalmes,** junction box. 11. *(Com. Fin.)* Cash-box, safe-deposit box (de caudales). **Caja de compensación,** equalization fund. **Hacer caja,** to make up the accounts for the day. **Ingresar en caja,** to pay in. 12. *(Cono Sur)* Riverted (lecho seco de río).

Caja de Ahorros [cah'-hah day ah-or'-ros], *f.* Savings Bank.

caja de cambios [cah'-hah day cam'-be-os], *f.* Transmission, gear box.

caja de caudales [cah'-hah day cah-oo-dah'-les], *f.* Strong box.

caja fuerte [cah'-hah foo-err'-tay], *f.* Safe, vault.

caja registradora [cah´-hah ray-hes-trah-do'-rah], *f.* Cash register.

cajear [cah-hay-ar'], *va. (CAm.)* To beat up.

cajero [cah-hay'-ro], *m.* 1. Cashier. **Cajero automático,** cash-dispenser. 2. Boxmaker.

cajeta [cah-hay'-tah], *f.* 1. Snuffbox. 2. *(Prov.)* Poorbox. **Cajetas,** *(Naut.)* Caburns. 3. *(Mex.)* Box of jelly. 4. *(And. CAm.)* Lip (de animal). 5. *(CAm. Mex.)*

cajete [cah-hay'-tay], *m. (Mex.)* 1. A flat bowl of unburnished clay, in which the *pulque* (the juice of the century plant or maguey) is sold to people. 2. Toilet, loo. 3. Bottom; arse (culo).

cajetilla [cah-hay-teel'-lyah], *f.*

cajetín [cah-hay-teen'], *m. dim.* 1. Very small box. 2. *(Typ.)* Fount-case, letter-case. 3. Spindle-case.

cajista [cah-hees-tah], *m.* Compositor (in printing).

cajo [cah'-ho], *m.* Among bookbinders, groove for the pasteboards in which*(Aer.)* are bound.

cajón [cah-hone'], *m.* 1. Box or chest for goods. 2. Chest of drawers; drawer under a table; locker; moneydrawer. 3. Mould for casting the pipes of an organ. 4. Space between the shelves of a bookcase. 5. Tub in which wet cloth is laid. 6. Wooden shed for selling provisions; *(Mex.)* Dry-goods store. 7. Crib, caisson. **Ser de cajón,** or **una cosa de cajón,** to be a matter of course, or a common thing. **Ser un cajón de sastre,** *(Met.)* 1. To have one´s brain full of confused ideas. 2. To know a great many things. **Cajones de cámara,** *(Naut.)* Lockers in the cabins of ships.8. Stall, booth. **Cajón de ropa** *(Mex.),* Draper´s (shop), dry-goods store. 9. *(Tec.)* **Cajón hidráulico, cajón de suspensión,** caisson. 10. *(CAm. Cono Sur)* Ravine.

cajonada [cah-ho-nah'-dah], *f. (Naut.)* Lockers.

cajoncito [cah-hon-thee'-to], *m. dim.* 1. A small box, chest, or drawer. 2. Compartments or pigeon-holes.

cajonera [cah-ho-nay'-rah], *f.* A box in which flowers or shrubbery are grown; a wood and glass frame for hot-houses.

cajonería [cah-ho-nay-ree'-ah], *f.* Chest of drawers.

cajuela [cah-hoo-ay'-lah], *f. (Mex.) (Aut.)* Boot, trunk,

cal [cahl], *f.* Lime. **Cal viva,** quick or unslaked lime. **Pared de cal y canto,** a wall of rough stone and mortar. **Ser de cal y canto,** *(Met.)* to be as strong as if built with lime and stone. **Dar una de cal y otra de arena,** to apply a policy of the carrot and the stick.

cala [cah'-lah], *f.* 1. *(Naut.)* Creek, a small bay. 2. Small piece cut out of a melon or other fruit to try its flavor. 3. Hole made in a wall to try its thickness. 4. *(Med.)* Suppository. **Hacer cala y cata,** to examine a thing to ascertain its quantity and quality.

calabacear [cah-lah-bah-thay-ar'], *va. (Univ.)* To fail, plough; to jilt.

calabacera [cah-lah-bah-thay'-rah], *f. (Bot.)* Pumpkin or gourd-plant. *V.* CALABAZA.

calabacero [cah-lah-bah-thay'-ro], *m.* Retailer of pumpkins.

calabacica, illa, ita [cah-lah-bah-thee'-cah, eel'-lyah, ee'-tah], *f. dim.* Small pumpkin.

calabacilla [cah-lah-bah-theel'-lyah], *f.* 1. Core, piece of wood in the shape of a gourd, around which a tassel of silk or worsted is formed. 2. Earring made of pearls in the shape of a gourd.

calabacín [cah-lah-bah-theen'], *m.* 1. A small, young, tender pumpkin. 2. *(Coll.)* Doll, a silly person.

calabacinate [cah-lah-bah-the-nah'-tay], *m.* Fried pumpkins.

calabacino [cah-lah-bah-thee'-no], *m.* Dry gourd or pumpkin scooped out, in which wine is carried; a calabash.

calabacita [cah-lah-bah-the'-tah], *f. (Esp.)* Courgette.

calabaza [cah-lah-bah'-thah], *f.* 1. *(Bot.)* The fruit of the pumpkin or gourd. **Calabaza anaranjada,** orange-fruited gourd. **Calabaza verruguera** or **verrugosa,** warted gourd. 2. Calabash. 3. Small button joining the ring of a key. **Dar calabazas,** 1. to reprove, to censure. 2. To give a denial; to give the mitten: applied to a woman who rejects a proposal of marriage. **Llevar calabazas,** to be dismissed, to be sent away. **Salir calabazas,** to be plucked, to fail in an examination. 4. *(fig.)* Dolt (idiota). 5. Bonce, head (cabeza).

calabazada [cah-lah-bah-thah-dah], *f.* 1. Knock one's against something. **Darse de calabazadas,** *(Met.)* To labor in vain to ascertain something. 2. Liquor drunk from a calabash.

calabazar [cah-lah-bah-thar'], *m.* Piece of ground planted with pumpkins.

calabazate [cah-lah-bah-thah'-tay], *m.* 1. Preserved pumpkin candied with sugar. 2. Piece of a pumpkin steeped in honey or must. 3. Knock of the head against a wall.

calabazazo [cah-lah-bah-thah'-tho], *m.* Bump on the head.

calabazo [cah-lah-bah-tha'-tho], *m.* Prison; prison cell; *(Hist.)* Dungeon; glasshouse.

calabazón [cah-lah-bah-thone'], *m. aug.* Large winter pumpkin.

calabobos [cah-lah-bo'-bos], *m.* Small, gentle, continued rain; drizzle.

calabozo [cah-lah-bo'-tho], *m.* 1. Dungeon, cell, calaboose: generally applied to such as are below ground. 2. *(Prov.)* Pruning-hook or knife.

calabriada [cah-lah-bre-ah´-dah], *f.* 1. A mixture of different things. 2. A mixture of white and red wine.

calabrote [cah-lah-bro´-tay], *m. (Naut.)* Stream cable, cable-rope.

calache [cah-lah'-chay], *m. (CAm.)* Thing. **Reúne tus calaches,** get your things.

calada [cah-lah´-dah], *f.* 1. Rapid flight of birds of prey. 2. Introduction. 3. Narrow, craggy road. 4. Reprimand. **Dar una calada,** to reprimand. 5. Soaking (mojada). 6. Lowering (de red). 7. Puff (cigarrillo).

caladero [cah-lah-day-ro], *m.* Fishing-grounds.

caladio [cah-lah'-de-o], *m. (Bot.)* Caladium, an ornamental-leaved plant.

calado [cah-lah-do], *m.* 1. Open work in metal, stone, wood, or linen; fretwork. 2. *(Naut.)* Draught, the depth of water which a vessel draws; **calados,** lace; **calado, da,** *pp.* of CALAR. **-a. Estar calado** (hasta los huesos), to be soaked.

calador [cah-lah-dor'], *m.* 1. Perforator, borer. 2. *(Naut.)* Caulking-iron. 3. A surgeon's probe.

caladre [cah-lah´-dray], *f.* A bird of the family of larks.

calafate, calafateador [cah-lah-fah' tay, cah-lah-fah-tay-ah-dor'], *m.* Caulker.

calafateadura [cah-lah-fah-tay-ah-doo'-rah], *f.* Caulking.

calafatear, calafetear [cah-lah-fah-tay-ar'], *va. (Naut.)* To caulk.

calafateo [cah-lah-fah-tay'-o], *m.* Caulking.

calafatería [cah-lah-fah-tay-ree'-ah], *f.* The act of caulking.

calafetín [cah-lah-fay-teen'], *m.* Caulker's boy or mate.

calafraga [cah-lah-frah'-gah], *f. (Bot.)* Saxifrage.

calagozo [cah-lah-go'-tho], *m.* Bill or hedging-hook.

calaguala [cah-lah-goo-ah'-lah], *f. (Bot.)* A medicinal fern.

calaguasca [cah-lah-goo-ah'-sah], *f. (LAm.)* Rum.

calaje [cah-lah'-hay], *m. (Prov.)* Chest, trunk, or coffer.

calaluz [cah-lah-looth'], *m. (Naut.)* Kind of East Indian vessel.

calamaco [cah-lah-mah-co], *m.* Calamanco, woollen material. **Calamacos, floreados,** flowered calamancoes. **Calamacos lisos,** plain calamancoes. **Calamacos rayados,** striped calamancoes.

calamar [cah-lah-mar'], *m.* Squid, or sea-sleeve: a variety of cuttle-fish which has the power of emitting an inky fluid. It contains an internal horny plate shaped much like a quill-pen, and which gives rise to its name.

calambrazo [cah-lam-brah'-tho], *m.* Attack of cramp, spasm.

calambre [cah-lam'-bray], *m.* Spasm, cramp.

calambuco [cah-lam-boo'-co], *m. (Bot.)* Calaba-tree.

calambuco, ca [cah-lam-boo'-co, cah], *a. (Cuba)* Pharisaical, hypocritical.

calambur [cah-lam-boor'], *m. (LAm.)* Pun.

calamento, *m.* **calaminta,** *f.* [cah-lah-men'-to, meen'-tah]. *(Bot.)* Mountain balm or calamint.

calamidad [cah-lah-me-dahd'], *f.* Misfortune, calamity, misery, grievousness, mishap, oppression. **Es una calamidad,** it´s a great pity (suceso); it´s a nuisance (persona). **Estar hecho una calamidad,** to be in a very bad way.

calamina, or **piedra calaminar** [cah- lah-mee´-nah], *f.* Calamine, zinc ore, a hydrous silicate of zinc. The carbonate, once known as calamine, is now called smithsonite.

calaminado [cah-lah-me-nah-do], *a. (LAm.)* Firm, bumpy, uneven.

calamís [cah-lah-mees'], *m. V.* CÁLAMO AROMÁTICO.

calamita [cah-lah-mee'-tah], *f.* 1. Loadstone. 2. *V.* CALAMITE. 3. A fossil, equisetaceous plant of coal formations.

calamite [cah-lah-mee'-tay], *m.* Kind of small green frog. The little green tree-frog.

calamitosamente [cah-lah-me-to-sah- men'-tay], *adv.* Unfortunately, disastrously.

calamitoso, sa [can-lah-me-to'-so, sah], *a.* Calamitous, unfortunate, wretched.

cálamo [cah'-lah-mo], *m.* 1. *(Bot.)* Sweet-flag. **Cálamo aromático,** calamus, sweet cane, sweet flag. 2. Pen; **empuñar el cálamo,** to take up one´s pen. **Menear el cálamo,** to wield a pen. 3. Sort of flute.

calamocano [cah.-lah-mo-cah'-no], *a.* **Estar** or **ir calamocano,** to be somewhat fuddled (ancianos).

calamoco [cah-lah-mo'-co], *m.* Icicle.

calamón [cah-lah-mone'], *m.* 1. *(Orn.)* Purple water hen or gallinule. 2. Round-headed nail. 3. Stay which supports the beam of an oil-mill.

calamorra [cah-lah-mor´-rah], *f. (Coll.)* The head.

calamorrada [cah-lah-mor-rah'-dah], *f.* Butt of horned cattle.

calandraco [cah-lahn-drah-co], *a. (And. Cono Sur)* Annoying (fastidioso), tedious; scatterbrained (casquivano).

calandrajo [cah-lan-drah'-ho], *m.* 1. Rag hanging from a garment. 2. Ragamuffin.

calandria [cah-lahn'-dre-ah], *f.* 1. *(Orn.)* Bunting, calendra lark. 2. Calender, a clothier's press, beetle mill, rolling-press. 3. A genus of rhyncophorous beetles. 4. Mangle.

calaña [cah-lah'-nyah], *f.* 1. Pattern, sample. 2. Character, quality. **Es hombre de buena** or **mala calaña,** he is a good- or ill-natured man. **Es una cosa de mala calaña,** it is a bad thing.

cálao [cah'-lah-o], *m. (Orn.)* Hornbill.

calapatillo [cah-lah-pah-teel'-lyo], *m.* A weevil, or its grub, very destructive to grains, nuts, and roots.

calar [cah-lar'], *va.* 1. To penetrate, to pierce, to perforate, to plug. 2. *(Met.)* To discover a design, to comprehend the meaning or cause of a thing. 3. To put,

to place. 4. To imitate net or lace work in linen or cotton. 5. *(Mech.)* To wedge. **Calar el timón,** *(Naut.)* to hang the rudder; 6. *(Tec.)* To do fretwork on (metal); to do openwork. 7. To size up; to see through *(fig.)* (penetrar). **A éstos los tengo muy calados,** I´ve got them thoroughly weighed up. 8. To lower, to let down (puente); to lower (vela). 9. To crush, to flatten, to sit on; *(fig.)* To humiliate. 10. *(Naut.)* To draw. **El buque cala 12 metros,** the ship draws 12 meters, the ship has a draught of 12 meters. -*vn.* 1. To sink in, soak in; to lead (zapato). 2. *(fig.)* **Calar en,** to go deeply into. **Hay que calar más hondo,** this must be investigated further. -*vr.* 1. To enter, to introduce oneself; to insinuate oneself into. 2. To be wet through, to soak, to imbibe. 3. To stoop, to dart down on prey. **Calarse el sombrero,** to stick one´s hat down; to put one´s hat on firmly.

calar [cah-lar'], *a.* Calcareous.

calatear [cah-lah-tay-ar'], 1. *va. (And. Cono Sur)* To undress, to strip. 2. *vr.* To get undressed, to strip off.

calato [cah-lah-to], *a. (And.)* Naked, bare; *(fig.)* Penniless, broke.

calatraveño, ña, or **calatravo** [cah-lah-trah-vay'-nyo, nyah, or cah-lah-trah'-vo], *a.* Pertaining to Calatrava.

calavera [cah-lah-vay'-rah], *f.* 1. Skull. 2. *(Met.)* A wild, hot-brained fellow. 3. *(Ent.)* Death´s-head moth. 4. *(Mex.) (Aut.)* Rear light. -*m.* Gay dog (juerguista); madcap (locuelo); rotter (canalla).

calaverada [cah-lah-vay-rah'-dah], *f.* Ridiculous, foolish, or ill-judged action.

calaverear [cah-lah-'vay-ray-ar], *vn.* To live it up; to have one´s fling.

calaverilla, ita [cah-lah-vay-reel'-lyah, ee'-tah], *f. dim.* 1. Little skull. 2. *m. (Met.)* Little crazy fellow.

calbote [cal-bo'-tay], *m. (Prov.)* Bread made from acorns or chestnuts.

calca [cal'-cah], *f. (And.) (Agri.)* Barn, granary. 2. *(LAm.)* copy (copia).

calcado [cal-cah'-do], *m.* A counter-drawing, tracing.

calcamar [cal-cah-mar'], *m.* Sea-fowl on the coast of Brazil.

calcañal, calcañar [cal-cah-nyahl´, cal-cah-nyar], *m.* Heel, heel bone, to be stupid.

calcaño [cal-cah'-nyo], *m.* Heel of the foot.

calcáneo [cal-cah'-nay-o], *m. (Anat.)* Calcaneum, the largest bone in the tarsus, which forms the heel.

calcañuelo [cal-cah-nyoo-ay'-lo], *m.* A disease of bees.

calcar [cal-car'], *va.* 1. To counterdraw, or to copy a design by means of pressure, to trace. 2. *(Prov.)* To trample on.

calcáreo, rea [ca-cah'-ray-o, ah], *a.* Calcareous.

calce [cahl-thay], *m.* 1. The tyre of a wheel. 2. A piece of iron or steel added to the coulter of a plough, when it is worn. 3. A wedge. 4. Wheel-shoe, a form of brake. 5. *(Naut.)* Top. 6. A cup, a chalice. 7. Small canal for irrigation. 8. *(CAm. Carib. Mex.)* Foot, lower margin (of a document). **Firmar el calce,** to sign at the foot of the page.

calcedonia [cal-thay-do'-ne-ah], *f.* Chalcedony, a precious stone.

calcés [cal-thess'], *m. (Naut.)* Masthead.

calceta [cal-thay'-tah], *f.* 1. Understocking, generally of thread. 2. *(Met.)* Fetters worn by criminals.

calcetería [cal-thay-ree'-ah], *f.* 1. Hosiery (oficio). 2. Hosier´s (shop).

calcetero, ra [cal-thay-tay'-ro, rah], *m. & f.* 1. One who makes, mends, or sells thread stockings. 2. Knitter of stockings.

calcetilla, calcilla [cal-thay-teel'-lyah, cal-theel-lyah], *f. dim.* Small stocking, sock.

calcetín [cal-thay-teen'], *m. V.* CALCETILLA. Half-hose, sock.

calcetón [cal-thay-tone'], *m. aug.* Large stocking worn under boots.

calciditos [cal'-the-dee'-tose], *m. pl.* Chalcididae, a family of hymenopterous insects, many parasitic, and useful to the husbandman.

calcificar [cal-the-fe-car'], *va.* To calcify.

calcificarse [cal-the-fe-car'-say], *vr.* To calcify, to turn into calcium.

calcina [cal-thee'-nah], *f.* Mortar, concrete.

calcinación [cal-the-nah-the-on'], *f. (Chem.)*, Calcination.

calcinar [cal-the-nar'], *va.* 1. To calcine; to burn, to reduce to ashes. **Las ruinas calcinadas del edificio**, the blackened ruins of the building. 2. To bother, annoy (fastidiar). *-vr.* To calcine.

calcinatorio [cal-the-nah-to'-re-o], *a.* **Vaso calcinatorio**, calcinatory.

calcio [cahl'-the-o], *m.* Calcium, a metallic element, widely distributed in limestone, gypsum, etc.

calco [cahl'-co], *m.* A counter-drawing copied by means of pressure: a drawing made from another by means of a transparent paper; a tracing.

calcografía [cal-co-grah-fee'-ah], *f.* 1. Chalcography, art of engraving. 2. Shop where engravings are sold and the place where they are engraved.

calcógrafo [cal-co'-grah-fo], *m.* Engraver.

calcomanía [cal-co-mah-nee'-ah], *f.* Decalcomania, a process of transfering prints from paper and making them adhere to porcelain, etc.

calcopirita [cal-co-pe-ree'-tah], *f.* Copper pyrites, chalcopyrite, native copper sulphide.

calculable [cal-coo-lah'-blay], *a.* Calculable.

calculación [cal-coo-lah-the-on'], *f.* Computation, calculation.

calculador, ra [cal-coo-lah-dor', rah], *m. & f.* 1. Calculator. **Calculador electrónico**, electronic calculator. **Calculadora**, adding machine. 2. *(LAm.)* Selfish, mercenary (egoísta).

calcular [cal-coo-lar'], *va.* To calculate, to reckon.

calculista [cal-coo-lees'-tah], *m.* Schemer

cálculo [cahl'-coo-lo], *m.* 1. Calculation, computation, the result of an arithmetical operation; estimate, count, account. 2. *(Med.)* Calculus, gravel, stone. 3. Small stone used by the ancients in arithmetical operations. **Cálculo diferencial**, *(Math.)* Differential calculus. **Cálculo integral**, integral calculus. **Según mis calculos**, according to my calculations.

calculoso, sa [cal-coo-lo-so, sah], *a.* Calculose, calculous.

Calcuta [Cal-coo'-tah], *f.* Calcutta.

calcha [cal'-cha], *f.* 1. *(Cono Sur)* clothing (ropa), bedding (de cama); harness (arreos). 2. *(Cono Sur)* fetlock; fringe.

calchona [cal-cho-nah], *f. (Cono Sur)* ghost, bogey (fantasma); *(fig.)* Hag (bruja).

calchudo [cal-choo'-do], *a. (Cono Sur)* shrewd, cunning.

calda [cahl'-dah], *f.* 1. Warmth, heat. 2. Act of warming or heating. **Caldas**, natural hot mineral-water baths.

caldaria [cal-dah'-re-ah], *f.* **Ley caldaria**, water ordeal.

caldeamiento [cal-day-ah-me-ayn'-to], *m.* Warming, heating.

caldear [cal-day-ar'], *va.* 1. To weld iron, and render it fit to be forged. 2. To warm, to heat. **Estar caldeado**, to be very hot. *-vr.* to get very hot, to get overheated.

caldeo [cal-day-o], *m.* Chaldaic, warming; heating; *(Tec.)* Welding.

caldera [cal-day'-rah], *f.* Caldron, boiler, sugar-kettle. **Caldera de Pedro Botero**, *(Coll.)* Davy Jones's locker; devil's boiler, hell. **Caldera de vapor**, steamboiler

calderada [cal-day-rah'-dah], *f.* A caldronful, a capperful.

calderería [cal-day-ray-ree'ah], *f.* 1. Brazier's shop. 2. Trade of a brazier.

calderero [cal-day ray'-ro], *m.* 1. Brazier, coppersmith, blacksmith. 2. Tinker. 3. Among wool-washers, one charged with keeping the fire burning under the boiler.

caldereta [cal-day-ray'-tah], *f.* 1. *(dim.)* Small caldron, a kettle, a pot. **Caldereta de agua bendita**, holy-water pot. 2. Kettleful. **Caldereta de pescado guisado**, kettleful of stewed fish. 3. *(Mex.)* Chocolate-pot. 4. Stew of meat.

calderico, ica, illo, illa [cal-day-ree'-co, cah, eel'-lyo, lyah], *m. & f. dim.* A small kettle.

calderilla [cal-day-reel'-lyah], *f.* 1. Holywater pot. 2. Any copper coin. 3. The lowermost part of a well, in the shape of a caldron.

caldero [cal-day-ro], *m.* 1. A caldron or boiler in the form of a bucket, a copper. 2. **Caldero de brea**, *(Naut.)* pitch-kettle.

calderón [cal-day-rone'], *m.* 1. Copper, large caldron or kettle. 2. Mark of a thousand. 3. *(Print.)* Paragraph. 4. *(Mus.)* Sign denoting a suspension of the instruments.

calderuela [cal-day-roo-ay'-lah], *f.* 1. *(dim.)* Small kettle. 2. Small pot or dark-lantern, used by sportsmen to drive partridges into the net.

caldillo, caldito [cal-deel'-lyo, cal- dee'-to], *m.* 1. Sauce of a ragout or fricassee. 2. Light broth.

caldu [cahl'-do], *m.* Broth, beef-tea, bouillon. **Caldo de carne**, consommé. **Cambiar el caldo a las aceitunas**, to have a leak; **Dar un caldo a uno**; *(Cono Sur)* to torture somebody. **Poner a uno a caldo**, to give somebody a bashing. **Caldos**, wine, oil, and all spirituous liquors which are transported by sea. **Los caldos jerezanos**, the wines of Jerez, sherries. 3. Fag, gasper (cigarrillo). 4. *(Mex.)* Sugar cane juice.

caldosito [cal-do-see'-to], *a. (Coll.)* Not too thick.

caldoso, sa [cal-do'-so, sah], *a.* Having plenty of broth, thin. *-a.* Watery, weak.

calducho [cal-doo'-cho], *m.* 1. *(Coll.)* Broth ill-seasoned and without substance, hog-wash. 2. *(Cono Sur)* day off.

cale [cah'-lay], *m.* Slap, smack.

calé [cah-lay'], 1. *a.* Gipsy. 2. *m.* f. Gipsy.

calecico [cah-lay-thee'-co], *m. dim.* Small chalice.

Caledonia [cah-lay-do'-ne-ah], *f.* Caledonia, ancient name of Scotland.

caledonio, ia [cah-le-do'-ne-o, ah], *a.* Caledonian, Scotsman, Scottish, Scots.

calefaciente [cah-lay-fah-the-en'-tay], *a. (Med.)* Heating.

calefacción [cah-lay-fac-the-on'], *f.* Calefaction, heating. **Calefacción central**, central heating.

calefactorio [cah-lay-fac-to'-re-o], *m.* Stove or place in convents designed for warming.

calefán [cah-lay-fan'], *m. (Cono Sur)* Water heater.

calefón [cah-lay-fon'], *m. (Cono Sur)* Hot water heater.

caleidoscopio [cah-lay-e-dos-co'-pee-o], *m.* Kaleidoscope.

calencas [cah-len'-cas], *f.* Kind of East India calico.

calenda [cah-len'-dah], *f.* The part of the martyrology which treats of the acts of the saints of the day. **Calendas**, calends, first day of every month; **a las calendas griegas**, i. e. never, because the Greeks had no calends; **a** or **en estas calendas**, at that time.

calendar [cah-len-dar'], *va.* To date, to programme.

calendario [cah-len-dah'-re-o], *m.* 1. Almanac, calendar. **Calendario de pared**, wall calendar. 2. Date. **Hacer calendarios**, *(Met.)* To make almanacs; to muse, to be thoughtful. **Calendario de Flora**, floral calendar, a table of the time of flowering of plants. **Calendario electrónico**, *(Inform.)* electronic calendar.

caléndula [cah-len'-doo-lah], *f. (Bot.)* Marigold.

calentador [cah-len-tah-dor'], *m.* Heater. **Calentador de agua**, water-heater. **Calentador eléctrico**, electric fire. **Calentador a gas**, gas heater. **Calentador de inmersión**, immersion heater.

calentamiento [cah-len-ta-me-en'-to], *m.* 1. Calefaction, warming, heating 2. Disease incidental to horses. 3. Warm-up (deporte).

calentar [cah-len-tar'], *va.* 1. To warm, to heat; to glow, to make warm. 2. To roll and heat a ball in one's hand before it is played. 3. *(Met.)* To urge, to press forward, to despatch speedily. **Calentar a alguno las orejas**, to chide or reprove one severely. **No calentar el asiento**, to retain office for but a short time. 4. **Calentar al rojo**, to make red-hot. 5. To arouse (excitar). *-vr.* 1. To be in heat (animales). 2. To mowburn, to ferment and heat in the mow (grano, trigo). 3. To grow hot, to dispute warmly, to be hurried by the ardor of debate. **Calentársele a uno la boca**, to speak incoherently from excessive ardor.

calentón [cah-len-tone'], *m*. **Darse un calentón**, *(Coll.)* To take a bit of a warming; to feel randy (sexy). -a. Sexy, randy.

calentura [cah-len-too'-rah], *f*. 1. A fever. **Estar con calentura**, to be feverish, have a temperature. 2. Warmth, gentle heat. *3. (Cono Sur)* tuberculosis. 4. *(And. Cono Sur)* Randiness, sexual excitement. 5. *(And.)* Fit of rage, tantrum (rabieta). 6. **Calentura de pollo**, *(Mex.)* Imaginary illness.

calenturiento ta, [cah-len-too-re-en'-to, tah], *a*. 1. Feverish; fever-sick. 2. *(Cono Sur)* comsumptive, tubercular. 3. Dirty, prurient (mente indecente). 4. Rash, impulsive (exaltado). **Las mentes calenturientas**, the hotheads.

calenturilla [cah-len-too-reel'-lyah], *f. dim.* Slight fever.

calenturón [cah-len-too-rone'], *m. aug.* Violent fever.

calanturoso, sa [cah-len-too-ro'-so, sah], *a*. Feverish. *V.* CALENTURIENTO.

calepino [cah-lay-pee'-no], *m. (Coll.)* Vocabulary, dictionary (de latín).

calera [cah-lay-rah], *f*. Lime-kiln; lime-pit.

calería [cah-lay-ree'-ah], *f.* House, place, or street, where lime is burnt and sold.

calero, ra [cah-lay-ro, rah], *a*. Calcareous.

calero [cah-lay'-ro], *m*. Lime-burner, lime-maker, or seller.

calés [cah-lays'], *m. & pl.* Bread, money.

calesa [cah-lay'-sah], *f.* Calash, a Spanish chaise.

calesera [cah-lay-say´-rah], *f.* 1. Type of bolero jacket. 2. Andalusian song.

calesero [cah-lay-say'-ro], *m*. Driver of a calash.

calesín [cah-lay-seen'], *m*. Single-horse chaise, a gig.

calesita [cah-lay-see'-tah], *f. (And. Cono Sur)* merry-go-round, carousel.

caleta [cah-lay'-tah], *f*. 1. *(Naut.)* Cove, creek, fleet, a small bay or inlet. 2. *(And.) (Naut.)* Coasting vessel, coaster. 3. *(And.)* Hiding-place (escondite).

caletero [cah-lay'-ro], *m*. 1. *(Carib.)* Docker, port worker (estibador). 2. *(LAm.) (Ferro.)* Milk-train. 3. *(Carib.)* Shop assistant.

caletre [cah-lay'-tray], *m*. 1. *(Coll.)* Understanding, judgment, discernment. **No le cabe en el caletre**, he can´t get it into his thick head. 2. In abusive language, the head.

cali [cah'-le], *m. (Chem.) V.* ÁLCALI.

calibeado, da [cah-le-bay-ah' do, dah], *a. (Med.)* 1. Chalybean, relating to steel. 2. Chalybeate, impregnated with iron.

calibración [cah-le-brah-the-on'], *f.* Calibration.

calibrador [cah-le-brah-dor´], *m*. Gauge, caliper, calipers.

calibrar [cah-le-brar'], *va*. To examine the calibre of a ball or fire-arm; to gauge, to size.

calibre [cah-lee'-bray], *m*. 1. Calibre. 2. Diameter of a column. 3. *(Met.)* Calibre, sort, kind. **Ser de buen o mal calibre**, to be of a good or bad quality. 4. *(Cono Sur)* **Palabras de grueso calibre**, crude language; swearing.

calicanto [cah-le-cahn'-to], *m*. 1. *(Bot.)* Allspice. 2. *(Carib. Cono Sur)* stone wall; jetty (muelle).

calicata [cah-le-cah'-tah], *f. (Min.)* A trial-pit; the test of a piece of ground by auger, or tools, or mere inspection.

cálice [cah'-le-thay], *m. (Obs.) V.* CÁLIZ.

calicinal [cah-le-the-nahl'], *a*. Relating to a calyx, calycine, or calycinal.

caliche [cah-lee'-chay], *m*. 1. Pebble or small piece of limestone accidentally introduced into a brick or tile at the time of its being burnt. 2. A crust of lime which flakes from a wall. 3. *(Peru and Chile)* Native saltpeter, or crude sodium nitrate.

calicó [cah-le-co'], *m*. Calico.

calicud, calicut [cah-le-cood', cah-le-coot'], *f.* Silk stuff from India.

calidad [cah-le-dahd'], *f*. 1. Quality; condition, character; kind or particular nature. **De calidad**, of quality. **De mala calidad**, of bad quality. 2. Importance or consequence of a thing. 3. Nobility, quality, condition, rank, fashion. 4. Condition, stipulation, requisite. **Calidades**, conditions in playing a game. **En calidad de**, in the capacity of. 5. Stipulation, term (contrato). **A calidad de que...**, provided that.

calidez [cah-le-deth'], *f. V.* ENCENDIMIENTO.

cálido, da [cah'-le-do, dah], *a*. 1. Hot (clima, país), Piquant, calid. 2. Crafty, artful.

calidoscópio o caleidoscopio [cah-lee-dos-co'-pe-o], *a*. Kaleidoscopic. *m.* Kaleidoscope.

calientacamas [cah-lee-ayn-tah-cah'-mas], *m*. Electric blanket.

calientapiernas [cah-lee-ayn-tah-pe-ayr'-nas], *m*. Leg-warmer.

calientapiés [cah-lee-ayn-tah-pe-ays'], *m*. Hot-water bottle; foot warmer.

calientaplatos [cah-lee-ayn-tah-pla'-tos], *m*. Hotplate.

caliente [cah-le-en'-tay], *a*. 1. Warm, hot; scalding. 2. Warm, fiery, feverish, vehement. **Tener la sangre caliente**, *(Met.)* To face dangers with great spirit. **En caliente**, Piping hot, on the spot, immediately, instantaneously. **Caliente de cascos**, hot-headed. **Estar caliente**, to be in heat (animales); to feel randy. *(Yo caliento, yo caliente, from Calentar. V.* ACERTAR.

calieta [cah-le-ay'-tah], *f.* Kind of mushroom.

califa [cah-lee'-fah], *m*. Caliph, successor: a title assumed by the successors of Mohammed.

califato [cah-le-fah'-to], *m*. Caliphate, the dignity of caliph.

calificación [cah-le-fe-cah-the-on'], *f.* 1. Qualification. 2. Judgment, censure. 3. Proof 4. Habilitation. 5. Grade, mark (escuela). **Calificación de sobresaliente**, first-class mark.

calificado, da [cah-le-fe-cah´-do, dah], *a*. 1. Qualified, authorized, competent. 2. Well-known, eminent (conocido); undisputed; proven, manifest. 3. *(Mex.) (Jur.)* Qualified, conditional. *-pp.* of CALIFICAR.

calificador [cah-le-fe-cah-dor'], *m*. 1. One who is qualified to spy and do something. 2. **Calificador del Santo Oficio**, officer of the Inquisition, appointed to examine books and writings.

calificar [cah-le-fe-car'], *va*. 1. To qualify. 2. To authorize, to empower. 3. To certify, to attest. 4. To illustrate, to ennoble. 5. To assess; to rate; to grade, to mark (examen). 6. **Calificar a uno**, to distinguish somebody, to give somebody his standing (reputación). 7. **Calificar a uno de tonto**, to call somebody silly, to describe somebody as silly, to label somebody silly. *-vr.* To prove one's noble birth and descent according to law. 2. *(LAm.)* To register as a voter.

calificativo [cah-le-fe-cah-te-vo], *a*. Qualifying.

California [cah-le-for'-nee-ah], *f.* California.

california [cah-le-for'-nee-ah], *f. (Cono Sur)* Horse-race (carrera). 2. *(Cono Sur) (Tec.)* Wire-stretcher.

californiano, na [cah-le-for-ne-ah'-no, nah], *a. & m. & f.* Californian, from California.

californio, ia [cah-le-for'-ne-o, ah], *a*. Native of California.

caliga [cah-lee'-gah], *f.* A kind of half-boots worn by Roman soldiers.

calígine [cah-lee'-he-nay], *f.* Mist, obscurity, darkness.

caliginoso, sa [cah-le-he-no'-so, sah], *a*. 1. Caliginous, dark, dim. 2. Intricate, obscure, difficult to be understood.

caligrafía [cah-le-grah-fee'-ah], *f.* Caligraphy, elegant penmanship.

caligráfico [cah-le-grah'-fee-co], *a*. Calligraphic.

calígrafo [cah-lee'-grah-fo], *m*. One who writes a beautiful hand: a penman.

calilla [cah-leel'-lyah], *f. dim.* 1. A small suppository. 2. *(CAm. Mex.)* Bore, nuisance. 3. Hoax (engaño); boring (joke).

calima [cah-lee'-mah], *f.* 1. *V.* CALINA. 2. A rosary of corks employed in seafishing.

calimaco [cah-le-mah'-co], *m. (Prov.) V.* CALAMACO.
calimocho [cah-le-mo'-cho], *m.* Drink of mixed Coca-cola and wine.
calín [cah-leen'], *m.* A metallic composition resembling lead.
calina [cah-lee'-nah], *f.* Thick vapor, resembling a mist or fog.
calinda [cah-leen'-dah], *f. (Cuba)* A popular dance of the creoles.
calino, na [cah-lee'-no, nah], *a.* Chalky, or containing chalk.
calinoso [cah-lee-no'-so], *a.* Hazy, misty.
calio [cah'-le-o], *m.* Kalium or potassium, a metallic element.
calíope [cah-lee'-o-pay], *f.* Calliope, muse of epic poetry.
calípedes [cah-lee'-pay-des], *m.* A slow-paced animal.
calipso [cah-leep'-so], *m.* 1. *(Bot.)* Calypso. 2. *(Mus.)* Calypso, musical rhythm from Trinidad.
caliqueño [cah-le-kay'-nyo], *m.* Prick. **Echar un caliqueño**, to have a screw.
calis [cah'-lis], *f.* l. *(Bot.)* Alkanet or orchanet.
calisaya [cah-le-sah'-yah], *f. (Bot.)* Calisaya, a highly prized variety of cinchona bark, indigenous to Peru.
calistenia [cah-lees-tay-ne-ah], *f.* Cal(l)isthenics.
calisténica [cah-lees-tay'-ne-cah], *f.* Calisthenics, gymnastics.
calixto [cah-leex'-to], *m. (Astr. and Poet.)* The constellation of the Great Bear.
cáliz [cah-leeth], *m.* 1. Chalice, a communion cup. 2. Bitter cup of grief and affliction.3. *(Bot.)* Calyx of a flower. **Cáliz de amargura, cáliz de dolor**, cup of sorrow.
caliza [cah-lee'-thah], *f.* Calcium carbonate in its various forms, whether limestone, marble, gypsum, or other.
calizo, za [cah-lee'-tho, thah], *a.* Calcareous, limy: calc (spar).
callada [cal-lyah'-dah], *f.* 1. Dish of tripe. 2. Silence: employed only in certain phrases. **A las calladas** or **de callada**, without noise, privately, on the quiet. **Dar la callada por respuesta**, to answer by silence.
calladamente [cal-lyah-dah-men'-tay], *adv.* Silently, tacitly, secretly, privately, in a reserved manner.
calladaris [cal-lyah-dah'-ris], *f.* A kind of cotton stuff.
callado, da [cal-lyah'-do, dah], *a.* 1. Silent, reserved, noiseless. 2. Discreet. **Todo estaba muy callado**, everything was very quiet. **Tener algo callado**, to keep quiet about something. **Pagar para tener callado a uno**, to pay to keep somebody quiet. **Nunca te quedas callado**, you always have an answer for everything. *-pp.* of *CALLAR.*
callamiento [cal-lyah-me-en'-to], *m. (Obs.)* Imposing and keeping silence.
callampa [cahl-lyam-bah], *f. (Cono Sur) (Bot.)* Mushroom; umbrella; **callampas**, big ears.
callana [cahl-lyah'-nah], *f. (LAm, Cono Sur)* Flat earthenware pan; *(Cono Sur)* pocket watch.
callandico, ito [cal-lyah-dee'-co, to], *adv.* In a low voice; silently; without noise, slyly, softly.
callar [cal-lyar'], *vn.* 1. To keep silence, to be silent. 2. To omit speaking of a thing, to pass it over in silence, to conceal, to hush.3. To cease singing: said of birds. 4. To dissemble.5. *(Poet.)* To abate, to become moderate, to grow calm (viento, mar). **Callar el pico**, to hold one's tongue, to pretend not to have heard or seen anything of the matter in question. **Mátalas callando**, by crafty silence he obtains his ends. **Quien calla otorga**, silence implies consent. *- vr.* To be silent, to be quiet, to remain silent. **¡Calla! ¡cállate!**, shut up!, be quiet!. **Hacer callar a uno**, to make somebody be quiet. **Sería mejor callarse**, it would be best to say nothing. **Callar como un muerto**, to shut up like a clam.
calle [cahl'-lyay], *f.* 1. Street, paved way. 2. Lane, a narrow way between hedges. 3. Lane, a passage between men standing on each side 4. *(Coll.)* Gullet. 5. (Kant) Liberty. 6. Pretext, excuse, means for evading a promise. **Calle de árboles**, alley or walk in a garden. **Calle mayor**, main street. **Calle sin salida**, dead-end street. **Alborotar la calle**, to cause an uproar in the street. **Dejar a uno en la calle**, to strip one of his all, also to turn one out of doors. **Echar algún secreto en la calle**, to proclaim a secret in the streets. **Hacer calle,**

a) to make way, to clear the passage. b) *(Met.)* to overcome difficulties. **Pasear** or **rondar la calle**, to court a woman, flirt on the street. **Pasear las calles**, to loiter about. **Quedar en la calle**, to be in the utmost distress. **Calles públicas** , the public streets. **Calle abajo**, down the street. **Calle de dirección única**, one-way street. **Calle peatonal**, pedestrian precinct. **Hacer la calle**, to be on the streets (prostituta). **Llevarse a uno de calle**, to bowl somebody over. **Poner a uno de patitas en la calle**, to kick somebody out. *-int.* 1. Strange! Wonderful! You don't say so! 2. Make way!
callear [cal-lyay-ar'], *va.* To clear the walks in a vineyard of loose branches.
calleja [cal-lyay'-hah], *f. V.* CALLEJUELA.
callejear [cal-lyay-hay-ar'], *vn.* To walk or loiter about the streets, to gad, to ramble.
callejero, ra [cal-lyay-hay'-ro, rah], *a.* 1. Applied to a loiterer; a gadder. 2. Street. **Accidente callejero**, street accident. **Disturbios callejeros**, trouble in the streets. **Perro callejero**, stray dog. *-m.* Street directory.
callejo, calleyo [cal-lyay'-ho, cal-lyay'-yo], *m. (Prov.)* Pit into which game falls when pursued.
callejón [cal-lyay-hone'], *m.* 1. Narrow lane. 2. Narrow pass between mountains. **Callejón sin salida**, 1. Blind alley. 2. Impasse, predicament. **Gente de callejón**, *(And.)* Low-class people.
callejoncillo [cal-lyay-hon-theel'-lyo], *m. dim.* A little narrow passage.
callejuela [cal-lyay-hoo-ay'-lah], *f.* 1. Lane or narrow passage. 2. *(Met.)* Shift, subterfuge, evasion. **Dar pan y callejuela**, to help one in his flight.
callemandra [cal-lyay-mahn'-drah], *f.* Kind of woollen stuff.
callialto, ta [cal-lye-ahl'-to, tah], *a.* Having swelling welts or borders (herraduras).
callicida [cahl-lye-the'-dah], *m.* Corn cure.
callista [cal-lyees'-tah], *m. & f.* A corn-doctor, chiropodist.
callizo [cal-lyee'-tho], *m. (Prov.) V.* CALLEJÓN and CALLEJUELA.
callo [cahl'-lyo], *m.* 1. Corn, a callous substance on the feet. 2. Wen. **Criar callos**, to become inured, become hardened. **Pisar los callos a uno**, to tread on somebody's toes. 3. *(Esp.) (Culin.)* **Callos**, tripe. **Callos al ajo**, tripe with garlic. 4. Old bat, old cow; ugly woman. 5. **Dar el callo**, *(Esp.)* to work hard.
callón [cal-lyone'], *m.* 1. *(aug.)* Big corn or wen. 2. Among shoemakers, rubber, a whetstone for smoothing the blades of awls.
callosidad [cal-lyo-se-dahd'], *f.* Callosity, callus.
calloso, sa [cal-lyo'-so, sah], *a.* Callous: corny, corneous horny.
calma [cahl'-mah], *f.* 1. *(Naut.)* A calm. **Estar en calma**, to be calm. 2. Calmness, tranquility, composure. 3. Suspension of business, cessation of pain. **Estar en calma**, to be steady (mercado). **En calma**, *(Naut.)* Smooth sea. **Calma muerta** or **chicha**, *(Naut.)* Dead calm. 4. Slowness in speaking or doing *(Coll.)*. **Hacer algo con calma**, to do something calmly. **Perder la calma**, to get ruffled, to lose one's composure.
calmadamente [cal-mah-dah-men'-tay], *adv.* Quietly, calmly.
calmado, da [cal-mah'-do, dah], *a.* Quiet, calm. *-pp.* of CALMAR.
calmante [cal-mahn'-tay], *m. (Med.)* Anodyne; sedative; tranquillizer, *pa. & m. & f.* 1. Mitigating, mitigant. 2. *(Med.)* Narcotic, anodyne, sedative.
calmar [cal-mar'], *va.* 1. To calm, to quiet, to compose, to pacify, to still, to hush. 2. To alleviate, to allay, to lay, to mitigate, to lull, to moderate, to soothe, to soften. *-vn.* To fall calm, to be becalmed. *-vr. (Met.)* To be pacified, to calm down oneself; to improve (tiempo), to settle down; **¡Cálmate!**, calm down!
calmazo [cal-mah-tho], *m.* Dead calm.
calmécac [cal-may-cahc'], *m. (Mex.) (Hit.)* Aztec school for priests.

calmia [cahl'-me-ah], *f.* Kalmia, a genus of shrubs of the heath family.

calmo, ma [cahl'-mo, mah], *a.* 1. Uncultivated, untilled; without trees or shrubbery (tierras). 2. Slow, steady, measured.

calmoso, sa [cal-mo'-so, sah], *a.* 1. Calm. 2. *(Met.)* Tranquil, soothing. 3. Slow, tardy.

caló [cah-lo'], *m.* 1. Gipsy language. 2. Cant.

calocar [cah-lo-car'], *m.* Kind of white earth or clay.

calocha [cah-lo'-chah, *f.* 1. Clog or wooden shoe. 2. Overshoe, galosh.

calofillo, lla [cah-lo-feel'-lyo, lyah], *a.* Having handsome leaves.

calofriado, da [cah-lo-fre-ah'-do, dah], *a.* Chilly, shivering with cold. *-pp.* of CALOFRIARSE.

calofriarse, calosfriarse [cah-lo-fre- ar'-say], *vr.* To be chilly, to shudder or shiver with cold; to be feverish or with shiverings. *V.* ESCALOFRIARSE.

calofrío, calosfrío [cah-lo-free'-o], *m.* Shiver, shudder, cold sweat.

caloma [cah-lo'-mah], *f. (Naut.)* Singing out of sailors when they haul a rope.

calomel or **calomelanos** [cah-lo-may-lah'-nos], *m. pl. (Med.)* Calomel.

calón [cah-lone'], *m.* 1. Rod for spreading nets. 2. Perch for measuring the depth in shallow water.

calóptero, ra [cah-lop'-tay-ro, rah], *a.* Which has beautiful wings.

calor [cah-lor'], *m.* 1. Heat; hotness, calidity; glow. 2. Burning, blazing. 3. *(Met.)* Warmth, ardor, fervor, fieriness (sentimientos, acciones). 4. Brunt of an action or engagement. 5. Favor, kind reception. **Dar calor a la empresa,** to encourage an undertaking. **Dar calor,** among tanners, to raise the color of a hide by heating it. **Un calor agradable,** a pleasant warmth. **Un calor excesivo,** an excessive heat. **Entrar en calor,** to get warm. **Hace mucho calor,** it's very hot.

caloría [cah-lo-ree'-ah], *f.* Calorie.

calórico, ca [cah-lo'-re-co, cah], *a.* Caloric.

calorífero, ra [cah-lo-ree'-fe-ro, rah], *a.* Heat-producing. *-m.* Furnace, heater. **Calorífero de aire caliente,** hot-air heater.

calorífico, ca [cah-lo-ree'-fe-co, cah], *a.* Heat-producing, calorific.

calorifugar [cah-lo-ree-foo-gar'], *va.* To lag (caldera, tubo).

calorífugo, ga [cah-lo-ree'-foo-go, gah], *a.* 1. Heat-resistant. 2. Incombustible.

calorímetro [cah-lo-ree'-may-tro], *m.* Calorimeter.

caloroso, sa [cah-lo-ro'-so, sah], *a. V.* CALUROSO.

calorro, rra [cah-lor'-ro], *a. m. & f.* Gipsy.

calostro [cah-los'-tro], *m.* Colostrum.

calote [cah-lo-tay], *m. (Cono Sur)* Con, swindle. **Dar calote,** to skip payments, leave without paying.

calotear [cah-lo-tay-ar'], *va. (Sp. Amer.)* To con, to swindle.

caloyo [cah-lo'-yo], *m.* Newborn lamb or kid.

calpense [cal-pen'-say], *a.* From Gibraltar, Gibraltarian.

calpul [cal-pool'], *m. (Sp. Amer.)* Gathering, get-together.

calseco, ca [cal-say'-co, cah], *a.* Cured with lime.

calta [cahl-tah], *f.* Marsh marigold.

caluga [cah-loo'-gah], *f. (Cono Sur)* Toffee.

caluma [cah-loo'-mah], *f. (And.)* Mountain pass (in the Andes).

calumbrecerse [ca-loom-bray-therr'-say], *vr.* To grow mouldy.

calumnia [cah-loom'-ne-ah], *f.* Calumny, false charge, slander. **Afiazar de calumnia,** *(Law.)* Applied to an accuser giving security to subject himself to legal penalties if he cannot prove his allegations.

calumniador, ra [cah-loom-ne-ah-dor', rah], *m. & f.* Calumniator, a slanderer.

calumniar [cah-loom-ne-ar'], *va.* To calumniate, to slander, to accuse falsely.

calumniosamente [cah-loom-ne-o'-sah- men'-tay], *adv.* Calumniously, slanderously.

calumnioso, sa [cah-loom-ne-o'-so, sah], *a.* Calumnious, slanderous.

calurosamente, *adv.* Warmly, ardently, hotly.

caluroso, sa [cah-loo-ro-so, sah], *a.* 1. Warm, hot, hearty, enthusiastic. 2. Heating.

calva [cahl'-vah], *f.* 1. Bald crown of the head, bald pate, bare spot, worn place.

calvar [cal-var'], *va.* 1. To impose upon one, to deceive.

Calvario [cal-vah'-re-o], *m.* 1. *(Met. Coll.)* Debts, tally, score. **Pasar un Calvario,** to suffer agonies. 2. a charnel-house. 3. Calvary, hill or elevation on which are crosses representing the stations at Mount Calvary.

calvatrueno [cal-vah-troo-ay'-no], *m.* 1. Baldness of the whole head. 2. *(Met.)* A wild person.

calvaza [cal-vah'-thah], *f. aug.* Large bald pate.

calvero, calvijar, calvitar [cal-vay'-ro, cal-ve-har', tar'], *m.* 1. Barren ground among fruitful lands. 2. Chalkpit, marlpit.

calvez, calvicie [cal-veth', cal-vee'-the-ay], *f.* Baldness. **Calvicie precoz,** premature baldness.

calvinismo [cal-ve-nees'-mo], *m.* Calvinism.

calvinista [cal-ve-nees'-tah], *m. f.* Calvinist.

calvo, va [cahl'-vo, vah], *a.* 1. Bald, without hair. **Quedarse calvo,** to go bald. 2. Barren, uncultivated (terreno). **Tierra calva,** barren soil.

calza [cahl'-thah], *f.* 1. Long, loose breeches, trousers. 2. Hose, stockings. **Medias calzas,** short stockings, reaching only to the knees. **Estar en calzas prietas,** to be in a fix. 3. *(LAm.)* Filling (de diente).

calzada [cal-thah'-dah], *f.* 1. Causeway, a paved highway. 2. The high road. 3. Gravel-walk. 4. Avenue.

calzadera [cal-thah-day'-rah], *f.* 1. Hempen cord for fastening the *albarcas,* a coarse kind of leather shoes. 2. Net twine.

calzadillo, ito [cal-thah-deel'-lyo, dee'-to], *m. dim.* Small shoe.

calzado, da [cal-thah'-do, dah], *a.* Calceated, shod, wearing shoes. **Calzado de,** shod with. **Conviene ir calzado,** it´s better to wear shoes. *-pp.* of CALZAR.

calzado [cal-thah'-do], *m.* 1. Footwear of all kinds. 2. Horse with four white feet. 3. All articles serving to cover the legs and feet. **Tráeme el calzado,** bring me my stockings, garters, and shoes.

calzador [cal-thah-dor'], *m.* 1. Shoeing leather, a piece of leather used to draw up the hind quarters of tigh shoes. 2. Shoe-horn, a piece of horn used for the same purpose as the shoeing-leather. **Entrar con calzador,** *(Met.)* To find great difficulties in entering a place.

calzadura [cal-thah-doo'-rah], *f.* 1. Act of putting on the shoes. 2. Felloe of a cart-wheel.

calzar [cal-thar'], *va.* 1. To put on shoes. 2. To strengthen with iron or wood.3. To scot or scotch a wheel. 4. To carry a ball of a determined size (armas de fuego). 5. To wedge, chock, key. 6. *(Typ.)* To overlay, to raise, underlay. 7. *(LAm.)* To fill (diente). 8. To pit, to put an iron tip on. **Calzar las herramientas,** to put a steel edge to iron tools. **Calzar los guantes,** to put on gloves. **Calzaba zapatos verdes,** she was wearing green shoes. **¿Qué numero calza Vd?,** what size do you take? **El primero que llega se calza,** first come first served. **Me ayudó a ponerme las botas,** he helped me to put my boots on. *-vn.* **Calza bien,** he wears good shoes. *-vr.* **1. Calzarse los zapatos,** to put on one´s shoes. **¿Qué zapatos calzaba?,** what shoes was he wearing?. 2. **Calzarse un empleo,** to get a job. **Calzarse a uno,** to keep somebody under one´s thumb.

calzatrepas [cal-thah-tray'-pas], *f.* Snare, trap.

calzo [cahl'-tho], *m. V.* CALCE. 1.*(Typ.)* Frisket-sheet, overlay. 2. Block, brake-shoe (ferrocarril). 3. *(Mech.)* Wedge, quoin. 4. Shoe of a felloe. 5. *(Naut.)* Skid, chock, bed, shoe.

calzón [cal-thone'], *m.* 1. Ombre, a game of cards. 2. Breeches, small clothes, hose: commonly used in the plural.

3. *(Mex.)* A disease of the sugar-cane from lack of irrigation. **Calzones marineros,** pants worn by sailors. **Calzones de baño,** bathing suit. **Amarrarse los calzones,** *(LAm.)* to get stuck in. **Ponerse los calzones,** *(fig.)* To wear the pants (mujer). **Tener muchos calzones,** *(Mex.)* to be tough. **Calzones de vinilo,** plastic pants (de plástico). - *pl. (Naut.)* Goose-wings: applied to sails when furled in a peculiar manner.

calzonarias [cal-tho-nah'-re-ahs], *f. pl. (Sp. Amer.)* Suspenders.

calzonario [cal-tho-nah'-re-o], *m. (LAm.)* Pants, underwear.

calzonazos [cal-tho-nah'-thos], *m.* 1. *(Coll.)* Mollycoddle, jellyfish. 2. Stupid fellow (tonto); weak-willed fellow (débil); henpecked husband (marido).

calzoncillos [cal-thon-theel'-lyos], *m. pl.* Shorts, drawers, pants, underpants, slips.

calzoneras [cal-tho-nay'-ras], *f. pl. (Mex.)* Pants open down both sides and the openings closed by buttons.

calzoneta [cal-tho-nay'-tah], *f. (CAm. Mex.)* Swimming suit (traje de baño).

calzonudo [cal-tho-noo-do], *a. (And. CAm. Cono Sur)* Stupid, weak-willed (débil), timid; *(Mex.)* energetic; bold, brave.

cama [cah'-mah], *f.* 1. Bed, couch, a place of repose. **Cama con ruedas,** a truck-bed. 2. Bed hangings and furniture. 3. Seat or couch of wild animals. 4. Floor or body of a cart. 5. *V.* CAMADA. 6. Litter, the straw laid under animals or on plants. 7. Slice of meat put upon another, to be both dressed together. 8. The axle of a wheel. 9. Branch of a bridle to which the reins are fastened; the cheek. 10. Piece of cloth cut slopewise, to be joined to another to make a round cloak. 11. Layer of dung and earth for raising plants; a garden-bed. 12. *(Mech.)* CAm. cog, catch, tooth. 13. Bed plate, base. 14. *(Geol.)* Layer, stratum. **Hacer cama,** to keep one's bed, to be confined to one's bed on account of sickness. **Hacer la cama,** to make the bed. **Caer en cama,** to fall sick. **Cama elástica,** trampoline. **Camas gemelas,** twin beds. **Cama de matrimonio,** double bed. **Cama plegable,** folding bed. **Cama redonda,** group sex. **Cama turca,** divan bed.

camachuelo [cah-may-choo-ay-lo], *m.* Bullfinch.

camada [cah-mah'-dah], *f.* 1. Brood of young animals, a litter. 2 Layer (of eggs, etc.). **Camada de ladrones,** den of thieves, nest of rogues.

camafeo [cah-mah-fay'-o], *m.* Cameo, a gem on which figures are engraved in basso-relieve.

camagua [cah-mah'-goo-ah], *f. (CAm.)* Ripening corn; *(Mex.)* Unriped corn.

camal [cah-mahl'], *m.* 1. Hempen halter. 2. Camail, a piece of chain mail attached to a basinet. 3. Slaughterhouse (matadero).

camaleón [cah-mah-lay-on´], *m.* 1. Chameleon. **Camaleón negro,** *(Bot.)* Corymbed carline thistle; *(Mex.)* The horned toad, properly lizard, of the U. S. Phrynosoma. 2. A flatterer who changes his language according to the presumed tastes of the person addressed.

camaleónico [cah-mah-lay-o'-ne-co], *a.* Chamaleon-like.

camaleopardo [cah-mah-lay-o-par'-do], *m.* Cameleopard, giraffe.

camalote [cah-mah-lay-o'-tay], *m.* Camalote (planta acuática).

camamila, camomila [cah-mah-mee´-lah, cah-mo-mee'-lah], *f. (Bot.)* Camomile. *V.* MANZANILLA.

camanance [cah-mah-nahn'-thay], *m. (CAm.)* Dimple.

camanchaca [cah-mahn-chah'-cah], *f. (Cono Sur)* thick fog, pea-soup.

camándula [cah-mahn'-doo-lah], *f.* Chaplet or rosary of one or three decades. **Tener muchas camándulas,** *(Coll.)* To make use of many tricks and artifices, to shuffle.

camandulear [cah-mahn-doo-lay-ar'], *vn.* To be a hypocrite, be falsely devout; *(LAm.)* to intrigue, scheme; to bumble (vacilar), avoid taking decisions.

camandulense [cah-man-doo-len'-say], *a.* Belonging to the religious order of Camandula or reformed Benedictines.

camandulería [cah-man-doo-lay-ree'-ah], *f.* Hypocrisy, insincerity, dissimulation.

camandulero, ra [cah-man- doo-lay'-ro, rah], *a. & n.* Full of tricks and artifices, dissembling, hypocritical; *(LAm.)* Intriguing (enredador), scheming; fawning (zalamero).

cámara [ca'-mah-rah], *f.* 1. Hall or main room of a house. 2. Granary, mow, a store-house of threshed corn. 3. Stool, evacuation by stool, laxity, laxness. 4. *V.* CILLA. 5. *(Naut.)* Cabin of a ship. 6. **Cámara alta,** *(Naut.)* Roundhouse of a ship. 7. Chamber in a mine. 8. Chamber of great guns and other fire-arms. 9. Bed-chamber. 10. Residence of the king and court. **Cámara del rey,** 1. Room in which the king holds a levee for gentlemen of the bedchamber, etc. 2. Exchequer. 11. The legislative body of foreign nations. 12. A photographic camera. **Cámara plegadiza,** a folding camera. **Cámara de mano,** a hand camera. **Cámara estereoscópica,** stereoscopic camera. **Pie de la cámara** (oscura), camera-stand. **Cámara de bolsillo,** pocket-camera. **Cámara con frente de quita y pon,** removable front camera. **Cámara baja o de los comunes,** the House of Commons. **Cámara nupcial,** bridal suite. **Música de cámara,** chamber music. **Médico de cámara,** royal doctor. **Cámara de comercio,** chamber of commerce; **Cámara de los Lores,** House of Lords. **Cámara de gas,** gas-room. **Cámara de aire;** tire, inner tube. **Cámara de cine,** movie-camera. **Cámara de televisión,** television camera. -*m.* Cameraman.

camarada [cah-mah-rah'-dah], *m.* 1. Comrade, partner, companion, mate, buddy, fellow; crony, chum. -*f.* 2. Society or company of people united; assembly. 3. **Camaradas de rancho,** messmates. **Camaradas de navío,** shipmates.

camaradería [cah-mah-rah-day-ree'-ah], *f.* Comradeship, fellowship.

camaraje [cah-mah-rah-hay], *m.* Granary, rent for a granary.

camaranchón [cah-mah-ran-chone'], *m.* 1. Garret. 2. Retired place, recess.

camarera [cah-mah-ray'-rah], *f.* Waitress, stewardess (azafata).

camarero [cah-mah-ray'-ro], *m.* 1. Waiter. 2. Steward (aviones); (camarero principal), head waiter.

camareta [cah-mah-ray'-tah], *f. dim. (Naut.)* Small cabin, deck-cabin; midshipmen's cabin.

camarico [cah-mah-re'-co], *m. (Cono Sur)* 1. Favorite place. 2. Love affair (amor).

camariento, ta [cah-mah-re-en'-to, tah], *a.* Troubled with diarrhoea.

camarilla [cah-mah-reel'-lyah], *f.* 1. *(dim.)* Small room. 2. The coterie of private advisers of the king. 3. *(Pol.)* Pressure group.

camarín [cah-mah-reen'], *m.* 1. Place behind an altar where the images are dressed, and the ornaments destined for that purpose are kept. 2. Closet. 3. A dressing-room in a theatre. 4. *(Naut.)* Cabin. 5. Elevator car (de ascensor).

camariña [cah-mah-ree'-nyah], *f.* Copse, short wood, a low shrub.

camarógrafo [cah-mah-roh'-grah-fo], *m.* Camera man.

camarón [cah-mah-rone'], *m.* 1. Shrimp; prawn. 2. *(CAm.)* Tip, gratuity. 3. *(And.)* Turncoat (traidor); **hacer camarón,** to change sides. 4. *(CAm.)* Casual word (trabajo). 5. *(Cono Sur)* Bunk (bed).

camaronear [cah-mah-ro-nay-ar'], *vn.* 1. *(Mex.)* To go shrimping (pescar camarones). 2. *(And.) (Pol.)* To change sides.

camaronero [cah-mah-ro-nay'-ro], *m.* Shrimper.

camarote [cah-mah-ro'-tay], *m. (Naut.)* Room on board a ship, a berth.

camarotero [cah-mah-ro-tay'-ro], *m. (LAm.)* Steward, cabin servant.

camaruta [cah-mah-roo'-tah], *f.* Bar girl.

camastro [cah-mahs'-tro], *m.* Poor, miserable bed.

camastrón [cah-mas-trone'], *m.* Sly, artful, cunning fellow. 2. *(CAm.)* Large bed.

camastronazo [cah-mas-tro-nah'-tho], *m. aug.* Great impostor, hypocrite or dissembler.

camastronería [cah-mas-tro-nay-ree'-ah], *f.* Cunning, artifice.

camatones [cah-mah-to'-nes'], *m. pl. (Naut.)* Iron fastenings of the shrouds.

camayo(c) [cah-mah'-yo], *m. (And.)* Foreman, overseer (finca).

cambado [cam-bah'-do], *a. (And. Cono Sur, Carib.)* Bow-legged.

cambalache [cam-bah-lah'-chay], *m.* 1. *(Coll.)* Barter. 2. Swap, exchange. 3. *(LAm.)* Second-hand shop.

cambalachear [cam-bah-lah-chay-ar'], *va.* To barter, to swap, to exchange.

cambalachero [cam-bah-lah-chay'-ro], *m.* Barterer.

cambaleo [cam-bah-lay'-o], *m.* An ancient company of comedians consisting of five men and a woman; the latter sang.

cambalés [cam-bah-less'], *a.* Relating to a *cambaleo.*

cambar [cam-bar'], *va. (Carib. Cono Sur) V.* COMBAR.

cámbaro [cahm'-bah-ro], *m.* The crabfish. *V.* CANGREJO. *(Acad.).*

cambas [cahm'-bas], *f. pl.* Pieces put into a cloak, or other round garment, to make it hang round.

cambayas [cam-bah'-yas], *f. pl.* Kind of cotton stuff.

cambiable [cam-be-ah'-blay], *a.* Fit to be bartered or exchanged.

cambiadiscos [cam-be-aha-dees-cos], *m.* Record-changer.

cambiadizo [cam-be-ah-tho], *a.* Changeable.

cambiador [cam-be-ah-dor'], *m.* 1. One who barters. 2. Money changer, money-broker. 3. *(Mex.)* Switchman (ferrocarril).

cambial [cam-be-ahl'], *m.* Bill of exchange.

cambiamano [cam-be-ah-mah'-no], *f.* A railroad switch.

cambiante [cam-be-ahn'-tay], *a.* 1. Bartering, exchanging. **Cambiante de letras**, a banker, exchanger. 2. *(Pey.)* Fickle, temperamental.

cambiante, *m.* Fabrics changeable in color according to the manner in which the light is reflected.

cambiar [cam-be-ar'], *va.* 1. To barter, to commute, to exchange one thing for another. 2. To change, to alter. **Cambiar de mano**, to change from the one side to the other (caballos). 3. To give or take money on bills, to negotiate bills and exchange them for money. 4. To transfer, to make over, to remove. **Cambiar las velas**, *(Naut.)* to shift the sails. 5. To carry on the business of a banker. **Cambiar dólares por pesos**, to change dollars for pesos. **Cambiar saludos**, to exchange greetings. **¿Lo cambiamos a otro lado?**, shall we move it somewhere else? -*vn.* To change, to alter. **Cambiar a un nuevo sistema**, to change to a new system. **No ha cambiado nada**, nothing has changed. **Está muy cambiado**, he´s changed a lot. -*vr.* 1. To be translated or transferred, to change, to change round. 2. **Cambiarse en**, to change into.

cambiario [cam-be-ah'-re-o], *a. (Fin.)* Exchange. **Liberización cambiario a**, freeing of exchange controls.

cambiavía [cam-be-ah-vee'-ah], *m. (Carib. Mex.) (Ferro.)* 1. Switch man (persona). 2. Switch, points.

cambiazo [cam-be-ah'-tho], *m. (Com.)* Switch (dishonest). **Dar el cambiazo**, to switch the goods.

cámbija [cahm'-be-hah], *f.* Reservoir, basin of water.

cambio [cahm'-be-o], *m.* 1. Barter, commutation. 2. Giving or taking of bills of exchange. 3. Rise and fall of the course of exchange. 4. Public or private bank. 5. Alteration, change; flux. 6. Compensation. 7. *(Vet.)* A tumor contained in the small veins of an animal. 8. Return of a favor, recompense. **Libre cambio**, free trade. **Cambio manual**, note of hand. **Dar o tomar a cambio**, to lend or borrow money on interest. **Cambio por letras**, trade in bills of exchange. **Ha habido muchos cambios**, there have been many changes. **Cambio de domicilio**, change of address. **Cambio de guardia**, changing of the guard. **Cambio de velocidades**, *(Aut.)* Gear change. **Cambio radical**, turning point. **Cambio de vía**, *(Ferro.)* Points. **¿Tienes cambio?**, have you got any change? **A las primera de cambio**, *(fig.)* at the very start. **Cambio de frecuencia**, *(Inform.)* frequency shift, keying

cambista [cam-bees'-tah], *m.* Banker, trader in money, broker, cambist; goldsmith.

cambiunte [cam-be-oon'-tay], *m.* 1. Changeable silk stuff. 2. A kind of camlet.

cambogio [cam-bo'-he-o], *m.* The tree which yields gamboge; garcinia. **Camboya** [Cam-bo'-yah], *f. (Hist.)* Cambodia.

camboyano, na [cam-bo-yah-no], *a. m. & f. (Hist.)* Cambodian.

cambrón [cam-brone'], *m. (Bot.)* Common buckthorn.

cambrona [cam-bro'-nah], *f. (Cono Sur)* Tough cotton cloth.

cambronal [cam-bro-nahl'], *m.* Thicket of briers, brambles, and thorns.

cambronera [cam-bro-nay'-rah], *f. (Bot.)* Boxthorn, a genus of plants. **Cambronera europea** or **común**, European boxthorn. **Cambronera africana**, African boxthorn. **Cambronera berberisca**, willow-leaved boxthorn.

cambucho [cam-boo'-cho], *m. (Cono Sur)* paper cone (cono); straw basket for waste paper or dirty clothes; straw cover (envase); miserable little room (cuartucho).

cambuj [cam-booh'], *m.* 1. Child's cap tied close to its head to keep it straight. 2. Mask, veil.

cambujo, ja [cam-boo'-ho, hah], *a.* An Indian mestizo; offspring of an Indian woman and a negro, or of a negress and an Indian; dark (persona), black (animal).

cambullón [cam-bool-lyone´], *m. (Peru)* Imposition, swindle.

cambur [cam-boor'], *m.* 1. *(Carib.)* Banana (plátano). 2. Government post, soft job, cushy number; windfall (dinero).

cambuto [cam-boo'-to], *a. (And.)* Small, squat; chubby.

cambuy [cam-boo'-e], *m.* American myrtle-tree.

camedrio [cah-may´-dre-o], *m. (Bot.)* Wall germander.

camedris [cah-may'-dris], *m. (Bot.)* Germander, speedwell, wild germander. **Camedris de agua**, water germander.

camelar [cah-may-lar'], *va.* 1. To court, to woo. 2. *(Coll.)* To seduce, to deceive by flattering. 3. *(Mex.)* To look into.

camelea [cah-may-lay'- ah], *f. (Bot.)* Widow-wail, a shrub.

camelete [cah-may-lay'-tay], *m. (Obs.)* Kind of great gun.

cameleuca [cah-may-lay'-oo-cah], *f. (Bot.)* Colt´s-foot.

camelia [cah-may'-le-ah], *f.* Camellia, an Asiatic genus of small shrubs.

camelista [ ], *m. & f.* Flatterer, creep.

camella [cah-mayl-'lyah], *f.* 1. She-camel. 2. Ridge in ploughed land. 3. A milk-pail. 4. Yoke.

camellar [cah-mayl-lyar'], *vn. (Carib.)* To work (hard).

camellear [cah-mayl-lay-ar'], *vn.* To push drugs, to be a pusher.

camellejo [cah-mel-lyay'-ho], *m. dim.* Small camel.

camelleo [cah-mahl-lay-o], *m.* Drug-pushing.

camellería [cah-mel-lyay-ree'-ah], *f.* 1. Stable or stand for camels. 2. Employment of a camel-driver.

camellero [cah-mel-lyay'-ro], *m.* Keeper or driver of camels.

camello [cah-mayl'-lyo], *m.* 1. Camel. 2. Ancient cannon. 3. Engine for setting ships afloat in shoal water. 4. Drug pusher. *V.* GIRAFA.

camellón [cah-mel-lyone'], *m.* 1. Ridge turned up by the plough or espade. 2. *(Prov.)* Long wooden drinking-trough for cattle. 3. Carpenter's horse. 4. Bed of flowers. 5. *(Prov.)* Camlet. **Camellones listados**, camleteens.

camelo [cah-may'-lo], *m.* 1. Gallant, wooer. 2. *(Coll.)* A joke, jest. **Dar camelo a uno**, to make fun of somebody. **Me huele a camelo**, it smells fishy.

camelote [cah-may-lo'-tay], *m.* Camlet.

camelotillos, camelloncillos [cah-may-lo-teel'-lyos, cah-may-lyon-theel´-lyos], *m.* Light or thin camlets.

camemoro [cah-may-mo'-ro], *m. (Bot.)* Cloud berry bramble.

camepitios [cah-may-pee'-te-os], *m. (Bot.)* Common ground pine.

camerino [cah-may-re'-no], *m. (Theat.)* Dressing room; *(Mex.)* roomette (ferrocarril).

camero [cah-may'-ro], *m.* 1. Upholsterer. 2. One who lets beds for rent.

camero [cah-may'-ro], *a.* Belonging to a bed or mattress

camerododendro [cah-may-ro-do-den'-dro], *m.* (*Bot.*) Rusty-leaved rhododendron.

Camerún [cah-may-roon'], *m.* Cameroon.

camilla [cah-meel'-lyah], *f.* 1. (*dim.*) Small bed, pallet, or cot; litter, stretcher. **Camilla baja**, low frame, on which cloth-shearers put their work.

camillero, ra [cah-mel-lay'-ro], *m. & f.* Stretcher-bearer.

camilucho [cah-me-loo'-cho], *m.* (*Cono Sur, Mex.*) Indian day laborer.

caminada [cah-me-nah'-dah], *f.* V. JORNADA.

caminador [cah-me-nah-dor'], *m.* Good walker.

caminante [cah-me-nahn'-tay], *m.f.* Traveler, walker.

caminar [cah-me-nar'], *vn.* 1. To travel, to walk, to go, to march. 2. To move along (ríos, objetos). **Caminar con pies de plomo**, (*Met.*) to act with prudence. **Caminar derecho**, (*Met.*) to act uprightly. **Venir caminando**, (*LAm.*) to come on foot. **Caminar derecho**, to behave properly. 3. (*LAm.*) (*Mech.*) To work.

caminata [cah-me-nah'-tah], *f.* (*Coll.*) 1. Long walk for exercise. 2. Excursion, jaunt.

caminera [cah-me-nay'-rah], *f.* (*And.*) Flask containing liquor carried by travelers.

caminero [cah-me-nay'-ro], 1. *a.* Road; V. PEON. 2. *m.* (*LAm.*) Road builder.

caminito [cah-me-ne'-to], *m.* **Caminito de rosas**, (*fig.*) Primrose path.

camino [cah-mee'-no], *m.* 1. Path, beaten road; high road. 2. Journey. 3. Turn of a boat or cart, for removing goods from place to place. 4. Gate, way, passage, road. 5. (*Met.*) Profession, station, calling. 6. (*Met.*) Way, manner or method of doing a thing. 7. (*Min.*) Drift, gait. 8. (*Naut.*) Ship's way, rate of sailing. **Camino cubierto**, (*Mil.*) Covert-way. **Camino carretero**, road for carriages and wagons. **Camino de Santiago**. (*Astr.*) Galaxy, the Milky Way; **ir fuera de camino**, (*Met.*) to be put out of one's latitude, to act contrary to reason. **Procurar el camino**, to clear the way. **Salir al camino**, 1. to go to meet a person. 2. (*Met.*) To go on the highway to rob. **De camino**, in one's way, going along. **Fui a Los Angeles y de camino hice una visita**, I went to Los Angeles, and on my way there I paid a visit. **Echarse al camino**, to take to the roads, to become a highway robber. **Ponerse en camino**, set out, start off. **Camino vecinal**, country road. **El camino a seguir**, the road. **Vamos camino de la muerte**, death awaits us all. **Después de tres horas de camino**, after traveling for three hours. **Es mucho camino**, it's a long way. **Ir por el buen camino**, (*fig.*) to be on the right track. **Traer a uno por buen camino**, (*fig.*) to put somebody on the right way. **Todos los caminos van a Roma**, all roads lead to Rome.

camino de acceso [cah-mee'-no day ac-thay'-so], *m.* Access road.

camión [cah-me-on'], *m.* Truck; lorry; van. **Camión de basura**, trash truck. **Camión de bomberos**, fire engine. **Camión cisterna**, tanker. **Camión de reparto**, delivery truck. **Camión de riego**, water cart.

camionaje [cah-me-o-nah'-hay], *m.* Haulage, cartage.

camionero [cah-me-o-nay'-ro], *m.* Truck-driver, teamster.

camioneta [cah-me-o-nay'-tah], *f.* 1. Station wagon. 2. Small truck.

camionista [cah-me-o-nees' tah], *m.* V. CAMIONERO.

camión-tanque [cah-me-on' tan-kay], *m. pl.* **Camiones-tanque**, (*Aut.*), tanker.

camisa [cah-mee'-sah], *f.* 1. Shirt. 2. Shift, chemise, the undergarment of women. 3. Alb or surplice, worn by priests and deacons. 4. Thin skin of almonds and other fruit. 5. Slough of a serpent. 6. (*Mil.*) Chemise, side of a rampart toward the field. 7. Stock of counters used at a game of cards. 8. Catamenia. 9. Rough casting or plastering of a wall before it is whitewashed. 10. Jacket, case, casing, in steam-engines (motores). 11. Internal lining of a furnace (hornos). **Camisa de una vela**, (*Naut.*) the body of a sail. **Meterse en camisa de once varas**, to interfere in other people's affairs; to undertake very difficult or dangerous business, or above one's power or means. **Vender hasta la camisa**, to sell all to the last shirt. **No llegarle a uno la camisa al cuerpo**, to be frightened, to be anxious. **Dejar a uno sin camisa**, to leave somebody destitute. **Camisa de dormir**, night gown. **Camisa de gas**, gas mantle. **Camisa de agua**, water jacket.

camisería [cah-me-say-ree'-ah], *f.* Shirt-store.

camisero [cah-me-say'-ro], *m.* Shirt-maker.

camiseta [cah-me-say'-tah], *f.* 1. Undershirt. V. ELASTICA. 2. (*Obs.*) Short shirt or shift with wide sleeves. 3. Chemisette.

camisilla [cah-me-seel'-lyah], *f.* (*Carib. Cono Sur*) V. CAMISETA.

camisola [cah-me-so'-lah], *f.* 1. Ruffled shirt. 2. Dicky. **Camisola de fuerza**, a strait-jacket.

camisolín [cah-me-so-leen'], *m.* Shirt-front, tucker, wimple.

camisón [cah-me-sone'], *m.* 1. (*aug.*) Long and wide shirt. 2. Frock worn by laborers and workmen. 3. (*Amer.*) Gown, a woman's upper garment. 4. (*Cuba and Puerto Rico*) Chemise. 5. Nightdress.

camisote [cah-me-so'-tay], *m.* Ancient armor.

camita [cah-mee'-tah], *f. dim.* Small bed, pallet, or cot.

camita [cah-me-tah], *a.* Hamitic.

camomila [cah-mo-me'-lah], *f.* Camomile.

camón [cah-mone'], *m.* Frame of laths, which serves to form an arch. **Camón de vidrios**, partition made by a glass frame. -*pl.* 1. Felloes of cartwheels, shod with evergreen oak instead of iron. 2. Incurvated pieces of timber in the wheels of corn-mills.

camoncillo [cah-mon-theel'-lyo], *m.* State stool in a drawing-room; cricket richly garnished.

camorra [cah-mor'-rah], *f.* (*Coll.*) Quarrel, dispute. **Armar camorra**, to kick up a row. **Buscar camorra**, to go looking for trouble.

camorrear [cah-mor-ray-ar'], *vn.* (*Coll.*) To dispute often.

camorrero [cah-mor-ray'-ro], *m.* V. CAMORRISTA.

camorrista [cah-mor-rees'-tah], *com.* (*Coll.*) Noisy, quarrelsome person, hooligan.

camote [cah-mo'-tay], *m.* (*Bot.*) A variety of sweet potato. 2. (*CAm. Cono Sur*) (*Med.*) Dump, swelling. 3. (*Cono Sur*) large stone. 3. (*Cono Sur*) bore, tedious person (persona). 4. (*CAm.*) Calf of the leg. 5. (*CAm.*) Nuisance, bother (molestia). 6. (*LAm.*) Love; crush (amor). **Tener camote con uno**, to have a crush on somebody. 7. (*And. Cono Sur*) Lover, sweetheart. 8. (*Cono Sur*) fib (mentirilla). 9. (*And. Cono Sur*) fool (tonto).

camotear [cah-mo-tay-ar'], *va.* 1. (*Cono Sur*) To rob, to fleece. 2. (*CAm.*) To annoy. -*vn.* (*CAm.*) To be trying, to cause trouble.

campa [cam-pah], 1. *a.* Tierra campa, treeless land. 2. *f.* Open land.

campal [cam-pahl'], *a.* Belonging to the field and encampments. **Batalla campal**; pitched battle.

campamentista [cam-pah-mayn-tees'-tah], *m. & f.* Camper.

campamento [cam-pah-men'-to], *m.* Encampment, camp. **Campamento para prisioneros**, prison camp. **Campamento de verano**, summer camp.

campana [cam-pah'-nah], *f.* 1. Bell. 2. Bell glass, receiver; anything which has the shape of a bell. 3. (*Met.*) Parish church, parish. 4. Bottom of a well made in the form of a bell. 5. In woollen factories, iron hoop, serving to keep the yarn from the bottom of the dyeing copper. 6. (*Arch.*) Drum, corbel. 7. (*LAm.*) Thieves' look out. **Hacer de campana**, to keep watch, to be on the lookout. **Campana de vidrio**, a bell-shaped glass vessel. **Campana de chimenea**, mantel, the funnel of a chimney when made in the form of a bell. **A toque de campana**, at the sound of the bell. **Oír campanas y no saber dónde**, to have heard of a fact, but not to be well informed of its true nature and complexion. **No haber oído campanas**, not to be informed of the most common things. **Echar las campanas al vuelo,** to peal the bells. **Campana de bucear,** diving bell.

campanada [cam-pah-nah'-dah], *f.* Sound produced by the clapper striking against the bell. **Dar campanada,** *(Met.)* to cause scandal, to make a noise.

campanario [cam-pah-nah'-re-o], *m.* 1. Belfry, bell tower. 2. *(Coll.)* Noddle, head. 3. Rack in velvet-looms.

campanazo [cam-pah-nah'-tho], *m.* 1. *V.* CAMPANADA. 2. *(And.)* Warning.

campaneado [cam-pah-nay-ah'-do], *a. (fig.)* Much talked of.

campanear [cam-pah-nay-ar'], *va.* 1. To ring the bell frequently. 2. To divulge, to noise about. 3. *(LAm.)* To keep watch (ladrón).

campanela [cam-pah-nay'-lah], *f.* Sudden motion of the feet in dancing.

campaneo [Cam-pah-nay'-o], *m.* 1. Bell ringing, chime. 2. *V.* CONTONEO,

campanero [cam-pah-nay-ro], *m.* 1. Bell-founder. 2. Bellman.

campaneta [cam-pah-nay'-tah], *f. dim.* Small bell.

campaniforme [cam-pa-ne-for'- may], *a.(Bot.)* Campaniform, bell-shaped. *V.* CAMPANUDO.

campanil [cam-pah-neel'], *m.* 1. Small belfry.- *a.* 2. **Metal campanil,** bell-metal.

campanilla [cam-pah-neel'-lyah], *f.* 1.*(dim.)* Small bell, hand-bell. 2. Small bubble. 3. *(Anat.)* Uvula. 4. Little tassel for ladies' gowns. 5. *(Naut.)* Cabin-bell. 6. *(Bot.)* Bell flower. 7. **Campanillas de otoño** *(Bot.)* Fall snowflake, garden daffodil. **De campanillas** or **de muchas campanillas,** of importance or consideration.

campanillazo [cam-pah-neel-lyah'-tho], *m.* 1. Violent ringing of a bell. 2. Signal given with a bell.

campanillear [cam-pah-neel-lyay-ar']. *va.* To ring a small bell often.

campanilleo [cam-pah-neel-lyay'-o], *m.* Ringing, tinkling.

campanillero [cam-pah-neel-lyay´-ro], *m.* Bellman, public crier.

campanino [cam-pah-nee'-no], *a.* Applied to a kind of marble.

campanólogo, ga [cam-pah-no'-lo-go], *m. & f.* Campanologist, bell-ringer.

campante [cam-pahn'-tay], *pa.* 1. Excelling, surpassing. 2. Buoyant, triumphant, cheerful. 3. Intrepid, robust. **Siguió tan campante,** he went on cheerfully. **Allí estaba tan campante,** there he was as large as life.

campanudo, da [cam-pah-noo'-do, dah], *a.* l. Wide, puffed up, bell-shaped (ropa). 2. *(Bot.)*

campánula [cam-pah'-noo-lah], *f. (Bot.)* Bell-flower, campanula.

campanulado, da [cam-pah-noo-lah' do, dah], **a**. *(Bot.)* Campanulate, bell-shaped.

campaña [cam-pah'-nyah], *f.* 1. Campaign, level country. 2. Campaign of an army. **Campaña naval,** *(Naut.)* Cruise. 3. *(Agri.)* Season. **Hacer campaña,** to campaign. **Hacer campaña en contra de,** to campaign against. **Hacer campaña a favor,** to campaign for.

campañola [cam-pah-nyo'-lah], *f.* Water rat.

campar [cam-par'], *vn.* 1. To encamp, to be encamped. 2. To excel in abilities, arts, and sciences. **Campar con su estrella,** to be fortunate or successful.

campeador [cam-pay-ah-dor'], *m.* 1. Combater, warrior. 2. A surname applied particularly to the Cid, Rodrigo Diaz de Vivar.

campear [cam-pay-ar'], *vn.* 1. To be in the field; to go out to pasture. 2. To frisk about (animales). **Campear de sol a sombra,** to be at work from morning to night. 3. To be eminent; to excel. 4. **Ir campeando,** to carry on. 5. *(LAm.)* To camp, to go camping. 6. *(And.)* To make one´s way through. 7. *(And.)* To bluster. **Campea por sus respetos,** he acts as if he were lord of the manor.

campechanería [campay-chah-nay-ree'-ah], *f. (LAm.)*, **Campechanía** *f.* , Frankness, openness; heartiness, cheerfulness.

campechano, na [cam-pay -chah´- no, nah], *a.* 1. Frank, hearty, ready for amusement. 2. *(Mex, Carib.)* Cocktail.

campeche [cam-pay'-chay], *m.* Campeachy-wood, log-wood.

campeón [cam-pay-on'], *m.* 1. Champion, combatant. 2. Champion, a judicial combatant, either in his own case or another's.

campeonato [cam-pay-o-nay'-to], *m.* Championship. **De campeonato,** *(fig.)* absolute, out-and-out; huge.

campero, ra [cam-pay'-ro, rah], *a.* 1. Exposed to the weather in the open field. 2. *(Mex.)* Having a gait like gentle trotting, pacing. 2. *(LAm.)* Knowledgeable about the countryside; expert in farming matters.

campero [cam-pay'-ro], *m.* 1. Friar who superintends a farm. 2. One who inspects another's lands and fields. 3. Pig brought up in the fields.

camperuso [cam-pay-roo'-so], *(Carib.)* *a.* 1. Rural, rustic. 2. Reserved, stand-offish. -*m.* f. Peasant.

campesino, na, campestre [cam-pay-see'-no, nah, cam-pes´-tray], *a.* Rural, campestral, rustic. -*m. & f.* A countryman, countrywoman.

campillo [cam-peel'-lyo], *m. dim.* Small field.

camping [cam'-peen], *m. pl.* 1. Campings, camping. **Hacer camping,** to go camping. 2. Camping site (sitio).

campiña [cam-pee'-nyah], *f.* Flat tract of arable land, field, campaign.

campirano [cam-pee-rah'-no], *m.* *(LAm.)* 1. Peasant (campesino); rustic, country bumpkin. 2. *(Agri.)* Expert in farming matters; guide, pathfinder; skilled horseman; stock-breeding expert (ganadero).

campista [cam-pees'-tah], *m. & f.* Camper. *a.* 1. *(CAm. Carib.)* Rural, country. 2. *(LAm.)* *V.* CAMPERO. -*m.* *(CAm.)* Herdsman.

campisto [cam-pees'-to], *a.* *(CAm.)* Rural, country. -*m.* 1. *(CAm.)* Peasant. 2. *(CAm.) (Agri.)* Amateur vet.

campo [cahm'-po], *m.* 1. Country. 2. Any tract of flat and even country. 3. Field, space, range of things. 4. Crops, trees, plantations. 5. Ground of silks and other stuffs. 6. Camp. 7. Ground on which an army is drawn up. 8. Ground of a painting. 9. **Campo santo,** burial-ground, cemetery. **Campo abierto,** plain, open country. **Campo de batalla,** battlefield. **Hacerse al campo,** to retreat, to flee from danger. **Dejar el campo abierto, libre,** to decline an undertaking where there are competitors. **Hombre de campo** or **del campo,** one who leads a country life. **Ir campo a través,** to take a short cut. **El campo está espléndido,** the countryside looks lovely. **Campo de aterrizaje,** landing field. **Campo de deportes,** sports ground. **Campo de fútbol,** football ground. **Campo de golf,** golf course. **Campo de minas,** minefield. **Campo de tiro,** firing range. **Levantar el campo,** *(Mil.)* to retire from the field. **Se le hizo el campo orégano,** *(Cono Sur)* it all turned out nicely for him. **No hay campo,** there´s no room. **Hay campo para más,** there´s scope for more. **Campo de concentración,** Concentration camp.

camposantero [cam-po-sahn-tay'-ro], *m.* Cemetery official.

campusano [cam-poo-sah'-no], *m.* Campus. -*m.* *(CAm.)* Peasant.

camuesa [cah-moo-ay'-sah], *f.* Pippin, an apple. **Camuesa blanca,** white pippin.

camueso [cah-moo-ay'-so], *m.* 1. *(Bot.)* Pippin tree. 2. Simpleton, fool.

camuflado [cah-moo-flah'-do], *a.* Camouflaged.

camuflaje [cah-moo-flah'-hay], *m.* Camouflage.

camuflar [cah-moo-flar'], *va. (fig.)* To camouflage.

camuza [cah-moo'-thah], *f.* Chamois goat. *V.* GAMUZA.

camuzón [cah-moo-thone'], *m. aug.* Large chamois-skin.

can [cahn], *m.* 1. *(Ant.)* Dog. 2. *(Arch.)* Bracket, shoulder, modillion, corbel. 3. *(Poet.)* Dog-star. 4. Ace in dice. 5. Trigger of guns, etc. 6. Ancient piece of ordnance. **Can rostro,** Pointer or setting-dog. **Can de busca,** terrier. **Can que mata al lobo,** wolfdog.

cana [cah'-nah], *f.* 1. Long measure, containing about two ells. 2. Gray or white hair. **Peinar canas,** to grow old. **Tener**

canas, to be old, to have white hair. **Echar una cana al aire,** to paint the town red, to have a good time, to go on a spree.
cana [cah'-nah], *f.* *(LAm.)* Jail; prison cell. 2. *(LAm.)* Police. **Caer en cana,** to land in jail. -*m.* Policeman (persona).
canaballa [cah-nah-bahl'-lyah], *f. (Naut.)* Fishing-boat.
canabis [cah-nah-bees'], *m.* Cannabis.
canaca [cah-nah'-cah], *m. & f. (And. Cono Sur)* chink; Chinese. 2. *(Cono Sur)* brothel keeper (dueño).
Canadá [Cah-nah-dah'], *m.* **El Canadá,** Canada.
canadiense [cah-nah-de-en'-say], *a.* Canadian.
canal [cah-nahl], *f.* 1. Channel, canal. Any of the paths by which the waters and vapors circulate in the bosom of the earth. 2. Drinking-trough for cattle. 3. Gutter, eaves-trough, pantile. 4. Duct or tube by which secretions of the body are conducted. 5. Comb of the loom, among weavers. 6. A domestic animal killed and dressed; particularly the hog. 7. Hemp which has been once hackled. 8. Front edge of a book. 9. Crease, slot (metales). **Canal de Panamá,** Panama Canal. **Canal de riego,** irrigation channel. **Canal de la Mancha,** English Channel. **Canal digestivo,** digestive tract, alimentary canal. -*m.* 10. Canal, an artificial waterway. 11. Channel, a strait between islands or continents. 12. Channel, navigable entrance to a harbor. 13. Channel, bed of a river. 14. Bed of a hot-press. 15. Pole of copper. **En canal,** from top to bottom. **Canal de desagüe,** *(And.)* Sewer. **Canal de humo,** *(Mex.)* Flue. **Canal inclinado,** chute. **Canal de entrada/salida,** input/output channel.
canalado, da [cah-nah-lah'-do, dah], *a.* V. ACANALADO.
canaleja [cah-nah-lay'-hah], *f.* 1. *(dim.)* Small drinking-trough for cattle. 2. In corn-mills, small channel to convey grain from the hopper to the millstones; mill-spout. 3. A priest's hat shaped like a trough.
canalera [cah-nah-lay'-rah], *f. (Prov.)* Gutter.
canaleta [cah-nah-lay'-tah], *f. (Cono Sur)* pipe, conduit; roof gutter.
canalete [cah-nah-lay'-tay], *m.* Paddle, a small oar.
canalita [cah-nah-lee'-tah], *f. dim.* Small channel or canal.
canalización [cah-nah-lee-tha-the-on'], *f.* 1. Canalization, chanelling. 2. *(Tec.)* Piping; *(Elec.)* Wiring; mains (de gas); *(LAm.)* Sewerage system, drainage (de cloacas).
canalizar [cah-nah-le-thar'], *va.* To channel, to canalize, provide an outlet.
canalizo [cah-nah-lee'-tho], *m.* Narrow channel between two islands or sand-banks.
canalón [cah-nah-lon'], *m.* 1. *(Arch.)* Gutter, guttering; spout; drainpipe. 2. Shovel hat (sombrero). 3. **Canalones** *(Culin.),* Canelloni.
canalla [cah-nahl'-lyah], *f.* Mob, rabble, multitude, populace, canaille. 2. Pack of hounds.
canallada [cah-nahl-lyah-dah], *f.* **canallería** *f. (LAm.)* Dirty trick, mean thing (to do), despicable act; nasty remark.
canallesco [cah-nahl-lyays'-co], *a.* Mean, rotten, despicable. **Diversión canallesca,** low form of amusement.
canalluza [cah-nal-lyoo'-thah], *f.* Roguery, vagrancy.
canalón [cah-nah-lone'], *m.* Large gutter or spout, eaves-trough, leader, waterway, rain-conductor.
canameño [cah-nah-may'-nyo], *m.* A traveling hammock. *(Cent. Amer.)*
canana [cah-nah'-nah], *f.* 1. A kind of cartridge-belt. 2. Fricassee of chicken. 3. *(LAm.)* *(Med.)* Goitre. 4. *(Carib.)* Mean trick, low prank.
canapé [cah-nah-pay'], *m.* 1. Couch or seat with a mattress, to sit or lie on. 2. Settee. 3. Lounge. 4. *(Culin.)* Canapé.
canario [cah-nah'-re-o], *m.* 1. Canarybird. 2. A native of the Canary Islands. 3 *(Naut.)* Barge used in the Canary Islands. 4. *(LAm.)* Yellow (amarillo).
canasta [cah-nahs'-tah], *f.* 1. Basket, hamper. **Canasta para los papeles,** wastepaper basket. 2. Canasta, card game.
canastero, ra [cah-nas-tay'-ro, rah], *m. & f.* Basket-maker.
canastilla [cah-nas-teel'-lyah], *f.* 1. *(dim.)* Small basket. **Canastilla de costura,** sewing basket. 2. An infant's basket; wardrobe for a baby. 3. A bride's trousseau.

canastillo [cah-nas-teel'-lyo], *m.* 1. Wicker tray; pannier. 2. Small basket. 3. Maund, a hand-basket.
canasto, canastro [cah-nahs'-to, cah-nahs'-tro], *m.* 1. Large basket. 2. **¡Canastos!** *int.* Denoting surprise or annoyance. 3. *(And.)* Servant.
cáncamo [cahn'-cah-mo], *m.* 1. *(Naut.)* Bolt-ring, to which the breeches and tackle of guns are fixed. **Cáncamos de argolla,** ring-bolts. **Cáncamos de gancho,** hook-bolts. **Cáncamos de ojo,** eye-bolts. 2. Blending of gums resembling myrrh.
cancamurria [cahn-cah-moor'-ree-ah], *f.* Blues, gloom.
cancamusa [can-cah-moo'-sah], *f.* Trick to deceive. **Ya le entiendo la cancamusa,** I am aware of the device.
cancán [cahn-cahn'], *m.* Cancan, a French dance.
cáncana [cahn'-cah-nah], *f.* Cricket, a kind of stool. 2. *(And.)* Thin person.
cancanco [cahn-cah'-no], *m. (Carib.)* *(Aut.)* Breakdown.
cancanear [cahn-cah-nay-ar'], *vn.* 1. To loiter, loaf about. 2. *(Cono Sur)* to dance the cancan. 3. *(And. CAm. Cono Sur)* to express oneself with difficulty, to stammer; to read haltingly.
cancaneo [cahn-cah-nay'-o], *m. (And. CAm. Mex.)* Faltering (al leer); stammering (tartamudeo).
cancanilla [can-cah-neel'-lyah], *f.* 1. Thing to play a trick with. 2. Deception, fraud.
cáncano [cahn'-cah-no], *m.* *(Coll.)* Louse. **Andar como cáncano loco,** to go round in circles.
cancel [can-thel'], *m.* 1. Wooden screen at the doors of churches and halls. 2. Glass-case in chapel behind which the king stands. 3. Limits or extent of a thing. 4. Windproof door, storm door.
cancela [can-thay'-lah], *f.* A grating or screen of open ironwork between the porch and the yard.
cancelación, canceladura [can-thay-lah-the-on', can-thay-lah-doo'-rah], *f.* Cancellation, expunging, obliteration, closing up.
cancelar [can-thay-lar'], *va.* To cancel or annul a writing. **Cancelar de la memoria,** *(Met.)* To efface from the memory.
cancelaría, cancelería [can-thay-lah-ree'-ah, lay-ree'-ah], *f.* Papal chancery, the court at Rome, whence apostolic grants and licenses are expedited.
cancelario [can-thay-lah'-re-o], *m.* Chancellor in universities who grants degrees.
cancellería [can-thel-lyay-ree'-ah], *f.* Chancery.
cáncer [cahn'-ther], *m.* 1. Cancer, virulent ulcer. 2. Cancer, one of the signs of the zodiac.
cancerado [cahn-thay-rah'-do], *a.* Cancerous; *(fig.)* Corrupt.
cancerarse [can-thay-rar'-say], *vr.* 1. To be afflicted with a cancer. 2. To cancerate or become a cancer.
cancerbero [can-ther-bay'-ro], *m.* 1. Cerberus, the three-headed dog which guarded the gate of the nether world. 2. *(Met.)* A severe and incorruptible guard. 3. A worthless gatekeeper.
cancerígeno, na [can-thay-ree'-hay-no, nah], *a.* Carcinogenic, cancerogenic.
cancerólogo, ga [cahn-thay-ro'-lo-go], *m. & f.* Cancer specialist.
canceroso, sa [can-thay-ro'-so, sah], *a.* Cancerous.
cancha [cahn'-chah], *f.* 1. Field, ball park, court. **Cancha de tenis,** tennis court. **Cancha de pelota,** pelota court. **Estar en su cancha,** *(Cono Sur)* to be in one's element. **En la cancha se ven los pingos,** *(LAm.)* Deeds speak louder than words. 2. Toasted corn. 3. *(Peru)* Popcorn.
canchar [can-char'], *va. (And. Cono Sur)* to toast.
canche [cahn'-chay], *a.* 1. *(CAm.)* Blonde (rubio). 2. *(And.)* Poorly seasoned, tasteless.
canchero, ra [cahn-chay-ro], *m. & f.* 1. Experienced person. 2. *(LAm.)* Groundsman, groundswoman (cuidador); experienced player. 3. *(Cono Sur)* layabout, loafer (vago).
canchilagua [can-chah-lah'-goo-ah], *f. (Bot.).* A medicinal herb growing in Peru.
canchón [cahn-chon'], *m. (And.)* Enclosed field.

cancilla [can-theel'-lyah], *f. (Prov.)* Wicker-door or wicker-gate.

canciller [can-theel-lyerr'], *m.* Chancellor.

cancilleresco, ca [can-theel-lyay-res´-co, cah], *a.* 1. Belonging to the writing characters used in chancery business. 2. *(Admin.)* Chancellery.

cancillería [can-theel-lyay-ree'-ah], *f. (Obs.)* V. CHANCILLERÍA.

canción [can-the-on'],*f.* 1. Song, verses set to music. **Canción de cuna**, lullaby, cradle song. 2. Poem of one or more stanzas, a lay. **Volver a la misma canción**, to return to the old tune, to repeat the old story. **Volvemos a la misma canción**, here we go again.

cancioncica, illa, ita [can-the-on-thee'-cah, eel´-lyah, ee'-tah],*f. dim.* Canzonet, a little song.

cancionero [can-the-o-nay'-ro], *m.* 1. Song-book. 2. Songwriter.

cancionista [can-the-o-nees'-tah], *m.* Author or singer of songs.

canco [can'-co], *m. (Chile)* 1. Earthen pot. 2. Flower pot. 3. Big hip.4. *(Bol.)* Buttocks, hips.

cancriforme [can-cre-for´-may], *a.* Cancriform, having the shape of a crab.

cancrinita [can-cre-nee´-tah], *f.* Cancrinite, a variously colored silicate, which crystallizes in the hexagonal system.

cancro [cahn'-cro], *m.* V. CÁNCER.

cancrófago, ga [can-cro´-fah-go, gah], *a.* Crab-eating.

cancroideo, ea [can-cro-e-day'-o, ah], *a.* Cancroid, resembling cancer.

candado [can-dah'-do], *m.* 1. Padlock. 2. Pendant, earring. **Echar** or **poner candado a los labios**, *(Met.)* To keep a secret, to be silent. 3. *(And.)* Beard.

candanga [cahn-dahn'-gah], *m.* El candanga, the devil.

candar [can-dar´], *va.* To lock, to shut.

cándara [cahn'-dah-rah],*f. (Prov.)* Frame of laths for sifting sand, earth, and gravel.

cande [cahn'-day], *a.* Sugar-candy. V. AZÚCAR.

candeal [can-day-ahl´], *a.* **Trigo candeal**, white wheat, summer wheat. **Pan candeal**, bread made of the white wheat.

candeda [can-day'-dah],*f.* Blossom of the walnut-tree.

candela [can-day'-lah],*f.* 1. Candle. 2. Flower or blossom of the chestnut-tree. 3. Candlestick. 4. Inclination of the balance-needle to the thing weighed. 5. *(Prov.)* Light, fire. **Arrimarse a la candela**, *(Prov.)* To draw near the fire. **Acabarse la candela**, *(Met.)* To be near one's end. **Estar con la candela en la mano**, to be dying. **Dar candela**, to be a nuisance. **Echar candela** to sparkle (ojos). **Prender candela**, to set fire.

candelabro [can-day-lah'-bro], *m.* Candlestick. V. CANDELERO.

candelada [can-day-lah'-dah], *f. (Prov.)* Sudden blaze from straw or brushwood. V. HOGUERA.

candelaria [can-day-lah'-re-ah], *f.* 1. Candlemas. 2. *(Bot.)* Mullein. V. GORDOLOBO.

candelejón [can-day-lay-hone´], *a. (So. Amer.)* Candid, simple-minded, dumb.

candelerazo [can-day-lay-rah'-tho], *m.* 1. *(aug.)* Large candlestick. 2. Stroke or blow given with a candlestick

candelería [can-day-lay-ree'-ah], *f.* Tallow and wax chandler's shop. V. VELERÍA.

candelero [can-day-lay'-ro], *m.* 1. Candlestick. **Candelero con muchos brazos**, chandelier. 2. *(Obs.)* Wax or tallow chandler. 3. Lamp. 4. Fishing-torch. **Estar en candelero**, *(Met.)* To be high in office, to hold an exalted station. **Candeleros**, *(Naut.)* Stanchions or crotches, pieces of timber which support the waist-trees. **Candeleros de trincheras y parapetos**, quarter-netting stanchions. **Tema en candelero**, hot subject. **Poner en candelero a uno**, to give somebody a high post. **Poner algo en candelero**, to bring something into the limelight.

candeletón [can-day-lay-tone'], *m.* Large stanchion.

candelilla [can-day-leel'-lyah], *f.* 1. *(Surg.)* Bougie, catheter. 2. Blossom of poplars and other trees. Catkin, ament. **Hacer la candelilla**, to stand on the hands and head, as boys do in play. **Le hacen candelillas los ojos**, *(Coll.)* He is half-seas over, or his eyes sparkle with the fumes of wine. 3. Small candle. 4. *(Carib. Cono Sur)* hem, border.

candelizas [can-day-lee'-thas], *f. pl. (Naut.)* Brails, small ropes reeved trough a block. **Candelizas de barlovento**, weather-braces. **Candelizas de sotavento** , lee-braces.

candelizo [cahn-day-lee'-tho], *m.* Icicle.

candelo [cahn-day'-lo], *a. (And.)* Reddish-blonde.

candencia [can-den'-the-ah], *f.* Incandescence, white heat.

candente [can-den'-tay], *a.* 1. Incandescent, red-hot, tending to a white heat. 2. *(fig.)* Burning (cuestión).

candi [cahn'-de], *a.* **Azúcar candi**, sugar-candy, rock-candy.

candial [can-de-ahl'], *a.* V. CANDEAL.

cándidamente [cahn'-de-dah-men-tay], *adv.* Candidly.

candidato, ta [can-de-dah'-to], *a.m. & f.* 1. Candidate; applicant for. 2. *(Cono Sur)* sucker.

candidatura [can-de-dah-too'-rah], *f.* 1. Candidacy; candidature; soliciting votes. 2. A list of those who aspire to some elective position.

candidez [can-de-deth'],*f.* 1. Whiteness. 2. Candor, sincerity, purity of mind. 3. Candidness, ingenuousness. 4. Simplicity.

cándido, da [cahn'-de-do, dah], *a.* 1. White, snowy, gray, pale. 2. Candid, guileless. 3. Simple.

candil [can-deel'], *m.* 1. A kitchen or stable lamp. 2. Lamp with oil, etc. 3. Cock of a hat. 4. Long irregular fold in petticoats. 5. Fishing-torch. V. CANDELERO. 6. *(Mex.)* A chandelier. **Puede arder en un candil**, it would burn in a lamp (vino generoso, personas brillantes); it is used ironically in the last sense. 7. Top of a stag's horn. **Baile de candil**, ball held by the light of a poor lamp. **Dar candil a uno**, *(fig.)* to be very strong.

candileja [can-de-lay'-hah],*f.* 1. Inner part of a kitchen lamp. 2. The foot-lights of a theater. 3. *(Bot.)* Willows, deadly carrot.

candilejera [can-de-lay-hay'-rah], *f. (Bot.)* Spanish birth wort.

candilejo [can-de-lay'-ho], *m. dim.* 1. Small kitchen lamp. 2. *(Bot.)* V. LUCÉRNULA .

candilera [can-de-lay'-rah], *f. (Bot.)* Lamp-wick.

candilón [can-de-lone'], *m. aug.* Large open lamp.

candinga [cahn-deen'-dah], *f.* 1. *(Cono Sur)* impertinence, insistence. **El candinga**, *(Mex.)* the devil.

candiota [can-de-o'-tah],*f.* 1. Barrel or keg for carrying wine in vintage time. 2. Large earthen jar, the inside of which is pitched, wherein wine is fermented. 3. An inhabitant of the island of Candia.

candiotera [can-de-o-tay'-rah],*f.* A wine-cellar: storage place of casks, tuns.

candiotero [cahn-dee-o-tay'-ro], *m.* Cooper.

candonga [can-don'-gah],*f.* 1. Mean, servile civility, intended to deceive. 2. Merry, playful trick. 3. Old mule unfit for service. 4. An old, ugly woman. 5. *(Col.)* Earring.

candongo, ga [can-don'-go, gah], *a.* 1. A cunning, fawning person. 2. Smooth oily (zalamero); sly (taimado), crafty; lazy. 2. *m.* Creep, toady, flatterer; sly sort; shirker, idler, lazy blighter.

candonguear [can-don-gay-ar´], *va. (Coll.)* To jeer, to sneer, to turn into ridicule.

candonguero, ra [can-don-gay'-ro, rah], *a. (Coll.)* The one who is mischievous or plays bad tricks. V. CANDONGO.

candor [can-dor'], *m.* 1. *(Obs.)* Supreme whiteness. 2. *(Met.)* Candor, purity of mind, ingenuousness fairness, frankness, openness.

candoroso, sa [can-do-ro'-so, sah], *a.* Ingenuous, frank, honest, straightforward.

canear [cah-nay-ar'*], va.* To bash, to hit (con vara).

caneca [cah'-nay-cah],*f.* 1. Glazed liquor bottle made of clay. 2. *(Arg.)* Wooden tub. 3. *(Cuba)* Hot-water bottle made of earthenware. 4. *(Cuba)* Liquid measure of 19 liters.

caneco [cah-nay'-co], *a. (And.)* Tipsy.

canecillo [cah-nay-theel'-lyo], *m. (Arch.)* Corbel, modillion, truss, cantilever; console.

canela [cah-nay'-lah], *f.* 1. *(Bot.)* Cinnamon. **Agua de canela**, cinnamon-water. 2. *(fig.)* Lovely thing, exquisite object. **Es canela fina**, she's wonderful. 3. *Interj.* Good gracious!

canelado, da [cah-nay-lah'-do, dah], *a. V.* ACANELADO.

canelero [cah-nay-lay'-ro], *m.* Cinnamon tree.

canelo [cah-nay'-lo], *m.* 1. *(Bot.)* Cinnamon-tree or cinnamon laurel. 2. *m.* Cinnamon-colored.

canelón [cah-nay-lone'], *m.* 1. Gutter. *V.* CANALÓN. 2. Sweetmeat. 3. Icicle. 4. *(Bot.)* A kind of bastard cinnamon, commonly called **Canelón de Santa Fe**. **Canelones**, end of a cat of nine-tails, thicker and more twisted than the rest. 5. *(CAm.)* Corkscrew curl.

canesú [cah-nay-soo'], *m.* 1. A bodice. 2. Upper part of a shirt for either sex. 3. *(Cos.)* Yoke.

caney [cah-nay'-e], *m.* 1. A logcabin. 2. Bight; riverbend.

canez [cah-neth'], *f.* Hair hoary or gray with age; old age. (*Yo canezco, yo canezca,* from *Canecer.* *V.* CONOCER).

canfín [cahn-feen'], *m. (CAm. Carib.)* Petrol, gasoline.

canforero [can-fo-ray'-ro], *m.* The camphor-tree.

canga [cahn'-gah], *f.* Cangue, a heavy wooden collar or yoke, worn around the neck by convicts in China as a punishment.

cangalla [can-gahl'-lyah], 1. *(Salv.)* Tattered shred of clothing. 2. *(Col.)* *m.* or *f.* Thinned-out animal or person. 3. *(Arg. & Peru)* A coward. 4. *(Bol.)* Packsaddle. 5. *(Arg. & Chile)* Mineral wastings.

cangallar [can-gahl-lyar'], *va. (Arg. & Chile)* To ransack metal in the mines.

cangilón [can-he-lone'], *m.* 1. Earthen jar or pitcher. 2. Oblong earthen jar fastened to the rope of a draw-well, or to a wheel for lifting water. 3. Metal tankard for wine or water. 4. *(LAm.)* Cart track.

cangreja [can-gray'-hah], *a.* **Vela cangreja**, *(Naut.)* boom sail, brig-sail, or gaffsail.

cangrejal [can-gray-hahl'], *m. (Amer.)* A spot frequented by crabs.

cangrejo [can-gray'-ho], *m.* 1. *(Zool.)* Craw-fish, crab. 2. Truckle-cart. 3. Trolley. **Andar como el cangrejo**, to go backward. 4. *(Naut.)* Gaff. 5. *(And.)* Idiot, crafty person. 6. *(LAm.)* Mystery, enigma.

cangrejuelo [can-gray-hoo-ay'-lo], *m. dim.* Small crawfish.

cangrena [can-gray'-nah], *f.* Gangrene, mortification. *V.* GANGRENA.

cangrenarse [can-gray-nar'-say], *vr.* To be afflicted with gangrene or mortification. *V.* GANGRENARE.

cangrenoso, sa [can-gray-no'-so, sah], *a.* Gangrenous, mortified.

cangri [cahn'-gree], *m.* 1. Nick (cárcel), prison. 2. Church.

cangro [cahn'-gro], *m. (And. CAm. Mex.)* Cancer.

canguelo [cahn-goo-ay'-lo], *m.* Canguis *m.* Funk.

canguro [cahn-goo'-ro], *m.* 1. *(Zool.)* Kangaroo. 2. Babysitter. **Hacer de canguro**, to baby-sit. 3. Light jacket, light coat.

cania [cah'-ne-ah], *f. (Bot.)* Small nettle.

caníbal [ca-nee'-bal], *m.* Cannibal, a man-eater.

canibalismo [cah-nee-bah-lees'-mo], *m.* Cannibalism; *(fig.)* fierceness, savageness.

canicas [cah-nee'-cahs], *f. pl.* Marbles.

caniche [cah-nee-chay], *m.* Poodle.

canicie [ca-nee'-the-ay], *f.* Whiteness of the hair

canícula [ca-nee'-coo-lah], *f.* 1. *(Astr.)* Dog-star. 2. *V.* CANICULARES. **Entra la canícula**, the hot days begin. **Canícula marina**, *(Zool.)* lesser spotted dog-fish.

canicular [ca-ne-coo-lar'], *a.* 1. Canicular belonging to the dog-star. 2. **Calores caniculares**, midsummer heat.

caniculares [ca-nee-coo-lah'-res], *m. pl.* Dog-days.

canido [ca-nee'-do], *m.* Kind of parrot found in the West Indies.

canijo, ja [ca-nee'-ho, hah], *a. & m. & f.* Weak, infirm, sickly. **Es un canijo**, he is a weak, puny being.

canilla [ca-nee'-lyah_, *f.* 1. A long bone of either extremity. **Canilla de la pierna**, shin-bone. **Canilla del brazo**, arm-bone. 2. Any of the principal bones of the wing of a fowl 3. Stopcock, faucet, spigot. 4. Reel, bobbin, spool; quill put into a shuttle on which the woof is wound. 5. Unevenness or inequality of the wool in point of thickness or color. **Irse como una canilla**; to let the tongue run like the clapper of a mill. 6. Rib (paño). 7. *(Carib.)* Cowardice. 8. *(Mex.)* **Tener canilla**, to have great physical strengh.

canillado, da [ca-neel-lyah'-do, dah], *a. V.* ACANILLADO.

canillento [ca-neel-lyayn'-to], *a. (And.)* Long-legged.

canillera [ca-nee'-lyay'-rah], *f.* 1. Ancient armor for the shin-bone. 2. Woman who distributes thread to be wound on spools. 3. *(LAm.)* Fear; cowardice.

canillero [ca-neel-lyay'-ro], *m.* 1. Hole in a cask or vat to draw off its contents. 2. Weaver's quill-winder.

canillita [cah-neel-lyee'-tah], *m. (Arg.)* A newsboy; a newsvendor.

canillón [cah-neel-lyone'], *a. (LAm.)*, **Canilludo** *a. (LAm.)* Long-legged.

canina [ca-nee-nah], *f.* Excrement of dogs.

caninamente [ca-ne-nah-men'-tay], *adv.* In a passionate, snarling manner; like a dog.

canino, na [ca-nee'-no, nah], *a.* Canine. **Hambre canina**, canine appetite, inordinate hunger. **Dientes caninos**, eye-teeth or canine-teeth. **Músculo canino**, canine muscle, which serves to elevate the upper lip.

canje [cahn'-hay], *m.* Exchange, used in speaking of prisoners, ratified treaties, or the credentials of diplomats.

canjear [can-hay-ar'], *va.* To exchange prisoners of war, treaties, or credentials, to change over, to interchange; to cash in.

cano, na [cah'-no, nah], *a.* 1. Hoary, hoar, frosty, gray-headed. 2. *(Met.)* Deliberate, prudent, judicious.

canoa [ca-no'-ah], *f.* 1. Canoe, a boat used by the Indians. **Canoa automóvil**, motor boat. 2. *(LAm.)* Conduit, pipe; feeding trough (comedero); chicken coop (de gallinas); dovecot (de palomas).

canódromo [cah-no'-dro-mo], *m.* Dog track.

canoero [ca-no-ay'-ro], *m.* One who conducts a canoe.

canoi [ca-no'-e], *m. (Amer.)* Basket used by Indians on a fishing party.

canoita [ca-no-ee'-tah], *m. dim.* Small canoe.

canon [cah'-non], *m.* 1. Canon, the decision of an ecclesiastical council relative to the doctrines or discipline of the church. 2. Catalogue of the books which compose the Holy Scriptures. 3. *(Law.)* Fee paid in acknowledgment of superiority in a higher lord. **Canon de tránsito**, *(Aut.)* Toll. **Como mandan los cánones**, as the rules require, in accordance with sound principles. 4. Catalogue, list. 5. *(Print.)* Canon, a large sort of type. **Cánones**, canons or canonical law. 6. *(Mus.)* Canon. A composition in which the music sung by one part, after a short rest, sung by another part, note for note.

canonesa [ca-no-nay'-sah], *f.* Canoness, a woman who lives in a religious house and observes its rules, without having taken the vows of a monastic life.

canonical [ca-no-ne-cahl'], *a.* Canonical, relating to canons, *(fig.)* Easy.

canónicamente [ca-no'-ne-cah-men-tay], *adv.* Canonically.

canonicato [ca-no-ne-cah'-to], *m.* Canonry, sinecure, cushy job. *V.* CANONJÍA.

canónico, ca [ca-no'-ne-co, cah], *a.* 1. Canonical canonic. **Iglesia o casa canónica**, house or monastery of regular canons. 2. Canonical; applied to the books which compose the Holy Scriptures.

canónigo [ca-no'-ne-go], *m.* Canon or prebendary.

canonista [ca-no-nees'-tah], *m.* Canonist, a professor or student of the canon law.

canonizable [ca-no-ne-thah'-blay], *a.* Worthy of canonization.

canonización [ca-no-ne-thah-the-on'], *f.* Canonization, consecration.

canonizar [ca-no-ne-thar'], *va.* 1. To canonize, to consecrate, to declare one a saint. 2. *(Met.)* To applaud or praise a thing. 3. *(Met.)* To prove a thing good.

canonjía [ca-non-hee'-ah], *f.* Canonry canonship, prebend or benefice of a canon: canonicate.

canoro, ra [ca-no'-ro, rah], *a.* 1. Canorous, melodious, musical. 2. Shrill, loud.

canoso, sa [ca-no'-so, sah], *a.* 1. Hoary, hoar, frosty, grayheaded. 2. Old.

canotaje [cah-no-tah'-hay], *m.* Boating.

canotier [cah-no-te-ayr'], *m.* **canotié** *m.* Straw hat, boater.

cansadamente [can-sah-dah-men'-tay], *adv.* 1. Importunely, troublesomely. 2. Wearily, in a tired way.

cansado, da [can-sah'-do, dah], *a.* 1. Weary, wearied, exhausted, tired. 2. Tedious, tiresome, troublesome. **Una vista cansada**, an impaired eyesight. **Con voz cansada**, in a weary voice. **Estoy cansado de hacerlo**, I'm tired of doing it. 3. Performed with pain or fatigue. -*pp.* of CANSAR. -*vr.* To tire, to get tired, to grow weary, to get bored. **Cansarse de hacer algo**, to get tired of doing something.

cansado [can-sah'-do], *m.* Bore.

cansancio [can-sahn'-the-o], *m.* Weariness, lassitude, fatigue.

cansar [can-sar'], *va.* 1. To weary, to tire, to fatigue, to overcome. 2. To harass, to molest, to bore. 3. To exhaust land.-*vr.* To tire oneself, to be fatigued, to grow weary.

cansera [can-say'-rah_, *f.* Fatigue, weariness.

casinamente [cahnn-see-nah-mayn'-tay], *adv.* Wearily; lifeless.

cansino, na [can-see'-no, nah], *a.* Worn by work (animales).

cantable [can-tah'-blay], *a.* 1. Tunable, harmonious, musical. 2. Pathetic, affecting.

Cantábrico, ca [can-tah'-bre-co, cah], **cántabro, bra** [cahn'-tah-bro, brah], *a.* 1. Cantabrian, of Cantabria 2. Name given to the part of the Atlantic Ocean which washes the northern coast of Spain.

cantada [can-tah'-dah], *f.* Cantata, a musical composition.

cantadera [cahn-tah-day'-rah], *f. (LAm.)* Loud singing, prolonged singing.

cantador, ra [can-tah-dor'], *m. & f.* V. CANTOR.

cantal [cahn-tahl'], *m.* 1. Boulder (piedra); stone block. 2. Stony ground.

cantaleta [can-ta-lay'-tah], *f.* 1. Charivari, a confused noise of voices or instruments. 2. Pun, jest, joke, humbug. **Dar cantaleta**, to deride, to laugh at, to turn into ridicule.

cantaloup [can-tah-loop'], *m.* Cantaloup or cantaloupe.

cantante [can-tahn'-tay], *m. & f.* A singer, especially one who sings for a livelihood.

cantaor, ora [cahn-tah-or'], *m. & f.* V. CANTADOR, RA. (De cante flamenco).

cantar [can-tar'], *m. (Coll.)* Song set to music. **Cantares**, canticles or Song of Solomon. **Cantares de gesta**, old metrical romances.

cantar [can-tar'], *va.* 1. To sing. 2. To recite in a poetical manner. 3. *(Met. Coll.)* To creak, to make a harsh, grinding noise. 4. *(Coll.)* To divulge a secret 5. At cards, to announce the trump. **Cantar a libro abierto**, to sing offhand. **Cantar de plano**, to make a plain and full confession. **Cantar la victoria**, *(Met.)* To triumph. **Cantar misa**, to say the first mass. **Ése es otro cantar**, that is another kind of speech. **¿Lo digo cantado o rezado ?** how would you have me say it? **Al fin se canta la gloria**, do not triumph till all is over, don't whistle before you are out of the woods. **Cantar las claras**, to speak out. **Cantar a dos voces**, to sing a duet.

cántara [cahn'-ta-rah_, *f.* 1. Large, narrow-mouthed pitcher. V. CÁNTARO 2. Wine measure containing about thirty-two pints.

cantarcico, illo, ito [can-tar-thee'-co, theel'-lyo, thee'-to], *m. dim.* Little song.

cantarera [can-ta-ray'-rah], *f.* Shelf for jars, pitchers, etc.

cantarería [cahn-tah-ray-ree'-ah], *f.* 1. Pottery shop, earthenware shop. 2. Pottery (shop).

cantarero, ra [can-ta-ray'-ro, rah], *m. & f.* A dealer in earthen jars, pitchers, pans, etc.

cantárida [can-tah'-re-dah], *f.* 1. Cantharis, Spanish-fly, the blistering fly. 2. Blistering plaster made with the blistering fly. 3. Blister, the vesicle raised on the skin by the blistering plaster.

cantarillo [can-ta-reel'-lyo], *m.* 1. *(dim.)* Small jar or pitcher. 2. *(Bot.)* Oval-leaved androsace. **Cantarillo que muchas veces va a la fuente, o deja el asa o la frente**, the pitcher which goes often to the well gets broken in the end.

cantarín [can-ta-reen'], *m. (Coll.)* One who sings constantly.

cantarina [can-ta-ree'-nah], *f.* A woman who sings on the stage.

cántaro [cahn'-ta-ro], *m.* 1. Large, narrow-mouthed pitcher, and the liquid contained in it. 2. Wine measure of different sizes. **Llover a cántaros**, to rain by bucketfuls, to pour, to rain cats and dogs.

cantata [cahn-tah'-tah], *f.* Cantata.

cantazo [can-tah'-tho], *m.* Wound given by flinging a stone.

cante [cahn'-tay], *m.* **Cante flamenco, conte jondo,** Andalusian gipsy singing.

cantegriles [cahn-tay-gree-lays], *m. pl. (Cono Sur)* Shanty-town.

canteles [can-tay'-les], *m. pl. (Naut.)* Ends of old ropes put under casks to keep them steady.

cantera [can-tay'-rah], *f.* 1. Quarry where stones are dug. **Cantera de arena**, sandpit. **Cantera de piedra**, stone quarry. 2. *(Met.)* Talents or genius.

canterear [can-tay-ray-ar'], *va.* To hang up flitches of bacon, that the brine may run off.

cantería [can-tay-ree'-ah], *f.* 1. Art of hewing stone, the trade of a stone-cutter. 2. Building made of hewn stone 3. Quarry. 4. Parcel of hewn stone.

cantero [can-tay'-ro], *m.* 1. Stone-cutter. 2. The extremity of a hard substance which can be easily separated from the rest. **Cantero de pan**, crust of bread. 3. *(Cono Sur)* bed, plot (sembradío). 4. *(Mex. And.)* Plot of sugar.

canterón [can-tay-rone'], *m. (Prov.)* Large tract of land.

canticio [can-tee'-the-o], *m. (Coll.)* Constant or frequent singing.

cántico [cahn'-te-co], *m.* Canticle. **Cántico de los cánticos**, the Song of Solomon.

cantidad [can-te-dahd'], *f.* 1. Quantity. 2. Measure, number, time used in pronouncing a syllable. 3. Quantity, large portion of a thing. **Por una cantidad alzada**, for a sum of money agreed upon. **Hacer buena alguna cantidad**, to pay a sum of money due. **En cantidad**, in quantity. **Tengo una cantidad de cosas que hacer**, I've got lots of things to do. **Este coche mola cantidad**, that car is really nice; **esto está degenerando cantidad**, this is really going down hill.

cantiga [can-tee'-gah], *f. (Obs.)* V. CANTAR. A poetical composition divided into strophes; after each follows a refrain.

cantil [can-teel'], *m.* Steep rock; shelf; ledge, coastal shelf (de costa); cliff (risco).

cantilagua [can-te-lah'-goo-ah], *f. (Prov.)* Purging flax.

cantilena [can-te-lay'-nah], *f.* Ballad, song, chant. V. CANTINELA.

cantillo [can-teel'-lyo], *m. dim.* A little stone.

cantimarones [can-te-mah-ro'-nes], *m. pl. (Naut.)* Kind of boats.

cantimplora [can-tim-plo'-rah], *f.* 1. Siphon, a crooked tube or pipe. 2. Vessel for cooling liquors; liquor-case.

cantina [can-tee'nah], *f.* 1. Saloon, tavern, bar, barroom. 2. Cellar for wine. 3. Canteen, shop where liquors and provisions are sold in barracks or military camps. 4. Canteen (used to carry water on a journey or march).

cantinela [can-te-nay'-lah], *f.* 1. Ballad. 2. Irksome repetition of a subject. **¿Ahora se viene con esa cantinela?**, does he come again with that old story?

cantinero [can-te-nay'-ro], *m.* 1. Bartender. 2. Keeper of a tavern or saloon.

cantinflismo [cahn-teen-flees'-mo], *m.* *(Mex.)* Babble, empty chatter.

cantiña [can-tee'-nyah], *f.* A song in Galicia and Asturias.

cantió [cahn-tee-o'], *m.* *(Carib.)* Folksong, popular song.

cantiral [cahn-tee-rahl'], *m.* Stony ground, stony place.

cantizal [can-te-thahl'], *m.* Stony ground, place full of stones.

canto [cahn'-to], *m.* 1. Singing. 2. A short poem, of heroic type. 3. Canto, a division of a long poem. 4. A chant or canticle. **Al canto del gallo,** at midnight. **El canto de los pájaros,** the singing of the birds. 5. End, edge, or border. 6. Extremity, point. 7. The crust (of a loaf). 8. Thickness of any thing; back of a knife. 9. The front edge of a book. 10. Dimension less than square. **Al canto,** by the side of. **De canto,** on edge. **El ladrillo está de canto y no de plano,** the brick stands on edge, and not flatwise. **Ni un canto de uña,** absolutely nothing. **Faltó el canto de un duro,** he had a close shave.

canto, *m.* 1. A stone, pebble. 2. Game of throwing the stone (duck on a rock). 3. Quarry-stone, block, dressed ashlar.

cantón [can-tone'], *m.* 1. Corner. 2 *(Her.)* Part of an escutcheon. 3. Canton, region, tract of land, district. 4. *(LAm.) (Cost.)* Cotton (material).

cantonada [can-to-nah'-dah], *f.* *(Prov.)* Corner. **Dar cantonada,** to laugh at a person on turning a corner; to disappoint a person by not taking notice of what he says or does.

cantonal [can-to-nahl'], *a.* Cantonal, relating to the canton or district.

cantonar [can-to-nar'], *va.* *V.* ACANTONAR.

cantonear [cahn-to-nay-ar'], *vn.* To loaf around.

cantonease [can-to-nay-ar'-say], *vr.* *V.* CONTORNEARSE.

cantoneo [can-to-nay'-o], *m.* *V.* CONTONEO.

cantonera [can-to-nay'-rah], *f.* 1. Plate nailed to the corners of a chest, etc., to strengthen it. 2. Corner cabinet (rinconera). 3. Angle-iron, corner bracket. 4. Wench, a woman of the town.

cantonero, ra [can-to-nay'-ro, rah], *a.* *(Obs.)* Standing idle at the corner of a street.

cantor, ra [can-tor', rah], *m. & f.* 1. Singer; minstrel. 2. One who composes hymns or psalms. 3. Small singing-bird.

cantorcillo [can-tor-theel'-lyo], *m. dim.* Petty, worthless singer.

cantoría [can-to-ree'-ah], *f.* Musical canto; singing.

cantorral [can-tor-rahl'], *m.* Stony ground, place full of stones.

cantueso [can-too-ay'-so], *m.* *(Bot.)* French lavender, spike.

cantuja [cahn-too'-hah], *f.* *(And.)* Slang.

cantúo [cahn-too'-o], *a.* **Una mujer cantúa,** a woman with a smashing figure.

canturía [can-too-ree'-ah], *f.* 1. Vocal music. 2. Musical composition. 3. Method of performing musical compositions. **Esta composición tiene buena canturía,** this piece of music may be easily sung.

canturrear, canturriar [can-toor-ray-ar', re-ar'], *vn.* To hum, to sing in a low voice.

canturreo [cahn-too-ray'-o], *m.* Humming, crooning, soft singing; chanting; droning.

cantusar [can-too-sar'], *va.* *V.* ENGATUSAR.

canudo, da [ca-noo'-do, dah], *a.* Hoary, gray; ancient.

canula [cah'-noo-lah], *f.* *(Med.)* Canula, a metal tube for withdrawing fluids; often fitted with a trocar.

canutazo [cah-noo-tah'-tho], *m.* Telephone call.

canutero [cah-noo-tay'-ro], *m.* *(LAm.)* Barrel (of pen).

canutillo [cah-noo-teel'-lyo], *m.* *V.* CANUTILLO.

canuto [cah-noo'-to], *a.* 1. Super, smashing. 2. **Pasarlas canutas,** to have a rough time of it. *-m.* 1. Small tube, small container. 2. *(Bot.)* Internode. 3. Tell-tale (persona). 4. Joint (porro). 5. Telephone.

canzonetista [cahn-tho-nay-tees'-tah], *f.* Vocalist, crooner.

caña [cah'-nyah], *f.* 1. Cane, reed. Arundo. 2. Stem, stalk. **La caña del trigo,** stem of corn 3. Walking-stick. **Caña común,** cultivated reed. **Caña dulce** or **de azúcar,** or **cañamiel,** common sugar-cane. 4. *V.* CANILLA for a bone. 5. Subterranean passage in the mines of Almadén. 6. Shaft of a column or pillar. 7. Marrow. 8. Tournament 9. *(Naut.)* Helm. 10. Lever drill, ratchet drill. 11. Glass-blower's pipe. 12. *(Carp.)* Shank. 13. Reed of wind instruments. **Caña del timón,** *(Naut.)* tiller. **Caña de pescar,** fishing-rod. **Hubo toros y cañas,** *(Met.)* there was the devil to pay. **Caña de cerveza,** glass of beer. **¡Dos cañas!,** two beers please.

cañada [cah-nyah'-dah], *f.* 1. Glen or dale between mountains; glade. 2. **Cañada real,** sheep-walk for the flocks passing from the mountainous and colder parts of Spain to the flat and warmer parts. 3. *(Prov.)* Measure of wine. 4. *(Amer.)* Rivulet, brook.

cañadicas, cañaditas [cah-nyah-dee'-cass, dee'-tas], *f. pl.* *(Prov.)* Small measures for wine.

cañadón [cah-nyah-done'], *m.* *(Cono Sur)* Low-lying part of a field.

cañafístula [cah-nyah-fees'-too-lah], *f.* Cassia fistula, the fruit of the purging cassia.

cañafístulo [can-nyah-fees'-too-lo], *m.* *(Bot.)* Purging cassia-tree.

cañaheja, cañaherla [ca-nyah-ay'-hah, cah-nyah-err'-lah], *f.* *(Bot.)* Common fennel-giant, or gigantic fennel.

cañahuate [cah-nyah-oo-ah'-tay], *m.* A species of lignum-vitae which grows in Colombia.

cañal [cah-nyahl'], *m.* 1. Weir or wear for fishing, made of canes or reeds. 2. Plantation of canes or reeds. 3. Small sluice or channel, for catching fish. 4. Conduit of water.

cañaliega [cah-nyah-le-ay'-gah], *f.* Wear or weir for fishing.

cáñama [cah'-nyah-mah], *f.* Assessment of taxes, paid by a village or other place. **Casa cáñama,** house exempt from taxes. **Cogedor de cáñama,** tax gatherer.

cañamar [cah-nyah-mar'], *m.* Hempfield.

cañamazo [cah-nyah-mah'-tho], *m.* 1. Tow of hemp. 2. Coarse canvas made of hemp-tow. 3. Painted or checkered stuff for table-carpets, made of hemp.

cañamelar [cah-nyah-may-lar'], *m.* Plantation of sugar-cane. Cane-field.

cañameño, ña [cah-nyah-may'-nyo, nyah], *a.* Hempen, made of hemp.

cañamero [cah-nyah-may'-ro], *a.* Hemp.

cañamiel [cah-nyah-me-el'], *f.* *(Bot.)* Sugar-cane. *V.* CAÑA DULCE.

cañamiz [cah-nyah-meeth'], *m.* Kind of Indian vessel.

cañamiza [cah-nyah-mee'-thah], *f.* Stalk of hemp; bullen, bun. *V.* AGRAMIZA.

cáñamo [cah'-nyah-mo], *m.* 1. *(Bot.)* Hemp. **Cáñamo silvestre,** bastard hemp. 2. Cloth made of hemp. 3. *(Poet.)* Slings, rigging, and other things made of hemp. **Cáñamo en rama,** undressed hemp.

cañamón [cah-nyah-mone'], *m.* Hempseed.

cañar [cah-nyar'], *m.* 1. Plantation of canes or reeds. 2. Weir for catching fish.

cañareja [cah-nyah-ray'-hah], *f.* *V.* CAÑAHEJA.

cañariego, ga [cah-nyah-re-ay'-go, gah], *a.* **Pellejos cañariegos,** skins of sheep which die on the road.

cañarroya [cah-nyah-ro'-yah], *f.* *(Bot.)* Pellitory, wall-wort.

cañavera [cah-nyah-vay'-rah], *f.* *(Bot.)* Common reed-grass.

cañaveral [cah-nyah-vay-rahl'], *m.* Plantation of canes or reeds. **Recorrer los cañaverales,** to go from house to house, to get something.

cañaverero [cah-nyah-vay-ray-ro], *m.* Retailer of canes or reeds.

cañavete [cah-nyah-vay'-tay], *m.* The knife with which shepherds slaughter their animals.

cañazo [cah-nyah'-tho], *m.* 1. Hostile blow with a cane. **Dar cañazo,** *(Met.)* To confound one by a rude comnunication. 2. Rum. *(Peru)*.

cañear [cah-nyay-ar'], *vn.* To drink, to carouse.

cañeo [cah-nyay'-o], *m.* Drinking, carousal.

cañengo [cah-nyayn'-go], *a.* cañengue *a.* *(And. Carib.)* Weak, sickly; skinny.

cañería [cah-nyay-ree'-ah], *f.* 1. Aqueduct, a water-pipe. 2. Water-main, gas-main. Cañería maestra, (gas) main. 3. *(Naut.)* Bilge-holes.

cañero [cah-nyay'-ro], *m.* 1. Conduit-maker, director of waterworks. 2. *(Prov.)* Angler.

cañero [cah-nyay'-ro], *a.* 1. *(LAm.)* Sugar-cane. Machete cañero, sugar-cane knife. 2. *(And. Carib.)* Lying (mentiroso); buffler, boaster.

cañete [cah-nyay'-tay], *m.* Small pipe.

cañilavado, da [cah-nye-la-vah'-do, dah], *a.* Small-limbed (caballos, mulas).

cañilla, ita [cah-nyeel'-lyah, ee'-tah], *f.* dim. Small cane or reed.

cañillera [cah-nyeel-lyay'-rah], *f.* Ancient armor for the shin-bone.

cañivete [cah-nye-vey'-tay], *m.* Small knife, penknife.

cañita [cah-nyee'-tah], *f.* *(And.)* (Drinking) straw.

cañiza [cah-nyee'-thah], *f.* Coarse linen.

cañizal, cañizar [cah-nye-thahl', thar'], *m.* V. CAÑAVERAL

cañizo [cah-nyee´-tho], *m.* 1. Hurdle, a frame for rearing silk-worms 2. Hurdle, used by hatters for shearing hats. 3. *(Naut.)* Flake.

caño [cah'-nyo], *m.* 1. Tube, pipe, or cylinder, of wood, glass, or metal. 2. Common sewer, gutter. 3. Spring; spout or conduit for spring-water. 4. Cellar or other place for cooling water. 5. Mine. 6. Subterranean passage. 7. *(Prov.)* Warren or burrow. V. VIVAR. Caños or cañones del órgano, tubes or pipes of an organ. 8. The channel which forms at the entrance to seaports.

cañocazo [cah-nyo-cah'-tho], *m.* Coarse flax.

cañón [cah-nyone'], *m.* 1. Cylindrical tube or pipe. 2. In glass-houses, tube or pipe for blowing glass. 3. Quill. 4. Down, or soft feathers. 5. Hollow folds in clothes. 6. Part of the beard next to the root. 7. Cannon, gun. Escopeta de dos cañones, doubled-barrelled gun. Cañon rayado, rifled barrel. 8. *(Min.)* Gallery. 9. *(Mech.)* Socket. 10. Gorge, ravine, canyon. 11. Quill pen (de pluma). 12. *(And.) (Bot.)* Trunk. 13. *(And. Mex.)* Mountain path. V. CAÑADA. A boca de cañón, at the mouth of a cannon. Canón reforzado, a re-enforced cannon. Cañón de agua, water cannon. Cañón antiaéreo, anti-aircraft gun. Cañón de campaña, field gun.14. One of the four spindles of the bar of a velvetloom. -*a.* Fabulous, marvelous. ¡La función estaba cañón!, the show was great! Una noticia cañón, a stunning piece of news.

cañonazo [cah-nyo-nah'-tho], *m.* 1. *(aug.)* Large piece of ordnance. 2. Cannon-shot. Cañonazo de advertencia, *(Naut.)* warning shot. 3. Report of a gun or shot.

cañoncico, illo, ito [cah-nyon-thee'-co, eel'-lyo, ee'-to], *m. dim.* Small cannon: small tube or pipe.

cañonear [cah-nyo-nay-ar'], *va.* To cannonade, to shell, to bombard. -*vr.* To cannonade each other; to exchange guns.

cañoneo [cah-nyo-nay'-o], *m.* Cannonade, shell fire.

cañonera [cah-nyo-nay'-rah], *f.* 1. Embrasure for cannon. 2. Large tent. 3. V. PISTOLERA. 4. *(Naut.)* A gunboat.

cañonería [cah-nyo-nay-ree'-ah], *f.* The pipes of an organ collectively.

cañonero, ra [cah-nyo-nay'-ro, rah], *a.* *(Naut.)* Mounting cannon; a gun boat.

cañota [cah-nyo'-tah], *f.* *(Bot.)* Panicled sorghum. Cañota suave, yellow-seeded soft grass.

cañucela [cah-nyoo-thay'-lah], *f.* A slender cane or reed.

cañuela [cah-nyoo-ay'-lah], *f.* *(Bot.)* Fescue grass, a genus of grasses. Cañuela ovina or ovejuna, sheep's fescue grass. Cañuela durilla, hard fescue grass.

cañusero [cah-nyoo-say'-ro], *m.* *(And.)* Owner of sugar-cane plantation.

canutazo [cah-nyoo-tah'-tho], *m.* *(Low.)* Information, private accusation, suggestion, whisper, tale. Fue con el cañutazo, he went to carry his tale.

cañutería [cah-nyoo-tay-ree'-ah], *f.* 1. V. CAÑONERÍA. 2. Gold or silver twist for embroidery.

cañutero [cah-nuoo-tay'-ro], *m.* Pincushion.

cañutillo [cah-nyoo-teel'-lyo], *m.* 1. *(dim.)* Small tube or pipe. 2. Bugle, small glass ornamental tubes stitched to the tassels and flounces of women's gowns. Cañutillo de hilo de oro o de plata para bordar, quill of gold or silver twist for embroidery. 3. A mode of grafting. *(Acad.)*

cañuto [cah-nyoo'-to], *m.* 1. Part of a cane, from knot to knot, internode. 2. Pipe made of wood or metal. 3 *(Prov.)* Pin-case. 4. Blast, gust. V. SOPLO. 5. Informer, tale-bearer. V. SOPLÓN. 6. Cañutos helados, *(Mex.)* Small ice-cream cylinders. 7. V. CANUTO.

caoba, caobana [cah-o'-bah, cah-o-bah'-nah], *f.* *(Bot.)* Mahogany-tree.

caolín [cah-o-leen'], *m.* Kaolin, chinaclay.

caos [cah'-os], *m.* 1. Chaos. 2. Confusion.

caótico, ca [cah-o'-te-co, cah], *a.* Chaotic; in disorder and confusion.

caoup [cah-o-oop'], *m.* *(Bot.)* Caoup, an American tree with fruit like an orange.

cap [cap], *abr.* de capítulo *(Chapter.)*.

capa [cah'-pah], *f.* 1. Cloak. 2. Mantle. 3. Layer, strata, lamina. 4. Coat or hair of a horse. 5. Cover, anything laid over another. 6. *(Met.)* Cloak, pretence or pretext, mask, cover. 7. Hider, harborer. 8. Property, fortune. V. CAUDAL. 9. An American rodent; the spotted cavy. V. PACA. 10. Among bell-founders, the third mould used in casting bells. 11. Coat of paint. 12. Bed, stratum, vein, seam, ledge. 13. *(Mas.)* Bed, course. 14. Wrapper for tobacco. Capa del cielo, *(Met.)* canopy of heaven. Capa pluvial, a pluvial or choircope, worn by prelates in processions. Capa y sombrero, *(Naut.)* hat-money, allowance per ton to the captain on his cargo; ponerse a la capa, *(Naut.)* to lie to. Andar or ir de capa caída, to be down in the mouth, crestfallen. Echar la capa al toro, *(Met.)* to expose oneself to danger. Estar o estarse a la capa, *(Met.)* to have a good or sharp lookout. Sacar bien su capa, *(Met.)* to disengage oneself from difficulties; (capa rota), *(fig.)* secret emissary. Capa torera, bullfighter's cape. Hacer de su capa un sayo, to do what one likes with one's own things, act freely. Comedia de capa y espada, cloak-and-dagger play. Primera capa, undercoat. Capas sociales, social layers. Madera de tres capas, three-ply wood.

capá [cah-pah'], *m.* Capá, a tree which grows in Cuba and Porto Rico; often used in building vessels.

capaburro [cah-pah-boor'-ro], *m.* *(LAm.)* Piranha.

capacete [cah-pah-chay´-tay], *m.* Helmet, casque.

capacha [cah-pah'-chah], *f.* 1. Frail, hamper. V. CAPACHO. 2. Frail, a basket made of rushed 3. *(Coll.)* The religious order of St. John of God. 4. *(And. Cono Sur)* jail. *(Cono Sur)* Caer en la capacha, to fall into the trap.

capacheca [cah-pah-chay-cah], *f.* *(And. Cono Sur)* Street-vendor's barrow.

capacho [cah-pah'-cho], *m.* 1. Frail, hamper, large basket. 2. Capacho de albañil, bricklayer's hod. 3. In oilmills, the bass, or willow frail through which oil is filtered. 4. Mendicant hospitaller, who collects charity for the sick. 5. *(Orn.)* Common owl, barn owl. 6. *(And. Cono Sur)* Old hat.

capacidad [cah-pah-che-dad'], *f.* 1. Capacity, capability. Capacidad de compra, purchasing power. Capacidad de arrastre, drawing power (de orador etc.). Capacidad de carga, carrying capacity. 2. Extent, extensiveness of a place. Una sala con capacidad para 900, a hall with room for 900. Un avión con capacidad para 20 plazas, a 20-seater plane 3. Opportunity or means of executing a thing. 4. *(Naut.)* Bulk or burden of a ship. 5. *(Met.)* Talent, genius, mental ability. Tener capacidad para, to have an aptitude for. **No tiene capacidad para los negocios**, he has no business sense. 6. *(LAm.)* Able person (persona hábil).

capacitación [cah-pah-the-tah-the-one'], *f.* Capacitation (jurado); Training, education.

capacitado [cah-pah-the-tah'-do], *a.* Qualified. **Estar capacitado para**, to be qualified to.

capacitar [cah-pah-the-tar'], *va.* 1. **Capacitar a uno para algo**, to fit somebody for something; to train (educate) somebody for something. 2. *(And. Cono Sur, Mex.)* **Capacitar a uno para hacer algo**, to empower somebody to do something. *-vr.* **Capacitarse para algo**, to fit oneself for something.

capador [cah-pah-dor'], *m.* 1. One whose business is to geld or castrate. 2. A kind of whistle employed by those whose business is to geld.

capadura [cah-pah-doo'-rah], *f.* 1. Castration. 2. Scar which remains after castration. 3. Leaf of tobacco of the second cutting; used for filling.

capar [cah-par'], *va.* 1. To geld, to castrate. 2. *(Met. Low.)* To castrate, to take away a part; to curtail, to diminish one's authority, income, etc. 3. *(And. Carib.)* To start on (comida). 4. *(Carib. Mex.)* To cut back, to prune.

caparazón [cah-pah-ra-thone'], *m.* 1. Carcass of a fowl. 2. Caparison, a sort of cover over the saddle of a horse. 3. Cover of a coach, or other things made of oilcloth. 4. *(Prov.)* Frail made of grass, in which horses feed when out of the stable. 5. *(Zool.)* Shell.

caparra [cah-par'-rah], *f.* 1. Sheeplouse. *V.* GARRAPATA. 2. Earnest money given to confirm a bargain. 3. *V.* ALCAPARRA.

caparrón [cah-par-rone'], *m.* *(Obs.)* Bud of a vine or tree.

caparrós [cah-par-ros'], *m.* *(Prov.)* *V.* CAPARROSA.

caparrosa [cah-par-ro'-sah], *f.* Copperas, or vitriol, ferrous sulphate. **Caparrosa azul**, blue vitriol, copper sulphate. **Caparrosa blanca**, white vitriol, zinc sulphate. **Caparrosa verde**, green vitriol, copperas.

capataz [cah-pah-tath'], *m.* 1. Overseer, superintendent. 2. One charged with receiving the marked metal to be coined in the mint. 3. Steward who superintends a farm. 4. Warden of a company or guild. 5. Conductor. 6. Foreman.

capaz [cah-path'], *a.* 1. Capacious, capable, able to hold other things. 2. Capacious, ample, spacious, roomy, wide. **Capaz para**, with a capacity of. **Coche capaz para 4 personas**, a car with room for 4 people. 3. *(Met.)* Fit, apt, suitable, competent. **Ser capaz de algo**, to be capable of something. **Es capaz de cualquier tontería**, he is able of any stupidity. **Capaz de funcionar**, operational. **Ser capaz para un trabajo**, to be qualified for a job. 4. *(Met.)* Learned, ingenious, capable, clever. **Hacerse capaz de alguna cosa**, *(Met.)* To render oneself master of a thing. 5. *(LAm.)* **Es capaz que venga**, he´ll probably come. *-adv.* *(LAm.)* ¿**Vendrá?**...**capaz que sí**, will he come?

capaza [cah-pah'-thah], *f.* *(Prov.)* *V.* CAPACHO.

capazmente [cah-path-men'-tay], *adv.* Capaciously, amply.

capazo [cah-pah'-tho], *m.* 1. Large frail or basket made of rushes.

capazón [cah-pah-thone'], *m.* *aug.* Very large frail made of brass.

capción [cap-the-on'], *f.* *(Obs.)* *V.* CAPTURA.

capciosamente [cap-the-o-sah-men'-tay], *adv.* Insidiously, captiously, artfully, cunningly.

capcioso, sa [cap-the-o'-so, sah], *a.* Captious, insidious, artful, cunning, faultfinding, wily, deceitful.

capea [cah-pay'-ah], *f.* Bullfighting with young bulls.

capeador [cah-pay-ah-dor'], *m.* 1. A bull-fighter who challenges the bull with his cloak. 2. Cloak-stealer.

capear [cah-pay-ar'], *va.* 1. To strip or rob one of a cloak in an inhabited place. 2. *(Naut.)* To try or lay to. 3. To challenge a bull with one's cloak. 4. To dodge (esquivar). 5. *(Naut.)* *(fig.)* To ride out, weather (temporal). *-vn.* *(Naut.)* To ride out the storm.

capeja [cah-pay'-hah], *f.* *(dim.* of depreciation) A poor or mean cape.

capel [cab-pel'], *m.* *(Prov.)* Cocoon or ball of a silkworm.

capela [cah-pay'-lah], *f.* *(Astr.)* Capella, the brightest star in Auriga.

capelina [cah-pay-lee'-nah], *f.* Capelline, a bandage especially fitted to the head.

capelo [cah-pay'-lo], *m.* 1. Dues received in ancient times by bishops from their clergy. 2. Hat. *V.* SOMBRERO. 3. Cardinal's hat. 4. Dignity of a cardinal, cardinalate.

capellán [cah-pel-lyahn'], *m.* 1. Chaplain, a clergyman who has obtained a chaplaincy: *V.* CAPELLANÍA. 2. Chaplain, a clergyman that officiates in domestic worship. **Capellán de navío**, chaplain of the navy. **Capellán de altar**, the priest who chants the mass. **Capellán de honor**, the king´s private champlain. **Capellán mayor de los ejércitos**, the vicar-general of the army.

capellar [cah-pel-lyar'], *m.* A kind of Moorish cloak.

capellina [cah-pel-lyee'-nah], *f.* 1. Head piece of a helmet or casque. 2. Hood worn by country people. 3. Trooper armed with a helmet.

capeo [cah-pay'-o], *m.* Act of challenging a bull with a cloak.

caperuceta, illa [cah-pay-roo-thay'-tah, theel'-lyah], *f.* *dim.* Small hood.

Caperucita Roja [cah-pay-roo-the'-tah ro-hah], *f.* Red Ridding Hood.

caperuza [cah-pay-roo'-thah], *f.* Hood or cap ending in a point, holster-cap. **Caperuza de chimenea**, covering of the top of a chimney. **Caperuza de palo**, hood of a mast-head when the ship is unrigged.

caperuzón [cah-pay-roo-thone'], *m.* *aug.* Large hood.

capeta [cah-pay'-tah], *f.* A short cape not reaching below the knee, and without collar.

capialzado [cah-pe-al-thah'-do], *a.* *(Arch.)* Applied to an arch, widening outward; arched cap-piece, back arch.

capi [cah'-pe], *f.* *(And. Cono Sur)* White cornflour (harina); corn; vaina unripe pod.

capia [cah'-pe-ah], *f.* *(And. Cono Sur)* White cornflour (harina); corn.

capiango [cah-pee-ahn'-go], *m.* *(Cono Sur)* Clever thief.

capibara [cah-pe-bah'-rah], *m.* Capybara, a large South American rodent, about three and a half feet long.

capichola [cah-pe-cho'-lah], *f.* Ribbed silk stuff.

capicúa [cah-pee-coo'-ah], *m.* Reversible number, symmetrical number; palindrome.

capidengue [cah-pe-den'-gay], *m.* Small cloak worn by ladies.

capiello [cah-pe-ayl'-lyo], *m.* *(Prov.)* *V.* CAPILLO.

capigorra [cah-pe-gor'-rah], *m.* Idler.

capigorrón [cah-pe-gor-rone'], *m.* 1. *(Coll.)* Vagabond; a parasite. 2. *(Prov.)* Student who has taken the minor orders.

capil [cah-peel'], *m.* *(Prov.)* Little cap or hood.

capiláceo, cea [cah-pe-lah'-thay-o, ah], *a.* *(Bot.)* Capillaceous, hair-like.

capilar [cah-pe-lar'], *a.* Capillary; slender as hair. *-m.* A capillary blood vessel; capillaries intervene between arteries and veins.

capilaridad [cah-pe-lah-re-dahd'], *f.* Capillarity, capillary attraction.

capilla [cah-peel'-lyah], *f.* 1. Hood. 2. Cowl of a monk or friar. 3. Chapel. 4. Chapel, a small church. 5. The priests and others employed in chapel service. 6. Chapter or assembly of collegians. 7. Among printers, the proof-sheet. 8. Portable chapel for military corps. **Caja de capilla**, *(Naut.)* Chest for chapel ornaments. **Estar en capilla**, a) to prepare for death: spoken of criminals, b) *(Coll.)* to await with impatience the issue of an affair. 10. Group of supporters, following; informal club (peña).

capillada [call-peel-lyah'-dah], *f.* A hoodful of something.

capilleja, ita [cah-peel-lyay'-hah, lyee'-tah], *f.* *dim.* Small chapel.

capillejo [cah-peel'-lyay'-ho], *m.* 1. (*dim.*) Small hood. 2. Skein of sewing-silk.

capiller, capillero [cah-pee1-lyerr', cah-peel-lyay'-ro], *m.* Clerk or sexton of a chapel; a churchwarden.

capilleta [cah-pee'-lyay'-tah], *f.* 1. (*dim. Obs.*) Small chapel. 2. Hood used by the knights of Calatrava.

capillo [cah-peel'-lyo], *m.* 1. Child's cap. 2. Hood of a hawk. 3. Bud of a rose. 4. Lining under the toepiece of a shoe. 5. Cap of distaff. *V.* ROCADERO. 9. Net for catching rabbits. 6. Colander through which wax is strained. 7. Cocoon of the silkworm. *V.* CAPULLO. 8. The covering or cloth which covered the offering of bread which used to be presented to the church. 9. The prepuce. 10. A kind of hood and cape worn by women.

capilludo, da [cah-peel-lyoo'-do, dah], *a.* Resembling the hood or cowl of a monk.

capirotada [cah-pe-ro-tah'-dah], *f.* Sort of American paste made of herbs, eggs, etc.

capirotazo [cah-pe-ro-tah'-tho], *m.* A blow on the nose with the finger; a flip.

capirote [cah-pe-ro'-tay], *m.* 1. Hood, ancient cover for the head. **Tonto de capirote**, blockhead, ignorant fool. 4. **Capirote de colmena**, cover of a bee-hive when full of honey. 5. (*Culin.*) Cloth strainer (for coffee etc.). *V.* PAPIROTE.

capirotero [cah-pe-ro-tay'-ro], *a.* Accustomed to wearing a hood: applied to a hawk.

capirucho [cah-pe-roo'-cho], *m.* (*Coll.*) *V.* CAPIROTE.

capiruchu [cah-pe-roo'-choo], *m.* (*CAm.*) Child's toy consisting of wooden cup and ball.

capisayo [cah-pe-sah'-yo], *m.* 1. Garment which serves both as a cloak and riding-coat. 2. A vesture proper to bishops.

capiscol [cah-pis-col'], *m.* The precentor: sub-chanter.

capiscolía [cah-pis-co-lee'-ah], *f.* Office and dignity of a preceptor.

capistrato, to [cah-pis-trah'-to, tah], *a.* Capistrate, epithet applied to animals whose snout appears to have a muzzle or halter.

capistrato, *m.* A squirrel of Carolina.

capistro [cah-pees'-tro], *m.* 1. Capistrum, a bandage for the head. 2. Tonic spasm of the muscles of the lower jaw. 3. (*Zool.*) Capister, the part of a bird's head about the base of the bill.

capitación [cah-pe-tah-the-on'], *f.* Poll tax, capitation.

capital [cah-pe-tahl'], *m.* 1. Sum of money put at interest. 2. Capital stock of a merchant or trading company. 3. (*Mil.*) Line drawn from the angle of a polygon to the point of the bastion and the middle of the gorge. 4. A capital letter; upper case of printers. **Capital de explotación**, working capital. **Capital físico**, (*Cono Sur*) capital assets. -*f.* Capital city (ciudad) of a country. **Capital de provincia**, provincial capital. **En Méjico capital**, in the city of Mexico.

capital [cah-pe-tahl'], *a.* 1. Capital, relating to the head. 2. Principal, leading; capital, essential. **Enemigo capital**, mortal enemy. **Error capital**, capital error. **Pecados capitales**, deadly sins. **Pena capital**, capital punishment.

capitalidad [cah-pe-tah-le-dahd'], *f.* The state of being capital, whether city or thing.

capitalino [cah-pe-tah-lee'-no], (*LAm.*) 1. *a.* Of capital. 2. *m. f.* Native of the capital; **los capitalinos**, the people of the capital. 3. City slicker.

capitalismo [cah-pe-tah-lees'-mo], *m.* Capitalism.

capitalista, [cah-pe-tah-lees'-tah], *com.* Capitalist.

capitalización [cah-pe-tah-le-thah-the-on'], *f.* Capitalization, conversion of property into money.

capitalizar [cah-pe-tah-le-thar'], *va.* To capitalize, convert into capital; to put a value on; to add overdue dividends to the capital stock, in order to obtain increased interest.

capitalmente [cah-pe-tal-men'-tay], *adv.* Capitally, mortally.

capitán [cah-pe-tahn'], *m.* 1. Captain, a military officer. 2. (*Obs.*) Commander-in-chief of an army. 3. Ringleader of a band of robbers. 4. Leader. 5. The commander of a ship of war or merchant vessel. **Capitán a guerra**, the mayor or chief magistrate of a place, invested with military power. **Capitán de fragata**, the commander of a frigate, with the rank of lieutenant-colonel. **Capitán de navío**, the commander of a man-of-war, with the rank of colonel. **Capitán general de ejército**, field-marshal. **Capitán general de provincia**, the commander-in-chief of a military district. **Capitán de puerto**, (*Naut.*) Port-captain. **Capitán del puerto**, (*Naut.*), harbor-master, water-bailiff. 6. In the wool trade, the overseer, who superintends the washing of wool.

capitana [cah-pe-tah'-nah], *f.* 1. Admiral's ship. 2. A captain's wife.

capitanear [cah-pe-tah-nay-ar'], *va.* 1. To have the command in chief of an army. 2. To head a troop of people.

capitanía [cah-pe-tah-nee'-ah], *f.* 1. Captainship, captaincy. 2. Company of officers and soldiers commanded by a captain. 3. A tax paid to the port captain by ships anchored in the harbor. 4. Military government of a province. 5. Chief authority, power, command.

capitel [cah-pe-tel'], *m.* 1. Spire over the dome of a church. 2. (*Arch.*) Capital of a column or pilaster. 3. Lid of a refining-furnace.

capitolino, na [cah-pe-to-lee'-no, nah], *a.* Belonging to the capitol.

capitolio [cah-pe-to'-le-o], *m.* 1. Capitol, a temple of Jupiter in Rome. 2. The Capitol, legislative building in Rome. 3. Any lofty or majestic public building.

capitón [cah-pe-tone'], *m.* (*Zool.*) Pollard, chub.

capitoné [cah-pe-to-nay'], *m.* 1. Removal van, furniture van. 2. (*Cono Sur*) Quilt, quilted blanket.

capitonear [cah-pe-to-nay-ar'], *va.* (*Cono Sur*) To quilt.

capitoso, sa [cah-pe-to'-so, sah], *a.* Obstinate, capricious, whimsical.

capitoste [cah-pe-tos'-tay], *m.* Chief, boss; petty tyrant.

capítula [cah-pee'-too-lah], *f.* Part of the prayers read at divine service.

capitulación [cah-pe-too-lah-the-on'], *f.* 1. Capitulation, stipulation, agreement. **Capitulación de matrimonio**, articles of marriage. 2. (*Mil.*) Capitulation, surrender of a place.

capitulante [cah-pe-too-lahn'-tay], *pa.* Capitulator.

capitular [cah-pe-too-lar'], *m.* Capitular, member of a chapter.

capitular [cah-pe-too-lar'], *a.* Capitulary, belonging to a chapter. **Sala capitular**, chapter house.

capitular [cah-pe-too-lar'], *va.* 1. To conclude an agreement, to draw up the articles of a contract; to compound. 2. (*Mil.*) To capitulate, to settle the terms of surrender. 3. (*Law.*) To impeach. -*vn.* 1. To sing prayers at divine service. 2. To come to terms, to make an agreement. 2. To capitulate, to surrender.

capitulario [cah-pe-too-lah'-re-o], *m.* Book of prayers for divine service.

capitularmente [cah-pe-too-lar-men'-tay], *adv.* Capitulary, according to the rules of a chapter.

capitulear [cah-pe-too-lay-ar'], *vn.* (*And. Cono Sur*) To lobby.

capituleo [cah-pe-too-lay'-o], *m.* (*And. Cono Sur.*) (*Parl.*) Lobbying.

capitulero [cah-pe-too-lay'-ro], *m. & a.* Capitular.

capítulo [cah-pee'-too-lo], *m.* 1. (*Prov.*) Chapter of a cathedral. 2. A meeting of the prelates of religious orders, and the place where they meet. 3. Meeting of a secular community or corporation. **Llamar a uno a capítulo**, to take somebody to task. 4. Chapter of a book or other writing. 5. Charge preferred for neglect of duty. 6. **Capítulos matrimoniales**, articles of marriage. 7. A public reproof for some fault. (*Acad.*) **Ganar o perder capítulo**, (*Met.*) to carry or lose one's point.

capnomancia [cap-no-mahn'-the-ah], *f.* Capnomancy, divination by the flying of smoke.

capnomante [cap-no-mahn'-tay], *m.* Fortune-teller by smoke.

capo [cah'-po], *(Cono Sur)* 1. *a.* Great, fabulous. 2. *m.* Boss, bigwig (persona de influencia).

capó [cah-po'], *m. (Aut.)* Bonnet, hood; *(Aer.)* Cowling.

capoc [cah-poc'], *m.* **capoca,** *f.* A sort of cotton so short and fine that it can not be spun: used for mattresses.

capolado [cah-po-lah'-do], *m. (Prov.)* 1. Minced meat. *V.* PICADILLO. 2. Act of cutting or tearing into ends and bits. -**Capolado, da,** *pp.* of CAPOLAR.

capolar [cah-po-lar'], *va. (Prov.)* 1. To mince or chop meat. 2. To behead, to decapitate.

capón [cah-pone'], *m.* 1. Eunuch. 2. Gelding. 3. Capon (pollo). 4. *(Coll.)* Rap with the knuckles on the head. 5. *(Prov.)* A bundle of brush-wood. 6. *(Naut.)* Anchor-stopper at the cat-head. 7. Sheep (carnero).

capón [cah-pone'], *a.* Castrated.

capona [cah-po'-nah], *f.* Shoulder-knot. **Capona** or **charretera capona,** an epaulet without fringe.

caponado, da [cah-po-nah'-do, dah], *a.* Tied together, as branches of vines. - *pp.* of CAPONAR.

caponar [cah-po-nar'], *va.* 1. *(Prov.)* To tie the branches of vines. 2. To cut, to curtail, to diminish.

caponera [cah-po-nay'-rah], *f.* 1. Coop, inclosure to fatten poultry. 2. *(Met. Coll.)* Place where one lives well at other people's expense. *(Met. and Coll.)* A Jail. 3. *(Mil.)* Caponier, a passage under a dry moat to the outworks. **Estar metido en caponera,** to be locked up in jail. 4. *V.* YEGUA CAPONERA 5. Stew-pan for oressing fowls.

capoquero [cah-po-kay'-ro], *m. (Bot.)* Capoc-tree.

caporal [cah-po-rahl'], *m.* 1. Chief, ringleader. 2. *(Obs.)* Corporal 3. *(Mex.)* Keeper of horned cattle. 4. *(Cant.)* A cock.

capot [cah-pot'], *m. (Aut.) V.* CAPÓ.

capota [cah-po'-tah], *f.* 1. Car top. 2. Cape without a hood. 3. A light bonnet.

capotar [cah-po-tar'], *vn. (Aut.)* To turn over, to turn turtle; to somersault.

capote [cah-po'-tay], *m.* 1. Sort of cloak with sleeves to keep off rain. 2. A short cloak, without hood, of bright color, used by bullfighters. 3.. *(Met.)* Austere, angry look or mien. 4. *(Coll.)* Thick cloud or mist over a mountain. 5. In games at cards, capot, when one player wins all the tricks. **Dar capote,** 1. To leave a guest without dinner, for coming late. 2. To win all the tricks at cards. **A mi capote,** in my opinion. **Dije para mi capote,** I said in my sleeve. **Capote de monte,** poncho. **Car un capote a,** *(Mex.)* to give up one´s job. **Decir para su capote,** to say to oneself.

capotear [cah-po-tay-ar'], *va.* 1. To trick a bull with a capote; to hold a cloak before oneself for him to spring at. 2. To whcedle, bamboozle. 3. To evade cleverly difficulties and promises.

capotera [cah-po-tay'-rah], *f.* 1. *(CAm.)* Clothes peg. 2. *(Cono Sur)* beating. 3. *(CAm.)* Tarpaulin (lona).

capotudo, da [cah-po-too'-do, dah], *a.* Frowning. *V.* CEÑUDO.

capra-capela [cah'-pra-cah-pay-lah], *f.* Cobra, a very venomous snake of tropical Asia.

capricho [cah-pree'-cho], *m.* 1. Caprice, whim, fancy, mood, humor, conceit. 2. *(Mus.)* Irregular but pleasing composition. 3. *(Art.)* Invention or design of a painting. **Hombre de capricho,** queer, whimsical fellow. **Capricho extravagante,** a crotchet or odd fancy, a capricious prank. **Por puro capricho,** just to please oneself. **Es un capricho nada más,** it´s just a passing whim.

caprichosamente [cah-pre-cho-sah-men'-tay], *adv.* Fantastically, fancifully, humorously, moodily, whimsically.

caprichoso, sa [cah-pre-cho'-so, sah], *a.* 1. Capricious, whimsical, obstinate. 2. Fanciful.

caprichudo, da [cah-pre-choo'-do, dah], *a.* Obstinate, stubborn, capricious.

capricornio [cah-pre-cor'-ne-o], *m.* 1. Capricorn, a sign of the zodiac. 2. *(Zool.)* A Capricorn beetle, one of the long-horned cerambycids.

caprimulga [cah-pre-mool'-gah], *f.* Goat-sucker, a kind of owl.

caprino, na [cah-pree'-no, nah], *a. (Poet.)* Goatish. *V.* CABRUNO.

cápsula [cap'-soo-lah], *f.* 1. *(Bot.)* Capsule, a seed-vessel in plants. 2. *(Anat.)* Capsule, a sac enveloping a joint or other region of the body. 3. *(Chem.)* Capsule, a vessel for the evaporation of liquids. 4. The cap or top of a bottle. 5. *(Mil.)* Cartridge. **Cápsula de emergencia** *(Aer.)*, escape capsule. **Cápsula espacial,** space capsule. **Cápsula fulminante,** detonator, percussion cap.

capsular [cap-soo-lar'], *a.* Capsular, capsulary. **En forma capsular,** in capsule form.

captador [cap-tah-dor'], *m. (Tec.)* Sensor.

captafaros [cap-tah-fah'-ros], *m.* **Placa de captafaros,** reflector.

captar [cap-tar], *va.* 1. To captivate, to win, to capture. 2. To grasp, to get, to catch. 3. To collect; to dam, to harness (aguas). 4. To tune in to; to pick up, to receive (emisora).

captividad [ca-te-ve-dahd'], *f. V.* CAUTIVIDAD,

captura [cap-too'-rah], *f. (Law.)* Capture, seizure.

capturar [cap-too-rar'], *va.* To capture; to seize; to arrest.

capuana [cah-poo-ah'-nah], *f.* A whipping.

capucha [cah-poo-chah], *f.* 1. *(Print.)* Circumflex (^), an accent. 2. Hood of a woman's cloak. 3. Cowl or hood of a friar.

capuchina [cah-poo-chee'-nah], *f.* 1. Capuchin nun. 2. *(Bot.)* Great Indian cress. **Capuchinas,** *(Naut.)* crotches and knees. 3. A small lamp of metal with extinguisher in the form of a hood. 4. Confection of egg yolk. *(Acad.)*

capuchino [cah-poo-chee'-no], *a.* 1. Capuchin monk. 2. *(LAm.)* Capuccino (coffee).

capuchino, na [cah-poo-chee'-no, nah], *a.* Relating to Capuchin friars or nuns. **Chupa capuchina,** waistcoat.

capucho [cah-poo'-cho], *m.* Cowl or hood.

capuchón [cah-poo-chone'], *m.* 1. *aug.* of CAPUCHO. 2. A lady's cloak with hood, especially one worn at night. 3. **Capuchón de válvula** *(Aut.)*, valve cap.

capujar [cah-poo-har'], *va. (Cono Sur)* To catch in the air (atrapar); to snatch (arrebatar); to say what somebody else was about to say.

capulí [cah-poo-lee'], *(Mex.)* **Capulín** [cah poo-leen'], *m. (Bot.)* An American fruit resembling a cherry.

capullada [cah-pool-lyah'-dah], *f.* Silly thing, piece of nonsense.

capullito [cah-pool-lyee'-to], *m. dim.* Small pod of a silkworm.

capullo [cah-pool-lyo], *m.* 1. Cocoon of a silkworm. 2. Flax knetted at the end; *(Com.)* a bunch of boiled flax. 3. Germ or bud of flowers. 4 Coarse stuff of spun silk. **Seda de capullos,** ferret-silk, grogram yarn. 5. Cup of an acorn. 6. Burr of a chestnut. 7. *(Anat.)* Prepuce.

capumpeba [cah-poom-pay'-bah], *f. (Bot.)* A Brazil plant.

capuz [cah-pooth'], *m.* 1. The act of ducking a person. *V.* CHAPUZ. 2. Old-fashioned cloak.

capuzar [cah-poo-thar'], *va.* **Capuzar un bajel,** *(Naut.)* to sink a ship by the head. *V.* CHAPUZAR.

caquéctico, ca [cah-kayc'-te-co, cah], *a.* Cachectical, cachectic, affected by cachexia.

caquexia [cah-kayc'-se-ah], *f. (Med.)* Cachexia, a condition of general bad health, especially from a specific morbid process, such as cancer or tuberculosis.

caqui or **kaki** [cah'-ke], *a.* Khaki. **Marcar el caqui,** to finish military service.

caqui [cah'-ke], *m. (Cono Sur)* date plum; *(fig.)* Red.

caquimia [cah-kee'-me-ah], *f.* An imperfect metallic substance.

caquino [cah-ke'-no], *m.* **Reírse a caquinos,** *(Mex.)* To laugh uproariously, cackle.

car, *f. (Naut.)* Extreme end of the mizzen-yard and mizzen.

cara [cah'-rah], *f.* 1. Face, visage, countenance. **Me recibió con buena cara,** he received me with a cheerful countenance.

Ella me mostró mala cara, I was received by her with a frown. 2. Head (de una moneda). 3. Presence of a person. 4. Face, front, surface, facing, side. 5. Boldness, nerve (valor). **Cara de acelga,** pale sallow face. **Cara de pocos amigos,** churlish look. **A cara descubierta,** openly, plainly. **Andar con la cara descubierta,** to act openly; to proceed with frankness, and without evasion or reserve. **Dar a alguno con las puertas en la cara,** to shut the door in one's face. **Jugar a cara o cruz,** to toss up a coin. **Dar en cara,** *(Met.)* to reproach, to upbraid. **Dar el sol de cara,** to have the sun in one's face. **Decírselo en su cara,** *(Met.)* to tell one to his face. **Hacer cara,** to face an enemy. **Hombre de dos caras,** double dealer, an insidious, artful fellow. **La cara se lo dice,** his face betrays him. **Lavar la cara a alguno,** *(Met.)* to flatter, to please with blandishments. **Lavar la cara a alguna cosa,** to brush up, to clean; e. g. a painting, house or coach. **No tener cara para hacer o decir alguna cosa,** not to have the face or courage to do or say a thing. **Saltar a la cara,** to answer reproof or admonition, etc., angrily. **Sacar cara por otro,** to sustain or defend another. **No volver la cara atrás,** *(Met.)* to pursue with spirit and perseverance; not to flinch. **Salir a la cara el contento, la enfermedad, la vergüenza,** satisfaction, infirmity, shame, expressed in the face. **Cara a cara,** face to face. **De cara,** opposite, over against, regarding in front. **El bien o el mal, a la cara sale,** the face is the mirror of the soul. **Cruzar la cara,** to give a blow or a cut with a whip on the face. **Echar a la cara,** to throw in one's face; to tell one his faults; also to remind of some benefit done. **Nos veremos las caras,** we will meet again (amenaza). **Cara adelante,** facing forwards. **Cara al norte,** facing north. **Cara al futuro,** with an eye to the future. **Tener cara de,** to look like. **Poner al mal tiempo buena cara,** to put a brave face on. **Cara de vinagre,** sour expression. **Tener más cara que...,** to have more nerve than...

caraba [cah-ra'-bah], *f.* **Esto es la caraba;** it´s the absolute tops; it´s the last straw, the limit.

carabao [cah-rah-bah'-o], *m.* Philippine buffalo.

cárabe [cah'-ra-bay], *m.* Amber.

carabela [cah-ra-bay'-lah], *f.* 1. *(Naut.)* Caravel, a three-masted vessel. 2. *(Prov.)* Large basket or tray for provisions.

carabelón [cah-ra-bay-lone'], *m. (Naut.)* Brig or brigantine.

carabina [cah-ra-bee'-nah], *f.* 1. Rifle. 2. Carbine or carabine. **Carabina rayada,** rifle carabine. **Es lo mismo que la carabina de Ambrosio,** it is not worth a straw. 3. Chaperon. **Hacer de carabina, ir de carabina,** to go as chaperon; to play gooseberry.

carabinazo [cah-ra-be-nah'-tho], *m.* Report of a carbine, effect of a carbine-shot.

carabinero [cah-ra-be-nay'-ro], *m.* 1. Carabineer, rifleman. 2. *(Obs.)* Light horse attached to cavalry. 3. *(Zool.)* Prawn.

cárabo [cah'-ra-bo], *m.* 1. *(Zool.)* Sort of a crab or cockle. 2. *(Orn.)* Large horned owl. V. AUTILLO. 3. Kind of setter-dog. 4. A ground beetle: a carabid; it is insectivorous.

carabú [cah-ra-boo'], *m.* A handsome tree of India.

Caracas [cah-rah'-cahs], *n.* Caracas.

caracoa [cah-ra-co'-ah], *f.* Small row-barge used in the Philippine Islands.

caracol [cah-ra-col'], *m.* 1. Fusee of an early watch or clock. 2. Snail. **Caracol marino,** periwinkle. **Caracol comestible,** edible snail. 3. **Escalera de caracol,** winding or spiral staircase. **Subir en caracol,** to spiral up (humo). 4. Caracole, the prancing of a horse. 5. A wide though short nightdress, used by women in Mexico. 6. Cochlea, of the ear. **Hacer caracoles,** *(Met.)* To caracole. **No importa un caracol,** it does not matter, it is not worth a rush. 7. **¡Caracoles!,** good heavens! (sorpresa). 8. Curl (de pelo).

caracola [cah-ra-co'-lah], *f.* 1. *(Prov.)* A small snail with a whitish shell. 2. A conch-shell used as a horn.

caracolear [cah-ra-co-lay-ar'], *vn.* To caracole.

caracolejo [cah-ra-co-lay'-ho], *m. dim.* Small snail, snail shell.

caracoleo [cah-ra-co-lay'-o], *m.* The act of caracoling.

caracolero, ra [cah-ra-co-lay'-ro, rah], *m. & f.* One who gathers snails.

caracoles!, [cah-ra-co'-les], *int.* V. CARAMBA.

caracoli [cah-ra-co'-lee], *m. (Min.)* Metallic composition resembling pinchbeck.

caracolilla [cah-ra-co-leel'-lyah], *f. dim.* Small snail shell.

caracolillo [cah-ra-co-leel'-lyo], *m.* 1. *(dim.)* Small snail. 2. *(Bot.)* Snail-flowered kidney bean. 3. Purple colored thread. **Caracolillos,** shell-work wrought on the edgings of clothes, for ornament. 4. A prized variety of coffee, smaller than the ordinary sort. 5. A much veined kind of mahogany.

caracolito [cah-ra-co-lee'-to], *m. dim.* Small snail.

caracón [cah-ra-cone'], *m. (Obs.)* Small vessel.

carácter [cah-rahc'-ter], *m.* 1. A written sign. 2. Character, condition, mark. **De medio carácter,** of an ill-defined nature. **De carácter totalmente distinto,** of quite a different kind. 3. Character, consequence, note, adventitious quality impressed by a post or office. 4. Character, handwriting. 5. Character, type, any letter used in writing or printing. 6. Character, personal qualities, particular constitution of mind, humor, manners. **Una persona de carácter,** a person with character. **De carácter duro,** hard-natured. **No tiene carácter,** he lacks firmness. 7. Temper, nature, genius. 8. Spiritual stamp impressed upon the soul by the sacraments of baptism and confirmation. Mark put upon sheep; brand. 9. Character, loftiness of soul, firmness, energy. 10. Style of speaking or writing. 11. **Caracteres de imprenta,** printing types. **Carácter elite / pica,** *(Inform.)* elite / pica-sized character.

característica [cah-rahc-tay-rees-te-cah], *f.* 1. Characteristic; trait, quality. 2. *(Theat.)* Character actress. 3. *(Inform.)* **Característica de recálculo,** recalculation feature.

característicamente [cah-rac-tay-rees'-te-cah-men-tay], *adv.* Characteristically.

característico, ca [cah-rac-tay-rees'-te-co, cah], *a.* 1. Characteristic, typical. 2. *m. (Theat.)* Character actor.

caracterizado, da [cah-rac-tay-re-thah´-do, dah], *a.* Characterized. **Es hombre muy caracterizado,** he is a man conspicuous either for his qualities or for the posts he fills, typical. - *pp.* of CARACTERIZAR.

caracterizar [cah-rac-tay-re-thar'], *va.* 1. To characterize, to distinguish by peculiar qualities. **Le caracterizaron de sabio,** he was classed among wise men. 2. To confer a distinguished employment, dignity, or office. 3. To mark, to point out. 4. *(Theat.)* To play with great effect. *-vr. (Theat.)* To make up, to dress for the part.

caracú [cah-rah-coo'], *m. (LAm.)* Bone marrow.

caracumbé [cah-rah-coom-bay'], *m.* Popular Afro-Latin dance.

caracha [cah-rah'-chah], *f.* or **Carache** [ca-rah'-chay], *m.* Itch, mange, scab.

carachento [cah-rah-chayn'-to], 1. *a.* **Carachoso** *a. (LAm.)* Mangy, scabby.

caracho [cah-rah'-cho], 1. *a.* Violet-colored. 2. *interj.* Good heavens!

caradelante [cah-ra-day-lahn'-tay], *adv.* 1. *(Obs.)* V. EN ADELANTE. 2. *(Prov.)* Forward.

carado, da [cah-rah'-do, dah], *a.* Faced. This adjective is always joined to the adverbs *bien* or *mal -e. g.* **Biencarado,** pretty-faced; **malcarado,** ill-faced.

cadura [cah-rah-doo'-rah], 1. *m. & f.* Rotter, cad, shameless person; you swine! 2. V. CARA.

caraguata [cah-ra-goo-ah´-tah], *f.* A kind of hemp in Paraguay from a plant of the same name.

caraja [cah-rah'-hah], *f.* A certain sail used by fishermen at Vera Cruz. **Tener la caraja,** to look absolutely knackered.

carajear [cah-rah-hay-ar'], *va. (Cono Sur)* to insult, to swear at.

carajiento [cah-rah-he-ayn'-to], *a. (And.)* Foul-mouthed.

carajillo [cah-rah-hel'-lyo], *m.* Coffee with a dash of brandy.

carajito [cah-rah-he'-to], *m. (LAm.)* Kid, small child.

carajo [cah-rah-ho], *m.* 1. prick. 2. **De carajo**, tremendous, awful. **Ese conductor del carajo**, that shit of a driver. **En el quinto carajo**, miles away. **No entiende un carajo**, he doesn´t know a damned thing about it. **Me importa un carajo**, I don´t give a damn. **Irse al carajo**, to fail, to go down the drain. **Mandar a uno al carajo**, to tell somebody to go to hell.

caramallera [cah-ra-mal-lyay'-rah], *f.* A rack, a toothed bar. *Cf.* CREMALLERA.

caramanchel [cah-ra-man-chel'], *m.* A covering like a shed over the hatchways ships, fixed or movable.

caramanchón [cah-ra-man-chone'], *m.* Garret. *V.* CAMARANCHÓN.

¡caramba! [cah-rahm'-bah], *int. (Coll.)* Goodness me! (asombro, sorpresa); damn it! (enfado). **¡Caramba con él!**, to hell with him!

carámbano [cah-rahm'-bah-no], *m.* Icicle, a shoot of ice.

carambillo [cah-ram-beel'-lyo], *m. (Bot.)* Saltwort, a source of barilla.

carambola [cah-ram-bo'-lah], *f.* 1. Cannon, the impact, in billiards, of the cue-ball against two other balls in succession. 2. Device or trick to cheat or deceive. **Lo hizo por carambola**, he accomplished it by mere chance, through luck, etc.

carambolear [cah-ram-bo-lay-ar'], *va.* To play the *carambola;* to carom.

carambolero [cah-ram-bo-lay'-ro], *m.* Player at *carambola.*

carambú [cah-ram-boo'], *m. (Bot.)* Willow herb, tall jussiena.

caramel [cah-ra-mel], *m. (Zool.)* Kind of pilchard or sardine.

caramelear [cah-rah-may-lay-ar'], *va. (And.)* To con, to deceive; to suck up to (engatusar).

caramelización [cah-ra-may-le-thah-the-one'], *f.* The reduction of sugar to candy by heat.

caramelo [cah-ra-may'-lo], *m.* Lozenge made of sugar and other ingredients; sugar-candy.

caramente [cah-ra-men'-tay], *adv.* 1. Dearly. 2. Exceedingly, highly. 3. *(Law.)* Rigorously.

caramillar [cah-ra-meel-lyar'], *vn. (Obs.)* To play on the flageolet, a small flute.

caramilleras [cah-ra-meel-lyay'-ras], *f. pl. (Prov.)* Pot-hooks.

caramillo [cah-ra-meel'-lyo], *m.* 1. Flageolet, a small flute. 2. *(Bot.)* V. BARRILLA. 3. Confused heap of things. 4. Deceit, fraudulent trick. 5. A piece of gossip. **Armar un caramillo**, to cause disturbances. 6. *(Bot.)* A wild shrub of the rose kind.

caramilloso [cah-rah-mel-lyo'-so], *a.* Fussy.

cáramo [cah'-ra-mo], *m.* Wine.

caramuyo [cah-ra-moo'-yo], *m.* Kind of sea-snail.

caramuzal [cah-ra-moo-thahl'], *m.* Transport vessel used by the Moors.

caranchear [cah-rahn-chay-ar'], *va. (Cono Sur)* To irritate, to annoy.

carancho [cah-rahn'-cho], *m. (And.)* Owl; *(Cono Sur)* vulture (buitre).

caranga [cah-rahn'-gah], *f. (And. CAm.)*, **Carango** *m. (LAm.)* Louse.

carángano [cah-rahn'-gah-no], *m.* 1. *(Sp. Amer.)* Louse. 2. *(Col.)* Native musical instrument.

carangue [cah-rahn'-gay], *m.* **Caranga** [cah-rahn'-gah], *f. (Amer.)* Kind of flat-fish in the West Indies.

carantamaula [cah-ran-ta-mah'-oo-lah], *f. (Coll.)* 1. Hideous mask or visor. 2. *(Met.)* Ugly hard-featured person.

carantoña [cah-ran-to'-nyah], *f.* 1. Hideous mask or visor. 2. Old coarse woman, who paints and dresses in style. 3. Ugly mug. *-pl.* Caresses, soft words and acts of endearment to wheedle or coax a person. **Hacer carantoñas a uno**, to make faces at somebody (muecas).

carantoñera [cah-ran-to-nyay'-rah], *f.* Coquette.

carantoñero [cah-ran-to-nyay'-ro], *m.* Flatterer, wheedler, cajoler.

caraña [cah-rah'-nyah], *f.* Kind of resinous American gum.

caraos [cah-rah'-os], *m. (Obs.)* Act of drinking a full bumper to one's health.

carapa [cah-rah'-pah], *f.* Oil of an American nut, which is said to cure the gout.

carapacho [cah-ra-pah'-cho], *m.* Carapace, shell (tortugas, crustáceos). **Meterse en un carapacho**, to go into one´s shell.

caraqueño, ña [cah-ra-kay'-nyo, nyah], *a.* Of or relating to Caracas.

caráspita [cah-rahs'-pe-tah], *Excl. (Cono Sur)* damn!

carátula [cah-rah'-too-lah], *f.* 1. Mask of pasteboard. 2. A wire cover for the face to defend it from bees, mosquitoes, etc. 3. The title-page of a book. 4. *(Met.)* The stage, the theater. 5. *(CAm. Mex.)* Face, dial (de reloj). 6. Sleeve (de disco).

caratulero [cah-ra-too-lay'-ro], *m.* One who makes or sells masks.

cárava [cah'-ra-vah], *f. (Obs.)* Meeting of country people on festive occasions. **Quien no va a Cárava no sabe nada**, he who would know what is going on must mix in the world.

caravana [cah-ra-vah'-nah], *f.* 1. *(Naut.)* Sea-campaign performed by the Knights of Malta. 2. Caravan, a company of traders, pilgrims, and the like; a camel-train in the desert. **Hacer** or **correr caravanas**, *(Met.)* To take a variety of steps for obtaining some end. **Caravana de automóviles**, autocade, motorcade. *(Pers. caruán.)*. 3. Group, band; crowd of trippers (excursionistas). 4. *(Aut.)* Stream of cars; jam, tailback. 5. *(Carib.)* Bird tramp (trampa). 6. *(LAm.)* Long earrings.

caravanera [cah-ra-vah-nay'-rah], *f.* Caravansary.

caravanero [cah-ra-vah-nay'-ro], *m.* 1. Leader of a caravan. 2. *(Prov.)* A wild fellow.

caray [cah-rah'-e], *m.* 1. Tortoise-shell. *V.* CAREY. 2. *(Amer.) int.* An exclamation denoting surprise or impatience, equivalent to *caramba;* good heavens!; well I am blowed!

caraza [cah-rah'-thah], *f. aug.* Broad large face.

carbohidrato [car-bo-e-drah'-to], *m.* Carbohydrate.

carbol [car-bole'], *m.* A certain Turkish vessel.

carbólico [car-bo'-le-co], *a.* Carbolic.

carbón [car-bone'], *m.* 1. Coal. 2. Charcoal. 3. Black pencil. **Carbón animal**, animal charcoal. **Carbón de leña** or **carbón vegetal**, charcoal. **Papel carbón**, carbon paper. **Al carbón**, charcoal grilled. 4. *(Elec.)* Carbon. 5. *(Agri.)* Smut.

carbonada [car-bo-nah'-dah], *f.* 1. Load of coal (para horno). 2. A native meat stew. 3. Kind of pancake. 4. Grilled meat ball.

carbonadilla [car bo-nah-deel'-lyah], *f. dim.* Small *carbonada.*

carbonario [car-bo-nah'-re-o], *m.* An individual of a secret society formed to destroy absolutism. *(Acad.)*

carbonatado, da [car-bo-nah-tah'-do, dah], *a.* Carbonated.

carbonato [car-bo-nah'-to], *m. (Chem.)* Carbonate. **Carbonato de calcio**, calcium carbonate. **Carbonato sódico**, sodium carbonate.

carboncillo [car-bon-theel'-lyo], *m.* 1. *(dim.)* Small coal. 2. Black crayon. 3. *(Aut.)* Carbon deposit.

carbonear [car-bo-nay-ar'], *va.* 1. To reduce to charcoal by the action of fire. 2. *(Cono Sur)* to push, to egg on.

carbonera [car-bo-nay'-rah], *f.* 1. Place where charcoal is made 2. Coalhouse, coalhole, or coal-cellar. 3. Coal-pit, colliery, coal-mine.

carbonería [car-bo-nay-ree'-ah], *f.* Coal-yard; coal-shed; coal-mine.

carbonero [car-bo-nay'-ro], *m.* 1. Charcoal-maker. 2. Collier, coal-man, coal-miner. 3. Coal-merchant, collier. 4. *(Naut.)* Coal-ship, collier. **Barco carbonero**, collier. **Estación carbonera**, coaling station.

carbónico, ca [car-bo'-ne-co, cah], *a.* 1. *(Chem.)* Carbonic. 2. *m. (Cono Sur)* **Papel carbónico**, carbon paper.

carbonífero [car-bo-nee'-fay-ro], *a.* Carboniferous. **Industria carbonífera**, coal industry.

carbonilla [car-bo-neel'-lyah], *f.* 1. *(Min.)* Small coat, coaldust; cinder. 2. *(Aut.)* Carbon, carbon deposit. 3. *(LAm.)* Charcoal.

carbonización [car-bo-ne-thah-the-on'], *f.* Carbonization.

carbonizado, da [car-bo-ne-thah'-do, dah], *a.* Carbonated. *-pp.* of CARBONIZAR.

carbonizar [car-bo-ne-thar'], *va.* 1. To combine carbon with another body. 2. To char. **Quedar cabornizado,** to be charred; *(Elec.)* To be electrocuted; to be burnt down (edificio). *-vr. (Quim.)* To carbonize.

carbono [car-bo'-no], *m. (Chem.)* Carbon.

carbonoso [car-bo-no'-so], *a.* Carbonaceous.

carborundo [car-bo-roon'-do], *m.* Carborundum.

carbuncal [car-boon-cahl'], *a.* Resembling a carbuncle.

carbunclo, carbunco [car-boon´-clo], *m.* 1. Carbuncle, a precious stone, 2. Red pustule or pimple. *V.* CARBÚNCULO.

carbuncoso, sa [car-boon-co'-so, sah], *a.* Of the nature of a carbuncle.

carbúnculo [car-boon'-coo-lo], *m. V.* RUBÍ.

carburador [car-boo-rah-dor´], *m.* Carburettor.

carburante [car-boo-rahn'-tay], *m.* Fuel.

carburar [car-boo-rahr'], *vn.* 1. To go, to work (funcionar). 2. To think over (pensar).

carbureto [car-boo-ray'-to], or **carburo** [car-boo'-ro], *m. (Chem.)* Carburet, or carbide.

carca [car'-cah], *a.* Square; narrow-minded, having a closed mind; ancient; dead-beat. *-m. & f.* 1. Square; narrow-minded person; old fogey; reactionary; *(And.)* Muck, filth.

carcacha [car-cah'-chah], *f. (Mex.) (Aut.)* Old crock, old banger.

carcaj [car-cah'], *m.* Quiver (para flechas); *(LAm.)* Rifle case, pistol holster. *V.* CARCAX.

carcajada [car-ca-hah-dah], *f.* Loud laughter, hearty laughter, cachinnation. **Hubo carcajadas,** there was loud laughter. **Reírse a carcajadas,** to laugh heartily.

carcajear [car-cah-hay-ar'], *vn.* **carcajearse** *vr.* To roar with laughter, to have a good laugh.

carcajú [car-ca-hoo'], *m.* The glutton, wolverine, a ravenous carnivorous animal.

carcamal [car-ca-mahl'], *m.* 1. Nickname of old people, especially of old women. 2. Old crock (vejestorio). **Es un carcamal;** he´s a wreck.

carcamán [car-ca-mahn'], *m.* 1. Tub, a heavy, big, unseaworthy vessel; *(And. Carib.)* Old crock, wreck. 2. Carcamana *f.* 3. *(Carib.)* Low- class person; *(And. Carib.)* Poor immigrant. 4. *(Cono Sur)* reactionary.

cárcamo [car'-ca-mo], *m. (Amer.)* Riffle, a cleated trough.

carcancha [car-chahn'-chah], *f. (Mex.)* Bus.

carcañal, carcañar [car-ca-nyal´, car-ca nyar'], *m.* Heelbone, calcaneum. *V.* CALCAÑAR.

carcaño [car-cah'-nyo], *m.* Heel of the foot.

carcápuli [car-cah'-poo-le], *m.* 1. *(Bot.)* Indian yellow orange of Java and Malabar. 2. *(Bot.)* The large carcapulla-tree in America, which produces a fruit resembling a cherry.

carcasa [car-cah'-sah], *f. (Aut.)* Chassis, grid; carcass (de neumático); *(Tec.)* Casing.

cárcava [car´-ca-vah], *f. (Obs.)* 1. Inclosure, mound, hedge, ditch. 2 Pit or grave for the dead. 3. Gully made by torrents of water.

carcavera [car-ca-vay'-rah], *f.* A bad woman; a witch.

cárcavo [car'-ca-vo], *m.* 1. The cavity of the abdomen 2. The hollow in which a water-wheel turns. 3. The footprint of an animal

carcavón [car-ca-vone´], *m.* Large and deep ditch.

carcavuezo [car-cah-voo-ay'-tho], *m.* A deep pit.

carcax [car-cahx'], *m.* 1. Quiver. 2. Ribbon with a case at the end, in which the cross is borne in a procession. 3. *(Amer.)* A leather case in which a rifle is carried at the saddle-bow. 4. Ornament of the ankle worn by the Moors. *V.* AJORCA.

carcayú [car-cah-yoo'], *m.* Wolverine.

cárcel [car-thel], *f.* 1. Prison, goal, jail. **Salir de la cárcel,** to come out of prison. 2. Among carpenters, a wooden clamp

to keep glued. 4. Cheek of a printing-press. **Cárceles,** among weavers, cog-reeds of a loom.

carcelaje, carcerje [car-thay-lah-hay, car-thay-rah´-hay], *m.* Prison-fees, jailer's fees, paid on leaving.

carcelario [car-thay-lah'-re-o], *a.* Prison.

carcelería [car-they-lay-ree'-ah], *f.* 1. Imprisonment. 2. Bail given for the appearance of a prisoner.

carcelero [car-thay-lay'-ro], *m.* Jailkeeper, jailer. **Fiador carcelero,** one who is bail, or surety for a prisoner.

carcinogénico [car-the-no-hay'-ne-co], *a.* Carcinogenic.

carcinógeno [car-the-no'-hay-no], *m. (Med.)* Carcinogen.

carcinoma [car-the-no'-mah], *f.* Carcinoma, cancer.

carcinomatoso [car-the-no-mah-to'-so], *a.* Carcinomatous, cancerous.

carcoa [car-co'-ah], *f.* Row-barge used in India.

cárcola [car'-co-lah], *f.* Treadle of a loom.

carcoma [car-co´-mah], *f.* 1. Woodborer, the larva of various beetles which burrow in wood. 2. Dust made by the wood-borer. 3. *(Met.)* Grief, anxious concern. 4. *(Met.)* One who runs by degrees through his whole fortune.

carcomer [car-co-merr'], *va.* 1. To gnaw, to corrode (carcoma). 2. To consume a thing by degrees. 3. *(Met.)* To gradually impair health, virtue, etc. *-vr.* 1. To decay, to decline in health, virtue, etc. 2. To get worm-eaten.

carcomido, da [car-co-mee'-do, dah], *a.* 1. Worm-eaten, consumed. 2. *(Met.)* Decayed, declined, impaired. *-pp.* of CARCOMER.

carcoso [car-co'-so], *a. (And.)* Dirty, mucky.

carda [car'-dah], *f.* 1. Teasel, for raising the nap on cloth. 2. Card, with which wool is combed. 3. Hatter's jack. 4. *(Met.)* Severe reprimand or censure. **Dar una carda a uno,** to rap somebody over the knuckes. 5. *(Naut.)* Small vessel built like a galley.

cardador [car-dah-dor´], *m.* Carder, comber.

cardadura [car-dah-doo´-rah], *f.* Carding, combing wool.

cardamomo [car-dah-mo'-mo], *m. (Bot.)* Cardamom, a medicinal seed.

cardán [car-dahn'], *m.* 1. *(Mech.)* Universal joint. 2. *(Cono Sur) (Aut.)* Propellor shaft; *(LAm.) (Aut.)* Axle.

cardar [car-dar'], *va.* 1. To card or comb wool. 2. To raise the nap on cloth with a teasel. **Cardarle a uno la lana,** *(Met.)* To win a large sum at play. **Cardarle a alguno la lana,** *(Met.)* To reprimand severely.

cardelina [car-day-lee´-nah], *f. (Orn.)* Goldfinch, thistle-finch. *V.* JILGUERO.

cardenal [car-day-nahl´], *m.* 1. Cardinal. 2. *(Orn.)* Virginian nightingale, cardinal grosbeak. 3. Discoloration from a lash or blow; lividity, bruise, mark. *V.* EQUIMOSIS.

cardenalato [car-day-na-lah´-to], *m.* Cardinalate, cardinalship.

cardenalicio, cia [car-day-na-lee'-the-o, ah] *a.* Belonging to a cardinal.

cardencha [car-den´-chah], *f.* 1. *(Bot.)* Teasel, a genus of plants. **Cardencha cardadora,** manured or fuller´s teasel. **Cardencha silvestre,** wild teasel. **Cardencha laciniada,** laciniated teasel. **Cardencha pelosa,** small teasel, shepherd's staff. 2. Card or comb, for carding or combing of wool.

cardenchal [car-den-chahl'], *m.* Place where teasels grow.

cardenillo [car-day-neel'-lyo], *m.* 1. Verdigris. 2. (Painting) Verditer, a green paint made of verdigris; Paris green.

cárdeno, na [car´-day-no, nah], *a.* Livid, of a dark purple color.

cardería [car-day-ree´-ah], *f.* Cardery, the workshop where combs or cards are made.

cardero [car-day'-ro], *m.* Card-maker.

cardíaca [car-dee´-ah-cah], *f. (Bot.)* Common motherwort.

cardíaco, ca [car-dee'-ah-co, cah], *a. (Med.)* 1. Cardiac (enfermedades del corazón). 2. Cardiac, cardiacal, cordial, having the quality of invigorating (medicinas).

cardial [car-de-ahl'], *a.* Cardiacal, cardiac.

cardialgía [car-de-al-hee'-ah], *f. (Med.)* Cardialgia, heartburn.

cardias [car'-de-as], *m.* The upper or cardiac orifice of the stomach.

cardillo [car-deel'-lyo], *m.* 1. (*Bot.*) Golden thistle. **Cardillo español,** (*Bot.*) perennial golden thistle or star-thistle. **Cardillo manchado,** annual golden thistle. 2. (*Mex.*) *V.* VISO. 3. Thistle-down.

cardinal [car-de-nahl'], *a.* Cardinal, principal, fundamental. **Vientos cardinales,** winds from the four cardinal points. **Virtudes cardinales,** cardinal virtues. **Números cardinales,** cardinal numbers.

cardiógrafo [car-de-o'-grah-fo], *m.* Cardiograph.

cardiograma [car-de-o-grah'-mah], *m.* Cardiogram.

cardiología [car-de-o-lo-hee'-ah], *f* Cardiology.

cardiológico [car-de-o-lo'-he-co], *a.* Cardiological.

cardiólogo, ga [car-de-o'-lo-go], *m. & f.* Cardiologist, heart specialist.

cardiovascular [car-de-o-vas-coo-lar'], *a.* Cardiovascular.

carditis [car-dee'-tis], *f.* Inflammation of the muscular tissue of the heart.

cardizal [car-de-thahl'], *m.* Land covered with thistles.

cardo [car'-do], *m.* (*Bot.*) Thistle, a genus of plants. **Cardo silvestre** or **borriqueño;** (*Bot.*) Spear-plume thistle. **Cardo de comer,** cardon artichoke. **Cardo alcachofero,** garden artichoke. **Cardo santo,** blessed thistle, centaury, holy thistle, carduus benedictus. **Cardo de burro** or **crespo,** curled thistle. **Cardo lechero** or **cardo mariano,** milk thistle. **Más áspero que un cardo,** rougher than a thistle (personas).

cardón [car-done'], *m.* 1. (*Bot.*) *V.* CARDENCHA. **Cardón de cochinilla,** cochineal, fig cactus. **Cardón lechal** or **lechar,** *V.* CARDILLO DE COMER. **Cardón cabezudo,** turk's-cap cactus. 2. The act and effect of carding.

cardoncillo [car-don-theel'-lyo], *m.* (*Bot.*) Mountain carthamus.

carducha [car-doo'-chah], *f.* Large comb for wool.

cardume, cardumen [car-doo'-may, car-doo'-men], *m.* 1. Shoal of fishes. 2. (*And. Cono Sur*) great number, mass. **Un cardumen de gente,** a lot of people.

carduza [car-doo'-thah], *f.* (*Obs.*) *V.* CARDA.

carduzador [car-doo-thah-dor'], *m.* Carder. *V.* CARDADOR.

carduzal [car-doo-thahl'], *m. V.* CARDIZAL.

carduzar [car-doo-thar'], *va.* 1. To card or comb wool. 2. To shear cloth.

careador [cah-ray-ah-dor'], *a.* **Perro careador,** a shepherd-dog, watchdog. *V.* CAREAR.

carear [cah ray-ar'], *va.* 1. (*Law.*) To confront criminals. 2. To compare. 3. To tend a drove of cattle or flock of sheep. -*vn.* To come face to face. -*vr.* To assemble or meet for business, to come face to face.

carecer [car-ray-therr'], *vn.* 1. To want, to be in need, to lack. **Carece de talento,** he lacks talent. **No carecemos de dinero,** we don´t lack money. **Eso carece de sentido,** that doesn´t make sense. 2. (*Cono Sur*) **Carece hacerlo,** it is necessary to do it.

carel [cah-rayl'], *m.* Side, edge.

carena [cah-ray'-nah], *f.* (*Naut.*) 1. Careening or repairing of a ship. **Carena mayor,** thorough repair. 2. (*Poet.*) Ship. 3. (*Obs.*) Forty days' penance on bread and water. **Dar carena,** (*Met.*) to blame, to find fault with, to reprimand; to banter, to joke.

carenaje [cah-ray-nah'-hay], *m. V.* CARENERO.

carenar [cah-ray-nar'], *va.* To careen a ship, to pay a ship's bottom. **Aparejo de carenar,** careening gear.

carencia [cah-ren'-the-ah], *f.* Want, need, lack.

carencial [cah-rayn-the-al'], *a.* **Estado carencial,** state of want. **Mal carencial,** deficiency disease.

carenero [cah-ray-nay'-ro], *m.* Careening-place.

carente [cah-rayn-tay], *a.* **Carente de,** lacking, devoid of.

carentón [cah-rayn-tone'], *a.* (*Cono Sur*) large-faced.

careo [cah-ray'-o], *m.* 1. (*Law.*) confrontation, the act of bringing criminals or witnesses face to face. 2. Comparison. 3. (*Fort.*) Front of a bastion or fortress.

carero, ra [cah-ray'-ro, rah], *a.* (*Coll.*) Selling things dear.

carestía [cah-res-tee'-ah], *f.* 1. Scarcity, want. 2. Famine, famishment; jejuneness. 3. Dearness, or high price originating from scarcity. **Carestía de la vida,** period of shortage.

careta [cah-ray'-tah], *f.* 1. Mask made of pasteboard. 2. Wire cover of the face worn by bee-keepers. 3. *V.* JUDÍA. 4. (*Med.*) Breathing apparatus, respirator. **Careta antigás,** gasmask. **Careta de esgrima,** fencing mask.

careto, ta [cah-ray'-to, tah], *a.* 1. Having the forehead marked with a white spot or stripe (caballos). 2. Ugly.

carey [cah-ray'-e], *m.* Tortoise-shell. (*Malay, carah.*).

careza [cah-ray'-thah], *f. V.* CARESTÍA. (*Yo carezco, yo carezca,* from *Carecer. V.* CONOCER.)

carga [car'-gah], *f.* 1. Load, burden, freight, lading. 2. Cargo, the lading of a ship. 3. Charge of a cannon or other firearm, and the nozzle of the flask which measures the powder of such charge. **Carga muerta,** over-loading, dead load. 4. Old corn measure, containing four *fanegas* or bushels. 5. Medical preparation for curing sprains and inflammation in horses and mules, composed of flour, whites of eggs, ashes, and Armenian bole, all beaten up with the blood of the sane animal. 6. Impost, duty toll, tax. **Carga fiscal,** tax burden. **Carga de pago,** payload 7. (*Met.*) Burden of the mind, heaviness. 8. Load, weight, hindrance, pressure, cumbrance, or encumbrance. **Bestia de carga,** a beast of burden; a mule or sumpter-horse. 9. (*Obs.*) Discharge of firearms. 10. Charge, an attack upon the enemy, responsibility. **Echar la carga a otro,** (*Met.*) to throw the blame upon another. **Llevar la carga,** to be the one responsible. **Carga de familia,** dependent relative. **Carga personal,** personal commitments. **Llevar los soldados a la carga,** (*Mil.*) to lead soldiers to the charge. **Volver a la carga sobre el enemigo,** to return to the charge; **navío de carga,** (*Naut.*) Ship of burden, a merchant ship. **Andén de carga,** loading platform. **Permitido carga y descarga,** loading and unloading. **A cargas,** abundantly, in great plenty. **A cargas le vienen los regalos,** he receives loads of presents. **Carga útil,** (*Aer.*) Payload.

cargada [car-gah'-dah], *f.* 1. (*Cono Sur*) unpleasant practical joke. 2. (*Mex.*) *V.* CARGA. 3. **Ir a la cargada,** (*Mex.*) To jump on the bandwagon.

cargadera [car-gah-day'-rah], *f.* (*Naut.*), Down-hauls, brails. **Cargaderas de las gavias,** topsail brails. **Aparejo de cargadera de recamento,** down-haul tackle.

cargadero [car-gah-day'-ro], *m.* 1. Place where goods are loaded or unloaded. 2. (*Arquit.*) Lintel.

cargadilla [car-gah-deel'-lyah], *f.* (*Coll.*) Increase of a debt newly contracted.

cargado, da [car-gah'-do, dah], *a.* 1. Loaded, full, fraught. **Cargado de espaldas,** round-shouldered, stooping. **Estar cargado de vino,** to be top-heavy, or half-seas over. **Un árbol cargado de fruto,** a tree laden with fruit. **Tener los ojos cargados de sueño,** to have eyes heavy with sleep. 2. (*Elec.*) Live; charged. 3. Strong (café). 4. Overcast (cielo). -*pp.* of CARGAR.

cargador [car-gah-tor'], *m.* 1. Loader, he who loads; porter. 2. Rammer, ramrod. **Cargador de acumuladores, cargador de baterías,** battery charger. 3. He that loads great guns. 4. A large pitchfork for straw. 5. (*Arch.*) A post put in a doorway or window. 6. Magazine (recámara). -*pl.* 1. (*Naut.*) Tackles. *V.* PALANQUINES. 2. Plates of copper or pallets used in gilding.

cargadora [car-gah-do'-rah], *f.* (*And. Carib.*) Nursemaid.

cargamento [car-gah-men'-to], *m.* 1. (*Naut.*) Cargo. **Cargamento de retorno,** return cargo. 2. Loading.

cargante [car-gahn'-tay], *a.* Demanding (persona), fussy; annoying, troublesome; tiring (niño); irksome (tarea).

cargar [car-gar'], *va. & vn.* 1. To load, to burden, to freight; to carry a load (hombres, animales). 2. To charge, to attack the enemy. 3. To ship goods for foreign markets. 4. To load or charge a gun. 5. To overload or overburden, to clog; to lay in an abundant stock. 6. To charge in account, to book. 7. To impose or lay taxes. 8. To impute, to impeach. 9. To incline with the whole body towards a point or place. 10. To rest, to recline for support. 11. To take a charge, a duty, or any trust. 12. To crowd. 13. In cards, in some games, to take a card by playing one higher. **Cargar con**, to carry, take. **Cargar sobre**, to be responsible for another's deficiencies. *(Gram.)* For one letter or syllable to have more value in prosody than another. **Cargar arriba una vela**, *(Naut.)* to clew up a sail. **Cargar sobre uno**, to importune, tease, or molest. **Cargar a uno de deudas**, to encumber somebody with debts. 14. *(LAm.)* To carry, to have use; to wear. **Cargar anteojos**, to wear glasses. ¿**Cargas dinero?**, have you got any money on? 15. To bore, to annoy. **Esto me carga**, this annoys me. 16. To fall (acento). 17. **Cargar en**, to lean on. *-vr.* 1. To recline, to rest, or to lean against anything. **El viento se ha cargado al norte**, the wind has veered to the north. 2. To charge one's own account with the sums received. 3. To maintain, to support, or take a new duty upon oneself. **Cargarse de algo**, to be full of something. **Cargarse de hijos**, to overburden oneself with children. **El árbol se carga de manzanas**, the tree produces apples in abundance. 4. ¡**Algún día me lo cargaré!**, I'll get him one day. 5. **Cargarse algo**, to break something. **Cargar energía**, *(Inform.)* to eat an energizer.

cargareme [car-ga-ray-may], *m.* Receipt, voucher. *(Cargaré*, future, and *me*, pronoun.)

cargazón [car-ga-thone'], *f.* 1. Cargo of a ship. 2. **Cargazón de cabeza**, heaviness of the head. 3. **Cargazón de tiempo**, cloudy, thick weather. 3. *(Med.)* Heaviness (estómago). 4. Abundance.

cargo [car'-go], *m.* 1. Burden, loading. 2. *(Prov.)* Load of stones which weighs forty *arrobas*. 3. A number of baskets piled one on the other and put in the oil-press. 4. A load of pressed grapes. 5. Wood measure, about a cubic yard. 6. Total amount of what has been received, in a general account. 7. *(Met.)* Employment, dignity, office, honor, ministry. **Desempeñar un cargo**, to fill an office. **Jurar el cargo**, to take the oath of office. 8. Charge, keeping, care. 9. *(Met.)* Obligation to perform something. 10. *(Met.)* Command or direction of a thing 11. Fault or deficiency in the performance of one's duty. 12. Charge, accusation. *(Law.)* Count. **Cargo de conciencia**, remorse, sense of guilt. **Hacer cargo a alguno de una cosa**, to charge one with a fault, to hold him responsible; to accuse, to impeach. **Apenas si pude hacerme cargo de ello**, I could scarcely grasp what was going on. 13. A merchant ship that carries goods from one port to another. 1. To take into consideration; to reflect. 2. To make oneself acquainted with a thing. **Hacerse uno cargo de algo**, to take upon oneself. **Ser en cargo**, to be debtor.

cargosear [car-go-say-ar'], *va. (And. Cono Sur)* To pester, to keep on at.

cargoso, sa [car-go'-so, sah], *a.* 1. Heavy. 2. Bothersome, annoying.

cargue [car'-gay], *m.* 1. Loading a vessel 2. License to load.

carguero, ra [car-gay'-ro, ra], *a.* 1. He who bears a burden, cargo boat, transport plane. **Carguero militar**, air-force transport. 2. *f. (And. Carib.)* Nursemaid.

carguica, illa, ita [car-gee'-cah, eel'-lyah, ee-tah], *f. dim.* Small, or light load.

carguío [car-gee-o], *m.* 1. Cargo of merchandise. 2. A load.

cari [cah'-re], *m.* Caraway-seed.

carí [cah-re'], *m. (Amer. Bot.)* Black berry-bush.

cari [cah-re']*a. (Cono Sur)* Gray.

caria [cah'-re-ah], *f. (Arch.)* 1. The shaft (or fust) of a column. 2. *V.* CARIES.

cariacedo, da [cah-re-ah-thay'-do, dah], *a.* Having a sour-looking countenance.

cariacontecido, da [cah-re-ah-con-tay-thee'-do, dah], *a.* Sad, mournful; expressive of grief.

cariacuchillado, da [cah-re-ah-coo-cheel-lyah'-do, dah], *a.* Having the face marked with cuts or gashes.

cariado, da. [cah-re-ah'-do, dah], *a.* Carious, rotten. *-pp.* of CARIARSE.

cariadura [cah-re-ah-doo-rah], *f. (Med.)* Caries, decay.

cariaguileño, ña [cah-re-ah-gee-lay'-nyo, nyah], *a. (Coll.)* Long-faced, with an aquiline or hooked nose.

carialegre [cah-re-ah-lay'-gray], *a.* Smiling, cheerful.

cariampollado, da [cah-re-am-pol-lyah'-do, dah], *a.* Round-faced, plump cheeked.

cariancho, cha [cah-re-ahn'-cho, chah], *a.* Broad-faced, chubby, chub-faced, bull-faced.

cariar [cah-re-ar'], *v.* To cause to decay.

cariarse [cah-re-ar'-sayh], *vr. (Med.)* To grow carious (huesos).

cariarú [cah-re-ah-roo'], *m.* A liana of the Antilles yielding a crimson dye.

cariátide [cah-re-ah'-te-day], *f. (Arch.)* Caryatides, columns or pilasters under the figure of women.

Caribe [cah-ree'-bay], *m.* Carib. *-pl.* Caribs, Indians of the Antilles. *a.* Caribbean. **Mar Caribe**, Caribbean Sea.

caribeño [cah-re-bay'-nyo], *V.* CARIBE.

caribito [cah-re-bee'-to], *m.* A river fish of the bream species.

caribobo, ba [cah-re-bo'-bo, bah], Having a stupid look.

caribú [cah-re-boo'], *m.* Caribou.

carica [cah-ree'-cah], *f. (Prov.)* Sort of kidney beans.

caricato [cah-re-cah'-to], *m. (Cono Sur. Mex.) V.* CARICATURA.

caricatura [cah-re-cah-too'-rah], *f.* 1. Caricature. 2. Cartoon. **Caricatura animada**, animated cartoon film.

caricaturar [cah-re-cah-too-rar'], *va.* To caricature.

caricaturesco, ca [cah-re-cah-too-res'-co, cah], *a.* Caricaturist, caricatural; belonging to caricature.

caricaturista [cah-re-cah-too-rees'-tah], *m.* Caricaturist.

caricaturizar [cah-re-cah-too-ree'-sahr], *va.* To caricature.

caricia [cah-ree'-the-ah], *f.* Caress, act of endearment, endearing expression.

cariciosamente [cah-re-the-o-sah-men'-tay], *adv.* In a fondling or endearing manner.

caricioso, sa [cah-re-the-o'-so, sah], *a.* Fondling, endearing, caressing.

caricuerdo, da [cah-re-coo-err'-do, dah], *a.* Having a serene or composed mien.

caridad [cah-re-dahd'], *f.* 1. Charity, charitableness, kindness, good-will, benevolence. 2. Alms. **La caridad empieza por nosotros mismos**, charity begins at home. **Hacer caridad a uno**, to give alms to somebody.

caridoliente [cah-re-do-le-en'-tay], *a.* Having a mournful countenance.

caries [cah'-re-es], *f.* Caries or cariosity, ulceration of bone.

cariescrito [cah-re-es-cree'-to], *a.* Corrugated, shrivelled.

carifruncido, da [cah-re-froon-thee'-do, dah], *a.* Having a face contracted into wrinkles.

carigordo, da [cah-re-gor'-do, dah], *a.* Full-faced.

carijusto, ta [cah-re-hoos'-to, tah], *a.* Dissembling, hypocritical.

carilampiño [cah-re-lam-pe'-nyo], *a.* Clean-shaven; smooth-faced beardless.

carilargo, ga [cah-re-lar'-go, gah], *a.* Long-faced.

carilla, [cah-reel'-lyah], *f.* 1. *(dim.)* Little or small face. 2. Mask used by bee-keepers. *V.* CARETA.

carilleno, na [cah-reel-lyay'-no, nah], *a. (Coll.)* Plump-faced.

carillero, ra [cah-rel-lyay'-ro], *a.* Round-faced.

carillo, lla [cah-reel'-lyo, lyah], *a. dim.* Dear, high-priced.

carillón [cah-rel-lyone'], *m.* Carillon.

carilucio, cia [cah-re-loo'-the-o, ah], *a.* Having a shining or glossy face.

carimbo [cah-reem'-bo], *m. (LAm.)* Branding iron.

carina [cah-ree'-nah], *f.* 1. *(Arch.)* Building raised by the Romans in form of a ship. 2. *(Bot.)* The two power petals of papilionaceous flowers; the keel, carina.

carinegro, gra [cah-re-nay'-gro, grah], *a.* Of a swarthy complexion.

carininfo [cah-re-neen'-fo], *a.* Having a womanish face (hombres).

cariño [cah-ree'-nyo], *m.* 1. Love, fondness, tenderness, affection, kindness; concern. **Por el cariño que le tengo**, because I am fond of him. **Tomar cariño a**, to take a liking to. 2. Soft or endearing expression. 3. *(Obs.)* Anxious desire of a thing. 4. *(LAm.)* Caress, stroke; gift (regalo). **Hacerle cariños a uno**, to caress somebody.

cariñosamente [cah-re-nyo-sah-men'-tay], *adv.* Fondly, affectionately; kindly; good-naturedly.

cariñoso, sa [cah-re-nyo'-so, sah], *a.* 1. Affectionate, endearing, lovely, benevolent, kind, good, good-natured, natural. 2. Anxious, desirous, longing.

carioca [cah-re-o'-cah], *a.* Of Rio de Janeiro.

cariocar [cah-re-o-car'], *m. (Bot.)* A remarkable tree of tropical America, which yields an oil which replaces butter in Guiana.

cariofíleo, ea [cah-re-o-fee'-lay-o, ah], *a.* Caryophyllaceous; like a pink or carnation in structure or habits.

cariofilo [cah-re-o-fee-lo], *m.* 1. The garden pink. 2. The clove.

carioso, sa [cah-re-o'-so, sah], *a.* Carious, liable to corruption.

cariota [cah-re-oh'-tah], *f. (Bot.)* Wild carrot.

caripando, da [cah-re-pahn'-do, dah], *a. (Prov.)* Idiot-like, stupid-faced.

cariparejo, ja [cah-re-pa-ray'-ho, hah], *a. & m. & f. (Low.)* Resembling, having a similar face; likeness.

carirraído, da [cah-rir-rah-ee'-do, dah], *a. (Coll.)* Brazen-faced, impudent.

carirredondo, da [cah-rir-ray-don'-do, dah], *a.* Round-faced.

caris [cah'-ris], *m.* Kind of ragout or fricassee.

carisellado [cah-re-sayl-lyah'-do], *m. (And.)* Toss of a coin. **Echar un carisellado**, to toss a coin.

carisma [cah-rees'-mah], *m. (Divin.)* Divine gift or favor.

carismático [cah-res-mah'-te-co], *a.* Charismatic.

carita [cah-ree'-tah], *f. dim.* Little or small face.

caritativamente [cah-re-tah-te-vah-men'-tay], *adv.* Charitably.

caritativo, va [cah-re-tah-tee'-vo, vah], *a.* Charitable, hospitable.

cariucho [cah-re-oo'-cho], *m.* An Indian national dish of Ecuador.

cariz [cah-reeth'], *m.* 1. The face of the sky; the aspect of the atmosphere or of the horizon, or of a business. 2. *(fig.)* Outlook. **Poner mal cariz**, to scowl. **En vista del cariz que toman las cosas**, in view of the way things are going.

carlán [car-lahn'], *m. (Prov.)* He who owns the duties and jurisdiction of a district.

carlanca [car-lahn'-cah], *f.* 1. A mastiff's collar. **Tener muchas carlancas**, to be very cunning or crafty. 2. *(CAm. Cono Sur)* bore, pest, drag (persona); boredom, tedium (aburrimiento). 3. **Carlancas**, tricks, cunning.

carlancón [car-lan-cone'], *m. (Met. Coll.)* Person very subtle and crafty.

carlear [car-lay-ar'], *vn.* To pant. *V.* JADEAR.

carlina [car-lee'-nah], *f. (Bot.)* Carline thistle.

carlinga [car-leen'-gah], *f.* 1. *(Naut.)* Step of a mast. 2. Pilot's cabin.

Carlomagno [car-lo-mahg'-no], *m.* Charlemagne.

carlovingio, gia [car-lo-veen'-he-o, he-ah], *a.* Carlovingian, relating to Charlemagne.

carmañola [car-ma-nyo-lah], *f.* 1. A French republican song, composed in 1792. 2. A kind of jacket with narrow neck and short skirt, much used in the time of the revolution.

carmel [car-mel'], *m. (Bot.)* Ribwort, plantain, rib grass.

carmelita [car-may-lee'-tah], *m. & f.* 1. Carmelite. 2. *f.* Flower of the great Indian cress.

carmelitano, na [car-may-le-tah'-no, nah], *a.* Belonging to the Carmelite order.

Carmen [car'-men], *m.* 1. *(Prov.)* Country-house and garden. 2. Carmelite order. 3. Verse. 4. Woman' name.

carmenador [car-may-nah-dor'], *m.* Teaser, one who scratches cloth to raise the nap.

carmenadura [car-may-nah-doo'-rah], *f.* Act of teasing or scratching cloth, to raise the nap.

carmenar [car-may-nar'], *va.* 1. To prick or card wool. 2. To scratch cloth for the purpose of raising the nap. 3. To pull out the hair of the head. **Carmenar el pelo a uno**, to pull somebody's hair. *V.* REPELAR. 4. To win another's money at play.

carmes [car'-mes], *m.* Kermes, the cochineal insect.

carmesí [car-may-see'], *m.* Cochineal powder.

carmesí [car-may-see'], *m. & a.* Crimson, bright red, somewhat darkened with blue; purple.

carmín [car-meen'], *m.* 1. Carmine, the coloring matter of cochineal. **Carmín bajo**, pale rose color; lipstick. 2. *(Bot.)* Pokeweed; phytolacca.

carminar [car-me-nar'], *va.* To expel wind.

carminativo [car-me-nah-tee'-vo], *m.* Carminative, relieving wind.

carmíneo [car-me'-nay-o], *a.* Carmine, crimson.

carnada [car-nah'-dah], *f.* Bait.

carnaje [car-nah'-hay], *m.* 1. Salt beef. 2. Carnage, slaughter.

carnal [car-nahl'], *a.* 1. Carnal, fleshy. 2. Sensual, carnal, fleshly, lustful, lecherous. 3. *(Met.)* Worldly, outward: opposed to spiritual. 4. United by kindred. **Hermano carnal**, full brother. **Primo carnal**, first cousin.

carnal, *m.* Time of the year in which meat may be eaten: opposed to Lent and other fast-days.

carnalidad [car-nah-le-dahd'], *f.* Carnality, lustfulness.

carnalmente [car-nal-men'-tay], *adv.* Carnally, sensually.

carnaval [car-nah-val'], *m.* Carnival, the feast held before Shrovetide. *V.* CARNESTOLENDAS.

carnavalero [car-nah-vah-lay'-ro], *a.* Carnival.

carnaza [car-nah'-thah], *f.* 1. Fleshy part of a hide or skin. 2. *(Coll.)* Meal consisting of an abundance of meat.

carne [car'-nay], *f.* 1. Flesh. 2. Meat or flesh-meat, for food, in contradistinction to fish. 3. The pulp of fruit. 4. A boyish game with a hollow bone. **Carne de membrillo**, pulp of quinces, boiled, cooled, and preserved. **Carne de gallina**, gooseflesh, goose pimples. **Carne asada en horno**, baked meat. **Carne asada en parrillas**, broiled meat. **Carne fiambre**, cold meat. **Color de carne**, flesh color. **Caldo de carne**, meat broth. **Poner toda la carne en el asador**, *(Met.)* to hazard one's all. **Ser uña y carne**, *(Met.)* to be hand and glove, to be intimate or familiar. **Entrado en carnes**, *(LAm.)* plump, overweight. **En carne viva**, on the raw. **Se me abrieron las las carnes**, I was terrified. **Ser de carne y hueso**, to be only human. **Carne de cerdo**, pork. **Carne congelada**, frozen meat. **Carne molida**, *(LAm.)* Mince. **Carne picada**, mince. **Carne de ternera**, veal. **Carne de vaca**, beef.

carné [car-nay'], *m. V.* CARNET.

carneada [car-nay-ah'-dah], *f. (Cono Sur)* slaughter (de animales); slaughter, massacre (masacre).

carnear [car-nay-ar'], *va.* 1. *(Cono Sur)* to slaughter (animal); *(fig.)* To murder, to butcher. 2. *(Cono Sur)* To cheat, to swindle.

carnecería, carnescería [car-nay-thay-ree'-ah, car-nes-thay-ree'-ah], *f. V.* CARNICERIA.

carnecilla [car-nay-theel'-lyah], *f.* Small excrescence in some part of the body; caruncle.

carnerada [car-nay-rah'-dah], *f.* Flock of sheep.

carneraje [car-nay-rah'-hay], *m.* Tax or duty on sheep.

carnerario [car-nay-rah'-re-o], *m. (Prov.)* Charnel-house.

carnereamiento [car-nay-ray-ah-me-en'-to], *m.* Poundage, penalty for the trespass of sheep.

carnerear [car-nay-ray-ar'], *va.* To fine the proprietor of sheep for damage done. *-vn. (Cono Sur)* To blackleg, to be a strikebreaker.

carnerero [car-nay-ray'-ro], *m.* Shepherd. *V.* PASTOR.

carneril [car-nay-reel'], *m.* Sheep-walk, pasture for sheep.

carnero [car-nay'-ro], *m.* 1. Sheep, mutton. 2. Mutton, the flesh of sheep dressed for food. 3. *(Prov.)* Sheepskin dressed or tanned. 4. Family vault, burying-place; charnel-house. 5. Larder. **Carnero manso para guía**, bellwether. **Carnero marino**, *(Zool.)* white shark. **Carnero de la sierra**, *(LAm.)*

Llama, alpaca, vicuña. **No hay tales carneros,** there´s no such thing. 6. *(Cono Sur)* Weak-willed person (débil); blackleg, strikebreaker.

carneruno, na [car-nay-roo'-no, nah], *a.* Resembling or belonging to sheep.

carnestolendas [car-nes-to-len'-das], *f. pl.* Three carnival days before Shrovetide or Ash-Wednesday.

carnet [car-net'], *m.* 1. Notebook. 2. Account book. 3. Dance program. 4. Identification card. **Carnet de conducir,** driving licence. **Carnet de identidad,** identity card. **Carnet sindical,** union card.

carnicería [car-ne-thay-ree'-ah], *f.* 1. Meat-market, meat shop. 2. Slaughterhouse; butcher´s (shop). 3. Carnage, havoc, slaughter. **Hacer carnicería,** 1. To cut away a great quantity of flesh. 2. To wound in many places. **Carnicería en las carreteras,** *(fig.)* Carnage on the roads.

carnicero [car-ne-thay'-ro], *m.* Butcher.

carnicero, ra [car-ne-thay'-ro, rah], *a.* 1. Carnivorous (animales). 2. Bloodthirsty, sanguinary. 3. Applied to pasture-grounds for cattle. 4. *(Coll.)* Applied to a person who eats much meat. 5. Belonging to shambles. **Libra carnicera,** pound for butcher's meat, which varies from twenty-four to thirty-six ounces.

cárnico [ ], *a.* Meat. **Industria cárnica,** meat industry.

carnicol [car-ne-cole'], *m.* Hoof of cloven-footed animals. V. TABA.

carnificación [car-ne-fe-ca-the-on'], *f.* Carnification, a morbid change of a tissue to the consistency of flesh, as in hepatization of the lungs.

carnificarse [car-ne-fe-car'-say], *vr.* To carnify, to breed flesh.

carnitas [car-nee'-tas], *f. pl. (Mex.)* Barbecue pork.

carnívoro, ra [car-nee'-vo-ro, rah], *a.* Carnivorous, flesh-eating; meat-eating.

carniza [car-nee-thah´], *f. (Low.)* 1. Refuse of meat. 2. Cats' or dogs' meat.

carnosidad [car-no-se-dahd'], *f.* 1. Carnosity, proud flesh, growing on a wound, or a fleshy excrescence of any part of the body. 2. Fatness, abundance of flesh and blood. 3. Fleshiness.

carnoso, sa [car-no'-so, sah], *a.* 1. Fleshy, carnous, carneous. 2. Full of marrow; pulpous (fruta). 3. Papescent, containing pap.

carnudo, da [car-noo'-do, dah], *a.* V. CARNOSO.

carnuza [car-noo'-thah], *f.* Abundance of meat, producing loathing.

caro, ra [cah'-ro', rah], *a.* 1. Dear, high-priced, costly. 2. Dear, beloved, affectionate. **Las cosas que nos son tan caras,** the things which are so dear to us. 3. Dear, expensive. **Lo barato es caro,** cheap things are dearest. **Un coche carisimo,** a terribly expensive car.

caro [cah'-ro], *adv.* Dearly, at a high price, at too great a price. **Le costó muy caro,** it cost him dear. **Éso sale bastante caro,** that comes rather expensive.

carobo [ca-ro'-bo], *m.* 1. Weight of the twenty-fourth part of a grain. 2. Kind of Turkish vessel.

caroca [ca-ro'-cah], *f. (Coll.)* Caress, endearing action or expression made with a selfish purpose, commonly used in the plural; flattery (exaggerated); soft soap (jabón).

carocha [ca-ro'-chah], *f.* 1. White glutinous secretion (probably from the appendicular glands) of the queen bee, in which she lays her eggs; this with the egg in each cell. 2. *(Mex.)* Old banger, old crock.

carochar [ca-ro-char'], *va.* To hatch eggs (colmenas).

caroleno [cah-ro-lay'-no], *m. (Mex.)* Back slang.

Carolina [ca-ro-le'-nah], *f. (Geog.)* **Carolina del Norte,** North Carolina; **Carolina del Sur,** South Carolina.

carolingio [cah-ro-leen'-ge-o], *a.* Carolingian.

caromomia [ca-ro-mo'-me-ah], *f.* The dry flesh of a mummy.

carón [ca-rone'], *a. (LAm.)* Broad-faced.

carona [ca-ro'-nah], *f.* 1. Padding of the saddle, which touches the animal's back. 2. Part of the animal's back on which

the saddle lies. **Esquilar la carona,** to shear the back of a mule; **andar con las caronas ladeadas,** *(Cono Sur)* to have problems. 3. *(Cono Sur)* Bed.

caronada [ca-ro-nah'-dah], *f.* Carronade, an absolete naval gun of short barrel and large bore.

caroñoso. sa [ca-ro-nyo'-so, sah], *a.* Old, galled, and cast off (bestias de carga).

caroquero, ra [ca-ro-kay'-ro, rah], *m. & f.* Wheedler, flatterer; caressing.

carosiera [ca-ro-se-ay'-rah], *f.* 1. *(Bot.)* Species of the palm-tree. 2. Date, the fruit of that species of the palm.

carota [cah-ro'-tah], *a.* 1. Barefaced, brazen. 2. *m. & f.* Rotter; shameless person.

carotas [ca-ro´-tas], *f. pl.* Rolls of tobacco ground to powder.

carótida [ca-ro'-te-dah], *f. (Prov.)* The carotid artery.

carozo [ca-ro'-tho], *m.* 1. *(Prov.)* Core of a pomegranate, or other fruit. 2. Cob of corn.

carpa [car'-pah], *f.* 1. *(Zool.)* Carp, a fresh-water fish. 2. Part of a bunch of grapes which is torn off. 3. *(Peru)* A tent of canvas or cloth.

carpanel [car-pa-nel´], *m. (Arch.)* Arch in a semi-elliptic form.

carpanta [car-pahn'-tah], *f.* Ravenous hunger.

carpe [car'-pay], *m. (Bot.)* Common horn-beam tree, witch-hazel.

carpedal [car-par-dahl'], *m.* Plantation of common horn-beam trees.

carpelo [car-pay'-lo], *m.* Carpel.

carpeta [car-pay'-tah], *f.* 1. Table-cover, covering of a table. 2. Portfolio, portable writing-desk. **Carpeta de información,** information folder. **Cerrar la carpeta,** to close the file. 3. Label, or indorsement, upon a bundle of papers; a wrapper.

carpetazo [car-pay-tah'-tho], *m.* A blow or stroke with a *carpeta.* **Dar carpetazo a,** to shelve, to put on one side.

carpetovetónico [car-pay-to-vay-to'-ne-co], *a.* Terribly Spanish, Spanish to the core.

carpidor, ra [car-pe-dor'], *m. & f. (LAm.)* Weeding hoe.

carpintear [car-pin-tay-ar'], *vn.* To do carpenter's work.

carpintería [car-pin-tay-ree'-ah], *f.* 1. Carpentry. 2. Carpenter's shop.

carpintero [car-pin-tay'-ro], *m.* 1. Carpenter, joiner. **Carpintero de prieto** or **de carretas,** cartwright, wheelwright. **Carpintero de ribera** or **de navío,** ship carpenter, shipwright. **Mestro carpintero de remos,** master oar-maker. **Segundo carpintero,** carpenter's mate. 2. **Pájaro carpintero,** *(Orn.)* Woodpecker. **Carpintero real,** ivory-billed woodpecker.

carpión [car-pe-on'], *m.* Large carp resembling a trout.

carpir [car-peer'], *vn.* To tear, to scrape, to scratch, to scold. *-vn. (LAm.)* To weed, to hoe.

carpo [car'-po], *m. (Anat.)* Carpus, wrist.

carpobálsamo [car-po-bahl'-sah-mo], *m.* Carpobalsamum, fruit of the tree which yields the balm of Gilead.

carpófago [car-po'-fah-go], *m.* One who lives on fruit.

carqueja, or **carqueija** [car-kay'-hah, car-kay'-e-hah], *f. (Bot.)* V. CARQUESA, for a plant.

carquesa, carquesia [car-kay'-sah, car- kay'-se-ah], *f.* In glass-houses, the annealing furnace.

carquexia [car-kek'-se-ah], *f.* A species of broom-plant.

carraca [car-rah'-cah], *f.* 1. Carrack, large and slow-sailing cargo ship. 2. Rattle (instrumento). 3. A rachet brace. 4. Old crock (coche).

carraco, ca [car-rah'-co, cah], *a.* Old, withered, decrepit.

carracón [car-rah-cone'], *m.* 1. Large cargo ship. 2. *(aug.)* Large rattle. 3. Animal worn out with age and fatigue.

carrada [cahr-rah'-dah], *f. (Cono Sur)* V. CARRETADA.

carral [car-rahl'], *m.* Barrel, butt, vat, pipe for transporting wine in carts and wagons.

carraleja [car-rah-lay'-hah], *f.* 1. Black beetle with yellow stripes; the oil-beetle, meloe. 2. Spanish blistering beetle. *(Acad.)*

carralero [car-rah-lay'-ro], *m.* Cooper.

carranclán [car-ran-clahn'], *m.* Gingham.

carranque [car-rahn'-kay], *m.* A Peruvian bird resembling a crane.

carrasca [car-rahs'-cah], *f. (Bot.) V.* CARRASCO; **ser de carrasca,** *V.* AÚPA.

carrascal [car-ras-cahl'], *m.* Plantation of evergreen oaks.

carrasco [car-rahs'-co], *m. (Bot.)* Ever green oak. *V.* COSCOJA.

carrascoloso [cahr-ras-co-lo'-so], *a. (LAm.)* Grumpy, touchy, irritable.

carrascon [car-ras-cone], *m. (Bot.)* Large evergreen oak.

carraspada [car-ras-pah'-dah], *f.* Negus, a beverage made of red wine, honey, and spice.

carraspante [car-ras-pahn'-tay], *a. (Prov.)* Harsh, acrid, strong.

carraspear [car-ras-pay-ar'], *vn.* To be hoarse, to have a frog in one´s throat.

carraspeo [car-ras-pay'-o], *m.* Sore throat.

carraspera [car-ras-pay'-rah], *f.* 1. Hoarseness. 2. Sore throat, attended with hoarseness.

carraspique [car-ras-pee'-kay], *m. (Bot.)* Candytuft.

carrasposo [car-ras-po'-so], *a.* 1. Hoarse, having a sore throat. 2. *(LAm.)* Rough, harsh.

carrasqueño, ña [car-ras-kay'-nyo, nyah], *a.* 1. Harsh, sharp, biting. 2. Rough, rude, sullen. 3. Belonging to the evergreen oak 4. *(Prov.)* Strong, nervous.

carrasquilla [car-ras-keel'-lyah], *f. (Bot. Prov.)* A species of the genus Rhamnus; a buckthorn.

carrear, carrejar [car-ray-ar', car-ray-har'], *va. (Obs.) V.* ACARREAR.

carrera [car-ray'-rah], *f.* 1. Race (deportes), course. **Carrera ciclista,** cycling. **Carrera de caballos,** horse racing. **Carrera pedestre,** footrace. **Carrera de sacos,** sack race. **Carrera de fondo,** long-distance race. 2. Run (béisbol, cricket). 2. The course of the stars. 3. Career (estudios). 4 High-road, from one town to another. 5. In Madrid, a broad and long street, as, **la carrera de San Francisco,** St. Francis street. 6. Alley, a walk in a garden; an avenue leading to a house, planted with trees. 7. Row of things, ranged in a line. 8. Range of iron teeth in combing-cards. 9. Line made by dividing and separating the hair. 10. Girder, in a floor. 11. Stitch in a stocking which has broken or fallen. 12. Course and duration of life. 13. Profession of arms or letters. 14. Course, method of life, train of actions. 15. Course, conduct, manner of proceeding, mode of action. *V.* CARRERILLA. **Carrera de Indias,** trade from Spain to South America. **No poder hacer carrera con alguno,** not to be able to bring one to reason. **A carrera abierta,** at full speed. **De carrera,** without thinking, rashly. **Carrera de armamentos,** arms race. **Carrera de relevos,** relay race. **Carrera de vallas,** hurdles. **Tomar carrera,** to back up in order to get a running start. **No poder hacer carrera con,** not to be able to do a thing with, not to make any headway with. **Dar carrera libre a,** to give free rein to. **Hacer el trabajo a la carrera,** to race through one´s work. **Carrera de despegue,** take-off run. **Carrera por carretera,** road race. **Carrera de coches,** car race. **Carrera de medio fondo,** middle-distance race. **Carrera de maratón,** marathon. **Carrera ascendente,** upstroke. **Diplomático de carrera,** career diplomat. **No hago carrera con este niño,** I can´t make any headway with this child. **No tiene carrera,** he has no profession.

carrerilla, ta [car-ray-reel'-lyah, ree'-tah], *f.* 1. *(dim.)* Small race or course. 2. Rapid motion in a Spanish dance. 3. *(Mus.)* Rise or fall of an octave. 4. Non-stop, continuosly. **Lo dijo de carrerilla,** he reeled it off.

carrerista [car-ray-rees'-tah], *m. & f.* 1. Fond of racing. 2. Racing cyclist. 3. *f.* Street walker.

carrero [car-ray'-ro], *m.* Carter, cart driver.

carreta [car-ray'-tah], *f.* 1. Long narrow cart, wagon. **Carreta de mano,** *V.* CARRETILLA. **Tener la carreta llena,** *(Carib.)* to be weighted down by problems. 2. **Carreta cubierta,** gallery of a siege, or the covered passage to the walls of a fortress.

carretada [car-ray-tah´-dah], *f.* 1. Cartful, cart-load. 2. Great quantity. **A carretadas,** *(Coll.)* copiously, in abundance.

carretaje [car-ray-tah'-hay], *m.* Cartage, haulage.

carrete [car-ray'-tay], *m.* 1. Spool, bobbin, reel. 2. Small reel for winding silk or gold and silver twist. 3. Reel of a fishing-rod. 4. *(Elec.)* Bobbin, wire coil. **Carrete de encendido,** induction coil. **Dar carrete a uno,** to keep somebody guessing.

carretear [car-ray-tay-ar'], *va.* 1. To cart, to convey in a cart. 2. To drive a cart. *-vr.* To draw unevenly (bueyes, mulos).

carretel [car-ray-tel'], *m.* 1. Spool, reel, bobbin. 2. *(Prov.)* A fishing-reel, line-reel. 3. *(Naut.)* Log-reel. 4. Spun-yarn winch. 5. Ropewalk reel. 6. **Carretel de carpintero,** carpenter's marking-line.

carretela [car-ray-tay'-lah], *f.* Caleche, calash, a four-wheeled carriage on springs.

carretera [car-ray-tay'-rah], *f.* Highway, road. **Por carretera,** by road. **Carretera nacional,** Arterial highway. **Carretera secundaria,** secondary road. **Carretera de circunvalación,** bypass. **Red de carreteras,** road network. **Mapa de carreteras,** road map.

carretería [car-ray-tay-ree'-ah], *f.* 1. Number of carts. 2. Trade of a carman. 3. Cartwright's yard; wheel wright's shop.

carretero [car-ray-tay'-ro], *m.* 1. Cartwright 2. Carman carrier, carter. **Voz de carretero,** harsh, loud, and unpleasant voice; **jurar como un carretero,** to swear like a trooper. 3. *(Astr.)* Wagoner, a northern constellation. *-a.* **Camino carretero,** vehicular road.

carretil [car-ray-teel'], *a.* Suitable for carts.

carretilla [car-ray-teel'-lyah], *f.* 1. Wheelbarrow. 2. Hand truck. 3. Hand cart. 4. Walker (for babies). 5. Firecracker. 6. Cake decorator. **Carretilla elevadora,** fork-lift truck. **Saber de carretilla una cosa,** to know something perfectly. 7. *(And.)* Lot, series. 8. *(Cono Sur)* jaw, jawbone (quijada).

carretón [car-ray-tone'], *m.* 1. Small cart, in the shape of an open chest, wagon. 2. Go-cart. 3. *(Obs.)* Gun-carriage. 4. **Carretón de lámpara,** pulley for raising or lowering lamps. 5. In Toledo, stage for religious plays. 6. Truck, dray, van.

carretoncillo [car-ray-ton-theel'-lyo], *m. dim.* Small go-cart for children.

carretonero [car-ray-to-nay'-ro], *m.* Driver of the *carretón;* drayman, truckman.

carricoche [car-re-co'-chay], *m.* 1. Cart with a box like a coach. 2. *(Prov.)* Old-fashioned coach, wagonette. 3. *(Prov.)* Muck-cart, dungcart.

carricuba [car-re-coo'-bah], *f.* Water cart.

carricureña [car-re-coo-ray'-nyah], *f. (Mil.)* Carriage of a light field-piece.

carriego [car-re-ay'-go], *m.* 1. Osier basket used for fishing. 2. Large rough basket used in bleaching flaxyarn.

carriel [car-re-ayl'], *m. (And. CAm.)* Leather case.

carril [car-reel'], *m.* 1. Rut, cart-way, cart-rut. 2. Narrow road where one cart only can pass at a time. 3. Furrow opened by the plough. 4. A rail of a railway. **Carril de autobús,** bus lane.

carrilada [cah-re-lah'-dah], *f.* Rut, the track of a cart or coach.

carrilano [car-re-lah'-no], *m. (Cono Sur)* 1. Robber, hold up man. 2. Railwayman (ferroviario).

carrilera [car-re-lay'-rah], *f.* 1. Rut, track (rodera). 2. *(Carib.)* *(Ferro.)* Siding.

carrilero [car-re-lay'-ro], *m. (And.) (Ferro.)* Railwayman; *(Cono Sur)* con man (embaucador).

carrillada [car-reel-lyah'-dah], *f.* Oily or medullar substance of a hog´s cheek. **Carrilladas de vaca o carnero,** *(Prov.)* Cow or sheep's head without the tongue.

carrillar [car-reel'-lyar], *va. (Naut.)* To hoist light things out of the hold with a tackle.

carrillera [car-reel-lyay'-rah], *f.* 1. The jaw. 2. Each of two straps, covered with metal scales used to fasten a soldier´s helmet; chin-strap.

carrillo [car-reel'-lyo], *m.* 1. *(dim.)* Small cart. 2. Cheek, the fleshy part of the face. 3. *(Naut.)* Tackle for hoisting light things. **Comer a dos carrillos**, to eat greedily. 4. *(Tec.)* Pulley. 5. Trolley, pushcart (mesa para servir).

carrilludo, da [car-reel-lyoo'-do, dah], *a.* Plump or round checked.

carrindanga [car-reen-dahn'-ga], *f. (Cono Sur)* old crock, old banger.

carriola [car-re-o-lah], *f.* 1. Trundle-bed. 2. Small chariot; curricle.

carrito [car-ree'-to], *m.* 1. Trolley, shopping cart (de supermercado); tea trolley, serving trolley. 2. *(Carib.)* Taxi.

carrizal [car-re-thahl'], *m.* Land which is full of reed-grass.

carrizo [car-ree'-tho], *m.* 1. *(Bot.)* Common reed-grass. 2. *(And. Mex.)* **Carrizos**, thin legs; *(And.)* **Hacer carrizos**, to cross one's legs. 3. *(Carib.)* **No nos ayudan en un carrizo**, they do nothing at all to help us. 4. *(And. CAm. Carib.), V.* CARAMBA.

carro [car'-ro], *m.* 1. Cart, a carriage with two wheels, chariot, cart. **Varas del carro**, shafts of a cart. **Toldo del carro**, tilt, the cloth thrown over the hoops of a cart. 2. A railway car. 3. The running gear of a carriage without the body. 4. *(Astr.)* The Greater Bear, a northern constellation. **Carro menor**, the Lesser Bear. **Carro de oro**, Brussels camlet, fine camlet. 5. *(Naut.)* Manufactory for cables and other ship cordage. 6. Measure for wood; a cartload. **Medio carro de leña**, a cord of wood. **Un carro de problemas**, *(fig.)* a whole load of problems. 7. The bed of a printing-press. **Carro de combate**, tank. **Carro fúnebre**, hearse. **Aguantar carros y carretas**, to put up with anything. **Apearse del carro**, to back down.

carrocería [car-ro-thay-re'-ah], *f.* 1. Coachbuilder's (taller); carriage repair shop. 2. *(Aut.)* Body work, coachwork.

carrocero [car-ro-thay'-ro], *m.* Coachbuilder, carriage builder.

carrocilla [car-ro-theel'-lyah], *f. dim.* Small coach.

carrocín [car-ro-theen'], *m.* Chaise, curricle.

carrocha [car-ro'-chah], *f.* Seminal substance in bees and other insects. Eggs.

carrochar [car-ro-char'], *vn.* To lay eggs, to shed the seminal substance (abejas, insectos).

carrofuerte [car-ro-foo-er'-tay], *m.* A strong cart or truck for transporting artillery or heavy weights.

carromatero [car-ro-mah-tay'-ro], *m.* Carter, charioteer, carman.

carromato [car-ro-mah´-to], *m.* A long, narrow cart with two wheels and tilt, for transporting goods, etc.

carroña [car-ro'-nyah], *f.* Carrion, putrid flesh.

carroñar [car-ro-nyar'], *va.* To infect sheep with the scab.

carroñero [car-ro-nyay'-ro], *m.* Rotten, vile, foul. **Animal carroñero**, animal which feeds on carrion.

carroño, ña [car-ro'-nyo, nyah], *a.* Putrefied, putrid, rotten.

carroza [car-ro'-thah], *f.* 1. Large coach; superb state coach. **Carroza fúnebre**, hearse. 2. *(Naut.)* Awning over a boat, or part of a ship. 3. *(Naut.)* Kind of cabin on the quarter-deck of a ship. *-m.* 1. Old geezer (viejo); old boy; square (carca); old reactionary. 2. Gay, queer, old queen (homosexual). *-a.* Archaic, passé; square.

carruaje [car-roo-ah'-hay], *m.* All sorts of vehicles for transporting persons or goods.

carruajero [ca-roo-ah-hay'-ro], *m.* Carrier, carter, wagoner.

carruco [car-roo- co], *m.* Small cart used in mountainous parts.

carrujado, da [car-roo-hah'-do, dah], *a.* Corrugated, wrinkled. *V.* ENCARRUJADO.

carrujo [car-roo'-ho], *m. (LAm.)* Joint, reefer.

carrusel [car-roo-sayl'], *m.* Merry-go-round, roundabout.

carry-all [car-ree-ol'], *m. (Cono Sur)* estate car, station wagon.

carta [car'-tah], *f.* 1. Letter; *(Com.)* Favor. 2. Royal ordinance. 3. Map, chart. 4. Card for playing. 5. A written constitution, charter. 6. *(Obs.)* Writing-paper. **Carta blanca**, letter or commission with a blank for the name to be inserted at pleasure; full powers given to one. **Carta abierta**, *(Obs.)* open order,

addressed to all persons. **Carta certificada**, a registered letter. **Carta cuenta**, bill or account of sale. **Carta credencial** or **de creencia**, credentials. **Carta de crédito**, letter of credit. **Carta de dote**, articles of marriage. **Carta de encomienda**, letter of safe conduct. **Carta de espera** or **moratoria**, letter of respite given to a debtor. **Carta de guía**, passport; **carta de naturaleza**, letters of naturalization. **Carta de pago**, acquittance, receipt, discharge in full. **Carta de portes**, booking ticket. **Carta de presentación**, letter of introduction. **Carta de seguridad**, safeguard, protection. **Carta de sanidad**, bill of health. **Carta de venta**, bill of sale. **Carta devuelta**, a deadletter. **Carta pastoral**, pastoral letter. **Carta receptoria**, warrant, voucher. **Perder con buenas cartas**, *(Met.)* To fail although protected or deserving. **Traer** or **venir con malas cartas**, *(Met.)* to attempt to enforce an ill-grounded claim. **Carta de pésame**, letter of condolence. **Carta postal**, *(LAm.)* Post-card. **Carta urgente**, special delivery letter. **Echar una carta al correo**, to post a letter. **Carta Magna**, Magna carta. **Carta verde**, green card. **Carta marítima**, chart. **Carta meteorológica**, weather map. **Echar las cartas**, to tell somebody's fortune. **Poner las cartas sobre la mesa**, to put one's cards on the table. **Tomar cartas en el asunto**, to intervene in a matter.

carta aérea [car'-tah ah-ay'-ray-ah], *f.* Airletter.

carta-bomba [car-tah-bom'-bah], *f. pl.* Letter-bomb.

cartabón [car-tah-bone´], *m.* 1. A carpenter's square, rule, an instrument to measure and form angles. **Echar el cartabón**, *(Met.)* to adopt measures for attaining one's end. **Cartabón de cola**, small square piece of glue. 2. Shoemaker's slide, size-stick. 3. Quadrant, a gunner's square, or instrument for elevating and pointing guns.

cartaginense [car-tah-he-nen'-say], *a.* Carthaginian: of Carthage.

cartaginés [car-tah-ge-nays'], *a.* Carthaginian.

Cartago [car-tah'-go], *f.* Carthage.

cártama [car'-tah-mah], *f. (Bot.)* Officinal carthamus. *V.* ALAZOR.

cártamo [car'-tah-mo], *m. (Bot.)* 1. A generical name of plants. 2. *V.* CÁRTAMA. Safflower.

cartapacio [car-tah-pah'-the-o], *m.* 1. Memorandum-book. 2. A student's note-book. 3. Satchel.

cartapartida [car-tah-par-tee'-dah], *f.* Charter-party. **Cartapartida bajo forma**, memorandum of charter-party.

cartapel [car-tah-pel'], *m.* 1. Memorandum filled with useless matter. 2. Edict, ordinance.

cartazo [car-tah'-tho], *m. (Coll.)* Letter or paper containing a severe rebuke.

cartear [car-tay-ar'], *vn.* To play low cards, in order to try how the game stands. *-va.* 1. *(Naut.)* To steer by the sea-chart. 2. To turn over the leaves of a book. *-vr.* To correspond by letters. **Se cartearon durante 2 años**, they wrote to each other for 2 years.

cartel [car-tel'], *m.* 1. Placard, handbill, poster. **Torero de cartel**, star bullfighter. **Se prohibe fijar carteles**, post no bills. 2. Cartel, a written agreement made by belligerent powers relative to the exchange of prisoners. 3. *(Obs.)* Challenge sent in writing. 4. *(Naut.)* Cartel-ship or flag of truce. 5. A fishing-net which spreads eighty fathoms.

cartela [car-tay'-lah], *f.* 1. Slip of paper, piece of wood, or other materials on which a memorandum is made. 2. Console, bracket, or stay on which carved work rests. 3. Iron stay, which supports a balcony.

cartelear [car-tay-lay-ar,], *va.* To publish libels.

cartelera [car-tay-lay'-rah], *f.* Billboard; notice (tablón); list of plays, theater section. **Mantenerse en la cartelera**, to be on. **Se mantuvo en la cartelera durante 3 años**, it ran for 3 years.

catelero [car-tay-lay'-ro], *m.* Billsticker, billposter.

cartelón [car-tay-lone'], *m. aug.* 1. Long edict. 2. Show-bill.

carteo [car-tay'-o], *m.* Frequent intercourse by letters.

carter [car'-ter], *m.* Crank case (of an auto).

cartera [car-tay'-rah], *f.* 1. Wallet. 2. Portfolio, briefcase. 3. Lettercase, letter-box. 4. Portfolio, the office of a cabinet minister. **Cartera de bolsillo,** wallet. **Cartera de herramientas,** saddlebag. **Cartera de pedidos,** order-book. **Proyecto en cartera,** plane in the pipeline. **Ministro sin cartera,** minister without portfolio. 5. *(Fin.)* Portfolio, holdings. **Efectos en cartera,** holdings, stocks.

carterero [car-tay-ray'-ro], *m. (Cono Sur)* pickpocket; bag-snatcher.

carteriana [car-tay-re-ah'-nah], *f.* Sort of silk.

carterista [car-tay-rees'-tah], *m.* Pickpocket.

carterita [car-tay-ree'-tah], *f.* **Carterita de fósforos,** book of matches.

cartero [car-tay'-o], *m.* Letter-carrier, postman.

carteta [car-tay'-tah], *f.* A game at cards. *V.* PARAR.

cartibanas [car-te-bah'-nas], *f. pl.* Pieces of paper glued to the leaves of a book to facilitate the binding; fly-sheets

cartica, ita [car-tee'-cah, ee'-tah], *f. dim.* Small letter or note.

cartilaginoso, sa [car-te-lah-he-no'-so, sah], *a.* Cartilaginous, gristly.

cartílago [car-tee'-lah-go], *m. (Anat.)* 1. A cartilage, gristle. 2. Parchment. *V.* TERNILLA.

cartilla [car-teel'-lyah], *f.* 1. *(dim.)* Small or short letter or note. 2. The first book of children, horn-book. 3. Certificate of a clergyman duly ordained. **Leerle a uno la cartilla,** *(Met.)* to give one a lecture. **No saber la cartilla,** *(Met.)* to be extremely ignorant. 4. *V.* AÑALEJO. 5. Savings bank book; deposit book. **Cartilla de ahorros,** savings bank book. **Cartilla de racionamiento,** ration book. **Cartilla de seguro,** social security card.

cartografía [car-to-grah-fee'-ah], *f.* Chartography, the art of map-drawing.

cartográfico, ca [car-to-grah'-fe-co, cah], *a.* Chartographic, relative to the drawing of maps.

cartógrafo [car-to'-grah-fo], *m.* Chartographer, a drawer of maps.

cartomancia [car-to-man'-the-ah], *f.* Fortune-telling.

cartón [car-tone'], *m.* 1. Pasteboard, binders' board. **Cartón de bingo,** bingo card. **Cartón de encuadernar,** millboard. **Cartón piedra,** papier mâché. 2. Kind of iron ornament, imitating the leaves of plants. 3. Cartoon, a painting or drawing on strong paper. **Parece de cartón,** he is as stiff as a poker. 4. Artist's cartoon.

cartoné [car-to-nay'], *m. (Typ.)* En cartoné, in boards.

cartonera [car-to-nay'-rah], *f.* A papermaking wasp, a social wasp. So called from the appearance of its cells. *-pl.* Pasteboard cases for filing papers.

cartonero [car-to-nay'-ro], *m.* One whose business is to make pasteboard.

cartuchera [car-too-chay'-rah], *f.* Cartridge-box, pouch, belt.

cartucho [car-too'-cho], *m.* 1. Cartouch, a cartridge, a charge of powder contained in paper. **Cartucho de fusil,** musket-cartridge. **Cartucho de fogeo,** blank cartridge. **Luchar hasta quemar el último cartucho,** to fight on the last ditch. 2. Small target. *V.* TARJETA.

cartuja [car-too'-hah], *f.* Carthusian order.

cartujano, na [car-too-hah'-no, nah], *a.* Carthusian.

cartujo [car-too'-ho], *m.* 1. Carthusian monk. 2. Kind of skin first used by Carthusian monks.

cartulaje [car-too-lah'-hay], *m.* Pack of cards.

cartulario [car-too-lah'-re-o], *m.* 1. Archives or registry. 2. The archivist. 3. Coucher, a register book in monasteries.

cartulina [car-too-lee'-nah], *f.* Bristol-board, cardboard. **Cartulina común,** Mill-board. **Cartulina en hojas,** sheet card.

carúncula [cah-roon'-coo-lah], *f.* 1. Caruncle. 2. Crustaceous excrescence on an ulcer or wound. **Carúncula lagrimal,** the lachrymal caruncle, a reddish elevation at the inner angle of the eye.

carunculado, da [cah-roon-coo-lah'-do, dah], *a.* Carunculated (pájaros).

carunculoso, sa [ca-roon-coo-lo'-so, sah], *a.* Relating to or like a caruncle.

carura [cah-roo-rah], *f.* 1. *(And. CAm. Cono Sur)* high price, dearness. 2. *(And. CAm. Cono Sur)* expensive thing. **En esta tienda sólo hay caruras,** everything in this shop is dear.

carvallo [car-vahl'-lyo], *m. (Bot.)* Common British oak.

carvi [car'-ve], *m.* 1. *(Bot.)* Common caraway. 2. Caraway, seed.

casa [cah'-sah], *f.* 1. House, edifice, dwelling. 2. Home, our own house, the private dwelling. 3. House, household, the family residing in a house. 4. Line or branch of a family. 5. Checkers, or squares, of a chess or draught-board. 6. Firm, business house. **Casa de campo,** country house. **Casa de socorro,** a receiving or emergency hospital. **Casa de locos,** 1. Mad-house. 2. *(Met.)* Noisy or riotous house. **Casa de posada, casa de huéspedes** or **casa de pupilos,** lodging-house, or lodging and boarding-house. **Casa pública,** brothel, bawdy-house. **Casa de sanidad,** office of the board of health. **Guardar la casa,** to stay at home. **Hacer su casa** *(Met.),* to raise or aggrandize one's own family. **No tener casa ni hogar,** to have neither house keeping nor home. **Poner casa,** to establish house, to begin housekeeping. **Ponerle a uno casa,** to furnish a house for another. **Ser muy de casa,** to be very intimate in a house, to be on familiar terms. **Casa del Señor, de Dios** or **de oración,** church or temple. **Casa Santa,** Church of the Holy Sepulchre at Jerusalen. **Casa de alquiler,** block of flats. **Casa de baños,** public baths. **Casas baratas,** low-costing housing. **Casa de citas,** brothel. **Casa consistorial,** city hall. **Casa de correos,** post office. **Casa cuna,** nursery. **Casa de maternidad,** maternity hospital. **Un complejo como una casa,** a massive complex. **Casa y comida,** board and lodging. **Casa paterna,** parent's house. **Es una casa alegre,** it's a happy home. **Ir a casa,** go home. **Estar en casa,** to be at home. **Zapatos de andar por casa,** shoes for wearing around the house. **Ser de la casa,** to be like one of the family. **Echar la casa por la ventana,** to go to enormous expense. **Empezar la casa por el tejado,** to put the cart before the horse. **Cada uno manda en su casa,** one's home is one's castle. **Sentirse como en casa,** to feel at home. **Casa bancaria,** banking house. **Casa editorial,** publishing house; **Casa Blanca,** White House. **Casa real,** royal house.

casabe [cah-sah'-bay], *m. (LAm.)* Cassava.

casablanca [cah-sah-blahn'-cah], *f.* Casablanca.

casaca [ca-sah'-cah], *f.* 1. Coat, upper garment of a man; dress-coat; **casaca de mujer,** a woman's jacket. **Cambiar de casaca,** to turn one's coat. 2. The marriage contract.

casación [cah-sah-the-on'], *f. (Law.)* Cassation, abrogation, the act of annulling or repealing a law or reversing a judicial sentence.

casacón [cah-sah-cone'], *m.* 1. Greatcoat, worn over other clothes. 2. Cassock.

casada [cah-sah'-dah], *f.* 1. *(Prov.)* Ancient family mansion. 2. Married woman.

casadero, ra [cah-sah-day'-ro, rah], *a.* Marriageable, fit for marriage.

casado [cah-sah'-do], *m.* 1. Imposition (imprenta). 2. Married. **Los casados,** married men. **Los recién casados,** the newlyweds. *a.* Married. **Bien casado,** happily married. **Casado y arrepentido,** marry in haste and repent at leisure. **Estar casado,** to be married.

casador [cah-sah-dor'], *m.* One who annuls or repeals.

casal [cah-sahl'], *m.* 1. Countryhouse of an ancient family. 2. *(Cono Sur)* Married couple.

casalero [cah-sah-lay'-ro], *m.* One who resides in his country-house.

casalicio [cah-sah-lee'-the-o], *m.* House, edifice.

casamata [cah-sah-mah'-tah], *f. (Mil.)* Casemate.

casamentero, ra [cah-sah-men-tay'-ro, rah], *m. & f.* Match or marriage-maker.

casamiento [cah-sah-me-en'-to], *m.* 1. Marriage, marriage contract; matrimony; match. **Casamiento de conveniencia,** marriage of convenience. **Casamiento a la fuerza,** forced marriage. 2. In games, betting money on a card. 3. A wife's fortune.

casampolga [cah-sahm-pol'-gah], *f. (CAm.) (Zool.)* Black widow spider.

casamuro [cah-sah-moo'-ro], *m. (Mil.)* Single wall without a terreplein.

casapuerta [cah-sah-poo-err'-tah], *f.* Porch; entrance of a house.

casaquilla [cah-sah-keel'-lyah], *f.* Kind of short and loose jacket, worn over other clothes.

casar [cah-sar'], *m.* 1. Hamlet, a small village. 2. *(Prov.)* Country-house for laborers to sleep in.

casar, *va.* 1. To marry, to join a man and woman in marriage or in wedlock (sacerdotes). 2. To marry, to dispose of in marriage; to couple, to unite in marriage. 3. *(Met.)* To sort things so as to match one another, to mate, to suit or proportion one thing to another. 4. To repeal, to abrogate, to annul. 5. *(Paint.)* To blend. 6. *(Typ.)* To impose. **Antes de que te cases mira lo que haces**, look before you leap. *-vr.* To marry, to take a wife or husband, to get married. **Ana se casó con Pedro**, Anne married Peter. **¿Cuándo te vas a casar?,** when are you getting married? **Volver a casarse en segunda nupcias**, to marry again.

casatienda [cah-sah-te-en'-dah], *f.* Tradesman's shop.

casave [cah-sah'-vay], *m.* Cassava, tapioca. Also CASABE and CAZABE.

casazo [cah-sah'-tho], *m. (Coll. aug.)* Great event.

casca [cahs'-cah], *f.* 1. Skins of grapes after the wine has been pressed out. 2. *(Prov.)* Bad wine or liquor. 3. Bark for tanning leather. 4. Kind of sweetbread.

cascabel [cas-cah-bel'], *m.* 1. Hawksbell, bell used for hawks, cats, or dogs, and also for beasts of burden. 2. Knob at the end of the breech of a cannon, cascabel. 3. Rattlesnake. **Echar a uno el cascabel,** *(Met.)* to throw off a burden and lay it on another. **Echar** or **soltar el cascabel,** *(Met.)* to drop a hint in conversation, to see how it takes. **Ser un cascabel,** *(Met.)* to be a crazy or rattle-brained fellow.

cascabela [cas-cah-bay'-lah], *f. (LAm.)* Rattlesnake.

cascabelada [cas-cah-bay-lah'-dah], *f.* 1. Jingling with small bells. 2. Inconsiderate speech or action. 3. Noisy feast.

cascabelear [cas-cah-bay-lay-ar'], *va.* To feed one with vain hopes, to induce one to act on visionary expectations. *-vn.* 1. To act with levity, or little forecast and prudence. 2. *(LAm.)* To jingle, to tinkle (tintinear). 3. *(Cono Sur)* to moan, to grumble (refunfuñar).

cascabeleo [cas-cah-bay-lay'-o], *m.* Jingle, jingling, tinkling.

cascabelero, ra [cas-cah-bay-lay'-ro, rah], *a.* Light-witted, scatterbrained.

cascabelillo [cas-cah-bay-leel'-lyo], *m. dim.* Small black plum.

cascabillo [cas-cah-beel'-lyo], *m.* 1. Hawk's bell. *V.* CASCABEL. 2. Chaff of wheat or other grain. 3. Husk of an acorn.

cascaciruelas [cas-cah-the-roo-ay'-las], *m.* Mean, despicable fellow.

cascada [cas-cah'-dah,], *f.* Cascade, water-fall. **Cascadas,** small plaits or folds in the drapery of paintings.

cascado, da [cas-cah'-do, dah], *a.* Broken, burst, decayed, infirm; crazy. **Vidrio cascado,** *(Met.)* singer who has lost his voice. **Estar muy cascado,** to be in a precarious state of health. *-pp.* of CASCAR.

cascadura [cas-cah-doo'-rah], *f.* Act of bursting or breaking asunder.

cascajal [cas-cah-hahl'], 1. Place full of gravel and pebbles. 2. Place in which the husks of grapes are thrown.

cascajar [cas-cah'-har], *m.* Place full of gravel and pebbles.

cascajo [cas-cah'-ho], *m.* 1. Pebble. 2. Fragments of broken vessels. 3. Rubbish. 4. *(Lit. us.)* Old and useless furniture. 5. Pod or silique; shell of a nut. 6. *(Met.)* Copper coin. 7. Bit of a bridle. **Estar hecho un cascajo,** to be very old and infirm.

cascajoso, sa [cas-cah-ho'-so, sah], *a.* Gravelly.

cascallo [cas-cahl'-lyo], *m.* Brazilian name of a diamond-field.

cascamajar [cas-cah-ma-har'], *va. (Prov.)* To break, bruise, or pound a thing slightly.

cascamiento [cas-cah-me-en'-to], *m.* Act of breaking or bruising.

cascanueces [cas-cah-noo-ay'-thes], *m.* Nut-cracker.

cascar [cas-car'], *va.* 1. To crack burst, or break into pieces. 2. To crunch. 3. To lick, to beat, or strike. 4. *(Prov.)* To talk much. 5. To shatter, to undermine. 6. To belt, to smack (pegar). 7. To belt, to smack. **Cascarla,** to kick the bucket. *- vr.* 1. To be broken open. 2. To crack up; to break (salud). *-vn.* To talk too much.

cáscara [cahs'-ca-rah], *f.* 1. Rind, peel, hull, or husk of various fruits, etc. **Cáscara de limón,** lemmon peel. **Patatas cocidas con cáscara,** potatoes in their jackets. 2. Bark of trees. **Cáscara sagrada,** dried bark of a tree which is used as a laxative. 3. *(CAm.)* **Tener cáscara,** to have a cheek, to be shameless.

¡cáscaras! [cahs'-ca-ras], *int.* Oh! exclamation expressive of astonishment or admiration.

cascarazo [cas-cah-rah'-zo], *m.* 1. *(And. Carib.)* Punch; lash. 2. *(Carib.)* Swig, slug.

cascarear [cas-cah-ray-ar'], *va. (And. CAm.)* To belt, smack. *-vn. (Mex.)* To scrape a living.

cascarilla, cascarita [cas-cah-reel'-lyah, ree'-tah], *f.* 1. *(dim.)* Small thin bark. 2. Peruvian bark, Jesuit's bark. 3. Cascarilla bark. 4. *(And. Cono Sur) (Med.)* Medicinal herb; dried cacao husks (used as tea). *-a. (Carib. Cono Sur)* touchy, quick-tempered.

cascarillero [cas-cah-reel-lyay'-ro], *m.* A gatherer of Peruvian bark.

cascarillo [cas-car-reel'-lyo], *m.* The cinchona shrub.

cascaroja [cas-cah-ro'-hah], *f.* Woodborer, shipworm, shippiercer. *V.* BROMA.

cascarón [cas-cah-rone'], *m.* 1. Egg-shell of a fowl or bird. 2. *(Arch.)* Arch or vault which contains the fourth part of a sphere; calotte. 3. Niche where the sacrament is placed for adoration in Roman Catholic churches.

cascarrabias [cas-car-rah'-be-as], *com.* A testy, irritable person.

cascarrabieta [cas-car-rah-be-ay'-tah], *a. V.* CASCARRABIAS.

cacarrabio, ia [cas-car-rah'-be-o, ah], *a.* Grumbling, testy, irritable.

cascarria [cas-car'-ree-ah], *f. (Cono Sur)* filth, muck; sheep droppings (ovejas).

cascarriento [cas-car-re-ayn'-to], *a. (Cono Sur)* filthy, mucky.

cascarrón, na [cas-car-rone', nah], *a. (Coll.)* Rough, harsh, rude. **Vino cascarrón,** wine of a rough flavor. **Voz cascarrona,** harsh, unpleasant tone of voice.

cascarudo, da [cas-ca-roo'-do, dah], *a.* Hully, having a thick rind or shell.

cascaruleta [cas-ca-roo-lay'-tah], *f. (Coll.)* Noise made by the teeth in consequence of patting under the chin.

casco [cahs'-co], *m.* 1. Skull, cranium, the bone which incloses the brain. 2. Potsherd, fragments of an earthen vessel. 3. Quarter of an orange, lemon, or pomegranate. 4. Coat or tegument of an onion. 5. Helmet, casque, or headpiece of ancient armor. 6. *(Prov.)* Cask, pipe, vat, or other wooden vessel in which wine is preserved. 7. **Casco de un navío,** *(Naut.)* Hull or hulk, of a ship. 8. Crown of a hat. 9. Printer's inking-ball. 10. Sheep-skin stripped of the wool. 11. Hoof of a horse. 12. **Casco** or **tapa de un barril,** the head of a cask. 13. **Casco de una silla de montar,** the tree of a saddle. **Cascos,** heads of sheep or bullocks without the tongues and brains. **Tener los cascos a la jineta,** *(Met.)* to be on the high horse. **Tener malos cascos,** *(Met.)* to be crazy or hare-brained. **Romperse los cascos,** to rack one's brain. **Ligero de cascos,** scatterbrained, frivolous. 14. Inner part, central area (de ciudad); **Casco comercial,** business quarter. **El casco antiguo de la ciudad,** the old part of the city. 15. *(LAm.)* Empty building.

cascolote [cas-co-lo'-tay], *m. (Mex.)* Thick bark of oaks, etc.; a fragment of thick bark.

cascorros [cas-cor'-ros], *m. & pl. (Mex.)* Shoes.

cascorvo, va [cas-cor'-vo, vah], *a. (Mex.)* Bowlegged.

cascote [cas-co'-tay], *m.* Rubbish, rubble, ruins of buildings, fragments of matter used in building.

cascotería [cas-co-tay-ree'-ah], *f.* Wall or work made of rubbish.

cascudo, da [cas-coo'-do, dah], *a.* Large-hoofed (animales).

cascundear [ ], *va. (CAm.)* To beat, to thrash.

caseación [cah-say-ah-the-on'], *f.* Coagulation of milk to form cheese.

caseína [cah-say-ee'-nah], *f.* Casein, the albuminous proximate principle of milk.

cáseo [cah'-say-o], 1. *a.* Cheesy. 2. *m.* Curd.

caseoso, sa [cah-say-o'-so, sah], *a.* Caseous, cheesy.

casera [cah-say'-rah], *f. (Prov.)* House-keeper, a woman servant that has the care of a single man. *V.* CASERO.

caseramente [cah-say-rah-men'-tay], *adv.* Homely, in a plain manner.

casería [cah-say-ree'-ah], *f.* 1. Isolated farm house. 2. Economical household management. 3. *(Sp. Amer.)* Clientele, customers.

caserío [cah-say-ree'-o], *m.* 1. A series of houses; village or very small town. 2. Country house, farmhouse.

caserna [cah-serr'-nah], *f. (Mil.)* Casern, a bomb-proof vault below a rampart; barracks.

casero, ra [cah-say'-ro, rah], *m. & f.* Landlord or steward of a house.

casero, ra [cah-say'-ro, rah], *a.* 1. Domestic, homely, in a family way. 2. Home-bred. **Familia**, house-keeping. **Baile casero**, family-dance. **Mujer casera**, A good housewife. **Remedio casero**, domestic medicine. **Pan casero**, household bread. 3. *(LAm.)* Customer, client.

caserón [cah-say-rone'], *m. aug.* 1. A large house. 2. A large house, ill-proportioned and without order.

caseta [cah-say'-tah], *f. dim.* Small house, hut, cottage, stall, booth; pavillion; changing-room (de piscina); bathing hut (de playa). **Caseta de perro**, kennel, doghouse. **Caseta del timón**, *(Naut.)* Wheelhouse.

casetera [cah-say-tay'-rah], *f. (LAm.)* Cassette deck.

caset(t)e [cah-say'-tay], 1. *m.* Cassette. 2. *f.* Cassette-player.

cash [cash], *m. pl.* Cash-and-carry store.

casi [cah'-se], *adv.* Almost, nearly, somewhat, more or less; just. **Casi casi**, very nearly. **Está casi acabado**, it´s almost finished. **Casi nada**, next to nothing. **Casi nunca**, almost never.

casia [cah'-se-ah], *f. (Bot.)* Bastard cinnamon, cassia.

casica, illa, ita [cah-see'-cah, eel'-lyah, ee'-tah], *f. dim.* Small house, cabin.

casilla [cah-see'-lyah], *f.* 1. Ticket office. 2. Booth, cockpit, cubbyhole. **Casilla de correos** or **Casilla postal**, post-office box. 3. *(Aut. Ferro.)* Cab. 4. *(And.)* Laboratory.

casillas [cah-seel'-lyas], *f.pl.* 1. Pigeon-holes: ruled columns in accounts, books or papers. 2. Points or houses of a backgammon table. 3. Square or checkers of a chess or draftboard. **Sacarle a uno de sus casillas**, *(Met.)* to molest, tease, or harass. **Salir de sus casillas**, to deviate from one's accustomed mode, especially through anger.

casillero [cah-seel-lyay'-ro], *m.* A desk fitted with pigeon-holes. *-pl. V.* CASILLAS.

casillo [cah-seel'-lyo], *m.* 1. *(dim.)* Trifling or slight cause. 2. A momentous affair, matter of consequence.

casimba [cah-seem-bah], *f. (LAm.) V.* CACIMBA.

casimbas [cah-seem'-bas], *f. pl. (Naut.)* Buckets for baling the water made by a ship, which the pumps are unable to discharge.

casimiro [cah-se-mee'-ro], *m.* Cashmere, kerseymere. **Casimir doble**, double-twilled kerseymere. **Casimir sencillo**, single-twilled kerseymere.

casimiro [cah-see-me'-ro], *a. (LAm.)* Cross-eyed.

casimodo [cah-se-mo'-do], *m. V.* CUASIMODO.

casinista [cah-see-nes'-tah], *m.* Clubman, member of a casino.

casino [cah-see'-no], *m.* 1. Casino, a room or building used as a public resort, for dancing, social, or club meetings, etc. 2. A club.

Casiopea [cah-se-o-pay-ah], *f.* Cassiopeia, the name of a northern constellation.

casís [cah-sees'], *f. (Bot.)* The blackcurrant.-*m. (Zool.)* A mollusk of the Mediterranean and the Indian Ocean.

casita [cah-see'-tah], *f.* Small house; cottage (de campo).

casiterita [cah-se-tay-ree'-tah], *f.* Cassiterite, oxide of tin; its chief ore.

caso [cah'-so], *m.* 1. Event, case, occurrence. 2. Case, contingency, hap, casualty, unexpected accident. 3. Occasion, opportunity. 4. Case stated to lawyers, physicians, etc. 5. *(Gram.)* Case. **Caso de conciencia**, case of conscience. 6. Peculiar figure of written characters. **En ese caso**, in that case. **En todo caso**, in any case. **Estar o no estar en el caso**, to comprehend or not comprehend something. **Hacer caso de una persona**, to esteem or respect a person. **Hacer caso de una cosa**, to take notice. **Ser o no ser al caso**, to be or not to be to the purpose. **Vamos al caso**, let us come to the point. **No estoy en el caso**, I do not understand the matter. **Dado el caso** or **demos el caso**, supposing that. **Caso negado**, proposition admitted only to be refuted. **Caso de que venga**, in case he should come. **En el mejor de los casos,** at best. **En último caso**, as a last resort. **Ponte en mi caso**, put yourself in my position. **Venir al caso**, to be relevant. **Verse en el caso de**, to be compelled to. **Maldito el caso que me hace**, a fat lot of notice he takes of me. **Hacer caso omiso de**, to ignore.

casona [cah-so'-nah], *f.* Large house.

casoar [cah-so-ar'], **casobar** [cah-so-bar'], *m.* The cassowary.

casorio [cah-so'-re-o], *m.* 1. *(Coll.)* Inconsiderate marriage. 2. A wedding.

caspa [cahs'-pah], *f.* Dandruff, scurf.

Caspio, ia [cahs'-pe-o, ah], *a.* Caspian.

¡cáspita! [cahs'-pe-tah], *int.* Wonderful!

caspitoso [cas-pe-to'-so], *a.* 1. Full of dandruff, scurfy. 2. *(fig.)* Shoddy, tawdry.

casposo, sa [cas-po'-so, sah], *a.* Full of dandruff, lentiginous.

casquería [cas-kay-ree'-ah], *f.* Tripe and offal shop.

casquero, ra [cas-kay'-ro], *m. & f.* Seller of tripe and offal.

casquetazo [cas-kay-tah'-tho], *m.* Blow given with the head.

casquete [cas-kay'-tay], *m.* 1. Helmet, casque; skull-cap, cap. **Casquete de hielo**, icecap. **Casquete polar**, polar cap. 2. Scull, wig, scratch. 3. Helmet shell. 4. Cataplasm to take the scurf off the heads of children. 5. **Echar un casquete**, to have a screw.

casquiblando, da [cas-ke-blahn'-do, dah], *a.* Soft-hoofed (caballos).

casquiderramado, da [cas-ke-der-rah-mah'-do, dah], *a.* Wide-hoofed (caballos).

casquijo [cas-kee'-ho], *m.* Gravel; ballast material.

casquilla [cas-keel'-lyah], *f.* Cell of the queen bee.

casquillo [cas-keel'-lyo], *m.* 1. *(dim.)* Small steel helm. 2. Tip, cap, ferule, socket. 3. An iron arrow-head.

casquilucio, cia [cas-ke-loo'-the-o, ah], *a.* Gay, frolicsome.

casquimuleño, ña [cas-ke-moo-lay'-nyo, nyah], *a.* Narrow-hoofed like mules (caballos).

casquinona [cas-ke-no'-nah], *f. (And.)* Beer bottle; beer (cerveza).

casquivano, na [cas-ke-vah'-no, nah], *a.* Impudent, inconsiderate, acting with levity; foolishly conceited.

cassette [cah-sayt'], *V.* CASET(T)E.

casta [cahs'-tah], *f.* 1. Caste, race, generation, lineage, particular breed, clan; offspring, kindred. 2. Kind or quality of a thing. **Hacer casta**, to get a particular breed of horses or other animals. **De casta**, of quality. **Carecer de casta**, to lack breeding.

castalia [cas-tah'-le-ah], *f.* Castalia, a fountain of Mount Parnassus, and the nymph whose name it received.

castamente [cas-tah-men'-tay], *adv.* Chastely, purely.

castaña [cas-tah´-nyah], *f.* 1. *(Bot.)* Chestnut. 2. Bottle, jug, or jar, in the shape of a chestnut. 3. Club of hair; chignon. 4. An abandoned mine. **Castaña pilonga** or **apilada**, dried chestnut. **Sacar las castañas del fuego**, to pull somebody´s chestnuts out of the fire for him. 5. **Coger una castaña**, to get drunk. 6. Bash, bow (golpe).

castañal, castañar [cas-ta-nyahl´, cas-ta-nyar´], *m.* Grove or plantation of chestnut-trees.

castañazo [cas-ta-nyah´-tho], *m.* 1. Blow from a chestnut. 2. *(Cono Sur)* punch, thump.

castañedo [cas-ta-nyay´-do], *m.* *(Prov.)* Chestnut-grove or plantation.

castañera [cas-ta-nyay´-rah], *f.* *(Prov.)* Country abounding with chestnut-trees.

castañero, ra [cas-ta-nyay´-ro, rah], *m. & f.* Dealer in chestnuts.

castañeta [cas-ta-nyay´-tah], *f.* 1. Snapping of the fingers 2. Castanet. *V.* CASTAÑUELA.

castañetazo [cas-ta-nyay-tah´-tho], *m.* 1. Blow with a castanet. 2. Sound of a chestnut bursting in the fire. 3. Cracking of the joints.

castañeteado [cas-ta-nyay-tay-ah-do], *m.* Sound of castanets. -*pp.* of CASTAÑETEAR.

castañetear [cas-ta-nyay-tay-ar´], *vn.* 1. To rattle the castanets. 2. To crackle, to clack (rodillas). 3. To cry (perdices). -*va.* 1. To snap (dedos). 2. To play on the castanets.

castañeteo [cas-tah-nyay-tay´-o], *m.* 1. Snap(ping); click(ing); clatter(ing); chatter(ing); rattling; crack(ing) (huesos). 2. *(Mus.)* Sound of the castanets.

castaño [cas-tah´-nyo], *m.* *(Bot.)* Common chestnut-tree. **Castaño de Indias**, horse-chestnut-tree. **Esto pasa de castaño oscuro**, this is really too much, this is beyond a joke.

castaño, ña [cas-tah´-nyo, nyah], *a.* Hazel.

castañuela [cas-ta-nyoo-ay´-lah], *f.* Castanet. **Estar como unas castañuelas**, to be very gay.

castañuelo, la [cas-ta-nyoo-ay´-lo, lah] *a. dim.* Of a light chestnut color (caballos).

castellanía [cas-tel-lyah-nee´-ah], *f.* Castellany, district belonging to a castle. **castellanizar** [cas-tel-lyah-ne-thar´], *ra.* To adapt a foreign word for use in Spanish: to castilianize.

castellano [cas-teil-lyah´-no], *m.* 1. Ancient Spanish coin. 2. Fiftieth part of a mark of gold. 3. Spanish language. 4. *(Obs.)* Castellan, the governor or warden of a castle.

castellano, na [cas-tel-lyah´-no, nah], *a.* 1. Castilian. 2. Applied to a mule got by a jackass and a mare. 3. *(Prov.)* Applied to the foremost mule in a cart or wagon.

castellar [cas-tel´-lyar´], *m.* 1. *(Obs.)* Place fortified with a castle. 2. *(Bot.)* St. John's wort, tutsan, park-leaves.

casticidad [cas-te-the-dahd´], *f.* 1. *(Ling.)* Purity, correctness. 2. Traditional character; thoroughbred charter, true-born nature; authenticity, genuineness.

casticismo [cas-te-thees´-mo], *m.* 1. *(Ling.)* Purity, correctness. 2. Love of tradition, traditionalism.

casticista [cas-te-thes-tah], *m. & f.* Purist.

castidad [cas-te-dahd´], *f.* Chastity, purity, honor.

castigación [cas-te-gah-the-on´], *f.* 1. Castigation. 2. Correction of errors of the press.

castigadera [cas-te-gah-day´-rah], *f.* 1. Rope with which a bell is tied to a mule, or other beast of burden. 2. Small cord with which the ring of a stirrup is tied to the girth.

castigador, ra [cas-te-gah-dor´, rah], *m. & f.* 1. A punisher or chastiser, castigator. 2. *(Obs.)* One that reproaches. 3. Seducer, libertine.

castigar [Cas-te-gar´], *va.* 1. To chastise, to punish, to castigate. 2. To afflict to put to pain, to grieve. **Castigar mucho a un caballo**, to ride a horse hard. 3. To advise, to inform. 4. *(Met.)* To correct proof-sheets or writings. 5. To reduce (gastos). 6. *(Mex.)* *(Mech.)* To tighten up. -*vr.* To mend.

castigo [cas-tee´-go], *m.* 1. Chastisement, punishment, correction, penalty. 2. Censure, animadversion, reproach. 3. Example, instruction. 4. Alteration or correction made in a work. **Castigo de Dios**, God's judgment. **Castigo de la miseria**, miser, skinflint.

Castilla [cas-teel´-lyah], *f.* Castile. **Castilla la Nueva**, New Castile. **Castilla la Vieja**, Old Castile.

castillejo [cas-teel´-lay´-ho], *m.* 1. *(dim.)* A small castle. 2. Go-cart. 3. *(Arquit.)* Scaffolding.

castillería [cas-teel-lyay-ree´-ah], *f.* 1. Toll paid on passing through a district which belongs to a castle. 2. Government of a castle.

castillo [cas-teel´-lyo], *m.* 1. Castle, fort. 2. The mounting of a velvetloom. 3. Cell of the queen-bee. 4. **Castillo de proa**, *(Naut.)* Forecastle. **Hacer castillos en el aire**, *(Met.)* to build castles in the air or in Spain. **Castillo de fuego**, firework set piece. **Castillo de naipes**, house of cards.

castilluelo [cas-teel-lyoo-ay´-lo], *m. dim.* Castlet, a small castle.

castizo, za [cas-tee´-tho, thah], *a.* 1. Of a noble descent, of a good breed, pure-blooded. **Caballo castizo**, blood-horse. **Estilo castizo**, a chaste, pure style.

casto, ta [cahs´-to, tah], *a.* 1. Pure, chaste, honest, modest, continent, cold, clean. 2. Perfect. 3. Pure (estilo).

castor [cas-tor´], *m.* 1. Castor, a beaver, an amphibious quadruped. Castor. 2. Beaver, a heavy cloth, of smooth surface, made for overcoats. 3. *(Mex.)* Fine red baize. 2. The two brightest stars in the constellation Gemini.

castorcillo [cas-tor-theel´-lyo], *m.* Kind of rough serge like cloth.

castoreño [cas-to-ray´-nyo], *m.* Beaver (hat); picador´s hat.

castra [cahs´-trah], *f.* Act of pruning trees or plants.

castración [cas-trah-the-on´], *f.* 1. Castration, gelding, spaying. 2. *(Agri.)* Extraction of honeycombs.

castradera [cas-trah-day´-rah], *f.* Iron instrument with which honey is taken from a hive.

castrado [cas-trah´-do], *m.* A eunuch. -*a.* Castrated.

castrador [cas-trah-dor´], *m.* One that gelds or castrates.

castradura [cas-trah-doo´-rah], *f.* 1. Castration. 2. Scar which remains after an animal has been castrated.

castrametación [cas-trah-may-tah-the-on´], *f.* Castrametation, encamping

castrapuercas [cas-trah-poo-err´-cas], *m.* Sow-gelder's whistle.

castrar [cas-trar´], *va.* 1. To geld, to castrate, to spay. 2. To cut away the proud flesh about a wound. 3. To prune trees or plants. 4. **Castrar las colmenas**, to cut the honey-combs from bee-hives.

castrazón [cas-trah-thone´], *f.* 1. Act of cutting honey-combs out of hives. 2. Castrating or gelding season.

castrense [cas-tren´-say], *a.* Belonging to the military profession. **Las glorias castrenses**, military glories.

castro [cahs´-tro], *m.* 1. Place where an army is encamped. 2. *(Prov.)* Ruins of ancient fortified places. 3. Game played by boys. 4. Act of taking honey-combs out of hives.

castrón [cas-trone´], *m.* Castrated goat; a gelded animal.

casual [cah-soo-ahl´], *a.* Casual, accidental, contingent, fortuitous, occasional, circumstantial. **Desinencia casual**, case ending.

casualidad [cah-soo-ah-le-dahd´], *f.* Casualty, hazard, contingency, occasion, coincidence, accident; **por casualidad**, by chance. **Me encontraba allí por casualidad**, I happened to be there. **Un día entró por casualidad**, one day he dropped in. **Dio la casualidad que**, it happened that.

casualmente [cah-soo-al-men´-tay], *adv.* Casually, accidentally, contingently, haply. **Le vi ayer casualmente**, I happened to see him yesterday.

casuca [cah-soo´-cah], *f.* Hovel, shack; slum.

casucha [cah-soo´-chah], *f.* *(Coll.)* Miserable hut or cottage, crib.

casucho [cah-soo´-cho], *m. V.* CASUCHA.

casuel [cah-soo-el'], *m. (Orn.)* Cassowary, emeu.

casuísta [cah-soo-ees'-tah], *m.* Casuist.

casuístico, ca [cah-soo-ees'-te-co, cah], *a.* Casuistical.

casulla [cah-sool'-lyah], *f.* Chasuble, vestment worn by priests.

casullero [cah-sool-lyay'-ro], *m.* One who makes chasubles and other vestments for priests.

casus belli [cah'-soos, bayl'-lee], *(Lat.)* Cause for war (lenguaje diplomático).

cata [cat'-tah], *f.* 1. Act of trying a thing by the taste. **Dar a cata,** to give upon trial. 2. Plummet for measuring heights. 3. *(LAm.) (Min.)* Trial excavation, test bore. 4. *(And. Cono Sur, Mex.)* Parrot.

cata [cah'-tah], *adv. (Coll.)* Mark, beware. *(Imp.* of CATAR.)

catabolismo [cah-tah-bo-lees'-mo], *m. (Biol.)* Catabolism.

catabre [cah-tah'-bray], *m.* 1. *(Naut.)* Sheep-shank. 2. *(And. Carib.)* Gourd; basket.

catacaldos [cah-tah-cahl-dos], *m.* 1. Taster of wine, liquors, soup, etc. 2. Rolling stone; quitter; person who starts things but gives up easily (persona inconstante).

cataclismo [cah-tah-clees'-mo], *m.* Cataclysm, deluge, inundation: a convulsion of nature.

catacumbas [cah-tah-coom'-bas], *f. pl.* Catacombs.

catacústica [cah-tah-coos'-te-cah], *f.* Catacoustics.

catadióptrico, ca [cah-tah-de-op'-tre-co-cah], *a.* Catadioptric, relating to light reflected and refracted.

catador, ra [cah-tah-dor'], *m. f.* Taster, blender, sampler.

catadura [cah-tah-doo'-rah], *f.* 1. Trying by the taste, tasting. 2. *(Coll.)* Gesture, face, countenance. 3. Mode of guarding or inspecting criminals.

catafalco [cah-tah-fahl'-co], *m.* A temporary cenotaph to celebrate funeral rites, catafalque.

catafotos [cah-tah-fo'-tos], *m. pl. (Aut.)* Cat's eyes.

catajarría [cah-tah-hahr-re'-ah], *f. (Carib.)* String, series.

catalán, na [cah-tah-lahn', lah'-nah], *a.* Catalonian.

catalejo [cah-tah-lay'-ho], *m.* Telescope,

cataléctico [cah-tah-layc'-te-co], *a. (Poet.)* Catalectic.

catalepsia [cah-tah-lep'-se-ah], *f.* Catalepsy, trance.

cataléptico, ca [ ], *a. m. & f.* Cataleptic.

catalicón [cah-tah-le-cone'], *m.* Catholicon, universal medicine.

catálisis [cah-tah'-le-sis], *f. (Chem.)* Catalysis.

catalizador [cah-tah-le-thah-dor'], *m. (Chem.)* Catalyst.

catalizar [cah-tah-le-thar'], *va.* To catalyse.

catalogación [cah-tah-lo-gah-the-one'], *f.* Cataloguing.

catalogar [cah-tah-lo-gar'], *va.* To catalog, to list, to catalogue.

catálogo [cah-tah'-lo-go], *m.* Catalog, catalogue, roll, file, matricula.

catalpa [cah-tahl'-pah], *f.* The catalpa, a genus of American and East Indian flowering trees, bearing long, cylindrical pods.

catalufa [cah-tah-loo'-fah], *f.* Kind of floor carpet.

catamarán [cah-tah-mah-rahn'], *m.* Catamaran.

catamiento [cah-tah-me-en'-to], *m.* Observation, inspection.

catamito [cah-tah-mee'-to], *m.* Catamite. V. SODOMITA.

catán [cah-tahn'], *m.* Indian sabre or cutlass.

catanance, catananque [ch-tah-nahn'-thay, kay], *f. (Bot.)* Lion's-foot. **Catanance azul,** blue catananche.

cataplasma [cah-tah-plahs'-mah], *f.* Poultice. **Cataplasma de mostaza,** mustard plaster.

cataplines [cah-tah-ple-nays], *m. pl.* Balls.

cataplum [cah-tah-ploom'], *interj.* Bang!, crash!

catapucia menor [cah-tah-poo'-the-ah may-nor'], *f. (Bot.)* Lesser or caper spurge. **Catapucia mayor,** castor-oil plant.

catapulta [cah-tah-pool'-tah], *f.* Catapult, an ancient war machine for throwing stones.

catapultar [cah-tah-pool-tar'], *va.* To catapult.

catapún [cah-tah-poon'], *a.* **Una cosa del año catapún,** an antiquated thing. **Películas del año catapún,** very old films.

catar [cah-tar'], *va.* 1. To taste, to try by the taste. 2. To view, to inspect, to inquire, to investigate, to examine. 3. To judge,

to form an opinion. 4. To esteem, to respect. 5. To bear in mind. 6. To cut the combs out of bee-hives; **¡cátale!,** just look at him!

catarata [cah-ta-rah'-tah], *f.* 1. Cataract, opacity of the crystalline lens of the eye. 2. Cataract, waterfall, cascade. **Extraer las cataratas,** to remove or extract cataracts. **Tener cataratas,** *(Met.)* not to understand clearly. **Cataratas del Niágara,** Niagara falls.

catarral [cah-tar-rahl'], *a.* Catarrhal.

catarribera [cah-tar-re-bay'-rah], *m.* 1. Man-servant appointed to follow the hawk on horseback, and bring it down with its prey. 2. *(Joc.)* Lawyer appointed to examine into the proceedings of magistrates charged with the administration of justice.

catarriento, ta [cah-tar-re-en'-to, tah], *a. V.* CATARROSO.

catarro [cah-tar'-ro], *m.* Catarrh. **Catarro epidémico,** influenza. **Catarro crónico del pecho,** chest trouble.

catarroso, sa [cah-tar-ro'-so, sah], *a.* 1. Catarrhal. 2. Subject to or troubled with a cold.

catarsis [cah-tar'-sees], *f.* Catharsis.

catártico, ca [cah-tar'-te-co, cah], *a.* Cathartic, purging.

catasalsas [cah-tah-sal'-sahs], *m. V.* CATACALDOS.

catastro [cah-tahs'-tro], *m.* 1. A tax-list of the real property in every district of a country. 2. The office of this tax-list.

catástrofe [cah-tahs'-tro-fay], *f.* 1. Catastrophe. 2. Catastrophe, dénouement.

catastrófico [cah-tas-tro'-fe-co], *a.* Catastrophic.

catastrofismo [cah-tas-tro-fes'-mo], *m.* Alarmism; doomwatching.

catastrofista [cah-tas-tro-fes'-tah], *m. & f.* Alarmist, doomwatcher.

catatán [cah-tah-tahn'], *m. (Chile)* Punishment.

catatar [cah-tah-tar'], *va. (And.)* To ill-treat.

catauro [cah-tah'-oo-ro], *m. (Carib.)* Basket.

cataviento [cah-tah-ve-en'-to], *m. (Naut.)* Dogvane. Weathercock.

catavino [cah-tah-vee'-no], *m.* 1. Small jug or cup used to taste wine. 2. *(Prov.)* Small hole at the top of large wine-vessels for tasting the wine. -*pl.* Tipplers who run from tavern to tavern to drink.

catavinos [cah-ta-vee'-nos], *m.* A winetaster, expert sampler. *V.* CATACALDOS.

cate [cah'-tay], *m.* 1. A weight, common in the Philippine Islands, equivalent to 1 lb. 6 oz. Spanish, or gm. 632.60. 2. Punch, bash (golpe). **Dar cate a uno,** to plough somebody. 3. *m.f.* Teacher.

catear [cah-tay-ar'], *va.* 1. To inquire after, to investigate, to discover. 2. *(Min.)* To prospect. 3. *(Univ.)* To plough, to fail (candidato). 3. *(Cono, Sur, Mex.)* To make test borings in, to explore. 4. *(Mex.)* To search, to make a search.

catecismo [cah-tay-thees'-mo], *m.* Catechism.

catecú [cah-tay-coo'], *m.* Catechu, an astringent extracted from East Indian plants, particularly from an acacia. *V.* CATO.

catecúmeno, na [cah-tay-coo'-may-no, nah] *m. & f.* Catechumen.

cátedra [cah'-tay-drah], *f.* 1. Seat or chair of a professor. 2. Professorship, office and functions of a professor or teacher; **Pedro regentó la cátedra tantos años,** Peter filled the professor's chair so many years. **Libertad de cátedra,** freedom to teach. **Explicar una cátedra,** to hold a chair. 3 See, the seat of pontifical or episcopal power. 4. Subject (asignatura). 5. Lecture room. 6. Group of students, class. 7. *(Carib.)* Wonder, marvel. **Es cátedra,** it's marvellous.

catedral [cah-tay-drahl'], *a. & f.* Cathedral.

catedralicio [cah-tray-lah-le'-the-o], *a.* Cathedral.

catedrático [cah-tay-drah'-te-co], *m.* 1. Professor in a university, or any other literary establishment. 2. Contribution formerly paid by the inferior clergy to bishops and prelates.

catedrilla [cah-tay-dreel'-lyah], *f.* 1. *(dim.)* Small or poor professor's chair. 2. In some universities, the less important professorship.

categoría [cah-tay-go-ree'-ah], *f.* 1. Predicament or category. 2. Character of a person. **Ser hombre de categoría**, to be a man of estimable qualities and talents; a man of rank. **De categoría**, important. **Hombre de cierta categoría**, he is a man of some standing. **De baja categoría**, of low quality.

categóricamente [cah-tay-co'-re-cah-men'-tay], *adv.* Categorically.

categórico, ca [cah-tay-go'-re-co, cah], *a.* Categorical, categoric.

catenaria [cah-tay-nah'-re-ah], *f.* (*Elec.*) (*Ferro.*) Overhead power cable.

catequesis [cah-tay-kay'-sis], *f.* A brief and simple explanation of a doctrine.

catequismo [cah-tay-kees'-mo], *m.* 1. Catechizing, instruction in religious doctrine. 2. (*Obs.*) V. CATECISMO.

catequista [cah-tay-kees'-tah], *m.* Catechizer.

catequístico, ca [cah-tay-kees'-te-co, cah], *a.* Catechetical, catechetic, catechistical.

catequizante [cah-tay-ke-thahn-tay], *pa.* Catechiser, catechist.

catequizar [cah-tay-ke-thar'], *va.* 1. To catechise, to instruct in the Christian faith. 2. (*Met.*) To persuade.

caterva [cah-terr'-vah], *f.* A great number, a swarm, a throng, a crowd; the vulgar.

catete [cah-tay'-tay], *m.* (*Chile Coll.*) The devil.

catéter [cah-tay'-ter], *m.* Catheter, a tube of metal, rubber, or woven material for surgical uses; as for drawing off urine, or for introducing air into the middle ear.

cateterismo [cah-tay-tay-rees'-mo], *m.* Catheterism, employment of the catheter.

cateterizar [cah-tay-tay-re-thar,], *va.* To catheterize, to use a catheter remedially.

cateto [cah-tay'-to], *m.* 1. (*Arch.*) Cathetus, perpendicular line which intersects the volute by passing through its centre. 2. *pl.* The sides which form the right angle of a right angled triangle. 3. Peasant, country bumpkin.

catimbao [cah-teem-bah'-o], *m.* 1. Clown. 2. (*Chile*) Someone ridiculously garbed. 3. (*Peru*) Short and stout person.

catinga [cah-teen'-gah], *f.* (*Sp. Amer.*) 1. Bad odor exuded by some plants and animals. 2. Name which sailors give to soldiers.

catingoso [cah-ten-go'-so], *a.* (*And. Cono Sur*), **catingudo** *a.* (*And. Cono Sur*) skinting, foul-smelling.

catisumba(da) [cah-te-soom'-bah, dah], *f.* (*CAm.*) Lot, great number. **Una catisumba de**, lots of.

catire [cah-tee'-ray], *m. & f.* (*Sp. Amer.*) Blond mulatto.

catita [cah-tee'-tah], *f.* (*Arg. Bol.*) Type of parrot.

catite [cah-tee'-tay], *m.* Loaf of the best refined sugar.

catitear [cah-te-tay-ar'], *vn.* (*Cono Sur*) to dodder, to shake (with old age).

cato [cah'-to], *m.* Japan earth, an extract obtained by the decoction of vegetable substance in water. V. CATECÚ.

catoche [cah-to'-chay], *m.* (*Mex.*) Bad humor.

catódico, ca [cah-to'-de-co, cah], *a.* (*Phy. & Chem.*) Cathodic.

cátodo [cah'-to-do], *m.* (*Phy. & Chem.*) Cathode.

católicamente [cah-to'-le-cah-men-tay], *adv.* In a catholic manner.

catolicidad [cah-to-le-the-dahd], *f.* Catholicity.

catolicismo [cah-to-le-thees'-mo], *m.* 1. Catholicism. 2. Catholicism, the orthodox faith of the Catholic church.

católico, ca [cah-to'-le-co, cah], *a.* 1. Catholic 2. General or universal. 3. True, infallible. **El rey católico**, his catholic majesty. **No estar muy católico**, not to be in good health, not to be very well.

católico [cah-to-le-co'], *m.* 1. Catholic, a Roman Catholic. 2. (*Chem.*) Chemical furnace.

catolicón [cah-to-le-cone'], *m.* Catholicon, a panacea.

catón [cah-tone'], *m.* 1. A very wise man or one who affects wisdom. 2. A reading-book for children. **Eso está en el catón**, that is absolutely elementary. 3. (*Met.*) A severe censor.

catoniano, na [cah-to-ne-ah'-no, nah], *a.* Catonian, relating to Cato.

catóptrica [cah-top'-tre-cah], *f.* Catoptrics, the science of reflected light.

catóptrico, ca [cah-top'-tre-co, cah], *a.* Catoptrical.

catorce [cah-tor'-thay], *a.* Fourteen.

catorcena [cah-tor-thay'-nah], *f.* The conjunction of fourteen units.

catorceno, na [cah-tor-thay'-no, nah], *a.* Fourteenth. V. PAÑO.

catorrazo [cah-tor-rah'-tho], *m.* (*Mex.*), **Catarro** *m.* (*Mex.*) Punch, blow.

catorzavo, va [cah-tor-thah'-vo, vah]. One of the fourteen parts of a unit, fourteenth.

catre [cah'-tray], *m.* 1. Small bedstead. **Catre de mar**, hammock or cot. **Catre de tijera**, camp bed. (*fig.*) **Cambiar el catre**, to change the subject. 2. **Catre de balsa**, (*Cono Sur*) raft (barquito).

catrecillo [cah-tray-thel-lyo], *m.* Camp stool, folding seat.

catrera [cah-tray-rah], *f.* (*Cono Sur*) Bunk, bed.

catricofre [cah-tre-co'-fray], *m.* Press-bed which shuts up; a folding-bed, bed-lounge.

catrín [cah-treen'], *m.* (*CAm. Mex.*) Toff, dude.

caucarse [cah-oo-car'-say], *vr.* (*Cono Sur*) To grow old (persona); to go stale (comida).

caucáseo, ea [cah-oo-cah'-say-o, ah], **Caucásico, ca,** *a.* Caucasian.

Cáucaso [cah'-oo-cah-so], *m.* Caucasus.

cauce [cah'-oo-thay], *m.* 1. The bed of a river. 2. Trench. irrigation ditch, for conveying water to fields, gardens, etc.

caución [cah-oo-the-on'], *f.* 1. Security or pledge given for the performance of an agreement; gage, guarantee. 2. (*Law.*) Bailbond. **Caución juratoria**, oath taken by a person having no bail to return to prison. 3. Caution, warning, foresight, prevention.

caucionar [cah-oo-the-o-nar'], *va.* (*Law.*) To guard against an evil or loss; to bail, to prevent.

cauchal [cah-oo-chah'], *m.* Rubber plantation.

cauchar [cah-oo-char'], 1. *m.* (*And.*) Rubber plantation. 2. *vn.* (*And.*) To tap (trees for rubber).

cauchero, ra [cah-oo-chay'-ro, rah], *a.* Pertaining to rubber. *-m.* Rubber worker. *-f.* Rubber plant.

caucho [cah'-oo-cho], *m.* 1. Rubber. **Árbol del caucho**, rubber plant. **Caucho sintético**, synthetic rubber. **Caucho esponjoso**, foam rubber. 2. (*LAm.*) Raincoat, mac; (*And.*) Waterproof blanket.

cauchutado [cah-oo-choo-tah'-do], *a.* Rubberize.

caudal [cah-oo-dahl'], *m.* 1. Property, fortune, wealth, means, fund: especially in money. 2. Capital or principal sum, stock. 3. (*Met.*) Plenty, abundance. **Hacer caudal de alguna cosa**, to hold a thing in high esteem.

caudal [cah-oo-dahl'], *a.* (*Zool.*) Caudal, relating to the tail. **Águila caudal**, the red-tailed eagle.

caudalejo [cah-oo-dah-lay-ho], *m. dim.* Middling fortune.

caudaloso, sa [cah-oo-da-lo'-so, sah], *a.* 1. Carrying much water (ríos). 2. Rich, wealthy (personas).

caudatario [cah-oo-dah-tah'-re-o], *m.* Clergyman who carries the train of an officiating bishop's robe.

caudato, ta [cah-oo-dah'-to, tah], *a.* 1. Having a tail (cometa). 2. Bearded, hairy.

caudatrémula [cah-oo-dah-tray'-moo-lah], *f.* (*Orn.*) The wagtail.

caudillaje [cah-oo-de-lyah'-hay], *m.* 1. Leadership. **Bajo el caudillaje de**, under the leadership of. 2. (*LAm.*) Tyranny, rule by political bosses.

caudillo [cah-oo-deel'-ly], *m.* 1. Commander of an armed troop. 2. Chief, leader, or director of a company.

caudón [cah-oo-done'], *m.* A bird of prey, a kind of falcon. V. PEGA REBORDA.

caula [cah'-oo-lah], *f.* (*CAm. Cono Sur*) plot, intrigue.

caulícolo [cah-oo-lee'-co-lo], *m.* (*Arch.*) Ornament of the capital of columns.

cauri [cah'-oo-re], *m.* Cowrie.

causa [cah´-oo-sah], *f.* 1. Cause; occasion. 2. Consideration, motive of action, motive or reason of doing a thing. 3. Causality. 4. Cause, side, or party, affair in which one takes an interest. 5. Lawsuit, trial 6. Criminal cause or information. **Causa pública**, public good. **A causa de**, considering, on account of. **Veamos cuál es la causa de esto**, let us see what is the reason for this. **Causa primera**, first cause. **Por mi causa**, for my sake. **Fuera de causa**, irrelevant.

causa [cah´-oo-sah], *f. (Cono Sur)* snack, light meal; picnic lunch. 2. *(And.)* Potato salad.

causador, ra [cah-oo-sah-dor´, rah], *m. & f.* Occasioner, causer.

causal [cah-oo-sahl´], *a.* Causal, ground on which something is done.

causalidad [cah-oo-sah-le-dahd´], *f.* Causality.

causante [cah-oo-sha´-ta,], *pa. & m.* Occasioner, causer. 2. *(Law.)* The person from whom a right is derived; constituent, principal. *-a.* Causing, originating. **El coche causante del accidente**, the car which caused the accident.

causar [cah-oo-sar´], *va.* 1. To cause, to produce, to generate, to create, to gender, to make. 2. To sue, to enter an action. 3. To occasion, to originate. **Causar risa a uno**, to make somebody laugh.

causear [cah-oo-s-ay-ar´], *vn. (Cono Sur)* to have a snack; to have a picnic.

causídico [cah-oo-see-de-co], *m.* Advocate, counsellor.

causídico, ca [cah-oo-see´-de-co, cah], *a. (Law.)* Relative to causes or litigation.

castor [cas-tor´], *m.* 1. Castor, a beaver, an amphibious quadruped.

cáustico, ca [cah´-oos-te-co, cah], *a.* 1. Caustic, caustical. 2. Applied to a ray of reflected light which unites with others in one point.

cautamente [cah-oo-tah-men´-tay], *adv.* Cautiously, warily, carefully.

cautchuc [cah-oot-chooc´], **Cauchuco** [cah-oo-choo´-co], *m.* Caoutchouc, the tree and the gum. **Cautchuc vulcanizado**, vulcanized rubber.

cautela [cah-oo-tay´-lah], *f.* 1. Caution, prudence, foresight, prevention, precaution and reserve. 2. Heed, heedfulness, guard. 3. Artfulness, craft, cunning. **Tener cautela de**, to take the precaution of.

cautelar [cah-oo-tay-lar´], *va.* To take the necessary precaution, to proceed with prudence. *-vr.* To be on one´s guard.

cautelosamente [cah-oo-tay-lo-sah-men´-tay], *adv.* Cautiously, warily, guardedly.

cauteloso, sa [cah-oo-tay-lo´-so, sah], *a.* Cautious, heedful, cunning, crafty.

cauterio [cah-oo-tay´-ree-o], *m.* 1. *(Med.)* Cautery. **Cauterio actual**, actual cautery, burning with hot iron. **Cauterio potencial**, potential cautery procured by chemicals. 2. *(fig.)* Remedy.

cauterización [cah-oo-tay-re-thah-the-on´], *f.* Cauterization, cauterizing.

cauterizador [cah-oo-tay-re-thah-dor´], *m.* He who cauterizes.

cauterizar [cah-oo-tay-re-thar´], *va.* 1. To cauterize. 2. To correct or reproach with severity.

cautín [cah-oo-teen´], *m.* A soldering-iron.

cautivante [cah-oo-te-vahn´-tay], *a.* Captivating.

cautivar [cah-oo-te-var´], *va.* 1. To make prisoners of war. 2. To imprison. 3. *(Met.)* To captivate, to charm, to subdue.

cautiverio, *m.* **cautividad**, *f.* [cah-oo-te-vay´-re-o, cah-oo-te-ve-dahd´]. 1. Captivity. 2. Confinement.

cautivo, va [cah-oo-tee´-vo, vah], *m. &. f.* Captive among infidels. 2. Captive, one charmed by beauty.

cauto, ta [cah´-oo-to, tah], *a.* Cautious, wary.

cava [cah´-vah], *f.* 1. Digging and earthing of vines. 2. Cellar where wine and water are kept. 3. Ditch. 4. *(Prov.)* Subterraneous vault. 5. *(Carib.)* Closed truck, lorry. *-m.* Sparkling wine.

cavacote [cah-vah-co´-tay], *m.* Mound of earth made with the hoe to serve as a mark or temporary boundary.

cavadiza [cah-vah-dee´-thah], *a.* Dug out of a pit (arena).

cavado, da [cah-vah´-do, dah], *a.* Hollow, concave. *-pp.* of CAVAR.

cavador [cah-vah-dor´], *m.* 1. Digger, excavator. **Cavador de greda**, chalk-cutter. **Cavador de oro**, gold digger. 2. Grave-digger.

cavadura [cah-vah-doo´-rah], *f.* Digging, excavation.

cavallillo [cah-val-lyeel´-lyo], *m.* Water-furrow between ridges.

caván [cah-vahn´], *m.* A measure used in the Philippine Islands equivalent to seventy-five liters.

cavar [cah-var], *va.* 1. To dig, to excavate. 2. To paw (caballos). *-vn.* 1. To penetrate far into a thing. 2. To penetrate, to think intensely or profoundly.

cavatina [cah-vah-tee´-nah], *f.* Cavatina, a melody of a more simple form than the aria; a song without a second part.

cavazón [cah-vah-thone´], *f.* Digging, excavation.

caverna [cah-verr´-nah], *f.* 1. Cavern, cave. 2. Hollow inside or depth of wounds; cavity resulting from tuberculous ulceration or from an abscess.

cavernícola [cah-vayr-ne´-co-lah], 1.*a.* Cave dwelling. **Hombre cavernícola**, caveman. 2. Reactionary. *-m. & f.* Cave dweller, caveman, troglodyte. 3. Reactionary, backwoodsman.

cavernilla [cah-ver-neel´-lyah], *f. dim.* small cavern.

cavernoso, sa [cah-ver-no´-so, sah], *a.* 1. Cavernous, caverned. **Cuerpo cavernoso**, *(Anat.)* Corpus cavernosum. 2. Resounding, deep, hollow (sonido).

caveto [cah-vay´-to], *m. (Arch.)* Flute, fluting, groove, hollow moulding.

caví [cah-vee´], *m.* A Peruvian root, called *oca.*

cavia [cah´-ve-ah], *f.* Circular excavation at the foot of a tree to collect water.

cavial, or **caviar** [cah-ve-ahl´, cah-ve-ar´], *m.* Caviar, the roe of the sturgeon pressed and salted.

cavidad [cah-ve-dahd´], *f.* Cavity, excavation, space.

cavidos [cah-vee´-dos], *m.* Portuguese measure of length.

cavilación [cah-ve-lah-the-on´], *f.* 1. Cavilling, deep thought, rumination. 2. Suspicion, apprehension.

cavilar [cah-ve-lar´], *va.* 1. To cavil, find fault. 2. To find subtle excuses to escape from a difficulty.

cavilosear [ ], *vn. (Carib.)* To harbor illusions; *(Carib.)* To vacillate, to hesitate; *(CAm.)* To gossip.

cavilosamente [cah-ve-lo-sah-me´-tay], *adv.* Cavillously.

cavilosidad [cah-ve-lo-se-dahd´], *f.* Captiousness; cavillingness.

caviloso, sa [cah-ve-lo´-so, sah], *a.* 1. Captious, cavillous. 2. *(CAm.)* Gossipy, backbiting. 3. *(And.)* Quarrelsome, touchy; fussy (agresivo).

cavilla [cah-veel´-lyah], *f.* 1. *(Bot.)* Sea-holly. 2. *(Naut.)* Tree-nail. *V.* CABILLA.

cavillador [cah-veel-lyah-dor´], *m. (Naut.)* Treenail maker.

cavillar [cah-veel-lyar´], *va. (Naut.)* To use treenails. **Cavillar un bajel**, to drive treenails into a ship.

cavo, va [cah´-vo, vah], *a.* 1. Concave. 2. Having only twenty-nine days (meses).

cayadilla [cah-yah-deel´-lyah], *f. dim.* Small shepherd's hook.

cayado [cah-yah´-do], *m.* 1. Shepherd's hook, crook. 2. Crozier of a bishop. 3. Walking-staff.

cayán [cah-yahn´], *m.* 1. *V.* TAPANCO. 2. A covering of matting put on certain Philippine boats to protect the person within.

cayanto [cah-yahn´-to], *m.* A kind of stuff.

cayelac [cah-yay-lahc´], *m.* Sweet-scented wood of Siam.

cayeput [cah-yay-poot´], *m.* Cajeput-oil.

cayo [cah´-yoh], *m.* A rock, shoal or islet in the sea; key.

cayote [cah-yo´-tay], *m. (Bot.) V.* CIDRACAYOTE.

cayou [cah-yo´-oo], *m.* Cashew-nut.

cayubro [cah-yoo´-bro], *a, (And.)* Reddish-blonde, red-haired.

cayuca [cah-yoo´-cah], *f. (Carib.)* Head, bean.

cayuco [cah-yoo'-co], *m. (Naut.)* Small fishing-boat used in Venezuela.

caz [cath], *m.* Canal, trench, or ditch, near rivers for irrigation; mill-race, conduit.

caza [cah'-thah], *f.* 1. Chase, hunting, fowling, field-sports. 2. Game. 3. *(Naut.)* Chase, pursuit of a vessel at sea. 4. Thin linen resembling gauze. **Caza mayor,** hunting wild-boars, stags, wolves, etc. **Caza menor,** shooting or fowling; chasing hares, rabbits partridges, etc. **Andar a caza,** to hunt. **Andar a caza de alguna cosa,** *(Met.)* to go in pursuit of a thing. **Andar a caza de gangas,** to spend one's time uselessly. **Dar caza,** *(Naut.)* to give chase to a vessel. **Espantar la caza,** *(Met.)* to injure one's claim by an untimely application. **Caballo de caza,** hunter, hunting horse. **Trompa de caza,** hunting horn. **Partida de caza,** hunting party. **Caza del tesoro,** treasure hunt. **Caza de patos,** duck shooting.

caza [cah'-thah], *m. (Aer.)* Fighter plane, pursuit plane.

cazabe [cah-thah'-bay], *m. (Sp. Am.).* Cassava bread.

caza-bombardeo [cah-tha bom-bahr-day'-o], *m.* Fighter-bomber.

cazaclavos [cah-thah-clah'-vos], *m.* Nail puller.

cazadero [cah-thah-day'-ro], *m.* Hunting ground.

cazador [cah-tha-dor'], *m.* 1. Hunt, hunter, chaser, huntsman, sportsman. 2. Animal which gives chase to another. 3. *(Naut.)* Vessel which gives chase to another. 4. *(Met.)* One who prevails upon another, and brings him over to his party. **Cazador de pieles,** trapper. **Cazador de cabezas,** head-hunter.

cazadora [cah-tha-do'-rah], *f.* 1. Huntress. 2. Windcheater, hunting jacket, jerkin (prenda). **Cazadora de piel,** leather jacket.

cazadotes [cah-tha-do'-tays], *m.* Fortune-hunter.

cazafortunas [cah-tha-for-too'-nas], *f.* Fortune hunter, gold digger.

cazagenios [cah-thah-hay'-ne-os], *m.* Talent scout, talent spotter.

cazamoscas [cah-tha-mos'-cas], *m. (Orn.)* Flycatcher, a bird.

cazar [cah-thar'], *va.* 1. To chase, to hunt, to fowl, to sport, to course. 2. *(Met.)* To gain a difficult point by dexterity and skill. 3. *(Met.)* To gain one's friendship by caresses and deceitful tricks. 4. *(Naut.)* To give chase to a ship. 5. **Cazar una vela,** *(Naut.)* to tally a sail, to haul the sheet aft. **Cazar moscas,** *(Met.)* to waste one's time in idle amusements. **Le cacé por fin en la tienda,** I eventually ran him down in the shop.

cazasubmarinos [cah-tha-soob-mah-re'-nos], *m.* Submarine chaser.

cazatalentos [cah-tha-tah-layn'-tos*]*, *m.* Talent scout, talent spotter.

cazatorpederos [cah-thah-tor-pay-day'-ros], *m* Torpedo-boat destroyer.

cazcalear [cath-cah-lay-ar'], *vn.* 1. *(Coll.)* To go from one place to another affecting diligence. 2. To fidget.

cazcarria [cath-car'-re-ah], *f.* Splashings of dirt on clothes: used commonly in the plural.

cazcarriento [cah-thahr-re-ayn'-to], *a.* Splashed with mud, mud-stained.

cazo [cah'-tho], *m.* 1. Copper saucepan with an iron handle. 2. Copper or iron ladle for taking water out of a large earthen vessel. 3. Large kettle or boiler. 4. Back part of a knife-blade.

cazoleja, eta [cah-tho-ley'-hah, tah], *f.* 1. *(dim.)* Small saucepan. 2. Pan of a musket-lock.

cazolero [cah-tho-lay'-ro], *m. (Coll.)* Mean person who does women's work in the kitchen; milksop.

cazolero, ra [cah-tho-lay'-ro, rah], *a.* Applied to a person too officious. *V.* COMINERO.

cazoleta [cah-tho-lay'-tah], *f.* 1. Pan of a musket-lock. 2. Boss or defence of a shield. 3. Hand-guard or languet of a sword. 4. Kind of perfume. 5. *V.* CAZOLEJA.

cazolilla [cah-tho-leel'-lyah], *f. dim.* small earthen pan.

cazolón [cah-tho-lone'], *m. aug.* Large earthen pot or stew-pan.

cazón [cah-thone'], *m.* 1. *(Zool.)* Dogfish or small shark. 2. *(Obs.)* Brown sugar.

cazonal [cah-tho-nahl'], *m. (Prov.)* Fishing-tackle for the shark-fishery.

cazonete [cah-tho-nay'-tay], *m. (Naut.)* Toggle, a pin used to fasten a portrope.

cazú [cah-thoo'], *m.* An edible African fruit resembling cacao.

cazudo, da [cah-thoo'-do, dah], *a.* Having a thick back (cuchillos).

cazuela [cah-thoo-ay-lah], *f.* 1. An earthen pan to dress meat in, stewing-pan, crock. 2. Meat dressed in an earthen pan, the gallery of playhouses in Spain reserved for women. 4. **Cazuela mojí** or **mojil,** *(Prov.)* Tart made of cheese, bread, apples, and honey. 5. Earthen pans for baking pies. *V.* TARTERA.

cazumbrar [cah-thoom-brar'], *va.* To join staves together with hempen cords.

cazumbre [cah-thoom'-bray], *m.* Hempen cord with which the staves of wine-casks are joined and tightened.

cazembrón [cah-thoom-brone'], *m.* Cooper.

cazurro, ra [cah-thoor'-ro, rah], *a.* 1. *(Coll.)* Taciturn, sulky, sullen. 2. *(Obs.)* Making use of low language. 3. Thick-headed.

cazuz [cah-thooth'], *m. (Bot.)* Ivy.

c/c abr de **cuenta corriente** (current account).

C.D. *m.* 1. *abr.* de **Cuerpo Diplomático** (Diplomatic Corps). 2. *abr.* de **Club Deportivo** (sports club).

c/d 1. *abr.* de **en casa de** (care of). 2. *(Cono Sur) abr.* de **descuento** (discount).

CDR *m. (Cuba)* **Comité de Defensa de la Revolución**.

CD ROM . CD ROM (Compact Disc Read Only Memory).

CDS *m.*1. *(Esp.) abr.* de **Centro Democrático y Social**. 2. (Nicaragua) *abr.* de **Comité de defensa Sandinista**.

CDU *f. abr.* de **Clasificación Decimal Universal** (Dewey decimal system).

CE *m. abr.* de **Consejo Europeo** (Council of Europe).

Ce [thay]. 1. *f.* Name of the third letter of the alphabet. 2. *int.* Hark, here, come hither. **Ce por be,** or **ce por ce,** minutely, circumstantially; **por ce o por be,** in one way or another.

cea [thay'-ah], *f.* Thigh-bone. *V.* CÍA.

ceanoto [thay-ah-no'-to], *m.* Ceanothus, a genus of American and Oceanic shrubs of the buckthorn family; Jersey tea, redroot, etc.

ceática [thay-ah'-te-cah], *f. (Med.)* Sciatica, a disease.

ceático, ca [thay-ah'-te-co, cah], *a. (Med.)* Sciatical, *V.* CIÁTICO.

ceba [thay'-bah], *f.* 1. The fattening of fowls or other domestic animals. 2. *(LAm.)* Charge priming. 3. Stoking (de horno).

cebada [thay-bah'-dah], *f. (Bot.)* Barley. **Cebada común,** spring barley. **Cebada común blanca,** a variety of the spring barley with white seeds. **Cebada negra,** black barley. **Cebada perlada,** pearl barley.

cebadal [thay-bah-dahl'], *m.* Field sown with barley.

cebadar [thay-bah-dar'], *va.* To feed barley to horses.

cebadazo, za [thay-bah-dah'-tho, thah], *a.* Belonging to barley.

cebadera [thay-bah-day'-rah], *f.* 1. Kind of bag in which feed is given in the field to working cattle. 2. *(Naut.)* Spritsail.

cebadería [thay-bah-day-ree'-ah], *f.* Barley-market.

cebadero [thay-bah-day'-ro], *m.* 1. Place where game or fowls are fed. 2. One whose business is to breed and feed hawks. 3. Mule which on a journey carries barley for the rest. 4. Bell-mule which takes the lead. 5. Painting which represents domestic fowls in the act of feeding. 6. Entrance of a tile-kiln. 7. Dealer in barley.

cebadilla [thay-bah-deel'-lyah], *f.* 1. *(Bot.)* Indian caustic barley or cevadilla. 2. *(Bot.)* Sneezewort. 3. *(Bot. Prov.)* Prickly oxeye. 4. Hellebore powdered and used as snuff.

cebado [thay-bah'-do], *a.* Fattened (un animal). Very fat. Fatted (becerro en la Biblia). -**Cebado, da,** *pp.* of CEBAR.

cebador [thay-bah-dor'], *m.* 1. One who fattens fowls or other animals. 2. Priming-horn, powder-horn. 3. *(Cono Sur) (Aut.)* Choke.

cebadura [thay-bah-doo'-rah], *f.* 1. Act of feeding or fattening fowls or other domestic animals. 2. Priming, stoking.

cebar [thay-bar,], *va. & vn.* 1. To feed amimals, to stuff; to cram. 2. To fatten fowls and other domestic animals. 3. *(Met.)* To keep up a fire. 4. To grapple, or to lay fast hold on one thing. 5. *(Met.)* To excite and cherish a passion or desire. 6. To prime a gun. 7. To let off a rocket or squib. 8. **Cebar un anzuelo**, to bait a fish-hook. *-vr.* 1. To be firmly bent upon a thing. 2. *(CAm. Mex.)* To fail to go off (tiro, fuegos artificiales); *(fig.)* to go wrong. 3. **Cerbarse en**, to vent one´s fury on, to prey upon. 4. **Cebarse en un estudio**, to devote oneself to study. 5. **Cebarse en la sangre**, to gloat over the blood (shed).

cebato [thay-bah'-to], *m.* A climbing plant of Arabia.

cebellina [thay-bel-lyee'-nah], *f.* 1. Sable. 2. Sable, the skin of the sable.

cebica [thay-bee'-cah], *f.* V. CIBICA.

cebiche [thay-bee'-chay], *m. (And.)* Marinaded fish.

cebo [thay'-bo], *m.* 1. Food given to animals; fodder. 2. Fattening of fowls and other animals. 3. Bait for wolves and birds of prey. 4. *(Met.)* That which excites or foments a passion. 5. Kind of monkey. *V.* CEFO. 6. Cart-grease. **Cebo de pescar**, bait for fishing. 7. Priming of guns. **Cebo** or **ceba fulminante**, percussion-cap.

cebolla [thay-bol'-lyah], *f.* 1. *(Bot.)* Onion. 2. The bulb of the onion. 3. Any kind of bulbous root. 4. The round part of a lamp into which oil is put. **Cebolla albarrana**, *(Bot.)* Squill. **Cebolla ascalonia**, *(Bot.)* Shallot garlic or ascalonian garlic.

cebollado [cay-bol-lye-ah'-do], *a. (LAm.)* Cooked with onions.

cebollana [thay-bol-lyah'-nah], *f. (Bot.)* Three-toothed globularia, chive.

cebollar [thay-bol-lyar'], *m.* Plot of ground sown with onions.

cebollero, ra [thay-bol-lyay'-ro, rah], *m. & f.* Dealer in onions.

cebolleta [thay-bol-lyay'-tah], *f. dim.* A tender onion.

cebollino [thay-bol-lyee'-no], *m.* 1. A young onion fit to be transplanted. 2. The onion's seeds. 3. *(Bot.)* Chive or cive; a plant allied to the leek and the onion.

cebollón [thay-bol-lyone'], *m. aug.* 1. A large onion. 2. *(Cono Sur)* old bachelor.

cebollona [thay-bol-lyo'-nah], *f. (Cono Sur)* old maid, spinster.

cebolludo, da [thay-bol-lyoo'-do, dah], *a.* 1. Among gardeners, applied to any plant with a big bulb. 2. *(Coll.)* Ill-shaped (personas).

cebón [thay-bone'], *m.* A fat bullock or hog. **Cebones de Galicia**, stall-fed bullocks.

ceboncillo [thay-bon-theel'-lyo], *m.* Fatling, a young animal fed for slaughter, particularly a pig.

ceboruco [thay-bo-roo'-co], *m.* 1. *(Carib.)* Reef. 2. *(Mex.)* Rough rocky place (terreno quebrado). 3. *(Carib.)* Brush, scrub *(land.)*

cebra [thay'-brah], *f.* 1. Zebra, a kind of ass whose body is marked with dark bands. 2. (Cebras), zebra crossing.

cebratana [thay-brah-tah'-nah], *f.* 1. A long wooden tube or pipe. V. CERBATANA. 2. *(Art.)* Piece of ordnance resembling a culverin.

cebruno, na [thay-broo'-no, nah], *a.* Having the color of deer or hares.

cebú [thay-boo'], *m.* Zebu.

ceburro [thay-boor'-ro], *a.* V. MIJO CEBURRO and CANDEAL.

CECA *f. (Esp.) (Hist.) abr.* de **Comunidad Europea del Carbón y del Acero**, (European Coal and Steel Community, ECSC).

ceca [thay'-cah], *f.* 1. A mint for the coining of money. 2. *m.* Name of the mosque which the Arabs had in Cordova, the most venerated after Mecca. **Andar de ceca en meca**, to rove, to wander about, hither and thither.

ceceo [thay-thay'-o], *m.* 1. Lisping, lisp. 2. Act of calling someone by the word *ce-ce*, which corresponds to *I say*.

ceceoso, sa [thay-thay-o'-so, sah], *m. & f.* Lisper. *-a.* Lisping.

cecial [thay-the-ahl'], *m.* Hake or similar fish cured and dried in the air.

cecias [thay'-the-as], *m.* North-west wind.

cecina [thay-thee'-nah], *f.* Hung beef, smoked meat, dry meat. **Echar en cecina**, to salt and dry meat.

cecinar [thay-the-nar'], *va.* To make hung beef. V. ACECINAR.

ceda [thay'-dah], *f.* . V. ZEDA. *-m.* **Ceda el paso**, *(Aut.)* Priority, right of way.

cedacería [thay-dah-thay-ree'-ah], *f.* Shop where sieves or cribs are made or sold.

cedacero [thay-dah-thay'-ro], *m.* One who makes or sells sieves, cribs, etc.

cedacillo, ito [thay-dah-theel'-lyo, ee´-to], *m. dim.* A small sieve. **Cedacito nuevo tres días en estaca**, a new broom sweeps clean.

cedazo [thay-dah'-tho], *m.* Hair sieve or strainer; tamis, flour-sieve, bolting-cloth.

cedazuelo [thay-dah-thoo-ay'-lo], *m. dim.* A small hair sieve or strainer.

ceder [thay-derr'], *va.* To grant, to cede, to resign, to yield, to deliver up, to make over, to give up. *-vn.* 1. To yield or yield to, to submit, to comply, to give out, to give over, to give way, to come in, to go back. *(Mech.)* To sag, slacken. **No ceden fácilmente a las innovaciones**, they do not give in easily to innovations. **No cede a nadie en experiencia**, he is inferior to none in experience. 2. To happen, to turn out ill or well. 3. To abate, to grow less.

cedilla [thay-deel'-lyah], *f.* Cedilla, a mark formerly placed under a **c** to show that it sounded like **z** (ç). V. ZEDILLA.

cediza [thay-dee'-thah], *a.* Tainted (carne).

cedizo [thay-de'-tho], *a.* High, tainted.

cedoaria [thay-do-ah'-re-ah], *f.* Zedoary, a medicinal root.

cedras [thay'-dra], *f. pl.* Saddle-bags of skin, in which shepherds carry bread and other provisions.

cedría [thay-dree'-ah], *f.* Cedria, cedrium, a resin distilled from the cedar.

cédride, cedrio [thay'-dree-day, thay'-dre-o], *m.* Fruit of the cedar-tree.

cedrino, na [thay-dree'-no, nah], *a.* Cedrine, cedarn.

cedro [thay'-dro], *m. (Bot.)* 1. Cedar. **Cedro de América**, Barbadoes bastard cedar. **Cedro del Líbano**, cedar of Lebanon. 2. *(Prov.)* Spanish juniper.

cédula [thay'-doo-lah], *f.* 1. Document. 2. Order, bill, degree. 3. I.O.U. (reconocimiento de deuda). 4. Lot. 5. Schedule; warrant, share, scrip. **Cédula de aduana**, a permit. **Cédula de abono**, order to remit a tax in a town or a province. **Cédula de cambio**, bill of exchange. **Cédula de diligencias**, a warrant which was issued by the Council of the Chamber, commissioning a judge to make some investigation. **Cédula personal** or **de vecindad**, an official document declaring the name, occupation, domicile, etc., of each citizen, and to serve for identification. **Car cédula de vida**, to show bravery by sparing the life of one who is in his opponent's power. **Cédula de inválidos**, warrant for the reception of invalids. **Echar cédulas**, to draw or cast lots.

cedulaje [thay-doo-lah'-hay], *m.* Fees or dues paid for the expedition of decrees or grants.

cedulilla, ita [thay-doo-leel'-lyah, ee'-tah], *f. dim.* A small slip of paper.

cedulón [thay-doo-lone'], *m. aug.* A large bill, long edict, a large libellous bill or paper. **Poner cedulones**, to post up bills, edicts, or libels.

CE *f. abr.* de **Comunidad Europea**, (European Community, EC).

cefalalgia [thay-fah-lahl'-he-ah], *f. (Med.)* Cephalalgia, headache.

cefalea [thay-fah-lay'-ah], *f.* Violent headache, generally one-sided, like migraine.

cefálico, ca [thay-fah'-le-co, cah], *a.* Cephalic, belonging to the head; cephalic (vein).

céfalo [thay-fah-lo], *m.* (*Zool.*) Mullet, a kind of perch.

cefalina [thay-fah-lee'-nah], *f.* The root of the tongue.

cefalópodo [thay-fah-lo'-po-do], *m.* Cephalopod, the highest class of mollusks.

cefalotomía [thay-fah-lo-to-mee'-ah], *f.* Cephalotomy, the act of opening or dividing the head of the foetus, to facilitate delivery.

cefeo [thay-fay'-o], *m.* Cepheus, a constellation of the northern hemisphere, near Cassiopeia and Draco.

céfiro [thay'-fe-ro], *m.* Zephyr.

cefo [thay'-fo], *m.* A large African monkey.

cegador [thay-gah-dor'], *a.* Blinding. **Brillo cegador,** blinding glare.

cegajo [thay-gah'-ho], *m.* A he-goat, two years old.

cegajoso, sa [thay-gah-ho'-so, sah], *a.* Bleary-eyed.

cegar [thay-gar'], *vn.* To grow blind. *-va.* 1. To blind, to make blind. 2. (*Met.*) To deprive of good sense, reason, or judgement. 3. To shut a door or window. **Cegar los conductos, los pasos o caminos,** to stop up channels, passages, or roads. **Le ciega la pasión,** he is blinded by passion. *-vr.* (*fig.*)To become blinded.

cegarra [thay-gar'-rah], *a. Coll.* for CEGATO.

cegarrita [thay-gar-ree'-tah], *m.* (*Coll.*) One who contracts the eye to see at a distance.

cegato, ta [thay-gah'-to, tah], *a.* (*Coll.*) Short-sighted.

cegatoso, sa [thay-gah-to'-so, sah], *a. V.* CEGAJOSO.

ceguecillo, ceguezuelo [thay-gay-theel'-lyo, thay-gay-thoo-ay'-lo], *m. dim.* Little blind fellow.

ceguedad [thay-gay-dahd'], *f.* 1. Blindness, cecity. 2. (*Met.*) Blindness, ignorance, intellectual darkness.

ceguera [thay-gay'-rah], *f.* 1. Disorder in the eye. 2. Absolute blindness.

cegueríes [thay-gay-ree'-es], *m.* Kind of marten or the fur of this animal.

ceguiñuela [thay-gee-nyoo-ay'-lah], *f.* (*Naut.*) Whip-staff of the helm. *V.* PINZOTE.

ceiba [thay'-e-bah], *f.* 1. (*Bot.*) Five-leaved silk-cotton tree. 2. By the seashore, sea-moss, alga.

Ceilán [thay-e-lahn'], *m.* (*Hist.*) Ceylon.

ceilanés, esa [thay-e-lahn-days'], *a. m. & f.* Ceylones(*Geog.*) [thay'-hah], *f.* 1. Eye-brow. 2. Edging of clothes; projecting part, as in the binding of books. 3. In stringed instruments, bridge on which the cords rest. 4. Summit of a mountain. 5. Circle of clouds round a hill; cloud-cap. 6. (*Arch.*) Weather-moulding, rim. 7. (*Naut.*) An opening in a cloudy horizon; **dar entre ceja y ceja,** (*Met.*) To tell one to his face unpleasant truths. **Tomar a uno entre cejas,** to take a dislike to anyone. **Quemarse las cejas,** (*Met.*) to study with intense application. **Fruncir las cejas,** to knit one´s brows.

cejadero [thay-hah-day'-ro], *m.* Traces of a harness.

cejar [thay-har'], *vn.* 1. To retrograde, to go backward. 2. (*Met.*) To slacken, to relax. **Sin cejar,** unflinchingly, undaunted. **No cejar en sus esfuerzos,** to keep (*Aer.*)´s efforts.

cejijunto, ta [thay-he-hoon'-to, tah], *a.* Having eyebrows which meet.

cejo [thay'-ho], *m.* 1. Thick fog which rises from rivers. 2. A cord tied around a bundle of esparto-grass, made of the same. 3. Frown, a look of displeasure.

cejudo, da [thay-hoo'-do, dah], *a.* Having heavy and long eyebrows.

cejuela [thay-hoo-ay'-lah], *f. dim.* A small eyebrow.

celada [thay-lah'-dah], *f.* 1. Helm, helmet. **Celada borgoñona,** burgundy helmet. 2. Ambuscade, ambush, lurch. 3. Artful trick. 4. Part of the key of the crossbow. 5. Horse soldier formerly armed with a crossbow. 6. (*Naut.*) Decoy or stratagem used by a small ship of war to bring an inferior vessel within gunshot. **Caer en la celada,** to fall into the trap.

celadilla [thay-lah-deel'-lyah], *f. dim.* Small helmet.

celador, ra [thay-lah-dor', rah], *m. & f.* 1. Curator. 2. Monitor in schools. 3. Warden.

celaje [thay-lah'-hay], *m.* 1. Color of the clouds 2. Small cloud moving before the wind, scud. 3. Painting which represents the rays of the sun breaking through clouds. 4. Presage, prognostic. 5. Skylight; upper part of a window; the sky of a picture. **Celajes,** light swiftly moving clouds, scud.

celán [thay-lahn'], *m.* A kind of herring.

celar [thay-lar'], *vn. & va.* 1. To fulfill the duties of an office with care. 2. To keep a watchful eye on. 3. To cover, to conceal. 4. *V.* RECELAR. (To conceal.) 5. To engrave; to cut in wood. (To grave).

celda [thel'-dah], *f.* 1. Cell in a convent. 2. Cell in beehives. 3. (*Naut. Obs.*) Small cabin. 4. (*Obs.*) Small room. **Celda de castigo,** solitary confinement cell. 5. (*Inform.*) **Celda actual,** current cell. **Celda de almacenamiento de datos,** memory cell, storage cell. **Celda de memoria,** memory cell, storage cell.

celdilla [thel-deel'-lyah], *f.* . (*Bot.*) Cell, the part of a pericarp or capsule in which seeds are lodged.

cele [thay-lay], *a.* (*CAm.*) Light green; unripe (inmaduro).

celebérrimo, ma [thay-lay-ber'-re-mo, mah], *a. sup.* Most celebrated.

celebración [thay-lay-brah-the-on'], *f.* 1. Celebration, solemn performance. 2. Celebration, praise, applause, acclamation.

celebrador, ra [thay-lay-brah-dor', rah], *m. & f.* Applauder, praiser, celebrator.

celebrante [thay-lay-brahn'-tay], *m.* 1. Celebrator. 2. A priest celebrating the mass.

celebrar [thay-lay-brar'], *va.* 1. To celebrate, to perform in a solemn manner. **Celebrar misa,** to say mass. 2. To hold, take place. **Celebrar un contrato,** to draw up a contract; **celebrar una reunión,** to hold a meeting. 3. To celebrate, to praise, to applaud, to commend. **Lo celebro mucho por él,** I´m very happy for his sake. 4. (*Carib.*) To fall in love. *-vr.* To fall, to occur, to be celebrated, to take place.

célebre [thay'-lay-bray], *a.* 1. Celebrated, famous, renowned, noted. 2 (*Met. Coll.*) Gay, facetious, agreeable in conversation.

célebremente [thay'-lay-bray-men-tay], *adv.* Facetiously, merrily.

celebridad [thay-lay-bre-dahd'], *f.* 1. Celebrity. 2. Renown, fame. 3. Pomp, magnificence, or ostentation, with which a feast or event is celebrated. 4. Public demonstration to commemorate some event.

celebrillo [thay-lay-breel'-lyo], *m. dim.* Small brains.

celebro [thay-lay'-bro], *m.* 1. Skull. 2. Brain. *V.* CEREBRO. 3. (*Met.*) Fancy imagination. 4. Prudence.

celemín [thay-lay-meen'], *m.* 1. Dry measure, the 12th part of a *fanega*, about an English peck. 2. The quantity of grain contained in a **celemín.**

celeminero [thay-lay-me-nay'-ro], *m.* (*Obs.*) Hostler who measures grain in inns.

celeque [thay-lay'-kay], *a.* (*CAm.*) Green, unripe.

celerado, celerario [thay-lay-rah'-do. thay-lay-rah'-re-o], *a. V.* MALVADO.

célere [thay'-lay-ray], *a.* Quick, rapid. *-m.* One of the select three hundred knights of ancient Roman nobility.

celeridad [thay-lay-re-dahd'], *f.* Celerity, velocity. **Con celeridad,** quickly.

celerímetro [thay-lay-ree'-may-tro], *m.* Speedometer.

celeste [thay-les'-tay], *a.* 1. Celestial. 2. Heavenly. 3. Sky-blue.

celestial [thay-les-te-ahl'], *a.* 1. Celestial, heavenly. 2. (*Met.*) Perfect, agreeable, delightful, excellent. 3. Silly.

celestialmente [thay-les-te-al-men'-tay], *adv.* Celestially, heavenly; perfectly.

celestina [thay-lays-te'-nah], *f.* Bawd, procuress; madam (burdel).

celestinazo [thay-lays-te-nah'-tho], *m.* Pimping, procuring.

celfo [thel'-fo], *m. V.* CEFO.

celíaco, ca [thay-lee'-ah-co, cah], *a. (Med.)* 1. Coeliac, relating to the coeliac passion. 2. Applied to a person afflicted with the coeliac passion.

celibato [thay-le-bah'-to], *m.* 1. Celibacy. 2. A bachelor. a single man.

célibe [thay'-le-bay], *m. f.* Single, unmarried.

célico, ca [thay'-le-co, cah], *a.* Celestial, heavenly.

celidonia [thay-le-do'-ne-ah], *f.* 1. *(Bot.)* Common celandine, swallowwort, tether-wort. 2. Swallow-stone, a small stone with several impressions.

celindrate [thay-lin-drah'-tay], *m.* Ragout made with coriander-seed.

celita [thay-lee'-tah], *f.* A fish caught in the Straits of Gibraltar.

celo [thay'-lo], *m.* 1. Zeal, ardor, devotion. 2. Heat, rut. 3. Religious zeal, fervor. **Caer en celo,** to come into rut. -*pl.* 1. Jealousy. **Dar celos,** to give grounds for jealousy. **Tener celos de uno,** to be jealous of somebody. 2. Suspicious. **Dar celos,** to excite suspicions.

celofán [thay-lo-fahn'], *m.* Cellophane.

celosamente [thay-lo-sah-men-tay], *adv.* 1. Zealously; eagerly; fervently. 2. *(fig.)* Suspiciously, distrustfully.

celosía [thay-lo-see'-ah], *f.* Lattice of a window, Venetian blind.

celoso, sa [thay-lo'-so, sah], *a.* 1. Jealous. 2. Light and swift-sailing (pequeños barcos). 3. Crank, unsteady, top-heavy: spoken of vessels and boats. 4. *(LAm.) (Mec.)* Highly sensitive; *(And.)* Unsteady, easily upset; *(LAm.)* Delicate (arma). **Éste es un fusil celoso,** this gun is quite liable to go off.

celotipia [thay-lo-tee'-pe-ah], *f.* Jealousy.

celsitud [thel-see-tood'], *f.* 1. Elevation, grandeur. 2. Highness, a title now expressed by *Alteza.*

celta [thel'-tah], *com.* Celt, Celtic. -*m.* The Celtic language.

celtibérico, ca [thel-te-bay'-re-co, cah], *a.* Celtiberian.

céltico ca [thel'-te-co, cah], *a.* Celtic.

celtista [thel-tees'-tah], *com.* Celtist, one who cultivates Celtic language and literature.

célula [thay'-loo-lah], *f. (Med.)* Cellule. **Célula nerviosa,** nerve cell. **Célula sanguínea,** blood cell.

celular [thay-loo-lar'], or **celulario, ia** [thay-loo-lah'-re-o, ah], *a.* 1. *(Med.)* Cellular. 2. A system of isolation among those imprisoned for grave crimes. 3. Cell, *V.* COCHE.

celulilla [thay-loo-leel'-lyah], *f. dim.* A very small cell or cavity.

celulitis [they-loo-le'-tes], *f.* Cellulitis.

celuloide [thay-loo-lo'-e-day], *m.* Celluloid.

celulosa [thay-loo-lo'-sah], *f.* Cellulose, woody fibre.

celuloso, sa [thay-loo-lo'-so, sah], *a.* Cellulose, containing cells.

cellenco, ca [thel-lyen'-co, cah], *a. (Coll.)* Decrepit.

cellisca [thel-lyees'-cah], *f. V.* VENTISCA. Fine rain or snow, sleet, driven by a heavy wind.

cellisquear [thel-lyees-kay-ar'], *vn.* To sleet, to be squally with fine snow or rain.

cembellina [them-bel-lyee'-nah], *f.* Hartshorn.

cementación [thay-men-tah-the-on'], *f.* Cementation.

cementar [thay-men-tar'], *va.* To cement. *V.* CIMENTAR.

cementerio [they-men-tay'-re-o], *m.* Cemetery, churchyard, graveyard; **cementerio de coches,** used car dump.

cemento [thay-men'-to], *m.* 1 Cement, concrete. **Cemento armado,** reinforced concrete. 2. *(Anat.)* Cement (de dientes).

cemita [thay-me'-tah], *f. (LAm.)* White bread roll.

cena [they'-nah], *f.* 1. Dinner, supper. 2. Scene, stage. **Jueves Santo** or **de la Cena,** Maundy Thursday, Thursday before Good Friday. **La Última Cena,** The Last Supper.

cenáculo [thay-nah'-coo-lo], *m.* The dining-hall in which our Lord celebrated The Last Supper with his disciples.

cenacho [thay-nah'-cho], *m.* Basket or hamper for fruit and greens.

cenadero [thay-nah-day'-ro], *m.* 1. A place for supping. 2. Summerhouse in a garden.

cenador [thay-nah-dor'], *m.* 1. One fond of suppers, or who eats in excess. 2. Summer-house in a garden, an arbor, bower.

cenaduría [they-nah-doo-ree'-ah], *f. (Mex.)* Eating house, restaurant.

cenagal [thay-nah-gahl'], *m.* Quagmire. **Meterse en un cenagal,** *(Met.)* To be involved in an unpleasant, arduous affair. **Salir de un cenagal,** to get rid of an unpleasant affair.

cenagoso, sa [thay-nah-go'-so, sah], *a.* Muddy, miry, marshy.

cena-homenaje [they-nah-o-may-nah'-hay], *f. pl.* **Cenas homenajes,** formal dinner. **Ofrecer una cena-homenaje,** to hold a dinner for somebody.

cenar [thay-nar'], *va.* To dine, to have dinner or supper. **Invitar a uno a cenar,** to invite someone to dinner. **Quedarse sin cenar,** to go without dinner or supper. -*vn.* To have one's supper; **vengo cenado,** I've had dinner.

cenata [thay-nah'-tah], *f. (Col.)* Merry banquet or dinner.

cenceño, ña [then-thay-nyo, nyah], *a.* Lean, thin, slender. 2. Pure, simple. **Pan cenceño,** unleavened bread.

cencerra [then-ther'-rah], *f.* 1. Bell worn by the leading mule. *V.* CENCERRO. 2. Clack of a mill which strikes the hopper and promotes the running of the corn. 3. The meat between the throttle and ribs of a saddle of mutton.

cencerrada [then-ther-rah'-dah], *f.* 1. Noise with bells and horns at the door of an old bridegroom or widower, the night of his marriage; charivari, din.

cencerrear [then-ther-ray-ar'], *vn.* 1. To jangle continually (mulas, caballos). 2. To clack. 3. To play on an untuned guitar. 4. To make a dreadful noise, as by windows and doors shaken by the wind.

cencerreo [then-ther-ray'-o], *m.* 1. Noise made by mule or horse bells. 2. Dreadful noise.

cencerril [then-ther-reel'], *a.* Resembling the noise of horse-bells.

cencerrilla, illo [then-ther-reel'-lyah, eel'-lyo], *f. & m. dim.* A small wether, horse, or mule bell.

cencerro [then-ther'-ro], *m.* 1. Bell worn by the leading wether, or mule. 2. Ill-tuned guitar. 3. *(Orn.)* Woodcrow. **No quiero perro con cencerro,** I do not want a dog with a bell; that is, I do not like to engage in a business that is more troublesome than profitable. **A cencerros tapados,** privately, stealthily. **Estar como un cencerro,** to be crazy.

cencerrón [then-ther-rone'], *m.* A small bunch of grapes which remains after the vintage.

cencerruno, na [then-ther-roo'-no, nah], *a. V.* CENCERRIL.

cencido, da [then-thee'-do, dah], *a.* Untilled, uncultivated (tierra).

cencro [theen'-cro], *m.* A serpent of Brazil.

cendal [theen-dahl'], *m.* 1. Light thin stuff made of silk or thread. 2. Furbelow, flounce or trimming of gowns, etc. 3. *(Poet.)* Garter.

cendea [then-day'-ah], *f. (Prov.)* In Navarre, meeting of the inhabitants of several villages to deliberate on public business.

cendolilla [then-do-leel'-lyah], *f.* A forward girl acting with little judgment.

cendra [then'-drah], *f.* 1. Paste used to clean silver. 2. Cupel. **Ser una cendra,** *(Met.)* to be lively as a cricket.

cendrar [then-drar'], *va. V.* ACENDRAR.

cenefa [thay-nay'-fah], *f.* 1. Frame of a picture. 2. Border or list of any kind of stuff. 3. Valance, fringes and drapery of a bed. 4. Trimming. 5. Middle piece of a priest's garment, called chasuble. 6. *(Poet.)* Bank of a river or lake, the brim of a ond. 7. **Cenefa de un toldo,** *(Naut.)* center of an awning. *(Arab.).*

ceñí [thay-nee'], *m.* A kind of fine brass or bronze.

cenicero [thay-ne-thay'-ro], *m.* Ashtray.

Cenicienta [they-ne-the-ayn'-tah], *f.* Cinderella. **La Cenicienta de la casa,** I'm always the one left out.

ceniciento, ta [thay-ne-the-en'-to, tah], *a.* Ash-colored, cinereous. -*m.* Scullion.

cenit [thay-neet'], *m. (Astr.)* Zenith; vertex.

cenital [thay-ne-tahl'], *a.* Vertical, relating to the zenith.

ceniza [thay-nee'-thah], *f.* 1. Ashes, cinders. 2. Coarse ashes, which remain in the strainer when the lye is made. *V.* CERNADA. 3. Ashes, the remains of the dead. **Cenizas de estaño**; putty. **Día de ceniza** or **Miércoles de ceniza**, ash-Wednesday. **Hacerse ceniza** or **cenizas alguna cosa**, *(Met.)* to be reduced to nothing, to come to nothing. **Reducir algo a cenizas**, to reduce something to ashes.

cenizal [thay-ne-thahl'], *m.* Heap of ashes.

cenizo [thay-nee'-tho], *m.* 1. *(Bot.)* White goosefoot. 2. *(Coll.)* Jinx, bearer of ill luck. **Es un avión cenizo**, it´s a plane with a jinx on it. **Entrar el cenizo en casa**, to have a spell of bad luck. *-a.* 1. Ashen, ash-colored. 2. Ill-omened; alarming.

cenizo, za [thay-nee'-tho, thah], *a. V.* CENICIENTO.

cenizoso, sa [thay-nee-tho'-so, sah], *a.* Covered with ashes, cineritious.

cenobio [thay-no'-be-o], *m.* Cenobium. *V.* MONASTERIO.

cenobita [thay-no-bee'-tah], *m.* Cenobite, a monk.

cenobítico, ca [thay-no-bee'-te-co, cah], *a.* Cenobitical.

cenotafio [thay-no-tah'-fe-o], *m.* Cenotaph, a monument.

cenote [thay-no'-tay], *m.* Deposit of water, generally at a great depth in the center of a cavern.

censal [then-sahl'], *m. & f. & a. (Prov.) V.* CENSO and CENSUAL.

censalista [then-sah-lees'-tah], *m. (Prov.) V.* CENSUALISTA.

censar [thayn-sar'], *va. (Cono Sur)* to take a census (población).

censatario, censero [then-sah-tah'-re-o, then-say'-ro], *m.* One who pays an annuity out of his estate to another person.

censista [thayn-thes'-tah], *m. & f.* Census official, census taker.

censo [then'-so], *m.* 1. An agreement by which a person acquires the right of receiving an annual pension. 2. Quit-rent. 3. Census, censual roll or book, where all the inhabitants of a kingdom or of a state are enumerated. **Censo electoral**, electoral roll. 4. Poll-tax, formerly in use among the Romans. 5. **Censo al quitar** or **reservativo**, a quit-rent or annuity which can be paid at once by a certain sum. **Censo de por vida**, annuity for one or more lives. 6. **Ser un censo**, to be a constant drain.

censontli, censontle [then-son'-tlee, then-son'-tlay], *m. (Mex.)* The Mexican mocking-bird. *Cf.* SINSONTE.

censor [theen-sor'], *m.f.* 1. Censor, an officer appointed to examine new books and publications, to see if they contain something contrary to religion and good manners. 2. Critic, reviewer of literary compositions. 3. Censorious person. 4. *(Com. fin.)* **Censora de cuentas**, auditor. **Censor jurado de cuentas**, chartered accountant.

censual [then-soo-ahl'], *a.* 1. Pertaining to a quit-rent, annuity, or any other annual rent paid for the possession of land. 2. Pertaining to interest on money invested. 3. *(Pol.)* Relating to the electoral roll.

censualista [then-soo-ah-lees'-tah], *m.* 1. A person in whose favor an annuity has been imposed, and who has the right to enjoy it until his death. 2. A copyholder.

censualmente [then-soo-al-men'-tay], *adv.* With a right to enjoy an annuity.

censuario [then-soo-ah'-re-o], *m. V.* CENSUALISTA.

censura [then-soo'-rah], *f.* 1. A critical review of literary productions. 2. Censure, blame, reproach, reprimand, reprehension, objurgation. 3. Reproach without foundation, gossiping. 4. Censure, a spiritual punishment inflicted by an ecclesiastical judge; fulmination or denunciation of censure. 5. Register, list. 6. Censorship. **Someter a la censura**, to censor. 7. *(Com. fin.)* **Cesura de cuentas**, auditing.

censurable [then-soo-rah'-blay], *a.* Censurable, reprehensible.

censurador [then-soo-rah-dor'], *m.* Censurer, fault-finder.

censurante [then-soo-rahn'-tay], *pa.* Censurer, censuring.

censurar [then-soo-rar'], *va.* 1. To review, to criticise, to judge. 2. To censure, to blame, to find fault with, to expose. 3. To accuse, to note, to reprehend. 4. To

record, to enter into a list or register. 5. To correct, to reprove.

censurista [thayn-soo-res'-tah], 1. *a.* Censorious. 2. *m. & f.* Critic, faultfinder.

centaura, centaurea [then-tah'-oo-rah], *f. (Bot.)* Centaury. **Centaurea mayor**, great centaury. **Centaurea menor**, common erythraea.

centauro [theen-tah'-oo-ro], *m.* 1. Centaur. 2. *(Astr.)* Centaur, a southern constellation.

centavo [then-tah´-vo], *m.* The hundredth part of something; a cent, as the hundredth of a dollar.

centella [then-tayl'-lyah], *f.* 1. Lightning. 2. Flash of a flint struck with steel; flake of fire. 3. Remaining spark of passion or discord. **Ser vivo como una centella** or **ser una centella**, to be all life and spirit.

centellante [then-tel-lyahn'-tay], *pa.* Sparkling, flashing.

centellar, centellear [then-tel-lyar´, then-tel-lyay-ar'], *vn.* To sparkle, to throw out sparks.

centelleante [thayn-tayl-lyay-ahn'-tay], *a.* 1. Sparkling, gleaming, glinting *(Aer.)(fig.)* Sparkling.

centelleo [then-tel-lyay´-o], *m.* Sparkle, scintillation, glinting, flashing.

centellón [then-tel-lyone'], *m. aug.* A large spark or flash.

centena [then-tay'-nah], *f.* 1. Hundred. 2. Centenary, the number of a hundred. 3. Stubble of rye.

centenadas [then-tay-nah´-das] *adv.* **A centenadas** or **a centenares**, by hundreds.

centenal [then-tay-nahl'], *m.* 1. Field sown with rye. 2. Centenary, the number of a hundred.

centenar [then-tay-nar'], *m.* 1. A hundred. 2. Field sown with rye. *V.* CENTENARIO.

centenario, ria [then-tay-nah´-re-o, ah], *a.* 1. Centenary, secular, happening but once in a century. 2. *m.* Centennial, feast celebrated every hundred years.

centenazo, za [then-tay-nah'-tho, thah], *a.* Belonging to rye. **Paja centenaza**, rye-straw.

centeno [then-tay'-no], *m. (Bot.)* Common rye.

centeno, na [then-tay´-no, nah], *a.* A numeral adjective which signifies hundred.

centenoso, sa [then-tay-no'-so, sah], *a.* Mixed with rye.

centésimal [thayn-tay'-se-mahl], *a.* Centesimal.

centésimo, ma [then-tay'-se-mo, mah], *a.* Centesimal, hundredth.

centi [then-te]. A prefix from the Latin, signifying the one one-hundredth.

centiárea [then-te-ah'-ray-ah], *f.* Centiare, the one one-hundredth of an acre, square measure.

centígrado, da [then-tee'-grah-do, dah], *a.* Centigrade, a scale divided into one hundred degrees.

centigramo [then-te-grah'-mo], *m.* Centigramme, 0.01 gramme, about one-sixth of a grain.

centilitro [then-te-lee´-tro], *m.* Centilitre.

centiloquio [then-te-lo´-ke-o], *m.* A work divided into a hundred parts or chapters.

centímano, na [then-tee'-mah-no, nah], *a. (Poet.)* Having a hundred hands.

centímetro [then-tee'-may-tro], *m.* Centimeter: 0.01 meter.

céntimo [then´-te-mo], *m.* Cent.

céntimo, ma [then´-te-mo, mah], *a.* The one-hundredth. **No tiene un céntimo**, he hasn´t got a penny. **No vale un céntimo**, it´s worthless.

centinela [then-te-nay'-lah], *com.* 1. *(Mil.)* Sentry or sentinel. 2. *(Met.)* One who pries into another's actions. **Centinela a caballo**, vedette, a sentinel on horseback. **Hacer centinela** or **estar de centinela**, to stand sentry, to be on guard.

centinodia [then-te-no'-de-ah], *f. (Bot.)* Knotgrass, persicaria.

centiplicado, da [then-te-ple-cah'-do, dah], *a.* Centuple, a hundred-fold.

centiplicar [then-te-ple-car'], *va. V.* CENTUPLICAR.

centollo, centolla [then-to'-lah, then-tol -lyah], *f.* Spider crab.

centón [then-tone´], *m.* 1. Crazy quilt. 2. Cento, a literary composition.

centrado; da [then-trah´-do, dah], *a.* Centered, balanced. **Una persona bien centrada,** a well balanced person.

central [then-trahl´], *f.* Main office (compañía telefónica). **Central telefónica,** telephone exchange, telephone office. **Central de correos,** main post office. **Central azucarera,** sugar mill. **Central nuclear,** nuclear power station. **Central de bombeo,** pumping station.

central, centrical [then-trahl', then-tre-cahl'], *a.* Central, centric.

centralidad [then-trah-le-dhad´], *f.* Centrality.

centralismo [thayn-trah-les'-mo], *m.* Centralism.

centralita [then-trah-lee'-tah], *f.* Telephone exchange.

centralización [then-trah-le-tha-the-on'], *f.* Centralization.

centralizar [then-trah-le-thar´], *va.* To centralize. *-vr.* To be centralized.

centralmente [then-tral-men'-tay], *adv.* Centrally.

centrar [thayn-trar'], *va.* 1. To center; to concentrate (esfuerzos). 2. To concentrate (fuego), *(fot.)* To focus on. *-vr.* **Centrarse en,** to center on, to be centered. 2. To settle in (en un empleo).

céntrico, ca [then'-tre-co, cah], *a.* Focal. **Punto céntrico,** object, end of one's views. *V.* CENTRO. **Es muy céntrico,** it´s very central; it´s very convenient. **Un restaurante céntrico,** a restaurant in the center of town.

centrífugo, ga [then-tree'-foo-go, gah], *a.* Centrifugal.

centrifugar [thayn-tre-foo-gar'], *va.* To centrifuge; to spin (colada).

centrífugo [thayn-tre'-foo-go], *a.* Centrifugal.

centrípeto, ta [thayn-tree'-pay-to, tah], *a.* Centripetal.

centro [then'-tro], *m.* 1. Center (medio), middle, root, origin. **El centro del círculo,** the center of the circle. **El centro de la ciudad,** the city center. 2 Height and depth of a thing. 3 *(Met.)* The principal object of desire and exertion 4. *(Bot.)* Disk of flowers. 5. A short dress of flannel which Indian women and half-breeds use in Ecuador. **Estar en el centro de la batalla,** to be in the center of the action. **El mando es el centro a que aspira la ambición,** command is the point to which ambition aspires. **Centro de salud,** health center. **Centro social,** community center. **Centro de gravedad,** center of gravity. **Centro docente,** teaching institution. 6. *(Dep.)* Center. **Centro del campo,** midfield. **Delantero centro,** center-forward. **Medio centro,** half-back.

Centroamérica [then-tro-ah-may´-re-cah], *f.* Central America.

centroamericano, na [tehn-tro-ah-may-re-cah'-no], *a. m. & f.* Central American.

centro comercial [then'-tro-co-mer-the-ahl'], *m.* Shopping center.

centrocampista [then-tro-cahm-pes'-tah], *m. & f. (Dep.)* Midfield player.

centrocampo [then-tro-cahm-po], *m. (Dep.)* Midfield.

Centroeuropa [then-tro-e-oo-ro'-pah], *f.* Central Europe.

centuplicar [then-too-ple-car'], *va.* To centuplicate, increase enormously.

céntuplo, pla [then'-too-plo, plah], *a.* Centuple, hundredfold.

centuria [tehn-too´-re-ah], *f.* 1. Century. 2. Among the Romans, one hundred soldiers, commanded by a centurion.

centurión [then-too-re-on'], *m.* Centurion.

centurionazgo [then-too-re-o-nath'-go], *m.* The office of a centurion.

cenutrio [the-noo'-trio] *m* Twit twerp

cenzalino, na [then-tha-lee'-no, nah], *a.* Pertaining to a *cénzalo.*

cénzalo [then'-tha-lo], *m.* Mosquito.

ceñido, da [thay-nyee´-do, dah], *a.* 1. Moderate in pleasure or expense. **Ceñido al tema,** keeping close to the point. **Ceñido y corto,** brief and to the point. 2. Ringed (abejas, insectos). 3. Tight, close-fitting, clinging. *-pp.* of CENIR.

ceñidor [thay-nye-dor'], *m.* Belt, girdle, girdle-belt, sash.

ceñidura [thay-nye-doo'-rah], *f.* The act of girding.

ceñir [thay-nycer'], *va.* 1. To gird, to surround, to circle, to girdle. **La muralla ciñe la ciudad,** the wall surrounds the

city. 2. To environ, to hem in. 3. *(Met.)* To reduce, to abbreviate, to contract. 4. To fasten round one´s waist. **Ceñir espada,** to wear a sword. **El vestido ciñe bien el cuerpo,** the dress fits well. 5. *(fig.)* To shorten, to cut down. *-vr.* 1. To reduce one's expenses, to tighten one´s belt. **Ceñirse a un tema,** to limit oneself to a subject. 2. To put something on. **Ceñirse la corona,** to take the crown.

ceño [thay'-nyo], *m.* 1. Frown, a supercilious look. **Arrugar el ceño,** to frown. **Mirar con ceño,** to frown, to scowl at. 2. Ring or ferrule. 3. *(Vet.)* Circle round the upper part of a horse's hoof. 4. *(Poet.)* A gloomy aspect, as of the sea, clouds, etc.

ceñoso, sa [thay-nyo-so, sah], *a.* 1. Hoof surrounded with rings. 2. *V.* CEÑUDO.

ceñudo, da [thay-nyoo'-do, dah], *a.* Frowning, supercilious; grim; gruff, sour of aspect.

cepa [thay´-pah], *f.* 1. The stump of a tree. 2. Stock of a vine 3. *(Met.)* Stock or origin of a family. **De buena cepa,** of good stock. 4. *(Met.)* Bud or root of the horns and tails of animals. 5. Root of the wool. 6. Foundation of columns, pilasters, or arches. 7. *(Mex.)* Pit, trench (hoyo).

cepeda [thay-pay´-dah], or **cepedera** [thay-pay-day'-rah], *f.* A spot where heath abounds.

cepejón [thay-pay-hone'], *m.* The largest part of a branch torn from the trunk.

cepillado [they-peel-lyah'-do], *m.* Brush. **Se elimina con un suave ceñido,** it goes away with a gentle brush.

cepilladuras [thay-peel-lyah-doo´-ras], *f. pl.* Shavings.

cepillar [thay-peel-lyar´], *va.* 1. To brush (trajes); to plane (carpintería). 2. To plane. *V.* ACEPILLAR. 3. To rip off (robar). 4. To win (ganar). 5. To bump off (matar). 6. To spank (pegar azotes). *-vr.* 1. **Cepillarse a uno,** to bump somebody off. 2. **Cepillarse algo,** to rip something off. 3. **Cepillarse a una,** to screw somebody.

cepillo [thay-peel'-lyo], *m.* 1. Plane, carpenter's tool. 2. Brush for clothes. 3. Poor-box; corban. **Cepillo de dientes,** toothbrush, **cepillo para las uñas,** nailbrush. **Cepillo para el suelo,** scrubbing brush. 4. *(Tec.)* Plane. 5. *(LAm.)* Flatterer, creep (adulador).

cepillón [thay-peel-lyone'], *a.* Soapy. *-m.* cepillona *f.* Creep.

cepita [thay-pee'-tah], *f. dim.* A small stock of a vine.

cepo [thay'-po], *m.* 1. Block on which an anvil is put. 2. Stocks, for punishment; on board of ships they are called *bilboes.* 3. Reel on which silk is wound. 4. Trap for wolves or other animals. 5. Charity, box in churches and public places. 6. *V.* CEFO. 7. The stocks with which a gun is made fast in the carriage. 8. Clamp, joining-press; horse (herreros). **Cepo del ancla,** *(Naut.)* anchor-stock. **Cepo de molinete,** *(Naut.)* Knight head of the windlass. **Cepos,** notched cleats or timbers fixed across other timbers to strengthen or secure them where they are pierced; anchor-stocks.

cepón [thay-pone'], *m. aug.* The large trunk of a tree or vine-stock.

ceporro [thay-por'-ro], *m.* 1. An old vine pulled up by the roots. 2. Twit (idiota).

cequiaje [thay-ke-ah'-hay], *m.* Annual contribution paid for irrigation rights by the towns of a community.

cequión [they-ke-one'], *m. (Cono Sur)* Large irrigation channel.

cera [thay'-rah], *f.* 1. Candle (vela), wax. 2. Tapers and candles of wax. **Cera virgen,** virgin wax. **Cera de dorar,** gold-size. **Cera de los oídos,** ear-wax. **Ceras,** the cells of wax and honey formed by bees. **Cera para suelos,** floor polish.

ceráceo, ea [thay-rah'-thay-o, ah], *a.* Of the consistency of wax.

ceración [thay-rah-the-on'], *f.* Ceration, preparation of a metal for fusion.

cerachates [thay-rah-chah'-tes], *f. pl.* Wax-stones, a yellow agate.

cerafolio [thay-rah-f'-le-o], *m. (Bot.)* Common chervil. *V.* PERIFOLLO.

cerámica [thay-rah'-me-cah], *f.* The ceramic art; ceramics, art of making pottery.

cerámico, ca [thay-rah'-me-co, cah], *a.* Ceramic, relating to pottery.

ceramista [they-rah-mes'-tah], *m. & f.* Potter.

cerapez [thay-rah-peth'], *f.* Cerate, a plaster of wax and pitch.

cerasina [thay-rah-see'-nah], *f.* Cerasin, the insoluble part of cherry, peach, and similar gums.

cerasta, *f.* **ceraste, cerastes,** *m.* [thay-rahs'-tah, thay-rahs'-tay, thay-rahs'-tes]. Horned serpent.

cerato [thay-rah'-to], *m. (Pharm.)* Cerate.

ceratófilo, ceratófilon [thay-rah-to'-fe-lo, thay-rah-to'-fe-lone], *m. (Bot.)* Hornwort, or pondweed.

ceraunia, or **ceraunita** [thay-rah'-oo-ne-ah, thay-rah-oo-nee'-tah], *f.* Ancient name of jasper or flint, oriental jade.

cerbatana [ther-bah-tah'-nah], *f.* 1 Blowpipe, popgun, pea-shooter, acoustic trumpet for the deaf. 3. Ancient culverin of small calibre.

cerca [therr'-cah], *f.* 1. Inclosure, hedge, or wall which surrounds a garden, park, or corn-field; fence. 2. Yard. *-m. pl.* **Los cercas**, among painters, objects in the foreground of a painting.

cerca [therr'-cah], *adv.* Near, at hand, not far off, close by, preceding the noun or pronoun to which it refers, it demands the preposition *de*. **Estar cerca de**, to be near. 1. **Aquí cerca, cerca de aquí**, just by. 2. **Cerca de**, close, near. **Hay cerca de 8 toneladas**, there are about 8 tons. 3. **Tocar de cerca**, 1. *(Met.)* To be nearly allied to, or near akin. 2. To be concerned in, to be interested.

cercado [ther-cah'-do], *m.* 1. A garden or field enclosed with a fence (valla); an enclosure (terreno cercado), a lock, a close or small enclosed field.

cercado, da, *pp.* of. CERCAR. 2. *(And.)* Communal lands. 3. *(And.) (Hist.)* State capital and surrounding towns.

cercador [ther-cah-dor'], *m.* 1. Hedger, one who encloses. 2. An iron graver marking-iron.

cercadura [ther-cah-doo'-rah], *f.* Enclosure, wall, fence.

cercamiento [ther-cah-me-en'-to], *m.* Act of enclosing.

cercanamente [ther-cah-nah-men'-tay], *adv.* Nearby, close by (a poca distancia); nearly.

cercanía [ther-ca-nee'-ah], *f.* 1. Proximity, neighborhood, vicinity, closeness. 2. **Cercanías**, outskirts, outer suburbs. **Tren de cercanías**, suburban train.

cercano, na [ther-cah'-no, nah], *a.* Near, close by, neighboring, adjoining.

Cercano Oriente, Near East.

cercar [ther-car'], *va.* 1. To inclose, to environ, to hem, to circle, to compass, to gird, to wall in (rodear con una cerca). 2. To fence, to secure by an inclosure; to surround with a hedge or wall, to pale. 3. *(Mil.)* To siege a town, to block up a fortress. 4. To crowd about a person. 5. To bring or put near. **Cercado de desdichas y trabajos**, involved in troubles and distress.

cercén [ther-then'], *adv.* **A cercén**, at the root. **Cercén a cercén**, from end to end, completely. **Cortar un brazo a cercén**, to cut an arm off completely.

cercenadamente [ther-thay-nah-dah-men'-tay], *adv.* In a clipping manner, with retrenchment.

cercenadera [ther-thay-nah-day'-rah], *f.* Clipping-knife used by wax-chandlers.

cercenador [ther-thay-nah-dor'], *m.* Clipper.

cercenadura [ther-thay-nah-doo'-rah], *f.* Clipping, retrenchment. *-pl.* Cuttings.

cercenar [ther-thay-nar'], *ra.* 1. To pare, to retrench, to clip. 2. To lop off the ends or extremities. 3. To lessen (gastos). 4. To curtail, to cut away; to abridge.

cercera [ther-thay'-rah], *f.* Air-tube of a vault to extract the foul air.

cerceta [ther-thay'-tah], *f.* 1. *(Orn.)* Widgeon, garganey, a species of duck. 2. Among sportsmen, the first pearl which grows about the bur of a deer's horn: an antler.

cercillo [ther-theel'-lyo], *m.* 1. Earring. *V.* ZARCILLO. 2. Tendril of a vine. *V.* TIJERETA. 3. Hoop.

cercio, cerción [therr'-the-o, ther-the-on'], *m.* An Indian mocking-bird.

cerciorar [ther-the-o-rar'], *va.* To assure, to ascertain, to affirm.

cerco [therr'-co], *m.* 1. Hoop or ring. 2. *(Mil.)* Blockade of a place. 3. Circular motion. 4. Circle, a private assembly. 5. Frame or case of a door or window. **En cerco**, round about. **Poner cerco a una plaza**, to block up a place. **Levantar el cerco**, to raise a blockade. **Echar cerco**, to surround game with dogs. **Cerco de puerta o ventana**, the frame of a door or window. **Hacer un cerco**, to strike a circle.

cercón [thayr-kone'], *adv. (LAm.)* Rather close.

cercopiteco [ther-co-pe-tay'-co], *m.* Cercopithecus, a kind of long-tailed monkey.

cercha [therr'-chah], *f.* A wooden rule for measuring convex or concave objects.

cerchar [ther-char'], *va. V.* ACODAR.

cerchón [ther-chone'], *m. V.* CIMBRIA.

cerda [therr'-dah], *f.* 1. Strong hair in a horse's tail or mane; a bristle. 2. *(Prov.)* Corn just cut and formed into sheaves. 3. *(Prov.)* Bundle of flax broken but not yet hackled. 4. Sow. **Cerda de puerco**, hog's bristle. 5. Slut, whore.

cerdada [thayr-dah'-dah], *f.* Dirty trick; nasty thing.

cerdamen [ther-dah'-men], *m.* Handful of bristles.

cerdana [ther-dah'-nah], *f.* Kind of dance in Catalonia.

cerdazo [ther-dah'-tho], *m.* 1. *(aug.)* A large hog or pig. 2. Hair sieve. *V.* CEDAZO.

cerdear [ther-day-ar'], *vn.* 1. To be weak in the forequarter (animales). 2. To emit a harsh and inharmonious sound (instrumentos de cuerda). 3. To decline a request or demand by subterfuges and evasions. 4. *(Mus.)* To scratch, to rasp, to grate; *(Mech.)* To work badly. 2. To hedge, to jib, to hold back. 3. To play a dirty trick.

Cerdeña [ther-day'-nyah], *f.* Sardinia.

cerdillo [ther-deel'-lyo], *m. dim.* A small hog or pig.

cerdito, ta [ther-dee'-to], *f. & m.* Piglet.

cerdo [therr'-do], *m.* 1. Hog or pig. **Cerdo salvaje**, wild pig. 2. **Cerdo marino**, porpoise. 3. *(Culin.)* Pork. 4. *(fig.)* Dirty person, slovenly fellow. *-a.* 1. Dirty, filthy. 2. Rotten.

cerdoso [ther-do'-so], *m.* Bristly.

cereal [thay-ray-ahl'], *a.* Cereal, relating to the food-producing grasses. *-m. pl.* Cereals.

cerebelo [thay-ray-bay'-lo], *m. (Anat.)* Cerebellum, the hindbrain.

cerebral [thay-ray-brahl'], *a.* Cerebral, brain; calculating.

cerebro [thay-ray'-bro], *m.* 1. Cerebrum, the front brain. 2. The entire brain. 3. Intelligence. **Cerebro electrónico**, electronic brain. **Estrujar el cerebro**, to rack one's brains.

cerecilla [thay-ray-theel'-lyah], *f. dim. V.* GUINDILLA.

cerecita [chay-ray-thee'-tah], *f. dim.* A small cherry.

ceremonia [thay-ray-mo'-ne-ah], *f.* 1. Ceremony, outward rite, external form of religion. 2. Ceremony, formality, forms of civility. 3. Ceremony, outward form of state. 4. Course, empty form, an affected compliment paid to a person. **Lo hace de pura ceremonia**, he does it out of mere ceremony. **De ceremonia**, with all ceremony or pomp. **Reunirse de ceremonia**, formal meeting, ceremonial meeting.

ceremonial [thay-ray-mo-ne-ahl'], *m.* A book of ceremonies for public occasions.

ceremonial [thay-ray-mo-ne-ahl'], *a.* Ceremonial, ceremonious.

ceremonialmente [thay-ray-mo-ne-all-men'-tay], *adv. V.* CEREMONIOSAMENTE.

ceremoniáticamente [thay-ray-mo-ne-ah'-te-cah-men-tay], *adv.* Ceremoniously.

ceremoniático, ca [thay-ray-mo-ne-ah'-te-co, cah], *a.* Ceremonious.

ceremoniosamente [thay-ray-mo-ne-o-sah-men'-tay], *adv.* Ceremoniously; formally; stiffly; with an excess of politeness.

ceremonioso, sa [thay-ray-mo-ne-o'-so, sah], *a.* Ceremonious, polite, formal, complimental.

céreo [thay'-ray-o], *m.* *(Bot.)* Torchthistle. *-a.* Wax, waxen.

cereolita [thay-ray-o-lee'-tah], *f.* A soft, waxy-looking lava.

cerería [thay-ray-ree'-ah], *f.* 1. Wax-chandler's shop.

cerero [thay-ray'-ro], *m.* 1. Waxchandler. 2. *(Prov.)* An idle person, a vagrant.

cereza [thay-ray'-thah], *f.* Cherry. **Cereza silvestre,** wild cherry.

cerezal [thay-ray-thahl'], *m.* Plantation of cherry-trees; cherry orchard.

cerezo [thay-ray'-tho], *m.* *(Bot.)* Cherry-tree, cherry-wood.

ceribón, ceribones [thay-re-bone', bo'-ness], *m.* A kind of an insolvent debtor surrendering his estate to his creditors. **Hacer ceribones,** To make submissive and affected compliments.

cérico, ca [thay'-re-co, cah], *a.* Ceric, relating to cerium.

ceriflor [thay-re-flor'], *f.* *(Bot.)* Honey-wort, honey-flower Cerinthe. *V.* CERINTO.

cerilla [thay-reel'-lyah], *f.* 1. Thin wax tapers rolled up in different forms. 2. Ball of wax and other ingredients used formerly by women as a kind of paint. 3. Wax-tablet. 4. Wax of the ear. 6. A wax-match.

cerillo [thay-reel'-lyo], *m.* *(Mex.)* Match.

cerina [thay-ree'-nah], *f.* A variety of wax (or waxlike material) extracted from the cork-tree.

cerinto [thay-reen'-to], *m.* *(Bot.)* Wax-flower, honey-wort, a plant of the borage family.

cerio, cererio [thay'-re-o, thay-ray'-re-o], *m.* *(Chem.)* Cerium or cererium Cerio, an annual solanaceous plant of Cochin China.

cerita [thay-ree'-tah], *f.* Cerite, a resinous brown silicate of cerium found in copper mines.

cermeña [ther-may'-nyah], *f.* A small early pear called the muscadine.

cermeño [ther-may'-nyo], *m.* *(Bot.)* Muscadine pear-tree.

cernada [ther-nah'-dah], *f.* 1. Coarse ashes which remain in the strainer after the lye is put on. 2. Size laid on canvas to prepare it for painting. 3. Plaster of ashes and other ingredients used by farriers in the cure of horses.

cernadero [ther-nah-day'-ro], *m.* 1. Coarse linen which serves as a strainer for the lye to buck clothes with 2. Thread and silk skeins for making ribbon. 3. Apron worn sifting flour. 4. Place for sifting flour.

cernedor [ther-nay-dor'], *m.* Sieve.

cerneja [ther-nay'-hah], *f.* Fetlock of a horse growing behind the pastern joints.

cernejudo, da [ther-nay-hoo'-do, dah], *a.* Having large fetlocks.

cerner [ther-nerr'], *va.* 1. To sift, to bolt. 2. *(fig.)* To scan, to watch. *-vn.* 1. To bud and blossom. 2. To drizzle, to fall in small drops. *-vr.* 1. To waggle, to wiggle, to move from side to side. 2. To soar (pájaros). 3. To hover (subir); to circle (helicóptero); to hang over.

cernícalo [ther-nee'-cah-lo], *m.* 1. *(Orn.)* Kestrel, sparrowhawk, windhover. 2. A person of scanty abilities. **Coger or pillar un cernícalo,** to be fuddled, to be tight, to be drunk.

cernidillo [ther-ne-deel'-lyo], *m.* 1. Thick mist or small rain; mizzle, drizzle. 2. A short and waddling gait.

cernido [ther-nee'-do], *m.* 1. Sifting. 2. The flour sifted. **Cernido, da,** *pp.* of CERNER.

cernidor [ther-nee-dor'], *m.* Sieve.

cernidura [ther-nee-doo'-rah], *f.* Sifting.

cernir [ther-neer'], *va.* 1. *V.* CERNER. 2. To examine, to purify.

cero [thay'-ro], *m.* 1. Zero, cipher, an arithmetical symbol, nothing, nought. **Ser un cero,** to be a mere cipher. **Por 3 goles a cero,** by three goals to nill. **Estamos a 40 a 0,** the game stands at 40-love. **Yo en eso estoy cero,** I'm not good at that. **Tendremos que partir nuevamente de cero,** *(fig.)* we shall have to start from scratch again. 2. Police car.

ceroferario [thay-ro-fay-rah'-re-o], *m.* The acolyte who carries the *cirial* or large candle-stick.

cerografía [thay-ro-grah-fee'-ah], *f.* Cerography, the art or process of engraving or writing on wax.

cerollo, lla [thay-rol'-lyo, lyah], *a.* Reaped when green and soft (grano).

cerón [thay-rone'], *m.* Dregs of pressed wax formed into a cake.

ceroso [thay-ro'-so], *a.* Waxen, waxy, waxlike.

cerote [thay-ro'-tay], *m.* 1. Shoemaker's wax, shoeblacking. 2. *(Coll.)* Panic, fear. 3. Cerate, a plaster. 4. *(CAm. Mex.)* Piece of human excrement, stool. **Estar hecho un cerote,** to be covered in dirt.

cerotear [thay-ro-tay-ar'], *va.* To wax (hilo).

ceroto [thay-ro'-to], *m.* A soft cerate of oil and wax.

ceroya [thay-ro'-yah], *f.* Crops of corn which begin to grow yellow.

cerquillo [ther-keel'-lyo], *m.* 1. *(dim.)* A small circle or hoop. 2. The seam or welt of a shoe. 3. The ring of hair or tonsure on the head; fringe (fleco).

cerquita [ther-kee'-tah], *f.* *dim.* Small inclosure.

cerquita [ther-kee'-tah], *adv.* At a small distance, nigh or near in point of time or place. **Aquí cerquita,** just by.

cerrada [ther-rah'-dah], *f.* 1. The strongest part of a hide or skin which covers the backbone of an animal. 2. *(Obs.)* Shutting or locking up of a thing. **Hacer cerrada,** to commit a gross fault or palpable mistake.

cerradero [ther-rah-day'-ro], *m.* 1. Staple which receives the bolt of a lock. 2. Any hole made to receive the bolt of a lock. 3. *(Obs.)* Purse-strings.

cerradero, ra [ther-rah-day'-ro, rah], *m.* & *f.* & *a.* Applied to the place locked, and to the thing with which it is locked, locking, fastening. **Echar la cerradera,** to lend a deaf ear, to refuse. **Caja cerradera,** box that can be locked.

cerradizo, za [ther-rah-dee'-tho, thah], *a.* That which may be locked or fastened.

cerrado [ther-rah'-do], *m.* *V.* CERCADO.

cerrado, da [ther-rah'-do, dah], *a.* 1. Close, reserved, dissembling. 2. Secret, concealed. 3. Obstinate, inflexible. **A ojos cerrados,** without examination. **A puerta cerrada,** privately, secretly. **Cerrado por obras,** closed for repair. **Aquí huele a cerrado,** it smells stuffy in here. 4. Obscure, incomprehensible. 5. Sharp, tight (curva). 6. Thick, full. 7. Reserved, quiet, uncommunicative; secretive. **Cerrado de mollera,** dense, dim (poco inteligente). 8. Typical, all-too-typical. 9. With a broad accent, marked, strong (persona); **habló con cerrado acento,** he spoke with a strong accent. *-pp.* of CERRAR.

cerrador [ther-rah-dor'] *m.* 1. Shutter, one that shuts. 2. Porter or doorkeeper. 3. Tie, fastening. 4. Bond, obligation.

cerradura [ther-rah-doo'-rah], *f.* 1. Closure, the act of shutting or locking up. 2. Lock. **Cerradura de golpe** or **de muelle,** springlock. **Cerradura de combinación,** combination lock. **Cerradura de seguridad,** safety lock. 3. Park or piece of ground surrounded with an inclosure.

cerradurilla, ita [ther-rah-doo-reel'-lyah, ee'-tah], *f. dim.* A small lock.

cerraja [ther-rah'-hah], *f.* 1. Lock of a door. 2. *(Bot.)* Common sow thistle. **Todo es agua de cerrajas,** it is all good for nothing, or it is nothing but empty words.

cerrajear [ther-rah-hay-ar'], *vn.* To carry on the trade of a locksmith.

cerrajería [ther-rah-hay-ree'-ah], *f.* 1. Trade of a locksmith. 2. Locksmith's shop or forge.

cerrajero [ther-rah-hay'-ro], *m.* Locksmith.

cerramiento [ther-rah-me-en-to], *m.* 1. Closure, occlusion, the act of shutting or locking up. 2. Costiveness. 3. Inclosure. 4. The finishing of the roof of a building. 5. Partition walls of a house. 6. *(For.)* Conclusion of an argument; inference.

cerrar [ther-rar], *va.* & *vn.* 1. To close, to shut, to occlude, to foreclose, to shut up the inlets or outlets of a place, to obstruct a passage. 2. To fit a door or window in its frame or case. 3. To lock, to fasten with a bolt or latch. 4. To include, to contain. 5. To fence or inclose a piece of ground. 6. *(Met.)*

gal

ate or finish a thing. 7. To stop up, to obstruct. 8. mbit, to forbid, to interdict. 9. To engage the enemy. rar la carta, to fold a letter. Cerrar algo con llave, to ck something. Han cerrado la frontera, they've closed the border. 10. To turn off (grifo, agua, gas). 11. To bring up the rear. Cerrar la marcha, to come last, to bring up the rear. La carretera está cerrada por la nieve, the road is blocked by snow. Cerrar la cuenta, to close an account. Cerrar la boca, (Met.) to be silent. Cerrar la mollera, (Met.) to begin to get sense. Cerrar la puerta, (Met.) to give a flat denial. Cerrar a alguno la puerta para que no entre, to lock one out, to shut out. Cerrar los ojos, 1. To die. 2. To sleep. 3. (Met.) Blindly, to submit to another's opinion. Al cerrar del día, at the close of day, at nightfall. -vn. Esta puerta cierra bien, this door closes tightly. Cerramos a las 9, we close at 9. Dejar una puerta sin cerrar, to leave a door open. -vr. 1. To remain firm in one's opinion. 2. To be shut or locked up. 3. To grow cloudy and overcast. 4. To close up (tropas). Cerrarse todas las puertas, to be completely destitute.

cerraurgal [ther-rah-oor-gahl], m. Water conduit.

cerrazón [ther-rah-thone´], f. 1. Fog preceding a storm. 2. Ignorant stubbornness, intolerance, etc.

cerrejón [ther-ray-hone'], m. Hillock.

cerrero, ra [ther-ray'-ro, rah], a. 1. Running wild. Caballo cerrero, an unbroken horse. 2. Haughty, lofty. 3. (And. Carib.) Unsweetened; bitter; ordinary; simple.

cerreta [ther-ray'-tah], f. (Naut.) Spar, rough tree. V. PERCHA.

cerril [ther-reel'], a. 1. Mountainous, rough, uneven (terreno). 2. Wild, untamed (ganado). Puente cerril, a small narrow bridge for cattle. 3. (Met.) Rude, unpolished, unmannerly.

cerrilismo [thayr-re-les'-mo], m. Roughness, uncouthness; obstinacy; small-mindedness.

cerrilla [ther-reel'-lyah], f. A die for milling coins.

cerrillar [ther-reel'-lyr], va. To mill coined metal, or to mark it at the edge.

cerrillo [ther-reel'-lyo], m. dim. A little eminence. Cerrillos, the dies for milling coined metal.

cerrión [ther-re-on'], m. 1. Icicle. 2. Fresh cheese.

cerro [therr'-ro], m. 1. Hill or high land. 2. Neck of an animal. 3. Backbone, or the ridge it forms. 4. Flax or hemp which is hackled and cleaned. 5. Lot, heap. Un cerro de, a heap of. Cerro enriscado, a steep and inaccessible mountain. En cerro, nakedly, barely. Como por los cerros de Úbeda, (Coll.) his mind is far away.

cerrojazo [thayr-ro-hah'-tho], m. Slamming. Dar cerrojazo, to slam the bolt; to end unexpectedly; to close unexpectedly. Dar cerrojazo a uno, to slam the door in somebody´s face.

cerrojillo [ther-ro-heel'-lyo], m. 1. (Orn.) A wagtail warbler. 2. (dim.) A small bolt.

cerrojo [ther-ro'-ho], m. Bolt, latch. Táctica de cerrojo, defensive play, negative play. Echar el cerrojo, to bolt the door.

cerrotino [ther-ro-tee'-no], m. Carded hemp.

cerruma [ther-roo'-mah], f. Weak or defective quarter in horses.

certamen [ther-tah'-men], m. 1. Duel; battle. 2. Literary controversy, disputation; competition. Certamen de belleza, beauty contest.

certeramente [ther-tay-rah-men-tay], adv. Accurately, unerringly.

certero, ra [ther-tay'-ro, rah], m. & f. 1. Sharpshooter. -a. 2. An excellent shot, well-aimed. 3. Accurate, sure, certain. 4. Well-informed.

certeza [ther-tay'-thah], f. Certainty, certitude. Tener la certeza de que..., to know for certain that..

certidumbre [ther-te-doom'-bray], f. 1. V. CERTEZA. 2. Security, obligation to fulfil a thing.

certificación [ther-te-fe-cah-the-on´], f. 1. Certificate, attesting the truth of a fact or event. 2. Return of a writ. 3. Certainty, security.

certificado [ther-te-fe-cah'-do], m. Certificate. Certificado de actitud, testimonial. Certificado de ciudadanía, naturalization papers. Certificado médico, medical certificate. Certificado de vacuna, vaccination certificate. V. CERTIFICACIÓN. -Certificado, da, pp. of CERTIFICAR.

certificador, ra [ther-te-fe-cah-dor', rah], m. & f. Certifier.

certificar [ther-te-fe-car'], va. 1. To assure, to affirm, to certify. Certificar la carta, in the post-office, to assure that a letter will reach its destination; to register a letter. 2. To prove by a public instrument.

certificativo, va, or certificatorio, ria [ther-te-fe-cah-tee´-vo, vah, ther-te-fe cah-to'-re-o, ah], a. That which certifies or serves to certify.

certísimo [ther-tee'-se-mo], a. sup. of CIERTO; most certain.

certitud [ther-tee-tood'], f. Certainty, certitude.

cerúleo, lea [thay-roo'-lay-o, ah], a. Cerulean, skyblue.

cerumen [thay-roo'-men], m. Earwax, cerumen.

ceruminoso, sa [thay-roo-me-no'-so, sah], a. Ceruminous, producing cerumen.

cerusa [thay-roo´-sah], f. Ceruse, whitelead.

cerval [ther-vahl'], a. Belonging to a deer. Miedo cerval, great fear.

cervantesco, ca [ther-van-tes'-co, cah], Cervántico [thervahn'-te-co], a. In the style of Cervantes.

cervantino [thayr-van-tee'-no], a. Cervantine; relating to Cervantes. Estilo cervantino, Cervantine style. Estudios cervantinos, Cervantes studies.

cervantista [ther-van-tees'-tah], a. Admiring Cervantes, specialist in Cervantes

cervático, illo [ther-vah-tee'-co, eel'-lyo], m. dim. A small deer.

cervato [ther-vah´-to], m. A fawn.

cervecería [ther-vay-thay-ree'-ah], f. 1. Brewery. 2. Alehouse.

cervecero [ther-vay-thay'-ro], m. 1. Brewer. 2. Beer-seller. a. La industria cervezera, the brewing industry.

cerveda [ther-vay'-dah], f. Extremity of the ribs of pork.

cerveza [ther-vay'-thah], f. Beer or ale, malt liquor. Cerveza de barril, draught beer, beer on draught. Cerveza de botella, bottled beer. Cerveza clara, light beer. Cerveza negra, brown beer. Cerveza de sifón, draught beer.

cervicabra [ther-ve-cah'-brah], f. Gazelle.

cervical [ther-ve-cahl'], a. (Anat.) Cervical.

cerviguido, da [ther-ve-goo'-do, dah], a. 1. High or thick-necked. 2. Obstinate, stubborn.

cerviguillo [ther-ve-geel'-lyo], m. Nape of the neck.

cervino, na [ther-vee'-no, nah], a. Resembling a deer.

cerviolas [ther-ve-oh'-las], f. pl. (Naut.) Catheads. V. SERVIOLAS.

cerviz [ther-veeth'], f. Cervix, nape of the neck. Ser de dura cerviz, to be incorrigible. Doblar or bajar la cerviz, (Met.) to humble oneself. Levantar la cerviz, (Met.) to be elated, to grow proud.

cervuno, na [ther-voo'-no, nah], a. 1. Resembling or belonging to a deer. 2. Of the color of a deer.

CES m. (Esp.) abr. de Consejo Económico y Social.

cesacio or Cesación a Divinis, [thay-sah'-the-o or thay-sa-the-on' ah de-vee'-nis], f. (Lat.) Suspension from religious functions.

cesación, f. cesamiento, m. [thay-sah-the-on', they-sah-me-en'-to]. Cessation, ceasing, pause.

cesante [thay-sahn'-tay], m. A public officer dismissed for economical or political reasons, but left in some cases with a portion of his salary until he obtains a new position; a retired official. -pa. Ceasing.

cesante [thay-sahn'-tay], a. Jobless, dismissed from a position.

cesantía [thay-san-tee'-ah], f. 1. The state of being a cesante, and the salary he receives. 2. Retirement pension, redundancy compensation.

cesar [thay-sar'], vn. 1. To cease, to give over, to forbear. 2. To leave or leave off, to desist. Cesar de hacer algo, to stop doing something. No cesa de hablar, she never stops talking.

Sin cesar, ceaselessly. -va. 1. To cease, to stop; to stop, to suspend. 2. To sack, to fire, to remove from office; **le cesaron en el trabajo,** they sacked him from his work.

César [thay'-sar], *m.* Caesar (emperador).

cesáreo, rea [thay-sah'-ray-o, ah], *a.* Imperial. **Operacion cesárea,** *(Surg.)* Cesarean operation.

cesariano, na [thay-sah-re-ah'-no, nah], *a.* Relating to Julius Caesar.

cesariense [thay-sah-re-en'-say], *a.* Pertaining to Caesar.

cese [thay'-say], *m.* 1. Cease: a mark put up against the names of persons who receive payment from the public treasury, that their pay should cease. **Dar el cese a uno,** to retire somebody. 2. Cessation; suspension, stoppage. **Cese de alarma,** all-clear signal. **Cese de fuego,** cease fire. **Cese de pagos,** suspension of payments.

cesible [thay-see'-blay], *a. (Law.)* That which may be ceded.

cesión [thay-se-on'], *f.* Cession, or tranfer of goods or estates made in one's favor; resignation, concession. **Cesión de bienes,** surrender of the estate of an insolvent debtor into the hands of his creditors.

cesionario, cesonario, ria [thay-se-onah'-re-o, thay-so-nah'-re-o, ah], *m. & f.* Cessionary, one in whose favor a tranfer is made, granted, assign.

cesionista [thay-se-o-nees'-tah], *m.* Transferer, assigner.

césped, céspede [thes´-ped, thes'-pay-day], *m.* 1. Lawn, grass. **Cortar el césped,** to mow the lawn. 2. Pitch (para juegos). Green (bochas), Sod, turf (trozo de tierra con hierba).

cespedera [thes-pay-day´-rah], *f.* Field where green sods are cut.

cesta [thes'-tah], *f.* Basket, pannier. **Cesta de la compra,** shopping basket. **Cesta de costura,** sewing basket. **Cesta para papeles,** wastepaper basket. **Llevar la cesta,** to go along as chaperon.

cestada [thes-tah'-dah], *f.* A basketful.

cestería [thes-tay-ree'-ah], *f.* Place where baskets are made or sold.

cestero, ra [thes-tay'-ro], *m. & f.* Basket maker or seller.

cestica, illa, ita [thes-tee'-cah, eel'-lyah, ee'tah], *f. dim.* A small basket, handbasket.

cestico, illo, ito [thestee'-co, eel' lyo, cc'-to], *m. dim.* A little basket.

cesto [thes'-to], *m.* A handbasket, hutch. **Estar hecho un cesto,** to be overcome by sleep or liquor. **Cesto de la colada,** clothes basket. **Cesto para papeles,** wastepaper basket.

cestón [thes-tone'], *m.* 1. A large pannier or basket. 2. *(Mil)* Gabion.-*pl.* Corbeils.

cestonada [thes-to-nah'-dah], *f.* Range of gabions.

cesura [thay-soo'-rah], *f.* Caesura, a figure or pause in poetry.

cetáceo, cea [thay-tah'-thay-o, ah], *a.* Cetaceous, of the whale kind.

cetárea, cetaría [ ], *f.* Shellfish farm.

cetís [thay-tees'], *m.* An old Galician coin.

cetorrino [thay-tor-re'-no], *m.* Basking shark.

cetre [thay'-tray], *m.* A small brass or copper bucket. *V.* ACETRE.

cetrería [thay-tray-ree'-ah], *f.* 1. Falconry. 2. Hawking; fowling with falcons.

cetrero [thay-tray'-ro], *m.* 1. Verger. 2. Falconer, sportsman.

cetrífero [thay-tree´-fay-ro], *m. (Poet.)* One who bears a sceptre.

cetrino, na [thay-tree'-no, nah], *a.* 1. Citrine, lemon-colored, greenish-yellow. 2. *(Met.)* Jaundiced, melancholy. 3. Belonging to citron,

cetro [thay'-tro], *m.* 1. Sceptre. 2. *(Met.)* Reign of a prince. **Empuñar el cetro,** to ascend the throne. 3. Verge carried by chaplains on solemn occasions. 4. Wand or staff borne by the deputies of confraternities.

chabacana [chah-bah-cah´-nah], *f.* An insipid kind of plum.

chabacanada [chah-bah-ca-nah´-dah], *f.* A very vulgar expression or observation.

chabacanamente [chah-bah-ca-na-nah-men´-tay], *adv.* In a bungling manner.

chabacanear [chah-bah-cah-nay-ar'], *vn. (LAm.)* To say coarse things.

chabacanería [chah-bah-ca-nay-ree'-ah], *f.* 1. Want of cleanliness and elegance. 2. Vulgarity, bad taste; commonness. 3. Coarse thing, vulgar remark.

chabacano, na [chah-bah-cah'-no, nah], *a.* Coarse, unpolished, ill-finished. -*m.* *(Mex.)* A kind of apricot.

chabán [chah-bahn'], *m.* A month corresponding to May among the ancient orientals.

chabeta [chah-bay'-tah], *f.* 1. Forelock key. 2. *(Coll.)* Judgment, reason. **Perder la chabeta,** *(Met.)* to lose one's senses, to run crazy. 3. *(Cuba)* A kind of knife used by cigar-makers.

chabola [chah-bo'-lah], *f.* Shack, shanty. **Chabolas** *(LAm.),* Shanty town.

chabolismo [cha-bo-les'mo], *m.* Shanty towns.

chabolista [cha-bo-les'-tah], *m. & f.* Shanty town dweller.

chabón [chah-bone'], *a.* Daft, stupid. -*f.* Twit.

chaborra [chah-bor'-rah], *f. (Coll. Prov.)* A young lass, fifteen to twenty years old.

chaborreta [chah-bor-ray'-tah], *f. dim. (Coll. Prov.)* A very young lass.

chaca [chah'-cah], *f.* **Estar en chaca,** *(Carib.)* to be flat broke.

chacal [chah-cahl´], *m.* Jackal.

chacalín, na [chah-cah-leen'], *m. f.* 1. *(CAm.)* Kid, child. 2. Shrimp (camarón).

chacanear [chah-cah-nay-ar'], *va.* 1. *(Cono Sur)* To spur violently. 2. *(Cono Sur)* To pester, to annoy. 3. *(And.)* To use daily.

chacaneo [chah-cah-nay'-o], *m.* **Para el chacaneo,** *(And.)* For daily use.

chácara [chah'-ca-rah], *f.* 1. *(S. Amer.)* A small plantation. *V.* CHACRA. 2. *(And. CAm. Cono Sur)* Sore, ulcer. 3. *(And. CAm. Carib.)* Large leather bag.

chacarería [chah-cah-ray-ree'-ah], *f.* 1. *(LAm.) (Agri.)* Market gardens, truck farms. 2. *(And. Cono Sur)* horticulture, market gardening, truck farming.

chacarero [chah-cah-ray'-ro], *m.* 1. *(LAm.)* Farmer, grower; market gardener, truck farmer. 2. *(Cono Sur)* Sandwich.

chacina [chah-thee'-nah], *f. (Prov.)* Pork seasoned with spice for sausages and balls.

chacinería [chah-thee-nay-ree'-ah], *f.* Pork butcher´s.

chacó [chah-co'], *m.* A high military cap, shako.

chacolí [chah-co-lee'], *m.* A light white wine made in the Basque Country.

chacolotear [chah-co-lo-tay-ar], *vn.* To clatter (caballos).

chacoloteo [chah-co-lo-tay'-o], *m.* The clapping of a loose horseshoe.

chaconá [cha-con-nah'], *m.* **chaconada** [cha-co-nah'-dah], *f.* Jaconet, a soft cotton cloth for summer dresses.

chacota [chah-co'-tah], *f.* Noisy mirth. **Echar a chacota alguna cosa,** to carry a thing off with a joke. **Hacer chacota de alguna cosa,** to turn a thing into ridicule.

chacotear [chah-co-tay-ar'], *vn.* To indulge in noisy mirth, to scoff, to have fun. -*vr.* **Chacotearse de algo,** to make fun of something.

chacotero, ra [chah-co-tay'-ro, rah], *a.* Waggish, ludicrous, acting the merry-andrew. *m.* fond of a laugh.

chacra [chah´-crah], *f. (Amer.)* An Indian rustic habitation, plantation, or farm.

chacuaco [chah-coo-ah'-co], *m.* 1. *(Mex.)* A small furnace for melting metals. 2. *(CAm.)* Roughly-made cigar. 3. *(Coll.)* Rustic, boorish, clownish.

chacual [chah-coo-ahl'], *m. (Mex.)* A gourd-cup.

chacha [chah'-chah], *f.* Familiar abbreviation of *muchacha,* maid, nurse maid. Girly." *V.* CHACHO.

chachacaste [chah-chah-cas´-tay], *m. (CAm.)* Liquor, brandy.

chachal [chah-chahl'], *m.* 1. *(Peru)* Graphite, plumbago. 2. *(CAm.)* Charm necklace.

chachalaca [chah-cha-lah'-cah], *f. (Mex.)* A grouse, a bird which cries continually while flying; *(Met.)* A chatterer.

chachar [chah-char'], *va. (And.)* To chew (coca).

cháchara [chah'-cha-rah], *f.* 1. *(Coll.)* Chitchat, idle talk, garrulity. **Todo eso no es más que cháchara,** that is all mere chitchat. 2. *(And.)* Joke. 3. *(Cono Sur. Mex.)* **Cháscharas,** things, bits and pieces.

chacharadas [chah-chah-rah'-das], *f. pl.* *(Cono Sur)* Useless ornaments; trinkets.

chacharear [chah-cha-ray-ar'], *vn.* *(Coll.)* To prate. *-va.* *(Mex.)* To deal in, to sell.

chacharera [chah-cha-ray'-rah], *f.* & *a.* Forward, talkative woman.

chacharería [chah-cha-ray-ree'-ah], *f.* *(Prov.)* Verbosity, verbiage, garrulity.

chacharero, chacharón [chah-chah-ray'-ro, chah-cha-rone'], *m.* & *: a.* 1. Prater, gabbler. 2. Chattering, garrulous. *-m.* Chatterbox (parlanchín). 3. *(Mex.)* Rag-and-bone man.

chache [chah'-chay], *m.* Oneself, me, the speaker. **El perjudicado es el chache,** I'll be the one to suffer.

chachi [chah'-che], *V.* CHANCHI.

chacho [chah'-cho], *m.* Boy, kid, lad (muchacho). Girl, lass (muchacha). **¡Ven aquí, chacho!,** come here, lad!

Chad [chad], *m.* Chad.

chafa [chah'-fah], *a.* *(Mex.)* Useless.

chafadura [chah-fah-doo'-rah], *f.* 1. Act of matting velvet. 2. Rumpling; soiling clothes.

chafaldetes [chah-fal-day'-tes], *m.* *(Naut.)* Clew lines.

chafaldita [chah-fa-dee'-tah], *f.* Joke, fun, repartee.

chafalla [chah-fahl'-lyah], *f.* *(Prov.)* A tattered suit of clothes.

chafallar [chah-fal-lyar'], *va.* To botch, to mend in a clumsy manner.

chafallo [chah-fahl'-lyo], *m.* Coarse patch, place mended in a botching and clumsy manner.

chafallón, na [chah-fal-lyone', nah], *m.* & *f.* A botcher.

chafalonía [chah-fa-lo-nee'-ah], *f.* 1. *(Amer. Peru)* Old plate, or broken articles of silver for remelting. 2. *(And.)* Worn-out gold jewellery.

chafalote [chah-fah-lo'-tay], *a.* *(Cono Sur)* common, vulgar. *-m.* *V.* CHAFAROTE. 3. *(LAm.)* Prick (pene).

chafar [chah-far'], *va.* 1. To make velvet or plush lose its lustre by pressing or crushing the pile. 2. To crease, to rumple, to soil clothing. 3. *(Met.)* To cut one short in his discourse. **Quedó chafado,** he was speechless. 4. To mess up, to make a hash of. **Le chafaron el negocio,** they messed up the deal for him. 5. *(Cono Sur)* To hoax, to deceive.

chafarote [chah-fa-ro'-tay], *m.* 1. A short, broad Turkish sword. 2. *(CAm.)* Cop.

chafarrinada [chah-far-re-nah'-dah], *f.* 1. Blot or stain in clothes or other things. 2. *(Met.)* Spot in reputation and character.

chafarrinar [chah-far-re-nar'], *va.* To blot, to stain.

chafarrinón [chah-far-re-none'], *m.* Blot, stain. **Echar un chafarrinón,** *(Met.)* To disgrace one's family by a mean or dishonorable action.

chafir(r)o [chah-fe'-ro], *m.* *(CAm. Mex.)* Knife.

chaflán [chah-flahn'], *m.* 1. Bevel, obtuse angle, chamfer. 2. Corner house. 3. *(Aut.)* Street corner.

chaflanar [chah-fla-nar'], *va.* To form a bevel, to cut a slope.

chagila [chah-hee'-lah], *f.* *(Amer.)* A slender reed which serves as a weapon among Indians of Ecuador.

chagra [chah'-grah], *m.* 1. Farm (chacra). 2. Peasant.

chagua [chah'-goo-ah], *f.* *(And.)* Gang; system of gang labor.

chaguar [chah-goo-ar'], *va.* *(Cono Sur)* To milk (vaca); to wring out (ropa).

chaguar [chah-goo-ar'], *m.* *(And.)* Agave fiber, hemp; rope of agave fiber.

chagüe [chah'-goo-ay], *m.* *(CAm.)* Swamp, bog.

chagüite [chah-goo-e'-tay], *vn.* *(CAm. Mex.)* Swamp; flooded field; banana plantation.

chagüitear [chah-goo-e-tay-ar'], *vn.* *(CAm. Mex.)* To chatter, to natter.

chai [chah'-e], *f.* Bird, dame.

chai(ne) [chah-e'-nay], *m.* *(And. CAm.)* Shoeshine.

chainear [chah-e-nay-ar'], *va.* *(CAm.)* To shine, to polish.

chair [chah-ear'], *m.* The inner side of a skin, among tanners.

chaira [chah'-e-rah], *f.* 1. A shoemaker's steel knife for sharpening. 2. Sharpener (para afilar).

chairar [chah-e-rahr'], *va.* *(Cono Sur)* To sharpen.

chal [chahl], *m.* Shawl. **Chal angosto,** long scarf.

chala [chah'-lah], *f.* 1. Leaf of corn, serving as fodder, chiefly while green. 2. *(And. Cono Sur)* money, dough. 3. *(Cono Sur)* sandal.

chalado, da [chah-lah'-do, dah], *a.* Dotty, round the bend; crazy, mad. **¡Estás chalado!,** you're mad! **Estar chalado por Jane, jazz,** to be crazy about Jane, jazz.

chaladura [chah-lah-doo'-rah], *f.* Crankiness.

chalán, na [chah-lahn', nah], *m.* & *f.* 1. Hawker, huckster. 2. Jockey, a dealer in horses.

chalana [chah-lah'-nah], *f.* A scow, lighter; square boat.

chalanear [chah-lah-nay-ar'], *va.*

chalaneo [chah-lah-nay-o], *m.* Hard bargaining, horse trading; trickery, deception.

chalanería [chah-lah-nay-ree'-ah], *f.* Artifice and cunning used by dealers in buying and selling.

chalaquear [chah-lah-kay-ar'], *(CAm.)* 1. *vn.* To chatter away, to rabbit on. 2. *va.* To trick, to con.

chalar [chah-lar'], *va.* To drive crazy, to drive round the bend. *-vr.* To go crazy, to go off one's rocker. **Chalarse por,** to be crazy about.

chalaza [chah-lah'-thah], *f.* 1. Chalaza, one of the ligaments uniting the yolk of an egg to the ends; treadle. 2. *(Med.)* Chalazion, a sebaceous tumor of the eyelid, resembling a stye.

chalcosina [chal-co-see'-nah], *f.* Modern name of copper pyrites; chalcopyrite.

chalchigüite, chalchihuite [chal-che-goo-ee'-tay], *m.* *(Amer.)* Stone of the color and fineness of the emerald. *(Mex.)* Jade.

chale [chah'-lay], *m.* & *f.* *(Mex.)* Chink.

chalé [chah-lay'], *m.* *V.* CHALET.

chaleco [chah-lay'-co], *m.* A waistcoat, vest. **Chaleco anti-balas,** bulletproof, vest. **Chaleco salvavidas,** life jacket.

chalecón [chah-lay-cone'], 1. *a.* *(Mex.)* Tricky, deceitful. 2. *m.* Conman.

chalequear [chah-lay-kay-ar'], *va.* *(Cono Sur. Mex.)* Trick.

chalet [chah-layt'], *m.* *pl*

chalí [chah-lee'], *m.* *(Com.)* 1. Mohair: a fabric of goat's hair, which is sometimes mixed with silk. 2. Challis, shalli; delaine.

chalina [chah-lee'-nah], *f.* Cravat, scarf.

chalón, chalún [chah-lone', chah-loon'], *m.* Shaloon, a kind of woollen stuff.

chalona [chah-lo'-nah], *f.* *(Peru)* Mutton cured on ice without salt.

chalupa [chah-loo'-pah], *f.* 1. *(Naut.)* Shallop, launch, a small light vessel, a longboat. 2. *(Mex.)* A canoe for one or two persons. *(Mex.)* *(Culin.)* Stuffed tortilla.

chalupa [chah-loo'-pah], 1. *a.* Crazy. **Volver chalupa a uno,** to drive somebody crazy. 2. *m.* Madman, crackpot.

chalupero [chah-loo-pay'-ro], *m.* A boatman, canoeman.

chamaca [chah-mah'-cah], *f.* *(Mex.)* Girl; girlfriend, sweetheart.

chamaco [chah-mah'-co], *m.* *(Mex.)* Boy, lad; boyfriend.

chamada [chah-mah'-dah], *f.* Chips, splinters of wood, to quicken a fire.

chamagoso, sa [chah-ma-go'-so, sah], *a.* *(Mex.)* 1. Greasy, filthy. 2. Ill-performed. 3. Vulgar (cosas).

chamaleón [chah-ma-le-on'], *m.* *V.* CAMALEÓN.

chamano [chah-mah'-no], *m.* A shrub of the Andes.

chamar [chah-mar'], To smoke.

chámara [chah'-mah-ra], *f.* Kindling, brushwood; brush fire, blaze.

chamarasca [chah-ma-rahs'-cah], *f.* 1. A brisk fire, made of brushwood. 2. *(Bot.)* Annual costmary.

chamaraz [chah-ma-rath'], *m.* *(Bot.)* Water-germander.

chamarilero, chamarillero [chah-ma-re-lay'-ro, chah-ma-reel-lyay'-ro], *m.* 1. Broker who deals in old pictures and furniture. 2. Gambler.

chamarillón [chah-ma-reel-lyone'], *m.* A bad player at cards.

chamariz [chah-ma-reeth'], *m. (Orn. Prov.)* Blue titmouse.

chamarón [chah-ma-rone'], *m. (Orn.)* Long-tailed titmouse.

chamarra [chah-mar'-rah], *f.* 1. Lumber jacket, mackinaw. 2. *(CAm. Carib.)* Blanket, poncho. 3. *(CAm.)* Con, swindle (engaño).

chamarrear [chah-mahr-ray-ar'], *va. (CAm.)* To con, to swindle.

chamarrero [chah-mahr-ray'-ro], *m. (Carib.)* Quack doctor.

chamarreta [chah-mar-ray'-tah], *f.* A short loose jacket with sleeves.

chamarro [chah-mahr'-ro], *m. (CAm. Cono Sur, Mex.)* Coarse woollen blanket; poncho, woollen cap.

chamba [cham'-bah], *f.* 1. *(And.)* Turf, sod. 2. *(And.)* Pond, pool (charca); *(And.)* Ditch (zanja). 3. *(CAm. Mex.)* Work; business; occupation. 4. *(Mex.)* Wages, pay (sueldos); low pay; soft job. 5. *(Carib. Mex.)* Dough, bread.

chamba [chahm'-bah], *f.* Fluke, lucky break. **Por chamba**, by a fluke.

chambeador [cham-bay-ah-dor'], *(Mex.) a & m.f.* Hard-working.

chambear [cham-bay-ar'], *(Mex.) va.* To exchange, to swap, to barter. *-vn.* To work; to slave (inútilmente).

chambelán [cham-be-lahn'], *m.* Chamberlain.

chambergo, ga [cham-ber'-go, gah], *a.* Slouched, uncocked (sombrero); coat worn by the regiment of *Chamberga,* and ever since a round uncocked hat has retained that name.

chambero [cham-bay'-ro], *m. (Mex.)* Draughtsman.

chambira [cham-bee'-rah], *f.* A forest palm.

chambón, na [cham-bone', nah], 1. *a.* Awkward, unhandy (person); botcher, lucky. 2. *m. f.* Fluky player, lucky player. **Hacer algo a la chambona,** *(And.) (fig.)* To do something in a rush.

chambonada [cham-bo-nah'-dah], *f.* A blunder, piece or stupidity; at billiards, a fluke.

chambonear [cham-bo-nay-ar'], *vn. (LAm.)* To have a stroke of luck, to win by a fluke.

chamborote [cham-bo-ray'-tay], *a. (And. CAm.)* Long-nosed.

chambra [cham'-brah], *f.* Morning-jacket, a short white blouse used by women over the chemise.

chambra [cham'-brah], *f.* 1. *(Carib.)* Din, hubbub. 2. *(Carib.)* Broad knife.

chambrana [cham-brah'-nah], *f.* 1. Doorcase, jamb-dressing. 2. *(And. Carib.)* Row, uproar, brawl.

chambre [cham'-bray], *m. (CAm.)* Tittle-tattle, gossip.

chambroso [cham-bro'-so], *a. (CAm.)* Gossipy.

chamburgo [cham-boor'-go], *m. (And.)* Pool, stagnant water.

chamelicos [chah-may-lee'-cos], *m. pl. (And. Cono Sur)* lumber, junk, old clothes; *(And.)* Old clothes.

chamelote [chah-may-lo'-tay], *m.* Camlet. **Chamelote de aguas,** clouded camlet. **Chamelote de flores,** flowered camlet.

chamelotina [chah-may-lo-tee'-nah], *f.* Kind of coarse camlet.

chamicera [chah-me-thay'-rah], *f.* A piece of forest where the wood has been scorched by fire.

chamicero, ra [chah-me-thay'-ro, rah], *a.* Belonging to scorched wood.

chamiza [chah-mee'-thah], *f.* Kind of wild cane or reed; chemise.

chamizal [chah-mee-thahl'], *m.* A thicket.

chamizo [chah-mee'-tho], *m.* 1. A piece of wood half burnt. 2. Thatched hut; shack, slum. 3. Den, joint.

chamo, ma [chah'-mo], *m. & f. (LAm.)* Kid, child.

chamorra [chah-mor'-rah], *f.* A shaved or shorn head.

chamorrada [chah-mor-rah'-dah], *f. (Low.)* Butt given with a shorn head.

chamorrar [chah-mor-rar'], *va.* To cut the hair with shears.

chamorro, ra [chah-mor'-ro, rah], 1. *a.* Shorn, bald, shorn. 2. *m.* Chamorro de cerdo, *(Mex.)* leg of pork.

champa [cham-pah], *f. (LAm.)* Sod, turf; ball of earth. 2. Mop of hair (greña). 3. *(fig.)* Tangled mass. 4. *(CAm. Mex.)* Roughly-built hut.

champán [cham-pahn'], *m.* 1. Kind of vessel in South America of seventy or eighty tons. 2. Champagne.

champaña [cham-pah'-nyah], *m.* Champagne.

champañazo [cham-pah-nyah'-tho], *m. (Cono Sur)* Champagne party.

champiñón [cham-pee-nyone'], *m.* Mushroom.

champiñones [cham-pe-nyo'-ness], *m. pl.* Edible mushrooms.

champú [cham-poo'], *m.* Shampoo. **Champú anticaspa**, anti-dandruff shampoo.

champudo [cham-poo'-do], *a. (LAm.)* Dishevelled, messy; long-haired (persona).

champurrado [cham-poor-rah'-do], *m. (Coll.)* 1. Jargon. 2. *(Prov.)* A mixture of different liquors. 3. *(Mex.)* Chocolate made in *atole* instead of water. **-Champurrado, da,** *pp.* of CHAMPURRAR.

champurrar [cham-poor-rar'], *va. (Coll.)* 1. To mix liquors. 2. *(Met.)* To speak with a mixture of words of different languages.

champurreado [cahm-poor-ray-ar'], *m.* 1. *(Cono Sur) (Culin.)* Hastily-prepared dish; *(fig.)* Hash, botch. 2. *V.* CHAMPURRADO.

chamuchina [chah-moo-chee'-nah], *f. (Peru)* Populace, rabble.

chamullar [chah-mool-lyar'], *va. vn.* To speak, to talk. **Yo también chamullo el caló,** I can talk slang too. **Chamullaban en Árabe,** they were jabbering away in Arabic.

chamuscado, da [chah-moos-cah-do, dah], *a.* 1. Tipsy, flustered with wine; tinged, inclined, addicted to vice. 2. Smitten, scorched, burnt with a passion. *(Met.)* Contaminated, tainted. *-pp.* of CHAMUSCAR.

chamuscar [chah-moos-car'], *va.* 1. To singe or scorch; to sear. 2. *(Mex.)* To sell cheap. *-vr.* To get scorched, singed.

chamusco [chah-moos'-co], *m. V.* CHAMUSQUINA.

chamuscón [chah-moos-cone'], *m. aug.* A large singe or scorch.

chamusquina [chah-moos-kee'-nah], *f.* 1. Scorching or singeing. 2. *(Met.)* Scolding, wrangling, high words. **Oler a chamusquina,** *(Met.)* to come from hot words to hard blows. 3. *(And. CAm.)* Bunch of kids.

chan [chan], *m. (CAm.)* Local guide.

chanada [chah-nah'-dah], *f.* Trick, joke, deceit.

chanar [chah-nar'], *va.* To understand.

chanate [chah-nah'-tay], *m. (Mex.)* A blackbird.

chanca [chan'-cah], *f.* 1. *(And. Cono Sur)* Grinding, crushing. 2. *(And. Cono Sur)* Beating (paliza).

chancaca [chan-cah'-cah], *f.* 1. **Azúcar de chancaca,** the refuse of the sugar in the boiler; raw sugar. 2. *(CAm.) (Culin.)* Maize cake, wheat cake.

chancadora [chan-cah-do'-rah], *f. (LAm.)* Grinder, crusher.

chancal [chan-cahl'], *m.* The moraine of a glacier.

chancar [chan-car'], *va.* 1. *(LAm.)* To grind, to crush (moler); to beat; to beat up; to ill-treat (maltratar). 2. *(And. Cono Sur)* to botch, to bungle.

chance [chan'-thay], *m. (LAm.)* 1. Chance (oportunidad). **Dale chance,** let him have a go. 2. Good luck (suerte).

chancear [chan-thay-ar'], *vn.* To jest, to joke. *-vr.* To jest, to joke, to fool.

chancero, ra [chan-thay'-ro, rah], *a.* Jocose, sportful, merry; fond of a joke.

chancha [chan'-chah], *f.* 1. *(LAm.) (Zool.)* Sow. 2. *(Cono Sur)* Small wooden cart (carro); bike. 3. *(And.)* Mouth. **Hacer la chancha,** to play truant.

chánchamo [chan'-cha-mo], *m. (Mex.) (Culin.)* Tamale.

cháncharras máncharras [chahn'-char-rahs mahn'-char-ras], *f. pl. (Low.)* **No andemos en cháncharras máncharras,** let us not beat about the bush, or use subterfuges and evasions.

panchería [chan-chay-ree'-ah], *f. (LAm.)* Pork-butcher's shop.

chanchero [chan-chay'-ro], *m. (LAm.)* Pork butcher.

chanchi [chan'-che], 1. *a.* Marvelous, smashing, jolly good; dishy (chica), smashing. **¡Estás chanchí!**, I think you are marvelous. *-adv.* Marvelously, jolly well. **Me fue chanchi,** I had a smashing time.

chancho [chan'-cho], *a.* (*LAm.*) Dirty, filthy. *-m.* 1. (*LAm.*) Pig, hog; pork (carne). **Chancho salvaje,** wild boar. 2. (*LAm.*) Blocked piece. 3. (*Cono Sur*) *V.* CHANCADORA. 4. (*LAm.*) (*fig.*) **Son como chanchos,** they´re as thick as thieves. **Quedar como chancho,** to come off badly.

chanchono [chan-cho'-no], *m.* Lie.

chanchullear [chan-chool-lyay-ar'], *va.* 1. To be guilty of crooked or underhand actions; to do vile things. 2. (*Coll.*) To smuggle.

chanchullero [chan-chool-lyay'-ro], *a.* Crooked, bent. *-m.* Crook, twister.

chanchullo [chan-chool'-lyo], *m.* Unlawful conduct to attain an end, and especially to get gain. Sharp practice, vile trick. (*Amer.*) Contraband.

chancica, illa [chan-thee'-cah, eel'-lyah], *f. dim.* A little fun or jest.

chanciller [chan-theel-lyerr'], *m.* (*Ant.*) *V.* CANCILLER, chancellor.

chancilleresco, ca [chan-theel-lyay-res'-co, cah], *a.* Belonging to the court of chancery.

chancillería [chan-theel-lyay-ree'-ah], *f.* 1. Chancery. 2. Chancellorship. 3. The right and fees of a chancellor.

chancita [chan-thee´-tah], *f. dim.* A little fun.

chancla [chan'-clah], *f.* 1. An old shoe with worn-down heel. 2. *V.* CHANCLETA.

chancleta [chan-clay'-tah], *f.* 1. Slipper. *V.* CHINELA. **Andar en chancleta,** to go slipshod. 2. (*LAm.*) Baby girl. 3. (*Carib.*) (*Aut.*) Accelerator. *-m f.* Muggings, charlie.

chancletear [chan-clay-tay-ar'], *vn.* To go slipshod.

chancletero [chan-clay-tay'-ro], *a.* (*And. Carib.*) **Chancletudo** *a.* 1. Common, low-class. 2. Scruffy.

chanclo [chahn´-clo], *m.* 1. Patten worn under the shoes by women. 2. Strong leather clog worn over shoes to guard against moisture and dirt. 3. Clog, galosh, overshoe.

chancón, cona [chan-cone'], *m. & f.* (*And.*) Swot.

chancro [chan'-cro], *m.* Chancre.

chandal [chan'-dal], *m.* Tracksuit.

chanelar [cha-nay-lar'], *va.* To catch on to, to twig.

chanfaina [chan-fah´-e-nah], *f.* 1. Ragout of livers and lights. 2. A trifling, worthless thing.

chanfle [chan'-flay], *m.* (*Cono Sur*) Bobby, cop.

chanflón, na [chan-flone', nah], *m. & f.* Bungler. *-a.* Bungling; made in a bungling manner.

changa [chahn´-gah], *f.* 1. (*Cuba*) Jest, joke, diversion. 2. Odd job, occasional job.

changador [chan-gah-dor'], *m.* (*S. Amer.*) Porter, carrier of burdens.

changamé [chan-gah-may'], *m.* (*Orn.*) A thrush of Panama.

changango [chan-gan'-go], *m.* (*Cono Sur*) Small guitar.

changarro [chan-gar'-ro], *m.* 1. (*Agri.*) A small cowbell. 2. (*Aut.*) Old car, jalopy. 3. *m.* (*Mex.*) Small shop.

changarse [chan-gar'-say], *vr.* To break down, to go wrong.

chango [chan'-go] *a.* 1. (*Mex.*) Quick, sharp; alert. 2. (*Carib. Mex.*) Mischievous, playful. 3. (*Carib.*) Silly, brainless (tonto); affected. 4. (*Cono Sur*) Annoying (molesto). 5. **La gente está changosa,** (*Mex.*) There are a lot of people. *-m.* **Changa** *f.* 1. (*Mex.*) Small monkey. 2. (*Cono Sur. Mex.*) Child; young servant. 3. (*Mex.*) Cunt (vagina).

changote [chan-go'-tay], *m.* An oblong bar of iron.

changuear [chan-gay-ar'], *vn.* To be jocose with others.

changüí [chan-goo-ee'], *m.* 1. (*Vulg.*) Jest, trick. 2. (*Cuba*) A dance.

changurro [chan-goor'-ro], *m.* Crab.

chanquete [chan-kay'-tay], *m.* White bait.

chanta [chan'-tah], *m. & f.* (*Cono Sur*) Loudmouth (fanfarrón); fraud.

chantado [chan-tah'-do], *m.* (*Prov. Gal.*) Wall or fence of slate in upright rows.

chantaje [chan-tah'-hay], *m.* Blackmail.

chantajismo [chan-tah-hees'-mo], *m.* Blackmailing.

chantajista [chan-tah-hees'-tah], *m. & f.* Blackmailer.

chantar [chan-tar'], *va.* 1. **Chantar a alguno una cosa,** to brave a person to his face. 2. To put on (vestido). 3. To thrust, to stick. 4. (*And. Cono Sur*) to throw, to chuck. 5. (*And. Cono Sur*) To put, to throw. **Chantar a uno en la calle,** to throw somebody out. 6. (*And. Cono Sur*) To give, to deal. 7. (*Cono Sur*) to leave in the lurch (abandonar).

chantre [chahn´-tray], *m.* Precentor, a dignified canon of a cathedral church. **chantría** [chan-tree'-ah], *f.* Precentorship.

chanza [chan'-thah], *f.* Joke, jest, fun. **Chanza pesada,** a sarcastic taunt, a bad trick. **Hablar de chanza,** to joke, to jest, to speak in jest.

chanzoneta [chan-tho-nay'-tah], *f.* 1. Joke, jest. 2. A little merry song, a ballad.

chanzonetero [chan-tho-nay-tay'-ro], *m.* Writer of ballads, a petty poet.

chañaca [chah-nyah-cah], *f.* (*Cono Sur*) 1. (*Med.*) Itch, rash. 2. (*fig.*) Bad reputation.

chao [chah'-o], *m.* Chow.

chao [chah'-o], *excl.* (*Cono Sur*) bye-bye!, so long!.

chapa [chah'-pah], *f.* 1. Plate, sheet (of metal). Bodywork (coche). **Chapa acanalada, chapa ondulada,** corrugated iron. 2. A kind of rosy shot on the cheek. 3. Rouge used by ladies. 4. A small bit of leather laid by shoemakers under the last stitches to prevent the binding from giving way. 5. **Chapas de freno,** the two bosses on each side of the bit of a bridle. 6. Transom and trunnion plates in gun carriages; judgment, good sense. **Chapas de caoba,** mahogany veneers. **Hombre de chapa,** a man of judgment, abilities, and merit. **Chapa de matricula,** licence plate. **Estar sin placa,** to be broke.

chapado [chah-pah'-do], *a.* 1. Covered with sheet metal (adornos, muebles). **Chapado de roble,** with an oak veneer. **Chapado de oro,** gold-plated.

chapaleo [chah-pah-lay'-o], *m. vn.* 1. Splash(ing); lap(ping). 2. Clatter(ing).

chapaleta [chah-pah-lay'-tah], *f.* (*Naut.*) A valve of strong leather put at the bottom of a ship's pump, which serves as a sucker.

chapapote [chah-pah-po'-tay], *m.* A tar from Cuba and Santo Domingo.

chapar [chah-par'], *va.* 1. To plate, to coat, to cover; to tile (pared). 2. To throw out, to come out with (observación). 3. To learn, to memorize. 4. To shut, to close. 5. To spy on. 6. (*And.*) To catch (atrapar); to catch up with, to overtake; to seize, to grasp; to kiss.

chaparra [cah-par'-rah], *f.* 1. Species of oak. *V.* CHAPARRO. 2. A coach with a low roof. 3. (*Amer.*) Bramblebush.

chaparrada [chah-par-rah'-dah], *f. V.* CHAPARRÓN.

chaparral [chah-par-rahl'], *m.* 1. Plantation of evergreen oaks. 2. (*Amer.*) Thick bramble-bushes entangled with thorny shrubs in clumps.

chaparrear [chah-pahr-ray-ar'], *vn.* To spur in torrents.

chaparreras [chah-par-ray'-ras], *f. pl.* Leather leggings for horseback riders.

chaparro [chah-par'-ro], *m.* (*Bot.*) Evergreen oak tree. *-a.* Squat, short and chubby. *-m. f.* (*fig.*) Short chubby person; (*Mex.*) Child, kid.

chaparrón [chah-par-rone'], *m.* A violent shower of rain.

chapatal [chah-pa-tahl'], *m.* A mire; muddy place. *V.* LODAZAL.

chape [chah'-pay], *m.* (*And. Cono Sur*) trees, pigtail.

chapear [chah-pay-ar'], *va.* 1. To adorn with metal plates. 2. (*LAm.*) (*Agri.*) To weed. 3. **Chapear a uno,** (*Carib.*) to cut somebody´s throat. *-vn. V.* CHACOLOTEAR.

chapeleta [chah-pah-lay'-tah], *f.* Flap valve, clack valve (válvula).

chapelete [chah-pay-lay'-tay], *m.* (*Prov.*) An ancient cover for the head.

chapeo [chah-pay'-o], *m.* (*Coll.*) Hat.

chapería [chah-pay-ree'-ah], *f.* Ornament of metal plates.

chapero [chah-pay'-ro], *m.* Queer (homosexual); male prostitute.

chaperón [chah-pay-rone'], *m.* Ancient hood or cowl.

chapeta [chah-pay'-tah], *f.* 1. A small metal plate. 2. Red spot on the cheek. 3. A stud for shirts or other articles.

chapetón [chah-pay-tone'], *m. (Amer.)* A wheel of silver to adorn a riding harness.

chapetón, na [chah-pay-tone', nah], *a.* A European lately arrived in America V. POLIZÓN.

chapetonada [chah-pay-to-nah'-dah], *f.* 1. A disease incident to Europeans in America, before they become accustomed to the climate. 2. *(And. Cono Sur)* awkwardness, clumsiness. 3. *(Carib.)* Sudden downpour.

chapín [chah-peen'], *m.* 1. Clog with a cork sole, worn by women. **Chapín de la reina**, tax formerly levied in Spain on the occasion of the king's marriage. **Poner en chapines** (a una hija), to marry off a daughter. **Ponerse en chapines**, to raise oneself above one's conditions. 2. *(CAm.) (Hum.)* Guatemalan.

chapinada [chah-pe-nah'-dah], *f. (CAm.) (Hum.)* Action typical of a Guatemalan, dirty trick.

chapinería [chah-pe-nay-ree'-ah], *f.* Shop where clogs and pattens are made and sold, and the art of making them.

chapinero [chah-pe-nay'-ro], *m.* Clog maker or seller.

chapinito [chah-pe-nee´-to], *m. dim.* A small clog.

chapiri [chah-pe'-re], *m.* Titfer, hat.

chápiro [chah'-pe-ro], *m.* A word of annoyance or menace used only in the phrases: **¡Por vida del chápiro (verde)! ¡Voto al chápiro!** about equal to "By Jupiter!"

chapisca [chah-pes'-cah], *f. (CAm.)* Corn harvest.

chapista [chah-pes'-tah], *m.* Tinsmith; *(Aut.)* Car-body worker, panel-beater.

chapistería [chah-pes-tay-ree'-ah], *f.* Car-body works, panel-beating shop.

chapita [chah-pe'-tah], *f. (And.)* Cop.

chapitel [chah-pe-tel'], *m.* 1. The upper part of a pillar rising in a pyramidal form. 2. A small movable brass plate over the compass. 3. V. CAPITEL.

chaple [chah'-play], *m.* Graver, the tool used in engraving.

chapo [chah'-po], *m.* 1. A short, stout person. *(Mex.)* 2. Corn porridge.

chapodar [chah-po-dar'], *va.* 1. To lop off the branches of trees and vines. 2. *(fig.)* To cut down, to reduce.

chapola [chah-po'-lah], *f. (And.)* Butterfly.

chapón [chah-pone'], *m.* A great blot of ink.

chapona [chah po' nah], *f. V.* CHAMBRA.

chapo(po)te [chah-po'-tay], *m. (Carib. CAm. Mex.)* Pitch, tar (pez); asphalt.

chapotear [chah-po-tay-ar'], *va.* To wet with a sponge or wet cloth. -*vn.* To paddle in the water; to dabble.

chapoteo [chah-po-tay'-o], *m.* 1. Sponging; moistening (limpieza con esponja). 2. Splashing; paddling; dabbling.

chapucear [chah-po-thay-ar'], *va.* 1. To botch, to bungle, to cobble, to fumble, to clout. 2. *(Mex.)* To swindle (estafar).

chapuceramente [chah-poo-thay-rah-men'-tay], *adv.* Fumblingly, clumsily, bunglingly.

chapucería [chah-poo-thay-ree'-ah], *f.* A clumsy, bungling work.

chapucero [chah-poo-thay'-ro], *m.* 1. Blacksmith, who makes nails, trivets, shovels, etc.; nailer. 2. Bungler, botcher.

chapucero, ra [chah-poo-thay'-ro, rah], *a.* Rough, unpolished, clumsy, bungling, rude.

chapulín [chah-poo-leen'], *m.* 1. *(Prov. Mex.)* A grasshopper, locust. 2. Trickster. 3. Child, kid.

chapupa [chah-poo'-pah], *f.* **Me salió de pura chapupa**, *(CAm.)* it was pure luck, it was a sheer fluke.

chapuro [chah-poo'-ro], *m. (CAm.)* Asphalt.

chapurrado [chah-poor-rah'-do], *m. (Coll.)* Jargon, broken language.

chapurr(e)ar [chah-poor-rar'], *va. (Coll.)* To speak gibberish. **Chapurrea el Italiano**, he speaks broken Italian. V. CHAMPURRAR.

chapuz [chah-pooth'], *m.* 1. The act of ducking one. 2. A clumsy performance. **Chapuces**, *(Naut.)* Mast spars.

chapuza [chah-poo'-thah], *f.* 1. Botched job, shoddy piece of work, mess; odd job (trabajillo), spare time job; small job about the house. 2. *(Mex.)* Trick, swindle.

chapuzar [chah-poo-thar'], *va.* 1. To duck. 2. To paddle with the oars. - *vn. & vr.* To dive; to draggle, to duck.

chapuzón [chah-poo´-thone'], *m.* 1. Dip, swim; ducking. **Darse un chapuzón**, to go for a dip. 2. Splashdown (de cápsula). 3. *(LAm.)* Cloudburst, downpour.

chaqué [chah-kay'], *m.* Morning coat.

chaquet [chah'-kayt], *m. pl.* **Chaqueta.** *V.*CHAQUE.

chaqueta [chah-kay'-tah], *f.* 1. Jacket. **Chaqueta de cuero**, leather jacket. 2. *(fig.)* Cambiar la chaqueta, *V.* CHAQUETEAR. 3. **Volarse la chaqueta**, *(CAm.)* to toss off.

chaquetar [chah-kay-tar'], *vn. (Mex.),* **Chaquetear** *vn.* To change sides, to be a turncoat, to turn traitor; to go back on one´s word.

chaquete [chah-kay'-tay], *m.* Game resembling backgammon.

chaquetero, ra [chah-kay-tay'-ro], *m. & f.* Turncoat. **Es una chaquetera,** she is always changing sides.

chaquetón [chah-kay-tone'], *m.* Long jacket, reefer, shooting jacket; three-quarter coat.

chaquira [chah-kee'-rah], *f.* Seedglass beads of all colors. *(Peru)*

charada [chah-rah'-dah], *f.* Charade, enigma.

charadrio [chah-rah´-dre-o], *m. (Orn.)* Common roller. *V.* GÁLGULO.

charaludo [chah-rah-loo'-do], *a. (Mex.)* Thin.

charamusca [chah-ra-moos'-cah], *f. (Mex.)* Twisted candy. 2. *(Peru) V.* CHAMARASCA. 3. *(Carib.)* Noise, row.

charamusquero [chah-ra-moos-kay'-ro], *m. (Mex.)* A seller of twisted candy.

charanchas [cha-rahn'-chas], *f. pl. (Naut.)* Battens used as supporters on board a ship.

charanga [chah-rahn'-gah], *f.* A military band of wind instruments only, fanfare, informal dance.

charango [chah-rahn'-go], *m. (And. Cono Sur)* A small five-stringed guitar.

charanguero, ra [chah-ran-gay'-ro, rah], *a.* 1. Clumsy, unpolished, artless (chapucero). 2. Applied to a bungler or bad workman.

charanguero [chah-ran-gay'-ro], *m. (Prov.)* 1. Peddler, hawker. 2. A kind of ship for the coast trade. 3. *(Coll.)* A lucky person.

charape [chah-rah'-pay], *m. (Mex.)* Type of pulque.

charca [char'-cah], *f.* Pool of water collected to make it congeal into ice.

charcanas [char-cah'-nas], *f.* Stuff of silk and cotton.

charco [char'-co], *m.* Pool of standing water; small lake. **Pasar el charco**, to cross the seas.

charcón [char-cone'], *a. (And. Cono Sur)* Thin, skinny.

charcoso, sa [char-co'-so, sah], *a. (Prov.)* Fenny, moorish, watery.

charcutería [char-coo-tay-ree'-ah], *f.* 1. Cooked pork products. 2. Pork butcher's, delicatessen (tienda).

charchina [char-che'-nah], *f. (LAm.)* Old crock, old banger.

charla [char'-lah], *f.* 1. *(Orn.)* Bohemian chatterer, silktail. 2. Idle chitchat or prattle, garrulity, gossip, loquaciousness. **Charla literaria**, literary talk. **Es de charla común**, it´s common knowledge. **Echar una charla**, to have a chat.

charlado [char-lah'-do], *m.* **Echar un charlado**, to have a chat.

charlador, ra [char-lah-dor', rah], *m. & f.* Gabbler, prater, a chattering fellow, a garrulous person, a chatterer.

charladuría [char-lah-doo-ree'-ah], *f.* Garrulity, gossip.

charlante [char-lahn'-tay], *m. & ; pa.* Gabbler, chatterer.

charlantín [char-lan-teen'], *m. (Coll.)* A mean prattler or gossip.

charlar [char-lar'], *vn.* To prattle, to babble, to chatter, to prate, to gabble, to gossip, to jabber, to clack, to chat.

charlatán, na [char-lah-tahn', nah], *m. & f.* 1. Prater, babbler, idle talker, gabbler. 2. Charlatan, a quack, a mountebank. *a.* Empirical.

charlatanear [char-lah-tah-nay-ar'], *vn.* To chatter away, to babble on. *V.* CHARLAR.

charlatanería [char-lah-tah-nay-ree'-ah], *f.* Garrulity, verbosity; quackery, charlatanism.

charlatanismo [char-lah-tah-nees´-mo], *m.* Charlatanry, quackery, empiricism, verbosity.

charleta [char-lay'-tah], *m. & f. (Cono Sur)* Chatterbox; gossip.

Charlot [Char-lot'], *m.* Charlie Chaplin.

charlotear [char-lo-tay-ar'], *vn.* To chatter, to talk a lot.

charmilla [char-meel'-lyah], *f. (Bot.)* Common hornbeam-tree.

charneca [char-nay'-cah], *f. (Bot.)* Mastic-tree, pistachia-tree. *V.* LENTISCO.

charnecal [char-nay-cahl], *m.* Plantation of mastic-trees.

charnel [char-nel'], *m.* 1. Two *maravedís.* 2. Small change.

charnela [char-nay'-lah], *f.* Hinge (bisagra); hinge-joint knuckle.

charneta [char-nay'-tah], *f.* Iron plate.

charol [chah-rol'], *m.* 1. Varnish (barniz). 2. Patent leather (cuero barnizado). Tray (bandeja). **Darse charol,** to boast, to blow one's trumpet, to brag.

charola [chah-ro'-lah], *f.* 1. *(LAm.)* Tray. 2. **Charolas,** *(CAm.)* Eyes.

charolado [chah-ro-lah-do], *a.* Polished, shiny.

charolar [chah-ro-lar'], *va.* To varnish.

charolista [chah-ro-lees'-tah], *m.* Gilder, varnisher, or japanner.

charpa [char'-pah], *f.* 1. Leather belt with compartments for pistols and poniards. 2. Sling for a broken arm. 3. *(Naut.)* Sling.

charpar [char-par'], *va.* To scarf, to lap one thing over another.

charque, or **charquí** [char'-kay, char-kee'], *m.* Meat dried in the sun; jerked beef. *V.* TASAJO.

charquear [char-kay-ar'], *va.* 1. To jerk beef; to dry it in the air. 2. To carve up, to slash, to wound severely.

charquecillo [char-kay-thel/lyo], *m. (And.) (Culin.)* Dried salted fish.

charqueo [char-kay'-o], *m.* Act of cleaning holywater fonts.

charqui [char'-ke], *m. (LAm.)* Dried beef, jerked meat; *(Cono Sur)* dried fruit, dried vegetables. **Hacer charqui a uno,** *(fig.) V.* CHAQUEAR.

charquicán [char-ke-cahn'], *m.* Sauce prepared with charquí.

charquillo [char-keel'-lyo], *m. dim.* A small pool or puddle.

charra [chahr'-rah], *f.* 1. *(fig.)* Peasant woman, coarse woman. 2. *(CAm.)* Broad-brimmed hat. 3.*(And.)* Itch, pimple. 4. *(CAm.)* Prick, tool.

charrada [char-rah'-dah], *f.* 1. Speech or action of a clown. 2. A dance. 3. *(Coll.)* Tawdriness, tinsel, finery. 4. Flashy ornament, vulgar adornment; tastelessly decorated object. 5. Coarse thing, piece of bad breeding.

charral [chahr-rahl'], *m. (CAm.)* Scrub, scrubland.

charramente [char-rah-men'-tay], *adv.* Clownishly, tastelessly, ostentatiously fine.

charrán [char-rahn'], *a.* Rascally, knavish.

charrán [chahr-rahn'], *m. (Orn.)* Tern.

charranada [chahr-rah-nah'-dah], *f.* Dirty trick.

charranear [char-rah-nay-ar'], *vn.* To play the knave, the rascal.

charranería [char-rah-nay-ree'-ah], *f.* Rascality, knavery.

charrar [chahr-rar'], *vn.* To talk, to burble; to blab.

charrasca [chahr-ras'-cah], *f.* Trailing sword; *(And. Cono Sur, Mex.)* Knife, razor.

charrasquear [chahr-ras-kay-ar'], *va.* 1. *(Mex.)* To knife, to stab (apuñalar). 2. *(And. CAm. Carib.)* To strum (rasguear).

charrería [chahr-ray-ree'-ah], *f. (Mex.)* Horsemanship.

charretera [char-ray-tay'-rah], *f.* 1. Strip of cloth, silk, etc., placed on the lower part of pants to fasten them with a buckle. 2. The buckle with which the strips are fastened. 3. Epaulet. **Charretera mocha,** shoulder-knot.

charro, ra [char'-ro, rah], *m. & f.* 1. A coarse, ill-bred, person. 2. A tawdry, showy person. 3. A name given to the peasants of the province of Salamanca in Spain. 4. Mexican. 5. *(Mex.)* Picturesque, quaint; traditional. 6. Rustic, boor, coarse, individual; flashy sort, overdressed individual. 7. *(Mex.)* Horseman, cowboy; typical Mexican. 8. *(Mex.)* Wide-brimmed hat. 9. *(Mex.) (Pol.)* Corrupt union boss.

charro, ra [char'-ro-rah], *a.* Gaudy, tawdry.

chárter [char'-tayr], *atrib.* **Vuelo chárter,** charter flight.

chas [chas], *m.* A low word, denoting the noise made by the cracking of wood or tearing of linen.

chasca [chahs'-cah], *f. (Amer.)* Disordered hair.

chascar [chas-car'], *vn.* To crackle, sputter: said of wood which sends off little pieces from a fire. *-va.* 1. To click (lengua etc.); to snap (dedos); to crack (látigo); to crunch (grava). 2. To gobble (comida), to gulp down.

chascarrillo [chas-car-reel'-lyo], *m.* Spicy anecdote, gossipy story.

chasco [chahs'-co], *m.* 1. Fun, joke, a trick, a sham. 2. Foil, frustration, disappointment. 3. Lash, the thong or point of the whip. **Dar un chasco,** to play a trick. **Dar chasco,** to disappoint. **Llevarse chasco,** to be disappointed.

chascón [chas-cone'], *a. (And. Cono Sur)* 1. Dishevelled, matted, entangled (pelo). 2. Slow, clumsy (torpe).

chasí [chah-see'], *m.* A photographic plateholder.

chasis [chah'-sis], *m.* Chassis (of a vehicle). **Quedarse en el chasis,** to be terribly thin.

chasque [chas'-kay], *m. (LAm.) V.* CHASQUI.

chasquear [chas-kay-ar'], *va.* To crack with a whip or lash. *-vn.* 1. To crack as timber at the approach of dry weather: to snap; to crepitate. 2. To fool, to play a waggish trick. 3. To disappoint, to fail, to fall short; to cheat.

chasqui [chahs'-kee], *m. (Peru)* Postboy, or messenger on foot.

chasquido [chas-kee'-do], *m.* 1. Crack of a whip or lash. 2. Crack, the noise made by timber when it breaks or splits.

chasquista [chas-kees'-tah], *m. (Low.)* A person fond of playing tricks; a sycophant.

chata [chah´-tah], *f.* 1. *(Naut.)* A flatbottomed boat. **Chata alijadora,** lighter. **Chata de arbolar,** sheerhulk. **Chata de carenar,** careening-hulk. 2. *(Cono Sur) (Aut.)* Lorry, truck.

chatarra [chah-tahr'-rah], *f.* Scrap, iron, junk; coppers (dinero), small change; medals. **Vender para chatarra,** to sell for scrap.

chatarrero [chah-tar-ray'-ro], *m.* Junkman, dealer, scrap merchant.

chate [chah'-tay], *m. (Bot.)* Roundleaved Egyptian or hairy cucumber.

chatear [chah-tay-ar'], *vn.* To go drinking, to have a few drinks.

chateo [chah-tay'-o], *m.* Drinking expedition.

chatí [chah-te'], *f.* Girl, bird; ¡oye chati!, hey beautiful!.

chato, ta [chah'-to, tah], *a.* 1. Flat, flattish: flatnosed. **Embarcación chata,** a flatbottomed vessel. 2. **¡Oye chata!,** hey, beautiful! 3. *(Carib. Cono Sur)* mean, wretched. 4. *(LAm.)* **Dejar chato a uno,** to crush somebody (anonadar); to embarrass somebody; *(Mex.)* To swindle somebody (estafar). *-m.* Wine glass. **Tomarse unos chatos,** to have a few drinks.

chatón [chah-tone'], *m.* 1. Bezel, the bevelled part of a ring in which a diamond is set. 2. Kind of coarse diamond. 3. Ornamental nail or button. 4. *pl.* Knobs which fasten one thing to another.

chatre [chah'-tray], *a.* 1. (Ecuador) Richly decked out. 2. *(And. Cono Sur)* smartly-dressed. **Está hecho un chatre,** he´s looking very smart.

chatungo [chah-toon'-go], *a. V.* CHATO.

chau [chah'-oo], *interj. (Cono Sur)* So long!

chaucha [chah'-oo-chah], a. 1.*(And. Cono Sur)* early; unripe (inmaduro), not fully grown; premature (nacimiento). 2. *(Cono Sur)* poor-quality; insipid, tasteless; characterless; in poor taste. *-f.* 1. Early potato, small potato; *(And. Cono Sur)* string bean; *(And.)* Food. **Pelar la chaucha**, to brandish one's knife. 2. *(And. Cono Sur)* 20-cent coin. 3. *(Cono Sur)* **Chauchas**; peanuts.

chauchau [chah'-oo-chah'-oo], *m. (And. Cono Sur)* Grub, chow.

chauchera [chah-oo-chay'-rah], *f. (And. Cono Sur)* Purse, pocket-book.

chauchero [chah-oo-chah'-ro], *m. (Cono Sur)* Errand boy; odd-jobman; poorly-paid worker.

chaúl [chah-ool'], *m.* A kind of blue silk material manufactured in China.

chauvinismo [chah-oo-ve-nees'-mo], *m.* Chauvinism.

chauvinista [chah-oo-ve-nees'-tah], *a. & m. & f.* Chauvinist.

chava [chah'-vah], *f. (CAm. Mex.)* Lass, girl.

chaval [chah-vahl'], *a.* Among the common people, young. **Estar hecho un chaval**, to feel very young again.

chavala [chah-vah'-lah], *f.* Girl, kid. **Mi chavala**, my bird; my girlfriend.

chavalo [chah-vah'-lo], *m. (CAm.)* Street urchin; boy.

chavalongo [chah-vah-lon'-go], *m. (Cono Sur)* fever; sunstroke; drowsiness (modorra).

chavea [chah-vay'-ah], *m. & f.* Kid, youngster.

chaveta [chah-vay'-tah], *f.* Bolt, cotter pin. **Perder la chaveta**, to lose one's head, to become rattled.

chavetear [chah-vay-tay-ar'], *va. (And. Carib.)* To knife.

chavo [chah'-vo], *m.* **1**. **No tener un chavo**, to be stone-broke. 2. Kid, boy. 3. *(CAm. Mex.)* Guy.

chayote [chah-yo'-tay], *m. (Mex.)* Mexican fruit. *V.* CHIOTE.

chayotera [chah-yo-tay'-rah], *f.* Chayote (plant).

chaza [chah'-thah], *f.* 1. Point where the ball is driven back, or where it stops, in a game at balls. 2. *(Naut.)* Berth on board a ship. **Hacer chaza**, to walk on the hind feet (caballos).

chazador [chah-thah-dor'], *m.* A person employed to stop the ball and mark the game.

chazar [chah-thar'], *va.* 1. To stop the ball before it reaches the winning point. 2. To mark the point whence the ball was driven back.

che [chay], *interj.* Oh Dear!; *(Cono Sur)* hey!, hi!; *(CAm.)* Who cares!

checa [chay'-cah], *f.* 1. Secret police. 2. Secret police headquarters.

cheche [chay'-chay], *m. (Carib.)* bully, braggart.

chechear [chay-chay-ar'], *va. (Cono Sur)* V. VOSEAR.

chécheres [chay'-chay-rays], *m. pl. (And. CAm.)* Things, gear; junk.

chechón [chay-chaone'], *a. (Mex.)* Spoilt, pampered.

checo, ca [chay'-co], *a. m. & f.* Czech.

checoslovaco, ca [chay-cos-lo-vah'-co, cah], *a.* Czechoslovakian. *-m. & f.* Czechoslovak.

Checoslovaquia [chay-cos-lo-vah'-ke-ah], Czechoslovakia.

chelear [chay-lay-ar'], *va. (CAm.)* To whiten, to whitewash.

chele [chay'-lay], *a. (CAm.)* Fair, blond.

cheli [chay'-le], *m.* Guy; boyfriend; **ven cheli acá**, come here, man.

chelín [chay-leen'], *m.* Shilling, an old English coin.

chelista [chay-les'-tah], *m. & f.* Cellist.

chelo [chay'-lo], *a. (Mex.)* Fair, blond(e).

chenil [chay-neel'], *m.* Chenille.

chepa [chay'-pah], *f.* A hump, hunch.

cheque [chay'-kay], *m.* Check, cheque. **Cheque de caja**, cashier's check. **Cheque en blanco**, blank check. **Cheque al portador**, bearer check. **Cheque de viaje**, traveler's check.

chequear [chay-kay-ar'], *va.* To check (cuenta, documento); to check (persona); to register, to check in; *(Mex.) (Aut.)* To service.

chequeo [chay-kay'-o], *m. (LAm.)* Check; checking up; *(Med.)* Check-up; *(Aut.)* Service.

chequera [chay-kay'-rah], *f. (LAm.)* Check book.

cherife [chay-reef'], *m. (LAm.)* Sheriff.

cherna [cherr'-nah], *f. (Zool. Prov.)* Ruffle, a fish resembling a salmon.

chero [chay'-ro], *m. (CAm.)* Pal, mate; buddy.

cheruto [chay-roo'-to], *m.* Cheroot.

cherva [cherr'-vah], *f. (Bot.)* The castoroil plant.

cheurón [chay-oor-rone'], *m. (Her.)* Chevron, a representation of two rafters of a house in heraldry.

chévere [chay-vay'-re], *a. (And. Carib. Mex.)* Smashing, super. *-m. (Carib.)* Bully, bragart.

chevronado, da [chay-vro-nah'-do, dah], *a. (Her.)* Chevroned, coat of arms charged with chevrons.

chía [chee'-ah], *f.* 1. A short black mantle, formerly worn in mournings. 2. Cowl of fine cloth, formerly worn by the nobility for distinction. 3. A white medicinal earth. 4. *(Bot.)* Limeleaved sage.

chiar [che-ar'], *vn.* To chirp (pájaros). *V.* PIAR.

chibcha [cheeb'-chah], *m.* A dweller of the clevated territory about Bogotá.

chibola [che-bo'-lah], *f. (CAm.)* 1. Fizzy drink, pop. 2. **Chibolo**, marble.

chibolo [che-bo'-lo], *m. (And. CAm.)* Bump, swelling; wen.

chibón [che-bone'], *m.* 1. A young cock-linnet. 2. Sort of gum from America.

chic [cheec], *a. m.* Chic, smart, elegant, elegance; composure.

chica [chee'-cah], *f.* 1. Girl (muchacha). **Es una linda chica**, *(Coll.)* she is a pretty girl. 2. Maid, servant.

chicada [che-cah'-dah], *f.* Herd of sickly kids.

chicalote [che-cah-lo'-tay], *m.* Mexican argemone.

chicana [che-cah'-nah], *f. (LAm.)* Chicanery.

chicanear [che-cah-nay-ar'], *vn.* To use trickery, to be cunning. *-va.* To trick, to take in.

chicanería [che-cah-nay-re'-ah], *f. (LAm.)* Chicanery.

chicanero [che-cah-nay'-ro], *a.* 1. *(LAm.)* Tricky, crafty. 2. *(And.)* Mean (tacaño).

chicano, na [che-cah'-no, nah], *a.* (Of) Mexican American. *-m. & f.* Mexican American, Chicano.

chicar [che-car'], *vn. (And.)* To booze, to drink.

chicarrón [che-cahr-rone'], *a.* Strapping, sturdy. *-m. f.* Strapping lad; sturdy lass.

chicato [che-cah'-to], *a. (Cono Sur)* short-sighted.

chicha [chee'-chah], *f.* 1. Meat: used only with children. **De chicha y nabo**, Insignificant. 2. Beverage made of pineapple rinds, sugar, or molasses. **Tener pocas chichas**, to be very lean or weak. 3. *(And. CAm.)* **Estar de chichas**, to be in a bad mood. 4. *(And.)* Thick-soled shoe. a. *(Naut.)* **Calma chicha**, dead calm.

chícharo [chee'-chah-ro], *f. (Bot.)* Pea.

chicharra [che-char'-rah], *f.* 1. Cicada (cigarra). 2. A talkative woman. **Hablar como una cicada**, to be a real chatterbox. 3. Kazoo, a child's plaything making a harsh, grating noise. **Cantar la chicharra**, *(Coll.)* to be scorching hot. 4. Bell, buzzer. 5. Reefer.

chicharrear [che-char-ray-ar'], *vn.* To creak, to chirp.

chicharrero [che-char ray'-ro], *m.* 1. A hot place or climate. 2. One who makes or sells kazoos.

chicharro [che-char'-ro], *m.* 1. A young tunnyfish. 2. Horsemackerel.

chicharrón [che-char-rone'], *m.* 1. Crackles, morsel of fried lard left in the pan. **Estar hecho un chicharrón**, to be burnt to a cinder, to be as red as a lobster (persona). 2. *(fig.)* Sunburnt person. 3. *(Carib.)* Flatterer (adulador).

chiche [chee'-chay], *m.* 1. *(Amer. Prov.)* A kind of sauce. 2. *(LAm.)* Precious thing, delightful object; fancy jewel (joya); trinket; small boy (juguete); clever person; well-dressed person (pulcro); elegant place, nice room. *-a. -adv. (CAm.)* Easy, simple, easily. **Está chiche**, it's a cinch. *-f. (Mex.)* Nursemaid.

chichear [che-chay-ar'], *va & vn.* To hiss.

chicheo [che-chay'-o], *m.* Hissing a speaker.

chichera [che-chay'-rah], *f. (CAm.)* Jail, clink.

chichería [che-chay-ree'-ah], *f.* Tavern where *chicha* is sold.

chichi [che-che], 1. *m.* Cunt. - *f. (Mex.)* 1. Teat (teta). 2. Nursemaid (niñera).

chichicaste [che-che-cas'-tay], *m. (CAm.) (Bot.)* Nettle; *(Med.)* Nettle rash.

chichigua [che-chee'-goo-ah], *f.* 1. *(Mex. vulg.)* Wet nurse. 2. *(Carib.)* Kite. 3. *(Mex.)* Tame animal; nursing animal. 4. *(Mex.)* Pimp.

chichimeco, ca [che-che-may'-co, cah], *a.* Of Chichimec.

chichisbeador [che-chis-bay-ah-dor'], *m.* Gallant, wooer.

chichisbear [che-chis-bay-ar'], *va.* To woo, to court.

chicho [che'-cho], *m.* 1. Curl, ringlet. 2. Curler, roller.

chichón [che-chone'], *m.* 1. Bump, on the head. 2. Bruise. *V.* ABOLLADURA.

chichón [che-chone'], *a.* 1. *(Cono Sur)* Merry, jovial. 2. *(CAm.)* Easy, straightforward. **Está chichón**, it´s a cinch, a piece of cake.

chichoncillo, cito [che-chon-theel'-lyo, thee'-to], *m. dim.* Small lump.

chichonear [che-cho-nay-ar'], *vn. (Cono Sur)* To joke.

chichonera [che-cho-nay_-rah], *f.* Tumblingcap, helmet.

chichota [che-cho'-tah], *f.* **Sin faltar chichota**, it wants not an iota; it is all complete.

chichus [che'-chus], *m. (CAm.)* Flea.

chicle [che'-clay], *m. (Bot.)* (Chicle), chewing gum.

chiclear [che-clay-ar'], *vn. (CAm. Mex.)* 1. To extract gum. 2. To chew gum (mascar).

chico, ca [chee'-co, cah], *m. & f.* 1. Boy, girl. **Es un buen chico**, *(Coll.)* he is a good boy. **Es una chica guapa**, she is a pretty girl. 2. Son, boy (hijo). 3. Daughter, girl (hija)

chico, ca [chee'-co, cah], *a.* Little, small. **Los chicos de la oficina**, the fellows at the office. **Es un buen chico**, he´s a good lad. **Chicos de la calle**, street urchins. **Como chico con zapatos nuevos**, as happy as a lark. -*a.* Small-size, tiny. **Dejar chico a uno**, to put somebody in the shade.

chicolear [che-co-lay-ar'], *va.* To joke or jest in gallantry. -*vn.* 1. To flirt, to murmur sweet nothings, to say nice things. 2. To amuse oneself, to have a good time. -*vr. (And.)* To amuse oneself.

chicoleo [che-co-lay'-o], *m.* 1. *(Coll.)* Joke, jest in gallantry. 2. Compliment, flirtatious remark. **Decir chicoleos**, to say nice things. 3. Flirting (acto). **Estar de chicoleo**, to be in a flirtatious mood. 4. *(And.)* Childish thing. **No andemos con chicoleos**, let´s be serious.

chicolero [che-co-lay'-ro], *a.* Flirtatious.

chicoria [che-co'-re-ah], *f. V.* ACHICORIA.

chicorrotico, ca [che-cor-ro-tee'-co, cah], *a. dim.* Very little or small (niños).

chicorrotín [che-cor-ro-teen'], *a.* Very small (niños).

chicotazo [che-co-tah'-tho], *m. (LAm.)* Lash, swipe.

chicote, ta [che-co'-tay, tah], *m. & f.* 1. *(Coll.)* A fat strong boy or girl. 2. *(Naut.)* End of a rope or cable. 3. *(Coll.)* End of a cigar partly smoked.

chicotear [che-co-tay-ar'], *va. (LAm.)* To whip, to lash (azotar); *(LAm.)* To beat up (pegar); *(And.)* To kill. -*vn. (LAm.)* To lash about (cola).

chicozapote [che-co-thah-po'-tay], *m.* A delicious American fruit. *V:* ZAPOTE.

chifa [chee'-fah], *(And.) f.* Chinese restaurant. -*a.* Chinky, Chinese.

chifla [chee'-flah], *f.* 1. Whistle. 2. With bookbinders, a paring-knife. 3. Hissing in a theater or public meeting.

chiflacayote [che-flah-cah-yo'-tay], *m.* A large kind of pumpkin in America.

chifladera [che-flah-day'-rah], *f.* 1. Whistle. 2. *(CAm. Mex.)* Crazy idea.

chiflado [che-flah'-do], *a.* Daft, barmy, cranky, crackpot. **Estar chiflado con, estar chiflado por**, to be crazy about. -*m. f.* Crank, crackpot.

chifladura [che-flah-doo'-rah], *f.* 1. Whistling. 2. *(Coll.)* Craziness. 3. Crazy idea, whim, fad, mania. **Su chifladura es el ajedrez**, he is crazy about chess. **Ese amor no es más que una chifladura**, what he calls love is just a foolish infatuation.

chiflar [che-flar'], *va.* 1. To pare, to skive (cuero). 2. To hiss, to whistle at, to boo. 3. To drink, to knock back, to gulp (beber). 4. To captivate; to drive crazy. **Me chifla ese conjunto**, I rave about that group. **Me chiflan los helados**, I just adore ice cream. **Esa chica le chifla**, he´s crazy about that girl. -*vn.* 1. To whistle. 2. To mock, to jest. 3. To tipple, to drink to excess. -*vr.* 1. *(Coll.)* To run mad, to be crazy. 2. **Chiflárselas** *(CAm.)* To peg out, to kick the bucket.

chiflato [che-flah-to], *m. V.* SILBATO.

chifle [chee'-flay], *m.* 1. Whistle. 2. Call, an instrument used to decoy birds. 3. *(Naut.)* Priming-horn used by the gunners of the navy. 4. *(Naut.)* Tide. **Aguas chifles**, neaptide.

chiflete [che-flay'-tay], *m. V.* CHIFLA.

chiflido [che-flee'-do], *m.* Whistling, shrill sound.

chiflo [chee'-flo], *m. V.* CHIFLA.

chiflón [che-flone'], *m.* 1. Draft, draught (current of air). 2. *(CAm. Carib, Cono Sur)* rapids, violent current; *(CAm.)* Waterfall; *(Mex.)* Flume, race; *(Mex.)* Nozzle (tobera).

chihuahuense [che-hooa-hoo'en-say], *(Mex.) m. & f.* Of Chihuahua.

chilaba [che-lah'-bah], *f.* Jellabah.

chilacayote [che-lah-cah-yo'-tay], *m. (Bot.)* American or bottle gourd.

chilanco [che-lahn'-coh], *m.* Pool or well of water remaining in a river when it has lost its current through drought.

chilango, ga [che-lahn'-go], *(Mex.) m. & f.* Of Mexico city.

chilar [che-lar'], *m.* A spot planted with Chile peppers.

chile [chee'-lay], *f. (Bot.)* American red pepper. **Chile ancho**, dried-up pepper in a broad shape. **Chile relleno**, *(Mex.)* Green pepper stuffed with minced meat, coated with eggs, and fried.

Chile [chee'-lay], *m.* Chile.

chilear [che-lay-ar'], *vn. (CAm.)* To tell jokes.

chileno, na, chileño, ña [che-lay'-nyo, nya], *a.* Chilean; of Chile.

chilera [che-lay'-rah], *f. (Naut.)* Rowlock hole.

chilicote [che-le-co'-tay], *m. (And. Cono Sur)* Cricket.

chilindrina [che-lin-dree'-nah], *f.* 1. *(Coll.)* Trifle, a thing of little value. **Meterse en chilindrinas**, to meddle in unimportant, but ticklish business. 2. Joke, fun, witticism.

chilindrinero, ra [che-lin-dre-nay'-ro, rah], *a.* Meddling in trifles.

chilindrón [che-lin-drone'], *m.* 1. Game at cards for four persons. 2. *(Low.)* Cut in the head. 3. **Al chilindrón**, cooked with tomatoes and peppers.

chilla [cheel'-lyah], *f.* 1. Call for foxes, hares, or rabbits. 2. *(Mex.)* 1. *(Theat.)* Gallery. 2. Poverty. **Estar en la chilla**, to be flat broke. 3. Decoy, call (caza).

chillado [cheel-lyah'-do], *m. (Prov.)* Roof of shingles or thin boards. - **Chillado, da**, *pp.of* CHILLAR.

chillador, ra [cheel-lyah-dor', rah], *m. & f.* Person who shrieks or screams; a thing that creaks.

chillante [cheel-lyahn´-tay], *pa.* Screaming, shrieking, screeching.

chillar [cheel-lyar'], *vn.* 1. To scream, to shriek. 2. To crackle, to creak. 3. To imitate the notes of birds. 4. To hiss: applied to things frying in a pan. **Chillar a uno**, to yell at somebody, to be loud. 5. To scream, to be loud (colores). 6. *(LAm.)* To shout, to protest. **No chillar** *(Carib. Cono Sur)*, to keep one´s mouth shut, not to say a word. **El cochino chilló**, *(Carib. Mex.)* They let the cat out of the bag. 7. *(LAm.)* To sob (llorar). -*vr.* 1. *(LAm.)* To complain, to protest. 2. *(And. Carib. Mex.)* To get cross; to take offence. 3. *(CAm.)* To get embarrassed (sofocarse).

chilleras [cheel-lyay'-ras], *f. pl. (Naut.)* Shotlockers for balls.

chillería [chel-lay-ree'-ah], *f.* Row, hubbub.

chillido [cheel-lyee'-do], *m.* 1. Squeak or shriek; a shrill, disagreeable sound. 2. Bawling of a woman or child. **Dar un chillido**, to utter a scream.

chillo [cheel'-lyo], *m.* 1. Call. *V.* CHILLA. 2. *(CAm.)* Debt. 3. *(Carib.)* Rabble, mob (muchedumbre). 4. Anger; loud protest.

chillón [cheel-lyone'], *m.* 1. *(Coll.)* Bawler, screamer, shrieker. 2 *(Prov.)* Common crier. 3. Nail, tack. **Chillón real**, spike used to fasten large timbers or planks. **Clavo chillón**, tack or small nail.

chillón, na [cheel-lyone', nah], *a.* Applied to showy or tawdry colors.

chilote [che-lo'-tay], *m. (Mex.) V.* JILOTE.

chilposo [chel-po'-so], *a. (Cono Sur)* Ragged, tattered.

chiltipiquín, chiltepín [cheel-te-pe-keen', cheel-tay-peen'], *m. (Mex.)* A red pepper, the size of a caper, and very pungent.

chimal [che-mahl'], *m. (Mex.)* Dishevelled hair, mop of hair.

chimar [che-mahr'], *va.* 1. *(CAm.)* To scratch. 2. *(CAm. Mex.)* To annoy, to bother (molestar). 3. *(CAm.)* To fuck, to screw.

chimate [che-mah'-tay], *m. V.* CHANCACA.

chimba [chem'-bah], *f.* 1. *(And. Cono Sur)* opposite bank (orilla); *(Cono Sur)* poor quarter (barrio); *(And.)* Ford (vado). 2. *(And.)* Pigtail.

chimbar [chem-bar'], *va. (And.)* To ford (río).

chimbero [cehm-bay'-ro], *a. (Cono Sur)* Slum (de chimba); coarse, rough (grosero).

chimbo [chem'-bo], *a.* 1. *(And. Carib.)* Worn-out, wasted, old. 2. *(And.)* Bad (cheque). *-m. (And.)* Piece of meat.

chimenea [che-may-nay'-ah], *f.* 1. Chimney. 2. *(Met. Coll.)* Head. 3. Hearth, fireplace. **Se le subió el humo a la chimenea**, the vapor has mounted to his head (borracho).

chimiscolear [che-mes-co-lay-ar'], *vn. (Mex.)* To gossip; to poke one's nose in (curiosear).

chimiscolero, ra [che-mes-co-lay'-ro], *m. & f. (Mex.)* Gossip.

chimpancé [chim-pan-thay'], *m.* Chimpanzee.

chimpín [chem-peen'], *m. (And.)* Brandy, liquor.

chimpipe [chim-pee'-pay], *m. (Nicaragua)* Turkey.

chimuelo [che-moo-ay'-lo], *a. (LAm.)* Toothless.

China [chee'nah], **f.** China.

china [chee'-nah], *f.* 1. Pebble, a small stone. 2. Chinaroot, a medicinal root. 3. Porcelain, china, chinaware. 4. China silk or cotton stuff. **Media china**, cloth coarser than that from China. 5. Boyish game of shutting hands, and guessing which contains the pebble. **Le tocó la china**, he had bad luck. 6. *(LAm.)* Woman (Indian); *(And. Cono Sur)* Nursemaid; *(And. Cono Sur)* servant girl; *(LAm.)* Mistress, concubine.

chinaca [che-nah'-cah], *f.* **La chinaca** *(Mex.)*, the plebs, the proles.

chinado [che-nah'-do], *a.* Crazy.

chinaloa [che-nah-lo'-ah], *f. (Mex.)* Heroin, smack.

chinampa [che-nahm'-pah], *f.* A small garden tract in lakes near the city of Mexico; anciently a floating garden.

chinampero [che-nam-pay'-ro], *m.* The tiller of a *chinampa*.

chinar [che-nar'], *vn.* To carve up, to slash. *(Obs.) V.* RECHINAR.

chinarro [che-nar'-ro], *m.* A large pebble.

chinateado [che-nah-tay-ah'-do], *m.* Stratum or layer of pebbles.

chinazo [che-nah'-tho], *m.* 1. *(aug.)* A large pebble. 2. Blow with a pebble. **le tocó el chinazo**, he had bad luck.

chincate [chin-cah'-tay], *m. (Amer.)* The last brown sugar which comes from the caldrons.

chinchada [chin-chah'-dah], *f. (Cono Sur)* Tug-of-war.

chinchal [chin-chahl'], *m. (Carib.)* Tobacco stall; small shop.

chinchar [chin-char'], *va.* To pester, to bother, to annoy; to upset. **Me chincha tener que**, it upsets me to have to. *-vr.* To get cross, to get upset. **¡Para que te chinches!**, so there!

chincharrazo [chin-char-rah'-tho], *m. (Coll.)* Thrust or cut with a sword. *V.* CINTARAZO.

chincharrero [chin-char-ray'-ro], *m.* Place swarming with bugs.

chinche [cheen'-chay], *f.* 1. Bedbug. **Caer como chinches**, to die like flies. 2. Thumbtack. 3. *(Cono Sur)* Pique, irritation (rabieta). *-m. & f. (fig.)* Nuisance; annoying person, pest, bore; *(And. CAm.)* Naughty child.

chinchero [chin-chay'-ro], *m.* Bugtrap made of twigs.

chincheta [chin-chay'-tah], *f.* Drawing pin, thumbtack.

chinchilla [chin-cheel'-lyah], *f.* Chinchilla, a small quadruped in Peru, well known for its fur.

chinchín [chin-cheen'], *m.* 1. *(Cuba)* Drizzling rain, mizzle. 2. Street music, tinny music. 3. *(CAm.)* Baby's rattle.

chincho [cheen-cho], *m. (Naut.)* A small plumb-line used by constructors of curved timbers.

chinchón [chin-chone'], *m.* Bump. *V.* CHICHÓN.

chinchona [chin-cho'nah], *f.* Quinine.

chinchorreo [chin-chor-ray'-o], *m. (Prov.)* Tiresome importunity or solicitation.

chinchorrería [chin-chor-ray-ree'-ah], *f.* 1. Lying jest. 2. *(Coll.)* Mischievous tale. 3. Fussiness; critical nature, disrespectful manner. *V.* CHISME.

chinchorrero, ra [chin-chor-ray'-ro, rah], *m. & f.* 1. A gossip. 2. *V.* CHINCHARRERO.

chinchorro [chin-chor'-ro], *m.* 1. Fishingboat used in America. 2. Kind of fishing-net. 3. A hammock used by Indians, suspended from trees. 4. The smallest rowboat on board a ship.

chinchoso, sa [chin-cho'-so, sah], *a.* 1. Peevish, fastidious, tiresome. 2. Full of bugs (chinches). 3. Tiresome, annoying (pesado). 3. *(And. Carib.)* Touchy, irritable (quisquilloso).

chinchudo [chin-choo'-do], *a.* **Estar chinchudo**, *(Cono Sur)* to be in a huff.

chindar [chin-dar'], *va.* To chuck out.

chinear [che-nay ar'], *va. (CAm.)* To carry in one's arms (niño); to care for. *-vn. (Cono Sur)* To have an affair with a half-breed girl.

chinel [che-nayl'], *m.* Guard.

chinela [che-nay'-lah], *f.* 1. Slipper. 2. Kind of pattens or clogs worn by women in dirty weather.

chinero [che-nay'-ro], *m.* A china-closet, or cupboard.

chinero [che-nay'-ro], *a. (And. Cono Sur)* fond of the (half-breed) girls.

chinesco, ca [che-nes'-co, cah], *a.* Chinese; relating to China.

chinetero [che-nay-tay'-ro], *a. (Cono Sur) V.* CHINERO.

chinflaina [chin-flah'-e-nah], *f.* Felt of a silk hat.

chinga [chin'-gah], *f.* 1. *(CAm. Carib.)* Fag end; cigar stub; *(fig.)* Drop, small amount. **Una chinga de agua**, a drop of water. 2. *(Carib.)* Drunkenness.

chingada [chin-gah'-dah], *f. (CAm. Mex.)* Fuck (acto sexual), screw; bloody nuisance (molestia).

chingana [chin-gah'-nah], *f. (Peru, Bol.)* 1. A small dramshop, where low people resort to dance and to get drunk; a " dive." 2. A tunnel, underground gallery.

chinganear [chin-gah-nay-ar'], *vn. (And. Cono Sur)* to go on the town, to live it up.

chinganero [chin-gah-ray'-ro], *(And. Cono Sur)* a. Fond of living it up, wildly social. *-m.* **chinganera**, the owner of a chingana.

chingar [chin-gar'], *va.* 1. To drink a lot. 2. *(CAm.)* To dock (animal); to cut off the tail. 3. *(LAm.)* To fuck, to screw. **Hijo de la chingada**, bastard. 4. *(Cono Sur)* To aim badly, to miss with (tiro). 5. *(Carib.)* To carry on one's shoulder. *-vn.* 1. To drink too much. 2. *(LAm.)* To fuck, to screw. 3. *(CAm.)* To joke. *-vr.* 1. To get intoxicated. 2. *(LAm.)* To fail, to fall through, to come to nothing. **La fiesta se chingó**, the party was a failure.

chingo [chin'-go], *a.* 1. *(CAm.)* Short (vestido); blunt (cuchillo); docked (animal). 2. *(And. Carib.)* Small (chico). 3. *(Cam, Carib.)* Snub-nosed (persona); flat, snub (nariz). 3. **Estar chingo por algo**, *(Carib.)* To be crazy about. *-m.* 1. *(And.)* Colt (potro). 2. *(And. CAm.)* Small boat. 3. **Chingos**, *(CAm.)* Underclothes. 4. **Un chingo de**, *(Mex.)* Lots of, loads of.

chingue [chin'-gay], *a. (Cono Sur)* Stinking, repulsive. *-m. (Cono Sur)* skunk.

chinguear [chin-gay-ar'], *va. (CAm.) V.* CHINGAR.

chinguirito [chin-ge-ree´-to], *m.* (*Mex. and Cuba*) 1. Rum from lees of sugar. 2. Draught, swallow. 3. Rough liquor.

chinilla, ita [che-neel´-lyah, ee´-tah], *f. dim.* A small pebble.

chinita [che-nee´-tah], *f.* 1. (*Amer.*) *V.* NIÑA. 2. Small stone, pebble. **Poner chinas a uno,** (*fig.*) to make trouble for somebody.

chinito, ta [che-nee´-to], *m. & f.* 1. (*Cono Sur*) servant. 2. (*LAm.*) Dear, dearest (en oración directa). 3. (*And. Carib. Cono Sur*) Indian boy, indian girl.

chino, na [chee´-no, nah], *a.* Chinese. **¿Somos chinos?,** do you think me a simpleton? **Ni que hablara en chino,** don't you understand?

chino, *m.* Chinese.

chino [che´-no], *a.* 1. (*CAm.*) Bald, hairless. 2. (*Mex.*) Curly, kinky (pelo); Curly-haired. 3. (*CAm. Carib.*) Angry, furious. 4. (*LAm.*) Young. -*m.* 1. (*LAm.*) Half-breed (mestizo); (*Cono Sur, Carib.*) Indian; offspring of Indian and Negress; (*Carib.*) Offpring of mulatto and Negress; (*And. Carib, Cono Sur*) servant; street urchin (golfo). **Quedarse como un chino,** (*Carib. Cono Sur*) to come off badly. **Trabajar como un chino,** (*Carib. Cono Sur*) to work like a slave. 2. (*And. CAm.*) Pig. 3. Chinos, curls. 4. (*CAm. Carib.*) Anger. **Le salió el chino,** he got angry.

chinoidina [che-no-e-dee´-nah], *f.* Quinoidine, an alkaloid from cinchona bark.

chinorri [che-nor´-re], *f.* Bird, chick.

chip [chip], *m. pl.* Chips. **Chip de silicio,** silicon chip. **Chip informático con conjunto de instrucciones reducidas (RISC),** reduced instruction set computer (RISC) chip.

chipa [chee´-pah], *f.* (*Amer.*) 1. Wooden basket in which Indians carry fruits. 2. Strap of leather.

chipe [chee´-pay], *a.* (*CAm.*) 1. Weak, sickly. 2. Whining (llorón), snivelling. -*m. & f.* (*And. CAm. Mex.*) Baby of the family.

chipé(n) [che-pay´], *a.* Super, smashing. -*adv.* Marvellously, really well. **Comer de chipé(n),** to have a super meal. -*f.* **La chipé(n),** the truth.

chipear [chee-pay-ar´], *va.* (*CAm.*) To bother, to pester. -*vn.* (*And. CAm.*) To moan, to whine (quejarse).

chipichipi [chee-pe-chee´-pe], *m.* (*Mex.*) Mist, drizzle, mizzle.

chipichusca [che-pe-choos´-cah], *f.* Whore.

chipión [che-pe-one´], *m.* (*CAm.*) Telling off.

chipirón [che-pe-rone], *m.* Small cuttlefish.

chipotear [che-po-tay-ar´], *va.* (*CAm.*) To slap.

Chipre [che-pray], *f.* Cyprus.

chiprino, na [che-pree´-no, nah], *a.* (*Poet.*) Proper to or proceeding from Cyprus.

chipriota [che-pre-o´-tah], *a. m. & f.* Native of Cyprus.

chiqueadores [che-kay-ah-do´-res], *m. pl.* Ring of tortoise-shell formerly used in Mexico as a feminine ornament.

chiquear [che-kay-ar´], *va.* (*Carib. Mex.*) To spoil, to indulge; to flatter, to suck up to (dar coba). -*vr.* 1. (*Mex.*) To be spoiled (mimarse). 2. (*CAm.*) To swagger along.

chiqueo [che-kay´-o], *m.* 1. (*Carib. Mex.*) Flattery, toadying. 2. (*CAm.*) Swagger (contoneo).

chiquero [che-kay´-ro], *m.* 1. Pigsty. 2. (*Prov.*) Hut for goats and kids. 3. (*Prov.*) Place where bulls are shut up in bull-feasts.

chiquichaque [che-ke-chah´-kay], *m.* 1. (*Coll.*) awer, sawyer. 2. Noise made by things rubbing against each other.

chiquichuite [che-ke-choo-ee´-tay], *m.* (*Mex.*) A willow basket.

chiquilicuatro [che-ke-le-coo-ah´-tro], *m.* Dabber, meddler. *V.* CHISGARABÍS.

chiquilín [che-ke-leen´], *m.* (*CAm. Cono Sur, Mex.*) Tiny tot, small boy.

chiquillada [che-keeh-lyah´-dah], *f.* A childish speech or action.

chiquillería [che-keel-lyay-ree´-ah], *f.* A great number of small children.

chiquillo, illa [che-keel´-lyo], *m. & f. dim.* A small child.

chiquirritico, ica, illo, illa, ito, ita [che-keer-re-tee´-co, ee´-cah], *a. dim.* Very small, very little.

chiquirritín, chiquitín [che-keer-re-teen´, che-ke-teen´], *m.* (*Coll.*) A small boy.

chiquitico, ca, chiquitillo, lla [che-ke-tee´-co, cah, che-ke-teel´-lyo, lyah], *a. dim.* Very small or little.

chiquitear [che-kee-tay-ar´], *vn.* 1. To play like a child. 2. To tipple (beber).

chiquito, ta [che-kee´-to, tah], *a. dim.* Little, small. **Hacerse chiquito,** (*Met.*) To dissemble or to conceal one's knowledge or power.

chiquitura [che-kee-too´-rah], *f.* 1. (*CAm.*) Small thing; insignificant detail. 2. (*CAm.*) *V.* CHIQUILLADA.

chira [che-rah], *f.* 1. (*And.*) Rag, tatter. 2. (*CAm.*) Wound, sore (llaga).

chirajos [che-rah´-hos], *m. pl.* 1. (*CAm.*) Lumber, junk (trastos). 2. (*And.*) Rasgs, tatters (andrajos).

chiribitas [che-re-bee´-tas], *f. pl.* 1. (*Coll.*) Particles which wander in the interior of the eyes and obscure the sight; spark (chispa). **Echar chiribitas, estar que echa chiribitas,** to be furious, to blow one´s top. **Le hacían chiribitas los ojos,** her eyes sparkled. 2. (*Bot.*) Daisy.

chiribitil [che-re-be-teel´], *m.* 1. Den, garret, cubbyhole. 2. A small room or chamber.

chirigaita [che-re-gah´-e-tah], *f.* (*Prov.*) Kind of gourd.

chirigota [che-ree-go´-tah], *f.* Joke; fun. **Hacer de uno una chirigota,** to poke fun at somebody.

chirigotero [che-ra-go-tay´-ro], *a.* Full of jokes, facetious.

chirimbolo [che-rem-bo´-lo], *m.* Thingummyjig; strange object, odd-looking implement. **Chirimbolos,** things, gear, equipment; lumber (trastos); junk; (*Culin.*) Kitchen things.

chirimía [che-re-mee´-ah], *f.* Oboe, a musical, wind instrument. -*m.* Oboe-player.

chirimiri [che-re-me´-re], *m.* Drizzle.

chirimoya [che-re-mo´-yah], *f.* Most delicious American fruit.

chirimoyo [che-re-mo´-yo], *m.* The tree which yields the *chirimoya.*

chirinada [che-re-nah´-dah], *f.* 1. (*Cono Sur*) failure, disaster. 2. *V.* CHIRINOLA.

chiringuito [che-ren-ge´-to], *m.* Small shop, stall; open air restaurant, open air drinks stall; bar; night club.

chirinola [che-re-no´-lah], *f.* l. Game played by boys. 2. Trifle, a thing of little importance or value. **Estar de chirinola,** to be in good spirits. 3. Fight, scrap; heated discussion; lengthy conversation, lively talk. **Pasar la tarde de chirinola,** to spend the afternoon deep in conversation.

chiripa [che-ree´-pah], *f.* (*Coll.*) Fortunate chance; windfall, good bargain, in billiards, a lucky stroke; a scratch, a fluke. **Por chiripa,** by chance.

chiripá [che--re-pah´], *m.* (*And. Cono Sur*) kind of blanket worn as trousers. **Gente de chiripá,** country people, peasants.

chiripear [che-re-pay-ar´], *va.* 1. To make a lucky hit; to procure a windfall. 2. To make a scratch or fluke at billiards.

chiripero [che-re-pay´-ro], *m.* A lucky person by chance.

chirís [che-rees´], *m. & f.* (*CAm.*) Kid, child.

chirivía [che-re-vee´-ah], *f.* 1. (*Bot.*) Parsnip. 2. (*Orn.*) Wagtail. *V.* AGUZANIEVE.

chirivisco [che-re-ves´-co], *m.* (*CAm.*) Firewood, kindling.

chirla [cheer´-lah], *f.* Mussel. *V.* ALMEJA.

chirlador, ra [chir-lah-dor´, rah], *m. & f.* A clamorous prattler, a talkative person.

chirlar [chir-lar´], *vn.* To prattle, to talk much and loud.

chirle [cheer´-lay], *m.* 1. The dung of sheep and goats. 2. A wild grape. 3. Watery, wishy-washy (sopa). 4. Flat, dull, wishy-washy.

chirlo [cheer´-lo], *m.* A large wound in the face, and the scar it leaves when cured.

chirola [chee-ro'-lah], *f. (CAm. Carib.)*, **chirona** *f.* Jug, jail. **Estar en chirola**, to be in the jug.

chiros [che'-ros], *m. pl. (And.)* Rags, tatters.

chiroso [che-ro-so], *a. (And. CAm.)* Ragged, tattered.

chirota [che-ro'-tah], *f. (CAm.)* Tough woman.

chirote [che-ro'-tay], *a. (And.)* Daft.

chirriado [chir-re-ah'-do], *m. V.* CHIRRIDO. *-a. (And.)* Witty (gracioso). **-Chirriado, da**, *pp.* of CHIRRIAR.

chirriador, ra [chir-re-ah-dor', rah], *a.* 1. Hissing (en la sartén). 2. Creaking (puerta). 3. Chirper.

chirriar [chir-re-ar'], *vn.* 1. To hiss (en la sartén). 2. To creak (puerta). 3. To crepitate; to creep. 4. To chirp, or to chirk. 5. To sing out of tune or time. 6. *(And.)* To shiver with cold. 7. *(And.)* To go on a spree.

chirrichote [chir-re-cho'-tay], *m. (Prov.)* A presumptuous man.

chirrido [chir-ree'-o], *m.* Chirping of birds; crick; chattering, shrill, sound; screech(ing); squeal(ling).

chirrío [chir-ree'-o], *m.* The creaking noise made by carts and wagons; crick; crepitation.

chirrión [chir-re-on'], *m.* 1. Tumbrel, a strong muck or dung cart; one-horse cart. 2. A whiphandle and lash. 3. Scraping on a violin by one who cannot play rightly. 4. *(CAm.)* String, line (sarta). 5. *(CAm.)* Chat, conversation.

chirrionar [cher-re-o-nar'], *va. (And. Mex.)* To whip, to lash.

chirrionero [chir-re-o-nay'-ro], *m.* Scavenger, dungcart driver.

chirrisco [cher-res'-co], *a.* 1. *(CAm. Carib.)* Very small, tiny. 2. *(Mex.)* Flirtatious. **Viejo chirrisco**, dirty old man.

chirumbela [che-room-bay'-lah], *f. V.* CHURUMBELA.

chirumen [che-roo'-men], *m.* Judgment. *V.* CALETRE.

chirusa [che-roo'-sah], *f. (Cono Sur)* girl, kid; poor woman.

chis [chis], *interj.* Hey!, psst! (pidiendo silencio); *(LAm.)* Ugh! (asco).

chischás [chis-chahs'], *m. (Coll.)* Clashing of swords or other sidearms.

chiscón [chis-cone'], *m.* Shack, hovel, slum.

chischís [chis-chees'], *m. (And. CAm. Carib.)* Drizzle.

chisgarabís [chis-gah-ra-bees'], *m.* A dabbler, an insignificant, noisy fellow, who meddles and interferes in everything.

chisguete [chis-gay'-tay], *m. (Coll.)* A small draft of wine; a small spout of any liquid.

chisguetear [chis-gay-te-ar'], *va.* To drink a small draught.

chisme [chees'-may], *m.* 1. Gossip, misreport, misrepresentation; any account maliciously false; a tale or story intended to excite discord and quarrels. **No me vengas con esos chismes**, don't bring those tales to me 2. Variety of lumber of little value; thing, whatnot. **Dame el chisme ese**, give me that whatsit, please. 3. *(Tec.)* Gadget, contrivance, jigger.

chismear [chis-may-ar'], *va.* To tattle, to carry tales, to misrepresent, to misreport, to tell tales.

chismería [chis-may-ree'ah], *f.* **chismerío** *m. (Cono Sur, Carib.)* Gossip, tittle-tattle, scandal.

chismero, ra [chis-may'-ro, ah], **chismoso, sa** [chis-mo'-so, sah], *a.* Tattling, tale-bearing, propagating injurious rumors.

chismorrear [chis-mor-ray-ar'], *vn. V.* CHISMEAR.

chismorreo [chis-mor-ray'-o], *m. V.* CHISMEAR.

chispa [chis'-pah], *f.* 1. Spark (centella); *(fig.)* Sparkle, gleam. **Echar chispas**, *(fig.)* To be hopping mad. 2. Drop (gota de lluvia). **Caen chispas**, there are a few drops falling. 3. *(fig.)* Bit, tiny amount. **Ni chispa**, not the least bit. **Eso no tiene ni chispa de gracia**, that's not in the least bit funny. **Si tuviera una chispa de inteligencia**, if he had an atom of intelligence. 4. *(fig.)* Sparkle, wit; life (ingenio). **El cuento tiene chispa**, the story has some wit. **Dar chispas**, to show oneself to be bright. **Tener mucha chispa**, to be a lively sort. 5. Drunkenness. **Coger una chispa**, to get tight. 6. *(And.)* Rumor. 7. *(And.)* Gun, weapon. *-a.* 1. *(Mex.)* Funny, amusing. 2. **Estar chispa**, to be tight. *-m.* Electrician.

chisparse [chis-par'-say], *vr.* 1. *(Amer.)* To become intoxicated, to get drunk. 2. *(CAm. Mex.)* To run away (huir).

¡chispas! [chees'-pas], *int.* Fire and tow! Blazes!

chispazo [chis-pah'-tho], *m.* 1. Spark. **Me saltó un chispazo a la cara**, a spark flew into my face. 2. *(Met.)* Tale or story mischievously circulated.

chispeante [chis-pay-ahn'-tay], *a. (fig.)* Sparkling, scintillating.

chispear [chis-pay-ar'], *vn.* 1. To sparkle, to emit sparks. 2. To rain gently or in small drops. 3. *(And.)* To gossip, to spread scandal. *-vr. (Carib. Cono Sur)* to get drunk.

chispeo [chis-pay'-o], *m.* Sparkle, brilliancy.

chispero [chis-pay'-ro], *m.* 1. Smith who makes kitchen utensils. 2. *(And. Carib.)* Gossiping, scandal-mongering. 3. *(CAm.)* Lighter; *(Aut.)* Sparkling plug.

chisporo, ra [chis-pay'-ro, rah], *a.* Emitting a number of sparks.

chispita [chis-pee'-tah], *f.* **Una chispita de vino**, a drop of wine.

chispo [chees'-po], *m.* 1 *(Coll.)* Tipsy. 2. *V.* CHISGUETE.

chisporrotear [chis-por-ro-tay-ar'], *vn. (Coll.)* To hiss and crackle, as burning oil or tallow mixed with water; to sputter.

chisporroteo [chis-por-ro-tay'-o], *m. (Coll.)* Sibilation, hissing, crackling.

chisposo, sa [chis-po'-so, sah], *a.* Sparkling, emitting sparks.

chisquero [chis-kay-ro], *m.* Pocket lighter.

chist [chist], **interj** *V.* CHIS.

chistar [chis-tar'], *vn.* To mumble, to mutter. **No chistó palabra**, he did not open his lips.

chiste [chees'-tay], *m.* 1. A fine witty saying 2. Facetiousness. 3. Fun, joke, jest. **Dar en el chiste**, to hit the nail on the head. **Chiste pesado**, scurvy trick. **No veo el chiste**, I don't get it. **Tomar algo a chiste**, to take something as a joke.

chistera [chis-tay'-rah], *f.* 1. Angler's basket, narrow basket for fish. 2. *(Coll.)* Top hat, topper (sombrero de copa).

chistosamente [chis-to-sah-men-tay], *adv.* Facetiously, wittily, merrily, gaily.

chistoso, sa [chis-to'-so, sah], *a.* Gay, cheerful, lively, facetious, humorous; funny.

chistu [chis-too], *m.* Flute (Basque).

chistulari [chis-too-lah'-re], *m.* (Basque) Flute player.

chita [chee'-tah], *f.* 1. The anklebone in sheep and bullocks. 2. Game with this bone. **No vale una chita**, it is not worth a rush. **Dar en la chita**, *(Met.)* to hit the nail on the head. **A la chita callando**, secretly, very quietly, by stealth. 3. *(Mex.)* Net bag; money; small savings, nest egg.

chite [chee'tay], *m.* Kind of cotton stuff, chintzes; India calico.

chiticalla [che-te-cal'-lyah], *f. (Coll.)* One who keeps silence.

chiticallar [chetecal-lyar'], *vn. (Coll.)* To keep silence. **Ir or andar chiticallando**, to go on one's tiptoes, not to make a noise.

chito [chee'-to], *m.* A piece of wood, bone, or other substance, on which the money is put in the game of *chita*. **Irse a chitos**, *(Coll.)* to lead a debauched life.

¡chito, chitón ! [chee'-to, che-tone'], *int.* Hush! not a word! hist! silence! mum!

chiva [chee'-vah], *f.* 1. Kid, a female goat. 2. *(LAm.)* Goatee (barba). 3. *(And. CAm.)* Bus; car. 4. *(CAm.)* Blanket, bedcover. 5. *(Carib. Cono Sur)* Naughty little girl, *(CAm. Cono Sur)* mannish woman; *(And. Carib, Cono Sur)* immoral woman. 6. *(CAm. Cono Sur)* Fib, tall story. 7. *(Carib.)* Grass, informer (delator). *-a. (CAm.) (excl.)* Look out!

chival [che-vahl'], *m. (Obs.)* Herd of goats.

chivalete [che-vah-lay'-tay], *m.* Chest of drawers with a desk for writing. *V.* ESCRITORIO.

chivar [che-var'], *(LAm.) (Prov.) va.* To annoy, to upset (molestar), to swindle. *-vr.* 1. To get annoyed. 2. To tell, to split. **Chivarse de algo al maestro**, to tell the teacher, to split to the teacher.

chivata [che-vah'-tah], *f.* 1. *(Prov.)* Shepherd's club or staff. 2. Torch.

chivatazo [che-vah-tah-tho], *m.* Tip-off. **Dar chivatazo,** to inform, to give a tip-off.

chivatear [che-vah-tay-ar'], *vn.* 1. To split (soplar); to inform, to squel; to blow the gaff. 2. *(And. Cono Sur)* To shout, to make a hullabaloo; to jump about; to indulge in horseplay (retozar). 3. *(Carib.)* To create a big impression. *-vr. (Carib.)* To get scared.

chivato [che-vah'-to], *m.*

chivera [che-vay'-rah], *f. (And. CAm.)* Goatee (beard).

chivero [che-vay'-ro], *m.* 1. *(Amer.)* The puma, American lion. 2. *(And.)* Bus-driver. 3. *(And.)* Brawler (matón). 4. *(Carib.)* Intriguer.

chivetero, chivital [che-vay-tay'-ro, che-ve-tahl'], *m.* Fold for kids.

chivo [chee'-vo], *m.* 1. Kid, he-goat. 2. *(Prov.)* Pit, a place for the lees of oil. 3. *(CAm.)* Dice; game of dice. 4. *(Carib.)* Fraud (estafa); plot, intrigue (intriga); smuggling; illegal trading; contraband (géneros). 5. *(And. CAm. Carib, Cono Sur)* fit of anger. 6. *(Mex.)* Day's wages (jornal); advance (anticipo); back-hander (soborno). 7. *(Carib.)* Punch, blow (golpe). 8. *(And. CAm.)* Naughty boy. 9. *(CAm.)* Guatemalan. 10. *(CAm.)* Pimp (chulo). *-a. (CAm.)* Guatemalan.

chivón [che-vone'], *(Carib.)* 1. *a.* Annoying, irritating. 2. *m.* **Chivona** *f.* Bore.

¡cho! [cho], *int.* A word used by the drivers of mules or horses to make them stop: whoa!

choca [cho'-cah], *f.* 1. Part of the game given to a hawk. 2. Stick or paddle used by soapboilers.

chocallo [cho-cahl'-lyo], *m. (Obs.)* V. ZARCILLO.

chocante [cho-cahn'-tay], *a.* 1. Startling, striking (sorprendente); odd, strange; note-worthy. **Es chocante que...,** it is odd that..... 2. Shocking, scandalous. 3. *(LAm.)* Tiresome, tedious, annoying; cheeky (fresco), impertinent.

chocantería [cho-cahn-tay-ree'-ah], *f. (LAm.)* 1. Impertinence. 2. Coarse joke (chiste).

chocar [cho'car'], *vn.* 1. To strike, to knock, to dash against one another. **Chocar con,** to collide with. **El buque**

chocarrear [cho-car-ray-ar'], *vn.* To joke, to jest, to act the buffoon.

chocarrería [cho-car-ray-ree'-ah], *f.* 1. Buffoonery, low jests, scurrilous mirth. 2. Deceiving, cheating at play. V. FULLERÍA.

chocarrero [cho-car-ray'-ro], *m.* 1. Buffoon, low jester, merry-andrew, mimic. 2. *(Obs.)* Cheat, or sharper at at play. 3. Vulgar. V. FULLERO.

chocarrero, ra [cho-car-ray'-ro, rah], *a.* Practising indecent raillery; scurrilous, buffoonlike.

chocarresco, ca [cho-car-res'-co, cah], *a. (Obs.)* V. CHOCAR-RERO.

chocha, chochaperdiz [cho'-chah, cho-chah-per-deeth'], *f. (Orn.)* Woodcock.

chochada [cho-chah'-dah], *f.* 1. Cunt (vagina). 2. *(CAm.)* Triviality. **Chochas,** bits and pieces.

chochear [cho-chay-ar'], *vn.* 1. To dodder, to be doddery, to be senile; to be in one's dotage. 2. *(fig.)* To be soft, to go all sentimental.

chochera, chochez [cho-chay'-rah, cho-cheth'], *f.* 1. Dotage, the speech and action of a dotard. 2. Silly thing. 3. *(And. Cono Sur)* favorite, pet. **Tener chochera por una,** to dote on somebody.

chochín [cho-cheen'], *m.* 1. Wren. 2. Bird; girl-friend.

chochita [cho-che'-tah], *f.* Wren.

chocho, cha [cho'-cho, chah], *a.* 1. Doting, having the intellect impaired by age. 2. Doddering, doddery, senile. 3. *(Cono Sur)* happy. 4. *(CAm.)* Nicaraguan.

chocho [cho'-cho], *m.* 1.*(Bot.)* Lupine V. ALTRAMUZ. 2. A sweetmeat or confection. **Chochos,** all sorts of sweetmeats given to children; dainties. 3. Drug addict. 4. *(CAm.)* Nicaraguan. 5. *(CAm.) Excl.* No kidding!, Really!. 6. *(Anat.)* Cunt.

chochoca [cho-cho-cah], *f. (CAm.)* Nut, head.

chocholear [cho-cho-lay-ar'], *va. (And.)* To spoil, to pamper.

chocilla [cho-theel'-lyah], *f. dim.* A small hut, a low cottage.

choclar [cho-clar'], *vn.* 1. In the Spanish game of *argolla,* to drive the ball out by the rings. 2. To bolt into a room.

choclo [cho'-clo], *m.* 1. V. CHANCLO. 2. *(Amer.)* Green ear of corn in a state fit for eating. 3. *(Cono Sur)* **choclos,** children's arms; children's legs. 4. *(And.) (fig.)* **Un choclo de,** a group of. 5. *(Cono Sur)* difficulty, trouble.

choco [cho'-co], *m. (Prov.)* 1. The small cuttlefish. 2. Hiding place (children) V. JIBIA.

choco [cho'-co], *a. (And. Cono Sur)* Dark red; chocolate-colored; swarthy dark (moreno). 2. *(CAm. Cono Sur, Mex.)* One-armed (manco); one-legged (cojo); one-eyed (tuerto); *-m.* 1. *(Cono Sur)* stump. 2. *(And.)* Top hat. 3. *(Mex.)* Cunt, fanny.

chocolate [cho-colah'tay], *m.* 1. Chocolate. 2. Chocolate the liquor made by a solution of chocolate in water, milk, or atole. 3. *(LAm.)* Blood. **Dar a uno agua de su propio chocolate,** to give somebody a taste of his own medicine. 4. Hash, pot. **Darle al chocolate,** to be hooked on drugs.

chocolatera [cho-co-lah-tay'rah], *f.* Chocolate pot.

chocolatería [cho-co-lah-tay-ree'-ah], *f.* Shop where only chocolate is sold; chocolate factory.

chocolatero [cho-colah-tay'-ro], *m.* 1. One who grinds or makes chocolate. 2. The seller of chocolate. 3. *(Mex.)* A stiff north wind, but not tempestuous like that of winter. *-a.* Fond of chocolate.

chocolatina [cho-co-lah-te'-nah], *f.* Chocolate.

chocolear [cho-co-lay-ar'], *(And.) -va.* To dock, to cut off the tail of. *-vn.* To get depressed.

chode [cho'-day], *m. (Prov.)* Paste of milk, eggs, sugar and flour.

chofer [chofer'], *m.* Chauffeur, automobile driver, motorist.

chofero [cho-fay'-ro], *m.* V. CHOFISTA.

chofes [cho'-fess], *m. pl.* Lungs. V. BOFES.

chofeta [cho-fay'-tah], *f.* Chafing-dish, firepan; a portable grate for coals.

chofista [chofees'tah], *m.* One who lives upon livers and lights.

cholada [cho-lah'-dah], *f. (And.)* Action typical of a cholo.

cholería [cho-lay-ree'-ah], *f. (And.),* **cholerío** *m. (And.),* Group of cholos.

cholga [chol-gah], *f. (LAm.)* Mussel, clam.

cholla [chol'-lyah], *f.* 1. *(Coll.)* Skull. 2. *(Met.)* Faculty, powers of the mind, judgment. **No tiene cholla,** he has not the brains of a sparrow; he is bird-brained. 3. *(CAm.)* Wound, sore. 4. *(And. CAm.)* Laziness, slowness.

chollo [chol'-lyo], *m.* 1. *(Com.)* Bargain, snip. **Es un chollo,** it's a doddle. 2. Love affair.

cholludo [chol-loo'-do], *a. (And. CAm.)* Lazy, slow.

cholo, la [cho'-lo, lah], *a. (Amer.)* 1. Halfbreed of European and Indian parentage. 2. Familiar diminutive in kindly tone, equivalent to son, deary. 3. *(Cono Sur)* coward.

chongo [chon'-go], *m.* 1. *(Cono Sur)* blunt knife, worn-out knife. 2. *(Carib.)* Old horse. 3. Chongos *(CAm. Mex.)* Pigtails, tresses (trenzas); bun (moño).

chonta [chon'-tah], *f.* A kind of palmtree, the wood of which is harder than ebony. *Cf.* CHORITA.

chontal [chon-tahl'], *m.* 1. A grove of chonta-trees. 2. *(Mex. and CAm.)* An Indian with no training, uncivilized; coarse, rough.

chop [chop], *m. (LAm.)* Tankard, mug.

chopa [cho'-pah], *f.* 1. *(Zool.)* Kind of seabream. 2. *(Naut.)* Topgallant poop, or poop royal. 3. Jacket.

chopazo, chope [cho-pah'-tho], *m. (Cono Sur)* punch, bash.

chopera [cho-pay'-rah], *f.* Poplar grove.

chopo [cho'-po], *m.* 1. *(Bot.)* Black poplar-tree. 2. Gun. **Cargar con el chopo,** *(fig.)* To join up, to do one's military service.

choque [cho'-kay], *m.* 1. Shock, clash, dash, collision. 2. Congress, encounter. 3. *(Mil.)* Skirmish, a slight engagement. 4. Difference, dispute, contest; jar. **Entrar choque**, to clash. 5. *(Naut.)* Chock, fur. **Choques de entremises**, *(Naut.)* Faying-chocks. 6. Crash, collision. **Choque de frente**, head-on collision. 7. *(Med.)* Shock.

choquear [cho-kay-ar'], *va.* To beat the soda-ash with the paddle in order to secure soap in fine pieces.

choquecilla [cho-kay-theel'-lyah], *f.* V. CHOQUEZUELA.

choqueo [cho-kay'-o], *m.* The act of beating the soapashes.

chorar [cho-rar'], *va.* To burgle (casa); to rip off (objeto).

chorba [chor'-bah], *f.* Bird, girlfriend.

chorbo [chor'-bo], *m.* 1. Boyfriend, guy, bloke (tío). 2. Pimp.

chorca [chor'-cah], *f. (Prov.)* Pit or hole dug in the ground. *V.* HOYO.

chorcha [chor'-chah], *f.* 1. *(Mex.)* Noisy party. **Una chorcha de amigos**, a group of friends. 2. *(CAm.)* Crest, comb. 3. *(CAm.) (Med.)* Goitre. 4. *(CAm.)* Clitoris. *V.* CHOCHA.

chorchero [chor-chay'-ro], *a. (Mex.)* Party-loving.

chorchi [chor'-che], *m.* Soldier.

chorear [cho-ray-ar'], *vn. (Cono Sur)* To grumble, to complain. *-va.* 1. **Me chorea**, it gets up my nose. 2. To pinch (robar).

choreo [cho-ray'-o], *m. (Cono Sur)* Grouse, complaint.

chori [cho'-re], *m.* 1. Knife. 2. Thief.

choricear [cho-re-thay-ar'], *va.* To rip off, to lift.

choricería [cho-re-thay-ree'-ah], *f. V.* SALCHICHERÍA.

choricero [cho-re-thay'-ro], *m.* 1. Sausage maker or seller. 2. Crook.

chorillo [cho-reel'-lyo], *m. (Peru)* Mill for coarse fabrics without fulling-stocks.

chorita [cho-ree'-tah], *m. (Amer.)* A palm-tree, the wood of which is black, solid, and heavier than ebony. *V.* CHONTA.

chorizar [cho-re-thar'], *va.* To nick, to rip off.

chorizo [cho-ree'-tho], *m.* 1. Pork sausage. 2. Balancing pole (circo). 3. *(Anat.)* Prick. 4. *(And. Cono Sur)* rump steak. 5. *(And. Cono Sur) (Arquit.)* Mixture of clay and straw used in plastering. 6. Thug, lout (matón). 7. *(And.)* Idiot. 8. *(Carib.)* Mulatto.

chorlito [chor-lee'to], *m.* 1. *(Orn.)* Curlew or gray plover. 2. *(Orn.)* Red shank. **Cabeza de chorlito**, hare-brained, frivolous.

chorlo [chor'-lo], *m.* 1. Schorl, tourmaline, especially the black variety. 2. *(And. CAm. Carib.)* Great-grand-grandchild.

choro [cho'-ro], *m.* 1. Thief, burglar. 2. *(And. Cono Sur) (Zool.)* Mussel.

chorote [cho-ro'-tay], *m.* A certain chocolate which the poor people of Venezuela take.

chorra [chor-rah], *f.* 1. Luck, jam. **¡Qué chorra tiene!**, look at that for jam! 2. *(Cono Sur)* underworld slang. 3. *(Anat.)* Prick. 4. *adv.* By chance.

chorreado, da [chor-ray-ah'-do, dah], *a.* Applied to a kind of satin. *-pp.* of CHORREAR.

chorreadura [chor-ray-ah-doo'-rah], *f.* Dripping, dropping, welling.

chorrear [chor-ray-ar'], *va.* 1. To fall or drop front a spout, to outpour, to gush, to drip. 2. *(Met.)* To come successively, or one by one. 3. To tick off (regañar). 4. *(And.)* To soak (mojar). *-vn.* 1. To gush, to spout. **Chorrear de sudor**, to run with sweat. **La ropa chorrear todavía**, his clothes are still wringing wet. 2. *(Fit.)* To trickle. **Chorrean todavía las solicitudes**, the applications are still trickling in. *-vr.* **Chorrearse algo**, to pinch something.

chorreo [chor-ray'-o], *m.* 1. The act and effect of dropping, dripping. 2. *(fig.)* Constant drain (de fuentes) 3. Ticking off (reprimenda). 4. **Chorreo mental**, nonsense.

chorrera [chor-ray'-rah], *f.* 1. Spout or place whence liquids drop. 2. Mark left by water or other liquids 3. Ornament formerly appended to crosses or badges of military orders. 4. Frill of a shirt. 5. *(LAm.) (fig.)* String, stream, lot. **Una chorrera de**, a whole string of, a lot of. 6. *(Carib.)* Ticking off. 7. *V.* JAMON.

chorrero [chor-ray'-ro], *a.* Jammy, lucky.

chorretada [chor-ray-tah'-dah], *f. (Coll.)* Water or other liquid rushing from a spout.

chorrillo [chor-reel'-lyo], *m.* 1. *(dim.)* A small spout of water or any other liquid. 2. The continual coming in and out going of money. **Irse por el chorrillo**, *(Met.)* to drive with the current, to conform to custom.

chorrito [chor-ree'-to], *m. dim.* A small spout of water or any other liquid.

chorro [chor'-ro], *m.* 1. Water or any other liquid, issuing from a spout or other narrow place, gush. **Beber a chorro**, to drink a jet of wine (from a wineskin). **Salir a chorros**, to gush forth. 2. A jet of water. 3. A strong and coarse sound emitted by the mouth. **Un chorro de palabras**, a stream of words. **Hablar a chorros**, to talk nineteen to the dozen. 4. Hole made in the ground for playing with nuts. **Soltar el chorro**, *(Met.)* to burst out into laughter. **A chorros**, abundantly, copiously. 5. Strand (látigo). 6. *(CAm.)* Tap (grifo) 7. *(Cono Sur)* thief, pickpocket. 8. *(Carib.)* Ticking off (ladrón).

chorro de arena [chor'-ro day ah-ray'-nah], *m.* Sandblast.

chorrón [chor-rone'], *m.* Hackled or dressed hemp.

chortal [chor-tahl´], *m.* Fountain or spring at the surface of the ground.

chota [cho'-tah], *f.* 1. A sucking kid. 2. Heifer calf. *-m. & f.* Hanger-on; creep, toady.

chotacabras [cho-tah-cah'-bras], *f. (Orn.)* Goatsucker, churnowl.

chotar [cho-tar'], *va. (Obs.)* To suck. *V.* MAMAR.

chote [cho'-tay], *m. V.* CHAYOTE.

chotear [cho-tay-ar´], *va.* 1. To tease. 2. To spoil, to pamper (mimar). 3. *(CAm.)* To shadow, to tail (sospechoso). *-vr.* 1. To joke, to take things as a joke. 2. To cough, to inform.

choteo [cho-tay'-o], *m.* Raillery, badinage, teasing.

chotis [cho'-tees], *m.* 1. Scottische. 2. Traditional dance of Madrid. 3. **Ser más agarrado que un chotis**, to be tight-fisted.

choto [cho'-to], *m.* 1. A sucking kid. 2. A calf. 3. Stupid old git.

choto [cho'-to], *a.* 1. *(CAm.)* Abundant, plentiful. **Estar choto de**, to be full of.

chotuno, na [cho-too'-no, nah], *a.* 1. Sucking (cabritas). 2. Poor, starved (corderos). 3. Goatish. **Oler a chotuna**, to stink like a goat.

chova [cho'-vah], *f. (Orn.)* Jay, chough.

chovinismo [cho-ve-nees'-mo], *m.* etc. *V.* CHAUVINISMO.

choya [cho'-yah], *f. (Orn.)* Jackdaw, crow. *V.* CORNEJA.

choz [choth], *m. (Coll.)* Sound of a blow or stroke. **Esta especie me ha dado choz**, *(Coll.)* I was struck with amazement at this affair.

choza [cho'-thah], *f.* Hut, cottage, hovel.

chozna [choth'-nah], *f.* Great-granddaughter.

chozno [choth'-no], *m.* Great-grandchild.

chozo [cho'-tho], *m.* A small hut; hovel.

chozuela [cho-thoo-ay'-lah], *f. dim.* A small hut or cottage.

chrisma, christma, christmas [chris'-mas], *f. m. pl.* Christmas card.

chual [choo-ahl'], *m.* A wild plant of California; a pigweed or goosefoot.

chualar [choo-ah-lar'], *m.* A spot abounding in chual plants.

chubarba [choo-bar'-bah], *f. (Bot.)* Stonecrop.

chubasco [choo-bahs'-co], *m. (Naut.)* Squall, a violent gust of wind and rain.

chubascoso, sa [choo-bas-co´-so, sah], *a.* Squally, gusty, stormy.

chubasquero [choo-bas-kay'-ro], *m.* 1. Oilskin; light raincoat (gabardina). 2. French letter.

chuca [choo´-cah], *f.* The concave part of a ball used by boys in play.

chucán [choo-cahn'], *a. (CAm.)* Buffoonish (bufón); coarse (grosero), rude.

chucallo [choo-cahl'-lyo], *m. (Obs.) V.* ZARCILLO.

chúcaro [choo'-cah-ro], *a. (LAm.)* Wild, untamed (animal); shy (persona).

chucear [choo-thay-ar'], *va. (LAm.)* To prick, to goad.

chucero [choo-thay'-ro], *m. (Mil.)* Pikeman.

chucha [choo'-chah], *f.* 1. A female dog, bitch. 2. **¡Chucha!** exclamation to restrain her.

chucha [choo'-chah], *f.* 1. Opossum. 2. *(And.)* Body odour. 3. *(And. Cono Sur)* Cunt.

chuchada [choo-chah'-dah], *f. (CAm.)* Trick, swindle.

chuchear [choo-chay-ar'], *va.* To fowl with calls, gins, and nets.-*vn.* To whisper. *V.* CUCHICHEAR.

chuchería [choo-chay-ree'-ah], *f.* 1. Gewgaw, bauble, a pretty trifle, a toy. 2. Tidbit which is nice, but not expensive. 3. Mode of fowling with calls, gins, and nets.

chuchero [choo-chay'-ro], *m.* Birdcatcher.

chucho [choo'-cho], *m.* 1. *(Orn.)* Longeared owl. 2. A dog. 3. **¡Chucho!** exclamation used to call a dog. 3. Sweetheart. 4. *(Carib.)* Switch; siding. 5. *(Carib.)* Rawhide whip (látigo). 6. *(Cono Sur)* jail. 7. *(LAm.)* Shakes, shivers. **Entrarle a uno el chucho,** to get the jitters. 8. *(CAm.)* Spiv (ostentoso) 9. *(LAm.)* Reefer; joint. 10. *(And. CAm. Mex.) (Culin.)* Tamale. -*a.* 1. *(And.)* Soft, watery (fruta); wrinkled (persona). 2. *(CAm.)* Mean (tacaño). 3. *(Mex.)* Gossipy.

chuchumeco [choo-choo-may'-co], *m.* 1. A sorry, contemptible little fellow. 2. Mean person (tacaño). 3. *(Cono Sur)* sickly person. 4. *(And. Carib.)* Toff, dude. 5. *(Carib.)* Idiot.

chuchupate [choo-choo-pah'-tay], *m.* A plant of the umbelliferae, indigenous to the Pacific coast.

chueca [choo-ay'-cah], *f.* 1. Pan or hollow of the joints of bones. 2. A small ball with which country people play at crickets. 3. *(Coll.)* Fun, trick. *V.* CHASCO. A soap-maker's paddle. 4. *(Bot.)* Stump.

chuecazo [choo-ay-cah'-tho], *m.* Stroke given to a ball.

chueco [choo-ay'-co], *a.* 1. *(LAm.)* Knock-kneed; *(And. Cono Sur)* pigeon-toed (patituerto); *(And.)* Lame (cojo); *(Mex.)* One-armed (manco); one-legged; *(CAm. Carib. Mex.)* Crooked, twisted, bent (torcido); bent, crooked (corrupto); left-handed (zurdo). **Un negocio chueco,** a crooked deal.

chufa [choo'-fah], *f.* 1. *(Bot.)* The edible cyperus; a sedge, the root of which is used as a substitute for coffee. 2. *(Obs.)* Rodomontade, an empty boast. **Echar chufas,** to hector, to act the bully.

chufeta [choo-fay'-tah], *f.* 1. Jest, joke. 2. *(Prov.)* Small pan used to hold live coals.

chufla [choo-flah], *f.* Joke, merry quip. **Tomar algo a chufla,** to take something as a joke.

chuflarse [choo-flar'-say], *vr.* To joke, to make jokes; to take things as a joke.

chufleta [choo-flay'tah], *f.* Taunt, jeer, gibe, fling, scoff.

chufletear [choo-flay-tayar´], *vn.* To sneer, to taunt, to show contempt, to joke.

chufletero, ra [choo-flay-tay'-ro, rah], *a.* Taunting, sneering.

chula [choo'-lah], *f.* 1. Woman from the back streets, low-class woman. 2. Loud wench, flashy female; brassy girl (charra). 3. *(LAm.)* girlfriend.

chulada [choo-lah'-dah], *f.* 1. Droll speech or action, pleasant conversation. 3. Indecorous action of persons of bad breeding or low condition. 3. Contemptuous word or action.

chulear [choo-layar'], *va..* To jest, to joke. 2. To sneer, to taunt, to ridicule. -*vr.* **Chulearse de,** to take the mickey out of.

chulería [choo-lay-ree'-ah], *f.* 1. A pleasing manner of acting and speaking, vulgarity, natural charm. 2. *V.* CHULADA.

chulesco [choo-lays'-co], *a. V.* CHULO.

chuleta [choo-lay'-tah], *f.* 1. Chop, cutlet. 2. *(Cos.)* Insert, piece let in. 3. Punch, bash (golpe). 4. *(Univ.)* Crib, trot; (TV) Autocue, teleprompter. 5. Side whiskers, sideboards (patillas). 6. Toff (persona). 7. Divot (golf).

chulillo [choo-leel-lyo], *m. (And.)* Tradesman´s assistant.

chulo, la [choo'-lo, lah], *m. & f.* 1. Punster, jester, merry-andrew. 2. An artful, sly, and deceitful person. 3. A funny person. 4. Butcher´s mate or assistant. 5. Bullfighter's assistant. 6. *V.* PÍCARO. A playful term of endearment. 7.

Smart, attractive (aspecto). 8. Proud, jaunty, swaggering. **Con el sombrero a lo chulo,** with his hat at a rakish angle. **Iba muy chulo,** he walked with a swagger. 9. Brilliant, super. 10. Villain, rascal. **Chulo de putas,** pimp, pander.

chulla [chool'-lyah], *f. (Prov.)* Slice of bacon.

chumacera [choo-mah-thay'-rah], *f.* 1 *(Mech.)* Bearing, journal bearing; cushion. 2. *(Naut.)* Rowlock, a strip of wood put on the gunwale of a boat to prevent the oars from wearing it.

chumarse [choo-mar'-say], *vr. (And.)* To get drunk.

chumbar [choom-bar'], *va.* 1. *(Cono Sur)* To attack, to go for (perro). 2. *(And.)* To shoot (fusilar). 3. To swaddle (bebé).

chumbo or **higo chumbo** [choom-bo], *m.* 1. Indian fig, pricky pear. 2. *(Cono Sur)* shot, pellet.

chumeco [choo-may'-co], *m. (CAm.)* Apprentice.

chuminada [choo-me-nah'-dah], *f.* 1. Silly thing, piece of nonsense. 2. Petty detail.

chumpipe [choom-pee'-pay], *m. (Costa Rica and Nicaragua)* Turkey.

chuncaca [choon-cah'-cah], *f. (Amer.)* Cane sirup boiled, but unclarified, of which coarse sugar is made. *V.* CHANCACA.

chuncho [choon'-cho], *(And.)* 1. *a.* Savage; uncivilized; bashful, shy. 2. *m. f.* Savage, bashful, shy.

chunga [choon'gah], *f.* Jest, joke. **Estar de chunga,** to be merry or in good humor.

chungo [choon-go], *a.* Bad, rotten; nasty (desagradable); ugly; dicey (dudoso), dodgy; dud (falso, billete).

chungón, gona [choon-gone'], *m. & f.* Joker.

chunguear [choon-gay-ar'], *vn. (Coll.)* To be merry, to be in good humor. -*vr.* To gag, to crack jokes; to be in a merry mood; to banter. **Chunguearse de uno,** to have a bit of fun with somebody.

chunguero, ra [choon-gay-ro, rah], *a* Diverting, amusing, humorous, fun-loving.

chunopa [choo-no'-pah], *f. (Peru) V.* YUCA.

chuño, chuno [choo'-nyo, choo'-no], *m. (Peru)* Dried potatoes cured on ice, for making vegetable soup.

chupa [choo'-pah], *f.* 1. Waistcoat; jacket *(fr.* Aljuba). 2. Drunkenness. 3. *(CAm.)* Bag.

chupa [choo'-pah], *f.* **Poner a uno como una chupa de dómine,** to give somebody a tremendous ticking off.

chupachupa [choo-pah-choo'-pah], *m. & f.* Sucker.

chupada [choo-pah'-dah], *f.* Suck; pull, puff; chupadas; sucking. **Dar chupadas a la pipa,** to puff away at one´s pipe.

chupadero, ra [choo-pah-day'-ro, rah], *a.* Sucking, sucker, drawing out milk or other liquids with the lips; absorbent.

chupado, da [choo-pah'-do, dah], *a.* 1. *(Coll.)* lean, emaciated. 2. Tight (falda). 3. **Estar chupado,** *(LAm.)* to be drunk. 4. **Está chupado,** it´s dead easy. -*pp.* of CHUPAR. -*m. (Cono Sur)* Missing person.

chupador, ra [choo-pah-dor', rah], *m. & f.* 1. Sucker, one who sucks or draws out with the lips. **Chupador de niños,** a sucking-bottle; a child's coral. 2. *(Amer.)* Tippler, one who gets intoxicated often, drunkard.

chupadura [choo-pah-doo'-rah], *f.* Sucking, suction, the act and effect of sucking.

chupaflores, chupamiel, chupamirtos, chuparomeros, [choo-pah-flo´-res, choo-pah-me-el', choo-pah-mir'-tos, choo-pah-ro may'-ros], *m. & f. (Orn.)* Humming-birds.

chupalandero [choo-pah-lan-day'-ro], *m. (Prov.)* A kind of snail that lives on trees and plants.

chupalla [choo-pahl'-lyah], *f. (Cono Sur. Mex.)* Straw hat.

chupamangas [choo-pah-mahn'-gas], *m. (And. Cono Sur),* **chupamedias,** creep, bootlicker.

chupar [choo-par'], *va.* 1. To suck. 2. To imbibe moisture (vegetales). 3. *(Met. Coll.)* To sponge, to hang upon others for subsistence; to fool. **Chuparse los dedos,** to eat with much pleasure, to be overjoyed. **Chupar la sangre,** *(Met.)* to suck one's blood, to stick to him like a leech, living at his expense. 4. *(LAm.)* To smoke. 5. To drink, to knock back. 6. *(fig.)* To milk, to sap. **Le chupan el dinero,** they are milking him of his money. **El trabajo le chupa la salud,** his work is undermining his health. 7. To put up with (aguantar). -vn. 1. To suck. 2. To booze (beber). 3. *(LAm.)* To smoke. -vr. 1. **¡Chúpate ésa!,** put that in your pipe and smoke it. 2. **Chuparse el dedo,** to suck one's finger; V. DEDO. 3. **Chuparse un insulto,** *(LAm.)* To put up with an insult. 4. *(Med.)* To waste away, to decline.

chupatintas [choo-pah-teen'-tas], *m.* Penpusher; petty clerk; minor bureaucrat; toady, creep.

chupativo, va [choo-pah-tee'-vo, vah], *a.* Of a sucking nature.

chupe [choo'-pay], *m.* A stew prepared with potatoes, eggs, cheese, etc.

chupeno, na [choo-pay'-no, nah], *a.* Attractive, delightful.

chupeta, illa, ita [choo-pay'-tah, eel'-lyah, ee'tah], *f.* *dim.* A short jacket or waistcoat.

chupete [choo-pay'-tay], *m.* 1. **Ser alguna cosa de chupete,** to possess great delicacy and good taste. 2. Dummy, pacifier. 3. Teat (de biberón); *(LAm.)* Lollipop (pirulí). 4. *(LAm.)* Suck (chupada). 5. V. RECHUPETE.

chupetada [choo-pay-tah'-dah], *f.* V. CHUPADURA.

chupetear [choo-pay-tay-ar'], *va.* To suck gently; to suck over and over.

chupeteo [choo-pay-tay'-o], *m.* Gentle sucking.

chupi, chupinudo [choo'-pe], *a.* Super, brilliant.

chupilote [choo-pe-lo'-tay], *m.* *(Amer.)* A vulture.

chupinazo [choo-pe-nah-tho], *m.* 1. Loud bang. 2. *(Dep.)* Hard kick, fierce shot.

chupo [choo-po], *m.* 1. *(LAm.)* *(Med.)* Boil. 2. *(And.)* Baby's bottle.

chupón [choo-pone'], *m.* 1. Sucker, a young twig. 2. The act of sucking. V. Doublet. V. CHUPETÍN. 3. Lollipop, sucking sweet (dulce). **Chupón de caramelo,** toffee apple. 4. *(LAm.)* Dummy, pacifier; baby's bottle. 5. *(And. Carib.)* Puff, pull (de pipa etc.). 6. *(And.)* *(Med.)* Boil. 7. *(Mex.)* Teat (biberón).

chupón, na [choo-pon', nah], *a.* *(Coll.)* One who cunningly deprives another of his money.

chuquelas [choo-kay'-las], *m.* A cotton cloth of India.

churdón [choor-done'], *m.* Raspberry jam.

churi [choo'-re], *m.* Chiv, knife.

churo [choo'-ro], *a.* *(And. Cono Sur)* handsome, attractive.

churo [choo'-ro], *m.* 1. *(And.)* *(Mus.)* Coiled wind instrument. 2. *(And.)* Spiral staircase. 3. *(And.)* Curl (rizo). 4. *(And.)* Jail.

churra [choor'-rah], *f.* The little pintailed grouse. -a. One year old heifer.

churrasco [choor-rahs'-co], *m.* *(Amer.)* Piece of meat broiled over coals.

churrascón [choor-ras-cone'], *m.* Act and effect of scorching.

churrasquear [choor-ras-kay-ar'], *vn.* *(Cono Sur)* To eat steak.

churre [choor'-ray], *m.* 1. *(Coll.)* Thick dirty grease. 2. Bloke, guy.

churrería [choor-ray-re'-ah], *f.* Fritter stall.

churrero, ra [choo-ray'-ro], *a. m. & f.* 1. Lucky, jammy. 2. Fritter seller.

churrete [choo-ray'-tay], *m.* Grease spot, dirty mark.

churretear [choo-ray-tay-ar'], *va.* *(LAm.)* To spot, to stain.

churretoso, sa [choor-ray-to'-so, sah], *a.* *(Prov.)* Gushing, spouting (líquidos).

churriento, ta [choor-re-en'-to, tah], *a.* 1. Greasy. 2. *(LAm.)* *(Med.)* Loose.

churillero, ra [choor-reel-lyay'-ro, rah], *m. & f.* *(Obs.)* Tattler, prattler, gossip.

churro, ra [choor'-ro, rah], *a.* Applied to sheep that have coarse wool, and to their wool. *m.* 1. A sort of fritter. 2. Botch, mess. **El dibujo ha salido un churro,** the sketch came out all wrong. 3. Fluke (chiripa). 4. *(Anat.)* Prick. 5. **Juan es un churro,** *(And. Cono Sur)* Juan is a dish. 6. *(Mex.)* Bad film.

churrullero, ra [choor-rool-lyay'-ro, rah], *m. & f.* Tattler, prattler, gossip.

churrupear [choor-roo-pay-ar'], *vn.* To sip, to drink by small draughts.

churrús [choor-roos'], *m.* Kind of silk stuff interwoven with a little gold and silver.

churruscar [choor-roos-kay-ar'], *va.* To burn, to scorch.

churruscarse [choor-roos-car'-say], *vr.* To be scorched, as bread, etc.

churrusco [choor-roos'-co], *m.* Bread too toasted or scorched. -a. *(And. CAm.)* Kinky, curly.

churruscón [choor-roos-cone'], *m.* V. CHURRASCÓN.

churumbela [choo-room-bay'-lah], *f.* Flageolet, wind instrument resembling an oboe; shawm.

churumen, *m.* V. CHIRUMEN.

churumo [choo-roo'-mo], *m.* Juice or substance of a thing. **Hay poco churumo,** there is little cash, little judgment.

chus ni mus [choos ne moos]. *(Coll.)* **No decir chus ni mus,** not to say a word.

chuscada [choos-cah'-dah], *f.* Pleasantry, drollery, buffoonery, fun, joke.

chusco, ca [choos'-co, cah], *a.* Pleasant, droll, merry.

chusma [choos'-mah], *f.* 1. The crew and slaves of a row-galley. 2. Rabble, mob.

chuspa [choos'-pah], *f.* *(Amer.)* A pouch of skin used among the country folk of the La Plata to carry maté, coca, money, and suchlike things.

chusquero [choos-kay'-ro], *m.* *(Mil.)* Ranker.

chut [choot], *m.* 1. *(Dep.)* Shot (at goal). 2. Shot (droga).

chuta [choo'-tah], *f.* V.CHUT. 2. *excl.* *(Cono Sur)* Good God! Good heavens!

chutar [choo-tar'], *vn.* 1. To shoot (at goal). 2. **Está que chuta,** he's hopping mad. 3. To go well. **Esto va que chuta,** it's going fine. -vr. To give oneself a shot (of drugs).

chute [choo'-tay], *m.* V. CHUT. -a. *(Cono Sur)* Spruce, natty.

chuza [choo'-thah], *f.* *(Mex.)* A stroke in the game of pigeonholes knocking all at once with one ball.

chuzar [choo-thar'], *va.* *(And.)* To prick; to sting, to hurt.

chuzazo [choo-thah'-tho], *m.* 1. A large pike. 2. The blow or stroke given with it.

chuzo [choo'-tho], *m.* 1. Pike. 2. *(Naut.)* Boarding-pike. **Chuzos,** abundance of rain, snow, or hail. **A chuzos,** abundantly, impetuously. **Llover a chuzos,** to rain pitchforks, or bucketfuls. **Echar chuzos,** to brag.

chuzón, na, [choo-thone', nah], *m. & ; f.* 1. A crafty, artful person. 2. Wag punster, jester.

C.I. *m. abr.* de **Coeficiente de inteligencia** (intelligence quotient).

cía [thee'-ah], *f.* Hipbone, huckle bone.

Cía, *abr.* de **Compañia** (Company, Co.).

ciaboga [the-ah-bo'-gah], *f.(Naut.)* The act of putting a row-galley about with the oars. **Hacer ciaboga,** to turn the boat (treineras)

ciánido [the-ah'-ne-do], *m.* Cyanide, a compound of cyanogen.

ciano [the-ah'-no], *m.* *(Bot.)* The bluebottle.

cianógeno [the-ah-no'-hay-no], *m.* Cyanogen, a colorless, poisonous, liquefiable gas.

cianosis [the-ah-no'-sis], *f.* Cyanosis, a livid hue resulting from insufficient oxygenation of the blood.

cianotipia [thc-ah-no-tee'-pe-ah], *f.* Blueprint. **Copiar a la cianotipia,** to blueprint.

cianuro [the-ah-noo'-ro], *m.* Cyanide, a compound of cyanogen.

ciar [the-ar'], *va.* 1. *(Naut.)* To hold water, to back a row-galley, to stop with oars. 2. To retrograde. 3. *(Met.)* To slacken in the pursuit of an affair

ciática [the-ah'-te-cah], *f.* Sciatica, or hip-gout.

ciático, ca [the-ah'-te-co, cah], *a.* Sciatic, sciatical.

ciato [the-ah'-to], *m.* *(Bot.)* A tree-fern of tropical regions.

cibario, ria [the-bah'-re-o, ah], *a.* Cibarious, relating to food.

cibera [the-bay'-rah], *f.* 1. Quantity of wheat put at once in the hopper. 2. All seeds or grains fit for animal food. 3. Coarse remains of grain and fruit, husks, etc. 4. Every operation which engages the powers of imagination and fancy. 5. *(Prov.)* Hopper in a cornmill.

cibernética [the-behr-nay'-te-cah], *f. (Med. & Elec.)* Cybernetics.

cibica. [the-bee'-cah], *f.* Clout, the iron plate nailed to an axle-tree, to prevent friction.

cibicón [the-be-cone'], *m.* A large kind of clout.

cíbolo, la [thee'-bo-lo, lah], *m. & f.* The Mexican bull, with horns turned backward; apparently the bison.

cibrú [the-broo'], *m.* Peruvian name of the cedar-tree.

cicaba [the-cah'-bah], *f.* A nocturnal bird of prey.

cicatear [the-cah-tay-ar'], *vn. (Coll.)* To be sordidly parsimonious.

cicatería [the-cah-tay-ree'-ah], *f.* Niggardliness, parsimony.

cicatero, ra [the-cah-tay'-ro, rah], *a.* Niggardly, sordid, parsimonious, mean.

cicateruelo [the-cah-tay-roo-ay'-lo], *m. dim.* An avaricious or niggardly little fellow, a little miser.

cicatricera [the-cah-tre-thay'-rah], *f.* A woman who used to follow troops and care for wounds.

cicatriz [the-cah-treeth'], *f.* 1. Cicatrice or cicatrix, a scar. 2. Gash, mark of a wound. 3. *(Met.)* Impression remaining on the mind.

cicatrización [the-cah-tre-thah-the-on'], *f.* Cicatrization.

cicatrizal [the-cah-tre-thahl'], *a.* Belonging to a cicatrice or scar.

cicatrizar [the-cah-tre-thar'], *va.* To cicatrize, to heal a wound. *-vr.* To heal.

cícero [thee'-thay-ro], *m. (Typ.)* Pica.

Cicerón [thee-thay-rone'] *m.* Cicero.

cicerone [the-thay-ro'-nay], *m.* A guide.

cicindela [the-thin-day'-lah], *f. (Zool.)* 1. A carabid beetle, tiger-beetle; the name is sometimes carelessly used for a firefly. 2. *(Obs.)* Glow-worm.

cición [the-the-on'], *m. (Prov.)* An intermittent fever.

cíclada [thee'-clah-dah], *f.* Kind of dress formerly worn by ladies.

ciclamor [the-clah-mor'], *m.* The sycamore, buttonwood, plane-tree.

ciclán [the-clahn'], *m.* 1. Ridgel. 2. A cryptorchid (or cryptorchis), an individual whose testicles have not descended into the scrotum (hombres, animales). 3. *(Met.)* Single, having no companion.

ciclatón [the-clah-tone'], *m.* A tunic once used by women.

cíclico, ca [thee'-cle-co, cah], *a.* Cyclical, belonging to a cycle.

ciclismo [the-clees'-mo], *m.* Bicycling, cycling; cycle racing.

ciclista [the-clees'-tah], *m. & f.* Cyclist.

ciclo [thee'-clo], *m.* 1. Cycle, a round of time. 2. *(Univ.)* Year, course. **Ciclo vital**, life-cycle. **Ciclo de reloj**, clock cycle. **Ciclo instrucción-decodificación-carga**, *(Inform.)* instruction-decoding-loading cycle

ciclo-cross [thee'-clo-cros'], *m.* Cycle-cross.

ciclodiatomía [the-clo-de-ah-to-mee'-ah], *f. (Mil.)* Calculation of the direction of a projectile.

cicloidal [the-clo'-e-dal], *a.* Cycloidal.

cicloide [the-clo'-e-day], *f. (Math.)* Cycloid.

ciclómetro [the-clo'-may-tro], *m.* Cyclometer.

ciclomotor [the-clo-mo-tor'], *m.* Motorbike, autocycle.

ciclón [the-clon'], *m.* 1. Cyclone. 2. Hurricane.

ciclonal, ciclónico, ca [the-clo-nahl', the-clo'-ne-co, cah], *a.* Cyclonic, cyclonical.

cíclope [thee'-clo-pay], *m.* Cyclops.

ciclópeo, ea [the-clo'-pay-o, ah], *a.* Cyclopean, gigantic.

ciclorama [the-clo-rah'-mah], *m.* Cyclorama, pictorial representation.

ciclotrón [the-clo-trone'], *m.* Cyclotron.

cicuta [the-coo'-tah], *f.* 1. *(Bot.)* Hemlock. **Cicuta acuática**, *(Bot.)* waterhemlock. **Cicuta virosa, cicuta de España**, Spanish hemlock. 2. Pipe or flute made of reed, a flageolet.

Cid [theed], *m.* 1. Chief, commander. 2. Surname of the Spanish hero, Rodrigo Díaz de Vivar.

C.I.D. *m. abr.* de **Centro Internacional para el Desarrollo**.

cidra [thee'-drah], *f.* 1. Citron. 2. Conserve of citrons.

cidracayote [the-drah-cah-yo'-tay], *f. (Bot.)* The American gourd.

cidrada [the-drah'-dah], *f.* A conserve made of citrons.

cidral [the-drahl'], *m.* Plantation of citron-trees.

cidria [thee'-dreah], *f. V.* CEDRIA.

cidro [thee'-dro], *m. (Bot.)* Citron-tree.

cidronela [the-dro-nay'-lah], *f. (Bot.)* Common balm.

ciegamente [the-ay-gah-men'-tay], *adv.* Blindly.

ciego, ga [the-ay'-go, gah], *a.* 1. Blind. 2. *(Met.)* Swayed by violent passion. **Ciego de ira**, blind with passion. 3. Choked or shut up (corredor). **A ciegas** 1. Blindly, in the dark. 2. Thoughtlessly, carelessly. **Quedar ciego**, to go blind. **Más ciego que un topo**, as blind as a bat. **Ciego para**, blind to. **Con una fe ciega**, with a blind faith.

ciego, *m.* 1. *(Anat.)* Caecum or blind gut. 2. Large black-pudding. *V.* MORCÓN. (*Yo ciego, yo ciegue*, from *Cegar. V.* ACERTAR.)

cielo [the-ay'-lo], *m.* 1. The sky, firmament, heaven(s). 2. Heaven, the habitation of God and pure souls departed. 3. Heaven, the supreme power, the sovereign of heaven. 4. Climate; atmosphere. **Éste es un cielo benigno**, this is a mild climate. 5. Roof, ceiling. 6. Glory, felicity; paradise. **Cielo raso**, flat roof or ceiling. **El cielo de la cama**, tester or cover of a bed. **Bajado del cielo**, prodigious, excellent, complete. **Cerrarse el cielo**, to cover over with clouds. **Dormir a cielo raso**, to sleep in the open air. **Estar hecho un cielo**, to be splendid, to be most brilliant. **Tomar el cielo con las manos**, *(Met.)* to be transported with joy, grief, or passion. **Venirse el cielo abajo**, the sky falling, i. e. to rain heavily. **Ver el cielo abierto**, to find an unforeseen opportunity. **Se le juntaron el cielo con la tierra**, *(LAm.)* he lost his nerve. **Poner a uno en el cielo**, to praise somebody to the over-optimistic.

cielo máximo [the-ay'-lo-mahc'-se-mo], *m. (Aer.)* Ceiling.

ciempiés, *m. V.* CIENTOPIES.

cien [the-en'], *a.* One hundred; used before nouns instead of *ciento*. **Cien hombres**, a hundred men. **Cien mujeres**, a hundred women. **Cien mil**, a hundred thousand. **Me pone a cien**, it drives me up the wall. **10 por cien**, ten per cent. **Lo apoyo cien por cien**, I support it a hundred per cent.

ciénaga [the-ay'-nah-gah], *f.* Marsh moor, a miry place. *V.* CENEGAL.

ciencia [the-en'-the-ah], *f.* 1. Science. 2. Knowledge, certainty. **A ciencia y paciencia**, by one's knowledge and permission. **Ciencias exactas**, mathematics. **Apostar** or **hacer alguna cosa a ciencia cierta**, to bet, or to do any thing with certainty, knowingly. **Ciencias naturales**, natural sciences. **Ciencias ocultas**, occult sciences.

ciencia-ficción [the-ayn-the-ah feec-the-aone'], *f.* Science fiction.

cienmilésimo, ma [the-en-me-lay'-se-mo, mah], *a.* The hundred thousandth.

cienmilmillonésimo, ma [the-en-mil-mil-lyo-nay'-se-mo, mah], *a.* The hundred thousand millionth.

cienmillonésimo, ma, *a.* The hundred millionth.

cieno [the-ay'-no], *m.* Mud, mire, a marshy ground.

cienoso [the-ay-no'-so], *a.* Muddy, miry; slimy.

cientemente [the-en-tay-men'-tay], *adv.* In a knowing, sure, and prudent manner.

científicamente [the-en-tee'-fe-cah-men-tay], *adv.* Scientifically.

científico, ca [the-en-tee'-fe-co, cah], *m. & f.* Scientific.

cientista [the-ayn-tes'-tah], *m. & f. (LAm.)* Scientist.

ciento [the-en'-to], *a.* One hundred. *V.* CIEN.

ciento [the-en'-to], *m.* 1. A hundred. **Un ciento de huevos**, a hundred eggs. 2. A hundredweight. **Diez por ciento**, ten per cent. **Un tanto por ciento**, a percentage. **Estar al ciento por ciento**, to be in top form. **Por cientos**, in hundreds. **Había ciento y la madre**, there were far too many.

cientopiés [the-en-to-pe-ess'], *m.* Wood-louse, milleped, sowbug.

cierna [the-err'-nah], *f.* The staminate blossom of vines, corn, and some other plants.

cierne [the-err'-ney],*m.* **En cierne,** in blossom. **Estar en cierne,** to be in its infancy. (*Yo cierno, yo cierne,* from *Cerner. V.* ATENDER.)

cierre [the-err'-ray], *m.* 1. Closing, shutting, locking. 2. Lock, clasp. **Cierre automático,** zipper. **Cierre de cremallera,** zipper. **Cierre hidráulico,** water seal. **Echar el cierre,** to shut.

cierro [the-err'-ro], *m.* 1. Inclosure. (*Yo cierro, yo cierre,* from *Cerrar.).*2. (*Cono Sur*) Wall; envelope.

ciertamente [the-er-tah-men'-tay], *adv.* Certainly, forsooth, surely.

cierto, ta [the-err'-to, tah], *a.* 1. Certain, doubtless, evident, constant. 2. Used in an indeterminate sense: **cierto lugar,** a certain place. **Me dan por cierto que,** I have been credibly informed that. **Por cierto,** for certain, for sure. **Es cierto que...,** it is certain that... **Lo cierto es que..,** the thing is that... **Estar cierto de,** to be sure of. **Estar en lo cierto,** to be right. **Por cierto...,** by the way... -*adv. V.* CIERTAMENTE.

cierva [the-err'-vah],*f.* Hind, the female stag, or red deer.

ciervo [the-err'-vo], *m.* Deer, hart, stag.

ciervo volante [the-err'-vo vo-lahn'-tay], *m.* Stagbeetle.

cierzo [the-err'-tho], *m.* A cold northerly wind. **Tener ventana al cierzo,** (*Met.*) To be haughty, lofty, elated with pride.

cifac, cifaque [the-fahc', the-fah'-kay], *m.* (*Obs. Anat.*) The peritoneum.

cifra [thee'-frah],*f.* 1. Cipher, the symbol 0. 2. Cipher, a secret or occult manner of writing. 3. Cipher, monogram engraved on seals or stamped upon stationery, etc. 4. Contraction, abbreviation. 5. Any arithmetical mark. 6. Music written with numbers. **Cifra arábiga,** Arabic numeral. **Escribirlo en cifras y palabras,** to write it down in figures and words. **Cifra global,** lump sum. **La cifra de este año es elevada,** the quantity this year is large. **La cifra de los muertos,** the number of dead.

cifradamente [the frah-dah-mayn'-tay], *adv.* 1. In code. 2. In brief, in a shortened form.

cifrado [the-frah'-do], *a.* Coded, in code.

cifrar [the-frar'], *va.* 1. To cipher or write in ciphers. 2. To abridge a discourse. 3. To inclose. **Una duración cifrada en miles de años,** a duration reckoned in thousands of years.

cigala [the-gah'-lah],*f.* Norway lobster.

cigarra [the-gar'-rah],*f.* Balmcricket, cicada, harvestfly.

cigarrera [the-gar-ray'-rah],*f.* Cigar-case.

cigarrero [the-gar-ray'-ro], *m.* Cigar maker; cigar-seller.

cigarrillo [the-gar-reel'-lyo], *m.* Cigarette.

cigarrista [the-gar-rees'-tah], *m.* Person who smokes many cigars.

cigarro [the-gar'-ro], *m.* Cigar, cigarette.

cigarrón [the-gar-rone'], *m.* 1. (*aug.*) A large cigar. 2. A large balm-cricket.

cigatera [the-gah-tay'-rah],*f.* (*Low.*) Prostitute.

cigoñino [the-go-nyee'-no], *m.* (*Orn.*) A young stork.

cigoñuela [the-go-nyoo-ay'-lah], *f.* (*Orn.*) A small bird resembling a stork.

cigoto [the-go'-to], *m.* (*Biol.*) Zygote.

ciguatera [the-goo-ah-tay'-rah],*f.* (*Amer.*) Kind of jaundice, from eating fish diseased with an affection like jaundice.

ciguato, ta [the-goo-ah'-to, tah], *a. V.* ACIGUATADO.

cigüente [the-goo-en'-tay], *a.* Applied to a kind of white grape.

cigüeña [the-goo-ay'-nyah],*f.* 1. (*Orn.*) White stork, a bird of passage; crane. 2. Crank of a bell to which a cord is fastened to ring it. 3. **Cigüeña de piedra de amolar,** the iron winch of a grindstone. 4. **Cigüeña de cordelería,** (*Naut.*) A laying hook or winch.

cigüeñal [the-goo-ay-nyahl'], *m.* (*Mech.*) Crankshaft.

cigüeño [the-goo-ay'-nyo], *m.* A male stork.

cigüeñuela [the-goo-ay-nyoo-ay'-lah], *f. dim.* Small crank of a bell.

cigüeñuelo de la Caña del Timón [the-goo-ay-nyco-ay'-lo]. (*Naut.*) The gooseneck of the tiller.

cija [thee'-hah], *f.* 1. (*Prov.*) Dungeon. 2. (*Obs.*) Granary. 3. Sheep shed.

cilampa [the-lam'-pah], *f.* (*CAm.*) Drizzle.

cilampear [the-lam-pay-ar'], *vn.* (*CAm.*) To drizzle.

cilanco [the-lahn'-co], *m.* A deep pool in bends, or slack water, of rivers.

cilantro [the-lahn'-tro], *m.* (*Bot.*) Coriander. *V.* CULANTRO.

ciliado, da [the-le-ah'-do, dah], *a.* Ciliated, provided with cilia.

ciliar [the-le-ar'], *a.* Ciliary, belonging to the eyelids.

cilicio [the-lee'-the-o], *m.* 1. Haircloth, very rough and prickly. 2. A cilicium or hair covering for the body, worn as penance. 3. Girdle of bristles or netted wire, with points, worn in mortification of the flesh. 4. (*Mil. Obs.*) Haircloth laid on a wall to preserve it.

cilífero, ra [the-lee'-fay-ro, rah], *a. V.* CILIADO.

ciliforme [the-le-for'-may], *a.* Like an eyelash in form; ciliform.

cilindrada [the-leen-drah'-dah], *f.* Cylinder capacity.

cilindradora [the-leen-drah-do'-rah], *f.* Steamroller, road roller.

cilindrar [the-leen-drar'], *va.* To roll, to roll flat.

cilíndrico, ca [the-leen'-dre-co, cah], *a.* Cylindric or cylindrical.

cilindrín [the-leen-dreen'], *m.* Fag, cigarette.

cilindro [the-leen'-dro], *m.* Cylinder; a roller. **Cilindro de escarchar,** silversmiths' rolls. **Cilindro compresor, cilindro de caminos,** steamroller, road roller. **Cilindro de datos,** (*Inform.*) data cylinder.

cilla [theel'-lyah],*f.* Granary for tithes and other grain.

cillerero [theel-lyay-ray'-ro], *m.* In some religious houses, the cellarist or butler.

cilleriza [theel-lyay-ree'-thah], *f.* A nun who directs the domestic affairs of the convent.

cillerizo [theel-lyay-ree'-tho], *m.* Keeper of a granary.

cillero [theel-lyay'-ro], *m.* 1. Keeper of a granary or storehouse for tithes. 2. Granary. 3. Vault, cellar, storeroom.

cima [thee'-mah],*f.* 1. Summit of a mountain or hill. 2. Top of trees. 3. Heart and tender sprouts of cardoons. 4. End or extremity of a thing. 5. Acme. **Por cima,** at the uppermost part, at the very top. **Dar cima,** to conclude happily.

cimacio [the-mah'-the-o], *m.* (*Arch.*) Cymatium, ogee, ogive, moulding which is half convex and half concave. **Cimacio del pedestal,** cornice of a pedestal.

cimar [the-mar'], *va.* To clip the tops of dry things, as plants, hedges.

cimarrón, na [the-mar-rone', nah], *a.* (*Amer.*) Wild, unruly (hombres, animales). -*m. & f.* A runaway slave, maroon. -*m.* (*Cono Sur*) Unsweetened maté.

cimba [theem'-bah],*f.* 1. (*And.*) Plaited rope of hard leather. 2. (*And.*) Pigtail. 3. (*And.*) Rope ladder (escala).

cimbalaria [thim-bah-lah'-re-ah],*f.* Ivywort, a plant which grows on old walls.

cimbalillo [thim-bah-leel'-lyo], *m. dim.* A small bell.

címbalo [theem'-bah-lo], *m.* 1. Cymbal. 2. A small bell.

cimbanillo [thim-bah-neel'-lyo], *m. V.* CIMBALILLO.

címbara [theem'-bah-rah],*f.* (*Prov.*) A large sickle, used to cut shrubs and plants.

cimbel [thim-bel'], *m.* 1. Decoy-pigeon. 2. Rope with which decoy-pigeons are made fast. 3. Prick (pene).

cimborio, cimborrio [thim-bo'-re-o, thim-bor'-re-o], *m.* Cupola. *v.* CÚPULA.

cimbornales [thim-bor-nah'-les], *m. pl.* (*Naut.*) Scupperholes. *V.* IMBORNALES.

cimbra [theem'-brah],*f.* 1. A wooden frame for constructing an arch. 2. **Cimbra de una tabla,** (*Naut.*) the bending of a board.

cimbrar, cimbrear [thim-brar', thim-bray-ar'], *va.* To brandish a rod or wand. **Cimbrar a alguno,** to give one a drubbing. **Cimbrar a uno,** to clout somebody. -*vr.* 1. To bend, to vibrate. 2. To walk gracefully.

cimbreño, ña [thim-bray'-nyo, nyah], *a.* Pliant, flexible (vara, caña).

cimbreo [thim-bray'-o], *m.* Crookedness, curvature, bending or moulding of a plank, shaking.

cimbria [theem'-bre-ah], *f. V.* CIMBRA.

cimbrón [theem-brone'], *m. (And. CAm. Cono Sur)* shudder; *(And.)* Sharp pain; *(Cono Sur. Mex.)* Blow with the flat of a sword; *(LAm.)* Crack (de lazo etc.); jerk, yang (tirón).

cimbronada [theem-bro-nah-dah], *f. (And. Cono Sur) V.* CIMBRON; *(Carib.)* Earthquake (terremoto).

cimbronazo [thim-bro-nah'-tho], *m.* Stroke given with a foil. *V.* CINTARAZO.

cimentación [the-mayn-tah-the-one'], *f.* 1. Foundation. 2. Laying of foundations.

cimentado [the-men-tah'-do], *m.* Refinement of gold. **Cimentado, da,** *pp.* Of CIMENTAR.

cimentador [the-men-tah-dor'], *m.* He who lays the foundation of a thing.

cimentar [the-men-tar'], *va.* 1. To lay the foundation of a building, to found, to ground. 2. *(Met.)* To establish the fundamental principles of religion, morals, and science. 3. To refine metals.

cimentera [the-men-tay'-rah], *f.* The art of laying the foundation of a building.

cimento [the-men'-to], *m.* Cement. *V.* CEMENTO.

cimera [the-may'-rah], *f.* Crest of a helmet, or coat of arms.

cimerio, ria [the-may-re-o, ah], *a.* Cimmerian; of a tribe which dwelt on the shores of the sea of Azov.

cimero, ra [the-may'-ro, rah], *a.* Placed at the height of some elevated spot.

cimiento [the-me-en'-to], *m.* 1. Foundation of a building. 2. *(Met.)* Basis, origin. **Abrir los cimientos,** to make the trenches for laying foundations. *(Yo cimiento, yo cimiente, from Cimentar. V.* ACRECENTAR.)

cimillo [the-meel'-lyo], *m.* Decoy-pigeon.

cimitarra [the-me-tar'-rah], *f.* Scimitar, falchion.

cimófana [the-mo'-fah-nah], *f.* Cymofane, the oriental cat's eye; a variety of chrysoberyl.

cimorra [the-mor'-rah], *f. (Vet.)* Glanders, a disease in horses.

cinabrio [the-nah'-bre-o], *m.* 1. Kind of gum, distilled from a tree in Africa. 2. Cinnabar. 3. Vermilion or artificial cinnabar.

cinamómino [the-nah-mo'-me-no], *m. (Med.)* An aromatic ointment, the chief ingredient of which is taken from the bead-tree.

cinamomo [the-nah-mo'-mo], *m. (Bot.)* The bead-tree.

cinc [think], *m. (Acad.)* Zinc, a metallic element.

cincel [thin-thel'], *m.* Chisel.

cincelado [thin-thay-lah'-do], *m.* Chiselling; engraving.

cincelador [thin-thay-lah-dor'], *m.* Engraver, sculptor, stone-cutter.

cincelar [thin-thay-lar'], *va.* To chisel, to engrave, to emboss.

cincelito [hin-thay-lee'-to], *m. dim.* Small chisel.

cinco [theen'-co], *m. & a.* Five. **Decir cuántas son cinco,** to threaten with reproof or punishment. **Él te dirá cuántas son cinco,** *(Met.)* he will oblige you to do it in spite of you. **No sabe cuántas son cinco,** *(Coll.)* he is a fool. **¡Vengan esos cinco!,** ¡shake it! -*m.* 1. *(And. CAm. Carib.)* 5-stringed guitar. 2. *(Mex.)* Bottom, backside. 3. *(CAm. Mex.)* 5-peso piece (moneda).

cincoañal [thin-co-ah-nyahl'], *a.* Five years old (animales).

cincoenrama [theen-co-en-rah'-mah], *f. (Bot.)* Common cinquefoil.

cincografía [thin-co-grah-fee'-ah], *f.* Zincography, a process of etching printing plates upon zinc.

cincomesino, na [thin-co-may-see'-no, nah], *a.* Five months old.

cincuenta [thin-coo-en'-tah], *m. & a.* Fifty, fiftieth.

cincuentavo [thin-coo-en-tah'-vo], *a.* The one-fiftieth part.

cincuentañero, a [thin-coo-ayn-tah-nyay'-ro, ah], *m.* Man, woman of about fifty.

cincuentavo [thin-coo-ayn-tah'-vo], *a.m.* Fiftieth.

cincuentén [thin-coo-en-ten'], *m.* A piece of wood, fifty palms in length (50 x 3 x 2).

cincuenteno, na [thin-coo-en-tay'-no, nah], *a.* Fiftieth.

cincuentón, na [thin-coo-en-tone', nah], *a.* Fifty years old.

cincha [theen'-chah], *f.* 1. Girth, cingle, cinch. **Ir rompiendo cinchas,** to drive on full speed. 2. *(Cos.)* Webbing (para sillas). 3. **Tener cincha;** *(And.)* To have a strain of Negro blood.

cinchada [thin-chah'-dah], *f. (Cono Sur. Mex.)* Tug-of-war.

cinchadura [thin-chah-doo'-rah], *f.* The act of girting.

cinchar [thin-char'], *va.* To girt, to bind with a girth.

cinchera [thin-chay'-rah], *f.* 1. Girthplace, the spot where the girth is put on a mule or horse. 2. Vein which horses or mules have in the place where they are girted. 3. Disorder incident to horses and mules, which affects the place where they are girted.

cincho [theen'-cho], *m.* 1. Belt or girdle used by laborers to keep their bodies warm. 2. The tire of a wheel. 3. Vessel of bassweed, in which cheese is moulded and pressed. 4. Disorder in the hoofs of horses. *V.* CEÑO.

cinchón [thin-chone'], *m. aug.* A broad girdle.

cinchona [thin-cho'-nah], *f. (LAm.)* Quinine bark.

cinchuela [thin-choo-ay'-lah], *f.* 1. *(dim.)* A small girth. 2. A narrow ribbon.

cine [thee'-nay], *m.* Motion pictures, movies; cinema. **Hacer cine,** to make films. **Cine mudo,** silent films. **Ir al cine,** to go to the cinema.

cineasta [the-nay-as'-tah], *m. & f.* Film fan, movie fan; film buff (experto); film critic (crítico); film maker, director.

cine-club [the-nay-cloob'], *m. pl.* Cine club, film society.

cinefilia [the-ney-fe'-le-ah], *f.* Love of the cinema.

cinéfilo, la [the-nay'-fe-lo], *m. & f.* Film fan, movie fan.

cinegética [the-nay-hay'-te-cah], *f.* Hunting, the chase.

cinegético [the-nay-hay'-te-co], *a.* Hunting, of the chase.

cinema [the-nay'-mah], *m.* Cinema, moving pictures, movies.

cinemateca [the-nay-mah-tay'-cah], *f.* Film library.

cinemática [the-nay-mah'-te-cah], *f.* Cinematics, the study of motion as limited only by space.

cinemático [the-nay-mah'-te-co], *a.* Cinematic.

cinematografía [the-nay-ma-to-grah-fe'-ah], *f.* Films, film-making, cinematography.

cinematografiar [the-nay-mah-to-grah-fe-ar'], *va.* To film.

cinematográfico, ca [the-nay-mah-to-grah'-fe-co, cah], *a.* Cinematographic.

cinematógrafo [the-nay-mah-to'-grah-fo], *m.* Motion pictures, movies, cinema.

cineración [the-nay-rah-the-on'], *V.* INCINERACIÓN.

cinerama [the-nay-rah-mah], *m.* Cinerama.

cinerario, ia [the-nay-rah'-re-o, ah], *a.* 1. *V.* CINÉREO. Ashy. 2. Cinerary.

cinéreo [the-nay'-ray-o], *a.* Ashy; ash-grey, ashem.

cinescopio [the-nes-co'-pe-o], *m.* Kinescope.

cineteca [the-nay-tay'-cah], *f. (LAm.)* Film archive.

cinético, ca [the-nay'-te-co, cah], *a.* Kinetic, pertaining to motion. **Energía cinética,** Kinetic energy.

cíngaro, ra [theen'-gah-ro, rah], *m. & f.* Gipsy. *V.* GITANO.

cinguería [then-gay-re'-ah], *f. (Cono Sur)* Sheet metalwork; sheet metal-shop.

cinguero [then-gay'-ro], *m. (Cono Sur)* Sheet metalworker.

cíngulo [theen'-goo-lo], *m.* 1. Girdle or band with which a priest's alb is tied up. 2. Cordon, band, a wreath. 3. A military badge. 4. Ring or list at the top and bottom of a column.

cínicamente [the'-ne-cah-mayn-tay], *adv.* 1. Cynically. 2. Brazenly, shamelessly, impudently.

cínico, ca [thee'-ne-co, cah], *a.* Cynic, cynical; satirical.

cínico [hee'-ne-co], *m.* Cynic, a philosopher of the sect of Diogenes.

cínife [thee'-ne-fay], *m.* The longshanked buzzing gnat.

cinismo [the-nees'-mo], *m.* 1. Cynicism, the philosophy of the Cynics. 2. Shamelessness in defending or practicing blamable actions or doctrines.

cinnámico, ca [thin-nah'-me-co, cah], *a.* Cinnamic; derived from cinnamon.

cinocéfalo [the-no-thay'-fah-lo], *m.* 1. Kind of monkey or baboon. 2. The name of the inhabitants of a fantastic country, who had dogs' heads.

cinosura [the-no-soo'-rah], *f.* 1. Cynosure, the constellation of the Lesser Bear, which contains the polar star. 2. An object strongly challenging attention.

cinta [theen'-tah], *f.* 1. Ribbon, tape. **Cinta de seda,** silk ribbon. **Cinta aisladora,** *(CAm. Mex.)* insulating tape. **Cinta de freno,** brake lining. **Cinta para máquina de escribir,** typewriter ribbon. **Cinta del cartucho,** *(Inform.)* cartridge ribbon. Cinta **magnética,** magnetic tape. 2. A strong net used in the tunny-fishery. 3. The lowest part of the pastern of a horse. 4. **Cinta para cinchas,** girth-web. 5. **Cintas de navío,** *(Naut.)* Wales. 6. *(Obs.)* Girdle. *V.* CINTO. 7. First course of floor-tiles. 8. *(LAm.)* Tin, can. 9. *(Mex.)* Shoelaces. 10. Kerb; tile skirting (de habitación).

cintadero [thin-tah-day'-ro], *m.* Part of a crossbow to which the string is fastened.

cintagorda [thin-tah-gor'-dah], *f.* Coarse hempen net for the tunny-fishery.

cintajos, cintarajos [thin-tah'-hos, thin-tah-rah'-hos], *m. pl.* 1. Knot or bunch of tumbled ribbons. 2. Tawdry ornaments in female dress.

cintar [thin-tar'], *va. (Prov.)* To adorn with ribbons.

cintarazo [thin-tah-rah'-tho], *m.* 1. Stroke or blow with the flat part of a broadsword. 2. Chastisement of a horse with the stirrup-leather.

cinta transportadora [theen'-tah trans-por-tah-dor'-rah], *f. (Mech.)* Conveyor belt.

cinteado, da [thin-tay-ah'-do, dah], *a.* Adorned with ribbons.

cintero [thin-tay'-ro], *m.* 1. One who weaves or sells ribbons. 2. Harness-maker. 3. Belt, girdle. 4. *(Prov.)* Truss. 5. Rope with a running knot thrown on a bull's head.

cintilla [thin-teel'-lyah], *f. dim.* 1. Small ribbon. 2. Narrow tape.

cintillo [thin-teel'-lyo], *m.* 1. Hat. band. 2. Ring set with precious stones.

cinto [theen'-to], *m.* Belt, girdle. *V.* CINTURA and CÍNGULO.

cintrel [thin-trel'], *m. (Arch.)* Rule or line placed in the center of a dome to adjust the ranges of brick or stone.

cintura [thin-too'-rah], *f.* 1. The waist. **Cintura de avispa,** wasp waist. 2. Small girdle for the waist. **Meter en cintura,** *(Met.)* To keep one in a state of subjection. 3. Narrow part of a chimney. *V.* CANAL.

cinturero [thin-too-ray'-ro], *m. (Prov.)* Girdler.

cinturica, illa, ita [thin-too-ree'-cah, eel'-lyah, ee'-tah], *f. dim.* 1. A small girdle. 2. Small or delicate waist.

cinturón [thin-too-rone'], *m.* 1. Belt. 2. Sash. **Cinturón salvavidas,** life-belt. **Cinturón de seguridad,** safety belt. 3. *(fig.)* Belt, zone. **El cinturón industrial de Buenos Aires,** Buenos Aires industrial belt.

cipayo [the-pah'-yo], *m.* Sepoy, a native of India, serving in the British troops.

cipero [the-pay'-ro], *m. (Bot.)* Cyperus or sedge.

cipo [thee'-po], *m.* Cippus, a short stone pilar used as a burial monument, as a boundary mark or as a signpost or milestone.

cipote [the-po'-tay], *a.* 1. *(And. Carib.)* Stupid, thick. 2. *(CAm.)* Plump, chubby. -*m.* 1. *(CAm. Carib.)* Lad, youngster; urchin 2. *(CAm.)* Indian club. 3. Chump, blockhead (idiota). 4. *(And.)* **Cipote de chica,** smashing girl.

cipotear [the-po-tay-ar'], *va.* To screw.

ciprés [the-press'], *m. (Bot.)* Cypress tree.

cipresal [the-pray-sahl'], *m.* Grove or plantation of cypress trees.

cipresino, na [the-pray-see'-no, nah], *a.* Resembling or belonging to cypress.

ciprino, na [the-pree'-no, nah], *a.* Relating to or made of cypress wood.

ciprio, ia [thee'-pre-o, ah], *a.* Cyprian; of the island of Cyprus.

ciquiricata [the-ke-re-cah'-tah], *f. (Coll.)* Caress, act of endearment; flattery.

circasiano, na [theer-cah-se-ah´-no, nah], *a.* Circassian.

circense [theer-then'-say], *a.* Circensial or circensian, relating to the exhibitions in the amphitheaters of Rome; circus, of the circus.

circo [theer'-co], *m.* 1. Circus, amphitheater. 2. *(Orn.)* The moorbuzzard.

circón [theer-cone'], *m. (Acad.)* Zircon, a zirconium silicate, of various colors' transparent to opaque.

circonio [theer-co-ne-o], *m.* Zirconium, an earthy metallic element, of no practical application, derived from zircon.

circuir [theer-co-eer´], *va.* To surround, to compass, to encircle.

circuito [theer-coo-ee'-to], *m.* 1. Circuit, circle, extent. 2. Circumference. 3. *(Elec.)* Circuit. **Corto circuito,** short circuit. 4. Radio hookup. **En circuito cerrado,** closed-circuit. 5. *(Inform.)* **Circuito aritmético MSI,** MSI arithmetic circuit. **Circuito basculante,** flip-flop. **Circuito combinacional,** combinatory, combinatorial, combinational circuit. **Circuito de Integración a Muy Gran Escala,** Very Large Scale Integration Circuit. **Circuito de Integración a Pequeña Escala,** Small Scale Integration Circuit. **Circuito de Integración a Gran Escala,** Large Scale Integration Circuit. **Circuito de Integración a Media Escala,** Medium Scale Integration circuit. **Circuito en caja QUIP,** Quad Inline Package circuit. **Circuito multiplexor MSI,** MSI multiplexer circuit. **Circuito secuencial,** sequential circuit. **Circuito SSI,** SSI circuit.

circulación [theer-coo-lah-the-on'], *f.* 1. Circulation, currency. **Circulación sanguínea,** circulation of the blood. **Estar fuera de circulación,** to be out of circulation. **Poner algo en circulación,** to issue something. 2. Traffic, movement of traffic. **La circulación es por la derecha,** they drive on the right. **Calle de gran circulación,** busy street. **Circulación única,** *(Mex.)* One way traffic.

circulante [theer-coo-lahn'-tay], *pa. & a.* Circulatory, circling, circulating.

circular [theer-coo-lar´], *a.* Circular, circulatory circling. **Carta circular,** a circular letter.

circular [theer-coo-lar´], *vn.* 1. To circulate, to surround, to travel round, to go from hand to hand. **Hacer circular una carta,** to circulate a letter. 2. To move about, to walk around (personas). **Hacer circular a la gente,** to move people along. 3. To drive. **Circular por la izquierda,** to drive on the left. 4. To run (transporte). **No circula los domingos,** it does not run on Sundays.

circularmente [theer-coo-lar-men´-tay], *adv.* Circularly.

círculo [theer'-coo-lo], *m.* 1. Circle. **Círculo máximo,** great circle. **Círculo polar antártico,** Antarctic Circle. 2. Orb, circlet; compass. 3. A superstitious ring or circle. 4. District. 5. Figure of speech, wherein a sentence begins and ends with the same words. 6. Circle, club. 7. *(fig.)* Scope, compass, extent.

circumambiente [theer-coom-am-been'-tay], *a.* Circumambient, surrounding.

circumcirca [theer-coom-theer'-cah], *adv. (Coll. Lat.)* About, thereabout; almost.

circumpolar [theer-coom-po-lar'], *a.* Circumpolar, near the pole.

circun...*pref.* circum...

circuncidante [theer-coon-the-dahn'-tay], *m. & pa.* Circumciser.

circuncidar [theer-coon-the-dar'], *va.* 1. To circumcise. 2. *(Met. Coll.)* To diminish, to curtail or modify.

circuncisión [theer-coon-the-se-on'], *f.* 1. Circumcisión. 2. A religious festival celebrated on the 1st of January, or New Year's day.

circunciso, sa [theer-coon-thee'-so, sah], *pp. irr.* of CIRCUNCIDAR. Circumcised.

circundante [ther-coon-dahn'-tay], *a.* Surrounding.

circundar [theer-coon-dar'], *va.* To surround, to circle, to compass.

circunferencia [theer-coon-fay-ren'-the-ah], *f.* Circumference.

circunferencial [theer-coon-fay-ren-the-ahl'], *a.* Circumferential, circular, surrounding.

circunferencialmente [theer-coon-fay-ren-the-al-men'-tay], *adv.* In a circular manner.

circunflejo, ja [theer-coon-flay'-ho, hah], *a.* **Acento circunflejo**, circumflex accent (^), composed of the acute and grave.

circunlocución [theer-coon-lo-coo-the-on'], *f.* Circunlocution, periphrasis, roundabout expression.

circunloquio [theer-coon-lo'-ke-o], *m.* Circumlocution, circle.

circunnavegación [theer-coon-nah-ve-gah-the-on'], *f.* Circumnavigation.

circunnavegar [theer-coon-nah-ve-gar'], *va.* To circumnavigate, sail round the world.

circunscribir [theer-coons-cre-beer'], *va.* To circumscribe, to inclose. *-vr. (fig.)* To limit oneself.

circunscripción [theer-coons-crip-the-on'], *f.* Circumscription, division.

circunscriptivo, va [theer-coons-crip-tee'-vo, vah], *a.* Circumscriptive, inclosing superficies.

circunspección [theer-coons-pec-the-on'], *f.* Circumspection, prudence, watchfulness, general attention.

circunspectamente [theer-coons-pec-tah-men'-tay], *adv.* Circumspectly.

circunspecto, ta [theer-coons-pec'-to, tah], *a.* Circumspect, cautious, considerate, judicious, grave.

circunstancia [theer-coons-tahn'-the-ah], *f.* 1. Circumstance. **Refirió el caso con todas sus circunstancias**, he gave a full and minute account of the case. 2. Incident, event. 3. Condition, state of affairs. **En las circunstancias presentes**, in the actual state of things. **En las circunstancias**, in the circumstances. **Las circunstancias cambian los casos**, circumstances alter cases.

circunstanciadamente [theer-coons-tan-the-ah-dah-men'-tay], *adv.* Circumstantially, minutely.

circunstanciado, da [theer-coons-tan-the-ah'-do, dah], *a.* 1. According to circumstances. 2. Circumstantial, minute. *-pp.* of CIRCUNSTANCIAR.

circunstancial [theer-coons-tahn-the-ahl'], *a.* 1. Circumstantial. 2. Emergency; incidental. **Mi estancia en Lima era circunstancial**, I just happened to be in Lima.

circunstante [theer-coons-tahn'-tay], *a.* circumstant, surrounding.

circunstantes [theer-coons-tahn'-tes], *m. pl.* By standers, persons present.

circunvalación [theer-coon-vah-lah-the-on'], *f.* Circumvallation, the act of surrounding a place.

circunvalar [theer-coon-vah-lar'], *va.* 1. To surround, to encircle. 2. *(Mil.)* To circumvallate, to surround with trenches.

circunvecino, na [theer-coon-vay-thee'-no, nah], *a.* Neighboring, adjacent, contiguous.

circunvención [theer-coon-ven-the-on'], *f.* Circumvention, overreaching, deceit.

circunvenir [theer-coon-vay-neer'], *va.* To circumvent, to overreach.

circunvolución [theer-coon-vo-loo-the-on'], *f.* Circumvolution.

circunyacente [theer-coon-yah-then'-tar], *a.* Circumjacent, lying near.

cirial [the-re-ahl'], *m.* Church candlestick (candelero). Processional candlestick (en procesiones)

cirílico [the-re'-le-co], *a.m.* Cyrillic.

cirineo [the-re-nay'-o], *m. (Coll.)* Mate, assistant.

cirio [thee'-re-o], *m.* A thick and long wax-candle; **cirio pascual**, paschal candle.

cirquero, ra [theer-kay'-ro], *m. & f. (Mex.)* Circus performer, acrobat; circus impresario.

cirro [theer'-ro], *m.* 1. *(Med.)* Schirrus. 2. Tuft of mane hanging over a horse's face

cirrosis [theer-ro'-sis], *f.* Cirrhosis, a morbid deposit of connective tissue in an organ, especially the liver, resulting in contraction and impaired function.

cirroso, sa [theer-ro'-so, sah], *a.* 1. Scirrhous. 2. Fibrous. **Raíces cirrosas**, fibrous roots.

ciruela [the-roo-ay'-lah], *f.* Plum, prune. **Ciruela pasa**, a dried plum; a prune. **Ciruela verdal**, a green gage.

ciruelar [the-roo-ay-lar'], *m.* A large plantation of plumtrees.

ciruelica, illa, ita [the-roo-ay-lee'-cah], *f. dim.* A small plum.

ciruelico, illo, ito [the-roo-ay-lee'-co], *m. dim.* A dwarf plum-tree.

ciruelo [the-roo-ay'-lo], *m.* 1. *(Bot.)* Plum-tree. 2. Dolt, idiot.

cirugía [the-roo-hee'-ah], *f.* Surgery. **Cirugía dental**, dental surgery. **Cirugía plástica**, plastic surgery, anaplasty.

cirujano [the-roo-hah'-no], *a.* Surgeon. **Cirujano dentista**, dental surgeon.

cis. A Latin prefix meaning on this side of, toward Rome.

cisalpino, no [this-al-pee'-no'-nah], *a.* Cisalpine, on this side of the Alps: between the Alps and Rome.

cisca [thees'-cah], *f. (Prov.)* Reed for roofing huts and cottages. *V.* CARRIZO.

ciscar [this-car'], *va.* 1. *(Coll.)* To besmear, to make dirty. 2. *(Carib. Mex.)* To shame, to put down. 3. *(Carib, Mex.)* To provoke, to needle. *-vr.* **Ciscarse de miedo**, to dirty oneself from fear, to soil oneself; to do one's business. **Los que ciscan en las teorías**, those who thumb their noses at theories.

cisco [thees'-co], *m.* 1. Coaldust, broken coal. **Hacer algo cisco**, to tear something to bits. **Estar hecho cisco**, to be a wreck. 2. Row, shindy. **Armar un cisco**, to kick up a row, to make trouble. 3. *(Mex.)* Fear, fright.

ciscón [thees-cone'], *a. (Carib. Mex.)* Touchy.

cisión [the-se-on'], *f.* Incision. *V.* CISURA or INCISION.

cisma [thees'-mah], *m.* 1. Schism. 2. Disturbance in a communnity.

cismático, ca [this-mah'-te-co, cah], *a.* 1. Schismatic. 2. Applied to the author of disturbances in a community.

cismontano, na [this-mon-tah'-no, nah], *a.* Living on this side of the mountains.

cisne [thees'-nay], *m.* 1. *(Orn.)* Swan. 2. Cygnus, the Swan, constellation in the northern hemisphere. 3. *(Met.)* A good poet or musician. 4. *(Low.)* Prostitute. 5. *(Cono Sur)* Powder puff (borla).

cisquero [thees-kay'-ro], *m.* A small linen bag with coaldust, used by painters and draftsmen.

ciste [thees'-tay], *m.* Cyst, bladder. *V.* QUISTE.

cistel, cister [this-tel', this-terr'], *m.* Cistercian order of St. Bernard.

cisterciense [this-ter-the-en'-say], *a.* Cistercian.

cisterna [this-terr'-nah], *f.* 1. Cistern. 2. Reservoir, an inclosed fountain.

cístico [thees'-te-co], *a. (Surg.)* Cystic.

cistitis [this-tee'-tis], *f.* Cystitis, inflammation of the bladder.

cisto [thees'-to], *m. (Bot.)* Cistus.

cistotomía [this-to-to-mee'-ah], *f. (Surg.)* Cystotomy.

cistótomo [this-to'-to-mo], *m.* Cystotome; now called lithotome.

cisura [the-soo'-rah], *f.* Incisure, incision.

cita [thee'-tah], *f.* 1. Appointment, engagement, a meeting appointed; rendez-vous. **Acudir a una cita**, to keep an appointment, turn up for an appointment. **se dieron una cita para las 8**, they agreed to meet at 8. **Faltar a una cita**, to miss an appointment. 2. Citation, quotation of a passage of a book.

citable [the-tah'-blay], *a.* Worthy of being cited, quoted.

citación [the-tah-the-on'], *f.* 1. Citation, quotation. 2. Summons, judicial notice. **Citación judicial**, summons. **Citación a licitadores**, invitation to bidders.

citado [the-tah'-do], *a.* Afore mentioned. **En el país citado,** in the afore mentioned country; in this country.

citador, ra [the-tah-dor', rah], *m. & f.* Citer.

citano, na [the-tah'-no, nah], *m. & f. (Coll.) V.* ZUTANO.

citar [the-tar'], *va.* 1. To make a business appointment. **Le cité para las 8,** I arranged to meet her at 8. 2. To convoke, to convene, to cite. 3. To quote, to cite. 4. To cite, to summon before a judge; to give judicial notice. **Dijo que se da por citado,** he declared that he was duly summoned. 5. *(Taur.)* To incite, to provoke, to stir up. *-vr.* **Citarse con uno,** to arrange to meet somebody. **Citémonos delante del estadio,** let´s meet outside the stadium.

cítara [thee'-ta-rah], *f.* 1. Cithara or cithern, a musical instrument; a guitar strung with wire, zither. 2. Body of troops covering the flanks of those advancing to the charge.

citara [the-tah'-rah], *f.* Partition-wall of the thickness of a brick.

citarista [the-ta-rees'-tah], *m. & f.* 1. A player of the cithern. 2. A maker or seller of citherns.

citarístico, ca [the-ta-rees'-te-co, cah], *a. (Poet.)* Belonging to poetry, adapted to the cithara.

citarizar [the-ta-re-thar'], *vn.* To play the cithara.

citatorio, ria [the-ta-to'-re-o, ah], *a. (Law.)* Citatory: applied to a summons.

citerior [the-tay-re-or'], *a.* Hither, nearer, toward this part. **España citerior,** the higher or northeastern part of Spain.

cítola [thee'-to-lah], *f.* 1. In cornmills, clack or clapper, a piece of wood which strikes the hopper and promotes the running of the corn. 2. *V.* CÍTARA. **La cítola es por demás, cuando el molinero es sordo,**

citología [the-to-lo-hee'-ah], *f.* Cytology.

citote [the-to'-tay], *m. (Coll.)* Summons, a judicial citation.

citramontano, na [the-trah-mon-tah'-no, nah], *a.* On this side of the mountains.

citrato [the-trah'-to], *m. (Chem.)* Citrate.

cítrico [thee'-tre-co], *a. (Chem.)* Citric.

citrícola [the-tre'-co-lah], *a.* Citrus.

cítrino, na [the-tree'-no, nah], *a. (Obs.)* Lemon-colored. *V.* CETRINO.

citrón [the-tronc'], *m.* Lemon.

ciudad [the-oo-dahd'], *f.* 1. City, town. **Ciudad del Cabo,** Cape Town. **Ciudad del Vaticano,** Vatican City. **Es el mejor café de la ciudad,** it´s the best café in town. 2. Corporation, civic body.

ciudadanía [the-oo-dah-dah-nee'-ah], *f.* Citizenship. **Ciudadanía de honor,** freedom of a city.

ciudadano, na [the-oo-da-dah'-no, nah], *a.* 1. City, relating to a city. 2 Civil, relating to any man, as member of a community. 3. Citizen-like.

ciudadano, m. 1. Citizen, freeman. 2. Inhabitant of a city. 3. A degree of nobility inferior to that of *caballero,* and superior to the condition of a tradesman.

ciudadela [the-oo-da-day'-lah], *f.* 1. *(Mil.)* Citadel, a small fortress. 2. *(LAm.)* Tenement block (casa pobre).

ciudad-estado [ ], *f. pl.* **Ciudades-estado,** city-state.

civeta [the-vay'-tah], *f.* Civet-cat. *V.* Gato de algalia.

civeto [the-vay´-to], *m.* Civet, the perfume.

cívico, ca [thee'-ve-co, cah], *a.* Civic. *V.* DOMÉSTICO.

civil [the-veel'], *a.* 1. Civil, relating to the community. 2. Civil, relating to man, as a member of a community. 3. Civil, polite, courteous, gentleman-like. 4. Civil, not military or ecclesiastical. **Derechos civiles,** civil rights. 5. Of low rank or extraction. 6. In law, civil, not criminal. **Población civil,** civilian population. *-m.* 1. Civil guard. 2. Civilian.

civilidad [the-ve-le-dahd'], *f.* 1. Civility, politeness, urbanity, good manners (cortesía).

civilista [the-ve-lees'-tah], *m.* 1. An attorney skilled in the civil law, especially the Roman law. 2. *(Amer.)* Partisan of civil government, opponent of militarism.

civlización [the-ve-le-thah-the-on'], *f.*

civilizador, ra [the-ve-le-thah-dor', rah], *a.* Civilizing.

civilizar [the-ve-le-thar´], *va.* To civilize. *-vr.* To become civilized.

civilmente [the-veel-men'-tay], *adv.* 1. Civilly, courteously, politely. 2. According to the common law.

civismo [the-vees'-mo], *m.* Patriotism, zeal for one's country.

cizalla [the-thahl'-lyah], *f.* Fragments or filings of gold, silver, or other metal clippings.*-pl.* **Cizallas,** Cutting-pliers, or strong shears for clipping metal or wire.

cizallar [the-thahl-lyar'], *va.* To use cutting pliers, or shears, in cutting wire or metal.

cizaña [the-thah'-nyah], *f. (Acad.)* 1. *(Bot.)* Darnel. 2. Discord. **Sembrar cizaña,** to sow discord. *V.* ZIZAÑA.

cizañar [the-thah-nyar'], *va.* To sow discord among.

cizañero, ra [the-thah-nyay'-ro], *m. & f.* Troublemaker, mischief-maker.

cl. *abr.* de **centilitro** (centiliter, cl.).

clac [clahc'], *m.* 1. A clapping of the hands. 2. A hat of tall crown provided with springs for shutting close; opera-hat.

clacote [clah-co'-tay], *m. (Mex.)* Pimple, pustule.

claitonia [clah-e-to'-ne-ah], *f. (Bot.)* Claytonia.

clamar [clah-mar'], *va.* 1. To call. *V.* LLAMAR. 2. To cry out in a mournful tone. 3. *(Met.)* To show a want of something (sustancias inanimadas). **La tierra clama por agua,** the ground wants water. *-vn.* To cry out, to clamor. **Clamar contra,** to cry out against. **Clamar por,** to clamor for. **Esto clama al cielo,** this cries out to heaven.

clámide [clah'-me-day], *f.* A short cape, the chlamys of the Greeks.

clamor [clah-mor'], *m.* 1. Clamor, outcry, scream, shriek, cry. 2. Sound of passing bells. 3. The public voice.

clamorear [clah-mo-ray-ar'], *va.* To clamor, to implore assistance.*-vn.* To toll the passing bell.

clamoreo [clah-mo-ray'-o], *m.* 1. Knell, clamor(ing), shouting. 2. *(fig.)* Sustained outcry, vociferous protests. **Clamoreo de protesta,** vigorous protests.

clamorosamente [clah-mo-ro-sah-men'-tay], *adv.* Clamorously.

clamoroso, sa [clah-mo-ro'-so, sah], *a.* 1. Clamorous, loud, noisy. 2. *(fig.)* Resounding, enormous (éxito). *V.* VOCINGLERO.

clamoso, sa [clah-mo'-so, sah], *a.* That which calls out, or solicits.

clan [clan], *m.* Clan; faction, group.

clandestinamente [clan-des-te-nah men´-tay], *adv.* Clandestinely, secretly.

clandestinidad [clan-des-te-ne-dahd´], *f.* Clandestinity, privacy, or secrecy. **en la clandestinidad,** in secrecy. **Movimiento en la clandestinidad,** *(Pol.)* in secrecy. **Pasar a la clandestinidad,** to go into hiding.

clandestino, na [clan-des-tee'-no, nah], *a.* Clandestine, secret, private.

clanga [clahn'-gah], *f. V.* PLANGA.

clangor [clan-gor'], *m. (Poet.)* The sound of a trumpet.

claque [clah'-kay], *f. (Theat.)* Claque, paid applauders.

claqué [clah-kay'], *m.* Tap-dancing.

claqueta [clah-kay'-tah], *f.* Clapperboard.

clara [clah´-rah], *f. (Coll.)* A short interval of fair weather on a rainy day. **Me aproveché de una clara para salir,** I availed myself of a fair moment to go out. **Clara de huevo,** white of an egg. **Claras,** pieces of cloth ill-woven, through which the light can be seen. **A las claras,** clearly, evidently.

clarabela [clah-ra-bay'-lah], *f.* Clarabella, an organstop of open wood pipes, soft and sweet.

claraboya [clah-ra-bo'-yah], *f.* Skylight, bull's-eye, window; dormer-window.

claramente [clah-ra-men'-tay], *adv.* Clearly, openly, manifestly, conspicuously, obviously, fairly.

clarea [clah-ray'-ah], *f.* White wine with cinnamon, sugar and spices added.

clarear [clah-ray-ar'], *vn.* To dawn, to grow light. **va.** 1. To brighten; to light up. 2. *(fig.)* To clarify, to make clear. 3. *(Mex.)* To go right through, to penetrate (atravesar). *-vr.* 1.

To be transparent, translucent. 2. *(Met.)* To be cleared up by conjectures or surmises.

clarecer [clah-ray-therr'], *vn.* To dawn, to grow light.

clareo [clah-ray'-o], *m.* **Darse un clareo**, to take a stroll (pasear).

clarete [clah-ray'-tay], *m.* Claret. *-a.* **Vino clarete**, claret wine.

claridad [clah-re-dahd'], *f.* 1. Clarity, brightness, splendor, light. 2. Clearness, distinctness, freedom from obscurity and confusion. 3. That which is said resolutely, to upbraid. **Lo explicó todo con claridad**, he explained it all very clearly. 4. Glory of the blessed. 5. *(Met.)* Celebrity, fame.

claridoso [clah-re-do'-so], *a.* *(CAm. Mex.)* Blunt, plain-spoken.

clarificación [clah-re-fe-cah-the-on´], *f.* Clarification, refining.

clarificar [clah-re-fe-car'], *va.* 1. To brighten, to illuminate. 2. To clarify, to purify, to refine.

clarificativo, va [clah-re-fe-cah-tee'-vo, vah], *a.* Purificative or purificatory.

clarimentos [clah-re-men'-tose], *m. pl.* The lights in a picture.

clarín [clah-reen'], *m.* 1. Trumpet, bugle (insturmento). 2. In organs, a trumpet or clarion stop. *-V.* CLARÓN. 3. Trumpeter. 4. Kind of batiste (tela).

clarinada [clah-re-nah'-dah], *f.* 1. Trumpet-call. 2. *(Met. and Coll.)* Extravagant answer.

clarinado, da [clah-re-nah'-do, dah], *a. (Her.)* Applied to animals with bells in their harness.

clarinazo [clah-re-nah-tho], *m. (fig.)* Trumpet call.

clarinero [clah-re-nay'-ro], *m.* Trumpeter.

clarinete [clah-re-nay'-tay], *m.* 1 Clarinet. 2. Player on the clarinet; clarinetist.

clarinetista [clah-re-nay-tees'-tah], *m.* Clarinetist, player upon the clarinet.

clarión [clah-re-on'], *m.* Crayon.

clarisa [clah-ree'-sah], *f.* Clare, a nun of the order of St. Clara.

clarísimo, ma [clah-ree'-se-mo, mah], *a.* Super, of *Claro*, most illustrious.

clarividencia [clah-re-ve-dayn'-the-ah], *f.* 1. Clairvoyance. 2. *(fig.)* Far-sightedness (previsión); discernment (discernimiento); intuition.

clarividente [clah-re-ve-dayn'-tay], *a.* Far-sighted, far-seeing; discerning. *- m. & f.* Clairvoyant.

claro, ra [clah'-ro, rah], *a.* 1. Clear, bright, transparent, lightsome. 2. Clear, transparent, pellucid, crystalline, fine, limpid. 3. Clear, thin, rare, not dense. 4. Clear, thin, not close. 5. Clear, free from clouds, serene, fair. 6. Light, not deeply tinged. **Azul claro**, light blue. 7. Clear, perspicuous, intelligible, not obscure. 8. Clear, obvious, explicit, evident, manifest, indisputable, apparent. **Es una verdad clara**, it is an undeniable truth. **Tan claro como la luz del día**, as plain as a day. **Más claro que el sol**, as clear as day light. 9. Open, frank, ingenuous. 10. Celebrated, illustrious. 11. *(Met.)* Sagacious, quick of thought.

claro [clah'-ro], *m.* 1. A kind of skylight. 2. Break in a discourse or writing; spacing in printing. 3. Rays of light falling on a painting. 4. Opening or space between the columns of a building or other things. 5. *(Naut.)* A clear spot in the sky. **Poner** or **sacar en claro** *(Met.)* to place a point in its true light, to explain, to expound, or interpret. **Pasar la noche de claro en claro**, to have not a wink of sleep all night. **De claro en claro**, evidently, manifestly. **Por lo claro**, clearly, manifestly, conspicuously. 6. Opening (abertura); gap, break, space (brecha, espacio); opening (en bosque); gap (en tráfico); bald patch (en pecho). 7. *(Arquit.)* Light, window; skylight. 8. *(Carib.) (Culin.)* Guava jelly. 9. *(Carib.)* Sugar-cane brandy. 10. **Clara de huevo**, eggwhite.

claro, *adv.* V. CLARAMENTE.

¡claro! [clah-ro], *interj.* Of course! naturally. **¡Claro que sí!** yes, definitely, of course.

clarol [clah-rol´], *m.* Inlaid work (muebles).

clarón [clah-rone'], *m.* Clarion, a register of the organ.

claroscuro [clah-ros-coo'-ro], *m.* Monochrome, a painting in one color.

clarucho, cha [clah-roo'-cho, chah], *a.* Too watery, too liquid.

clase [clah'-say], *f.* 1. Class or rank of the people, order of persons. 2. Division of schoolboys. 3. Classis, kind, generical class, a set of beings or things. **Con toda clase de**, with all kinds of. **De otra clase**, of another sort. **De primera clase**, first class. 4. Class, species, family. 5. *(Com.)* Sort, description, quality. **Navío de primera clase**, a first class ship. **Primera clase**, first class. **Clase intermedia**, *(Naut.)* cabin class. 6. *(Escol.)* Class; lecture. **Clase de geografía**, geography class; geography lesson. **Clase nocturna**, evening class. **Dar clases**, to teach. **Faltar a clase**, to miss class. 7. *(Escol.)* Classroom. 8. *(Pol.)* Class. **Clase alta**, upper class. **Clase obrera**, working class. **Las clases pudientes**, the well-to-do classes.

clase acomodada [clah'-say ah-co-mo-dah'-dah], *f.* Well-to-do class, people of wealth.

clase media [clah'-say may'-de-ah], *f.* Middle class.

clásicamente [clah-se-cah-mem´-tay], *adv.* Classically.

clasicismo [clah-se-thees'-mo], *m.* Classic style; classicism.

clásico, ca [clah'-se-co, cah], *a.* 1 Classical, classic. 2. Principal, remarkable, of the first order or rank. **Error clásico**, a gross error. **Autores clásicos**, classics. **Le dio el clásico saludo**, he gave him the time-honored salute.

clasificable [clah-se-fe-cah'-blay], *a.* Classifiable.

clasificación [clah-se-fe-cah-the-one'], *f.* Classification; sorting (Correos); *(Naut.)* Rating. **Clasificación nacional del disco**, top twenty, record hit parade.

clasificador [clah-se-fe-cah-dor'], *m.* 1. Classifier (persona). 2. Filing cabinet (mueble). **Clasificador de cartas**, letter file.

clasificar [clah-se-fe-car'], *va.* To clasify, to arrange, to class. *-vr.* 1. *(Dep.)* To win a place; to occupy a position; **Meca se clasificó después de la Ceca**, Meca came after Ceca. 2. *(Dep.)* To qualify. **No se clasificó el equipo para la final**, the team did not qualify for the final.

clasismo [clah-sees'-mo], *m.* Class, feelings; class-consciousness; class structure.

clasista [clah-sees'-tah], *a.* *(Pol.)* Class; class-conscious; snobbish.

claudia [clah'-oo-de-ah], *f.* Greengage.

claudicación [clah-oo-de-cah-the-on'], *f.* Claudication, halting or limping.

claudicante [clah-oo-de-cahn´-tay], *a. & pa.* Claudicant, claudicating, halting, limping.

claudicar [clah-oo-de-car'], *vn.* 1. To claudicate, to halt or limp. 2. *(Met.)* To proceed in a bungling manner, without rule or order.

Claudio [clah'-oo-de-o], *m.* Claudius.

clauquillar [clah-oo-keel-lyar'], *va. (Obs. Prov.)* To put the customhouse seal on bales of goods.

claustral [clah-oos-trahl'], *a.* 1. Claustral. 2. Claustral (monjes). *-m. & f. (Univ.)* Member of the Senate.

claustrico, illo, ito [clah-oos-tree'-co, eel'-lyo, ee'-to], *m. dim.* Small cloister.

claustro [clah'-oos-tro], *m.* 1. Cloister, piazza, or gallery around the court of a convent. 2. Assembly or meeting of the principal members of a university. 3. Womb. 4. *(Obs.)* Room, chamber.

claustrofobia [clah-oos-tro-fo'-be-ah], *f.* Claustrophobia.

claustrofóbico [clah-oos-tro-fo'-fe-co], *a.* Claustrophobic.

cláusula [clah'-oo-soo-lah], *f.* 1. Period, clause of a discourse. 2. Clause, condition, an article or particular stipulation.

clausular [clah-oo-soo-lar'], *va.* To close a period; to terminate a speech.

clausulilla [clah-oo-soo-leel'-lyah], *f. dim.* A little clause.

clausura [clah-oo-soo'-rah], *f.* 1. Cloister, the inner recess of a convent. **Convento de clausura**, enclosed convent. 2. Clausure, confinement, retirement. **Guardar clausura** or **vivir en clausura**, to lead a monastic or retired life.

clausurar [clah-oo-soo-rar'], *va.* 1. To close, to bring to a close; to adjourn, to close. 2. *(LAm.)* To close (casa).

clava [clah'-vah], *f.* 1. Club. 2. (*Naut.*) Scupper.

clavada [clah-vah'-dah], *f.* **Pegar una clavada a uno,** to rip somebody off, overcharge somebody.

clavado [clah-vah'-do], *m.* (*Mex.*) Fancy dive. **Echarse un clavado,** to dive.

clavado, da [clah-vah'-do, dah], *a.* 1. Exact, precise. **El reloj está clavado a las cinco,** it is just five by the clock. **Venir clavada una cosa a otra,** to fit exactly. 2. Nailed, armed or furnished with nails. 3. Relating to a club, especially to that of Hercules. 4. Just right, exactly fitting (vestido). 5. **Dejar a uno clavado,** to leave somebody speechless. 6. **Está clavado a su padre,** (*LAm.*) he´s the spitting image of his father. *-pp.* of CLAVAR.

clavador [clah-vah-dor'], *m.* Nail-driver.

clavadura [clah-vah-doo'-rah], *f.* Nailing, driving a nail to the quick in horse-shoeing.

clavar [clah-var'], *va.* 1. To nail; to fasten with nails; to fasten in, to force in. 2. To stick, to prick, to gore; to introduce a pointed thing into another. **Se clavó un alfiler,** he pricked himself with a pin. **Me clavé una espina,** I pricked myself with a thorn. **Clavar los ojos** or **la vista,** to stare, to look with fixed eyes. 3. To cheat, to deceive. **Me clavaron 50 dólares,** they stung me for 50 dollars. 4. To set in gold or silver. 5. (*Mil.*) To ground. *-vr.* 1. To penetrate, to go in. 2. **Clavarse una astilla en el dedo,** to get a splinter in one´s finger. 3. (*fig.*) To be mistaken. 4. **Clavársela,** to get drunk. 5. **Clavarse algo,** (*Mex.*) To pocket something.

clavaria [clah-vah'-re-ah], *f.* V. LLAVERA.

clavario [clah-vah'-re-o], *m.* 1. Treasurer, cashier. 2. A dignitary of the military order of Montesa.

clavazón [clah-va-thone'], *f.* 1. Set of nails. 2. (*Naut.*) Assortment of the different nails used in the construction of ships.

clave [clah'-vay], *f.* 1. Code, key. **El telegrama está en clave,** the telegram is in code. 2. (*Mus.*) Key, clef. **Clave de sol,** treble clef. 3. (*Arch.*) Keystone of an arch. 4. Harpsichord. *-m.* (*Mus.*) Harpsichord.

clavecín [clah-vay-theen'], *m.* Spinet.

clavel [clah-vel'], *m.* Carnation. **No tener un clavel,** to be broke.

clavelina [clah-vay-lee'-nah], *f.* (*Bot.*) 1. The plant which bears the common pink. 2. Mignonette.

clavelón [clah-vay-lone'], *m.* (*Bot. aug.*) Marigold; African marigold.

clavellina [clah-vel-lyee'-nah], *f.* 1. (*Bot.*) The pink, carnation.

claveque [clah-vay'-kay], *m.* Rock crystal.

clavera [clah-vay'-rah], *f.* 1. Mould for nail-heads. 2. Hole through which a nail is fastened. 3. Nail-hole in a horse-shoe. 4. (*Prov. Ext.*) Boundary where landmarks are set up.

clavería [clah-vay-ree'-ah], *f.* Office and dignity of the key-bearer in the military orders of Calatrava and Alcántara.

clavero, ra [clah-vay'-ro, rah], *m. & f.* 1. Keeper of the keys, treasurer, cashier. 2. (*Bot.*) Aromatic clove-tree. 3. Key-bearer, the knight of the orders of Calatrava and Alcantara, who takes care of the castle, convent, and archives.

clavete [clah-vay'-tay], *m. dim.* Tack, a small nail.

claveteado [clah-vay-tay-ah'-do], *m.* Studs, studding.

clavetear [clah-vay-tay-ar'], *va.* 1. To nail, to garnish with brass or other nails. 2. To point or tag a lace. 3. (*fig.*) To clinch, to close, to wind up (trato).

clavicémbalo [clah-ve-them'-bah-lo], *m.* Harpsichord.

clavicordio [clah-ve-cor'-de-o], *m.* Harpsichord, manichord.

clavícula [clah-vee'-coo-lah], *f.* (*Anat.*) Clavicle, the collarbone.

clavidista [clah-ve-dees'-tah], *m. & f.* (*Mex.*) (*Dep.*) Diver.

clavija [clah-vee'-hah], *f.* Pin, peg, or tack of wood or iron, thrust into a hole for rolling or winding something around. 2. A peg for hanging something on. 3. Peg of a stringed instrument. **Clavija maestra,** the fore axle-tree pintle. **Apretar a uno las clavijas,** (*Met.*) to push home an argument.

clavijera [clah-ve-hay'-rah], *f.* (*Prov.*) Opening in mud walls to let in the water.

clavijero [clah-ve-hay'-ro], *m.* 1. Bridge of a harpsichord. 2. Rack or perch for clothing or hats.

clavillo, ito [clah-vee'-lyo, ee'-to], *m. dim.* A small nail. **Clavillo de hebilla,** Rivet of a buckle. **Clavillos,** cloves.

claviórgano [clah-ve-or'-gah-no], *m.* An organized harpsichord, composed of strings and pipes, like an organ.

clavo [clah'-vo], *m.* 1. Nail, an iron spike. **Clavo de herradura,** hobnail. **Clavo plateado,** tinned nail, a nail dipped in lead or solder. 2. Corn, a hard and painful excrescence on the feet. 3. Spot in the eye. 4. Hurt for wounds or sores; a tent. (*Surg.*) 5. **Clavo** or **clavo de especia,** clove, a valuable spice. 6. (*Naut.*) Rudder of a ship. 7. (*Met.*) Severe grief or pain. 8. Tumor between the hair and the hoof of a horse. 9. (*Prov.*) Headache. V. JAQUECA. 10. **Clavos romanos,** (*Amer.*) Curtain knobs. **Clavo,** in the mines of Mexico, a bunch of rich ore. **Arrimar el clavo,** in horse-shoeing, to strike the quick and make the horse limp. **Dar en el clavo,** (*Met.*) to hit the mark, to succeed in a doubtful matter. **Agarrarse a un clavo ardiendo,** to clutch. **Estar como un clavo,** to be terribly thin. **Llegar como un clavo,** to arrive on the dot. **Remachar el clavo,** (*fig.*) to make matters worse. 11. (*CAm. Mex.*) Problem, snag. 12. (*And. Cono Sur*) unpleasant thing; nasty situation; unsaleable article.

clavulina [clah-voo-lee'-nah], *f.* A microscopic shell.

claxon [klak'-son], *s.* (*Mex.*) Auto horn. **Tocar el claxon,** to sound one´s horn, to hoot.

claxonar [clak-so-nar'], *vn.* To sound one´s horn, to hoot.

claxonazo [clak-so-nah'-tho], *m.* (*Aut.*) Hoot, toot (on the horn).

clemátide [clay-mah'-te-day], *f.* (*Bot.*) Traveler's-joy, virgin´s-bower, or the upright lady's-bower, clematis.

clemencia [clay-men'-the-ah], *f.* Clemency, mercy, forbearance.

clemente [clay-men'-tay], *a.* Clement, merciful.

clementemente [clay-men-tay-men'-tay], *adv.* Mercifully, clemently.

clementina [clay men-tee'-nah], *f.* 1. The canons of Pope Clement V, contained in the collection called *Clementinas,* published by Pope John XXII. 2. Tangerine.

clementísimo, ma [clay-men-tee'-se-mo, mah], *a. sup.* of CLEMENTE.

Cleopatra [Clay-o-pah-trah], *f.* Cleopatra.

clepsidra [Clep-see'-drah], *f.* Clepsydra, waterclock, an hour-glass.

cleptomanía [clep-to-mah-nee'-ah], *f.* Kleptomania.

cleptómano, na [clep-to'-mah-no, nah], *m. & f. & a.* Klepto-maniac.

clerecía [clay-ray-thee'-ah], *f.* 1. Clergy. 2. The body of clergymen who attend with surplices at religious festivals.

clergyman [clayr-he-man], *a.* Clergyman (clérigo protestante). **Traje clergyman,** clergyman's suit.

clerical [clay-re-cahl'], *a.* Clerical.

clericalismo [clay-re-cah-lees'-mo], *m.* Clericalism.

clericalmente [clay-re-cal-men'-tay], *adv.* In a clerical manner.

clericato [clay-re-cah'-to], *m.* State and dignity of a clergyman. **Clericato de cámara,** some distinguished offices in the palace of the Pope.

clericatura [clay-re-cah-too'-rah], *f.* State of a clergyman.

clericó [clay-re-co'], *m.* (*Cono Sur*) Mulled wine.

clérigo [clay'-re-go], *m.* A clergyman, a cleric, a clerk. **Clérigo de misa,** a presbyter.

clero [clay'-ro], *m.* Clergy. **Clero secular,** secular clergy, who do not make the three solemn vows of poverty, obedience, and chastity. **Clero regular,** regular clergy who profess a monastic life, and make the above vows.

clerofobia [clay-ro-fo'-be-ah], *f.* Anticlericalism.

clerófobo [clay-ro'-fo-bo], *a.* Anticlerical.

cliché [cle-chay'], *m.* 1. (*Typ.*) Cliché, stereotype plate. 2. (*Liter.*) Cliché; V. CLISE.

cliente [cle-en'-tay], *m. & f.* com. 1. Client, a person under the protection and tutorage of another. 2. Customer, patient.

clientela [cle-en-tay'-lah], *f.* 1. A body of clients or dependents; a following; clientele. 2. Protection or patronage. 3. Clientship, condition of a client.

cliéntulo, la [cle-en'-too-lo, lah], *m. & f. (Obs.) V.* CLIENTE.

clima [clee'-mah], *m.* Climate, clime. **Clima artificial** or **acondicionamiento del aire**, air conditioning. **Clima cálido,** warm climate. **Clima templado,** temperate climate.

climatérico, [cle-mah-tay'-re-co, cah], *a.* Climatic, climatical. **Estar climatérico,** *(Coll.)* to be ill-humored.

climático [cle-mah'-te-co], *a.* Climatic.

climatización [cle-mah-te-thah-the-one'], *f.* Air-conditioning.

climatizado [cle-mah-te-thah'-do], *a.* Air-conditioned.

climatizador [cle-mah-te-thah-dor'], *m.* Air-conditioner.

climatología [cle-mah-to-lo-hee'-ah], *f.* Climatology, that part of meteorology which deals with climate.

climatológico, ca [cle-mah-to-lo'-he-co, cah], *a.* Climatological, relating to climate.

clímax [clee'-max], *m.* Climax, a rhetorical figure.

clin [cleen], *f. (Coll.) V.* CRIN. The part of a horse's neck from which the mane grows. **Tenerse a las clines,** *(Met.)* to make every effort not to decline in rank or fortune.

clínica [clee'-ne-cah], *f.* Clinic.

clínico, ca [clee'-ne-co, cah], *a.* Clinical. **Termómetro clínico,** clinical thermometer.

clínico, *m.* 1. *(Med.)* Clinician, physician. 2. The medical student who attends clinical lectures in hospitals.

clinométrico, ca [cle-no-may'-tre-co, cah], *a.* Clinometric, pertaining to the clinometer.

clinómetro [cle-no'-may-tro], *m.* Clinometer, generic name of the instruments used for measuring the inclination of any line or plane to the horizontal.

clip [clip], *m.pl.* **Clips;** paper clip; clip (para pelo); pant clip (de pantalón); clip (joya); *(LAm.)* Earing.

cliper [cle'-payr], *m. (Naut.)* Clipper (barco, avión).

clisado [cle-sah'-do], *m.* Stereotyping the act and effect.

clisar [cle-sar'], *va.* To stereotype, to make a cliché or stereotype plate.

clisé [cle-say'], *m.* 1. The matrix for a stereotype plate. 2. A stereotype plate.

cliso [clee'-so], *m.* 1. *(Med.)* Medicament obtained by the vapors of nitre burned with other substances. 2. *(Chem.)* Product of the distillation of antimony, nitre, and sulphur previously mixed.

clisos [cle-sos], *m. pl.* Peepers, eyes.

clistel, clister [clis-tel', clis-tayr'], *m.* Clyster, an injection into the rectum. *V.* AYUDA.

clítoris [clee'-to-ris], *m.* Clitoris, a small erectile organ at the summit of the vulva.

clivoso, sa [cle-vo'-so, sah], *a. (Poet.)* Declivous, gradually descending.

clo clo, *m.* Clucking of a hen when she is hatching or calling her chickens.

cloaca [clo-ah'-cah], *f.* Sewer, drain (alcantarilla).

cloacal [clo-ah-cahl'], *a.* Lavatorial (chiste, etc.).

clocar [clo-car'], *va.* To cluck. *V.* CLOQUEAR.

cloche [clo'-chay], *m. (CAm. Carib.) (Aut.)* Clutch.

clon [clone], *m.* Clone.

clonación, clonaje [clo-nah-the-on'], *f. m.* Cloning.

clonar [clo-nar'], *va.* To clone.

cloque [clo'-kay], *m.* 1. *(Naut.)* Grapnel, a grappling-iron. *V.* COCLE. 2. Harpoon.

cloquear [clo-kay-ar'], *vn.* 1. To cluck, to chuck. to make a noise like a hen. -*va.* 2. To angle.

cloqueo [clo-kay'-o], *m.* Cluck, chuck, the voice of a hen.

cloquera [clo-kay'-rah], *f.* The state of hatching in fowls.

cloquero [clo-kay'-ro], *m.* A person who manages the harpoon in the catching of tunas.

cloral [clo-rahl'], *m.* Chloral.

cloramfenicol [clo-ram-fay-ne-col'], *m. (Med.)* Chloramphenicol.

cloremia [clo-ray'-me-ah], *f. (Med.)* Chloremia.

clorhidrato [clor-e-drah'-to], *m.* Hydrochlorate, clorhydrate.

clorhídrico [clor-ee'-dre-co], *m.* Clorhydric, hydrochloric.

clórico [clo'-re-co], *a.* Chloric, pertaining to or obtained from chlorine.

clorinar [clo-re-nar'], *va.* To chlorinate.

clorinda [clo-ren-dah], *f. (Cono Sur)* Bleach.

cloris [clo'-ris], *f. (Orn.)* Greenfinch.

cloro [clo'-ro], *m.* Chlorine, a yellowish green pungent gas; an element allied to iodine and bromine.

clorofila [clo-ro-fee'-lah], *f.* Chlorophyll, green coloring matter in plants.

cloroformar [clo-ro-for-mar'], *va.* To chloroform.

cloroformización [clo-ro-for-me-thah-the-on'], *f.* Chloroformization, anaesthesia by chloroform.

cloroformizar [clo-ro-for-me-thar'], *va.* To anaesthetize by chloroform; to chloroform.

cloroformo [clo-ro-for'-mo], *m.* Chloroform.

cloromicetina [clo-ro-me-thay-tee'-nah], *f. (Med.)* Chloromycetin.

clorosis [clo-ro'-sis], *f. (Med.)* Chlorosis, greensickness.

clorótico, ca [clo-ro'-te-co, cah], *a.* Chlorotic, affected by chlorosis.

cloruro [clo-roo'-ro], *m.* Chloride, a compound of chlorine.

closet [clo'-set], *m. (LAm.)* Built-in cupboard, wardrobe (armario).

clown [clo'-oon], *m. pl.* **Clowns,** clown.

club [cloob], *m.* Club, an association of persons. **Club campestre,** country club. **Club nocturno,** night club.

clueca [cloo-ay'-cah], *a.* Clucking and hatching (gallinas).

clueco, ca [cloo-ay'-co, cah], *a.* 1. *(Coll.)* Decrepit, worn out with age. 2. Broody (gallina). 3. *(Cono Sur)* Sickly, weak. 3. *(Carib.)* Stuck-up (engreído).

cm abr de **centímetro** (centimeter, cm).

CN *f. abr.* de **Carretera Nacional.**

coa [co'-ah], *f.* 1. Hoe.

coacción [co-ac-the-on'], *f.* Coercion, compulsion.

coaccionar [co-ac-the-o-nar'], *va.* To coerce, to compel, to put great pressure on.

coacervar [co-ah-ther-var'], *va.* To heap together.

coactivo, va [co-ac-tee'-vo, vah], *a.* Coactive, coercive; compulsive.

coacusar [co-ah-coo-sar'], *va.* *(For.)* To accuse jointly with another or others.

coadjutor [co-ad-hoo-tor'], *m.* 1. Coadjutor, assistant. 2. Coadjutor, a person elected or appointed to a prebend without enjoying the benefit thereof until the death of the incumbent. **Obispo coadjutor,** assistant bishop.

coadjutora [co-ad-hoo-to'-rah], *f.* Coadjutrix.

coadjutoría [co-ad-hoo-to-ree'-ah], *f.* 1. Coadjuvancy, help, assistance. 2. Right of survivorship of a coadjutor. 3. Office or dignity of a coadjutor.

coadjuvar [co-ad-hoo-var'], *va.* To help, to assist; to help in, to contribute to.

coadministrador [co-ad-me-nis-trah-dor'], *m.* One who governs a diocese by virtue of a bull, or by appointment of a bishop.

coadunación [co-ah-doo-nah-the-on'], *f.* Coadunation, the conjunction of different substances into one mass.

coadunamiento [co-ah-doo-nah-me-en'-to], *m. V.* COADUNACIÓN.

coadunar [Co-ah-doo-nar'], *va.* To jumble things together.

coadyudador [co-ad-yoo-dah-dor'], *m. V.* COADYUVADOR.

coadyutor [co-ad-yoo-tor'], *m. V.* COADJUTOR.

coadyutorio, ria [co-ad-yoo-to'-re-o, ah], *a.* That which assists.

coadyuvador [co-ad-yoo-vah-dor'], *m.* Fellowhelper, assistant.

coadyuvante [coad-yoo-vahn'-tay], *a. & pa.* Coadjutant, helper, assistant.

coadyuvar [co-ad-yoo-var'], *va.* To help, to assist.

coagulable [co-ah-goo-lah'-blay], *a.* Coagulable.

coagulación [co-ah-goo-la-the-on'], *f.* Coagulation; clotting.

coagulador, ra [co-ah-goo-lah-dor', rah], *a.* Causing coagulation; coagulatory, coagulative.

coagulante [co-ah-goo-lahn'-tay], *pa.* Coagulant, that which coagulates.

coagular [co-ah-goo-lar'], *va.* To coagulate, to curd. *-vr.* To coagulate, to condense, to become concrete, to clod, to curdle.

coagulativo, va [co-ah-goo-lah-tee'-vo, vah], *a.* Coagulative.

coágulo [co-ah'-goo-lo], *m.* 1. Coagulum, coagulated blood. 2. Coagulation, the body formed by coagulation. 3. Coagulator, that which causes coagulation.

coalabar [co-ah-lah-bar'], *va.* To join in praising.

coalescencia [co-ah-les-then'-the-ah], *f.* Coalescence, union of parts.

coalición [co-ah-le-the-on'], *f.* Coalition, confederacy.

coalla [co-ahl'-lya], *f. (Orn.)* Woodcock. *V.* CHOCHA and CODORNIZ.

coamante [co-ah-mahn'-tay], *a.* A partner or companion in loving.

coarmador [co-ar-mah-dor'], *m.* Part owner of a vessel.

coarrendador [co-ar-ren-dah-dor'], *m.* A joint partner in renting something.

coartación [co-ar-tah-the-on'], *f. (Law.)* Obligating to be ordained within a certain time to enjoy a benefice.

coartada [co-ar-tah'-dah], *f.* Alibi. **Probar la coartada**, to prove an alibi.

coartar [co-ar-tar'], *va.* To limit, to restrain, to restrict.

coatí [co-ah-tee'], *m. (Zool.)* Coati raccoon.

coautor, ra [co-ah-oo-tor', rah], *m. &. f.* Coauthor, joint author.

coaxial [co-ac-se-al'], *a. (Mech.)* Coaxial.

coba [co'-bah], *f. (Coll.)* Ingenious fib. 2. Flattery. **Dar coba**, to flatter, to softsoap.

cobaltífero, ra [co-bal-tee'-fay-ro, arh], *a.* Cobalt-bearing, cobaltiferous.

cobalto [co bahl'-to], *m.* Cobalt, a grayish semi-metal.

cobanillo [co-bah-neel'-lyo], *m.* A small basket used by vintners during the vintage.

cobarde [co-bar'-day], *a.* Coward, cowardly, timid, fearful, fainthearted.

cobardear [co-bar-day-ar], *vn.* To be a coward, to be timid or fearful.

cobardemente [co-bar-day-men'-tay], *adv.* Cowardly.

cobardía [co-bar-dee'-ah], *f.* Cowardice, dastardy, dastardness, abjectness.

cobardón [co-bar-done'], *m.* Shameful coward, great coward.

cobayismo [co-bah-ees'-mo], *m.* Use of animals in medical experiments.

cobayo [co-bah'-yo], *m.* The guinea pig, a familiar rodent.

cobea [co-bay'-ah], *f.* Coboea, a climbing plant, having purple bell-shaped flowers; it is a garden plant native of Mexico.

cobertera [co-ber-tey'-rah], *f.* 1. Cover, Pot-lid. 2. *(Met.)* Bawd, procuress. 3. *(Prov. Tol.)* White waterlily. *V.* NENÚFAR. **Coberteras**, the two middle feathers of a hawk´s tail.

cobertizo [co-ber-tee'-tho], *m.* 1. A small roof jutting out from the wall, to shelter people from the rain. 2. A covered passage. **Cobertizo para automóvil**, carport.

cobertor [co-ber-tor'], *m.* Coverlet, quilt, cloth, counterpane.

cobertura [oo ber too'-rah], *f.* 1. Cover, covering, coverlet. 2. **Cobertura de seguro**, insurance cover.

cobija [co-bee'-hah], *f.* 1. A gutter tile. 2. A small cloak for women. 3. Fire screen. 4. *(Arquit.)* Coping tile. 5. Bedclothes. **Pegársele a uno las cobijas**, to oversleep.

cobijador, ra [co-be-hah-dor', rah], *a.* Covering, protective.

cobijadura [co-be-hah-doo'-rah], *f.* The act of covering.

cobijamiento, cobijo [co-be-hah-me-en'-to, co-bee'-ho], *m.* 1. The act of covering. 2. Lodging.

cobijar [co-be-har'], *va.* 1. To cover, to overspread, to shelter. **Quien a buen árbol se arrima, buena sombra le cobija**,

(Prov.) he who gets under a good tree, has a good shelter. 2. To protect, to lodge. *-vr.* To take shelter.

cobijo [co-be-ho], *m.* 1. *(Lit.)* Shelter, lodging. 2. *(fig.)* Cover.

cobil [co-beel'], *m.* Corner, angle.

cobista [co-bees'-tah], *a.* Soapy, smarmy. *-m.* Soapy individual.

cobo [co'-bo], *m. (Carib.)* 1. *(Zool.)* Sea snail. 2. Unsociable person, shy person. **Ser un cobo**, to be shy.

cobol [co'-bol], . *(Inform.)* Cobol (Common Business-Oriented Language)

cobra [co'-brah], *f.* 1. *(Zool.)* Cobra. 2. Rope for yoking oxen. 3. Retrieving (in hunting).

cobrable [co-brah'-blay], *a.* Retrievable. 2. Chargeable (dinero).

cobradero, ra [co-brah-da'-ro, rah], *a.* That which may be recovered or collected.

cobrado, da [co-brah'-do, dah], *a. & pp.* of COBRAR. 1. Recovered, received. 2. Complete, undaunted.

cobrador [co-brah-dor'], *m.* 1. Receiver or collector of rents and other money. 2. Conductor, collector.

cobradora [co-brah-do'-rah], *f.* Conductress.

cobramiento [co-brah-me-en'-to], *m.* 1. Recovery, restoration. 2. Utility, profit, emolument.

cobranza [co-brahn'-thah], *f.* 1. Recovery or collection of money. 2. Act of fetching game which is killed or wounded.

cobrar [co-brar'], *va.* 1. To recover, to collect, or receive what is due. 2. To recover what is lost. 3. To fetch game that is wounded or killed. 4. To gain affection or esteem. **Cobrar ánimo** or **corazón**, to take courage. **Cobrar fuerzas**, to gather strength. **El accidente se cobró la vida de 50 personas**, the accident took the lives of 50 people. 5. To charge (precio). **Cobran 200 dólares por componerlo**, they charge 200 dollars to repair it. **Me han cobrado demasiado**, they´ve charged me too much. To collect, to receive. **Fue a la oficina a cobrar el sueldo**, he went to the office to get his wages. **Cuenta por cobrar**, unpaid bill. *-vn* 1. *(Fin.)* To draw one´s pay, to get one´s wages; to collect one´s salary. **Cobra los viernes**, he gets paid on Fridays. **Vino el lechero a cobrar**, the milkman came for his money. 2. **Cobrar al número llamado**, to reverse the charges. *-vr.* 1. To recover, to return to oneself. 2. To gain celebrity or fame. **Contra reembolso**, C. O. D., collect on delivery. 3. **Cobrar de una pérdida**, to make up for a loss.

cobratorio, la [co-bra-to'-re-o, ah], *a.* Pertaining to the collection of money; collectible.

cobre [co'-bray], *m.* 1. Copper, a red-colored metal. 2. Kitchen furniture. 3. *(Obs.)* String of onions or garlic. 4. **Batir el cobre**, *(Met.)* to pursue with spirit and vigor. 5. *(LAm.)* Cent, small copper coin. 6. *(LAm.)* **Enseñar el cobre**, to show one´s true colors.

cobreado [co-bray-ah'-do], *a.* Copperplated.

cobrero [co-bray'-ro], *m.* Coppersmith.

cobrizo, za [co-bree'-tho, thah], *a.* Coppery, cupreous, copperish.

cobro [co'-hro], *m.* 1. Collection, payment (deudas). **Cargo por cobro**, collection charge. **Deuda de cobro difícil**, debt that is hard to collect. **Cobro a la entrega**, collect on delivery. 2. Safe place. **Poner algo en cobro**, to put something in a safe place. **Ponerse en cobro**, to take refuge. *V.* COBRANZA.

coca [co'-cah], *f.* 1. Coca (arbusto). The dried leaves of a South American shrub (Erythroxylon coca) of the flax family, chewed by the natives as a stimulant, yields cocaine, a local anaesthetic. 2. Indian berry. 3. A bugbear; figure of a serpent borne at the festival of Corpus Christi. 4. *(Naut.)* A sort of small vessel 5. Two puffs of hair of women put back from forehead and fastened behind the ears. 6. A rap with the knuckles on the head. 7. Nut, head. 8. Cake, loaf.

cocacolo, la [cah-cah-co'-lo], *m. & f. (And.)* Frivolous teenager, idle young person.

cocacho [co-cah'-cho], *m. (And. Cono Sur)* Tap on the head.

cocada [co-cah'-dah], *f.* 1. Type of coconut jam (dulce). 2. Lump of coca for chewing. 3. Nougat (turrón).

cocador, ra [co-cah-dor', rah], *a.* Wheedling, coaxing, flattering.

cocaína [co-cah-ee'-nah], *f.* Cocaine, the alkaloid and active principle of the coca-plant, remarkable for its anaesthetic power locally.

cocainomanía [co-cah-e-no-mah-ne'-ah], *f.* Addiction to cocaine.

cocainómano, na [co-cah-e-no'-mah-no], *m. & f.* Cocaine addict.

cocal [co-cahl'], *m.* 1. *(Ven.)* V. COCOTAL. 2. *(Peru)* The cocoa-tree and the spot where it abounds.

cocar [co-car'], *va.* 1. To make grimaces or wry faces. 2. *(Met. Coll.)* To coax, to gain by wheedling and flattering.

cocarar [co-ca-rar'], *va.* To gather the leaves of the plant called coca.

cocción [coc-the-on'], *f.* 1. Coction. 2. *(Tec.)* Baking, firing.

coce [co'-thay], *f. (fibs.)* A kick. V. Coz.

coceador, ra [co-thay-ah-dor', rah], *m. & f.* Kicker.

coceadura [co-thar-ah-doo'-rah], *f.* **Coceamiento,** *m.* Kicking.

cocear [co-thay-ar'], *va.* 1. To kick, to fling out. V. ACOCEAR. 2. *(Met.)* To repugn, to resist. 3. *(Obs.)* To trample, to tread under foot.

cocedero, ra [co-thay-day'-ro, rah], *a.* Easily boiled.

cocedero, *m.* Place where bread is kneaded or baked, or where anything is boiled.

cocedor [co-thay-dor'], *m.* A person whose business it is to boil must and new wine.

cócedra [co'-thay-drah], *f.* Featherbed. V. CÓLCEDRA.

cocedura [co-thay-doo'-rah], *f.* The act of boiling.

cocer [co-therr'], *va.* 1. To boil, to dress victuals. 2. To bake bricks, tiles, or earthenware. 3. To digest.-*vn.* 1. To boil: to ferment. 2. To seethe, ferment, without fire, as wine. -*vr.* To suffer intense and continued pain.

cocido, da [co-thee'-do, dah], *a. & pp.* Of COCER. 1. Boiled, baked. **Carne bien cocida,** meat well done. 2. *(Met.)* Skilled, experienced. **Estar cocido en alguna cosa,** to understand business well. 3. **Estar cocido,** to be plastered, to be drunk.

cocido [co-thee'-do], *m.* V. OLLA.

cociente [co-the-en'-tay], *m. (Math.)* Quotient. **Cociente intelectual,** intelligence quotient, I.Q.

cocimiento [co-the-me-en-to], *m.* 1. Coction, decoction. 2. *(Med.)* Decoction. 3. With dyers, a bath or mordant preparatory to dyeing. 4. A quick, lively sensation. V. ESCOZOR.

cocina [co-thee'-nah], *f.* 1. Kitchen. 2. Cookery, the art of cooking. 3. Range, stove. **Cocina económica,** stove, cooking range. **Libro de cocina,** cookbook. **Utensilios de cocina,** cooking utensils. **Cocina eléctrica,** electric cooker.

cocinar [co-the-nar'], *va.* 1. To cook or dress victuals. 2. *(Met.)* To meddle in other people's affairs. -*vn.* 1. To cook, to do the cooking. 2. *(fig.)* To meddle.

cocinera [co-the-nay'-rah], *f.* Cook, cookmaid, kitchenmaid.

cocinería [co-the-nay-ree'-ah], *f. (Chile & Peru)* Cheap restaurant.

cocinero [co-the-nay'-ro], *m.* Cook. **Haber sido cocinero antes que fraile,** a guarantee of success in one who directs a thing from having practised it himself.

cocinilla [co-the-neel'-lyah], *f.* 1. Chafing dish, cooker. 2. Small kitchen.

cocinita [co-the-nee'-tah], *f.* Small kitchen.

cocker [co'-kayr], *m.* Cocker spaniel, cocker (perro).

cocle [co'-clay], *m. (Naut.)* Grapnel, a grappling-iron.

cóclea [co'-clay-ah], *f.* 1. An ancient machine for raising water. 2. An endless screw. 3. The inner cavity of the ear.

coclear [co-clay-ar'], *va.* To harpoon. -*vn.* To cluck or hatch. V. CLOQUEAR.

coclearia [co-clay-ah'-re-ah], *f. (Bot.)* Common scurvygrass.

coco 1 [co'-co], *m.* 1. *(Bot.)* Coconut-tree (árbol); Indian palm-tree. 2. Coconut, coconut (fruto). 3. Chocolate-cup made of the coconut. 4. *(LAm.)* Cup made from a coconut palm (vasija). 5. Noodle, brain. **Me estoy comiendo el coco,** I am try-

ing to think. 6. Derby, bowler (sombrero). 7. *(And. Cono Sur)* percale. 8. **Cortarse el pelo a coco,** *(And.)* To have one's head shaved. 9. **Cocos,** Diamonds (Naipes). -*a.* 1. *(Carib.)* Hard, strong. 2. Obstinate.

coco 2 *m.* 1. Worm or grub bred in seeds and fruit. 2. Coccus; scale insect. 3. Coccus, a bacterium of spherical form.

coco 3 *m.* 1. Boogie-man for frightening children, phantasm. **Ser un coco,** or **parecer un coco,** to be an ugly-looking person.

coco 4 *m.* (from COCA, 1st *art.*). Cocos, India berries from which rosaries are made.

coco 5 *m.* Gesture, grimace, a flattering gesture; **hacer cocos,** *(Met.)* To flatter, wheedle, gain one's affections. *(Coll.)* To make signs of affections, to flirt.

cocobolo [Co-co-bo'-lo], *m. (Bot.)* A species of coconut-tree, much used by cabinet-makers.

cococha [co-co'-chah], *f.* Barbel (de bacalao).

cocodrilo [co-co-dree'-lo], *m.* Crocodile.

cocoí [co-co-ee'], *m.* A crested heron, of the size of a stork.

cocoliche [co-co-le-chay], *m. (Cono Sur)* pidgin Spanish; Italian.

cocoliste [co-co-lees'-tay], *m.* In New Spain or Mexico, an epidemic fever.

cócona [co'-co-nah], *f. (Carib.)* Tip.

coconote [co-co-no'-tay], *m. (Mex.)* Child, chubby child; squat person.

cócora [co'-co-rah], *com.* An impertinent and annoying person.

cocoroco [co-co-ro'-co], *a. (Cono Sur)* Vain, stuck-up; insolent, cheeky.

cocoso, sa [co-co'-so, sah], *a.* Worm-eaten, gnawed by grubs.

cocota [co-co'-tah], *f.* V. COGOTERA.

cocotal [co-co-tahl'], *m.* A clump of coconut-trees.

cocote [co-co'-tay], *m. (Prov.)* Occiput. V. COGOTE.

cocotero [co-co-tay'-ro], *m. (Bot.)* Cocoa-tree. V. COCO1.

cóctel [cok-tell'], *m.* 1. Cocktail. 2. Cocktail party. **Ofrecer un cóctel en honor de uno,** to hold a cocktail party in somebody's honor.

coctelera [cok-tay-lay'-rah], *f.* Cocktail shaker.

cocuyo [co-coo'-yo], or **cocuyo,** *m.* The fire-fly or fire-beetle of the West Indies, about an inch and a half long.

cocha [co'-chah], *f.* In mines, a small reservoir of water.

cochambre [co-chahm'-bray], *m.* A greasy, dirty, stinking thing.

cochambrería [co-cham-bray-ree'-ah], *f. (Coll.)* Heap of filthy things.

cochambroso, sa [co-cham-bro'-so,sah], *a. (Coll.)* Nasty, filthy, stinking.

cocharro [co-char'-ro], *m.* A wooden dish, cup, or platter.

cocharse [co-char'-say], *vr.* To hasten, to accelerate.

cochastro [co-chahs'-tro], *m.* A little sucking wild boar.

coche 1 [co'-chay], *m.* 1. Coach carriage. 2. Car, motor-car, automobile. **Coche de alquiler,** car for hire. **Coche de línea,** long-distance bus. **Ir en coche,** to go by car. **Coche patrulla,** patrol car. **Coche de bomberos,** fire engine. 3. Coach, carriage. 4. *(Mex.)* Taxi, cab.

coche 2 [co'-chay], *m. (CAm. Mex.)* Pig, hog; pork. **Coche de monte,** wild pig.

cochear [co-chay-ar'], *vn.* To drive a coach.

coche-bomba [co'-chay bom'-bah], *m.* Car bomb.

coche-cama [co'-chay-cah-mah], *m.* Sleeping car.

cochecillo [co-chay-thee'-lyo], *m.* Small carriage, child's carriage, baby buggy.

cochecito [co-chay-thel'-lyo], *m.* Baby carriage. **Cochecito de niño,** go-cart.

coche-correo [co-chay cor-ray'-o], *m.* Mail van.

coche-cuba [co-chay-coo-bah], *m.* Tank lorry, water wagon.

cochera [co-chay'-rah], *f.* 1. Carriage. 2. Garage (para coches). Coach house (para carruajes). Depot. **Cochera de autobuses,** bus depot.

cocherada [cho-ray-dah'-dah], *f. (Mex.)* Coarse expression.

coche-restaurante [co-chay res-tah-oo-rahn'-tay], *m.* Dining car, restaurant car.

cocheril [co-chay-reel'], *a. (Coll.)* Relating to coachmen.

cocherillo [co-chay-reel'-lyo], *m. dim.* A little coachman.

cochero [co-chay'-ro], *m.* 1. Coachman. 2. Coachmaker. 3. Wagoner, a northern constellation.

cochero, ra [co-chay'-ro, rah], *a. (Prov.)* Easily boiled.

cocherón [co-chay-rone'], *m. (aug.)* 1. Large coach-house. 2. Engine-house; roundhouse.

cochevira [co-chay-vee'-rah], *f.* Lard.

cochevís [co-chay-vees'], *m.* The crested shorelark.

coche-vivienda [co-chay ve-ve-ayn'-dah], *m.* Caravan, trailer.

cochifrito [co-che-free'-to], *m.* Fricassee of lamb, mutton, etc.

cochigato [co-che-gah'-to], *m.* A bird of Mexico, having the head and neck black, with a red collar and green belly; the bill seven inches long.

cochina [co-chee'-nah], *f.* Sow.

cochinada [co-che-nah´-dah], *f.* 1. Herd of swine. 2. Hoggishness; any mean, dirty action. **Eso fue una cochinada**, that was a beastly thing to do. **Hacer una cochinada a uno**, to play a dirty trick on somebody.

cochinamente [co-che-nah-men'-tay], *adv.* 1. Foully, hoggishly, filthily, nastily. 2. Meanly, basely.

cochinata [co-che-nah'-tah], *f. (Naut.)* Rider, a piece of timber to strengthen a vessel.

cochinería [co-che-nay-ree'-ah], *f.* 1. Dirtiness, foulness, filthiness, nastiness. 2. Meanness, niggardliness.

cochinero, ra [co-che-nay'-ro, rah], *a.* Use of fruits poor in quality, given to hogs.

cochinilla [co-che-neel'-lyah], *f.* 1. Woodlouse, a small insect. 2. Cochineal, an insect of commercial value. 3. *(Carib. Mex.)* Trivial, unimportant.

cochinilla, illa [co-che-neel'-lyo, lyah], *m. & f. dim.* A little pig. **Cochinillo**, *m.* An animal in Brazil resembling a pig. **Cochinillo de Indias**, guinea pig.

cochino, na [co-chee'-no, nah], *a.* Dirty, nasty, filthy. **Esta vida cochina**, this wretched life.

cochino [co-chee'-no], *m.* Pig. *V.* PUERCO.

cochio, ia, cochizo, za [co-chee'-o, ah, co-chee'-tho, thah], *a.* Easily boiled.

cochiquera [co-che-kay´-rah], *f.* Hog-sty, pigsty.

cochite hervite [co-chee'-tay er-vee´-tay]. *(Coll.)* Helter-skelter: applied to something done hastily.

cochitril [co-che-treel'], *m. (Coll.)* 1. A pigsty. 2. A filthy room, quarters.

cocho, cha [co'-cho, chah], *a.* 1. *V.* COCIDO. 2. Old, past. *-m. f.* Old man; old woman.

cochón, ona [co-chone'], *m. & f.* Poof (hombre); dyke.

cochoso [co-cho'-so], *a. (And.)* Filthy.

cochura [co-choo'-rah], *f.* 1. Act of boiling. 2. Dough for a batch of bread.

cod. *m. abr.* de **código** (code).

coda [co'-dah], *f. (Prov.)* 1. Tail. *V.* COLA. 2. Burden of a song or other piece of music.

codadura [co-dah-doo'-rah], *f.* Part of an old vine laid in the ground, from which young buds shoot forth.

codal [co-dahl], *m.* 1. Piece of ancient armor for the elbow. 2. A short and thick wax-candle, of the size of the elbow. 3. Shoot issuing from a vine. 4. Frame of a handsaw. **Codales**, a carpenter's square, 5. Prop, shore, stay strut, staybolt.

codal [co-dahl'], *a.* Cubital, containing only the length of a cubit. **Palo codal**, a stick of the length of a cubit, hung round the neck as a penance.

codaste [co-dahs'-tay], *m. (Naut.)* Sternpost.

codazo [co-dah'-tho], *m.* 1. Blow with the elbow: a hunch. 2. *(Mex.)* Tip-off (consejo).

codear [co-day-ar´], *vn.* 1. To elbow. **Codearse con**, to rub elbows with. 2. *(And. Cono Sur)* To live off somebody (vivir de gorra). *-va.* 1. To elbow, to nudge, to jostle. 2. *(And. Cono Sur)* **Codear a uno**, to keep on at somebody,

pester somebody. *-vr.* **Codearse con**, to hobnob with, to rub shoulders with.

codecillar, codicilar [co-day-theel-lyar', co-de-the-lar'], *vn.* To make a codicil.

codeína [co-day-ee'-nah], *f.* Codeine, an alkaloid obtained from opium.

codena [co-day'-nah], *f.* Body or thickness required in cloth.

codeo [co-day'-o], *m. (And.)* Sponging; pesterings (insistencia).

codera [co-day'-rah], *f.* 1. Itch or scabbiness on the elbow. 2. A piece reinforcing the elbows of jackets. **Codera en un cable**, *(Naut.)* A spring on a cable.

codesera [co-day-say'-rah], *f.* A spot grown over with hairy cytisus.

codeso [co-day'-so], *m. (Bot.)* Hairy cytisus. **Codeso de los Alpes**, laburnum, ebony of the Alps.

códice [co'-de-thay], *m.* Old manuscript, dealing with remarkable points of antiquity; codex.

codicia [co-dee'-the-ah], *f.* 1. Covetousness, cupidity. 2. *(Obs.)* Sensual appetite, lust. 3. *(Met.)* Greediness, an ardent desire of good things. **La codicia rompe el saco**, covet all, lose all.

codiciable [co-de-the-ah'-blay], *a.* Covetable.

codiciado [co-de-the-ah'-do], *a.* Widely desired; much in demand; sought-after, coveted.

codiciador [co-de-the-ah-dor,], *m.* Coveter.

codiciante [co-de-the-ahn'-tay], *pa.* Coveting.

codiciar [co-de-the-ar'], *va.* To covet.

codicilar [co-de-the-lar'], *a.* Pertaining to a codicil.

codicilo [co-de-thee'-lo], *m.* Codicil, a supplement to a last will.

codiciosamente [co-de-the-o-sah-men'-tay], *adv.* Covetously, greedily.

codiciosito, ita [co-de-the-o-see'-to, tah], *a. dim.* Somewhat covetous.

codicioso, sa [co-de-the-o'-so, sah], *a.* 1. Greedy, covetous, avericious 2. *(Met. Coll.)* Diligent, laborious, assiduous.

codificación [co-de-fe-cah-the-one'], *f.* 1. Codification. 2. *(Inform.)* Encryption.

codificar [co-de-fe-car'], *va.* To codify laws; reduce to a code.

código [co'-de-go], *m.* Code (of laws). **Código de comercio**, mercantile law. **Código de señales**, signal code. **Código de circulación**, highway code. **Código de leyes**, law code. **Código territorial**, area code. **Mensaje en código**, message in code. **Código ASCII**, *(Inform.)* American Standard Code for Information Interchange. **Código de control de la impresora**, *(Inform.)* printer control code. **Código EBCDIC**, *(Inform.)* Extended Binary Coded Decimal Interchange Code. **Código reutilizable**, *(Inform.)* reusable code. **Código de corrección de errores**, error-correcting code.

codillera [co-deel-lyay'-rah], *f. (Vet.)* Tumor on the knee of horses.

codillo [co-deel´-lyo], *m.* 1. Knee of horses and other quadrupeds. 2. Angle. 3. Codille. 4. That part of a branch of a tree which joins the trunk. 5. **Codillo de una curva**, *(Naut.)* breech of a knee 6. Stirrup of a saddle. **Jugársela a uno de codillo**, *(Met.)* to trick or outwit a person. **Codillos**, file used by silversmiths. **Tirar a uno al codillo**, to endeavor to destroy one; doing him all possible damage.

codo [co'-do], *m.* 1. Elbow. 2. Cubit, a measure of length equal to the distance from the elbow to the end of the middle finger. **Alzar de codo** or **el codo**, to drink too much wine. **Comerse los codos de hambre**, to be starved with hunger. **Dar de codo**, to elbow, to push with the elbow, to treat with contempt. **Hablar por los codos**, to chatter, to prattle. **Levantar de codo**, *(Cono Sur Mex.)* to booze; to drink. **Morderse el codo**, *(Cono Sur Mex.)* to restrain oneself, to bite one´s lip. **Trabajar codo con codo**, to work side by side.

codón [co-done´], *m.* A leather cover of a horse's tail.

codoña [co-do'-nyah], *f.* Quince.

codoñero [co-do-nyay'-ro], *m.* Quince-tree.

codorniz [co-dor-neeth'], *f. (Orn.)* Quail.

coecual [co-ay-coo-ahl'], *a. (Div.)* Coequal.

coeducación [co-ay-doo-cah-the-on'], *f.* Coeducation.

coeducacional [co-ay-doo-cah-the-o-nahl'], *a.* Coeducational.

coeficiente [co-ay-fe-the-en'-tay], *a.* Coefficient. **Coeficiente de inteligencia,** intelligence quotient.

coepíscopo [co-ay-pees'-co-po], *m.* Contemporary bishop.

coercer [co-er-therr'], *va.* To coerce, to check, to restrain.

coercibilidad [co-er-the-be-le-dahd'], *f.* Coercibility: liability to restraint.

coercible [co-er-thee'-blay], *a.* Coercible; subject to check.

coerción [co-er-the-on'], *f.* Coercion, restraint, check.

coercitivo, va [co-er-the-tee'-vo, vah], *a.* Coercive, restraining.

coesencial [co-ay-sen-the-ahl'], *a.* Coessential, consubstantial.

coetáneo, nea [co-ay-tah´-nay-o, ah], *a.* Coetaneous, contemporary.

coevo, va [co-ay'-vo, vah], *a.* Coeval.

coexistencia [co-ek-sis-ten'-the-ah], *f.* Coexistence.

coexistente [co-ek-sis-ten´-tay], *pa.* Coexistent.

coexistir [co-ek-sis-teer'], *vn.* To coexist.

coextenderse [co-ex-ten-der'-say], *vr.* To coextend.

cofa [co'-fa], *f. (Naut.)* Top. **Cofa mayor,** main top.

cofia [co´-fe-ah], *f.* 1. A net of silk or thread worn on the head; a kind of cowl, head-dress, headgear, coif. 2. An iron case in which the die is fastened for coining.

cofiezuela [co-fe-ay-thoo'-lah], *f. dim.* A small net.

cofín [co-feen´], *m.* A small basket for fruit.

cofina [co-fee'-nah], *f.* Cofino, *m.* V. COFÍN.

cofrade, da [co-fraih-day, dah], *m. & f.* Confrier, a member of any confraternity or brotherhood.

cofradía [co-frah-dee'-ah], *f.* 1. Confraternity, brotherhood, or sisterhood. 2. Association of persons for any purpose.

cofre [co'-fray], *m.* 1. Trunk for clothes. 2. Fish found in the West Indies. 3. *(Mil.)* Coffer, a hollow lodgement across a dry moat. 4. *(Print.)* Coffin of a printing press.

cofrecico, illo, ito [co-fray-thee´-co], *m. dim.* A small trunk.

cofrero [co-fray'-ro], *m.* Trunk-maker or seller of trunks.

cofundador, ra [co-foon-dah-dor; rah], *m. & f.* Cofounder, a joint founder.

cogedera [co-hay-day'-rah], *f.* A sort of beehive used to gather a swarm which has quit the stock.

cogedero, ra [co-hay-day'-ro, rah], *m. & f.* Collector, gatherer. *-a.* Ripe, ready to be picked (fruto).

cogedizo, za [co-hay-dee'-thoh, thah], *a.* That which can be easily collected or gathered.

cogedor [co-hay-dor'], *m.* 1. Collector, gatherer. 2. Dustbox or dustpan. 3. *(Obs.)* Tax-gatherer. 4. Among velvet-weavers, a box in which the woven velvet is put.

cogedura [co-hay-doo'-rah], *f.* Act of gathering or collecting.

coger [co-herr'], *va.* 1. To take, to catch, to grasp, to seize with the hand, to get, to lay hold of, to come upon. 2. To imbibe, to soak. **La tierra no ha cogido bastante agua,** the earth has not drawn in sufficient water. 3. To gather the produce of the ground. 4. To have room to hold. **Esta cámara coge mil fanegas de trigo,** this granary holds a thousand bushels of wheat. 5. To occupy, to take up. **Cogió la alfombra toda la sala,** the carpet covered the whole room. 6. To find, to procure. **Me cogió descuidado,** he took me unawares. **Procuré cogerle de buen humor,** I endeavored to see him when in a good mood. 7. To surprise, to attack unexpectedly. **La tempestad me cogió por sorpresa,** the storm overtook me unexpectedly. **Coger en mentira,** to catch in a lie. 8. To intercept, to obstruct. **Coger la calle,** to flee, to escape. **Coger a deseo,** to obtain one's wishes. **Coger una mona,** to be intoxicated. 9. To take, to pinch (robar). **En la aduana le cogieron una radio,** they found a radio on him at customs. **Me coge siempre las cerillas,** he always takes my matches. 10. To catch (persona); to arrest; to take prisoner. **Coger un buen marido,** to catch oneself a good husband. **La guerra nos cogió en Francia,** the war caught us in France. **Coger a uno detrás de la puerta,** to catch somebody at a disadvantage. 11. To take, to accept. **Cogió la noticia sin interés,** he received the news without interest. 12. To catch (enfermedad, resfriado). **El niño cogió sarampión,** the child got measles. **Los perros cogen pulgas,** dogs get fleas. 13. To get, to understand, to pick up (radio); to learn. **Con esta radio cogemos Praga;** with his set we can get Prague. 14. To take down. **Le cogieron el discurso taquigráficamente,** they took his speech down in shorthand. To take, to catch, to go by. **Vamos a coger el tren,** let´s take the train. *-vn.* 1. *(Bot.)* To take, to strike. 2. To fit, to go, to have room (caber). **Aquí no coge,** it doesn´t fit in here. 3. **Cogió y se fue,** he just upped and left. 4. *(LAm.)* To fuck, to screw. *-vr.* 1. To catch. **Cogerse los dedos en la puerta,** to catch one´s fingers in the door. 2. **Cogerse algo,** to steal something. 3. *(Carib.)* **Cogerse con uno,** to get on with somebody.

cogestión [co-hays-te-on'], *f.* Co-partnership (en industria, etc.).

cogida [co-hee'-dah], *f.* 1. The gathering or harvesting of fruits. 2. The yield of fruits. 3. The act of the bull's catching the bullfighter.

cogido, da [co-hee'-do, dah], *a.* Joined, united. *-m.* Fold, accidental or designed, made in women´s clothing, curtains, etc.

cogienda [co-he-ayn'-dah], *f.* 1. *(And. Carib.)* V. COGIDA. 2. *(Mil.)* Forced enlistment. 3. *(Mex.)* Fucking, screwing (acto sexual).

cogimiento [co-he-me-en´-to], *m.* Gathering, collecting, or catching.

cogitabundo, da [co-he-tah-boon'-do, dah], *a.* Pensive, thoughtful, musing.

cogitación [co-he-tah-the-on'], *f.* Reflection, meditation, cogitation.

cogitar [co-he-tar'], *va.* To reflect, to meditate, to muse.

cogitativo, va [co-he-tah-tee'-vo, vah], *a.* Cogitative, given to meditation.

cognación [cog-nah-the-on'], *f.* Cognation, kindred.

cognado, da [cog-nah'-do, dah], *a.* Cognate, related by consanguinity.

cognaticio , ia [cog-nah-tee'-the-o, ah], *a.* Order of succession of the collateral relatives by the female line, through lack of male succession.

cognición [cog-ne-the-on'], *f.* V. CONOCIMIENTO.

cognitivo [cog-ne-te'-vo], *a.* Cognitive.

cognomento [cog-no-men'-to], *m.* Cognomination, surname.

cognoscible [cog-nos-thee'-blay], *a.* Cognoscible, that may be known.

cognoscitivo, va [cog-nos-the-tee'-vo, vah], *a.* Cognitive, having the power of knowing.

cogollico, ito [co-gol-yee'-co, ee´-to], *m. dim.* A small heart or flower of garden plants, such as cabbage, etc.

cogollo [co-gol´-lyo], *m.* 1. Heart of garden plants, such as lettuce, cabbage, etc. 2. Shoot of a plant. 3. Top, summit. **Cogollos,** ornaments of the friezes of Corinthian capitals. 4. *(fig.)* Best part, cream. **El cogollo de la sociedad,** the cream of society. 5. *(fig.)* Centre, core, nucleus. 6. *(Carib.)* Straw hat.

cogolmar [co-gol-mar'], *va.* To fill up a vessel. V. COLMAR.

cogombradura [co-gom-brah-doo´-rah], *f. (Obs.)* Digging and earthing about plants.

cogombro [co-gom'-bro], *m.* V. COHOMBRO.

cogorza [co-gor'-thah], *f.* **Pescar una cogorza,** to get very drunk.

cogotazo [co-go-tah'-tho], *m.* Blow on the back of the neck; rabbit punch (boxeo).

cogote [co-go'-tay], *m.* 1. Occiput, hind part of the head. 2. Crest at the back of the helmet. **Coger a uno por el cogote,** to take somebody by the scruff of the neck. **Estar hasta el cogote,** *(Carib.)* to have had it up to here.

cogotera [co-go-tay'-rah], *f.* The hair combed down on the neck.

cogotudo [co-go-too'-do], *a. (And. Cono Sur)* Well-heeled, filthy rich; *(Carib.)* Powerful in politics. *-m. (LAm.)* Self-made man.

cogucho [co-goo'-cho], *m.* The most inferior sort of sugar.

cogujada [co-goo-hah'-dah], *f. (Orn.)* Crested lark.

cogujón [co-goo-hone'], *m.* Corner of a mattress or bolster.

cogujonero, ra [co-goo-ho-nay'-ro, rah], *a.* Pointed, as the corners of mattresses or bolsters.

cogulla [co-gool'-lyah], *f.* Cowl, monk's hood or habit.

cogullada [co-gool-lyah'-dah], *f. V.* PAPADA DE PUERCO.

cohabitación [co-ah-be-tah-the-on'], *f.* Cohabitation, living together as man and wife, whether lawfully or illicitly.

cohabitar [co-ah-be-tar'], *vn.* To cohabit, to accustom, to live together.

cohecha [co-ay'-chah], *f. (Agri.)* Cultivating the land the last time before sowing the crop.

cohechador [co-ay-chah-dor'], *m.* 1. Bribed, suborner. 2. Bribed judge.

cohechamiento [co-ay-chah-me-en'-to], *m. V.* COHECHO.

cohechar [co-ay-char'], *va.* 1. To bribe, to gain by bribes, to suborn, to hire, to daub, to fee. 2. To force, to oblige. 3. *(Agri.)* To plough the ground the last time before it is sown.

cohechazón [co-ay-chah-thone'], *f. (Prov.)* 1. Act of breaking up the ground for cultivation. 2. The last ploughing of the ground before it is sown.

cohecho [co-ay'-cho], *m.* 1. Bribery. 2. *(Agri.)* Season for ploughing the ground.

cohén [co-en'], *m. & f.* 1. Soothsayer. 2. Procurer, pimp.

coheredera [co-ay-ray-day'-rah], *f.* Co-heiress, joint-heiress.

coheredero [co-ay-ray-day'-ro], *m.* Co-heir, fellow heir, joint-heir.

coherencia [co-ay-ren'-the-ah], *f.* 1. Co-herence, the relation of one thing to another; connection. 2. Adhesion of molecules.

coherente [co-ay-rent-tay], *a.* Coherent, consistent, cohesive.

coherentemente [co-ay-ren-tay-men'-tay], *adv.* Cohesively.

cohermano [co-er-mah'-no], *m.* First cousin. *V.* PRIMO.

cohesión [co-ay-se-on'], *f.* Cohesion.

cohesionar [co-ay-se-o-nar'], *va.* To unite.

cohesivo [co-ay-se'-vo], *a.* Cohesive.

cohete [co-ay'-tay], *m.* 1. Sky-rocket; fire-cracker. 2. Fuse. **Cohete de ignición múltiple,** *(Aer.)* multistage rocket. **Cohete de señales,** flare. **Cohete impulsor,** *(Aer.)* Booster rock-et. **Cohete espacial de combustible sólido,** solid-fueled space rocket. 3. *(CAm. Mex.)* Pistol. 4. *(Mex.)* Blasting fuse (mecha). 5. **Al cohete,** *(And. Cono Sur)* without rhyme or reason. *-a. (Mex. CAm.)* Drunk, tight.

cohetería [co-hay-tay-ree'-ah], *f.* Rocketry.

cohetero [co-hay-tay'-ro], *m.* Rocketeer.

cohibición [co-e-be-the-on'], *f.* Prohibition, restraint.

cohibido [co-e-be-do], *a.* Restrained, restricted; full of inhibitions (de temperamento); shy, timid. **Sentirse cohibido,** to feel shy.

cohibir [co-e-beer'], *va.* To cohibit, to prohibit, to restrain. *-vr.* 1. To restrain oneself. 2. To fell inhibited; to get uneasy, to become shy.

cohobar [co-o-bar'], *va.* To redistil, cohobate. (Early chemistry.)

cohombral [co-om-brahl'], *m.* Cucumberbed.

cohombrillo [co-om-breel'-lyo], *m. dim.* Gherkin **Cohombrillo amargo,** the bitter cucumber, squirting cucumber.

cohombro [co-om'-bro], *m.* 1. Cucumber, or snake cucumber. **Cohombro marino,** or **de mar,** sea-cucumber, a holothurian. 2. A fritter made of the same mass as used for buns, and after being fried cut into pieces like a cucumber.

cohonder [co-on-derr'], *va.* To corrupt, to vilify.

cohondimiento [co-on-de-me-en'-to], *m.* Corruption, reproach, infamy.

cohonestar [co-o-nes-tar'], *va.* 1. To give an honest or decent appearance to an action. 2. To blend, to harmonize.

cohorte [co-or'-tay], *f.* Cohort, a body of Roman infantry, numbering usually five hundred.

COI *m. abr.* de **Comité Olímpico Internacional** (International Olympic Committee, IOC).

coi, or **Coy,** *pl.* **Coyes** [co'-e], *m. (Naut.)* Hammock.

coima [co'-e-mah], *f.* 1. Perquisite received by the keeper of a gaming-table. 2. *(Low.)* A prostitute.

coime, coimero [co'-e-may, co-e-may'-ro], *m.* 1. Keeper of a gaming table. 2. Pimp, ponce (chulo). 3. *(And.)* Waiter.

coimero [co-e-may'-ro], *a. (And. Cono Sur)* Easily bribed, bribable, bent.

coincidencia [co-in-the-den'-the-ah], *f.* 1. Coincidence; concurrence. 2. Agreement. **En coincidencia con,** in agreement with.

coincidente [co-in-the-den'-tay], *pa.* Coincident, concurrent, consistent.

coincidir [co-in-the-deer'], *vn.* 1. To fall upon or meet in the same point, to fall in. **Todos coinciden en que...,** everybody agrees that... 2. To concur, to coincide.

coindicación [co-in-de-cah-the-on'], *f. (Med.)* Coindication.

coindicante [co-in-de-cahn'-tay], *m. & a. (Med.)* Coindicant.

coinquinarse [co-in-ke-nar'-say], *vr.* To be stained. *V.* MANCHARSE.

cointeresado, da [co-in-tay-ray-sah-do, dah], *a.* Jointly interested.

coitivo, va [co-e-tee'-vo, vah], *a.* Relating to the act of generation or coition.

coito [co'-e-to], *m.* Coitus, coition, carnal copulation,

coja [co'-hah], *f.* 1. Back of the knee; popliteal space. 2. A lewd woman.

cojear [co-hay-ar'], *vn.* 1. To limp, to halt, to hobble. 2. To deviate from virtue. **Cojear del mismo pie,** to have the same defect or passion. **Saber de qué pie cojea,** to know a person's weak points.

cojera, cojez [co-hay'-rah, co-heth'], *f.* Lameness, halt, hobble, limp.

cojijoso, sa [co-he-ho'-so, sah], *a.* Peevish, irritable.

cojín [co-heen'], *m.* Cushion; soft pad placed on a saddle. **Cojines de bote,** *(Naut.)* Boat cushions.

cojincillo [co-hin-thee'-lyo], *m. dim.* Small cushion or pillow.

cojinete [co-he-nay' tay], *m.* 1. Small cushion, pad. 2. *(Mech.)* **Coginete de bolas,** roller bearing. 3. *(Ferro. etc.)* Chair. 3. *(And. Carib. Mex.)* Saddlebags.

cojinillos [co-he-nel-lyos], *m. pl. (CAm. Mex.)* Saddlebags.

cojitranco, ca [co-he-trahn'-co, cah], *a.* Applied as a nickname to evil-disposed lame persons.

cojo, ja [co'-ho, hah], *n. & a.* 1. Cripple, halter. 2. Lame, cripple, halt (personas, sillas, mesas). **No ser cojo ni manco,** to have all the necessary requisites to do something: to be very intelligent and skilled in the matter at hand. 4. *(fig.)* Lame, weak, shaky. **El verso queda cojo,** the line is defective. **La frase está coja,** the sentence is incomplete.

cojón [co-hone'], *m.* 1. *(Low.)* Testicle. *V.* TESTÍCULO. **Una película de cojones,** a tremendous film. **Me lo paso por los cojones,** I just laugh at it. 2. *(fig.)* Guts. **Es un tío con cojones,** he's got guts. **Hace falta tener cojones,** you've got to have guts. 3. *adv.* **Hace un frío de cojones,** it's terribly cold. **Me importa un cojón,** I don't give a damn.

cojonudamente [co-ho-noo-dah-mayn'-tay], *adv.* Marvelously, splendidly.

cojonudo [co-ho-noo'-do], *a.* 1. Strong; brave; full of guts. 2. Huge, colossal; very important. 3. Marvelous, splendid; smashing bird. **Un tío cojonudo,** a great guy. 4. Very funny, highly amusing.

cojudo, da [co-hoo'-do, dah], *a.* Entire, not gelt, or castrated.

cojuelo, ela [co-hoo-ay'-lo, lah], *a. dim.* A small cripple.

cok [coke], *m.* Coke, retorted coal.

cokera [co-kay'-rah], *f.* A hod for coke.

col [cole], *f.* Species of cabbage with large leaves and short stalk. **Entre col y col, lechuga,** variety is pleasing. **Coles de Bruselas,** sprouts. **Col roja,** red cabbage.

cola [co´-lah], *f.* 1. Tail (animales, aviones). 2. Train (vestido). **La cola del traje de la novia,** the train of the wedding dress. 3. Tail (chaqué, cometa). 4. In music, the prolonged sound of the voice at the end of a song. **A la cola,** backwards, behind. **Cola de caballo,** *(Bot.)* horsetail. **Cola de rata,** rattail file. **Estar en la cola de clase,** to be at the bottom of the class. **Venir a la cola,** to come last. **Vagón de cola,** last truck. 5. Line. **Hacer cola,** to form a line. 6. *(fig.)* Consequences. **Traer cola,** to have serious consequences. **Menea la cola el can, no por ti, sino por el pan,** the dog wags his tail, not for the love of you but for what you will give him.

Cola, *f.* 1. Glue. **Cola fuerte,** strong glue made of oxhides. **Cola de pescado,** isinglass; **eso no pega ni con cola,** that has nothing whatsoever to do with it. 2. *(And.)* Fizzy drink.

cola [co-lah], *f.* Coke, Coca-Cola.

colaboración [co-lah-bo-rah-the-on'], *f.* Collaboration, working together.

colaboracionismo [co-la-bo-rah-the-o-nees'-mo], *m.* Collaboration.

colaboracionista [co-lah-bo-rah-the-o-nees'-tah], *m. & f.* (Political) Collaborator.

colaborador, ra [co-lah-bo-rah-dor', rah], *m.& f.* 1. Collaborator, associate 2. Contributor (periódico). **Colaboradores de un libro,** joint authors of a book.

colaborar [co-lah-bo-rar'], *va.* To collaborate; to help, to assist. **Colaborar con uno en un trabajo,** to callaborate with somebody on a piece of work.

colación [co-lah-the-on'], *f.* 1. Collation, comparing of one thing with another. 2. Collation, act of bestowing an ecclesiastical benefice, or conferring degrees in universities. 3. Conference or conversation between the monks on spiritual affairs. 4. Collation, a slight repast. 5. Potation, the act of drinking. 6. Sweetmeats given to servants on Christmas eve. 7. Precinct or district of a parish. **Sacar a colación,** to make mention of a person or thing. **Traer a colacion,** to produce proofs or reasons to support a cause; to introduce, in conversation, something irrelevant.

colacionar [co-lah-the-o-nar'], *va.* 1. To collate one thing of the same kind with another, to compare. 2. To collate, to place in an ecclesiastical benefice.

colada [co-lah´-dah], *f.* 1. Washing (ropa). **Tender la colada,** to hang out the washing. 2. The linen thus bucked. 3. An open ground. 4. Road for cattle over a common.

coladera [co-lah-day´-rah], *f.* 1. Strainer, colander. 2. Sieve or scarce used by wax-chandlers.

coladero [co-lah-day´-ro], *m.* 1. Colander, a sieve through which liquors are poured, a strainer. 2. A narrow passage. 3. Bucking of clothes.

colado [co-lah´-do], *a.* 1. Metal cast (molde). 2. **Aire colado,** draught. 3. **Estar colado,** to be in love. *-m. f.* Intruder; uninvited guest, gate-crasher.

colador [co-lah-dor'], *m.* 1. Colander. *V.* COLADERO. 2. Collator, one who confers ecclesiastical benefices. 3. In printing-offices, a leach-tub for making lye.

coladora [co-lah-do'-rah], *f.* A woman who bucks.

coladura [co-lah-doo'-rah], *f.* 1. Straining, filtration. 2. **Coladuras,** dregs or bees of clarified wax. 3. Absurdity, piece of nonsense.

colaire [co-lah'-e-ray], *m. (Prov.)* Place through which a current of air passes.

colambre, *f. V.* CORAMBRE.

colanilla [co-lah-neel'-lyah], *f.* A small bolt.

colaña [co-lah'-nyah], *f.* Joist about twenty palms long and six inches broad.

colapez, colapiscis [co-lah-peth', co-la-pees'-thees], *f.* Isinglass. *V.* COLA DE PESCADO.

colapsar [co-lahp-sar'], *va.* 1. To overthrow, cause to collapse. 2. *(Aut.)* To jam, to block; to disrupt. *-vn.* To collapse, to go to pieces.

colapso [co-lap'-so], *m. (Med.)* Collapse, prostration, destruction. **Colapso nervioso,** nervous breakdown.

colar [co-lar'], *va. & vn.* 1. To strain. to filter. 2. To bleach clothing after washing. 3. To collate or confer ecclesiastical benefices. 4. To obtain some difficult matter. 5. *(Coll.)* To spread false news as certain facts; to pass counterfeit money. 6. To pass through a strait place. **Colar algo por un sitio,** to slip something through a place. **Colar unos géneros por la aduana,** to slip goods through the customs. 7. To drink wine. *-vr.* 1. To strain or to be filtered. 2. To steal into a place, to creep in by stealth. 3. To be displeased with a jest. 4. To jump the queue. **La moto se cuela por entre la circulación,** the motorcycle slips through the traffic. **Se ha colado algún indeseable,** some undesirable has slipped in.

colateral [co-lah-tay-rahl'], *a.* 1. Collateral. 2. Standing equal in relation to some ancestor.

colativo, va [co-lah-tee'-vo, vah], *a.* 1.

colca [col'-cah], *f. (And.)* Barn, granary (troje); storeroom (almacén); attic store.

colcha [col'-chah], *f.* 1. Coverlet, counterpane. 2. *(Naut.)* V. COLCHADURA.

colchadura [col-chah-doo'-rah], *f.* 1. Quilting. 2. *(Naut.)* Laying or twisting ropes.

colchar [col-char'], *va.* 1. To quilt. *V.* ACOLCHAR. 2. **Colchar cabos,** *(Naut.)* To lay or twist ropes. **Carro de colchar,** a rope-maker's sledge.

colchero [col-chay'-ro], *m.* Quiltmaker.

cólchico [col'-che-co], *m. (Bot.)* Colchicum, meadow saffron. *V.* CÓLQUICO.

colchón [col-chone'], *m.* Mattress. **Colchón de pluma,** feather-bed. **Colchón de aire** airbed. **Colchón de muelles,** spring mattress. **Servir de colchón a,** *(fig.)* to act as a buffer for.

colchoncico, illo, ito [col-chon-thee'-co], *m. dim.* A small mattress.

colchonero, ra [col-cho-nay'-ro, rah], *m. & f.* Mattress-maker, feather-bed-maker.

colchoneta [col-cho-nay'-tah], *f.* Mat.

colcótar [col-co'-tar], *m. (Chem.)* Colcothar, crocus, rouge.

colcrén [col-crayn'], *m.* Cold cream.

cole [co'-lay], *m. V.* COLEGIO.

coleada [co-lay-ah'-dah], *f.* Wag or motion of the tail of fishes or other animals.

coleadura [co-lay-ah-doo'-rah], *f.* 1. Wagging of the tail. 2. Wriggling, a ridiculous motion of women in walking.

colear [co-lay-ar'], *vn.* 1. To wag the tail (as dogs). 2. To wriggle or move in walking. **Todavía colea,** it's still pending (referring to a business not yet settled). *-va. (Sp. Amer.)* 1. To annoy, to nag. 2. To pursue (a person). 3. In bullfights, to take the bull by the tail, and while running, to overturn him. *-vr. (Carib.)* 1. *(Aut.)* To skid (sin control). 2. To arrive unexpectedly (huésped).

colección [co-lec-the-on'], *f.* Collection, an assemblage of things, collation, knot, compilement. **Es de colección,** it´s a collector´s item.

coleccionador, ra [co-lec-the-o-nah-dor'], *m. & f.* Collector.

coleccionar [co-lec-the-o-nar,], *va. vn.* To collect. **Coleccionar sellos de correo,** to collect postage stamps.

coleccionista [co-lec-the-o-nees'-tah], *m. & f.* Collector.

colecitas de Bruselas [co-lay-thee'-tahs day broo-say'-lahs], *f. pl. (Bot.)* Brussel sprouts.

colecta [co-lec'-tah], *f.* 1. Distribution of a tax levied on a town. 2. Collect, a prayer of the mass. 3. Collection of voluntary offerings for pious uses. 4. Assemblage of the faithful in churches for the celebration of divine service.

colectación [co-lec-tah-the-on'], *f.* Levy, the act of collecting rents, taxes, or other dues. *V.* RECAUDACIÓN.

colectar [co-lec-tar'], *va.* To collect taxes. *V.* RECAUDAR.

colecticio, cia [co-lec-tee'-the-o, ah], *a.* Collectitious, applied to troops without discipline.

colectivamente [co-lec-te-vah-men´-tay], *adv.* Collectively.

colectivero [co-lec-te-vay'-ro], *m. (Cono Sur)* bus driver.

colectividad [co-lec-te-ve-dahd´], *f.* Community.

colectivismo [c-lec-te-vees'-mo], *m.* Collectivism.

colectivización [co-lec-te-ve-thah-the-on'], *f.* Collectivization.

colectivizar [co-lec-te-ve-thar'], *va.* To collectivize.

colectivo, va [co-lec-tee'-vo, vah], *a.* Collective. **Contrato colectivo**, closed shop (laboral). *-m.* 1. (*Pol.*) Collective. 2. (*And. Cono Sur*) bus, minibus; (*And.*) Taxi.

colector [co-lec-tor'], *m.* 1. Collector, gatherer. 2. Tax or rent-gatherer. 3. Collector of the contributions for religious services. 4. (*Mech.*) Sump, trap, container; sewer (albañil).

colecturía [co-lec-too-ree'-ah], *f.* 1. Collectorship. 2. Office of the collector.

colega [co-lay'-gah], *m.* Colleague; chum, mate, pal.

colegatario, ria [co-lay-gah-tah´-re-o, ah], *m. & f.* Collega-tary, colegatee.

colegiado, da [co-lay-he-ah´-do], *a. m. & f.* Collegiate, a member of a college or corporation, etc.

colegial [co-lay-ge-ahl'], *m.* Collegian, collegiate, a member of a college, schoolboy; inexperienced person.

colegial [co-lay-he-ahl'], *a.* Collegial, relating to a college. **Iglesia colegial**, a collegiate church composed of dignitaries and canons, who celebrate divine service.

colegiala [co-lay-he-ah'-lah], *f.* A woman who is a member of a college; schoolgirl.

colegialmente [co-lay-he-al-men'-tay], *adv.* In a collegial manner.

colegiarse [co-lay-he-ar'-say], *vr.* To unite in a college those of the same profession or class.

colegiata [co-lay-he-ah'-tah], *f.* A collegiate church.

colegiatura [co-lay-he-ah-too'-rah], *f.* Fellowship or estab-lishment in a college.

colegio [co-lay'-he-o], *m.* 1. College, school. **Colegio de internos**, boarding school. **Colegio de pago**, fee-paying school. 2. College, the house in which collegians reside. 3. A seminary of education for young ladies. 4. College, a society of men of the same profession. **Colegio de abogados**, bar association. **Colegio electoral**, electoral college.

colegir [co-lay-heer'], *va.* 1. To collect or gather things which are scattered. 2. To collect, to deduce, to infer.

colegislador, ra [co-lay-his-lah-dor', rah], *a.* Colegislative (body).

coleo [co-lay'-o], *m.* (*Coll.*) V. COLEADURA.

coleóptero, ra [co-lay-op'-tay-ro, rah], *a.* Coleopterous, belonging to the division of insects named coleoptera. *-m. pl.* The coleoptera.

cólera [co'-lay-rah], *f.* 1. Choler, bile. 2. Choler, anger, fury, rage, passion. **Montar en cólera**, to be angry, to be in a pas-sion. **Descargar la cólera en**, to vent one´s anger on. *-m.* 3. **Cólera asiática**, Asiatic cholera.

colera [co-lay'-rah], *f.* Ornament for the tail of a horse.

coléricamente [co-lay'-re-cah-men-tay], *adv.* Fumingly, pas-sionately.

colérico, ca [co-lay'-re-co, cah], *a.* 1. Choleric. 2. Passionate, hasty; hotheaded.

coleriforme [co-lay-re-for'-may], *a.* Choleriform.

colerina [co-lay-ree'-nah], *f.* Cholerine, a diarrhoea, sometimes premonitory of cholera.

colesterina [o-les-tay-ree'-nah], *f.* Cholesterol.

colesterol [co-les-tay-role'], *m.* Cholesterol.

coleta [co-lay'-tah], *f.* 1. Pigtail. **Gente de coleta**, bullfighters. **Cortarse la coleta**, to quit the ring, give up bullfighting 2. (*Coll.*) A short addition to a discourse or writing; postscript. 3. (*Bot.*) Nineleaved coronilla. 4. Nankin, or nankeen.

coletánea, nea [co-lay-tah´-nay-o, ah], *a.* (*Obs.*) V. CO-LACTÁNEO.

coletazo [co-lay-tah'-tho], *m.* 1. Lash, blow with the tail. 2. Sway, swaying movement (de vehículo). **Dar coletazos**, to sway about. 3. (*fig.*) Sting with the tail; unexpected after-effect.

coletero [co-lay-tay'-ro], *m.* One who makes buff doublets and breeches.

coletilla [co-lay-teel'-lyah], *f. dim.* Filler phrase or cliched phrase added at the end of sentences.

coletillo [co-lay-teel'-lyo], *m. dim.* A small doublet of buff or other skins.

coleto [co-lay'-to], *m.* 1. Buff doublet or jacket. 2. (*Coll.*) Body of a man; interior of a person. **Dije para mi coleto**, I said to myself. **Echarse al coleto**, (*Coll.*) to read from cover to cover (libro). **Echarse algo al coleto**, to eat or drink something.

colgadero [col-gah-day'-ro], *m.* Hook to hang things upon.

colgadero, ra [col-gah-day'-ro, rah], *a.* Fit to be hung up.

colgadizo [col-gah-dee'-tho], *m.* 1. Shed, a temporary covering from the weather. 2. Flat roof.

colgadizo, za [col-gah-dee'-tho, thah], *a.* Pendent, sus-pended.

colgado, da [col-gah'-do, dah], *a.* 1. Suspended. **Dejar a al-guno colgado** or **quedarse alguno colgado**, to frustrate one's hopes or desires. 2. **Estar colgado**, to have withdrawal pains (drogas). **Quedar colgado**, to get hooked (drogas). *-pp.* of COLGAR.

colgador [col-gah-dor´], *m.* Peel-hanger (imprenta). Hook (gancho). Coat hanger (percha).

colgadura [col-gah-doo'-rah], *f.* Tapestry, hanging or drapery. **Colgadura de cama**, bed furniture. **Colgaduras de papel pintado**, paper hangings.

colgajo [col-gah'-ho], *m.* 1. Tatter or rag hanging from clothes. 2. **Colgajo de uvas**, bunch of grapes hung up to be preserved. *-3. pl.* The fleshy tissues left in some amputations to form the stump.

colgante [col-gahn'-tay], *pa.* Hanging, pending, clinging. **Colgantes**, earrings, trinkets; (*Carib. Cono Sur*) watch chain; (*Arquit.*) Festoon; **colgantes**, fringe.

colgar [col-gar'], *va.* 1. To hang up, to suspend in the air, to flag, to flow, to hover. 2. To adorn with tapestry or hangings. 3. To hang or kill by hanging. *-vn.* 1. To hang from, to be suspended. 2. To be in a state of dependence. **Colgar los habitos**, to doff the cassock. **Ella está siempre colgada de la ventana**, she is always fixcd at the window. **Colgar los libros**, to abandon one´s studies.

colia [co´-le-ah], *f.* **colias** [co´-le-as], *m.* A small fish resembling a pilchard.

coliblanca [co-le-blahn'-cah], *f.* (*Zool.*) An eagle of South America.

coliblanco, ca [co-le-blahn'-co, cah], *a.* White-tailed.

colibre, colibrí [co-lee'-bray, co-le-bree'], *m.* (*Orn.*) Colibri, a beautiful American humming-bird, especially one with a curved beak.

cólica [co´-le-cah], *f.* Colic.

colicano, na [co-le-cah'-no, nah], *a.* Having gray hair in the tail (caballos).

cólico or **dolor cólico** [co'-le-co], *m.* 1. Colic, a condition caused by acute spasmodic abdominal pain. 2. (*Cono Sur*) **energía cólico**, wind power.

colicorto ta [co-le-cor'-to, tah], *a.* Short-tailed.

collcuación [co-le-coo-ah-the-on'], *f.* Colliquation, the act of melting or dissolving.

colicuante [co-le-coo-ahn'-tay], *pa.* Colliquant, colliquative.

colicuar [co-le-coo-ar'], *va.* To colliquate, to melt, to dissolve.*-vr.* To colliquate, to become liquid.

colicuativo, va [co-le-coo-ah-tee´-vo, vah], *a.* Colliquative, colliquescent.

colicuecer [co-le-coo-ay-therr´], *va.* To fuse or melt.

coliculoso, sa [co-le-coo-lo'-so, sah], *a.* (*Bot.*) Presenting knobs, rounded prominences in a small space.

colidir [co-le-deer'], *va.* (*Obs.*) To collide, to dash or knock together.

colifato [co-le-fah'-to], (*Cono Sur*) 1. *a.* Nuts. 2. *m.* Madman, nutcase.

colífero, ra [co-lee'-fay-ro, rah], *a.* (*Bot.*) Cauliferous: said of the ovary of plants when it has a neck.

coliflor [co-le-flor'], *f.* (*Bot.*) Cauliflower. *-pl.* Cauliflower excrescences, venereal warts.

coligación [co-le-gah-the-on'], *f.* 1. Colligation, the binding of things together. 2. Connection of one thing with another. 3. Union, alliance.

coligado, da [co-le-gah´-do; dah], *m. & f.* Leaguer, covenanter. *-a.* Agreed and associated for some purpose. *-pp.* of COLIGARSE.

coligadura [co-le-gah-doo'-rah], *f.* Combining or connecting of one thing with another.

coligamiento [co-le-gah-me-en'-to], *m.* V. COLIGACIÓN,

coligancia [co-le-gahn'-the-ah], *f.* Connection, relation, correspondence of one thing with another.

coligarse [co-le-gar'-say], *vr.* To colligate, to colleague, to unite; to join together. *(Yo colijo, yo colija; él colijió,* from Colegir. V. PEDIR.).

colilla [co-leel'-lyah], *f.* 1. *(dim.)* A small tail. 2. Train of a gown. 3. Stub of a cigar or cigarette. **Ser una colilla,** to be past it, to be all washed up.

colimba [co-leem'-bah], *(Cono Sur)* 1. *m.* Conscript. 2. *f.* Military service; **hacer la colimba,** to do military service.

colimbo [co-leem'-bo], *m.* Diver.

colimense, colimeño, *m. & f.* V. COLIMOTE.

colimote [co-le-mo'-tay], *m. & f.* Of Colima province.

colín [co-leen'], *m. (Carib.)* Machete, cane knife.

colina [co-lee'-nah], *f.* 1. Hill, hillock, hummock. 2. Seed of cabbage. 3. V. COLINO.

colinabo [co-le-nah'-bo], *m. (Bot.)* Turnip.

colindante [co-lin-dahn'-tay], *a.* Contiguous, adjacent.

colindar [co-lin-dar'], *vn.* To be contiguous, to be adjacent.

colino [co-lee'-no], *m.* Small cabbage not transplanted.

colinsia [co-leen'-se-ah], *f.* Collinsia, a garden plant of the figwort family, native of California.

colirio [co-lee'-re-o], *m.* Collyrium, a wash for the eyes.

colirrojo [cor-ro'-ho], *m.* Redstart.

colís [co-lees'], *m. (And.)* Machete, cane knife.

colisa [co-lee'-sah], *f.* A swivel gun.

Coliseo [co-le-say'-o], *m.* Theater, opera-house, playhouse, Coliseum.

colisión [co-le-se-on'], *f.* 1. Collision, crush, clash. 2. A gall, fretting, chafing. 3. Opposition, clash of ideas.

colisionar [co-le-se-o-nar'], *vn.* To collide. **Colisionar con,** to collide with.

colista [co-lees'tah], 1. *m.* Bottom club (liga). 2. *m. & f.* Person who stands in line.

colitea [co-le-tay'-ah], *f. (Bot.)* Judas tree.

colitigante [co-le-te-gahn'-tay], *m.* One who carries on a lawsuit with another.

colitis [co-le'-tes], *f.* Colitis.

colla [col-lyah], *f.* 1. Collet, a piece of ancient armor for the neck. 2. Continuous squalls preceding the monsoons, at times followed by a hurricane. 3. Channel of an auger. 4. Last oakum placed in a seam.

collado [col-lyah'-do], *m.* Hill, fell, a small eminence.

collage [col-lya'-hay], *m.* Collage (arte).

collar [col-lyar'], *m.* 1. Necklace. 2. Chain or cord from which hang certain insignia of honor. 3. Collar, collet. 4. **Collar de un estay,** *(Naut.)* collar of a stay. 5. *(Mech.)* Collar, ring. 6. **Collar de fuerza,** strangle-hold.

collarcito [col-lyar-thee'-to], *m. dim.* A small necklace, string of beads, or chain.

collarín [col-lyah-reen'], *m.* 1. A black collar, edged with white, worn by the Roman Catholic clergy. V. ALZACUELLO. 2. Collar of a coat. 3. Surgical collar.

collarino [col-lyah-ree'-no], *m. (Arch.)* Ring or list at the top and bottom of the shaft of a column; a half round, torus. V. ASTRÁGALO.

collazo [col-lyah'-tho], *m.* Ploughman who tills the ground for a master, for which he gets some small tenement or ground to till for himself. **Collazos,** poles on which barill-plants are carried to the pit to be burnt.

colleja [col-lyay'-hah], *f.* 1. *(Bot.)* Lamb's-lettuce, or cornsalad. **Collejas,** slender nerves found in a sheep's neck. 2. Dandelion.

collera [col-lyay'-rah], *f.* 1. Collar, breastharness of leather stuffed with hay or straw for draught cattle. 2. Horse collar. 3. Chain gang. 4. Pair (de animales). 5. *(Arg.)* Cufflinks.

collerón [col-lyay-rone'], *m.* Harness collar, hame.

colleta [col-lyay'-tah], *f. (Bot. Prov.)* A small kind of cabbage.

collín [col-lyeen'], *m. (CAm.)* Cane Knife.

collón [col-lyone'], *m. (Coll.)* Coward, a poltroon, mean fellow.

collonada [col-lyo-nah'-dah], *f.* Cowardliness.

collonería [col-lyo-nay-ree'-ah], *f.* 1. Cowardice. 2. *(Coll. Vul.)* Nonsense.

colmadamente [col-mah-dah-men-tay], *adv.* Abundantly. plentifully.

colmado, da [col-mah'-do, dah], *a.* Filled, heaped. **Una cucharada colmada,** one heaped spoonful. **Una tarde colada de incidentes,** an afternoon full of incidents. *-pp.* of COLMAR. *-m.* Cheap seafood restaurant.

colmar [col-mar'], *va.* 1. To heap up to fill to the brim. 2. To fulfil, to make up. V. LLENAR. 3. *(Met.)* To confer great favors. **Colmar a uno de honores,** to shower honors upon somebody. **Colmar a uno de alabanzas,** to heap praises on somebody. **Colmar a uno de favores,** to lavish favors on somebody.

colmataje [col-ma-tah'-hay], *m.* A heaping up, brimming.

colmena [col-may'-nah], *f.* Beehive. **Tener la casa como una colmena,** to have one's house well stocked with provisions.

colmenar [col-may-nar'], *m.* Apiary.

colmenero, ra [col-may-nay'-ro], *m.f.* Bee-keeper, bee-master. **Oso colmenero,** a bear who eats the honey of bee-hives.

colmenilla [col-may-neel'-lyah], *f.* Morel or moril, a kind of mushroom.

colmillada [col-meel-lyah'-dah], *f.* An injury made by an eye tooth.

colmillazo [col-meel-lyah'-tho], *m.* 1. *(aug.)* A large eye tooth. 2. A wound made by an eye tooth or fang.

colmillo [col-meel'-lyo], *m.* 1. Eye tooth, canine-tooth. 2. Fang, the long tusk of a boar or other animal. **Mostrar los colmillos,** *(Met.)* to show spirit and resolution. **Tener colmillos,** *(Mex.)* to be long in the tooth. **Tener el colmillo torcido,** to be an old fox.

colmilludo, da [col-meel-lyoo'-do, dah], *a.* 1. Having eye teeth fangs, or tusks (personas, animales). 2. Sagacious, quick-sighted, not easily imposed upon.

colmo [col'-mo], *m.* 1. Heap, that which rises above the brim of a measure of grain, flour, etc. 2. Complement, finishing, completion, crown. 3. Over-measure, full; height. **Ella llegó al colmo de sus deseos,** she attained the summit of her wishes. **El colmo de la elegancia,** the height of elegance. **El colmo de lo absurdo,** the height of absurdity. **Para colmo de desgracias,** to make matters worse. **Sería el colmo si...,** it would be the last straw if...

colmo, ma [col'-mo, mah], *a.* V. COLMADO.

colo [co'-lo], *m.* A coleopterous, tetramerous, curculionid insect of South America.

colobo [co-lo'-bo], *m.* 1. A kind of linen tunic worn by Egyptian monks. 2. *(Zool.)* Colobus, an African monkey, having the thumb absent or rudimentary.

coloboma [co-lo-bo'-mah], *m.* Coloboma, defect of substance; specifically, of the iris of the eye.

colocación [co-lo-cah-the-on'], *f.* 1. Employment, place, office. **No encuentro colocación,** I can´t find a job. 2. Arrangement of the parts of a building, speech, etc., collocation, location. 3. Position, situation.

colocado [co-lo-cah'-do*],* *a.* **Apostar para colocado,** to back (a horse) for a place; **estar colocado,** to be high (on drugs).

colocar [co-lo-car'], *va.* 1. To arrange, to put in due place or order, to place. **Colocar la quilla de un buque,** to lay down a ship. **Colocar un satélite en órbita,** to put a satellite in orbit. 2. To place, to put in any place, rank, condition, or office, to provide one with a place or employment. 3. To collocate, to locate to lay. 4. **Colocar una responsabilidad a uno,** to saddle somebody with a responsibility. 5. To nick, to arrest. -vr. 1. To place oneself, to station oneself; *(Dep.)* to get a place. **El equipo se ha colocado en quinto lugar,** the team has climbed to fifth position. 2. To get a job.

colocasia [co-lo-cah´-se-ah], *f. (Bot.)* The Egyptian bean, a plant with thick, tuberous rootstocks, large leaves, and rose-colored blossoms.

colocho [co-lo´-cho], *(CAm.)* 1. *a.* Curly-haired. 2. *m. pl.* Curls (rizos); wood shavings.

colocutor, ra [co-lo-coo-tor´, rah], *m. & f.* He who holds colloquial intercourse with another; collocutor.

colodión [co-lo-de-on´], *m.* Collodion.

colodra [co-lo´-drah], *f.* 1. Milkpail, a kit; a pailful. 2. A wooden can with which wine is measured and retailed. 3. A wooden can with a handle, used for drinking. 4. A horn with a cork bottom, used as a tumbler. **Ser una colodra,** *(Coll.)* to be a toper or tippler. 5. *(Prov. Sant.)* A wooden case tied about the waist, in which the mower carries a whetstone.

colodrazgo [co-lo-drath´-go], *m.* Tax or excise on wine sold in small quantities.

colodrillo [co-lo-dreel´-lyo], *m.* Occiput, hind part of the head.

colodro [co-lo´-dro], *m.* 1. A wooden shoe. 2. *(Prov.)* Wine measure.

colofón [co-lo-fone´], *m.* Colophon, an inscription or device put at the end of a book, giving the printer´s name and date and place of printing.

colofonia [co-lo-fo-nee-ah], *f.* Colophony, a kind of resin.

colofonita [co-lo-fo-nee´tah], *f.* A garnet of a light-green or rosy-red color, the least fusible of all garnets.

coloide [co-lo´-e-day], *m.* Colloid.

Colombia [co-lom´-be-ah], *f.* Colombia.

colombiano, na [co-lom-be-ah´-no, nah], *a.* Columbian, of Colombia.

colombicultura [co-lom-bee-cool-too´-rah], *f.* Pigeon-breeding.

colombino, na [co-lom-bee´-no, nah], *a.* Pertaining to Columbus or his family.

colombofilia [co-lom-bo-fee´-lee-ah], *f.* Pigeon-fancying.

colombófilo, la [co-lom-bo´-fe-lo], *m. & f.* Pigeon-fancier.

colombroño [co-lom-bro´-nyo], *m.* Namesake. *V.* TOCAYO.

colon [co´-lone], *m.* 1. Colon (:) (dos puntos). Semicolon (;) (punto y coma). 2. Colon, the largest of the intestines. 3. *(Gram.)* Principal part or member of a period.

colón [co-lone´], *m.* Colon (unit of currency of Costa Rica and El Salvador).

colonche [co-lone´-chay], *m.* An intoxicating drink made in Mexico from the sap of the red prickly pear (cactus) and sugar.

colonia [co-lo´-ne-ah], *f.* 1. Colony. **Colonia escolar,** summer camp for school-children. **Colonia obrera,** working-class. **Colonia penal,** penal settlement. **Colonia veraniega,** holiday camp. 2. Colony, a plantation. 3. *(Mex.)* Each subdivision in which cities are divided. **Colonia residencial,** residential district.

colonia [co-lo´-ne-ah], *f.* Eau-de-Cologne.

coloniaje [co-lo-ne-ah´-hay], *m. (LAm.)* Colonial period; system of colonial government; slavery, slave status.

colonial [co-lo-ne-ahl´], *a.* Colonial.

colonialismo [co-lo-ne-ah-lees´-mo], *m.* Colonialism.

colonialista [co-lo-ne-ah-lees´-tah], *a. & m. & f.* Colonialist.

colonización [co-lo-ne-thah-the-on´], *f.* Colonization, the making of a colony.

colonizador, ra [co-lo-ne-tha-dor´], *m. & f.* Colonist, colonizer. -*a.* Colonizing.

colonizar [co-lo-ne-thar´], *va.* To colonize, form a settlement.

colono [co-lo´-no], *m.* 1. Colonist, planter. 2. Laborer, who cultivates a piece of ground and lives on it. 3. A farmer.

coloqueta [co-lo-kay´-tah], *f.* 1. Arrest. 2. Police sweep (redada).

coloquial [co-lo-ke-al´], *a.* Colloquial, familiar.

coloquio [co-lo´-ke-o], *m.* Discussion, colloquy, chat, conversation, talk.

color [co-lor´], *m.* 1: Color, hue, dye. 2. Rouge. 3. *(Met.)* Color, pretext, pretence, false show or appearance. 4. Color, the tint of the painter. -*pl.* 1. Color, the freshness or appearance of blood in the face. 2. *(Pict.)* Color, or mixture of paint. **Color lleno** or **cargado,** a deep color. **Color vivo,** a bright color. **Mudar de colores,** *(Met.)* to change color. **Sacarle los colores a una persona,** *(Met.)* to make a person blush. **Gente de color,** colored people. **Zapatos de color,** brown shoes. **Color muerto,** dull color. **Verlo todo color de rosa,** to see everything through rose-colored spectacles. 5. **Colores,** colors. **Los colores nacionales,** the national colors.

coloración [co-lo-rah-the-on´], *f.* 1. Coloring, coloration. 2. Blush. **Coloración protectora,** protective coloring, mimetism.

coloradamente [co-lo-rah-dah-men´-tay], *adv.* Speciously, under a pretext.

colorado, da [co-lo-rah´-do, dah], *a.* 1. Ruddy, florid, red. 2. Indelicate, smutty (historias, frases). 3. Colored, specious. **Ponerse colorado,** to blush with shame. **Poner a alguno colorado,** to put one to the blush. -*pp.* of COLORAR. -*m.* 1. Bread, money. 2. *(Carib.)* Scarlet fever. 3. **Los Colorados,** Uruguayan political party.

coloradote [co-lo-rah-do´-tay], *a.* Red-faced, ruddy.

coloramiento [co-lo-rah-me-en´-to], *m. V.* ENCENDIMIENTO.

colorante [co-lo-rahn´tay], *m.* Dye, coloring. -*a.* Dyeing, coloring. **Materia colorante,** dyeing matter, coloring substance.

colorar [co-lo.rar´], *va.* 1. To dye, to color. 2. To make plausible. *vn.* To blush with shame. -*vr.* To be ashamed.

colorativo, va [co-lo-rah-tee´-vo, vah], *a.* Colorific, tingeing.

colorear [co-lo-ray-ar´], *va.* To color, to make plausible, to palliate, to excuse. -*vn.* To redden, to grow red.

colorete [co-lo-ray´-tay], *m.* Rouge.

colorido [co-lo-ree´-do], *m.* 1. Coloring or color. 2. Pretext, pretence.

colorido , da [co-lo-ree´-do, dah], *a.* Colorate. -*pp.* of COLORIR.

colorín [co-lo-reen´], *m.* 1. *(Orn.)* Linnet. 2. Bright, vivid color. **Gustar de colorines,** to like showy colors. **Colorín, colorado, este cuento se ha acabado,** traditional ending of children's stories. 3. *(Orn.)* Goldfinch. 4. *(Med.)* Measles. 5. Magazine of love stories.

colorir [co-lo-reer´], *va.* 1. To color, to mark with some hue or dye. 2. *V.* COLOREAR.

colorista [co-lo-rees´-tah], *m.* Colorist.

colosal [co-lo-sahl´], *a.* Colossal, giant, huge.

coloso [co-lo´-so], *m.* 1. Colossus, a statue of enormous magnitude. 2. *(Cono Sur)* Trailer.

colpa [col´-pah], *f.* A whitish sort of copperas, a flux.

colpez [col-peth´], *f.* Isinglass; fish glue.

cólquico [cole´´-ke-co], *m.* Colchicum meadow saffron; used in medicine as a remedy for gout.

coludir [co-loo-deer´], *va.* 1. To collude. 2. To collide.

columbio [co-loom´-be-o], *m. (Min.)* Columbium, a metal.

columbino, na [co-loom-bee´-no, nah], *a.* Dovelike, innocent, candid.

columbo [co-loom´-bo], *m.* Columbo root. Radix coculi palmati.

columbrar [co-loom-brar´], *va.* 1. To discern at a distance, to see far off. 2. *(Met.)* To pursue or trace a thing by conjectures.

columelar [co-loo-may-lar´], *m.* Incisor. *V.* CORTADORES.

columna [co-loom´-nah], *f.* 1. Column, a round pillar. **Columna ática, compuesta, corintia, dórica, jónica,** etc. Attic Composite, Corinthian, Doric, Ionic, etc., column. 2. Column of air. 3. **Columna fosfórica,** lighthouse, built on a rock. **Columna hueca,** a hollow column, in which is a spiral staircase. 4. *(Met.)* Supporter or maintainer. **La justicia, la paz y la religión son las columnas del estado,** justice, peace, and religion are the supporters of the state. 5. Column, a long file of troops. 6. Column, part of a page. 7. *(Anat.)* **Columna vertebral**, spine.

columnario, ria [co-loom-nah'-re-o, ah], *a.* Columnar: applied to the money coined in Spanish America, with the impressions of two columns. *-m. & f. (Obs.) V.* COLUMNATA.

columnata [co-loom-nah'-tah], *f.* Colonnade.

columnista [co-loom-nees'-tah], *m. & f.* Columnist.

columpiar [co-loom-pe-ar'], *va.* To swing.*-vr.* 1. To swing, to fly forward or backward on a rope. 2. *(Met.)* To waddle, to shake in walking from side to side.

columpio [co-loom'-pe-o], *m.* A swing. **Columpio basculante**, seesaw.

colurión [co-loo-re-on'], *m. (Orn.)* Lesser butcher-bird, flusher.

coluro [co-loo'-ro], *m. (Astr.)* Colure, one of the two great circles of the celestial sphere which pass from the pole through the equinoxes and solstices respectively.

colusión [co-loo-se-on'], *f.* 1. Collusion, deceitful agreement. 2. Shock, collision.

colusoriamente [co-loo-so-re-ah-men'-tay], *adv.* Collusively, fraudulently.

colusorio, ria [co-loo-so'-re-o, ah], *a.* Collusory, collusive.

colza [cole'-thah], *f.* Colza, summer rape, a variety of turnip.

colzal [col-thahl'], *f.* Colewort seed.

coma [co'-mah],*f.* 1. Comma (,). 2. Each of the parts into which a tone divided. 3. **Sin faltar una coma**, or **sin faltar punto ni coma**, without a title being wanting in the account or narrative.

coma [co'-mah], *m.* Coma, profound insensibility.

comadre [co-mah'-dray],*f.* 1. Midwife (partera). 2. The name by which the godfather and godmother address the mother of their godson or daughter, and by which she also always addresses the godmother. 3. *(Coll.)* A gossip. **Un grupo de comadres**, a group of gossips. 4. Pansy (maricón). 5. Neighbor (vecina).

comadrear [co-mah-dray-ar'], *vn.* To gossip, to tattle.

comadreja [co-mah-dray'-hah], *f.* Weasel. **Comadreja marina**, weaselblenny.

comadreo [co-mah-dray'-o], *m.* **comadrería** [co-mah-dray-ree'-ah], *f.* Gossip, gossiping, chattering.

comadrero, ra [co-mah-dray'-ro, rah], *a.* Gossiping from house to house.

comadrón [co-mah-drone'], *m.* Man-midwife, accoucheur.

comadrona [co-mah-dro'-nah], *f.* Midwife.

comal [co-mahl'], *m. (Mex.)* A flat earthen ware pan for cooking corn cake.

comalía, comalición [co-mah-lee'-ah, co-man-le-the-on'],*f.* An epizootic disease, not contagious, among the wool-bearing animals, characterized by (chronic) dropsy.

comandado, da, *a. (Mil.)* Officered. *-pp.* of COMANDAR.

comandamiento [co-man-dah-me-en'-to], *m. (Obs.) V.* MANDO and MANDAMIENTO.

comandancia [co-man-dahn'-the-ah], *f.* 1. Command, the office of a commander. 2. The province or district of a commander. **Comandancia militar**, a military command. **Comandancia general de Marina**, the High Court of Admiralty. 3. Commander's headquarter.

comandanta [co-mahn-dah'-tah],*f.* 1. *(Mil.)* Major (woman); *(Hist.)* Mayor's wife. 2. *(Naut.)* Flagship.

comandante [co-man-dahn'-tay], *m.* Commander, a chief, a commandant, a leader. **Comandante en Jefe**, commander-in-Chief.

comandar [co-man-dar'], *va.* 1. To command, to govern. 2. *(Obs.)* To commend, to recommend.

comandita [co-man-dee'-tah],*f.* A silent partnership.

comanditario [co-man-de-tah'-re-o], *m.* A sleeping partner.

comando [co-mahn'-do], *m.* 1. Command. 2. *(Mil.)* Commando. **Comando suicida**, suicide squad.

comarca [co-mar'-cah], *f.* 1. Territory, district. 2. Border, boundary, limit.

comarcal [co-mar-cahl'], *a.* Local, regional.

comarcano, na [co-mar-cah'-no, nah], *a.* Neighboring, near, bordering upon.

comarcar [co-mar-car'], *va.* To plant trees in a straight line, so as to form paths. *-vn.* To border, to confine upon; to be on the borders.

comato ta [co-mah'-to, tah], *a.* **Cometa comato**, hairy or comate comet.

comatoso, sa [co-ma-to'-so, sah], *a.* Comatose, in a profound stupor.

comaya [co-mah'-yah], *f.* 1. A large basket, a pannier. 2. *(Orn.)* The white owl or barn owl. *V.* ZUMAYA.

comba [com'-bah], *f.* 1. Curvature or inflexion of timber when warped, or iron when bent; a curve, a bend; convexity. 2. The game of jumping or skipping rope. 3. The skipping rope itself. **Hacer combas**, to bend and twist the body from one side to the other. 4. **No pierde comba**, he doesn't miss a trick.

combadura [com-bah-doo'-rah], *f.* Curvature, convexity, warping, bending.

combar [com-bar'], *va.* To bend, to curve. *-vr.* To warp, to become crooked, to jut.

combate [com-bah'-tay], *m.* 1. Combat, conflict, engagement, fray, fight. **Combate naval**, naval battle. **Estar fuera de combate**, to be out of action. 2. Agitation of the mind.

combatidor [com-bah-te-dor'], *m.* Combatant, champion.

combatiente [com-bah-te-en'-tay], *m. pa.* Combatant, fighter.

combatir [com-bah-teer'], *va. & vn.* 1. To combat, to fight. 2. To contend, to contest, to meet or meet with. 3. To attack, to invade. 4. To contradict, conflict with. 5. *(Met.)* To agitate the mind, to rouse the passions. **Combatir a la retreta**, *(Naut.)* To keep up a running fight.

combatividad [com-ba-te-ve-dahd'], *f. (Phren.)* Combativeness; aggressiveness.

combativo [com-bah-te-vo], *a.* Full of fight, spirited; aggressive, combative.

combazo [com-bah-tho], *m. (Cono Sur)* punch.

combeneficiado [com-bay-nay-fe-the-ah-do], *m.* Prebendary of the same church as another.

combés [com-bess'], *m. (Naut.)* Waist of a ship.

combi [com'-be],*f.* 1. Fiddle (ardid), wangle. 2. Slip (prenda).

combinable [com-be-nah'-blay], *a.* Combinable.

combinación [com-be-nah-the-on'], *f.* 1. Combination. 2. Aggregate of several words which begin with the same syllable. 3. Concurrence. 4 *(Chem.)* A compound; cocktail (bebida). 5. Arrangement, set-up, scheme; plan (proyecto). 6. *(Ferro. etc.)* Connection. **Hacer combinación con**, to connect with.

combinado [com-be-nah'-do], *m.* Cocktail.

combinar [com-be-ner'], *va.* 1. To combine, to join, to unite, to connect. 2. To compare. *-vr.* To combine; to get together, to join together.

combinatorio, ria [com-be-nah-to'-re-o, ah], *a.* Combining, uniting.

combo, ba [com'-bo, bah], *a.* Bent, crooked, warped.

combo [com'-bo], *m.* 1. Stand or frame for casks. 2. *(LAm.)* Sledge-hammer (martillo). 3. *(And. Cono Sur)* slap; punch (puñetazo).

combustibilidad [com-boos-te-be-le-dahd'], *f.* Combustibility.

combustible [com-boos-tee'-blay], *a.* Combustible.

combustible [com-boos-tee'-blay], *m.* 1. Combustible, a combustible material. 2. Fuel. **Combustible de alta potencia**, exotic fuel.

combustion [com-boos-te-on'], *f.* Combustion, burning.

comebolas [co-may-bo'-lahs], *m. (Carib.)* Simple soul, gullible individual.

comedero [co-may-day'-ro], *m.* 1. Dining-room. 2. A feeding trough for fowls and other animals. 3. *(Carib.)* Brothel (prostíbulo). 4. *(And.)* Haunt, hang-out (sitio favorito).

comedero, ra [co-may-day'-ro, rah], *a.* Eatable, edible.

comedia [co-may'-de-ah], *f.* Comedy. **Es una comedia**, it is a complete farce: applied to ridiculous speeches or actions. **Comedia de enredo**, that whose merit consists principally in the ingenuity and complexity of the plot. **Hacer la comedia**, to make believe, to pretend.

comedianta [co-may-de-ahn'-tah], *f. V.* ACTRIZ. Comedienne.

comediante [co-may-de-ahn'-tay], *m.* Player, actor, comedian. **Comediante de la lengua**, strolling player; hypocrite, fraud.

comediar [co-may-de-ar'], *va.* 1. To divide into equal shares. 2. To regulate, to direct.

comédico, ca [co-may'-de-co, cah], *a.* Comical. *V.* CÓMICO.

comedidamente [co-may-de-dah-men'-tay], *adv.* Gently, courteously, moderately.

comedido, da [co-may-dee'-do, dah], *a.* 1. Civil, polite, gentle, courteous. 2. Kind, obsequious, obliging.-*pp.* of COMEDIRSE.

comedimiento [co-may-de-me-en'-to], *m.* 1. Civility, politeness, urbanity, moderation. 2. Kindness, obsequiousness.

comedio [co-may'-de-o], *m.* 1. Middle of a kingdom or place. 2. Intermediate time between epochs.

comediógrafo, fa [co-may-de-o'-grah-fo], *m. & f.* Playwright.

comedión [co-may-de-on'], *m.* A poor or long and tedious comedy.

comedirse [co-may-deer'-say], *vr.* 1. To govern oneself, to regulate one's conduct, to be civil, obliging, kind. 2. *(LAm.)* **Comedirse a**, to offer to.

comedón [co-may-done'], *m.* Blackhead.

comedor, ra [co-may-dor', rah], *m. & f.* 1. Eater (personas). 2. *m.* Dining-room.

comefuego [co-may foo-ay'-go], *m.* Fire-eater (circo).

comegente [co-may-hayn-tay], *m. (And. Carib.)* Glutton.

comején [co-may-hen'], *m.* 1. Kind of termite or white ant, very destructive to houses and their contents in tropical America. 2. A sort of woodborer which pierces pipe-staves. 3. *(And.)* Nagging worry (preocupación). 4. *(And.)* Glutton.

comelina [co-may-lee'-nah], *f. (Bot.)* Commelina, a large genus of herbs of the spiderwort family.

comelitona [co-may-le-to'-nah], *f. (Mex.) V.* COMILONA.

comelón [co-may-lone'], *a. (LAm.) V.* COMILON.

comendable [co-men-dah'-blay], *a.* Commendable. *V.* RECOMENDABLE.

comendador [co-men-dah-dor'], *m.* 1. Knight commander of a military order. 2. Prelate or prefect of religious houses.

comendadora [co-men-dah-do'-rah], *f.* The superior of a nunnery of a military order, and also of other nunneries.

comendamiento [co-men-dah-me-en'-to], *m. V.* ENCOMIENDA and MANDAMIENTO.

comendar [co-men-dar'], *va. V.* RECOMENDAR.

comendatario [co-men-dah-tah'-re-o], *m.* Commendator, commendatory, a secular clergyman who enjoys a benefice belonging to a military order.

comendatorio, ria [co-men-dah-to'-re-o, ah], *a.* Relating to letters of introduction or recommendation.

comensal [co-men-sahl'], *com.* Commensal, one that eats at the same table. *V.* CONMENSAL. -*m. & f.* 1. Fellow guest. **Habrá 13 comensales**, there will be 13 to dinner. **Me lo dijo mi comensal**, the man sitting next to me at dinner told me so.

comensalía [co-men-sah-lee'-ah], *f.* Fellowship of house and table.

comentador, ra [co-men-tah-dor', rah], *m. & f.* 1. Commentator, expositor, annotator, expounder, glosser. 2. Inventor of falsehoods.

comentar [co-mentar'], *va.* To comment, to explain, to expound, to gloss.

comentario [co-men-tah'-re-o], *m.* 1. A commentary. 2. Commentary, an historical work written in a familiar manner. 3.

Comment, remark, observation. **Y ahora sin más comentario...**, and now without further comment... 4. **Comentarios**, gossip, talk. **Dar lugar a comentarios**, to cause gossip.

comentarista [co-men-tah-rees'-tah], *m. & f.* Commentator. **Comentarista deportivo**, sports commentator.

comento [co-men'-to], *m.* Comment, exposition, or explanation of some writing or circumstance.

comenzar [co-men-thar'], *va.vn.* To commence, to start, to begin (empezar). **Comenzar a hacer algo**, to begin to do something. **Comenzar por**, to begin with.

comer [co-merr'], *va.* 1. To eat, to chew or swallow something, to feed. 2. To dine. 3. *(Coll.)* To be in possession of an income. **Él se come diez mil dólares de renta**, he spends ten thousand dollars a year. 4. To run through a fortune. 5. To have an itching all over one's body. 6. *vr.* To suppress some letter or syllable in the pronunciation of words. **Se lo comió todo**, he ate it all up. **Se come las palabras**, he mumbles. **Tiene muchos nombres y se come el García**, she has lots of names and drops the García. 7. *(Met.)* To corrode, to consume. 8. **Comerse una dama**; to take a queen in the game of chess. **Comerse un peón**, to take a pawn in the same game. **Comerse de risa**, to refrain from laughing. **Comerse unos a otros** *(Met.)*, to be constantly at drawn daggers. **Comerse a uno con los ojos**, to look daggers at any one. **¿En qué bodegón hemos comido juntos?** where have we eaten together? (a rebuke for undue familiarity). **Tener que comer**, to have a competency to live upon. **Ganar de comer**, to earn a livelihood. 9. *(fig.)* **Le come la envidia**, she is eaten up with envy. -*vn.* 1. To eat; (comer de), to eat, to partake. **Comer como una vaca**, to eat like a horse. 2. *(fig.)* **El mismo que come y viste**, the very same. **Este pescado es de buen comer**, this fish is good eating. **No tienen qué comer**, they don't have enough to live on.

comer [co-merr'], *m. (Obs.) V.* COMIDA.

comerciable [co-mer-the-ah'-blay], *a.* 1. Saleable, marketable. 2. Sociable, social, affable.

comercial [co-mer-the-ahl'], *a.* Commercial, trading. **Barrio comercial**, business quarter. **Centro comercial**, business center.

comercialización [co-mer-the-ah-le-tha-the-on'], *f.* 1. Commercialization. 2. Marketing.

comercializar [co-mer-the-ah-le-thar'], *va.* 1. To commercialize. 2. To market.

comercialmente [co-mer-te-al-men'-tay], *adv.* Commercially.

comerciante [co-mer-the-ahn'-tay], *m. pa.* Trader, merchant, trafficker.

comerciar [co-mer-the-ar'], *va. f.* To trade, to traffic. 2. *(Met.)* To commerce, to have intercourse with (personas, lugares).

comercio [co-merr'-the-o], *m.* 1. Trade, commerce, traffic; mart. **Comercio de**, trade in. **El comercio español**, Spanish trade. **Comercio exterior**, foreign trade. **Comercio de exportación**, export trade. 2. Communication, intercourse. 3. An unlawful connection between the sexes. 4. Body or company of merchants. 5. The most frequented place in large towns. 6. A kind of card game.

comestible [co-mes-tee'-blay], *a.* Eatable, edible. **Comestibles**, *m. pl.* Provisions, groceries. **Tienda de comestibles**, grocery store.

cometa [co-may'-tah], *m.* 1. Comet. **Cometa comado** or **crinito**, hairy comet. -*f.* 2. Kite, a plaything for boys. 3. Kind of card game in which the nine of diamonds is called **cometa**. 4. *(Her.)* Allegorical figure in form of a star. 5. *(Zool.)* A longicorn beetle of Brazil.

cometario, ia [co-may-tah'-re-o, ah], *a.* Relating to comets, cometary.

cometedor [co-may-tay-dor'], *m.* 1. Offender, a criminal. 2. Assaulter. *V.* ACOMETEDOR.

cometer [co-may-terr'], *va.* 1. To commit, to charge, to entrust. 2. To undertake, to attempt. 3. To attack, to assault. 4. To commit some criminal act or error. 5. *(Gram.)* To use tropes and figures. 6. *(Com.)* To order. -*vr.* 1. To expose oneself. 2.

To take something to one's charge. 3 To commit oneself, to make a mistake (equivocación).

cometido [co-may-tee'-do], *m.* Commission, charge, trust.

cometografía [co-may-to-grah'-fee-ah], *f.* Cometography.

comezón [co-may-thone'], *f.* 1. Itch or itching. **Siento comezón en el brazo,** my arm itches. 2. *(Met.)* The anxiety or trouble of mind produced by a longing desire.

comible [co-me'-blay], *a.* Edible, fit to eat.

cómicamente [co'-me-cah-men-tay], *adv.* Comically.

comic [co'-meec], *m.* **comics** *pl.* Comic.

cómica [co'-me-cah], *f.* Actress; comedian (comediante).

comicastro [co-me-cahs-tro], *m.* Ham, third-rate actor (actor).

comicial [co-me-the-ahl'], *a.* Pertaining to the Roman comitia; comitial.

comicidad [co-me-the-dahd'], *f.* Humor, comedy, comicalness.

comicios [co-mee'-the-ose], *m. pl.* 1. Comitia, Roman assembly. 2. Government elections, voting.

cómico, ca [co'-me-co, cah], *a.* 1. Comic, comical, relating to the stage. 2. Comic, comical, ludicrous, funny, mock.

cómico, *m.* **cómica.** *f.* [co'-me-co, cah] 1. Player, actor, comedian. *V.* COMEDIANTE. 2. *(Obs.)* Comedian, a writer of comedies.

comida [co-mee'-dah], *f.* 1. Eating, food, dressed victuals. 2. Dinner; fare, feed. 3. The board. **Comida y alojamiento,** board and lodging. **Hacer una buena comida,** to make a good meal. **Comida rápida,** fast food. **Bendecir la comida,** to say grace.

comidilla [co-me-deel'-lyah], *f.* 1. *(dim.)* A slight repast. 2. Peculiar pleasure afforded by something which strikes our fancy. 3. **Ser la comidilla de la ciudad,** to be the talk of the town.

comido, da [co-mee'-do, dah], *a.* Satiate, full to satiety. **Comido por servido,** meat for work signifying the small value of any employ. *-pp.* of COMER. *(Yo me comido, él se comidió,* from *Comedirse. V.* PEDIR.)

comience [co-me-ayn'-thay], *m. (And.) V.* COMIENZO.

comienzo [co-me-en´-tho], *m.* Origin, beginning, initiation. **Al comienzo,** from the beginning. **En los comienzos de este siglo,** at the beginning of this century. *(Yo comienzo, yo comience,* from *Comenzar. V.* ACERTAR.)

comilitón [co-me-le-tone'], *m.* Parasite, sponger. *V.* CON-MILITÓN.

comilitona, comilona [co-me-le-to'-nah, co-me-lo'-nah], *f. (Coll.)* A splendid and plentiful repast.

comilón, na [co-me-lone', nah], *m. & f.* A great eater, a glutton.

comilla [co-meel'-lyah], *f. dim.* fr. COMA. *-pl.* Quotation marks (" "). Also guiding marks (,,).

cominillo [co-me-neel'-lyo], *m.* Darnel. *V.* JOYO.

comino [co-mee'-no], *m. (Bot.)* Cumin plant, cuminseed. **Cominos,** cuminseed. **No vale** or **no monta un comino,** it is not worth tuppence. **No se me da un comino.** *(Coll.)* It's not worth a damn. **No me importa un comino,** I don´t care two hoots.

comisar [co-me-sar´], *va.* To confiscate (confiscar), to declare a thing confiscated; to sequestrate (secuestrar), to attach.

comisaría [co-me-sah-ree'-ah], *f.* **comisariato,** *m.* Commissaryship, commissariat, police station; sheriff's office.

comisario [co-me-sah'-re-o], *m.* Commissary, delegate, deputy, manager; **comisario de entradas,** in some hospitals, the person charged with taking an account of the patients who enter. **Comisario de cuartel** or **de barrio,** justice of the peace of a ward. **Comisario de policía,** police super-intendent.

comiscar [co-mes-car'], *va.* To nibble from time to time.

comisión [co-me-se-on´], *f.* 1. Trust, commission, warrant by which a trust is held. 2. Mandate, charge, precept, or commission sent or transmitted; ministration, ministry. 3. Commission, perpetration, act of committing a crime. **Pecado de comisión,** a sin of commission. 4. Commission,

committee. **Comisión de preparativos y disposiciones,** committee of arrangements. **Comisiones obreras,** worker´s unions. **Comisión permanente,** standing committee. 5. Commission (pago). **Comisión sobre las ventas,** sales commission.

comisionado, da [co-me-se-o-nah'-do, dah], *a. & pp.* of COMISIONAR. 1. Commissional or commissionary. 2. Commissioned, deputed, empowered. *-m. & f.* 1. Commissioner. 2. *(Com.)* Agent, proxy.

comisionar [co-me-se-o-nar'], *va.* To commission, to depute, to empower, to appoint.

comisionista [co-me-se-o-nees'-tah], *m.* 1. Commissioner. 2. Commission merchant. 3. Commission agent.

comiso [co-mee'-so], *m.* 1. *(Law.)* Confiscation of prohibited goods, and the goods when confiscated. 2. *(Com.)* Seizure, attachment.

comisorio, ria [co-me-so-re-o, ah], *a.* Obligatory for a time or valid for a fixed day.

comisquear [co-mes-kay-ar'], *va. V.* COMISCAR.

comistión [co-mis-te-on´], *f. V.* CONMISTIÓN.

comistrajo [co-mis-trah´-ho], *m. (Coll.)* Hodgepodge, a medley of eatables.

comisura [co-me-soo'-rah], *f.* 1. *(Anat.)* Commissure, suture. **Comisura de los labios,** corner of the mouth. 2. Corner, angle.

comital [co-me-tahl'], *a. V.* CONDAL.

cómite [co'-me-tay], *m.* Count. *V.* CONDE.

comité [co-me-tay'], *m.* Committee; **Comité de No Intervención,** Non Intervention Committee.

comitente [co-me-ten'-tay], *pa.* Constituent.

comitiva [co-me-tee'-vah], *f.* Suite, retinue, followers.

cómitre [co'-me-tray], *m. (Naut.)* 1. Boatswain on board a galley. 2. A sea-captain under orders of the admiral of the fleet.

comiza [co-mee'-thah], *f. (Zool.)* A kind of barbel.

como [co'-mo], *adv.* 1. How, in what manner, to what degree. **¿Cómo estamos de cosecha?** how is the harvest? 2. **As,** in a sense of comparison, e. g. **Es tan fuerte como un león,** he is as strong as a lion. 3. Why? 4. In such a manner. **Hago como tú haces,** I do as you do. 5. In what manner. **Diga Vd. cómo hemos llegado,** please, say in what condition we arrived. 6. If. **Como sea todo así...,** if it is all like this... 7. Like, in the same manner, in the same manner as. 8. So that. 9. Used in a causal sense it precedes *que.* 10. Used with the subjunctive it is equivalent to the gerund of the same verb. **Dar como** or **dar un como,** *(Coll.)* to play a trick, to joke. **Como quiera que sea,** however, at any rate. **Como quiera,** however, notwithstanding, nevertheless, yet: used with the negative *no.* **Como quiera que,** notwithstanding that, although, yet, howsoever. **Como** used interrogatively or as an exclamation receives the accent: **¡Cómo! ¿Cómo son?,** what are they like? **¿Cómo es de alto?,** how tall is it? **No veo cómo,** I don´t see how. *-conj.* 1. As, since. **Como no tenía dinero,** as I had no money. **Como que...,** because.... **Hacía como que no nos veía,** he pretended not to see us.

cómoda [co'-mo-dah], *f.* A chest of drawers, bureau.

comodable [co-mo-dah'-blay], *a.* That which can be lent or borrowed.

cómodamente [co'-mo-dah-men-tay], *adv.* Conveniently, commodiously, comfortably.

comodante [co-mo-dahn'-tay], *m. (For.)* One who lends gratuitously for a limited time.

comodatario [co-mo-dah-tah´-re-o], *m. (Law.)* 1. Borrower. 2. Pawnbroker.

comodato [co-mo-dah'-to], *m. (Law.)* Loan; a contract of loan and restitution at a stipulated time.

comodidad [co-mo-de-dahd'], *f.* 1. Comfort, convenience, accommodation. **Pensar en su propia comodidad,** to consider one´s own convenience. **Venga a su comodidad,** come at your convenience. 2. Convenience, ease, or cause of ease freedom from want. 3. Leisure: opportunity. 4. Profit, interest, advantage. 5. **Comodidades**, comforts, amenities, pleasant things.

comodín [co-mo-deen'], *m.* 1. *(Coll.)* Something of general utility; in cards, to make a suit. 2. *(Mec. etc.)* Useful gadget. 3. Pretext, excuse, standby. 4. *(Ling.)* Catch-all, useful vague word, all-purpose word. a. *(And. Carib. Mex.)* V. COMODON.

cómodo [co'-mo-do], *m.* Utility, profit, convenience.

cómodo, da [co'-mo-do, dah], *a.* Convenient, commodious, suitable, comfortable. **Así estarás cómodo**, you'll be comfortable this way. **Ponerse cómodo**, to make oneself comfortable.

comodón [co-mo-done'], *a.* Comfort-loving (regalón); easy-going (pasivo); spoiled, spoilt. **Es muy comodón**, he'll do anything for a quiet life.

comodonería [co-mo-do-nay-re'-ah], *f.* Love of comfort; liking for a quiet life.

comodoro [co-mo-do'-ro], *m.* Commodore.

comoquiera [co-mo-ke-ay'-rah], *conj. (Liter.)* 1. **Comoquiera que**..., since...., in view of the fact that. 2. **Comoquiera que sea eso**, however that may be, in whatever way that may be.

comorar [co-mo-rar'], *vn.* To cohabit, to live together.

compa [com'-pah], *m. (CAm.)* 1. *(Pol.)* Comrade. 2. Pal (amigo).

compacidad [com-pah-the-dahd'], *f.* Compactness.

compactación [com-pac-tah-the-on'], *f.* Compacting, compression.

compactar [com-pac-tar'], *va.* To compact, to press together.

compacto, ta [com-pac'-to, tah], *a.* Compact, close, dense.

compadecer [com-pah-day-thayr'], *va.* To pity, to be sorry for.

compadecerse [com-pah-day-therr-say], *vr.* 1. To pity, to be compassionate; in this sense it is now very often used in an active sense, as **compadezco a Vd.**, I pity you, I feel for you, I commiserate your distress. 2. To agree with each other. *(Yo me compadezco, yo me compadezca, from Compadecerse. V. CONOCER.)*

compadrada [com-pah-drah'-dah], *f. (Cono Sur)* Cheek, insolence.

compadrar [com-pah-drar'], *vn.* To become a godfather or mother, to contract a spiritual affinity.

compadrazgo [com-pah-drath'-go], *m.* 1. In canon law, a spiritual affinity or connection contracted by a godfather with the parents of a child for which he stands sponsor. 2. *(LAm.)* Close relationship.

compadre [com-pah'-drary], *m.* 1. Godfather, the word by which the godfather and godmother address the father of their godson or daughter, and by which the father and mother address him. 2. Protector, benefactor. 3. Friend. *4. (Cono Sur)* Braggart; show-off (engreído); bully (matón).

compadrear [com-pah-dray-ar'], *vn.* 1. To be pals (ser amigos). 2. *(Cono Sur)* to brag, to show off (presumir); to give threatening looks (amenazar).

compadrería [com-pah-dray-ree'-ah], *f.* Friendly intercourse between godfathers, friends, or companions.

compadrito [com-pah-dre'-to], *m. (LAm.)* V. COMPADRE.

compage [com-pah'-hay], *f.* Compages, a system of many parts united.

compaginación [com-pah-he-nah-theon'], *f.* Compagination, union, structure.

compaginador [com-pah-he-nah-dor'], *m.* One who joins, unites, or couples.

compaginar [com-pah-he-nar'], *va.* To join, to unite, to couple, to compact, to compaginate. -*vr.* To agree, to tally. **Compaginarse con**, to agree with. **No se compagina esa conducta con su cáracter**, such conduct does not fit in with his character.

companage [com-pah-nah'-hay], *m.* A cold lunch; bread, cheese, raisins, etc.

compaña [com-pah'-nyah], *f.* 1. Out-house, office. 2. Company of soldiers. 3. Family. 4. Company.

compañería [com-pah-nyay-ree'-ah], *f.* V. MANCEBÍA.

compañerismo [com-pah-nyay-rees'-mo], *m.* Harmony, good-fellowship; team spirit.

compañero, ra [com-pah-nyay'-ro, rah], *m. & f.* 1. Companion, friend, consort, an equal, a match, a compère, a mate, one with whom a person frequently converses; fellow. **Compañero de viaje**, fellow traveler. **Compañero de juego**, playmate. 2. **Compañero de cuarto**, roommate; chum, a roommate in the universities. 3. Comrade, colleague, fellowmember, condisciple. **Compañero de armas**, comrade-in-arms. **Compañero de trabajo**, workmate. 4. Partner, associate, coadjutor. 5. Follower, one who shares the lot and fortune of another. 6. One thing suited to another. **Dos calcetines que no son compañeros**, two socks which do not match. **¿Dónde está el compañero de éste?**, where is the one that goes with this?

compañía [com-pah-nyee'-ah], *f.* 1. Company or society of persons, an assembly or meeting together, fellowship. 2. Partnership, fellowship; copartnership, company. **Hacer compañía a uno**, to keep somebody company. **Andar en malas compañías**, to keep bad company. 3. Company, troop, a body of soldiers. 4. Company, a number of players. 5. Company, conversation of a companion. 6. Family confederacy. **Compañía de Jesús**, Order of Jesuits, founded by Ignatius de Loyola.

compaño, compañón [Com-pah-nyo], *m.* V. COMPAÑERO.

compañón [com-pah-nyone'], *m.* Testicle. V. TESTÍCULO.

comparable [com-pah-rah'-blay], *a.* Comparable.

comparación [com-pah-rah-the-on'], *f.* 1. Comparison, conference. **En comparación con**, in comparison with. **No tiene comparación**, it is beyond compare. 2. Compare; collation, conferring.

comparado [com-pah-rah'-do], *a.* 1. **Comparado con**, compared with, in comparison. 2. Comparative (estudio).

comparador [com-pah-rah-dor'], *m.* An instrument serving to show the smallest difference in the length of two rules; comparing-rule.

comparanza [com-pah-rahn'-thah], *f. (Coll.)* V. COMPARACIÓN.

comparar [com-pah-rar'], *va.* To compare, to estimate, to confront, to confer, to collate.

comparativamente [com-pah-rah-te vah-men'-tay], *adv.* Comparatively.

comparativo, va [com-pah-rah-tee'-vo, vah], *a.* 1. Comparative. 2. Comparative, a degree of comparison in grammar.

comparecencia [com-pah-ray-then'-theah], *f.* Appearance before a judge.

comparecer [com-pah-ray-therr'], *vn.* To appear before a judge.

compareciente [com-pah-ray-the-en'-tay], *pa.* of COMPARECER.

comparendo [com-pah-ren'-do], *m.* Summons, citation, admonition to appear. *(Yo comparezco, yo comparezca, from Comparecer.)*

comparición [com-pah-re-the-on'], *f. (Law.)* Appearance.

comparsa [com-par'-sah], *f.* 1. Retinue of characters represented on the stage. 2. A party composed of persons masked and costumed as students, Moors, soldiers, etc. -*m. & f. (Theat.)* Extra, supernumerary; *(Carib.)* Dance team.

comparsería [com-par-say-re'-ah], *f. (Theat.)* Extras, supernumeraries.

comparte [com-par'-tay], *m. & f. (Law.)* Joint party or accomplice in a civil or criminal cause.

compartimiento [com-par-te-me-en'-to], *m.* 1. Compartment, the division of a whole into proportionate parts. 2. Inclosure, department. **Compartimiento interior de un navío**, accommodations on board a ship. **Compartimiento de carga**, hold.

compartir [com-par-teer'], *va.* 1. To compart or divide into equal parts. 2. *(Art.)* To arrange or dispose the different parts of a painting. -*vn.* To divide, to share. **No comparto ese criterio**, I do not share that view.

compás [com-pahs'], *m.* 1. Pair of compasses, a mathematical instrument. *V.* PANTÓMETRA. **Compás de relojero**, clockmaker's compass. 2. A territory and district assigned to a monastery. 3. Power of the voice to express the notes of music. 4. Measure, time in music. **A compás**, in right musical time. **Al compás de la música**, in time to the music. **Entraron a los compases de un vals**, they came in to the strains of a waltz. 5. Motion of the hand of a conductor of an orchestra. 6. Measure, the space upon the staff between two bars. 7. Size, compass. 8. *(Met.)* Rule of life, principle to be governed by, pattern. 9. **Compás de muelle**, springs compass, springs of metal to raise or lower a coachroof. 10. **Compás de mar**, mariner's compass. *V.* BRÚJULA and BITACÓRA. 11. **Compás mixto**, *(Fenc.)* Mixed movement, partly direct and partly curved; a feint.

compasadamente [com-pah-sah-da.-men'-tay], *adv.* By rule and measure.

compasado [com-paah-sah'-do], *a.* Measured, moderate.

compasar [com-pah-sar'], *va.* 1. To measure with a rule and compass. 2. *(Met.)* To regulate things so that there may be neither too much nor too little. 3. *(Mus.)* To divide a musical composition into equal parts. 4. To adjust (tiempo).

compasible [com-pah-see'-blay], *a.* 1. Lamentable, deserving pity. 2. Compassionate.

compasillo [com-pah-seel'-lyo], *m.* Quick musical time.

compasión [com-pah-se-on'], *f.* Compassion, pity, commiseration, mercifulness; **tener compasión de**, to feel sorry for; **¡por compasión!,** for pity's sake!

compasivamente [com-pah-se-vah-mayn'-tay], *adv.* Compassionately; pityingly; sympathetically.

compasivo, iva [com-pah-see'-vo, vah], *a.* Compassionate, merciful, tender-hearted, humane.

compaternidad [com-pah-ter-ne-dahd'], *f. V.* COMPADRAZGO.

compatibilidad [com -pah-te-be-le-dahd'], *f.* Compatibility, consistency, conjuncture.

compatibilizar [com-tah-be-le-thar'], *va.* To harmonize, to bring into line, to make compatible.

compatible [com-pah-tee'-blay], *a.* Compatible, suitable to, fit for, consistent with.

compatricio [com-pah-tree'-the-o], or **compatriota** [com-pah-tre-o'-tah], *com.* Countryman or countrywoman, compatriot, fellow-citizen.

compatronato [com-pah-tro-nah'-to], *m.* Common right of patronage, the right of conferring a benefice in common with another.

compatrono, na [com-pah-tro'-no, nah], *m. & f.* Fellow-patron or patroness, joint-patron.

compeler, compelir [com-pay-lerr', coin-pay-leer'], *va.* 1 To compel, to constrain. 2. To extort.

compendiador [com-pen-de-ah-dor'], *m.* Epitomizer, abridger.

compendiar [com-pen-de-ar'], *va.* To epitomize, to shorten, to abridge, to extract, to contract; to cut short.

compendio [com-pen'-de-o], *m.* Compendium, epitome, abridgment, summary, compend, abstract.

compendiosamente [com-pen-de-o-sah-men'-tay], *adv.* Briefly, compendiously, in a concise manner.

compendioso, sa [com-pen-de-o'-so, sah], *a.* Brief, abridged, compendious, laconic or laconical, compact.

compendizar [com-pen-de-thar'], *va. V. COMPENDIAR.*

compenetración [com-pay-nay-trah-the-on'], *f.* Mutual understanding, fellow feeling, natural sympathy; mutual influence.

compenetrarse [com-pay-nay-trar'-say], *vr.* 1. *(Quim. etc.)* To interpenetrate, to fuse. 2. *(fig.)* To share each other's feelings; to undergo mutual influence; to enter into the spirit of.

compensable [com-pen-sah-blay], *a.* Compensable.

compensación [com-pen-sah-the-on], *f.* 1. Compensation, recompense. 2. Handicap (en deportes). 3. *(Com.)* Clearing; **bolsa** or **banco de compensación**, clearing house.

compensador [com-pen-sah-dor'], *m.* Compensator, a mechanical device of two or more metals to counteract the effect of variations of temperature.

compensar [com-pen-sar'], *va. & vn.* 1. To compensate, to counterbalance, to countervail. 2. To make amends, to make up. **Los malos años se compensan con los buenos**, good years make amends for bad ones. 3. To enjoy an equivalent for any loss or injury, to compensate. **Le compensaron con 100 dólares por los cristales rotos**, they gave him 100 dollars' compensation for the broken windows.

compensatorio [com-pen-sah-to'-re-o], *a.* Compensatory.

competencia [com-pay-ten'-the-ah], *f.* 1. Competition, rivalry, contest, contention. **Competencia desleal**, unfair competition. **En competencia con**, in competition with. 2. Competence, cognizance, the power or competency of a court or judge. 3. Incumbency. 4. Aptitude, fitness. **A competencia**, contentiously, contesting. 5. Domain, field, province. **Y otras cosas de su competencia**, and other things which concern him. **No es de mi competencia**, that is not my responsibility.

competente [com-pay-ten'-tay], *a.* Competent, sufficient, fit for, consistent with, applicable to; adequate. **Esto se elevará al ministerio competente**, this will be sent to the appropriate ministry. **De fuente competente**, from a reliable source.

competentemente [com-pay-ten-tay-men'-tay], *adv.* Competently, appropriately.

competer [com-pay-terr'], *vn.* To be one's due, to have a fair claim to something.

competición [com-pay-te-the-on'], *f.* Competition, rivalry. *V.* COMPETENCIA.

competidor, ra [com-pay-te-dor', rah], *m. & f.* Competitor, rival, opponent, contender; competitrix.

competir [com-pay-teer'], *vn.* 1. To vie, to contest, to contend, to strive. 2. To stand in competition, to rival, to cope. 3. To be on a level or par with another, to rival, to vie with. **Los dos cuadros compiten en belleza**, the two pictures vie with each other in beauty.

competitividad [com-pay-te-te-ve-dahd'], *f.* Competitiveness.

competitivo [com-pay-te-te'-vo], *a.* Competitive.

compilación [com-pe-lah-the-on'], *f.* 1. Compilation. 2. Compilement.

compilador, ra [com-pe-lah-dor', rah], *m. & f.* Compiler, compilator, collector.

compilar [com-pe-lar'], *va.* To compile.

compincharse [com-peen-chahr'-say], *vr.* To band together, to team up.

compinche [com-peen'-chay], *m. (Coll.)* Bosom friend, comrade, confidant, crony. *(Yo compito, yo compita,* from *Competir. V.* PEDIR.)

complacedero, ra [com-plah-thay-day'-ro, rah], *a. V.* COMPLACIENTE.

complacencia [com-plah-then'-the-ah], *f.* Pleasure, satisfaction, gratification; complacency, compliance, condescendence. **Lo hizo con complacencia**, he did it gladly.

complacer [com-plah-therr'], *va.* To please, to humor, to content. **Nos complace que sea así**, we are glad it is so. *-vr.* To be pleased with or take delight in a thing. **El Banco se complace en comunicar a su clientela que...**, the Bank is glad to tell its clients that...

complacido [com-plah-the-do], *a.* Pleased, satisfied. **Me miró complacido**, she gave me a grateful look.

complaciente [com-plah-the-en'-tay], *pa.* Pleasing, one who pleases.

complañir [com-plah-nyeer'], *vn. (Obs.)* To weep, to be compassionate. *(Yo complazco, yo complazca,* from *Complacer. V.* CONOCER.).

complejidad [com-play-he-dahd'], *f.* Complexity.

complejo, ja [com-play'-ho, hah], *a.* Complex. *V.* COMPLEXO.

complementario, ia [com-play-men-tah'-re-o, ah], *a.* Complementary, serving to complete.

complemento [com-play-men'-to], *m.* 1. Complement, perfection, accomplishment, completion; accomplishment. 2. *(Ling.)* Complement, object; complemento directo, direct object. 3. Essential part, natural concomitant. **El vino es un complemento de la buena comida**, wine is an essential complement to good food. 4. *(Aut.)* Accessories. 5. *(Mil.)* Oficial de complemento, reserve officer.

completa [com-play'-tah], *f. (Carib.) (Culin.)* Full meal.

completamente [com-play-tah-men'-tay], *adv.* Completely, perfectly, finally.

completar [com-play-tar'], *va.* To complete, to perfect, to finish, to accomplish, to crown, to consummate, to make up.

completas [com-play'-tas], *f. pl.* Compline, the last of the canonical hours or evening prayers.

completivamente, *adv.* V. COMPLETIVO.

completivo, va [com-play-tee'-vo, vah], *a.* Completive, absolute.

completo, ta [com-play'-to, tah], *a.* Complete, perfect, finished; concluded; full, absolute, all-out. **Por completo**, completely, totally. **Fue un completo fracaso**, it was a complete failure.

complexión [com-plek-se-on'], *f.* Constitution, temperament of the body, habit, nature.

complexionado, da [com-plek-se-o-nah'-do, dah], *a.* Constituted. **Bien o mal complexionado**, of a good or bad constitution.

complexional [com-plek-se-o-nahl,], *a.* Constitutional, temperamental.

complexo [com-plek'-so], *m.* Complex.

complexo [com-plek'-so], *a.* 1. Arduous, difficult, complicated. 2. Complex, not simple; of several parts. 3. *(Anat.)* Applied to one of the muscles of the head.

complicación [com-ple-cah-the-on'], *f.* Complication, complex, complexure; **una persona sin complicación**, an uncomplicated person.

complicadamente, *adv.* V. COMPLICADO.

complicado, da, *a.* Complicated, complex. *-pp.* of COMPLICAR.

complicar [com-ple car'], *va.* To complicate, to jumble things together. *-vr.* 1. To get complicated. 2. **Complicarse en un asunto**, to get involved in a matter.

cómplice [com'-ple-thay], *com.* Accomplice, cooperator, associate, complice, abetter, accessory.

complicidad [com-ple-the-dahd'], *f.* Accessoriness, complicity.

compló [com-plo'], *m.* V. COMPLOT.

complot [com-plot'], *m.* Plot, conspiracy, a joint agreement to commit crime.

complutense [com-ploo-ten'-say], *a. & n.* Native of or belonging to Alcalá de Henares.

componedor, ra [com-po-nay-dor', rah], *m. m. & . f.* Composer, writer, author 2. Arbitrator.

componenda [com-po-nen'-dah], *f.* 1. Compromise (acuerdo); settlement (provisional), arrangement (temporalmente). 2. Shady deal.

componente, *pa.* [com-po-nayn'-tay], *a.* Component. *-m. (Quim. etc.)* Component; ingredient (de bebida etc.). **Componentes lógicos**, software *(Inform.).* **Un viento de componente norte**, a northerly wind.

componer [com-po-nerr'], *va.* 1. To compose, to compound. 2. To construct. 3. To sum up. 4. To frame, to devise, to invent 5. To mend, to repair, to heal, to restore. 6. To strengthen, to fortify, to restore. 7. To furnish, to fit up, to garnish. 8. To compose, to reconcile, to accommodate, to adjust, to settle, to compose differences. 9. To ward off a danger. 10. To compose, to calm, to quiet. 11. *(Mus.)* To note, to set down the notes of a tune, to form a tune. 12. To compose or compile a boo. 13. To compose or write verses. **Él compone muy bien**, he writes very good verses. 14. *(Print.)* To compose types. *-vr.* 1. To deck oneself with clothes. 2. **Componerse de**, to consist of. **Se compone de seis partes**, it consists of 6 parts. 3. **Componerse con uno**,

to come to terms with somebody. 4. **Componérselas**, to manage, to get along. 5. *(LAm.) (Med.)* To recover, to get better. **Las cosas se compondrán**, everything will be all right.

componible [com-po-nee'-blay], *a.* Compoundable, accommodable, mendable,

comporta [com-por'-tah], *f. (Prov.)* A large basket in which grapes are carried during the vintage.

comportable [com-por-tah'-blay], *a.* Supportable, tolerable.

comportamiento [com-por-tah-me-en'-to], *m. (Prov.)* Behavior, conduct.

comportar [com-por-tar'], *va.* 1. To carry or bring together. 2. To suffer, to tolerate. 3. To involve, to carry with it. **Ello no comporta obligación alguna**, it carries no obligation. *-vr.* To comport, to behave or conduct oneself. **Comportarse como es debido**, to behave properly.

comporte [com-por'-tay], *m.* 1. *V.* SUFRIMIENTO. 2. Proceeding, conduct. 3. Air, manner.

comportilla [com-por-teel'-lyah], *f. dim.* A small basket:

composición [com-po-se-the-on'], *f.* 1. Composition, the act of composing something, composure, making up. 2. Composition of a difference, adjustment, agreement, compact. 3. A literary, scientific, or musical work. 4. *(Print.)* Arrangement of types. 5. Calm, modest, or sedate appearance.

compositivo, va [com-po-se-tee'-vo, vah], *a.* Compositive, synthetic; used of a preposition or particle forming a compound word.

compositor, ra [com-po-se-tor'], *m. & f.* 1. Composer of musical compositions. 2. *(Print.)* Compositor. 3. *(Cono Sur)* Quack doctor, bone-settler.

compostura [com-pos-too'-rah], *f.* 1. Composition, composure. 2. Mending or repairing. **Estar en compostura**, to be undergoing repairs. 3. Cleanliness, neatness of dress. 4. Composition of a difference, composure, accommodation, adjustment, agreement, compact. **Perder la compostura**, to lose one's composure. 5. Modesty, circumspection, sedateness, composure. 6. A mixture with which something is adulterated.

compota [com-po'-tah], *f.* Preserves, sweetmeats, compote. **Compota de manzanas**, stewed apples.

compotera [Com-po-tay'-rah], *f.* Vessel in which jams are served up for the table.

compra [com'-prah], *f.* 1. Purchase. **Compra al contado**, cash purchase; **compra a plazos**, hire purchase. 2. Collection of necessaries bought for daily use, shopping. **Hacer las compras**, to do the shopping.

comprable [com-prah'-blay], *a.* Purchasable.

comprador, ra [com-prah-dor'-rah], *m.&.f.* 1. Buyer, purchaser. 2. Caterer.

comprante [com-prahn'-tay], *pa.* Buyer, purchaser.

comprar [com-prar'], *va.* 1. To buy, to purchase, to shop; to acquire. **Comprar al contado**, to pay cash for. **Comprar a plazos**, to buy on installments. 2. *(fig.)* To buy off, to bribe; to win over.

compraventa [com-prah-ven'-tah], *f.* Buying and selling. *V.* CONTRATO DE COMPRAVENTA.

comprendedor, ra [com-pren-day-dor', rah], *m. & f.* One who comprehends or understands.

comprender [com-pren-derr'], *va.* 1. To embrace, to encircle, to comprehend. 2. To comprise, to include, to contain. **Servicio no comprendido**, service not included. **Todo comprendido**, everything included. 3. To comprehend, to understand, to conceive, to know. **No comprendo cómo**, I don't see how. **Comprendo su actitud**, I understand his attitude. **Hacerse comprender**, to make oneself understood.

comprensibilidad [com-pren-se-be-le-dahd'], *f.* Comprehensibleness, comprehensibility.

comprensible [com-pren-see'-blay], *a.* Comprehensible, conceivable.

comprensiblemente, *adv.* Comprehensibly.

comprensión [com-pren-se-on'], *f.* 1. Comprehension, comprisal, conceiving, conception. 2. Comprehensiveness. 3. Act of comprising or containing. 4. Understanding; sympathy, tolerance, kindness.

comprensivo, va [com-pren-see'-vo, vah], *a.* 1. Comprehensive, having the power to comprehend. 2. Comprehensive, having the quality of comprising much.

comprensor, ra [com-pren-sor', rah], *m. & f.* 1. (*Theol.*) The blessed, one who enjoys the presence of God in the heavenly mansions. 2. One that understands, attains, or embraces a thing.

compresa [com-pray'-sah], *f.* Compress, folded linen put under a bandage. **Compresa higiénica,** sanitary towel.

compresibilidad [com-pray-se-be-le-dahd'], *f.* Compressibility.

compresible [com-pray-see'-blay], *a.* Compressible.

compresión [com-pray-se-on'], *f.* 1. Compression, pressing together, compressure. 2. (*Gram.*) V. SINÉRESIS.

compresivamente [com-pray-se-vah-men'-tay], *adv.* Compressibly, contractedly.

compresivo, va [com-pray-see'-vo, vah], *a.* Compressive, compressing or reducing to a smaller compass.

compresor [com-pray-sor'], *m.* Compressor.

comprimible [com-pre-mee'-blay], *a.* 1. Compressible. 2. Repressible.

comprimido [com-pre-me'-do], *a.* Compressed. -*m.* Tablet, pill. **Comprimido para dormir,** sleeping pill.

comprimir [com-pre-meer'], *va.* 1. To compress; to constrain; to condense. 2. To repress, to restrain, to keep in awe. -*vr.* 1. To subdue one's passion. **Tuve que comprimirme para no reír,** I had to keep myself from laughing.

comprobable [com-pro-bah'-blay], *a.* Verifiable, capable of being checked. **Un alegato fácilmente,** an allegation which is easy to check.

comprobación [com-pro-bah-the-on'], *f.* 1. Comprobation, attestation. 2. Comparison, verification of printer's proof corrections. **En comprobación de ello,** in proof whereof, as proof of what I stay. **De difícil comprobación,** hard to check. **Comprobación de paridad par,** (*Inform.*) even parity check.

comprobador [com-pro-bah-dor'], *m.* Tester.

comprobante [com-pro-bahn'-tay], *pa.* 1. Proving, one who proves. 2. Voucher, schedule, document. **Documento comprobante,** supporting document.

comprobar [com-pro-bar'], *va.* 1. To verify, to confirm by comparison. 2. To comprobate; to compare. 3. To prove, to give evidence.

comprofesor [com-pro-fay-sor'], *m.* Colleague.

comprometedor, ra [com-pro-may-tay-dor', rah], *m. & f.* Compromiser, one who compromises. -*a.* Compromising.

comprometer [com-pro-may-terr'], *va.* 1. To compromise. **Aquellas cartas le comprometieron,** those letters compromised him. 2. To engage, to bind by an appointment or contract; to render one accountable or answerable. 3. To expose, to put in danger. **Comprometer la reputación,** to risk one's reputation. 4. To agree formally. 4. **Comprometer a uno a algo,** to hold somebody to something. -*vr.* 1. To comprise oneself, to get involved. 2. To undertake, to promise to. **Se compromete a todo,** he'll say yes to anything.

comprometido, da [com-pro-may-tee'-do, dah], *a.* 1. Obligated, obliged. 2. Engaged to be married. -*m. & f.* Fiancé, fiancée.

comprometimiento [com-pro-may-te-me-en'-to], *m.* Compromise, a compact or adjustment.

compromisario, ria [com-pro-me-sah'-re-o], *m.f.* Arbitrator, umpire, compromiser, referee.

compromiso [com-pro-mee'-so], *m.* 1. Compromise. 2. Arbitration bond. 3. Difficulty, embarrassment. **Estar en un fuerte compromiso,** to be in real difficulty. **Poner a uno en un compromiso,** to place somebody in an embarrassing situation. 4. An obligation contracted. **Poner en compromiso,** to compromise, to render doubtful. **Libre de compromiso,** without

obligation. **Atender sus compromisos,** to meet one's obligations. **Tener muchos compromisos,** to have many commitments. 5. Agreement. **Compromiso matrimonial,** engagement. **Compromiso verbal,** verbal agreement.

compropietario, in [com-pro-pe-ay-tah'-re-o, ah], *m. & f. & a.* Joint owner, owning jointly with another, or others. *V.* COPROPIETARIO.

comprotector [com-pro-tec-tor'], *m.* A joint protector.

compuerta [com-poo-err'-tah], *f.* 1. Hatch or halfdoor. 2. Lock or sluice, floodgate. **Compuerta de marea,** (*Naut.*) tidegate, tiderace.

compuestamente [com-poo-es-tah-nen'-tay], *adv.* Regularly, orderly.

compuesto [com-poo-es'-to], *m.* Compound, commixture, composition. **Compuesto químico,** chemical compound.

compuesto, ta [com-poo-es'-to, tah], *a. & pp.* of COMPONER. Composed, compound, complex, made up; fresh, repaired. **Orden compuesto,** the composite order in architecture. **Flores compuestas,** composite flowers; the family of Compositae. **Estar compuesto de,** to be composed of.

compulsa [com-pool'-sah], *f.* 1. (*Law.*) An authentic or attested copy of some instrument or writing. 2. To collate, to compare.

compulsar [com-pool-sar'], *va.* 1. (*Obs.*) To compel, to force. 2. (*Law.*) To make an authentic copy or transcript. 3. To compare, to collate.

compulsión [com-pool-se-on'], *f.* 1. Compulsion, forcing. 2. Compulsion.

compulsivo, va [com-pool-see'-vo, vah], *a.* Compulsive, compulsory.

compulso, sa [com-pool'-so, sah], *pp. irr.* of COMPELER.

compulsorio, ria [com-pool-so'-re-o, ah], *a.* 1. Compulsory, compulsatory. 2. Ordering an authentic copy to be made: applied to the decree of a judge or magistrate.

compunción [com-poon-the-on'], *f.* Compunction, repentance, contrition.

compungido, da [com-poon-hee'-do, dah], *a.* Compunctious, sorry. -*pp.* of COMPUNGIR.

compungir [com-poon-heer'], *va.* To make remorseful, to arouse feelings of contrition in.

compungirse [com-poon-heer'-say], *vr.* To feel compunction, to be pierced with remorse.

compungivo, va [com-poon-hee'-vo, vah], *a.* Compunctive, pricking, stinging.

compurgación [com-poor-gah-the-on'], *f.* Compurgation.

compurgador [com-poor-gah-dor'], *m.* Compurgator.

compurgar [com-poor-gar'], *va.* To prove one's veracity or innocence by the oath of another.

computable [com-poo-tah'-blay], *a.* Computable.

computación [com-poo-tah-the-on'], *f.* Computation, manner of calculating time.

computador, ra [com-poo-tah-dor', rah], *m. & f.* 1. One who computes (persona). Computer (aparato). **Computadora digital,** (*Mech.*) digital computer.

computar [com-poo-tar'], *va.* To compute, to estimate by years or ages.

computerización [com-poo-tay-re-thah-the-on'], *f.* Computerization.

computerizar [com-poo-tay-re-thar'], *va.* To computerize.

computista [com-poo-tees'-tah], *m.* Computist, computer, user.

cómputo [com'-poo-to], *m.* Computation, calculation account. **Según nuestros cómputos,** according to our calculations.

comulación [co-moo-lah-the-on'], *f.* Cumulation. *V.* ACUMULACIÓN.

comulgar [co-mool-gar'], *va.* To administer the holy Eucharist. -*vn.* To communicate or to receive the sacrament.

comulgatorio [co-mool-gah-to'-re-o], *m.* Communion altar.

común [co-moon'], *a.* 1. Common. **Los intereses comúnes,** common interests. **A no tiene nada de común con B,** A has nothing in common with B. 2. Common, usual, general, customary, ordinary, familiar, generally received. **Es costumbre muy común,** it is a very widespread custom. 3. Common, much used, frequent, current, habitual. 4. Vulgar, mean, low. **Por lo común,** in general, genenerally.

común [co-moon'], *m.* 1. Community, public. 2. V. SECRETA. **En común,** conjointly, collectively; **por lo común,** commonly, frequently. 3. Toilet. 4. **Los Comunes,** the Commons (Britain).

comuna [co-moo'-nah], *f.* 1. *(Prov.)* The principal canal of irrigation. 2. Commune (comunidad). 3. *(LAm.)* Municipality, city council.

comunal [co-moo-nahl'], *m.* Commonalty, common people. -*a.* Common, commonable.

comunalmente [co-moo-nahl'-men-tay], *adv.* Communally; as a community.

comunaleza [co-moo-nah-lay'-thah], *f.* 1. Mediocrity. 2. Communication, intercourse. 3. Common.

comunero, ra [co-moo-nay'-ro, rah], *a.* 1. Popular, common, and pleasing to the people. 2. Commoner, one of the common people, as distinguished from the nobility.

comunero *m.* 1. A joint holder of a tenure of lands. 2. An individual of the party that upheld Spanish liberty against the encroachments of Charles V.

comunicabilidad [co-moo-ne-cah-be-le-dahd'], *f.* Communicability.

comunicable [co-moo-ne-cah'-blay], *a.* 1. Communicable. 2. Sociable, affable.

comunicación [co-moo-ne-cah-the-on'], *f.* 1. Communication. **Las comunicaciones están rotas,** communications are broken. **No hemos tenido más comunicación con él,** we have had no further contact with him. **Comunicaciones interactivas remotas** *(Inform.),* remote interactive communications. 2. Communication, intercourse, converse. 3. Junction or union of one thing with an other. 4. Message; report. 5. *(Liter.)* Rhetorical question. 6. **No hay comunicación entre los dos pueblos,** *(Mex.)* there´s no way of getting from one town to the other.

comunicado [co-moo-ne-cah'-do], *m.* An article of a personal nature sent to a periodical for publication.

comunicante [co moo ne cahn'-tay], *pa.* Communicating, a communicant; letter writer.

comunicar [co-moo-ne-car'], *va.* 1. To communicate, to impart, to extend, to discover or make known. **Nos comunicó su miedo,** he affected us with his fear. 2. To communicate with another either by word or writing. 3. To consult or confer upon a subject. 4. To communicate, to take the Lord's Supper. 5. To connect, to join, to open a way between. **Cuartos comunicados,** connecting rooms. -*vr.* To be joined, united, or contiguous to each other. **Comunicarse entre sí,** to interchange sentiments or ideas. -*vn.* 1. To send a report. **Comunican desde Lisboa que...,** it is reported from Lisbon that... 2. *(Telec.)* **Estar comunicando,** to be engaged. 3. *(Arch.)* **Comunicarse con,** to connect with.

comunicativo, va [co-moo-ne-cah-tee'-vo, vah], *a.* Communicative, liberal, not reserved.

comunidad [co-moo-ne-dahd'], *f.* 1. Commonness. 2. Commonalty, the common people. 3. Community, corporation, guild, society. **De comunidad,** conjointly, collectively; **Comunidad Europea,** European Community. **Comunidad Británica de Naciones,** British Commonwealth. **Comunidad de vecinos,** residents´ association. 4. The cities of Castile, which at the beginning of the reign of Charles V rose against his government, in support of Spanish liberty.

comunión [co-moo-ne-on'], *f.* 1. Communion, fellowship, common possession. 2. Familiar intercourse. 3. Communion, the act of receiving the blessed sacrament. 4. Congregation of persons who profess the same religious faith.

comunismo [co-moo-nees'-mo], *m.* Communism, the doctrine of the community of property.

comunista [co-moo-nees'-tah], *m. & f.* Communist, an advocate of communism.

comunistoide [co-moo-nees-toy'-day], *m.* Fellow traveler, communist sympathizer.

comunitario [co-moo-ne-tah-re-o], *a.* 1. Community. 2. Member of the European Community. -*m.* Member nation of the EC.

comúnmente [co-moon-men'-tay], *adv.* 1. Commonly, customarily, usually, generally. 2. Frequently, often.

comuña [co-moo'-nyah], *f.* 1. Mixed grain; as wheat and rye, mashlim, or meslin. **Comuñas,** seeds. V. CAMUÑAS.

con [cone], *prep.* 1. With, by. **Atado con cuerda,** tied with string. **Con su ayuda,** with his help. 2. Although. **Con tal que** or **con que,** so that, provided that, on condition that. **Yo lo haré, con tal que,** etc., I will do it, provided that, etc. 3. **Con que,** then, so then. **Con que Vd. ha hecho esto,** you have done this, then. **Con todo** or **con todo eso,** nevertheless, notwithstanding. **Con que vámonos,** well, then, let us go. **Con que, adiós, señoras,** then goodbye, ladies. **Con que sí, con que no,** Shillyshally. **Con tantas dificultades, no se descorazonó,** in spite of all the difficulties he was not discouraged. **Amable con todos,** kind to everybody. **Con decirle que no voy,** when I tell you I´m not going.

con que, *m. (Coll.)* Condition, stipulation, circumstance.

conato [co-nah'-to], *m.* 1. Conatus, endeavor, effort, exertion. 2. *(Law.)* Crime attempted but not executed. **Conato de hurto,** attempt at robbery.

conaviero [co-nah-ve-ay'-ro], *m.* Copartner, or part owner in a ship.

concadenar [con-cah-day-nar'], *va. (Met.)* To concatenate; to chain or link together.

concambio [con-cahm'-be-o], *m.* Exchange. V. CAMBIO.

concanónigo [con-ca-no'-ne-go], *m.* A fellow canon.

concatedralidad [con-cah-tay-drah-le.-dahd'], *f.* Union of two cathedral churches.

concatenación [con-cah-tay-nah-the-on´], *f.* Concatenation, linking. **Concatenación de circunstancias,** chain of circumstances.

concatenar [con-cah-tay-nar'], *va.* To link together, to concatenate.

concausa [con-cah'-oo-sah], *f.* A joint cause, a shared cause.

cóncava, concavidad [con'-cah-vah], *f.* Concavity, hollowness, hollow.

cóncavo, va [con'-cah-vo, vah], *a.* Concave, hollow.

cóncavo [con'-cah-vo], *m.* Concavity. V. CONCAVIDAD.

concebible [con-thay-bee'-blay], *a.* V. COMPRENSIBLE. **No es concebible que..,** it is unthinkable that.

concebimiento [con-thay-be-me-en'-to], *m.* Conception.

concebir [con-thay-beer'], *va. & vn.* 1. To conceive, to become pregnant. 2. To conceive, to imagine, to have an idea of. 3. To conceive, to comprehend, to think to understand; to look on. **La cláusula está concebida en estos términos,** the clause is expressed in these terms. **Concebir esperanzas,** to nourish hopes. **No concibo que...,** I cannot understand how...

concedente [con-thay-den'-tay], *pa.* Conceding, one who concedes.

conceder [con-thay-derr'], *va.* 1. To give, to grant, to bestow a boon or gift. 2. To concede, to allow, to grant. to admit.

concedido, da [con-thay-dee'-do, dah], *a. & pp.* of CONCEDER. Conceded, granted. **Dado y no concedido,** admitted but not agreed.

conceial, la [con-thay-hal'], *m. & f.* Member of a council or board.

concejal [con-thay-hal'], *a.* Relating to public boards or councils.

concejalía [con-thay-hah-le'-ah], *f.* Post of town councillor; seat on the city council.

concejil [con-thay-heel'], *m.* 1. An alderman, or member of a corporation. 2. *(Prov.)* Foundling, a child found without parent or owner.

concejil, *a.* Common, public, belonging to the public.

concejo [con-thay'-ho], *m.* 1. The civic body of a small town or village, and the house where its members hold their meetings. 2. District composed of several parishes with one common jurisdiction. 3. Foundling. **Concejo abierto**, a meeting of the inhabitants of a small town or village presided over by the *alcalde,* deliberate upon public affairs.

concelebrar [con-thay-lay-brar'], *va.* To celebrate jointly, together.

concento [con-then'-to], *m.* 1. Concord, a concert of voices, harmony. 2. Meter, verse, cadence.

concentración [con-then-trah-the-on´], *f.* 1. Concentration. 2. Gathering, meeting, rally. 3. *(LAm.) (Com.)* Merger.

concentrado, da [con-then-trah'-do, dah], *a.* Concentrated, tending to the center. *-pp.* of CONCENTRAR.

concentrar [con-then-trar'], *va.* To concentrate. *V.* RECONCENTRAR. *-vr.* 1. *(Mil.)* To gather together. 2. **Concentrarse a**, to concentrate on. **El interés se concentra en esta lucha,** the interest is centered on this fight.

concéntrico, ca [con-then'-tre-co, cah], *a.* Concentric, concentrical.

concepción [con-thep-the-on'], *f.* 1. Conception, the act of conceiving. 2. Conception, idea, comprehension, conceit, image in the mind, fancy.

conceptáculo [con-thep-tah´-coo-lo], *m.* 1. Conceptacle, a cavity containing the spores of cryptogamous plants. 2. Fruit, follicle.

conceptear [con-thep-tay-ar'], *vn.* To give smart repartees, to abound in witty sayings.

conceptible [con-thep-tee'-blay], *a.* Conceivable, that may be imagined.

conceptillo [con-thep-teel'-lyo], *m. dim.* A witty trifle, an attempt at wit.

conceptista [con-thep-tees'-tah], *m.* 1. A wit. 2. A man of genius, a man of fancy. 3. A humorist. 4. Punster.

concepto [con-thep'-to], *m.* 1. Conceit, thought, idea, conception. **Un concepto grandioso,** a bold conception. **Formarse un concepto de algo,** to get an idea of something. 2. Foetus. *V.* FETO. 3. Sentiment, striking thought, flash of wit, pun. 4. Judgment, opinion. 5. Estimation, favorable opinion. 6. Heading, section. **Bajo todos los conceptos,** from every point of view. **Por dicho concepto,** for this reason. **Se le pagó esa cantidad por concepto de derechos,** he was paid that amount as royalties. 7. *(Inform.)* **Concepto de Von Neumann,** Von Neumann concept.

conceptual [con-cep-too-ahl'], *a.* Conceptual.

conceptualismo [con-thep-too-ah-lees'-mo], *m.* A philosophical system, designed to reconcile nominalism and realism, dating from 12th century.

conceptualizar [con-thep-too-ah-le-thar'], *va.* To conceptualize.

conceptuar [con-thep-too-ar'], *va.* To conceive, judge, think or be of opinion. **Conceptúo que debe hacerse esto,** I am of opinion that this should be done. **Conceptuar a uno de,** to regard somebody as.

conceptuosamente [con-thep-too-o-sah-men'-tay], *adv.* Ingeniously, wittily.

conceptuoso, sa [con-thep-too-o'-so, sah], *a.* Witty, conceited.

concernencia [con-ther-nen'-the-ah], *f.* Concernment, relation, influence.

concerniente [con-ther-ne-en'-tay], *pa.* Concerning. **Por lo concerniente,** concerning.

concernir [con-ther-neer'], *v. imp.* To regard, to concern, to belong or appertain to. *V.* ATAÑER.

concertación [con-ther-tah-the-on'], *f.* Harmonizing; coordination; reconciliation.

concertadamente, *adv.* 1. Regularly, orderly, methodically. 2. By agreement.

concertado [con-ther-tah-do], 1. *a.* Methodical, systematic. 2. *m. f.* Contract worker.

concertador [con-ther-tah-dor'], *m.* Regulator, adjuster, expediter.

concertante [con-ther-tahn'-tay], *a. (Mus.)* Concerted, arrangement for two or more voices or instruments.

concertar [con-ther-tar'], *va.* 1. To concert, to settle by mutual communication, to adjust, to harmonize. **Concertar a varias personas para que...,** to get several people. 2. To settle the price of things. 3. To bargain, to covenant, to conclude an agreement. **Concertar una venta en 20 dólares,** to agree to sell something for 20 dollars. 4. To tune musical instruments. 5. To compare, to estimate the relative qualities of things. 6. To beat about the bush, to start or rouse the game. *-vn.* To agree, to accord, to suit one another. *-vr.* 1. To dress or deck oneself. 2. To go hand in hand; to concert, to contrive, to form or design.

concertina [con-ther-te'-nah], *f.* Concertina (instrumento).

concertino, na [con-ther-te'-no], *m. & f.* First violin, leader (de la orquesta); concertmaster.

concertista, [con-ther-tis'-tah], *m. & f.* Soloist, solo performer.

concesión [con-thay-se-on'], *f.* Concession, grant, granting or yielding acknowledgment.

concesionario [con-thay-se-o-nah'-re-o], *m.* 1. *(Law.)* Grantee. 2. Concessionary, one to whom a special privilege is granted.

concesivo [con-the-se'-vo], *a.* Concessive.

concha [con'-chah], *f.* 1. Shell. 2. Oyster. 3. Tortoise-shell. 4. An ancient copper coin, worth about three farthings, or eight maravedis. **Concha de nácar,** mother-of-pearl shell. 5. *(Arch.)* Volute, any ornament in the form of a shell, conch. 6. The external ear. 7. Shell of a dagger or cutlass. 8. The shell-shaped covering of the spike of Indian corn. 9. **Concha de cabrestante,** *(Naut.)* socket of the capstan. **Tener muchas conchas,** *(Met.)* to be very reserved, artful, cunning. 10. Flake, chip (porcelana). 11. Prompt, box (teatro.). 12. *(And. Carib.)* Nerve, cheek (descaro). **¡Qué concha la tuya!,** you´ve got a nerve! 13. *(And.)* Sloth, sluggishness (pereza). 14. *(Carib.)* Cartridge case (cartucho). 15. **Concha de su madre,** *(Cono Sur)* son of a bitch, bastard.

conchabado, da [con-chah-bah'-do], *m. & f. (LAm.)* Servant.

conchabanza [con-chah-bahn'-thah], *f.* 1. The manner of making oneself easy and comfortable. 2. *(Coll.)* The act of meeting or collecting in unlawful assemblies. 3. Plotting, conspiracy.

conchabar [con-chah-bar'], *va.* 1. To join, to unite. 2. To mix inferior wool with the superior or middling quality instead of separating it into three kinds at shearing-time. 3. *(LAm.)* To hire, to engage, to employ (criado). 4. *(LAm.)* To barter (trocar). *-vr.* 1. To unite, to join or unite for some evil purpose; to plot, to conspire. 2. *(LAm.)* To hire oneself out, to get a job (como criado).

conchabo [con-chah-bah-do], *m.* 1. *(LAm.)* Hiring, engagement (contratación). **Oficina de conchabo,** employment agency for domestics. 2. *(Cono Sur)* bater(ing).

conchado, da [con-chah'-do, dah], *a.* Scaly, crustaceous, shelly.

conchal [con-chahl´], *a. V.* SEDA CONCHAL.

cónchale [con'-chah-lay], *interj. (Carib.)* Well!, goodness!

conchil [con-cheel'], *m.* Rockshell. Murex, the mollusk which yielded the purple of the ancients. *Cf.* PÚRPURA.

conchilla, ita [con-cheel'-lyah, chee -tah], *f. dim.* A small shell.

conchite [con-chee'-tay], *f.* Conchite, a sort of petrified shell.

conchito [con-che'-to], *m. (And. Cono Sur)* youngest child, baby of the family.

concho [con'-cho], *m. (Carib.)* 1. Taxi. 2. *(CAm.) a.* Crude, vulgar. 3. *m.* Peasant; rustic. 4. Dregs, sediment; residue; left-overs (drogas). **Hasta el concho,** to the very end. 5. *(And. Cono Sur). (Anat.) V.* COÑO.

conchología [con-cho-lo-hee'-ah], *f.* Conchology.

conchudo, da [con-choo'-do, dah], *a.* 1. Scaly, crustaceous, ostraceous. 2. Cunning, crafty, close, reserved. -*m.* **Conchuda,** *f.* 1. *(And. Mex.)* Shameless person, cheeky bastard. 2. *(LAm.)* Stubborn person.

conchuela [con-choo-ay'-lah], *f. dim. V.* CONCHILLA.

concibimiento [con-the-be-me-en'-to], *m.* 1. Conceit, thought, idea, conception. 2. Act of conceiving.

conciencia [con-the-en'-the-ah], *f.* 1. Conscience. **Conciencia doble,** double personality. **Tener mala conciencia,** to have a bad conscience. 2. Scrupulosity, conscientiousness. 3. Consciousness, knowledge of one's personality. **Tener plena conciencia de,** to be fully aware of. **Tomar conciencia de que,** to become aware that. **Hacer conciencia de alguna cosa,** to be scrupulous about a thing. **A conciencia,** conscientiously. **En conciencia,** in earnest, in truth.

concienciación [con-the-ayn-the-ah-the-on'], f. Arousal, awakening.

concienciar [con-the-ayn-the-ar'], *va.* To arouse, to awaken, to make aware. -*vr.* To be aroused, to become aware of.

concienzudamente [con-the-ayn-thoo-dah-men'-tay], *adv.* Conscientiously, painstakingly, thoroughly.

concienzudo, da [con-the-en-thoo'-do, dah], *a.* Conscientious, scrupulous, exactly just: applied generally to a person too scrupulous.

concierto [con-the-err'-to], *m.* 1. The good order and arrangement of things. 2. Concert, communication of designs: bargain, agreement, or contract between two or three persons. **Quedar de concierto a cerca de,** to be in agreement with regard to. 3. Accommodation. 4. Act of beating the wood with hounds to start the game. 5. Concert, an assembly of musicians performing a musical composition. 6. Concert, a piece of music composed for a concert. **De concierto,** according to agreement, by common consent. *(Yo concierto, yo concierto from Concertar. V.* ACERTAR.*)*

conciliable [con-the-le-ah'-blay], *a.* Reconcilable, capable of conciliation.

conciliábulo [con-the-le-ah'-boo-lo], *m.* Secret meeting (reunión); unlawful assembly; confabulation (entrevista).

conciliación [con-the-le-ah-the-on'], *f.* 1. Conciliation. 2. Resemblance or affinity which different things bear to each other. 3. Act of obtaining esteem, friendship, or favor.

conciliador, ra [con-the-le-ah-dor', rah], *m. & f.* Conciliator, peacemaker, reconciler. -*a.* Conciliatory.

conciliar [con-the-le-ar'], *va.* 1. To conciliate or compose differences. 2. To conciliate, to gain, to win the affection or esteem of others; to reconcile. 3. To accord, to reconcile two or more doctrines or propositions seemingly contraries. **Conciliar el sueño,** to induce sleep. **Conciliar las amistades,** to make friends.

conciliar [con-the-le-ar'], *a.* Conciliar, relating to councils.

conciliar [con-the-le-ar'], *m.* Member of a council.

conciliativo, va [con-the-le-ah-tee'-vo, vah], *a.* Conciliatory.

conciliatorio [con-the-le-ah-to'-re-o], *a.* Conciliatory.

concilio [con-thee'-le-o], *m.* 1. Council. 2. Council, an assembly of bishops to deliberate upon points of religion. 3. Collection of decrees of a council. **Hacer** or **tener concilio,** *(Coll.)* to keep or hold unlawful meetings.

concinidad [con-the-ne-dahd'], *f.* Harmony, just proportion of sound.

concino, na [con-thee'-no, nah], *a.* Harmonious, agreeable to number and harmony.

concisamente [con-the-sah-men'-tay], *adv.* Concisely, briefly, shortly, laconically.

concisión [con-the-se-on'], *f.* Conciseness, brevity, terseness.

conciso, sa [con-thee'-so, sah], *a.* Concise, brief, short, laconic.

concitación [con-the-tah-the-on'], *f.* Incitation, the act of stirring up.

concitador [co-the-tah-dor'], *m.* Instigator, troublemaker.

concitar [con-the-tar'], *va.* To excite; to stir up commotions, to incite.

concitativo, va [con-the-tah-tee'-vo, vah], *a.* Inciting; stirring up commotions.

conciudadano [con-the-oo-da-dah'-no], *m.* Fellow citizen, townsman, countryman.

cónclave [con-clah´-vay], *or* **cónclave,** *m.* 1. Conclave, place in which the cardinals meet to elect a pope. 2. Conclave, the meeting held for that purpose by the cardinals. 3. Conclave, a close meeting or assembly.

conclavista [con-clah-vees'-tah], *m.* Conclavist, a domestic of a cardinal.

concluir [con-cloo-eer'], *va.* 1. To conclude, to end, to terminate, to finish, to close, to complete, to make up. 2. To complete a thing suddenly. 3. To convince with reason, to make evident. 4. To decide finally, to determine. 5. To infer, to deduce. 6. To close judicial proceedings; to submit to a final decision. 7. *(Fenc.)* To disarm an adversary by laying hold of the hilt of his sword. -*vn.* To end, to conclude, to finish. **Concluir de,** to finish; **todo ha concluido,** it´s all over. -*vr.* To end, to conclude.

conclusión [con-cloo-se-on'], *f.* 1. Conclusion. 2. Conclusion, end, close or closure, date, issue. 3. *(Fenc.)* Act of laying hold of the hilt of an adversary's sword. 4. The conclusion of the proceedings in a suit of law. 5. Conclusion, consequence. 6. Thesis controverted and defended in schools. **En conclusión,** finally.

conclusivo, va [con-cloo-see´-vo, vah], *a.* Conclusional, conclusive, final.

concluso, sa [con-cloo'-so, sah], *a.* 1. Concluded, closed, terminated. 2. *(Obs.)* Inclosed, contained. -*pp. irr.* of CONCLUIR.

concluyente [con-cloo-yen´-tay], *pa.* Concluding; conclusive.

concluyentemente [con-cloo-yen-tay-men'-tay], *adv.* Conclusively. *(Yo concluyo, yo concluyera. el concluyó, from Concluir. V.* INSTRUIR.*)*

concofrade [con-co-frah'-day], *m.* He who belongs to the same brotherhood as another.

concoidal [con-co-e-dahl'], *a. V.* CONCOIDEO.

concoide [con-co'-e-day], *f. (Math.)* Conchoid.

concoideo, a [con-co-e-day'-o-, ah], *a.* Conchoidal, resembling a shell.

concolega [con-co-lay'-gah], *m.* Fellow-collegian.

concolón [con-co-lone'], *m. (LAm.) (Culin.)* Scrapings.

concomerse [con-co-merr'-say], *vr.* To shrug the shoulders.

concomimiento, concomio [con-co-me-me-en´-to, con-co'-me-o], *m.* Shrugging of the shoulders.

concomitancia [con-co-me-tahn'-the-ah], *f.* 1. Concomitance, existence together with some other thing. 2. Circumstantial evidence.

concomitante [con-co-me-tahn'-tay], *pa.* 1. Concomitant, concurrent, accompanying. 2. Accessory.

concomitar [con-co-me-tar´], *va.* To concomitate, to attend, to accompany.

conconete [con-co-nay'-tay], *m. (Mex.)* Child, little one.

concordable [con-cor-dah'-blay], *a.* Concordant, conformable, agreeable, accommodating, consistent with.

concordación [con-cor-dah-the-on'], *f.* Coordination, combination, conformation.

concordador [con-cor-dah-dor'], *m.* Conciliator, peacemaker.

concordancia [con-cor-dahn'-the-ah], *f.* 1. Concordance, concord, agreement between persons and things. 2. Harmony, concord of sounds. 3. A concordance of Scripture texts or words. 4. Grammatical concord.

concordante [con-cor-dahn'-tay], *pa.* Concordant, agreeing.

concordar [con-cor-dar'], *va.* 1. To accord, to regulate, to make one thing agree with another; to compromise. -*vn.* 1. To accord, to agree, to comport, to concord. 2. To be congenial, be in accord. **La copia concuerda con su original,** the copy agrees with the original. **Esto no**

concuerda con los hechos, this does not square with the facts.

concordato [con-cor-dah´-to], *m.* Concordat, a covenant made by a state or government with the Pope upon ecclesiastical matters.

concorde [con-cor´-day], *a.* Concordant, agreeable, agreeing. **Poner a dos personas concordes**, to bring about agreement between two people.

concordemente [con-cor-day-men'-tay] *adv.* With one accord.

concordia [con-cor'-de-ah], *f.* 1. Concord, conformity, union, harmony. 2. Agreement between persons engaged in a lawsuit. **De concordia**, jointly, by common consent.

concorpóreo, rea [con-cor-po'-ray-o, ah], *a.* Concorporeal, of the same body.

concreción [con-cray-the-on'], *f.* Concretion.

concrecionar [cone-cray-the-o-nar'], *vn.* To form concretions.

concrescencia [con-cres-then'-the-ah], *f.* *(Phys.)* Concrescence, growing by the union of separate particles.

concretamente [con-cray-tah-men'-tay], *adv.* Concretely, specifically; exactly. **Se refirió concretamente a dos**, he referred specifically to two. **No es concretamente una fiesta**, it's not exactly a party.

concretar [con-cray-tar'], *va.* To combine, to unite, to concrete. **Concreta sus esperanzas a ganar el premio**, he is concentrating all his hopes on winning the prize. **Vamos a concretar los puntos esenciales**, let sum up the essential points. *-vr.* To be reduced to speaking or treating of one subject only.

concreto, ta [con-cray-to´, tah], *a.* 1. Concrete, in logic, not abstracted: applied to a subject. 2. Concrete, formed by concretion: in this last sense it is used as a substantive. **En este caso concreto**, in this particular instance. **No me dijo ninguna hora concreta**, he didn´t tell me any definite time. **En concreto había 7**, there were 7 to be exact. *-m.* 1. Concretion. 2. *(LAm.)* Concrete (hormigón).

concubina [con-coo-bee´-nah], *f.* Concubine, mistress.

concubinario [con-coo-be-nah'-re-o], *m.* One who keeps a mistress.

concubinato [con-coo-be-nah'-to], *m.* Concubinage.

concúbito [con-coo´-be-to], *m.* Coition, copulation. (*Yo concuerdo, yo concuerde*, from *Concordar*. *V.* ACORDAR.)

conculcación [con-cool-cah-the-on'], *f.* Trampling.

conculcar [con-cool-car'], *va.* 1. To trample under foot. 2. To mock, despise, break to pieces, heap abuse upon. 3. To infringe.

concuñado, da [con-coo-nyah'-do, dah], *m. & f.* Brother or sister-in-law; a term confined to persons who are married to two brothers or sisters.

concupiscencia [con-coo-pis-then'-the-ah], *f.* 1. Concupiscence, lust, cupidity. 2. Avarice, Inordinate desire.

concupiscente [con-coo-pis-then'-tay], *a.* 1. Greedy (avaro), acquisitive. 2. Lewd (lujurioso), lustful, concupiscent.

concupiscible [con-coo-pis-thee'-blay], *a.* Concupiscible; impressing desire.

concurrencia [con-coor-ren'-the-ah], *f.* 1. Convention or assembly of persons. **Había una numerosa concurrencia**, there was a big attendance. 2. Concurrence, coincidence. 3. Conspiracy, tendency of many causes to one event.

concurrente [con-coor-ren'-tay], *pa.* Concurrent, coincident. **Concurrente cantidad**, the quantity necessary to make up the deficiency of a determinate sum. *-m.* 1. Person present, person attending. **Concurrente al cine**, cinema goer. **Los concurrentes**, those present. 2. Competition.

concurrido [con-coor-re'-do], *a.* Crowded (lugar); much frequented; busy, crowded; popular, well-attended; full (of people).

concurrir [con-coor-reer'], *vn.* 1. To concur, to meet in one point, time, or place. **Concurrir a un baile**, to go to a

dance. 2. To concur, to contribute, to coincide, to conspire, to agree with or to agree together, to assist. **Concurrir a la derrota**, to contribute to the defeat. **Concurrir al éxito de una empresa**, to contribute to the success of an enterprise. **Concurrir con una empresa**, to cooperate in an undertaking. 3. To be found. **Concurren de ella muchas buenas cualidades**, she has many good qualities. 4. To compete. **Concurrir a un mercado**, to compete in a market.

concursado, da [con-coor-sah'-do], *m. & f.* Insolvent debtor, bankrupt.

concursante [con-coor-sahn'-tay], *m. & f.* Competitor, contestant, participant.

concursar [con-coor-sar´], *va.* 1. To lay an injunction on the goods and chattels of an insolvent debtor. 2. To compete in, to compete for. **Va a concursar a la vacante**, he is going to compete for the vacancy. *-vn.* To compete, to participate.

concurso [con-coor´-so], *m.* 1. Concourse or confluence of persons or things; crowd, congregation, assembly. 2. Aid, assistance. **Con el concurso de**, with the help of. 3. Contest, competition. **Concurso de belleza**, beauty contest. **Concurso hípico**, horse show. **Concurso radiofónico**, radio quiz. **Concurso literario**, literary competition. 4. Proceedings against an insolvent debtor.

concusión [con-coo-se-on'], *f.* Concussion, shaking, the act of shaking. **Concusión violenta**, extortion.

concusionario, ia [con-coo-se-o-nah'-re-o. ah], *a.* Concussive, shaking, extortioner.

condado [con-dah'-do], *m.* 1. Earldom, county. 2. Dignity of a count or earl. 3. County, a political division.

condal [con-dahl'], *a.* Relating to the dignity of an earl or count.

conde [con´-day], *m.* 1 Earl, count. 2. *(Prov.)* Overseer. 3. Head or chief of the gypsies, appointed by election.

condecoración [con-day-co-rah-the-on'], *f.* Decoration, embellishing or decorating.

condecorar [con-day-co-rar'], *va.* To ornament, to adorn, to embellish, to honor, to reward.

condena [con-day'-nah], *f.* 1. The clerk of the court's attestation of the sentence of a condemned criminal. 2. Sentence. **Condena de reclusión perpetua**, life sentence. **Cumplir una condena**, to serve a sentence.

condenable [con-day-nah´-blay], *a.* Condemnable, blamable, culpable, damnable.

condenación [con-day-nah-the-on'], *f.* 1. Condemnation, sentence to punishment. 2. Punishment. **Es una condenación**, *(Coll.)* It is unbearable, intolerable. 3. *(Met.)* Eternal damnation.

condenadamente [con-day-nah-dah-men'-tay], *adv.* **Una mujer condenadamente lista**, a darned clever woman. **Es un trabajo condenadamente duro**, it´s darned hard work.

condenado, da [con-day-nah'-do, dah], *m. & f.* One condemned to eternal punishment. **El condenado a muerte**, the condemned man. **El condenado de mi tío**, that ruddy uncle of mine.

condenado, da [con-day-nah'-do, dah], *a. & pp.* 1. of CONDENAR. Condemned, damned, sentenced. **Ser or salir condenado en costas**, to be sentenced to pay the costs of a suit at law. **Puerta condenada**, a door boarded up and no longer used. **Aquel condenado teléfono**, that ruddy telephone. 2. Naughty, mischievous (niño). 3. *(Ecl.)* Dammed soul.

condenador, ra [con-day-nah-dor', rah], *m. & f.* Condemner, blamer, censurer.

condenar [con-day-nar'], *va.* 1. To condemn, to pronounce judgment, to sentence. **Condenar a uno a una multa**, to sentence somebody to pay a fine. **Le condenaron por ladrón**, they found him guilty of robbery. 2. To damn. 3. To condemn, to censure, to blame. 4. To refute a doctrine or opinion, to disapprove. **Condenar una puerta, una ventana** or **un pasadizo**, to stop or shut a door, window, or passage, to nail or wall up a door, etc. 5. To vex, to annoy (fastidiar). -*vr.* 1. To condemn oneself, to acknowledge one's fault. 2. To incur eternal punishment in a future state. 3. To be dammed.

condenatorio, ria [con-day-nah-to'-re-o, ah], *a.* Condemnatory, damnatory.

condensabilidad [con-den-sah-be-le-dahd'], *f.* The quality of being condensable.

condensable [con-den-sah'-blay], *a.* Condensable.

condensación [con-den-sah-the-on'], *f.* Condensation, compression.

condensado, da [con-den-sah'-do, dah], *a.* Condensed. **Leche condensada**, condensed milk.

condensador, ra [con-den-sah-dor', rah], *m. & f.* Condenser.

condensamiento [con-den-sah-me-en'-to], *m.* V. CONDENSACIÓN.

condensante [con-den-sahn'-tay], *pa.* Condensing.

condensar [con-den-sar'], *va.* To thicken, to condense. -*vr.* To be condensed, to gather.

condensativo, va [con-den-sah-tee´-vo, vah], *a.* Condensative.

condensidad [con-den-se-dahd'], *f.* Condensity, condensation.

condesa [con-de'-sah], *f.* Countess, the wife of a count or the heiress to an earldom.

condescendencia [con-des-then-den'-the-ah], *f.* Condescendence, condescension, condescending, compliance, complacency, flexibility.

condescender [con-des-then-derr'], *vn.* To condescend, to yield, to submit, to comply; **condescender a algo**, to consent to something. **Condescender en**, to agree to.

condescendiente [con-des-then-de-en´-tay], *a. & pa.* Complacent, compliant, acquiescent.

condescendientemente, *adv.* Condescendingly. *(Yo condesciendo, yo condescienda*, from *Condescender.* V. ATENDER.)

condesita [con-day-see'-tah], *f. dim.* A little or young, countess.

condesito [con-day-see'-to], *m. dim.* A little earl, a little count.

condestable [con-des-tah'-blay], *m.* 1. Constable, a lord high constable. 2 **Condestable de arsenales**, *(Naut.)* Gunner of a dockyard. **Segundo condestable**, gunner's mate. 3. *(Naut.)* Sergeant of marine artillery.

condestablía [con-des-tah-blee'-ah], *f.* Constableship.

condición [con-de-the-on'], *f.* 1. Condition, quality. 2. Condition, state, footing, habit. 3. Condition, natural quality of the mind, natural temper or constitution. 4. Quality, rank, or class in society; fashion, especially implying nobility. 5. Condition, clause, stipulation. **Tener mala condición** or **tener condición**, to be of a peevish or irritable disposition; bad tempered. **Tener** or **poner en condición**, to hazard, to expose to danger. **De condición** or **con condición**, so as, on the condition that. **Persona de condición**, person of rank. **La condición humana**, the human condition. **De excelentes cualidades**, of splendid qualities. **Condiciones de trabajo**, working conditions. **Las condiciones del contrato**, the terms of the contract. **Ayuda sin condiciones**, help with no strings attached.

condicionado, da [con-de-the-o-nah'-do, dah], *a.* 1. Conditioned; well or bad conditioned. 2. V. CONDICIONAL. -*pp.* of CONDICIONAR.

condicional [con-de-the-o-nahl'], *a.* Conditional, not absolute.

condicionalmente [con-de-the-o-nal-men'-tay], *adv.* Conditionally, hypothetically.

condicionante [con-de-the-o-nahn'-tay], *m.* Determining factor, determinant.

condicionar [con-de-the-o-nar'], *vn.* To agree, to accord, to condition. -*vr.* To be of the same nature, condition, or temper.

condicionaza [con-de-the-o-nah'-thah], *f. aug.* A violent disposition or temper.

condicioncilla, ita [con-de-the-on-theel'-lyah, ee'-tah], *f. dim.* 1. A hasty or passionate disposition or temper. 2. A small clause, or stipulation.

condignamente [con-dig-nah-men'-tay], *adv.* Condignly, deservedly.

condigno, na [con-deeg'-no, nah], *a.* Condign, suitable, deserved, merited.

cóndilo [cone'-de-lo], *m. (Anat.)* Condyle.

condimentar [con-de-men-tar'], *va.* To dress or season victuals.

condimento [con-de-men'-to], *m.* Condiment, seasoning, sauce.

condiscípulo, la [con-dis-thee'-poo-lo], *m.f.* Condisciple, school-fellow, fellow-scholar or fellow-student.

condistinguir [con-dis-tin-geer'], *va.* To distinguish, to make a distinction.

condolecerse, condolerse [con-do-lay-therr´-say, con-do-lerr'-say], *vr.* To condole, to be sorry for, to sympathize with.

condolencia [con-do-layn'-the-ah], *f.* Condolence, sympathy.

condominio [con-do-mee'-ne-o], *m.* 1. Joint ownership. 2. Condominium.

condómino [con-do'-me-no], *m.* A joint owner.

condón [con-done'], *m.* Condom, preservative, sheath.

condonación [con-do-nah-the-on'], *f.* Remission, pardoning, forgiving.

condonar [con-do-nar'], *va.* To pardon, to forgive.

cóndor [con'-dor], *m. (Orn.)* Condor.

condrila [con-dree'-lah], *f. (Bot.)* Common gum-succory. Chondrilla juncea.

condrín [con-dreen'], *m.* A weight for precious metals in the Philippines = 0.3768 gramme.

condritis [con-dree'-tis], *f.* Inflammation of cartilage, chondritis.

condrografía [con-dro-grah-fee'-ah], *f.* A description of cartilages.

conducción [con-dooc-the-on'], *f.* 1. Conveyance. 2. Carriage, the act of carrying. 3. The act of conveying or conducting. 4. Leading, guiding, conduct. 5. Reward for conducting. **Conducción a la derecha**, right-handed drive. **Conducción de agua**, water pipe. **Conducción principal de agua**, water main.

conducencia [con-doo-then'-the-ah], *f.* The conducing to or promoting any end, conducement.

conducente [con-doo-then'-tay], *a. & pa.* Conducive, conducent, conducible; official.

conducidor [con-doo-the-dor'], *m.* Conductor, leader.

conducir [con-doo-theer'], *va. & vn.* 1. To drive (coches), to convey, to carry, or conduct a thing from one place to another. 2. To conduct, to guide or direct to a place, to show the way, to lead (un ejército). 3. To direct, to manage, to conduct or adjust any affair or business. **Los cables conducen la electricidad**, the cables carry the electricity; **me condujeron por un pasillo**, they led me along a passage. 4. *vn.* To conduce, to contribute, to favor, to be fitted for.-*vr.* To behave, to act, to conduct oneself.

conducta [con-dooc'-tah], *f.* 1. Conduct, management, course, manner of proceeding. 2. Conduct, behavior, comportment, conversation. 3. Life, conduct. 4. Number of mules or horses carrying money from one place to another. 5. Government, command, direction. 6. Party of recruits conducted to the regiment.

conductibilidad [con-dooc-te-be-le-dahd'], *f.* Conductibility.

conductible [con-dooc-tee'-blay], *a.* Conveyable, conductible.

conductividad [con-dooc-te-ve-dahd'], *f.* Conductivity (electricidad).

conductivo, va [con-duc-tee'-vo, vah], *a.* Having the power of conveying or transporting.

conducto [con-dooc'-to], *m.* 1. Conduit, sewer, drain, sink. **Conducto alimenticio**, alimentary canal. **Conducto de humo**, flue. 2. Channel, mediation. **Por conducto de**, via, through. **Salvo conducto**, Safe-conduct.

conductor [con-dooc-tor'], *m.* 1. Conductor, leader, usher, conduct, guide, conveyer. **Conductor de embajadores**, one whose business is to introduce ambassadors. 2. **Conductor eléctrico**, electric rod. 3. *(Aut.)* Driver, motorist. **Aprendiz de conductor**, learner-driver. 4. *(LAm.) (Mus.)* Conductor. **Conductor de autobuses**, bus driver.

conductora [con-dooc-to'-rah], *f.* 1. Conductress, directress. 2. Woman driver (coches). *(Yo me conduelo, yo me conduela, from Condoler. V.* MOVER.)

condueño [con-doo-ay'-nyo], *m. (Com.)* Joint owner.

condumio [con-doo'-me-o], *m.* 1. *(Coll.)* Meat dressed to be eaten with bread. 2. Plenty of food.

conduplicación [con-doo-ple-cah-the-on], *f.* The rhetorical figure of reduplication; the repetition of the last word of the clause just preceding.

condutal [con-doo-tahl'], *m.* Spout to carry off the rainwater from the houses. *V.* CANAL. *(Yo conduzco, yo conduzca; él condujo, el condujera; from Conducir. V.* CONDUCIR.)

conectado [co-nec-tah'-do], *a.* Connected. **Estar conectado**, to be on; to be live.

conectar [co-nec-tar'], *va.* 1. *(Mech.)* To connect, to couple up. **Conectar un aparato a tierra**, to earth a piece of apparatus. **Conectar a uno con otra persona**, to put somebody in touch with somebody else. **Yo les puedo conectar**, I can put you in touch. *-vn.* **Conectar con**, to communicate with. **Ellos conectan bien**, they get on well. **Ahora conectamos con Londres**, now we´re going over to London. *-vr.* To make a connection.

conectículo [co-nec-tee'-coo-lo], *m. (Bot.)* Connective, elastic ring or ferns.

conectivo [co-nec-te'-vo], *a.* Connective.

conector [co-nec-tor'], *m.* Connector.

coneina [co-nay-ee'-nah], *f.* Conein, coneia, an alkaloid obtained from hemlock.

coneja [co-nay'-hah], *f. V.* CONEJO.

conejal [co-nay-hahl'], *m.* 1. Rabbit warren. *V.* CONEJERA. 2. *(Met.)* Suburb inhabited by the common people.

conejar [co-nay-har'], *m.* Rabbit warren.

conejera [co-nay-hay'-rah], *f.* 1. Warren for breeding rabbits. 2. *(Met.)* Brothel. 3. *(Met.)* Den or cavern inhabited by poor people.

conejero [co-nay-hay'-ro], *m.* Warrener, the keeper of a rabbitwarren.

conejero [co-nay-hay'-ro, rah], *a.* That which hunts rabbits (perros).

conejito [co-nay-hee'-to], *m. dim.* A little rabbit.

conejo [co-nay'-ho], *a.* **Alambre conejo**, Rabbit wire, copper wire.

conejo, ja [co-nay'-ho, hah], *m. & f.* 1. Rabbit. **Es una coneja**, *(Met.)* She breeds like a rabbit. 2. *(CAm.)* Detective; (andar de conejo), *(LAm.)* To be undercover (policía). 3. *(Mil.)* Recruit, squaddle.

conejuna [co-nay-hoo'-nah], *f.* Rabbit down or fur.

conejuno, na [co-nay-hoo'-no, ah], *a.* Relating to the rabbit kind.

cóneo, a [co'-nay-o, ah], *a.* Like a cone; conical.

conexidades [co-nek-se-dah'-des], *f. pl.* Rights annexed to the principal.

conexión [co-nek-se-on'], *f.* 1. Connection, conjunction, union, conjucture, cohesion, closeness, coherence. 2. *(fig.)* Relationship.

conexionarse [co-nec-se-o-nar'-say], *vr.* To get in touch; to make connections.

conexivo, va [co-nek-see'-vo, vah], *a.* Connective.

conexo, xa [co-nek'-so, sah], *a.* Connected, united.

confabulación [con-fah-boo-lah-the-on'], *f.* 1. Confabulation, easy conversation, chat. 2. Leaguing, conspiracy, collusion.

confabulador, ra [con-fah-boo-lah-dor', rah], *m. & f.* A storyteller, gossip; schemer.

confabular [con-fah-boo-lar'], *vn.* 1. To confabulate, to talk easily together, to chat. 2. To tell stories. 3. *vr.* To league, to enter into conspiracy.

confalón [con-fah-lone'], *m.* Gonfalon, standard, an ensign.

confalonier [con-fah-lo-ne-err'], **Confaloniero,** *m.* Gonfalonier, chief standardbearer.

confección [con-fec-the-on'], *f.* Confection, making, construction. **Confección de vestidos**, dressmaking. **Traje de confección**, ready-to-wear suit. **Es una confección Pérez**, it´s a Pérez creation.

confeccionado [con-fec-the-o-nah'-do], *a.* Ready-made, ready-to-wear.

confeccionador, ra [con-fec-the-o-nah-dor', rah], *m. & f.* Confectioner.

confeccionar [con-fec-the-o-nar'], *va.* 1. To make, to prepare, to put together, to complete. 2. To confect.

confecciones, *(Sp. Amer.)* Readymade dresses.

confederación [con-fay-day-rah-the-on'], *f.* 1. Confederacy, league, union, confederation, federation, coalition. 2. Agreement or mutual treaty between monarchs or republics.

confederado, da [con-fay-day-rah'-do, dah], *a. & m. & f.* Confederate, allied, conjoint, federate, covenanter, federal, consociate. *-pp.* of CONFEDERAR.

confederar [con-fay-day-rar'], *va.* To confederate. to join in a league. *-vr.* To confederate, to conjoin, to league.

conferencia [con-fay-ren'-the-ah], *f.* 1. Conference, meeting, conversation, collocution; congress. **Conferencia de desarme**, disarmament conference. **Conferencia de prensa**, press conference. 2. Daily lecture studied by students in universities. **Dar una conferencia**, to give a lecture. 3. Telephone call. **Conferencia de cobro invertido**, reversed-charge call. **Conferencia de persona a persona**, personal call.

conferenciante [con-fay-ren-the-ahn-tay], *m. & f.* Lecturer, speaker.

conferenciar [con-fay-ren-the-ar'], *va.* To confer; to hold a conference.

conferencista [con-fay-ren-thees'-tah], *m. & f.* Lecturer, orator, speaker.

conferir [con-fay-reer'], *va.* 1. To confer, to compare, to estimate the relative qualities of things. 2. To confer, to deliberate, to commune. 3. To give, to bestow; to confer; **conferir un beneficio**, to confer a benefice.

conferva [con-ferr'-vah], *f. (Bot.)* Conferva, a filamentous freshwater alga.

confesa [con-fay'-sah], *f. V.* CONFES0.

confesado, da [con-fay-sah'-do, dah], *a. & pp.* of CONFESAR, Confessed.-*n. (Coll.)* Penitent, one under the spiritual direction of a confessor.

confesante [con-fay-sahn'-tay], *pa.* He who confesses by word or writing before a judge, penitent.

confesar [con-fay-sar'], *va.* 1. To manifest or assert one´s opinion. 2. To confess, to acknowledge, to own, to avow, to grant. 3. To confess, to hear or receive confessions. 4. To confess to the priest. **Confesar sin tormento**, to confess, to acknowledge or avow a fault, a crime, etc., freely and readily. *-vr.* To confess, or make confession; to shrive. **Confesarse de sus pecados**, to confess one´s sins.

confesión [con-fay-se-on'], *f.* 1. Confession, acknowledgment. 2. Confession to a priest. **Hijo** or **hija de confesión,** a person who has a certain constant confessor. 3. Declaration of a criminal either denying or confessing the charges against him.

confesional [con-fay-se-o-nahl'], *a.* 1. Confessional. **Secreto confesional**, secrecy of confession. 2. Confessional, denominational.

confesionario [con-fay-se-o-nah'-re-o], *m.* 1. Treatise which lays down rules for confessing or hearing confessions, confessional box. 2. Confessional.

confeso, sa [con-fay'-so, sah], *m. & . f.* Jewish proselyte. 2. A lay brother; a nun who was before a widow.

confeso, sa [con-fay'-so, sah], *a. (Law.)* Confessed: applied to the person who has acknowledged a crime. *pp. irr.* Of CONFESAR.

confesonario [con-fay-so-nah'-re-o], *m.* Confessional.

confesor [con-fay-sor'], *m.* 1. Confessor, a priest of the Roman church authorized to hear confession of sins and to grant absolution. 2. A title given to holy men by the Roman Catholic church; as, **San Juan Crisóstomo, Doctor, Obispo y Confesor,** St. John Crysostom, B. C. D.

confeti [con-fay'-te], *m.* Confetti.

confiabilidad [con-fe-a-be-le-dahd'], *f.* Reliability, trustworthiness.

confiable [con-fe-ah'-blay], *a.* Trusty.

confiadamente [con-fe-ah-dah-men', tay], *adv.* Confidently, trustingly, hopefully.

confiado, da [con-fe-ah'-do, dah], *a.* Confident, secure, unsuspicious, trusting; presumptuous, arrogant, forward.

confiador [con-fe-ah-dor'], *m.* 1. A joint surety, a fellow-bondsman. 2. He who confides or expects.

confianza [con-fe-ahn'-thah], *f.* 1. Confidence, trust, reliance, firm belief. **Persona de toda confianza,** reliable person. **Puesto de confianza,** responsible post. **Poner su confianza en,** to put one's trust in. 2. Confidence, honest boldness, firmness of opinion. **Con toda confianza,** with complete confidence. **Estar lleno de confianza,** to be full of confidence. 3. Confidence, presumptuousness, forwardness, assurance. **En confianza,** privately, secretly, confidentially. 4. Confidences; familiarities. **Se toma demasiadas confianzas,** he is too familiar, he's too fresh. 5. Intimacy, familiarity. **Amigo de confianza,** close friend. **Reunión de confianza,** intimate gathering. **Tener confianza con uno,** to be on close terms with somebody.

confianzudo [con-fe-ahn-thoo'-do], *a.* 1. Overfamiliar, fresh. 2. *(LAm.)* Meddlesome (entrometido).

confiar [con-fe-ar'], *va. & vn.* 1. To confide, to trust in. 2. To confide, to credit, to commit to the care of another. 3. To hope; to feed with hope. **Confiar algo en uno,** to entrust something to somebody. **Confiar el éxito de algo,** to feel confident about the success of something. -*vr.* 1. **Confiarse a algo,** to entrust oneself to something. 2. **Confiarse a uno,** *(fig.)* To open one's heart to somebody.

confidencia [con-fe-den'-the-ah], *f.* 1. Confidence. V. CONFIANZA. 2. Secret information.

confidencial [con-fe-den-the-ahl'], *a.* Confidential.

confidencialidad [con-fe-den-the-a-le-dahd'], *f.* Confidentiality, confidential nature.

confidencialmente [con-fe-den-the-al-men'-tay], *adv.* Confidentially.

confidente [con-fe-den'-tay], *m.* 1. Confident, intimate, neighbor, counsellor. 2. A spy.

confidente [con-fe-den'-tay], *a.* True, faithful, trusty.

confidentemente [con-fe-den-tay-men'-tay], *adv.* 1. Confidently, faithfully. 2. Faithfully. *(Yo confiero, yo confiera; él confirió, él confiriera;* from *Conferir.* V. ASENTIR.) *(Yo confieso, yo confiese,* from *Confesar.* V. ACERTAR.)

configuración [con-fe-goo-rah-the-on'], *f.* Configuration. **La configuración del futuro,** the shape of things to come.

configurado, da [con-fe goo rah'-do, dah], *a.* Configurated -*pp.* of CONFIGURAR.

configurar [con-fe-goo-rar'], *va.* To configure, to arrange the parts of something; to configurate: also used reciprocally.

confín [con-feen'], *m.* Limit, boundary, confine, border.

confín, confinante [con-feen', con-fe-nahn'-tay], *a.* Bordering upon, conterminous. -**Confinante,** *pa.* of CONFINAR.

confinar [con-fe-nar'], *va. & vn.* 1. To banish, to exile. 2. To confine, to imprison or immure. 3. To confine, to border upon, to abut. -*vr.* To shut oneself away.

confirmación [con-feer-mah-the-on'], *f.* 1. Confirmation, corroboration, attestation. 2. Evidence; additional proof. 3. Confirmation, a sacrament of the Catholic church.

confirmadamente [con-feer-mah-dah-men'-tay], *adv.* Firmly, unalterably.

confirmador, ra [con-feer-mah-dor', rah], *m. & f.* Confirmator, attester, confirmer.

confirmante [con-feer-mahn'-tay], *pa.* Confirmer.

confirmar [con-fer-mar'], *va.* 1. To confirm, to corroborate, to fortify. 2. To strengthen or support a person or thing. 3. To confirm, to admit to the full privileges of a Christian by the solemn imposition of hands. **La excepción confirma la regla,** the exception proves the rule.

confirmativamente [con-feer-mah-te-vah-men'-tay], *adv.* Confirmingly.

confirmatorio, ria [con-feer-mah-to'-re-o, ah], *a.* Confirmatory, confirmative.

confiscable [con-fis-cah'-blay], *a.* Confiscable, forfeitable.

confiscación [con-fis-cah-the-on'], *f.* Confiscation, forfeiture.

confiscado, da [con-fis-cah'-do, dah], *a. & pp.* of CONFISCAR. Confiscate, confiscated.

confiscar [con-fis-car'], *va.* To confiscate, to transfer private property to the public use.

confiscado [con-fes-cah'-do], *a. (CAm.)* Mischievous, naughty.

confitado [con-fe-tah'-do], *a.* **Fruta confitada,** crystallised fruit.

confitar [con-fe-tar'], *va.* 1. To confect, to candy with melted sugar. 2. To make up into sweetmeats. 3. *(Met.)* To dulcify, to sweeten.

confite [con-fee'-tay], *m.* Sweet, candy, sugarplum. **Confites.** 1. Dainties, sugarplum.

confitera [con-fe-tay'-rah], *f.* Candy dish, bonbon dish. V. CONFITERO.

confitería [con-fe-tay-ree'-ah], *f.* 1. A confectioner's shop. 2. Confectionery, sweets, candies.

confitero, ra [con-fe-tay'-ro, rah], *m. & f.* 1. Confectioner. 2. Tray in which sweetmeats are served up.

confitillo [con-fe-teel'-lyo], *m.* 1. Decoration on coverlets. 2. *(dim.)* Small comfit; a sugar-coated sweet containing a nut or seed.

confitón [con-fe-tone'], *m. (aug.)* A large comfit.

confitura [con-fe-too'-rah], *f.* Confiture, comfit, confection, sweetmeats.

conflación [con-flah-the-on'], *f.* Fusion, melting metals, smelting.

conflagración [con-flah-grah-thee-on'], *f.* 1. Conflagration. 2. A sudden and violent perturbation of towns and nations.

conflátil [con-flah'-teel], *a.* Fusible.

conflictividad [con-fleec-te-ve-dahd'], *f.* 1. Tensions and disputes; strains; potentiality for conflict. 2. Controversial nature.

conflictivo [con-fleec-te'-vo], *a.* Troubled (sociedad), filled with conflict; unstable (sistema); controversial. **La edad conflictiva,** the age of conflict. **Zona conflictiva,** area of conflict.

conflicto [con-fleec'-to], *m.* 1. Conflict, struggle, a violent combat or contest. 2. *(Met.)* Struggle, agony, pang.

confluencia [con-floo-en'-the-ah], *f.* Confluence, conflux, flux.

confluente [con-floo-en'-tay], *pa.* Confluent.

confluir [con-floo-eer'], *vn.* 1. To join or meet (ríos, corrientes). 2. *(Met.)* To meet or assemble in one place (muchedumbre).

conformación [con-for-ma-the-on'], *f.* Conformation, shape, form.

conformado [con-for-mah-do], *a.* 1. **Bien conformado,** well-made, well-shaped. 2. Patient, resigned, long-suffering.

conformar [con-for-mar'], *va.* To conform, to adjust, to fit. -*vn.* 1. To suit, to fit, to conform, to cohere, to level. 2. To comply with, to agree in opinion. -*vr.* To yield, to submit, to accommodate. **Se conforma con cualquier cosa,** he agrees to anything. **No me conformo con hacerlo así,** I do not agree to doing it that way.

conforme [con-for'-may], *a.* 1. Conformable, correspondent, suitable, congruent, consonant, convenient, accordant. 2. Consistent, similar. 3. Compliant, resigned. **Conforme a,**

consistent with, agreeable to. **Son muy conforme en todo**, they are very similar in every respect. **Un premio conforme a sus méritos**, a prize consistent with his merits. **Estar conformes**, to agree. **Estamos conformes en que...**, we agree that... **No se quedó conforme con la propina**, he was not satisfied with the tip. *-prep.* **Conforme a**, in conformity with. **Lo hicieron conforme a sus instrucciones**, they acted according to their intructions.

conforme [con-for'-may], *adv.* 1. In proportion, or according to proportion. **Conforme lo iban sacando**, as they were taking it out. 2. Agreeably, according to. *-m.* Agreement. **Dar el conforme**, to agree.

conformemente [con-for-may-men'-tay], *adv.* Conformably, unanimousy.

conformidad [con-for-me-dahd'], *f.* 1. Similitude, resemblance, likeness, conformity. 2. Agreement, consistence, consonance, congruence. 3. Union, concord, concordance. 4. Symmetry. 5. A close attachment of one person to another. 6. Submission, acquiescence, patience, resignation. **De conformidad**, by common consent; together, in company. **En conformidad**, agreeably, suitably, according to. **Dar su conformidad**, to consent.

conformismo [con-for-mes'-mo], *m.* Conformism.

conformista [con-for-mees'-tah], *m.f.* Conformist.

confort [con-fort'], *m. pl.* **Conforts** 1. Comfort. 2. *(Cono Sur)* Toilet paper.

confortable [con-for-tah'-blay], *a.* Comfortable. *-m.* Sofa.

confortablemente [con-for-tah-blay-men'-tay], *adv.* Comfortably.

confortación [con-for-tah-the-on'], *f.* Comfort, consolation.

confortador, ra [con-for-tah-dor', rah], *m. & f.* Comforter.

confortante [con-for-tahn'-tay], *pa.* Comforting, soothing. *-m.* Calmative, a soothing remedy; stomachic, relating to food. *-pl.* Mitts.

confortar [con-for-tar'], *pa.* 1. To comfort, to corroborate, to strengthen, to enliven, to invigorate. 2. To console.

confortativo, va [con-for-tah-tee'-vo, vah], *a.* Comfortable, corroborative, cordial; it is frequently used as a substantive. *-m.* 1. Comfort, consolation; encouragement. 2. *(Med.)* Tonic, restorative.

confracción [con-frac-the-on'], *f.* Fraction, breaking.

confraguación [con-frah-goo-ah-the-on'], *f.* The act of mixing, uniting, or incorporating metals with each other.

confraternidad [con-frah-ter-ne-dahd'], *f.* Confraternity, brotherhood.

confraternizar [con-frah-ter-ne-thar'], *vn.* To fraternize.

confrontación [con-fron-tah-the-on'], *f.* 1. Confrontation. 2. Comparing one thing with another. 3. *(Met.)* Sympathy, natural conformity.

confrontante [con-fron-tahn'-tay], *pa.* Confronting, confronter.

confrontar [con-fron-tar'], *va.* 1. To confer, to collate, to confront. 2. To compare one thing with another. *-vn.* 1. To agree in sentiments and opinion. 2. To border upon. *-vr.* **Confrontarse con**, to confront, to face.

confundible [con-foon-de'-blay], *a.* **Fácilmente confundible**, easily mistaken, confused.

confundir [con-foon-deer'], *va.* 1. To confound, to jumble. 2. To confound, to perplex, to confuse, to darken, to throw into disorder. **Confundimos el camino**, we mistook our way. **Ha confundido todos los sellos**, he has mixed up all the stamps. 3. To confute by arguement. **Confundir a uno con atenciones**, to overwhelm somebody with kindness. 4. To abase, humiliate. *-vr.* 1. To be bewildered, perplexed, or confounded. **Usted se ha confundido de número**, you have the wrong number. 2. To be ashamed and humbled by the knowledge of one's own character. 3. To mix, to blend. **Se confundió con la multitud**, he became lost in the crowd.

confusamente [con-foo-sah-men'-tay], *adv.* Confusedly, mingledly, helterskelter.

confusion [con-foo-se-on'], *f.* 1. Confusion, tumult, disorder, misrule. 2. Confusion, perplexity, perturbation of mind. 3. Confusedness, indistinct combination, obscurity. 4. Humiliation, debasement of mind. 5. Shame, ignominy, reproach. **Echar la confusión a alguno**, *(Law. Obs.)* To imprecate or curse someone.

confusional [con-foo-se-o-nahl'], *a.* **Estado confusional**, confused state, state of confusion.

confusionismo [con-foo-se-o-nes'-mo], *f.* Confusion; uncertainty; confused state. **Sembrar el confusionismo y el desconcierto**, to spread alarm and despondency.

confuso, sa [con-foo'-so, sah], *a.* 1. Confused, mixed, confounded, jumbled together. 2. Obscure, doubtful, indistinct. 3. Fearful, timorous. 4. Perplexed. **En confuso**, confusedly, obscurely, indistinctly.

confutación [con-foo-tah-the-on'], *f.* Confutation, disproof.

confutar [con-foo-tar'], *va.* To confute, to disprove, to falsify, to convict.

conga [con'-gah], *f. (LAm.) (Mus.)* To confute.

congal [con-gahl'], *m. (Mex.)* Brothel.

congelación [con-hay-lah-the-on'], *f.* Freezing, congealing. **Congelación rápida**, deep freezing. **Congelación de salarios**, wage freeze.

congelado [con-hay-lah'-do], *a.* 1. Frozen, chilled (carne). 2. *(Med.)* Frostbitten. 3. *(Fin. etc.)* Frozen, blocked.

congelador [con-hay-lah-dor], *m.* or **congeladora** [con-hay-lah-do'-rah], *f.* Freezer, deepfreeze. **Almacenar en congeladora**, to deepfreeze.

congelar [con-hay-lar], *va.* 1. To freeze, to congeal. **Congelar alimentos**, to freeze food. 2. *(Med.)* To freeze, affect with frostbite. 3. *(Fin. etc.)* To freeze, to block; to suspend, to freeze. *-vr.* 1. To freeze, to be very cold. 2. *(Med.)* To get frostbitten.

congelativo, va [con-hay-lah-tee'-vo, vah], *a.* Having the power of congealing.

congénere [con-hay'-nay-rayl **congenérico, ca** [con-hay-nay'-re-co, cah], *a.* Congeneric, of like kind.

congenial [con-hay-ne-ahl'], *a.* Congenial, analogous.

congeniar [con-hay-ne-ar'], *vn.* To be congenial, to sympathize. **Congeniamos con los dos hermanos**, we hit it off with the two brothers.

congenital [con-hay-ne-tahl'], *a. (LAm.)* Congenital.

congénito [con-hay'-re-to], *a.* Congenital, connate.

congerie [con-hay'-re-ay], *f.* Congeries, heap, mass.

congestión [con-hes-te-on´], *f.* Congestion.

congestionado [con-hays-te-o-nah'-do], *a.* 1. Congested. 2. *(Med.)* Congested, chesty; flushed (cara).

congestionamiento [con-hays-te-o-nah-me-ayn'-to], *m. (Aut.)* Traffic jam.

congestionar [con-hes-te-oh-nar'], *vn. & vr.* To congest, become congested.

congio [con'-he-o], *m.* Ancient Roman liquid measure: gallon.

conglobación [con-glo-bah-the-on'], *f.*

conglobar [con-glo-bar'], *va.* To conglobate; to heap together.

conglomeración [con-glo-may-rah-the-on'], *f.* Conglomeration, heterogeneous mixture.

conglomerado, da [con-glo-may-rah'-do, dah], *a.* Conglomerate. *-pp.* of CONGLOMERAR.

conglomerar [con-glo-may-rar'], *va.* To conglomerate. *-vr.* To conglomerate.

congloriar [con-glo-re-ar'], *va.* To fill or cover with glory.

conglutinación [con-gloo-te-nah-the-on´], *f.* Conglutination, glutination: gluing together.

conglutinado, da [con-gloo-te-nah'-do, dah], *a.* Conglutinate. *-pp.* of CONGLUTINAR.

conglutinar [con-gloo-te-nar'], *va.* To conglutinate, to cement, to reunite. *-vr.* To conglutinate.

conglutinativo, va [con-gloo-te-nah-tee´-vo, vah], **Conglutinoso, sa**, *a.* Viscous, glutinous.

Congo [con'-go], *m.* The Congo.

congoja [con-go'-hah], *f.* Anguish, dismay, anxiety of mind.

congojar [con-go-har'], *va*. To oppress, to afflict. *V.* ACON-GOJAR.

congojosamente [con-go-ho-sah-men'-tay], *adv.* Anxiously, painfully.

congojoso, sa [con-go-ho'-so, sah], *a.* 1. Afflictive, painful, tormenting, distressing. 2. Afflicted.

congola [con-go-lah], *f. (And.)* Pipe.

congoleño, ña [con-go-lay'-nyo, nyah], *a.* Relating to or native of the Congo region, in Africa.

congolés [con-go-lays'], *V.* CONGOLEÑO.

congosto [con-gos'-to], *m.* Narrow pass, canyon.

congraciador, ra [con-grah-the-ah-dor', rah], *m. & f.* Flatterer, fawner, wheedler, congratulator.

congraciamiento [con-grah-the-ah-me-en'-to], *m.* Flattery, false praise, mean obsequiousness.

congraciante [con-grah-the-ahn'-tay], *a.* Ingratiating.

congraciar [con-grah-the-ar'], *va.* To ingratiate, to flatter, to win over. *-vr.* To get into one's good graces.

congratulación [con-grah-too-lah-the-on´], *f.* Congratulation.

congratular [con-grah-too-lar'], *va.* To congratulate, to compliment upon any happy event, to greet. *-vr.* To congratulate, to be pleased. **De eso nos congratulamos,** we congratulate ourselves on that.

congratulatorio, ria [con-grah-too-lah-to'-reo, ah], *a.* Congratulatory, congratulant.

congregación [con-gray-gah-the-on'], *f.* 1. Congregation, a meeting or assembly. 2. Fraternity, brotherhood. 3. Congregation, an assembly met to worship God. 4. In some religious orders, union of many monasteries under the direction of a superior general. **Congregación de los fieles,** the catholic or universal church.

congregacionalismo [con-gray-gah-the-o-nah-lees'-mo], *m.* Congregationalism.

congregacionalista [con-gray-gah-the-o-nah-lees'-tah], *com.* Congregationalist.

congregante, ta [con-gray-gahn'-tay, tah], *m. & f.* Member of a congregation, fraternity, or brotherhood.

congregar [con-gray-gar'], *va.*

congresal [con-gray-sahl'], *m. & f. V.* CONGRESISTA.

congresista [con-gray-sees'-tah], *m. & f.* Delegate, member of a congress.

congreso [con-gray´-so], *m.* 1. Congress. 2. Consistory, convention, any solemn assembly or congress. 3. Congress, a meeting of commissioners to settle terms of peace between powers at war. 4. Congress, carnal union of man and woman.

congresual [con-gray-soo-ahl'], *a.* **Reunión congresual,** meeting of parliament.

congrio [con'-gre-o], *m. (Zool.)* Conger-eel, or sea-eel.

congrua [con'-groo-ah], *f.* A stipend paid to someone who is to be ordained a priest.

congruamente [con-groo-ah-men'-tay], *adv.* Conveniently, becomingly.

congruencia [con-groo-en'-the-ah], *f.* Convenience, fitness, congruence.

congruente [con-groo-en'-tay], *a.* Congruent, agreeing, corresponding.

congruentemente [con-groo-en-tay-men'-tay], *adv.* Suitably, congruously.

congruidad [con-groo-e-dahd'], *f. V.* CONGRUENCIA.

congruismo [con-groo-ees'-mo], *m.* Congruism, a religious doctrine which explains the efficacy of grace by its appropriateness.

congruista [con-groo-ees'-tah], *m.* A supporter of the foregoing theory.

congruo, ua [con'-groo-o, ah], *a.* Congruous, apt, fit, suitable.

conicidad [co-ne-the-dahd'], *f.* Conicity, the figure which the tire of a wheel presents in machines and railroad carriages.

cónico, ca [co´-ne-co, cah], *a.* Conical or conic.

conífero, ra [co-nee'-fay-ro, rah], *a. (Bot.)* Coniferous (plantas, árboles).

coniza [co-nee'-thah], *f. (Bot.)* Great fleabane. *V.* ZARAGATONA.

conjetura [con-hay-too'-rah], *f.* Conjecture, surmise, guess. **Por conjetura,** by guess-work.

conjeturable [con-hay-too-rah'-blay], *a.* Conjecturable.

conjeturador, ra [con-hay-too-rah-dor', rah], *m. & f.* Conjecturer, guesser.

conjetural [con-hay-too-rahl'], *a.* Conjectural.

conjeturalmente [con-hay-too-ral-men'-tay], *adv.* Conjecturally, guessingly.

conjeturar [con-hay-too-rar'], *va.* To conjecture, to guess.

conjuez [con-hoo-eth'], *m.* A judge jointly with another upon the same matter.

conjugación [con-hoo-gah-the-on'], *f.* 1. Conjugation, the form of inflecting verbs. 2. The act of comparing one thing with another.

conjugado, da [con-hoo-gah'-do, dah], *a. & pp.* of CONJUGAR. Conjugated, inflected; compared. **Nervios conjugados,** *(Anat.)* Conjugate nerves, those which discharge analogous functions or serve for the same sensation.

conjugar [con-hoo-gar'], *va.* 1. To conjugate or inflect verbs. 2. To compare, to bring together. **La obra conjuga cualidades y defectos,** the work has both qualities and defects. **Es difícil conjugar los deseos de los dos,** it is difficult to fit their wishes together. *-vr.* 1. *(Ling.)* To be conjugated. 2. To fit together, to blend.

conjunción [con-hoon-the-on'], *f.* 1. Conjunction, union, association, league, conjugation, copulation, the act of coupling or joining together; consolidation. 2. Conjunction, a part of speech. 3. *(Astr.)* Conjunction of two planets in the same degree of the zodiac.

conjuntamente [con-hoon´-tah-men-tay]. *adv.* Conjunctly, jointly.

conjuntero, ra [con-hoon-tay'-ro], *m. & f.* Member of a musical group.

conjuntiva [con-hoon-tee'-vah], *f.* Conjunctiva, the mucous membrane of the eye.

conjuntivitis [con-hoon-te-vee'-tis], *f. (Med.)* Conjunctivitis.

conjuntivo, va [con-hoon-tee´-vo, vah], *a.* Conjunctive, copulative, connexive.

conjuntivo [con-hoon-tee'-vo], *m.* The conjunctive mood of a verb. *V.* SUBJUNTIVO.

conjunto, ta [con-hoon'-to, tah], *a.* 1. Conjunct, united, connected, conjunctive, contiguous. 2. Allied by kindred or friendship. 3. Mixed or incorporated with another thing.

conjunto [con-hoon'-to], *m.* 1. The whole, aggregate, entirety. **En conjunto,** as a whole. **Vista de conjunto,** all-embracing view. 2. *(Cos.)* Ensemble; costume. 3. *(Mus.)* Ensemble (de cámara); group (de pop); team. 4. *(Theat.)* Chorus. 5. *(Mech.)* Unit, assembly.

conjuntura [con-hoon-too'-rah], *f. V.* COYUNTURA and CONJUNCIÓN.

conjura [con-hoo'-rah], *f. V.* CONJURACIÓN.

conjuración [con-hoo-rah-the-on'], *f.* 1. Conspiracy, conjuration, plot, complot, machination. 2. Conjuration, the form or act of summoning another in some sacred name. 3. *V.* CONJURO.

conjurado, da [con-hoo-rah'-do, dah], *m. & f.* Conspirator; leaguer, covenanter. *-pp.* of CONJURAR.

conjurador [con-hoo-rah-dor'], *m.* 1. Conjurer, enchanter, impostor. 2. Exorcist. 3. Conspirator.

conjuramentar [con-hoo-rah-men-tar'], *va.* 1. To bind by an oath. 2. To take an oath to another. *-vr.* To bind oneself by an oath. *V.* JURAMENTARSE.

conjurante [con-hoo-rahn'-tay], *pa.* Conjuring, conspiring.

conjurar [con-hoo-rar'], *vn.* To conjure, to conspire, to plot, to hatch or concert treason. 2. To conspire. 3. To join in a conspiracy formed by others. 4. To swear or take an oath improperly with others. *-va.* 1. To exorcise. 2. To conjure, to summon in a sacred name. 3. To entreat, to implore, to ask anything in a solemn manner. 4. To avert, ward off, a mischief or danger.

conjuro [con-hoo'-ro], *m.* 1. Conjuration, exorcism. **Al conjuro de sus palabras,** under the magical effect of his words. 2. Incantation.

conllevador [con-lyay-vah-dor'], *va.* Helper, assistant.

conllevar [con-lyay-var'], *va.* 1. To aid or assist another in his labors; to bear with anyone. 2. To convey, to carry, to imply, to involve, to bring with it, to bring in its wake.

conmaterial [con-mah-tay-re-ahl'], *a.* (Rare) Of the same material.

conmemoración [con-may-mo-rah-theon'], *f.* 1. Remembrance of a person or thing. 2. Commemoration, public celebration. 3. **Conmemoración de los difuntos,** anniversary celebrated by the Roman Catholic church in memory of the deceased, Nov. 2; Allsouls' day.

conmemorar [con-may-mo-rar'], *va.* To commemorate by public acts.

conmemorativo, va [con-may-mo-rah-tee'-vo, vah], *a.* Commemorative. **Un sello conmemorativo,** a commemorative stamp.

conmensal [con-men-sahl'], *m.* Commensal, mate, messmate, one who lives and boards with another at his expense.

conmensalía [con-men-sah-lee'-ah], *f.* Commensality.

conmensurabilidad [con-men-soo-rah-be-le-dahd'], *f.* Commensurability.

conmensurable [con-men-soo-rah'-blay], *a.* Commensurable.

conmensuración [con-men-soo-rah-the-on'], *f.* Commensuration.

conmensurar [con-men-soo-rar'], *va.* To commensurate.

conmensurativo, va [con-men-soo-rah-tee'-vo, vah], *a.* Commensurable.

conmigo [con-mee'-go], *pron. pers.* With me, with myself.

conmilitón [con-me-le-tone'], *m.* Comrade, a fellow soldier.

conminación [con-me-nah-the-on'], *f.* Commination, a threat.

conminar [con-me-nar'], *va.* To threaten or denounce punishment to a criminal in order to make him declare the truth.

conminatorio. ria [con-me-nah-to'-re-o, ah], *a.* Comminatory, denunciatory, threatening.

conminuta [con-me-noo'-tah], *a.* Comminuted. V. FRACTURA.

conmiseración [con-me-say-rah-the-on'], *f.* Commiseration, pity, compassion.

conmistión, conmistura [con-mis-te-on'], *f.* Mixture.

conmisto, ta, or **conmixto, ta** [con-mees'-to, tah], *a.* Mixed, mingled, incorporated.

conmoción [con-mo-the-on'], *f.* 1. Commotion of the mind or body. 2. Excitement, stirring up; flurry, fretting. 3. Commotion, tumult, disturbance, convulsion. **Una conmoción social,** a social upheaval. **Producir una conmoción desagradable a uno,** to give somebody a nasty shock.

conmocionado [con-mo-te-o-nah'-do], *a.* (Med.) Shocked, concussed.

conmocionar [con-mo-the-o-nar'], *va.* 1. To move, to affect deeply. 2. (Med.) To put into shock.

conmonitorio [con-mo-ne-to'-re-o], *m.* 1. A written narration of an event. 2. Order from a superior to an inferior judge, reminding him of his duty.

conmovedor [con-mo-vay-dor'], -*a.* Touching, moving; poignant.

conmover [con-mo-verr'], *va.* 1. To move, to touch, to disturb, to affect (persona). 2. To shake, to disturb (edificio). -*vr.* 1. To shake, to be shaken. 2. (fig.) To be moved.

conmovimiento [con-mo-ve-me-en'-to], *m.* V. CONMOCIÓN. *(Yo conmuevo, yo conmueva, from Conmover. V. MOVER.).*

conmuta [con-moo'-tah], *f. (And. Cono Sur)* Change, alteration.

conmutabilidad [con-moo-tah-be-le-dahd'], *f.* Commutability.

conmutable [con-moo-tah'-blay], *a.* Commutable.

conmutación [con-moo-tah-the-on'], *f.* Commutation, exchange.

conmutador [con-moo-tah-dor'], *m.* Electric switch, telegraph key, cutout, commutator.

conmutar [con-moo-tar'], *va.* To commute, to change, to barter.

conmutativo, va [con-moo-tah-tee'-vo, vah], *a.* Commutative.

connato, ta [con-nah'-to, tah], *a.* 1. (Med.) Connate, congenital, innate. 2. (Bot.) Connate, conjoined.

connatural [con-nah-too-rahl'], *a.* Connatural, inborn.

connaturalización [con-nah-too-rah-le-thah-the-on'], *f.* Naturalization, investing aliens with the privileges of native subjects.

connaturalizar [con-nah-too-rah-le-thar'], *va.* To naturalize, to invest with the privileges of native subjects. -*vr.* To accustom oneself to labor, climate, or food; to inure.

connaturalmente [con-nah-too-ral-men'-tay], *adv.* Connaturally.

conexidad [con-nek-se-dahd,], *f. V.* CONEXIDAD.

connivencia [con-ne-ven'-the-ah], *f.* 1. Connivance. 2. Action of confabulating.

connotación [con-no-tah-the-on'], *f.* 1. Connotation. 2. A distant relation.

connotado [con-no-tah'-do], *m.* Relationship, kindred. *Connotado, da pp.* of CONNOTAR. -*a.* Notable, famous.

connotar [con-no-tar'], *va.* To connote, to connotate, to imply.

connotativo, va [con-no-tah-tee'-vo, vah], *a.* (Gram.) Connotative or connotive, applied to nouns which signify the quality of the object designated by the primitive noun, or the office of the subject from which it is derived, as *aquilino, caballar, bacanal, lírico,* etc.

connovicio, cia [con-no-vee'-the-o, ah], *m. & f.* A fellow-novice.

connubial [con-noo-be-ahl'], *a.* Connubial, matrimonial, conjugal.

connubio [con-noo'-be-o], *m. (Poet.)* Matrimony, marriage, wedlock.

connumerar [con-noo-may-rar'], *va.* To enumerate; to include in a number.

cono [co'-no], *m.* 1. (Geom.) Cone. 2. (Zool.) Genus of mollusks which has the spiral of the shell flattened. 3. (Bot.) Cone, the fruit of the pine family. 4. **El Cono Sur** = Argentina, Chile, Uruguay.

conocedor, ra [co-no-thay-dor', rah], *m. & f.* 1. Connoisseur, expert. 2. Judge or critic in matters of taste. **Es buen conocedor de ganado,** he´s a good judge of cattle.

conocencia [co-no-then'-the-ah], *f. (LAm.)* Girlfriend, sweetheart.

conocer [co-no-therr'], *va.* 1. To know, to be acquainted with. 2. To possess a clear or distinct idea of a person's physiognomy, or the figure of a thing, to feel. 3. To perceive, to comprehend. 4. To experience, to observe. 5. To conjecture, to surmise. 6. To know carnally. 7. To acknowledge a crime, or debt. **Conocer de una causa** or **pleito,** to try a cause (jueces). **Conocer a uno de vista,** to know somebody by sight. **Conozco las dificultades,** I know the difficulties. **Vengo a conocer Portugal,** I have come to get to know Portugal. **Dar a conocer,** to introduce. **Conocer a uno por su modo de andar,** to know somebody by his walk. **No me conoce de nada,** he doesn´t know me from Adam. -*vr.* 1. To know one another. **Se conocieron en un baile,** they met at a dance. 2. To appreciate one's own good or bad qualities. -*vn.* **Conocer de,** to know about. 2. **Conocer de una causa,** *(Jur.)* To try a case.

conocible [co-no-thee'-blay], *a.* Cognoscible, knowable.

conocidamente [co-no-the-dah-men'-tay], *adv.* Knowingly, evidently, confessedly.

conocido, da [co-no-thee'-do, dah], 1. *m. & f.* Acquaintance. 2. *a.* Person of family or distinction. -*pp.* of CONOCER.

conocimiento [co-no-the-me-en'-to], *m.* 1. Knowledge, understanding, skill. **Hablar con conocimiento de causa,** to know what one is talking about. **Ha llegado a mi conocimiento que...,** it has come to my attention that... **Mis pocos conocimientos de filosofía,** my small knowledge of philosophy. **Conocimientos avanzados,** expert knowledge. 2. Acquaintance, the person with whom we are acquainted. 3. Acquaintance, a slight or initial knowledge, a sort of friendship. 4. Cognizance, judicial notice. 5. *(Com.)* Bill of lading. 6. A note of identification, relative to business matters. 7. *(Amer.)* A check for baggage. 8. *(Med.)* Consciousness. **Estar sin conocimiento,** to be unconcious. *-pl.* Accomplishments, science. **Venir en conocimiento,** to remember or recollect a thing distinctly, to comprehend a thing clearly after thinking of it.

conoidal [co-no-e-dahl'], *a.* Conoidal, conoidical.

conoide [co-no'-e-day], *f.* Conoid.

conopial, conopio [co-no-pe-ahl', co-no-pe-o], *m. (Arch.)* Ogee arch *(Yo conozco, yo conozca,* from *Conocer. V.* ABORRECER.).

conque [con-kay'], *m. (Coll.)* Condition, quality.

conquiforme [con-ke-for´-may], *a.* Conchiform, shaped line onehalf of a bivalve shell.

conquista [con-kees'-tah], *f.* 1. Conquest, subjection. 2. Conquest, acquisition by victory; the thing gained. 3. Act of winning another's affections.

conquistador [con-kees-tah-dor'], *m.* 1. Conqueror. 2. Wolf, lady-killer. *-a.* Conquering.

conquistadora [con-kees-tah-do´-rah], *f.* Conqueress.

conquistar [con-kees-tar'], *va.* 1. To conquer, to overcome, to subdue. 2. To acquire, to win another person's affections.

conrear [con-ray-ar'], *va.* 1. In manufactories, to grease wool. 2. To hoe the soil. *V.* BINAR.

conregnante [con-reg-nahn'-tay], *a.* Reigning with another.

conreinar [con-ray-e-nar'], *vn.* To reign with another.

consabido, da [con-sah-bee'-do, dah], *a.* Already known; alluded to, in question: applied to persons or things already treated of. *-pp.* of CONSABER.

consabidor, ra [con-sah-be-dor', rah], *m. & f.* One who possesses knowledge jointly with others.

consagración [con-sah-grah-the-on'], *f.* Consecration.

consagrado, da [con-sah-grah-do, dah], *a. & pp.* of CONSAGRAR. 1. Consecrate, consecrated, sacred, devoted. 2. *(fig.)* Time-honored, hallowed, ritual, traditional. **Actor consagrado,** an established actor.

consagrante [con-sah-grahn'-tay], *m. & pa.* Consecrator.

consagrar [con-sa-grar'], *va.* 1. To consecrate, to hallow, to make sacred. 2. Among the Romans, to deify their emperors. 3. To consecrate, to devote, to dedicate. 4. To erect a monument. 5. To confirm. **Este triunfo le consagra como un cirujano excepcional,** this success confirms him as a really exceptional surgeon. *-vr.* To devote oneself.

consanguíneo, nea [con-san-gee'-nay-o, ah], *a.* Consanguineous, cognate, kindred.

consanguinidad [con-san-gee-ne-dahd'], *f.* Consanguinity.

consciencia, *f.* Consciousness; awareness. *V.* CONCIENCIA.

consciente [cons-the-en'-tay], *a.* 1. Conscious, in possession of one's faculties. **Ser consciente de,** to be conscious of. 2. *(Med.)* **Estar consciente,** to be conscious. 3. *(Jur.)* Fully responsible for one´s actions. *-m.* Conscious, conscious mind.

conscientemente [cons-the-ayn-tay-men-tay], *adv.* Consciously.

conscripción [cons-crip-the-on'], *f.* Conscription.

conscripto [cons-creep´-to], *m.* Conscript, taken by lot, or compulsorily enrolled to serve in the army or navy. *a.* Conscript (senadores romanos).

consectario [con-sec-tah´-re-o], *m.* Consectary, corollary.

consectario [con-sec-tah´-re-o], *a.* Consectary, consequent.

consecución [con-say-coo-the-on'], *f.* Attainment of a benefice, employment, or other desirable object, obtaining, acquisition. **De difícil consecución,** hard to

obtain. **Para la consecución de estos objetos,** for the attainment of these aims.

consecuencia [con-say-coo-en'-the-ah], *f.* 1. Consequence, conclusion, inference. **Por consecuencia,** therefore. 2. Result or effect of a cause, issue. **En consecuencia de eso,** as a result of that. **Aceptar las consecuencias,** to take the consequences. 3. Consistence, firmness, coherence. **Guardar consecuencia,** to be consistent. 4. Consequence, importance, moment, concern, matter; consideration, note. **De consecuencia,** of importance. **Ser de consecuencia,** to be important. **Ser de consecuencia,** to be very important. **En consecuencia,** consequently, therefore, in consequence of.

consecuente [con-say-coo-en'-tay], *m.* 1. Consequent, consequence. 2. Effect. 3. Important. **No demasiado consecuente,** not very important.

consecuente, [con-say-coo-ayn'-tay], *a.* 1. Consequent, following by rational deduction. 2. Following, as the effect of a cause. 3. Consistent, coherent. **Ser consecuente en sus operaciones,** to act with consistency.

consecuentemente [con-say-coo-en-tay-men´-tay], *adv.* 1. Consequently. 2. By consequence, necessarily, inevitably.

consecutivamente [con-say-coo-te-vah-men'-tay], *adv.* Consecutively.

consecutivo, va [con-say-coo-tee'-vo, vah], *a.* Consecutive, consequential.

conseguible [con-say-gee'-blay], *a.* Obtainable, attainable.

conseguimiento [con-say-gee-me-en'-to], *m.* Attainment, obtainment. *V.* CONSECUCIÓN.

conseguir [con-say-geer'], *va.* To attain, to get, to gain, to obtain, to succeed. **Conseguir que uno haga algo,** to manage to make somebody do something. **Lo consigue como mi abuela,** he has as much chance of getting it as the man in the moon.

conseja [con-say'-hah], *f.* A fable, tale, story, legend.

consejera [con-say-hay'-rah], *f.* Counsellor's wife; woman who gives advice.

consejería [con-say-hay-ree'-ah], *f.* Council, commission.

consejero, ra [con-say-hay´-ro], *m. & f.* 1. Counsellor, member of a council. 2. Counsellor, adviser. 3. Anything which may give warning. 4. **Consejero de estado,** a counsellor of state.

consejo [con-say'-ho], *m.* 1. Counsel, advice, opinion. **Agradezco el consejo,** I am grateful for your advice. **Pedir consejo a uno,** to ask somebody for advice. 2. Council, an assembly of magistrates. 3. Councilhouse. **Consejo directivo,** board of directors. **Consejo de ministros,** cabinet. **Consejo de guerra,** court-martial. **Consejo de disciplina,** disciplinary board.

consejuela [con-say-hoo-ay'-lah], *f. dim.* A little tale or story.

conseminado, da [con-say-me-nah'-do, dah], *a. (Agri.)* Sown with different kinds of grain.

consenciente [con-sen-the-en'-tay], *pa.* Consenting, conniver.

consenso [con-sen'-so], *m.* A general assent, agreement of opinion: consensus.

consensual [con-sen-soo-ahl'], *a.* Agreed. **Unión consensual,** common-law marriage.

consensuar [con-sen-soo-ar'], *va.* To agree on, to reach an agreement on, to reach a consensus on.

consentido [con-sen-tee' do], *a.* 1. Applied to a spoiled child 2. Applied to a cuckold by his own consent. - **consentido, da,** *pp.* of CONSENTIR.

consentidor, ra [con-sen-te-dor', rah], *m. & f.* Complier, conniver.

consentimiento [con-sen-te-me-en'-to], *m.* 1. Consent, connivance, compliance, acquiescence, concurrence, consenting, acknowledgment. 2. *(Med.)* Consent.

consentir [con-sen-teer'], *va.* 1. To consent, to agree. **Aquí no se consiente hablar,** they don´t let you speak. 2. To comply, to acquiesce, to accede, to condescend, to admit. **La plata-**

forma no consiente más peso, the platform will not bear any more weight. 3. To believe for certain, to rely, to depend. 4. To coddle, spoil, overindulge children or servants. *(Acad.).* *-vn.* To agree, to consent, to say yes; to give in. **Consentir en hacer algo,** to agree to. *-vr.* To break, to give; to split, to crack.

conserje [con-serr'-hay], *m.* Keeper or warden of a royal palace, castle, or public building. (*Cf.* Concierge.)

conserjería [con-ser-hay-ree'-ah], *f.* 1. Wardenship of a royal palace or castle. 2. Warden's dwelling.

conserva [con-serr'-vah], *f.* 1. Conserve, preserve. **Conservas alimenticias,** canned foods. **Conservas de carne,** canned meat. **En conservas,** preserved. 2. Pickles. 3. Fleet of merchant men under convoy of a ship of war. **Ir** or **navegar de conserva,** to sail under convoy, to navigate in company with other ships. - *pl.* Tinned, canned food.

conservación [con-ser-vah-the-on'], *f.* 1. Conservation, preservation. 2. Maintenance, upkeep. **Conservación del suelo,** soil conservation. **Conservación de la naturaleza,** nature conservation. **Instinto de conservación,** instinct of self-preservation.

conservacionismo [con-ser-vah-the-o-nes'-mo], *m.* Conservationist; conservation; conservation movement.

conservacionista [con-ser-vah-the-o-nes-tah], *a. m. & f.* Conservationist.

conservador [con-ser-vah-dor,], *m.* Conservator, preserver.

conservadora [con-ser-vah-do'-rah], *f.* 1. Conservatrix. 2. Curator, keeper (de museo).

conservadurismo [con-ser-vah-doo-res'-mo], *m. (Pol. etc.)* Conservatism.

conservante [con-ser-vahn'-tay], *pa.* Conserving, conserver, preservative.

conservar [con-ser-var'], *va.* 1. To conserve, to maintain, to preserve, to keep, to hold. 2. To guard, to observe, to continue. 3. To preserve or pickle fruit. **Conservo varias cartas suyas,** I have a few letters of his. **Conserva todavía la señal,** he still has the mark. *-vr.* 1. To survive, to remain; to be retained, to be kept. 2. To keep (persona); to take good care of; **conservar con salud,** to keep well.

conservatismo [con-ser-vah-tes'-mo], *m.* Conservatism.

conservativo, va [con-ser-vah-tee'-vo, vah], *a.* Conservative, preservative.

conservativos [con-ser-vah-tee'-vos], *m. pl.* Glasses with preservative lenses.

conservatoría [con-ser-vah-to-ree'-ah], *f.* 1. Place and office of a *Juez conservador,* who is responsible for preserving and defending the rights and privileges of a community. 2. Indult or apostolical letters granted to communities, by virtue of which they choose their own judges conservators; **conservatorías,** letters patent granted by conservatory judges in favor of those under their jurisdiction.

conservatorio [con-ser-vah-to'-re-o], *m.* 1. Conservatory, a place for instruction in the fine arts. 2. *(Cono Sur)* Greenhouse. 3. *(Cono Sur)* private school.

conservatorio, ria [con-ser-vah-to'-re-o, ah], *a.* Conservatory, having a preservative quality.

conservero, ra [con-ser-vay'-ro, rah], *m. & f.* Conserver, a preparer of conserves.

considerable [con-se-day-rah'-blay], *a.* 1. Considerable. 2. Great, large, plentiful.

considerablemente [con-se-day-rah.-blay-men'-tay], *adv.* Considerably.

consideración [con-se-day-rah-the-on'], *f.* 1. Consideration, regard, notice, sake, account. **Hablar sin consideración,** to speak disrespectfully. **Tratar a uno sin consideración,** to treat somebody without consideration. 2. Consideration; reflection, contemplation, meditation. 3. Consideration, importance, claim to notice, worthiness of regard. **Una casa de cierta consideración,** a sizeable house. **Una herida de consideración,** a serious wound. 4. Urbanity, respect. **Ser de consideración,** to be of great importance. **En**

consideración, considering, in consideration, in proportion.

consideradamente [con-se-day-rah-dah-men'-tay], *adv.* Considerately, calmly.

considerado [con-se-day-rah'-do], *a.* Prudent, considerate. - **Considerado, da,** *pp.* of CONSIDERAR.

considerador, ra [con-se-day-rah-dor', rah], *m. & f.* Considerer, considerator, a person of prudence or reflection.

considerando [con-se-day-rahn'-do], *m. (Jur.)* Word with which each item in a judgement begins; point, item, statement.

considerante [con-se-day-rahn'-tay], *pa.* Considering.

considerar [con-se-day-rar'], *va.* 1. To consider, meditate. 2. To treat with urbanity, respect, consideration. 3. To take into acount. **Considera que...,** bear in mind that... **Bien considerado, es razonable,** on reflection, that is reasonable. **Lo considero imposible,** I consider it impossible. **Considerar poco a,** to scorn, to despise.

consigna [con-seeg'-nah], *f.* 1. *(Mil.)* Watchword, countersign, order, instruction. **Consignas de un vuelo,** operating instructions for a flight. 2. *(Ferro. etc.)* Cloakroom, left-luggage office, check-room.

consignación [con-sig-nah-the-on'], *f.* 1. Consignation. 2. Sum of money destined to serve for a certain time some peculiar purpose. 3. Consignment, cargo of goods.

consignador, ra [con-sig-nah-dor'], *m. & f.* Consignor, one who consigns goods or merchandise to a foreign correspondent.

consignar [con-sig-nar'], *va.* 1. To consign, assign, or make over the rent of a house or any other sum for the payment of a debt. 2. To consign, to yield, to entrust, to lay to. 3. To lay by, to deposit. 4. To deliver, 5. To consign goods or merchandise to a foreign correspondent, to be sold on behalf of the consigner. 6. To sign with the mark of a cross. 7. *(CAm. Mex.) (Jur.)* To remand, to hold for trial. **Olvidé consignar mi nombre,** I forgot to write my name in, I forgot to state my name. **El hecho no quedó consignado en ningún libro,** the fact was not recorded in any book.

consignatario, ria [con-sig-nah-tah'-re-o], *m. & f.* 1. Trustee, who receives money in trust for another. 2. Mortgagee, who possesses and enjoys the lands or tenements mortgaged, until the debt be paid out of the proceeds. 3. Consignee, a merchant or factor to whom a ship or cargo, or merely part of the latter, is consigned.

consigo [con-see'-go], *pro.pers.* With oneself, with himself, herself, themselves, yourself, or yourselves. **Consigo mismo,** alone, by oneself. (**Yo consigo, yo consigo, from Conseguir.** *V.* PEDIR.)

consiguiente [con-se-gee-en'-tay], *m. (Log.)* Consequence, result.

consiguiente [con-se-gee-en'-tay], *a.* Consequent, consecutive, consequential. **De consiguiente, por consiguiente,** or **por el consiguiente, consequently,** by consequence, pursuantly.

consiguientemente [con-se-ge-en-tay-men'-tay], *adv.* Consequently.

consiliario [con-se-le-ah'-re-o], *m.* Counsellor or assistant to the heads of colleges, convents, etc. *V.* CONSEJERO.

consintiente [con-sin-te-en'-tay], *pa.* Consenting, agreeing.

consistencia [con-sis-ten'-the-ah], *f.* 1. Consistence, or consistency, degree of density or rarity. 2. Consistency, stability, duration; coherence, conformity. 3. Consistency, firmness, solidity, intellectual strength.

consistente [con-sis-ten'-tay], *a.* 1. Consistent, firm, solid. 2. **Consistente en,** consisting of.

consistir [con-sis-teer'], *vn.* 1. To consist, to subsist, to continue fixed; to lie. 2. To consist, to be comprised, to be contained. 3. To consist, to be composed. **Consistir en,** to be due to, to be accounted for by. **No consiste en eso la dificultad,** the difficulty does not lie in that. **Su atractivo consiste en su naturalidad,** her charm lies in her naturalness.

consistorial [con-sis-to-re-ahl'], *a.* 1. Consistorial, belonging or relating to an ecclesiastical court. 2. **Casa consistorial,** or **casas consistoriales,** senatehouse, guildhall, townhouses or townhalls, courthouse.

consistorio [con-sis-to'-re-o], *m. (Ecl.)* Consistory; *(Pol.)* Town council; town hall (edificio).

consocio [con-so'-the-o], *m.* Partner, companion, fellow-partner.

consol [con-sol'], *m. (Peru)* = CONSOLA.

consola [con-so'-lah], *f.* Console, bracket-shelf.

consolable [con-so-lah'-blay], *a.* Consolable, relievable, comfortable.

consolación [con-so-lah-the-on'], *f.* Consolation, comfort.

consolado, da [con-so-lah'-do, dah], *a.* Consoled, comforted. *pp.* of CONSOLAR.

consolador, ra [con-so-lah-dor', rah], *m. & f.* 1. Consolator, comforter. 2. *m.*Comforter, a name of the Holy Spirit.

consolador, ra [con-so-lah-dor', rah], *a.* Consolatory, comfortable.

consolante [con-so-lahn´-tay], *pa.* Comforting, consoling, comfortable.

consolar [con-so-lar´], *va.* To console, to comfort, to cheer. **Me consuela de no haber ido,** it consoles me for not having gone. *-vr.* To console oneself; to find consolation, to take comfort.

consolativo, va [con-so-lah-tee´-vo, vah], **consolatorio, ria,** *a.* consolatory, comfortable.

consoldamiento, *m. (Obs.) V.* CONSOLIDACIÓN.

consólida [con-so'-le-dah],*f. (Bot.) V.* CONSUELDA. **Consólida real,** larkspur.

consolidación [con-so-le-dah-the-on'], *f.* Consolidation.

consolidado, da [con-so-le-dah'-do, dah], *a.* Consolidated. *-pl.* Consolidated annuities, consols, government securities.

consolidar [con-so-le-dar'], *va.* To consolidate, to compact, to close, to harden, to strengthen. *-vr.* 1. To consolidate, to grow firm, hard, or solid. 2. *(Law.)* To unite the interest with the principal.

consolidativo, va [con-so-le-dah-tee'-vo, vah], *a.* Consolidant, consolidative.

consommé [con-so-may´], *m.* Consommé, beef broth.

consonancia [con-so-nahn'-the-ah], *f.* 1. Consonance, harmony, accord of sound. 2. Consistency, congruence, consent. 3. *(Met.)* Conformity.

consonante [con-so-nahn'-tay], *m.* 1. Rhyme, a word, the last syllable or syllables of which, from the vowel where the accent is, corresponds with that of another. 2. *(Mus.)* A consonous or corresponding sound. 3. *f. (Gram.)* A consonant.

consonante [con-so-nahn'-tay], *a.* Consonant, agreeable, consistent, concordant, conformable. **Letras consonantes,** the consonants.

consonantemente [con-so-nan-tay-men'-tay], *adv.* Consonantly, agreeably.

consonántico [con-so-nahn'-te-co], *a.* Consonantal.

consonar [con-so-nar'], *vn.* 1. To make a body sound; to play on musical instruments. 2. To rhyme. 3. *(Met.)* To agree, to resemble.

cónsones [con'-so-nes], *m. pl. (Mus.)* Concordant sounds.

cónsono, na [con'-so-no, nah], *a.* Consonous, harmonious, consonant.

consorcio [con-sor'-the-o], *m.* 1. Consortium, partnership, society. 2. Friendly intercourse, mutual affection.

consorte [con-sor´-tay], *com.* 1. Consort, companion, partner; mate. 2. Consort, a person joined in marriage with another. **Príncipe consorte,** prince consort. 3. One who enters or defends an action jointly with another.

conspicuamente [cons-pe-coo-ah-men'-tay], *adv.* Conspicuously.

conspicuo, cua [cons-pee'-coo-o, ah], *a.* 1. Conspicuous, obvious, observable. 2. Conspicuous, eminent, famous, distinguished.

conspiración [cons-pe-rah-the-on'],*f.* Conspiracy, plot, complot, conjuration, conspiration: an agreement of men to do anything evil or unlawful.

conspirado [cons-pe-rah'-do], *m. V.* CONSPIRADOR. **-Conspirado, da,** *pp.* of CONSPIRAR.

conspirador, ra [cons-pe-rah-dor'], *m.f.* Conspirator, one who plots, traitor.

conspirante [cons-pe-rahn'-tay], *pa.* Conspiring. **Fuerzas conspirantes,** conspiring powers, co-operating mechanical powers which concur in producing the same effect.

conspirar [cons-pe-rar'], *va.* To implore the assistance or solicit the favor of another.*-vn.* 1. To conspire, to concert a crime, to plot. 2. To conspire, to agree, to cooperate, to combine.

conspirativo [cons-pe-rah-te'-vo], *a.* Conspiratorial.

constancia [cons-tahn'-the-ah], *f.* 1. Constancy, steadiness, immutability. 2. Certainty; proof, evidence. **No hay constancia de ello,** there is no certainty of it. **Dejar constancia de algo,** to place something on record. **Para que quede constancia de la fecha,** in order to give proof of the date. 3. *(LAm.)* Documentary proof, written evidence. **Dar constancia,** to give proof.

constante [cons-tahn'-tay], *a.* 1. Constant, firm, unalterable, immutable. 2. Loyal, constant. 3. Manifest, apparent, clear. 4. *m. & f.* One who is constant. *-pa.* Composed of, consisting in. 5. *(Inform.)* **Constante numérica,** numeric constant.

constantemente [cons-tan-tay-men'-tay], *adv.* 1. Constantly, firmly, unalterably. 2. Evidently, undoubtedly.

Constantino [cons-tahn-te'-no], *m.* Constantine.

constantinopolitano, na [cons-tan-te-no-po-le-tah'-no, nah], *a.* Of Constantinople.

constar [cons-tar'], *v. imp.* 1. To be clear, evident, certain. **Consta en autos** or **de autos,** it appears from the judicial proceedings. **Consta que...,** it is clear that. **Conste que yo no lo aprobé,** let it be clearly understood that I did not approve it. **Que conste que lo hice por ti,** believe me, I did it for your own good. 2. To be composed of, to consist in. 3. Of verses, to have the measure and accent corresponding to their class. 4. To exist in recorded form, to be on record. **No consta en el catálogo,** it is not listed in the catalog.

constatable [cons-tah-tah-blay], *a.* Observable, evident. **Es constatable que...,** it can be observed that...

constatación [cons-tah-tah-te-on'], *f.* Confirmation, verification.

constatar [cons-tah-tar'], *va.* To confirm, to verify, to check, to show.

constelación [cons-tay-lah-the-on'], *f.* 1. Constellation, a cluster of fixed stars. 2. Climate, temperature of the air.

constelado [cons-tay-lah-do], *a.* Starry, full of stars.

consternación [cons-ter-nah-the-on'],*f.* Consternation, perturbation of mind, amazement, horror, distress.

consternado [cons-ter-nah-do], *a.* **Estar consternado,** to be dismayed

consternar [cons-ter-nar'], *va.* To terrify, to strike with horror or amazement, to confound. *-vr.* To be dismayed, to be shattered; to be aghast.

constipación [cons-te-pah-the-on'], *f.* 1. Cold (resfriado). 2. Constipation (estreñimiento).

constipado [cons-te-pah'-do], *m.* Cold (resfriado). **-Constipado, da,** *pp.* of CONSTIPAR; **coger un constipado,** to catch a cold.

constipar [cons-te-par'], *va.* To cause a cold, to obstruct the perspiration.*-vr.* 1. To catch cold. 2. To be costive.

constipativo, va [cons-te-pah-tee'-vo, vah], *a.* Constrictive.

constitución [cons-te-too-the-on'], *f.* 1. Constitution. 2. Constitution, corporeal frame, temper of body with respect to health or disease, habit of the body. 3. Constitution, established form of government; system of laws and customs. 4. Constitution, particular law or established usage. 5. Any of the by-laws by which a body or corporation is governed.

constitucional [cons-te-too-the-o-nahl'], *m.* Constitutionalist, constitutionist. *a.* Constitutional.

constitucionalidad [cons-te-too-the-o-nah-le-dahd'],*f.* Constitutionality.

constitucionalismo [cons-te-too-the-o-nah-lees'-mo], *m.* Constitutionalism, love of the constitution of a country.

constitucionalmente, *adv.* Constitutionally.

constituir [cons-te-too-eer'], *va.* 1. To constitute, to produce. **Eso no constituye estorbo,** that isn´t an obstacle. 2. To erect, to establish, to make; to create. **Lo constituyen 12 miembros,** it consists of 12 members. **Constituir una nación en república,** to make a country into a republic. **Constituir a uno en árbitro,** to set somebody up as an arbiter. 3. To appoint, to depute. 4. **Constituir la dote,** to pay off a woman´s portion, either by installments or in one sum. 6. **Constituirse en obligación de alguna cosa,** to bind oneself to perform anything. *-vr.* 1. **Constituirse en juez,** to set oneself up as a judge. 2. **Constituirse en un lugar,** to present oneself at a place.

constitutivo, va [cons-te-too-tee'-vo, vah], *a.* Constitutive, essential, productive, formal, hypostatical. *-m. & f.* Constituent.

constituto [cons-te-too'-to], *m.* A legal fiction of alienation and transference.

constituyente [cons-te-too-yen'-tay], *m.* 1. Constituent. 2. *V.* COMITENTE. *-a.* Constituent, that which makes a thing what it is *pa.* of CONSTITUIR.

constreñidamente [cons-tre-nye-dah-men'-tay], *adv.* Compulsively.

constreñimiento [cons-tray-nyee-me-en'-to], *m.* Constraint or compulsion.

constreñir [cons-tray-nyeer'], *va.* 1. To constrain, to compel, to force, to constrict. **Constreñir a uno a hacer algo,** to compel somebody to do something. 2. *(Med.)* To bind or make costive (comida).

constricción [cons-tric-the-on'],*f.* Constriction, contraction.

constrictivo, va [cons-tric-tee'-vo, vah], *a.* Binding, astringent, or constringent.

constrictor [cons-tric-tor'], *m. & a.* Constrictor.

constringente [cons-trin-hen'-tay], *a.* **&** *pa.* Constringent: constrictor.

constriñir, *va.* *(Obs.)* V. CONSTREÑIR. *(Yo constriño, yo constriña; él constriñó, constriñera*; from *Constreñir.* V. PEDIR.)

Construcción [cons-trooc-the-on'],*f.* 1. Construction. **Construcción de carreteras,** road building. 2. Construction, the putting of words together. 3. Construction, arranging terms in their proper order; the sense or the meaning. 4. Interpretation, version, translation. 5. Shipbuilding, naval architecture. **Construcción de buques,** ship-building.

constructivamente [cons-trooc-te-vah-men-tay], *adv.* Constructively.

constructivo [cons-trooc-te-vo], *a.* Constructive.

constructor, ra [cons-trooc-tor', rah], *a.* Building, constructing. **Ingeniero constructor,** constructing engineer. *-m.* Constructor. **Constructor de caminos,** road builder.

constructora [cons-trooc-to-rah],*f.* Construction company.

construir [cons-troo-eer'], *va.* 1. To form, to build, to construct, to fabricate, to frame. 2. To construe, to range words in their natural order. 3. To translate literally. *-vr. (Ling.)* **Este verbo se construye con subjuntivo,** this verb goes into the subjunctive.

constuprador [cons-too-prah-dor'], *m.* A debaucher, a defiler, a corruptor.

constuprar [cons-too-prar'], *va.* To defile, to corrupt.

consubstanciación [con-soobs-tan-the-ah-the-on'],*f.* 1. The mingling of one thing with another. 2. Consubstantiation, the doctrine of the Lutherans upon the Eucharist.

consubstanciador [con-soobs-tan-the-ah-dor'], *a.* Epithet applied by the Catholics to the Lutherans, who hold the doctrine of consubstantiation.

consubstancial, [con-soobs-tahn-the-ahl'], *a.* Consubstantial: applied to the Holy Trinity; of one and the same substance.

consubstancialilad [con-soobs-tan-the-ah-le-dahd'],*f.* Consubstantiality.

consuegrar [con-soo-ay-grar´], *vn.* To become joint fathers or mothers-in-law.

consuegro, gra [con-soo-ay'-gro, grah], *m. & f.* Father-in-law or mother-in-law of one's child.

consuelda [con-soo-el´-dah], *f. (Bot.)* Comfrey. **Consuelda media,** common bugle, bugleweed.

consuelo [con-soo-ay'-lo], *m.* 1. Consolation, comfort, relief, comfortableness. 2. Joy, merriment. 3. Charity. 4. *(Coll.)* **Sin consuelo,** out of rule or measure. **Premio de consuelo,** consolation prize. *(Yo consuelo, yo consuele,* from *Consolar.* V. ACORDAR.) *(Yo consueno, yo consuene,* from *Consonar.* V. ACORDAR.)

consueta [con-soo-ay'-tah], *m. &.f.* 1. *(Prov.)* Stage prompter. 2. *(Prov.)* Directory, which contains the order for divine service. **Consuelas,** short prayers used on certain days in divine service.

consuetudinario, ria [con-soo-ay-too-de-nah'-re-o, ah], *a.* 1. Customary, generally practised. 2. *(Theol.)* In the habit of sinning. 3. **Derecho consuetudinario,** common law.

cónsul [cone'-sool], *m.* 1. Consul, the chief magistrate in ancient Rome. 2. Member of the tribunal of commerce. 3. Consul, an officer commissioned in foreign countries to protect the commerce of his country.

consulado [con-soo-lah'-do], *m.* 1. Consulate. 2. Term of office as consul. 3. Tribunal of commerce, appointed to try and decide causes which concern navigation and trade. 4. Office of consul and territory of same.

consulaje [con-soo-lah'-hay], *m.* Fees paid to consuls by all merchant vessels.

consular [con-soo-lar'], *a.* Consular. **Varón consular,** one who has been consul.

consulta [con-sool'-tah],*f.* 1. A question proposed, or a proposal made in writing. 2. Consultation, conference, meeting for deliberation. 3. Report made and advice given to the king in council. 4. Advice to the king by the supreme tribunals and officers of state, with regard to persons proposed to fill public employments. 5. *(Med.)* Consulting room. **Consulta externa,** out-patients department. 6. *(Med.)* Examination. **Horas de consulta,** surgery hours. **El doctor no pasa consulta a domicilio,** the doctor does not make home visits.

consultable [con-sool-tah'-blay], *a.* Worthy or necessary to be deliberated upon.

consultación [con-sool-tah-the-on'], *f.* Consultation, conference, meeting.

consultante [con-sool-tahn´-tay], *pa.* Consulting, consulter. **Ministro consultante,** minister who lays before the king the opinion of his council.

consultar [con-sool-tar´], *va.* 1. To consult, to ask or take another's advice. **Consultar a un médico,** to consult a doctor. 2. To advise, to give advice. 3. To consult, to deliberate, to take counsel together. **Consultar con la almohada,** to take into mature consideration: literally, to consult the pillow. 4. To consult (libro); to look up.

consultivo, va [con-sool-tee´-vo, vah], *a.* 1. Consultative. 2. Applied to matters which the councils and tribunals are obliged to lay before the king, accompanied with their advice.

consultor, ra [con-sool-tor', rah], *m. &.f.* 1. Consultor, adviser, counsel. 2. *(Inform.)* Consultant. **Consultor del centro de información,** information center consultant

consultoría [con-sool-to-re'-ah], f. Consultancy.

consultorio [con-sool-to´-ryo], *m.* 1. Consulting office. 2. Doctor's office.

consumación [con-soo-mah-the-on'], *f.* 1. Consummation, perfection, end, finishing, accomplishment. 2. Destruction, suppression. **Consumación de los siglos**, consummation, the end of the present system of things.

consumadamente [con-soo-mah-dah-men-tay], *adv.* Perfectly, completely, consummately.

consumado, da [con-soo-mah'-do, dah], *a.* Consummate, complete, perfect, accomplished, exquisite. *-pp.* of CONSUMAR. *-m.* 1. Loot, swag (cosas robadas). 2. Hash (droga).

consumador, ra [con-soo-mah-dor', rah], *m. & f.* Finisher, one who consummates, perfects, or finishes.

consumar [con-soo-mar'], *va.* 1. To consummate, to finish, to perfect, to complete. 2. *(And. CAm.)* To submerge.

consumativo, va [con-soo-mah-tee'-vo, vah], *a.* Consummate, that which consummates or completes (sacramentos).

consumible [con-soo-mee'-blay], *a.* Consumable.

consumición [con-soo-me-the-on'], *f. (Com.)* V. CONSUMO. **Consumición mínima**, minimum charge. **Pagar la consumición**, to pay for what one has had.

consumido , da [con-soo-mee'-do, dah], *a.* 1. Lean, meagre, exhausted, spent. 2. Easily afflicted.-*pp.* of CONSUMIR.

consumidor, ra [con-soo-me-dor', rah], *m. & f.* Consumer, destroyer. **Consumidor de drogas**, drug-taker. **Productos al consumidor**, consumer products.

consumimiento [con-soo-me-me-en'-to], *m.* Consumption.

consumir [con-soo-meer], *va.* 1. To consume, to destroy. to waste, to exhaust; to lick up: to obliterate; to melt. **Le consumen los celos**, he is eaten up with jealously. **Ese deseo le consume**, that desire is burning him up. **Me consume su terquedad**, his obstinacy is getting on my nerves. 2. In the sacrifice of the mass, to swallow the elements of bread and wine in the Eucharist. *-vr.* 1. To be spent, to be exausted. **Se ha consumido la vela**, the candle is finished. 2. To fret, to be uneasy, to be vexed. **Consumirse de envidia**, to be eaten up with jealously. **Consumirse de rabia**, to fume with rage. 3. To wear away, to waste away, to languish, to consume, to linger, to fail.

consumismo [con-soo-mes'-mo], *m.* Consumerism (tendencia); consumer society.

consumista [con-soo-mes'-tah], *a.* **El sector consumista**, the consumer section. *-m. & f.* Consumer.

consumo [con-soo' mo], *m.* The consumption of provisions and merchandise. **Consumo de drogas**, drug-taking. **Sociedad de consumo**, consumer society. 2. A tax upon the traffic in provisions and other merchandise.

consunción [con-soon-the-on'], *f.* 1. Consumption, waste. 2. Consumption, the state of wasting. 3. *(Mod.)* Consumption.

consuno (De) [con-soo'-no], *adv.* V. JUNTAMENTE.

consuntivo, va [con-soon-tee'-vo, vah], *a.* Consumptive.

consurrección [con-soor-rec-the-on'], *f.* Revival, revivification.

consustanciación [con-soos-tan-the-ah.-the-on'], *f.* V. CONSUBSTANCIACIÓN.

consustancial [con-soos-tahn-the-ahl'], *a.* Consubstantial. **Ser consustancial con**, to be inseparable from.

contabilidad [con-tah-be-le-dahd'], *f.* Accounting, bookkeeping, the art of keeping accounts.

contabilizar [con-tah-be-le-thar'], *va.* To enter in the accounts.

contable [con-tah'-blay], *a.* Countable. *-m. & f.* Accountant, book-keeper.

contactar [con-tac-tar'], *va. vn.* To contact, to get in touch.

contacto [con-tac'-to], *m.* 1. Contact, touch, union. **Estar en contacto con**, to be in touch with. **Ponerse en contacto con**, to get in touch with. **Lo hizo el municipio en contacto con el gobierno**, the city did it in collaboration with the government. 2. Means by which a contagious or epidemic disease is communicated to the healthy. 3. A soft iron guard for bar-magnets. 4. Intersection of two lines. 5. Switch, contact breaker.

contadero, ra [con-tah-day'-ro, rah], *a.* Countable, numerable, that which may be numbered.

contadero, [con-tah-day-ro] *m.* A narrow passage where sheep or cattle are counted. **Salir** or **entrar por contadero**, to go in or out through a narrow passage.

contado, da [con-tah'-do, dah], *a.* 1. Scarce, rare, uncommon, infrequent. **De contado**, instantly, immediately; in hand. **Al contado**, with ready money, for cash. 2. Designed, marked, or pointed out. **En contadas ocasiones**, on rare ocasions. **Contadas veces**, seldom. *-pp.* of CONTAR. *-m.* 1. Naturally, of course. 2. *(And.)* Installment (plazo).

contador, ra [con-tah-dor', rah], *m. &; f.* 1. Computer, reckoner, one skilled in accounts, accountant. 2. Numberer, numerator. 3. Counter, tell-tale a device attached to a machine for counting its strokes or revolutions, a meter for gas or water. **Contador de gas**, gas meter. **Contador de revoluciones**, tachometer. 4. Counter, the table on which money is told in a shop. 5. Desk. 6. An auditor. 7. Counting-house. 8. Counter, a false piece of money used for marking the game. **Contador de marina**, purser in the navy. **Contador en serie**, *(Inform.)* serial counter.

contador Geiger [con-tah-dor', gay'-ger], *m.* Geiger counter.

contaduría [con-tah-doo-ree'-ah], *f.* 1. Accountant's or auditor's office at the exchequer. 2. Auditorship, place and employment of a public auditor of receipts.

contagiar [con-tah-he-ar'], *va.* 1. To infect, to communicate disease, to hurt by contagion. 2. *(Met.)* To corrupt one's morals by a bad example, to pervert. *-vr.* 1. *(Med.)* To be contagious. **El mal ejemplo se contagia**, a bad example is contagious. **La anarquía se contagia a otros**, anarchy spreads to others.

contagio [con-tah'-he o], *a.* 1. Contagion. 2. *(Met.)* Contagion, corruption of morals.

contagión [con-tah-he-on'], *f.* 1. The progressive malignity of a disease, as cancer. 2. *(Met.)* Propagation of vice and evil habits. 3. V. CONTAGIO.

contagioso, sa [con-tah-he-o'-so, sah], *a.* 1. Contagious, malign, infectious. 2. *(Met.)* Infectious (doctrinas peligrosas, malos ejemplos). 3. *(Coll. Mex.)* Odd, particular.

contáiner [con-tah'-e-nayr], *m.* Container.

contal de cuentas [con-tahl'-day-coo-en'-tas], *m.* A string of beads for counting or reckoning.

contaminación [con-tah-me-nah-the-on'], *f.* Contamination, pollution, defilement; stain, blot. **Contaminación de aire**, air pollution. 2. *(fig.)* Taint, corrupting.

contaminado, da [con-tah-me-nah'-do, dah], *a. & pp.* of CONTAMINAR. Contaminated, corrupted, polluted.

contaminante [con-tah-me-nahn'-tay], *m.* Pollutant.

contaminar [con-tah-me-nar'], *va.* 1. To contaminate, to defile or pollute. 2. To infect by contagion 3. To corrupt, to vitiate or destroy the integrity of a text or original. 4. *(Met.)* To profane, to violate anything sacred. *-vr.* To be contaminated.

contante [con-tahn-tay], *a.* That can be counted. **Dinero contante y sonante**, ready cash.

contar [con-tar'], *va.* 1. To count, to reckon, to number, to enumerate, to relate, to mention. **Contar con los dedos,** to count on one's fingers. **Le cuento entre mis amigos**, I reckon him among my friends. **Sin contar**, not counting. 2. To calculate, to compute. 3. To book, to place to account. 4. To class, to range according to some stated method of distribution. 5. To consider, to look upon. 6. To depend, to rely. **Contar con la amistad de uno**, to rely upon one's friendship. **Mire a quién se lo cuenta**, an expression signifying that he who hears knows more than he who relates the particulars of an event. *-vn.* 1. *(Math.)* To count, to count up. **Hay que contar mucho para llegar con la paga al final del mes**, we have to go carefully in order to get to the end of the month. 2. *(fig.)* To count, to matter. **Unas pocas equivocaciones no cuentan**, a few errors don't matter. 3. To rely on. **Contar con**, to rely on. **Cuenta conmigo**, trust me. **Contaban por segura su ay-**

uda, they were relying absolutely on his help. *-vr.* 1. To be counted. **Se le cuenta entre los más famosos,** he is reckoned among the most famous. 2. To be told. **Cuéntese que...,** it is said that... **Cuenta y no acaba de hablar,** he never stops talking.

contemperante [con-tem-pay-rahn'-tay], *pa.* Tempering; moderator.

contemperar [con-tem-pay-rar'], *va.* To temper, to moderate. *V.* ATEMPERAR.

contemplación [con-tem-plah-the-on'], *f.* 1. Contemplation, meditation. 2. Holy meditation, a holy exercise of the soul. 3. Compliance, complaisance. **No andarse con contemplaciones,** not to stand on ceremony. **No tiene contemplaciones en eso,** he makes no compromises with that sort of things. **Sin contemplaciones, without ceremony, without any explanation.**

contemplador [con-tem-plah-dor'], *m.* Contemplator. *V.* CONTEMPLATIVO.

contemplar [con-tem-plar'], *va.* 1. To contemplate, to consider with conntinued attention, to study. 2. To view, to behold, to look upon. 3. To contemplate, to meditate, to muse. 4. To assent, to condescend, to yield a point. *-vn.* To meditate.

contemplativamente [con-tem-plah-te-vah-men'-tay], *adv.* Attentively, thoughtfully.

contemplativo, va [con-tem-plah-tee'-vo, vah], *a.* Contemplative, studious, meditative. **Vida contemplativa,** a life spent in contemplation and study.

contemplativo [con-tem-plah-tee'-vo], *m.* 1. Contemplator; one employed in contemplation and study. 2 A pious devotee.

contemporáneamente, *adv.* At the same time, contemporaneously.

contemporaneidad [con-tem-po-nay-e-dahd'], *f.* Contemporariness.

contemporáneo, nea [con-tem-po-rah´-nay-o, ah], *a.* Contemporary, coetaneous, coeval.

contemporización [con-tem-po-re-thah-the-on'], *f.* Temporizing, compliance.

contemporizador [con-tem-po-re-tha-dor'], *a.* Excessively compliant; temporizing; lacking firm principles. *-m. f.* Timeserver, compromiser; person who lacks firm principles.

contemporizar [con-tem-po-re-thar'], *vn.* To temporize, to comply with the will and opinion of another.

contención [con-ten-the-on'], *f.* 1. Contention, emulation. 2. Contest, dispute, strife, fighting.

contenciosamente, *adv.* Contentiously, contestingly.

contencioso, sa [con-ten-the-o'-so, sah], *a.* 1. Contentious, concertative, contradictious, quarrelsome, disputatious. 2. Being the object of strife or dispute; contestable. 3. Quarrelsome, litigious.

contendedor [con-ten-day-dor'], *m. V.* CONTENDOR.

contender [con-ten-derr'], *vn.* 1. To contend, to strive, to struggle, to contest, to conflict, to debate, to litigate. 2. *(Met.)* To argue, to discuss, to expostulate.

contendiente [con-ten-de-en'-tay], *pa.* Disputant, litigant.

contendor [con-ten-dor'], *m.* Contender, antagonist, opponent.

contenedor, ra [con-tay-nay-dor', rah], *m. & f.* Holder; a tenant, container.

contenencia [con-tay-nen'-the-ah], *f.* 1. Suspension in the flight of birds, especially birds of prey. 2. *(For.)* A demurrer: a written denial of the cause of action.

contener [con-tay-nerr'], *va.* 1. To contain, as a vessel: to comprise, as a writing; to comprehend. 2. To refrain, to curb, to restrain, to coerce. 3. To repress, to check the motion or progress of a thing.*-vr.* 1. To keep one´s temper, to refrain, to hold. 2. To contain. **Él no puede contenerse,** he has no command of himself. *(Yo contengo, yo contuve,* from *Contener.* *V.* TENER.

contenido, da [con-tay-nee'-do, dah], *a.* Moderate, prudent, temperate, modest. 2. Contained, suppressed. **Risa contenida,** contained laughter. *-pp.* of CONTENER.

contenido [con-tay-nee'-do], *m.* Contents, context.

conteniente [con-tay-ne-en'-tay], *pa.* Containing, comprising.

contenta [con-ten'-tah], *f.* 1. Endorsement. *V.* ENDOSO. 2. Reception or present which satisfies anyone. 3. Certificate of good conduct, given by the magistrate of a place to the commander of troops which have been quartered there; also, a similar certificate, given by the commanding officer to the magistrate.

contentadizo, za [con-ten-tah-dee'-tho, thah], *a.* **Bien contentadizo,** easily contented; **mal contentadizo,** hard to please.

contentamente [con-ten-tah-men'-tay], *adv.* Contentedly.

contentamiento [con-ten-tah-me-en´-to], *m.* Contentment, joy, satisfaction, content.

contentar [con-ten-tar'], *va.* 1. To content, to satisfy, to gratify, to please, to fill. 2. To indorse. *V.* ENDOSAR. *-vr.* To be contented, pleased, or satisfied. **Ser de buen o mal contentar,** to be easily pleased, or difficult to be pleased.

contentible [con-ten-tee'-blay], *a.* Contemptible.

contentivo, va [con-ten-tee'-vo, vah], *a.* Containing, comprising.

contento, ta [con-ten'-to, tah], *a.* 1. Glad, pleased, full of joy, mirthful. **Estar contento con,** to be satisfied with. **Están contentos con el coche,** they are pleased with the car. **Viven muy contentos,** they live very happily. 2. Contented, satisfied, content. 3. Moderate, temperate, prudent.

contento con-ten'-to], *m.* 1. Contentment, joy, satisfaction, content, mirth. **No caber en sí de contento,** to be overjoyed. 2. Receipt, discharge.

conteo [con-tay'-o], *m.* Countdown (deporte). Used also in rocket launchings.

contera [con-tay'-rah], *f.* 1. Chape, a piece of brass, tin, or silver, put at the end of a cane, stick, or scabbard. 2. Button of the cascabel of a gun. 3. *(Poet.)* Prelude of a song, or other musical composition. **Por contera,** ultimately, finally.

contérmino, na [con-terr'-me-no, nah], *a.* Contiguous, bordering upon.

conterráneo, nea [con-ter-rah'-nay-o, ah], *m. & f.* Countryman, countrywoman.

contertuliano, na [con-ter-too-le-ah'-no, nah], or **contertulio,** *a.* Belonging to the same social circle; of the same set.

contesta [con-tays'-tah], *f. (LAm.)* Answer.

contestable [con-tes-tah'-blay], *a.* Contestable, disputable, controvertible.

contestación [con-tes-tah-the-on'], *f.* 1. Answer, reply. 2. Contestation, the act of contesting: debate, strife. 3. Altercation, disputation, contention. **Contestación a la demanda,** *(Jur.)* Defence plea. **Mala contestación,** sharp report.

contestador [con-tays-tah-dor'], *a.* Cheeky, saucy. *-m.* **Contestador automatico,** answering machine.

contestar [con-tes-tar'], *va.* 1. To confirm the deposition of another. 2. To prove, to attest. 3. To answer, to reply. **Contestar una pregunta,** to answer a question. **Contestar una carta,** to reply to a letter. *-m.* To agree, to accord. *-vn.* 1. *(Mex.)* To chat, to talk. 2. *(Pol.)* To protest.

contestatario [con-tes-tah-tah'-re-o], *a.* Rebellious; non-conformist, anti-establishment. *-m. f.* Rebel; nonconformist.

conteste [con-tes'-tay], *a.* Confirming the evidence of another, making the same deposition as another witness.

contesto [con-tays-tao], *m. (And. Cono Sur, Mex.)* Answer, reply.

contexto [con-tex'-to], *m.* 1. Intertexture, diversification of things mingled or interwoven. 2. Context of a discourse.

contextura [con-tex-too´-rah], *f.* 1. Contexture. 2. Context, the general series of a discourse. 3. *(Met.)* Frame and structure of the human body.

conticinio [con-te-thee´-ne-o], *m.* Dead of night.

contienda [con-te-en'-dah], *f.* 1. Contest, dispute, debate, expostulation. 2. Conflict, contention, clashing, fray, jarring. *(Yo contiendo, yo contienda,* from *Contender. V.* ENTENDER.)

contigo [con-tee'-go], *pron. pers.* With you.

contiguamente, *adv.* Contiguously, closely.

contigüidad [con-te-goo-e-dad'], *f.* Contiguity, closeness.

contiguo, gua [con-te'-goo-o, ah], *a.* Contiguous, close.

continencia [con-te-nen'-the-ah], *f.* 1. Continence, self-command. 2. Continence, abstinence from carnal pleasures. 3. Continence, moderation in lawful pleasures. 4. The act of containing. **Continencia de la causa,** *(Law.)* Unity which should exist in every judgment or sentence.

continental [con-te-nen-tahl'], *a.* Continental.

continente [con-te-nen'-tay], *m.* 1. Continent, that which contains something. 2. Countenance, air, mien, gait. 3. Continent, a large extent of land; mainland.

continente [con-te-nen'-tay], *a.* Continent, chaste, abstinent, moderate in pleasures. **En continente,** *(Obs.)* Immediately.

continentemente [con-te-nen-tay-men'-tay], *adv.* Moderately, abstemiously, chastely.

contingencia [con-tin-hen'-the-ah], *f.* Contingence or contingency, possibility, risk.

contingentación [con-tin-hen-tah-the-on'], *f.* Quota system.

contingentar [con-tin-hen-tar'], *va.* To make subject to quotas; to fix quotas for.

contingente [con-tin-hen'-tay], *a.* Contingent, fortuitous, accidental.

contingente [con-tin-hen'-tay], *m.* Contingent, a proportion that falls to any person upon a division.

contingentemente [con-tin-hen-tay-men'-tay] *adv.* Casually, accidentally, contingently.

continuación [con-te-noo-ah-the-on'], *f.* 1. Continuation, protraction, an uninterrupted succession, lengthening. 2. Continuity, connection uninterrupted. 3. Continuance, stay. **Según lo expuesto a continuación,** as set out below.

continuadamente [con-te-noo-ah-dah-men'-tay], *adv.* Continually.

continuador [con-te-noo-ah-dor'], *m.* Continuer, continuator.

continuamente [con-te-noo-ah-men'-tay], *adv.* Continually.

continuar [con-te-noo-ar'], *va. & vn.* 1. To continue, to remain in the same state, to hold. **La puerta continúa cerrada,** the door is still shut. 2. To continue, to last, to endure. **Continuaba en Noruega,** he was still in Norway. **Continuar con salud,** to keep in good health. 3. To continue, to pursue, to protract, to carry on.

continuativo, va [con-te-noo-ah-tee'-vo, vah], *a.* Denoting continuation: said of a conjunction; continuative.

continuidad [con-te-noo-e-dahd'], *f.* Continuity, cohesion, continuance.

continuismo [con-te-noo-ees'-mo], *m.* Politics of continuity; wish for everything to go on as before.

continuo, nua [con-tee'-noo-o, ah], *a.* 1. Continuous, joined together without intervening space; continual. 2. Constant, lasting. **Sus continuas quejas,** his continual complaints. 3. Assiduous, persevering; perennial.

continuo, *m.* 1. A whole, composed of united parts. **Continuo** or **de continuo,** *adv.* Continually, constantly.

contómetro [con-to'-may-tro], *m.* Comptometer, calculating machine.

contonearse [con-to-nay-ar'-say], *vr.* To walk with an affected air or manner, to waggle.

contoneo [con-to-nay'-o], *m.* An affected gait or manner of walking.

contorcerse [con-tor-therr'-say], *vr.* To distort, twist, or writhe one's body.

contorción [con-tor-the-on'], *f. V.* RETORCIMIENTO and CONTORSIÓN.

contornado [con-tor-nah'-do], *a. (Her.)* Applied to the heads of animals, turned toward the sinister side of the shield. -**Contornado, da,** *pp.* of CONTORNAR.

contornar, contornear [con-tor-nar', con-tor-nay-ar'], *va.* 1. To trace the contour or outline of a figure. 2. To form according to a proposed model or design.

contorneo [con-tor-nay'-o], *m. V.* RODEO.

contorno [con-tor'-no], *m.* 1. Environs or vicinity of a place. **Caracas y sus contornos,** Caracas and its environs. **En estos contornos,** in these parts. 2. Contour, outline. 3. Every line in a spiral or volute. **En contorno,** round about. 4. Measurement round, distance round. **El contorno de cintura es de 26 pulgadas,** her waist measurement is 26 inches.

contorsión [con-tor-se-on'], *f.* 1. Contortion, twist, wry motion. 2. A grotesque gesture.

contorsionarse [con-tor-se-o-nar'-say], *vr.* To contort oneself.

contorsionista [con-tor-se-o-nes'-tah], *m. & f.* Contorsionist.

contra [cohn'-trah], *prep.* Against, in opposition to, counter, contrary to, opposite to. **En contra,** against or in opposition to another thing. **Ni a favor ni en contra,** neither pro nor con. -*adv.* Against. **Puntos en contra,** points against. **Votar en contra,** to vote against. **Opinar en contra,** to disagree. -*m.* 1. Opposite sense. 2. *(Mus.)* The pedal organ; the pipes forming the lowest bass, more common in plural. 3. Trouble, inconvenience. 4. **Hacer la contra,** to be consistently obtrusive. 5. *(LAm.) (Med.)* Antidote. 6. (Bridge) double. -*f.* 1. Difficulty, inconvenience. 2. Counter, in fencing, a parry in which one foil follows another in a small circle.

contraabertura [con-trah-ah-ber-too'-rah], *f. (Med.)* Counter-opening.

contraábside [con-trah-ahb'-se-day'], *m. & f.* Western apse or apsis.

contraaletas [con-trah-ah-lay'-tas], *f. pl. (Naut.)* Counterfashion pieces, the outermost timbers of the stern of the ship on both sides.

contraalmirante or **contralmirante** [con-trah-al-me-rahn'tay], *m.* Rear admiral.

contraamantillas [con-trah-ah-man-teel'-lyas], *f. pl. (Naut.)* Preventer-braces which serve to succour the main or foreyard of a ship.

contraamura [con-trah-ah-moo'-rah], *f. (Naut.)* Preventertack, which serves to support the tacks.

contraaproches [con-trah-ah-pro'-chess], *m. pl.* Counter-approaches made by the besieged against the besiegers.

contraarmiños [con-trah-ar-mee'-nyos], *m. pl. (Her.)* Contrary to ermine, i. e. black field and white spots.

contraatacar [con-trah-ah-tah-car'], *va. vn.* To counterattack.

contraataques [con-trah-ah-tah'-kes], *m. pl.* Counter attacks made by the besieged.

contrabajo [con-trah-bah'-ho], *m.* 1. Counterbass, the deepest of all musical sounds. 2. Bass, or baseviol; double bass.

contrabalancear [con-trah-bah-lan-thay-ar'], *va.* To counterbalance, to counterpoise.

contrabalanza [con-trah-bah-lahn'-thah], *f. V.* CONTRAPESO and CONTRAPOSICIÓN.

contrabanda [con-trah-bahn'-dah], *f. (Her.)* 1. A band divided into two of different metals, one of them colored. 2. The piece which crosses the shield in a sense contrary to the bend.

contrabandear [con-trah-bahn-day-ar'], *vn.* To smuggle.

contrabandista [con-trah-ban-dees'-tah], *m.* Smuggler, contrabandist.

contrabando [con-trah-bahn'-do], *m.* 1. A prohibited commodity. **Géneros de contrabando,** smuggled prohibited article. 2. Contraband trade, smuggling. **Contrabando de armas,** gun-runner. 3. *(Met.)* Any unlawful action. **Ir** or **venir de contrabando,** to go or come by stealth.

contrabarrado da [con-trah-bar-rah'-do, dah], *a. (Her.)* A shield counterbarred.

contrabasa, *f. (Arch.) V.* PEDESTAL.

contrabatería [con-trah-bah-tay-ree'-ah], *f.* Counterbattery.

contrabatir [con-trah-bah-teer'], *va.* To fire upon the enemy's batteries.

contrabitas [con-trah-bee'-tas], *f. pl. (Naut.)* Standards of the bitts.

contrabolina [con-tra-bo-lee'-nah], *f. (Naut.)* Preventer bowline.

contrabovedilla [con-trah-bo-vay-deel'-lyah], *f. (Naut.)* Second counter, upper counter.

contrabracear [con-trah-brah-thay-ar'], *va. (Naut.)* To counterbrace.

contrabranque [con-trah-brahn'-kay], *m. (Naut.)* Stemson, a strong piece of timber intended to re-enforce the stem.

contrabraza [con-trah-brah'-thah], *f. (Naut.)* Preventer-brace.

contrabrazola [con-trah-brah-tho'-lah], *f. (Naut.)* Head ledge.

contracalcar [con-trah-cal-car'], *va.* To print a drawing backward, in order to obtain another in the same position as the original.

contracambiada [con-trah-cam-be-ah'-dah], *f.* Changing of the forefoot by a horse.

contracambio [con-trah-cahm'-be-o], *m.*

contracanal [con-trah-cah-nahl'], *m.* Channel or conduit leading from another; counterchannel.

contracarril [con-trah-car-reel'], *m.* Checkrail, guardrail, safety-rail, wingrail.

contracción [con-trac-the-on'], *f.* 1. Contraction, shrinking, shriveling, contractedness, constriction; corrugation. 2. Contraction, the state of being contracted. 3. Abbreviation, abridgment.

contracebadera [con-trah-thay-bah-day´-rah], *f. (Naut.)* Sprit topsail.

contracédula [con-trah-thay'-doo-lah], *f.* A decree which reverses or annuls another of an anterior date.

contracepción [con-trah-thep-the-on'], *f.* Contraception.

contraceptivo [con-trah-thep-tee´-vo], *m.* Contraceptive. **Contraceptivo bucal**, oral contraceptive.

contrachapado [con-trah-chah-pah'-do], *a.* **Madera contrachapado,** *V.* PLYWOOD.

contracifra [con-trah-thee'-frah], *f.* Countercipher, the key to a secret manner of writing.

contraclave [con-trah-clah'-vay], *f. (Arch.)* The voussoir next to the keystone.

contracodaste interior [con-trah-co-dahs'-tay in-tay-re-or'], *m. (Naut.)* The inner sternpost. **Contracodaste exterior,** *(Naut.)* The back of the sternpost.

contracorriente [con-trah-cor-re-en'-tay], *f. (Naut.)* Countercurrent, stop-water.

contracosta [con-trah-cos'-tah], *f.* Coast opposite to another.

contráctil [con-trahc'-teel], *a.* 1. Contractile. 2. Contractible.

contractilidad [con-trac-te-le-dahd'], *f.* Contractility, contractibility.

contractual [con-trac-too-ahl'], *a.* Contractual.

contractura [con-trac-too'-rah], *f. (Med.)* Contracture, rigidity of muscles in a state of flexion, from whatever cause.

contracuerdas [con-trah-coo-err'-das], *f. pl. (Naut.)* The outward deckplanks or platforms.

contradancista [con-trah-dan-thees'-tah], *m. & f.* A person very fond of dancing country dances.

contradanza [con-trah-dahn'-thah], *f.* Square dance, country dance.

contradecir [con-trah-day-theer'], *va.* To contradict, to gainsay.

contradicción [con-trah-dic-the-on'], *f.* 1. Contradiction, controversy. 2. Control, controlment. 3. Clashing, oppugnancy, hostile resistance. 4. Contradiction, inconsistency with itself; incongruity in words or thoughts. 5. Contradic-

tion, opposition, gainsaying. **Espíritu de contradicción,** contradictory temper. **Contradicción de términos,** contradiction in terms.

contradicho, cha, [con-trah-de'-cho], *pp. irr.* of CONTRADECIR.

contradictor, ra [con-trah-dic-tor', rah], *m. & f.* Contradictor, gainsayer.

contradictoria [con-trah-dic-to'-re-ah], *f. (Log.)* Contradictory.

contradictoriamente, *adv.* Contradictorily, inconsistently.

contradictorio, ria [con-tra-dic-to´-re-o, ah], *a.* Contradictory. *(Yo contradigo, yo contradije, yo contradiga, from Contradecir. V.* DECIR.)

contradique [con-trah-dee'-kay], *m.* Counterdike, a second dike.

contradriza [con-trah-dree'-thah], *f. (Naut.)* Second halliard.

contraeje [con-trah-ay'-hay], *m.* A countershaft.

contraemboscada [con-trah-em-bos-cah'-dah], *f.* Counterambuscade.

contraemergente [con-trah-ay-mer.-hen'-tay], *a. (Her.)* Countersalient.

contraempuje [con-trah-em-poo-hay], *m.* Counter-thrust.

contraempuñadura [con-trah-em-poo-nyah-doo´-rah], *f. (Naut.)* Preventer earring.

contraendosar [con-trah-en-do-sar'], *va.* To reindorse, indorse back.

contraer [con-trah-err'], *va. & vn.* 1. To contract, to knit, to furl, to shrink, to join, to unite. 2. To bring two parties together, to make a bargain. 3. To procure, to incur, to get. *-vr.* 1. To contract, to shrink up, as nerves, etc., to crumple. 2. To reduce a discourse to an idea or phrase. **Contraer deudas,** to run into debt. **Contraer enfermedad,** to contract a disease. **Contraer matrimonio,** to marry. **Contrae su teoría a ciertos puntos,** he limits his theory to certain points.

contraescarpa [con-trah-es-car'-pah], *f. (Mil.)* Counterscarp.

contraescota [con-trah-es-co'-tah], *f. (Naut.)* Preventer-sheet.

contraescotín [con-trah-es-co-teen'], *m. (Naut.)* Preventer topsail sheet.

contraescritura [con-trah-es-cre-too'-rah], *f.* Counterdeed, instrument granted to protest against what had been previously given.

contraesmaltar [con-trah-es-mal-tar'], *va.* To enamel the back part.

contraespaldera [con-trah-es-pal-day´-rah] *f.* A kind of hedge or fence of trees in front of a hedge; a second espalier.

contraespionaje [con-trah-es-pe-o-nah'-hay], *m.* Counter-intelligence, counterespionage.

contraestay del mayor, or **del trinquete** [con-trah-es-tah'-e del mah-yor', or del treen-kay'-tay], *m. (Naut.)* Preventer stay of the main or foremast.

contrafajado, da [con-trah-fah-hah´-do, dah], *a. (Her.)* A shield having faces opposed in metal or color.

contrafallar [con-trah-fal-lyar'], *va.* At cards, to trump after another, to overtrump.

contrafaz [con-trah-fath'], *f.* The reverse of every face.

contrafianza [con-trah-fe-ahn'-thah], *f.* Indemnity bond.

contrafigura [con-trah-fe-goo'-rah], *f.* A person or dummy which imitates a personage in the theater.

contrafilo [con-trah-fee'-lo], *m.* Back edge (near the point).

contrafirma [con-trah-feer'-mah], *f. (Law. Prov.)* Inhibition of an anterior decree.

contrafirmante [con-trah-feer-mahn'-tay], *pa. (Law. Prov.)* The party who obtains an inhibition or injunction.

contrafirmar [con-trah-feer-mar'], *va. (Law. Prov.)* To obtain a countermanding decree or inhibition. .

contraflorado, da [con-trah-flo-rah'-do, dah], *a. (Her.)* Having flowers opposed in color and metal.

contrafoque [con-trah-fo'-kay], *m. (Naut.)* The foretop staysail; also the jib or flying-jib of a smack.

contraforjar [con-trah-for-har'], *va.* To hammer alike on the flat and on edge.

contrafoso [con-trah-fo'-so], *m.* The outer ditch of a fortress.

contrafractura [con-trah-frac-too'-rah], *f.* A fracture made by counter-stroke or contre-coup.

contrafuero [con-trah-foo-ay'-ro], *m.* Infringement or violation of a charter or privilege.

contrafuerte [con-trah-foo-err'-tay], *m.* 1. Counterfort, a fort constructed in opposition to another. 2. Abutment, buttress, spur, a pillar of masonry serving to prop and support a wall. 3. Strap of leather to secure the girths on a saddle-tree. 4. Stiffener of a shoe.

contragambito [con-trah-gahm-be'-to], *m.* Counter-gambit.

contragolpe [con-trah-gole'-pay], *m. (Med.)* A counter-stroke (contrecoup), lesion produced in a part other than that which received the blow.

contraguardia [con-trah-goo-ar'-de-ah], *f.* Counterguard, a work erected to cover a bastion or ravelin.

contraguía [con-trah-gee'ah], *f.* In a pair of draught animals, the mule which goes forward, to the left.

contraguiñada [con-trah-gee-nyah'-dah], *f. (Naut.)* Counter-yaw, a movement of the tiller to correct the course of a ship.

contrahacedor, ra [con-trah-ah-thay-dor', rah], *m. & f.* Imitator, counterfeiter.

contrahacer [con-trah-ah-ther'], *va.* 1. To counterfeit. 2. To falsify, to forge. 3. To imitate, to copy. 4. To pirate the works of an author. 5. To mimic.

contrahacimiento [con-trah-ah-the-me-en'-to], *m. (Obs.)* Counterfeit. *(Yo contrahago, yo contrahaga,* from *Contrahacer. V.* HACER.)

contrahaz [con-trah-ath'], *m.* The wrong side of cloth and some other things.

contrahecho, cha [con-trah-ay'-cho, chah], *a.* 1. Humpbacked, deformed. 2. Counterfeit, counterfeited, fictitious. *-pp.* of CONTRAHACER.

contrahechura [con-trah-ay-choo'-rah], *f.* Counterfeit; forgery, fake; pirated edition, spurious edition.

contrahierba [con-trah-e-err'-bah], *f.* 1. *(Bot.)* Dorstenia contrayerba, a South American medicinal plant. 2. Antidote.

contrahilera [con-trah-e-lay'-rah], *f.* A second line formed to defend another.

Contrahojas de las ventanas [con-trah-o'-has day las ventah'-nas], *f. pl. (Naut.)* Deadlights of the cabin.

contrahoradar [con-trah-o-rah-dar'], *va.* To bore on the opposite side. *(Yo contraigo, yo contraiga* from *Contraer. V.* TRAER.

contraído [con-trah-e'-do], *a.* 1. Contracted, shrunken, wasted. 2. *(And.)* Diligent, industrious.

contraindicación [con-trah-in-de-cah-the-on'], *f. (Med.)* Contraindication.

contraindicante *m. (Med.)* Contra-indicant.

contraindicar [con-trah-in-de-car'], *va. (Med.)* To contraindicate.

contrainteligencia [con-trah-en-te-le-hen'-the-ah], *f.* Counter-intelligence.

contralizo [con-trah-lee'-tho], *m.* A rod of wood to move the threads in a loom; a back leash.

contralor [con-trah-lor'], *m.* Comptroller, inspector.

contraloría [con-trah-lo-ree'-ah], *f.* Comptrollership.

contralto [con-trahl'-to], *m.* Contralto, countertenor, middle voice between the treble and tenor.

contraluz [con-trah-looth'], *f.* 1. View against the light. 2. Backlight. 3. Bad light. **A contraluz,** against the light, into the sun.

contramaestre [con-trah-mah-es'-tray], *m.* 1. *(Naut.)* Boatswain. 2. Overseer of a manufactory. 3. **Contramaestre de construcción,** the foreman of a dockyard.

contramalla, contramalladura [con-trah-mahl'-lyah, con-trah-mahl-lyah-doo'-rah], *f.* A double net for catching fish.

contramallar [con-trah-mal-lyar'], *va.* To make nets with double meshes.

contramandar [con-trah-man-dar'], *va.* To countermand.

contramangas [con-trah-mahn'-gas], *f. pl.* Oversleeves.

contramaniobra [con-trah-mah-ne-o'-brah], *f.* Counter-maneuver, a sudden change of tactics.

contramano [con-trah-mah'-no], *adv.* **A contramano,** in the wrong direction, the wrong way.

contramarca [con-trah-mar'-cah], *f.* 1. Countermark, a particular or additional mark. 2. A duty to be paid on goods which have no custom house mark. 3. A mark added to a medal or other piece of coined metal long after it has been struck, by which the curious know the several changes in value. 4. **Cartas** or **patentes de contramarca,** letters of marque.

contramarcar [con-trah-mar-car'], *va.* To countermark, to put a second or additional mark on bale goods, etc.

contramarco [con-trah-mar'-co], *m.* Counterframe of a glass window.

contramarcha [con-trah-mar'-cha], *f.* 1. Countermarch, retrocession. 2. Part of a weaver's loom. *V.* VIADERA. 3. *(Mil. and Naut.)* Evolution, by means of which a body of troops or division of ships change their front.

contramarchar [con-trah-mar-char'], *vn.* To countermarch.

contramarea [con-trah-mah-ray'-ah], *f. (Naut.)* Countertide, or springtide.

contramatar [con-trah-mah-tar'], *va.* **Contramatar a uno,** *(LAm.)* To hang somebody against the wall. *-vr. (LAm.)* To crash into something.

contramedida [con-trah-may-de'-dah], *f.* Counter-measure.

contramesana [con-trah-may-sah'-nah], *f. (Naut.)* Mizzenmast.

contramina [con-trah-mee'-nah], *f.* 1. Countermine, a mine intended to seek out and destroy the enemy's mines. 2. A subterraneous communication between two or more mines of metals or minerals.

contraminar [con-tra-me-nar'], *va.* 1. To countermine. 2. To counterwork, to defeat by secret measures.

contramolde [con-trah-mole'-day], *m.* 1. Countermould: an enveloping mould. 2. A kind of pasteboard on which is moulded, in relief or depression, what it is desired to represent.

contramotivo [con-trah-mo-tee'-vo], *m. (Mus.)* A motive or subject opposed to another; countersubject.

contramuelle [con-trah-moo-ayl'-lyay], *m. (Mech.)* A duplicate spring.

contramuralla [con-trah-moo-rahl'-lyah], *f. (Mil.)* Countermure, a low rampart.

contramuro [con-trah-moo'-ro], *m.* 1. Countermure.

contranatural [con-trah-nah-too-rahl'], *a.* Counternatural, contranatural, unnatural.

contraofensiva [con-trah-o-fen-see'-vah] *f.* Counteroffensive.

contraoferta [con-trah-o-fer'-tah], *f.* Counter-offer.

contraorden [con-trah-or'-den], *f.* Countermand; counter or revoking order.

contraordenar, *va. V.* CONTRAMANDAR

contrapares [con-trah-pah'-es], *m. pl. (Arch.)* Counter rafters in a building.

contraparte [con-trah-par'-tay], *f.* 1. Counterpart. 2. A duplicate copy of a deed.

contrapartida [con-trah-par-tee'-dah], *f.* 1. In book-keeping, corrective entry. 2.*(fig.)* Compensation; counterweight. **Pero como contrapartida añade que...,** but in contrast she adds that... **Como contrapartida de,** as compensation for.

contrapás [con-trah-pahs'], *m.* Kind of dance or step in dancing.

contrapasamiento [con-trah-pah-sah-me-en'-to], *m.* The act and effect of passing to the opposite side or party.

contrapasar [con-trah-pah-sar'], *vn.* To join the opposite party.

contrapaso [con-trah-pah'-so], *m.* 1. A backstep in walking or dancing. 2. Counterpace, contrary measure to any scheme. 3. *(Mus.)* Counternote.

contrapelear [con-trah-pay-lay-ar'], *vn. (Obs.)* To defend oneself in an engagement.

contrapelo (a) [con-trah-pay´-lo], *adv.* Against the grain; the wrong way. **Todo lo hace a contrapelo**, he does everything the wrong way around. **Acariciar un gato a contrapelo**, to stroke a cat the wrong way.

contrapesar [con-trah-pay-sar´], *va.* 1. To counterpoise, to counterbalance, to counterweigh 2. To countervail, to be equivalent to. 3. To act with equal power against any person or cause.

contrapeso [con-trah-pay´-so], *m.* 1. Counterpoise, equiponderance, counterbalance, countervail. 2. A rope dancer´s pole. 3. *(Met.)* Equipollence, equivalence of power. 4. Counterpoise in a velvet-loom 5. An addition of inferior quality thrown to complete the weight of meat, fish, etc.

contrapeste [con-trah-pes´-tay], *m.* Remedy against pestilence.

contrapié [con-trah-pe-ay´], *m.* 1. The loss by a dog of the scent or the trail of what it was following. 2. Stratagem, trick.

contrapilastra [con-trah-pe-lahs´-trah], *f.* 1. *(Arch.)* Counterpilaster 2. Moulding on the joints of doors or shutters, to keep out the wind.

contraponedor [con-trah-po-nay-dor´], *m.* He who compares one thing with another.

contraponer [con-trah-po-nerr´], *va.* To compare, to oppose. **Contraponer A a B**, to set up A against B. **A esta idea ellos contraponen su teoría de que...**, against this idea they set up their theory that...

contraportada [cocn-trah-por-tah-dah], *f.* Inside cover (de libro).

contraposición [con-trah-po-se-the-on´], *f.* 1. Contraposition, the placing over against. 2. Counterview, contrast, a position in which two dissimilar things illustrate each other. 3. An act by which the execution of a sentence is barred.

contrapresión [con-trah-pray-se-on´], *f.* Counterpressure, back pressure.

contraprincipio [con-trah-prin-thee´-pe-o], *m.* Assertion contrary to a principle known as such.

contraproducente [con-trah-pro-doo-then´-tay], *a.* Self-defeating, counterproductive, defeating its own purpose. **Tener un resultado contraproducente**, to have a boomerang effect.

contrapromesa [con-trah-pro-may´-sah], *f.* 1. Declaration annulling a thing promised. 2. Conflict of one promise with another.

contraproposición [con-trah-pro-po-se-the-on´], *f.* Counterproposition.

contrapropuesta [con-trah-pro-poo-ays'-tah], *f.* Counterproposal.

contraprueba [con-trah-proo-ay´-bah], *f.* Counterproof, a second impression of a print taken off by printers; counterdrawing.

contrapuerta [con-trah-poo-err´-tah], *f.* 1. Storm door. 2. Inner large door of a house.

contrapuesto, ta [con-trah-poo-es´-to, tah], *a. & pp.* of CONTRAPONER. Compared.

contrapunta [con-trah-poon´-tah], *f.* Cutting part of the edge of a sabre´s blade.

contrapuntante [con-trah-poon-tahn´-tay], *m.* He who sings in counterpoint.

contrapuntear [con-trah-poon-tay-ar´], *va.* 1. *(Mus.)* To sing in counterpoint. 2. To compare. 3. To taunt, to revile. -*vr.* To treat one another with abusive language, to wrangle, to dispute.

contrapunteo [con-trah-poon-tay'-o], *m. (And. Carib, Cono Sur)* argument, quarrel; *(And. Cono Sur)* improvised verse duel.

contrapuntista [con-trah-poon-tees´-tah], *m.* Contrapuntist, one skilled in counterpoint.

contrapunto [con-trah-poon´-to], *m.* 1. *(Mus.)* Counterpoint, harmony. 2. *(Lit.)* Counterpoint.

contrapunzón [con-trah-poon-thone´], *m.* 1. Puncheon for driving in a nail. 2. Counterpunch, an instrument wich serves

to open others. 3. The gunsmith's countermark on guns, to prevent their being exchanged for others, or purloined.

contraquerella [con-trah-kay-rayl´-lyah], *f.* A cross-complaint.

contraquilla [con-trah-keel´-lyah], *f. (Naut.)* False keel. *V.* ZAPATA DE LA QUILLA.

contrariamente [con-trah-re-ah-men-tay], *adv.* Contrarily, contrariously. **Contrariamente a lo que habíamos pensado**, contrary to what we had thought.

contrariar [con-trah-re-ar´], *va.* To contradict, to oppose, to counteract, to counterwork; to vex.

contrariedad [con-trah-re-ay-dahd´], *f.* 1.Contrariety, repugnance, opposition, contradiction. 2. Vexation, annoyance. **Producir a uno contrariedad**, to upset somebody.

contrario [con-trah´-re-o], *m.* 1. Opponent, antagonist. 2. Competitor, rival. 3. Impediment, obstacle, obstruction.

contrario, ria [con-trah´-re-o, ah], *a.* 1. Contrary, repugnant, opposite, contradictory, contrarious. **En sentido contrario**, the other way. **Se ha interpretado en sentido contrario**, it has been interpreted in the opposite sense. 2. Contrary, adverse, abhorrent, cross. 3. Harmful, mischievous. **Tiempo contrario**, *(Naut.)* Foul weather. **Echar al contrario**, to cross the breed. **Al contrario** or **por el contrario**, on the contrary. **En contrario**, against, in opposition to. **Llevar la contraria**, to contradict, to oppose. **Contrario a los intereses del país**, contrary to the nation´s interests. **Al contrario de lo que habíamos pensado**, against what we had thought. **Todo lo contrario**, quite the reverse.

contrarracamento [con-trar-rah-cah-men´-to], *m. (Naut.)* Preventerparrel.

contrarrampante [con-trar-ram-pahn´-tay], *a. (Her.)* Rampant, and face to face.

contrarreclamación [con-trar-ray-clah-mah-the-on´], *f.* Counterclaim.

contrarreforma [con-trar-re-for'-mah], *f.* Counter-Reformation.

contrarregistro [con-trar-ray-hess´-tro], *m.* Control, a register or account kept to be compared with any other.

contrarreguera [con-trar-ray-gay-rah], *f.* A lateral drain, to prevent mischief to the tilled land, and to aid in even distribution of irrigation.

contrarreparo [con-trar-ray-pah´-ro], *m. (Mil.)* Counterguard, or counterdefence.

contrarréplica [con-trar-ray´-ple-cah], *f.* Rejoinder, reply to an answer: it is sometimes also rebutter, or an answer to a rejoinder.

contrarrestar [con-trar-res-tar´], *va.* 1. To strike back a ball, to counterbuff. 2. To resist, to oppose, to check, to countercheck, to counterwork.

contrarresto [con-trar-res´-to], *m.* 1. A player who is to strike back the ball. 2. Check, opposition, contradiction.

contrarrevolución [con-trar-ray-vo-loo-the-on´], *f.* Counterrevolution.

contrarrevolucionario ria [con-trar-ray-vo-loo-the-o-nah´-re-o, ah], *m. & f. & a.* 1. Counterrevolucionist. 2. Belonging to a counterrevolution.

contrarroa, contrarroda [con-trar-ro´-ah, con-trar-ro´-dah], *f. (Naut.)* Stemson.

contrarronda [con-trar-ron´-dah], *f.* 1. *(Mil.)* Counterround, which follows the first round for greater safety's sake, to visit the different posts. 2. Round made by officers to inspect the posts, guards, and sentinels.

contrarrotura [con-trar-ro-too´-rah], *f. (Vet.)* Plaster or poultice applied to fractures or wounds by veterinarians.

contras [cone´-trass], *m. pl. (Mus.)* The bass pipes of a large organ. *V.* CONTRA.

contrasalida [con-trah-sah-lee´-dah], *f.* Countersally; resistance of besiegers to a sally.

contrasalva [con-trah-sahl´-vah], *f. (Mil.)* Countersalute.

contrasellar [con-trah-sayl-lyar´], *va.* To counterseal, to seal with others.

contrasentido [con-trah-sen-tee´-do], *m.* 1. Countersense, opposed meaning. 2. A deduction opposed to the logical antecedents. **Aquí hay un contrasentido**, there is a contradiction here. **Es un contrasentido que él actúe así**, it doesn't make sense for him to act like that.

contraseña [con-trah-say´-nyah], *f. L* Countersign or countermark. 2. *(Mil.)* Watchword. 3. Password.

contrasol [con-trah-sole´], *m.* Sunshade, a tub in greenhouses to protect certain plants likely to be injured by full sunlight.

contrastable [con-tras-tah´-blay], *a.* Contrastable, capable of contrast.

contrastante [con-tras-tahn´-tay], *pa.* Contrasting.

contrastar [con-tras-tar´], *va.* 1. To contrast, to place in opposition: to oppose. 2. To resist, to contradict. 3. To assay metals. 4. To examine measures and weights. 5. *(Naut.)* To endure misfortunes, or contrary winds, and resist them mechanically. -*vn.* 1. To contrast, to form a contrast (hacer contraste). 2. **Contrastar con, contrastar contra,** to resist, to face up.

contraste [con-trahs´-tay], *m.* 1. Assayer of the mint. 2. Assayer´s office where gold and silver are tried and marked. 3. Assayer of weights and measures. 4. *(Prov.)* A public office where raw silk is weighed. 5. Counterview contrast, a position in which two dissimilar things illustrate each other. **Hacer contrastar con,** to contrast with. 6. Opposition and strife between persons and things. 7. Contrast, opposition and dissimilitude of figures. 8. *(Nat.)* Sudden change of the wind, by which it becomes foul or contrary.

contrata [con-trah´-tah], *f.* 1. Contract, a deed in which the terms of a contract, bargain, or agreement are set forth. 2. Territory, district.

contratación [con trah-tah-the-on´], *f.* 1. Trade, commerce, traffic, enterprise, undertaking, business transaction. 2. Contract (contrato), hiring. **Contrato temporal,** temporary contract. 3. Engagement, taking-on.

contratante [con-trah-tahn´-say], *pa.* Contracting; contractor, one of the parties to a contract.

contratar [con-trah-tar´], *va.*1. To trade, to traffic. 2. To contract or bargain. 3. To contract, to stipulate, to covenant. -*vr.* To sign on. **Contratarse para hacer algo,** to contract to do something.

contratela [con-trah-tay´-lah], *f.* Second inclosure of canvas, within which game is enveloped or wild boars are fought.

contratiempo [con-trah-te-em´-po], *m.* Disappointment, misfortune, calamity, trouble, frustration.

contratista [con-trah-tees´-tah], *m.f.* Contractor, lessee, patentee, conventionist, covenanter. **Contratista de obras,** building contractor.

contrato [con-trah´-to], *m.* 1. Contract, convention, or mutual agreement, pact; stipulation, covenant. 2. Contract, a deed in which the terms of a contract or bargain are set forth. **Entrar en contrato,** to make a covenant. **Contrato temporal o indefinido,** definite or indefinite contract. **Contrato aleatorio,** aleatory contract. **Contrato de compraventa,** a contract of bargain and sale.

contratrancaniles [con-trah-tran-ca-nee´-les], *m. pl. (Naut.)* Inner waterways, serving to carry off the water by the scuppers.

contratreta [con-trah-tray´-tah], *f.* Counterplot.

contratrinchera [con-trah-trin-chay´-rah], *f. (Mil.)* Countertrench, an intrenchment made by the besieged against the besiegers.

contratuerca [con-trah-too-ayr´-cah], *f.* Locknut.

contravalación [con-trah-vah-la-the-on´], *f. (Mil.)* Contravallation.

contravalar [con-trah-vah-lar´], *va.* To form a line of contravallation.

contravalor [con-trah-vah-lor´], *m.* Countervalue, equivalent. *(Com.)*

contravención [con-trah-ven-the-on´], *f.* Contravention, violation of a law.

contraveneno [con-trah-vay-nay´-no], *m.* 1. Counterpoison, antidote. 2. *(Met.)* Precaution taken to avoid some infamy or mischief.

contravenir [con-trah-vay-neer´], *va.* 1. To contravene, to transgress a command, to violate a law. 2. To oppose, to obstruct, to baffle, to countermine.

contraventana [con-trah-ven-tah´-nah], *f.* 1. Storm window. 2. Outside window shutter.

contraventor, ra [con-trah-ven-tor´, rah], *m. & f.* 1. Transgressor, offender. 2. Contravener, he who opposes another.

contravidriera [con-trah-ve-dre-ay´-rah], *f.* A second glass window, to keep off cold or heat.

contravirar [con-trah-ve-rar´], *va.* To turn in the opposite direction.

contray [con-trah´-e], *m.* Sort of fine cloth.

contrayente [con-trah-yen´-tay], *pa.* Contracting (matrimonios).

contrayugo [con-trah-yoo´-go], *m. (Naut.)* Inner transom.

contrecho, cha [con-tray´-cho, chah], *a.* Crippled, maimed.

contrete [con-tray´-tay], *m.* 1. *(Naut.)* Breastshore. 2. Crochet, angle iron, stay. 3. Gusset.

contribución [con-tre-boo-the-on´], *f.* 1 Contribution. **Poner a contribución,** to make use of. 2. Contribution, tax. **Única contribución,** income tax. **Contribución directa,** direct tax. **Exento de contribuciones,** free of tax.

contribuidor, ra [con-tre-boo-e-dor´, rah], *m. & f.* Contributor.

contribuir [con-tre-boo-eer´], *va.* 1. To contribute, to pay one's share of a tax. 2. To contribute, to give to some common stock. **Contribuir con una cantidad**, to contribute with a sum. **Contribuir al éxito de algo,** to contribute to the success of something. 3. To contribute, to bear a part in some common design.

contribulado, da [con-tre-boo-lah´-do, dah], *a.* Grieved, afflicted.

contributario [con-tre-boo-tah´-re-o], *m.* Contributor, taxpayer.

contribuyente [con-tre-boo-yen´-tay], *pa.* Contributing; contributor; cooperative, contributory.

contrición [con-tre-the-on´], *f.* Contrition, penitence, compunction.

contrincante [con-trin-cahn´-tay], *m.* Competitor, rival, opponent.

contristar [con-trees-tar´], *va.* To afflict, to sadden. -*vr.* To grow sad, to grieve.

contrito, ta [con-tree´-to, tah], *a.* Contrite, compunctious, penitent.

control [con-trol], *m.* Control, check, regulation. **Control remoto,** remote control. **Control de natalidad,** birth control. **Control de precios,** price control. **Perder el control,** to lose control. **Control de la circulación,** traffic control. **Control de sí mismo,** self-control. **Control nuclear,** nuclear inspection.

controlador, ra [con-tro-laah-dor´], *m. & f.* Controller; *(LAm.) (Ferro.)* Inspector, ticket-collector. **Controlador de estacionamiento,** traffic warden. Driver *(Comput.).* **Controlador de pantalla,** monitor controller. **Controlador del dispositivo,** device controller. **Controlador de la impresora,** printer driver. **Controlador del ratón,** mouse driver.

controlar [con-tro-lar´], *va.* 1. To control, to regulate. 2. To restrain to hold in check. 3. To monitor to verify; to check.

controversia [con-tro-verr´-se-ah], *f.* Controversy, debate.

controversial [con-trah-ver-se-ah], *a.* Controversial.

controversista [con-tro-ver-sees´-tah], *m.* Controversialist, disputant, controverter.

controvertible [con-tro-ver-tee´-blay], *a.* Controvertible, disputable, litigious.

controvertido [con-trah-ver-tee'-do], *a.* Controversial.
controvertir [con-tro-ver-teer'], *va.* To controvert, to dispute a thing in writing. 2. To discuss, to argue against. *-vn.* To argue. *(Yo controvierto, yo controvierta; él controvirtió, él controvirtiera; from Controvertir. V. ASENTIR.)*
contubernal [con-too-ber-nahl'], *m.* Chamberfellow, companion in the same apartment.
contubernio [con-too-berr'-ne-o], *m.* 1. Cohabitation, inhabiting the same place with another. 2. Concubinage, living with a woman not married.
contumacia [con-too-mah'-the-ah], *f.* 1. Obstinacy; perverseness, stubbornness. 2. *(Law.)* Contumacy, a wilful contempt and disobedience to any lawful summons or judicial order, nonappearance; contempt of court; default.
contumaz [con-too-math'], *a.* 1. Obstinate, stubborn. perverse. 2. Contumacious, disobedient. 3. *(Med.)* Disease-carrying, germ-laden.
contumazmente, *adv.* Contumaciously, obstinately.
contumelia [con-too-may'-le-ah], *f.* Contumely, reproach, contumeliousness, abuse.
contumeliosamente, *adv.* Contumeliously, reproachfully.
contumelioso, sa [con-too-may-le-o'-so, sah], *a.* Contumelious, reproachful, sarcastic.
contumerioso [con-too-may-re-o-so], *a. (CAm.)* Finicky, fussy.
contundencia [con-toon-den'-the-ah], *f.* Forcefulness, power, conclusive nature; crushing nature; strictness, severity; toughness; aggressive nature.
contundente [con-toon-den'-tay], *pa.* 1. Producing a contusion (armas); (instrumento contundente), blunt instrument. 2. *(fig.)* Forceful, convincing, powerful (argumento); conclusive (prueba); forceful (tono); crushing (derrota); strict, severe.
contundir [con-toon-deer'], *va.* To contuse, to contund; to bruise; to cause a contusion.
conturbación [con-toor-bah-the-on'], *f.* Perturbation, uneasiness of mind.
conturbado, da [con-toor-bah'-do, dah], *a.* Turbulent, troublesome.*-pp.* of CONTURBAR.
conturbador [con-toor-bah-dor'], *m.* Perturber, disturber.
conturbamiento [con-toor-bah-me-en'-to], *m.* Perturbation, disquietude.
conturbar [con-toor-bar'], *va.* To perturb, to disquiet, to disturb. *-vr.* To be troubled, to be dismayed, to become perturbed.
conturbativo, va [con-toor-bah-tee'-vo, vah], *a.* That which perturbs or disquiets.
contusión [con-too-se-on'], *f.* Contusion, bruise.
contusionar [con-too-se-o-nar'], *va.* To bruise; to hurt, to damage.
contuso, sa [con-too'-so, sah], *a.* Bruised.*-pp* irr. of CONTUNDIR.
contutor [con-too-tor'], *m.* Assistant tutor, fellow-tutor.
conuco, or **cunuco** [co-noo'-co, coo-noo'-co], *m.* 1. *(Amer.)* A very small farm or plantation, often given by masters to their slaves to cultivate for themselves. 2. Cornfield.
conuquero [co-noo-kay'-ro], *m. (And. Carib.)* Smallholder, farmer.
conusco, *pron. pers. (Obs.)* With us.
conusfusorio [co-noos-foo-so'-re-o], *m.* A metallic crucible, shaped like an inverted cone, used in smelting.
convalaria [con-vah-lah'-re-ah], *f.* Lily of the valley.
convalariado, da, convalárico, ca, *a.* Resembling the lily of the valley.
convalecencia [con-vah-lay-then'-the-ah], *f.* Convalescence, recovery from disease. **Casa de convalecencia** or only **convalencencia,** a hospital for convalescent patients.
convalecer [con-vah-lay-therr'], *vn.* 1. To recover from sickness. 2. *(Met.)* To recover lost prosperity and power.
convaleciente [con-vah-lay-the-en'-tay], *pa.* Convalescent.
convalidación [con-vah-le-dah-the-on'], *f.* Acceptance, recognition; validation; ratification, confirmation.

convalidar [con-vah-le-dar'], *va.* To accept, to recognize; to validate; to ratify, to confirm (documento).
convección [con-vec-the-on'], *f.* Convection.
convecino, na [con-vay-thee'-no, nah], *a.* Neighboring, conterminous.
convelerse [con-vay-lerr'-say], *vr.* To twitch, to be contracted: applied to muscular fibers, membranes, blood-vessels, etc.
convencedor, ra [con-ven-thay-dor', rah], *m. & f.* One who demonstrates and convinces.
convencer [con-ven-therr'], *va.* To convince, to convict, to demonstrate. **Convencer a uno de que algo es mejor,** to convince somebody something is better. **No me convence del todo,** I´m not fully convinced. *-vn.* To convince. **El argumento no convence,** the argument does not convince. *-vr.* To be assured, to become convinced ¡**Convéncete!,** believe me!
convencible [con-ven-thee'-blay], *a.* Convincible, convictible.
convencido, da [con-ven-thee'-do, dah], *a.* Convict.*-pp.* of CONVENCER.
convencimiento [con-ven-the-me-en'-to], *m.* Conviction, confutation. **Llegar al convencimiento de,** to become convinced of. **Tener el convencimiento de que...,** to be convinced that...
convención [con-ven-the-on'], *f.* 1. Convention, contract, agreement, pact, composition. 2. Convenience, convening.
convencional [con-ven-the-o-nahl'], *a.* Conventional, conventionary.
convencionalismo [con-ven-the-o-nah-les'-mo], *m.* Conventionalism.
convencionalmente, [con-ven-the-o-nahl'-men-tay] *adv.* Conventionally.
convencionero [con-ven-the-o-nay-ro], *a. (And. Mex.)* Comfort-loving, self-indulgent.
convenible [con-vay-nee'-blay], *a.* 1. Docile, tractable, compliant, obsequious. 2. Convenient. 3. Of a moderate or reasonable price.
convenido, da, *a. & pp.* of CONVENIR. Settled by consent, agreed, done.
conveniencia [con-vay-ne-en'-the-ah], *f.* 1. Conformity, congruity, consistence. 2. Utility, profit, advantage, comfort. **A la primera conveniencia,** at one´s earliest opportunity. 3. Agreement, convention, adjustment. 4. Service, a servant´s place in a house or family. 5. Convenience, ease or cause of ease, commodiousness, accommodation, commodity. **Es amigo de conveniencia,** he loves his ease or comfort. 6. Convenience, fitness, expedience. **Conveniencias,** 1. Emoluments, perquisites. 2. Income, property.
conveniente [con-vay-ne-en'-tay], *a.* 1. Useful, profitable, advantageous, good. **Sería conveniente que..,** it would be a good thing if... 2. Accordant, conformable. 3. Fit, suitable, agreeable. **Nada conveniente,** unsuitable. 4. Convenient, expedient, correspondent, opportune. 5. Commodious, timely. 6. Decent.
convenientemente, [con-vay-ne-en-tay-men'-tay], *adv.* Conveniently, fitly, suitably, expediently.
convenio [con-vay'-ne-o], *m.* 1. Convention, contract, agreement, pact, concert, consent. **Convenio colectivo,** collective bargain. **Convenio salarial,** wages agreement. 2. Contrivance. 3. Plot.
convenir [con-vay-neer'], *vn.* 1. To agree, to be of the same opinion to coincide to cohere, to consist, to compromise. **Convenir en hacer algo,** to agree to do something. 2. To agree, to fit, to harmonize, to comport, to suit. **Si le conviene,** if it suits you. **No me conviene,** it´s not in my interest. **Lo que más le conviene es un reposo completo,** the best thing for him is complete rest. 3. To correspond, to belong to. 4. To assemble, to convene. 5. To cohabit carnally. 6. To litigate. *-v. imp.* To suit, to be to the purpose. *-vr.* To compound, to agree, to close, to suit one's interests. **Convenir**

en, to close upon, to close with, to settle. **Conviene saber,** that is, to wit.

conventazo [con-ven-tah´-tho], *m. aug.* A large convent or monastery.

conventículo [con-ven-tee´-coo-lo], *m.* Conventicle, a secret assembly or meeting for some unlawful purpose.

conventillero [con-ven-tel-lyay´-ro], *(And. Cono Sur)* 1. a. Gossipy. 2. *m, f.* Sandalmonger, gossip, telltale.

conventillo [con-ven-tel´-lyo], *m. (And. Cono Sur)* Tenement, inner city slum.

convento [con-ven´-to], *m.* 1. Convent of monks or nuns, monastery, nunnery. 2. Community of religious men or women.

conventual [con-ven-too-ahl´], *a.* Conventual, monastic.

conventual [con-ven-too-ahl´], *m.* 1. Conventual, a monk, one that lives in a convent. 2. Franciscan friar possessing estates or property.

conventualidad [con-ven-too-ah-le-dahd´], *f.* 1. The state of living together as religious persons in a convent or monastery. 2. Assignment of a monk to a determined convent.

conventualmente *adv.* Monastically, reclusely.

convergencia [con-ver-hen´-the-ah], *f.* 1. Convergence. 2. *(fig.)* Common tendency, common direction; concurrence. **Convergencia de izquierdas,** grouping of left-wing forces.

convergente [con-ver-hen´-say], *a.* Convergent, converging.

convergentemente [con-ver-hen-tay-men´-tay], *adv.* **Convergentemente con,** together with, jointly with.

converger [con-ver-herr´], *vn. V.* CONVERGIR *(Acad.)* 1. To converge. 2. *(fig.)* To have a common tendency, to tend in the same direction; to concur, to be in accord. **Sus esfuerzos convergen a un fin común,** their efforts have a common purpose.

convergir [con-ver-heer´], *vn.* 1. To converge. 2. To agree in opinions.

conversa [con-ver´-sah], *f.* 1. *(Geom.)* Converse. 2. *(LAm.)* Talk, chat; smooth talk.

conversable [con-ver-sah´-blay], *a.* 1. Conversable, sociable. 2. *(Theology)* Communicable.

conversación [con-ver-sah-the-on´], *f.* 1. Conversation, easy talk, chat, converse, conference, communication, colloquy. **Cambiar de conversación,** to change the subject. **Tratar conversación con uno,** to get into conversation with somebody. 2. Conversation, commerce, intercourse, society, company. 3. *(Obs.)* Room, bedroom. 4. Criminal intercourse. 5. Club, an assembly. *V.* TERTULIA.

conversacional [con-ver-sah-the-o-nahl´], *a.* Conversational; colloquial (estilo).

conversador [con-ver-sah-dor´], 1. *a. (LAm.)* Talkative, chatty. 2. *m. (LAm.)* Smooth talker (zalamero).

conversar [con-ver-sar´], *vn.* 1. To converse, to have a chat, to discourse familiarly, to commune, to talk together. 2. To live together in the company of others. 3. *(Mil.)* To change front, wheel.

conversata [con-ver-sah´-tah], *f. (Cono Sur)* Talk, chat.

conversión [con-ver-se-on´], *f.* 1. Conversion. 2. Conversion, change from one state to another. 3. *(Rhet.)* Apostrophe. 4. *(Mil.)* Wheel, wheeling. **Cuarto de conversión,** quarterwheeling. **Conversión paralelo-serie,** *(Inform.)* parallel-to-serial conversion.

conversivo, va [con-ver-see´-vo, vah], *a.* Having the power of converting or changing one thing into another.

converso [con-verr´-so], *m.* 1. Convert, a person converted from one religion or opinion to another. 2. Lay brother, a man admitted for the service of a religious house without being ordained. *-a.* Converted.

conversón [con-ver-sone´], *(And.)* 1. *a.* Talkative, gossiping. 2. *m. f.* Talkative person.

conversor [con-ver-sor´], *m. (Rad.)* Converter.

convertibilidad [con-ver-te-be-le-dahd´], *f.* Convertibility, capability of being exchanged.

convertible [con-ver-tee´-blay], *a.* 1. Convertible. 2. Movable, transferable. *-m.* Convertible (automobile).

convertido, da [con-ver-tee´-do, dah], *a. & pp.* of CONVERTIR. Converted, changed, transformed.

convertidor [con-ver-te-dor´], *m.* Converter, transformer.

convertir [con-ver-teer´], *va.* 1. To convert, to change into another substance, to permute. 2. To convert, to change from one religion or opinion to another. **Convertir a uno al catolicismo,** to convert somebody to Catholicism. 3. To convert, to turn from a bad to a good life. 4. To apply things to a use for which they were not intended. 5. To convert, to direct, to appropriate. **Todo lo convierte en substancia,** *(Met.)* He minds nothing, nothing makes the least impression upon him; he wants nothing but real facts. *-vr.* To be converted, to undergo a change either in religion or life.

convexidad [con-vek-se-dahd´], *f.* Convexity.

convexo, xa [con-vek´-so, sah], *a.* Convex, convexed.

convicción [con-vic-the-on´], *f.* Conviction, convincement.

convicto, ta [con-veec´-to, tah], *pp. irr.* of CONVENCER. Convicted, guilty.

convidada [con-ve-dah´-dah], *f.* An invitation to drink; a treat. **Dar una convidada,** to buy around.

convidante [con-ve-dahn´-tay], *m. & f.* One who invites, host.

convidado, da [con-ve-dah´-do, dah], *a. & pp.* of CONVIDAR. Invited, it is often used as a substantive for a guest, or a person invited to a dinner, party, etc.

convidador, ra [con-ve-dah-dor´, rah], *m. & f.* Inviter.

convidar [con-ve-dar´], *va.* 1. To invite, to bid, to ask or call to anything pleasing, to treat. **Convidar a uno a hacer algo,** to invite somebody to do something. **Convidar a uno a una cerveza,** to buy somebody a beer. 2. To treat someone to something. 3. *(Met.)* To allure, to invite, to persuade. **El ambiente convida a la meditación,** the setting invites one to indulge in meditation. *-vr.* To offer one's services spontaneously.

convincente [con-vin-then´-tay], *a.* Convincing, convincible.

convincentemente, *adv.* Convincingly, convictively.

convite [con-vee´-tay], *m.* 1. Invitation. 2. Feast to which persons are invited.

convivencia [con-ve-ven´-the-ah], *f.* Living together, life together; good fellowship, socializing.

conviviente [con-ve-ven´-tay], *a.* Living together. *-m. & f. (LAm.)* Live-in lover.

convivir [con-ve-ver´], *vn.* To live together; to share the same life; *(Pol.)* To coexist; *(fig.)* To exist side by side.

convocación [con-vo-cah-the-on´], *f.* Convocation, calling.

convocadero, ra [con-vo-cah-day´-ro, rah], *a.* That is to be convened or convoked.

convocador, ra [con-vo-cah-dor´, rah], *m. & f.* Convener, convoker.

convocar [con-vo-car´], *va.* 1. To convene, to convoke, to call together, to congregate. 2. To shout in triumph or exultation. *-vn.* Convocar a, to call for.

convocatoria [con-vo-cah-to´-re-ah], *f.* Letter of convocation, an edict.

convocatrio, ria [con-vo-cah-to´-re-o, ah], *a.* That which convokes.

convoluto, ta [con-vo-loo´-to, tah], *a.* Convolute, wrapped around itself.

convolvuláceo, cea [con-vol-voo-lah´-thay-o, ah], *a.* Convolvulaceous, of the convolvulus family.

convólvulo [con-vol´-voo-lo], *m.* 1. *(Bot.)* Convolvulus, bindweed. 2. A small worm which destroys the vines and wraps itself in their leaves. 3. A vinefretter.

convoy [con-vo´-e], *m.* 1. Convoy, conduct, an escort or guard. 2. The things conveyed with an escort or convoy. 3. *(Coll.)* Retinue, suite. 4. A railway train. 5. *(Carib.)* Salad (ensalada).

convoyante [con-vo-yahn´-tay], *pa.* Convoying.

convoyar [con-vo-yar´], *va.* 1. To convoy, to escort, or guard. 2. *(Cono Sur)* to back, to sponsor (financiar). *-vr. (Carib.)* To connive together, to plot.

convulsar [con-vool-sar'], *vn.* (*Vet.*) To feel an involuntary contraction of the nerves.-*vr.* To be convulsed.

convulsión [con-vool-se-on'], *f.* Convulsion.

convulsionar [con-vool-se-o-nar'], *va.* (*Med.*) To produce convulsions in; (*fig.*) To convulse, to cause an upheaval in.

convulsivamente [con-vool-se-vah-men'-tay], *adv.* Convulsively.

convulsivo, va [con-vool-see'-vo, vah], *a.* Convulsive, disturbed.

convulso, sa [con-vool'-so, sah], *a.* Convulsed.

convusco [con-voos'-co], *pron. pers.* With you.

conyúdice [con-yoo'-de-thay], *m.* (*Obs.*) V. CONJUEZ.

conyugal [con-yoo-gahl'], *a.* Conjugal, connubial, married.

conyugalmente, *adv.* Conjugally, matrimonially.

cónyuge [con'-yoo-hay], *m. & f.* Spouse; partner; husband, wife.

cónyuges [con'-yoo-hess], *m. pl.* A married couple, husband and wife.

conyunto, ta [con-yoon'-to, tah], *a.* CONJUNTO.

coña [co'-nyah], *f.* 1. Humor, humorous tone, joking way. **Estar de coña,** to be in a joking mood. **Tomar algo a coña,** to take something as a joke. 2. Annoyance, bind.

coñac [co-nyac'], *m.* Cognac.

coñazo [co-nyah'-tho], *m.* 1. Pain (persona, cosa). 2. **Dar el coñazo,** to be a real pain.

coñe [co'-nyay], *excl.* V. COÑO.

coñearse [co-nyay-ar'-say], *vr.* To speak in a joking way, to adopt a humorous tone. **Coñearse de,** to make fun of.

coñete [co-nyay'-tay], *a.* (*And. Cono Sur*) stingy, tighfisted.

coño [co'nyo], *m.* 1. (*Anat.*) Cunt. 2. excl. Hell!, damn!, damn it all!; well I´m damned! (sorpresa). **¡Esto hay que celebrarlo, coño!,** we jolly well must celebrate this! 3. *adv.* ¿Qué coño haces aquí?, what in hell´s name are you up to? 4. **¡Qué libro ni qué coño!,** what a goddamned book! **Viven en el quinto coño,** they live way out. 5. (*Cono Sur. Mex.*) pejorative term applied to Spaniards.

cooperación [co-o-pay-rah-the-on'], *f.* Cooperation, conspiracy, coefficiency.

cooperador, ra [co-o-pay-rah-dor', rah], *m. & f.* Cooperator.

cooperante [co-o-pay-rahn'-tay], *pa. & a.* Cooperating, cooperator, cooperative, coactive, contributive.

cooperar [co-o-pay-rar'], *va.* To cooperate, to labor jointly with another, to concur. **Cooperar a un mismo fin,** to work for a common aim. **Cooperar en,** to collaborate in. **Los factores que cooperaron al fracaso,** the factors which together led to failure.

cooperario [co-o-pay-rah'-re-o], *m.* V. COOPERADOR.

cooperativa [co-o-pay-rah-te'-vah], *f.* Cooperative, mutual association. **Cooperativa agrícola,** agricultural cooperative.

cooperativamente, *adv.* Coefficiently.

cooperativista [co-o-pay-rah-te-ves'-tah], *m. & f.* Member of a cooperative.

cooperativo, va [co-o-pay-rah-tee'-vo, vah], *a.* Cooperative.

coopositor [co-o-po-se-tor'], *m.* He who is a candidate with another for a prebend, professorship, etc., which is obtained by a public trial of skill; competitor, rival.

coordenada [co-or-day-nah'-dah], *f.* (*Math.*) Coordinate.

coordinación [co-or-de-nah-the-on'], *f.* Coordination; classification; collateralness.

coordinadamente [co-or-day-na-dah-men'-tay] *adv.* Coordinately.

coordinado, da [co-or-de-nah'-do, dah], *a.* Coordinate.-*pp.* of COORDINAR.

coordinador, ra [co-or-de-nah-dor'], *m. & f.* Coordinator.

coordinadora [co-or-de-nah-do'-rah], *f.* Coordinating, committee.

coordinar [co-or-de-nar'], *va.* To coordinate, to arrange, to adjust, to class, to coordinate.

copa [co'-pah], *f.* 1. Cup, a small drinking vessel; goblet, wineglass. **Copa Mundial,** World Cup. **Llevar una copa de más,** to have one over the eight. 2. Meeting of the branches of a tree, a bower. 3. Crown of a hat. 4. Brazier, firepan. 5. Gill liquid measure, the fourth part of a pint; teacupful. 6. Each of the cards with a heart. 7. (*fig.*) **Copa de la amargura,** cup of sorrow. **Apurar la copa,** to know the utmost depths of suffering. -*pl.* 1. Hearts, one of the four suits at cards. 2. Bosses of a bridle.

copado, da [co-pah'-do, dah], *a.* Tufted, copped.-*pp.* of COPAR.

copaiba [co-pah'-e-bah], *f.* 1. (*Bot.*) The copaiba-tree, from which the copaiba gum or balsam distils. 2. Balsam copaiba.

copal [co-pahl'], *m.* Copal, a transparent resin.

copaljocol [co-pal-ho-cohl'], *m.* (*Bot.*) Tree in New Spain resembling a cherrytree.

copar [co-par'], *va.* 1. In monte, to put on a card a sum equal to what there is in the bank. 2. (*Met. and Coll.*) To possess oneself of many persons and things united; to corner. **Quedar copado en un trabajo,** to get bogged down in a place of work. 3. (*Mil.*) To surprise, cut off the retreat of a military force, making it prisoner. 4. (*Mex.*) To monopolize.

coparticipación [co-par-te-the-pah-the-on'], *f.* Joint participation.

copartícipe [co-par-tee'-the-pay], *com.* Participant, copartner, collaborator.

copaza [co-pah'-thah], *f. aug.* A large cup or glass with a foot.

copazo [co-pah'-tho], *m. aug.* A large fleece of wool. 2. Large snowflake.

copear [co-pay-ar'], *vn.* 1. To booze, to tipple; to go on a drinking spree. 2. (*Com.*) To sell wine by the glass.

copela [co-pay'-lah], *f.* Cupel or coppel, a vessel used in assaying precious metals.

copelación [co-pay-lah-the-on'], *f.* Cupellation, the act of refining metals.

copelar [co-pay-ar'], *va.* To refine or purify metals.

copeo [co-pay-o], *m.* **Ir de copeo,** to go drinking.

copera [co-pay'-rah], *f.* Cupboard: closet for glassware.

coperillo [co-pay-reel'-lyo], *m. dim.* A little cupbearer or attendant at a feast to serve wine.

Copérnico [co-per'-ne-co], *m.* Copernicus.

copero [co-pay'-ro], *m.* Cupbearer, one who serves drink at a feast.

copeta [co-pay'-tah], *f.dim.* A small cup or drinking-vessel.

copete [co-pay'-tay], *m.* 1. A crest, a tuft, aigret, toupee. **Estar hasta el copete,** (*Carib. Mex.*) To be fed up to the back teeth. 2. Forelock of a horse. 3. Crownwork of a looking-glass frame, made in the shape of a shell. 4. Top of the shoe which rises over the buckle. 5. Top, summit. 6. The projecting top or cop of sherbets or ice cream. **Hombre de copete,** a man of respectability and character. **Tener copete** or **mucho copete,** to assume an air of authority, to be lofty, supercilious, and haughty. **Asir la ocasión por el copete,** (*Prov.*) To profit by the opportunity.

copetín [co-pay-teen'], *m.* (*Arg.*) A before dinner drink; aperitif; liquor glass.

copetón [co-pay-tone'], *a.* 1. (*LAm.*) V. COPETUDO. 2. (*And.*) **Estar copetón,** to be tight.

copetudo, da [co-pay-too-do, dah], *a.* 1. Copped, rising to a top or head. 2. High, lofty, supercilious, on account of one's noble descent.

copey [co-pay'-e], *m.* 1. American tree, of excellent wood for engraving. 2. A bitumen found in Ecuador, and employed in repairing ships.

copia [co'-pe-ah], *f.* 1. Copiousness, plenty, abundance, fulness; fertility. 2. Copy, transcript; counterpart. 3. Portrait from an original design; copy of a picture. 4. Rate or valuation of tithe. 5. (*Gram.*) List of nouns and verbs, and the cases they govern. **Sacar una copia de,** to make a copy of. **Copia en limpio,** fair copy. **Copia carbónica,** (*Cono Sur*) carbon copy. **Copia impresa,** hard copy.

copiador [co-pe-ah-dor'], *m.* Copyist, copier, transcriber. **Copiador** or **libro copiador.** among merchants, book in which letters are copied, a copybook.

copiante [co-pe-ahn'-tay], *m.* Copyist, copier, an imitator.
copiar [co-pe-ar'], *va.* 1. To copy, to transcribe, to exemplify. 2. To imitate, to draw after life. 3. To write on the same subject with another, and nearly in the same manner. 4. *(Poet.)* To describe, to depict. **Copiar del natural**, to copy from life; among artists, to design from the naked body.
copilador [co-pe-lah-dor'], *m.* Compiler, collector. *V.* COMPILADOR.
copilar [co-pe-lar'], *va.* To compile; to collect. *V.* COMPILAR.
copilla [co-pee'-lyah], *f.* 1. *dim.* of COPA. 2. Cigar-lighter.
copiloto [co-pe-lo'-to], *m. & f. (Aut.)* Co-driver; *(Aer.)* Co-pilot.
copín [co-peen'], *m.* In Asturias, a Spanish measure, equal to half a *celemín*, or the twelfth part of a quintal or *fanega*.
copina [co-pee'-nah], *f. (Mex.)* A skin taken off whole.
copinar [co-pe-nar'], *va.* To remove an entire skin.
copiosamente [co-pe-o-sah-men'-tay], *adv.* Copiously, abundantly, plentifully, largely.
copioso, sa [co-pe-o'-so, sah], *a.* Copious, abundant, full, fruitful, plentiful, fluent, large.
copista [co-pees'-tah], *m.* 1. Copyist, transcriber. 2. A copying-machine.
copita [co-pee'-tah], *f. dim.* A small cup or drinking vessel. **Tomarse unas copitas**, to have a drink or two.
copito [co-pee'-to], *m. dim.* A small fleece or flake.
copla [co'-plah], *f.* 1. A certain number of consonant verses, a couplet; a stanza of four lines, of eight or eleven syllables, the second and fourth lines rhyming; by extension, short rhymes. 2. A sarcastic hint or remark, a lampoon. 3. *(Prov.)* Ballad. **Echar coplas de repente**, to talk nonsense. **Andar en coplas**, to be on everyone's lips. **Echar coplas a uno**, to speak ill of someone.
copleador [co-play-ah-dor'], *m. (Obs.)* Poetaster, rhymer.
coplear [co-play-ar'], *vn.* To versify, to make couplets.
coplero [co-play'-ro], *m.* 1. Poetaster, petty poet. 2. Ballad-seller.
coplica, illa, ita [co-plee'-cah, eel'-lyah, ee'-tah], *f. dim.* A little couplet.
coplista [co-plees'-tah], *m. V.* COPLERO.
coplón [co-plone'], *m. aug.* Low, vile poetry: generally used in the plural number, **coplones**.
copo [co'-po], *m.* 1. A small bundle of cotton, hemp, flax, or silk, put on the distaff to be spun. **Copo de algodón**, cotton ball. **Copos de avena**, oatmeal, rolled oats. 2. Snow flake. 3. Thick part of a fishing-net. 4. *(Prov.)* Odor of the flower of the aromatic myrrh-tree. 5. *(And. Carib.)* Tree-top (de árbol). 6. *(Cono Sur)* Piled-up clouds.
copón [co-pone'], *m.* 1. *(aug.)* A large cup or drinking vessel. 2. Ciborium, a large cup used in Catholic churches. 3. *(Naut.)* A small cable for weighing the anchor. **Y todo el copón**, and all the rest. **Un susto del copón**, a tremendous fright.
coposo, sa [co-po'-so, sah], *a. V.* COPADO.
copra [co'-prah], *f.* Copra, dried coconut meat.
coproducción [co-pro-dooc-the-one'], *f.* Joint production.
copropietario, ia [co-pro-pe-ay-tah'-re-o, ah], *a.* Jointly owning, coproprietor.
cóptico, ca [cop'-te-co, cah], *a.* Coptic, ancient Egyptian, or from that stock.
copto [cop' to], *m.* Coptic, the language of the Copts.
copucha [co-poo'-chah], *f. (Cono Sur)* lie, fib (mentira); gossip (chismes).
copuchar [co-poo-chahr'], *vn. (Cono Sur)* To lie, to fib; to gossip.
copudo, da [co-poo'-do, dah], *a.* Tufted, bushy, thick-topped.
cópula [co'-poo-lah], *f.* 1. The joining or coupling two things together. 2. Copulation, carnal union. 3. *(Arch.) V.* CÚPULA. 4. *(Log.)* Copula, the word which unites the predicate with the subject.
copular [co-poo-lar'], *va.* To connect, to join, or unite.-*vr.* To copulate, to come together.

copulativamente [co-poo-lah-te-vah-men'-tay], *adv.* Jointly.
copulativo, va [co-poo-lah-tee'-vo, vah], *a.* 1. *(Gram.)* Copulative. 2. Joining or uniting together.
coque [co'-kay], *m.* Coke.
coqueluche [co-kay-loo'-chay], *f.* Whooping cough.
coqueta [co-kay'-tah], *f.* 1. *(Prov.)* Feruling or blow with a ferule on the hand by school teachers. 2. *(Prov.)* A small loaf. 3. Coquette, flirt.
coquetear [co-kay-tay-arr'], *vn.* To coquet, to flirt.
coqueteo [co-kay-tay'-o], *m.* 1. Flirtatiousness, flightiness, coquetry; flirtatious disposition; *(fig.)* affection. 2. Flirtation.
coquetería [co-kay-tay-ree'-ah], *f.* Coquetry, flirtation.
coqueto, coquetón [co-key-tone'] [ ], *m.* A male flirt, ladykiller. *-a.* Smart, natty (vestido).
coquilla [co-keel'-lyah], *f. (Cono Sur)* shell.
coquillo [co-keel'-lyo], *m.* 1. Vinefretter, an insect which destroys vines. *V.* CONVÓLVULO. 2. Jean, a twilled fabric.
coquina [co-kee´-nah], *f.* 1. *(Prov.)* Shellfish in general. 2. Cockle.
coquinero [co-ke-nay´-ro], *m. (Prov.)* Fishmonger, one who deals in shellfish.
coquito [co-kee´-to], *m.* 1. *(dim.)* A small coconut. 2. Grimace to amuse children. **Hacer coquitos**, to make faces. 5. A turtle dove of Mexico, having a song like the cuckoo´s.
cor [cor], *m.* . 1. *V.* CORAZÓN. 2. *V.* CORO. **De cor**, By heart.
coráceo, cea [co-rah'-thay-o, ah], *a. V.* CORIÁCEO.
coracero [co-rah-thay'-ro], *m.* 1. Cuirassier. 2. *(Coll.)* A poor cigar.
coracha [co-rah'-chah], *f.* A leather bag.
corachín [co-rah-cheen'], *m. dim.* A little leather bag.
coracilla [co-rah-theel'-lyah], *f. dim.* A small coat of mail.
coracina [co-rah-thee'-nah], *f.* A small breast-plate, anciently worn by soldiers.
corada, coradela [co-rah'-dah, co-rah-day' -lah], *f. V.* ASADURA.
coraje [co-rah'-hay], *m.* 1. Courage, bravery, fortitude, mettle. 2. Anger, passion. 3. **Eso me da tanto coraje**, *(Met.)* That puts me in such a rage.
corajina [co-rah-he'-nah], *f.* Fit of temper, explosion of rage.
corajudo, da [co-rah-hoo'-do, dah], *a.* 1. Angry, passionate, easily irritated. 2. Spirited; tough; bold; *(Cono Sur)* brave.
coral [co-rahl'], *m.* 1. Coral, a marine calcareous production. **Corales**, strings of corals. 2. The polyp which produces the substance known as coral; these polyps are mostly anthozoan or hydroid. 3. *(Naut.)* A large knee which fastens the sternpost to the keel.
coral [co-rahl'], *a.* Choral, belonging to the choir.
coralero [co-rah-lay'-ro], *m.* A worker or dealer in corals.
coralífero, ra [co-rah-lee'-fay-ro, rah], *a.* Coralbearing.
coralillo [co-rah-leel´-lyo], *m.* The coral-colored snake, extraordinarily venomous.
coralina [co-rah-lee'-nah], *f.* 1. Sea-coralline or white wormseed. 2. *(Naut.)* A coral fishing-boat. 3. Every sea animal resembling coral.
coralino, na [co-rah-lee'-no, nah], *a.* Coralline.
corambre [co-rahm'-bray], *f.* All hides and skins of animals, dressed or undressed; pelts.
corambrero [co-ram-bray'-ro], *m.* Dealer in hides and skins.
coramvobis [co-ram-vo'-bis], *m. (Coll.)* A corpulent person, strutting about with affected gravity.
Corán [co-rahn'], *m.* Koran, the sacred book of the Mohammedans. *V.* ALCORÁN.
corana [co-rah'-nah], *f. (And. Cono Sur) (Hist.)* Sickle.
coránico [co-rah'-ne-co], *a.* Koranic.
corascora [co-ras-co'-rah], *f. (Naut.)* Corascora, a coasting vessel in India.
coraza [co-rah'-thah], *f.* 1. Cuirass, an ancient breast-plate. 2. **Coraza** or **caballo coraza**, cuirassier. 3. A plate of armor, iron or steel, for men-of-war. 4. Shell or carapace of a turtle, or other defensive armor of some reptiles.

coraznada [co-rath-nah'-dah], *f.* 1. Pith of a pine-tree. 2. Fricassee of the hearts of animals.

corazón [co-rah-thone'], *m.* 1. Heart, core. 2. Heart, benevolence, affection. 3. Heart, spirit, courage. 4. Will, mind. 5. Heart, the middle or center of anything. 6. In a loom, cam. 7. Pith of a tree. 8. **Corazón de un cabo**, *(Naut.)* Heartstrand. **Llevar** or **tener el corazón en las manos**, to be sincere and candid; to wear one´s heart on one's sleeve. **De corazón**, *adv.* 1. Heartily, sincerely. 2. From memory. **Clavarle (a uno) en el corazón**, to cause or to suffer great affliction. **Estar enfermo del corazón**, to have heart trouble. **Revista del corazón**, magazine of love stories. **Encoger a uno el corazón**, to fill somebody with fear. **No tener corazón**, to have no heart.

corazonada [co-rah-tho-nah'-dah], *f.* 1. Courage, an impulse of the heart to encounter dangers. 2. Presentiment, foreboding. 3. Entrails.

corazonazo [co-rah-tho-nah'-tho], *m. aug.* A great heart.

corazoncico, illo, ito [co-rah-thon-thee'-co], *m. dim.* A little heart, a pitiful or faint-hearted person.

corazoncillo [co-rah-thon-theel'-lyo], *m. (Bot.)* Perforated St. John´s wort.

corbachada [cor-bah-chah´-dah], *f.* A stroke or lash given with a *corbacho.*

corbacho [cor-bah'-cho], *m.* The tendon or aponeurosis of an ox or a bull, with which the boatswain of a galley punished the convicts.

corbás [cor-bahs'], *f. pl. (Falc.)* The four largest feathers of a hawk.

corbata [cor-bah'-tah], *f.* 1. Tie, cravat, a neckcloth, neck handkerchief. 2. A sash or ribbon ornamented with gold or silver fringe tied to banners. 3. Ribbon, insignias of an order. *-m.* Magistrate not brought up to the law; also a layman who has neither studied the civil nor canon law.

corbatín [cor-bah-teen'], *m.* 1. Cravat. *V.* CORBATA. 2. Stock, a close neckchoth.

corbato [cor-bah'-to], *m.* Cooler, a vat filled with water in which the worm of a still is placed to cool.

corbatón [cor-bah-tone'], *m. (Naut.)* A small knee used in different parts of a ship.

corbe [cor'-bay], *m.* An ancient measure for baskets.

corbeta [cor-bay'-tah], *f.* 1. Corvette, a light vessel with three masts and squaresails. 2. **Corbeta de guerra**, a sloop of war.

corca [cor'-cah], *f.* Woodworm.

Córcega [cor'-the-gah], *f.* Corsica.

corcel [cor-thel'], *m.* A steady horse, a charger.

corcesca [cor-thes´-cah], *f.* Ancient pike or spear.

corcha [cor'-chah], *f. V.* CORCHO and CORCHERA.

corche [cor'-chay], *m.* A sort of sandal or shoe, open at the top, and tied with latchets.

corchea [cor-chay'-ah], *f. (Mus.)* Crochet, half a minim.

corchear [cor-chay-ar'], *va.* Among curriers, to grain leather with a cork.

corchera [cor-chay'-rah], *f.* Vessel of pitched cork or staves, in which a bottle or flask is put with ice or snow, to cool liquor.

corchero [cor-chay'-ro], *a.* Cork. **Industria corchera**, cork industry.

corcheta [cor-chay'-tah], *f.* Eye of a hook or clasp.

corchete [cor-chay'-tay], *m.* 1. Clasp, a hook and eye: commonly used in the plural. **Corchetes**, hooks and eyes. 2. Locket, a small lock; crotch. 3. *(Coll.)* An arresting officer. 4. An iron instrument for flattening tin plates. 5. Brace used to connect lines in writing or printing. 6. Benchhook of a carpenter's bench.

corchetear [cor-chay-ar'], *va. (Cono Sur)* to staple.

corchetera [cor-chay-tay'-rah], *f. (Cono Sur)* stapler.

corcho [cor'-cho], *m.* 1. Cork, the bark of the corktree. 2. Icevessel. *V.* CORCHERA. 3. Beehive. *V.* COLMENA. 4. Cork, the stopple of a bottle, flask, or jar. 5. Box made of cork, for carrying eatables. 6. Corkboard, put before beds and tables to serve as a shelter. **Sacar el corcho**, to draw the cork. **Cor-**

cho virgen, virgin cork. *-pl.* 1. Clogs, a sort of pattens used by women to keep their shoes clean and dry. 2. *(Mil.)* Tampion or tompion, a plug placed in a gun's muzzle when the gun is not in use.

córcholis [cor'-cho-les], *excl.* Good lord!, dear me!

corchoro [cor-cho'-ro], *m. (Bot.)* Corohorus, a genus of plants.

corchoso, sa [Cor-cho'-so, sah], *a.* Like cork in appearance or condition.

corcillo, illa [cor-theel'-lyo, lyah], *m. & f. dim.* A small deer or little fawn.

corcino [cor-thee'-no], *m.* A small deer.

corcor [cor-cor'], *m. (CAm. Carib.)* Gurgle. **Beber corcor**, to swig, to knock it back.

corcova [cor-co'-vah], *f.* 1. Hump, a crooked back, hunch. 2. Convexity, protuberance, curvature, gibbosity. 3. *(And. Cono Sur)* all night party (fiesta).

corcovado, da [cor-co-vah'-do, dah], *a.* Hump-backed, gibbous, crooked. *-pp.* of CORCOVAR.

corcovar [cor-co-var'], *va. (Obs.)* To crook.

corcovear [cor-co-vay-ar'], *vn.* 1. To curvet, to cut capers. 2. *(And. Carib, Cono Sur)* to grumble, to grouse. 3. *(Mex.)* To be frightened.

corcoveta [cor-co-vay'-tah], *com.* A crookbacked person.

corcovilla, ita [cor-co-veel'-lyah], *f. dim.* Little hump or crooked back.

corcovo [cor-co'-vo], *m.* 1. Spring, or curvest, made by a horse on the point of leaping. 2. A wrong step, unfair proceeding.

córculo [cor'-coo-lo], *m.* Heartshell, an aquatic insect.

corcusido, da [cor-coo-see'-do, dah], *a.* Clumsily mended or sewed on. *-pp.* of CORCUSIR.

corcusir [cor-coo-seer´], *va. (Coll.)* To darn holes in cloth or stuff, to patch.

corda [cor'-dah], *f.* **Estar el navío a la corda**, *(Naut.)* To be closehauled, or lying to (barco).

cordada [cor-dah'-dah], *f.* Team, roped team (alpinismo).

cordaje [cor-dah'-hay], *m. (Naut.)* Cordage, all sorts of rope used in the rigging of ships; strings (raqueta).

cordal [cor-dahl´], *m.* Double tooth. **Cordales**, grinders.

cordato, ta [cor-dah'-to, tah], *a.* Wise, prudent, discreet, judicious, considerate.

cordel [cor-del'], *m.* 1. Cord, a rope of several strands. 2. *(Naut.)* A thin rope or line used on board a ship; a line. **Cordel alquitranado**, a tarred line. **Cordel blanco**, an untarred line. **Cordel de corredera**, logline. **Mozo de cordel**, porter, one who carries burdens for hire. **Apretar los cordeles**, to oblige one to say or do a thing by violence. **Echar el cordel**, 1. To mark with a line or cord. 2. *(Met.)* To administer justice impartially. 3. *(Met.)* To draw lines in order to consider the manner of executing a thing. **Estar a cordel**, to be in a right line.

cordelado, da [cor-day-lah'-do, dah], *a.* Twisted for ribbons or garters: applied to silk.

cordelazo [cor-day-lah'-tho], *m.* Stroke or lash with a rope.

cordelejo [cor-day-lay'-ho], *m.* 1. *(dim.)* A small rope. 2. Fun, jest joke. 3. **Dar cordelejo**, *(Met.)* To pump out a secret artfully.

cordelería [cor-day-lay-ree'-ah], *f.* 1. Cordage, all sorts of ropes. 2. Ropewalk. 3. *(Naut.)* Rigging.

cordelero [cor-day-lay'-ro], *m.* Rope-maker, cordmaker.

cordelito [cor-day-lee´-to], *m. dim.* A small rope, cord, or line.

cordellate [cor-del-lyah'-tay], *m.* Grogram, a sort of stuff.

cordera [cor-day'-rah], *f.* 1. Ewe lamb. 2. Meek, gentle, or mild woman.

cordería [cor-day-ree'-ah], *f.* 1. Cordage, cords, ropes. 2. Place where cordage is kept.

corderica, illo, ito [cor-day-ree'-cah], *f. dim.* Little lamb.

corderico, illo, ito [cor-day-ree'-co], *m. dim.* A young or little lamb.

corderillo [cor-day-reel'-lyo], *m.* Lambskin dressed with the fleece.

corderina [cor-day-ree'-nah], *f.* Lambskin.

corderino, na [cor-day-ree'-no, nah], *a.* Of the lamb kind, belonging to lambs.

cordero [cor-day'-ro], *m.* 1. Lamb. 2. A dressed lambskin. 3. Meek, gentle, or mild man. **Cordero lechal**, houselamb. **Cordero asado**, roast lamb. **Cordero de Dios**, Lamb of God.

corderuna [cor-day-roo'-nah], *f.* Lambskin.

cordeta [cor-day'-tah], *f. (Prov.)* A small rope made of the platted strands of bassweed.

cordezuela [cor-day-thoo-ay'-lah], *f. dim.* A small rope .

cordíaco, ca [cor-dee'-ah-co, cah], *a.* V. CARDÍACO.

cordial [cor-de-ahl'], *a.* 1. Cordial, affectionate, sincere. 2. Cordial, invigorating, reviving.

cordial [cor-de-ahl'], *m.* Cordial, a strengthening medicine.

cordialidad [cor-de-ah-le-dahd'], *f.* Cordiality, intimacy.

cordialmente [cor-de-ahl-men'-tay], *adv.* Cordially, sincerely, affectionately, heartily.

cordila [cor-dee'-lah], *f.* Spawn of a tunnyfish

cordilo [cor-dee'-lo], *m.* An amphibious animal resembling a crocodile.

cordilla [cor-deel'-lyah], *f.* Guts of sheep, given to cats to eat.

cordillera [cor-deel-lyay'-rah], *f.* Chain or ridge of mountains. In particular, the Andes.

cordillerano [cor-del-lay-rah'-no], *a. (Cono Sur)* Andean.

cordita [cor-dee'-tah], *f.* Cordite.

Córdoba [cor'-do-bah], *f.* 1. Standard monetary unit of Nicaragua. 2. Cordova (city).

cordobán [cor-do-bahn'], *m.* Cordovan, cordwain, morocco or Spanish leather, tanned goatskin.

cordobana [cor-do-bah'-nah], *f.* Nakedness, nudity. **Andar a la cordobana**, to go stark naked.

cordobés, sa [cor-do-bess', bay'-sah], *f.* Native of or belonging to Cordova.

cordojo [cor-do'-ho], *m. (Obs.)* Anguish, anxiety, affliction.

cordón [cor-done'], *m.* 1. Cord or string made of silk, wool, hemp, etc. 2. Twisted or platted lace. 3. Cord or girdle with which monks tie up their habits. 4. A military cordon, formed by a line of troops to prevent any communication. **Cordón sanitario**, sanitary cordon. 5. *(Naut.)* Strand of a cable or rope. **Cabo de tres o cuatro cordones**, a three or four stranded rope or cable. 6. *(Mil.)* Cordon, a row of stones jutting out between the rampart and the basis of the parapet, where the wall begins to be perpendicular. 7. *(Arch.)* V. BOCEL. 8. The milled edge of coined metal. 9. *(Anat.)* Cord. **Cordón umbilical**, umbilical cord. 10. *(Cono Sur)* kerb. 11. *(And. Carib, Cono Sur)* **Cordón de cerros**, chain of hills. 12. *(And. Carib.)* Liquor, brandy. 13. *(Cono Sur)* **Cordón detonante**, fuse. -*pl.* 1. Silver or gold cords from the right shoulder to the breast, worn by the cadets and other military men. 2. Harness cords of a velvetloom.

cordonazo [cor-do-nah'-tho], *m.* 1. Stroke with a cord or rope. 2. *(aug.)* Large cord.

cordoncico, illo, ito [cor-don-thee'-co], *m. dim.* A small cord or line.

cordoncillo [cor-don-theel'-lyo], *m.* 1. A twisted cord, round lace, lacing, braid. 2. Milling round the edge of coin.

cordonería [cor-do-nay-ree'-ah], *f.* 1. All the work of twisters or lacemakers in general. 2. A lacemaker's shop.

cordonero, ra [cor-do-nay'-ro, rah], *m. & f.* 1. Lacemaker, lace-man, or woman. 2. Ropemaker.

cordura [cor-doo'-rah], *f.* Prudence, practical wisdom; judgment. **Hacer cordura**, To act in a prudent manner.

Corea [co-ray'-ah], *f.* Korea; **Corea del Norte**, North Korea; **Corea del Sur**; South Korea.

corea [co-ray'-ah], *f.* 1. Dance, accompanied with a chorus. 2. Chorea, St. Vitus's dance. 3. Corea *(Geog.)*.

coreano, na [co-ray-ah'-no], *m. & f.* Korean.

corear [co-ray-ar'], *va.* To sing or play in a chorus. **Música coreada**, chorus music. -*vn.* To speak all together; *(Mus.)* To sing all together, to join in.

corecico [co-ray-thee'-co], *m. dim.* of CUERO, Small hide or skin.

corecillo [co-ray-theel'-lyo], *m.* A roasted sucking pig.

coreo [co-ray'-o], *m.* 1. A foot in Latin verse. 2. Connected harmony of a chorus.

coreografía [co-ray-o-gra-fee'-ah], *f.* 1. The art of dancing. 2. Choreography, the art of arranging dances and ballets.

coreográfico [co-ray-o-gra'-fe-co], *a.* Choreographic.

coreógrafo, fa [co-ray-o'-gra-fo], *m. & f.* Choreographer.

corezuelo [co-ray-thoo-ay'-lo], *m.* 1. *(Prov.)*

corisáceo, cea [co-re-ah'-thay-o, ah], *a.* Coriaceous, leathery.

coriámbico, ca [co-re-ahm'-be-co, cah], *a.* Applied to Latin verses written with coriambics.

coriambo [co-re-ahm'-bo], *m.* Coriambic, a foot of prosody; a troche and an iambus combined.

coriana [co-re-ah'-nah], *f. (And.)* Blanket.

coriandro [co-re-ahn'-dro], *m. (Bot.)* Coriander, or common coriander.

coribante [co-re-bahn'-tay], *m.* Corybantes, priests of Cybele.

coribantismo [co-re-ban-tees'-mo], *m.* A kind of frenzy accompanied by many contorsions.

coríceo [co-ree'-thay-o], *m.* A hall for playing ball in ancient gymnasiums.

córida [co'-re-dah], *f.* 1. A substance which the Arabs use against small pox. 2. Cowry, a kind of shell used for money by some African tribes. 3. *(Bot.)* A perennial plant of the cowslip family.

corifeo [co-re-fay'-oh], *m.* 1. Coryphaeus, the leader of the ancient dramatic chorus. 2. Coryphaeus, leader of a sect or party.

corillo [co-reel'-lyo], *m. dim.* A small choir, an organ loft.

corimbífero [co-rim-bee'-fay-ro], *a. (Bot.)* Corymbiferous, bearing fruit or berries in clusters.

corimbo [co-reem'-bo], *m. (Bot.)* Corymb, a flower cluster of indeterminate florescence.

corindón [co-rin-done'], *m.* Corundum, the hardest known substance, next to the diamond.

corintio, tia [co-reen'-te-o, ah], *a.* 1. Native of or belonging to Corinth. 2. Corinthian (arquitectura).

corinto [co-reen'-to], *a. m.* Maroon, purplish.

corion [co'-re-on], *m. (Anat.)* Chorion, the exterior membrane that envelopes the foetus.

corisanto [co-re-sahn'-to], *m. (Bot.)* Perennial orchidaceous plant cultivated in European botanical gardens, native of Chili and California.

corista [co-rees'-tah], *com.* Chorist or chorister; *(Mus.)* Member of the chorus.

coristerión [co-ris-tay-re-on'], *m.* An organ secreting the glutinous material with which insects fasten their eggs to one another.

corito [co-ree'-to], *a.* 1. Timid, pusillanimous. 2. Naked. -*m.* A workman who treads grapes in the winepress.

coriza [co-ree'-thah], *f.* 1. A kind of shoe of undressed leather, laced from the toe to the instep, worn by common people in some parts of Spain. 2. Coryza, a copious running from the nose. V. ROMADIZO.

corladura [cor-lah-doo'-rah], *f.* Goldvarnish.

corlar, corlear [cor-lar'-cor-lay-ar'], *va.* To put on goldvarnish.

corma [cor'-mah], *f.* 1. The stocks. 2. *(Met.)* Trouble, uneasiness.

cormorán [cor-mo-rán'], *m.* Cormorant, a waterfowl.

cornac, or **cornaca** [cor-nah'-cah], *m.* A keeper of domesticated elephants: native name.

cornada [cor-nah'-dah], *f.* 1. Thrust with a bull's or cow's horn. 2. Thrust with a foil in a cunning manner, with the vulgar.

cornadillo [cor-nah-deel'-lyo], *m.* A small piece of money of little value. **Emplear su cornadillo**, to attain one´s end by low means.

cornadura [cor-nah-doo'-rah], *f.* Horns; antlers (de ciervo).

cornal [cor-nahl'], *m.* A strap or thong with which oxen are tied to the yoke by the horns.

cornalina [cor-nah-lee'-nah], *f.* Cornelian, a red variety of chalcedony.

cornamenta [cor-nah-men'-tah], *f.* Horns of any animal; antlers (de ciervo); cuckold´s horns (de marido). **Poner la cornamenta a uno**, to cuckold somebody.

cornamusa [cor-nah-moo'-sah], *f.* 1. Cornemuse, a wind instrument; a sort of long trumpet (metal). 2. *(Naut.)* A belaying cleat. **Cornamusas de los palos**,

cornas [cor'-nas], *f. pl. (Naut.)* Backstays. V. BRANDALES.

cornatillo [cor-nah-teel'-lyo], *m.* A kind of olive.

córnea [cor'-nay-ah], *f.* 1. Cornea, the transparent part of the eye: applied also, in Spanish, to the sclerotic or white of the eye. 2. A stone like jasper.

corneador, ra [cor-nay-ah-dor', rah], *m. & f.* A horned animal, which butts or plays with the horns.

corneal [cor-nay-ahl'], *a.* Corneal.

conear [cor-nay-ar'], *va.* To butt or play with the horns. V. ACORNEAR.

cornecico, illo, ito [cor-nay-thee'-co], *m. dim.* Cornicle, a small horn.

corneja [cor-nay'-hah], *f. (Orn.)* Crow, fetlock, dow.

cornejal [cor-nay-hahl'], *m.* A collection of dogwood-trees.

cornejalejo [cor-nay-hah-lay'-ho], *m.* A kind of pod in which some seed or fruit is contained.

cornejo [cor-nay'-ho], *m. (Bot.)* Hound-tree or cornel-tree, dogwood.

cornelina [cor-nay-lee'-nah], or **cornerina**, *f.* V. CORNALINA.

córneo, ea [cor'-nay-o, ah], *a.* Horny, corny, callous.

córner [cor'-nayr], *m. pl.* **córnes** [cor'-nays], Corner, corner kick.

cornerina [cor-nay-re'-nah], *f.* Cornelian, carnelian.

cornero [cor-nay'-ro], *m.* **Cornero de pan**, *(Prov.)* Crust of bread.

corneta [cor-nay´-tah], *f.* 1. A wind instrument in the shape of a horn; **corneta acústica**, ear trumpet. 2. A French horn. 3. A postillion's horn; hunting-horn. 4. Cornet, an ensign of horse who carries the standard. 5. Troop of horse. 6. *(Naut.)* Broad pennant; a rear admiral's flag. 7. Horn used by swineherds to call their hogs. *-m. & f.* Burgler; cornet player.

cornete [cor-nay'-tay], *m. dim.* A small musical horn, or buglehorn. *-pl.* 1. *(Anat.)* Small bony plates of the nasal fossae. 2. A surgical instrument.

cornetear [cor-nay-tay-ar'], *vn. (Carib.) (Aut.)* To sound the horn.

cornetín [cor-nay-teen'], *m.* 1. *dim.* of CORNETA. 2. Cornet, a brass instrument of the trumpet family, now provided with three valves.

corneto [cor-nay'-to], *a. (CAm.)* Bow-legged.

cornezuelo [cor-nay-thoo-ay'-lo], *m.* 1. Ergot of rye. 2. An instrument for bleeding horses. 3. *(Bot.)* V. CORNICABRA.

cornflaques [con'-flayks], *m. pl.* cornflakes.

corniabierto, ta [cor-ne-ah-be-err'-to, tah], *a.* Having widespread horns.

cornial [cor-ne-ahl'], *a.* In the shape of a horn.

corniapretado, da [cor-ne-ah-pray-tah'-do, dah], *a.* Having close set horns.

cornicabra [cor-ne-cah'-brah], *f.* 1. *(Bot.)* Turpentine-tree, pistachia-tree, of which the *Orihuela* snuff-boxes are made in Spain. 2. A sort of olives.

corniculata [cor-ne-coo-lah'-tah], *a.* Horned, as the new moon.

cornículo [cor-nee'-coo-lo], *m.* Old name for the antenna of insects.

corniforme [cor-ne-for'-may], *a.* In the shape of horns.

cornigacho, cha [cor-ne-gah'-cho, chah], *a.* Having the horns turned slightly downward.

cornígero, ra [cor-nee'-hay-ro, rah], *a. (Poet.)* Horned.

cornija [cor-nee'-hah], *f. (Arch.)* Cornice, a horizontal moulding.

cornijal [cor-ne-hahl'], *m.* Angle or corner of a building.

cornijamento, cornijamiento [cor-ne-hah-men'-to], *m. (Arch.)* V. CORNIJÓN.

cornijón [cor-ne-hone'], *m. (Arch.)* The third of the three principal pieces on the tops of columns, consisting of the architrave, frieze, and cornice; the entablature.

cornil [cor-neel'], *m.* V. CORNAL.

corniola [cor-ne-o'-lah], *f.* V. CORNALINA.

cornisa [cor-nee'-sah], *f. (Arch.)* Cornice.

cornisamento, cornisamiento [cor-nee-sah-men'-to], *m.* V. CORNIJÓN.

cornisica, illa, ita [cor-ne-see'-cah], *f. dim.* Small cornice.

corniveleto, ta [cor-ne-vay-lay'-to, tah], *a.* Having horns turned strongly upward.

corno [cor'-no], *m.* 1. *(Bot.)* Cornel-tree. V. CORNEJO. 2. Corno, English horn, a reed instrument resembling the oboe, pitched onefifth lower.

cornucopia [cor-noo-co'-pe-ah], *f.* 1. Cornucopia, the horn of plenty. 2. Sconce, a branched candlestick. 3. A pierglass.

cornudico, illo, ito [cor-noo-dee'-coh], *m. dim.* A little cuckold.

cornudo, da [cor-noo'-do, dah], *a.* Horned.-*m.* Cuckold.

cornúpeta [cor-noo'-pay-tah], *a.* Attacking with the horns. *(Acad.)*

coro [co'-ro], *m.* 1. Choir, a part of a church where the service is sung. 2. Choir, chorus, an assembly or band of singers; also a quartette of voices, or even a trío. **La chica del coro**, a girl from the chorus. 3. Choir, the singers in divine worship. 4. Chorus of a song. **Cantar a coros**, to sing alternately. 5. Memory. **Decir** or **tomar de coro**, to say or get by heart. 6. Chorus of a Greek tragedy. 7. Dance. 8. *(Poet.)* Summer solstitial wind. 9. Choir of angels. **Hablar a coros**, to speak alternately. 10. A dry measure of the Hebrews, about six bushels.

corocha [co-ro'-chah], *f.* 1. *(Prov.)* Vinefretter or vinegrub, an insect destructive to vines. 2. Coat.

corografía [co-ro-grah-fee'-ah], *f.* Chorography, the art of describing particular regions.

corográficamente, *adv.* Chorographically.

corográfico, ca [co-ro-grah'-fe-co, cah], *a.* Chorographical.

corógrafo [co-ro´-grah-fo], *m.* Chorographer.

coroidea [co-ro-e-day'-ah], *f.* The choroid coat of the eye.

corola [co-ro'-lah], *f. (Bot.)* Corolla, the envelope of a flower next to the stamens and pistils; usually colored.

corolario [co-ro-lah'-re-o], *m.* Corollary, inference, deduction.

corona [co-ro'-nah], *f.* 1. Crown, the emblem of royalty. **Ceñirse la corona**, to take the crown. 2. Coronet, an inferior crown worn by the nobility. 3. Crown, the top of the head. 4. A clerical tonsure. 5. An old Spanish gold and silver coin. 6. Crown, an English silver coin. 7. Crown, regal power, royalty. 8. Kingdom, monarchy. 9. Crown, reward, distinction. 10. Crown, honor, splendor, ornament, decoration. 11. Aureola with which saints are crowned. 12. Rosary of seven decades offered to the Holy Virgin. 13. End of a work. 14. Corona, a luminous halo about the sun, seen in total eclipses. **Corona de espinas**, crown of thorns. 15. Crown, completion, reward. 16. *(Naut.)* Pendant; a rope used for various purposes. **Coronas de palos**, maintackle pendants. 17. *(Bot.)* Appendices of a corolla, resembling a crown; the persistent, dry limb of the calyx of a flower. 18. Glory, triumph. **Corona de rosas**, chaplet of roses. 19 *(Mil.)* Crownwork. 20. *(Arch.)* Corona, a large flat member of the cornice, which crowns the entablature. 21. *(Her.)* The ornament painted in the upper part of a coat of arms, and which denotes the rank of nobility or distinction of the family to which it belongs. **Corona de fraile**, *(Bot.)* Three-toothed globularia. V. CABOLLANA. **Corona de rey**, *(Bot.)* Common melilot trefoil.

coronación [co-ro-nah-the-on'], *f.* 1. Coronation. 2. The end of any work. 3. *(Arch.) V.* CORONAMIENTO. 4. Queening (ajedrez).

coronado [co-ro-nah'-do], *m.* A Roman Catholic clergyman who received the tonsure. -**Coronado, da**, *pp.* of CORONAR.

coronador, ra [co-ro-nah-dor', rah], *m. & f.* 1. Crowner. 2. Finisher.

coronal [co-ro-nahl'], *m. & f. & a. (Anat.)* 1. Frontal bone. 2. Belonging to the frontal bone.

coronamiento [co-ro-nah-me-en'-to], *m.* 1. Ornament placed on the top of a building. 2. *(Obs.)* Coronation. 3. *(Naut.)* Taffrail.

coronar [co-ro-nar'], *va.* 1. To crown, to invest with the crown. **Coronar a uno rey**, to crown somebody king. 2. *(Met.)* To crown, to complete, to perfect, to finish. **Coronar algo con éxito**, to crown something with success. 3. *(Met.)* To decorate the top of a building. 4. To fill a glass up to the brim. 5. To queen (ajedrez). 6. *(And. Carib, Cono Sur)* to cuckold, to make a cuckold of.

coronaria [co-ro-nah'-re-ah], *a.* 1 *(Anat.)* Coronary. 2. Applied to the crownwheel of a watch.

coronario, ria [co-ro-nah'-re-o, ah], *a.* 1. Coronary, relating to a crown. 2. *(Bot.)* Coronary. 3. Extremely refined (oro).

corondel [co-ron-del], *m.* (Printing) Column-rule; reglet.

coronel [co-ro-nel'], *m.* 1. Colonel. **Coronel de aviación**, group captain, colonel. 2. *(Her.)* Crown.-*pl.* In paper-mills, the worked little sticks which there are to sustain the mould.

coronela [co-ro-nay'-lah], *f.* Colonel's wife; colonel.

coronela [co-ro-nay'-lah], *a.* Applied to the company, flag, etc., supposed to belong to the colonel of a regiment.

coronelía [co-ro-nay-lee'-ah], *f.* Colonelship. *V.* REGIMIENTO.

coronilla [co-ro-neel'-lyah], *f.* 1. Crown, top of the head, coxcomb. 2. Among bellfounders, the car by which a bell is suspended. 3. A genus of plants. **Coronilla** or **coronilla de rey**, *(Bot.)* nine-leaved coronilla. **Coronilla de fraile**, *(Bot.)* the French daisy. 4. In Castile, the kingdoms of Aragon, Valentia, Catalonia, and Majorca, which composed the ancient kingdom of Aragon. **Andar de coronilla**, to slog away. **Dar de coronilla**, to bump one's head. **Estar hasta la coronilla**, to be utterly fed up.

coroto [co-ro'-to], *m. (And. CAm. Carib.)* Gourd, vessel (vasija).

corotos [co-ro'-tos], *m. pl. (Sp. Amer. Coll.)* Belongings, things.

corozo [co-ro'-tho], *m. (Bot.)* A species of high palm-tree in Africa and America.

corpacho, corpanchón, corpazo [cor-pan-chone', cor-pah'-tho], *m. aug.* A very big body or carcass. **Corpanchón de ave**, carcass of a fowl.

corpecico, illo, ito, corpezuelo [cor-pay-thee'-co], *m. dim.* A little or small body, or carcass.

corpezuelo [cor-pay-thoo-ay'-lo], *m.* An under waiscoat without sleeves or skirts.

corpiño [cor-pee'-nyo], *m.* Waist, bodice. *V* JUSTILLO.

corporación [cor-po-rah-the-on'], *f.* Corporation, guild; community.

corporal [cor-po-rahl'], *a.* Corporal, belonging to the body. **Castigo corporal**, corporal punishment.

corporal [cor-po-rahl'], *m.* Corporal, altar linen on which the communion bread and wine are put to be consecrated.

corporalidad [cor-po-rah-le-dahd'] *f* 1 Corporality, the quality of being embodied. 2. Any corporeal substance.

corporalmente [cor-po-rahl-men'-tay], *adv.* Corporally, bodily.

corporativismo [cor-po-rah-te-ves'-mo], *m.* Corporate nature; corporate spirit.

corporativo [cor-po-rah-te'-vo], *a.* Corporate.

corporeidad [cor-po-ray-e-dahd'], *f.* Corporeal nature.

corpóreo, rea [cor-por'-ray-o, ah], *a.* Corporeal, corporeous.

corps [corps], *m.* Corps, a French term, implying body. **Los guardias de corps**, the lifeguards.

corpudo da [cor-poo'-do, dah], *a.* Corpulent, bulky.

corpulencia [cor-poo-len'-the-ah], *f.* Corpulence, corpulency. **Cayó con toda su corpulencia**, he fell with his full weight.

corpulento, ta [cor-poo-len'-to, tah], *a.* Corpulent, fleshy, fat.

corpus [cor'-poos], *m.* Corpus Christi day, or the procession held on that day in Roman Catholic countries.

corpuscular [car-poos-coo-lar], *a.* Corpuscular.

corpusculista [cor-poos-coo-lees'-tah], *m.* Atomist.

corpúsculo [cor-poos'-coo-lo], *m.* Corpuscle, atom, molecule.

corral [cor-rahl'], *m.* 1. Yard, inclosure; a poultry-yard (aves). 2. Court, open space before a house. 3. Fishpond. 4. Playhouse. 5. Blank left by students in writing lectures. **Aves de corral**, poultry. 6. Square formed by a body of foot. **Corral de madera**, timber yard. **Corral de ganado, corral del concejo**, pound. *(Naut.)* Place where cattle are kept on board a ship. **Hacer corrales**, *(Met.)* to loiter about in school or business hours. **Corral de vecindad**, tenement.

corralera [cor-rah-lay'-rah], *f.* 1. A brazenfaced impudent woman.

corralero [cor-rah-lay'-ro], *m.* Keeper of a dungyard.

corralillo, ito [cor-rah-leel'-lyo], *m. dim.* A small yard.

corraliza [cor-rah-lee'-thah], *f.* Yard, court.

corralón [cor-rah-lone'], *m. aug.* A large yard.

correa [cor-ray'-ah], *f.* 1. Leather strap or thong. 2. Leash. 3. Among saddlers, strap which fastens the holsters to the saddle. 4. Flexibility or extension of anything. 5. Leather belting, belt (cinturón), for machinery. **Besar la correa**, *(Met.)* to be obliged to humble oneself to another. **Tener correa**, to bear wit or raillery without irritation. **Correa de seguridad**, safety belt. **correaje** [cor-ray-ah'-hay], *m.* Heap of leather straps or thongs.

correal [cor-ray-al'], *m.* Dressed deerskin. **Coser correal**, or **labrar de correal**, to sew with small leather thongs instead of thread.

correar [cor-ray-ar'], *va.* To draw out wool and prepare it for use.

correazo [cor-ray-ah'-tho], *m.* Blow with a leather strap or thong.

correcalles [cor-ray-cahl'-lyes], *m.* Idler, lounger.

corrección [cor-rec-the-on'], *f.* 1. Correction, reprehension, lecture. 2. Correction, amendment, alteration to a better state. 3. Correction, that which is substituted in the place of anything wrong, emendation; **correción de pruebas**, *(Typ.)* Proofreading, proof-correction.

correccional [cor-rec-the-o-nahl'], *a.* Correctional, corrective, reformatory.

correcorre [cor-re-cor-re], *m. (Carib.)* Headlong rush, stampede.

correctamente [cor-rec'-tah-men-tay], *adv.* 1. Correctly; accurately. 2. Regularly. 3. Politely; properly, fittingly.

correctivo, va [cor-rec-tee'-vo, vah], *a.* Corrective.

correctivo [cor-rec-te'-vo], *m.* 1. Corrective, that which has the power of altering or correcting. 2. *(Med.)* Corrective, a medicine which abates the force of another.

correcto, ta [cor-rec'-to, tah], *a.* 1. Exact, correct, conformable to the rules. 2. Regular, well-formed (rasgos). 3. Correct; courteous, polite, well-mannered (persona). -*pp. irr.* of CORREGIR.

corrector, ra [cor-rec-tor'], *m. & f.* 1. Corrector, amender. 2. Corrector of the press, proofreader. 3. *m.* Superior, or abbot, in the convent of St. Francis de Paula. 4. *(Inform.)* **Corrector gramatical**, grammar checker. **Corrector ortográfico**, spell checker.

corredentor, ra [cor-ray-den-tor, rah], *m. & f.* One who redeems from captivity, jointly with another.

corredera [cor-ray-day'-rah], *f.* 1. Race-ground. 2. A small wicket or backdoor. 3. Runner or upper grinding stone in a cornmill. 4. Street. 5. *(Coll.)* Pimp, procuress.

6. *(Naut.)* Log or logline. 7. In glasshouses, roller, a metal cylinder for rolling plate grass. 8. Cockroach. *V.* CUCARACHA. 9. A slide-valve. 10. *(Typ.)* Track, slide, rail. **Puerta corredera**, sliding door. 11. *(Mech.)* Tongue, rail, guide, runner. 12. *(Mint.)* A milling-machine. 13. *(Astr.)* A thread which crosses the field of a lens and serves to measure the apparent diameter of a star.

corredizo, za [cor-ray-dee'-tho, thah], *a.* Easy to be untied, like a running knot.

corredor, ra [cor-ray-dor', rah], *m. & f.* 1. Runner. **Corredor automovilista**, racing driver. **Corredor de fondo**, long-distance runner. 2. Racehorse. 3. Corridor, a gallery. 4. *(Mil.)* Corridor, covertway, lying round a fortress. 5. *(Mil.)* Scout. 6. Forerunner. 7. Broker, one who does business for another. 8. A certain net, upon some coasts, which drags at the surface of the water, and is drawn into an oared boat. 9. *-f.* A name given to certain wandering, non-web-weaving spiders. **Corredor de popa**, *(Naut.)* balcony, or stern gallery of a ship. **Corredor de Bolsa**, stockbroker.

corredorcillo [co-ray-dor-theel'-lyo], *m. dim.* A small corridor.

corredura [cor-ray-doo'-rah], *f.* 1. Liquor which flows over the brim of a vessel with which liquids are measured. 2. Incursions into enemy's country.

correduría [cor-ray-doo-ree'-ah], *f.* 1. Brokerage. 2. *(Coll.)* Fine, penalty.

correería [cor-ray-ay-ree'-ah], *f.* Trade of a strapmaker.

correero [cor-ray-ay'-ro], *m.* Strap-maker.

corregencia [cor-ray-hen'-the-ah], *f.*Co-regency.

corregente [cor-ray-hen'-tay], *m.* Co-regent.

corregibilidad [cor-ray-he-be-le-dahd'], *f.* Correctibleness, susceptibility to being corrected.

corregible [cor-ray-hee'-blay], *a.* Corrigible, docile.

corregidor [cor-ray-he-dor'], *m.* 1. Corrector, one who punishes and corrects. 2. Corregidor, a Spanish magistrate in old days; a mayor of a town.

corregidora [cor-ray-he-do'-rah], *f.* Chief magistrate.

corregimiento [cor-ray-he-me-en'-to], *m.* The place, office, and district of a *corregidor.*

corregir [cor-ray-heer'], *va.* 1. To correct, to amend, to mend, to take away faults. 2. To correct, to remark faults, to reprehend, to admonish. 3. To correct, to temper, to mitigate, to make less active. 4. To adorn, to embellish. *-vr.* To mend; to mend one's way. **Corregirse su terquedad**, to stop being obstinate.

corregnante [cor-reg-nahn'-tay], *a.* Reigning with another.

corregüela, or **correhüela** [cor-ray-goo-ay´-lah], *f.* 1. *(dim.)* A small strap or thong. 2. Game among boys with a stick and small strap. 3. *(Bot.)* Bindweed.

correinante [cor-ray-e-nahn´-tay], *a.* *(Acad.)* *V.* CORREGNANTE.

correlación [cor-ray-lah-the-on´], *f.* Correlations analogy.

correlacionar [cor-ray-lah-the-o-nar'], *va.* To corretale.

correlativamente [cor-re-lah-te-vah-men'-tay], *adv.* Correlatively.

correlativo, va [cor-ray-lah-tee'-vo, vah], *a.* Correlative.

correligionario, ia [cor-ray-le-he-o-nah'-re-o, ah], *a.* 1. Of the same religion with another, fellow-believer. 2. Of the same politics.

correlón [cor-ray-lone'], *a.* 1. *(LAm.)* Fast, good at running. 2. *(CAm. Mex.)* Cowardly.

correncia [cor-ren-the-ah], *f.* *(Coll.)* Looseness, diarrhoea.

correndilla [cor-ren-deel'-lyah], *f.* *(Coll.)* Incursion. *V.* CORRERÍA.

correntada [cor-ren-tah'-dah], *f.* *(Cono Sur)* Rapids, strong current.

correntía [cor-ren-tee'-ah], *f.* 1. *(Prov.)* An artificial irrigation of stubble ground, to make the stalks rot, and convert them into manure. 2. *V.* CORRENCIA.

correntiar [cor-ren-te-ar'], *va.* *(Prov.)* To irrigate stubble ground.

correntío, tía [cor-ren-teo'-o, ah], *a.* 1. Current, running. 2. Light, free, unembarrassed.

correntón, na [cor-ren-tone', nah], *a.* 1. Gay, fond of company, pleasant; cheerful. 2. Taking a great deal of snuff. 3. A clever fellow. 4. Busy, active (activo). *-m. (And. Carib.)* Strong current.

correntoso [cor-ren-to'-so], *a.* *(LAm.)* Fast-flowing, rapid (río); in flood, in spate; torrential (agua).

correo [cor-ray'-o], *m.* 1. Post, mail. 2. Post office. **Correo aéreo**, air mail. **Correo marítimo**, mail via steamer. **Correo ordinario**, regular mail. **Casilla** or **apartado de correos**, post office box. **Correo de primera clase**, first-class mail. **Echar al correo**, to post. **Por correo**, by post. **Correo electrónico**, *(Inform.)* electronic mailbox. **Correo**, mailing.

correón [cor-ray-on'], *m. aug.* A large leather strap for holding up the body of ancient coaches.

correosidad [cor-ray-o-se-dahd'], *f.* Toughness, leatheriness; flexibility.

correoso, sa [cor-ray-o´-so, sah], *a.* Ductile, flexible, easily bent.

correr [cor-rerr'], *va. & vn.* 1. To run, to move at a quick pace. 2. To run, to flow, or to stream (líquidos). 3. To blow (viento). 4. To run, to pass away: as time and life. 5. To hasten to put anything in execution. 6. To solicit one's protection. 7. *(Met.)* To take the proper course, to pass through the proper channel (negocios). 8. To snatch away. 9. *(Coll.)* To persecute. 10. To extend, to expand. 11. To put one to the blush. 12. To arrive: said of the time fixed for payments. 13. To receive or admit a thing. 14. To flourish, to prevail for the time. 15. To tend, to guard, to take care of anything. 16. To be said, to be related. 17. Preceded by *con,* to charge oneself with a matter. 18. To travel. 19. To pursue a course. 20. To file right or left. 21. To have relations with, acquaintance with someone: used with *bueno* or *malo.* 22. To be smooth, fluent in style. **Correr los mares**, *(Naut.)* to follow the sea, to lead a mariner's life. **Correr en el mismo rumbo**, to stand onward in the same course. **Correr viento en popa**, to sail before the wind. **Correr la cortina**, to draw the curtain; to discover anything; to conceal, to quash. **Correr a rienda suelta**, 1. To ride full speed. 2. *(Met.)* To give a loose rein to one's passions. **Corre la voz**, it is reported, it is said, the story goes. **Correr la voz,** to pass the word, to be divulged. **Correr mal tiempo**, the times are evil. **A más correr, a todo correr**, as swiftly as possible. **Correrse**, to be ashamed or confused; to run away. **A todo correr**, happen what may. **El que no corre, vuela**, he who is observant while pretending indifference. **Quien más corre, menos vuela**, the more haste, the less speed. **Corre la flecha**, the arrow flies (said when Indian tribes agree to make war upon a common enemy). **Correr el velo**, to discover a secret; to take off the mask. **Correr la palabra**, *(Mil.)* to give the word. **Ha corrido medio mundo**, he has been round half the world. **Correr a uno**, *(CAm. Carib. Mex.)* To throw somebebody out. **Echar a correr**, to start to run. **Dejar correr las cosas**, to let things run on. **Dejar correr la sangre**, to let the blood flow. **Su sueldo correrá desde el primer día del mes**, his salary will be payable from the first of the month. **Correr con los gastos**, to pay the expenses. **Esto correr por tu cuenta**, *(fig.)* that's your problem. **Correrse una juerga**, *V.* JUERGA.

correría [cor-ray-ree'-ah], *f.* 1. A hostile incursion, a foray. 2. Leather strap.

correspondencia [cor-res-pon-den´-the-ah], *f.* 1. Correspondence relation. 2. Correspondence, commerce, intercourse. **Correspondencia particular**, private correspondence. **Curso por correspondencia**, correspondence course. **Estar en correspondencia con uno**, to be in correspondence with somebody. 3. Correspondence, friendship, interchange of offices or civilities. 4. Proportion, symmetry, congruity. 5. Consentaneousness, consent, agreement. **Mis ofertas no tuvieron correspondencia**, my

offers met with no response. **Yo esperaba más correspondencia,** I had expected a greater response.
corresponder [cor-res-pon-derr'], *va. & vn.* 1. To return a favor, to make a suitable return. 2. To correspond, to answer, to fit, to suit, to belong to, to regard. **Ese libro no corresponde aquí,** that book doesn't belong here. **La llave corresponde a esa cerradura,** the key fits this lock. **Corresponder dignamente a,** to make a fitting reply to. **Ella le correspondió con una corbata,** she gave him a tie in return. 3. To agree. 4. To fall to the lot of. **Le dieron lo que le correspondía,** they gave him his share. 5. To concern; to rest with, to devolve upon. **Me corresponde hacerlo,** it is my job to do it. **Me corresponde jugar a mí,** it's my turn to play. -*vr.* 1. To correspond, to keep up commerce by alternate letters. 2. To respect or esteem each other. **A todos aquéllos a quienes corresponda,** *(Met.)* to all whom it may concern.
correspondiente [cor-res-pon-de-en'-tay], *a.* Correspondent, conformable, agreeable, suitable.
correspondiente [cor-res-pon-de-en'-tay], *m.* V. CORRESPONSAL.
corresponsal, *m.* 1. Correspondent, one with whom intelligence is kept up by messages or letters. 2. One who deals with another that resides in a different place. **Corresponsal de guerra,** war correspondent.
corretaje [cor-ray-tah'-hay], *m.* 1. Brokerage, money paid to a broker for making sales or purchases. 2. *(Coll.)* Money paid to a pimp or procurer.
corretear [cor-ray-tay-ar'], *va.* 1. To walk the streets, to rove, to ramble, to go up and down, to jaunt, to gad, to flirt. 2. *(CAm.)* To scare off (ahuyentar). 3. *(Cono Sur)* to sell on behalf of. 4. *(Cono Sur)* to hurry along (trabajo). -*vn.* 1. To run about. 2. To loiter, to hang about the streets (vagar).
correteo [cor-ray-tay'-o], *m.* **Andar en correteos,** *(CAm.)* To rush about.
corretero [cor-ray'-tay-ro], *m.* Gadder.
corretora [cor-ray-to'-rah], *f.* In some convents, the nun who directs the choir.
correvedile, correveidile [cor-ray-vey-dee'-lay], *m. (Coll.)* l. Talebearer, mischiefmaker. 2. Procurer, pimp, go between.
correverás [cor-ray-vay-rahs'], *m.* 1. A child's toy, representing a coach or a living figure, and moved by a spring. 2. Something offered to a child to induce it to take medicine, or comply with its parents' wishes. *(Acad.)*
corricorriendo [cor-re-cor-re-en'-do], *adv. (Coll.)* In haste, at full speed.
corrida [cor-ree'-dah], *f.* 1. Course, race, career. 2. Incursion. 3. **Corrida de toros,** bullfighting. 4. Flow of any liquid. **De corrida,** at full speed, swiftly, in haste. 5. *(Carib. Cono Sur)* party, rave-up. 6. *(Cono Sur)* row, line, file. 7. *(Mex.)* Run, journey. 8. *(Geol.)* Outcrop.
corridamente [cor-re-dah-men'-tay], *adv.* Currently, easily, plainly.
corridita [cor-re-dee-tah], *f. dim.* A small course.
corrido [cor-ree'-do], *m.* 1. Romance, a merry song, accompanied with a guitar, in the *fandango* style. **Corridos,** Rents due and not paid. V. CAIDOS. 2. *(And.)* Fugitive from justice.
corrido, da [cor-ree'-do, dah], *a.* 1. Expert, experienced, artful. **Es una mujer corrida,** she's a woman who has been around. 2. Abashed, ashamed.-*pp.* of CORRER. 3. **Tres noches corridas,** three nights running. 4. *(Arch. etc.)* Continuous. 5. Fluent, confident (estilo). **Decir algo de corrido,** to rattle something off. 6. Excellent, splendid (fiesta). 7. Cursive (escritura).
corriente [cor-re-en'-tay], *f.* 1. Course of rivers. **Corriente del Golfo,** Gulf Stream. **Corriente submarina,** undercurrent. 2. Current, a running stream. 3. Current, course, progression. 4. *(Elec.)* Current. **Corriente alterna,** alternating current. **Corriente directa,** direct current. **Corriente de aire,** draft or draught, current of air. 5. Course, tendency; drift. **Dejarse llevar de la corriente,** to drift along. **Las corrientes modernas del arte,** modern trends in art.

corriente [cor-re-en'-tay], *pa.* Runner, running.
corriente [cor-re-en'-tay], *a.* 1. Current, plain, easy. 2. Current, generally received, uncontradicted. 3. Current, common, general. **Aquí es corriente ver eso,** it's common to see that here. **Es una chica corriente,** she's an ordinary sort of girl. 4. Current, what is now passing; the present month or year; instant. **El año corriente,** the current year. 5. Fluent (estilo). 6. Current, running. **Moneda corriente,** current coin. 7. Marketable, merchantable. **Géneros de consumo corriente,** staple commodities. **Ir corriente en los pagos,** to be up to date in one's payments.
corrientemente [cor-re-ayn-tay-men'-tay], *adv.* Currently.
corrillero, ra [cor-reel-lyay'-ro], *m.f.* Braggadocio, idle person, person with time to gossip.
corrillo [cor-reel'-lyo], *m.* A circle of persons standing to talk of the news of the day, or to censure the conduct of others.
corrimiento [cor-re-me-en'-to], *m.* 1 *(Met.)* Shame, bashfulness. 2. An acrid humor. 3. Concourse, act of assembling. 4. Act of running; course or flow of waters. **Corrimiento de tierras,** landslide. 5. V. CORRERÍA. 5. *(Med.)* Discharge; *(Carib. Cono Sur)* rheumatism; *(And.)* Tooth abscess.
corrincho [cor-reen'-cho], *m.* Meeting of low, vulgar people.
corrivación [cor-re-vah-the-on'], *f.* A diversion of brooks, and storing their water in a reservoir.
corro [cor'-ro], *m.* 1. Circle, ring formed by people who meet to talk or see a show. **Hacer corro,** to clear the way, to make room. 2. Sort of dance. 3. Small area, part, piece; *(Agri.)* Plot, small field, patch.
corroboración [cor-ro-bo-rah-the-on'], *f.* Corroboration.
corroborante [cor-ro-bo-rahntay], *m. & pa.* Corroborative, corroborant.
corroborar [cor-ro-bo-rar'], *va.* 1. To corroborate, to strengthen, to fortify, to confirm. 2. *(Met.)* To give new force to an argument or opinion.
corroborativo, va [cor-ro-bo-rah-tee'-vo, vah], *a.* V. CORROBORANTE.
corrobra [cor-ro'-brah], *f.* Treat or entertainment given at the conclusion of a bargain or contract. V. ALBOROQUE.
corroer [cor-ro-err'], *va.* To corrode, to eat away by degrees. **Le corroen los celos,** he is eaten up with jealously. -*vr.* To corrode, to become corroded.
corrompedor, ra [cor-rom-pay-dor', rah], *m. & f.* Corrupter.
corromper [cor-rom-perr'], *va.* 1. To corrupt, to vitiate, to mar, to turn from a sound to a putrescent state, to mortify. 2. To seduce a woman. 3. To corrupt, to bribe, to suborn. -*vn.* To stink, to emit an offensive smell.-*vr.* 1. To corrupt, to rot, to become putrid. 2. *(fig.)* To become corrupted, to become perverted.
corrompidamente [cor-rom-pe-dah-men'-tay], *adv.* Corruptly, viciously.
corrompido [cor-rom-pe'-do], **da.** *a.* Corrupt, spoiled, unsound. -*pp.* of CORROMPER.
corrompimiento [cor-rom-pe-me-en'-to], *m.* 1. Corruption, depravation, depravity. 2. Bribery. V. CORRUPCIÓN.
corroncha [cor-ron'-chah], *f. (And. CAm.)* Crust, scale.
corroncho [cor-ron'-cho], *a.* 1. *(Carib.)* Slow, sluggish. 2. *(fig.)* Corrupted, corrupt; depraved, degenerate.
corronchoso [cor-ron-cho'-so], *a. (And. CAm. Carib.)* Rough, coarse; crusty, scaly (escamoso).
corrongo [cor-ron'-go], *a. (CAm. Carib.)* First-rate, splendid; charming (encantador), attractive.
corrosca [cor-ros'-cah], *f. (Col.)* Wide straw hat for the sun.
corrosible [cor-ro-see'-blay], *a.* Corrosible.
corrosión [cor-ro-se-on'], *f.* Corrosion, exulceration.
corrosivo, va [cor-ro-see'-vo, vah], *a.* Corrosive, acrid, corrodent, acrimonious.
corroyente [cor-ro-yen'-tay], *pa.* Corroding, corrodent.
corroyera [cor-ro-yay'-rah], *f.* A kind of sumac which is employed in tanning.

corrugación [cor-roo-gah-the-on'], *f.* Corrugation, contraction into wrinkles.

corrugador [cor-roo-gah-dor'], *m.* Corrugater, a small muscle of the face which wrinkles the skin.

corrugar [cor-roo-gar'], *va. V.* ARRUGAR.

corrulla [cor-rool'-lyah], *f. (Naut.)* Room under deck in a row galley.

corrupción [cor-roop-the-on'], *f.* 1. Corruption, putrefaction, corruptness, corrupting. 2. Corruption, pollution, filth. 3. A spurious alteration in a book or writing. 4. Looseness of the bowels. 5. Destruction. 6. Corruption, depravity, depravation or perversion of manners or principles. **En el gobierno existe mucha corrupción**, there is a lot of corruption in the government. 7. Complete disorganization of any substance.

corruptamente [cor-roop'-tah-men-tay], *adv.* Corruptly, viciously.

corruptela [cor-roop-tay'-lah], *f.* 1. Corruption, depravation, corruptness. 2. *(Law.)* Bad habit or practice contrary to law; abuse.

corruptibilidad [cor-roop-te-be-le-dahd'], *f.* Corruptibility, corruptibleness.

corruptible [cor-roop-tee´-blay], *a.* 1. Corruptible (persona). 2. Perishable (alimentos).

corruptivo, va [cor-roop-tee'-vo, vah], *a.* Corruptive.

corrupto, ta [cor-roop'-to, tah], *pp. irr.* Of CORROMPER, and *a.* Corrupted, corrupt; defiled, perverse.

corruptor [cor-roop-tor'], *m.* Corrupter, misleader, one who taints or vitiates. *-a.* Corrupting.

corrusco [cor-roos'-co], *m. (Coll.)* Offal, broken bread. *V.* MENDRUGO.

corsa [cor'-sah], *f. (Naut. Obs.)* A coasting voyage, a cruise.

corsario [cor-sah'-re-o], *m.* Corsair, privateer, pirate.

corsario, ria [cor-sah'-re-o, ah], *a.* Cruising: applied to a privateer or letter or marque, authorized to cruise against the enemy.

corsé [cor-say'], *m.* Corset, stays for women.

corsear [cor-say-ar'], *va.* To cruise against the enemy.

corsetera [cor-say-tay'-rah], *f.* A woman who makes or sells corsets.

corsí [cor-see'], *m.* The second of the thrones of God, according to Mohammedan belief, from which he is to judge men at the last day.

corsia [cor´-se-ah], *f.* Passage between the sails in a row-galley.

corso [cor'-so], *m. (Naut.)* Cruise, cruising, privateering.

corso [cor'-so], *a. m. & f.* Corsican.

corta [cor'-tah], *f.* Felling of wood, said also of reeds.

cortaalambres [cor-tah-a-lam'-brays], *m.* Wire cutters.

cortabolsas [cor-tah-bol'-sas], *m.* Pick-pocket, filcher, petty robber.

cortacésped [cor-tah-thes'-ped], *m.* Lawnmower.

cortacircuitos [cor-tah-theer-coo-ee'-tose], *m. (Elec.)* Circuit breaker.

cortacorriente [cor-tah-cor-re-ayn'-tay], *m.* Switch.

cortacutícula [ ], *f.* Cuticle scissors.

cortada [cor-tah'-dah], *f.* 1. *(LAm.)* Cut, slash; trench (zanja); short cut (atajo). 2. Slice (de pan).

cortadera [cor-tah-day´-rah], *f.* 1. Chisel for cutting hot iron. 2. Knife or instrument used by beekeepers to cut out the honey-combs.

cortadero, ra [cor-tah-day'-ro, rah], *a.* Cutting readily; easily cut.

cortadillo [cor-tah-deel'-lyo], *m.* 1. A small drinking glass, a tumbler. 2. A liquid measure, about a gill, the quantity which the glass will hold. 3. The block of iron which, with others, forms grapeshot. 4. A clipped piece of money. **Echar cortadillos**. 1. To speak in an affected manner. 2. To drink wine. 5. Lump of sugar. 6. Affair (ligue).

cortado [cor-tah'-o], *m.* 1. Caper; a leap or jump in dancing. 2. Coffee with a little milk.

cortado, da [cor-tah'-do, dah], *a.* 1. Adapted, proportioned, accommodated, fit exact. 2. Sculptured. 3. *(Her.)* Parted in the middle. 4. Confounded. 5. Short, interrupted (estilo de escritura). 6. **Estar cortado,** *(Cono Sur)* to be broke. 7. **Tener el cuerpo cortado,** *(Mex.)* to feel off color. *-pp.* of CORTAR. **Quedarse cortado** or **cortarse**, to be out of countenance.

cortador, ra [cor-tah-dor', rah], *m. & f.* 1. Cutter, one who cuts. 2. That which cuts. *-a.* **Cortadora de césped,** lawnmower.

cortador [cor-tah-dor'], *m.* 1. Butcher. *V.* CARNICERO. 2. Slicing-machine, cutter. 3. *(Tel.)* Interrupter. 4. *(Zool.)* Scissorbill. *-pl.* Incisor teeth.

cortadora [cor-tah-do'-rah], *f.* Cutting board in a velvet loom.

cortadura [cor-tah-doo'-rah], *f.* 1. Cut, the action of a sharp instrument. 2. Cut, the separation of continuity by a sharp instrument; cutting, abscission. 3. Incision, cut, a wound made by cutting. 4. Fissure, or scissure 5. *(Mil.)* Parapet with embrasures and merlons, made in a breach to prevent the enemy from taking possession of it. 6. *(Mil.)* Work raised in narrow passes to defend them. **Cortaduras,** 1. Shreds of cloth, cuttings of paper, parings. 2. Figures cut in paper.

cortafrío [cor-tah-free'-o], *m.* A cold chisel; chisel for cutting cold iron.

cortafuego [cor-tah-foo-ay'-go], *m.* Fire-break, fire lane.

cortahierro [cor-tah-e-err'-ro], *m. V.* CORTAFRÍO.

cortahuevos [cor-tah-oo-ay'-vos], *m.* Egg-slicer.

cortahumedades [cor-tah-oo-may-dah'-days], *m.* Damp course.

cortalápiz [cor-tah-lah'-peeth], *m.* Pencil-sharpener.

cortamalla [cor-tah-mahl'-lyah], *f. (Agri.)* Alternate pruning of vineshoots when they are close.

cortamechas [cor-tah-may'-chas], *m.* A cuttingboard or table.

cortamente, *adv.* Sparingly, frugally, scantily.

cortamiento [cor-tah-me-en'-to], *m. (Obs.)* The act of cutting or amputating.

cortán [cor-tahn'], *m.* 1. *(Prov.)* Measure for grain, containing about a peck. 2. Oil measure, containing 8 lbs. 5 oz.

cortante [cor-tahn'-tay], *m.* Cutter, butcher.

cortante [cor-tahn'-tay], *pa.* Cutting, edged, sharp.

cortapapel [cor-tah-pa-pel], *m.* Papercutter, paperknife.

cortapicos y callares [cor-tah-pee'-cos ee cal-lyah'-res]. 1. *(Coll.)* Keep quiet! No more questions! (usado con niños). 2. *-m.* Earwig.

cortapiés [cor-tah-pe-ess´], *m. (Coll.)* Thrust made at the legs in fencing.

cortapisa [cor-tah-pee´-sah], *f.* 1. Obstacle, hindrance, impediment. **Sin cortapisas**, without strings attached. 2. Elegance and grace in speaking. 3. Condition or restriction with which a thing is given.

cortaplumas [cr-tah-ploo'-mas], *m.* 1. Penknife. 2. Earwig.

cortapuros [cor-tah-poo'-ros], *m.* Cigar cutter.

cortar [cor-tar'], *va.* 1. To cut, to cut off, to cut out, to curtail. 2. To cut, to disjoin, to separate, to hew, to chop. **Cortar por la mitad**, to cut down the middle. 3. *(Mil.)* To cut off part of the enemy's army. 4. To cut, to divide packs of cards in card-playing. 5. To interrupt the course of things. 6. To cut or interrupt a conversation, to cut short. 7. To cut, to form by cutting. 8. To abridge a speech or discourse. 9. To take a short cut, shorten the way. 10. To suspend, to restrain, to keep back. **Cortar el agua**, 1. To cut off the water. 2. *(Met.)* To navigate or sail through water. 11. To arbitrate or decide. 12. To cut figures in paper. 13. *(Naut.)* To cut away a mast or cable. **Cortar la corriente**, *(Elec.)* to break contact. **Cortar la lengua**, to speak a language with propriety and elegance. **Aire que corta**, a cutting, piercing, or nipping wind. **Cortar a alguno**, *(Met.)* to put one to the blush. *-vn.* 1. To cut. **Este cuchillo no corta**, this knife doesn´t cut. 2. To cut (cartas). 3. **Cortar con el pasado**, to break with the past. 4. **¡Corta!**, get away! *-vr.* 1. To be daunted, ashamed, or confounded, to stop short, not to know what to say. 2. To open out the folds or wrinkles in cloth. 3. To separate, as the serous part of milk from the butter. 4. Of geometrical figures, to cross, intersect. 5. To interpose one's forces, dividing those of the enemy. 6. To add to a liquid another to subdue its properties. 7. *(Vet.)*

To injure the forefeet with the shoes, in walking. 8. **Cortarse el pelo**, to have one's hair cut. 9. *(Cono Sur)* to be out of breath (caballo). 10. *(And. Carib. Mex.) (Med.)* To shiver, to get the shivers. 11. *(Cono Sur)* to die.

cortaúñas [cor-tah-oo'-nyas], *m*. Nail clippers.

cortavapor [cor-tah-vah-por'], *m*. Cut off of a steam-engine.

cortavidrios [cor-tah-ve'-dre-os], *m*. Glass cutter.

corte [cor'-tay], *m*. 1. Edge of a sword, knife, or any other cutting instrument. 2. Exsection, abscission, the act of cutting. **Corte de pelo**, haircut. 3. Cut, the effect of a cutting instrument. 4. Felling of trees. 5. Mediation or reconciliation of persons at variance. 6. Measure, expedient, or step taken in an affair. 7. Notch, hack, a hollow cut in something, the stuff necessary for a garment. **Corte de chaleco**, a vest pattern. **Un corte de vestido**, the stuff required for a full dress. 8. The surface which all the edges of the leaves of a book form. **Con cortes dorados**, with gilt edges. 9. (Mining) A shaft made in searching for a vein of mineral. 10. *(Arch.)* A sectional view of a building. *(Acad.)* 11. Resolutions which states adopt when they cannot satisfy overdue obligations. *(Acad.)* 12. Closing an account by a debtor without the assent of the creditor *(fr.* Cortar). 13. *(Elec. etc.)* Cut, failure. **Corte de corriente**, power cut. **Hay corte de agua**, the water has been cut off. 14. Start, surprise. 15. Snub, rebuff (desaire). 16. Sharp answer (réplica).

corte [cor'-tay], *f*. 1. Court, the town or place where the sovereign resides. 2. Court, persons who compose the retinue of a monarch. 3. Levee. 4. **Corte Suprema**, Supreme court. 5. Retinue, suite. 6. Yard, court. 7. Court, courtship, art of pleasing, civility. **Hacer la corte**, 1. To court, to endeavor to please. 2. To attend the levees of the sovereign or of men in power, to pay court. 8. Stable for cattle; sheepfold. 9. *(Obs.)* District of five leagues round the court. *-pl.* **Cortes**, the senate and congress of deputies of Spain.

cortecica, illa, ita [cor-tay-thee'-cah], *f. dim*. A small crust, peel, or bark.

cortedad [cor-tay-dahd'], *f*. 1. Smallness, littleness, minuteness. 2. Dulness, stupidity, want of intellect or instruction. 3. Pusillanimity, timidity, diffidence. **Cortedad de medios**, poverty, indigence, want of means.

cortejador [cor-tay-hah-dor'], *m*. Wooer.

cortejante [cor-tay-hahn'-tay], *pa*. Courting; courtier, he who makes love, gallant.

cortejar [cor-tay-har'], *va*. 1. To accompany, to assist another 2. To court, to pay homage. 3. To make love; **cortejar una dama**, to pay one's addresses to a lady. **Cortejar a alguno**, *(Coll.)* To stand treat.

cortejo [cor-tay'-ho], *m*. 1. Court, homage paid to another, courtship. 2. Gift, present, gratification. 3. Gallant, beau, lover, sweetheart. 4. Lady courted or sued for love; paramour. 5. Procession; solemn gathering. **Cortejo fúnebre**, funeral procession.

cortés [cor-tess'], *a*. Courteous, gentle, mild, civil, complaisant, complacent, gracious, courtly, mannerly, genteel, polite.

cortesanamente [cor-tay-sah-nah-men'-tay], *adv*. Courteously, politely.

cortesanazo, za [cor-tay-sa-nah'-tho, thah], *a. aug*. Awkwardly or fulsomely civil.

cortesanía [cor-tay-sa-nee'-ah], *f*. Courtesy, civility, politeness, complaisance, good manners.

cortesano, na [cor-tay-sah' no, nah], *a*. 1. Courtlike. 2. *V.* CORTÉS. 3. Courteous, gentle, mild, obliging; courtly. **Cortesana** or **dama cortesana**, courtesan.

cortesano [cor-tay-sah'-no], *m*. Courtier.

cortesía [cor-tay-see'-ah], *f*. 1. Courtesy, an act of civility and respect, obeisance, courteousness; good manners. **Visita de cortesía**, formal visit. 2. Compliment, an expression of civility; a title of courtesy. 3. Gift, present, gratifications. 4. Days of grace allowed by custom for the payment of a bill of exchange, after it becomes due. 5. Mercy, favor. **Título o tratamiento de cortesía**, a title or appellation of honor, not

of right, but by courtesy. **Hacer una cortesía**, to drop a courtesy.

cortésmente [cor-tays-men'-tay], *adv*. Courteously, civilly, genteelly, politely, obligingly.

corte transversal [cor'-tay trans-ver-sahl'], *m*. Cross section.

corteza [cor-tay'-thah], *f*. 1. Bark of a tree. 2. Peel, skin, or rind of many things. **Añadir una corteza de limón**, to add a bit of lemon peel. 3. Crust of bread pies, etc. 4. A wild fowl of the family of widgeons. 5. *(Met.)* Outward appearance of things. 6. *(Met.)* Rusticity, want of politeness, crustiness.

cortezón [cor-tay-thone'], *m. aug*. Thick bark, rind, crust, or peel.

cortezoncito [cor-tay-thon-thee'-to], *m. dim*. Thin bark, rind, crust, or peel.

cortezudo, da [cor-tay-thoo'-do, dah], *a*. 1. Corticose, barky; having a strong rough bark. 2. Rustic, unmannerly, unpolished.

cortezuela [cor-tay-thoo-ay'-lah], *f. dim. V.* CORTENZOCITO.

cortical [cor-te-cahl'], *a*. Cortical.

cortijada [cor-te-hah'-dah], *f*. A collection of houses put up by the laborers or owners of a grange.

cortijo [cor-tee'-ho], *m*. Farmhouse, grange, manse.

cortil [cor-teel'], *m. V.* CORRAL.

cortina [cor-tee'-nah], *f*. 1. Curtain, shade, screen, portiere. 2. *(Mil.)* Curtain, part of a wall or rampart which lies between two bastions. 3. Any veil or covering. **Cortina de hierro**, iron curtain. **Cortina de humo**, smoke screen. **Correr la cortina**, *(fig.)* to draw a veil over something. **Descorrer la cortina**, *(fig.)* To draw back the veil.

cortinado [cor-tee-nah'-do], *m. (Cono Sur)* curtains.

cortinaje [cor-te-nah'-hay], *m*. Set of curtains for a house.

cortinal [cor-te-nahl'], *m*. A piece of ground near a village or farmhouse, which is generally sown every year.

cortinilla [cor-te-neel'-lyah], *f*. Screen, shade, portiere, thin curtain.

cortinón [cor-te-none'], *m. aug*. A large curtain to keep out the air.

cortiña [cor-te'-nyah], *f*. A plot of vegetables and cereals.

cortisona [cor-te-soh'-nah], *f. (Med.)* Cortisone.

corto, ta [cor'-to, tah], *a*. 1. Short, not long, scanty, narrow, curt. **El vestido le ha quedado corto**, the dress has got too short for her. **El niño va todavía de corto**, the child is still wearing short trousers. 2. Small. 3. Short, not of long duration. 4. *(Met.)* Dull, stupid, weak of intellect. 5. *(Met.)* Timid, pusillanimous, fearful. **Quedarse corto**, to say less than one should say. 6. *(Met.)* Short of words, concise. 7. Imperfect, defective. **Corto de vista**, short-sighted. **Corto de oído**, hard of hearing. **Corto de manos**, slow at work, unhandy, not handy, not dexterous. **Pongamos 50 dólares y me quedo corto**, let's say 50 dollars and that's an underestimate. **Se quedó corta en la comida**, she did not provide enough food. *-m. (Cine)* Short (cine).

cortocircuito [cor-to-theer-coo-e'-to], *m*. Short-circuit, shift circuit. **Poner en cortocircuito**, to short-circuit.

cortometraje [cor-to-may-trah'-hay], *m*. Short (cine).

cortón [cor-tone'], *m*. Worm, ringworm which destroys plants in gardens.

cortón [cor-tone'], *a*. 1. Bashful, timid. 2. **Es muy cortón**, *(CAm.)* He's always interrupting.

cortopunzante [cor-to-poon-than'-tay], *a. (Cono Sur)* sharp.

corulla [co-rool'-lyah], *f*. In galleys, place for the stoppers of cables.

coruscante, corusco, ca [co-roo-cahn-tay, co-roos'-co, cah], *a. (Poet.)* Coruscant, glittering by flashes, brilliant.

corva [cor'-vah], *f*. 1. Ham, a part of the leg. 2. Curb, a disease in horses' knees.

corvadura [cor-vah-doo'-rah], *f*. 1. Curvature, crookedness, inflexion; gibbousness. 2. *(Arch.)* Bend of an arch or vault.

corval [cor-vahl'], *a*. Of an oblong shape: applied to olives.

corvato [cor-vah'-to], *m*. A young crow or rook.

corvaza [cor-vah'-thah], *f*. Curb, a disease in horses' knees.

corvecito [cor-vey-thee'-to], *m. dim.* A young little crow or rook.

corvejón [cor-vay-hone'], *m.* 1. Hough, the joint of the hind leg of beasts. 2. Spur of a cock.

corvejos [cor-vay'-hose], *m. pl* An articulation of six bones joined by ligaments with which animals make movements of flexion and extension.

corveta [cor-vey´-tah], *f.* Curvet, corvetto, leap or bound of a horse.

corvetear [cor-vey-tay-ar'], *vn.* To curvet, to bound, to leap.

corvídeo, ea [cor-vee´-day-o, ah], *a.* Like or belonging to a crow.

córvidos [cor´-ve-dose], *m. pl. (Zool.)* The family of crows, jays, etc.; corvidae.

corvillo [cor-veel'-lyo], *m.* 1. Bill, a kind of hatchet with a hooked point. 2. **Corvillo de podón**, pruning-knife. 3. **Corvillo de zapatero**, a shoemaker's paring-knife. 4. A small sickle to cut thread and form velvet in velvet looms. **Miércoles corvillo**, Ash Wednesday.

corvina [cor-vee'-nah], *f.* 1. A kind of conger or sea-eel in the Mediterranean. 2. White sea bass of California.

corvino, na [cor-vee´-no, nah], *a.* Rook-like, belonging to a rook.

corvo, va [cor´-vo, vah], *a.* 1. Bent, crooked arched. 2. Stingy, mean.

corvo [cor'-vo], *m.* 1. *(Zool. Prov.)* Crawfish, a kind of sea-fish. 2. Pot-hook.

corza [cor'-thah], *f.* Doe.

corzo, za [cor'-tho, thah], *m. & f.* Roe deer, fallow deer.

corzuelo [cor-thoo-ay'-lo], *m.* Wheat left in the husks by the thrashers.

cosa [co'-sah], *f.* 1. Thing, substance, that which has being or existence; **cosa de entidad**, an important thing. **Cosa de risa** or **cosa ridícula**, laughing-stock. **Cosa de ver**, a thing worth seeing. **No hay tal cosa** or **no es así,** no such thing. **Alguna cosa**, something. **No me queda otra cosa,** I have no alternative. **Es poca cosa**, it´s not important. **Tal como están las cosas**, as things stand. **Decir cuatro cosas a uno**, to give somebody a piece of one´s mind. **Es cosa de nunca acabar**, there´s no end to it. **Es cosa distinta**, that´s another matter. **Es cosa fácil**, it´s easy. **Cosa rara**, strange thing. **Las cosas de palacio van despacio,** (*fig.*) it all takes time. 3. Affair, business. **Ésa es cosa tuya**, that´s your affair. 4. **Cosas**, odd ideas. **¡Tienes unas cosas!,** what dreadful things you say! 5. *(LAm.) (conj.)* **No le digas nada, como que no se ofenda**, don´t say anything to him, that way he won´t get offended.

cosa de, *adv.* About, little more or less. **Cosa de media legua,** half a league, more or less.

cosaco, ca [co-sah´-co, cah], *a.* 1. Cossack. 2. *(Cono Sur)* mounted policeman.

cosar [co-sar'], *m. (Com.)* Kind of cotton stuff made in India.

cosario [co-sah'-re-o], *m.* 1. Privateer, corsair, pirate, cruiser. 2. Carrier, one who carries goods. 3. Huntsman by profession.

cosario, ria [co-sah´-re-o, ah], *a.* 1. Belonging or relating to privateers or corsairs. 2. Beaten, frequented (carreteras).

coscacho [cos-cah-cho*]*, *m. (And. Cono Sur)* Rap on the head.

coscarana [cos-ca-rah´-nah], *f. (Prov.)* Cracknel, a crisp cake.

coscarse [cos-car'-say], *vr.* To catch on. *(Coll.)* V. CONCOMERSE.

coscoja [cos-co'-hah], *f.* 1. *(Bot.)* Kermes or scarlet-oak. 2. Dry leaves of the kermes oak. 3. Ring or knob on the crossbit of a bridle.

coscojal, coscojar [cos-co-hahl', cos-co-har'], *m.* Plantation of kermes or scarlet oaks.

coscojo [cos-co'-ho], *m.* Scarlet or kermes grain, after the worn or insect has left it. **Coscojos**, bits of iron composing the chain fastened to the mouthpiece of a horse's bridle.

coscolino [cos-co-le'-no], *a.* 1. *(Mex.)* Peevish, touchy; naughty (niño). 2. Of loose morals (moralmente).

coscón, na [cos-cone', nah], *a.* Crafty, sly.

coscorrón [cos-cor-rone'], *m.* 1. Contusion, a blow or bruise on the head 2. Bruise in a loaf. 3. *(fig.)* Set-back, disappointment, knock.

coscorronera [cos-cor-ro-nay'-rah], *f.* A kind of bonnet put upon children to avoid blows upon the head. *V.* CHICHONERA.

coscurro [cos-coor'-ro], *m.* Flat loaf.

cosecante [co-say-cahn'-tay], *m. (Geom.)* Cosecant.

cosecha [co-say'-chah], *f.* 1. Harvest, harvest time. 2. Harvest, the corn ripened and gathered. 3. The season of reaping and gathering olives, etc. 4. The act of gathering the harvest. **Cosecha de vino**, vintage. 5. *(Met.)* Collection of immaterial things, as virtues, vices, etc. **De su cosecha**, of one´s own invention.

cosechadora [co-say-chah-do'-rah], *f.* Combine-harvester.

cosechar [co-say-char'], *va.* 1. *(Prov.)* To crop, to reap, to gather the corn at harvest time, cultivate, grow. **Aquí no cosechan sino patatas**, the only thing they grow here is potatoes. 2. *(fig.)* To reap, to reap the reward of. **No cosechó sino disgustos**, all he got was troubles.

cosechero, ra [co-say-chay'-ro], *m. & f.* The person who has corn, olives, etc., of his own to reap and gather: commonly used to designate the proprietor of the produce.

cosechón [co-say-chone'], *m.* Bumper crop.

cosederos de los tablones, *m. pl. (Naut.)* Plank seams.

cosedora [co-say-do'-rah], *f.* Seamstress, stitcher.

coselete [co-say-lay'-tay], *a.* 1. Corselet, ancient coat of armor. 2. A light corselet. 3. Pikeman, anciently armed with a corselet. 4. The thorax of insects.

coseno [co-say'-no], *m. (Geom.)* Cosine. **Coseno verso**, the coversed sine. **coser** [co-serr'], *va.* 1. To sew. 2. To join and unite things. **Coser a puñaladas**, *(Coll.)* to stab or give wounds with a pointed weapon. **Coser y cantar**, to offer no difficulties; or, more fully. **Ya no queda más que coser y cantar**, what remains to be done is a trifle. **Coserse la boca**, not to speak a word.

cosera [co-say'-rah], *f. (Prov.)* Piece of ground which can be irrigated at once.

cosetada [co-say-tah'-dah], *f.* Race, a violent course.

cosiaca [co-se-ah'-cah], *f. (LAm.)* Small thing, trifle.

cosible [co-see'-blay], *a. (Obs.)* That which may be sewed.

cosido [co-see'-do], *m.* 1. Clothing collectively, and needle work. 2. Action of sewing. **Cosido de cama**, quilt and blankets of a bed stitched together to prevent their separation. -**Cosido da**, *pp.* of COSER, Devoted to, wedded to.

cosiduras [co-see-doo'-ras], *f. pl. (Naut.)* Lashings, ends of ropes used in ships to secure movable things.

cosignatario, ria [co-seg-nah-tah'-re-o], *m. & f.* Cosignatory.

cosijoso [co-se-ho'-so], *a.* 1. *(CAm. Mex.)* Bothersome (molesto). 2. *(CAm. Mex.)* Peevish, irritable.

cosita [co-see'-tah], *f. dim.* A small thing, a trifle.

cosmético [cos-may'-te-co], *m.* Cosmetic.

cósmico, ca [cos'-me-co, cah], *a.* 1. Cosmic, belonging to the universe. 2. A rising or setting star, which coincides with the rising of the sun.

cosmocracia [cos-mo-crah'-the-ah], *f.* Cosmocracy, a system of universal monarchy.

cosmócrata [cos-mo'-crah-tah], *a.* Cosmocratic, aspiring to universal monarchy.

cosmocrático, ca [cos-mo-crah'-te-co, cah], *a.* Cosmocratic, relating to cosmocracy.

cosmódromo [cos-mo'-dro-mo], *m.* Space station.

cosmogonía [cos-mo-go-nee'-ah], *f.* Cosmogony.

cosmografía [cos-mo-grah-fee'-ah], *f.* Cosmography.

cosmográfico, ca [cos-mo-grah'-fe-co, cah], *a.* Cosmographical.

cosmógrafo, fa [cos-mo'-grah-fo], *m. & f.* Cosmographer.

cosmología [cos-mo-lo-hee'-ah], *f.* Cosmology.

cosmonauta [cos-mo-nah''-oo-tah], *m. & f.* Astronaut, spaceman, cosmonaut (astronauta).

cosmopolita [cos-mo-po-lee'-tah], *com.* Cosmopolite.

cosmorama [cos-mo-rah'-mah], *a.* Cosmorama.

cosmos [cose'-mose], *m.* The universe, cosmos.

cosmotrón [cos-mo-trone'], *m.* Cosmotron.

cosmovisión [cos-mo-ve-se-on'], *f.* World view.

coso [co'-so], *m.* 1. (*Prov.*) Place or square for bullfights or other public entertainments. 2. Worm which lodges in the trunks of some fruit-trees. 3. *V.* COSA.

cospe [cose'-pay], *m.* Chipping with an adze or hatchet.

cospel [cos-pel'], *m.* Coin blank, in the mint.

cospillo [cos-peel'-lyo], *m.* Lees of the olive, after expression.

cosquillar [cos-ke-lyar'], *va.* To tickle.

cosquillas [cos-keel'-lyas], *f. pl.* Tickling, titillation. **Hacer cosquillas alguna cosa,** (*Met.*) to be tickled by anything; to excite desire, curiosity, or suspicion. **No sufrir cosquillas,** (*Met.*) to understand or suffer no jokes. **Tener malas cosquillas,** (*Met.*) to be easily offended, to be ill-tempered. **Siento cosquillas en el pie,** my foot tickles. **Tener cosquillas,** to be ticklish.

cosquillear [cos-keel-lyay-ar'], *va.* To tickle.

cosquilleo [cos-keel-lyay'-o], *m.* Sensation of tickling.

cosquilloso, sa [cos-keel-lyo'-so, sah], *a.* 1. Ticklish. 2. Susceptible, easily offended.

costa [cos'-tah], *f.* 1. Cost, the price paid for a thing. 2. Cost, charge, expense. 3. Expensiveness. 4. Expense or charges of a lawsuit: in this sense it is almost always used in the plural. **Condenar en costas,** to sentence a party to pay the costs of a suit. 5. (*Met.*) Labor, expense, fatigue. **A costa de,** at the expense of. **A toda costa,** at all hazards, at all events. 6. Coast; the shore. **Dar a la costa,** or **en la costa,** to get on shore. **Arrimado a la costa,** close inshore.

costado [cos-tah'-do], *m.* 1. Side, the lateral part of animals. 2. *V.* LADO. 3. (*Mil.*) Flank. 4. (*Obs.*) Hind or back part. 5. Side of a ship. **Presentar el costado a un enemigo,** to bring the broadside to bear upon an enemy's ship. **Costados,** race, lineage, succession of ancestors. **Español por los 4 costados,** Spanish on both sides of the family. **Es un gandul por los 4 costados,** he´s an absolute idler.

costal [cos-tahl'], *m.* 1. Sack or large bag. **Estar hecho un costal de huesos,** to be all skin and bones. 2. Rammer, to beat down the earth of a mud wall or rampart.

costal [cos-tahl'], *a.* Costal, belonging to the ribs.

costalada [cos-tah-lah'-dah], *f.* A fall flat on the ground.

costalazo [cos-tah-lah'-tho], *m.* Blow with a sack. **Dar un costalazo,** to fall flat on the ground like a sack; to fail.

costalero [cos-tah-lay'-ro], *m.* (*Prov.*) Porter, who carries goods.

costalito [cos-tah-lee'-to], *m. dim.* A small sack.

costanera [cos-tah-nay'-rah], *f.* 1. Side, flank. 2. Slope (cuesta). 3. (*Cono Sur*) jetty; paved area beside the sea. 4. (*Carib.*) Firm ground (alrededor de un pantano).

costaneras [cos-tah-nay'-ras], *f. pl.* In building, rafters.

costanero, ra [cos-tah-nay'-ro, rah], *a.* 1. Belonging to a coast. 2. Declivous, inclining downward. **Buque** or **bajel costanero,** coaster, a vessel employed in the coasting trade. **Navegación costancra,** coasting navigation.

costanilla [cos-tah-neel'-lyah], *f. dim.* Gentle declivity, side of a small hill; a steep street.

costar [cos-tar'], *vn.* 1. To cost, to be bought for, to be had at a price. **Me cuesta tanto,** it's such an effort. 2. To suffer detriment or loss. **Cuesta poco,** it´s easy. **Le ha costado caro,** it has cost him dear. **Es un trabajo que cuesta unos minutos,** it´s a job which takes a few minutes. **Me cuesta hablar alemán,** I find it difficult to speak German.

Costa Rica [cos-tah-ree'-cah], *f.* Costa Rica.

costarricense [cos-tar-re-then'-say], or **costarriqueño, ña** [cos-tar-re-kay'-nyo, nyah], *a.* Costa Rican, of Costa Rica.

coste [cos'-tay], *m.* cost, expense, price paid for a thing. **Coste humano,** (*fig.*) human cost.

costeable [cos-tay-ah'-blay], *a.* Financially feasible.

costear [cos-tay-ar'], *va.* 1. To pay the cost of. **Costea los estudios a su sobrino,** he is paying for his nephew´s

education. 2. To skirt. 3. (*Naut.*) To sail along the coast of. -*vr.* 1. To pay its own way, to cover the costs involved.

costeño [cos-tay'-nyo], *a.* 1. **Barco costeño,** a small boat wed only in the coasting trade. 2. *m. & f.* Coastal.

costera [cos-tay'-rah], *f.* 1. Side of a bale of goods. 2. A fisherman's basket. 3. Each of the two parts of the mould into which tubes of lead or tin empty. 4. Time of fishing for surmullets. 5. Outside quire of a ream of paper. 6. Sea coast.

costero [cos-tay'-ro], *m.* First plank cut from a pinetree.

costero, ra [cos-tay'-ro, rah], *a.* 1. Outward; **papel costero,** outside quires. 2. Oblique: applied to a cannonshot or a declivity. 3. Coastal.

costezuela [cos-tay-thoo-ay'-lah], *f. dim.* Slight declivity or coast.

costífero, ra [cos-tee'-fay-ro, rah], *a.* (*Zool.*) Ribbed longitudinally.

costilla [cos-teel'-lyah], *f.* 1. Rib. 2. Stave, the board of a barrel. 3. A piece of timber which serves to strengthen joists. 4. The rib of a cupola, springer. 5. (*Met. Coll.*) Property, support, wealth. 6. (*Coll.*) Rib (esposa). 7. (*Bot.*) A thick nervure or rib of a leaf. 8. Chop (carne). **Costilla de cerdo,** pork chop. -*pl.* 1. Shoulders, back. **Todo carga sobre mis costillas,** I get all the burdens, everything is put on my back. 2. (*Agri.*) Wooden strips to which horses are tied in ploughing. 3. (*Mech.*) Cramp irons, chimney ties for securing chimney flues. **Medirle a uno las costillas,** to cudgel him.

costillaje, costillar [cos-teel-lyah'-hay cos-teel-lyar'], *m.* 1. The whole of the ribs, and their place in the body. 2. The ribs in a flitch of bacon. 3. (*Naut.*) The timbers or frame of a ship.

costilludo, da [cos-teel-lyoo'-do, dah], *a.* (*Coll.*) 1. Broad shouldered. 2. Clownish, unmannerly.

costípedo, da [cos-tee'-pay-do, dah], *a.* Said of birds which arc perfectly balanced upon their legs.

costo [cos'-to], *m.* 1. Cost, price. **Costo efectivo,** actual cost. 2. Charges, expense. **Costo de expedición,** shipping charges. 3. Labor, fatigue. **Hacerse el costo de hacer algo,** (*Cono Sur*) to take the trouble to do something. 4. (*Bot.*) Costus arabicus, or sweet and bitter costus. 5. Costus root. 6. Drugs, dope (drogas).

costosamente [ ], *adv.* Costly, at a high price, expensively; extravagantly.

costoso, sa [cos-to' so, sah], *a.* 1. Costly, dear, expensive. 2. (*Met.*) Dear, difficult to be obtained. 3. Dear, sad, grievous.

costra [cos'-trah], *f.* 1. Crust. 2. Crust, scab. 3. Broken biscuit given to the people on board of galleys. 4. An encrusted part of a wick.

costrada [cos-trah'-dah], *f.* Seedcake, candied with melted sugar, beaten eggs, and grated bread.

costribar [cos-tre-bar'], *va.* To indurate, to harden; to make strong.

costringir [cos-trin-heer'], *va.* To constrain, to compel.

costroso, sa [cos-tro'-so, sah], *a.* Crusty, covered with a crust.

costumbre [cos-toom'-bray], *f.* 1. Custom, habit, haunt, habitude, familiarity. **Las costumbres de esta provincia,** the customs of this province. **He perdido la costumbre,** I have got out of the habit. 2. Custom, a law which has obtained force by usage. 3. Custom, the common way of acting, fashion, established manner. **Persona de buenas costumbres,** respectable person. 4. Periodical indisposition of women, catamenia, courses. **Costumbres,** customs, the characteristic manners and habits of a nation or a person.

costumbrismo [cos-toom-bres'-mo], *m.* Literary genre of customs and manners.

costumbrista [cos-toom-bres'-tah], *a.* Customs and manners (novela etc.). -*m. & f.* Writer of customs and manners.

costura [cos-too'-rah], *f.* 1. Seam, seamless. **Sin costuras,** seamless. **Sentar las costuras,** to press the seams. 2. Needlework, especially upon white goods: sheets, shirts, etc. **Alta costura,** haute couture. **La costura italiana,** Italian fashion. 3. (*Naut.*)

Splicing of a rope. *(Carp.)* A joint between two pieces of wood. **Costuras de los tablones de un navío,** *(Naut.)* the seams of the planks of a ship. **Costuras abiertas,** seams of a ship from which the oakum has been washed out.

costurar [cos-too-rar'], *va. vn. (LAm.) V.* COSER.

costurera [cos-too-ray'-rah], *f.* Seamstress, dressmaker.

costurero [cos-too-ray'-ro], *m.* 1. A lady's workbox. 2. *(Obs.)* Tailor.

costurón [cos-too-rone'], *m.* 1. Seam, a coarse suture which joins two edges. 2. A large scar.

cota [co'-tah], *f.* 1. Coat of mail. 2. Coat of arms, formerly worn by the kings at arms. 3. *(Topog.)* A number indicating the height of a point above the sea or some other level. **Misil de baja cota,** low-flying missile. 4. Quota, a share assigned to each. 5. The back and callous part of a boar's hide.

cotana [co-tah'-nah], *f.* Mortise, mortise hole.

cotangente [co-tan-hen'-tay], *f. (Geom.)* Cotangent.

cotanza [co-tahn'-thah], *f.* Sort of linen, medium fineness.

cotar [co-tar'], *va. V.* ACOTAR.

cotarrera [co-tar-ray'-rah], *f. (Coll.)* A gadding woman.

cotarro [co-tar'-ro], *m.* 1. Charity hut for the reception of beggars. **Andar de cotarro en cotarro,** to wander about. **Alborotar el cotarro,** to cause disturbance. 2. *(Cono Sur)* mate, pal.

cote [co'-tay], *m. (Naut.)* Half hitch, knot. **Dos cotes,** clove-hitch.

coteja [co-tay'-hah], *f. (And. CAm.)* Equal, match.

cotejar [co-tay-har'], *va.* 1. To compare one thing with another, to confront, to confer. 2. *(And. Carib.)* To arrange.

cotejo [co-tay'-ho], *m.* 1. Comparison, collation, parallel. 2. *(Dep.)* Match, game. -*a. (LAm.)* Similar, same.

cotelé [co-tay-lay'], *m. (Cono Sur)* Corduroy.

cotense [co-ten'-say], *m. (Mex.)* Coarse brown linen wrapper.

cotí [co-tee'], *m.* 1. Sort of linen. 2. Ticking used for mattresses.

cotidianamente [co-te-de-ah-nah-men'-tay], *adv.* Daily.

cotidiano, na [co-te-de-ah'-no, nah], *a.* Daily, each day; quotidian.

cotiledón [co-te-lay-done'], *m.* 1. *(Bot.)* Cotyledon, seedleaf. 2. *(Anat.)* Cotyledon, a lobule of the placenta.

cotiledonado, da, or **cotiledóneo, ea** [co-te-lay-do-nah'-do, dah, co-te-lay-do'-nay-o, ah], *a.* Cotyledonous.

cotiliforme [co-te-le-for'-may], *a. (Bot.)* Cotyliform, having a wide cylindrical tube and straight limb.

cotilo [co-tee'-lo], *m. (Antiq.)* Cotyle, a cup-like cavity.

cotilóidea [co-te-loi'-day-ah], *f.* The cotyloid cavity which receives the head of the thighbone.

cotilóideo, ea [co-te-loi'-day-o, ah], *a.* Cotyloid, cup-like.

cotilla [co-teel'-lyah], *f.* 1. Stays, corsets. **Varillas de cotilla,** whalebones. -*m. & f.* Busybody, gossip.

cotillear [co-teel-lyay-ar'], *vn.* To gossip.

cotilleo [co-teel-lay'-o], *m.* Gossip(ing).

cotillero [co-teel-lyay'-ro], *m.* 1. Staymaker. 2. *V.* COTILLA.

cotillo [co-teel'-lyo], *m.* The peen of a hammer: end opposite to flat surface; claw of hammer.

cotillón [co-teel-lyone'], *m.* A dance, generally a waltz, at the end of a society ball.

cotín [co-teen'], *m.* 1. A back stroke given in the air to a ball. 2. Bedticking.

cotiza [co-tee'-thah], *f.* 1. *(Her.)* Band of a shield, fret. 2. *(Mech.)* Each of the grooves for the warp of the silk fabric called lustering. 3. *(And. Carib.)* Sandal.

cotizable [co-te-thah'-blay], *a.* Quotable, valued at.

cotización [co-te-thah-the-on'], *f. (Com.)* Quotation; price-current, price-list. **Cotización de apertura,** opening price. **Cotización de cierre,** closing price.

cotizado, da [co-te-thah'-do, dah], *a.* 1. *(Her.)* Banded, having bands. 2. In demand, popular, sought-after. 3. *(fig.)* Valued, esteemed.

cotizante [co-te-thahn'-tay], *m. & f.* Contributor.

cotizar [co-te-thar'], *va.* 1. To quote prices; to cry out the current prices in the exchange. 2. To fix (cuota); to pay (suscripción). 3. *(Carib. Cono Sur)*

coto [co'-to], *m.* 1. Inclosure of pasture-grounds. **Coto de caza,** game preserve. 2. Landmark. 3. *(Prov.)* Territory, district. 4. Combination among merchants not to sell goods under a certain rate. 5. Measure of a handbreadth. 6. *(Prov.)* Fine. 7. Chub, a small freshwater fish. 8. Rate or price of a thing. 9. *(Amer.)* A morbid swelling in the throat, goitre. *V.* PAPERA. 10. Boundary stone; *(fig.)* Limit. **Poner coto a,** to put a stop to.

cotobelo [co-to-bay'-lo], *m.* Opening in the branch of a bridle.

cotón [cotone'], *m.* 1. Printed cotton. 2. *(LAm.)* Shirt (camisa); *(Mex.)* Blouse.

cotona [co-toh'-nah], *f.* 1. *(Mex.)* Chamois jacket. 2. *(LAm.)* Strongly-made shirt. 3. *(Carib.)* Child's nightdress.

cotonada [co-to-nah'-dah], *f.* Sort of cotton cloth, striped and flowered; calico, prints.

cotoncillo [co-ton-theel'-lyo], *m.* Button of a maulstick or painters staff.

cotonete [co-to-nay'-tay], *m. (Mex.) (Med. etc.)* Cotton bud.

cotonía [co-to-nee'-ah], *f.* Dimity, fine fustian.

cotorina [co-to-re'-nah], *f. (Mex.)* Jerkin.

cotorra [co-tor'-rah], *f.* 1. *(Orn.)* A parrot of the smallest kind. 2. *(Orn.)* Magpie. 3. *(Met.)* A loquacious woman. 4. *(Mex.)* Chamber-pot (orinal). 5. *(Mex.)* Whore (puta).

cotorrear [co-tor-ray-ar'], *vn.* To chatter, to gabble.

cotorreo [co-tor-ray'-o], *m.* 1. Chattering, gossiping. 2. *(Mex.)* fun, good time.

cotorrera [co-tor-ray'-rah], *f.* 1. A hen parrot. 2. *(Met.)* A prattling woman.

cotorrería [co-tor-ray-ree'-ah], *f. (Coll.)* Loquacity: speaking of women.

cotorro [co-tor'-ro], *a. (Mex.)* Chatty, talkative; loud, noisy (alborotado).

cototo [co-to'-to], *m. (Cono Sur)* Bump, bruise (on the head).

cotrai [co-trah'-e], *m.* Sort of linen.

cotral [co-trahl'], *m.* An old worn-out ox, set to graze.

cotudo, da [co-too'-do, dah], *a.* 1. Hairy, cottony. 2. *(LAm.) (Med.)* Suffering from goitre. 3. *(And.)* Stupid.

cotufa [co-too'-fah], *f.* 1. *(Bot.)* Jerusalem artichoke. 2. Tidbits, delicate food. **Pedir cotufas en el golfo,** to require impossibilities. 3. **Cotufas,** *(LAm.)* Popcorn.

cotufero, ra [co-too-fay'-ro, rah], *a.* Producing tidbits or delicate food.

cotunio [co-too'-ne-o], *m.* A transparent and viscous fluid which fills the cavities of the internal ear.

cotunnio, cotunnito [co-toon'-ne-o, nee'-to], *m.* Cotunnite, a lead chloride found in volcanic craters.

coturno [co-toor'-no], *m.* Cothurnus, buskin, a kind of high boot worn by the ancient actors of tragedy. **Calzar el coturno,** *(Met.)* to make use of pompous language in poetry.

coutelina [co-oo-tay-lee'-nah], *f.* A blue or white cotton cloth imported from India.

covacha [co-vah'-chah], *f.* 1. A small cave or hollow underground; a grot or grotto. 2. *(And. Carib, Cono Sur)* lumber room (trastera). 3. *(CAm. Carib.)* Hut. 4. *(And.)* Vegetable stall. 5. *(Carib.)* Kennel (perrera).

covachuela [co-vah-choo-ay'-lah], *f.* 1. *(dim.)* A small cave or grot. 2. *(Coll.)* Office of secretary of state.

covachuelista, or **covachuelo** [co-vah-choo-ay-lees'-tah], *m. (Coll.)* Clerk in one of the offices of the secretaries of state.

covadera [co-vah-day'-rah], *f. (And. Cono Sur)* Guano deposit.

covanillo [co-vah-neel'-lyo], *m. dim.* Basket with a wide mouth, used for gathering grapes.

covin [co-veen'], *m. (Cono Sur)* popcorn.

coxalgia [coc-sahl'-he-ah], *f.* Hip-joint disease, coxalgia.

coxcojilla, ita [cox-co-heel'-lyah, hee'-tah], *f.* A children's play; hopscotch.

coxcoj (a), or **coxcojita (a)** [ah cox-coh, or ah cocs-co-hee'-tah], *adv.* Lamely, haltingly, limpingly.

coxis [coc'-sees], *m.* The coccyx.

coy [co'-e], *m. (Naut.)* Hammock, cot, a sailor's bed. **Afuera coys**, all hammocks up.

coya [co'-yah], *f. (Peru)* The queen, wife, and sister of the inca.

coyote [co-yo'-tay], *a.* 1. *(Amer.)* Native, of the country; domestic. **Cidra coyote, indio coyote.** 2. *(Mex.)* Astute person; guide of illegal immigrants; *(Com. Fin.)* Speculator, dealer in shares; middleman (intermediario). 3. *(Mex.)* Youngest child (hijo). -*m. (Mex.)* A kind of wolf; coyote.

coyotear [co-yo-tay-ar'], *vn. (CAm. Mex.)* 1. To be smart, to be clever. 2. *(Com. Fin.)* To deal in shares.

coyoteo [co-yoh-tay'-oh], *m. (Mex. Coll.)* Lobbying.

coyunda [co-yoon'-dah], *f.* 1. A trap or cord with which oxen are tied to the yoke. 2. *(Met.)* Dominion, power. 3. Matrimonial union.

coyundado, da [co-yoon-dah'-do, dah], *a.* Tied to the yoke with a strap or cord.

coyundilla [co-yoon-deel'-lyah], *f. dim.* A small strap or cord.

coyuntura [co-yoon-too'-rah], *f.* 1. Joint, articulation. 2. Occasion, conjuncture, juncture; a critical point of time, a seasonable opportunity. **La coyuntura política**, the political situation. **Esperar una coyuntura favorable**, to await a favorable moment.

coyuntural [co-yoon-too-ral'], *a.* Relating to the moment. **Datos coyunturales**, relevant data. **Medidas coyunturales**, immediately relevant measures.

coz [coth], *f.* 1. Kicking with the hind leg (caballos, mulas). **Dar cozes**, to kick. 2. Kick or blow with the foot. 3. Recoil of a gun 4. Flowing back of a flood. 5. *V.* CULATA. 6. The back of a pistol from the guard to the end of the tip 7. *(Coll.)* Churlishness, unprovoked brusqueness. **A coces**, by dint of kicking. **Tirar coces contra el aguijón**, to kick against the pricks, to spurn at superiority. 8. Insult, rude remark. **Tratar a uno a coces**, to be rude to somebody.

C.P.A. *f. abr.* de **Caja Postal de Ahorros** (Post Office Savings Bank).

CNP *m. (Esp.) abr.* de **Cuerpo de la Policía Nacional.**

cra [crah], *m.* Caw of the crow.

crabrón [crah-brone'], *m.* Hornet.

crac 1 [crac], *m.* 1. *(Com. fin.)* Failure, crash; bankruptcy. **Crac financiero**, financial crash. 2. *(fig.)* Crack-up.

crac 2 [crac], *interj.* Snap! **Hizo ¡crac! y se abrió**, it went crack! and it opened up.

crac 3 [crac], *m. & f. (LAm.)* Star player, star performer; best horse.

crambo [crahm'-bo], *m.* Name formerly common to all cabbages and kales.

crameria [crah-may-re-ah], *f.* Krameria, rhatany, a medicinal plant of the polygala family indigenous to Peru. It is astringent.

crampón [cram-one'], *m.* Crampon.

cran [crahn], *m. (Typ.)* Nick, one of the grooves cast upon the front of the shank of a type to aid the compositor in rightly placing it.

craneano, na [crah-nay-ah'no, nah], *a.* Cranial, relating to the skull.

cráneo [crah'nay-o], *m.* The skull; cranium. **Ir de cráneo con uno**, to be on bad terms with somebody.

craneología [crah-nay-olo-he'-ah], *f.* Craniology, phrenology.

crápula [crah'-poo-lah], *f.* Inebriation, intoxication, crapulence.

crapuloso, sa [crah-poo-lo'-so, sah], *a.* 1. Drunken; gluttonous, surfeited. 2. Dissolute, dissipated.

craquear [cra-kay'ar'], *va.* To crack.

craqueo [cra-kay'-o], *m. (Quim.)* Cracking.

crasamente [cra-sah-men'-tay], *adv.* Grossly, rudely.

crascitar [cras-the-tar'], *vn.* To crow, to croak.

crasiento, ta, *a.* Greasy. *V.* GRASIENTO.

crasino [crah-see'-no], *m. (Orn.)* *V.* Hoco.

crasitud [crah-se-tood'], *f.* 1. Fatness, corpulency, crassitude, obesity. 2. Ignorance, stupidity, dullness.

craso, sa [crah'-so, sah], *a.* 1. Fat, greasy, oily, unctuous. 2. Thick, gross, crass. **Ignorancia crasa**, gross ignorance. **Error craso**, gross error. 3. *(And. Cono Sur)* coarse (grosero).

cráter [crah'tayr], *m.* Crater of a volcano.

crátera [crah'tayrah], *f.* Krater or crater, amphora, type of Grecian urn.

cratícula [crah-tee'-coo-lah], *f.* A small wicket or window, through which nuns receive the communion.

crawl [crol], *m.* Crawl.

crayón [crah-yone'], *m.* Crayon, chalk.

craza [crah'-thah], *f.* A receptacle for melted metal.

crea [cray'-ah], *f.* Linen.

creable [crayah'blay], *a.* Creative, creatable.

creación [cray-ah-the-on'], *f.* Creation.

creado, da [crey-ah'do, dah], *a.* Created, begotten, made. -*pp.* of CREAR.

creador [cray-ah-dor'], *m.* The Creator, God. -*a.* Creative.

crear [cray-ar'], *va.* 1. To create, to make, to cause to exist. 2. *(Met.)* To institute, to establish; to compose, produce literary or artistic works of relative merit. 3. To nourish, to support.

creatividad [cray-ah-te-ve-dahd'], *f.* Creativity.

creativo [cray-ah-te'-vo], *a.* Creative.

crébol [cray'-bol], *m.* Hollytree. *V.* ACEBO.

crece [cray'-thay], *m, f. (Cono Sur)* *V.* CRECIDA.

crecedero, ra [cray-thay-day'-ro, rah], *a.* Able to grow, that which can grow.

crecepelos [cray-thay-pay'-los], *m.* Hair restorer.

crecer [cray-therr'], *vn.* 1. To grow, to increase. **Dejar crecer la barba**, to grow a beard. 2. To grow or increase in stature. 3. To become larger. 4. To grow, to swell: a sea term. 5. To augment the extrinsic value of money. -*vr.* 1. *(Cos.)* **Se crece un punto**, increase by one stitch. 2. To grow bolder, to acquire greater confidence; to get conceited, to have an exaggerated sense of one's importance.

creces [cray'thes], *f. pl.* 1. Augmentation, increase; excess, in some things. **Para los niños se hace ropa con creces**, children's clothes are made to be let out. 2. The additional quantity of corn paid by a farmer to a public granary, besides what he borrowed from it.

crecida [cray-thee'-dah], *f.* Freshet, swollen state of rivers in consequence of heavy fulls of rain. *V.* AVENIDA.

crecidamente [cray-the-dah-men'-tay], *adv.* Plentifully, copiously, abundantly.

crecidito, ta [cray-the-dee'-to, tah], *a. dim.* Somewhat increased or grown.

crecido, da [cray-thee'do, dah], *a.* 1. Grown, increased. **Ya eres crecido para eso**, you're too big for that now. 2. Grave, important. 3. Large, great. -*pp.* of CRECER. 4. **Estar crecido**, to be in flood. 5. *(fig.)* Vain, conceited.

crecidos [craythee'-dos], *m pl.* Widening stitches with knitting needles, to enlarge the width of a stocking.

creciente [cray-the-en'tay], *pa.* 1. Growing, increasing, crescent. 2. Susceptible of increase. 3. *(Her.)* A halfmoon with points upward.

creciente [cray-the-ayn'-tay], *f.* 1. Swell, freshet of waters. 2. *(Prov.)* Leaven. 3. Crescent, the moon in her state of increase.

crecimiento [cray-the-me-en'-to], *m.* 1. Increase or increment, growing, growth. **Crecimiento de la marejada**, *(Naut.)* Swell of the sea. 2. Increase of the value of money.

credencia [cray-den'-the-ah], *f.* 1. Sideboard of an altar, on which all the necessaries are placed for celebrating high mass. 2. Credentials.

credencial [cray-den-the-ahl'], *f.* Credential, that which gives a title to credit, accreditation. **Credenciales** or **cartas credenciales**, credentials or credential letters. -*a.* Accrediting; *V.* CARTA.

credibilidad [cray-de-be-le-dahd'], *f.* Credibility.

crediticio [cray-de-te'-the-o], *a. (Fin.)* Credit.

crédito [cray'-de-to], *m.* 1. Acquiescence, assent. 2. Credit, a sum of money due to any one. **Abrir un crédito a**, to open a credit for. 3. Credence, credit, belief, faith. **Dar crédito a**, to believe. 4. Reputation, character, name. 5. Credit, trust, confidence, esteem, authority. **Persona de crédito**, reliable person. 6. Note, bill, order for payment. **Créditos activos**, assets. **Créditos pasivos**, liabilities.

credo [cray'-do], *m.* Creed, articles of faith. **Cada credo**, every moment. **En un credo**, in a trice, in a moment.

credulidad [cray-doo-le-dahd'], *f.* 1. Credulity. 2. *V.* CREENCIA.

crédulo, la [cray'-doo-lo, lah], *a.* Credulous.

creedero, ra [crayay-day'ro, rah], *a.* Credible. **Tener buenas creederas**, to be easy of belief, to swallow the bait.

creedor, ra [cray-ay-dor', rah], *a.* Credulous

creencia [cray-en'the-ah], *f.* 1. Credence, belief, credit. 2. Credence, belief of the truths of religion, creed, persuasion. 3. *V.* MENSAJE and SALVA.

creer [cray-err'], *va.* 1. To believe, to give faith and credit to a thing. **Creo que sí**, I think so **¡Ya lo creo!**, I should think so! 2. To believe, to have a firm persuasion of the revealed truths of religion. 3. To credit, to receive a thing as probable. **Ver y creer**, to believe only what we see. 4. To think, to deem, to consider. **No le creo tan culpable**, I don´t think him so much to blame. **Lo creo de mi deber**, I consider it my duty. *-vn.* **Creer en**, to believe in. *-vr.* 1. To believe oneself, to consider oneself. **Se cree muy astuto**, he thinks he´s pretty clever. **¿Qué se ha creído?**, who does he think he is? 2. **No me lo creo**, I don´t believe it. **Se cree todo lo que le dicen**, he swallows everything he´s told. **Hace falta que yo me lo crea**, I still have to be convinced.

crehuela [cray-oo-ay´-lah], *f.* Sort of linen, osnaburgs.

creíble [cray-e'blay], *a.* Credible, likely.

creíblemente [cray-e'-blay-men-tay], *adv.* Credibly.

creído [cray-e'-do], *a.* 1. *(LAm.)* Gullible, trusting. 2. *(And. Cono Sur)* Vain, conceited.

crema [cray'-mah], *f.* 1. Cream of milk (nata). **Crema batida**, whipped cream. **Un coche color crema**, a cream-colored. 2. Custard. 3. Diaeresis. 4. Cream, the select of society. **La crema de la sociedad**, the cream of society. 5. Cream, cosmetic of creamy consistency. **Crema de afeitar**, shaving cream. **Crema dental**, toothpaste. **Crema hidratante**, moisturizing cream. 6. **Crema para el calzado**, shoe polish.

cremación [cray-mah-the-on'], *f.* 1. Cremation, the act of burning. 2. Incineration of dead bodies.

cremallera [cray-mahl-lyay'-rah], *f.* 1. *(Mech.)* Rack. 2. Zipper. 3. Cog railway.

cremar [cray-mar'], *va.* To cremate.

crematística [cray-mah-tees´-te-cah], *f.* Science of acquiring and preserving wealth.

crematístico [cray-mah-tes'-te-co], *a.* Financial, economic.

crematólogo [cray-mah-to'-lo-go], *m.* Political economist.

crematología [cray-mah-tolo-he'-ah], *f.* Political economy.

crematológico, ca [cray-mah-to-lo'-he-co, cah], *a.* Economical, relating to political economy.

crematorio [cray-mah-to'-re-o], *a.* **Horno crematorio**. *-m.* Crematorium; incinerator.

cremonés, sa [cray-mo-ness', sah], *a.* Relating to Cremona.

crémor [cray'-mor], *m.* **Crémor** or **crémor tártaro**, cream of tartar.

cremoso [cray-mo'-so], *a.* Creamy.

crencha [cren'-chah], *f.* The parting of the hair into two equal parts; each of these parts.

creosota, creosoto [cray-o-so'tah, to], *f. & m.* Creosote.

crep [crayp], *m.* **Crepa** *f. (LAm.)* Pancake, crêpe.

crepar [cray-par'], *vn. (Cono Sur)* To peg out, to kick the bucket.

crepitación [cray-pe-tah-the-on'], *f.* 1. Crepitation, crackling. 2. Crepitus of fractures.

crepitante [cray-pe-tahn'-tay], Crackling, crepitant.

crepitar [cray-pe-tar'], *vn.* To crackle, crepitate.

crepuscular [cray-poos-coo-lar'], *a.* Crepuscular; **luz crepuscular**, twilight.

crepúsculo [cray-poos'-coo-lo], *m.* Crepuscule, twilight, dawn.

cresa [cray'-sah], *f.* Flyblow, the egg of a fly; maggot.

crescendo [crays-then'-do], *m.* Crescendo.

Creso [cray'-so], *m.* Croesus.

crespar [cres-par'], *va.* To curl the hair. *-vr.* To grow angry, to be displeased.

crespilla [cres-peel'-lyah], *f.* An agaric. *V.* CAGARRIA.

crespina [cres-pee'-nah], *f.* Net used by women for holding up their hair.

crespino [cres-pee'-no], *m. (Bot.)* The barberry tree.

crespo, pa [cres'-po, pah], *a.* 1. Crisp, curled, crispy. 2. *(Bot.)* Crisp-leaved. 3. *(Met.)* Obscure and bombastic (estilo). 4. *(Amer.)* A curl. 5. *(Met.)* Angry, displeased, vexed. *-m.* Hair, head of hair.

crespón [cres-pone'], *m.* Crape. **Crespón de Cantón**, Canton crape.

cresta [cres'tah], *f.* 1. Comb, cock's comb. 2. Crest of birds. 3. Crest of a helmet. 4. Crest or summit of lofty mountains. 5. Cramp iron supporting the runner. *(Mil.)* **Alzar** or **levantar la cresta**, *(Met.)* To be elated with pride. 6. Wig, toupée (peluca).

crestado, da [cres-tah-do, dah], *a.* Crested.

crestería [crays-tay-re'-ah], *f. (Arch.)* Crenellations, battlements.

crestomatía [cres-to-mah-tee'-ah], *f.* Chrestomathy, a selection of pieces from various authors arranged for study.

crestón [cres-tone'], *m.* 1. Crest of a helmet in which the feathers are placed. 2. *(Min.)* An outcropping of a vein, ore.

creta [cray'-tah], *f.* Chalk.

Creta [cray'-tah], *f.* Crete.

cretáceo, cea [cray-tah'-theo, ah], *a.* Cretaceous, chalky.

cretense, or **crético, ca** [cray-ten'-say, cray'te-co, cah], *a.* Cretan, belonging to Crete.

crético [cray'-te-co], *m.* A verse of three syllables, the first and third long, the second short.

cretinismo [crey-te-nees´-mo], *m.* Cretinism, a kind of idiocy, with deformity.

cretino, na [cray-tee'-no, nah], *a.* A cretin, one affected with cretinism.

cretona [cray-to´-nah], *f.* Sort of linen, cretonne.

cretoso [cray-to'-so], *a.* Chalky.

creyente [cray-yen´-tay], *pa.* Believing, he who believes.

crezneja [creth-nay'-hah], *f.* Streak of bleached bassweed.

CRI *f. abr.* de **Cruz Roja Internacional** (International Red Cross).

cría [cree'-ah], *f.* 1. Brood of animals. **Cría de ganado**, cattle breeding. **Cría de peces**, fish farming. **Hembra de cría**, breeding female. 2. Suckling. 3. *(Coll.)* Child reared by a nurse. 4. A concise and pathetic narrative.

criada [cre-ah´-dah], *f.* 1. Female servant, maid or maidservant, hand-maid. **Criada de menaje**, housemaid. **Criada por horas**, hourly-paid woman. **Criada para todo**, maid of all work. 2. Wash bat, with which washer-women used to beat clothes.

criadero [cre-ah-day'-ro], *m.* 1. Plantation of young trees taken from the nursery. 2. Place for breeding animals. 3. Cocoon-bed.

criadero, ra [cre-ah-day'-ro, rah], *a.* Fruitful, prolific.

criadilla [cre-ah-deel'-lyah], *f.* 1. Testicle of an animal. 2. A small loaf. 3. *(dim.)* A little worthless servant-maid. 4. *(Bot.)* Truffle, a kind of mushroom.

criado [creah'do], *m.* Servant, menial, groom. **Criado capitulado**, a person who, wishing to go to a colony, engages to serve it a certain time in payment for his passage.

criado, da [cre-ah'-do, dah], *a.* Educated, instructed, bred.-*pp.* of CRIAR.

criador, ra [cre-ah-dor', rah], *m. & f.* 1. One who rears and trains domestic animals and fowls; a breeder. 2. The Creator.

criadora [cre-ah-do'-rah], *a.* Fruitful, fecund (tierra).

criamiento [cre-ah-me-en'-to], *m.* Renovation and preservation of something.

criandera [cre-an-day'-rah], *f. (Amer.)* Wet nurse.

crianza [cre-ahn'-thah], *f.* 1. Creation, act of creating. 2. Lactation. 3. Breeding, manners, education, nursery. **Dar crianza,** to breed, to educate, to bring up. **Mala crianza,** bad breeding. **Sin crianza,** ill-bred.

criar [crear'], *va.* 1. To create, to give existence, to feed. **Criar a los pechos,** to breast-feed, to nurse. 2. To breed, to procreate, to produce. **Esta tierra no produce hierba,** this land does not grow grass. **Está criando pelo,** he´s getting some hair. 3. To rear, to bring up from infancy. 4. To nurse, to suckle, to foster, to nourish. 5. To rear or fatten fowls and other animals. 6. To breed, to educate, to instruct. 7. To institute a new office or employment. *V.* CREAR. **Criar carnes,** to grow fat and lusty. -*vn.* To have young, to produce. -*vr.* To grow. **Se criaron juntos,** they were brought up together. **Criarse en buena cuna,** to be born with a silver spoon in one´s mouth.

criatura [cre-ah-too'rah], *f.* 1. Creature. 2. A newborn child, a baby. 3. An unborn child, a foetus. 4. Creature, a person who owes his rise or fortune to another. **Es una criatura,** he is but an infant, or like an infant. **Tengo lástima de la pobre criatura,** I pity the poor thing.

criba [cree'-bah], *f.* 1. Cribble, sieve, crib, riddle, screen. 2. *(fig.)* Sifting, selection; screening. **Hacer una criba,** *(fig.)* to sort out the sheep from the goats.

cribador, ra [cre-bah-dor', rah], *m. & f.* Sifter.

cribadura [cre-bah-doo'-rah], *f.* Sifting.

cribar [cre-bar'], *va.* 1. To sift with a sieve, to screen. 2. *(fig.)* To sift, to select; to screen.

cribo [cree'-bo], *m. V.* CRIBA.

cric [creek], *m.* Jackscrew, lifting-jack. *V.* GATO.

crica [cree'-cah], *f.* 1.Fissure. 2. *(Med.)* The female pudenda.

Crimea [cree may'-ah], *f.* Crimea.

crimen [cree'-men], *m.* 1. Crime, offence, guilt. **Crimen de guerra,** war crime. 2. *(Theol.)* A mortal sin. **Sala del crimen,** a criminal tribunal.

criminal [creme-nahl'], *a.* 1. Criminal, guilty of a crime. 2. Criminal, not civil. 3. Censorious.

criminalidad [cre-me-nah-le-dahd'], *f.* 1. Criminality, guiltiness. 2. Crime rate (índice).

criminalista [cre-me-nah-lees'-tah], *m.* 1. An author who has written on criminal matters. 2. A criminal lawyer.

criminalística [cre-me-nah-les'-te-cah], *f.* Criminology; study of the criminal.

criminalmente [cre-me-nal-men'-tay], *adv.* Criminally, guiltily.

criminar [cre-me-nar'], *va.* To accuse, to incriminate.

criminología [cre-me-no-lo-hee'-ah], *f.* Criminology.

criminólogo, ga [cre-me-no'-lo-go], *m. & f.* Criminologist.

criminoso, sa [cre-me-no'so, sah], *m. & f.* Delinquent, criminal. *a.* Criminal.

crimno [creem'-no], *m.* Sort of coarse flour generally used in making a certain kind of fritters.

crin [creen], *f.* 1. Mane, horse hair. 2. A loom, specially constructed for weaving horse hair.

crinado, da, crinito, ta [cre-nah'do, dah, cre-nee'-to, tah], *a.* Crinite, maned, having long hair. **Cometa crinito,** a long-bearded comet.

crinífero, ra [cre-nee'-fay-ro, rah], *a.* Mane-bearing; having a mane.

crinóideo [cre-no-i'-day-o], *m. (Geol.)* A crinoid.

crinolina [cre-no-lee'-nah], *f.* 1. Crinoline, a coarse fabric. 2. Crinoline, a hoop-skirt.

crinudo [cre-noo'-do], *a. (LAm.)* Long-maned (caballo).

criogenía [cre-o-hay-nee'-ah], *f.* Cryogenics.

criógeno, na [cre-o'-hay-no, nah], *a.* Cryogenic. -*m.* Cryogen.

criollismo [cre-ol-lyees'-mo], *m. (Amer.)* 1. Feature of the New World culture. 2. Inclination for the New World culture.

crío [cre'-o], *m.* Kid, child; brat.

criollaje [cre-ol-lyah'-hay], *m. (LAm.)* Creoles; peasantry.

criollo, lla [cre-ol'-lyo, lyah], *a. & n.* 1. Creole, one born in America or the West Indies, of European parents. 2. The Negro born in America, as opposed to one brought from Africa. -*a.* Indigenous, national.

crioterapia [cre-o-tay-rah'-pe-ah], *f.* Crymotherapy.

cripta [creep'-tah], *f.* Crypt.

cripto....*pref.* crypt....

criptógamo, ma [crip-to'gah-mo, mah], *a. (Bot.)* Cryptogamous, of concealed fertilization.

criptografía [crip-to-grah-fee'-ah], *f.* Cryptography, the art of writing secret characters.

criptográfico [crip-to-grah'-fe-co], *a.* Cryptographic.

criptógrafo, fa [crip-to'-grah-fo], *m. & f.* Cryptographer.

criptograma [crip-to-gra'-mah], *m.* Cryptogram.

criptología [crip-to-lo-hee'-ah], *f.* Cryptology, enigmatical language.

cris [crees], *m.* A dagger of a wavy blade used in the Philippines and Malay peninsula.

crisálida [cre-sah'-le-dah], *f. (Ent.)* Pupa, the chrysalis of a caterpillar.

crisalidar [cre-sah-le-dar'], *vn.* To pupate.

crisantemo [cre-san-tay'-mo], *m. (Bot.)* Chrysanthemum, a genus of plants.

crisis [cree'-sis], *f.* 1. Crisis, the point in which a disease kills or changes for the better. 2. Judgment, criterion. 3. The decisive moment. **Crisis económica,** economic crisis. **Llegar a la crisis,** to reach crisis point.

crisma [crees'-mah], *m.* 1. Chrism, oil mixed with balsam and consecrated by bishops, used in baptism, confirmation, and the consecration of bishops. 2. *(Coll.)* As synonym of head; in this sense it is feminine. **Romper la crisma,** to break (bruise) the head. 3. Christmas card.

crismar [cris-mar'], *va.* 1. To perform the rite of confirmation. 2. *(Coll.)* To break one's skull.

crismera [cris-may'-rah], *f.* Vial or urn, commonly of silver, in which the chrism or consecrated oil is preserved.

crisoberilo [cre-so-bay-ree'-lo], *m.* Chrysoberyl, a precious stone.

crisol [cre-sole'], *m.* 1. Crucible for melting metals, croslet or crosslet. 2. Cruset, a goldsmiths melting pot.

crisolada [cre-so-lah'-dah], *f.* Crucible full of metal; a charge.

crisólito [cre-so'-le-to], *m.* Chrysolite, a precious stone.

crisopeya [cre-so-pay'-yah], *f.* Alchemy, the transmutation of metals.

crispación [cris-pah-the-one'], *f. (fig.)* Tension, nervousness; increase of tension; outrageous nature. **Una escena de absoluta crispación,** an utterly shattering scene.

crispamiento [cris-pah-me-en'-to], *m.* Contraction, twitching. *V.* CRISPATURA.

crispante [cris-pahn'-tay], *a.* Infuriating; outrageous; shattering.

crispar [cris-par'], *va.* 1. To cause muscles to contract convulsively; to twitch or contract convulsively. **Con el rostro crispado por la ira,** with his face contorted with anger. 2. **Crispar a uno,** to annoy somebody intensely. -*vr.* To twitch, to contract (músculo).

crispatura [cris-pah-too'-rah], *f. (Med.)* Crispation, a spasmodic contraction of the muscles.

crispetas [cris-pay'-tahs], *f. pl. (And.)* Popcorn.

crispir [cris-peer'], *va.* To spatter with a hard brush, to imitate granite, porphyry, or grained stone.

crista [crees'-tah], *f. (Her.)* Crest, the ornament of a helmet.

cristal [cris-tahl'], *m*. 1. Glass, crystal. 2. *(Chem.)* Crystal or crystals, salts congealed in the manner of crystal. 3. Crystal, the best and clearest glass manufactured in glasshouses, flint-glass. **Cristal ahumado**, smoked glass. 4. Looking-glass. **Cristal de aumento**, lens. 5. *(Poet.)* Water. 6. **Cristal tártaro**, cream of tartar. 7. Fine shining woollen stuff. **Cristal de roca**, rock crystal, transparent quartz. **Cristal cilindrado**, plate glass.

cristalera [cris-tah-lay'-rah], *f*. China closet.

cristalería [cris-tah-lay-ree'-ah], *f*. 1. Glassware. 2. Repository of glass-ware.

cristalero [cris-tah-lay'-ro], *m*. *(Cono Sur)* glass cabinet.

cristalino, na [cris-tah-lee'-no, nah], *a*. 1. Crystalline, crystal, transparent, glassy, pellucid, bright. 2. *(Anat.)* Crystalline lens of the eye.

cristalizable [cris-tah-lethah'-blay], *a*. Crystallizable.

cristalización [cris-tah-le-thah-the-on'], *f*. Crystallization.

cristalizador [cris-tah-le-thah-dor'], *m*. *(Chem.)* A vessel in which crystals are made.

cristalizar [cris-tah-le-thar'], *va*. To crystallize, to cause to congeal in crystals.-*vr*. To crystallize, to coagulate or concrete into crystals.

cristalografía [cris-tah-lo-grah-fee'-ah], *f*. Crystallography.

cristel [cris-tel'], *m*. Clyster. V. CLISTER.

cristianamente [cris-te-ah-nah-men'-tay], *adv*. Christianly. **Morir cristianamente**, to die as a Christian.

cristianar [cris-te-ah-nar'], *va*. *(Coll.)* To baptize, to christen.

cristiandad [cris-te-an-dahd'], *f*. 1. Christianity, the body of professing Christians. 2. Christendom. 3. Observance of the law of Christ.

cristianismo [cris-te-ah-nees'-mo], *m*. 1. Christianity. 2. The body of Christians. 3. Christening. V. BAUTIZO.

cristianización [cris-te-ah-ne-thah-the-on'], *f*. Christianization.

cristianizar [cris-te-ah-ne-thar'], *va*. To Christianize.

cristiano, na [cris-te-ah'-no, nah], *a*. 1. Christian. 2. Watered wine. 3. *(LAm.)* Simple minded.

cristiano, na [cris-te-ah'-no, nah], *m. & f*. 1. A Christian. 2. The Spanish language, opposed to Arabic or other foreign tongues; *(Acad.)* **A ley de cristiano**, upon the word of a Christian. **Hablar en cristiano**, to speak straightforwardly. -*m*. Person, soul. **Eso lo sabe cualquier cristiano**, any idiot knows that. **Eso no hay cristiano que lo entienda**, that is beyond anyone's comprehension.

Cristo [crees'-to], *m*. 1. Christ, Messiah, our blessed Savior. 2. Image of Christ crucified. **Ni por un Cristo**, by no means, not for the world. **El año 41 antes de Cristo**, 41 BC. **Donde Cristo perdió la gorra**, at the back of beyond. **Eso no lo sabe ni Cristo**, nobody knows that. **Todo Cristo**, every mortal soul.

Cristobal [cris-to'-bal], *m*. Christopher.

Cristus [crees'-toos], *m*. 1. Cross printed at the beginning of the alphabet. 2. The alphabet; crisscross row *(Obs.)*. **No saber el Cristus**, to be very ignorant. **Estar en el Cristus**, *(Met.)* to be the ABC of something.

crisuela [cre-soo-ay'-lah], *f*. The dripping-pan of a lamp.

criterio [cre-tay'-re-o], *m*. 1. Criterion, a standard by which a judgment can be formed. **Lo dejo a su criterio**, I leave it to your discretion. **Tiene buen criterio**, his taste is admirable. 2. Judgment, discernment. 3. View, opinion. **En mi criterio**, in my opinion. **Cambiar de criterio**, to change one's mind. 4. Viewpoint, attitude, approach. **Depende del criterio de cada uno**, it depends on the individual viewpoint.

crítica [cree'-te-cah], *f*. 1. Criticism. 2. Critique, critic, critical examination of any writing or publication. **Crítica literaria**, literary criticism. 3. Censure. 4. Refutation.

criticable [cre-te-cah'-blay], *a*. V. CENSURABLE.

criticador, ra [cre-te-cah-dor'], *m. & f*. Critic, censurer.

criticar [cre-te-car'], *va*. 1. To criticize. 2. To criticise, to judge.

criticastro, tra [cre-te-cahs'-tro], *m. & f*. Would be critic.

crítico [cree'-te-co], *m*. 1. Critic, criticizer. 2. *(Coll.)* An affected refiner of style and language. 3. Critic, a censurer, a man apt to find fault.

crítico, ca [cree'-te-co, cah], *a*. 1. Critical, critic, decisive. 2. Hypercritical, nicely judicious. 3. *(Med.)* Critical, producing a crisis in a disease.

criticón, ona [cre-te-cone', nah], *a*. Eager to criticize, fault-finding. -*m. & f*. Would be critic, fault-finder.

critiquear [cre-te-kay-ar'], *va*. To criticize, to play the critic, to censure.

critiquizar [cre-te-ke-thar'], *va*. *(Coll.)* To criticize, to censure, to find fault.

crizneja [crith-nay'-hah], *f*. Trace or rope of hair or osiers.

Croacia [co-ah'-the-ah], *f*. Croatia.

croar [cro-ar'], *vn*. To croak like a frog.

croata [cro-ah'-tah], *a*. Croatian.

crocante [cro-cahn'-tay], *m*. Brittle. **Crocante de cacahuate o maní**, peanut brittle.

croché [cro-chay'], *m*. *(Cos.)* Crochet. **Hacer croché**, to crochet.

crochet [cro-chayt'], *m*. 1. *(Cos.)* V. CROCHÉ. 2. Hook (boxeo).

crocino, na [cro-thee'-no, nah], *a*. Of crocus, saffron.

crocitar [cro-the-tar'], *vn*. To crow, to caw.

crocodilo [cro-co-dee'-lo], *m*. Crocodile. V. COCODRILO.

crol [crol], *m*. Crawl (natación).

cromado [cro-mah'-do], *a*. Chromiun-plated. -*m*. Chromium plating, chrome.

cromático, ca [cro-mah'-te-co, cah], *a*. 1. *(Mus.)* Chromatic, proceeding by semitones. 2. *(Opt.)* Chromatic, showing prismatic colors; uncorrected.

cromatismo [cro-mah-tees'-mo], *m*. Chromatic aberration.

cromato [cro-mah'-to], *m*. Chromate, a salt of chromic acid.

crómico, ca [cro'-me-co, cah], *a*. Chromic, belonging to chromium.

cromo [cro'-mo], *m*. 1. Chromium, a metallic element; discovered in 1797. 2. Chromo: a chromolithograph.

cromolitografía [cro-mo-le-to-grah-fee'-ah], *f*. 1. Chromolithograph, a print in colors. 2. The art of printing in colors; chromolithography.

cromolitográfico, ca [cro-mo-le-to-grah'-fe-co, cah], *a*. Chromolithographic, printed in colors.

cromoso, sa [cro-mo'-so, sah], *a*. Relating to chromium; chrome, chromous.

cromosoma [cro-mo-so'-mah], *m*. *(Biol.)* Chromosome.

crómula [cro'-moo-lah], *f*. The green coloring-matter of leaves, chlorophyll.

cromurgia [cro-moor'-he-ah], *f*. Treatise on coloring-matters industriously applied.

cromúrgico, ca [cro-moor'-he-co, cah], *a*. Relating to dyes or coloring-matters.

crónica [cro'-ne-cah], *f*. Chronicle, a register of events. **Crónica literaria**, literary page. **Crónica de sociedad**, society page.

crónico, ca [cro'-ne-co, cah], *a*. Chronic, applied to diseases.

cronicón [cro-ne-cone'], *m*. Chronicle, a succinct account of events.

cronista [cro-nees'-tah], *m*. Chronicler, annalist. **Cronista de radio**, radio commentator.

crono [cro'-no], *m*. V. CRONOMETRO.

cronografía [cro-no-grah-fee'-ah], *f*. Chronography, the science of time.

cronografista [cro-no-grah-fes'-tah], *m. & f*. *(Cono Sur)* Timekeeper.

cronógrafo [cro-no'-gra-fo], *m*. Chronograph.

cronograma [cro-no-grah-mah], *f*. Chronogram, an inscription including the date of any action.

cronología [cro-no-lo-hee'-ah], *f*. Chronology.

cronológicamente [cro-no-lo'-he-cah-men-tay], *adv*. Chronologically.

cronológico, ca [cro-no-lo'-he-co, cah], *a.* Chronological, chronologic.

cronologista, cronólogo [cro-no-lo-hees´-tah, crono'logo], *m.* Chronologist, chronologer.

cronometrador, ra [cro-no-may-trah-dor'], *m. & f.* Timekeeper.

cronometraje [cro-no-may-trah'-hay], *m.* Timing.

cronometrar [cro-no-may-trar'], *va.* To time.

cronometría [cro-no-may-tree'-ah], *f.* Chronometry, measurement of time.

cronométrico, ca [cro-no-may´-tree-co, cah], *a.* Chronometlic, chronometrical.

cronometrista [cro-no-may-trees'-tah], *m.* Chronometer-maker.

cronómetro [cro-no'-may-tro], *m.* 1. Chronometer. 2. Stopwatch.

croque [cro'-kay], *m.* Hook or crook, used in the tunny-fishery.

croquet [cro-kayt], *m.* Croquet.

croqueta [cro-kay'-tah], *f.* A croquette.

croquis [cro'-kees], *m.* 1. A light sketch, of some ground or military position. 2. Any sketch, rough draft.

croscitar [cros-the-tar'], *vn.* V. CRASCITAR.

cross [cros], *m.* Cross-country race; cross-country running.

crotafal [cro-tah-fahl'], *a.* (*Anat.*) Crotaphite: applied to the elementary bony pieces of the head.

crotáfico, ca [cro-tah'-fe-co, cah], *a.* Relative to the temples or temporal region; crotaphic.

crótalo [cro'-tah-lo], *m.* 1. Castanet. 2. The rattlesnake (Crotalus).

crotalogía [cro-tah-lo-hee'-ah], *f.* The art of playing the castanets.

croto [cro-to], *m.* (*Cono Sur*) Bum, layabout.

crotón [crotone'], *m.* A great genus of the spurge family.

CRT. (*Inform.*) CRT (cathode ray tube).

cruasán [croo-ah-sahn'], *m.* Croissant.

cruce [croo´-thay], *m.* 1. Crossing. 2. Crossroads. **Cruce de carreteras**, crossroads. **Cruce giratorio**, roundabout. **Cruce de peatones**, pedestrian crossing. 3. (*Telec.*) Crossing of lines. **Hay un cruce en las líneas**, the wires are crossed. 4. (*Ling.*) Cross, mutual interference.

crucera [croo-thay'-rah], *f.* Withers of a horse. **Cruceras**, the two large pins which fasten the body of a cart or wagon to the axle-tree; bolling pine.

crucería [croo-thay-ree'-ah], *f.* Gothic architecture.

crucero [croo-thay'-ro], *m.* 1. Crossvault of a church under the dome. 2. Crossbearer, one who carries the cross before the archbishop in a procession. 3. Piece of timber which lies across the rafters in a building 4. A crossing of two streets or roads; a railway crossing. 5. (*Print.*) Crossbar of a chase. 6. (*Naut.*) Cruising station. 7. (*Naut.*) Cruiser. **Crucero de paseo**, pleasure cruise. 8. (*Astr.*) Cross, a southern constellation.

cruceta [croo-thay´-tah], *f.* Crosspiece, headstick.

crucial [croo-the-ahl'], *a.* Crucial, making the shape of a cross.

cruciata [croo-the-ah'-tah], *f.* (*Bot.*) Crosswort, vallantia.

cruciferario [croo-the-fay-rah'-reo], *m.* Crossbearer.

crucífero [croo-thee'-fay-ro], *m.* 1. Crossbearer. 2. Crouched, cruched, or crutched friar, a friar of the order of the Holy Cross.

crucífero, ra [croo-thee'-ro] *a.* 1. Cruciferous or crucigerous, bearing a cross. 2. (*Bot.*) Having petals in the form of a cross.

crucíferas [croo-the-fay-rahs] *f. pl.* The cruciferae, mustard family.

crucificado, da [croo-the-fe-cah'-do, dah], *pp.* of CRUCIFICAR. Crucified; **el Crucificado**, Jesus Christ.

crucificar [croo-the-fe-car'], *va.* 1. To crucify. 2. To molest, to vex, to torment.

crucifijo [croo-the-fee'-ho], *m.* Crucifix.

crucifixión [croo-the-fik-se-on'], *f.* Crucifixion.

cruciforme [croo-the-for'-may], *a.* Cruciform.

crucígero, ra [croo-thee'-hay-ro, rah], *a.* Carrying or bearing the sign of the cross.

crucigrama [croo-the-grah'-mah], *m.* Crossword puzzle.

crucillo [croo-theel'lyo], *m.* Push-pin, a play.

cruda [croo'-dah*], f. (LAm.)* Hangover.

crudamente [croo-dah-men'-tay], *adv.* Rudely, crudely.

crudeza [croo-day'-thah], *f.* 1. Crudity, crudeness, unripeness. 2. (*Met.*) Rudeness, severity, cruelty. 3. (*Coll.*) Vapor, vain boasting. **Crudezas del estómago**, the crudities or indigestions of the stomach.

crudo [croo'-do], *m.* 1. Packing or wrapping cloth. 2. (*Mex.*) Hangover. 3. Crude (petróleo).

crudo, da [croo'-do, dah], *a.* 1. Raw, crude. 2. (*Prov.*) Green, unripe (fruta). 3. Rude, cruel, pitiless, grievous. 4. Crude, unfinished, immature. 5. Crude, hard of digestion. 6. A blustering, hectoring person. 7. (*Med.*) Unripe, not mature (tumores). **Tiempo crudo**, bleak, raw weather.

cruel [croo-el'], *a.* 1. Cruel, hard-hearted. 2. (*Met.*) Intolerable, insufferable; **un frío cruel**, an intense cold. **Dolores crueles**, severe pains. 3. Hard, oppressive. 4. (*Met.*) Bloody, violent, murderous, merciless, fierce, fiendlike.

crueldad [croo-el-dahd´], *f.* 1. Cruelty, inhumanity, savageness, mercilessness, ferociousness. 2. Hardness, oppression, acerbity. 3. Cruelty, a barbarous action, outrage.

cruelmente [croo-el-men'-tay], *adv.* Cruelly, mercilessly.

cruentamente [croo-en-tah-men'-tay], *adv.* Bloodily, with effusion of blood.

cruento, ta [croo-en'-to, tah], *a.* Bloody, cruel, inhuman.

crufia [croo'-fe-ah], *f.* Sign by which obscure passages are marked in literary works, in form of a semicircle with a point in the middle.

crujía [croo-hee'-ah], *f.* 1. (*Naut.*) The midship gangway of a galley. 2. A large open hall or passage in a building. **La crujía de un hospital**, the great hall of a hospital, with beds on each side; the aisle of a ward. 3. Passage with rails on each side, from the choir to the high altar in cathedral churches; **pasar crujía**, 1. To run the gantlet. 2. (*Met.*) To suffer great fatigue and misery.

crujido [croo-hee'-do], *m.* Crack, noise made by wood, creak, clash, crackling.

crujidor [croo-he-dor'], *m.* A glass trimmer.

crujiente [croo-he-ayn'-tay], *a.* Rustling; creaking; crunchy; grinding; cracking.

crujir [croo-heer'], *vn.* 1. To crackle, to rustle. 2. To grind (one's teeth). **Hacer crujir los nudillos**, to crack one's knuckles.

crúor [croo-or'], *m.* 1. Cruor, a blood clot, gore, congealed blood. 2. The coloring-matter of the blood; also the blood-globules.

cruórico, ca [croo-o´-re-co, cah], **a.** Bloody.

crup [croop], *m.* Croup, membranous or true croup.

crupal [croo-pahl'], *a.* Croupal, croupous, belonging to croup. (*Acad.*)

crupier [croo-pe-ayr'], *m.* Croupier.

crural [croo-rahl'], *a.* Crural, belonging to the leg.

crustáceo, cea [croos-tah'-thay-o, ah], *a.* Crustaceous, shelly, having jointed shells or carapaces.

cruz [crooth], *f.* 1. Cross. 2. Cross, a line drawn through another. 3. The sign of the cross, the ensign of the Christian religion. 4. Cross, the badge of some military order. 5. Cross, trial of patience, anything that thwarts; toil, trouble, vexation. 6. Withers, the upper juncture of the shoulder bone in beasts. 7. Dagger, in printing; obelisk. **Cruz y botón**, (*Naut.*) Frapping, the crossing and drawing together the several parts of a tackle. **Cruz Roja**, Red Cross; **en cruz**, cross-shaped. **Firmar con una cruz**, to make one's mark. **Con los brazos en cruz**, with arms crossed.

cruza [croo'-tha], *f.* (*Cono Sur*) 1. (*Agri.*) Second ploughing. 2. (*Biol.*) Cross, crossing.

cruzada [croo-thah'-dah], *f.* 1. Crusade. 2. Tribunal of the crusade. 3. Indulgences granted to those who support the crusade.

cruzado [croo-thah'-do], *m.* 1. Cruzado, an old Spanish coin of gold, silver, or brass. 2. Crusado, a Portuguese coin of gold or silver. 3. Crusader, a soldier enlisted under the banners of the crusade. 4. Knight who wears the badge of some military order. 5. Manner of playing on the guitar. 6. Figure in dancing.

cruzado, da [croo-thah'-do, dah], *a.* 1. Crucial, transverse, twilled. **Estarse con los brazos cruzados**, To be idle.-*pp.* of CRUZAR. 2. *(Cos.)* Double-breasted. 3. *(Zool.)* Crossbred, hybrid. 4. *(And.)* Hopping mad, furious.

cruzador, ra [croo-thah-dor', rah], *a.* Crossing from one side to another. -*m. & f. (Mex.)* Shoplifter.

cruzamen de una vela [croo-thah'-men day oo'-nah vay'-lah], *m. (Naut.)* Square or width of a sail.

cruzamiento [croo-thah-me-ayn'-to], *m.* 1. *(Biol.)* Crossing. 2. *(Ferro.)* Crossover.

cruzar [croo-thar'], *va.* 1. To cross, to lay one body across another. **Cruzar un palo sobre otro**, to place a stick across another. 2. To cross a street or road. **Cruzar el lago a nado**, to swim across the lake. 3. *(Naut.)* To cruise. 4. To cross the breed. 5. To twill. **Cruzar la cara a alguno**, to cut and hack one's face. -*vr.* 1. To be knighted, to obtain the cross or badge of a military order. 2. To cross and trip, as horses do when they are weak in their pasterns and quarters; **Cruzarse con uno**, *(And. Cono Sur)* to fight somebody. **Cruzarse con uno en la calle**, to pass somebody in the street.

CSD *m. abr.* de **Consejo Superior de Deportes**.

c.s.f. *abr.* de **coste, seguro y flete** (cost, insurance and freight).

CSN *m. (Esp.) abr.* de **Consejo de Seguridad Nuclear** (nuclear safety council).

CSP *m. abr.* de **Cuerpo Superior de Policía**.

cta. *abr.* de **cuenta** (account, a/c).

cta. cto. *abr.* de **Carta de crédito** (letter of credit, L.C.).

cte. *abr.* de **corriente, de los corrientes** (of the present months, instant, inst.).

c/u *abr.* de **cada uno** (each, ea.).

Cu [coo], *m.* Name which the ancient historians give to the Mexican temples.

cuacar [coo-ah-car'], *va. (And. Carib, Cono Sur)* **no me cueca**, I don't want to.

cuácara [coo-ah'-cah-rah], *f. (And.)* Frock, coat; *(Cono Sur)* workman's blouse

cuaco [coo-ah'-co], *m.* 1. *(Carib. Mex.)* Nag (caballo). 2. Bag snatcher (bolsista).

cuaderna [coo-ah-derr'-nah], *f.* 1. *(Prov.)* The fourth part of something, especially of bread and of money. 2. *(Naut.)* Frame, the timber work which forms the ribs of a ship. 3. Double fours, in the game of backgammon. **Cuaderna maestra**, *(Naut.)* Midship frame. **Cuaderna del cuerpo popes**, *(Naut.)* Stern frame. **Cuadernas a escuadra**, *(Naut.)* Square timbers.

cuadernal [coo-ah-der-nahl'], *m. (Naut.)* Block, a piece of wood with sheaves and pulleys, on which the running rigging is reeved. **Cuadernales de carenar**, *(Naut.)* Careening gears.

cuadernalete [coo-ah-der-nah-lay'-tay], *m. (Naut.)* Short and double block.

cuadernillo [coo-ah-der-neel'-lyo], *m.* 1. Five sheets of paper placed within each other. 2. Clerical directory, containing the daily order of divine service.

cuadernillo, ito, *m. dim.* Small parcel of paper stitched together.

cuaderno [coo-ah-derr'-no], *m.* 1. Parcel of paper stitched together. 2. Small memorandum book. 3. In printing-offices, four printed sheets placed within each other. **Cuaderno de bitácora**, *(Naut.)* Logbook.

cuadra [coo-ah'-drah], *f.* 1. Hall, saloon; drawing-room. 2. Stable, a house for beasts. 3. *(Amer.)* A block of houses. 4.

(Naut.) Quarter of a ship. 5. *(Mil.)* Hut. 6. Hall, large room. 7. Ward (hospital). 8. *(And. Cono Sur)* 125.50 meters (medida).

cuadrada [coo-ah-drah-dah], *f. (Mus.)* Breve.

cuadrado, da [coo-ah-drah'do, dah], *a.* 1. Square, quadrate. 2. Perfect, without defect. 3. With squares. 4. Broad, square-shouldered (persona). 5. *(Carib. Cono Sur)* coarse, rude. 6. *(And.)* Elegant, graceful. -*pp.* of CUADRAR.

cuadrado [coo-ah-drah-do] , *m.* 1. Square, quadrate. 2. Clock, the flowers or inverted work in stockings. 3. Gusset of a shirt sleeve. 4. Die. V. TROQUEL. 5. *(Print.)* Quadrat, quad. **De cuadrado**, in front, opposite, face to face; squared.

cuadragenario, ria [coo-ah-drah-hay-nah'-reo, ah], *a.* Forty years old, of forty years.

cuadragésima [coo-ah-drah-hay'-se-mah], *f.* Lent. V. CUARESMA.

cuadragesimal [coo-ah-drah-hay-se-mahl´] *a.* 1. Quadragesimal. 2. Lenten, used in Lent.

cuadragésimo, ma [coo-ah-drah-hay'-se-mo, mah], *a.* Fortieth.

cuadral [coo-ah-drahl´], *m. (Arch.)* Piece of timber which crosses two others diagonally.

cuadrangular [coo-ah-dran-goo-lar'], *a.* Quadrangular.

cuadrángulo [coo-ah-drahn'-goo-lo], *m. & a.* Quadrangle, a surface with four angles.

cuadrantal [coo-ah-dran-tahl'], *a. (Math.)* Quadrantal.

cuadrante [coo-ah-drahn'-tay], *m.* 1. Quadrant, the fourth part of a circle. 2. Quadrant, a mathematical instrument for taking the latitude. 3. Dial plate of a sundial; dial of a clock or a watch. 4. A square board put up in churches, pointing out the order of masses to be celebrated. 5. The fourth part of an inheritance. 6. The smallest coin current in a country. **Hasta el último cuadrante**, to the last farthing.

cuadrar [cooahdrar'], *va. & vn.* 1. To square, to form into a square. 2. To square, to reduce to a square. 3. To square timbers. 4. *(Arith.)* To multiply a number by itself. 5. *(Pict.)* V. CUADRICULAR. 6. To square, to fit, to suit, to correspond. **Si le cuadra**, if it suits you. 7. To regulate, to adjust. 8. To please, to accommodate. -*vr.* 1. To square up, to square one's shoulders, to stand to attention. 2. *(fig.)* To dig one's heels in; to refuse to budge. 3. **Cuadrarse con uno**, to become very solemn towards somebody. 4. *(Carib.)* To make one's pile (enriquecerse). 5. *(Carib.)* To come out on top (tener éxito).

cuadrática [coo-ah-drah'-te-cah], *f.* Quadratic (equation); containing the square of a quantity.

cuadratín [coo-ah-drah-teen'], *m. (Typ.)* Quadrat (commonly abreviated to quad); quotation, piece of type metal used to fill up blanks.

cuadratura [coo-ah-drah-too,-rah], *f.* 1. Quadrature. 2. First and last quarter of the moon. 3. Pantograph, an instrument for copying designs. 4 (Watch) The dial train work; interior works of a watch.

cuadrete [coo-ah-dray'-tay], *m. dim.* A small square.

cuadricenal [coo-ah-dre-thay-nahl'], *a.* Done every forty years.

cuadrícula [coo-ah-dree'-coo-lah], *f.* A series of squares, uniform in size used by painters and sculptors to plot their studies in due proportion.

cuadricular [coo-ah-dre-coo-lar'], *va. (Pict.)* To copy a drawing with the pantograph; to copy by means of squares. -*a.* Ruled in squares (papel), divided into squares.

cuadrienal [coo-ah-dre-ay-nahl'], *a.* Quadrennial, comprising four years.

cuadrienio [coo-ah-dre-ay'-neo], *m.* Time and space of four years.

cuadriforme [coo-ah-dre-for'-may], *a.* Fourfaced.

cuadriga [coo-ah-dree'-gah], *f.* Carriage drawn by four horses.

cuadril [coo-ah-dreel'], *m.* Haunch-bone in beasts.

cuadrilátero, ra [coo-ah-dre-lah'-tay-ro, rah], *a.* Quadrilateral.

cuadriliteral [coo-ah-dre-le-tay-rahl'], *a.* Consisting of four letters

cuadrilongo [coo-ah-dre-lon'-go], *m.* 1. Rectangle; right-angled parallelogram. 2. Formation of a corps of infantry into an oblong form.

cuadrilongo, ga [coo-ah-dre-lon´-go, gah], *a.* Having the shape or form of a rectangle.

cuadrilla [coo-ah-dreel'-lyah], *f.* 1. Meeting of four or more persons, for some particular purpose. 2. Gang, crew, herd, troop. 3. Bullfighter´s team. **Cuadrilla de demolición,** demolition squad. **Cuadrilla de noche,** night shift.

cuadrillazo [coo-ah-dreel-lah-tho], *m. (And. Cono Sur)* Gang attack.

cuadrillero [coo-ah-dreel-lyay´-ro], *m.* 1. Group leader; chief; gang leader. 2. The commander of an armed band.

cuadrillo [coo-ah-dreel'-lyo], *m.* 1. *(dim.)* A small square. 2. A kind of dart formerly used by the Moors.

cuadrimestre [coo-ah-dre-mes'-tray], *m.* Space of four months.

cuadringentésimo, ma [coo-ah-din-hen-tay'-se-mo, mah], *a.* One four-hundredth.

cuadrinomio [coo-ah-dre-no'-me-o], *m. (Alg.)* Quadrinomial.

cuadripartido [coo-ah-dre-par-tee'-do], *a.* Quadripartite, divided in four.

cuádriple [coo-ah'-dre-play], *a. V.* CUÁDRUPLE.

cuadriplicado, da [coo-ah-dre-ple-cah´-do, dah], *a.* Quadrupled.

cuadrisílabo, ba [coo-ah-dre-see'-lah-bo, bah], *a.* Quadrisyllable.

cuadrito [coo-ah-dre'-to], *m. (Culin. etc.)* Cube. **Cortar en cuadrito,** to dice.

cuadrivio [coo-ah-dree'-ve-o], *m.* 1. Quadrivium, place where four roads meet. 2. Anything which may be undertaken four different ways.

cuadríyugo [coo-ah-dree'-yoo-go], *m.* Cart with four horses.

cuadro, dra [coo-ah'-dro, drah], *a. V.* CUADRADO.

cuadro [coo-ah'-dro], *m.* 1. Square, figure having four equal sides and four angles. **En cuadro,** squared, in a square form. 2. Picture, painting. **Dos cuadros de Velázquez,** two Velazquez' paintings. 3. A square bed of earth in a garden. 4. Picture frame, frame of a window. 5. *(Mil.)* Square body of troops. **Formar el cuadro,** to close ranks. 6. *(Print.)* Platen, part of a printing press which makes the impression. 7. Scene, a division of an act of a play or of a poem. *(Acad.).* **Fue un cuadro desgarrador,** it was a heart-breaking scene. 8. *(Arch. Téc.)* Frame. **Cuadro de bicicleta,** bicycle frame. 9. Description, picture. **Cuadro de costumbres,** description of customs. 10. *(Elec.)* Panel. **Cuadro de conexión manual,** switchboard. **Cuadro de instrumentos,** instrument panel. 11. *(And.)* Blackboard (pizarra). 12. *(Cono Sur)* slaughterhouse (matadero). 13. Cadre, staff, establishment of officials (personas).

cuadrumano, na [coo-ah-droo-mah'-no, nah], *a.* Quadrumanous; fourhanded. *-m. pl.* The quadrumana.

cuadrupedal [coo-ah-droo-pay-dahl'], *a.* Quadrupedal, four-footed (animales).

cuadrupedante [coo-ahdroo paydahn'-tay], *a. (Poet.)* Quadrupedant.

cuadrúpede, cuadrúpedo, da [coo-ah-droo'-pay-day], *a.* Quadruped, having four feet.

cuádruple [coo-ah'-droo-play], *a.* Quadruple, composed of four parts, four-fold.

cuadruplicación [coo-ah-droo-ple-cah-the-on'], *f.* Quadruplicating.

cuadruplicado [coo-ah-droo-ple-cah'-do], *a.* Quadruplicate. **Por cuadruplicado,** in quadruplicate.

cuadruplicar [coo-ah-droo-ple-car'], *va.* To quadruplicate. *-vr.* To quadruple.

cuádruplo, pla [coo-ah'-droo-plo, plah], *a.* Quadruple, fourfold, quadripartite; **al cuádruplo,** quadruply.

cuaga [coo-ah'-gah], *m.* Quagga, a South African animal of the horse tribe.

cuaja [coo-ah'-hah], *f.* 1. The act of fructifying a tree or plant. 2. In some countries the mire collected after the sun has dried a pond.

cuajada [coo-ah-hah'-dah], *f.* Curd of the milk separated from the whey.

cuajadillo [coo-ah-hah-deel'-lyo], *m.* Sort of silk gauze with flowers.

cuajado [coo-ah-hah'-do], *m.* A dish made of meat, herbs, or fruits, with eggs and sugar, dressed in a pan. *-a.* 1. Immobile, paralyzed with astonishment. *(Acad.)* 2. Curdled, set, coagulated. 3. *(fig.)* **Cuajado de,** full of. **Un texto cuajado de problemas,** a text bristling with problems. **Una corona cuajada de joyas,** a crown covered with jewels. 4. **Estar cuajado,** To fall asleep. 5. **Quedarse cuajado,** *(fig.)* To fall asleep. -**Cuajado, da,** *pp.* of CUAJAR.

cuajaleche [coo-ah-hah-lay, chay], *f.* 1. *(Bot.)* Lady's bedstraw, yellow goosegrass, cheese rennet. 2. Cheese rennet.

cuajamiento [coo-ah-hah-meen'-to], *m.* Coagulation.

cuajar [coo-ah-har'], *m.* Rennet bag, maw or stomach of a calf or sucking animal, the crop of a fowl; the fourth stomach, abomasum, of a ruminant animal.

cuajar [coo-ah-har'], *va.* 1. To coagulate, to concrete, to curd. 2. To ornament or decorate with too many ornaments. **Cuajó el tablero de cifras,** he covered the board with figures. 3. **Cuajar con azúcar,** to ice with sugar. *-vn. (Coll.)* 1. To succeed, to have the desired effect. 2. To please, to like, to choose. 3. *(fig.)* To become set, to become firm, to become established; to jell, to take shape; to come off, to work. **El noviazgo no cuajó,** the engagement did not work. *-vr.* 1. To coagulate, to run into concretions, to curdle. 2. *(fig.)* **Coagularse de,** *(fig.)* To fill with, to fill up with; to become crowded with. 3. *(fig.)* To go fast asleep.

cuajarón [coo-ah-hah-rone'], *m.* Grume, clot, gore.

cuajo [coo-ah'-ho], *m.* 1. A lacteal substance found in the stomach of animals before they feed. 2. Rennet, a liquor made by steeping the stomach of a calf in hot water, and used to coagulate milk for curds and cheese. 3. Concretion, coagulation. **Tener buen cuajo,** to be too dull and patient. **Arrancar de cuajo,** to eradicate, to tear up by the roots. **Hierba del cuajo,** cheese rennet. 4. *(Mex.)* Chat; chatter. 5. *(Mex.)* Fib (mentira). 6. *(Mex.)* Pipe dream (proyecto). 7. *(Mex.)* Playtime (en escuela).

cuakerismo, or **cuaquerismo** [coo-ah-kay-rees'-mo], *m.* Quakerism.

cuákero, ra, or **cuáquero, ra** [coo-ah'-kay-ro, rah], *m. & f.* A Quaker.

cual [coo-ahl'], *pron.* 1. Which; he who. **Cada cual,** each one, everyone. *V.* EL QUE. **¿Cuál de los dos quiere usted?,** which of the two will you have? **¿Cuál es el que dices?,** which one are you talking about? **Ignora cuál será el resultado,** he does not know what the result will be. 2. Same, like, such. *V.* CUALQUIERA. 3. One, other, partly. *Cual o cual, V.* TAL CUAL. **El cual,** which. **Ése es el policía el cual me puso una multa,** that's the policeman who gave me a fine. *-adv.* As. *V.* COMO. **Cual el padre tal el hijo,** like father like son. **Cual llega el día tras la noche,** just as day follows night.*-int.* How then.

cualesquiera [coo ah les ke ay' rah], *pl.* of CUALQUIERA, *q. v.*

cualidad [coo-ha-le-dahd'], *f.* Quality. *V.* CALIDAD. **Tiene buenas cualidades,** he has good qualities.

cualificado [coo-ah-le-fe-cah'-do], *a.* 1. Skilled, qualified. **Obrero no cualificado,** unskilled worker. 2. **Estar cualificado para,** to be entitled to.

cualitativamente [coo-ah-le-tah-te-vah-men'-tay], *adv.* Qualitatively.

cualitativo, va [coo-ah-le-tah-tee'-vo, vah], *a.* Qualitative. **Análisis cualitativo,** qualitative analysis.

cualquier [coo-al-ke-err'], *a.* Any. **Cualquier hombre de los de aquí,** any man from these parts. **En cualquier sitio donde los busques,** in whatever place you look for it. 2. **Hay cualquier cantidad,** *(LAm.)* There´s a large quantity, there´s any amount. 3. Any. **Ella no es una mujer cualquiera,** she´s not just any woman.

cualquiera [coo-al-ke-ay'-rah], *pron.* 1. Anyone, someone, either one or the other, whichever, whoever. **Te lo diría cualquiera,** anyone would tell you the same. **Cualquiera puede hacer eso,** anybody can do that. 2. **Cualquiera que sea,** whoever he is. 3. **Es un cualquiera,** he´s a nobody. 4. **Una cualquiera,** a whore.

cuan [coo-ahn'], *adv.* How, as. *V.* CUANTO.

cuando [coo-ahn'-do], *adv.* 1. When, pointing out a certain time. 2. In case that; if. 3. Though, although; even. **Incluso cuando no hubiera más razón,** even if there were no other reasons. 4. Sometimes, at times. **De cuando en cuando,** from time to time; now and then. **Cuando más** or **cuando mucho,** at most, at best. **Cuando menos,** at least. **Cuando quiera,** when you please, whenever. **¿Hasta cuándo?,** when shall I see you again? literally, until when? **Cuando no sea así,** even if it is not so. **Eso fue cuando la guerra,** that was during the war. **Cuando niño,** as a child.

cuantía [coo-an-tee'-ah], *f.* 1. Quantity, amount. **De mayor cuantía,** first-rate. **De poca cuantía,** second-rate. *V.* CANTIDAD. 2. Rank, distinction. **Hombre de gran cuantía,** a man of high rank.

cuantiar [coo-an-te-ar'], *va.* To estimate or appraise possessions; to fix a price.

cuántico [coo-ahn'-te-co], *a.* **Teoría cuántica,** quantum theory.

cuantidad [coo-an-te-dahd'], *f.* Quantity; a word especially used by mathematicians. *V.* CANTIDAD.

cuantificación [coo-ahn-te-fe-cah-the-on'], *f.* Quantifying.

cuantificar [coo-ahn-te-fe-car'], *va.* To quantify.

cuantimás. *(Obs.) V.* CUANTO MÁS.

cuantiosamente [coo-ahn-te-o'-sah-men-tey], *adv.* Copiously.

cuantioso, sa [coo-an-te-o'-so, sah], *a.* Numerous, copious, rich.

cuantitativamente [coo-ahn-te--tah-te'-vah-men-tey], *adv.* Quantitatively.

cuantitativo, va [coo-an-te-tah-tee'-vo, vah], *a.* Quantitative, estimable, according to quantity. *(Chem.)* **Análisis cuantitativo,** quantitative analysis.

cuanto, ta [coo-ahn'-to, tah], *a.* 1. Containing quantity or relating to it, susceptible of quantity. **Daremos cuantos créditos se precisen,** we will give all the credits that may be necessary. **Unos cuantos libros,** a few books. 2. **¿Cuánto?** how much? **¿Cuánto has gastado?,** how much have you spent? **¿Cuánto durará esto?,** how long will this last? **¿Cuántos?,** how many? 3. As many as, as much as, the more; correlative of *tanto.* **Cuanto uno es más pobre, se le debe socorrer más,** the poorer a person is the more should he be supported. **Cuanto usted quiera,** as much as you like. 4. All, whatever. 5. Excessive, great in some way. (Note. *-Cuanto,* signifying " how much," receives an accent, thus: **cuánto.** **¡Cuánta sabiduría!,** how much wisdom! *-adv.* Respecting, whilst. **Cuanto antes,** immediately, as soon as possible. **Cuanto más,** moreover, the more as. **En cuanto a,** with regard to, as to, in the meantime. **Cuanto quiera,** although. **Por cuanto,** inasmuch as. **En cuanto lo supe me fui,** as soon as I heard it I left. **Cuanto más difícil parezca,** the more difficult it may seem.

cuaquerismo [coo-ah-kay-res'-mo], *m.* Quakerism.

cuáquero, ra [cooah'kayro, rah], *m. & f. & a.* Quaker.

cuarango [coo-ah-rahn'-go], *m.* The vulgar name of the *Cinchona* or Peruvian bark tree.

cuarenta [coo-ah-ren'-tah], *a. & m.* Forty. **Cantar a uno las cuarenta,** to tell someone a few home truths.

cuarentañera [coo-ah-ren-tay'-nyah], *f.* Woman of about forty.

cuarentañero [coo-ah-ren-tay'-nyah], *m.* Man of about forty.

cuarentavo, va [coo-ah-ren-tah'-vo, vah], *a.* Fortieth.

cuarentena [coo-ah-ren-tay'-nah], *f.* 1. Space of forty days, months, or years; the fortieth part. 2. Lent, the forty days of fast prescribed by the Church. 3. *(Met.)* Suspension of assent to anything. 4. The number 40 in general. 5. *(Naut.)* Quarantine, the time when a ship, suspected of infection, is obliged to abstain from intercourse with the inhabitants of a country. **Hacer cuarentena,** *(Naut.)* To perform quarantine.

cuarentón, na [coo-ah-ren-tone', nah], *a. & m. & f.* Person forty years old.

cuaresma [coo-ah-res'-mah], *f.* 1. Lent, the forty days' fast prescribed by the Church. 2. Collection of Lent sermons.

cuaresmal [coo-ah-res-mahl'], *a.* Lenten.

cuarta [coo-ar'-tah], *f.* 1. Fourth, fourth part; a quarter. 2. Quadrant, fourth part of a circle. 3. *(Naut.)* Quarter point of the compass. 4. Sequence of four cards in the game of piquet. 6. *(Fen.)* Quart, or carte. 7. Palm, a handbreadth. 8. Quart, a liquid measure. 9. *(Mil.)* Quarter of a company of soldiers. 10. *(Mus.)* A fourth. 11. A piece of timber square in section. 12. *(Prov.)* A guide mule. 13. *(Hex.)* A sort of whip. 14. *(Cono Sur)* Extra pair of oxen. 15. **Andar de la cuarta al pértigo,** *(Cono Sur),* **vivir a la cuarta,** *(Cono Sur. Mex.)* to be on the bread line.

cuartago [coo-ar-tah'-go], *m.* Nag, pony, hack.

cuartal [coo-ar-tahl'], *m.* 1. Kind of bread weighing the fourth part of a loaf. 2. Quarter, dry measure, fourth part of a fanega.

cuartán [coo-ar-tahn'], *m.* *(Prov.)* A grain measure, equal to 18 litres and 8 centilitres.

cuartanal [coo-ar-tah-nahl'], *a.* Intermittent.

cuartanario, ria [coo-ar-tah-nah'-reo, ah], *a.* Laboring under a quartan.

cuartar [coo-ar-tar'], *va.* To plough the ground the fourth time.

cuartazo [coo-ar-tah'-tho], *m. aug.* A large room; a large quarter. **Cuartazos,** a coarse, corpulent person; a stroke with a whip.

cuartear [coo-ar-tay-ar'], *va.* 1. To quarter, to divide into four parts. 2. To bid a fourth more at public sales. 3. To make a fourth person at a game. 4. To zigzag up steep places. 5. *(Naut.)* **Cuartear la aguja,** to box the compass. 6. *(Carib. Mex.)* To whip, to beat (azotar). *-vn.* 1. To make a fourth (naipes). 2. *(Taur.)* To dodge, to step aside. *vr.* 1. To split into pieces. 2. *(Taur.)* To dodge, to step aside. 3. *(Mex.)* To go back to one´s word.

cuartel [coo-ar-tell'], *m.* 1. Quarter, the fourth part of a garden or other thing. 2. Quarter, district, ward of a city. 3. Quarter, the place where soldiers are lodged and stationed. 4. Dwelling, habitation, home. 5. Quarter, remission of life granted by hostile troops. 6. *V.* CUARTETO. 7. *(Naut.)* Hatch, the lid of a hatchway. **Cuartel de la salud,** a safe place free from hazard and danger. **Cuartel de bomberos,** fire station. **Estar de cuartel,** to be on half-pay. **Guerra sin cuartel,** war without mercy. **Dar cuartel a,** to support, to encourage.

cuartelada, cuartelazo [coo-ar-tay-lah'-dah], *f. m.* Military uprising, mutiny, coup.

cuartelar [coo-ar-tay-lar'], *va.* *(Her.)* To quarter.

cuartelero [coo-ar-tay-lay'-ro], *m.* *(Mil.)* Soldier in each company appointed to keep the apartments clean.

cuartera [coo-ar-tay'-rah], *f.* A dry measure in Catalonia, containing about fifteen pecks.

cuartería [coo-ar-tay-re'-ah], *f.* *(Carib. Cono Sur)* Bunkhouse (en un rancho).

cuartero, ra [coo-ar-tay´-ro, rah], *a.* *(Prov.)* Applied to those who collect the rents of the grain of farms, which pay the fourth part to the landlords.

cuarterola [coo-ar-tay-ro'-lah], *f.* Quarter cask of liquors or fluids.

cuarterón [coo-ar-tay-rone´], *m.* 1. Quartern, quarter, the fourth part of a whole; quarter of a pound. 2. Upper part of windows which may be opened and shut. **Cuarterones,** squares of wainscot in a door or window shutter. 3. *(LAm.)* Quadroon.

cuarterón, na, [coo-ar-tay-rone' *a. (Amer.)* Applied to a child begotten of a creole and a native of Spain; quadroon.

cuarteta [coo-ar-tay'-tah], *f. (Poet.)* Quatrain, a metrical composition of four lines.

cuartete, cuarteto [coo-ar-tay'-tay, coo-ar-tay-to], *m.* 1. *(Poet.)* Quatrain, a stanza of four verses. 2. *(Mus.)* Quartet.

cuartilla [coo-ar-teel'-lyah], *f.* 1. Fourth part of an *arroba*, or sixteenth part of a quintal. 2. Fourth part of a sheet of paper. 3. Pastern of horses.

cuartillo [coo-ar-teel'lyo], *m.* 1. Pint, the fourth part of a bottle in liquids. 2. The fourth part of a peck in grain. 3. Fourth part of a real. **Ir de cuartillo,** to share the profits or losses in any business.

cuartilludo, da [coo-ar-teel-lyoo'-do, dah], *a.* Applied to a horse with long pasterns.

cuartito [coo-ar-tee'-to], *m. dim.* A small room.

cuarto [coo-ar'-to], *m.* 1. Fourth part, quadrant, quarter. **Cuarto creciente,** first quarter. **Tardó tres cuartos de hora,** he took three-quarters of an hour. 2. Habitation, dwelling, room, apartment. **Cuarto de baño,** bathroom. **Cuarto de juego,** playroom. **Cuarto de los niños,** nursery. *V.* APOSENTO; **cuarto bajo,** room on the ground floor. 3. Copper coin worth four *maravedís.* 4. Series of paternal or maternal ancestors. 5. Crack in horses' hoofs. 6. Quarter of clothes, quarter of animals or of criminals whose body is quartered and exposed in public places. **De tres al cuarto,** of little moment. **Poner cuarto,** to take lodgings; to furnish apartments. **Cuarto principal,** first floor. **No tener un cuarto,** not to be worth a cent; **cuartos,** 1. Cash, money. 2. Well proportioned members of an animal's body. **Por 5 cuartos,** for a song. **Estar sin un cuarto,** to be broke.

cuarto, ta [coo-ar'-to, tah], *a.* Fourth, the ordinal of four.

cuartogénito, ta [coo-ar-to-hay´-ne-to, tah], *a.* The fourth born child.

cuartón [coo-ar-tone´], *m.* 1. Quarter, a large joist or girder, a beam sixteen feet long. 2. *(Prov.)* Measure of wine and vinegar.

cuartucho [coo-ar-too'-cho], *m.* Hovel; poky little room.

cuarzo [coo-ar´-tho], *m.* Quartz, a crystallized silicious stone. **Cuarzo citrino,** occidental topaz.

cuarzoso, sa [coo-ar-tho'-so, sah], *a.* Quartzose.

cuás [coo-ahs'], *m. (Mex.)* Bosom pal.

cuásar [coo-ah'-sahr], *m.* Quasar.

cuasi [coo-ah'-se], *adv.* Almost. *V.* CASI and COMO.

cuasicontrato [coo-ah-se-con-trah´-to], *m. (Law.)* Quasi-contract; a contract though not formal, yet effectual. *Cuasidelito, (Law.)* Quasi-crime or delict.

cuasimodo [coo-ah-semo'-do], *m.* First Sunday after Easter.

cuate [coo-ah'tay], *m. (Mex.) V.* GEMELO. **Eso no tiene cuate,** *(Coll.)* that has no match.

cuaterna [coo-ah-terr'-nah], *f.* 1. Union of four things. 2. *V.* CUADERNA. 3. Lesson for four.

cuaternario, ria [coo-ah-ter-nah'-re-o, ah], *a.* Quaternary.

cuaternidad [coo-ah-tar-ne-dahd'], *f.* Quaternity, quaternary.

cuaternión [coo-ah-ter-ne-on'], *m.* Union of four things, of four sheets in printing.

cuatralbo [coo-ah-trahl'-bo], *a.* Having four white feet (animales). *m.* Commander of four galleys.

cuatre(re)ar [coo-ah-tray-ar'], *va. (Cono Sur)* To rustle (ganado), to steal. *-vn. (Cono Sur)* To act treacherously.

cuatrero [coo-ah-tray'-ro], *m.* Thief who steals horses, sheep, or other beasts. *-a.* Treacherous, disloyal.

cuatridial, cuatridiano [coo-ah-tre-de-ahl'], *a.* Lasting four days.

cuatrienal [coo-ah-tre-ah-nahl'], *a.* Four-year.

cuatrienio [coo-ah-tre-ay'-ne-o], *m. V.* CUADRIENIO.

cuatrillizos, zas [coo-ah-trel-lye'-thos], *m, f. & pl.* Quadruplets.

cuatrimestre [coo-ah-tre-mes'-tray], *a.* Lasting four months. *-m.* The space of four months.

cuatrimotor [coo-ah-tre-mo-tor'], *a.* Four-engined. *-m.* Four-engined plane.

cuatrinca [coo-ah-treen'-cah], *f.* 1. Union of four persons or things. 2. Four cards of the same print in the game of *báciga.*

cuatrisílabo, ba, [coo-ah-tre-se'-lah-bo], *a. V.* CUADRISÍLABO.

cuatro [coo-ah'tro], *a.* 1. Four, twice two. 2. *V.* CUARTO. **Más de cuatro,** *(fig.)* quite a few. **Sólo había cuatro muebles,** there were only a few pieces of furniture. **Cayeron cuatro gotas,** a few drops fell.

cuatro, *m.* 1. Character or figure 4. 2. One who votes for four absent persons. 3. Musical composition sung by four voices. 4. Card with four marks. 5. *f.* Four o'clock. **Más de cuatro,** a great number of persons.

cuatrocientos, tas [coo-ah-tro-theen'-tos, tas], *a.* Four hundred.

cuatrodial [coo-ah-tro-de-ahl´], *a.* That which is of four days.

cuatrodoblar [coo-ah-tro-do-blar'], *va.* To quadruple.

cuatropear [coo-ah-tro-pay-ar'], *vn.* To run on all fours.

cuba [coo'-bah], *f.* 1. Cask for wine or oil. 2. *(Met.)* Toper, drunkard. **Estar hecho una cuba,** to be as drunk as a skunk. 3. Tub. **Cuba para el agua de lluvia,** rainwater butt.

Cuba [coo'-bah], *f.* Cuba.

cubaje [coo-bah'-hay], *m. (LAm.)* Volume, contents.

cuba-libre [coo'-bah le'-bray], *m. pl.* **cubas-libres,** drink of rum and Coca Cola.

cubanismo [coo-bah-nes'-mo], *m.* Cubanism, word peculiar to Cuba.

cubano, na [coo-bah´-no, nah], *a.* Cuban.

cubar [coo-bar'], *va.* To cube, to raise to the third power.

cubata [coo-bah-tah], *m. V.* CUBA LIBRE.

cubaza [coo-bah'-thah], *f. aug.* A large pipe, a hogshead.

cubeba [coo-bay'-bah], *f. (Bot.)* Cubeb or cubebs, the berries of the Piper.

cubero [coo-bay´-ro], *m.* A cooper.

cubertería [coo-ber-tay-re'-ah], *f.* Cutlery.

cubertura [coo-ber-too´-rah], *f.* Cover, Covering. *V.* COBERTURA.

cubeta [coo-bay'-tah], *f.* 1. A small barrel or cask. 2. Tub, pail. 3. Back, vat of brewers. 4. Beck, or trough of dyers. **Cubeta** or **bidón donde se come,** *(Naut.)* mess bucket. **Cubeta para alquitrán,** *(Naut.)* tar bucket.

cubetilla, ita [coo-bay-teel'-lyah], *f. dim.* A small bucket.

cubeto [coo-bay'-to], *m.* A small barrel.

cúbica [coo´-be-cah], *f.* A woollen stuff finer than serge.

cubicación [coo-be-cah-the-on'], *f.* 1. Measurement of edifices. 2. Act of cubing.

cubicaje [coo-be-cah'-hay], *m. (Aut.)* Cylinder capacity.

cúbicamente [coo'-be-cah-men-tay], *adv.* Cubically.

cubicar [coo-be-car'], *va.* 1. To cube, to raise to the third power. 2. To determine the volume of.

cubichete [coo-be-chay'-tay], *m. (Naut.)* Waterboards or weatherboards, on the upper part of a ship's side, to keep off a rough sea.

cúbico, ca [coo´-be-co, ca] *a.* Cubical, cubic, cubiform.

cubiculario [coo-be-coo-lah'-re-o], *m.* Groom of the bedchamber, valet-de-chambre.

cubículo [coo-be'-coo-lo], *m.* Cubicle.

cubierta [coo-be-err'-tah], *f.* 1. Cover, covering, covert. **Cubierta de cama,** coverlet. **Cubierta de lona,** tarpaulin, canvas. **Cubierta flexible o de plástico corrugado** *(Inform.),* flexible or rugged plastic-coated cover. 2. *(Met.)* Pretext or pretence. 3. *(Naut.)* Deck of a ship. **Cubierta primera** or **principal,** the lower or gundeck. **Segunda cubierta,** the middle deck. **Cubierta arqueada,** a cambering deck. **Cubi-**

erta de vuelo, flight deck. **Cubierta de paseo**, promenade deck. 4. Cover of a letter, envelope. 5. Casing, coat, facing: roofing. 6. Hood of a carriage.

cubiertamente [coo-be-ayr-tah-men'-tay], *adv.* Privately, secretly.

cubierto [coo-be-err´-to], *m.* 1. Cover, part of a table service, consisting of a plate, fork, spoon, knife, and napkin, for every one who sits down to table. **Cubiertos**, cutlery. 2. Roof of a house, or any other covering from the inclemency of the weather; covert, coverture, cover. 3. Allowance of a soldier billeted in a house. 4. Course, a number of dishes set at once on a table. 5. A meal at a fixed price. **Cubiertos de 80 pesos**, 80-peso meal. *(Acad.)* **Ponerse a cubierto**, to shelter oneself from an apprehended danger. *-pp. irr.* of CUBRIR; 1. Covered; overcast. 2. **La vacante está ya cubierta**, the place has already been filled.

cubil [coo-beel'], *m.* 1. Lair or couch of wild beasts. 2. *(Prov.)* Hogsty.

cubilar [coo-be-lar´], *vn.* To take shelter. *V.* MAJADEAR.

cubilete [coo-be-lay'-tay], *m.* 1. A copper pan for baking pies and other pastry, and the pie or pastry made on it; used also by jugglers. 2. *(Ant.)* Tumbler, goblet, a drinking-cup. 3. A cup made of a medicinal wood, such as quassia. 4. Cup (en juegos); dice box (de dados). 5. *(LAm.)* Intrigue. 6. *(LAm.)* Top hat (chistera); bowler hat (hongo).

cubiletear [coo-be-lay-tay-ar'], *vn.* 1. To shake the dice box. 2. *(fig.)* To intrigue, to scheme.

cubiletero [coo-be-lay-tay'-ro], *m.* 1. Pastemould. 2. A large mug. *-m. & f.* Conjurer.

cubilote [coo-be-lo'-tay], *m.* Cupola smelting furnace, smelting-pot.

cubillo [coo-beel'-lyo], *m.* 1. Spanish-fly, blister-beetle. 2. A piece of table-service for keeping water cool. 3. A small box near the stage. 4. *(Naut.)* A socket for the flagpole. **Cubillos**, the ladles or receptacles of a millwheel.

cubismo [coo-bees´-mo], *m.* Cubism.

cubista [coo-bes'-tah], *a.* Cubist. *- m. & f.* Cubist.

cubital [coo-be-tahl'], *a.* Cubital, the length of a cubit.

cúbito [coo'-be-to], *m.* *(Anat.)* Ulna, the largest bone of the forearm.

cubito [coo-be'-to], *m.* 1. Bucket, beach pail (de niño). 2. **Cubito de hielo**, ice cube.

cubo [coo'-bo], *m.* 1. Cube, a solid body of six equal sides. 2. A wooden pail with an iron handle, bucket. **Cubo de la basura**, trash can. 3. Millpond. 4. Barrel of a watch or clock. 5. *(Mil.)* A small tower formerly raised on old walls. 6. Cube, product of the multiplication of a square number by its root. 7. Nave or hub of a wheel. 8. Bayonet socket. 9. Among masons, a hodful of mixed mortar. 10. *(Com.)* Tongue way, socket, shaft-case.

cuboide [coo-bo'-e-day], *m.* 1. Cuboid bone of the tarsus. 2. Rhomboid, little differing from a cube.

cubreasientos [coo-bray-ah-se-en'-tose], *m.* Seatcover.

cubrebocas [coo-bray-bo'-cas], *m.* *(Med.)* Mask.

cubrecama [coo-bray-cah'-mah], *f.* Bedspread, coverlet.

cubrellanta [coo-bray-lyahn'-tah], *m.* Tire covering, tire casing.

cubremesa [coo-bray-may'-sah], *f.* *(LAm.)* Table cover.

cubreobjetos [coo-bray-ob-hay'-tos], *m*

cubrepán [coo-bray-pahn'], *m.* Sort of fire-shovel, used by shepherds.

cubriente [coo-bre-en'-tay], *pa.* Covering, hiding.

cubrimiento [coo-bre-me-en'-to], *m.* 1. Covering, act of covering. 2. Roofing.

cubrir [coo-breer'], *va.* 1. To cover, to lay, to spread one thing over another. **Lo cubrieron las aguas**, the waters closed over it. **El agua casi me cubría**, the water almost covered me. 2. To face, or cover with additional superficies. 3. *(Met.)* To cover, to screen, to consent, to palliate. **Cubrir a uno de improperios**, to shower insults on somebody. **Cubrir a uno de atenciones**, to overwhelm some-

body with kindness. 4. To cover, to disguise, to dissemble, to cloak. **Cubre su tristeza con una falsa alegría**, she covers up her sadness with a false cheerfulness. 5. To cover or protect a post, to prevent its being attacked by the enemy. **Cubrir su retirada**, to cover one's retreat. 6. To roof a building. 7. To cover, to copulate; to fecundate (animales, plantas). 8. **Cubrir la mesa**, to lay the table. **Cubrir la cuenta**, to balance an account. 9. To cover, to travel. *-vr.* 1. To take measures to insure oneself against loss. **Cubrirse contra un riesgo**, to cover oneself against a risk. 2. To put a place in a state of defence. 3. To be covered, to put on one's hat. 4. To become overcast.

cuca [coo'-cah], *f.* 1. A kind of root-tubercle of a sedge, used in place of coffee. *V.* CHUFA. 2. A Peruvian plant. *V.* COCA. 3. Sort of caterpillar. *V.* Cuco. 4. **Cuca y matacán**, sort of card game. **Mala cuca**, *(Coll.)* A wicked person. **Cuca de aquí**, *(Coll.)* Begone! 5. Sweets. 6. *(CAm.)* Cunt (vagina).

cucambé [coo-cam'-bay], *m.* *(And.)* Hide-and-seek.

cucamonas [coo-ca-mo´-nas], *f. pl.* Sweet nothings (palabras); caresses (caricias); fondling (mageo). **Ella me hizo cucamonas**, she gave me a come-hither look. *(Coll.)* *V.* CARANTOÑAS.

cucaña [coo-cah'-nyah], *f.* 1. A public amusement, climbing a greased pole. 2. Anything acquired with little trouble, and at other people's expense. 3. Soft job; bargain; easy thing.

cucañero, ra [coo-ca-nyay'-ro], *m. & f.* Parasite, one who lives at other people's expense.

cucar [coo-car´], *va.* 1. To wink. 2. To deride, to mock. 3. *(LAm.)* To urge on, to incite.

cucaracha [coo-ca-rah'-chah], *f.* 1. Cockroach. 2. Hazel-colored snuff. 3. Scare-crow. 4. *(Mex.)* *(Aut.)* Old crock. *-m.* Priest.

cucarachera [coo-ca-rah-chay'-rah], *f.* *(Vulg.)* Luck, good fortune. **Hallarse buena cucarachera**, to be lucky or fortunate.

cucarachero [coo-ca-rah-chay'-ro], *m.* *(And. Carib.)* Parasite, hanger-on; *(And.)* Flatterer, creep (adulador).

cuceranita [coo-thay-rah-nee'-tah], *f.* *(Min.)* A certain silicate of aluminum.

cuchar [coo-char'], *f.* 1. Tax or duty on grain. 2. *(Prov.)* Spoon. 3. Ancient corn measure, the twelfth part of a *celemín* or peck. **Cuchar herrera**, iron spoon.

cuchara [coo-chah'-rah], *f.* 1. Spoon. **Cuchara de café**, coffee spoon. **Cuchara de gas**, spoonful. **Despacharse con la cuchara grande**, *(LAm.)* to give oneself a big helping. 2. An iron ladle, for taking water out of a large earthen jar. 3. *(Mas.)* A trowel. **Cuchara para brea**, *(Naut.)* pitchladle. **Cuchara para sacar el agua de los barcos**, *(Naut.)* scoop for baling boats. **Cucharas**, ladleboards of a waterwheel in an overshot mill. 4. *(LAm.)* Flat trowel. **Albañil de cuchara**, skilled bricklayer. 5. *(CAm. Carib, Cono Sur)* Pout. **Hacer cuchara**, to pout. 6. *(Mex.)* Pickpoket (carterista). **cucharada** [coo-chah-rah'-dah], *f.* Spoonful, ladleful. **Meter su cucharada**, to meddle in other people's conversation, to have a linger in the pie.

cucharadita [coo-chah-rah-dee'-tah], *f.* Teaspoonful.

cucharal [coo-chah-rahl], *m.* Bag in which shepherds preserve their spoons.

cucharazo [coo-chah-rah'-tho], *m.* Stroke or blow with a spoon.

cucharear [coo-chah-ray-ar'], *va.* *(Culin.)* To spoon out, to ladle out; *(Agri.)* To pitch.

cuchareta [coo-chah-ray'-tah], *f. dim.* 1. A small spoon. 2. A variety of wheat. 3. Inflammation of the liver in sheep. *(Acad.)*

cucharetear [coo-chah-ray-tay-ar'], *vn.* *(Coll.)* 1. To stir with a spoon. 2. *(Met.)* To busy oneself with other people's affairs.

cucharetero [coo-chah-ray-tay´-ro], *m.* 1. Maker or retailer of wooden spoons. 2. List or linen, nailed to a board, with small interstices to hold spoons. 3. Fringe sewed to under petticoats.

cucharilla [coo-chah-reel'-lyah], *f.* 1. Liver disease in swine. *(Acad.)* 2. *(Surg.)* A scoop. 3. Small spoon, teaspoon.

cucharita [coo-chah-ree'-tah], *f.* Tea-spoon.

cucharón [coo-chah-rone'], *m.* 1. Ladle for the kitchen, a soup-spoon for the table. 2. *(aug.)* A large spoon, dipper; scoop, bucket. **Tener el cucharón por el mango,** to be the boss.

cucharro [coo-char'-ro], *m.* 1. *(Naut.)* Harping. **Tablones de cucharros,** *(Naut.)* serving-planks. 2. *(Agri.)* A vessel made from a gourd used for watering plants by hand.

cuche [coo'-chay], *m. (CAm.)* Pig.

cuchichear [coo-che-chay-ar'], *vn.* To whisper.

cuchicheo [coo-che-chay'o], *m.* Whisper, whispering.

cuchichero, ra [coo-che-chay'-ro', rah], *m. & f. (Coll.)* Whisperer.

cuchichiar [coo-che-che-ar'], *vn.* 1. To call like a partridge. 2. To whisper.

cuchilla [coo-cheel'-lyah], *f.* 1. A large kitchen-knife; a chopping-knife. 2. Sort of ancient poniard. 3. *(Poet.)* Sword. **Cuchilla de afeitar,** razor blade. 4. *(Geog.)* Ridge, crest; *(LAm.)* Line of low hills; *(Carib.)* Mountain top.

cuchillada [coo-cheel-lyah'-dah], *f.* 1. Cut or clash with a knife or other cutting instrument. 2. Gash, a deep wound. 3. Slash, a cut in cloth, formerly made to let the lining open to view: it was commonly used in the plural. 4. *-pl.* Wrangles, quarrels. 5. Galley-stick, sidestick. 6. Truss, girder.

cuchillar [coo-cheel-lyar'], *a.* Belonging or relating to a knife.

cuchillazo [coo-cheel-lah-tho], *m. (LAm.) V.* CUCHILLADA.

cuchillejo [coo-cheel-lyay'-ho], *m.* 1. *(dim.)* A small knife; a paring-knife (herreros). 2. *(Bot.)* Cockleweed.

cuchillera [coo-cheel-lyay'-rah], *f.* Knife-case or scabbard.

cuchillería [coo-cheel-lyayree'-ah], *f.* Cutler's shop, and the place or street where there are many cutlers' shops; cutlery.

cuchillero [coo-cheel-lyay'-ro], *m.* Cutler. *-a. (LAm.)* Quarrelsome.

cuchillo [coo-cheel'-lyo], *m.* 1. Knife of one blade, with a handle. 2. Gore, a triangular piece of cloth sewed into a garment. 3. *(Met.)* Right of governing and putting the laws in execution. 4. A beam, girder. 5. *(Naut.)* Every plank cut on the bevel. 6. A cut, crevice, fissure. 7. Every triangular sail, leg-of-mutton sail. 8. *(Arch.)* Upright, support. 9. Fang, tusk (de jabalí etc.). **Cuchillo de monte,** a hunter's cutlass. **Pasar a cuchillo,** to put to the sword. **Cuchillo de hoja automática,** switch-blade. **Cuchillo de postres,** fruit knife. **Cuchillo mantequillero,** butter knife.

cuchillón [coo-cheel-lyone'], *m. aug.* A large or big knife.

cuchipanda [coo-che-pahn'-dah], *f.* A cheerful dinner shared by several persons.

cuchitril [coo-chee-treel'], *m.* A narrow hole or corner; a very small room; a hut.

cucho [coo'-cho], *m.* 1. *(CAm.)* hunchback; *(Mex.)* limbless (manco). 2. *(Cono Sur)* Puss. 3. *(And.) V.* CUCHITRIL.

cuchuche [coo-choo'-chay], *m.* **Ir de cuchuche,** *(CAm.)* To ride piggyback.

cuchuchear [coo-choo-chay-ar'], *vn. (Coll.)* 1. To whisper, to speak with a low voice. 2. *(Met.)* To carry tales.

cuchufleta [coo-choo-flay'-tah], *f.* 1. Joke, jest, fun. 2. *(Mex.)* Trinket (baratija).

cuchuflí [coo-choo-fle'], *m. (Carib.)* Uncomfortable place; cell.

cuchugos [coo-choo'-cho], *m. & pl. (And. Carib.)* Saddlebags.

cuchumbo [coo-choom'-co], *m. (CAm.)* Funnel (embudo); bucket, pail; dice box (de dados); game of dice.

cucioso, sa [coo-the-oh'-so, sah], *a.* Diligent. *V.* SOLÍCITO.

cucita [coo-thee'-tah], *f.* Lapdog.

cuclear [coo-clay-ar'], *m.* To sing like the cuckoo.

cuclillas (En) [coo-cleel'-lyas], *adv.* In a cowering manner. **Sentarse en cuclillas,** to squat, to sit cowering, to sit close to the ground.

cuclillo [coo-cleel'-lyo], *m.* 1. *(Orn.)* Cuckoo. 2. *(Met.)* Cuckold.

cuco [coo'-co], *m.* 1. Sort of caterpillar. 2. Person of a swarthy complexion. 3. Sort of game at cards. 4. Cuckoo. 5. A gambler. **Reloj de cuco,** cuckoo clock. 6. *(Mex.)* **Hacer cuco a uno,** to poke fun at somebody. 7. *(And. Cono Sur)* bogeyman (fantasma).

cuco, ca [coo'-co, cah], *a. (Coll.)* Cunning, crafty, astute, shrewd.

cucú [coo-coo'], *m.* Word imitative of the cuckoo's note.

cucuche [coo-coo'-chay], *(CAm.)* **Ir de cucuche,** to ride astride.

cucufato [coo-coo-fah'-to], *m. (And. Cono Sur)* Hypocrite; prude (mojigato); nut (loco).

cucuiza [coo-coo-ee'-thah], *f. (Amer.)* Thread of the agave.

cuculí [coo-coo-le'], *m. (And. Cono Sur)* Wood pigeon.

cuculla [coo-cool'-lyah], *f.* Cowl, a kind of hood formerly worn by men and women.

cucuma [coo-coo'-mah], *f.* Kind of bread made in Colombia from a root like yucca.

cucumeráceo, cea [coo-coo-may-rah'-thay-o, ah], *a.* Cucumberlike.

cucúrbita [coo-coor'-be-tah], *f.* 1. A retort, for distilling. 2. Scientific name of the gourd.

cucurbitáceo, cea [coo-coor-be-tah'-thay-o, ah], *a. (Bot.)* Cucurbitaceous.

cucurucho [coo-coo-roo'-cho], *m.* 1. A paper cone, used by grocers; cornucopia. 2. *(Ecl.)* Hooded garment; pointed hat. 3. *(And. CAm. Carib.)* Top, summit, apex. 4. *(Carib.)* Hovel, shack (cuchitril).

cudria [coo'-dre-ah], *f.* A flat woven bassrope.

cueca [coo-ay'-cah], *f. (Cono Sur)* Handkerchief dance.

cuelga [coo-el'-gah], *f.* 1. Cluster of grapes or other fruit hung up for use. **Cuelga** or **ristra de cebollas,** bunch of onions. 2. A birthday present. 3. *(And. Cono Sur) (Geog.)* Fall.

cuelgacapas [coo-el-gah-cah'-pas], *m.* A cloak-hanger. *(Yo cuelgo, yo cuelgue,* from *Colgar. V.* ACORDAR.)

cuelgue [coo-ayl'-gay], *m.* **Llevar un cuelgue,** to be broke; to be all at sea (confuso); to need a fix (drogas).

cuelmo [coo-el'-mo], *m.* Candlewood, a piece of pine, or other seasoned wood, which burns like a torch. *V.* TEA.

cuellicorto, ta [coo-el-lye-cor'-to, tah], *a.* Shortnecked.

cuellierguido, da [coo-el-lyee-er-gee'-do, dah], *a.* 1. Stiff-necked. 2. Elated with pride.

cuellllargo, ga [coo-el-lyee-lar'-go, gah], *a.* Longnecked.

cuello [coo-el'-lyo], *m.* 1. The neck. **Cuello de botella,** *(fig.)* Bottleneck. 2. *(Met.)* Neck of a vessel, the narrow part near its mouth. 3. Collar of a priest's garment. 4. Small end of a waxcandle. 5. A large plaited neckcloth, formerly worn. 6. Collar-band of a cloak, coat, shirt, etc. **Cuello alto,** high collar. **De cuello blanco,** white-collar. 7. Collar of a beam in oilmills. **Levantar el cuello,** *(Met.)* to be in a state of prosperity.

cuenca [coo-on'-cah], *f.* 1. A wooden bowl. 2. Socket of the eye. 3. The basin of a river. 4. Deep valley surrounded by mountains.

cuenco [coo-en'-co], *m.* 1. An earthen bowl. 2. *(Prov.)* Hod.

cuenda [coo-en'-dah], *f.* 1. End of packthread, which divides and keeps together a skein of silk or thread. 2. End of a skein of silk or thread.

cuenta [coo-en'-tah], *f.* 1. Computation, calculation. 2. Account, count, reckoning. 3. Account, narrative. 4. Obligation, care, duty. 5. One of the beads of a rosary. 6. Answerableness; reason, satisfaction. 7. Consideration, merit, importance. *(interj.)* **¡Cuenta!** take care! **Cuenta corriente,** *(Com.)* Current account ; *(Com.)* **Cuenta de venta,** account sales. **A buena cuenta** or **a cuenta,** on account, in part payment. **A esa cuenta,** at that rate. **Dar cuenta de su persona,** to answer, or give a justificatory account of what has been intrusted to any one. **Dar cuenta,** to answer, to give account. **Dar cuenta de algo,** *(Coll.)* to waste or destroy something. **Estar fuera de cuenta,** to have completed the full term of pregnancy. **Tomar en cuenta**, to take into account. **Tomar por su cuenta**, to take care of. **En resumidas cuentas**, in short. **Perder la cuenta**, to lose track (count). **Cuenta de la vieja**, counting on one´s fingers. **Contar al revés**, countdown. **Cuenta de ahorros**, savings account. **Abrir una cuenta**, to open an account. **La cuenta del sastre**, the tailor´s bill. **Cuenta de gastos**, expense account. **Echar las cuentas**, to reckon up. **Llevar la cuenta de**, to keep an account of. **Vivir a cuenta de**, to live at the expense of. **Ajustar cuentas**, to settle up. **Tener cuentas pendientes con uno**, to have a matter to settle with somebody. **Rendir cuentas de uno**, to report to somebody. **De cuenta y riesgo de uno**, at one´s own risk. **Por mi cuenta**, in my opinion. **No querer cuentas con uno**, to want nothing to do with somebody. **No tiene cuenta**, there is no point in. **Por la cuenta que le tiene**, because it is to his benefit.

cuenta correntista [coo-ayn-tah-cor-ren-tes'-tah], *m. & f.* Depositor.

cuenta corriente [coo-en'-tah cor-reen´-tay], *f.* 1. Charge account. 2. Checking account.

cuentagotas [coo-en-tah-go'-tahs], *m.* Dropper, medicine dropper.

cuentahilos [coo-en-tah-ee'-los], *m.* Thread counter, a kind of microscope for counting the threads in a fabric.

cuenta inversa [coo-en-tah in-ver'-sah], *f. (Aer.)* Countdown.

cuentakilómetros [coo-en-tah-ke-lo'-may-tros], *m.* A milometer; speedmeter.

cuentapasos [coo-en-tah-pah'-sos], *m.* Odometer, an instrument for measuring distances.

cuentarrevoluciones [co-en-tahr-re-vo-loo-the-o-nays], *m.* Tachometer.

cuentear [coo-en-tay-ar'], *va. (And.)* To court (pretender); to compliment. -*vn. (CAm.)* To gossip.

cuenterete [coo-en-tay-ray'-tay], *m. (CAm.)* Piece of gossip; tall story, tale.

cuentero, ra, [coo-en-tay'-ro], *m. & f. & a.* V. CUENTISTA.

cuentista [coo-en-tees'-tah], *m.* Tale-bearer, informer, misrepresenter.

cuento [coo-en'-to], *m.* 1. Relation of an event, tale, story. 2. Fable, fictitious story for children. **Cuento de viejas**, old women's stories, idle story. 3. Variance, disagreement between friends. **Andar en cuentos**, to be at loggerheads; to carry tales, to breed quarrels. 4. Articulation of the wing. 5. Account, number. **A cuento**, to the purpose, seasonably, opportunely. **Ése es el cuento**, there is the rub, that is the difficulty. **Dejarse de cuentos**, or **quitarse de cuentos**, to come to the point. **En cuento de**, in place of, instead of. **Poner en cuentos**, to expose, to risk. **Ser mucho cuento**, to be excessive, exaggerated. **Cuento de hadas**, fairy tale. **Es un cuento largo**, it´s a long story. **Eso no viene a cuento**, that´s off the point. **Sin cuento**, countless. **Tener más cuento que siete viejas,** to be given to fibbing. **Han tenido no se qué cuentos entre ellos**, they´ve had some upset among themselves. **Tiene mucho cuento**, he makes a lot of fuss.

cuento 2 [coo-en'-to], *m.* 1. The butt-end of a pike, spear, or like weapon. 2. Prop, shore, support. *(Yo cuento, yo cuente, from Contar. V.* ACORDAR.*)*

cuera [coo-ay'-rah], *f.* 1. A leather jacket. 2. *(LAm.)* Hide (piel); strap (correa). 3. **Cueras,** *(CAm.)* Leggings. 4. *(And. Carib. CAm.)* Flogging (paliza).

cuerazo [coo-ay-rah'-tho], *m. (LAm.)* Lashing.

cuerda [coo-err'-dah], *f.* 1. Cord, rope, halter, string, (fishing) line. 2. A string for musical instruments, catgut or wire. 3. Compass, number of notes which a voice reaches; the four fundamental voices *(Acad.)* 4. *(Geom.)* Chord, a right line which joins the two ends of an arc. 5. Match for firing a gun. 6. Chain of a watch or clock. 7. *(Anat.)* Tendon. **Aflojar la cuerda**, to ease up. **Bajo cuerda**, underhandedly. **Cuerdas vocales**, vocal cords. **Dar cuerda a**, 1. To wind. 2. *(Coll.)* to give free rein to. **De cuerda automática**, selfwinding. **Tocar la cuerda sensible**, to get through to. **Cuerda floja**, tightrope. **Cuerda de tendedero**, clothesline. **Bailar en la cuer-**

da floja, to keep in with both parties. **Dar cuerda al reloj**, to wind up one´s watch. **Tienen cuerda para rato**, they´ve something to keep them going.

cuerdamente [coo-ayr-dah-men'-tay], *adv.* Prudently, advisedly, deliberately.

cuerdo, da [coo-err'-do, dah], *a.* 1. Prudent, discreet, sensible, judicious. 2. In his senses, not mad.

cuereada [coo-ay-ray-ah'-dah], *f. (LAm.)* Beating, tanning.

cuerear [coo-ay-ray-ar'], *va.* 1. *(LAm.)* To skin, to flay. 2. *(LAm.)* To whip (persona). 3. **Cuerear a uno**, *(Carib. Cono Sur)* to tear a strip off somebody.

cuerezuelo [coo-ay-ray-thoo-ay'-lo], *m.* A sucking pig. V. COREZUELO.

cuerito [coo-ay-re'-to], **De cuerita**, *adv. (LAm.)* From end to end.

cueriza [coo-ay-re-tha], *f. (LAm.)* Beating, tanning.

cuerna [coo-err'-nah], *f.* 1. A horn vessel, not which cows or goats are milked. 2. Stag's or deer's horn. 3. Sportsman's horn.

cuernecico, illo, ito [coo-er-nay-thee'-co], *m. dim.* Cornicle, a small horn.

cuernezuelo [coo-er-nay-thoo-ay'-lo], *m.* 1. *(dim.)* Cornicle, a small horn. 2. A farrier's paring-knife.

cuerno [coo-err'-no], *m.* 1. Horn, the horn of quadrupeds. 2. Feeler, the horn or antenna of insects. 3. Horn, pointed end of the moon. 4. A button at the end of a rod about which a manuscript was rolled. 5. A huntsman´s horn. 6. *(Bot.)* A spur or outgrowth resembling a horn. 7 *(Naut.)* An outrigger. 8. *(Vet.)* A disease of horses, occurring below where the saddle rests; callosity, presumably. 9. **Cuerno de ciervo**, hart's horn. **Verse en los cuernos del toro**, to be in the most imminent danger. **Poner los cuernos**, to cuckold: applied to a wife who wrongs her husband by unchastity. **Saber a cuerno quemado**, to be suspicious. **Irse al cuerno**, to fail, to fall through. **Mandar a uno al cuerno**, to tell somebody to go to hell. **Mandar algo al cuerno**, to consign something to hell.

cuero [coo-ay'-ro], *m.* 1. Pelt, the skin of an animal. 2. Leather. 3. Goat skin dressed entire, which serves as a bag to carry wine or oil. 4. *(Met.)* Toper, a great drinker. 5. *(And. Carib.)* Whore; *(And.)* Old maid (soltera); *(Carib.)* Old bag (vieja); *(And. Mex.)* Mistress (amante). 6. *(CAm. Carib.)* Cheek (descarado). 7. Wallet (cartera). **Cuero de suela**, sole leather. **En cueros** or **cueros vivos**, stark naked. **Cueros**, hangings or drapery of gilded or painted leather. **Cuero cabelludo**, scalp. **Estar hecho un cuero**, to be as drunk as a Lord. **Arrimar el cuero a uno**, *(LAm.)* to give somebody a beating.

cuerpada [coo-ayr-pah'-dah], *f.* **Tiene buena cuerpada**, *(Cono Sur)* she´s got a good body.

cuerpear [coo-ayr-pay-ar'], *vn. (Cono Sur)* To dodge.

cuerpecico, illo, ito, cuerpezuelo [coo-er-pay-thee'-co], *m. dim.* A small body or carcass.

cuerpo [coo-err'-po], *m.* 1. Body, material substance. 2. Body of an animal; also more narrowly, the trunk. 3. Cadaver, a corpse, a dead body. 4. Body, matter; opposed to spirit. 5. Body, corporation, guild, any corporate body. 6. *(Geom.)* Body, any solid figure. 7. *(Arch.)* Floor or story in a building. 8. Volume, book. **Su librería contiene dos mil cuerpos de libros**, his library contains two thousand volumes. 9. The whole of a book, except the preface and index. 10. *(Law.)* Body, a collection of laws. **Cuerpo de doctrina**, body of teaching. **Cuerpo de leyes**, body of laws. 11. Degree of thickness of silks, woollens, or cottons. 12. Body, size; strength, thickness of liquids. **Un vino de mucho cuerpo**, a strongbodied wine. 13. Body; a collective mass. Body, in several other senses; as a body of a musical instrument, of ore, of scientific or diplomatic persons, etc. 14. Personal disposition; *(Acad.)* **Cuerpo del ejército**, the main body of an army. **Cuerpo de batalla de una escuadra**, the center division of a fleet. **Cuerpo a cuerpo**, hand to hand; in single combat. **A cuerpo descubierto**, 15. without cover or shelter.

16. manifestly. **Cuerpo del delito**, corpus delicti. **Cuerpo de Dios, de mí, de tal**; an exclamation denoting anger or vexation. **Cuerpo de guardia**, a guardroom. **Tratar a cuerpo de rey**, to feast like a king. **Tomar cuerpo**, to increase to enlarge. **En cuerpo y alma**, *(Coll.)* totally, wholly. **Estar de cuerpo presente**, to be actually present; also, to lie in state after death. **Misa de cuerpo presente**, a mass said while the corpse of the deceased is present in the church. **Cantar cuando lo pide el cuerpo**, to sing when one has a mind to. **Luchar cuerpo a cuerpo**, to fight hand-to-hand. **Con el cuerpo en tierra**, to fall down. **Ir a cuerpo**, to go without a coat. **Cuerpo estatal**, public body. **Cuerpo de intendencia**, service corps. **Cuerpo compuesto**, compound.

cuerpo aéreo [coo-err'-po ah-ay'-ray-o], *m.* Air corps.

cuerudo [coo-ay-roo'-do], *a.* 1. *(LAm.)* Slow, sluggish (caballo); lazy. 2. *(LAm.)* Annoying (persona). 3. *(Cono Sur)* brave, tough. 4. *(CAm. Carib.)* Impudent, cheeky.

cuerva [coo-err'-vah], *f.* 1. *(Orn.)* Crow, rook. 2. A fish very common on the Cantabrian, Biscay, coasts.

cuervo [coo-err'-vo], *m.* 1. *(Orn.)* Raven, crow. 2. **Cuervo marino**, cormorant. 3. *(Astr.)* A southern constellation. **No poder ser el cuervo más negro que las alas**, the crow cannot be blacker than its wings; greater evil is not to be feared; the worst is over.

cuesco [coo-es'-co], *m.* 1. Kernel, the stone or core of pulpy fruit. 2. Millstone of an oilmill. 3. Wind from behind. 4. Punch, bash. 5. Loud fart (pedo).

cuesquillo [coo-es-keel'-lyo], *m. dim.* A small kernel or stone of fruit.

cuesta [coo-es'-tah], *f.* 1. Hill, mount. 2. Any ground rising with a slope. 3. Quest, gathering, charity, money collected by begging. 4. Coast. **Ir cuesta abajo**, to go downhill. **Ir cuesta arriba**, to go uphill. **Cuesta arriba**, painfully; with great trouble and difficulty. 5. **A cuestas**, on one's shoulders or back. 6. To one's charge or care. **Hemos vencido la cuesta ya**, we're over the hump now. **Echar algo a cuestas**, to put something on one's back, *(fig.)* to take on the burden of something.

cuestación [coo-es-tah-the-on'], *f.* Petition, solicitation for a charitable purpose.

cuestero [coo-es-tay'-ro], *m.* One who collects alms or charity.

cuestión [coo-es-te-on'], *f.* 1. Question, inquiry. **Cuestión clave**, key question. **La cosa en cuestión**, the matter at issue. **Eso es otra cuestión**, that's another matter. 2. Question, dispute, quarrel. **La cuestión es que...**, the trouble is that... **No quiero questiones con los empleados**, I don't want trouble with the staff. 3. Problem. 4. Dough, money.

cuestionable [coo-es-te-o-nah'-blay], *a.* Questionable, problematical.

cuestionamiento [coo-es-te-o-nah-me-ayn'-to], *m.* Questioning.

cuestionar [coo-es-te-o-nar'], *va.* To question, to dispute.

cuestionario [coo-es-te-o-nah'-re-o], *m.* Questionnaire.

cuestor [coo-es-tor'], *m.* 1. Questor, a magistrate of ancient Rome. 2. Mendicant, one who collects alms.

cuestor, ra [coo-ays-tor'], *m. & f.* Charity collector.

cuestuoso, sa [coo-es-to-o-so, sah], *a.* Lucrative, productive.

cuete [coo-ay'-tay], *a. (Mex.)* Drunk. *-m.* 1. *(And. CAm. Mex.)* Pistol. 2. *(CAm. Mex.)* V. COHETE. 3. *(Mex.)* Drunkenness. 4. *(Mex.) (Culin.)* Steak.

cuetearse [coo-ay-tar' say], *vr. (And.)* 1. To go off, to explode. 2. To kick the bucket.

cueto [coo-ay'-to], *m.* A lofty place, defended.

cuetzale [coo-et-thah'-lay], *m. (Orn.)* A large Mexican bird of golden green plumage. V. QUETZAL.

cueva [coo-ay'-vah], *f.* 1. Cave, grot, grotto, a subterraneous cavity. 2. Cellar. **Cueva de ladrones**, nest of thieves. **Cueva de fieras**, den of wild beasts.

cuévano [coo-ay'-vah-no], *m.* 1. A basket, or hamper, somewhat wider at the top than below. 2. *(Min.)* Sump basket.

cuevero [coo-ay-vay'-ro], *m.* One who makes caves and grottoes.

cuezo [coo-ay'-tho], *m.* 1. Hod for carrying mortar. 2. Skirt, petticoat; *(Acad.)* **Meter el cuezo**, to put in an oar, to intrude.

cúfico, ca [coo'-fe-co, cah], *a.* Cufic, relating to Cufa; said of the characters in which Arabic was written before the 10th century.

cuguar [coo-goo-ar'], *m. (Zool.)* Puma, cougar.

cugujada [coo-goo-hah'-dah], *f. (Orn.)* Common field-lark, skylark.

cugulla [coo-gool'lyah], *f.* Cowl. V. COGULLA.

cuí [coo-e'], *m. (LAm.)* Guinea-pig.

cuica [coo-e-cah], *f. (And.)* Earthworm.

cuico [coo-e'-co], *a. (And.)* Thin; *(Carib.)* Rachitic, feeble. *-m.* 1. *(Cono Sur)* foreigner, outsider. 2. *(And. Cono Sur)* Bolivian. 3. *(Carib.)* Mexican. 4. *(Mex.)* Policeman.

cuida [coo-ee'-dah], *f.* In ladies' seminaries, a young lady who takes care of another of tender age.

cuidadero, ra [coo-e-day'-ro], *m. & f. (Zool.)* Keeper.

cuidado [coo-e-dah'-do], *m.* 1. Care, solicitude, attention, heed, heedfulness. 2. Care, keeping, custody, charge or trust conferred. 3. Care, caution, fear, apprehension, anxiety. 4. Followed by prep. *con* and the name of a person, denotes vexation. **Estar con cuidado**, to be anxious. **Eso me trae sin cuidado**, I'm not worried about that. **Andarse con cuidado**, to go carefully. **Poner mucho cuidado en algo**, to take great care over something. **Hay que tener cuidado con él**, you have to handle him carefully. *-int.* **¡Cuidado!** Look out! stop! beware! **Está al cuidado de la computadora**, he's in charge of the computer. **Los niños están al cuidado de la abuela**, the children are in their grandmother's charge.

cuidador [coo-e-dah-dor'], *m.* Second (boxeo); trainer. **Cuidador de campo**, groundsman.

cuidadora [coo-e-dah-do'-rah], *f. (Mex.)* Nursemaid, nanny.

cuidadosamente [coo-e-dah-do-sah-men'-tay], *adv.* Carefully, attentively, heedfully, mindfully, cautiously, providently.

cuidadoso, sa [coo-e-dah-do'-so, sah], *a.* Careful, solicitous; vigilant, heedful, mindful, painstaking, curious, observing.

cuidaniños [coo-e-dah-nee'-nyos], *m. & f.* Babysitter.

cuidar [coo-e-dar'], *va.* To heed, to care; to execute with care, diligence, and attention; to keep, to mind, to look after. **Ella cuida a los niños**, she looks after the children. **No cuidan la casa**, they don't look after the house. *-vn.* 1. **Cuidar de**, to take care of. **Cuide de que no pase nadie**, see that nobody gets in. **Cuide de no caer**, take care not to fall. 2. **Cuida con esa gente**, be wary of those people. *-vr.* 1. To look after oneself. 2. **Cuidarse de algo**, to worry about something. 3. **Cuidar muy bien de**, to take good care not to.

cuido [coo-e'-do], *m.* Care, minding. **Para su cuido**, for your own good.

cuita [coo-e'-tah], *f.* (1.) Care, grief, affliction, trouble. 2. *(Ant.)* Ardent desire, craving. **Contar sus cuitas**, to tell one's troubles.

cuitadamente [coo-e-tah-dah-men'-tay], *adv.* Slothfully, afflictedly.

cuitadico, ica, illo, illa, ito, ita [coo-e-tah-dee'-co], *a. dim.* 1. Timid, chicken-hearted. 2. Having some slight trouble or affliction.

cuitado, da [coo-e-tah'-do, dah], *a.* 1. Anxious, wretched, miserable. 2. Chicken-hearted, pusillanimous, timid.

cuja [coo'-hah], *f.* 1. Bag, formerly fastened to the saddle, into which a spear or flagstaff was put for easier carriage. 2. Bedstead. 3. *(Obs.)* Thigh. 4. *(CAm. Mex.)* Envelope.

cujarda [coo-har-dah], *f. (Bot.)* V. CORONILLA DE FRAILE.

cuje [coo'-hay], *m. (Cuba)* Withe, each of three slender flexible rods, made of any wood, of which a kind of crane, or gallows, is made for suspending the stems in gathering tobacco. **Cujes** *pl.* Hoop-poles.

cujinillos [coo-he-nel-lyos], *m. & pl. (Mex.)* Saddlebags.

culada

culada [coo-lah'-dah], *f.* 1. Stroke with the backside or breech of anything. 2. Fall on one's backside. **Culadas**, *(Naut.)* Shocks and rollings of a ship.

culamen [coo-lah'-men], *m.* Bottom.

culandrón [coo-lahn-drone'], *m.* Queer.

culantrillo, or **Culantrillo de pozo** [coo-lan-treel'-lyo], *m.* Maiden's hair.

culantro [coo-lahn'-tro], *m. (Bot.)* Coriander. *V.* CORIANDRO and CILANTRO.

culata [coo-lah'-tah], *f.* 1. Breech of a gun, buttend of a musket. 2. Screwpin, which fastens the breech of a gun to the stock. 3. The back part of anything. **Dar de culata**, to recoil, among coachmen and carriage makers. **Dar la culata**, means to lift the back of the vehicle in order to remove it without disturbing the front part. 4. *(Cono Sur)* Shelter, hut.

culatada [coo-lah-tah'-dah], *f.* Kick, recoil of a firearm.

culatazo [coo-lah-tah'-tho], *m.* Recoil of a gun or musket.

culazo [coo-lah'-tho], *m. aug.* A large backside.

culcusido [cool-coo-see'-do], *m.* Botch-work, anything clumsily sewed. *V.* CORCUSIDO.

culear [coo-lay-ar'], *va. (And. Cono Sur, Mex.)* To fuck. -*vn.* 1. To waggle one's bottom (mover el culo). 2. *(And. Cono Sur, Mex.)* To fuck.

culebra [coo-lay'-brah], *f.* 1. Snake. 2. Trick, fun, joke. *V.* CULEBRAZO. 3. The worm, spiral part of a still. 4. Disorder, confusion suddenly made by a few in a peaceful assembly. **Sabe más que las culebras**, *(Coll.)* he is very crafty and cunning. **Culebra de cascabel**, a rattlesnake. 5. *(And.)* Debt, bill. 6. *(Mex.)* Waterspout. 7. *(Mex.)* Hosepipe (manga).

culebrear [coo-laybray-ar'], *vn.* 1. To move like a snake; to crankle. 2. *(Carib.)* To stall, to hedge.

culebreo [coo-lay-bray'-o], *m.* Wriggling; zigzag; winding, meandering.

culebrilla [coo-lay-breel'-lyah], *f.* 1. Tetter, ringworm; a cutaneous disease. 2. Rocking-staff of a loom. 3. Fissure in a gunbarrel.

culebrina [coo-lay-bree'-nah], *f. (Mil.)* Culverin.

culebrino, na [coo-lay-bree'-no, nah], *a.* Snake, snaky.

culebrón [coo-lay-brone'], *m.* 1. A crafty fellow; a double dealer. 2. A long T.V. serial.

culebrona [coo-lay-bro'-nah], *f.* An intriguing woman.

culeco [coo-lay'-co], *a.* 1. *(LAm.)* Broody (gallina). 2. *(LAm.)* Home-loving. 3. **Estar culeco**, *(And. Carib, Cono Sur)* to be head over heels in love. 4. **Estar culeco con algo**, *(And. CAm. Carib, Mex.)* To be very pleased about something.

culera [coo-lay'-rah], *f.* 1. Stain of urine in children's underwear. 2. A patch on the seat of drawers or trousers. *(Acad.)*.

culeras [coo-lay'-ras], *m. & f.* Coward.

culero [coo-lay'-ro], *m.* 1. Clout, diaper, a cloth for keeping children clean. 2. Disease in birds. 3. *(Mex.)* Coward. 4. *(CAm.)* Poof (maricón).

culero, ra [coo-lay'-ro, rah], *a.* Slothful, lazy.

culí [coo-le'], *m.* Coolie.

culibajo [coo-le-bah'-ho], *a.* Short, dumpy.

culícidos [coo-lee'-the-dose], *m. pl.* Culicidae, the family of gnats and mosquitoes.

culillera [coo-lel-lay'-rah], *f. (CAm.)*, **culillo** *m.* 1. *(And. CAm. Carib.)* Fear, fright. 2. **Tener culillera**, *(Carib.)* To be in a hurry.

culinario, ia [coo-le-nah'-reo, ah], *a.* Culinary, belonging to the kitchen.

culipandear [coo-le-pan-day-ar'], *vn. vr. (Carib.)* To stall, to hedge.

culito [coo-lee'-to], *m. dim.* A small breech or backside.

culmífero, ra [cool-mee'-fay-ro, rah], *a. (Bot.)* Culmiferous.

culminación [cool-me-nah-the-on'], *f.* 1. *(Astr.)* Culmination, the transit of a planet through the meridian. 2. *(Naut.)* High tide.

culminancia [cool-me-nahn'-the-ah], *f. (Poet.)* Height, elevation, peak.

culminante [cool-me-nahn'-tay], *a.* Highest, topmost, culminating; culminating (momento); outstanding.

culminar [cool-me-nar'], *vn.* 1. *(Astr.)* To culminate, to be in the meridian. 2. To be raised or elevated. 3. *(Naut.)* To reach high water.

culo [coo'-lo], *m.* 1. Breech, backside, buttock. 2. Bottom, socket. 3. Anus. 4. The lower or hinder extremity of anything. **Culo de mona**, very ugly and ridiculous thing. **Ser un culo de mal asiento**, to be restless. **Ir con el culo a rastras**, to be in a jam. **Ir de culo**, to be overloaded with work. **Ser culo de vaso**, to be false.

culón [coo-lone'], *m. (Coll.)* An invalided or retired soldier. -*a. V.* CULIGORDO.

culpa [cool'-pah], *f.* Fault, offence, slight crime, failure, guilt. **Por culpa de**, through the fault of. **Echar la culpa a uno**, to blame somebody. **Nadie tiene la culpa**, nobody is to blame. **La culpa fue de los frenos**, the brakes were to blame. **Pagar las culpas ajenas**, to pay for somebody else's sins.

culpabilidad [cool-pah-be-le-dahd'], *f.* Culpability.

culpable [cool-pah'-blay], *a.* Culpable; faulty, condemnable, accusable. **Declarar culpable a uno**, to find somebody guilty. **Es culpable no hacerlo**, it is criminal not to do it. -*m. & f.* Culprit; offender, guilty party.

culpablemente, *adv.* Culpably.

culpadamente [cool-pah-dah-men'-tay], *adv.* Culpably.

culpado, da [cool-pah'-do, dah], *n. & a.* Guilty. -*pp.* of CULPAR.

culpar [cool-par'], *va.* To blame, to impeach, to accuse, to condemn, to reproach. **Culpar a uno de algo**, to blame somebody for something.

cultamente [cool-tah-men'-tay], *adv.* 1. Neatly, elegantly, affectedly, politely.

cultedad [cool-tay-dahd'], *f.* Affected elegance and purity of style.

culteranismo [cool-tayrah-nees'-mo], *m.* Sect of purists who are affectedly nice in the use of words and phrases.

culterano, na [cool-tay-rah'-no, nah], *m. & f.* Purist with affectation.

culterano, na [cool-tay-rah'-no, nah], *a.* Relating to affected elegance and purity of style.

cultero [cool-tay'-ro], *m.* Purist with affectation.

cultiparlar [cool-te-par-lar'], *vn.* To speak with affected elegance.

cultiparlista [cool-te-par-lees'-tah], *a.* Speaking much with affected elegance and purity of language.

cultipicaño, ña [cool-te-pe-cah'-nyo, nyah], *a.* (Humorous) Speaking with affected elegance, and in a jeering manner.

cultismo [cool-tes'-mo], *m. (Ling.)* Learned word (palabra culta); gongorism.

cultivable [cool-te-vah'-blay], *a.* Cultivable, manurable, capable of cultivation.

cultivación [cool-te-vah-the-on'], *f.* Cultivation, culture.

cultivador, ra [cool-te-vah-dor'], *m. & f.* 1. Cultivator. **Cultivador de vino**, winegrower. 2. Kind of plough.

cultivar [cool-te-var'], *va.* 1. To cultivate the soil, to farm, to husband; to manure, to labor. 2. To cultivate, to preserve, to keep up: speaking of friendship, acquaintances, etc. 3. To cultivate, to exercise the memory, the talent, etc. 4. To cultivate the arts or sciences.

cultivo [cool-tee'-vo], *m.* 1. Cultivation, cultivating and improving the soil. 2. Cultivation, improvement. 3. Act of cultivating one's acquaintance or friendship. 4. Culture of the mind, elegance of manners. **El cultivo principal de la región**, the chief crop of the area. **Cultivo de secano**, dry farming.

culto, ta [cool'-to, tah], *a.* 1. Pure, elegant, correct (estilo, lenguaje). 2. Affectedly elegant. 3. Polished, enlightened, civilized (persona bien informada, nación).

culto [cool'-to], *m.* 1. Speaking in general, respect or veneration paid to a person, as a testimony of his superior excellence and worth. 2. Worship, adoration, religious act of reverence. **Culto divino**, public worship in churches. **Culto externo**, external demonstrations of respect to God and his saints, by processions, sacrifices, offerings, etc. **Culto sagrado o religioso**, honor or worship to God and the saints. **Culto superfluo**, worship by means of vain useless things. **Culto supersticioso**, worship paid either to whom it is not due, or in an improper manner.

cultro [cool'-tro], *m. (Prov.)* Plough with which the first fallow ploughing is performed.

cultrún [cool-troon'], *m. (Cono Sur) (Mus.)* Drum.

cultura [cool-too'-rah], *f.* 1. Culture, improvement or amelioration of the soil. 2. Culture and improvement of the mind. 3. Elegance of style or language. 4. Urbanity, polish of manner, politeness. **Cultura física**, physical culture. **La cultura popular**, popular culture. **Persona de cultura**, cultured person. **No tiene cultura**, he has no manners.

cultural [cool-too-rahl'], *a.* Cultural.

culturar [cool-too-rar'], *va. (Prov.)* To cultivate. V. CULTIVAR.

culturismo [cool-too-res'-mo], *m.* Body-building.

culturista [cool-too-res'-tah], *m. & f.* Body-builder.

culturizar [cool-too-re-thar'], *va.* To educate, to enlighten. *-vr.* To educate oneself.

cuma [coo'-mah], *f. (S. Amer.)* 1. Godmother. 2. Crony, female friend or neighbor. 3. *(CAm.)* Long knife.

cumarú [coo-mah-roo'], *m.* The Tonquin or Tonka bean, used for flavoring tobacco and perfuming snuff.

cumbancha [coo-bahn'-chah], *f. (Carib.)* Spree, drinking bout.

cumbé [coom-bay'], *m.* Sort of dance among the negroes, and the tune to which it is performed.

cumbia [coom-be-ah], *f. (And.)* Colombian dance music; popular Colombian dance.

cúmbila [coom'-be-lah], *m. (Carib.)* Pal, buddy.

cumbo [coom'-bo], *m.* 1. *(CAm.)* Top hat; bowler hat (hongo). 2. *(CAm.)* Narrow-mouthed cup.

cumbre [coom´-bray], **cumbrera** [coom-bray'rah], *f.* 1. Ridgepole, tiebeam, summit, top. 2. Top, summit, cop, culmination. 3. *(Met.)* The greatest height of favor, fortune, science, etc. **Conferencia cumbre**, summit conference. **está en la cumbre de su poderío**, he is at the height of his power. **Momento cumbre**, culminating point.

cume [coo'-may], *m.* **cumiche** *m. (CAm.)* Baby of the family.

cumero [coo-may'-ro], *m.* A tree of Guiana.

cumia [coo´-me-ah], *f.* Fruit of the cumero-tree, and the resin which is used for incense in the churches of Guiana.

cumíneo, nea [coo-mee´-nay-o, ah], *a.* Cumin-like.

cuminol [coo-me-nole'], *m.* Oil of cumin.

cumpa [coom'-pah], *m. (LAm.)* 1. Godfather. 2. Comrade, companion.

cúmplase [coom'-plah-say], *m.* 1. The countersign of a superior officer upon commissions in the army, or certificate of retirement. 2. A permit.

cumpleaños [coom-play-ah'-ny-os], *m.* Birthday.

cumplidamente [coom-ple-dah-men'-tay], *adv.* Completely, complimentarily.

cumplidero, ra [coom-ple-day'-ro, rah], *a.* 1. That which must be fulfilled or executed. 2. Convenient, fit, suitable, accomplishable.

cumplido, da [coom-plee'-do, dah], *a.* 1. Large, plentiful, high. **Un abrigo cumplido**, a full coat. **Una comida cumplida**, a plentiful dinner. 2. Gifted with talents, worthy of esteem, faultless. 3. Polished, polite, civil, courteous. 4. **Tiene 60 años cumplidos**, he is 60 (years old). *-pp.* of CUMPLIR.

cumplido, *m.* 1. Compliment; courtesy. **Visita de cumplido**, formal visit. **Andarse con cumplidos**, to stand on ceremony. **He venido por cumplido**, I came out of a sense of duty. 2. *(Naut.)* The length of the thing in question compared with the unit, as a cable's length.

cumplidor [coom-ple-dor'], *m.* One who executes a commission or trust.

cumplimentar [coom-ple-men-tar'], *va.* 1. To compliment or congratulate. 2. *(Law.)* To carry out superior orders.

cumplimentero, ra [coom-ple-men-tay'-ro, rah], *a. & n.* 1. *(Coll.)* Full of compliments, complimental, complaisant. 2. *complimentary.*

cumplimiento [coom-ple-meen'-to], *m.* 1. Act of complimenting or paying a compliment, complaisance, civility. 2. Compliment, accomplishment, completion, perfection, fulfilling. **Al cumplimiento del tiempo** or **del plazo**, at the expiration of the time. 3. Compliment, an expression of civility, course. **No se ande Vd. en cumplimientos**, do not stand upon compliments. 4. Complement.

cumplir [coom-pleer'], *va.* 1. To execute, discharge, or perform one's duty, fulfil. 2. To have served the time required in the militia. **Cumplir años** or **días**, to reach one's birthday. **Hoy cumple 8 años**, she´s 8 today. **Cuando cumplas los 21 años**, when you´re 21. **Cumplir de palabra**, keep one's word. **Cumplir por otro**, to do something in the name of another. **Cumpla Vd. por mí**, do it in my name. *-vn.* 1. To be fit or convenient. 2. To suffice, to be sufficient. 3. To mature, to be the time (or day) when an obligation, undertaking, ends. 4. To be realized, verified. **Por cumplir**, for mere courtesy, outward show. **El plazo se ha cumplido**, the time has expired. **Cumplir con la iglesia**, to fulfil one´s religious obligations. *-vr.* 1. To be fulfilled. 2. To expire, to end (plazo). 3. **Se obedece pero no se cumple**, the letter of the law is observed but not its spirit.

cumucho [coo-moo'-cho], *m. (Cono Sur)* 1. Gathering, mob, crowd (multitud). 2. Hut, hovel (cabaña).

cumulador [coo-moo-lah-dor'], *m.* V. ACUMULADOR.

cumular [coo-moo-lar'], *va.* To accumulate, to compile or heap together. V. ACUMULAR.

cumulativamente [coo-moo-lah-te-vah-men'-tah] , *adv.* In heaps.

cumulativo, va [coo moo-lah-tee'-vo, vah], *a.* Cumulative.

cúmulo [coo'-moo-lo], *m.* 1. Heap or pile; congeries. 2. *(Met.)* Throng of business; variety of trouble and difficulties.

cuna [coo'-nah], *f.* 1. Cradle. **Cuna portátil**, carrycot. 2. *(Prov.)* Foundling hospital 3. *(Met.)* The native soil or country. 4. Family, lineage. **De humilde** or **de ilustre cuna**, of an humble or illustrious family. 5. Origin, beginning of anything. **Cuna del famoso poeta**, the birthplace of the famous poet.

cunar, cunear [coo-nar', coo-nay-ar'], *va.* To rock a cradle. To move, rock, like a cradle.

cunasiri [coo-nah-see'-ree], *m.* Peruvian tree of pinkish aromatic wood.

cuncuna [coon-coo'-nah], *f.* Caterpillar of Chili, resembling the silkworm.

cunchos [coon'-chose], *m. pl.* Indigenous independent race in Chili.

cundido [coon-dee'-do], *m.* 1. The provision of oil, vinegar, and salt given to shepherds. 2. Honey or cheese given to boys to eat with their bread -**Cundido, da**, *pp.* of CUNDIR.

cundir [coon-deer'], *va. (Obs.)* To occupy, to fill.-*vn.* 1. To spread (líquidos). 2. To yield abundantly. 3. To grow, to increase, to propagate. **Cunde el rumor que...**, there´s a rumor going round that... **Hoy no me ha cundido el trabajo**, work did not go well for me today.

cunear [coo-nay-ar'], *va.* To rock, to craddle. *-vr.* To rock, to sway; to swing along, to walk with a roll.

cuneario, ia [coo-nay-ah'-reo, ah], *a. (Bot.)* Wedge-shaped.

cuneco [coo-nay'-co], *m. (Carib.)* Baby of the family.

cuneiforme [coo-nay-e-for'-may], *a.* Cuneiform, in the form of a wedge.

cúneo [coo'-nay-o], *m.* 1. *(Obs. Mil.)* Triangular formation of troops. 2. Space between the passages in ancient theaters.

cuneo [coo-nay´-o], *m.* 1. Rocking. 2. *(Naut.)* Rolling, pitching.

cunero ra [coo-nay'-ro, rah], *m. & f. (Prov.)* A foundling.

cuneta [coo-nay´-tah], *f. (Mil.)* A small trench made in a dry ditch or moat of a fortress, to drain off the rainwater, side culvert.

cunicultura [coo-ne-cool-too-rah], *f.* Rabbit breeding.

cuña [coo´-nyah], *f.* 1. Wedge, quoin. 2. Any object employed in splitting or dividing a body. 3. A chip, splinter, driven with a hammer. **Cuñas de mango**, *(Naut.)* Horsing-irons. **Cuñas de puntería**, *(Mil.)* Gun-quoins. 4. **Meter cuña**, to sow discord. 5. *(LAm.)* Influential person. 6. Influence, pull. **Tener cuñas**, to have pull. 7. *(CAm. Carib.) (Aut.)* Two-seater car. 8. (Rad, TV) spot, slot.

cuñadería [coo-nyah-day-ree´-ah], *f.* Spiritual affinity contracted by being godfather to a child.

cuñadía, *f.* **cuñadío,** *m.* [coo-nyah-dee'-ah, coo-nyah-dee'-o]. Kindred by affinity.

cuñadismo [coo-nay-des'-mo], *m.* Nepotism, old boys network.

cuñado da [coo-nyah'-do, dah], *m. & f.* A brother or sister-in-law.

cuñete [coo-nyay'-tay], *m.* Keg, firkin.

cuño [coo'-nyo], *m.* 1. Die for coining money. 2. Impression made by the die. 3. Mark put on silver. 4. A triangular formation of troops.

cuociente [cwo-the-en'-tay], *m.* V. COCIENTE.

cuedlibético, ca [kwod-le-bay'-te-co, cah], *a.* Quodlibetic, not restricted to a particular subject.

cuodlibeto [kwo-dle-bay'-to], *m.* 1. A debatable point; discussion upon a scientific subject chosen by the author. 2. A thesis, scholastic dissertation in ancient universities. 3. A pungent saying, sharp sometimes, trivial and flat at others, not directed to a useful end.

cuota [coo-o´-tah], *f.* Quota, contingent, fixed share. **Cuota de enseñanza**, school fees. **Cuota de socio**, membership fee.

cuotidiano [coo-o-te-de-ah'-no], *a.* V. COTIDIANO.

cupano [coo-pah'-no], *m.* A great tree of the Philippine Islands, the bark yielding a dye-stuff and the wood fit for building.

cupé [coo-pay'], *m.* 1. Landau, a fourwheeled carriage. 2. Coupé, a car with two doors.

cupido [coo-pee'-do], *m.* 1. Bit of steel taken out of the eye of a needle. 2. Cupid. 3. A gallant, wooer, lover.

cupitel [coo-pe-tel'] **Tirar de cupitel**, to throw a bowl archwise.

cuplé [coo-play'], *m.* Pop song.

cupletista [coo-play-tes'-tah], *f.* Cabaret singer.

cupo [coo'-po], *m.* 1. Quota; share. **Cupo de azúcar**, sugar quota. 2. *(Mex.)* Space, room, capacity; *(And. Carib. Mex.)* Empty seat, vacancy. **No hay cupo**, there´s no room.

cupón [coo-pone'], *m.* Coupon, a voucher for interest attached to a bond. **Cupón de los ciegos**, ticket for the lottery for the blind. **Cupón de dividendos**, dividend voucher.

cuprero [coo-pray'-ro], *a. (Cono Sur)* copper.

cupresino na [coo-pray-see'-no, nah], *a. (Poet.)* Belonging to the cypress-tree, or made of cypress-wood.

cúprico, ca [coo'-pre-co, cah], *a.* Cupric, belonging to copper.

cuproso, sa [coo-pro´-so, sah], *a.* Cuprous, like copper. Cuprous, combining in a lower equivalence than cupric.

cúpula [coo'-poo-lah], *f.* 1. Cupola, dome. 2. The turret of a monitor. 3. *(Bot.)* Cupule, cup, a sort of involucre. 4. *(Pol.)* Party, leadership, leading members.

cupulífero, ra [coo-poo-lee'-fay-ro, rah], *a.* Cupuliferous, cupbearing.

cupulino [coo-poo-lee'no], *m.* Lantern a small cupola raised upon another, which serves to light the vault.

cuquería [coo-kay-re'-ah], *f.* Craftiness.

cuquillero [coo-keel-lyay'-ro], *m. (Prov.)* Baker's boy, who fetches the paste of bread, and carries it back when baked.

cuquillo [coo-keel'lyo], *m.* 1. *(Orn.)* Cuckoo. V. CUCLILLO. 2. *(Ent.)* Insect which consumes the vines.

cura [coo´-rah], *m.* 1. Parish priest, rector, curate. **Cura párroco**, parish priest. 2. In Castile, it is commonly used to denote any clergyman, priest, or parson. -*f.* 1. Cure, healing, the act and effect of healing or of restoring to health. **Primera cura**, first aid. **Cura de reposo**, rest cure. **No tiene cura**, there´s no remedy. 2. Guardianship. 3. Parsonage, the benefice of a parish. **Los derechos de cura,** the dues or fees of a rector, parson, or curate, with a parochial charge.

curable [coo-rah'-blay], *a.* Curable, healable.

curaca [coo-rah-cah], *f.* 1. *(And.)* Priest´s housekeeper. 2. *(And.)* Indian chief, Indian native authority.

curación [coo-rah-the-on'], *f.* Cure, healing.

curadero [coo-rah-day'-ro], *m.* Place for bleaching woven goods and other objects.

curadillo [coo-rah-deel'-lyo], *m.* 1. *(Prov.)* Codfish, lingfish. 2. *(Tec.)* Bleached linen.

curado, da [coo-rah'-do, dah], *a.* Rectorial, belonging to the rector of a parish; relating to a rectory or parsonage.-*a. & pp.* of CURAR. 1. Cured, strengthened, restored to health. 2. Hardened, strengthened, or tanned. 3. Cured, salted.

curador [coo-rah-dor'], *m.* 1. Overseer. **Curador de bacalao**, codsalter. 2. Guardian, one who has the care of minors and orphans. 3. Physician, surgeon, healer. 4. Curator, administrator.

curadora [coo-rah-do´-rah], *f.* 1. Guardianess, a female guardian. 2. Healer.

curaduría [coo-rah-doo-ree'-ah], *f.* Guardianship.

curalle [coo-rahl'-lyay], *m.* Physic administered to a hawk.

curanderismo [coo-rahn-day-res'-mo], *m.* Quack medicine.

curandero [coo-ran-day'-ro], *m.* Quack, medicaster, an artful and tricking practitioner in physic.

curar [coo-rar'], *va. & vn.* 1. To cure, to heal, to restore to health, to administer medicines. 2. To prescribe the medicine or diet of a patient. 3. To salt, to cure meat or fish, to preserve. 4. To bleach thread, linen, or clothes. 5. To season timber. 6. To recover from sickness. 7. *(Met.)* To remedy an evil. **Curarse en salud**, *(Coll.)* 1. To guard against evil, when there is little or no danger. 2. To defend oneself, without being accused. 3. To confess a fault, to avoid reproach. -*vr.* 1. *(Med.)* To recover, to get better; to heal up (herida etc.). 2. **Curarse de**, to take notice of. 3. *(And. Cono Sur)* to get drunk, to get tight.

curare [coo-rah'-ray], *m.* Curare, or woorari, an extract obtained from Strychnos toxifera, a powerful blood-poison, used by South American Indians as an arrow-poison.

curatela [coo-rah-tay'-lah], *f. (Legal.)* V. CURADURÍA.

curativo, va [coo-rah-tee'-vo, vah], *a.* Curative.

curato [coo-rah'-to], *m.* 1. The charge of souls. 2. Parish, the district committed to the care of a rector or parson. **Curato anejo**, a small parish, annexed to another.

curca [coor-cah], *f. (And. Cono Sur)* Hump.

curco [coor'-co], *a. (And. Cono Sur)* Hunchbacked.

curculiónido, da [coor-coo-le-o'-ne-do, dah], *a.* Curculionid, like the curculio.

cúrcuma [coor'-coo-mah], *f.* 1. Turmeric, a root resembling ginger. 2. Turmeric, the yellow coloring-matter obtained from curcuma, useful in chemistry for testing for alkalies, which turn it brown.

curcumáceo, cea [coor-coo-mah'-thay-o, ah], *a.* Resembling turmeric.

curcumina [coor-coo-mee'-nah], *f.* Turmeric yellow, the coloring-matter of curcuma.

curcuncho [coor-coon-cho], *a.* 1. *(LAm.)* Hunchbacked (jorobado). 2. Fed up; annoyed (molesto). -*m. (LAm.)* Hunchback.

curda [coor'-dah], *m.* Drunk, sot. -*f.* Drunkenness. **Agarrar una curda**, to get sozzled. **Estar en curda**, *(Cono Sur)* to be sozzled.

cureña [coo-ray'-nyah], *f.* 1. Guncarriage. 2. Stay of a crossbow. 3. A gunstock in the rough. **A cureña rasa**, 4. Without a parapet or breastwork (militar). 5. *(Coll. Met.)* without shelter or defence. **Tirar a cureña rasa**, to fire at random.

cureñaje [coo-ray-nyah'-hay], *m.* Collection of gun carriages.

curesca [coo-res'-cah], *f.* Shearwool cut off by a clothier with shears when the cloth has been combed.

curia [coo'-reah], *f.* 1. A tribunal, court, more often used of ecclesiastical matters. 2. Care, skill, nice attention. 3. An ancient Roman division of people.

curial [coo-re-ahl'], *a.* Relating to the Roman *curia,* or tribunal for ecclesiastical affairs.

curial [coo-re-al], *m.* 1. A member of the Roman *curia.* 2. One who employs an agent in Rome to obtain bulls or rescripts. 3. One in a subaltern employ in the tribunals of justice, or who is occupied with other's affairs.

curiana [coo-re-ah'-nah], *f.* A cockroach. *V.* CUCARACHA.

curiche [coo-re'-chay], *m. (Cono Sur)* negro.

curiosamente [coo-re-o-sah-men'-tay], *adv.* 1. Curiously. 2 Neatly, cleanly. 3. In a diligent; careful manner.

curiosear [coo-re-o-say-ar'], *vn.* To busy oneself in discovering what others are doing and saying. **Curiosear por las tiendas,** to wander round the shops. **Curiosear por los escaparates,** to go window-shopping. *-va.* To glance at, to look over.

curiosidad [coo-re-o-se-dahd'], *f.* 1. Curiosity, inquisitiveness, curiousness. **Despertar la curiosidad de uno,** to arouse somebody´s curiosity. **Estar muerto de curiosidad,** to be dying of curiosity. 2. Neatness, cleanliness. 3. An object of curiosity, rarity.

curioso, sa [coo-re-oh'-so, sah], *a.* 1. Curious, inquisitive, desirous of information. **Estar curioso por,** to be curious to. 2. Neat, clean. 3. Careful, attentive, diligent. 4. Odd, curious, exciting attention.

curiosón, sona [coo-re-o-sone'], *m. & f.* Busybody.

curita [coo-re'-tah], *f. (LAm.)* Plaster.

currante [coor-rahn'-tay], *m. & f.* Worker, laborer.

currar, currelar [coor-rahr'], *vn.* To work.

currele, currelo [coor-ray-lo], *m.* Work; job; activity.

currículo [coor-re'-coo-loom], *m.* Curriculum.

currinche [coor-ren'-chay], *m.* 1. *(Typ.)* Apprentice journalist, cub reporter. 2. Little man (persona insignificante).

curro [coor-ro], *a.* 1. Smart; showy, flashy. 2. Cocky, brashy, confident. *-m.* 1. Work; job. 2. Bashing, beating (golpes). **Dar un curro a uno,** to beat somebody up.

curroadicto, ta [coor-ro-a-dec'-to], *m. & f.* Workaholic.

curruca [coor-roo'-cah], *f. (Orn.)* Linnet, babbling warbler.

currutaca [coo-roo-tah'-cah], *f.* A woman fond of show, dress, and flutter.

currutaco [coor-roo-tah'-co], *m.* 1. Beau, fop, dandy, coxcomb, dude. 2. Insignificant little man. 3. *(CAm.)* Curratos, diarrhoea.

currutaco, ca, *a.* 1. Belonging to a person affectedly nice in his or her dress. 2. Loud, showy, flashy (ostentoso). 3. Short, squat (bajito).

currutaquería [coo-roo-tah-kay-ree'-ah], *f.* Dandyism, coxcombry.

cursado, da [coor-sah' do, dah], *a.* Accustomed, habituated, inured. *-pp.* of CURSAR.

cursante [coor-san'-tay], *pa.* 1. Frequenting; assiduous. 2. One who hears lectures in a university; student, scholar.

cursar [coor-sar'], *va.* 1. To frequent a place, to repeat a thing. 2. To follow the schools, or to follow a course of lectures in the universities. *-vn.* **El mes que cursa,** the present month.

curseta [coor-say'-tah], *f.* A snake of the island of Martinique.

cursi [coor'-se], *a.* Pretentious, vulgar, shoddy.

cursilería [coor-se-lay-re'-ah], *f.* Bad taste, vulgarity; pretentiousness; loudness, showiness, flashiness; poshness, gentility.

cursillo [coor-seel'-lyo], *m. dim.* A short course of lectures on any science in a university.

cursilón, ona [coor-se-lone'], *m. & f.* Common but pretentious person; flashy type; posh sort, genteel individual.

cursivo, va [coor-see'vo, vah], *a.* Relating to Italic characters in printing; cursive, script.

curso [coor'-so], *m.* 1. Course, direction, career. 2. Course of lectures in universities. **Los de segundo curso,** those in the second year. **Curso por correspondencia,** correspondence course. 3. Course, a collection of the principal treatises used in instruction in some branch in the universities. 4. Course, a series of sucessive and methodical procedures. 5. Laxity or looseness of the body: generally used in the plural. **Curso de la corriente,** *(Naut.)* The current's way. **Curso de la marea,** *(Naut.)* the tide's way. 6. *(fig.)* Course. **El curso de la enfermedad,** the course of the disease. **Dejar que las cosas sigan su curso,** to let matters take their course. **El proceso está en curso,** the process is going on.

cursor [coor-sor'], *m.* Slider, slide.

curtación [coor-tah-the-on'], *f. (Astr.)* The curtate distance. *V.* ACORTAMIENTO.

curtidero [coor-te-day'-ro], *m.* Ground tanbark.

curtido, da [coor-tee'-do, dah], *a.* 1. Accustomed; dexterous, expert. 2. Weather-beaten, tanned. 3. **Estar curtido en,** *(fig.)* To be expert at. *-m.* 1. Tanning (acto). 2. Tanned leather, tanned hides.

curtidor [coor-te-dor'], *m.* Tanner, Currier, leather-dresser.

curtidos [coor-tee'-dose], *m. pl.* Tanned leather; sometimes singular.

curtiduría [coor-te-doo-ree'-ah], *f.* Tanyard, tannery.

curtiente [coor-te-en'-tay], *a.* A powdery astringent substance serving to tan hides.

curtimbre [coor-teem'-bray], *f.* 1. Tanning 2. The total of the hides tanned.

curtimiento [coor-te-meen'-to], *m.* Tanning.

curtir [coor-teer'], *va.* 1. To tan leather. 2. To imbrown by the sun, to tan the complexion: commonly used in its reciprocal sense. 3. To inure to hardships, to harden. **Estar curtido,** *(Coll.)* to be habituated, accustomed, or inured. *-vr.* 1. To become tanned, to become bronzed. 2. To become inured. 3. *(LAm.)* To get oneself dirty.

curto, ta [coor'-to, tah], *a. (Prov.)* Short docktailed.

curú [coo-roo'], *m. (Peru)* Clothes moth.

curuca, curuja [coo-roo'-cah' coo-roo-hah], *f. (Orn.)* Eagle-owl.

curucucú [coo-roo-coo-coo'], *m.* A disease caused by the bite of a certain South American snake.

curul [coo-rool'], *a.* Curule, belonging to a senatorial or triumphal chair in ancient Rome. Edile.

curva [coor'-vah], *f.* 1. Curve, a curved line. 2. *(Naut.)* Knee, timber hewed like a knee. **Curva cuadrada,** square knee. **Curvas verticales de las cubiertas,** hanging knees of the decks. **Curva de la felicidad,** paunch, beer belly. **Curva de nivel,** contour line.

curva cerrada [coor'-vah ther-rah'-dah], *f.* Sharp bend (road sign).

curva doble, curva completa or **curva en U,** *f.* U-turn (road sign).

curvativo, va [coor-vah-tee'-vo, vah], *a. (Bot.)* Involute, rolling inward.

curvato [coor vah'-to], *m.* Bastinado, whipping the feet, an oriental punishment.

curvatón [coor-vah-tone'], *m. (Naut.)* Little knee or small knee.

curvatura, curvidad [coor-vah-too'-rah, coor-ve-dahd'], *f.* 1. Curvature, inflexion. 2. *(Naut.)* Curvature of any piece of timber.

curvilíneo, nea [coor-ve-lee'-nay-o, ah], *a. (Geom.)* Curvilinear.

curvo, va [coor'-vo, vah], *a.* 1. Curved, crooked, bent. 2. *(And.)* Bow-legged. 3. *(Carib.)* Left-handed.

cusca [coos'-cah], *f.* 1. **Hacer la cusca a uno**, to play a dirty trick on somebody; to harm somebody. 2. *(CAm.)* To flirt (coqueta). 3. *(Mex.)* Whore.

cuscurrante [coor-roos-cahn'-tay], *a.* Crunchy, crisp.

cuscurro [coos-coor'-ro], *m.* Crouton.

cuscus [coos-coos]. Couscous.

cuscha [coos'-chah], *f. (CAm.)* Liquor, rum.

cusir [coo-seer'], *va. (Coll.)* To sew or stitch clumsily.

cusita [coo-see'-tah], *a.* Cushite, descended from Cush, son of Ham.

cusma [coos-mah], *f. (And.)* Sleeveless shirt, tunic.

cuspa [coos-pah], *f. (And.) (Agri.)* Weeding.

cuspar [coos-pahr], *va. (And.) (Agri.)* To weed.

cúspide [coos'-pe-day], *f.* 1. Cusp, the sharp end of a thing; vertex of a pyramid or cone. 2. Peak of a mountain.

cuspídeo, dea [coos-pee'-day-o, ah], *a. (Bot.)* Cuspidate.

custodia [coos-to'-de-ah], *f.* 1. Custody, keeping; hold. **Bajo la custodia de**, in the care of. 2. Monstrance, the casket or reliquary in which the consecrated Host is manifested to public veneration in Catholic churches. 3. Guard, keeper. 4. Tabernacle. 5. In the order of St. Francis, a number of convents not sufficient to form a province.

custodiar [coos-to-de-ar'], *va.* Take care of; to guard, to watch over. *V.* GUARDAR.

custodio [coos-to'-de-o], *m.* Guard, keeper, watchman. **Ángel custodio**, guardian angel.

cususa [coo-soo'-sah], *f. (CAm.)* Home-made liquor.

cutama [coo-tah'-mah], *f. (Cono Sur)* bag, sack.

cutáneo, nea [coo-tah'-nay-o, ah], *a.* Cutaneous; of the skin.

cutaras [coo-tah'-rahs], *f. pl. (CAm. Carib. Mex.)* Sandals, rough shoes.

cúter [coo'-ter], *m. (Naut.)* Cutter, a small vessel rigged as a sloop.

cutí [coo-tee'], *m.* Bed-ticking. *V.* COTÍ.

cutícula [coo-tee'-coo-lah], *f.* The cuticle, epidermis.

cuticular [coo-te-coo-lar'], *a.* Cuticular. *V.* CUTÁNEO.

cutio [coo'-te-o], *m.* Labor, work. **Trabajo cutio**, short work.

cutir [coo-teer'], *va.* To knock or dash one thing against another.

cutis [coo'-tis], *m. & f.* The skin of the human body.

cutitis [coo-tee'-tis], *f.* Dermatitis, inflammation of the skin.

cuto, ta [coo'-to, tah], *a. (LAm.)* Handless, one-handed, maimed.

cutral [coo-trahl'], *com.* An old wornout ox, or cow, past usefulness, generally, destined to the slaughterhouse.

cutre [coo'-tray], *m. (Coll.)* A pitiful, miserable fellow.

cuyo, ya [coo'-yo, yah], *pron. pos.* Of which, of whom, whose, whereof. **El asunto, cuyos detalles conoces**, the matter of which you know the details. **En cuyo caso**, in which case.

cuyo [coo'-yo], *m. (Coll.)* Gallant, lover, wooer, sweetheart.

cuz, cuz [cooth, cooth], *m.* A term for calling dogs.

cuzma [cooth'-mah], *f. (Peru)* A sleeveless shirt used by some forest Indians of Peru. (Kechuan.)

cuzqueño, ña [cooth-kay'-nyo, nyah], or **cuzquense**, *a.* Belonging to Cuzco and its inhabitants.

C.V. *abr.* de **caballos de vapor** (horsepower).

czar [thar], *m. V.* ZAR.

czarevitz [thah-ray-veets'], *m. V.* ZAREVITZ.

czariano, na [thah-re-ah'-no, nah], *a. V.* ZARIANO.

czarina [thah-ree'-nah], *f. V.* ZARINA.

D

d [day] is the fourth letter of the Spanish alphabet. **D** has the same unvaried sound it has in English in the words *dedicate, fed*. In pronouncing this letter the tongue must not touch the palate at all, and barely come in contact with the teeth. In some provinces of Spain it is wrongly sounded as

th in *although*, and at the end of a word as *th* lisped in *path*, or as *t*. In Andalusia and some parts of America it is by some made silent in the termination *ado, ido*, and they say *compráo, vendío*, instead of *comprado, vendido*. **D**. is a contraction for *Don, Doña*, and Doctor; **DD.**, doctors. As a Roman numeral, **D**. is 500.

dabaji [dah-bah'-he], *m.* An Arabic word used by Cervantes, meaning corporal of a squad.

dable [dah'-bray], *a.* Possible, feasible, practicable. **No es dable hacerlo**, it is not possible to do it.

dabna [dahb'-nah], *f. (Zool.)* A kind of African viper, which attacks venomous serpents and destroys pernicious insects.

dabuti [dah-boo'-te], *a.* Funny, killing; super, smashing. *-adv.* **Pasarlo dabuti**, to have a great time.

dacá [dah-cah'], *adv.* This here, this side, on this side here. **Dacá**, or **de acá**, from this.

daca [dah'-cah], *v. def.* Give here. **Daca acá**, give hither. **Daca**, or **da acá**, or **dame acá**, give me here.

dacio, cia [dah'-the-o, the-ah], *a.* Dacian, relating to Dacia. *-m.* Tribute, tax.

dación [dah-the-on'], *f. (Law.)* Yielding something or giving something up, esp. in payment of a debt; delivery.

dacriocistitis [dah-cre-o-this-tee'-tis], *f.* Inflammation of the lachrymal sac; dacryocystitis.

dacrióideo, dea [dah-cre-o'-i-day-o, dayah], *a.* Like a tear: applied to seeds.

dacrón [dah-crone'], *m.* Dacron (trademark); polyester fiber.

dactílado, da [dac-te'-lah'-do, dah], *a.* Finger-shaped.

dactilar [dahc-te-lar'], *a.* Finger. **Huella dactilar**, fingerprint.

dactílico, ca [dac-tee'-le-co, cah], *a.* Dactylic.

dactilio [dac-tee'-le-o], *m. (Zool.)* A worm parasitic in man, found in the bladder.

dactilión [dac-te-leon'], *m.* 1. Webbed fingers or toes. 2. An apparatus devised for finger-gymnastics.

dáctilo [dahc'-te-lo], *m.* 1. Dactyl, a poetic foot. 2. Kind of shell.

dactilografía [dac-te-lo-grah-fee'-ah], *f.* Typewriting.

dactilógrafo, fa [dac-te-lo-grah'-fo], *m & f.* Typist.

dactilograma [dac-te-lo-grah'-mah], *m. (Mex.)* Fingerprints.

dactitología [dac-te-tolo-hee'-ah], *f.* Dactylology, the art of talking by manual signs.

dactilóptero [dac-te-lop'-tay-ro], *m.* The flyingfish.

dactiloscopia [dac-te-los-co'-pe-ah], *f.* Dactyloscopy, identification and classification of fingerprinting.

dadaísmo [dah-dah-es'-mo], *m.* Dadaism.

dadaíso [dah-dah-ees'-mo], *m.* Dadaism, a literary movement.

dadista [dah-des'-tah], *m. (Mex.)* Gambler.

dádiva [dah'-de-vah], *f.* Gift, present, gratification, grant, keepsake.

dadivosamente [dah-de-vo-sah-men'-tay], *adv.* Liberally, plentifully, bountifully

dadivosidad [dah-de-vo-se-dahd'], *f.* Liberality, magnificence, bounty.

dadivoso, sa [dah-de-vo'-so, sah], *a.* Bountiful, magnificent, liberal, free, generous.

dado [dah'-do], *m.* 1. Die, *pl.* dice. **Dado falso**, cogged or false dice, filled with quicksilver, with which sharpers play. **A una vuelta de dado**, at the cast of a die. 2. *(Arch.)* Dado. *V.* NETO. 4. *V.* DONACIÓN. **Dados de las velas**, *(Naut.)* tablings of the bowline cringles. *-pp.* of DAR. **Dado a su corta edad**, in view of his youth. **Dadas estas circunstancias**, since these circumstances exist. **Ser dado a**, to be given to. **Dado que...**, provided that....

dador, ra [dah-dor', rah], *m. & f.* 1. Donor, giver; one who gives or bestows; God. 2. Drawer of a bill of exchange. 3. *m.* Carrier of a letter from one individual to another, bearer.

dafnáceo, cea [daf-nah'-thay-o, thay-ah], *a.* Like the daphne, or laurel.

dafne [dahf'-nay], *m. (Bot.)* Daphne, laurel.

daga [dah'-gah], *f.* 1. Dagger. 2. Stove or furnace of a brick-kiln.

dagazo [dah-gah-tho], *m. (Carib. Mex.)* Stab wound.

daguerrotipia [dah-gher-ro-tee'-pe-ah], *f.* The art of making daguerreotypes.

daguerrotipo [dah-gher-ro-tee'-po], *m.* Daguerreotype, a portrait made upon a prepared metal plate, and the process by which it was obtained. Important, historically, as the precursor of the photograph.

daguilla [dah-geel'-lyah], *f.* 1. *(Dim.)* Small dagger. 2. *(Prov.)* V. PALILLO.

daifa [dah'-e-fah], *f.* Mistress, concubine.

daiquirí [dah-e-ke-ree], *m.* Daiquiri, mixed alcoholic drink.

dala [dah'-lah], *f. (Naut.)* Pump-dale of a ship.

dale [dah'-lay], *int.* A word expressive of displeasure at the obstinacy of another. V. DAR.

dalgo. Hacer mucho dalgo, to receive anyone with great attention and respect.

dalia [dah'-le-ah], *f. (Bot.)* The dahlia.

dálmata [dahl'-ma-tah], or **dalmático, ca** [dal-mah'-te-co, cah], *a.* Dalmatian, belonging to or native of Dalmatia.

Dalmacia [dal-mah'-the-ah], *f.* Dalmatia.

dalmática [dahl-mah'-te-cah], *f.* Dalmatica, vestment worn by the deacons in the Roman Catholic church.

daltoniano, na [dahl-to-ne-ah'-no, nah], *a.* Affected with daltonism, color-blind.

daltonismo [dahl-to-nees'-mo], *m.* Color-blindness, especially red-blindness; daltonism.

dallá, *adv. (Obs.)* V. DE ALLÁ.

dallador [dal-lyah-dor'], *m. (Prov.)* A mower of grass.

dallar [dal-lyar'], *va. (Prov.)* To mow.

dalle [dahl'-lyay], *m.* Scythe, sickle.

dallén [dal-lyen'], *adv.* From the other side there, from the other side.**dama** [dah'-mah], *f.* 1. Lady, dame; a noble or distinguished woman. 2. Lady courted by a gentleman. 3. A lady of honor at court. 4. A mistress or concubine. 5. Queen in the game of chess: king in the game of draughts or checkers. **Dama de palacio**, lady of honor at court. 6. Any woman affectedly nice. **Es muy dama**, she is excessively nice, difficult, or scrupulous. 7. American fallow deer. **Juego de damas**, game of draughts. 8. The actress who performs the principal parts: she is also called. **Primera dama**, or first actress, to distinguish her from *la segunda*, the second, or even *la* **tercera dama**, the third actress, who acts the secondary female parts in a play.

damajuana [dah-ma-hoo-ah'-nah], *f.* Demijohn.

damascado, da [dah-mas-cah'-do, dah], *a.* V. ADAMASCADO.

damascena [dah-mas-thay'-nah], *f.* Damson, damascene, damaskplum, a small black plum.

damasceno, na [dah-mas-thay'-no, nah], *a.* Damascene, native of or belonging to Damascus.

damasco [dah-mahs'-co], *m.* 1. Damask, figured silk stuff. **Damasco de lana**, woollen damask. 2. The Brussels apricot. 3. Damson, a small black plum.

damasina [dah-ma-see'-nah], *f.* Silk stuff resembling damask.

damasquillo [dah-mas-keel'-lyo], *m.* 1. Kind of cloth, of silk or wool, resembling damask. 2. *(Prov.)* V. ALBARICOQUE.

damasquinado [dah-mahs-ke-nah'-do], *m. (Tec.)* Damascene.

damasquinar [dah-mas-ke-nar'], *va.* To damascene, to ornament (steel) by etching or by inlaying, usually with gold or silver.

damasquino, na [dah-mas-kee'-no, nah], *a.* 1. Damaskeened (hierro y acero). 2. Belonging to Damascus. **A la damasquina**, damascus fashion.

damero [dah-may'-ro], *m.* Checkerboard, draughtboard.

damesana [dah-may'-sah], *f. (LAm.)* Demijohn.

damil [dah-meel'], *a. (Obs.)* Female, feminine.

damisela [dah-me-say'-lah], *f.* 1. A young gentlewoman: applied to girls that give themselves the air of high ladies. 2. *(Coll.)* A courtesan.

damita [dah-me'-tah], *f. (CAm.)* Young lady.

damnificador, ra [dam-ne-fe-cah-dor', rah], *m. & f.* One who damnifies.

damnificar [dam-ne-fe-car'], *va.* To hurt, to damage, to injure.

danchado, da [dan-chah'-do, dah], *a. (Her.)* Dentate, indented.

dandí [dahn--de'], *m.* Dandy, fop.

dandismo [dahn-des'-mo], *m.* Foppishness, foppish ways; extreme elegance.

danés, sa [dahness', sah], *a.* Danish.

dánico, ca [dah'ne-co, cah], *a.* Dane, Danish.

dango, *m. (Orn.)* V. PLANOA.

danta [dahn'-tah], *f. (Zool.)* Tapir.

dantellado, da [dan-tayl-lyah'-do, dah], *a.* Dentated, having the form of teeth.

dantesco [dahn-tes'-co], *a.* 1. *(Liter.)* Of Dante, relating to Dante. 2. *(Fig.)* Dantesque; horrific, weird, macabre.

Danubio [dah-noo'-be-o], *m.* Danube.

danza [dahn'-thah], *f.* 1. Dance. **Danza de espadas**, sword dance. 2. A set, or number of dancers. 3. *(Coll.)* A quarrel. 4. An entangled affair. **Meter en la danza**, *(Met.)* to involve another in some business or dispute. **¿Por dónde va la danza?** *(Met.)* to which side does the wind blow? 5. Row, rumpus. **Armar una danza**, to kick up a row. **No metas los perros en danza**, let sleeping dogs lie.

danzador, ra [dan-thah-dor', rah], *m. & f.* Dancer.

danzante, ta [dan-thahn'-tay, tah], *m. & f.* 1. Dancer. 2. A knowing person. 3. A fickle, airy person. **Hablar danzante**, to stammer.

danzar [dan-thar'], *vn.* 1. To dance. 2. To whirl a thing round. **Sacar a danzar**, a) to invite or engage a lady to dance. b) to cite or to oblige one to take part in any business. 3. to make public the share which a person has taken in a business. 4. *(Coll.)* To introduce oneself into any business.

danzarín, na [dan-thah-reen', nah], *m. & f.* 1. A fine dancer. 2. *(Met.)* Giddy, meddling person.

dañable [dah-nyah'-blay], *a.* Prejudicial, condemnable.

dañado, da [dah-nyah'-do, dah], *a.* Eternally damned. -*pp.* of DAÑAR.

dañador, ra [dah-nyah-dor',rah], *m. & f.* Offender.

dañar [dah-nyar'], *va.* 1. To hurt, to harm. 2. To damage, to injure, to mar, to impair; to spoil. 3. To weaken, to damnify. 4. To condemn. -*vr.* To get damaged, to get hurt.

dañinear [dah-nye-nay-ar'], *va.* 1. *(Cono Sur)* V. DAÑAR. 2. *(Cono Sur)* To steal.

dañino, na [dah-nyee'-no, nah], *a.* Noxious, hurtful, injurious, mischievous, harmful. -*m. (Cono Sur)* Thief.

daño [dah'-nyo], *m.* 1. Damage, hurt, injury, prejudice, harm, mischief, maim, nuisance, loss, hindrance. **Hacer daño a**, to damage. **El ajo me hace daño**, garlic disagrees with me. **Los médicos no saben donde está el daño**, the doctors cannot tell where the trouble is. 2. *(LAm.)* Spell, curse (maleficio).

dañosamente [dah-nyo-sah-men'-tay], *adv.* Hurtfully, mischievously, harmfully.

dañoso, sa [dah-nyo'-so, sah], *a.* Hurtful, noxious, injurious, mischievous, harmful.

DAO *abr.* de **Diseño Asistido por Ordenador** (Computer Aided Design).

dar [dar], *va. & vn.* 1. To give. 2. To give, to supply, to minister, to afford. 3. To minister, to give medicines, to administer a remedy. 4. To give, to deliver, to confer, to bestow. 5. To consign, to give to another in a formal manner. 6. To hit, to strike, to beat, to knock. 7. To give, to impart, to extend, to communicate. 8. To suppose erroneously. 9. To consider an affair as concluded. 10. To give, to allow, to grant a position, to coincide in opinion. 11. To persist obstinately in doing a thing. 12. To appoint. 13. To sacrifice.

14. To explain, to elucidate. 15. To be situated, to look toward. 16. With *creer, imaginar,* and analogous verbs, to simply execute the action implied. **Dar contra alguna cosa,** to hit against. **Dar crédito,** a) to accredit, to believe. b) to trust, to sell on trust. **Dar cuenta de,** to account. **Dar de comer,** to feed. **Dar de,** to fall in the manner shown by the noun. **Dar en,** to engage, bind oneself, persist in. **Dar bien,** to have good fortune. **Dar consigo,** to cause to fall, to throw down, to stop. **Dar en el blanco,** to hit the mark. **Dar fiado,** to give credit. **Dar que hacer,** to give trouble. **Dar licencia,** to give leave. **Dar memorias,** to give one´s respects. **Dar razón,** to inform, to give an account of anything. **Dar prestado,** to lend. **Dar que reír,** to set laughing. **Dar que llorar,** to fall crying. **Mi ventana da al campo,** my window overlooks the field. **Dar de traste,** *(Naut.)* to run aground. **Dar al traste,** to give up a thing, an undertaking; to lose, to destroy. **Dar largas,** to prolong an affair. **Dar que decir,** to give occasion to censure. **Dar de barato,** to allow it for peace' sake. **Dar fuego,** *(Naut.)* to bream a ship. **Dar calda,** to heat the iron. **Dar con uno,** to meet a person one is looking out for. **Dar de comer al diablo,** to wrangle, to quarrel; literally, to prepare food for the devil. **Dar de sí,** to stretch. **Dar el sí,** to grant anything; to consent to marry a person. **Dar fiador** or **fianza,** to find bail, to give security. **Dar guerra,** to wage war; to torment; to be very troublesome. **Dar la cara,** to go to the defence of someone. **Dar** or **echar luz,** to recover health. **Dar margen,** to occasion, to cause, to give opportunity. **Dar la enhorabuena,** to rejoice in another's happiness, to congratulate. **Dar la paz,** to give an embrace, to give an image to be kissed as a token of peace and fraternity. **Dar los días,** to congratulate one on his birthday. **Dar los buenos días,** to wish good day. **Dar madrugón,** to get up early. **Dar mal rato,** to give uneasiness. **Dar parte,** to share with. **Dar puerta y silla,** to invite a person to come in and sit down. **Dar señal,** to give earnest money, in token that a bargain is ratified. **Dar tras uno,** to persecute one. **Dar vez,** to give one his turn. **Dar voces,** to call, cry, or scream. **Dar vuelco a un coche,** to overturn a car. **Dar golpe alguna cosa,** to be surprised or struck with the beauty or rarity of a thing. **Dar de mano,** to depreciate or despise. **Dar a luz,** a) to be delivered of a child. b) to print, to publish. **Dar de baja,** to dismiss from the army. **No dar pie, ni patada,** to take no trouble to gain an end. **Dar entre ceja y ceja,** to strike between the eyes; to make an unpleasant announcement. **Dar pie con bola,** to guess rightly. **Dar el pésame,** to express condolence. **Dado que,** supposing that . . ., granted that . . . (argumentos). **Lo que cada uno cada puede dar de sí,** what each one can contribute. **Dan un 7 por 100 de interés,** they yield 7% interest. **Le dio un fuerte dolor de costado,** he felt a sharp pain in his side. **El reloj dio las 3,** the clock struck 3. **Lo podemos dar por terminado,** we shall be able to consider it finished. **Le ha dado por no venir a clase,** he has begun to cut classes. **Han dado en llamarle Boko,** they´ve taken to calling him Boko.

dardabasí [dar-dah-bah-see'], *m. (Orn.)* Hawk, kite.

dardada [dar-dah'-dah], *f.* Blow with a dart.

dárdano, na [dar'-dah-no, nah], *a.* Trojan, Dardanian.

dardo [dar'-do], *m.* 1. Dart, a missile. 2. A freshwater fish, about a foot long, easy of digestion, but full of spines. **Dardo de pescador,** fishgig, fizgig, a kind of harpoon.

dares y tomares [dah'-rays e to-mah'-rays], *m. pl.* 1. Quantity given and received. *(Acad.)* 2. *(Coll.)* Altercations, disputes.

darse [dar'-say], *vr.* 1. To yield, to cease resistance, to give in. **Darse a,** with noun or infinitive, to execute quickly or repeatedly the action of the verb. 2. To give oneself up to virtue or vice. 3. **Darse a la vela,** *(Naut.)* to set sail. 4. **Darse a merced,** *(Mil.)* to surrender at discretion, in hunting (pájaros), to halt fatigued. 5. To concern, to interest. **Darse por vencido,** to surrender. **Me doy por vencido,** I give it up. **Darse las manos,** to shake hands. **Darse maña,** to manage one's affairs in an able manner; to contrive. **Darse**

prisa, to make haste, to hasten, to accelerate. **Darse una panzada,** *(Coll.)* to be fed to satiety and sickness. **Darse una vuelta,** to scrutinize one's own conduct, to find out one´s own faults. **Si se da el caso,** if that happens. **El cultivo se da bien este año,** the crop is coming on well this year. **Darse por perdido,** to give oneself up for lost. **Se le dan muy bien las matemáticas,** she´s pretty good at maths. **Dársela a uno,** to fool somebody.

dársena [dar'-sa-nah], *f.* Place in a harbor for preserving and repairing ships; dock, basin.

darvinista, darwinista [dahr-ve-nes'-tah], *a.* Darwinist; Darwinian. *-m & f.* Darwinist.

data [dah'-tah], *f.* 1. Date the time at which a letter is written, or any instrument drawn up. 2. Item or article in an account. 3. An aperture or orifice made in reservoirs in order to let out a definite quantity. **La cosa está de mala data,** the affair is in a bad state. 4. Written permission to do anything.

datable [dah-tah'-blay], *a.* Datable, that can be dated.

datación [dah-tah-the-on'], *f.* Date, dating. **De difícil datación,** hard to date.

datáfono [dah-tah'-fo-no], *m.* Dataphone.

datar [dah-tar'], *va. & vn.* 1. To date, to note with the time at which anything is written or done. 2. To date, to reckon. **Esto data de muy atrás,** this dates back a long time.

dataría [dah-tah-ree'-ah], *f.* Datary, an office of the chancery at Rome where the Pope's bulls are expedited.

datario [dah-tah'-re-o], *m.* The principal officer of the datary.

dátil [dah'-teel], *m.* 1. *(Bot.)* Date, the fruit of the common date-palm. **Dátil de raposa,** the fruit of the dwarf fan palm. 2. Belemnites, arrow-head or finger stone.

datilado, da [dah-te-lah'-do, dah], *a.* Resembling a date.

datilera [dah-te-lay'-rah], *f.* Common datepalm.

datilillo [dah-te-leel'lyo], *m. dim.* A small date.

dativa, *f.* The thing given.

dativo [dah-tee'-vo], *m.* Dative, the third case of nouns.

dato [dah'-to], *m.* 1. Datum, a fact, a truth granted and admitted, the basis of an opinion. **Un dato interesante,** an interesting fact. **No tenemos todos los datos,** we do not have all the facts. 2. A title of high dignity in some oriental countries. 3. *(Comput.)* **Datos de entrada,** input data. **Datos de salida,** output data. **Datos semipermanentes,** semipermanent data.

daturina [dah-too-ree'-nah], *f.* Daturine, the alkaloid of datura. V. ATROPINA.

dauco [dah'-oo-co], *m. (Bot.)* Carrot.

DC *f. (Pol.)* abr. de **Democracia Cristiana.**

dcha. *abr.* de **derecha** (right hand).

d. de J.C. *abr.* de **después de Jesucristo** (Anno Domini, in the year of our Lord).

de [day], *prep.* 1. Of, the sign of a genitive or possessive case, as **La ley de Dios,** the law of God. **El poder de la mente,** mind's power. 2. It serves to point out the matter of which a thing is made. **Vaso de plata,** a silver cup. 3. It is the sign of the ablative case. **Vengo de Flandes,** I come from Flanders. 4. It serves sometimes instead of the preposition con. **De intento,** on purpose. 5. It is used in place of por. **De miedo,** from fear. 6. It is of the same import as *desde.* **Vamos de Madrid a Toledo,** we go from Madrid to Toledo. 7. It sometimes governs the infinitive mood. **Hora de comer,** dinner time. 8. It is placed before adverbs of time. **De día,** by day. **De noche,** by night. 9. Sometimes marks an inference. 10. In familiar style it is used to give energy to an expression. 11. It is used after many verbs to denote some, a little, a portion, etc. **Comió del pescado,** he ate some fish. **Bebió del vino,** he drank some wine. 12. It is prefixed to many verbs, nouns, etc., altering their sense, as from *poner,* to put or to place, is formed *deponer,* to depose, etc. 13. *(Obs.)* To. **Bueno de comer,** good to eat. **De balde,** for nothing, free. **El coche de mi amigo,** the car of my friend, my friend´s car. **Es de ellos,** it´s theirs. **El peor alumno de la clase,** the worst pupil in the class. **Dolores no es de aquí,** Dolores is not from here. **De esto se deduce que...,** from this one deduces that. **Tiene tres hijos de su primera mujer,** he has 3 children by his first wife. **Hablaba de política,** he was talking about politics. **Una tacita de café;** a cup of coffee. **Un libro de Cela,** a book by Cela. **Máquina de coser,** sewing machine. **Pintado de negro,** painted in black. **De puerta en puerta,** from door to door. **Dar un salto,** in one bound. **Estar loco de contento,** to be crazy with joy. **Paralizado de las dos piernas,** paralysed in both legs. **De niño,** as a child. **Una persona amada de todos,** a person loved by all. **El bueno de Juan,** good old John

dea [day'-ah], *f. (Poet.)* Goddess. *V.* DIOSA.

deal [day-ahl,], *a.* Like a goddess, divine (rare).

dealbación [day-ahl-bah-the-on'], *f.* (Chem.) Making white by means of fire.

deambular [day-ahn-boo-lar'], *vn.* To saunter, to stroll, to wander.

deán [day-ahn'], *m.* Dean, an ecclesiastical dignitary.

deanato, deanazgo [day-ah-nah'-to, day-ah-nahth´-go], *m.* Deanship.

debacle [day-bah'-clay], *f.* Disaster.

debajo [day-bah'-'ho], *adv.* Under, underneath, below. **Debajo de la mesa,** under the table. **Por debajo de,** under. Underhand, privately. *-prep.* Under, subordinate, dependent.

debate [day-bah'-tay], *m.* Debate, altercation, expostulation, discussion, contention.

debatir [day-bah-teer'], *va.* 1. To debate, to argue, to discuss. 2. To combat, to engage with arms. 3. To expostulate. *-vr, vn.* To struggle.

debe [day'-bay], *m. (Com.)* The debtor-side of an account, debit. **Debe y haber,** debit and credit.

debelar [day-bay-lar'], *va.* To debellate, to conquer.

deber [day-berr´], *m.* 1. Obligation, duty. 2. Debt. **Hacer su deber,** to fulfil one's duty.

deber [day-berr'], *va.* To owe, no. to pay a debt which is due. **Me debes cinco dólares,** you owe me five dollars. **Esto lo debe a la influencia francesa,** he owes this to French influence. *-vn.* To be obliged to, to be to, must, ought, would, have to. **Debía ser,** must have been. **Deber de,** must. **Debo hacerlo,** I must do it. **He debido perderlo,** I must have lost it. **Debe de ser así,** it must be like that. **No debe de ser muy caro,** it can´t be very dear. *-vr.* **Deberse a,** to be owing to. **Se debe al mal tiempo,** it´s on account of the bad weather. **Puede deberse a que...,** it may be because....

debidamente [day-be-dah-men´-tay], *adv.* 1. Justly, with moderation and justice. 2. Duly, exactly, perfectly. **Un documento debidamente redactado,** a properly drawn up document.

debido, da [day-bee'-do, dah], *a.* Due, proper. **En forma debida,** in due or proper form. **Como es debido,** as is proper. **Debido a las circunstancias,** due to circumstances. **Debido a la falta de agua,** because of the water shortage.

débil [day'-beel], *a.* 1. Feeble, weak, extenuated, debilitated, faintly, sickly, infirm. 2. Feeble, weak. 3. Fragile, frail. 4. Pusillanimous, mean spirited.

debilidad [day-be-le-dahd'], *f.* 1. Debility, weakness, languor. 2. Weakness, feebleness, want of strength. 3. *(Met.)* Pusillanimity, fondness, craziness: frailty. **Tener una debilidad por el chocolate,** to have a weakness for chocolate.

debilitación [day-be-le-tah-the-on'], *f.* Debilitation, extenuation.

debilitar [day-be-le-tar'], *va.* To debilitate, to weaken, to extenuate, to enfeeble, to enervate. *-vr.* To grow weak(er), to weaken.

débilmente [day'-beel-men-tay], *adv.* Weakly, feebly, faintly, lamely.

débito [day'-be-to], *m.* Debt. **Débito** or **débito conyugal,** conjugal duty.

debitorio [day-be-to'-re-o], *m.* Contract of bargain and sale upon credit, by virtue of a partial payment, until settlement of the debt.

debó [day-bo'], *m.* Instrument used for scraping skins, scraper.

debocar [day-bo-car'], *va. vn.* To vomit.

debut [day-boo'], *m.* Debut.

debutanta, tante [day-boo-tahn'-tah], *m & f.* Debutant.

debutar [day-boo-tar'], *vn.* To make one's debut, to present for the first time.

deca [day'-cah], Greek prefix, meaning ten.

década [day'-cah-dah], *f.* Decade, the number or sum of ten.

decadencia [day-cah-den'-the-ah], *f.* Decay, decline, fading, failing, decaying. **Ir en decadencia,** to be on the decline.

decadente [day-cahn'-tay], *pa.* Decaying, declining.

decáedro, dra [day-cah'-ay-dro, drah], *m. & f.* Decahedron, a solid of ten faces.

decaer [day-cah-err'], *vn.* 1. To decay, to decline, to fail, to languish, to grow weak, to fade. **Ella ha decaído en belleza,** her beauty is not what it was. 2. *(Naut.)* To fall to leeward. *(Yo decaigo, yo decaí, yo decaiga,* from *Decaer. V.* CAER.)

decágono [day-cah'-go-no], *m.* Decagon, a polygon of ten sides or angles.

decagramo [day-cah-grah´-mo], *m.* Decagram, the weight of ten grams.

decaído, da [day-cah-ee'-do, dah], *a.* Crestfallen, dejected, dispirited.

decaimiento [day-cah-e-me-an'to], *m.* Decay, failing, decline, weakness.

decalitro [day-cah-lee'-tro], *a.* Decaliter, ten liters.

decálogo [day-cah'logo], *m.* Decalogue, the Ten Commandments.

decámetro [day-cah'-may-tro], *m.* Decameter, the length of ten meters.

decampamento [day-cam-pahmen'to], *m.* Decampment, the act of shifting the camp.

decampar [day-cam-par'], *vn.* To decamp.

decanato [day-cahnah'to], *m.* Dignity of the senior of any community.

decandrio, dria [day-cahn´-dreo, ah], *a.* Decandrous, having ten stamens. *-f. pl.* Decandria, plants whose flowers have ten stamens.

decano [daycah'no], *m.* Senior, the most ancient member of a community or corporation.

decantación [daycantah-the-on'], *f.* Decantation, pouring off.

decantar [day-can-tar'], *va.* 1. To cry up, to exaggerate or magnify a thing. **El tan decantado edificio,** this building which has been so effusively praised. 2. To turn anything from a right line and give it an oblique direction. 3. To decant, to draw off liquor. *-vr.* **Decantarse hacia,** to move towards. **Decantarse por algo,** to show preference for something.

decapétalo, la [day-cah-pay'-tah-lo, lah], *a.* Having ten petals; decapetalous.

decapitación [day-cah-pe-tah-theon'], *f.* Decapitation, beheading.

decapitar [day-cah-pe-tar'], *va.* To behead, to decapitate.

decasílabo [day-cah-see'-lah-bo], *a. (Poet.)* Having ten syllables.

decastilo [day-cas-tee´-lo], *m. (Arch.)* Decastyle, an assemblage of ten pillars.

deceleración [day-thay-lay-rah-the-on´], *f. (Phys.)* Deceleration.

decena [day-thay'-nah], *f.* 1. Ten. **Una decena de barcos,** about ten ships. **Contar por decenas,** to count in tens. 2. *(Prov.)* Company or party of ten persons. 3. *(Mus.)* Consonance made of an octave and a third; a tenth.

decenal [day-thay-nahl'], *a.* Decennial, a space of ten years.

decenar [day-they-nar'], *m.* A squad or crew of ten.

decencia [day-then'-the-ah], *f.* 1. Decency, propriety of form or conduct. 2. Decency, reservedness, honesty, modesty.

decenio [day-thay'-neo], *m.* Space of ten years; decennial.

deceno, na [day-thay-no, nah], *a.* Tenth, ordinal of ten.

decentar [day-then-tar'], *va.* 1. To commence the use of things not before used. 2. To begin to lose that which had been preserved. -vr. To wound, to gall or injure the skin or body; to be bedridden.

decente [day-then'-tay], a. 1. Decent, just, honest, becoming, fit, suitable, decorous. 2. Convenient, reasonable. 3. Decent, modest, grave, genteel. 4. Of honest, but not noble parents.

decentemente [day-tehn-t-ay-men'-tay], adv. 1. Decently, fairly, honorably. 2. Decently, without immodesty, comely. 3. Abundantly.

decenvirato [day-then-ve-rah'-to], m. Decemvirate.

decepción [day-thep-the-on'], f. Deception, illusion; disappointment.

decepcionante [day-thep-the-o-nahn'-tay], a. Disappointing.

decepcionar [day-thep-the-onar], va. To disappoint, to disillusion. -vr. To be disappointed.

deceso [day-thay'-so], m. Decease, a natural death.

dechado [day-chah'-do], m. 1. Sample, pattern, design, standard. 2. Linen, on which young girls perform several sorts of needlework. 3. Example, pattern, or model of virtue and perfection.

deci [day'-the], A Latin prefix, signifying one tenth.

deciárea [day-the-ah'-ray-ah], f. Decire, one tenth of an âre: 10 sq. meters.

decibel [day-the-bel], or **decibelio** [daythe-bay'-le-o], m. (Phys.) Decibel.

decible [day-thee'-blay], a. Expressible, that which may be expressed.

decidero, ra [day-the-day'-ro, rah], a. What may be said without inconvenience or impropriety.

decididamente [day-ce-de-dah-men'-tay], adv. Decidedly.

decidido, da [day-the-dee'-do, dah], a. Determined, decided. **De carácter decidido**, firm, strong-willed.

decidir [day-the-deer'], va. To decide, to determine, to resolve, to conclude. **Esto le decidió a dejarlo**, this decided him to give it up. -vn. To decide, to make one's mind. **Decidir en favor de uno**, to decide in somebody's favor. -vr. To decide, to be determined.

decidor, ra [day-the-dor', rah], m. & f. 1. One who speaks with fluency and elegance. 2. A wit. 3. Versifier, poet.

decigramo [day-the-grah'-mo], m. Decigram, one tenth of a gram.

decilitro [day-the-lee'-tro], m. Decilitre, one-tenth of a liter.

décima [day'the-mah], f. 1. (Poet.) A Spanish stanza consisting of ten verses of eight syllables. 2. Tenth, tithe, the tenth part.

decimal [day-the-mahl], a. 1. Decimal. 2. Pertaining to tithes. **Rentas decimales**, tithes or tithe rents. **Decimal codificado en binario**, (Comput.) binary coded decimal.

décimanovena [day'-the-mah-no-vay'-nah], f. One of the registers of the pipes of an organ.

decimar [day-the-mar'], va. V. DIEZMAR.

decímetro [day-thee'-may-tro], m. Decimeter, one-tenth of a meter.

décimo, ma [day'-the-mo, mah], a. Tenth, ordinal of ten.

décimoctavo va [day'-the-moc-tah'-vo, vah], a. Eighteenth.

décimocuarto, ta [day-the-mo-koo-ahr'-to], a. Fourteenth.

decimonónico [day-the-mo-no'-ne-co], Nineteenth-century; Victorian; (fig.) outdated, antiquated.

décimonono, na [day'-the-mo-no-no, nah], a. Nineteenth.

décimonoveno, na [day'-the-mo-no-vay' no, nah], a. V. DÉCIMONONO.

décimoquinto, ta [day'-the-mo-keen'-to, tah], a. Fifteenth.

decimoséptimo, ma [day'-the-mo-sep'-temo, mah], a. Seventeenth.

décimosexto, ta [day'-the-mo-sex'-to, tah], a. Sixteenth.

decimotercio, cia [day'-the-mo-terr'-theo, ah], a. Thirteenth.

deciochono, na [day-the-o-chay'-no, nah], a. 1. Eighteenth. 2. Kind of cloth having a warp of 1,800 threads. 3. V. DIECIOCHENO.

decir [day-theer'], va. 1. To say or utter, to tell, to speak, to express by words. 2. To assure, to persuade. 3. To name, to give a name to a person or place. 4. To be conformable, to correspond. 5. To denote, to mark, to be a sign of. 6. To declare or depose upon oath. 7. To verify. **Decir bien**, to

speak fluently or gracefully; to explain a thing well. **¡Digo!** I say; hark; used in calling or speaking to. **Decir que sí**, to affirm something. **Decir que no**, to deny. **Decir por decir**, to talk for the sake of talking. **Como dijo el otro**, used of an unknown author, or when a name cannot be recalled. **Decir alguna cosa con la boca chica**, to offer a thing merely for form's sake. **No sé qué decir**, how can I tell?. **¿Qué quiere decir eso?**, what does that mean?. **Por más que Vd. diga**, you may say what you will. **No dijo nada**, he said nothing. **Decir a uno que se calle**, to tell somebody to be quiet. **Pero dice mal**, but he is wrong. **Como quien no dice nada**, quite casually. **Me dijo de todo**, he called me all the names under the sun. **Es mucho decir**, that's saying a lot. **Querer decir**, to mean. **Dar que decir**, to make people talk. **Por decirlo así**, so to speak. **El qué dirán**, public opinion. **Digan lo que digan**, whatever they say. **No estuvo muy cortés que digamos**, actually he wasn't all that polite. **No es que digamos muy guapa**, she's not really that pretty. **Su cara dice lo que es**, his face shows him up for what he is. -vr. 1. **Yo sé lo que me digo**, I know what I'm talking about. 2. To be called, to be named. **Esta plaza se dice de la Revolución**, this is called Revolution Square. 3. **Se dice**, it is said. **Se me ha dicho que...**, I have been told that. 4. **Esto es lo que se dice un queso**, this is a real cheese.

decir [day-theer'], m. A notable saying. **Decires**, idle talk, false rumors, scandal, slander. **Es un decir**, it's just a phrase.

decisión [day-the-se-on'], f. 1. Decision, determination, resolution, issue. **Tomar una decisión**, to make a decision. 2. Decision, judgment by court of justice. 3. Verdict by a jury. 4. Disposition.

decisivamente [day-the-se-vah-men'-tay], adv. Decisively.

decisivo, va [day-the-see'-vo, vah], a. Decisive, final, conclusive, decretory.

decisorio, ria [day-the-so're-o, ah], a. (Law.) Decisive, concluding, decisory.

declamación [day-clah-mah-the-on'], f. 1. Declamation, harangue, oration, discourse. 2. A speech delivered, an oratorial invective. 3. Declamation, a discourse addressed to the passions. 4. Delivery. 5. The manner of reciting theatrical compositions. 6. Panegyric.

declamador, ra [day-clah-mah-dor', rah], m. & f. Declaimer, exclaimer.

declamar [day-clah-mar'], vn. To declaim, to harangue. -va. To declaim, to recite (versos).

declamatorio, ria [day-clah-ma-to're-o, ah], a. Declamatory.

declaración [day-clah-rah-the-on'], f. 1. Declaration. 2. Declaration, interpretation, exposition. **Declaración conjunta**, joint declaration. **Declaración de derechos**, bill of rights 3. Manifest, manifestation; account. 4. Overture, proposal. 5. (Law.) Deposition. **Declaración de culpabilidad**, confession of guilt. **Prestar declaración**, to make a statement.

declaradamente [day-clah-rah-dah-men'-tay], adv. Declaredly, avowedly.

declarado, da [day-clah-rah'-do, dah], a. & pp. of DECLARAR. 1. Declared. 2. Applied to a person who speaks too plainly.

declarador, ra [day-clah-rah-dor, rah], m. & f. Declarer, expositor.

declarante [day-clah-rahn'-tay], m. 1. Declarer, one who declares or explains; a witness in the act of being examined. **Juan declarante**, a talkative person, who speaks his mind too freely. 2. Bidder (naipes).

declarar [day-clah-rar'], va. 1. To declare, to manifest, to make known. 2 To expound, to explain, to exemplify. 3. (Law.) To determine and decide, to find. **Declarar culpable a uno**, to find somebody guilty. 4. (Law.) To witness or depose upon oath. -vn. 1. To declare. **Según él mismo declara**, as he himself declares. 2. To bid, to declare (naipes). 3. To make a statement; to testify. -vr. 1. To declare one's opinion, to explain one's mind. **Declararse a una joven**, to say to a girl that one loves her. 2. **Declararse culpable**, to plead guilty.

declarativo, va [day-clah-ra-tee'-vo, vah], *a.* Declarative, assertive.

declaratorio, ria [day-clah-rah-to'-re-o, ah], *a.* Declaratory, explanatory.

declinable [day-cle-nah'-blay], *a.* *(Gram.)* Declinable, having variety of terminations.

declinación [day-cle-nah-the-on'], *f.* 1. Declination, descent, decay, fall, decline, falling. 2. *(Gram.)* Declination, the declension of nouns. 3. *(Astr.)* Declination, distance of a star or planet from the equator. 4. Deviation of a wall or building from facing one of the cardinal points of the compass. 5. Magnetic variation of the needle from the pole.

declinante [day-cle-nahn'-tay], *a.* Declining, bending down.

declinar [day-cle-nar'], *vn.* 1. To decline, to lean downward. 2. To decline, to sink, to be impaired, to decay, to degenerate, to abate, to diminish (de enfermedad). 3. To be finished or reach the last. 4. *(Naut.)* To vary from the true magnetic meridian. **Va declinando el día**, it is near twilight. -*va.* 1. *(Gram.)* To decline a word by various determinations. 2. To challenge a judge, to transfer a cause to another tribunal: in this last sense it is always used with the word *jurisdicción*.

declinatoria [day-cle-nah-to'-re-ah], *f.* *(Law.)* Plea which attacks the competency of a judge.

declinatorio [day-cle-nah-to´-re-o], *m.* Declinator, or declinatory, an instrument used in dialing.

declive, declivio [day-clee'-vey, day-clee'-veo], *m.* 1. Declivity, inclination downward, slope, fall. 2. Gradient, grade. **Tierra en declive**, sloping ground. **Estar en declive**, to slope.

declividad [day-cle-ve-dahd'], *f.* Declivity.

decocción [day-co-co-the-on'], *f.* Decoction.

decoctivo, va [day-coc-tee'-vo, vah], *a.* Digestive.

decodificador [day-co-de-fe-cah-dor], *m.* *(Comput.)* Decoder.

decolación [day-co-lah-the-on'], *f.* 1. Separation of the parts of an organ which ought to act together. 2. Decapitation of the foetus.

desoloración [day-colo-rah-the-on'], *f.* Decoloration, loss of color; decolorization, bleaching, blanching.

decolorante [day-co-lo-rahn'-tay], *m.* Bleaching agent.

decolorar [day-colo-rar'], *va.* To remove the color from any substance, to decolorize. -*vr.* To lose color.

decolorímetro [day-co-lo-re-e'-may-tro], *m.* Decolorimeter.

decombustión [day-com-boos-te-on'], *f.* An operation to destroy the oxidation of a body which has undergone combustion.

decomisar [day-co-me-sar'], *va.* To confiscate, to seize, to forfeit.

decomiso [day-co-me-e'-so], *m.* Confiscation, forfeiture, seizure.

decoración [day-co-rah-the-on'], *f.* Decoration, ornament. **Decoración de escaparate**, window display. **Decoración de interiores**, interior decorating. -*pl.* The scenery and curtains of a theater.

decorado [day-co-rah-do], *m.* Scenery, set (cine, teatro).

decorador, ra [day-co-rah-dor'] , *m.f.* Decorator.

decorar [day-co-rar'], *va.* 1. To decorate, to adorn, to embellish, to furnish. 2. To illustrate, to ennoble, to honor, to exalt. 3. To learn by heart. 4. To recite, to repeat.

decorativo [day-co-rah-te-vo], *a.* Decorative, ornamental.

decoro [day-co'-ro], *m.* 1. Honor, respect, reverence due to any person. 2. Circumspection, gravity, integrity. 3. Purity, honesty. 4. Decorum, decency, civility.

decorosamente [day-co-ro-sah-men'-tay], *adv.* Decently, decorously.

decoroso, sa [day-co-ro'-so, sah], *a.* Decorous, decent.

decorticación [day-cor-tee-cah-the-on'], *f.* Decortication, the act of stripping the bark or husk.

decrecer [day-cray-therr'], *vn.* To decrease, to diminish.

decreciente [day-cray-the-ayn'-tay], *a.* Decreasing, diminishing.

decrecimiento [day-cray-the-me-ayn'-to], *m.* Decrease, diminution; fall; shortening.

decremento [day-cray-men'-to], *m.* Decrement, decrease, diminution, declension, wane.

decrepitación [day-cray-pe-tah-the-on'], *f.* *(Chem.)* Decrepitation, a crackling noise as made by suit when heated.

decrepitante [day-cray-pe-tahn'tay], *pa.* *(Chem.)* Decrepitant.

decrepitar [day-cray-pe-tar'], *va. & vn.* 1. To decrepitate, to calcine salt until it has ceased to crackle in the fire. 2. To decrepitate, to crackle when put over the fire (sal).

decrépito, ta [day-cray'-pe-to, tah], *a.* Decrepit, worn with age.

decrepitud [day-cray-pe-tood'], *f.* Decrepitude, the last stage of decay; old age.

decretación [day-cray-tah-the-on'], *f.* Determination, establishment.

decretal [day-cray-tahl'], *f.* Decretal, letter or rescript of the Pope. **Decretales**, decretals, a collection of letters and decrees of the Popes.—*a.* Docretal.

decretalista [day-cray-tah-lees'-tah], *m.* Decretist, one that draws up or studies the rescripts, letters, and decrees of Popes.

decretar [day-cray-tar'], *va.* 1. To decree, to determine, to resolve. 2. *(Law.)* To give a decree or a determination in a suit. 3. To award (premio). -*vn.* To deliver a judgment.

decretero [day-cray-tay'-ro], *m.* 1 Catalogue or list of the names and offences of criminals. 2. Decretal, collection of decrees.

decretista [day-cray-tees'-tah], *m.* Decretist, one who expounds or explains the decretals.

decreto [day-cray'-to], *m.* 1. Decree, decision resolution. 2. Decree, order or determination issued in the king´s name. 3. A judical decree. **Por real decreto**, royal decree. 4. In canon law, decree or ordinance enacted by the Pope with the advice of his cardinals. 5. Opinion, vote, advice.

decreto-ley [cay-cray'-to lay-e], *m. pl.* **decretos-leyes**, decree law.

decretorio, ria [day-cray-to'-re-o, ah], *a.* Decretory, critical: applied to the days when a judgment may be formed on the issue of a fit of illness.

decúbito [day-coo'-be-to], *m.* 1. *(Med.)* Decubitus, the position of a patient in bed. **Decúbito prono**, prone position. **Úlcera de decúbito**, bedsore.

décuplo, pla [day'-coo-plo, plah], *a.* Decuple, tenfold.

decuria [day-coo'-re-ah], *f.* Ten Roman soldiers under a decurion.

decurrente [day-coor-ren'-tay], *a.* Decurrent, applied to the stem: said of leaves.

decursas [day-coor'-sa], *f. pl.* *(Law.)* Arrears of rent.

decurso [day-coor'-so], *m.* Course, succession of movement or time. **En el decurso de los años**, over the years.

decusación [day-coo-sah-the-on'], *f.* 1. Decussation, intercrossing of nervefibers. 2. The spot of intersection of such fibers.

decusado, da [day-coo-sah'-do, dah], *a.* Intersected.

dedada [day-dah'-dah], *f.* 1. That which can be taken up with the finger at once, a pinch. **Dedada de miel**, adulation, flattery, wheedling. **Dar a uno una dedada de miel**, *(Met.)* to put a cheat on one, to deceive; literally, to give one a fingerful of honey 2. Triglyph of a Doric frieze.

dedal [day-dahl'], *m.* 1. Thimble. 2 A leather fingerstall used by calkers on the little finger of the left hand.

dedalera [day-dah-lay'-rah], *f.* *(Bot.)* Foxglove.

dédalo [day'-dah-lo], *m.* 1. A labyrinth, an entanglement. 2. *(Fig.)* Tangle, mess.

dedicación [day-de-cah-the-on'], *f.* Dedication, the act of dedicating, consecration; inscription. **Estar en dedicación exclusiva**, to work full-time; **dedicación plena**, full-time.

dedicante [day-de-cahn´-tay], *pa.* Dedicating, dedicator.

dedicar [day-de-car'], *va.* 1. To dedicate, to devote, to consecrate. **Dedico un día a la semana a pescar,** I spend one day a week fishing. 2. To dedicate a literary work to someone. **Dedicarse a alguna cosa,** to apply oneself to a thing. **Se dedicó a la cerámica,** he devoted himself to pottery.
dedicativo, va [day-de-cah-tee'-vo, vah], *a.* V. DEDICATORIO.
dedicatoria [day-de-cah-to'-re-ah], *f.* Dedication, an address by which a literary composition is inscribed to a patron or friend.
dedicatorio, ria [day-de-cah-to'-re-o, ah], *a.* Dedicatory, containing or serving as a dedication.
dedición [day-de-the-on'], *f.* Unconditional surrender of a town to ancient Rome.
dedil [day-deel'], *m.* Thumbstall of linen or leather used by reapers.
dedillo, ito [day-deel'-lyo], *m. dim.* A little finger. **Saber una cosa al dedillo,** to know a thing perfectly.
dedo [day'-do], *m.* 1. Finger. 2. Toe. 3. The forty-eighth part of a Spanish yard, or *vara.* 4. A finger's breadth, a small bit. **Meter los dedos,** to pump one. **Señalarle con el dedo,** to point at another with the finger. **Dedo pulgar,** thumb. **Dedo índice** or **saludador,** the index or forefinger. **Dedo del corazón, cordial** or **de en medio,** middle finger. **Dedo anular,** the ringfinger. **Dedo meñique** or **auricular,** the little finger. **A dos dedos de,** very near to. **Chuparse los dedos,** to eat, say, do, or hear something with delight. **Meter a uno los dedos,** to pretend to believe the contrary of what one knows certainly. **Morderse los dedos,** to be revengefully angry. **Se le escapó entre los dedos,** it slipped through his fingers. **Pillarse los dedos,** *(fig.)* to get caught red-handed. **No tienes dos dedos de frente,** he's pretty dim.
deducción [day-dooc-the-on'], *f.* 1. Deduction, derivation, origin, consequence. 2. Deduction, that which is deducted. 3. *(Mus.)* The natural progression of sounds.
deducible [day-doo-thee'-blay], *a.* Deducible, inferable.
deducir [day-doo-theer'], *va.* 1. To deduce, to collect, to infer as a consequence; to fetch, to devise, to draw. 2. To allege in pleading, to offer as a plea. 3. To subtract, to deduct, to extract.
deductivo, va [day-dooc-tee'-vo, vah], *a.* Deductive.
defácile [day-fah'-the-lay], *adv.* Easily.
defacto [day-fac'-to], *adv.* In fact, actually, effectually. = DE HECHO.
defalcar [day-fal-car'], *va.* V. DESFALCAR.
defecación [day-fay-cah-the-on'], *f.* 1. Defecation, purification of a liquid from lees or sediment. 2. Defecation, voiding of excrement.
defecadora [day-fay-cah-do'-rah], *f.* In sugar refining, defecating pan, second boiler.
defecar [day-fay-car'], *va.* 1. To defecate, purify from lees, dregs, or polluting matter. 2. To defecate, void excrement.
defección [day-fec-the-on'], *f.* Defection, apostasy; revolt.
defectible [day-fec-tee'-blay], *a.* Defectible, imperfect, deficient.
defectillo [day-fec-teel'-lyo], *m. dim.* Slight fault or defect.
defectivo, va [day-fec-tee'-vo, vah], *a.* Defective, imperfect.
defecto [day-fec-to], *m.* 1. Defect, failing, fault. 2. Defect, any natural imperfection. **Defecto físico,** physical defect. **Defecto de palabra,** speech defect. *-pl.* *(Print.)* Sheets remaining after a day's work in order to complete the full number. **Poner defectos,** to find fault.
defectuosamente [day-fec-too-o-sah-men'-tay], *adv.* Defectively, faultily, deficiently.
defectuoso, sa [day-fec-too-oh'-so, sah], *a.* Defective, imperfect, faulty.
defendedoro, ra [day-fen-day-day'-ro, rah], *a.* Defensible.
defendedor, ra [day-fen-day-dor', rah], *a. & m. & f.* V. DEFENSOR.
defender [day-fen-derr'], *va.* 1. To defend, to protect, to guard. 2. To defend, to make good, to justify, to assert, to maintain. 3. To defend, to vindicate. 4. To veto, to prohibit,

to forbid. 5. To resist, to oppose. 6. To defend a place, a cause, etc.; to fence. *-vr.* 1. To defend oneself. **Defenderse bien,** to resist firmly. 2. *(Fig.)* **Me defiendo en inglés,** I can manage in English. **Gana poco pero se defiende,** she doesn't earn much but she manages.
defendible [day-fen-dee'-blay], *a.* Defensible.
defendido, da [day-fen-dee'-do], *m.f.* A client.
defenecimiento [day-fay-nay-the-me-en'-to], *m.* *(Com. Prov.)* Settlement of an account.
defensa [day-fen'-sah], *f.* 1. Defence, safeguard, arms. **Defensa de,** defence against. 2. Defence, vindication, justification, apology. 3. Defence, guard, shelter, protection; fence. 4. Defence, in law, the defendant's reply. 5. (Sports) Defense. 6. Tusk. 7. Horn. **Legítima defensa,** *(For.)* self defense. **Defensas,** 1. Fortifications, defenses. 2. *(Naut.)* Skids. 3. *(Naut.)* Fenders.
defensa [day-fen'-sah], *m.* (Sports) Back.
defensa civil [day-fen'-sah the-veel'], *f.* Civil defense.
defensión [day-fen-se-on'], *f.* Safeguard, defence.
defensiva [day-fen-see'-vah], *f.* Defensive. **Estar a la defensiva,** or **ponerse sobre la defensiva,** to be upon the defensive, to put oneself upon the defensive.
defensivo [day-fen-see'-vo], *m.* 1. Defence, safeguard, preservative. 2. Piece of linen steeped in any medicated liquor, and applied to some part of the body, to refresh and strengthen it.
defensivo, va [day-fen-see'-vo, vah], *a.* Defensive, that which serves as a defence or safeguard; justificatory, defensory.
defensor, ra [day-fen-sor', rah], 1. Defender or keeper, maintainer, conservator, protector, supporter. **Defensor del pueblo,** public defender. 2. *(Law.)* A lawyer appointed by a court of justice to defend one absent, or one who cannot pay a defender. V. ABOGADO DE POBRES.
defensoría [day-fen-so-ree'-ah], *f.* The duty and office of a lawyer appointed by a judge to defend a person who is absent, or who has no defender.
defensorio [day-fen-so-re'-o], *m.* Defence, an apologetic writing in favor of any person or thing; a memoir, a manifesto.
deferencia [day-fay-ren'-the-ah], *f.* Deference, complaisance, condescension.
deferente [day-fay-ren'-tay], *a.* Assenting, deferring to the opinion of another; deferent.
deferir [day-fay-reer'], *vn.* To defer, to pay deference to another's opinion, to yield to another's judgment. *-va.* To communicate, or share in the jurisdiction or power.
defibríneo, a [day-fe-bree'-nay-o, ah], *a.* Defibrinated.
deficiencia [day-fe-the-en'-the-ah], *f.* Deficiency, imperfection. *(Antiq.).* **Deficiencia mental,** mental deficiency.
deficiente [day-fe-the-en'-tay], *a.* Defective, faulty, deficient. **Deficiente mental,** mental defective.
déficit [day'-fe-theet], *m.* Deficit. **Déficit comercial,** trade deficit.
deficitario [day-fe-the-ah'-re-o], *a.* 1. *(Fin.)* Deficit; in deficit, showing a deficit. 2. **Ser deficitario en,** to be short of.
definible [day-fe-nee'-blay], *a.* Definable.
definición [day-fe-ne-the-on'], *f.* 1. Definition. 2. Decision, determination. **Definiciones,** statutes of military orders.
definido, da [day-fe-nee'-do, dah], *a.* Definite. **Bien definido,** well defined. **Definido por el usuario,** user defined. *-pp.* of DEFINIR.
definidor [day-fe-ne-dor'], *m.* 1. Definer. 2. In some religious orders, one of the members who compose, under the presidency of their superior, a chapter or assembly to govern the order.
definir [day-fe-neer'], *va.* 1. To define, to describe, to explain. 2. To decide, to determine. 3. *(Pict.)* To conclude any work, finishing all its parts, even the least important, with perfection.
definitivamente [day-fe-ne-te-vah-men'-tay], *adv.* Definitively
definitivo, va [day-fe-ne-tee'-vo, vah], *a.* Definitive, determinate. **En definitiva,** definitively.

definitorio [day-fe-ne-to're-o], *m.* 1. Chapter or assembly of the chiefs of religious orders, to deliberate on the affairs of the order. 2. House or hall where the above chapters are held.

deflagración [day-flah-grah-the-on'], *f.* Deflagration, sudden burning.

deflagrador [day-flah-grah-dor'], *m.* Deflagrator, ignitor.

deflagrar [day-fla-grar'], *va.* To deflagrate, to cause to burn.

deflegmación [day-fleg-mah-the-on'], *f. (Med.)* Expectoration.

deflegmar [day-fleg-mar'], *vn.* To become free from water, as spirituous liquors; to dephlegmate, concentrate.

deflujo [day-floo'-ho], *m. (Astr.)* The recession of the moon from any planet.

defoliación [day-fo-le-ah-the-on'], *f.* Defoliation, the shedding of leaves.

defoliante [day-fo-lle-ahn'-tay], *m.* Defoliant.

deformación [day-for-mah-the-on'], *f.* Deformation; defacing.

deformador [day-for-mah-dor'], *m.* One who deforms or disfigures.

deformar [day-for-mar'], *va.* To deform, to disfigure, to misshape. *-vr.* To become deformed; to get distorted.

deformatorio, ria [day-for-mah-to'-re-o, ah], *a.* Deforming, disfiguring.

deforme [day-for'-may], *a.* Deformed, disfigured, ugly, hideous.

deformemente [day-for-may-men'-tay], *adv.* Deformedly.

deformidad [day-for-me-dahd'], *f.* 1. Deformity, hideousness, ugliness. 2. A gross error.

defraudación [day-frah-oo-dah-the-on'], *f.* Defraudation, fraud, deceit, usurpation. **Defraudación de impuestos**, tax evasion.

defraudador [day-fra-hoo-dah-dor'], *m.* Defrauder, defaulter.

defraudar [day-fra-hoo-dar'], *va.* 1. To defraud, to rob or deprive by wile or trick. 2. To defraud, to cheat, to trick, to usurp what belongs to another. 3. *(Met.)* To intercept the light of the sun; to spoil the taste; to disturb the sleep.

defuera [day-foo-ay'-rah], *adv.* Externally, outwardly on the outside.

defunción [day-foon-the-on'], *f. (Prov.)* 1. Death. 2. Extinction, transition from being to not being.

degeneración [day-hay-nay-rah-the-on'], *f.* Degeneration, degeneracy.

degenerado, da [day-hay-nay-rah'-do, dah], *a.* Degenerate. *-pp.* of DEGENERAR.

degenerar [day-hay-nay-rar'], *vn.* 1. To degenerate, to fall from its kind, to grow wild or base (plantas). 2. To degenerate, to fall from the virtue of our ancestors. 3. *(Pict.)* To disfigure anything. **La manifestación degeneró en una sangrienta revuelta**, the demonstration degenerated into a bloody riot.

deglución [day-gloo-the-on'], *f. (Med.)* Deglutition, swallowing.

deglutir [day-gloo-teer'], *va.* To swallow.

degollación [day-gol'-lyah-the-on'], *f.* Decollation, beheading.

degolladero [day-gol-lyah-day'-ro], *m.* 1. Throttle, windpipe. 2. Shambles, slaughterhouse. 3. In theaters, a place in the pit farthest from the stage, with no seats, where men are admitted at a very low price. It is separated from the pit by a partition as high as one's neck, from which it takes its name. **Degolladero de bolsas**, cut purse; also a shop where goods are sold at an extravagant price, or bad measure or weight is given. **Llevar al degolladero**, *(Met.)* to put one in very great danger.

degolladura [day-gol-lyah'-do], *m.* A dart in women's waists or jackets.

degollador [day-gol-lyah-dor'], *m.* Executioner.

degolladura [day-gol-lyah-doo'-rah], *f.* 1. Cutting of the throat. 2. Interstice between two bricks filled up with mortar. 3. A slope out of women's jackets. 4. Slender part of balusters.

degollar [day-gol-lyar,], *va.* 1. To behead, to decapitate; to guillotine. 2. *(Met.)* To destroy, to ruin, to annihilate. 3. *(Coll.)* To tease, to importune. **Esta persona me degüella**, this person troubles and harasses me.

degollina [day-gol-lyee'-nah], *f. (Coll.)* Slaughter, butchery.

degradación [day-grah-dah-the-on'], *f.* 1. Degradation, dismission from an office or dignity; fall. 2. Degradation, degeneracy. 3. *(Pict.)* Degradation, diminution.

degradante [day-grah-dahn'-tay], *a.* Degrading.

degradar [day-grah-dar'], *va.* To degrade, to deprive one of his place, dignity, or honors. *-vr.* To degrade or demean oneself.

degüello [day-goo-ayl'-lyo], *m.* 1. Decollation, the act of beheading or cutting one's throat. 2. Neck or narrow part of many things. 3. Destruction, ruin. **Tirar a degüello**, to endeavor to destroy a person; to seek one's ruin.

degustación [day-goos-tah-the-on'], *f.* Tasting, sampling.

degustar [day-goos-tar'], *va.* To taste, to sample; to drink, to take.

dehesa [day-ay'-sah], *f.* Pasture-ground. **Dehesa concejil**, common, a pasture-ground.

dehesar [day-ay-sar'], *va.* To turn arable land into pasture-ground.

dehesero [day-ay-say'-ro], *m.* Keeper of a pasture-ground.

dehiscencia [day-is-then'-the-ah], *f. (Bot.)* Dehiscence.

deicida [day-e-thee'-dah], *m.* Deicide: a term applied by some writers to those who concurred in the crucifixion of Jesus.

deicidio [day-e-thee'-deo], *m.* Deicide, murder of Christ.

deidad [day-e-dahd'], *f.* 1. Deity, divinity. 2. Deity, goddess: a term of flattery addressed to women.

deificación [day-e-fe-ca-the-on'], *f.* Deification, apotheosis.

deificar [day-e-fe-car'], *va.* To deify, or praise excessively or extravagantly.

deífico [day-ee'-fe-co], *a.* Deifical, making divine; belonging to God.

deiforme [day-e-for'-may], *a.* Deiform, of a godlike form; godlike.

deípara [day-ee'-pa-rah], *f.* Deiparous, that brings forth a God: applied to the blessed Virgin.

deisidemonía [day-e-se-day-mo-nee'-ah], *f.* Superstitious fear.

deismo [day-ees'-mo], *m.* Deism.

deista [day-ees'-tah], *m.f.* Deist.

deja [day'-hah], *f.* Prominence between two fissures.

dejación [day-hah-the-on'], *f.* 1. Act of leaving, relinquishing, or giving up. 2. Abdication, resignation. **Dejación de bienes**, the act of resigning one's property to his creditors.

dejada [day-hah'-dah], *f. V.* DEJACIÓN.

dejadez [day-hah-deth'], *f.* Slovenliness, neglect, laziness, lassitude.

dejado, da [day-hah'-do, dah], *a.* 1. Slovenly, idle, indolent. 2. Dejected, low-spirited. *-pp.* of DEJAR.

dejamiento [day-hah-me-en'-to], *m.* 1. Act of leaving, relinquishing, or giving up. 2. Indolence, idleness, carelessness. 3. Languor, decay of spirits. 4. Abdication, resignation.

dejar [day-har'], *va.* 1. To leave, to let, to relinquish, to quit, to come from, to go from. 2. To omit saying or doing anything. 3. To permit, to allow, not to obstruct. 4. To leave, to forsake, to desert. 5. To yield, to produce. 6. To commit, to give in charge. 7. To nominate, to appoint. **Dejar cargado**, to debit. **Dejar dicho**, to leave word or orders. **Dejar escrito**, to leave in writing. **Déjale que venga**, let him come. 8. To fling up, to give up. 9. To lay away. 10. To forbear, to leave off, to cease. 11. To leave a legacy to one absent. **Dejar atrás**, to excel, to surpass. **Dejar a uno a oscuras**, not to grant a request; to leave one in doubt. **Dejarse de cuentos**, to come to the point. **Dejar en cueros**, to strip one of his property. **Dejar para mañana**, to delay, to procrastinate. *-vn.* **Dejó de cantar**, she stopped singing. **No puedo dejar de fumar**, I can't give up smoking. *-vr.* 1. Not to take care of oneself. 2. To allow or suffer oneself to. 3. To become languid. 4. To abandon oneself to. **Dejarse llevar**, to suffer oneself to be led by another. **Dejarse rogar**, to extend the concession required, that the favor may be more estimable. **Dejarse vencer**, to yield oneself to the opinion of another. **Dejarse caer abajo por un río**, *(Naut.)* to drop down a river. **Dejarse caer a la popa**, *(Naut.)* to fall astern. **Dejarse caer a sotavento**, *(Naut.)* to fall to leeward. **Dejarse alguna cosa en el tintero**, to omit something necessary to the subject.

dejillo [day-heel'-lyo], *m. dim.* Slight relish or taste which remains after eating or drinking.

dejo [day'-ho], *m.* 1. End, termination. Negligence, carelessness, laziness. *V.* ABNEGACIÓN. 4. Relish or taste which remains after eating or drinking. 5. Result, effect, or remains of a passion 6. Particular accentuation on the last syllable of words, of each province or country. 7. Recollection, echo.

dejugar [day-hoo-gar'], *va.* To extract the juice or substance of something.

del [del]. Of the, a contraction of the preposition *De* and the masculine article *el;* as, **el mérito del libro**, instead of *el mérito* de el *libro*.

Del. *abr.* de **Delegación**.

delación [day-lah-the-on'], *f.* 1. Delation, accusation, impeachment. 2. Information.

delantal [day-lan-tahl'], *m.* Apron; dashboard of a carriage. **Delantal de cuero**, leather apron.

delante [day-lahn'-tay], *adv.* 1. Before, in the presence of, in the sight of, in front of. **La casa no tiene nada delante**, the house has nothing opposite. **La parte de delante**, the front part. 2. Before, anteriorly, preceding in time. **Tenemos todavía 4 horas por delante**, we still have 4 hours in front of us. 3. Before, in preference to, prior to.

delantera [day-lan-tay'-rah], *f.* 1. Fore front, fore end, the fore part of anything. 2. The front seats, behind the barriers of a place, where bullfeasts are held. 3. Fore skirts of clothes. 4. Advantage obtained over another. 5. Vanguard of an army. **Coger la delantera**, to get the start of a person. **Ir en la delantera**, to take the lead. 6. *(Anat.)* Tits. 7. **Delanteras**, chaps (calzones).

delantero, ra [day-lan-tay'-ro, rah], *a.* Foremost, first.

delantero [day-lahn-tay'-ro], *m.* The first, one who takes the lead. **Delantero centro**, center forward, **delantero extremo**, outside forward. —*m. pl.* Linemen (en fútbol).

delatable [day-lah-tah'-blay], *a.* Accusable, blamable.

delatante [day-lah-tahn'-tay], *pa.* Informer, accuser.

delatar [day-lah-tar'], *va.* To inform, to accuse, to denounce, to impeach.

delator, ra [day-lah-tor'], *m. f.* Accuser, informer, denouncer.

delco [dayl'-co], *m. (Aut.)* Distributor.

del crédere [del cray'-day-ray], *m.* A guarantee by a merchant for another's payment.

delectación [day-lec-tah-the-on´], *f.* Delectation, pleasure, delight. **Delectación morosa**, the deliberate indulgence of some sensual pleasure.

delectar [day-lec'-tar], *va.* To delight.

delecto [day-lec'-to], *m.* Election, choice. *V.* ELECCIÓN.

delegación [day-lay-gah-the-on'], *f.* 1. Delegation, substitution. 2. Power conferred upon someone to act in behalf of others; a proxy. **Delegación de poderes**, devolution. **La delegación fue a cumplimentar al Ministro**, the delegation went to pay its respects to the minister.

delegado, da [day-lay-gah'-do], *m.f.* Delegate, deputy, commissioner, minister. —**Delegado; da**, *pp.* of DELEGAR.

delegante [day-lay-gahn'-tay], *pa.* Constituent, one that delegates.

delegar [day-lay-gar'], *va.* To delegate, to substitute.

deleitabilidad [day-lay-e-tah-be-le-dahd'], *f.* Delectableness, delightfulness.

deleitable [day-lay-tah'-blay], *a.* Delectable, delightful.

deleitación [day-lay-tah-the-on'], *f.* Delectation, pleasure, delight.

deleitamiento [day-lay-tah-me-en'-to], *m.* Delight, pleasure.

deleitante [day-lay-tahn´-tay], *pa.* Delighting.

deleitar [day-lay-tar'], *va.* To delight to please, to content. - *vr.* To delight, to have delight or pleasure in.

deleite [day-lay'-e-tay], *m.* 1. Pleasure, delight, gratification. **Deleite sexual**, sexual pleasure. 2. Lust, carnal appetite.

deleitosamente [day-lay-te-so-sah-men'-tay], *adv.* Delightfully, pleasantly, cheerfully.

deleitoso, sa [day-lay-e-to'-so, sah], *a.* Delightful, agreeable, pleasing.

deletéreo, ea [day-lay-tay'-ray-o, ah], *a. (Med.)* Deleterious, deletory.

deletreador [day-lay-tray-ah-dor'], *m.* Speller.

deletrear [day-lay-tray-ar'], *va.* 1. To spell, to read by spelling. 2. To find out and explain the meaning of what is difficult and obscure; to examine. to scrutinize.

deletreo [day-lay-tray'-o], *m.* 1. Spelling. 2. Teaching to read by spelling the letters.

deleznable [day-leth-nah'-blay], *a.* 1. Slippery, smooth. 2. Brittle, fragile.

deleznadero [day-leth-nah-day'ro], *m.* A slippery place.

deleznamiento [day-leth-nah-me-en'-to], *m.* Act of slipping.

délfico, ca [day-'fe-co, cah], *a.* Delphic, of Delphi.

delfín [del-feen'], *m.* 1. Dolphin, a cetaceous animal. 2. Dolphin, a northern constellation. 3. Dauphin, formerly the title of the eldest son of the King of France. 4. *(Pol.)* Heir apparent, designated successor.

delfina [del-fee'-nah], *f.* 1. Dauphiness, the wife or widow of the dauphin of France. 2. An alkaloid extracted from larkspur and stavesacre.

delfinela [del-fe-nay'-lah], *f. (Bot.) V.* DELFINIO.

delfinio [del-fee'-neo], *m. (Bot.)* Larkspur.

delgadez [del-gah-deth'], *f.* 1. Thinness, tenuity. 2. *(Met.)* Acuteness, ingenuity. 3. Slenderness, leanness, smallness.

delgado, da [del-gah'-do, dah], *a.* 1. Thin, tenuous, delicate, light. **Delgado como un fideo**, as thin as a rake. 2. Thin, exiguous, slender, lean, lank, gaunt. 3. *(Met.)* Acute, fine, ingenious. 4. Short, little, scanty, poor, extenuate. **Delgados de un navío**, *(Naut.)* the narrowing or rising of a ship's floor.

delgado [del-gah'-do], *m.* A strait place. **Delgados**, flanks of animals.

delgaducho, cha [del-gah-doo'-cho, chah], *a.* Thin, delicate (with a sense of depreciation).

delgazar, *va. (Obs.) V.* ADELGAZAR.

deliberación [day-lebay-rah-the-on'], *f.* 1. Deliberation, consideration, reflection. 2. Resolution, determination. 3. Liberation.

deliberadamente [day-le-be-rah-dah-men'-tay], *adv.* Deliberately.

deliberado [day-le-bay-rah'-do], *a.* Deliberate.

deliberador [day-le-bay-rah-dor'], *m.* Deliverer.

deliberamiento [day-le-bay-rah-me-en'-to] *m.* Deliverance.

deliberar [day-le-bay-rar'], *vn.* 1. To consider, to deliberate, to discourse. 2. To consult or take counsel together. -*vr.* To have delight or pleasure in.-*va.* 1. To deliberate, to think in order to choose, to ponder. 2. To rescue from captivity. 3. *(Obs.)* To emancipate.

deliberativo, va [day-le-bay-rah-tee'-vo, vah], *a.* Deliberative.

delibrar [day-le-brar'], *va.* 1. To deliberate, to determine. 2. To liberate. 3. *V.* DESPACHAR.

delicadamente [day-le-cah-dah-men'-tay], *adv.* Delicately.

delicadez [day-le-cah-deth'], *f.* 1. Delicacy, weakness of constitution. 2. *(Met.)* Delicacy, tenderness, scrupulousness, mercifulness. 3. Gentleness of manners, sweetness of temper.

delicadeza [day-le-cah-day´-thah], *f.* 1 Delicateness, tenderness, softness, effeminacy; nicety, exquisiteness. 2. Delicacy, nicety in the choice of food, daintiness. 3. Subtlety, dexterity. 4. Fineness, tenuity. 5. *(Met.)* Acuteness of understanding, refinement of wit; perspicacity; curiosity; mellifluence. 6. Idleness, negligence.

delicado, da [day-le-cah'-do, dah], *a.* 1. Delicate, sweet, pleasing, tender. 2. Weak, faint, effeminate, finical, feminine, ladylike. 3. Delicate, exquisite, nice, delicious, dainty, pleasing to the taste; of an agreeable flavor. 4. Thin, slender, subtile. 5. Nice, scrupulous, fastidious. 6. Arduous, difficult, perplexing. 7. Captious, easy of annoyance, suspicious. **Está delicado del estómago**, he has a delicate stomach. **Es muy delicado en el comer**, he´s very choosy about food. **Es muy delicada para la limpieza**, she´s very particular about cleanliness.

delicia [day-lee'-the-ah], *f.* 1. Delight, comfort, satisfaction. **El país es una delicia**, the country is delightful. 2. A lively sensual pleasure. *(Acad.).* **El libro que ha hecho las delicias de muchos niños**, a book which has been the delight of many children.

deliviarse [day-le-the-ar'-say], *vr.* To delight, to have delight or pleasure in. *(Acad.)*

deliciosamente [day-le-the-o-sah-men'-tay], *adv.* Deliciously, daintily, delightsomely.

delicioso, sa [day-le-the-oh'-so, sah], *a.* Delicious, delightful, pleasing.

delictivo [day-lec-te-vo], *a.* Criminal.

delicuescencia [day-le-coo-es-then'-the-ah], *a.* *(Chem.)* Deliquescence.

delicuescente [day-le-coo-es-then'-tay], *a.* *(Chem.)* Deliquescent.

deligación [day-le-gah-the-on'], *f.* The art of preparing and applying bandages and other external applications.

deliminación [day-le-me-nah-the-on'], *f.* Delimitation.

delimitar [day-le-me-tar'], *va.* To delimit.

delincuencia [day-lin-coo-en'-the-ah], *f.* Delinquency, offence, failure in duty. **Delincuencia de menores**, juvenile delinquency. **Cifras de la delincuencia**, figures of crimes committed.

delincuente [day-lin-coo-en-tay], *pa.* Delinquent, offender. **Delincuente habitual**, hardened criminal. **Delincuente juvenil**, juvenile delinquent.

delineación [day-le-nay-ah-the-on'], *f.* Delineation, draft, sketch.

delineador, ra [day-le-nay-ah-dor', rah], *m. & f.* Delineator, draftsman.

delineamento, delineamiento [day-le-nay-ah-men' to], *m.* Delineament. *V.* DELINEACIÓN.

delineante [day-le-ne-ahn'-tay], *m.* Draughtsman.

delinear [day-le-nay-ar'], *va.* 1. To delineate, to draw the first draft of a thing; to sketch, to figure. 2. *(Met.)* To describe, in prose or verse.

delinquimiento [day-lin-kee-me-en'-to], *m.* Delinquency, fault, transgression.

delinquir [day-lin-keer'], *vn.* To transgress the law, to offend.

delintar, delinterar, *va.* *(Obs.)* V. CEDER and TRASPASAR.

delio [day'-leo], *m.* Of Delos. (Applied to Apollo.)

deliquio [day-lee'-keo], *m.* 1. Swoon, a fainting-fit, ecstasy. 2. State of a body wich has become more or less fluid; deliquescence.

deliramento [day-le-rah-men'-to], *m.* Delirium.

delirante [day-le-rahn'-tay], *pa.* Delirious, light-headed; raving.

delirar [day-le-rar'], *vn.* 1. To be delirious, to dote, to rave. 2. *(Met.)* To rant, to talk nonsense.

delirio [day-lee'-re-o], *m.* 1. Delirium, alienation of mind, dotage. 2. *(Met.)* Rant, nonsense, idle talk. 3. Frenzy; mania. **Delirio de grandezas**, megalomania. 4. **Con delirio**, madly. **Me gusta con delirio**, I´m crazy about it.

delirium tremens [day-lee'-re-oom tray'-mens], *m.* Delirium tremens (provoked by alcoholism).

delitescencia [day-le-tes-then'-the-ah], *f.* 1. Delitescence, a sudden subsidence of a local inflammation. 2. *(Chem.)* A sudden loss, by a crystallized body, of its water of crystallization, and consequent bursting asunder.

delito [day-lee'-to], *m.* Transgression of a law; fault, crime, guilt, delinquency. **Delito de mayor cuantía**, felony. **Delito de sangre**, violent crime. **Delitos informáticos**, *(Comput.)* computer-related crime.

della, dello [dayl'-lyah, dayl'-lyo]. Contractions of the words *de ella, de ello*, of her, of it. **Della con dello**, reciprocally, alternatively, one with the other, good and bad as they come.

delta, *f.* Delta, the fourth letter of the Greek alphabet. *-m.* A triangular island at the mouth of certain rivers, named from resembling the Greek letter of same name.

deltoides, dea [del-to'-e-des, day-ah], *a.* Deltoid, like a Greek delta.

delusivo, va [day-loo-see'-vo, vah], *a.* Delusive, fallacious.

delusor [day-loo-sor'], *m.* Cheat, impostor, deluder.

delusoriamente, *adv.* Delusively, deceitfully.

delusorio, ria [day-loo-so'-reo, ah], *a.* Deceitful, fallacious.

demacración [day-mah-crah-the-on'], *f.* Wasting away in flesh (of men and animals) marasmus.

demacrado, da [day-mah-rah'-do, dah], *a.* Emaciated. **Rostro demacrado**, wan, haggard countenance.

demacrar [day-mah-crar'], *vr.* To waste away. *-va.* To cause wasting.

demagogia [day-mah-go'-heah], *f.* 1. Demagogism, ambition to rule in a popular faction. 2. The predominance of the rabble.

demagógico, ca [day-mah-go'-he-co, cah], *a.* Demagogical.

demagogo [day-mah-go'-go], *m.* Demagogue.

demagrar [day-mah-grar'], *vn.* To waste away. *V.* DEMACRAR.

demanda [day-mahn'-dah], *f.* 1. Demand, claim, pretension, complaint. **Demanda de pago**, demand for payment. 2. Judicial suit, lawsuit. **Entablar una demanda**, to sue. **Salir a la demanda**, to appear in one's own defense. 3. Request petition. 4. Interrogation. **La ley de la oferta y la demanda**, the law of demand and supply. **Ese producto no tiene demanda**, there is no demand for that product.

demandadero, ra [day-man-dah-day'-ro, rah], *m. & f.* 1. A servant man or woman who attends at the door of a nunnery or convent, to run errands. 2. A servant in a jail.

demandado, da [day-man-dah'-do, dah], *m. & f.* Defendant, the person accused. *-pp.* of DEMANDAR.

demandador [day-man-dah-dor'], *m.* 1. One who goes about asking charity for pious uses. 2. Claimant, plaintiff. 3. One who solicits a woman in marriage.

demandadora [day-man-dah-do'-rah], *f.* A female plaintiff or petitioner.

demandante [day-man-dahn'-tay], *pa.* Claimant, complainant, plaintiff.

demandar [day-man-dar'], *va.* 1. To demand, to ask, to petition. 2. To claim, to enter an action. **Demandó al periódico por calumnia**, he sued the paper for libel. **Demandar a uno por daños y perjuicios**, to sue somebody for damages.

demarcación [day-mar-cah-the-on'], *f.* Demarcation.

demarcador [day-mar-cah-dor´], *m.* Designator, surveyor.

demarcar [day-mar-car'], *va.* To mark out confines or limits, to survey. **Demarcar el terreno de un campamento**, to trace out the ground of a camp.

demarrarse [day-mar-rar'-say], *vr.* To mislead, to deviate from the right way.

demás [day-mahs'], *adv.* Over and above a certain quantity, measure, or number; besides, moreover.

demás [day-mahs'], *a.* It is almost always used with the article prefixed to it, except sometimes in the plural. **Lo demás**, the rest. **Los demás** or **las demás**, the rest, the others. **Y así de lo demás**, and so on; so with the rest. **Estar demás**, to be over and above; to be useless or superfluous. **Por demás**, uselessly, in vain, to no purpose. *V.* ADEMÁS.

demases [day-mah'-ses], *m. pl.* *(Prov.)* Abundance, copiousness.

demasía [day-mah-see'-ah], *f.* 1. Excess, superabundance. 2. Badness, iniquity, quilt. 3. A bold, arduous undertaking. **En demasía**, excessively.

demasiadamente [day-mah-se-ah-dah-men'-tay], *adv.* Excessively; too.

demasiado, da [day-mah-se-ah'-do, dah], *a.* 1. Excessive, more than enough, too much. **Eso es demasiado**, that's too much. **Con demasiado cuidado**, with excessive care. 2. Bold, daring, enterprising.

demasiado [day-mah-seah'-do], *adv.* Enough, too, sufficiently, excessively. **Comer demasiado**, to eat too much. **Es demasiado pesado para levantar**, it is too heavy to lift.

demasié [day-mah-se-ay'], *adj, adv.* V. DEMASIADO.

dembo [dem'-bo], *m.* A kind of drum which the natives of the Congo use.

demediar [day-may-de-ar'], *va.* 1. To split, to divide into halves. 2. To wear a thing until it has lost half its value. 3. To complete half its age, or course. *-vn.* To reach half the duration of a thing. **Demediar la confesión**, to confess but half one's sins.

demencia [day-men'-the-ah], *f.* Dementia, loss of mind, insanity.

demencial [day-men-the-al'], *a.* Mad, crazy, demented.

dementar [day-men-tar'], *va.* To render insane: almost always used in its reciprocal sense. *-vr.* to go mad, to become demented.

demente [day-men'-tay], *a.* Demented, mad, distracted, infatuated, insane.

demergido [day-mer-hee'-do], *a.* V. ABATIDO.

demérito [day-may'-re-to], *m.* 1. Demerit. 2. The act of demeriting.

demeritorio, ria [day-may-re-to'-re-o, ah], *a.* Without merit.

demisión [day-me-se-on'], *f.* Submission, humility.

demiurgo [day-me-oor'-go], *m.* Demiurge, in Plato's philosophy, a spirit intermediate between God and the creature.

demo [day'-mo], *m. (Prov.)* Demon, a spirit; generally an evil spirit.

democracia [day-mo-crah'-the-ah], *f.* Democracy.

damócrata [day-mo'-cra-tah], *m.* Democrat.

democráticamente [day-mo-crah'-te-cah-men-tay], *adv.* Democratically.

democrático, ca [day-mo-crah'-te-co, cah], *a.* 1. Democratical, popular, liberal. 2. *(Met.)* Modest, without pretensions. 3. Rabble.

democratización [day-mo-crah-te-thah-the-on'], Democratization.

democratizar [day-mo-cra-te-thar'], *va.* To propagate or spread democratic ideas.

demografía [day-mo-grah-fee'-ah], *f* Demography.

demográfico, ca [day-mo-grah'-fe-co, cah] *a.* Demographic. **La explosión demográfica**, the population explosion.

demógrafo, fa [day-mo'-grah-fo], *m & f.* Demographer.

demoledor [day-mo-lay-dor'], *a. (Fig.)* Powerful, overwhelming; shattering (ataque).

demoler [day-mo-lerr'], *va.* To demolish, to overthrow.

demonche [day-mo-ne'-chay], *m.* Little devil: a vulgarism in form of the diminutive.

demolición [day-mo-le-the-on'], *f.* Demolition.

demoniaco, ca [day-mo-ne-ah'-co, cah], *a.* 1. Demoniacal, devilish. 2. Demoniacal. 3. Demonian.

demonio [day-mo'-ne-o], *m.* 1. Demon, familiar. 2. The devil. **Ir como el demonio**, to go like the devil. **Tener el demonio en el cuerpo**, to be always on the go. **Esto sabe a demonios**, this tastes awful. 3. *int.* The deuce! **Estudiar con el demonio**, to show signs of great genius and acuteness for evil, or of great knavery. **¿Dónde demonios lo habré dejado?**, where the devil can I have left it?.

demontre [day-mone'-tray], *m.* V. DEMONIO. Used as an exclamation: The deuce!

demoñuelo [day-mo-nyoo-ay'-lo], *m. dim.* A little demon or devil.

demora [day-mo'-rah], *f.* 1. Delay, procrastination, protraction, demurrer. 2. Demurrage, an allowance made for the detention of a ship in a port. **Sin demora**, without delay.

demorar [day-mo-rar'], *vn.* 1. To remain, to continue long in a place. 2. *(Naut.)* To bear, to be situated in regard to a ship. **La costa demora norte**, the coast bears north. 3. *va.* To retard, to delay. *-vr.* To take a long time.

demostrable [day-mos-trah'-blay], *a.* Demonstrable, manifestable.

demostrablemente [day-mos-trah-blay-men'-tay], *adv.* Demonstrably, ostensibly.

demostración [day-mos-trah-the-on'], *f.* 1. Demonstration; manifestation. **Demostración de cariño**, show of affection. 2. *(Mil.)* Demonstration, a feigned attack upon an enemy, to divert his attention.

demostrador, ra [day-mos-trah-dor', rah], *m. & f.* Demonstrator.

demostrar [day-mos-trar'], *va.* 1. To demonstrate, to prove, to manifest, to lay open, to make out. 2. To teach. **Demostrar cómo se hace algo**, to demonstrate how something is done. **Demostrar que...**, to show that....

demostrativamente [day-mos-trah-te-vah-men'-tay], *adv.* Demonstratively.

demostrativo, va [day-mos-trah-tee'-vo, vah], *a.* Demonstrative.

demótico, ca [day-mo'-te-co, cah], *a.* Demotic, belonging to the common people: especially used of Egyptian writing.

demudación [day-moo-dah-the-on'], *f.* Change, alteration.

demudar [day-moo-dar'], *va.* 1. To alter, to change, vary. 2. To cloak, disguise. *-vr.* To be changed; to change color suddenly, or the expression of countenance. **Continuó sin demudarse**, he went on quite unaffected.

demulcente [day-mool-then'-tay], *a. & m. (Med.)* Demulcent, emollient.

demultiplexor [day-mool-te-playc-sor], *m. (Comput.)* Demultiplexer.

denante, denantes [day-nan'-tay], *adv. (Prov. Obs.)* V. ANTES.

denario [day-nah'-re-o], *m.* 1. Roman denarius, the penny of the New Testament, a small silver coin. 2. Denary, decimal or tenth number. 3. Money paid to laborers for one day's labor.

denario, ria [day-nah'-re-o, ah], *a.* Tenth, containing the number of ten.

dende [den'-day], *adv.* Hence, from V. DESDE.

dendrita, dendrite [den-dree'-tah, den-dree'-tay], *f.* Dendrite, a mineral representing the figures of plants.

dendrítico, ca [den-dree'-te-co, cah], *a.* Dendritic, showing markings like foliage.

dendrografía [den-dro-grah-fee'-ah], *f.* Dendrology, a description of trees.

dendrómetro [den-dro'-may-tro], *m. (Math.)* An instrument which resolves in a graphic manner problems of plane geometry.

denegación [day-nay-gah-the-on'], *f.* Denial, refusal, denegation.

denegar [day-nay-gar'], *va.* To deny, to refuse, to denegate.

denegrecer [day-nay-gray-therr'], *va.* 1. To blacken, to darken, to denigrate. 2. V. DENIGRAR.

denegrido, da [day-nay-gree'-do, dah], *a.* Blackened, denigrated. *-pp.* of DENEGRIR.

denegrir [day-nay-greer'], *va.* V. DENEGRECER.

dengoso, sa [den-go'-so, sah], *a.* Fastidious, overnice, scrupulous.

dengue [den'-gay], *m.* 1. Fastidiousness. 2. Prudery. 3. A sort of woman's cape with long points. 4. A boat used in the sardine fishery. 5. Dengue, or breakbone fever. 6. Affectation. **Andar en dengues**, to be overnice, to be too punctilious. **No andar en dengues**, not to mind trifles.

denguero, ra [den-gay'-ro, rah], *a.* Prudish, affected. V. DENGOSO.

denigración [day-ne-grah-the-on'], *f.* Denigration, stigma, disgrace.

denigrante [day-ne-grahn-tay], *a.* Insulting; degrading.

denigrar [day-ne-grar'], *va.* 1. To denigrate or blacken the character of a person, to calumniate, to defame, to expose, to censure. 2. To insult.

denigrativamente [day-ne-grah-te-vah-men'-tay], *adv.* Injuriously, infamously.

denigrativo, va [day-ne-grah-tee'-vo, vah], *a.* Blackening, stigmatizing.

denigratorio [day-ne-grah-to-re-o], *a.* Denigratory.

denodado, da [day-no-dah'-do, dah], *a.* Bold, intrepid, audacious.

denominable [day-no-me-nah'-blay], *a.* Denominable.

denominación [day-no-me-nah-the-on'], *f.* Denomination. **Moneda de baja denominación**, low value coin. **Denominación social**, *(Mex.)* Firm´s official name. **Denominación de origen**, mark of origin.

denominadamente [day-no-me-nah-dah-men'-tay], *adv.* Distinctly, definitively.

denominado [day-no-me-nah'-do], *a.* Named, called; so-called.

denominador [day-no-me-nah-dor'], *m. (Arith.)* Denominator. **Denominador común**, *(Math.)* Common denominator.

denominar [day-no-me-nar'], *va.* To denominate, to give a name.

denominativo, va, *a.* Denominative.

denostadamente [day-nos-tah-dah-men'-tay], *adv.* Ignominiously, insultingly.

denostador [day-nos-tah-dor'], *m.* Vilifier, railer, reviler.

denostar [day-nos-tar'], *va.* To insult a person with foul language, to revile, to abuse.

denotación [day-no-tah-the-on'], *f.* Designation, denotation.

denotar [day-no-tar'], *va.* 1. To denote, to signify, to express. 2. To explain.

denotativo, va [day-no-tah-tee'-vo, vah], *a.* Denoting, denotative.

densamente [dayn-sah-men'-tay], *adv.* Closely, densely.

densidad [den-se-dahd'], *f.* 1. Density, closeness, compactness, grossness. 2. Obscurity, confusion, darkness. **Densidad de integración**, integration density.

densifoliado, da [den-se-fo-le-ah'-do, dah], *a.* Thick-leaved, of crowded foliage.

densímetro [den-see'-may-tro], *m.* Densimeter, an apparatus for determining the relative density of a substance.

denso, sa [den'-so, sah], *a.* 1. Dense, thick. 2. Close, compact. **El argumento es algo denso**, the reasoning is somewhat confused.

dentado, da [den-tah'-do, dah], *a.* 1. Furnished with teeth. 2. Denticulated, dentated, toothed. 3. Crenated, indented. *-pp.* of DENTAR. **Dentado** is sometimes used as a substantive.

dentadura [den-tah-doo'-rah], *f.* 1. A set of teeth. **Dentadura postiza**, false teeth. **Tener mala dentadura**, to have bad teeth. 2. Number and quality of the cogs or teeth of a wheel.

dentagra [den-tah´-grah], *f.* Toothache.

dental [den-tahl'], *m.* 1. Bed to which the plough-share is fixed. 2. A wooden fork, used to separate the straw from corn.

dental [den-tahl'], *a.* 1. Dental, belonging to the teeth. 2. *(Gram.)* Dental pronounced principally by the agency of the teeth.

dentar [den-tar´], *va. & vn.* 1. To tooth, to furnish with teeth, to indent; to cut into teeth. 2. To teeth, to cut teeth.

dentaria [den-tah'-re-ah], *f. (Bot.)* Toothwort.

dentecillo [den-tay-theel'-lyo], *m. dim.* Small tooth.

dentejón [den-tay-hone'], *m.* Yoke-tree, with which oxen are yoked to the cart.

dentelaria [den-tay-lah'-re-ah], *f. (Bot.)* Leadwort.

dentelete [den-tay-lay'-tay], *m.* Dentil, or dental, of a cornice of some Ionic entablatures.

dentellada [den-tel-lyah'-dah], *f.* 1. Gnashing of teeth. 2. Nip, a pinch with the teeth. 3. Impression made by the teeth. **A dentelladas**, snappishly, peevishly. **Dar o sacudir dentelladas**, to speak surlily and uncivilly.

dentellado, da [den-tel-lyah'-do, dah], *a.* 1. Denticulated, dented. 2. Bit or wounded with the teeth. *-pp.* of DENTELLAR.

dentellar [den-tel-lyar'], *vn.* To gnash, to grind or collide the teeth. **Estaba dentellando**, his teeth were chattering.

dentellear [den-tel-lyay-ar'], *va.* To bite, to fix the teeth in anything.

dentellón [den-tel-lyone'], *m.* 1. Moulding or ornament of the Corinthian cornice. 2. Piece of a doorlock which represents a large tooth.

dentera [den-tay'-rah], *f.* 1. An unpleasant sensation, or tingling pain in the teeth. **Dar dentera a uno**, to set somebody´s teeth on edge. 2. *(Met.)* V. ENVIDIA. **Le da dentera que hagan fiestas al niño**, it makes him jealous when they make a fuss of the baby.

dentezuelo [den-tay-thoo-ay'-lo], *m. dim.* A little tooth.

dentición [den-te-the-on'], *f.* 1. Dentition, cutting the teeth. 2. Dentition, the time at which children's teeth are cut.

denticular [den-te-coo-lar'], *a.* Like teeth, as a tooth; denticulated, toothed.

dentículo [den-tee'-coo-lo], *m. (Arch.)* Denticle, dentil.

dentífrico [den-tee'-fre-co], *m.* Dentifrice, toothpaste.

dentirrostros [den-teer-ros'-tros], *m. pl. (Zool.)* An order of birds with the upper mandible notched near the tip.

dentista [den-tees'-tah], *m & f.* Dentist.

dentivano, na [den-te-vah'-no, nah], *a.* Having long and large teeth: applied to horses.

dentolabial [den-to-lah-be-ahl'], *a. (Gram.)* Dentilabial, articulated by placing the lips and teeth together, as f.

dentón, na [den-tone', nah], *a.* Having large uneven teeth.

dentón [den-tone'], *m. (Zool.)* 1. Dental, a small shellfish. 2. A seafish of the sparus family, like a bream, remarkable for its strong, conical teeth.

dentrambos [den-trahm'-bos]. Contraction of *De entrambos*.

dentro [den'-tro], *adv.* Within. **Dentro del año**, in the course of the year. **Dentro de poco**, shortly. **Allí dentro**, in there. **Vamos dentro**, let´s go in. *-prep.* 1. **Dentro de**, in, inside. **Dentro de la casa**, inside the house. 2. **Lo metió dentro del cajón**, he put it into the drawer. 3. Into, inside (tiempo). **Dentro de tres meses**, inside three months. 4. **Dentro de lo posible**, as far as one can.

dentudo, da [den-too'-do, dah], *a.* Having large uneven teeth.

denudación [day-noo-dah-the-on'], *f.* 1. Denudation, laying bare. 2. *(Geol.)* Erosion of mineral matters which form beds of auriferous sands.

denuedo [day-noo-ay'-do], *m.* Boldness, audaciousness, courage, intrepidity.

denuesto [day-noo-es'-to], *m.* Affront, insult.

denuncia [day-noon'-the-ah], *f.* 1. Denunciation. 2. Information laid against another person. **Hacer una denuncia**, to report an accident. **Falsa denuncia**, false accusation.

denunciable [day-noon-the-ah'-blay], *a.* Fit to be denounced. V. DELATABLE.

denunciación [day-noon-the-ah-the-on'], *f.* Denunciation, accusation. V. DENUNCIA and DELACIÓN.

denunciador [day-noon-the-ah-dor'], *m.* Denunciator, informer, accuser.

denunciar [day-noon-the-ar'], *va.* 1. To report, to give notice. 2. To denounce, to lay an information against another. 3. To prognosticate, to foretell. 4. To pronounce, to denounce, to proclaim, to publish solemnly. **El accidente fue denunciado a la policía**, the accident was reported to the police.

denunciatorio, ria [day-noon-the-ah-to´-re-o, ah], *a.* Denunciatory.

denuncio [day-noon'-the-o], *m. (Prov.) V.* DENUNCIA.

deñar [day-nyar'], *va.* To deign, to deem worthy.

deontología [day-on-to-lo-hee'-ah], *f.* Deontology, ethics, the science of moral obligation.

deontólogo [day-on-toh'-lo-go], *m.* A writer on ethics or deontology.

deoperculado, da [day-o-per-coo-lah'-do, dah], *a.* Deoperculate, deprived of the operculum.

Dep. 1. *abr.* de **Departamento** (Department, Dept.). 2. *abr.* de **Depósito** (deposit, depot, dep.).

deparar [day-pa-rar'], *va.* To offer, to furnish, to present. **Los placeres que el viaje nos deparó**, the pleasures which the trip afforded us.

departamento [day-par-tah-men'-to], *m.* 1. Apartment. 2. Department, separate part, office or division. **Departamento de primera**, first-class compartment. 3. A part or division of the executive government. 4. A province, district, or subdivision of a country.

departidor, ra [day-par-te-dor', do'-rah], *m. & f.* Distributor, divider.

departimiento [day-par-te-me-en'-to], *m. (Obs.)* 1. Division, separation. 2. Distance; difference. 3. Dispute.

departir [day-par-teer'], *vn.* To speak, to converse, to commune. *-a.* 1. To divide, to separate. 2. To distinguish by notes of diversity. 3. To argue, to contend, to dispute. 4. To teach, to explain; to mark out, to impede, to obstruct.

depauperar [day-pah-oo-pay-rar'], *va.* 1. To impoverish. 2. To debilitate, to weaken, to exhaust.

dependencia [day-pen-den'-the-ah], *f.* 1. Dependence, dependency, the state of dependence on another. 2. Dependence, subordination to superior power. 3. Relations by consanguinity or affinity. 4. Business, affair, trust, charge. **Pedro tiene muchas dependencias**, Peter has a deal of business on his hands. 5. Dependence, relation of one thing to another.

depender [day-pen-derr'], *vn.* 1. To depend, to rest upon anything as its cause. 2. To depend, to be in a state of dependence or servitude. 3. To hang, to be dependent on. **Depender de**, to depend on. **Depende de lo que haga él.** it depends on what he does. **Todos dependemos de ti**, we are all relying on you.

dependienta [day-pen-de-ayn'-tah], *f.* Salesgirl, saleswoman, shop assistant.

dependiente [day-pen-de-en'-tay], *pa. & m.* 1. A dependent, one subordinate to or at the disposal of another. 2 *(Amer.)* A clerk.

dependientemente [day-pen-de-ayn-tay-men'-tay], *adv.* Dependently.

depilación [day-pe-lah-the-on'], *f.* Depilation.

depilar [day-pe-lar'], *va.* To strip of hair, to depilate.

depilatorio, a [day-pe-lah-to'-re-o, ah], *a.* Depilatory, used to remove hair.

depletivo, va [day-play-tee'-vo, vah], *a.* Depletive, evacuant.

deplorable [day-plo-rah'-blay], *a.* Deplorable, lamentable, calamitous, hopeless, mournful.

deplorablemente [day-plo-rah-blay-men'-tay], *adv.* Deplorably, mournfully, sorrowfully.

deplorar [day-plo-rar'], *va.* To deplore, to lament, to bewail, to bemoan, to condole, to mourn.

deponente [day-po-nen'-tay], *m. & f.* Deponent, a witness.

deponer [day-po-nerr'], *va.* 1. To lay by, separate, to put aside from oneself. 2. To depose, to remove from office. 3. To declare judicially, to depose, to declare upon oath. 4. To take down, to remove a thing from the place in which it is. 5. To evacuate the bowels. *-vn.* 1. *(Jur.)* To give evidence, to make a statement. 2. *(CAm. Mex.)* To vomit. *(Yo depongo, yo deponga,* from *Deponer. V.* PONER.)

deponible [day-po-nee'-blay], *a.* Declarable, capable of affirmation.

depopulador [day-po-poo-lah-dor'], *m.* Depopulator, devastator of a country or city.

deportación [day-por-tah-the-on'], *f.* Deportation, transportation, banishment.

deportar [day-por-tar'], *va.* To transport, to exile, to banish. *-vr.* 1. To take a diversion. 2. To rest.

deporte [day-por'-tay], *m.* 1. Sports, athletics. 2. Diversion, pastime, recreation. **Deportes acuáticos**, water sports. **El fútbol es un deporte**, football is a game. **Es muy aficionado a los deportes**, he is very fond of sport.

deportista [day-por-tees'-tah], *m.* Sportsman, athlete. *-f.* Sportswoman, athlete.

deportividad [day-por-te-ve-dahd'], *f.* Sportmanship.

deportivo, va [day-por-tee'-vo, vah], *a.* Athletic, connected with sports. **Espíritu deportivo**, sportsmanship.

deposición [day-po-se-the-on'], *f.* 1. Deposition, testimony upon oath. 2. Declaration, assertion, affirmation. 3. Deposition, degradation from dignity or station. 4. Alvine evacuation. 5. *(Med.)* Depression.

depositador, ra [day-po-se-tah-dor'], *m. f.* One who leaves anything in trust with another, depositor.

depositante [day-po-se-tahn'-tay], *pa.* Depositor.

depositar [day-po-se-tar'], *pa.* 1. To deposit, to confide, to trust. 2. To commit or to put in any place for safekeeping. 3. To put a person in a position where he may freely manifest his will. 4. To inclose, to contain. *-vr.* To settle.

depositaría [day-po-se-tah-ree'-ah], *f.* Depository, the place where a thing is lodged.

depositario, ria [day-po-se-tah´-re-o, ah], *m. & f.* Depositary, the person with whom a thing is lodged in trust; trustee, receiver.

depositario, ria [day-pose-tah'-re-o, ah], *a.* Relating to a depository.

depósito [day-po'-se-to], *m.* 1. The thing deposited; deposit, trust. 2. Depository, the place where a thing is lodged. 3. The wind chest and windtrunks of organs. 4. *(Gil.)* A recruiting station. 5. *(Chem.)* Deposit, precipitate. 6. *(Geol.)* Layers of aqueous rocks formed by sluggish waters. **Depósito de animales perdidos**, pound. **En depósito**, in bond. **Depósito bancario**, bank deposit. **Depósito de libros**, book stack. **Depósito de basura**, rubbish dump. **Depósito de agua**, water tank. **Depósito de gasolina**, gas tank. **Depósito adicional**, bonus tank.

depravación [day-prah-vah-the-on'], *f.* Depravation, depravity.

depravado, da [day-prah-vah'-do, dah], *a.* Bad, depraved, lewd. *-pp.* of DEPRAVAR.

depravador [day-prah-vah-dor'], *m.* Depraver, corrupter.

depravar [day-prah-var'], *va.* To deprave, to vitiate, to corrupt, to contaminate, used chiefly of immaterial things. *-vr.* To become depraved.

depre [day-pray], *f.* Depression. **Tiene la depre**, she´s feeling a bit low.

deprecación [day-pray-cah-the-on'], *f.* Petition, prayer, deprecation, conjuration.

deprecar [day-pray-car'], *va.* To entreat, to implore, to deprecate.

deprecativo, va, deprecatorio, ria [day-pray-cah-tee'-vo, vah], *a.* Deprecative, deprecatory .

depreciación [day-pray-the-ah-the-on'], *f.* Depreciation, decrease in price.

depreciar [day-pray-the-ar'], *va.* To depreciate, to reduce the value of. *-vr.* To depreciate, to lose value.

depredación [day-pray-dah-the-on'], *f.* 1. Depredation, plundering, laying waste, pillage. 2. Malversation committed by guardians or trustees.

depredador, ra [day-pray-dah-dor', rah], *m. & f.* A robber, destroyer, predator.

depredar [day-pray-dar'], *va.* To rob, to pillage, to defraud, to be predatory on.

deprensión [day-pren-se-on´], *f.* A basement, humiliation.

depresión [day-pray-se-on'], *f.* 1. Depression, pressing down. 2. Depression, abasement. 3. Lowering; drop, fall. **Depresión del mercurio**, fall in temperature.

depresivo, va [day-pray-see'-vo, vah], *a.* Depressive, lowering.

depresor [day-pray-sor'], *m.* 1. Depressor, an oppressor. 2. *(Anat.)* Depressor, a name given to muscles which depress the part on which they act.

depresorio, ria [day-pray-so'-re-o, ah], *a.* Depressor.

depreterición [day-pray-tay-re-the-on'], *f. (Obs. Law)* Preterition. *V.* PRETERICIÓN.

deprimación [day-pre-mah-the-on'], *f.* Act and effect of cropping frostbitten grass.

deprimado, da [day-pre-mah'-do, dah], *a.* Applied to the fields or meadow in which the animals have eaten the tips of grass frostbitten by dews.

deprimar [day-pre-mar'], *va.* To make horses crop off the ends of grass frostbitten by the first spring dews.

deprimente [day-pre-men'-tay], *a.* Depressing. *-m.* Depressant.

deprimido, da [day-pre-mee'-do, dah], *a.* 1. Compressible, disappearing under the pressure of the finger, said of the pulse. 2. Flattened or hollowed at the middle; said of a tumor. 3. Depressed.

deprimir [day-pre-meer'], *va.* To depress, to humble, to deject, to sink; to depreciate, to belittle. *-vr.* To get depressed.

depurable [day-poo-rah'blay], *a.* Purifiable, capable of cleansing.

depuración [day-poo-rah-the-on'], *f.* Depuration, purification.

depurado, da [day-poo-rah'-do, dah], *a.* Depurate, cleansed, purified. *-pp.* of DEPURAR.

depuradora [day-poo-rah-do'-rah], *f.* Purifying plant.

depuramiento [day-poo-rah-meen'-to], *m. V.* DEPURACIÓN.

depurar [day-poo-rar'], *va.* To depurate, to cleanse, to purify, to filter.

depurativo, va [day-poo rah tee' vo, vah], *a.* Depurant, depurative, purifying; antiscorbutic. *-m.* Blood tonic.

depuratorio, ria [day-poo-rah-to'-re-o, ah], *a.* Depuratory, purifying.

derecha [day-ray-chah], *f.* 1. Right hand, right side. 2. *(Obs.)* Pack of hounds, or the path they pursue in the chase. **A derechas** or **a las derechas**, right; well done, as it ought to be, honestly, rightly, justly. **No hacer cosa a derechas**, not to do anything right; to do everything wrong. **Torcer a la derecha**, to turn right **Seguir por la derecha**, to keep right.

derechamente [day-ray-chah-men'-tay], *adv.* 1. Directly, full, straight. 2. Rightly, prudently, justly. 3 Expressly, formally, legally.

derechera [day-ray-chay'-rah], *f.* The direct road.

derechero [day-ray-chay'-ro], *m.* Clerk appointed to collect taxes.

derechista [day-ray-chees'-tah], *m.* Rightist (in political tendencies); rightwing.

derecho, cha [day-ray'-cho, chah], *a.* 1. Right, straight. **Todo derecho**, straight-forward. 2. Just, lawful, well-grounded, reasonable. legitimate. **Hecho y derecho**, perfect, absolute, complete; true, certain; without doubt. 3. Right, opposite to the left. *(Obs.)* Certain; directed.

derecho [day-ray'-cho], *m.* 1. Right, justice, law, equity. **Derecho civil**, civil law. **Derecho penal**, criminal law. 2. A just claim. 3. Tax, duty, impost, custom, toll. **Sujeto a derechos**, subject to duty. **Derechos de aduana**, **derechos arancelarios**, customs duty. 4. Due, fee, payment claimed by persons in office; in the last two senses it is almost always used in the plural. 5. The right side of cloth. 6. Exemption, freedom, privilege. 7. *(Obs.)* Road, path. **Derecho administrativo**, a collection of ordinances, regulations, etc.. **En derecho de su dedo** or **sus narices**, selfish care for one's own interest. **Derecho de gentes**, natural law, such as prevails among outside nations, as contrasted with the Roman law. **Derecho no escrito**, unwritten law, established custom. **Derecho de propiedad**

literaria, copyright. **Derecho de visita**, right of search. **Tener derechos a**, to have a right to.

derecho [day-ray'-cho], *adv. V.* DERECHAMENTE.

derecho de vía [day-ray'-cho day vee'-ah], *m.* Right of way.

derechuelo, derechuelos [day-ray-choo-ay'-lo], *m.* One of the first seams taught to little girls.

derechura [day-ray-choo'-rah], *f.* 1. Rectitude; right way. 2. Salary, pay. 3. *(Obs.)* Right; dexterity. **En derechura,** 1. By the most direct road. 2. Without delay, directly, immediately.

deriva [day-ree'-vah], *f.* 1. *(Naut.)* Ship's course. **Ir a la deriva**, to be adrift. 2. *(Aer.)* Deviation, drift.

derivable [day-re-vah'-blay], *a.* Derivable, deducible.

derivación [day-re-vah-the-on'], *f.* 1. Derivation, descent. 2. Derivation, a draining of water, a turning of its course. 3. *(Gram.)* Derivation, the tracing of a word from its original. 4. Shunt (en electricidad). 5. The act of separating one thing from another. 6. Diversion, turn-off (de una carretera).

derivado [day-re-vah-do], *m.* 1. Derivative. 2. Byproduct.

derivar [day-re-var'], *va.* 1. To derive, to separate one thing from another. 2. To derive, to deduce, or to trace anything from its origin. *-vn. (Naut.)* To derive or deflect from the course. *-vr.* To derive, to come from, to descend from.

derivativo, va [day-re-vah-tee'-vo, vah], *a.* Derivative.

dermalgia [der-mahl'-he-ah], *f.* Neuralgia of the skin.

dermatitis [der-mah-tee'-tis], *f.* Dermatitis, inflammation of the skin.

dermatología [der-mah-to-lo-hee'-ah], *f. (Anat.)* Dermatology, science of skin diseases.

dermatológico, ca [der-mah-to-lo'-he-co, cah], *a.* Dermatological, skin (as adjective).

dermatologista, or **dermatólogo** [der-mah-to-lo-hees'-tah, der-mah-toh'-lo-go], *m.* Dermatologist, specialist in skin diseases.

dermatoponte [der-mah-to-pon'-tay], *a. (Zool.)* Breathing by the skin.

dermesto [der-mes'-to], *m.* Dermestid, a genus including the bacon beetle and carpet beetle; very destructive warehouse pests.

dérmico, ca [dayr'-me-co, cah], *a.* Dermic, relating to the skin.

dermis [dayr'-mis], *f.* Derma, dermis, the corium or true skin.

dermitis [der-mee'-tis], *f.* Inflammation of the skin.

dermodonte [der-mo don' tay], *a. (Zool.)* With teeth set below the skin.

dermografía [der-mo-gra-fee'-ah], *f.* Dermography, a scientific description of the skin.

dermóideo, a [der-mo'-e-dayo, ah], *a.* Dermoid, resembling skin.

dermología, dermologista [der-mo-lo-he'-ah], etc. *V.* DERMATOLOGÍA, etc.

derogable [day-ro-gah'-blay], *a.* Abolishable, annullable.

derogación [day-ro-gah-the-on'], *f.* 1. Derogation or abolition of a law, or of one of its clauses. 2. Deterioration, diminution.

derogado, da [day-ro-gah'-do, dah], *a. pp.* of DEROGAR. Derogate, abrogated.

derogar [dar-ro-gar'], *va.* 1. To derogate, to abolish or annul any legal disposition. 2. To reform, to remove.

derogatorio, ria [day-ro-gah-to'-re-o, ah], *a.* Derogatory, derogative.

derrabadura [der-rah-bah-doo'-rah], *f.* The wound made in docking the tail of an animal.

derrabar [der-rah-bar'], *va.* To dock the tail.

derraigar [dayr-rah-e-gar'], *va. V.* DESARRAIGAR.

derrama [der-rah'-mah], *f.* Assessment of a tax, duty, or impost.

derramadamente [dar-rah-mah-dah-men'-tay], *adv.* 1. Profusely, lavishly. 2. Depravedly, corruptly.

derramadero, ra [der-rah-mah-day'-ro, rah], *a. V.* VERTEDERO.

derramador [der-rah-mah-dor'], *m.* Prodigal, waster, spendthrift.

derramamiento [der-rah-mah-me-en´-to], *m*. 1. Pouring out, wasting, or lavishing something. 2. Effusion, waste, spilling or shedding. 3. Dispersion, scattering, spreading. **Derramamiento de lágrimas**, flood of tears.

derramar [der-rah-mar´], *va*. 1. To pour, to-let out of a vessel, as liquids. 2. To leak, to let any liquid in or out. 3. To publish, to spread. 4. To spill, to scatter, to waste, to shed. **Derramar una taza de café**, to spill a cup of coffee. 5. To assess taxes. **Derramar doctrina**, *(Met.)* to diffuse a doctrine. *-vr*. 1. To be scattered or spread, to fly abroad. 2. To abandon oneself to sensual pleasures. 3. To disembogue itself (río), as a river. 4. *(Obs.)* To escape.

derrame [der-rah´-may], *m*. 1. The portion of liquor or seed lost in measuring. 2. Leakage, allowance for accidental loss in liquid measures. 3. Bevel of a wall at a window or door, to facilitate the entrance of light. 4. Declivity. 5. Subdivision of a ravine or valley in narrow outlets. 6. *(Mod.)* Accumulation of a liquid in a cavity, or its issuing from the body. **Derrame cerebral**, brain haemorrhage.

derramo [der-rah´-mo], *m*. The sloping of a wall in the aperture for door or window.

derrapar [dayr-rah-par´], *vn*. *(Aut.)* To skid. *-vr*. To slip.

derrape [dayr-rah´-pay], *m*. 1. *(Aut.)* Skip. 2. *(Carib.)* Uproar (alboroto).

derraspado [der-ras-pah´-do], *a*. Beardless (trigo).

derredor [der-ray-dor´], *m*. Circumference, circuit; round about: generally used in the plural, or with the article *al*, or the preposition *en*. **Al derredor** or **en derredor**, round about.

derrenegar [der-ray-nay-gar´], *vn*. *(Coll.)* To hate, to detest.

derrengada [der-ren-gah´-dah], *f*. *(Prov.)* Step in dancing.

derrengado, da [der-ren-gah´-do, dah], *a*. Incurvated, bent, crooked, lame, crippled. *-pp*. of DERRENGAR.

derrengadura [der-ren-gah-doo´-rah], *f*. Weakness in the hip, dislocation of the hip; lameness.

derrengar [der-ren-gar´], *va*. 1. To sprain the hip, to hurt severely the spine or loins of a person or animal; to cripple. 2. *(Prov.)* To knock off the fruit of a tree. *-vn*. *(Low.)* To abominate, to detest.

derrengo [der-ren´-go], *m*. *(Prov.)* Stick with which fruits are knocked off.

derretido, da [der-ray-tee´-do, dah], *a*. Melted (hielo, mantequilla). Madly in love (enamorado). *-pp*. of DERRETIR.

derretimiento [der-raytemeen´-to], *m*. 1. Thaw, liquefaction, fusion, melting (nieve). 2. Violent affection.

derretir [der-ray-teer´], *va*. 1. To liquefy, to melt (hielo, manteca), to dissolve, to fuse. 2. *(Coll.)* To change money. 3. To consume, to expend. *-vr*. 1. To be deeply in love. 2. To fall in love very easily. 3. To liquefy, to fuse, to melt or to be melted, to become liquid. 4. To melt, to grow tender or loving. 5. To be full of impatience. *(Acad.)* 6. To smelt, to found.

derribado [der-re-bah´-do], *a*. Applied to horses having the croup or buttocks rounder and lower than usual.*-pp*. of DERRIBAR.

derribar [der-re-bar´], *va*. 1. To demolish, to level with the ground. 2. To throw down, to knock down, to fell, to bring to the ground; to flatten; to lay flat, to lodge, to prostrate. **Fue derribado sobre el Canal**, he was shot down over the Channel. 3. To depose, to displace, to divest, to make a person lose protection, estimation, or acquired dignity. 4. *(Met.)* To subject, to subdue disordered passions of the mind. *-vr*. To tumble down, to throw oneself on the ground.

derribo [der-ree´-bo], *m*. 1. Demolition, as of a building. 2. Ruins of a demolished building.

derrisorio, a [der-re-so´-reo, ah], *a*. Derisive. V. IRRISORIO.

derrocadero [der-ro-cah-day´-ro], *m*. A very rocky and precipitous place, whence there is danger of falling.

derrocar [der-ro-car´], *va*. 1. To precipitate or fling down from a rock. 2. To pull down, to demolish, to fell, to lay. 3. *(Met.)* To rob one of his fortune or happiness. 4. To precipitate, to distract from anything spiritual or intellectual. *-vn*. To tumble, to fall down. -

vr. **Derrocarse por un precipicio**, to throw oneself over a cliff.

derrochador, ra [der-ro-chah-dor´,rah], *m*. *f*. A prodigal, a spendthrift.

derrochamiento [der-ro-chah-me-en´-to], *m*. *(Antiq.)* Waste, squandering. V. DERROCHE.

derrochar [der-ro-char´], *va*. To dissipate, to waste or destroy property, to make way with.

derroche [der-ro´-chay], *m*. Waste, dissipation, destruction. **No se puede tolerar tal derroche**, such extravagance is not to be tolerated.

derrota [der-ro´-tah], *f*. 1. *(Naut.)* Ship's course, the tack on which a ship sails; **seguir en directa derrota**, *(Naut.)* to steer a straight course. 2. Road, path. 3. Rout or defeat of an army; overthrow. **Sufrir una grave derrota**, to suffer a serious defeat.

derrotado [dayr-ro-tah´-do], *a*. 1. Defeated (vencido); defeated (equipo), beaten, losing. 2. Shabby (persona). **Un actor derrotado**, a shabby old actor.

derrotar [der-ro-tar´], *va*. 1. *(Naut.)* To cause to drive or fall off (viento, tormentas). 2. To destroy health or fortune. 3. To rout, to defeat. *-vn*. To arrive in a place in a ruined state, or in the utmost confusion and disorder. *-vr*. To cough (delincuente), to sing.

derrote [der-ro´-tay], *m*. 1. Defeat, rout, destruction. 2. *(Prov.)* Dilapidation.

derrotero [der-ro-tay´-ro], *m*. 1. *(Naut.)* Collection of sea-charts. 2. *(Naut.)* Ship's course. 3. *(Met.)* Course, way or plan of life, conduct, or action.

derrotismo [der-ro-tees´-mo], *m*. Defeatism.

derrotista [der-ro-tees´-tah], *m*. & *f*. Defeatist.

derrubiar [der-roo-be-ar´], *va*. To break the bounds of a river or rivulet insensibly; to undermine or wash away the ground.

derrubio [der-roo´-be-o], *m*. The insensible overflow of water from a river or rivulet over the level grounds near to its bed, and the earth which falls or moulders away by this means.

derruir [der-roo-eer´], *va*. To demolish, to destroy, to ruin. V. DERRIBAR.

derrumbadero [der-room-bah-day´-ro], *m*. 1. Precipice; craggy, steep, and broken ground. 2. *(Met.)* A thorny or arduous affair.

derrumbamiento [der-room-bah-me-en´-to], *m*. Precipitation.

derrumbar [der-room-bar´], *va*. To precipitate, to throw down headlong. *-vr*. 1. To precipitate oneself head-long. 2. To sink down, crumble away, tumble down (edificio). 3. *(Fig.)* **Se han derrumbado los precios**, prices have tumbled.

derrumbe [der-room-bay´], *m*. 1. A tumbling down, collapse. 2. A landslide.

derviche [der-vee´-chay], *m*. Dervish, a Mohammedan monk or friar.

des [dess]. 1. A preposition, corresponding with the Latin *dis*; never used but in compound words. 2. *(Obs.)* A contraction of *de ese*, of this, of that.

desabarrancar [des-ah-bar-ran-car´], *va*. 1. To drag, to draw, or to pull out of a ditch. 2. *(Met.)* To disentangle from a state of perplexity, to extricate from difficulties.

desabastecer [des-ah-bas-tay-therr´], *va*. Not to supply a place with provisions, either through neglect or in consequence of a prohibition.

desabastecido [des-ah-bas-tay-the´-do], *a*. **Estar desabastecido de,** to be out of. **Nos cogió desabastecidos de gasolina**, it caught us without gas.

desabastecimiento [des-ah-bas-tay-the-me-ayn´-to], *m*. Shortage, scarcity.

desabejar [des-ah-bay-har´], *va*. To remove bees from their hive.

desabido, da [day-sah-bee´-do, dah], *a*. *(Obs.)* 1. Ignorant, illiterate. 2. Excessive, extraordinary.

desabillé [des-ah-beel-lyay´], *m*. Dishabille, undress; a loose dress for women.

desabitar [des-ah-be-tar'], *va. (Naut.)* To unbitt. **Desabitar el cable**, to unbitt a cable; that is, to remove the turns of a cable from the bitts.

desabollador [des-ah-bol-lyah-dor'], *m.* 1. An instrument used by tinworkers to take bulges out of pewter dishes, plates, or vessels. 2. Tinker.

desabollar [des-ah-bol-lyar], *va.* To tinker.

desabonarse [des-ah-bo-nar'-say], *vr.* To revoke a season-ticket or subscription.

desabono [des-ah-bo'-no], *m.* 1. Prejudice, injury. 2. Cancellation of one's subscription.

desabor [day-sah-bor'], *m.* 1. Insipidity, want of taste. 2. *(Met. Obs.)* Dullness, dejection, lowness of spirits.

desaborar [day-sah-bo-rar'], *va.* 1. To render a thing tasteless, to make it insipid or disgusting. 2. *(Met.)* To disgust, to vex.

desabordarse [des-ah-bor-dar'-say], *vr. (Naut.)* To get clear of a ship which has run foul of one's vessel.

desaborido, da [day-sah-bo-ree'-do, dah], *a.* 1. Tasteless, insipid. 2. Without substance.

desabotonar [des-ah-bo-to-nar'], *va.* To unbutton. *-vn.* To blow, to bloom, to blossom. *-vr.* To come undone.

desabozar [des-ah-bo-thar'], *va. (Naut.)* To unstopper.

desabrazar [des-ah-brah-thar], *va.* To separate one thing from another; to loosen, release what is embraced.

desabridamente [day-sah-bre-dah-men'-tay], *adv.* Bitterly, rudely, harshly.

desabrido, da [day-sah-bree'-do, dah], *a.* 1. Tasteless, insipid. 2. Sour, peevish, severe. 3. Hard, difficult (armas de fuego). 4. Bleak, sharp (aire, viento). 5. Disgusted, dissatisfied, at variance with.

desabrigadamente [de-sah-bri-gah-dah-men'-tay], *adv.* 1. Nakedly, without covering 2. Without shelter, without harbor.

desabrigado, da [des-ah-bre-gah'-do, dah], *a.* 1. Uncovered, wanting covering or clothes. 2. Shelterless; harborless, unsheltered. *-f.* An open roadstead. 3. *(Met.)* Abandoned, without support. *-pp.* of DESABRIGAR.

desabrigar [des-ah-bre-gar'], *va.* 1. To uncover, to divest of covering; to strip, or to take off covering. 2. To deprive of shelter or harbor. *-vr.* To take off one's clothing; to leave oneself bare. **Desabrigarse en la cama**, to throw off one's bedcovers.

desabrigo [des-ah-bree'-go], *m.* 1. Nudity, nakedness. 2. Want of shelter or harbor. 3. *(Met.)* Destitution, want of support or protection.

desabrimiento [day-sah-bre-me-en'-to], *m.* 1. Insipidity, want of taste or flavor, flatness. 2. Severity or asperity of temper, rudeness of manners, acerbity. 3. Despondency, dejection, lowness of spirits. 4. The rebound of guns when discharged.

desabrir [day-sah-breer'], *va.* To vex, to plague, to torment, to harass.

desabrochar [des-ah-bro-char'], *va.* 1. To unclasp. 2. To unbutton. 3. To open, to burst open. *-vr.* To unbosom, to reveal in confidence, to disclose.

desacabalar [des-ah-cah-bah-lar'], *va.* To pilfer. *V.* DESCABALAR.

desacalorarse [des-ah-cah-lo-rar'-say], *vr. (Met.)* To grow less warm.

desacatadamente [des-ah-cah-tah-dah-men'-tay], *adv.* Disrespectfully.

desacatado, da [des-ah-cah-tah'-do, dah], *a.* Acting in a disrespectful manner. *-pp.* of DESACATAR.

desacatador, ra [des-ah-cah-tah-dor', rah], *m. & f* An irreverent, uncivil, or disrespectful person.

desacatamiento [des-ah-cah-tah-me-en'-to], *m.* Disrespect.

desacatar [des-ah-cah-tar'], *va.* 1. To treat in a disrespectful manner: generally used in its reciprocal sense. 2. To desecrate, to profane, to dishonor.

desacato [des-ah-cah'-to], *m.* 1. Disrespect, incivility, want of reverence. 2. Desecration, profanation, dishonor. **Desacato de la autoridad**, contempt.

desaceitado, da [des-ah-thay-e-do, dah], *a.* Destitute of the necessary quantity of oil.

desaceitar [des-ah-thay-e-tar'], *va.* To remove oil from wollen stuffs; to remove fat.

desaceleración [des-ah-teh-lay-rah-the-on'], *f.* Deceleration, slowing down. **desacelerar** [des-ah-teh-lay-rar'], *vn.* To decelerate, to slow down.

desacerar [des-ah-thay-rar'], *va.* To unsteel, reduce from the state of steel.

desacerbar [des-ah-ther-bar'], *va.* 1. To temper, to sweeten, to take away harshness and bitterness. 2. *(Met.)* To pacify, to tranquillize, to calm.

desacertadamente [des-ah-ther-t-ah-dah-men'-tay], *adv.* Inconsiderately.

desacertado, da [des-ah-ther-tah'-do, dah], *a.* Inconsiderate, imprudent, without reflection. *-pp.* of DESACERTAR.

desacertar [des-ah-ther-tar'], *va.* To be wrong, to make a mistake.

desacidificar [des-ah-the-de-fe-car'], *va.* To remove the acid from a substance, to neutralize an acid state; to deacidify.

desacierto [des-ah-the-err'-to], *m.* Error, mistake, blunder. **Ha sido un desacierto elegir tal sitio**, it was a mistake to choose such a place. *(Yo desacierto, from Desacertar. V.* ACERTAR.)

desacobardar [des-ah-co-bar-dar'], *va.* To remove fear or cowardice, to inspire courage.

desacollar [des-ah-col-lyar'], *va. (Prov.)* To dig up the ground about vines, to cultivate vines.

desacomodadamente [des-ah-como-dah-dah-men'-tay], *adv.* Incommodiously, inconveniently.

desacomodado, da [des-ah-co-mo-dah'-do, dah], *a.* 1. Destitute of the conveniences of life. 2. Out of place or employment; out of service. 3. That which causes trouble or inconvenience. *-pp.* of DESACOMODAR.

desacomodar [des-ah-co-mo-dar'], *va.* 1. To incommode, to molest. 2. To deprive of ease or convenience. 3. To turn out of place. *-vr.* To lose one's place, to be out of place.

desacomodo [des-ah-co-mo'-do], *m.* Loss of a place or position.

desacompañamiento [des-ah-com-pa-nyah-me-en'to], *m.* Want of company or society.

desacompañar [des-ah-com-pa-nyar'], *va.* To leave the company, to retire.

desaconsejado, da [des-ah-con-say-hah'-do, dah], *a.* Acting without prudence or reflection, inconsiderate, ill-advised -*pp.* of DESACONSEJAR.

desaconsejar [des-ah-con-say-har'], *va.* To dissuade, to disapprove of.

desacoplar [des-ah-co-plar'], *va.* To unfasten, to separate two similar things.

desacordadamente [des-ah-cor-dah-dah-men'-tay], *adv.* Inconsiderately, unadvisedly.

desacordado, da [des-ah-cor-dah'-do, dah], *a. (Art.)* Discordant. *-pp.* of DESACORDAR.

desacordamiento [des-ah-cor-dah-me-ayn'-to], *m. V.* DESACUERDO.

desacordanza, *f. V.* DISCORDANCIA.

desacordar [des-ah-cor-dar'], *va.* To untune; said of musical instruments. *-vn. V.* DISCORDAR. *-vr.* 1. To be forgetful, or of short memory. 2. To be at variance, to disagree.

desacorde [des-ah-cor'-dar], *a.* Discordant.

desacordonar [des-ah-cor-do-nar'], *va.* To uncord, to remove strings; to untie, to unfasten.

desacorralar [des-ah-cor-rah-lar'], *va.* 1. To let the flock or cattle out of the penfold. 2. To bring a bull into the open field. 3. *(Met.)* To inspirit, to animate, to encourage.

desacostumbradamente [des-ah-cos-toom-brah-dah-men'-tay], *adv.* Unusually.

desacostumbrado, da [desah-cos-toom-brah´-do, dah], *a.* Unusual, unaccustomed. *-pp.* of DESACOSTUMBRAR.

desacostumbrar [des-ah-cos-toom-brar'], *va.* To disuse, to drop or to lose the custom. *-vr.* **desacostumbrarse de,** to break oneself of the habit of.

desacotar [des-ah-co-tar'], *va.* 1. To lay open a pasture-ground which was before inclosed. 2. To raise or withdraw a prohibition. 3. To relinquish a contract, to withdraw from an agreement. 4. Among boys, to play without conditions or rules.

desacoto [des-ah-co'-to], *m.* The act of withdrawing the prohibition to enter a pasture-ground.

desacreditar [des-ah-cray-de-tar´], *va.* 1. To discredit, to impair one's credit or reputation, to cry down. 2. To dissemble or conceal the merits of anything. *-vr.* To become discredited.

desactivar [des-ac-te-var´], *va.* To desactivate, to switch off.

desactualizado [des-ac-too-ah-le-tah'-do], *a.* Out of date.

desacuerdo [des-ah-coo-err'-do], *m.* 1. Forgetfulness, oblivion. 2. Derangement of the mental faculties. 3. Discordance, disagreement, disunion. **Estar en desacuerdo,** to be out of keeping. 4. Error, mistake, blunder. 5. Want of accuracy and exactness. *(Yo desacuerdo, yo desacuerde,* from *Desacordar.* V. ACORDAR.)

desacuñador [des-ah-coo-nyah-dor'], *m.* *(Typ.)* A shooting-stick.

desacuñar [des-ah-coon-yar'], *va.* To unwedge, to remove the quoins.

desachispar [des-ah-chees-par'], *va.* *(Coll.)* To remove intoxication.

desaderezar [des-ah-day-ray-thar'], *va.* To undress, to divest of ornaments, to ruffle, to disarrange.

desadeudar [des-ah-day-oo-dar'], *va.* To pay one's debts.

desadorar [des-ah-do-rar'], *va.* To cease to worship or love.

desadormecer [des-ah-dor-may-therr'], *va.* 1. To wake, to rouse from sleep. 2. To rouse from mental stupor. *(Yo desadormezco, yo desadormezca,* from *Desadormecer.* V. ABORRECER.)

desadornar [des-ah-dor-nar´], *va.* To divest of ornaments or decorations.

desadorno [des-ah-dor'-no], *m.* Want of embellishments and charms.

desadvertidamente [des-ad-ver-te-dah-men'-tay], *adv.* Inadvertently, inconsiderately.

desadvertido, da [des-ad-ver-tee'-do, dah], *a.* Inconsiderate, imprudent. *-pp.* of DESADVERTIR.

desadvertimiento [des-ad-ver-te-me-en'-to], *m.* Want of prudence and reflection.

desadvertir [des-ad-ver-teer'], *va.* To act inconsiderately, to proceed without judgment or prudence.

desafear [des-ah-fay-ar'], *va.* To remove, or to diminish ugliness.

desafección [des-ah-fec-the-on'], *f.* Disaffection.

desafectación [des-ah-fec-tah-the-on'], *f.* Unaffectedness.

desafecto, ta [des-ah-fec'-to], *a.* Disaffected.

desafecto [des-ah-fec'-to], *m.* Disaffection, disaffectedness.

desaferrar [des-ah-fer-rar'], *va.* 1. *(Naut.)* To raise, weigh the anchors, so that the ship may sail. 2. To loosen anything which was tied or fastened. 3. To make one change an opinion which he has strenuously maintained.

desafiador, ra [des-ah-fe-ah-dor'], *m. f.* 1. A challenger, duellist. 2. Darer, one who dares or defies.

desafiante [des-ah-fe-ahn'-tay], *a.* Challenging; defiant (actitud).

desafianzador, ra [des-ah-fe-ahn-thah-dor', rah], *m. & f.* One who withdraws security.

desafianzar [des-ah-fe-ahn-thar'], *va.* 1. To withdraw the security given in favor of someone. 2. *vr.* To become impaired, to deteriorate.

desafiar [des-ah-fe-ar'], *va.* 1. To challenge, to defy, to dare. 2. To try one´s strength against another. 3. To rival, to oppose, to struggle. 4. To decompose, to dissolve; to rescind; to discharge.

desafición [des-ah-fe-the-on'], *f.* Disaffection.

desaficionar [des-ah-fe-the-onar'], *va.* To destroy one's desire, wish, or affection for a thing. *-vr.* To come to dislike, to take a dislike to.

desafijar [des-ah-fe-har'], *va.* 1. *V.* DESFIJAR. 2. To deny the filiation of a son.

desafilado [des-ah-fe-lah'-do], *a.* Blunt.

desafilar [des-ah-fe-lar'], *va.* To blunt, to dull. *-vr.* To get blunt.

desafinadamente [des-ah-fe-nah-dah-men'-tay], *adv.* Dissonantly, discordantly.

desafinado [des-ah-fe-nah-do], *a.* Flat, out of tune.

desafinar [des-ah-fe-nar'], *va. & vn.* 1. To be inharmonious, to be out of tune. 2. To untune.

desafío [des-ah-fee'-o], *m.* 1. Challenge, duel. **Es un desafío a todos nosotros,** it is a challenge to us all. 2. Struggle, contest, combat. 3. Dismissal.

desaforado, da [des-ah-fo-rah'-do, dah], *a.* 1. Huge, uncommonly large. 2. Disorderly, lawless, impudent, outrageous. *-pp.* of DESAFORAR.

desaforar [des-ah-fo-rar'], *va.* 1. To encroach upon one's rights, to infringe one's privileges. 2. To deprive anyone of the rights or privileges belonging to his birth, profession, or character. *(Mil.)* To cashier. 3. To redeem a property. *-vr.* 1. To relinquish one's rights and privileges. 2. To be outrageous or disorderly.

desaforo [des-ah-fo´-ro], *m.* The act and effect of redeeming a perpetual lease.

desaforrar [des-ah-for-rar'], *va.* 1. To remove the lining of anything. 2. **Desaforrar los cables,** *(Naut.)* to unserve the cables.

desafortunado, da [des-ah-for-too-nah'-do, dah], *a.* Unfortunate, unlucky.

desafuero [des-ah-foo-ay'-ro], *m.* Excess; outrage, open violence, downright injustice, infraction of law.

desagarrar [des-ah-gar-rar'], *va.* *(Coll.)* To release; to let loose.

desagitadera [des-ah-he-tah-day'-rah], *f.* *(Agri.)* An instrument used in separating honeycombs from the hive.

desagitar [des-ah-he-tar'], *va.* To remove honeycombs from the hive with the *desagitadera.*

desagotar [des-ah-go-tar'], *va.* *V.* DESAGUAR.

desagraciado, da [de-sah-grah-the-ah'-do, dah], *a.* Ungraceful, inelegant. *-pp.* of DESAGRACIAR.

desagraciar [des-ah-grah-the-ar'], *va.* To deform, to disfigure, to make ungraceful or inelegant.

desagradable [des-ah-grah-dah´-blay], *a.* Disagreeable, unpleasant; uncomfortable.

desagradablemente [des-ah-grah-dah-blay-men'-tay], *adv.* Disagreeably.

desagradar [des-ah-grah-dar'], *va.* To displease, to offend, to make angry. **Me desagrada ese olor,** I don´t like that smell. *-imp.* It does not suit.

desagradecer [des-ah-grah-day-therr'], *va.* To be ungrateful.

desagradecidamente [des-grah-the-ah-dah-men'-tay], *adv.* Ungratefully.

desagradecido, da [des-ah-grah-day-thee'-do, dah], *a.* Ungrateful. *-pp.* of DESAGREDECER.

desagradecimiento [des-ah-grah-day-the-me-en'-to], *m.* Ingratitude.

desagrado [des-ah-grah'-do], *m.* 1. Asperity, harshness. 2. Discontent, displeasure. **Ser del desagrado del rey,** to have incurred the king's displeasure.

desagraviar [des-ah-grah-ve-ar'], *va.* 1. To give satisfaction, or make amends for an injury done; to relieve. 2. To vindicate. *-vr.* To get one´s own back; to exact an apology.

desagravio [des-ah-grah'-veo], *m.* 1. Relief, satisfaction, or compensation for an injury done. 2. Vindication, justice, vengeance.

desagregación [des-ahgraygah-the-on'], *f.* 1. Separation, disintegration. *(Min.)* Separation of the mineral parts by means of a force which reduces the metal to grains or powder. 2. Separation of the molecules of a body.

desagregar [des-ah-gray-gar'], *va.* To disjoin, to separate. *-vr.* To desintegrate.

desagriar [des-ah-gre-ar'], *va.* 1. To neutralize acidity. 2. To sweeten, mollify, soften the character of someone. 3. To appease, remove anger.

desaguadero [des-ah-goo-ah-day'-ro], *m.* 1. Channel, drain for drawing off superfluous water. 2. *(Met.)* Drain of money.

desaguador [des-ah-goo-ah-dor'], *m.* Waterpipe, channel or conduit for water.

desaguar [des-ah-goo-ar'], *va.* 1. To drain, to draw off water. 2. *(Met.)* To waste money in extravagant expenses. *-vn.* To empty or flow into the sea (ríos). *-vr. (Met.)* To discharge by vomits or stools.

desaguazar [des-ah-goo-ah-thar'], *va.* To drain the water from any part.

desagüe [des-ah'-goo-ay], *m.* 1. Channel, drain, outlet. 2. Extraordinary expense. 3. Drainage.

desaguisado, da [des-ah-gee-sah'-do, dah], *a.* 1. Injurious, unjust. 2. Disproportionate, exorbitant. 3. Intrepid, bold.

desaguisado [des-ah-ges-ah'-do], *m.* Offence, injury, wrong.

desahijar [des-ah-eh-ar'], *va.* To wean, to separate the young from the dams. *-vr.* To swarm (abejas).

desahitarse [des-ah-e-tar'-say], *vr.* To relieve indigestion, to unload the stomach.

desahogadamente [des-ah-o-gah-dah-men'-tay], *adv.* 1. Freely, without embarrassment or obstruction. 2. In an impudent or brazen-faced manner.

desahogado, da [des-a-ho-gah'-do, dah], *a.* 1. Petulant, impudent, brazen-faced, licentious. 2. Having plenty of room, free, unencumbered (lugares). 3. *(Naut.)* Having sea room. *-pp.* of DESAHOGAR.

desahogamiento [des-ah-o-gah-me-ayn'-to], *m.* V. DESAHOGO.

desahogar [des-ah-o-gar'], *va.* To ease pain, to alleviate distress. *-vr.* 1. To recover from fatigue or disease. 2. To unbosom, to disclose one's grief. 3. To expostulate or debate with one against wrong received. 4. To vent, to utter. 5. To extricate oneself from debt. 6. To give a horse liberty, so that he may vent his passion and become obedient to the bridle.

desahogo [des-aho'-go], *m.* 1. Ease, alleviation from pain or affliction. **Es un desahogo de tantas cosas malas**, it´s an outlet for so many unpleasant things. 2. The unbosoming or disclosing one's troubles or grief. 3. Freedom of speech, vent. **Expresarse con cierto desahogo**, to express oneself with a certain freedom. 4. Laxity. 5. Domestic convenience.

desahuciado, da [des-ah-oo-the-ah'-do, dah], *a.* Given over, despaired of. — *pp.* of DESAHUCIAR.

desahuciar [des-ah-oo-the-ar'], *va.* 1. To despair, to take away all hopes of obtaining a thing. **Con esa decisión le desahuciaron definitivamente**, by that decision they finally put an end to his hopes. 2. To give over, to declare a patient past recovery. 3. To dismiss a tenant or renter, at the expiration of his agreement. 4. To drive away cattle from a pasture-ground, at the expiration of a fixed term. *-vr.* To lose all hopes.

desahucio [des-ah-oo'-theo], *m.* The act of dismissing a tenant, or of driving away cattle from a pasture-ground, at the expiration of the stipulated time.

desahumado, da [des-ah-oo-mah'-do, dah], *a.* Mild, faded, vapid, applied to liquor which has lost its strength. *-pp.* of DESAHUMAR.

desahumar [des-ah-oo-mar'], *va.* To free from smoke, to expel smoke.

desainadura [day-sah-e-nah-doo'-rah], *f. (Vet.)* Disease in horses, occasioned by liquefying their fat through overheating them.

desainar [day-sah-e-nar'], *va.* To remove the fat of an animal; to lessen or diminish the thickness or substance of anything. *-vr.* To lose a great quantity of blood.

desairadamente [des-ah-e-rah-dah-men´-tay], *adv.* Unhandsomely, gracelessly.

desairado, da [des-ah-e-rah'-do, dah], *a.* 1. Unattractive, graceless. 2. *(Met.)* Disregarded, slighted, unrewarded. *-pp.* of DESAIRAR.

desairar [des-ah-e-rar'], *va.* To disregard, to slight, to take no notice, to disrespect, to rebuff.

desaire [des-ah'-ee-ray], *m.* 1. Slight, rebuff, disdain, disrespect. **Fue un desaire sin precedentes**, it was an unprecedented snub. **Sufrir un desaire**, to suffer a rebuff. 2. Awkwardness. 3. *(Met.)* Frown of fortune or power.

desaislarse [des-ah-is-lar'-say], *vr.* To cease to be insulated.

desajustar [des-ah-hoos-tar'], *va.* To mismatch, to unfit, to make unsuitable; not to adjust, not to be fit. *-vr.* 1. To disagree, to withdraw from an agreement. 2. To be out of order; as a door, a shutter, etc.

desajuste [des-ah-hoos'-tay], *m.* 1. The act of making a thing unfit, unsuitable, or out of order. 2. Disagreement, breaking of a contract.

desalabanza [des-ah-la-bahn'-thah], *f.* Vituperation, depreciation.

desalabar [des-ah-lah-bar'], *va.* To dispraise, to censure, to depreciate.

desalabear [des-ah-lah-bay-ar'], *va.* To straighten a warped plank or board.

desaladamente [des-ah-lah-dah-men'-tay], *adv.* Anxiously, swiftly.

desaladura [day-sah-lah-doo'-rah], *f. (Chem.)* V. DESALAZÓN.

desalar [des-ah-lar'], *va.* To cut off the wings. *-vr.* 1. *(Met.)* To run up to one with open arms. 2. To toil with excess to obtain something: to hurry. 3. *(Naut.)* To take away the stowage or heavy part of the cargo which served as ballast .

desalar [day-sah-lar'], *va.* To take the salt out of fish, meat, etc., by steeping it in fresh water. *-vr.* 1. *(Chem.)* To precipitate from solutions (as salts), to fall as a precipitate. 2. *(Naut.)* To make sea-water drinkable.

desalazón [day-sah-lah-thone'], *f. (Chem.)* Removal from a liquid of a part or all of its contained salts.

desalbardar [des-al-bar-dar'], *va.* To take off the packsaddle from a beast of burden.

desalentador, ra [des-ah-len-tah-dor', rah], *a.* Dispiriting, discouraging.

desalentar [des-ah-len-tar'], *va.* 1. To put one out of breath by dint of labor. 2. *(Met.)* To discourage, to dismay, to damp. *-vr.* To jade, to lose heart.

desalfombrar [des-al-fom-brar'], *va.* To remove carpets from a room or house.

desalforjar [des-al-for-har'], *va.* To take off the saddlebags from horses or mules. *-vr. (Met. Coll.)* To take off one's accoutrements, to make oneself easy.

desalhajar [des-al-ah-har'], *va.* To strip a house or room of furniture.

desaliento [des-ah-le-en'-to], *m.* 1. Dismay, depression of spirits, discouragement, dejection. 2. Faintness, languor. *(Yo desaliento, yo desaliente,* from *Desalentar. V.* ACERTAR.)

desalinear [des-ah-le-nay-ar'], *va.* To destroy the lineation, to disorder, to separate from the line.

desaliñadamente [des-ah-le-nyah-dah-men'-tay], *adv.* Slovenly, uncleanly.

desaliñado [des-ah-le-nyah-do], *m.* 1. Slovenly, dirty, down-at-heel; shabby (raído); untidy. 2. Careless (negligente).

desaliñar [des-ah-le-nyar'], *va.* To disarrange, to disorder, to ruffle; to make one slovenly or dirty.

desaliño [des-ah-lee'-nyo], *m.* 1. Slovenliness, indecent negligence of dress. 2. Carelessness, want of attention.

desalivación [day-sah-le-vah-the-on'], *f.* Salivation, profuse flow of saliva.

desalivar [day-sah-le-var'], *vn.* To salivate.

desalmadamente [de-sal-mah-dah-men'-tay], *adv.* Soullessly, inhumanly.

desalmado, da [de-sal-mah'-do, dah], *a.* 1. Soulless, inhuman, merciless. 2 Impious, profligate. 3. Inanimate, abject. *-pp.* of DESALMAR.

desalmamiento [de-sal-mah-me-en'-to], *m.* Inhumanity, impiety, profligacy. *(Ant.)*

desalmar [des-al-mar'], *va. (Met.)* To speak with ingenuity and candor. *-vr.* To desire something very anxiously.

desalmenado, da [de-sal-may-nah'-do, dah], *a.* 1. Stripped of turrets (castillos, fortalezas). 2. Wanting an ornament or capital.

desalmidonar [des-al-me-do-nar'], *va.* To take the starch out of linen.

desalojamiento [des-ah-lo-hah-me-en'-to], *m.* 1. Dislodging, ejection, ousting. 2. Evacuation; abandonment; clearing.

desalojar [des-ah-lo-har'], *va.* 1. To dislodge the enemy's troops, to dispossess them of a place or post. 2. To remove, to expel (gas etc.). 3. To evacuate, to abandon, to move out of, to move away from. **Desalojar un tribunal de público**, to clear a court, to clean the public from a court. *-vn.* To quit one's house or apartments.

desalquilado, da [de-sal-ke-lah'-do, dah], *a.* Untenanted, unrented.

desalquilar [de-sal-kee-lar'], *va. & vr.* To leave a room or house for which a rent was paid.

desalterar [de-sal-tay-rar'], *va.* To allay, to assuage, to settle.

desalumbradamente [de-sah-loom-brah-dah-men'-tay], *adv.* Blindly, erroneously.

desalumbrado, da [des-ah-loom-brah'-do, dah], *a.* 1. Dazzled, overpowered with light; stricken with astonishment; surprised with splendor. 2. *(Met.)* Groping in the dark.

desalumbramiento [des-ah-loom-brah-me-en'-to], *m.* Blindness, want of foresight or knowledge, error.

desamable [des-ah-mah'-blay], *a.* Unamiable.

desamador [de-sah-mah-dor'], *m.* One who does not love, or has ceased loving; one who dislikes persons or things.

desamar [des-ah-mar'], *va.* 1. To love no more, not to love or esteem as formerly. 2. To hate, to detest.

desamarrar [des-ah-mar-rar'], *va. (Naut.)* To unmoor a ship. 2. To untie. **Desamarrar un cabo**, *(Naut.)* to unbend a rope.

desamasado, da [des-ah-mah-sah'-do, dah], *a.* Dissolved, disunited, unkneaded.

desamelgamiento [des-ah-mel-ah-me-en'-to], *m.* Rotation, variation of crops.

desamelgar [des-ah-mel-gar'], *va. (Agri.)* To rotate crops, to vary the order of cultivation, alternating with lying fallow.

desamigado, da [des-ah-me-gah'-do, dah], *a.* Unfriendly, unconnected.

desamistad [des-ah-mis-tahd'], *f.* Unfriendliness.

desamistarse [des-ah-mis-tar'-say], *vr.* To fall out, to quarrel.

desamodorrar [des-ah-mo-dor-rar'], *va.* To remove lethargy or drowsiness. *-vr.* To emerge from lethargy or drowsiness; to recover oneself.

desamoldar [des-ah-mol-dar'], *va* 1. To unmould, to change as to the form. 2. *(Met.)* To change the proportion or symmetry of a thing; to disfigure.

desamor [des-ah-mor'], *m.* 1. Disregard, disaffection. 2. Lack of sentiment and affection which certain things generally inspire. 3. Enmity, hatred.

desamoradamente [des-ah-mo-rah-dah-men'-tay], *adv. (Obs.)* Unfriendly, harshly.

desamorado, da [des-ah-mo-rah'-do, dah], *a.* 1. Loveless, cold-hearted. 2. Harsh, rude, disdainful. *-pp.* of DESAMORAR.

desamorar [des-ah-mo-rar'], *va.* To extinguish love, to cease loving.

desamoroso, sa [des-ah-mo-ro'-so, sah], *a.* Unloving, destitute of regard or love.

desamorrar [des-ah-mor-rar'], *va. (Coll.)* To cheer up, to make one give up his obstinacy.

desamortajar [des-ah-mor-tah-har'], *va.* To unshroud, to remove the shroud.

desamortecer [des-ah-mor-tay-therr'], *va.* To remove torpor; to recover from a swoon.

desamortización [des-ah-mor-te-thah-the-on'], *f. (Jur.)* Disentailment.

desamortizar [des-ah-mor-te-thar'], *va.* To disentail, to break an entail.

desamotinarse [des-ah-mo-te-nar'-say], *vr.* To withdraw from mutiny and sedition.

desamparado, da [des-am-pah-rah'-do], *a.* 1. Helpless, defenceless; abandoned (niño, etc.). **Los niños desamparados de la ciudad**, the city's waifs and strays. 2. Exposed (lugar). 3. Lonely, deserted (lugar).

desamparador, ra [des-am-pa-rah-dor', rah], *m. & f.* Deserter, one who abandons.

desamparar [des-am-pa-rar'], *va.* 1. To forsake, to abandon, to leave, to relinquish, to desert. 2. To quit a place. 3. *(Naut.)* To dismantle, dismast a ship. **Desamparar los bienes**, to give up one's property, in order to avoid being molested by creditors.

desamparo [des-am-pah'-ro], *m.* 1. Abandonment, desertion, want of protection, helplessness, forlornness. 2. Dereliction, the state of being forsaken.

desamueblado, da [des-ah-moo-ay-blah'-do, dah], *a.* Unfurnished. *-pp.* of DESAMUEBLAR.

desamueblar [des-ah-moo-ay-blar'], *va.* To unfurnish, to deprive or strip of furniture.

desanclar, desancorar [des-an-clar'-de-san-co-rar'], *va. (Naut.)* To weigh anchor.

desandadura [des-an-dah-doo'-rah], *f.* Going back over the same road.

desandar [des-an-dar'], *va.* To retrograde, to go back the same road by which one came. **Desandar lo andado**, to undo what has been done.

desandrajado, da [des-an-drah-hah'-do, dah], *a.* Ragged, in tatters.

desangramiento [day-san-grah-me-en'-to], *m.* Bleeding to excess.

desangrar [day-an-grar'], *va.* 1. To bleed one to excess. 2. To draw a large quantity of water from a river. 3. *(Met.)* To exhaust one's means, to make poor. *-vr.* To lose much blood.

desanidar [des-ah-ne-dar'], *vn.* To forsake the nest (pájaros). *-va.* 1. *(Met.)* To dislodge from a post. 2. To apprehend fugitives in their place of concealment.

desanimadamente [des-ah-ne-mah-dah-men'-tay], *adv.* Spiritlessly.

desanimado, da [des-ah-ne-mah'-do, dah], *a.* 1. Despondent, dejected, discouraged. 2. Dull, lifeless, flat. **Fue una fiesta de lo más desanimada**, it was a terrible, dull party.

desanimar [des-ah-ne-mar'], *va.* 1. To dishearten, to dispirit, to discourage; to put a damper upon one's spirits. 2. To damp, to pall, to daunt. *-vr.* To jade. **No hay que desanimarse**, we must not lose heart.

desánimo [des-ah-ne-mo], *m.* 1. Despondency, depression, dejection. 2. Dullness, lifelessness (flojedad).

desanudar [des-ah-noo-dar'], *va.* 1. To untie, to loosen a knot. 2. *(Met.)* To extricate, to disentangle, to clear up what was obscure. **Desanudar la voz**, to pronounce clearly and distinctly, to articulate freely.

desañudadura [des-ah-nyoo-dah-doo'-rah], *f.* The untying or loosening of a knot; disentanglement.

desapacibilidad [des-ah-pa-the-be-le-dahd'], *f.* Rudeness, churlishness, peevishness.

desapacible [des-ah-pa-thee'-blay], *a.* Sharp, rough, disagreeable, unpleasant, harsh.

desapaciblemente [des-ah-pa-the-blay-men'-tay], *adv.* Sharply, disagreeably.

desapadrinar [des-ah-pah-dre-nar'], *va. (Met.)* To disprove, to contradict.

desaparear [des-ah-pa-ray-ar'], *va.* To unmatch, to disjoin.

desaparecer [des-ah-pa-ray-therr'], *va.* To remove from sight, to hide. *-vn. & vr.* To disappear.

desaparecido [des-ah-pah-r-ay-the'-do], *a.* Missing; extinct (especie). **El libro desaparecido,** the missing book. **Uno de los animales desaparecidos,** one of the extinct animals. 2. *m. pl.* **Los desaparecidos,** the missing.

desaparecimiento [des-ah-pa-ray-the-me-en'-to], *m.* The act of disappearing or vanishing out of sight.

desaparejar [des-ah-pa-ray-har'], *va.* 1. To unharness beasts of draught or burden. 2. *(Naut.)* To unrig a ship.

desaparición [des-ah-pah-re-the-on'], *f.* Disappearance, vanishing from sight. *(Astr.)* Occultation.

desaparroquiar [des-ah-par-roke-ar´], *va.* To remove someone from his parish.-*vr.* 1. To change one´s parish, to remove from one parish to another. 2. *(Met.)* To cease to be a customer of a shop.

desapasionadamente [des-ah-pah-se-o-nah-dah-men'tay], *adv.* Impartially.

desapasionado [des-ah-pah-se-o-nah'-do], *a.* Dispassionate, impartial.

desapasionarse [des-ah-pah-se-o-nar´-say], *vr.* To root out a passion, or strong affection for anything.

desapegarse [des-ah-pay-gar'-say], *vr.* To be alienated from natural affection.

desapego [des-ah-pay'-go], *m.* 1. Alienation of love or affection, coolness. 2. Impartiality, disinterestedness, indifference.

desapercibidamente [des-ah-per-the-bah-men'-tay], *adv.* Inadvertently, carelessly.

desapercibido, da [des-ah-per-the-bee'-do, dah], *a.* 1. Unprovided, unprepared, unguarded, careless. 2. **Pasar desapercibido,** to go unnoticed.

desapercibimiento, desapercibo [des-ah-per-the-be-me-en'-to, des-ah-per-the-e'-bo], *m.* Unpreparedness.

desapestar [des-ah-pes-tar'], *va.* 1. To cure persons infected with the plague. 2. To disinfect.

desapiadadamente [des-ah-pe-ah-dah, dah-men'-tay], *adv.* Unmercifully, impiously.

desapiadado, da [des-ah-pe-ah-dah'-do, dah], Merciless, impious, inhuman.

desapiolar [des-ah-pe-o-lar'], *va.* To loosen the strings with which game is tied.

desaplicación [des-ah-ple-cah-the-on'], *f.* Inapplication, indolence.

desaplicadamente [des-ah-ple-cah-dah-men'-tay], *adv.* Indolently.

desaplicado, da [des-ah-ple-cah'-do, dah], *a.* Indolent, careless, neglectful, lazy.

desaplomar [des-ah-plo-mar´], *va.* To put out of plumb.

desapoderado, da [des-ah-po-day-rah´-do, dah], *a.* Furious, impetuous, ungovernable. -*pp.* of DESAPODERAR.

desapoderamiento [des-ah-po-day-rah-me-en'-to], *m.* 1. The act of depriving or ejecting. 2. Excessive boldness, extreme audacity.

desapoderar [des-ah-po-day-rar'], *va.* 1. To dispossess, to rob one of his property. 2. To repeal or revoke a power of attorney.

desapolillar [des-ah-po-leel-lyar'], *va.* To free and clear of moths. -*vr.* 1. *(Coll.)* To take the air when it is cold and sharp. 2. To get rid of moths.

desaporcar [des-ah-por-car'], *va.* To take away from plants earth which had been heaped about them.

desaposentar [des-ah-pos-en-tar'], *va.* 1. To turn one out of his lodgings, to force him to move. 2. To expel a thing from one's mind.

desaposesionar [des-ah-po-say-se-o-nar'], *va.* To dispossess.

desapostura [des-ah-pos-too'-rah], *f.* Inelegance, deformity, indecency.

desapoyar [des-ah-po-yar], *va.* To remove the foundation of something. *V.* DESAPUNTALAR.

desapreciar [des-ah-pray-the-ar'], *m.* To depreciate, to undervalue, to cry down.

desaprecio [des-ah-pray-theo], *m. (Prov.)* Depreciation, lessening the worth or value of a thing.

desaprender [des-ah-pren-derr'], *va.* To unlearn, to forget what one has learned by heart.

desaprensar [de-sah-pren-sar'], *va.* 1. To take away the gloss which clothes or other things obtain in the press. 2. *(Met.)* To extricate oneself from a pressing difficulty.

desaprensión [des-ah-pren-se-on'], *f.* Unscrupulousness, lack of scruple.

desaprensivamente [des-aph-pren-se-vah-men'-tay], *adv.* Unscrupulously.

desaprensivo [des-ah-pren-se'-vo], *a.* Unscrupulous.

desapretador [des-ah-pray-tah-dor'], *m.* Screwdriver.

desapretar [des-ah-pray-tar'], *va.* 1. To slacken, to loosen, to loose. 2. *(Met.)* To ease, to free from anxiety or uneasiness. *(Yo desaprieto, yo desapriete,* from *Desapretar. V.* ACERTAR.)

desaprisionar [des-ah-pre-se-onar'], *va.* To release from confinement, to set at liberty. -*vr. (Met.)* To extricate oneself from difficulties, to remove an impediment.

desaprobación [des-ah-pro-bah-the-on'], *f.* Disapprobation, censure.

desaprobar [des-ah-pro-bar'], *va.* To disapprove, to censure, to reprove, to condemn, to find fault.

desapropiación, *f.* **desapropiamiento,** *m.* [des-ah-pro-pe-ah-the-on', me-en'-to]. Alienation. *V.* ENAJENAMIENTO.

desapropiar [des-ah-pro-pe-ar'], *va.* To deprive someone of ownership. -*vr.* To alienate, to transfer one's right and property to another, to expropriate.

desapropio [des-ah-pro'-peo], *m.* Alienation, transfer of property.

desaprovechadamente [des-ah-pro-vay-chah-dah-men'-tay], *adv.* Unprofitably.

desaprovechado, da [des-ah-pro-vay-chah'-do, data], *a.* 1. Unprofitable, useless. 2. Backward. -*pp.* of DESAPROVECHAR.

desaprovechamiento [des-ah-pro-vay-chah-me-en'-to], *m.* 1. Backwardness, waste. 2. Inapplication, negligence.

desaprovechar [des-ah-pro-vay-char'], *va.* To waste, to misspend, to turn to a bad use. -*vn.* To be backward, to make little or no progress.

desapuntalar [des-ah-poon-tah-lar'], *va.* To take away the props or supports.

desapuntar [des-ah-poon-tar'], *va.* 1. To unstitch, to rip up. 2. To aim badly. 3. To efface the days of absence from the choir.

desarbolar [des-ar-bo-lar'], *va.* 1. *(Naut.)* To unmast a ship, to cut down the masts. 2. -*vn. (Naut.)* To loosen the masts by accident. 3. *(Agri.)* To root up or cut down the trees of a grove.

desarbolo [des-ar-bo'-lo], *m.* The act of unmasting a ship or laying her up in ordinary.

desarenar [des-ah-ray-nar'], *va.* To take away sand, to clear a place of sand.

desareno [des-ah-ray'-no], *m.* Clearing a place of sand.

desarmable [des-ar-mah'-blay], *a.* Demountable, collapsible.

desarmado, da [des-ar-mah'-do, dah], *a.* Unarmed, defenceless, bare.-*pp.* of DESARMAR.

desarmador [des-ar-mah-dor'], *m.* He, who discharges a gun.

desarmadura, *f.* **desarmamiento,** *m.* [des-ar-mah-doo'-rah, des-ar-mah-me-on' to], Disarming, the act and effect of disarming.

desarmar [des-ar-mar'], *va.* 1. To disarm. 2. To prohibit the carrying of arms. 3. To undo a thing, to take it asunder. 4. To disband a body of troops. 5. To dismount a crossbow; to dismount cannon. 6. To butt, to strike with the horns. 7. *(Met.)* To pacify, to disarm wrath or vengeance. -*vn.* To disarm.

desarme [des-ar'-may], *m.* 1. Disarming of ships or troops. 2. Disarmament. **Desarme total,** total disarmament. **Desarme nuclear,** nuclear disarmament.

desarraigar [des-ar-rah-e-gar'], *va*. 1. To eradicate, to root out, to deracinate. 2. *(Met.)* To extirpate, to destroy, to exterminate. 3. *(Law.)* To expel from the country.

desarraigo [des-arrah-'e-go], *m*. 1. Eradication. 2. *(Law.)* Expulsion from a country.

desarrancarse [des-ar-ran-car'-say], *vr*. To desert, to separate from a body or association.

desarrapado, da [des-ar-rah-pah'-do, dah], *a*. Ragged.

desarrebozar [des-ar-ray-bo-thar'], *va*. 1. To unmuffle. 2. *(Met.)* To lay open, to manifest, to discover.

desarrebujar [des-ar-ray-boo-har'], *va*. 1. To unfold, to spread out. 2. To uncover. 3. To explain, to clear up.

desarregladamente [des-ahr-re-glah-dah-men'-tay], *adv*. Disorderly.

desarreglado, da [des-ar-ray-glah'-do, dah], *a*. 1. Immoderate, intemperate. 2. Extravagant, excessive. 3. Lawless, unruly. 4. Out of order; upset (estómago etc.). *-pp*. of DESARREGLAR.

desarreglar [des-ar-ray-glar'], *va*. To disorder, to discompose; to disarrange. **El viento le desarregló el peinado**, the wind made a mess of her hairdo. **No desarregles la cama**, don´t mess up your bed. *-vr*. To get disarranged; to get untidy.

desarreglo [des-ar-ray'-glo], *m*. 1. Disorder, confusion, irregularity, mismanagement. 2. Licentiousness, license, disorder. 3. Derangement.

desarrendarse [des-ar-ren-dar'-say], *vr*. To shake off the bridle applied to a horse.

desarrimar [des-ar-re-mar'], *va*. 1. To remove, to separate. 2. To dissuade, to move away.

desarrimo [des-ar-ree'-mo], *m*. Want of props or support.

desarrollado [des-ahr-rolyah'-do], *a*. Well-developed.

desarrollar [des-ar-rol-lyar'], *va*. 1. To unroll, to unfold. 2. To develop (fotos). 3. To expand. 4. *(Mech.)* **El coche desarrolla 30 caballos**, the engine develops 30 hp. *-vr*. 1. To unfold, to develop (semillas). 2. To develop, expand, acquire growth and vigor. **La industria se desarrolla rápidamente**, the industry is developing rapidly. **La acción se desarrolla en Roma**, the scene is set in Rome.

desarrollo [de-sar-rol'-lyo], *m*. Unfolding, development, evolution. **Un país en desarrollo**, a developing country. **La industria está en pleno desarrollo**, the industry is making rapid growth.

desarropar [des-ar-ro-par'], *va*. To uncover, to undress. *-vr*. To undress, to uncover oneself. **Todavía el tiempo no es para desarroparse**, it´s not yet weather for leaving off any clothes.

desarrugar [des-ar-roo-gar'], *va*. To take out wrinkles.

desarrumar [des-ar-roo-mar'], *va*. *(Naut.)* 1. To unload a ship, to discharge the cargo. 2. To remove the ballast in order to inspect the bottom.

desarticulación [des-ar-te-coo-lah-the-on'], *f*. Taking to pieces; separation; dislocation; breaking up.

desarticulado [des-ar-te-coo-lah'-do], *a*. Disjointed.

desarticular [des-ar-te-coo-lar'], *va*. To disarticulate, sever a joint. *(Naut.)* To loosen.

desartillar [des-ar-teel-lyar'], *va*. To take the guns out of a ship or a fortress.

desarzonar [des-ar-tho-nar'], *va*. To throw from the saddle, to unhorse.

desasado, da [des-ah-sah'-do, dah], *a*. 1. Without handles. 2. *(Cant.)* Without ears. *(Acad.).*

desaseadamente [des-ah-say-ah-dah-men'-tay], *adv*. Uncleanly.

desasear [des-ah-say-ar'], *va*. To make dirty or unclean; to discompose, to disorder.

desasegurar [des-ah-say-goo-rar'], *va*. 1. To lose the security of something. 2. *(Amer.)* To cancel life or fire insurance.

desasentar [des-ah-sen-tar'], *va*. *(Met.)* To disagree with, to displease, not to suit or not to set well. *-vr*. To stand up.

desaseo [des-ah-say'-o], *m*. Uncleanliness, dirtiness, carelessness.

desasimiento [des-ah-se-me-en'-to], *m*. 1. The act of loosening or letting loose. 2. *(Met.)* Alienation of affection or love, disregard. 3. Disinterestedness.

desasir [des-ah-seer'], *va*. To loosen, to disentangle, to give up. *-vr*. 1. To disengage or extricate oneself. 2. *(Met.)* To disregard, to look with indifference or contempt. 3. To give up the possession of property.

desasnar [des-as-nar'], *va*. *(Met. Coll.)* To instruct, to polish one's manners. *-vr*. To grow sharp, to learn wit, to become polite.

desasociable [des-ah-so-the-ah'-blay], *a*. Unsociable.

desasosegadamente [des-ah-so-say-gah-dah-men'-tay], *adv*. Uneasily.

desasosegado [des-ah-so-say-gah'p-do], *a*. Uneasy, anxious; restless.

desasosegar [des-ah-so-say-gar'], *m*. To disquiet, to disturb. *-vr*. To become uneasy, to get perturbed.

desasosiego [des-ah-so-se-ay'-go], *m*. Restlessness, want of tranquility, uneasiness. (*Yo desasosiego,* from *Desasosegar. V.* ACERTAR.)

desastrado, da [des-as-trah'-do, dah], *a*. 1. Wretched, miserable, unfortunate. 2. Ragged, tattered.

desastre [des-ahs'-tray], *m*. Disaster, catastrophe, misfortune. **La boda fue un desastre**, the wedding was a disaster.

desastroso, sa [des-as-tro'-so, sah], *a*. Unfortunate, disastrous.

desatacar [des-ah-tah-car'], *va*. To loosen, to untie.

desatado, da [des-ah-tah'-do, dah], *a*. Loose, unbound, untied.*-pp*.. of DESATAR.

desatador [des-ah-tah-dor'], *m*. He who unties, absolver.

desatadura, *f*. **desatamiento**, *m*. [des-ah-tah-doo'-rah, des-ah-tah-me-en'-to]. Untying, loosening.

desatancar [des-ah-tan-car'], *va*. 1. To clear sewers and conduits.

desatar [des-ah-tar'], *va*.1. To untie, to undo, to unfasten, to loosen or unbind, to separate, to detach. 2. To loosen, to separate. 3. To solve, to find out, to unravel. 4. To liquefy, to dissolve.*-vr*. 1. To give loose rein to one's tongue. 2. To lose all reserve, fear, or bashfulness. 3. **Desatarse de un compromiso**, to get out of an agreement. 4. *(Fig.)* To break, to burst; to break out. **Desatarse en injurias**, to let rip with a torrent of abuse. 5. *(Fig.)* To spark off, give rise to, unleash.

desatascar [des-ah-tas-car'], *va*. 1. To pull or draw out of the mud. 2. V. DESATANCAR.. 3. *(Met.)* To extricate one from difficulties.

desataviar [des-ah-tah-ve-ar'], *va*. To strip off ornaments and decorations.

desatavio [des-ah-tah-vee'-o], *m*. Uncleanliness, negligence in dress.

desate [des-ah'-tay], *m*. 1. Disorderly proceeding. 2. Loss of fear, of reserve, of bashfulness. **Desate de vientre**, looseness of the bowels.

desatención [des-ah-ten-the-on'], *f*. 1. Inattention, absence of mind, abstraction. 2. Disrespect, want of respect 3. Incivility, want of politeness.

desatender [des-ah-ten-derr'], *va*. 1. To pay no attention to what is said or done. 2. To disregard, to neglect. 3. To take no notice of a person or thing.

desatendible [des-ah-ten-dee'-blay], *a*. What ought to be neglected or disregarded; mean, despicable, inconsiderate.

desatentado, da [des-ah-ten-tah'-do, dah], *a*. 1. Inconsiderate, unadvised, acting in an absurd and unreasonable manner. 2. Excessive, rigorous, disordered. *-pp*. of DESATENTAR.

desatentamente [des-ah-ten-tah-dah-men'-tay], *adv*. Disrespectfully, uncivilly.

desatentar [des-ah-ten-tar'], *va*. To perturb the mind, to perplex the understanding.

desatento, ta [des-ah-ten'-to, tah], *a*. 1. Inattentive, careless, heedless, thoughtless. 2. Rude, unmannerly, uncivil.

desatesorar [des-ah-tay-so-rar'], *va.* To remove or spend the treasure.

desatestar [des-ah-tes-tar'], *va.* To contradict a testimony. *-vr.* To retract from the testimony given.

desatiento [des-ah-te-en'-to], *m.* Inconsiderateness, thoughtlessness, absence of mind. *(Yo desatiento, yo desatiente, from Desatentar. V. ACRECENTAR.)*

desatinadamente [des-ah-te-nah-dah-men'-tay], *adv.* 1. Inconsiderately, indiscreetly. 2. Extravagantly, disproportionately.

desatinado, da [des-ah-te-nah'-do, dah], *a.* Extravagant, nonsensical, crazy, foolish, irregular, wild. *-pp.* of DESATIMAR.

desatinado [des-ah-te-nah-do], *m.* Idiot, fool, madman.

desatinar [des-ah-te-nar'], *va. & vn.* 1. To do foolish things, to act in an incoherent manner. 2. To disorder or derange one's mind. 3. To throw into a violent passion, to make one mad. 4. To talk nonsense. 5. To reel, to stagger, to totter, to dote.

desatino [des-ah-tee'-no], *m.* 1. Extravagance, irregularity, wildness; headiness. 2. Reeling, staggering. 3. Madness, craziness; nonsense.

desativar [des-ah-te-var'], *va.* To free a mine from heaps of rubbish.

desatolondrado, da [des-ah-to-lon-drah'-do, dah], *a.* 1. Recovery from stupor. 2. *(Peru.)* Extravagant, foolish. *-pp.* of DESATOLONDRAR.

desatolondrar [des-ah-to-lon-drar'], *va.* To bring one to his senses. *-vr.* To recover one's senses.

desatollar [des-ah-tol-lyar'], *va.* To pull out of the need or mire. V. DESATASCAR.

desatontarse [des-ah-ton-tar'-say], *vr.* To recover oneself from stupefaction.

desatornillador [des-tor-neel-lyah-dor'], *m. (LAm.)* Screwdriver.

desatornillar [des-ah-tor-neel-lyar'], *va.* To unscrew, to remove the screws.

desatrabillar [des-ah-trah-beel-lyar'], *va.* To unstrap, to unbuckle.

desatracar [des-ah-trah-car'], *va. (Naut.)* To sheer off, to bear away.

desatraer [des-ah-trah-err'], *va.* To disjoin, to separate, to remove one thing from another.

desatraillar [des-ah-trah-eel-lyar'], *va.* To uncouple hounds, to untie the leash with which they are coupled.

desatrampar [des-ah-tram-par'], *va.* 1. To clear a conduit, sink, or sewer. 2. V. DESATASCAR.

desatrancar des-ah-tran-car'], *va.* 1. To unbar. 2. To clear a well or spring.

desatufarse [des-ah-too-far'-say], *vr.* To grow calm, to allay one's passion.

desaturdir [des-ah-toor-deer'], *va.* To rouse from a state of dizziness or stupor, to animate.

desautoridad [des-ah-oo-to-re-dahd'], *f.* Want of authority.

desautorización [des-ah-oo-to-re-thah-the-on], *f.* 1. Discrediting; disapproval; repudiation. 2. Denial.

desautorizado [des-ah-oo-to-re-thah'-do], *a.* Unauthorized; unofficial.

desautorizar [des-ah-oo-to-re-thar'], *va.* To disauthorize.

desavahado, da [des-sah-va-hah'-do, dah], *a. (Ant.)* Uncovered, free from fogs, clouds, or vapors: applied to places where the sky is commonly very clear. *-pp.* of DESAVAHAR.

desavahar [des-ah-vah-ar'], *va. (Ant.)* To expose to the air, to evaporate, to send forth a fume or vapor. *-vr.* To grow lively or sprightly.

desavecindado, da [des-ah-vay-thin-dah'-do, dah], *a.* Deserted, unpeopled: applied to a place abandoned by its inhabitants. *-pp.* of DESAVECINDARSE.

desavecindarse [des-ah-vay-thin-dar'-say], *vr.* To change one's domicile; to leave the place where one was living.

desavenencia [des-ah-vay-nen-the-ah], *f.* Discord, disagreement, misunderstanding, misintelligence.

desavenido, da [des-ah-vay-nee'-do, dah], *a.* Discordant, disagreeing. *-pp.* of DESAVENIR.

desavenimiento [des-ah-vay-ne-me-en'-to], *m. (Obs.)* V. DESAVENENCIA.

desavenir [des-ah-vay-neer'], *va.* To discompose, to disconcert, to unsettle. *-vr.* To disagree, to quarrel.

desaventajadamente [des-ah-vayn-tah-hah-dah-men'-tay], *adv.* Disadvantageously, unprofitably.

desaventajado, da [des-ah-ven-tah-hah'-do, dah], *a.* Disadvantageous, unprofitable.

desaviar [des-ah-ve-ar'], *va.* 1. To deviate from the high road, to lead astray. 2. To strip of necessaries or conveniences. *-vr.* 1. To go astray, to miss one's way. 2. To lose the means of acquiring necessaries, conveniences, etc.

desavío [des-ah-vee'-o], *m.* 1. The act of going astray, or losing one's road. 2. Want of the necessary means for attaining some end or purpose.

desavisado, da [des-ah-ve-sah'-do, dah], *a.* Ill-advised, unadvised, misguided. *-pp.* of DESAVISAR.

desavisar [des-ah-ve-sar'], *va.* To give a contrary account, to contradict former advice, to countermand.

desayudar [des-ah-yoo-dar'], *va.* Not to assist, but oppose one with regard to his claims or rights. *-vr.* To be negligent or careless in the performance of one's duty.

desayunar [des-ah-yoo-nar'], *va.* To give the first intelligence of something unknown *-vr.* 1. To have breakfast. 2. *(Met.)* To have the first intelligence of anything.

desayuno [des-ah-yoo'-no], *m.* Light breakfast.

desayuntamiento [des-ah-yoon-tah-me-en'-to], *m. (Agri.)* Unyoking, uncoupling.

desayuntar [des-ah-yoon-tar'], *va.* To disunite, to dissolve, to separate; to uncouple a working span.

desayustar [des-ah-yoos-tar'], *va. (Naut.)* To unbend a rope or cable.

desazogar [des-ah-tho-gar'], *va.* To take off the quicksilver from a looking-glass or any other thing. *-vr. (Peru.)* To become unquiet, restless.

desazón [days-ah-thone'], *f.* 1. Insipidity, want of taste or flavor. 2. Disgust, displeasure. 3. *(Met.)* Disquietness, uneasiness, affliction, restlessness. 4. Unfitness of a soil for agricultural purposes.

desazonado, da [days-ah-tho-nah'-do, dah], *a.* 1. Ill-adapted, unfit for some purpose (tierra). 2. Peevish, impertinent, passionate, ill-humored. 3. Poorly, indifferent in health. *-pp.* of DESAZONAR.

desazonar [days-ah-tho-nar'], *va.* 1. To render tasteless, to infect with an unpleasant taste. 2. To disgust, to vex, to mortify. *-vr.* To become indisposed in health, to be sick.

desazufrar [des-ah-thoo-frar'], *va. (Chem.)* To desulphurize, to desulphur.

desbabador [des-bah-bah-dor'], *m.* A mouthing bit, put on a horse to excite salivation.

desbabar [des-bah-bar'], *vn.* To drivel, to slaver. *-vr. (Coll.)* To be deeply in love, to regard with excessive fondness, to dote upon.

desbagar [des-bah-gar'], *va.* To extract the flaxseed from the capsule.

desbalijamiento [des-bah-le-hah-me-en'-to], *m.* The plundering of a portmanteau.

desbalijar [des-bah-le-har'], *va.* To plunder a portmanteau of its contents.

desballestar [des-bal-lyes-tar'], *va.* To unbend a crossbow, to take it asunder.

desbancar [des-ban-car'], *va.* 1. To clear a room of the benches, etc. 2. To win all the money staked by a gambler, who holds a basset or faro-table. 3. *(Met.)* To circumvent one in the frienship and affection of another.

desbandada [des-bahn-dah'-dah], *f.* Rush. **Hubo una desbandada general de turistas**, there was a mass exodus of tourists. **A la desbandada**, in disorder.

desbandarse [des-ban-dar'-say], *vr.* 1. To disband, to desert the colors (soldados). 2. To flee in disorder; to go off in all directions.

desbarajustar [des-bah-rah-hoos-tar'], *va.* To disorder, to confuse, to mix things.

desbarajuste [des-bah-rah-hoos'-tay], *m.* Disorder, confused medley of things.

desbaratadamente [des-bah-rah-tah-dah-men'-tay], *adv.* Disorderly.

desbaratado, da [des-bah-rah-tah'-do, dah] *a.* Debauched, corrupted with lewdness and intemperance. *-pp.* of DESBARATAR.

desbaratador, ra [des-bah-rah-tah-dor', rah], *m. & f.* 1. Destroyer, confounder, disturber. 2. Debaucher.

desbaratamiento [des-bah-rah-tah-me-en'to], *m.* Perturbation, commotion descomposition.

desbaratar [des-bah-rah-tar'], *va.* 1. To destroy or break up anything. 2. To defeat or rout an army. 3. To waste, to misspend, to dissipate, to cross. 4. To impede, disturb. **Desbaratar la paz**, to break the peace. *-vn.* To speak foolishly, to talk nonsense. *-vr.* To be confounded, to be disordered in mind, to be deranged.

desbarate, desbarato [des-bah-rah´-tay, des-bah-rah'-to], *m.* 1. The act of routing or defeating. 2. Ignorance, folly, madness, misgovernment.

desbarbado, da [des-bar-bah'-do, dah], *a.* Beardless. *pp.* of DESBARBAR.

desbarbar [des-bar-bar'], *va.* 1. (*Coll.*) To shave. 2. (*Met.*) To trim, to cut off the filaments of plants, to loosen threads of stuff, or other things. *-vr.* To shave.

desbarbillar [des-bar-beel-lyar'], *va.* (*Agri.*) To prune the roots which spring from the stems of young vines.

desbardar [des-bar-dar'], *va.* To uncover a wall or fence, to remove the brushwood or straw placed on the top of a mud wall to preserve it from injury.

desbarrar [des-bar-rar'], *vn.* 1. To throw (with an iron bar) as far as the strength permits, without taking aim. 2. To slip, to rove, to go beyond limits. 3. (*Met.*) To ramble beyond proper bounds. 4. To err, mistake in what is said or done.

desbarretar [des-bar-ray-tar'], *va.* To unbar, to unbolt.

desbarrigado, da [des-bar-re-gah'-do, dah], *a.* Little-bellied. *-pp.* of DESBARRIGAR,

desbarrigar [des-bar-re-gar'], *va.* To rip open the belly.

desbarro [des-bar'-ro], *m.* 1. The act of slipping or falling into fault or error. 2. Nonsense, madness, extravagance, frenzy.

desbastadura [des-bas-tah-doo'-rah], *f.* The act of planing, trimming, or polishing.

desbastar [des-bas-tar'], *va.* 1. To plane, to smooth the surface of boards. 2. To trim, to polish. 3. To waste, to consume, to weaken. 4. To purify one's morals and manners. *-vr.* (*Fig.*) To acquire some polish.

desbaste [des-bahs'-tay], *m.* The act of hewing, polishing, or trimming.

desbastecido, da [des-bas-tay-thee´-do, dah], *a.* Unprovided.

desbautizarse [des-bah-oo-te-thar'-say], *vr.* 1. (*Coll. Met.*) To be irritated, to fly into a passion. 2. To change one's name, to renounce the baptismal name. 3. (*Coll.*) To fall from a height and break one's head.

desbazadero [des-bah-thah-day'-ro], *m.* Humid, slippery place.

desbeber [des-bay-berr'], *va.* (*Coll.*) To urinate.

desbecerrar [des-bay-ther-rar'], *va.* To wean young animals.

desbituminación [des-be-too-me-nah-the-on'], *f.* Removal of bitumen from a body.

desbituminizar [des-be-too-me-ne-thar'], *va.* To remove bitumen.

desblandir [des-blan-deer'], *va.* To remove grease from skins in running water in order to curry them better.

desblanquecido, da [des-blan-kay-thee'-do, dah], *a.* Blanched. *V.* BLANQUECINO.

desblanquiñado [des-blan-ke-nyah'-do], *m. V.* DESBLANQUECIDO.

desbloquear [des-blo-kay-ar'], *va.* 1. (*Mil.*) To break the blockade of. 2. (*Com. Fin.*) To unfreeze, to unblock. 3. To unblock (caño etc.), to free (tráfico).

desbocadamente [des-bo-cah-dah-men'tay], *adv.* Impudently, ungovernedly.

desbocado, da [des-bo-cah'-do, dah], *a.* 1. Open-mouthed, wide at the mouth. 2. Wild (caballo). 3. Broken-lipped or mouthed, mouthless. 4. (*Met.*) Foul-mouthed, indecent. *-pp.* of DESBOCAR.

desbocamiento [des-bo-cah-me-en'-to], *m.* Impertinence, impudence.

desbocar [des-bo-car'], *va.* To break the brim of a mug, jar, or other vessel. *-vn.* To disembogue. *V.* DESEMBOCAR. *-vr.* 1. To be hard-mouthed, to be insensible of the bridle. 2. To use injurious or abusive language. 3. To be wild, not to obey the bridle (caballo).

desbonetarse [des-bo-nay-tar'-say], *vr.* (*Coll.*) To take off the cap or bonnet, to be uncovered.

desboquillar [des-bo-keel-lyar'], *va.* To break the mouth of a vessel.

desbordamiento [des-bor-dah-me-en'-to], *m.* 1. Inundation. 2. Overflowing. 3. (*Fig.*) Eruption, outburst. **Un tremendo desbordamiento de entusiasmo**, a great upsurge of enthusiasm.

desbordante [des-bor-dahn'-tay], *a.* Overflowing; (*fig.*) Overwhelming; excessive.

desbordar [des-bor-dar'], *vn.vr.* 1. To overthrow, to inundate, to run over the brim of a vessel. 2. To erupt, to burst forth (entusiasmo etc.). 3. To give free rein to one´s feelings (persona); to get carried away (pasarse); to lose one´s self-control. *-va.* To pass, to go beyond; to exceed, to surpass. **Desbordaron las líneas enemigas**, they burst through the enemy lines.

desboronar [des-bo-ro-nar'], *va.* (*Prov.*) *V.* DESMORONAR.

desborrar [des-bor-rar´], *va.* 1. To cut off the loose threads of stuff when it comes out of the loom. 2. (*Prov.*) To lop off the branches of trees, particularly of the mulberry.

desboscar [des-bos-car'], *va.* To deforest, to destroy the trees and woods of mountains particularly.

desbozar [des-bo-thar'], *va.* To take off the reliefs, carvings, or mouldings of a statue.

desbragado, da [des-brah-gah'-do, dah], *a.* Unbreeched.

desbraguetado, da [des-brah-gay-tah'-do, dah], *a.* 1. Having the forepart of the breeches unbuttoned and open. 2 Careless, heedless.

desbravar, desbravecer [des-brah-var'], *va.* To break in, to tame. *-vn.* 1. To tame, to break in (caballos). 2. To diminish the strength or force of anything, to mollify, to moderate; to lose some part of the fierceness.

desbrazarse [des-brah-thar'-say], *vr.* To extend one's arms, to stretch out the arms violently.

desbrevarse [des-bray-var'-say], *vr.* To evaporate, to lose body and strength (vino, licores).

desbridar [des-bre-dar'], *va.* 1. To break or remove a bridle. 2. (*Med.*) To pare away parts which prevent widening a wound and allowing pus to escape.

desbriznar [des-brith-nar'], *va.* 1. To chop or mince meat. 2. To cut or divide a thing, into small parts. 3. To pluck the stamens of saffron.

desbroce [des-bro'-thay], *m.* Clippings, cuttings from pruning trees; and the clearing of lands or trenches.

desbrozar [des-bro-thar'], *va.* To clear away rubbish.

desbrozo [des-bro'-tho], *m.* The act of clearing away rubbish.

desbruar [des-broo-ar'], *va.* To clean cloth of grease, to put it in the fulling-mill.

desbrujar [des-broo-har'], *va. V.* DESMORONAR.

desbuchar [des-boo-char'], *va.* 1. To disclose one's secrets, to tell all one knows. 2. To ease the stomach (pájaros). 3. *V.* DESAINAR.

desbulla [des-bool'-lyah], *f.* The part of an oyster that remains on the shell.

desbullar [des-bool-lyar'], *va.* To extract an oyster from its shell.

descabal [des-cah-bahl'], *a.* Imperfect, incomplete.

descabaladura [des-cah-bah-lah-doo'-rah], *f.* Diminution, impairment of a thing.

descabalar [des-cah-bah-lar'], *va.* 1. To make incomplete, to take away some necessary part; to unmatch. 2. To pilfer; to diminish the weight, quantity, or number of things, by petty thefts. 3. To impair the perfection of anything.

descabalgadura [des-cah-bal-gah-doo'-rah], *f.* The act of dismounting or alighting from a horse.

descabalgar [des-cah-bal-gar'], *vn.* To dismount, to alight from a horse. *-va.* To dismount. **Descabalgar la artillería de las cureñas**, to dismount the guns, to take them from carriages.

descaballar [des-cah-bal-lyar'], *va.* Among gardeners, to take away the leaves and superfluous buds of plants.

descabelladamente [des-cah-bayl-lyah-dah-men'-tay], *adv.* Without order or regularity.

descabellado, da [des-cah-bel-lyah'-do, dah], *a.* 1. Dishevelled (pelo). 2. *(Met.)* Disorderly, out of all rule and order. 3. Lavish, wild, unrestrained. 4. Disproportional. 5. Preposterous, absurd. *-pp.* of DESCABELLAR.

descabelladura [des-cah-bel-lyah-doo'-rah], *f.* The act and effect of tossing the hair.

descabellamiento [des-cah-bel-lyah-me-en-to], *m.* V. DESPROPÓSITO.

descabellar [des-cah-bel-lyar'], *va.* 1. To disorder and undress the hair; commonly used as reciprocal. 2. To kill the bull by pricking it in the back of the neck with the point of the sword.

descabestrar [des-cah-bes-trar'], *va.* To unhalter. V. DESENCABESTRAR.

descabezado, da [des-cah-bay-thah'-do, dah], *a.* 1. Beheaded. 2. Lightheaded, injudicious, void of judgment, giddy. *-pp.* of DESCABEZAR.

descabezamiento [des-cah-bay-thah-me en'-to], *m.* 1. The act of beheading. 2. The state of a person who is bewildered, or does not know how to act.

descabezar [des-cah-bay-thar'], *va.* 1. To behead. 2. To revoke an assessment which towns have made. 3. To cut the upper parts or points of some things; to head, top, poll. 4. To begin, to let the beginning of a thing pass over. 5. *(Naut.)* To break a mast through its neck. **descabezar la misa**, to let the beginning of the mass be over, before one enters church. *vn.* To terminate, to join another property: speaking of the part of an estate or piece of land which adjoins another, belonging to a different person. *-vr.* 1. To screw one's wits, to batter one's brains. 2. To take the grain from the ears of corn.

descabritar [des-cah-bre-tar'], *va.* To wean goats.

descabullirse [des-cah-bool-lyeer'-say], *vr.* 1. To sneak off, to steal away, to scamper. 2. *(Met.)* To elude the strength of an argument, to avoid a difficulty by artifice.

descacilar [des-cah-the-lar'], *va. (Prov.)* To cut the extreme ends of bricks equally.

descaderar [des-cah-day-rar'], *va.* To hip, to sprain or dislocate the hip.

descadillar [des-cah-deel-lyar'], *va.* In woollen factories, to cut off the loose threads of the warp.

descaecer [des-cah-ay-therr'], *vn.* 1. To decline, to droop, to languish, to decay. 2. *(Naut.)* To edge away.

descaecido, da [des-cah-ay-thee-'do, dah], *a.* Weak, feeble, languishing. *-pp.* of DESCAECER.

descaecimiento, descaimiento [des-cah-ay-the-me-en'-to], *m.* 1. Weakness, debility, decay. 2. Despondency, lowness of spirits, languor.

descafeinado [des-cah-fay-e-nah'-do], *a.* Decaffeinated.

descalabazarse [des-cah-lah-bah-thar'-say], *vr. (Coll.)* To puzzle one's brains, to screw one's wits.

descalabrado, da [des-cah-lah-brah'-do, dah], *a. & pp.* of DESCALABRAR. Injured; wounded on the head. **Salir descalabrado**, to be a loser in any suit, game, or business.

descalabradura [des-cah-lah-brah-doo'-rah], *f.* 1. Contusion or wound in the head. 2. The scar remaining after such wound.

descalabrar [des-cah-lah-brar'], *va.* 1. To break or wound the head slightly. 2. To attack or impeach one's character. 3. To hurt, to injure. *(Naut.)* To cause a ship considerable damage. To occasion losses to the enemy 4. To cause annoyance. 5. To annoy by screams. *-vr.* To fall from a height and break one's skull. *(Peru.)* To be ruined, violently destroyed. **Vd. me descalabra con esto**, you will neither do what you offer nor give what you promise. Literally: you break my head with your proposal.

descalabro [des-cah-lah'-bro], *m.* A calamitous event, a considerable loss; misfortune.

descalandrajar [des-cah-lan-drah-har'], *va.* To rend or tear one's clothes.

descalar [des-cah-lar'], *va. (Naut.)* To unship the helm, to unhang the rudder.

descalcador [des-cal-cah-dor'], *m. (Carp.)* Ripping-iron, claw; *(Naut.)* ravehook.

descalcar [des-cal-car'], *va.* To take out old oakum from the seams of a boat.

descalcañalar [des-cal-cah-nyah-lar'], *va.* 1. *(Prov.)* To smooth, to take out the flutings or furrows. 2. *(Coll.)* To run shoes down at the heel.

descalcez [des-cal-theth'], *f.* 1. Nudity of the feet. 2. Barefootedness (monjes descalzos).

descalcificación [des-cal-the-fe-cah-the-on'], *f. (Med.)* Lack of calcium, calcium deficiency.

descalificación [des-cal-le-fe-cah-the-on'], *f.* Discrediting; *(Dep.)* Disqualification.

descalificar [des-cal-le-fe-car'], *va.* To discredit; *(Dep.)* To disqualify.

descalorarse [des-cah-lo-rar'-say], *vr. (Prov.)* V. DESACALORARSE.

descalostrado, da [des-cal-los-trah'-do, dah], *a.* Having passed the days of the first milk (bebés).

descalzadero [des-cal-thah-day'-ro], *m. (Prov.)* Little door of a pigeon-house.

descalzado, da [des-cal-thah'-do, dah] *a. & pp.* of DESCALZAR. Barefooted.

descalzador [des-cal-thah-dor'], *f.* Bootjack. 2. *(Mas.)* Crowbar.

descalzadura [des-cal-thah-doo'-rah], *f* Laying bare, the uncovering (pies, fundación, raíces).

descalzamiento [des-cal-thah-me-en'-to], *m.* 1. The act of baring the feet. 2. *(Agri.)* Removal of soil, in part, about the roots of plants.

descalzar [des-cal-thar'], *va.* 1. To take off shoes and stockings. 2. To remove an impediment, to surmount an obstacle: applied only to the impediment or obstacle used to prevent the motion of a wheel. 3. To take away the bits of thin boards put under tables to make them stand fast. 4. To lose or cast a shoe or shoes (caballos). *-vr.* To pull off one's own shoes and stockings. **Descalzarse los guantes**, to pull off one's gloves.

descalzo, za [des-cahl'-tho, thah], *a.* 1. Barefoot, barefooted, shoeless. **Estar con los pies descalzos**, to be barefooted, to have one's shoes off. 2. Barefooted (monjes). In this last sense it is frequently used as a substantive. 3. *(Fig.)* Destitute. **Su padre le dejó descalzo**, his father left him without a dime.

descamación [des-cah-mah-the-on'], *f.* 1. Removal of scales or layers from bulbous roots. 2. *(Med.)* Desquamation of epidermis.

descambiar [des-cam-be-ar'], *va.* To cancel an exchange or barter. V. DESTROCAR.

descambio [des-cam'-bio], *m.* Swap, change back; *(Com.)* Exchange.

descaminadamente [des-c-ah-me-nah-dah-men'-tay], *adv.* Absurdly, unreasonably, out of order.

descaminado, da [des-cah-me-nah'-do, dah], *a. & pp.* of DESCAMINAR. Ill-advised; misguided. **Ir descaminado,** to deviate from rectitude, reason, or truth; to take a wrong way.

descaminar [des-cah-me-nar'], *va.* 1. To misguide, to mislead, to lead astray. 2. To seduce one from his duty. 3. To seize upon smuggled goods. -*vr.* To go astray.

descamino [des-cah-mee'-no], *m.* 1. Seizure of smuggled goods. 2. The goods thus seized. 3. Deviation from the high road. 4. Error, blindness: deviation from justice, truth, and reason. 5. Duty imposed on things seized.

descamisado, da [des-cah-me-sah'-do, dah], *a.* Shirtless, naked (pobres). -*m.* **Es un descamisado,** *(Coll.)* He is a mean, poor fellow, a ragamuffin.

descampado, da [des-cam-pah'-do, dah], *a.* Disengaged, free, open, clear. **En descampado,** in the open air, exposed to wind and weather.-*pp.* of DESCAMPAR.

descansadamente [des-cahn-sah-dah-men'-tay], *adv.* Easily, without toil or fatigue.

descansadero [des-can-sah-day-ro], *m.* Resting place.

descansado, da [des-can-sah'-do, dah], *a.* Rested, refreshed. **Vida descansada,** a quiet, easy life. -*pp.* of DESCANSAR.

descansar [des-can-sar'], *vn.* 1. To rest from labor and fatigue, to recover strength by repose. **Necesito descansar un rato,** I need to rest a bit. **Podemos descansar aquí,** we can rest here. 2. To have some relief from cares, to give respite (said of evils). 3. To rest, to lean upon, as a joist does upon a beam. 4. To rest, to be satisfied, to trust or place confidence in the power, kindness, activity, etc., of another. 5. To repose, to sleep. **El enfermo ha descansado dos horas,** the patient has slept two hours. **Descansar las tierras,** to lie at rest (tierras). 6. To repose in the sepulchre. -*va.* 1. To aid or alleviate another in labor or fatigue. **Esto descansa la vista más,** this rests one´s eyes better. 2. To help. -*vr.* **Descansarse en uno,** to rely on somebody.

descansillo [des-can-seel'-lyo], *m. (Arquit.)* Landing.

descanso [des-cahn'-so], *m.* 1. Rest, repose from labor or fatigue. **Tomarse unos días de descanso,** to take a few days´ rest. **Trabajar sin descanso,** to work without a rest. 2. Quiet, tranquility, peace, stillness, sleep. 3. Cause of tranquility and rest. 4. Landing-place of stairs; seat, bench, or support of anything. 5. Day of rest. 6. Parade rest. 7. *(Naut.)* A strong chock in which the claw of the anchor rests. 8. *(Naut.)* Partner of the bowsprit. **Descanso exterior del bauprés,** *(Naut.)* pillow of the bowsprit.

descantar [des-can-tar'], *va.* To clear from stones.

descantear [des-can-tay-ar'], *va.* To smooth angles or corners.

descanterar [des-can-tay-rar'], *va.* To take off the crust of anything (pan).

descantillar, descantonar [des-can-teel-lyar'], *va.* 1. To pare off, to break off part of a thing. 2. To subtract part from a total. 3. *(Met.)* To lessen, to speak ill of someone, to murmur at one's neighbor.

descantillón [des-can-teel-lyone'], *m.* A small line marking the proper scantling to which anything is to be cut.

descañar [des-cah-nyar'], *va.* To pull up by the roots the canes from a piece of ground in order to utilize it; to break the stem or branch of something.

descañonar [des-cah-nyo-nar'], *va.* 1 To pluck out the feathers of a bird or fowl. 2. To shave close. 3. *(Met.)* To trick one out of his money at gambling or otherwise.

descaperuzar [des-cah-pay-roo-thar'], *va.* To take off the cowl or hood from another's head.-*vr.* To take off one's cowl or hood to salute another; to uncover one's head.

descaperuzo [des-cah-pay-roo'-tho], *m.* Taking off the cowl, hood, or huntingcap, in saluting.

descapillar [des-cah-peel-lyar'], *va.* To take off the hood. *V.* DESCAPERUZAR.

descapirotar [des-cah-pe-ro-tar'], *va.* To take off the *capirote* or ancient headcover, now used by doctors of some universities.

descapotable [des-cah-po-tah'-blay], *(Aut.) a.* Convertible. -*m.* Convertible.

descaradamente [des-cah-rah-dah-men'-tay], *adv.* Impudently, saucily, barefacedly.

descarado, da [des-cah-rah'-do, dah], *a.* Impudent, barefaced, saucy, pert, petulant. -*pp.* of DESCARARSE.

descararse [des-cah-rar'-say], *vr.* To behave in an impudent or insolent manner.

descarburar [des-car-boo-rar'], *va.* To decarbonize, to remove carbon from a body containing it.

descarcañalar [des-car-cah-nyah-lar'], *va. & vr.* To run down the heel of a shoe.

descarga [des-car'-gah], *f.* 1. Unburdening, unloading. 2. The act of mitigating the pressure. 3. Volley, a general discharge of great or small guns, flight, shooting. 4. **Descarga de aduana,** *(Com.)* clearance at the custom-house, permit to unload a vessel. **Descarga general del costado del navío,** *(Naut.)* broadside of a man-of-war. 5. Unloading or discharge of the cargo of a ship. 6. Exoneration.

descargadero [des-car-gah-day'-ro], *m.* Wharf, unloading-place.

descargado [des-car-gah'-do], *a.* Empty, unloaded; flat (pila).

descargador [des-car-gah-dor'], *m.* Discharger, unloader.

descargadura [des-car-gah-doo'-rah], *f.* Taking bones out of meat, to render it more useful.

descargar [des-car-gar'], *va.* 1. To unload, to discharge, to disburden, to ease, to take off or alleviate a burden, to lighten. 2. To take off the flap and bones of meat. 3. To fire, to discharge firearms, to unload firearms, to draw out the charge of powder and ball. **Descargar un golpe en uno,** to let fly a blow at somebody. 4. To unload a cargo. *(Naut.)* 5. To brace a lee, to clear the sails or yards. 6. To put the rudder in the middle or on an even keel, in a line with the keel. 7. To lower slightly the sheets, so as to diminish the surface and angle which the sails present to the wind. 8. To make port by degrees. 9. To acquit, to clear from a charge of guilt. 10. To acquit, to exonerate, to liberate from a charge, obligation, or debt. -*vn.* To disembogue or disgorge waters into the sea. **Descargar o meter en viento una vela,** *(Naut.)* to fill a sail again. -*vr.* 1. *(Law.)* To give a plea or answer to an impeachment or accusation; to assign or allege a cause of nonappearance when summoned. 2. To resign one's place or employment. 3. In painting, to lose brightness and lustre: applied to colors.

descargo [des-car'-go], *m.* 1. Exoneration, discharge, acquittal. 2. Acquittance, receipt. 3. Plea or answer to an impeachment or action, acquitted from blame. 4. *(Jur.)* **Pliego de descargo,** evidence, depositions.

descargue [des-car´-gay], *m.* 1. Unloading. 2. License to discharge vessels. 3. The last and largest metal plate of those which come from the furnace.

descariñarse [des-cah-ree-nyar'-say], *vr.* To withdraw the love or affection for a thing, to become cool.

descariño [des-cah-ree'-nyo], *m.* Coolness, indifference.

descarnado [des-car-nah'-do], *a.* Thin (flaco), lean, scrawny; cadaverous; *(fig.)* Bare.

descarnador [des-car-nah-dor'], *m.* Scraper, an instrument with which the flesh is removed from a tooth that is to be drawn.

descarnadura [des-car-nah-doo, rah], *f.* Excarnification, clearing from flesh.

descarnar [des-car-nar'], *va.* 1. To excarnate, to clear from flesh. 2. To take away part of a thing. **Descarnar los pellejos,** among curriers, to scrape hides or skins with the drawing-knife. 3. To remove one from earthly things. -*vr.* 1. To lose flesh, emaciate. 2. *(Naut.)* To destroy, undermine a spot of ground (mar). 3. To become uncovered (tierras, playas). 4. *(Agri.)* To prune too severely.

descaro [des-cah'-ro], *m.* 1. Impudence, barefacedness, effrontery. 2. Sauciness, forwardness, assurance.

descarriamiento [des-carre-ah-meen'-to], *m.* 1. The act of losing one's way or going astray. 2. The act of making anyone lose his way.

descarriar [des-car-rear'], *va.* 1. To take out of the right road, to lead astray, to misguide, to mislead. 2. To separate cattle. **Ser una oveja descarriada**, to be like a lost sheep. -*vr.* 1. To be disjoined or separated. 2. *(Met.)* To deviate from justice or reason. 3. To go astray, to become vitiated, corrupted; to acquire bad habits.

descarrilamiento [des-car-relah-me-en'-to], *m.* Derailment of cars.

descarrilar [des-car-re-lar'], *va. & vr.* To derail a train; to run off the track.

descarrilo [des-cahr-re'-lo], *m.* Derailment.

descarrillar [des-car-reel-lyar'], *va.* To tear the jaws asunder.

descarrío [des-car-ree'-o], *m.* The act of losing one's way or going astray.

descartar [des-car-tar'], *va.* To discard, to fling away, to dismiss, to eject, to put aside, to lay out. -*vr.* 1. To discard, or to throw out of the hand such cards as are useless. 2. To excuse oneself; to refuse doing what is solicited or required.

descarte [des-car'-tay], *m.* 1. The cards discarded or thrown out as useless. 2. The act of discarding. 3. *(Met.)* Evasion, subterfuge.

descarzar [des-car-thar'], *va.* 1. To remove fungous matter from the trunks of trees. 2. To remove empty combs from a beehive.

descasamiento [des-cah-sah-me-en'-to], *m.* 1. Unmarrying. 2. Divorce, repudiation.

descasar [des-cah-sar'], *va.* 1. To unmarry, to divorce: to declare a marriage null. 2. *(Met.)* To remove or disturb the order of things. 3. *(Typ.)* To alter the position of the pages of a sheet, in order to suitably rearrange them.

descascar [des-cas-car'], *va.* To decorticate. -*vr.* To break into pieces.

descascarador [des-cas-cah-rah-dor'], *m.* Sheller, husker.

descascarar [des-cas-cah-rar'], *va.* 1. To peel, to decorticate, to flay. 2. *(Met.)* To boast or talk much, to bluster, to bully. -*vr.* To fall or come off (superficies).

descaspar [des-cas-par'], *va.* 1. Among curriers, to scrape off the fleshy parts of a half-dressed hide. 2. To take dandruff from the head.

descastado, da [des-cas-tah'-do, dah], *a.* Showing little natural affection to relatives, or others to whom it is due.

descastar [des-cas-tar'], *va.* 1. To lose caste, to deteriorate a race or lineage. 2. To make an end of a caste (hormigas, chinches). *V.* DESENCASTAR.

descaudalado, da [des-cah-oo-dah-lah'-do, dah], *a.* Penniless.

descebar [des-thay-bar'], *va.* To unprime firearms, to take away the priming of guns.

descendencia [des-then-den'-the-ah], *f.* Descent, origin, offspring, extraction, house. **Morir sin dejar descendencia**, to die without issue.

descendente [des-then-den'-tay], *pa.* Descending.

descender [des-then-derr'], *va. & vn.* 1. To descend, to get or to go down, to walk downward. 2. To flow or run as liquids. 3. To descend to, to proceed from, to be derived from. 4. To let down, to lower anything. 5. To descend from. **La tribu desciende de la región central**, the tribe comes from the central region. **De esa palabra descienden otras muchas**, many other words derive from that one.

descendida [des-then-dee'-dah], *f.* 1. Descent. 2. Maritime expedition and disembarkment.

descendiente [des-then-de-en'-tay], *pa. & m.* 1. Descending. 2. Descendant, the offspring of an ancestor. 3. Lineal, allied by lineal descent.

descendimiento [des-then-de-me-en'-to], *m.* 1. Descent. 2. Descension. 3. Defluxion from the head to the breast.

descensión [des-then-se-on'], *f.* 1. Descension, descent. 3. *V.* DESCENDENCIA.

descenso [des-then'-so], *m.* 1. Descent. **Las cifras han experimentado un brusco descenso**, the figures show a sharp fall. 2. The act of putting one from his degree or of reducing from a higher to a lower state; degradation. 3. The rapid flight of a bird of prey in order to fall upon its prey. 4. A conducting tube. 5. *(Med.)* Hernia, rupture. 6. Prolapse of the womb.

descentración [des-then-trah-the-on'], *f.* Maladjustment.

descentrado [des-tehn-trah'-do], *a.* 1. *(Lit.)* Off-center. 2. *(Fig.)* Out of focus; wrongly adjusted, maladjusted. **Parece que el problema está descentrado**, the problem seems to be out of focus.

descentralización [des-then-trah-le-thah-the-on'], *f.* Decentralization.

descentralizar [des-then-trah-le-thar'], *va.* 1. To decenter. 2. To decentralize, to divide the powers and authority of the state. 3. To grant local autonomy.

desceñir [des-thay-nyeer'], *va.* To ungird, to loosen or take off the girdle or belt with which clothes are tied.

descepar [des-thay-par'], *va.* 1. To eradicate, to pull up by the roots. 2. *(Naut.)* To remove the anchor-stocks.

descerar [des-thay-rar'], *va.* To take the empty combs from a beehive.

descercado, da [des-ther-cah'-do, dah], *a.* Open, unfortified, undefended (lugares). *pp.* of DESCERCAR.

descercador [des-ther-cah-dor'], *m.* He that forces the enemy to raise a siege.

descercar [des-ther-car], *va.* 1. To destroy or pull down a wall. 2. To oblige the enemy to raise a siege.

descerco [des-therr'-co], *m.* The act of raising a siege.

descerebrado [des-they-ray-brah-do], *a.* Brainless.

descerrajado, da [des-ther-rah-hah'-do, dah], *a.* Corrupt, vicious, wicked, ill-disposed.-*pp.* of DESCERRAJAR.

descerrajadura [des-ther-rah-hah-doo'-rah], *f.* The act of taking off locks or bolts.

descerrajar [des-ther-rah-har'], *va.* 1. To take off the lock of a door, chest, trunk, etc. 2. To discharge fire-arms.

descerrumarse [des-ther-roo-mar'-say], *vr.* To be wrenched or distorted (músculos).

descifrable [des-the-frah'-blay], *a.* Decipherable.

descifrador [des-the-frah-dor'], *m.* Decipherer.

descifrar [des-the-frar], *va.* 1. To decipher, to explain writings in cipher. 2. *(Met.)* To unravel, to interpret the obscure, intricate, and of difficult understanding. 3. To translate a language or an unknown, strange inscription.

descinchar [des-thin-char'], *a.* To ungirt a horse.

desclasificación [des-cla-se-fe-cah-the-on'], *f. (Dep.)* Disqualification.

desclasificar [des-cla-se-fe-car'], *va.* To disqualify.

desclavador [des-cla-vah-dor], *m.* Nailpull, drawer.

desclavar [des-clah-var'], *va.* To draw out nails; to unnail.

descoagulable [des-co-ah-goo-lah'-blay], *a.* Redissolvable after coagulation.

descoagulación [des-co-ah-goo-lah-the-on'], *f.* Solution, liquefaction of a clot or curd.

descoagular [des-co-ah-goo-lar,], *va.* To liquefy, to dissolve.

descobajar [des-co-bah-har'], *va.* To pull the stem from a grape.

descobijar [des-co-be-har'], *va.* To uncover, to undress.

descocadamente [des-co-cah-dah-men'-tay], *adv.* Impudently, boldly, brazen-facedly.

descocado, da [des-co-cah'-do, dah], *a.* Bold, impudent, licentious (mujeres). -*pp.* of DESCOCAR.

descocar [des-co-car'], *va.* To clean, to clear trees from insects. -*vr.* To be impudent, saucy, or petulant.

descocer [des-co-therr'], *va.* To digest, to concoct in the stomach.

descoco [des-co'-co], *m.* Barefacedness, impudence, boldness, sauciness.

descodar [des-co-dar'], *va. (Prov.)* To rip, to unstitch.
descodificar [des-co-de-fi-car'], *va. (Ling.)* To decode.
descoger [des-co-herr'], *va.* To unfold, to extend, to spread, to expand.
descogollar [des-co-gol-lyar'], *va.* To take out the heart or bud of a plant; to strip the summit.
descogotado, da [des-co-go-tah'-do, dah], *a.* Having the neck naked and exposed. *-pp.* of DESCOGOTAR.
descogotar [des-co-go-tar'], *va. (Obs.)* 1. To kill a beast by one blow on the nape. 2. To knock off with one blow on the nape. 3. To knock off the horns of a stag at one blow.
descojonante [des-co-ho-nahn'-tay], *a.* 1. Wildly funny (gracioso). 2. Immensely impressive (impresionante).
descojonarse [des-co-ho-har'-say], *vr.* 1. To die laughing. 2. To kill oneself.
descolar [des-co-lar'], *va.* 1. To cut off an animal's tail, to dock. 2. To cut off the fag-end of a piece of cloth.
descolchar [des-col-char'], *va. (Naut.)* To untwist a cable.
descolgar [des-col-gar'], *va.* 1. To take down what has been hung up. 2. To unhang, to take down hangings or tapestry. *-vr.* 1. To come down gently, to slip down by means of a rope or any other thing. **Descolgarse por una pared,** to climb down a wall. 2. *(Met.)* To glide flow, or run down (ríos, riachuelos). 3. **Descolgarse con una estupidez,** to come out with a silly remark.
descolmar [des-col-mar'], *va.* 1. To strike corn in a measure with strickle. 2. *(Met.)* To diminish.
descolmillar [des-col-meel-lyar'], *va.* To pull out or break the eye-teeth.
descolocado [des-co-lo-cah'-do], *a.* Out of a place.
descoloración [des-co-lo-rah-the-on'], *f.* 1. Discoloration. 2. *(Chem.)* Discolorizing.
descoloramiento [des-co-lo-rah-me-en'-to], *m.* Paleness, discoloration.
descolorar [des-co-lo-rar'], *va.* To discolor, to pale, to change from the natural hue. *-vr.* To lose the natural hue, to become discolored or pale.
descolorido, da [des-co-lo-ree'-do, dah], *a.* Discolored, pale, colorless, pallid. *-pp.* of DESCOLORIR.
descolorir [des-co-lo-reer'], *va.* To discolor, to change from the natural hue.
descolladamente [des-col-lyah-dah-men'-tay], *adv.* Loftily, haughtily; with an air of authority.
descollamiento [des-col-lyah-me-ayn'-to], *m. V.* DESCUELLO.
descollar [des-col-lyar'], *vn.* To overtop, to excel, to surpass. *-vr.* To exceed, to outdo, to be superior to others.
descombrar [des-com-brar'], *va.* To remove obstacles or encumbrances.
descomedidamente [des-co-may-de-dah-men'-tay], *adv.* 1. Rudely, coarsely, unmannerly; haughtily. 2. Excessively, immoderately.
descomedido, da [des-co-may-dee'-do, dah], *a.* 1. Excessive, disproportionate, immoderate. 2. Rude, impudent, insolent. *-pp.* of DESCOMEDIRSE.
descomedimiento [des-co-may-de-me-en'-to], *m.* Rudeness, incivility.
descomedirse [des-co-may-deer'-say], *vr.* To be rude or disrespectful, to act or speak unmannerly.
descomer [des-co-merr'], *vn. (Coll.)* To evacuate waste matter from the bowels; to shit.
descomodidad [des-co-mo-de-dahd'], *f.* Incommodity, inconvenience, uncomfortableness.
descompadrar [des-com-pah-drar'], *vn.* To disagree, to fall out with one.
descompaginar [des-com-pah-ge-nar'], *va.* To disarrange, to disorganize, to mess up.
descompás [des-com-pahs'], *m.* Excess, redundance, want of measure or proportion.
descompasadamente [des-com-pah-sah-dah-men'-tay], *adv. V.* DESCOMEDIDAMENTE.

descompasado, da [des-com-pah-sah'-do, dah], *a.* 1. Excessive, extravagant, beyond rule and measure, disproportionable. 2. Out of tune or time. *-pp.* of DESCOMPASARSE.
descompasarse [des-com-pah-sar'-say], *vr.* 1. To exceed all rule and measure, to transgress all bounds and proportion. 2. To be out of tune or time. 3. *(Met.)* To insult a person.
descompensar [des-com-pen-sar'], *va.* To unbalance.
descomponer [des-com-po-nerr'], *va.* 1. To discompose, to alter the order or composition of a thing. **Descomponer el peinado a una,** to mess up somebody's hair. 2. To discompose, to destroy harmony and friendship, to set at odds, to disconcert. 3. To decompound. 4. *(Chem.)* To decompose bodies. *-vr.* 1. To be out of temper, to transgress the rules of modesty and good behavior. **Descomponerse con uno,** to fall out with somebody. 2. To be indisposed or out of order. 3. To change for the worse (tiempo). 4. **Se le descompuso la cara,** her face fell. *(Yo descompongo,* from *Descomponer. V.* PONER.)
descomposición [des-com-po-se-the-on'], *f.* 1. Disagreement, disaccord. 2. Discomposure, disorder, confusion. 3. *(Chem.)* Breakdown, analysis. 4. **Descomposición de vientre,** *(Med.)* Upset stomach.
descompostura [des-com-pos-too'-rah], *f.* 1. Disagreement. 2. Discomposure, disorder, confusion, perturbation. 3. Slovenliness, uncleanliness. 4. Forwardness, impudence, want of modesty, disrespectful conduct.
descompresión [des-com-pray-se-on'], *f.* Decompression.
descompuestamente [des-com-poo-ays-tah-men'-tay], *adv.* Audaciously, impudently, insolently.
descompuesto, ta [des-com-poo-es-to, tah], *a.* 1. Audacious, impudent, insolent, immodest, out of order. 2. *(Bot.)* Branching much at the base (tallos); decompound (hojas, pétalos). *-pp.* of DESCOMPONER.
descomulgado, da [des-co-mool-gah'-do, dah], *a.* Perverse, nefarious, wicked. *-pp.* of DESCOMULGAR.
descomulgador [des-co-mool-gah-dor'], *m.* Excommunicator. *V.* EXCOMULGADOR.
descomulgar [des-co-mool-gar'], *va.* To excommunicate.
descomunal [des-co-moo-nahl'], *a.* Extraordinary, monstrous, enormous, colossal.
descomunalmente [des-co-moo-nahl'-men-tay], *adv.* Uncommonly, immoderately, extraordinarily.
descomunión [des-co-moo-ne-on'], *f.* Excommunication. *V.* EXCOMUNIÓN.
desconcentración [des-con-then-trah-the-on'], *f.* Decentralization, breaking-up.
desconcentrar [des-con-then-trar'], *va.* To decentralize (industria); to break up; to distribute over a wider area.
desconcertadamente [des-con-ther-tah'-dah-men-tay], *adv.* Disorderly, confusedly.
desconcertado, da [des-con-ther-tah'-do, dah], *a.* Disorderly, slovenly. *-pp.* Of DESCONCERTAR.
desconcertador [des-con-ther-tah-dor'], *m.* Disturber, disconcerter.
desconcertante [des-con-ther-tahn'-tay], *a.* Disconcerting.
desconcertar [des-con-ther-tar'], *va.* 1. To discompose, to disturb the order of things, to confound, to confuse. 2. To disconcert, to defeat machinations, measures, etc. *-vr.* 1. To disagree. 2. To luxate, to put out of joint, to disjoint. 3. To exceed the limits of prudence. 4. To be disconcerted, to be upset, to get embarrassed. **Siguió sin desconcertarse,** he went on quite unruffled.
desconcierto [des-con-the-err'-to], *m.* 1. Discomposure, disagreement of parts. 2. Discomposure, disorder, confusion. 3. Want of prudence and circumspection. 4. Flux, or looseness of the body. 5. *(Fig.)* Uneasiness; uncertainty; embarrassment; bewilderment (perplejidad). **Sembrar el desconcierto en el partido,** to sow confusion in the party. *(Yo desconcierto,* from *Desconcertar. V.* ACERTAR.)
desconchado [des-con-chah'-do], *m.* Place where plaster has broken away.

329

descorrer

desconchar [des-con-char'], *va.* To strip off a surface of varnish, stucco, plaster. etc. -*vr.* To peel off, to flake off, to chip.

desconcordia [des-con-cor'-de-ah], *f.* Discord, disagreement, variance, disunion.

desconectar [des-co-nec-tar'], *va.* To disconnect; to uncouple; to switch off.

desconfiadamente [des-con-fe-ah-dah-men'-tay], *adv.* Diffidently, mistrustfully.

desconfiado, da [des-con-fe-ah'-do, dah], *a.* Diffident, distrustful, mistrustful, jealous. -*pp.* of DESCONFIAR.

desconfianza [des-con-fe-ahn'-thah], *f.* 1. Diffidence, distrust, mistrust. 2. Jealousy, suspicious fear.

desconfiar [des-con-fe-ar'], *vn.* 1. To distrust, to have no confidence in. 2. To mistrust, to suspect, to regard with distrust. **¿Desconfía Vd. de mi integridad?**, do you doubt my integrity? **Desconfía de las imitaciones,** beware of imitations.

desconformar [des-con-for-mar'], *vn.* To dissent, to disagree, to differ in opinion. -*vr.* To discord, to disagree, not to suit with.

desconforme [des-con-for-may], *a.* 1. Discordant, disagreeing, contrary. 2. Unequal, unlike.

desconformidad [des-con-for-me-dahd'], *f.* 1. Disagreement, opposition, contrariety of opinion, non-conformity. 2. Inequality, dissimilitude, unlikeness.

descongelación [des-con-hay-lah-the-on'], *f. (Aer.)* De-icing; freeing (de salarios), unfreezing.

descongelador [des-con-hay-la-dor'], *m.* Defroster, deicer.

descongelar [des-con-hay-lar'], *va.* To defrost. -*vn.* To melt.

descongestionar [des-con-hays-te-o-nar'], *va.* To relieve; to clear (cabeza); to make less crowded (ciudad); to relieve the traffic problems, to make less crowded.

desconocer [des-co-no-therr'], *va.* 1. Not to preserve the idea which was held of something. 2. To recognize the notable change which is found in some person or thing. 3. To disown, to disavow. 4. To mistake, to be totally ignorant of a thing, not to know a person. **Desconocer la tierra,** to be unacquainted with a country. **Desconocer a uno por hijo,** not to own one as a son. **Desconocer el beneficio,** not to acknowledge a favor received; to be ungrateful.

desconocidamente [des-co-no-the'-dah-men-tay], *adv.* 1. Ignorantly. 2. Ungratefully.

desconocido, da [des-co-no-thee'-do, dah], *a.* 1. Strange, unknown, ungrateful. **Por razones desconocidas,** for reasons which are not known. 2. Much changed. **Está desconocido,** he is much altered. -*m. & f.* Stranger.

desconocimiento [des-co-no-the-me-en'-to], *m.* 1. Ungratefulness, ingratitude. 2. Ignorance.

desconsentir [des-con-sen-teer'], *va.* To dissent, to disagree, not to acquiesce.

desconsideradamente [des-con-se-day-rah'-dah-men-tay], *adv.* Inconsiderately, rashly.

desconsiderado, da [des-con-se-day-rah'-do, dah], *a.* Inconsiderate, imprudent, thoughtless, rash.

desconsolación [des-con-so-lah-the-on'], *f.* Disconsolateness.

desconsoladamente [des-con-so-lah'-dah-men-tay], *adv.* Inconsolably, disconsolately.

desconsolado, da [des-con-so-lah'-do, dah], *a.* 1. Disconsolate, comfortless. 2. Disconsolate, heartsick, sorrowful, melancholy

desconsolador, ra [des-con-so-lah-dor', rah], *a.* Disconsolate, disappointing, disconcerting, lamentable.

desconsolar [des-con-so-lar'], *va.* To afflict, to put in pain, to treat rudely. -*vr.* To lose one's cheerfulness; to become low-spirited or afflicted.

desconsuelo [des-con-soo-ay'-lo], *m.* 1. Affliction, trouble, disconsolateness. *(Yo desconsuelo,* from *Desconsolar.* V. ACORDAR.

descontado [des-con-tah'-do], *a.* **Por descontado,** of course.

descontagiar [des-con-tah-he-ar'], *va.* To purity, to disinfect.

descontaminación [des-con-tah-me-nah-the-on'], *f.* Decontamination.

descontaminar [des-con-tah-me-nar'], *va.* To decontaminate.

descontar [des-con-tar'], *va.* 1. To discount. 2. *(Met.)* To abate, to lessen, to diminish. 3. To detract from merit or virtues.

descontentadizo, za [des-con-ten-tah-dee'-tho, thah], *a.* Fastidious, too nice.

descontentamiento [des-con-ten-tah-me-en'-to], *m.* Discontentment, displeasure, grief.

descontentar [des-con-ten-tar'], *va.* To discontent, to dissatisfy, to displease.

descontento [des-con-ten'-to], *m.* Discontent, uneasiness, dissatisfaction, disgust, grumbling. **Estar descontento de,** to be dissatisfied with.

descontento, ta [des-con-ten'-to, tah], *a.* Discontent, dissatisfied, uneasy, displeased.

descontinuar [des-con-te-noo-ar'], *va.* To discontinue, to leave off, to forbear, to give over.

descontinuo, ua [des-con-tee'-noo-o, ah], *a.* Disjoined, discontinued.

descontrol [des-con-trol], *m.* Lack of control.

descontrolado [des-con-tro-lah-do], *a.* 1. Wild, undisciplined (desordenado). **Desarrollo descontrolado,** uncontrolled development. 2. *(LAm.)* Upset, irritated (perturbado).

descontrolarse [des-con-tro-lar'-say], *vr.* 1. To lose control. 2. To blow one's top, to go up the wall (enojarse).

desconveniencia [des-con-vay-ne-en'-the-ah], *f.* Inconvenience, incommodity, disadvantage, prejudice.

desconveniente [des-con-vay-ne-en'-tay], *pa.* Inconvenient, discording; incongruous.

desconvenir [des-con-vay-neer']' *vn.* 1. To disagree, to discord. 2. To be unlike, to dissimilar; not to suit.

desconvidar [des-con-ve-dar'], *va.* 1. To cancel or to retract an invitation. 2. To revolve, to annul, to rescind.

desconvocación [des-con-vo-cah-the-on'], *f.* Calling-off, cancellation.

desconvocar [des-con-vo-car'], *va.* To call off, to cancel.

desconvocatoria [des-con-vo-cah-to'-re-ah], *f.* Calling off, cancellation.

descopar [des-co-par'], *va.* To lop off the branches of a tree.

descorazonado, da [des-co-rah-tho-nah'-do, dah], *a.* Depressed, dejected, dispirited.

descorazonamiento [des-co-rah-tho-nah-me-ayn'-to] , *m.* Lowness of spirits, depression, dejection.

descorazonar [des-co-ra-tho nar'], *va.* 1. To tear out the heart 2. *(Met.)* To dishearten, to discourage. -*vr.* To lose heart, to get discouraged.

descorchador [des-cor-chah-dor'], *m.* Uncorker. **Descorchador de colmena,** one who breaks the hive to steal the honey.

descorchar [des-cor-char'], *va.* 1. To decorticate a corktree, to uncork. 2. To break a beehive to steal the honey. 3. To break open a chest or trunk to take out the contents. 4. To uncork (botellas).

descordar [des-cor-dar'], *va.* To uncord an instrument.

descorderar [des-cor-day-rar'], *va.* To wean lambs.

descordonar [des-cor-do-nar'], *va.* To remove or strike off by blows of a hammer the crusty string which sticks to the mallets in a fulling-mill,

descornar [des-cor-nar'], *va.* 1. To dishorn, to knock off the horns of an animal. -*vr.* 1. To break the skull by a fall. 2. *(Fig.)* To work like a slave.

descoronar [des-co-ro-nar'], *va.* To take away the top or crown from a thing.

descorrear [des-cor-rayar'], *vn.* To loosen the skin that covers the tenderlings of a deer.

descorregido, da [des-cor-ray-hee'-do, dah], *a.* Incorrect, disarranged.

descorrer [des-cor-rerr'], *va.* 1. To flow, as liquids. 2. To retrograde. **Descorrer la cortina,** to draw the curtain.

descorrimiento [des-cor-re-me-en'-to], *m.* The fluxion of any liquid.

descortés [des-cor-tes'], *a.* Impolite, uncivil, unmannerly, ill-bred, coarse, misbehaved, impudent.

descortesía [des-cor-tay-see'-ah], *f.* Incivility, impoliteness, churlishness.

descortésmente [des-cor-tays'-men-tay], *adv.* Uncivilly, discourteously, rudely.

descortezador [des-cor-tay-thah-dor'], *m.* One who strips off the bark; decorticator.

descortezadura, *f.* **descortezamiento,** *m.* [des-cor-tay-thah-doo'rah]. Decortication, excortication.

descortezar [des-cor-tay-thar'], *va.* 1. To decorticate, to divest of the bark or husk. 2. To flay, to take off the crust of bread, to strip off the bark of trees, etc. 3. *(Met.)* To polish or civilize. -*vr.* To become civil and polite.

descosedura [des-co-say-doo'-rah], *f.* Ripping, unseaming.

descoser [des-co-serr'], *va.* 1. To rip, to unseam, to cut open. 2. *(Met.)* To separate, to disjoin. **No descoser los labios,** to keep a profound silence. -*vr.* 1. *(Met.)* To loosen one's tongue, to babble incessantly and indiscreetly. 2. *(Coll.)* V. VENTOSEAR

descosidamente [des-co-se'-dah-men-tay], *adv.* Excessively, immoderately.

descosido [des-co-see'-do], *m.* 1. Babler, an idle talker, a teller of secrets. 2. V. DESCOSEDURA. **Comer o beber como un descosido,** to eat or drink immoderately.

descosido, da [des-co-see'-do, dah], *a. & pp.* of DESCOSER. Ripped, unseamed, unstitched.

descostillar [des-cos-til-lyar'], *va.* 1. To give many blows to anyone on the ribs. 2. To take out the ribs; to break the ribs. -*vr.* To fall with violence on one's back.

descostrar [des-cos-trar'], *va.* To take off the crust.

descotar [des-co-tar'], *va.* 1. To remove a restriction from the use of any road, boundary, or property. 2. *vr.* To expose the neck and shoulders.

descote [des-co'-tay], *m.* The nakedness or exposure of the neck and shoulders. V. ESCOTE.

descoyuntamiento [des-co-yoon-tah-me-en'-to], *m.* 1. Luxation, the act of disjointing bones. 2. Dislocation, a joint put out. 3. A pain or uneasiness felt in many parts of the body, in consequence of over-exertion.

descoyuntar [des-co-yoon-tar'], *va.* 1. To luxate or disjoint bones. **Descoyuntarse un hueso,** to put a bone out of joint. 2. To vex, to molest, to displease. -*vr.* To experience some violent motion. **Descoyuntarse de risa,** to split one's sides with laughing.

descrecencia [des-cray-then'-the-ah], *f.* Decrement, decreasing.

descrecer [des-cray-therr'], *va. & vn.* 1. To decrease, to make less, to diminish. 2. To decrease, to grow less. 3. To fall, to subside (mareas, ríos). 4. To grow short (día).

descrecimiento [des-cray-the-me-en'-to], *m.* Decrease, diminution, decrement.

descrédito [des-cray'-de-to], *m.* Discredit, loss of reputation. **Caer en descrédito,** to fall into disrepute.

descreer [des-cray-err'], *va.* 1. To disbelieve. 2. To deny due credit to a person; to disown or abjure.

descreído, da [des-cray-ee'-do, dah], *a.* Incredulous, infidel, miscreant. -*pp.* of DESCREER.

descreimiento [des-cray-ee-me-en'-to], *m.* Infidelity, unbelief, want of religious faith.

descremar [des-cray-mar'], *va.* To skim (leche).

descrestar [des-cres-tar'], *va.* To take off the crest.

descriarse [des-cre-ar'-say], *vr.* To weaken, to extenuate; to pine with desire or anxiety.

describir [des-cre-beer'], *va.* 1. To draw, to delineate. 2. To describe, to relate minutely. 3. *(Log.)* To give a description.

descripción [des-crip-the-on'], *f.* 1. Delineation, design. 2. Description, narration, account, relation. 3. *(Log.)* Description, imperfect definition. 4. *(Law.)* V. INVENTARIO.

descriptible [des-crep-te-blay], *a.* Describable.

descriptivo, va [des-crep-tee'-vo, vah], *a.* Descriptive.

descripto, ta [des-creep'-to, tah], *pp.* of DESCRIBIR. Described.

descriptor, ra [des-crip'-tor, rah], *m. & f.* Describer, narrator.

descrismar [des-cris-mar'], *va.* 1. *(Coll.)* To knock someone's block off. 2. To remove the chrism. -*vr.* To lose patience, to be enraged.

descristianar [des-cris-te-ah-nar'], *va.* V. DESCRISMAR.

descrito, ta [des-cre'-to], *pp. irr.* of DESCRIBIR. Described.

descruzar [des-croo-thar'], *va.* To undo the form or figure of a cross: used chiefly by the hands.

descuadernar [des-coo-ah-der-nar'], *va.* 1. To unbind (libros). 2. *(Met.)* To discompose, to disconcert, to disorder.

descuadrillado [des-coo-ah-dril-lyah'-do], *m.* *(Vet.)* Sprain in the haunch of animals.

descuadrillado, da [des-coo-ah-drel-lyah'-do], *a.* Separated from the rank or lines.-*pp.* of DESCUADRILLAR.

descuadrillarse [des-coo-ah-dril-lyar'-say], *vr.* To be sprained in the haunches (animales).

descuajado, da [des-coo-ah-hah'-do, dah], *a.* Dispirited, disheartened.

descuajar [des-coo-ah-har'], *va.* 1. To dissolve, to liquefy. 2. To eradicate, to pluck up weeds. 3. *(Met.)* To extirpate, to uproot.

descuajo [des-coo-ah'-ho], *m.* Eradication, destroying or eradicating weeds.

descuartelado [des-coo-ar-tay-lah'-do]. **A un descuartelado,** *(Naut.)* abaft the beam (viento fuerte).

descuartelar [des-coo-ar-tay-lar']. *va.* 1. To remove troops from winter quarters. 2. *(Naut.)* To undo the quartering of the sails.

descuartizar [des-coo-ar-te-thar'], *va.* 1. To quarter. 2. To carve, to cut eatables at the table.

descubierta [des-coo-be-err'-tah], *f.* 1. Pie without an upper crust. 2. *(Mil.)* Recognition, inspection made in the morning, before opening the gates of a citadel, or the passes of an encampment, to prevent surprises or ambuscades. 3. *(Naut.)* Scanning of the horizon at sunrise and sunset. **A la descubierta,** openly, clearly.

descubiertamente [des-coo-be-ay'r-tah-men-tay], *adv.* Manifestly, openly.

descubierto [des-coo-be-err'-to], *m.* 1. The solemn exposition of the sacrament. 2. Balance of accounts. **Vender al descubierto,** to sell short. 3. A deficit. **Al descubierto,** openly, manifestly. **Dejar en descubierto,** to leave others to pay a debt. **Estar** or **quedar en descubierto,** to be a defaulter.

descubierto, ta [des-coo-be-err'-to, tah], *a.* Patent, manifest, unveiled. **A descubierto,** *(Com.)* in blank.-*pp.* of DESCUBRIR.

descubridero [des-coo-bre-day'-ro], *m.* Eminence from which the adjacent country can be overlooked.

descubridor, ra [des-coo-bre-dor´, rah], *m. & f.* 1. Discoverer, finder. 2. Investigator, searcher, seeker. 3. *(Mil.)* Scout, spy. 4. A vessel on a voyage of discovery.

descubrimiento [des-coo-bre-me-en'-to], *m.* 1. Discovery. 2. Discovery, disclosure. 3. Country or thing discovered.

descubrir [des-coo-breer'], *va.* 1. To discover, to disclose, to show, to bring, to light, to uncover. 2. To discover, to make visible, to expose to view, to lay open. 3. To discover, to find out. 4. To discover, to reveal, to communicate, to make known. 5. To discover things or places before unknown. 6. To expose the sacrament to public adoration or worship. 7. *(Mil.)* To overlook any place in a fortification. **Descubrir una vía** or **abertura de agua** *(Naut.)* to discover a leak. **Descubrir la tierra,** *(Naut.)* To make the land. **Descubrir por la popa** or **por la proa,** *(Naut.)* to descry astern or ahead. **Descubrir su pecho,** to unbosom, to communicate secrets to another. **Descubrir el cuerpo.** 1. To expose to danger any part of the body. 2. *(Met.)* To favor a perilous undertaking. **Descubrir quién es,** to find out who he is. **Descubrir sus intenciones,** to reveal one's intentions.

Fue la criada la que les descubrió a la policía, it was the servant who gave them away to the police. -vr. To uncover oneself, to take off the hat to anyone. 2. **Descubrirse a uno,** to confess to somebody. 3. To come out.

descuello [des-coo-ayl´-lyo], m. 1. Excessive stature or height. 2. *(Met.)* Pre-eminence, superiority. 3. *(Met.)* Loftiness, haughtiness.

descuento [des-coo-en´-to], m. 1. Deduction. 2. Discount. 3. Allowance. **Descuento en efectivo,** cash discount. **Descuento por no declaración de siniestro,** no claims bonus. *(Yo descuento, from Descontar. V. ACORDAR.)*

descuernacabras [des-coo-er-nah-cah-bras], m. Cold north wind.

descuerno [des-coo-err´-no], m. *(Coll.)* V. DESAIRE.

descuidadamente [des-coo-e-dah-dah-men´-tay], adv. Carelessly, negligently, idly.

descuidado, da [des-coo-e-dah´-do, dah], a. 1. Careless, negligent, thoughtless, heedless, absent, listless, forgetful. 2. Slovenly, unclean. 3. V. DESPREVENIDO.-pp. of DESCUIDAR. 4. Easy in one´s mind, without worries. **Puedes estar descuidado,** you needn´t worry.

descuidar [des-coo-e-dar´], va. & vn. 1. To neglect, to forget, to overlook, to lay aside. 2. To relieve from care, to make easy. 3. To render careless or indolent; to want attention or diligence. **Ha descuidado mucho su negocio,** he has neglected his business a lot. **A poco que te descuides te cobran el doble,** you´ve got to watch them all the time or they´ll charge you double. -vr. 1. To be forgetful of duty. 2. To make oneself easy. **Descuide Ud.,** make yourself easy. **Descuidarse de hacer algo,** not to bother to do something.

descuido [des-coo-ee´-do], m. 1. Carelessness, indolence, negligence, omission, forgetfulness. 2. Heedlessness, abstraction, absence. 3. Oversight. 4. Want of attention, incivility, coldness, disesteem. 5. Improper or disgraceful action. 6. Imprudence, immodesty. **Al descuido,** affectedly or dissemblingly careless. **Al descuido y con cuidado,** studiously careless, a dissembling carelessness.

descular [descoolar´], va. To break the bottom or end of a thing.

descumbrado, da [des-coom-brah´-do, dah], a. Level, plain.

descurtir [des-coor-teer´], va. To remove tan from the complexion.

desdar [des-dar´], va. Among ropemakers, to untwist a rope.

desde [des´-day], prep. From, since, after, as soon as. **Desde aquí,** from this place. **Desde luego,** thereupon, immediately. **Desde entonces,** from that time forward, ever since. **Desde niño,** from or since one's childhood. **Desde allí,** thence, from that period. **Desde abajo,** from below. **Desde el martes,** since Tuesday. **Desde hace 2 años no le vemos,** we haven´t seen him for 2 years. -adv. V. DESPUÉS DE.

desdecir [des-day-theer´], va. To give the lie to, to charge with falsehood. -vn. 1. To fail to live up to, not to be equal to. 2. To differ, to disagree. **Esta novela no desdice de las otras,** this novel is well up to the standard of the others. -vr. To renege, to retract, to recant. **Desdecirse de algo,** to go back on something.

desdén [des-dayn´], m. 1. Disdain, scorn, contempt, fastidiousness, neglect. **Al desdén,** affectedly careless. 2. Affront, insult. **Desdenes de la fortuna,** *(Met.)* the frowns of fortune.

desdentado, da [des-den-tah´-do, dah], a. Toothless.

desdentados, m. pl. The edentates; mammals having no cutting teeth, e.g. sloths, anteaters. -pp. of DESDENTAR.

desdentar [des-den-tar´], va. To draw teeth.

desdeñable [des-day-nyah´-blay], a. Contemptible; despicable.

desdeñadamente [des--day-nyah´-dah-men-tay], adv. Disdainfully, scornfully.

desdeñador, ra [des-day-nyah-dor´, rah], m. & f. *(Obs.)* Scorner.

desdeñar [des-day-nyar´], va. 1. To disdain, to scorn. **La tierra le desdeña,** he is universally despised. 2. To vex, to exasperate. -vr. To be disdainful; to be reserved.

desdeñosamente [des-day-nyo-sah-men´-tay], adv. Disdainfully, contemptuously.

desdeñoso, sa [des-day-nyo´-so, sah], a. Disdainful; fastidious; contemptuous.

desdevanar [des-day-vah-nar´], va. To unwind or to undo a clew.

desdibujado [des-de-boo-hah´-do], a. Blurred (contorno); unclear (nada claro); faded (descolorado).

desdibujar [des-de-boo-har´], va. To blur. -vr. To blur, to get blurred, to fade away. **El recuerdo se ha desdibujado,** the memory has become blurred.

desdicha [des-dee´-chah], f. Misfortune, calamity, unhappiness, ill luck, misery, infelicity.

desdichadamente [des-de-chah-dah-men´-tay], adv. Unfortunately, unhappily.

desdichado, da [des-de-chah´-do, dah], a. Unfortunate, unhappy, unlucky, distressed, wretched, miserable, calamitous. **Es un desdichado,** *(Coll.)* he is a sorry, pitiful creature; he is a good-for-nothing fellow.

desdicho, cha [des-dee´-cho, chah], pp. irr. of DESDECIR.

desdoblado [des-po-blah´-do], a. *(Fig.)* Split (personalidad); two-lane (carretera).

desdoblar [des-do-blar´], va. 1. To unfold, to spread open. 2. To resume the thread of a speech or discourse. 3. *(Prov.)* To explain, to clear up. 4. *(Fig.)* To double, to divide. 5. *(Quim.)* To break down. -vr. To divide, to split into two.

desdorar [des-do-rar´], va. 1. To take off the gilding of a thing. 2. *(Met.)* To tarnish or sully one's reputation.

desdoro [des-do´-ro], m. Dishonor, blemish, blot, stigma.

deseable [day-say-ah´-blay], a. Desirable.

deseablemente [des-ay-ah´-blay], adv. Desirously.

desear [day-say-ar´], va. To desire, to wish, to long for, to covet. **Os deseo toda clase de éxito,** I wish you every success. **Estoy deseando que esto termine,** I wish this would end.

desecación [day-say-cah-the-on´], f. Desiccation, drying up; withering (plantas).

desecado, da [day-say-cah´-do, dah], a. Dried, desiccated.

desecador [day-say-cah-dor´], m. A room destined for drying medicinal substances.

desecamiento [day-say-cah-me-en´-to], m. Desiccation, drying.

desecante [day-say-cahn´-tay], pa. & m. & f. Drying, drier; desiccant.

desecar [day-say-car´], va. 1. To dry, to draw the moisture from anything, to desiccate. 2. To stop, to detain.

desecativo, va [day-say-cah-tee´-vo, vah], a. Desiccative. -m. Healing plaster.

desechable [des-ay-chah-blay], a. Disposable, throwaway. **Envases desechables,** non-returnable empties.

desechadamente [des-ay´-chah-men-tay], adv. Vilely, despicably.

desechado, da [des-ay-chah´-do, dah], a. & pp. of DESECHAR. Refused, excluded, expelled, rejected; outcast.

desechar [des-ay-char´], va. 1. To exclude, reprobate. 2. To depreciate, undervalue, disesteem. 3. To renounce, not admit. 4. To refuse not to admit. 5. To put aside sorrow, fear, etc. 6. To lay aside, fling away, not to use or wear; to reject.

desecho [des-ay´-cho], m. 1. Depreciation, renunciation. 2. Residue, overplus, remainder, rubbish. **Desecho de hierro,** scrap iron. **Producto de desecho,** waste product. 3. Refuse, offal. 4. *(Met.)* Disregard, contempt. **El desecho de la sociedad,** the scum of society. **Ese tío es un desecho,** that fellow is a disaster.

desedificación [des-ay-de-fe-cah-the-on´], f. Scandal, bad example.

desedificar [des-ay-de-fe-car´], va. To scandalize, to offend by some criminal or disgraceful action.

desegregación [day-say-gray-gah-the-on´], *f.* Desegregation.

desegregar [day-say-gray-gar´], *va.* To desegregate.

desejecutar [des-ay-hay-coo-tar´] *va.* *(Law.)* To raise a sequestration, execution, or seizure.

deselladura [day-sel-lyah-doo´-rah], *f.* Unsealing or taking off the seals.

desellar [day-sel-lyar´], *va.* To unseal, to take off the seals.

desembalaje [des-em-bah-lah´-hay], *m.* Unpacking, opening of bales.

desembalar [des-em-bah-lar´], *va.* To unpack, to open bales of goods.

desembaldosar [des-em-bal-do-sar´], *va.* To take away the flagstones or tiles.

desemballestar [des-em-bal-lyes-tar´], *va.* *(Falc.)* To prepare to bring a hawk down when it is ascending.

desembanastar [des-em-bah-nas-tar´], *va.* 1. To take out the contents of a basket. 2. *(Met.)* To talk much and at random. 3. *(Coll.)* To draw the sword. *-vr.* To break out or break loose (escapar).

desembarazadamente [des-em-bah-rah-thah-dah-men´-tay], *adv.* Freely, without embarrassment.

desembarazado, da [des-em-bah-ra-thah´-do, dah], *a.* Free, disengaged; unrestrained. **Modales desembarazados**, easy manners. *-pp.* of DESEMBARAZAR.

desembarazar [des-em-bah-ra-thar´], *va.* 1. To disembarrass, to free, to disengage, to remove an impediment or obstruction. 2. To remove an encumbrance. 3. To extricate. 4. To disencumber. 5. To unburden, to expedite. *-vr.* To be extricated from difficulties or embarrassments.

desembarazo [des-em-bah-rah´-tho], *m.* 1. Disembarrassment. 2. Disencumbrance, extrication. 3. Disengagement. 4. Freedom or liberty to do anything.

desembarcadero [des-em-bar-cah-day´-ro], *m.* Landing-place; dock, quay; platform.

desembarcar [des-em-bar-car´], *va.* To unship, to disembark. *-vn. vr.* 1. To land, to go on shore. 2. *(Met.)* To alight from a coach. 3. *(Coll.)* To be confined, to lie in. 4. To end at a landing place: said of a staircase.

desembarco [des-em-bar´-co], *m.* 1. Landing, disembarkation, unshipment. 2. Landing-place at the top of stairs.

desembargador [des-em-bar-gah-dor´], *m.* Chief magistrate and privy councillor in Portugal.

desembargar [des-em-bar-gar´], *va.* 1. *(Law.)* To raise an embargo or attachment. 2. To remove impediments, or clear away obstructions.

desembargo [des-em-bar´-go], *m.* *(Law.)* The act of raising an embargo or sequestration; removal of an attachment.

desembarque [des-em-bar´-kay] *m.* Landing, the act of coming onshore; clearance.

desembarrancar [des-em-bar-rahn-car´], *va.* V. DESABARRANCAR

desembarrar [des-em-bar-rar´], *va.* To clear a thing from mud or clay.

desembastar [des-em-bas-tar´], *va.* 1. To give a suitable form to any object of metal, filing it to suit. 2. *(Mil.)* To remove the packsaddles from the horses which draw the field-pieces.

desembaste [des-em-bahs´-tay], *m.* Trimming a metallic object.

desembaular [des-em-bah-oo-lar´], *va.* 1. To empty a trunk, to take out its contents. 2. To empty a box, bag, chest, etc. 3. *(Met.)* To speak one's mind freely; to disclose one's secret thoughts.

desembebecerse [des-em-bay-bay-therr´-say], *vr.* To recover the use of one's senses.

desembelesarse [des-em-bay-lay-sar´-say], *vr.* To recover from amazement or abstraction.

desemblanza [day-sem-blahn´-thah], *f.* V. DESEMEJANZA.

desembocadero [des-em-bo-cah-day´-ro], *m.* 1. Exit, outlet. 2. The mouth of a river or canal, or the point where it empties into the sea; disemboguement.

desembocadura [des-em-bo-cah-doo´-rah], *f.* V. DESEMBOCADERO.

desembocar [des-em-bo-car´], *vn.* 1. *(Naut.)* To disembogue, to sail out of a strait. 2. To disembogue, to flow out at the mouth (río). **Desembocar la calle**, to go from one street into another. **Todas las calles que desembocan en la plaza estaban empalizadas**, all the streets that terminate in the square were barricaded. 3. *(Fig.)* To end in, to result in, to produce. **Esto desembocó en una tragedia**, this ended in tragedy.

desembolsar [des-em-bol-sar´], *va.* 1. To empty a purse. 2. To disburse, to expend, to lay out.

desembolso [des-em-bol´-so], *m.* 1. Disbursement, expenditure. 2. An advance with the object of speculating.

desemboque [des-em-bo´-kay], *m.* V. DESEMBOCADERO.

desemborrachar [des-em-bor-rah-char´], *va.* To sober up, to make sober, to cure of intoxication. *-vr.* To grow sober.

desemborrar [des-em-bor-rar´], *va.* To take away the nap from wool, silk, cotton, etc.

desemboscada [des-em-bos-cah´-dah], *f.* 1. The coming out of the game into the open. 2. Sound of horns to give notice that the game has gone into the open.

desemboscarse [des-em-bos-car´-say], *vr.* To get out of the woods, to get clear of an ambuscade.

desembotar [des-em-bo-tar´], *va.* To remove dullness from the understanding.

desembozar [des-em-bo-thar´], *va.* 1. To unmuffle or uncover the face. 2. To unmask, show oneself in one's true colors. Also *vr.*

desembozo [des-em-bo´-tho], *m.* Uncovering or unmuffling the face.

desembragar [des-em-brah-gar´], *va.* 1. To unbind from the cable. 2. *(Mech.)* To ungear, disconnect. *-pp.* **desembragado**, out of gear.

desembrague [des-em-brah-gay], *m.* Disengagement; *(Aut.)* Declutching; clutch release (pieza).

desembravecer [des-em-brah-vay-therr´], *va.* To tame, to domesticate. *-vr.* To calm down.

desembravecimiento [des-em-brah-vay-the-me-en´-to], *m.* Taming, or reclaiming from wildness.

desembrazar [des-em-brah-thar´], *va.* 1. To dart or throw weapons; to throw from the arms. 2. To take anything from the arms.

desembriagar [des-em-bre-ah-gar´], *va.* To sober up, to cure from intoxication. *-vr.* To grow sober, to recover from drunkenness.

desembridar [des-em-bre-dar´], *va.* To unbridle a horse.

desembrollar [des-em-brol-lyar´], *va.* To unravel, to disentangle, to clear, to extricate.

desembuchar [des-em-boo-char´], *va.* 1. To disgorge, to turn out of the maw (pájaros). 2. *(Met.)* To unbosom, to disclose one's sentiments and secrets. *-vn. (Fig.)* To reveal a secret, to spill the beans.

desemejable [day-say-may-hah´-blay], *a.* 1. Dissimilar. 2. Strong, large, violent.

desemejado, da [day-say-may-hah´-do, dah], *a. & pp.* of DESEMEJAR.

desemejante [day-say-may-hahn´-tay], *a.* Dissimilar, unlike.

desemejantemente [day-say-may-han´-tah-men-tay], *adv.* Dissimilarly.

desemejanza [day-say-may-hahn´-thah] *f.* Dissimilitude, unlikeness, dissimilarity.

desemejar [day-say-may-har´], *vn.* To be dissimilar or unlike. *-va.* V. DESFIGURAR.

desempacar [des-em-pah-car´], *va.* To unpack. *-vr. (Coll.)* To grow calm, to be appeased.

desempachar [des-em-pah-char´], *va.* To make the stomach discharge crudities or undigested material. *-vr. (Met.)* To grow bold, to lose all bashfulness.

desempacho [des-em-pah´-cho], *m.* Ease, alleviation.

desempalagar [des-em-pah-lah-gar'], va. 1. To remove nausea or loathing, to restore the appetite. 2. To clear a mill of stagnant water.

desempañar [des-em-pah-nyar'], va. 1. To take away the swaddling-clothes of children. 2. To clean a glass, looking-glass, or anything which is tarnished.

desempapelar [des-em-pah-pay-lar,], va. To unwrap, to unfold anything wrapped up in paper.

desempaquetar [des-em-pah-kay-tar'], va. To unpack, to open a packet.

desemparejar [des-em-pah-ray-har'], va. To unmatch, to make things unequal. -vn. 1. To become inimical. 2. To part, to be separated.

desemparentado, da [des-em-pah-ren-tah'-do, dah], a. Without relatives.

desemparvar [des-em-par-var'], va. To gather the thrashed corn in heaps.

desempastelar [des-em-pas-tay-lar'], va. (Print.) 1. To compose disarranged type. 2. To distribute, or mix letters. 3. To undo a secret meeting, political machination. 4. To disentangle, to extricate, to clear up.

desempatar [des-em-pah-tar'], va. 1. To make unequal, to do away existing equality. **Volvieron a jugar para desempatar**, they held a play-off (to resolve the earlier tie). 2. (Met.) To explain, to clear up, to facilitate.

desempate [des-em-pah'-tay], m. Play-off (fútbol, etc.).

desempedrar [des-em-pay-drar'], va. To unpave.

desempeñado, da [des-em-pay-nyah'-do dah], a. & pp. of DESEMPEÑAR, Free or clear of debt.

desempeñar [des-em-pay-nyar'], va. 1. To redeem, to recover what was in another's possession, to take out of pawn. 2. To clear or extricate from debt. **Sus estados están desempeñados**, his estates are clear of debt. 3. To perform any duty or promise, to discharge, to transact. **Desempeñar el asunto**, to prove a subject completely. **Desempeñó el negocio a satisfacción**, he accomplished the business satisfactorily. 4. To acquit, to free from an obligation. 5. To disengage from a difficult or arduous affair. -vr. 1. To extricate oneself from debt, to pay all debts. 2. In bullfighting, to disengage oneself from the attack of a bull.

desempeño [des-em-pay'-nyo], m. 1. The act of redeeming a pledge. 2. (Met.) Proof or confirmation of a statement. 3. Performance of an obligation or promise; fulfilment, discharge.

desemperezar [des-em-pay-ray-thar'], va. To relinquish habits of laziness and indolence.

desempernar [des-em-per-nar'], va. To take out the bolts or spikes.

desempiolar [des-em-pe-o-lar'], va. To remove the leash from falcons.

desempleada [des-em-play-dah'-dah], f. Unemployed woman.

desempleado [des-em-play-dah'-do], a. Unemployed, out of work. -m. Unemployed man.

desempleo [des-em-play'-o], m. Unemployment.

desemplomar [des-em-plo-mar'], va. To remove a leaden seal placed on goods (aduanas).

desemplumar [des-em-ploo-mar'], va. V. DESPLUMAR.

desempobrecer [des-em-po-bray-therr'], va. To relieve from poverty. -vr. To extricate oneself from poverty.

desempolvar [des-em-pol-var'], va. To remove dust or powder.

desempolvoradura [des-em-pol-vo-rah-doo'-rah], f. Dusting.

desempolvorar [des-em-pol-vo-rar'], va. To crust, to remove dust.

desemponzoñar [des-em-pon-tho-nyar'], va. 1. To heal from the effects of poison, to expel poison. 2. (Met.) To cure any disordinate passion or affection.

desempotrar [des-em-po-trar'], va. To remove the stays or props which support anything.

desempulgadura [des-em-pool-gah-doo'-rah], f. The unbending of a bow.

desempular [des-em-pool-gar'], va. To unbend a bow.

desenalbardar [des-ay-nal-bar-dar'], va. To take off a packsaddle.

desenamorar [des-ay-nah-mo-rar'], va. To destroy love or affection. -vr. 1. To lose love or affection. 2. To relinquish or yield up one's opinion.

desenastar [des-ay-nas-tar'], va. To remove the handle of a weapon or iron tool.

desencabalgar [des-en-cah-bal-gar'], va. (Mil.) To dismount cannon.

desencabestradura [des-en-cah-bes-trah-doo'-rah], f. The disentangling of a beast from the halter.

desencabestrar [des-en-cah-bes-trar'], va. To disentangle a beast from the halter, in which the forefeet are entangled.

desencadenamiento [des-en-cah-day-nah-me-ayn'-to], f. (Fig.) Unleashing; bursting. **Desencadenamiento de hostilidades**, outbreak of hostilities.

desencadenar [des-en-cah-day-nar'], va. 1. To unchain, to break the chain, to break loose. 2. (Met.) To dissolve all connection or obligation. -vr. 1. To break loose, to free oneself from chains. 2. To become infuriated (personas, pasiones, elementos). **Se desencadenaron los aplausos**, a storm of clapping broke out.

desencajado [des-en-cah-hah'-do], a. Twisted (cara), contorted; wild (ojos).

desencajadura [des-en-cah-hah-doo', rah], f. The part or place which remains unjoined, when the connection is removed; unjointing.

desencajamiento, desencaje [des-en-cah-hah-me-en'-to, des-en-cah'-hay], m. Disjointedness, luxation.

desencajar [des-en-cah-har'], va. 1. To disjoint, to take a thing out of its place; to disfigure. 2. To luxate. -vr. To become distorted (cara); to look wild (ojos).

desencajonar [des-en-cah-ho-nar'], va. 1. To unpack, to take out the contents of a box. 2. (Mil.) To separate the wings from the main body in a line of battle.

desencalabrinar [des-en-cah-lah-bre-nar'], va. 1. To remove dizziness, to free from stupidity. 2. To remove wrong impressions.

desencalcar [des-en-cal-car'], va. To loosen or dissolve what was caked, or close pressed.

desencallar [des-en-cal-lyar'], va. (Naut.) To set a ship afloat which has struck on rocky ground.

desencaminar [des-en-cah-me-nar'], va. 1. To lose one's way, to go astray. 2. To deviate from rectitude.

desencantamiento [des-en-cahn-tah-me-ayn'-to], m. V. DESENCANTO.

desencantar [des-en-can-tar'], va. To disenchant, to counter-charm.

desencantaración [des-en-can-ta-rah-the-on'], f. Act and effect of drawing lots or balloting for anything.

desencantarar [des-en-can-ta-rar'], va. 1. To draw lots for candidates. 2. To be withdrawn as incompetent, to withdraw a name on account of incapacity or privilege.

desencanto [des-en-cahn'-to], m. Disenchantment.

desencapillar [des-en-cah-pil-lyar'], va. (Naut.) To unrig, to take off the rigging.

desencapotadura [des-en-cah-po-tah-doo'-rah], f. Act of stripping on a cloak or a greatcoat.

desencapotar [des-en-cah-po-tar'], va. 1. To strip one of his cloak or greatcoat. 2. (Met. Coll.) To uncover, to make manifest. 3. (Met.) To raise and keep up the head of a horse. **Desencapotar las orejas**, to cock up the ears. -vr. 1. To lay aside frowns; to put on a pleasing countenance. 2. To clear up (cielo).

desencaprichar [des-en-cah-pre-char'], va. To dissuade from error or prejudice, to cure one of conceit. -vr. To desist, to yield, to get over a whim.

desencarcelar [des-en-car-thay-lar'], *va.* 1. To disincarcerate, to release from confinement, to set at liberty. 2. *(Met.)* To free from oppression, to extricate from difficulties.

desencarecer [des-en-cah-ray-therr'], *va.* To lower the price of anything offered for sale.

desencarnar [des-en-car-nar'], *va.* 1. To prevent dogs from eating game. 2. *(Met.)* To lose an affection for anything, or to divert the mind from it. 3. *(Art.)* To soften flesh color in figures.

desencastar [des-en-cas-tar'], *va.* To destroy insects, to end their race.

desencastillar [des-en-cas-til-lyar'], *va.* 1. To expel or drive out of a castle. 2. To manifest, to make appear, to discover.

desencenagar [des-en-thay-nah-gar'], *va.* 1. *V.* DESATASCAR. 2. To extricate one from a den of vice or crime.

desencentrar [des-en-then-trar'], *va.* To take anything from its center: to decenter.

desenceparse [des-en-thay-par'-say], *vr.* To unloosen folds of cable from the anchor stock.

desencerrar [des-en-ther-rar'], *va.* 1. To free from confinement. 2. To open, to unclose. 3. To disclose what was hidden or unknown. *(Yo desencierro, from Desencerrar. V.* ALENTAR.).

desenchufar [des-en-choo-far'], *va.* To disconnect, to unplug. *-vr.* To relax, to unwind, to switch off.

desencintar [des-en-thin-tar'], *va.* To untie, to loosen.

desenclavar [des-en-clah-var'], *va.* 1. To draw out nails. *V.* DESCLAVAR. 2. To put one violently out of his place.

desenclavijar [des-en-clah-ve-har'], *va.* To take out pins or pegs of a musical instrument.

desencoger [des-en-co-herr'], *va.* To unfold. *-vr.* 1. *(Met.)* To lay aside bashfulness or reserve, to grow bold. 2. To make merry.

desencogimiento [des-en-co-he-me-en'-to], *m.* Disembarrassment, freedom from perplexity.

desencolar [des-en-co-lar'], *va.* To unglue.

esencolerizarse [des-en-co-lay-re-thar'-say], *vr.* To grow calm, to be appeased.

desenconar [des-en-co-nar'], *va.* 1. To remove an inflammation. 2. *(Met.)* To moderate, to check or appease one's passion. 3. To make mild and begging. *-vr.* To become milder, to be appeased, to forget injuries.

desencono [des-en-co'-no], *m.* Mitigating anger or passion.

desencordar [des-en-cor-dar'], *va.* To unstring, to loosen or untie strings.

desencordelar [des-en-cor-day-lar'], *va.* To loosen, to untie or take away ropes.

desencorvar [des-en-cor-var'], *va.* To straighten, to untwist.

desencrudecer [des-en-croo-day-therr'], *va.* 1. To prepare silk or thread for receiving the dye. 2. To boil cocoons so as to be able to unwind the silk more readily. 3. To clean fabrics from matter which might alter them.

desencrudecimiento [des-en-croo-day-the-me-en'-to], *m.* Cleansing of silk (with lye).

desencuadernar [des-en-coo-ah-der-nar'], *va.* 1. To unbind, to take off the binding of a book. 2. *V.* DESCUADERNAR.

desendemoniar, desendiablar [des-en-day-mo-ne-ar', des-en-de-ah-blar'], *va.* To exorcise, to drive out an evil spirit. **Desendiablarse**, *(Met.)* to moderate one's fury or passion.

desendiosar [des-en-de-o-sar'], *va.* To humble vanity, to pull down presumption and haughtiness

desenfadaderas [des-en-fah-dah-day'-ras], *f. pl.* **Tener desenfadaderas**, *(Coll.)* to take means to extricate oneself from difficulties, or to liberate oneself from oppression.

desenfadado, da [des-en-fah-dah'-do-dah], *a.* 1. Free, unembarrassed. 2. Wide, spacious, capacious (lugares). *-pp.* of DESENFADAR.

desenfadar [des-en-fah-dar'], *va.* To abate anger, to appease passion. *-vr.* To be entertained or amused.

desenfado [des-en-fah'-do], *m.* 1. Freedom, ease, facility. 2. Calmness, relaxation.

desenfaldar [des-en-fal-dar'], *va.* To let fall the train of a gown.

desenfamar, [des-en-fa-mar'] *va. V.* DISFAMAR.

desenfangar [des-en-fan-gar'], *va.* To cleanse, to clear from mud, mire, car filth.

desenfardar, desenfardelar [des-en-far-dar', des-en-far-day-lar'], *va.* To unpack bales of goods.

desenfardelamiento [des-en-far-day-lah-me-en'-to], *m.* Unpacking of bales.

desenfardo [des-en-far'-do], *m. V.* DESENFARDELAMIENTO.

desenfatuar [des-en-fah-too-ar'], *va. (Prov.)* To undeceive, to free from error.

desenfilada [des-en-fe-lah'-dah], *a. (Mil.)* Under cover from fire. *-f.* Part of a fortification protected against being fired upon from adjoining high lands.

desenfilar [des-en-fe-lar'], *va.* 1. To put the troops under cover from flank fire . 2. To unthread.

desenfocado [des-en-fo-cah'-do], *a.* Out of focus.

desenfrailar [des-en-frah-e-lar'], *vn. (Coll.)* To leave the monastic life, to become secularized. *-vr.* 1. To come out from subjection. 2. To rest from business for a time. *-va. (Prov. Agri.)* To lop off, to mutilate trees.

desenfrenadamente [des-en-fray-nah-dah-men'-tay], *adv.* Ungovernably, licentiously.

desenfrenado, da [des-en-fray-nah'-do, dah], *a. & pp.* of DESENFRENAR. Ungoverned, unbridled, outrageous, licentious, wanton.

desenfrenamiento [des-en-fray-nah-me-en'-to], *m.* Unruliness, rashness, wantonness, licentiousness, boundless liberty or license; libidinousness.

desenfrenar [des-en-fray-nar'], *va.* To unbridle. *-vr.* 1. To give loose rein to one's passions and desires. 2. To fly into a violent passion. 3. To be mad or wild.

desenfreno [des-en-fray'-no], *m. V.* DESENFRENAMIENTO. **Desenfreno de vientre**, sudden and violent looseness.

desenfundar [des-en-foon-dar'], *va.* To take out of a bag, bolster, pillow-case, etc.

desenfurecerse [des-en-foo-ray-therr'-say], *vr.* To grow calm or quiet, to lay aside anger.

desengalanar [des-en-gah-lah-nar'], *va.* To remove trappings or adornments.

desengalgar [des-en-gal-gar'], *va.* 1. To remove the (wooden) brake of a cart, to unscotch. 2. *(Naut.)* To remove anchorstakes.

desenganchar [des-en-gan-char'], *va.* To unhook, to take down from a hook. **Desenganchen los caballos** (del coche), let the horses be unharnessed. *-vr.* To come off drugs, to free oneself from drug addiction.

desengañadamente [des-en-gah-nyah-dah-men'-tay], *adv.* 1. Truly, clearly, ingenuously. 2. Awkwardly, without care or address, scurvily.

desengañado, da [des-en-gah-nyah'-do, dah], *a.* 1. Undeceived, disabused, knowing from experience. **Él está desengañado de eso**, he is aware of that. 2. Despicable, ill-executed. *-pp.* of DESENGAÑAR.

desengañador [des-en-gah-nyah-dor'], *m.* Undeceiver.

desengañar [des-en-gah-nyar'], *va.* 1. To undeceive, to free from error, to disabuse, to set right. **Es mejor no desengañarla**, it is best not to disillusion her. 2. *(Tec.)* To accustom a horse to every kind of noise, and to objects which frighten him.

desengañilar [des-en-gah-nye-lar'], *va.* To free or disengage from grasp claws, or fangs of a person or beast.

desengaño [des-en-gah'-nyo], *m.* 1. Detection or discovery of an error by which one was deceived: undeceiving, the disabusing or freeing from error, disillusion; disappointment. **Sufrir un desengaño amoroso**, to be disappointed in love. 2. Censure, reproof, reproach, upbraiding. 3. Warning, admonition.

desengarrafar [des-en-gar-rah-far'], *va.* To unfasten or disengage from claws or clinched fingers.

desengarzar [des-en-gar-thar'], *va.* To unravel, to unstring.

desengastar [des-en-gas-tar'], *va.* To take a stone out of its setting.

desengoznar [des-en-goth-nar'], *va.* To unhinge; to disjoint. *V.* DESGOZNAR.

desengranar [des-en-grah-nar'], *va.* To uncog, to separate two cog-wheels; to ungear. *-vr.* To get out of gear.

desengrasador [des-en-grah-sah-dor'], *m.* A wringing-machine; scourer, wiping clout.

desengrasar [des-en-grah-sar'], *va.* 1. To take out the grease. 2. To remove the taste of fat.

desengrase [des-en-grah'-say], *m.* Removal of grease.

desengrosar [des-en-gro-sar'], *va.* To extenuate, to make lean, to debilitate, to make thin or fine.

desengrudamiento [des-en-groo-dah-me-en'-to], *m.* The rubbing off of cement or paste.

desengrudar [des-en-groo-dar'], *va.* To scrape or rub off paste.

desenhebrar [des-en-ay-brar'], *va.* To unthread.

desenhornar [des-en-or-nar'], *va.* To take out of the oven.

desenjaezar [des-en-hah-ay-thar'], *va.* To unharness mules or horses, to unsaddle.

desenjalmar [des-en-hal-mar'], *va.* To unharness mules or horses; to take off a packsaddle from a beast of burden.

desenjaular [des-en-hah-oo-lar'], *va.* 1. To uncage. 2. To remove someone from a jail.

desenlabonar [des-en-lah-bo-nar'], *va.* To unlink.

desenlace [des-en-lah'-thay], *m.* 1. (*Poet.*) Catastrophe of a play or dramatic poem. 2. (*Met.*) Conclusion, end, unravelling of an affair. **Desenlace trágico**, tragic ending. **Desenlace feliz**, happy ending.

desenladrillar [dcs-en-lah-dril-lyar'], *va.* To take up floor-tiles or bricks.

desenlazar [des-en-lah-thar'], *va.* 1. To unlace, to untie knots; to loosen. 2. To distinguish. 3. (*Fig.*) To solve (problema). *-vr.* 1. To come undone (desatarse). 2. (*Liter.*) To end, to turn out.

desenlodar [des-en-lo dar'], *va.* 1. To remove, to clean off mud. 2. To separate earthy parts from any mineral or ore.

desenlosar [des-en-lo-sar'], *va.* To take up a floor made of flags.

desenlutar [des-en-loo-tar'], *va.* 1. To leave off mourning. 2. To banish sorrow.

desenmangar [des-en-mahn-gar'], *va.* To unhaft, to remove the handle of something. *V.* DESENASTAR.

desenmarañar [des-en-mah-ra-nyar'], *va.* 1. To disentangle. 2. (*Met.*) To extricate from impediments or difficulties, to explain.

desenmascarar [des-en-mas-cah-rar'] *va.* 1. To remove the mask. 2. To reveal the hidden intentions of someone.

desenmohecer [des-en-mo-ay-therr'], *va.* 1. To clear from rust. 2. (*Met.*) To clear up, to make manifest.

desenmudecer [des-en-moo-day-therr'], *va.* 1. To remove an impediment of speech. 2. To break a long silence.

desenojar [des-ay-no-har'], *va.* To appease anger, to allay passion. *-vr.* To recreate, to amuse oneself. (*Coll.*) To make friends.

desenojo [des-ay-no'-ho], *m.* Reconcilableness, appeasableness.

desenojoso, sa [des-ay-no-ho'-so, sah], *a.* Appeasing, reconciling

desenredar [des-en-ray-dar'], *va.* 1. To disentangle, to free from perplexities, to outwind, to extricate, to loosen, to clear. 2. To put in order, to set to rights. *-vr.* To extricate oneself from difficulties.

desenredo [des-en-ray'-do], *m.* 1. Disentanglement. 2. (*Poet.*) Catastrophe of a play or poem.

desenrizar [des-en-re-thar'], *va.* To uncurl hair, to take out the curls.

desenrollar [des-en-ro-lyar'], *va.* To unroll. *V.* DESARROLLAR.

desenroñecer [des-en-ro-nyay-therr'], *va* 1. To remove rust from metal. 2 (*Met.*) To polish manners, to cultivate the mind.

desenronquecer [des-en-ron-kay-therr'], *va.* To free from hoarseness.

desenroscar [des-en-ros-car'], *va.* To untwist.

desensabanar [des-en-sah-ba-nar'], *va.* 1. (*Coll.*) To change or take off the sheets. 2. (*Met. Coll.*) To remove an impediment or obstacle.

desensañar [des-en-sah-nyar'], *va.* 1. To appease, to pacify. 2. To mitigate irritation.

desensartar [des-en-sar-tar'], *va.* To unthread, to unstring.

desensebar [des-en-say-bar'], *va.* 1. To strip of fat. 2. (*Met.*) To change occupation in order to render one's work more endurable, to draw breath. 3. (*Met.*) To take away the taste of fat of a thing just eaten.

desensenar [des-en-say-nar'], *va.* To take out of the breast of bosom.

desensillar [des-en-se-lyar'], *va.* To unsaddle.

desensoberbecer [des-en-so-ber-bay-therr'], *va.* To humble, to take away pride. *-vr.* To become humble, to moderate one's pride.

desensortijado, da [des-en-sor-te-hah'-do, dah], *a.* Dislocated, displaced.

desentablar [des-en-tah-blar'], *va.* 1. To rip up or off planks or boards. 2. (*Met.*) To discompose, to disturb, to confuse. 3. To embroil an affair, to break off a bargain, to interrupt friendly intercourse. *-vr.* **Una discusión se desentabló**, a row broke out.

desentalengar [des-en-tah-len-gar'], *va.* (*Naut.*) To unbend a cable.

desentarquinar [des-en-tar-ke-nar'], *va.* To free a ditch or trench from mud, mire, or filth.

desentenderse [des-en-ten-derr'-say], *vr.* 1. To feign not to understand a thing. 2. To pass by a thing without taking notice of it. **Se ha desentendido de todo eso**, he has ceased to take any part in that.

desentendido, da [des-en-ten-dee'-do, dah], *a.* Unmindful, pretending or feigning ignorance. *-pp.* of DESENTENDERSE. **Hacerse el desentendido** or **darse por desentendido**, (*Coll.*) to wink at a thing; to pretend not to have taken notice, or to be ignorant of it.

desenterrador [des-en-ter-rah-dor'], *m.* He who disinters or digs up.

desenterramiento [des-en-ter-rah-me-en'-to], *m.* Disinterment.

desenterrar [des-en-ter-rar'], *va.* 1. To disinter, to unbury, to exhume, to dig up, to unearth. 2. (*Met.*) To recall to one's memory things forgotten. **Desenterrar los muertos** (*Met.*) to slander the dead.

desentierramuertos [des-en-te-er-rah-moo-err'-tos], *m.* Calumniator of the dead.

desentoldar [des-en-tol-dar'], *va.* 1. To take away awning. 2. (*Met.*) To strip a thing of its ornaments.

desentonación [des-en-to-nah-the on'], *f.* Dissonance.

desentonadamente [des-en-to-nah-dah-men'-tay], *adv.* Unharmoniously.

desentonado, da [des-en-to-nah'-do, dah], *a. & pp.* of DESENTONAR. Out of tune, inharmonical, discordant.

desentonamiento [des-en-to-nah-me-en'-to], *m.* Dissonance, excess in the tone of the voice.

desentonar [de-sen-to-nar'], *va.* To humble, to wound the pride of anyone. *-vn.* To be out of tune, to be inharmonious. *-vr.* To be of a coarse address, to be rude or uncouth; to raise one's voice in disrespect.

desentono [des-en-toh'-no], *m.* 1. Disharmony, discord. 2. A harsh, rude tone of voice. 3. Musical discord; false note.

desentornillar [des-en-tor-nil-lyar'], *va.* To unscrew.

desentorpecer [des-en-tor-pay-therr'], *va.* To free from torpor, to restore motion to torpid limbs. *-vr.* 1. To be freed from torpor, to be restored from numbness. 2. To become lively, smart, or pert. *(Yo desentorpezco.* from *Desentorpecer. V.* ABORRECER.)

desentrampar [des-en-tram-par'], *va.* To free from debts; or to take away traps set for mischievous animals. *-vr.* To get out of the red.

desentrañamiento [des-en-tra-nyah-me-en'-to], *m.* The act of giving anything as a proof of love and affection.

desentrañar [des-en-tra-nyar'], *va.* 1. To eviscerate, to disembowel. 2. *(Met.)* To penetrate or to dive into the most hidden and difficult matters. 3. *(Naut.)* To remove loops, twists, from ropes. *-vr. (Met.)* To give away all one's fortune and property, out of love and affection for a person.

desentrenado [des-en-tray-nah'-do], *a.* Out of practice; off form; untrained (soldado).

desentristecer [des-en-tris-tay-therr'], *va.* To banish sadness and grief.

desentronizar [des-en-tro-ne-thar'], *va.* 1. *V.* DESTRONAR. 2. To deprive anyone of his power or authority.

desentumecer [des-en-too-may-therr'], *va. V.* DESENTORPECER. *-vr.* To be freed from numbness.

desentumir [des-en-too-meer'], *va.* To free from torpor.

desenvainar [des-en-vah-e-nar'], *va.* To unsheath, as a sword. 2. *(Coll.)* To expose to view anything which was hidden or covered. 3. To stretch out the claws: applied to animals having talons.

desenvelejar [des-en-vay-lay-har'], *va. (Naut.)* To strip a vessel of her sails.

desenvendar [des-en-ven-dar'], *va.* To take off fillets or bands.

desenvenenar [des-en-vay-nay-nar'], *va.* To extract, to remove poison; to destroy the poisonous qualities of a substance.

desenvergar [des-en-ver-gar'], *va. (Naut.)* To unbend a sail.

desenvoltura [des-en-vol-too'-rah], *f.* 1. Sprightliness, cheerfulness. 2. Impudence, effrontery, boldness. 3. A lewd posture or gesture in women. 4. A graceful and easy delivery of one's sentiments and thoughts.

desenvolvedor [des-en-vol-vay-dor'], *m.* Unfolder, investigator.

desenvolver [des-en-vol-verr'], *va.* 1. To unfold, to unroll. 2. *(Met.)* To decipher, to discover, to unravel. *-vr.* To be forward, to behave with too much assurance. *(Yo desenvuelvo,* from *Desenvolver. V.* ABSOLVER.)

desenvueltamente [des-en-voo-el-ta-men'-tay], *adv.* 1. Impudently, licentiously. 2. Expeditiously.

desenvuelto, ta [des-en-voo-el-to, tah], *a.* Forward, impudent, licentious. *-pp.* of DESENVOLVER.

desenyesar [des-en-yay-sar'], *va.* To remove plaster from a wall. *-vr.* To fall, as plaster, from a wall.

desenzarzar [des-en-thar-thar'], *va.* 1. To disentangle from brambles. 2. To appease, to reconcile those who quarrel. *-vr.* To get well out of some entangled matter.

deseo [day-say'-o], *m.* Desire, wish, mind, liking. **A medida del deseo**, according to one's wish. **Arder de deseos de algo**, to yearn for something. **Tener deseos de**, to want, to yearn for.

deseoso, sa [day-say-oh'-so, sah], *a.* 1. Desirous, longing. 2. Greedy, eager.

desequilibrado [des-ay-ke-le-brah'-do], *a.* 1. Unbalanced; badly balanced, out of true. 2. *(Med.)* Unbalanced (mentalmente).

desequilibrar [des-ay-ke-le-brar'], *va.* To unbalance.

desequilibrio [des-ay-ke-lee'-bre-o], *m.* Unstable equilibrium; an unbalanced state.

deserción [day-ser-the-on'], *f.* 1. Desertion. 2. *(Law.)* Abandonment of a suit by a plaintiff.

desertar [day-ser-tar'], *va.* 1. To desert. **Desertar de sus deberes**, to neglect one's duties. 2. To go over to another party. 3. To separate from a body or company. 4. *(Law.)* To abandon a cause. **Desertarse a**, to fall over.

desértico [de-sayr'-te-co], *a.* Arid, desert-like; deserted (vacío).

desertización [de-sayr-te-thah-the-on'], *f.* Turning land into a desert; *(fig.)* Depopulation.

desertor, ra [day-ser-tor'], *m. f.* 1. Deserter. 2. Deserter, forsaker, fugitive, the person that has forsaken his cause, post etc.

deservicio [day-ser-vee'-the-o], *m.* Disservice, fault committed against a person who has a claim to services or devotion.

deservidor [day-ser-ve-dor'], *m.* He who fails in serving another.

deservir [day-ser-veer'], *va. (Ant.)* Not to perform one's duty, to disserve.

desescamar [des-es-cah-mar'], *va.* To scale, to remove scales.

desescombrar [des-es-com-brar'], *va.* To remove the garbage.

desescombro [des-es-com-bro], *m.* Clearing-up, clean-up.

desesalabonar [des-es-lah-bo-nar'], *va.* To cut the links of a chain.

desespaldar [des-es-pal-dar'], *va.* To wound the shoulder.

desespaldillar [des-es-pal-dil-lyar'], *va.* To wound in the shoulder blade. *-vr.* To receive a lesion in this bone.

desesperación [des-es-pay-rah-the-on'], *f.* 1. Despondency, despair, desperation. 2. *(Met.)* Displeasure, anger, passion, fury. **Es una desesperación**, *(Coll.)* It is unbearable. **Nadar con desesperación**, to swim furiously.

desesperadamente [des-es-pay-ra-dah-men'-tay], *adv.* 1. Despairingly, hopelessly. 2. Desperately, furiously, madly.

desesperado, da [des-es-pay-rah'-do, dah], *a. & pp.* of DESESPERAR. 1. Desperate, despaired, hopeless. 2. Desperate, furious. *-f.* **Hacer algo a la desesperada**, to do something as a last hope.

desesperado [des-es-pay-rah'-do], *m.* Desperate, despairer, desperado, a desperate man. **Como un desesperado**, like mad.

desesperante [des-es-pay-rahn'-tay], *a.* Maddening, infuriating.

desesperanzar [des-es-pay-ran-thar'], *va.* To deprive one of hope, to make him despair, to deprive of all hope. *-vr.* To lose hope.

desesperar [des-es-pay-rar'], *vn.* To despair, to be cast down. *-va.* To make one despair, to deprive him of all hope. *-vr.* 1. To sink into the utmost despair, to despond. 2. To fret, to be desperate.

desespigar [des-es-pe-gar'], *va.* To thrash grain.

desespigo, desespigue [des-es-pee'-go, gay], *m.* Thrashing of grain by the trampling of animals, or of suitable instruments.

desesponjarse [des-es-pon-har'-say], *vr.* To lose porosity or sponginess.

desestabilizar [des-es-tah-be-le-thar'], *va.* To destabilize.

desestacar [des-es-tah-car'], *va.* To take away stakes or props from vines, after the vintage.

desestancar [des-es-tan-car'], *va.* To take away a monopoly; to declare an article open to trade.

desesterar [des-es-tay-rar'], *va.* 1. To take off the mats. 2. *(Met.)* To lay aside winter clothes.

desestimación [des-es-te-mah-the-on'], *f.* Disesteem, disrespect; crying down.

desestimador, ra [des-es-te-mah-dor', rah], *m. & f.* Contemner, despiser.

desestimar [des-es-te-mar'], *va.* 1. To disregard, to contemn, to undervalue. 2. To reject, to deny.

desestivar [des-es-te-var'], *va. (Naut.)* To alter the stowage.

desfacedor [des-fah-thay-dor'], *m. (Obs.)* Destroyer. **Desfacedor de entuertos**, undoer of injuries.

desfacer [des-fah-therr'], *va. V.* DESHACER.

desfachatado, da [des-fah-chah-tah'-do, dah], *a.* Impudent, saucy.

desfachatez [des-fah-chah-teth'], *f. (Neol. Coll.)* Impudence, effrontery.

desfajar [des-fah-har'], *va.* To ungird.

desfalcador, ra [des-fahl-cah-dor'], *m & f.* Embezzler.

desfalcar [des-fal-car'], va. 1. To take away part of something, to cut off, to lop. 2. To peculate, to defalcate. 3. To oust one from his protection or patronage.

desfalcazar [des-fal-ca-thar'], va. (Naut.) To untwist a rope to make oakum.

desfalco [des-fahl'-co], m. 1. Defalcation, shortage, deficit. 2. Diminution, diminishing, detracting.

desfallecer [des-fal-lyay-therr'], vn. 1. To pine, to fall away, to grow weak. 2. To swoon, to faint. -va. To weaken, to debilitate.

desfallecido [des-fahl-lyay-the'-do], a. Weak; faint.

desfalleciente [des-fal-lyay-the-en'-tay], pa, Pining, languishing.

desfallecimiento [des-fal-lyay-the-me-en'-to], m. 1. Languor, fainting, decline; dejection of mind. 2. A swoon, fainting fit.

desfasado [des-fah-sah'-do], a. (Mech.) Out of phase, badly adjusted; (fig.) Out of step; behind the times, antiquated. **Estar desfasado,** (Aer.) To be suffering from jet lag.

desfasar [des-fah-sar'], va. To change the phase of; (fig.) To put out of phase; to unbalance, to upset.

desfase [des-fah-say], m. Being out of phase; imbalance; gap, difference; (Aer.) Jet lag.

desfavor [des-fah-vor'], m. Disfavor.

desfavorable [des-fah-vo-rah'-blay], a. Unfavorable, contrary.

desfavorecedor, ra [des-fah-vo-ray-thay-dor', rah], m. & f. Disfavorer: contemner.

desfavorecer [des-fah-vo-ray-therr'], va. 1. To disfavor, to discountenance. 2. To despise, to contemn. 3. To injure, to hurt;. 4. To contradict, to oppose.

desfertilizar [des-fer-te-le-thar'], va. To destroy fertility. -vr. To lose fertility.

desfiguración, f. **desfiguramiento,** m. [des-fe-goo-rah-the-on'], Deformation, disfiguration, disfigurement.

desfigurado [des-fe-goo-rah'-do], a. Disfigured; deformed; distorted (sentido), misrepresentation.

desfigurar [des-fe-goo-rar'], va. 1. To disfigure, to deform, to misshape, to misform. **Una cicatriz le desfigura la cara,** a scar disfigures his face. 2. To disguise. 3. To misrepresent, to misstate. 4. (Met.) To cloud, to darken. -vr. To be disfigured by passion, or an accident.

desfijar [des-fe-har'], va. To remove a thing from its place.

desfilachar [des-fe-lah-char'], va. V. DESHILACHAR.

desfilada [des-fe-lah'-dah], f. (Mil.) Single file.

desfiladero [des-fe-lah-day'-ro], m. 1. Narrow passage where troops pass, single file. 2. Canyon.

desfilar [des-fe-lar'], va. (Obs.) To ravel, to unweave, to parade. **Desfilaron ante el general,** they paraded before the general. -vn. (Mil.) 1. To defile; to march off by files; to file off. 2. To march in review before an officer of high rank.

desfile [des-fee'-lay], m. 1. Parade, procession, marching in files. 2. (Moda) Fashion show.

desflecar [des-flay-car'], va. To remove the flakes of wool or frettings of cloth.

desflemación [des-flay-mah-the-on'], f. (Chem. Obs.) Dephlegmation.

desflemar [des-flay-mar'], va. To dephlegmate.-vn. (Prov.) To brag, to boast.

desflocar [des-flo-car'], va. To ravel out the ends of stud. V. DESFLECAR.

desfloración [des-flo-rah-the on'], f. Defloration.

desfloramiento [des-flo-rah-me-en'-to], m. Violation, constupration, ravishment.

desflorar [des-flo-rar'], va. 1. To pull up or cut up flowers. 2. To constuprate, to violate, to deflower. 3. To tarnish, to stain or sully. 4. To write or speak very superficially.

desflorecer [des-flo-ray-therr'], vn. To lose its bloom.

desflorecimiento [des-flo-ray-the-me-en'-to], m. Falling of flowers.

desfogar [des-fo-gar'], va. 1. To vent, to make an opening for fire. 2. To vent the violence of passion. 3. To temper or

moderate passion or desire. 4. To give loose rein to a horse. -vr. To vent one's anger.

desfogonadura [des-fo-go-nah-doo', ran], f. Disproportionate width of the vent of a cannon.

desfogonar [des-fo-go-nar'], va. To widen or burst the vent of a cannon.

desfogue [des-fo'-gay], m. The venting or foaming out of passion.

desfollonar [des-fol-lyo-nar'], va. To strip off useless leaves.

desfondar [des-fon-dar'], va. 1. To break or take off the bottom of a vessel. 2. (Naut.) To penetrate the bottom of a ship. -vr. (Fig.) To go to pieces.

desforado, da [des-fo-rah'-do, dah], a. Outlawed; unjudicial. V. DESAFORADO.

desforestación [des-fo-rays-tah-the-on'], f. Deforestation.

desforestar [des-fo-rays-tar'], va. To deforest.

desformar [des-for-mar'], va. To disfigure, to deform. V. DEFORMAR.

desfortalecer, or **desfortificar** [des-for-tah-lay-therr'], va. (Mil.) To dismantle, to demolish the works of a fortress.

desfrenar [des-fray-nar'], va. To unbridle. V. DESENFRENAR.

desfundar [des-foon-dar'], va. V. DESENFUNDAR.

desfusión [des-foo-se-on'], f. Dilution, diffusion, attenuation. Quaint and rare form for Difusión.

desgaire [des-gah'-e-ray], m. 1. A graceless mien or deportment, slovenliness, affected carelessness in dress. 2. Gesture, indicating scorn or contempt. **Al desgaire,** affectedly careless, disdainfully, contemptuously.

desgajado [des-gah-hah-do], a. Separated, unconnected.

desgajadura [des-gah-hah-doo'-rah], f. Disruption, tearing off the branch of a tree.

desgajar [des-gah-har'], va. 1. To lop off the branches of trees. 2. To break or tear in pieces. -vr. 1. To be separated or disjointed. 2. To be rent or torn in pieces (ropa). 3. To tear oneself away from.

desgalgadero [des-gal-gah-day'-ro], m. A rugged declivitous place.

desgalgado, da [des-gal-gah'-do, dah], a. & pp. of DESGALGAR. 1. Precipitated. 2. Light, thin, small-waisted.

desgalgar [des-gal-gar'], va. To precipitate; to throw headlong.-vr. To flee by rough roads.

desgalichado, da [des-gah-le-chah'-do, dah], a. (Coll.) Ungainly, ungraceful.

desgana [des-gah'-nah], f. 1. Disgust, want of appetite. 2. Aversion, repugnance, reluctance. **Hacer algo a desgana,** to do something reluctantly. 3. V. CONGOJA.

desganado [des-gah-nah'-do], a. **Estar desganado,** to have no appetite.

desganar [des-gah-nar'], va. To deprive of the idea, desire, or pleasure of doing something. -vr. 1. To do with reluctance what was done before with pleasure. 2. To lose the appetite or desire for food.

desganchar [des-gan-char'], va. To lop off the branches of trees.

desgañifarse, desgañitarse [des-gah-nye-far'-say, des-gah-nye-tar'-say], vr. To shriek, to scream, to bawl.

desgarbado, da [des-gar-bah'-do, dah], a. Ungraceful, ungenteel, inelegant, ungainly.

desgargamillado, da [des-gar-gah-mil-lyah'-do, dah] a (Prov.) V. DESIDIOSO and MANDRIA.

desgargantarse [des-gar-gan-tar'-say], vr. (Coll.) To become hoarse with bawling or screaming.

desgargolar [des-gar-go-lar'], va. To shed the seed (cáñamo).

desgaritar [des-gah-re-tar], vn. (Naut.) To lose the course (barco). -vr. 1. (Naut.) To lose the course. 2. (Met.) To give up a design or undertaking.

desgarradamente [des-gar-rah-dah-men'-tay], adv. Impudently, barefacedly, shamelessly.

desgarrado, da [des-gar-rah'-do, dah], a. 1. Licentious, dissolute: impudent, shameless, bold. -pp. of DESGARRAR.

2. Irregularly segmented upon the border (hojas, alas de insectos).

desgarrador, ra [des-gar-rah-dor', rah], *m. & f.* Tearer, heart-breaking (escena), uncontrollable (emoción), piercing (grito).

desgarradura [des-gar-rah-doo'-rah], *f. (Prov.)* Rent, laceration, break.

desgarrar [des-gar-rar'], *va.* 1. To rend, to tear; to claw. 2. (Cuba) To expectorate, to cough up (phlegm). -*vr.* 1. To withdraw from one's company; to retire. 2. To give a loose rein to one's passions, to lead a licentious life.

desgarro [des-gar'-ro], *m.* 1. Laceration, rent, break, breach. 2. Impudence, effrontery. 3. Looseness, criminal levity. 4. Fanfaronade, idle boast, brag. 5. Solution of continuity, in a tissue by being overstretched.

desgarrón [des-gar-rone'], *m.* 1. (aug.) A large rent. 2. Piece of cloth torn off. 3. A big tear.

desgastamiento [des-gas-tah-me-en'-to], *m.* Prodigality, profusion.

desgastar [des-gas-tar'], *va.* 1. To consume, to waste by degrees. 2. To corrode, to gnaw, to eat away. 3. (Met.) To pervert, to vitiate. 4. To wear down. -*vr.* To ruin oneself by extravagant expenses; to debilitate oneself. 2. To wear away; to erode; to chafe, to fray; to corrode; to get worn out.

desgavilado, da [des-gah-ve-lah'-do, dah], *a. (Coll.)* Unkempt, ungainly.

desglosar [des-glo-sar'], *va.* 1. To blot out a note or comment on a thing. 2. To take off; to separate.

desglose [des-glo'-say], *m.* Act of blotting out a comment or gloss.

desgobernado, da [des-go-ber-nah'-do, dah], *a.* Ill-governed or regulated, ungovernable (personas). -*pp.* of DESGOBERNAR.

desgobernadura [des-go-ber-nah-doo'-rah], *f. (Vet.)* Act of confining a vein in animals.

desgobernar [des-go-ber-nar'], *va.* 1. To disturb or overturn the order of government; to misgovern. 2. To dislocate or disjoint. 3. To bar a vein on a horse's leg. 4. *(Naut.)* Not to steer steadily the right course. -*vr.* To affect ridiculous motions in dancing.

desgobierno [des-go-be-err'-no], *m.* 1. Mismanagement, misgovernment, misrule, want of conduct and economy; ill administration of public affairs. 2. *(Vet.)* Act of barring a vein on a horse's leg.

desgolletar [des-gol-lyay-tar'], *va.* 1. To break off the neck of a bottle or other vessel. 2. To cut off slopingly the fore part of a woman´s gown.

desgonzar [des-gon-thar'], *va.* 1. V. DESGOZNAR. 2. To uncase, to unhinge, to discompose, to disjoint.

desgorrarse [des-gor-rar'-say], *vr.* To pull off one's bonnet, hat, or huntingcap.

desgotar [des-go-tar'], *va.* To drain off water. V. AGOTAR.

desgoznar [des-goth-nar'], *va.* To unhinge, to disjoint. -*vr.* 1. To be dislocated or disjointed. 2. To be torn to pieces. 3. To distort the body with violent motions.

desgrabar [des-grah-bar'], *va.* To wipe (cinta).

desgracia [des-grah'-the-ah], *f.* 1. Misfortune, adversity, mishap, fatality. 2. Misadventure, mischance, harm. 3. Enmity, unfriendly disposition. 4. Disgrace, state of being out of favor. 5. Unpleasantness, rudeness of language and address. **Correr con desgracia**, to be unfortunate in a design or undertaking. **Caer en desgracia**, to be disgraced or put out of favor. **La familia ha tenido una serie de desgracias**, the family has had a series of misfortunes.

desgraciadamente [des-grah-the-ah-dah-men'-tay], *adv.* Unfortunately, unhappily.

desgraciado, da [des-grah-the-ah'-do, dah], *a.* 1. Unfortunate, unhappy, unlucky, miserable, subject to misfortunes. **Desgraciado en amores**, unlucky in love. 2. Misadventured, luckless, hapless. 3. Out of work. 4. Disagreeable, ungrateful. -*m. f.* Wretch, poor devil. -*pp.* of DESGRACIAR.

desgraciar [des-grah-the-ar'], *va. (Obs.)* To displease, to disgust, to offend. -*vn.* V. MALOGRAR. -*vr.* 1. To disgrace, to fall out with one. 2. To be out of order; not to enjoy good health. 3. To lose the perfection formerly possessed, to degenerate; to die young. **Este negocio se desgració a sus principios**, this business failed at its commencement. **Se desgració con esta acción**, by this action he disgraced himself.

desgramar [des-grah-mar'], *va.* To pull up the panic-grass by the root.

desgranadera [des-grah-nah-day'-rah], *f.* An instrument for separating grapes from the stems.

desgranamiento [des-grah-nah-me-en'-to], *m.* 1. (Agri.) Shaking out grain. 2. (Mil.) Grooves which the expansive force of powder forms on the inner orifice of the vent-hole.

desgranar [des-grah-nar'], *va.* 1. To shake out the grain from the ears of corn, or other fruits. 2. (Met.) To kill. 3. (Met.) To scatter about. 4. **Desgranar mentiras**, to come out with a string of lies. 5. (Fig.) To sort out, to distinguish between. 6. (Fig.) To spell out (sentido). -*vr.* To wear away: applied to the vent of firearms.

desgranzar [des-gran-thar'], *va.* 1. To separate the husks or chaff from the grain. 2. (Pict.) To give colors the first grinding.

desgrasar [des-grah-sar'], *va.* To remove the fat (from).

desgravable [des-grah-vah'-blay], *a.* Tax-deductible.

desgravación [des-grah-vah-the-on'], *f.* **Desgravación fiscal**, tax relief.

desgravar [des-grah-var'], *va.* To reduce the tax on; to exempt from tax.

desgreñadura [des-gray-nyah-doo'-rah], *f.* The act and effect of dishevelling.

desgreñar [des-gray-nyar'], *va.* 1. To dishevel hair, to pull it out by the roots. 2. To discompose, to disturb.

desguace [des-goo-ah'-they], *m.* 1. Breaking up; scrapping; stripping. 2. Scrapyard (parque).

desguarnecer [des-goo-ar-nay-therr'], *va..* 1. To strip clothes of trimmings and other ornaments. 2. To deprive something of its strength, to strip it of all accessories; to take away what is necesary for the use of some mechanical instrument. 3. To disgarnish, to deprive of ornament or lustre. 4. To disgarrison. *(Yo desguarnezco, yo desguarnezca* from *Desguarnecer.* V. CONOCER.)

desguarnir [des-goo-ar-neer´], *va. (Naut.)* To unrig the capstan.

desguazar [des-goo-ah-thar´], *va.* To cut asunder timber or wood.

desguince [des-geen'-thay], *m.* 1. The knife which cuts lags in paper-mills. 2. V. ESQUINCE.

desguindar [des-geen-dar'], *va. (Naut.)* To take and bring down. -*vr.* To slide down a rope.

desguinzar [des-geen-thar'], *a.* To cut cloth or rags in papermills.

deshabitado [des-ah-be-tah-do], *a.* Uninhabited; deserted; empty, vacant.

deshabitar [des-ah-be-tar'], *va.* 1. To quit one's house or habitation. 2. To unpeople, to depopulate, to desert a place.

deshabituación [des-ah-be-too-ah-the-on'], *f.* Disuse, disusage, desuetude.

deshabituar [des-ah-be-too-ar], *va.* To disaccustom, to disuse, to destroy the force of habit. -*vr.* To lose the habit, to get out of the habit.

deshacedor [des-ah-thay-dor'], *m.* **Deshacedor de agravios**, undoer of injuries.

deshacer [des-ah-ther], *va.* 1. To undo or destroy the form or figure of a thing; to undo what has been done. 2. To consume, to diminish. 3. To cancel, to blot or scratch out, to efface. 4. To rout an army, to put to flight. 5. To melt, to liquefy. 6. To cut up, to divide. 7. To dissolve in a liquid. 8. To violate a treaty or agreement. 9. To discharge troops from service. **Deshacer algo en agua**, to dissolve something in water. **Deshacer el camino**, to go back over one´s route. -*vr.* 1. To be wasted or destroyed. 2. To grieve, to mourn. 3. To disappear, to get out of one's sight. 4. To do anything with vehemence. 5. To grow feeble or meagre. 6. To be crippled, grievously maltreated. 7. To remove a hindrance to the carrying out of a project. 8. To transfer, to sell. **Deshacerse como el humo,** to vanish like smoke. **Deshacerse en lágrimas,** to burst into a flood of tears. **Deshacerse de una cosa,** to give a thing away, to dispose of. **Cuando se deshizo la reunión,** when the meeting broke up. **Deshacerse de algo,** to get rid of something. **Deshacerse por hacer algo,** to strive to do something, to struggle to do something. *(Yo deshago, yo deshice, yo deshaga,* from *Deshacer. V.* HACER.)

desharrapado, da [des-ar-rah-pah'-do, dah], *a.* Shabby, ragged, in tatters.

desharrapamiento [des-ar-rah-pah-me-en'-to], *m.* Misery, meanness.

deshebillar [des-ay-bil-lyar'], *va.* To unbuckle.

deshebrar [des-ay-brar'], *va.* 1. To unthread, to ravel into threads. 2. *(Met.)* To separate into filaments. 3. *(Met.)* To shed a flood of tears.

deshecha [des-ay'-chah], *f.* I. Simulation, fiction, evasion, shift. 2. A genteel departure, a polite farewell. 3. Step in a Spanish dance. **A la deshecha,** dissemblingly; deceitfully.

deshechizar [des-ay-che-thar'], *va.* To disenchant.

deshechizo [des-ay-chee'-tho], *m.* Disenchantment.

deshecho, cha [des-ay'-cho´, chah], *a. & pp.* of DESHACER. 1. Undone, destroyed, wasted; melted: in pieces. 2. Perfectly mixed (colores). **Borrasca deshecha,** a violent tempest. **Tener un brazo deshecho,** to have a badly injured arm.

deshelador [des-ay-lah-dor'], *m.* De-icer.

deshelar [des-ay-lar'], *va.* 1. To thaw. 2. To overcome one's obstinacy. 3. *(Met.)* To invite, to inspirit. *-vr.* To thaw, to melt.

desherbar [des-er-bar'], *va.* To pluck up or extirpate herbs.

desheredación [des-ay-ray-dah-the-on´], *f.* Disheritance, disinheriting.

desheredamiento [des-ay-ray-dah-me-en'-to], *m.* Disinheriting.

desheredar [des-ay-ray-dar'], *va.* 1. To disinherit, to deprive of an inheritance; to disinherit, to cut off from an hereditary right. 2. *(Met.)* To deprive of influence or favor. *-vr.* To degenerate, to fall from the dignity and virtue of one's ancestors.

deshermanar [des-er-mah-nar'], *va. (Met.)* To unmatch things which were similar or equal. *-vr.* To violate the love due to a brother.

desherradura [des-er-rah-doo´-rah], *f. (Vet.)* Surbating, injury done to a horse's foot by being unshod.

desherrar [des-er-rar'], *va.* 1. To unchain. 2. To rip off the shoes of horses.

desherrumbrar [des-er-room-brar'], *va.* To clear a thing of rust.

deshidratado, da [des-e-drah-tah'-do, dah], *a.* Dehydrated.

deshidratación [des-e-drah-tah-the-on'], *f.* Dehydration.

deshidratado [des-e-drah-tah'-do], *u.* Dehydrated.

deshidratar [des-e-drah-tar'], *va.* To dehydrate.

deshielo [des-e-ay'-lo], *m.* Thaw. *(Yo deshielo,* from *Deshelar. V.* ACRECENTAR.)

deshilachar [des-e-lah-char'], *va.* To ravel, to uncord.

deshilado [des-e-lah'-do], *m.* Openwork, a kind of embroidery; drawn work

deshilado, da [des-e-lah'-do dah], *a.* Marching in a file. **A la deshilada,** 1. In file, one after another, stealthily. 2. Deceitfully, dissemblingly.*-pp.* of DESHILAR.

deshiladura [des-e-lah-doo'-rah], *f.* Ripping, ravelling out.

deshilar [des-e-lar'], *va.* 1. To draw out threads from cloth, to ravel. 2. To reduce, to convert into filaments or lint. 3. To distract bees, in order to lead them from one hive to another. *-vn.* To grow thin, by reason of sickness.

deshilo [des-e-e'-lo], *m.* Obstructing the communication of bees, to get them into a new hive.

deshilvanar [des-eel-vah-nar'], *va.* To remove the basting-threads.

deshincadura [des-in-cah-doo'-rah], *f.* Act of drawing out anything nailed or fixed.

deshincar [des-in-car'], *va.* To draw a nail, to remove what is fixed.

deshinchadura [des-in-chah-doo'-rah], *f.* Act of abating a swelling.

deshinchar [des-in-char'], *va.* 1. To reduce a swelling. 2. To let out the air, or fluid, with which something is inflated. 3. To appease anger or annoyance. *-vr.* 1. To be removed (inflamación). 2. *(Met.)* To abate presumption.

deshipotecar [des-e-po-tay-car'], *va.* To lift, to satisfy a mortgage.

deshojado [des-o-hah'-do], *a.* Leafless (rama etc.); Stripped of its petals (flor).

deshojador [des-oh-hah-dor'], *m.* A stripper of leaves.

deshojadura [des-oh-hah-doo'-rah], *f.* Stripping a tree of its leaves.

deshojar [des-oh-har'], *va.* 1. To strip off the leaves. 2. *(Met.)* To display rhetorical elegance in discussion. 3. *(Met.)* To deprive of all hopes.

deshoje [des-oh'-hay], *m.* The fall of leaves from plants.

deshollejar [des-ol-lyay-har'], *va.* To peel, to pare, to strip off the husk.

deshollinador [des-ol-lyee-nah-dor´], *m.* 1. Chimney-sweeper. 2. Any instrument for sweeping chimneys. 3. *(Met. Coll.)* He who examines and inspects carefully and curiously.

deshollinar [des-ol-lyee-nar'], *va.* 1. To sweep or clean chimneys. 2. To clean what is dirty. 3. *(Met.)* To shift, to change clothes. 4. *(Met. Col.)* To view and examine with attention.

deshombrecerse [des-om-bray-therr'-say], *vr. (Prov.)* To shrug up the shoulders.

deshonestamente [des-o-nes-tah-men-tay], *adv.* 1. Dishonorably, disgracefully. 2. Lewdly, dishonestly.

deshonestar [des-o-nes-tar'], *va.* 1. To dishonor, to disgrace. 2. *(Obs.)* To disfigure, to deform. *-vr.* To be insolent, to be saucy.

deshonestidad [des-o-nes-te-dahd'], *f.* Immodesty, indecency, lewdness in actions or words.

deshonesto, ta [des-o-nes'-to, tah], *a.* 1. Immodest, lewd, unchaste, libidinous, lustful, dishonest. 2. Unreasonable, not conformable to reason. 3. *(Obs.)* Saucy, rude, rustic.

deshonor [des-o-nor'], *m.* 1. Dishonor, disgrace. 2. Injury, insult, affront.

deshonorar [des-o-no-rar'], *va.* 1. To deprive of office or employment. 2. *(Obs.)* To dishonor, to disgrace.

deshonra [des-on'-rah], *f.* 1. Dishonor, discredit. 2. Disgrace or infamy, obloquy, opprobrium. 3. Seduction or defloration of a woman. **Tener a deshonra alguna cosa,** to consider a thing unworthy, and beneath the rank or character of a person.

deshonradamente [des-onr-rah'-dah-men-tay], *adv.* Dishonorably, shamefully, disgracefully.

deshonrador [des-on-rah-dor'], *m.* 1. One who dishonors, violator of chastity. 2. One who disgraces.

deshonrar [de-son-rar'], *va.* 1. To affront, to insult, to defame, to dishonor, to disgrace. 2. To scorn, to despise. 3. To seduce an honest woman.

deshonrible [des-on-ree'-bley], *a.* Shameless, despicable.

deshonroso, sa [des-on-ro'-so, sah], Dishonorable, indecent, disgraceful, low.

deshora [des-oh'-rah], *f.* An unseasonable or inconvenient time. **A deshora** or **a deshoras,** untimely, unseasonably; extemporary.

deshorado, da [des-o-rah'-do, dah], *a.* Untimely, unseasonable; unpropitious, fatal.

deshornar [des-or-nar´], *va.* To take out of the oven. *V.* DESENHORNAR.

deshuesamiento

deshuesamiento [des-oo-ay-sah-me-en'-to], *m.* Removal of bones.

deshuesar [des-oo-ay-sar'], *va.* To rid of bones.

deshumanizar [des-oo-mah-ne-thar'], *va.* To dehumanize.

deshumedecer [des-oo-may-day- therr'], *va.* To dehumidify, to deprive of humidity. *-vr.* To grow dry.

desiderable [day-se-day-rah'-blay], *a.* Desirable.

desiderativo, va [day-se-day-rah-tee'-vo, vah], *a.* Desiderative, expressing desire.

desidia [day-see'-de-ah], *f.* Idleness, laziness, indolence.

desidiosamente [day-se-de-o-sah-men'-tay], *adv.* Indolently, idly.

desidioso, sa [day-se-de-oh'-so, sah], *a.* Lazy, idle, indolent, heavy.

desierto, ta [day-se-err'-to, tah], *a.* Deserted, uninhabited, lonesome, solitary, desert, waste. **La calle estaba desierta,** the street was deserted.

desierta [day-se-ayr'-tah], *f. (Law.)* Withdrawal of an appeal.

desierto [day-se-err'-to], *m.* Desert, wilderness.

designación [day-sig-nah-the-on'], *f.* Designation.

designar [day-sig-nar'], *va.* 1. To design, to purpose, to intend anything. 2. To appoint a person for some determined purpose. 3. To express, to name.

designativo, va [day-sig-nah-tee'-vo, vah], *a.* Designative.

designio [day-sig'-ne-o], *m.* Design, purpose, intention, contrivance, mind.

desigual [des-e-goo-ahl'], *a.* 1. Unequal, dissimilar, unlike. 2. Uneven, unlevelled, broken, craggy, cragged. 3. Arduous, difficult, perious. 4. Variable; abrupt. 5. Excessive, extreme.

desigualar [des-e-goo-ah-lar'], *va.* To make unequal or to mismatch. *-vr.* To excel, to surpass.

desigualdad [des-e-goo-al-dahd'], *f.* 1. Inequality, odds, dissimilitude. 2. Variableness, levity, inconstancy. 3. Wrong, injury, injustice. 4. Knottiness, unevenness, craggedness, cragginess, unevenness of the ground, anfractuosity.

desigualmente [day-se-goo-ahl-men'-tay], *adv.* **Unequally,** oddly.

desilusión [des-e-loo-se-on'], *f.* Disillusion, disappointment. **Sufrir una desilusión,** to suffer a disappointment.

desilusionar [des-e-loo-se-o-nar'], *va.* 1. To destroy an illusion, to cause it to vanish. 2. To undeceive. *-vr.* 1. To lose an illusion. 2. To be disabused, undeceived.

desimaginar [des-e-mah-he-nar'], *va.* To blot out or obliterate in the mind. *-vn.* To be thoughtless or unconcerned about what may happen.

desimanarse [des-e-mah-nar'-say], *vn.* To lose its magnetism.

desimpresionar [des-im-pray-se-o-nar'], *va.* To undeceive.

desinclinar [des-in-cle-nar'], *va.* To disincline.

desincorporación [des-in-cor-po-rah-the-on'], *f.* Disincorporation, end of corporate existence.

desincorporar [des-in-cor-po-rar'], *va. & vr.* To separate what was before united or incorporated; to disincorporate.

desinencia [day-se-nen'-the-ah], *f. (Gram.)* Termination, ending.

desinfatuación [des-in-fah-too-ah-the-on'], *f.* Disinfatuation.

desinfatuar [des-in-fah-too-ar'], *va. & vr.* To disinfatuate, to become freed from infatuation.

desinfección [des-in-fec-the-on'], *f.* Disinfection, act of disinfecting.

desinfectante [des-in-fec-tahn'-tay], *pa. & m.* Disinfectant; capable of destroying or neutralizing infection.

desinfectar [des-in-fec-tar'], *va.* To disinfect, to destroy the poison of disease.

desinficionar [des-in-fe-the-o-nar'], *va.* To free from infection.

desinflación [des-in-flah-the-on'], *f.* 1. Deflation. 2. Depression, dejection.

desinflado [des-en-flah-do], *a.* Flat (neumático).

desinflamar [des-in-flah-mar'], **va.** To cure or remove an inflammation.

desinflar [des-in-flar'], *va.* To deflate. **Desinflarse,** *(fig.)* to be deflated, to come down to earth.

desinformación [des-in-for-mah-the-on'], *f.* 1. Desinformation, misleading information. 2. Ignorance, lack of information.

desinformado [des-in-for-mah-do], *a.* Uninformed.

desinformar [des-in-for-mar'], *va.* To misinform.

desintegrable [des-in-tay-grah'-blay], *a.* Fissionable.

desintegración [des-in-tay-grah-the-on'], *f.* Disintegration. **Desintegración del átomo,** splitting of the atom.

desintegrador de átomos [des-in-tay-grah-dor' day ah'-to-mos], *m. (Phys.)* Atom smasher.

desintegrar [des-in-tay-grar'], *va.* To disintegrate, to decompose. *-vr.* To disintegrate; to split.

desinterés [des-in-tay-res'], *m.* Disinterest, indifference.

desinteresadamente [des-in-tay-ray-sah'-da-men-tay], *adv.* Disinterestedly.

desinteresado, da [des-in-tay-ray-sah'-do, dah], *a.* Disinterested, impartial.

desintoxicación [des-in-toc-se-cah-the-on'], *f.* Curing of poisoning; curing of drug addiction.

desintoxicar [des-in-toc-se-car'], *va.* To cure of poisoning.

desinvernar [des-in-ver-nar'], *vn.* To leave winter quarters: used of troops.

desistimiento [day-sis-te-me-en'-to], *m.* Desistance, the act of desisting.

desistir [day-sis-teer'], *vn.* 1. To desist, to cease, to give out, to go back. 2. To leave, to abandon, to flinch. 3. *(For.)* To abdicate a right.

desjarretar [des-har-ray-tar'], *va.* 1. To hough, to hamstring. 2. *(Met. Coll.)* To weaken, to debilitate, to leave powerless.

desjarrete [des-har-ray'-tay], *m.* Act of houghing.

desjugar [des-hoo-gar'], *va.* To extract the juice from anything.

desjuntamiento [des-hoon-tah-me-en'-to], *m.* Separation, disjunction.

desjuntar [des-hoon-tar], *va.* To divide, to separate,to part.

desjurar [des-hoo-rar'], *va.* To retract an oath, to forswear.

deslabonar [des-lah-bo-nar'], *va.* 1. To unlink, to separate one link from another. 2. *(Met.)* To disjoin, to destroy. *-vr.* To withdraw from a company, to retire.

desladrillar [des-lah-dril-lyar'], *va. V.* DESENLADRILLAR.

deslamar [des-lah-mar'], *va.* To clear of mud.

deslastrar [des-las-trar'], *va.* To unballast a ship.

deslatar [des-lah-tar'], *va.* To take the laths or small joists out of a house or other building.

deslavado, da [des-lah-vah'-do, dah], *a.* Impudent, barefaced. *-pp.* of DESLAVAR.

deslavadura [des-lah-vah-doo'-rah], *f.* Washing, rinsing.

deslavar [des-lah-var'], *va.* 1. To wash or cleanse superficially, to rinse. 2. To wet, to spoil by wetting. 3. To take away the color, force, or vigor of a thing. **Cara deslavada,** a pale, puny face.

deslavazar [des-lah-vah-thar'], *va.* 1. *V.* DESLAVAR. 2. *(Agri.)* To expose hay to the action of rain.

deslave [des-lah'-vay], *m.* Washout, overflowing.

deslazamiento [des-lah-thah-me-en'-to], *m.* Disjunction, dissolution.

deslazar [des-lah-thar'], *va.* To unlace, to untie a knot.

desleal [des-lay-ahl'], *a.* Disloyal; perfidious, faithless; traitorous.

deslealmente [des-lay-ahl'-men-tay], *adv.* Disloyally, treacherously.

deslealtad [des-lay-al-tahd'], *f.* Disloyalty, treachery, faithlessness.

deslechar [des-lay-char'], *va. (Prov.)* To remove the leaves and dirt from silkworms.

deslecho [des-lay'-cho], *m. (Prov.)* Act of cleansing silkworms.

deslechugador [des-lay-choo-gah-dor'], *m.* Vine-dresser, pruner.

deslechugar, deslechuguillar [des-lay-choo-gar'], *va. (Agri.)* To cut and prune the branches of vines.

desleidura [des-lay-e-doo'-rah], *f.* **desleimiento,** *m.* Dilution, making thin or weak.

desleír [des-lay-eer'], *va.* To dilute, to make thin or weak, to dissolve. *-vr.* To dissolve; to become diluted; to get weaker. *(Yo deslío, yo desleí, el deslió, el disliera; from Desleír. V.* PEDIR.)

deslendrar [des-len-drar'], *va.* To clear the hair of nits.

deslenguado, da [des-len-goo-ah'-do, dah], *a.* Loquacious, impudent, foul-mouthed, scurrilous. *-pp.* of DESLENGUAR.

deslenguamiento [des-len-goo-ah-me-en'-to], *m.* Loquacity, impudence.

deslenguar [des-len-goo-ar'], *va.* To cut out the tongue. *-vr.* To talk ill of, to slander.

desliar [des-le-ar'], *va.* To untie, to loose. *-vr.* To come undone.

desligadura, *f.* or **desligamiento,** *m.* [des-le-gah-doo'-rah]. Disjunction, untying.

desligar [des-le-gar'], *va.* 1. To loosen, to untie, to unbind. 2. *(Met.)* To disentangle, to extricate, to unravel something not material. 3. *(Met.)* To absolve from ecclesiastical censure. 4. To remove from a ship part of its knees, or futtock timbers, or the spikes which hold them. 5. *(Med.)* To unfasten bandages or ligatures. 6. *(Mus.)* To separate notes very clearly. **Desligar el maleficio,** to dissolve a spell which prevented a husband from enjoying the marriage rights. **Desligar el primer aspecto del segundo,** to separate the first aspect from the second. *-vr.* To come undone, to get unfastened; to extricate oneself.

deslindable [des-lin-dah'-blay], *a.* Surveyable, capable of demarcation.

deslindador [des-lin-dah-dor'], *m.* He who marks limits or boundaries.

deslindamiento [des-lin-dah-me-en´-to], *m.* Demarcation.

deslindar [des-lin-dar'], *va.* 1. To mark the limits and bounds of a place or district. 2. *(Met.)* To clear up a thing.

deslinde [des-leen'-day], *m.* 1. Demarcation. 2. *(Fig.)* Definition.

deslingar [des-lin-gar'], *va.* To unsling.

desliñar [des-le-nyar'], *va.* To clean cloth before it goes to the press.

desliz [des-leeth'], *m.* 1. Slip, the act of slipping or sliding. 2. *(Met.)* Slip, a false step, frailty, weakness, failure, fault. **Los deslizes de la juventud,** the indiscretions of youth. 3. The mercury which escapes in melting silver ore.

deslizable [des-le-thah'-blay], *a.* That which can slip or slide.

deslizadero [des-le-thah-day'-ro], *m.* A slippery place.*-a. V.* DESLIZADIZO.

deslizadero, ra, or **deslizadizo, za** [des-le-thah-dee'-tho, thah], *a.* Slippery, slippy, lubricous.

deslizador [des-le-thah-dor'], *m.* 1. *(Aer.)* Glider. 2. Scooter (de niño). 3. *(Naut.)* Small speedboat. 4. *(Dep.)* Surfboard, aquaplane, water ski.

deslizamiento [des-le-thah-me-en'-to], *m.* 1. Slip, slipping. 2. Gliding.

deslizar [des-le-thar'], *vn. & vr.* 1. To slip, to slide, to glide. **Deslizar una mesa por el suelo,** to slide a table along the floor. **El insecto se deslizó fuera del agujero,** the insect wriggled out of the hole. **Deslizar la mano por la mesa,** to run one´s hand over the table. **Deslizarse en un cuarto,** to slip into a room. 2. To act or speak carelessly, to make a slip of the tongue.

deslodaje [des-lo-dah'-hay], *m.* Cleansing of a mineral substance from mud which enwraps it.

deslomadura [des-lo-mah-doo'-rah], *f.* Act of breaking the back. *(Vet.)* Violent extension and even rupture of the fleshy fibres or of the aponeuroses of the muscles of the loins of horses.

deslomar [des-lo-mar'], *va.* To break the back, to distort or strain the loins, to chine. **No se deslomará,** he is sure not to overwork himself. *-vr. (Fig.)* To get worn out.

deslucidamente [des-loo-the'-dah-men-tay], *adv.* Ungracefully, inelegantly.

deslucido, da [des-loo-thee'-do, dah], *a.* 1. Unadorned, ungraceful, inelegant, awkward. 2. Useless, fruitless. 3. Flat, dull, lifeless. **Hizo un papel deslucido,** he was dull in the part. 4. **Quedó muy deslucido,** he did very badly, he made a very poor showing. *-pp.* of DESLUCIR.

deslucimiento [des-loo-the-me-en'-to], *m.* Disgrace, dishonor, want of splendor.

deslucir [des-loo-theer'], *va.* 1. To tarnish or impair the lustre and splendour of a thing. **La lluvia deslució el acto,** the rain ruined the ceremony. 2. *(Met.)* To obscure one's merit. *-vr. (Fig.)* To do badly; to make a poor showing.

deslumbrador, ra [des-loom-brah-dor', rah], *a.* Dazzling, brilliant, glaring.

deslumbramiento, deslumbre [des-loom-brah-me-en'-to], *m.* 1. Glare, overpowering lustre; dazzling. 2. Confusion of sight or mind; hallucination.

deslumbrante [des-loom-brahn'-tay], *a.* Dazzling.

deslumbrar [des-loom-brar'], *va.* 1. To dazzle the sight, to glare. 2. *(Met.)* To puzzle, to leave in doubt and uncertainty. **Deslumbró a todos con su oratoria,** he captivated everyone with his oratory.

deslustrador, ra [des-loos-trah-dor', rah], *m. & f.* Tarnisher.

deslustrar [des-loos-trar'], *va.* 1. To tarnish or sully the brilliancy of a thing, to take away the lustre. 2. To obscure, to make less beautiful or illustrious. 3. *(Met.)* To blast one's reputation, to impeach one's character or merit.

deslustre [des-loos'-tray], *m.* 1. Spot or stain which obscures the lustre or splendor of a thing. 2. Disgrace, ignominy, stigma.

deslustroso, sa [des-loos-tro'-so, sah], *a.* Unbecoming, ugly.

desmadejamiento [des-mah-day-hah-me-en'-to], *m.* Languishment, languidness.

desmadejar [des-mah-day-har'], *va.* To enervate, to produce languor. *-vr.* To languish, to be enervated and weak.

desmadrado [des-mah-drah-do], *a.* 1. Unruly (desenfrenado), rebellious; uninhibited (desinhibido). 2. Confused; disoriented, lost.

desmadrarse [des-mah-drahr'-say], *vr.* To rebel; to get out of control, to go too far, to run wild. **Los gastos se han desmadrado,** costs have gone right over the top.

desmadre [des-mah'-dray], *m.* 1. Excess; excess of emotion. **Esto va de desmadre total,** this is really getting out of hand. 2. Chaos, confusion; mess; outrage. 3. Wild party, rave-up.

desmajolar [des-mah-ho-lar'], *va.* 1. To pull up vines by the roots. 2. To loosen or untie the shoestrings.

desmallador [des-mal-lyah-dor'], *m.* He who breaks a coat of mail.

desmalladura [des-ma-lyah-doo'-rah], *f.* Act of ripping up or breaking a coat of mail.

desmallar [des-mal-lyar'], *va.* To cut and destroy a coat of mail.

desmamar [des-mah-mar'], *va. V.* DESTETAR.

desmamonar [des-mah-mo-nar'], *va.* To cut off the young shoots of vines or trees.

desmán [des-mahn'], *m.* 1. Misfortune, disaster, mishap, calamity. 2. Misbehavior. 3. Excess in actions or words. 4. Shrewmouse.

desmanarse [des-mah-nar' say], *vr.* To stray from a flock or herd.

desmanche [des-mahn'-chay], *m.* Excessive movement in a rider, want of firmness in the saddle.

desmandado, da [des-man-dah'-do, dah], *a. V.* DESOBEDIENTE.*-pp.* of DESMANDAR.

desmandamiento [des-man-dah-me-en'-to], *m.* 1. Act of countermanding or disbanding. 2. Disorder, irregularity, neglect of rule.

desmandar [des-man-dar'], *va.* 1. To repeal an order, to countermand, to revoke an offer. 2. To revoke a legacy. *-vr.*

1. To transgress the bounds of justice and reason. 2. To disband (tropas). 3. To stray from the flock. 4. To go astray.
desmanear [des-mah-nayar'], va. To unfetter, to take off fetters or shackles (caballos, mulas).
desmangamiento, desmangue [des-man-gah-me-en'-to], m. Taking off the handle of a thing.
desmangar [des-man-gar'], va. To take off the handle of a thing.
desmanotado, da [des-mah-no-tah'-do, dah], a. Unhandy, awkward.
desmantecar [des-man-tay-car'], va. To take off the butter.
desmantelado, da [des-man-tay-lah'-do, ah], a. & pp. of DESMANTELAR. Dismantled, ruinous, dilapidated.
desmantelamiento [des-mahn-tay-lah-me-ayn'-to], m. 1. Dismantling; abandonment. 2. Dilapidation.
desmantelar [des-man-tay-lar'], va. 1. To dismantle. 2. To abandon, to desert, to forsake. 3. (Naut.) To unmast. -vr. To fall into disrepair, to become dilapidated.
desmaña [des-mah'-nyah], f. 1. Awkwardness, clumsiness. 2. Idleness, laziness.
desmañado, da [des-mah-nyah-do, dah], a. 1. Unhandy, clumsy, awkward, clownish. 2. Lazy, idle, indolent.
desmañar [des-mah-nyar'], va. (Ant.) To impede, to obstruct.
desmaquillador [des-mah-kel-lyah-dor'], m. Make-up remover.
desmarañar [des-mah-rah-nyar'], va. To disentangle. V. DESENMARAÑAR.
desmarcar [des-mar-car'], va. To remove, to efface, to obliterate marks. -vr. To shake off one's attacker; to avoid an opponent; to get clear; (fig.) To step out of line.
desmaridar [des-mah-re-dar'], va. To separate husband and wife.
desmarojador [des-mah-ro-hah-dor'], m. He who takes off the rind of olives.
desmarojar [des-mah-ro-har'], va. To take the glutinous rind from olives.
desmarrido, da [des-mar-ree'-do, dah], a. Sad, languid, dejected, exhausted.
desmayadamente [des-mah-yah'-dah-men-tay], adv. Weakly, dejectedly.
desmayado da [des-mah-yah'-do dah], a. & pp. of DESMAYAR. 1. Pale, weak, faint of lustre. 2. Dismayed, appalled.
desmayar [des-mah-yar'], vn. To be dispirited or faint-hearted, to want strength and courage. -vn. To dismay, to depress, to discourage. -vr. To faint, to swoon.
desmayo [des-mah'-yo], m. 1. Swoon, fainting fit. **Sufrir un desmayo**, to have a fainting fit. 2. Decay of strength and vigor. **Hablar con desmayo**, to speak falteringly. **Tenía un desmayo en todo el cuerpo**, he felt limp all over. 3. Dismay, discouragement.
desmazalado, da [des-mah-thah-lah'-do, dah], a. Weak, dejected, faint-hearted, spiritless.
desmedidamente [des-may-de'-dah-men-tay], adv. Disproportionably, disproportionately.
desmedido, da [des-may-dee'-do, dah], a. Unproportionable, out of proportion or measure. -pp. of DESMEDIRSE.
desmedirse [des-may-deer'-say], vr. V. DEMANDARSE and EXCEDERSE.
desmedrar [des-may-drar'], vn. To decrease, to decay.-va. To impair, to deteriorate.
desmedro [des-may'-dro], m. Diminution. decay, detriment.
desmejora [des-may-ho'-rah], f. Deterioration, depreciation, diminution, loss.
desmejorado [des-may-ho-rah'-do], a. **Queda muy desmejorada**, she's lost her looks.
desmejorar [des-may-ho-rar'], va. 1. To debase, to make worse. 2. (Med.) To weaken, to affect the health of. -vr. 1. To decay, to decline, to grow worse. 2. To lose one's looks, to look less attractive; (Med.) To lose one's health.
desmelancolizar [des-may-lan-co-le-thar'], va. To cheer, to enliven, to gladden.

desmelar [des-may-lar'], va. To take the honey from a hive.
desmelenado [des-may-lay-nah'-do], a. Dishevelled, tousled.
desmelenar [des-may-lay-nar'], va. To dishevel, to disarrange the hair. -vr. 1. To spruce up, to pull one's socks up. 2. To sail into action.
desmembración, desmembradura [des-mem-brah-the-on', des-mem-brah-doo'-rah], f. Dismemberment, division.
desmembrador, ra [des-mem-brah-dor', rah], m. & f. Divider, one who dismembers or divides.
desmembrar [des-mem-brar'], va. 1. To dismember, to divide limb from limb, to tear asunder, to curtail. 2. To separate, to divide.
desmemoriado, da [des-may-mo-re-ah'-do, dah], a. Forgetful, having a poor memory.
desmemoriarse [des-may-mo-re-ar'-say], vr. To be forgetful, to forget.
desmenguar [des-men-goo-ar'], va. 1. To lessen; to defalcate. 2. V. MENGUAR.
desmentida [des-men-tee'-dah], f. or **desmentido**, m. The act of giving the lie.
desmentidor, ra [des-men-te-dor', rah], m. & f. One who convicts of a falsehood.
desmentir [des-men-teer'], va. 1. To give the lie to, to convince of a falsehood. 2. To counterfeit, to conceal, to dissemble. 3. To do things unworthy of one's birth, character, or profession. 4. To lose the right line, to warp or to change from the true situation. 5. To fold a lady's handkerchief so that one point may fall short of the other. **Desmentir rotundamente una acusación**, to deny a charge flatly. -vr. 1. To recant, retract. 2. Not to behave in accord with what has been said, to be lie.
desmenuzable [des-may-noo-thah'-blay], a. Friable, brittle, crisp, crimp, easily crumbled.
desmenuzador, ra [des-may-noo-thah-dor', rah], m. & f. A scrutator or investigator; a purifier.
desmenuzar [des-may-noo-thar'], va. 1. To crumble, to comminute, to crumb, to chip, to mill, to fritter. 2. (Met.) To sift, to examine minutely. -vr. To crumble, to fall into small pieces.
desmeollado, da [des-may-ol-lyah'-do, dah], a. Silly, simple, crackbrained.
desmeollar [des-may-ol-lyar'], va. To take out the marrow or pith.
desmerecedor [des-may-ray-thay-dor'], m. An unworthy, undeserving person.
desmerecer [des-may-ray-therr']. va. To demerit, to become unworthy or undeserving of a thing. -vn. 1. To lose part of its worth. 2. To grow worse, to deteriorate. 3. **Desmerecer de,** to compare unfavorably with.
desmerecimiento [des-may-ray-the-me-en'-to], m. Demerit, unworthiness.
desmesura [des-may-soo'-rah], f. 1. Excess, want of moderation and order. 2. Impudence, insolence; rudeness.
desmesuradamente [des-may-soo-rah'-dah-men-tay], adv. 1. Immeasurably. 2. Uncivilly, impudently.
desmesurado, da [des-may-soo-rah'-do, dah], a. 1. Immeasurable. 2. Huge, of gigantic stature or size. 3. Unmeasurable. -pp. of DESMESURAR.
desmesurar [des-may-soo-rar'], va. To disorder, to discompose, to perturbate. -vr. To be forward, to act or talk with impudence or insolence, to be rude.
desmidiáceo, cea [des-me-de-ah'-thay-o, theah], a. Like a desmid, desmidaceous.
desmigajar [des-me-gah-har'], va. To crumble, to comminute. -vr. To crumble.
desmigar [des-me-gar'], va. To crumble bread.
desmilitarización [des-me-le-tah-re-thah-the-on'], m. Demilitarization.
desmilitarizar [des-me-le-tah-re-thar'], va. To demilitarize.
desmirriado, da [des-mir-re-ah-do, dah], a. (Coll.) 1. Lean, extenuated, exhausted. 2. Melancholy.

desmocha [des-mo'-chah], *f.* 1. Lopping or cutting off. 2. Diminution or destruction of a great part of a thing.

desmochadura [des-mo-chah-doo'-rah], *f.* V. DESMOCHE.

desmochar [des-mo-char'], *va..* 1. To lop or cut off, to mutilate. 2. To unhorn (venado).

desmoche [des-mo'-chay], *m.* Truncation, mutilation.

desmocho [des-mo'-cho], *m.* Heap of things lopped or cut off.

desmogar [des-mo-gar'], *vn.* To cast the horns (venados).

desmografía [des-mo-grah-fee'-ah], *f.* Desmography, a description of the ligaments.

desmogue [des-mo'-gay], *m.* Act of casting the horns (vendados).

desmolado, da [des-mo-lah'-do, dah], *a.* Toothless, having no grinders.

desmoldamiento [des-mo-le-dah-me-en'-to], or **desmolde** [des-mo-le'-day], *m.* Removal of a casting from the mould.

desmoldar [des-mo-le-dar'], *va.* To remove from the mould, to strike the frame.

desmología [des-mo-lo-hee'-ah], *f.* Desmology, anatomical description of ligaments.

desmonetizar [des-mo-nay-te-thar'], *va.* 1. To convert money into bullion for other purposes. 2. To demonetize, deprive of legal-tender value.

desmontable [des-mon-tah'-blay], *a.* Detachable; sectional, in sections, which takes apart. *-m.* Tire level.

desmontador, ra [des-mon-tah-dor', rah], *m. & f.* 1. One who fells wood. 2. Dismounter.

desmontadura [des-mon-tah-doo'-rah], *f.* Felling timber, clearing from shrubbery.

desmontar [des-mon-tar'], *va.* 1. To fell or cut down wood. 2. To remove a heap of dirt or garbage. 3. To uncock firearms, to take an instrument to pieces. 4. To dismount a troop of horse, to dismount cannon. 5. **Desmontar el timón**, *(Naut.)* To unhang the rudder.*-vn.* To dismount, to alight from a horse, mule, etc.

desmonte [des-mon'-tay], *m.* 1. Felling, the act of cutting down, as timber. 2. The timber remaining on the spot. 3. Clearing a wood from trees, shrubbery, etc.

desmonterado, da [des-mon-tay-rah'-do, dah], *a.* Without the sort of cap named *montera*.

desmoñar [des-mo-nyar'], *va. (Coll.)* To undo the toupee of the hair, to loosen the hair.

desmoralización [des-mo-rah-le-thah-the-on'], *f.* Demoralization, corruption or depravation of morals; depravity.

desmoralizado, da [des-mo-rah-le-thah'-do, dah], *a. & pp.* of DESMORALIZAR. Demoralized, depraved, corrupted.

desmoralizador [des-mo-rah-le-thah-dor'], *a.* Demoralizing.

desmoralizar [des-mo-rah-le-thar'], *va.* To demoralize, to corrupt, to deprave. *-vr. (Mil.)* To relax the discipline of an army.

desmoronadizo, za [des-mo-ro-nah-dee'-tho, trah], *a.* Easily mouldered.

desmoronado [des-mo-ro-nah'-do], *a.* Tumbledown, ruinous, dilapidated.

desmoronamiento [des-mo-ro-nah-me-ayn'-to], *m.* Crumbling, dilapidation, decay; collapse.

desmoronar [des-mo-ro-nar'], *va.* 1. To destroy little by little, to ruin by insensible degrees. 2. *(Met.)* To cause to dwindle or moulder off. *-vr.* To moulder, to fall, to decay.

desmoso, sa [des-mo'-so, sah], *a.* Ligamentous.

desmostar [des-mos-tar'], *va.* To separate the must from the grapes. *-vn.* To ferment.

desmotadera [des-mo-tah-day'-rah], *f.* 1. Woman employed to take off knots and coarse naps from cloth. 2. An instrument used for removing knots from cloth; cloth nipper.

desmotar [des-mo-tar], *va.* To clear cloth of knots and coarse naps.

desmovilización [des-mo-ve-le-thah-the-on'], *f.* Demobilization.

desmovilizar [des-mo-ve-le-thar'], *va.* To demobilize.

desmueblar [des-moo-ay-blar'], *va.* V. DESAMUEBLAR.

desmuelo [des-moo-ay'-lo], *m.* Want or loss of grinders.

desmugrador [des-moo-grah-dor'], *m.* Instrument which serves to clean wool or cloth of grease.

desmugrar [des-moo-grar'], *va.* To clean wool or cloth of grease.

desmuir [des-moo-eer'], *va.* To pick olives.

desmullir [des-mool-lyeer'], *va.* To discompose anything soft or bland.

desnacionalizar [des-nah-the-o-nah-le-thar'], *va. (Neol.)* To denationalize, to cause the loss of national characteristics.

desnarigar [des-nah-re-gar'], *va.* To cut off the nose.

desnatadora [des-nah-tah-do'-rah], *f.* Cream separator.

desnatar [des-nah-tar'], *va.* 1. To skim milk. **Leche sin desnatar**, whole milk. 2. To take the flower or choicest part of a thing.

desnaturalización [des-nah-too-rah-le-tha-the-on'], *f.* Expatriation, denaturalization.

desnaturalizado, da [des-nah-too-rah-le-thah'-do, dah], *a.* 1. Denatured. **Alcohol desnaturalizado**, denatured alcohol. 2. Unnatural; cruel, inhuman (persona).

desnaturalizar [des-nah-too-rah-le-thar'], *va.* To divest of the rights of naturalization, to deprive of the privileges of a citizen. *-vr.* To abandon one's country.

desnegar [des-nay-gar'], *va.* To contradict, to retract. *-vr.* To unsay, to retract, to recant.

desnervar [des-ner-var'], *va.* To enervate.

desnevado, da [des-nay-vah'-do, dah], *a.* Thawed, free from snow. *-pp.* of DESNEVAR.

desnevar [des-nay-var'], *va.* To thaw, to dissolve.

desnivel [des-ne-vel'], *m.* 1. Unevenness, inequality of the ground. 2. *(Fig.)* Inequality, difference, gap; lack of adjustment.

desnivelación [des-ne-vay-lah-the-on'], *f.* Making uneven.

desnivelado [des-ne-vay-lah'-do], *a.* 1. Uneven (terreno). 2. *(Fig.)* Unbalanced, badly adjusted (instrumento).

desnivelar [des-ne-vay-lar'], *va.* To make uneven or unequal. *-vn.* To lose its level.

desnucar [des-noo-car'], *va.* 1. To break the neck, to disjoint the nape. 2. To kill by a blow upon the nape. *-vr.* To break one's neck.

desnuclearizar [des-noo-clay-ah-re-thar'], *va.* To denuclearize. **Región desnuclearizada**, nuclear-free area.

desnudador [des-noo-dah-dor'], *m.* One that denudes.

desnudamente [des-noo-dah-men'-tay], *adv.* Nakedly; manifestly, plainly.

desnudar [des-noo-dar'], *va.* 1. To denudate, to denude, to strip off clothes or coverings; to fleece. 2. *(Met.)* To discover, to reveal. 3. *(Naut.)* To unrig. *-vr.* 1. To undress, to take off one's clothes. **Desnudarse hasta la cintura**, to strip to the waist. 2. *(Met.)* To deprive oneself of a thing.

desnudez [des-noo-deth'], *f.* Nudity, nakedness.

desnudismo [des-noo-dees'-moh], *m.* Nudism.

desnudo, da [des-noo'-do, dah], *a.* 1. Naked, bare, uncovered, ill-clothed. **En las paredes desnudas**, on the bare wall. **La ciudad quedó desnuda**, the town was flattened. 2. *(Met.)* Plain, evident, apparent. **Estar desnudo de**, to be devoid of. 3. Empty-handed, destitute of merit, interest, etc. **Y ahora están desnudos**, and now all they've got is what they stand up in.

desnudo [des-noo'-do], *m.* 1. *(Pict.)* A picture or statue without drapery; the nude. 2. Metal free from all foreign matter.

desnutrición [des-no-tre-the-on'], *f.* Malnutrition.

desnutrido [des-noo-tre'-do], *a.* Undernourished.

desobedecer [des-o-bay-day-therr'], *va.* To disobey. *(Yo desobedezco, yo desobedezca, from Desobedecer. V. CONOCER.)*

desobedecimiento [de-so-bay-day-the-me-en'-to], *m.* 1. Disobedience, incompliance. 2. Contempt of court.

desobediencia [de-so-bay-de-en'-the-ah], *f.* Disobedience; lawlessness. **Desobediencia civil**, civil disobedience.

desobediente [de-so-bay-de-en'-tay], *pa.* Disobedient.

desobedientemente [des-o-bay-de-ayn'-tay], *adv.* Disobediently.

desobligar [des-o-ble-gar'], *va.* 1. To release from an obligation. 2. To disoblige, to offend; to alienate the affections.

desobstruir [des-obs-troo-eer'], *va.* 1. To remove obstructions. 2. *(Med.)* To deobstruct.

desocupación [des-o-coo-pah-the-on'], *f.* Leisure, want of business or occupation.

desocupadamente [des-o-coo-pah'-dah-men-tay], *adv.* Deliberately, leisurely.

desocupado [des-o-coo-pah'-do], *a.* 1. Empty, vacant, unoccupied (silla, etc.). 2. Spare, free (tiempo). 3. Free, not busy; at leisure (persona).

desocupar [des-o-coo-par'], *va.* To evacuate, to quit, to empty. *-vr.* To disengage oneself from a business or occupation, to withdraw from.

desodorante [des-o-do-rahn'-tay], *m. & a.* Deodorant.

desofuscar [des-o-foos-car'], *va.* 1. To remove obscurity. 2. *(Met.)* To remove anyone's confusion.

desoir [des-o-eer'], *va.* To pretend not to hear.

desojar [des-o-har'], *va.* To break or burst (ojo de aguja). *-vr.* To strain one's eyes by looking steadily at a thing; to look intently.

desolación [day-so-lah-the-on'], *f.* 1. Desolation, destruction, havoc, extermination; fall. 2. Want of consolation or comfort, affliction.

desolado, da [day-so-lah'-do, dah], *a.* Desolate, disconsolate. **Estoy desolado por aquello,** I´m terribly grieved about that. *-pp.* of DESOLAR.

desolador, ra [day-so-lah-dor', rah], *m. & f.* Grieving.

desolar [day-so-lar'], *va.* To desolate, to lay waste, to harass. *-vr.* To grieve, to be distressed, to be disconsolate.

desolladamente [des-ol-lyah-dah-men'-tay], *adv. (Coll.)* Impudently, petulantly.

desolladero [des-ol-lyah-day'-ro], *m.* 1. A place where hides are taken off; slaughter-house. 2. An inn or shop, where exorbitant prices are charged.

desollado, da [day-sol-lyah'-do, dah], *a. (Coll.)* Forward, impudent, insolent. *-pp.* of DESOLLAR.

desollador [day-sol-lyah-dor'], *m.* 1. Flayer. 2. *(Prov.)* Slaughterhouse, a place where beasts are skinned. 3. *(Met.)* Extortioner. 4. Butcher-bird.

desolladura [day-sol-lyah-doo'-rah], *f.* Excoriation.

desollar [day-sol-lyar'], *va.* 1. To flay, to skin, to strip off the skin, to excoriate. 2. *(Met.)* To extort an immoderate price. 3. *(Naut.)* To pull at the creases of a sail, to reduce them to regular folds. 4. **Desollar vivo a uno,** *(fig.)* To fleece somebody, to make somebody pay through the nose.

desonce [des-on'-thay], *m.* The discount of an ounce or ounces in each pound. *(Ant.)*

desonzar [des-on-thar'], *va.* To discount or deduct an ounce or ounces in the pound. *(Ant.)*

desopilar [des-o-pel-ar'], *va.* 1. To clear away obstructions. 2. *(Med.)* To remove retention or suppression of menstruation.

desopilativo, va. [des-o-pe-lah-tee'-vo, vah], *a.* Deobstruent.

desopinar [des-o-pe-nar'], *va.* To impeach one's characer, to defame.

desoprimir [des-o-pre-meer'], *va.* To free from oppression.

desorbitado [des-or-be-tah-do], *a.* 1. Disproportionate, excessive; exorbitant (precio); exaggerated (pretension etc.). 2. **Con los ojos desorbitados,** wild-eyed, pop-eyed.

desorbitante [des-or-be-tah'-dah-men-tay], *a.* Excessive, overwhelming.

desorbitar [des-or-be-tar'], *va.* 1. To carry to extremes; to exaggerate. 2. **Desorbitar un asunto,** to misinterpret. *-vr.* To go to extremes (persona).

desorden [desor'den], *m.* 1. Disorder, confusion, irregularity. 2. Lawlessness, license, excess, abuse. 3. Lack of symmetry of connection, in lyric poetry.

desordenadamente [des-or-day-nah-dah-men'-tay], *adv.* Disorderly, irregularly, confusedly.

desordenado, da [des-or-day-nah'-do, dah], *a.* 1. Disorderly, irregular, disordered, orderless. 2. Disorderly, lawless, licentious. *-pp.* of DESORDENAR.

desordenar [des-or-day-nar'], *va.* To disorder, to throw into confusion, to disturb, to confound or confuse. *-vr.* 1. To exceed or go beyond all rule: to be out of order, to be irregular. 2. To get unruly, to be unmanageable (caballo).

desorejado, da [des-o-ray-hah'-do, dah], *a. (Coll.)* Licentious, dissolute, degraded.

desorejador, ra [des-o-ray-hah-dor', ran], *m. & f.* One who crops off the ears.

desorejamiento [des-o-ray-hah-me-en'-to], *m.* Cropping the ears.

desorejar [des-o-ray-har'], *va.* To crop ears.

desorganización [des-or-gah-ne-thah-the-on'], *f.* Disorganization.

desorganizador [des-or-gah-ne-thah-dor'], *m.* Disorganizer.

desorganizar [des-or-gah-ne-thar'], *va.* 1. To disorganize. 2. To disconcert in the highest degree. 3. *(Chem.)* To decompose. 4. *(Mil.)* To disband an army. 5. To relax discipline. *-vr. (Med.)* To be altered, changed in texture, disorganized.

desorientado, da [des-o-re-en-tah'-do, dah], *a.* Disorientated, turned from the right direction. *-pp.* Of DESORIENTAR.

desorientar [des-o-re-en-tar'], *va.* 1. To lose or cause to lose one's bearings so as not to know one's position, geographically or morally. 2. To turn from the right direction, confuse. 3. To lose the way. **El nuevo cruce me desorientó,** the new junction made me lose my bearings. *-vr.* 1. To lose one´s way, to lose one´s bearings. 2. *(Fig.)* To go wrong, to go astray, to get off the track.

desorillar [des-o-reel-lyar'], *va.* 1. To cut off the selvage of cloth or other things. 2. To stretch skins well, so as not to form folds at the ends.

desortijado, da [day-sor-te-hah'-do, dah], *a. (Vet.)* Sprained (músculos de mulas y caballos). *-pp.* of DESORTIJAR.

desortijar [day-sor-te-har'], *va. (Agri.)* To hoe or weed plants the first time.

desosado, da [des-o-sah'-do, dah], *a.* Deprived of the bones. *-pp.* of DESOSAR.

desosar [des-o-sar'], *va.* To deprive of the bones. *-vn.* To be cowardly or fearful.

desoterrar [day-so-tayr-rahr'], *va.* To unbury, to dig up.

desovar [des-o-var'], *va.* To spawn.

desove [des-o'-vay], *m.* 1. Spawning. 2. The time in which fishes cast their spawn.

desovillar [des-o-vil-lyar'], *va.* 1. To unclew. 2. *(Met.)* To unravel, to disentangle, to clear up. 3. *(Met.)* To encourage, to animate.

desoxidación [des-ok-se-dah-the-on'], *f.* Deoxydization, removal of oxygen.

desoxidar [des-ok-se-dar'], *va.* To deoxydize, to remove oxygen from any compound.

desoxigenación [des-ok-se-hay-nah-the-on'], *f.* Deoxydation.

desoxigenar [des-ok-se-hay-nar'], *va.* To remove from a body the oxygen which it holds, to deoxydize.

despabiladeras [des-pah-be-lah-day'-ras], *f. pl.* Snuffers.

despabilado, da [des-pah-be-lah'-do, dah], *a. & pp.* of DESPABILAR. 1. Snuffed (velas). 2. *(Met.)* Watchful, vigilant in sleeping hours. 3. Lively, active, smart.

despabilador, ra [des-pah-be-lah-dor', rah], *m. & f.* Candle-snuffer; he who snuffs.

despabiladura [des-pah-be-lah-doo'-rah], *f.* Snuff of the candle.

despabilar [des-pah-be-lar'], *va.* 1. To snuff a candle. 2. *(Met.)* To cut off a superfluity. 3. *(Met.)* To despatch briefly or expeditiously. 4. *(Met.)* To rouse, to enliven. 5. *(Coll.)* To kill. **Despabilar el ingenio,** to sharpen the wits. *-vr.* To rouse, to wake from slunder, to be excited. **Vd. le verá despabilarse,** you will see him brighten up.

despacio [des-pah'-the-o], *adv.* 1. Slowly, leisurely; gently. 2. Insensibly, little by little. 3. Continually, without interruption.

¡despacio! *int.* Softly, gently.

despacito [des-pah-thee'-to], *adv.* 1. Very gently, softly. 2. Leisurely, very slowly.

despachado, da [des-pah-chah'-do, dah], *a.* 1. *(Coll.)* Impudent, bold-faced, brazen. 2. Resourceful, quick; business-like; practical. **Ir bien despachado de,** to be well off for. -*pp.* of DESPACHAR.

despachador [des-pah-chah-dor'], *m.* Expediter, one who despatches.

despachar [des-pah-char'], *va.* 1. To despatch, to expedite, to abridge, to facilitate. 2. To despatch, to pack, to send in a hurry; to lay by. 3. To despatch, to perform a business quickly, to cut off delays. 4. To decide and expedite suits and causes. 5. To dispose of goods and merchandise, to sell. 6. *(Met.)* To despatch, to send out of the world. **Despachar un barco,** to clear a vessel at the custom-house. **Despachar géneros** or **mercaderías en la aduana,** to clear, or take out goods or merchandise at the custom-house. **Despachar asuntos con el gerente,** to do business with the manager. -*vr.* 1. To accelerate, to make haste. 2. To finish off. **Suelo despacharme a las 5,** I finish at 5. **Despacharse a su gusto con uno,** to say what one really thinks to somebody. -*vn.* 1. In offices, to carry papers drawn up for the signature of the principal. 2. *(Com.)* To expend, to let goods go for money or barter. 3. To serve a shop. **No despacha los domingos,** he doesn't do business on Sundays. 4. To hurry up. 5. To finish things off.

despacho [des-pah'-cho], *m.* 1. Expedient, determination. 2. Despatch expedition. 3. Custom, application from buyers. 4. Cabinet, office, counting-house. 5. Commission, warrant, patent. 6. Despatch, correspondence by telegraph. **Secretario del despacho,** secretary of state. 7. Resourcefulness, quickness of mind; business sense; efficiency. **Tener buen despacho,** to be very efficient. 8. Sale. **Géneros sin despacho,** unsaleable goods.

despachurrado, da [des-pah-choor-rah'-do, dah], *a.* Pressed together. **Dejar a uno despachurrado,** *(Coll.)* to leave one stupefied. **Es un despachurrado,** *(Coll.)* he is a ridiculous, insipid fellow. -*pp.* of DESPACHURRAR.

despachurrar [des-pah-choor-rar'], *va.* *(Coll.)* 1. To press together, to squash, to rush. 2. *(Met.)* To make a speech, to obscure a subject by a bad explanation. 3. *(Met.)* To confound one by a smart repartee. **Despachurrar el cuento,** to interrupt a story and prevent its conclusion.

despajador, ra [des-pah-hah-dor', rah], *m. & f.* One who winnows.

despajadura [des-pah-hah-doo-rah], *f.* Winnowing.

despajar [des-pah-har'], *va.* To winnow.

despaje [des-pah'-hay], **despajo** [des-pah'ho], *m.* Winnowing or cleaning grain.

despaldillar [des-pal-dil-lyar'], *va.* To dislocate or break the shoulder or back of an animal. -*vr.* To disjoint or dislocate one's shoulder-blade.

despalillar [des-pah-leel-lyar'], *va.* To remove the stems from raisins, to strip tobacco, etc.

despalmador [des-pal-mah-dor'], *m.* *(Naut.)* Careening-place, dockyard.

despalmadura [des-pahl-mah-doo'-rah], *f.* or **despalme** [des-pahl'-may], *m.* Calking, paying the bottom.

despalmar [des-pal-mar'], *va.* 1. *(Naut.)* To grave, to calk. 2. To pare off a horse's hoof.

despampanador [des-pam-pah-nah-dor'], *m.* Pruner of vines.

despampanadura [des-pam-pah-nah-doo'-rah], *f.* Act of pruning vines.

despampanante [des-pahm-pah.-nahn'-tay], *a.* Stunning.

despampanar [des-pam-pah-nar'], *va.* 1. To prune vines. 2. *(Met. Coll.)* To unbosom, to give vent to one's feelings. 3. *vr. (Coll.)* To pity much, to be very sorry, to grieve.

despampanillar [des-pam-pah-nil-lyar'], *va.* To prune grape-vines.

desplamonador, ra [des-pam-plo-nah-dor', rah], *m. & f.* One who separates vine-stems.

desplamonar [des-pam-plo-nar'], *va.* To make space between the shoots of the vine or shrub when they are very close. -*vr. (Met.)* To get dislocated (mano).

despanado da [des-pah-nah'-do, dah], *a.* *(Prov. Coll.)* Breadless, in want of bread. -*pp.* of DESPANAR.

despanar [des-pah-nar'], *va.* *(Prov.)* To remove the reaped corn from the field.

despancijar, despanzurrar [des-pan-the-har', des-pan-thoor-rar'], *va. (Coll.)* To burst the belly.

despapar [des-pah-par'], *vn.* To carry the head too high (caballo).

desparcir [des-par-theer'], *va.* *(Prov.)* To scatter, to disseminate.

desparecer [des-pah-ray-therr'], *vn.* To disappear. *V.* DESAPARECER.-*vr.* To be unlike or dissimilar.

desparejar [des-pah-ray-har'], *va.* To make unequal or uneven.

desparpajado, da [des-par-pah-hah'-do, dah], *a. & pp.* of DESPARPAJAR. Pert, petulant, garrulous.

desparpajar [des-par-pah-har'], *va.* 1. To undo in a disolderly manner. 2. *(Coll.)* To rant, to prattle at random.

desparpajo [des-par-pah'-ho], *m.* 1. *(Coll.)* Pertness of speech or action, self-confidence; naturalness; charm. 2. Savoir-faire, practical know-how; sharpness, quickness of mind. 3. *(CAm.)* Disorder, muddle. 4. *(And.)* Flippant remark (comentario).

desparramado, da [des-par-rah-mah'-do, dah], *a.* Wide, open.-*pp.* of DESPARRAMAR.

desparramador, ra [des-par-rah-mah-dor', rah], *m. & f.* Disperser, dilapidator; prodigal, waster, spendthrift.

desparramamiento [des-par-rah-ma-me-en'-to], *m.* Squandering, extravagance, dissipation.

desparramar [des-par-rah-mar'], *va.* 1. To scatter, to disseminate, to overspread. 2. To squander, to dissipate, to lavish. -*vr.* To give oneself up to pleasures with extravagance and excess, to be dissipated.

despartidor [des-par-te-dor'], *m.* Pacificator.

despartir [des-par-teer'], *va.* 1. To dispart, to part, to divide. 2. To conciliate.

desparvar [des-par-var'], *va.* To take the sheaves of corn out of the stack or rick to be thrashed.

despasar [des-pah-sar'], *va.* 1. To draw a cord or ribbon from a button-hole or seam. 2. *(Naut.)* To unreeve a cable from the blocks. 3. When sailing along the coast to keep the course until the wind is received in the same position on the opposite side.

despasmarse [des-pas-mar'-say], *vr.* To recover oneself from a stupor or spasm.

despatarrado, da [des-pah-tar-rah'-do, dah], *a.* **Quedar** or **dejar a uno despatarrado,** *(Coll.)* to leave one astonished, abashed, or stupefied. -*pp.* of DESPATARRAR.

despatarrar [des-pah-tar-rar'], *va.* To silence, to oblige one to be silent. -*vr.* 1. To slip and fall on the ground. 2. To be stupefied, to remain motionless.

despavorido [des-paha-vo-re'-do], *a.* **Estar despavorido,** to be utterly terrified.

despatillar [des-pah-til-lyar'], *va.* 1. To cut grooves or mortises in wood. 2. *(Naut.)* To break off the arm of an anchor by its getting caught in rocks on the bottom. 3. -*vr. (Coll.)* To shave oneself.

despavesadura [des-pah-vay-sah-doo'-rah], *f.* The act of snuffing the candle.

despavesar [des-pah-vay-sar'], *va.* To snuff the candle.

despavoridamente [des-pah-vo-red-ah-men'-tay], *adv.* Terrifiedly, aghast.

despavorir [des-pah-vo-reer'], *vn. & vr.* To be terrified, to be frightened, to be aghast. Defective verb: it is used only in the infinitive and past participle.

despearse [des-pay-ar'-say], *vr.* To bruise the feet or make them sore by much walking.

despectivamente [des-pec-tee'-vah-men-tay], *adv.* Contemptuously, scornfully; in derogatory terms.

despectivo, va [des-pec-tee'-vo, vah], *a.* Depreciatory; denoting contempt.

despechadamente [des-pay-chah-dah-men'-tay], *adv.* Angrily, spitefully.

despechado [des-pay-chah-do], *a.* Angry, indignant; spiteful.

despechador [des-pay-chah-dor'], *m.* Extortioner, tormentor, oppressor.

despechamiento [des-pay-chah-me-en'-to], *m.* Act of enraging or overburdening.

despechar [des-pay-char'], *va.* 1. To enrage, to excite indignation. 2. To overwhelm with taxes.-*vr.* 1. To fret, to be peevish. 2. To lose all hope, to despair.

despecho [des-pay'-cho], *m.* 1. Indignation, displeasure, wrath. 2. Asperity, harshness of temper. 3. Despite spite, defiance. **Por despecho,** out of spite. 4. Dejection, dismay, despair. 5. Disrespect, insolence. 6. Deceit, infidelity. 7. Derision, scores. **A despecho,** in spite of, in defiance of, against one's will.

despechugadura [des-pay-choo-gah-doo'-rah], *f.* Act of cutting of or uncovering the breast.

despechugar [des-pay-choo-gar'], *va.* To cut off the breast of a fowl. -*vr.* To uncover the breast, to walk with the breast open.

despedazador, ra [des-pay-dah-thah-dor', ah], *m. & f.* Dissector, lacerator, mangler.

despedazamiento [des-pay-dah-thah-me-en'-to], *m.* Laceration, dissection, cutting to pieces; mangling.

despedazar [des-pay-dah-thar'], *va.* 1. To cut into bits, to tear into pieces, to cut asunder, to limb, to claw. 2. *(Met.)* To lacerate, to destroy, to mangle. **Despedazarse de risa,** to burst into a fit of laughter.

despedida [des-pay-dee'-dah], *f.* 1. Leave-taking, farewell, leave. **Cena de despedida,** farewell dinner. **Regalo de despedida,** parting gift. 2. Dismission, dismissal. 3. *(Liter. etc.)* Envoi; *(Mus.)* Final verse; closing formula (en carta).

despedir [des-pay-deer'], *va.* 1. To emit, to discharge, to dart. 2. To dismiss from office, to discard. 3. To remove, to lay by. 4. To accompany through courtesy a departing guest. **Fuimos a despedirle a la estación,** we went to see him off at the station. 5. To diffuse, disperse odour, rays of light, etc. **Despedir la vida,** to die. -*vr.* 1. To take leave, to say, some expression of courtesy. **Se despidieron,** they said goodbye to each other. 2. To renounce something temporarily or perpetually. 3. To go out from service, to leave one's occupation.

despedrar [des-pay-drar'], *va. (Prov.)* V. DESPEDREGAR.

despedregar [des-pay-dray-gar'], *va.* To clear a field or other place of stones.

despegable [des-pay-gah'-blay], *a.* Dissoluble, dissolvable.

despegadamente [des-pay-gah-blay], *adv.* Roughly, harshly, disgustingly.

despegado, da [des-pay-gah'-do, dah], *a. & pp.* of DESPEGAR. Rough, morose, sullen, sour of temper, disgusting, unpleasant, harsh; separated.

despegadura [des-pay-gah-doo'-rah], *f.* Dissolving, separating.

despegamiento [des-pay-gah-me-en'-to], *m.* V. DESAPEGO.

despegar [des-pay-gar'], *va.* To unglue, to separate, to disjoin. **Despegar los labios,** to speak, to open one's lips, to break silence. -*vn.* To take off (avión). -*vr.* 1. To grow apart, to withdraw one's affections (from someone). 2. To become alienated, to become detached. **Despegarse de los amigos,** to break with one's friends.

despego [des-pay'-go], *m.* 1. Asperity, moroseness, coyness. 2. Displeasure, aversion. 3. Coldness, indifference.

despegue [des-pay'-gay], *m. (Aer.)* 1. Take off. 2. Blast-off. **Despegue de emergencia,** *(Aer.)* scramble. **Despegue vertical,** vertical take-off.

despeinado [des-pay-e-nah'-do], *a.* Dishevelled, tousled; unkempt.

despeinar [des-pay-e-nar'], *va.* To disarrange the hair of. -*vr. (Fig.)* To make a great effort, to get really involved.

despejadamente [des-pay-hah-dah-men'-tay], *adv.* Expeditiously, readily, freely

despejado, da [des-pay-hah'-do, dah], *a.* 1. Sprightly, smart, quick, vivacious, sagacious, dexterous, clean. 2. Clear, disengaged. 3. Wide-awake; *(Med.)* Free of fever; lucid. -*pp.* of DESPEJAR.

despejar [des-pay-har'], *va.* To remove impediments, to surmount obstacles to clear away obstructions. **Despejen la sala,** clear the room. **Los bomberos despejaron el teatro,** the firemen cleared the theater. -*vr.* 1. To cheer up, to amuse oneself. 2. To acquire or show looseness in behavior. 3. To be relieved of pain (paciente). 4. *(Math.)* To discover the unknown. **Despejarse el cielo, el día, el tiempo,** to become clear, serene weather.

despeje [des-pay-hay], *m.* 1. *(Dep.)* Clearance. 2. Clarity (de mente).

despejo [despay'ho], *m.* 1. The act of removing obstacles or clearing away impediments. 2. Sprightliness, smartness, liveliness, vivacity, briskness; grace, ease.

despelotar [des-pay-lo-tar'], *va.* 1. To dishevel the hair. 2. To strip, to undress. -*vr.* To strip off, to undress.

despelote [des-pay-lo-tay], *m.* 1. Nudity, nakedness; strip. 2. *(Carib.)* Big spree (juerga).

despeluzamiento [des-pay-loo-thah-me-en'-to], *m.* Act of making hair stand on end, horripilation.

despeluzar, despeluznar [des-pay-loo-thar', des-pay-looth-nar'], *va.* To make hair stand on end (miedo, terror). -*vr.* 1. To stand on end (pelo). 2. To be horrified (persona).

despellejadura [des-pel-lyay-hah-doo'-rah], *f.* 1. Scratch, slight wound. 2. Skinning.

despellejar [des-pel-lyay-har'], *va.* 1. To skin. **Despellejar un conejo,** to uncase a rabbit. 2. *(Fig.)* To flay, to criticize unmercifully (criticar). 3. **Despellejar a uno,** to fleece somebody.

despenador, ra [des-pay-nah-dor', rah], *m. & f.* One who relieves pain.

despenalización [des-pay-nah-le-thah-the-on'], *f.* Legalization; decriminalization.

despenalizar [des-pay-nah-le-thar'], *va.* To legalize; to decriminalize.

despenar [des-pay-nar'], *va.* 1. To relieve from pain. 2. *(Met.)* To kill.

despendedor, ra [des-pen-day-dor', rah]. *m. & f.* Spendthrift, prodigal.

despender [des-pen-derr'], *va.* To spend, to expend, to waste, to squander.

despensa [des-pen'-sah], *f.* 1. Pantry, larder. 2. Store of provisions for a journey. 3. Butlership. 4. The provisions that are bought for daily use; marketing. 5. Contract to provide a horse with hay, straw, and barley, all year. 6. *(Naut.)* Steward's room.

despensería [des-pen-say-ree'-ah], *f.* Office of steward.

despensero, ra [des-pen-say'-ro, rah], *m. & f.* 1. Butler, caterer; *(Naut.)* steward on board of ships. 2. Dispenser, distributer.

despeñadero [des-pay-nyah-day'-ro], *m.* 1. Precipice, crag. 2. *(Met.)* A bold and dangerous undertaking.

despeñadero, ra [des-pay-nyah-day-ro, rah], *a.* Steep, precipitous, headlong.

despeñadizo, za [des-pay-nyah-dee'-tho, thah], *a.* 1. Steep, precipitous. 2. Glib, slippery.

despeñar [des-pay-nyar'], *va.* To precipitate, to fling down a precipice. -*vr.* To precipitate oneself, to throw oneself headlong.

despeño, despeñamiento [des-pay'-nyo, des-pay-nyah-me-en'-to], *m.* 1. A precipitate fall. 2. Destruction of character or credit. 3. Diarrhoea.

despepitador [des-pay-pe-tah-dor'], *m.* An instrument for removing cores or stones of fruit. -*va.* To remove the seeds from a melon or other fruit; to stone.

despepitar [des-pay-pe-tar'], *vr.* To give license to one's tongue, to vociferate, to speak rashly and inconsiderately, to act imprudently. -*va.* To remove the pips from.

despercudir [des-per-coo-deer'], *va.* To clean or wash what is greasy.

desperdiciadamente [des-per-de-the-ah'-dah-men-tay], *adv.* Profusely, wastefully.

desperdiciado, da [des-per-de-the-ah'-do, dah], *a. & pp.* of DESPERDICIAR. Wasted, destroyed, squandered.

desperdiciador, ra [des-per-de-the-ah-dor', rah], *m. & f.* Spendthrift, squanderer, lavisher.

desperdiciar [des-per-de-the-ar'], *va.* 1. To squander, to misspend, to fling away. 2. To lose, not to avail oneself of, not to utilize.

desperdicio [des-per-dee'-the-o], *m.* 1. Prodigality, profusion, waste. 2. Residuum, relics, remains, garbage. **Desperdicios de cuero,** furrier's waste. **El muchacho no tiene desperdicio,** he´s a fine lad.

desperdigar [des-per-de-gar'], *va.* To separate, to disjoin, to scatter. -*vr.* To scatter, to separate.

desperecerse [des-pay-ray-therr'-say], *vr.* To crave, to desire eagerly. **Desperecerse de risa,** to laugh heartily.

desperezarse [des-pay-ray-thar'-say], *va.* To put away sloth. -*vr.* To stretch one's limbs on being roused from sleep.

desperezo [des-pay-ray'-tho], *m. V.* ESPEREZO.

desperfecto [des-per-fec'-to], *m.* 1. Deterioration, loss. 2. Injury which possessions suffer by the neglect or fault of the owner. **Sufrió algunos desperfectos en el accidente,** it suffered slight damage in the accident.

desperfilar [des-per-fe-lar'], *va. (Pict.)* To soften the lines of a painting. -*vr.* To lose the posture of a profile line or contour.

despergaminar [des-per-gah-me-nar'], *va.* To hull, to decorticate.

despernada [des-per-nah' ah], *f.* A motion in dancing.

despernado, da [des-per-nah'-do, dah], *a.* Weary, fatigued, tired. -*pp.* of DESPERNAR.

despernar [des-per-nar'], *va.* To maim, to cripple, or cut off one's legs. -*vr.* To be worn out, to crippled from walking.

desperpentar [des-per-pen-tar'], *va. (Prov.)* To cut off with one stroke.

despertador, ra [des-per-tah-dor', rah], *m. & f.* 1. Awakener, one who awakes or rouses out of sleep. 2. Alarm bell in clocks: an alarm-clock. 3. Causing wakefulness, care, or anxiety.

despertamiento [des-per-tah-me-en'-to], *m.* Awakening. 2. Excitation, the act of rousing or awakening.

despertar [des-per-tar'], *va.* 1. To awake, to awaken. 2. To awaken, to excite, to put in motion. 3. To enliven, to make lively or sprightly. 4. To call to recollection. -*vn.* 1. To awake, to break from sleep. 2. To revive, to grow lively or sprightly.

despesar [des-pay-sar'], *m.* Displeasure, aversion, dislike.

despestañarse [des-pes-tah-nyar'-say], *va.* To pluck out eyelashes. -*vr.* 1. To look steadfastly at anything, to inspect it closely. 2. *(Met.)* To apply oneself attentively to business.

despezar [des-pay-thar'], *va.* 1. To dispose and arrange stones at a proper distance. 2. To make thinner at the end, applied to tubes and pipes.

despezo [des-pay'-tho], *m.* Diminution of one end of a tube or pipe. **Despezos,** faces of stone, where they join each other.

despezonar [des-pay-tho-nar'], *va.* 1. To cut off the end of a thing, to break off the stalk of fruit. 2. To divide, to separate. -*vr.* To break off (tallos de fruta).

despiadadamente [des-pe-ah-dah-dah-men-tay], *adv.* Cruelly; mercilessly, relentlessly; heartlessly.

despiadado, da [des-pe-ah-dah'-do, dah], *a.* Impious, cruel. *V.* DESAPIADADO.

despicar [des-pe-car'], *va.* To satisfy, to gratify. -*vr.* To take revenge.

despicarazar [des-pe-cah-ra-thar'], *va. (Prov.)* To pick figs (pájaros).

despichar [des-pe-char'], *va.* 1. *(Prov.)* To pick grapes; to seed grapes before pressing them. 2. To expel or discharge moisture or humor. 3. *(Coll.)* To die.

despidida [des-pe-dee'-dah], *f. (Prov.)* Gutter, a passage for water.

despido [des-pee'-do], *m.* 1. Despatch. 2. Dismissal. **Despido improcedente**, wrongful dismissal. *(Yo despido, él despidió, yo despida, from Despedir. V.* PEDIR.).

despiertamente [des-pe-er-tah-men'-tay], *adv.* Acutely, ingeniously, cleverly.

despierto, ta [des-pe-err'-to, tah], *a.* 1. Awake. 2. Vigilant, watchful, diligent. 3. Brisk, sprightly, lively, smart, clearsighted. *(Yo despierto, yo despierte, from Despertar. V.* ACERTAR.)

despiezo [des-pe-ay'-tho], *m. (Arch.)* Juncture or bed of one stone on another.

despilarar [des-pe-lah-rar'], *va. (Min.)* To take away the pillars of ore-bearing rock.

despilfarradamente [des-pel-fahr-rah-dah'-men-tay], *adv.* Wastefully; slovenly.

despilfarrado, da [des-peel-far-rah'-do, dah], *a.* 1. Prodigal, wasteful. 2. Ragged, in tatters. -*pp.* of DESPILFARRAR.

despilfarrador, ra [des-peel-far-rah-dor', rah], *a.* Spendthrift, wasteful.

despilfarrar [des-peel-far-rar'], *va.* To destroy or waste with slovenliness, of prodigality.

despilfarro [des-peel-far'-ro], *m.* 1. Slovenliness, uncleanliness. 2. Waste, mismanagement, lavishness. 3. Misgovernment in public affairs.

despimpollar [des-pim-pol-lyar'], *va.* To prune away useless stems from plants.

despinces [des-peen'-thays], *m. pl.* Tweezers. *V.* PINZAS.

despintar [des-pin-tar'], *va.* 1. To blot or efface what is painted. 2. *(Met.)* To obscure things or make them less intelligible; to mislead. -*vn.* To degenerate. -*vr.* 1. To be deceived by mistaking one card for another. **No despintársele a uno alguna persona o cosa,** not to forget the appearance of a person or thing. 2. To wash off (con la lluvia etc.); To lose its color.

despinzadera [des-pin-thah-day'-rah], *f.* 1. Woman that plucks the knots off cloth. -*pl.* 2. Tweezers.

despinzar [des-pin-thar'], *va.* To pick off the knots, hair, or straw from clothes.

despiojar [des-pe-o-har'], *va.* 1. To louse, to clean of lice. 2. *(Met. Coll.)* To trim or dress, to relieve from misery.

despique [des-pee'-kay], *m.* Vengeance, revenge.

despiritado, da [des-pe-re-tah'-do, dah], *a.* Languid, spiritless.

despistado, da [des-pis-tah-do], *a, m & f.* Vague, absent-minded; unpractical; hopeless. 2. Confused, out of touch; off the beam. **Ando muy despistado con todo esto,** I´m terribly muddled about all this.

despistar [des-pis-tar'], *va.* 1. To turn from the right trail. 2. *(Fig.)* To put off the scent; to mislead. **Esa pregunta está hecha para despistar,** that question is designed to mislead people. -*vr. (Fig.)* To go wrong; to take the wrong route.

despiste [des-pis'-tay], *m.* 1. *(Aut. etc.)* Swerve. 2. Mistake. 3. Absent-minded; muddle; confusion, bewilderment. **Tiene un terrible despiste,** he´s terribly absent-minded.

despizcar [des-pith-car'], *va.* To comminute, to break or cut into small bits. -*vr.*To make the utmost exertions, to use one's best endeavors.

desplacer [des-plah-therr'], *m.* Displeasure, disgust, disobligation.

desplacer [des-plah-therr'], *va.* To displease, to disgust.

desplantación [des-plan-tah-the-on'], *f.* Eradication, displantation.

desplantador, ra [des-plan-tah-dor', rah], *m. & f.* One who eradicates, eradicator. -*m.* A trowel, scoop trowel.

desplantar [des-plan-tar'], *va.* To eradicate. V. DESARRAIGAR. -*vr.* To lose one's erect posture in fencing or dancing; to dismount artillery.

desplante [des-plahn'-tay], *m.* 1. An oblique posture in fencing. 2. Outspoken remark; impudent remark, cutting remark. **Me dio un desplante,** he left me stunned. 3. Lack of respect.

desplatar [des-plah-tar'], *va.* To separate silver from other substances with which it is mixed.

desplate [des-plah'-tay], *m.* The act of separating silver from other metals or substances.

desplazado, da [des-plah-thah-do], *a. m & f.* 1. Displaced, wrongly placed (objeto). 2. Badly adjusted (persona). **Sentirse un poco desplazado,** to feel rather out of place.

desplazamiento [des-plah-thah-me-en'-to], *m.* 1. *(Obs.)* Displacement, change of place. 2. *(Naut.)* Displacement of a vessel. 3. Journey, trip. **Reside en Madrid aunque con frecuentes desplazamientos,** she lives in Madrid but is often away.

desplazar [des-plah-thar'], *va.* 1. *(Ant.)* To displace. 2. *(Naut.)* To displace. 3. To displace (persona). -*vr.* 1. To move (objeto). 2. To go, to travel; to move away, to move out. **Tiene que desplazarse todos los días 25 kms,** he has to travel 25 kms every day.

desplegable [des-play-gah-blay], *m.* Folder, brochure.

desplegadura [des-play-gah-doo'-rah], *f.* Explication, unfolding, elucidation.

desplegar [des-play-gar'], *va.* 1. To unfold, to display, to expand, to spread, to lay out, to lay before. 2. *(Met.)* To explain, to elucidate. 3. *(Naut.)* To unfurl. **Desplegar las velas,** to unfurl the sails. **Desplegar la bandera,** to hoist the flag. -*vr.* 1. To open, unfold (flores). 2. To spread out (tropas). 3. To execute a maneuvre. 4. To acquire ease and freedom in his movements by good teaching (caballos).

despleguetear [des-play-gay-tay-ar'], *va. (Agri.)* To remove the folds from the tendrils of vines.

despliegue [des-ple-ay'-gay], *m.* 1. Unfurling, unfolding. 2. *(Mil.)* Change from the order of march to that of battle, or to form in line fronting a given position. 3. *(Fig.)* Manifestation, display, show.

desplomar [des-plo-mar'], *va.* To make a wall, building, etc., to bulge out. -*vr.* 1. To deviate from a perpendicular line, to sag (pared). **Se ha desplomado el techo,** the ceiling has fallen in. 2. *(Met.)* To fall flat to the ground.

desplome [des-ploh'-may], *m.* Collapse, downfall, toppling.

desplomo [des-plo'-mo], *m.* The bulging or jutting out of a wall.

desplumadura [des-ploo-mah-doo'-rah], *f.* Deplumation.

desplumar [des-ploo-mar'], *va.* 1. To deplume, to pluck, to strip off feathers. 2. *(Met.)* To despoil or strip one of his property. 3. *(Naut.)* To dismast an enemy's ship. -*vr.* To moult feathers.

despoblación, despoblada [des-po-blah-the-on'], *f.* Depopulation. **Desplobación rural,** rural depopulation.

despoblado [des-po-blah-do'], *m.* Desert, an uninhabited place. **Despoblado, da,** *a. & pp.* of DESPOBLAR, Depopulated.

despoblador, ra [des-po-blah-dor', rah], *a.* Which depopulates.

despoblar [des-po-blar'], *va.* 1. To depopulate, to dispeople. 2. To despoil or desolate a place. **Despoblar una zona de árboles,** to clear an area of trees. -*vr.* To depopulate, to become deserted.

despojador, ra [des-po-hah-dor', rah], *m. & f.* Despoiler, spoiler.

despojar [des-po-har'], *va.* 1. To despoil or strip one of his property. 2. To deprive of, to cut off from, judicially. 3. To dismiss, to turn out of a place or employment. -*vr.* 1. To undress. 2. To relinquish, to forsake.

despojo [des-po'-ho], *m.* 1. Despoliation, spoliation. 2. Plunder, spoils. **La hermosura es despojo del tiempo,** beauty is the spoil of time. 3. Slough, the cast-off skin of a serpent. 4. Head, pluck, and feet of animals.-*pl.* 1. Leavings, scraps of the table. **Despojos de hierro,** scrap iron. 2. Giblets, the wings, neck, heart, and gizzard of fowls

despolarización [des-po-lah-re-thah-the-on'], *f.* Depolarization.

despolarizar [des-po-lah-re-thar'], *va.* To depolarize.

despolitización [des-po-le-te-thah-the-on'], *f.* Depoliticization.

despolitizar [des-po-le-te-thar'], *va.* To depoliticize.

despolvar [des-pol-var'], *va.* To remove the dust.

despolvorear [des-pol-vo-ra-yar'], *va.* 1. To dust. 2. *(Met.)* To separate, to scatter, to dissipate. *(Coll.)* To sprinkle.

desponerse [des-po-nerr'-say], *vr.* To cease laying eggs (aves).

despopularizar [des-po-poo-lah-re-thar'], *va. & vr.* To deprive of; or to lose one's popularity.

desportillar [des-por-til-lyar'], *pa.* To break the neck of a bottle, pot, etc. *(Arch.)* To splay.

desposado, da [des-po-sah'-do, dah], *a.* Handcuffed. -*pp.* of DESPOSAR.

desposar [des-po-sar'], *va.* To marry, to betroth, to mate, to match. -*vr.* 1. To be betrothed, to get married. 2. *(Met.)* To be paired or coupled.

desposeer [des-po-say-err'], *va.* To dispossess, to oust. **Desposeer a uno de su autoridad,** to remove somebody's authority. -*vr.* **Desposeerse de algo,** to give something up.

desposeimiento [des-po-say-e-me-en'-to], *m.* Dispossession.

desposorio [des-po-so'-re-o], *m.* 1. A mutual promise to contract marriage: almost always used in the plural. 2. Betrothal, the act of betrothing.

déspota [des'-po-tah], *m.* 1. A despot, absolute sovereign. 2. A tyrant.

despóticamente [des-po'-te-cah-men-tay], *adv.* Despotically.

despótico, ca [des-po'-te-co, cah], *a.* Despotic, despotical.

despotismo [des-po-tees'-mo], *m.* Despotism, absoluteness.

despotricar [des-po-tre-car'], *vn. (Coll.)* To talk inconsiderately.

despreciable [des-pre-the-ah'-blay] *a.* Contemptible, despicable or despisable, worthless, abject, mean, paltry, miserable, lowly.

despreciador, ra [des-pray-the-ah-dor', rah], *m. & f.* Depreciator, asperser, despiser, scorner, contemner.

despreciar [des-pray-the-ar'], *va.* To depreciate, to despise, to scorn, to contemn, to reject, to lay aside, to neglect. **No hay que despreciar tal posibilidad,** one should not understimate such a possibility. -*vr.* **Despreciarse de,** to think it beneath oneself.

despreciativo, va [des-pray-the-ah-tee'-vo, vah], *a.* 1. Depreciative, depreciatory. 2. Offensive.

desprecio [des-pray'-the-o], *m.* 1. Disregard, scorn, contempt, despising, neglect, contumely, irrision. **Lo miró con desprecio,** he looked at it contemptuously. 2. Dispraise.

desprender [des-pren-derr'], *va.* To unfasten, to loose, to disjoin, to separate. -*vr.* 1. To give way, to fall down. 2. To extricate oneself, to dispossess oneself, to give away. **Desprenderse de un estorbo,** to extricate oneself from a difficulty. **Desprenderse de algo,** to give something up. **Tendremos que desprendernos del coche,** we shall have to get rid of the car. 3. To be deduced, to be inferred. **Se desprende de esta declaración que...,** it is clear from this statement that...

desprendido, da [des-pren-dee'-do, dah], *a.* Disinterested, generous, uncovetous.

desprendimiento [des-pren-de-me-en'-to], *m.* 1. Alienation, disinterestedness. 2. A landslide, landslip.

desprensar [des-pren-sar'], *va.* To remove from the press.

despreocupación [des-pray-o-coo-pah-the-on'], *f.* Nonprejudice, freedom from bias, enlightenment.

despreocupado, da [des-pray-o-coo-pah'-do, dah], *a. pp.* of DESPREOCUPAR. Unconcerned, carefree, unconventional. **Despreocupado en el vestir,** careless in his attire.

despreocupar [des-pray-o-coo-par'], *va.* To unprepossess, to unpreoccupy. *-vr.* To be disabused of a prejudice or error, be set right.

desprestigiar [des-pres-te-he-ar'], *va.* To remove reputation, prestige. *-vr.* To lose prestige; to lose caste.

desprestigio [des-pres-tee'-he-o], *m.* Loss of reputation or prestige. **Campaña de desprestigio,** smear campaign. **Esas cosas que van en desprestigio nuestro,** those things which are to our discredit.

desprevención [des-pray-ven-the-on'], *f.* Improvidence, improvision, want of caution.

desprevenidamente [des-pray-vay-ne'-dah-men-tay], *adv.* Improvidently.

desprevenido, da [des-pray-vay-nee'-do, dah], *a.* 1. Unprovided, unprepared. 2. Improvident.

desproporción [des-pro-por-the-on'], *f.* Disproportion, want of symmetry, disparity; disproportionableness.

desproporcionadamente [des-pro-por-the-o-nah-dah-men'-tay], *adv.* Disproportionately.

desproporcionado, da [des-pro-por-the-o-nah'-do, dah], *a. & pp.* of DESPROPORCIONAR. Disproportionate, disproportional, unsymmetrical, unsuitable, unbecoming.

desproporcionar [des-pro-por-the-o-nar'], *va.* To disproportion, to mismatch things, to misproportion.

despropositado, da [des-pro-po-se-tah'-do, dah], *a.* Absurd.

despropósito [des-pro-po'-se-to], *m.* Absurdity, oddity.

desprotección [des-pro-tec-the-on'], *f.* Deprotection.

desprotegido [des-pro-tay-he-do], *a.* Unprotected.

desproveer [des-pro-vay-err'], *va.* To deprive of provisions, to despoil of the necessaries of life.

desproveído, da [des-pro-vey-ee'-do, dah], *a.* Unprovided, unprepared. *-pp.* of DESPROVEER.

desproveimiento [des-pro-vay-e-me-en'-to], *m.* Penury, poverty.

desprovisto, ta [des-pro-vees'-to, tah], *a. & pp. irreg.* of DESPROVEER. *V.* DESPROVEÍDO.

despueble [des-poo-ay'-blay], or **despueblo** [des-poo-ay'-blo], *m.* Depopulation.

después [des-poo-es'], *adv.* After, posterior in time; afterward, next, then. **Después de Dios,** under or after God. **Primero lo negó y después lo confesó,** he first denied it, then he confessed it. **Después de esa fecha,** since that date. **Mi nombre está después del tuyo,** my name comes next to yours. **Después que lo escribí,** after I wrote it.

despulir [des-poo-leer'], *va.* To tarnish. to frost, to grind (glass). **Vidrio despulido,** ground glass.

despulsar [des-pool-sar'], *va.* To leave without vigor or pulse. *-vr.* 1. To be sorely vexed. 2. To be violently affected with any passion; to eagerly desire.

despumación [des-poo-mah-the-on'], *f.* Despumation, the skimming of liquors.

despumar [des-poo-mar'], *va. V.* ESPUMAR.

despuntado [des-poon-tah'-do], *a.* Blunt.

despuntadura [des-poon-tah-doo'-rah], *f.* The act of blunting or taking off the point.

despuntar [des-poon-tar], *va.* 1. To blunt. 2. To cut away the dry combs in a beehive. 3. *(Naut.)* To double a cape. *-vn.* 1. To advance or make progress in the acquisition of talents and knowledge: to manifest wit and genius. **Despunta en matemáticas,** he shines at math. **Despunta por su talento,** her talent shines out. 2. To begin to sprout or bud, as plants.

3. To surpass, excel, morally. 4. To begin to dawn: said of the day or the sun.

desque [des'-key], *adv. (Vulg.)* Since, then, presently. *V.* DESDE QUE.

desquebrajar [des-kay-brah-har'], *va. & vr.* To break, to split, to crack.

desquejar [des-kay-har'], *va.* To pluck up a shoot near the root of a plant.

desqueje [des-kay'-hay], *m.* Pulling up a shoot near the root of a plant.

desquiciamiento [des-kee-the-ah-me-en'-to], *m.* Unhingeing, disjoining.

desquiciado [des-kee-the-ah-do], *a. (Fig.)* Deranged, unhinged.

desquiciar [des-ke-the-ar'], *va.* 1. To unhinge. 2. *(Met.)* To discompose, to disorder. 3. *(Met.)* To deprive of favor or protection.

desquijaramiento [des-ke-ha-rah-me-en'-to], *m.* Act of breaking the jaws.

desquijarar [des-ke-ha-rar'], *va.* 1. To break the jaws. 2. *(Naut.)* To break the cheek of a block.

desquijerar [des-ke-hay-rar'], *va.* To cut timber on both sides to make a tenon.

desquilatar [des-ke-lah-tar'], *va.* To diminish the intrinsic value of gold.

desquitar [des-ke-tar'], *va.* To retrieve a loss. *-vr.* 1. To win one's money back again. **Desquitarse de una pérdida,** to make up for a loss. 2. To retaliate, to take revenge; to meet with one.

desquite [des-kee'-tay], *m.* 1. Compensation, recovery of a loss. 2. Revenge, satisfaction retaliation. **Tomar el desquite,** to have one's revenge.

desrabotar [des-rah-bo-tar'], *va.* To cut off the tails of lambs or sheep, in order to fatten them.

desrancharse [des-ran-char'-say], *vr.* To withdraw oneself from a mess.

desramillar [des-rah-mil-lyar'], *va. (Agri.) V.* DESLECHUGAR.

desraspado [des-ras-pah'-do], *a. V.* CHAMORRO, as a kind of wheat. *-pp.* of DESRASPAR.

desraspar [des-ras-par'], *va. V.* RASPAR.

desrastrojar [des-ras-tro-har'], *va. (Agri.)* To remove the stubble.

desrastrojo [des-ras-tro'-ho], *m.* Removal, collection of stubble.

desrayadura [des-rah-yah-doo'-rah], *f.* 1. The last furrow of tillage in a field. 2. A deep boundary furrow between two fields.

desrayar [des-rah-yar'], *va.* 1. To open furrows for irrigation of a tilled field. 2. To make a boundary furrow to divide one field from another.

desrazonable [des-rah-tho-nah'-blay], *a.* Unreasonable, idle-headed.

desreglado, da [des-ray-glah'-do, dah], *a.* Disorderly, irregular. *V.* DESARREGLADO.

desreglarse [des-ray-glar'-say], *vr.* To be irregular, or ungovernable.

desrelingar [des-ray-lin-gar'], *va.* To take away the boltropes from the sails. *-vr. (Naut.)* To be blown from the boltrope (velas).

desreputación [des-ray-poo-tah-the-on'], *f.* Dishonor, ignominy.

desriñonarse [des-re-nyo-nahr'-say], *vr.* To slog one's guts out, *(fig.)* To break one's back.

desrizar [des-re-thar'], *va.* To uncurl.

desroblar [des-ro-blar'], *va.* To take off the rivets.

desroñar [des-ro-nyar'], *va. (Agri.)* To lop off decayed branches.

destacado [des-tah-cah'-do], *a.* Notable, outstanding, distinguished.

destacamento [des-tah-cah-men'-to], *m.* 1. Detachment, a body of troops detached on some particular service. 2. Station, or military post.

destacar [des-tah-car'], *va.* 1. To detach a body of troops from the main army on some particular service. 2. To make stand out; *(fig.)* To emphasize, to show up, to point up, to bring out. **Quiero destacar que...**, I wish to emphasize that... *-vr.* 1. To stand out. **Destacarse en**, to stand out against.

destaconar [des-tah-co-nar'], *va.* To wear out, or to break, the heels of footwear.

destajador [des-tah-hah-dor'], *m.* A kind of smith's hammer.

destajamiento [des-tah-hah-me-en'-to], *m.* *(Obs.)* 1. *(Met.)* Diminution, reduction. 2. Current taking a new course.

destajar [des-tah-har'], *va.* 1. To hire or undertake a job by the bulk, to do task work. 2. To stipulate the terms and conditions on which an undertaking is to be performed. 3. *(Obs.)* To prevent, to interrupt, to mislead.

destajero [des-tah-hay'-ro], *m.* One who undertakes a work by task or by the job.

destajista [des-tah-hes'-tah] *m.* V. DESTAJERO.

destajo [des-tah'-ho], *m.* 1. Job. 2. Undertaking the completion of a job within a certain time. **A destajo**, by the job, by the lump: earnestly, diligently. **Hablar a destajo**, to talk much and at random.

destallar [des-tal-lyar'], *va.* V. DESBORRAR.

destalonar [des-tah-lo-nar'], *va.* 1. To deprive of talons or heels. 2. *(Vet.)* To level horses' hoofs.

destapada [des-tah-pah'-dah], *f.* A kind of pie.

destapar [des-tah-par'], *va.* To uncover.-*vr.* 1. To be uncovered. 2. *(Fig.)* To cause surprise, to do something unexpected. 3. *(Fig.)* To speak frankly, to come into the open. 4. To lose control.

destape [des-tah-pay], *m.* 1. State of undress, nudity. 2. *(Fig.)* Permissiveness; process of liberalization.

destapiar [des-tah-pe-ar'], *va.* To pull down mud walls.

destapo [des-tah'-po], *m.* *(Prov.)* Act of uncovering or unstopping.

destaponar [des-tah-po-nar'], *va.* To uncork, to remove the stopper.

destarar [des-tah-rar'], *va.* To diminish the tare allowed in weighing a thing.

destartalado, da [des-tar-tah-lah'-do, dah], *a.* Huddled, rambling, in disorder, ruinous, tumbledown.

destazador [des-tah-thah-dor'], *m.* He who cuts dead things in pieces.

destazar [des-tah-thar'], *va.* To cut things in pieces.

deste, ta, to [des'-tay, tah], *pron.* A contraction formerly used for *De este, de esta, de esto.*

destechar [des-tay-char'], *va.* To unroof.

destejar [des-tay-har'], *va.* 1. To untile, to take off the tiles. 2. To leave a thing defenceless.

destejer [des-tay-herr'], *va.* To unweave, to ravel, to undo a warp prepared for the loom.

destellar [des-tel-lyar'], *va.* To throw out or scatter rays of light.

destello [des-tayl'-lyo], *m.* 1. The act of flowing out drop by drop. 2. Sparkle; flash; gleam; glint. 3. *(Fig.)* Atom, particle. **No tiene un destello de verdad**, there's not an ounce of truth in it. 4. **Destellos**, *(fig.)* Glimmer. **Tiene a veces destellos de inteligencia**, he sometimes shows a glimmer of intelligence.

destempladamente [des-tem-plah-dah-men'-tay], *adv.* Intemperately.

destemplado, da [des-tem-plah'-do, dah], *a.* 1. *(Art.)* Inharmonious, incongruous (cuadros). 2. Disharmonious, unharmonious, out of tune. 3. Intemperate. *-pp.* of DESTEMPLAR.

destemplanza [des-tem-plahn'-thah], *f.* 1. Unsettledness. 2. Disorder, intemperance; excess in the desires, or in the use of certain things. 3. Indisposition, an alteration in the pulse, not approaching fever symptoms. 4. Disorder, alteration in words or actions, lack of moderation.

destemplar [des-tem-plar'], *va.* 1. To distemper, to alter, to disconcert. 2. To put to confusion. 3. To untune. *-vr.* 1. To be ruffled, to be discomposed. 2. To be out of order (pulso). 3.

To grow blunt, to lose the temper (instrumentos). 4. To act improperly or rashly; to lose moderation in actions or words. 5. To melt glue or other cement. 6. To anneal, to take out the temper of metals.

destemple [des-tem'-play], *m.* 1. Discordance, disharmony. 2. Discomposure, disorder. 3. Intemperance, distemperature. 4. *(Pict.)* Distemper. 5. Distemper, a slight indisposition.

destender [des-ten-derr'], *va.* *(Prov.)* To fold, to double.

desteñido [des-tay-ñye-do], *a.* Faded, discolored.

desteñir [des-tay-nyeer'], *va.* To discolor, to change from the natural hue. *-vn & vr.* 1. To fade, to discolor, to take the color out of. 2. To run (colores de tela). **Esta tela no destiñe**, this fabric will not run.

desternillarse [des-ter-nil-lyar'-say], *vr.* To break one's cartilage or gristle. **Desternillarse de risa**, to laugh violently.

desterradero [des-ter-rah-day'-ro], *m.* A retired part of the town.

desterrado, da [des-ter-rah'-do, dah], *a. & pp.* of DESTERRAR. Banished, outcast.

desterrado, da [des-ter-rah'-do, dah], *m. & f.* Exile, outcast.

desterrar [des-ter-rar'], *va.* 1. To banish, to transport, to exile. 2. To lay, or put aside. **Desterrar una sospecha**, to banish a suspicion from one's mind. 3. To take the earth from a thing. **Desterrar del mundo**, to be the outcast of the world.

desterronador, ra [des-ter-ro-nah-dor', rah], *m. & f.* Clodcrusher.

desterronar [des-ter-ro-nar'], *va.* To break clods with a harrow or spade.

destetadera [des-tay-tah-day'-rah], *f.* Pointed instrument placed on the teats of cows, to prevent calves from sucking.

destetar [des-tay-tar'], *va.* To wean, to ablactate.*-vr.* To wean oneself from an evil habit or custom.

destete [des-tay'-tay], *m.* The act of weaning from the breast.

desteto [des-tay'-to], *m.* 1. Number of weanlings (ganado). 2. The place where newly weaned mules are kept.

destiempo [des-te-em'-po], *m.* An unseasonable time. **A destiempo**, unseasonably, untimely.

destierro [des-te-er'-ro], *m.* 1. Exile, banishment, transportation. 2. The place where the exile lives. 3. Any remote and solitary place. 4. Judicial banishment. *(Yo destierro, yo destierre,* from *Desterrar. V.* ACERTAR.)

destilación [des-te-lah-the-on'], *f.* 1. Distillation, act of dropping or falling in drops. 2. Distillation, the act of extracting by the fire or still. 3. Distillation, the substance drawn by the still.

destiladera [des-te-lah-day'-rah], *f.* 1. Still, alembic, a vessel for distillation. 2. An ingenious device or stratagem for obtaining one's end.

destilador [des-te-lah-dor'], *m.* 1. Distiller. 2. Filtering-stone. 3. Alembic, retort.

destilar [des-te-lar'], *va.* 1. To distil. 2. *(Fig.)* To exude; to reveal. **La carta destilaba odio**, the letter exuded hatred. *-vn.* 1. To distil, to drop, to fall in drops. 2. To distil, to filter though a stone.

destilatorio [des-te-lah-to'-reo], *m.* 1. Distillery. 2. Alembic.

destinación [des-te-nah-the-on'], *f.* 1. Destination. 2. Destiny, fate.

destinar [des-te-nar'], *va.* 1. To destine, to appoint for any use or purpose. **Ir destinado a**, to be bound for. **Una carta que viene destinada a ti**, a letter for you. 2. To destinate, to design for any particular end; to allot, assign. **Le han destinado a Lima**, they have appointed him to Lima. 3. *(Naut.)* To station strips.

destinatario, ria [des-te-nah-tah'-re-o], *m & f.* Addressee.

destino [des-tee'-no], *m.* 1. Destiny. 2. Fate, doom, fortune, force. **Es mi destino no encontrarlo**, I am fated not to find it. 3. Destination, appointment for any use or purpose. **Van con destino a Londres**, they are going to London. **Salir con destino a**, to leave for. 4. Profession, business. **Buscarse un destino de cartero**, to look for a job as a postman. 5. *(Naut.)* Station. **Con destino a**, bound for.

destiño [des-tee'-nyo], *m.* Piece of unfinished yellow or green and dry honeycomb in a beehive. *(Yo destiño, él destiñó,* from *Desteñir. V.* PEDIR.)

destitución [des-te-too-the-on'], *f.* 1. Privation of an employment, office or charge. 2. Destitution, dereliction, abandonment.

destituido, da [des-te-too-ee'-do, dah], *a. & pp.* of DESTITUIR. Destitute, forsaken, friendless, helpless.

destituir [des-te-too-eer'], *va.* To deprive, to make destitute. **Destituir a uno de algo,** to deprive somebody of something.

destocar [des-to-car'], *va.* 1. To uncoif, to pull off the cap or headdress. 2. *(Prov.)* To uncover the head.

destorcedura [des-tor-thay-doo'-rah], *f.* Untwisting, uncurling.

destorcer [des-tor-therr'], *va.* 1. To untwist, to uncurl. 2. To rectify what was not right. *-vr. (Naut.)* To deviate from the track, to lose the way.

destorgar [des-tor-gar'], *va. (Prov.)* To break the branches of evergreen oaks, taking off their acorns.

destornillado, da [des-tor-nil-lyah'-do, dah], *a.* Inconsiderate, heedless, rash. *-pp.* of DESTORNILLAR.

destornillador [des-tor-nil-lyah-dor'], *m.* Unscrewer, he or that which unscrews; screwdriver, wrench, turn-screw.

destornillar [des-tor-nil-lyar'], *va.* To unscrew. *-vr.* To act rashly, or without judgment or prudence.

destoserse [des-to-serr'-say], *vr.* To feign a cough, to cough needlessly.

destostarse [des-tos-tar'-say], *vr.* To gradually remove the tanning of the skin by the sun.

destrabar [des-trah-bar'], *va.* 1. To unfetter, to unbind. 2. To untie, to loosen, to separate; to break the barriers.

destrados [des-trah'-dos], *m. pl. (Prov.)* A coarse sort of woollen carpets, or rugs.

destraillar [des-tra-hil-lyar'], *va.* To unleash dogs.

destral [des-trahl'], *m.* A small axe or hatchet.

destraleja [des-trah-lay'-hah], *f.* A very small hatchet.

destralero [des-trah-lay'-ro], *m.* One who makes axes and hatchets.

destramar [des-trah-mar'], *va.* 1. To unweave, to undo the warp. 2. *(Mil.)* To dissolve a conspiracy or intrigue.

destrenzar [des-tren-thar'], *va.* To undo a tress of hair.

destreza [des-tray'-thah], *f.* 1. Dexterity, address, handiness, expertness, mastery, knowledge, cunning. 2. Nimbleness, adroitness. 3. Skill in fencing.

destrincar [des-trin-car'], *va. & vr. (Naut.)* To loose, to unlash.

destripacuentos [des-tre-pah-coo-en'-tos], *com.* One who often interrupts the person who is talking.

destripador [des-tre-pah-dor'], *m. (Fig.)* Butcher; murderer.

destripar [des-tre-par'], *va.* 1. To disembowel, to gut, to eviscerate. 2. V. DESPACHURRAR. 3. *(Met.)* To draw out the inside of a thing. **Destripar una botella,** to crack a bottle.

destripaterrones [des-tre-pah-ter-ro'-nes], *m. (Coll.)* Harrower, day laborer who harrows the land, clodbeater.

destripular [des-tre-poo-lar'], *va.* To discharge the crew of a vessel.

destriunfar [des-tre-oon-far'], *va.* To extract all the trumps in games at cards.

destrizar [des-tre-thar'], *va.* To mince, to crumble.*-vr.* To break the heart, to wear away with grief

destrocar [des-tro-car'], *va.* To return a thing bartered.

destrocos [des-tro'-cose], *m. pl.* Ruins, remains.

destrón [des-trone'], *m.* A blind man's guide.

destronamiento [des-tro-nah-me-en'-to], *m.* Dethronement.

destronar [des-tro-nar'], *va.* To dethrone, to divest of legality.

destroncamiento [des-tron-cah-me-en'-to], *m.* Detruncation, amputation, lopping trees.

destroncar [des-tron-car'], *va.* 1. To detruncate, to lop, to cut short. 2. To maim, to dislocate, to cut a body in pieces. 3.

(Met.) To ruin, to destroy anyone; obstruct his affairs or pretensions. 4. *(Met.)* To cut short a discourse.

destronque [des-tron'-kay], *m.* DESTRONCAMIENTO.

destroquerio [des-tro-kay'-re-o], *m. (Her.)* The right arm, clothed or bare, but always armed, upon crests of arms.

destrozado, da [des-tro-thah'-do], *a.* Smashed, shattered, ruined.

destrozador, ra [des-tro-thah-dor', rah], *m. & f.* Destroyer, mangler.

destrozar [des-tro-thar'], *va.* 1. To destroy, to break into pieces. 2. To rout, to defeat to massacre. 3. *(Met.)* To spend much inconsiderately. **Destrozar la armonía,** to ruin the harmony. **Le ha destrozado el que no quisiera casarse con él,** he was shattered when she wouldn't marry him.

destrozo [des-tro'-tho], *m.* 1. Destruction. 2. Havoc, rout, defeat, massacre.

destrozón, na [des-tro-thone', nah], *m. & f.* One who is destructive of apparel, shoes, etc.

destrucción [des-trooc-the-on'], *f.* 1. Destruction, extermination, extinction, overthrow. 2. Destruction, ruin, havoc, loss.

destructible [des-trooc-te-blay], *a.* Destructible.

destructivamente [des-trooc-te-vah-men'-tay], *adv.* Destructively.

destructividad [des-trooc-te-vee-dahd'], *f.* Destructiveness, a phrenological term: its supposed seat is above the auditory canal.

destructivo, va [des-trooc-tee'-vo, vah], *a.* Destructive, wasteful, consumptive.

destructor, ra [des-trooc-tor', rah], *m. & f.* Destructor, destroyer (barco), consumer, harasser.

destructorio, ria [des-trooc-toh'-re-o, ah], *a.* Destroying.

destrueco, destrueque [des-troo-ay'-co, des-troo-ay'-kay], *m.* The mutual restitution of things bartered or exchanged. *(Yo destrueco, yo destrueque,* from *Destrocar. V.* ACORDAR.)

destruible [des-troo-ee'-blay], *a.* Destructible.

destruidor, ra [des-troo-e-dor', rah], *m. & f.* Destroyer, devastator.

destruir [des-troo-eer'], *va.* 1. To destroy, to ruin, to lay level. 2. To destroy, to waste or lay waste, to harass; to overthrow. 3. To misspend one's fortune. 4. To deprive one of the means of earning a livelihood.

destruyente [des-troo-yen'-tay], *va.* Destroying.

desturbar [des-toor-bar'], *va.* To turn out, to drive away. V. ECHAR.

destutanarse [des-too-tah-nar'-say], *va. (Amer. Cuba)* To kill oneself with work, either physical or mental.

desubstanciar [day-soobs-tan-the-ar'], *va.* To enervate, to deprive of strength and substance.

desucación [day-soo-ca-the-on'], *f.* Act of extrating the juice.

desucar [day-soo-car'], *va.* V. DESJUGAR. *(Lat. succus,* juice.)

desudar [day-soo-dar'], *va.* To wipe off sweat.

desuelar [day-soo-ay-lar'], *va.* To take off the sole. *-vr.* To be wrenched off or fall off (suela de zapato).

desuellacaras [day-soo-el-lyah-cah'-ras], *m.* 1. *(Prov. Coll.)* A bad barber. 2. *(Coll.)* An impudent, shameless person.

desuello [day-soo-ay'-lyo], *m.* 1. The act of flaying, fleecing, or skinning. 2. Forwardness, impudence, insolence. 3. Extortion, or an exorbitant price. *(Yo desuello, yo desuelle,* from *Desollar. V.* ACORDAR.)

desulfuración [day-sool-foo-rah-the-on'], *f.* Removal of sulphur from a compound.

desulfurar [day-sool-foo-rar'], *va.* To desulphurize.

desuncir [des-oon-theer'], *va.* To unyoke, to abjugate.

desunidamente [des-oo-ne-dah-men-tay], *adv.* Separately, severally.

desunión [des-oo-ne-on'], *f.* 1. Separation disunion, disjunction. 2. Discord, disunion, dissension, feud.

desunir [des-oo-neer'], *va.* To separate, to part, to disunite; to occasion discord. *-vr.* To loosen, to come asunder; to set at odds; to disunite, to become separated.

desuñar [des-oo-nyar], *va.* 1. To tear off the nails. 2. To pull out the roots of trees. *-vr.* To plunge into vice and disorder.

desurcar [day-soor-car'], *va.* To remove or undo furrows.

desurdir [des-oor-deer'], *va.* 1. To unweave cloth. 2. To unravel a plot.

desusadamente [des-oo-sah'-dah-men-tay], *adv.* Unusually, out of use, contrary to custom.

desusado, da [des-oo-sah'-do, dah], *a. & pp.* of DESUSAR. Disused, obsolete, out of date, archaic.

desusar [des-oo-sar'], *va.* To disuse, to discontinue the use of. *-vr.* To become disused or obsolete.

desuso [des-oo'-so], *m.* Disuse, obsoleteness, desuetude.

desustanciar [day-soos-tan-the-ar'], *va.* 1. To enervate. 2. To deprive of strength and substance.

desvahar [des-vah-ar'], *va. (Agri.)* To take away the dry or withered part of a plant.

desvaído, da [des-vah-ee'-do, dah], *a.* 1. Tall and graceless. 2. Dull, lustreless, matt (of colors). 3. *(Naut.)* Gaping: applied to the sheathing of ships; when its joints separate.

desvainar [des-vah-e-nar'], *va.* 1. To husk, to strip off the outward integument. 2. To unsheath.

desvalido, da [des-vah-lee'-do, dah], *a.* Helpless, destitute, unprotected. **Niñez desvalida**, underprivileged children.

desvalijar [des-vah-leh-ar'], *va.* 1. To take out the contents of a valise or gripsack. 2. To rob one of what he was carrying in a valise or satchel.

desvalimiento [des-vah-le-me-en'-to], *m.* Dereliction, abandonment, want of favor or protection.

desvalorar [des-vah-lo-rar'], *va.* 1. To devalue, to depreciate. 2. To discredit.

desvalorización [des-vah-lo-re-thah-the-on'], *f.* Devaluation.

desvalorizar [des-vah-lo-re-thar'], *va.* To devalue, to depreciate. *-vr.* 2. To depreciate.

desván [des-vahn'], *m.* Garret; loft. **Desván gatero**, cockloft, a room over the garret.

desvanar [des-vah-nar'], *va.* To wind to a skein. V. DEVANAR.

desvanecer [des-vah-nay-therr'], *va.* 1. To divide into imperceptible parts. 2. To cause to vanish or disappear, to take away from the sight. 3. To undo, to remove. 4. To swell with presumption or pride. *-vr.* 1. To pall, to grow vapid, to become insipid. 2. To vanish, to evaporate, to exhale. 3. To be effected with giddiness or dizziness; to fall. *(Yo me desvanezco, or desvanezca, from Desvanecerse. V.* CONOCER.)

desvanecidamente [des-vah-nay-the-dah-men'-tay], *adv.* Vainly, haughtily, proudly.

desvanecido [des-vah-nay-the'-do], *a.* 1. *(Med.)* Faint; giddy, dizzy. **Caer desvanecido**, to fall in a faint. 2. *(Fig.)* Vain (engreido); proud (orguñoso).

desvanecimiento [des-vah-nay-the-me-en'-to], *m.* 1. Pride, haughtiness, loftiness. 2. Giddiness, dizziness. 3. *(Med.)* Fainting fit, swoon. 4. *(Quim.)* Evaporation; melting.

desvano [des-vah'-no], *m.* Garret. V. DESVÁN.

desvaporizar [des-vah-po-re-thar'], *va.* V. EVAPORAR.

desvarar [des-vah-rar'], *va. vn. & vr.* 1. V. RESBALAR. 2. *(Naut.)* To set afloat a ship that was aground.

desvariadamente [des-vah-re-ah'-dah-men-tay], *adv.* 1. Ravingly, foolishly, madly. 2. Differently, diversely, dissimilarly.

desvariado, da [des-vah-re-ah'-do, dah], *a.* 1. Delirious, raving. 2. Disorderly, irregular. 3. Extravagant, nonsensical. 4. Long, luxuriant: applied to the branches of trees. *-pp.* of DESVARIAR.

desvariar [des-vah-re-ar'], *vn.* 1. To rave, to be delirious, to dote. 2. To make extravagant demands. *-vr.* To deviate, go wrong, go astray.

desvarío [des-vah-ree'-o], *m.* 1. An extravagant action or speech. 2. Delirium, raving, giddiness. 3. Inequality, inconstancy, caprice. 4. Monstrousness, extravagancy; derangement; disunion.

desvedado, da [des-vay-dah'-do, dah], *a.* Unprohibited, free from prohibition, having been prohibited before. *-pp.* of DESVEDAR.

desvedar [des-vay-dar'], *va.* To remove or revoke a prohibition against a thing.

desveladamente [des-vay-lah'-dah-men-tay], *adv.* Watchfully, vigilantly.

desvelado, da [des-vey-lah'-do, dah], *a.* Watchful, vigilant, careful. *-pp.* of DESVELAR.

desvelamiento [des-vay-lah-me-en'-to], *m.* Watchfulness. V. DESVELO.

desvelar [des-vay-lar'], *va.* 1. To keep awake. 2. To solve, to explain (misterio). *-vr.* To be or watchful or vigilant or zealous. 2. To stay awake, to keep awake; to go without sleep.

desvelo [des-vay'-lo], *m.* 1. Watching, want or privation of sleep. 2. Watch, forbearance of sleep. 3. Watchfulness, vigilance. 4. Anxiety, uneasiness.

desvenar [des-vay-nar'], *va.* 1. To separate or clear the veins of flesh. 2. To extract anything from the veins of mines or the filaments of plants. 3. To raise the bit of a bridle, so as to form an arch of mouth.

desvencijado, da [des-ven-the-hah´-do, dah], *a.* Rickety, loose-jointed.

desvencijar [des-ven-the-har'], *va.* To disunite, to weaken, to divide, to break. *-vr.* 1. To be ruptured; to be relaxed. 2. *(Coll.)* To be exhausted.

desvendar [des-ven-dar'], *va.* To take off a bandage, to unbandage.

desveno [des-vay´-no], *m.* Arch of the mouth; a kind of bridle-bit.

desventaja [des-ven-tah'-hah], *f.* 1. Disadvantage, misfortune, damage, loss: **Estar en desventaja con respecto a otros**, to be at a disadvantage compared with others. 2. Disfavor, which results from comparing two persons or things.

desventajado [des-ven-tah-hah'-do], *a.* Disadvantaged.

desventajosamente [des-ven-tah-ho-sah-men-tay], *adv.* Disadvantageously, unprofitably.

desventajoso, sa [des-ven-tah-ho´-so, sah], *a.* Disadvantageous, unfavorable, unprofitable, detrimental.

desventar [des-ven-tar'], *va.* To vent, to let out air.

desventura [des-ven-too'-rah], *f.* Misfortune, calamity, mishap, mischance; misery.

desventuradamente [des-ven-too-rah-dah-men'-tay], *adv.* Unhappily, unfortunately.

desventurado, da [des-ven-too-rah'-do, dah], *a.* 1. Unfortunate, calamitous, wretched, unlucky, unhappy, miserable. 2. Chicken-hearted, pusillanimous, timid. 3. Mean (tacaño). *-m. f.* Wretch, unfortunate.

desvergonzadamente [des-ver-gon-thah-dah-men'-tay], *adv.* Impudent, shamelessly.

desvergonzado, da [des-ver-gon-thah-do, dah], *a.* Impudent, shameless, immodest.

desvergonzarse [des-ver-gon-thar'-say], *vr.* To speak or act in an impudent or insolent manner. **Desvergonzarse a pedir algo**, to have the nerve to ask for something.

desvergüenza [des-ver-goo-en'-thah], *f.* 1. Impudence, effrontery, assurance, grossness. 2. Shameless word or action. **Esto es una desvergüenza**, this is disgraceful. *(Yo me desvergüenzo, yo me desvergüence, from Desvergonzarse. V.* ACORDAR.).

desvertebrar [des-ver-tay-brar'], *va. (Fig.)* To dislocate; to disturb, to upset, to throw off balance.

desvestir [des-ves-ter'], *va.* To undress. *-vr.* To undress.

desvezar [des-vay-thar'], *va. (Agr. Prov.)* To cut the young shoots of vines near the roots.

desviación [des-ve-ah-the-on'], *f.* 1. Deviation, deflection, separation. **Es una desviación de sus principios**, it is a deviation from his principles. 2. *(Med.)* Vicious direction of some parts of the body, especially the limbs and the bones: applied also to extravasation of fluids. 3. *(Astr.)* Wrong position of a telescope out of the plane of the meridian. 4. The quantity by which a body, falling freely, deviates from the perpendicular, and the variation of the magnetic needle. 5. Shunt (ferrocarril). 6. Detour; diversion (tráfico); bypass, ring road. **Desviación de circulación,** traffic diversion.

desviadero [des-ve-ah-day'-ro], *m.* A railway switch, siding, side-track, passing-place.

desviado, da [des-ve-ah'-do, dah], *a.* Devious, out of the common trach askew. *-pp.* of DESVIAR.

desviar [des-ve-ar'], *va.* 1. To divert from the right way, to lead off, to avert, to turn aside. **Desviar el cauce de un río,** to alter the course of a river. **Desviar a uno del buen camino,** to lead somebody astray. 2. To dissuade, to discourage someone, to put someone off. 3. To parry a thrust (esgrima). *-vr.* To deviate, to turn away, to turn off. **Desviarse de un tema,** to digress from a theme.

desviejar [des-ve-ay-har'], *va.* Among shepherds, to separate the old ewes or rams from the flock.

desvigorizar [des-ve-go-re-thar'], *va.* To take away or diminish vigor.

desvincular [des-ven-coo-lar'], *va.* To detach; to disentail (finca). *-vr.* **Desvincularse con,** to break with.

desvío [des-vee'-o], *m.* 1. Turning away, going astray, deviation, aberrance. 2. The act of diverting. 3. Aversion, displeasure. 4. Coldness, indifference.

desvirar [des-ve-rar'], *va.* 1. To pare of the fore part of a sole. 2. In book-binding to trim a book. 3. *(Naut.)* To turn the capstan the other way from that used in winding, the cable; to reverse the capstan.

desvirgar [des-virr-gar'], *va. (Low.)* To deflower a maid.

desvirtuar [des-virr-too-ar'], *va.* To pall, to make insipid or vapid, to take the substance, virtue, or strength from anything. *-vr.* To spoil, to go off, to decline in quality.

desvivirse [des-ve-veer'-say], *vr.* To love excessively; to desire anxiously. **Desvivirse por los amigos,** to do one's utmost for one's friends.

desvolvedor [des-vol-vay-dor'], *m.* A screw tap.

desvolver [des-vol-verr'], *va.* 1. To alter a thing, to give it another shape. 2. To plough, to till the ground.

desyemar [des-yay-mar'], *va.* 1. *(Agri.)* To remove buds from plants. 2. To separate the yolk from the white of an egg.

desyerbar [des-yer-var'], *va.* To pluck up herbs, to weed, to grub.

desyuncir [des-yoon-theer'], *va.* 1. To unyoke. 2. To free from oppression or servitude.

deszafrar [des-thah-frar'], *va.* To carry away the ore from an excavation.

deszocar [des-tho-car'], *va.* To wound or hurt the foot.

deszumar [des-thoo-mar'], *va.* To extract the juice or substance.

detalladamente [day-tahl-lyah-dah'-men-tay], *adv.* In detail.

detallado [day-tahl-lyah'-do], *a.* Detailed.

detallar [day-tal-lyar'], *va.* To detail, to relate particularly or minutely, to particularize, to enumerate.

detalle [day-tahl'-lyay], *m.* 1. Detail, enumeration. **Con todos los detalles,** in detail. **Hasta en sus menores detalles,** down to the last detail. **No pierde detalle,** he misses nothing. 2. *(Fig.)* Token, gesture. **Tiene muchos detalles,** he is very considerate.

detectable [day-tec-tah'-blay], *a.* Detectable.

detectar [day-tec tar'], *va.* To detect.

detective [day-tec-tee'-vay], *m. & f.* Detective, sleuth.

detector [day-tec-tor'], *m.* Detector. **Detector de humo,** smoke detector. **Detector de metales,** metal detector.

detención [day-ten-the-on'], *f.* 1. Detention, delay, stopping. **Detención de juego,** stoppage of play. 2. *(Naut.)* Demurrage. 3. Arrest. **Detención sin procedimiento,** imprisonment without trial.

detenedor, ra [day-tay-nay-dor', rah], *m. & f.* Detainer, one that detains.

detener [day-tay-nerr'], *va.* 1. To stop, to detain, to hinder, to fix. **Detener el progreso de,** to hold up the progress of. 2. To arrest, to imprison, to constrain. 3. To keep, to keep back, to retain, to reserve. *-vr.* 1. To tarry, to stay, to continue, to forbear, to give over. 2. To be detained, to stop, to be at leisure. **Se detuvo a mirarlo,** he stopped to look at it. 3. To consider a thing maturely. *(Yo detengo, yo detuve,* from *Detener. V.* TENER.)

detenidamente [day-tay-ne-dah-men'-tay], *adv.* Dilatorily, cautiously, attentively.

detenido, da [day-tay-nee'-do, dah], *a.* 1. Sparing, niggardly, parsimonious. 2. Embarrassed, of little resolution, dilatory, *-pp.* of DETENER.

detenimiento [day-tay-ne-me-en'-to], *m.* 1. *V.* DETENCIÓN. 2. Care, circumspection, reflection, tact.

detentación [day-ten-tah-the-on'], *f. (Law.)* Deforcement, detention, the act of keeping what belongs to another.

detentar [day-ten-tar'], *va.* To detain, to retain, to keep unlawfully the property or rights belonging to another.

detentor [day-ten-tor'], *m. (Com.)* Holder.

detergente [day-ter-hen'-tay], *a.* Detergent. **Jabón detergente,** detergent soap. *-m.* Detergent.

deterger [day-ter-herr'], *va.* To wash or cleanse an ulcer, a wound, etc.

deterior [day-tay-re-or'], *a.* Worse, of an inferior quality.

deterioración [day-tay-re-orah-the-on'], *f.* Deterioration, detriment, damage.

deteriorado [day-tay-re-o-rah'-do], *a.* Spoiled, damaged; worn; shopsoiled (géneros).

deteriorar [day-tay-re-o-rar'], *va. & vr.* To deteriorate, to impair.

deterioro [day-tay-re-oh'-ro], *m.* Deterioration, impairment, injury. **En caso de deterioro de las mercancías,** should the goods be damaged in in any way.

determinable [day-ter-me-nah'-blay], *a.* Determinable, conclusible.

determinación [day-ter-me-nah-theon'], *f.* 1. Determination, resolution, decision. 2. Conclusion or final decision. 3. Resolution, firmness, boldness, audaciousness.

determinadamente [day-ter-me-nah-dah-men'-tay], *adv.* 1. Determinately, resolutely. 2. Definitively, expressly, especially.

determinado, da [day-ter-me-nah'-do, dah], *a.* 1. Determinate, determined, resolved, decided; fixed, resolute. **Un día determinado,** on a certain day. **En momentos determinados,** at certain times. 2. Determinate, settled, definite, determined.*-pp.* of DETERMINAR.

determinante [day-ter-me-nahn'-tay], *pa.* Determining. *-a.* Determinate, determinative.

determinante [day-ter-me-nahn'-tay], *m.* 1. *(Gram.)* The determining verb. 2. Determiner, determinator, he who determines.

determinar [day-ter-me-nar'], *va.* 1. To determine, to resolve, to fix in a determination. **Determinar el peso de algo,** to determine the weight of something. 2. To distinguish, to discerns. 3. To appoint, to assign. 4. To cause, to produce. **Aquello determinó la caída del gobierno,** that brought about the fall of the government. 5. To classify. 6. To decide, to conclude. **Determinar un pleito,** to decide a lawsuit. *-vr.* To determine, to resolve, to take a resolution, or to come to a resolution.

determinativo, va [day-ter-me-nah-tee'-vo, vah], *a.* Determinative.

determinismo [day-ter-me-nees'-mo], *m.* Determinism, fatalism; a philosophy according to which the actions of men obey irresistible motives, mostly not suspected by the individual.

determinista [day-ter-me-nees'-tah], *m.* A fatalist.

detersión [day-tar-se-on'], *f.* 1. Detersion, the act of cleansing a sore. 2. Cleansing. 3. The act and effect of cleansing.

detersivo, va [day-ter-see'-vo, vah], *a.* Detersive, fit for a cleansing surgical application.

detersorio, ria [day-ter-so'-reo, ah], *a.* Detersive, cleansing.

detestable [day-tes-tah'-blay], *a.* Detestable, hateful, heinous, loathsome.

detestablemente [day-tes-tah'-blay-men-tay], *adv.* Detestably, hatefully, confoundedly.

detestación [day-tes-tah-the-on'], *f.* Detestation, hatred, abhorrence, horror, abomination.

detestar [day-tes-tar'], *va.* To detest, to abhor, to hate, to abominate, to loathe.

detienebuey [day-te-ay-nay-boo-ay'-e], *m. (Bot.)* Common rest-harrow, cammoc, groundfurze.

detonación [day-to-nah-the-on'], *f.* Detonation, noise.

detonador [day-to-nah-dor'], *m.* Detonator.

detonar [day-to-nar'], *va. (Chem.)* To flash, to detonate.

detorsión [day-tor-se-on'], *f.* Violent extension, wrenching of a muscle, tendon, or ligament.

detracción [day-trac-the-on'], *f.* 1. Detraction, defamation, slander, obloquy. 2. Detraction, a withdrawing, a taking away.

detractar [day-trac-tar'], *va.* To detract, to defame, to slander.

detractor, ra [day-trac-tor´, rah], *m. & f.* Detractor, slanderer.

detraer [day-tra-herr'], *va.* 1. To detract, to remove, to take away, to withdraw. 2. To detract, to slander to vilify.

detrás [day-trahs'], *adv.* 1. Behind. **Detrás de la puerta**, behind the door. **Por detrás**, behind. **Salir de detrás de un árbol**, to come out from behind a tree. 2. In the absence.

detrimento [day-tre-men'-to], *m.* Detriment, damage, loss, harm.

detrítico, ca [day-tree'-te-co, cah], *a.* Composed of detritus; detrital, detritic.

detritus [day-tree'-toos], *m. (Neol.)* 1. Detritus, remnants of the destruction of rocks and plants. 2. Inorganic residue replacing tissue in degenerated parts of the body. 3. Filth, excrements.

detumescencia [day-too-mes-then'-the-ah], *f.* Detumescence, resolution of a swelling.

detumescente [day-too-mes-then'-tay], *a.* Having power to disperse a swelling.

deturbadora (Fuerza) [day-toor-bah-do'-rah], *a.* 1. A force perpendicular to the plane of the orbit of the disturbed planet. 2. *V.* PERTURBACIÓN.

deuda [day'-oo-dah], *f.* 1. Debt, that which one man owes to another. 2. Fault, offence. 3. That which has relationship or affinity. **Deudas activas**, assets. **Deudas pasivas**, liabilities. **Deuda a largo plazo**, long-term debt. **Contraer deudas**, to contract debts. **Estar en deuda**, to be in debt.

deudo, da [day'-oo-do, dah], *m. & f.* 1. Parent, relative. 2. Kindred, relation. *V.* DESDÉN and PARENTESCO.

deudor, ra [day-oo-dor', rah], *m. & f.* Debtor. **Deudor moroso**, slow payer.

deuterio [day-oo-tay'-re-o], *m. (Chem.)* Deuterium.

deuterogamia [day-oo-tay-ro-gah'-me-ah], *f.* State of second marriage.

deuterógamo, ma [day-oo-tay-ro'-gah-mo, mah], *a.* One who marries a second time.

deuteronomio [day-oo-tay-ro-no'-me-o], *m.* Deuteronomy, the fifth book of the Pentateuch.

devalar [day-vah-lar'], *vn. (Naut.)* To be driven out of the right course by a current (barcos).

devaluación [day-vah-loo-ah-the-on'], *f. (Fin.)* Devaluation.

devaluar [day-vah-loo-ar'], *va.* To devaluate, to depreciate.

devanadera [day-vah-nah-day'-rah], *f.* 1. A reel, spool, bobbin. **Devanadera de golpe**, clockreel, snapreel. 2. A movable picture or decoration on the stage. 3. *(Naut.)* Logreel.

devanador, ra [day-vah-nah-dor', rah], *m. & f.* 1. Winder, one who reels yarn. 2. Quill, bit of paper, or other thing, on which yarn is wound; spool.

devanar [day-vah-nar'], *va.* 1. To reel, as yarn. 2. *(Met.)* To wrap up one thing, in another. **Devanar las tripas**, to importune one with some impertinent affair. **Devanarse los**

sesos, to screw one's wits, to fatigue oneself with intense thinking, to hammer one's brains.

devanear [day-vah-nay-ar'], *vn.* To rave, to talk nonsense; to dote, to be delirious.

devaneo [day-vah-nay'-o], *m.* 1. Delirium, alienation of mind, giddiness; frenzy. 2. Idle or mad pursuit; dissipation.

devantal [day-van-tahl'], *m.* Apron. *V.* DELANTAL.

devastación [day-vas-tah-the-on'], *f.* Devastation, destruction, desolation, waste.

devastador, ra [day-vas-tah-dor', rah], *m. & f.* Desolator, harasser, spoiler. *-a.* Devastating.

devastar [day-vas-tar'], *va.* To desolate, to waste or to lay waste, to harass.

develar [day-vay-lar'], *va.* To blockade a port.

devengar [day-ven-gar'], *va.* To obtain as the reward of labor, to deserve, to acquire a right to a thing as a reward for services, etc.

devisa [day-vee'-sah], *f.* 1. *V.* DIVISA. 2. Part of the tithes which belong to a plebeian heir. 3. Ancient patriots in Castile.

devoción [day-vo-the-on'], *f.* 1. Devotion, piety. **Con devoción**, devoutly; piously. 2. Godliness, observance of religious duties. 3. Prayer, act of religion. 4. *(Met.)* Strong affection, ardent love. **Sienten devoción por su general**, they feel devotion to their general. 5. *(Div.)* Devoutness, promptitude in obeying the will of God. **Estar a la devoción de alguno**, to be at one's disposal, to attend his orders.

devocionario [day-vo-the-o-nah'-re-o], *m.* Prayer-book.

devocionero, ra [day-vo-the-o-nay'-ro, rah], *a.* Devotional.

devolución [day-vo-loo-the-on'], *f. (Law.)* Devolution, restitution. **Pidió la devolución de los libros**, he asked for the books to be given back. **No se admiten devoluciones**, no refund will be given.

devoluta [day-vo-loo'-ta], *f.* In canonical law, the bestowal by the Pope of a vacant benefice.

devolutario [day-vo-loo-tah'-re-o], *m.* A person who receives a benefice from the Pope.

devolutivo [day-vo-loo-tee'-vo], *a. (Law.)* 1. What may be returned (causas). 2. What may be restored to a former state (derechos).

devolutorio, ria [day-vo-loo-toh'-re-o, ah], *a. V.* DEVOLUTIVO.

devolver [day-vol-verr'], *va.* To return, to refund, to restore. **Devolver el estómago**, *(coll.)* to vomit. **Devolver una carta al remitente**, to return a letter to the sender. **El espejo devuelve la imagen**, the mirror sends back the image. **Han devuelto el castillo a su antiguo esplendor**, they have restored the castle to its former glory.

devorador, ra [day-vo-rah-dor', rah], *m. & f.* Devourer. **Una mujer devoradora de hombres**, a man-eating woman.

devorar [dayvorar'], *va.* To devour, to swallow up, to consume ravenously, to glut. **Todo lo devoró el fuego**, the fire consumed everything. **Le devoran los celos**, he is consumed with jealously.

devotamente [day-vo-tah-men'-tay], *adv.* Devoutly, piously.

devoto, ta [day-vo'-to, tah], *a.* 1. Devout, pious, devotional, religious, godly. 2. Exciting devotion. 3. Strongly attached. **Devoto de monjas**, he who frequently visits and converses with nuns. **Su devoto amigo**, your devoted friend. **Es devoto de ese café**, he is much attached to that café.

devuelto, ta [day-voo-el'-to, tah], *pp. irr.* of DEVOLVER. Returned, restored.

dexiocardia [dek-se-o-car-de-ah], *f.* Deviation of the heart to the right side of the thoracic cavity.

dextrina [dex-tree'-nah], *f.* Dextrine.

dextrosa [dex-tro'-sah], *f. (Chem.)* Dextrose.

dezmable [deth-mah'-blay], *a.* Tithable, subject to tithes.

dezmar [deth-mar´], *va. V.* DIEZMAR

dezmatorio [deth-mah-to'-re-o], *m.* 1. Place in which tithes are collected. 2. Tithing.

dezmero, ra [dayth-may'-ro], *a.* Belonging to tithes.

dezmería, dezmía [deth-may-ree'-ah, deth-mee'-ah], *f.* Titheland.

dezmero [deth-may'-ro], *m.* 1. One who pays tithes. 2. Tithe-gatherer; a tither.

día [dee'-ah], *m.* 1. Day: the space of twenty-four hours. 2. Day: the time between the rising and setting of the sun. 3. Daylight, sunshine. -*pl.* 1. Certain lapse of time, a certain epoch. 2. Existence, life. **Día de cumpleaños**, birthday. **Día de ayuno o de vigilia**, fasting-day or fastday. **Día de viernes**, day on which fish is eaten instead of meat. **Día de trabajo**, working-day. **Día de descanso**, 1. Day of rest. 2. The Sabbath-day. **Día del juicio**, doomsday. **Día laborable**, working-day. **Día natural**, from midnight to midnight. **De día**, by day. **De un día para otro** or **de día en día**, from day to day. **Un día sí y otro no**, or **cada tercer día**, every other day. **Hasta el día de hoy**, to this day. **El día de hoy** or **hoy en día**, the present day. **El mejor día**, some fine day. **Día pesado**, a dull, gloomy day. **Luz del día**, daylight. **Entre día**, in the daytime. **Tener días**, *(Coll.)* 1. To vary in one's physiognomy or countenance. 2. To be full of days, to be old. **De hoy en ocho días**, this day week. **Días complementarios**, complementary days which the Aztecs added at the end of the year to complete it. **Días de gracia**, days of grace allowed for the payment of bills. **Buenos días**, good morning. **En cuatro días**, in a short time. **Hace buen día**, it's a fine day. **Parece que no pasan por ti los días**, you don't look a day older. **Un día de éstos**, one of these days. **Todos los días**, every day. **7 veces al día**, 7 times a day. **Poner al día**, to enter up, to write up. **Día festivo**, vacation. **Día libre**, free day, day off. **Día señalado**, special day.

diabetes [de-ah-bay'-tes], *f.* Diabetes, a disease whose chief symptom is the abundant excretion of sugar in the urine.

diabético, ca [de-ah-bay'-te-co, cah], *a.* Diabetic, relating to diabetes.

diabla (A la) [de-ah'-blah (ah'lah)], *adv.* Carelessly; rudely. *f.* 1. A machine for carding wool or cotton. **Cosido a la diabla**, bound in paper. 2. A truck.

diablazo [de-ah-blah'-tho], *m. aug.* A great devil.

diablear [de-ah-blay-ar'], *vn. (Coll.)* To commit deviltries, play pranks.

diablesa [de-ah-blay'-sah], *f. (Coll.)* A she-devil.

diablillo [de-ah-bleel'-lyo], *m.* 1. *(Dim.)* Deviling, devilkin, a little devil. 2. An acute, clever man.

diablo [de-ah'-blo], *m.* 1. Devil, Satan. **Ése es el diablo**, that's the devil of it. 2. Person of a perverse temper. 3. An ugly person. 4. A cunning, subtle person. **Ser la piel or de la piel del diablo**, to be a limb of the devil. **Pobre diablo**, poor devil. **Algún pobre diablo de cartero**, some poor devil of a postman.

diablotín, diabolín [de-ah-blo-teen', de-ah-bo-leen'], *m.* A sort of sweetmeat.

diablura [de-ah-bloo'-rah], *f.* A diabolical undertaking, devilishness, deviltry, mischief, wild prank.

diabólicamente [de-ah-bo'-le-cah-men-tay], *adv.* Diabolically, devilishly.

diabólico, ca [de-ah-bo'-le-co, cah], *a.* Diabolical, devilish.

diabrosis [de-ah-bro'-sis], *f.* Ulceration, erosion, corrosion.

diabrótico, ca [de-ah-bro'-te-co, cah], *a.* Corrosive, erosisve. -*m.* **Diabrótico**, a beetle destructive to vegetation.

diacasis [de-ah-blah'-sis], *m.* A purgative prepared from Cassia fistula (related to senna).

diacatalicón [de-ah-cah-tah-le-cone'], *m.* Diacatholicion, a universal medicine or purge.

diacitrón [de-ah-the-trone'], *m.* Lemon-peel preserved in sugar.

diaco [de-ah'-co], *a. & m.* A cleric of the order of Malta, who reached a chaplaincy only after twelve years of service.

diaconado [de-ah-co-nah'-do], *m. V.* DIACONATO.

diaconal [de-ah-co-nahl'], *a.* Diaconal.

diaconato [de-ah-co-nah'-to], *m.* Deanconship.

diaconía [de-ah-co-nee'-ah], *f.* Deaconry.

diaconisa [de-ah-co-nee'-sah], *f.* Deaconess.

diácono [de-ah'-co-no], *m.* Deacon, clergyman next in order below a priest.

diácope [de-ah'-co-pay], *m.* 1. *(Glam.)* Hyperbaton. 2. Incision, longitudinal fracture of a bone.

diacorético, ca [de-ah-co-ray'-te-co, cah], *a.* Having the property of producing evacuations.

diacrítico, ca [de-ah-cree'-te-co, cah], *a.* Diacritic, diacritical; distinguishing, diagnostic.

diacroción [de-ah-cro-the-on'], *m.* A collyrium prepared from saffron.

diacústica [de-ah-coos'-te-cah], *f.* Diacoustics, the doctrine of sounds.

diadelfia [de-ah-del'-fe-ah], *f.* A plant having the stamens united into two sets.

diadelfo, fa [de-ah-del'-fo, fah], *a.* Diadelphous, with stamens in two sets.

diadema [de-ah-day'-mah], *f.* l. Diadem, crown. 2. Crown, glory, a circle of metal put round the heads of images; represented in pictures by luminous circles.

diademado, da [de-ah-day-mah'-do, dah], *a. (Her.)* Diademed, adorned with a diadem.

diafanidad [de-ah-fah-ne-dahd'], *f.* Disphaneity, transparency, pellucidness.

diáfano, na [de-ah'-fah-no, nah], *a.* 1. Transparent, pellucid, clear, lucid, diaphanous. 2. *(Amer.)* Finical, timid, and affected.

diafiláctico, ca [de-ah-fe-lahc'-te-co, cah], *a. (Med.)* Prophylactic.

diaforesis [de-ah-fo-ray'-sis], *f.* Diaphoresis, gentle perspiration.

diaforético. ca [de-ah-fo-ray'-te-co, cah], *a. (Med.)* Diaphoretic.

diafragma [de-ah frahg'-mah], *m.* 1. Diaphragm, the midriff. 2. Cartilaginous partition of the nostrils. 3. A perforated disk used to cut off marginal rays in some optical instruments, or the vibrating disk of a telephone. 4. The porous cup of a voltaic cell.

diafragmático, ca [de-ah-frag-mah'-to-co, cah], *a.* Diaphragmatic, relating to the diaphragm.

diagnosis [de-ahg-no'-ses], *f.* Diagnosis.

diagnosticar [de-ag-nos-te-car'], *va.* To diagnosticate, form the diagnosis.

diagnóstico [de-ag-nos'-te-co], *m. & a. (Med.)* Diagnostic, a distinguishing symptom; diagnosis.

diagonal [de-ah-go-nahl'], *a.* Diagonal.

diagonalmente [de-ah-go-nal-men'-tay], *adv.* Diagonally.

diagráfica [de-ah-grah'-fe-cah], *f.* Sketch, design.

diagráfico, ca [de-ah-grah'-fe-co, cah], *a.* Diagraphic, showing by lines.

diagrafita [de-ah-grah-fee'-tah], *f.* Graphite, from which drawing-pencils are made.

diagrama [de-ah-grah'-mah], *f.* Diagram. **Diagrama de barras**, bar chart. **Diagrama circular** *(Comput.)*, pie chart. **Diagrama de Venn** *(Comput.)*, Venn diagram.

dialage [de-ah-lah'-hay], *m.* Diallage, the use of many arguments to prove one proposition.

dialéctica [de-ah-lec'-te-cah], *f.* Logic, dialectic.

dialéctico [de-ah-lec'-te-co], *m.* Dialectician, logician.

dialéctico, ca [de-ah-lec'-te-co, cah], *a.* Dialectical, logical.

dialecto [de-ah-lec'-to], *m.* Dialect, phraseology, speech.

diálisis [de-ah'-le-sis], *f.* Dialysis.

dialogal [de-ah-lo-gahl'], *a.* Relating to dialogue; written in dialogue.

dialogar [de-ah-lo-gar'], *vn.* 1. To speak a dialogue. 2. To sing responsively.

dialogismo [de-ah-lo-he-es'-mo], *m.* Dialogism.

dialogístico, ca [de-ah-lo-hees'-te-co, cah], *a.* Colloquial.

dialogizar [de-ah-lo-he-thar'], *vn.* To dialogize, to discourse in dialogue.

diálogo [de-ah'-lo-go], *m.* Dialogue.

dialoguista [de-ah-lo-gees'-tah], *m.* Dialogist.

diamantazo [de-ah-man-tah'-tho], *m. aug.* A large diamond.

diamante [de-ah-mahn'-tay], *m.* 1. Diamond. **Diamante en bruto**, uncut diamond. **Ser un diamante en bruto,** *(fig.)* To be a rough diamond. 2. Hardness, resistance.

diamantino, na [de-ah-man-tee'-no, nah], *a.* Adamantine, diamantine.

diamantista [de-ah-man-tees'-tah], *m. V.* LAPIDARIO.

diametral [de-ah-may-trahl'], *a.* Diametrical.

diametralmente [de-ah-may-tral-men'-tay], *adv.* Diametrically.

diámetro [de-ah'-may-tro], *m. (Geom.)* Diameter.

diana [de-ah'-nah], *f. (Mil.)* 1. Reveille, the beating of the drum at daybreak. 2. The moon.

dianche, diantre [de-ahn'-chay, de-ahn'-tray], *m. & int. (Coll.)* Deuce, the devil.

diantero [de-an-tay'-ro, rah], *a.* Having two anthers.

dianto, ta [de-ahn'-to, tah], *a.* Having two flowers, biflorous.

diapasón [de-ah-pah-so-ne'], *m.* 1. Diapason, an octave (from ancient Greek music). 2. A rule provided with scales of equal parts. 3. A tuning-fork, or the standard pitch given by the tuningfork. 4. Measure, compass.

diapente [de-ah-pen'-tay], *m. (Mus.)* A perfect fifth.

diapiema, diapiesis [de-ah-pe-ay'-mah, deah-peay'sis], *f.* Suppuration.

diapositiva [de-ah-po-se-tee'-vah], *f. (Phot.)* Plate, slide. **Diapositiva en color**, color slide.

diaprea [de-ah-pray-ah], *f.* Sort of round plum.

diaquea [de-ah-kay´-ah], *f.* A small fungus which grows on decayed wood.

diaquilón [de-ah-ke-lo-ne'], *m.* Lead plaster, diachylon.

diaria [de-ah'-re-ah], *f. (Naut.)* Supply of provisions and arms for a fortnight.

diariamente [de-ah-re-ah-men'-tay], *adv.* Daily.

diario, ria [de-ah'-re-o, ah], *a.* Daily.

diario, *m.* 1. Journal, diary; daily newspaper. **Diario dominical**, Sunday paper. 2. Diary, a daily account. **Nuestro mantel de diario**, our tablecloth for everyday. **Para diario**, for everyday use. 3. Daily expense. 4. Log. **Diario de navegación**, log-book.

diarista [de-ah-rees'-tah], *com.* Journalist.

diarrea [de-ar-ray'-ah], *f.* Diarrhoea.

diasfixia [de-as-feek'-se-ah], *f. (Med.)* Rapid pulse, palpitation of the heart.

diáspero, diaspro [de-ahs'-pay-ro, de-ahs'-pro], *m.* Jasper.

diastasia [de-as-tah'-se-ah], *f.* Diastase, a proximate principle discovered in cereals after germination.

diastema [de-as-tay'-mah], *m.* 1. Diasteme, name of pores scattered over the surface of bodies, which can be demonstrated only by the penetration of liquids. 2. *(Mus.)* A simple interval, in contrast to a complex. 3. Interspace between two consecutive teeth.

diástole [de-ahs'-to-lay], *m.* 1. *(Anat.)* Diastole, the dilatation of the heart. 2. *(Rhet.)* Diastole, a figure by which a short syllable is made long.

diastólico, ca [de-as-toh'-le-co, cah], *a.* Diastolic, relating to the diastole.

diatérmano, na [de-ah-terr'-mah-no, nah], *f.* Diathermanous, allowing free passage to rays of heat.

diatermia [de-ah-ter'-me-ah], *f.* Diathermy.

diatesarón [de-ah-tay-sah-ron'], *m.* 1. The harmony of the four Gospels. 2. *(Mus.)* Diatessaron, the interval of a fourth.

diatéstico, ca [de-ah-tay'-se-co, cah], *a. (Med.)* Diathetic, belonging to a diathesis.

diátesis [de-ah'-tay-sis], *f. (Med.)* Diathesis, organic disposition to contract certain diseases.

diatónico [de-ah-toh'-ne-co], *a. (Mus.)* Diatonic.

diatriba [de-ah-tree'-bah], *f.* Diatribe, a dissertation or discourse on polemic matters; a severe criticism on works of genius.

dibit [de-beet], *(Comput.)* Dibit.

dibujador, ra [de-boo-hah-dor', rah], *m. & f.* 1. Delineator. 2. Graver, a tool used in graving.

dibujante [de-boo-hahn'-tay], *m. & pa.* Designer, sketching. **Comerciante de publicidad**, commercial artist.

dibujar [de-boo-har'], *va.* 1. To draw, to design, to delineate, to sketch. 2. *(Met.)* To paint any passion of the mind. *-vr.* 1. To throw a shadow upon a surface. 2. To show, to appear. **El sufrimiento se dibuja en su cara**, suffering showed in his face.

dibujo [de-boo'-ho], *m.* 1. Design, drawing, sketch, draught. 2. Delineation, description. **Es un dibujo**, it is a picture (cara bonita). **Dibujos animados**, cartoon. **Un papel con dibujos a rayas**, a wallpaper with a stripped pattern.

dicacidad [de-ca-the-dahd'], *f.* 1. Pertness, sauciness, loquacity. 2. Jesting sarcasm.

dicaz [de-cath'], *a.* Keen, biting (said of speech).

dicción [dic-the-on'], *f.* Diction, style, language, expression.

diccionario [dic-the-o-nah'-re-o], *m.* Dictionary, lexicon. **Diccionario de bolsillo**, pocket dictionary.

dicha [dee'-chah], *f.* Happiness, felicity, fortune, good luck, good fortune. **Por dicha** or **a dicha**, by chance. **Para completar su dicha**, to complete her happiness.

dicharacho [de-chah-rah'-cho], *m. (Coll.)* A vulgar, low, or indecent expression.

dichido, dichito [de-chee'-do, de-chee'-to], *m. (Coll.)* A sharp or pert expression, small talk.

dicho [dee'-cho], *m.* 1. Saying, expression, sentence. 2. Declaration, deposition. 3. Promise of marriage. **Dicho y hecho**, no sooner said than done. **Del dicho al hecho hay gran trecho,** (prov.) saying and doing are two very different things. **Es un dicho**, it´s just a saying. *-a.* Said. **Dichos animales**, the said animals. **En dicho país**, in this country. —**Dicho, cha**, *pp. irr.* of DECIR.

dichosamente [de-cho-sah-men-tay], *adv.* Happily, fortunately, luckily.

dichoso, sa [de-cho'-so, sah], *a.* Happy, fortunate, prosperous, successful, lucky. **Hacer dichoso a uno**, to make somebody happy. **Me siento dichoso de**, I feel happy to.

diciembre [de-the-em'-bray], *m.* December.

diciente [de-the-en'-tay], *pa.* of DECIR. Saying, talking.

dicotiledón, dicotiledóneo, a [de-co-te-lay-done'], *a. (Bot.)* Dicotyledonous, having two seedleaves.

dicotomal [de-co-to-mahl'], *a.* Dichotomal.

dicotomía [de-co-to-mee'-ah], *f.* 1. State of the moon when the sun illuminates no more than half its disk. 2. The angle formed by two dichotomous branches.

dicotómico, ca or **dicótomo, ma** [de-co-to'-me-co], *a. (Bot.)* Subdividing into two; dichotomous. *(Astr.)* Halflighted (Moon, Venus y Mercury).

dicroismo [de-cro-ees'-mo], *m.* Dichroism, the property of showing different colors when viewed in different directions.

dicrónico, ca [de-cro'-ne-co, cah], *a.* Having two epochs or seasons in vegetation.

dicroto, ta [de-cro'-to, tah], *a. (Med.)* Dicrotic, dicrotous, showing two beats to each systole.

dictado [dic-tah'-do], *m.* 1. A title of dignity or honor. **Dictado, da**, *pp.* of DICTAR. 2. Dictation. **Escribir al dictado**, to take dictation.

dictador [dic-tah-dor'], *m.* Dictator, an ancient magistrate of Rome, invested with absolute authority.

dictadura [dic-tah-doo'-rah], *f.* Dictatorship, dictature.

dictáfono [dic-tah'-fo-no], *m.* Dictaphone, dictating machine.

dictamen [dic-tah'-men], *m.* 1. Opinion, sentiments, notion, judgment, mind. 2. Suggestion, insinuation, dictate.

dictaminar [dic-tah-me-nar'], *va.* To pass (sentencia). *-vn.* To pass judgement, to give an opinion.

díctamo [deec'-tah-mo], *m. (Bot.)* Dittany. **Díctamo blanco** or **real**, white flaxinella. **Díctamo crético**, dittany of Crete, marjoram. **Díctamo bastardo**, shrubby white horehound.

dictar [dic-tar'], *va.* 1. To dictate, to deliver one´s opinions with authority. **Lo que dicta el sentido común**, what common sense suggests. 2. To dictate, to pronounce what another is to say or write.

dictatorio, ria [dic-tah-to'-re-o, ah], *a.* Dictatorial.

dicterio [dic-tay'reo], *m.* Sarcasm, taunt, keen reproach, insult.

didáctica [de-dahc'-te-cah], *a.* The art of teaching, pedagogy.

didáctico, ca, didascálico, ca [de-dahc'-te-co, cah, de-das-cah'-le-co, cah], *a.* Didactic, didactical, preceptive, giving precepts.

didascalia [de-das-cah'-le-ah], *f.* Pedagogy, the science and rules of teaching.

didelfo [de-del'-fo], *m.* The opossum.

didínamo, ma [de-dee'-nah-mo, mah], *a.* Didynamous: said of stamens arranged in two pairs of different sizes.

diecinueve [de-ay-the-noo-ay'-vay], *a.* & *m.* Nineteen.

diecinueveavo, va [de-ay-the-noo-ay-vay-ah'-vo, vah], *a.* Nineteenth.

dieciochavo, va [de-ay-the-o-chah´-vo, vah], *a.* & *m.* 1. An eighteenth part. 2. *(Typ.)* 18°, octodécimo, a sheet folding into 18 parts, or 36 pages.

dieciocheno, na [de-ay-the-o-chay'-no, nah], *a.* & *m.* 1. Eighteenth 2. A kind of cloth.

dieciséis [de-ay-the-say'-es], *a.* Sixteen; sixteenth.

diecisiete [de-ay-the-se-ay'-tay], *a.* Seventeen; seventeenth.

dieciseisavo [de-ay-the-say-es-ah'-vo], *m.* Décimo-sexto: applied to a book printed on a sheet folded into 16 leaves.

dieciseiseno, na [de-ay-the-say-es-ay'-no, nah], *a.* Sixteenth.

diecisieteavo, va [de-ay-the-se-ay-tay-ah'-vo, vah], *a.* Seventeenth.

diedro, dra [de-ay'-dro, drah], *a.* Dihedral, formed by or having two plane faces, as a dihedral angle.

diente [de-ayn'-tay], *m.* 1. Tooth. 2. Prop used by founders to secure the founding-frame. 3. Fang or tusk of wild boars. **Diente molar,** *V.* MUELA. **Diente incisivo,** incisor, foretooth. 4. Jag, a protuberance or denticulation. **Diente de lobo,** burnisher, a burnishing or polishing instrument. **Dientes de elefante,** elephant's tusks. **Dientes de jabalí,** wild boar's teeth. **Dientes postizos,** artificial teeth. **Diente de perro,** sampler, a piece worked by young girls. **Diente de león,** *(Bot.)* dandelion or lion's tooth. **Diente de perro,** *(Bot.)* dog's tooth violet. *-pl.* 1. The indented edges of different instruments, jags. 2. The prominent parts of wheels. **Dientes de ajo,** cloves of garlic. **Crujir de dientes,** to grind the teeth. **Tomar a uno entre dientes,** to have an antipathy against a person. **Pelear hasta con los dientes,** *(Coll.)* to fight tooth and nail. **Hablar** or **decir entre dientes,** to mumble, to mutter. **Hincar el diente,** to appropriate property to oneself. *(Coll.)* To censure, to grumble at. **Mostrar los dientes,** to oppose a person, to growl at him, to show spunk. **Diente de leche,** milk tooth.

dientecico, illo, ito [de-en-tay-thee´-co, theel'-lyo, ee'-to], *m. dim.* Little tooth.

diéresis [de-ay'-ray-sis], *f.* 1. *(Rhet.)* Diaeresis, poetical figure. 2. The two points placed over a vowel to show that it does not form a diphthong with the following vowel, as flu *argüir.*

diesel [de-ay'-sayl], **Motor diesel,** diesel engine.

diesi [de-ay'-se], *f. (Mus.)* The smallest and simplest part into which a tone is divided.

diestra [de-es'-trah], *f.* 1. The right hand. 2. *(Met.)* Favor, support, protection. **Juntar diestra con diestra,** To shake hands, to make up matters.

diestramente [de-es-trah-men-tay], *adv.* Dexterously, cleverly, neatly.

diestro, tra [de-es-tro, trah], *a.* 1. Right, dexter. 2. Dexterous, skillful, handy. 3. Sagacious, prudent, knowing, learned. 4. Sly, artful, cunning. 5. Favorable, propitious. **A diestro y siniestro,** right or wrong. **Llevar del diestro,** to lead a beast by the helter or bridle. **Repartir golpes a diestro y siniestro,** to lash out wildy.

diestro [de-es-tro], *m.* 1. A skilful fencer. 2. Halter or bridle for horses.

dieta [de-ay'-tah], *f.* 1. Diet, regimen, food regulated by the rules of medicine. **Dieta láctea,** milk diet. 2. Diet, the assembly of the ministers of the states of Germany. 3. *(Law.)*

One day's journey of ten leagues by land. 4. Daily salary of judges and other officers of the law. **Dietas,** *(Naut.)* cattle put on board a fleet, to furnish fresh provisions for the sick.

dietética [de-ay-tay'-te-cah], *f.* Dietetics, that branch of hygiene which treats of diet.

dietético, ca [de-ay-tay'-te-co, cah], *a.* Dietetic, dietetical.

diéxodo [de-ek'-so-do], *m.* Every secretory passage; emunctory, some use this term as synonymous of dejection, evacuation.

diez [de-eth'], *m.* Ten. **Las diez,** ten oclock.

diezma [de-eth'-mah], *f. (Prov.) V.* DÉCIMA and DIEZMO.

diezmador [de-eth-mah-dor'], *m. (Prov.) V.* DIEZMERO.

diezmal [de-eth-mahl'], *a.* Decimal tenth.

diezmar [de-eth-mar'], *va.* 1. To decimate, to take the tenth, to tithe. 2. To tithe, to pay the tithe to the church. 3. *(Mil.)* When there are many offenders, to punish one in ten.

diezmero [de-eth-may´-ro], *m.* 1. He who pays the tithe. 2. Tither, he who gathers the tithe.

diezmesino, na [de-eth-may-see'-no, nah], *a.* That which is ten months, or belongs to that tine.

diezmo [de-eth'-mo], *m.* 1. Tithe, the tenth part. 2. Duty of ten per cent paid to the king. 3. Tithe, the tenth part of the fruits of the earth assigned to the maintenance of the clergy. 4. Decimation.

difamación [de-fah-mah-the-on'], *f.* Defamation, libelling.

difamador [de-fah-mah-dor'], *m.* Defamer, libeller.

difamar [de-fah-mar'], *va.* To defame, to discredit; to libel. To divulge.

difamatorio, ria [de-fah-mah-to'-re-o, ah], *a.* Defamatory, scandalous, calumnious, contumelious, libellous.

difarreación [de-far-ray-ah-the-on'], *f.* Diffarreation, the parting of a cake, a sacrifice performed between man and wife at their divorce, among the Romans.

diferencia [defay-ren'-the-ah], *f.* 1. Difference. 2. Dissimilarity, dissimilitude. 3. Controversy, contrariety, mutual opposition. **A diferencia,** with the difference. **Diferencia de edades,** difference in ages. **Hacer diferencia entre,** to make a distinction between. **Partir la diferencia,** to split the difference.

diferencial [de-fay-ren-the-ahl´], *a.* Differential, different. **Cálculo diferencial,** differential calculus. *-m. (Mech.)* Differential, differential gear. *-f. (Math.)* Differential.

diferenciar [de-fay-ren-the-ar'], *va.* 1. To differ, to make different, to differentiate. 2. To change or alter the use or destination of things. *-vn.* To differ, to dissent, to disagree in opinion. *-vr.* 1. To differ, to be distinguished from. 2. To distinguish oneself. **No se diferencian en nada,** they do not differ at all. **Se diferencian en que...,** they differ in that...

diferente [de-fay-ren'-tay], *a.* Different, dissimilar, unlike. **Por diferentes razones,** for various reasons.

diferentemente [de-fay-ren-tay-men'-tay], *adv.* Differently, diversely.

diferido [de-fay-re-do], *a.* **Emisión diferida, emisión en diferido,** recorded program.

diferir [de-fay-reer'], *va.* To defer, to delay, to put off. **Diferir algo para otro tiempo,** to defer anything to another time. *-vn.* 1. To differ, to be different. 2. *(Naut.)* To remove the gaskets of a sail.

difícil [de-fee'-theel], *a.* 1. Difficult, arduous, hard, laborious. **Difícil de vencer,** hard to beat. **Creo que lo tiene difícil,** I think he´s got a tough job on. **Es un hombre difícil,** he is a difficult man. 2. Unlikely. **Es difícil que...,** it is unlikely that.... 3. Odd, ugly (cara).

difícilmente [de-fee'-theel-men-tay], *adv.* Difficultly, hardly.

dificultad [de-fe-cool-tahd'], *f.* 1. Difficulty, embarrassment, hardness. 2. Difficulty, objection, adverse argument. **Sin dificultad alguna,** without the least difficulty. **Ha tenido dificultades con la policía,** he´s been in trouble with the police. **Poner dificultades,** to raise objections.

dificultador [de-fe-cool-tah-dor'], *m.* One who starts or raises difficulties.

dificultar [de-fe-cool-tar'], *va.* 1. To start or raise difficulties. 2. To render difficult.

dificultosamente [de-fe-cool-to-sah-men'-tay], *adv.* Difficultly.

dificultoso, sa [de-fe-cool-to-so, sah], *a.* 1. Difficult, hard, troublesome, tiresome, laborious, painful. 2. Ugly, deformed: applied to the face.

difidación [de-fe-dah-the-on'], *f.* Manifesto, a declaration issued in justification of a war.

difidencia [de-fe-den'-the-ah], *f.* Distrust, doubtfulness.

difidente [de-fe-den'-tay], *a.* Disloyal, distrustful.

difluir [de-floo-eer'], *vn.* To be diffused, to spread out, to be shed.

difracción [de-frac-the-on'], *f.* Diffraction.

difractar [de-frac-tar'], *va.* To diffract a ray of light.

difractivo, va [de-frac-tee'-vo, vah], *a.* Diffractive, causing diffraction.

difrige [de-free'-hay], *m.* Dross of melted copper, gathered in the furnace.

difteria [dif-tay'-reah], *f.* Diphteria, a disease characterized by the formation of false membranes.

diftérico, ca [dif-tay'-re-co, cah], *a.* Diphtheritic, belonging to diphtheria.

difugio [de-foo'-he-o], *m.* V. EFUGIO.

difuminado [de-foo-me-nah'-do], *a.* Slurred, husky (voz).

difuminar [de-foo-me-nahr'], *va.* To blur. -*vr.* 1. To shade into. 2. *(Fig.)* To fade away.

difumino [de-foo-mee'-no], *m.* V. ESFUMINO.

difundido, da [de-foon-dee'-no, nah], *a. & pp.* of DIFUNDIR. Diffuse, diffused, scattered.

difundir [de-foon-deer'], *va.* 1. To diffuse, to extend, to outspread. **Difundir la alegría,** to spread happiness. 2. *(Met.)* To divulge, to publish. -*vr.* To spread; to become diffused.

difunto, ta [de-foon'-to, tah], *a.* 1. Defunct, dead; late. **El difunto ministro,** the late minister. 2. *(Met.)* Decayed, withered. **Día de los difuntos,** all-souls' Day, celebrated on Nov. 2nd by the Roman church. Instituted in 998. -*m.* V. CADÁVER.

difusamente [de-foo-sah-men'-tay], *adv.* Diffusely, diffusedly.

difusible [de-foo-see'-blay], *a.* Diffusible, of rapid diffusion.

difusión [de-foo-se-on'], *f.* 1. Diffusion, diffusiveness, dispersion. 2. *(Met.)* Diffusion, copiousness or exuberance of style.

difusivo, va [de-foo-see'-vo, vah], *a.* Diffusive.

difuso, sa [de-foo'-so, sah], *a.* Diffuse, diffusive, copious, ample, wide-spread.

digástrico, ca [de-gahs'-tre-co, cah], *a.* Digastric, of two muscular bands.

digerible [de-hay-ree'-blay], *a.* Digestible.

digerir [de-hay-reer'], *va.* 1. To digest. 2. *(Met.)* To bear with patience any loss or affront. 3. *(Met.)* To examine carefully into a thing. 4. *(Met.)* To digest, to adjust, to arrange methodically in the mind. **No puedo digerir a ese tío,** I can't stand that chap. 5. *(Them.)* To digest, to soften by heat, as in a boiler.

digestible [de-hes-tee'-blay], *a.* Digestible.

digestión [de-hes-te-on'], *f.* 1. Digestion. 2. Digestion, preparation of matter by chemical heat. **Hombre de mala digestión,** a man of a peevish, fretful temper. **Negocio de mala digestión,** a perplexed affair.

digestivo [de-hes-tee'-vo], *m.* *(Surg.)* Digestive, an application which disposes a wound to generate matter.

digestivo, va [de-hes-tee'-vo, vah], *a.* Digestive, assisting digestion.

digesto [de-hes'-to], *m.* Digest.

digino, na [de-hee'-no, nah], *a.* Digynous, having two pistils.

digitación [de-he-tah-the-on'], *f.* The art which teaches the use of the fingers upon some instrument.

digitado, da [de-he-tah'-do, dah], *a.* Digitate, arranged like fingers. *(Bot. and Zool.)*

digital [de-ne-tahl'], *a.* Digital, belonging to or like fingers. **Huellas digitales,** fingerprints. -*f.* Digitalis, foxglove, a medicinal plant.

digitalina [de-he-tah-lee'-nah], *f.* Digitalin, a poisonous alkaloid procured from digitalis.

digitígrado, da [de-he-tee'-grah-do, dah], *a.* Digitigrade, walking on the toes; opposed to plantigrade.

dígito [dee'-he-to], *m.* *(Ast.)* Digit, the twelfth part of the diameter of the sun or moon.

dignación [dig-nah-the-on'], *f.* Condescension, voluntary humiliation.

dignamente [dig-nah-men'-tay], *adv.* 1. Worthily; fittingly, properly, appropriately. 2. Honorably. 3. With dignity. 4. Decently.

dignarse [dig-nar'-say], *vr.* To condescend, to deign, to vouchsafe.

dignatario [dig-nah-tah'-re-o], *m.* A dignitary, one who holds high rank, especially ecclesiastical.

dignidad [dig-ne-dahd'], *f.* 1. Dignity, rank, honor, greatness. **Herir la dignidad de uno,** to offend somebody's self-respect. 2. Dignity, grandeur of mien, nobleness. 3. Dignity, advancement, high place. 4. Among ecclesiastics, the prebend of a cathedral superior to a simple canonry, and the dignitary who possesses it. 5. The dignity of an archbishop or bishop. 6. *(Astrol.)* Dignity, the state of a planet being in any sign.

dignificante [dig-ne-fe-cahn'-tay], *pa.* *(Theol.)* Dignifying, that which dignifies.

dignificar [dig-ne-fe-car'], *va.* To dignify.

digno, na [deeg'-no, nah], *a.* 1. Meritorious, worthy, deserving. **Digno de,** worthy of. **Digno de mención,** worth a mention. 2. Condign, suitable, correspondent. **Digno de alabanza,** worthy to be praised. **Es digno,** it is worthwhile.

digresión [de-gray-se-on'], *f.* 1. Digression, deviation from the main scope of a speech or treatise. 2. *(Astr.)* Departure of a planet from the equinoctial line.

digresivamente [de-gray-se'-vah-men-tay], *adv.* Digressively.

digresivo, va [de-gray-see'-vo, vah], *a.* Digressive.

dije (or **dij**) [dee'-hay], *m.* 1. A trinket put upon a child. 2. *pl.* Trinkets relics, used for personal adornment. **Dije,** 1st pers. sing. past tense, of **decir:** I said.

dilaceración [de-lah-thay-rah-the-on'], *f.* Dilaceration.

dilacerar [de-lah-thay-rar'], *va.* To dilacerate, to tear.

dilación [de-lah-theon'], *f.* 1. Delay, dilation, procrastination. 2. Dilatation, expansion.

dilapidación [de-lah-pe-dah-the-on'], *f.* Dilapidation.

dilapidador [de-lah-pe-dah-dor'], *m.* Dilapidator.

dilapidar [de-lah-pe-dar'], *va.* To dilapidate, to waste.

dilatable [de-lah-tah'-blay], *a.* Dilatable.

dilatación [de-lah-tah-the-on'], *f.* 1. Dilatation, extension, amplification. 2. Evenness, greatness of mind, calmness.

dilatadamente [de-lah-tah-dah-men'-tay], *adv.* With dilatation.

dilatado, da [de-lah-tah'-do, dah], *a. & pp.* of DILATAR. 1. Large, numerous, great. 2. Prolix, long, not concise. 3. Spacious, extensive, vast.

dilatador, ra [de-lah-tah-dor', rah]. *m. & f.* 1. One who dilates or extends. 2. Dilator, an instrument for stretching.

dilatar [de-lah-tar'], *va.* 1. To dilate, to expand, to enlarge, to lengthen, to spread out. 2. To defer, to retard to delay, to put off, to protract. 3. *(Met.)* To comfort, to cheer up. -*vr.* To expatiate or enlarge on any subject. **El valle se dilata en aquella parte,** the valley widens at that point.

dilatativo, va [de-lah-tah-tee'-vo, vah], *a.* That which dilates.

dilatoria [de-lah-to'-re-ah], *f.* V. DILACIÓN. A term given by a court of judge to a debtor. **Andar con dilatorias,** to waste time by deceiving with false promises.

dilatorio, ria [de-lah-to'-re-o, ah], *a.* Dilatory, delaying, long.

dilección [de-lec-the-on'], *f.* Love, affection.

dilecto, ta [de-lec'-to, tah], *a.* Loved beloved.

dilema [de-lay'-mah], _m._ Dilemma, an argument equally conclusive by contrary suppositions. **Estar en un dilema,** to be in a dilemma.

dilemático, ca [de-lay-mah'-te-co, cah], _a._ Belonging to a dilemma, dilemmatic.

diligencia [de-le-hen'-the-ah], _f._ 1. Diligence, assiduity, laboriousness. 2. Haste, hastiness, speed, diligence, activity, briskness in the performance of a thing. 3. _(Coll.)_ Affair, business, something to be transacted, obligation. **Tengo que ir a una diligencia,** I must go upon some business. **Hacer diligencias,** to do business. 4. Return of a writ, judicial formalties procedure. **Hacer las diligencias de cristiano,** to perform the duty of a Christian. **Hacer diligencia,** to try, to endeavor. 5. Stage-coach, diligence.

diligenciar [de-le-hen-the-ar'], _va._ To exert oneself; to endeavor.

diligenciero [de-le-hen-the-ay'-ro], _m._ 1. Agent, attorney. 2. Apparitor, summoner; the lowest officer of an ecclesiastical court.

diligente [de-le-hen'-tay], _a._ 1. Diligent, assiduous, careful, laborious, active. 2. Prompt, swift, ready. **Diligente en aprender,** diligent to learn.

diligentemente [de-le-hen'-tay-men-tay], _adv._ Diligently, assiduously.

dilíndilín [de-leen'-de-leen'], _m._ The sound of a bell; ding-dong. (Imitative.)

dilogía [de-lo-hee'-ah], _f._ 1. Ambiguity, double sense. 2. Drama with two actions at once.

dilucidación [de-loo-the-dah-the-on'], _f._ Elucidation, explanation, illustration.

dilucidador [de-loo-the-dah-dor'], _m._ Elucidator.

dilucidar [de-loo-the-dar'], _va._ To elucidate, to explain.

dilucidario [de-loo-the-dah'-re-o], _m._ Explanatory writing.

dilución [de-loo-the-on'], _f._ Dilution, solution.

diluente [de-loo-en'-tay], _pa._ Diluent.

diluición [de-loo-e-the-on'], _va._ Dilution.

diluido [de-loo-e'-do], _a._ Dilute; diluted, weak; watered-down.

diluir [de-loo-eer'], _va._ To dilute anything.

diluviano [de-loo-ve-ah'-no], _a._ Diluvian, relating to the deluge.

diluviar [de-loo've-ar'], _vn. imp._ To rain like a deluge.

diluvio [de-loo'-ve-o], _m._ 1. Deluge overflow, inundation, flood. 2. _(Met.)_ Vast abundance.

dimanación [de-mah-nah-the-on'], _f._ Act of springing or issuing from, origin.

dimanante [de-mah-nahn'-tay], _pa._ Springing or proceeding from, originating.

dimanar [de-mah-nar'], _vn._ To spring or proceed from; to originate, to flow. **Dimanar de,** to originate from.

dimensión [de-men-se-on'], _f._ 1. Dimension, extent, capacity, bulk. **De grandes dimensiones,** of great size. 2. _(Mus.)_ Compass, range. 3. _(Math.)_ Either of the three geometrical properties, length, breadth, and depth. 4. Power, or grade of an equation. 5. Quaintity which enters as a factor of an algebraic expression.

dimensional [de-men-se-o-nahl'], _a_ Belonging to the dimension.

dimes [dee'-mes], _m. pl._ **Andar en dimes y diretes,** to use _ifs_ and _buts,_ or quibbles and quirks; to contend, to use altercations.

dimidiar [de-me-de-ar'], _va._ To dimidiate, to divide into halves. _V._ DEMEDIAR.

diminución [de-me-noo-the-on'], _f._ 1. Diminution, losing; exhaustion. 2. Contraction of the diameter of a column as it ascends. **Ir en diminución,** 1. To grow tapering to the top. 2. _(Met.)_ To be losing one's character or credit.

diminuir [de-me-noo-eer'], _va._ To diminish. _V._ DISMINUIR.

diminutamente [de-me-noo-te-vah-men-tay], _adv._ 1. Diminutively. 2. Minutely, by retail.

diminutivo, va [de-me-noo-tee'-vo vah], _a._ Diminutive. -_m._ A noun which decreases the meaning of the primitive.

diminuto, ta [de-me-noo'-to, tah], _a._ Defective, faulty; tiny, minute.

dimisión [de-me-se-on'], _f._ Resignation, the act of resigning a place, employment, or commission. **Hacer dimisión de su empleo,** to resign one's place or employment.

dimisorias [de-me-so'-re-as], _f. pl._ Dimissory letters, given by the bishop to a candidate for holy orders that he may be lawfully ordained. **Dar dimisorias,** _(Coll.)_ to dismiss anyone, driving him away ungraciously. **Llevar dimsorias,** to get dismissed, to get packed off.

dímite [dee'-me-tay], _m._ Dimity. _V._ COTONÍA.

dimitir [de-me-teer'], _va._ 1. To give up, to relinquish, to resign, to abdicate. **Dimitir la jefatura del partido,** to resign the party leadership. 2. To dismiss, to sack.

dimoño [de-mo'-nyo], _m._ _(Coll.)_ Demon. _V._ DEMONIO.

dimorfismo [de-mor-fees'-mo], _m._ Dimorphism, two different crystallizations.

dina [dee'-nah], _f._ _(Phys.)_ Dyne.

dinamarques, sa [de-nah-mar-kes', sah], _a._ Dane, Danish.

dinamia [de-nah'-me-ah], _f._ 1. Dynam, a foot-pound; a unit of effective force. 2. _(Med.)_ Dynamia, vigor, robustness.

dinámica [de-nah'-me-cah], _f._ Dynamics, the science of moving powers.

dinámico, ca [de-nah'-me-co, cah], _a._ Dynamic.

dinamita [de-nah-mee'-tah], _f._ Dynamite; nitroglycerine combined with inert matter, a terrific explosive.

dinamo [de-nah'-mo], _m._ A dynamo-electric machine; a dynamo.

dinamómetro [de-nah-mo'-me-tro], _m._ Dynamometer, an instrument for measuring force exerted or power expended.

dinastía [de-nas-tee'-ah], _f._ Dynasty, sovereignty, race or family of rulers; time of their rule.

dinerada [de-nay-rah'-dah], _f._ _(Coll.)_ A large sum of money.

dineral [de-nay-rahl'], _m._ 1. A large sum of money. **Habrá costado un dineral,** it must have cost a fortune. 2. Weight used by assayers to fix the purity of precious metals; a gold **dineral** is divided into 24 _quilates_ or carats, each of which is 4 grains, a silver **dineral** is divided into 12 _dineros_ of 24 grains each.

dinerillo [de-nay-reel'-lyo], _m._ _(Coll.)_ A round sum of money.

dinero [de-nay'-ro], _m._ 1. Money. 2. An ancient Spanish copper coin. 3. Standard of silver, the twelfth of a dineral, penny-weight. **Dinero llama dinero,** money gets money. **Tener dinero,** to be rich. **Por el dinero baila** or **salta el perro,** _(Prov.)_ Money makes the mare go. **Dinero contante,** cash. **El dinero lo puede todo,** money can do anything. **Andar mal de dinero,** to be badly off. **El negocio no da dinero,** the business does not pay.

dineroso, sa [de-nay-ro-so, sah], _a._ Moneyed, rich.

dineruelo [de-nay-roo-ay'-lo], _m. dim._ Small coin.

dinosaurio, or **dinosauro** [de-no-sah'-oo-re-o], _m._ Dinosaur, a fossil reptile, or reptile of enormous size.

dinoterio [de-no-tay'-re-o], _m._ Dinotherium, a gigantic mammal of the miocene epoch.

dintel [din-tel'], _m._ Lintel, part of a doorframe.

dintelar [din-tay-lar'], _va._ To make lintels.

dintorno [din-tor'-no], _m._ _(Art.)_ Delineation of the parts of a figure contained within the contour.

diocesano, na [de-o-thay-sah'-no, nah], _a._ Diocesan.

diocesano [de-o-thay-sah'-no], _m._ Diocesan, a bishop as he stands related to his own clergy or flock.

diócesi, diócesis [de-o'-thay-se, de-o'-thay-sis], _f._ Diocese, the circuit of a bishop's jurisdiction.

diodo [de-o-do], _m._ _(Comput.)_ Diode. **Diodo emisor luz,** light emitting diode.

diodón [de-o-don'], _m._ Sea-urchin.

dióico, ca [de-o'-e-co, cah], _a._ 1. Dicecious, plants whose reproductive organs are borne upon different individuals. 2. Similarly applied to cephalopod mollusks.

diónea [de-o'-nay-ah], _f._ Dioaena, the Venus's flytrap of North Carolina.

dionisia [de-o-nee'-se-ah], *f.* Blood stone, a black stone, variegated with red spots; hematites.

dióptrica [de-op'-tre-cah], *f.* Dioptrics.

dióptrico, ca [de-op'-tre-co, cah], *a* Dioptric.

diorama [de-o-rah'-mah], *m.* Diorama, an optical contrivance consisting of a series of views placed vertically, in which by means of arranged lights, objects are seen of natural size and distance without lenses.

diorámico, ca [de-o-rah'-me-co, cah], *a.* Dioramic, relating to a diorama.

diorita [de-o-ree'-tah], *f.* Diorite, a crystalline plutonic rock, very esteemed by the ancient Egyptians.

Dios [de-os'], *m.* 1. God, the Supreme Being. 2. God, a false god, an idol. 3. *(Met.)* God, any person or thing passionately beloved or adored. **A Dios** or **anda con Dios**, farewell, adieu. **Después de Dios**, under God. **Vaya usted con Dios**, farewell, God be with you. **Dios dará**, God will provide: used to stimulate alms-giving. **Oh, santo Dios**, oh, gracious God. **Por Dios**, for God's sake. **No lo quiera Dios**, God forbid. **Quiera Dios**, please God. **Sea como Dios quiera**, God's will be done. **Dios los cría y ellos se juntan**, birds of a feather flock together. **Dios lo quiera** or **lo haga**, God grant. **Mediante Dios**, God willing. **¡Válgame Dios!**, bless me!, **¡Válgate Dios!**, God preserve you or bless you. **A Dios rogando y con el mazo dando**, trust in God but keep your powder dry. **Vaya con Dios**, goodbye.

diosa [de-o'-sah], *f.* Goddess.

diosecillo, diosecito [de-o-say-theel'-lyo, de-o-say-thee'-to], *m. dim.* A godling, a little divinity.

diosecita [de-o-say-thee'-tah], *f. dim.* A little goddess.

diostedé [de-os-tay-day'], *m. (Amer.)* A bird of the toucan family whose note sounds like *¡Dios te dé!* it abounds in Venezuela, Peru, etc.

dióxido (or **bioxido**) **de carbono** [de-oc'-se-do, be-oc'-se-do day car-bo'-no], *m.* Carbon dioxide

dipétalo, la [de-pay-tah-lo, lah], *a.* Dipetalous, having two petals.

diplaco [de-plah'-co], *m.* A scrophulariaceous plant from California, highly esteemed in the gardens of Europe for the beauty of its flowers.

diplejia espástica [de-play'-he-ah es-pahs'-te-ca], *f.* Cerebral palsy.

diploe [de-plo'-ay], *m.* Diploe.

diploma [de-plo'-mah], *m.* 1. Diploma, patent, license. 2. *(Chem.)* A double-walled vessel in which water is put, and can replace the waterbath.

diplomacia [de-plo-may-the-ah], *f.* 1. Diplomacy, the management of international relations. 2. *(Coll.)* Simulated and interested courtesy.

diplomado, da [de-plo-mah'-do], *a. m & f.* Qualified, trained, having a diploma.

diplomarse [de-plo-mar'-say], *vr.* To graduate, to obtain a diploma.

diplomática [de-plo-mah'-te-cah], *f.* Diplomatics, the science of diplomas, or of ancient writings, literary and public documents, etc., especially concerned with their authenticity.

diplomáticamente [de-plo-mah'-te-cah-men-tay], *a.* Diplomatically.

diplomático, ca [de-plo-math'-te-co, cah], *a.* 1. Diplomatic, relating; to diplomas. 2. Diplomatical. -*m.* 3. Diplomatist.

diplónomo, ma [de-plo'-no-mo, mah], *a.* Obeying two laws simultaneously.

diplóstomo [de-plos'-to-mo], *m.* A worm found in the eyes of certain fishes, but more often among the whales.

dípneo, nea, dipneumóneo, nea [deep'-na-yo, ah, dip-na-yoo-mo'-nay-o, ah], *a.* Having two lungs.

dípodo, da [dee'-po-do, dah], *a.* Dipodous, biped, having two (hind) feet.

diprósopo, pa [de-pro'-so-po, pah], *a.* A term applied to fishes having both eyes on the same side.

dipsaca [dip-sah'-cah], *f. (Bot.)* Teasel. *V.* CONDENCHA.

dipsas [deep'-sas], *m.* Serpent whose bite is said to produce great thirst.

díptero, ra [deep'-tay-ro, rah], *a.* 1. *(Arch.)* Having two wings, or a double colonnade. 2. *(Entom.)* Dipterous, two winged. -*m. pl.* The diptera, two-winged insects, embracing the host of flies, mosquitoes, midges, etc.

dipterólogo [dip-tay-ro'-lo-go], *m.* Dipserologist, a naturalist who devotes himself to the study of the diptera.

díptica [deep'-te-cah], *f.* Diptych, register of bishops and martyrs.

díptico [deep'-te-co], *m. V.* DÍPTICA.

diptongar [dip-ton-gar'], *va.* 1. To unite two vowels. 2. *(Met.)* To combine two or more things so as to form one whole.

diptongo [dip-ton'-go], *m.* Diphthong.

diputación [de-poo-tah-the-on'], *f.* 1. Deputation, the act of deputing on a special commission. 2. Deputation, the body of persons deputed; committee. 3. The object of a deputation. **Diputación permanente**, standing committee. **Diputación provincial**, county council.

diputado [de-poo-tah'-do], *m.* 1. Deputy, one appointed or elected to act for another, a representative, delegate. **Diputado a Cortes**, parliamentary deputy. 2. *(Com.)* Assignee. **Diputado, da**, *pp.* of DIPUTAR.

diputar [de-poo-tar'], *va.* 1. To depute, to commission, to constitute. 2. To depute, to empower one to act for another.

dique [dee'-kay], *m.* 1. Dike, dam. 2. Dock. **Dique de carena** or **dique seco**, dry dock. **Dique flotante**, floating dock.

dirección [de-rec-the-on'], *f.* 1. Direction, guiding or directing; tendency of motion. 2. Guidance, direction, administration. 3. Direction, order, command, prescription. 4. The board of directors appointed to supervise the management of some business or organization. **De dos direcciones**, two-way. **Dirección de viento**, wind direction. **Dirección prohibida**, no entry. **Calle de dirección obligatoria**, one-way street. **Cambiar de calle**, to change direction. **Bajo la dirección de**, under the direction of. **Me han confiado la dirección de la obra**, I have been put in charge of the work. **Dirección asistida**, power steering. **Dirección General de Turismo**, State Tourist Office. **Dirección de memoria**, *(Comput.)* memory adress.

directamente [de-rec-the-on'], *adv.* Directly.

directamento [de-rec-tah-men'-tay], *adv.* Directly, rectilineally.

directiva [de-rec-tee'-vah], *f.* 1. Governing body; management. 2. Directive.

directivo, va [de-rec-tee'-vo, vah], *a.* Managing, governing. -*m.* Manager, executive. **Un congreso de los directivos de la industria**, a conference of executives from the industry.

directo, ta [de-rec-to, tah], *a.* 1. Direct, in a straight line, non-stop. 2. Clear, open, apparent, evident. 3. Live. **Transmitir en directo**, to broadcast live. -*m.* Straight punch (boxeo); forehand shot (tenis).

director [de-rec-tor´], *m.* 1. Director, one that has authority over others. 2. Conductor, controller, guide, corypheus. 3. President in some institutions for public business. 4. Director, manager, one who has the management of the concerns of a trading company. 5. Overruler, overseer. **Director** or **director espiritual**, confessor, who guides the conscience of a person. **Director gerente**, managing director. **Director de hotel**, hotel manager. **Director de personal**, personnel manager. **Director de automatización de la oficina**, *(Comput.)* office automation director. **Director de procesamiento de datos**, director of data processing. **Director del centro de información**, *(Comput.)* information center director. **Director del departamento de informática**, *(Comput.)* computer manager.

directora [de-rec-to'-rah], *f.* 1. Directress, governess. 2. *(Geom.)* Directrix, a line determining the motion of another line or point in order to produce a definite curve or surface.

directorial [de-rec-to-re-ahl'], *a.* Relating to a directory.

directorio, ria [de-rec-to'-re-o, ah], *a.* 1. Directive, directorial.
directorio [de-rec-to'-re-o], *m.* 1. Directory, a book which serves as a guide in certain sciences or business matters. 2. The governing body of five men organized in the fourth year of the French republic, Oct., 1795. 3. *(Com.)* A body of directors, directorate. 4 . Directors, board of directors. 5. Directory. **Directorio de teléfonos**, telephone directory. 6. Directory *(Comput.)* **Directorio principal**, root directory.
dirigible [de-re-hee'-blay], *m.* Dirigible. *-a.* Pliable, manageable, easily directed.
dirigido [de-re-he'-do], *a.* Guided.
dirigir [de-re-heer'], *va.* 1. To direct, to aim, to lead or to drive in a straight line; to level. 2. To guide, to direct, to conduct. 3. To dedicate a work. 4. To direct, to regulate, to head, to govern, to give rules or laws for the management of anything. 5. **Dirigir el rumbo**, *(Naut.)* to steer. *-vr.* 1. To address, to apply, to resort to. **Se dirigió a mí en la calle**, he spoke to me in the street. 2. To go to (ir hacia), to make one´s way to; to head for. **Dirigirse hacia**, to head for.
dirimente [de-re-men'-tay], *pa.* Breaking off, dissolving.
dirimir [de-re-meer'], *va.* 1. To dissolve, to disjoin, to separate. 2. To adjust or accommodate differences. 3. To annul, to declare void.
dirradiación [dir-rah-de-ah-the-on'], *f.* Radiation of the light proceeding, from a body.
dirradiar [dir-rah-de-ar'], *va.* To radiate, to scatter luminous rays.
dirruir [dir-roo-eer'], *va.* To ruin, to destroy. *V.* DERRUIR.
dis [dees], *prep.* From the Latin, changed often into **Des**; it is used only in compound words; it has the meaning of the English prefixes **Dis** and **Un,** and implies separation, division, but commonly privation or negation; as, *armar,* to arm; *desarmar,* to disarm; *atar,* to tie; *desatar,* to untie; *gusto,* pleasure; *disgusto,* displeasure.
disafia [de-sah'-fe-ah], *f. (Met.)* Alteration of the sense of touch.
discantar [dis-can-tar'], *va.* 1. To chant, to sing. 2. To compose or recite verses. 3. To descant, to discourse copiously. 4. To quaver upon a note.
discante [dis-cahn'-tay], *m.* 1. Treble. *V.* TIPLE. 2. Concert, especially of stringed instruments. 3. A small guitar.
discapacitado [dis-cah-pah-the-tah'-do], *a.* Incapacitated, handicapped.
discapacitar [dis-cah-pah-the-tar'], *va.* To incapacitate, to handicap.
discataposis [dis-cah-tah-po'-sis], *f. (Med.)* Dysphagia, difficulty in swallowing.
disceptación [dis-thep-tah-the-on'], *f.* Argument, controversy, dispute.
disceptar [dis-thep-tar'], *va.* To dispute, to argue.
discernidor [dis-ther-ne-dor'], *m.* Discerner.
discernimiento [dis-ther-ne-me-en'-to], *m.* 1. Discernment, judgment. 2. Choice, the power of distinguishing. 3. Appointment of a guardian by the proper magistrates.
discernir [dis-ther-neer'], *va.* 1. To discern, to distinguish, to comprehend, to judge, to know. 2. To appoint a guardian.
disciforme [dis-the-for'-may], *a.* Disciform, having the shape of a disk.
discinesia [dis-the-nay'-se-ah], *f. (Med.)* Paralysis of voluntary movements.
disciplina [dis-the-plee'-nah], *f.* 1. Discipline, education, instruction. 2. Discipline, any art or science taught. 3. Discipline, rule of conduct, order. 4. Correction or punishment inflicted upon oneself. **Disciplinas**, scourge, a cat-of-nine-tails. 5. Flagellation.
disciplinable [dis-the-ple-nah'-blay], *a.* Disciplinable, capable of instruction.
disciplinadamente [dis-the-ple-nah'-dah-men-tay], *adv.* With discipline.
disciplinado, da [dis-the-ple-nah'-do dah], *a.* Marbled, variegated. *-pp.* of DISCIPLINAR.

disciplinal [dis-the-ple-nahl'], *a.* Relative to discipline, disciplinal.
disciplinante [des-the-ple-nahn'-tay], *pa.* Flagellator.
disciplinar [dis-the-ple-nar'], *va.* 1. To discipline, to educate, to instruct, to bring up. 2. To drill, to teach the manual exercise or the military regulations. 3. To chastise, to correct. *-vr.* To scourge oneself as penance.
disciplinario, ria [dis-the-ple-nah'-re-o, ah], *a.* Disciplinary, belonging to discipline.
discipulado [dis-the-poo-lah'-do], *m.* 1. Number of scholars who frequent the same school. 2. Education, instruction.
discípulo, la [dis-thee'-poo-lo, lah], *m. & f.* Disciple, scholar, learner, follower.
disco [dees'-co], *m.* 1. Disk, a round piece of iron thrown in the ancient sports; a quoit. **Disco volante**, flying saucer. 2. Face of the sun or moon, as it appears to the eye. 3. A plate of glass, of circular form, which serves for an electric machine, etc. **Disco de larga duración**, long-playing record. **Disco de marcar**, dial. 4. A cylinder whose base is very large as compared with its height: as the telescope lens. 5. A railway signal-disk, semaphore. 6. *(Comput.)* **Disco de arranque**, boot disk. **Disco duro**; **disco flexible**, floppy disk, diskette, floppy; **disco** virtual, RAM disk. **Disco grabable**, writable disk. **Disco magnético desmontable**, removable magnetic disk. **Disco óptico digital**, digital optical disk. **Disco WORM**, WORM disk (Write Once Read Many). **Disco de Winchester**, Winchester disk.
disco [dis-co], *f.* Disco (sala de baile).
discóbolo [dis-co'-bo-lo], *m.* Discus thrower.
discografía [dis-co-grah-fe'-ah], *f.* 1. Records; collection of records. **La discografía de Ecles**, the complete recordings of Eccles. 2. Record company.
discográfico [disd-co-grah'-fc-co], *a.* Record. **Casa discográfica**, record company. **El momento discográfico actual**, the present state of the record industry.
díscolo, la [dees'-co-lo, lah], *a.* Ungovernable; wayward, peevish, froward.
disconforme [dis-con-for'-may], *a.* Differing. **Estar disconforme**, to be in disagreement.
disconformidad [dis-con-for-me-dahd'], *f.* Disagreement.
discontinuar [dis-con-te-noo-ar'], *va. V.* DESCONTINUAR.
discontinuo, a [dis-con-tee'-noo-o, ah], *a.* Discontinued.
disconveniencia [dis-con-vay-ne-en'-the-ah], *f.* Discord, disunion.
disconveniente [dis-con-vay-ne-en'-tay], *a. V.* DESCONVENIENTE.
discordancia [dis-cor-dahn'-the-ah], *f.* Disagreement, contrariety of opinion; discordance.
discordante [dis-cor-dahn'-tay], *pa. & a.* Dissonant, discordant.
discordar [dis-cor-dar'], *vn.* To discord, to disagree.
discorde [dis-cor'-day], *a.* 1. Discordant, contrary, not conformable. 2. *(Mus.)* Dissonant.
discordia [dis-cor'-de-ah], *f.* 1. Discord, disagreement, mis-intelligence. 2. Contrariety of opinion, opposition.
discoteca [dis-co-tay'-cah], *f.* 1. Record library. 2. Record store. 3. Discotheque.
discrasia [dis-crah'-se-ah], *f. (Med.)* Dyscrasia, ill-health due to constitutional disease; general bad health.
discreción [dis-cray-the-on'], *f.* 1. Discretion, prudence, judgment. 2. Acuteness of mind, sharpness of wit, liveliness of fancy. **Con vino a discreción**, with as much wine as one wants. **Comer a discreción**, to eat as much as one likes. 3. Discretion, liberty of acting at pleasure. **A discreción**, 1. At the discretion or will of another. 2. According to one's own will or fancy.
discrecional [dis-cray-the-o-nahl'], *a.* Discretional, discretionary.
discrepancia [dis-cray-pahn'-the-ah], *f.* Discrepancy, difference, contrariety.

discrepante [dis-cray-pahn'-tay], *pa.* Disagreeing, discrepant. **Hubo varias voces discrepantes**, there were some dissenting voices.

discrepar [dis-cray-par'], *vn.* To differ, to disagree.

discretamente [dis-cray-tah-men'-tay],*adv.* Discreetly, sensibly, prudently.

discretear [dis-cray-tay-ar'], *vn.* To be discreet, to talk with discretion: used ironically.

discreto, ta [dis-cray'-to, tah], *a.* 1. Discreet, circumspect, considerate, prudent. 2. Ingenious, sharp, witty, eloquent. 3. Discrete, distinct, separate. **Es más delicado que discreto**, he is more nice than wise. **Le daremos un plazo discreto**, we'll allow him a reasonable time.

discreto, ta [dis-cray'-to, tah], *m. & f.* A person elected assistant in the council of some religious houses.

discretorio [dis-cray-to'-re-o], *m.* Meeting or council of the seniors of religious bodies.

discriminación [dis-cre-me-nah-the-on'], *f.* Discrimination. **Discriminación racial**, racial discrimination.

discriminado [dis-cre-me-nah'-do], *a.* **Sentirse discriminado**, to feel that one has been unfairly treated.

discriminar [dis-cre-me-nar'], *va.* To discriminate.

disculpa [dis-cool'-pah],*f.* 1. Apology, excuse, exculpation. 2. *(Law.)* Plea.

disculpabilidad [dis-cool-pah-be-le-dahd'], *f.* Excusability, palliation, pardonableness.

disculpable [dis-cool-pah'-blay], *a.* Excusable, pardonable.

disculpablemente [dis-cool-pah'-blay-men-tay], *adv.* Pardonably, excusably.

disculpadamente [dis-cool-pah'-dah-men-tay], *adv.* Excusably.

disculpar [dis-cool-par'], *va.* To exculpate, to excuse, to palliate. **Disculpa el que venga tarde**, forgive me for coming late. *-vr.* To excuse oneself. **Disculparse con uno por haber hecho algo**, to apologize to somebody for having done something.

discurrir [dis-coor-reer'], *vn.* 1. To gad, to ramble about, to run to and fro, to pass, to flow by. **El verano discurrió sin grandes calores**, the summer passed without great heat. 2. To discourse upon a subject. 3. To discuss. **Discurre menos que un mosquito**, he just never thinks. *-va.* 1. To invent, to plan, to contrive, to consult, to meditate, to scheme. 2. To discourse, to infer, to deduce.

discursar [dis-coor-sar'], *vn.* To discourse, to treat upon, to converse.

discursista [dis-coor-sees'-tah], *m.* One who discusses a subject.

discursivo, va [dis-coor-see'-vo, vah], *a.* Discursive, reflective; cogitative.

discurso [dis-coor'-so], *m.* 1. Discourse. 2. Ratiocination, reasoning. 3. Discourse, conversation, speech. **Discurso de clausura**, closing speech. **Pronunciar un discurso**, to make a speech. 4. Discourse, dissertation, treatise, tract. 5. Space of time. **En el discurso del tiempo**, with the passage of time. 6. Ramble.

discusión [dis-coo-se-on'],*f.* Discussion, argument, dispute. **Tener una discusión**, to have an argument.

discusivo, va [dis-coo-see'-vo, vah], *a. (Med.)* Resolvent.

discutible [dis-coo-tee'-blay], *a.* Susceptible of discussion or examination; controvertible.

discutidor, ra [dis-coo-te-dor', rah], *m. & f.* Prone to discuss, fond of disputing.

discutir [dis-coo-teer'], *va.* To discuss, to investigate, to examine, to debate. **Discutir a uno lo que está diciendo**, to contradict what somebody is saying. *-vn.* To discuss, to talk; to argue. **Discutir de política**, to argue about politics.

disecación [de-say-cah-the-on'], *f.* Dissection, anatomist.

disecador [de-say-cah-dor'], *m.* Dissector, anatomist.

disecar [de-say-car'], *va.* 1. To dissect (cuerpos de animales). 2. To make an autopsy for study. 3. To preserve dead animals

with the appearance of life. 4. *(Met.)* To analyze minutely; to criticise.

disecativo, va [de-say-cah-tee'-vo, vah], *a.* Desiccative, desiccant, drying.

disección [de-sec-the-on'], *f.* Dissection, anatomy.

disector [de-sec-tor'], *m.* Dissector, anatomist.

diseminable [de-say-me-nah'-blay], *a.* Disseminable, capable of being spread or propagated.

diseminación [de-say-me-nah-the-on'], *f.* Dissemination, publishing; scattering of ripe seeds.

diseminador, ra [de-say-me-nah-dor, rah], *m. & f.* Disseminator, spreader.

diseminar [de-say-me-nar'], *va.* To disseminate, to propagate.

disensión [de-sen-se-on'],*f.* 1. Dissension, misunderstanding, contention, contest, strife. 2. The cause or motive of dissension.

disenso [de-sen'-so], *m.* Dissent, disagreement.

disentería [de-sen-tay-ree'-ah], *f.* Dysentery, a disease.

disentérico, ca [de-sen-tay'-re-co, cah], *a.* Belonging to dysentery.

disentimiento [de-sen-te-me-en'-to], *m.* Dissent, disagreement, declaration of difference of opinion.

disentir [de-sen-teer'], *vn.* To dissent, to disagree, or to differ in opinion.

diseñador, ra [de-say-nyah-dor'], *m & f.* Designer, delineator.

diseñar [de-say-nyar'], *va.* To draw, to design.

diseño [de-say'-nyo], *m.* 1. Design, sketch, draft, plan. 2. Delineation, description. 3. Picture, image. *V.* DESIGNIO. 4. Pattern, model. **Diseño asistido por ordenador**, *(Comput.)* Computer Aided Design (CAD).

disépalo, la [de-say'-pah-lo, lah], *a.* Having two sepals.

disepimento [de-say-pe-men'-to], *m.* Dissepiment, a partition of a compund ovary.

disertación [de-ser-tah-the-on'], *f.* Dissertation, a discourse, a disquisition, discussion.

disertador [de-ser-tah-dor'], *m.* Dissertator, debater.

disertar [de-ser-tar'], *va.* To dispute, to debate, to argue.

disestesia [di-ses-tay'-se-ah], *f.* Dysmaesthesia, numbness, loss of sensation.

disfagia [des-fah'-ge-ah], *f.* Dysphagia, difficulty in swallowing.

disfamación [dis-fah-mah-the-on'], *f.* Defamation, slander: censure.

disfamador, ra [dis-fah-mah-dor', rah], *m. & f.* Defamer, detractor, slanderer.

disfamar [dis-fah-mar'], *va.* 1. To defame, to slander. 2. To discredit.

disfamatorio, ria [dis-fah-mah-to'-re-o, ah], *a.* Defamatory, calumnious, libellous.

disfavor [dis-fah-vor'], *m.* 1. Disregard, want of favor. 2. Discountenance, cold treatment.

disfonía [dis-fo-nee'-ah], *f. (Med.)* Sensible alteration of the voice and speech, dysphonia.

disformar [des-for-mar'], *va. V.* DEFORMAR and AFEAR.

disforme [dis-for'-may], *a.* 1. Deformed, ugly, monstrous, formless. 2. Huge, big.

disformidad [dis-for-me-dahd'], *f.* Deformity, excessive bigness.

disfraz [dis-frath'], *m.* 1. Mask, disguise. **Baile de disfraces**, fancy-dress ball. 2. *(Met.)* Dissimulation, dissembling.

disfrazado [dis-frah-thah'-do], *a.* **Disfrazado de**, disguised as. **Ir disfrazado de duque**, to be made up like a duke.

disfrazar [dis-frah-thar'], *va.* 1. To disguise, to conceal. **Disfrazar a uno de lavandera**, to disguise somebody as a washerwoman. 2. To cloak, to dissemble, to cover; to misrepresent. *-vr.* 1. To masquerade, to go in disguise. 2. To feign.

disfrutar [dis-froo-tar'], *va.* 1. To gain fruit or advantage, to gather the fruit or products. 2. To enjoy, to reap benefit from a thing, without caring for its preservation or betterment. 3.

To enjoy health, convenience. 4. To avail oneself of, to profit by, the favor, friendship, or protection of some one. -*vn*. 1. To enjoy oneself; to have a good time. **Disfrutar con algo**, to enjoy something. **Siempre disfruto con los libros así**, I always enjoy books of that sort. 2. **Disfrutar de**, to enjoy; to have, to possess. **Disfrutar de una buena salud**, to enjoy good health.

disfrute [des-froo'-tay], *m*. Use, enjoyment.

disgregable [dis-gray-gah'-blay], *a*. Separable, segregable.

disgregación [dis-gray-gah-the-on'], *f*. 1. Separation, disjunction. 2. Dispersion of light rays.

disgregar [dis-gray-gar'], *va*. 1. To separate, to disjoin. 2. To disperse the rays of light.

disgregativo, va [dis-gray-gah-tee'-vo, vah], *a*. Disjunctive.

disgustadamente [dis-goos-tah'-dah-men-tay], *adv*. Disgustingly.

disgustar [dis-goos-tar'], *va*. 1. To disgust, to distaste, to disrelish. 2. To disgust, to strike with dislike, to offend. **Es un olor que me disgusta**, it´s a smell which upsets me. **Me disgusta tener que repetirlo**, it annoys me to have to repeat it. -*vr*. 1. To be displeased, to fall out, to be at variance with another. 2. To get tired, fatigued, to be bored.

disgustillo [dis-goos-teel'-lyo], *m*. *dim*. Displeasure, slight disgust.

disgusto [dis-goos'-to], *m*. 1. Disgust, aversion, of the palate, loathing. 2. Ill-humor; offence conceived. 3. Grief, sorrow. **A disgusto**, in spite of, contrary to one's will and pleasure. **Me causó un gran disgusto**, it was a great blow to me. **Nunca nos dio un disgusto**, he never gave us any trouble. **Matar a uno a disgustos**, to wear somebody out with burdens.

disidencia [de-se-den'-the-ah], *f*. Dissidence, non-conformity.

disidente [de-se-den'-tay], *a. & m. & f*. Dissident, dissenter, non-conformist, schismatic.

disidio [de-see'-de-o], *m*. *(Poet.)* Discord.

disidir [de-se-deer'], *vn*. 1. To dissent, to separate from a (religious) belief before held. 2. To be of a distinct opinion, especially in matters of belief.

disilábico, ca [de-se-lah'-be-co, cah], *a*. Dissyllabic, of two syllables. Also **disílabo, ba**.

disílabo [de-see'-lah-bo], *m*. Dissyllable.

disímil [de-see'-mil], *a*. Dissimilar.

disimilar [de-se-me-lar'], *a*. Unequal, dissimilar.

disimilitud [de-se-me-le-tood'], *f*. Dissimilitude.

disimulable [de-se-moo-lah'-blay], *a*. What may be dissembled or feigned.

disimulación [de-se-moo-lah-the-on'], *f*. 1. Dissimulation, the act of dissembling; simulation, hypocrisy, mask, feint. 2. Reserve, reservedness.

disimuladamente [de-se-moo-lah-dah-men'-tay], *adv*. Dissemblingly; reservedly.

disimulado, da [de-se-moo-lah'-do, dah], *a*. 1. Dissembling. 2. Reserved, sullen, not open, not frank. 3. Dissembled, sly, cunning. -*pp*. of DISIMULAR. **A lo disimulado**, dissemblingly; reservedly. **Hacer la disimulada**, to feign ignorance.

disimulador, ra [de-se-moo-lah-dor', rah], *m. & f*. Dissembler.

disimular [de-see-moo-lar'], *va*. 1. To dissemble, to conceal one's real intentions. 2. To cloak, to conceal artfully any bent of the mind. 3. To hide. 4. To tolerate, to allow so as not to hinder, to overlook, to let pass. **Disimula mi atrevimiento**, forgive me if I have been too bold. 5. To color, to misrepresent.

disimulo [de-se-moo'-lo], *m*. 1. Dissimulation, reservedness. **Con disimulo**, cunningly, craftily. V. DISMULACIÓN. 2. Tolerance.

disipable [de-se-pah'-blay], *a*. Dissipable, easily scattered, easily dissipated.

disipación [de-se-pah-the-on'], *f*. 1. Separation of the parts which composed a whole. 2. Resolution of anything into

vapor. 3. Dissolute living. 4. Dissipation, the act of spending one´s fortune; licentiousness, extravagance, waste.

disipado, da [de-se-pah'-do, dah], *a*. 1, Dissipated, devoted to pleasure. 2. Prodigal, lavisher. 3. Licentious, dissolute. -*pp*. of DISIPAR.

disipador, ra [de-se-pah-dor', rah], *m. & f*. Spendthrift, a prodigal, a lavisher.

disipar [de-se-par'], *va*. 1. To dissipate, to disperse, to scatter. 2. To misspend, to lavish. 3. To drive away, to put to flight. -*vr*. To vanish; to evaporate.

disjunto, ta [dis-hoon'-to, tah], *a*. *(Mus.)* Disjoined, not followed but separated by another interval.

diskette [dis-kay-tay], *m*. *(Comput.)* Floppy disk.

dislacerar [dis-lah-thay-rar'], *va*. To lacerate.

dislate [dis-lah'-tay], *m*. Nonsense, absurdity. V. DISPARATE.

dislexia [dis-lec'-se-ah], *f*. Dyslexia.

dislocación, dislocadura [dis-lo-ca-the-on', dis-lo-ca-doo'-rah], *f*. 1. Dislocation. 2. Dislocation, a luxation, a joint put out. 3. Separation of the different parts which form a machine.

dislocar [dis-lo-car'], *va*. To dislocate, to displace; to luxate, to disjoint. -*vr*. To be dislocated, to come asunder.

dismembración [dis-mem-brah-the-on'], *f*. V. DESMEMBRACIÓN.

dismenia [dis-may'-ne-ah], *f*. V. DISMENORREA.

dismenorrea [dis-may-no-rray'-ah], *f*. Dysmenorrhoea, painful menstruation.

disminución [dis-me-noo-the-on'], *f*. 1. V. DIMINUCIÓN. **Proceso de disminución de réditos**, law of diminishing returns. 2. Disease in horses' hoofs.

disminuido, da [dis-me-noo-ee'-do], *a. m & f*. *(Med.)* Crippled, handicapped.

disminuir [dis-me-noo-eer'], *va*. 1. To diminish, to lessen, to lower, to abridge, to cut short. 2. To detract from. -*vr*. To lessen, to lower, to grow less.

disnea [dis-nay'-ah], *f*. Dyspnoea, difficulty in respiration.

disociación [dis-so-the-ah-the-on'], *f*. Disjunction, separation.

disociar [de-so-the-ar'], *va*. To disjoin, to separate things.

disodila [de-so-dee'-lah], *f*. *(Min.)* A papyraceous coal, kind of bituminous earth in plates, found in Sicily.

disolubilidad [de-so-loo-be-le-dahd'], *f*. Dissolubility.

disoluble [de-so-loo'-blay], *a*. Dissoluble.

disolución [de-so-loo-the-on'], *f*. 1. Dissolution, the resolution of a body into its constituent elements. 2. Dissoluteness, dissipation, libertinism, lewdness, licentiousness.

disolutamente [de-so-loo-tah-men'-tay], *adv*. Dissolutely, licentiously.

disolutivo, va [de-so-loo-tee'-vo, vah], *a*. Dissolvent, solvent.

disoluto, ta [de-so-loo'-to, tah], *a*. Dissolute, loose, licentious, lewd, libidinous, libertine.

disolvente [de-sol-ven'-tay], *m*. Dissolvent, dissolver.

disolver [de-sol-verr'], *va*. 1. To loosen, to untie. 2. To dissolve, to liquate, to disunite. 3. To melt, to liquefy. 4. To interrupt. -*vr*. To dissolve, to be melted.

disoma [de-so'-mah], *f*. An arsenosulphide of nickel; greynickel.

disón [de-sone'], *m*. *(Mus.)* Harsh, dissonant tone; discord.

disonancia [de-so-nahn'-the-ah], *f*. 1. Dissonance. 2. Disagreement, discord. **Hacer disonancia a la razón**, to be contrary to reason.

disonante [de-so-nahn'-tay], *a*. 1. Disonant, inharmonious, discrepant. 2. *(Met.)* Discordant, unsuitable.

disonar [de-so-nar'], *vn*. 1. To disagree in sound, to be disharmonious. 2. To discord, to disagree. 3. To be contrary or repugnant.

dísono, na [dee'-so-no, nah], *a*. Dissonant, inconstant.

dispar [dis-par'], *a*. Unlike, unequal.

disparado [dis-pah-r-ah'-do], *a*. **Entrar disparado**, to shoot in. **Salir disparado**, to shoot out, to be off like a shot.

disparador

disparador [dis-pah-rah-dor'], *m.* 1. Shooter. 2. Trigger of a gunlock. 3. Ratch, ratchet, or ratchet-wheel, in clock-work. 4. *(Naut.)* Anchor-tripper. 5. A machine like a musket for setting off rockets.

disparar [dis-pa-rar'], *va. & vn.* 1. To shoot, to discharge a thing with violence. **Disparar desde un sitio oculto,** to snipe. 2. To fire, to discharge fire-arms; to let off. 3. To cast or throw with violence. 4. *(Coll.)* To talk nonsense, to blunder. *-vr.* 1. To run headlong. 2. To stoop, to dart down on prey (halcón). 3. To run away disobeying the bridle (caballo). 4. *(Naut.)* To turn violently (cabr. estante). 5. To get loose from tiller ropes (timón).

disparatadamente [dis-paah-rah-tah'-dah-men-tay], *adv.* Absurdly, nonsensically.

disparatado, da [dis-pa-rah-tah'-do, dah], *a.* Inconsistent, absurd, extravagant, silly, foolish. *-pp.* of DISPARATAR.

disparatar [dis-pa-rah-tar'], *va.* 1. To act or talk in an absurd and inconsistent manner. 2. To blunder, to talk nonsense.

disparate [dis-pa-rah´-tay], *m.* Nonsense, blunder, absurdity, extravagance. **Hiciste un disparate protestando,** it was silly of you to complain.

disparatón [dis-pa-rah-tone'], *m. aug.* A great piece of nonsense, a very great blunder.

disparatorio [dis-pa-rah-to'-re-o], *m.* Speech or discourse full of nonsense.

disparidad [dis-pa-re-dahd'], *f.* Disparity, inequality, dissimilitude

disparo [dis-pah'-ro], *m.* 1. Shot (tiro). 2. Firing (acción de disparar un arma). 3. Shot (fútbol) 4. Discharge, explosion. 5. Nonsense, absurdity.

dispendio [dis-pen'-de-o], *m.* 1. Excessive or extravagant expense. 2. *(Met.)* Voluntary loss of life, honor, or fame.

dispendioso, sa [dis-pen-de-o'-so, sah], *a.* Costly, expensive.

dispensa [des-pen'-sah], *f.* 1. Dispense, exemption, dispensation. 2. Diploma granting a dispensation.

dispensable [dis-pen-sah'-blay], *a.* Dispensable.

dispensación [dis-pen-sah-the-on'], *f.* 1. Dispensation, exception. 2. *V.* DISPENSA.

dispensador, ra [dis-pen-sah-dor', rah], *m. & f.* 1. One who grants a dispensation. 2. Dispenser, distributor.

dispensar [dis-pen-sar'], *va.* 1. To dispense, to exempt, to absolve or set free from an engagement. 2. *(Coll.)* To excuse, to dispense with, to do without. **Dispensar a uno de una obligación,** to excuse somebody from an obligation. **Dispensar a uno de,** to excuse somebody from. 3. To deal out, to distribute. *-vr.* **No puedo dispensarme de esa obligación,** I cannot escape that duty.

dispensario [des-pen-sah'-re-o], *m.* 1. Pharmacopoeia. 2. Laboratory of medicaments. 3. Dispensary, clinic.

dispepsia [dis-pep'-se-ah], *f.* Dyspepsia.

dispéptico, ca [dis-pep'-te-co, cah], *a.* Dyspeptic.

dispermo, ma [dis-perr'-mo, mah], *a.* *(Bot.)* Having only two seeds.

dispersar [des-per-sar'], *va.* 1. To separate the things or persons who were joined. 2. *(Mil.)* To put to flight, to disperse. 3. *(Comput.)* To scramble *-vr.* To disperse, to scatter.

dispersión [dis-per-se-on'], *f.* Dispersion.

disperso, sa [dis-per´-so, sah], *a.* 1. Dispersed, separated. 2. Applied to military men who do not belong to a body of forces, and reside where they please.

dispertador, ra [dis-per-tah-dor', rah], *m. & f.* *V.* DESPERTADOR.

dispertar [dis-per-tar'], *va.* *V.* DESPERTAR. *(Yo dispierto, yo dispierte,* from *Dispertar. V.* ACERTAR.)

displacer [dis-plah-therr'], *va.* *V.* DESPLACER.

displicencia [dis-ple-then'-the-ah], *f.* Displeasure, discontent, dislike.

displicente [dis-ple-then'-tay], *a.* 1. Displeasing, unpleasing. 2. Angry, peevish, fretful.

dispondeo [dis-pon-day'-o], *m.* *(Poet.)* Dispondee, a foot of prosody consisting of four long syllables.

disponedor, ra [dis-po-nay-dor', rah], *m. & f.* Disposer; distributer.

disponer [dis-po-nerr'], *va. & vn.* 1. To arrange, to order, to place things in order. 2. To dispose, to make fit, to prepare. 3. To dispose of, to give, to distribute. 4. To deliberate, to resolve, to direct, to command. 5. To act freely, to dispose of property. **Disponer sus cosas,** to make a last will. **Disponer las velas al viento,** to trim the sails to the wind (barcos). **La ley dispone que...,** the law provides that... **Disponemos de poco tiempo,** we have very little time. *-vr.* To prepare oneself, to get ready, to resolve. *(Yo dispongo, yo dispuse,* from *Disponer. V.* PONER.)

disponible [dis-po-nee'-blay], *a.* Disposable (propiedad).

disposición [dis-po-se-the-on'], *f.* 1. Disposition, arrangement or distribution of things, ordering. 2. Disposition, natural fitness. 3. Disposition, tendency to any act or state. 4. Proportion, symmetry, measure. 5. Resolution, order, command. 6. Power, authority 7. Disposition, inclination, temper of mind. 8. *(Naut.)* Trim of a ship. 9. Elegance of person. 10. Despatch of business. **A la disposición,** at the disposal or will of another. **Según las disposiciones del código,** according to the provisions of the statue. **Tener algo a su disposición,** to have something at one´s disposal. **Estar en disposición de,** to be ready to. **No tener disposición para,** to have no aptitude for. **Disposición de la página,** *(Comput.)* page layout.

dispositivo, va [dis-po-se-tee'-vo, vah], *a.* Preparatory, readying, preliminary. *-m.* Device, mechanism. **Dispositivo de arranque,** starting mechanism. **Dispositivo de seguridad,** safety catch. **Dispositivo de lecturas multiventana,** *(Comput.)* multiwindow readout device. **Dispositivo de comportamiento,** *(Comput.)* behavioral device. **Dispositivo de devolución de llamada,** *(Comput.)* callback device. **Dispositivo de seguridad biométrico,** *(Comput.)* biometric security device. **Dispositivo fisiológico,** *(Comput.)* physiological device.

dispositorio, ria [dis-po-se-to'-re-o, ah], *a.* *V.* DISPOSITIVO.

dispuesto, ta [dis-poo-es'-to, tah], *a.* 1. Disposed, fit, ready, minded. **Dispuesto según ciertos principios,** arranged according to certain principles. 2. Comely, genteel, graceful. **Bien dispuesto,** quite well, with regard to health. **Mal dispuesto,** indisposed, ill. 3. **Estar dispuesto a,** to be prepared to. **Estar poco dispuesto a,** to be reluctant to. *-pp. irr.* of DISPONER.

disputa [dis-poo'-tah], *f.* 1. Dispute, controversy, arguement. 2. Dispute, contest, conflict; contention, clash, fray, odds. **Sin disputa,** beyond dispute.

disputable [dis-poo-tah'-blay], *a.* Disputable, controvertible, contestable.

disputador [dis-poo-tah-dor'], *m.* Disputant, disputer.

disputar [dis-poo-tar'], *va. & vn.* 1. To dispute, to controvert, to contend, to contest. 2. To dispute, to question, to reason about. 3. To dispute, to debate, to argue. 4. To dispute, to jar, or to clamor. 5. To strive; to resist. **Disputar sobre algo,** to dispute on something. **Disputar con uno por un premio,** to contend with somebody for a prize. *-vr.* **Disputarse un premio,** to contend for a prize.

disputativamente [dis-poo-tah-te-vah-men'-tay], *adv.* Disputingly.

disquete [dis-ke-tay], *m.* Floppy disk, diskette, floppy.

disquisición [dis-ke-se-the-on'], *f.* Disquisition, examination.

distancia [dis-tahn'-the-ah], *f.* 1. Distance, interval of time or place. 2. Remoteness, length. 3. Difference, disparity. **Acortar distancias,** to reduce the distance. **Tomar distancias,** to calculate the longitude of a vessel. **Distancia del suelo,** height of the ground. **A larga distancia,** long-distance. **Mantener a uno a distancia,** to keep somebody at a distance. **Guardar las distancias,** to keep one´s distance. **Distancia de Hamming,** *(Comput.)* Hamming distance.

distanciado [dis-tahn-the-ah'-do], *a.* 1. Remote; widely separated, isolated (aislado). 2. *(Fig.)* Far apart. **Estamos algo distanciados**, we are not particularly close. **Ella está distanciada de su familia**, she has grown apart from her family.

distanciar [dis-tahn-the-ar'], *va.* 1. To space out (objetos), to separate; to put further apart. 2. To out-distance (rival). 3. To cause a rift between. *-vr.* 1. **Distanciarse de un rival**, to get ahead of a rival. 2. To fall out, to become estranged; to become remote from each other.

distante [dis-tahn'-tay], *a.* 1. Distant, remote. 2. *(Naut.)* Off, offward.

distar [dis-tar'], *vn.* 1. To be distant or remote with regard to time or place. **Dista 5 kms de aquí**, it is 5 kms from here. 2. To be different, to vary.

distender [dis-ten-derr'], *va. (Med.)* To cause violent stretching in tissues, membranes, etc.

distensión [dis-ten-se-on'], *f.* Violent stretching.

distesia [dis-tay'-se-ah], *f. (Med.)* General discomfort and impatience in disease; dysthesia.

dístico [de-es'-te-co], *m.* Distich, couplet.

distilo, la [dis-tee'-lo, lah], *a.* Having two styles or pistils.

distinción [dis-tin-the-on'], *f.* 1. Distinction, difference, diversity. **Obrar sin distinción**, to act arbitrarily. **Sin distinción de edades**, irrespective of differences of age. 2. Prerogative, privilege. 3. Distinction, honorable note of superiority. 4. Order, clarity, precision. **Persona de distinción**, a person of superior rank. **A distinción**, in contradistinction.

distinguible [dis-tin-gee'-blay], *a.* Distinguishable.

distinguido, da [dis-tin-gee'-do, dah], *a. & pp.* of DISTINGUIR. 1. Distinguished, conspicuous. *-m.* 2. **Distinguido**, refined (modales). Gentlemanly (caballero). **Distinguido** or **soldado distinguido**, a nobleman serving as a private, who was allowed to wear a sword, and was exempted from menial labor.

distinguir [dis-tin-geer'], *va.* 1. To distinguish. **No distingo cuál es el mío**, I can't tell which is mine. 2. To distinguish. 3. To see clearly, and at a distance. 4. To discern, to discriminate, to know; to judge. 5. To set a peculiar value on things or persons. **Me distingue con su amistad**, he honors me with his friendship. 6. To clear up, to explain. *-vn.* **No distinguir**, to have no critical sense. **Es un hombre que sabe distinguir**, he is a discerning person. *vr.* 1. To distinguish oneself, especially by warlike exploits. 2. To differ, to be distinguished from.

distintamente [dis-tin-tah-men'-tay], *adv.* Distinctly, diversely.

distintivo, va [dis-tin-tee'-vo, vah], *a.* Distinctive.

distintivo *m.* 1. A distinctive mark, as the badge of a military order. 2. A particular attribute, characteristic feature.

distinto, ta [dis-teen'-to, tah], *a.* 1 Distinct, different, diverse. **Son muy distintos**, they are very different. 2. Distinct, clear; intelligible. 3. **Distintos**, several, various.

distracción [dis-trac-the-on'], *f.* 1. Distraction, want of attention; heedlessness, absence; ecstasy, reverie. **Por distracción**, through sheer forgetfulness. 2. Amusement, pastime, sport. **Es mi distracción favorita**, it's my favorite amusement. 3. Licentiousness, dissolute living; want of constraint.

distráctil [dis-trahc'-teel], *a. (Bot.)* Applied to the connective, when it sensibly divides the cells of the anthers, as in the sage; distractile.

distraer [dis-trah-err'], *va.* 1. To distract, to harass the mind; to perplex, to divert. **Distraer a uno para robarle algo**, to distract somebody's attention so as to steal something from him. 2. To seduce from a virtuous life. 3. To amuse, to relax, to entertain. **La música me distrae**, music relaxes me. *-vr.* 2. To amuse, to be absent of mind, inattentive. **Me distraigo pescando**, I relax when I fish. **Me distraje un momento**, I allowed my attention to wander for a moment.

distraídamente [dis-trah-ee'-dah-men-tay], *adv.* Distractedly, licentiously.

distraído, da [dis-trah-ee'-do, dah], *a.* 1. Absent, inattentive, heedless, mopish. **Iba yo algo distraído**, I was rather absorbed in other things. **Con aire distraído**, idly, casually. 2. Dissolute, licentious. 3. Amusing, entertaining. 4. Dissolute (vida). *-pp.* of DISTRAER. (*Yo distraigo, yo distraje,* from *Distraer.* V. TRAER.)

distraimiento [dis-trah-e-me-en'-to], *m.* 1. Distraction. V. DISTRACCIÓN. 2. A licentious life.

distribución [dis-tre-boo-the-on'], *f.* 1. Distribution; division, separation. **Distribución de premios**, prize giving. 2. Proper collocation, arrangement. 3. Distribution of type in the printer's cases. 4. *(Arch.)* The art of economical employment and good selection of building materials.

distribuido [dis-tre-boo-ee'-dah], *a.* **Una casa bien distribuida**, a well-designed house.

distribuidor, ra [dis-tre-boo-e-dor', rah], *m. & f.* Distributor, divider.

distribuir [dis-tre-boo-eer'], *va.* 1. To distribute, to divide, to deal out. 2. To dispose, to range; to compart; to lot. 3. To allot, to measure. 4. *(Print.)* To distribute types.

distributivamente [dis-tre-boo-tee'-vah-men-tay], *adv.* Distributively.

distributivo, va [dis-tre-boo-tee'-vo, vah], *a.* Distributive.

distributor, ra [dis-tre-boo-tor', rah], *m. & f.* Distributer.

distribuyente [dis-tre-boo-yen'-tay], *pa.* Distributer, giver.

distrito [dis-tree'-to], *m.* 1. District, circuit of authority, province. 2. District, region, country, territory. **Distrito postal,** postal district.

distrofia muscular [dis-tro'-fe-ah moos-coo-lar], *f.* Muscular dystrophy.

disturbar [dis-toor-bar'], *va.* To disturb, to interrupt, to perturb.

disturbio [dis-toor'-be-o], *m.* Disturbance, outbreak, interruption. **Los disturbios**, the disturbances.

disuadir [de-soo-ah-deer'], *va.* To dissuade, to deter.

disuasión [de-soo-ah-se-on'], *f.* Dissuasion, determent.

disuasivo, va [de-soo-ah-see'-vo, vah], *a.* Dissuasive.

disuelto, ta [de-soo-el'-to, tah], *a. & pp. irr.* of DISOLVER. Dissolved, melted.

disuria [de-soo'-re-ah], *f. (Med.)* Dysuria, difficulty in urinating.

disyunción [dis-yoon-the-on'], *f.* 1. Disjunction, separation. 2. *(Gram.)* A disjunctive particle.

disyunta [dis-yoon'-tah], *f. (Mus.)* Change of the voice.

disyuntivamente [dis-yoon-tee'-vah-men-tay], *adv.* Disjunctively, separately.

disyuntivo, va [dis-yoon-tee'-vo, vah], *a.* 1. Disjunctive. 2. Disjunctive, applied to the insertion of stamens when the petals are united below the receptacle, but not to it.

disyunto, ta [dis-yoon'-to, tah], *a.* Separated, disjoined, distant.

disyuntor [dis-yoon-tor'], *m. (Elec.)* Circuit breaker.

dita [dee'-tah], *f.* 1. Securer, bonds-man; security, bond. 2. *(Prov. Amer.)* Debt.

ditirámbica [de-te-rahm'-be-cah], *f.* Dithyrambic, a hymn in honor of Bacchus, sung, danced, and placed at the same time.

ditirámbico, ca [de-te-rahm'-bee-co, cah], *a.* Dithyrambical.

ditirambo [de-te-rahm'-bo], *m.* 1. *(Poet.)* Dithyrambie, a dithyramb. 2. Exaggerated eulogy.

dito [dee'-to], *m. & pp. obs.* V. DICHO.

dítono [dee'-to-no], *m. (Mus.)* An interval of two tones, ditone, major third.

ditorno [de-tor'-no], *m.* A name which engravers give to the intermediate parts of a figure.

diuresis [de-oo-ray'-sis], *f.* Diuresis.

diurético, ca [de-oo-ray'-teco, cah], *a. (Med.)* Diuretic; also used as a substantive.

diurno, na [de-oor'-no, nah], *a.* Diurnal. *-f. pl.* Butterflies, lepidoptera. *-m. pl.* Insects which live but twenty-four hours; dayflies.

diurno [de-oor'-no], *m.* Diurnal, prayerbook, among Roman Catholics, which contains the canonical hours, except matins.

diuturnidad [de-oo-toor-ne-dahd'], *f.* Diuturnity, long duration.

diuturno, na [de-oo-toor'-no, nah], *a.* Diuturnal, lasting.

diva [dee'-vah], *f.* 1. (*Poet.*) Goddess. 2. (*Neol.*) A prima donna, star.

divagación [de-vah-gah-the-on'], *f.* Wandering, digression.

divagante [de-vah-gahn'-tay], *pa.* Rambling.

divagar [de-vah-gar'], *vn.* 1. To ramble. *V.* VAGAR. 2. To digress.

diván [de-vahn'], *m.* 1. Divan, the supreme council among the Turks. 2. The place of its meetings. 3. By extension, the Sublime Porte, the Ottoman govermnent. 4. Divan, a low, cushioned sofa.

divaricado, da [de-vah-re-cah'-do, dah] *a.* (*Bot.*) Divaricate, widely diverging.

divaricar [de-vah-re-car'], *va.* To separate, to cause to spread.

divergencia [de-ver-hen´-the-ah], *f.* 1. Divergence. 2. Diversity or difference in opinions.

divergente [de-ver-hen'-tay], *a.* 1. Divergent. 2. Dissenting, opposed, contrary.

divergir [de-ver-heer'], *vn.* 1. (*Phys.*) To diverge. 2. To differ, to be opposed, to clash (opiniones).

diversamente [de-ver-sah-men'-tay] *adv.* Diversely, differently.

diversidad [de-ver-se-dahd'], *f.* 1. Diversity, dissimilitude, unlikeness. 2. Diversity, distinct being. 3. Diversity, variety of things, abundance, plenty.

diversificar [de-ver-se-fe-car'], *va.* To diversify, to vary.

diversión [de-ver-se-on'], *f.* 1. Diversion. 2. Diversion, sport, merriment, fun, amusement. 3. (*Mil.*) Diversion, an attack made upon the enemy, to withdraw his attention from the real attack.

diversivo, va [de-ver-see'-vo, vah], *a.* Divertive.

diverso, sa [de-ver'-so], *a.* 1. Diverse, different from another. **Se trata de diverso asunto**, it is about a different matter. 2. Diverse, different from itself; various; multiform. *-pl.* Several, sundry, many. **Está en diversos libros**, it figures in several books.

divertículo [de-ver-tee'-coo-lo], *m.* A blind pouch, a diverticulum; a vertical appendix.

divertido, da [de-ver-tee'-do, dah], *a. & pp.* of DIVERTIR. Amused, amusive, merry, divertive, diverted, festive, funny, absent, inattentive. **Andar divertido**, to be engaged in love affairs.

divertimiento [de-ver-te-me-en'-to], *m.* 1. Diversion, sport, merriment, fun. 2. Amusement, entertaiment of the mind, pastime, sport.

divertir [de-ver-teer'], *va.* 1. To turn aside, divert, turn away. 2. To amuse, to entertain, to exhilarate, to divert, to make merry. 3. (*Mil.*) To draw the enemy off from some design, by threatening or attacking a distant part.*-vr.* To sport, to play, to frolic, to wanton, to dally, to fool, to amuse. **Divertirse haciendo algo**, to amusc oneself doing something. **Divertirse con el amor de uno**, to toy with somebody´s affections.

dividendo [de-ve-den'-do], *m.* 1. (*Arith.*) Dividend, the number to be divided. 2. Dividend, share, the interest received for money placed in the public stocks or in a partnership.

dividir [de-ve-deer'], *va.* 1. To divide, to disjoin, to disunite, to cut. 2. To divide, to distribute, to separate. 3. To divide, to disunite by discord. **Dividir 12 por 4**, to divide 12 by 4. *-vr.* 1. To divide, to part, to cleave. 2. To divide, or to be of different opinions. 3. To divide, to break friendship, to withdraw oneself from the company and friendship of anyone. **Dividir por la mitad**, to divide into halves.

dividuo, dua [de-vee-doo-o, ah], *a.* (*Law.*) Divisible.

divieso [de-ve-ay'-so], *m.* (*Med.*) Furuncle, boil.

divinamente [de-ve-nah-men'-tay], *adv.* Divinely, heavenly, admirably.

divinidad [de-ve-ne-dahd'], *f.* 1. Divinity; deity, godhead, godship, divine nature. **Divinidad marina**, sea god. 2. The Supreme Being. 3. False god.

divinizable [de-ve-ne-thah´-blay], *a.* Worthy of being deified.

divinizado. da [de-ve-ne-thah'-do, dah], *a. & pp.* of DIVINIZAR. Deified.

divinizar [de-ve-ne-thar'], *va.* 1. To deify. 2. (*Met.*) To sanctify.

divino, na [de-vee'-no, nah], *a.* 1. Divine. 2. Heavenly, heaven-born, godlike. 3. Excellent in a supreme degree. **Es un ingenio divino**, he is a man of uncommon talents.

divino, na [de-vee'-no, nah], *m. & f. V.* ADIVINO.

divisa [de-vee'-sah], *f.* 1. Badge, emblem, identifying mark. 2. (*Her.*) Motto, device. 3. (*For.*) Share of the paternal inheritance. 4. Foreign exchange. **Control de divisas**, exchange control.

divisar [de-ve-sar'], *va.* 1. To distinguish at a distance, to perceive indistinctly, to make out, to discern. 2. (*Her.*) To make a difference, to vary.

divisero [de-ve-say'-ro], *m.* Heir who is not of noble extraction.

divisibilidad [de-ve-se-be-le-dahd'], *f.* Divisibility .

divisible [de-ve-see'-blay], *a.* Divisible.

división [de-ve-se-on'], *f.* 1. Division, the act of dividing a thing into parts. 2. Division, partition, distribution. compartment. 3. Division, disunion, difference, diversity of opinion. 4. Hyphen. 5. Division; one of the parts into which a thing is divided: used technically, especially in the army and navy. 6. (*Arith.*) Division, a rule in arithmetic.

divisional [de-ve-se-o-nahl'], *a.* Divisional.

divisivo, va [de-ve-see'-vo, vah], *a* Divisible, divisive.

diviso, sa [de-vee'-so, sah], *a. & pp. & rr.* of DIVIDIR. Divided, disunited.

divisor [de-ve-sor'], *m.* 1. Divisor. 2. Anything which divides another.

divisorio, ria [de-ve-o'-re-o, ah], *a.* Divisive, forming division.

divo, va [dee'-vo, vah], *a.* (*Poet.*) Divine, godlike. *-m.* Movie star.

divorciado, da [de-vor-the-ah'-do], *a. m & f.* 1. Divorced. 2. **Las opiniones están divorciadas**, (*fig.*) Opinions are divided.

divorciar [de-vor-the-ar'], *va.* To divorce, to separate, to part, to divide. *-vr.* To be divorced.

divorcio [de-vor'-the-o], *m.* 1. Divorce, separation, disunion. 2. Rupture among friends.

divulgable [de-vool-gah'-blay], *a.* That which may be divulged.

divulgación [de-vool-gah-the-on'], *f.* Divulgation, publication.

divulgador, ra [de-vool-gah-dor', rah] *m. & f.* Divulger.

divulgar [de-vool-gar'], *ra.* To publish, to divulge, to report, to give out, to reveal. *-vr.* To go abroad.

divulsión [de-vol-se-on'], *f.* Divulsion, rupture.

DMA (*Comput.*) DMA (Direct Memory Access).

do [doh], *m.* First note of the musical scale.

dobla [do'-blah], *f.* An ancient Spanish gold coin.

dobladamente [do-blah-dah-men'-tay], *adv.* 1. Doubly. 2. Deceitfully, artfully.

dobladilla [do-blah-deel'-lyah], *f.* Ancient game of cards. **A la dobladilla**, doubly, repeatedly.

dobladillo, lla [do-blah-deel'-lyo, lyah], *a.* Squat and broad, short and thick.

dobladillo [do-blah-deel'-lyo], *m.* 1. Hem, the edge of a garment. 2. A strong thread commonly used to make stockings.

doblado [do-blah'-do], *m.* l. Measure of the fold in cloth. 2. (*Med.*) A sort of asphyxia which attacks those who clean out privies.

doblado, da [do-blah'-do, dah], *a.* 1. Strong, robust, thickset. 2. *(Met.)* Deceitful, dissembling. **Tierra doblada**, a broken, mountainous country. *-pp.* of DOBLAR.

doblador [do-blah-dor'], *m.* A machine which serves to pass sugarcane a second time between the cylinders of the mill.

dobladura [do-blah-doo'-rah], *f.* 1. Fold, mark of a fold. 2. Anciently, an extra horse, for emergencies, which warriors had to take along. 3. Dish consisting of fried meat, bread, onions, nuts, etc. 4. *(Obs.)* Malicious fabrication.

doblaje [do-blah'-hay], *m.* Dubbling (cine).

doblamiento [do-blah-me-en'-to], *m.* Doubling, bending, as act and effect.

doblar [do-blar'], *va. & vn.* 1. To double, by addition of the same quantity. **Doblar el sueldo a uno**, to double somebody's salary. 2. To double, to fold. 3. To double, to contain twice the quantity. 4. To bend, to make crooked, to crook. 5. To toll or ring the passing bell. 6. To induce someone to do the contrary of what he had thought. **Doblar la rodilla**, to kneel. 7. To turn, to go round. 8. **Doblar dos papeles**, to take two parts (teatro). *-vr.* 1. To bend, to flow, to stoop, to submit. 2. To be led away by the opinion of another. 3. To change one's opinion.

doble [do'-blay], *a.* 1. Double, twice as much, duplicate; *(Chem.)* binary. 2. Thick and short. 3. Strong, robust. 4. Double, artful, deceitful. **Al doble**, doubly. *(Mus.)* **Espacios dobles** are intervals which exceed octaves. **Doble o nada**, double or quits. **Doble densidad** *(Comput.)*, double density.

doble [do'-blay], *m.* 1. Fold, crease. 2. Dissimulation, double-dealing. 3. Toll of the passing-bell. 4. Step in Spanish dance. 5. Double. **El doble**, twice the quantity. **Su sueldo es el doble del mío**, his salary is twice mine. 6. **Dobles,** doubles (tenis). **Dobles masculinos,** men's doubles. **Dobles mixtos,** mixed doubles. *-m & f.* Double. **Ser el doble de uno**, *(fig.)* to be somebody's double (cine).

doblegable [do-blay-gah'-blay], *a.* 1. Flexible, flexile. 2. Pliant. 3. That which may be doubled.

doblegar [do-blay-gar'], *va.* 1. To bend, to incurvate, to inflect. 2. To gain by persuasion, to reclaim. **Doblegar a uno**, *(fig.)* To be somebody's double. *-vr.* 1. To bend, to be incurvated. 2. To bend, to submit, to be submissive.

doblel [do-blel'], *m.* Bag, satchel.

doblemano [do-blay-mah'-no], *f. (Mus.)* Octave-coupler.

doblemente [do-blay-men'-tay], *adv.* Deceitfully, doubly, artfully.

doblcro [do-blay'-ro], *m. (Prov.)* A small loaf of bread.

doblete [do-blay'-tay], *a.* That which is between double and single. *-m.* 1. Factitious gem. 2. A play in billiards.

doblez [do-bleth'], *m.* 1. Crease, a mark made by folding; fold; duplication, duplicature. *(Anat.)* A fold which forms a membrane by being turned back upon itself. 2. Duplicity, doubleness, disingenuity, dissimulation, double-dealing.

doblo [do'-blo], *m. (Law.)* Double.

doblón [do-blone'], *m.* 1. Doubloon, a Spanish gold coin. **Doblón de oro**, gold coin. 2. **Doblón de vaca**, tripes of a bullock or cow.

doblonada [do-blo-nah'-dah], *f.* Heap of doubloons or money. **Echar doblonadas**, to exaggerate one's revenues.

dobrao [do-brah'-o], *m.* A Portuguese gold coin, corresponding to the doubloon.

doce [do'-thay], *m.& a.* 1. Twelve. 2. Twelfth, as **El doce de Abril**, the 12th of April.

doceavo [do-thay-ah'-vo], *a.* Twelfth. *-m.* Twelfth.

docena [do-thay'-nah], *f.* Dozen. **Docena de fraile**, baker's dozen. **A docenas**, abundantly, in great quantities. **Por docenas**, by the dozen.

docenal [do-thay-nahl'], *a.* That which is sold by dozens.

docenario, ria [do-thay-nah'-re-o, ah], *a.* Containing twelve.

docente [do-then'-tay], *a.* Teaching. **Iglesia docente**, the body of prelates and clergy. **Personal docente**, teaching staff.

doceno, na [do-thay'-no, nah], *a.* Twelfth.

doceno [do-thay'-no], *m. & a.* A kind of cloth, the warp of which consists of twelve hundred threads.

doceñal [do-thay-nyahl'], *a.* That which consists of twelve years.

dócil [do'-theel], *a.* 1. Docile, mild, tractable, gentle. 2. Obedient, pliant, flexible, governable. 3. Ductile, pliable, malleable, flexible.

docilidad [do-the-le-dahd'], *f.* 1. Docility. 2. Flexibleness, compliance, easiness to be persuaded. 3. Manageableness, tractableness. 4. Gentleness, meekness.

dócilmente [do'-theel-men-tay], *adv.* Tractably, obediently.

docimástica [do-the-mahs'-te-cah], *f.* Assay, the docimastic art, the art of assaying minerals or ores.

doctamente [doc-tah-men'-tay], *adv.* Learnedly.

doctilocuo, cua [doc-te-lo'-coo-o, ah], *a.* Fluent and elegant in speech.

docto, ta [doc'-to, tah], *a.* Learned.

doctor [doc-tor'], *m.* 1. Doctor in medicine, law, physics, or philosophy. **Doctor en derecho**, doctor of laws. 2. Any able or learned teacher. 3. *(Coll.)* A physician.

doctora [doc-to'-rah], *f.* 1. Doctoress, she who professes the skill of a doctor; a vain, impertinent, or assuming woman. 2. A female medical practitioner. 3. Title given to Saint Theresa.

doctorado [doc-to-rah'-do], *m.* Doctorate, doctorship. **Estudiante de doctorado**, research student.

doctoral [doc-to-rahl'], *a.* Doctoral.

doctoral [doc-to-rah'], *f.* The canonry called **doctoral** in the Spanish cathedrals. *-m.* The canon who possesses the **doctoral** canonry, councillor of the cathedral.

doctoramiento [doc-to-rah-me-en'-to] *m.* 1. The act of taking the degree of doctor. 2. Doctorate, doctorship.

doctorando [doc-to-rahn'-do], *m.* One who is on the point of taking out his degree as doctor.

doctorar [doc-to-rar'], *va.* To doctorate, to dignify with the degree of a doctor. *vr.* To take one's doctor's degree.

doctorcillo [doc-tor-theel'-lyo], *m. dim.* 1. A little doctor: commonly used in a jocular style. 2. Quack, a petty physician.

doctorismo [doc-to-rees'-mo], *m. (Hum.)* The body of doctors.

doctrina [doc-tree'-nah], *f.* 1. Doctrine, instruction, lore. 2. Doctrine, the principles or positions of any sect or master. 3. Science, wisdom. 4. Discourse on the tenets of the Christian faith.

doctrinador, ra [doc-tre-nah-dor', rah], *m. & f.* Instructor, teacher.

doctrinal [doc-tre-nahl'], *m.* Catechism, an abridgment of Christian doctrine. *-a.* Doctrinal, relating to doctrine.

doctrinar [doc-tre-nar'], *pa.* 1. To teach, to instruct. 2. To break in horses.

doctrinero [doc-tre-nay'-ro], *m.* 1. Teacher of Christian doctrine. 2. Curate or parish priest in America. 3. One who accompanies a missionary in his teaching.

doctrino [doc-tree'-no], *m.* 1. An orphan child received into some college. 2. *(Met.)* A person of small talent and too free manners.

documentación [do-coo-men-tah-the-on'], *f.* 1. Documentation. 2. Papers, documents. **Documentos del barco**, ship's papers.

documental [do-coo-men-tahl'], *a.* Documental. *-m.* Documentary.

documentar [do-coo-men-tar'], *va.* 1. To document. 2. To inform, to acquaint. *-vr.* To get the necesary information.

documento [do-coo-men'-to], *m.* 1. Instruction, advice to avoid evil. 2. Document; writing, record. 3. Voucher, schedule. 4. *(Com.)* Any transferable paper, representing value; security. **Documentos del coche**, car papers, insurance papers of the car. **Documento de trabajo**, working paper.

dodecaedro [do-day-cah-ay'-dro], *m.* Dodecahedron.

dodecágono [do-day-cah'-go-no], *m.* Dodecagon.

dodecasílabo, ba [do-day-cah-see'-lah-bo, bah], *a.* Dodecasyllable, having twelve syllables.

dogal [do-gahl´], *m.* 1. Rope tied round the neck. 2. Halter, a rope to hang malefactors.

dogma [dog´-mah], *m.* 1. Dogma, established principle. 2. Act article of faith.

dogmáticamente [dog-mah´-te-cah-men tay], *adv.* Dogmatically, in a dogmatic manner.

dogmático, ca [dog-mah´-te-co, cah], *a.* Dogmatical or dogmatic.

dogmático [dog-mah´-te-co], *m.* Dogmatic.

dogmatismo [dog-mah-tees´-mo], *m.* 1. Dogmatism, disposition to affirm and believe in contrast to scepticism. Dogmatism admits an absolute certainty. 2. Dogmatic assertion, affirmation without proof. 3. Name of an ancient medical theory.

dogmatista [dog-mah-tees´-tah], *m.* 1. Dogmatist; a teacher of new dogmas. 2. An upholder of dogmatism.

dogmatizador, dogmatizante [dog-mah-te-thah-dor´, dog-mah-te-thahn´-tay], *m.* Dogmatizer, dogmatist.

dogmatizar [dog-mah-te-thar´], *va.* To dogmatize, to teach or assert false dogmas.

dogo [do´-go], *m.* 1. Terrier. 2. A kind of small dog.

dogre [do´-gray], *m.* A Dutch boat for the herring-fishery, two-masted and like a smack; a dogger.

doladera [do-lah-day´-rah], *a.* A cooper's adze.

dolador [do-lah-dor´], *m.* Joiner, one who planes and polishes wood or stone.

doladura [do-lah-doo´-rah], *f.* Adzing, shavings from planing.

dolaje [do-lah´-hay], *m.* The wine imbibed by pipe-staves.

dolamas, *f. pl.* **dolames,** *m. pl.* [do-lah´-mas, do-lah´-mes], Hidden vices and defects incident to horses.

dolar [do-lar´], *va.* To plane or smooth wood or stone.

dólar [do´lar], *m.* Dollar.

dolencia [do-len´-the-ah], *f.* 1. Disease, affliction. 2. *(Met. Obs.)* Danger; dishonor. **La dolencia de la economía**, the ills of the economy.

doler [do-lerr´], *vn.* 1. To feel pain, to ache or be in pain. **Me duele el brazo**, my arm hurts. **No me ha dolido nada**, it didn´t hurt at all. 2. To cause sorrow or distress in the mind. **Le duele aún la pérdida**, the loss still grieves him. **No me duele el dinero**, I don´t mind about the money. *-vr.* 1. To be in pain about anything, to be sorry; to repent. 2. To feel for the sufferings of others. 3. To lament, to complain. **Dolerse de**, to grieve. **Lo sufre todo sin dolerse**, he puts up with everything without complaining.

dolerita [do-lay-ree´-tah], *f.* Dolerite, an igneous rock.

dolerítico, ca [do-lay-ree´-te-co, cah], *a.* Doleritic, containing dolerite or resembling it.

doliente [do-le-en´-tay], *a.* Suffering or laboring under a complaint or affliction; sorrowful.—*m.* 1. Pall-bearer 2. Mourner.

dolimán [do-le-mahn´], *m.* Kind of long robe worn by the Turks.

dolo [do´-lo], *m.* Fraud, deceit, imposition, vulgarly, humbug. **Poner dolo**, to judge ill of a person.

dolomía [do-lo-mee´-ah], *f.* Dolomite, a brittle marble, phosphorescent upon rubbing.

dolomítico, ca [do-lo-mee´-te-co, cah], *a.* Dolomitic.

dolor [do-lor´], *m.* 1. Pain, sensation of uneasiness, aching, ache. **Dolor de cabeza**, headache. **Dolor de muelas**, toothache. **Dolor de tripas**, gripping. **Dolor de oídos**, earache. **Dolor de estómago**, stomachache. **Tener mucho dolor**, to be in great pain. 2. Affliction, anguish, grief, painfulness. **Le causa mucho dolor**, it causes him great distress. 3. Repentance, contrition. 4. Pain, the throes of childbirth. **Estar con dolores**, to be in labor.

dolorcillo, ito [do-lor-theel´-lyo, thee´-to], *m. dim.* A slight pain.

dolorido, da [do-lo-ree´-do, dah], *a.* Doleful, afflicted, painful, heartsick. V. DOLIENTE.

dolorido [do-lo-ree´-do], *m.* 1. The chief mourner, the nearest relation of a person deceased. 2. One in pain.

dolorosamente [do-lo-ro-sah-men´-tay], *adv.* Painfully, sorrowfully, miserably.

doloroso, sa [do-lo-ro´-so, sah], *a.* Sorrowful, afflicted, dolorous, dismal, doleful; painful.

dolosamente [do-lo´-sah-men-tay]**,** *adv.* Deceitfully.

doloso, sa [do-loh´-so, sah], *a.* Deceitful, knavish.

domable [do-mah´-blay], *a.* Tamable, conquerable.

domador, ra [do-mah-dor´, rah], *m. & f.* 1. Tamer, subduer. 2. Horse-breaker.

domadura [do-mah-doo´-rah], *f.* Act of taming or subduing.

domar [do-mar´], *va.* 1. To tame: to break or to break in. 2. To subdue, to overcome, to master, to conquer.

dombo [dom´-bo], *m.* Dome, cupola.

domeñar [do-may-nyar´], *va.* To reclaim, to make tractable, to tame, to master, to subdue.

domesticable [do-mes-te-cah´-blay], *a.* Tamable.

domesticado [do-mes-te-cah´-do], *a.* Tame; pet.

domésticamente [do-mes´-te-cah-men-tay], *adv.* Domestically.

domesticar [do-mes-te-car´], *va.* To render gentle, to domesticate. *-vr.* To grow tame.

domesticidad [do-mes-te-the-dahd´], *f.* Domesticity, affability.

doméstico, ca [do-mes´-te-co, cah], *a.* 1. Domestic, domestical. **Economía doméstica**, home economy. **Gastos domésticos**, household expenses. 2. Domestic, inhabiting the house. 3. Domesticant, forming part of the same family.

doméstico [do-mes´-te-co], *m.* Domestic, menial.

domestiquez [do-mes-te-keth´], *f.* Meekness, tameness.

domiciliación [do-me-the-le-ah-the-on´], *f. (Fin.)* Automatic payment (a través de banco).

domiciliado, da [do-me-the-le-ah´-do, dah], *a. & pp.* of DOMICILIARSE. Received as a denizen or citizen of a place; domiciliated.

domiciliar [do-me-the-le-ar´], *va.* 1. To domicile, to establish; to house. 2. *(Com.)* To place. 3. **Domiciliar su cuenta**, to give the number of one´s account. *-vr.* To establish oneself, to take up residence.

domiciliario [do-me-the-le-ah´-re-o], *m.* Inhabitant, citizen.

domiciliario, ria [do-me-the-le-ah´-re-o ah], *a.* Domiciliary, intruding into private houses.

domiciliarse [do-me-the-le-ar´-say], *vr.* To establish oneself in a residence.

domicilio [do-me-thee´-le-o], *m.* Habitation, abode, domicile, home, dwelling-house. **Domicilio particular**, private residence. **Servicio a domicilio**, delivery service.

dominación [do-me-nah-the-on´], *f.* 1. Dominion, domination, authority, power. 2. *(Mil.)* Commanding ground. *-pl.* Dominations, some angelic beings.

dominador, ra [do-me-nah-dor´, rah], *m. & f.* Dominator.

dominante [do-me-nahn´-tay], *a.* 1. Dominant, domineering, dictatory ascendant; prevailing, excelling. **La tendencia dominante**, the dominant tendency. 2. Dominative, imperious, masterful. 3. *(Mus.)* Dominant, the fifth in the scale.

dominar [do-me-nar´], *va.* 1. To dominate, to rule, to act without control, to oversway. **Le domina la envidia**, he is ruled by envy. 2. To master, to lord, to lead, to command. 3. *(Met.)* To moderate one's passions, to correct one's evil habits. 4. To have a good grasp of. **Domina 7 idiomas**, he knows 7 languages well. *-vn.* To dominate (edificio); to tower above, to look down on. *-vr.* 1. To rise above others (colinas). 2. To control oneself.

dominativo, va [do-me-nah-tee´-vo, vah], *a.* Dominative. V. DOMINANTE.

dómine *m.* Latin teacher.

domingo [do-meen´-go], *m.* Sunday, the first day of the week, the Christian Sabbath. **Domingo de Adviento**, Advent Sunday. **Domingo de Pasión** or **de Lázaro**, Passion Sunday. **Domingo de Ramos**, Palm Sunday. **Domingo de Resurrección**, Easter Sunday. **Hacer domingo**, to pass a working day idling.

dominguero, ra [do-min-gay'-ro, rah], *a.* Belonging to the Sabbath, done or worn on Sunday. **Traje dominguero**, Sunday clothes, Sunday suit.

dominguillo [do-min-geel'-lyo], *m.* Figure of a boy made of straw, and used at bull-feasts to frighten the bulls. **Hacer su dominguillo de uno**, *(Coll.)* to make one a laughing-stock; to sport at some one's expense.

domínica [do-mee'-ne-cah], *f.* Sunday, in ecclesiastical language. **Domínica in Albis**, Low Sunday. *V.* Domingo.

dominical [do-me-ne-cahl'], *a.* 1. Manorial (derechos feudales). 2. Dominical, belonging to the Lord's day. **Oración dominical**, lord's prayer. 3. A veil used by women in the old days for receiving communion. 4. Sunday. **Periódico dominical**, Sunday newspaper. *f.* Discourse of the Sundays of Advent and Lent.

dominicano, na, dominico, ca [do-me-ne-cah'-no, nah], *a.* 1. Dominican, belonging to the Dominican friars. 2. Native of the island of Santo Domingo.

dominico [do-me-nee-co], *m.* Jacobin, a friar of the order of Saint Dominic.

dominicatura [do-me-ne-cah-too'-rah] *f. (Prov.)* Certain duty of vassalage paid to the lord of the manor.

dominio [do-mee'-ne-o], *m.* 1. Dominion, domination, power, right of possession or use. **Dominio público**, public property. 2. Dominion, authority. 3. Dominion, territory, region. 4. Domain, possession, estate.

dominó [do-me-no'], *m.* 1. Domino, a masquerade garment. 2. The game of dominoes. **Juego de dominó**, dominoes.

Don [don], *m.* 1. Don, the Spanish title for a gentleman. It is equivalent to *Mr.* in English, but used only before Christian names, as **Don Juan** or **Don Andrés Pérez**, Mr. John or Mr. Andrew Perez. 2. **Don** alone or with an adjective or epithet, was formerly equivalent to *Señor.* **Don Guindo**, one who boasts of learning which he does not possess. **Don Lindo**, a dandy.

don, *m.* 1. Gift, present. 2. Gift, faculty, dexterity, knack, gracefulness, ability. **Dones sobrenaturales**, supernatural gifts, as prophecy, etc. **Don de gentes**, an habitual skill to win the goodwill of those persons with whom anyone is acquainted. **Don de acierto**, habitual dexterity in doing everything in the most successful manner. **Don de lenguas**, gift for languages. **Don de palabra**, gift of oratory.

dona [do'-nah], *f.* 1. Woman, lady. 2, *pl.* Wedding presents which the groom makes to the bride. *(Acad.)*

donación [do-nah-the-on'], *f.* 1. Donation. 2. Donation, gift, grant. **Donación piadosa**, pious donation.

donadío [do-nah-dee'-o], *m.*1. *(Obs.) V.* DON. 2. *(Prov.)* Property derived from royal donations.

donado, da [do-nah'-do, dah], *m. & f.* Lay brother or lay sister of a religious community. *-pp.* of DONAR.

donador, ra [do-nah-dor', rah], *m. & f.* Donor, bestower, giver.

donaire [do-nah'-e-ray], *m.* 1. Grace, elegance, gracefulness, gentility. 2. Witty saying, facetiousness. 3. Gracefulness, ease, activity in walking. **Hacer donaire de alguna cosa**, to make little of anything.

donairosamente [do-nah-e-ro'-sah-men-tay], *adv.* Facetiously, wittily.

donairoso, sa [do-nah-e-ro'-so, sah], *a.* 1. Pleasant. 2. Graceful, elegant. 3. Witty, facetious.

donante [do nan' tay], *pa.* Donor, giver.

donar [do-nar'], *va.* To make free gifts, to bestow.

donatario [do-nah-tah'-re-o], *m.* Donee, grantee, a person in whose favor a donation is made.

donativo [do-nah-tee'-vo], *m.* Donative.

doncel [don-thel'], *m.* 1. An appellation formerly given to the king's pages. 2. A man who has not carnally known a woman. 3. *(Obs.)* The son of noble parents. 4. The youth who was not yet armed as a knight. **Pino doncel**, timber of young pines without knots. *-adj.* Mild, mellow in flavor. **Vino doncel**, wine of a mild flavor.

doncella [don-thayl'-lyah], *f.* 1. Maid, virgin, maiden, lass. 2. Lady's maid, waiting-maid. 3. **Doncella de Numidia**, *(Or.)* the Numidian heron. 4. *(Zool.)* Snakefish. 5. *(Bot.)* The sensitive plant, humble plant. **Doncella jamona**, an old maid.

doncelleja [don-thel-lyay'-hah], *f. dim.* Little maid.

doncellería [don-thel-lyay-ree'-ah], *f. (Coll.)* Maiden-head, virginity.

doncellez [don-thel-lyeth'], *f.* Virginity, maidenhood.

doncellica, ita [don-thel-lyee'-cah, ee'-tah], *f. dim.* A young maid, a girl.

donde [don-day], *adv.* 1. *V.* ADONDE. 2. Where, in what place? 3. Whither, to what place? **¿De dónde?**, from what place? **Dondequiera**, Anywhere. **¿Hacia dónde?**, towards what place? **¿Por dónde?**, by what way or road?, by what reason or cause? **Fue adonde estaban**, he went to where they were. **No hay por donde cogerle**, there´s no way to catch him. *-inter.* **¿Dónde lo dejaste?**, where did you leave it? **¿Adónde vas?**, where are you going?

dondequiera [don-day-ke-ay'-rah], *adv.* Anywhere. **Por dondequiera**, everywhere. *-conj.* Anywhere, wherever. **Dondequiera que lo busques**, wherever you look for it.

dondiego [don-de-ay'-go]. *(Bot.)* The morning-glory; jalap, marvel of Peru.

donecillo [do-nay-theel'-lyo], *m. dim.* A small present.

dongola [don-go'-lah], *f.* A beverage, like beer, made in Ethiopia.

dongón [don-gone'], *m.* A tree of the Philippine Islands, whose wood is of stony hardness and serves to make keels and other resisting parts of vessels.

donguindo [don-geen'-do], *m.* A pear-tree of larger fruit than the ordinary.

donillero [do-nil-lyay´-ro], *m.* Swindler, sharper, a tricking gambler.

donjuán [don-hoo-ahn'], *m. (Bot.) V.* DONDIEGO.

donosamente [do-no'-sah-men-tay], *adv.* Gracefully, pleasing, comelily.

donosidad [do-no-se-dahd'], *f.* Gracefulness, wittiness, festivity.

donosilla [do-no-seel'-lyah], *f.* Piece of plaited muslin, which ladies used to wear around their necks.

donoso, sa [do-no'-so, sah], *a.* Gay, witty, pleasant.

donosura [do-no soo' rah], *f.* Gracefulness, grace, elegance, gentility.

donpedro [don-pay'-dro], *m.* Morning glory. *V.* DOMPEDRO.

doña [do'-nyah], *f.* Lady, mistress.

doñear [do-nyay-ar'], *vn. (Coll.)* To pass the time or converse much with women.

doñegal, doñigal [do-nyay-gahl', do-nye-gahl'], *a.* Applied to a kind of figs, red inside.

dopado [do-pah'-do], *a.* Doped, doped-up.

dopar [do-par'], *va.* To dope, to drug.

doping [do'-peen], *m.* Doping, drugging.

doquier, doquiera [do-ke-err', do-ke-ay´-rah], *adv. V.* DONDEQUIERA.

dorada, doradilla [do-rah'-dah, do-rah-deel'-lyah], *f. (Zool.)* Gilthead, giltpoll.

doradilla [do-rah-deel'-lyah], *f.* 1. *(Bot.)* Common ceterach. 2. Gilthead (fish).

doradillo [do-rah-deel'-lyo], *m.* 1. Fine brass wire. 2. Wagtail, a small bird.

dorado, da [do-rah'-do, dah], *a.* Gilt. **Sopa dorada**, a high-colored soup. *-pp.* of DORAR.

dorado [do-rah'-do], *m.* 1.Gilding. *V.* DORADURA. 2. *(Zool.) V.* DORADA.

dorador [do-rah-dor'], *m.* Gilder.

doradura [do-rah-doo'-rah], *f.* Gilding.

doral [do-rahl'], *m. (Orn.)* Flycatcher.

dorar [do-rar'], *va.* 1. To gild, as with gold. 2. *(Met.)* To palliate, to excuse. 3. *(Poet.)* To gild, to illuminate with the rays of the sun, as a mountain top. 4. To coat pastry with the yolk of egg, to yellow it.

dórico, ca [do'-re-co, cah], *a.* Doric.

dorífora [do-ree'-fo-rah], *f.* The Colorado potato beetle, a noxious pest.

doríforo [do-ree'-fo-ro], *m.* A beetle of the chrysomelid group, of equinoctial America, of brilliant coloring.

dormán [dor-mahn'], *m.* Dolman, a lady's jacket; named from a huzzar's jacket.

dormida [dor-mee'-dah], *f.* 1. Time during which the silkworm sleeps and rests before each molt. In general, time spent in sleep. 2. The place where animals repose. 3. *(Amer.)* Alcove, bed.

dormidera [dor-me-day'-rah], *f.* *(Bot.)* Garden-poppy. -*pl.* Sleepiness, drowsiness. *V.* ADORIMIDERA.

dormidero, ra [dor-me-day'-ro, rah], *a.* Sleepy, soporiferous, narcotic, somniferous.—*m.* Place where cattle repose.

dormidor [dor-me-dor'], *m.* A great sleeper.

dormidos [dor-mee'-dos], *m. pl. V.* DURMIENTES.

dormiente [dor-me-en'-tay], *pa. V.* DURMIENTE.

dormilón, na [dor-me-lone', nah], *m. & f.* A dull, sleepy person, one who sleeps much.

dormir [dor-meer'], *vn.* 1. To sleep. 2. To sleep, to be inattentive, to neglect one's business. 3. To be calm or still or torpid. 4. *(Naut.)* Used of the magnetic needle, to lose its virtue. 5. To be slow and heavy in moving (barcos). 6. To be in the pupa state. 7. Among Freemasons, to cease to be an active member of any lodge. **Dormir la siesta**, to take a nap after dinner. **Dormir al sereno**, to sleep in the open. **Dormir a pierna suelta, a pierna tendida** or **a sueño suelto**, *(Coll.)* To sleep carelessly. **Dormir como un lirón**, to sleep like a log. **Dormir con uno**, to sleep with somebody. -*vr.* To be overcome by sleep, to fall asleep.

dormitar [dor-me-tar'], *vn.* To doze, to nap, to mope.

dormitivo [dor-me-tee'-vo], *m.* Domitive, a soporiferous potion.

dormitorio [dor-me-to'-re-o], *m.* 1. In convents and colleges, a large room where novices or collegians sleep. 2. Dormitory, bedroom.

dornajo [dor-nah'-ho], *m.* A trough.

dorsal [dor-sahl'], *a.* Dorsal, belonging to the back.

dorsífero, ra [dor-see'-fay-ro, rah], *a.* *(Bot.)* Dorsiferous, dorsiparous.

dorso [dor'-so], *m.* The back part of anything; dorsum. **Al dorso**, on back, on the other side. **Escribir algo al dorso**, to write something on the back.

dos [dose], *m. & a.* 1. Two. 2. Second. **Dos de Abril**, the 2nd of April. 3. Deuce. 4. **A dos manos**, with both hands, with open arms. **Dos a dos**, two by two. **De dos en dos**, two by two, by couples. **Dos veces**, twice, double. **Las dos**, two o'clock. **Como ése no hay dos**, they don't come any better than that.

dosañal [dos-ah-nyahl'], *a.* Biennial, of two years.

doscientos, tas [dos-the-en'-tos, tas], *a. pl. & n.* Two hundred.

dosel [dosel'], *m.* A canopy.

doselera [do-say-lay'-rah], *f.* Valance, the drapery of a canopy.

doselico [do-say-lee'-co], *m. dim.* A small canopy.

dosier [do-se-ayr'], *m.* Dossier.

dosificación [do-se-fe-cah-the-on'], *f.* Dosage.

dosificar [do-se-fe-car'], *va.* To measure out (medicina); to put up in doses.

dosis [do'-sis], *f.* 1. Dose, as of medicine. 2. Quantity.

dotación [do-tah-the-on'], *f.* 1. Dotation, endowment, foundation, a revenue established for any purpose. 2. Dotation, the act of giving a dowry. **Dotación de navíos**, *(Naut.)* fund appropriated to the repairing of ships. 3. **Dotación de un buque**, the complement of a crew. 4. *(Prov.)* Stock. 5. Munition and garrison of a fortress.

dotado, da [do-tah'-do, dah], *a. & pp.* of DOTAR. Dowered, portioned. **Dotado de**, endowed with, gifted with. **Bien dotado**, highly talented.

dotador, ra [do-tah-dor', rah], *m. & f.* One who portions or endows; donor, instituter.

dotal [do-tahl'], *a.* Dotal, relating to a portion or dowry.

dotar [do-tar'], *va.* 1. To portion, to endow with a fortune, to give a portion. **La dotó con un millón**, he gave her a million as a dowry. 2. To gift, to endow with powers or talents. **La naturaleza le dotó de buenas cualidades**, nature endowed him with good qualities. 3. To settle a sum for a particular purpose (beca); to endow: **La Academia ha dotado 2 premios**, the Academy has established 2 prizes. 4. *(Mech. etc.)* To supply, to fit, to provide. **Dotar un avión de todos los adelantos modernos**, to equip a plane with all the latest devices.

dote [doh'tay], *m. & f.* 1. Dower, dowry, the fortune or portion given with a wife. 2. Stock of counters to play with. -*m. pl.* 1. The choicest gifts of the blessed. 2. Gifts, blessings, talents received from nature. **Tiene excelentes dotes**, she has great gifts. 3. Endowments.

dovela [do-vey'-lah], *f.* The curved sides of the keystone of an arch; keystone.

dovelaje [do-vay-lah'-hay], *m.* Series of curved stones for an arch.

dovelar [do-vay-lar'], *va.* To hew a stone in curves for an arch or keystone.

dozavado, da [do-thah-vah'-do, dah], *a.* Twelve-sided.

dozavo, va [do-thah'-vo, vah], *m. & f.* The twelfth part.

Dpto. *abr.* de **Departamento** (department, dept.).

Dr. *abr.* de **doctor** (Doctor, Dr.).

Dra. *abr.* de **doctora** (Doctor, Dr.).

draba [drah'-bah], *f.* *(Bot.)* Whitlow.

dracena [drah-thay'-nah], *f.* Dracaena, a palm-like plant belonging to the lily family.

dracma [drahc'-mah], *f.* 1. Drachm, the eighth part of an ounce. 2. Greek silver coin.

draconiano, na [drah-co-ne-ah'-no, nah], *a.* Draconian, hence barbarous and cruel.

dracúnculo [drah-coon'-coo-lo], *m.* *(Ent.)* Dracunculus, long worm which breeds between the skin and flesh, guinea-worm.

draga [drah'-gah], *f.* Dredge, dredger: applied to the machine and the barge which carries it.

dragaminas [drah-gah-mee'-nas], *m.* *(Mil., Naut.)* Mine sweeper.

dragar [drah-gar'], *va.* To dredge, to use the dredging-machine to deepen a channel.

dragante [drah-gahn'-tay], *m.* 1. *(Bot.)* Goat's thorn. 2. Tragacanth, a sort of gum. 3. *(Naut.)* Pillow of the bowsprit.

drago [drah'-go], *m.* *(Bot.)* Dragon-tree, a tree of America and the Canary Islands, from which the resin called dragon's blood is obtained.

dragomán [drah-go-mahn'], *m.* Dragoman, an interpreter among the Turks.

dragón [drah-gone'], *m.* 1. An old serpent; a fabulous monster. 2. An herb, about three feet high, of red or white flowers, which serves for ornament. 3. *(Mil.).* Dragoon, a horse-soldier who serves occasionally on foot. 4. White spots in the pupils of horses' eyes. 5. Kind of exhalation or vapor. 6. A chimney of a reverberatory furnace. 7. *(Astr.)* A constellation of the northern hemisphere, consisting of forty-nine stars. 8. (Head and tail of the dragon.) The two opposite points in which the orbit of the moon cuts the ecliptic.

dragona [drah-go'-nah], *f.* 1. Shoulder-knot worn by military officers. 2. Female dragon.

dragonal [drah-go-nahl'], *m.* *(Bot.)* V. DRAGO.

dragonazo [drah-go-nah'-tho], *m. aug.* A large dragon.

dragoncillo [drah-gon-theel'-lyo], *m.* 1. Drake, a kind of ancient gun. 2. *(Dim.)* A little dragon or dragoon.

dragonero [drah-go-nay'-ro], *m. V.* DRACENA.

dragontea, dragontía [drah-gon-tay'-ah, drah-gon-tee'-ah], *f.* *(Bot.)* Common dragon.

dragontino, na [drah-gon-tee'-no, nah], *a.* Dragonish.

drama [drah'-mah], *m.* Drama.

dramática [drah-mah'-te-cah], *f.* The dramatic art.

dramáticamente [drah-mah-te-cah-men-tay], *adv.* Dramatically.

dramático, ca [drah-mah'-te-co, cah], *a.* Dramatical, dramatic.

dramatizar [drah-mah-te-thar'], *va.* To dramatize.

dramaturgo, ga [drah-ma-toor'-go, gah], *m. & f.* An author of dramas especially if tragic.

drao [drah'-o], *m. (Naut.)* A monkey, ram, pile-driver.

drapa [drah'-pah], *f. (Arch.)* V. GRAPA.

drástico, ca [drahs'-te-co, cah], *a.* Drastic, acting powerfully.

drecera [dray-thay'-rah], *f.* A row of houses, trees, etc., which form a straight line.

drenaje [dray-nah'-hay], *m.* Drainage by means of subterranean pipes, subsoil drainage.

dríada, dríade [dree'-ah-dah, dree'-ah-day], *f.* Dryad, wood-nymph.

dril [dreel], *m.* Drilling, a strong cloth; drill.

drino [dree'-no], *m.* Kind of venemous serpent.

drizar [dre-thar'], *va. (Naut.)* To hoist up the yards.

driza [dree'-thah], *f. (Naut.)* Halliard. **Drizas del foque mayor,** throat-halliards.

droga [dro'-gah], *f.* 1. Drug, any ingredient used in physic. **Droga dura,** hard drug. **El peligro de las drogas,** the drug menace. 2. *(Met.)* Stratagem, artifice, deceit. 3. Nuisance (molestia). 4. Drug on the market, unsaleable article.

drogadicción [dro-gah-deec-the-on'], *f.* Drug addiction.

drogadicto, ta [dro-gah-deec'-to], *m & f.* Drug addict.

drogado [dro-gah'-do], *m.* Drugging; drug taking.

drogar [dro-gar'], *va.* To drug. *-vr.* To drug oneself, to take drugs.

drogmán [drog-mahn'], *m.* Dragoman.

drogodependencia [dro-go-day-pen-den'-the-ah], *f.* Dependence on drugs, drug addiction.

drogodependiente [dro-go-day-pen-de-ayn'-tay], *m & f.* Person dependent on drugs.

droguería [dro-gay-ree'-ah], *f.* A druggist's shop; trade in drugs.

droguero [dro-gay'-ro], *m.* 1. Druggist. 2. Cheat, bad paymaster.

droguete [dro-gay'-tay], *m.* Drugget, kind of woollen stuff.

droguista [dro-gees'-tah], *m.* 1. Druggist. 2. Cheat, impostor.

dromedario [dro-may-dah'-re-o], *m.* 1. Dromedary. 2. *(Met.)* An unwieldy horse or mule.

dropacismo [dro-pah-thees'-mo], *m.* Ointment for taking off hairs.

drope [dro'-pay], *m. (Coll.)* Vile, despicable man.

druida [droo-ee'-dah], *m.* Druid.

drupa [droo'-pah], *f. (Bot.)* Drupe, a stone fruit with fleshy exterior and nut within.

drusa [droo'-sah], *f. (Min.)* A kind of incrustation in a mineral formed of distinct crystals.

Dtor. *abr.* de **Director** (Director, Dir.).

Dtora. *abr.* de **Directora** (Director, Dir).

dúa [doo'-ah], *f. (Obs.)* Kind of personal service.

dual [doo-ahl'], *a. (Gram.)* Dual, belonging to two. **Duales,** Incisors. V. CORTADORES.

dualismo [doo-ah-lees'-mo], *m.* 1. A philosophy which recognizes two active principles in the universe, a spirit of good and one of evil, in perpetual conflict. 2. Antagonism.

duba [doo'-bah], *f. (Prov.)* Wall or inclosure of earth.

dublo [doo'-beo], *m. (Law.)* Doubt.

dubitable [doo-be-tah'-blay], *a.* Doubtful, dubitable, dubious.

dubitación [doo-be-tah-the-on'], *f.* Dubitation, doubt.

dubitativo, va [doo-be-tah-tee'-vo, vah], *a. (Gram.)* Used to express a doubt, doubtful, dubious (conjunciones).

ducado [doo-cah-do], *m.*1 Duchy, dukedom. 2. Ducat, an ancient gold and silver coin.

ducal [doo-cahl'], *a.* Ducal.

ducentésimo, ma [doo-then-tay'-se-mo, mah], *a.* Two-hundredth.

ducha [doo'-chah], *f.* 1. Shower. 2. Straight piece of land reaped by a reaper. 3. Douche, a jet of water, used for medicinal effect upon the body. **Tomarse una ducha,** to have a shower. 4. The instruments by which the jet is applied.

duchar [doo-chahr'], *va.* To give a shower, to douche. *-vr.* To have a shower.

ducho, cha [doo'-cho, cha], *a.* Dexterous, accustomed, skillful.

dúcil [doo'-theel], *m. (Prov.)* V. ESPITA.

dúctil [doc'-teel], *a.* Ductile.

ductilidad [dooc-te-le-dahd'], *f.* Ductility.

ductivo, va [dooc-tee'-vo, vah], *a.* Conducing. *(Acad.)*

ductor [dooc-tor'], *m.* 1. Guide, conductor. 2. *(Med.)* Probe.

ductriz [dooc-treeth'], *f.* Conductress

duda [doo'-dah], *f.* 1. Doubt, uncertainty of mind, suspense, fluctuation, hesitation, irresolution. **Fuera de toda duda,** beyond all doubt. **Ello constituye una duda importante,** this is a big question mark. 2. Doubtfulness, dubiousness. 3. Doubt, question, point unsettled. **Sin duda** or **sin duda alguna,** certainly, doubtlessly, without doubt. **No cabe duda,** there is no doubt about it.

dudable [doo-dah'-blay], *a.* Dubitable, dubious, doubtful.

dudar [doo-dar'], *vn. & va.* 1. To doubt, to hesitate, to be in suspense; to fluctuate. **No dudo de su talento,** I don't question his talent. **No lo dudo,** I don't doubt it. 2. To doubt, to fear. **Dudar de algo,** to doubt something.

dudosamente [doo-do-sah-mayn-tay], *adv.* Doubtfully, dubiously.

dudoso, sa [doo-do'-so, sah], *a.* 1. Doubtful, dubious, uncertain. 2. Dubious, hazardous.

duela [doo-ay'-lah], *f.* Stave. **Duelas para toneles,** hogshead staves. **Duelas para pipas,** pipe staves. **Duelas para barriles,** barrel staves.

duelaje [doo-ay-lah'-hay], *m.* V. DOLAJE.

duelista [doo-ay-lees'-tah], *m.* 1. Duellist. 2. Duellist, fighter, a single combatant.

duelo [doo-ay'-lo], *m.* 1. Duel, challenge. **Batirse en duelo,** to fight a duel. 2. Sorrow, pain, grief, affliction. 3. Mourning, funeral; lamentation, condolement. **Duelos,** troubles, vexations, afflictions. **Sin duelo,** abundantly. *(Yo me duelo, yo me duela, from Dolerse.* V. MOVER.)

duende [doo-en'-day], *m.* 1. Elf, fairy, goblin or hobgoblin, ghost. **Tener duende,** to be hypocondriac, to be restless. 2. A kind of glazed silk.

duendecillo [doo-en-day-theel'-lyo], *m. dim.* A little fairy.

duendo, da [doo-en'-do, dah], *a.* Domestic, tame (palomas).

dueña [doo-ay'-nyah], *f.* 1. Owner proprietress, mistress. 2. Duenna, a widowed woman who used to be in the principal houses for authority, respect, and care of the maid-servants. 3. A married lady. 4. A single woman who has lost her virginity.

dueña de casa [doo-ay'-nyah day cah'-sah], *f.* 1. Housewife. 2. Lady of the house.

dueñaza [doo-ay-nyah'-thah], *f. aug.* A very old duenna, and also the duenna who was very strict.

dueñesco [doo-ay-nyes'-co], *a. (Coll.)* Belonging to a duenna.

dueño [doo-ay'-nyo], *m. & f.* Owner, proprietor, master or mistress. *-m.* Master, with respect to a servant. **Ser dueño de,** to be the owner of. **Ser dueño de sí mismo,** to be self-possessed. **Ser dueño de,** to be free to. **Hacerse dueño de,** to take over.

duermevela [doo-err-may-vay'-lah], *m. (Acad.)* 1. *(Coll.)* Dozing, a nap. 2. *(Coll.)* Labored, interrupted sleep; a catnap.

duerna [doo-err'-nah], *f.* V. ARTESA.

duerno [doo-err'-no], *m.* Double sheet, two, sheets of printed paper, one within another.

dueto [doo-ay'-to], *m.* Duet, a short composition for two voices or two instruments.

dula [doo'-lah], *f. (Prov.)* 1. Herd of black cattle belonging to different persons. 2. Horses and mules which graze on the same pasture. **Vete a la dula,** *(Coll.)* begone, get out of my sight.

dulcamara [dool-cah-mah'-rah], *f. (Bot.)* Woody night-shade.

dulce [dool'-thay], *a.* 1. Sweet, pleasing to the taste, luscious, honeyed. 2. Sweet, not salty; not sour; fresh; without flavor. 3. Sweet, mild, soft, gentle, meek. 4. Confortable, pleasing, sweet, pleasant, agreeable. 5. Soft, ductile. **Un instrumento dulce**, a sweet-sounding instrument. **Con el acento dulce del país**, with the soft accent of the region. *-m.* 1. Confiture, sweetmeat, confection, candied or dried fruits. **Dulce de almíbar**, preserves, fruit preserved in sirup. 2. *V.* DULZURA.

dulcecillo, illa, ito, ita [dool-thay-theel'-lyo], *a. dim.* Sweetish, somewhat sweet.

dulcedumbre [dool-thay-doom'-bray], *f.* Sweetness. *V.* DULZURA.

dulcémele [dool-thay'-may-lay], *m.* Dulcimer, a musical instrument.

dulcemente [dool-thay-men'-tay], *adv.* Sweetly, delightfully, mildly, gently.

dulcenta [dool-cen'-tah], *f.* A large kind of apple, red and savory, suited for making cider.

dulcería [dool-thay-ree'-ah], *f.* Confectionery-shop.

dulcera [dool-thay'-rah], *f.* A preserve dish, generally of glass.

dulcero, ra [dool-thay'-ro, rah], *m. & f.* Confectioner.

dulcificación [dool-the-fe-cah-the-on'], *f.* Dulcification.

dulcificante [dool-the-fe-cahn'-tay], *pa.* Dulcifying; sweetener.

dulcificar [dool-the-fe-car'], *va.* To sweeten, to dulcify. *-vr.* To turn mild.

dulcinea [dool-the-nay'-ah], *f.* Mistress, beloved one, in allusion to the celebrated character of this name in Don Quixote.

dulcir [dool-theer'], *va.* To grind plate-glass, to remove the inequalities of the surface, to polish.

dulcísono, na [dool-thee'-so-no, nah], *a.* Sweet toned.

dulero [doo-lay'-ro], *m. (Prov.)* Herdsman.

dulía [doo-lee'-ah], *f.* Dulia, worship of the saints.

dulimán [doo-le-mahn'], *m.* Long robe worn by the Turks.

dulzaina [dool-thah'-e-nah], *f.* 1. A musical wind instrument. 2. *(Mex.)* A lute. 3. *(Coll.)* Quantity of sweetmeats.

dulzamara [dool-thah-mah'-rah], *f. (Bot.) V.* DULCAMARA.

dulzarrón, na [dool-thar-rone', nah], *a.* Cloying, sickening, by being too sweet.

dulzor [dool-thorr'], *m. V.* DULZURA.

dulzorar [dool-tho-rar'], *va. (Prov.)* To sweeten, to dulcify.

dulzura [dool-thoo'-rah], *f.* 1. Sweetness. 2. Sweetness, meekness, gentleness, graciousness, agreeableness. 3. Confortableness, pleasure. 4. Forbearance. 5. A graceful and pleasing manner of speaking or writing.

dulzurar [dool-thoo-rar'], *va.* 1. *(Chem.)* To free from saltness, to dulcify. 2. *(Obs.)* To soften, to mitigate.

dulleta [dool-lyay'-tah], *f.* A loose wrapper, for use in cold weather over the house-dress.

duna [doo-nah], *f.* Dune.

dunas [doo'-nas], *f. pl.* Downs, banks of sand which the sea forms on a coast, dunes.

duneta [doo-nay'-tah], *f. (Naut.)* The highest part of the poop.

dungarra [doon-gar'-rah], *f.* A sort of white cotton stuff, made in Persia.

dúo [doo'-o], *m. (Mus.)* Duo, duet, a musical composition.

duodecaedro [doo-o-day-cah-ay'-dro], *m. (Geom.)* Dodecahedron, a solid body of twelve faces.

duodecágono, na [doo-o-day-cah'-go-no, nah], *a. & m. & f.* Dodecagon, a polygon of twelve sides.

duodecasílabo, ba [doo-o-day-cah-see'-lah-bo, bah], *a.* Consisting of twelve syllables.

duodécima [doo-o-day'-the-mah], *f. (Mus.)* A twelfth, octave of the fifth.

duodecimal [doo-o-day-the-mahl'], *a.* 1. The last of twelve. 2. Duodecimal, a sistem of enumeration employing twelve

distinct characters, and having more common divisors than the decimal.

duodecimo, ma [doo-o-day'-the-mo, ma], *a.* Twelfth.

duodécuplo, pla [doo-o-day'-coo-plo, plah], *a.* Duodecuple, twelve fold.

duodenal [doo-o-day-nahl'], *a.* Duodenal, relating to the duodenum.

duodenario, ria [doo-o-day-nah'-re-o, ah], *a.* 1. Lasting twelve days. 2. Divided into twelve parts.

duodeno, na [doo-o-day'-no, nah], *a.* Twelfth.

duodeno [doo-o-day'-no], *m. & a. (Anat.)* Duodenum, the first of the small intestines.

duomesino, na [doo-o-may-see'-no, nah], *a.* Of two months, or relating to that space of time.

dupa [doo'-pah], *m.* Dupe.

dupla [doo'-plah], *f.* In colleges, an allowance of provision larger than usual.

duplex [doo-plex], *m.* 1. Split level flat; semidetached house. 2. *(Telec.)* Link up. 3. *(Comput.)* Duplex.

dúplica [doo'-ple-cah], *f.* A writing in which the defendant replies to the complaint of the plaintiff.

duplicación [doo-ple-cah-the-on'], *f.* 1. Duplication; the act of multiplying by two. 2. Conduplication, a doubling.

duplicadamente [doo-ple-cah-dah-men'-tay], *adv.* Doubly.

duplicado [doo-ple-cah'-do], *m.* Duplicate, counterpart. **Por duplicado**, in duplicate.

duplicado, da [doo-ple-cah'-do, dah], *a. & pp.* of DUPLICAR. Duplicate, doubled.

duplicador [doo-ple-cah-dor'], *m.* An instrument for estimating the particular state of a given volume of air, and its electricity, positive or negative.

duplicar [doo-ple-car'], *va.* 1. To double, to duplicate. 2. To repeat, to do or say the same thing twice. *-vr.* To double.

duplicatura [doo-ple-cah-too'-rah], *f. V.* DOBLADURA.

dúplice [doo'-ple-thay], *a.* Double: applied to ancient monasteries with separate cells for friars and nuns.

duplicidad [doo-ple-the-dahd'], *f.* Duplicity, deceit, foul dealing, falseness.

duplo [doo'-plo], *m.* Double, twice as much; duple.

duque [doo'-kay], *m.* Duke.

duquecito [doo-kay-thee'-to], *m. dim.* A pretty duke; a young duke.

duquesa [doo-kay'-sah], *f.* 1. Duchess. **La señora Duquesa**, Her Grace the Duchess. 2. Sort of couch.

dura [doo'-rah], *f.* Duration, continuance.

durable [doo-rah'-blay], *a.* Durable, lasting.

duración, durada [doo-rah-the-on', doo-rah-dah'], *f.* Duration, continuance, durableness, durability. **De larga duración**, long-lasting.

duraderamente [doo-rah-day'-rah-men-tay], *adv.* Durably.

duraderas [doo-rah-day'-ras], *f. pl.* Lasting; lasting prunella.

duradero, ra [doo-rah-day'-ro, rah], *a.* Lasting, durable.

duramater [doo-rah-mah'-ter], *f. (Anat.)* Dura mater, membrane inclosing the brain.

duramente [doo-rah-men'-tay], *adv.* Hardy, rigorously.

durando [doo-rahn'-do], *m.* Kind of cloth formerly used in Spain.

durante [doo-rahn'-tay], *prep.* During, in the meantime. **Durante muchos años**, for many years. **Habló durante una hora**, he spoke for an hour.

durar [doo-rar'], *vn.* To last, to continue, to endure. **Duró 5 años**, it lasted 5 years.

duraznero [doo-rath-nay'-ro], *m. (Bot.) V.* DURAZNO for the tree.

durazno [doo-rath'-no], *m.* 1. *(Bot.)* Common peach-tree. 2. Peach, the fruit of a peach-tree.

dureto [doo-ray'-to], *m.* A variety of apple.

dureza [doo-ray'-thah], *f.* 1. Hardness, solidity, firmness. 2. Acerbity or sharpness of temper, obduracy, hardness of heart, cruelty. 3. Steadiness, perseverance, obstinacy. 4. Want of softness or delicacy in paintings. 5. Tumor or callosity.

Dureza de vientre, costiveness. **Dureza de oído**, dullness of hearing. **Dureza de estilo**, harshness of style.

duriagra [doo-re-ah'-grah], *f.* A sort of cotton striped stuff, white and blue.

durillo, lla [doo-reel'-lyo, lyah], *a. dim.* Rather hard, hardish. -*m.* 1. (*Bot.*) Common laurustine, viburnum. 2. Callosity upon a horse, arising from the rubbing of some part of the harness or saddle. 3. **Durillo relevante**, bombast, fustian.

durmiente [door-me-en'-tay], *pa.* Sleeping, sleeper, dormant. -*m.* 1. In buildings, dormant or dormer, a piece of timber which rests on another; girder, stringer. 2. A sleeper (ferrocarril) 3. (*Naut.*) Clamp, shelf, a thick plank nailed to the ship's side within.

duro, ra [doo'-ro, rah], *a.* 1. Hard, solid, firm, knotty. **Más duro que una piedra**, as hard as nails. Tough (alimentos). Stale (pan). **Más duro que un mendrugo**, as tough as old boots. 2. Hard, vexatious, unbearable, unjust. 3. Hard, oppressive, rigorous, cruel, hard-hearted, unmerciful. **Ser duro con uno**, to be tough with somebody. 4. Stubborn, obstinate. **Duro de mollera**, dense (lerdo); pig-headed (terco). 5. Miserable, avaricious. 6. Rude, ill-natured, harsh, peevish, rough, rugged of temper. 7. (*Naut.*) Carrying a stiff sail (barco). 8. (*Pict.*) Harsh and rough, opposite of delicate and soft. Harsh, unsonorous (música). **A duras penas**, with difficulty and labor.

duro [doo'-ro], *m.* A five-peseta coin. **Estar sin un duro**, to be broke.

dutka [doot'-kah], *f.* A double flute, with three holes in each of the tubes, which are unequal. Used in Rusia.

duunvir [doo-oon-veer'] *m.* Roman judge.

duunvirato [doo-oon-ve-rah'-to], *m.* Duumvirate.

dux [doocs], *m.* Doge, magistrate in the republics of Venice and Genoa.

duz [dooth], -*a.* Sweet (dulce). Mild, gentle.

dzohara [dtho-ah'-rah], *f.* An Arabian divinity, corresponding to Venus.

E

e [A or ay] is the fifth letter of the alphabet, and the second of the vowels. **E** is pronounced in Spanish as in the English words they, **eh**; when unaccented, much like **e** in red. **E** was formerly used as a copulative conjunction, corresponding to **and**, but it is now in general replaced by *y*, yet retained when it precedes a word which begins with the vowel *i* or *hi;* as, **Sabios e ignorantes**, wise and ignorant men. **Padre e hijo**, father and son.

ea [ay'-ah], *m.* A kind of aspiration used to awaken attention. **Ea pues**, an interjection of inference or inquiry, equal to, *well then! Let us see.*

ebanista [ay-bah-nees-tah], *m.* Cabinet-maker, ebonist.

ebanistería [ay-bah-nees-tay-ree'-ah], *f.* Cabinet-work, cabinet-maker's shop.

ebanizar [ay-bah-ne-thar'], *va.* To ebonize, to give wood the color of ebony .

ébano [ay'-bah-no], *m.* Ebony, a hard, black wood.

ebonita [ay-bo-nee'-tah], *f.* Vulcanite, ebonite.

ebriedad [ay-bre-ay-dahd'], *f.* V. EMBRIAGUEZ.

ebrio, ria [ay'-bre-o, ah] *a* Inebriated, intoxicated, tipsy.

ebrioso, sa [ay-bre-o'so, sah], *a.* Intoxicated, drunken.

ebullición [ay-bool-lye-the-on'], *f.* 1. Ebullition. **Punto de ebullición**, boiling point. 2. (*Fig.*) Movement, activity. **La juventud está en ebullición**, young people are in a state of ferment.

ebúrneo, nea [ay-boor'-nay-o, ah], *a.* (*Poet.*) Made of ivory, resembling ivory.

eccehomo [ec-thay-oh'-mo], *m.* Ecce Homo. Behold the man: the name of any painting which represents Jesus given up to the mob by Pilate.

eccema, *f.* or **eczema,** *m.* [ec-thay'-mah], (*Med.*) Eczema, a disease of the skin.

ecdémico, ca [ec-day'-me-co, cah], *a.* (*Med.*) Non-contagious.

ecdora [ec-do'-rah], *f.* (*Med.*) Excoriation.

ecfora [ec-fo'-rah], *f.* (*Arch.*) Ecphora, the projection of any member beyond that immediately below it.

eclécticamente [ay-clec'-te-cah-men-tay], *adv.* Eclectically.

eclecticismo [ay-clec-te-thees'-mo], *m.* Eclecticism.

ecléctico [ay-clec'-te-co], *m.* Eclectic, ancient philosophers who professed not to belong to any sect but who chose what was good from all sects.

ecléctico, ca [ay-clec'-te-co, cah], *a.* Eclectic.

eclesiástico [ay-clay-se-ahs'-te-co], *m.* 1. Clergyman, ecclesiastic, priest. 2. Ecclesiasticus, one of the books of Scripture.

eclesiástico, ca [ay-clay-se-ahs'-te-co, cah], *a.* Ecclesiastical, ecclesiastic.

eclesiastizar [ay-clay-se-as-te-thar'], *va.* V. ESPIRITUALIZAR.

eclipsable [ay-clip-sah'-blay], *a.* That may be eclipsed.

eclipsar [ay-clip-sar'], *va.* To eclipse, to darken a luminary, to outshine.

eclipse [ay-cleep'-say], *m.* Eclipse.

eclipsis [ay-cleep'-sis], *f.* Ellipsis.

eclíptica [ay-cleep'-te-cah], *f.* Ecliptic, a circle supposed to run obliquely through the equator.

eclíptico, ca [ay-cleep'-te-co, cah], *a.* Ecliptic, belonging to the eclipse.

eclisa [ay-clee'-sah], *f.* A rail coupling fishplate, shin.

écloga [ay'-clo-gah], *f.* Eclogue, pastoral poem. V. EGLOGA.

eco [ay'-co], *m.* 1. Echo. **Hacer eco**, to echo. 2. The repetition of the last syllables of verse. 3. A confused remembrance or idea of the past. 4. Hole or hollow in a horse's sole, occasioned by a frush or other humor. **Hacer eco**, to accord, to agree; to do something great or notable. **Hacerse eco de una opinión**, to echo an opinion. **Encontrar un eco**, to produce a response.

ecóico, ca [ay-co'-e-co, cah], *a.* (*Poet.*) Relating to echoes.

ecología [ay-co-lo-ge'-ah], *f.* Ecology.

ecológico, ca [ay-co-lo'-he-co, cah], *a.* Ecological.

ecologista [ay-co-lo-hes'-tah], *a. m & f.* Conservation; environmental, conservationist; environmentalist.

ecólogo, ga [ay-coh'-lo-go, gah], *m. & f.* Ecologist.

ecometría [ay-co-may tree'-ah], *f.* Arch. Echometry.

ecómetro [ay-co'-may-tro], *m.* Echometer.

economato [ay-co-no-mah'-to], *m.* 1. Guardianship, trusteeship. 2. Cooperative store.

economía [ay-co-no-mee'-ah], *f.* 1. Economy, prudent management, moderation, frugality. **Economía de mercado**, market economy. **Economía dirigida**, planned economy. 2. Economy, the disposition of time and many other things. 3. (*Pict.*) The disposition of figures. 4. Scantiness, misery. 5. Economy, a political science.

economía doméstica [ay-co-no-mee'-ah do-mes'-te-cah], *f.* Home economics; domestic science.

económica [ay-co-no'-me-cah], *f.* Economics, household management.

económicamente [ay-co-no'-me-cah-men-tay], *adv.* Economically.

económico, ca [ay-co-no'-me-co, cah], *a.* 1. Economical, economic. 2. Economical frugal, avaricious.

economista [ay-co-no-mees'-tah], *m.* 1. Economist. 2. One who is a good manager of affairs.

economizar [ay-co-no-me-thar'], *va.* To economize. -*vn.* To economize, to save; to save up.

ecónomo [ay-co'-no-mo], *m.* 1. Curator or guardian, trustee. 2. An administrator of ecclesiastical livings which are under litigation.

ecosistema [ay-co-ses-tay'-mah], *m.* Ecosystem.

éctasis [ec'-tah-sis], *f.* (*Gram.*) Ectasis, the lengthening of a short syllable for the due measure of the verse.

ectipo [ec-tee'-po], *m.* Ectype, copy from an original.

ectropión [ec-tro-pe-on'], m. (Med.) Ectropion, eversion of the eyelids, as a morbid state.

ecuable [ay-coo-ay'-blay], a. 1. Equable, equal to itself. 2. (Obs.) Just, right.

ecuación [ay-coo-ah-the-on'], f. 1. Equation. the difference between the time marked by the sun´s apparent motion, and that measured by its real motion. 2. Equation, expression of equality between two algebraic quantities. **Ecuación de segundo grado**, quadratic equation. 3. Equalization.

ecuador, ecuator [ay-coo-ah-dor', ay-coo-ah-tor'], m. 1. Equator, a great circle of the celestial and terrestrial spheres. 2. The line.

ecualizador [ay-coo-ah-le-thah-dor'], m. (Tec.) Equalizer.

ecualizar [ay-coo-ah-le-thar'], va. To equalize.

ecuanimidad [ay-coo-ah-ne-me-dahd'], f. Equanimity; evenness of mind.

ecuatorial [ay-coo-ah-to-re-ahl'], a. Equatorial, relating to the equator. -m. Equatorial telescope.

ecuatoriano, na [ah-coo-ah-to-re-ah'-no, nah], a. Ecuadorian, belonging to Ecuador.

ecuestre [ay-coo-es'-tray], a. Equestrian.

ecuménico, ca [ay-coo-may'-ne-co, cah], a. Ecumenical, universal.

ecuóreo, rea [ay-coo-o'-ray-o, ah], a. (Poet.) Belonging to the sea.

eczema [ec-thay'-mah], m. V. ECCEMA.

echacantos [ay-chah-cahn'-tos], m. (coll.) A rattlebrained fellow.

echacorvear [ay-chah-cor-vay-ar'], vn. (coll.) To pimp, to procure.

echacuervos [ay-chah-coo-err'-vos], m. (coll.) 1. Pimp, procurer. V. ALCAHUETE. 2. Cheat, impostor.

echada [ay-chah'-dah], f. 1. Cast, throw. 2. The act of throwing oneself on the ground.

echadero [ay-chah-day'-ro], m. Place of rest or repose.

echadillo [ay-chah-deel'-lyo], m. A foundling.

echadizo, za [ay-chah-dee'-tho, thah], m. & f. 1. A Spy. 2. One who is employed in cautiously circulating reports. 3. Foundling.

echadizo, za [ay-chah-dee'-tho, thah], a. 1. That which is indirectly reported with the object of discovering some secret. 2. Applied to a person suborned to pry into other people's actions. 3. Supposititious, fictitious.

echador, ra [ay-chah-dor', rah], m. & f. Thrower, boaster, braggart.

echadura [ay-chah-doo'-rah], f. 1. The act of laying oneself down in a place. 2. Brooding, hatching, the act of sitting on eggs.

echamiento [ay-chah-me-en'-to], m. 1. Cast, throw, casting or throning. 2. Projection, the act of throwing away, rejection. 3. Ejection, casting out, expulsion.

echapellas [ay-chah-pel'-lyas], m. A woolsoaker.

echar [ay-char'], va. 1. To cast, to throw, to dart, to jet. 2. To turn or drive away, to eject, to reject, to cast away, to throw out or expel from an office or profession. 3. To shoot, to bud, to issue, to sprout, to burst out. 4. To put, to apply. 5. To lay on or impose as a tax. 6. (coll.) To eat, to drink. 7. To couple male and female animals for procreating. 8. To impute, to ascribe. 9. To perform for a wager. 10. To deal out, to distribute. 11. To publish, to give out, to issue. 12. With por and the name of a calling, to follow it. 13. With the words rayos, centellas, fuego, etc., to show much annoyance, to be very angry. 14. With the name of a punishment, to condemn to it. 15. With the infinitive of a verb and the preposition a, it signifies to begin the action denoted by the verb. **Echar a reír**, to burst out laughing. 16. **Echar por**, to go by one side or the other. 17. Speaking of horses, coaches, clothing, to use them, put into service. The verb **echar** is well described by a Spanish lexicographer as a verb of general utility. It serves frequently to assist the meaning of another verb, and enters into many phrases. **Echar carnes**, to become fat.

Echar por otra parte, to differ in opinions from another. **Echar de menos**, to miss. **Echar a perder**, to lose its good taste, to spoil. **Echar fuego**, to be the cause of a dispute. **Echar los hígados**, to be very much fatigued. **Echar a alguno a patadas**, to kick one out. **Echar al camino**, to take to the road, to become a highway robber. **Echar a fondo or a pique**, (Naut.) to sink a vessel. **Echar abajo, en tierra, por tierra or por el suelo**, to throw down, to demolish. **Echar el agua a un niño**, to baptize a child. **Echar en saco roto**, (Met.) to labor to no purpose, not to follow one's advice. **Echar de menos una persona o cosas**, to miss a person or thing. **Echar a uno la pierna encima**, to surpass or outshine a person. **Echar tierra a alguna cosa**, to bury an affair in oblivion. **Echar al mundo**, to create, to bring forth. **Echar mano**, to give assistance. **Echar a uno a pasear**, to send one abruptly about his business. **Echar suertes**, to draw lots. **Echar a correr**, to run away. **Echar en cara, a la cara or en la cara**, to reproach to one's face, to throw something in one's teeth. **Echar la ley a uno**, to judge and condemn a person to the utmost rigor of the law. **Echar a perder**, to spoil, to mar, not to utilize a thing. **Echarlo todo a rodar**, to spoil or mar utterly an affair. **Echar mano**, to lay hold of a thing; to make use of it, to seize, to catch. **Echar por en medio**, to cut short any difference. **Echar el pie adelante**, (Met.) to progress, to be foremost. **Echar el pie atrás**, to retrograde, to be last. **Echar una mano**, to lend a hand, to assist. **Echar un jarro de agua**, (Met.) to cut short a person´s discourse, or throw a damper on it by an unexpected dry remark. **Echar or echarse un borrón**, (Met.) to disgrace oneself. **Echar el guante**, to arrest a person. **Echar en tierra**, (Naut.) to land, to disembark. **Echar raíces**. a) to take root. b) to become fixed or established in a place. c) to be rooted or confirmed in something by inveterate habit or custom. -vr. 1. To lie, to rest, to stretch oneself to full length; of birds, to sit on eggs. 2. To throw oneself down. 3. To apply oneself to a business. 4. To yield, to desist; of the wind, to grow calm, to abate. **Echarse un pitillo**, to have a smoke. **Echarse una siestecita**, to have a doze. **Echarse atrás**, to throw oneself back. **Echarse en brazos de uno**, to throw oneself into somebody´s arms. **Echárselas de**, to boast of.

echazón [ay-chah-thon'], f. (Law.) Jetson or jettison, act of throwing goods overboard.

echeno [ay-chay'-no], m. In foundries, the pouring hole.

edad [ay-dahd'], f. 1. Age, the length of life. 2. Age, a particular generation or epoch of time. 3. Era, the time when a particular group of men or animals lived. **Edad de la aviación**, air age. **Edad atómica**, atomic age. **Edad media**, the Middle Ages. **Mayor de edad**, of age. **Menor edad**. a) minority. b) infancy. **Ser menor de edad**, to be a minor; to be under age. **Un señor de edad**, an older man. **Tener la edad de diez años**, to be ten years old. **Edad adulta**, adult age. **Persona de la tercera edad**, senior citizen. **Edad escolar**, school age. **Ella no aparenta la edad que tiene**, she doesn´t look her age. **De edad**, elderly.

edecán [ay-day-cahn'], m. (Mil.) Aide-de-camp.

edema [ay-day'-mah], f. Oedema, a general puffiness of parts, due to effusion of serum.

Edén [ay-dayn'], m. Eden, paradise.

edeografía [ay-day-o-grah-fee'-ah], f. Description of the organs of generation.

éder [ay'-der], m. (Zool.) Eider-duck.

edición [ay-de-the-on'], f. 1. Edition. **Edición aérea**, airmail edition. **Edición de bolsillo**, pocket edition. **Edición semanal**, weekly edition. 2. Publication, issue. 3. **Ediciones Ramírez**, Ramírez Publications. 4. (Fig.) Event, occasion. **Es la tercera edición de este festival**, this is the third occasion on which this festival has been held. **Edición asistida por ordenador**, (Inform.) desktop publishing. **Edición informática**, (Inform.) desktop publishing.

edicto [ay-deec'-to], m. 1. Edict, proclamation. 2. Poster, placard.

edificación [ay-de-fe-cah-the-on,], *f.* 1. Construction, the art of raising any building. 2. Edification, edifying.

edificador, ra [ay-de-fe-cah-dor', rah], *m. & f.* Edifier, constructor, builder.

edificante [ay-de-fe-cahn'-tay], *a.* Edifying; erecting.

edificar [ay-de-fe-car'], *va.* 1. To edify, to build, to raise or construct a building. 2. To edify, to instruct.

edificativo. va [ay-de-fe-cah-tee'-vo, vah], *a.* Exemplary, instructive.

edificatorio, ria [ay-de-fe-cah-to'-re-o, ah], *a.* Edificatory.

edificio [ay-de-fee'-the-o], *m.* Edifice, structure, fabric.

edil [ay-deel'], *m.* 1. Edile, a Roman magistrate. 2. *(Neol.)* V. CONCEJAL.

edilidad [ay-de-le-dahd'], *f.* Edileship.

editar [ay-de-tar'], *va.* 1. To publish. 2. To edit, to correct. 3. To edit (texto). 4. *(Inform.)* To edit.

editor, ra [ay-de-tor', rah], *a.* Publishing.-*m. & f.* 1. Publisher. **Casa editora**, publishing house. 2. Editor. **Editor responsable**, editor (article). **Editor de textos**, *(Inform.)* text editor.

editorial [ay-de-to-re-al'], *a.* Publishing. 2. Editorial. -*m.* (Article) Editorial. -*f.* Publishing house.

edredón [ay-dray-done'], *m.* 1. Eiderdown, the down of an eiderduck. 2. Feather-pillow.

educación [ay-doo-cah-the-on'],*f.* 1. Education (enseñanza), instruction. **Educación física**, physical education. **Educación sexual**, sex education. 2. Manners (modales). **Falta de educación**, bad manners. **Es una persona sin educación**, he´s a badly-bred person. **No tener educación**, to have no manners, to lack breeding. **Tiene muy mala educación**, he has very bad manners.

educado [ay-doo-cah'-do], *a.* Well-mannered, polite; nicely behaved; cultivated (culto). **Mal educado**, ill-mannered.

educador, ra [ay-doo-cah-dor', rah], *m. & f.* Instructor, educator, teacher (profesor).

educando, da [ay-doo-cahn'-do, dah], *m. & f.* Young person that enters a college to be educated.

educar [ay-doo-car'], *va.* To educate, to instruct, to nourish.

educativo, va [ay-doo cah-tee'-vo, vah], *a.* Educational.

educción [ay-dooc-the-on'], *f.* Eduction, the act of bringing out.

educir [ay-doo-theer'], *va.* To educe, to extract, to bring out.

edulcoración [ay-dool-co-rah-the-on´], *f.* Edulcoration, removal of acidity.

edulcorar [ay-dool-co-rar'], *va. (Chem.)* To sweeten, to remove acidity or acridity.

efe [ay'-fay], *f.* Spanish name of the letter F.

efebo, ba [ay-fay'-bo, bah], *a.* Name which the Athenians gave to youths of eighteen to twenty years.

efectivamente [ay-fec-te-vah-men'-tay], *adv.* Effectually, powerfully: certainly, actually.

efectividad [ay-fec-te-ve-dahd'], *f.* Effectiveness.

efectivo, va [ay-fec-tee'-vo, vah], *a.* 1. Effective, true, certain, effectual. 2. *(Com.)* Specie, cash, in coin. **Efectivo en caja**, cash on hand. **Hacer efectiva una letra**, to cash a draft. **Con 50 libras en efectivo**, with 50 pounds in cash.

efecto [ay-fec'-to], *m.* 1. Effect, result (resultado); operation. **Efectos sonoros**, sound effects. **Hacer efecto**, to take effect (medicina). 2. Effect, consequence. **Tener por efecto**, to have as a result. 3. Effect, purpose, meaning; general intent. **A este efecto**, to this end. **Al efecto de que**, in order that... -*pl.* 1. Assets. 2. Effects, goods, movables.-*pl.* *(Com.)* Drafts. **Efectos públicos**, public securities. **Efectos en cartera**, bills in hand. **Efectos a pagar**, bills payable. **Efectos a recibir**, bills receivable. **En efecto**, in fact, in truth, actually.

efectuar [ay-fec-too-ar], *va.* To effectuate, to bring to pass, to accomplish, to effect.

efemérides [ay-fa'-may'-re-des], *f. pl.* Ephemeris, a journal; an account of daily transactions.

efémero [ay-fay'-may-ro], *m. (Bot.)* Iris. Iris sylvestris.

efervescencia [ay-fer-ves-then'-the-ah],*f.* 1. Effervescence, ebullition. 2. *(Met.)* Ardor, fervor.

efervescente [ay-fer-vays-then'-tay], *a.* 1. Effervescent. 2. Seething.

eficacia [ay-fe-cah'-the-ah],*f.* Efficacy, activity.

eficaz [ay-fe-cath'], *a.* Efficacious, active, powerful, forcible, effective.

eficazmente [ay-fe-cath-men'-tay], *adv.* Efficaciously, actively, effectively.

eficiencia [ay-fe-the-en'-the-ah], *f.* Efficiency, effectiveness.

eficiente [ay-fe-the-en'-tay], *a.* Efficient, effective, effectual.

eficientemente [ay-fe-the-ayn'-tay-men-tay], *adv.* Efficiently, effectively.

efigie [ay-fee'-he-ay], *f.* Effigy, image.

efímera [ay-fee'-may-rah], *f.* 1. Ephemera, a fever that terminates in one day. 2. Ephemera, ephemerid, dayfly or Mayfly, an insect that lives but a day.

efímero, ra [ay-fee'-may-ro, rah], *a.* Ephemeral, ephemerous, diurnal, beginning and ending in one day.

eflorecer [ay-flo-ray-therr], *vr. (Chem.)* To effloresce, to fall into powder when exposed to air.

eflorescencia [ay-flo-res-then'-the-ah], *f.* *(Chem.)* Efflorescent.

eflorescente [ay-flo-res-then'-tay], *a. (Chem.)* Efflorescent.

efluencia [ay-floo-en'-the-ah], *f.* Effluence, emanation.

efluente [ay-floo-en'-tay], *f.* Effluent, emanant.

efluvio [ay-floo'-veo], *m.* 1. Effluvium or effluvia. 2. Exhalation.

efugio [ay-foo'-he-o], *m.* Subterfuge, evasion, shift.

efundir [ay-foon-deer'], *va.* To effuse, to pour out, to spill.

efusión [ay-foo-se-on'],*f.* 1. Effusion, efflux. 2. Confidential disclosure of sentiments. **Efusiones amorosas,** amorous excesses.

efusivo [ay-foo-se-vo], *a.* Effusive; extrusive, warm; effusive (manera). **Mis más efusivas gracias,** my warmest thanks.

efuso, sa [ay-foo'-so, sah], *a. & pp. irr.* of EFUNDIR. Effused

égida [ay'-he-dah],*f.* 1. Egis, the shield of Minerva 2. *(Met.)* Protection, defense.

egílope [ay-hee'-lo-pay], *f. (Bot.)* Wild bastard oat.

egipcio [ay-hip-the-o], *a.* Egyptian.

egiptólogo [ayhiptoh'logo], *m.* Egyptologist.

égira [ay'-he-rah], *f.* Hegira, the Mohammedan epoch.

égloga [ay'-glo-gah], *f.* Eclogue, a pastoral poem.

egocéntrico [ay-go-then'-tre-co], *a.* Egocentric, self-centered,

egoísmo [ay-go-ees'-mo], *m.* 1. Selfishness, self-love. 2. Egoism.

egoísta [ay-go-ees'-tah], *a.* Selfish, attentive only to one's own interest or case. -*m.* Egoist, one of a class of philosophers who professed to be sure of nothing but their own existence.

egotismo [ay-go-tees'-mo], *m.* Egotism, selfishness.

egotista [ay-go-tees'-tah], *m. & a.* Egotist, one who talks too much of himself.

egregiamente [ay-gray'-he-ah-men-tay], *adv.* Illustriously, egregiously.

egregio, gia [ay-gray'-heo, ah], *a.* Egregious, eminent.

egrena [ay-gray'-nah], *f.* An iron clamp.

egreso [ay-gray'-so], *m.* Item of expense, outgo.

egrisador [ay-gre-sah-dor'], *m.* A box in which lapidaries preserve the powder for grinding diamonds.

egrisar [ay-gre-sar'], *va.* To grind and polish diamonds.

eidero [ay-e-day'-ro], *m.* Eider-duck

ej. abr de **ejemplo** (example, ex.).

ejarrar [ay-har-rar'], *va.* To scrape the bristles from a hide.

eje [ay'-hay], *m.* 1. Axis. 2. Axle tree, axle. **Eje delantero**, front axle. 3. Center. 4. Wrist pin. **Eje vertical**, *(Aer.)* vertical axis. **Naciones del Eje**, axis Nations.

ejecución [ay-hay-coo-the-on'],*f.* 1. Execution, completion, performance. **Poner en ejecución**, to carry out, to carry into effect. **Ejecución secuencial,** *(Inform.)* sequential execution. 2. Execution, the act of the law, by which possession is given of body or goods. 3. Death inflicted by forms of law. **Pelotón de ejecución**, firing squad. 4. *(Mus.)* Execution, technical skill in playing or singing. **Poner en ejecución,** to put into execution, to carry out.

ejecutable [ay-hay-coo-tah'-blay], *a.* Executable, performable.

ejecutante [ay-hay-coo-tahn'-tay], *m. & a.* One who compels another to pay a debt by legal execution.

ejecutar [ay-hay-coo-tar], *va.* 1. To execute, to perform, to make, to do, to act, to carry out (proyecto). 2. *(Met.)* To impel, to urge to importune, to incite. 3. To oblige one to pay what he owes. 4. To put to death according to the form of justice (condenado).

ejecutivamente [ay-hay-coo-te-vah-men'-tay], *adv.* Executively, promptly.

ejecutivo, va [ay-hay-coo-tee'-vo, vah] *a.* 1. Executive, active. 2. Executory.

ejecutor, ra [ay-hay-coo-tor', rah], *m. & f.* 1. Executor or executer, one that performs or executes something. 2. Officer of justice who serves executions. **Ejecutor or ejecutor de la justicia,** executioner, executer. *V.* VERDUGO.

ejecutoria [ay-hay-coo-to'-re-ah], *f.* 1. *(Law.)* A writ or decree of execution. 2. Letters patent of nobility, pedigree. 3. Executorship.

ejecutoría [ay-hay-coo-to-ree'-ah], *f.* The post or office of an executioner.

ejecutorial [ay-hay-coo-to-re-ahl'], *a.* Applied to the execution of the sentence of an ecclesiastical tribunal.

ejecutoriar [ay-hay-coo-to-re-ar'], *va.* 1. To obtain a verdict or judgment in one's favor. 2. To establish the truth of a thing.

ejecutorio, ria [ay-hay-coo-to'-re-o, ah] *a.* *(Law.)* Executory, belonging to an execution or seizure.

ejemplar [ay-hem-plar'], *m.* 1. Exemplar, a pattern, model; original, prototype. **Ejemplar gratuito,** free copy. 2. Precedent, example. 3. Copy of a work. 4. An example warning. *-a.* Exemplary, worthy of imitation. **Sin ejemplar,** a) not to be a precedent: used in conceding special grants. b) without precedent.

ejemplarmente [ay-hem-plar-men-tay], *adv.* 1. Exemplarily. 2. Exemplarily, in a manner to warn others. 3. Edifyingly

ejemplificación [ay-hem-ple-fe-cah-the-on'], *f.* Exemplification, illustration by examples.

ejemplificar [ay-hem-ple-fe-car'], *va.* To exemplify.

ejemplo [ay-hem'-plo], *m.* 1. Example, precedent, instance; comparison. 2. Pattern, copy; exemplar, exemplarity, footstep. **Por ejemplo,** for instance. **Dar ejemplo,** to set an example for the imitation of others.

ejercer [ay-her-therr'], *va.* To exercise, to practice, to perform, to use. *-vn.* To practise; to be in office, to hold office.

ejercicio [ay-her-thee'-the-o], *m.* 1. Exercise. 2. Employment, exercise, office, task; ministry. **Durante el ejercicio actual,** during the current financial year. 3. Exercise, labor of the body, labor considered as conducive to health. 4. Military evolutions. **Hacer ejercicio.** 1. To drill troops, to train to military operations. **Ejercicio de defensa contra incendios,** fire drill. 2. To take a walk; to labor for health. **Estar en or tomar ejercicios,** to be in a spiritual retreat; to devote some days to meditation, prayer, etc. **El ejercicio hace maestro,** practice makes perfect.

ejercitación [ay-her-the-tah-the-on'], *f.* Exercitation, practice.

ejercitador, ra [ay-her-the-tah-dor', rah], *m. & f.* 1. Exerciser, practiser.

ejercitante [ay-her-the-tahn'-tay], *m.* 1. The person who is in a spiritual retreat. 2. One who maintains a thesis in disputation or for an academic degree. *-pa.* Exerciser, exercising.

ejercitar [ay-her-the-tar'], *va.* 1. To exercise, to put into practice. 2. To exercise troops, to teach by practice. **Ejercitar la paciencia de alguno,** to try the patience of someone. *-vr.* To practise, to do repeatedly in order to acquire skill.

ejercitativo, va [ay-her-the-tah-tee'-vo vah], *a.* That which may be exercised.

ejército [ay-herr'-the-to], *m.* An army. **Ejercito de ocupación,** army of occupation.

ejido [ay-hee'-do], *m.* Common, a public inclosed space of land.

ejión [ay-he-on'], *m.* *(Arch.)* Corbel, purlin.

ejotes [ay-ho'-tes], *m. pl.* (Mexican) String-beans.

el [el]. An article of the masculine gender. The. **El General Prim,** General Prim. **El tío ese,** that guy. **El de Pepe es mejor,** Joe´s is better.

él, ella, ello [ayl´ ayl'-lyah, ayl'-lyo], *pron.* He, she, it. **Él es alto,** he is tall. **Ella es guapa,** she is pretty.

elaboración [ay-lah-bo-rah-the-on'], *f.* Elaboration.

elaborado, da [ay-lah-bo-rah'-do, dah], *a.* Elaborate.-*pp.* of ELABORAR.

elaborador, ra [ay-lah-bo-rah-dor', rah], *m. & f.* One who or that which elaborates.

elaborar [ay-lah-bo-rar´], *va.* To elaborate, to finish with care.

elación [ay-lah-the-on'], *f.* 1. Elation, haughtiness, pride. 2. Magnanimity generosity. 3. Affected elevation or sublimity of style.

elaína [ay-lah-ee'-nah], *f.* Olein or triolein; absolute oil.

elaiometría [ay-lah-e-o-may-tree´-ah], *f.* The measurement of the density of oils.

elaiómetro [ay-lah-e-o'-may-tro], *m.* Elaeometer, a hydrometer for determining the density of oils.

elaiso [ay-lah'-e-so], *m.* 1. Greek name of the olive-tree. 2. A kind of palm, from the fruit of which in S. America an oil is obtained.

elamí [ay-lah-mee'], *m.* The note in music named mi. *(Ant.)*

elamita [ay-lah-mee'-tah], *a. & m.* Elamite, belonging to Elam.

elasticidad [ay-las-te-the-dahd'], *f.* 1. Elasticity. 2. Facility of being adapted to every use and necessity.

clástico, ca [ay-lahs'-te-ço, cah], *a.* Elastic, elastical. *-f.* An undershirt. *-m.* A spring. *(Mech.)*

elaterina [ay-lah-tay-ree'-nah], *f.* Elaterin, a crystallizable principle obtained from elaterium.

elaterio [ay-lah-tay-re-o], *m.* Elaterium, violent purge.

elatine [ay-lah-tee'-nay], *f.* *(Bot.)* Smooth speedwell.

elche [el'-chay], *m.* Apostate, renegade.

eldorado [el-do-rah'-do], *m.* An imaginary paradise of riches and abundance.

ele [ay'-lay], *f.* Spanish name of the letter L.

eleborina [ay-lay-bo-ree-nah], *f.* *(Bot.)* Helleborine.

eléboro, elebor [ay-lay'-bo-ro, ay-lay-bor'], *m.* *(Bot.)* Hellebore.

elección [ay-lec-the-on'], *f.* 1. Election, the act of choosing. **Una elección acertada,** a sensible choice. 2. Election, the ceremony of a public choice. **Elecciones generales,** general election. 3. Election, voluntary preference, liberty of action. 4. Election, discernment, choice, distinction, mind.

electivo, va [ay-lec-tee'-vo, vah], *a.* Elective.

electo, ta [ay-lec'-to, tah], *a. & pp. irr.* of ELEGIR. Elect, chosen.

electo [ay-lec'-to], *m.* Elect, a person chosen, nominee.

elector [ay-lec-tor'], *m.* 1. Elector, voter (elecciones). 2. Elector (antiguo príncipe alemán).

electoral [ay-lec-to-rahl'], *a.* Electoral.

electricidad [ay-lec-tre-the-dahd'], *f.* Electricity.

electricista [ay-lec-tre-thees'-tah], *m.* Electrician.

eléctrico, ca [ay-lec'-tre-co, cah], *a.* Electric or electrical.

electrificación [ay-lec-tre-fe-cah-the-on´], *f.* Electrification.

electrificar [ay-lec-tre-fe-car'], *va.* To electrify.

electrización [ay-lec-tre-tha-the-on´], *f.* *(Phys.)* Electrification, electrization.

electrizar [ay-lec-tre-thar'], *va.* 1. To electrify (cargar de electricidad), to make electric, to impart electricity. 2. To fill with enthusiasm. *-vr.* To electrize.

electro [ay-lec'-tro], *m.* 1. Electron or amber. 2. Electrum, a mixed metal of gold and silver.

electrocardiógrafo [ay-lec-tro-car-de-o'-grah-fo], *m.* Electrocardiograph.

electrocardiograma [ay-lec-tro-car-de-o-grah'-mah], *m.* Electrocardiogram.

electrocución [ay-lec-tro-coo-the-on'], *f.* Electrocution.

electrocutar [ay-lec-tro-coo-tar'], *va.* To electrocute.

electrochoque [ay-lec-tro-cho'-kay], *m.* Electroshock therapy.

electrodinámica [ay-lec-tro-de-nah'-me-cah], *f.* Electrodynamics.

electrodinámico, ca [ay-lec-tro-de-nah'-me-co, cah], *a.* Electrodynamic.

electrodo [aylectro'-do], *m.* Electrode.

electrodoméstico, ca [ay-lec-tro-do-mes'-te-co, cah], *a.* **Aparato electrodoméstico**, home appliance.

electróforo [ay-lec-tro'-fo-ro], *m.* Electrophorus.

electrógrafo [ay-lec-tro'-grah-fo], *m.* Electrograph.

electroimán [ay-lec-tro-ee-mahn'], *m.* Electromagnet.

electrólisis [ay-lec-tro'-le-sis], *f.* Electrolysia

electrólito [ay-lec-tro'-le-to], m. Electrolyte.

electrolizable [ay-lec-tro-le-thah'-blay] a. Electrolyzable, decomposable by electricity.

electrolización [ay-lec-tro-le-thah-the-on'], f. Electrolyzation, decomposing by electricity.

electrolizar [ay-lec-tro-le-thar'], *va.* To electrolyze, to decompose a chemical compound by electricity.

electromagnético, ca [ay-lec-tro-mag-nay'-te-co, cah], *a.* Electromagnetic.

electromagnetismo [ay-lec-tro-mag-nay-tees'-mo], *m.* Electromagnetism.

electrometría [ay-lec-tro-may-tree'-ah], *f.* Electrometry, the science or art of making electrical measurements.

electrómetro [ay-lec-tro'-may-tro], *m.* Electrometer, an instrument for measuring electricity.

electromotor, ra [ay lec-tro-mo-tor', rah], *a.* Electromotor. *-m.* An electric motor.

electrón [ay-lec-trone'], *m.* Electron.

electronegativo, va [ay-lec-tro-nay-gah-te'-vo, vah], *a.* Electronegative.

electrónica [ay-lec-tro'-nee-cah], *f.* Electronics.

electrónico, ca [ay-lec-tro'-ne-co, cah], *a.* Electronic.

electropositivo, va [ay-lec-tro-po-se-tee'-vo, vah], Electropositive.

electropuntura [ay-lec-tro-poon-too'-rah], *f.* Electropuncture.

electroscopio [ay-lec-tros-co'-peo], *m.* Electroscope.

electrotecnia [ay-lec-tro-tec'-ne-ah], *f.* Electrotechnics.

electroterapia [ay-lec-tro-tay-rah'-pe-ah], *f.* Electrotherapy.

electrotipia [ay-lec-tro-tee'-pe-ah], *f.* Electrotyping.

electrotípico, ca [ay-lec-tro-tee'-pe-co, cah], *a.* Electrotypic, relating to electrotyping.

electrotipista [ay-lec-tro-te-pees'-tah], *m.* Electrotyper.

electuario [ay-lec-too-ah'-re-o], *m.* Electuary, a kind of medicinal conserve.

elefancía [ay-lay-fan-thee'-ah], *f.* Elephantiasis.

elefante, ta [ay-lay-fahn'-tay, tah], *m. & f.* Elephant.

elefantíasis [ay-lay-fan-tee'-ah-sis], *f.* Elephantiasis.

elefantino, na [ay-lay-fan-tee'-no, nah], *a.* Elephantine.

elegancia [ay-lay-gahn'-the-ah], *f.* 1. Elegance, smartness, beauty of style. 2. Elegance, gracefulness; neatness.

elegante [ay-lay-gahn'-tay], *a.* Elegant, smart, gallant, fine, accomplished, nice, dainty, man of fashion (hombre). Fashionable woman (mujer).

elegía [ay-lay-hee'-ah], *f.* Elegy.

elegibilidad [ay-lay-he-be-le-dahd'], *f.* Eligibility.

elegible [ay-lay-hee'-blay], *a.* Eligible, preferable.

elegido, da [ay-lay-hee'-do, dah], *a.* 1. Elected, chosen. 2. Select, choice (selecto). **El presidente elegido**, the president-elect. *-m. & f.* Elected person. One chosen (escogido). *-pp.* of ELEGIR.

elegir [ay-lay-heer'], *va.* To choose, to elect, to name, to nominate. **Te toca elegir a ti**, the choice is yours.

élego, ga [ay'-lay-go, gah], *a.* Mournful, plaintive.

elemental [ay-lay-men-tahl'], *a.* 1. Elemental. 2. Essential, fundamental. 3. Constitutive, constituent.

elemento [ay-lay-men'-to], *m.* 1. Element. **Los cuatro elementos**, the four elements. 2. Element, the first or constituent principle of something. 3. Element, the proper sphere of something. **Elementos**, elements, rudiments (literatura, ciencia).

elemí [ay-le-mee'], *m.* Elimi, a resin.

elenco [ay-len'-co], *m.* I. Table index. **Elenco de artistas**, cast of characters (obra teatral).

elevación [ay-lay-vah-the-on'], *f.* 1. Elevation, the act of raising something. 2. Highness, loftiness. 3. Elevation, exaltation, dignity, advancement. 4. Elevation, rise, ascent; height. 5. Elevation, exaltation of mind, ecstasy, rapture. 6. Haughtiness, presumption, pride. 7. Altitude, the elevation of the pole above the horizon.

elevadamente [ay-lay-vah'-dah-men-tay], *adv.* With elevation, loftily.

elevado, da [ay-lay-vah'-do, dah], *a. & pp.* of ELEVAR. 1. Elevate, elevated, exalted, raised aloft. 2. Elevated, sublime, majestic, high, grand, lofty.

elevador [ay-lay-vah-dor'], *m.* Elevator. **Elevador de granos**, grain elevator.

elevalunas [ay-lay-vah-loo'-nahs], *m. (Aut.)* Electrically-operated window system.

elevamiento [ay-lay-vah-me-en'-to], *m.* Elevation, ecstasy, rapture.

elevar [ay-lay-var'], *va.* 1. To raise, to elevate, to heave, to lift up. 2. *(Met.)* To elevate, to exalt to a high station. *-vr.* 1. To be enraptured. 2. To be elated with presumption or pride. **La cantidad se eleva a...**, the quantity amounts to... **Los precios se han elevado mucho**, prices have risen a lot.

elidir [ay-le-deer'], *va.* 1. To weaken, to enervate, to debilitate. 2. *(Gram.)* To elide.

elijar [ay-le-har'], *va. (Pharm.)* To seethe or digest vegetable substances.

eliminación [ay-le-me-nah-the-on'], *f.* Elimination, exclusion.

eliminador, ra [ay-le-me-nah-dor', rah], *m. & f.* One who or that which eliminates.

eliminar [ay-le-me-nar'], *va.* 1. To eliminate, to remove one thing from another. 2. To remove a name from a list, a quantity from a calculation, etc.

elipse [ay-leep'-say], *f. (Geom.)* Ellipse, a conic section.

elipsis [ay-leep'-sis], *f. (Gram.)* Ellipsis.

elíptico, ca [ay-leep'-te-co, cah], *a.* Elliptic or elliptical.

elíseos [ay-lee'-say-os], *m. pl.* Elysian. **Campos Elíseos**, Elypsean fields.

elisión [ay-le-se-on'], *f. (Gram.)* Elision.

elite [ay'-le-tay], *f.* Élite.

élitro [ay'le-tro], *m.* 1. Elytron, a thickened wing-cover. 2. *(Bot.)* A common conceptacle.

elixir [ay-lic-seer'], or **elíxir** [ay-leec'-seer], *m.* Elixir (medicina).

ella [ayl'-lyah], *pr. f.* She (sujeto, personas). **Ella vino anoche**, she came last night. 2. Her, herself (enfático, personas). **Es ella**, it's her. **Lo hizo ella**, she did it herself. **Hablo de ella**, I'm talking about her. **Mañana será ella**, there will be trouble tomorrow. **Mi libro y el de ella**, my book and hers.

ellas pron. pers. pl. V. ELLOS.

elle [ayl'-lyay], *f.* Name of the letter *Ll*.

ello [ayl'-lyo], *pron.* 1. It; this business, that whole affair. **Ello es difícil**, it's awkward. **Ello no me gusta**, I don't like it. 2. **Es que ello...**, the fact is that. **Es por ello que...**, that is why... **Por ello no quiero**, that's why I don't want to.

ellos [ayl-lyos], *pron pers. m. pl.* 1. They. 2. Them (tras prep.). 3. Theirs (tras de).

elocución [ay-lo-coo-the-on'], *f.* 1. Elocution. 2. Language, expression, style.

elocuencia [ay-lo-coo-en'-the-ah], *f.* Eloquence.

elocuente [ay-lo-coo-en'-tay], *a.* Eloquent. **Un dato elocuente**, a significant fact.

elocuentemente [ay-lo-coo-en-tay-men'-tay], *adv.* Eloquently.

elogiador, ra [ay-lo-he-ah-dor', rah], *m & f.* Eulogist, encomiast, praiser. *-a.* laudatory, eulogitic.

elogiar [ay-lo-he-ar'], *va.* To praise, to extol, to eulogize, to laud.

elogio [ay-lo'-he-o], *m.* Eulogy, panegyric. **Hacer elogio de**, to praise. **Hizo un caluroso elogio del héroe**, he paid a warm tribute to the hero.

elote [ay-lo'-tay], *m. (Mex.)* A tender ear of maize. Also written *Helote.*

elucidación [ay-loo-the-dah-the-on'], *f.* Elucidation, explanation.

eludible [ay-loo-de-blay], *a.* Avoidable.

eludir [ay-loo-deer'], *va.* To elude, to avoid by artifice.

elzevir [ayl-thay-veer'], *m.* Elzevir (libro).

emaciación [ay-mah-the-ah-the-on'], *f. (Med.)* Emaciation, emaceration.

emanación [ay-mah-nah-the-on'], *f.* 1. Emanation. 2. Emanation, effluvium.

emanante [ay-mah-nahn'-tay], *pa.* Emanating, emanant, emanative.

emanar [ay-mah-nar'], *vn.* To emanate, to proceed from.

emancipación [ay-man-the-pah-the-on'], *f.* Emancipation.

emancipador, ra [ay-man-the-pah-dor', rah], *m. & f.* Emancipator.

emancipar [ay-man-the-par'], *va.* To emancipate. *-vr.* 1. To recover liberty. 2. To go out from tutelage. 3. To shake off a yoke.

emasculación [ay-mas-coo-lah-the-on'], *f.* Emasculation, castration.

emascular [ay-mas-coo-lar'], *va.* To castrate, to emasculate.

embabiamiento [em-bah-be-ah-me-en'-to], *m.* 1. Stupidity, foolishness. 2. Distraction, absence of mind.

embachar [em-bah-char'], *va.* To pen sheep, to be shorn.

embadurnar [em-bah-door-nar'], *va.* To besmear, to bedaub.

embaidor, ra [em-bah-e-dor', rah], *m. & f.* Sharper, impostor, swindler.

embaimiento [em-bah-e-me-en'-to], *m.* 1. Delusion, illusion. 2. Deceit, imposition, imposture.

embair [em-bah-eer'], *va.* To impose upon, to deceive.

embajada [em-bah-hah'-dah], *f.* 1. Embassy, a public or solemn message, legation. 2. Embassy, an ambassador's house.

embajador [em-bah-hah-dor'], *m.* Ambassador.

embajadora, embajatriz [em-bah-hah-do'-rah, em-bah-hah-treeth'], *f.* Ambassadress, ambassador's lady.

embajatorio, ria [em-bah-hah-to'-re-o, ah], *a.* Belonging to an ambassador.

embalador [em-bah-lah-dor'], *m.* Packer.

embalar [em-bah-lar'], *va.* To bale, to make up into bundles, to pack.

embalaje [em-bah-lah'-hay], *m.* Packing, package, baling.

embaldosado [em-bal-do-sah'-do], *m.* Tiled floor. *-a.* Tiled. **Embaldosado, da**, *pp.* of EMBALDOSAR.

embaldosar [em-bal-do-sar'], *va.* To floor with tiles, to tile (con baldosas).

embalijar [em-bah-le-har'], *va.* To pack up into a portmanteau.

emballenador [em-bal-lyay-nah-dor'], *m.* Staymaker.

emballenar [em-bal-lyay-nar'], *va.* To stiffen with whalebone (ballenas).

emballestado [em-bal-lyes-tah'-do], *m.* Contraction of the nerves in the feet of animals. -**Emballestado, da**, *pp.* of EMBALLESTARSE.

emballestarse [em-bal-lyes-tar'-say], *vr.* To be on the point of discharging a cross-bow.

embalsadero [em-bal-sah-day-ro], *m.* Pool of stagnant rainwater.

embalsamador, ra [em-bal-sah-mah-dor', rah], *m.* Embalmer.

embalsamadura, *f.* **embalsamamiento,** *m.* [em-bal-sah-mah-doo'-rah] Embalming.

embalsamar [em-bal-sah-mar], *va.* To embalm, to dam up; to retain, to collect.

embalsamiento [em-bal-sah-me-en-to], *m.* 1. Act of putting something into a pool of water. 2. The stoppage of water, forming a pool.

embalsar [em-bal-sar'], *va.* 1. To dam, to dam up (agua). 2. To sling, to hoist (izar). 3. To put something into a pool of still water. 4. To drive cattle into a pool of water to refresh them.

embalse [em-bahl'-say], *m.* 1. Dam (presa), damming, damming up (acción de embalsar); reservoir, dam (lago artificial) 2. Slinging, hoisting (izar). 3. Act of putting anything into a pool of water. 4. Act of driving cattle into water.

embalumar [em-bah-loo-mar'], *va.* To load a horse unequally.*-vr.* To embarrass oneself with business.

embanastar [em-bah-nas-tar'], *va.* To put into a basket.

embancadura [em-ban-cah-doo'-rah], *f.* The benches, collectively, of a rowboat.

embancar [em-ban-car'], *va.* To move to the center the spool of the spindles in looms, in order to begin to lay the warp. *-vr.* to run aground.

embaracillo [em-bah-rah-theel'-lyo], *m. dim.* A slight embarrassment.

embarazada [em-bah-rah-thah'-dah], *a.* Pregnant. **Dejar embarazada a una**, to get a girl pregnant. *-f.* Pregnant woman.

embarazadamente [em-bah-rah-thah-dah-men'-tay], *adv.* Perplexedly, with embarrassment, awkwardly.

embarazado, da [em-bah-rah-thah'-do, dah], *a.* Embarrassed, perplexed, mazy. *-pp.* of EMBARAZAR. **Embarazada**, pregnant.

embarazador, ra [em-bah-rah-thah-dor', rah], *m. & f.* Embarrasser.

embarazar [em-bah-rah-thar'], *va.* 1. To embarrass, to perplex, to hinder, to obstruct, to cumber. 2. To make pregnant.

embarazo [em-bah-rah´-tho], *m.* 1. Impediment, embarrasament, vexation, obstruction, obstacle. 2. Confusion, perplexity. 3. Pregnancy, time of gestation.

embarazosamente [em-bah-rah-tho'-sah-men-tay], *adv.* Difficultly, cumbersomely.

embarazoso, sa [em-bah-rah-tho-so, sah], *a.* Difficult, intricate, entangled, cumbersome, troublesome, vexatious, obstructive.

embarbascado, da [em-bar-bas-cah'-do, dah], *a.* Difficult, intricate, involved, complicated. *-pp.* of EMBARBASCAR.

embarbascar [em-bar-bas-car'], *va.* 1. To throw hellebore, mullein, etc., into water, to stupefy fish. 2. *(Met.)* To perplex, to confound, to embarrass. *-vr.* To be entangled among the roots of plants.

embarbecer [em-bar-bay-therr'], *vn.* To have a beard appearing, at the age of puberty.

embarbillar [em-bar-beel-lyar'], *va.* To join planks or beams together.

embarcación [em-bar-cah-the-on'], *f.* 1. Vessel or ship of any size or description. **Embarcación de arrastre**, trawler. 2. Embarkation. *V.* EMBARCO. 3. Navigation.

embarcadero [em-bar-cah-day'-ro], *m.* 1. Wharf, quay, or key. 2. Port, harbor.

embarcador [em-bar-cah-dor'], *m.* One who embarks or ships goods.

embarcar [em-bar-car'], *va.* 1. To embark, to ship, to put on shipboard. 2. *(Met.)* To embark, to engage another in an affair or enterprise. **Embarcar a uno en una empresa**, to involve somebody in an enterprise. *-vr.* 1. To embark, to go on shipboard. 2. *(Met.)* To embark, to engage in an affair. **Embarcarse en un asunto**, to get involved in a matter.

embarco [em-bar-co], *m.* Embarcation (personas), embarking, shipping (mercancías).

embargador [em-bar-gah-dor'], *m.* One who sequestrates or lays on an embargo; sequestrator.

embargante [em-bar-gahn'-tay], *pa.* Arresting, impeding, restraining. **No embargante,** notwithstanding, nevertheless.

embargar [em-bar-gar'], *va.* 1. (*Law.*) To sequestrate, to seize (juzgado), to attach, to lay an embargo upon. 2. (*Met.*) To impede, to restrain, to suspend. 3. To overcome (emoción, dolor)

embargo [em-bar'-go], *m.* 1. Embargo on shipping, sequestration. 2. (*Law.*) Extent, execution, distraint, seizure attachment. 3. Access (emoción). 4. Indigestion. **Sin embargo,** notwithstanding. **Sin embargo de,** despite the fact that.

embarnecer [em-bar-nay-therr'], *vn.* (*Obs.*) To grow plump, full, or fat.

embarnizador [em-bar-ne-thah-dor´], *m.* Varnisher.

embarnizadura [em-bar-ne-thah-doo'-rah], *f.* Varnishing.

embarnizar [em-bar-ne-thar'], *va.* 1. To varnish, to japan, to glaze. 2. (*Met.*) To adorn, to embellish, to set off.

embarque [em-bar'-kay], *m.* Putting goods and provisions on shipboard.

embarrado [em-bar-rah'-do], *a.* Muddy.

embarrador [em-bar-rah-dor'], *m.* Plasterer, dauber.

embarradura [em-bar-rah-doo'-rah], *f.* Overlaying with plaster or mortar.

embarrancarse [em-bar-ran-car'-say], *vr.* 1. To get mired in a deep hole. 2. (*Naut.*) To run aground.

embarrar [em-bar-rar'], *va.* 1. To daub or overlay with plaster, clay, or mortar. 2. (*Met.*) To confound or perplex an affair. 3. To besmear with mud. 4. To cover with plaster. -*vr.*, To collect or mount upon trees, as partridges when pursued.

embarrillar [em-bar-re-lar'], *va.* To barrel, to put in a barrel.

embarrotar [em-bahr-ro-tar'], *va.* V. ABARROTAR.

embarullar [em-bah-rool-lyar'], *va.* (*coll.*) 1. To confuse, to mix things in disorder. 2. To act without order or plan. -*vr.* To be confounded, overwhelmed.

embasamiento [em-bah-sah-me-en'-to]. *m.* (*Arch.*) Basis or foundation of a building.

embastar [em-bas-tar'], *va.* 1. To baste linen, silk, etc., to secure it in a frame to be embroidered. 2. To put stitches in a mattress. 3. (*Prov.*) To put a packsaddle on a beast of burden.

embaste [em-bahs'-tay], *m.* Basting.

embastecer [em-bas-tay-therr'], *vn.* To become corpulent; to become fat or gross. -*vr.* To become gross.

embatada [em-bah-tah'-dah], *f.* (*Naut.*) A sudden dash of the sea or wind against the course being followed.

embate [em-bah'-tay], *m.* 1. The dashing of the sea against something. 2. A sudden impetuous attack. **Embates,** sudden reversal of fortune.

embaucador, ra [em-bah-oo-cah-dor], *m & f.* Sharper, impostor, abuser.

embaucamiento [em-bah-oo-cah-me-en'-to], *m.* Deception, illusion.

embaucar [em-bah-oo-car´], *va.* To deceive, to delude, to humbug, to impose upon.

embaular [em-ba-hoo-lar'], *va.* 1. To pack in a trunk. 2. (*Met. coll.*) To cram with food.

embausamiento [em-bah-oo-sah-me-en'-to], *m.* Amazement, astonishment, absence of mind.

embazador [em-bah-thah-dor'], *m.* One who shades or darkens a color.

embazadura [em-bah-thah-doo'-rah], *f.* 1. The art of shading or darkening colors. 2. (*Met.*) Amazement, astonishment.

embazar [em-bah-thar'], *va.* 1. To tinge, to shade. 2. (*Met.*) To astonish, to strike with amazement. 3. (*Met.*) To impede the execution of a thing. -*vn.* To be amazed or astonished, to remain without action. -*vr.* 1. To become tired, disgusted, or satiated. 2. To blush.

embebecer [em-bay-bay-therr'], *va.* 1. To astonish, to stupefy. 2. To entertain, to amuse. -*vr.* To be struck with amazement.

embebecidamente [em-bay-bay-the'-dah-men-tay], *adv.* Amazedly.

embebecimiento [em-bay-bay-the-me-en'-to], *m.* Amazement, astonishment.

embebedor, ra [em-ba'-bay-dor', rah], *m. & f.* Imbiber.

embeber [em-bay-berr']. *va.* 1. To imbibe, to drink in. 2. To imbibe, to drench, to saturate. 3. To incorporate, to introduce, to include. 4. To shrink or make to shrink, to squeeze, to press. 5. Among curriers, to oil a hide. -*vn.* 1. To shrink, to contract itself. 2. To row thick and close. -*vr.* 1. To be enraptured or ravished, to be wrapt up in thought. 2. To imbibe, to admit or retain firmly in the mind.

embebimiento [em-bay-be-me-en'-to], *m.* Imbibition.

embecaduras [em-bay-cah-doo'-ras], *f. pl.* (*Arch.*) Spandrel.

embelecador, ra [em-bay-lay-cah-dor rah], *m. & f.* Impostor, sharper.

embelecar [em-bay-lay-car'], *va.* To impose upon, to deceive, to humbug.

embeleco [em-bay-lay'-co], *m.* Fraud, delusion, imposition, humbug.

embeleñado, da [em-bay-lay-nyah´-do, dah], *a. & pp.* of EMBELEÑAR. 1. Enraptured, ravished. 2. Stupefied, besotted.

embeleñar [em-bay-lay-nyar'], *va.* To stupefy, to besot.

embelesamiento [em-bay-lay-sah-me-en'-to], *m.* Amazement, astonishment, rapture.

embelesar [em-bay-lay-sar'], *va.* 1. To amaze, to astonish. 2. To charm, to subdue the mind by pleasure. -*vr.* To be charmed, ravished or delighted.

embeleso [em-bay-lay'-so], *m.* 1. Amazement, astonishment, ravishment. 2. Charm, charmer.

embellaquecerse [em-bel-lyah-kay-therr'-say], *vr.* To become low-minded or mean-spirited; to have wicked or worthless ideas.

embellecedor [em-bel-lyay-the-dor'], *m.* (*Aut.*) Hub cap.

embellecer [em-bel-lyay-therr'], *va.* To embellish, to adorn, to decorate, to flourish.

emberar [em-bay-rar'], *vn.* (*Prov.*) To begin to have a ripe color (uvas).

embermejar [em-ber-may-har'], *va.* To give a red color.

embermejecer [em-ber-may-hay-therr'] *va.* 1. To dye red. 2. To put to blush, to shame.-*vr.* To blush.

embermellonar [em-ber-mayl-lyo-nar'], *va.* To apply vermilion, to paint scarlet.

embere [em-bay'-ray], *m.* (*Prov.*) Color of grapes which are ripening.

emberrincharse [em-ber-rin-char'-say] *vr.* (*coll.*) To fly into a violent passion (niños).

embestida [em-bes-tee-dah], *f.* 1. Assault, violent attack, onset. 2. (*Met.*) Importunate demand by way of charity, loan, etc.

embestidor [em-bes-te-dor'], *m.* One who makes importunate demands.

embestidura [em bes-te-doo'-rah], *f.* Attack, assault, onset.

embestir [em-bes-teer'], *va.* 1. To assail, to attack, to offend. 2. To importune with unseasonable demands. 3. (*Naut.*) To collide against something, or against another vessel. -*va. & vr.* 1. To entangle the parts of a harness or to get entangled. 2. (*Mil.*) To invest a place.

embetunar [em-bay-too-nar'], *va.* To cover with gum-resin or bitumen.

embicador [em-be-cah-dor'], *m.* (*Amer.*) Cup and ball.

embicar [em-be-car'], *va.* **Embicar las vergas,** (*Naut.*) To top the yards. -*vn.* 1. To be inclined toward the horizon: said of something which has arms. 2. To steer straight upon the shore or beach with the lifeboat. 3. To luff, to haul to the wind. 4. (*Mil.*) To point downward the mouths of cannon as much as possible.

embijar [em-be-har'], *va.* To paint with minium or red lead.

embión [cm-be-on'], *m.* A shove.

embioncillo [em-be-on-theel'-lyo], *m. dim.* A slight shove.

embizarrarse [em-be-thar-rar'-say], vr. In the jocular style, to brag, to boast of courage, to bully.

emblandecer [em-blan-day-therr'], va. To moisten, to soften with moisture. -vn. (Met.) To soften, or move to pity. -vr. To soften, to get soft.

emblanquecer [em-blan-kay-ther'], va. To bleach or whiten. -vr. To grow white, to be bleaching.

emblanquecimiento, emblanquimiento [em-blan-kay-the-me-en'-to, em-blan-ke-me-en'to], m. (Obs.) Whitening, bleaching.

emblema [em-blay'-mah], m. 1. Emblem. 2. All occult representation, an allusive picture.

emblemático, ca [em-blay-mah'-te-co, cah], a. Emblematic.

embobamiento [em-bo-bah-me-en'-to], m. Admiration, astonishment, enchantment; stupefying.

embobar [em-bo-bar'], va. To amuse, to entertain the mind, to divert from, to distract. -vr. To be in suspense, to stand gaping or gazing, to muse. **Reírse embobado**, to laugh like mad.

embobecer [em-bo-bay-therr'], va. To stultify, to stupefy, to make foolish. -vr. To become stupefied or stultified.

embobecimiento [em-bo-bay-the-me-en'-to], m. Stupefaction.

embocadero, embocador [em-bo-cah-day'-ro, em-bo-cah-dor'], m. Mouth of a channel, by which water is conveyed through a mill-dam. **Estar al embocadero**, to be at the point of attaining something.

embocado, da [em-bo-cah'-do, dah], a. Applied to wine which is pleasant to the taste. -pp. of EMBOCAR.

embocadura [em-bo-cah-doo'-rah], f. 1. The mouth or entrance by a narrow passage. 2. Mouthpiece of a bridle. 3. Mouthpiece of a musical instrument.

embocar [em-bo-car'], va. 1. To enter by the mouth. **Embocar una cosa en un agujero**, to insert something into a hole. 2. (Met.) To enter by a pass or narrow passage. 3. To swallow in haste, to cram food. **Embocar la comida**, to cram one's food. 4. (Met.) To give news agreeable or sad, without preparation or warning.

embocinado, da [em-bo-the-nah'-do, dah], a. V. ABOCINADO.

embodarse [em-bo-dar'-say], vr. (Obs.) To be married.

embojar [em-bo-har'], va. To arrange branches for silkworms, for forming their webs and cocoons.

embojo [em-bo'-ho], m. The operation of arranging branches for silkworms, and the branches so arranged.

embolar [em-bo-lar'], va. 1. To put balls on the tips of bulls' horns. 2. To apply the gilding-size.

embolia [em-bo'-lee-ah], f. Embolism, obstruction of a blood-vessel by a clot or plug. **Embolia cerebral**, clot on the brain.

embolismador, ra [em-bo-lis-mah-dor', rah], m. & f. & a. Detractor, reviler, reviling.

embolismal [em-bo-lis-mahl'], a. Applied to the intercalary year, composed of thirteen lunations.

embolismar [em-bo-lis-mar'], va. To propagate malicious sarcasms and rumors.

embolismo [em-bo-lees'-mo], m. 1. Embolism, intercalation; insertion of days or years to produce regularity and equation of time. 2. The time inserted, intercalary time. 3. Confusion, mixture of things. 4. Maze. 5. Falsehood.

émbolo [em'-bo-lo], m. 1. Embolus, the piston or plunger in a pump. 2. Forcer, the embolus of a force-pump.

embolsar [em-bol-sar'], va. 1. To put money into a purse. 2. To reimburse, to recover money advanced.

embolso [em-bol'-so], m. The act of putting money into a purse.

embonar [em-bo-nar'], va. 1. To make good or firm. 2. (Naut.) To cover a ship's bottom and sides with planks.

embones [em-bo'-nes], m. pl. (Naut.) Planks which are employed in covering the ship's bottom.

embono [em-bo'-no], m. 1. (Naut.) The act of doubling a ship's bottom and soles with planks. 2. Lining, stiffening.

emboñigar [em-bo-nye-gar'], va. To plaster with cow-dung.

emboque [em-bo'-kay], m. 1. Passage of a thing through an arch or strait part. 2. Deception, cheat, fraud. **Eso no tiene emboque**, (Amer.) that has not the least appearance of truth.

emboquillar [em-bo-keel-lyar'], va. To make the entrance of a shaft in mines.

embornal [em-bor-nahl'], m. (Naut.) Scupperhole.

emborrachador, ra [em-bor-rah-chah-dor', rah], a. Intoxicating, producing drunkenness. -n. One who makes drunk.

emborrachamiento [em-bor-rah-chah-me-en'-to], m. (coll.) Intoxication, drunkenness.

emborrachar [em-bor-rah-char'], va. To intoxicate, to inebriate, to fuddle, to get drunk. -vr. To inebriate, to be intoxicated, to overdrink oneself.

emborrada [em-bor-rah'-dah], f. Portion of wool which is passed through the carder.

emborradura [em-bor-rah-doo'-rah], f. 1. Recarding of wool. 2. What serves to recard.

emborrar [em-bor-rar'], va. 1. To stuff with goat's hair. 2. In woollen manufactories, to card the wool a second time.

emborrascar [em-bor-ras-car'], va. &; vr. To provoke, to enrage.

emborrazamiento [em-bor-rah-thah-me-en'-to], m. Act of basting a fowl while roasting.

emborrazar [em-bor-rah-thar'], va. To tie pieces of pork on a fowl, to serve as basting.

emborricarse [em-bor-re-car'-say], vr. (coll.) To be stupefied, or to grow stupid.

emborrizar [em-bor-re-thar'], va. To give the first combing to wool.

emborrullarse [em-bor-rool-lyar'-say], vr. In jocular style, to be at variance, to dispute noisily.

emboscada [em-bos-cah'-dah], f. 1. Ambuscade. 2. (Mil.) Ambush, ambuscade. **Tender una emboscada**, to lay an ambush for.

emboscadura [em-bos-cah-doo'-rah], f. Ambush, ambuscade.

emboscar [em-bos-car'], va. 1. (Mil.) To place in ambush. 2. To emboss. 3. (Met.) To conceal in some secret place. -vr. 1. To retire into the thickest part of a forest. 2. To ambush, to lie in ambush. **Estaban emboscados cerca del camino**, they lay in ambush near the road.

embosquecer [em-bos-kay-therr'], vn. To become woody, to convert into shrubberies.

embotado, da [em-bo-tah'-do, dah], a. Blunt, dull. -pp. of EMBOTAR.

embotador [em-bo-tah-dor'], m. He who blunts the points or edges of swords, etc.

embotadura [em-bo-tah-doo'-rah], f. Blunting (acción), dullness, bluntness (estado) of swords and other edged weapons.

embotamiento [em-bo-tah-me-en'-to], m. 1. Blunting edged weapons; obtusion. 2. Bluntness, obtuseness, dullness. 3. (Met.) Stupefaction, the act of making dull or stupid.

embotar [em-bo-tar'], va. 1. To blunt, to dull an edge or point, to break off the edges or points of edged tools or weapons, to foil. 2. (Met.) To enervate, to debilitate. 3. To dull, to stupefy. -vr. 1. To dull, to become dull. 2. (coll.) To put on the boots.

embotellado [em-bo-tayl-lyah'-do], a. Bottled; prepared (discurso). -m. Bottling.

embotellamiento [em-bo-tayl-lyah-me-ayn'-to], m. 1. (Aut.) Traffic jam. 2. (Fig.) Bottleneck.

embotellar [em-bo-tel-lyar'], va. To bottle wine or other liquors.

embotijar [em-bo-te-har'], va. 1. To lay a stratum of small earthen jars, before a tile flooring is put down. 2. To fill jars with oil or other liquids. -vr. 1. To swell, to expand. 2. To be in passion, to be inflated with arrogance.

embovedado, da [em-bo-vay-dah'-do, dah], a. Arched, vaulted.

embovedar [em-bo-bay-dar'], *va.* To cover with an arch or vault.

emboza [em-bo'-thah], *f.* Inequalities in the bottom of barrels or casks.

embozado, da [em-bo-thah'-do, dah], *a.* Covered, involved. *-pp.* of EMBOZAR.

embozalar [em-bo-thah-lar'], *va.* To muzzle animals.

embozar [em-bo-thar'], *va.* 1. To muffle the greater part of the face. 2. To cloak, to dissemble. 3. To muzzle. *-vr.* To muffle oneself by throwing the right fold of the cape over the left shoulder.

embozo [em-bo'-tho], *m.* 1. The part of a cloak, veil, or any other thing with which the face is muffled. 2. The act of muffling the greater part of the face. 3. *(Met.)* An artful way of expressing one's thoughts, so as to keep them in part concealed.

embozo (De) [em-bo'-tho], *adv.* Incognito, unknown, private.

embracilado, da [em-brah-the-lah'-do, dah], *a. (coll.)* Constantly carried about in one's mother's arms.

embragar [em-brah-gar'], *vn.* To let out the clutch. *-va.* 1. *(Naut.)* To sling. 2. To put in gear, to engage.

embrague [em-brah'-gay], *m.* 1. Clutch. 2. Letting out the clutch. **Embrague automático**, Automatic transmission.

embravar, embravecer [em-brah-vay', em-brah-vey-therr'], *va.* To enrage, to irritate, to make furious. *-vn.* To become strong (plantas). *-vr.* 1. To become furious, to enraged. 2. *(Naut.)* To be extremely boisterous (el mar).

embravecimiento [em-brah-vey-the-me-en'-to], *m.* Fury, rage, passion.

embrazadura [em-brah-thah-do'-rah], *f.* 1. Clasping of a shield or buckler. 2. Embracing, clasping.

embrazar [em-brah-thar'], *va.* 1. To clasp a shield, as in the posture of fighting. 2. To engage the teeth of two wheels in each other.

embreado [em-bray-ah'-do], *m.* **embreadura** [em-bray-ah-doo'-rah], *f. (Naut.)* Tarring, paying a ship with pitch.

embrear [em-bray-ar'], *va. (Naut.)* To pay with pitch, to tar.

embregarse [em-bray-gar'-say], *vr.* To quarrel, to wrangle, to dispute.

embreñarse [em-bray-nyar'-say], *vr.* To hide oneself among brambles or in thickets.

embriagado, da [em-bre-ah-gah'-do, dah], *a. & pp.* of EMBRIAGAR. Intoxicated, drunk.

embriagador [em-bre-ah-gah-dor'], *a.* Intoxicating (olor); Heady, strong (vino etc.).

embriagar [em-bre-ah-gar'], *va.* 1. To intoxicate, to inebriate. 2. To transport, to enrapture. *-vr.* To inebriate, to grow drunk.

embriaguez [em-bre-ah-geth'], *f.* 1. Intoxication, drunkenness, inebriety. 2. *(Met.)* Rapture, transport of the mind.

embridar [em-bre-dar'], *va.* 1. To bridle, to guide by a bridle. 2. *(Met.)* To govern, to restrain.

embriogenia [em-bre-o-hay'-ne-ah], *f.* Formation and development of the foetus in its intrauterine existence.

embriología [em-bre-o-lo-hee'-ah], *f.* Embryology.

embriologo, ga [em-bre-o'-lo-go, gah], *m. & f.* Embryologist.

embrión [em-bre-on'], *m.* 1. Embryo or embryon, the first rudiment of a plant or an animal. 2. The beginning of a thing, still shapeless. 3. *(Met.)* Assemblage of confused ideas, without method or order.

embrionario, ria [em-bre-o-nah'-re-o, ah], *a.* Embryonal, rudimentary,

embroca, embrocación [em-bro'-cah, em-bro-cah-the-on'], *f. (Pharm.)* Embrocation.

embrocar [em-bro-car'], *va.* 1. To pour out of one vessel into another. 2. With embroiderers, to wind thread or twist upon quills. 3. To fasten with tacks to the last (zapateros). 4. To catch the bull between the horns.

embrochado, da [em-bro-chah'-do, dah], *a.* Embroidered.

embrochalar [em-bro-chah-lar'], *va.* To sustain with a crosspiece or a bar of iron the beams which rest on the walls.

embrolla [em-brol'-lyah], *f. (coll.)* V. EMBROLLO.

embrollador, ra [em-brol-lyah-dor', rah], *m. & f.* 1. Entangler, confounder. 2. V. EMBROLLÓN.

embrollar [em-brol-lyar'], *va.* 1. To entangle, to twist, to overlace, to comber. 2. *(Met.)* To entangle, to ensnare, to confound with artful subtleties, to embroil. *-vr.* To get into a muddle, to get into a mess. **Embrollarse en un asunto**, to get involved in a matter.

embrollo [em-brol'-lyo], *m.* Fraud, imposture, snare, deception; embroiling; knot.

embrollón, na [em-brol-lyone', nah], *m. & f.* 1. Liar, tale-bearer; impostor. 2. Entangler.

embromada, da [em-bro-mah'-do, dah], *a. (Prov. Naut.)* Misty, hazy, foggy. *-pp.* of EMBROMAR.

embromador, ra [em-bro-mah-dor', rah], *m. & f. & a.* 1. Applied to one who is tumultuously merry. 2. Wheedler, one who deceives by artful tricks.

embromar [em-bro-mar'], *va.* 1. To make fun, to tease (burlarse de). 2. To hoax, to fool (engañar). 3. To jest, to joke. 4. To repair provisionally the damaged seams of a ship, to chinse.

embroquelarse [em-bro-kay-lar'-say], V. ABROQUELARSE.

embroquetar [em-bro-kay-tar'], *va.* To skewer the legs of birds, in order to roast them.

embrujado [em-broo-hah'-do], *a.* Bewitched (persona); Haunted (lugar). **Una casa embrujada**, a haunted house.

embrujar [em-broo-har'], *va.* To bewitch. **La casa está embrujada**, the house is haunted. V. HECHIZAR.

embrujo [em-broo'-ho], *m.* 1. Bewitching (acto). 2. Curse (maldición). 3. Spell, charm (ensalmo). **El embrujo de la Alhambra**, the enchantment of the Alhambra.

embrutecer [em-broo-tay-therr'], *va.* To stupefy. *-vr.* 1. To grow stupid, to become brutish. 2. To lose refined manners.

embrutecimiento [em-broo-tay-the-me-en'-to], *m.* The act of making brutish stupefaction.

embuchado [em-boo-chah'-do], *m.* Large sausage made of pork, with salt and spice. **—Embuchado, da**, *pp.* Of EMBUCHAR.

embuchar [em-boo-char'], *va.* 1. To stuff with minced meat: to make pork sausages. 2. To cram the maw of animals. 3. *(Met.)* To swallow food without chewing.

embudador [em-boo-dah-dor'], *m.* Filler, one who fills vessels with a funnel.

embudar [em-boo-dar'], *va.* 1. To put a funnel into a vessel to pour liquors through. 2. *(Met.)* To scheme, to ensnare.

embudista [em-boo-dees'-tah], *m.* Intriguer, deceiver.

embudito [em-boo-dee'-to], *m. dim.* A little funnel.

embudo [em-boo'-do], *m.* 1. Funnel. 2. Among wax-chandlers, tail of a wax-candle mould. 3. The basin of a water-closet. 4. *(Met.)* Fraud, deceit artifice.

embullarse [em-bool-lyar'-say], *vr. (Prov. Cuba and Canary Islands.)* To carouse, to revel, to be gay.

embullo [em-bool'-lyo], *m.* Carousal, gaiety, revelry. *(Cuba and Canary Islands.)*

emburujar [em-boo-roo-har'], *va. (coll.)* To jumble, to mix confusedly.

embuste [em-boos'-tay], *m.* 1. An artful tale; a lie, fiction. 2. Fraud, imposition. 3. *(Met.)* Pleasing quibble of children. **Embustes**, gewgaws, baubles, trinkets.

embustear [em-boos-tay-ar'], *vn.* 1. To lie, to impose upon, to gab. 2. To make frequent use of frauds, tricks, and deceits.

embustería [em-boos-tay-ree'-ah], *f* Deceit, imposture, trick.

embustero, ra [em-boos-tay'-ro, rah], *m. & f.* 1. Liar, tale-bearer, tale-teller. 2. Impostor, cheat. 3. Hypocrite, dissembler. 4. *(coll.)* Cajoler, coaxer.

embusterón, na [em-boos-tay-rone', nah], *a. aug.* V. EMBUSTERO.

embutidera [em-boo-te-day'-rah], *f.* Instrument for riveting tin-work.

embutido [em-boo-tee'-do], *m.* Inlaid work.*-pl.* Large sausage filled with minced meat. **—Embutido, da**, *pp.* of EMBUTIR.

embutidor [em-boo-te-dor'], *m.* A riveting set, a punch.

embutidura [em-boo-te-doo'-rah], *f. (Naut.)* Worming, filling the grooves of a rope with material.

embutir [em-boo-teer'], *va.* 1. To inlay, to encase. 2. To mix confusedly, to jumble, to insert. 3. *(Met.)* To cram, to eat much. 4. *(Obs.)* To imbue. **Embutir algo a uno,** to make somebody swallow something. *-vr.* To stuff oneself.

eme [ay'-may], *f.* Spanish name of the letter M.

emenagogo [ay-may-nah-go'-go], *m.* Emmenagogue, an agent promoting the menstrual flow.

emendable [ay-men-dah'-blay], *a. (Ant.)* Amendable, corrigible.

emendación [ay-men-dah-the-on'], *f.* 1. Emendation, amendment, correction. 2. Satisfaction, chastisement.

emendador [ay-men-dah-dor'], *m. (Ant.)* Emendator.

emendadura, *f.* **emendamiento,** *m.* [ay-men-dah-doo'-rah, ay-men-dah-me-en'-to]. *(Obs.)* V. ENMIENDA.

emendar [ay-men-dar'], *va. (Ant.)* 1. To amend, to correct, to emend. 2. **Emendar un aparejo,** *(Naut.)* to overhaul a tackle.

emergencia [ay-mer-hen'-the-ah], *f.* 1. Emergency. 2. Emergence. **Aterrizaje de emergencia,** forced landing, emergency landing.

emergente [ay-mer-hen'-tay], *a.* Emergent, resulting, issuing from something.

emerger [ay-mer-her'], *a.* 1. To emerge; to appear; to surface (submarino).

emérito [ay-may'-re-to], *a.* 1. Emeritus, an epithet applied to a professor in a university, public institution, or religious order, who, having well discharged his duties for a stated time, is allowed to retire, receiving the whole or part of his appointment, and retaining the honors and exemptions belonging to it. 2. A Roman soldier allowed to retire after having done sufficient public service.

emersión [ay-mer-se-on'], *f. (Ast.)* Emersion.

emético, ca [ay-may'-te-co, cah], *m. & a.* Emetic. *-m.* Tartar emetic, tartrate of antimony and potassa.

emetina [ay-may-tee'-nah], *f.* Emetin, an alkaloid procured from ipecacuanha.

emetizar [ay-may-te-thar'], *va.* 1. To add an emetic to any substance whatever. 2. To produce vomiting.

emienda [ay-me-en'-dah], *f. (Ant.)* V. ENMIENDA.

emigración [ay-me-grah-the-on'], *f.* 1. Emigration, immigration. 2. Sum total of emigrants. 3. Periodical migration of certain animals.

emigrado [ay-me-grah'-do], *m.* Emigrant, immigrant.

emigrado, da [ay-me-grah'-do, dah], *a. & m. & f.* Emigrated, immigrated. *-pp.* of EMIGRAR.

emigrante [ay-me-grahn'-tay], *m.* Emigrant.

emigrar [ay-me-grar'], *vn.* To emigrate, to immigrate.

emina [ay-mee'-nah], *f.* 1. Measure containing the fourth part of a Spanish bushel. 2. Ancient tax.

eminencia [ay-me-nen'-the-ah], *f.* 1. Eminence, eminency, height, a hill. 2. *(Met.)* Eminence, excellence, conspicuousness. 3. Eminence, greatness, power. 4. Eminence, title given to cardinals. **Con eminencia,** eminently.

eminencial [ay-me-nen-the-ahl'], *a.* Eminential.

eminente [ay-me-nen'-tay], *a.* 1. Eminent, high, lofty. 2. Eminent, eximious, conspicuous.

eminentemente [ay-me-nen'-tay-men-tay], *adv.* Eminently, conspicuously.

eminentísimo [ay-me-nen-tee'-se-mo], *a.* Most eminent (título de cardenales).

emir [ay-meer'], *m.* 1. Emir, or ameer. 2. Prince, lord 3. A title of dignity among the Turks.

emisario [ay-me-sah'-re-o], *m.* 1. Emissary, spy. 2. Outlet, discharge. 3. *(Med.)* Emunctory.

emisión [ay-me-se-on'], *f.* 1. Emission, vent. 2. Issue of paper money. 3. Scattering of atoms. 4. *(Med.)* Emission. 5. Broadcasting (radio); broadcast (programa). **Emisión deportiva,** sports program.

emisivo, va [ay-me-see'-vo, vah], *a.* Having the faculty of spreading or scattering warmth or light.

emisor, ra [ay-me-sor, rah], *a.* Emitting, issuing. *-f.* Broadcasting station (radio).

emitir [ay-me-teer'], *va.* 1. To emit, to send forth, to let go. 2. To issue, to put into circulation (dinero). 3. To show, manifest an opinion, to give a vote. 4. To broadcast (radio, TV).

emoción [ay-mo-the-on'], *f.* 1. Emotion, agitation of mind. **Nos comunica una emoción de nostalgia,** it gives us a nostalgic feeling. 2. Excitement, thrill; tensión, suspense. **Al abrirlo sentí gran emoción,** I felt very excited on opening it.

emocionado [ay-mo-the-o-nah-do], *a.* Deeply moved, deeply stirred.

emocional [ay-mo-the-o-nahl'], *a.* Emotional.

emocionalismo [ay-mo-the-o-nah-lees'-mo], *m.* Emotionalism.

emocionante [ay-mo-the-o-nahn'-tay], *a.* Emotional, thrilling, exciting.

emocionar [ay-mo-the-o-nar'], *va.* To excite, to thrill. *-vr.* To get excited, to be thrilled. **¡No te emociones tanto!,** don´t get so excited.

emoliente [ay-mo-leen'-tay], *m. & a.* Emollient, softening, healing.

emolumento [ay-mo-loo-men'-to], *m.* 1. Emolument, fee, profit, advantage. 2. Perquisite. Mostly used in the plural.

emotivo [ay-mo-tee'-vo], *a.* Emotional.

empacar [em-pah-car'], *va.* To pack up in chests; to wrap up in hides or skins. *-vr.* To be sullen, to be displeased.

empachadamente [em-pah-chah'-dah-men-tay], *adv. (Prov.)* Cumbersomely

empachado, da [em-pah-chah'-do, dah], *a. & pp.* of EMPACHAR. 1. Clumsy, awkward (torpe). 2. Surfeited, glutted, fed to satiety. **Estar empachado,** to have indigestion (estómago).

empachar [em-pah-char'], *va.* 1. To impede, to embarrass, to clog, to disturb. 2. To perplex, to confound. 3. To overload, to cram, to cause indigestion (estómago). 4. To disguise. *-vr.* 1. To be ashamed, to be confounded. 2. To be fed to satiety.

empacho [em-pah'-cho], *m.* 1. Bashfulness, timidity. 2. Embarrassment, obstacle. 3. Surfeit, indigestion.

empachoso, sa [em-pah-cho'-so, sah], *a.* V. VERGONZOSO.

empacón [em-pah-cone'], *a. (Prov. S. Amer.)* Obstinate, stubborn, contumacious.

empadronador [em-pah-dro-nah-dor'] *m.* Enroller, census-taker.

empadronamiento [em-pah-dro-nah-me-en'-to], *m.* 1. Census, an official enumeration of the inhabitants of a country. 2. List or register of persons liable to pay taxes. V. PADRÓN.

empadronar [em-pah-dro-nar'], *va.* 1. To make, or take the census of a country. 2. To enter in a register the names of those who are liable to pay taxes. *-vr.* To register.

empajar [em-pah-har'], *va.* To cover something or to fill it with straw.

empalagamiento [em-pah-lah-gah-me-en'-to], *m.* Loathing, surfeit, cloying.

empalagar [em-pah-lah-gar'], *va.* 1. To loathe, to cause the disgust of satiety, to cloy. 2. To disgust in a high degree, to offend, to trouble. *-vr.* 1. To loathe, to feel abhorrence or disgust. 2. To be cloyed, to be disgusted or displeased.

empalago [em-pah-lah'-go], *m.* V. EMPALAGAMIENTO.

empalagoso, sa [em-pah-lah-go'-so, sah], *a.* Squeamish, cloying, loathsome, loathful, fastidious, troublesome.

empalamiento [em-pah-lah-me-en'-to], *m.* Empalement, empaling.

empalar [em-pah-lar'], *va.* To empale.

empaliar [em-pah-le-ar'], *va. (Prov.)* To hang with tapestry a church cloister, or other place, through which a procession passes.

empalizada [em-pah-le-thah'-dah], *f. (Mil.)* Palisade or palisado.

empalizar [em-pah-le-thar'], va. 1. To palisade, to inclose with palisades. 2. To pale.

empalmadura [em-pal-mah-doo'-rah], f. Dovetailing, the junction of two pieces of wood. V. EMPALME.

empalmar [em-pal-mar'], va. 1. To scarf, to dovetail. 2. (Naut.) To splice cables. 3. To join, to connect; to splice (cuerdas). -vn. To join, to meet, to come together (ferrocarril).

empalme [em-pahl'-may], m. 1. Scarf, joining, connection (conexión). 2. A splicing. 3. Junction of a branch line of railway with the main line.

empalmillar [em-pal-mil-lyar'], m. (Arch.) A wall of stone, unhewed, for procuring the filtering of river water, which is to be turned into irrigating trenches.—va. To glue the inner sole of the shoe.

empalmo [em-pahl'-mo], m. Shank, a piece of wood which goes under the head of a beam.

empalomadura [em-pah-lo-mah-doo'-rah], f. (Naut.) Marline.

empalomar [em-pah-lo-mar'], va. (Naut.) To sew the bolt-rope to the sail.

empalletado [em-pal-lyay-tah'-do], m. (Naut.) A kind of quilting as a defence in fight to those who are on deck.

empalletar [em-pal-lyay-tar'], va. To form the parapet called empalletado.

empamparse [em-pam-par'-say], vr. (Amer.) 1. To be absent of mind, to be in suspense. 2. To get lost on a pampa.

empanada [em-pah-nah'-dah], f. 1. Meat pie. 2. **Empanada mental,** confusion.

empanadilla [em-pah-nah-deel'-lyah], f. 1. (dim.) A small pie. 2. (Prov.) Movable footstep put in coaches.

empanado [em-pah-nah'-do], a. 1. Receiving light from another room. 2. Covered in breadcrumbs (cocina). **Empanados,** limber boards; planks laid over the well in a ship. —**Empanado, da,** pp. of EMPANAR.

empanar [em-pah-nar'], va. 1. To cover with paste, to bake in paste. 2. To sow grain. -vr. To be choked by too much seed having been sown (agricultura).

empandar [em-pan-dar'], va. To bend into an arch.

empandillar [em-pan-dil-lyar'], va. To remove by stealth, to hide.

empantanado [em-pahn-tah-nah'-do], a. Flooded, swampy.

empantanar [em-pan-tah-nar'], va. 1. To submerge, to make a pond or lake. 2. To bemire. 3. To embarrass the course of an affair. -vr. 1. To be flooded, to get swamped. 2. (Fig.) To be obstructed, to be held up.

empañado [em-pah-nyah'-do], a. Misty, steamy, steamed-up (ventana); dim, blurred (contorno); tarnished (superficie); faint (voz).

empañadura [em-pah-nyah-doo'-rah], f. Swaddling of children.

empañar [em-pah-nyar'], va. 1. To swaddle, to wrap in swaddling clothes. 2. (Met.) To soil a glass with one's breath, to darken, to obscure. 3. (Met.) To denigrate, to impeach one's character or reputation. -vr. 1. To film over, to get misty; to cloud over.

empañilcar [em-pah-nye-car'], va. (Naut.) To hand or furl (barcos).

empapar [em-pah-par'], va. To imbibe, to saturate, to soak, to drench. -vr. 1. To imbibe, to be soaked, to be surfeited. 2. To imbue oneself with the principles of doctrine, science etc. 3. To surfeit. 4. To boast of something without reason.

empapelado [em-pah-pay-lah'-do], m. Papering, paperhanging.

empapelador [em-pah-pay-lah-dor'], m. A person who wraps something up in paper.

empapelar [em-pah-pay-lar'], va. 1. To wrap up in paper. 2. (Prov.) To waste paper. 3. **Empapelar a uno,** (Jur.) To lay a charge against somebody.

empapirolado, da [em-pah-pe-ro-lah'. do, dah], a. (coll.) Full, satisfied.

empapirotado, da [em-pah-pe-ro-tah'. do, dah], a. (coll.) Lofty, haughty, puffed up.-pp. of EMPAPIROTAR.

empapirotar [em-pah-pe-ro-tar'], va. (coll.) To adorn carefully, to deck nicely.

empapujar [em-pah-poo-har'], va. To make one eat too much. (Acad.)

empaque [em-pah'-kay], m. 1. Packing. 2. (And. and Amer.) Air, semblance, look: generally in bad part. Appearance and aspect of a person, according to which he pleases us, or displeases, at first sight. (Acad.)

empaquetador, ra [em-pah-kay-tah-dor', rah], m. & f. Packer. -f. Packing machine.

empaquetadura [em-pah-kay-tah-doo'-rah], f. Packing, gasket.

empaquetar [em-pah-kay-tar'], va. To pack, to bind goods into bales; to clap together.

emparamentar [em-pah-rah-men-tar'], va. To adorn, to set off.

emparchar [em-par-char'], va. To cover with a plaster.

emparedado, da [em-pah-ray-dah'-do, dah], m. & f. 1. Cloisterer: applied to a devotee who lives in a cloister without the vows. 2. A sandwich. 3. Confinement. -pp. of EMPAREDAR.

emparedamiento [em-pah-ray-dah-me-en'-to], m. 1. Confinement, the act of shutting up between walls. 2. Cloister, religious retirement.

emparedar [em-pah-ray-dar'], va. To confine, to immure, to shut up between walls.

emparejador [em-pah-ray-hah-dor'], m. Matcher, fitter.

emparejadura [em-pah-ray-hah-doo'-rah], f. Equalization.

emparejamiento [em-pah-ray-hah-me-en'-to], m. Act of matching or making equal.

emparejar [em-pah-ray-har'], va. & vn. 1. To level, to reduce to a level. 2. To match, to fit, to equal. 3. To put abreast, to put on a level, to be equal. -vr. To pair off.

emparentar [em-pah-ren-tar'], vn. To be related by marriage.

emparentado, da [em-pah-ren-tah'-do, dah], a. & pp. of EMPARENTAR. Related by marriage. **Estar bien or muy emparentado,** have respectable relatives.

emparentar [em-pah-rayn-tar'], vn. To become related by marriage. **Emparentar con una familia,** to marry into a family.

emparrado [em-par-rah'-do], m. Arbor or bower made with the branches of primped vines. —**Emparrado, da,** pp. of EMPARRAR.

emparrar [em-par-rar'], va. To embower, to form bowers with the branches of vines.

emparrillar [em-par-reel-lyar'], va. To broil on the grill.

emparvar [em-par-var'], va. To put grain in order to be thrashed.

empasma [em-pahs'-mah], m. A perfumed toilet powder.

empastado [em-pas-tah'-do], a. 1. (Typ.) Clothbound, bound. 2. Filled (diente).

empastador [em-pas-tah-dor'], m. 1. A painter who gives a liberal coat of color to his works. 2. Pastebrush. 3. (Amer.) Binder of books in leather.

empastadura [em-pas-tah-doo'-rah], f. Dental filling.

empastar [em-pas-tar'], va. 1. To bind (books, etc.) 2. To fill with paste. 3. To fill (muela). 4. To cover with paint.

empaste [em-pahs'-tay], m. 1. Filling (diente). 2. (Typ.) Binding.

empastelar [em-pas-tay-lar'], va. & vr. (Fig. and coll.) 1. To transact a matter without regard to justice in order to get out of a difficulty. 2. (Typ.) To pie, to distribute wrongly, to jumble together.

empatadera [em-pah-tah-day'-rah], f. (coll.) Checking, impeding; suspension of anything.

empatar [em-pah-tar'], va. 1. To draw, to tie. **Empatar a dos,** to tie two to two. **Smith empató en el minuto veinte,** Smith equalized in the twentieth minute. To tie, to have a dead hit (carreras). **Han empatado a dos,** they tied two to two. **Estar empatados,** to be equal or tying. **Han empatado,** they tied, or drew.

empate [em-pah´-tay], *m.* 1. Equality, equal number of votes. 2. Stop, suspension.

empatronamiento [em-pah-tro-nah-me-en'-to], *m.* Stamping as standard.

empatronar [em-pah-tro-nar'], *va.* To stamp a certain mark upon weights and measures, to certify that they are standard.

empavesada [em-pah-vay-sah'-dah], *f. (Naut.)* Waist clothes, painted linen or close netting spread on the sides of ships to obstruct the enemy's sight.

empavesar [em-pah-vay-sar'], *va.* 1. *(Naut.)* To spread waist clothes on the sides of a ship. 2. *(Naut.)* To dress ships.

empecatado, da [em-pay-cah-tah'-do, dah], *a.* Very wily, evil-minded, incorrigible. *(Acad.)*

empecer [em-pay-therr'], *va.* 1. To hurt, to offend, to injure. 2. To prevent.

empecinado [em-pay-the-nah'-do], *m. (Acad.)* 1. *V.* PEGUERO. 2. *(Peru)* Stubborn, inexorable, incorrigible.

empecinar [em-pay-the-nar'], *va.* 1. To fill with mud. 2. *V.* EMPEGAR.-*vr. (Amer.)* To be obstinate, to be given over to vice. **Empecinarse en algo,** to be stubborn.

empedernido [em-pay-der-ne'-do], *a.* 1. Heartless; obdurate (persona); flinty, stony (corazón). 2. Hardened, inveterate (en un vicio). **Un fumador empedernido,** a strongly addicted smoker.

empedernimiento [em-pay-der-ne-me-en'-to], *m.* Hardness of heart.

empedernir [em-pay-der-neer'], *va.* To indurate, to harden. -*vr.* 1. To be petrified, to grow hard as stone. 2. *(Met.)* To be obstinate, to be inflexible.

empedrado [em-pay-drah'-do], *m.* Pavement. **Empedrado, da,** *pp.* of EMPEDRAR.

empedrador [em-pay-drah-dor'], *m.* Paver or pavier.

empedrar [em-pay-drar'], *va.* 1. To pave, to floor with stones. 2. To form small holes or cavities in any superficies.

empega [em-pay'-gah], *f.* 1. Varnish of pitch. 2. Mark of pitch.

empegadura [em-pay-gah-doo'-rah], *f.* The varnish of pitch which is put on vessels.

empegar [em-pay-gar'], *va.* 1. To pitch, to cover with pitch. 2. To mark sheep with pitch.

empego [em-pay'-go], *m.* 1. Marking sheep with pitch. 2. *(Amer.)* The disagreeable taste which some wines have.

empeguntar [em-pay-goon-tar'], *va.* To mark sheep with pitch.

empeine [em-pay'-e-nay], *m.* 1. The groin. 2. The instep. 3. Hoof of a beast. 4. Tetter, ringworm. 5. *(Prov.)* Flower of the cotton plant. 6. *(Bot. Ant.)* Lichen, an order of cryptogramous plants.

empeinoso, sa [em-pay-e-no'-so, sah], *a.* Full of fetters or ringworms.

empelar [em-pay-lar'], *vn.* To get hair, to begin to be hairy.

empelechar [em-pay-lay-char'], *va.* To join or unite marble blocks.

empelotarse [em-pay-lo-tar'-say], *vr.* 1. To be at variance, to quarrel. 2. To be vexed, to be uneasy.

empeltre [em-pel'-tray], *m. (Prov.)* Small olive-tree or sapling springing from an old trunk.

empella [em-pel'-lyah], *f.* 1. The fat of fowls, the lard of swine. 2. Upper leather of a shoe.

empellar, empeller [em-pel-lyar' em-pel-lyerr'], *va.* To push, to impel.

empellejar [em-pel-lyay-har'], *va.* To cover with skins.

empellón [em-pel-lyone'], *m.* Push, heavy blow. **A empellones,** rudely, with pushes.

empenachar [em-pay-nah-char'], *va.* To adorn with plumes.

empenar [em-pay-nar'], *va.* To feather an arrow, to dress with feathers.

empenta [em-pen'-tah], *f.* Prop, stay, shore.

empentar [em-pen-tar'], *va. (Prov.)* To push, to impel. *V.* EMPUJAR.

empeña [em-pay'-nyah], *f. (Obs.)* Upper leather of a shoe. *V.* PELLA.

empeñadamente [em-pay-nyah-dah-men'-tay], *adv.* Strenuously, in a courageous or spirited manner.

empeñado [em-pay-nyo], *a.* 1. Pawned (objeto). 2. **Estar empeñado hasta los ojos,** to be deeply in debt. 3. Determined (persona). **Estar empeñado en,** to be determined to.

empeñar [em-pay-nyar'], *va.* 1. To pawn, to pledge, to gage, to impignorate. 2. To engage, to oblige. -*vr.* 1. To bind oneself, to fulfil a contract or to pay debts. 2. To persist in a determination or resolution. 3. To encounter dangers with courage and spirit. 4. To intercede, to mediate. 5. *(Naut.)* To be embayed on a leeshore. **Empeñarse por alguno,** to recommend anyone, or to exert oneself in favor of anyone. **Empeñarse en algo,** to take a fancy, to undertake a thing eagerly.

empeño [em-pay'-nyo], *m.* 1. Obligation contracted by pledging. 2. Engagement, contract. 3. Earnest desire, ardent love. 4. Boldness; courage and perseverance in overcoming difficulties. 5. Firmness, constancy. 6. Protection, favor, recommendation. 7. Recommender, the person who protects or favors. **Con empeño,** with great ardor, diligence, eagerness. **Tengo un empeño con Vd,** I have a particular favor to ask you. **Tiene empeño en que su amigo salga bien,** he is bent on his friend's success.

empeoramiento [em-pay-o-rah-me-en'-to], *m.* Deterioration.

empeorar [em-pay-o-rar'], *va.* To impair, to deteriorate. -*vn.* -*vr.* To grow worse.

empequeñecer [em-pay-kay-nyay-therr'], *va.* To make smaller, to diminish.

emperador [em-pay-rah-dor'], *m.* 1. An emperor. 2. A name given to certain animals on account of their great size and beauty; for example, the golden-crested wren, the emperor moth, etc.

emperatriz [em-pay-rah-treeth'], *f.* Empress.

empercharr [em-per-char'], *va.* To suspend on a perch.

emperdigar [em-per-de-gar'], *va. V.* PERDIGAR.

emperejilar [em-pay-ray-he-lar'], *va.* To adorn, or to dress with a profusion of ornaments. -*vr.* To be adorned, to be dressed out.

emperezar [em-pay-ray-thar'], *vn. & vr.* 1. To be lazy or indolent. 2. To be dilatory, tardy, slow.

empericado, da [em-pay-re-cah'-do, dah], *a.* To be dressed in style; to wear false hair.

emperifollar [em-pay-re-fol-lyar'], *va. & vr.* To decorate excessively, to cover with ribbons and bows, to deck with flowers, to ornament a discourse with flowers of rhetoric.

empernar [em-per-nar'], *va.* 1. To nail, to spike, to peg. 2. *(Naut.)* To bolt, to fasten with bolts.

empero [em-pay'-ro], *conj.* Yet, however. *V.* PERO.

emperramiento [em-per-rah-me-ayn'-to], *m.* Stubbornness.

emperrar [em-per-rar'], *va.* To irritate, to enrage. -*vr.* To grow mad or furious, to be obstinate or stubborn. **Emperrarse en algo,** to be stubborn about something.

empesador [em-pay-sah-dor'], *m.* Handful of rushes used by weavers for trimming their yarn.

empetro [em-pay'-tro], *m. (Bot.)* Crow-berry. **Empetro blanco,** white-berried crowberry. **Empetro negro,** Blackberried crowberry.

empezar [em-pay-thar'], *va.* To begin, to commence. **Obra empezada, medio acabada,** well begun is half done. **Empezar por,** to begin by. **Empezó diciendo que...,** he began by saying that...

empicarse [em-pe-car´-say], *vr.* To be too much attached to something.

empicotadura [em-pe-co-tah-doo, rah], *f.* Act of pillorying.

empicotar [em-pe-co-tar'], *va.* To pillory, to put in the pillory; to picket.

empiedro [em-pe-ay'-dro], *m.* Paving: a dry wall. *(Yo empiedro, yo empiedre,* from *Empedrar. V.* ACERTAR.)

empiema [em-pe-ay'-mah], *m.* 1. A serous, bloody, or purulent accumulation in any part of the body, but especially in the thoracic region. 2. Name of the surgical operation employed to withdraw such fluid, it is called also paracentesis of the thorax.

empiezo [em-pe-ay'-tho], *m.* *(Prov.)* Beginning of a thing. *(Yo empiezo, yo empiece,* from *Empezar.* V. ACERTAR.).

empinado [em-pe-nah'-do], *a.* 1. Steep (cuesta); high, lofty (edificio). 2. *(Fig.)* Proud (orgulloso); stiff (tieso).

empinador, ra [em-pe-nah-dor', rah], *m. & f. (coll.)* One who drinks much wine or liquors.

empinadura [em-pe-nah-doo'-rah], *f.* Exaltation, elevation, raising.

empinamiento [em-pe-nah-me-en'-to] *m.* Erection, elevation.

empinar [em-pe-nar'], *va.* 1. To raise to exalt. 2. *(coll.)* To drink much. *-vr.* 1. To stand on tiptoe. 2. To tower, to rise high.

empingorotar [em-pin-go-ro-tar'], *va. (coll.)* To raise something and put it upon another.

empino [em-pee'-no], *m.* Elevation, height.

empiolar [em-pe-o-lar'], *va.* 1. To tie the legs of hawks with jesses. 2. *(Met.)* To bind, to subject, to imprison. 3. V. APIOLAR.

empíreo [em-pee'-ray-o], *m.* 1. Empyrean, the highest heaven. 2. Happiness, paradise.

empíreo, rea [em-pee'-ray-o, ah], *a.* Empyreal, celestial.

empireuma [em-pe-ray'-oo-mah], *f. (Chem.)* Empyreum, empyreuma.

empireumático, ca [em-pe-ray-oo-mah'-te-co, cah], *a. (Chem.)* Empyreumatic, empyreumatical.

empírico [em-pee'-re-co], *m.* Quack, empiric, medicaster.

empírico, ca [em-pee'-re-co, cah], *a.* Empiric, empirical.

empirismo [em-pe-rees'-mo], *m.* 1. Empiricism, quackery. 2. A philosophical doctrine according to which all human knowledge is due to experience.

empizarrado [em-pe-thar-rah'-do], *m.* All of the slates which cover a building.—**Empizarrado, da,** *pp.* of EMPIZAR

empizarrar [em-pe-thar-rar'], *va.* To slate, to roof a building with slates.

emplastadura, *f.* **emplastamiento,** *m.* [em-plas-tah-doo'-rah]. Plastering.

emplastar [em-plas-tar'], *va.* 1. To plaster, to apply plasters. 2. To paint the face. 3. To suspend, to obstruct. *-vr.* V. EMBADURNARSE.

emplastecer [em-plas-tay-therr'], *va. (Art.)* To level the surface in order to paint something.

emplasto [em plahs' to], *m.* 1. Plaster or emplaster. **Estar hecho un emplasto,** to be in a bad state of health. 2. A sickly and extremely delicate person.

emplástrico, ca [em-plahs'-tre-co, cah], *a.* 1. Glutinous, resembling a plaster. 2. *(Med.)* Suppurative.

emplazador [em-plah-thah-dor'], *m. (Law.)* Summoner; messenger of a court who serves summonses.

emplazamiento, emplazo [em-plah-thah-me-en'-to, em-plah'-tho], *m. (Law.)* Summons, citation.

emplazar [em-plah-thar'], *va.* 1. *(Law.)* To summon, to cite. 2. To convene, to summon judicially. **Emplazar la caza,** to arrange or set the chase. 3. *(coll.)* To cite to appear before the judgment seat of God.*-vr.* In bullfights, for the bull to plant himself in the midst of the ring, and to show no disposition to charge.

empleado [em-play-ah'-do], *m.* Employee, clerk (oficinista). **Funcionarios o empleados del estado,** civil servants. **Empleado, da,** *pp.* of EMPLEAR. **Empleado de confianza,** confidential clerk. **Empleado bancario,** bank clerk.

empleador [em-play-ah-dor'], *m.* Employer.

emplear [em-play-ar'], *va.* 1. To employ, to use (usar), to exercise, to occupy. 2. To employ, to give a place or employment, to commission, to entrust with the management of affairs. 3. To purchase, to lay out, to employ one's money in the purchase of property. 4. To make use of. 5. To employ, to fill up, to lead, to pass, or spend in a certain manner (tiempo). **Emplear mal el tiempo,** to waste time. *-vr.* To be employed, to occupy, to follow business.

Emplearse haciendo algo, to occupy oneself doing something.

empleita [em-play'-e-tah], *f.* V. PLEITA.

emplenta [em-plen'-tah], *f.* 1. Piece of mudwall made at once. 2. *(Obs.)* Impression.

empleo [em-play'-o], *m.* 1. Employ, job, employment, business, occupation. 2. Employment or employ, public place or station, office. 3. Employment, calling, vocation, profession. 4. Aim or object of our desires. 5. Lady courted, sweetheart. **Empleo del dinero or fondos, en algún negocio,** investment of money or capital in some business. **Buscar un empleo,** to look for a job. **Estar sin empleo,** to be unemployed.

empleomanía [em-play-o-mah-nee'-ah], *f.* Rage for public office.

emplomado [em-plo-mah'-do], *m.* Roof covered with lead. **Emplomado, da,** *pp.* of EMPLOMAR.

emplomador [em-plo-mah-dor'], *m.* Plumber, he who fits with lead in any way.

emplomar [em-plo-mar'], *va.* To lead, to fit with lead.

emplumar [em-ploo-mar'], *va.* 1. To feather, or dress in feathers, as a punishment. 2. To feather, to adorn with feathers or plumes. 3. To swindle (estafar). *-vr.* To mew, to moult, to shed the feathers.

emplumecer [em-ploo-may-ther'], *vn.* To begin to get feathers, to fledge. *(Yo emplumezco, yo emplumezca,* from, *Emplumecer.* V. CONOCER.)

empobrecer [em-po-bray-therr'], *va.* To impoverish.*-vr.* To become poor. *(Yo empobrezco, yo empobrezca,* from *Empobrecer.* V. CONOCER.

empobrecimiento [em-po-bray-the-me-en'-to], *m.* Impoverishment, depauperation.

empodrecer [em-po-dray-therr'], *vn.* To corrupt, to reduce to a state of putrefaction.—*vr.* To corrupt, to become putrid.

empolvar [em-pol-var'], *va. & vr.* 1. To cover with dust. 2. To sprinkle powder upon, as the hair; to powder.

empolvoramiento [em-pol-vo-rah-me-en'-to], *m.* The act of covering with dust.

empolvorizar [em-pol-vo-re-thar'], **empolvorar** [em-pol-vo-rar'], *va.* To cover with dust or powder.

empollado, da [em-pol-lyah'-do, dah], *a.* 1. Hatched. 2. *(Met.)* Confined, pent up in the house. *-pp.* of EMPOLLAR

empolladura [em-pol-lyah-doo'-rah], *f.* Brood of bees.

empollar [em-pol-lyar'], *va.* 1. To brood, to hatch. 2. V. AMPOLLAR.

empollón, ona [em-pol-lyon'], *m & f.* Swot, bookworm (estudiante).

emponzoñador, ra [em-pon-tho-nyah-dor', rah], *m. & f.* Poisoner.

emponzoñamiento [em-pon-tho-nyah-me-en'-to], *m.* Poisoning, the act of administering or killing by poison.

emponzoñar [em-pon-tho-nyar'], *va.* 1. To poison, to infect with poison. 2. *(Met.)* To poison, to taint, to corrupt one's morals.

empopar [em-po-par'], *va. (Naut.)* To give the stern to the wind. *-vn. & vr.* To sail before the wind.

emporcar [em-por-car'], *va.* To soil, to dirty, to foul.

emporio [em-po'-re-o], *m.* 1. Emporium, a mart for the sale of merchandise. 2. A place which has made itself famous for sciences, arts, etc.

emporrado [em-por-rah'-do], *a.* **Estar emporrado,** to be high (drogas).

empotrado, da [em-po-trah'-do, dah], *a.* Built-in. **Muebles empotrados,** built-in furniture.

empotramiento [em-po-trah-me-en'-to], *m.* The act of scarfing two timbers together.

empotrar [em-po-trar'], *va.* 1. To mortise, to join with a mortise. 2. To scarf, to splice. 3. To put beehives in a pit (to divide the hives). 4. *(Naut.)* To fasten the cannon so that they shall not run back on firing. 5. To prevent the turning of the wheels of a guncarriage. *-vr.* **El coche se empotró en la tienda,** the car embedded itself in the shop.

empozar [em-po-thar'], *va.* To throw into a well. To stagnate, (estancarse). -*vr.* To be pigeonholed (papel normal).

empradizarse [em-prah-de-thar'-say], *vr.* To become a meadow.

emprendedor [em-pren-day-dor'], *m.* 1. Enterpriser, one who undertakes a great thing. 2. Undertaker, one who engages in projects and affairs.

emprender [em-pren-derr'], *va.* 1. To undertake, to engage in an arduous undertaking. 2. To attempt, to go about any business. **Emprender con alguno,** to address or accost one, either to trouble, to reprimand, to supplicate, or to quarrel with him. **Emprender la retirada,** to begin to retreat.

empreñar [em-pray-nyar'], *va.* To impregnate; to beget.

empresa [em-pray'-sah], *f.* 1. Symbol, motto. 2. Enterprise, undertaking. **Empresa privada,** private enterprise. **Empresa funeraria,** undertaker's. **Empresa de servicios públicos,** public utility company. 3. Design, an intention, a purpose. **Empresa de venta por correspondencia,** mail-order firm.

empresarial [em-pray-sah'-re-ah], *a.* Owners', manager's; managerial (función, clase). **Estudios empresariales,** business studies.

empresario [em-pray-say'-re-o], *m.* 1 The person who undertakes to do or perform, on his own account, some business of great importance. **Pequeño empresario,** small businessman. 2. Manager of a theater.

emprestillar [em-pres-til-lyar'], *va.* To borrow frequently, to ask the use of any thing.

empréstito [em-prays'-te-to], *m.* Loan, something lent. **Un empréstito del gobierno,** a government loan. **Lanzar un empréstito,** to float a loan.

emprimado [em-pre-mah'-do], *m.* Last combing to wool. —**Emprimado, da,** *pp.* of EMPRIMAR.

emprimar [em-pre-mar'], *va.* 1. To print linen or cotton. 2. In woollen manufactories, to card the wool several times, to prepare it for spinning. 3. *(coll.)* To abuse one's candor, to deceive, to mock.

emprimerar [em-pre-may-rar'], *va.* To place one in the first rank at a feast, or on any other occasion.

empringar [em-prin-gar'], *va. V.* PRINGAR.

emprisionar [em-pre-se-o-nar'], *vn. V.* APRISIONAR.

empsícosis [emp-see'-co-sis], *f. (Phil.)* 1. Animation. 2. Union of the soul with the body.

empuchar [em-poo-char'], *va.* To cut skeins of thread into a lye, or to buck them before they are bleached.

empujamiento [em-poo-hah-me-en'-to], *m.* 1. The act of pushing away. 2. The force employed for that purpose.

empujar [em-poo-har'], *va.* 1. To push, to force by constant violence, to press forward. **Empujar el botón a fondo,** to press the button down hard. 2. To push away, to shove off. -*vn. (Fig.)* To intrigue, to work behind the scenes.

empuje [em-poo'-hay], *m.* 1. Impulse, push, driving force. 2. *(Aer.)* Thrust. 3. *(Fig.)* Push, drive. **Le falta empuje,** he hasn't got any go to him, he lacks drive.

empujón [em-poo-hone'], *m.* Push, a violent shove. **A empujones,** pushingly, rudely.

empulgar [em-pool-gar'], *va.* To stretch the cord of a crossbow.

empulgueras [em-pool-gay-ras], *f. pl.* 1. Wings of a crossbow, through which the ends of the cord run. 2. Instrument with which the thumbs were tied together. **Apretar las empulgueras a uno,** to put one in a difficult situation, to compel him.

empuntador [em-poon-tah-dor'], *m.* One who makes the points of needles or pins.

empuntadura [em-poon-tah-doo'-rah], *f.* Pointing of needles or pins.

empuntar [em-poon-tar'], *va.* To point, form the point of a needle or pin.

empuñador, ra [em-poo-nyah-dor', rah], *m. & f.* Grasper.

empuñadura [em-poo-nyah-doo'-rah], *f.* Hilt of a sword. **Empuñaduras,** *(Naut.)* earrings, thin ropes fastened to the four corners of a sail, in the form of a ring.

empuñar [em-poo-nyar'], *va.* 1. To clinch, to clutch, to grasp, to gripe with the fist. **Empuñar el bastón,** *(Fig.)* To take command.

empuñir [em-poo-nyeer'], *va. (Naut.)* To pull on the sheets until the fists touch the block where the topsail sheet works.

emulación [ay-moo-lah-the-on'], *f.* Emulation, envy, jealousy.

emulador, ra [ay-moo-lah-dor', rah], *m.* Emulator, rival.

emular [ay-moo-lar'], *va.* To emulate, to rival, to contest.

emulgente [ay-mool-hen'-tay], *a.* Emulgent.

émulo [ay'-moo-lo], *m.* Competitor, rival, emulator.

emulsina [ay-mool-see'-nah], *f.* Emulsin or synaptase, an albuminous principle of almonds, which forms an emulsion with water and acts as a ferment.

emulsión [ay-mool-se-on'], *f.* Emulsion.

emulsivo, va [ay-mool-see'-vo, vah], *a.* Emulsive.

emunctorio [ay-moonc-to'-re-o], *m.* Emunctory, excretory gland.

emundación [ay-moon-dah-the-on'], *f.* Cleansing.

emuselado, da [ay-moo-say-lah-do', dah], *a.* Muzzled to prevent biting (oso, perro).

en [en], *prep.*

1. Tiempo. -IN. **Estar en 1999,** to be in 1999. **En un año,** in a year's time. **Estamos en invierno,** we are in winter. **Estábamos en enero,** we were in January. **In mis tiempos,** in my time. **En vísperas de,** on the eve of. **En esto,** thereupon. **No dormí en toda la noche,** I didn't sleep a wink all night. **En 1997,** in 1997. **En agosto,** in August. -ON. **Lo hicimos el domingo,** we did it on Sunday. **El día de Nochebuena,** on Christmas eve. -AT. **En aquella época,** at that time. **En el momento de su llegada,** at the time of his arrival. **Al anochecer,** at nightfall.

2. Lugar. -IN. **Está en la habitación,** it's in the room. **Trabaja en la tienda,** she works in the shop. **En la cama,** in bed. **En un sillón,** in an armchair. **En un coche,** in a car. **En la calle del Oeste,** in West street. **en los Alpes,** in the Alps. -ON. **En el autobús,** on the bus. **En el avión,** on the plane. **En la costa,** on the coast. **Sobre el río,** on the river. **Sobre la mesa,** on the table. **En la silla,** on the chair. -AT. **Está en casa,** he is at home. **En el semáforo,** at the traffic lights. **Nos encontramos en la estación,** we met at the station. **La vi en el supermercado,** I saw her at the supermarket.

3. Modo. -IN. **En pantalones cortos,** in shorts. **En voz alta,** in a loud voice. -BY. **La conocí al andar,** I recognized her by her gait. **Ir en tren, bicycleta, autobús,** to go by train, bicycle, bus.

4. Locuciones. En cuanto podamos, as soon as we can. **En un rincón,** in a corner. **En la esquina,** on/at the corner. **En la parte de atrás,** at the back. **En el concierto,** at the concert. **En la peluquería,** at the hairdresser's. **De vez en cuando,** from time to time. **De casa en casa,** from house to house. **En la colina,** on the hill.

enaceitarse [ay-nah-thay-e-tar'-say], *vr.* To become oily or rancid.

enacerar [ay-nah-thay-rar'], *va.* To steel, to edge with steel.

enaguachar [ay-nah-goo-ah-char'], *va.* To fill or load with water; used only to denote the state of the stomach after drinking a great deal.

enaguas [ay-nah'-goo-as], *f.pl.* 1. Petticoat, underskirt. **Enaguas blancas,** the inner skirt. 2. A gown or tunic of black baize, formerly worn by men as mourning.

enaguar [ay-nah-goo-ar'] *va.* To flood, to drench, to soak.

enaguazar [ay-nah-goo-ah-thar'], *va.* To irrigate; to cover with water (la tierra).

enagüillas, tas [ay-nah-goo-eel'-lyas, ee'-tas], *f. pl.* 1. *(dim.)* Short linen under-petticoats. 2. *V.* ENAGUAS for a gown or tunic.

enajenable [ay-nah-hay-nah'-blay], *a.* Alienable.

enajenación, *f.* **enajenamiento,** *m.* [ay-nah-hay-nah-the-on', ay-nah-hay-nah-me-en'-to]. 1. Alienation, the act of transferring property. 2. Change of affection, want of friendly intercourse. 3. Absence of mind; distress of mind; rapture, astonishment; overjoy. 4. Disorder of the mental faculties. **Enajenación mental,** mental derangement.

enajenar [ay-nah-hay-nar'], *va.* 1. To alienate, to transfer or to give away property. 2. To transport, to enrapture. *-vr.* 1. To withdraw one's affection. 2. To be deprived of reason. 3. To be restless or uneasy.

enálage [ay-nah-'lah-hay], *f.* *(Gram.)* Enallage, the use of one part of speech or inflection for another.

enalbar [ay-nal-bar'], *va.* To heat iron to a white heat.

enalbardar [ay-nal-har-dar'], *va.* 1. To lay a packsaddle on beasts of burden. 2. To cover meat or any other dish with a batter of eggs, flour, and sugar, and fry it afterward in oil or butter.

enalforjar [ay-nal-for-har'], *va.* To put into a saddlebag.

enalmagrado, da [ay-nal-mah-grah'-do, dah], *a.* & *pp.* of ENALMAGRAR. 1. Colored with ochre. 2. Vile, despicable.

emalmagrar [ay-nal-mah-grar'], *va.* To cover with ochre.

enalmenar [ay-nal-may-nar'], *va.* To crown a wall with indented battlements.

enaltecer [ay-nal-tay-therr'], *va.* V. ENSALZAR.

enamarillecer [ay-nah-mah-reel-lyay-therr'], *va.* To dye yellow, to make yellow. *-vr.* *(Ant.)* 1. To become yellow. 2. To grow pale.

enamoradamente [ay-nah-mo-rah-dah-men'-tay], *adv.* Lovingly, in a loving manner.

enamoradizo, za [ay-nah-mo-rah-dee'-tho, thah], *a.* Inclined to love, of an amorous disposition.

enamorado, da [ay-nah-mo-rah'-do-dah], *a.* & *pp.* of ENAMORAR. In love, enamoured, lovesick. **Es muy enamorado de ella,** he is madly in love with her. *-m.* *y f.* Sweetheart, lover. **Es un enamorado de la buena música,** he is a lover of good music.

enamorador [ay-nah-mo-rah-dor'], *m.* Lover, wooer.

enamoramiento [ay-nah-mo-rah-me-en'-to], *m.* Act of enamouring, lovesuit.

enamorar [ay-nah-mo-rar'], *va.* 1. To excite or inspire love. 2. To make love, to woo, to court, to enamour. **Por fin la enamoró,** eventually he got her to fall in love with him. *vr.* To fall in love.

enamoricarse [ay-nah-mo-re-car'-say], *vr.* *(coll.)* To be slightly in love.

enanchar [ay-nan-char'], *va.* *(coll.)* To widen, to enlarge.

enangostar [ay-nan-gos-tar'], *va.* V. ANGOSTAR.

enanito, ita [ay-nah-nee'-to, tah], *a. dim.* Little, minute.

enano, na [ay-nah'-no, nah], *a.* Dwarfish, low, small, little.

enano [ay-nah'-no], *m.* Dwarf.

enarbolar [ay-nar-bo-lar'], *va.* To hoist, to raise high; to hang out. **Enarbolar la bandera,** *(Naut.)* to hoist the colors. *-vr.* V. ENCABRITARSE.

enarcar [ay-nar-car'], *va.* 1. To hoop barrels. 2. V. ARQUEAR.

enardecer [ay-nar-day-therr'], *va.* To fire with passion, to kindle, to inflame. *-vr.* To be kindled, inflamed, or animated, with anger.

enarenación [ay-nah-ray-nah-the-on'], *f.* Lime and sand, or plaster, used to whiten walls before painting them.

enarenar [ay-nah-ray-nar'], *va.* To fill with sand, to choke with sand. *-vr.* *(Naut, Obs.)* To run onshore.

enarme [ay-nar'-may], *m.* *(Prov.)* A framework in fishing-nets, or the method of fitting them up.

enarmonar [ay-nar-mo-nar'], *va.* To raise, to rear. *-vr.* To rise on the hind feet.

enarmonía [ay-nar-mo-nee'-ah], *f.* *(Mus.)* Enharmonic modulation, a change in notation without a change in sound.

enarmónico, ca [ay-nar-mo'-ne-co, cah], *a.* Enharmonic, proceeding by quarter tones.

enarración [ay-nar-rah-the-on'], *f.* Narration, relation.

enarrar [ay-nar-rar'], *va.* To narrate.

enastar [ay-nas-tar'], *va.* To put a handle to an instrument.

enastillar [ay-nas-teel-lyar'], *va.* To put handles to forging-hammers.

encabalgamiento [en-cah-bal-gah-me-en'-to], *m.* Gun-carriage.

encabalgar [en-cah-bal-gar'], *vn.* 1. To be upon (something else); to be mounted. 2. *(Obs.)* To parade on horseback. *-va.* To provide horses.

encaballadura [en-cah-bal-lyah-doo-rah], *f.* Lapping over.

encaballar [en-cah-bal-lyar'], *va.* To lap over, to imbricate, to lay so that the object rests upon the end of another, as tiles or shingles upon a roof.

encabellecer [en-cah-bel-lyay-therr'], *vn.* & *vr.* To begin to have hair on a part of the head where there was none before. *(Yo encabellezco, yo encabellezca,* from *Encabellecer. V.* CONOCER.)

encabestradura [en-cah-bes-trah-doo´-rah], *f.* An injury to a horse by a halter.

encabestrar [en-cah-bes-trar'], *va.* 1. To put a halter to a beast. 2. *(Met.)* To force to obedience. *-vr.* To be entangled in the halter.

encabezador [en-cah-bay-thah-dor'], *m.* Header, a reaping-machine which removes the heads of grain.

encabezadura [en-cah-bay-thah-doo'-rah], *f.* Scarfing, heading.

encabezamiento, encabezonamiento [en-cah-bay-thah-me-en'-to], *m.* 1. List, roll, or register of persons liable to pay a tax; census. 2. The act of enrolling persons liable to pay taxes. 3. Tax tribute, or imposts. 4. Headline, heading.

encabezar, encabezonar [en-cah-bay-thar'], *va.* 1. To make a roll or register of all those subject to any tax or tribute, to take a census of the inhabitants. 2. To register, to enroll, to set down in a list of taxes. *-vr.* 1. To compound for taxes. 2. To compound, to bargain in the lump. 3. To put the beginning of a formula to certain writings, as a will. 4. *(Amer.)* To put at the head, or in the first line. 5. To strengthen a wine, to add other stronger, or some brandy. 6. **Encabezar un terreno,** *(Agr.)* To put fresh earth at the top of a slope. 7. *(Carp.)* To join top and top, to scarf, to head. 8. *(Naut.)* To mend the furring of a ship.

encabillar [en-cah-beel-lyar'], *va.* *(Naut.)* To scotch, to pin, to bolt.

encabrahigar [en-cah-brah-e-gar'], *va.* V. CABRAHIGAR.

encabriar [en-cah-bre-ar'], *va.* To preserve and fashion timber for roofing.

encabritarse [en-cah-bre-tar'-say], *vr.* To rise on the hind feet (caballos).

encachar [en-cah-char'], *va.* To thrust anything in a wall or box, to imbed.

encadenadura, *f.* **encadenamiento,** *m.* [en-cah-day-nah-doo'-rah, en-cah-day-nah-me-en'-to]. 1. Catenation, the act of linking together. 2. State of being linked or connected, concatenation. 3. Chaining. **Encadenamiento en margarita,** daisy chaining.

encadenar [en-cah-day-nar'], *va.* 1. To chain, to link, to fetter, to enchain, to shackle. 2. To concatenate, to link together. 3. *(Met.)* To leave anyone without movement or action. **Los negocios le encadenan al escritorio,** business ties him to his desk. 4. To subject, to subjugate, to oppress. 5. To captivate, to gain the will. 6. To cast the chains which close the entrance of harbors, docks, etc.

encajador [en-cah-hah-dor'], *m.* 1. He who encases or inserts. 2. Instrument for encasing.

encajadura [en-cah-hah-doo'-rah], *f.* Encasing, inserting or inclosing one thing into another.

encajar [en-cah-har'], *va.* 1. To encase, to infix, to drive in, to inclose one thing in another, to insert. 2. To thrust with violence one into another. 3. *(Met.)* To do or say something inopportunely. 4. Of firearms, to shoot, fire. **Encajar bien,** to be to the purpose, to come to the point, to be opportune. **Encajar las manos,** *(coll.)* to join or shake hands. *-vn.* 1. To fit well. 2. To chuck (lanzar). 3. *(Fig.)* To fit, to match, to correspond. **Esto no encaja con lo que dijo antes**, this does not square with what he said before. -*vr.* 1. To thrust oneself into some narrow place. 2. To intrude. 3. To squeeze in; to intrude.

encaje [en-cah'-hay], *m.* 1. The act of adjusting or fitting one thing to another. 2. The place or cavity in which anything is inlaid or inserted; groove. 3. The measure of one thing to adjust with another. 4. Encasing. 5. Joining together. 6. Lace. **Encaje de oro, de plata, de kilo, etc.**, gold silver, thread lace, etc. 7. Inlaid work. **Ley del encaje**, an arbitrary law.

encajera [en-cah-hay'-rah], *f.* Lace-woman, she who makes lace.

encajerado, da [en-cah-hay-rah'-do dah], *a. (Naut.)* Fouled or entangled on the sheave of a block or pulley (cuerda).

encajerarse [en-cah-hay-rar'-say], *vr. (Naut.)* To get caught between the brook and the pulley-wheel (cuerda).

encajonado [en-cah-ho-nah'-do], *m.* Mudwall supported by pillars of bricks and stones.—**Encajonado, da**, *pp.* of ENCAJONAR.

encajonamiento [en-cah-ho-nah-me-en'-to], *m.* Act of packing up in a box.

encajonar [en-cah-ho-nar'], *va.* 1. To box, to pack up in a box, to lay up in a chest. 2. To squeeze in (meter con dificultad). -*vr.* To run through a narrow place (río).

encalabozar [en-cah-lah-bo-thar'], *va. (coll.)* To put one into a dungeon.

encalabrinado, da [en-cah-lah-bre-nah'-do, dah], *a.* Headstrong, stubborn, obstinate. -*pp.* ENCALABRINAR.

encalabrinar [en-cah-lah-bre-nar'], *va.* To affect the head with some unpleasant smell or vapor. -*vr.* To become headstrong, obstinate, or stubborn; to be confused.

encalada [en-cah-lah'-dah], *f.* Piece of the trimmings of a saddle.

encalador [en-cah-lah-dor'], *m.* In tanneries, the lime pit or vat, into which hides are put.

encaladura [en-cah-lah-doo'-rah], *f.* The act of whitening with lime; whitewashing.

encalar [en-cah-lar'], *va.* 1. To whitewash. 2. To cover with plaster or mortar. 3. To thrust into a pipe or tube. 4. To put hides into the lime vats or pits.

encalipto [en-cah-leep'-to], *m.* A kind of moss belonging to the northern hemisphere.

encalmadura [en-cal-mah-doo'-rah], *f.* A disease in horses occasioned by much work in times of great heat.

encalmarse [en-cal-mar'-say], *vr.* 1. To be worn out with fatigue. 2. *(Naut.)* To be becalmed (barco).

encalostrarse [en-cah-los-trar'-say], *vr.* To make the young sick by sucking the first milk.

encalvecer [en-cal-vay-therr'], *vn.* To grow bald. *(Yo encalvezco, yo encalvezca, from Encalvecer. V.* CONOCER.)

encallada [en-cal-lyah'-dah], *f.* V. ENCALLADURA.

encalladero [en-cal-lyah-day'-ro], *m. (Naut.)* Shoal, sandbank.

encalladura [en-cal-lyah-doo'-rah], *f. (Naut.)* Striking on a sandbank.

encallar [en-cal-lyar'], *vn.* 1. *(Naut.)* To run aground, to stand, to hit against. 2. To be checked in the progress of an enterprise, not to be able to proceed.

encalle [en-cahl'-lyay], *m. V.* ECALLADURA.

encallecer [en-cal-lyay-therr'], *vn.* To get corns on the feet. 2. To attain much experience in something. -*vr.* To harden, to be confirmed in wickedness.

encallecido, da [en-cal-lyay-thee'-do, dah], *a. & pp.* of ENCALLECER. 1. Troubled with corns. 2. *(Met.)* Hardened in wickedness and iniquities.

encallejonar [en-cal-lyay-ho-nar'], *va.* To enter or put something into a narrow street.

encamación [en-cah-mah-the-on'], *f.* Scaffolding for sustaining the galleries in mines.

encamarados [en-cah-mah-rah'-dos], *m. pl.* Chambers in cannon and mortars.

encamarar [en-cah-mah-rar'], *va. (Colt.)* To store up grain in granaries.

encamarse [en-cah-mar'-say], *vr.* 1. *(coll.)* To keep oneself in bed. 2. To lie down, to stretch themselves out to rest (animales). 3. To be laid or laid flat by rain, wind, etc. (maíz).

encambijar [en-cam-be-har'], *va.* To conduct water by means of arched reservoirs.

encambrar [en-cam-brar'], *va.* To put in a store.

encambrillonar [en-cam-breel-lyo-nar], *va.* To put the first narrow sole, called *encambrillonado*, upon a shoe.

encambronar [en-cam-bro-nar'], *va.* 1. To inclose witty hedges of briers and brambles. 2. To strengthen with iron.

encaminadura [en-cah-me-nah-doo'-rah], *f.* **Encaminamiento,** *m.* The act of putting on the right road.

encaminar [en-cah-me-nar'], *va.* 1. To guide, to put on the right road, to show the way. 2. *(Met.)* To direct or manage an affair or business. **El proyecto está encaminado a,** the plan is directed towards. -*vr.* To take a road, to proceed in a road, to go to.

encamorrarse [en-cah-mor-rar'-say], *vr.* To embroil oneself in disputes.

encampanado, da [en-cam-pah-nah'-do, dah], *a.* Bellshaped (morteros).

encanalar, encanalizar [en-cah-nah-lar', en-cah-nah-le-thar'], *va.* To convey through pipes or conduits.

encanallarse [en-cah-nal-lyar'-say], *vr. (Acad.)* 1. To contract a habit of committing mean and vile acts. 2. To associate with depraved and base people.

encanarse [en-cah-nar'-say], *vr.* To grow senseless with fear or crying (niños).

encanastar [en-cah-nas-tar'], *va.* 1. To pack up in canisters, baskets or hampers. 2. *(Naut.)* To put the topsails In the roundhouse or top.

encancerarse [en-can-thay-rar'-say], *vr. V.* CANCERARSE.

encandecer [en-can-day-therr'], *va.* To heat something white-hot.

encandelar [en-can-day-lar'], *vn.* To bud, as trees, instead of flowering.

encandiladera, encandiladora [en-can-de-lah-day'-rah, en-can-de-lah-do'-rah], *f.* Procuress, bawd.

encandilado, da [en-can-de-lah'-do dah], *a.* 1. Sharp or high-cocked (sombreros). **Trae el sombrero muy encandilado,** he wears his hat fiercely cocked. 2. *(Naut.)* Raised vertically. -*pp.* of ENCANDILAR.

encandilar [en-can-de-lar'], *va.* 1. To dazzle with the light of a candle or lamp. 2. *(Met.)* To dazzle or deceive with false appearances. 3. *(coll.)* To stir the fire. -*vr.* 1. To inflame one's eyes, as with drink, to be dazzled. 2. To get excited, to become emotional (persona).

encanecer [en-cah-nay-therr'], *vn.* 1. To grow gray. 2. To mould. 3. To grow old. 4. To possess much experience and knowledge. *(Yo encanezco, yo encanezca, from Encanecer. V.* CONOCER.)

encanijamiento [en-cah-ne-hah-me-en'-to], *m.* Weakness, meagreness; the act of growing weak and lean; extenuation.

encanijar [en-cah-ne-har'], *va.* To weaken a baby by giving him bad milk. -*vr.* 1. To pine, to be emaciated, to grow weak and thin, to fall away (niños mal amamantados). 2. To grow weak.

encanillar [en-cah-nil-lyar'], *va.* To wind silk, wool, or linen on a quill made of cane.

encantado, da [en-can-tah'-do, dah], *a.* 1. Haunted, enchanted, charmed. **Casa encantada,** a haunted house. **Hombre encantado,** a man who is habitually absent or musing. 2. Delighted, pleased (persona). **Estoy encantado de conocerle,** I´m delighted to meet you. -*pp.* of ENCANTAR.

encantador [en-can-tah-dor'], *m.* Enchanter, sorcerer, conjurer; charmer.

encantadora [en-can-tah-doo-rah], *f.* Sorceress, enchantress; charming, bewitching.

encantamiento [en-can-tah-me-en'-to], *m*. 1. Magic (mágia). **Como por encantamiento,** as if by magic. 2. Bewitchment, witchcraft (hechizo). 3. Spell, charm, enchantment, incantation (invocación mágica).

encantar [en-can-tar'], *va*. 1. To enchant, to charm, to conjure, to bewitch, to cast a spell on (con magia). 2. To fascinate, to delight in a high degree. **Nos encanta la casa,** we are delighted with the house.

encantarar [en-can-tah-rar'], *va*. To put something into a jar or pitcher.

encante [en-cahn'-tay], *m*. Auction, public sale: the place where it is held.

encanto [en-cahn'-to], *m*. Enchantment, charm, spell. 2. Fascination. **Es un encanto,** it is truly charming, it is bewitching. **El niño es un encanto,** the child is a little treasure.

encantorio [en-can-to'-re-o], *m*. *(coll.)* Enchantment.

encantusar [en-can-too-sar'], *va*. To coax, to wheedle, to deceive by flatteries.

encañado [en-cahn-yah'-do], *m*. 1. Conduit of water. 2. Hedge formed with canes or reeds. -*a*. Piped, tubed. **Encañado, da,** *pp*. of ENCAÑAR.

encañador, ra [en-cah-nyah-dor', rah], *m*. & *f*. One who spools or winds silk on quills made of cane.

encañadura [en-cah-nyah-doo'-rah], *f*. 1. Hedge made of cane or reeds. 2. Strong rye-straw not broken.

encañar [en-cah-nyar'], *va*. 1. To inclose a plantation with a hedge of cane. 2. To convey water through conduits or pipes. 3. To wind silk on quills of reed or cane. -*vn*. To form or grow into stalks (maíz).

encañizada [en-cah-nye-thah'-dah], *f*. Inclosure made of cane and reeds for catching mullets.

encañonado [en-cah-nyo-nah'-do], *a*. 1. Goffering, crimping (planchado). 2. Applied to the wind blowing through a narrow passage. — **Encañonado, da,** *pp*. of ENCAÑONAR.

encañonar [en-cah-nyo-nar'], *va*. & *vn*. 1. To begin to grow fledged, to get feathers and wings (aves). 2. To put into tubes or pipes (agua). 3. To plait, to fold. 4. To wind silk on quills of cane. 5. To aim at, to point at (armas).

encañutar [en-cah-nyoo-tar'], *va*. To flute, to mould into the form of tubes and pipes.

encapacetado, da [en-cah-pah-thay-tah'-do, dah], *a*. Covered with a helmet.

encapachadura [en-cah-pah-chah-doo'-rah], *f*. In oil-mills, number of baskets full of olives to be pressed.

encapachar [en-cah-pah-char'], *va*. 1. To put into a flail or basket. 2. *(Agr. Prov.)* To guard bunches of grapes from the sun by covering them with the shoots.

encapado, da [en-cah-pah'-do, dah], *a*. Cloaked, wearing a cloak.

encapazar [en-cah-pah-thar'], *a*. To collect and put into a basket.

encaperuzado, da [en-cah-pay-roo-thah'-do, dah], *a*. Hooded, wearing a hood.

encaperuzarse [en-cah-pay-roo-thar'-say], *vr*. To cover one's head with a hood.

encapilladura [en-cah-pil-lyah-doo'-rah], *f*. *(Naut.)* Tie of a shroud or stay; top-rigging.

encapillar [en-cah-pil-lyar'], *va*. 1. *(Naut.)* To fix the standing rigging to the mast-head. 2. To rig the yards. **Encapillarse ol agua,** *(Naut.)* to ship a head sea.-*vr*. To put on clothes over the head.

encapirotado, da [en-cah-pe-ro-tah'-do, dah], Wearing a cloak of hood.-*pp*. of ENCAPIROTAR.

encapirotar [en-cah-pe-ro-tar'], *va*. To hood a hawk.

encapotado [en-cah-po-tah'-do], *a*. 1. Cloaked, wearing a cloak. 2. Cloudy, overcast (cielo).

encapotadura [en-cah-po-tah-doo'-rah], *f*. **encapotamiento** [en-cah-po-tah-me-en'-to], *m*. Lower, frown, cloudiness.

encapotar [en-cah-po-tar'], *va*. 1. To cloak, to cover with a cloak or great-coat. 2. To cover with a veil, to muffle the face. -*vr*. 1. To lower, to gloom, to be clouded (cielo). 2. To lower the head too much and press upon the bit (caballos).

encaprichamiento [en-cah-pre-chah-me-en'-to], *m*. Headstrongness, stubbornness.

encapricharse [en-cah-pre-char'-say], *vr*. 1. To indulge in whims and fanciful desires, to become obstinate or stubborn. 2. *(coll.)* To be somewhat enamoured.

encapsulado [en-cap-soo-lah-do], *a*. *(Inform.)* Encapsulated.

encapuchar [en-cah-poo-char'], *va*. To cover a thing with a hood.

encapuzado, da [en-cah-poo-thah'-do, dah], *a*. Covered with a hood or cowl. -*pp*. of ENCAPUZAR.

encapuzar [en-cah-poo-thar'], *va*. To cover with a long gown.

encarado, da [en-cah-rah'-do, dah], *a*. 1. Faced. **Bien or mal encarado,** well or ill faced. 2. *(Amer.)* Haughty, threatening. -*pp*. of ENCARAR.

encaramadura [en-cah-rah-mah-doo'-. rah], *f*. *(Obs.)* 1. Height, eminence. 2. The act of climbing up an eminence.

encaramar [en-cah-rah-mar'], *va*. & *vr*. 1. To raise; to elevate. 2. To extol, to exaggerate. 3. To climb. 4. To reach an eminent post.

encaramiento [en-cah-rah-me-en'-to], *m*. The act of facing or aiming.

encarar [encahrar'], *vn*. To face, to confront, to be opposite. **Encararse con,** to face. **Tendrá que encararse con los electores,** he will have to face the electorate. -*va*. 1. To aim, to point or level a firelock. 2. To face, to confront (problema). 3. To bring face to face (dos cosas).

encaratularse [en-cah-rah-too-lar'-say], *vr*. To mask or disguise oneself.

encaraxis [en-ca-rahk'-sis], *f*. Scarification.

encarbo [en-car'-bo], *m*. Pointer, a pointer dog.

encarcavinar [en-car-cah-ve-nar'], *va*. 1. To infect with a pestilential smell. 2. To put one into a ditch.

encarcelación [en-car-thay-lah-the-on'], *f*. Incarceration.

encarcelado, da [en-car-thay-lah'-do dah], *a*. & *pp*. of ENCARCELAR. Confined, imprisoned.

encarcelar [en-car-thay-lar'], *va*. 1. To imprison, to commit to prison. 2. To compress newly glued timbers in a clamp. 3. To fasten something with mortar (jambas de puerta). 4. *(Naut.)* To woold; to fasten two cables which cross each other.

encarecedor [en-cah-ray-thay-dor'], *m*. Praiser, extoller; one who exaggerates.

encarecer [en-cah-ray-therr'], *va*. & *vn*. & *vr*. 1. To raise the price of commodities, to overrate, to overvalue. 2. *(Met.)* To enhance, to exaggerate. 3. To recommend earnestly.

encarecidamente [en-cah-ray-the-dah-men'-tay], *adv*. Exceedingly, highly, hyperbolically.

encarecimiento [en-cah-ray-the-me-en'-to], *m*. 1. Enhancement, augmentation of value. 2. Exaggeration, hyperbolical amplification. **Con encarecimiento,** ardently, earnestly.

encargado [en-car-gah'-do], *a*. **El empleado encargado de estos géneros,** the employee in charge of these stocks. -*m* & *f*. Agent, representative. **Encargado de campo,** groundsman. **Encargado de vestuario,** costume designer.

encargado de negocios [en-car-gah'-do day nay-go'-the-os], *m*. 1. Chargé d'affaires 2. *(Mex.)* Agent, attorney, commissioner.

encargar [en-car-gar'], *va*. To recommend, to charge, to commission, to commit. **Encargarse de alguna cosa,** to take charge of something.

encargo [en-car'-go], *m*. 1. Charge, command, trust conferred, commission, request. **Hacer encargos,** to run errands. 2. Office, place, employ. 3. *(Com.)* Order.

encariñado [en-c-ah-re-nyah'-do], *a*. **Estar encariñado con,** to be fond of.

encariñar [en-cah-re-nyar'], *va*. To inspire affection, fondness or love. -*vr*. To become passionately fond of.

encarna [en-car'-nah], *f.* Act of giving the entrails of dead game to the dogs.

encarnación [en-car-nah-the-on'], *f.* 1. Incarnation, the act of assuming a body (Jesucristo). 2. Carnation, the natural flesh color. 3. A certain adhesive cement which serves to repair chinaware, etc. 4. *(Med.)* Making of tissue in a wound.

encarnadino, na [en-car-nah-dee'-no, nah], *a.* Incarnadine, of a reddish color.

encarnado, da [en-car-nah'-do, dah], *a. & pp.* of ENCARNAR. 1. Incarnate, anything tinged of a deep red color. 2. Dyed flesh color. 3. Covered with flesh.

encarnado [en-car-nah'-do], *m.* Flesh color given to pieces of sculpture.

encarnadura [en-car-nah-doo'-rah], *f.* 1. The natural state of flesh in living bodies, with respect to the cure of wound. 2. The effect produced by an edged weapon on the flesh.

encarnamiento [en-car-nah-me-en'-to], *m.* Incarnation, the act of breeding flesh (herida).

encarnar [en-car-nar'], *vn.* To incarn, to incarnate, to breed flesh. *-va.* To incarnadine, to give a flesh color to pieces of sculpture. 2. To make a strong impression upon the mind. 3. To fill a wound with new flesh. 4. To wound, to pierce the flesh with a dart. 5. To embody. 6. To entice or allure dogs; to feed sporting dogs with flesh.*-vr.* To unite or incorporate one thing with another.

encarnativo [en-car-nah-tee'-vo, vah], *m. & a.* Incarnative, a medicine suposed to generate flesh.

encarne [en-car'-nay], *m.* First feed given to dog of the entrails of game.

encarnecer [en-car-nay-therr'], *vn.* To grow fat and fleshy.

encarnizado, da [en-car-ne-thah'-do, dah], *a.* Bloodshot, inflamed (ojos). *-pp.* of ENCARNIZAR.

encarnizamiento [en-car-ne-thah-me-en'-to], *m.* 1. The act of fleshing or satiating with flesh. 2. Cruelty, rage, fury.

encarnizar [en-car-ne-thar'], *va.* To flesh, to satiate with flesh. 2. To provoke, to irritate. *-vr.* 1. To be glutted with flesh. 2. To be cruelly bent against one; to fall foul upon one.

encaro [en-cah'-ro], *m.* 1. The act of viewing steadfastly. 2. *(Prov.)* Blunderbuss, a wide-mouthed short handgun. **Encaro de escopeta**, aiming, the act of levelling a musket or fire-lock aim.

encarrilar, or **encarrillar** [en-car-ril-yar'], *va.* 1. To direct, to guide, to put on the right road, to conduct a carriage in a proper track, to place in the rails. 2. *(Met.)* To arrange again what had been deranged. *-vr. (Naut.)* To be fouled or entangled on the sheave of a block (cuerda).

encarroñar [en-car-ro-nyar'], *va. (coll.)* To infect, to corrupt. *-vr.* To be infected or corrupted.

encarrujado [en-car-roo-hah'-do], *m.* Ancient kind of silk stuff.*-pp.* of ENCARRUJAR.

encarrujar [en-car-roo-har'], *va.* To plait, to flute, to mangle. *-vr.* To be corrugated, curled, or wrinkled.

encartación [en-car-tah-the-on'], *f.* 1. Enrolment. V. ENPADRONAMIENTO. 2. Vassalage, the state of a vassal; tenure at will; servitude. 3. The people or places which enter into a state of vassalage, or knowledge one as a lord.

encartamiento [en-car-tah-me-en'-to], *m.* 1. Outlawry, proscription. 2. Vassalage. V. ENCARTACIÓN.

encartar [en-car-tar'], *va.* 1. To outlaw, to proscribe. 2. To summon to judgment. 3. To include, to enrol. 4. To enter in the register of taxes. *-vr.* To be unable to discard in a game (naipes).

encarte [en-car'-tay], *m.* In cards, the fortuitous order in which the cards remain at the close of a hand.

encartonador [en-car-to-nah-dor'], *m.* One who applies boards to books for binding.

encartonar [en-car-to-nar'], *va.* 1. To apply (binder's) boards to books. 2. To bind in boards only.

encartuchar [en-car-too-char'], *va.* To fill cartridges with powder.

encasamento [en-cah-sah-men'-to], *m.* Niche, place in a wall for a statue.

encasamiento [en-cah-sah-me-en'-to], *m.* 1. An ornament of fillets and mouldings. 2. Reparation of ruinous houses. 3. Niche.

encasar [en-cah-sa'], *va.* To set a dislocated bone.

encascabelado, da [en-cas-cah-bay-lah'-do, dah], *a.* Filled or adorned with bells.

encascotar [en-cas-co-tar'], *va.* To cover with a layer of rubbish.

encasillado [en-cah-se-lyah'-do], *m.* Set of pigeon-holes.

encasillar [en-cah-se-lyar'], *va.* 1. To place in pigeon-holes. 2. To classify persons or things and assign them to their places.

encasquetar [en-cas-kay-tar'], *va.* 1. To clap on one's hat close to the head. 2. *(Met.)* To induce one to adopt an opinion. *-vr.* To persist, to be head-strong.

encastar [en-cas-tar'], *va.* 1. To improve a race of animals. 2. V. PROCREAR.

encastillado, da [en-cas-til-lyah'-do, dah], *a. (Met.)* Elated, lofty, haughty.*-pp.* of ENCASTILLAR.

encastillador, ra [en-cas-til-lyah-dor', rah], *m. & f.* 1. One who shuts himself up in a castle. 2. A potter's workman who piles up the pieces which ought to be aired before going into the furnace.

encastillamiento [en-cas-til-lyah-me-en'-to], *m.* Act of shutting up in a castle.

encastillar [en-cas-til-lyar'], *va.* To fortify with castles.*-vn.* To make the cell of the queen-bee in beehives.*-vr.* 1. To shut oneself up in a castle, by way of defence. 2. *(Met.)* To persevere obstinately in maintaining one´s opinion.

encastrar [en-cas-trar'], *va.* 1. *(Naut.)* To mortise or scarf pieces of timber. 2. To let in, to imbed.

encastre [en-cahs'-tray], *m.* Fitting in, groove; socket.

encatusar [en-cah-too-sar'], *va.* V. ENGATUSAR.

encauchado [en-cah-oo-chah'-do], *m.* An India-rubber poncho.

encauma [en-cah'-oo-mah], *f. (Med.)* 1. A pustule produced by a burn, and the scar which remains. 2. Corroding ulcer of the cornea.

encausado, da [en-cah-oo-sah'-do], *m & f. (Jur.)* Accused, defendant.

encausar [en-cah-oo-say], *va.* To prosecute, to sue; to put on trial.

encáustico, ca [en-cah'-oos-te-co, cah] *a.* Encaustic, belonging to enamel-painting.

encausto [en-cah'-oos-to], *m.* 1. *(Pict.)* Enamelling. **Pintar al encausto**, to paint in colors requiring firing. 2. A red ink with which emperors alone used to write.

encauzar [en-cah-oo-thar'], *va.* 1. To channel (agua). 2. *(Fig.)* To channel, to direct, to guide. **Las protestas se pueden encauzar a fines buenos**, the protests can be directed towards good objectives.

encavarse [en-cah-var'-say], *vr.* To incave oneself, to hide in a hole.

encebadamiento [en-thay-bah-dah-me-en'-to], *m.* Surfeit, repletion of horses.

encebadar [en-thay-bah-dar'], *va.* To surfeit with barley, and water drunk immediately after it. (animales). *-vr.* To be surfeited by eating barley and drinking water (caballos).

encebollado [en-thay-bol-lyah'-do], *m.* Fricassee of beef or mutton and onions seasoned with spice.

encefálico, ca [en-thay-fah'-le-co, cah], *a.* Encephalic, relating to the brain.

encefalitis [en-thay-fah-lee'-tis], *f.* Encephalitis, inflammation of the brain. **Encefalitis letárgica**, sleeping sickness.

encéfalo [en-thay'-fah-lo], *m.* The encephalon, the brain as a whole; cerebrum, cerebellum, and medulla oblongata.

encefalograma [en-thay-fah-lo-grah'-mah], *m.* Encephalogram.

encefalóideo, dea [en-thay-fah-lo'-e-day-o, ah], *a.* Encephaloid, resembling brain matter in aspect. *-f.* Encephaloid, a variety of cancer resembling the brain in consistency.

encelar [en-thay-lar'], va. To excite jealousy. -vr. To become jealous or suspicious in love.

encelitis [en-thay-lee'-tis], f. (Med.) Intestinal inflammation.

encellar [en-thel-lyar'], va. To mould curds or cheese in a wattle.

encenagado, da [en-thay-nah-gah'-do, dah], a. Mixed or filled with mud.-pp. of ENCENAGARSE.

encenagar [en-thay-nah-gar'], va. To mull, to mire.-vr. 1. To wallow in dirt or mire, to dirty oneself with mud or mire. 2. (Met.) To wallow in crimes and vices: it is seldom used but in its reflexive sense.

encencerrado, da [en-then-ther-rah'-do, dah], a. Carrying a wetherbell.

encendedor, ra [en-then-day-dor', rah], a. Lighting. -m. 1. Lighter. 2. Cigarette lighter. **Encendedor de gas**, gas lighter.

encender [en-then-derr'], va. 1. To light (vela, cigarrillo), to make burn. 2. To set fire to, to set on fire. 3. To heat, to produce heat, to glow. 4. (Met.) To inflame, to inspirit, to incite. 5. (Met.) To foment a party, to sow discord. 6. To switch on, to turn on, to put on (luz, aparato eléctrico). 7. To strike, to light (cerilla). -vr. To fire, to take fire, to be kindled. **Encenderse en cólera**, to fly into a passion. **Encenderse en ira**, to kindle with anger. **¿Cuándo se encienden las luces?**, when is lighting up time?

encendidamente [en-then-de-dah-men'-tay], adv. Vividly, ardently; efficaciously.

encendido, da [en-then-dee'-do, dah], a. & pp. of ENCENDER. 1. Lit (fuego, cigarrillo). 2. On, switched on (luz, aparato eléctrico). **La luz está encendida**, the light is on. 3. Flushed, red, inflamed. **Encendido de color**, high colored. -m. 1. Lighting. **El encendido de las farolas**, the lighting of the lamps. 2. Ignition (coche). Firing (cohete).

encendimiento [en-then-de-me-en'-to] m. 1. Incension, the act of kindling and the state of being on fire. 2. Incandescence, glow. 3. (Met.) Inflammation. 4. (Met.) Liveliness and ardor of human passions and affections.

encenizar [en-thay-ne-thar'], va. To fill or cover with ashes.

encensar, encensuar [en-then-sar', en-then-soo-ar'], va. To give or take at lawful interest, to lease.

encentador [en-then-tah-dor'], m. The person who begins to use things not before used.

encentadura [en-then-tah-doo'-rah], f. **encentamiento**, m. The act of beginning the use of a thing not before used.

encentar [en-then-tar'], va. . To start, to begin.

encepador [en-thay-pah-dor'], m. Stocker, gun-stocker.

encepar [en-thay-par'], va. 1. (coll.) To put in the stocks. 2. To stock a gun; to stock the anchor. -vn. To take root (planta).

encerado [en-thay-rah'-do], m. 1. Oil-cloth, oilskin. 2. Window-blind. 3. (Naut.) Tarpauling. 4. Sticking-plaster. 5. A square of oil-skin, used as a slate or black board in schools.

encerado, da [en-thay-rah'-do, dah], a. Waxed, like wax. -pp. de Encerar. **Papel encerado**, wax paper.

enceramiento [en-thay-rah-me-en'-to], m. Act of waxing, paper, cloth, etc.

encerar [en-thay-rar'], va. 1. To fasten or stiffen with wax. 2. To fill or stain with wax.

encernada [en-ther-nah-dar'], va. V. ACERNADAR.

encerotar [en-thay-ro-tar'], va. To wax thread.

encerradero [en-ther-rah-day'-ro], m. 1. Place for keeping sheep before or after shearing. 2. V. ENCIERRO.

encerrado, da [en-ther-rah'-do, dah], a. (Obs.) Brief, succinct.-pp. of ENCERRAR.

encerrador [en-ther-rah-dor'], m. 1. One who shuts or locks up. 2. Driver of black cattle.

encerradura [en-ther-rah-doo'-rah], f. Cloister, enclosure, closure.

encerramiento [en-ther-rah-me-en'-to], m. 1. Cloister, retreat, place of retirement. 2. Prison, jail, dungeon. 3. The locking up of a thing.

encerrar [en-ther-rar'], va. 1. To lock or shut up, to confine, to get in or to close in. 2. To emboss. 3. To contain, to conclude, to comprehend. **El libro encierra profundas**

verdades, the book contains deep truths. -vr. 1. To retire or withdraw from the world. 2. To be locked or shut up, to be closeted. **Se encerró en el cuarto**, she shut herself in her room.

encerrona [en-ther-ro'-nah], f. A voluntary retreat, a spontaneous retirement.

encespedar [en-thes-pay-dar'], va. (Mil.) To line or cover the sides of a moat with sods.

encestar [en-thes-tar'], va. 1. To gather and put in a basket; to toss in basket, to hamper. 2. To make a basket (basketball).

enchabetar [en-chah-bay-tar'], va. **Enchabetar un perno**, (Naut.) to forelock a bolt.

enchalecar [en-chah-lay-car'], va. (Prov. Amer.) To put in the straitjacket (locos).

enchamarrado, da [en-chah-mar-rah'-do, dah], a. Clothed in coarse frieze or sheepskin.

enchancletar [en-chan-clay-tar'], va. 1. To put on slippers. 2. To wear shoes in the manner of slippers.

enchapar [en-chah-par'], va. To veneer; to plate (con metal).

enchapinado, da [en-chah-pe-nah'-do dah], a. 1. Made in the manner of patters. 2. Built and raised upon a vault or arch.

encharcada [en-char-cah'-dah], f. A pool of water.

encharcar [en-char-car'], va. To swamp, to flood (terreno); to cover with puddles, to turn into pools.

encharcarse [en-char-car'-say], vr. To be covered with water, to be inundated.

enchicar [en-che-car'], va. V. ACHICAR.

enchilada [en-che-lah'-dah], f. A cake of corn dressed with peppers, a Mexican dish.

enchiquerar [en-che-kay-rar'], va. 1. To shut the bull in the pen called chiquero. 2. (Met. coll.) To imprison.

encía [en-thee'-ah], f. The gum of the mouth.

enciclia [en-thee'-cle-ah], f. Concentric circles formed in water when a solid and heavy body falls into it.

encíclica [en-thee'-cle-cah], f. An encyclical letter from the Pope to all the world.

encíclico, ca [en-thee'-cle-o, cah], a. Encyclic, circular (cartas pastorales).

enciclopedia [en-the-clo-pay'-de-ah], f. Encyclopedia, cyclopedia, the circle of sciences.

enciclopédico, ca [en-the-clo-pay'-de-co, cah], a. Encyclopedic.

enciclopedista [en-the-clo-pay-dees'-tah], a. & n. Encyclopedist.

encierro [en-theer'-ro], m. 1. Closure, confinement, closeness. 2 Inclosure. 3. Cloister, religious retreat. 4. Prison, close confinement, custody. 5. The act of driving bulls into the penfold for the bullfighting. (Yo encierro, yo encierre, from Encerrar. V. ACRECENTAR.)

encima [en-thee'-mah], adv. 1. Above, over. 2. At the top. 3. Over and above, besides. 4. On. 5. Overhead. **Encima de la mesa**, over the table. **El avión pasó encima**, the plane passed over. **Echarse algo encima**, to take something upon oneself. **La guerra está encima**, war is upon us. **Por encima de**, over.

encimar [en-the-mar'], va. (Obs.) To place at the top, to raise high. -vr. To raise oneself upon.

encimero, ra [en-the-may'-ro, rah], a. That which is placed over or upon.

encina [en-thee'-nah], f. (Bot.) Evergreen oak, live oak.

encinal, encinar [en-the-nahl', enthe-nar'], m. Wood, consisting of evergreen oak.

encinta [en-theen'-tah], a. Pregnant.

encintado [en-thin-tah'-do], m. Curb.

encintar [en-thin-tar'], va. 1. To ribbon. 2. To curb (acera).

encismar [en-this-mar'], va. (coll.) To set a schism or division.

encisto [en-thees'-to], m. An encysted tumor.

enclaustrado, da [en-clah-oos-trah'-do, dah], a. Shut up in cloisters.

enclaustrar [en-clah-oos-trar'], va. To cloister; to hide away.

enclavación [en-clah-vah-the-on'], *f. (Obs.)* Act of nailing or fixing.

enclavadura [en-clah-vah-doo'-rah], *f.* 1. The part where two pieces of wood are joined. 2. *V.* CLAVADURA.

enclavar [en-clah-var'], *va.* 1. To nail, to fasten with nails. 2. To prick horses in shoeing. *V.* TRASPASAR. **Enclavar la artillería**, to spike up guns.

enclavijar [en-clah-ve-har'], *va.* To unite or join closely. **Enclavijar un instrumento**, to put pegs in a musical instrument. *(Naut.) V.* EMPERNAR.

enclenque [en-clen'-kay], *m. & a.* One who is of a weak or feeble constitution, an emaciated person.

encliquitaje [en-cle-ke-tah'-hay], *m.* Gearing, cogging.

enclítico, ca [en-clee'-te-co, cah], *a.* Enclitic.

encloclar, encloquecer [en-clo-clar', en-clo-kay-therr'], *vn. & vr.* To cluck, to manifest a desire to hatch eggs (aves).

encobar [en-co-bar'], *vn.* To cover or hatch eggs.

encobijar [en-co-be-har'], *va. V.* COBIJAR.

encobrado, da [en-co-brah'-do, dah], *a.* Coppery; copper-colored, copper-plated.

encoclar [en-co-clar'], *vn.* To cluck, to show a desire; to lay eggs (aves).

encocorar [en-co-co-rar'], *va. (coll.)* To molest, to vex, to annoy.

encofrado [en-co-frah'-do], *m. (Min.)* Plank lining timbering.

encofrar [en-co-frar'], *va. (Min.)* To plank, to line with sheeting.

encoger [en-co-herr'], *va.* 1. To contract, to draw together, to shorten. 2. To shrink, to make to shrink. 3. *(Met.)* To discourage, to dispirit. *-vr.* 1. To be low-spirited, to be dismayed. 2. To humble oneself, to be dejected. 3. To shrink, to contract itself into less room. **Encogerse de hombros**, to shrink the shoulders with fear; to put an end to a debate, to occasion silence.

encogidamente [en-co-he'-dah-men-tay], *adv.* Meanly, abjectly.

encogido, da [en-co-hee'-do, dah], *a.* Pusillanimous, timid, fearful, narrow-minded.-*pp.* of ENCOGER.

encogimiento [en-co-he-me-en'-to], *m.* 1. Contraction, contracting, drawing together or shortening; constriction, corrugation. 2. Pusillanimity, want of resolution. 3. Lowness of spirits. 4. Humility, submission, resignation. **Encogimiento de los costados**, *(Naut.)* the tumbling home or housing in of the sides of a ship.

encojar [en-co-har'], *va.* To cripple, to lame, to make lame. *-vr.* 1. To grow lame. 2. To feign sickness in order to avoid doing some business.

encoladura [en-co-lah-doo´-rah], *f.* **encolamiento** [en-co-lah-me-en'-to], *m.* Gluing, the act and effect of gluing.

encolar [en-co-lar'], *va.* To glue, to fasten with cement; to glutinate.

encolerizar [en-co-lay-re-thar'], *va.* To provoke, to anger, to irritate. *-vr.* To be in a passion, to be vexed or displeased; to be in a rage.

encolpismo [en-col-pees'-mo], *m. (Med.)* Vaginal injection.

encomendable [en-co-men-dah'-blay], *a.* Recommendable, commendable.

encomendado [en-co-men-dah'-do], *m.* Vassal of a military chief. —**Encomendado. da**, *pp.* of ENCOMENDAR.

encomendamiento [en-co-men-dah-me-ayn'-to], *m. V.* ENCOMIENDA.

encomendar [en-co-men-dar'], *va.* 1. To recommend, to commend, to commit, to charge. 2. To praise, to applaud. *-vn.* To hold a commandery in a military order. *-vr.* 1. To commit oneself to another's protection. 2. To send compliments and messages. **Sin encomendarse a Dios ni al diablo**, proverb used to signify foolhardiness in throwing oneself into some desperate affair: literally, without commending oneself to God or the devil.

encomendero [en-co-men-day'-ro], *m.* 1. Agent who receives and executes commissions and orders. 2. Pensioner or annuitant. 3. One who holds a commandery in a military order.

encomiador, ra [en-co-me-ah-dor', rah], *m. & f.* One who praises.

encomiar [en-co-me-ar´], *va.* 1. To offer encomiums or praises. 2. To eulogize, to extol.

encomiasta [en-co-me-ahs'-tah], *m.* Encomiast.

encomiástico, ca [en-co-me-ahs'-te-co, cah], *a.* Encomiastic, panegyrical, laudatory.

encomienda [en-co-me-en'-dah], *f.* 1. Commission, charge. 2. Message, compliment sent to an absent person. 3. Commandery in a military order: land or rent belonging to a commandery. 4. The embroidered cross worn by knights of military orders. 5. Patronage, protection, support. 6. Recommendation. 7. *(Com.)* Charge or commission for negotiation. **Encomiendas**, compliments, invitations, respects. **Encomienda de Santiago**, *(Bot.)* daffodil.

encomio [en-co'meo], *m.* Praise, encomium, eulogy, commendation.

encompadrar [en-com-pah-drar'], *vn. (coll.)* 1. To contract affinity by godfather. 2. To be close friends.

enconado, da [en-co-nah'-do, dah], *a. & pp.* of ENCONAR. 1. Inflamed, swollen. 2. Tainted, stained, spotted.

enconamiento [en-co-nah-me-en'-to], *m.* 1. Inflammation, a morbid swelling. 2. *(Met.)* Provocation, the act of exciting passion or anger. 2. *(Obs.)* Venom.

enconar [en-co-nar'], *va.* 1. To inflame, to irritate, to provoke. 2. To increase the state of inflammation in a wound. *-vr.* To rankle, to fester (herida).

encono [en-co'-no], *m.* Malevolence, rancor, ill-will, steadfast implacability.

enconoso, sa [en-co-no'-so, sah], *a.* 1. Apt to cause or produce an inflammation. 2. Hurtful, prejudicial, malevolent.

enconrear [en-con-ray-ar'], *va.* To oil wool that is to be carded.

encontradizo, za [en-con-trah-dee'-tho, thah], *a.* That which may be met on the way. **Hacerse encontradizo con alguno**, to go to meet someone as if by chance.

encontrado, da [en-con-trah'-do, dah], *a.* 1. Opposite, in front. 2. Hostile, opposed. 3. *(Naut.)* One of the classes of blocks, the contrary course of two vessels, and everything, which is moved or is situated opposite to that with which it is compared. *-pp.* of ENCONTRAR.

encontrar [en-con-trar'], *va. & vn.* 1. To meet, to encounter. 2. To meet, to encounter unexpectedly, to hit upon, to find by chance, to fall in with, to light upon. 3. To meet, to assemble, to come together. **Lo encontró bastante fácil**, he found it pretty easy. **No lo encuentro en ninguna parte**, I can´t find it anywhere. *-vr.* 1. To meet, to encounter in a hostile manner, to clash. 2. To be of opposite opinions. 3. To meet at the same place, to meet with. **Encontrarse con uno**, to meet somebody. **Encontrarse con un obstáculo**, to run into an obstacle.

encontrón [en-con-trone'], *m.* Collision, clash, push, shock, violent concourse, a sudden stroke.

encopetado, da [en-co-pay-tah'-do, dah], *a.* Presumptuous, boastful.-*pp.* of ENCOPETAR.

encopetar [en-co-pay-tar'], *va. (Obs.)* To raise the hair high, as in a toupee.

encorachar [en-co-rah-char'], *va.* To put in a leather bag.

encorado, da [en-co-rah'-do, dah], *a. & pp.* of ENCORAR. Wrapped up in leather.

encorajado, da [en-co-rah-hah'-do, dah], *a. & pp.* of ENCORAJAR. 1. Bold, audacious, adventurous. 2. Angry, furious, in a rage.

encorajar [en-co-rah-har'], *va.* To animate, to give courage, to inflame. *-vr.* To be furious, to be in a rage.

encoramentar [en-co-rah-men-tar'], *va. (Naut.)* To bolt, to coak, to fay.

encoramento, encoramiento [en-co-rah-me-en'-to], *m. (Naut.)* Bolting, coaking, faying.

encorar [en-co-rar'], *va. & vn.* 1. To cover with leather. 2. To wrap up in leather. 3. To get a skin (heridas). 4. To skin, to heal the skin.

encorazado, da [en-co-rah-thah'-do, dah], *a.* 1. Covered with a cuirass. 2. Covered with leather in the cuirass fashion. 3. Iron-clad, armored. *Acorazado* is more commonly used.

encorchadura [en-cor-chah-doo'-rah], *f.* 1. The act of hiving bees. 2. The corks or floats, collectively, of fishing nets.

encorchar [en-cor-char'], *va.* 1. To hive bees, to put them into hives made of cork. 2. To buck (caballo).

encorchetar [en-cor-chay-tar'], *va.* To hook, to put on hooks or clasps.

encordar [en-cor-dar'], *va.* 1. To string or chord musical instruments. 2. To halter, to lash or bind with cords or ropes. **Encordelar una cama**, to cord a bed.

encordelar [en-cor-day-lar'], *va..* To bind with cords. **Encordelar una cama**, to cord a bed.

encordonado, da [en-cor-do-nah'-do, dah], *a.* Adorned with cords. *-pp.* of ENCORDONAR.

encordonar [en-cor-do-nar'], *va.* To put running strings to a purse or other thing; to tie with strings.

encorecer [en-co-ray-therr'], *va. & vn.* 1. To skin, to heal the skin. 2. To get a skin (heridas).

encoriación [en-co-re-ah-the-on'], *f.* Act of skinning over a sore, healing a wound.

encornar [en-cor-nar'], *va.* 1. To inlay with horn. 2. To gore or wound with the horns. 3. *(Arch.)* To ornament the ends of an arch with tips of horn.

encornijamiento [en-cor-ne-hah-men'-to], *m.* V. CORNIJAMENTO.

encornudar [en-cor-noo-dar'], *vn.* To begin to get horns (ganado). *-va.* To cuckold, to hornify.

encorozar [en-co-ro-thar'], *va.* To cover the head with a *coraza*, or cone-shaped cap, worn by criminals as a punishment.

encorralar [en-cor-rah-lar'], *va.* To inclose and keep in a yard (ganado).

encortinar [en-cor-te-nar'], *va.* To provide with curtains.

encorvada [en-cor-vah'-dah], *f.* 1. The act of bending or doubling the body. 2. A graceless and awkward manner of dancing. 3. *(Bot.)* Hatchet wetch coronilla. **Hacer la encorvada**, *(Met.)* to feign disease to avoid something.

encorvadura, *f.* **encorvamiento**, *m.* [en-cor-vah-doo'-rah]. 1. Act of bending or reducing to a crooked shape, crouching. 2. Crookedness; falcation, hookedness.

encorvar [en-cor-var'], *va.* To bend, to incurvate, to crook, to curve. *-vr.* To bend, to curb; to go crooked.

encosadura [en-co-sah-doo'-rah], *f. (Prov.)* The act of sewing or joining fine linen to some of a coarser sort.

encostarse [en-cos-tar'-say], *(Naut.)* To stand inshore, to near the coast.

encostradura [en-cos-trah-doo'-rah], *f.* Incrustation, crust.

encostrar [en-cos-trar'], *va.* 1. To crust, to incrust, to envelope or cover with a crust. 2. To roughcast with mortar, made of lime and sand.

encovadura [en-co-vah-doo´-rah], *f.* Act of depositing in a cellar.

encovar [en-co-var'], *va.* 1. To put or lay up in a cellar. 2. *(Met.)* To guard, to conceal, to inclose. *-vr.* 1. To go down into a cellar or cave. 2. To hide oneself.

encrasar [en-crah-sar'], *va.* To fatten; to thicken.

encrespado [en-cres-pah'-do], *a.* Curly (pelo); choppy (mar).

encrespador [en-cres-pah-dor'], *m.* Crisping-pin, crisping-iron, curling-iron.

encrespadura [en-cres-pah-doo'-rah], *f.* Crispation, the act of curling.

encrespamiento [en-cres-pah-me-en'-to], *m.* Crispation, crispness, curliness, curledness.

encrespar [en-cres-par'], *va.* 1. To curl, to frizzle, to crimp. *-vr.* 1. *(Naut.)* To become rough and boisterous (mar). 2. To be rude or unpolite. 3. To be involved in quarrels and disputes.

encrespo [en-cres-po], *m. (Obs.)* Crispation, the act and effect of curling.

encrestado, da [en-cres-tah'-do, dah], *a. & pp.* of ENCRESTARSE. 1. Adorned with a crest or comb. 2. *(Met.)* Haughty, lofty.

encrestarse [en-cres-tar'-say], *vr.* 1. To get the crest or comb (gallo). 2. *(Met.)* To be proud, elated, or haughty.

encrinita [en-cre-nee'-tah], *f.* Encrinite, a fossil crinoid.

encruce [en-croo-thay], *m.* 1. Crossing of threads. 2. Shed, lease, the plane in which the warp-threads cross.

encrucijada [en-croo-the-hah'-dah], *f.* Crossway, crossroad, intersection, junction. *(Fig.)* **Estamos en la encrucijada**, we are at the crossroads.

encrudecer [en-croo-day-therr'], *va.* 1. To make a wound worse or raw. 2. To exasperate, to irritate. *-vr.* To be enraged, to become furious with passion. *(Yo me encrudezco, yo me encrudezca, from Encrudecerse. V. CONOCER.)*

encruelecer [en-croo-ay-lay-therr'], *va.* To excite to cruelties, to make cruel. *(Yo me encruelezco, yo me encruelezca, from Encruelecer. V. CONOCER.)*

encruzar [en-croo-thar'], *va.* To cross the threads of the warp, to twill.

encuadernación [en-coo-ah-der-nah-the-on'], *f.* Binding (libros) **Encuadernación en cantoné**, paste-board binding. **Encuadernación en tela**, cloth binding.

encuadernador [en-coo-ah-der-nah-dor'], *m.* Binder or bookbinder.

encuadernar [en-coo-ah-der-nar'], *va.* 1. To bind books, pamphlets, etc. 2. *(Met.)* To join again what was disjoined. 3. To reconcile.

encuadrar [en-coo-ah-drar'], *va.* 1. To frame, to encase. 2. To fit, to insert (encajar). 3. *(Fig.)* To contain, to comprise.

encubar [en-coo-bar'], *va.* 1. To put liquids into casks, barrels, etc. 2. *(Ant.)* To put a criminal into a butt, by way of punishment.

encubertado [en-coo-ber-tah'-do], *m. (Zool.)* A kind of South American armadillo.

encubertar [en-coo-ber-tar'], *va.* To overspread with a covering of cloth or silk. *-vr.* To dress and arm oneself for defence of the body.

encubierta [en-coo-be-err'-tah], *f.* Fraud, deceit, imposition.

encubiertamente [en-coo-be-ayr'-tah-men-tay], *adv.* 1. Hiddenly, secretly. 2. Deceitfully, fraudulently.

encubierto, ta [en-coo-be-err'-to, tah], *a. & pp.* of ENCUBRIR. 1. Hidden concealed. 2. V. CUBIERTO. *(Yo encubierto, yo encubierta, from Encubertar. V. ACRECENTAR.)*

encubridor, ra [en-coo-bre-dor', rah], *m. & f.* Concealer, hider, harborer. **Encubridor de hurtos**, receiver of stolen goods.

encubrimiento [en-coo-bre-me-en'-to], *m.* Concealment, hiding, the act of hiding or concealing.

encubrir [en-coo-breer'], *va.* To hide, to conceal, to cloak, to mask, to palliate.

encucar [en-coo-car'], *va. (Prov.)* To gather nuts and filberts, and store them up.

encuentro [en-coo-en'-tro], *m.* 1. Knock, a sudden stroke, chock, jostle, clash. 2. Encounter, accidental congress; sudden meeting. 3. Encounter, fight. 4. The act of going to meet and see anyone. 5. Opposition, difficulty. 6. Joint of the wings, in fowls or birds, next to the breast. 7. In the larger quadrupeds, the points of the shoulder-blades. 8. *(Arch.)* An angle formed by two beams, two walls, etc. **Salir al encuentro**, a) to go to meet a person in a certain place. b) to encounter. c) to prevent a person in what he is to say or observe. **Encuentros**, temples of a loom. **Un encuentro fortuito**, a chance meeting. **Ir al encuentro de lo desconocido**, to go out to face the unknown. *(Yo encuentro, yo encuentre, from Encontrar. V. ACORDAR.)*

encuesta [en-coo-ays'-tah], *f.* Poll, opinion poll, survey (opinión pública). **Hacer una encuesta**, to carry out an opinion poll. 2. Inquiry, investigation (investigación).

encuestador, ra [en-coo-ays-tah-dor'], *m & f.* Pollster.

encuestar [en-coo-ays-tar'], *va.* To poll, to take a poll of.

encuitarse [en-coo-e-tar-say], *vr.* To grieve, to afflict oneself.

enculatar [en-coo-lah-tar'], *va.* To put on the covering or cap of a hive.

encumbrado, da [en-coom-brah'-do, dah], *a.* High, elevated, lofty, stately.-*pp.* of ENCUMBRAR.

encumbramiento [en-coom-brah-me-en'-to], *m.* 1. The act of raising or elevating. 2. Height, eminence.

encumbrar [en-coom-brar'], *va.* 1. To raise, to elevate. 2. To mount or ascend a height. 3. *(Met.)* To elevate to dignities or honors. -*vr.* 1. To be raised or elevated. 2. To be proud, to rate himself high.

encunar [en-coo-nar'], *va.* 1. To put a child in the cradle. 2. *(Met.)* To catch the bullfighter between the horns (toro).

encuñar [en-coo-nyar'], *va.* To coin. V. ACUÑAR.

encureñado, da [en-coo-ray-nyah'-do, dah], *a.* Put into the carriage or stock.

encurtidos [en-coor-tee'-dos], *m. pl.* Pickles of small cucumbers and peppers.

encurtir [en-coor-teer'], *va.* To souse in pickle or vinegar.

enchironar [en-che-ro-nar'], *va.* To jug, to jail.

enchufado, da [en-choo-fah'-do], *m & f.* Creep; teacher´s pet (en escuela).

enchufar [en-choo-far'], *vn.* To fit, as the orifice of a tube into another. -*va.* 1. To join, to connect, to fit together (técnica). 2. *(Com, Fin.)* To merge. -*vr.* To wangle oneself a job (puesto).

enchufe [en-choo'-fay], *m.* 1. Socket joint (unión). 2. Plug (clavija). 3. *(coll.)* Additional job obtained through political influence. **Tiene un enchufe en el ministerio**, he´s got a contact in the ministry. **Hay que tener enchufes**, you´ve got to have contacts.

endeble [en-day'-blay], *a.* Feeble, weak, flaccid, flimsy, forceless.

endeblez [en-day-bleth´],*f.* Feebleness, flaccidity, flimsiness.

endecágono [en-day-cah'-gono], *m.* Hendecagon, a figure of eleven angles or sides.

endecasílabo, ba [en-day-cah-see'-lah-bo, bah], *a.* Applied to metrical lines consisting of eleven syllables. **Verso endecasílabo**, hendecasyllable verse.

endecha [en-day'-chah], *f.* Dirge, a doleful ditty.

endechar [en-day-char'], *va.* To sing funeral songs in honor and praise of the dead. -*vr.* To grieve, to mourn.

endemia [en-day'-me-ah],*f.* Endemia, any disease produced and propagated by local conditions.

endémico, ca [en-day'-me-co, cah], *a.* Endemic, chronic, peculiar to a climate.

endemoniado, da [en-day-mo-ne-ah'-do, dah], *a.* 1. Possessed with the devil, fiendful (poseído). 2. Devilish, extremely bad, perverse or hurtful (endiablado).-*pp.* of ENDEMONIAR.

endemoniar [en-day-mo-ne-ar'], *va.* 1 To possess with a devil (endiablar). 2. *(Met.)* To irritate, to provoke, to enrage. -*vr.* To get riled.

endentar [en-den-tar'], *va.* 1. To join with a mortise. 2. *(Naut.)* To insert one thing in another. 3. To snake the teeth on a wheel.

endentecer [en-den-tay-therr'], *vn.* To cut teeth, to teeth, to tooth. *(Yo endentezco, yo endentezca,* from *Endentecer.* V. CONOCER.)

endeñado, da [en-day-nyah'-do, dah], *a.* Damaged, hurt, inflamed.

enderezadamenete [en-day-ray-thah-dah-men'-tay], *adv.* Justly, rightly; directly.

enderezado [en-day-ray-thah'do], *a.* Appropriate; favorable, opportune.

enderezador [en-day-ray-thah-dor'], *m.* Guide, director; governor.

enderezadura [en-day-ray-thah-doo'-rah],*f.* The straight and right road.

enderezamiento [en-day-ray-thah-me-en'-to], *m.* Guidance, direction, the act of guiding or setting right.

enderezar [en-day-ray-thar'], *va.* 1. To erect, to place perpendicularly to the horizon what is not upright, to make

straight (poner vertical). 2. To rectify, to set right. 3. To address, to dedicate (dedicar). 4. To go and meet a person. **Las medidas están enderezadas a corregirlo**, the measures are designed to correct it. -*vn.* To take the direct road. -*vr.* 1. To erect, to rise upright. 2. *(Met.)* To fix or establish oneself in a place or employment. **Enderezar el genio**, to break a bad temper.

endérmico, ca [en-derr'-me-co, cah], *a.* Endermic, said of a remedy applied directly to the skin.

endeudarse [en-day-oo-dar'-say], *vr.* To get in debt, to contract debts. V. ADEUDARSE. **Endeudarse con uno**, to become indebted to somebody.

endiablada [en-de-ah-blah'-dah],*f.* Masquerade, a diversion in which the company is dressed in masks.

endiabladamente [en-de-ah-blah-dah-men-tay], *adv.* Uglily, abominably, devilishly.

endiablado, da [en-de-ah-blah´-do, dah], *a. & pp.* of ENDIABLAR. 1. Devilish, diabolical, diabolic (diabólico). 2. Ugly, deformed (feo); perverse, wicked. 3. Furious, angry (enojado).

endiablar [en-de-ah-blar'], *va.* 1. *(Obs.)* To possess with the devil (endemoniar). 2. *(Met.)* To pervert, to corrupt (corromper). -*vr.* 1. To be possessed with a devil. 2. *(Met.)* To be furious, to be beside oneself.

endíadis [en-dee'-ah-dis], *f. (Rhet.)* Hendiadys, a figure by which two words are used to express a single idea.

endibia [en-dee'-be-ah], *f. (Bot.)* Endive, succory.

endilgador, ra [en-deel-gah-dor', rah] *m. &f. (coll.)* Pander; inducer, adviser.

endilgar [en-deel-gar'], *va. (coll.)* 1. To pander, to induce, to persuade. 2. To procure, to facilitate, to accommodate. 3. To show the way, to direct (encaminar).

endiñar [en-dee-nyahr'], *va.* 1. To fetch (tortazo), to deal, to land (golpe). 2. **Endiñarla**, to put it in.

endiosamiento [en-de-o-sah-me-en´-to] *m.* 1. Haughtiness, loftiness, pride (engreimiento). 2. Ecstasy, abstraction; disregard of worldly concerns.

endiosar [en-de-o-sar'], *va.* To deify, to adore as a god, to glorify. -*vr.* 1. To be elated, to be puffed up with pride (engreírse). 2. To be in a state of religious abstraction or fervent devotion.

endoblado, da [en-do-blah'-do, dah], *a.* Applied to a lamb that sucks its own mother and another ewe.

endocardio [en-do-car'-de-o], *m.* Endocardium, the serous lining membrane of the heart.

endocarditis [en-do-car-dee'-tis], *f.* Endocarditis, inflammation of the lining of the heart.

endocarpo [en-do-car'-po], *m. (Bot.)* Endocarp, the inner membrane of the pericarp.

endógeno, na [en-do'-hay-no, nah], *a.* Endogenous, growing by internal additions.

endorsar, endosar [en-dor-sar', en-do-sar'], *va.* To endorse a bill of exchange.

endorso, endoso [en-dor'-so, en-do'-so], *m.* Endorsement of a bill of exchange.

endosador, endosante [en-do-sah-dor', en-do-sahn'-tay], *m.* Endorser.

endoselar [en-do-say-lar'], *va.* To hang, to make hangings or curtains.

endósmosis [en-dos'-mo-sis], *f.* Endosmosis, transudation.

endospermo [en-dos-perr'-mo], *m.* Endosperm, the albumen of a seed.

endotérmico, ca [en-do-terr'-me-co, cah], *a. (Chem.)* Endothermic.

endragonarse [en-drah-go-nar'-say], *vr.* In the jocular style, to grow furious as a dragon.

endriago [en-dre-ah'-go], *m.* A kind of fabulous monster.

endrina [en-dree'-nah],*f.* Sloe, the fruit of the blackthorn or sloetree.

endrino [en-dree'-no], *m. (Bot.)* Black-thorn, sloetree.

endrino, na [en-dree'-no, nah], *a.* Of a sloe-color.

endulzamiento [en-dool-thah-me-en'-to], *m.* **endulzadura** [en-dool-thah-doo'-rah], *f.* Dulcification, act of sweetening.

endulzante [en-dool-than'-tay], *m.* Sweetening, sweetener.

endulzar, endulzorar [en-dool-thar', en-dool-tho-rar'], *va.* 1. To sweeten, to make sweet. 2. *(Met.)* To soften, to make mild; to alleviate the toils of life.

endurador, ra [en-doo-rah-dor', rah], *m. & f. & a.* Miser, a mean, avaricious person.

endurar [en-doo-rar'], *va* l. To harden, to indurate, to make hard. 2. To live in a parsimonious manner. 3. To endure, to bear, to suffer. 4. To delay, to put off.

endurecer [en-doo-ray-therr'], *va.* 1. To harden, to indurate, to make hard. 2. *(Met.)* To accustom the body to labor and hardships, to inure. 3. *(Met.)* To render one steady in his sentiments and opinions. 4. To exasperate, to irritate. **Endurecer a uno a los peligros**, to inure somebody to dangers. *-vr.* 1. To harden, to grow hard, to grow cruel. 2. To hammer metals. 3. In the manufacture of needles, to temper then. *(Yo endurezco, yo endurezca, from Endurecer. V.* CONOCER.)

endurecidamente [en-doo-ray-the-dah-men'-tay], *adv.* Pertinaciously.

endurecido, da [en-doo-ray-thee'-do, dah], *a. & pp.* of ENDURECER. 1. Hard (duro), hardy. 2. Indurated, hardened (lodo), obdurate. 3. Tutored by experience, inured.

endurecimiento [en-doo-ray-the-me-en-to], *m.* Hardness; obstinacy, tenacity, hardness of heart, obdurateness. **Endurecimiento de las arterias**, hardening of the arteries.

ene [ay'-nay], *f.* Spanish name of the letter N.

enea [ay-nay'-ah], *f. (Bot.)* Cat's tail, reedmace, rush.

eneágono [ay-nay-ah'-go-no], *m.* A plain figure with nine sides and nine angles.

eneático, ca [ay-nay-ah'-te-co, cah], *a.* Belonging to the number nine.

enebral [ay nay brahl'], *m.* Plantation, of the juniper-tree.

enebrina [ay-nay-bree'-nah], *f.* Fruit of the juniper-tree.

enebro [ay-nay'-bro], *m. (Bot.)* Common juniper.

eneida [ay-nay'-e-dah], *f.* The Aeneid, an epic poem by Virgil.

enejar [ay-nay-har'], *va.* 1. To put an axle-tree to a cart or carriage. 2. To put anything in an axle-tree.

eneldo [ay-nel'-do], *m. (Bot.)* Common dill.

enema [ay-nay'-mah], *f.* Enema, injection, clyster.

enemiga [ay-nay-mee'-gah], *f.* Enmity, malevolence, aversion, ill-will.

enemigamente [ay-nay-mee'-gah-men-tay], *adv.* Inimically, in a hostile manner.

enemigarse [ay-nay-me-gar'-say], *vr.* To be in a state of enmity.

enemigo, ga [ay-ne-mee'-go, gah], *a.* Inimical, hostile, contrary, unfriendly, adverse. **Ser enemigo de**, to be hostile to.

enemigo, ga [ay-nay-mee'-go, gah], *m. & f.* Enemy, antagonist, foe, foeman. **El enemigo**, the fiend, the devil.

enemistad [ay-nay-mis-tahd'], *f.* Enmity, hatred.

enemistar [ay-nay-mis-tar'], *va.* To make an enemy. *-vr.* To become an enemy. **Enemistarse con uno**, to become an enemy of somebody.

eneo, ea [ay-na-yo, ah], *a. (Poet.)* Brazen, belonging to brass.

enerar [ay-nay-rar'], *va.* To kill plants by frost.

energético [ay-nayr'-he-co], *a.* 1. *(Tec.)* Energy, fuel, power. **La crisis energética**, the energy crisis.

energía [ay-ner-hee'-ah], *f.* 1. Energy, power, vigor (vigor). **Obrar con energía**, to act energetically. 2. Strength of expression, force of meaning. 3. Comprehensiveness. 4. Pep *(coll.)*. **Energía atómica**, atomic energy. **Energía solar**, Solar power. **Energía eólica**, wind power.

enérgicamente [ay-nerr'-he-cah-men-tay], *adv.* Energetically, expressively.

enérgico, ca [ay-nerr'-he-co, cah], *a.* Energetic, energetical, energic (persona), forcible, active, vigorous (esfuerzo), expressive, lively, strenuous (esfuerzo).

energúmeno, na [ay-nayr-goo'-may-no], *m & f.* Person possessed of the devil; *(Fig.)* demon, wild person, madman. **Ponerse como un energúmeno**, to get mad (enfadarse).

enero [ay-nay'-ro], *m.* January, the first month of the year.

enervación [ay-ner-vah-the-on'], *f.* 1. Enervation. 2. *(Vet.)* Section of two tendons in the head of a horse.

enervado, da [ay-ner-vah'-do], *a. & pp.* of ENERVAR. Enervate, enervated, weakened.

enervador, ra [ay-ner-vah-dor', rah], *a.* Weakening, enervating.

enervamiento [ay-ner-vah-me-en'-to], *m.* 1. Enervation. 2. Effeminacy.

enervar [ay-ner-var'], *va.* 1. To enervate, to deprive of force. 2. To weaken the reasons or arguments. *-vr.* 1. To grow weak, to lose force. 2. To become effeminate. 3. To become dull (sentidos). 4. To cut the tendon of the muscles which raise the upper lip of horses.

enésimo, ma [ay-nay'-se-mo], *a. m & f.* **Por enésima vez**, for the umpteenth time.

enético, ca [ay-nay'-te-co, cah], *a.* Lethal, mortal.

enfadadizo za [en-fah-dah-dee'-tho, thah], *a.* Irritable, irascible, peevish, waspish, easily offended, soon angry.

enfadar [en-fah-dar'], *va.* To vex, to molest, to trouble, to fret, to offend (ofender), to make angry, to cut to the heart, to anger (enojar). *-vr.* To fret, to become angry (enojarse). **No te enfades**, don't be cross. **De nada sirve enfadarse**, it's no good getting cross.

enfado [en-fah'-do], *m.* 1. Trouble, vexation, molestation, fret, crossness, anger, gall, fastidiousness (enojo). 2. *V.* AFÁN and TRABAJO.

enfadoso, sa [en-fah-do'-so, sah], *a.* Vexatious, troublesome, heavy, cumbersome, molestful.

enfaldar [en-fal-dar'], *va.* To lop off the lower branches of trees. *-vr.* To tuck or truss up the skirts of one's clothes.

enfaldo [en-fahl'-do], *m.* Act of tucking up one's clothes.

enfangar [en--fahn-gar'], *va.* To cover with mud.

enfangarse [en-fan-gar'-say], *vr. (Naut.)* To touch ground in a miry or muddy place. *(coll.)* To get into difficulties.

enfardador [en-far-dah-dor], *m.* Packer, a person who packs up bales and packages.

enfardar [en-far-dar'], *va.* To pack, to bale, to make packages.

enfardelador [en-far-day-lah-dor'], *m.* Packer, one who makes up bales.

enfardeladura [en-far-day-lah-doo'-rah], *f.* Packing, act of packing merchandise.

enfardelar [en-far-day-lar'], *va.* To bale, to make up into bales, to pack.

énfasis [en'-fah-sis], *m.* Emphasis, a remarkable stress laid on a word or sentence. **Hablar con énfasis**, to speak emphatically.

enfáticamente [en-fah'-te-cah-men-tay], *adv.* Emphatically.

enfático, ca [en-fah'-te-co, cah], *a.* Emphatical, emphatic, impressive, heavy (discurso).

enfatizar [en-fah-te-thar'], *va.* To emphasize, to stress. *-vn.* To emphasize.

enfelpar [en-fel-par'], *va. V.* AFELPAR.

enfermamente [en-fer-mah-men'-tay], *adv.* Weakly, feebly.

enfermar [en-fer-mar'], *vn.* To be seized with a fit of illness, to fall ill. *-va.* 1. To make sick. 2. To cause damage or loss. 3. To weaken, to enervate.

enfermedad [en-fer-may-dahd'], *f.* 1. Infirmity, indisposition (indisposición), illness, complaint, disease, malady, distemper. **Durante esta enfermedad**, during this illness. **Enfermedad de la piel**, skin disease. **Enfermedad de transmisión sexual**, sexually transmitted disease. 2. Damage, disorder, risk.

enfermería [en-fer-may-ree'-ah], *f.* Infirmary, lodgings for the sick, sanatorium; hospital.

enfermero, ra [en-fer-may'-ro, rah], *m. & f.* Overseer or nurse, who has the care of the sick.

enfermizo, za [en-fer-mee'-tho, thah], *a.* 1. Infirm, sickly, in bad health. 2. Morbifical, morbific, causing diseases.

enfermo, ma [en-ferr'-mo, mah], *a.*1. Sick, diseased, infirm, indisposed, unhealthy. 2. Weak, feeble. 3. Of little importance or consideration. 4. Corrupted, tainted. **Enfermo de amor,** love-sick. **Ponerse enfermo,** to fall ill. *m. & f.* Sick person, invalid; patient (hospital).

enfervorizar [en-fer-vo-re-thar'], *va.* To heat, to inflame, to incite. *-vr.* To overheat oneself.

enfeudación [en-fay-oo-dah-the-on'], *f.* Infeudation, enfeoffment, the act of putting one in possession of a fee or estate.

enfeudar [en-fay-oo-dar'], *va.* To feoff, to enfeoff, to invest with a right or estate.

enfielar [en-fe-ay-lar'], *va.* To put in balance.

enfilar [en-fe-lar'], *va.* 1. To continue as if united in a file or line (alinear). 2. To enfilade, to pierce in a right line; to carry off by a cannon shot a whole file of the enemy's troops; to keep straight forward (rumbo). **El piloto trató de enfilar la pista,** the pilot tried to line the aircraft up with the runway.

enfisema [en-fe-say'-mah], *m.* Emphysema, infiltration of the cellular tissue with air.

enfisematoso, sa [en-fe-say-ma-to'-so, sah], *a.* Emphysematous, affected by emphysema.

enfiteusis, enfitéosis [en-fe-tay'-oo-sis, en-fe-tay'-o-sis], *m. & f.* A species of alienation, by which the use and usufruct are transferred, but not the whole right of property.

enfiteuta [en-fe-tay'-oo-tah], *m.* A tenant by emphyteusis.

enfitéutico, ca [en-fe-tay'-oo-te-co, cah], *a.* Emphyteutic, taken on hire.

enflaquecer [en-flah-kay-therr'], *va.* To weaken, to diminish, to make thin and lean, to extenuate, to fade. *-vr.* To become thin and lean (adelgazarse), to fall away or fall off.

enflaquecidamente [en-flah-kay-the-dah-men'-tay], *adv.* Weakly, feebly, faintly, without strength.

enflaquecimiento [en-flah-kay-the-me-en'-to], *m.* 1. Extenuation, a general decay in the muscular flesh of the whole body (adelgazamiento). 2. Attenuation, debilitation, maceration.

enflautado, da [en-flah-oo-tah'-do, dah] *a.* Turgid, inflated. *-m.* 1. *(Naut.)* The row of cannon mouths which show upon a vessel's side. 2. *(Amer.)* The flutestops of act organ, collectively. 3. A sound which imitates the flute.

enflautador, ra [en-flah-oo-tah-dor', rah], *m. & f.* Procurer, pimp.

enflautar [en-flah-oo-tar'], *va.* To procure.

enflechado, da [en-flay-chah'-do, dah], *a.* Applied to a bent bow or arrow ready to discharge.

enflechastes [en-flay-chahs'-tes], *m. pl. (Naut.)* Ratlines.

enfocar [en-fo-car'], *va.* 1. To focus. 2. To size up or weigh the aspects (de un problema o negocio). **Podemos enfocar este problema de tres maneras,** we can approach this problem in three ways.

enfoque [en-fo'-kay], *m.* Focus.

enfornar [en-for-nar'], *va.* V. ENHORNAR.

enfoscado, da [en-fos-cah'-do, dah], *a. & pp.* of ENFOSCARSE. 1. Brow-beaten. 2. Confused, entangled.

enfoscar [en-fos-car'], *va. & vr.* 1. To be uneasy, to be troubled or perplexed. 2. To be immersed in business. 3. To be cloudy (cielo). 4. To stop up the holes in a wall after it is constructed.

enfrailar [en-frah-e-lar'], *va. & vr.* To make one a monk or a friar, to induce him to take the vows of a religious order; to become a friar.

enfranquecer [en-fran-kay-therr'], *va.* To frank, to make free.

enfrascamiento [en-fras-cah-me-en'-to], *m.* The act of being entangled between brambles and briers.

enfrascar [en-fras-car'], *va.* To put liquid in a flask or bottle. *-vr.* 1. To be entangled between brambles and briers. 2. *(Met.)* To be involved in difficulties and to troubles, to engage deeply in an object. **Enfrascarse en un problema,** to get deeply involved in a problem. **Estaba enfrascado en la lectura,** he was buried in a book.

enfrenador [en-fray-nah-dor'], *m.* Bridler, one who puts on a bridle.

enfrenamiento [en-fray-nah-me-en'-to], *m.* 1. Putting on the brake (automóvil). 2. Bridling (caballo).

enfrenar [en-fray-nar'], *va.* 1. To put on the brake (automóvil) 2. To curb, to restrain. 3. To bridle, to put on the bridle (caballo).

enfrentamiento [en-fren-tah-me-ayn'-to], *m.* Clash, confrontation.

enfrentar [en-fren-tar'], *va.* 1. To put face to face (carear). 2. To face, to confront (problema). *-vn.* To face. *-vr.* **enfrentarse con,** to face, to confront. **Hay que enfrentarse con el peligro,** one must face up to the danger.

enfrente [en-fren'-tay], *adv.* Over against, opposite, in front, front to front. **Enfrente de casa,** opposite to the house.

enfriadera [en-fre-ah-day'-rah], *f.* Back, cooler or keelfat, the vessel for cooling any liquid; refrigerator.

enfriadero, enfriador [en-fre-ah-day'-ro, en-fre-ah-dor'], *m.* Cooling-place; refrigerator.

enfriamiento [en-fre-ah-me-en'-to], *m.* Refrigeration, the act of cooling, the state of being cooled (refrigeración).

enfriar [en-fre-ar'], *va.* 1. To cool (helar), to make cool, to allay, to heat out of, to refrigerate. 2. *(Met.)* To cool, to allay the heat of passion, to calm the mind. *-vr.* 1. To cool, to grow less hot. 2. *(Met.)* To cool, to grow less warm with regard to passion.

enfundar [en-foon-dar'], *va.* 1. To case, to put into a case (instrumento); to sheathe (espada). 2. To fill up to the brim, to cram, to stuff (llenar).

enfuñarse [en-foo-nyar'-say], *vr. (Prov. Cuba)* To get excited, worried. V. AMOHINARSE.

enfurecer [en-foo-ray-therr'], *va.* 1. To irritate, to enrage, to madden, to make furious. V. ENSOBERBECER.*-vr.* 1. To rage, to grow boisterous or furious (viento y mar). 2. To become furious or enraged. *(Yo me enfurezco, yo me enfurezca, from Enfurecerse. V. CONOCER.)*

enfurruñarse [en-foor-roo-nyar'-say], *vr. (coll.)* To grow angry, to tiff, to sulk (enfadarse), to frown.

enfurtir [en-toor-teer'], *va.* 1. To full or mill clothes. 2. Among hatters; to felt.

engace [en-gah'-thay], *m.* Catenation, connection. V. ENGARCE.

engaitador, ra [en-gah-e-tah-dor', rah], *m. & f.* Coaxer, wheedler.

engaitar [en-gah-e-tar'], *va.* To coax, to wheedle.

engalanado [en-gah-lah-nah'-do], *m.* The banners and bunting with which a ship is adorned.

engalanar [en-gah-lah-nar'], *va.* 1. To adorn, to deck. 2. *(Naut.)* To dress a ship, to display a variety of colors, ensigns, or pendants. *-vr.* To adorn oneself; to dress up.

engalgar [en-gal-gar'], *va.* To pursue closely, not to lose sight of (galgos).

engallado, da [en-gal-lyah'-do, dah], *a.* 1. Erect, upright. 2. Haughty, elated, arrogant (arrogante).

engalladura [en-gal-lyah-doo'-rah], *f.* V. GALLADURA.

engallarse [en-gal-lyar'-say], *vr.* To affect gravity.

enganchador [en-gan-chah-dor'], *m.* One who decoys others into military service, vulgarly a crimp.

enganchamiento [en-gan-chah-me-en'-to], *m.* 1. Accroachment, the act of drawing as with a hook, hooking. 2. The act of entrapping, alluring, or decoying someone, particularly to make him enlist in the military service.

enganchar [en-gan-char'], *va.* 1. To hook, to catch with a hook, to accroach (con gancho). 2. To entrap, to ensnare. 3. To decoy into the military service, vulgarly to crimp. 4. To couple, to connect. **Enganchar los caballos al coche,** to harness the horses to the carriage. *-vr.* 1. To engage, to enlist or enroll in military service. 2. **Engancharse a las drogas,** to get hooked (prenderse).

enganche [en-gahn'-chay], *m.* 1. Enlistment, enrollment. 2. Bounty money (pago). 3. Coupler, coupling, connecting link. 4. *(Mex. coll.)* Down payment on a purchase.

engañabobos [en-gah-nyah-bo'bos], *m. (coll.)* 1. Impostor. 2. Fooltrap, a snare to catch fools in.

engañadizo, za [en-gah-nyah-dee'-tho, thah], *a.* Deceptible, easily deceived.

engañado, da [en-gah-nyah'-do, dah] *a. & pp.* of ENGAÑAR. Mistaken, deceived, overseen.

engañador, ra [en-gah-nyah-dor', rah] *m. & f.* Cheat, impostor, deceiver, cozener, colluder, abuser.

engañadura [en-gah-nyah-doo'-rah], *f. (Naut.)* Seizing truck, shroud, double wall knot.

engañapastor [en-gah-nyah-pas-tor'], *m. (Orn.)* Wagtail, a bird.

engañar [en-gah-nyar'], *va.* 1. To deceive (embaucar), to cheat, to mock, to mislead (despistar). **A mí no me engaña nadie,** you can´t fool me. **Engaña a su marido,** she´s unfaithful to her husband. 2. To cheat, to delude, to impose upon, to trick. 3. To fool, to hoax, to abuse, to gull. *-vr.* To be deceived, to mistake, to make a mistake. **Ser malo de engañar,** *(coll.)* to be not easily deceived, to be sagacious. **Se engaña con falsas esperanzas,** she deludes herself with false hopes.

engañifa [en-gah-nyee'-fah], *f. (coll.)* 1. Deceit, trick, fraudulent action. 2. A catchpenny.

engaño [en-gah'-nyo], *m.* 1. Mistake, mistaking, misunderstanding (malentendido), misapprehension, misconception. 2. Deceit (cualidad), fraud, imposition, falsehood (cosa fingida). 3. Hoax, lure. **Todo es engaño,** it´s all a sham. **Aquí no hay engaño,** there is no attempt to deceive anybody here. **Padecer engaño,** to labor under a misunderstanding.

engañosamente [en-gah-nyo'-sah-men-tay], *adv.* Deceitfully, fraudfully, guilefully; mistakenly.

engañoso, sa [en-gah-nyo'-so, sah], *a.* Deceitful (persona), artful, fallacious, false, fraudulent, mendacious.

engarabatar [en-gah-ra-bah tar'], *va. (coll.)* To hook, to seize with violence. *-vr.* To grow crooked.

engarabitarse [en-gah-ra-be-tar'-say], *vr. (coll.)* To climb, to mount, to ascend (subir).

engarbarse [en-gar-bar'-say], *vr.* To perch on the highest branch of a tree (pájaros).

engarbullar [en-gar-bool-lyar'], *va. (coll.)* To entangle, to involve.

engarce [en-gar-thay], *m.* 1. Catenation, link. 2. Close union or connection. 3. Setting, mount of jewellery.

engargantar [en-gar-gan-tar'], *va.* 1. To put something into the throat. 2. To thrust the foot into the stirrup, quite at the instep. 3. *vn.* To gear, to fit into each other: used of cogwheels.

engargolar [en-gar-go-lar'], *va.* To fit the end of one waterpipe into that of another.

engaripolar [en-gah-re-po-lar'], *va. (coll.)* To adorn with trifles and baubles.

engaritado, da [en-gah-re-tah'-do, dah], *a.* 1. Cheated, deceived. 2. Surrounded with sentry-boxes. *-pp.* of ENGARITAR.

engaritar [en-gah-re-tar'], *va.* 1. To fortify, to adorn with sentry-boxes. 2. To impose upon or deceive in an artful or dexterous manner.

engarrafador [en-gar-rah-fah-dor'], *m.* Grappler.

engarrafar [en-gar-rah-far'], *va. (coll.)* 1. To claw, to seize with the claws or talons. 2. To grapple with hooks.

engarrotar [en gar-ro-tar'], *va.* To squeeze and press hard. V. AGARROTAR. *-vr. (LAm.)* To get stiff, to go numb (pierna).

engarzador [en-gar-thah-dor'], *m.* One who links or enchains; stringer of beads.

engarzar [en-gar-thar'], *va.* To enchain, to link; to curl (pelo), to set (joya).

engastador [en-gas-tah-dor'], *m.* Encaser, incloser.

engastar [en-gas-tar'], *va.* To inclose one thing in another without being screened, such as a diamond in gold; to set, to mount.

engaste [en-gahs'-tay], *m.* 1. The setting of stones, the act of setting or infixing. 2. The hoop or envelope. 3. A pearl flat on one side.

engatado, da [en-gah-tah'-do, dah], *a. & n.* A petty robber, a sharper, a petty thief. *-pp.* of ENGATAR.

engatar [en-gah-tar'], *va. (coll.)* To cheat in a dexterous manner, to wheedle.

engatillado, da [en-gah-til-lyah'-do, dah], *a.* Thick, high-necked (caballos y toros). *-pp.* of ENGATILLAR.

engatillar [en-gah-til-lyar'], *va. (Arch.)* To bind with a crampiron.

engatusador, ra [en-gah-too-e-ah-dor', rah], *m. & f.* One who coaxes; wheedler.

engatusamiento [en-gah-too-sah-me-en'-to], *m. (coll.)* Deception, cheat, coaxing.

engatusar [en-gah-too-sar'], *va. (coll.)* To trick without intention; to rob or hurt, to coax. **Engatusar a uno para que haga algo,** to coax somebody into doing something.

engavillar [en-gah-vel-lyar'], *va.* V. AGAVILLAR.

engazador, ra [en-gah-thah-dor', rah], *m. & f.* V. ENGARZADOR.

engazadura [en-gah-tha-doo'-rah], *f. (Naut.)* 1. Splicing in form of a ring. 2. Spot in a cable where a round splice is made.

engazamiento [en-gah-thah-me-ayn'-tao], *m.* V. ENGARCE.

engazar [engahthar'], *va.* 1. To enchain, to link. 2. *(Naut.)* To stop or splice an end of a rope in a circular form about a block. 3. To dye in the cloth.

engendrable [en-hen-drah'-blay], *a.* That may be engendered.

engendramiento [en-hen-drah-me-en'-to], *m.* Begetting, generating.

engendrador, ra [en-hen-drah-dor', rah], *m. & f.* Engenderer, one who engenders or produces.

engendrar [en-hen-drar'], *va.* 1. To beget, to engender, to gender, to generate. 2. To produce, to bear fruit; to create.

engendro [en-hen'-dro], *m.* 1. Foetus, a shapeless embryo. 2. Abortive. **Mal engendro,** a low breed; a perverse youth. 3. Bungled job (chapuza); idiotic scheme (proyecto); brain-child (idea).

engestado [en-hes-tah'-do], *a. (Amer.)* **Bien or mal engestado,** well or gruff-looking.

engestarse [en-hes-tar'-say], *vr. (Amer.)* To address abruptly and uncivilly.

engibar [en-he-bar'], *va.* To crook, to make gibbous.

engilmar [en-heel-mar'], *va. (Naut.)* To pick up a mast which is floating in the sea.

engimelgar [en-he-mel-gar'], *va. (Naut.)* To fish a mast, to mend a spar.

englandado, da [en-glan-dah'-do, dah], *a. (Her.)* Covered with acorns (roble).

englobar [en-glo-bar'], *va.* 1. To include, to comprise (abarcar). 2. To lump together, to put all together (unir).

engolado, da [en-go-lah'-do, dah], *a.* Collared, wearing a collar.

engolfar [en-gol-far'], *vn. (Naut.)* To enter a gulf or deep bay. *-vr.* 1. To be engaged in arduous undertakings or difficult affairs. 2. To be lost in thought, to be absorbed in meditation.

engolondrinarse [en-go-lon-dree-nar'-say], *vr.* 1. *(coll.)* To be elated, to be puffed up with pride. 2. *(Low.)* To fall in love, to be smitten with love (amorosamente).

engolosinar [en-go-lo-se-nar'], *va.* To tempt, to entice. *-vr.* To delight, or to have delight or pleasure in.

engollar [en-gol-lyar'], *va.* To make a horse carry his head and neck by means of the bridle.

engolletado da [en-gol-lyay-tah'-do, dah], *a. (coll.)* Elated, puffed up, presumptuous, haughty. *-pp.* of ENGOLLETARSE.

engolletarse [en-gol-lyay-tar'-say], *vr.* To elate, to become haughty.

engomadero, ra [en-go-mah-day'-ro, rah], *a.* That may be stiffened with starch or gum.

engomadura [en-go-mah-doo-rah], f. 1. Gumming, act of gumming. 2. Coat which bees lay over their hives before making the wax.

engomar [en-go-mar'], va. To gum, to stiffen with gum.

engominar [en-go-me'-nah], va. To put hair-cream on (pelo).

engorar [en-go-rar'], va. To addle. V. ENHUERAR.

engordadero [en-gor-dah-day'-ro], m. 1. Stall or sty to fatten hogs. 2. Time for fattening them.

engordador [en-gor-dah-dor'], m. One who makes it his sole business to pamper himself.

engordar [en-gor-dar'], va. To pamper, to fatten, to lard, to make fat. -vn. 1. To grow fat, to feed (ponerse gordo). 2. To grow rich, to amass a fortune (enriquecerse). 3. Of waves, to increase in size, to swell.

engorde [en-gor'-day], m. Fattening of herds, especially of hogs.

engorgetado, da [en-gor-hay-tah´-do, dah], a. Palisaded breast-high.

engorro [en-gor'-ro], m. (coll.) Impediment, embarrassment, obstacle.

engorroso, sa [en-gor-ro'-so, sah], a. Troublesome, tiresome, vexatious, cumbersome, cumbrous.

engoznar [en-goth-nar'], va. To hinge, to put hinges on doors and windows.

engranaje [en-grah-nah'-hay], m. 1. Gear, transmission gear. **Caja de engranaje**, gear case. 2. (Fig.) Adjustment, interlocking of ideas, circumstances, etc.

engranar [en-grah-nar'], va. To tooth, to connect; to gear, to throw into gear.

engrandar [en-grahn'-day], va. V. AGRANDAR.

engrandecer [en-gran-day-therr'], va. 1. To augment, to aggrandize, to increase. 2. To promote to a higher station, to exalt, to extol (ensalzar). 3. (Met.) To exaggerate, to magnify (exagerar). (Yo engrandezco, yo engrandezca, from Engrandecer. V. CONOCER.)

engrandecimiento [en-gran-day-the-me-en´-to], m. 1. Increase, aggrandizement; aggrandization. 2. Exaggeration, hyperbolical amplification.

engranerar [en-grah-nay-rar'], va. To enclose in a granary.

engranujarse [en-grah-noo-har'-say], vr. 1. To be covered with pimples. 2. To become a rogue.

engrapar [en-grah-par'], va. To secure, to unite or bind with cramp-irons.

engrasación [en-grah-sah-the-on´], f. or **engrasamiento**, m. Lubrication, oiling, greasing.

engrasador [en-grah-sah-dor'], m. Oiler, lubricator (aceitera).

engrasar [en-grah-sar'], va. 1. To grease, to oil, to fat, to lubricate. 2. To stain with grease (manchar). 3. To dress cloth. 4. (Met.) To pickle. 5. (Prov.) To manure, to hearten.

engrase [en-g-rah'-say], m. 1. Greasing, lubrication. 2. Bribe.

engravedar [en-grah-vay-dar'], va. To assume an air of dignity, to affect gravity.

engredar [en-gray-dar'], va. To bedaub with marl or fuller's earth.

engreído, da [en-gray-ee'-do, dah], a. & pp. of ENGREÍR. Elated, lofty, haughty; petulant.

engreimiento [en-gray-e-me-en'-to], m. 1. Presumption, vanity, elation. 2. Vain pomp in dress.

engreír [en-gray-eer'], va. To encourage someone's pride and petulance, to make him pert and saucy, to lift, to flush, to pride. -vr. 1. V. ENSOBERBECERSE and ENVANECERSE. 2. To deck or attire oneself in style, to be extravagant in dress. (Yo me engrío, yo me engría, from Engreirse. V. PEDIR.)

engrifarse [en-gre-far'-say], vr. To tiff, to be in a pet, to be displeased, to sulk.

engrosar [en-gro-sar´], va. 1. To make a thing fat and corpulent, to increase its bulk. 2. To make strong or vigorous. 3. To augment, to make more numerous (cantidad). -vn. To grow strong, to increase in vigor and bulk. -vr. 1. To fatten. 2. (Naut.) To increase in cloudiness, to increase in size (olas). (Yo engrueso, yo engruese, from Engrosar. V. ACORDAR.)

engrudador [en-groo-dah-dor'], m. Paster, one who pastes; gluer.

engrudamiento [en-groo-dah-me-en'-to], m. 1. Act of pasting. 2. Gluing.

engrudar [en-groo-dar'], va. To paste, to fasten with paste.

engrudo [en-groo'-do], m. 1. Paste, flour and water boiled together so as to make a cement. 2. (Naut.) Cement, made chiefly of pounded glass and cow-hair, used to stanch the planks of a ship.

engruesar [en-groo-ay-sar'], va. V. ENGORDAR and ENGROSAR.

engrumecerse [en-groo-may-therr'-say], vr. To clot.

engualdar [en-goo-ahl-dar'], va. To make like woad, or the color of woad.

engualdrapar [en-goo-al-drah-par'], va. To caparison a horse with rich trappings.

enguantado, da [en-goo-an-tah'-do, dah], a. Wearing gloves. -pp. of ENGUANTARSE.

enguantarse [en-goo-an-tar-say], vr. To put on gloves.

enguedejado, da [en-gay-day-hah'-do dah], a. 1. Curl-pated, having hair curled or braided, and growing in tufts and locks. 2. Crisped, curled.

enguijarrar [en-gee-har-rar'], va. To pave with pebbles.

enguillar [en-geel-lyar´], va. (Naut.) To wind a thin rope around a thicker one.

enguirnaldado, da [en-geer-nal-dah'-do, dah], a. Adorned with garlands.

enguirnaldar [en-geer-nal-dar'], va. To garland, to engarland, to adorn with garlands.

enguizgar [en-geeth-gar'], va. To excite, to incite, to set on.

engullidor, ra [en-gool-lye-dor', rah], m. & f. 1. Devourer, one who swallows without mastication. 2. Gobbler, one who devours in haste.

engullir [en-gool-lyeer'], va. To devour meat without chewing it, to gobble, to glut, to gorge.

engurriñarse [en-goor-re-nyar'-say], vr. (coll.) To be melancholy (pájaros).

engurruñarse [en-goor-roo-nyar'-say], vr. To get sad, to grow gloomy.

enharinar [en-ah-re-nar'], va. To cover or besprinkle with flour.

enhastiar [en-as-te-ar'], va. To disgust, to excite disgust, to cloy.

enhastillar [en-as-til-lyar'], va. To put arrows in a quiver.

enhatijar [en-ah-te-har'], va. To cover the mouths of hives with bassweed, in order to move them from one place to another.

enhebrar [en-ay-brar'], va. 1. To thread a needle. 2. (Met. coll.) To link, to unite or connect closely.

enhenar [en-ay-nar'], va. To cover with hay, to wrap up in hay.

enherbolar [en-er-bo-lar'], va. To poison with venomous herbs.

enhestador [en-es-tah-dor'], m. He who erects.

enhestadura [en-es-tah-doo'-rah], f. Erection.

enhestar [en-es-tar'], va. 1. To erect to set upright. -vr. To erect, to rise upright.

enhidro, dra [en-ee'-dro, drah], a. (Miner.) Hyaline quartz or fluorine which contains some drops of water.

enhielar [en-e-ay-lar'], va. To mix with gall or bile.

enhiesto, ta [en-e-ays'-to, tah], a. & pp. irr. of ENHESTAR. Erect, upright, erected.

enhilado, da [en-e-lah'-do, dah], a. Well arranged, disposed in good order. -pp. of ENHILAR.

enhilar [en-e-lar'], va. 1. To thread (aguja). 2. To direct, to tend; to take the way or road to anything or place. 3. To arrange. 4. (coll.) To enter or go through a long story.

enhorabuena [en-o-rah-boo-ay'-nah], f. Congratulation, felicitation, joy for the happiness or success of another. **Dar la enhorabuena a uno**, to congratulate somebody. **Estar de enhorabuena**, to be in luck. -adv. Well and good; all right.

enhoramala [en-o-rah-mah'-lah], *f.* A word used to express the act of scorning, despising, or contemning a thing. -*adv.* Its an evil hour. **Vete enhora mala,** *(coll.)* go to the devil.

enhornar [en-or-nar'], *va.* To put into an oven to be baked.

enhuecar [en-oo-ay-car'], *va. V.* AHUECAR.

enhuerar [en-oo-ay-rar'], *va.* To lay addle eggs, to addle.

enigma [ay-neeg'-mah], *m.* Enigma, a riddle; an obscure question; cross-purpose.

enigmático, ca [ay-nig-mah'-te-co, cah], *a.* Enigmatical, dark, obscure, ambiguously or darkly expressed.

enigmatista [ay-nig-mah-tess'-tah], *m.* Enigmatist.

enigmatizar [ay-nig-mah-te-thar'], *va.* To make enigmas. -*vn.* To talk ambiguously.

enipiotismo [ay-ne-pe-o-tees'-mo], *m.* Magnetic sleep, hypnotism.

enjabegarse [en-hah-bay-gar-say], *vr. (Naut.)* 1. To get entangled (cuerdas). 2. Among fishers, to be twisted.

enjabonadura [en-hah-bo-nah-doo'-rah], *f. V.* JABONADURA.

enjabonar [en-hah-bo-nar'], *va.* 1. To soap, to wash with soap. 2. *(Met.)* To insult with foul language and blows. 3. *(coll.)* To soft-soap one (dar coba a).

enjaezar [en-hah-ay-thar'], *va.* To caparison a horse with rich trappings; to harness.

enjagüe [en-hah'-goo-ay], *m.* Adjudication required by the creditors of a ship.

enjalbegador, ra [en-hal-bay-gah-dor', rah], *m. & f.* Whitewasher, a plasterer.

enjalbegadura [en-hal-bay-gah-doo'-rah], *f.* Act of whitewashing walls.

enjalbegar [en-hal-bay-gar'], *va.* 1. To whitewash walls. 2. *(Met.)* To paint, to paint the face.

enjalbiego [en-hal-be-ay'-go], *m.* Whitewashing.

enjalma [en-hahl'-mah], *f.* Kind of packsaddle.

enjalmar [en-hal-mar'], *va.* 1. To put the packsaddle on a horse. 2. To make pack-saddles.

enjalmos [en-hal'-mos], *m. (Bot.)* Crooked-meadow saxifrage.

enjalmero [en-hal-may'-ro], *m.* Packsaddle maker.

enjambradera [en-ham-brah-day'-rah], *f.* 1. *(Prov.)* Queenbee of a hive. 2. *V.* CASQUILLA.

enjambradero [en-ham-brah-day'-ro], *m.* Place where bees collect to form their hives.

enjambrar [en-ham-brar'], *va.* 1. To gather a scattered swarm of bees. 2. To form a new hive of bees, which left another hive. -*vn.* To breed a new hive of bees, to produce abundantly.

enjambrazón [en-ham-brah-thone'], *f.* Generation or swarming of bees.

enjambre [en-hahm'-bray], *m.* 1. Swarm of bees. 2. Crowd, multitude of people.

enjambrillo [en-ham-breel'-lyo], *m. dim.* A small swarm of bees.

enjarciadura [en-har-the-ah-doo'-rah], *f.* The act of rigging a ship.

enjarciar [en-har-the-ar'], *va.* To put the tackle aboard a ship.

enjardinar [en-har-de-nar'], *va.* 1. To set and trim the trees as they are in gardens. 2. *(Fal.)* To put a bird of prey into a meadow or green field.

enjaretado [en-hah-ray-tah'-do], *m. (Naut.)* Gratings, nettings, a kind of lattice-work between the main and foremast. **Enjaretado de proa,** the beak or head gratings.

enjaretar [en-hah-ray-tar'], *va.* 1. To draw through a seam. 2. *(Met.)* To order, to dispose a matter. -*vr. (Met. coll.)* To creep in by stealth, to be introduced subtly into some place, conversation, etc.

enjaular [en-ha-oo-lar'], *va.* 1. To cage. 2. *(Met.)* To imprison, to confine, to mew, to crib, to coop.

enjebar [en-hay-bar'], *va.* To steep in lye, to buck.

enjebe [en-hay'-bay], *m.* Lye in which cloth is put to be cleansed or scoured; act of bucking.

enjergar [en-her-gar'], *va. (Colt.)* To set about a business, to bring a thing on the tapis.

enjero [en-hay'-ro], *m. (Prov.)* Beam of a plough.

enjertación [en-her-tah-the-on'], *f.* Insertion, inoculation, budding.

enjertal [en-her-tahl'], *m.* Nursery of grafted fruit-trees.

enjertar [en-her-tar'], *va. V.* INJERTAR.

enjerto [en-herr'-to], *m.* 1. *V.* INJERTO 2. *(Met.)* Mixture of diverse things. -*pp. irr.* of ENJERTAR.

enjorguinar [en-hor-gee-nar'], *va.* To smear or cover with soot. -*vr.* To be blackened with soot.

enjoyado [en-ho-yah'-do], *a.* Bejewelled, set with jewels.

enjoyar [en-ho-yar'], *va.* 1. To adorn with jewels. 2. To set a ring with diamonds or other precious stones. 3. *(Met.)* To heighten the lustre and brilliancy of a thing, to give additional splendor.

enjoyelado, da [en-ho-yay-lah'-do, dah], *a.* Applied to gold or silver used in jewellery.

enjoyelador [en-ho-yay-lah-dor'], *m.* Enchaser, he who enchases.

enjuagadientes [en-hoo-ah-gah-de-en'-tes], *m. (coll.)* Mouthful of water or wine for rinsing the mouth after a meal.

enjuagadura [en-hoo-ah-gah-doo'-rah], *f.* Act of rinsing the mouth.

enjuagar [en-hoo-ah-gar'], *va.* 1. To rinse the mouth and teeth 2. To rinse clothes.

enjuague [en-hoo-ah'-gay], *m.* 1. Water, wine, or other liquid, used to rinse the mouth and teeth, and the act of rinsing the mouth with a liquid. 2. Finger-bowl. 3. *(Met.)* Plot to obtain an object, which cannot be attained openly.

enjugadero [en-hoo-gah-day'-ro], *m.* 1. *V.* ENJUGADOR, 1st def. 2. A place in which something is dried.

enjugador, ra [en-hoo-gah-dor', rah], *m.* 1. Drier, one who dries. 2. Round-house for airing linen.

enjugar [en-hoo-gar'], *va.* 1. To dry in the air or at the fire, to make dry. 2. To wipe on moisture.-*vr.* To dry up; to grow lean.

enjuiciamiento [en-hoo-ee-the-ah-me-en'-to], *m.* 1. Preparation of a lawsuit. 2. A judge's charge; legal instruction upon the subject of a suit. **Enjuiciamiento criminal,** trial, criminal prosecution.

enjuiciar [en-hoo-e-the-ar'], *va. (Law.)* 1. To prepare a lawsuit for judgment (juzgar). 2. To make a pleading. 3. To pass judgment (sentenciar).

enjulio, or **enjullo** [en-hoo'-leo, en-hool'-lyo], *m.* The clothbeam of a loom.

enjuncar [en-hoon-car'], *va.* To tie with rush ropes. **Enjuncar un barco,** to ballast a vessel with kentledge or stones.

enjundia [en-hoon'-de-ah], *f.* 1. Fat in the ovary of fowls, and also the grease or fat of an animal. 2. Substance, force.

enjundioso, sa [en-hoon-de-o'-so, sah], *a.* Fat, fatty.

enjunque [en-hoon'-kay], *m. (Naut.)* The heaviest part of a cargo which serves as ballast.

enjuta [en-hoo'-tah], *f. (Arch.)* 1. Each of the spaces left by a circle inscribed within a square. 2. *V.* PECHINA.

enjutar [en-hoo-tar'], *va.* To dry.

enjutez [en-hoo-teth'], *f.* Dryness, aridity.

enjuto, ta [en-hoo'-to, tah], *a. & pp. irr.* of ENJUTAR. 1. Dried. 2. Lean, spare, slender. **A pie enjuto,** without pain or labor.

enjutos [en-hoo'-tos], *m. pl.* 1. Dry brushwood for lighting a fire. 2. Dry crust of bread.

enlabiador, ra [en-lah-be-ah-dor'-rah], *m. & f.* Wheedler, cajoler, seducer.

enlace [en-lah'-thay], *m.* 1. Connection or coherence of one thing with another; link, lacing (vinculación). 2. *(Met.)* Kindred, affinity. **El enlace de las dos familias,** the linking of the two families by marriage. **Enlace telefónico,** telephone link-up.

enlaciar [en-lah-the-ar'], *vn.* To be lax or languid. -*vr.* To wither, to become dry, to decay (plantas, fruta).

enladrillado [en-lah-dril-lyah'-do], *m.* Pavement made of bricks; brickwork. —**Enladrillado, da**, *pp. of* ENLADRILLAR.

enladrillador [en-lah-dril-lyah-dor'], *m.* One who bricks or paves with bricks.

enladrilladura [en-lah-dreel-lyah-doo'-rah], *f.* 1. The act and effect of paving with brick. 2. *V.* ENLADRILLADO.

enladrillar [en-lah-dril-lyar'], *va.* To pave a floor with bricks.

enlamar [en-lah-mar'], *va.* To cover land with slime (inundaciones).

enlanado, da [en-lah-nah'-do, dah], *a.* Covered or supplied with wool.

enlardar [en-lar-dar'], *va.* To rub with grease, to baste. *V.* LARDAR.

enlargues [en-lar'-gays], *m. pl.* (*Naut.*) Rope-ends fastened to the head of a sail, with which it is tied to the yard.

enlatado [en-lah-tah'-do], *a.* Canned, tinned; (*Mus.*) canned. -*m.* Canning, tinning.

enlatar [en-lah-tar'], *va.* To can, to tin; to pre-record (televisión).

enlazable [en-lah-thah'-blay], *a.* Which can be bound or fastened together.

enlazador, ra [en-lah-thah-dor', rah], *m. & f.* Binder, uniter.

enlazadura [en-lah-thah-doo'-rah], *f. V.* ENLAZAMIENTO.

enlazamiento [en-lah-thah-me-en'-to], *m.* 1. Connection, binding, uniting. 2. (*Met.*) *V.* ENLACE.

enlazar [en-lah-thar'], *va.* 1. To bind, to join, to unite; to connect. 2. To knit, to lace. -*vr.* To link, to be linked; to be connected; to join; to interlock; to entwine; to marry (novios).

enlechuguillado, da [en-lay-choo-gil-lyah'-do, dah], *a.* Applied to one who wears a ruff round the neck.

enlejiar [en-lay-he-ar'], *va.* To make into lye.

enligarse [en-legar'-say], *vr.* To be joined by means of a glutinous substance, to stick, to adhere.

enlistonado [en-lis-to-nah'-do], *m.* Lathing, lath work.

enlistonar [en-lis-to-nar'], *va.* To lath, to batten.

enlizar [en-lee-thar'], *va.* To provide a loom with leashes.

enllantar [en-lyan-tar'], *va.* To rim, to shoe a wheel.

enllentecer [en-lyen-tay-therr'], *va.* To soften, to blandish.

enlodadura [en-lo-dah-doo'-rah], *f.* Act of daubing and filling up with mud.

enlodar [en-lo-dar'], *va.* 1. To bemire, to mire, to soil or bedaub with mud. 2. To stop up a vessel with loam or clay; to lute. 3. (*Met.*) To tarnish one's reputation.

enloquecer [en-lo-kay-therr'], *va.* To enrage, to madden.-*vn.* or *vr.* 1. To madden, to become mad, to become enraged. 2. To be vexed, to be annoyed. 3. To grow barren (árbol). (*Yo enloquezco, yo enloquezca,* from *Enloquecer. V.* CONOCER.)

enloquecimiento [en-lo-key-the-me-en'-to], *m.* Enraging, maddening.

enlosado [en-lo-sah'-do], *m.* Pavement made of flags; flagging. —**Enlosado, da**, *pp.* of ENLOSAR.

enlosar [en-lo-sar'], *va.* To lay a floor with flags.

enlozanarse [en-lo-thah-nar'-say], *vr.* To boast of one's dexterity or strength.

enlucido da [en-loo-thee'-do, dah], *a.* Whitewashed, plastered. -*m.* Whitewash, coat of plaster.

enlucidor [en-loo-the-dor'], *m.* Whitener.

enlucimiento [en-loo-the-me-en'-to], *m.* 1. The whitewashing of a wall. 2. The scouring of plate.

enlucir [en-loo-theer'], *va.* 1. To whitewash a wall (pared). 2. To scour plate with whiting or chalk. (*Yo enluzco, yo enluzca,* from *Enlucir.*)

enlustrecer [en-loos-tray-therr'], *va.* To clean, to brighten, to render bright.

enlutar [en-loo-tar'], *va.* 1. To put in mourning (persona). 2. To veil, to cover with a veil (vestido etc.) 3. To darken. -*vr.* To go into mourning.

enmacetar [en-mah-thay-tar'], *va.* To pot, to put in a pot (planta).

enmachambra [en-man-cham-brar'], *va.* To scarf pieces of timber together.

enmaderado [en-mah-day-rah-do], *va.* Timbered; boarded.

enmaderamiento, *m.* **enmaderación,** *f.* [en-mah-day-rah-me-en'-to], Work or cover of wood, wains-cotting.

enmaderar [en-mah-day-rar'], *va.* To roof a house with timber, to floor with boards.

enmadrado [en-mah-drah'-do], *a.* **Está enmadrado,** he´s a mama´s boy.

enmagrecer [en-mah-gray-therr'], *vn.* To grow lean; to lose fat.

enmalecer [en-mah-lay-therr'], *vn.* To fall sick.

enmallar [en-mahl-lyar'], *va.* (*Naut.*) To put meshes, to border a net.

enmalletado, da [en-mahl-lyay-tah'-do dah], *a.* (*Naut.*) Fouled (cables, cuerdas). *V.* ENREDADO.

enmalletar [en-mahl-lyay-tar'], *va.* (*Naut.*) 1. To set partners; to secure masts. 2. *V.* ENDENTAR.

enmangar [en-man-gar'], *va.* To put a handle to an instrument.

enmantar [en-man-tar'], *va.* To cover with a blanket. -*vr.* To be melancholy (pájaros).

enmarañamiento [en-mah-ra-nyah-me-en'-to], *m.* Entanglement, perplexity.

enmarañar [en-mah-ra-nyar'], *va.* 1. To entangle, to perplex (persona), to involve in difficulties (asunto). 2. (*Met.*) To puzzle, to confound. **Sólo logró enmarañar más el asunto,** he only managed to make a still worse mess of the matter. -*vr.* 1. To get tangled. 2. (*Fig.*) To get more involved; to get into a mess; to get confused.

enmararse [en-mah-rar'-say], *vr.* (*Naut.*) To get or take sea-room.

enmarcar [en-mar-car'], *va.* 1. To frame (cuadro). 2. (*Fig.*) To fit into a framework, to set in a framework.

enmaridar [en-mah-reel-dar'], *vn.* To marry, to take a husband.

enmarillecerse [en-mah-reel-lyay-therr'-say], *vr.* To become yellow.

enmaromar [en-mah-ro-mar'], *va.* To tie with a rope.

enmascarado, da [en-mas-cah-rah'-do], *m & f.* Masked person.

enmascarar [en-mas-cah-rar'], *va.* 1. To mask, to cover the face with a mask. 2. (*Met.*) To cloak, to give a false appearance. -*vr.* To masquerade, to go in disguise.

enmasillar [en-mah-seel-lyar'], *va.* To putty, to cement.

enmechar [en-may-char'], *va.* (*Naut.*) To rabbet, to fit and join two pieces of timber.

enmelar [en-may-lar'], *va.* 1. To bedaub or besmear with honey. 2. (*Met.*) To sweeten, to give a pleasing taste.

enmendación [en-men-dah-the-on'], *f.* Emendation, correction.

enmendadamente [en-men-dah-da-men'-tay], *adv.* Accurately, exactly.

enmendado [en-men-dah-dor'], *m.* Corrector, emendator, mender.

enmendar [en-men-dar'], *va.* 1. To correct, to reform (texto). 2. To repair, to compensate (pérdida). 3. (*Law.*) To revoke, to abrogate. 4. To put back a thing in the spot which it had before occupied. -*vr.* To mend, to grow better, to lead a new life. (*Yo enmiendo, yo enmiende,* frown *Enmendar. V.* ACRECENTAR.)

enmienda [en-me-en'-dah], *f.* 1. Emendation, correction, amendment. 2. Correction, emendation, that which is substituted in the place of something wrong. 3. Reward, premium. 4. (*Law.*) Satisfaction, compensation.

enmohecer [en-mo-ay-therr'], *va.* To mould, to must, to mildew, to make mouldy. -*vr.* 1. To mould, to grow mouldy or musty. 2. To rust, to gather rust (metal).

enmohecido, da [en-mo-ay-thee'-do, dah], *a. & pp.* of ENMOHECER. Musty, mouldy, spoiled with damp.

enredar

enmoldado, da [en-mol-dah'-do, dah], *a.* 1. Moulded, cast in a mould. 2. Figured, modelled.

enmollecer [en-mol-lyay-therr'], *va.* To soften, to make tender.

enmondar [en-mon-dar'], *va.* To clear cloth from knots.

enmoquetar [en-mo-kay-tar'], *va.* To carpet.

enmordazar [en-mor-dah-thar'], *va.* To gag. V. AMORDAZAR.

enmudecer [en-moo-day-therr'], *vn.* 1. To grow dumb, to be deprived of speech. 2. To be silent, to be still. *-va.* To impose silence, to hush. *-vr.* To be silent; to remain silent, to say nothing (callarse). *(Yo enmudezco, yo enmudezca, from Enmudecer. V. CONOCER.)*

ennatado, da [en-nah-tah'-do, dah], *a. (Agr.)* Recuperated: said of a field which has recovered its fertility by lying fallow.

ennegrecer [en-nay-gray-therr'], *va.* 1. To blacken, to make black (poner negro). 2. *(Met.)* To darken, to obscure (oscurecer). *-vr. -vn.* To turn black. *(Yo ennegrezco, yo ennegrezca, from Ennegrecer. V. CONOCER.)*

ennoblecer [en-no-blay-therr'], *va.* 1. To ennoble, to illustrate, to make noble. 2. *(Met.)* To adorn, to embellish. *(Yo ennoblezco, yo ennoblezca, from Ennoblecer. V. CONOCER.)*

ennoblecimiento [en-no-blay-the-me-en'-to], *m.* Ennoblement, the act of ennobling.

ennoviar [en-no-ve-ar'], *vn.* To contract marriage.

ennudecer [en-noo-day-therr'], *vn.* V. ANUDARSE.

enodación [ay-no-dah-the-on´], *f.* Illustration, explanation.

enodio [ay-no'-de-o], *m.* Fawn, a young deer.

enodrida [ay-no-dree'-dah], *a.* Barren (gallinas).

enoema [ay-no-ay'-mah], *f.* Fantastic idea, product of simple conception.

enofobia [ay-no-fo'-be-ah], *f.* Dread of wine.

enófobo, ba [ay-no'-fo-bo, bah], *m. & f.* One who hates wine.

enóforo [ay-no'-fo-ro], *m.* 1. A vessel for wine. 2. Name of a handsome statue of Praxiteles . 3. One charged with the service of wines or who used to sell them.

enojadamente [ay-no-hah-dah-men'-tay], *adv.* Fretfully, crossly, peevishly.

enojadizo, za [ay-no-hah-dee'-tho, thah], *a.* Fretful, peevish, fractious.

enojado, da [ay-no-hah'-do, dah], *a.* Angry, fretful, peevish, out of humor. *-pp.* of ENOJAR.

enojante [ay-no-hahn'-tay], *pa.* He who vexes.

enojar [ay-no-har'], *va.* 1. To vex, to irritate, to anger, to fret, to make angry (enfadar). 2. To tease, to molest, to trouble. 3. To offend, to displease, to injure.*-vr.* 1. To be fretful or peevish. 2. To be boisterous. 3. To be offended, displeased.

enojo [ay-no'-ho], *m.* 1. Fretfulness, peevishness. 2. Anger, choler, passion (irritación). **Decir con enojo**, to say angrily.

enojosamente [ay-no-ho-sah-men'-tay], *adv.* Vexatiously, crossly.

enojoso, sa [ay-no-ho'-so, sah], *a.* Offensive, vexatious.

enojuelo [ay-no-hoo-ay'-lo], *m. dim.* Slight peevishness.

enología [ay-no-lo-hee'-ah], *f.* The art of making wine; enology.

enómetro [ay-no'-may-tro], *m.* Enometer, a hydrometer for determining the alcoholic strength of wines by their specific gravity.

enorgullecer [en-or-gool-lyay-therr'], *va.* To make proud or haughty.*-vr.* To be filled with pride or arrogance. **Enogullecerse de**, to be proud of.

enorgullecimiento [en-or-gool-lyay-the-me-en'-to], *m.* Arrogance, haughtiness.

enorgullecido, da [en-or-gool-lyay-thee'-do, dah], *a.* Haughty, arrogant, very proud.

enorme [ay-nor'-may], *a.* 1. Enormous, vast, huge, mighty, exorbitant. 2. Horrible, crying, grievous. 3. Wicked beyond common measure, heinous. **Delito enorme**, enormity.

enormemente [ay-nor'-may-men-tay], *adv.* Immoderately, enormously, hugely, horridly.

enormidad [ay-nor-me-dahd'], *f.* 1. Enormity, enormousness, monstrousness, exorbitance (inmensidad). 2. Grievousness, horridness, gravity. 3. An enormous deed, an atrocious crime (crimen).

enótera [ay-no'-tay-rah], *f. (Bot.)* Enothera, a generic name of plants, typical of the evening primrose family. **enótera bienal**, the evening-primrose. **Enótera florichica**, small-flowered enothera.

enuiciado, da [en-ke-the-ah'-do, dah], *a.* 1. Hung upon hinges. 2. *(Met.)* Built upon a solid foundation. *-pp.* of ENQUICIAR.

enquiciar [en-ke-the-ar'], *va.* To hinge, to put on hinges.

enquillotrarse [en-kil-lyo-trar'-say], *vr.* 1. To be jumbled together. 2.*(coll.)* To fall in love, to be enamoured.

enquimosis [en-ke-mo'-sis], *f. (Med.)* A sudden effusion of blood in the cutaneous vessels.

enquiridión [en-ke-re-de-on'], *m.* Compendium, summary, abridgment.

enquistado, da [en-kis-tah'-do, dah], *a. (Surg.)* Cysted, encysted.

enquistar [en-kis-tar'], *va. (Fig.)* To seal off, to shut off, to enclose. *-vr.* To develop a cyst.

enrabiarse [en-rah-be-ar'-say], *vr. (coll.)* To grow furious, to become enraged.

enraigonar [en-ra-he-go-nar'], *va. (Prov.)* To fix bassweed in the walls of sheds, for the silkworms to begin to spin.

enraizar [en-rah-e-thar'], *vn.* To take root.

enralecer [en-rah-lay-therr'], *va. (Agr.)* 1. To thin plants, to pluck away leaves or branches. 2. To prune.

enramada [en-rah-mah'-dah], *f.* 1. A decoration formed with the branches of trees. 2. A covering of branches for shade, a bower (cobertizo). 3. *(Poet.)* A thicket, a wood. 4. Undergrowth.

enramar [en-rah-mar'], *va.* 1. To cover with branches of trees. 2. To cover the ground with flowers, branches, and aromatic herbs in some festival. 3. *(Naut.)* To mast a vessel.

enranciarse [en-ran-the-ar'-say], *vr.* To grow rancid, to be stale.

enrarecer [en-rah-ray-therr'], *va.* To thin, to rarefy, to extenuate. *-vr.* 1. To become rarefied (aire). 2. To become scarce, to grow rare (escasear). 3. To deteriorate, to become tense (relaciones). *(Yo enrarezco, yo enrarezca, from Enrarecer. V. CONOCER.)*

enrarecido [en-rah-ray-the-do], *a.* 1. Rarefied. 2. Tense, difficult (relaciones).

enrarecimiento [en-rah-ray-the-me-en'-to], *m.* Rarefaction.

enrás [en-rahs'], *m.* 1. *(Arch.)* Bed, seat. 2. *(Mas.)* Last or levelling course.

enrasado, da [en-rah-sah'-do, dah], *a. & pp.* of ENRASAR. Smoothed, flush. **Puertas enrasadas**, plain doors.

enrasar [en-rah-sar'], *va.* 1. To smooth, to plane. 2. To even, to make even or level, to flush. *-vn.* To be bald.

enrastrar [en-ras-trar'], *va. (Prov.)* To string the silk cocoons.

enrayar [en-rah-yar'], *va.* To fix spokes in a wheel.

enredadera [en-ray-dah-day'-rah], *f. (Bot.)* 1. A name applied to all twining plants, particularly to the convolvulus, cultivated in gardens. 2. Small bindweed, bell-bind.

enredado, da [en-ray-dah'-do, dah], *a.* 1. Entangled, matted. 2. *(Naut.)* Foul (cables y cuerdas). *-pp.* of ENREDAR.

enredador, ra [en-ray-dah-dor', rah], *m. & f.* 1. Entangler, one who entangles, ensnares, or involves in difficulties. 2. Tattler, tale-bearer; busybody (entrometido), intermeddler, gossip (chismoso).

enredar [en-ray-dar'], *va.* 1. To entangle, to ensnare, to hamper, to lime, to knot. 2. To confound, to perplex, to involve in difficulties, to puzzle (asunto). 3. To catch in the net (animal etc.) 4. To lay snares for birds. 5. To sow discord. 6. To fumble, to play childishly. *-vr.* 1. To tangle or to be entangled (enmarañarse). **No te enredes**, don´t you get mixed up in this. **Enredarse de palabras**, to get involved in an argument. 2. *(coll.)* To live in concubinage.

enredo [en-ray'-do], *m.* 1. Entanglement, entangling, ensnaring (lío). 2. Perplexity, embarrassment, puzzle. 3. Complexity, complicateness. 4. Imposition, falsehood, intricate or mischievous lies (mentiras), circumvention. 5. Plot of a play. **Comedia de enredo**, comedy of intrigue.

enredoso, sa [en-ray-do'-so, sah], *a.* Full of snares and difficulties.

enrehojar [en-ray-o-har'], *va.* Among wax-chandlers, to remove the bleached leaves and thin cakes of wax.

enrejado [en-ray-hah'-do], *m.* 1. Trellis (de jardín), lattice (de ventana); grate, grillework. 2. Kind of open embroidery or lace worn by ladies. **Enrejado, da**, *pp.* of ENREJAR.

enrejar [en-ray-har'], *va.* 1. To fix a grating to a window. 2. To fix the ploughshare to the plough. 3. To make a trellis, to grate, to lattice. 4. To wound cattle's feet with a ploughshare.

enrevesado, da [en-ray-vay-sah'-do, dah], *a.* *V.* REVESADO.

enriado [en-re-ah'-do], *m.* Maceration, retting of flax or hemp.

enriador [en-re-ah-dor'], *m.* One who steeps or submerges.

enriar [en-re-ar'], *va.* To steep hemp and flax in water, in order to macerate its stalky parts; to ret.

enrielar [en-re-ay-lar'], *va.* To make ingots of gold or silver.

enripiado [en-re-pe-ah'-do], *m.* Filling, packing, rubble work.

enripiar [en-re-pe-ar'], *va.* To fill the chinks of a wall with small stones and mortar.

enriquecedor, ra [en-re-kay-thay-dor', rah], *m. & f.* One who enriches.

enriquecer [en-re-kay-therr'], *va.* 1. To enrich, to aggrandize. 2. To adorn.-*vn.* To gain, to grow rich. -*vr.* To get rich; to prosper; to enrich oneself. **Enriquecerse a costa ajena**, to do well at other people's expense. *(Yo enriquezco, yo enriquezca,* from *Enriquecer. V.* CONOCER.)

enriquecimiento [en-re-kay-the-me-ayn'-to], *m.* Enrichment.

enriscado, da [en-ris-cah'-do, dah], *a.* Mountainous, craggy; full of rocks and cliffs.-*pp.* of ENRISCAR.

enriscamiento [en-ris-cah-me-en'-to], *m.* Taking refuge among rocks.

enriscar [en-ris-car'], *va.* To place on the top of mountains or rocks. *(Met.)* To lift, to raise.-*vr.* To take refuge, among rocks.

enristrar [en-ris-trar'], *va.* 1. To couch the lance, or to fix it in the posture of attack. 2. To range, to file, to string (cebollas, ajos). 3. *(Met.)* To go directly to a place, to meet a difficulty. 4. To succeed finally in a difficult matter (dificultad).

enristre [en-rees'-tray], *m.* Act of couching a lance.

enrizamiento [en-re-thah-me-en'-to], *m.* 1. Act of curling. 2. Irritating.

enrizar [en-re-thar'], *va.* *(Ant. and Amer.)* 1. To curl, to turn into ringlets. 2. To irritate. *V.* RIZAR.

enrobrescido, da [en-ro-bres-thee'-do, dah], *a.* Hard and strong, like an oak.

enrobustecer [en-ro-boos-tay-therr'], *va.* To make robust.

enrocar [en-ro-car'], *va.* At chess, to castle the king.

enrodar [en-ro-dar'], *va.* To break on the wheel. *(Yo enruedo, yo enruede,* from *Enrodar. V.* ACORDAR.)

enrodelado, da [en-ro-day-lah'-do, dah], *a.* Armed with a shield.

enrodrigonar [en-ro-dre-go-nar'], *va.* To prop vines with stakes.

enrojar, enrojecer [en-ro-har', en-ro-hay-therr'], *va.* 1. To tinge, to dye, or to give a red color (volver rojo). 2. To put to the blush (persona). -*vn.* -*vr.* To blush, to redden.

enrojecido, da [en-ro-hay-thee'-do, dah], *a.* Red.

enrollado [en-rol-lyah'-do], *a.* **Un tío muy enrollado**, a thoroughly turned-on guy.

enrollar [en-rol-lyar'], *va.* To wrap a thing within another or round about it (cuerda) -*vr.* 1. To go on a long time (al explicarse). **Cuando se enrolla no hay quien lo pare,**

when he gets going there's no stopping him. 2. **Enrollarse en**, to get involved in.

enromar [en-ro-mar'], *va.* To blunt, to dull an edge or point.

enronar [en-ro-nar'], *va.* *(Prov.)* To throw rubbish in a place.

enronquecer [en-ron-kay-therr'], *va.* To make hoarse.-*vn.* To grow hoarse.

enronquecimiento [en-ron-kay-the-me-en'-to], *m.* Hoarseness. *V.* RONQUERA.

enroñar [en-ro-nyar'], *va.* To fill with scabs or scurf.

enrosar [en-ro-sar'], *va.* To tinge, to dye or give a rose color.

enroscadamente [en-ros-cah-da-men'-tay], *adv.* Intricately.

enroscado [en-ros-cah-do], *a.* 1. Coiled; twisted; kinky. 2. *(And.)* Angry.

enroscadura [en-ros-cah-doo'-rah], *f.* Act of twisting; convolution, sinuosity, twist.

enroscar [en-ros-car'], *va.* 1. To twine, to twist (torcer). 2. To screw in (tornillo). -*vr.* To curl or twist itself.

enrubescer [en-roo-bes-therr'], *va.* To make red.

enrubiador, ra [en-roo-be-ah-dor', rah], *m. & f.* That which has the power of making red.

enrubiar [en-roo-be-ar'], *va.* To tinge, to dye, or give a bright reddish color.

enrubio [en-roo'-be-o], *m.* Rubefaction, reddening.

enrudecer [en-roo-day-therr'], *va.* To weaken the intellect, to make dull.

enruinecer, enruinescer [en-roo-e-nay-therr', en-roo-e-nes-therr'], *vn.* To become vile.

ensabanar [en-sah-ba-nar'], *va.* To wrap up in sheets.

ensacar [en-sah-car'], *va.* To sack up, to inclose or put in a sack.

ensaí [en-sa-hee'], *m.* *(Naut.)* A clear space between the frames.

ensalada [en-sah-lah'-dah], *f.* 1. Salad, a food of raw herbs, seasoned with salt, oil, vinegar, etc. **Ensalada de patatas**, potato salad. 2. Hodge-podge, medley.

ensaladera [en-sah-lah-day'-rah], *f.* Salad-dish or bowl.

ensaladilla [en-sah-lah-deel'-lyah], *f.* 1. Dry sweetmeats of different sorts and sizes. 2. Jewel made up of different precious stones.

ensalmador, ra [en-sal-mah-dor', rah], *m. & f.* 1. Bone-setter. 2. One who pretends to cure by charms.

ensalmar [en-sal-mar'], *va.* 1. To set dislocated or broken bones (hueso). 2. To enchant, to charm, to bewitch; to cure by spells (enfermedad). **Ensalmar a alguno**, to break the head.

ensalmo [en-sahl'-mo], *m.* Enchantment, spell, charm.

ensalobrarse [en-sah-lo-brar'-say], *vr.* To become putrid and corrupt, as stagnant water.

ensalvajar [en-sal-vah-har'], *va.* To brutalize, to brutify.

ensalzador [en-sal-thah-dor'], *m.* Exalter, praiser, extoller.

ensalzamiento [en-sal-thah-me-en'-to], *m.* Exaltation.

ensalzar [en-sal-thar'], *va.* 1. To extol, to exalt, to aggrandize. 2. To magnify, to exaggerate.-*vr.* To boast, to display one's own worth or actions.

ensambenitar [en-sam-bay-ne-tar'], *va.* To put on the *sambenito*, a gown worn by penitent convicts of the Inquisition.

ensamblado [en-sam-blah-do], *m.* Assembly (coches).

ensamblador [en-sam-blah-dor'], *m.* Joiner, worker in wood.

ensambladura [en-sam-blah-doo'-rah], *f.* 1. Joinery, the trade of a joiner. 2. Art of joining boards, planks, and timbers together.

ensamblaje [en-sam-blah'-hay], *m.* *V.* ENSAMBLADURA.

ensamblar [en-sam-blar'], *va.* To join or unite pieces of wood; to scarf, to dovetail, to mortise.

ensamble [en-sahm'-blay], *m.* *V.* ENSAMBLADURA.

ensancha [en-sahn'-chah], *f.* Extension, enlargement. *V.* ENSANCHE. **Dar ensanchas**, to give too much license or liberty.

ensanchador, ra [en-san-chah-dor', rah], *m. & f.* One who or that which makes a thing larger; stretcher, widener, expander, reamer.

ensanchamiento [en-san-chah-me-en'-to], *m.* 1. Widening, enlarging. 2. Dilation, augmentation.

ensanchar [en-san-char'], *va.* To widen, to extend, to enlarge. **Ensanchar el corazón**, to cheer up, to raise one's spirits, to unburden the mind. *-vr.* 1. To assume an air of importance, to affect grandeur and dignity. 2. To get wider, to spread, to expand.

ensanche [en-sahn'-chay], *m.* 1. Dilatation, augmentation, widening, extension. 2. Gore, a slip of cloth or linen to widen a garment. 3. Suburbs which are joined to the city (de ciudad). 4. Reaming.

ensandecer [en-san-day-therr'], *vn.* To grow crazy, to turn mad.

ensangrentado [en-san-grayn-tah'-do], *a.* Blood-stained; bloody, gory.

ensangrentamiento [en-san-gren-tah-me-en´-to], *m.* Bloodiness.

ensangrentar [en-san-gren-tar'], *va.* To imbrue, to stain with blood. *-vr.* To be too irritated, vexed, in a dispute. *(Yo ensangriento, yo ensangriente,* from *Ensangrentar. V.* ACRECENTAR.)

ensañar [en-sah-nyar'], *va.* To irritate, to enrage. *-vr.* **Ensañarse con**, to vent one´s anger on.

ensarnecer [en-sar-nay-therr'], *vn.* To get the itch.

ensarta [en-sar'-tah], *f.* A string (perlas). *V.* SARTA.

ensartar [en-sar-tar´], *va.* 1. To string, to file on a string; to link (cuentas etc.) 2. *(Met.)* To make a string of observations (larga historia) *.-vr.* To be shut up in a narrow place; to be piled one upon another.

ensay [en-sah'-e], *m.* Assay, trial, proof.

ensayado, da [en-sah-yah'-do, dah], *a.* Tested, tried, practiced.

ensayador [en-sah-yah-dor'], *m.* 1. Assayer, an officer of the mint. 2. Rehearser, prompter on the stage.

ensayar [en-sah-yar'], *va.* 1. To assay precious metals. 2. To instruct, to teach, to make dexterous. 3. To rehearse, to practise. 4. To examine, to prove, to try, to test (probar). *-vr.* To exercise oneself, or to train oneself by use to any act.

ensaye [en-sah'-yay], *m.* Assay, trial, proof.

ensayo [en-sah'-yo], *m.* 1. Assay, trial, proof (prueba). 2. Rehearsal of a play. **Ensayo general**, dress rehearsal. 3. Essay, a trial, an experiment (experimento), liking. **Viaje de ensayo**, trial run. **Vuelo de ensayo**, test flight. 4. Exercise, preparatory practice (ejercicio). 5. *(Com.)* Sample.

ensebar [en-say-bar'], *va.* To grease, to tallow.

ensedar [en-say-dar'], *va.* To join the thread with the bristle in order to sew shoes.

enseguida [en-say-gee'-dah], *adv.* Straight off; at once, right away. **Enseguida termino**, I´ve very nearly finished. **enseguida**, at once.

enselvado, da [en-sel-vah'-do, dah], Full of trees. *-pp.* of ENSELVAR.

enselvar [en-sel-var'], *va. V.* EMBOSCAR.

ensenada [en-say-nah'-dah], *f.* Creek, cove, fleet, a small bay.

ensenado, da [en-say-nah'-do, dah], *a.* Having the form of a bay, creek, or gulf. *-pp.* of ENSENAR.

enseña [en-say'-nyah], *f.* Standard, colors, ensign.

enseñable [en-say-nyah'-blay], *a.* Teachable.

enseñado [en-say-nyah'-do], *a.* Trained; informed; educated. **Bien enseñado**, house-trained (perro).

enseñador, ra [en-say-nyah-dor', rah], *m. & f.* Teacher, instructor.

enseñanza [en-say-nyahn'-thah], *f.* 1. Teaching, instruction, doctrine (doctrina), the act of teaching, the way or manner of teaching (acto, profesión). 2. Public instructions. **Enseñanza primaria**, elementary education. **Enseñanza universitaria**, university education. **Enseñanza programada**, programmed learning.

enseñar [en-say-nyar'], *va.* 1. To teach, to instruct, to lecture, to lesson (asignatura). **Enseñar a uno a hacer algo**, to teach somebody to do something. 2. To show the way (mostrar), to point out the road (señalar), to lead. **Nos enseñó el museo**, he showed us the museum. **Esto nos enseña las dificultades**, this reveals the difficulties to us. *-vr.* To accustom or habituate oneself; to be inured.

enseño [en-say'-nyo], *m. (coll.) V.* ENSEÑANZA.

enseñoreador [en-say-nyo-ray-ah-dor'], *m.* He who domineers.

enseñorear [en-say-nyo-ray-ar'], *va.* To lord, to domineer. *-vr.* To possess oneself of a thing.

enserar [en-say-rar'], *va.* To cover with bassweed.

enseres [en-say'-res], *m. pl.* Chattels (efectos personales), marketable effects, fixtures, furniture, utensils. **Enseres de cocina**, kitchen utensils.

enseriarse [en-say-re-ar'-say], *vr. (Cuba and Amer.)* To become serious, to affect seriousness.

enserpentado, da [en-ser-pen-tah'-do, dah], *a.* Enraged, furious.

enserrinar [en-ser-re-nar'], *va.* To varnish.

ensifoliado, da [en-se-fo-le-ah'-do, dah], *a.* Having sword-shaped or ensiform leaves.

ensiforme [en-se-for'-may], *a.* Ensiform, having the shape of a sword.

ensilaje [en-se-lah'-hay], *m.* Ensilage, the process of preserving green fodder in a silo, and the fodder so stored.

ensilar [en-se-lar'], *va.* To preserve grain in a place under ground.

ensillado, da [en-sil-lyah'-do, dah], *a.* Hollow-backed (caballos).*-pp.* of ENSILLAR.

ensilladura [en-sil-lyah-doo'-rah], *f.* The part on which a saddle is placed on a horse or mule.

ensillar [en-sil-lyar'], *va.* 1. To saddle.

ensimismado [en-se-mis-mah'-do], *a.* 1. Selfish. 2. Absorbed in thought.

ensimismarse [en-se-mis-mar'-say], *vr.* To be centred in oneself, to be abstracted.

ensoberbecer [en-so-ber-bay-therr'], *va.* To make proud, to puff up with haughtiness and pride. *-vr.* 1. To become proud and haughty, to be arrogant. 2. *(Naut.)* To become boisterous (mar). *(Yo me ensoberbezco, yo me ensoberbezca,* from *Ensoberbecerse. V.* CONOCER.)

ensoberbecimiento [en-so-ber-bay-the-me-en'-to], *m.* Haughtiness, arrogance, pride.

ensogar [en-so-gar'], *va.* To fasten with a rope.

ensolapar [en-so-lah-par´], *va.* To lap over, to overlap (de solapa).

ensolerar [en-so-lay-rar'], *va.* To fix stools to beehives.

ensolver [en-sol-verr´], *va.* 1. To jumble, to mix confusedly together. 2. *(Med.)* To resolve, to discuss, to dissipate.

ensombrecer [en-som-bray-ther'], *va.* 1. To darken. 2. *(Fig.)* To overshadow, to put in the shade. *-vr.* 1. To darken, to get dark. 2. *(Fig.)* To get gloomy.

ensoñar [en-so-nyar'], *va. V.* SOÑAR.

ensopar [en-so-par'], *va.* To make soup by steeping bread in wine.

ensordecedor [en-sor-day-the-dor'], *a.* Deafening.

ensordecer [en-sor-day-therr'], *va.* To deafen, to make deaf, to cause deafness (persona). *-vn.* 1. To grow deaf, to be deprived of hearing. 2. To become silent, to observe silence.

ensordecimiento [en-sor-day-the-me-en'-to], *m.* Deafness, the act of deafening.

ensortijadura [en sor-te-hah-doo'-rah], *f.* 1. A ring which looms have in the middle of the netting called *perchado*. 2. *(Vet.)* Dislocation.

ensortijamiento [en-sor-te-hah-me-en-to], *m.* Act of curling the hair, or ringing animals.

ensortijar [en-sor-te-har'], *va.* 1. To ring, to form into a ring, to encircle; to curl (pelo). 2. To ring hogs, buffaloes, or other beasts. 3. To fix a ring in (nariz).

ensotarse [en-so-tar'-say], *vr.* To conceal oneself in a thicket.

ensuciador, ra [en-soo-the-ah-dor', rah], *m. & f.* Stainer, defiler.

ensuciamiento [en-soo-the-ah-me-en'-to], *m.* Act of dirtying, staining, or polluting.

ensuciar [en-soo-the-ar'], *va.* 1. To stain, to dirty, to soil, to smear, to file, to daub, to sully, to focal. 2. *(Met.)* To defile, to pollute with vicious habits. *-vr.* To dirty one's bed, clothes, etc.

ensueño [en-soo-ay'-nyo], *m.* Sleep, fantasy. **Una cocina de ensueño,** a dream kitchen. **Mundo de ensueño,** dream world.

entablación [en-tah-blah-the-on'], *f.* A register in churches.

entablado [en-tah-blah'-do], *m.* Floor made of boards. **-Entablado, da,** *pp.* of ENTABLAR

entabladura [en-tah-blah-doo'-rah], *f.* Act of flooring with boards; wains-cotting.

entablamento [en-tah-blah-men'-to], *m.* 1. *(Arch.)* Entablature, entablement. 2. Roof of boards.

entablar [en-tah-blar'], *va.* 1. To cover with boards, to floor with boards. 2. To bring an affair on the tapis, to take the preparatory steps for attaining one's end (conversación). 3. *(coll.)* To claim something without right and with pretence. *(Amer.)* 4. To set up (ajedrez). 5. To enter into (contrato).

entable [en-tah'-blay], *m.* 1. V. ENTABLADURA. 2. *(Amer.)* Exaggerated pretence.

entablillado [en-tah-ble-lyah'-do], *m.* *(Surg.)* Splint.

entablillar [en-tah-ble-lyar'], *va.* To secure with small boards, to bind up a broken leg; to splint.

entalamado, da [en-tah-lah-mah'-do, dah], *a.* Hung with tapestry.*-pp.* of ENTALAMAR.

entalamadura [en-tah-lah-mah-doo'-rah], *f.* Awning of a boat, carriage, etc.

entalegar [en-tah-lay-gar'], *va.* To put in a bag or sack.

entalingar [en-tah-lin-gar'], *va.* *(Naut.)* To clinch the cable, to fasten it to the anchor.

entalpía [en-tal-pee'-ah], *f.* Enthalpy .

entallable [en-tal-lyah'-blay], *a.* Capable of being sculptured.

entallado, da [en-tal-lyah'-do, dah], *a.* Close fitting, tight fitting.

entallador [en-tal-lyah-dor'], *m.* 1. Sculptor, a cutter in wood or stone. 2. Engraver. 3. Carter.

entalladura [en-tal-lyah-doo'-rah], *f.* 1. Sculpture, carving (arte, objeto); engraving. 2. Slot (corte), notch, cut, groove.

entallamiento [en-tal-lyah-me-en'-to], *m.* 1. Sculpture, act of sculpturing, carving. 2. Among carpenters, a mortise or groove for receiving a piece. 3. *(Med.)* A deep incision by a cutting instrument.

entallar [en-tal-lyar'], *va.* 1. To sculpture, to carve; to cut figures in wood or stone (esculpir). 2. To engrave, to picture by incisions in copper (gravar).*-vn.* To cut or shape a thing so as to fit it to the body. **Traje que entalla bien,** a suit that fits well.

entalle [en-tahl'-lyay], *m.* The work of a sculptor or engraver; intaglio.

entallecer [en-tal-lyay-therr'], *vn.* To shoot, to sprout (plantas).

entamar [en-tah-mar'], *va. (Prov.)* 1. V. DECENTAR. 2. In woollen factories to label the cloth which belongs to a purchaser.

entapizado [en-tah-pe-thah'-do], *a.* 1. Upholstered; hung; covered. 2. *(Bot.)* Overgrown. *-m. (Mex.)* Wall-coverings, tapestries.

entapizar [en-tah-pe-thar'], *va.* 1. To hang or adorn with tapestry (pared). 2. To upholster (mueble). 3. To cover with fabric (butaca)

entarascar [en-ta-ras-car'], *va. (coll.)* To cover with too many ornaments.

entarimado [en-tah-re-mah'-do], *m.* Boarded floor (tablas), parquetry, inlaid floor (taracea).—**Entarimado, da,** *pp.* of ENTARIMAR.

entarimar [en-tah-re-mar'], *va.* To cover a floor with boards.

entarquinar [en-tar-ke-nar'], *va.* To bemire, to cover with mud or mire; to manure land with mud.

entasis [en'-tah-sis], *m.* The increase of diameter which some columns present in their first third: entasis.

ente [en'-tay] *m.* 1. Entity, being. 2. Ridiculous man.

enteco, ca [en-tay'-co, cah], *a.* 1. Infirm, weak, languid. 2. Timid, pusillanimous.

entejado, da [en-tay-hah'-do, dah], *a. (Prov.)* Made in the form or shape of tiles.

entelararse [en-tay-lah-ra-nyar'-say], *vr. (Prov.)* To be clouded or overcast (cielo).

entelequía [en-tay-lay-kee'-ah], *f. (Phil.)* Entelechy, (in the philosophy of Aristotle) actuality as opposed to potentiality.

entelerido, da [en-tay-lay-ree'-do, dah] *a.* Fearful (atemorizado), timid.

entena [en-tay'-nah], *f. (Naut.)* Lateen yard.

entenada [en-tay-nah'-dah], *f.* A step-daughter, a daughter of a former marriage.

entenado [en-tay-nah'-do], *m.* A stepson, a son of a former marriage.

entenallas [en-tay-nahl'-lyas], *f. pl.* A small hand-vise.

entendederas [en-ten-day-day'-ras], *f. pl. (coll.)* Understanding, judgment. **Ser corto de entendederas,** to be pretty dim, to be slow on the uptake. **Sus entendederas no llegan a más,** he has a brain the size of a pea, he's a bird-brain.

entendedor, ra [en-ten-day-dor', rah] *m. & f.* Understander, one who understands.

entender [en-ten-derr'], *va.& vn.* 1. To understand, to comprehend (comprender), to conceive, to relieve, to hear. 2. To remark, to take notice of, to realize (darse cuenta). 3. To reason, to think (creer), to judge. 4. To be employed about or engaged in something. **A mi entender,** in my opinion. **Lo mismo se debe entender este artículo,** the same construction is to be given to this article. **Entenderse con alguno,** to address or correspond with someone. **Tenga usted entendido,** I warn you, or you must be aware, you must keep in mind. **Sólo me he entendido con él,** I have applied only to, or had correspondence only with him, I have known no other person but him. **No entiendo palabra,** it's Greek to me. **Hacer entender algo a uno,** to make somebody understand something. **Entender de carpintería,** to know all about carpentry. **Ella no entiende de coches,** she's hopeless with cars. *-vr.* 1. To have some motive for doing a thing (tener razones). **Él se entiende,** he knows what he is about. 2. To agree or be agreed. 3. To understand each other (dos personas). **Entender de alguna cosa,** to be skilful in anything. **Entenderse con alguna cosa,** to take the charge or management of a chair. **Ya te entiendo,** I know your intention. **Se entiende que...,** it is undertood that... **Entenderse con una mujer,** to have an affair with a woman. *(Yo entiendo, yo entienda,* from *Entender.* V. ATENDER.)

entendidamente [en-ten-de-dah-men'-tay], *adv.* Knowingly, prudently.

entendido, da [en-ten-dee'-do, dah], *a.* Wise (sabio), learned, prudent, knowing. **Darse por entendido,** to manifest by signs or words that the thing is understood; to answer any attention or compliment in the customary manner. **Tenemos entendido que...,** we understand that... **Según tenemos entendido,** as far as we can gather. **Según el juicio de los entendidos,** in the opinion of those who know.

entendimiento [en-ten-de-me-en'-to], *m.* 1. Understanding (comprensión), knowledge, judgment, mind (inteligencia); conceiving. 2. Explanation, illustration.

entenebrecer [en-tay-nay-bray-therr'], *va.*To obscure, to darken.

enténola [en-tay'-no-lah], *f. (Naut.)* A spare spar.

enteomanía [en-tay-o-mah-nee'-ah], *f..* A kind of religious insanity, which consists in believing oneself inspired by Heaven.

enterado [en-tay-rah'-do], *a.* 1. Knowledgeable; well-informed. **Estar enterado,** to be informed. **No darse por enterado,** to pretend not to understand. *-m. f.* Know-all.

enteralgia [en-tay-rahl'-ge-ah], *f.* Enteralgia, neuralgia of the intestines.

enteramente [en-tay-rah-men'-tay], *adv.* Entirely, fully, completely, full; clear, clean; quite.

enterar [en-tay-rar´], *va.* 1. To inform thoroughly, to acquaint, to instruct, to give intelligence. 2. *(Amer.)* To complete, to make entire. *-vr.* To find out, to get to know. **Enterarse de,** to find out about. **Seguir sin enterarse,** to remain ignorant. **Ya me voy enterando,** I´m beginning to understand.

entereza [en-tay-ray'-thah], *f.* 1. Entireness, integrity. 2. Rectitude, uprightness; perfection. 3. Fortitude, firmness. **Entereza virginal,** virginity.

enteritis [en-tay-ree'-tis], *f. (Med.)* Enteritis, inflammation of the mucous coat of the bowels.

enterizo, za [en-tay-ree'-tho, thah], *a.* Entire, complete; of one piece.

enternecedor, ra [en-ter-nay-the-dor', rah], *a.* Compassionate, pitiful.

enternecer [en-ter-nayt-herr'], *va.* 1. To soften, to make fonder or soft, to melt, to affect. 2. *(Met.)* To move to compassion. *-vr.* To be moved to compassion, to pity, to commiserate, to be affected. *(Yo enternezco, yo enternezca,* from *Enternecer.* V. CONOCER.)

enternecidamente [en-ter-nay-the-dah-men'-tay], *adv.* Compassionately.

enternecimiento [en-ter-nay-the-me-en'-to], *m.* Compassion, pity, melting.

entero, ra [en-tay'-ro, rah], *a.* 1. Entire, undiminished. 2. Perfect, complete. 3. Sound, without a flaw. 4. Just, right. 5. Honest, upright, pure, uncorrupted (honesto). 6. Strong, robust, vigorous. 7. Informed, instructed. 8. Uncastrated. 9. Strong, coarse (ropa de casa). 10. *(Arith.)* Whole. **Números enteros,** whole numbers. 11. Constant, firm. **Por entero,** entirely, fully, completely. *-m.* 1. *(Mat.)* Integer, whole number. 2. *(Com., Fin.)* Point. **Las acciones han subido dos enteros,** the shares have gone up two points.

enterorrafia [en-tay-ror-rah'-fe-ah, *f.* Enterorraphy, a suture for maintaining the edges of a wound of the intestines.

enterótomo [en-tay-ro'-to-mo], *m.* Enterotome.

enterrado [en-tayr-rah'-do], *a.* Buried; ingrowing (uña).

enterrador [en-ter-rah-dor'], *m.* 1. Gravedigger, burier, sexton. 2. The sexton beetle; necrophorus.

enterraje [en-ter-rah'-hay], *m.* In foundries, a bank of earth around a mould.

enterramiento [en-ter-rah-me-en'-to], *m.* 1. Interment, burial, funeral. 2. Tomb, burying place.

enterrar [en-ter-rar'], *va.* 1. To inter, to bury. 2. V. SOBREVIVIR.

enterronar [en-ter-ro-nar'], *va.* To cover with clods.

entesamiento [en-tay-sah-me-en'-to], *m.* The act of stretching, the effect of being stretched, fullness.

entesar [en-tay-sar'], *va.* To extend, to stretch out, to give greater force or vigor to a thing.

entestado, da [en-tes-tah'-do, dah], *a.* Obstinate, stubborn.

entibador [en-te-bah-dor'], *m.* One who shores up mines.

entibar [en-te-bar'], *vn.* To rest, to lean upon. *-va.* To prop, to shore up mines.

entibiadero [en-te-be-ah-day'-ro], *m.* Cooler, a bath in which something is cooled.

entibiar [en-te-be-ar'], *va.* 1. To cool, to make cool, to damp. 2. To temper, to moderate the passions. *-vr. (Met.)* To become cool, to slacken, to relax, to languish.

entibo [en-tee'-bo], *m.* 1. Stay, prop, shore. 2. Foundation.

entidad [en-te-dahd'], *f.* 1. Entity, a real being. 2. *(Met.)* Consideration, extimation, value, moment, consequence, import, matter, importance.

entierro [en-teer'-ro], *m.* 1. Burial, interment (acto), funeral (funeral). **Asistir al entierro,** to go to the funeral. 2. Tomb, grave (tumba), sepulture. *(Yo entierro, yo entierre,* from *Enterrar.* V. ACERTAR.)

entigrecerse [en-te-gray-therr'-say], *vr.* To be as enraged or furious as a tiger.

entimema [en-te-may'-mah], *f.* Enthymem, a syllogism which consists of two propositions.

entinar [en-te-nar'], *va.* 1. To tinge, to color. 2. To put wool into the clearing bath.

entintar [en-tin-tar'], *va.* 1. To stain with ink (manchar). 2. To tinge or give a different color.

entiznar [en-teeth-nar'], *va.* To revile, to defame. V. TIZNAR.

entoldado [en-tol-dah'-do], *m.* An awning.—**Entoldado, da,** *pp.* of ENTOLDAR.

entoldamieto [en-tol-dah-me-en'-to], *m.* Act of covering with an awning.

entoldar [en-tol-dar'], *va.* 1. To cover with an awning (cubrir con toldo). 2. To hang walls with cloths or silks (decorar). *-vr.* 1. To dress pompously. 2. To grow cloudy or overcast.

entomizar [en-to-me-thar'], *va.* To tie bass cords around posts or laths, that the plaster may stick to them.

entomófago, ga [en-to-mo'-fah-go, gah], *a.* Insectivorous, entomophagous.

entomófilo, la [en-to-mo'-fe-lo, lah], *a.* Entomophilous, fond of insects.

entomología [en-to-mo-lo-hee'-ah], *f.* Entomology.

entomológicamente [en-to-mo-lo'-he-cah-men-tay], *adv.* Entomologically.

entomológico, ca [en-to-mo-lo'-he-co, cah], *a.* Entomological, relating to the study of insects.

entomologista [en-to-mo-lo-hees'-tah], *m.* or **entomólogo,** *m.* An entomologist.

entomostráceo, cea [en-to-mos-trah'-thay-o, ah], *a.* Entomostracan.*-m. pl.* The entomostracans.

entonación [en-to-nah-the-on´], *f.* 1. Modulation, intonation. 2. The act of blowing the bellows of an organ. 3. *(Met.)* Haughtiness, presumption, pride.

entonadera [en-to-nah-day'-rah], *f.* The blow-lever of an organ.

entonado [en-to-nah'-do], *m.* The process of toning in photography.

entonado, da [en-to-nah'-do, dah], *a. & pp.* of ENTONAR. Haughty, puffed with pride (orgulloso).

entonador [en-to-nah-dor'], *m.* 1. Organ-blower. 2. One who tunes the first verse of a psalm. 3. One that sets the tune. 4. *(Med.)* A tonic.

entonamiento [en-to-nah-me-en'-to], *m.* 1. V. TONO. 2. Intoning. 3. Arrogance, haughtiness.

entonar [en-to-nar'], *va.* 1. To tune to modulate, to intonate (canción) 2. To commence or set a tune. 3. *(Pict.)* To harmonize colors. *(Phot.)* To tone prints. 4. To blow the bellows of an organ (órgano). 5. *(Med.)* To strengthen the muscular fibers by means of tonic medicines. *-vr. (Met.)* To grow haughty, to be puffed up with pride; to look big.

entonatorio [en-to-nah-to'-re-o], *m.* A book of sacred music used in Catholic churches.

entonces [en-ton'-thes], *adv.* Then, at that time, on that occasion. **Desde entonces,** since then. **Las costumbres de entonces,** the customs of the time. **Fue entonces que...,** it was then that... **No fue hasta entonces,** it wasn't till then.

entonelar [en-to-nay-lar'], *va.* To barrel.

entono [en-toh'-no], *m.* 1. The act of intoning. 2. V. ENTONACIÓN. 3. *(Met.)* Arrogance, haughtiness, pride.

entontecer [en-ton-tay-therr'], *va.* To mope, to fool, to craze. *-vn. & vr.* To grow foolish, to be stupid. *(Yo me entontezco, yo me entontezca,* from *Entontecerse.* V. CONOCER.)

entontecimiento [en-ton-tay-the-me-en'-to], *m.* Act of growing foolish or stupid.

entorchado [en-tor-chah'-do], *m.* A twisted gold or silver cord, for embroideries. **Entorchados,** cords for a musical instrument covered with silver wire, bass strings.

entorchar [en-tor-char'], *va.* 1. To twist a cord. 2. To cover cords for musical instruments with wire.

entorilar [en-to-re-lar'], *va.* To put the bull in the *toril,* or stall.

entornar [en-tor-nar'], *va.* To turn, to half-close (ojos); to half-close (puerta); to upset (volcar).

entornillar [en-tor-nil-lyar'], *va.* To make something in the form of a screw or ring.

entorno [en-tor'-no], *m.* Setting, milieu, ambience; climate; scene. **El entorno cultural,** the cultural scene.

entorpecer [en-tor-pay-therr'], *va.* 1. To benumb (entendimiento), to dampen, to render torpid (aletargar). 2. To stupefy, to obscure the understanding. *(Yo me entorpezco, yo me entorpezca,* from *Entorpecerse. V.* CONOCER.

entorpecimiento [en-tor-pay-the-me-en'-to], *m.* 1. Torpor, benumbedness, numbness, stupefaction, dullness. 2. Stupidity, thickness.

entortadura [en-tor-tah-doo'-rah], *f.* Crookedness, curvity.

entortar [en-tor-tar'], *va.* 1. To bend, to make crooked. 2. To pull out an eye.

entortijar [en-tor-te-har'], *va. V.* ENSORTIJAR.

entosigar [en-to-se-gar'], *va. V.* ATOSIGAR.

entozoario, ria [en-to-tho-ah'-re-o, ah], *a. & n.* Entozoarian, entozoic; entozoa.

entrada [en-trah'-dah], *f.* 1. Entrance, entry (lugar). 2. Entrance, entry, coming in, ingress (acto). **La entrada de las tropas en 1940,** the entry of the troops in 1940. **Su entrada en la Academia,** his admission to the Academy. 3. Entrance, prerogative of certain authorities to enter places forbidden to the public (público). 4. Beginning of a musical clause. 5. Entry, the act of publicly entering a city. 6. The act of admitting a person into a community or society. 7. Concourse of people. **Hubo una grande entrada aquel día en la comedia,** the play-house was crowded on that day. 8. Entrance fee, admission, ticket (billete). **Entrada de regalo,** complimentary ticket. 9. The means or power to do something. 10. Familiar access, intimacy. 11. *(Naut.)* The rising, beginning of a wind, a soft breeze, or a storm. 12. A good hand at cards. 13. Each of the more substantial dishes which are served at table (comidas). 14. Receipts, property vested in any concern. **Derechos de entrada,** import duty. **Entradas,** temples, the upper parts of the sides of the head. 15. **Entrada furtiva en una casa, forzándola para robar,** *(Law.)* burglary. 16. Beginning. **La entrada de la primavera,** the start of spring. 17. *(Fin.)* Receipts, takings; income. **Entradas familiares,** family income. **Entradas brutas,** gross receipts. **Entradas y salidas,** income and expenditure. **Entrada de reloj (validación, muestreo),** *(Inform.)* clock input, enable, strobe.

entradero [en-trah-day'-ro], *m. (Prov.)* A narrow entrance.

entrado [en-trah'-do], *a.* 1. **Entrado en años,** elderly, advanced in years. 2. **Hasta muy entrada la noche,** until late at night.

entramado [en-tra-mah'-do], *m. (Carp.)* Framework, studwork, bay-work.

entramar [en-tra-mar'], *va.* To make stud-work, framework.

entrambos, bas [en-trahm'-bos, bas], *pron. pl.* Both. *V.* AMBOS.

entrampar [en-tram-par'], *va.* 1. To entrap, to ensnare, to catch in a trap. 2. *(Met.)* To involve in difficulties, to perplex. 3. To ensnare, to deceive; to noose, to circumvent, to hamper. 4. *(Met.)* To encumber an estate with debts, to contract debts. *-vr.* To borrow money, to become indebted.

entrante [en-trahn'-tay], *pa.* 1. Entering, coming in. **El mes entrante,** the coming month.-*m.* 1. One who is entering (persona). 2. The coming month. - *m & pl.* **Entrantes y salientes,** people coming to and leaving a house.

entraña [en-trah'-nyah], *f.* An entrail, a bowel, any principal organ or part which has an appropriate use; very seldom used in the singular in either language. *-pl.* 1. Entrails, bowels. 2. *(Met.)* Entrails, the internal parts of anything; center of a city, heart of a country. 3. *(Met.)* Mind, affection (sentimientos); disposition (temperamento); idiosyncrasy. 4. The inmost recess of something. **Dar las entrañas,** or

dar hasta las entrañas, to give one's very heart-blood away. **Esto me llega a las entrañas,** that goes to my heart.

entrañable [en-trah-nyah'-blay], *a.* Intimate, affectionate (afectuoso), charming (simpático).

entrañablemente [en-trah-nyah-blay-men'-tay], *adv.* Affectionately.

entrañar [en-trah-nyar'], *vn.* To penetrate to the core, to know profoundly. *-vr.* 1. To contract intimacy and familiarity. 2. *V.* EMBUTIR. *(Naut.)*

entrapada [en-trah-pah'-dah], *f.* A coarse crimson cloth.

entrapajar [en-trah-pah-har'], *va.* To tie with rags.

entrapar [en-trah-par'], *va.* 1. To powder the hair to clean it. 2. *(Agr.)* To put woollen rags to the roots of plants, as manure. *-vr.* To be covered with dust.

entrar [en-trar'], *va. & vn.* 1. To enter, to go in, to march in, to come in and *fig.*, to penetrate. 2. To inclose one thing in another, to introduce it (objeto). 3. To commence, to begin, to win a trick at cards. 4. To undertake. 5. *(Geog.)* To disembogue, to join (ríos). 6. To thrust or put one thing upon another. 7. To take possession of a place by force of arms. 8. To set down, or place to account. **Entrar en una partida de trigo, lana, etc.,** to purchase a quantity of wheat, wool, etc. 9. To be classed or ranked, to conduce, or to be employed for some end (número de cosas). 10. Followed by the prepositions *a* or *en,* it signifies to begin or commence, as, **entrar a cantar,** to begin to sing in concert. **Entrar en recelo,** to begin to suspect. **Este abrigo no entra en la maleta,** this coat doesn't fit in the suitcase. **Entrar de por medio,** to settle a scuffle, to adjust, to reconcile disputants. 11. To dedicate or consecrate oneself to something. 12. To find place, to take possession of the mind (pasión, afecto). 13. In fencing to advance a step. 14. *(Naut.)* To gain upon a vessel steering the same course, to begin to rise (la marea) or to blow (el viento). **Entrar bien alguna cosa,** to come to the point. **Entrar dentro de sí** or **en sí mismo,** to reflect upon one's own conduct in order to improve it. **No entrar (a alguno) alguna cosa,** not to believe a thing; to have a repugnance for it. **Entrar y salir,** to be clever in business or conversation. **Entrar como por su casa,** to fit loosely. **Juan entró tercero,** John came in third. **El paquete no entra en el saco,** the parcel won't go into the bag. **Entrar en detalles,** to go into details. **Le entraron deseos de,** he felt a sudden urge to. **Estos zapatos no me entran,** these shoes don't fit. **No me entra la lógica,** I can't get the hang of logic. **La letra con sangre entra,** those who would succeed must work with a will. **Me entra por un oído y por el otro me sale,** it goes in one ear and out of the other.

entre [en'tray], *prep.* 1. Between (dos cosas). **Entre año, semana, día, etc.,** in the course of the year, week, day, etc. **Entre dos aguas,** wavering, irresolute. **Trae a uno entre dientes,** to take a dislike to somebody. 2. In, or in the number of things, among (más de dos cosas). **Entre tanto,** in the interim. **Entre manos,** in hand. **Traer una cosa entre manos,** to be doing something. **Tomar entre manos,** to take in hand. 3. In composition with another word it weakens or limits the signification, as **entrefino,** middling fine. **Lo cogió entre sus manos,** he took it in his hands. **Dicho sea entre nosotros,** between ourselves. **Estaba entre la vida y la muerte,** he was at death's door. **Entre tanto,** meanwhile, in the meantime. **Entre el ruido y el calor no he dormido,** what with the noise and the heat I didn't sleep. **Entre todos había 30 personas,** there were 30 people all together.

entreabierto [en-tray-ah-be-ayr'-to], *a.* Half-open; ajar.

entreabrir [en-tray-ah-breer'], *va.* To half open a door, to leave it ajar.

entreacto [en-tray-ahc'-to], *m.* Interval.

entreancho, cha [en-tray-ahn'-cho, chah], *a.* Neither wide nor narrow.

entrecalle [en-tray-cahl'-lyay], *m.* Clear between two mouldings, quirk.

entrecanal [en-tray-cah-nahl'], *f. (Arch.)* Space between the striae or flutings of a column.

entrecano, na [en-tray-cah'-no, nah], *a.* Between black and gray, grayish (pelo, barba).

entrecava [en-tray-cah'-vah], *f.* A very shallow digging.

entrecavar [en-tray-cah-var'], *va.* To dig shallow, not to dig deep.

entrecejo [en-tray-thay'-ho], *m.* 1. The space between the eyebrows. 2. A frowning, supercilious look, show of annoyance. **Arrugar el entrecejo,** to frown.

entrecerca [en-tray-ther'-cah], *f.* Space between inclosures.

entrecielo [en-tray-the-ay'-lo], *m.* Awning. *V.* TOLDO.

entreclaro, ra [en-tray-clah'-ro, rah], *a.* Slightly clear.

entrecogedura [en-tray-coh-ay-doo'-rah], *f.* Act of catching.

entrecoger [en-tray-co-herr'], *va.* 1. To catch, to intercept. 2. To compel by arguments or threats.

entrecomillar [en-tray-co-mel-lyar'], *va.* To place in inverted commas, to put inverted commas, quotes.

entrecoro [en-tray-co'-ro], *m.* Space between the choir and the chief altar; chancel.

entrecortado, da [en-tray-cor-tah'-do, dah], *a.* 1. *(Med.)* Short of breath, dyspneal (respiración). 2. *(Geol.)* Broken.

entrecortadura [en-tray-cor-tah-doo'-rah], *f.* Cut made in the middle of anything without dividing it.

entrecortar [en-tray-cor-tar'], *va.* To cut a thing in the middle without dividing (cortar).

entrecorteza [en-tray-cor-tay'-thah], *f.* An imperfection in timbers through the union of the branches to the trunk, with interior defects.

entrecot [en-tray-cot'], *m. (Culin.)* Sirloin steak.

entrecriar [en-tray-cre-ar'], *va.* To rear plants among others.

entrecruzar [en-tray-croo-thar'], *va.* To interlace, to interweave. *-vr. (Bio.)* To interbreed.

entrecubiertas, entrepuentes [en-tray-coo-be-err'-tas, en-tray-poo-en'-tes], *m. & f. pl. (Naut.)* Between decks.

entrecuesto [en-tray-coo-es'-to], *m.* Back-bone.

entredecir [en-tray-day-theer'], *va.* To interdict, to prohibit.

entredicho [en-tray-dee'-cho], *m.* 1. Interdiction, prohibition. **Estar en entredicho,** to be under a ban (prohibido). 2. Ecclesiastical censure or interdict.—**Entredicho, cha**, *pp. irr.* of ENTREDECIR.

entredoble [en-tray-do'-blay], *a.* Neither double nor single.

entredós [en-tray-dose'], *m.* 1. A strip of lace between two hems; insertion. 2. The size of type called long primer. 3. *(Arch.)* The keystone of an arch. Plancher.

cntrcfino, na [cn-tray-fcc'-no, nah], *a.* Middling fine.

entreforro [en-tray-for'-ro], *m.* 1. Doublet, waistcoat, jerkin. 2. *(Naut.)* Parceling, a canvas wrapping, usually tarred, applied to protect a rope.

entrega [en-tray'-gah], *f.* 1. Delivery, the act of delivering, conveyance. **Entrega contra reembolso,** cash on delivery. **Hacer entrega de,** to hand over. 2. Part, installment (novela); part, number, fascicule (revista).

entregadamente [en-tray-gah-dah'-men-tay], *adv.* Really, perfectly.

entregadero, ra [en-tray-gah-day-ro, rah], *a. (Com.)* To be supplied; deliverable.

entregado [en-tray-gah'-do], *a.* Committed, devoted. **Entregado a,** absorbed in. **Entregado en,** committed to.

entregador [en-tray-gah-dore'], *m.* 1. Deliverer. 2. Executor.

entregamiento [en-tray-gah-me-en'-to], *m.* Delivery.

entregar [en-tray-gar'], *va.* 1. To deliver, to put into the hands of another (dar); to give, to give way, or to give up (ceder): *(Ćom.)* to transfer, to pay. **Entregar algo a un abogado,** to refer something to a lawyer. **No quiso entregármelo,** he refused to hand it over to me. 2. To insert by the point or sidewise, part of one body into another.*-vr.* 1. To deliver oneself up into the hands of another. **Entregarse a vicios**, to abandon oneself to vices. 2. To devote oneself wholly to something (dedicarse). **A entregar,** to be supplied; supply expected.

entregerir [en-tray-hay-reer'], *va.* To insert, to intermix.

entrego [en-tray'-go], *m.* Delivery.

entrejuntar [en-tray-hoon-tar'], *va.* To nail or join the panels of a door to the crossbars or ledges.

entrelazado [en-tray-lah-tha'-do], *a.* Entwined, interlaced; criss-crossed; interlocking.

entrelazar [en-tray-lah-thar'], *va.* To interlace, to intermix, to interweave, to entwine. *-vr.* To entwine, to interlace; to interlock.

entreliño [en-tray-lee'-nyo], *m.* Space of ground between the rows of vines or olives.

entrelistado, da [en-tray-lis-tah'-do, dah], *a.* Striped or variegated.

entrelucir [en-tray-loo-theer'], *vn.* To glimmer, to shine faintly (relucir). (*Yo entreluzco, yo entreluzca,* from *Entrelucir. V.* DESLUCIR).

entremedias [en-tray-may'-de-as], *adv.* In the meantime.

entremés [en-tray-mess'], *m.* 1. A playlet, an interlude, entertainment. 2. Entrée, side dish. **Entremés salado,** savory. **Entreméses,** hors d'oeuvres.

entremesear [en-tray-may-say-ar'], *va.* To act a part in a farce or interlude.

entremesista [en-tray-may-sees'-tah], *m.* Player of farces or interludes.

entremeter [en-tray-may-terr'], *va.* 1. To put one thing between others. 2. To put on a clean cloth without undressing children, or taking off the swaddling clothes. *-vr.* 1. To thrust oneself into a place without being called or invited. 2. To take charge of. 3. To intermeddle, to meddle, to pry, to interpose officiously.

entremetido [en-tray-may-tee'-do], *m.* Meddler, obtruder, intermeddler; a busy-body, a go-between.

entremetido, da [en-tray-may-tee'-do, dah], *a. & pp.* of ENTREMETER. Meddling or intermeddling, officious, meddlesome.

entremetimiento [en-tray-may-te-me-en'-to], *m.* Interposition, interjection, intermeddling, meddlesomeness, obtrusion.

entremezcladura [en-tray-meth-clah-doo'-rah], *f.* Intermixture.

entremezclar [en-tray-meth-clar'], *va.* To interweave, to intermix.

entremiso [en-tray-mee'-so], *m.* A long bench on which cheeses are formed.

entremorir [en-tray-mo-reer'], *vn.* To die away by degrees, to be nearly extinguished (llama).

entrenador, ra [en-tray-nah-dor', rah], *m. & f.* Coach, trainer, instructor, instructress.

entrenamiento [en-tray-nah-me-ayn'-to], *m.* Training, coaching.

entrenar [en-tray-nar'], *va. (Dep.)* To train, to coach; to exercise (caballo). **Estar entrenado,** to be in training. *-vr.* To train.

entrencar [entren-car'], *va.* To put rods in a beehive.

entrenervios [en-tray-nerr'-ve-ose], *m. pl.* Among bookbinders the spaces between the bands of the back of a book.

entrenudos [en-tray-noo'-dos], *m. pl. (Bot.)* Internodes, the spaces between the nodes of a stem.

entrenzar [en-tren-thar'], *va.* To plait hair.

entreoír [en-tray-o-eer'], *va.* To hear without perfectly understanding what is said. (*Yo entreoigo, yo entreoiga; él entreoiga, entreoyera;* from *Entreoír, V.* OÍR.)

entreordinario, ria [en-tray-or-de-nah'-re-o, ah], *a.* Middling, between good and bad.

entrepalmadura [en-tray-pal-mah-doo'-rah], *f. (Vet.)* Disease in horses, hoofs.

entrepanes [en-tray-pah'-nes], *m. pl.* Pieces of unsown ground between others that are sown.

entrepañado, da [en-tray-pa-nyah'-do, dah], *a.* Composed of several panels (puertas).

entrepaño [en-tray-pah'-nyo], *m.* 1. Panel. 2. Space between pilasters. 3. Pier.

entreparecerse [en-tray-pa-ray-therr'-say], *vr.* 1. To be transparent, to shine through. 2. To have traces of resemblance to some other thing, to be like.

entrepechuga [en-tray-pay-choo'-gah], *f.* Small piece of flesh on the breast of birds.

entrepeines [en-tray-pay'-e-nes], *m. pl.* The wool which remains in the comb after combing.

entrepelado, da [en-tray-pay-lah'-do, dah], *a.* Spotted with white upon a dark ground, pied (colores de mulas y caballos).

entrepelar [en-tray-pay-lar'], *va.* To variegate hair, or mix it with different colors.

entrepernar [en-tray-per-nar'], *vn.* To put legs between those of others for ease in sitting.

entrepiernas [en-tray-pe-er'-nas], *f. pl.* 1. Opening between the legs; the inner surface of the thighs. 2. Pieces put into the fork of a pair of breeches.

entreponer [en-tray-po-nerr'], *va.* To interpose.

entrepretado, da [en-tray-pray-tah'-do, dah], *a. (Vet.)* Applied to a mule or horse with a weak breast or shoulder.

entrepuentes [en-tray-poo-en'-tes], *m. pl. (Naut.)* Between decks.

entrepunta [en-tray-poon'-tah], *f.* One of the pieces of a crane.

entrepuzadura [en-tray-poon-thah-doo'-rah], *f.* Pricking pain of an unripe tumor.

entrerrenglón [en-tray-ren-glone'], *m.* Interline, space between lines.

entrerrenglonadura [en-tray-ren-glo-nah-doo'-rah], *f.* Something written within lines: interlineal note.

entrerrenglonar [en-tray-ren-glo-nar'], *va.* To interline.

entresaca, entresacadura [en-tray-sah'-cah, en-tray-sah-cah-doo'-rah], *f.* 1. The act of cutting down trees, in order to thin a wood. 2. Selection of branches at the time of pruning.

entresacar [en-tray-sah-car'], *va.* 1. To pick or choose out of a number or parcel of things (seleccionar). 2. *(Agr.)* To cut away branches of trees, to make a clearing. 3. To clip hair close to the head.

entrescuro, ra [en-tres-coo'-ro, rah], *a. (Prov.)* Somewhat obscure.

entresemana [en-tray-say-mah'-nah], *f.* Midweek; working days of the week. **Cualquier día de entresemana,** any day midweek.

entresijo [en-tray-see'-ho], *m.* 1. Mesentery (mesenterio); secret, mystery (misterio). **Tener muchos entresijos,** to be very complicated. 2. *(Met.)* Something occult, hidden (parte oculta).

entresuelo [en-tray-soo-ay'-lo], *m.* A small room between two stories; floor between the first floor and the second floor; entresol, mezzanine.

entresurco [en-tray-soor'-co], *m.* Space between furrows.

entretalla, entretalladura [en-tray-tahl'-lyah, en-tray-tal-lyah-doo'-rah], *f.* Sculpture in bas-relief.

entretallar [en-tray-tal-lyar'], *va.* 1. To sculpture or carve in bas-relief. 2. To cut, to slash, or to mangle. 3. *(Met.)* To intercept or obstruct the passage.

entretanto [en-tray-tahn'-tao], *a.* Meanwhile, meantime. *-m.* Meantime. *-conj.* **Entretanto esto se produce,** until this happens.

entretejedura [en-tray-tay-hay-doo'-rah], *f.* Intertexture, a work interwoven with another.

entretejer [en-tray-tay-herr'], *va.* 1. To tissue, to variegate. 2. To interweave, to intermix, to knit. 3. To insert words, verses, etc., in a book or writing.

entretejimiento [en-tray-tay-he-me-en'-to], *m.* Intertexture, interweaving; variegation.

entretela [en-tray-tay'-lah], *f.* Interlining (sastrería).

entretelar [en-tray-tay-lar'], *va.* To put buckram between the lining and cloth.

entretenedor [en-tray-tay-nay-dor'], *m.* Entertainer, he that pleases, diverts, or amuses.

entretener [en-tray-tay-nerr'], *va.* 1. To feed or to keep in hope or expectation. 2. To allay pain, to make less troublesome. 3. To amuse (distraer), to entertain (divertir). 4. To delay (demorar), to put off, to postpone (aplazar). **Nos entretuvo en conversación,** he engaged us in conversation. *-vr.* To amuse oneself. *(Yo entretengo, yo entretuve; yo entretenga, entretuviera;* from *Entrener.* V. TENER.)

entretenido, da [en-tray-tay-nee'-do, dah], *a.* 1. Entertaining, pleasant, amusing. 2. Doing business in an office, in hopes of obtaining a place. 3. *(Naut.)* The prisoner who cannot set foot on land. **Dar a uno con la entretenida,** to put one off with excuses, for not giving what is asked for. *-pp.* of ENTRETENER.

entretenimiento [en-tray-tay-ne-me-en'-to], *m.* 1. Amusement, entertainment. **Es un entretenimiento más,** it's just an amusement. 2. Pay, allowance, appointment. 3. Delay, procrastination. 4. Game or sport of any kind, fun, jest, joke.

entretiempo [en-tray-te-em-po], *m.* The middle season between the beginning and end of spring or autumn.

entreuntar [en-tray-oon-tar'], *va.* To anoint slightly.

entrevenarse [en-tray-vay-nar'-say], *vr.* To diffuse through the veins.

entreventana [en-tray-ven-tah-nah], *f.* Space between windows.

entrever [en-tray-verr'], *va.* To have a glimpse of, to see imperfectly.

entreverado, da [en-tray-vey-rah'-do, dah], *a.* Interlined with fat and lean (carne). *-pp.* of ENTREVERAR.

entreverar [en-tray-vay-rar'], *va..* To intermix, to insert one thing in another, to mix with others.

entrevía [en-tray-vee'-ah], *f.* Railway gauge, space between rails.

entrevista [en-tray-vees'-tah], *f.* 1. Interview. 2. Conference. **Entrevista de fondo,** interview in depth.

entrevistador, ra [en-tray-vees-tah-dor', rah], *m. & f.* Interviewer.

entrevistar [en-tray-vees-tar'], *va.* To interview.

entrevistarse [en-tray-vees-tar'-say], *vr.* To confer. **Entrevistarse con,** to interview, to have an interview with.

entrincado, da [en-trin-cah'-do, dah], *a.* Intricate. V. INTRINCADO.

entripado, da [en-tree-pah'-do, dah], *m.f.* Contained in the entrails or intestines.

entripado [en-tree-pah'-do], *m.* 1. *(coll.)* Dissembled anger or displeasure. 2. An indigestion. 3. *(Mex.)* A game of cards. 4. A dead animal from which the intestines have not been removed.

entristecer [en-tris-tay-therr'], *va.* To sadden, to grieve, to afflict, to make melancholy. *-vr.* 1. To grieve, to fret, to grow sad. 2. To wither, to decay (plantas). *(Yo entristezco, yo entristezca,* from *Entristecer.* V. CONOCER.)

entristecimiento [en-tris-tay-the-me-en'-to], *m.* Gloominess, heaviness of mind, sadness (tristeza), sorrowfulness; mournfulness, dejection; fretting.

entrojar [en-tro-har'], *va.* 1. To gather grain in barns. 2. To mow, to gather the harvest.

entrometer [en-tro-may-terr'], *va. & vn.* V. ENTREMETER in all its meanings.

entrometido [en-tro-may-tee'-do], *a.* Meddlesome, interfering. *-m. f.* Meddler, intruder.

entrometimiento [en-tro-may-te-me-en'to], *m.* Intermeddling.

entronar [en-tro-nar'], *va.* To enthrone. V. ENTRONIZAR.

entroncar [en-tron-car'], *vn.* 1. To be descended from the same stock, to belong to the same family. 2. To contract relationship.

entronerar [en-tro-nay-rar'], *va.* To drive the ball into the hole of a truck or billiard-table.

entronización [en-tro-ne-thah-the-on'], *f.* Elevation to a throne.

entronizar [en-tro-ne-thar'], *va.* 1. To enthrone, to place on the throne. 2. To exalt, to raise to a distinguished rank or station. *-vr.* 1. To be elated or puffed up with pride. 2. To take possession of, to seat oneself in a post.

entronque [en-tron'-kay], *m.* 1. Cognation, relationship with the chief of a family. 2. A railway junction.

entropía [en-tro-pee'-ah], *f.* Entropy.

entruchada [en-troo-chah'-dah], *f.* Clandestine operation, an underhand business *(coll.)* Plot, intrigue.

entruchar [en-troo-char'], *va.* To decoy, to lure into a snare.

estruchón, na [es-troo-chone', nah], *m. & f.* Decoyer, plotter.

entruejo [en-troo-ay'-ho'], *m.* V. ANTRUEJO.

entruesca [en-troo-es'-cah], *f.* In some mills, the cogged wheel.

entrujar [en-troo-har'], *va.* 1. To keep olives in the storeroom. 2. V. ENTROJAR. 3. *(Fig. Coll.)* To reimburse.

entuerto [en-too-err'-to], *m.* V. AGRAVIO and TUERTO. *-pl.* Afterpains.

entullecer [en-tool-lyay-therr'], *vn.* To be crippled or maimed. *-va.* To stop, to check, to obstruct. *(Yo entullezco, yo entullezca, from Entullecer. V. CONOCER.)*

entumecer [en-too-may-therr'], *va.* 1. To swell, to make tumid. 2. To benumb, to make torpid (miembro). *-vr.* To swell, to surge (mar), to rise high.

entumecimiento [en-too-may-the-me-en'-to], *m.* 1. Swelling. 2. Torpor, deadness, numbness.

entumescencia [en-too-mes-then'-the-ah], *f. (Med.)* Intumescence, swelling.

entumirse [en-too-meer'-say], *vr.* To become torpid.

entunicar [en-too-ne-car'], *va.* To give two coats of plaster to a wall before painting it (fresco).

entupir [en-too-peer'], *va.* 1. To obstruct, to block up. 2. To compress, to tighten, to press.

enturbiar [en-toor-be-ar'], *va.* 1. To muddle, to make muddy or turbid (agua). 2. To obscure, to confound (asunto). *-vr.* To disorder or derange a thing.

entusiasmado, da [en-too-se-as-mah'-do, dah], *a. & pp.* of ENTUSIASMAR Enthusiastical, enthusiastic.

entusiasmar [en-too-se-as-mar'], *va.* To transport, to enrapture, to fill with enthusiasm. **No me entusiasma mucho la idea,** I´m not very keen on the idea. *-vr.* To become enthusiastic, to be enraptured. **Se ha quedado entusiasmada con el vestido**, she was delighted with the dress.

entusiasmo [en-too-se-ahs'-mo], *m.* Enthusiasm, heat of imagination, ardor; fanaticism, caprice.

entusiasta [en-too-se-ahs'-tah], *m. & f.* Enthusiast, a visionary.

entusiástico, ca [en-too-se-ahs'-te-co, cah], *a.* Enthusiastic, fanatical.

enucleación [ay-noo-clayah-the-on'], *f.* 1. Enucleation, extraction of the kernel of a stone-fruit. 2. Enucleation, extirpation of a tumor. 3. Excision of a bone.

enuclear [ay-noo-clay-ar'], *va.* 1. To enucleate. 2. To excise a bone.

énula campana [ay'-noo-lah cam-pah'-nah], *f. (Bot.)* Elecampane, a tall herb of the aster family.

enumerable [ay-noo-may-rah'-blay], *a.* Numerable, capable of being counted.

enumeración [ay-noo-may-ra-the-on'], *f.* 1. Enumeration. 2. Recapitulation of the points of a discourse.

enumerar [ay-noo-may-rar'], *va.* 1. To enumerate (nombrar). 2. To count (contar).

enunciación [ay-noon-the-ah-the-on'], *f.* Enunciation, declaration.

enunciar [ay-noon-the-ar'], *va.* To enunciate, to declare, to proclaim.

enunciativo, va [ay-noon-the-ah-tee'-vo, vah], *a.* Enunciative.

enuresis, or **enuresia** [ay-noo-ray'-sis], *f.* Enuresis, incontinence of urine.

envagarar, or **envagrar** [en-vah-ga-rar'], *va. (Naut.)* To set the cross-pawls, or rib-bands, upon the frames of a ship.

evainador, ra [en-vah-e-nah-dor', rah], *a.* Sheathing. *(Bot.)* Clasping the stem.

envainar [en-vah-e-nar'], *va.* To sheathe (espada); to plunge.

envalentonar [en-vah-len-to-nar'], *va.* To encourage, to inspirit, to render bold. *-vr.* To become courageous.

envanecer [en-vah-nay-therr´], *va.* To make vain; to lift, to swell with pride.*-vr.* To become proud or haughty. *(Yo envanezco, yo envanezca, from Envanecer. V. CONOCER.)*

envarado, da [en-vah-rah'-do, dah], *a. & pp.* of ENVARAR. Deadened, benumbed, numbed (entumecido).

envaramiento [en-vah-rah-me-en'-to], *m.* 1. Deadness, stiffness, numbness 2. A number of bailiffs or petty officers of justice.

envarar [en-vah-rar'], *va.* To benumb, to numb (entumecer) to make torpid, to stupefy. *-vn.* To go numb (entumecerse) to go stiff (ponerse tieso).

envasado [en-vah-sah'-do], *m.* Packaging.

envasador [en-vah-sah-dor'], *m.* 1. Filler, one whose employment is to fill vessels of carriage. 2. Funnel.

envasar [en-vah-sar'], *va.* 1. To funnel, to put liquor into casks, to barrel (en tonel), to bottle. 2. To drink liquor to excess. 3. To put grain into sacks (en saco). 4. To pack, to wrap (en paquete).

envase [en-vah'-say], *m.* 1. The recipient or vessel in which liquids are preserved or transported. 2. Packing, wrapping; packaging (acto). 3. Container (recipiente); package (papel), wrapping; bottle. **Recipiente de hojalata,** tin can. **Géneros sin envase,** unpackaged goods.

envedijarse [en-vay-de-har'-say], *vr.* 1. To get entangled. 2. *(coll.)* To wrangle.

envejecer [en-vay-hay-therr'], *va.* To make old, to make a person or thing look old. *-vn.* To grow old (persona).*-vr.* 1. To be of an old date or fashion (objeto). 2. To hold out a long time, to be of long duration. 3. To grow out of use. **En dos años ha envejecido mucho,** he´s got very old these last two years. *(Yo envejezco, yo envejezca, from Envejecer. V. CONOCER.)*

envejecido, da [en-vay-hay-thee'-do, dah], *a. & pp.* of ENVEJECER. 1. Grown old, looking old. 2. Accustomed, habituated.

envejecimiento [en-vay-hay-the-me-en'-to], *m.* Oldness, age.

envenenador, ra [en-vay-nay-nah-dor', rah], *m. & f.* A poisoner.

envenenamiento [en-vay-nay-nah-me-en'-to], *m.* Poisoning.

envenenar [en-vay-nay-nar'], *va.* 1. To envenom, to poison; to infect with poison, to pollute (el aire). 2. To reproach, to judge ill of one. 3. To embitter one's own talk or another's. *-vr.* To poison oneself, to take poison.

enverdecer [en-ver-day-therr'], *vn.* To grow green. *(Yo enverdezco, yo enverdezca, from Enverdecer. V. CONOCER.)*

enveredar [en-vay-ray-dar'], *va.* To put on the right road, to guide.

envergadura [en-ver-ga-doo'-rah], *f.* 1. Bending the sails. 2. The rope bands of a sail collectively. 3. Breadth of the sails. 4. V. GRATIL. 5. Expanse, spread, extent. 6. *(Fig.)* Scope, compass; magnitude. **Un programa de gran envergadura,** a program of considerable scope. **La obra es de envergadura,** the plan is ambitious.

envergar [en-ver-gar'], *va. (Naut.)* To bend the sails.

envergues [en-ver'-gays], *m. pl. (Naut.)* Rope-bands, used to fasten sails to the yards.

envés [en-vays'], *m.* 1. The wrong side of anything (tela) V. REVÉS. 2. Back, shoulders.

envesado [en vay nah' do], *m.* Among leather-dressers, the fleshy part of hides.

envestidura [en-ves-te-doo'-rah],*f.* Act of investing one with an office or place.

envestir [en-ves-teer'], *va.* 1. To invest, to put in possession of a place or office. 2. To adorn, to set off. 3. To illuminate, to enlighten. 4. To cover. V. REVESTIR. *-vr.* 1. To accustom or habituate oneself, to contract a habit. 2. To introduce oneself, or to interfere in something. 3. V. REVESTIRSE. *(Yo envisto, yo envista, envistiera or envistiese, from Envestir. V. PEDIR.)*

enviada [en-ve-ah'-dah], *f.* 1. Message, errand. 2. Skiff, or smack, for carrying fish to land.

enviadizo, za [en-ve-ah-dee'-tho, thah], *a.* Missive, designed to be sent.

enviado [en-ve-ah'-do], *m.* 1. Envoy, representative, a public minister sent from one power to another. 2. Envoy, messenger (periodista).

enviador [en-ve-ah-dor'], *m.* A sender.

enviajado, da [en-ve-ah-hah'-do, dah], *a. (Arch.)* Oblique, sloped.

enviar [en-ve-ar'], *va.* 1. To send, to transmit, to convey. 2. To send, to give, to bestow. 3. To exile. **Enviar a pasear**, *(Met.)* to send someone about his business; to give one his walking-ticket; to dismiss contemptuously. **Enviar de vuelta**, *(Com.)* to return. **Enviar a uno a hacer algo**, to send somebody to do something.

enviciar [en-ve-the-ar'], *va.* To vitiate, to corrupt, to make vicious. *-vn.* To have luxurious foliage and little fruit (plantas). *-vr.* To be immoderately addicted to, to be excessively fond of.

envidador [en-ve-dah-dor'], *m.* He who invites at cards, or opens the game by staking a sum.

envidar [en-ve-dar'], *va.* Among gamesters, to invite, or to open the game by staking a certain sum.

envidia [en-vee'-de-ah], *f.* 1. Envy. 2. Emulation.

envidiable [en-ve-de-ah'-blay], *a.* Enviable.

envidiador, ra [en-ve-de-ah-dor', rah], *m. & f.* Envier, envious person.

envidiar [en-ve-de-ar'], *vn.* 1. To envy, to feel envy, to grudge, to malign. 2. *(Met.)* To covet, to desire what is lawful and honorable.

envidiosamente [en-ve-de-o'-sah-men-tay], *adv.* Enviously.

envidioso, sa [en-ve-de-oh'-so, sah], *a.* Envious; invidious, jealous, malignant.

envigotar [en-ve-go-tar'], *va. (Naut.)* To strap dead-eyes.

envilecer [en-ve-lay-therr'], *va.* To vilify, to debase, to make contemptible. *-vr.* To degrade oneself, to be disgraced.

envilecimiento [en-ve-lay-the-me-en'-to], *m.* Vilification, debasement.

envinado, da [en-ve-nah'-do, dah], *a.* Having the taste of wine.*-pp.* of ENVINAR.

envinagrar [en-ve-nah-grar'], *va.* To put vinegar into something.

envinar [en-ve-nar'], *va.* To mix wine with water.

envío [en-ve-e'-o], *m.* Remittance (dinero), consignment of goods (mercancías), sending (acto), dispatch. **Gastos de envío**, postage and packing. **Envío contra reembolso**, cash on delivery. Shipment *(Inform.)*

enviperado, da [en-ve-pay-rah'-do, dah], *a.* In jocular style, viperlike, enraged, furious.

envirar [en-ve-rar'], *va.* To clasp or unite together cork wood to form a beehive.

enviscamiento [en-vis-cah-me-en'-to], *m.* Act of gluing.

enviscar [en-vis-car'], *va.* 1. To glue, to fasten with glue. 2. To irritate, to anger.*-vn* To be glued with birdlie (pájaros e insectos).

envite [en-vee'-tay], *m.* 1. The act of inviting at cards, or opening the game by staking a certain sum (apuesta). 2. Invitation; any kind of polite offer (oferta).

enviudar [en-ve-oo-dar'], *vn.* To become a widower or widow. **Enviudar de su primera mujer**, to lose one´s first wife.

envoltorio [en-vol-to'-re-o], *m.* 1. Bundle of clothes. 2. Fault in cloth, arising from the mixture of inferior material.

envoltura [en-vol-too'-rah], *f.* 1. Wrapper, jacket (libro). 2. Wrapping, covering.

envolturas [en-vol-too'-ras], *f. pl.* 1. Swaddling cloth, swaddling band, cloth wrapped round a baby. 2. *(Anat.)* The coverings, commonly membranous, which serve as a protection to certain organs.

envolvedero, envolvedor [en-vol-vay-day'-ro, en-vol-vay-dor'], *m.* Wrapper, wrapping, envelope, cover.

envolver [en-vol-verr'], *va.* 1. To wrap up, to wrap around with paper, cloth, or other analogous thing: to convolve; to inwrap. **Dos paquetes envueltos en papel**, two parcels wrapped in paper. 2. *(Met.)* To convince by reasoning. 3. To put things into confusion. 4. *(Mil.)* To attack an enemy on all sides, to surround, so as to force a surrender. *-vr.* 1. To be implicated in an affair. 2. To be unlawfully connected with women. *(Yo envuelvo, yo envuelva*, from *Envolver. V.* MOVER.)

envolvimiento [en-vol-ve-me-en'-to], *m.* 1. Envelopment, inwrapping or enveloping. 2. V. REVOLCADERO.

envuelto, ta [en-voo-el'-to, tah], *pp. irr.* of ENVOLVER. 1. Wrapped. 2. **Envuelta**, a cord matted.

enyerbarse [en-yer-bar'-say], *vr. (Amer. Cuba)* To be clothed or covered with grass.

enyesado [en-yay-sah'-do], *m.* Plastering; plaster cast.

enyesadura [en-yay-sah-doo'-rah], *f.* Plastering with gypsum.

enyesar [en-yay-sar'], *va.* To plaster, to cover with plaster; to whitewash.

enyugar [en-yoo-gar'], *va.* To yoke cattle.*-vr. (Met. Obs.)* To marry.

enzamarrado, da [en-thah-mar-rah'-do, dah], *a.* Dressed in a shepherd's greatcoat, made of sheep skins with the wool on.

enzarzada [en-thar-thah'-dah], *f. (Mil.)* A light fortification; breastworks at the entrance of forests, defiles, and crags, aiding to defend an important pass.

enzarzado, da [en-thar-thah'-do, dah], *a.* Curled, matted (pelo).*-pp.* Of ENZARZAR.

enzarzar [en-thar-thar'], *va.* 1. To throw among brambles and briers. 2. *(Met.)* To sow discord, to excite dissensions. 3. To put hurdles for silkworms. *-vr.* 1. To be entangled among brambles and briers. 2. *(Met.)* To be involved in difficulties. 5. To squabble, to wrangle.

enzima [en-thee'-mah], *f.* Enzyme.

enzimático, ca [en-the-mah'-te-co, cah], *a.* Enzymic, enzymatic.

enzimología [en-the-mo-lo-hee'-ah], *f.* Enzymology.

enzootía [en-thoo-tee'-ah], *f.* Epizootic, a contagious disease among cattle.

enzurdecer [en-thoor-day-therr'], *vn.* To become left-handed.

enzurronar [en-thoor-ro-nar'], *va.* 1. To put in a bag. 2. *(Met.)* To inclose one thing in another.

eñe [ay'nyay], *f.* Spanish name of the letter Ñ.

eoceno, na [ay-o-thay'-no, nah], *a. (Geol.)* Eocene.

eólico [ay-o'le-co], *a.* æolian, æolic. 2. The æolian dialect.

eolio, lia [ay-o'-leo, ah], *a.* æolian, Eolian; used of the dialect.

eolipilo [ay-o-le-pee'-lo], *m.* A ventilator for cleaning chimneys.

eón [ay-on´], *m. (Geol.)* Eon.

epacta [ay-pahc'-tah], *f.* 1. Epact, the excess of the solar year over twelve lunar months. 2. V. AÑALEJO

epactilla [ay-pac-teel'-lyah], *f.* A small calendar for the performance of divine service, which is published every year.

epagómeno [ay-pa-go'-may-no], *a.* Epagomenal, intercalary: said of the five days which the Egyptians and Chaldeans added to the 360 of the vague year, after the establishment of the lunar cycle.

epéntesis [ay-pen'-tay-sis], *f. (Gram.)* Epenthesis.

eperlano [ay-per-lah'-no], *m. (Zool.)* Smelt, a small sea-fish.

epi, a Greek preposition signifying on, used as a prefix.

épicamente [ay-pe'-cah-rah-men-tay], *adv.* In an epic or heroic manner.

epicarpo [ay-pe-car'-po], *m.* Epicarp, a membrane which covers the pericarp.

epicedio [ay-pe-thay'-de-o], *m.* Epicedium, elegy, eulogy of the dead.

epiceno, na [ay-pe-thay'-no, nah], *a.* Epicene, belonging to both genders.

epicentro [ay-pe-then'-tro], *m.* Epicenter.

epiciclo [ay-pe-thee'-clo], *m.* Epicycle, a small circle, whose center is supposed to be upon the circumference of another.

epicicloide [ay-pe-the-clo'-e-day], *f. (Goons.)* Epicycloid.

épico, ca [ay'-pe-co, cah], *a.* Epic, narrative, containing narrations. **Poema épico**, epic, epopee, an epic poem.

epicúreo, rea [ay-pe-coo'-ra-yo, ah], *a.* Epicurean.

epidemia [ay-pe-day'-me-ah], *f.* 1. An epidemic disease. 2. A multitude of ills or misfortunes.

epidémico, ca [ay-pe-day'-me-co, cah], *a.* Epidemical, epidemic.

epidendro [ay-pe-den'-dro], *m.* Epidendrum, a large genus of tropical American epiphytic orchids often cultivated for their beautiful flowers.

epidérmico, ca [ay-pe-derr'-me-co, cah], *a.* Epidermic, belonging to the outer covering.

epidermis [ay-pe-derr'-mis], *f.* Epidermis, the scarf-skin, the cuticle.

epidídimo [ay-pe-dee'-de-mo], *m. (Anat.)* Epididymis.

epifanía [ay-pe-fah-nee'-ah], *f.* Epiphany.

epifaringe [ay-pe-fah-reen'-hay], *f.* Epipharynx, a little valve which closes the pharynx of certain hymenoptera.

epifillo, lla [ay-pe-feel'-lyo, lyah], *a. (Bot.)* Budding and growing upon the surface of leaves.

epifilospermo, ma [ay-pe-fe-los-perr'-mo, mah], *a. (Bot.)* Epiphyllospermous.

epífisis [ay-pee'-fe-sis], *f. (Anat.)* Epiphysis.

epífito, ta [ay-pee'-fe'-to, tah], *a.* Epiphytal, growing upon other plants, but not extracting nutriment from them.

epifonema [ay-pe-fo-nay'-ma], *f. (Rhet.)* Epiphonema, an exclamation made after recounting something.

epífora [ay-pee'-fo-rah], *f.* 1. Epiphora, watering of the eye. 2. *(Rhet.)* A kind of amplification.

epigástrico, ca [ay-pe-gahs'-tre-co, cah], *a.* Epigastric.

epiglotis [ay-pe-glo'-tis], *f.* Epiglottis, a cartilage of the larynx.

epígrafe [ay-pee'-grah-fay], *m.* Epigraph, title (encabezamiento), inscription (inscripción); motto (lema).

epigrama [ay-pe-grah'-mah], *m. & f.* Epigram.

epigramatario, ria, or **epigramático, ca** [ay-pe-grah-mah-tah'-re-o, ah], *a.* Epigrammatic.

epigramático, epigramatista, epigramista [ay-pe-grah-mah'-te-co, ay-pe-grah-mah-tees'-tah], *m.* Epigrammatist.

epilepsia [ay-pe-lep'-se-ah], *f.* Epilepsy.

epiléptico, ca [ay-pe-lep'-te-co, cah], *a.* Epileptic epileptical.

epilogación [ay-pe-lo-gah-the-on'], *f. V.* EPÍLOGO.

epilogal [ay-pe-lo-gahl'], *a.* Epilogistic, compendious, summary.

epilogar [ay-pe-lo-gar'], *va.* To recapitulate, to sum up.

epilogismo [ay-pe-lo-hees'-mo], *m.* Epilogism, calculation, computation.

epílogo [ay-pee'-lo-go], *m.* 1. A conclusion or close of a speech. 2. Epilogue. 3. Recapitulation, a brief or compendious statement.

epipedometría [ay-pe-pay-do-may-tree'-ah], *f.* Epipedometry, the mensuration of figures standing on the same base.

epiqueya [ay-pe-kay'-yah], *f.* A mild and prudent interpretation of the law.

episcopado [ay-pis-co-pah'-do], *m.* Episcopacy; episcopate (período), bishopric (oficio), the dignity of a bishop.

episcopal [ay-pis-co-pahl'], *a.* Episcopal, relating to bishops.

episódico, ca [ay-pe-so'-de-co, cah], *a.* Episodic, episodical.

episodio [ay-pe-so'-de-o], *m.* 1. Episode, an incidental narrative or digression in a poem. 2. *V.* DIGRESIÓN.

epispástico, ca [ay-pis-pahs'-te-co, cah], *a.* Epispastic, blistering, reddening the skin.

epispermo [ay-pis-perr'-mo], *m.* Episperm, an envelope which inwraps the seed.

epistaxis [ay-pis-tak'-sis], *f.* Epistaxis, nose-bleed.

epistemología [ay-pis-tay-mo-lo-hee'-ah], *f.* Epistemology.

epistilo [ay-pis-tee'-lo], *m. (Arch.)* Epistyle.

epístola [ay-pees'-to-lah], *f.* 1. Epistle, letter. 2. Epistle, a part of the mass. **Epístola** or **orden de epístola**, subdeaconship, subdeaconry.

epistolar [ay-pis-to-lar'], *a.* Epistolary.

epistolario [ay-pis-to-lah'-re-o], *m.* 1. Collection of epistles read or sung at the mass. 2. Volume of letters.

epistolero [ay-pis-to-lay'-ro], *m.* Epistler, the subdeacon or any priest who sings the epistle.

epitafio [ay-pe-tah'-fe-o], *m.* Epitaph, inscription on a tomb.

epitalamio [ay-pe-tah-lah'lmelo], *m.* Epithalamium, a nuptial song; a compliment upon marriage.

epítasis [aylpee'ltahlsis], *f.* Epitasis the most complex part of the plot of a play.

epitelio [aylpeltay'llelo], *m.* Epithelium, the epidermis of mucous membranes.

epítema, or **epítima** [ay-pee'-te-mah], *f.* Epithem, a lotion.

epíteto [ay-pee'-tay-to], *m.* Epithet.

epitimar [ay-pe-te-mar'], *va.* To apply an epithem.

epítimo [ay-pee'-te-mo], *m. (Bot.)* Lesser dodder.

epitomar [ay-pe-to-mar'], *va.* To epitomize, to abstract, to contract into a narrow space.

epítome [ay-pee'-to-may], *m.* Epitome, abridgment, extract, summary, compend or compendium.

epizoario, a [ay-pe-tho-ah'-re-o, ah], *a. (Zool.)* Epizoic, epizoan, parasitic on the body of other animals, like lice.

epizóico, ca [ay-pe-tho'-eco, cah], *a.* 1. *V.* EPIZOARIO. 2. *(Geol.)* Denoting upper primitive lands which contain remain of organized bodies.

epizootia [ay-pe-tho-o'-te-ah], *f. (Vet.)* Epizooty, epidemic influenza.

época [ay'-po-cah], *f.* 1. Epoch. 2. Date of an event. **En la época de Carlos III**, in Charles III´s time. **En aquella época**, at that time. **Coche de época**, vintage car. **Todos tenemos épocas así**, we all go through spells like that.

épodo [ay'-po-do], *m.* Epode.

epopeya [ay-po-pay'-yah], *f.* Epopee, an epic poem.

epsomita [ep-so-mee'-tah], *f.* Epsom salts.

epulia, epúlida [ay-poo'-le-ah, ay-poo´-le-dah], *f.* Epulis, a tumor of the gums.

epulón [ay-poo-lon'], *m.* An epicure or great eater.

equeno [ay-kay'-no], *m.* A rectangular earthen trough, for pouring melted metal into a mould, used in casting statues.

equiángulo, la [ay-ke-ahn'-goo-lo, lah], *a. (Geom.)* Equiangular.

equiáxeo, a [ay-kee-ak'-say-o, ah], *a.* Equiaxe, having equal axes.

equidad [ay-ke-dahd'], *f.* 1. Equity, equitableness, right, honesty. 2. Equity, impartiality, justice. 3. Conscionableness; conscientiousness. 4. Moderation in the execution of laws, or in the price of things bought or sold (precio)

equidistancia [ay-ke-dis-tahn'-the-ah], *f.* Equidistance.

equidastante [ay-ke-dis-tahn'-tay], *pa.* Equidistant.

equidistar [ay-ke-dis-tar'], *vn.* To be equidistant.

equidna [ay-keed'-nah], *m.* Echidna, the porcupine ant-eater.

equidnita [ay-keed-nee'-tah], *f.* A kind of agate with spots like those of the viper.

equilateral [ay-ke-lah-tay-rahl'], *a. V.* EQUILÁTERO.

equilátero, ra [ay-ke-lah'-tay-ro, rah], *a.* Equilateral.

equilibrado, da [ay-ke-le-brah'-do, dah], *a.* 1. Balanced. 2. Sensible, fair, just, **Dieta equilibrada**, balanced diet.

equilibrar [ay-ke-le-brar'], *va.* 1. To equilibrate, to balance in a scale. 2. *(Met.)* To balance equally. 3. To counterpoise, to counterbalance.

equilibre [ay-ke-lee'-bray], *a.* Balanced, equilibrious.

equilibrio [ay-ke-lee'-bre-o], *m.* Equilibrium, equilibrity, equipoise (social), equality of weight, counterpoise, counterbalance, equilibration. **Perder el equilibrio**, to lose one´s balance. **Equilibrio político**, balance of power.

equilibrista [ay-ke-le-brees'-tah], *m.* 1. Balancer, tight-rope walker. 2. Turn-coat, one who changes political opinions often.

equimosis [ay-ke-mo'-sis], *m. (Med.)* Ecchymosis, subcutaneous effusion of blood, caused by a blow.

equinita [ay-ke-nee'-tah], *f.* Sea-urchin, sea-hedgehog, echinus.

equino, na [ay-kee'-no, nah], *a. (Poet.)* Belonging to a horse, equine.

equino [ay-kee'-no], *m.* 1. *(Zool.)* Echinus, a shellfish set with prickles. 2. *(Arch.)* Echinus, an ornament.

equinoccial [ay-ke-noc-the-ahl'], *a.* Equinoctial. **Línea equinoccial**, the equinoctial line.

equinoccio [ay-ke-noc'-the-o], *m.* The equinox. **Equinoccio otoñal**, autumnal equinox.

equinodermo, ma [ay-ke-no-derr'-mo, mah] *a.* Echinodermatous.

equipaje [ay-ke-pah'-hay], *m.* 1. Luggage, baggage. **Equipaje de mano**, hand luggage. **Facturar el equipaje**, to register one's luggage. 2. *(Naut.)* The crew (tripulación). 3. *(Mil.)* Baggage train, supply wagons. 4. Storehouse. 5. Equipment (avíos).

equipamento [ay-ke-pah-men'-to], *m. (Naut.)* Fitting out, accoutrement, for navigation and military operations.

equipamiento [ay-ke-pah-me-ayn'-to], *m.* Equipment.

equipar [ay-ke-par'], *va.* 1. To fit out, to supply with everything necessary. 2. To equip, to furnish, to accoutre; to gird.

equiparable [ay-ke-pah-rah'-blay], *a.* Comparable; applicable.

equiparación [ay-ke-pa-rah-the-on´], *f.* Comparison, collation.

equiparar [ay-ke-pa-rar'], *va.* To compare (comparar), to match. *-vr.* **Equipararse con**, to be on a level with.

equipo [ay-kee'-po], *m.* 1. *(Mil.)* Fitting out, accoutrement, equipment (conjunto de cosas). 2. Trappings. **Equipo de alpinismo**, climbing kit. **Equipo de caza**, hunting gear. **Equipo de primeros auxilios**, first-aid kit. **Equipo de reparaciones**, repair kit. *(Ferro.)* **Equipo rodante**, rolling stock. 3. Team (personas); side. **Equipo de fútbol**, football team. 4. *(Comput.)* **Equipo interferente**, infringing equipment. **Equipo para copias de seguridad**, backup equipment.

equipolencia [ay-ke-po-len'-the-ah], *f.* Equipollence, equality of force or power.

equipolente [ay-ke-po-len'-tay], *a.* Equivalent, equipollent.

equiponderación, or **equiponderancia** [ay-ke-pon-day-rahn'-the-ah], *f.* Equality of weight, balance.

equiponderante [ay-ke-pon-day-rahn'-tay], *pa. & a.* Equiponderating; equiponderant.

equiponderar [ay-ke-pon-day-rar'], *vn.* To equiponderate.

equis [ay'-kis], *f.* Spanish name of the letter X. **Estar hecho una equis**, to be intoxicated and staggering. **Tenía que hacer equis cosas**, I had to do any amount of things.

equitación [ay-ke-tah-the-on'], *f.* Horsemanship (arte): equitation.

equitativamente [ay-ke-tah-te-vah-men'-tay], *adv.* Equitably.

equitativo, va [ay-ke-tah-tee'-vo, vah], *a.* 1. Equitable (juicio justo). 2. Just, honorable. **A precio muy equitativo**, very cheap.

equivalencia [ay-ke-vah-len'-the-ah], *f.* Compensation; equivalence.

equivalente [ay-ke-vah-len'-tay], *a.* 1. Equivalent. 2. Compensatory, compensative.

equivaler [ay-ke-vah-lerr'], *vn.* 1. To be of equal value and price. 2. To equiponderate, to be equal to. *(Yo equivalgo, yo equivalga; equivaliera, equivaliese, equivaliere; from Equivaler. V.* VALER.)

equivocación [ay-ke-vo-cah-the-on'], *f.* 1. Mistake (error), misconception, error, misapprehension, misunderstanding (malentendido), oversight (olvido). 2. Blunder, hallucination.

equivocadamente [ay-ke-vo-cah'-dah-men-tay], *adv.* Mistakenly, by mistake.

equivocado, da [ay-ke-vo-cah'-do, dah], *a. & pp.* of EQUIVOCAR. Mistaken. **Estás equivocado**, you're mistaken.

equívocamente [ay-kee'-vo-cah-men-tay], *adv.* Ambiguously, equivocally.

equivocar [ay-ke-vo-car'], *va.* To mistake, to take one thing for another; to conceive wrong. **Equivocar el camino**, to take the wrong road. *-vr.* To mistake, to be mistaken, to make a mistake. **Pero se equivocó**, but he was wrong.

equívoco, ca [ay-kee'-vo-co, cah], *a.* Equivocal, ambiguous.

equívoco [ay-kee'-vo-co], *m.* Equivocation (ambigüedad), equivoque, a quibble.

equivoquillo [ay-ke-vo-keel'-lyo], *m. dim.* A quibble, a slight cavil; a sort of pun.

era [ay'-rah], *f.* 1. Era, computation from any date or epoch. 2. Age, or long space of time. **Era atómica**, atomic age. **Era cristiana**, Christian era. 3. Thrashing-floor. 4. Bed or plot in a garden, sown with salad-seeds, etc.

eradicación [ay-rah-de-cah-the-on'], *f.* Eradication, thorough cure.

eradicativo, va [ay-rah-de-cah-tee'-vo, vah], *a.* Eradicative, radically curative.

eraje [ay-rah'-hay], *m. (Prov.)* Virgin honey.

eral [ay-rahl'], *m.* A two-year-old ox.

erar [ay-rar'], *va.* To lay out ground for growing garden-stuff.

erario [ay-rah'-re-o], *m.* Exchequer public treasury.

erección [ay-rec-the-on'], *f.* 1. Foundation, erection, establishment. 2. Erection, erectness, elevation.

eréctil [ay-rayk'-teel], *a.* Erectile, capable of erection.

erectilidad [ay-rec-te-le-dahd'], *f.* Erectility, power of erection.

erector, ra [ay-rec-tor', rah], *m. & f.* Erecter, founder.

eremita [ay-ray-mee'-tah], *m. V.* ERMITAÑO.

eremítico, ca [ay-ray-mee'-te-co, cah], *a.* Hermitical, eremitical, solitary.

eretismo [ay-ray-tees'-mo], *m.* Erethism, abnormal excitability.

ergio [er'-he-o], *m. (Phys.)* Erg.

ergotear [er-go-tay-ar'], *vn. (coll.)* To argue, to debate without reason.

ergoteo [er-go-tay'-o], *m. (coll.)* Sophistry, debate on trifling things.

erguido, da [er-gee'-do, dah], *a.* 1. Erect, straight. 2. Swelled with pride.

erguir [er-geer'], *va.* To erect, to raise up straight (enderezar). *(Fig.)* **Erguir la cabeza**, to hold one's head high. *-vr.* To be elated or puffed up with pride.

erial, eriazo, za [ay-reahl´, ay-re-ah'-tho, thah], *a.* Unploughed, untilled, uncultivated: it is commonly used as a substantive to express a piece of uncultivated ground.

erica [ay-ree´-cah], *f. (Bot.)* Heath, heather.

ericáceo, cea [ay-re-cah'-thay-o, ah], *a.* Ericaceous of the heath family.

ericera [ay-re-thay'-rah], *f. (Prov.)* Kind of hut without a roof.

erigeron [ay-re-hay'-ron], *m. (Bot.)* Erigeron.

erigir [ay-re-heer'], *va.* 1. To erect, to raise, to build. 2. To erect, to establish anew.

eringe [ay-reen'-hay], *f. (Bot.) V.* ERINGIO.

eringio [ay-reen'-he-o], *m. (Bot.)* Field eringo.

erío, ría [ay-ree'-o, ah], *a.* Unploughed, untilled. *V.* ERIAL.

erísimo [ay-ree'-se-mo], *m. (Bot.)* Hedgemustard.

erisipela [ay-re-se-pay'-lah], *f. (Med.)* Erysipelas, a disease.

erisipelar [ay-re-se-pay-lar'], *va.* To cause erysipelas.

erisipelatoso, sa [ay-re-se-pay-lah-to´-so, sah], *a. (Med.)* Erysipelatous, belonging to erysipelas.

eristalo [ay-ris-tah'-lo], *m.* The dronefly, eristalis; much resembling a drone-bee in appearance.

eritema [ay-re-tay'-mah], *f. (Med.)* Erythema, congestion of the skin.

eritematoso, sa [ay-re-tay-ma-to'-so, sah], *a*. Erythematous, relating to or characterized by erythema.

eritreo, trea [ay-ree-tray'-o, ah], *a*. *(Poet.)* Erythraean, belonging to the Red Sea.

erizado da [ay-re-thah'-do, dah], *a*. Covered with bristles. -*pp*. of ERIZAR.

erizamiento [ay-re-thah-me-en'-to], *m*. Act of setting on end, as the hair.

erizar [ay-re-thar'], *va*. To set on end; to bristle (pelo). **El gato erizó el pelo**, the cat bristled. -*vr*. 1. To stand on end (pelo). 2. To bristle, to stand erect.

erizo [ay-ree'-tho], *m*. 1. Hedgehog. 2. Sea-hedgehog, or urchin. 3. Echinus, the prickly husk of a chestnut and other fruits. 4. *(Mech.)* In weaving, an urchin, a carding roller; a sprocket wheel, a rag wheel, spar-toothed wheel.

ermita [er-mee'-tah], *f*. Hermitage.

ermitaña [er-me-tah'-nyah], *f*. Hermitess.

ermitaño [er-me-tha'-nyo], *m*. Hermit, one who takes care of a hermitage.

ermitorio [er-me-to're-o], *m*. V. EREMITORIO.

ermunia [er-moo'-ne-ah], *f*. A certain kind of earth which needs constant moisture in order to be productive.

ermunio [er-moo'-ne-o], *m*. Name formerly given to persons exempted from every kind of tribute and service.

erogar [ay-ro-gar'], *va*. To distribute (bienes), to divide, to apportion, to spend in fees or judicial proceedings.

erogatorio [ay-ro-gah-to'-re-o], *m*. Pipe through which liquor is drawn.

erosión [ay-ro-se-on'], *f*. Erosion, corosion.

erosionar [ay-ro-se-o-nar'], *va*. To erode. -*vr*. To erode, to be eroded.

eróticamente [ay-ro'-te-cah-men-tay], *adv*. Erotically, in an erotic manner.

erótico, ca [ay-ro'-te-co, cah], *a*. Erotical, erotic, belonging to love (pocsía); voluptuous, sensual.

erótilo [ay-ro'-te-lo], *m*. A beetle of Mexico and South America.

erótema [ay-ro'-tay-mah], *f*. *(Rhet.)* Interrogation.

erotismo [ay-ro-tees'-mo], *m*. 1. A violent love. 2. Sensuality.

erotomanía [ay-ro-to-mah-nee'-ah], *f*. Erotomania, love-madness.

erpetología [er-pay-to-lo-hee'-ah], *f*. Herpetology, that branch of zoology which treats of reptiles.

errabundo, da [er-rah boon' do, dah], *a*. Wandering, strolling about.

errada [er-rah'-dah], *f*. A miss, in billiards.

erradamente [er-rah-da-men'-tay], *adv*. Erroneously, falsely, faultily, mistakenly, erratically.

erradicación [er-rah-de-ca-the-on'], *f*. Eradication, extirpation.

erradicar [er-rah-de-car'], *va*. To eradicate, to pull up by the roots.

erradizo, za [er-rah-dee'-tho, thah], *a*. Wandering to and fro.

errado, da [ar-rah'-do], *a*. & *pp*. of ERRAR. Mistaken, erring, erroneous.

erraj [er-rah'], *m*. Fine coal made from the stones of olives.

errante [er-rahn'-tay], *pa*. & *a*. Errant, erring, roving, wandering, rambling; excursive, nomadic.

errar [er-rar'], *va*. 1. To err, to commit errors. 2. To misjudge, to make mistakes, to mistake. 3. To offend anyone. -*vn*. To wander about without knowing one's way (vagar). **Errar el camino**, to miss the right way. **Errar el golpe**, to miss a blow. *(Met.)* To miss one's aim.

errata [er-rah'-tah], *f*. Error in writing or printing; erratum. **Erratas** or **fe de erratas**, errata, the faults of the printer.

errático, ca [er-rah'-te-co, cah], *m*. Wandering, vagabond, vagrant, erratic or erratical.

errátil [er-rah'-teel], *a*. *(coll.)* Wavering, not firm or steady.

erre [er'-ray], *f*. The Spanish name of the letter R. **Erre que erre**, pertinaciously, obstinately.

erróneamente [er-ro'-nay-ah-men-tay], *adv*. Erroneously, mistakenly, faultily, falsely.

erróneo, nea [er-ro'-nay-o, ah], *a*. Erroneous, mistaken, not conformable to truth (doctrinas y opiniones).

erronía [er-ro-ne'-ah], *f*. *(coll.)* Opposition, hatred.

error [er-ror'], *m*. 1. Error, stale, involuntary deviation from truth, misapprehension, misbelief, misconception, hallucination, fallacy (de teoría) 2. Mispersuasion, misguidance. 3. Deceit, falsity, illusion, fault (defecto). 4. Deficiency, fault, defect. **Error de copia**, clerical error. **Error de imprenta**, writing error. **Por error**, by mistake. **Caer en un error**, to fall into error. **Error de paridad**, *(Inform.)* parity error. **Error intencionado**, *(Inform.)* willful misconduct.

erubescencia [ay-roo-bes-then'-the-ah], *f*. Erubescence, the act of blushing. **eructación** [ay-rooc-tah-the-on'], *f*. Eructation, belching.

eructar [ay-rooc-tar'], *vn*. To belch, to eructate.

eructo [ay-rooc'-to], *m*. Belching, eructation.

erudición [ay-roo-de-the-on'], *f*. Erudition, learning, knowledge, letters.

eruditamente [ay-roo-de'-tah-men-tay], *adv*. Learnedly.

erudito, ta [ay-roo-dee'-to, tah], *a*. Erudite, learned, lettered.

eruginoso sa [ay-roo-he-no'-so, sah], *a*. That which is thick, coarse, and knotty.

erupción [ay-roop-the-on'], *f*. Eruption, outbreak, bursting forth. **Estar en erupción**, to be erupting.

eruptivo, va [ay-roop-tee'-vo, vah], *a*. Eruptive.

erutación [ay-roo-tah-the-on'], *f*. Eructation, belching.

erutar [ay-roo-tar'], *vn*. V. ERUCTAR.

eruto [ay-roo'-to], *m*. V. ERUCTO.

ervato [er-vah'-to], *m*. *(Bot.)* Sea sulphur-wort, hog's-fennel.

ervellada [er-vel-lyah'-da], *f*. *(Bot.)* Bean-trefoil.

ésa [ay'-sah], A demonstrative pronoun of the feminine gender. That, that one.

esa [ay-sah], Demonstrative adjective, feminine. That.

esbatimentar [es-bah-te-men-tar'], *va*. *(Art.)* To delineate a shadow. -*vn*. To cast the shadow of one body on another.

esbatimento [es-bah-te-men'-to], *m*. Shade in a picture.

esebeltez [es-bel-teth'], *f*. Slenderness, gracefulness.

esbelto, ta [es-bel'-to, tah], *a*. Slender, svelte, graceful.

esbirro [es-bir'-ro], *m*. Bailiff (alguacil), apparitor; a petty officer of courts of justice, a myrmidon, henchman (ayudante), killer (sicario).

esbozar [es-bo-thar'], *va*. To outline, to sketch, to make a plan.

esbozo [es-bo'-tho], *m*. *(Pict.)* Sketch, outline; a rough draught.

esca [ays'-cah], *f*. 1. Food, nourishment. 2. Bait for hunting or fishing.

escabechar [es-cah-bay-char'], *va*. To souse, to steep in pickle, to pickle.

escabeche [es-cah-bay'-chay], *m*. Souse pickle (de escabechar); pickled fish (pescado).

escabel [es-cah-bel'], *m*. 1. Foot-stool; small seat. 2. A small seat of boards without back.

escabelillo [es cah-bay-leel'-lyo], *m*. *dim*. A small foot-stool.

escabelón [es-cah-be-lone'], *m*. *(Arch.)* A kind of pedestal.

escabiosa [es-cah-be-o'-sah], *f*. *(Bot.)* Field-scabious.

escabioso, sa [es-cah-be-o'-so, sah], *a*. *(Med.)* Scabious; relating to scabies, or the itch.

escabro [es-cah'-bro], *m*. 1. A kind of scab, itch, or mange in sheep. 2. The large amphibious crab. 3. A roughness, like mange, which grows upon the bark of trees and vines.

escabrosamente [es-cah-bro-sah-men'-tay], *adv*. Roughly, ruggedly.

escabrosidad [es-cah-bro-se-dahd], *f*. 1. Roughness, unevenness. 2. Difficulty, hardness. 3. Sharpness.

escabroso, sa [es-cah-bro'-so, sah], *a*. 1. Rough, uneven (terreno). 2. Very difficult, thorny (problema). 3. Scabrous.

escabullimiento [es-cah-bool-lyee-me-en'-to], *m*. Evasion, slipping away, act of escaping.

escabullirse [es-cah-bool-lyeer'-say], *vr*. To escape, to evade; to slip away, to slip through one's hands.

escacado, da [es-cah-cah'-do, dah], *a. (Her.)* Checkered, variegated, like a chess-board.

escachar [es-cah-char'], *va. (Prov.)* To smash, to squash. *-vr.* To prick.

escacharrar [es-cah-char-rar'], *va.* 1. To break, to smash. 2. *(Fig.)* To ruin, to wreck

escachifollar [es-cah-che-fol-lyar'], *va.* To humiliate.

escafandra, *f.* **escafandro,** *m.* [es-cah-fahn'-drah, es-cah-fahn'-dro], Diving suit. **Escafandra autónoma,** scuba. **Escafandra espacial,** space suit. **Escafandra rígida,** rigid diving suit.

escafandrero [es-cah-fan-dray'-ro], *m.* Deep-sea diver.

escafóideo, dea [es-cah-fo´-day´-o, ah], *m.* Scaphoid, skiff-like.

escala [es-cah-lah], *f.* 1. Ladder, scale. 2. Scale, a figure subdivided by lines to measure proportions. 3. Scale, the series of harmonic or musical proportions. 4. Scale, regular graduation. 5. Any port, bay, or road for stripe to ride in, in order to get provisions, etc (parada). **Modelo a escala,** scale model. **A escala nacional,** on a national scale. **Un plan en gran escala,** a large-scale plan. **Vuelo sin escalas,** non-stop flight.

escalada [es-cah-lah'-dah], *f.* 1. Escalade (con escalera de mano), scaling (pared, acantilado). **Escalada a escala vista,** a daylight escalade. **Escalada de precios,** price escalade. 2. Climb (alpinismo) **Escalada en rocas,** rock climbing.

escalado, da [es-cah-lah´-do, dah], *a.* Applied to fish cut open to be salted or cured.*-pp.* of ESCALAR.

escalador, ra [es-cah-lah-dor'], *m & f.* Climber, person who scales walls (alpinista).

escalafón [es-cah-lah-fon´], *m.* 1. Seniority scale, grade scale (de personas). 2. Company roster.

escalamera [es-cah—lah-may´-rah], *f.* Bar rowlock.

escalamiento [es-cah-lah-me-en'-to], *m.* Act of scaling walls.

escálamo [es-cah'-lah-mo], *m. (Naut.)* Thole or thowl, or tholepin; row-lock.

escalamotes [es-cah-lah-mo´-tes], *m. pl. (Naut.)* Timber-heads, kevelheads.

escalante [es-cah-lahn'-tay], *pa.* Scaling, climbing.

escalar [es-cah-lar'], *va.* 1. To scale, to climb (montaña) *(Fig.)* **Escalar puestos,** to move up. 2. To burgle, to break into (casa). *-vn.* To climb; *(Fig.)* to climb the social ladder.

escaldada [es-cal-dah'-dah], *f.* A woman very abusive, loose, and lewd in her behavior.

escaldado, da [es-cal-dah'-do], *a.* Cautious, suspicious, wary.*-pp.* of ESCALDAR.

escaldar [es-cal-dar´], *va.* 1. To burn, to scald (quemar); to bathe with very hot water. 2. To make iron red-hot. *-vr.* 1. To get scalded. 2. To chafe.

escaldrantes [es-cal-drahn´-tes], *m. pl. (Naut.)* Kevels, wooden pin on which tackle and sails are put to dry.

escaldufar [es-cal-doo-far´], *va. (Prov.)* To take broth out of the pot when it is too full.

escaleno [es-cah-lay'-no], *a. (Geom.)* Scalene.

escalentamiento [es-cah-len-tah-me-en'-to], *m.* Inflammation, disease in the feet of animals.

escalera [es-cah-ley'-rah], *f.* 1. Staircase. 2. Stair (de casa). **Escalera de caracol,** a winding stair. **Escalera de incendios,** fire escape. 3. Ladder (escalera de mano). 4. Sloats of a cart.

escalera mecánica [es-cah-lay'-rah may-cah'-ne-cah], *f.* Escalator.

escalereja, escalerilla [es-cah-la-ray'-hah, es-cah-lay-reel'-lyah], *f.* 1. *(dim.)* A small ladder. 2. *(Mech.)* Rack. 3. Drenching instrument. **En escalerilla,** in degrees.

escalerón [es-cah-lay-rone'], *m. aug.* A large staircase.

escaleta [es-cah-lay'-tah], *f.* Engine for raising cannons and mortars on their carriages.

escalfado, da [es-cal-fah'-do, dah], *a.* Applied to whitewashed walls full of blisters.*-pp.* of ESCALFAR.

escalfador [es-cal-fah-dor'], *m.* 1. A barber's pan for keeping water warm. 2. Chafing-dish.

escalfar [es-cal-far'], *va.* 1. To poach eggs. 2. To warm. **Escalfar el pan,** to put bread into an oven which is too hot, and scorches it.

escalfarote [es-cal-fah-ro'-tay], *m.* A kind of wide boot lined with hay.

escalfeta [es-cal-fay'-tah], *f.* 1. Small pan, used to hold live coals. 2. Chafing-dish. *V.* ESCALFADOR. 3. Water-dish or water-plate, for keeping meat hot.

escalimarse [es-cah-le-mar'-say], *m. (Naut.)* To be split or worked out of the seams of a ship (estopa).

escalinata [es-cah-le-nah'-tah], *f.* A stone staircase in front of an edifice.

escalio [es-cah'-le-o], *m.* Land abandoned for tillage.

escalmo [es-cahl'-mo], *m. V.* ESCÁLAMO.

escalofriado, da [es-cah-lo-fre-ah'-do, dah] *a.* Shivering.

escalofriante [es-cah-lo-fre-ahn'-tay], *a.* Hair-raising, chilling, frightening.

escalofrío [es-cah-lo-free'-o], *m.* Indisposition attended with shivering; cold stage of a fever.

escalón [es-cah-lo-ne´], *m.* 1. Step of a stair (peldaño). 2. Degree of dignity. 3. *(Mil.)* Echelon.

escalonar [es-cah-lo-nar´], *va.* 1. *(Mil.)* To echelon. 2. To scale, to place at intervals. 3. To stagger (horas de trabajo, etc.)

escalope [es-cah-lo'-pay], *m. (Culin.)* Escalope. **Escalope de ternera,** escalope of veal.

escalpelo [es-cal-pay'-lo], *m. (Med.)* Scalpel, a surgeon's instrument.

escalplo [es-cahl'-plo], *m.* Currier's knife.

escaluña [es-cah-loo'-nyah], *f. (Bot.)* Eschalot, shallot, scallion.

escama [es-cah'-mah], *f.* 1. Scale, horny plate, forming the coat of fishes (pez) 2. Scale, something exfoliated, a thin lamina. 3. A small scaly piece, many of which, lapping one over another form a coat of mail. 4. *(Met.)* Resentment, grudge, deep sense of injury. 5. *(Bot.)* Scale, an abortive, rudimentary leaf.

escamada [es-cah-mah'-dah], *f.* Embroidery in figure of scales.

escamado [es-cah-mah'-o], *m.* Work wrought with the figure of scales.

escamado, da [es-cah-mah'-do, dah], *a. & pp.* of ESCAMAR. Tutored by experience.

escamdura [es-cah-mah-doo'-ra], *f.* Act of embroidering like scales.

escamar [es-cah-mar'], *va.* 1. To scale fish. 2. *(Met.)* To offend, to irritate, to molest. **Eso me escama,** that makes me suspicious. *-vn.* To embroider scale or shell fashion. *-vr.* To be tutored by painful experience, to resent, to take ill. **Y luego se escamó,** and after that he was on his guard.

escambronal [es-cam-bro-nahl'], *m.* Plantation of buckthorns.

escamel [es-cah-mel'], *m.* Instrument used by sword-makers; long arm of an anvil on which the sword is laid to beat it out.

escamilla, ita [es-cah-meel'-lyah, ee'-tah], *f. dim.* A little scale.

escamochear [es-cah-mo-chay-ar'], *vn. (Prov.)* V. PAVORDEAR.

escamocho [es-cah-mo'-cho], *m.* 1. Broken victuals, leavings. 2. *(Prov.)* A rickety and languid person.

escamonda [es-cah-mon'dah], *f.* The act of pruning trees.

escamondadura [es-cah-mon-dah-doo'-rah], *f.* Useless branches of trees.

escamondar [es-cah-mon-dar'], *va.* 1. To prune or clear trees of noxious excrescences. 2. To clean, to cleanse.

escamondo [es-cah-mon'-do], *m.* Clearing trees of useless branches.

escamonea [es-cah-mo-nay´-a], *f. (Bot.)* Scammony.

escamoneado, da [es-cah-mo-nay-ah'-do, dah], *a.* Relating to scammony.*-pp.* of ESCAMONEARSE.

escamonearse [es-cah-mo-nay-ar'-say], *vr. (coll.)* To resent, to take ill, to be offended.

escamoso, sa [es-cah-mo'-so, sah], *a.* Scaly (pez), ostraceous, squamous.

escamotar [es'-cah-mo-tar'], *va.* In jugglery, to palm, to make a thing disappear from among the hands.

escamoteador, ra [es-cah-mo-tay-ah-dor', rah], *m.* & *f.* A juggler, prestidigitateur.

escamotear [es-cah-mo-tay-ar'], *va.* V. ESCAMOTAR.

escamoteo [es-cah-mo-tay'-o], *m.* Jugglery, sleight of hand (destreza).

escampada [es-cam-pah'-dah], *f.* Stampede.

escampado, da [es-cam-pah'-do, dah], *a.* V. DESCAMPADO. *-pp.* of ESCAMPAR.

escampar [es-cam-par'], *vn.* 1. To cease raining. 2. To leave off working. *-va.* To clean or clear out a place.

escampavía [es-cam-pa-vee'-ah], *f.* (Naut.) A light craft.

escamudo, da [es-cah-moo'-do, dah], *a.* V. ESCAMOSO.

escamujar [es-cah-moo-har'], *va.* To prune olive trees, to lop off the superfluous branches.

escamujo [es-cah-moo'-ho], *m.* 1. A lopped-off branch of an olive tree. 2. Time of pruning olive trees.

escanciador, ra [es-can-teah-dor', rah], *m.* & *f.* Cup bearer, the person that serves wine at feasts.

escanciar [es-can-the-ar'], *va.* To pour wine, to serve wine.

escanda [es-cahn'-dah], *f.* (Bot.) Spelt-wheat.

escandalar [es-can-dah-lar'], *m.* Apartment for the compass.

escandalizador, ra [es-can-dah-le-thah-dor', rah], *m.* & *f.* One who scandalizes.

escandalizante [es-can-dah-le-thahn'-tay], *a.* Scandalous , shocking.

escandalizar [es-can-dah-le-thar'], *va.* To scandalize, to offend by a scandalous action. *-vr.* 1. To be scandalized. 2. To be irritated. 3. To be amazed, to wonder (at). **Se escandalizó ante la pintura**, he threw up his hands in horror at the picture.

escandalizativo, va [es-can-dah-le-tha-tee'-vo, vah], *a.* Scandalous.

escandallar [es-can-dal-lyar'], *va.* (Naut.) To sound.

escandallo [es-can-dahl'lyo], *m.* 1. (Naut.) Deep sea lead. 2. (Met.) Proof, trial.

escándalo [es-cahn'-dah-lo], *m.* 1. Scandal, offence given by the faults of others. 2. Admiration, astonishment (asombro). 3. Tumult, commotion (alboroto). **El escándalo del año**, the scandal of the year. **Es un escándalo cómo suben los precios**, it is scandalous the way prices are rising. **Armar un escándalo a uno**, to give someone a dressing down.

escandalosa [es-can-dah-lo'-sah], *f.* (Naut.) Gaff-sail.

escandalosamente [es-can-dah-lo'-sah-men-tay], *adv.* Scandalously, shamefully.

escandaloso, sa [es-can-dah-lo'-so, sah], *a.* 1. Scandalous, giving public offence. 2. Scandalous (vida), shameful, disgraceful. 3. Turbulent, flagrant (crimen)

escandecencia [es-can-day-then'-the-ah], *f.* 1. Candescence, the state of growing hot. 2. Heat, anger, passion. V. EXCANDECENCIA.

escandecer [es-can-day-therr'], *va.* V. EXCANDECER.

escandelar [es-can-day-lar'], *m.* (Naut.) The second cabin in a row-galley.

escandelarete [es-can-day-lah-ray-tay], *m.* (Naut.) A small cabin in a row-galley.

escandia [es-cahn'-deah], *f.* (Bot.) Cienfuegos wheat.

escandinavo, va [es-can-de-nah'-vo, vah], *a.* Scandinavian.

escáner [es-cah'-nayr], *m.* (Med.) Scanner.

escantillar [es-can-til-lyar'], *va.* To trace lines on walls, to make them of different colors.

escantillón [es-can-teel-lyon'], *m.* 1. Gauge, pattern, template, rule. 2. Angle forested by two walls. 3. (Mil.) Semi-circular modelling-board to measure the exterior diameters of pieces of artillery.

escaña [es-cah'-nyah], *f.* (Bot.) Saint Peter's corn, or one-grained wheat.

escañero [es-cah-nyay'-ro], *m.* Seat-keeper, one who takes care of seats and benches in council chambers or courts.

escañillo [es-cah-nyeel'-lyo], *m. dim.* A small bench or form with a back.

escaño [es-cah'-nyo], *m.* 1. Bench or form with a back. 2. (Naut.) Sheer-rail, which divides the quick works from the dead works. 3. (Parl.) Seat.

escañuelo [es-cah-nyoo-ay'-lo], *m.* Small bench placed at the feet.

escapada, *f.* escapamiento, *m.* [es-cah-pah'-dah]. Escape (huida), flight, escapade. **Haré la comida en una escapada**, I'll get the meal right away.

escapar [es-cah-par'], *va.* To liberate from danger; to slip from the memory, to ride hard (caballo). *-vn.* & *vr.* To escape (persona), to flee, to get out of danger, to avoid punishment, to flee away or to get away off, to make off, to make one's escape. **Escapar de la cárcel**, to escape from prison. **Escaparse con algo**, to make off with something. **Escaparse por un pelo, to have a narrow escape.**

escaparate [es-cah-pa-rah'-tay], *m.* 1. Press, case, cupboard (vitrina). 2. Shop window (de tienda).

escaparatico [es-cah-pa-rah-tee'-co], *m. dim.* A little cupboard.

escaparatista [es-cah-pa-rah-tees'-tah], *m* & *f.* Window dresser.

escapatoria [es-cah-pa-to'-re-ah], *f.* 1. Escape, flying, flight. 2. Escape, excuse, evasion, subterfuge, loophole.

escape [es-cah'-pay], *m.* 1. Escape, flight, escaping (huida). 2. Flying, flight. 3. Escape, subterfuge, evasion. 3. Leak, leakage (de gas) **A todo escape**, at full speed. 4. Leak. 5. Exhaust valve, exhaust. **Tubo de escape**, exhaust pipe.

escapo [es-cah'-po], *m.* 1. (Arch.) Shaft of a column without base or capital. 2. (Bot.) Scape, a stem rising from the root, and bearing nothing but flowers.

escápula [es-cah'-poo-lah], *f.* (Anat.) Scapula, shoulder blade.

escapular [es-cah-poo-lar'], *va.* (Naut.) To double or clear a cape. *-a.* Scapular, relating to the shoulder blade.

escapulario [es-cah-poo-lah'-re-o], *m.* 1. Scapulary, a part of the habit of various religious orders. 2. Scapular. 3. (Med.) Shoulder-strap.

escaque [es-cah'-kay], *m.* 1. Any of the squares of a chess-board. 2. (Her.) Any of the squares of a coat of arms. *-pl.* 1. Checker work of a draught or chessboard. 2. Any work resembling the checkers of a draught or chess-board. 3. The game of chess.

escaqueado, da [es-cah-kay-ah'-do, dah], *a.* Checkered, variegated with alternate colors.*-pp.* of ESCAQUEAR.

escara [es-cah'-rah], *f.* (Med.) 1. The scurf or crust of a sore. 2. Eschar, a hard crust or scar made by caustics.

escarabajear [es-cah-rah-bah-ha-yar'], *vn.* 1. To crawl to and fro like insects. 2. To scrawl, to scribble (escribir mal). 3. (coll.) To give pain, to disquiet, to harass.

escarabajo [es-cah-rah-bah'-ho], *m.* 1. (Ent.) The common black beetle, tumble bug, dung beetle. 2. Nickname given to a thick, short, ill-shaped person (enano). 3. Flaw (en un tejido); fault in the bore (de un cañón).

escarabídeo, dea [es-cah-rah-bee'-day-o, ah], *a.* Scarabaeid, like a tumble bug.

escarafullar [es-cah-rah-fool-lyar'], *vn.* To deceive, to gloss over.

escaramucear [es-cah-rah-moo-thay-ar'], *vn.* To skirmish.

escaramujo [es-cah-rah-moo'-ho], *m.* 1. (Bot.) Dog rose. 2. (Zool.) A kind of small marine snail which clings to the hull of vessels.

escaramuza [es-cah-rah-moo'-thah], *f.* 1. Skirmish, slight engagement. 2. (Met.) Skirmish, contest, dispute, quarrel, contention.

escaramuzador [es-cah-rah-moo-thah-dor'], *m.* 1. Skirmisher. 2. (Met.) Disputer.

escaramuzar [es-cah-rah-moo-thar'], *vn.* 1. To skirmish, to fight loosely. 2. *(Met.)* To dispute, to quarrel; rarely used in this sense.

escarapela [es-cah-rah-pay'-lah], *f.* 1. Dispute which terminates in blows: applied commonly to a fray among women. 2. Cockade worn in the hat.

escarapelar [es-cah-rah-pay-lar'], *vn. & vr.* 1. To dispute (discutir), to wrangle, to quarrel (mujeres). 2. *vr. (Peru. and S. A.)* To have hair stand on end; to cringe upon hearing sharp noises.

escarbadero [es-car-bah-day'-ro], *m.* Place where boars, wolves, and other animals scrape or scratch the ground.

escarbadientes [es-car-bah-deen'-tes], *m. V.* MONDADIENTES.

escarbador [es-car-bah-dor'], *m.* Scratcher, scraper.

escarbadura [es-car-bah-doo'-rah], *f.* Act and effect of scratching.

escarbajuelo [es-car-bah-hoo-ay'-lo], *m. (Ent.)* Vine-fretter.

escarbaorejas [es-car-bah-o-ray'-has], *m.* Earpick.

escarbar [es-car-bar'], *va.* 1. To scrape or scratch the earth, as fowls (tierra). 2. *(Met.)* To inquire minutely, to investigate.

escarbo [es-car'-bo], *m.* Act and effect of scraping or scratching.

escarcela [es-car-thay'-lah], *f.* 1. A large pouch fastened to the belt; sportsman's net for catching game. 2. Cuisse, armor which covers the thigh. 3. Kind of head-dress for women.

escarceo [es-car-thay'-o], *m.* Small broken waves occasioned by currents (olas). **Escarceos**, bounds and windings of spirited horses.

escarcha [es-car'-chah], *f.* 1. Hoar frost, rime. 2. The frozen watery vapors observable on windows and other articles of glass; frost work.

escarchada [es-car-chah'-dah], *f. (Bot.)* Ice plant, *fig.* marigold.

escarchado [es-car-chah'-do], *m.* 1. A kind of gold or silver twist. 2. Frosting upon cakes and confectionery.

escarchado, da [es-car-chah'-do], *a. & pp.* of ESCARCHAR. Hoary, white with frost.

escarchador [es-car-chah-dor'], *m.* Freezing tool, a device in mints for thinning the nibs of ingots so as to make them pass through the gauge plate.

escarchar [es-car-char'], *vn.* To be frozen or congealed (rocío, vapor).-*va.* 1. To dilute potter's clay with water. 2. To put frostwork, shining points, upon confections. 3. To thin nibs of ingots, in mints.

escarche [es-car'-chay], *m.* A kind of gold or silver flat wire for embroidery.

escarcho [es-car'-cho], *m. (Zool.)* Red surmullet.

escarchosa [es-car-cho'-sah], *f. (Bot.)* Ice plant, fig-marigold.

escarda [es-car'-dah], *f.* 1. Weed hook (herramienta). 2. The act of weeding cornfields.

escardadera [es-car-dah-day'-rah], *f.* 1. Woman employed to clear cornfields of weeds or noxious herbs. 2. A gardener's hoe.

escardador, ra [es-car-dah-dor', rah], *m. & f.* Weeder, a man or woman who weeds cornfields.

escardadura [es-car-dah-doo'-rah], *f.* or **escardamiento**, *m.* Weeding.

escardar [es-car-dar'], *va.* 1. To weed cornfields. 2. *(Met.)* To weed, to part good from bad; to root out vice. **Enviar a escardar**, *(coll.)* to refuse harshly.

escardillar [es-car-deel-lyar'], *va. V.* ESCARDAR.

escardillo, lla [es-car-deel'-lyo, lyah], *m. & f.* 1. Small weed hook. 2. Thistledown.

escariador [es-car-reah-dor'], *m.* Kind of punch used by coppersmiths; reamer.

escariar [es-cah-re-ar'], *va.* To ream, to widen a hole or the interior of a tube, by using the reamer.

escarificación [es-cah-re-fe-cah-the, on'], *f. (Med.)* Scarification.

escarificador [es-cah-re-fe-cah-dor'], *m. (Med.)* Scarifier, scarificator; cupping glass.

escarificar [es-cah-re-fe-car'], *va. (Surg.)* To scarify.

escarioso, sa [es-cah-re-o´-so, sah], *a. (Both.)* Scarious, like a thin scale.

escarizar [es-cah-re-thar'], *va. (Surg.)* To clean a sore by taking away the scurf or scab.

escarlador [es-car-lah-dor'], *m.* Iron instrument for polishing combs.

escarlata [es-car-lah'-tah], *f.* 1. Scarlet (color). 2. Scarlet, cloth dyed with a scarlet color. 3. Scarlet fever, scarlatina (emfermedad).

escarlatina [es-car-lah-tee'-nah], *f.* 1. *(Com.)* A red or crimson woollen fabric. 2. *(Med.)* Scarlatina, scarlet fever, a contagious eruptive fever.

escarmenador [es-car-may-nah-dor'], *m. V.* ESCARPIDOR.

escarmenar [es-car-may-nar'], *va.* 1. To comb, to pick wool, silk, etc.; to disentangle what is twisted. 2. To punish anyone by depriving him of his money. 3. To cheat.

escarmentado, da [es-car-men-tah'-do, dah], *a.* Punished (por experiencia).

escarmentar [es-car-men-tar'], *vn.* To be tutored by experience, to take warning. **Yo escarmenté y no lo volví a hacer**, I learned my lesson and never did it again. -*va.* 1. To correct severely, to inflict an exemplary punishment.

escarmiento [es-car-me-en'-to], *m.* 1. Warning, caution, lesson (aviso), punishment (castigo). 2. Fine, chastisement. **Que esto te sirva de escarmiento**, let this be a lesson to you. *(Yo escarmiento, yo escarmiente,* from *Escarmentar. V.* ACRECENTAR.)

escarnecedor, ra [es-car-nay-thay-dor', rah], *m. & f.* Scoffer, scorner, jeerer, giber, mocker, flinger.

escarnecer [es-car-nay-therr'], *va.* To scoff; to mock, to ridicule, to jeer, to gibe, to laugh at. *(Yo escarnezco, yo escarnezca,* from *Escarnecer. V.* CONOCER.)

escarnecidamente [es-car-nay-the'-dah-men-tay], *adv.* Scornfully.

escarnecimiento [es-car-nay-the-me-en'-to], *m.* Scoffing; derision.

escarnido, da [es-car-nee'-do, dah], *a. V.* DESCARNADO.

escarnio [es-car'-ne-o], *m.* 1. Scoff, contemptuous, ridicule. 2. Gibe, jeer, jeering, mock, flout.

escaro [es-cah'-ro], *m.* 1. *(Zool.)* A kind of mutton fish. 2. One who has crooked feet.

escarola [es-cah-ro'-lah], *f.* 1. *(Bot.)* Endive, garden-succory. 2. Plaited frill round the neck, ruff.

escarolado, da [es-cah-ro-lah'-do, dah], *a.* 1. Of the endive color. 2. Curled.-*pp.* of ESCAROLAR.

escarolar [es-cah-ro-lar'], *va. V.* ALECHUGAR.

escarolero, ra [es-cah-ro-lay'-ro, rah], *m. & f.* One who sells endives.

escarolita [es-cah-ro-lee'-tah], *f. dim.* A small endive.

escarótico, ca [es-cah-ro'-te-co, cah], *a.* Escharotic, caustic.

escarpa [es-car'-pah], *f.* 1. Declivity or gradual descent of a place. 2. *(Mil.)* Scarp, or escarp, the talus or slope on the inside of a ditch toward the rampart.

escarpado, da [es-car-pah'-do, dah], *a.* Sloped, craggy, rugged, crabbed. -*pp.* of ESCARPAR. -*m.(Arch.) V.* ESCARPE.

escarpar [es-car-par'], *va.* 1. *(Naut.)* To scarf or join timbers. 2. To rasp or cleanse works of sculpture. 3. *(Mil.)* To escarp, to slope down.

escarpe [es-car'-pay], *m.* 1. Declivity, sloped bank. 2. *(Arch.)* The scarf of a wall, a lapped joint. 3. *(Naut.)* A scarf joint.

escarpelar [es-car-pay-lar'], *va. (Anat.)* To scalp.

escarpelo [es-car-pay'-lo], *m.* Rasp, a coarse file.

escarpia [es-car'-pe-ah], *f.* 1. Tenterhook. 2. Meat hook, flesh hook.

escarpidor [es-car-pe-dor'], *m.* Comb with large wide teeth.

escarpín [es-car-peen'], *m.* 1. Sock, half hose (calcetín). 2. Shoe with a thin sole and low heel, a pump (zapatilla).

escarpión [es-car-pe-on'], *adv.* In the form of a tenter or hook.

escartivana [es-car-te-vah'-nah], *f.* A strip of paper or linen for binding maps or engravings.

escarza [es-car´-thah], *f.* 1. A sore in the hoofs of horses or mules. 2. An opening for discovering a tumor.

escarzamiento, *m.* or **escarzadura,** *f.* [es-car-thah-me-en'-to, es-car-thah-doo'-rah]. Act and effect of removing honey-combs.

escarzano, na [es-car-thah'-no, nah], *a. (Arch.)* Applied to an arch which is less than a semicircle.

escarzar [es-car-thar'], *va.* To remove the honeycomb from a hive in February.

escarzo [es-car´-tho], *m.* 1. Blackish green honeycomb found in the hive without honey. 2. Operation and time of removing honey from a hive. 3. Fungi on the trunks of trees. 4. Floss silk.

escarzo, za [es-car'-tho, thah], *a.* Lame on account of sores in the hoof (mulas, caballos).

escasamente [es-cah-sah-men'-tay], *adv.* 1. Scantily, sparingly, miserably. 2. Hardly, scarcely, difficultly; narrowly.

escaseada [es-cah-say-ah'-dah], **escaseadura,** *f. (Naut.)* Lack of wind.

escasear [es-cah-say-ar'], *va.* 1. To give sparingly and grudgingly. 2. To spare, to live in a frugal manner.-*vn.* 1. To grow less, to decrease, to be wanting. 2. *(Naut.)* To grow scanty (viento).

escasez, escaseza [es-cah-seth', es-cah-say'-thah], *f.* 1. Scantiness, meagreness; hardiness. 2. Want, lack (falta). 3. Poverty (pobreza).

escaso, sa [es-cah´-so, sah], *a.* 1. Small, short, limited, little. 2. Sparing, parsimonious, not in us. 3. Scanty, defective, narrow; hard; churlish. **Escaso de población,** thinly populated. **Escaso de recursos naturales,** poor in natural resources. **Andar escaso de dinero,** to be short of money.

escatimado, da [es-cah-te-mah'-do, dah], *a.* Little, scanty.-*pp.* of ESCATIMAR.

escatimar [es-cah-te-mar'], *va.* 1. To curtail (reducir), to lessen, to clip. 2. To haggle, to be tedious in a bargain. 3. To corrupt the meaning of words.

escatimosamente [es-cah-te-mo'-sah-men-tay], *adv.* Maliciously, viciously.

escatimoso, sa [es-cah-te mo'-so, sah], *a.* Cunning, malicious.

escatofagio, gia [es-cah-to-fah'-heo, ah], *a.* Scatophagous, dungeating.

escaupil [es-cah-oo-peel'], *m.* Armor used by the Mexicans before the conquest.

escayola [es-cah-yo'-lah], *f.* 1. Paste or composition resembling marble in appearance. 2. *(Med.)* Plaster.

escayolar [es-cah-yo-lar'], *va.* To put in plaster. **Con la pierna escayolada,** with his leg in plaster. **Tener el cuello escayolado,** to have one´s neck in plaster.

escena [es-thay'-nah], *f.* 1. The stage (escenario). **Entrar en escena,** to enter. **Poner en escena,** to stage. 2. Scene, part of a play. **Escena muda,** by-play. 3. *(Met.)* Revolution, vicissitude. 4. Bed and shepherd's hut made of branches. 5. A spectacle.

escenario [es-thay-nah'-re-o], *m.* 1. The stage. 2. *(Fig.)* Scene; setting. **El escenario del crimen,** the scene of the crime. **Desapareció del escenario político,** he disappeared from the political scene.

escénico, ca [es-thay´-ne-co, cah], *a.* Scenic, belonging to the stage.

escenificación [es-thay-ne-fe-cah-the-on'], *f.* Dramatization, adapting for stage or movies.

escenificar [es-thay-ne-fe-car'], *va.* To dramatize (novela), to stage (comedia).

escenita [es-thay-nee'-tah], *f. dim.* A short scene.

escenografía [es-thay-no-grah-fee'-ah], *f.* Scenography, the art of perspective.

escenográfico, ca [es-thay-no-grah'-fe-co, cah], *a.* Scenographic, perspective.

escenógrafo [es-thay-no´-grah-fo], *m.* An instrument for representing perspective views.

escépticamente [es-thep'-te-cah-men-tay], *adv.* Sceptically.

escepticismo [es-thep-te-thees'-mo], *m.* Scepticism.

escéptico, ca [es-thep'-te-co, cah], *a.* Sceptic, sceptical.

esciadofillo, lla [es-the-ah-do-feel'-lyo, lyah], *a.* Having parasol-shaped leaves.

esciagrafía [es-the-ah-grah-fee'-ah], *f.* 1. *(Arch.)* Sciagraph, the plan of a building in vertical section. 2. The art of correct shading. 3. *(Ast.)* Sciagraphy, the art of finding the hour by the shadows of heavenly bodies.

esciágrafo [es-the-ah'-grah-fo], *m.* Sciagrapher.

esciarro [es-the-ar'-ro], *m.* A stream of lava.

esciatérico, ca [es-the-ah-tay'-re-co, cah], *a.* Sciatheric, relative to a sundial.

esciatorio [es-the-ah-tay'-reo], *m.* 1. Gnomon, triangular piece of a sundial. 2. Among quarrymen, a dialplate.

esciátero [es-the-ah'-tay-ro], *m.* A kind of sundial of the ancients.

escibalario, ria [es-the-bah-lah'-re-o, ah], *a.* Living in excrement.

escible [es-thee'-blay], *a.* Worthy of being known.

esciena [es-the-ay'-nah], *f. (Zool.)* A species of crawfish.

escífula [es-thee'-foo-lah], *f.* A kind of funnel with which certain lichens are provided.

escila marítima [es-thee'-lah ma-ree'-te-mah], *f. (Bot.)* Squill.

esciografía [es-the-o-grah-fe'-ah], etc. *V.* ESCIAGRAFÍA, etc.

escisión [es-these-on´], *f.* Scission, splitting, fission.

esclarecedor [es-cla-ray-they-dor'], *a.* Illuminating (explicación).

esclarecer [es-clah-ray-therr'], *va.* 1. To lighten, to produce light; to illuminate. 2. *(Met.)* To illustrate, to ennoble (ennoblecer). -*vn.* To dawn.

esclarecidamente [es-clah-ray-the'-dah-men-tay], *adv.* Illustriously, conspicuously.

esclarecido, da [es-clah-ray-thee´-do, dah], *a.* Illustrious, noble, conspicuous, eminent, honorable. *pp.* of ESCLARECER.

escalarecimiento [es-clah-ray-the-me-en'-to], *m.* 1. Dawn, the morning dawn. 2. Ennoblement, illustriousness, conspicuousness.

esclava [es-clah'-vah], *f.* 1. Slave, drudge. **Esclava blanca,** white slave. 2. Slave bangle (pulsera).

esclavillo, illa; ito, ita [es-clah-veel'-lyo, lyah, vee'-to, vee'-tah], *m. & f. dim.* A little slave.

esclavina [es-clah vee' nah], *f.* 1. A long robe worn by pilgrims. 2. Pilgrim's pall, to which shells are fixed. 3. Collar formally worn by priests. 4. Kind of cloth formally worn over women's shoulders in winter; tippet. 5. Cape of a cloak.

esclavista [es-clah-vees'-tah], *a.* Proslavery.

esclavitud [es-clah-ve-tood'], *f.* 1. Slavery, bondage, servitude, enslavement, mancipation, slavishness. 2. *(Met.)* Brotherhood, congregation. 3. *(Met.)* Servile subjection of passions and sentiments. 4. Ornament of jewels, worn by women on the breast.

esclavizar [es-clah-ve-thar'], *va.* 1. To enslave, to reduce to slavery. 2. *(Met.)* To drive, to overwork.

esclavo, va [es-clah'-vo, vah], *m. & f.* 1. Slave, captive, helot. **Vender a uno como esclavo,** to sell somebody into slavery. 2. Member of a brotherhood or confraternity. 3. Fag, one who works hard. 4. *(Met.)* Slave of one's own desires and passions. **Ser esclavo del tabaco,** to be a slave to tobacco.

esclavón, na [es-clah-vo-ne', nah], *a.* Slavonian, belonging to Slavonia, Slavonic language.

esclerosis [es-clay-ro'-sis], *f. (Med.)* Sclerosis. **Esclerosis múltiple,** multiple sclerosis.

esclerótica [es-clay-ro'-te-cah], *f.* Sclerotic, the exterior white coat of the eye.

esclusa [es-cloo'-sah], *f.* Lock, sluice, floodgate, milldam.

escoa [es-co'-ah], *f. (Naut.)* Rung-head, floor-head, floor-timber of the head.

escoba [es-co'-bah], *f.* 1. Broom, a besom. 2. A tall shrub from which brooms are made.

escobada [es-co-bah'-dah], *f.* The act of sweeping slightly.

escobadera [es-co-bah-day'-rah], *f.* A woman who sweeps, or cleans, with a broom.

escobajo [es-co-bah'-ho], *m.* 1. The remains of an old broom. 2. The stalk of a bunch of grapes.

escobar [es-co-bar'], *m.* A place where broom grows.

escobar [es-co-bar'], *va.* To sweep with a broom.

escobazar [es-co-bah-thar'], *va.* To sprinkle water with a broom or brush.

escobazo [es-co-bah'-tho], *m.* Stroke or blow with a broom (golpe). **Dar un escobazo**, to have a quick sweep-up (barrido).

escobera [es-co-bay'-rah], *f.* V. RETAMA.

escobenes [es-co-bay'-nes], *m. pl. (Naut.)* Hawses or hawseholes.

escobero, ra [es-co-bay'-ro, rah], *m.* 1. One who makes or sells brooms. 2. A broom used by masons for cleaning stones. *-f.* V. RETAMA.

escobeta [es-co-bay'-tah], *f.* 1. A small brush. 2. *(Bot.)* Sweet sultan centaury.

escobilla [es-co-beel'-lyah], *f.* 1. Brush. 2. A small broom or besom; a whisk. 3. *(Bot.)* The head of the plume-thistle with which silk is carded. 4. Sweepings of gold or silver in the workshop of a gold or silversmith 5. A swab for cleaning the touch-hole of a gun.

escobillón [es-co-beel-lyone'], *m. (Mil.)* Sponge of a cannon.

escobina [es-co-bee'-nah], *f.* Chips or dust made in boring something.

escobo [es-co'-bo], *m.* Brushwood, briers, brambles.

escobón [es-co-bone'], *m.* 1. *(Aug.)* A large broom (escoba). 2. Brush, with which a smith sprinkles the fire in his forge (bruza). *-pl. (Naut.)* Hawses.

escocer [es-co-therr'], *va.* 1. To cause a sharp pain, as if the part had been burnt. 2. *(Met.)* To make one smart or feel a poignant pain. 3. *(Met.)* To irritate, to provoke. *-vr.* To smart.

escocés, sa [es-co-thes', thay'-sah], *a.* Scotch, Scottish.

Escocia [es-co'-the-ah], *f. (Arch.)* Scotia, a semicircular concave moulding around the base of a column. Scotland.

escoda [es-co'-dah], *f.* An edged hammer, used by stone-cutters.

escodadero [es-co-dah-day'-ro], *m.* Place where cattle rub their horns.

escodar [es-co-dar'], *va.* To hew stones with an edged hammer.

escofia [es-co'-fe-ah], *f.* V. COFIA.

escofiar [es-co-fe-ar'], *va.* To dress the head with a net.

escofieta [es-co-fe-ay'-tah], *f.* Coif, head-tire, women's head-dress.

escofina [es-co-fee'-nah], *f.* 1. Rasp, a coarse file used by carpenters. 2. Nailfile, file for corns.

escofinar [es-co-fe-nar'], *a.* To rasp, to mould wood with a large file.

escogedor, ra [es-co-hay-dor', rah], *m. & f.* Selecter, chooser.

escoger [es-co-herr'], *va.* To choose (entre), to select, to pick out, to excerpt, to cull, to elect (por voto).

escogidamente [es-co-he-dah-men'-tay], *adv.* 1. Choicely, selectly. 2. Elegantly, nicely.

escogido, da [es-co-hee'-do, dah], *a.* 1. Select, choice (en calidad). 2. Chosen.

escolar [es-co-lar'], *m.* Scholar, student, clerk, learner. *-a.* Scholastic, scholastical.

escolar [es-co-lar'], *vn.* V. COLAR.

escolaridad [es-co-lah-re-dahd'], *f.* Schooling. **Escolaridad obligatoria**, compulsory schooling.

escolarizar [es-co-lah-re-thar'], *va.* To enrol in school. **Niños sin escolarizar**, children not in school.

escolásticamente [es-co-lahs'-te-cah-men-tay], *adv.* Scholastically.

escolasticismo [es-co-las-te-thees'-mo], *m.* Scholasticism, Aristotelian philosophy.

escolástico, ca [es-co-lahs'-te-co, cah], *a.* Scholastic, scholastical, pertaining to schools.

escolástico [es-co-lahs´-te-co], *m.* A professor of theology.

escoliador [es-co-le-ah-dor'], *m.* Scholiast, a writer of explanatory notes.

escoliar [es-co-le-ar'], *va.* To gloss, to explain, to comment.

escolimado, da [es-co-le-mah'-do, dah], *a.* Weak, delicate.

escolimoso, sa [es-co-le-mo'-so, sah], *a.* Difficult, severe, hard to please.

escolio [es-co'-leo], *m.* 1. Scholion or scholium, a brief explanatory observation. 2. Gloss, commentary. 3. *(Geom.)* Note which refers to a preceding proposition.

escoliosis [es-co-le-o'-sis], *f. (Med.)* Scoliosis, lateral curvature of the spinal column.

escolopendra [es-co-lo-pen´-drah], *f.* 1. *(Ent.)* Scolopendra, centipede, a myriapod insect. 2. A fish. 3. *(Bot.)* Spleenwort, common hart's tongue.

escolta [es-col'-tah], *f.* Escort (persona), convoy, guard. **Dar escolta a**, to escort.

escoltar [es-col-tar'], *va.* To escort, to convoy, to guard (proteger).

escollera [es-col-lyay'-rah], *f. (Naut.)* Rocky place or cliff.

escollo [es-col'-lyo], *m.* 1. A shelf in the sea, or a rock under shallow water; a reef. 2. *(Met.)* Embarrassment, difficulty, danger (peligro oculto).

escombra [es-com'-brah], *f.* Purgation, removal of obstacles.

escombrar [es-com-brar'], *va.* To remove obstacles, to free from obstructions; to purify.

escombro [es-com'-bro], *m.* 1. Rubbish, fragments of materials used in building. 2. *(Zool.)* Mackerel.

escomerse [es-co-merr'-say], *va.* To be wasted or worn out with use or time.

esconce [es-con'-thay], *m.* Corner, angle.

esconderero [es-con-day-ray'-ro], *m.* A hiding or lurking place.

esconder [es-con-derr'], *va.* 1. To hide, to conceal, to keep in, to keep out of sight. 2. *(Met.)* To disguise, to dissemble. 3. To include, to contain. *-vr.* To hide, to lie hid, to be concealed, to skulk.

escondidamente [es-con-de-dah-men'-tay], *adv.* Privately, secretly, hiddenly.

escondidas (A), A escondidillas [es-con-dee'-das, ah es-con-de-deel'-lyas], *adv.* Privately, in a secret manner.

escondimiento [es-con-de-me-en'-to], *m.* Concealment, concealing, the act of hiding or concealing something.

escondite [es-con-dee'-tay], *m.* Concealment, hold, a lurking place, a hiding place (escondrijo). **Juego de escondite**, hide and seek.

escondrijo [es-con-dree'-ho], *m.* Concealment, a hiding or lurking place.

escontrete [es-con-tray'-tay], *m. (Naut.)* Prop, stay, shore.

esconzado, da [es-con-thah'-do, dah], *a.* Angular, oblique.

escoñarse [es-co-nyar'-say], *vr.* 1. To hurt oneself (persona). **Estoy escoñado**, I´m knackered. 2. *(Med.)* To break, to get broken.

escopa [es-co'-pah], *f.* A kind of a chisel for chipping or cutting stones.

escoperada [es-co-pay-rah'-dah], *f.* Gunwale.

escopero [es-co-pay'-ro], *m. (Naut.)* Pitch-brush for paying the seams of ships; swab.

escopeta [es-co-pay'-tah], *f.* A shotgun, a gun. **Escopeta de viento**, an air-gun. **A tiro de escopeta**, 1. Within gunshot. 2. *(Met.)* At first view, easily. **Escopeta de aire comprimido**, popgun. **Escopeta de dos cañones**, double-barrelled gun.

escopetar [es-co-pay-tar'], *va.* To dig out goldmines.

escopetazo [es-co-pay-tah'-tho], *m.* 1. Gun or musket-shot (disparo). 2. Wound made by a gunshot (herida).

escopetear [es-co-pay-tay-ar'], *va.* To discharge a firelock or gun repeatedly. *-vr.* 1. To discharge firelocks at each other. 2. *(Met.)* To insult each other with foul language.

escopeteo [es-co-pay-tay'-o], *m.* Act of discharging volley of shots (disparos).

escopetería [es-co-pay-tay-ree'-ah], *f.* 1. Infantry armed with muskets. 2. Multitude of gunshot wounds.

escopetero [es-co-pay-tay'-ro], *m.* Gunsmith, armorer.

escopetilla [es-co-pay-teel'-lyah], *f. dim.* A small gun.

escopetón [es-co-pay-tone'], *m. aug.* A large gun.

escopleadura [es-co-play-ah-doo'-rah], *f.* Mortise-hole.

escoplear [es-co-play-ar'], *va.* To chisel, to cut with a chisel.

escoplillo, ito [es-co-pleel'-lyo, ee'-to], *m. dim.* A small chisel.

escoplo [es-co'-plo], *m.* Chisel.

escora [es-co'-rah], *f.* 1. Stanchion, prop, outrigger. 2. *(Naut.)* That part of a ship's side which makes the most resistance (apoyo); the central line of a vessel (línea). **Navío de escora baja,** a ship which carries a stiff sail. **Escoras,** *(Naut.)* shores, outriggers.

escorar [es-co-rar'], *va.* 1. *(Naut.)* To prop, to shore up. 2. To bank (avión). 3. *(Naut.)* To wedge. *-vn.* To reach low tide.

escorbútico, ca [es-cor-boo'-te-co, cah], *a.* Scorbutic, scorbutical; it is sometimes used as a substantive for a person affected with scurvy.

escorbuto [es-cor-boo'-to], *m.* Scurvy, a disease.

escorchapín [es-cor-chah-peen'], *m.* Passageboat, ferry.

escorchar [es-cor-chahr'], *va.* V. DESOLLAR.

escorche [es-cor'-chay], *m.* Decrease of a tuberous body.

escordio [es-cor'-deo], *m. (Bot.)* Water germander.

escoria [es-co'-re-ah], *f.* 1. Dross slags, scoria (metal). 2. Lee. 3. *(Met.)* Any mean or worthless thing. *-pl.* Scoriae, volcanic ashes.

escoriáceo, cea [es-co-re-ah'-thay-o, ah], *a.* Scoriaceous, ensembling scoria.

escoriación [es-co-re-ah-the-on'], *f.* Incrustation, scurf formed on a sore. V. EXCORIACIÓN.

escorial [es-co-re-ahl'], *m.* 1. Place where a mine has been exhausted. 2. Place where the dross of metals is thrown.

escoriar [es-co-re-ar'], *va.* V. EXCORIAR.

escorificación [es-co-re-fe-cah-the-on'], *f.* Scorification, smelting an ore with lead.

escorificar [es-co-re-fe-car'], *va.* To scarify, to separate (oro y plata) by the process of scorification.

escorificatorio [es-co-re-fe-cah-to-tre-o], *m.* Scorifier. 1. A small flat dish used for scarifying. 2. A furnace for the same purpose.

escorodonia [es-co-ro-do'-ne-ah], *f. (Bot.)* Wood sage termander.

escorpena, escorpina [es-cor-pay'-nah, es-cor-pee'-nah], *f.* Grouper, a small sea food fish.

escorpiaco [es-cor-pe-ah'-co], *m.* An antidote against scorpion bites.

escorpioide [es-cor-pe-o'-e-day], *f. (Bot.)* V. ALACRANERA.

escorpión [es-cor-pe-on'], *m.* 1. Scorpion. Scorpio. 2. Scorpion (pez). 3. An ancient war-like machine. 4. Scorpion (zodíaco). 5. Instrument of torture, armed with metal points.

escorpiónido, da [es-cor-pe-o'-ne-do, dah], *a.* Scorpion-like. *-m. pl.* Scorpionidea, the scorpion family.

escorpiuro [es-cor-pe-oo'-ro], *m.* Scorpiurus, an herb of the bean family.

escorroso [es-cor-ro'-so], *m. (Prov. Cuba)* 1. Clamor, vociferation. 2. V. CACAREO.

escorrozo [es-cor-ro'-tho], *m. (coll.)* Pleasure, enjoyment.

escorzado [es-cor-thah'-do], *m. (Art.)* V. ESCORZO. **Escorzado, da,** *pp.* of ESCORZAR. Fore-shortened.

escorzar [es-cor-thar'], *va.* 1. *(Pict.)* To contract the size of a figure; to fore-shorten. 2. To form a depressed arch.

escorzo [es-cor'-tho], *m. (Art.)* Contraction or decrease of a figure in perspective.

escorzón [es-cor-thone'], *m.* V. ESCUERZO.

escorzonera [es-cor-tho-nay'-rah], *f. (Bot.)* Viper-root or garden viper-grass. **Escorzonera laciniada,** cut-leaved viper-grass.

escoscarse [es-cos-car'-say], *vr.* V. CONCOMERSE.

escota [es-co'-tah], *f.* 1. *(Agr. Prov.)* A kind of mattock or grubbing axe. 2. *(Naut.)* Sheet, a rope fastened to the lower corners of a sail for the purpose of extending or retaining it in a particular position. **Escotas mayores,** main-sheets. **Escotas de las velas de estay,** stay-sail sheets. **Escotas volantes,** flowing-sheets.

escotado [es-co-tah'-do], *m.* Neck, neckline (escotadura). *-a.* low-necked, low-cut (vestido). **Iba muy escotada,** she was wearing a very low-cut dress.

escotadura [es-co-tah-doo'-rah], *f.* 1. Sloping of a jacket or a corset. 2. The large trap-door of a theater or stage. 3. *(Mil.)* In the breast-plate of armor, the armhole to enable the arms to be moved.

escotar [es-co-tar'], *va.* 1. To cut out a thing so as to make it fit. 2. To slope. 3. To hollow a garment about the neck. 4. To club, to contribute to a common expense. 5. To draw water from (río).

escote [es-co'-tay], *m.* 1. Neck, neckline (corte del cuello). Low cut, low neckline. 2. Tucker, lace frill (adorno). 3. One's share (cuota). **Comprar algo a escote,** to club together to buy something. **Pagar a escote,** to pay Dutch (una pareja). **Cada uno pagó su escote,** each one paid his share.

escotera [es-co-tay'-rah], *f. (Naut.)* Sheet-hole, through which the main and fore-sheets are reeved.

escotero, ra [es-co-tey'-ro, rah], *a.* Free, disengaged.

escotilla [es-co-teel'-lyah], *f. (Naut.)* Hatchway. **Escotilla mayor,** the main hatchway. **Escotilla de proa,** fore-hatchway. **Escotilla de popa,** magazine hatchway.

escotillón [es-co-teel-lyone'], *m.* Scuttle, trap-door.

escotín [es-co-teen'], *m. (Naut.)* Tow sail-sheet, fastened to the lower corners of top-sails and topgallant-sails.

escotomía [es-co-to-mee'-ah], *f.* Dizziness or swimming in the head.

escoznete [es-coth-nay'-tay], *m. (Prov.)* A nutpick.

escozor [es-co-thor'], *m.* 1. A smart pungent pain. 2. *(Met.)* A lively sensation or perception of the mind.

escriba [es-cree'-bah], *m.* Scribe, among the Hebrews.

escribanía [es-cre-bah-nee'-ah], *f.* 1. Office or employment of a notary or scrivener (oficina). 2. Office or place where contracts and other notarial deeds and instruments are drawn up. 3. Secretary, escritoire, a case of drawers for writings, with a desk (mueble). 4. Portable writing-case (enseres).

escribano [es-cre-bah'-no], *m.* 1. Notary public; scrivener. **Escribano de cámara,** the clerk of a high court of justice, who must be also a notary public. **Escribano de número, or del número,** one of a certain number of notaries public, before whom only certain deeds can be executed. 2. Purser of a vessel. 3. *(Zool.)* An insect, shaped like a small spider, which is in continual movement upon the surface of slow streams or fountains. A (agua) skater. Gerris. **Es un gran escribano,** he writes a very neat hand, he writes like copper plate. **Escribano or escribanillo del agua,** water-skater.

escribiente [es-cre-be-en'-tay], *m.* Amanuensis, a clerk.

escribir [es-cre-beer'], *va.* 1. To write. **Escribir a mano,** to write in longhand. **Escribir a máquina,** to type. 2. To write, to compose literary works (escritor). 3. To write, to tell by letters. *-vr.* 1. To enrol oneself, to enter one's name in a register or roll. 2. To keep up an epistolary correspondence. **Escribir en la arena,** to bury in oblivion.

escriño [es-cree'-nyo], *m.* 1. Sort of hamper made of straw, and matted together with osier. 2. *(Prov.)* A jewel box, casket of jewels.

escrita [es-cree'-tah], *f.* A kind of fish, having marks like letters upon the back. V. ESCUADRO.

escritillas [es-cre-teel'-yas], *f. pl.* Lamb's testicles.

escrito [es-cree'-to], *m.* 1. Book or other literary composition. 2. *(Law.)* Allegation or petition exhibited in a court of justice. **Acuerdo por escrito,** written agreement. **Poner algo por escrito,** to commit something to paper. **—Escrito, ta,** *pp. irr.* of ESCRIBIR.

escritor, ra [es-cree-tor´], *m & f.* 1. Writer, author, composer. 2. Copyist.

escritorcillo [es-cre-tor-theel´-lyo], *m. dim.* A bad writer.

escritorillo [es-cre-to-reel´-lyo], *m. dim.* A small scrutoire.

escritorio [es-cre-to´-re-o], *m.* 1. A writing desk (mueble), secretary. 2. Counting-house, office (despacho). 3. Press, a large chest of drawers, or sort of cupboard, adorned with inlaid ivory, ebony, etc. 4. In printing offices every composing-case.

escritorzuelo, la [es-cre-tor-thoo-ay´-lo, lah], *m. & f. dim.* A poor writer.

escritura [es-cre-too´-rah], *f.* 1. Writing, the act of putting something on paper. 2. Deed, instrument, bond, contract. 3. Writing, a work or treatise written. **Escritura de seguro**, policy of insurance. 4. Art of writing. **Tiene malísima escritura**, her writing is terrible. **No acierto a leer su escritura**, I can´t read his writing.

escriturar [es-cre-too-rar'], *va.* To bind oneself by a public instrument; to sign articles, to formalize legally (documentos). **Estar escriturado**, to be under articles.

escriturario [es-cre-too-rah'-re-o], *m.* One who professes to explain the holy Scripture, a professor of divinity.

escrófula [es-cro'-foo-lah], *f.* Scrofula, king´s evil.

escrofularia [es-cro-foo-lah'-re-ah], *f. (Bot.)* Figwort.

escrofuloso, sa [es-cro-foo-lo'-so, sah], *a.* Scrofulous.

escrotal [es-cro-tahl'], *a.* Scrotal, relating to the scrotum.

escroto [es-cro'-to], *m.* Scrotum.

escrudriñar [es-croo-de-nyar'], *va. V.* ESCUDRIÑAR.

escrupulear [es-croo-poo-lay-ar'], *v. V.* ESCRUPULIZAR.

escrupulete [es-croo-poo-lay'-tay], *m. dim. (coll.)* A slight doubt or scruple.

escrupulillo [es-croo-poo-leel'-lyo], *m.* 1. *(dim.)* Slight doubt, scruple, or hesitation. 2. Small piece of metal put into a hollow brass globe, to ring as a bell for animals.

escrupulizar [es-croo-poo-le-thar'], *vn.* To scruple, to doubt, to hesitate.

escrúpulo [es-croo'-poo-lo], *m.* 1. Doubt, scruple, hesitation (duda). **Falta de escrúpulos**, unscrupulousness. 2. Scrupulosity, a great nicety or tenderness of conscience; conscience (cualidad). 3. Scruple, a small weight, the third part of a drachm. 4. *(Ast.)* Minute on a graduated sphere.

escrupulosamente [es-croo-poo-lo'-sah-men-tay], *adv.* Scrupulously.

escrupulosidad [es-croo-poo-lo-se-dah'], *f.* 1. Scrupulosity, minute and nice doubtfulness. 2. Scrupulosity, conscientiousness.

escrupuloso, sa [es-croo-poo-lo'-so, sah], *a.* 1. Scrupulous, characterized by careful observation of what is morally right, conscientious. 2. Scrupulous, nice, cautious, exact; narrow; critical.

escrutador, ra [es-croo-ta-dor'], *m & f.* 1. Examiner, scrutator, inquirer, searcher. 2. Inspector of an election.

escrutar [es-croo-tar´], *va.* 1. To count votes (votos). 2. To search (examinar), to pry into.

escrutinio [es-croo-tee'-ne-o], *m.* Scrutiny, inquiry, close examination. **Escrutinio electoral**, election returns, counting of electoral votes (votación).

escrutiñador [es-croo-te-nyah-dor'], *m.* Scrutator, censor.

escuadra [es-coo-ah'-drah], *f.* 1. Square, an instrument for measuring right angles. 2. Socket in which the pivot or spindle of a door turns. 3. A small number of horses or foot soldiers commanded by a corporal; a squad. 4. Squadron, fleet (de coches etc.), or more properly a part of a fleet. **A escuadra**, in a square manner. **Jefe de escuadra**, *(Naut.)* rear-admiral.

escuadrador [es-coo-ah-drah-dor'], *m.* Groover, a tool for opening the moulds of wax-candles.

escuadrar [es-coo-ah-drar'], *va.* 1. To square; to reduce to a square. 2. To fix the trunnions horizontally in a piece of ordenance.

escuadreo [es-coo-ah-dray'-o], *m.* Dimension, valuation of the square contents of a piece of ground.

escuadría [es-coo-ah-dree'-ah], *f.* Square, a measure having or forming right angles.

escuadrilla [es-coo-ah-dree'-lyah], *f.* Squadron of ships or planes.

escuadro [es-coo-ah'-dro], *m.* Species of dogfish.

escuadrón [es-coo-ah-dro-ne'], *m.* Squadron, troop of horses, a small body of horses. **Escuadrón de la muerte**, death squad.

escuadronar [es-coo-ah-dro-nar'], *va.* To draw up troops in rank and file, to form troops in squadrons.

escuadroncillo, ito [es-coo-ah-dron-theel'-lyo, ee'-to], *m. dim.* A small party of troops.

escuadronista [es-coo-ah-dro-nees'-tah] *m. (Mil.)* He who forms squadrons.

escualidez [es-coo-ah-le-deth'], *f.* Squalor, wretchedness.

escuálido, da [es-coo-ah'-le-do, dah], *a.* 1. Very weak, languid (débil). 2. Squalid, filthy (sucio), nauseous. 3. Like the spotted dogfish.

escualino, na [es-coo-ah-lee'-no, nah], *a. V.* ESCUÁLIDO, 3d def.

escualo [es-coo-ah'-lo], *m.* The spotted dogfish; a shark.

escucha [es-coo'-hah], *f.* 1. Sentinel, sentry. 2. **Escucha, or madre escucha**, a nun who is sent with another to the grate, to listen to what is said. 3. Scout, one who is sent privily to observe the motions of the enemy. 4. A small window, made for listening. 5. Servant who sleeps near her mistress, in order to wait on her. 6. Listening (acto). **Escucha telefónica**, telephone tapping. **Estar a la escucha**, to listen in.

escuchador, ra [es-coo-chah-dor', rah], *m. & f.* Hearer, hearkener, listener.

escuchante [es-coo-chahn'-tay], *pa. & m. & f.* Listener; hearkening.

escuchar [es-coo-char'], *va.* To listen (consejo), to give ear, to attend, to hear. *-vr.* To hear oneself with complacency, to be highly gratified with one's eloquence.

escudar [es-coo-dar'], *va.* 1. To shield, to defend with a shield. 2. To guard from danger. *-vr. (Met.)* To depend on some means of evading danger.

escuderaje [es-coo-day-rah'-hay], *m.* The office and service of a lady´s page.

escuderear [es-coo-day-ray-ar'], *va.* To perform the service of a page; to perform the functions of a squire.

escudería [es-coo-day-ree'-ah], *f.* Service of a squire or shield-bearer.

escuderil [es-coo-day-reel'], *a.* Belonging to the office of a shield bearer, or to the place of a page.

escudero [es-coo-day'-ro], *m.* 1. Shield-bearer, squire or attendant on a warrior, a custrel. 2. Gentleman descended from an illustrious family. 3. Page who attends a lady. 4. A maker of shields and other defensive armor. **Escudero de a pie**, a servant kept to carry messages.

escuderón [es-coo-day-rone'], *m.* Squire puffed up with vanity and pride.

escudete [es-coo-day'-tay], *m.* 1. Gusset, a piece of lace sewn on a surplice under the armpit, to strengthen it. 2. A stain on the olive's fruit, from damage received in consequence of falls of rain. 3. Budding or inoculating. 4. *(Bot.)* White waterlily. *V.* NENÚFAR.

escudilla [es-coo-deel'-lyah], *f.* Bowl (recipiente), bowlful (contenido), crock; a soup-plate, porringer.

escudillar [es-coo-deel-lyar'], *va.* 1. To pour broth into porringers, to distribute broth. 2. *(Met.)* To lord, to domineer.

escudillo, ito [es-coo-deel'-lyo, ee'-to], *m. dim.* A small shield.

escudo [es-coo'-do], *m.* 1. Shield, buckler. 2. Plate on which arms are engraved. 3. Scutcheon of a lock. 4. Shield, patronage, protection, defense. 5. Back of a wild boar. 6. The bandage used in bleeding. 7. Sideplate of a gun. **Escudo de bote**, *(Naut.)* The backboard of a boat. 8. Crown, a coin of a different value in different countries.

escudriñador, ra [es-coo-dre-nyah-dor', rah], *m. & f.* Prier, scrutator; a person who inquires into the secrets of others.

escudriñamiento [es-coo-dre-nyah-me-en'-to], *m.* Investigation, scrutiny.

escudriñar [es-coo-dre-nyar'], *va.* To search, to pry into; to inquire after (investigar), to examine into (examinar); to consult.

escudriño [es-coo-dree'-nyo], *m. V.* ESCUDRIÑAMIENTO.

escuela [es-co-ay'-lah], *f.* 1. School, a house of discipline and instruction. 2. School, university, a place of literary education. 3. School, a state of instruction or the instruction given in schools. 4. School, a system of doctrine; style of a teacher. **Escuela de párvulos**, infant school. **Escuela de Bellas Artes**, Art school. **Escuela automovilista**, driving school. **Escuela elemental**, primary school. **Escuela naval**, naval academy. **Escuela de equitación**, riding school. **Estar en la escuela**, to be at school. **Formarse en una escuela dura**, to learn in a tough school. **Tener buena escuela**, to be well trained.

escuerzo [es-coo-err'-tho], *m.* Toad.

escueto, ta [es-coo-ay'-to, tah], *a.* 1 Concise (conciso), simple, unadorned, plain. **Un informe muy escueto**, a very concise report. **La verdad escueta**, the plain truth. 2. *(Amer. Peru)* Solitary, uninhabited.

escueznar [es-coo-eth-nar'], *va. (Prov.)* To extract the kernel of nuts.

escuezno [es-coo-eth'-no], *m. (Prov.)* Pulp or soft kernel of a nut fit for eating.

esculina [es-coo-lee'-nah], *f.* Esculin, a substance obtained from the horse-chestnut.

escullador [es-cool-lyah-dor'], *m.* In oilmills, a vessel for carrying off the oil.

escullirse [es-cool-lyeer'-say], *V. (Prov.)* To slip, to slide.

esculpir [es-cool-peer'], *va.* To sculpture, to engrave in wood or stone, to cut (inscripción).

esculto, ta [es-cool'-to, tah], *pp. irr. obs.* of ESCULPIR.

escultor [es-cool-tor'], *m.* Sculptor, carver.

escultora [es-cool-to'-rah], *f.* Female sculptor, sculptress.

escultura [es-cool-too'-rah], *f.* 1. Sculpture, the art of cutting wood or stone into images. 2. Carved work, the work made by a sculptor. **Escultura en madera**, wood carving.

escultural [es-cool-too-rahl'], *a.* Sculptural; belonging to the art of sculpture.

escupidera [es-coo-pe-day'-rah], *f.* Spittoon, cuspidor.

escupidero [es-coo-pe-day'-ro], *m.* 1. Spitting place. 2. *(Met.)* Despicable or abject situation.

escupido [es-coo-pee'-do], *m. V.* ESPUTO.—**Escupido, da**, *pp.* of ESCUPIR.

escupidor, ra [es-coo-pe-dor', rah], *m. & f.* A great spitter (persona).

escupidura [es-coo-pe-doo'-rah], *f.* 1. The act of spitting. 2. Spittle. 3. (En labios) Cracking.

escupir [es-coo-peer'], *va.* 1. To spit, to spit out (palabra, comida). **Escupir en el suelo**, to spit on the ground. 2. To break out in the skin (sangre). 3. *(Met. Poet.)* To discharge balls from firearms. 4. *(Met.)* To dart, to flash. 5. *(Met.)* To depreciate, to underrate the value of a thing. **Escupir en la cara**, to deride to the face, to ridicule. 6. To cough (confesar). 7. To cough up (pagar).

escupita, escupitina [es-coo-pee'-tah, es-coo-pe-tee'-nah], *f. (coll.) V.* SALIVA.

escupitajo [es-coo-pee-tah-ho], *m.* Spit.

escurar [es-coo-rar'], *va.* To scour cloth, to cleanse it from grease before it is milled.

escurina [es-coo-ree'-nah], *f. (Prov.)* Obscurity, darkness.

escurreplatos [es-coor-ray-plah'-tos], *m.* Plate rack.

escurribanda [es-coor-re-bahn'-dah], *f.* 1. Evasion, subterfuge. 2. Diarrhoea (vientre), bowel complaint. 3. Scuffle, bustle.

escurridizo, za [es-coor-re-dee'-tho, thah], *a.* 1. Slippery, not affording firm footing (superficie). 2. Hard to hold, hard to keep, easily escaping (objeto). **Lazo escurridizo**, a running knot.

escurridor [es-coor-re-dor'], *m.* Wringer (ropa); plate rack (de loza); colander, strainer (cocina).

escurriduras, escurrimbres [es-coor-re-doo´-ras, es-coor-reem'-bress], *f. pl.* Dregs, the sediment of liquors; the lees, the grounds. **Llegar a las escurriduras**, to reach the end of a festival, the remains of a dinner.

escurrimiento [es-coor-re-me-ayn'-to], *m. V.* DESLIZ.

escurripa [es-coor-ree'-pah], *f. (Bot.)* Cardinal flower.

escurrir [es-coor-reer'], *va.* To drain off liquor to the dregs (líquido). *-vn.* 1. To drop, to fall in drops (líquido). 2. To slip, to slide (objeto). 3. To lapse, to glide slowly. *-vr.* To escape from danger (persona); to slip out (observación), or to slip away; to creep, to skulk. **Se me escurrió de entre las manos**, it slipped out of my hands.

escutas, escutillas [es-coo´-tas, es-coo-teel-lyas], *f. pl. (Naut.)* Scuttles. *V.* ESCOTILLAS.

escutelaria [es-coo-tay-lah'-re-ah], *f.* (Scutellaria), skullcap, a herb of the mint family.

escuteliforme [es-coo-tay-le-for'-may], *a. (Bot.)* Shield-shaped, platter-shaped.

escúter [es-coo'-tayr], *m.* Scooter (motor).

escutiforme [es-coo-tefor'-may], *a.* Shield-shaped. *m.* The thyroid cartilage.

escuyer [es-coo-yerr'], *m.* Purveyor of meat to the palace.

esdrújula [es-droo'-hoo-lo], *f.* A Spanish word of more than two syllables, the last two of which are short, e. g. *cántaro.*

ese [ay'-say], *f.* 1. Spanish name of the letter **S.** 2. Link of a chain of the figure of this letter. **Hacer eses**, to zigzag.

ése, ésa, eso [ay´-say], *dem. pron.* That, that one. (plural: **ésos, ésas;** those). **Ni por ésas**, on no account. **No es una chica de ésas**, she´s not one of those. **Ésos son tus padres**, those are your parents. **Éste lo sabe**, he knows. **Llegaremos a ésta mañana**, we'll get there tomorrow. **¡No me vengas con ésas!**, don't come to me with that story! **¡Conque ésas tenemos!**, so that's it! **Eso es lo que me dijo**, that's what he told me. **Ésa es la que vino**, that's the one who came.

ese, esa, *dem. adj.* That. (plural: **esos, esas;** those). **Esa mujer**, that woman. **Ese hombre**, that man. **Esos hombres**, those men. **Esos libros**, those books.

esecilla [ay-say-theel'-lyah], *f. dim.* Small link of a chain.

esencia [ay-sen'-the-ah], *f.* 1. Essence, formal existence (problema) 2. *(Chem. and Phar.)* Essence, a volatile oil; a solution in alcohol of an aromatic, or volatile oil. **Quinta esencia**, quintessence, an extract. **Ser de esencia**, to be indispensable, necessary.

esencial [ay-sen-the-ahl'], *a.* 1. Essential, necessary, constituent. 2. Essential, important in the highest degree; material; principal, main: formal.

esencialmente [ay-sen-the-ahl'-men-tay], *adv.* Essentially, principally, naturally, materially.

esenciarse [ay-sen-the-ar'-say], *vr.* To be intimately united, to grow essential.

esfacelado, da [es-fah-thay-lah'-do, dah], *a. (Med.)* Sphacelated, gangrenous.

esfacelar [es-fah-thay-lar'], *va.* To cause sphacelus, or gangrene.

esfacelo [es-fah-thay'-lo], *m. (Med.)* Sphacelus, gangrene of an entire member.

esfeciforme [es-fay-the-for'-may], *a.* Wasp-shaped, like a sphex (avispa).

esfenoidal [es-fay-no-ee-dahl'], *a.* Sphenoidal, belonging to the sphenoid bone.

esfenoides [es-fay-no'-e-days], *m.* The sphenoid bone.

esfera [es-fay'-rah], *f.* 1. Sphere, a globe or orb. 2. Globe, representing the earth or sky. 3. Quality, character, condition, state, rank. 4. *(Post.)* Heaven. **Está fuera de mi esfera**, that is out of my reach. **En forma de esfera**, spherical.

esferal [es-fay-rahl'], *a. V.* ESFÉRICO.

esféricamente [es-fay'-re-cah-men-tay], *adv.* Spherically.

esfericidad [es-fay-re-the-dahd'], *f.* Sphericity, rotundity, orbicularness, globosity.

esférico, ca [es-fay'-re-co, cah], *a.* Spherical, globular, globous, globated.

esferoidal [es-fay-ro-e-dahl'], *a.* Spheroidical, spheroidal.

esferoide [es-fay-ro'-e-day'], *f.* Spheroid. **Bóveda esferoide**, elliptical arch.

esférula [es-fay'-roo-lah], *f.* A rounded conceptacle, whether oblong or conical, which is porous in its upper part.

esfinge [es-feen'-hay], *f.* Sphinx, a fabulous monster. *-m.* Sphinx, hawk-moth, or humming bird moth.

esfíngido, da [es-feen'-he-do, dah], *a.* Sphinx-like.

esfínter [es-feen'-ter], *m. (Anat.)* Sphincter.

esflorecer [es-flo-ray-therr'], *vn. (Chem.)* To effloresce, to fall into powder when exposed to the air.

esforrocino [es-for-ro-thee'-no], *m.* Sprig shooting from the trunk of a vine.

esforzadamente [es-for-thah-dah'-men-tay], *adv.* Strenuously, vigorously, valiantly.

esforzado [es-for-thah'-do], *m.* One of the books of the civil law which deals with testaments and last wills.

esforzado, da [es-for-thah'-do, dah], *a.* Strong (fuerte), vigorous, valiant (valiente). *-pp.* of ESFORZAR.

esforzador, ra [es-for-thah-dor', rah], *m. & f.* Exciter, animater.

esforzar [es-for-thar'], *va.* 1 To strengthen (fortalecer), to invigorate, to exert, to enforce or to force. 2. *(Met.)* To aid, to corroborate, to encourage (animar). *-vr.* 1. To exert oneself, to make efforts. **Hay que esforzarse más,** you must try harder. 2. To be confident, to assure oneself.

esfuerzo [es-foo-err'-tho], *m.* 1 Courage (valentía), spirit, vigor (vigor), heart, manfulness. 2. Effort (imaginación), strong endeavor, exertion, contention, laboring. **Sin esfuerzo,** effortlessly, without strain. **Bien vale el esfuerzo,** it´s well worth the effort. 3. Confidence, faith. 4. Help, aid. *(Yo esfuerzo, yo esfuerce, from Esforzar. V. ACORDAR.)*

esfumado [es-foo-mah'-do], *m.* The first sketch of a painting, drawn with a pencil or charcoal. *-a.* Sfumato, having hazy outlines. **Esfumado, da,** *pp.* of ESFUMAR.

esfumar [es-foo-mar'], *va. (Pict.)* To shade over the pencilled outlines of a picture.

esfumarse [es-foo-mar'-say], *vr.* To disappear, to fade away (esperanzas)

esfumino [es-foo-mee'-no], *m. (Art.)* A stump for shading with charcoal or powdered pigments. *Cf.* DIFUMINO.

esgarrar [es-gar-rar'], *m. (Prov. Amer.)* V. GARGAJEAR.

esgarro [es-gar'-ro], *m. (Amer.)* V. GARGAJO.

esgorbia [es-gor'-be-ah], *f.* An auger for tin workers.

esgrima [es-gree'-mah], *f.* Fencing, the art of manual defence (arte). **Maestro de esgrima,** fencing master.

esgrimidor [es-gre-me-dor'], *m.* Fencer or fencing master. **Casa de esgrimidor,** *(Met.)* house without furniture.

esgrimidura [es-gre-me-doo'-rah], *f.* The act of fencing.

esgrimir [es-gre-meer'], *va.* 1. To practise the use of weapons (espada). 2. To fence, to fight according to art.

esguazable [es-goo-ah-thah'-blay], *a.* Fordable.

esguazar [es-goo-ah-thar'], *va.* To ford, as a river.

esgucio [es-goo'-the-o], *m. (Arch.)* Concave moulding.

esguín [es-geen'], *m.* Young salmon before entering the sea.

esguince [es-geen'-thay], *m.* 1. Movement of the body to avoid a blow or a fall (movimiento). 2. Frown (ceño). 3. A twist or sprain of a joint.

esgüízaro [es-goo-ee'-thah -ro], *a.* A miserable fellow, a ragamuffin.

eskol [es'-kole], *m.* A fabulous wolf.

eslabón [es-lah-bone'], *m.* 1. Link of a chain, chain links (cadena). 2. Steel for striking fire with a flint. 3. Steel for sharpening knives. 4. A very poisonous scorpion.

eslabonador [es-lah-bo-nah-dor'], *m.* Chain maker.

eslabonamiento [es-la-bo-nah-me-en'-to], *m.* 1. Linking, uniting. 2. A chain, concatenation of various things.

eslabonar [es-lah-bo-nar'], *va.* 1. To link, to join one ring to another. 2. *(Met.)* To add, to unite.

eslavo, va [es-lah'-vo, vah], *a.* Slavic, Slavonic *-m. & f.* Slav *-m.* Slavic language.

eslinga [es-leen'-gah], *f. (Naut.)* Sling, a rope with which bales or casks are hoisted.

eslingar [es-lin-gar'], *va. (Naut.)* To sling, to throw with a sling.

eslogan [es-lo'-gahn], *m.* V. SLOGAN.

eslora [es-lo'-rah], *f.* Length of a ship on the deck from the stem to the sternpost. **Esloras,** beams running from stem to stern.

esmaltador [es-mal-tah-dor'], *m.* Enameller.

esmaltadura [es-mal-tah-doo'-rah], *f.* 1. Enamelling. 2. Enamel work.

esmaltar [es-mal-tar'], *va.* 1. To enamel (metal), to be scattered over, to varnish (uñas) 2. *(Met.)* To adorn, to embellish.

esmalte [es-mal'-tay], *m.* 1. Enamel, something enamelled. 2. An azure color, made of paste. 3. Smalt. **Esmalte de uñas,** nail polish. V. LUSTRE.

esmarchazo [es-mar-chah'-tho], *m.* A bully.

esmectita [es-mec-tee'-tah], *f.* Name of some clays like fuller's earth.

esmeradamente [es-may-rah-dah-men'-tay], *adv.* Nicely, correctly, accurately.

esmerado, da [es-may-rah'-do,dah], *a.* Careful, neat, executed with care, painstaking, precise (trabajo). *-pp.* of ESMERAR.

esmeralda [es-may-rahl'-dah], *f.* Emerald, a precious stone.

esmerar [es-may-rar'], *va.* To polish, to brighten by attrition. *-vr.* To endeavor, to attain eminence or excellence, to take great pains.

esmerejón [es-may-ray-hone'], *m.* 1. *(Orn.)* Merlin, the yellow-legged falcon. 2. Small piece of artillery.

esmeril [es-may-reel'], *m.* 1. Emery, a mineral used in polishing. 2. Small piece of ordnance.

esmerilar [es-may-re-lar'], *va.* To burnish, to polish with emery.

esmerilazo [es-may-re-lah'-tho], *m.* Shot of a gun called *esmeril.*

esmero [es-may'-ro], *m.* Careful attention, elaborate effort, niceness, correctness, accuracy. **Poner esmero en algo,** to take great care over something.

esmilacina [es-me-lah-thee'-nah], *f.* 1. *(Bot.)* Smilacina, false Solomon's seal. 2. An alkaloid obtained from the inner pith of the sarsaparilla.

esmirriado [es-mer-re-ah'-do], *a.* Puny, thin (enclenque); scraggy.

esmodita [es-mo-dee'-tah], *f.* A pulverulent material produced by volcanoes.

esmoladera [es-mo-lah-day'-rah], *f.* Whetstone.

esmoquin [es-mo'-keen], *m.* Dinner jacket.

esmuciarse [es-moo-the-ar'-say], *vr. (Prov.)* To slip from the hands.

esnifar [es-ne-far'], *va.* To sniff.

esnob or **snob** [es-nob'], *m.* Snob (persona); posh (coche, restaurante).

esnobismo [es-no-bees'-mo], *m.* Snobbery, snobbishness.

esnón [es-none'], *m. (Naut.)* A spencer mast, trysail mast.

eso [ay'-so], *dem. pron.* That. (plural: **Esos,** those). **Eso es,** that is it. **No es eso,** it is not that. **A eso de,** toward, about. **No me gusta eso,** I don´t like that. **Nada de eso,** nothing of the kind. **Antes de eso,** before that. **Después de eso,** after that. **Es por eso que no vino,** that´s why she didn´t come.

esófago [ay-so'-fah-go], *m. (Anat.)* Esophagus, gullet; the throat.

esotérico, ca [ay-so-tay'-re-co, cah], *a.* Esoteric; confidential, secret.

esotro, tra [ay-so'-tro, ay-so'-trah], *pron dem.* This or that other; pointing out not the first, but the second, third, etc., person or thing.

espabiladeras [es-pah-be-lah-day-ras], *f. pl.* Snuffers.

espabilar [es-pah-be-lar'], va. 1. To snuff a candle (vela). 2. To nick (robar). 3. To do in (matar). -vr. To wake up; to look lively, to get a move on; to pull one's socks up. V. DESPABILAR.

espachurrar [es-pah-choor-rhar'], va. To squash, to flatten.

espaciador [es-pah-the-ah-dor'], m. Spacer (máquina de escribir).

espacial [es-pah-the-al'], a. Relating to space. Cápsula espacial, space capsule.

espaciar [es-pah-the-ar'], va. 1. To extend, to dilate, to spread. 2. To space, to separate the lines in writing or printing. 3. To stagger (horas de trabajo).-vr. 1. To expand (en escritura y hablado). Espaciarse en un tema, to enlarge on a subject. 2. To amuse oneself.

espacio [es-pah'-the-o], m. 1. Space, capacity; distance between objects. Espacio libre, clear space. 2. Space, interval of time. En el espacio de tres generaciones, in the space of three generations. 3. Slowness, delay (tardanza), procrastination. 4. (Obs.) Recreation, diversion. 5. Musical interval. 6. In printing, space, type which separates words. A dos espacios, doubled-space. 7. (Ast.) V. DESCAMPADO.

espacio interastral [es-pah-the-o in-ter-as-trahl'], m. Outer space.

especiosamente [es-pay-the-o'-sah-men-tay], adv. Deliberately, spaciously.

espaciosidad [es-pah-the-o-se-dahd'], f. Spaciousness, capacity.

espacioso, sa [es-pah-the-oh'-so, sah], a. 1. Spacious, capacious, wide, roomy, large, extensive (cuarto). 2. Blow, deliberate (movimiento).

espada [es-pah'-dah], f. 1. Sword (arma). 2. Swordsman (persona). 3. Ace of spades, or any card in the suit of spades. 4. (Zool.) Swordfish. 5. The bullfighter who kills the bull with a sword. Espada blanca, sword. Espada negra or de esgrima, foil, a blunt sword used in fencing. Entrar con espada en mano, to attack sword in hand; to enter upon an affair supporting one's own business strongly. Hombre de capa y espada, a person of no profession. Primer espada, the head bullfighter. Verse entre la espada y la pared, to be driven to the wall, to be surrounded by danger. Es una buena espada, he is a good or dexterous swordsman. Espada ancha or espada de a caballo, Broadsword; dragoon's sabre.

espadachín [es-pah-dah-cheen'], m. Bully, hackster, one who affects valor.

espadadero [es-pah-dah-day'-ro], m. Braking floor, scutch-blade, a table for braking flax or hemp.

espadado, da [es-pah-dah'do, dah], a. Armed with a sword. -pp. of ESPADAR.

espadador [es-pah-dah-dor'], m. One who brakes flax or hemp with a swingle.

espadaña [es-pah-dah'-nyah], f. 1 (Bot.) Reedmace, great cat-tail. 2. Spire.

espadaña [es-pah-dah-nya], f. Sudden flow of blood, water, etc., from the mouth.

espadañal [es-pah-dah-nyahl'], m. The place where reedmace is growing.

espadañar [es-pah-dah-nyar'], va. To divide into long thin slips, resembling flags.

espadar [es-pah-dar'], va. To brake hemp or flax with a swingle.

espadarte [es-pah-dar'-tay], m. (Zool.) Swordfish. V. ESPADA.

espadazo [es-pah-dah-tho], m. Sword thrust, slash with a sword.

espadería [es-pah-day-ree'-ah], f. Sword-cutler's shop.

espadero [es-pah-day'-ro], m. Swordsmith.

espádice [es-pah'de-thay], m. Spadix, a common receptacle of several flowers inclosed in a spathe.

espadilla [es-pah-deel'-lyah], f. 1. Red insignia of the order of Santiago in the shape of a sword. 2. Swingle used in braking hemp and flax, a scutching handle. 3. (Naut.) A small oar, or helm for boats. 4. Ace of spades. 5. (Bot.) Cornflag.

espadillar [es-pah-deel-lyar'], va. To brake or scutch hemp or flax with a swingle.

espadillazo [es-pah-dil-lyah'-tho], m. Adverse fortune at cards, where the ace is lost.

espadín [es-pah-deen'], m. A small short sword (espada).

espadita [es-pah-dee'-tah], f. dim. A small sword.

espadón [es-pah-done'], m. 1. (Aug.) A large sword. 2. Eunuch, one that is castrated.

espadrapo [es-pah-drah'-po], m. V. ESPARADRAPO.

espagírica [es-pah-hee'-re-cah], f. Metallurgy, the art of refining metals.

espagírico, ca [es-pah-he'-re-co, cah], a. Belonging to the art of metallurgy.

espaguetis [es-pah-gay'-tees], m. pl. Spaghetti.

espalda [es-pahl'-dah], f. 1. Shoulder, the upper part of the back. 2. (Mil.) Shoulder of a bastion. Espaldas, a) back or back part. b) (Met.) aid, protection. A espaldas, at one's back, in one's absence. Echar a las espaldas, to forget on purpose, to abandon. Sobre mis espaldas, at my expense. Tornar or volver las espaldas, 1. To avoid someone; to turn one's back in contempt. 2. To fly, to run away. A espaldas de uno, behind somebody's back. Atar las manos a la espalda, to tie somebody's hands behind his back. Cubrir las espaldas, (Fig.) to cover oneself.

espaldar [es-pal-dar'], m. 1. Back piece of an armor, shoulder piece of a coat of mail. 2. Place where one puts his back to rest against (silla). 3. Espalier in gardens. Espaldares, pieces of tapestry against which chairs lean.

espaldarazo [es-pal-dah-rah'-tho], m. Blow with the flat of a sword, or of the hand, on the shoulders.

espaldarón [es-pal-dah-rone'], m. Ancient armor for the shoulders.

espaldear [es-pal-day-ar'], va. (Naut.) To break (olas) with impetuosity against the poop of a vessel.

espalder [es-pal-derr'], m. The first of stern rower in a galley.

espaldera [es-pal-day' rah], f. Espalier, trees planted and cut so as to join; wall trees.

espaldilla [es-pal-deel'-lyah], f. 1. Shoulder blade. 2. Hind quarter of a waistcoat or jacket. 3. (Anat.) Omoplate, scapula.

espalditendido, da [es-pal-de-ten-dee'-do, dah], a. (coll.) Stretched on one's back.

espaldón [es-pal-done'], m. 1. (Arch.) V. RASTRO. 2. Intrenchment or barrier to defend one from an attack. 3. (Naut.) A hawsepiece. 4. A barrier of, baskets, bags, etc., to guard the artillery and sappers during a siege. 5. Half bulwark, generally of one face and one flank.

espaldonarse [es-pal-do-nar'-say], vr To get under cover, to guard oneself from the fire of the enemy.

espaldudo, da [es-pal-doo'-do, dah], a. Broad-shouldered.

espalmadura [es-pal-mah-doo'-rah], f. Hoofs of quadrupeds.

espalmar [es-pal-mar'], va. (Naut.) To clean and pay a ship's bottom. V. DESPALMAR.

espalto [es-pahl'-to], m. 1. Dark-colored paint. 2. (Mil.) Esplanade. 3. Spalt, a scaly whitish mineral used as a flux for metals.

espantable [es-pan-tah'-blay], a. 1. Frightful, horrid, terrible. 2. Marvellous, wonderful.

espantablemente [es pan tah blay men'-tay], adv. Horribly, terribly, frightfully.

espantadizo, za [es-pan-tah-dee'-tho, thah], a. Timid, easily frightened.

espantado [es-pan-tah'-do], a. Frightened, scared, terrified.

espantador, ra [es-pan-tah-dor', rah], m. & f. Bugbear, one that frightens or terrifies (espantador).

espantajo [es-pan-tah'-ho], m. 1 Scarecrow, set up to frighten birds. 2. One who cuts grimaces for the purpose of frightening.

espantalobos [es-pan-tah-lo'-bos], *m.* *(Bot.)* Bladder or bastard senna. **Espantalobos arborescente**, common bladder senna.

espantamocas [es-pan-tah-mos'-cas], *m.* Net put on horses to scare away flies.

espantanublados [es-pan-tah-noo-blah'-dos],*m.* Rake, vagabond begging in long robes, who is thought by the vulgar to have power over the clouds.

espantapájaros [es-pan-tah-pah'-hah-ros], *m.* Scarecrow.

espantar [es-pan-tar'], *va.* 1. To frighten (asustar), to terrify, to fright, to daunt, to shock. 2. To chase or drive away (ahuyentar). *-vr.* To be surprised or astonished, to marvel (asombrarse).

espantavillanos [es-pan-tah-vil-lyah', nos], *m.* Sort of shining or glittering gaudy stuff.

espanto [es-pahn'-to], *m.* 1 Fright (miedo), consternation (consternación), frightfulness. 2. Menace, threat (amenaza). 3. Admiration, wonder, surprise; horror. 4. Hideousness, grimness. **Hace un frío de espanto**, it´s terribly cold.

espantosamente [es-pah-to'-sah-men-tay], *adv.* Dreadfully, marvellously, frightfully, ghastfully.

espantoso, sa [es-pan-to'-so, sah], *a.* 1. Frightful, dreadful, horrid, horrible; fearful. 2. Marvelous, wonderful.

español, la [es-pah-nyole', lah], *a.* Spanish, relating to Spain. **A la española**, in the Spanish manner.

español [es-pah-nyole'], *m.* Spanish language.

españolado, da [es-pah-nyo-lah'-do, dah], *a.* Applied to a foreigner who in his manners, etc., is like a Spaniard, or who follows Spanish customs.*-pp.* of ESPAÑOLAR.

españolar [es-pah-nyo-lar´], *va.* V. ESPAÑOLIZAR.

españolería [es-pah-nyo-lay-ree´-ah],*f.* *(Obs.)* Spanish taste, manners, and customs.

españoleta [es-pah-nyo-lay'-tah], *f.* Ancient Spanish dance.

españolismo [es-pah-nyo-lees'-mo], *f.* Love, devotion, to Spain; patriotism.

españolizado, da [es-pah-nyo-lee-thah'-do, dah], *a. & pp.* of *Españolizar*. V. ESPAÑOLADO.

españolizar [es-pah-nyo-le-thar'], *va.* To make Spanish, to render conformable to the Spanish language or Spanish analogies. *-vr.* To adopt the customs and manners of Spain.

espar [es-par'], *m.* Spar, a kind of aromatic drug.

esparadrapo [es-pah-rah-drah'-po], *m.* Adhesive plaster, court plaster.

esparagón [es-pah-rah-gone'], *m.* Grogram, a coarse stuff.

esparamarín [es-pah-rah-ma-reen'], *m.* Serpent which mounts trees to dart on its prey.

esparaván [es-pah-rah-vahn'], *m.* 1 *(Vet.)* Bone-spavin, tumor in the legs of horses. 2. *(Orn.)* Sparrow-hawk.

esparavel [es-pah-rah-vel´], *m.* 1. Kind of fishing net. 2. Carpenter's mortarboard.

esparceta [es-par-thay´-tah], *f.* *(Bot.)* Saintfoin hedysarum.

esparciata [es-par-the-ah'-tah] *,a.* Spartan.

esparcidamente [es-par-the'-dah-men-tay], *adv.* Distinctly, separately; gayly.

esparcido, da [es-par-thee'-do, dah], *a.* 1. Scattered (desparramado). 2. *(Met.)* Merry, festive, gay (alegre). *-pp.* of ESPARCIR.

esparcilla [es-par-theel'-lyah], *f.* *(Bot.)* Spurrey. **Esparcilla arvense**, rough-seeded spurrey.

esparcimiento [es-par-the-me-en'-to], *m.* 1. Scattering, dissemination. 2. Amusement (recreo). 3. *(Met.)* Frankness, openness (franqueza). 4. *(Met.)* Liberality of sentiments, generosity of mind.

esparcir [es-par-theer'], *va.* 1. To scatter (desparramar), to disseminate (divulgar), to fling. 2. *(Met.)* To divulge, to spread abroad. *-vr.* To amuse oneself (distraerse), to make merry.

espardeña [es-par-day´-nyah], *f.* *(Prov.)* V. ESPARTEÑA.

esparganio [es-par-gah'-ne-o], *m.* *(Bot.)* Bur-reed.

esparo [es-pah'-ro], *m.* *(Zool.)* Gilt-head, a seafish.

esparragado [es-par-rah-gah'-do], *m.* A dish of asparagus.

esparragador [es-par-rah-gah-dor'], *m.* He who collects and takes care of asparagus.

esparragar [es-par-rah-gar'], *va.* To guard or collect asparagus. **Anda or vete a esparragar**, *(coll.)* expression, to dispatch or dismiss one contemptuously or angrily.

esparragíneo, nea [es-par-rah-hee'-nay-o, ah], *a.* Asparagoid, like asparagus.

espárrago [es-par´-rah-go], *m.* 1. *(Bot.)* Sprout of asparagus. **Solo como el espárrago**, *(coll.)* As lonely as asparagus; every stalk growing by itself. **Espárrago triguero**, wild asparagus. **Mandar a uno a freír espárragos**, to tell somebody to go to hell. 2. Pole to support an awning.

esparragón [es-par-rah-gone'], *m.* Silk stuff that forms a cord thicker and stronger than taffeta.

esparraguera [es-par-rah-gay´-rah], *f.* 1. Asparagus plant; stem of this plant. 2. An asparagus bed.

esparraguero, ra [es-par-rah-gay'-ro, rah], *m. & f.* One who gathers and sells asparagus.

esparrancado, da [es-par-ran-cah´-do, dah], *a.* Bow-legged, bandy-legged, divaricated. *-pp.* of ESPARRANCARSE.

esparrancarse [es-par-ran-car'-say], *vr.* *(coll.)* To straddle, to bestride.

espartal [es-par-tahl'], *m.* Field on which feathergrass is growing.

espartano, na [es-par-tah'-no, nah], *a.* Spartan, belonging to Sparta.

esparteña [es-par-tay'-nyah], *f.* A sort of sandal made of feathergrass.

espartería [es-par-tay-ree'-ah], *f.* Place where mats of tough feather-grass are made or sold.

espartero, ra [es-par-tay'-ro, rah], *m. & f.* One who makes and sells articles of feathergrass.

espartilla [es-par-teel'-lyah], *f.* Handful of feathergrass which serves as brush for cleaning animals.

espartizal [es-par-te-thahl'], *m.* Field on which feathergrass is growing.

esparto [es-par'-to], *m.* *(Bot.)* Feather grass; Spanish grass hemp. **Esparto basto**, rush-leaved lygeum.

espasmo [es-pahs'-mo], *m.* V. PASMO. Spasm.

espasmódico, ca [es-pas-mo´-de-co, cah], *a.* Spasmodic, convulsive.

espástico, ca [es-pahs'-te-co, cah], *a.* Spastic, spasmodic.

espata [es-pah'-tah], *f.* *(Bot.)* Spathe, a large bract sheathing a fowercluster.

espático, ca [es-pah'-te-co, cah], *a.* Spathic, of spar.

espato [es-pah'-to], *m.* Spar, a calcareous mineral.

espátula [es-pah'-too-lah], *f.* 1. Spatula, or slice used by apothecaries and surgeons. 2. A palette knife. 3. *(Bot.)* A kind of fetidiris. 4. *(Zool.)* The spoonbill, a long-shanked bird common in S. America.

espaviento [es-pah-ve-en'-to], *m.* V. ASPAVIENTO.

espavorido, da, espavorecido, da [es-pah-vo-ree'-do, dah, es-pah-ro-ray-thee'-do, dah], *a.* V. DESPAVORIDO.

especería [es-pay-thay-ree'-ah],*f.* The more colloquial form. V. ESPECIERÍA. Spicery.

especia [es-pay'-the-ah], *f.* Spice.*-pl.* Medicinal drugs.

especial [es-pay-the-ahl'], *a.* Special, particular (persona). **En especial**, specially.

especialidad [es-pay-the-ah-le-dahd'], *f.* Speciality or specialty, particularity.

especialista [es-pay-the-ah-lees'-tah], *a. & m.* Specialist, one who cultivates or excels in a science. **Especialista en telecomunicaciones**, *(Inform.)* telecommunications specialist.

especialización [es-pay-the-ah-le-thah-the-on'], *f.* Specialization.

especializado, da [es-pay-the-ah-le-thah-do], *a.* Specialized; skilled (obrero), trained. **Mano de obra especializada**, skilled labor.

especializarse [es-pay-the-ah-le-thar'-say], *vr.* To specialize.

especialmente [es-pay-the-al-men'-tay], *adv.* Especially, in particular, namely, nominally.

especiar [es-pay-the-ar'], *va.* To spice broth or food.

especie [es-pay'-the-ay], *f.* 1. Species; a kind, a sort; a sub-division of a general term; nature (clase). 2. Species, any sensible representation. 3. Image or idea of any object in the mind (idea). 4. Event, incident. 5. Pretext, show. 6. *(Chem.)* A collection of properties which only belong to one body. 7. Feint in fencing. 8. *pl.* *(Phys.)* Luminous rays diversely reflected. 9. *pl.* **Especies sacramentales**, the accidents of color, taste, and smell, which remain in the sacrament, after the conversion of the bread and wine into the body and blood of Christ.

especiería [es-pay-the-ay-ree'-ah], *f.* 1. A grocer's shop, grocery. 2. A shop where spices are sold. 3. Spices and all sorts of aromatic drugs. *(Acad.)*

especiero [es-pay-the-ay'-ro], *m.* A dealer in spices and aromatic drugs, a grocer.

especificación [es-pay-the-fe-ca-the-on'], *f.* Specification, a minute enumeration of things.

específicamente [es-pay-the'-fe-cah-men-tay], *adv.* Specifically, distinctly, expressly.

especificar [es-pay-the-fe-car'], *va.* To specify, to state minutely, to name; to show by some particular mark of distinction.

especificativo, va [es-pay-the-fe-cah-tee'-vo, vah]. *a.* That which has the power of specifying or distinguishing.

específico [es-pay-thee'-fe-co], *m.* Specific, a remedy for some particular disease.

específico, ca [es-pay-thee'-fe-co, cah], *a.* Specific.

espécimen [es-pay'-the-men], *m.* *(Neol.)* Specimen, sample. -*pl.* The known kinds of letters in ancient times.

especioso, sa [es-pay-thc-oh'-so, sah], *a.* 1. Neat, beautiful, gay; finished with care. 2. Superficial, apparent, specious, plausible, colorable; glossy.

espectacular [es-payc-tah-coo-lar'], *a.* Spectacular.

espectacularmente [es-payc-tah-coo-lahr'-men-tay], *adv.* Spectacularly, in spectacular fashion.

espectáculo [es-pec-tah'-coo lo], *m.* 1. Spectacle, show; a pageant. **Espectáculo de variedades**, variety show. 2. Spectacle, anything to be looked on, or anything exhibited as eminently remarkable. **Dar un espectáculo**, to make a scene.

espectador [es-pec-tah-dor'], *m.* Spectator. **Los espectadores**, the spectators.

espectral [es-pec-trahl'], *a.* 1. Spectral, phantom-like, ghost-like. 2. *(Phys.)* Spectral.

espectro [es-pec'-tro], *m.* 1. Specter, phantom, ghost (fantasma). 2. A vampire bat.

espectroscópico, ca [es-pec-tros-co'-pe-co, cah], *a.* Spectroscopic, relating to the solar spectrum.

espectroscopio [es-pec-tros-co'-pe-o], *m.* Spectroscope.

especulación [es-pay-coo-lah-the-on'], *f.* 1. Speculation, contemplation (meditación), mental view. 2. A commercial scheme or adventure. 3. Theory, as opposed to practice.

especulador, ra [es-pay-coo-lah-dor', rah], *m. & f.* Speculator.

especular [es-pay-coo-lar'], *va.* 1. To behold, to view, to examine (examinar). 2. To speculate, to meditate (meditar), to contemplate. 3. To form commercial schemes.

especular, *adj.* 1. Specular, relating to a mirror. 2. Transparent, diaphanous

especulativa [es-pay-coo-lah-tee'-vah], *f.* Faculty of viewing or speculating understanding.

especulativamente [es-payc-tah-coo-lah-te'-vah-men-tay], *adv.* Speculatively.

especulativo, va [es-pay-coo-lah-tee'-vo, vah], *a.* Speculative, thoughtful.

espéculo [es-pay'-coo-lo], *m.* 1. Speculum, an instrument to aid in the inspection of cavities of the body. 2. A code of laws compiled by order of Alfonso the Wise.

espejado, da [es-pay-hah'-do, dah], *a.* Mirror-like, resembling or consisting of looking glasses.

espejería [es-pay-hay-ree'-ah], *f.* 1. Glass-shop, a place where looking glasses are sold. 2. Glasshouse, where plate-glass is made.

espejero [es-pay-hay'-ro], *m.* One whose trade is to make or sell mirrors.

espejico, illo, ito [es-pay-hee'-co, eel'-lyo, ee'to], *m. dim.* Little mirror.

espejismo (or **espejeo**) [es-pay-hees'-mo, es-pay-hay'o], *m.* Looming, mirage.

espejo [es-pay'-ho], *m.* 1. Looking glass, mirror; a glass which shows forms reflected. **Limpio como un espejo**, as clean as a penny. **Espejo de cuerpo entero**, full-length mirror. **Espejo retrovisor**, driving mirror. 2. **Espejo de popa**, *(Naut.)* Sternframe.

espejuela [es-pay-hoo-ay'-lah], *f.* A kind of sharp bit for a horse, forming an arch.

espejuelo [es-pay-hoo-ay'-lo], *m.* 1. *(dim.)* A small looking glass. 2. Specular stone, selenite, a kind of transparent lamellated gypsum. 3. Transparent leaf of mica. 4. Instrument used by bird catchers in catching larks. **Espejuelos**, crystal lenses, of which spectacles are made; glasses.

espelta [es-pel'-tah], *f.* *(Bot.)* 1. V. ESCANDIA. 2. V. ESCAÑA.

espélteo, ea [es-pel'-tay-o, ah], *a.* Belonging to spelt.

espeluznante [es-pay-looth-nahn'-tay], *a.* Hair-raising, horrifying.

espeluznarse [es-pay-looth-nar'-say], *vr.* To have the hair dishevelled, or set on end with fear.

espeque [es-pay'-kay], *m.* Handspike, wooden lever.

espera [es-pay'-rah], *f.* 1. Expectation, the act of expecting. 2. Expectance or expectancy, the state of expecting. 3. Stay, the act of waiting (período). 4. Pause, stop. 5. Stay, restraint, prudence, caution, steadiness. 6. *(Law.)* Respite, adjournment, pause, interval. 7. A kind of heavy ordnance. 8. A letter of license. **Estar a la espera**, to be in expectation of. **En espera de su contestación**, awaiting your reply. **La cosa no tiene espera**, the matter brooks no delay. **Sala de espera**, waiting room.

esperable [es-pay-rah'-blay], *a.* That which may be expected or hoped.

esperador, ra [es-pay-ra-dor', rah], *a.* Expectant.

esperanza [es-pay-rahn'-thah], *f.* Hope, expectance, expectancy. **No hay esperanza**, there is no chance. **Esperanza de vida**, life expectancy. **Hay pocas esperanzas de que venga**, there is little prospect of his coming. **Tener esperanzas de**, to have hopes of.

esperanzador [es-pay-ran-thah-dor'], *a.* Hopeful, encouraging.

esperanzar [es-pay-ran-thar'], *va.* To give hope.

esperar [es-pay-rar'], *va.* 1. To hope (tener esperanza). **Esperar que**, to hope that... **Espero que sea así**, I hope it is so. **Espero que vengas**, I hope you'll come. 2. To expect, to have a previous apprehension of either good or evil. **Esperamos que llegue a la hora**, we expect it to arrive on time. 3. To wait, to stay, to wait for (aguardar, esperar a), to attend the coming, to look for. **Esperar el avión**, to wait for the plane. **Ir a esperar a uno**, to go and meet somebody. **No me esperes después de las 7**, don't wait for me after 7. 4. To fear. *-vr.* To expect, to wait, to stay (aguardar). **Como podía esperarse**, as it might be expected. **Se espera que todo esté listo**, it is hoped that all will be ready.

esperezarse, or **desperezarse** [es-pay-ray-thar'-say], *vr.* To stretch oneself.

esperezo [es-pay-ray'-tho], *m.* The act of stretching one's arms and legs after being roused from sleep.

esperiego, ga [es-pay-re-ay'-go, gah], *a.* V. ASPERIEGA. **Esperiego**, tart apple-tree, pippin.

esperlán [es-per-lahn'], *m.* *(Zool.)* Smelt, a small sea-fish.

esperma [es-perr'-mah], *f.* Sperm. V. SEMEN. **Esperma de ballena**, spermaceti.

espermeceti [es-per-may-thay'-te], *m.* Spermaceti.

espermático, ca [es-per-mah'-te-co, cah], *a.* Spermatic, seminal, belonging to the sperm.

espermatorrea [es-per-ma-tor-ray'-ah], *f.* Spermatorrhoea, involuntary loss of semen.

espermatozoide [es-per-mah-to-thoy'-day], *m.* Spermatozoid.

espérmido, da [es-perr'-me-do, dah], Producing seeds.

espernada [es-per-nah'-dah], *f.* End of a chain.

espernible [es-per-nee-blay], *a. (Prov.)* Despicable.

esperón [es-pay-rone'], *m. (Naut.)* The forecastle head.

esperonte [es-pay-ron'-tay], *m.* Kind of ancient fortification.

esperpento [es-per-pen'-to], *m.* 1. Fright, sight (persona). 2. Absurdity (disparate), nonsense. 3. Macabre story (cuento), grotesque tale. 4. *(Teat.)* Play which focuses on the grotesque.

esperriaca [es-per-re-ah'-cah], *f. (Prov.)* The last must or juice drawn from grapes.

espesamiento [es-pay-sah-me-en´-to], *m. (Prov.)* Coagulation.

espesar [es-pay-sar'], *va.* 1. To thicken, to inspissate, to condense what is fluid (líquido). 2. To coagulate, to curdle, to concrete. 3. To mass, to assemble. 4. To close, to join, as silk or stuff does (tejido). *-vr.* To condensate, to grow thicker.

espesartina [es-pay-sar-tee'-nah], *f.* Spessartite or spessartin, a hyacinthred garnet.

espesativo, va [es-pay-sah-tee'-vo, vah], *a.* That which has the power of thickening.

espeso, sa [es-pay'-so, sah], *a.* 1. Thick, condensed, dense (bosque), gross, crass; curdy. 2. Close, contiguous. 3. Frequent, often repeated. 4. Slovenly, dirty (sucio).

espesor [es-pay-sor'], *m.* Thickness, grossness, crassitude; corpulence.

espesura [es-pay-soo'-rah], *f.* 1. Thickness (espesor), density, closeness, crassitude. 2. *(Fort.)* Thickness, solidity of the works of a fortress. 3. Thicket, a close wood. **Se refugiaron en las espesuras**, they took refuge in the forest. 4. Slovenliness, negligence of dress.

espetamiento [es-pay-tah-me-en'-to], *m. (coll.)* Stiffness, formality, stateliness of mien or deportment.

espetar [es-pay-tar'], *va.* 1. To spit, to put upon a spit. 2. To run through with a sword (persona). 3. To tell, to relate (lección, sermón). **Le espetó fuertes razones**, he gave strong reasons. *-vr.* 1. To be stiff and stately, to be puffed up with pride. 2. *(Met. coll.)* To slide or thrust oneself into some narrow place.

espatera [es-pay-tay'-rah], *f.* 1. Rack, a board with hooks, on which kitchen utensils are hung. 2. Kitchen furniture.

espetón [es-pay-tone'], *m.* 1. Spit, a long iron prong (broqueta). 2. A large pin (clavija). 3. *(Zool.)* Seapike, spit-fish. 4. Blow given with a spit.

espía [es-pee'-ah], *m. & f.* 1. A spy. **Espía doble**, double agent. 2. *(Naut.)* Warp, a rope used in moving a ship, a tow-rope of twisted bark (cabo).

espiar [es-pe-ar'], *va.* 1. To spy, to watch closely (vigilar). 2. To lurk, to lie in wait. 3. *(Naut.)* To warp, to move a ship by means of a warp.

espibia [es-pee'-be-ah], *f. (Vet.)* Incomplete dislocation of the vertebrae.

espibio, espibión [es-pee'-be-o, es-pe-be-on'], *m. (Vet.)* Dislocation or contraction in the nape of the neck of animals.

espicanardi [es-pe-cah-nar'-de], *f. (Bot.)* Spikenard.

espichar [es-pe-char´], *va.* 1. To prick (pinchar). V. PINCHAR. 2.*(coll.)* To give up the ghost, to die (morir).

espiche [es-pee'-chay], *m.* A sharp-pointed weapon. **Espiches**, *(Naut.)* pegs, small pointed pieces of wood driven into the holes of the planks of ships, dowel, spire.

espichón [es-pe-chone'], *m.* Wound with a pointed weapon.

espicifloro, ra [es-pe-the-flo'-ro, rah], *a. (Bot.)* Spicate, having flowers arranged in spikes.

espicúleo, a [es-pe-coo'-lay-o, ah], *a. (Bot.)* Spiculate, divided into spikelets.

espiculífero, ra [es-pe-coo-lee'-fay-ro, rah], *a. (Bot.)* Spiculiferous, bearing spikelets.

espiga [es-pee'-gah], *f.* 1. Ear, the spike or head of corn (trigo); that part which contains the seed. 2. Tenon, the end of a piece of timber fitted into another (clavija). 3. Fuse of a bomb or shell. 4. *(Naut.)* Distance between the last collar of the top-gallant masts and the summit or acorn; sail of a galley. **Espiga céltica**, a valerian. **Espiga de agua**, *(Bot.)* pondweed.

espigadera [es-pe-gah-day'-rah], *f.* Gleaner, a woman who gathers corn after the reapers.

espigado, da [es-pe-gah'-do, dah], *a.* 1. Tall, graceful, slender (delgado, esbelto) . 2. Acrospired.*-pp.* of ESPIGAR.

espigadora [es-pe-gah-do'-rah], *f. V.* ESPIGADERA.

espigar [es-pe-gar'], *vn.* 1. To ear, to shoot into ears (trigo). 2. *(Met.)* To grow, to increase in bulk and stature. *-va.* 1. To glean, to gather corn left by the reapers. 2. *(Prov.)* To make presents to a bride. 3. To make a tenon.

espigelia [es-pe-hay'-le-ah], *f.* Spigelia, pinkroot, an anthelmintic herb.

espigón [es-pee-gone'], *m.* 1. Ear of corn. 2. Sting, as of bees, wasps, etc. 3. Point of a dart or javelin. 4. Sharp point of a hill without trees. **Ir con espigón or llevar espigón**, *(Met.)* to retire indignant or irritated.

espiguilla, ta [es-pe-geel'-lyah, gee'-tah], *f.* 1. Small edging of lace, tape, or inkle. 2. Flower of some trees. 3. *(dim.)* A small ear of corn; spikelet.

espilo [es-pee'-lo], *m.* A small spot upon grasses below the first membrane, at its inner base.

espilorchería [es-pe-lor-chay-ree'-ah], *f. (Low.)* Sordid avarice.

espín [es-peen´], *m.* Porcupine.

espina [es-pee'-nah], *f.* 1. A thorn. 2. A fishbone (de pez). 3. Spine, the back bone. 4. A small splinter of wood, esparto, etc (astilla). 5. *(Met.)* Scruple, doubt, suspicion. **Espina blanca**, *(Bot.)* woolly cotton thistle. **Mala espina**, resentment. **Me da mala espina**, it worries me. **Sacarse la espina**, *(Fig.)* to pay off an old score, to get even. **Tener una espina en el corazón**, to have a spine in one's side.

espinaca es-pe-nah'-cah], *f. (Bot.)* Spinage.

espina dorsal [es-pee'-nah dor-sahl'], *f.* Spinal column.

espinadura [es-pe-nah-doo'-rah], *f.* Act of pricking with a thorn.

espinal, espinar [es-pe-nahl', es-pe-nar'], *m.* 1. Place full of thornbushes, brambles, and briers. 2. *(Met.)* A dangerous undertaking, an arduous enterprise.

espinal [es-pe-nahl'], *a.* Spinal, dorsal.

espinar [es-pe-nar'], *va.* 1. To prick with thorns (punzar). 2. To surround trees with briers and thornbushes. 3. *(Met.)* To nettle, to make uneasy, to abuse, to provoke.

espinazo [es-pe-nah'-tho], *m.* Spine, the backbone.

espinel [es-pe-nel'], *m.* A fishing-line with many hooks, to catch congereels and other large fishes.

espinela [es-pe-nay'-lah], *f.* 1. A piece of Spanish poetry, consisting of ten verses of eight syllables. 2. Spinel-ruby, a precious stone.

espineta [es-pe-nay'-tah], *f.* 1. Spinet, a small harpsichord. 2. The bit of a bridle.

espingarda [es-pin-gar'-dah], *f.* 1. A small piece of ordnance. 2. A long handgun or musket used in Morocco.

espinica, illa [es-pe-nee'-cah, eel'-lyah], *f. dim.* A small thorn.

espinilla [es-pe-nee'-lyah], *f.* 1. Shin or shin bone. 2. Blackhead.

espinita [es-pe-nee'-tah], *f. dim.* A little thorn.

espino [es-pee'-no], *m. (Bot.)* Thorn, a prickly tree of several kinds; hawthorn. **Espino albar or blanco**, white-thorn. **Espino negro**, boxthorn like buckthorn.

espinoso, sa [es-pe-no´-so, sah], *a.* 1. Spiny, thorny (planta). 2. *(Met.)* Arduous, dangerous. 3. Bony (pez).

espinoso [es-pe-no'-so], *m. (Zool.)* Three-spined stickleback.

espinulífero, ra [es-pe-noo-lee'-fay-ro, rah], *a. (Bot.)* Spinuliferous, thorn-bearing.

espinuloso, sa [es-pe-noo-lo'-so, sah], *(Bot.)* Spinulous, thorny.

espinzar [es-pin-thar'], *va.* To burl; to dress cloth after it has been milled.

espión [es-pe-on'], *m.* Spy. *V.* ESPÍA.

espionaje [es-pe-o-nah´-hay], *m.* Espionage, the action of spying. **Novela de espionaje,** spy story.

espiote [es-pe-o'-tay], *m.* A sharp pointed weapon.

espique [es-pee'-kay], *m. V.* ESPICANARDI.

espira [es-pee'-rah], *f.* 1. A spiral line, a spire, a helix. 2. Spire, a winding staircase. 3. Part of the base of a column, above the plinth. 4. Each turn of a conical shell.

espiración [es-pe-rah-the-on'], *f.* Expiration, respiration.

espiráculo [es-pe-rah´-coo-lo], *m.* Spiracle, breathing pore.

espiradero [es-pe-rah-day'-ro], *m. V.* RESPIRADERO.

espirador [es-pe-rah-dor'], *m.* He who expires or breathes.

espiral [es-pe-rahl'], *a.* Spiral, winding, helical, helispherical. *-f.* Spiral, corkscrew (forma); *(Tec.)* whorl; hairspring (reloj). **El humo subía en espiral,** the smoke went spiralling up.

espiralmente [es-pe-ral-men'-tay], *adv.* Spirally.

espirante [es-pe-rahn'-tay], *pa.* Expiring, respiring.

espirar [es-pe-rar'], *vn.* 1. To expire, to breathe the last. 2. To make an emission of the breath, to expire. 3. To finish, to come to an end. 4. To fly out with a blast. *-va.* 1. To exhale (aire). 2. To infuse a divine spirit.

espirativo, va [es-pe-rah-tee'-vo, vah], *a.* That which can breathe or respire.

espirea [es-pe-ray'-ah], *f. (Bot.)* Spiraea. **Espira ulmaria,** meadow sweet spiraea. **Espirea opulifolia,** guelder rose-leaved spiraled.

espiratar [es-pe-ra-tar'], *va.* 1. To irritate or agitate. 2. *V.* ENDEMONIAR. *-vr.* To be possessed with an evil spirit.

espiritillo [es-pe-re-teel'-lyo], *m. dim.* A little spirit.

espiritismo [es-pe-re-tees'-mo], *m.* Spiritualism, spiritism, the belief that the spirits of the dead communicate in various ways with men, usually through a medium.

espiritista [es-pe-re-tees'-tah], *m. & f.* A spiritualist.

espiritosamente [es-pe-re-to'-sah-men-tay], *adv.* Spiritedly, ardently.

espiritoso, sa [es-pe-re-to'-so, sah], *a.* 1. Spiritious (licor). 2. *(Met.)* Spirited, lively, active, ardent (persona).

espíritu [es-pee'-re-too], *m.* 1. Spirit, an immaterial substance. 2. Soul of man. 3. Genius, vigor of mind; power of mind, moral or intellectual. 4. Spirit, ardor, courage, life, manhood. 5. That which gives vigor or cheerfulness to the mind or body. 6. Inclination, turn of mind (talento). 7. Spirit, inflammable liquor, raised by distillation (alcohol). 8. True sense or meaning. **El Espíritu Santo,** the Holy Ghost. **Espíritu maligno,** the devil. **Dar el espíritu,** to give up the ghost, to die. **Cobrar espíritu,** to take courage. **Espíritus,** 1. Spirits, demons, hobgoblins. 2. Spirits, ether. **Pobre de espíritu,** poor in spirit. **Con espíritu amplio,** with an open mind.

espiritual [es-pe-re-too-ahl'], *a.* Spiritual, ghostly (fantasmal).

espiritualidad [es-pe-re-too-ah-le-dahd'], *f.* 1. Spirituality, incorporality, intellectual nature. 2. Principle and effect of what is spiritual. **Espiritualidades de un obispo,** revenue of a bishop arising from his jurisdiction.

espiritualismo [es-pe-re-too-ah-lees'-mo], *m.* Spiritualism, as a philosophic system, opposed to materialism.

espiritualista [es-pe-re-too-ah-lees'-tah], *m.* He who treats of the vital spirits.

espiritualizar [es-pe-re-too-ah-le-thar'], *va.* 1. To spiritualize, to purify from the feculencies of the world. 2. To refine the intellect.

espiritualmente [es-pe-re-too-al-men-tay], *adv.* Spiritually.

espirituoso, sa [es-pe-re-too-oh'-so, sah], *a.* 1. Spirituous, having the quality of spirit; ardent, inflammable. 2. Spirituous, vivid, airy, lively.

espirómetro [es-pe-ro'-may-tro], *m.* Spirometer, instrument for measuring the breathing capacity of the lungs.

espita [es-pee'-tah], *f.* 1. A faucet. 2. Tippler, a drunkard. 3. Span, the space from the end of the thumb to the end of the little finger extended.

espitar [es-pe-tar'], *va.* To put a faucet in a tub or other vessel.

espito [es-pee'-to], *m.* Peel, a piece of wood used to hang up paper to dry.

esplendente [es-plen-den'-tay], *pa. (Poet.)* Shining, glittering, resplendent.

espléndidamente [es-plen'-de-dah-men-tay], *adv.* Splendidly, nobly, magnificently, gloriously, brightly, glitteringly.

esplendidez [es-plen-de-deth'], *f.* Splendor, magnificence, ostentation.

espléndido, da [es-plen'-de-do, dah], *a.* 1. Splendid (magnífico), magnificent, grand, sumptuous, pompous. 2. *(Poet.)* Resplendent.

esplendor [es-plen-dor'], *m.* 1. Splendor, brilliancy, luster, glory, magnificence, grandeur. 2. Fulgency, glitter, lucidity. 3. Excellence, eminence, nobleness, gallantry. 4. Finery, fineness, gorgeousness. 5. White paint made of pounded egg-shells.

esplendoroso, sa [es-plen-do-ro'-so, sah], *a. (Poet.)* Brilliant, refulgent, luminous.

esplenético, ca [es-play-nay'-te-co, cah], *a.* Splenic, belonging to the spleen or milt.

espliego [es-ple-ay´-go], *m. (Bot.)* Lavender.

esplín [es-pleen'], *m. (coll.)* Spleen, melancholy.

esplique [es-plee'-kay], *m.* Machine for catching birds.

espodio [es-po'-deo], *m.* 1. Calx found in copper furnaces. 2. Ashes of burnt ivory or reeds.

espodito [es-po-dee'-to], *m.* Whitish ashes of volcanoes.

espodolenco, ca [es-po-do-len'-co, cah], *a. (Zool.)* Ashen in color, of a mixed gray and white.

espolada [es-po-lah-dah], *f.* Prick with a spur (espolazo). **Espolada de vino,** *(coll.)* a large draught of wine.

espolazo [es-po-lah'-tho], *m.* A violent prick with a spur.

espoleadura [es-po-lay-ah-doo'-rah], *f.* Wound made with a spur.

espolear [es-po-lay-ar'], *va.* 1. To spur, to drive with a spur (caballo). 2. To spur, to instigate, to incite, to urge forward.

espoleta [es-po-lay'-tah], *f.* 1. Fuse of a bomb or a handgrenade. **Espoletas de cubierta,** *(Naut.)* fuses of a fireship. 2. Small bone between the wings of birds.

espolín [es-po-leen'], *m.* 1. A small spool for raising flowers on stuff. 2. Silk stuff; on which flowers are raised, like brocade.

espolinado, da [es-po-le-nah'-do, dah], *a.* Flowered (material de seda). *-pp.* of ESPOLINAR.

espolinar [es-po-le-nar'], *va.* To weave flowers in silk.

espolio [es-po'-le-o], *m.* The property which a prelate leaves at his death.

espolique [es-poo-lee'-kay], *m.* Footman.

espolista [es-po-lees'-tah], *m.* 1. A servant who travels on foot before the horse or mule of his master, a running footman. 2. One who farms the fruits of the ecclesiastical benefice of a diseased bishop.

espolón [es-po-lone'], *m.* 1. Spur, the sharp point on the legs of a cock (gallo). 2. The acute angle of the pier of a stone bridge, to break the force of the current. 3. *(Arch.)* Stay, prop. 4. *(Naut.)* The ram of a man-of-war. 5. *(Naut.)* Fender-beam, knee of the head, a curve which is put upon vessels which lack a cut water, in order to fit the bowsprit to it. 6. Part of a causeway or dock which juts into the sea 7. *(Fort.)* Kind of a salient angle. 8. Chilblain.

espolvorear [es-pol-vo-ray-ar'], *va.* 1. To powder, to sprinkle with powder. 2. To dust, to brush off the dust. 3. *(Met.)* To separate, to scatter, to dissipate.

espolvorizar [es-pol-vo-re-thar'], *va.* To scatter powder.

espondaico, ca [es-pon-dah'-ee-co, cah], *a.* Spondaic, of spondees.

espondeo [es-pon-day'-o], *m.* Spondee, a foot of verse consisting of two long syllables.

espondilitis [es-pon-de-lee'-tis], *f. (Med.)* Spondylitis, inflammation of the spinal column.

espóndilo [es-pon'-de-lo], *m.* 1. Vertebra. 2. A ball which was used in ancient Greece for elections.

esponja [es-po-ne'-hah], *f.* 1. Sponge. **Esponja de baño,** bath sponge. **Beber como una esponja,** to drink like a fish. 2. *(Met.)* Sponger (gorrón), one who by mean arts lives on others.

esponjado [es-pon-hah'-do], *m. (Prov.)* A sponge made of sugar which instantly dissolves.—**Esponjado, da,** *pp.* of ESPONJAR.

esponjadura [es-pon-hah-doo'-rah], *f.* 1. Act of sponging. 2. Cavity or defect in cast metal.

esponjar [es-pon-har'], *va.* To sponge, to soak or imbibe. *-vr.* To be puffed up with pride (engreírse).

esponjilla [es-pon-hel'-lyah], *f. (Bot.)* A fruit of the size of a turkey's egg which abounds in Venezuela, Colombia, and Ecuador.

esponjilla, ita, uela [es-pon-heel'-lyah], *f. dim.* A small piece of sponge.

esponjosidad [es-pon-ho-se-dahd'], *f.* Sponginess.

esponjoso, sa [es-pon-ho'-so, sah], *a.* Spongy (materia), porous.

esponsales [es-pon-sah'-les], *m. pl.* Espousals, betrothal, a mutual promise of marriage.

esponsalicio, cia [es-pon-sah-lee'-the-o, ah], *a.* Belonging to espousals, nuptial, spousal.

esponsor [es-pon-sor'], *m. (Com. Dep. etc.)* Sponsor.

espontáneamente [es-pon-tah'-nay-ah-men-tay], *adv.* Spontaneously, voluntarily.

espontanearse [es-pon-tah-nay-ar'-say], *vr. & vn.* To avow or declare spontaneously (confesar).

espontaneidad [es-pon-tah-nay-e-dahd'], *f.* Spontaneity, spontaneousness, the state of being spontaneous, voluntariness.

espontáneo, nea [es-pon-tah'-nay-o, ah], *a.* Spontaneous, voluntary, willing.

espontón [es-pon-tone'], *m.* Spontoon, a half-pike.

espontonada [es-pon-to-nah'-dah], *f.* Salute to royal personages or generals with a spontoon.

esporádico, ca [es-po-rah'-de-co, cah], *a.* Sporadic, isolated (enfermedad).*-adv.* **Esporádicamente.**

espora, *f.* or **esporo,** *m.* [es-po-rah, roh], *(Bot.)* Spore.

esportear [es-por-tay-ar'], *va.* To carry something in frails, panniers, or baskets.

esportilla [es-por-teel'-lyah], *f. dim.* A small frail, pannier, or wicker vessel.

esportillero [es-por-til-lyay-ro], *m.* Porter, one who carries burdens for hire.

esportillo [es-por-teel'-lyo], *m.* Pannier, fail, a wicker vessel.

esportón [es-por-tone'], *m.* A large pannier.

espórtula [es-por'-too-lah], *f. (Prov.)* Judicial fees.

esposa [es-po'-sah], *f.* Spouse, wife, consort, matron. *-pl.* Manacles, handcuffs, fetters, or chains for the hands. **Poner las esposas a uno,** to handcuff somebody.

esposo [es-po'-so], *m.* Spouse, husband, consort.

esprilla [es-preel'-lyah], *f. (Both.)* V. ESCAÑA.

espuela [es-poo-ay'-lah], *f.* 1. Spur, a goading instrument worn off a horseman's heel. 2. *(Met.)* Spur, stimulus, incitement. **Mozo de espuela,** V. ESPOLISTA. **Poner espuela.** *(Met.)* to incite, to urge on.

espuenda [es-poo-en'-dah], *f. (Naut.)* Margin of a river.

espuerta [es-poo-err'-tah], *f.* Pannier, basket, frail, with two handles.

espulgar [es-pool-gar'], *va.* 1. To rid of, to clean from lice or fleas (quitar las pulgas). 2. To examine closely, to scrutinize.

espulgo [es-pool'-go], *m.* The act of cleaning from lice or fleas.

espuma [es-poo'-mah], *f.* 1. Froth (sobre cerveza), spume, foam (sobre agua); the bubbles caused in liquors by agitation.

Espuma de mar, meerschaum. **Crecer como la espuma,** to flourish like the green bay tree. 2. Scum (residuos). **Hacer espuma,** to foam.

espumadera [es-poo-mah-day'-rah], *f.* 1. Skimmer, a sort of ladle with holes. 2. Vessel used by confectioners to clarify sugar. 3. *(Naut.)* Pitchskimmer.

espumajear [es-poo-mah-hay-ar'], *vn.* To foam at the mouth.

espumajo [es-poo-mah'-ho], *m.* Froth, spume; saliva.

espumajoso, sa [es-poo-mah-ho'-so, sah], *a.* Foamy, frothy, spumous.

espumante [es-poo-mahn'-tay], *pa.* Foaming at the mouth, like enraged animals.*-a.* Sparkling.

espumar [es-poo-mar'], *va.* To skim or to scum, to take off the scum.*-vn.* To froth, to foam.

espumear [es-poo-may-ar'], *va.* To raise foam.

espumarajo [es-poo-ma-rah'-ho], *m.* Foam, frothy substance thrown from the mouth. **Echar espumarajos por la boca,** to foam at the mouth with passion.

espumero [es-poo-may-ro], *m.* Place where salt water is collected to crystallize.

espumescente [es-poo-mes-then'-tay], *a.* Spumescent.

espumilla [es-poo-meel'-lyah], *f.* Thread crape, a sort of thin cloth loosely woven.

espumillón [es-poo-mil-lyone'], *m.* Silk crape or gauze.

espumosidad [es-poo-mo-se-dahd'], *f.* Frothiness, foaminess.

espumoso, sa [es-poo-mo'-so, sah], *a.* Frothy, foamy, lathery (jabón), sparkling (vino).

espundia [es-poon'-de-ah], *f. (Vet.)* A cancerous ulcer.

espurcílocuo, cua [es-poor-thee'-lo-kwo, kwah], *a.* Of foul, disgusting talk.

espúreo, rea, or **espurio, ria** [es-poo'-ray-o, ah, re-o, ah], *a.* 1. Spurious, not legitimate. 2. *(Met.)* Spurious, adulterated, corrupted, not genuine.

espurriar, or **espurrear** [es-poor-re-ar'], *va.* To spurt, to moisten a thing with water.

espurrir [es-poor-reer'], *va.* To stretch out something, chiefly said of the feet.

esputo [es-poo'-to], *m.* Spittle, saliva; sputum.

esquebrajar [es-kay-brah-har'], *va.* To split, to cleave. *-vr.* To become open, to be split or full of chinks, as wood.

esqueje [es-kay'-hay], *m.* Among gardeners, a cutting, slip.

esquela [es-kay'-lah], *f.* Billet, a small letter or paper, a note (nota). **Esquela amatoria,** a love-letter.

esquelético [es-kay-lay'-te-co], *a.* Skeletal; thin, skinny.

esqueleto [es-kay-lay'-to], *m.* 1. Skeleton, the bones of the body preserved in their natural situation. 2. Person very thin and meager. 3. Watch, the works and movements of which are exposed to view. 4. *(Naut.)* Carcass or framework of a ship without cover or sheathing. **En esqueleto,** unfinished, in an incomplete manner. **Menear el esqueleto,** to shake a hoof. **Estar hecho un esqueleto,** to be like a skeleton.

esquelita [es-kay-lee'-tah], *f.* 1. A small note, a billet. 2. Tungstate of calcium.

esquema [es-kay'-mah], *m.* Plan (proyecto), sketch (esbozo), outline, diagram (diagrama). **Esquema del vuelo,** *(Aer.)* flight pattern.

esquemático, ca [es-kay-mah'-te-co, cah], *a.* Schematic. *-m. pl.* Sectarians who believed that the body of Jesus Christ was only apparent.

esquena [es-kay'-nah], *f.* Spine of fishes.

esquero [es-kay'-ro], *m.* A leather bag or pouch.

esquerro, ra [es-ker'-ro, rah], *a.* V. IZQUIERDO.

esquí [es-kee'], *m.* Ski. **Esquí acuático,** water ski. **Hacer esquí,** to go skiing.

esquiador, ra [es-kee-ah-dor'], *m & f.* Skier.

esquiar [es-ke-ar'], *vn.* To ski.

esquiciado, da [es-ke-the-ah'-do, dah], *a.* Sketched, traced, delineated. *-pp.* of ESQUICIAR.

esquiciar [es-ke-the-ar'], *va.* To sketch, to draw the outlines of a painting; to trace, to delineate.

esquicio [es-kee'-the-o], *m.* Sketch, outline, line.

esquifada [es-ke-fah'-dah], *f.* 1. A skiff or boat load. 2. Vault of a cistern.

esquifar [es-ke-far'], *va.* 1. *(Naut.)* To arm a boat with oars. 2. To fit out a ship.

esquifazón [es-ke-fah-thone'], *f. (Naut.)* 1. A boat's crew. 2. A set of sails, written also *Esquifación.*

esquife [es-kee'-fay], *m.* 1. A skiff, a small boat. 2. *(Arch.)* Cylindrical vault.

esquila [es-kee'-lah], *f.* 1. Hand bell, a small bell, also a bell carried by cattle (campanilla). 2. The act and time of sheep shearing. V. ESQUILEO. 3. *(Zool.)* Shrimp. 4. *(Ent.)* Water-spider. 5. *(Bot.)* V. ESCILLA.

esquilada [es-ke-lah'-dah], *f. (Prov.)* V. CENCERRADA.

esquilador [es-ke-lah-dor'], *m.* Sheep-shearer, clipper.

esquilar [es-ke-lar'], *va.* 1. To shear or to fleece sheep, to cut off the wool or hair of animals. 2. *(Prov.)* To climb a tree with the hands and feet only.

esquileo [es-ke-lay'-o], *m.* Sheep-shearing time; also, the act and place of shearing.

esquilimoso, sa [es-ke-le-mo'-so, sah], *a. (coll.)* Fastidious, over nice.

esquilmar [es-keel-mar'], *va.* To gather and get in the harvest (cosecha). **Esquilmar la tierra**, to impoverish the earth (árboles).

esquilmeño, ña [es-keel-may'-nyo, nyah], *a.* Fruitful, productive (árboles, plantas).

esquilmo [es-keel'-mo], *m.* 1. Harvest, the corn garnered. 2. Produce of vines. 3. Produce of cattle.

esquilo [es-kee'-lo], *m.* 1. Shearing time; also, the act of shearing. 2. Kind of squirrel.

esquilón [es-ke-lone'], *m.* 1. A small bell. 2. Large bell worn by cattle.

esquimal [es-kee-mahl'], *a.* Eskimo.

esquina [es-kee'-nah], *f.* Corner, the outward angle formed by two lines, coin, edge, angle. **En la esquina de la calle**, on the corner of the street. **La tienda de la esquina**, the corner shop.

esquinado, da [es-ke-nah'-do, dah], *a.* Cornered (que tiene esquinas), angled.-*pp.* of ESQUINAR.

esquinal [es-ke-nahl'], *m.* Corner plate, angle iron; iron knee, corner casting.

esquinante, esquinanto [es-ke-nahn'-tay], *m.* Kind of aromatic or medicinal rush.

esquinar [es-ke-nar'], *va.* 1. *(Prov.)* To make a corner (hacer esquina), to form into an angle. 2. To square (madera). 3. To swerve, to slice (pelota). 4. To set at odds (personas). -*vr.* 1. To quarrel, to fall out. 2. To get a chip on one's shoulder (estar resentido).

esquinazo [es-ke-nah'-tho], *m.* 1. Corner (esquina), a very acute outward angle. 2. *(coll.)* Quinsy. **Dar a uno esquinazo**, to dodge somebody.

esquinela [es-ke-nay'-lah], *f.* Armor for the legs.

esquinzador [es-kin-thah-dor'], *m.* Large apartment in paper-mills for putting the rags in, after cutting them.

esquinzar [es-kin-thar'], *va.* To cut rags in small pieces, in paper-mills.

esquipado, da [es-ke-pah'-do, dah], *a.* Made boat-fashion. -*pp.* of ESQUIPAR.

esquipar [es-ke-par'], *pa. (Naut.)* To equip, to fit out a ship. V. EQUIPAR.

esquiraza [es-ke-rah'-thah], *f.* Kind of ancient ship.

esquirla [es-keer'-lah], *f. (Surg.)* Splinter of a bone.

esquirol [es-ke-rol'], *m.* 1. Squirrel. 2. Strike-breaker.

esquirro [es-keer'-ro], *m. (Med.)* Scirrhus, hard cancer.

esquirrogastria [es-kir-ro-gahs'-tre-ah], *f.* Cancerous degeneration of the stomach.

esquisar [es-ke-sar'], *va. (Obs.)* To search, to investigate.

esquisto [es-kees'-to], *m.* Schist.

esquistoso, sa [es-kis-to'-so, sah], *a.* Schistose.

esquitar [es-ke-tar'], *va. (coll.)* To pardon, to remit a debt.

esquivar [es-ke-var'], *va.* To shun, to avoid, to evade, to escape. **Esquivar un golpe**, to dodge a blow. -*vr.* To disdain, to scorn, to view with contempt, to coy.

esquivez [es-ke-veth'], *f.* Disdain, scorn, asperity, coyness, coldness.

esquivo, va [es-kee'-vo, vah], *a.* 1. Scornful, severe, stubborn, fastidious. 2. Shy (tímido), reserved, difficult, coyish, cold, haggard.

esquizado, da [es-ke-thah'-do, dah], Applied to spotted marble.

esquizofrenia [es-ke-tho-fray'-ne-ah], *f.* Schizophrenia.

esquizofrénico, ca [es-ke-tho-fray'-ne-co cah], *a. & m. & f.* Schizophrenic.

esquizomicetes [es-ke-tho-me-thay'-tays], *m. pl.* Schizomycetes, a class of minute unicellular plants allied to the algae; it comprises the bacteria.

estabilidad [es-tah-be-le-dahd'], *f.* Stability, duration, permanence, constancy, firmness, consistence, fixedness.

estabilización [es-tah-be-le-thah the-on´], *f.* Stabilization.

estabilizar [es-tah-be-le-thar´], *va.* To stabilize, to hold steady, to prevent fluctuations. -*vr.* To become stable, to settle down (en la vida).

estable [es-tah'-blay], *a.* Stable (firme), permanent, durable, steady, firm, fast, consistent.

establear [es-tah-blay-ar'], *va.* To tame, to domesticate, to accustom to the stable.

establecedor [es-tah-blay-thay-dor'], *m.* Founder, he that establishes an institution or law; confirmer.

establecer [es-tah-blay-therr'], *va.* 1. To enact, to establish by law, to decree, to confirm. 2. To establish, to found, to fix immovably. 3. To fortify; to constitute. 4. To establish, to fix or settle in an opinion, to ground. -*vr.* To establish or fix oneself in a place. *(Yo establezco, yo establezca,* from *Establecer.* V. CONOCER.)

estableciente [es-tah-blay-the-en'-tay], *pa. & m. & f.* Establisher: establishing.

establecimiento [es-tah-blay-the me-en'-to], *m.* 1. Statute, law, ordinance. 2. Establishment, foundation, settlement. 3. Establishment, footing, settlement or fixed state of a person. 4. *(coll.)* Manufactory, place where handicraft business is carried out. **Establecimiento comercial**, commercial establishment.

establemente [es-tah'-blay-men-tay], *adv.* Stably, firmly.

establillo [es-tah-bleel'-lyo], *m. dim.* A small stable.

establo [es-tah'-blo], *m.* Stable for horses and mules; barn (granero).

estaca [es-tah'-cah], *f.* 1. A stake (poste), picket. 2. Slip of a tree put into the ground to grow. 3. Stick, cudgel, bludgeon. -*pl.* 1. *(Naut.)* Thowls or tholes. V. TOLETES. 2. Divisions or partitions made in mines. 3. Clampnails, large nails used by carpenters. **Estar a la estaca**, *(coll.)* to live very poorly, to be indigent or oppressed with want.

estacada [es-tah-cah'-dah], *f.* 1. *(Mil.)* Palisade or stockade. 2. Paling, a kind of fence-work for parks, gardens, and grounds (cerca). 3. A place to fight in, place for a duel. **Dejar en la estacada**, to abandon one in peril, to sacrifice him.

estacado [es-tah-cah'-do], *m.* Place for a duel.—**Estacado, da**, *pp.* of ESTACAR.

estacar [es-tah-car'], *va.* 1. To put stakes into the ground; to enclose a spot with stakes (tierra, propiedad). 2. To tie to a stake (animal). -*vr.* To be enclosed or surrounded with stakes.

estacazo [es-tah-cah'-tho], *m.* Blow given with a stake.

estacha [es-tah'-chah], *f.* Rope fastened to a harpoon, to give the whale room to dive.

estación [es-tah-the-on'], *f.* 1. State, situation, position. 2. Season of the year (temporada). **Las cuatro estaciones,** the four seasons. 3. Hour, moment, time. 4. Station, a railway stopping place. 5. Stations of the cross (Vía Crucis). 6. Apparent motion in the stars. 7. A party of persons posted at some place. 8. Business, duty, one's obligations. **Estación astral**, *(Aer.)* space station. **Estación de servicio**, car service station. **Estación de vehículos**, cab stand, parking lot. **Red de estaciones**, radio network. **Estación de ferrocarril**, railway station. **Estación de gasolina**, gas station. **Estación**

terminal, terminus. **Estación invernal,** winter sports resort. **Estación de autobuses,** bus station.

estacional [es-tah-theo-nahl'], *a.* 1. Pertaining to the seasons. 2. Seasonal, occurring at a specified time. 3. *(Ast.)* Stationary.

estacionamiento [es-tah-the-o-nah-me-en'-to], *m.* Parking (vehículo).

estacionar [es-tah-the-o-nar'], *va.* To park (vehículo). *-vn. & vr.* To be motionless or stationary.

estacionario, ria [es-tah-the-o-nah'-re-o, ah], *a.* Stationary, fixed, not progressive.

estacte [es-tahc'-tay], *m.* Odoriferous liquor extracted from fresh myrrh.

estada [es-tah'-dah], *f.* Stay, sojourn, residence.

estadal [es-tah-dahl'], *m.* 1. Land measure, containing about three square yards and two thirds, or eleven feet. 2. Kind of ornament or holy ribbon worn at the neck. 3. *(Prov.)* Fathom of wax taper.

estadía [es-tah-dee'-ah], *f.* 1. An instrument used for levelling. 2. *(Com. and Naut.)* Stay (estancia), detention; demurrage. Cost of such stay.

estadio [es-tah'-de-o], *m.* 1. Race-course. 2. Stadium (pl: stadia), ancient measure of 125 paces, furlong. 3. Stage, phase (fase).

estadista [es-tah-dees'-tah], *m.* Statist, statesman, politician.

estadística [es-tah-dees'-te-cah], *f.* Statistics, the science so called.

estadístico, ca [es-tah-dees'-te-co, cah], *a.* Statistical, statistic, political.

estadizo, za [es-tah-dee'-tho, thah], *a.* Stagnant, corrupted (agua).

estado [es-tah'-do], *m.* 1. State, the actual condition of a thing. 2. State, condition, circumstances of nature or fortune, footing, station in life. 3. Rank, state, estate, quality, condition (status). 4. State, the commonwealth. 5. Stature or height of a person. 6. Statement, account, report (informe). 7. Suite, attendants. **Estado general or llano,** community or peasantry of any district, not including the nobles. **Materias de estado,** state affairs. **Estado mayor,** *(Mil.)* staff, generals and commanders of an army. **Hombre de estado,** statesmam. **Estado de emergencia,** state of emergency. **Estado de sitio,** state of siege. **Estar en estado,** to be pregnant. **Estar en malísimo estado,** to be in a terrible condition. 8. *(Inform.)* **Estado de espera,** wait state. **Estado flotante,** floating state.

estadounidense, estadunidense [es-tah-do-oo-nee-denn'-say], *m. & f.* Native of United States of America. *-a.* From the United States.

estafa [es-tah'-fah], *f.* Trick, deceit, imposition.

estafador, ra [es-tah-fah-dor', rah], *m. & f.* Impostor, swindler, chiseler, cheat. *-a.* Chiseling, swindling.

estafar [es-tah-far'], *va.* 1. To deceive, to defraud. **Estafar algo a uno,** to swindle something out of somebody. 2. Among sculptors, to size a statue with a white coat in order to gild it.

estafermo [es-tah-ferr'-mo], *m.* 1. A wooden movable figure of an armed man. 2. *(Met.)* An idle fellow, who affects importance.

estafeta [es-tah-fay'-tah], *f.* 1. Courier (persona), express, estafet. 2. General postoffice for letters (oficina).

estafetero [es-tah-fay-tay'-ro], *m.* Postmaster, director of the post office.

estafilea piñada [es-tah-fe-lay'-ah pe-nyah'-dah], *f.* 1. *(Bot.)* Five-leaved bladder-nut. 2. **Estafilea,** a nymph converted by Bacchus into a cluster of grapes.

estafisagra [es-tah-fe-sah'-grah], *f.* *(Bot.)* Stavesacre, lousewort.

estagnación [es-tag-nah-the-on'], *f.* Stagnation, want of circulation in fluids or in business. V. ESTANCACIÓN.

estala [es-tah'-lah], *f.* 1. Stable. 2. Seaport.

estalación [es-tah-lah-the-on'], *f.* Class, rank, order.

estalactita [es-tah-lac-tee'-tah], *f.* Stalactite, a rocky concretion, in form of an icicle, hanging from the vaults of caves.

estalagmita [es-tah-lag-mee'-tah], *f.* Stalagmite, a cylindrical or conical deposit on the floor of a cavern, formed by a dropping from the roof.

estalingadura [es-tah-lin-gah-doo'-rah], *m.* *(Naut.)* The bending of a cable, or fastening it to the ring of the anchor

estalingar [es-tah-lin-gar'], *va.* *(Naut.)* To bend a cable.

estallar [es-tal-lyar'], *vn.* 1. To crack (látido), to burst into chinks with a loud sound (bomba, neumático), to creak. 2. *(Met.)* To break out into fury or rage. **Estallar en llanto,** to burst into tears. **Hacer estallar,** to set off; *(Fig.)* to spark off.

estallido, estallo [es-tal-lyee'-do, es-tahl'-lyo], *m.* 1. Crack, crackling, creaking, crashing, the sound of something bursting or falling. 2. The report of firearms. **Dar un estallido,** to publish, to expose; to make a noise or confusion. *(coll.)* To fail dishonestly.

estambor [es-tam-bor'], *m.* *(Naut.)* Sternpost.

estambrado [es-tam-brah'-do], *m.* *(Prov.)* Kind of cloth made of worsted.

estambrar [es-tam-brar'], *va.* To twist wool into yarn, to spin worsted.

estambre [es-tahm'-bray], *m.* 1. Fine worsted or woollen yarn. 2. Fine wool. 3. *(Bot.)* Stamen of flowers. **Estambre de la vida,** *(Poet.)* the thread of life. 4. Warp. V. URDIMBRE.

estamento [es-tah-men'-to], *m.* 1. Name given to each of the estates of Spain, or to the clergy, nobility, and commons, who composed the assembly of the Cortes. 2. Body (cuerpo); stratum (estrato); class (clase).

estameña [es-tah-may'-nyah], *f.* Serge , a kind of woollen stuff.

estaminal [es-tah-me-nahl'], *a.* Staminal, pertaining to stamens.

estamíneo, nea [es-tah-mee'-nay-o, ah], or **estaminífero, ra** [es-ta-me-nee'-fay-ro, rah], *a.* Staminate, having stamens.

estampa [es-tahm'-pah], *f.* 1. Print, a figure or image printed (imagen); stamp; cut. **De estampa poco agradable,** of disagreable appearance. 2. The first sketch or design of a drawing or painting. 3. Press or printing machine for printing books (imprenta). 4. Track, an impression left by the foot.

estampado [es-tam-pah'-do], *m.* Impression, act and effect of stamping (impresión).

estampado, da [es-tam-pah'-do, dah], *a.* 1. Stamped (lino, algodón). 2. Embossed, figured: in speaking of printed dry goods. *-pp.* of ESTAMPAR.

estampador [es-tam-pah-dor'], *m.* 1. One who makes or sells prints. 2. Printer.

estampar [es-tam-par'], *va.* 1. To print (imprimir), to stamp (marcar). 2. To leave in the ground an impression of the foot. 3. *(Met.)* To fix in one's mind or memory.

estampería [es-tam-pay-ree'-ah], *f.* Office for printing or selling prints.

estampero [es-tam-pay'-ro], *m.* He who makes or sells prints or stamps.

estampida [es-tam-pee'-dah], *f.* 1. *(Amer.)* Stampede, a general scamper of animals. 2. *(coll.)* **Dar una estampida,** to run away: to run away in debt.

estampido [es-tam-pee'-do], *m.* 1. Report of a gun or piece of ordinance. 2. Crack, crash, crashing, the sound of anything bursting or falling. **Dar estampido,** to publish, to propagate, to make a noise.

estampilla [es-tam-peel'-lyah], *f.* 1. *(dim.)* A small print. 2. A small press. 3. Signet, a seal manual, used instead of a signature. 4. *(Amer.)* A postage-stamp (sello).

estampita [es-tam-pee'-tah], *f. dim.* A small print or stamp.

estancación [es-tan-cah-the-on'], *f.* Stagnation of circulating fluids or of business matters.

estancado [es-tan-cah'-do], *a.* 1. Stagnant (agua). 2. *(Fig.)* Static. **Estar estancado,** to be held up.

estancamiento [es-tan-cah-me-ayn'-to], *m.* 1. Stagnancy, stagnation (de agua). 2. *(Fig.)* Stagnation; blockage, stoppage, suspension.

estancar [es-tan-car'], *va*. 1. To stop, to check, to stem a current. 2. *(Naut.)* To caulk a leak. 3. To monopolize, to hinder the free sale of merchandise. 4. To interdict, to prohibit, to suspend (negocio). *-vr.* 1. To stagnate, to become stagnant (agua). 2. *(Fig.)* To stagnate.

estancia [es-tahn'-the-ah], *f*. 1. Stay (permanencia), sojourn, continuance in a place. 2. Mansion, dwelling (domicilio), habitation; a sitting-room, a bedroom (cuarto). 3. *(Poet.)* Stanza, a division of a song or poem. 4. *(Amer.)* Farm; farm for grazing cattle; a country house. 5. *(Anger.)* Landed property.

estanciero [es-tan-the-ay'-ro], *m*. Overseer of a farm, mansion, or domain.

estanco [es-tahn'-co], *m*. 1. Forestalling, monopoly. 2. Place where privileged goods are sold exclusively. 3. Stop, stay, detention. 4. Repository, archives. 5. Tank.

estanco, ca [es-tahn'-co, cah], *a*. *(Naut.)* Stanch, well-repaired (barco).

estandar [es-tahn'-dar], *a. m*. Standard.

estandardización [es-tan-dar-de-thah-the-on'], *f*. Standardization.

estandarte [es-tan-dar'-tay], *m*. 1. Banner, standard, colors. 2. **Estandarte real**, *(Naut.)* Royal standard, used only by the commanding admiral of a fleet. 3. The upper petal of a papilionaceous corolla.

estangurria [es-tan-goor'-re-ah], *f*. 1. Strangury, difficulty in evacuating urine. 2. Catheter, an instrument to assist in voiding urine.

estánnico, estanífero [es-tahn'-ne-co], *a*. Stannic, containing tin.

estannolita [es-tan-no-lee'-tah], *f*. Oxide of tin.

estanque [es-tahn'-kay], *m*. Pond, basin, dam of water. **Estanque para chapotear**, paddling pool.

estanquero, ra [es-tan-kay'-ro], *m*. 1. Keeper of reservoirs. 2. Retailer of privileged goods, as tobacco in Spain.

estanquillero [es-tan-keel-lyay'-ro], *m*. A tobacconist.

estantal [es-tan-tahl'], *m*. Buttress. *V.* ESTRIBO.

estante [es-tahn'-tay], *m*. 1. Shelf, bookshelf (para libros). 2. *(Prov.)* He who carries, in company with others, images in processions. *-pa. & a*. 1. Being, existing in a place; extant. 2. Fixed, permanent: applied to sheep which are not driven to the mountains in summer.

estantería [es-tan-tay-ree'-ah], *f*. 1. A series of bookshelves. 2. Shelving.

estanterol [es-tan-tay-rol'], *m*. Center of a galley, where the captain stands in an engagement.

estantigua [es-tan-tee'-goo-ah], *f*. 1. Phantom, vision, hobgoblin. 2. A deformed person in a ridiculous garb.

estantío, tía [es-tan-tee'-o, ah], *a*. 1. Standing still and immovable on a spot. 2. *(Met.)* Dull, stupid; without life or spirit.

estañadera [es-tah-nyah-day'-rah], *f*. Soldering receiver or holder of tin plate.

estañado [es-tah-nyah'-do], *m*. Vessel or bath with melted pewter, in which copper or iron plates are immersed to be tinned.—**Estañado, da**, *pp*. of ESTAÑAR.

estañador [es-tah-nyah-dor'], *m*. Tinman, a manufacturer of tin or tinned iron.

estañadura [es-tah-nyah-doo'-rah], *f*. Act of tinning.

estañar [es-tah-nyar'], *va*. To tin, to cover with tin.

estañero [es-tah-nyay'-ro], *m*. A person who works and sells tinware, a metalman.

estaño [es-tah'-nyo], *m*. 1. Tin, a primitive metal. 2. Tin, iron plates covered with tin.

estaquero [es-tah-kay'-ro], *m*. Buck or doe of a year old.

estaquilla, ita [es-tah-keel'-lyah, ee'-tah], *f*. 1. In shoe making, a peg (madera). 2. Any wooden pin which fastens one piece of timber to another. 3. Beam of a velvet-loom.

estaquillador [es-tah-keel-lyah-dor'], *m*. An awl to bore for pegs.

estaquillar [es-tah-keel-lyar'], *va*. To peg, to fasten with pegs.

estaquis [es-tah'-kees], *f. (Bot.)* Stachys, hedge-nettle, a plant resembling hoarhound.

estar [es-tar'], *vn*. 1. To be in a place (permanecer). 2. To understand or comprehend (comprensión). **Estoy en lo que Vd. me dice,** I understand what you tell me. 3. To be in favor of, to answer for (acuerdo). 4. To be of the opinion. **Estoy en que,** I am of the opinion that. 5. To be: an auxiliary verb, derived from the Latin *stare*, to stand, and used always with reference to existing or being in a place. **Estar escribiendo,** to be writing. 6. To undertake, to oblige or subject oneself to. 7. To stand. 8. To cost (precio) 9. With the preposition *en*, it signifies cause, motive. **En eso está,** in this it consists, on this it depends. 10. With the preposition *por* and the infinitive of some verbs it sometimes means that something is not done, and sometimes that something will be done immediately. **Estar por** or **para partir,** to be ready to set out. 11. With *a* and some nouns it signifies to be obliged or disposed to execute what the noun signifies. 12. With *con* and a person's name, to live in company with. 13. To see another in order to treat with him of a matter. 14. With *de* to be executing a thing or understanding in it, in whatever way. **Estar de gaita,** to be merry, in high spirits. **Estar algo por suceder,** to expect something to happen. **Estar a erre,** to be doing something with the utmost care. **Estar alerta,** to be on the watch, to be vigilant. **Estar bajo de llave** or **cerrado con llave,** to be under lock and key. **Estar de buen humor,** to be in good humor or spirits. **Estar de mal humor,** to sulk, to be angry. **Estar de pie** or **en pie; estar levantado** or **derecho,** to stand. **Estar de prisa,** to be in haste, to haste, to hasten. **Estar de por medio,** to interpose, to mediate. **Estar sobre sí,** to be tranquil or serene; to be greatly elated. **Estar para ello,** to be ready, to be disposed to do anything. **¡Dónde estamos!** An expression of admiration or disgust at what we see or hear. **Estar bien con,** to have regard for a person, to be in concord with him. **Estar bien una cosa,** to suit, to agree, to fit. **Estar mal con,** to have a bad opinion of. **Estar mal,** not to suit, to show bad looks. **¿Está Vd.?** or **Estamos?** Are you aware? Have you understood well? **Estar con el pie en el aire,** to be unsettled. **Está enfermo,** he is ill. **Dos vueltas más y ya está,** two more turns and that´s it. **Para las cinco estará terminado,** it will be finished by 5 o´clock. **Las uvas están a 50 pesos,** grapes are 50 pesos. **Estar de vacaciones,** to be on vacation. **Está por llover,** it´s about to rain. **Están sin vender,** they remain unsold. *-vr.* To be detained; to stay (quedarse). **Estarse parado** or **quieto,** to stand still.

estarcido [es-tar-thee'-do], *m*. Stencil.

estarcir [es-tar-theer'], *va*. To stencil.

estarna [es-tar'-nah], *f. (Orn.)* Kind of small partridge.

estatal [es-tah-tahl'], *a*. State.

estatera [es-tah-tay'-rah], *f*. 1. Balance, steel-yard. 2. An ancient Grecian coin.

estática [es-tah'-te-cah], *f*. (Radio) Static.

estátice [es-tah'-te-thay], *f. (Bot.)* Sea-lavender. **Estátice sinuada,** scallop-leaved sea-lavender.

estático, ca [es-tah'-te-co, cah], *a*. 1. (Radio) Static. 2. Static, motionless. 3 Dumbfounded

estatificar [es-tah-te-fe-car'], *va*. To nationalize.

estatismo [es-tah-tees'-mo], *m*. 1. Static condition. 2. Statism, government control.

estatua [es-tah'-too-ah], *f*. 1. A statue. 2. A dull, stupid fellow.

estatuaria [es-tah-too-ah'-re-ah], *f*. Statuary.

estatuario [es-tah-too-ah'-re-o], *m*. Statuary, one who makes statues.

estatuir [es-tah-too-eer'], *va*. To establish (ordenar), to ordain, to enact, to prove (probar).

estatura [es-tah-too´-rah], *f*. Stature, the height of a person. **De regular estatura,** of average height.

estatutario, ria [es-tah-too-tah'-re-o, ah], *a.* Belonging to a statute or law.

estatuto [es-tah-too'-to], *m.* 1. Statute, law (de ciudad), ordinance. 2. Form of government established by laws and customs.

estay [es-tah'-e], *m. (Naut.)* Stay. **Estay mayor**, the main stay. **Estay de trinquete**, the fore stay. **Estay del mastelero mayor**, the maintop stay.

este [es'-tay], *m.* East, one of the four cardinal points of the compass. **Este cuarto** or **cuarta al nordeste**, East-by-north. **Este nordeste**, East-north-east. **Este cuarto al sudeste**, East-by-south. **Este sudeste**, East-south-east. **Viento del este**, easterly wind.

éste, ésta, esto [es'-tay, tah, to], *pron. dem.* This, this one (pl: **éstos, éstas**, these). **En esto**, at this time. **Ésta lo vio**, She saw it. **Nos gusta más esa casa que ésta**, we prefer that house to this one. **Ese problema es fácil, éste es más difícil**, that problem is easy, this one is more difficult.

este, esta *adj. dem.* (pl: **estos, estas;** these). **Este coche es el más grande**, this car is the biggest. **Esta casa es la más bonita**, this house is the nicest. **Estos hombres llevan aquí todo el día**, these men have been here all day. **Estas chicas son muy atractivas**, these girls are very attractive.

estearato [es-tay-rah'-to], *m.* Stearate, a salt of stearic acid.

esteárico, ca [es-tay-ah'-re-co, cah], *a.* Stearic, relating to stearine.

estearina [es-tay-ah-ree'-nah], *f. (Chem.)* Stearine, a white crystalline component of fats.

estearona [es-tay-ah-ro'-nah], *f.* Stearone, a crystalline compound the ketone of stearic acid.

esteatita [es-tay-ah-tee'-tah], *f.* Steatite, soap stone, massive talc.

esteba [es-tay-bah], *f.* 1. A plant of prickly leaves and stem, growing in ponds and marshy places. 2. A stout pole, used on boats for pushing bales of wool close together.

estebar [es-tay-bar'], *va.* With dyers, to put cloth into the caldron to dye it.

esteclar [es-tay-clar'], *va.* To change the combs of looms for silk fringe, when they can no longer serve.

esteirosis [es-tay-e-ro'-sis], *f. (Med.)* Barrenness, sterility.

estela [es-tay'-lah], *f.* 1. The wake of a ship. 2. The trail of a meteor. **Estela de vapor,** *(Aer.)* contrail.

estelar [es-tay-lar'], *a.* 1. Stellar, sideral. 2. *(Teat. etc.)* Star. **Cargo estelar,** star role. **Combate estelar,** star bout (boxeo).

estelaria [es-tay-lah'-re-ah], *f.* 1. *(Bot.)* An old name given to the silvery ladiesmantle.

estelión [es-tay-le-on´], *m.* 1. Stellion, a small spotted lizard. 2. Toadstone.

estelionato [es-tay-le-o-nah'-to], *m. (Law.)* Stellionate, the crime of maliciously defrauding the unwary.

estelón [es-tay-lone'], *m.* Toadstone.

estelulado, da [es-tay-loo-lah'-do, dah], *a.* Stellular, star-shaped.

estemenaras [es-tay-may-nah-ras], *f. pl. (Naut.)* Futtock timbers. *V.* LIGAZONES.

estemple [es-tem'-play], *m. (Mining.)* Stempel, a beam helping to support a platform.

estenografía [es-tay-no-grah-fee'-ah], *f.* Stenography, shorthand; in particular, phonography.

estenografiar [es-tay-no-grah-fe-ar'], *va.* To write in stenography.

estenográfico, ca [es-tay-no-grah'-fe-co, cah], *a.* Stenographic, relating to shorthand.

estenógrafo, fa [es-tay-no'-grah-fo, fah], *m. & f.* Stenographer, one who writes shorthand.

estenomecanografía [es-tay-no-may-cah-no-grah-fee'-ah], *f.* Stenotyping.

estenomecanógrafa [es-tay-no-may-cah-no'-grah-fah], *f.* Stenotypist.

estenotipía [es-tay-no-te-pee'-ah], *f.* Stenotyping.

estepa [es-tay'-pah], *f.* 1. *(Bot.)* Rock rose. **Estepa común,** laurel-leaved rock-rose. 2. Steppe, an immense uncultivated plain of Russia and certain regions of Asia.

estepar [es-tay-par'], *m.* Place filled with rock-roses.

estepilla [es-tay-peel'-lyah], *f. (Bot.)* White-leaved rock-rose.

ester [es'-ter], *m. (Chem.)* Ester.

estera [es-tay'-rah], *f.* Mat, a texture of sedge, flags, or rushes.

esterar [es-tay-rar'], *va.* To mat, to cover with mats. *-vn. (Met. coll.)* To keep oneself warm with clothes.

estercolar [es-ter-co-lar'], *va.* To dung, to muck, to manure, etc. *-vn.* To void the excrements (animales).

estercolero [es-ter-co-lay'-ro], *m.* 1. Boy or servant who drives the muckcart, or carries dung into the fields. 2. Dunghill, muckhill. 3. Laystall, a heap of dung.

estercorácea [es-ter-co-rah'-tha-yah], *f. adj.* Fistula of the anus.

estercuelo [es-ter-coo-ay-lo], *m.* The act of manuring the earth.

estéreo [es-tay'-ray-o], *m. (Arith.)* Stere, a unit of cubic measurement; one cubic meter. *-a.* Stereo. **Un disco estéreo,** a stereo record.

estereofónico, ca [es-tay-ray-o-fo'-ne-o, cah], *a.* Stereophonic. **Sonido estereofónico,** stereophonic sound.

estereografía [es-tay-ray-grah-fee'-ah], *f.* Stereography, representation of solids on a plane.

estereográfico, ca [es-tay-ray-o-grah'-fe-co, cah], *a.* Stereographic.

estereometría [es-tay-ray-o-may-tree'-ah], *f.* Stereometry, art of measuring solids.

estereómetro [es-tay-ray-o'-may-tro], *m.* Stereometer, an instrument for measuring the volume of a body.

estereoscópico [es-tay-ray-os-co'-pe-co], *m.* Stereoscope.

estereoscopio [es-tay-ray-os-co'-pe-o], *m.* Stereoscope, an optical instrument, showing two slightly different pictures, blended into one, in relief.

estereotipa [es-tay-ray-o-tee'-pah], *f. V.* ESTEREOTIPIA.

estereotipar [es-tay-ray-o-tee-par'], *va.* To stereotype or print with solid plates.

estereotipia [es-tay-ray-tee'-pe-ah], *f.* Stereotype, stereotyping.

estereotípico, ca [es-tay-ray-o-tee'-pe-co, cah], *a.* Stereotype, stereotypic, belonging to stereotype.

estereotipo [es-tay-re-o-te-po], *m.* Stereotype.

esterero [es-tay-ray'-ro], *m.* Mat-maker, mat-seller.

estéril [es-tay'-reel], *a.* Sterile, barren (terreno), unfruitful, unproductive, fruitless (esfuerzo).

esterilidad [es-tay-re-le-dahd'], *f.* 1. Sterility, barrenness (terreno), unfruitfulness, jejuneness. 2. Scarcity, the want of crops.

esterilización [es-tay-re-le-thah-the-on´], *f.* Sterilization, sterilizing.

esterilizar [es-tay-re-le-thar'], *va.* To sterilize, to make sterile.

esterilla [es-tay-reel'-lyah], *f.* 1. *(dim.)* Small mat (alfombrilla). 2. Ferret lace, made of gold, silver, or thread. **Paños de esterilla,** saved lists. **Esterilla de cerda para forrar sillas, etc.**, haircloth.

estérilmente [es-tay'-reel-men-tay], *adv.* Barrenly, unfruitfully, meagrely.

esterlino, na [es-ter-lee'-no, nah], *a.* Sterling (dinero).

esternón [es-ter-none'], *m. (Anat.)* Sternum, the breast-bone.

estero [es-tay'-ro], *m.* 1. A large lake near the sea, a salt marsh (pantano). 2. Matting, the act of covering with matting; also, the season in which matting is laid down. 3. *(Geog.)* A small creek, into which the tide flows (estuario). 4. A certain fishing-net.

esteroide [es-tay-ro'-e-day], *m.* Steroid.

estertor [es-ter-tor´], *m.* Rattle in the throat of agonizing persons; stertor.

estertoroso, sa [es-ter-to-ro'so, sah], *a.* Stertorous, accompanied by a snoring sound.

esteta [es-tay'-tah], *m. & f.* Aesthete or esthete.

estética [es-tay'-te-cah], *f.* aesthetics; the science of the beautiful.

esteticista [ess-tay-te-this'-tah], *m.* Beauty consultant, beauty specialist.

estético, ca [es-tay'-te-co, cah], *a.* æsthetic.

estetoscopio [es-tay-tos-co'-peo], *m. (Med.)* Stethoscope.

esteva [es-tay'-vah], *f.* 1. Plough-handle. 2. Curved bar of wood on the bottom, of coaches, connected with the shafts.

estevado, da [es-tay-vah'-do, dah], *a.* Bow-legged.

estezado [es-tay-thah'-do], *m.* V. CORREAL.

estiaje [es-te-ah'-hay], *m.* The lowest stage of water in a river, by reason of heat.

estiba [es-tee'-bah], *f.* 1. Rammer. V. ATACADOR. 2. Stowage, the arrangement of a ship's cargo. 3. Place where wool is compressed.

estibador [es-te-bah-dor'], *m.* Stevedore.

estibar [es-te-bar'], *va.* 1. To compress wool (lana). 2. To stow a cargo (meter).

estibio [es-tee'-be-o], *m.* Antimony stibium.

estíctico, ca [es-teec'-te-co, cah], *a. (Biol.)* Marked with points, punctate.

estiércol [es-te-ayr'-col], *m.* 1. Dung, excrement, ordure. 2. Dung or compost to fatten lands, manure.

estigma [es-teeg'-mah], *m.* 1. Stigma, brand (marca), mark of a slave or criminal. 2. Stigma, every mark of infamy. 3. *(Bot.)* Stigma, the upper extremity of the pistil for receiving the pollen. 4. A miraculous mark upon the body (marca de nacimiento).

estigmatizar [es-tig-ma-tee-thar'], *va.* To stigmatize, to mark with a brand.

estilar [es-te-lar'], *vn. & va.* 1. To use, to be accustomed (usar). 2. To draw up in writing according to the usual style or practice. *-vr.* To be in fashion. **Ya no se estila la chistera,** top hats aren't in fashion any more.

estilbita [es-teel-bee'-tah], *f.* Stilbite hydrous aluminum-calcium silicate.

estilista [es-te-lees'-tah], *m.* Stylist (escritor).

estilito [es-te-lee' to], *m. dim.* A small style or gnomon.

estilizar [es-te-lee-thar'], *va.* To stylize; to design, to style. *-vn.* To cut a dash, to show off.

estilo [es-tee'-lo], *m.* 1. Style, a pointed iron formerly used to write on tables of wax. 2. Gnomon or style of a dial (reloj del sol). 3. Style, the manner of talking or writing, with regard to language. 4. Form or manner of proceeding in suits at law. 5. Use, custom. 6. *(Bot.)* Style, prolongation of the ovary and support of the stigma. **Estilo castizo,** a correct style. **Estilo de vida,** life-style. **Al estilo antiguo,** in the old style. **Los dictadores y otros por el estilo,** dictators and others of that sort.

estilográfico, ca [es-te-lo-grah'-fe-co, cah], *a.* Stylographic. **Pluma estilográfica,** fountain pen.

estilóideo [es-te-lo'-e-day-o], *a.* Styloid, like a style.

estima [es-tee'-mah], *f.* 1. Esteem, respect (aprecio). 2. *(Naut.)* Dead reckoning.

estimabilidad [es-te-mah-be-le-dahd'], *f.* Estimableness.

estimable [es-te-mah'-blay], *a.* Estimable, valuable, creditable; worthy of honor and esteem; computable.

estimación [es-te-mah-the-on'], *f.* 1. Estimation, valuation (evaluación), esteem, regard (aprecio). 2. Estimation, estimate, valuation, account. **Estimación propia,** self-esteem.

estimador, ra [es-te-mah-dor', rah], *m. & f.* Esteemer, estimator.

estimar [es-te-mar'], *va.* 1. To estimate (evaluar), to value; to set a value on a thing; to compute or to computate (calcular), to make of. 2. To esteem, to respect (apreciar), to regard, to honor, to make account of, or to make much of. **Estimar a uno en mucho,** to have a high regard for somebody. **Se lo estimo mucho,** I am much indebted to you for it. 3. To judge, to form an opinion. 4. To thank, to acknowledge. 5. To look into.

estimativa [es-te-mah-tee'-vah], *f.* 1. Power of judging and forming an opinion. 2. Instinct, natural propensity or aversion.

estimulante [es-te-moo-lahn'-tay], *pa. & a.* Stimulating, exciting. *-m.* Stimulant, excitant.

estimular [es-tee-moo-lar'], *va.* 1. To sting, to stimulate (apetito), to irritate, to excite, to goad. 2. To incite, to encourage (esfuerzo, industria).

estímulo [es-tee'-moo-lo], *m.* Sting, stimulus; incitement; stimulation, encouragement.

estinco [es-teen'-co], *m.* Skink, kind of lizard.

estío [es-tee'-o], *m.* The summer.

estiomenado, da [es-te-o-may-nah'-do, dah], *a.* Mortified, corrupted.*-pp.* of ESTIOMENAR.

estiomenar [es-te-o-may-nar], *va.* To corrode, to mortify.

estiómeno [es-te-o' may-no], *m.* Mortification, gangrene.

estipa [es-tee'-pah], *f.* Stipa, a genus of tall, tufted grasses.

estipendiar [es-te-pen-de-ar'], *va.* To give a stipend.

estipendiario [es-te pen-de-ah'-re-o], *m.* Stipendiary, one who performs a service for a settled payment.

estipendio [es-te-pen'-de-o], *m.* Stipend, salary (sueldo), pay, wages, fee (derechos).

estípite [es-tee'-pe-tay], *m. (Arch.)* Plaster in form of a reversed pyramid.

estipticar [es-tip-te-car'], *va.* To use or apply a styptic.

estipticidad [es-tip-te-the-dahd'], *f.* 1. Stypticity, the power of stanching blood.

estíptico, ca [es-teep'-te-co, cah], *a.* 1. Styptic, astringent: having the power of stanching. 2. Costive, bound in the body. 3. *(Met.)* Miserly, avaricious. 4. *(Met.)* Difficult to be obtained.

estiptiquez [es-tip-te-keth'], *f.* 1. Costiveness. 2. Niggardliness.

estípula [es-tee'-poo-lah], *f. (Bot.)* Stipule, a foliaceous appendage at the base of the petiole.

estipulación [es-te-poo-lah-the-on'], *f.* Stipulation, promise, clause, covenant, bargain.

estipulante [es-te-poo-lahn'-tay], *pa.* Stipulator, stipulating.

estipular [es-te-poo-lar'], *va.* To stipulate, to contract, to bargain, to settle terms, to covenant.

estique [es-tee'-kay], *m.* Stick, a wooden instrument used by sculptors for modelling in clay.

estira [es-tee'-rah], *f.* Kind of knife used by curriers.

estirace [es-te-rah'-thay], *m. (Bot.)* Styrax, the typical genus of the storax family; one species yields benzoin, another storax.

estiracear [es-te-rah-thay ar'], *va. (coll.)* To pull, to tug, to stretch.

estiráceo, cea [es-te-rah'-thay-o, ah], *a.* Like styrax, styracaceous.

estiradamente [es-terah-dah-men'-tay], *adv.* 1. Scarcely, difficultly. 2. Violently, forcibly.

estirado, da [es-te-rah'-do, dah], *a.* 1. Extended, dilated, expanded. 2. Excellent. 3. *(Met.)* Grave, stiff (tieso), lofty; full of affected dignity. *pp.* of ESTIRAR.

estirador [es-te-rah-dor'], *m.* 1. Stretcher (cortinas) 2. Drawing table.

estirar [es-te-rar'], *va.* 1. To dilate, to stretch out (extender), to lengthen. 2. To fit, to adjust. 3. To extend a discourse, to enlarge upon a subject (discurso) 4. *(Naut.)* To row slowly, to continue the tack. **Estirar la pierna,** *(coll.)* to die. *-vr.* 1. To stretch, to be extended, to bear extension (cuerpo, miembro). 2. To hold up one's head with affected gravity.

estirón [es-te-rone'], *m.* 1. Pull, the act of pulling (tirón); pluck, haul or hauling. 2. Pain produced by the violent extension of any part. 3. *(Naut.)* The distance gained in the course pursued. **Dar un estirón,** *(coll.)* to grow rapidly.

estirpe [es-teer'-pay], *f.* Race, origin, stock.

estitiquez [es-te-te-keth'], *f.* Costiveness. V. ESTIPTIQUEZ.

estivador [es-te-vah-dor'], *m.* Packer of wool at shearing.

estival [es-te-vahl'], *a.* Estival, pertaining to the summer.

esto [es'-to], *pron. dem.* This. **A esto,** hereto, hereunto. **Con esto,** herewith. **En esto,** herein, hereinto. **Sobre esto,** hereon, hereupon. **Por esto,** hereby. **Todo esto es inútil,** all this is useless. **Antes de esto,** before this. **Esto es todo lo que sé,** this is all I know.

estocada [es-to-cah'-dah], *f.* Stab (golpe), a thrust with a sword, lunge. **Estocada de vino,** breath of a person intoxicated. **Estocada por cornada,** *(coll.)* injury which one receives in striking another.

estoequiometría [es-to-ay-ke-o-may-tree'-ah], *f.* Stoichiometry, the mathematics of chemistry.

estoequiométrico, ca [es-to-ay-ke-o-may'-tre-co, cah], *a.* Stoichiometric, belonging to chemical calculations.

estofa [es-toh'-fah], *f.* 1. Quilted stuff. 2. *(Met.)* Quality, condition. **Hombre de estofa,** a person of consideration.

estofado, da [es-to-fah'-do, dah], *a. & pp.* of ESTOFAR. 1. Quilted. 2. Stewed.

estofado, *m.* Stewed meat.

estofador [es-to-fah-dor'], *m.* Quilter.

estofar [es-to-far'], *va.* 1. To quilt. 2. To paint relievos on a gilt ground. 3. To stew meat with wine, spice, or vinegar.

estoicamente [es-to-e-cah-men'-tay], *adv.* Stoically.

estoicidad [es-to-e-the-dahd'], *f.* Imperturbability.

estoicismo [es-to-e-thees'-mo], *m.* 1. Stoicism, the doctrine and sect of the Stoics. 2. A philosophical school founded in Athens by Zeno, 308 B.C., and whose motto was, "Suffer and abstain."

estoico, ca [es-to'-e-co, cah], *a.* Stoic, stoical.-*m.* Stoic.

estola [es-to'-lah], *f.* 1. Stole, a garment worn by priests. **Derechos de estola,** surplice fees. 2. Stole, woman's scarf. **Estola de piel,** fur stole.

estolidez [es-to-le-deth'], *f.* Stupidity, incapacity.

estólido, da [es-toh'-le-do, dah], *a.* Stupid, foolish.

estolón [es-to-lone'], *m. aug.* 1. A large stole. 2. *(Bot.)* Stolon, a runner or offset.

estomacacia [es-to-ma-cah'-the-ah], *f. (Med.)* Ulceration of the mouth; also scurvy.

estomacal [es-to-mah-cahl'], *a.* Stomachic, belonging to the stomach.

estomagar [es-to-mah-gar'], *vn. &. va.* 1. To stomach, to resent, to remember with anger or malignity. 2. To enrage, to make angry.

estómago [es-toh'-mah-go], *m.* The stomach. **Tener buen estómago,** *(coll.)* to bear insults patiently. **Dolor de estómago,** stomach ache.

estomaguero [es-to-mah-gay'-ro], *m.* Stomacher, a piece of baize applied to the stomach of children.

estomaguillo [es-to-mah-geel'-lyo], *m.* 1. *(dim.)* A small stomach. 2. A weak stomach.

estomatical [es-to-mah-te-cahl'], *a.* Stomachic.

estomaticón [es-to-mah-te-cone'], *m.* Stomach-plaster.

estomatitis [es-to-mah-tee'-tis], *f.* Stomatitis, inflammation of the membranes of the mouth.

estopa [es-toh'-pah], *f.* 1. Tow, the coarsest part of hemp and flax. 2. Coarse cloth made of tow (del cáñamo). 3. *(Naut.)* Oakum.

estopada [es-to-pah'-dah], *f.* Quantity of tow for spinning.

estopear [es-to-pay-ar'], *va.* 1. To calk. 2. *(Naut.)* To stuff oakum in a sail to catch water.

estopeño, ña [es-to-pay'-nyo, nyah], *a.* Of tow; belonging to tow.

estopero [es-to-pay'-ro], *m.* That part of the piston of a pump round which tow is wound.

estoperol [es-to-pay-role'], *m.* 1. *(Naut.)* Short, round-headed tarpaulin nails. 2. Match or wick made of tow (mecha).

estopilla [es-to-peel'-lyah], *f.* 1. Cheese cloth. 2. Finest part of heron or flax.

estopín [es-to-peen'], *m.* Quick match, to fire off a gun.

estopón [es-to-pone'], *m.* Coarse tow.

estoposo, sa [es-to-po'-so, sah], *a.* Belonging to tow; filaceous, filamentous.

estoque [es-toh'-kay], *m.* 1. Estoc, rapier, a long, narrow sword (espada). 2. *(Bot.)* V. ESPADILLA.

estoqueador [es-to-kay-ah-dor'], *m.* Thruster (toreros) who use a long, narrow sword.

estoquear [es-to-kay-ar'], *va.* To thrust with a rapier.

estoqueo [es-to-kay'-o], *m.* Act of thrusting or stabbing.

estoraque [es-to-rah'-kay], *m.* 1. *(Bot.)* Officinal storax. 2. Gum of the storax-tree. **Estoraque líquido,** sweet gum tree, or sweet gum liquid ambar.

estorbador, ra [es-tor-bah-dor', rah], *m. & f.* Hinderer, obstructer.

estorbar [es-tor-bar'], *va.* To hinder (obstaculizar), to impede, to obstruct, to cumber, to hamper, to forbid, to lead off or out of, to be in one's way.

estorbo [es-tor'-bo], *m.* Impediment, hindrance, obstruction, nuisance. **No hay estorbo para que se haga,** there is no obstacle to its being done.

estornija [es-tor-nee'-hah], *f.* 1. An iron ring round the end and arms of an axle tree, which secures the linch-pin holes. 2. *(Prov.)* Boys' play.

estornino [es-tor-nee'-no], *m.* *(Orn.)* Starling.

estornudar [es-tor-noo-dar'], *vn.* To sneeze.

estornudo [es-tor-noo'-do], *m.* Sternutation, sneeze.

estornutatorio [es-tor-noo-tah-toh'-re-o], *m.* Sternutatory, medicine that provokes sneezing.

estotro, tra [es-to'-tro, trah]. A compound pronoun of *esto* and *otro,* this other.

estovar [es-to-var'], *va.* V. REHOGAR.

estrabismo [es-trah-bees'-mo], *m.* Squint, strabismus.

estracilla [es-trah-theel'-lyah], *f.* Kind of fine brown paper; fine blotting paper.

estrada [es-trah'-dah], *f.* Causeway, paved road; turnpike road (carretera). **Estrada encubierta,** *(Mil.)* covert-way.

estradiota [es-trah-de-o'-tah], *f.* 1. Ancient mode of riding with long stirrups and stiff legs. 2. Kind of lance.

estradiote, ta [es-trah-de-oh'-tay, tah], *a.* Relating to riding with long stirrups. **Estradiote,** soldier mounted with long stirrups.

estrado [es-trah'-do], *m.* 1. Drawing-room where company is received, guest chamber. 2. Carpets and other embellishments of a drawing-room. **Entrados,** halls where courts of justice hold their sittings. 3. Baker's table for holding the loaves to be put into the oven. 4. A platform on which the royal throne is placed.

estrafalariamente [es-trah-fah-lah-re-ah-men'-tay], *adv.* *(coll.)* Carelessly, slovenly, extravagantly, wildly.

estrafalario, ria [es-trah-fah-lah'-re-o, ah], *a.* 1. Slovenly, uncleanly dressed; indecently neglectful of dress; estravagant, wild (ropa). 2. Odd, queer, eccentric (excéntrico).

estragadamente [es-trah-gah-dah-men'-tay], *adv.* Depravedly.

estragador, ra [es-trah-gah-dor', rah], *m. & f.* Corrupter, destroyer.

estragamiento [es-trah-gah-meen'-to], *m.* 1. Ravage, waste, ruin. 2. *(Met.)* Disorder, corruption of morals.

estragar [es-trah-gar'], *va.* 1. To deprave, to vitiate, to corrupt, to spoil (gusto), to make less pure, to disfigure. 2. *(Obs.)* To destroy, to ruin, to waste, to harass.

estrago [es-trah'-go], *m.* 1. Ravage, waste, ruin, havoc. **Los estragos del tiempo,** the ravages of time. 2. Wickedness, corruption of morals, depravity.

estragón [es-trah-gone'], *m.* *(Bot.)* Tarragon wormwood.

estrambosidad [es-tram-bo-se-dahd'], *f.* Distortion of the eyes.

estrambote [es-tram-bo'-tay], *m.* Burden of a song.

estrambótico, ca [es-tram-bo'-te-co, cah], *a.* 1. Strange, extravagant, irregular. 2. Eccentric, eccentrical.

estramonio [es-trah-mo'-ne-o], *m.* *(Bot.)* Common thornapple; used as a remedy for asthmatic attacks.

estrangol [es-tran-gole'], *m.* *(Vet.)* Inflammation in a horse's tongue.

estrangul [es-tran-gool'], *m*. A reed for an oboe or any other winding strument, of cane or of metal.

estrangulación [es-tran-goo-lah-the-on´], *f*. 1. Strangling, as act and effect. 2. Strangulation, constriction of the neck by a circular ligature. 3. Stoppage of a hydraulic apparatus.

estrangulado, da [es-tran-goo-lah'-do, dah], *a*. *(Med.)* Strangulated.

estrangulador [es-tran-goo-lah-dor'], *m*. 1. Strangler (persona). 2. *(Mech.)* Throttle.

estrangulamiento [es-tran-goo-lah-me-ayn'-to], *m*. *(Aut.)* Narrow stretch of road, bottleneck.

estrangular [es-tran-goo-lar'], *va*. 1. To strangle (persona), to kill by compressing the trachea. 2. *(Med.)* To strangulate. 3. *(Mech.)* To throttle; to choke.

estraperlo [es-trah-payr-lo], *m*. Black market.

estrapontina [es-trah-pon-tee'-nah], *f*. Kind of hammock.

estratagema [es-trah-tah-hay'-mah], *f*. 1. Stratagem in war. 2. Trick, artful deception; craftiness; finesse; fetch.

estrategia [es-trah-tay'-he-ah], *f*. *(Mill.)* Strategy, military science.

estratégico, ca [es-trah-tay´-he-co, cah], *a*. *(Mil.)* Strategic, strategical, belonging to strategy.

estratificación [es-trah-te-fe-cah-the-on'], *f*. *(Min.)* Stratification, arrangement of layers.

estratificar [es-trah-te-fe-car'], *va*. *(Min.)* To stratify, to dispose in strata.

estratiforme [es-trah-te-for'-may], *a*. Stratiform, disposed in strata.

estrato [es-trah-to], *m*. *(Geol.)* Stratum, layer, bed.

estratosfera [es-trah-tos-fay'-rah], *f*. Stratosphere.

estrave [es-trah'-vey], *m*. *(Naut.)* End of a ship's keel.

estraza [es-trah'-thah], *f*. Rag, fragment of cloth. **Papel de estraza**, brown paper.

estrazar [es-trah-thar'], *va*. *(Obs.)* To tear or break into pieces.

estrechamente [es-tray-chah-men'-tay], *adv*. 1. Narrowly, tightly (apretadamente), closely, fast, compactly, close, nearly. 2. *(Met.)* Exactly, punctually. 3. *(Met.)* Strongly, forcibly. 4. *(Met.)* Strictly (severamente), rigorously. 5. *(Met.)* Scantily, penuriously.

estrechamiento [es-tray-chah-me-en'-to], *m*. Act of tightening, tightness, narrowing.

estrechar [es-tray-char'], *va*. 1. To tighten, to make narrow (hacer estrecho). 2. To contract, to constringe, to constrict, to curtail, to compress. 3. *(Met.)* To confine, to pin up. 4. *(Met.)* To constrain, to compel (presionar). 5. *(Met.)* To restrain, to obstruct. -*vr*. 1. To bind oneself strictly. 2. *(Met.)* To reduce one's expenses (gastos). **Estrecharse en los gastos**, to stint oneself, to economize. 3. *(Met.)* To act in concert with another. 4. *(Met.)* To relate or communicate in confidence (amistad). 5. *(Met.)* To be dejected. 6. To be intimate with. **Se estrecharon la mano**, they shook hands.

estrechez [es-tray-cheth'], *f*. 1. Straitness, narrowness, compactness, closeness. 2. *(Met.)* Intimate union. 3. *(Met.)* Intimacy, friendship (amistad). 4. *(Met.)* Arduous or dangerous undertaking. 5. *(Met.)* Austerity (austeridad), abstraction from worldly objects. 6. *(Met.)* Property. 6. Financial stringency. **Estrechez del dinero**, tightness of money. **Estrecheces**, financial difficulties. **Vivir con estrechez**, to live in straitened circumstances.

estrecho [es-tray'-cho], *m*. 1. Strait or frith, a narrow arm of the sea. 2. Pass, a narrow passage between two mountains. 3. *(Met.)* Peril, danger, risk.

estrecho, cha [es-tray'-cho, chah], *a*. 1. Narrow, close, dense. 2. Straight, tight. **Estos zapatos me están muy estrechos**, these shoes are too small for me. 3. *(Met.)* Intimate, familiar (relación). 4. *(Met.)* Rigid (actitud), austere (carácter). 5. *(Met.)* Exact, punctual. 6. *(Met.)* Narrow-minded, illiberal. **Es muy estrecha**, she´s very strait-laced. 7. *(Met.)* Poor, indigent, penurious, needy, necessitous. -*m*. Narrows, channel. **Estrecho de Gibraltar**, Straits of Gibraltar.

estrechura [es-tray-choh'-rah], *f*. 1. Narrowness, straitness; narrowing. 2. *(Met.)* Austerity, abstraction from the world. 3. *(Met.)* Distress, danger. 4. Intimate familiarity.

estregadera [es-tray-gah-day-rah], *f*. A kind of brush used for rubbing off dirt (fregasuelos, bruza).

estregadero [es-tray-gah-day'-ro], *m*. 1. Place where beasts rub themselves against a tree, stone, etc. 2. Place for washing clothes.

estregadura [es-tray-gah-doo'-rah], *f*. Friction, act of rubbing.

estregamiento [es-tray-gah-me-en'-to], *m*. Friction.

estregar [es-tray-gar'], *m*. 1. To rub one thing against another, to scour (con cepillo), to fray, to grind. 2. To scratch.

estrella [es-trayl'-lyah], *f*. 1. A star. **La estrella de Belén**, star of Bethlehem. **Estrella del norte**, north star. **Estrella polar**, polar star. 2. *(Met.)* A white mark on a horse's face. 3. Asterisk, a mark in printing. 4. *(Met.)* Fate, lot, destiny. **Tener estrella**, to be fortunate. 5. *(Mil.)* Star-fort, a work with five or more faces, having salient and re-entering angles. **Tomar la estrella**, *(Naut.)* to take the altitude of a star. **Estrellas errantes** or **erráticas**, planets, satellites. **Con estrellas**, after night or before sunrise.

estrellada [es-trehl-lyah'-dah], *f*. *(Bot.)* Ladies' mantle. *V*. ALQUIMILA.

estrelladera [es-trel-lyah-day'-rah], *f*. Kind of ladle for frying eggs.

estrelladero [es-trel-lyah-day'-ro], *m*. Kind of frying-pan for dressing eggs without breaking the yolks.

estrellado, da [es-trel-lyah'-do, dah], *a*. Starry (con estrellas). **Huevos, estrellados**, eggs fried in oil or butter; fried eggs. -*pp*. of ESTRELLAR.

estrellamar [es-trel-lyah-mar'], *f*. 1. *(Bot.)* Buckthorn plantain. 2. Starfish.

estrellar [es-trel-lyar'], *a*. Stellated, starry.

estrellar [es-trel-lyar´], *va*. 1. To smash, to dash to bits (romper). **Lo estrelló contra la pared**, he smashed it against the wall. **Estrelló el balón en el poste**, he crashed the ball into the goal-post. 2. To fry (huevos). -*vr*. 1. *(Aer. and Naut.)* To crash. 2. To smash, shatter. 3. *(Fig.)* To be ruined, to fail utterly. 4. To fill with stars. **Estrellarse con**, to conflict violently with.

estrellato [es-trel-lay-to], *m*. Stardom.

estrellera [es-trel-lyay'-rah], *f*. *(Naut.)* Plain rigging without runners.

estrellón [es-trel-lyone'], *m*. 1. *(Aug.)* Large star (estrella). 2. Star ball used in artificial fireworks (fuegos artificiales).

estremecedor, ra [es-tray-may-thay-dor', rah], *a*. Frightful, terrifying.

estremecer [es-tray-may-therr'], *va*. 1. To shake (sacudir), to make tremble. 2. *(Naut.)* To work or labor hard (barco) .-*vr*. To shake (edificio), to tremble (persona: miedo), to shudder (horror), to be uncommonly agitated. *(Yo me estremezco, yo me estremezca, from Estremecer. V.* CONOCER.*)*

estremecimiento [es-tray-may-the-me-en'-to], *m*. Trembling, quaking, shaking.

estremiche [es-tray-mee'-chay], *m*. *(Naut.)* A piece of timber which is notched into the knee of a ship.

estrena [es-tray'-nah], *f*. 1. A new year's gift. 2. *(Arch.)* Handsel, the first act of using anything; the first act of sale. 3. Treat on wearing a new suit of clothes.

estrenar [es-tray-nar'], *va*. 1. To handsel, to use or to do something the first time (ropa) 2. To commence, to begin. -*vr*. To begin to put something in execution. **No se estrena**, he hasn´t done a hand´s turn.

estreno [es-tray'-no], *m*. Debut (persona), premier, first presentation; new play (comedia), new film, new release (película). **Cine de estreno**, first-run cinema. **Su estreno como vendedor fue un éxito**, his debut as a salesman was quite a success.

estrenque [es-tren'-kay], *m*. *(Naut.)* Rope made of bass or sedge.

estrenuidad [es-tray-noo-e-dahd'], *f.* Strength, valor, strenuousness. (*Acad.*)

estrenuo, nua [es-tray'-noo-o, ah], *a.* Strong, agile, valorous, strenuous. (*Acad.*)

estreñido, da [es-tray-nyee'-do, dah], *a.* 1. Close bound, costive, hard bound. 2. Miserable, niggardly. -*pp.* of ESTREÑIR.

estreñimiento [es-tray-nye-me-en'-to], *m.* Obstruction: the act of binding or restraining; confine, confinement.

estreñir [es-trey-nyeer'], *va.* To bind, to tie close, to restrain. -*vn.* To restrain oneself. **Estreñirse el vientre**, to constipate, to be costive. (*Yo estriño, yo estriña, from Estreñir. V. PEDIR.*)

estrepa, estrepilla [es-tray'-pah, es-tray-peel'-lyah], *f.* (*Bot.*) V. ESTEPILLA.

estrepitarse [es-tray-pe-tar'-say], *vr.* (*Coll. Cuba.*) To be noisily merry, to carouse wildly.

estrépito [es-tray'-pe-to], *m.* Noise, clamor, bustle, noisiness, racket, din (ruido fuerte); clatter, clash (ruido brusco).

estrepitosamente [es-tre-pe-to'-sah-men-tay], *adv.* Noisily, with a din.

estrepitoso, sa [es-tray-pe-toh'-so, sah], *a.* Noisy, boisterous, loud, clamorous, deafening; rowdy (persona).

estreptococo [es-trep-to-co'-co], *m.* Streptococcus.

estreptomicina [es-trep-to-me-thee'-nah], *f.* (*Med.*) Streptomycin.

estrés [es-tress'], *m.* (*Med.*) Stress.

estresante [es-tray-sahn'-tay], *a.* Stressful.

estría [es-tree'-ah], *f.* (*Arch.*) Fluting, channel cut along half the length of shafts or pilasters. Stria.

estriadura [es-tre-ah-doo'-rah], *f.* (*Arch.*) Fluting.

estriar [es-tre-ar'], *va.* (*Arch.*) To flute, to cut columns into channels and grooves, to gutter.-*vr.* To be grooved, striated.

estribadero [es-tre-bah-day'-ro], *m.* Prop, stay.

estribar [es-tre-bar'], *vn.* 1. To prop, to support with props. 2. (*Met.*) To found, to build upon; to be supported. **La dificultad estriba en el texto**, the difficulty lies in the text.

estribera [es-tre-bay'-rah], *f.* 1. Buttress, arch, pillar. 2. Joiner's bench.

estribería [es-tre-bay-ree'-ah], *f.* Place where stirrups are kept.

estriberón [es-tre-bay-rone'], *m.* Prominences made on earth or wood by cross-bars, to serve as steps.

estribillo [es-tre-beel'-lyo], *m.* 1. Introduction or beginning of a song, chorus, refrain. 2. Tautology, a needless and superfluous repetition of the same words.

estribo [es-tree'-bo], *m.* 1. Buttress, abutment arch, pillar. 2. Stirrup (jinete). 3. Step on the side of a coach (apoyapié). 4. Staple fixed at the end of a cross-bow. 5. Bone of the ear resembling a stirrup; the stapes. 6. V. ESTRIBILLO. 7. (*Gunn.*) Clasp on the felloes of gun-carriage wheels. **Estribos,** (*Naut.*) stirrups of a ship, pieces of timber fastened to the keel with iron plates. **Perder los estribos,** (*Fig.*) to fly off the handle.

estribor [es-tre-bor'], *m.* (*Naut.*) Starboard.

estribordarios [es-tre-bor-dah'-re-os], *m. pl.* People on the starboard hand.

estricnina [es-tric-nee'-nah], *f.* (*Med.*) Strychnine, an alkaloid obtained from nux vomica; an important medicine and a violent poison.

estricote (Al) [es-tre-co'-tay], *adv.* Without rule or order. **Tener a uno al estricote**, to amuse one with vain promises.

estrictamente [es-treec'-tah-men-tay], *adv.* Strictly.

estricto, ta [es-treec'-to, tah], *a.* 1. Strict, exact, accurate, rigorously nice. 2. Strict, severe, rigorous, extreme.

estridente [es-tre-den'-tay], *a.* (*Poet.*) That which causes noise or creaking; strident.

estridor [es-tre-dor'], *m.* Noise, creak, screech, stridor.

estrige [es-tree'-hay], *f.* Night-bird, said to be an unlucky omen; screechowl, vampire.

estrigila [es-tre-hee'lah], *f.* Strigil, a scraper of bronze which Roman gladiators used to clean off the oil and dust of combat, and which passed for a specific for certain diseases.

estringa [es-treen'-gah], *f.* V. AGUJETA.

estripar [es-tre-par'], *va.* (*Prov.*) V. DESTRIPAR.

estriptís *m.* **estriptise** *m.* [es-trip-tees'], Striptease.

estrobilífero, ra [es-tro-be-lee'-fay-ro, rah], *a.* Cone-bearing, strobiliferous.

estróbilo [es-tro'-be-lo], *m.* Strobile, cone of the pine family.

estroboscopio [es-tro-bos-co'-pe-o], *m.* Stroboscope.

estrofa [es-tro'-fah], *f.* (*Poet.*) Strophe.

estrógeno [es-tro'-hay-no], *m.* (*Biol.*) Estrogen.

estronciana [es-tron-the-ah'-nah], *f.* Strontia, an alkaline earth.

estroncio [es-tron'-the-o], *m.* Strontium, a metallic element.

estropajear [es-tro-pah-hay-ar'], *va.* To clean a wall with a dry brush or rubber.

estropajo [es-tro-pah'-ho], *m.* 1. Dishcloth (trapo). 2. Brush, made of bass or sedge, to clean culinary vessels. **Estropajo de acero**, steel wool. 3. (*Met.*) A worthless, trifling thing (objeto inútil).

estropajosamente [es-tro-pah-ho'-sah-men-tay], *adv.* Stammeringly.

estropajoso, sa [es-tro-pah-ho'-so, sah], *a.* 1. Ragged, despicable, low, mean (vil). 2. (*Met.*) Troublesome, useless. 3. (*Met.*) Stuttering, stammering (habla).

estropalina [es-tro-pah-lee'-nah], *f.* Refuse of wool.

estropeado, da [es-tro-pay-ah'-do, dah], *a. & pp.* of ESTROPEAR. Lame. **Está muy estropeada**, she looks older than she is.

estropeamiento [es-tro-pay-ah-me-en'-to], *m.* Act of maining, wounding, or laming.

estropear [es-tro-pay-ar'], *va.* 1. To damage (objeto), to ruin, to cripple (persona), to mutilate, to mangle (texto etc.), to cut. 2. To mix lime and sand. -*vr.* To get damaged; to spoil, to go bad; to deteriorate, to fail (plan).

estropecillo [es-tro-pay-theel'-lyo], *m. dim.* A slight stumble or impediment.

estropeo [es-tro-pay'-o], *m.* (*Prov.*) Maim, hurt, injury.

estropicio [es-tro-pee'-the-o], *m.* (*Acad. Coll.*) 1. Clatter, crash (rotura estrepitosa), destruction, with noise, of table service, etc. 2. Damage (destrozo), rumpus (jaleo).

estrovo [es-tro'-vo], *m.* (*Naut.*) Strap, a piece of rope used for strapping blocks.

estructura [es-trooc-too'-rah], *f.* 1. Structure, constructure, manner of building or constructing an edifice. 2. Order, method, arrangement (orden).

estructurar [es-trook-too-rar'], *va.* 1. To distribute, to organize the parts (projecto). 2. To construct.

estruendo [es-troo-en'-do], *m.* 1. Clamor, noise (ruido), outcry, clatter. 2. Confusion, bustle, uproar (alboroto) 3. Pomp, ostentation (fig.: pompa), show.

estruendoso, sa [es-troo-en-do'-so, sah], *a.* 1. Noisy, clamorous. 2. Pompous, full of ostentation.

estrujadura [es-troo-hah-doo'-rah], *f.* Pressing, squeezing, pressure, compressing.

estrujamiento [es-troo-hah-me-en'-to], *m.* V. ESTRUJADURA.

estrujar [es-troo-har'], *va.* To press, to squeeze the juice (exprimir). **Estrujar el dinero**, to be avaricious or extremely covetous.

estrujón [es-troo-hone'], *m.* 1. The last pressing of grapes, which gives a miserable wine. 2. Pressing, squeezeing, expression.

estrupador [es-troo-pa-dor'], *m.* V. ESTUPRADOR.

estrupar [es-troo-par'], *va.* V. ESTUPRAR.

estuante [es-too-ahn'-tay], *a.* Very hot, boiling, scorching.

estuario [es-too-ah'-re-o], *m.* A low ground, overflowed by the sea at high tides; an estuary.

estucador [es-too-cah-dor'], *m.* A stucco-plasterer.

estucar [es-too-car'], *va.* To stucco or plaster something.

estuco [es-too'-co], *m.* Stucco, a kind of fine plaster.

estuche [es-too'-chay], *m.* 1. Case for scissors or other instruments (caja). **Estuche de aseo**, toilet case. **Estuche**

de joyas, jewel box. 2. The ace of spades, the deuce of spades or clubs, and ace of clubs in certain games of cards. 3. Small comb. 4. *(Met.)* One who knows a little of everything, or is capable of anything. **Ser estuche** or **es un estuche de habilidades,** *(Met. Coll.)* he is a very clever fellow.

estudiador [es-too-de-ah-dor'], *m. (coll.)* Student.

estudiantazo [es-too-de-an-tah'-tho], *m.* He who is reputed a great scholar.

estudiante [es-too-de-ahn'-tay], *m.* 1. Scholars; one who learns of a master (universidades); a student. **Estudiante de medicina,** medical student. 2. A kind of prompter to players.

estudiantil [es-too-de-an-teel'], *a. (coll.)* Scholastic, belonging to scholar.

estudiantillo [es-too-de-an-teel'lyo], *m. dim.* A little scholar.

estudiantino, na [es-too-de-an-tee'-no, nah], *a.* Belonging to a scholar or student. **A la estudiantina,** in the manner of students.

estudiantón [es-too-de-an-tone'], *m. aug.* A big student.

estudiar [es-too-de-ar'], *va.* 1. To study, to acquire knowledge. 2. To muse, to ponder, to contemplate, to commit, to memory. 3. To make a drawing after a model or nature. 4. To attend the clases in a university. **Estudiar para abogado,** to study to become a lawyer. **Tengo que ir a estudiar,** I must go and work.

estudio [es-too'-de-o], *m.* 1. Study, application to books and learning. 2. Study (dibujo, arte). 3. Study, apartment (cuarto). 4. Hall where models, prints, and plans are kept to be copied or studied. 5. *(Met.)* Study, attention, meditation, contemplation. **Hacer estudio de alguna cosa,** *(Met.)* to act with art, cunning, or crafty reflection. **Estudio general,** university. **Un estudio del mercado,** a market survey or reasearch. -*pl.* 1. Time, trouble, and core applied to the study of the sciences. 2. Sciences, letters. **Dar estudios a uno,** to maintain one at his studies. **Hizo sus estudios en París,** he studied in París. **Estudios de tiempo y movimiento,** time and motion study. 6. Studio (arte, cine). **Estudio de cine,** film studio. **Estudio de televisión,** television studio.

estudiosamente [es-too-de-o-sah-men'-tay], *adv.* Studiously, with care and reflection.

estudioso, sa [es-too-de-oh'-so, sah], *a.* 1. Studious, given to study and reflection. .2. *(Met.)* Studious, careful solicitous, contemplative.

estufa [es-too'-fah], *f.* 1. A stove, heater (calentador). **Estufa de gas,** gas heater. **Estufa eléctrica,** electric heater. 2. A warm, close room, a hothouse. 3. A drying-chamber, hot closet, dry bath. 4. A small brazier used to warm the feet.

estufador [es-too-fah-dor'], *m.* Vessel in which meat is stewed.

estufar [es-too-far'], *va. (Obs.)* 1. To warm something. 2. V. ESTOFAR.

estufero [es-too-fay'-ro], or **estufista,** *m.* He who makes stoves.

estufilla [es-too-feel'-lyah], *f.* 1. Muff a cover made of fur to keep the hands warm. 2. A small brasier, used to warm the feet on (brasero).

estultamente [es-tool-tah-men'-tay], *adv. (coll.)* Foolishly, sillily.

estulticia [es-tool-tee'-the-ah], *f. (coll.)* Folly, silliness.

estulto, ta [es-tool'-to, tah], *a. (coll.)* Foolish, silly.

estuosidad [es-too-o-se-dahd'], *f.* Burning, excessive hotness.

estuoso, sa [es-too-oh'-so, sah], *a.* Very hot, ardent, burnt by the heat of the sun.

estupefacción [es-too-pay-fac-the-on'], *f.* Stupefaction, numbness.

estupefacientes [es-too-pay-fah-the-en'-tess], *m. pl.* Narcotics, narcotic drugs.

estupefactivo, va [es-too-pay-fac-tee'-vo, vah], *a.* Stupefying.

estupefacto [es-too-pay-fahc´-to], *a. (coll.)* Motionless, petrified, immovable with astonishment.

estupendamente [es-too-pen-dah-men'-tay], *adv.* Wonderfully, stupendously.

estupendo, da [es-too-pen'-do, dah], *a.* Stupendous, wonderful, marvellous. **Esas chicas son estupendas,** those girls are terrific. **Tiene un coche estupendo,** he´s got a marvelous car.

estúpidamente [es-too'-pe-dah-men-tay], *adv.* Stupidly, dully, lumpishly.

estupidez [es-too-pe-deth'], *f.* Stupidity (cualidad), insensibility, dullness, sluggishness, stupidness.

estúpido, da [es-too'-pee-do, dah], *a.* Stupid, insensible, dull, crackbrained, gross, heavy, mopish.

estupor [es-too-por'], *m.* 1. Stupor, suspension of sensibility. 2. Amazement, admiration, astonishment.

estuprador [es-too-prah-dor'], *m.* Ravisher, deflowerer, violator.

estuprar [es-too-prar'], *va.* To ravish, to violate, to deflower.

estupro [es-too'-pro], *m.* Ravishment, rape, constuparation.

estuque [es-too'-kay], *m.* V. ESTUCO. **Estuquista** [es-too-kees´-tah], *m.* Plasterer, stucco-worker.

esturar [es-too-rar'], *va.* 1. To dry by the force of fire. 2. To overdo meat by the force of fire.

esturión [es-too-re-on'], *m. (Zool.)* Sturgeon.

ésula [ay'-soo-lah], *f. (Bot.)* Leafy-branched spurge.

esviaje [es-ve-ah'-hay], *m. (Arch.)* 1. The inclination of a vertical with respect to a line which crosses it. 2. Oblique direction of the sides of an arch or vault.

etanún [ay-tah-noon'], *m.* The seventh month of the Hebrew ecclesiastical year.

etapa [ay-tah'-pah], *f.* 1. *(Mil.)* The ration of necessaries to troops in the field or traveling (de viaje). **A cortas etapas,** in easy stages. 2. Stage (cohete). 3. *(Fig.)* Stage, phase. **En la segunda etapa del plan,** in the second phase of the plan. **Lo haremos por etapas,** we´ll do it in stages.

etcétera [et thay'-tay-rah], *f.* Etcetera, the rest, and so on. Commonly abbreviated to *etc.*

éter [ay'-ter], *m.* 1. *(Chem.)* Ether, ethyl ether. 2. Ether or aether, a supposed medium, filling all space, through which the vibrations of light, heat, and electricity are propagated. 3. Ether, the upper air, the sky.

etéreo, rea [ay-tay'-ray-o, ah], *a.* 1. Ethereal, etherous, formed of ether. 2. *(Poet.)* Ethereal, ethereous, heavenly.

eterióscopo [ay-tay-re-os-co-po], *m.* An instrument for measuring the force of solar radiation.

eterización [ay-tay-re-thah-the-on´], *f.* Etherization, the administration of ether for anaesthesia.

eterizar [ay-tay-re-thar'], *va.* 1. To etherize, to cause anaesthesia by inhalation of ether. 2. To convert into ether (eterificar).

eternal [ay-ter-nahl'], *a.* Eternal.

eternamente [ay-ter'-nah-men-tay], *adv.* 1. Eternally, forever, everlastingly, evermore. 2. *(Met.)* For a long time. 3. Never.

eternidad [ay-ter-ne-dahd'], *f.* 1. Eternity. 2. Duration or length of continuance, which comprehends many ages.

eternizar [ay-ter-ne-thar'], *va.* 1. To eternize, to perpetuate. 2. To prolong for a great length of time.

eterno, na [ay-tayr'-no, nah], *a.* 1. Eternal, endless, never-ending, everlasting. 2. Durable, lasting.

eteromancia [ay-tay-ro-mahn´-the-ah], *f.* Divination by the flight or song of birds.

ética [ay'-te-cah], *f.* Ethics, morals, morality, or the doctrine of morality.

ético, ca [ay'-te-co, cah], *a.* Ethical, moral, treating on morality.

etileno [ay-te-lay'-no], *m. (Chem.)* Ethylene.

etilo [ar-tee'-lo], *m. (Chem.)* Ethyl.

etimología [ay-te-mo-lo-hee'-ah], *f.* Etymology.

etimológicamente [ay-te-mo-lo'-he-cah-men-tay], *adv.* Etymologically.

etimológico, ca [ay-te-mo-lo'-he-co, cah], *a.* Etymological.

etimologista [ay-te-mo-lo-hees'-tah], *m.* Etymologist, etymologer.

etíope

etíope, etiópico, ca, etiopio, a [ay-tee'-pay, ay-te-o'-pe-co, cah], *a.* Ethiopian.

etiópide [ay-te-oh'-pe-day], *f. (Bot.)* Clary, Ethiopian mullein.

etiqueta [ay-te-kay'-tah], *f.* 1. Etiquette, ceremony, formality (formalistmo). **De etiqueta,** formal, full-dress. **Baile de etiqueta,** dress ball. 2. Compliments in conversation. 3. *(Com.)* Label showing price and class of merchandise (rótulo); in this sense it is Gallicism. 4. *(Inform.)* Label. **Etiqueta opaca,** opaque sticker.

etiquetado [ay-te-kay-tah'-do], *m.* Labelling.

etiquetar [ay-te-kay-tar'], *va.* To label.

etiquetero, ra [ay-te-kay-tay'-ro, rah], *a.* Ceremonious, civil and formal to a fault: it is used frequently as a substantive to express an observer of etiquette, or a very ceremonious person.

etites [ay-tee'-les], *f.* Eaglestone, hydroxide of iron.

etmoides [ayt-mo'-e-days], *m. (Anat.)* The ethmoid bone.

etnia [ayt'-nee-ah], *f.* Ethnic group; race.

étnico, ca [ayt'-ne-co, cah], *a.* Ethnic. V. GENTIL.

etnografía [et-no-grah-fee'-ah], *f.* Ethnography, the study of races of men.

etnográfico, ca [et-no-grah'-fe-co, cah], *a.* Ethnographic, relating to ethnography.

etnógrafo [et-no'-grah-fo], *m.* Ethnographer.

etnología [et-no-lo-hee'-ah], *f.* Ethnology, the science of the natural races or families of men. **Etnólogo,** *m.* Ethnologist.

etografía [ay-to-grah-fee'-ah], *f.* Ethology, the science of the formation of human character.

etólico, ca, or **etolio, lia** [ay-toh'-le-co, cah], *a.* Etolian.

etrusco, ca [ay-troos'-co, cah], *a.* Etruscan.

eubolia [ay-oo-bo'-leah], *f.* The act of expressing one's thoughts with propriety.

eucalipto [ay-oo-cah-leep'-to], *m.* Eucalyptus, the Australian gum tree.

Eucaristía [ay-oo-cah-ris-tee'-ah], *f.* The Eucharist.

eucarístico, ca [ay-oo-cah-rees'-te-co, cah], *a.* 1. Eucharistical, eucharistic. 2. Eucharistical, belonging to works in prose or verse containing acts of thanksgiving.

euclorina [ay-oo-clo-ree'-nah], *f.* Euchloring, chlorous oxide gas, an explosive mixture of chlorine dioxide and chlorine.

eucologio, eucólogo [ay-oo-co-lo'-he-o, ay-oo-co'-lo-go], *m.* Euchology, book containing the service for all the Sundays, and festivals in the year; euchologion.

eucrasia [ay-oo-crah'-se-ah], *f. (Med.)* Eucrasy, sound health.

eucrático, ca [ay-oo-crah'-te-co, cah], *a.* Euchratical.

eudiometría [ay-oo-de-o-may-tree'-ah], *f.* Eudiometry.

eudiómetro [ay-oo-de-o'-may-tro], *m. (Chem.)* Eudiometer.

eufemismo [ay-oo-fay-mees'-mo], *m.* Euphemism, a suave style in words and expressions; the toning down of what would otherwise sound harsh or offensive.

eufonía [ay-oo-fo-nee'-ah], *f.* Euphony.

eufónico, ca [ay-oo-fo'-nee-co, cah], *a.* Euphonic, euphonious.

eufono [ay-oo-fo'-no], *m.* Euphonium, a musical instrument composed of 42 glass cylinders.

euforbio [ay-oo-for'-beo], *m. (Bot.)* Officinal spurge.

euforia [ay-oo-fo'-re-ah], *f.* Euphoria; exuberance, elation.

eufórico [ay-oo-fo'-re-co], *a.* Euphoric; exuberant.

eufrasia [ay-oo-frah'-se-ah], *f. (Bot.)* Eyebright. **Euphrasia oficinal,** common eyebright.

eugenesia [ay-oo-hay-nay'-se-ah], *f.* Eugenics.

eumenes [ay-oo-may'-nes], *m.* Eumenes, a genus of solitary wasps.

eunuco [ay-oo-noo'-co], *m.* Eunuch.

eupatorio [ay-oo-pah-to'-re-o], *m. (Bot.)* Eupatorium. **Eupatorio cañameño,** hempagrimony eupatorium.

euritmia [ay-oo-reet-'me-ah], *f.* 1. *(Arch.)* Eurythmy, proportion and harmony in an edifice. 2. Happy selection of musical rhythm and movement. 3. Skill in the handling of surgical instruments. 4. Regularity in arterial pulsations, normal pulse.

euro [ay'-oo-ro], *m.* 1. Eurus, the east wind. **Euro austro** or **Euro noto,** southeast wind. 2. European currency.

eurodiputado, da [ay-oo-ro-de-poo-tah'-do], *m & f.* Euro MP, member of the European Parliament.

Europa [ay-oo-ro'-pah], *f.* Europe.

europeo, a [ay-oo-ro-pay'-o, ah], *a.* European.

éuscaro, ra [ay'-oos-cah-ro, rah], *a.* Pertainining to the Basques or their language. *-n.* A Basque, a native of Biscay.

eutanasia [ay-oo-tah-nah´-se-ah], *f.* 1. Euthanasia, a painless, peaceful death. 2. A means for producing a gentle, easy death. 3. Death in a state of grace.

eutaxia [ay-oo-tahc'-se-ah], *f. (Med.)* A perfectly organized constitution.

eutiquiano, na [ay-oo-te-ke-ah'-no, nah], *a.* Eutychian, belonging to the sect of Eutyches.

eutrapelia, eutropelia [ay-oo-trah-pay'-leah, ay-oo-tro-pay'-le-ah], *f.* 1. Moderation in jests, jokes, and pleasures. 2. Pastime, sport.

eutrapélico, ca, eutropélico, ca [ay-oo-trah-pay'-le-co, cah], *a.* Moderate, temperate.

evacuación [ay-vah-coo-ah-the-on'], *f.* Evacuation.

evacuante [ay-vah-coo-ahn'-tay], *pa. & a.* Evacuant, evacuating: it is used sometimes as a substantive.

evacuar [ay-vah-coo-ar'], *va.* 1. To evacuate, to empty. 2. To quit, to leave. **Evacuar un negocio,** to finish or complete a business.

evacuativo, va [ay-vah-coo-ah-tee'-vo, vah], *a.* Evacuative, that which has the power of evacuating.

evacuatorio, ria [ay-vah-coo-ah-to'-re-o, ah], *a.* 1. That which evacuates. 2. Public lavatory.

evadir [ay-vah-deer'], *va.* 1. To evade, to escape, to flee from danger. 2. To evade (dinero), to elude by sophistry, to avoid, to decline by subterfuge. *-vr.* 1. To evade, to escape, to slip away, to make one's escape. 2. To evade, to practise sophistry or evasions.

evagación [ay-vah-gah-the-on'], *f.* Evagation, the act of wandering; excursion.

evaluación [ay-vah-loo-ah-the-on'], *f.* 1. *(Gen.)* Evaluation. 2. *(Escol.)* Report, assessment.

evaluar [ay-vah-loo-arl´], *va.* To evaluate.

evalúo [ay-vah-loo'-o], *m. (Com.)* Valuation, appraisement.

evangélicamente [ay-vah-he'-le-cah-men-tay], *adv.* Evangelically.

evangélico, ca [ay-van-hay'-le-co, cah], *a.* Evangelical.

evangelio [ay-van-hay'-le-o], *m.* 1. Gospel. 2. Small book, containing the first chapters of St. John and the other evangelists, placed between relics, and formerly worn by children around their necks.

evangelismo [ay-van-hay-lees'-mo], *m.* 1. Evangelism, the religious and humanitarian system of the Gospel. 2. Spirit of reform among Protestant sects who call themselves evangelical.

evangelista [ay-van-hay-lees'-tah], *m.* 1. Evangelist. 2. Gospeller, one who chants the gospels in churches.

evangelistero [ay-van-hay-lis-tay'-ro], *m.* 1. Gospeller, a priest or deacon who chants the books of the evangelists at solemn masses. 2. Gospel bookstand, on which the gospel book is laid to sing the gospel at high mass.

evangelizar [ay-van-hay-le-thar'], *va.* To evangelize, to preach the gospel.

evaporable [ay-vah-po-rah'-blay], *a.* Evaporable, that may be evaporated.

evaporación [ay-vah-po-rah-the-on'], *f.* 1. Evaporation, exhalation of vapor. 2. Act of damping cloth, or placing it over steam, to render the wool softer.

evaporado, da [ay-vah-po-rah'-do, dah], *a.* Evaporated. **Leche evaporada,** evaporated milk.

evaporar [ay-vah-po-rar'], *vn.* To evaporate, to fly off in vapors or fumes. *-va.* To evaporate, to drive away in fumes, to disperse in vapors: to flat, to flatten, to pall, to make vapid. *-vr.* 1. To vanish, to pass away. 2. To pall, to grow vapid.

evaporatorio [ay-vah-po-rah-toh'-re-o], *a.* Having the power of evaporating.

evaporizar [ay-vah-po-re-thar'], *vn. & va.* To evaporate.

evasión [ay-vah-se-on'], *f.* Evasion, escape, subterfuge. **Evasión de impuestos,** tax evasion.

evasiva [ay-vah-see'-vah], *f.* Subterfuge, evasion; loophole (escapatoria), way out.

evasivamente [ay-vah-se'-vah-men-tay], *adv.* Evasively.

evasivo, va [ay-vah-see'-vo, vah], *a.* Evasive, elusive, sophistical.

evata [ay-vah'-tah], *f.* Kind of black wood resembling ebony.

evección [ay-vec-the-on'], *f. (Ast.)* Evection, the largest inequality in the motion of the moon, as an effect of solar attraction.

evento [ay-vayn'-to], *m.* Event, accident, issue, unforeseen happening (incidente).

eventración [ay-ven-trah-the-on'], *f.* 1. Eventration, ventral hernia, or relaxation of the abdominal walls. 2. Disemboweling.

eventual [ay-ven-too-ahl'], *a.* 1. Eventual, fortuitous (casual); possible (posible). 2. Temporary (obrero, trabajo); stopgap (solución).

eventualidad [ay-ven-too-ah-le-dahd'], *f.* Contingency.

eventualmente [ay-ven-too-al-men'-tay], *adv.* 1. Fortuitously, by chance (accidentalmente). 2. Possibly (posiblemente), depending upon circumstances.

eversión [ay-ver-se-on'], *f.* Eversion, destruction, ruin, desolation.

evicción [ay-vic-the-on'], *f.* Eviction, security, convictiveness.

evidencia [ay-ve-den'-the-ah], *f.* Evidence (pruebas), manifestation, proof, obviousness, conspicuity, nakedness, cogency. **Evidencia por pruebas** or **causas comitantes,** circumstantial evidence.

evidenciar [ay-ve-den-the-ar'], *va.* To evidence, to prove, to render evident.

evidente [ay-ve-den'-tay], *a.* Evident, clear, manifest, open, naked, palpable, obvious, plain, glaring.

evidentemente [ay-ve-den'-tay-men-tay], *adv.* Evidently, plainly, clearly, manifestly, glaringly, notoriously.

evilasa [ay-ve-lah'-sah], *f.* Kind of ebony which grows in the island of Madagascar.

evisceración [ay-vis-thay-rah-the-on'], *f.* Evisceration, removal of the viscera in an autopsy, or embalming.

eviscerar [ay-vis-thay-rar'], *va.* To eviscerate, to remove the viscera.

evitable [ay-ve-tah'-blay], *a.* Avoidable, extricable, evitable.

evitación [ay-ve-tah-the-on'], *f.* Evitation, act of avoiding.

evitado, da [ay-ve-tah'-do, dah], *a. & pp.* of EVITAR. Avoided.

evitar [ay-ve-tar'], *va.* To avoid, to escape (peligro), to forbear, to help; to fly, to shun, to decline, to avoid (peligro). **Para evitar tales dificultades,** in order to avoid such difficulties. *-vr.* **Para evitarse trabajo,** in order to save onself trouble.

eviterno, na [ay-ve-terr'-no, nah], *a. (Theol.)* Imperishable, lasting, without end.

evo [ay'-vo], *m.* 1. *(Poet.)* Age, a long period of time. 2. *(Theol.)* Eternity, endless duration.

evocación [ay-vo-cah-the-on'], *f.* Evocation, pagan invocation.

evocar [ay-vo-car'], *va.* 1. To call out. 2. To invoke, to solicit a favor, to implore assistance.

evolución [ay-vo-loo-the-on'], *f.* 1. Evolution, changing the position of troops or ships. 2. Evolution, gradual development of things and of ideas, slow transformation. 3. *(Met.)* Change of political ideas.

evolucionar [ay-vo-loo-the-o-nar'], *m. (Mil. Naut.)* To perform evolutions or tactical movements.

evoluta [ay-vo-loo'-tah], *f.* 1. *(Math.)* Volute. 2. *(Naut.)* A snail-shell.

evolutivo, va [ay-vo-loo-tee'-vo, vah], *a.* Evolutive.

evulsión [ay-vool-se-on'], *f. (Med.)* Evulsion, plucking out, forcible extraction.

ex [ex], *prep.* Used in Spanish only in composition, where it either amplifies, the signification, as exponer, or serves as a negative, as *exámine. Exprovincial,* Former or late provincial.

ex abrupto [ex ah-broop'-to], *adv.* Abruptly, violently.

exacción [ek-sac-the-on'], *f.* 1. Exaction, the act of levying taxes. 2. Impost, tax, contribution, levy.

exacerbación [ek-sah-ther-bah-the-on'], *f. (Med.)* Exacerbation, paroxysm.

exacerbar [ek-sah-ther-bar'], *va.* To irritate, to exasperate, to exacerbate.

exactamente [ek-sac-tah-men'-tay], *adv.* Exactly, minutely, just, justly, accurately, faithfully, circumstantially, critically, nicely, to a hair.

exactitud [ek-sac-te-tood'], *f.* Exactness, exactitude, punctuality, accuracy, correctness, justness, niceness.

exacto, ta [ek-sahc'-to, tah], *a.* Exact, punctual (puntual), assiduous, nice, heedful, faithful, observant, critical, just, precise (preciso), right (correcto).

exactor [ek-sac-tor'], *m.* Tax-gatherer, exactor.

exactora [ek-sac-to'-rah], *f.* Exactress.

exageración [ek-sah-hay-rah-the-on'], *f.* Exaggeration, hyperbolical amplification.

exageradamente [ek-sah-hay-rah'-dah-men-tay], *adv.* In an exaggerated way; excessively, exorbitantly; over-demonstratively, theatrically.

exagerado [ek-sah-hay-rah'-do], *a.* 1. Exaggerated (pretensión). 2. Highly-colored (relato). 3. Excessive (precio). 4. Theatrical.

exagerador, ra [ek-sah-hay-rah-dor', rah], *m. & f.* Amplifier, one that exaggerates.

exagerante [ek-sah-hay-rahn'-tay], *pa. & m. (Poet.)* Amplifier; exaggerating.

exagerar [ek-sah-hay-rar'], *va.* To exaggerate, to amplify, to heighten by misrepresentation, to magnify, to hyperbolize, to overstate.

exagerativamente [ek-sah-hay-rah-te'-vah-men-tay], *adv.* With exaggeration.

exagerativo, va [ek-sah-hay-rah-tee'-vo, vah], *a.* Exaggerating, exaggeratory.

exágono, na [ek-sah'-go-no, nah], *a.* Hexagonal. *V.* HEXÁGONO.

exaltación [ek-sal-tah-the-on'], *f.* 1. Exaltation (ensalzamiento), elevation. 2. *(Chem.)* Sublimation.

exaltado, da [ek-sal-tah'-do, dah], *a.* 1. *(Neol.)* Exaggerated and violent in political ideas (fanático). 2. Exalted (elevado). 3. Over-excited (humor), worked up; elated; excitable (carácter).

exaltar [ek-sal-tar'], *va.* 1. To exalt, to elevate (elevar); to magnify; to lift, to heave. 2. To praise, to extol (elogiar); to cry up. *-vr.* To get excited (emocionar), to get worked up; to get carried away; to get heated (discusión), to become very intense.

examen [ek-sah'-men], *m.* 1. Examination, disquisition, exploration, consideration. 2. Trial, inquiry (encuesta). 3. Examination. **Examen de conductor,** driving test. **Examen de fin de curso,** final examination. 4. Care and diligence in searching out something.

exámetro [ek-sah'-may-tro], *m.* Hexameter verse.

examinación [ek-sah-me-nah-the-on'], *f.* Examination.

examinado, da [ek-sah-me-nah'-do], *m. & f.* Examinee, candidate.

examinador, ra [ek-sah-me-nah-dor', rah], *m. & f.* Examiner, explorator; examinator.

examinando [ek-sah-me-nahn-'do], *m.* Examinant, he who is to be examined.

examinante [ek-sah-me-nahn'-tay], *pa. & n.* 1. Examining.

examinar [ek-sah-me-nar'], *va.* I. To examine (poner a prueba), to investigate (inspeccionar). 2. To consider (problema), to explore, to look into (indagar), to look over, to fathom; to feel, to consult. 3. To inquire into books or writings. *-vr.* To take an examination.

esangüe [ek-sahn'-goo-ay], *a.* 1. Bloodless, without blood; pale from the loss of blood, exsanguious. 2. *(Met.)* Weak, without strength.

exángulo, la [ek-sahn'-goo-lo, lah], *a.* Having six angles.

exanimación [ek-sah-ne-ma-the-on'], *f.* Examination.

exánime [ek-sah'-ne-may], *a.* Spiritless, exanimous, weak, without force or vigor.

exantema [ek-san-tay-mah], *f.* Exanthema, an eruptive disease of the skin.

exantemático, ca, or **exantematoso, sa** [ek-san-tay-mah'-co, cah, ek-san-tay-mah-to'-so, sah], *a.* Exanthematous, or exanthematic.

exantropía [ex-san-tro-pee'-ah], *f. (Med.)* The last stage of melancholy.

exápodo, da [ek-sah'-po-do, dah], *a.* Hexapod, six-footed. *-m. pl.* Hexapods, the true insects, with six feet.

exarcado [ek-sar-cah'-do], *m.* Exarchate or vice royalty.

exarco [ek-sar'-co], *m.* 1. Exarch, viceroy. 2. A dignitary in the Greek church.

exasperación [ek-sas-pay-rah-the-on'], *f.* Exasperation.

exasperado, da [ek-sas-pay-rah'-do, dah], *a. & pp.* of EXASPERAR. Exasperate, exasperated.

exasperante *a.* [ek-sas-pay-rahn'-tay], Exasperating, infuriating.

exasperar [ek-sas-pay-rar'], *va.* To exasperate, to irritate, to offend, to acerbate. *-vr.* To get exasperated.

exastilo [ex-sas-tee'-lo], *m. (Arch.)* Hexastyle, a portico of six columns in front.

excandencencia [ex-can-day-then'-the-ah], *f.* 1. Candescence, incandescence. 2. Anger, passion.

excandecer [ex-can-day-therr'], *va.* To irritate, to provoke, to put into a passion. *-vr.* To be in a passion.

excarcelación [ex-car-thay-lah-the-on'], *f.* Release (cárcel).

excarcelado, da [ex-car-the-lah'-do], *m & f.* Ex-prisoner, former prisoner.

excarcelar [ex-car-thay-lar'], *va.* To remove a prisoner from the jail by command of the judge.

ex cáthedra *(Acad.)* A phrase from Latin to denote a tone of mastery and finality. To speak, or decide, **ex cáthedra**.

excava, excavación [ex-cah'-vah, es-cah-vaht-he-on'], *f.* Excavation.

excavador, ra [es-cah-vah-dor'-rah], *a.* Excavating.*-f.* Excavating machine.

excavar [ex-cah-var'], *va.* To escavate, to dig out, to hollow.

excavillo [ex-cah-veel'-lyo], *m. (Prov.)* A little spade used in making excavations.

excedencia [ex-the-den'-the-ah], *f.* Leave of absence. **Excedencia por maternidad**, maternity leave.

excedente [ex-thay-den'-tay], *pa. & a.* Excessive, exceeding.

exceder [ex-thay-derr'], *va.* To exceed (superar), to surpass (sobrepasar), to excel, to go beyond, to outrun, to outgo, to overtop. *-vr.* To exceed, to overgo. **Excederse a sí mismo**, to surpass one's own actions. **Excederse en sus funciones**, to exceed one's duty.

excelencia [ex-thay-len'-the-ah], *f.* 1. Excellence, eminence, height, exquisiteness, superior worth or merit. 2. Excellency, a title of honor applied in Spain to grandees, councillors of state, etc. **Por excelencia**, *(coll.)* par exellence.

excelente [ex-thay-len'-tay], *a.* Excellent, exquisite.

excelentemente [ex-the-len'tay-men-tay], *adv.* Exceptionally.

excelentísimo, ma [ex-the-len-tee'-se-mo, mah], *a. superl.* Most excellent: applied in courtesy to persons receiving the title of *Excellency.*

excelsamente [ex-thel-sah-men'-tay], *adv.* Sublimely.

excelsitud [ex-thel-se-tood'], *f.* Excelsitude, loftiness.

excelso, sa [ex-thel'-so, sah], *a.* Elevated, sublime, lofty.

excéntrica [es-then'-tre-cah], *f. (Mech.)* Cam.

excéntricamente [ex-then'-tre-cah-men-tay], *adv.* Eccentrically.

excentricidad [ex-then-tre-the-dahd'], *f.* Eccentricity; deviation from the center; excursion from the proper orb.

excéntrico, ca [ex-then'-tre'-co, cah], *a.* 1. Eccentric, eccentrical, having a different center. 2. Extravagant, odd, eccentric.

excepción [ex-thep-the-on'], *f.* 1. Exception, exclusion from things comprehended. 2. Exception, thing excepted or specified in exception. 3. *(Law.)* Demurrer, exception, a stop or stay to an action. **Excepción de la regla**, exception to the rule. **A excepción de**, with the exception of.

excepcional [ex-thep-the-o-nahl'], *a.* Exceptional, unusual, contrary to rule.

excepcionar [ex-thep-theo-nar'], *va. (Law.)* To except, to object, to demur.

excepto [ex-thep'-to], *adv.* Except that, besides that, excepting.

exceptuación [ex-thep-too-ah-the-on'], *V.* EXCEPCIÓN.

exceptuar [ex-thep-too-ar'], *va.* To except, to exempt, to exclude, to leave out.

excerta [ex-therr'-tah], *f.* Excerpt, extract, citation.

excesivamente [ex-the-see'-vah-men-tay], *adv.* Excessively, excessive.

excesivo, va [ex-thay-see'-vo, vah], *a.* Excessive, inmoderate, exorbitant, overgreat, extreme, unreasonable (indebido).

exceso [ex-thay'-so], *m.* 1. Excess, overmuch; superfluity (de comida), excessiveness, exuberance. 2. Excess, intemperance in eating or drinking. 3. Excess, irregularity, transgression of due limits. 4. Great wickedness, enormity of crime. 5. Excess, violence of passion. **En exceso**, excessively. **Exceso de equipaje**, excess luggage. **Exceso de peso**, excess weight. **Cuidadoso en exceso**, excessively careful. **Llevar algo al exceso**, to carry something to excess.

excipiente [ex-the-pe-en'-tay], *m. (Med.)* Excipient, a substance serving to incorporate, or to dissolve others in a medicine; a vehicle.

excisión [ex-the-se-on'], *f.* 1. Uprising, mutiny. 2. Altercation, quarrel.

excitabilidad [ex-the-tah-be-le-dahd'], *f.* Excitability.

excitable [ex-the-tah'-blay], *a.* Excitable.

excitación [ex-the-tah-the-on'], *f.* Excitation, exciting, the act of exciting; excitement (estado).

excitante [ex-the-tahn'-tay], *a.* Exciting (emocionante), stimulating. *-m.* Stimulant, excitant.

excitar [ex-the-tar'], *va.* To excite, to move, to stimulate. 2. To excite (emoción), to stir up, to rouse, to animate, to fire, to flame. 3. To incite, to urge on (incitar). **Excitar al pueblo a la rebelión**, to incite the populace to rebellion.

excitativo, va [ex-the-tah-tee'-vo, vah], *a.* Exciting, stimulative, excitative.

esclamación [ex-clah-ma-the-on'], *f.* 1. Exclamation, vehement outcry, clamour. 2. Exclamation, an emphatical utterance.

exclamar [ex-clah-mar'], *vn.* To exclaim, to cry out, to clamor. *-vr.* To complain, to protest.

exclamativo, va [ex-clah-mah-tee'-vo, vah], *a.* Exclaiming.

exclamatorio, ria [ex-clah-mah-to'-re-o, ah], *a.* Exclamatory.

exclaustrado [ex-clah-oos-trah'-do, da], *m.* The cleric who has ceased to live in a cloister, chiefly by supression of his order; a secularized monk.

excluir [ex-cloo-eer'], *va.* 1. To exclude, to shut out, to expel, to foreclose, to cut out. 2. To exclude (posibilidad), to debar, to hinder from participation.

exclusión [ex-cloo-se-on'], *f.* 1. Exclusion, shutting out or denying admission, rejection, ejection. 2. Exclusion, exception.

exclusiva [ex-cloo-se'-vah], *f.* 1. Refusal of place or employment; rejection of an application to become member of a community (negativa); exclusion. 2. A special privilege. *(Acad.).* 3. *(Com.)* Sole right, sole agency. **Tener la exclusiva de un producto**, to have the sole right to sell a product. 4. **Trabajar en exclusiva para**, to work exclusively for.

exclusivamente, exclusive [ex-cloo-se-vah-men'-tay], *adv.* Exclusively.

exclusivo, va [ex-cloo-see'-vo, vah], *a.* Exclusive.

excluso [ex-cloo'-so], *pp. irr.* From EXCLUIR.

excogitable [ex-co-he-tah'-blay], *a.* Imaginable, possible to be conceived.

excogitar [ex-co-hetar'], *va.* To excogitate, to meditate; to strike out by thinking.

excombatiente [ex-com-bah-tee-ayn'-tay], *m.* Ex-service man, veteran.

excomulgación, excomunicación [ex-co-mool-gah-the-on', ex-co-moo-ne-cah-the-on'], *f. V.* EXCOMUNICACIÓN.

excomulgado, da [ex-co-mool-gah'-do, dah], *a. & pp.* of EXCOMULGAR. Excommunicate, excommunicated, accursed.

excomulgador [ex-co-mool-gah-dor'], *m.* Excommunicator.

excomulgar [ex-co-mool-gar'], *va.* 1. To excommunicate, to eject from the communion of the church, and the use of the sacraments. 2. To fulminate ecclesiastical censure. 3. *(Met.)* To treat with foul language, to use ill, to accurse (maldecir).

excomunión [ex-co-moo-ne-on'], *f.* Excommunication, exclusion from the fellowship of the church.

excoriación [ex-co-re-ah-the-on'], *f.* Excoriation, privation of skin, the act of flaying.

excoriar [ex-co-re-ar'], *va. (Med.)* To excoriate, to flay: it is almost always used in its reciprocal sense.

excrecencia [ex-cray-then'-the-ah], *f.* Excrescence or excrescency.

excreción [ex-cray-the-on'], *f.* Excretion.

excrementar [ex-cray-men-tar'], *va.* To excrementize, to purge, to void by stool.

excrementicio, cia [ex-cray-men-tee'-the-o, ah], *a.* Excrementitious, excremental.

excremento [ex-cray-men'-to], *m.* 1. Excrement, flux. 2. Particles separated from plants by putrefaction.

excrementoso, sa [ex-cray-men-to'-so, sah], *a.* Excremental, excrementitious.

excretar [ex-cray-tar'], *vn.* To excrete; to eject the excrements.

excreto, ta [ex-cray'-to, tah], *a.* That which is ejected.

excretor, ra, or **excretorio, ria** [ex-cray-to're-o, ah], *a.* Excretory, excretive, having the quality of ejecting superfluous parts.

excursión [ex-coor-se-on'], *f.* 1. Excursion, expedition into the enemy's country. 2. *(Law.)* Liquidation of the estate of a debtor for paying off his debts. 3. Excursion, outing, trip. **Excursión de caza,** hunting trip. **Ir de excursión,** to go on a trip.

excursionista [ex-coor-se-o nees'-tah] *m. & f.* Excursionist, traveler.

excusa [ex-coo'-sah], *f.* 1. Excuse, apology or plea offered in extenuation. 2. Excuse, the act of excusing or apologizing. 3. Excuse, cause for which one is excused. 4. Allowance, excusableness, color, cloak, loop-hole. **Excusas,** exemptions, immunities or emoluments granted to certain persons. **Buscar excusa,** to look for an excuse. **Presentar sus excusas,** to make one's excuses.

excusabaraja [ex-coo-sah-ba-rah'-hah], *f.* Basket or pannier with a cover of osiers.

excusable [ex-coo-sah'-blay], *a.* Excusable, pardonable.

excursación [ex-coo-sah-the-on'], *f. V.* EXCUSA.

excusadamente [ex-coo-sah-dah'-men-tay], *adv.* Uselessly, voluntarily, without necessity; not to the purpose.

excusado [ex-coo-sah'-do], *a.* 1. Exempted, privileged. 2. Superfluous, useless (inútil). 3. Preserved, laid up as useless.-*pp.* of EXCUSAR.

excusado [ex-coo-sah-do], *m.* Toilet.

excusador, ra [ex-coo-sah-dor', rah], *m. & f.* 1. One who performs another's functions in his stead. 2. Vicar or curate of a parish church. 3. *(Law.)* Excuser, one who excuses the non-appearance of a defendant in court.

excusalí [ex-coo-sah-lee'], *m.* Small apron.

excusar [ex-coo-sar'], *va.* 1. To excuse (disculpar), to extenuate by apology, to exculpate, to color, to palliate. 2. To exempt from taxes. 3. To obstruct, to hinder, to prevent. **Excusamos decirle que...,** we don't have to tell you that... 4. To shun, to avoid. -*vr.* To decline or reject a request, to

apologize. **Escusarse de haber hecho algo,** to apologize for having done something.

excusión [ex-coo-se-on'], *f. (Law.)* 1. Liquidation of the estate of a debtor for paying his debts. 2. *(Med.)* Concussion, a violent shaking.

ex diámetro [ex de-ah'-may-tro], *adv.* Diametrically.

execrable [ek-say-crah'-blay], *a.* Execrable, detestable, hateful, accursed.

execrablemente [ek-say-crah'-blay-men-tay], *adv.* Execrably.

execración [ek-say-crah-the-on'], *f.* Execration, detestation, cursing, abhorrence.

execrador, ra [ek-say-crah-dor', rah], *m. & f.* Execrater.

execrar [ek-say-crar'], *va.* To execrate, to detest, to curse, to imprecate ill upon. -*vr.* To mutually hate one another.

execratorio [ek-say-crah-to'-re-o], *a.* **Juramento execratorio,** execratory.

exégesis [ek-say'-hay-sis], *f.* Exegesis, explanation in general, and in particular of the Bible.

exegético, ca [ek-say-hay'-te-co, cah], *a.* Exegetical, explanatory.

exención [ek-sen-the-on'], *f.* 1. Exemption, immunity, privilege, freedom from imposts. 2. Franchise, exemption from any onerous duty.

exentado, da [ek-sen-tah'-do, dah], *a. & pp.* of EXENTAR. Exempt, exempted.

exentamente [ek-sen-tah-men'-tay], *adv.* 1. Freely. 2. Clearly, simply, sincerely.

exentar [ek-sen-tar'], *va.* 1. To exempt, to grant immunity from, to privilege, to franchise. 2. To absolve, to acquit, to excuse, to disengage from an obligation. -*vr.* To except oneself.

exento, ta [ek-sen'-to, tah], *a.* 1. Exempt (libre), free, freed, disengaged. 2. Exemptible, exempt, free, privileged. **Exento de derechos,** duty-free. 3. Clear, open, isolated, free from impediment. **Estar exento de cuidados,** to be free of worries. -*pp. irr.* of EXIMIR.

exequátur [ek-say-koo-ah' toor] *m.* Exequatur.

exequias [ek-say'-ke-as], *f. pl.* Exequies, funeral rites.

exequible [ek-say-kee'-blay], *a.* Attainable.

exerción [ek-ser-the-on'], *f. (Neol. Med.)* Irritation, animation, activity, or contraction of fibrous tissues.

exergo [ek-serr'-go], *m.* Exergue, the space left on the face sides of medals for the inscription.

exfoliación [ex-fo-le-ah-the-on'], *f. (Med.)* Desquamation, scaling.

exfoliar [ex-fo-le-ar'], *va. (Med.)* To exfoliate. -*vr.* To become exfoliated.

exfoliativo, va [ex-fo-le-ah-tee'-vo, vah], *a. (Surg.)* Exfoliative, producing exfoliation.

exhalación [ex-ah-lah-the-on'], *f.* 1 Exhalation, the act of exhaling. 2. Exhalation, that which rises in vapors. 3. An electrical or other fire accustomed to be seen in the atmosphere; a shooting star.

exhalador, ra [ex-ah-lah-dor', rah], *m. & f.* Exhaler, one who exhales.

exhalar [ex-ah-lar'], *va.* To exhale, to send or draw out vapors or fumes. -*vr.* 1. To exhale, to evaporate. 2. To be consumed or wasted gradually. 3. To be consumed or wasted by violent exercise of the body.

exhalatorio, ria [ex-ah-lah to' ro o, ah], *a.* Exhalant. -*m.* An apparatus for evaporating fresh water in salt-works.

exhaución [ex-ah-oo-the-on'], *f.* Exhaustion, a method of establishing the equality of two numbers by proving that they differ by less than any assignable quantity.

exhaustivo [ex-ah-oos-te'-vo], *a.* Exhaustive; comprehensive.

exhausto, ta [ex-ah'-oos-to, tah], *a.* Exhausted, totally drained or drawn out.

exheredación [ex-ay-ray-dah-the-on'], *f.* Disinheritance, privation of an inheritance.

exheredar [ex-ay-ray-dar'], *va.* To disinherit.

exhibición [ex-e-be-the-on'], *f*. Exhibition, the act of exhibiting, display, show (cine). **Exhibición folklórica,** folk festival. **Una impresionante exhibición de fuerza,** an impressive show of strength.

exhibicionismo [ex-e-be-the-o-nees'-mo], *m*. 1. Exhibitionism. 2. Indecent exposure (sexual).

exhibicionista [ex-e-be-the-o-nees'-tah], *a*. Exhibitionist. *-m & f*. Exhibitionist.

exhibir [ex-e-beer'], *va*. To exhibit, to prevent, to make manifest, to lay, to show, to show (pasaporte), to show off (mostrar con orgullo). *-vr*. 1. To show oneself. 2. To expose oneself (sexualmente).

exhortación [ex-or-tah-the-on'], *f*. 1. Exhortation, admonition. 2. A short and familiar sermon.

exhortador, ra [ex-or-tah-dor', rah], *m. & f*. Exhorter, monitor.

exhortar [ex-or-tar'], *va*. To exhort, to excite by words to a good action.

exhortatorio, ria [ex-or-tah-to'-re-o, ah], *a*. Exhortatory, hortative.

exhorto [ex-or'-to], *m*. Letters requisitorial sent by one judge to another.

exhumación [ex-oo-mah-the-on'], *f*. Exhumation, disinterment.

exhumar [es-oo-mar'], *va*. To disinter, to unbury, to exhume.

exigencia [ek-se-hen'-the-ah], *f*. Exigence, want, pressing necessity, exaction, demand (requerimiento). **Según las exigencias de la situación,** as the situation requires.

exigente [ek-se-hen'-tay], *a*. Demanding, exacting, exigent. **Ser exigente con uno,** to be hard on somebody. **Es muy exigente en la limpieza,** she is very particular about cleanliness.

exigible [ek-se-hee'-blay], *a*. Capable of being demanded or required.

exigir [ek-se-heer'], *va*. 1. To exact (contribución), to demand (requirir), to require. **Exigir el pago,** to demand payment. **Esto exige mucho cuidado,** this needs a lot of care. 2. To wish for, to desire, to beg of.

exigüidad [ek-se-goo-e-dahd'], *f*. Exiguity, smallness.

exiguo, ua [ek-see'-goo-o, a], *a*. Exiguous, small.

exiliado [ek-se-le-ah'-do], *a. m & f*. Exile, in exile.

exiliar [ek-se-le-ahr'], *va*. To exile.

exilio [ek-se'-le-o], *m*. Exile. **Estar en el exilio,** to be in exile.

eximio, mia [ek-see'-me-o, ah], *a*. Eximious, famous, eminent.

eximir [ek-se-meer'], *va*. 1. To exempt, to free from an obligation, to clear from a charge. **Esto me exime de toda obligación con él,** this frees me from any obligation with him. 2. To exempt, to privilege, to excuse, to except. *-vr*. **Eximirse de,** to excuse oneself from.

exinanición [ek-se-nah-ne-the-on'], *f*. Inanition, want of vigor and strength, debility.

exinanido, da [ek-se-nah-nee'-do, dah], *a*. Debilitated, very weak, very feeble.

existencia [ek-sis-ten'-the-ah], *f*. Existence (vida), existency, state of being; actual possession of being. **Existencias,** stock in hand, articles or goods remaining unsold. **Amargar la existencia a uno,** to make somebody's life a misery.

existencialismo [ek-sis-ten-the-ah-lees'-mo], *m*. Existentialism.

existente [ek-sis-ten'-tay], *pa. & a*. Existing, extant (texto), existent, on hand. **La situación existente,** the existing situation.

existimación [ek-sis-te-ma-the-on'], *f*. Estimation, opinion, esteem.

existimar [ek-sis-tee-mar'], *va*. To hold, to form an opinion, to judge.

existir [ek-sis-teer'], *vn*. To exist, to be, to have a being. **Dejar de existir,** to pass out of existence.

éxito [ek'-se-to], *m*. 1. Result (resultado), outcome. **Buen éxito,** happy outcome. 2. Success (logro), good fortune.

Con éxito, successfully. **Tener éxito en,** to be successful in. 3. *(Mus. Teat. fig.)* Success, hit. **Éxito editorial,** bestseller.

exitoso, sa [ek-se-to'-so, sah], *a*. Successful.

éxodo [ek'-so-do], *m*. Exodus, the second of Moses. **El éxodo rural,** the depopulation of the countryside.

exoftalmía [ex-of-tahl-me'-ah], *f*. Exophthalmia, or exophthalmus, abnormal protrusion of the eyeball from the orbit.

exoneración [ek-so-nay-rah-the-on'], *f*. Exoneration, the act of disburdening.

exonerar [ek-so-nay-rar'], *va*. To exonerate (de culpa), to unload; to disburden, to lighten, to exempt (de un impuesto). **Exonerar a uno de un deber,** to free somebody from a duty.

exopilativo, va [ek-so-pe-lah-tee'-vo, vah], *a*. Deobstruent.

exorable [ek-so-rah'-blay], *a*. Exorable, to be moved by entreaty.

exorbitancia [ek-sor-be-tahn'-the-ah], *f*. Exorbitance.

exorbitante [ek-sor-be-tahn'-tay], *a*. Exorbitant, enormous, excessive, extravagant.

exorbitantemente [ek-sor-be-tahn'-tay-men-tay], *adv*. Exorbitantly, extravagantly.

exorcismo [ek-sor-thees'-mo], *m*. Exorcism.

exorcista [ek-sor-thees'-tah], *m*. Exorciser, exorcist.

exorcizante [ek-sor-the-thahn'-tay], *pa. & com*. Exorcising; exorciser.

exorcizar [ek-sor-the-thar'], *va*. To exorcise, to adjure by some holy name, to drive away by adjurations.

exordio [ek-sor'-de-o], *m*. Exordium, the proemial part of a composition; origin, beginning.

exornación [ek-sor-nah-the-on'], *f. (Rhet.)* Exornation, ornaments in waiting or speaking.

exornar [ek-sor-nar'], *va*. To adorn or embellish a discourse with rhetorical figures.

exortación [ek-sor-tah-the-on'], *f*. Exhortation, familiar admonition to piety; monition.

exostosis [ek-sos-to'-sis], *f*. 1. Exostosis, a disease of the bones. 2. *(Bot.)* Excrescence on the trunk of trees of very hard wood, whose fibres cross in all directions.

exotérico, ca [ek-so-tay'-re-co, cah], *a*. Exoteric, public, common.

exótico, ca [ek-so'-te-co, cah], *a*. 1. Exotic, foreign, extraneous. 2. Extravagant, odd.

expandir [ex-pan-deer'], *va*. 1. To expand; to spread out (ropa); *(comm.)* to expand, to enlarge; *(Fig.)* to expand, to extend; to spread (noticia). **Expandir el mercado de un producto,** to expand the market for a product. *-vr*. To expand; to extend, to spread.

expansibilidad [ex-pan-se-be-le-dahd'], *f*. Expansibility.

expansión [ex-pan-se-on'], *f*. 1. Expansion, extension, spreading. **La expansión económica,** economic growth. 2. *(Fig.)* To relax (relajarse). 3. *(Fig.)* Expansiveness (efusión).

expansionar [ex-pan-see-o-nar'], *va*. To expand (mercado). *-vr*. 1. To expand. 2. *(Fig.)* To relax (relajarse). 3. *(Fig.)* To unbosom oneself (desahogarse).

expansivo, va [ox-pan-see'-vo, vah], *a*. 1. Expansive, capable of extension. 2. Affable, communicative.

expanso [ex-pahn'-so], *m*. 1. Expanse, a body widely expanded. 2. Space between the superior sphere of the air and the empyrean or highest heaven.

expatriación [ex-pah-tre-ah-the-on'], *f*. Expatriation.

expatriado, da [ex-pah-tre-ah-do], *m & f*. Expatriate; exile.

expatriar [ex-pah-tre-ar'], *va*. To expatriate, to go into exile. *-vr*. To be exiled.

expectable [ex-pec-tah'-blay], *a*. Conspicuous, eminent, illustrious.

expectación [ex-pec-tah-the-on'], *f*. Expectation (esperanza), expectance, expectancy, anxious desire, hope, looking. **Joven de expectación,** a hopeful youth. **Hombre de expectación,** a celebrated man.

expectativa [ex-pec-tah-tee'-vah], *f*. 1. Right or claim respecting some future thing. 2. Hope of obtaining a reward, employment, or other thing. 3. Expectation, expectance. **Estar a la expectativa,** to wait and see.

expectoración [ex-pec-to-rah-the-on'], *f.* Expectoration, the act and effect of expectorating; sputum.

expectorante [ex-pec-to-rahn'-tay], *pa.* Expectorting. -*a.* & *n.* (*Med.*) Expectorant, a medicine which provokes expectoration.

expectorar [ex-pec-to-rar'], *va.* To expectorate, to spit out.

expedición [ex-pay-de-the-on'], *f.* 1. Readiness, facility, or freedom in saying, or doing. 2. Expedition, haste, speed (prontitud), activity, nimbleness. 3. Brevet or bull despatched by the See of Rome. 4. Expedition, a warlike enterprise. **Expedición militar,** military expedition. 5. Excursion, jaunt, journey.

expedicionero [ex-pay-de-the-o-nay'-ro], *m.* He who superintends expeditions or despatches.

expedido [ex-pay-dee'-do], *a.* & *pp.* of EXPEDIR. Expedite, quick, prompt, nimble.

expedidor [ex-pay-de-dor'], *m.* (*Com.*) Agent, shipper.

expediente [ex-pay-de-en'-tay], *m.* 1. The collection of all the papers belonging to a business matter (dossier, ficha). 2. Despatch, course of business. 3. Expedient, measure, means to an end contrived in an exigency or difficulty. 4. Facility or dexterity in the management of affairs. 5. Dismissal (despido).

expedienteo [ex-pay-de-en-tay'-o], *m.* (*coll.*) Red tape.

expedir [ex-pay-deer'], *va.* 1. To expedite, to facilitate, to free from impediment. 2. To despatch (negocio), to issue from a public office (orden, pasaporte), to forward, to transit (mercancías).

expeditamente [ex-pay-de'-tah-men-tay], *adv.* Expeditiously, expeditely, easily.

expeditivo, va [cx-pay-de-tee'-vo, vah], *a.* Expeditive, performing with speed, expeditious, speedy, quick; apt in expedients.

expedito, ta [ex-pay-dee'-to, tah], *a.* Prompt, expeditious, speedy, quick (pronto).

expeler [ex-pay-lerr'], *va.* To expel, to eject, to throw with violence.

expeliente [ex-pay-leen'-tay], *pa.* & *m.* & *f.* Expelling, expulser.

expendedor, ra [ex-pen-day-dor', rah], *m.* & *f.* 1. Spendthrift, lavisher. 2. One who sells publicly and disposes of some merchandise. 3. One who passes counterfeit money, knowing it to be so. 4. Agent, commission merchant; one who sells goods for another (agente). **Expendedor de billetes,** ticket clerk.

expendeduría [ex-pen-day-doo-ree'-ah], *f.* A shop in which tobacco and other wares are retailed.

expender [ex-pen-derr'], *va.* 1. To expend, to spend, to lay out (dinero). 2. (*For.*) To pass counterfeit money or stolen goods in trade.

expendio [ex-pen'-de-o], *m.* Expense, outlay, consumption. (*Acad.*)

expensas [ex-pen'-sas], *f. pl.* Expenses, charges, costs. **Estar a expensas de otro,** to live by favor, at the cost of another, or to depend upon him.

experiencia [ex-pay-reen'-the-ah], *f.* 1. Experience, knowledge gained by practice. 2. Experience, experiment (experimento), practice, trial. **Una triste experiencia,** a sad experience. **Aprender por la experiencia,** to learn by experience.

experimentado, da [ex-pay-re-men-tah'-do, dah], *a.* & *pp.* of EXPERIMENTAR. Experienced, conversant.

experimentador, ra [ex-pay-re-men-tah-dor', rah], *m.* & *f.* Experimenter, experimentalist.

experimental [ex-pay-re-men-tahl'], *a.* Experimental; attained by experience.

experimentalmente [ex-pay-re-men-tahl'-men-tay], *adv.* Experimentally.

experimentar [ex-pay-re-men-tar'], *va.* 1. To experience, to learn or know by practice. 2. To experiment, to search out by

trial. **Están experimentando un nuevo helicóptero,** they are testing a new helicopter. 3. To experience, to undergo, to go through (sufrir cambio); to suffer (pérdida); to feel (emoción). **No experimenté ninguna sensación nueva,** I felt no new sensation.

experimento [ex-pay-re-men-to], *m.* Experiment, trial of something. **Hacer experimentos,** to experiment.

expertamente [ex-perr'-tah-men-tay], *adv.* Expertly, cunningly.

experto, ta [ex-perr'-to, tah], *a.* Expert, able, experienced, conversant, clever, cunning.

expiación [ex-pe-ah-the-on'], *f.* 1. Expiation, the act of atoning for any crime. 2. Atonement, purification. 3. Reparation, compensation for damage.

expiar [ex-pe-ar'], *va.* 1. To expiate, to pay for a crime. 2. To purify, to free from profanation.

expiativo, va [ex-pe-ah-tee'-vo, vah], *a.* That which serves for expiation, expiatory.

expiatorio, ria [ex-pe-ah-to'-re-o, ah], *a.* Expiatory.

explanación [ex-plah-nah-the-on'], *f.* Explanation, elucidation, exposition.

explanada [ex-plah-nah'-dah], *f.* (*Mil.*) 1. A slope. 2. Esplanade (paseo), glacis, raised area (plataforma); levelled area (zona nivelada).

explanar [ex-plah-nar'], *va.* 1. To level. V. ALLANAR. 2. (*Met.*) To explain, to elucidate, to clear up.

explayamiento [ex-plah-yah-me-en'-to], *m.* The act of dilating or dwelling upon a subject.

explayar [ex-plah-yar'], *va.* To extend, to dilate, to enlarge. -*vr.* 1. To enlarge or dwell upon a subject (discurso). 2. To amuse oneself, by taking a walk or any other amusement (relajarse). 3. To be extended or enlarged (extender).

expletivo, va [ex-play-tee'-vo, vah], *a.* Expletivo.

explicable [ex-ple-cah'-blay], *a.* Explicable, explainable. **Cosas no fácilmente explicables,** things not easily explained.

explicación [ex-ple-cah-the-on'], *f.* Explanation, explication, elucidation, exposition, interpretation, comment. **Sin dar explicaciones,** without giving any reason.

explicadamente [ex-ple-cah-dah-men'-tay], *adv.* Explicitly.

explicaderas [ex-ple-cah-day'-ras], *f. pl.* (*coll.*) Manner in which something is explained; facility of explaining. (Irónico.)

explicador, ra [ex-ple-cah-dor', rah], *m.* & *f.* 1. One who explains. 2. Commentator, glossarist, glossator.

explicar [ex-ple-car'], *va.* To explain, to clear up, to expound (teoría), to comment, to construe. -*vr.* 1. To explain or speak one's mind with propriety and freedom. **Explicar el porqué de una cosa,** to account. 2. To be explained (ser explicable). **Esto no se explica fácilmente,** this cannot be explained easily.

explicativo, va [ex-ple-cah-tee'-vo, vah], *a.* Explicative, explicatory, exegetical.

explícitamente [ex-ple'-the-tah-men-tay], *adv.* Explicitly, manifestly.

explícito, ta [ex-plee'-the-to, tah], *f.* Explicit, clear, distinct, manifest.

exploración [ex-plo-rah-the-on'], *f.* Exploration; scanning (radar); Skin diving (deporte).

explorador, ra [ex-plo-rah-dor', rah], *f.* 1. Explorator, explorer. 2. (*Med.*) Probe; scanner (radar)

explorar [ex-plo-rar'], *va.* To explore, to search into, to examine by trial.

exploratorio [ex-plo-rah-to'-re-o], *m.* Probe, catheter.

explosión [ex-plo-se-on'], *f.* 1. Explosion, outburst. **Explosión demográfica,** population explosion. 2. (*Fig.*) Explosion, blast. **Hacer explosión,** to explode.

explosivo, va [ex-plo-see-vo, vah], *a.* Explosive, capable of producing an explosion.

explotable [ex-plo-tah-blay], *a.* Workable, exploitable.

explotación [ex-plo-tah-the-on'], *f.* 1. Exploiting, exploitation, improvement of mines, or of lands. 2. Exploitation, unfair utilization (de algo, de alguien).

explotar

explotar [ex-plo-tar'], *va.* 1. To work or develop mines (veta). 2. To till lands. 3. *(Met.)* To exploit, to get all the benefit possible out of a thing (recursos etc). 3. To exploit (obreros); to exploit (situación). *-vn. (Mil. etc.)* To explode; to go off. **Explotaron 2 bombas**, 2 bombs exploded.

expoliación [ex-po-le-ah-the-on'], *f.* Despoiling, spoliation.

expolio [ex-po'-lee-o], *m.* 1. Pillaging, sacking. 2. **Armar un expolio**, to cause a hullaballoo.

exponencial [ex-po-nen-the-ahl'], *a. (Alg.)* Exponential.

exponente [ex-po-nen'-tay], *pa. & m. & f.* Expositor. 2. *(Arith.)* Exponent. 3. *(Com.)* Exhibitor; manufacturer, inventor or artist who exhibits a product in public exhibitions.

exponer [ex-po-nerr'], *va.* 1. To expose, to lay before the public. to show, to exhibit (cuadro) 2. To expound, to explain (argumento). 3. To expose, to, lay open, to make bare. 4. To expose, to put in danger, to hazard, to expose, to chance. 5. To expose a young child, or to cast him out to chance.-*vr.* To hazard, to adventure, to try the chance.

exportación [ex-por-tah-the-on'], *f.* 1. Exportation, sending commodities to other countries. 2. Export (artículo); exported article; exports (mercancías). **Géneros de exportación**, exports.

exportar [ex-por-tar'], *va.* To export, to carry out of a country.

exposición [ex-po-se-the-on'], *f.* 1. Exposition, explanation, interpretation (de hechos) 2. Making manifest. 3. Solicitude lifted into petition or allegation. 4. Exposition, a public display of industrial products, agricultural, artistic (arte). **Exposición de modas**, fashion show. 5. Peril, risk.

expositivo, va [ex-po-se-tee'-vo, vah], *a.* Explanatory, expositive.

expósito, ta [ex-po'-se-to, tah], *a.* Exposed (niños abandonados).

expositor, ra [ex-po-se-tor'], *m & f.* Expounder, interpreter, explainer, explicator, exhibitor (arte); exponent (de teoría).

expremijo [ex-pray-mee'-ho], *m.* Cheesevat, a wooden case in which cheeses are formed and pressed.

exprés [ex-press'], *m.* Black coffee.

expresado, da [ex-pray-sah'-do, dah], *a.* Before mentioned, cited, aforesaid. **Según las cifras expresadas**, according to these figures.

expresamente [ex-pray-sah-men'-tay], *adv.* Expressly, in direct terms, plainly.

expresar [ex-pray-sar'], *va.* 1. To express, to declare one's sentiments clearly and distinctly, to word (redactar); to state (declarar); to quote (citar). **Expresa las opiniones de todos**, he is voicing the opinions of us all. 2. To delineate, to sketch, to design. *-vr.* 1. To express oneself (persona). 2. To be stated (cifra, dato). **Como se expresa abajo**, as is stated below.

expresión [ex-pray-se-on'], *f.* 1. Expression, declaration of one's sentiments and opinions. **Esta expresión de nuestro agradecimiento**, this expression of our gratitude. 2. Expression, the form of language in which thoughts are uttered. 3. Expression phrase, a mode of speech. 4. Expression, the act of squeezing out the juice from succulent fruits. 5. Present, gift. 6. Expression, the act of representing something.

expresivamente [ex-pray-see'-vah-men'-tay], *adv.* 1. Expressively. 2. Tenderly, affectionately (cariñosamente).

expresividad [ex-pray-see-ve-dahd], *f.* Expressiveness.

expresivo, va [ex-pray-see'-vo, vah], *a.* 1. Expressive (personas, cosas). 2. Affectionate, kind, gracious (afectuoso).

expreso, sa [ex-pray'-so, sah], *a. & pp. irr.* of EXPRESAR. Expressed: express (explícito), clear, manifest, not dubious (exacto).

expreso [ex-pray'-so], *m.* 1. Express, extraordinary messenger, a courier (persona). 2. *(Naut.)* Packet-boat, advice-boat. 3. A rapid train for passengers and mails.

exprimidera [ex-pre-me-day'-rah], *f.* A small press used by apothecaries to squeeze out the juice of herbs.

exprimidero [ex-pre-me-day'-ro], *m.* A press or any other thing, by which, something is crushed or squeezed.

exprimido, da [ex-pre-mee'-do, dah], *a. & pp.* of EXPRIMIR Squeezed: dry, extenuated.

exprimidor [ex-pre-me-dor], *m.* Wringer, presser, squeezer. **Exprimidor de limones**, lemon squeezer.

exprimir [ex-pre-meer'], *va.* 1. To squeeze or press out (fruta). 2. To express, to declare clearly and distinctly.

ex profeso [ex-pro-fay'-so], *adv. (Lat.)* Avowedly, designedly, on purpose.

expropiación [ex-pro-pe-ah-the-on'], *f.* Expropriation, dispossession from ownership for public use.

expropiar [ex-pro-pe-ar'], *va.* To expropriate, to take property from a private owner for public use.

exprovincial [ex-pro-vin-the-ahl'], *m.* Exprovincial, a late provincial.

expuesto, ta [ex-poo-es'-to, tah], *a. & pp. irr.* of EXPONER. **Exponer; según lo arriba expuesto**, according to what has been stated above. Exposed, liable, obnoxious.

expugnable [ex-poog-nah'-blay], *a.* Expugnable.

expugnación [ex-poog-nah-the-on'], *f.* Expugnation.

expugnador [ex-poog-nah-dor'], *m.* Expugner, he who takes by assault.

expugnar [ex-poog-nar'], *va.* To expugn, to conquer, to reduce a place by force of arms.

expulsar [ex-pool-sar'], *va.* To expel, to eject, to drive out, to force away, to send off (jugador).

expulsión [ex-pool-se-on'], *f.* Expulsion, the act of driving out.

expulsivo, va [ex-pool-see'-vo, vah], *a.* Expulsive.

expulso, va [ex-pool-so, sah], *a. & pp. irr.* of EXPELER and EXPULSAR. *(Acad.)* Ejected, driven out, expelled: outcast.

expurgación [ex-poor-gah-the-on'], *f.* Expurgation, purification from bad mixture or error.

expurgar [ex-poor-gar'], *va.* 1. To expurgate, to expunge, to purge away, to cleanse, to purify. 2. *(Lit.)* To correct, to emend, to remove errors.

expurgativo, va [ex-poor-gah-tee'-vo, vah], *a.* Expurgatory, expurgatorious.

expurgatorio [ex-poor-gah-to'-re-o], *m.* Index of the books prohibited by the Inquisition.

expurgo [ex-poor'-go], *m. (Prov.)* Expurgation, purification from bad mixture.

exquisitamente [ex-ke-see'-tah-men-tay], *adv.* Exquisitely; deliciously, delightfully; excellently.

exquisitez [ex-ke-see-tayth'], *f.* 1. Exquisiteness; excellence. 2. Affection.

exquisito, ta [ex-ke-see'-to, tah], *a.* Exquisite, consummate, excellent, delicious (excelente).

éxtasis [ex'-tah-sis], *m.* 1. Ecstasy, enthusiasm. 2. *(Med.)* Catalepsy, or hypnotic sleep, with the eyes open (de médium).

extático, ca [ex-tah'-te-co, cah], *a.* 1. Ecstatic, absorbed. 2. *(Med.)* Cataleptic.

extemporáneamente [ex-tem-po-rah'-nay-ah-men-tay], *adv.* Extemporaneously, extempore, without premeditation.

extemporáneo, nea [es-tem-po-rah'-nay-o, ah], *a.* Extemporaneous, unpremeditated, out of time.

extender [ex-ten-derr'], *va.* 1 To extend, to stretch out or stretch forth, to hold out (brazo, mano), to stretch out, to spread (crema, mantequilla) 2. To extend, to expand, to unfold, to unwrap. 3. Speaking of a message, writing, etc. (documento), to record it in the ordinary form. *-vr.* 1. To be extended or enlarged; to increase in bulk; to propagate (en el espacio). **Delante de nosotros se extendía la mar**, the sea stretched out before us. **Sus terrenos se extienden sobre muchos kilómetros**, his lands spread over many miles. 2. To extend (tiempo). 3. To spread, to extend (conocimiento, costumbre); to escalate, to widen, to broaden (guerra). **Su venganza se extendió hasta matar a las mujeres**, in his vengeance he even killed the women.

extendidamente [ex-ten-de'-dah-men-tay], *adv.* Extensively.

extendido, da [ex-ten-dee'-do, dah], *a. & pp.* of EXTENDER. Extended, stretched out (brazos), extent, extensive, spacious, roomy.

extendimiento [ex-ten-de-me-en´-to], *m.* Extension, dilatation.

extensamente [ex-ten-sah-men-tay], *adv.* 1. Extensively (viajar, leer). 2. Fully, in full, with full details (tratar).

extensible [ex-ten-see'-blay], *a.* Extensible, extensile.

extensión [ex-ten-se-on´], *f.* 1. Extension (acto). 2. Extension, extent, length, space or degree to which something is extended; extensiveness (dimensiones). **Un solar de mayor dimensión**, a site of greater size. 3. Length, duration; span (de tiempo). 4. *(Mus.)* Range, compass. 5. **Extensión de cable**, extension lead.

extensivamente [ex-ten-see'-vah-men-tay], *adv.* Amply, extensively, widely, largerly.

extensivo, va [ex-ten-see´-vo, vah], *a.* Extensive, ample, wide, large, extensible. **Hacer extensivo a**, to extend to.

extenso, sa [ex-ten'-so, sah], *pp. irr.* of EXTENDER, and *a.* Extensive (grande). **Por extenso**, at large; clearly and distinctly.

extensor, ra [ex-ten-sor', rah], *a.* Extending. *(Med.)* Extensor, as used of certain muscles.

extenuación [ex-tay-noo-ah-the-on'], *f.* Extenuation, a general decay in the muscular flesh of the whole body; feebleness, wasting.

extenuado, da [ex-tay-noo-ah'-do, dah] *a. & pp.* of EXTENUAR. Extenuated, extenuate, weak.

extenuar [ex-tay-noo-ar'], *va.* To extenuate, to diminish, to debilitate, to make lean, to wear away. *-vr.* To languish, to grow feeble, to lose strength, to decay.

extenuativo, va [ex-tay-noo-ah-tee'-vo, vah], *a.* That which extenuates.

exterior [ex-tay-re-or'], *a.* Exterior, external, formal, extrinsic, extrinsical, outward (aspecto); outside (cuarto).

exterior [ex-tay-re-or'], *m.* 1. Exterior, outside (parte de casa etc.); composure. **Con el exterior pintado de azul**, with the outside painted blue. 2. Foreign parts (países extranjeros). **Noticias del extranjero**, foreign news. 3. *(Pol.)* **Exteriores**, foreign affairs.

exterioridad [ex-tay-re-o-re-dahd'], *f.* 1. Exteriority, outwardness, outward or external form; outward appearance. 2. Outside (superficies), surface, external part. 3. Pomp, ostentation, pageantry.

exteriorizar [ex-tay-re-o-re-thar´], *va.* To express (expresar), to reveal outwardly (mostrar).

exteriormente [ex-tay-re-or-men'-tay], *adv.* 1. Externally, outwardly. 2. Externally, in appearance. 3. Exteriorly.

exterminación [ex-ter-me-nah-the-on'], *f. V.* EXTERMINIO.

exterminador, ra [ex-ter-me-nah-dor' rah], *m. & f.* Exterminator.

exterminar [ex-ter-me-nar´], *va.* 1. To banish, to drive away. 2. To exterminate, to root out, to tear up, to destroy, to confound.

exterminio [ex-ter-mee'-ne-o], *m.* 1. Expulsion, banishment. 2. Extermination, desolation, extirpation, destruction.

externo, na [ex-terr´-no, nah], *a.* External, visible, outward. 2. A day-pupil, one who attends classes at a school or college, but does not board there.

extestamento [ex tes-tah-men'-to], By will or testament in contrast to ab intestato.

extinción [ex-tin-the-on'], *f.* 1. Extinction, quenching or extinguishing. 2. Extinction, suppression. 3. Extinguishment, obliteration.

extinguible [ex-tin-gee-blay], *a.* Extinguishable.

extinguido [ex-tin-gee'-do], *a.* 1. **Estar extinguido** (incendio), to be out, to be extinguished. 2. Extinct (animal, volcán).

extinguir [ex-tin-geer´], *va.* 1. To quench, to extinguish, to put out (incendio). 2. To extirpate, to suppress, to destroy. *-vr.* 1. To go out (fuego). 2. *(Bio.)* To die out, to become extinct.

extinto, ta [ex-teen'-to, tah], *a. & pp. irr.* of EXTINGUIR. Extinguished, extinct.

extintor [ex-tin-tor'], *m.* Extinguisher, fire extinguisher. **Extintor de incendios**, fire extinguisher.

extirpación [ex-teer-pah-the-on'], *f.* Extirpation, eradication, extermination, excision.

extirpador [ex-teer-pah-dor'], *m.* Extirpator.

extirpar [ex-teer-par'], *va.* 1. To extirpate, to root out, to eradicate, to exscind. 2. To destroy.

extorsión [ex-tor-se-on'], *f.* 1. Extortion. *(coll.)* Shake down. 2. Inconvenience (molestia).

extorsionar [ex-tor-se-o-nar'], *va.* 1. To extort (usurpar), to extract. 2. *(Fig.)* To pester, to bother.

extra [ex-trah], *prep.* Out, without, besides. *-a.* Extra. **Vino extra**, high-quality wine. **Extra de**, in addition to.

extracción [ex-trac-the-on'], *f.* 1. Exportation. 2. Extraction, the act ot drawing one part out of a compound. 3. *(Surg.)* Extraction, the taking of extraneous substances out of the body. 4. Drawing numbers in the lottery **Extracción de fondos**, *(Com.)* The secreting of effects. 5. *(Math.)* The procces of finding the root of a number.

extractador [ex-trac-tah-dor´], *m.* Extractor.

extractar [ex-trac-tar'], *va.* To extract, to abridge, to select an abstract from a longer writing (resumir).

extractivo, va [ex-trac-tee'-vo, vah], *a.* Extractive.

extracto [ex-trahc'-to], *m.* 1. Extract, an abridgment or compendium of a large work, book, or writing. 2. *(Pharm.)* Extract, any substance obtained by the evaporation of a vegetable solution. **Extracto de Saturno**, white lead. **Extractos**, excerpts. 3. A number drawn in a lottery.

extractor [ex-trac-tor'], *m.* Extractor.

extradición [ex tra-de-thc-on'], *f.* Extradition.

extraer [ex-trah-err'], *va.* 1. To extract, to remove, to export. 2. To extract, to draw out the chief parts of a compound. 3. *(Law.)* To extract from any document. 4. To discover the root of a number. *(Yo extraigo, yo extraiga, extraje, extrajera, from Extraer. V.* TRAER.)

extraescolar [ex-trah-ays-co lar'], *a.* **Actividad extraescolar**, out-of-school activity.

extrajudicial [ex-trah-hoo-de-the-ahl'], *a.* Extrajudicial.

extrajudicialmente [ex-trah-hoo-de-the-ahl-men-tay], *adv.* Extrajudicially.

extramuros [ex'-trah-moo'-ros], *adv.* Outside the walls of a town.

extranjería [ex-tran-hay-ree'-ah], *f.* 1. The quality of being a stranger or foreigner. 2. The manner, use, and customs of a foreigner. **Ley de extranjería**, law on aliens.

extranjerismo [ex-tran-hay-rees'-mo], *m.* Fondness for foreign customs.

extranjero [ex-tran-hay'-ro], *m.* Any foreign land. **En el extranjero**, abroad, in a foreign land. **No me siento a gusto en el extranjero**, I don´t feel at ease abroad.

extranjero, ra [ex-tran-hay'-ro, rah], *m. & f.* Stranger, foreigner, alien. *-a.* Foreign, outlandish, exotic.

extranjía [cx-tran-hee´-ah], *f.* or **Extranjis**. 1. *(coll.)* V. EXTRANJERÍA. **De extranjía or de extranjis**, foreign. 2. *(Fig.)* A strange or unexpected thing (secretamente).

extrañamente [ex-trah-nyah-men'-tay], *adv.* Wonderfully, extraordinarily, oddly.

extrañamiento [ex-trah-nyah-me-en'-to], *m.* 1. Alienation, rejection, aversion. 2. Expulsion.

extrañar [ex-trah-nyar'], *va.* 1. To alienate, to banish from one's sight and intercourse. 2. To admire, to wonder (asombrar). **Me extrañaba que no hubieras venido**, I was surprised that you had not come. 3. To censure, to chide, to reprimand. **No hay que extrañar**, no wonder. 4. To miss (echar de menos). *-vr.* 1. To refuse (negarse), to decline; to break off any engagement. 2. To be amazed, to be surprised (asombrarse); to marvel (maravillarse). **Extrañarse de que...**, to be surprised that...

extrañeza [ex-trah-nyay'-thah], *f.* 1. Alienation or change of affection, aversion (amigos). 2. Singularity, irregularity (rareza). 3. Admiration, surprise (asombro). **Me miró con extrañeza**, he looked at me in surprise.

extraño, ña [ex-trah'-nyo, nyah], *a*. 1. Foreign, extraneous (extranjero). 2. Rare, monstrous, singular, marvelous (raro). 3. Extravagant, irregular, wild. 4. Unwelcome, not well received. **Es muy extraño**, it is very odd. **País extraño**, Foreign country.

extraoficial [ex-trah-o-fe-the-ahl'], *a*. Unofficial.

extraordinariamente [ex-trah-or-de-nah'-re-ah-men-tay], *adv*. Extraordinarily, uncommonly, remarkably.

extraordinario, a [ex-trah-or-de-nah'-re-o, ah], *a*. Extraordinary, uncommon (insólito), rare, odd, outstanding (destacado). **Por sus servicios extraordinarios**, for his outstanding services.

extraordinario [ex-trah-or-de-nah'-re-o], *m*. The dish or dishes which are used only on a particular day or occasion. **Extraordinario** or **correo extraordinario**, an extraordinary courier.

extrapolar [ex-trah-po-lar'], *va. & vn. (Math.)* Extrapolate.

extrarradio [ex-trahr-rah'-de-o], *m*. Outer parts (ciudad).

extrasecular [ex-trah-say-coo-lar'], *a*. 1. Who has lived beyond a century. 2. Of another century, of remote times, antique.

extrasensorial [ex-trah-sen-so-re-ahl'], *a*. Extrasensory.

extrasensorio, ria [ex-tra-sen-so'-re-o, ah], *a*. Extrasensory. **Percepción extrasensoria**, extrasensory perception.

extratémpora [ex-trah-tem'-po-rah], *f*. Dispensation for receiving orders out of the time specified by the church.

extraterrestre [ex-trah-ter-res-tray], *a*. Extraterrestrial.

extraterritorial [ex-trah-ter-re-to-re-ah'], *a*. Extraterritorial, outside territorial limits of a jurisdiction.

extravagancia [ex-trah-vah-gahn'-the-ah], *f*. 1. Extravagance (cualidad), irregularity, oddness, folly, freak. 2. Extravagance, waste, vain and superfluous expense (capricho).

extravagante [ex-trah-vah-gahn'-tay], *a*. 1. Extravagant, irregular, wild, humorous, frantic, freakish. 2. *(coll.)* Odd (raro), out of the way, outlandish (estrafalario).

extravagante [ex-trah-vah-gahn'-tay], *f*. Extravagant, a papal constitution not included in the body of the canon law almost always used in the plural.

extravagantemente [ex-trah-vah-gahn'-tay-men-tay], *adv*. Extravagantly; eccentrically.

extravasación [ex-trah-vah-sah-the-on'], *f. (Med.)* Extravasation.

extravasarse [ex-trah-vah-sar'-say], *vr*. To extravasate, to exude.

extravenado, da [ex-trah-vay-nah'-do, dah], *a*. Extravenate, forced out of the veins. *-pp*. of EXTRAVENARSE.

extravenarse [ex-trah-vay-nar'-say], *vr*. To let out of the veins.

extraviar [ex-trah-vear'], *va*. To mislead, to lead out of the way; to embezzle (dinero), secrete. **Extraviados**, *(Mil.)* Men missing. *-vr*. 1. To lose one's way, to deviate from the right or common way (persona). 2. To stray from rectitude, to err.

extravío [ex-trah-vee'-o], *m*. 1. Misplacement, loss (pérdida). 2. Deviation. 3. Irregularity, disorder, misguidance. 4. Frenzy.

extremadamente [ex-tray-mah'-dah-men-tay], *adv*. Extremely, in the utmost degree, greatly, hugely.

extremadas [ex-tray-mah'-das], *f. pl*. The time of making cheese.

extremado, da [ex-tray-mah'-do, dah], *a*. 1. Extreme, absolute, consummate in good or bad, intense (intenso); extremely good (muy bueno); extremely bad (muy malo). 2. Facetious, cheerful, gay.*-pp*. of EXTREMAR.

extremamente [ex-tray-mah-men'-tay], *adv*. Extremely, exceedingly, mightily.

extremar [ex-tray-mar'], *va*. 1. To reduce to an extreme; generally used in a bad sense. 2. To finish, to complete, to give the finishing stroke. **Sin extremar el sentimentalismo**, without overdoing the sentimentality. *-vr*. 1. To be punctual or exact in the performance of something. 2. To persist

obstinately in an undertaking. *-vn*. To winter in Extremadura (oveja).

extremaunción [ex-tray-mah-oon-the-on'], *f*. Unction or extreme unction.

extremidad [ex-tray-me-dahd'], *f*. 1. The end or extremity of something (punta). 2. The edge, brink, border, or brim of any thing (borde).

extremismo [ex-tray-mees'-mo], *m*. Extremism.

extremista [ex-tray-mees'-tah], *a.m. & f*. Extremist.

extremo, ma [ex-tray'-mo, mah], *a*. 1. Extreme, last, that beyond which there is nothing (lugar). 2. Extreme, greatest, of the highest degree. 3. Extreme, excessive, utmost. **Con extremo, en extremo, por extremo**, extremely, in the utmost degree.

extremo [ex-tray'-mo], *m*. 1. Extreme, utmost point, highest degree (punto maás alto). **Hasta el extremo de**, to the point of. 2. Extreme, the point at the greatest distance from the center, extremity (cabo, limite). **Pasar de un extremo a otro**, to go from one end to another. 3. *(Met.)* Extreme care or application (asunto). **Hacer extremos**, to caress, to fondle; to manifest grief and displeasure. 4. The winter or summer of emigrating flocks.

extremoso, sa [ex-tray-mo'-so, sah], *a*. Extreme, impassioned, unbridled, gushing (persona); vehement (vehemente).

extrínseco, ca [ex-treen'-say-co, cah], *a*. Extrinsic, outward, external, eastern.

extrovertido [ex-tro-vayr-te'-do], *a*. Extrovert; outgoing. -*m. f*. Extrovert.

extumescencia [ex-too-me-then'-the-ah], *f. (Med.)* Swelling, tumefaction.

exuberancia [ek-soo-bay-rahn'-the-ah], *a*. Exuberance, utmost, plenty, abundance.

exuberante [ek-soo-bay-rahn'-tay], *a*. Exuberant, overabundant.

exuberar [ek-soo-bay-rar'], *vn*. To be exuberant, to exuberate.

exudación [ek-soo-dah-the-on'], *f*. Sweating, a critical sweat.

exudar [ek-soo-dar'], *vn*. To exude, to ooze like sweat.

exulceración [ek-sool-thay-rah-the-on'], *f*. Exulceration, ulceration.

exulcerar [ek-sool-thay-rar'], *va*. To exulcerate, to ulcerate, to disuse with sores.

exultación [ek-sool-tah-the-on'], *f*. Exultation, demonstration of joy.

exutorio [ek-soo-toh'-re-o], *m. (Med.)* Issue, an ulcer artificially made and maintained for a curative purpose.

exvoto [ex-vo'-to], *m. (Lat.)* Offering to God in consequence of a vow, consisting of relics, pictures, images, etc., hung up in churches.

eyaculación [ay-yah-coo-lah-the-on'], *f. (Neol.)* 1. *(Med.)* Ejaculation, the rapid emission of certain secretions. 2. *(Zool.)* Rapid expulsion of water from the gills of certain fishes (para escapar). 3. Rapidity with which the chameleon darts its tongue upon the insects which cling to it.

eyaculador, ra [ay-yah-coo-lah-dor', rah], *a*. Ejaculatory, serving for ejaculation.

eyacular [ay-yah-co-lar'], *va*. To ejaculate, to expel fluid secretions.

eyector [ay-yec-tor'], *m*. Ejector (maquina).

ézula [ay'-thoo-lah], *f. (Bot.)* Spurge. V. ÉSULA.

F

f [ay'-fay]. Sixth letter of the Spanish alphabet. Its name is *efe*. This letter is pronounced in Spanish, as in English. In law works, *ff* signifies digest or pandect of the civil law. F stood for 40 in the middle ages, and with a dash above, 40,000. In music, *f* stands for **fuerte**, loud. In works of art, **fecit** or **faciebat**.

fa [fah], *m. (Mus.)* Fourth note in the gamut.

faba [fah'-bah], *f.* *(Prov.)* V. HABA.

fabacrasa [fah-bah-crah'-sah], *f.* *(Bot.)* Common orpine, stone-crop.

fabada [fah-bah'-dah], *f.* Rich stew of beans, pork, etc.

faber [fah-bayr'], *m.* A fish, the gilthead.

fábrica [fah'-bre-cah], *f.* 1. Factory, works; still, distillery. **Fábrica de cerveza,** brewery. **Fábrica de papel,** paper mill. 2. Fabrication, manufacture (acto). **Marca de fábrica,** trademark. **Trabajo de fábricas,** factory work. 3. Make (origen). **De fábrica alemana,** of German make. 4. *(Arch.)* Building, structure.

fabricación [fah-bre-cah-the-on'], *f.* Manufacture, construction. **Fabricación en serie** or **en gran escala,** mass production. **Fabricación de coches,** car manufacture. **Estar en fabricación,** to be in production. **Fabricación asistida por ordenador,** *(Comput.)* computer-aided manufacturing.

fabricador, ra [fah-bre-cah-dor', rah], *m. & f.* 1. V. FABRICANTE. 2. Inventor, contriver, deviser, coiner, framer. 3. *(Naut.)* Constructor.

fabricante [fah-bre-cahn'-tay], *m.* 1. Builder, architect, fabricator. 2. Maker, manufacturer, master workman, artificer (industria). 3. Operative, artisan.

fabricar [fah-bre-car'], *va.* 1. To build (construir), to make, to construct, to frame, to fabricate. 2. To manufacture (producir). 3. To fabricate, to contrive, to devise. **Fabricar a piedra perdida,** to build upon a false foundation.

fabril [fah-breel'], *a.* 1. Belonging to manufacturers, artisans, or workmen. 2. Febrile, belonging to the craft of a smith, mason, or carpenter.

fabriquero [fah-bre-cay'-ro], *m.* 1. Manufacturer, artisan, artificer (fabricante). 2. Person charged with the care of cathedrals and church buildings.

fabuco [fah-boo'-co], *m.* Beechmast, the fruit of the beech tree.

fabueno [fah-boo-ay'-no], *m.* Westerly wind.

fábula [fah'-boo-lah], *f.* 1. Fable, a feigned story, to enforce some moral precept. 2. Rumor, report, common talk (rumor, chisme). 3. Fable, a fiction, a lie, a false-hood (mentira). 4. Fable, the series of events which constitute a poem: a legend. 5. Mockery, derision. **Está hecho la fábula del mundo,** he is become the laughing-stock of the whole world. 6. V. MITOLOGÍA. 7. **Un negocio de fábula,** a splendid piece of business.

fabulador [fah-boo-lah-dor'], *m.* Fabulist, author of fables, dealer in fictions.

fabular [fah-boo-lar'], *va.* To invent fables or deal in fictions.

fabulilla, ita [fah-boo-leel'-lyah, ee'-tah], *f. dim.* A little fable.

fabulista [fah-boo-lees'-tah], *m.* Fabulist, a writer of fables.

fabulosamente [fah-boo-lo-sah-men'-tay], *adv.* Fabulously.

fabuloso, sa [fah-boo-lo-so, sah], *a.* Fabulous (estupendo, mítico), feigned, fictitious (ficticio), legendary, romantic.

faca [fah'-cah], *f.* A curved knife.

facción [fac-the-on'], *f.* 1. Military exploit, engagement, action. 2. Faction, a turbulent party in a state. 3. Party, faction. 4. Feature, countenance, favor: in this last sense it is generally used in the plural. 5. An act of military service, as guard, patrol, etc. **Facción de testamento,** faculty of testating. **Facciones,** features; the lineaments, cast or form of the face.

faccionario, ria [fac-the-o-nah'-re-o, ah], *a.* Belonging to a party or faction. *-m. & f.* Factionary, a party man.

faccioso, sa [fac-the-o'-so, sah], *a.* Factious, turbulent, unruly, mutinous; it is used as a substantive. **Los facciosos,** the rebels.

faceta [fah-thay'-tah], *f.* Facet, face or side of a precious stone cut into a number of angles.

faceto, ta [fah-thay'-to, tah], *a.* Merry, witty, gay, lively.

facha [fah'-chah], *f. (coll.)* Appearance, aspect, look (aspecto), mien, face (cara). **Ser un facha** or **una facha,** to be ridiculous. **Tiene facha de poli,** he looks like a cop. **Tiene facha de buena gente,** he looks OK.

fachada [fah-chah'-dah], *f.* 1. Facade, face, front, or fore part of a building. 2. *(coll.)* V. PRESENCIA for figure. 3.

(Met.) Broad or plump face. 4. Frontispiece of a book. 5. Front-age (medida). **Con fachada al parque,** looking towards the park. 6. *(Fig.)* Facade, outward show. **No tiene más que fachada,** it´s all just show with him. 7. Mug, face (cara).

fachenda [fah-chen'-dah], *a. (coll.)* Vain, ostentatious (hombre de negocios). *-f.* Vanity, boasting.

fachendear [fah-chen-day-ar'], *va.* To affect having much important business, to make an ostentatious parade of business.

fachendista [fah-chen-dees'-tah], *a. & m. & f. (coll.)* A vain and ostentatious person, a busybody.

fachendón, na [fah-chen-done', nah], *a. aug.* Very vain and ostentatious

fachín [fah-cheen'], *m. (Prov.)* Porter carrier.

fachinal [fah-che-nahl'], *m. (Prov. Amer.)* A salt marsh, swamp, place liable to be overflowed.

facial [fah-the-ahl'], *a.* Facial, belonging to the face. **Ángulo facial,** the facial angle.

facie [fah'-the-ay], *f. (Min.)* A face of a crystal.

facies [fah'-the-ays], *m. (Med.)* Facies, physiognomy in disease.

fácil [fah'-theel], *a.* 1. Facile, easy, light, performable with little trouble (sencillo). **Fácil para el usuario,** user-friendly. **Fácil de hacer,** easy to do. 2. Pliant, flexible, compliant, familiar, easily persuaded (persona). 3. Easy of access (mujeres). 4. Frail, weak of resolution.

facilidad [fah-the-le-dahd'], *f.* 1. Facility, easiness to be performed; freedom from difficulty. **Con la mayor facilidad,** with the greatest ease. 2. Facility, easiness to be persuaded, vicious docility (docilidad), ready compliance. 3. **Facilidades,** facilities. **Facilidades de crédito,** credit facilities.

facilillo, illa, ito, ita [fah-the-leel'-lyo, eel'-yah, ee'-to, ce'-tah], *a. dim.* Rather easy. **Facilillo es eso,** (Iron.) that is easy enough: meaning that it is extremely difficult.

facilitación [fah-the-le-tah-the-on'], *f.* Facility, expedition, facilitation.

facilitar [fah-the-le-tar'], *va.* 1. To facilitate, to make easy (hacer fácil), to free from difficulties, to expedite (agilizar). 2. To supply, to deliver (proporcionar). **Me facilitó un coche,** he supplied me with a car.

fácilmente [fah'-theel-men-tay], *adv.* Easily, lightly, without difficulty, facilely.

facilitón, na [fah-the-le-tone', nah], *a.* One who assumes to make everything easy.

facineroso [fah-the-nay-ro'-so], *a.* Wicked, atrocious, flagitious: it is also used as a substantive, speaking of highwaymen.

facistol [fah-this-tole'], *m.* Chorister's desk or stand on which choirbooks are placed.

facistor, ra [fah-this-tor', rah], *a. (Cuban).* V. FACHENDA.

faco [fah'-co], *m.* (Coll.) 1. Pony, a little nag. 2. Francis (apodo).

facsímile [fac-see'-me-lay], *m.* Facsimile.

factible [fac-tee'-blay], *a.* Feasible, practicable.

facticio, cia [fac-tee'-the-o, ah], *a.* Factitious, made by art.

factor [fac-tor], *m.* 1. Factor, an agent for another. 2. Factor (aritmética). 3. Factor, constituting element (elemento). **Factor Rh,** *(Med.)* Rh factor. **Factor humano,** human factor. **El factor suerte,** the luck factor.

factoraje [fac-to-rah'-hay], *m.* Factorage, commission for agency in purchasing goods.

factoría [fac-to-ree'-ah], *f.* 1. Factory, foreign traders in a distant country; also the district where they reside; trading houses. 2. Factorage, the commission of factor, agency (agencia). 3. Foundry (fundición).

factorizar [fac-to-re-thar'], *va.* To establish commerce by factors.

factótum [fac-to'-toom], *m.* 1. Factotum, a man of all work (empleado). 2. One who officiously intermeddles in everything.

factura [fac-too´-rah], *f.* 1. Invoice of merchandise. **Según factura**, as per invoice. **Presentar factura**, to send an invoice. 2. Among organ-builders, the quality, length, breadth, and thickness of the pipes.

facturación [fac-too-rah-the-on´], *f.* 1. Invoicing (acto). 2. *(Com.)* Sales (ventas). 3. *(Aer.)* Check-in.

facturar [fac-too-rar´], *va.* 1. To note on merchandise the amount of the prime cost. 2. To check baggage.

fácula [fah´-coo-lah], *f. (Ast.)* Bright spot on the sun's disk.

facultad [fah-cool-tahd´], *f.* 1. Faculty, power of doing something. 2. Faculty, privilege, authority, right to do anything (autoridad). 3. Science, art. 4. Faculty, in a university, denotes the body of the professors teaching a science. 5. *(Med.)* Faculty, the power of performing an action, natural, vital, or animal (de mente). **Facultades metales**, mental powers. 6. License, permission.-*pl.* **Facultades**, fortune, wealth, means of living. **Facultades del alma**, powers of the mind. **Facultad mayor**, in universities, divinity, civil and canonical law, or medicine.

facultado, da [fah-cool-tah´-do, dah], *a.* Authorized, empowered.

facultador, ra [fah-cool-tah-dor´, rah], *m. & f.* One who commissions or empowers.

facultar [fah-cool-tar´], *va. (Law.)* To empower, to authorize, to commision.

facultativamente [fah-cool-tah-te-vah-men´-tay], *adv.* According to the principles, rules, or axioms of a science or art.

facultativo, va [fah-cool-tah-tee´-vo, vah], *a.* 1. Belonging to some faculty, art, or science. 2. Granting power, faculty, leave, or permision. 3. That which may be done or omitted at pleasure (opcional).

facultativo [fah-cool-tah-tee´-vo], *m.* 1. Master of a science or art (profesional). 2. A person skilful, intelligent, or conversant with an art, trade, or business; connoisseur (doctores).

facundia [fah-coon´-de-ah], *f.* Eloquence, the power of speaking with fluency and elegance.

facundo, da [fah-coon´-do, dah], *a.* Eloquent, fluent.

fada [fah´-dah], *f.* 1. A small apple of the pippin kind. 2. Witch.

fadiga [fah-dee´-gah], *f. (Prov.)* Leave granted to sell a feudal estate.

faena [fah-ay´-nah], *f.* 1. Work, labor, fatigue (trabajo). **Faena doméstica**, house-work. 2. *(Naut.)* Duty on board of ships. 3. **Mala faena**, dirty trick. **Hacer una faena a uno**, to lay a dirty trick on somebody. 4. Play with the cape; performance (tauromaquia). **Hizo una faena maravillosa**, he gave a splendid performance.

faenar [fah-ay-nar´], *va.* To slaughter (ganado). -*vn.* To fish (pescar), to work.

faetón [fah-ay-tone´], *m.* 1. Phaeton, a kind of open carriage. 2. An omnibus, with seats along the sides.

fagina [fah-hee´-nah], *f.* 1. Fascine, a small bundle of branches bound up. 2. Fagot, a bundle of sticks or brush-wood for fuel. 3. Stock or rick of corn piled up in sheaves. 4. Fatigue, work, labor. 5. *(Mil.)* A war-call.

faginada [fah-he-nah´-dah], *f.* Collection of fascines or fagots.

fagocitos [fah-go-thee´-tos], *m. pl. (Biol.)* Phagocytes, a type of white corpuscle.

fagot [fah-gote´], *m.* Bassoon (instrumento).

fagotista [fah-go-tees´-tah], *m.* Bassoon player.

faisán [fah-e-sahn´], *m & f.* Pheasant (pájaro).

faja [fah´-hah], *f.* 1. Band, bandage (tira de tela), roller, fillet; a swathing band. 2. Border, a line which divides any superficies. 3. *(Arch.)* Fascia, belt, fillet . 4. A belt, sash, girdle (prenda). **Faja pantalón**, panty girdle. 5. *(Mil.)* Scarf, the principal insignia of a general. 6. *(Naut.)* A reefband.

fajadura [fah-hah-doo´-rah], *f. (Naut.)* Patched clothes rolled round a rope to preserve it.

fajamiento [fah-hah-me-en´-to], *m.* Act of rolling or swathing.

fajar [fah-har´], *va.* 1. To swathe (envolver), to bind a child with bands and rollers; to fillet. 2. To fall on, to attack (atacar). 3. To bandage (vendar); to wrap up (correos). -*vr.* To put on one´s belt (ponerse una faja).

fajardo [fah-har´-do], *m.* A kind of minced pie.

fajeado, da [fah-hay-ah´-do, dah], *a.* That which has girdles, bands, or rollers.

fajero [fah-hay´-ro], *m.* A knitted swaddling band for children.

fajín [fah-heen´], *m.* Sash (militar). **El fajín rojo del general,** the general's red sash.

fajo [fah´-ho], *m.* 1. Bundle (papeles); roll (billetes). 2. Baby´s clothes (de bebé). V. HAZ.-*pl.* Swaddling clothes.

fajón [fah-hone´], *m. aug.* A large band or roller.

fajuela [fah-hoo-ay´-lah], *f. dim.* A small bandage or roller.

fakir [fah-keer´], *m.* Fakir (faquir).

falacia [fah-lah´-the-ah], *f.* Fallacy (error), fraud (engaño), sophism, deceitful argument, hollowness, fallaciousness.

falange [fah-lahn´-hay], *f.* 1.Phalanx, a closely embodied troop. 2. Phalanx, *pl.* phalanges, small bones of the fingers and toes.

falangia, *f.* **falangio,** *m.* [fah-lahn´-he-ah, fah-lahn´-he-o]. A venomous spider with a red head and a black body.

falangista [fah-lan-hees´-tah], *m. & f.* Falangist.

fálaris [fah´-la-ris], *f. (Orn. Acad.)* V. FOJA.

falaz [fah-lath´], *a.* Deceitful (persona), fraudulent; frustrative, fallacious (doctrina), disappointing, deceptive (aspecto)

falbalá [fal-bah-lah´], *m.* 1. Flounce, furbelow, an ornament sewed to a garment and hanging loose. V. FARCALÁ. 2. Skirt of a gown or coat plaited.

falca [fahl´-cah], *f.* 1. *(Naut.)* A waistboard, or washboard. 2. *(Prov.)* A small wedge of wood used by carpenters.

falcada [fal-cah´-dah], *f.* Falcade, a curvet made by horses.

falcado, da [fal-cah´-do, dah], *a. & pp.* of FALCAR. Hooked, curvated, falcated. A scythed chariot.

falcario [fal-cah´-re-o], *m.* Roman soldier armed with a falchion.

falce [fahl´-thay], *f.* 1. Sickle, reaping-hook, scythe, billhook. 2. Falchion, a short crooked sword.

falcidia [fal-thee´-de-ah], *f.* 1. Fourth part of an inheritance. 2. The Roman law which established such division.

falciforme [fal-the-for´-may], *a.* Falciform, sickle-shaped.

falcinelo [fal-the-nay´-lo], *m. (Orn.)* Gray ibis, sicklebill.

falcón [fal-cone´], *m.* Ancient piece of artillery.

falconete [fal-co-nay´-tay], *m.* Falconet, a small piece of ordnance.

falda [fahl´-dah], *f.* 1. Skirt (prenda), the loose edge of a garment: that part which hangs loose below the waist; train; flap. **Falda escocesa**, kilt. **Haberse criado bajo las faldas de mamá**, to have led a very sheltered life. 2. The lap. **Sentarse en la falda de una**, to sit on somebody´s lap. 3. Brow of a hill, that part of an eminence which slopes into the plain. 4. Loin of beef, mutton, etc. 5. The brim of a brazier where the hinge is fixed. 6. Brim (de sombrero). 7. Table cover (de camilla). **Perrillo faldero**, lap-dog.

faldamento [fal-dah-men´-to], *m.* Fold, flap, skirt. *V.* FALDA.

faldar [fal-dar´], *m.* Tassel, armor for the thighs.

faldellín [fal-del-lyeen´], *m.* 1. A skirt or underpetticoat used formerly by women (falda). 2. *V.* REFAJO.

falderillo, illa [fal-day-reel´-lyo, lyah], *a. dim.* 1. Small lap. 2. Little lap-dog.

faldero, ra [fal-day´-ro, rah], *a.* 1. Belonging to the lap. **Perrillo faldero**, lap-dog. 2. Fond of being constantly among women, and busy with women's affairs.

faldeta [fal-day´-tah], *f. dim.* Small skirt.

faldetes [fal-day´-tes], *f. pl.* 1. Tassels. 2. Fringes, trimmings.

faldicorto, ta [fal-de-cor´-to, tah], *a.* Having short skirts.

faldilla [fal-deel´-lyah], *f. dim. V.* FALDETA. -*pl.* Small skirts of a jacket.

faldistorio [fal-dis-to´-re-o], *m.* Stool on which bishops sit during the performance of church functions.

faldón [fal-done'], *m.* 1. A long flowing skirt, flap (de vestido). 2. The flap of a saddle. 3. A millstone of a horsemill put upon another to increase the weight. 4. *(Arch.)* A sloping, side, gable; also the cap-piece and walls of the entrance of chimneys.

faldriguera [fal-dre-gay'-rah], *f.* Pocket. *V.* FALTRIQUERA.

falena [fah-lay'-nah], *f. (Zool.)* Moth, a nocturnal lepidopterous insect; a tent-caterpillar.

falencia [fah-len'-the-ah], *f.* Want of security, uncertainty, mistake.

faleris [fah-lay'-ris], *m.* Coot, a bird of the family of the penguins. It inhabits Behring Strait and adjacent waters.

falibilidad [fah-le-be-le-dahd], *f.* Fallibility.

falible [fah-lee'-blay], *a.* Fallible.

falimiento [fah-le-meen'-to], *m.* Deception, deceit, falsehood.

falla [fahl´-lyah], *f.* 1. *(Naut.)* Defect, deficiency; lack of wood for the finishing of a certain figure. *V.* FALTA. 2. A sort of light loose cover, worn by women over their headdress at night. 3. *(Geol.)* Fault, dislocation of a seam or layer.

fallar [fal-lyar'], *va.* 1. *(Law.)* To give sentence, to judge. 2. To ruff (naipes), to trump, to win a trick with trumps. -*v. impers.* To be deficient or wanting. -*vn.* To fail (cosecha, freno, memoria); to go wrong (plan); to miss (tiro); to break (apoyo, cuerda); to misfire (fusil). **Algo falló en sus planes**, something went wrong with his plans.

falleba [fal-lyay'-bah], *f.* An iron bar for fastening doors and windows.

fallecedor, ra [fal-lyay-thay-dor', rah], *a.* Perishable.

fallecer [fal-lyay-therr'], *vn.* To die. *(Yo fallezco, yo fallezca, from Fallecer. V.* ABORRECER.)

fallecido, da [fahl-lay-the'-do], *m & f.* Deceased, person who has lately died.

fallecimiento [fal-lyay-the-me-en'-to], *m.* Decease, death.

fallido, da [fal-lyee'-do, dah], *a.* 1. Deceived, disappointed, frustrated. 2. Bankrupt.

fallo [fahl'-lyo], *m.* 1. Judgment, decision of a judge in a lawsuit or trial. 2. In some games of cards not to have a card of the suit played. 3. Shortcoming (defecto); *(Med.)* failure; error, mix-up. **Debido a un fallo de los frenos**, because of a break failure. **Fallo del equipo**, *(Comput.)* equipment failure.

falo [fah'-lo], *m.* 1. Phallus the generative organ, the penis (clítoris). 2. Phallus, a genus of fungi.

falordía [fah-lor-dee'-ah], *f. (Prov.)* Deception, imposition, deceit, fable.

falsa or **falsa escuadra** [fal'-sah, es-coo-ah'-drah], *f.* Bevel rule, bevel square.

falsamarra [fal-sah-mar'-rah], *f. (Naut.)* Preventer-rope, employed to support another which suffers an unusual strain.

falsamente [fal-sah-men'-tay], *adv.* Falsely; deceitfully, lyingly, fallaciously, counterfeitly, untruly.

falsario, ria [fal-sah-re-o, ah], *a.* 1. Falsifying, forging, counterfeiting. 2. Accustomed to tell falsehoods. -*m. & f.* 1. Falsifier (mentiroso); liar. 2. Forger (falseador), counterfeiter.

falsarregla [fal-sahr-ray'-glah], *f.* Bevel rule, bevel square.

falseable [fal-say-ah'-blay], *a.* Falsifiable, capable of being counterfeited.

falseador [fal-say-ah-dor'], *m.* Forger, counterfeiter, falsifier.

falsear [fal-say-ar'], *va.* 1. To falsify (falsificar), to adulterate, to counterfeit (moneda); to forge (firma). 2. To pierce, to penetrate. **Falsear la llave**, to counterfeit a key. -*vn.* 1. To slacken, to lose strength and firmness. 2. Not to agree in sound (instrumentos musicales). 3. To leave a hollow in saddles to make easy.

falsedad [fal-say-dahd´], *f.* 1. Falsehood, falsity, untruth, mendacity, fiction, fable, fib. 2. Deceit, malicious dissimulation.

falsete [fal-say'-tay], *m.* 1. Falsetto voice, the register of head tones. 2. *(Prov.)* Spigot.

falsía [fal-see'-ah], *f. V.* FALSEDAD.

falsificación [fal-se-fe-cah-the-on'], *f.* Falsification (acto), falsifying or counterfeiting forgery (objeto), counterfeit.

falsificador, ra [fal-se-fe-cah-dor'-rah], *m. & f.* Falsifier, counterfeiter, forger.

falsificar [fal-se-fe-car'], *va.* To falsify to counterfeit (moneda), to forge (cuadro, sello), to foist, imitation (joya); false (declaración, testimonio); hollow (persona).

falsilla [fal-seel'-lyah], *f.* Ruled pattern to guide in writing.

falsío [fal-see'-o], *m. (Prov.)* Kind of sausage.

falso, sa [fahl'-so, sah], *a.* 1. False (moneda), false, untrue (testimonio); uncertain, not real. 2. False, false-hearted, hypocritical, deceitful, treacherous, perfidious, traitorous (amigo). 3. False, counterfeit, supposititious, supposed. 4. Feint; mock. **Piedras falsas**, mock jewellery. 5. Vicious (caballos, mulas). 6. Producing no fruit (flores). 7. Defective, false. **De falso**, falsely deceitfully. **En falso**, without due security. **No levantarás falso testimonio**, thou shalt not bear false witness against thy neighbor. **Cerrar en falso la puerta**, to miss shutting the door, or to leave the door purposely unlocked. **Dar un paso en falso**, to step on something that is not there.

falta [fahl'-tah], *f.* 1. Fault, defect, want, absence, lack (carencia), mistake (dictado, escrito). **Falta de asistencia**, non-attendance. **Falta de peso**, short weight. **Echar algo en falta**. 2. Fault (culpa), offence, slight crime, defect (de fabricación), faultiness, failing, misdoing, failure, flaw. 3. Want or stoppage of the catamenia in pregnant women. **Tiene cuatro faltas**, she is in the fifth month of her pregnancy. 4. Deficiency in the weight of coin. 5. Default, non-appearance in court at day assigned. **Sin falta**, without fail. **A falta de**, in want or for want of. **Hacer falta**, to be absolutely necessary to anything; not to be punctual to the fixed time; to be in want of a thing, to disappoint. *(Com.)* **Falta de aceptación, de pago**, for non-acceptance. **Acusar de falta**, to find fault with.

faltar [fartar'], *vn.* 1. To be deficient, to be wanting (ser necesario). 2. To fail (fallar), to falter, to fault, to flinch. 3. To be consumed, to fall short. 4. Not to fulfil one's promise, not to perform one's engagement. 5. To need, to lack, to be in want of. 6. To die. **Faltar a su palabra**, to fall back. **Le falta dinero**, he lacks money. **Nos falta tiempo para hacerlo**, we lack the time to do it. **Faltaron 3 en la reunión**, there were 3 missing in the meeting. **Fatar al trabajo**, to stay away. **Faltar en hacer algo**, to fail to do something. **Faltan pocos minutos para el comienzo**, there's only a few minutes to go till the start. **Falta poco para terminar**, it´s almost over.

faltilla [fal-teel'-lyah], *f. dim.* A slight fault or defect.

falto, ta [fahl'-to, tah], *a.* 1. Wanting, deficient, defective (deficiente). **Estar falto de**, to be short of. 2. Miserable, wretched (moralmente). 3. Mad, insane.

faltrero, ra [fal-tray'-ro, rah], *f.* Pickpocket, petty thief.

faltriquera [fal-tre-kay-rah'], *f.* Pocket (bolsillo), as in clothes; fob, watch pocket (de reloj); handbag (bolso).

falúa, faluca [fah-loo'-ah, fah-loo'cah], *f. (Naut.)* Felucca, a small open boat, or a long boat with oars.

falucho [fah-loo'-cho], *m.* A small boat with oars, and one lateen sail.

fama [fah'-mah], *f.* 1. Fame, report, rumor (rumor). 2. Fame (renombre), reputation (reputación), repute, name; glory. **Mala fama**, bad reputation. **El libro que le dio fama**, the book which made him famous.

fame [fah'-may], *f. (Prov.)* Hunger. *V.* HAMBRE.

tamélico, ca [fah-may'leco, cah], *a.* Hungry. *V.* HAMBRIENTO.

familia [fah-mee'-le-ah], *f.* 1. Family, the people who live in the same house together. 2. Family, those that descend from one common progenitor: a race, a generation, a house, a clan. **Familia política**, relatives by marriage. **De buena familia**, of good family. **Ser como de la familia**, to be one of the family. 3. Religious order. 4. Number of servants or retainers.

familiar [fah-me-le-ar'], *a.* 1. Familiar, domestic, belonging to the family (de la familia). **Los lazos familiares**, the family bond. 2. Familiar, common, frequent. 3. Familiar, well known, well acquainted with (conocido). 4. Agreeable, conformable, useful, observant, conversant. **Estilo familiar**, colloquial, familiar style; an easy, unconstrained style.

familiar, *m.* 1. Domestic, one belonging to a family, one kept in the same house. 2. Servant, especially of the clergy. 3. College servant, who waits upon all the collegians collectively. 4. Demon, a familiar spirit. 5. Familiar or intimate friend, one long acquainted. 6. One of the officers of the Inquisition.

familiarcito [fah-me-le-ar-thee'-to], *m.* 1. *(dim.)* Servant-boy, a little servant. 2. One who affects great familiarity or intimacy.

familiaridad [fah-me-le-ah-re-dahd'], *f.* 1. Familiarity, easiness of conversation or intercourse. 2. Familiarity, acquaintance, habitude. 3. *V.* FAMILIATURA.

familiarizar [fah-me-le-ah-re-thar'], *va.* To familiarize, to render familiar, to make easy by habitude. *-vr.* To become familiar, to descend from a state of distant superiority.

familiarmente [fah-me-le-ar-men'-tay], *adv.* Familiarly.

familiatura [fah-me-le-ah-too'-rah], *f.* 1. Place and employment of *a familiar* of the Inquisition. 2. Place of one of the college-servants called *familiares.*

famis [fah'-mis], *f.* A kind of gold cloth or brocade from Smyrna.

famosamente [fah-mo-sah-men'-tay], *adv.* Famously, excellently.

famoso, sa [fah-mo'-so, sah], *a.* 1. Famous, celebrated, renowned, conspicuous, great, splendid (estupendo). 2. Noted (ladrones) 3. Notorious.

fámula [fah'-moo-lah], *f. (coll.)* Maid-servant.

famulato, famulicio [fah-moo-lah'-to, fah-moo-lee'-the-o], *m.* Servitude.

fámulo [fah'-moo-lo], *m.* Servant of a college.

fan [fahn], *m & f.* Fan *(Cine, Mus. etc.)*

fanal [fah-nahl'], *m.* 1. *(Naut.)* Pooplantern of a commodore's ship. 2. Lantern (linterna), a lighthouse to guide ships (faro). 3. A kind of lantern of crystal in the form of a conoid. 4. *(Met.)* Guide, friend, adviser in difficulties and dangers.

fanáticamente [fah-nah'-te-cah-men-tay], *adv.* Fanatically.

fanático, ca [fah-nah'-te-co, cah], *a.* Fanatic, fanatical, enthusiastic, superstitious. **Es un fanático del aeromodelismo**, he´s mad about model aeroplanes.

fanatismo [fah-nah-tees'-mo], *m.* Fanaticism, mysticism, religious frenzy.

fanatizar [fah-nah-te-thar'], *va.* To spread or instil fanaticism.

fandango [fan-dahn'-go], *m.* 1. Fandango, a lively Spanish dance; the music to this dance. 2. Festive entertainment; dance with castanets or balls in the hands. 3. Row (jaleo).

fandanguear [fan-dan-gayar'], *va. (coll.)* To revel, to carouse.

fandanguero [fan-dan-gay'-ro], *m.* 1. Fandango-dancer. 2. One fond of festive entertainments.

faneca [fah-nay'-cah], *f. (Zool.)* Pout, whiting pout.

fanega [fah-nay'-gah], *f.* 1. A measure of grain and seed of about a hundred weight, or an English bushel: it has been sometimes called faneague in English. 2. The quantity of seed contained in a **fanega** or Spanish bushel, and the vessel containing it. **Fanega de tierra**, extent of arable and, generally of four hundred fathoms square, and of pasture land five hundred. **Fanega de cacao**, a measure of one hundred and ten pounds of cocoa.

fanegada [fah-nay-gah'-dah], *f. V.* FANEGA DE TIERRA. **A fanegadas**, in great plenty or abundance.

faneranto, ta [fah-nay-rahn'-to, tah], *a.* Flowering, having visible flowers.

fanerocarpo, pa [fah-nay-ro-car'-po, pah], *a. (Biol.)* Having visible fruits or reproductive corpuscles.

fanerógamo, ma [fah-nay-ro'-gah-mo, mah], *a.* Phanerogamous, flowering.

fanfarrear [fan-far-ray-ar'], *vn.* To bully, to brag.

fanfarria [fan-far'-re-ah], *f.* 1. *(coll.)* Empty arrogance of a braggart. 2. *(Mus.)* Fanfare.

fanfarrón [fan-far-rone'], *m.* Fanfaron, a bully, a hector.

fanfarrón, na [fan-far-rone', nah], *a. (coll.)* Boasting, vaunting; inflated.

fanfarronada [fan-far-ro-nah'-dah], *f.* Fanfaronade, boast, brag, a bravado.

fanfarronazo, za [fan-far-ro-nah'-tho, thah], *a.* Applied to a great swank, boasting, vaunting.

fanfarronear [fan-far-ro-nay-ar'], *vn.* To bully, to brag, to show off, to swank.

fanfarronería [fan-far-ro-nay-ree'-ah], *f.* Fanfaronade, braggartism, bragging, show off.

fanfarronesca [fan-far-ro-ness'-cah], *f.* Manner of a fanfaron.

fanfurriña [fan-foor-ree'-nyah], *f.* Passion or displeasure, arising from a slight motive.

fangal [fan-gahl'], *m.* Slough, a miry place, a fen, a marsh, a place full of mud or mire.

fango [fahn'-go], *m.* 1. Mire, mud at the bottom of still water. 2. *(Naut.)* Oozy bottom of the sea.

fangoso, sa [fan-go'-so, sah], *a.* Muddy, miry.

fanón [fah-none'], *m.* 1. *(Med.)* A cylindrical splint made of barley-straw, and used in fractures of the thigh. 2. *(Vet.)* The tuft of hairs back of a horse's head. 3. A fold in the lower part of the neck of the ox and the sheep.

fantasear [fan-tah-say-ar'], *vn.* To fancy, to imagine.

fantasía [fan-tah-see'-ah], *f.* 1. Fancy, imagination. 2. Fantasy, the power of imagining. (facultad). 3. Fancy, caprice, humor, whim, conceit (capricho). 4. Fancy, an opinion bred rather by the imagination than the reason. 5. Fancy, fiction, conception, image. 6. Presumption, vanity (afectación). 7. *pl.* A string of pearls. 8. *(Naut.) V.* ESTIMA. *(Mus.)* A kind of composition whose origin dates from the 16th century.

fantasioso, sa [fan-tah-se-o'-so, sah], *a. (coll.)* Fantastic, vain, conceited.

fantasma [fan-tahs'-mah], *m.* 1. Phantom, a fancied vision. 2. A vain, presumptuous man (presumido). 3. Image of some object which remains impressed on the mind. *-f.* 1. Ghost, Specter, apparition, a scarecrow to frighten simple folks. 2. *(Med.)* Lesion or defect of the visual organs.

fantasmada [fan-tahs-mah'-dah], *f.* Bluster, bravado.

fantasmagoría [fan-tas-mah-go-ree´-ah], *f.* Phantasmagoria, an optical illusion.

fantasmagórico, ca [fan-tas-mah-go'-re-co, cah], *a.* Phantasmagoric.

fantasmal [fan-tahs'-mah], *a.* Ghostly; phantom.

fantasmón [fan-tas-mone'], *m. aug.* presumptuous coxcomb, a vain pretender.

fantásticamente [fan-tahs'-te-cah-men-tay], *adv.* Fantastically, fallaciously, pompously, conceitedly, grotesquely.

fantástico, ca [fan-tahs'-te-co, cah], *a.* 1. Fantastic, whimsical, fanciful (caprichoso). 2. Fantastic, imaginary, fantasied, subsisting only in the fancy. 3. Fantastic, unreal (extraño). 4. Fantastic, conceited, vain, presumptuous (vanidoso).

fantoche [fan-to-chay], *m.* 1. Puppet, marionette (muñeco). 2. Mediocrity, nonentity (mediocre); braggart (presumido).

faquín [fah-keen'], *m.* Porter, carrier.

faquir [fat-keer´], *m.* Fakir. *(Acad.)*

fara [fah'-rah], *f.* A kind of serpent of Africa.

farachar [fah-rah-char'], *va. (Prov.)* To beat or clean hemp.

faralá [fah-rah-lah'], *m.* 1. Flounce. *V.* FARFALÁ, VUELO. 2. Rufflet, frill.

farallón [fah-ral-lyone']. *m. (Naut.)* Small rocky island in the sea.

faramalla [fah-rah-mahl'-lyah], *f.* Bluff, deceitful chatter. *-m. & f.* Bluffer, deceitful person.

faramallear [fah-rah-mahl-lyay-ar'], *va.* To tattle, to babble.

faramallón, faramallón [fah-rah-mal-lyay´-ro, lyon'], *m. (coll.)* Tattling, deceitful man, busybody.

farándula [fah-rahn'-doo-lah], *f.* 1. Profession of a low comedian. 2. Artful trick, stratagem; humbug (labia); pack of lies (mentiras); confidence trick (trampa); wicked gossip (chisme).

farandulero [fah-ran-doo-lay'-ro], *m.* 1. Actor, player. 2. Idle tattler, deceitful talker (timador).

farandúlico, ca [fah-ran-doo'-le-co, ca], *a.* Relating to a low comedian.

faraón [fah-rah-on'], *m.* 1. Faro, game of cards. 2. An ancient dance. 3. Pharaoh, the scriptural name of Egyptian kings.

faraute [fah-rah'-oo-tay], *m.* 1. Messenger, he who carries messages. 2. *(coll.)* Principal manager or director. 3. *(coll.)* A noisy, meddling fellow. 4. Player who recites the prologue of a play.

farcinador [far-the-nah-dor'], *m. (Prov.)* One who stuffs or fills something.

farda [fahr'-dah], *f.* 1. A kind of tax or tribute formerly paid by foreigners in Spain. 2. Bundle of clothing. 3. Notch in a timber for joining with another.

fardacho [far-dah'-cho], *m. (Prov.)* V. LAGARTO.

fardada [far-dah'-dah], *f.* Show, display; piece of showmanship. **Pegarse una fardada,** to swank.

fardaje [far-dah'-hay], *m.* Luggage.

fardar [far-dar'], *va.* To furnish or supply with clothes. *-vn.* 1. To give tone, to be classy (objeto). **Es un coche que farda mucho,** it's a car with a lot of class. 2. To show off (persona). 3. To boast.

fardel [far-del'], *m.* 1. Bag, knapsack. 2. Parcel, bundle (bulto).

fardería [far-day-ree'-ah], *f.* A collection of bundles or packages, luggage. V. FARDAJE.

fardillo [far-deel'-lyo], *m. dim.* A small bundle, a parcel.

fardo [far'-do], *m.* Bale of goods, parcel, bundle, pack, package.

farellón [fah-rel-lyone'], *m.* 1. Point, cape, headland. 2. Rock, cliff in the sea.

farfalá [far-fah-lah'], *f.* Flounce, ornament of a gown or curtain; furbelow. V. VUELO.

farfallás [far-fal-lyahs'], *f. pl. (Bot. Prov.)* V. BARBAJAS.

farfalloso, sa [far-fal-lyo'-so, sah], *a. (Prov.)* Stammering.

farfán [far-fahn'], *m.* A name given to Christian horsemen who served Mohammedan princes.

farfante, farfantón [far-fahn'-tay, far-fan-tone'], *m.* A boasting babbler.

farfantonada, farfantonería [far-fan-to-nah'-dah], *f.* Idle boast.

fárfara [far'-fah-rah], *f.* 1. *(Bot.)* Colt's foot. 2. Membrane which covers the white of an egg.

farfulla [far-fool'-lyah], *m.* Mumbler, a stammering, talkative person (tartamudez).

farfulladamente [far-fool-lyah'-dah-men-tay], *adv.* Stammeringly.

farfullador, ra [far-fool-lyah-dor', rah], *m. & f.* Stammerer, mumbler, jabberer.

farfullar [far-foo-lyar'], *va.* 1 To talk quickly and stammeringly, to talk low and quick. 2. *(Met.)* To do in a hurry with confusion.

farfullero, ra [far-fool-lyay'-ro, rah], *a.* 1. Mumbling, talking unintelligibly 2. Hurried and confused in action.

fargallón, na [far-gal-lyone', nah], *a. & m. & f. (coll.)* Applied to those who are careless or dirty in their dress, and to those who do things hurriedly.

farináceo, [fah-re-nah-thay-o, ah], *a.* Farinaceous, mealy, starchy.

farinetas [fah-re-nay'-tas], *f. pl. (Prov.)* Fritters made of flour, honey, and water.

faringe [fah-reen'-hay], *f. (Anat.)* Pharynx.

faríngeo, gea [fah-reen'-hay-o, ah], *a.* Pharyngeal, relating to the pharynx.

faringitis [fah-rin-hee'-tis], *f. (Med.)* Pharingitis.

farisaico, ca [fah-re-sah´-e-co, cah], *a.* Pharisaical, pharisaic.

farisaismo [fah-re-sah-ees-mo], *m.* Pharisaism.

fariseo [fah-re-say'-o], *m.* 1. A Pharisee.

farmacéutico, ca [far-mah-thay'-oo-te-co, cah], *a.* Pharmaceutical.*-m.* Pharmacist.

farmacia [far-mah'-the-ah], *f.* 1. Pharmacy, the art of preparing medicines (ciencia). 2. Pharmacy, the shop where they are prepared and sold. 3. A collection of medications.

fármaco [far'-mah-co], *m.* V. MEDICAMENTO.

farmacología [far-mah-co-lo-hee'-ah], *f.* Pharmacology, the knowledge of medicines.

farmacológico, ca [far-mah-co-lo'-he-co, cah], *a.* Pharmacological, relating to drugs.

farmacólogo [far-mah-co'-lo-go], *m.* Pharmacologist, a writer upon medicines.

farmacopea [far-mah-co-pay'-ah], *f.* Pharmacopoeia.

farmacópola [far-mah-co'-po-lah], *m. (coll.)* Apothecary, pharmaceutist, pharmacopolist.

farmacopólico, ca [far-mah-co-po'-le-co, cah], *a. (coll.)* Pharmaceutical, pharmaceutic.

farnero [far-nay´-ro], *m. (Prov.)* Receiver of rents.

faro [fah'-ro], *m.* 1. Pharos, a lighthouse (torre); beacon (señal). 2. *(Naut.)* Light, lantern; *(Aut.)* headlamp, headlight. **Faro antiniebla,** fog-lamp. **Faro piloto,** rear light.

farol [fah-ro-le'], *m.* 1. A lantern (linterna); headlamp. **Farol de la calle,** streetlamp. 2. Lamppost (farola); handstand (gimnasia). 3. Wrapping of tobacco packet (envase). 4. Swank (ostentación). **Echarse un farol,** to shoot a line. 5. Lie, fib (mentira). 6. Bluff (juego).

farola [fah-ro'-lah], *f.* A lantern of great size.

farolear [fah-ro-lay-ar'], *vn. (coll.)* To strut, to make an ostentatious parade.

farolero [fah-ro-lay'-ro], *m.* 1. One who makes lanterns. 2. Lamplighter. *(coll.)* V. FAROLÓN.

farolico [fah-ro-lee'-co], *m. dim.* Small lantern. **Farolico de jardín,** Indian heartseed, smooth-leaved heartseed.

farolillo, ito [fah-ro-leel'-lyo, ee'to], *m. dim.* Small lantern. **Farolillo de jardín,** *(Bot.)* V. FAROLICO DE JARDÍN.

farolón [fah-ro-lone'], *m.* 1. *(coll.)* A boasting person 2. *(Aug.)* A large lantern.

farota [fah-ro-tah'], *f. (Prov.)* A brazen-faced woman, without sense or judgment.

farotón [fah-roh-tone'], *m. (Prov.)* A brazen-faced, stupid fellow.

farotona [fah-roh-to'-nah], *f.* Tall slovenly woman.

farpa [far'-pah], *f. pl.* Any of the notches, hollows, or segments of circles marked on the edge of a thing.

farpado, da [far-pah'-do, dah], *a.* Scalloped, notched.

farra [far´-rah], *f. (Zool.)* A kind of salmon.

farra [far-rah], *f.* 1. Spree, party, carousal (juerga). **Ir de juerga,** to go on a spree. 2. Mockery, teasing (mofa).

fárrago [far'-rah-go], or **farrago** [far-rah'-go], *m.* Farrago, a confused mass of ingredients; a medley.

farraguista [far-rah-gees'-tah], *m.* A pedantic scholar; one vain of useless learning.

farro [far'-ro], *m.* 1. Peeled barley, barley freed from the husk. 2. A sort of husked wheat.

farropea [far-ro-pay'-ah], *f. (Prov.)* V. ARROPEA.

farruco [far-roo'-co], *a.* Pig-headed (agresivo).

farsa [far'-sah], *f.* 1. Farce, a ludicrous dramatical composition, or representation 2. Company of players.

farsanta [far-sahn'-tah], *f.* An actress.

farsante [far-sahn'-tay], *m.* 1. An actor, a player. 2. A pretender, a deceiver.

farsista [far-sees'-tah], *com.* A writer of farces.

fartal, farte [far-tahl, far-tay], *m. (Prov.)* Fruit-tart or pie.

fartriquera [far-tre-kay'-rah], *f. (Prov.)* V. FALTRIQUERA.

fas (por), o por nefas [por fas oh por nay'-fas], *adv.* Justly or unjustly.

fascal [fas-cahl'], *m. (Prov.)* Shock, a pile of sheaves of corn.

fasciculado, da [fas-the-coo-lah'-do, dah], *a.* Fasciculate, composed of or growing in bundles.

fascicular [fas-the-coo-lar'], *a. (Bot.)* Fascicular, disposed in bundles.

fascículo [fas-thee'-coo-lo], *m*. 1. A bundle, armful, the quantity of plants which may be carried under the arm. 2. Fascicle, a number of printed sheets stitched together.

fascinación [fas-the-nah-the-on'], *f*. 1 Fascination, the power or act of bewitching; enchantment. 2. Imposition, deceit.

fascinador, ra [fas-the-nah-dor, rah], *m*. & *f*. Fascinator, charmer. *-a*. Fascinating.

fascinante [fas-the-nahn'-tay], *pa*. & *m*. ×& *f*. Fascinator, fascinating.

fascinar [fas-the-nar'], *va*. 1. To fascinate, to bewitch (hechizar), to enchant. 2. To deceive, to impose upon.

fascismo [fas-thees'-mo], *m*. Fascism.

fascista [fas-thees'-tah], *a*. & *m*. & *f*. Fascist.

fase [fah'-say], *f*: 1. (*Ast*.) Phase of the moon or planets. 2. (*Dep*.) Half. **Estar en fase ascendente**, to be on one's way up.

fasma [fahs'-mah], *f*. (*Zool*.) Walking stick, phasma.

fásoles [fah'-so-les], *m*. *pl*. Kidney-beans, haricots.

fastbus [fast-boos], *m*. Fastbus.

fastial [fas-te-ahl'], *m*. Pyramid placed on the top of an edifice.

fastidiar [fas-te-de-ar'], *va*. 1. To excite, to disgust. 2. To look on with dislike or abhorrence (dar asco a). 3. To grate, to offend by something harsh or vexatious. 4. To annoy, to bother, to vex (molestar); to bore (aburrir). **Eso me fastidia terriblemente**, it annoys me no end. *-vr*. 1. To loathe, to feel disgust or abhorrence, to weary, to be weary (aburrirse). 2. To suffer damage or loss. 3. To get cross (enojarse). **¡Para que te fastidies!** so there!

fastidio [fas-tee'-de-o], *m*. 1. Squeamishness, arising from a weak or disordered stomach, or from a bad smell. 2. Weariness, lassitude, fatigue, ennui. 3. Distaste, disgust, fastidiousness (molestia). 4. Disgust, repugnance (asco). 5. Loathing.

fastidiosamente [fas-te-de-o-sah-men´-tay], *adv*. Fastidiously.

fastidioso, sa [fas-te-de-o'-so, sah], *a*. 1 Fastidious, squeamish, delicate to a vice. 2. Loathsome, nauseous, mawkish. 3. Tedious, livelong (aburrido). 4. Disdainful, disgusted (asqueroso).

fastigio [fas-tee'-he-o], *m*. (*Arch*.) 1. Pinnacle, the top of anything which ends in a point. 2. The top of trees. 3. Summit, meridian.

fasto [fahs'-to], *m*. 1. Haughtiness, pride. 2. Splendor, pageantry, pomp, grandeur.

fastosamente [fas-to-sah-men´-tay], *adv*. Pompously, gaudily, magnificently.

fastoso, fastuoso, sa [fas-to'-so, fas-too-o' so, sah], *a*. Proud, haughty, ostentatious: gaudy.

fatal [fah-tahl'], *a*. 1. Fatal, ominous, proceeding by destiny. 2. Fatal (mortal), deadly, mortal, destructive. 3. Unfortunate. 3. Irrevocable; unavoidable (inevitable). 4. Awful, ghastly, rotten (horrible). **Tiene un inglés fatal**, he speaks awful English.

fatalidad [fah-tah-le-dahd'], *f*. 1. Fatality, predetermined order of things and events (destino). 2. Fatality, tendency to danger, mischance, ill luck, ill fortune (desdicha).

fatalismo [fah-tah-lees'-mo], *m*. Fatalism.

fatalista [fah-tah-lees´-tah], *m*. Fatalist, predestinarian.

fatalmente [fah-tal-men-tay], *adv*. Fatally, ominously.

fatídicamente [fah-tee'-de-cah-men-tay], *adv*. 1. Prophetically. 2. Fatefully, ominously.

fatídico, ca [fah-tee'-de-co, cah], *a*. Fatidical, prophetic of gloom (profético). 2. Fateful (de mal agüero).

fatiga [fah-tee'-gah], *f*. 1 Toil, hard labor, fatigue, lassitude (cansancio). 2. Hardship oppression. 3. Anguish, grief, painfulness, importunity. **Fatiga cerebral**, mental fatigue.

fatigadamente [fah-te-gah-dah-men'-tay], *adv*. With difficulty.

fatigador, ra [fah-te-gah-dor', rah], *m*. & *f*. Molester.

fatigar [fah-te-gar'], *va*. 1. To fatigue, to tire (cansar), to molest (molestar), to weary, to harass, to gall. 2. To desolate

or lay waste by warlike incursion or invasion. *-vr*. To tire or be tired, to fail with weariness.

fatigosamente [fah-te-go-sah-men-tay]. *adv*. Painfully, wearisomely, tediously.

fatigoso, sa [fah-te-go'-so, sah], *a*. 1. Tiresome (molesto), troublesome. 2. Anxious, painful. 3. Tiring, exhausting, fatiguing (que cansa).

fatuidad [fah-too-e-dahd'], *f*. 1. Fatuity, foolishness, weakness of mind. 2. A stupid speech, a foolish action.

fatuo, tua [fah'-too-o, ah], *a*. Fatuous (necio), stupid, foolish, coxcombical, foppish, conceited (vanidoso), crazy.

fauces [fah'-oo-thes], *f*. *pl*. Fauces, gullet.

fauna [fah'-oo-nah], *f*. 1. Fauna, the whole of the animals belonging to a region or country. 2. A work in which these are described.

fausto, ta [fah'-oos-to, tah], *a*. Happy, fortunate, prosperous, successful.

fausto [fah'-oos-to], *m*. Splendor, pomp, pageantry, ostentation, gaudiness, gaiety; grandeur, greatness; luxury.

faustoso sa [fah-oos-to'-so, sah], *a*. Fastuous, haughty, proud, ostentatious, gaudy.

fautor, ra [fah-oo-tor', rah], *m*. & *f*. Countenancer, abetter, furtherer, favorer, supporter.

fautoría [fa-oo-to-ree'-ah], *f*. Aid, favor, auxiliary.

favo [fah'-vo], *m*. (*Med*.) V. AVISPERO. Favus; carbuncle.

favonio [fah-vo-ne-o], *m*. Westerly wind, zephyr.

favor [fah-vor'], *m*. 1. Favor, protection, support (apoyo), countenance, help. 2. Favor, kindness granted, good turn, gift (regalo), grace (gracia); comfort. 3. Compliment, an expression of civility and kindness. 4. Favor, love-favor, something given by a lady to be worn. **A favor de**, on behalf of, on account of. **Por favor**, please. **Haga el favor de no fumar**, please be so good as to refrain from smoking. **Estar en favor**, to be in favor. **A favor de la marea**, helped by the tide. **Gozar del favor de alguien**, to be in somebody's favor. **Tener algo en su favor**, to have something in one's favor.

favorable [fah-vo-rah'-blay], *a*. Favorable, advantageous, propitious, kind, friendly, gracious.

favorablemente [fah-vo-rah-blay-men'-tay], *adv*. Favorably.

favorcillo [fah-vor-theel'-lyo], *m*. *dim*. A small favor.

favorecedor, ra [fah-vo-ray-thay-dor´, rah], *m*. & *f*. Favorer, countenancer, friend, helper, well-wisher.

favorecer [fah-vo-ray-therr'], *va*. 1. To favor, to protect, to help (amparar), to countenance, to accredit, to abet. 2. To grant favors. **Favorecerse de alguno or de alguna cosa**, to avail oneself of a person's favor or support, or of any other kind of protection. *-vr*. To help one another. (*Yo favorezco, yo favorezca*, from *Favorecer*. V. ABORRECER.)

favoritismo [fah-vo-re-tees'-mo], *m*. Favoritism, nepotism.

favorito, ta [fah-vo-ree'-to, tah], *a*. Favorite, beloved, regarded with favor, darling.

favorito, ta [fah-vo-ree'-to, tah], *m*. & *f*. 1. Favorite, one chosen as a companion by a superior. 2. Favorite, court minion. 3. Favorite, darling. fondling.

fax [fax], *m*. Fax.

fayado [fah-yah'-do], *m*. (*Prov*.) A small garret or lumber-room.

fayanca [fah-yahn'-cah], *f*. Position of the body, in which it does not stand firm and steady.

fayanco [fah-yahn'-co], *m*. A flat basket made of osier.

faz [fath], *f*. 1. Face. V. ROSTRO. 2. Front, the fore part of a building or any other thing. V. HAZ. **Faz a faz**, face to face. **A prima faz**, at first sight.

fe [fay], *f*. 1. Faith, belief of the revealed truths of religion. 2. Faith, trust in God. 3. Faith, testimony, credit, credence, confidence, trust. 4. Promise given. 5. Assertion, asseveration. 6. Certificate (certificado), testimony. **Dar fe**, to attest, to certify. **Poseedor de buena fe**, a bona fide possessor, one who thinks himself the right owner, although he is not. **De buena fe**, with truth and sincerity. **A fe**, in truth, in good earnest. **A fe mía** or **por mi fe**, upon my honor. **A la buena fe**, with candor and sincerity without malice. **En fe**, consequently. **De mala fe**, craftily, deceitfully, cunningly, fallaciously. **Fe de bautismo**, certificate of baptism.

fea [fay-ah], *f.* Ugly woman, plain girl. **Ser la fea del baile**, to be a wallflower.

fealdad [fay-al-dahd'], *f.* 1. Ugliness, deformity; disproportion of the parts which compose a whole. 2. Homeliness; hard favoredness: hideousness. 3. *(Met.)* Turpitude, dishonesty, foulness, moral depravity.

feamente [fay-ah-men'-tay], *adv.* 1. Uglily, deformedly. 2. *(Met.)* Brutally, inordinately.

feazo, za [fay-ah-tho, thah], *a. aug.* Very ugly or deformed.

febeo, bea [fay-bay'-o, ah], *a. (Poet.)* Relating to Phoebus, or the sun.

feble [fay'-blay], *a.* 1. Weak, faint, feeble. 2. Among jewellers, mintmen, and silversmiths, deficient in weight or quality (plata, diamantes).

feble [fay'-blay], *m.* Light money or coin.

feblemente [fay-blay-men'-tay], *adv.* Feebly.

febo [fay-bo], *m. (Poet.)* Phoebus, the sun.

febrero [fay-bray'-ro], *m.* February.

febricitante [fay-bre-the-tahn'-tay], *a. V.* CALENTURIENTO.

febrífugo, ga [fay-bree'-foo-go, gah], *a.* Febrifuge: also used as a substantive.

febril [fay-breel'], *a.* Febrile.

fecal [fay-cahl'], *a.* Feculent, excrementitious, fecal.

fécula [fay'-coo-lah], *f.* Fecula, a substance obtained by bruising vegetables in water; starch.

feculencia [fay-coo-len'-the-ah], *f.* Feculence, dregs, lees.

feculento, ta [fay-coo-len'-to, tah], or **feculoso, sa,** *a.* Feculent, foul, dreggy.

fecundación [fay-coon-dah-the-on'], *f* Fecundation, making fruitful or prolific.

fecundamente [fay-coon-dah-men'-tay], *adv.* Fertilely, fruitfully.

fecundante [fay-coon-dahn'-tay], *a. & pa.* Fructifying, making fruitful.

fecundar [fay-coon-dar'], *va.* To fertilize, to make fruitful, to fructify.

fecundativo, va [fay-coon-dah-tee'-vo, vah], *a.* Fertilizing, fructifying.

fecundidad [fay-coon-de-dahd'], *f.* Fecundity, fertility, fruitfulness.

fecundizar [fay-coon-de-thar], *va.* To fecundate, to fertilize, to fructify.

fecundo, da [fay-coon'-do, dah], *a.* 1. Fecund, fruitful, fertile, prolific. 2. *(Fig.)* Fruitful; copious (copioso), abundant; productive (productivo). **Fecundo de palabras**, fluent. **Un libro fecundo en ideas**, a book full of ideas.

fecha [fay'-chah], *f.* Date of a letter or other writing. **Fecha tope**, closing date. **A partir de esta fecha**, from today. **En fecha próxima**, soon. **¿Cuál es la fecha de hoy?** What is the date today? **El año pasado por estas fechas**, this time last year.

fechar [fay-char'], *va.* To date, to put the date to a letter or other writing.

fecho [fay'-cho], *m.* **Fecho de azúcar**, chest of sugar, containing not more than twelve *arrobas* or about three hundredweight.

fecho, cha [fay'-cho, chah], *pp. irr.* of FACER. Hecho.

fechoría [fay-cho-ree'-ah], *f.* Misdeed, misdemeanor. **Cometer fechorías**, to commit misdeeds; mischief. **Los niños hicieron fechorías**, the children got up to mischief.

fechuría [fay-choo-re'-ah], *f. V.* FECHORÍA.

federación [fay-day-rah-the-on'], *f.* Federation, confederation.

federado [fay-day-rah'-do], *m.* Federate. *a.* Federate, federated.

federal [fay-day-rahl'], *a.* Federal.

federalismo [fay-day-rah-lees-mo], *m.* Federalism, political autonomy of various provinces or states.

federativo, va [fay-day-rah-tee'-vo, vah], *a.* Federative.

fehaciente [fay-ah-the-en'-tay], *a.* Authentic.

feldespato, or **feldspato** [fel-des-pah'-to, or fel-des-pah'-to], *m.* Feldspar, a common constituent of rocks; silicate of aluminum and an alkali.

feldmariscal [feld-mah-ris-cahl'], *m. (Gil.)* Fieldmarshal.

felice [fay-lee'-thay], *a. (Poet.) V.* FELIZ.

felicidad [fay-le-the-dahd'], *f.* Felicity, happiness (alegría), success, luckiness, blissfulness, blessedness, prosperity. **Felicidades**, best wishes, congratulations. **Os deseo toda clase de felicidades**, I wish you every kind of happiness. **La curva de la felicidad**, potbelly.

felicitación [fay-le-the-tah-the-on] *f.* Congratulation, felicitation, professing, joy for the happiness or success of another.

felicitar [fay-le-the-tar'], *va.* To congratulate, to compliment upon any happy event, to felicitate.

feligrés, sa [fay-le-grays', sah], *m. & f.* Parishioner, one who belongs to a parish.

feligresía [fay-le-gray-see'-ah], *f.* District of a parish, and the inhabitants of the same.

felino [fay-le'-no], *a.* Feline, cat-like.

feliz [fay-leeth'], *a.* Happy, fortunate, lucky (afortunado), prosperous, felicitous. **Y vivieron felices**, and they lived happily. **La cosa tuvo un final feliz**, the affair had a happy ending. **¡Feliz Año Nuevo!** Happy New Year! **Feliz desenlace**, happy ending. **¡Feliz viaje!** have a good journey!

felizmente [fay-leeth'-men-tay], *adv.* Happily, fortunately, luckily, felicitously.

felonía [fay-lo-nee'-ah], *f.* Treachery, disloyalty, felony.

felpa [fayl'-pah], *f.* 1. Plush, a silk stuff. 2. In jocular style, a good drubbing.

felpado, da [fel-pah'-do, dah], *a.* Shaggy, villous.

felpilla [fel-peel-lyah], *f.* Corded silk for embroidering; chenille.

felposo, sa [fel-po'-so, sah], *a.* 1. Felted, with interlaced fibres. 2. Plush-covered.

felpudo [fel-poo'-do], *m.* Mat, doormat (alfombrilla).

felpudo, da [fel-poo'-do, dah], *a.* Plushy, velvety. *V.* FELPADO.

femenil [fay-may-neel'], *a.* Feminine, womanish, womanly.

femenilmente [fay-may-neel'-men-tay], *adv.* Effeminately, womanishly, womanly.

femenino, na [fay-may-nee'-no, nah], *a.* 1. Feminine, belonging to women, female (sexo). 2. Feminine, of the feminine gender. **Equipo femenino**, women's team. **Del género femenino**, of the feminine gender.

fementídamente [fay-men-tee'-dah-men-tay], *adv.* Falsely, fallaciously.

fementido, da [fay-men-tee'-do, dah], *a.* False, unfaithful, deficient in the performance of one's promise.

feminidad [fay-me-ne-dahd'], *f.* Femininity.

feminismo [fay-me-nees'-mo], *m.* Feminism, women's liberation.

feminista [fay-me-nees'-tah], *a. & m. & f.* Feminist.

femoral [fay-mo-rahl'], *a.* Femoral, belonging to the thighs.

fémur [fay'-mor], *m.* Femur.

fenacetina [fay-nah-thay-tee'-nah], *f. (Med.)* Phenacetin.

fenda [fen'-dah], *f.* A crack in the bark of trees.

fendiente [fen-de-en'-tay], *m.* Gash, a deep cut or wound.

fenecer [fay-nay-therr'], *vn.* 1. To terminate, to be at an end (terminar). 2. To degenerate, to decline, 3. To die (morir) -*va.* To finish, to conclude, to close. (*Yo fenezco, yo fenezca*, from *Fenecer. V.* ABORRECER.)

fenecimiento [fay-nay-the-me-en'-to], *m.* 1. Close, finish, termination, end. 2. Settling of an account. 3. Dying.

fenedal [fay-nay-dahl'], *m. (Prov.)* Hay-loft.

fenicio, cia [fay-nee'-the-o, ah], *a.* Phoenician.

fénico [fay'-ne-co], *a.* Phenic, carbolic. **Ácido fénico**, Phenol, carbolic acid.

fénix [fay'-nix], *m.* 1. Phoenix, fabulous bird. 2. *(Met.)* That which is exquisite or unique of its kind.

fenol [fay-nole'], *n.* Phenol, carbolic acid.

fenomenal [fay-no-may-nahl'], *a.* 1. Phenomenal. 2. Tremendous, terrific (estupendo).

fenomenalismo [fay-no-may-nah-lees'-mo], *m.* Phenomenalism, materialism, a doctrine which gives importance only to what can affect our senses.

fenomenalmente [fay-no-may-nal'-men-tay], *adv.* Terrifically.

fenómeno [fay-no'-may-no], *m.* Phenomenon. -*a.* Great, marvelous. **Una chica fenómena,** a smashing girl. -*adv.* **Lo hemos pasado fenómeno,** we had a terrific time.

feo, ea [fay'-o, ah], *a.* 1. Ugly, deformed, hideous (aspecto), haggard, grim: homely. **Más feo que Picio,** as ugly as sin. 2. Causing horror or adversion. 3. Bad, nasty (olor); dirty (jugada); nasty, awful (tiempo); nasty (situación). **Eso es muy feo,** that's nasty. **Esto se está poniendo feo,** this is beginning to look bad. -*m.* Insult, slight. **Hacer un feo a uno,** to insult somebody.

feracidad [fay-rah-the-dahd'], *f.* Feracity, fecundity, fruitfulness, fertility.

feral [fay-rahl'], *a.* Cruel, bloodthirsty.

feraz [fay-rath'], *a.* 1. Fertile, fruitful, feracious. 2. Abundant, copious, plentiful.

féretro [fay'-ray-tro], *m.* Bier, coffin, hearse.

feria [fay-re-ah], *f.* 1. Any day of the week, exempting Saturday and Sunday. 2. Fair, an annual or stated meeting of sellers and buyers (mercado). 3. Rest, repose. 4. Carnival (carnaval). **Feria de libros,** book fair. **Feria de muestras,** trade show. 5. Holiday (descanso). 6. Fun fair.

feriado, da [fay-re-ah'-do, dah], *a.* **Día feriado,** a holiday. -*pp.* of FERIAR.

ferial [fay-re-ahl'], *a.* 1. Belonging to fairs. 2. Ferial, relating to the days of the week. -*m. & f.* Market, fair.

feriante [fay-re-ahn'-tay], *m.* (*Prov.*) One who trades at fairs (vendedor).

feriar [fay-re-ar'], *va.* 1. To sell, to buy; to exchange one thing for another (comerciar). 2. To give fairings, to make presents at a fair. 3. *V.* SUSPENDER.

ferino, na [fay-ree'-no, nah], *a.* Ferine, wild, savage, ferocious.

fermata [fer-mah'-tah], *f.* (*Mus.*) A pause or hold.

fermentación [fer-men-tah-the-on'], *f.* Fermentation.

fermentar [fer-men-tar'], *vn. & vn.* To ferment. **Hacer fermentar,** to ferment or to cause to ferment, to heat.

fermentativo, va [fer-men-tah-tee'-vo, vah], *a.* Fermentative.

fermentescible [fer-men-tes-thee'-blay], *a.* Fermentable, capable of fermentation.

fermento [fer-men'-to], *m.* 1. Ferment. 2. Leaven, leavening. 3. Ferment, intestine motion, tumult.

fernambuco [fer-nah-mboo-'co], *m.* A dyewood of Brazil.

fernandina [fer-nan-dee'-nah], *f.* Kind of linen.

ferocidad [fay-ro-the-dahd'], *f.* Ferocity, wildness, ferociousness, fierceness, savageness, fury.

feróstico, ca [fay-ros'-te-co, cah], *a.* (*coll.*) Irritable, wayward.

feroz [fay-roth'], *a.* Ferocious, cruel, savage, fierce, ravenous, heathenish. **El lobo feroz,** the big bad wolf. **Tener un hambre feroz,** to be ravenous.

ferozmente [fay-roth-men'-tay], *adv.* Ferociously, folly, savagely.

ferrada [fer-rah'-dah], *f.* Iron club, used formerly as an offensive and defensive weapon.

ferrado [fer-rah'-do], *m.* (*Prov.*) 1. Measure for corn, which makes about the fourth part of a bushel. 2. Measure for land of twelve yards square.

ferrar [fer-rar'], *va.* 1. To garnish with points of iron; to strengthen with iron plates. 2. *V.* HERRAR.

férreo, rea [fer-ray-o, ah], *a.* 1. Ferreous, made of iron or containing iron. 2. Iron (época). 3. Iron, harsh, stern, severe. 4. (*Ferro.*) Rail. **Volutad férrea,** iron will. **Vía férrea,** railroad.

ferrería [fer-ray-ree'-ah], *a.* Iron works, where iron is manufactured.

ferrete [fer-ray'-tay], *m.* 1. Burnt copper or brass used to color glass. 2. Marking-iron.

ferretear [fer-ray-tay-ar'], *va.* To bind, to fasten, to mark, or work with iron.

ferretería [fer-ray-tay-ree-ah], *f.* Hardware store, ironmongery (objetos).

ferretero, ra [fer-ray-tay'-ro], *m & f.* Ironmonger, hardware dealer.

férrico, ca [fer'-re-co, cah], *a.* 1. Ferric, containing iron. 2. Ferric, pertaining to iron in its higher combinations.

férridos, das [fer'-re-dos, das], *a. pl.* Simple bodies whose type is iron.

ferro [fer'-ro], *m.* (*Naut.*) Anchor.

ferrocarril [fer-ro-car-reel'], *m.* Railroad, railway. **Ferrocarril funicular,** cable railroad. **Ferrocarril subterráneo,** subway. **Ferrocarril de vía estrecha,** narrow-gauge railroad.

ferrocarrilero, ra [fer-ro-car-re-lay'-ro, rah], *a.* Railway. -*m.* Railroad man, railroad worker.

ferrón [fer-rone'], *m.* (*Prod.*) 1. Iron manufacturer. 2. Ironmonger.

ferroso, sa [fer-ro'-so, sah], *a.* Ferrous, obtained from iron, pertaining to iron in its lower combinations.

ferrotipia [fer-ro-tee'-pe-ah], *f.* Tintype, ferrotype.

ferroviario, ria [fer-ro-ve-ah'-re-o, re-ah], *a.* Railroad, pertaining to a railroad. -*a.* Railroadman, railroad employee.

ferrugiento, ta [fer-roo-he-en'-to, tah], *a.* Irony, belonging to or containing iron.

ferrugíneo, nea [fer-roo-hee'-nay-o, ah], *a.* Ferruginous.

ferruginoso, sa [fer-roo-he-no'-so, sah], *a.* Ferruginous.

ferry [fer'-ree], *m.* Ferry.

fértil [fayr'-teel], *a.* Fertile, fruitful, copious, plentiful, fertile (imaginación).

fertilidad [fer-te-le-dahd'], *f.* Fertility, copiousness, plenty, fruitfulness.

fertilizantes [fer-te-le-thahn'-tess], *m. pl.* Fertilizers, fertilizing agents.

fertilizar [fer-te-le-thar'], *va.* To fertilize, to fructify, to make the soil fruitful.

fértilmente [fayr'-teel-men-tay], *adv.* Fertilely.

férula [fay'-roo-lah], *f.* 1. Ferule (del maestro), cane. 2. (*Met.*) Rule, yoke, authority 3. (*Bot.*) Ferula, a genus of umbelliferous plants.

feruláceo, ea [fay-roo-lah'-thay-o, ah], *a.* Like a ferule.

ferventísimo, fervientísimo [fer-ven-tee'-se-mo, mah], *a. sup.* Fervent, ardent in piety, warm in zeal.

férvido, da [fayr'-ve-do, dah], *a.* Fervid, ardent.

ferviente [fer-ve-en'-tay], *a.* Fervent, ardent. *V.* FERVOROSO.

fervor [fer-vor'], *m.* 1. Fervor, violent heat, warmth. 2. Fervor, fervidness, zeal, ardor, eagerness. 3. Fervor, fervency, ardor of piety.

fervorizar [fer-vo-re-thar'], *va.* To heat, to inflame, to incite.

fervorosamente [fer-vo-ro-sah-men'-tay], *adv.* Fervently, ardently.

fervoroso, sa [fer-vo-ro'-so, sah], *a.* Fervent, ardent in piety, warm in zeal; active, officious.

festejador, ra [fes-tay-hah-dor', rah], *m. & f.* Feaster, courtier, entertainer.

festejar [fes-tay-har'], *va.* 1. To entertain, to feast (persona). 2. To court, to woo (mujer), to make love. 3. To celebrate or solemnize an event (aniversario, ocasión etc).

festejo, festeo [fes-tay'-ho, fes-tay'-ho], *m.* 1. An expression of joy for the happiness of another. 2. (*Coll.*) Courtship, solicitation of a woman in marriage (cortejo). 3. Feast, entertainment (fiesta). 4. Obsequiousness. **Hacer festejos a uno,** to make a great fuss of somebody.

festero [fes-tay'-ro], *m.* Director of church music on festive occasions.

festín [fes-teen'], *m.* Feast, entertainment, banquet.

festinación [fes-te-nah-the-on'], *f.* Speed, haste, hurry.

festival [fes-te-vahl'], *m.* (*Neol.*) Festival, a great vocal and instrumental concert.

festivamente [fes-te-vah-men'-tay], *adv.* Festively, wittily, jovially.

festividad [fes-te-ve-dahd'], *f.* 1. Festivity, rejoicing, gaiety, merrymaking (actos). 2. Solemn manner of celebrating an event.

festivo, va [fes-tee'-vo, vah], *a.* 1. Festive, gay, joyful, light-hearted (alegre). 2. Festival, festal, pertaining to feasts. 3. Witty, facetious, humorous (gracioso). **Día festivo**, a holiday.

festón [fes-tone'], *m.* 1. Garland, wreath of flowers. 2. Festoon.

festonear [fes-to-nay-ar'], *va.* To embellish with festoons.

festuca [fes-too'-cah], *f. (Bot.) V.* CAÑUELA. Fescue-grass, valuable for pasturage.

fetal [fay-tahl'], *a.* Foetal.

fetichismo [fay-te-chees'-mo], *m.* Fetishism.

fetichista [fay-te-chees'-tah], *m & f.* Fetishistic.

fétido, da [fay'-te-do, dah], *a.* Fetid, stinking, foul-smelling.

feto [fay'-to], *m.* 1. *(Bio.)* Foetus. 2. Abortion, monster (monstruo).

feúcho, cha [fay-oo'-cho, chah], *a.* Ugly, repulsive.

feudal [fay-oo-dahl'], *a.* Feudal, feodal.

feudalidad [fay-oo-dah-le-dahd'], *f.* Feodality, feudality.

feudalismo [fay-oo-dah-lees'-mo], *m.* Feudalism.

feudar [fay-oo-dahr'], *va. V.* ENFEUDAR.

feudatario [fay-oo-dah-tah'-re-o], *m.* Feudatary, feodatary.

feudatario, ria [fay-oo-dah-tah'-re-o, ah], *a.* Feudatary, feudary.

feudista [fay-oo-dees'-tah], *m.* Feudist, a writer upon feudal law.

feudo [fay'-oo-do], *m.* 1. Fief, all lands or tenements held by acknowledgment of a superior lord, feod, feud, manor. 2. Tribute or rent paid to a feudal lord.

fez [feth]. *m.* Fez, a woollen cap, white or red, used in the Orient and in Northern Africa.

fiabilidad [fe-ah-be-le-dahd'], *f.* Reliability, trustworthiness; credibility.

fiable [fe-ah'-blay], *a.* Trustworthy, reliable.

fiado, da [fe-ah'-do, dah], *a. & pp.* of FIAR. Confident, trusting. **Al fiado**, upon trust. **En fiado**, upon bail. **Comprar géneros, al fiado**, to buy goods on credit. **Dar fiado**, to give credit.

fiador, ra [fe-ah-dor', rah], *m. & f.* 1. One who trusts another. 2. Bondsman, guarantor, surety, one who becomes security for another, *m,* 3. The loop of a cloak. 4. *(Falcon.)* Creance. 5. Bolt or instrument with which something is made fast; stop, catch, safety catch, ratchet, detent, tumbler of a lock.

fiambrar [fe-am-brar'], *va.* To boil or roast meat, and leave it to cool for eating.

fiambre [fe-ahm'-bray], *m.* 1. Cold meat preserved for use. 2. Corpse, stiff (cadáver). **El pobre está fiambre**, the poor chap is stone dead. 3. *-a.* 1. Cold (carne). 2. *(coll.)* Of a long standing.

fiambrera [fe-am-bray'-rah], *f.* 1. Pannier or basket in which cold meat is carried into the country (canasto). 2. *(coll.)* Stupid or foolish speech.

fiambrero [fe-am-bray'-ro], *m.* One who takes care of the larder, or of the cold meat preserved for use.

fiancilla [fe-an-theel'-lyah], *f.* Binding ring of a carriage.

fianza [fe-ahn'-thah], *f.* 1. Caution, guarantee, security given for the performance of engagements (garantía). 2. Reversion. 3. Bond, security, bail. **Fianza bancaria**, bank security given in Rome to insure pensions charged on ecclesiastical works. **Dar fianza**, to give bail or a pledge. **Bajo fianza**, on bail.

fiar [fe-ar'], *va.* 1. To bail, to give bail. 2. To trust, to sell upon trust to give credit. 3. To place confidence in another, to commit to another, to credit. *-vn.* To confide, to be sure of a thing. **Ser de fiar**, to be reliable. *-vr.* **Fiarse de uno**, to trust somebody. **No me fío de él**, I don´t trust him.

fiasco [fe-ahs'-co], *m.* Failure. **Hacer fiasco**, to result in humiliating failure (teatro).

fíat [fee'-at], *m.* Fiat, blessing. **Dar el fiat**, to give one's blessing.

fibra [fee'-brah], *f.* 1. Fiber, filament, staple. **Fibra artificial**, man-made fiber. 2. Fiber, a delicate root. 3. *(Met.)* Energy of character, firmness, vigor. **Despertar la fibra sensible**, to strike a sympathetic cord. 4. *(Min.)* Vein of ore.

fibrazón [fe-brah-thone'], *f.* The whole of the ore-veins of a mine.

fibrila [fe-bree'-lah], *f. (Bot.)* Fibril, a capillary rootlet.

fibrilar [fe-bre-lar'], *a.* Fibrillar, disposed in fibrils or fine fibers.

fibrina [fe-bree'-nah], *f. (Chem.)* Fibrin, fibrine.

fibrinoso, sa [fe-bre-no'-so, sah], *a.* Fibrinous.

fibroso, sa [fe-bro'-so, sah], *a.* 1. Fibrous. 2. Energetic, firm, or vigorous in character.

ficción [fic-the-on'], *f.* 1. Fiction, the act of feigning or inventing. 2. Fiction, figment, an invention, and the thing feigned or invented. 3. Fiction, falsehood, lie. 4. Grimace, gesture. 6. Stratagem, artifice.

fice [fee'-thay], *m. (Zool.)* Whiting.

ficha [fee'-chah], *f.* 1. Counter, used in reckoning (en juegos); chip (póquer); *(Com. Fin.)* token, tally. **Ficha del dominó**, domino. 2. Card (tarjeta); registration form (hotel). **Ficha policíaca**, police record.

fichaje [fee-chah'-hay], *m.* 1. *(Dep.)* Signing-up (nuevo jugador). 2. **Buenos fichajes**, new good players, new supporters.

fichar [fee-chahr'], *va.* 1. To file, to index (ficha). 2. To file the personal (persona); to record (dato). **Le tenemos fichado**, we have his record. 3. To play (dominó). 4. To sign up (deporte).

fichero [fee-chay-ro], *m.* File (informática); filling cabinet. **Fichero fotográfico de delincuentes**, photographic records of criminals.

ficticio, cia [fec-tee'-the-o, ah], *a.* Fictitious.

ficto, ta [feec'-to, tah], *a.* 1. Feigned, counterfeited. 2. Vain, useless, of no value.

fidedigno, na [fe-day-deeg'-no], *a.* Worthy or credit, deserving of belief.

fideicomisario [fe-day-e-co-me-sah'-re-o], *m.* Trustee, fiduciary, one who holds something in trust for another.

fideicomiso [fe-day-e-co-mee'-so], *m.* Trusteeship of any executor.

fidelidad [fe-day-le-dahd'], *f.* 1. Fidelity (lealtad), honesty, veracity, faith, constancy, honor. 2. Fidelity, faithful adherence, fealty, loyalty. 3. Punctuality in the execution or performance of anything. 4. Accuracy (exactitud). 5. *(Rad.)* **Alta fidelidad**, high fidelity.

fidelísimo, ma [fe-day-lee´-se-mo, mah], *a. aug.* of FIEL.

fideos [fe-day'-os], *m. pl.* Vermicelli, noodles, spaghetti.

fiducial [fe-do-the-ahl'], *a.* 1. *(Math.)* Passing through the center of graduation, referring to a fixed line. 2. Belonging to faith or credit.

fiduciario, ria [fe-doo-the-ah'-re-o, ah], *a.* Fiduciary, belonging to a position of trust or confidence.

fiebre [fe-ay'-bray], *f.* Fever. **Fiebre amarilla**, yellow fever. **Fiebre mediterránea o de Malta**, undulant fever. **Fiebre del oro**, gold rush. **Tener fiebre**, to have a temperature.

fiebrecilla [fe-ay-bray-theel'-lyah], *f. dim.* Feveret. *V.* CALENTURILLA.

fiel [fe-ayl'], *a.* 1. Faithful, honest (fiable), loyal, upright. 2. True, right. 3. Faithful, observant of compact or promise.

fiel [fe-ayl'], *m.* 1. Inspector, supervisor (verificador) of the market, a person appointed to inspect weights and measures. 2. Needle of a balance. 3. Pivot of a steelyard. 4. Pin which keeps the blades of scissors together. 5. Catholic Christian who lives in obedience to the Church.

fielmente [fe-ayl-men'-tay], *adv.* 1. Faithfully. 2. Accurately, exactly (exactamente).

fieltro [fe-ayl'-tro], *m.* 1. Felt, a stuff used to make hats (tela). 2. A kind of hat used to keep off rain. 3. Surtout, a large great coat.

fieme [fe-ay'-may], *m. (Vet.)* Fleam, a heart-shaped lancet.

fiemo [fe-ay'-mo], *m. (Prov.)* Dung, manure.

fiera [fe-ay´-rah], *f.* 1. A wild beast (animal). 2. An inhuman, haughty and excessively choleric man, a savage. *-m & f. (Fig.)* Fiend; virago, dragon; ball on fire (en buen sentido), highly energetic person. **Como una fiera enjaulada,** like a caged tiger. **Es un fiera para el trabajo,** he´s a demon for work.

fierabrás [fe-ay-rah-brahs'], *m. (coll.)* Bully, braggart, blusterer.

fieramente [fe-ay-rah-men'-tay], *adv.* Fiercely, savagely, ferociously, haughtily.

fiereza [fe-ay-ray´-thah], *f.* 1. Fierceness, cruelty, ferocity, hardness (ferocidad). 2. Fierceness, heat of temper. 3. *(Her.)* Attitude of an animal showing its teeth. 4. Deformity, ugliness (fealdad).

fiero, ra [fe-ay´-ro, rah], *a.* 1. Fierce (feroz), cruel (cruel), bloodthirsty; ferocious, fiery. 2. Ugly, deformed (feo). 3. Rough, rude. 4. Great, huge enormous. 5. Furious, terrible; wild, savage. *-m. pl.* **Fieros,** fierce threats and bravadoes.

fierro [fe-er´-ro], *m. V.* HIERRO Brand, the mark of ownership on an animal, and frequently on other articles.

fiesta [fe-ess´-tah], *f.* 1. Feast, entertainment, rejoicing, feasting, merriment (de la ciudad). 2. Feast, festivity, festival, a church feast holiday; the day of some ecclesiastical festival. 3. Merrymaking, festivities, fun and games (juerga). **Fiesta de guardar,** day of obligation to hear mass. **Estar de fiesta,** to be merry, to be in a good mood. **Aguar la fiesta,** to spoil the fun. **No sabe de qué va la fiesta,** he hasn´t a clue. **Fiesta nacional,** public holiday. **La fiesta continuó hasta muy tarde,** the festivities went on very late. *.-pl.* 1. Vacations. **No estar para fiestas,** to be out of humor. **Fiestas reales,** royal festivals. 2. **Fiestas de pólvora,** artificial fireworks; a bonfire. 3. Caresses, nets of endearment. **Hacer fiestas,** to caress, to wheedle, to fawn. **Hacer fiesta,** to take the day off. **Aguar la fiesta,** to be a wet blanket.

figala [fe-gah'-lah], *f.* An East Indian oared boat with one mast.

figle [fee'-glay], *m. (Mus.)* Ophicleide, a bass brass instrument of 12 keys.

figón [fe-gone'], *m.* Eating house, chop house.

figonero [fe-go-nay´-ro], *m.* Keeper of an eating house.

figueral [fe-gay-rahl´], *m.* Plantation of fig trees.

figulino, na [fe-goo-lee-no, nah], *a.* Made of potter's clay.

figura [fe-goo´-rah], *f.* 1. Figure, the form of anything. **De figura entera,** full-length. 2. The shape, the particular external appearance of a thing (forma). 3. Face, mien, countenance. 4. Figure, statue, image, anything formed in resemblance of something else. 5. *(Law.)* Form, mode. 6. *(Mus.)* A musical tone; 2. motive, theme, subject. 7. *(Gram.)* Figure, any deviation from the rules of analogy or syntax. 8. *(Geom.)* Figure, a space included in certain lines. 9. *(Rhet.)* Figure, any mode of speaking in which words are distorted from their literal and primitive sense (personaje). **Natural or genio y figura hasta la sepultura,** *(Prov.)* what is bred in the bone will never come out of the flesh. 10. Figure (baile, patinaje). 11. Marionette (títere). 12. Picture card (naipes). *-m.* A foolish person assuming an air of importance and dignity. **Ser un figura,** to be a big name. *-com.* Person of a mean or ridiculous appearance. *-f. pl.* In games of cards, the king, queen, and knave.

figurable [fe-goo-rah'-blay], *a.* Figurable, that which may be figured.

figuradamente [fe-goo-rah-dah-men-tay], *adv.* Figuratively.

figurado, da [fe-goo-rah'-do, dah], *a.* Figurative, typical; not literal; rhetorical. *-pp.* of FIGURAR.

figural [fe-goo-rahl'], *a.* Figural, belonging to figures; represented by delineation.

figuranza [fe-goo-rahn´-thah], *f. (Prov.)* Resemblance.

figurar [fe-goo-rar'], *va.* 1. To figure, to form into a determinate shape. 2. To adorn with figures. *-vn.* 1. To figure (incluirse). **Los nombres no figuran aquí,** the names do not appear here. 2. *(Fig.)* To show off, to cut a dash. *-vr.* To fancy, to imagine, to believe without being able to prove. **Ya**

me lo figuraba, I thought as much. **Me figuro que es caro,** I fancy it´s dear.

figurativamente [fe-goo-rah-te-vah-men'-tay], *adv.* Figuratively.

figurativo, va [fe-goo-rah-tee'-vo, rah], *a.* 1. Figurative, typical; not literal, explanatory. 2. Symbolical, emblematic. 3. Representational (arte).

figurería [fe-goo-ray-ree'-ah], *f. V.* MUECA.

figurero, ra [fe-goo-ray'-ro, rah], *m. & f.* Mimic, a ludicrous imitator; a buffoon who copies another's actions.

figurilla, ita [fe-goo-reel'-lyah, ee'tah], *f. dim.* A small figure.

figurín [fe-goo-reen'], *m.* Fashion plate, or small model for dresses.

figurón [fe-goo-rone'], *m.* 1. *(Aug.)* A huge or enormous figure of a ridiculous appearance. 2. A low-bred person assuming an air of dignity and importance (presumido).

fija [fee´-hah], *f.* Kind of hinge.

fijación [fe-hah-the-on'], *f.* 1. Fixation, stability, firmness. 2. The act of posting up printed bills, edicts, etc. 3. Fixation, the net of fixing mercury or any other volatile spirit.

fijador ra [fe-hah-dor', rah], *a.* 1. *(Phot.)* Fixer; fixing bath. 2. **Fijador para el pelo,** hair lotion.

fijamente [fe-hah-men-tay], *adv.* 1. Firmly, assuredly. 2. Intensely, attentively. 3. Fixedly, steadfastly.

fijar [fehar'], *va.* 1. To fix, to fasten (clavar), to make fast, firm, or stable. 2. To fix, to settle, to establish (residencia), to clinch. 3. To fix, to direct without variation. 4. To fix, to deprive of volatility. 5. *(Fig.)* To settle on, to decide, to determine (determinar). **La fecha no se puede fijar con precisión,** the date cannot exactly be determined. *-vr.* 1. To fix or settle itself in a place (establecerse), to stare at (observar). 2. To fix, to determine, to resolve. **Lo malo es que no se fija,** the trouble is he doesn´t pay attention. **Fíjese bien,** pay close attention. **Fijarse en algo,** to observe something.

fijenes [fe-hay'-nes], *m. pl.* Cheeks of a press.

fijeza [fe-hay´-thah], *f.* Firmness, stability.

fijo, ja [fee-ho, hah], *a. & pp. irr.* of FIJAR. 1. Fixed, firm, secure. 2. Settled, permanent.

fila [fee´-lah], *f.* 1. A long row or series of persons or things (cola, asientos) **Una fila de coches,** a line of cars. **En fila,** in a row. 2. A line of soldiers ranged abreast or side by side. **En fila,** in a line, in a row. **Estar en filas,** to be with the colors. **Llamar a uno a filas,** to call somebody up. **Romper filas,** to break ranks.

filacteria [fe-lac-tay'-re-ah], *f.* Phylactery.

filada [fe-lah-dah], *f.* A slaty, schistose, micaceous rock, at times containing other varieties.

filagrama [fe-lah-grah-mah], *f.* A wire mould for a watermark. *Cf.* FILIGRAMA.

filamento [fe-lah-men´-to], *m.* Filament, fiber, thread.

filamentoso, sa [fe-lah-men-to´-so, sah], *a.* Filamentous.

filandria [fe-lahn´-dre-ah], *f.* Worm bred in the intestines of birds of prey.

filantropía [fe-lan-tro-pee´-ah], *f.* Philanthropy, good nature.

filantrópicamente [fe-lan-tro´-pe-cah-men-tay], *adv.* Humanely.

filantrópico [fe-lan-tro'-pe-co], **ca,** *a.* Philanthropical, philanthropic.

filántropo [fe-lahn´-tro-po], *m.* Philanthropist.

filar [fe-lar'], *a.* **Triángulo filar,** a mathematical instrument serving as a sector, for various uses.

filarete [fe-lah-ray'-tay], *m. (Naut.)* Netting put on the waist or sides of a ship.

filariosis [fe-lah-re-o'-sis], *f. (Med.)* Filariasis.

filarmonía [fe-lar-mo-nee'-ah], *f.* Love of harmony, passion for music.

filarmónico, ca [fe-lar-mo'-ne-co, cah], *a.* Philharmonic, devoted to music.

filástica [fe-lahs'-te-cah], *f. (Naut.)* Rope-yarn, yarn made of untwisted ropes. **Filástica fina para maniobras,** fine rope-yarn for running rigging.

filatelia [fe-lah-tay'-le-ah], *f.* Philately, stamp collecting.

filatélico, ca [fe-lah-tay'-le-co, cah], *a.* Philatelic.

filatelista [fe-lah-tay-lees'-tah], *m. & f.* Philatelist, stamp collector.

filatería [fe-lah-tay-ree'-ah], *f.* Verbosity, exuberance or superfluity of words.

filatero [fe-lah-tay'-ro], *m.* A verbose speaker.

filatura [fe-lah-too'-rah], *f.* The art of spinning wool, cotton, etc.

filbán [feel-bahn'], *m.* The rough edge of a knife, scissors, etc.

filderretor [fil-der-ray-tor'], *m.* Sort of superfine camlet.

filelí [fe-lay-lee'], *m.* A very thin woollen stuff; superfine flannel. It comes from Barbary.

fileno, na [fe-lay'-no, nah], *a. (coll.)* Delicate, effeminate, soft.

filcra [fe-lay'-rah], *f.* 1. A fishing net apparatus with small weights at the ends. 2. Spinneret of weaving spiders.

filete [fe-lay'-tay], *m.* 1. *(Arch.)* Fillet, a small member which appears in ornaments and mouldings, otherwise called *listel.* 2. Hem, the edge of a garment doubled and sewed. 3. A thin and small spit for roasting. 4. Welt of a shoe. 5. A twist-like ornament raised on plate. 6. Tenderloin, loin of beef (carne), fillet (pescado). **Darse el filete con,** to feel, touch up.

filetear [fe-lay-tay-ar'], *va.* To adorn with fillets.

filetón [fe-lay-tone'], *m.* 1 *(Aug.)* In architecture, a large fillet or listel 2. Kind of embroidery.

filiación [fe-leah-the-on'], *f.* 1. Filiation, the relation of a son to a father (relación); connection, relationship (de ideas etc.) 2. Dependence of some things upon others. 3. *(Mil.)* Regimental register of a soldier's height, physiognomy, age, etc. 4. Personal description; characteristics (señas).

filial [fe-le-ahl'], *a.* Filial, befitting a son.

filiar [fe-le-arl], *vn.* To prove one's descent. *-va.* To enrol a soldier.

filiatra [fe-le-ah-trah], *a. & n.* Devoted to the study of medicine. Philiater.

filiatría [fe-le-ah-tree'-ah], *f.* Love of the study of medicine.

filibote [fe-le-bo-tay], *m.* Fly boat, light vessel of 100 tons burden.

filibustero [fe-le-boos-tay'-ro] *m.* 1. Name given to freebooters or buccaneers (bucanero), who plundered America in the 17th century. 2. Filibuster, an armed adventurer invading unlawfully other people's territory

filiforme [fe-le-for-may], *a.* Filiform, slender like a thread.

filigrana [fe-le-grah'-nah], *f.* 1. Filigree, filigrane, fine work made of gold and silver threads. 2. *(Met.)* Anything neatly wrought.

filípica [fe-lee'-pe-cah], *f.* Philippic, invective, declamation.

filipichín [fe-le-pe-cheen'], *m.* Kind of damask, moreen, woollen cloth.

filipino, na [fe-le-pee'-no, nah], *a.* Philippine, belonging to the Philippine Islands.

filis [fee'-lis], *f.* 1. Grace, a graceful manner of doing or saying a thing. 2. Gewgaw made of clay.

filisteo, tea [fe-lis-tay'-o, ah], *m. & f.* 1. *(coll.)* A very tall and corpulent person (gigante). 2. Philistine.

film, filme [feelm, feel'-may], *m.* Film, movie.

filmación [feel-mah-the-on'], *f.* Filming, shooting.

filmador [feel-mah-dor'], *m.* Film maker.

filmadora [feel-mah-do'-rah], *f.* Film studio (estudio); film camera (aparato)

filmar [feel-mar'], *va.* To film.

filmina [feel-mee'-nah], *f.* Slide (diapositiva); short film (película).

filmografía [feel-mo-graha-fee'-ah], *f.* 1. Study of the film (estudio). **La filmografía de la estrella,** the star's film history. 2. Films (filmes).

filmoteca [feel-mo-tay'-cah], *f.* Film library.

filo [fee'-lo], *m.* Edge of a sword or other cutting instrument (de herramienta), blade; dividing line (línea); ridge (cresta). **De doble filo,** double-edged. **Dar un filo a,** to sharpen.

filogenitura [fe-lo-hay-ne-too'-rah], *f.* Philoprogenitiveness.

filología, filológica [fe-lo-lo-hee'-ah, fe-lo-lo'-he-cah], *f.* Philology, linguistics.

filológico, ca [fe-lo-lo'-he-co, cah], *a.* Philological.

filólogo [fe-lo'-lo-go], *m.* Philologist.

filomena [fe-lo-may'-nah], *f.* Nightingale, philomel, philomela.

filón [fe-lone'], *m. (Geol.)* Vein, lode, mineral layer; gang.

filonio [fe-lo'-ne-o], *m. (Pharm.)* Kind of opiate.

filopos [fe-lo'-pos], *m. pl.* Pieces of linen used to drive game into a place assigned for that purpose.

filoseda [fe-lo-say'-dah], *f.* Vesting, silk and worsted or cotton cloth.

filosofador, ra [fe-lo-so-fah-dor', rah], *m. & f.* Philosopher.

filosofal [fe-lo-so-fahl'], *a.* **Piedra filosofal,** philosopher's stone. *(Ant.)*

filosofar [fe-lo-so-far'], *va.* 1. To philosophize, to examine as a philosopher. 2. To play the philosopher, to assume the critic.

filosofastro [fe-lo-so-fahs-tro], *m.* A pretended philosopher, a smatterer in philosophy, philosophaster.

filosofía [fe-lo-so-fee'-ah], *f.* 1. Philosophy, a science which treats of the essence and affections of things and beings. 2. Philosophy, a particular doctrine or system of opinions. **Filosofía moral,** ethics or moral philosphy. **Filosofía natural,** physics or natural philosophy.

filosóficamente [fe-lo-so'-fe-cah-men-tay], *adv.* Philosophically.

filosófico, ca [fe-lo-so'-fe-co, cah], *a.* Philosophical, philosophic.

filosofismo [fe-lo-so-fees'-mo], *m. (Iron.)* Philosophism, sophistry, free thinking.

filosofista [fe-lo-so-fees'-tah], *m. (Iron.)* Philosophist, sophist.

filósofo [fe-lo'-so-fo], *m.* Philosopher.

filósofo, fa [fe-lo'-so-fo, fah], *a.* 1. Philosophic, philosophical. 2. *V.* AFILOSOFADO.

filoxera [fe-loc-say'-rah], *f.* Phylloxera, an insect of the aphis family, terrible in the destruction it causes to vineyards.

filtración [fil-trah-the-on'], *f.* 1. Filtration, leakage, loss. 2. Leak(age), leaking (información).

filtrador [fil-trah-dor'], *a.* Filtering. *-m.* filter.

filtrar [fil trar'], *va.* 1. To filter, to filtrate, to detecate. 2. To filter, to strain. 3. To leak (información). *-vn. -vr.* 1. To filter. **Filtrarse por,** to filter through. 2. *(Fig.)* To dwindle, to disppear bit by bit.

filtro [feel'-tro], *m.* 1. Filter, a piece of cloth, linen, or paper, through which liquids are strained. **Filtro de aceite,** oil filter. **Filtro de aire,** air filter. 2. Philter, a love-potion.

fimbria [feem'-bre-ah], *f.* Edge or lower part of a garment doubled in.

fimo [fee'-mo], *m.* Manure. *V.* FIEMO.

fin [feen], *m.* 1. End (final), close, termination, conclusion, issue. 2. Limit, boundary. 3. End, object, purpose (objetivo). 4. Goal, the end to which a design tends. **Al fin,** at last, at length, upon the main. **En fin** or **por fin,** finally, lastly, in fine. **Dar fin,** to die. **Dar fin a alguna cosa,** to finish, to conclude a thing. **Dar fin de alguna cosa,** to destroy a thing completely. **A fin de,** in order that. **Por cualquier fin,** prompted by any motive, or end **Fin de fichero,** end-of-file. **Hacia finales del siglo,** towards the end of the century. **Poner fin** a, to stop. **A tal fin,** with this aim in view. **Con fines deshonestos,** with an immoral purpose.

finado, da [fe-nah'-do, dah], *a. & pp.* of FINAR. Dead, deceased. **Día de los finados,** All Souls' Day. *-m. & f.* Person dead.

final [fe-nahl'], *a.* Final, ultimate, conclusive.

final [fe-nahl'], *m.* End, termination, conclusion. **Por final,** in fine, ultimately, lastly. **Final feliz,** happy-ending. **Al final de la calle,** at the end of the street.

finalizar [fe-nah-le-thar'], *va.* To finish, to conclude. **Dar algo por finalizado,** to consider something finished. *-vn.* To be finished or concluded.

finalmente [fe-nal-men'-tay], *adv.* Finally, at last, ultimately, lastly.

finamente [fe-nah-men-tay], *adv.* Finely, nicely, delicately.

finamiento [fe-nah-me-en'-to], *m.* Death, decease.

financiamiento [fe-nan-the-ah-me-en'-to], *m.* Financing.

financiar [fe-nan-the-ar'], *va.* To finance.

financiero [fe-nan-the-ay-ro], *m.* & *a.* Financer, financial. **El mundo financiero,** the financial world.

finanzas [fe-nahn'-thas], *f. pl.* Finances.

finar [fe-nar'], *vn.* To die. *-vr.* To long for.

finca [feen'-cah], *f.* Any kind of property, but especially land, which yields a regular income; tenement, building, house, real estate (propiedad). **Propiedad urbana,** town property. **Propiedad cafetera,** coffee plantation. **Penetrar en propiedad ajena,** to trespass.

fincar [fin-car'], *vn.* & *va.* 1. To buy real estate. 2. *(Fig. Peru.)* To lean on, to have confidence in something.

fin de semana [feen day say-mah-nah], *m.* Weekend.

finés, sa [fe-nays, sah], *a.* Finnie, or Finnish, relating to the Finns.

fineza [fe-nay'-thah], *f.* 1. Fineness, goodness, purity, perfection (calidad). 2. Kindness, expression of friendship or love. 3. Delicacy, beauty. 4. Friendly activity and zeal. 5. A small, friendly gift (regalo), a favor.

fingidamente [fin-he-dah-men-tay], *adv.* Feignedly, fictitiously, counterfeitly.

fingido, da [fin-hee'-do, dah], *a.* Feigned, dissembled, false. **Nombre fingido,** false name.

fingidor, ra [fin-he-dor', rah], *m.* & *f.* Dissembler, simulator, feigner.

fingimiento [fin-he-me-en'-to], *m.* Simulation, deceit, false appearance.

fingir [fin-heer'], *va.* 1. To feign, to dissemble, to counterfeit, to pretend, to affect. 2. To fancy, to imagine what does not really exist. **Fingir mucha humildad,** to pretend to be very humble. *-vn.* To pretend, to feign. **Fingir dormir,** to pretend to be asleep.

finiquitar [fe-ne-ke-tar'], *va.* To give a final receipt, close an account (cuenta).

finiquito [fe-ne-kee'-to], *m.* 1. Quittance, close of an account. 2. Final receipt or discharge.

finítimo, ma [fe-nee'-te-mo, mah], *a.* Bordering, contiguous, near.

finito, ta [fe-nee'-to, tah], *a.* Finite, limited, bounded.

finlandés, sa [fin-lan-days', sah], *a.* Of Finland, Finnish. *-m.* A Finn.

fino, na [fee'-no, nah], *a.* 1. Fine, perfect, pure (de buena calidad). 2. Delicate, nice (sutil). 3 Excellent, eminent. 4. Affectionate, true. 5. Acute, sagacious, cunning (inteligencia). 6. Of polished education and choice manners (cortés).

finta [feen'-tah], *f.* 1. A tax formerly paid to government. 2. Feint, a deceptive movement in fencing.

finura [fe-noo'-rah], *f.* 1. Fineness (calidad de fino), purity, delicacy. 2. In horsemanship, attention and obedience of a horse to the least wish of the rider. 3. Politeness, courtesy, refinement (cortesía). 4. Shrewdness, acuteness (astucia).

fiordo [fe-or'-do], *m.* Fiord or fjord.

fique [fee'-kay], *m.* A filaceous substance, resembling hemp, made of the leaves of the maguey tree.

firma [feer'-mah], *f.* 1. Signature. 2. A commercial house and its firm name. 3. *(Law. Prov.)* Order or rescript of a tribunal for keeping possession. **Firma en blanco,** blank signature. **Buena firma,** a house of standing, solvent.

firmamento [fir-mah-men'-to], *m.* Firmament, sky, heaven. *V.* EMPÍREO.

firmán [fir-mahn'], *m.* Firman, a grant or license given by oriental potentates.

firmante [fir-mahn-tay], *pa.* & *m.* & *f.* Supporter, subscriber.

firmar [fir-mar'], *va.* To sign, to subscribe. **Firmado y sellado,** signed and sealed. *-vr.* To style oneself, to assume a title or appellation.

firme [feer'-may], *a.* 1. Firm, stable (estable), strong, secure, fast, hard (duro), compact. **Estar en lo firme,** to be in the right. 2. Firm, unshaken, constant, consistent, resolute. 3. Steady (mercado); firm (precio), stable. 4. Staunch (persona), steadfast, resolute. 5. **De firme,** firmly. **Batir de firme,** to strike hard. **Oferta en firme,** firm offer. **Ponerse firmes,** to come to attention. **Sentencia firme,** final judgement.

firmemente [fir-may-men-tay], *adv.* 1. Firmly, strongly, unmovably. 2. Firmly, faithfully, steadily, constantly. 3. Staunchly, steadfastly (lealmente).

firmeza [fir-may'-thah], *f.* 1. Firmness, stability, hardness, compactness. 2. Firmness, steadiness, constancy. 3. Gold or silver clasp, ornament made of a precious stone in a triangular form. 3. Firmness (moral); steadfastness, resolution.

fisalia [fe-sah'-le-ah], *f.* *(Zool.)* Physalia, an acaleph; the Portuguese man of-war.

fiscal [fis-cahl'], *m.* 1. Attorney-general, a ministerial officer, who acts for the government by which he is appointed, and who, *ex oficio* personates the state or the people. 2. **Fiscal** or **abogado fiscal,** a public attorney, a prosecutor. 3. *(coll.)* Censurer, critical.

fiscal [fis-cahl'], *a.* Fiscal, belonging to the exchequer. **Año fiscal,** fiscal year.

fiscalear [fis-cah-lay-ar'], *va.* *(coll.)* To become a public accuser, to censure.

fiscalía [fis-cah-lee'-ah], *f.* Office and business of the magistrate called *fiscal* .

fiscalizar [fis-cah-le-thar'], *va.* To accuse of a criminal offence, to criticize, to censure, to control (controlar).

fisco [fees'-co], *m.* National treasury, exchequer. **Declarar algo al fisco,** to declare something for tax purposes.

fiseter [fe-say-terr'], *m.* *(Zool.)* The small blunt-headed whale or cachalot.

fisga [fees'-gah], *f.* 1. Harpoon with three hooks for catching large fish. 2. *(Met.)* Raillery, jest, scoff. 3. *(Prov.)* Wheat of the finest quality; bread of spelt-wheat.

fisgador, ra [fis-gah-dor', rah], *m.* & *f.* Harpooner; one who burlesques. *V.* FISGÓN.

fisgar [fis-gar'], *va.* 1. To mock, to scoff, to jeer (mofarse). 2. To fish with a harpoon (pez). 3. To peep, to pry.

fisgón, one [fis-gone', nah], *a.* 1. Prying, peeping, snooping (curioso). 2. Jesting, mocking (mofador).-*m.* & *f.* 1. Busybody, Peeping Tom. 2. Jester, buffoon.

fisgonear [fis-go-nay-ar'], *va.* FISGAR.

física [fee'-se-cah], *f.* Physics. **Física de bajas energías,** high-energy physics. **Física de bajas temperaturas,** low-temperature physics. **Física del estado sólido,** solid-state physics. **Física del plasma,** plasma physics.

físicamente [fee'-se-cah-men-tay], *adv.* Physically; corporeally; really.

físico, ca [fee'-se-co, cah], *a.* 1. Physical, relating to nature or natural philosophy. 2. Natural, really existing.

físico [fee'-se-co], *m.* 1. Physicist. 2. Physique, constitution. 3. *(coll.)* Face, appearance (aspecto).

fisicoquímico, ca [fee-se-co-kee'-me-co, cah], *a.* Physicochemical.

fisiografía [fe-seo-grah-fee'-ah], *f.* Physiography, a description of nature.

fisiográfico, ca [fe-se-o-grah'-fe-co, cah], *a.* Physiographic.

fisiología [fe-se-o-lo-hee'-ah], *f.* Physiology, the science of vital phenomena. **fisiológico, ca** [fe-se-o-lo'-he-co, cah], *a.* Physiological. *-adv* **Fisiológicamente.**

fisiologista [fe-se-o-lo-hees'-tah], *m.* Physiologist.

fisiólogo [fe-se-o'-lo-go], *m.* Phisiologist: used also as adjective.

fisión [fe-se-on'], *f.* *(Phy.)* Fission. **Fisión nuclear,** nuclear fission.

fisionable [fe-se-o-nah'-blay], *a.* Fissionable.

fisionomía [fe-se-o-no-mee´-ah], V. FISONOMÍA. *(Acad.)*
fisioterapeuta [fe-se-o-tay-rah-pay´-oo-tah], *m & f.* Physiotherapist.
fisioterapia [fe-se-o-tay-rah´-pe-ah], *f.* Physiotherapy.
fisioterapista [fe-se-o-tay-rah-pees´-tah], *m & f.* Physiotherapist.
fisonomía [fe-so-no-mee´-ah], *f.* 1. Physiognomy, lineaments, features. 2. Physiognomy, the art of discovering the temper and talents by the features of the face.
fisonómico, ca [fe-so-no´-me-co, cah], *a.* Physiognomical.
fisonomista, fisónomo [fe-so-no-mees´-tah], *m.* Physiognomist.
fistol [fis-tole´], *m.* 1. A crafty person, specially a gambler. 2. *(Mex.)* A stickpin.
fístola [fees´-to-lah], *f.* 1. *(Surg.)* Fistula, a narrow channel not disposed to heal. 2. V. FÍSTULA for a pipe. 3. V. CAÑAFÍSTULA.
fístula [fees´-too-lah], *f.* 1. Waterpipe or conduit. 2. Musical wind-instrument, resembling a flute or flageolet. 3. *(Surg.)* Fistule.
fistular [fis-too-lar´], *a.* *(Med.)* Fistular, fistulous.
fistuloso, sa [fis-too-lo´-so, sah], *a.* Fistulous.
fisura [fe-soo-rah], *f.* 1. *(Geol.)* Fissure, cleft. 2. *(Med.)* Fissure, a shallow and narrow break of continuity. 3. Fissure, a longitudinal fracture of a bone.
fitobiología [fe-to-be-o-lo-hee´-ah], *f.* Phytobiology, the branch of biology which treats of plants.
fitogenesia [fe-to-hay-nay´-se-ah], *f.* Phytogenesis, the doctrine of the origin of plants.
fitografía [fe-to-grah-fee´-ah], *f.* Phytography, plant geography; description of plant life.
fitología [fe-to-lo-hee´-ah], *f.* Phytology, botany.
fitonisa [fe-to-nee´-sah], *f.* V. PITONISA.
flabelación [flah-bay-lah-the-on´], *f.* Action of agitating the air to refresh it.
flabelado, da [flah-bay-lah´-do, dah], *a.* 1. Like a flyflap. 2. *(Bot.)* Fan-shaped.
flacamente [flah-cah-men-tay], *adv.* Languidly, weakly, feebly.
flacidez [flah-the-deth´], *f.* *(Med.)* Flaccidity, laxity, limberness, want of tension.
flácido, da [flah´-the-do, dah], *a.* *(Med.)* Flaccid, limber, lax.
flaco, ca [flah´-co, cah], *a.* 1 Lank, lean, meagre, flaccid. 2. Feeble, languid. 3. Dejected, low-spirited. 4. Frail, weak of resolution. **Ponerse flaco**, to get thin.
flacura [flah-coo´-rah], *f.* 1. Meagreness, leanness, weakness (debilidad). 2. Thinness (delgadez).
flagelación [flah-hay-lah-the-on´], *f.* Flagellation, scourging.
flagelar [flah-hay-lar´], *va.* 1. To lash (azotar), to scourge. V. AZOTAR. 2. *(Fig.)* To flay, to criticize severely.
flagelo [flah-hay´-lo], *m.* 1. Lash (azote), scourge, chastisement. 2. *(Biol.)* Flagellum, a lash-like locomotive appendage of certain infusoria; a large cilium. 3. *(Amer.)* An epidemic.
flagicio [flah-hee´-the-o], *m.* Flagitiousness, wickedness; an enormous crime.
flagicioso, sa [flah-he-the-o´-so, sah], *a.* Flagitious, wicked.
flagrante [flah-grahn´-tay], *a. & pa.* Flagrant, resplendent. **En flagrante delito**, in the very act, red-handed (in fraganti).
flagrar [flah-grar´], *vn.* *(Poet.)* To flagrate, to burn, to glow, to flame.
flajolé [flah-ho-lay´], *m.* Flageolet, a beakflute.
flama [flah´-mah], *f.* 1. Flame, excessive ardor. 2. An ornament upon the upper part of caps, shakos, etc., in the army.
flamante [flah-mahn´-tay], *a.* 1. Flaming, bright, resplendent. 2. Quite new (nuevo), spick and span; luxurious (lujoso); superb (estupendo).
flamear [flah-may-ar´], *vn.* *(Naut.)* To shiver, to flutter (vela).
flamenco [flah-men´-co], *m.* *(Orn.)* Flamingo.
flamenco, ca [flah-men´-co, cah], *a.* 1. Flemish, relating to Flanders. 2. Andalusian gipsy. **Cantante flamenco,**

flamenco singer. 3. **Ponerse flamenco**, to get cocky (engreído); to get on one´s high horse (satisfecho).
flamenquilla [flah-men-keel´-lyah], *f.* *(Prov.)* 1. Dish of a middling size. 2. Marigold.
flámeo [flah´-may-o], *m.* A kind of yellow veil, with which the face of a bride was formerly covered during the marriage ceremony.
flameo [flah-may´-o], *m.* Flapping or fluttering of banners, sails, etc.
flamígero, ra [flah-mee´-hay-ro, ra], *a.* *(Poet.)* Flamiferous, emitting, flames.
flamín [flah-meen´], *m.* Flamen, a Roman priest.
flámula [flah´-moo-lah], *f.* 1. *(Bot.)* Sweet-scented virgin's bower. 2. *(Naut.)* Streamer, pennon
flan [flahn], *m.* Caramel custard (crema); baked custard (pastel).
flanco [flahn´-co], *m.* 1. *(Fort.)* Flank, flanker the part of a bastion which reaches from the curtain to the face. 2. *(Mil.)* Flank of an army. 3. *(Naut.)* Side of a ship.
Flandes [flahn´-des], *m.* Flanders.
flanela [flah-nay´-lah], *f.* Flannel.
flanquear [flan-kay-ar´], *va.* *(Fort.)* To flank; to defend by lateral fortifications.
flanqueo [flan-kay´-o], *m.* A flank attack.
flaón [flah-on´], *m.* 1. A custard. 2. Piece of gold or silver ready to be coined.
flaquear [flah-kay-ar´], *vn.* 1. To flag, to grow feeble, to lose vigor. 2. To grow spiritless or dejected, to be disheartened (moralmente). 3. To slacken in the ardor with which an enterprise was commenced (esfuerzo). 4. To decline (salud).
flaqueza [flah-kay´-thah], *f.* 1. Leanness, extenuation of the body, want of flesh, meagreness, lankness. 2. Feebleness, faintness, languishment. 3. Weakness, frailty, foible. 4. Importunity, molestation.
flash [flash], *m. pl.* Flashed, flashs 1. News flash (noticia). 2. Flash, flashlight. **Con flash**, by flashlight. 3. *(Fig.)* Surprise.
flato [flah´-to], *m.* Flatus, wind gathered in a cavity of the body.
flatoso, flatuoso, sa [flah-to´-so, flah-too-o´-so, sah], *a.* Flatuous, windy; full of wind.
flatulencia [flah-too-len´-the-ah], *f.* Flatulency.
flatulento, ta [flah-too-len´-to, tah], *a.* Flatulent, turgid with air, windy.
flauta [flah´-oo-tah], *f.* A flute (instrumento).
flautado, da [fla-hoo-tah´-do, dah], *a.* Resembling a flute.
flautado [flah-oo-tah-do], *m.* Stop in an organ, which produces the sound of a flute.
flautero [flah-oo-tay´-ro], *m.* One who makes flutes.
flautillo [flah-oo-teel´-lyo], *m.* V. CARAMILLO.
flautín [flah-oo-teen´], *m.* 1. Octave flute, piccolo, a small flute of high pitch. 2. *-m -f.* Piccolo player (persona).
flautista [flah-oo-tees´-tah], *m.* Player of the flute. **El flautista de Hamelin**, the Pied Piper of Hamelin.
flavo, va [flah´-vo, vah], *a.* Of a fallow or honey color.
flébil [flay´-beel], *a.* Mournful, deplorable, lamentable.
flebolito [flay-bo-lee´-to], *m.* Phlebolith, a concretion formed in a vein: vein-stone.
flebotomía [flay-bo-to-mee-ah], *f.* Phlebotomy, blood-letting.
flebotomiano [flay-bo-to-me-ah´-no], *m.* Phlebotomist, one who lets blood for medical purposes.
flebotomista [flay-bo-to-mees´-tah], *m.* V. FLEBOTOMIANO.
flebotomizar [flay-bo-to-me-thar´], *va.* To bleed, to let blood.
flebótomo [flay-bo´-to-mo], *m.* V. FLEBOTOMIANO.
fleco [flay´-co], *m.* 1. Fringe, an ornamental appendage to dress and furniture. 2. Flounce. 3. Fringe (pelo).
flecha [flay´-chah], *f.* 1. Arrow, dart. 2. A sign which serves to indicate the north, or the current of rivers, upon a map. 3. *(Fort.)* A work of two faces and two sides. 4. *(Naut.)* Front piece of the cutwater. 5. The principal piece of those which compose the beakhead of a galley. 6. *(Min.)* Variety of hydroxide of iron called "love's dart." 7. Sagitta, a northern

constellation. **Flecha de dirección**, Trafficator. **Como una flecha**, like an arrow.

flechador [flay-chah-dor'], *m.* Archer.

flechaduras [flay-chah-doo-ras'], *f. pl. (Naut.)* Ratlines. *V.* FLECHASTES.

flechar [flay-char'], *va.* 1. To dart, to shoot an arrow or dart (arco). 2. To wound or kill with a bow and arrow. 3. *(Prov. Mex.)* To point out, without fear, in gambling. *-vn.* To have a bow drawn ready to shoot.

flechaste [flay-chas'-tay], *m. (Naut.)* Ratline.

flechazo [flay-chah´-tho], *m.* 1. Blow or stroke given with a dart or arrow. 2. Love at first sight (amor). **Con nosotros fue el flechazo**, with us it was love at first sight.

flechera [flay-chay'-rah], *f. (S. Am.)* A long, narrow, sharp canoe.

flechería [flay-chay-ree´-ah], *f.* A number of darts or arrows darted at a time, shower of arrows.

flechero [flay-chay'-ro], *m.* 1. Archer, bowman. 2. Fletcher, an arrow maker.

flegmasía [fleg-mah-see'-ah], *f.* Inflammation, phlegmasia.

fleje [flay'-hay], *m.* Hoop. **Flejes de hierro** or **fierro**, iron hoops. **Flejes**, twigs for barrels.

flema [flay'-mah], *f.* 1. Phlegm. 2. Thick spittle ejected from the mouth. 3. Phlegm, coolness, dullness, sluggishness.

flemático, ca [flay-mah´-te-co, cah], *a.* 1. Phlegmatic, generating phlegm; abounding in phlegm. 2. Phlegmatic, dull, cold, sluggish.

fleme [flay'-may], *f.* Fleam, an instrument used to bleed cattle.

flemón [flay-mo-ne'], *m.* 1. Phlegmon, an inflammation of the cellular tissue. 2. A gumboil, a tumor of the gum ending in suppuration.

flemoso, sa [flay-mo'-so, sah], *a.* Mucous, consisting of phlegm.

flemudo, da [flay-moo'-do, dah], *a. (Prov.)* Dull, sluggish, cold, frigid.

flequillo [flay-keel'-lyo], *m.* Fringe.

flerecín [flay-ray-theen'], *m. (Med.)* Gout.

flet, flez [flet, fleth], *m. (Zool.)* Halibut.

fletador [flay-tah-dor'], *m.* Freighter, charterer of a ship.

fletamento [flay-tah-men'-to], *m.* Freightment, the act of freighting a ship; chartering. **Cerrar el fletamento**, to charter, to make out the charter-party.

fletante [flay-tahn'-tay], *m.* 1. Ship owner. 2. Shipper.

fletar [flay-tar´], *va.* To freight a ship, to charter (avión, barco).

flete [flay'-tay], *m.* 1. Charter (alquiler). **Vuelo flete**, charter flight. 2. Freight (carga). 3. Freightage (gastos).

flexibilidad [flec-se-be-le-dahd'], *f.* 1. Flexibility, pliableness, ductility, flexibleness. 2. Flexibility, easiness to be persuaded, ductility of mind, manageableness, obsequiousness, mildness of temper.

flexibilizar [flec-se-be-le-thar'], *va.* To make flexible; to adjust.

flexible [flec-see-blay], *a.* 1. Flexible, ductile, pliant, possible to be bent. 2. Flexible, manageable, docile. 3. Soft (sombrero). 3. Open-minded, open to argument (persona).

flexión [flec-se-on´], *f.* Flexion, flexure, act of bending.

flexionar [flec-se-o-nar'], *va.* To bend; to flex (músculo).

flexor [flec-sor'], *a.* Flexor, used of the muscles which bend a joint.

flexuoso, sa [flec-soo-o-so, sah], *a. (Bot.)* Flexuose, changing its direction in a curve from joint to joint or from bud to bud in the stem, or from flower to flower in the peduncle.

flibote [fle-bo´-tay], *m.* Flyboat, a small fast-sailing vessel.

flictena [flic-tay'-nah], *f. (Med.)* Phlyctena, a small blister, or vesicle, filled with a serous or watery fluid.

flin [fleen'], *m.* Stone used for edging and polishing steel; a kind of emery.

flinflón [flin-flon´], *m.* A fresh-colored, corpulent man.

flipante [fle-pahn-tay], *a.* Attractive, cool.

flipar [fle-pahr'], *vn.* 1. To freak out (desmadrarse); to go round the twist (volverse loco); to get stoned (drogarse,

emborracharse). 2. **Flipar por algo**, to be dying for something.

flirtear [flir-tay-ar'], *vn.* To flirt, to have a light-hearted affair.

flocadura [flo-cah-doo'-rah], *f.* A trimming made with fringes as an ornament of dress.

flogosis [flo-go'-sis], *f.* Inflammation, phlegmasia.

flojamente [floh-ah-men'-tay], *adv.* Slowly, carelessly, laxly, loosely (sueltamente), weakly (débilmente), lightly (ligeramente).

flojear [flo-hay-ar'], *vn.* To slacken, to grow weak. *V.* FLAQUEAR.

flojedad [flo-hay-dahd´], *f.* 1. Weakness, feebleness, laxity. 2. Sloth, laziness, negligence, slackness.

flojel [flo-hel'], *m.* 1. Wool shorn from cloth by the shearer. 2. Down, soil feathers.

flojera [flo-hay´-rah], *f. (coll.)* Weakness. *V.* FLOJEDAD.

flojo, ja [flo'-ho, hah], *a.* 1. Slack; loose (tuerca) **Vino flojo**, flaggy, insipid wine. 2. Feeble, weak, flaccid (esfuerzo). 3. Slack, remiss, lazy, slothful, negligent, cold, cool, spiritless (actitud). 4. Low, weak (precio). 5. Soft, limp (carne). **Me la trae floja**, it leaves me stone-cold.

floqueado, da [flo-kay-ah'-do, dah], *a.* Fringed.

flor [flor'], *f.* 1. Flower, that part of a plant which contains the organs of generation; a blossom. 2. The down of fruits newly gathered. 3. Flower, prime, the most excellent or valuable part of a thing; bloom. 4. Cuticle or thin skin formed, on the surface of liquors. 5. *(Chem.)* Flos, the most subtle part of mineral separated in sublimation. 6. Virginity, maidenhood. 7. The face or surface of the earth. 8. Smart or witty saying: commonly used in plural. 9. Grain, the outside of tanned leather. 10. Trick or artifice among gamesters or gamblers. 11. Figures of rhetoric. **Flor de canela**, cassia buds. **Flor de la miel**, *(Bot.)* great honeyflower. **Flor de lis**, 1. Flower-de-luce. 2. *(Bot.)* Jacobea lily, amaryllis. **Flor del sol**, *(Bot.) V.* CORONA REAL. **En flor**, in a state of infancy, imperfect, in blossom, in flower. **En la flor de su edad**, *(Met.)* in his bloom. **La flor y nata de la sociedad**, the cream of society. **En la flor de la vida**, in the prime of life. **Decir flores a una**, to pay pretty compliments to a girl (piropo). **A flor de agua**, awash, even with the surface of the water. **La flor y nata**, the cream, the best. **Tienda de flores**, florist's shop.

flora [flo'-rah], *f. (Bot.)* Flora, the description of the plants of some district, region, etc.

florada [flo-rah-da´h], *f. (Prov.)* The season of flowers with bee-masters.

florales [flo-rah'-les], *a. pl.* Floral; feasts in honor of Flora.

florar [flo-rar´], *vn.* To flower. *(Acad.)*

flordelisado, da [flor-day-le-sah'-do, dah], *a.* Adorned with iris. *-pp.* of FLORDELISAR.

floreado, da [flo-ray-ah´-do, dah], *a. & pp.* of FLOREAR. 1. Flowered (tela). 2. Applied to things made of the finest flour or meal. **Rasos, sedas, u otros efectos or géneros floreados**, silks, or any other figured goods.

florear [flo-ray-ar'], *va.* 1. To adorn with flowers (tela) 2. To flourish a sword. 3. *(Mus.)* To flourish, to play the guitar without rule. 4. *(Amer.) V.* FLORAR.

florecer [flo-ray-therr'], *vn.* 1. To flower, to bloom, to blossom. 2. To flourish, to thrive, to prosper. 3. To flourish in any age. *-vr.* To mould, to become mouldy.

florecica [flo-ray-thee'-cah], *f. dim.* Floweret.

floreciente [flo-ray-the-en'-tay], *pa. & a.* Flourishing, blossoming, flowery.

florecilla, ita [flo-ray-theel'-lyah, ee'-tah], *f.* 1. *(dim.)* A small flower. 2. *(Bot.)* The partial or separate little flower of an aggregate flower.

florentina, f. florentin, *m.* [flo-ren-tee'-nah, flo-ren-teen']. A silk stuff first manufactured at Florence; florentines.

floreo [flo-ray'-o], *m.* 1. Flourish made by fencers before they engage. 2. Flourish on the guitar; flourish (esgrima). 3. A luxuriant redundancy of words (cumplido). 4. Cross caper, a movement in dancing. 5. Idle pastime.

florera [flo-ray'-rah], *f.* Flower girl, female flower vendor.

florero [flo-ray'-ro], *m.* 1. Vase (recipiente). 2. One who makes or deals in artificial flowers. 3. Painting representing flowers. 4. Case destined for artificial flowers. 5. One who makes use of florid, empty language (persona). 6. A chaplet of flowers.

florescencia [flo-res-then'-the-ah], *f.* 1. (*Bot.*) Florescence or the flowering season. 2. Efflorescence, manner of flowering.

floresta [flo-res'-tah], *f.* 1. Forest, shrubbery, thicket. 2. A delightful, rural place (lugar atractivo). 3. Collection of fine things pleasing to the taste; beauties.

florestero [flo-res-tay'-ro], *m.* Forester, keeper of a forest.

floreta [flo-ray'-tah], *f.* 1. Border of morocco leather on the edge of a girth. 2. In paper mills, pile, heap.

florete [flo-ray'-tay], *m.* Foil, floret, a blunt sword used in learning to fence (esgrima).

florete [flo-ray'-tay], *a.* Very white and fine (papel).

floretear [flo-ray-tay-ar'], *va.* To garnish with flowers.

floricultura [flo-re-cool-too'-rah], *f.* Floriculture, cultivation of flowers.

floridamente [flo-re-dah-men'-tay], *adv.* Elegantly, floridly, flourishingly.

florídeas [flo-ree'-day-as], *f. pl.* Floridae, a very large class of marine algae, purple and red. The color is enhanced upon drying.

floridez [flo-re-deth'], *f.* Floridity, floridness.

florido, da [flo-ree'-do, dah], *a.* 1. Florid, flowery; full of flowers (campo) 2. Choice, elegant, select. 3. Flowery, florid (estilo).

florífero, ra [flo-ree'-fay-ro, rah], *a.* Floriferous, bearing flowers.

florilegio [flo-re-lay-he-o], *m.* Florilegium, anthology, select writings.

florín [flo-reen'], *m.* Florin, a silver coin.

floripondio, floripundio [flo-re-pon'-de-o, flo-re-poon'-de-o], *m.* 1. Magnolia, tree of great beauty, with very large white fragrant flowers. 2. (*Bot.*) Floripondium, smooth stalked brugmansia.

florisado, da [flo-re-sah'-do, dah], *a.* V. FLORDELISADO.

florista [flo-rees'-tah], *com.* 1. Florist. 2. One who makes or deals in artificial flowers.

floristería [flo-rees-tay-ree'-ah], *f.* Florist´s (tienda).

florón [flo-ro-ne'], *m.* 1. (*Aug.*) A large flower. 2. Flower work, an ornament resembling a large flower.

flósculo [flos'-coo-lo], *m.* (*Bot.*) The separate little flower of an aggregate one; floret.

flosculoso, sa [flos-coo-lo'-so, sah], *a.* (*Bot.*) Flosculous, composed of flowers or florets.

flota [flo'-tah], *f.* 1. (*Naut.*) Fleet of merchant ships. **Flota mercante**, merchant marine. **La flota pesquera**, the fishing fleet. 2. Fleet, squadron. Nowadays the term *escuadra* or *armada* is used.

flotable [flo-tah'-blay], *a.* 1. Capable of floating. 2. A navigable river. (*Acad.*)

flotación [flo-tah-the-on'], *f.* 1. Floating, the act of floating. 2. Friction, rubbing. 3. (*Min.*) Flotation. **Línea de flotación**, (*Naut.*) Waterline.

flotador, ra [flo-tah-dor', rah], *a.* Floating. *-m.* 1. Float. 2. (*Aer.*) Pontoon. 3. Ballcock (de cisterna). 4. Rubber ring (de niño).

flotamiento [flo-tah-me-en'-to], *m.* Stroking, gentle friction.

flotante [flo-tahn'-tay], *pa. & a.* 1. Floating, floaty. 2. (*Bot.*) Rooted upon the bottom of a stream and whose leaves follow the course of the current.

flotar [flo-tar'], *vn.* 1. To float. 2. To hang, to hang loose (pieza); to flutter (bandera) **Flotar en el aire**, to float in the air. **Flotar al viento**, to stream in the wind. *-va.* (*Ant.*) To stroke, to rub gently.

flote [flo-tay'], *m.* V. FLOTADURA. *Afloat*, afloat; (*fig.*) escaping happily. **Estar a flote**, to be afloat.

flotilla [flo-teel'-lyah], *f.* 1. Flotilla, a number of small vessels. 2. (*Dun.*) A small fleet.

flox [flox], *m.* (*Bot.*) Phlox.

fluatado, da [floo-ah-tah'-do, dah], *a.* Fluorid, fluorate.

fluato [floo-ah'-to], *m.* Fluorate, compound of hydrofluoric acid.

fluctuación [flooc-too-ah-the-on'], *f.* 1. Fluctuation, motion of the waves. 2. Fluctuation, uncertainty, indetermination, irresolution (indecisión). 3. (*Med.*) Fluctuation.

fluctuamiento [flooc-too-ah-me-ayn'-to], *m.* V. FLUCTUACIÓN.

fluctuante [flooc-too-ahn'-tay], *pa. & a.* Fluctuating, fluctuant; floating (población).

fluctuar [flooc-too-ar'], *vn.* 1. To fluctuate, to float backward and forward, to oscillate. 2. To be in danger of being lost or destroyed. 3. To fluctuate, to hesitate, to be irresolute, to vacillate (vacilar). 4. To fluctuate, to be in an uncertain state.

fluctícola [flooc-tee'-co-lah], *a.* (*Zool.*) Inhabiting the waters.

fluctígena [flooc-tee'-hay-nah], *a.* (*Zool.*) Born on the water.

fluctuoso, sa [flooc-too-o'-so, sah], *a.* Fluctuant, wavering.

fluente [floo-en'-tay], *pa. & a.* Fluent, flowing.

fluidez [floo-e-deth'], *f.* Fluidity, liquidity. **Fluidez de stilo**, fluency.

fluidificable [floo-e-de-fe-cah'-blay], *a.* Liquefiable.

fluidificación [floo-e-de-fe-cah-the-on'], *f.* Liquefaction, rendering fluid.

fluidificar [floo-e-de-fe-car'], *va. & vr.* To convert into fluid, to liquefy.

fluido, da [floo-ee'-do, dah], *a.* 1. Fluid, not solid (líquido). 2. (*Met.*) Fluent (estilo); fluent (lenguaje). **La circulación es bastante fluida**, traffic is moving quite freely. *-pp.* of FLUIR.

fluido [floo-ee'-do], *m.* 1. Fluid, not solid. 2. (*Med.*) Fluid, any animal juice.

fluir [floo-eer'], *vn.* To flow. **El fluir del agua**, the flow of water.

flujo [floo'-ho], *m.* 1. Flux, the motion of liquids. 2. (*Med.*) Flux, a flow or discharge. 3. Flowing, haemorrhage. 4. (*Naut.*) Flow, rising tide. 5. (*Chem.*) Flux, a substance aiding the fusion of another substance. **Flujo de palabras**, flow of words, volubility. **Flujo de risa**, fit of laughter. **Flujo de sangre**, haemorrhage. **Flujo de vientre**, diarrhoea.

fluor [floo'-or], *m.* Fluorine, a gaseous element.

fluorescencia [floo-o-res-then'-the-ah], *f.* Fluorescence.

fluorescente [floo-o-res-then-tay], *a.* Flourescente.

fluorhídrico, ca [floo-o-ree'-dre-co, cah], *a.* Fluorhydric, hydrofluoric.

fluórico, ca [floo-o'-re-co, cah], *a.* (*Chew.*) Fluoric, containing fluorine.

fluorita, fluorina [floo-o-ree'-nah, floo-ree'-nah], *f.* Fluor(spar), fluorite.

fluoroacopio [floo-oo-ros-co'-pe-o], *m.* Fluoroscope.

fluoruración [floo-o-roo-rah-the-one'], *f.* Fluoridation.

fluvial [floo-ve-ahl'], *a.* Fluvial, pertaining to rivers. **Navegación fluvial**, river navigation.

flux [floocs], *m.* Flush, a run of cards of the same suit (naipes). **Hacer flux**, (*Colt.*) to spend one's whole fortune without paying a debt.

fluxión [floocs-se-on'], *f.* 1. A flow or discharge: flux. 2. (*Amer.*) A cold, catarrh. 3. (*Hex.*) A very painful toothache.

Fo [fo], The Chinese name of Buddha.

foca [fo'-cah], *f.* Seal. **Foca de trompa**, sea elephant.

focal [fo-cal'], *a.* Focal.

foco [fo-co], *m.* 1. Focus, the point of convergence (centro). 2. The principal spot where an insurrection has broken out. 3. Center of action, origin, source (de calor, de luz). 4. The seat of a purulent process; core or center of an abscess (de incendio). 6. (*Mil.*) Touch-hole of a gun. 7. The focus of an ellipse. 7. (*Chom.*) Firebox, furnace; place for combustibles.

fóculo [fo'-coo-lo], *m.* A small fire place.

focha [fo'-chah], *f.* (*Zool.*) Rail; mudhen.

fodolí [fo-do-lee'], *a.* Meddlesome, intrusive.

fofo, fa [fo'-fo, fah], *a.* Spongy, soft, bland (esponjoso); flabby (carnes). 2. Fat, plump (rechoncho).

fogaril [fo-gah-reel'], *m.* Combustibles which serve for signal lights.

fogata [fo-gah'-tah], *f.* 1. Blaze, the light of a flame. 2. A small mine under some attackable point.

fogón [fo-gone'], *m.* 1. Hearth, the fireside. 2. Vent or touch-hole of a gun (de cañón, máquina). 3. *(Naut.)* Caboose, a cooking stove for a ship. 4. *(Naut.)* Galley, cook room, the kitchen in ships.

fogonadura [fo-go-nah-doo'-rah], *f. (Naut.)* Partner, piece of timber round the holes into which mats are set.

fogonazo [fo-go-nah'-tho], *m.* Flame of the priming of a gun, a flash in the pan (estallido).

fogonero [fo-go-nay'-ro], *m.* Fireman, stoker.

fogosidad [fo-go-se-dahd'], *f.* Excessive vivacity, fieriness, heat of temper.

fogoso, sa [fo-go'-so, sah], *a.* 1. Fiery, vehement, ardent. 2. Fervent, hot in temper, ardent in love, impetuous, lively, choleric.

fogote [fo-go'-tay], *m.* A live coal, match.

fogueación [fo-gay-ah-the-on'], *f.* Enumeration of hearths or fire.

foguear [fo-gay-ar'], *va.* 1. To habituate persons or horses to the discharge of fire-arms. 2. To cleanse fire-arms with a charge of gunpowder. -*vr.* To have one´s baptism of fire.

fogueo [fo-gay'-o], *m.* **Bala de foqueo**, blank cartridge.

foja [fo'-hah], *f.* 1. *(For.)* A sheet of paper. 2. *(Orn.)* Coot or common coot.

fole [fo'-lay], *m.* A leather bag, especially of the Galician bagpipe.

folgo [fol'-go], *m.* Foot-warmer, bag of skin to cover the feet and legs when sitting.

foliáceo [fo-le-ah'-the-o], *a. (Bot.)* Foliaceous.

foliación [fo-le-ah-the-on'], *f.* 1. Numbering the pages of a book. 2. The numeration of the pages of a book. 3. *(Bot.)* Foliation.

foliar [fo-le-ar'], *va.* To page, to number the leaves of a book.

foliatura [fo-le-ah-too'-rah], *f.* 1. Numbering the pages of a book. 2. Numeration of the pages of a book.

folículo [fo-lee'-coo-lo], *m.* 1. *(Bot.)* Follicle, a seed-vessel or pericarp. 2. *(Anat.)* Follicle, a membraneous sac.

folio [fo'-le-o], *m.* Folio, leaf of a book (hoja). **Al primer folio**, at first sight. **En folio**, in folio.

folklore [fo-clor'], *m.* Folklore.

folklórico [fol-clo'-re-co], *a.* Folklore; folk; popular, traditional. **Es muy folklórico**, it´s very quaint. -*m & f.* Folk singer.

folla [fol'-lyah], *f.* 1. An irregular conflict in a tournament. 2. Medley of a variety of things confusedly jumbled together; olio.

follada [fol-lyah'-dah], *f.* 1. Sort of hollow paste. 2. Fuck.

follados [fol-lyah'-dos], *m. pl.* Ancient kind of pants.

follaje [fol-lyah'-hay], *m.* 1. Foliage. 2. Leafiness: leafage. 3. Gaudy ornament of trifling value. 4. Fucking.

follar [fol-lyar'], *va.* 1. To blow with bellows. 2. To form in leaves. 3. To fuck. 4. To bother, to annoy. -*vr.* 1. *(coll.)* To discharge wind without noise. 2. To fuck.

follero [fol-lyay'-ro], *m.* One who makes or sells bellows.

folleta [fol-lyay'-tah], *f.* Wine measure nearly equal to an English pint.

folletín [fol-lyay-teen'], *m.* The story, novel, etc., inserted in many periodicals.

folletinista [fol-lyay-te-nees'-tah], *m.* One who edits *folletines*.

folletista [fol-lyay-tees'-tah], *m.* Pamphleteer, a writer of pamphlets.

folleto [fol-lyay'-to], *m.* A pamphlet; folder, brochure, leaflet.

follón, na [fol-lyone', nah], *a.* Feeble, inert, lazy (perezoso); negligent, mean, blustering (fanfarrón).

follón [fo-lyone'], *m.* 1. Rogue, villain, a mean, despicable fellow. 2. Rocket which discharges without noise (cohete).

3. Bud or branch from the root or trunk of a tree. 4. Breaking wind without noise. 5. Rumpus, row, shindy (jaleo); mess (lío).

follonería [fol-yo-nay-ree'-ah], *f.* Knavishness.

foma [fo'-mah], *f. (Bot.)* A fungus growing generally in small tubercles upon branches or leaves of plants.

fomentación [fo-men-tah-the-on'], *f.* Fomentation.

fomentador, ra [fo-men-tah-dor', rah], *m. & f.* Fomenter.

fomentar [fo-men-tar'], *va.* 1. To foment, to produce warmth by fomentation. 2. *(Met.)* To foment, to protect, to favor, to patronize, to countenance, to encourage.

fomento [fo-men'-to], *m.* 1. Fomentation. 2. Fuel. 3. Patronage, protection, support, encouragement.

fomes [fo'-mes], *m.* 1. Incentive, generally applied to that which excites to sin. 2. Lust, concupiscence.

fonación [fo-nah-the-on´], *f.* 1. Phonation, emission of the voice. 2. Pronunciation.

fonas [fo'-nas], *f. pl.* Pieces sewed to a cloak.

fonda [fon'-dah], *f.* Hotel, inn, tavern, lodging house (pensión), small restaurant (restaurante).

fondable [fon-dah'-blay], *a.* That may be sounded with a plummet.

fondado, da [fon-dah'-do, dah], *a.* Applied to pipes or barrels, the bottoms of which are secured with cords or nails.

fondeadero [fon-day-ah-day'-ro], *m. (Naut.)* Anchoring-ground.

fondear [fon-day-ar'], *va.* 1. To sound, to explore the depth of water (profundidad). 2. To bring up from the bottom of water. 3. *(Naut.)* To search a ship for prohibited goods (registrar). 4. To examine closely. -*vn. (Naut.)* To cast anchor.

fondeo [fon-day'-o], *m.* The act of searching a ship.

fondillón [fon-del-lyone'], *m.* 1. The dregs and lees at the bottom of a cask of liquor. 2. Rancid Alicant wine.

fondillos [fon-deel'-lyos], *m. pl.* The seat of underwear or wide pants. *(Acad.)*

fondista [fon-dees'-tah], *m.* Inn-keeper, hotel-keeper, tavern-keeper.

fondo [fon'-do], *m.* 1. Bottom of a hollow thing (de caja) 2. Bottom, the ground under the water (de mar). 3. Bottoms of a hill or valley. 4. Ground of silks and other stuffs. 5. Plain or cut velvet. 6. Thickness of a diamond. 7. Bottom, the extent of a man's capacity (carácter). 8. The principal or essential part of a thing. 9. Stock, quantity, store (virtudes, vicios) 10. Stock, fund, capital, effects. **Fondos públicos**, stute securities. 11. Every hollow to be gilded. 12. *(Mil.)* Space occupied by files of soldiers. **Dar fondo**, *(Naut.)* to cast anchor. **Echar a fondo**, to sink a vessel. **Irse a fondo**, to go to the bottom, to founder. **A fondo**, perfectly, completely. **Fondos vitalicios**, life annuities. **Fondos de un navío**, *(Naut.)* the floor or flat of a ship. **A fondo**, deeply. **El fondo**, the background. **Conocer algo a fondo**, to know something thoroughly. **Corredor de medio fondo**, middle-distance runner. **Bajos fondos sociales**, dregs of society. **Estar sin fondos**, to have no fund. **Reunir fondos**, to get money together.

fondón [fon-done'], *m.* 1. *V.* FONDILLÓN. 2. Ground of silk or velvet.

fondona [fon-do'-nah], *a.* Old and ungraceful (mujer).

fondura [fon-doo'-rah], *f.* Profundity, depth.

fonema [fo-nay'-mah], *m.* Phoneme.

fonética [fo-nay'-te-cah], *f.* Phonetics.

fonético, ca [fo-nay'-te-co, cah], *a.* Phonetic, relating to, or representing sounds.

fónica [fo'-ne-cah], *f.* Phonics, the science of articulate sound.

fónico [fo'-ne-co, cah], *a.* Phonic, relating to sound: phonetic. *(Arch.)* An elliptic arch for repeating echoes; the foci are called phonic, and there are placed the speaker and the listener. A whispering gallery.

fonil [fo-neel'], *m. (Naut.)* Funnel, an instrument for filling hogsheads of water.

fonje [fon'-hay], *a.* Bland, soft, spongy.

fonografía [fo-no-grah-fee'-ah], *f.* Phonography, representation of sound by signs: the chief mode of stenography.

fonográfico, ca [fo-no-grah'-fe-co, cah], *a.* Phonographic, belonging to phonography.

fonógrafo [fo-no'-grah-fo], *m.* Phonograph, an apparatus invented by Edison, for fixing and recording sounds.

fonología [fo-no-lo-hee'-ah], *f.* Phonology, the science of the letters and pronunciation of a language.

fonoteca [fo-no'-tay-cah], *f.* Record library, sound archive.

fontal [fon-tahl'], *a. (Ant.)* Main, chief, principal.

fontana [fon-tah'-nah], *f. (Poet.)* Fountain.

fontanal [fon-tah-nahl'], *m.* 1. Source or spring of water. 2. Place abounding in springs. -*a.* Belonging to fountain.

fontanar [fon-tah-nar'], *m.* A spring of water.

fontanela [fon-tah-nay'-lah], *f.* Surgeon's instrument for opening issues.

fontanería [fon-tah-nay-ree'-ah], *f.* 1. The art of conducting water through pipes to make fountains. 2. The collection of pipes and conduits through which water is conducted for a fountain. 3. Plumber's shop (tienda).

fontanero [fon-tah-nay'-ro], *m.* He that makes fountains, by conducting water through pipes and conduits.

fontezuela [fon-tay-thoo-ay'-lah], *f. dim.* A small fountain.

fontícola [fon-tee'-co-lah], *a. (Biol.)* Living in fountains or on their borders.

footing [foo'-teen], *m.* Jogging. **Hacer footing**, to jog, to go jogging.

foque [fo'-kay], *m. (Naut.)* Jib. **Foque mayor** or **foque de caza**, the standing jib.

forajido, da [fo-rah-hee'-do, dah], *a.* 1. Outlawed. 2. Wicked, villainous: used as a substantive.

foral [fo-rahl'], *a. (Law.)* Belonging to the statute law of a country, or to the civil rights of its inhabitants. **Bienes forales,** lands and tenements held by acknowledgment of superiority to a higher lord.

foralmente [fo-ral-men'-tay], *adv.* In the manner of courts.

foramen [fo-rah'-men], *m.* Hole in the under stone of a mill.

foraminíferos [fo-rah-me-nee'-fay-ros], *m. pl.* Foraminifera, microscopic protozoa, having calcareous shells.

foráneo, nea [fo-rah'-nayo, ah], *a.* Stranger, foreign.

forastería [fo-ras-tay-ree'-ah], *f.* Place for strangers, inn for strangers.

forastero, ra [fo-ras-tay'-ro, rah], *a.* 1. Strange, not living in the town or place. 2. Exotic, not produced in the country.

forastero, ra [fo-ras-tay'-ro, rah], *m. & f.* Stranger, guest: applied to persons belonging to another town, but of the same nation.

forbante [for-bahn'-tay], *m. V.* FILIBUSTERO.

forcejar [for-thay-har'], or **Forcejear,** *vn.* 1. To struggle, to strive, to labor. 2. To strive, to contest, to contend to struggle in opposition. -*va. V.* FORZAR.

forcejo [for-thay'-ho], *m.* Struggling, striving, laboring in opposition.

forcejón [for-thay-hone'], *m.* Push effort to disengage oneself from another.

forcejudo, da [for-thay-hoo'-do, dah], *a.* Strong, robust, of great strength.

fórceps [for'-theps], *m.* Forceps, ordinary and surgical.

forchina [for-chee'-nah], *f.* War-like instrument in shape of a fork.

forcina [for-thee'-nah], *f.* Swelling of a tree in the angle formed by a thick branch with the trunk.

forense [fo-ren'-say], *a.* Forensic, belonging to the courts.

forero, ra [fo-ray'-ro, rah], *a.* Conformable to the statute law of a country.

forestación [fo-rays-tah-the-on'], *f.* Afforestation.

forestal [fo-rays-tahl', *a.* Forest.

forja [for'-hah], *f.* 1. Forge, the place where silver is beaten into form (fundición). 2. Forging, fabricating, manufacturing. 3. Mortar, cement.

forjable [for-hah'-blay], *a.* Forgeable.

forjador [for-hah-dor'], *m.* Smith gold-beater; franker, forger.

forjadura [for-hah-doo'-rah], *f.* 1. Forging, beating a metal into form or shape. 2. Trap, snare, imposition. 3. Forgery; falsification.

forjar [for-har'], *va.* 1. To forge, to hammer, to bend metal into shape (hierro) 2. To finale, to form or fabricate by orderly construction. 3. To forge, to counterfeit, to falsify (falsificar). 4. To frame, to invent, to fabricate. **Forjar un plan**, to make a plan.

forlón [for-lone'], *m.* Old kind of coach with four seats.

forma [for'-mah], *f.* 1. Form, shape, a figure abstractedly considered, free, make, fashion. 2. Form, stated method, established practice, ritual, prescribed manner of doing something. 3. Hand, form or cast of waiting. 4. Form, the essential modification of matter, by which it has existence. 5. Form, regularity, method, order. 6. Form, particular model or modifation, mould, matrix. 7. *(Print.)* Form, a frame containing the pages arranged for press, as they appear on one side of a planted sheet. 8. The unleavened bread which serves for the communion of the laity. 9. Form, ceremony, external rights. **De forma que**, in such a manner that. **En forma** or **en debida forma**, formally, according to law or established rules, legally. **En forma** or **en toda forma**, perfectly, completely, carefully, heedfully, exactly. **Dar forma**, to regulate or arrange that which was disordered. **Tener buenas formas:** a) to be of fine figure, well-proportioned, especially said of women. b) to be polite, affable and discreet in speech and action. **La única forma de hacerlo es...**, the only way to do it is. **De esta forma**, in this way. **De todas formas**, at any rate. **Forma de pago**, means of payment.

formable [for-mah'-blay], *a.* That which may be formed.

formación [for-mah-the-on'], *f.* 1. Formation, the act of forming or generating. 2. Formation, the manner in which something is formed; form, shape, figure. 3. *(Mil.)* Array of troops. 4. Twisted cord of silk, gold, silver, etc., used by embroiderers. 5. Training, education (educación). **Sin la debida formación en la investigación,** without the proper research.

formador, ra [for-mah-dor', rah], *m. & f.* Former, one that forms, fashions, or shapes.

formaje [for-mah'-hay], *m.* Cheesevat, cheese. *Cf.* Fr. fromage.

formal [for-mahl'], *a.* 1. Formal, regular, methodical. 2. Proper, genuine. 3. Formal (promesa etc.), serious (serio), grave, steady, sedate, punctual (puntual), dignified (grave). **Es una persona muy seria**, he is a perfectly reliable sort. **Siempre estuvo muy formal conmigo,** he was always very correct towards me.

formalidad [for-mah-le-dahd'], *f.* 1. Formality, the quality by which something is what it is. 2. Exactness, punctuality. 3. Formality, ceremony; established mode of behavior. 4. Gravity, seriousness (seriedad), solemnity. 5. Established form of judicial proceedings, or legal precedent (requisito). **Son las formalidades de costumbre**, these are the usual formalities. **Con formalidad**, in earnest.

formalismo [for-mah-lees'-mo], *m.* 1. Formalism, a metaphysical system which denies the existence of matter and recognizes only the form. 2. Rigorous application of method, adhesion to routine; red tape (burocrático).

formalizar [for-mah-le-thar'], *va.* To form or make complete or perfect (cosas no materiales). -*vr.* 1. To grow formal (relación), to affect gravity, to be regulized (situación). 2. To grow serious (ponerse serio). 3. To take offence (ofenderse).

formalmente [for-mal-men'-tay], *adv.* 1. Formally, according to established rules. 2. Formally, seriously.

formar [for-mar'], *va.* 1. To form, to shape, to fashion, to frame, to make up, to cut out, to build up (existenciar, reserva). 2. To form, to make out of materials (integrar). 3. To form, to model to a particular shape. 4. To form or draw up troops; to put in order; to arrange in a particular manner. 5. To train, to educate (educar). -*vn.* 1. To adjust the edges of embroidery work. 2. To shape, to develop (desarrollarse). 3. To be trained, to be educated (educarse). **Formar concepto**, to form judgment. **Está formado por**, it is formed by. **Se formó en la escuela de Praga**, he was trained in the Prague school.

formatear [for-mah-tay-ar'], *va.* (*Comput.*) To format.

formateo [for-mah-tay'-o], *m.* (*Comput.*) Formating.

formativo, va [for-mah-tee'-vo, vah], *a.* Formative.

formato [for-mah'-to], *m.* 1. (*Tip.*) Format; size (tamaño de papel). **Periódico de formato reducido**, tabloid newspaper. 2. (*Comput.*) **Formato del hardware**, hardware formatting. **Formato del software**, software formatting. **Formato opcional**, optional formatting.

formatriz [for-mah-treeth'], *a.* Forming.

formejar [for-may-har'], *va.* (*Naut.*) To arrange things in order on board ships; to trim the hold.

formero [for-may'-ro], *m.* (*Arch.*) Side arch of a vault.

formicante [for-me-cahn'-tay], *a.* Applied to a low, weak, and frequent pulse.

formicarios, formícidos [for-me-cah'-re-os, for-mee'-the-dos], *m. pl.* (*Et.*) Hymenoptera which carry a sting; bees, wasps, sandwasps, etc.

fórmico [for'-me-co], *m.* 1. Formic, (ácido, éter). 2. A certain hard tumor like a wart.

formicular [for-me-coo-lar'], *a.* Relating to ants.

formidable [for-me-dah'-blay], *a.* 1. Formidable (terrible), dreadful, tremendous, terrific (estupendo). 2. Uncommonly large (enorme).

formidablemente [for-me-dah-blay-men'-tay], *adv.* Formidably.

formidoloso, sa [for-me-do-lo'-so, sah], *a.* 1. Timorous, timid, fearful. 2. Dreadful, frightful, horrible.

formillón [for-meel-lyon'], *m.* A hatform.

formón [for-mone'], *m.* 1. Paring chisel, used by carpenters and joiners. 2. Punch, an instrument used to cut wafers for consecration.

fórmula [for'-moo-lah], *f.* 1. Formula, a prescribed model or rule. 2. Recipe. 3. An algebraical expression. 4. Profession of faith. 5. Formulary. **Una fórmula para conseguir el éxito**, a formula to ensure success.

formular [for-moo-lar'], *va.* To formulate; to draw up, to make out; to frame, to pose (pregunta); to file, to put in (reivindicación).

formulario [for-moo-lah'-re-o], *m.* Formulary, a book containing models, rules, or formulas. **Formulario de inscripción**, application form.

formulista [for-moo-lees'-tah], *m.* One who punctually observes the prescribed models.

fornáceo, cea [for-nah'-thay-o, ah], *a.* (*Poet.*) Belonging to or like a furnace.

fornaz [for-nath'], *m.* (*Poet.*) V. FRAGUA.

fornecino, na [for-nay-thee'-no, nah], *a.* Bastard, illegitimate (niños).

fornelo [for-nay'-lo], *m.* A portable little oven or furnace.

fornicación [for-ne-cah-the-on'], *f.* 1. Fornication. 2. In Scripture, sometimes idolatry.

fornicador, ra [for-ne-cah-dor', rah], *m. & f.* Fornicator.

fornicar [for-ne-car'], *va.* To fornicate, to commit lewdness.

fornicario, ria [for-ne-cah'-re-o, ah], *a.* Relating to fornication.

fornicio [for-nee'-the-o], *m.* (*Ant.*) Fornication.

fornido, da [for-nee'-do, dah], *a.* Robust, corpulent, lusty, stout.

fornitura [for-ne-too'-rah], *f.* 1. Leather straps worn by soldiers. 2. (*Print.*) Types cast to complete sorts.

foro [fo'-ro], *m.* 1. Court of justice, the hall where tribunals hold their sittings. 2. Bar, the legal profession. 3. Lordship, the right of a superior lord, of whom lands or tenements are held. 4. Background of the stage or theatre. 5. Forum (reunión), meeting.

forofo, fa [fo-ro'-fo], *m & f.* Fan, supporter.

forrado [for-rah'-do], *a. & pp.* of FORRAR. Lined. **Un libro forrado de pergamino**, a book bound in parchment.

forraje [for-rah'-hay], *m.* 1. Forage (pienso); grain, hay, or grass for horses; foraging (acto). 2. (*coll.*) Abundance of things of little value.

forrajeador, forrajero [for-rah-hay-ah-dor'], *m.* Forager, a soldier detached in search of forage; fodderer.

forrajear [for-rah-hay-ar'], *va.* To forage, to collect forage for the horses of soldiers.

forrar [for-rar'], *va.* 1. To line (ropa). 2. To cover (libro). 3. To upholster (coche). 4. To lag (cubo, cisterna). -*vr.* 1. To line one's pocket (enriquecerse). 2. To stuff oneself (de comida).

forro [for'-ro], *m.* 1. Lining. 2.(*Naut.*) Furring of a ship, double planks laid on the sides, sheathing. 3. Cover of a book. **Con forro de piel**, with a fur lining. **Ni por el forro**, not in the slightest.

fortachón, na [for-tah-chon', nah], *a.* Applied to a person possessed of uncommon strength.

fortalecedor, ra [for-tah-lay-thay-dor', rah], *m. & f.* Fortifier.

fortalecer [for-tah-lay-therr'], *va.* 1. To fortify, to strengthen, to corroborate. 2. To fortify a place. 3. To aid, to encourage, to support (moralmente). -*vr.* 1. To fortify oneself. 2. To become stronger (opinión). (*Yo fortalezco, yo fortalezca*, from *Fortalecer.* V. ABORRECER.)

fortalecimiento [for-tah-lay-the-me-en'-to], *m.* 1. Act of fortifying. 2. Works raised for the defence of a place.

fortaleza [for-tah-lay'-thah], *f.* 1. Fortitude, firmness. 2. Fortitude, courage. 3. Strength, vigor, nerve, force, manhood (cualidad). 4. Stronghold, fortress.

forte [for'-tay], *int.* (*Naut.*) Avast! **-a.** (*Mus.*) Loud.

fortificable [for-te-fe-cah'-blay], *a.* Fortifiable.

fortificación [for-te-fe-cah-the-on'], *f.* 1. Fortification, the science of military architecture. 2. Fortification, place built for strength. 3. Works raised for the defence of a place.

fortificador [for-te-fe-cah-dor'], Fortifier.

fortificante [for-te-fe-cahn'-tay], *pa.* Fortifying.

fortificar [for-te-fe-car'], *va.* 1. To strengthen, to fortify, to corroborate, to invigorate. 2. To fortify a place.

fortín [for-teen'], *m.* 1. (*dim.*) Fortin, fortlet, a small fort. 2. Field or temporary fortifications for the defence of troops.

FORTRAN [for-tran], *m.* . (*Comput.*) FORTRAN (FORmula TRANslator).

fortuitamente [for-too-ee-tah-men'-tay], *adv.* Fortuitously; by chance.

fortuito, ta [for-too-ee'-to, tah], *a.* Fortuitous, accidental, unexpected.

fortuna [for-too'-nah], *f.* 1. Fortune, chance, fate. 2. Good luck (suerte), success. 3. Storm, tempest. 4. Chance, unforeseen event. **Probar fortuna**, to try one's fortune. **Por fortuna**, luckily.

fortunón [for-too-none'], *m.* (*Aug.*) Great fortune, immense riches.

forzadamente [for-thah-dah-men-tay], *adv.* Forcibly, violently, forcefully. **Sonreír forzadamente**, to force a smile.

forzado, da [for-thah'-do, dah], *a. & pp.* of FORZAR. 1. Forced, constrained, necessitated. 2. Indispensable, necessary. **Sonrisa forzada**, forced smile.

forzado [for-thah'-do], *m.* Criminal sentenced to the galleys.

forzador [for-thah-dor'], *m.* 1. Ravisher. 2. Forcer, one who commits acts of violence to attain some purpose.

forzal [for-thahl'], *m.* The middle part of a comb between the two rows of teeth.

forzamiento [for-thah-me-en'-to], *m.* The act of forcing.

forzar [for-thar'], *va.* 1. To force, to overpower by strength, to draw or push by main strength (obligar). 2. To force, to compel, to constrain. 3. To enforce, to urge. 4. To subdue by force of arms. 5. To force, to ravish, to commit a rape (mujer). 6. To force, to oblige or enforce, to urge. 7. To force (puerta); to break into (casa); to force (cerradura).

forzosa [for-tho'-sah], *f.* 1. A decisive move at the game of draughts. 2. Necessity of acting against one's will.

forzosamente [for-tho-sah-men'-tay], *adv.* Forcibly, necessarily; violently, forcedly. **Tuvieron forzosamente que venderlo**, they had no choice but to sell it.

forzoso, sa [for-tho'-so, sah], *a.* Indispensable, necessary (necesario), needful, requisite, compulsory (obligatorio); forced (aterrizaje)

forzudo, da [for-thoo'-do, dah], *a.* Strong, vigorous, potent, lusty, stout, able-bodied.

fosa [fo'-sah], *f.* 1. Grave, tomb (sepultura). **Fosa común**, common grave. 2. *(Anat.)* Fossa. **Fosa séptica**, septic tank.

fosar [fo-sar'], *va.* To make a pit, ditch, or fosse round something.

fosca [fos'-cah], *f. (Prov.)* A thick wood or grove.

fosco, ca [fos'-co, cah], *a.* Brow-beaten, frowning. *V.* HOSCO.

fosfático, ca [fos-fah'-te-co, cah], *a.* Phosphatic.

fosfato [fos-fah'-to], *m.* Phosphate, salt of phosphoric acid.

fosfito [fos-fee'-to], *m.* Phosphite, a salt of phosphorous acid.

fosforado, da [fos-fo-rah'-do, dah], *a.* Phosphated, containing phosphorus.

fosforera [fos-fo-ray'-rah], *f.* A match-box.

fosforero, ra [fos-fo-ray'-ro, rah], *m. & f.* A vender of matches.

fosforescencia [fos-fo-res-then'-the-ah], *f.* Phosphorescence.

fosforescente [fos-fo-res-then'-tay], *a.* Phosphorescent.

fosforescer [fos-fo-res-therr'], *vn.* To be phosphorescent, to shed a phosphoric light.

fosfórico, ca [fos-fo'-re-co, cah], *a.* Phosphoric.

fósforo [fos'-fo-ro], *m.* 1. Phosphorus, one of the elements. 2. A friction match (cerilla).

fosforoso, sa [fos-fo-ro'-so, sah], *a.* Phosphorous, relating to the lower equivalents of phosphorus.

fósfuro [fos-foo'-ro], *m.* Phosphide, a compound of phosphorus, not acid.

fosgeno [fos-hay'-no], *m. (Chem.)* Phosgene.

fósil [fo'-seel], *a.* Fossil, dug out of the earth, and mineral in nature. *-m* Fossil, petrifaction, organic remains.

fosilizarse [fo-se-le-thar'-say], *vr.* To become fossilized, petrified.

foso [fo'-so], *m.* 1. Pit, hole dug in the ground. *V.* HOYO. 2. Bog, a marshy ground covered with water. 3. Moat, ditch fosse. 4. Pit (escenario).

foto [fo-to], *f.* Photo; snap, snapshot. **Foto de conjunto**, group photo. **Sacar una foto**, to take a photo.

fotocélula [fo-to-thay'-loo'-lah], *f.* Electric eye.

fotocopia [fo-to-co'-pe-ah], *f.* 1. Photocopy. 2. Photocopying (acto).

fotocopiadora [fo-to-co-pe-ah'-do-rah], *f.* Photocopier.

fotocopiar [fo-to-co-pe-ar'], *va.* To photocopy.

fotoeléctrico, ca [fo-to-ay-lec'-tre-co, cah], *a.* Photoelectric.

fotofobia [fo-to-fo'-be-ah], *f.* Photophobia, dread of light (enfermedad).

fotogénico, ca [fo-to-hay'-ne-co, cah], *a.* Photogenic, light-producing.

fotograbado [fo-to-grah-bah'-do], *m.* A photo engraving, photo gravure.

fotografía [fo-to-grah-fee'-ah], *f.* 1. Photography, the art of fixing an image by the chemical rays of light. 2. A photograph, the picture obtained by this process. **Fotografía aérea**, aerial photography. **Fotografía en colores**, color photography.

fotografiar [fo-to-grah-fe-ar'], *va.* To photograph.

fotográfico, ca [fo-to-grah'-fe-co, cah], *a.* Photographic, relative to photography.

fotógrafo [fo-to'-grah-fo], *m.* Photographer. **Fotógrafo aficionado**, amateur photographer.

fotograma [fo-to-grah-mah], *m.* (Cine) Shot, still.

fotolitografía [fo-to-le-to-grah-fee'-ah], *f.* 1. Photolithography, the art of imprinting a photograph upon a lithographic stone. 2. Photolithograph, each of the prints obtained by this process.

fotomatón [fo-to-mah-tone'], *m.* 1. Photograph booth (quiosco). 2. Passport-type photo (foto).

fotometría [fo-to-may-tree'-ah], *f.* Photometry.

fotométrico, ca [fo-to-may'-tre-co, cah], *a.* Photometric, measuring light.

fotómetro [fo-to'-may-tro], *m.* Photometer.

fotonovela [fo-to-no-vay'-lah], *f.* Romance illustrated with photos.

fotosíntesis [fo-to-seen'-tay-sis], *f.* Photosynthesis.

fotostático, ca [fo-tos-tah'-te-co, cah], *a.* Photostatic.

fototipia [fo-to-tee'-pe-ah], *f.* Phototypy.

foulard [foo-lar'], *m.* Scarf (cabeza).

fovila [fo-vee'-lah], *f. (Bot.)* Fovilla, a substance emitted from the pollen of flowers.

foya [fo'-yah], *f. (Prov.)* An oven full of charcoal.

frac [frahc], *m.* A dress-coat.

fracasado, da [frah-cah-sah'-do], *a.* Unsuccessful, failed. *-m & f.* Failure, person who is a failure.

fracasar [frah-cah-sar'], *vn.* 1. To crumble, to break in pieces (barcos). 2. To be lost or destroyed. 3. To be unsuccessful.

fracaso [frah-cah'-so], *m.* 1. Downfall, ruin, destruction. 2. Calamity, an unfortunate event. **Es un total fracaso**, it's a complete disaster.

fracción [frac-the-on'], *f.* 1. Fraction, the act of breaking into parts. 2. Fraction, a broken part of an integral. 3. *(Math.)* Fraction. **Fracción decimal**, fraction.

fraccionar [frac-the-o-nar'], *va.* To divide into fractions, to break up, to split up.

fraccionario, ria [frac-theo-nah'-re-o, ah], *a.* Fractional. **Número fraccionario**, a mixed number.

fracmasón [frac-mah-son'], *m.* Freemason, mason.

fractura [frac-too'-rah], *f.* 1. Fracture, breach, separation of contiguous parts. 2. *(Surg.)* Fracture, the separation of the continuity of a bone. **Fractura complicada**, compound fracture.

fracturar [frac-too-rar'], *va.* To fracture, to break a bone. *-vr.* To fracture, to break

fraga, fragaria [frah'-gah, frah-gah'-re-ah], *f.* Species of raspberry.

fragancia [frah-gahn'-the-ah], *f.* 1. Fragrance, sweetness of smell. 2. Good name, good reputation. 3. Actual commission of a crime.

fragante [trah-gahn'-tay], *a.* 1. Fragrant, odoriferous. 2. Flagrant, notorious. **En fragante**, in the act itself, red-handed (en flagrante delito). *V.* FLAGRANTE.

franganti (in) *adv.* Red-handed, in the act.

fragata [frah-gah'-tah], *f.* 1. A frigate. **Fragata ligera**, a light fast-sailing vessel. 2. The frigate bird.

frágil [frah'-heel], *a.* 1. Brittle, tangible, fragile. 2. Frail, weak of resolution, liable to error or seduction. 3. Decaying, perishable.

fragilidad [frah-he-le-dahd'], *f.* 1. Fragility, brittleness. 2. Fragility, frailty, liableness to a fault. 3. Sin of infirmity, sensual pleasure, folly.

frágilmente [frah'-heel-men-tay], *adv.* Frailly.

fragmentación [frag-men-tah-the-on'], *f.* Fragmentation.

fragmento [frag-men'-to], *m.* 1. Fragment, a small part separated from the whole. 2. Fragment, a part of some book or writing.

fragor [frah-gor'], *m. (Archaic.)* Noise, clamor, crash.

fragoroso, sa [frah-go-so], *a. (Poet.)* Noisy, obstreperous.

fragosidad [frah-go-se-dahd'], *f.* Unevenness or roughness of the road; imperviousness of a forest; craggedness, cragginess.

fragoso, sa [frah-go'-so, sah], *a.* Craggy, rough, uneven; full of brambles and briers; noisy; difficult (terreno); dense (bosque).

fragua [frah'-goo-ah], *f.* 1. Forge, as for iron. 2. Place where intrigues are plotted.

fraguador [frah-goo-ah-dor'], *m.* Schemer, one who plans an intrigue; one who counterfeits or forges.

fraguar [frah-goo-ar'], *va.* 1. To forge, to reduce iron or other metal into shape (hierro) 2. *(Met.)* To plan, to plot, to contrive, to brew, to hatch.-*vr.* To unite in a mass (mortero)

fragura [frah-goo'-rah], *f.* Roughness of the road, imperviousness of a forest.

fraile [frah'-e-lay], *m.* 1. Friar, brother; appellation of the members of religious orders. **Fraile predicador**, friar preacher. *V.* RELIGIOSO. 2. Fold or plait in petticoats. 3. *(Print.)* That part of a printed page which is pale for want of ink. 4. The upright post of a floodgate in watermills.

frailecillo [fra-he-lay-theel'-lyo], *m.* 1. *(dim.)* A little friar, or a child which wears a friar's habit. 2. *(Orn.)* Lapwing. 3. Wedge securing the spindle of a silkreel.

frailería [fra-he-lay-ree'-ah], *f. (coll.)* Number of friars assembled together.

frailero, ra [frah-e-lay'-ro, rah], *a.* Very fond of friars.

frailesco, ca [frah-e-less'-co, cah], *a.* Monkish, belonging to friars, friar-like.

frailía [frah-e-lee'-ah], *f.* 1. State of monks, monastic life. 2. Regular clergy.

frailuno, na [frah-e-loo'-no, nah], Belonging or proper to a friar.

frambuesa [fram-boo-ay'-sah], *f.* The raspberry.

frambueso [fram-boo-ay'-so], *m. (Bot.)* Raspberry bush.

frámea [frah'-may-ah], *f. (Obs.)* Javelin, dart.

francachela [fran-cah-chay'-lah], *f. V.* COMILONA.

francalete [fran-cah-lay'-tay], *m.* Strap, slip of leather with a buckle.

francamente [fran-cah-men'-tay], *adv.* 1. Frankly, openly, freely, nakedly (hablar) 2. Frankly; really, definitely (realmente). **Francamente no lo sé**, frankly I don't know.

francés, sa [fran-thays', sah], *a.* French. -*m.* The French language. **A la francesa**, after the French fashion. **Despedirse a la francesa**, *(Coll.)* to take French leave.

francesilla [fran-thay-seel'-lyah], *f. (Bot.)* Common yard crowfoot.

franchipán [fran-che-pahn'], *m.* Frangipani, a perfume.

franciscano, na [fran-this-cah'-no, nah], *a.* 1. Franciscan, belonging to the order of St. Francis. 2. Gray-colored, like the dress of the Franciscans.

francmasón [franc-mah-sone'], *m.* (free) mason.

francmasonería [franc-mah-so-nay-ree'-ah], *f.* (Free) masonry, a secret society of mutual protection.

franco [frahn'-co], *m.* 1. Franc, a French coin. 2. Fairtime, when merchandise is sold free of duty.-*pl.* Franks, an appellation given by the Turks, Arabs, and Greeks to the people of the west of Europe.

franco, ca [frahn'-co, cah], *a.* 1. Frank, open, generous, liberal, open-hearted, bountiful (directo). **Si he de ser franco**, frankly, to tell the truth. 2. Free, disengaged. 3. Exempt, privileged. 4. Ingenuous, plain, sincere (sincero), fair, generous. 5. Free, exempt from duty. **Puerto franco**, a free port. **Franco de porte**, carriage-free.

francófono [fran-do-fo'-no], *a.* French-speaking. -*m & f.* French speaker.

franco-hispano [fran-co-ees-pah'-no], *a.* Franco-Spanish.

francolín [fran-co-leen'], *m. (Orn.)* Francolin, the African or Indian partridge. **francotirador** [fran-co-tee-rah-dor'], *m.* 1. Sniper, sharp shooter. 2. Freelance (periodista)

franela [frah-nay'-lah], *f.* Flannel (tela).

frange [frahn'-hay], *m. (Her.)* Division of the field of a shield.

frangente [fran-hen'-tay], *m.* Accident, disaster.

frangible [fran-hee'-blay], *a.* Brittle, frangible.

frangollar [fran-gol-lyar'], *va.* To do a thing carelessly.

frangollo [fran-gol'-lyo], *m.* 1. Pottage made of wheat boiled in milk. 2. *(Peru and Chili)* A stew of many ingredients or which is poorly made. 3. *(coll.)* Disorder, confusion.

frangote [fran-go'-tay], *m.* Bale of goods.

frángula [frahn'-goo-lah], *f. (Bot.)* Berrybearing alder, alder buckthorn.

franja [frahn'-hah], *f.* 1. Fringe, an ornamental border, stripe. 2. Fringe, strip, band (zona). **Franja de tierra**, strip of land.

franjar [fran-har'], *va.* To fringe, to trim with fringe, to adorn with fringes.

franjear [fran-hay-ar'], *va. V.* FRANJAR.

franquear [fran-kay-ar'], *va.* 1. To exempt, to grant immunity from, to enfranchise. 2. To pay the postage on letters, books, etc (Correos). **Una carta franqueada**, a post-paid letter. 3. To gratify, to make liberal grants or gifts. 4. To disengage, to extricate; to clear from obstacles or impediments (obstáculo). 5. To free a slave. *(Acad.) -vr.* 1. To give oneself easily to the desire of others. **Franquearse con uno**, to unbosom oneself to somebody. 2. To unbosom oneself, to reveal in confidence one's secrets or thoughts. 3. To become liberal. 4. *(Naut.)* To be ready for sailing.-*vn. (Naut.)* To be situated at a point whence may be seen clearly and openly a work, harbor-entrance, etc.

franqueo [fran-kay'-o], *m.* 1. Franking letters, printed matter, etc. 2. Postage, that is paid on mail matter; also postage stamps.

franqueza [fran-kay'-thah], *f.* 1. Freedom, liberty, exemption, enfranchisement, freeness. 2. Frankness, generosity, open-heartedness; liberality of sentiment. 3. Frankness, ingenuousness, sincerity. **Lo digo con toda franqueza**, I say so quite frankly. **Con franqueza**, frankly.

franquía [fran-kee'-ah], *f. (Naut.)* In the stream. Readiness for sailing.

franquicia [fran-kee'-the-ah], *f.* 1. Immunity or exemption from taxes, liberty, franchise (exención). 2. A privileged place, which enjoys exemption from taxes and imposts. **Franquicia postal**, privilege of franking letters.

fraque [frah'-kay], *m. V.* FRAC.

frasca [frahs'-cah], *f. (Prov.)* Dry leaves or small branches of trees.

frasco [frahs'-co], *m.* 1. Flask, a bottle with a narrow neck. **Frasco de bolsillo**, hip flask. **Frasco de perfume**, scent bottle. 2. Powder-horn or flask.

frase [frah'-say], *f.* 1. Phrase, a mode of speech (locución). 2. Idiomatic expression, style of any writer (oración). 3. An energetic expression, generally metaphorical, signifying more than is expressed. **Frase compleja**, complex sentence. **Diccionario de frases**, dictionary of quotations.

frasear [frah-say-ar'], *va.* 1. To phrase, to employ idiomatic expressions. 2. *(Mus.)* To phrase, to give the proper expression to each musical phrase.

fraseología [frah-say-olo-hee'-ah], *f.* 1. Phraseology, the style of a writer. 2. Verbosity, pomposity.

frasquera [fras-kay'-rah], *f.* Bottle-case, liquor-case.

frasquerilla, ita [fras-kay-reel'-lyah, ee'-tah], *f. dim.* Small bottle-case.

frasqueta [fras-kay'-tah], *f.* Frisket of a printing press.

frasquillo, ito [fras-keel'-lyo], *m. dim.* A small flask.

fraterna [frah-terr'-nah], *f. (coll.)* A severe reprimand, lecture, lesson.

fraternal [frah-ter-nahl'], *a.* Fraternal, brotherly.

fraternalmente [frah-ter-nal-men'-tay], *adv.* Fraternally.

fraternidad [frah-ter-ne-dahd'], *f.* Fraternity, the state or quality of a brother, brotherhood.

fraternizar [fra-ter-ne-thar'], *vn.* To live in harmony, to fraternize.

fraterno, na [frah-terr'-no, nah], *a.* Fraternal, brotherly.

frates [frah'-tes], *m.* 1. A glass instrument, mushroom-shaped, for polishing stockings after they are washed. 2. A mason's wooden trowel.

fratesar [frah-tay-sar'], *va.* To polish or smooth with the frates.

fratricida [frah-tre-thee'-dah], *m. & f.* Fratricide, murderer of a brother.

fratricidio [frah-tre-thee'-de-o], *m.* Fratricide, murder of a brother.

fraude [frah'-oo-day], *m.* Fraud, deceit, cheat, trick, artifice, imposture, craft, gull, dishonestly (cualidad).

fraudulencia [frah-oo-doo-len'-the-ah], *f.* Fraudulence, trickiness, deceitfulness.

fraudulentamente [frah-oo-doo-len-tah-men'-tay], adv. Fraudulently, knavishly.

fraudulento, ta [frah-oo-doo-len'-to, tah], a. Fraudulent, deceitful, artful, knavish.

fraudulosamente [frah-oo-doo-lo-sah-men'-tay], adv. Fraudulently, deceitfully, knavishly.

fraustina [frah-oos-tee'-nah], f. A wooden head for fashioning ladies' headdresses.

fraxinela [frac-se-nay'-lah], f. (Bot.) White dittany.

fray [frah'-e], m. A contracted appellation of respect addressed to religious men; brother. V. FRAILE.

frazada [frah-thah'-dah], f. A blanket.

frazadilla [frah-thah-deel'-lyah], f. dim. A small or light blanket.

frecuencia [fray-coo-en'-the-ah], f. Frequency. **Con frecuencia**, frequently.

frecuentación [fray-coo-en-tah-the-on'], f. Frequentation, frequenting, visiting often.

frecuentador, ra [fray-coo-en-tah-dor', rah], m. & f. Frequenter.

frecuentar [fray-coo-en-tar'], va. 1. To frequent, to haunt, to visit often. 2. To repeat an act often.

frecuentativo [fray-coo-en-tah-tee'-vo], a. (Gram.) Frequentative (verbos).

frecuente [fray-coo-en'-tay], a. Frequent, often done (costumbre) or seen, often occurring. -adv. V. FRECUENTEMENTE.

frecuentemente [fray-coo-en-tay-men', tay], adv. Frequently, often, commonly.

fregadero [fray-gah-day'-ro], m. Kitchen sink (recipiente).

fregado [fray-gah'-do], m. 1. The act of scouring or cleaning kitchen utensils (de cocina). 2. A complicated subject or matter (lío); nasty affair (asunto turbio). -**Fregado, da**, pp. of FREGAR.

fregador [fray-gah-dor'], m. 1. Scullery. V. FREGADERO. 2. Dishcloth (trapo).

fregadura [fray-gah-doo'-rah], f. The act of rubbing or scouring.

fregajo [fray-gah'-ho], m. V. ESTROPAJO.

fregamiento [fray-gah-me-en'-to], m. V. FRICACIÓN.

fregar [fray-gar'], va. 1. To rub one thing against another (estregar). 2. To scour kitchen utensils (platos).

fregatriz [fray-gah-treeth'], f. Kitchen maid, kitchen-wench.

fregona [fray-go'-nah], f. Kitchen maid (persona), kitchen-wench, mop (utensilio).

fregoncilla [fray-gon-theel'-lyah], f. dim. A little kitchen maid.

fregonil [fray-go-neel'], a. Belonging to or becoming a kitchen maid.

fregonzuela [fray-gon-thoo-ay'-lah], f. dim. A little kitchen-girl.

freidura [fray-doo'-rah], f. Act of frying or dressing in a pan.

freír [fray-eer'], va. 1. To fry or dress in a frying pan. 2. (Fig.) To annoy (molestar); to torment (atormentar); to bore (aburrir). -vr. To fry, to be frying. **Freírse de calor**, to be excessively hot.

freje [fray'-hay], m. (Prov.) A hoop of osier to bind things with.

fréjol [fray'-ho-le], m. French bean, kidney bean.

frejol [fray-ho-le'], m. (Amer.) V. FREJOL and FRÍSOL.

frelo, la [tray'-lo, lah], a. Delicate, weakly, sickly. (Prov. Andal.)

frémito [fray'-me-to], m. V. BRAMIDO.

frenar [fray-nar'], va. 1. (Aut.) To brake; to put the brake on. 2. (Fig.) To check.

frenazo [fray-nah-tho], m. Sudden braking; sudden halt. **Dar un frenazo**, to brake suddenly.

frenería [fray-nay-ree'-ah], f. 1. Business of bridle making. 2. Place in which bridles are made or sold.

frenero [fray-nay'-ro], m. One who makes the bits of a bridle, a bridle maker.

frenesí [fray-nay-see'], m. 1. Frenzy, madness, distraction. 2. (Met.) Folly, extravagant caprice.

frenéticamente [fray-nay'-te-cah-men-tay], adv. Madly, furiously, distractedly, franticly.

frenético, ca [fray-nay'-te-co, cah], a. Mad, distracted, frantic, furious, lunatic.

frénico, ca [fray'-ne-co, cah], a. 1. Phrenic, relating to the diaphragm. 2. Relating to the intelligence or thought (phrenic).

frenillar [fray-neel-lyar'], va. (Naut.) To bridle the oars.

frenillo [fray-neel'-lyo], m. 1. Frenum of the tongue; tongue-tie. 2. (Naut.) Bridle of the oars, a rope with which oars are tied.

frenitis [fray-nee'-tis], f. Inflammation of the diaphragm.

freno [fray'-no], m. 1. Brake (coche). **Meter el freno**, to put on the brake. **Soltar el freno**, to release the brake. 2. Curb, check, restraint. **Poner frenos a las malas lenguas**, to stop the gossip. 3. Bridle or bit (de caballo). 4. Brace (dientes).

frenología [fray-no-lo-hee'-ah], f. Phrenology, cranioscopy; (formerly) the branch of science concerned with localization of functions of the human brain, esp. by examination of the shape and size of the skull.

frenológico, ca [fray-no-lo'-he-co, cah], a. Phrenological.

frenólogo [fray-no'-lo-go], m. Phrenologist.

frental [fren-tahl'], a. Frontal (frente). V. FRONTAL.

frentaza [fran-tah'-thah], f. aug. A broad forehead.

frente [fren'-tay], f. 1. The forehead. **Arrugar la frente**, to knit one's brow. **Frente a frente**, face to face. **Ir de frente**, to go foward. **Hacer frente a unos grandes gastos**, to meet considerable expenses. 2. Blank space at the beginning of a letter or other document. (Acad.) 3. com. Front, the forepart of a building or any other thing (parte delantera). **Frente, en frente**, opposite, over the way. -m. 4. (Mil.) Front rank of a body of troops. **Frente de batalla**, battle front. 5. Face of a bastion. -prep. Opposite, facing; in front of; (fig.) as opposed to.

frentero [fren-tay'-ro], m. Band worn on the forehead of children, to protect their face in case of falling.

freo [fray'-o], m. (Naut.) 1. A narrow channel between an island and the mainland. 2. (Prov.) Gorge, canyon, ravine between mountains.

fresa [fray'-sah], f. Strawberry, the fruit of the strawberry plant.

fresada [fray-sah'-dah], f. A dish formerly made of flour, milk and butter.

fresadora [fray-sah-do'-rah], f. Milling or drilling machine.

fresal [fray-sahl'], m. 1. (Bot.) Strawberry plant. 2. Ground bearing strawberry plants.

fresca [fres'-cah], f. 1. V. FRESCO. **Tomar la fresca**, to take the air (aire). **Salir con la fresca**, to go out during the fresh air in the evening or very early in the morning (período). 2. (coll.) (impertinencia) A cheeky remark. 3. Shameless woman, brazen woman (descarada).

frescachón, na [fres-cah-chone', nah], a. 1. Stout, good looking (robusto). 2. (Naut.) Fresh, cool (viento).

frescal [fres-cahl'], a. Not entirely fresh, but preserved with little salt (pescado).

frescamente [fres-cah-men'-tay], adv. 1. Freshly, recently, lately. 2. Coolly, resolutely, without passion.

frescar [fres-car'], vn. (Naut.) V. REFRESCAR.

fresco, ca [fres'-co, cah], a. 1. Fresh, coolish, rather cool. 2. Fresh, recent, newly come, just made (nuevo). **Cosas todavía frescas en la memoria**, things still fresh in the memory. 3. Plump, ruddy. 4. Fresh, bold in manner (descarado). **Estar más fresco que una lechuga**, to be as cool as a cucumber. **Dinero fresco**, ready money, cash paid off-hand. **Viento fresco**, (Naut.) a fresh breeze. 5. Light, thin (vestido, tela) 6. Fresh, ruddy, healthy (tez).

fresco [fres'-co], m. 1. Cool, refreshing air (aire). **Tomar el fresco**, to get some fresh air. 2. Fresh guy (sinvergüenza). V. FRESCURA. 3. (Perú) A cold iced drink, prepared from pineapple.

frescón, na [fres-cone', nah], *a. aug.* Very fresh; blooming.

frescor [fres-cor'], *m.* **1.** Cool, refreshing air. 2. *V.* FRESCURA. 3. Flesh-color (pintura).

frescote, ta [fres-co'-tay, tah], *a.* 1. Aug. of FRESCO. 2. Ruddy, youthful, and strong.

frescura [fres-coo'-rah], *f.* 1. Freshness, coolness (frío), cool, gentle cold, cheek (descarado). 2. Amenity, agreeableness of situation. 3. Frankness, openness. 4. Freedom, ease, disengagement. 5. Serenity (serenidad), tranquility, coolness of mind. **Con la mayor serenidad**, with the greatest unconcern.

fresera [fray-say'-rah], *f.* A rosaceous plant with fibrous roots, resembling the strawberry and cinquefoil.

fresita [fray-see'-tah], *f.* The service-berry.

fresnal [fres-nahl'], *m. V.* FRESNEDA.

fresneda [fres-nay'-dah], *f.* Grove or plantation of ash trees.

fresnillo [fres-neel'-lyo], *m. V.* DÍCTAMO BLANCO. White fraxinella.

fresno [fres'-no], *m.* 1. (*Bot.*) Ash tree. 2. (*Poet.*) Staff of a lance, a spear. **Fresno florido or de flor**, (*Bot.*) Flowering ash tree.

fresón or **fresón de Chile** [fray-sone'], *m.* (*Bot.*) Chili strawberry (fruta).

fresquecito, ita, fresquillo, lla [fres-kay-thee'-to, ee'-tah, fres-keel'-lyo, lyah], *a. dim. V.* FRESQUITO.

fresquista [fres-kees'-tah], *m.* A painter employed in painting in fresco.

fresquito, ta [fres-kee'-to, tah], *a. dim.* Cool, foolish, approaching to cold.

fresquito [fres-kee'-to], *m.* Cool, fresh air.

frey [fray'-e], *m.* Father, if a religious person; or brother, if a secular man.

frez, freza [freth, fray'-thah], *f.* Dung, the excrement of animals.

freza [fray-thah], *f.* 1. The time when silkworms eat (estación). 2. Ground turned up by the snout of a hog or other animal. 3. Track, trace of fish in spawning (huevos).

frezada [fray-thah'-dah], *f.* A blanket. *V.* FRAZADA.

frezar [fray-thar'], *vn.* 1. To eject excrements (animales). 2. To eject the droppings of grubs from hives.

frezar [fray-thar'], *va.* 1. To nibble the leaves of mulberry trees (gusanos de seda). 2. To rub in order to spawn (peces). 3. To turn up the ground, as hogs. 4. To be disposed to rise like worms after moulting.

fría [free'-ah], *a.* (*Pros.*) Applied to dead fowls, paid as tribute.

friabilidad [free-ah-be-le-dahd'], *f.* Friability, brittleness.

friable [fre-ah'-blay], *a.* Friable, fragile, brittle.

frialdad [fre-al-dahd'], *f.* 1. Frigidity, coldness, want of warmth. 2. Frigidity, coldness, unconcern, coolness, want of affection. 3. Frigidity, insipidity, dullness. 4. A silly observation or saying. 5. (*Med.*) Impotence (impotencia), inability to procreate.

fríamente [free'-ah-men-tay], *adv.* In a heavy, stupid, and graceless manner; coldly, frigidly, coolly, flatly.

friático, ca [fre-ah'-te-co, cah], *a.* 1. Foolish, graceless, silly. 2. Chilly.

fricación [fre-cah-the-on'], *f.* Friction.

fricandó [fre-can-do'], *m.* Scotch collop; veal cut into small pieces and stewed.

fricar [fre-car'], *va.* To rub, to scour.

fricasé [fre-cah-say'], *m.* Fricassee.

fricción [fric-the-on'], *f.* 1. Friction. *V.* FRICACIÓN. 2. Embrocation, liniment.

friega [fre-ay'-gah], *f.* Friction, rubbing with flesh-brush, etc. (*Yo friego, yo friegue,* from *Fregar. V.* ACERTAR.)

friera [fre-ay'-rah], *f.* Chilblain.

frigidez [fre-he-dayth'], *f. V.* FRIALDAD.

frígido, da [free'-he-do, dah], *a.* (*Poet.*) Cold, frigid.

frigo [free'-go], *m.* Fridge, refrigerator.

frigorífero, ra [fre-go-ree'-fay-ro, rah], *a.* Cooling, chilling.

frigorífico, ca [fre-go-ree'-fe-co, cah], *a.* Cooling, refrigerating, chilling. **Cámara frigorífica**, cooler, freezer. *-m.* 1. Cold storage. 2. Refrigerator, freezer. 3. Refrigerator van or ship.

friísimo, ma [free-e'-se-mo, mah], *a. sup.* Extremely cold.

fríjol [free'-hol], *m.* Kidney bean, French bean. **Fríjol de soja**, soy bean.

frío, ía [free'-o, ah], *a.* 1. Cold, frigid, tepid. **Más frío que el hielo**, as cold as ice. 2. Cold, frigid, impotent by nature (impotente). 3. Cold, frigid, indifferent, heartless, without warmth of affection. **Eso me deja frío**, that leaves me cold. 4. Frigid, dull, graceless, inefficacious.

frío [free'-o], *m.* 1. Cold, the effect of coldness. 2. Cool, fresh air. 3. Iced drinks. **Hace frío**, it´s cold. **Pasar frío**, to be cold.

friolento, ta [fre-o-len'-to, tah], *a.* Chilly; very sensible to cold.

friolera [fre-o-lay'-rah], *f.* An insignificant speech or act; a trifle.

friolero, ra [fre-o-lay'-ro, rah], *a. V.* FRIOLENTO.

frisa [free'-sah], *f.* Frieze, a coarse woollen stuff (tela).

frisado [fre-sah´-do], *m.* Silk plush or shag. -**Frisado, da**, *pp.* of FRISAR.

frisador [fre-sah-dor'], *m.* Frizzler, one who frizzles or raises the nap on frieze or cloth.

frisadura [fre-sah-doo´-rah], *f.* Act of frizzling or shagging.

frisar [fre-sar'], *va.* To frizzle or frizz, to raise the nap on frieze or other woollen stuff (tela)*;* to rub against the grain. *-vn.* To resemble, to be like; to assimilate, to approach.

friso [free'-so], *m.* 1. (*Arch.*) Frieze, the part of a column between the architrave and cornice. 2. Wainscot.

frísol [free'-sol], *m.* (*Bot.*) French or kidney bean.

frisón [fre-sone'], *m.* 1. A large draught horse, a cart or dray horse. 2. Any animal of a large size.

frita [free´-tah], *f.* 1. Frit, the ingredients of which glass is made; partially fused sand and fluxes. 2. The time employed in fusing glass.

fritada [fre-tah'-dah], *f.* Dish of fried meat or fish.

fritilaria [fre-te-lah'-re-ah], *f.* (*Bot.*) Fritillary.

fritillas [fre-teel'-lyas], *f. pl.* (*Prov.*) Fritters, pancakes.

frito [free'-to], *m.* Fry, fried (plato). **Fritos variados**, mixed fry. *V.* FRITADA.

frito, ta [free'-to, tah], *pp. irr.* of FREÍR. Fried.

frito [free-to], *a.* 1. Fried. 2. **Tener frito a uno**, to worry somebody to death (acosar). 3. **Estar frito**, to be kipping (dormido); to be a goner (muerto).

frituras [fre-too'-rahs], *f. pl.* Fritters (plato frito). **Frituras de maíz**, (*Mex.*), corn fritters.

frívolamente [free'-vo-lah-men-tay], *adv.* Frivolously, triflingly, without weight.

frivolidad [fre-vo-le-dahd'], *f.* Frivolity, frivolousness, triflingness, emptiness, frothiness.

frivolité [fre-vo-le-tay'], *f.* Tatting.

frívolo, la [free'-vo-lo, lah], *a.* Frivolous, slight, trifling, vain, empty, frothy, light, futile.

froga [fro'-gah], *f.* Brickwork, masonry.

fronda [fron'-dah], *f (Bot.)* Frond, a name given to the leaves of ferns and hepaticae.

frondescencia [fron-des-then'-the-ah], *f.* 1. (*Bot.*) The leafing process, frondescence. 2. (*Zool.*) Disposition of a polipary in leafy branches.

frondescente [fron-des-then'-tay], *a.* (*Bot.*) Frondescent.

frondífero [fron-dee'-fay-ro], *a.* (*Bot.*) Frondiferous, bearing leaves.

frondosidad [fron-do-se-dahd'], *f.* 1. Luxuriance of the branches and leaves of trees; foliage. 2. Redundancy of words or phrases.

frondoso, sa [fron-do'-so, sah], *a.* Leafy, abounding with leaves, frondose or full of leaves, luxuriant.

frontal [fron-tahl'], *a.* Frontal, relating to the forehead. *-m.* 1. Frontlet, a fillet with the name of God or a biblical text, which the Jews used to wear upon the forehead. 2. Frontal, a rich hanging for the front of an altar. 3. Chisel used by guitar makers to finish the frets. 4. Headstall of a bridle. 5. Piece of black baize, put as mourning over a horse's head. **frontalmente** [fron-tal'-men-tay], *adv.* Frontally. **Chocar frontalmente**, to collide head-on.

frontalera [fron-tah-lay'-rah], *f.* Ornament for the front of an altar, and the place where such ornaments are kept.

frontera [fron-tay'-rah], *f.* 1. Frontier, limit, confine, the border (zona), the marches. 2. Fillet of a bridle; binder of a frail basket. 3. *V.* FACHADA. 4. Ornament for the control of a riding saddle.

fronterizo, za [fron-tay-ree'-tho, thah], *a.* 1. Limitaneous, belonging to a frontier. 2. Frontier, bounding or bordering upon. 3. Fronting, opposite, over against (en frente).

frontero [fron-tay'-ro], *m.* 1. Governor or magistrate of a frontier town. 2. Frontlet, frontal, or browband. - *adv.* In front.

frontero, ra [fron-tay'-ro, rah], *a.* Frontier, placed in front

frontil [fron-teel'], *m.* Bassweed matting on the foreheads of draught-oxen, to preserve them from injury.

frontino, na [fron-tee'-no, nah], *a.* Applied to animals marked in the face.

frontis [fron'-tis], *m.* Frontispiece, facade.

frontispicio [fron-tees-pe'-the-o], *m.* 1. Front, the fore part of a building, or any other thing which meets the eye. 2. *(coll.)* Face, visage (cara). 3. Title page of a book.

frontón [fron-tone'], *m.* 1. Pelota court; wall of a pelota court (pared). 2. Court where Jai alai is played. 3. *(Arch.)* Pediment, a triangular gable of the principal entrance of a building.

frontudo, da [fron-too'-do, dah], *a.* Broad-faced.

frontura [fron-too'-rah], *f.* Front of a stocking frame.

frotación, frotadura [fro-tah-the-on', fro-tah-doo'-rah], *f.* Friction.

frotador, ra [fro-tah-dor', rah], *m. & f.* 1. One who rubs. 2. Kind of old brushes which hatters use to clean the sadiron.

frotar [fro-tar'], *va.* 1. To rub one thing against another. **Quitar algo frotando**, to rub something off. 2. To stroke gently with the hand. 3. To strike (cerilla). -*vr.* To rub, to chafe. **Frotarse las manos**, to rub one's hands.

fructescencia [frooc-tes-then'-the-ah], *f. (Bot.)* Frutescence or the fruiting season, the time when vegetables scatter their ripe seeds.

fructíferamente [frooc-tee'-fay-rah-men-tay], *adv.* Fruitfully.

fructífero, ra [frooc-tee'-fay-ro, rah], *a.* Fructiferous, frugiferous, fruit-bearing, fruitful.

fructificación [frooc-te-fe-cah-the-on'], *f. (Bot.)* Fructification, fertilization.

fructificador, ra, [frooc-te-fe-cah-dor', rah], *m. & f.* Fertilizer.

fructificar [frooc-te-fe-car'], *va.* 1. To fructify, to fertilize, to make fruitful. 2. *(Met.)* To profit or give profit, to benefit. 3. *(Met.)* To edify, to promote piety and morality.

fructívoro, ra [frooc-tee'-vo-ro, rah], *a.* Frugivorous, fruit-eating.

fructosa [frook-to'-sah], *f.* Fructose.

fructuosamente [frooc-too-o-sah-men-tay], *adv.* Fruitfully.

fructuoso, sa [frooc-too-o'-so, sah], *a.* Fruitful, fructuous, useful.

frugal [froo-gahl'], *a.* Frugal, parsimonious, sparing, thrifty.

frugalidad [froo-gah-le-dahd'], *f.* Frugality, parsimony, thrift, economy.

frugalmente [froo-gal-men'-tay], *adv.* Frugally, sparingly, thriftily.

frugívoro, ra [froo-hee'-vo-ro, rah], *a.* Frugivorous, herbivorous, plant-eating.

fruición [froo-e-the-on'], *f.* 1. Fruition, enjoyment of possession. 2. Fruition, satisfaction, gratification, taste.

fruir [froo-eer'], *vn.* To live in happiness, to enjoy.

fruitivo, va [froo-e-tee'-vo, vah], *a.* Fruitive, enjoying.

frumentario, ria [froo-men-tah'-re-o, ah], *a.* Cereal, relating to cereal grains in respect to their supply and to commerce.

-*m.* A Roman official charged with conveying wheat to the army.

frumenticio, cia [froo-men-tee'-the-o, ah], *a. (Bot.)* Frumentaceous, cereal.

frunce [froon'-thay], *m.* Plait, fold.

fruncido, da [froon-thee'-do, dah], *a.* Frizzled, corrugated, wrinkled (frente); frowning (cara). -*pp.* of FRUNCIR.

fruncidor [froon-the-dor'], *m.* Plaiter, folder.

fruncimiento [froon-the-me-en'-to], *m.* 1. The act of pursing up into corrugations. 2. Fiction, deceit, imposture.

fruncir [froon-theer'], *va.* 1. To gather the edge of cloth into plaits. 2. *(Met.)* To reduce to a smaller compass. 3. *(Met.)* To conceal the truth. 4. To affect modesty and composure. 5. To wrinkle (frente); to purse (labios). **Fruncir las cejas**, to knit the eyebrows. **Fruncir los labios**, to curl the lips.

fruslera [froos-lay'-rah], *f.* Brass turnings or clippings.

fruslería [frus-lay-ree'-ah], *f.* Trifle, a thing of no value, frivolity.

fruslero, ra [froos-lay'-ro, rah], *a.* Trifling, frivolous, insignificant, futile.

frustración [fross-trah-the-on], *f.* Frustration.

frustráneo, nea [froos-trah'-nay-o, ah], *a.* Vain, useless, nugatory.

frustrante [froos-trahn-tay], *a.* Frustrating.

frustrar [froos-trar'], *va.* To frustrate, to disappoint, to balk, to defeat, to mock, to elude. -*vr.* To miscarry, to fail (plan), to be balked.

frustratorio, ria [froos-trah-to'-re-o', ah], *a. V.* FRUSTRÁNEO.

fruta [froo'-tah], *f.* Fruitage, fruit, the eatable fruit of a tree or plant. **Fruta del tiempo**, 1. Fruit eaten in the season in which it is produced. 2. *(Met.)* Anything incident or peculiar to a season. **Fruta prohibida**, forbidden fruit.

frutaje [froo-tah'-hay], *m.* A painting of fruits and flowers.

frutal [froo-tahl'], *a.* Fruitful, fruit bearing (árboles).-*m.* Fruit tree.

frutar [froo-ter'], *va. (Prov.)* To fertilize.

frutería [froo-tay-ree'-ah], *f.* Fruitery, place where fruit is kept or preserved (tienda).

frutero, ra [froo-tay'-ro, rah], *m. & f.* 1. Fruiterer, one who deals in fruit (persona). 2. Fruit basket served up at table (recipiente). 3. Piece of painting representing various sorts of fruit.

frutescente [froo-tes-then'-tay], *a. (Bot.)* Frutescent: applied to stems from herbaceous becoming shrubby.

frútice [froo'-te-thay], *m.* Any perennial shrub.

fruticultura [froo-te-cool-too-rah], *f.* Fruit growing, fruit farming.

fruticoso, sa [froo-te-co'-so, sah], *a.* 1. *(Bot.)* Fruticant, frutescent; applied to a plant with many branches from its root. 2. Shrubby: applied to vegetables bearing woody stems. **Tallo fruticoso**, shrubby stem.

frutilla [froo-teel'-lyah], *f.* 1. *(dim.)* Small fruit. 2. In Peru, strawberry. 3. Round shell or nut of which rosaries are made.

frutillar [froo-teel-lyar'], *m.* Strawberry bed.

fruto [froo'-to], *m.* 1. Fruit, the product of a tree or plant in which the seeds are contained. **Dar fruto**, bear fruit. 2. Any useful produce of the earth. 3. Fruit, benefice (beneficio), profit, advantage gained by an enterprise or conduct (resultado). **El fruto de esta unión**, the offspring of this marriage. -*pl.* 1. Seeds, grain. 2. Produce of an estate, place, or employment.

fu [foo], *interj.* 1. Of disgust. 2. Sound imitating the snarling of a cat.

fucáceo, cea [foo-cah'-thay-o, ah], *a.* Fucaceous, relating to fucus, or great sea weeds.

fúcar [foo'-car], *m.* A rich, opulent man.

fucsia [fooc'-se-ah], *f.* Fuchsia, an ornamental plant with pendent blossoms.

fucha [foo'-chah], *int. (Mex.)* Exclamation denoting neatness.

fuego [foo-ay'-go], *m.* 1. Fire. **Fuegos artificiales**, fireworks. **Apagar el fuego**, to put out the fire. **Jugar con fuego**, to play with fire. 2. Fire, anything burning. 3. Fire, a conflagration. 4. Signal given with smoke from the coast; beacon fire. 5. *(Met.)* Force, life, vigor, animation. 6. (Cocina) Burner, ring. 7. Firing of soldiers. 8. Hearth, fireplace (hogar). 9. Ardor, heat of an action. 10. Flame, heat (calor). **Hervir a fuego lento,** to simmer. 11. Light (para cigarro). **Le pedí fuego,** I asked him for a light. 12. Burner, ring (de gas). **Una cocina a gas de cuatro fuegos,** a gas cooker with 4 burners. **¡Fuego!** the military command to shoot. **Estar entre dos fuegos,** to be between two fires. **Jugar con fuego,** to play with fire. **Fuego nutrido,** heavy fire. **Marcar a fuego,** to brand (reses). **Fuego a discreción,** fire at will. **Arma de fuego,** firearm. **Poner las manos en el fuego por,** to stake one's life on. **Romper el fuego,** to open fire. **Echar leña al fuego,** to add fuel to the fire.

fuel [foo-ayl'], *m.* Paraffin, kerosene.

fuellar [foo-el-lyar'], *m.* Paper ornament around wax tapers

fuelle [foo-ayl'-lyay], *m.* 1. Bellows (de soplar). 2. *(coll.)* Tell-tale (soplón). 3. Leather curtain of an open chaise. 4. Puff for powdering hair. **Fuelles,** puckers or corrugations in clothes.

fuente [foo-en'-tay], *f.* 1. Fountain, fount, a spring of water (manantial). **Fuente de beber,** drinking fountain. 2. Jet, a spout of water. 3. *(Met.)* Original, first principle, first cause, source. **De fuente desconocida,** from an unknown source. 4. Dish, platter, a broad wide vessel in which food is served up at table (recipiente). 5. A small ulcer, an issue. 6. *(Comput.)* Character set. **Fuente de caracteres,** characters font.

fuentecica, illa, ita, zuela [foo-en-tay-thee'-cah, eel'lyah, ee'tah, thoo-ay'-lah], *f. dim.* A small fountain.

fuer (A) [foo-ayr'], *adv.* **A fuer de caballero,** upon the word of a gentleman.

fuera [foo-ay'-rah], *adv.* 1. Out, speaking of a person or thing which is not a place. 2. Without, out of the place where one is. 3. *V.* AFUERA. 4. Over and above. 5. **Estar fuera,** to be out of town (persona). 6. Away (de casa). **Los de fuera,** the away team. **Fuera de sí,** deranged, beside oneself, aghast. **De fuera,** exteriorly. **Fuera de,** out of, forth. **Fuera de eso,** besides, moreover. **Estar fuera,** not to be at home, not to be in some place. **Fuera de esto,** short of this, besides this. **Fuera de que,** besides over and above. -prep. 1. Outside (lugar). **Estaba fuera de su jaula,** it was outside its cage. 2. *(Fig.)* In addition to, besides, beyond.

¡fuera! [foo-ay'-rah], *int.* Away, get out!, out of the way, clear the way.

fuera-borda [foo-ay-rah bor'-dah], *m.* Outboard engine, outboard motor.

fuercecilla, ita [foo-er-thay-theel'-lyah], *f. dim.* Little strength.

fuero [foo-ay'-ro], *m.* 1. Statute law of a country. 2. Jurisdiction, judicial power (autoridad). 3. Privilege or exemption granted to a province (de grupo). 4. A compilation of laws. **Fuero exterior or externo,** canon and civil laws. **A fuero,** according to law.

fuerte [foo-err'-tay], *m.* 1. Fortification, intrenchment, fort, hold. *-f.* 2. Coin over weight. 3. *(Mus.)* Forte, the loudness of the voice or notes marked. *-f.* 4. The buckle from which the stirrup hangs.

fuerte [foo-err'-tay], *a.* 1. Vigorous, able, hardy, lusty, stout, healthy, hale. 2. Strong (defensa, fe, objeción). 3. Strong (té, vino), firm, compact. 4. Strong, forcible, resistless, cogent, efficacious. 5. Manly, manlike, firm. 6. Hard, not malleable. 7. Terrible, grave (crisis). **Eso es muy fuerte,** that's a very serious thing to say. **Fuerte como un roble,** as strong as a horse.

fuerte [foo-err'-tay], *adv.* Strongly; hard (golpear); loud (tocar, hablar). **Poner la radio más alta,** to turn the radio up. **Toca muy alto,** she plays very loud.

fuertecico, illo, ito [foo-er-tay-thee'-co, eel-lyo, ee'-to], *m. dim.* Small fortress, a block-house.

fuertemente [foo-er-tay-men'-tay], *adv.* Strongly, lustily, firmly, fast, forcible, vehemently.

fuerza [foo-err'-thah], *f.* 1. Force, strength (de persona), might, vigor, cogency. 2. Fortitude, valor, courage, manliness, constancy. 3. Force (obligación), violence, coercion, compulsion, constraint. 4. Force (argumento), violence (violencia), defloration, rape. 5. Force, virtue, efficacy, mental power or strength. 6. Force, moment, impulsive weight, actuating power. 7. Force, armament, war-like preparation: commonly used in the plural. 8. Fortress, a strong place: used commonly in the plural. 9. The natural force, power, or faculty of things. 10. *V.* RESISTENCIA. 11. The strongest part of a thing. 12. Proneness, strong propensity. 13. The third of a sword next the hilt. **A fuerza de,** by dint of; by force of. **Por fuerza** or **de por fuerza,** by force, head and shoulders, violently, forcibly; by sheer necessity, necessarily; without excuse. **Fuerza de voluntad,** will-power. **Írsele a uno la fuerza por la boca,** to be all talk and no action. **En fuerza de,** by virtue of. **Sin usar fuerza,** without using force. **Fuerzas aéreas,** air force. **Fuerzas armadas,** armed forces. **Fuerzas del orden público,** forces of law and order.

fuete [foo-ay'-tay], *m. (Cuba)* A whip.

fufú [foo-foo'], *m. (Cuba)* Mass made of yam, plantain, or other nutritious root, and pounded.

fuga [foo'-gah], *f.* 1. Flight, escape (huida), elopement (de amantes). 2. State of the utmost perfection of a thing. 3. *(Mus.)* Fugue, a musical composition in which a theme introduced by one part is repeated and imitated by the others in succession. 4. *(Naut.)* Force, violence, velocity of the wind. 5. Leak, escape (de gas) **Fuga de la cárcel,** escape from prison. **Darse a la fuga,** to flee.

fugacidad [foo-gah-the-dahd'], *f.* Fugacity, volatility, fugitiveness, fugaciousness, brevity.

fugado, da [foo-gah'-do, dah], *a.* Written in the style of a fugue, without following the strict rules for the latter.

fugar [foo-gar'], *va.* To cause to fly or escape.-*vr.* To escape, to fly, to run away, to get out of danger (huir).

fugaz [foo-gahth'], *a.* 1. Fugacious, volatile, apt to fly away. 2. Fugitive, running away. 3. *(Met.)* Perishable, decaying. 4. Fleeting (momento). 5. Elusive (esquivo).

fúgido [foo'-he-do], **da,** *a. (Poet.) V.* FUGAZ.

fugitivo, va [foo-he-tee'-vo, vah], *m. & f.* A fugitive.

fugitivo [foo-he-te'-vo], **va,** *a.* 1. Fugitive, running, from danger, flying from duty (que huye). 2. Fugitive, unsteady, unstable.

fuina [foo-ee'-nah], *f. V.* GARDUÑA.

fulanito, ta [foo-lah-nee'-to, tah], *m. & f. dim.* Little master, little miss.

fulano, na [foo-lah'-no, nah], *m. & f.* Such a one; so-and-so.

fulero [foo-lay'-ro], *a.* 1. Useless (inútil); sham (falso); poor-quality (pobremente hecho). 2. Tricky, sly (taimado). 3. Blundering (torpe).

fulgecer [fool-hay-therr'], *vn. (Poet.)* To shine, to be resplendent.

fulgente [fool-hen'-tay], *a. (Poet.)* Refulgent, brilliant.

fúlgido, da [fool'-he-do, dah], *a. (Poet.)* Resplendent.

fulgor [fool-gor'], *m.* Fulgency, resplendence, brilliancy.

fulgora [fool-go'-rah], *f.* Fulgora, the lantern-fly, a homopterous insect, with ocelli and antennae beneath the compound eyes.

fulgurante [fool-goo-rahn'-tay], *pa. & a. (Poet.)* Resplendent, shining (brillante).

fulgurar [fool-goo-rar'], *vn. (Poet.)* To fulgurate, to emit flashes of light, to yield splendor and brilliancy.

fuliginoso, sa [foo-le-he-no'-so, sah], *a.* Fuliginous, dark, obscure.

fullería [fool-lyay-ree'-ah], *f.* 1. Cheating at games (naipes, etc.) 2. Cunning, arts used to deceive (cualidad). 3. Cogging, cheat, fallacy (tramposo.)

fullerito [fool-lyay-ree'-to], *m. dim.* A little sharper.

fullero [fool-lyay'-ro], *m.* Sharper, cheater at games (naipes), gamester, gambler.

fullet [fool-lyet'], *m.* A very small saw.

fullona [fool-lyo'-nah], *f. (coll.)* Dispute, quarrel.

fulminación [fool-me-nah-the-on'], *f.* Fulmination, the act of thundering.

fulminado [fool-me-nah'-do], *a.* Wounded by lightning. -**Fulminado, da,** *pp. of* FULMINAR.

fulminador [fool-me-nah-dor'], *m.* Thunderer.

fulminante [fool-me-nahn'-tay], *pa. & a.* Fulminating (polvo), thundering. -*m.* Detonator, percussion cap (cápsula fulminante).

fulminar [fool-me-nar'], *va.* 1. To fulminute, to emit lightning (con rayo). 2. To throw out as an object of terror, to express wrath. **Fulminar a uno con la mirada,** to look daggers at somebody.

fulminato [fool-me-nah'-to], *m.(Chem.)* Fulminate, a salt of fulminic acid.

fulmíneo, nea [fool-mee'-nay-o, ah], *a. (Poet.)* Belonging to thunder and lightning.

fulmínico [fool-mee'-ne-co], *a. (Chem.)* Fulminic (ácido), a compound of cyano gen and oxygen; its salts are explosive.

fulminoso, sa [fool-me-no'-so, sah], *a. (Poet.)* Fulminatory, thundering, striking horror.

fumada [foo-mah'-dah], *f.* The quantity of smoke taken at once in smoking tobacco; whiff.

fumadero [foo-mah-day'-ro], *m. (coll.)* A place particularly used for smoking tobacco, smoking room.

fumador, ra [foo-mah-dor', rah], *m. & f. (coll.)* Smoker, one who smokes tobacco.

fumante [foo-mahn'-tay], *pa.* Fuming, smoking.

fumar [foo-mar'], *pa.* To disperse in vapors; to smoke (tabaco.) **Fumar como una chimenea,** to smoke like a chimney. **Está fumando su pipa,** he is smoking his pipe. -*vr.* To dissipate (dinero); to cut, to miss (clase).

fumarada [foo-mah-rah'-dah], *f.* 1. Blast of smoke (fumada). 2. A pipeful of tobacco (en pipa).

fumaria [foo-mah'-re-ah], *f. (Bot.)* Fumitory.

fumear [too-may-ar'], *va. (Prov.)* V. HUMEAR.

fumífero, ra [foo-mee'-fay-ro, rah], *a. (Poet.)* Smoking, emitting smoke.

fumífugo, ga [foo-mee'-foo-go, gah], *a.* Smoke dispersing.

fumigación [foo-me-gah-the-on'], *f.* 1. Fumigation, fumes raised by fire. 2. Fumigation, application of medicines to the body in fumes.

fumigador [foo-me-gah-dor'], *m.* Fumigator, one who or that which fumigates.

fumigar [foo-me-gar'], *va.* 1. To fumigate, to smoke. 2. To fumigate, to medicate or purify by vapors (cosecha).

fumigatorio, ria [foo-me-gah-to'-re-o, ah], *a.* Fumigatory.

fumívoro, ra [foo-mee'-vo-ro, rah], *a.* Smoke consuming.

fumorola [foo-mo-ro'lah], *f.* Cavity in the earth which emits a sulphureous smoke.

fumosidad [foo-mo-se-dahd'], *f.* Smokiness.

fumoso, sa [foo-mo'-so, sah], *a.* Full of smoke or fume, fumid, smoky.

funámbulo, la [foo-nahm'-boo-lo, lah], *m. & f.* Funambulist, a rope dancer.

función [foon-the-on'], *f.* 1. Function, fulfilling the duties of any employment, profession, or office (puesto). **Presidente en funciones,** acting president. 2. *(Med.)* Function, vital action. 3. Solemnity, festival, feast, party, rout. **Función de la tarde,** matinée. **Mañana no hay función,** there will be no performance tomorrow. 4. Festive concourse of people, a public act. 5. Fight, engagement, battle. 6. Function; functioning (de máquina). 5. *(Comput.)* **Función aritmética,** arithmetic function. **Función condicional,** conditional function. **Función de fecha,** date function. **Función de macro,** macro facility. **Función estadística,** statistical function. **Función financiera,** financial function. **Función "engaño",** cheat function.

funcionamiento [foon-the-nah-me-en'-to], *m.* Functioning, operation, action. **Máquina en funcionamiento,** machine in working order. **Entrar en funcionamiento,** to come into operation. **Funcionamiento erróneo,** *(Comput.)* defective operation.

funcionar [foon-the-o-nar'], *vn.* To work, to perform duly, to functionate (maquinarias, personas). **Hacer funcionar una máquina,** to operate a machine.

funcionario [foon-the-o-nah'-re-o], *m.* Functionary, a public official.

funda [foon'-dah], *f.* A case, a sheath, a covering, generally of linen or leather. **Funda de almohada,** pillow-case.

fundación [foon-dah-the-on'], *f.* 1. Foundation, groundwork. 2. Foundation, the act of fixing the basis of an edifice, etc. 3. Foundation, rise, beginning, or origin of a thing. 4. Foundation, revenue established for any purpose.

fundadamente [foon-dah-dah-men'-tay], *adv.* Fundamentally.

fundado [foon-dah-do], *a.* Firm, well-founded, justified.

fundador, ra [foon-dah-dor', rah], *m. & f.* Founder.

fundamental [foon-dah-men-tahl'], *a.* 1. Fundamental, serving for the foundation. 2. Fundamental, essential, principal.

fundamentalmente [foon-dah-men-tal-men'-tay], *adv.* Fundamentally.

fundamentar [foon-dah-men-tar'], *va.* 1. To found (sentar las bases), to lay the foundation of a building. 2. *(Met.)* To found (argumento), to establish, to fix firm.

fundamento [foon-dah-men'-to], *m.* 1. Foundation, groundwork. 2. Fundamental, lending proposition. 3. Foundation, ground, the principles on which any notion is raised. **Eso carece de fundamento,** that is groundless. 4. Reason, cause, ground or principle. 5. Source, origin, root. 6. Weft, the woof of cloth.

fundar [foon-dar'], *va.* 1. To found, to lay the foundation of a building. 2. To found, to establish (crear). 3. To found (teoría), to ground, to raise upon, as on a principle, maxim, or ground. **Fundarse en algo,** to go upon or to take as a principle.

fundible [foon-dee'-blay], *a.* Fusible.

fundibulario [foon-de-boo-lah'-re-o], *m.* In the Roman militia, the soldier who was armed with a sling.

fundíbulo [foon-dee'-boo-lo], *m.* An ancient war-like machine for throwing stones; a sling.

fundición [foon-de-the-on'], *f.* 1. Fusion, melting of metals (acto). **Fundición de hierro,** iron foundry. 2. Foundry, a place where melted metal is cast into form; a casting house (fábrica). 3. A complete set of printing types; font.

fundidor [foon-de-dor'], *m.* Founder, melter, one who casts metals.

fundilario [foon-de-lah'-re-o], *m.* Slinger, Roman soldier who used a sling.

fundir [foon-deer'], *va.* 1. To found or melt metals. 2. *(Met.)* To unmake a thing in order to make it anew. 3. To fuse (fusionar). 4. To melt (nieve). 5. To throw away (dinero). -*vr.* 1. To fuse; to join, to unite; to merge (colores, efectos) 2. To melt (derretirse).

fundo [foon'-do], *m.* 1. *(Law and Amer.)* V. HEREDAD. 2. A large estate.

funebre [foo'-nay-bray], *a.* 1. Mournful, sad, lamentable. 2. Funeral, funereal, mourning (sonido) 3. Funeral (pompa).

fúnebremente [foo'-nay-bray-men-tay], *adv.* Mournfully, sorrowfully, lamentably.

funeral [foo-nay-rahl'], *a.* Funeral.

funeral [foo-nay-rahl'], *m.* Funeral, the solemnization of a burial; generally used in the plural.

funeraria [foo-nay-rah'-re-ah], *f.* Funeral parlor.

funerario, ria [foo-nay-rah'-re-o, ah], *a.* Funeral, funereal.

funéreo, rea [foo-nay'-ray-o, ah], *a. (Poet.)* Mournful, sad. V. FÚNEBRE.

funestar [foo-nes-tar'], *va.* To blot, to stain, to profane.

funestamente [foo-nay'-tah-men-tay], *adv.* Mournfully.

funesto, ta [foo-ness'-to, tah], *a.* Funest, doleful, lamentable, untoward; mournful, sad, dismal.

fungiforme [foon-he-for'-may], *a.* Fungiform, like a mushroom.

fungir [foon-heer'], *vn. (Amer.)* To affect importance.

fungita [foon-hee'-tah], *f.* Fungite, a fossil like a fungioid coral.

fungívoro, ra [foon-hee'-vo-ro, rah], *a.* Fungivorous, devouring fungi.

fungo [foon'-go], *m. (Surg.)* Fungus, fleshy excrescence.

fungóideo, dea [foon-go'-e-day-o, ah], *a. (Med.)* Fungoid, like a fungus.

fungón [foon-gone'], *m. (coll.)* A great snuff-taker.

fungosidad [foon-go-se-dahd'], *f. (Surg.)* Fungosity, excrescence.

fungoso, sa [foon-go'-so, sah], *a.* Fungous, excrescent, spongy.

funicular [foo-ne-coo-lar'], *a.* l. Funicular, consisting of cords or fibres. 2. Funicular machine, machines with a cord attached at one point and passing over a pulley, weights being added to demonstrate certain mechanical principles. 3. *(Naut.)* Tackle, rigging.

funículo [foo-nee'-coo-lo], *m. (Bot.)* Funicle, or funiculus, a filament which connects the ovule or seed with the placenta.

funiculoso, sa [foo-ne-coo-lo'-so, sah], *a. (Zool.)* Provided with prominent lines (cáscaras).

funífero, ra [foo-nee'-fay-ro, rah], *a. (Bot.)* Having appendages like cords.

furcia [foor'-the-ah], *f.* Tart, whore, prostitute.

furgón [foor-gone'], *m.* 1. A military covered transport wagon. 2. A freight car or box car. **Furgón entero,** a car-load.

furgoneta [foor-go-nay'-tah], *f. (Com.)* Van; transit van, pick-up truck; estate car (coche particular).

furia [foo'-re-ah], *f.* 1. Fury, rage. 2. Fury, one of the deities of vengeance, and thence a stormy, violent woman. 3. Hurry, velocity and vigor, used in the performance of a thing. **A toda furia,** with the utmost speed. 4. Zeal, ardor. 5. A Roman law which prohibited the manumission of more than one hundred slaves at once.

furial [foo-re-ahl'], *a. (Poet.)* Belonging to the Furies.

furibundo, da [foo-re-boon'-do, daha], *a.* Furious, enraged, frantic, raging.

furiosamente [foo-re-o-sah-men'-tay], *adv.* Furiously.

furioso, sa [foo-re-o'-so, sah], *a.* 1. Furious, mad, frantic, frenetic. 2. Furious, raging, violent. 3. Very great, excessive. **Estar furioso,** to be furious.

furo, ra [foo'-ro, rah], *a.* 1. Shy, reserved. 2. *(Prov.)* Ferocious, fierce; severe.

furor [foo-ror'], *m.* 1. Fury (ira), madness, franticness. 2. Fury, rage, anger, approaching to madness (locura). 3. *(Poet.)* Fury, enthusiasm, exaltation of fancy.

furtivamente [foor-te-vah-men'-tay], *adv.* By stealth, clandestinely.

furtivo, va [foor-tee'-vo, vah], *a.* Furtive, clandestine; pirated (edición).

furúnculo [foo-roon'-coo-lo], *m. (Surg.)* Furuncle, boil.

furunculoso, sa [foo-roon-coo-lo'-so, sah], *a.* Furunculose, prone to suffer a succession of boils.

fusa [foo'-sah], *f.* Demi-semiquaver, a note in music.

fusado, da, fuselado, da [foo-sah'-do, dah], *a. (Her.)* Charged with fusils or spindles.

fusca [foos'-cah], *f.* A kind of dark-colored duck.

fusco, ca [foos'-co, cah], *a.* Fuscous, brown, of a dim or dark color.

fuselaje [foo-say-lah'-hay], *m.* Fuselage (avión).

fusible [foo-see'-blay], *m. (Elec.)* Fuse.

fusible, fúsil [foo-see'-blay, foo'-seel], *a.* Fusible.

fusiforme [foo-se-for'-may], *a.* Fusiform, spindle-shaped.

fusil [foo-seel'], *m.* Gun, rifle. **Fusil de juguete,** toy gun. **Fusil ametrallador,** automatic rifle. **Fusil de chispa,** flintlock. **Fusil de repetición,** magazine rifle.

fusilador, ra [foo-se-lah-dor', rah], *m. & f.* One who shoots and who commands to shoot.

fusilamiento [foo-se-lah-me-en'-to], *m.* The act and effect of shooting.

fusilar [foo-se-lar'], *va.* 1. To kill by shooting (ejecutar, matar). 2. To shoot, to execute by shooting.

fusilazo [foo-se-lah'-tho], *m.* Musket shot, blow with a musket.

fusilería [foo-se-lay-ree'-ah], *f.* Body of fusileers or musketeers.

fusilero [foo-se-lay'-ro], *m.* Fusileer, musketeer.

fusión [foo-se-on'], *f.* 1. Fusion, melting together (de metal). 2. Alliance, mingling of parties, systems, etc. 3. Liquefaction.

fusionar [foo-se-o-nar'], *va.* To fuse; to merge, to amalgamate. *-vr.* To fuse; to merge, to amagamate.

fusique [foo-see'-kay], *m.* Kind of snuff-box in the shape of a small bottle.

fuslina [foos-lee'-nah], *f.* Smelting works.

fuslor [foos-lor'], *m.* Smelting ladle, a vessel for melting.

fusta [foos'-tah], *f.* 1. Small vessel, with lateen sails. 2. Thin boards of wood (leña). 3 Kind of woollen cloth. 4. Whip (látigo).

fustán [foos-tahn'], *m.* 1. Fustian, a kind of cotton stuff (tela). 2. *(Peru)* A woman's white skirt (falda).

fustanero [foos-tah-nay'-ro], *m.* Fustian manufacturer.

fuste [foos'-tay], *m.* 1. Wood, timber (madera). 2. Tree and bows of a saddle (silla). 3. *(Poet.)* A saddle. 4. Shaft of a lance (arma). 5. Foundation of something, not material. 6. Substance of anything. 7. *(Arch.)* Fust or body of a column (columna, chimenea). 8. An instrument of silversmiths.

fustero, ra [foos-tay'-ro, rah], *a.* Belonging to a fuss, foundation, etc.

fustero [foos-tay'-ro], *m.* Turner or carpenter.

fustete [foos-tay'-tay], *m. (Bot.)* Red or Venice sumach-tree. Fustic, a wood from the West Indies, used in dyeing. V. FUSTOC.

fustigar [foos-te-gar'], *va.* To whip, to fustigate.

fustina [foos-tee'-nah], *f.* Place for fusing metals.

fustoc [foos-toc'], *m.* Fustic, a yellow dye-wood, Venie sumach.

fútbol [foot-ball'], *m.* Soccer. **Fútbol americano,** American football.

futbolín [foot-bo-leen'], *m.* Table soccer, bar soccer.

futbolista [foot-bo-lees'-tah], *m & f.* Soccer player.

futesa [foo-tay'-sah], *f. (coll.)* Trifle, bagatelle.

fútil [foo'-teel], *a.* Futile, trifling, worthless, flimsy.

futileza [foo-te-lay'-thah], *f.* V. FUTILIDAD.

futilidad [foo-te-le-dahd'], *f.* Futility, weakness, groundlessness.

futura [foo-too'-rah], *f.* 1. Survivor-ship, survival. 2. *(coll.)* Intended bride (novia).

futurismo [foo-too-rees'-mo], *m.* Futurism.

futurista [foo-too-rees'-tah], *a.* Futuristic.

futuro, ra [foo-too'-ro, rah], *a.* Future. **Futura madre,** mother-to-be.

futuro [foo-too'-ro], *m.* 1. Future, futurity. 2. *(Gram.)* Future tense. **Para el futuro,** for the future. **En un futuro próximo,** in the very near future.

futurología [foo-too-ro-lo-he'-ah], *f.* Futurology.

futurólogo, ga [foo-too-ro'-lo-go], *m & f.* Futurologist.

G

g [hay], before the vowels *a, o* and *u,* has the same sound in Spanish as in English, but before *e* and *i* is the same as the Spanish *j,* or the English *h* strongly aspirated, as in *hay, her, he.* Before the diphthongs *ue, ui,* as in **guerra, guión,** the *u* becomes liquid, and the *g* has the hard sound as in the English word *give;* with a diaeresis over the *ü,* both letters have their proper sound as in **agüero.**

gabacho, cha [gah-bah'-cho, chah], *a.* 1. Applied to the natives of some places at the foot of the Pyrenees; used also in derision to the French. 2. Frenchified (afrancesado), given to Gallicisms.

gabán [gah-bahn'], *m.* 1. Great-coat with a hood and close sleeves. 2. Overcoat.

gabanzo [gah-bahn'-tho], *m.* (*Bot.*) Dogrose. V. GAVANZO.

gabaonita [gah-bah-o-nee'-tah], *a. & n.* Gibeonite.

gabarda [gah-bar'-dah], *f.* Wild rose.

gabardina [gah-bar-dee'-nah], *f.* Gabardine (tela), cassock with close-buttoned sleeves (prenda).

gabarra [gah-bar'-rah], *f.* 1. (*Naut.*) Lighter, a large boat. 2. A ferry-boat. 3. A fishing boat.

gabarrero [gah-bar-ray'-ro], *m.* 1. Dealer in wood and timber. 2. (*Naut.*) Lighterman.

gabarro [gah-bar'-ro], *m.* 1. A morbid swelling on the pastern of horses. 2. Pip, a horny pellicle on the tongue of fowls (de gallina). 3. Flaw or defect in cloth (tela). 4. Error or mistake in accounts (error). 5. Defect discovered in goods after they have been bought. 6. (*Met.*) Obligation, burdensome change, error in accounts.

gábata [gah'-bah-tah], *f.* Bowl, a small wooden basin.

gabazo [gah-bah'-tho], *m.* In sugarmills, bruised sugar-cane. V. BAGAZO.

gabela [gah-bay'-lah], *f.* 1. Gabelle, tax or duty paid to government. 2. Load, heavy service.

gabesina [gah-bay-see'-nah], *f.* Ancient kind of arms.

gabinete [gah-be-nay'-tay], *m.* 1. Cabinet, a meeting of ministers of state and privy councillors. 2. Cabinet, a private room for consultation (estudio). 3. Cabinet, a closet or small room for retirement (cuarto de estar). 4. A dressing room for ladies (tocador). 5. Collection of curiosities, museum (museo). **Gabinete de historia natural**, natural history section. **Gabinete de lectura**, reading room.

gabón [gah-bon'], *m.* 1. (*Naut.*) Lodging quarters in the hold of a galley. 2. Powder magazine.

gabote [gah-bo'-tay], *m.* (*Prov.*) Shuttle-cock.

gacel [gah-thel'], *m.* **Gacela** [gah-thay'-lah], *f.* Gazelle, antelope.

gaceta [gah thay'-tah], *f.* Gazette (boletín), newspaper (diario); an official publication.

gacetero [gah-thay-tay'-ro], *m.* 1. Gazetteer, news-writer (periodista). 2. A seller of newspapers (vendedor).

gacetilla [gah-thay-tee'-lyah], *f.* 1. A section of a newspaper devoted to news generally non political (notas de sociedad). 2. *a. & n.* Newsmonger.

gacetillero [gah-thay-teel-lyay'-ro], *m.* 1. Editor of a *gacetilla*. 2. A wretched writer, penny-a-liner.

gacetista [gah-thay-tees'-tah], *m.* 1. One who delights in reading newspapers. 2. Newsmonger, gossip of news.

gacha [gah'-chah], *f.* (*Amer. Cuba*) 1. An unglazed crock for preparing salt, and which the Indians use for eating and drinking. 2. (*Naut.*) V. GATA.

gachas [gah'-chahs], *f. pl.* 1. Sort of fritters, made of flour, honey, and water. 2. Any sort of soft pap. 3. (*Prov. Andal.*) Caresses, pettings. **Hacerse unas gachas**, to manifest extraordinary emotion in the presence or at the recollection of something; also, to grant a favor first refused. **¡Ánimo a las gachas!** Cheer up! take courage!

gacheta [gah-chay-tah], *f.* 1. Spring in large locks. 2. (*Prov.*) V. ENGRUDO.

gacho, cha [gah' cho, chah], *a.* 1. Curvated, bent downward. 2. Having horns curved downward (ganado). 3. Slouching (sombreros).

gachón, na [gah-chone', nah], *a. & m & f.* 1. (*coll.*) Graceful, sweet, attractive. 2. (*Andal.*) Pampered, spoiled, petted (niños).

gachondo, da [gah-chon'-do, dah], *a.* V. GACHÓN, second definition.

gachonería, gachonada [gah-cho-na-ree'-ah], *f.* Caress, endearment, fondness.

gachumbo [gah-choom'-bo], *m.* (*Almer.*) The woody, tough rind of various fruits, from which cups and other vessels are made.

gachupín [gah-choo-peen'], *m.* Name given in Mexico to a native of Spain who in Lima is called *Chapetón* and in Buenos Ayres *Maturrango*.

gádidos [gah'-de-dos], *pl.* Gadidae, codfishes and allied species.

gaditano, na [gah-de-tah'-no, nah], *a.* Native of or belonging to Cadiz.

gaélico, ca [ga-hay'-le-co, cah], *a.* Gaelic.

gafa [gah'-fah], *f.* A kind of hook, used to bend a crossbow. -*pl.* 1. (*Naut.*) Can-hooks, used to raise or lower casks. 2. Spectacles. **Gafas ahumadas**, smoked glasses. **Gafas negras**, dark glasses. 3. Spectacle-bows. 4. Grapple (grapa); clamp (abrazadera).

gafar [gah-far'], *va.* 1. To hook (agarrar), to catch with a hook. 2. To bring bad luck (mala suerte).

gafe [gah-fay], *a.* **Ser gafe**, to have constant bad luck.

gafedad [gah-fay-dahd'], *f.* 1. Kind of leprosy. 2. Contraction of the nerves.

gafete [gah-fay'-tay], *m.* Clasp, a hook and eye. V. CORCHETE.

gafo, fa [gah'-fo, fah], *a.* 1. Infected with leprosy. 2. Indisposed with a contraction of the nerves. 3. (*Peru*) Paralytic, tremulous.

gafón [gah-fone'], *m.* (*Orn.*) Green-finch.

gago [gah-go], **ga**, *a.* V. TARTAMUDO.

gaguear [gah-gay-ar'], *vn.* (*Peru. Cuba*) V. TARTAMUDEAR.

gaillardia [gah-eel-lyar'-de-ah], *f.* (*Bot.*) Gaillardia, a showy composite flower of the gardens.

gaita [gah'-ee-tah], *f.* 1. Bagpipe; hornpipe. 2. Flageolet (flauta). 3. Hand-organ. 4. (*coll.*) The neck (cuello). 5. Bother, nuisance (molestia); tough job (trabajo) **Estar de gaita**, (*coll.*) to be very merry, in high spirits.

gaitería [gah-e-tay-ree'-ah], *f.* A gay and gaudy dress.

gaitero [gah-e-tay'-ro], *m.* Piper, one who plays the bagpipe (persona).

gaitero, ra [gah-e-tay'-ro, rah], *a.* Applied to a person who is more facetious or lively than is proper to his character or profession.

gaje [gah'-hay], *m.* 1. Challenge, a summons to fight. 2. Salary, pay, wages. -*pl.* Perquisites, fees, above the settled wages· sometimes used in the singular. **Los gajes del oficio**, the occupational hazards.

gajo [gah'-ho], *m.* 1. Branch of a tree (rama). 2. Part of a bunch of grapes torn off (uvas) 3. Pyramidal raceme of any fruit.

gajoso, sa [gah-ho'-so, sah], *a.* Branchy; spreading.

gala [gah'-lah], *f.* 1. Gala, full, or court-dress (traje de etiqueta). **Día de gala**, court day; holiday. 2. Graceful, pleasing address. 3. Parade, ostentation. 4. Choicest part of a thing. 5. In America, the present or premium given to anyone as a reward of merit. **Hacer gala**, to glory in having done something. 6. Finery, trappings; jewels, adornments (lujos). **Galas de novia**, bridal attire. 7. Elegance (elegancia). 8. Speciality (especialidad), special accomplishment.

galactite [gah-lac-tee'-tay], *f.* Fuller's-earth, alumina.

galactófago, ga [gah-lac-to'-fah-go, gah], *a.* Living upon milk in the first period of life.

galactóforo, ra [gah-lac-to'-fo-ro rah], *a.* 1. Galactiferous, conducting milk. 2. (*Med.*) Galactogog(ue), increasing the flow of milk. 3. *m.* Breast-pump.

galactómetro [gah-lac-to'-may-tro], *m.* Galactometer, lactometer, an instrument for determining the density of milk.

galafate [gah-lah-fah'-tay], *m.* 1. An artful thief, a cunning rogue. 2. Hangman, executioner. 3. Porter who carries burdens. 4. (*Naut.*) Calker. V. CALAFATE.

galafatear [gah-lah-fah-tay-ar'], (*Naut.*) V. CALAFATEAR.

galaico, ca [gah-lah'-e-co, cah], *a.* V. GALLEGO. (*Acad.*)

galamero, ra [gah-lah-may'-ro, rah], *a.* Dainty. V. GOLOSO.

galán [gah-lahn'], *m.* 1. Gallant, a spruce, well-made man (joven). 2. Gentleman in full dress. 3. Gallant (novio), suitor (pretendiente); lover, wooer. 4. Actors who perform serious characters in plays are distinguished in order, as first, second, etc., *galán.* **Primer galán**, leading man. **Joven galán**, juvenile lead.

galán, na [gah-lahn', nah], *a.* 1. Gallant, gay, fine, neat, well-dressed. 2. Elegant, lively, ingenious. 3. Gallant, courtly, with respect to ladies.

galana [gah-lah'-nah], *f.* 1. *(Bot.)* Flat-podded lathyrus. 2. A woman very showily dressed.

galanamente [gah-lah-nah-men'-tay], *adv.* Gallantly, elegantly.

galancete [gah-lan-thay'-tay], *m. dim.* A spruce little man, a buck, a spark, a little gallant.

galanga [gah-lahn'-gah], *f. (Bot.)* **Galanga mayor**, officinal galangal. **Galanga menor**, smaller galangal.

galano, na [gah-lah'-no, nah], *a.* 1. Gallant, fine, gay, genteel, splendidly dressed (gallardo). 2. Elegant (elegante), ingenious, lively, sprightly.

galante [ga-lan'-tay], *a.* 1. Gallant (hombre), courtly with respect to ladies. 2. Brave, generous, liberal. 3. Elegant, handsome; witty, facetious.

galanteador [gah-lan-tay-ah-dor'], *m.* Wooer, lover.

galantear [gah-lan-tay-ar'], *va.* To court, to woo (cortejar); to solicit favor, to flirt with (coquetear con).

galantemente [gah-lan-tay-men'-tay], *adv.* Gallantly, civilly.

galanteo [gah-lan-tay'-o], *m.* 1. The act of soliciting favor. 2. Gallantry, courtship, refined address to women.

galantería [gah-lan-tay-ree'-ah], *f.* 1. Gallantness, gallantry, elegance. 2. Splendor of appearance, show, magnificence; a graceful manner. 3. Liberality, munificence, generosity. 4. Compliment (cumplido); charming thing (piropo).

galanto [gah-lahn'-to], *m. (Bot.)* Snowdrop.

galanura [gah-lah-noo'-rah], *f.* 1. A showy, splendid dress or ornament. 2. Gracefulness, elegance.

galápago [gah-lah'-pah-go], *m.* 1. Fresh-water tortoise. 2. Bed of a plough-share. 3. Frame for boring guns. 4. A kind of shed which soldiers once formed with shields joined together. 5. A horns saddle. 6. A pig of copper, lead, or tin. 7. A convex frame, on which vaults are formed. 8. Cleft in a horse's foot. 9. Ancient military machine.

galapo [gah-lah'-po], *m.* Frame for twisting ropes.

galardón [gah-lar-done'], *m.* Guerdon, reward, recompense.

galardonador, ra [gah-lar-do-nah-dor', rah], *m. & f.* Remunerator, rewarder.

galardonar [gah-lar-do-nar'], *va.* To reward, to recompense, to requite. **Obra galardonada por la Academia**, work which won an Academy prize.

gálata [gah'-lah-tah], *a.* Galatian, of Galatia.

galatea [gah-lah-tay'-ah], *f.* 1. *(Bot.)* A composite plant common in North America and North Asia. 2. A crustacean of the Mediterranean and of the coasts of Chili.

galato [gah-lah'-to], *m. (Chem.)* Gallate.

galatite [gah-lah-te'-tay], *f. V.* GALACTITE.

galaxía [gah-lac-see'-ah], *f.* 1. *(Ast.)* Galaxy, the milky way. 2. Soap stone.

galbana [gal-bah'-nah], *f.* 1. *(Bot.) V.* GULANA. 2. Sloth, laziness, slothfulness, idleness, indolence.

galbanado, da [gal-bah-nah'-do, dah], *a.* Of the color of galbanum.

galbanero, ra [gal-bah-nay'-ro, rah], *a. (coll.)* Lazy, indolent, careless, inattentive.

gálbano [gahl'-bah-no], *m. (Pharm.)* Galbanum, a resinous gum.

galbanoso, sa [gal-bah-no'-so, sah], *a.* Indolent, lazy, shiftless.

gálbulo [gahl'-boo-lo], *m.* The nut of the cypress-tree.

galdrope [gal-dro'-pay], *m. (Naut.)* Wheel-rope, the rope of the steering-wheel.

gálea [gah'-lay-ah], *f.* An ancient morion or helmet.

galeato, ta [gah-lay-ah'-to, tah], *a.* Applied to the prologue or preface of any work, in which a reply or defence is made to the objections against it.

galeaza [gah-lay-ah'-thah], *f. (Naut.)* Galeas, a kind of vessel.

galega [gah-lay-gah], *f. (Bot.)* Officinal goat's-rue.

galena [gah-lay'-nah], *f.* Galena sulphur of lead.

galénico, ca [gah-lay'-ne-co, cah], *a.* Galenic, galenical.

galenismo [gah-lay-ness'-mo], *m.* Galenism, doctrine of Galen.

galenista [gah-lay-nees'-tah], *m.* Galenist, physician who follows the doctrine of Galen.

galeo [gah-lay'-o], *m. (Zool.)* Swordfish.

galeón [gah-lay-on'], *m. (Naut.)* Galleon, aimed ship of burden, formerly used in Spain for trade in time of war.

galeota [gah-lay-o'-tah], *f. (Naut.)* Galliot, a smaller galley of sixteen to twenty oars on a side.

galeote [gah-lay-o'-tay], *m.* Galley-slave.

galera [gah-lay'-rah], *f.* 1. Galley, a vessel with oars, in use in the Mediterranean. 2. Wagon (carro), a heavy covered carriage for burdens. 3. House of correction for women. 4. *(Print.)* Galley, an oblong square frame with ledges, to preserve together a column of types as they were composed. 5. *(Arith.)* Line cutting off the quotient in division. 6. *(Mil.)* A subterranean gallery under a fortress. 7. A room for keeping the common metals. 8. An organ-builder's plane. 9. A furnace for distilling sulphur.-*pl.* Punishment of rowing on board of galleys.

galerada [gah-lay-rah'-dah], *f.* 1. *(Print.)* Galley of types composed, or the proof of a galley for correction. 2. Wagon-load (carga).

galerero [gah-lay-ray'-ro], *m.* A wagoner.

galería [gah-lay-ree'-ah], *f.* 1. Gallery, lobby. 2. *(Fort.)* A narrow covered passage across a moat. 3. **Galería de popa**, *(Naut.)* stern-gallery or balcony, into which there is a passage out of the great cabin. **Galería secreta**, secret passage.

galerilla [gah-lay-reel'-lyah], *f. dim.* A small gallery.

galerín [gah-lay-reen'], *m. dim.* A wooden galley in printing offices.

galerita [gah-lay-ree'-tah], *f. (Orn.)* Crested lark.

galerna [gah-lerr'-nah], *f. (Naut.)* A stormy northwest wind which blows on hot summer days upon the northern coast of Spain.

galfarro [gal-far'-ro], *m.* 1. Rogue, swindler. 2. *(Prov.* León) *V.* GAVILÁN.

galga [gahl'-gah], *f.* 1. Greyhound bitch, the female of the *Canis grajus*, L. 2. Wheel of the stone of an oilmill. 3. Kind of itch. 4. *(Naut.)* Back of an anchor. 5. Drag, Scotch brake for a wheel.

galgo [gahl'-go], *m.* Greyhound (perro). **Correr como un galgo**, to run like a hare.

galgo [gahl-go], **ga**, *a. (Amer.)* Hungry, anxious for something.

galgueño, ña [gal-gay'-nyo, nyah], *a.* Resembling or concerning a greyhound.

gálugulo [gal'-goo-lo], *m. (Orn.)* Roller.

galiambo [gah-le-ahm'-bo], *m.* Song of the Gallic priest of Cybele.

galibar [gah-le-bar'], *va. (Naut.)* To mould.

gálibo [gah'-lee-bo], *m. (Naut.)* Model of a ship.

galicado, da [gah-le-cah'-do, dah], *a. (coll.) V.* GALICOSO.

galicana [gah-le-cah'-nah], *a.* **La iglesia galicana**, the Gallican church.

galicismo [gah-le-thees'-mo], *m.* Gallicism, French phraseology.

gálico [gah'-le-coh], *m.* Venereal disease, syphilis. -*a.* Gallic.

galicoso, sa [gah-le-co'-so, sah], *a. (coll.)* Infected with syphilis.

galileo, lea [gah-le-lay'-o, ah], *a.* Galilean, of Galilee.

galillo [gah-leel'-lyo], *m.* Uvula, hanging palate.

galimatías [gah-le-mah-tee'-ahs], *m. (coll.)* 1. Gibberish, confused speech, jive. 2. A tangled, confused matter.

galio [gah'-le-o], *m.* 1. (*Bot.*) Cheese-rennet bed-straw. 2. (*Chem.*) Galium.

galiopsis [gah-le-op'-sis], *f.* (*Bot.*) Common hedge-nettle.

galipodio [gah-le-po'-de-o], *m.* White frankincense, or the white rosin which distils from the pine-tree or fir; galipot.

galivos [gah-lee'-vos], *m. pl.* Compassings, bevellings, pieces of timber incurvated in the form of an arch.

galizabra [gah-le-thah'-brah], *f.* Kind of vessel with lateen sails in the Levant trade.

galladura [gal-lyah-doo'-rah], *f.* Tread, cicatricula, a ruddy spot in the yolk of an egg.

gallarda [gal-lyar'-dah], *f.* A kind of airy Spanish dance.

gallardamente [gal-lyar-dah-men-tay], *adv.* Elegantly, gracefully, gallantly.

gallardear [gal-lyar-day-ar'], *vn.* To do something with grace or elegance (con elegancia).

gallardete [gal-lyar-day'-tay], *m.* (*Naut.*) Pennant, streamer.

gallardetón [gal-lyar-day-tone'], *m.* (*Naut.*) Broad pennant.

gallardía [gal-lyar-dee'-ah], *f.* 1. A graceful air and deportment. 2. Genteelness, elegance, gracefulness. 3. Gallantry, bravery, nobleness. 4. Activity, briskness in the execution or performance of a thing. 5. Liberality of sentiments, disinterestedness. 6. Magnanimity, greatness of mind.

gallardo, da [gal-yar'-do, dah], *a.* 1. Gay, graceful, elegant, genteel (elegante). 2. Magnanimous, great of mind, exalted in sentiments. 3. Generous, disinterested, high-spirited; pleasant, lively. 4. Brave (valiente), daring, bold, gallant, noble (noble).

gallareta [gal-lyah-ray'-tah], *f.* (*Orn.*) Widgeon.

gallarón [gal-lyah-ron'], *m.* (*Orn.*) A kind of bustard.

gallarito [gal-lyah-ree'-to], *m.* (*Bot.*) Lousewort.

gallaruza [gal-lyah-roo'-thah], *f.* A coarse garment, worn by country people.

gallear [gal-lyay-ar'], *va.* 1. To tread, to copulate as birds (gallo). 2. (*Met.*) To assume an air of importance. -*vn.* 1. To raise the voice with a menace or call; to become irritated (gritar). 2. To crow, to bully (envalentonarse).

gallegada [gal-lyay-gah'-dah], *f.* 1. Number of natives of Galicia assembled together. 2. Manners or behavior of the natives of Galicia. 3. A Galician dance.

gallera [gal-lyay'-rah], *f.* (*Sp. Am.*) Cock fighting ring.

galleta [gal-lyay'-tah], *f.* 1. Cracker. 2. Cookie. 3. Sea biscuit. 4. (*coll.*) Slap in the face (puñetazo). 5. Small bowl with a spout.

gallillo [gal-lyeel'-lyo (generally pronounced gah-leel'-lyo)], *m.* (*Anat.*) Uvula. V. GALILLO.

gallina [gal-lyee'-nah], *f.* 1. Hen, a domestic fowl. **Gallina de agua,** coot. **Gallina clueca,** broody hen. 2. (*Met.*) Coward, a chicken-hearted fellow. In this sense used as masculine. **Eres un gallina,** you're chicken, you're yellow. 3. In some universities, second orator or student destined to deliver the eulogium at graduating. **Gallina ciega,** blind-man's-buff, or hoodman's blind: a play among children. **Gallina de río,** V. GALLINETA.

gallináceo, cea [gah-lye nah'-thay-o, ah], *a.* Gallinaceous, relating to domestic fowls.

gallinaza [gal-lye-nah'-thah], *f.* 1. Hendung. 2. (*Orn.*) Carrion vulture, kite.

gallinería [gal-lye-nay-ree'-ah], *f* I. (*Prov.*) Poulterer's shop (tienda). 2. Hen-coop or hen-house. 3. (*Met.*) Cowardice, pusillanimity.

gallinero, ra [gal-lrye-nay'-ro, rah], *a.* (*Falc.*) Praying or feeding upon fowls.

gallinero [gal-lye-nay'-ro], *m.* 1. Poulterer, one who deals in poultry (persona). 2. Henyard, hen-coop, henroost, hen-house (criadero). 3. Basket in which fowls are carried to market (cesta). 4. (*Met.*) Place where many women meet. 5. (*coll.*) The gallery of a Spanish play-house.

gallineta [gal-lye-nay'-tah], *f.* 1. (*Orn.*) Sand-piper. 2. Buffed grouse.

gallipavo [gal-lye-pah'-vo], *m.* 1. (*Orn.*) Turkey. 2. A false, unpleasant note in singing.

gallipollo [gal-lye-pol-lyo], *m.* Cockerel, a young cock.

gallipuente [gal-lye-poo-en'-tay], (*Prov.*) Bridge without rails.

gallito [gal-lyee'-to], *m.* 1. Beau, coxcomb. 2. (*Dim.*) Small cock. **Gallitos,** shaggy-leaved toad-flax. 3. The yellow violet of California.

gallo [gahl'-lyo], *m.* 1. (*Orn.*) Cock, rooster, the male to the hen. **Gallo de pelea,** game cock. **Estar como gallo en gallinero,** to be much esteemed. **Otro gallo me cantara,** that would be quite a different matter. 2. (*Zool.*) Dory, a seafish (pez). 3. (*Met.*) Chief of a village or parish (jefe). 4. Float of cork serving as a mark to fishers, so that they may draw their nets. 5. V. GALLIPAVO. 6. (*Carp.*) Wall-board in the roofing of a house. 7. (*Mus.*) False note, squeak, squawk. **Soltó un gallo,** his voice cracked.

gallobosque [gal-lyo-bos'-kay], *m.* (*Orn.*) Wood-grouse.

gallocresta [gal-lyo-cres'-tah], *f.* (*Bot.*) Annual clary sage.

gallofa [gal-lyo'-fah], *f.* 1. Morsel of bread or other food given to pilgrims. 2. Greens used for salad and pottage. 3. An idle tale. 4. (*Prov.*) Directory of divine service.

gallofear [gal-lyo-fay-ar'], *vn.* To saunter about and live upon alms.

gallofero, ra [gal-lyo-fay'-ro, rah], *a.* Idle, lazy, vagabond: applied to a beggar without a home.

gallofo, fa [gal-lyo'-fo, fah], *a.* V. GALLOFERO.

gallón [gal-lyo-ne'], *m.* 1. (*Prov.*) Green sod, turf; a clod covered with grass. 2. Local bass (cacique).

gallonada [gal-lyo-nah'-dah], *f.* Wall made of sods.

galluda [gal-lyoo'-dah], *f.* (*Zool.*) Tope, dogfish, a small shark.

gallumbos [gal-loom'-bos], *m. pl.* Pants, trousers.

galo, la [gah'-lo, lah], *a.* Gaul, native of Gaul; French (moderno).

galocha [gah-lo'-chah], *f.* 1. Galosh, clog, a wooden shoe. 2. Patten, an over-shoe of wood with an iron ring.

galón [gah-lone'], *m.* 1. Galloon, a texture of silk, thread, gold or silver. 2. Lace. 3. Gallon, a liquid measure (medida). 4. (*Naut.*) Wooden ornament on the sides of ships. **La acción le valió 2 galones,** the action got him a couple of stripes.

galonazo [gahlo-nah'-tho], *m.* 1. (*aug.*) Large galloon. 2. Excessive ornament.

galoneadura [gah-lo-nay-ah-doo'-rah], *f.* Garnishing with lace or galloons.

galonear [gah-lo-nay-ar'], *va.* To lace, to adorn with lace.

galonero [gah-lo-nay'-ro], *m.* Lace or galloon maker.

galop [gah-lop'], *m.* (*Acad.*) A Hungarian dance, and the music to which it is set.

galopada [gah-lo-pah'-dah], *f.* The space over which a horse gallops.

galopante [gah-lo-pahn'-tay], *a.* (*Med. fig.*) Galloping.

galopar [gah-lo-par'], *vn.* To gallop. **Echar a galopar,** to break into a gallop.

galope [gah-lo'-pay], *m.* 1. Gallop, motion of a horse. 2. Hasty execution of a thing. **A galope** or **de galope,** gallopingly.

galopeado, da [gah-lo-pay-ah'-do, dah], *a. & pp.* of GALOPEAR. Done in a hurry.-*m.* Whipping, flogging.

galopear [gah-lo-pay-ar'], *vn.* V. GALOPAR.

galopín [gah-lo-peen'], *m.* 1. (*Naut.*) Swabber, a boy who swabs the deck; a cabin boy. 2. Scullion, a kitchen boy. 3. A contemptible rogue. 4. Boy meanly dressed. 5. A clever knave. 6. Ragamuffin (pícaro). 7. Scroundel, rogue (bribón); smart-aleck (sabelotodo).

galopo [gah-lo'-po], *m.* Rogue.

galopinada [gah-lo-pe-nah'-dah], *f.* Action of a cunning, crafty person; knavery.

galpito [gal-pee'-to], *m.* A weak, sickly chicken.

galpón [gal-pone'], *m.* (*Peru*) dormitory for the laborers of a farm.

galván (proper name). **No lo entenderá Galván**, an intricate, difficult thing.

galvánico, ca [gal-vah'-ne-co, cah], *a. (Phys.)* Galvanic.

galvanismo [gal-vah-nees'-mo], *m.* Galvanism, electricity of metals.

galvanizar [gal-vah-ne-thar'], *(Phys.)* To galvanize.

galvanómetro [gal-vah-no'-may-tro], Galvanometer.

galvanoplastia, or **galvanoplástica** [galvah-no-plahs'-te-ah], *f.* Galvanoplasty, electrotypy.

gama [gah'-mah], *f.* 1. Gamut, the scale of musical notes. 2. Doe, the female to a buck.

gama globulina [gah'-mah glo-boo-lee'-nah], *f. (Med.)* Gammaglobulin.

gamalote [gah-mah-lo'-tay], *m.* A grass of South America; arrowgrass.

gamarra [gah-mar'-rah], *f.* Martingale, a strap used to prevent a horse from rearing.

gamarza [gah-mar'-thah], *f. (Bot.)* Wild Syrian rue, peganum.

gamba [gam'-bah], *f. (Zool.)* Prawn.

gambaj, or **gambax** [gam-bah', gam-box'], *m.* A quilted-jacket of wool.

gambalúa [gam-bah-loo'-ah], *f. (coll.)* A tall, ill-shaped man, without life or spirit.

gámbaro [gahm'-bah-ro], *m.* A kind of small craw-fish.

gambesina [gam-bay-see'-nah], *f.* or **gambesón** [gam-bay-son'], *m.* A kind of jacket worn under the armor for comfort.

gamberrada [gam-bayr-rah'-dah], *f.* Piece of hooliganism, loutish thing.

gamberrismo [gam-bayr-rees'-mo], *m.* Hooliganism; loutishness.

gamberro [gam-bayr'-ro], *f.* Ill-bread, loutish, rough. -*m.* Lout, hooligan, troublemaker.

gambeta [gam-bay'-tah], *f.* 1. Cross caper in dancing; ancient dolce. 2. Affected language or tone of voice. 3. **Gambeta de mar**, scaled center shell.

gambetear [gam-bay-tay-ar'], *vn.* To caper like a horse.

gambeto [gam-bay'-to], *m.* A quilted great-coat.

gambo [gahm'-bo], *m.* Cap for a new born child.

gambotes [gam-bo'-tes], *m. pl. (Naut.)* Counter timbers, arched timbers (Also **Gambotas**, *f.*)

gambux [gam-boocs'], *m.* A small bonnet or cap for children.

gamela [gah-may'-lah], *f.* Kind of basket.

gamelo [gah-may'-lo], *m.* Name given by the Indians to balsam copaiba.

gamella [gah-mel'-lyah], *f.* 1. Yoke for oxen and mules. 2. A large wooden trough. 3. V. **CAMELLÓN**. 4. She-camel. *(Acad.)*

gamelleja [gah-mel-lyay'-hah], *f. dim.* A small yoke.

gamellón [gah-mel-lyone'], *m.* 1. *(aug.)* A large yoke for oxen and mules. 2. *(Prov.)* Trough in which grapes are trodden.

gamezno [gah-meth'-no], *m.* Little young buck.

gamino [gah-mee'-no], *m. (Vet.)* A tumor which attacks sheep and goats.

gamo [gah'-mo], *m.* 1. Buck of the fullow-deer. 2. V. GAMINO. 3. An iron hook in a wooden handle for hooking fishes already caught. 4. *(coll.)* A restless, quick-moving individual.

gamogastro [gah-mo-gahs'-tro], *a. (Bot.)* Gamogastrous, having the ovaries united.

gamón [gah-mone'], *m. (Bot.)* Asphodel.

gamonal [gah-mo-nahl'], *m.* Place in which asphodels flourish.

gamoncillo [gah-mon-theel'-lyo], *m. (Bot.)* Onion-leaved asphodel.

gamonito [gah-mo-nee'-to], *m.* 1. Young shoots springing round trees or shrubs. 2. *(Dim.)* Young asphodel. 3. *(Bot.)* V. MARTAGÓN.

gamonoso, sa [gah-mo-no'-so, sah], *a.* Abounding in asphodels.

gamopétalo, la [gah-mo-pay'-tah-lo, lah], *a.* Gamopetalous.

gamosépalo, la [gah-mo—say'-pah-lo, lah], *a.* Gamosepalous.

gamucería [gah-moo-thay'-ree'-ah], *f.* The factory where chamois skins are curried and prepared.

gamuno, na [gah-moo'-no, nah], *a.* Skins (ciervos).

gamuza [gah-moo'-thah], *f.* 1. Chamois. 2. Chamois or chamois leather (piel).

gamuzado, da [gah-moo-thah'-do, dah], *a.* Chamois color.

gamuzón [gah-moo-thon'], *m. dim.* A kind of coarse chamois.

gana [gah'-nah], *f.* 1. Appetite (apetito), keenness of stomach; hunger. 2. *(Prov.)* A healthy disposition of body. 3. Inclination (afán), desire (deseo), mind, list. **De buena gana**, with pleasure, willingly, voluntarily. **De mala gana**, unwillingly, with reluctance, with dislike. **De gana**, designedly, on purpose. **Tener gana**, to have a mind. **Comer con gana**, to eat with an appetite. **Hacer algo con ganas**, to do something reluctantly. **Como te dé la gana**, just as you wish. **Quedarse con las ganas**, to fail. **Tengo pocas ganas de**, I don´t much feel like.

ganadería [gah-nah-day-ree'-ah], *f.* 1. Breeding cattle (raza). 2. Stock of cattle (crianza).

ganadero, ra [gah-nah-day'-ro, rah], *a.* Cattle (animal), stock; cattle-raising. -*m.* Stock-breeder (persona), rancher; cattle dealer.

ganado [gah-nah'-do], *m.* 1. Herd of domesticated animals of the same kind; flock, drove. **Ganado mayor**, cattle: it is also said of mules. **Ganado menor**, sheep. **Ganado asnal**, donkeys. **Ganado ovejuno**, sheep. **Ganado cabrío**, goats. 2. Cattle, word of contempt applied to men and women. 3. Collection of bees of a beehive.—**Ganado,da**, *pp.* of GANAR.

ganador, ra [gah-nah-dor', rah], *m. & f.* 1. Winner. 2. Gainer. 3. Earner. **El equipo ganador**, the winning team.

ganancia [gah-nahn'-the-ah], *f.* 1. Gain (beneficio), earnings, profit. 2. Winnings. 3. Earning, profiting. **Ganancia bruta**, gross profit. **Gananancias y perdidas**, profit and loss.

ganancial [gah-nan-the-ahl'], *a.* Lucrative. **Bienes gananciales**, property acquired during marriage.

ganancioso, sa [gah-nan-the-o'-so, sah], *a.* Lucrative, gainful (lucrativo).

ganapán [gah-nah-pahn'], *m.* 1. A porter (recadero). 2. A rude, coarse man (patán). *(Acad.)* A shiftless fellow, a ne'er-do-well.

ganapierde [gah-nah-pe-err'-day], *m.* A mode of playing draughts, where he who loses all his men wins the game; give away or losing game.

ganar [gah-nar'], *va.* 1. To gain, to get or obtain (adquirir), as profit or advantage. 2. To gain, to win (premio). 3. To gain, to have the overplus in comparative computation. 4. To win, to conciliate, to allure to kindness or compliance. 5. To attain, to acquire. 6. To conquer. 7. To surpass. **Ganar la vida**, to gain a living. **Ha ganado mucho dinero**, she has made a great deal of money. **Ganar unas oposiciones para un puesto**, to win a post by public competition. **No hay quien le gane**, there´s nobody who can beat him. -*vn.* 1. *(Dep. etc.)* To win; to gain. 2. To thrive, to improve; to do well (prosperar). **Ha ganado mucho en salud**, he has much improved in health.

ganchero [gan-chay'-ro], *m.* Conductor of a raft of timber.

ganchillo [gan-cheel'-lyo], *m. dim.* A little hook or crotch.

gancho [gahn'-cho], *m.* 1. Hook, which remains after a branch of a tree has been broken off. 2. Hook, an incurvated piece of iron; a crotch. 3. Crook, a sheep-hook. 4. An allurer, one who insinuates himself into the favor of another to attain some purpose. 5. Pimp, procurer, pander (persona). 6. *(Naut.)* An iron hook with an eye. 6. Appeal, attraction (atractivo). **Gancho de aparejo**, tackle-hook. **Gancho de carnicero**, butcher´s hook. **Echar el gancho a**, *(Fig.)* to hook.

ganchoso, sa [gan-cho'-so, sah], *a.* Hooked, curved.

ganchuelo [gan-choo-ay'-lo], *m. dim.* V. GANCHILLO.

gándara [gahn'-dah-rah], *f.* A low range of mountains, or rough, uncultivated ground.

gandaya [gan-dah'-yah], *f.* 1. Laziness, idleness. 2. *V.* COFIA.

gandido, da [gan-dee'-do, dah], *a.* 1. *(Prov.)* Seduced, led astray. 2. *(Amer. Peru.)* Hungry, gluttonous.

gandinga [gan-deen'-gah], *f. (Cuba)* A stew made from the liver of a hog or other animal.

gandir [gan-deer'], *va.* To eat.

gandujado [gan-doo-hah'-do], *m.* Ornament or ruffle of a woman's dress.—**Gandujado, da**, *pp.* of GANDUJAR.

gandujar [gan-doo-har'], *va.* To bend, to plait, to fold.

gandul, la [gan-dool', lah], *m. dim.* Vagabond, vagrant, tramp.

gandulear [gan-doo-lay-ar'], *vn.* To lounge, to be idle.

ganfalonero [gan-fah-lo-nay'-ro], *m.* Gonfalonier, Pope's standard-bearer.

ganfanón [gan-fah-non'], *m.* Gonfalon, ensign of the Romish church, and of some Italian states.

ganforro, ra [gan-for'-ro, rah], *m. & f. (coll.)* Vagrant, vagabond.

ganga [gahn'-gah], *f.* 1. *(Orn.)* The little pintailed grouse. 2. Anything valuable acquired with little labor (cosa fácil). 3. Bargain price. **Precio de ganga**, bargain price. **Esto es una ganga**, this is a cinch.

ganga [gahn'-gah], *f. (Min.)* Gangue, bed or matrix of minerals.

gangarilla [gan-gah-reel'-lyah], *f.* Ancient company of strolling players.

ganglio [gahn'-gle-o], *m.* 1. *(Anat.)* Ganglion. 2. *(Med.)* Ganglion, a small tumor of the sheath of a tendon.

ganglionar [gan-gle-o-nar'], *a.* Ganglionic, provided with ganglions.

gangoso, sa [gan-go'-so, sah], *a.* Snuffling, or speaking through the nose (acento).

gangrena [gan-gray'-nah], *f.* Gangrene, mortification.

gangrenar [gan-gray-nar'], *va.* To cause gangrene or mortification; to corrupt, to rot. *-vr.* To become gangrenous or mortified.

gangrenoso, sa [gan-gray-no'-so, sah], *a.* Gangrenous.

gán(g)ster [gahns'-tayr], *m.* Gangster, gunman.

ganguear [gan-gay-ar'], *vn.* To snuffle, to speak through the nose.

gánguil [gahn'-geel], *m.* 1. A barge used for fishing, or in the coasting trade; lighter. 2. A fishing net broader than that called *tartana*.

ganil [gah-neel'], *m.* A granular, calcareous rock.

ganoso, sa [gah-no'-so, sah], *a.* Desirous, full of desire; longing after (afanoso).

gansa [gahn'-sah], *f.* 1. *(Orn.)* Goose. 2. Goose, silly girl.

gansarón [gan-sah-ron'], *m.* 1. A gosling. 2. A tall, thin man.

gansería [gan-say-ree'-ah], *f.* Folly, stupidity.

ganso, sa [gahn'-so, sah], *m. & f.* 1. *(Orn.)* Gander, goose. 2. Tall, slender person. 3. *(coll.)* A goose or goose-cap, a silly person. *-pl.* Giblets of a goose.

gánster [gahns'-tayr], *m.* Gangster.

gante [gahn'-tay], *m.* A kind of linen manufactured in Ghent.

ganzúa [gan-thoo'-ah], *f.* 1. Picklock, an instrument with which locks are opened. 2. Thief who picks locks (ladrón).

ganzuar [gan-thoo-ar'], *va.* To pick a lock, to open it with a picklock.

gañán [gah-nyahn'], *m.* Day laborer; teamster, rustic.

gañanía [gah-nyah-nee'-ah], *f.* Number of day-laborers.

gañido [gah-nyee'-do], *m.* Yelping or howling of a dog. **Gañido, da**, *pp.* of GAÑIR.

gañiles [gah-nyee'-les], *m. pl.* The cartilaginous larynx, organ of the voice.

gañir [gah-nyeer'], *va.* 1. To yelp or howl (perro). 2. To croak (pájaro), to cackle, to crow. 3. To talk hoarsely (persona).

gañón, gañote [gah-nyon', gah-nyo'-tay], *m.* 1. The throat. 2. *(Prov.)* Kind of fritters.

gaón [gah-on'], *m.* 1. A substitute for the oar in the Indian vessels known as barangays and virreys. 2. Title of honor which was once given to rabbis or Jews who distinguished themselves in the sciences.

garabatada [gah-rah-bah-tah'-dah], *f. (coll.)* Act of throwing a hook.

garabatear [gah-rah-bah-tay-ar'], *va.* 1. To hook, to catch with a hook. 2. To scrawl, to scribble. 3. To use tergiversations. *-vn.* 1. To scribble, to scrawl (escribiendo). 2. To beat about the bush (andar con rodeos).

garabateo [gah-rah-bah-tay'-o], *m.* Act of hooking.

garabatillo [gah-rah-bah-teel'-lyo], *m.* 1. *(Dim.)* A small hook. 2. Difficulty of evacuating any peccant matter from the lungs.

garabato [gah-rah-bah'-to], *m.* 1. Pot-hook (escritura); grapnel, creeper. **Garabatos**, scribble. 2. Hook to hang meat on (gancho). 3. A graceful gait and deportment. *-pl.* 1. Ill-formed or scrawling letters or characters; pot-hooks. 2. Improper gestures or movements of the hands and fingers.

garabatoso, sa [gah-rah-bah-to'-so, sah], *a.* 1. Full of scrawls. 2. *(Met.)* Elegant charming, attractive.

garabeta [gah-rah-bay'-tah], *f.* A stick armed with one or more hooks at the end to catch cuttle-fish.

garabito [gah-rah-bee'-to], *m.* A linen cover spread over fruit stalls (mercado).

garaje [gah-rah'-hay], *m.* Garage.

garamón [gah-rah-mone'], *m.* In printing, a small Roman type.

garante [gah-rahn'-tay], *m.* 1. Guarantee, a power who undertakes to see stipulations performed (responsable). 2. Warranter. *V.* FIADOR.

garantía [gah-ran-tee'-ah], *f.* 1. Warranty, guaranty, the act of securing the performance of articles or stipulations (seguridad); undertaking (compromiso).

garantir [gah-ran-teer'], *va.* To guarantee.

garantizado [gah-rahn-tee-thah'-do], *a.* Guaranteed.

garantizar [gah-rahn-tee-thar'], *va.* To guarantee, to warrant; to vouch for. *V.* GARANTIR.

garañón [gah-rah-nyone'], *m.* 1. Jackass kept for breeding (asno). 2. A man much given to lust; lecher. 3. Male breeding camel. *(Acad.)*

garapacho [gah-rah-pah'-cho], *m.* Kind of dressed meat.

garapiña [gah-rah-pe'-nyah], *f.* 1. The congealed particles of any liquid. 2. A kind of black lace.

garapiñado, da [gah-rah-pe-nyah'-do, dah], *a.* Glacé, candied.

garapiñar [gah-rah-pe-nyar'], *va.* To ice, to turn, to ice (pastel), to cover with ice, to freeze (helado), to clot (nata).

garapiñera [gah-rah-pe-nyay'-rah], *f.* Vessel in which liquids are congealed; a cooler, refrigerator.

garapita [gah-rah-pee'-tah], *f.* Fishing net with small meshes.

garapito [gah-rah-pee'-to], *m.* Small insect, like a tick.

garapullo [gah-rah-pool'-lyo], *m.* 1. Dart made of paper (rehilete). 2. A shuttle-cock. 3. Banderilla (toros).

garatura [gah-rah-too'-rah], *f.* Scraper, an instrument used by curriers of leather.

garatusa [gah-rah-too'-sah], *f.* 1. A sort of card game. 2. *(coll.)* Caress, act of endearment.

garavito [gah-rah-vee'-to], *m.* Stall, a small shed, in which greens, fruit, etc., are sold at market.

garay [gah-rah'-e], *m.* A Philippine craft.

garba [gar'-bah], *f.* Sheaf, as of corn. *(Bot.)* Hairy bastard vetch.

garbancera [gar-ban-thay'-rah], *f. (Bot.)* V. GARBANCILLO.

garbanzal [gar-ban-thahl'], *m.* A piece of ground sown with chick-peas.

garbanzo [gar-bahn'-tho], *m. (Bot.)* Chick-pea or common chick-pea. **Ganarse los garbanzos**, to earn one's living.

garbanzuelo [gar-ban-thoo-ay'-lo], *m. dim.* 1. *(Dim.)* Small chick-pea. 2. *(Vet.)* Disease in horses' feet. *V.* ESPARAVÁN.

garbar [gar-bar'], *va. (Prov.)* To form sheaves, to tie stalks of corn into bundles.

garbear [gar-bay-ar'], *va.* 1. *(Prov.)* V. GARBAR. 2. To seize, to lay hold of something eagerly.-*vn.* To affect an air of dignity and grandeur (afectar garbo).

garbeo [gar-bay'-o], *m.* Affected elegance, show. **Darse un garbeo**, to go for a walk.

garbeña [gar-bay'-nyah], *f. (Bot.)* Common heath.

garbias [gar'-be-as], **pl.** A ragout, made of herbs, cheese, flour, eggs, sugar, and butter.

garbillador [gar-beel-lyah-dor'], *m.* Sifter, riddler.

garbillar [gar-beel-lyar'], *va.* To garble, to sift; to separate the bad from the good.

garbillo [gar-beel'-lyo], *m.* Riddle, a coarse sieve made of bass or sedge.

garbín [gar-been'], *m.* Coif made of net-work.

garbino [gar-bee'-no], *m.* South-west wind.

garbo [gar'-bo], *m.* 1. Gracefulness, gentility, elegance of manner, jauntiness (aire); grace (elegancia). 2. A clover and genteel way of doing things. 3. A gentleman-like air and deportment. 4. Frankness, disinterestedness, generosity (larqueza); liberality of sentiments; cleverness. **Andar con garbo**, to walk gracefully. **Hacer algo con garbo**, to do something with grace.

garbosamente [gar-bo-sah-men'-tay], *adv.* Gallantly, nobly, generously, liberally.

garboso, sa [gar-bo'-so, sah], *a.* 1. Genteel, graceful (elegante), elegant, comely, gallant, sprightly, gay. 2. Liberal, generous, magnanimous (generoso).

garbullo [gar-bool'-lyo], *m.* Crowd, a multitude confusedly pressed together.

garcero, ra [gar-thay'-ro, rah], *m. & f. (Orn.)* Heron-hawk.

garceta [gar-thay'-tah], *f.* 1. A young heron. 2. Hair which falls in locks on the cheeks and temples. 3. *(Naut.)* Point or reef-band, a small rope which serves to furl the sails. **Garcetas**, tenderlings, the first horns of a deer.

gardenia [gar-day'-nyah], *f. (Bot.)* Gardenia.

garduja [gar-doo'-hah], *f.* Barren stone thrown away in quicksilver mines.

garduña [gar-doo'-nyah], *f.* Marten.

garduño [gar-doo'-nyo], *m.* 1. He or male marten. 2. *(coll.)* Filcher, a petty thief.

garete [gah-ray'-tay], *m.* **Ir al garete**, to be adrift.

garfa [gar'-fah], *f.* 1. Claw, as of an animal or bird (sarcastically) a hand. 2. An ancient tax.

garfada, garfiada [gar-fah'-dah, gar-fe-ah'-dah], *f.* Clawing or seizing with the nails.

garfear [gar-fay-ar'], *vn.* To use a drag-hook for getting something out of a well or river.

garfio [gar'-feo], *m.* Hook, drag-hook; gaff, climbing iron (alpinismo).

gargajeada [gar-gah-hay-ah'-dah], *f.* Spitting, ejecting phlegm.

gargajear [gar-gah-hay-ar'], *vn.* To spit, to expectorate.

gargajeo [gar-gah-hay'-o], *m.* Spitting, ejecting phlegm.

gargajiento, ta [gar-gah-he-en'-to, tah], *a.* Spitting, ejecting expectorated matter.

gargajo [gar-gah'-ho], *m.* Phlegm or mucus brought up by coughing, expectorated matter, sputum.

gargajoso, sa [gar-gah-ho'-so, sah], *a.* V. GARGAJIENTO.

garganchón [gar-gahn-chone'], *m.* V. GARGÜERO.

garganta [gar-gahn'-tah], *f.* 1. Throat, gullet. 2. The instep (pie). 3. Mountain-flood, torrent. 4. A narrow pass between mountains or rivers. 5. The shaft of a column or balustrade. 6. Neck (botella). 7. Shaft (columna). **Tener buena garganta**, to be a good singer. **Tener el agua a la garganta**, to be in imminent danger.

gargantada [gar-gan-tah'-dah], *f.* Quantity of water, wine, or blood, ejected at once from the throat.

gargantear [gar-gan-tay-ar'], *vn.* To quaver, to warble.

garganteo [gar-gan-tay'-o], *m.* Quavering, a tremulous modulation of the voice.

gargantilla [gar-gan-teel'-lyah], *f.* Necklace worn by women.

gárgara [gar'-gah-rah], *f.* Noise made by gargling the throat. **Mandar a uno a hacer gárgaras**, to tell somebody to go to hell.

gargarismo [gar-gah-rees'-mo], *m.* 1. Gargarism, gargle (líquido). 2. Gargling.

gargarizar [gar-gah-re-thar'], *va.* To gargle, to gargarize.

gárgol [gar'-gol], *m.* Groove. V. RANURA. **Gárgoles**, grooves of casks, where the head and bottom pieces come in, chimes.

gárgol [gar'-gol], *a. (Prov.)* Empty, addle (huevos).

gárgola [gar'-go-lah], *f.* 1. Spout of a gutter in the form of a lion or other animal; gargoyle. 2. Linseed.

gargüero, garguero [gar-goo-ay'-ro, gar-gay'-ro], *m.* 1. The gullet. 2. Windpipe.

garico [gah-ree'-co], *m.* A kind of medicinal fungus of Canada which grows among the pines.

gariofilea [gah-re-o-fe-lay'-ah], *f. (Bot.)* Common avens or herb bennet.

garita [gah-ree-tah], *f.* 1. Sentry box. 2. A porter's lodge (consejería). 3. A seat in a privy. 4. Look-out post (de vigilancia).

garitear [gah-re-tay-ar'], *vn. (coll.)* To gamble.

garitero [gah-re-tay'-ro], *m.* 1. Owner of a gambling-house (dueño). 2. Gamester, gambler (jugador).

garito [gah-ree'-to], *m.* Gambling-house, gambling-den (casa), profits of gaming (ganancias).

garla [gar'-lah], *f. (coll.)* Talk, chatter.

garlador, ra [gar-lah-dor', rah], *m. & f. (coll.)* Babbler, prattler.

garlante [gar-lahn'-tay], *pa. (coll.)* Babbling, prater.

garlar [gar-lar'], *va. (coll.)* To babble, to prattle, to chatter.

garlito [gar-lee'-to], *m.* 1. A wicker snare or trap for fish. 2. Snare, trap, or gin.

garlocha [gar-lo'-chah], *f.* Goad, with which oxen are driven; oxgoad. V. GARROCHA.

garlopa [gar-lo'-pah], *f.* Jack plane, a long plane.

garnacha [gar-nah'-chah], *f.* 1. Robe, a dress worn by councillors. 2. Dignity or employment of a councillor. 3. A liquor made of honey and wine. 4. A large red grape and the wine made from it (vino). 5. Company of strolling players. V. GARGARILLA.

garo [gah'-ro], *m.* 1. A kind of lobster. 2. Brine for fish or meat.

garra [gar'-rah], *f.* 1. Claw of a wild beast, talon of a bird of prey, a clutch a fang. 2. Hand, in contempt. **Echarle a uno la garra**, *(coll.)* to grasp, to seize, to imprison anyone. 3. *(Tec.)* Claw, tooth, hook. 4. *(Fig.)* Bite, penetration; *(Dep.)* sharpness, edge. **Esta canción no tiene garra**, that song has no bite to it.

garrafa [gar-rah'-fah], *f.* Vessel for cooling liquors; carafe (de vino, licor).

garrafal [gar-rah-fahl´], *a.* 1. Applied to a kind of cherries larger and sweeter than the common ones. 2. Great, vast, huge; monumental (error).

garrafilla [gar-rah-feel'-lyah], *f. dim.* A small vessel for cooling liquids.

garrafinar [gar-rah-fee-nar´], *va. (coll.)* To grapple, to snatch away.

garrafón [gar-rah-fone'], *m. aug.* 1. A large vessel for cooling liquids. 2. Demijohn, carboy.

garrama [gar-rah'-mah], *f.* 1. Tax or duty anciently paid by the Moors. 2. Imposition, fraud, robbery.

garramar [gar-rah-mar'], *va.* 1. To rob, to plunder and pillage. 2. To collect an ancient tax.

garrancho [gar-rahn'-cho], *m.* Branch of a tree broken off; splinter.

garrapata [gar-rah-pah'-tah], *f.* 1. Tick, the louse of dogs and sheep. 2. A short, little person.

garrapatear [gar-rah-pah-tay-ar'], *vn.* To scribble, to scrawl.

garrapatilla [gar-rah-pah-teel'-lyah], *f. dim.* A small tick.

garrapato [gar-rah-pah'-to], *m.* Pot-hook, ill-formed character or letter.

garrar, garrear [gar-rar' gar-ray-ar'], *vn. (Naut.)* To drag, to be driven from the moorings (barco). **El ancla garra,** the anchor drags.

garridamente [gar-re-dah-men'-tay], *adv.* Gracefully, neatly.

garrido, da [gar-ree'-do, dah], *a.* Handsome (bien parecido), neat (elegante), graceful.

garroba [gar-ro-bah], *f. V.* ALGARROBA.

garrobal [gar-ro-bahl'], *m.* Plantation of carob-trees.

garrobilla [gar-ro-beel'-lyah], *f.* Chips of carob-trees used to tan leather.

garrobo [gar-ro'-bo], *m.* 1. *(Bot.)* Carob-tree, or St. Johns bread. 2. Small alligator (caimán).

garrocha [gar-ro'-chah], *f.* 1. A sort of javelin with a hooked head. 2. A kind of dart used to prick bulls.

garrochada [gar-ro-chah'-dah], *f.* or **Garrochazo,** *m.* Prick with a javelin or dart.

garrocheador [gar-ro-chay-ah-dor'], *m.* Goader, pricker.

garrochear [gar-ro-chay-ar'], *va. V.* AGARROCHAR.

garrochón [gar-ro-chone'], *m.* Spear, used by bullfighters on horseback.

garrofa, or **garroba** [gar-ro'-fah, gar-ro'-bah], *f. (Prov.)* A fruit of the carob-tree. *V.* ALGARROBA.

garrofal [gar-ro-fahl'], *m. V.* GARROBAL.

garrón [gar-rone'], *m.* 1. Spur of cocks and birds. 2. Talon of a bird of prey. 3. *V.* CALCAÑAR.

garrotazo [gar-ro-tah'-tho], *m.* 1. Blow with a cudgel. 2. *(aug.)* A large cudgel.

garrotal [gar-ro-tahl'], *m.* A plantation of olive-trees, made with crossed slips of large olive-trees put into the ground to grow.

garrote [gar-ro'-tay], *m.* 1. Cudgel, a strong stick (bastón). 2. A capital punishment used in Spain, consisting in strangling a criminal with an iron collar. 3. The scaffold where the capital punishment called **garrote** is inflicted. 4. *V.* GARROTAZO. 5. The act of tying a rope or cord very tight. 6. *(Prov.)* Hazel basket or pannier. **Dar garrote a uno,** to garrotte somebody.

garrotillo [gar-ro-teel'-lyo], *m.* Inflammation in the throat, croup, diphtheria.

garrubia [gar-roo'-be-ah], *f. V.* ALGARROBA.

garrucha [gar-roo'-chah], *f.* 1. Pulley, one of the mechanical powers. 2. Horse or board on which the card is fixed for combing wool.

garruchón [gar-roo-chone'], *m.* Body of a coach without straps and buckles.

garrucho [gar-roo'-cho], *m. (Naut.)* Cringle, a sort of ring for a variety of uses on board of ships.

garruchuela [gar-roo-choo-ay'-lah], *f. dim.* A small pulley.

garrudo, da [gar-roo'-do, dah], *a.* Nervous, brawny, strong.

garrulador, ra [gar-roo-lah-dor', rah], *m. & f.* A garrulous person.

garrulería [gar-roo-lay-re'-ah], *f.* Chatter.

gárrulo, la [gar'-roo-lo, lah], *a.* 1. Chirping, making a cheerful noise, as birds. 2. Chattering, prattling; garrulous (persona). 3. Noisy (viento).

garú [gah-roo'], *m.* A plant of the mozereum family, of disagreeable smell, whose bark is used as a sinapism or mustard plaster by moistening it in vinegar.

garúa [gah-roo'-ah], *f. (Peru)* Drizzle (lloviznar).

garuar [gah-roo-ar'], *vn. (Peru)* To drizzle.

garufo [gah-roo' fo], *m.* Concrete. *V.* HORMIGÓN.

garulla [gah-rool'-lyah], *f.* 1. Ripe grapes which remain in the basket (uvas). 2. *(coll.)* Rabble, crowd (gentío). *(Per.)*

garullada [gah-rool-lyah'-dah], *f.* Gang of rogues.

garvier [gar-ve-ayr'], *m.* A small pouch anciently in use.

garza [gar'-thah], *f. (Orn.)* Heron.

garzo [gar'-tho], *m.* Agaric.

garzo, za [gar-tho', thah], *a.* Blue-eyed (persona).

garzón [gar-thone'], *m.* Lad, boy; stripling.

garzonear [gar-tho-nay-ar'], *vn.* To make a parade of boyish actions; to solicit, to court.

garzota [gar-tho'-tah], *f.* 1. *(Orn.)* Night-heron. 2. Plumage worn as an ornament. 3. Crest of a helmet.

garzul [gar-thool'], *m. (Prov.)* A kind of wheat.

gas [gahs], *m.* Gas, fumes (vapores).**Gas combustible,** inflammable gas. **Gas lacrimógeno,** tear gas. **Gas venenoso,** poison gas. **Gas natural,** natural gas. **Asfixiar con gas,** to gas.

gasa [gah'-sah], *f.* Gauze, a very thin, transparent cloth, nappy-liner (pañal), crêpe (luto). **Gasa rayada,** striped muslin. **Gasa higiénica,** sanitary towel.

gascón, na, nés [gas-con', nah, nes'], *a.* Gascon, belonging to or native of Gascony.

gasconada [gas-co-nah'-dah], *f.* Gasconade, boast, a bravado.

gaseiforme [gah-say-e-for'-may], *a.* Aeriform, gaseous.

gaseoso, sa [gah-say-o'-so, sah], *a.* Gaseous gas. -*f.* Soda water.

gasífero, ra [gah-see'-fay-ro, rah], *a.* Gasconducting.

gasificable [gah-se-fe-cah'-blay], *a.* Convertible into gas.

gasificación [gah-se-fe-cah-the-on'], *f.* Gasification, conversion into gas.

gasificar [gah-se-fe-car'], *va.* To gasify, to convert into gas.

gas-oil [gah-so'-el], *m.* Diesel oil.

gasóleo [gah-so'-lay-o], *m.* Diesel oil.

gasolina [gah-so-lee'-nah], *f.* Gasoline, petrol, motor spirit. **Estación de gasolina,** gas station. **Gasolina super,** three star petrol.

gasolinera [gah-so-le-nay'-rah], *f.* 1. Motor launch. 2. Gas station.

gasómetro [gah-so'-may-tro], *m.* 1. Gasholder, gas-storage tank. 2. Gasometer.

gasoquimia [gah-so-kee'-me-ah], *f.* Gas chemistry.

gastable [gas-tah'-blay], *a.* That may be wasted or spent.

gastadero [gas-tah-day'-ro], *m.* 1. Waster, spender. 2. Wasting, spending.

gastado, da [gas-tah'-do, dah], *a. & pp.* of GASTAR. Worn-out (decaído), useless, shabby (ropa), hackneyed (trillado).

gastador, ra [gas-tah-dor', rah], *m. & f.* 1. Spendthrift (derrochador), prodigal. 2. Pioneer in military operations. 3. Persons sentenced to public labor. 4. *(Met.)* Corrupter, destroyer.

gastadura [gas-tah-doo'-rah], *f.* The murk which remains upon any object as an effect of friction.

gastamiento [gas-tah-me-en'-to], *m.* Consumption of something.

gastar [gas-tar'], *va.* 1. To expend, to lay out money, to spend (dinero, esfuerzo, tiempo) **Han gastado un** dineral, they've spent a fortune. 2. To waste or make way with, to melt, to consume or wear out gradually (ropa, zapatos) 3. To apply to some purpose. 4. To plunder, to pillage, to sack. 5. To digest, to concoct in the stomach. 6. **Gastar bromas,** to play practical jokes. **Gastar saliva,** to waste one's breath. **Ya verás tú cómo las gasto,** you'll see what stuff I'm made of. **Ya sé cómo las gasta usted.** I know what you are like. 7. To have, to wear (vestir). **Antes no gastaba gafas,** didn't use to wear glasses. -*vr.* 1. To be sold or disposed of. 2. To grow old or useless. 3. To become rotten or corrupted.

gasterópodo, da [gas-tay-ro'-po-do, dah], *a.* Gasteropod.

gasto [gahs'-to], *m.* 1. Expenditure, expense, cost, consumption (consumo). 2. Act of spending or consuming (acto). -*pl.* Expenses, charges, disbursements, outlay, commission. **Gastos de administración,** administrative costs. **Gastos comerciales,** business expenses. **Gastos de explotación,** operating costs. **Gastos de viaje,** traveling expenses.

gástrico, ca [gahs'-tre-co, cah], *a.* Gastric, belonging to the stomach.

gastritis [gas-tree'-tis], *f.* Gastritis, inflammation of the stomach.

gastroenteritis [gas-tro-en-tay-ree'-tees], *f.* Gastroenteritis.

gastrología [gas-tro-lo-hee'-ah], *f.* Gastrology, a treatise on the kitchen and culinary art.

gastronomía [gas-tro-no-mee'-ah], *f.* Gastronomy, epicurism.

gastronómico, ca [gas-tro-no'-me-co, cah], *a.* Gastronomic, belonging to epicurism.

gastrónomo, ma [gas-tro'-no-mo], *m & f.* 1. Epicure, gourmet, gastronomer, a judge of good eating. 2. A writer on epicurism.

gastrorrectomía [gas-tror-rec-to-mee'-ah], *f.* Gastrorectomy.

gastrotomía [gas-tro-to-mee'-ah], *f. (Surg.)* Gastrostomy.

gástrula [gahs'-troo-lah], *f. (Surg.)* Gastrula.

gata [gah'-tah], *f.* 1. She-cat, puss. 2. *(Bot.)* V. GATUÑA. 3. *(Naut.)* A toothed bar from which is suspended the flood-gate of a dam. 4. *(Mil.)* A machine which served to protect those who were scaling a wall against the besieged. 5. *(Naut.)* The crossjack yard. **A gatas**, on all fours.

gatada [gah-tah'-dah], *f.* 1. Clawing, wounding with claws (arañazo). 2. Turn of a hare which is closely pursued. 3. Theft or robbery effected in an artful manner (ladrón). 4. *(coll.)* An artful action or doing; scurvy trick (trampa).

gatafura [gah-tah-foo'-rah], *f.* Cake made of herbs and sour milk.

gatallón [gah-tal-lyone'], *m. (coll.)* Rogue, cheat.

gatatumba [gah-tah-toom'-bah], *f. (coll.)* Affected civility or submission.

gatazo [gah-tah'-tho], *m.* 1. *(aug.)* A large cat. 2. A clumsy joke. 3. An artful trick (trampa).

gateado, da [gah-tay-ah'-do, dah], *a.* Feline, catlike (gatuno).-*pp.* of GATEAR.-*m.* A very compact American wood, employed in rich furniture. 2. Crawl, crawling (movimiento). 3. Scratch, clawing (arañazos).

gateamiento [gah-tay-ah-me-en'to], *m.* Scratching, tearing with the nails.

gatear [gah-tay-ar'], *vn.* To climb up (trepar), to clamber, to go up upon all fours (andar a gatas).-*va. (coll.)* 1. To scratch or claw (arañar). 2. To steal, to rob (robar).

gatera [gah-tay'-rah], *f.* 1. A cat's hole, through which cats go in and out. (apertura) 2. *(Bot.)* Common catmint.

gatería [gah-tay-ree'-ah], *f.* 1. Number of cats brought together in a place (gatos). 2. Cringing submission, mean servility. 3. Rabble, assembly of low people; a number of mischievous ill-bred boys brought together (pandilla).

gatica, illa, ita [gah-tee'-cah, eel'-lyah, ee'-tah], *f. dim.* A little she-cat.

gaticida [gah-te-thee'-dah], *m.* Cat killer.

gatico, illo, ito [gah-tee'-co, eel'-lyo, ee'-to], *m. dim.* A little cat.

gatillazo [gah-teel-lyah'-tho], *m.* The noise made by a trigger at firing.

gatillo [gah-teel'-lyo], *m.* 1. *(Dim.)* A little cat, a kitten. 2. Pelican, an instrument for drawing teeth. 3. Trigger of a gun. 4. Nape of a bull or ox. 5. Filcher, a petty thief or robber.

gato [gah'-to], *m.* 1. Cat, tomcat. 2. Skin of a cat used as a purse, and its contents. 3. A pickpocket, petty thief (ladrón), filcher. 4. Tongs used for hooping casks. 5. Crampiron. 6. Instrument used for examining the bore of a cannon. 7. (de coche) Jack. **Gato montés** or **de clavo**, mountain cat. **Gato de Angora**, Angora cat. **Aquí hay gato encerrado**, I smell a rat. **Llevar el gato al agua**, to pull off something difficult.

gatuna, gatuña [gah-too'-nah, gah-too'-nyah], *f. (Bot.)* Rest-harrow, cammock.

gatunero [gah-too-nay'-ro], *m. (Prov.)* A person who sells smuggled meat.

gatuno, na [gah-too'-no, nah], *a.* Catlike, feline.

gatuperio [gah-too-pay'-re-o], *m.* 1. Mixture of liquors without art and proportion (mezcla). 2. Fraud (fraude), snare, intrigue.

gauchada [gah-oo-chah'-dah], *f. (Rep. Arg.)* 1. Artifice. 2. Action of a gaucho.

gaucho, cha [gah'-oo-cho, chah], *a. (Arch.)* Applied to unlevel superficies.-*m. & f. (Arg.)* 1. Rustic, herdsman, or

Indian of the pampas of the Argentine Republic. 2. A man of the humble people, of rude manners.

gaudeamus, gaudete [gah-oo-day-ah'-moos, gah-oo-day'-tay], *m.* Feast, entertainment, merry making.

gaulteria [gah-ool-tay'-re-ah], *f.* Gaultheria, a heath-plant of the hot lands of South America.

gavanza [gah-vahn'-thah], *f.* Flower of the dog-rose.

gavanzo [gah-vahn'-tho], *m.* Dog-rose. V. ESCARAMUJO.

gaveta [gah-vay'-tah], *f.* Drawer of a desk, locker.

gavetilla [gah-vay-teel'-lyah], *f. dim.* A small drawer of a desk.

gavia [gah'-ve-ah], *f.* 1. *(Naut.)* Main topsail. 2. Place where madmen are confined. 3. Pit or hole into which a tree is transplanted with its roots. 4. V. GAVIOTA.-*pl. (Naut.)* Topsails of the main and foremast.

gavial [gah-ve-ahl'], *m.* A crocodile of the Ganges.

gaviero [gah-ve-ay'-ro], *m. (Naut.)* Seaman who works at the top-masts.

gavieta [gah-ve-ay'-tah], *f. (Naut.)* Scuttle.

gaviete de las lanchas [gah-ve-ay'-tay], *m. (Naut.)* Davit in a long boat.

gavilán [gah-ve-lahn'], *m.* 1. *(Orn.)* Sparrow-hawk. 2. Fine hairstroke in letters; either side of the nib of a pen (plumilla). 3. An iron hook. 4. Among tailors, the point which each pant-leg forms at the crotch. 5. The part which projects under the chisel in turning with the lathe.-*pl.* 1. *(Naut.)* Tholes. V. TOLETES. 2. Dry flowers of artichokes or thistles.

gavilancillo [gah-ve-lan-theel'-lyo], *m.* 1. *(Dim.)* A young hawk. 2. The incurvated point of an artichoke leaf.

gavilla [gah-veel'lyah], *f.* 1. Sheaf of corn; a bundle of vine-shoots. 2. Gang of suspicious persons.

gavillero [gah-veel-lyay'-ro], *m.* 1. Place where suspicious persons assemble; a nest of thieves. 2. Place where the sheaves of corn are collected.

gavina [gah-ve-nah], *f. (Prov.)* V. GAVIOTA.

gavión [gah-ve-on'], *m.* 1. *(Mil.)* Gabion, a wicker basket filled with earth to protect against the fire of the enemy. 2. A large hat.

gavioncillo [gah-ve-on-theel'-lyo], *m. dim. (Mil.)* A small gabion.

gaviota [gah-ve-o'-tah], *f. (Orn.)* Gull, sea-gull.

gavitel [gah-ve-tel'], *m. (Naut.)* A small buoy.

gavota [gah-vo'-tah], *f.* Gavot, a French dance.

gaya [gah'-yah], *f.* 1. Stripe of different colors on stuffs, silks, ribbons, etc (tela). 2. V. PICAZA.

gayado, da [gah-yah'-do, dah], *a. & pp.* of GAYAR. Motley, mingled of various colors.

gayadura [gah-yah-doo'-rah], *f.* Garniture, an ornamental trimming of various colors.

gayar [gah-yar'], *va.* To garnish or adorn with trimming of a different color from the stuff; to variegate, to checker.

gayata [gah-yah'-tah], *f. (Prov.)* Crook, sheep-hook.

gayo [gah'-yo], *m.* 1. *(Orn.)* Jay. 2. Merry, gay (alegre). 3. Bright, showy (vistoso).

gayola [gah-yo'-lah], *f.* 1. *(Naut.)* V. JAULA. 2. *(Prov.)* Kind of hut raised for watching vineyards.

gayomba [gah-yom'-bah], *f. (Bot.)* White single-seed broom.

gayuba [gah-yoo'-bah], *f. (Bot.)* Strawberry-tree, red berried arbutus.

gayubal [gah-yoo-bahl'], *m.* Place where there is an abundance of the strawberry-tree.

gaza [gah'-thah], *f. (Naut.)* Strap, spliced in a circular form, and used to fasten blocks to the masts, yards, and rigging.

gazafatón, gazapatón [gah-thah-fah-tone', gah-thah-pah-tone'], *m.* Nonsense, foolish talk.

gazapa [gah-thah'-pah], *f. (Prov.)* Lie, falsehood.

gazapela [gah-thah-pay'-lah], *f.* Clamorous wrangling or quarrelling.

gazapera [gah-thah-pay'-rah], *f.* 1. Warren for rabbits (conejera). 2. A hiding place where people meet for unlawful purposes.

gazapico, illo, ito [gah-thah-pee'-co, eel'-lyo, ee'-to], *m. dim.* A small rabbit.

gazapina [gah-thah-pee'-nah], *f.* 1. Assembly of vile people. 2. Confusion, disorder, wrangling.

gazapo [gah-thah'-po], *m.* 1. A young rabbit. 2. A dissembling, artful knave. 3. *(coll.)* A great lie (mentira). 4. Sly fellow (taimado).

gazí [gah-thee'], *a.* Applied formerly to a Moor who changed his religion.

gazmiar [gath-me-ar'], *va.* To steal and eat tid-bits. -*vn. (coll.)* To complain, to resent.

gazmol [gath-mole'], *m.* Kind of cancer on the tongue of hawks.

gazmoñada, gazmoñería [gath-mo-nyah'-dah, gath-mo-nyay-re'-ah], *f.* Hypocrisy, false devotion.

gazmoñero, ra, gazmoño, ña [gath-mo-nyay' ro, rah, gath-mo'-ny-o, nyah], *a.* Hypocritical (hipócrita), dissembling, hypocrite.

gaznápiro [gath-nah' pe-ro], *a. & m.* Churlish, a simpleton, dolt, clown.

gaznar [gath-nar'], *vn. V.* GRAZNAR.

gaznatada [gath-nah-tah'-dah], *f.* Blow or stroke on the throttle.

gaznate [gath-nah'-tay], *m.* Throttle, windpipe, gorge. **Remojar el gaznate**, to have a drink.

gaznatón [gath-nah-tone'], *m.* 1. Blow on the throat. 2. Pancake, fritter.

gazofia [gath-tho'-fah], *f. V.* BAZOFIA.

gazpacho [gath-pah'-cho], *m.* 1. Dish made of bread, oil, vinegar, onions, salt, and red pepper, mixed together in water. 2. Crumbs of bread fried in a pan.

gazuza [gah-thoo'-thah], *f. (coll.)* Keenness of stomach, violent hunger.

ge [hey], *f.* Spanish name of the letter G.

geato [hay-ah'-to], *m. (Chem.)* Geate, or humate, a salt of humic acid.

gehena [hay-ay'-nah], *m.* Hell. *(Heb.)*

geico, ca [hay'-e-co, cah], *a. (Chem.)* Geic, humic, ulmic.

geiger, contador de [gah'-e-ger, con-tah-dor'-day], *m.* Geiger counter.

géiser [hay'-ser], *m.* Geyser, gusher.

gelasino, na [hay-lah-see'-no, nah], *a.* Seen on laughing (dientes frontales).

gelatina [hay-lah-tee'-nah], *f.* 1. Gelatine, jelly. 2. A compound jelly made of animal substances, with fruit and sugar.

gelatiniforme [hay-lah-te-ne-for'-may], *a.* Gelatiniform, like gelatine.

gelatinoso, sa [hay-lah-te-no'-so, sah], *a.* Gelatinous, glutinous.

gelatinudo, da [hay-lah-te-noo'-do, dah], *a. (Peru)* 1. Gelatinous. 2. Phlegmatic, lazy, without energy.

gelberda [hel-bayr'-dah], *f.* An argilaceous variety of ochre belonging to the silicates of iron.

gelenita [hay-lay-nee'-tah], *f. (Mill.)* Stilbite, a hydrous aluminum-calciumferrous silicate.

gelfe [hel'-fay], *m.* A black slave.

gélido, da [hay'-le-do, dah], *a. (Poet.)* Gelid, frigid.

gema [hay'-mah], *f.* 1. A short and deep cut in a piece of wood. 2. Gem, precious stone (joya). 3. *(Bot.)* Bud. *V.* YEMA. **Sal gema**, rock-salt.

gemación [hay-mah-the-on'], *f.* Gemation, the first development of the bud.

gemebundo, da [hay-may-boon'-do, dah], *a. (Poet.)* Groaning, moaning, howling.

gemela [hay-may'-lah], *f.* Flower exhaling the odour of orange and jessamine; jasmine.

gemelo, la [hay-may'-lo, lah], *a. & m. & f.* Twin. **Hermanas gemelas**, twin sisters. -*m. pl.* 1. Binocular telescope, opera glasses, field glasses. 2. Cuff links.

gemido [hay-mee'-do], *m.* 1. Groan. 2. Lamentation, moan. 3. Howl, the cry of a wolf or dog. **Gemido, da**, *pp.* of GEMIR.

gemidor, ra [hay-me-dor', rah], *m. & f.* Lamenter, mourner: also used as an adjective, applied to one who groans, or to anything which makes a noise like a groan.

gemificación [hay-me-fe-cah-the-on'], *f.* Gemmation, the mode or time of development of the buds of plants.

geminífloro, ra [hay-me-nee'-flo-ro, rah], *a.* Twin-flowered; bearing flowers set in pairs.

Géminis [hay'-me-nis], *m.* 1. Gemini, a sign of the zodiac. 2. A kind of resolving and healing plaster.

gemir [hay-meer'], *vn.* 1. To groan, to moan, to grieve (quejarse). 2. To howl, as a wolf or dog (animal). 3. To roar, to whistle, as the sea or wind. 4. To grunt.

gen [hen], *m. (Biol.)* Gene.

genciana [hen-the-ah'-nah], *f. (Bot.)* Gentian.

gencianáceo, cea [hen-the-ah-nah'-thay-o, ah], *a.* Gentianaceous, belonging to the gentian family.

genciáneo, a, gencianoideo, a, *a. V.* GENCIANÁCEO.

gendarme [hen-dar'-may], *m.* 1. Gendarme, French policeman. 2. Policeman.

gendarmería [hen-dar-may-ree'-ah], *f.* Gendarmery, French police.

gene [hay'-nay], *m.* Gene.

genealogía [hay-nay-ah-lo-hee'-ah], *f.* Genealogy (ascendientes), lineage.

genealógico, ca [hay-nay-ah-lo'-he-co, cah], *a.* Genealogical, heraldic.

genealogista [hay-nay-ah-lo-hees'-tah], *m.* Genealogist.

geneantropía [hay-nay-an-tro-pee'-ah], *f.* A treatise on the origin of the human race.

geneático, ca [hay-nay-ah'-te-co, cah], *a.* Genethliacal, relating to divination by nativities.

geneo [hay-nay'-o], *m.* A banana of Peru.

generable [hay-nay-rah'-blay], *a.* Generable, that may be produced or begotten.

generación [hay-nay-rah-the-on'], *f.* 1. Generation, act of begetting (acto). 2. Generation, progeny (descendencia), race, offspring. 3. Generation (grupo), age. **La generación del 98**, the 1898 generation. 4. *V.* NACIÓN. 5. Generation, succession (sucesión), lineage. 6. Generation, a single succession.

generador, ra [hay-nay-rah-dor', rah], *m. & f.* 1. Generator. **Generador de códigos**, *(Comput.)* code generator. 2. *(Math.)* Every extension which by its movement produces another. 3. *pl.* The genital organs.

general [hay-nay-rahl'], *a.* 1. General, comprehending many species or individuals. 2. General, universal, relating to a whole class or body of men. 3. General, common (común), usual (frecuente). **En general**, generally, in general. **Es general por todo Méjico**, it is common throughout Mexico. **El mundo en general**, the world in general.

general [hay-nay-rahl'], *m.* 1. Hall or room in a public school where the sciences are taught (habitación). 2. A general (militar). 3. *(Prov.)* Custom-house. 4. General, superior of a religious order.

generala [hay-nay-rah'-lah], *f.* 1. General (llamamiento), a beat of the drum, which calls troops to arms. 2. The wife of a general (mujer). 3. *(Naut.)* Signal to join convoy.

generalato [hay-nay-rah-lah'-to], *m.* 1. Generalship, commission or dignity of a general (órdenes religiosas). 2. Generals (personas).

generalero [hay-nay-rah lay'-ro], *m. (Prov.) V.* ADUANERO.

generalidad [hay-nay-rah-le-dahd'], *f.* 1. Generality, the whole, totality. **La generalidad de los hombres**, the mass of ordinary people. 2. *(Prov.)* Community corporation. 3. *(Prov.)* Custom duties on goods. **generalidades**, *(Prov.)* custom-house fees; discourse consisting of only general principles. 4. Vague answer (vaguedad).

generalísimo [hay-nay-rah-lee'-se-mo], *m.* 1. Generalissimo, the commander-in-chief of an army or of a fleet of ships of war. 2. *V.* GENERAL, for a superior of a religious order.

generalización [hay-nay-rah-le-thah-the-on'], *f.* 1. Generalization (acto). 2. Widening, escalation (conflicto).

generalizar [hay-nay-rah-le-thar'], *va.* To generalize. *-vr.* 1. To become general or usual. 2. To be divulged.

generalmente [hay-nay-ral-men'-tay], *adv.* Generally.

generante [hay-nay-rahn'-tay], *pa. & a.* Generating, engendering; generant.

generar [hay-nay-rar'], *va.* To generate.

generativo, va [hay-nay-rah-tee'-vo, vah], *a.* Generative, having the power of propagation.

generatriz [hay-nay-rah-treeth'], *a. (Math.)* Generatrix.

genéricamente [hay-nay'-re-cah-men-tay], *adv.* Generically.

genérico, ca [hay-nay'-re-co, cah], *a.* Generic.

género [hay'-nay-ro], *m.* 1. Genus, a class comprehending many species. 2. Kin, the same generical class: speaking of the relation between two or more different beings. **Género humano**, human nature, mankind. 3. Manner, way, kind, sort, or mode of doing something (manera). 4. Sex, gender. 5. *(Gram.)* Gender. 6. Something to be bought or sold (productos). **Géneros**, goods, merchandise, wares, or commodities. **Género para chalecos**, vestings. **Géneros de algodón fino**, cotton shirtings. 7. *(Arte, Liter.)* Genre; type. **Género novelístico**, novel genre.

generosidad [hay-nay-ro-se-dahd'], *f.* 1. Hereditary, nobility. 2. Generosity (largueza), magnanimity, liberality, frankness, munificence, open-heartedness. 3. Valor and fortitude in arduous undertakings.

generoso, sa [hay-nay-ro'-so, sah], *a.* 1. Noble (noble), generous, of good extraction. 2. Generous, magnanimous, honorable, freehearted. 3. Generous (liberal), liberal, frank, openhanded, munificent. 4. Generous, strong, vigorous (vinos). 5. Excellent.

genesíaco, ca [hay-ne-see'-ah-co, cah], *a.* 1. Genesiacal, belonging to Genesis. 2. Genesial, belonging to the origin or creation of something.

génesis [hay'-nay-sis], *m.* 1. Genesis, the first book of the Old Testament. 2. Origin.

genética [hay-nay'-te-cah], *f. (Biol.)* Genetics.

genético [hay-nay'-te-co], *a.* Genetic.

genetliaca [hay-net-leah'-cah], *f.* Genethliacs, the science of casting nativities.

genetliaco, ca [hay-net-leah'-co, cah], *a.* Genethliacal, prognosticating by nativities.

gengibre [hen-hee'-bray], *m. V.* JENGIBRE.

genial [hay-ne-ahl'], *a.* 1. Inspired, brilliant (brillante). **Escritor genial**, writer of genius. 2. Pleasant (agradable), cheerful, genial; cordial (afable); witty (divertido). 3. In character, characteristic (propio); individual (singular); typical (típico).

genialidad [han-ne-ah-le-dahd'], *f.* Habits or disposition of a person produced by his natural temper (genio).

genialmente [hay-ne-al-men'-tay], *adv.* Genially (con genio).

geniculación [hay-ne-coo-lah-the-on'], *f.* Geniculation, curvature in the shape of a knee.

geniculado, da [hay-ne-coo-lah-do, dah], *a.* Geniculate, bent like a knee-joint.

genio [hay'-ne-o], *m.* 1. Genius, peculiar mental power or faculties (talento). **¡Eres un genio!**, you´re a genius! 2. Genius, the protecting power of men, places, and things; its plural is genii. 3. Nature, genius, peculiar characteristic, disposition of a person, temper, character, inclination, humor (temperamento). **Genio alegre**, cheerful nature. **De mal genio**, bad-tempered. **Tiene genio**, he´s temperamental. **Estar de mal genio**, to be in a bad temper. 4. *(Pict.)* Little angel.

genipa [hay-nee'-pah], *f. (Bot.)* Silky mugwort or wormwood.

geniquén (or **henequén**) [hay-nee'-kayhn], *m. (Mex.)* Sisal hemp, the fibre of Agave Ixtli, of Mexico and Yucatan. *V.* HENEQUÉN.

genista [hay-nees'-tah], *f. (Bot.)* 1. *V.* RETAMA DE OLOR. 2. *V.* GINESTA.

genital [hay-ne-tahl'], *a.* Genital. *-m. V.* TESTÍCULO.

genitivo, va [hay-ne-tee'-vo, vah], *a.* Having the power of generation. *-m. (Gram.)* The genitive or possessive case.

genitura [hay-ne-too'-rah], *f.* 1. Generation, procreation. 2. *(Ast.)* Horoscope.

genízaro, ra [hay-nee'-thah-ro, rah], *a.* 1. Begotten by parents of different nations. 2. Composed of different species.

genocidio [hay-no-thee'-de-o], *m.* Genocide, extermination of a racial, political or cultural group.

génoli, génuli [hay'-no-le], *m.* A light yellow paste made of sandarach, used by painters.

genovés, sa [hay-no-vays', sah], *a.* Genoese.

gentalla [hen-tahl'-lyah], *f.* Rabble, mob. *V.* GENTUALLA.

gente [hen'-tay], *f.* 1. People, persons in general, folk. 2. Nation, those who compose a community (nación). 3. *(coll.)* A family (parientes). 4. Army, troops (séquito). **Gente de bien** or **de buen proceder**, honest people. **Gente común** or **gente vulgar**, common people. **Gente de pluma**, notaries, attorneys. **Gente fina**, well-educated persons. **Gente de razón**, educated persons. **Son gente inculta**, they´re rough people. **No me gusta esa gente**, I don´t like those people. **Gente de color**, colored people. **Gente de mar**, seafaring men, seamen. **Gente de pelo**, well-to-do people. **Gente gorda,** people of influence. **Gente menuda**, children. **Gente humilde,** humble people.

gentecilla [hen-tay-theel'-lyah], *f.* Mob, rabble.

gentil [hen-teel'], *m.* Gentile, pagan, heathen.

gentil [hen-teel'], *a.* 1. Genteel, elegant (elegante), graceful, handsome, charming (encantador). 2. Excellent, exquisite.

gentileza [hen-tee-lay'-thah], *f.* 1. Gentility, gracefulness of mien, elegance of behavior (elegancia), genteel deportment and address, charm (encanto). 2. Easiness, freedom from constraint. 3. Ostentation, pageantry. 4. Civility, politeness, genteelness.

gentil hombre [hen-teel' om'-bray], *m.* 1. Fine fellow: my good man. 2. Gentleman, the servant who waits about the person of a man of rank.

gentilicio, ia [hen-te-lee'-the-o, ah], *a.* 1. Gentilitious, peculiar to a nation. 2. Gentilitious, hereditary, entailed on a family; tribal.

gentílico, ca [hen-tee'-leco, cah], *a.* Heathen, gentile, pagan, heathenish, hellenic.

gentilidad [hen-te-le-dahd'], *f.* Gentilism, gentility, heathenism, paganism, religion of the heathens; the body of heathens or gentiles.

gentilismo [hen-te-lees'-mo], *m. V.* GENTILIDAD.

gentilizar [hen-te-le-thar'], *vn.* To observe the rites of gentiles or heathens; to gentilize.

gentilmente [hen-teel-men'-tay], *adv.* Genteelly; heathenishly, elegantly (con elegancia); charmingly (con encanto), prettily (con gracia).

gentío [hen-tee'-o], *m.* Crowd, multitude. **Había un gentío**, there were lots of people.

gentualla, gentuza [hen-too-ahl'-lyah, hen-too'-thah], *f.* Rabble, mob.

genuflexión [hay-noo-flec-se-on'], *f.* Genuflexion, bending the knee.

genuino, na [hay-noo-ee'-no, nah], *a.* Genuine, pure, real, legitimate, natural, good.

geocéntrico [hay-o-then'-tree-co], *a. (Ast.)* Geocentric.

geoda [hay-o'-dah], *f.* Geode, a nodule of stone containing crystals.

geodesia [hay-o-day'-se-ah], *f.* Geodaesia, the doctrine or art of measuring surfaces; land surveying.

geodésico, ca [hay-o-day'-se-co, cah], *a.* Geodesic. **Cúpula geodésica**, geodesic dome.

geófago, ga [hay-o'-fah-go, gah], *a.* Geophagous, earth-eating. *-m. f.* Geofagia.

geofísica [hay-o-fee'-se-cah], *f. (Geol.)* Geophysics.

geognosia [hay-og-no'-se-ah], *f.* Geognosy, structural geology.

geografía [hay-ograh-fee'-ah], *f.* Geography. **En toda la geografía nacional**, all over the country.

geográficamente [hay-o-grah'-fe-cah-men-tay], *adv.* Geographically.

geográfico, ca [hay-o-grah'-fe-co, cah], *a.* Geographical.

geógrafo, fa [hay-o'-grah-fo], *m & f.* Geographer.

geología [hay-o-lo-hee'-ah], *f.* Geology.

geológico, ca [hay-o-lo'-he-co, cah], *a.* Geologic(al); relating to geology.

geólogo, ga [hay-o'-lo-go], *m & f.* Geologist.

geomagnético, ca [hay-o-mag-nay'-te-co, cah], *a.* Geomagnetic.

geomancia [hay-o-mahn'-the-ah], *f.* Geomancy, foretelling by figures.

geomántico [hay-o-mahn'-te-co], *m.* Geomancer. **-a.** Geomantic.

geómetra [hay-o'-may-trah], *m.* Geometer, a geometrician.

geometral [hay-o-may-tral'], *a.* V. GEOMÉTRICO.

geometría [hay-o-may-tree´-ah], *f.* Geometry. **Geometría del espacio,** solid geometry. **Geometría plana,** plane geometry.

geométricamente [hay-o-may´-tre-cah-men-tay], *adv.* Geometrically.

geométrico, ca [hay-o-may'-tre-co, cah], *a.* Geometrical, geometric.

geometrinos [hay-o-may-tree'-nos], *m. pl.* The geometric moths, whose larva are called measuring worms.

geopolítica [hay-o-po-lee'-te-cah], *f.* Geopolitics.

geopónica [hay-o-po'-ne-cah], *f.* Geoponics, the science of agriculture; gardening.

georama [hay-o-rah'-mah], *f.* Georama, a large hollow globe, on the side of which are represented the natural divisions of the earth.

georgiano, na [hay-or-he-ah'-no, nah], *a.* Georgian, relating to Georgia.

geórgica [hay-or'-he-cah], *f.* Georgic, a poem upon husbandry.

geranio [hay-rah'-ne-o], *m.* *(Bot.)* Crane's-bill. Geranium.

gerapliega [hay-rah-ple-ay'-gah], *f.* *(Pharm.)* Hierapicra, a bitter purgative medicine.

gerbo [herr'-bo], *m.* The jerboa.

gerencia [hay-ren'-the-ah], *f.* 1. Administration. 2. Management (de negocios) 3. Management (dirección). 4. Managership (cargo). 5. Manager´s office (oficina).

gerente [hay-ren'-tay], *m.* *(Com.)* Manager, director. **Gerente de fábrica,** works manager.

geriatra [hay-re-ah'-trah], *m.* Geriatrician.

geriatría [hay-re-ah-tree'-ah], *f.* *(Med.)* Geriatrics.

geriátrico [hay-re-ah'-tre-co], *a. m & f.* Geriactric.

gericaya [hay-re-cah-yah], *f.* *(Mex.)* Custard.

gerifalto [hay-re-fahl'-tay], *m.* *(Orn.)* Gerfalcon.

germanesco, ca [her-mah-ness´-co, cah], *a.* Belonging to the jargon of the gipsies.

germanía [her-mah-nee'-ah], *f.* 1. Jargon or cant of the gipsies, thieves, etc.; slang. 2. Concubinage.

germánico, ca [her-mah'-ne-co, cah], *a.* Germanic, German; of Germany.

germanismo [her-mah-nees'-mo], *m.* Germanism, a German idiom employed in another language.

germen [her´-men], *m.* 1. Germ. **Germen plasma,** germ plasma. 2. Sprout, shoot.

germicida [her-me-thee'-da], *a.* Germicidal.**-m.** Germicide.

germicultura [her-me-cool-too'-rah], *f.* Culture or medium for the growth of bacteria.

germífugo, ga [her-mee´-foo-go, gah], *a.* Germicidal.

germinación [her-me-nah-the-on'], *f.* *(Bot.)* Germination, the first act of vegetation in a seed.

germinar [her-me-nar'], *vn.* To germinate, to bud.

germinativo, va [her-me-nah-tee'-vo, vah], *a.* Germinative.

gerundiada [hay-roon-deah'-dah], *f.* *(coll.)* An emphatical, pompous, and unmeaning expression.

gerundio [hay-roon'-de-o], *m.* 1. *(Gram.)* Gerund, a verbal noun. 2. The person who affects to speak or preach in a pompous and emphatical manner.

gesta [hess'-tah], *f.* *(Bot.)* V. RETAMA.

gestación [hes-tah-the-on'], *f.* 1. Gestation, the term of pregnancy. 2. An exercise practised among the Romans for the confirmation of health, and the place where it was carried out. 3. Superstition of wearing rings to preserve oneself from evil.

gestar [hes-tar'], *va.* *(Bio.)* To gestate; *(Fig.)* to prepare, to hatch. *-vr.* *(Bio.)* To gestate; *(Fig.)* to be in preparation.

gestatorio, ria [hes-tah-to'-re-o, ah], *a.* Proper to gestation (estado, ejercicio).

gestero, ra [hes-tay'-ro, rah], *a.* Playing antic tricks, making grimaces; it is also used as a substantive for one who distorts his countenance from habit or affectation; a gesticulator.

gesticulación [hes-te-coo-lah-the-on'], *f.* Gesticulation (ademán), gesture (mueca).

gesticular [hes-te-coo-lar'], *va.* To gesticulate (hacer ademanes), to make gestures or grimaces (hacer muecas).

gesticular [hes-te-coo-lar'], *a.* Relating to gestures or gesticulation; gesticulatory.

gestión [hes-te-on'], *f.* 1. *(Com. etc.)* Management, conduct. 2. Negotiation (negociación). 3. Measure (medida), step; action (acción); effort (esfuerzo); operation (operación). **Gestiones,** measures. **Hacer las gestiones preliminares,** to do the ground work.

gestionar [hes-te-o-nar'], *va.* 1. To manage (conducir). 2. To negotiate (negociar). 3. To try to arrange (procurar).

gesto [hess'-to], *m.* 1. Face (cara), visage. 2. Grimace (mueca), a distortion of the countenance, a gesture. 3. Aspect, appearance (semblante). 4. Likeness, resemblance. **Estar de buen gesto,** to be in good humor. **Hacer un gesto,** to make a face. **Hacer gestos,** to make gestures. **Con un gesto de cansancio,** with a weary gesture.

gestor [hes-tor'], *m.* 1. *(Com.)* Superintendent, manager. 2. *(for.)* Proxy, representative, one who executes another's business and require his principal's ratification.

gestora [hes-to'-rah], *f.* Committee of management.

gestoría [hes-to-ree'-ah], *f.* Agency.

gestudo, da [hes-too'-do, dah], *a.* Humored, cross.

gialomina [he-ah-lo mcc'-nah], *f.* Sort of yellow ochre.

giba [hee'-bah], *f.* 1. Hump, crooked back, hunch, gibbosity. 2. *(coll.)* Importunity, tiresomeness.

gibado, da [he-bah'-do, dah], *a.* Crooked, hump-backed. V. GIBOSO.*-pp.* of GIBAR.

gibar [he-bar'], *va.* V. JIBAR.

gibón [he-bon'], *m.* Gibbon, an anthropoid ape.

gibosidad [he-boo-se-dahd'], *f.* 1. *(Bot.)* A hump, gibbosity. 2. *(Med.)* A hump on the back.

giboso, sa [he-bo'-so, sah], *a.* Gibbous, crook-backed, hump-backed.

gicama [hee'-cah-mah], *f.* *(Mex.)* A palatable root resembling yucca.

giganta [he-gahn'-tah], *f.* 1. Giantess 2. *(Bot.)* Smooth bear's breech.

gigantazo, za [he-gan-tah'-tho, thah], *m. & f. aug.* A huge giant.

gigante [he-gahn'-tay], *m.* 1. Giant, one unnaturally large. 2. One superior in courage, talents, or virtues.*-a.* Gigantic.

gigantesco, ca [he-gan-tays´-co, cah], *a.* Gigantic, giant-like.

gigantez [he-gan-teth'], *f.* Gigantic tallness.

gigantilla [he-gan-teel'-lyah], *f.* A figure made of paste or paste-board, with a very large head.

gigantón, na [he gan tone', nah], *m. & f. aug.* Giant of enormous size. **Gigantones,** gigantic figures of pasteboard.

gijas [hee'-has], *f. pl.* *(Prov.)* V. GUIJAS.

gilí [he-lee'], *a.* 1. Stupid, silly (tonto). 2. Stuck-up (vanidoso); presumptuous (presumido). *-m & f.* 1. Berk (tonto), idiot. 2. Conceited individual (vanidoso).

gilia [hee'-leah], *f.* Gilia, a plant of the phlox family.

gilicopa [he-lo-co'-pah], *f.* V. JILOCOPO.

gilipollas [he-le-po'-yahs], *m & f.* V. GILÍ.

gilipollez [he-le-po-yeth'], *f.* 1. Idiocy (idiotez); silliness. 2. Conceit (vanidad), presumption.

gilvo, va [heel'-vo, vah], *a.* 1 Honey-colored, or between white and red.

gimelga [he-mel´-gah], *f.* *(Naut.)* Fish, a piece of timber used to strengthen masts and yards.

gimnanto, ta [him-nahn'-to, tah], *a. (Bot.)* Naked, without floral envelopes.

gimnasia [him-nah´-se-ah], *f.* Gymnastics; physical training. **Hacer gimnasia**, to do gymnastics. *V.* GIMNÁSTICA.

gimnasiarca [him-nah-se-ar´-cah], *m.* Gymnasiarch, head of an academy, college, or school.

gimnasio [him-nah´-se-o], *m.* 1. School, academy, gymnasium. 2. Gymnasium, a place for athletic training and exercises.

gimnasta [him-nahs'-tah], *m.* Master of athletic exercises.

gimnasterio [him-nas-tay'-re-o], *m.* Wardrobe of a gymnasium.

gimnástica [him-nahs´-te-cah], *f.* Gymnastics.

gimnástico, ca [him-nahs'-te-co, cah], *a.* Gymnastic, gymnastical.

gímnica [heem'-ne-cah], *f.* Gymnics, athletic exercises and the art of teaching them.

gímnico, ca [heem'-ne-co, cah], *a.* Gymnastical.

gimnobranquio, ia [him-no-brahn'-ke-o, ah], *a.* Having naked gills, gymnobranchiate.

gimnocarpeo, a [him-no-car'-pay-o, ah], *a.* Gymnocarpous, having naked fruit.

gimnoclado [him-no-clah'-do], *m.* The Kentucky coffee tree: gymnocladus.

gimnópodo, da [him-no'-po-do, dah], *a.* Gymnopodous, naked-footed.

gimnoto [him-no'-to], *m.* Gymnotus, the electrical eel.

gimnosofista [him-no-so-fees´-tah], *m.* Gymnosophist, one of a sect of Indian philosophers.

gimnospermo, ma [him-nos-perr'-mo, mah], *a.* Gymnospermous, having the seeds naked.

gimotear [he-mo-tay-ar'], *vn.* 1. *(coll.)* To be always crying (lamentar, lloriquear). 2. To whine (gemir), to whimper.

gimoteo [he-mo-tay'-o], *m.* 1. The act of crying very frequently (lamento, lloriqueo). 2. Whine, whining (gemido).

ginantropo [he-nan-tro'-po], *m.* Hermaphrodite.

ginebra [he-nay'-brah], *f.* 1. Rattle, an instrument popular among the Moors;. 2. Gin or geneva. 3. *(Met.)* Confusion, disorder. 4. A confused noise. 5. Game of cards. 6. Geneva.

ginebrada [he-nay-brah'-dah], *f.* Sort of puff paste.

ginebrés, sa, or **ginebrino, na** [he-nay-brays', sah, he-nay-bree´-no, nah], *a.* Genevan, relating to Geneva.

gineceo [he-nay-thay'-o], *m.* Gyneceum, the part of an ancient Greek house reserved for women.

ginecocracía [he-nay-co-crah-thee'-ah], *f.* Gynaeocracy or gynecocracy, gynarchy, female government.

ginecografía [he-nay-co-grah-fee'-ah], *f.* Gynecology, a treatise on the diseases of women.

ginecología [he-nay-co-lo-hee´-ah], *f.* *(Med.)* Gynecology, study of women's diseases.

ginecólogo, ga [he-nay-co'-lo-go, gah], *m. & f.* Gynecologist, specialist in women's diseases.

gineta [he-nay'-tah], *f.* Genet, a kind of weasel. *V.* JINETA.

ginete [he-nay'-tay], *m.* *V.* JINETE.

gingivitis [hin-he-vee'-tis], *f.* *(Med.)* Gingivitis.

ginizo [he-nee'-tho], *m.* The moist, viscous surface of the stigma of orchids.

ginología [he-no-lo-hee'-ah], *f.* Gynecology.

ginseng [hin-seng'], *m.* *(Bot.)* Ginseng, Aralia ginseng.

gipaeto [he-pah-ay'-to], *m.* A diurnal bird of prey resembling the vulture and the eagle.

gips [heeps], *m.* A bird of the vulture family, of a brownish color.

gipsífero, ra [hip-see'-fay-ro, rah], *a.* Gypseous, containing gypsum.

gira [hee'-rah], *f.* *V.* JIRA.

girada [he-rah'-dah], *f.* 1. Gyration; pirouette, a turn on one foot in dancing. 2. Reciprocal motion of a tuft of wool from one comb to another in wool-shops.

girado [he-rah'-do], *m.* *(Com.)* Drawee.

girador, girante [he-rah-dor', he-rahn'-tay], *m.* *(Com.)* Drawer.

girafa [he-rah'-fah], *f.* Giraffe, camelopard.

giralda [he-rahl'-dah], *f.* 1. Vane or weather-cock in the form of a statue; derived from the statue of a woman on the spire of the cathedral church of Seville. 2. Common name of this tower.

giralete [he-ral-day´-tay], *m.* Rochet or surplice without sleeves.

giraldilla [he-ral-deel'-lyah], *f.* *dim.* A small vane or weather-cock in the form of a statue.

girándula [he-rahn'-doo-lah], *f.* 1. In artificial fireworks, box of rockets, which turns swiftly and emits a quantity of rockets. 2. Girandole, a branched candle-stick.

girar [he-rar´], *vn.* 1. To turn round (voltearse), to make a gyre, to circumgyrate, to hurdle, to rotate (dar vueltas). **Girar hacia la derecha**, to turn right. **El satélite gira alrededor de la tierra**, the satellite circles the earth. 2. To remit, to draw bills of exchange, to draw. 3. To swing (balancear); to swivel; to pivot (en equilibrio). -*va.* To turn (dar vuelta a), to turn round, to rotate; to twist (torcer); to spin (revolverse). **Girar la manilla 2 veces**, to turn the crank twice.

girasol [he-rah-sole'], *m.* *(Bot.)* Sunflower.

giratorio, ria [he-rah-to'-re-o, ah], *a.* Rotating, gyrating, revolving (puerta) **Silla giratoria**, swivel chair.

girel [he-rel´], *m.* Caparison, trappings for a horse. *V.* JIREL.

girifalte [he-re-fahl'-tay], *m.* *V.* GERIFALTE.

girimiquiar [he-re-me-ke-ar'], *vn.* *(Cuba)* To sob.

girino [he-ree'-no], *m.* 1. Embryo of a frog. 2. Gyrinus, whirligig beetle.

giro [hee´-ro], *m.* 1. *(Com.)* Draft. **Giro a la vista**, sight draft. **Giro postal**, money order. 2. Gyration, rotation. 3. Turn (vuelta), trend (tendencia), turn of events. **Tomar otro giro**, to change intent or resolution, to change the aspect of the matter. **Giro regular de los negocios**, a fair run of business.

giromancia [he-ro-man'-the-ah], *f.* Gyromancy.

giroscopio [he-ros-co´-pe-o], *m.* Gyroscope.

gis [hees], *m.* *(Pict.)* Crayon.

gitana [he-tah-nah], *f.* Gipsy; fortune teller (de feria)

gitanada [he-tah-nah'-dah], *f.* Blandishment, wheedling like gipsies, caress, flattery.

gitanamente [he-tah-nah-men'-tay], *adv.* In a sly, winning manner.

gitanear [he-tah-nay-ar'], *va.* To flatter, to wheedle, to caress, to entice by soft words.

gitanería [he-tah-nay-ree'-ah], *f.* 1. Band of gipsies (gítanos). 2. Gipsy (vida). 3. Gipsy saying (dicho).

gitanesco, ca [he-tah-ness'-co, cah], *a.* Gipsy-like, gipsy.

gitanillo, lla [he-tah-neel'-lyo, lyah], *m. & f. dim.* Little gipsy.

gitanismo [he-tah-nees'-mo], *m.* The gipsies taken as a body, gipsyism, customs and manners which characterize gipsies.

gitano, na [he-tah'-no, nah], *m. & f.* 1. Gipsy. 2. A sly, artful fellow, of a genteel pleasing address (zalamero).

gitón [he-tone'], *m.* Ancient copper coin used only as the title of unity. *V.* GUITÓN.

glacial [glah-the-ahl'], *a.* Glacial. **Mar glacial**, the frozen sea.

glaciar [glah-the-ar'], *m.* Glacier.

glacis [glah'-this], *m.* 1. *(Mil.)* *V.* EXPLANADA. 2. Ends which join the bar in lacework. 3. Union of colors, scumbling, in a picture to give it tone and harmony (cuadro). 4. *(Arch.)* The slope of a cornice to turn off water.

gladiador [glah-de-ah-dor'], or **Gladiator** [glah-de-ah-tor'], *m.* Gladiator a sword-player; a prize-fighter.

gladiatorio, ria [glah-de-ah-to'-re-o, ah], *a.* Gladiatorial, gladiatory.

gladiolo [glah-de-o'-lo], *m.* *(Bot.)* Common corn-flag.

glaglar [glah-glar'], *va. (coll.)* To gaggle, to talk in a voice resembling the cry of a goose.

glande [glahn-day], *m.* The glans penis, or clitoridis.

glandífero, ra, glandígero, ro [glan-dee'-fay-ro, rah], *a.* 1. Glandiferous, bearing acorns. 2. Bearing tubercles in the form of acorns.

glándula [glan'-doo-lah], *f.* 1. Gland, a soft, spongy substance. 2. *(Bot.)* Gland, a little tumor discharging a fluid. **Glándula endocrina**, endocrine gland. **Glándula tiroides**, thyroid.

glandular [glan-doo-lar'], *a.* Glandular.

glandulífero, ra [glan-doo-lee'-fay-ro, rah], *a.* Glanduliferous, gland-bearing.

glandulilla [glan-doo-leel'-lyah], *f. dim.* Glandule, a small gland.

glanduloso, sa [glan-doo-lo'-so, sah], *a.* Glandulous, glandular, pertaining to the glands.

glasé [glah-say'], *m.* Glacé finish.

glaseado, da [glah-say-ah'-do, dah], *a.* Variegated, embroidered, glossy.

glasear [glah-say-ar'], *va.* To glaze (papel); to glaze (repostería).

glasto [glash'-to], *m. (Bot.)* Woad or common dyers' woad.

glaucio [glah'-oo-the-o], *m. (Bot.)* Celandine.

glauco, ca [glah'-oo-co, cah], *a. (Bot.)* Glaucous, sea-green, pale bluish green.

glauco [gah'-oo-co], *m.* A kind of oyster with equal shells.

glaucoma [glah-oo-co'-mah], *m.* Glaucoma, a disease of the eye characterized by increased tension, advancing farsightedness, dimness of vision and ultimate blindness.

gleba [glay'-bah], *f.* 1. Sod of earth turned up by the plough; glebe; fief; heritage. 2. A slave anciently joined to a piece of land and transferred with it to another owner.

gleboso, sa [glay-bo'-so, sah], *a. (Prov.)* Glebous, turfy.

glenóideo, dea [glay-no'-e-day-o, ah], *a.* Glenoid, every deep cavity which receives the head of a bonc.

glicerina [gle-thay-ree'-nah], *f.* Glicerine

glicónico [gle-co'-ne-co], *m.* A kind of Latin verse.

glifo [glee'-fo], *m. (Arch.)* Glyph, a concave ornament.

glíptica [gleep'-te-cah], *f.* Glyptics, the art of engraving fine stones and the like.

gliptografía [gleep-to-grah-fee'-ah], *f.* Glyptography, a description of the art of engraving upon gems.

global [glo-bahl'], *a.* Global (en conjunto); total (completo), complete, overall; full (investigación, informe), comprehensive; total (suma).

globalizar [glo-bah-le-thar'], *va.* To encompass, to include.

globalmente [glo-bahl'-men-tay], *adv.* As a whole (considerar, examinar).

globiforme [glo-be-for'-may], *a.* Globe shaped, globiform, spherical.

globo [glo'-bo], *m.* 1. Globe, a spherical body. 2. Sphere, a terrestrial or celestial globe on which the various regions of the earth are geographically delineated, or the constellations and stars depicted. 3. Orb. **Globo aerostático**, a balloon. **Globo terráqueo**, globe. **Globo dirigible**, dirigible.

globoso, sa [glo-bo'-so, sah, *a.* Globular, spherical, orbicular.

globular [glo-boo-lar'], *a.* Globular spherical.

glóbulo [glo'-boo-lo], *m.* 1. Globule. 2. Conceptacle of the reproductive bodies of certain lichens. **Glóbulo blanco**, white corpuscle.

globuloso, sa [glo-boo-lo'-so, sah], *u.* Globulous.

glomerula [glo-may'-roo-lah], *f. (Bot.)* Glomerule, head of flowers.

glomerulado, da [glo-may-roo-lah'-do, dah], *a.* Glomerulate, in small clusters.

gloria [glo'-re-ah], *f.* 1. Glory (fama), honor, fame. 2. Paradise, state of blessedness. 3. Pleasure, delight in something (delicia). 4. Majesty, splendor. 5. Glory, blessedness, that which ennobles or illustrates. 6. A sort of tart or pie. 7. In painting, an opening in the sky representing angels,

splendors, etc. **Oler a gloria**, to smell divine. **Saber a gloria**, to taste heavenly. **Una vieja gloria**, a has-been, a great figure.

gloriarse [glo-re-ar'-say], *vr.* 1. To glory, to boast in, to be proud of, to flourish. 2. To take a delight in something.

glorieta [glo-re-ay'-tah], *f.* Summer house (cenador), bower (pérgola), arbor. 2. Roundabout, traffic circle (encrucijada). 3. Square (plaza ajardinada).

glorificación [glo-re-fe-cah-the-on'], *f.* 1. Glorification, giving glory. 2. Praise.

glorificador [glo-re-fe-cah-dor'], *m.* Glorifier, he that glorifies: an appellation given to God.

glorificante [glo-re-fe-cahn'-tay], *pa. & m. & f.* Glorifying; glorifier.

glorificar [glo-re-fe-car'], *va.* 1. To glorify, to pay honor in worship. 2. To exalt to glory or dignity; to praise, to honor, to extol. -*vr.* V. GLORIARSE.

gloriosamente [glo-re-o-sah-men'-tay], *adv.* Gloriously.

glorioso, sa [glo-re-o'-so, sah], *a.* 1. Glorious, excellent, worthy of honor or praise. 2. Enjoying the bliss of heaven, blessed. 3. Glorious, boastful, ostentatious, proud, elate.

glosa [glo'-sah], *f.* 1. Gloss, a scholium; a comment or commentary. 2. Note added to a document, or inserted in a book of accounts, to explain its contents. 3. *(Poet.)* Amplification of a verse. 4. *(Mus.)* Variation in a tune.

glosador, ra [glo-sah-dor', rah], *m. & f.* Commentator, glosser, a writer of glosses.

glosalgia [glo-sahl'-he-ah], *f.* Glossalgia, neuralgia of the tongue.

glosantrace [glo-san-trah'-thay], or **Glosántrax**, *m.* Glossanthrax, carbuncle of the tongue.

glosar [glo-sar'], *va.* 1. To gloss, to explain by comment. 2. To palliate by specious exposition or representation. 3. *(Poet.)* To amplify the sense of a verse. 4. *(Mus.)* To vary notes.

glosario [glo-sah'-re-o], *m.* 1. A glossary; a special lexicon. 2. The mouth parts of insects.

glose [glo'-say], *m.* Act of glossing or commentating.

glosilla [glo-seel'-lyah], *f.* 1. *(Dim.)* A short gloss, comment, or note. 2. *(Print.)* Minion type. 7. Point.

glositis [glo scc'-tis], *f.* Glossitis, inflammation of the tongue.

glotis [glo'-tis], *f. (Anai.)* Glottis, opening of the larynx.

glotón, na [glo-to-ne', nah], *m. & f.* 1. A glutton, gormandizer. 2. Glutton wolverene, a carnivore. -*a.* Gluttonous, given to excessive feeding.

glotonazo, za [glo-to-nah'-tho, thah], *m & f. aug.* Great glutton, great eater.

glotoncillo, illa [glo-ton-theel'-lyoh, lyah], *m. & f. dim.* Little glutton.

glotonear [glo-to-nay-ar'], *vn.* To indulge too much in eating, to devour, to gormandize.

glotonería, glotonía [glo-to-nay-ree'-ah], *f.* Gluttony, greediness.

gloxinia [gloc-see'-ne-ah], *f.* Gloxinia, a perennial plant, having large, handsome flowers.

glucina [gloo-thee'-nah], *f.* Glucina, aluminum oxide.

glucinio [gloo-thee'-ne-o], *m.* Glucinum, a hard, silver, white metallic element.

glucosa [gloo-co'-sah], *f.* Glucose.

gluma [gloo'-mah], *f. (Bot.)* Glume, the chaff-like bract of the blossom of grasses and sedges.

glumáceo, cea [gloo-mah'-thay-o, ah], *a.* Glumaceous.

glumal [gloo-mahl'], *a.* V. GLUMÁCEO.

glumífero, ra [gloo-mee'-tay-ro, rah], *a.* Glumaceous, bearing glumes.

gluten [gloo'-ten], *m.* Gluten.

gluteo, tea [gloo-tay'-o, ah], *a.* Gluteal, relating to the buttocks.

glutinosidad [gloo-te-nose-dahd'], *f.* Glutinousness, viscosity.

glutinoso, sa [gloo-te-no'-so, sah], *a.* Glutinous, viscous, mucous.

gneis [nay'-is], *m.* Gneiss, a rock resembling granite, composed of quartz, feldspar, and hornblende.

gnómico, ca [no'-me-co, cah], *a.* Sententious, gnomic.
gnomo [no'-mo], *m.* 1. Aphorism, apothegm. 2. Gnome, a fabulous being.
gnomon [no'-mon], *m.* 1. Gnomon, the hand of a dial. 2. Bevel square, composed of two movable rules.
gnomónica [no-mo'-ne-cah],*f.* Gnomonics, the science which teaches the art of making sun-dials.
gnomónico, ca [no-mo'-ne-co, cah], *a.* Gnomonic, gnomonical, relating to dialing.
gnosticismo [nos-te-thees'-mo], *m.* Gnosticism, the philosophy of the gnostics, prevailing from the 1st to the 6th century.
gnóstico [nos'-te-co], *m. & a.* Gnostic: applied to one of the earliest heretics.
goa [go'-ah], *f.* Pig iron.
gobernable [go-bayr-nah'-blay], *a.* 1. *(Pol.)* Gobernable. **Un pueblo difícilmente gobernable,** people hard to govern. 2. *(Naut.)* Navigable.
gobernación [go-ber-nah-the-on'], *f.* 1. Government, governing (acto). **Ministro de la gobernación,** Department of the Interior. 2. Governor´s residence (residencia); governor´s office (oficina). *V.* GOBIERNO.
gobernado, da [go-ber-nah'-do, dah], *a. & pp.* of GOBERNAR. Governed.
gobernador [go-ber-nah-dor'], *m.* Governor, ruler, muster. **Gobernador civil,** civil governor.
gobernadora [go-ber-nah-do'-rah],*f.* Governess, directress.
gobernalle [go-ber-nahl'-lyay], *m.* Rudder, helm.
gobernante [go-ber-nahn'-tay], *m. (coll.)* A person assuming the management of a thing.-*pa.* Governing (que gobierna).
gobernar [go-ber-nar'], *va.* 1. To govern, to rule as a first magistrate. 2. To regulate to govern, to command, to lead, to head, to control (controlar), to manage: to guide (dirigir), to direct. 3. To entertain, to maintain. **Gobernar el timón,** to steer the ship.
gobernativo, va [go-ber-nah-tee'-vo, vah], *a. V.* GUBERNATIVO.
gobernoso, sa [go-bayr-no'-so, sah], *a.* Methodical, systematic, loving good order.
gobierno [go-be-ayr'-no], *m.* 1. Government, form of a community with respect to the disposition of the supreme authority. 2. Government, administration of public affairs, executive power. 3. Government, district or province under the command of a governor. 4. The space of time which the administration of a governor lasts, and the manner in which he governs. 5. Government, regularity of behavior, guidance (en general), conduct, management, direction. **Gobierno autónomo,** autonomous government. **Gobierno militar,** military government. **Gobierno de la casa,** house keeping. *(Yo gobierno, yo gobierne,* from *Gobernar. V.* ACERTAR.)
gobio [go'-be-o], *m. (Zool.)* Gudgeon.
goce [go'-thay], *m.* Enjoyment; possession.
gocete [go-thay'-tay], *m.* Ancient armor for the head.
gocha [go'-chah], *f.* Sow.
gocho [go'-cho], *m.* Pig (cerdo), hog.
gociano, na [go-the-ah'-no, nah], *a.* Goth, Gothic.
godeño, ña [go-day'-nyo, nyah], *a.* Rich, renowned.
godetia [go-day'-te-ah], *f.* Godetia, a genus of showy flowers, belonging to the evening-primrose family of California and Chili.
godo, da [go'-do, dah], *a. & m. & f.* Gothic; a Goth.
gofio [go'-fe-o], *m. (Cuba)* Parched corn-meal, maize, or other cereal.
gofo, fa [go'-fo, fah], *a.* Stupid; ignorant, rude. **Gofo,** *(Pict.)* a little figure or image.
gofrador [go-frah-dor'], *m. (Neol.)* Leaf-marker, a florist's copper tool for stamping in relief the veins of leaves. 2. The one who uses this tool.
gofrar [go-frar'], *va.* To mark leaves for artificial flowers.
gol [gol], *m.* Goal. **Meter un gol,** *(Fig.)* to score a point against somebody.

gola [go'-lah], *f.* 1. Gullet, throat, oesophagus. 2. Goriget, a piece of silver or brass worn by officers of foot when on duty. 3. *(Fort.)* Gorge, the entrance of a bastion, ravelin, or other work. 4. *(Arch.)* Gola, cymatium, a moulding, the profile of which represents an S.
goleada [go-lay-ah'-dah],*f.* Quantity of goals, high score.
goleador [go-lay-ah-dor'], *a. m & f.* **El equipo más goleador,** the team which has scored most goals.
golear [go-lay-ar'], *va.* To score a goal against. **El portero menos goleado,** the keeper who has let in fewest goals.
goleta [go-lay'-tah], *f. (Naut.)* A schooner.
golf [golf], *m.* Golf, golf game (juego); golf course (pista).
golfa [gol-fah], *f.* Tart, whore.
golfan [gol-fahn'], *m. V.* NENUFAR.
golfería [gol-fay-ree'-ah], *f.* 1. Loafers (golfos). 2. Loafing (acto); life of idleness (estilo de vida).
golfín [gol-feen'], *m. V.* DELFÍN.
golfista [gol-fees'-tah], *m & f.* Golfer.
golfo [gol'-fo], *m.* 1. Gulf, bay (bahía). 2. Gulf, abyss. 3. Hoodlum, rake, vagabond.
golilla [go-leel'-lyah],*f.* 1. A kind of collar, forming part of the dress of the magistrates of some superior courts of justice in Spain. 2. *(coll.)* The magistrate of said superior courts. **Levantar la golilla,** to become passionate. **Bajar la golilla,** to be pacified.
golillero, ra [go-leel-lyay'-ro, rah], *m. &. f.* Collar-maker.
gollería, golloría [gol-lyay-ree'-ah], *f.* 1. A dainty dish (golosina). 2. Delicacy, superfluity, excess.
gollete [gol-lyay'-tay], *m.* 1. Throttle, the superior part of the throat (garganta). 2. The neck of a bottle.
gollizo [gol-lyce'-tho], *m.* Narrow passage of mountains or rivers.
golmajo, ja [gol-mah'-ho, hah], *(Prov.) V.* GOLOSO.
golondrina [go-lon-dree'-nah], *f.* 1. *(Orn.)* Swallow. **Golondrina de mar,** tern. 2. *(Zool.)* Sapphire gurnard, tub-fish.
golodrinera [go-lon-dre-nay'-rah], *f. (Bot.)* Swallow-wort, celandine.
golondrino [go-lon-dree'-no], *m.* 1. A male swallow. 2. Vagrant, deserter (vagabundo). 3. Tub-fish. 4. A large tumor in the arm-pit.
golondro [go-lon'-dro], *m.* Desire, longing. **Campar de golondro,** *(coll.)* to live at another´s expense. **Andar en golondro,** *(coll.)* to feed on vain hopes.
golosamente [go-lo-sah-men'-tay], *adv.* Daintily.
goloserazo [go-lo-sah'-tho], *m. aug.* Applied to a person extremely fond of dainties or delicacies.
golosear [go-lo-say-ar'], *va. V.* GOLOSINAR.
golosina [go-lo-see'-nah], *f.* 1. Dainty, something nice or delicate, a titbit (manjar). 2. Daintiness, fondness of dainties. 3. Something more agreeable than useful. 4. Cupidity, desire (deseo). -*pl.* Niceties, dainties, delicacies.
golosinar, golosinear, golosmear [go-lo-se-nar', go-lo-se-nay-ar', golos-may-ar'], *va.* 1. To eat titbits, dainties, or sweatmeats, and also to look for them. 2. To be fond of tasting or trying the relish of nice things. 3. To guzzle dainties.
goloso, sa [go-lo'-so, sah], *a. & m. & f.* Applied to a person very fond of dainties, nicotine, or sweetmeats; sweet tooth, lickerish.
golpazo [gol-pah'-tho], *m. aug.* A great blow.
golpe [gol'-pay], *m.* 1. Blow (impacto), stroke, hit; knock, dash; wound, hurt. 2. Action, push, act. 3. Crowd, throng of people, abundance (multitud). 4. An unfortunate accident. 5. Spring bolt of a lock. 6. *V.* LATIDO. 7. A pocket flap (abrigo). 8. Movements of attack in fencing. 9. Admiration, surprise (sorpresa). 10. Opportunity concluding in some business. 11. With gardeners, a hole for planting; also the depth, of a foot or more, to which a thing is plumed. 12. *(Naut.)* Any point which does not follow rigorously the direction of a given line. 13. *(Mus.)* The action of striking a string, key, etc. **Golpe de música,** band of music. **Golpe de remo,** stroke in rowing. **Golpe de fortuna,** A fortunate

event, a jump. **El golpe del reloj**, the tick of the watch, or clock. **De golpe**, plump, all at once. **De un golpe**, once, all at once. **Golpe de Estado**, a stroke of policy, **Darse golpes de pecho**, to beat one's breast. **Golpe aplastante**, crushing blow. **Dar golpes en la puerta**, to thump the door. **No dar golpe**, not to do a stroke. **Preparaba su primer golpe**, he was planning his first job. **Golpe de viento**, gust of wind. **Cerrar una puerta de golpe**, to slam a door.

golpeadero [gol-pay-ah-day'-ro], *m*. 1. Place much beaten. 2. Noise made by striking a thing repeatedly.

golpeado, da [gol-pay-ah'-do, dah], *a*. Done a stroke, with a free brush and masterfully (pintura).

golpeador, ra [gol-pay-ah-dor', rah], *m. & f*. Striker, person or thing that strikes, beater.

golpeadura [gol-pay-ah-doo'-rah], *f*. Percussion, the act of beating, hammering or striking.

golpear [gol-pay-ar'], *va*. 1. To beat, to strike, to hit (desastre natural), to knock, to hammer, to give blows; to bruise, to tap (suavemente), to punch (puñetazos), to thump (mesa). 2. To tick, like a watch. *-vn*. To throb (latir), to tick.

golpecico, illo, ito [gol-pay-thee'-co], *m. dim*. A slight blow.

golpeo [gol-pay'-o], *m*. Striking, knocking, hitting; beating, pounding; punching. *V*. GOLPEADURA.

golpeteo [gol-pay-tay'-o], *m*. Lively and continued striking; constant hammering. *(Acad.)*

golusmear [go-loos-may-ar'], *vn. V*. GOLOSINEAR.

goma [go'-mah], *f*. 1. Gum. 2. Rubber. 3. Rubber band. **Goma arábiga**, arabic gum. **Goma de borrar**, eraser. **goma elástica**, rubber.

gomal [go-mahl'], *m. (Sp. Am.)* Grove of rubber trees.

gomero, ra [go-may'-ro, rah], *a*. Rubber.*-m. & f*. Rubber plantation worker (obrero).

gomía [go-mee'-ah], *f*. 1. Bugbear to frighten children. 2. Glutton, a voracious eater. **Gomía del caudal**, spendthrift.

gomífero, ra [go-mee'-fay-ro, rah], *a*. Bearing or containing gum; gummiferous.

gomina [go-mee'-nah], *f*. Hair cream (brillantina); gel (fijador).

gomorresina [go-mor-ray-see'-nah], *f*. Gum-resin.

gomosidad [go-mo-se-dahd'], *f*. Gumminess, viscosity.

gomos [go'-mos], *m*. A gummatous tumor.

gomoso, sa [go-mo'-so, sah], *a*. Gummy, productive of gum.

gomuto [go-moo'-to], *m*. An East Indian palm-tree yielding an edible fruit highly prized.

gonagra [go-nah'-grah], *f. (Med.)* Gout which attacks the knees.

gonce [gon'-thay], *m. V*. GOZNE.

góndola [gon'-do-lah], *f*. 1. Gondola, a Venetian flat boat with an awning. 2. A certain carriage in which several can ride together.

gondolero [gon-do-lay'-ro], *m*. Gondolier, rower of a gondola.

gonela [go-nay'-lah], *f*. A tunic or outer garment, sleeveless, and reaching to the calf of the leg, worn over the armor and bearing the arms, in embroidery, of the knight who wore it.

gonfalón [gon-fah-lon'], *m*. 1. Banner, pennant. 2. *(Her.)* Standard of the church.

gonfaloniero [gon-fah-lo-ne-ay'-ro], *m*. 1. Title of the chiefs of some of the small republics in Italy. 2. Standard bearer.

gongorino, na [gon-go-ree'-no, nah], *a. (coll.)* Applied to a pompous, lofty style of writing,

gongorismo [gon-go-rees'-mo], *m. (coll.)* Altiloquence, pompous language (poesía).

gongorista [gon-go-rees'-tah], *f*. One who affects to write poetry in a pompous style.

gongorizar [gon-go-re-thar'], *vn*. To affect loftiness of style in poetry.

goniometría [go-ne-o-may-tree'-ah], *f*. Goniometry, art of measuring angles.

goniométrico, ca [go-ne-may'-tre-co, cah], *a*. Goniometric, belonging to goniometry.

goniómetro [go-ne-o'-may-tro], *m*. Goniometer, instrument for measuring angles.

gonóideo, dea [go-no'-e-day-o, ah], *a*. Resembling sperm or semen.

gonorrea [go-nor-ray'-ah], *f. (Med.)* 1. Spermatorrhoea *(Acad.)* 2. Gonorrhoea, a venereal disease; specific urethritis.

gonorreico, ca [go-nor-ray'-e-co, cah], *a*. Gonorrhoeal, relating to gonorrhoea.

gorbión [gor-be-on'], *m*. 1. A kind of edging for embroidering. 2. Gum euphorbium.

gordal [gor-dahl'], *a*. Fat, big, fleshy.

gordana [gor-dah'-nah], *f*. Oil extracted in India from the testicles of oxen, and used for wool.

gordazo, za [gor-dah'-tho, thah], *a. aug*. Very fat and big.

gordico, ica, illo, illa, ito, ita [gor-dee'-co, cah, etc.], *m. & f. dim*. Not very fat, rather plump.

gordiflón, na [gor-de-flone', nah], *m. f*. A very corpulent, flabby person.

gordo, da [gor'-do, dah], *a*. 1. Fat, corpulent, plump, fleshy, obese (persona). **Está más gordo que nunca**, he´s fatter than ever. 2. Fat, rich, gray, oily (comida, sustancia). **Tocino gordo**, fat pork. 3. Coarse, thick (hilo, tela) **Lienzo gordo**, coarse linen. 4. Great, large, big. 5. Torpid, stupid. **Mentira gorda**, a gross falsehood. 6. Unpleasant. **Ese tipo me cae gordo**, that chap gets on my nerves. **Lo más gordo fue...**, the most outrageous was...

gordo [gor'-do], *m*. Fat, suet, lard.

gordolobo [gor-do-lo'-bo], *m. (Bot.)* Great-mullein.

gordón, na [gor-done', nah], *a. aug. (coll.)* Very fat and corpulent.

gordura [gor-doo'-rah], *f*. 1. Grease, fat (obesidad). 2. Fatness, corpulence (corpulencia).

gorfe [gor'-fay], *m*. A deep hole in a river forming a whirlpool or eddy.

gorga [gor'-gah], *f*. 1. Food of hawks. 2. *(Prov.)* Whirlpool.

gorgojarse [gor-go-har'-say], *vr. V*. AGORGOJARSE.

gorgojo [gor-go'-ho], *m*. 1. Grub, weevil. 2. A dwarfish little boy.

gorgojoso, sa [gor-go-ho'-so, sah], *a*. Full of grubs or weevils.

gorgona [gor-go'-nah], *f*. 1. Gorgonia, sea-fan, a zoophyte. 2. *(Amer.)* A whirlpool near the island of this name, S. W. of the coast of Columbia, in lat. 3° N.

gorgorán [gor-go-rahn'], *m*. Sort of silk program.

gorgorear [gor-go-ray-ar'], *en. (Prov.)* To cry like a turkey-cock.

gorgorita [gor-go-ree'-tah], *f*. Bubble formed on water by the fall of rain.

gorgoritear [gor-go-re-tay-ar'], *vn*. To warble, to gargle, to quiver the voice.

gorgoritos [gor-go-ree'-tos], *m. pl. (coll.)* Quivers of the voice.

gorgorotada [gor-go-ro-tah'-dah], *f*. The quantity of liquid swallowed at once.

gorgotero [gor-go-tay'-ro], *m*. Peddler, hawker.

gorguera [gor-gay'-rah], *f*. 1. A kind of neckcloth, formerly worn by ladies of fashion. 2. Armor of the neck.

gorguerín [gor-gay-reen'], *f*. Small kind of ruff or frill for the neck.

gorguz [gor-gooth'], *m*. Javelin, a missile weapon.

gorila [go-ree'-lah], *m*. 1. Gorilla. 2. Tough (matón), bruiser, thug; henchman (guardaespaldas), bodyguard.

gorja [gor'-hah], *f*. 1. Throat, throttle. 2. Rejoicing, merry making. 3. *(Naut.)* Head of the keel.

gorjal [gor-hahl'], *m*. 1. Collar of a doublet. 2. Armor to defend the neck or throat.

gorjeador, ra [gor-hay-ah-dor', rah], *m. & f*. Warbler, modulator.

gorjear [gor-hay-ar'], *vn*. To warble, to quaver, to shake the voice in a melodious manner; to chirp, to twitter.*-vr*. To gabble (niño).

gorjeo [gor-hay'-o], *m.* 1. Trilling, quaver; a melodious shake of the voice; chirp, twitter. 2. Chatter of a child which begins to talk.

gorjería [gor-hay-ree'-ah], *f. V.* GORJEO for chatter of a child.

gorra [gor'-rah], *f.* 1. Cap, bonnet (de bebé), a covering of the head. **Gorra de montar**, riding cap. **Gorra de visera,** peaked cap. 2. **Gorra de señora**, lady's hat or bonnet. 3. Hunting cap. 4. Intrusion at feasts without invitation. **Colarse de gorra**, to gatecrash. **Entrar de gorra**, to get in free. 5. Parasite, sponger.

gorrada [gor-rah'-dah], *f. V.* GORRETADA.

gorrero [gor-ray'-ro], *m.* 1. Cap-maker. 2. Parasite, sponger.

gorretada [gor-ray-tah'], *f.* Salute with a cap.

gorrete [gor-ray'-tay], *m. dim.* Small cap.

gorrica, ills, ita [gor-ree'-cah, eel'-lyah, ee'-tah], *f. dim.* Small cap or bonnet.

gorrico, illo, ito [gor-ree'-co, eel'-lyo, ee'-to], *m. dim.* Small round cap.

gorrín, gorrino [gor-reen', gor-ree'-no], *m.* 1. A small pig (cochinito), a sucking pig. 2. *(Prov.)* Pig (cerdo).

gorrinada, or **gorrinera** [gor-re-nah'-dah, gor-re-nay'-rah], *f.* 1. Pigs (cerdos). 2. Dirty trick (mala pasada).

gorrinería [gor-re-nay-ree'-ah], *f.* 1. A pigsty. 2. *(Met.)* Filthiness, bestiality. 3. A dirty trick (mala pasada). 4. A disgusting thing.

gorrinillo, ito [gor-re-neel'-lyo, ee'-to], *m. dim.* A small sucking pig.

gorrión [gor-re-on'], *m. (Orn.)* Sparrow.

gorrioncillo [gor-re-on-theel'-lyo], *m. dim.* A small sparrow.

gorrionera [gor-re-o-nay'-rah], *f.* Rendez-vous or hiding place of rogues.

gorrista [gor-rees'-tah], *m.* Parasite, sponger.

gorro [gor'-ro], *m.* A night-cap, bonnet (de mujer, niño). **Gorro de baño**, bathing cap. **Estar hasta el gorro de**, to be fed up with.

gorrón [gor-rone'], *m.* 1. A poor student who goes from house to house to get his dinner; parasite. 2. Spindle, pivot, or gudgeon of a gate or door; pillow, swing-block. 3. Lazy, unhealthy silkworm. 4. A round, smooth pebble (guijarro). 5. Man given to debauchery and lewdness. 6. An iron staff which aids in turning flee capstan. 7. Peg serving as a hinge in flood-gates.

gorrona [gor-ro'-nah], *f.* Strumpet, prostitute.

gorronal [gor-ro-nahl'], *m.* Place full of pebbles or coarse gravel.

gorronazo [gor-ro-nah'-tho], *m. (aug.)* A great lecher or rake.

gorronear [gor-ro-nay-ar'], va. To scrounge. **Gorronear algo a uno**, to scrounge something from somebody. *-vn.* To cadge, to sponge.

gorronería [gor-ro-nay-re'-ah], f. 1. Cadging (sablear), sponging. 2. Avarice, greed (avaricia).

gorullo [go-rool'-lyo], *m.* A small button or ball of wool, or other matter which sticks together.

gosipífero, ra [go-se-pee'-fay-ro, rah], *a.* Cotton producing.

gosipino, na [go-se-pee'-no, nah], *a.* Of a cottony surface.

gosipio [go-see'-pe-o], *m.* Goseypium, the cotton plant.

gota [go'-tah], *f.* 1. Drop, a globule of moisture which falls at once. 2. A small quantity of any liquor. 3. Gout, a disease. 4. A small portion taken from a smelting of gold or silver for assaying. 5. In clock work, the small steel plate put at the end of the fuse and sometimes of the barrel arbor. 6. A variety of topaz called "water drop." **Gota a gota**, drop by drop. **Sudar la gota gorda**, to sweat blood. **La gota que colma el vaso**, the straw that breaks the camel's back, the last straw. *-pl. (Arch.)* Ornaments of the Doric order. **Unas gotas de coñac**, a few drops of brandy.

goteado, da [go-tay-ah'-do, dah], *a. & pp.* of GOTEAR. Guttated, sprinkled, spotted, speckled.

gotear [go-tay-ar'], vn. 1. To drop, to fall drop by drop, to drip (destilar), to trickle (escurrir). 2. To give by driblets or intermittently: to leak (salirse).

goteo [go-tay'-o], *m.* 1. Leak, leakage. 2. Dribbling.

gotera [go-tay'-rah], *f.* 1. Gutter, a passage made by water on the roofs of houses. 2. Leak, the water which drops or runs through the passage, the place where the water falls, and the mark left by the dropping of rain (agujero). 3. Fringe of bed-hangings, valance (colgadura). 4. Invalidism. V. ACHAQUE.

goterón [go-tay-ron'], *m.* 1. A large drop of rain-water. 2. Throating in a cornice.

goteroncillo [go-tay-ron-theel'-lyo], *m.* A drop of rain-water not much larger than usual.

gotica, illa, ita [go-tee'-cah, eel'-lyah, ee'-tah], *f. dim.* Droplet, a small drop.

gótico, ca [go'-te-co, cah], *a.* Gothic: chiefly applied to the pointed style of building. **Letra gótica**, gothic characters.

gotón, na [go-ton', nah], *a. & m. pl.* Goth.

gotoso, sa [go-to'-so, sah], *a.* Gouty.

gozada [go-thah'-dah], *f.* Pleasure, delight.

gozador, ra [go-thah-dor', rah], *m. & f.* Enjoyer.

gozante [go-thahn'-tay], *pa.* Enjoying; enjoyer.

gozar [go-thar'], va. 1. To enjoy (disfrutar), to have possession or fruition of (poseer). 2. To enjoy, to seduce (mujer). *-vr.* To rejoice.

gozne [goth'-nay], *m.* Hinge.

gozo [go'-tho], *m.* 1. Joy (alegría), pleasure (placer), satisfaction, glee, merriment, mirth gladfulness, gladness, cheerfulness. **Es un gozo para los ojos**, it´s a joy to see. **No caber de gozo**, to be beside oneself with joy. 2. A sudden blaze of dry chips of wood. 3. *pl.* Verses in praise of the Virgin or the saints in which certain words are repeated at the end of every couplet.

gozosamente [go-tho-sah-men'-tay], *adv.* Joyfully, cheerfully.

gozoso, sa [go-tho'-so, sah], *a.* Joyful, cheerful, content, glad, festive, mirthful, merry.

gozque [goth'-kay], *m.* A cur-dog.

gozquejo [goth-kay'-ho], *m. dim.* A small cur-dog.

grabación [grah-bah-the-on'], *f.* Recording. **Grabación en cinta**, tape recording.

grabado [grah-bah'-do], *m.* 1. Engraving, the art of engraving. 2. Engraving, the copy printed from an engraved plate. **Grabado en madera**, woodcut. **Grabado al agua tinta**, aquatint. *-a.* Recorded (música); on tape (en cinta). **Grabado, da**, *pp.* of GRABAR.

grabador, ra [grah-bah-dor', rah], *m. & f.* Engraver, a cutter in stone, metal, or wood. *-m.* Tape recorder.

grabadura [grah-bah-doo'-rah], *f.* Act of engraving, sculpture.

grabar [grah-bar'], *va.* 1. To engrave (arte), to picture by incisions in stone, wood, or metal; to grave. **Grabar al agua fuerte** or **de agua fuerte**, to etch. 2. To record (cinta, disco).

grabazón [grah-bah-thone'], *f.* Engraving, sculpture.

gracejo [grah-thay'-ho], *m.* 1. Joke, jest, mirth, facetiousness, cheerful wit (chispa). 2. A graceful or pleasing delivery in speaking, charm (encanto).

gracia [grah´-the-ah], *f.* 1. Grace (garbo), favorable influence of God in the human mind, and the effect of this influence. 2. Grace, natural excellence, gracefulness, gentility, elegance of mien or manner; cleverness. 3. Grace, favor confered (favor), gift, benefaction, kindness, concession; graciousness (benevolencia), condescension. 4. Benevolence, courtesy, pleasing manners (agrado). 5. Grace, pardon, mercy. 6. Elegance (elegancia), beauty. 7. Remission of a debt. 8. A witty saying or expression. 9. *(coll.)* Name, the discriminative appellation of an individual. 10. Gratitude for favors received. **Dar gracias**, to thank, or to give thanks. **Caer en gracia**, to become a favorite. **Gracias**, grants or concessions. **Gracia de Dios**, *(coll.)* the bread. **En gracia de**, for the sake of. *-interj.* **¡Qué gracia!** What a wonder! A fine thing indeed!

Golpe de gracia, finishing stroke. **Me cayó en gracia**, I took to him. **Ahí está la gracia**, that's what's so funny about it. **Tener gracia**, to be funny. **Gracias a la ayuda de otros**, thanks to the help of others.

graciable [grah-theah'-blay], *a.* 1. Good natured, affable (afable). 2. Easily obtained (favor).

grácil [grah'-theel], *a.* Gracile, slender (esbelto), small (fino).

graciola [grah-the-o'-lah], *f. (Bot.)* Hedge hyssop.

graciosamente [grah-the-o-sah-men'-tay], *adv.* Graciously, gratefully, kindly, gratuitously.

graciosidad [grah-the-o-se-dahd'], *f.* 1. Gracefulness, beauty, perfection, elegance and dignity of manners. 2. Facetiousness, cheerful wit.

gracioso, sa [grah-the-o'-so, sah], *a.* 1. Graceful (garboso), beautiful, accomplished, 2. Facetious, witty, funny (chistoso), pleasing (atractivo). **Una situación muy graciosa**, a very amusing situation. 3. Benevolent, inclined to grant favors, gracious. 4. Gratuitous (gratuito), granted without claim. 5. Ridiculous, extravagant.

gracioso, sa [grah-the-o'-so, sah], *m. & f.* 1. Merry-andrew, buffoon, harlequin, mime. 2. Comic actor or actress, generally in the character of servants in Spanish plays.

grada [grah'-dah], *f.* 1. Step of a staircase (peldaño). 2. In nunneries, a room where the nuns are allowed to hold conversation with their friends through a grate. 3. An older of steps before a church, gradatory. 4. Harrow, to break the clods after ploughing. **Grada de construcción**, *(Naut.)* stocks for ship building. -*pl.* 1. Bar, the place where legal cases are tried. 2. Seats of an amphitheater.

gradación [grah-dah-the-on'], *f.* 1. A harmonious gradation (progresión) or scale of music. 2. *(Rhet.)* Climax.

gradado, da [grah-dah'-do, dah], *a.* Applied to the building with an order of steps around it. -*pp.* of GRADAR.

gradar [grah-dar'], *va. (Prov.)* To harrow, to break with the harrow.

gradatim [grah-dah'-tim], *adv. (Lat.)* Gradually, by degrees.

gradería [grah-day-ree'-ah], *f.* Series of seats or steps (asientos, escalones).

gradilla [grah-deel'-lyah], *f.* 1. *(Dim.)* Small step or seat. 2. Tile-mould. 3. A step-ladder, a small portable ladder.

gradinar [grah-de-nar'], *va.* To cut off with a chisel.

gradino [grah-dee'-no], *m.* 1. Chisel, an edged tool used by stone-cutters. 2. Graver, the tool used in graving.

gradlolo [grah-de-o'lo], *m. (Bot.)* V. GLADIOLO.

grado [grah'-do], *m.* 1. Step of a staircase (peldaño). 2. Value or quality of a thing (cualidad). 3. Degree of kindred, order of lineage (punto). 4. Will, pleasure. 5. Degree, an academical title of honor conferred by universities. 6. *(Mil.)* Rank. 7. *(Geom.)* Degree, the three hundred and sixtieth part of the circumference of a circle (medida). 8. Degree, the division of the lines upon mathematical instruments. 9. Degree, grade, the measure of the quality or state of a thing. 10. *(Mus.)* Degree, the intervals of sounds. **De grado en grado**, gradually, by degrees, in regular progression. **El grado que ahora hemos alcanzado**, the stage we have now reached. **Está en el segundo grado de elaboración**, it is now in the second stage of production. **Grado** universitario, university degree. **En un ángulo de 45 grados**, at an angle of 45 degrees. **De buen grado**, willingly.

graduación [grah-doo-ah-the-on'], *f.* 1. The act and effect of measuring or comparing different things. 2. Graduation, regular progression by succession of degrees. 3. Rank, condition or quality of a person. **De alta graduación**, of high rank. 4. *(Mil.)* Rank. 5. *(Univ.)* Gradation (acto). 6. Grading (regulación).

graduado, da [grah-doo-ah'-do, dah], *a. (Mil.)* Brevet: applied to officers enjoying higher rank than they possess. -*pp.* of GRADUAR.-*m.* Graduate, one who has obtained an academical degree.

graduador [grah-doo-ah-dor'], *m.* Graduator, graduating instrument, gauge.

gradual [grah-doo-ahl'], *a.* Gradual, proceeding by degrees.

gradual [grah-doo-ahl'], *m.* A verse read between the epistle and gospel at the celebration of mass.

gradualmente [grah-doo-al-men'-tay], *adv.* Gradually, by degrees.

graduando [grah-doo-ahn'-do], *m.* Candidate for academical degrees.

graduar [grah-doo-ar'], *va.* 1. To measure or compare different things (medir). 2. To graduate, to dignify with an academical degree. 3. To give military rank. 4. To divide into degrees. *(coll.)* To calculate, to appraise (evaluar).-*vr.* 1. To graduate, to take an academical degree. 2. *(Mil.)* To take a commission.

gráfica [grah'-fe-cah], *f.* Diagram (diagrama), sketch, illustration.

gráficamente [grah'-fe-cah-men-tay], *adv.* Graphically, in a picturesque manner.

gráfico, ca [grah'-fe-co, cah], *a.* Graphic, graphical, relating to engravings; well delineated.

gráfila [grah'-fe-lah], *f.* The little border on the edge of a coin.

grafio [grah'-fe-o], *m.* Graver, a tool used in making grafitto or scratch-work.

grafioles [grah-fe-o'-les], *m. pl.* Kind of biscuits made in the form of an S.

grafito [grah-fee'-to], *m.* Graphite, plumbago.

grafolita [grah-fo-lee'-tah], *f.* Grapholite, a variety of slate suitable for writing on.

grafología [grah-fo-lo-hee'-ah], *f.* Graphology, study of handwriting.

grafólogo, ga [grah-fo'-lo-go], *m & f.* Graphologist.

grafómetro [grah-fo'-may-tro], *m.* Graphometer, circumferentor, a surveying instrument with sights for measuring angles.

graja [grah'-hah], *f. (Orn.)* 1. Female jackdaw. 2. Jay.

grajal [grah-hahl'], *a.* Belonging to crows, ravens, or magpies.

grajea [grah-hay'-ah], *f.* A very small sugar-plum.

grajear [grah-hay-ar'], *vn.* To caw, as crows; to chatter, as magpies.

grajero, ra [grah-hay'-ro, rah], *a.* Applied to rookeries.

grajo [grah'-ho], *m.* 1. *(Orn.)* Jackdaw. 2. *(Peru. Coll.)* Strong sweat, particularly in the armpits.

grajuelo [grah-hoo-ay'-lo], *m. dim.* A small jackdaw

grama [grah'-mah], *f. (Bot.)* Creeping cynodon.

gramal [grah-mahl'], *m.* Place where couch-grass or dog's-grass grows.

gramalla [grah-mahl'-lyah], *f.* 1. A long scarlet gown anciently worn by the magistrates of Aragon. 2. Coat of mail.

gramallera [grah-mal-lyay'-rah], *f. (Prod.)* Pothanger. V. LLARES.

gramar [grah-mar'], *va. (Prov.)* To knead the dough of bread.

gramática [grah-mah'-te-cah], *f.* Grammar.

gramatical [grah-mah-te-cahl'], *a.* Grammatical, grammar.

gramaticalmente [grah-mah-te-cahl'-men-tay], *adv.* Grammatically.

gramático [grah-mah'-te-co], *m.* Grammarian.

gramaticón [grah-mah-te-cone'], *m.* One who believes himself a great grammarian, or he who knows nothing but grammar.

gramaticuelo [grah-mah-te-coo-ay'-lo], *m. dim.* Grammaticaster, a smatterer in grammar, a pedant.

gramatista [grah-mah-tees'-tah], *f.* Teacher of grammar.

gramil [grah-meel'], *m.* A joiner's marking gauge.

gramilla [grah-meel'-lyah], *f.* Brake, a wooden instrument for dressing hemp or flax.

gramíneo, ea [grah-mee'-nay-o, ah], *a. (Poet.)* Gramineous, grassy.

graminívoro, ra [grah-me-nee'-vo-ro, rah], *a.* Graminivorous, grass eating, living upon grass.

gramo [grah'-mo], *m.* Gram, unit of weight in the metrical system: the weight of a cubic centimeter of distilled water.

gramófono [grah-mo'-fo-no], *m.* Gramophone, talking machine.

gramómetro [grah-mo'-may-tro], *m.* A type-gauge.

grampa [grahm'-pah], *f. (Naut.)* A hook for sustaining light weights.

gramuro, ra [grah-moo'-ro, rah], *a.* Having a long, slender tail.

Gran [grahn], *a.* 1. Great. *V.* GRANDE. It is used only before substantives in the singular, as **Gran cosa**, great thing; **Gran miedo**, great fear. 2. Grand, as chief or principal: used also before substantives as **Gran maestre**, grand-master. **Gran señor**, grand signior.

grana [grah'-nah], *f.* 1. Grain, the seed of plants (semilla). 2. The time when corn, flax, etc., form their seed (estación). 3. Cochineal. 4. Scarlet grain. 5. Fine scarlet cloth (tela). 6. Fresh red color of the lips and checks (color). **Ponerse como la grana**, to turn scarlet.

granada [grah-nah-dah], *f.* 1. Pomegranate (fruta). 2. *(Mil.)* Hand-grenade. **Granada de mano**, hand grenade. **Granada de metralla**, shrapnel shell.

granadera [grah-nah-day-rah], *f. (Mil.)* A grenadier's pouch.

granadero [grah-nah-day´-ro], *m. (Mil.)* Grenadier, a foot-soldier, formerly employed to throw grenades.

granadilla [grah-nah-deel'-lyah], *f. (Bot.)* Passion-flower; passion fruit (fruta).

granadino, na [grah-nah-dee'-no, nah], *a.* Native of or belonging to Granada, or the U. S. of Colombia, formerly New Granada. *-m.* The flower of the pomegranate-tree.

granado, da [grah-nah'-do, dah], *a.* 1. Large, remarkable. 2. Principal, chief; illustrious; select (selecto). 3. Seedy, abounding with seed. *-pp.* of GRANAR.

granado [grah-nah'-do], *m. (Bot.)* Pomegranate-tree.

granador [grah-nah-dor'], *m.* A sieve for granulating gunpowder, and the spot destined for this operation.

granaje [grah-nah'-hay], *m.* The act of granulating powder.

granalla [grah-nahl'-lyah], *f.* Granulation, grains of metal.

granar [grah-nar'], *vn.* 1. To seed, to grow to maturity so as to shed the seed. 2. To seed, to shed the seed. 3. To grain, to granulate.

granate [grah-nah'-tay], *m.* Garnet, a precious stone resembling a ruby.

granático, ca [grah-nah'-te-co, cah], *a.* Scarlet, garnet; characteristic of cochineal or the garnet.

granatín [grah-nah-teen'], *m.* Kind of ancient cloth.

granazón [grah-nah-thone´], *f.* Seeding, shedding the seed.

gran bestia [gran bes'-te-ah], *f.* Tapir.

grancé [gran-thay'], *a.* Madder colored.

grande [grahn'-day], *a.* 1. Great, large in bulk or number, extensive, huge, big (tamaño), big, tall (estatura), old (persona). **Grande como una montaña**, as big as a house. **Los zapatos le están muy grandes**, the shoes are too big. 2. Great, having any quality in a high degree, impressive (impresionante). 3. Grand, principal. 4. As a whole (en conjunto), on a grand scale, in a big way. **Estar en grande**, to be going strong. **Pasarlo en grande**, to have a tremendous time.

grande [grahn'-day], *m.* 1. Grandee, Spanish nobleman of the first rank. 2. **Los grandes**, the great.

grandecico, ica, illo, illa, ito, ita, [gran-day-thee´-co], *a.* Growing rather big; pretty large or big.

grandemente [grahn-day-men-tay], *adv.* Greatly; very well; extremely; grandly.

grandeza [gran-day'-thah], *f.* 1. Greatness, bigness (gran tamaño). 2. Greatness (impresionante), grandeur, magnificence, grandness, nobleness. 3. Grandeeship, the preeminence and dignity of a grandee of Spain (rango). 4. The body of grandees (personas).

grandilocuencia [gran-de-lo-coo-en'-the-ah], *f.* Grandiloquence.

grandilocuente [gran-dee-lo-coo-en', tay], *a. V.* GRANDÍLOCUO.

grandílocuo, cua [gran-dee'-lo-coo-o, coo-ah], *a.* Grandiloquent, making use of a lofty or pompous style.

grandillón, na [gran-deel-lyone', nah], *a. aug.* Excessively large and big.

grandiosamente [gran-de-o-sah-men'-tay], *adv.* Magnificently.

grandiosidad [gran-de-o-se-dahd'], *f.* Greatness, grandeur; magnificence; abundance.

grandioso, sa [gran-de-o'-so, sah], *a.* Grand, great, magnificent, splendid.

grandísimo [gran-dee'-se-mo], *a.* Superl. **De grande**, great, big. **Un coche grandísimo**, a whacking great car.

grandor [gran-dor'], *m.* Size and bigness of things, magnitude, greatness, extensiveness.

grandullón, na [gran-dool-lyone', nah], *a.* Large in proportion to age.

graneado, da [grah-nay-ah'-do, dah], *a.* 1. Reduced to grains; spotted, granulous. 2. *(Peru)* Select, choice. *-pp.* of GRANEAR.

graneador [grah-nay-ah-dor'], *m.* A kind of graver or tool for engraving.

granear [grah-nay-ar'], *va.* 1. To sow grain in the earth. 2. To engrave.

granel [grah-nel'], *m. (Prov.)* Heap of corn (montón); in abundance (abundancia); by the score (a montones); lavishly; at random (al azar). **A granel**, 1. In a heap. 2. *(Naut.)* In bulk. 3. *(Amer. Peru.)* The *gacetilla* of some periodicals.

granelar [grah-nay-lar'], *va.* In tanneries, to grain leather.

graneo [grah-nay'-o], *m.* The act of shedding seed, or sowing seed.

granero [grah-nay´-ro], *m.* 1. Granary, grange, cornloft. 2. A fruitful country.

granete [grah-nay'-tay], *m. (Mech.)* Marking-awl; countersink punch.

granevano [grah-nay-vah´-no], *m. (Bot.)* Goat's-thorn.

granguardia [gran-goo-ar'-de-ah], *f. (Mil.)* Grandguard, an advanced guard in front of an army.

granico [grah-nee'-co], *m. dim.* Granule, small grain.

granífero, ra [gra-nee'-fay-ro rah], *a. (Bot.)* Bearing seeds in the form of grains.

granilla [grah-neel'-lyah], *f.* Rough nap on cloth.

granillero, ra [grah-neel-lyay'-ro, rah], *a. (Prov.)* Applied to hogs that feed on what they find in the fields.

granillo [grah-neel'-lyo], *m.* 1. *(Dim.)* Granule, small grain. 2. Gain or profit frequently obtained. 3. Pimple growing at the extremity of the rump of canary birds and linnets.

granilloso, sa [grah-neel-lyo'-so, sah], *a.* Granulous, granular.

granítico, ca [grah-nee'-te-co, cah], *a.* Granitic, formed of granite.

granito [grah-nee'-to], *m.* 1. Granite, a hard stone composed of quartz, feldspar, and mica. 2. Hairs, streaks, or points which diminish the brilliancy and price of diamonds. 3. (Pharmacy) Granule. 4. *(Prov. Murcia)* Small egg of a silkworm.

granitulino, na [grah-ne-too-lee'-no, nah], *a. (Min.)* Nodular; granulous.

granívoro, ra [grah-nee'-vo-ro, rah], *a.* Granivorous, eating grain, living upon grain.

granizada [grah-ne-thah´-dah], *f.* 1. Copious full of hail. 2. *(Met.)* Multitude of things which fall in abundance.

granizado, da [grah-ne-thah'-do, dah], *a.* 1. Fall of hail, destroyed by hail. 2. Iced drink. *-pp.* of GRANIZAR.

granizar [grah-ne-thar'], *vn.* 1. To hail. 2. To pour down with violence (lluvia).

granizo [grah-nee'-tho], *m.* 1. Hail, rain frozen in falling. 2. Cloud or web in the eyes. *V.* GRANIZADA.

granja [grahn'-hah], *f.* Grange, farm, farm-house (cortijo); a country-house, a villa, a manse, dairy (lechería). **Granja avícola**, chicken farm.

granjear [gran-hay-ar'], *va.* 1. To gain, to get, to obtain, to win. 2. To conciliate or gain the good-will of another.

granjeo [gran-hay'-o], *m*. 1. The act of getting or acquiring. 2. Gain, profit, advantage, advancement in interest, influence, etc.

granjería [gran-hay-ree'-ah], *f*. Gain, profit, advantage.

granjero, ra [gran-hay'-ro, rah], *m. & f*. 1. Farmer, husbandman, granger. 2. Dealer in profitable commodities.

grano [grah'-no], *m*. 1. Grain, the seed of corn (semilla). 2. Grain, a single seed of corn. 3. Grain, any minute particle (partícula). 4. Grain, the direction of the fibres of wood or other fibrous matter. 5. *(Pharm.)* Grain, the smallest weight in physic, twenty of which make an English scruple, and twenty four a Spanish one. 6. The bushing of a cannon. 7. Pimple, a pustule on the skin, furuncle. **Grano de arroz**, grain of rice. **Grano de café**, coffee bean. **Ir al grano**, to get to the point. **Poner su grano de arena**, *(Fig.)* to make one's contribution.

granoso, sa [grah-no'-so, sah], *a*. Granulous, grainy, granular.

granudo, da [grah-noo'-do, dah], *a. V.* GRANOSO.

granuja [grah-noo'-hah], *f*. 1. Ripe grapes separated from the branches. 2. Grapestone, the stone or seed contained in the grape. 3. Little rogue, scoundrel, knave, rascal (canalla). 4. Urchin (pilluelo).

granujado, da [grah-noo-hah'-do, dah], *a*. 1. Full of pimples. 2. Full of stones, full of seeds.

granujiento, ta [grah-noo-heen'-to, tah], *a*. Grainy, full of grain.

granujo [grah-noo'-ho], *m. (coll.)* Pimple or tumor in the flesh.

gránula [grah'-noo-lah], *f. (Bot.)* Spore, reproductive body of cryptogamous plants.

granulación [grah-noo-lah-the-on'], *f. (Chem.)* 1. Granulation, the act of being reduced into small particles. 2. Granulation, the act of reducing metal into grains by pouring it, when melted, into cold water.

granular [grah-noo-lar'], *va*. To granulate, to reduce to small pieces like grains.-*vr*. 1. To granulate. 2. To be covered with granules.

granular [grah-noo-lar'], *a*. Granular.

gránulo [grah'-noo-lo], *m*. 1. Granule, a small grain. 2. Pellet, a medicated granule.

granulosidad [grah-noo-lo-se-dahd'], *f*. Granularity, the state of being granular.

granuloso, sa [grah-noo-lo'-so, sah], *a*. Granulous, granular.

granza [grahn'-thah], *f*. Madder. *V.* RUBIA.-*pl*. 1. Siftings, the refuse of corn which has been winnowed and sifted. 2. Dross of metals.

granzón [gran-thone'], *m*. Fragment of ore which does not pass through the screen; screenings. *(Acad.)* -*pl*. Refuse of straw not eaten, but left by the cattle.

granzoso, sa [gran-tho'-so, sah], *a*. Applied to grain, having much refuse.

grañón [grah-nyone'], *m*. 1. Pap made of boiled wheat. 2. *V.* GRANO.

grao [grah'-o], *m*. Strand, shore.

grapa [grah'-pah], *f*. 1. Staple; clip, fastener (para papeles). 2. Kind of mangy ulcers in the joints of horses.

grapadora [grah-pah-do'-rah], *f*. Stapler, stapling machine.

grapar [grah-pahr'], *va*. To staple (papeles).

grapón [grah-pone'], *m. aug*. A large cramp-iron.

graptolita [grap-to-lee'-tah], *f*. Dendrite, generic name of stones exhibiting markings upon the surface.

grasa [grah-sah], *f*. 1. Suet (sebo), fat; grease; kitchen stuff. **Grasa de ballena**, blubber. **Grasa de pescado**, fish oil. 2. Gum of juniper-trees. 3. Grease of clothes. 4. *(Naut.)* Compound of rosin, pitch, and tallow used for preserving masts and yards. 5. Slag of metals. 6. The base of an ointment or pomade.

grasera [grah-say'-rah], *f*. 1. An ointment jar. 2. Vessel for fat or grease; a dripping pan.

grasería [grah-say-ree'-ah], *f*. 1. Tallow-chandler's shop. 2. A disease of silk-worms.

graseza [grah-say'-thah], *f*. Quality of fat or grease.

grasiento, ta [grah-seen'-to, tah], *a*. Greasy (grasoso); filthy, grimy.

grasilla [grah-seel'-lyah], *f*. 1. Pounce, a powder made of gum sandarach. 2. *(Bot.)* The odoriferous resin which the juniper produces.

graso, sa [grah'-so, sah], *a*. Fat, unctuous, lardy, oily (comida).

graso [grah'-so], *m*. Fat, grease.

grasones [grah-so'-nes], *m. pl*. 1. Fast dish, made of flour, milk of almonds, sugar, and cinnamon.

grasoso, sa [grah-so-so], *a*. Fatty (graso); greasy (grasiento).

grasura [grah-soo'-rah], *f. V.* GROSURA.

grata, grataguja [grah'-tah, grah-tah-goo'-hah], *f*. Instrument for burnishing silver or silver gilt.

gratamente [grah-tah-men'-tay], *adv*. Graciously, gratefully, in a kind and benevolent manner.

gratar [grah-tar'], *va*. To burnish silver or silver gilt.

gratel [grah-tel'], *m*. A braid, made by hand, with the number of skeins of yarn suited to its use.

gratificación [grah-te-fe-cah-the-on'], *f*. 1. Gratification, reward (recompensa), recompense, gratuity, fee, tip (propina), allowance to officers for expenses. 2. Indulgence.

gratificador, ra [grah-te-fe-cah-dor', rah], *m. & f*. Gratifier; pleasurable.

gratificante [grah-te-fe-cahn'-tay], *a*. Gratifying.

gratificar [grah-te-fe-car'], *va*. 1. To gratify, to reward, to requite, to recompense. 2. To gratify (satisfacer), to indulge (anhelo), to delight.

gratil [grah-teel'], *m*. 1. *(Naut.)* Head of a sail. 2. Body of the yard where the sail is tied.

gratis [grah'-tis], *adv*. Gratis, for nothing.

gratisdato, ta [grah-tis-dah'-to, tah], *a*. Gratuitous.

gratitud [grah-te-tood'], *f*. Gratitude, gratefulness.

grato, ta [grah'-to, tah], *a*. 1. Graceful, pleasing (placentero), pleasant, luscious; acceptable. 2. Grateful (agradecido). **Recibir una impresión grata**, to get a pleasing impression.

gratonada [grah-to-nah'-dah], *f*. Kind of ragout or fricassee, made of chickens half roasted, bacon, almonds, rich broth, fresh eggs, spice, and greens.

gratuitamente [grah-too-ee-tah-men'-tay], *adv*. Gratuitously, free (gratis).

gratuito, ta [grah-too-ee'-to, tah], *a*. 1. Gratuitous, gratis, free (gratis). 2. Gratuitous (observación), uncalled-for; unfounded; unjustified (acusación).

gratular [grah-too-lar'], *vn*. To congratulate.-*vr*. To rejoice.

gratulatorio, ria [grah-too-lah-to'-re-o, ah], *a*. Congratulatory.

grava [grah'-vah], *f*. Gravel (guijarros), coarse sand, crushed stone (piedra molida); road metal (carretera).

gravamen [grah-vah'-men], *m*. 1. Charge, obligation to perform or execute something. 2. Hardship, load, inconvenience, nuisance. 3. Encumbrance, burden. 4. *(Law.)* Mortgage.

gravar [grah-var'], *va*. To burden (cargar), to oppress, to fatigue, to molest, to assess for tax. **Gravar con impuestos**, to burden with taxes.

gravativo, va [grah-vah-tee-vo, vah], *a*. Grievous, injurious.

grave [grah'-vay], *a*. 1. Weighty, ponderous, heavy (pesado). 2. Grace, important (importante), momentous, of weight, of great consequence, dangerous *(Met.)* Mortal, deadly. 3. Great, huge, vast. 4. Grave, circumspect. 5. Haughty, lofty. 6. Troublesome, vexatious, grievous; arduous, difficult (pérdida). **Ponerse grave**, to assume an air of importance. 7. *(Mus.)* Grave tone (nota, tono). 8. *(Gram.)* Grave accent (acento). **Delito grave**, a heinous crime. **Enfermedad grave**, a dangerous disease. **Estar grave**, to be seriously ill. **La situación es grave**, the situation is grave.

gravear [grah-vay-ar'], *vn*. To weigh, to gravitate, to sink.

gravedad [grah-vay-dahd'], *f*. 1. Gravity, weight, heaviness. 2. Gravity, modesty, composure, circumspection. 3. Graveness, seriousness, sobriety of behavior, importance;

severity (severidad). 4. Gravity, enormity, atrociousness. 5. Vanity, pride (grandeza). 6. Seriousness, dignity (dignidad). **Estar de gravedad**, to be seriously ill. **Estar herido de gravedad**, to be severely injured.

gravemente [grah-vay-men'-tay], *adv.* Gravely, seriously. **Estar gravemente enfermo**, to be critically ill.

gravidez [grah-ve-deth´], *f.* Pregnancy.

grávido, da [grah'-ve-do, dah], *a.* 1. Full, abundant. 2. Gravid, pregnant (embarazado).

gravilla [grah-vel'-lyah], *f.* Gravel.

gravímetro [gra-vee'-may-tro], *m.* Gravimeter, an instrument for learning specific weight.

gravitación [grah-ve-tah-the-on'], *f.* Gravitation.

gravitar [grah-ve-tar'], *va.* To gravitate, to weigh down (caer sobre), to tend to some part slightly.

gravívolo, la [grah-vee'-vo-lo, lah], *a. (Zool.)* Of heavy flight.

gravoso, sa [grah-vo'-so, sah], *a.* 1. Grievous, offensive, afflictive, painful, onerous. 2. Unbearable.

graznador, ra [grath-nah-dor´, rah], *m. & f.* Croaker; cawing, cackling.

graznar [grath-nar'], *vn.* To croak, to caw (cuervo), to cackle (ganso), to quack (pato).

graznido [grath-nee'-do], *m.* 1. A croak, caw, or cackle. 2. Croaking.

greba [gray'-bah], *f.* Ancient armor for the leg; greave(s).

greca [gray´-cah], *f.* Grecian fret, ornament consisting of a line forming many right angles.

greciano, na [gray-the-ah'-no, nah], or **grecisco** [gray-thees'-co], *a.* Greek, Grecian (fuego griego).

grecismo [gray-thees'-mo], *m.* Grecism, Hellenism, Greekism.

grecizante [gray-the-thahn'-tay], *pa.* Grecianizing, Hellenizing.

grecizar [gray-the-thar'], *vn.* To Grecianize, to Hellenize, to play the Grecian, to speak Greek.

Greco, ca [gray'-co, cah], *a.* Greek. In the form *Greco* it enters into composition, as: **Grecolatino**, written in Greek and Latin. **A la greca**, in the Grecian style.

greda [gray´-dah], *f.* 1.Chalk, marl. 2. Fuller's earth.

gredal [gray-dahl'], *m.* Pit where chalk, marl or fuller's earth is found.

gredal [gray-dahl'], *a.* Chalky.

gredoso, sa [gray-do´-so, sah], *a.* Chalky, marly, cretaceous.

green [green], *m.* (Golf) Green.

gregal [gray-gahl´], *m.* Northeast wind in the Mediterranean.

gregal [gray-gahl'], *a.* Gregarious, going in flocks.

gregalizar [gray-gah-lee-thar'], *vn. (Naut.)* To be north-easting, to drive or decline to north-east.

gregario, ria [gray-gah´-re-o, ah], *a.* Gregarian, of the common sort, ordinary.

gregoriano, na [gray-go-re-ah'-no, nah], *a.* Gregorian.

gregorillo [gray-go-reel'-lyo], *m.* Neck cloth formerly worn by women.

greguería [gray-gay-ree'-ah], *f.* 1. Out-cry, confused clamor. 2. *V.* GUIRIGAY.

gregüescos [gray-goo-ays'-cos], *pl.* A wide sort of breeches made in the Grecian fashion.

greguisco, ca [gray-gees'-co, cah], *a.* Greek, belonging to Greece.

greguizar [gray-gee-thar'], *va.* 1. To Grecianize, to talk Greek. 2. To Grecize, to convert into Greek.

gremial [gray-me-ahl'], *m.* Lap cloth, used by bishops when they officiate at divine service.

gremial [gray-me-ahl'], *a.* Belonging or relating to a body, corporation, or guild; it is also used as a substantive for a member of the corporation. -m & f. Union member (miembro).

gremio [gray'-me-o], *m.* 1. The lap. 2. Body, society, company, guild, corporation; fraternity. 3. Trade-union (sindical). **El gremio de la iglesia**, the pale of the church. **El gremio de una universidad**, the professors, doctors, and scholars, belonging to a university, considered as a body.

greña [gray'-nyah], *f.* 1. Entangled or matted hair (cabellos revueltos). 2. Something entangled. 3. *(Prov.)* Heap of grain laid to be thrashed. 4. *(Prov.)* First leaves of a vine-shoot.

greñudo, da [gray-nyoo'-do, dah], *a.* Dishevelled, having entangled hair.

greñuela [gray-nyoo-ay'-lah], *f. (Prov.)* The first shoots of a vine.

gres [grays], *m.* Generic name of every rock of grainy texture.

gresca [grays'-cah], *f.* 1. Carousal, revelling, clatter. 2. Wrangle, quarrel.

grey [gray'-e], *f.* 1. Flock, as of sheep or goats. 2. *(Met.)* Flock, congregation of the faithful.

grial [gre-ahl'], *m.* Grail, the legendary holy chalice of the Last Supper.

griego, ga [gre-ay'-go, gah], *a.* Greek; belonging to or native of Greece.-*m.* 1. The Greek language. 2. Incomprehensible language.

grieta [gre-ay'-tah], *f.* 1. Crevice, crack, cleft. 2. Chink, fissure, cranny, flaw. 3. Scratch or fissure in the skin. **Grieta en las manos**, chapped hands.

grietado, da [gre-ay-tah'-do, dah], *a.* Fissured, cleft, showing flaws.

grietarse [gre-ay-tar'-say], *vr.* To crack in the form of a star: said of ingots or metal plates.

grietecilla [gre-ay-tay-theel'-lyah], *f. dim.* A small fissure or scratch; a small crevice.

grietoso, sa [gre-ay-to´-so, sah], *a.* Full of cracks or crevices, flawy.

grifa [gree'-fah], *f.* Italics, in printing.

grifado, da [gre-fah'-do, dah], *a.* Italic (type).

grifalto [gre-fahl'-to], *m.* Small kind of culverin.

grifo, fa [gree´-fo, fah], *a.* 1. Applied to the letters invented by Haldus Pius Manutius, which superseded the Gothic characters; Italic. 2. Kinky (pelo).

grifo [gree'-fo], *m.* 1. Griffin or griffon, a fabled animal. 2. *(Amer.)* The child of a negro and an Indian. **Grifos**, frizzled hair. 3. Tap, faucet. **Cerveza al grifo**, draught beer.

grifón [gre-fone'], *m.* A stop-cock for water; faucet, spigot.

gril [greel'], *m.* Grilse, Scotch name of a young salmon on its first return from sea.

griliforme [gre-le-for'-may], *a. (Zool.)* Shaped like a cricket.

grilla [greel'-lyah], *f.* 1. Female cricket. *V.* GRILLO. 2. A piece of the mechanism of a stocking loom. **Esa es grilla**, there is no such a thing: vulgar expression of doubt.

grillado [greel-lah'-do], *a.* Barmy.

grillar [greel-lyar'], *vn.* To chirp or squeak (grillo).-*vr.* To shoot, to sprout.

grillera [greel-lyay'-rah], *f.* Cricket cage, a place where crickets are kept (jaula).

grillero [greel-lyay'-ro], *m.* He who takes off prisoners' irons.

grillete [greel-lyay´-tay], *m.* Shackle, fetter.

grillo [greel´-lyo], *m.* 1. Cricket, an insect. 2. Shoot issuing from seed in the earth, germ. **Grillos**, 1. Fetters, irons, shackles or chains for the feet. 2. Any impediment which prevents motion.

grillones [greel-lyo'-nes], *m. pl. aug.* Large fetters or irons.

grillotalpa [greel-lyo-tahl'-pah], *m.* Mole-cricket, fen-cricket.

grima [gree'-mah], *f.* Fright, horror, astonishment, grimness, aversion (aversión), uneasiness (inquietud); annoyance (molestia).

grimazo [gre-mah'-tho], *m.* A grotesque posture, or contortion of the face.

grímpola [greem'-po-lah], *f. (Naut.)* Vane, a sort of weather-cock on the top-mast head. 1. Pennant, streamer.

grinalde [gre-nahl'day], *m.* Machine of artificial firework.

gringo [green´-go], *a. (coll.)* Unintelligible, gibberish (idioma).-*m. (Vulg.)* Yankee (norteamericano). **Hablar en gringo**, to speak double Dutch.

griñón [gre-nyone'], *m.* 1. A wimple worn by nuns and religious women.

gripe [gree'-pay], *f.* Influenza, flu, grippe.

gris [grees], *m.* 1. Mixture of white and black, grizzle, gray. 2. Miniver, a grizzle-colored squirrel or weasel. 3. *(coll.)* Cold, sharp air or weather.

gris [grees], *a.* Gray, grizzled (día, tiempo). **Gris marengo** (telas), dark gray. **Gris perla,** pearl-gray.

grisa [gree´-sah], *f. (Amer.)* V. CHINCHILLA.

grisáceo [gree-sah´-thay-o], *a.* Grayish.

grisalla [gre-sahl´-lyah], *f.* Grisaille, a style of painting in grayish tints imitating the effect of relief.

grisar [gre-sar´], *va.* To polish the diamond.

griseta [gre-say´-tah], *f.* 1. Kind of flowered silk. 2. *(Neol.)* A French grisette.

grisú [gre-soo´], *m.* A French and Belgian name of fire-damp, or methane gas, which in coal mines produces an explosive mixture with atmospheric air.

grita [gree´-tah], *f.* 1. Clamor, outcry, vociferation. 2. Halloo; a word of encouragement to dogs. 3. Exclamations of applause or censure.

gritador, ra [gre-tah-dor´, rah], *m. & f.* Clamorer, exclaimer; bawler.

gritar [gre-tar´], *vn.* 1. To exclaim, to cry out, to clamor, to clatter, to halloo, to shout, to hoot. 2. To talk very loud. 3. To bawl. 4. To shriek.

gritería [gre-tay-ree´-ah], *f.* 1. Outcry, clamor, confused noise, shout, exclamation, screaming; hooting. 2. Confused cry of many voices.

grito [gree´-to], *m.* Cry, scream, howling; hoot. **Estar en un grito,** to be in continual pain. **Dar un grito,** to raise an outcry, to set up a shout, a hurrah. **Llorar a gritos,** to weep and wail. **Es el último grito,** it´s the very latest.

gritón, na [gre-tone´, nah], *a.* Vociferous, clamorous.

gro [gro], *m.* Grosgrain, a twilled silk fabric; a stout silk.

groenlandés, sa [gro-en-lan-days´, sah], *a. m. & f.* Greenlander.

gromo [gro´-mo], *m. (Bot.)* Leafy bud, young shoot.

gropos [gro´-pos], *m. pl.* Cotton put in ink-stands or ink-horns.

gros [gros], *m.* Ancient coin of small value.

grosca [gros´-cah], *f.* Kind of venomous serpent.

grosella [gro-sayl´-lyah], *f. (Bot.)* The fruit of the red currant. **Grosella blanca,** white currant, the fruit of a variety of red currant. **Grosella negra,** fruit of the black currant.

grosellero [gro-sel-lyay´-ro], *m. (Bot.)* Currant. **Grosellero rojo or común,** red currant. **Grosellero blanco,** white red currant. **Grosellero negro,** black currant.

groseramente, [gro-say-rah-men´-tay], *adv.* Grossly, coarsely (ordinariamente), rudely (descortésmente), clownishly, in a rude, unmannerly way.

grosería [gro-say-ree´-ah], *f.* 1. Grossness, homeliness, plainness, coarseness (ordinariez), churlishness, clumsiness, clownishness, rudeness, ill-breeding. 2. Grossness, shameless word or action.

grosero, ra [gro-say´-ro, rah], *a.* 1. Gross, coarse (ordinario), rough (maleducado), plain, homely, homespun, not elegant, not fine. 2. Gross, thick, fat, bulky. 3. Gross, rude, unpolished, churlish, clownish, uncivil, rough, brutal. 4. Gross, indelicate (indecente), indecent, smutty.

grosísimo, ma [gro-see´-se-mo, mah], superlative of GRUESO.

groso [gro´-so], *a.* Coarse snuff, badly powdered.

grosor [gro-sor´], *m.* Thickness, density, closeness, compactness.

grosularina, or grosulina [gro-soo-lah-ree´-nah, gro-soo-lee´-nah], *f. (Chem.)* Grossaline, a vegetable jelly found in acid fruits.

grosura [gro-soo´-rah], *f.* 1. Suet, tallow, fat of animals. 2. Extremities, heart, liver, and lungs of an animal.

grotesco, ca [gro-tes´-co, cah], *a.* Grotesque, laughable.

grúa [groo´-ah], *f.* 1. Crane, a machine for raising heavy weights. 2. An ancient military machine. 3. *(Naut.)* Bend of a curved piece of timber. 4. Hoist, derrick. **Grúa corredera,** traveling crane. **Grúa de torre,** tower crane.

grueras [groo-ay´-ras], *f. pl. (Naut.)* Rope holes.

gruero, ra [groo-ay´-ro, rah], *a.* Belonging to birds of prey, trained to pursue cranes.

gruesa [groo-ay´-sah], *f.* 1. Gross, twelve dozen. 2. Chief part of a prebend. 3. Bottomry.

gruesamente [groo-ay-sah-men-tay], *adv.* Grossly, coarsely by wholesale.

grueso, sa [groo-ay´-so, sah], *a.* 1. Bulky (voluminoso), corpulent, thick (espeso), fleshy, fat, fullfed, plump, gross. 2. Large, great, big (grande, pesado). 3. Coarse, plain, homespun, not fine. 4. Dense, compact. 5. *(Met.)* Heavy, dull, stupid, dim, not quick in any of the senses.

grueso [groo-ay´-so], *m.* 1. Corpulence, bulkiness of body (tamaño). 2. Thickness (calidad), density, space taken up by matter interposed. 3. Gross, the main body, the bulk, the chief part (parte principal). 4. Size body of type.

gruir [groo-eer´], *vn.* To crank or crankle: to cry like a crane.

grujidor [groo-he-dor´], *m.* Steel instrument used by glaziers for rounding glass.

grujir [groo-heer´], *va.* To chip away angles and inequalities of glass with a *grujidor.*

grulla [grool´-lyah], *f.* 1. *(Orn.)* Crane. 2. Crane, the name of a southern constellation.

grullada [grool-lyah´-dah], *f. (coll.)* 1. Crowd of people going together to any place. 2. Crowd of constables or police officers.

grullero, ra [grool-lyay´-ro, rah], *a.* Applied to falcons or birds of prey in chase of cranes.

grumete [groo-may´-tay], *m. (Naut.)* Younker, ship´s boy.

grumillo [groo-meel´-lyo], *m. dim.* A small grume, clot, or curd.

grumo [groo´-mo], *m.* 1. Grume, a thick viscid consistence in a fluid; a clot (coágulo). **Grumo de leche,** curd. 2. Cluster, bunch (de uvas) 3. Heart or pith of trees. **Grumos,** pinions, the joints of the wings remotest from the body.

grumoso, sa [groo-mo´-so, sah], *a.* Grumy, grumous, clotty; full of grumes.

gruñido [groo-nyee´-do], *m.* 1. Grunt, the noise of a hog. 2. Growl, maundering, the murmur of a discontented person. **Gruñido, da,** *pp.* of GRUÑIR.

gruñidor, ra [groo-nye-dor´, rah], *m. & f.* Grunter, grumbler, murmurer, mutterer.

gruñimiento [groo-nye-me-en´-to], *m.* Grunting, murmuring, grumbling.

gruñir [groo-nyeer´], *vn.* 1. To grunt like a hog. 2. To creak (puerta) 3. *(Met.)* To grumble, to growl, to snarl.

gruñón, na [groo-nyone´, nah], *m. & f. (coll.)* V. GRUÑIDOR.

grupa [groo´-pah], *f.* 1. Croup, the buttocks of a horse. 2. A cavalry call to saddle the horses. **Cargar la grupa,** to pass the tail of a horse through the crupper.

grupada [groo-pah´-dah], *f.* 1. Squall or gust of wind. 2. Croupade, leap of a horse.

grupera [groo-pay´-rah], *f.* 1. Cushion at the back of a saddle for carrying a satchel, etc (de caballo). 2. Crupper, a looped strap for a horse´s tail. 3. V. RETRANCA.

grupo [groo´-po], *m.* 1. Group, assemblage. 2. Clump of sprigs growing out of the same root. 3. Cluster (árboles) **Reunirse en grupos,** to gather in groups. **Grupo de trabajo,** working party.

gruta [groo´-tah], *f.* Cavern, cavity between rocks; a grotto, a grot. **Gruta de fieras,** menagerie. **Grutas,** crypts, vaults, subterranean edifices.

grutesco [groo-tes´-co], *m.* Grotesque, a kind of ornament in painting, composed of leaves, shells, etc.

gruyere [groo-yerr´], *m.* A kind of rich cheese, made at Gruyere in France.

¡gúa! [goo´-ah]. Interjection of surprise and depreciation used in Peru and Bolivia. Come now!

guaba [goo-ah´-bah], *f.* Abbreviated form of *guayaba.*

guaca [goo-ah´-cah], *f.* A grave mound of the ancient Peruvians (tumba).

guacal [goo-ah-cahl'], *m. (Mex.)* An oblong hamper for carrying fruit (cajón).

guacamayo [goo-ah-cah-mah'-yo], *m. (Orn.)* Macao or macaw.

guacamole [goo-ah-cah-mo'-lay], *m. (Cuba)* Salad of alligator pear.

guachapear [goo-ah-chah-pay-ar'], *va.* To daddle, to play with the feet in water (agua) .-*vn.* To clap, as horses' shoes when loose; to clatter.

guachapelí [goo-ah-chah-pay-lee'], *m.* Solid strong wood, which grows in Guayaquil, used for ships.

guácharo, ra [goo-ah'-chah-ro, rah], *a.* 1. Sickly, not in health. 2. Dropsical, diseased with dropsy.

guachí [goo-ah-chee'], or **guají** [goo-ah-hee'], *m. (Mex.)* Fool, dolt, simpleton.

guachinango, ga [goo-ah-che-nahn'-go, gah], *m. & f.* A name given by the inhabitants of Cuba to the natives of Mexico, and in Vera Cruz to those of the interior (persona astuta).

guacho, cha [goo-ah'-cho, chah], *a. (W. S. Amer.)* 1. Orphan (huérfano), foundling. 2. Solitary, forlorn.-*m.* Birdling of a sparrow. *(Acad.)*

guacia [goo-ah'-the-ah], *f.* 1. *V.* ACACIA. 2. Gumarabic.

guaco [goo'-ah'-co], *m. (Amer.)* A plant of South America, eminent as an antidote for the bite of venomous snakes.

guadafiones [goo-ah-dah-fe-o'-nes], *m. pl.* Fetters with which the legs of horses are shackled.

guadamacil [goo-ah-dah-mah-theel'], *m.* Printed leather, gilt and adorned with figures.

guadamacilería [goo-ah-dah-mah-the-lay-ree'-ah], *f.* Manufactory of gilt or printed leather.

guadamacilero [goo-ah-dah-mah-the-lay'-ro], *m.* Manufacturer of printed leather.

guadaña [goo-ah-dah'-nyah], *f.* 1. Scythe for mowing. 2. *(Met.)* Death, as depicted with a scythe. 3. A knife used by manufacturers of leather wine-bags.

guadañadora [goo-ah-dah-nyah-do'-rah], *f.* Mowing machine.

guadañar [goo-ah-dah-nyar'], **or guadañear**, *va. (Prov.)* To mow, to cut grass.

guadañero [goo-ah-dah-nyay'-ro], *m.* 1. Mower, one who cuts grass. 2. The owner or manager of a *guadaño*.

guadañil [goo-ah-dah-nyeel'], *m.* Mower who cuts down hay; haymaker.

guadaño [goo-ah-dah'-nyo], *m.* 1. A small boat with an awning used in the traffic of the port of Havana. 2. Name given at Cadiz and other sea-ports to transport vessels.

guadañón [goo-ah-dah-nyone'], *m.* Mower. *V.* GUADAÑERO.

guadapero [goo-ah-dah-pay'-ro], *m.* 1. *(Bot.)* Wild common pear. 2. A boy who carries victuals to reapers or mowers.

guadarnés [goo-ah-dar-nays'], *m.* 1. Harness-room, a place where harness is kept. 2. Harness keeper, an officer of the king's mews.

guadijeño [goo-ah-de-hay'-nyo], *m.* Poniard, stiletto, knife. -*a.* Belonging to Guadix.

guadramaña [goo-ah-drah-mah'-nyah], *f.* Trick, deceit, imposition.

guadua [goo-ah'-doo-ah], *f.* Gadua bamboo-cane of Ecuador and Colombia. **guadual** [goo-ah-doo-ahl'], *m.* Plantation of large reeds.

guagua [goo-ah'-goo-ah]. 1. *f.* Nursing baby. (In *Ecuad.*) Both *f.* and *m.* 2. *(Cuba)* A kind of insect. 3. *(Cuba)* A kind of bus. 4. **(De)** *adv.* Free, for nothing (gratis).

guainambí [goo-ah-e-nam-bee'], *m. (Medic. C. A.)* A humming-bird.

guaira [go-ah'-e-rah], *f. (S. Amer.)* 1. A triangular sail. 2. A tall furnace which the Peruvians used in smelting metals.

guairo [goo-ah'-e-ro], *m. (Ecu.)* 1. One of the seven faces of a dice used by the Indians. 2. A small two-masted craft with sails called *guairas*. *V. supra.*

guajalote, or **guajolote** [goo-ah-hah-lo'-tay], *m. (Mex.)* Turkey.

guajamón, na [goo-ah-hah-mone', nah], *a. (Cuba)* Orange-colored, speaking of horses.

guájaras [goo-ah'-hah-ras], *f. pl.* Fastnesses, the roughest part of a range of mountains.

guaje [goo-ah'-hay], *m. (Mex.)* A calabash which serves for learning to swim. In Peru, called *mate*; in Cuba, *güiro*.

guajiro, ra [goo-ah-hee'-ro, rah], *a. (Cuba)* 1. Rustic, rural. 2. Rustic, rude, boorish.

gualá! [goo-ah-lah'], *int.* Assuredly.

gualatina [goo-ah-lah-tee'-nah], *f.* Dish made of boiled apples, milk of almonds and broth, and beaten up with spice and rose water.

gualda [goo-ahl'-dah], *f. (Bot.)* Weld, wild woad, dye's weed, reseda, a plant which dyer's yellow.

gualdado, da [goo-al-dah'-do, dah], *a.* Weld-colored, yellowish.

gualderas [goo-al-day'-ras], *f. pl.* The sides, cheeks or brackets of a gun-carriage. **Gualderas de las garlingas**, *(Naut.)* checks of the mast-steps.

gualdo, da [goo-ahl'-do, dah], *a.* Weld, yellow or gold color.

gualdón [goo-al-done'], *m. (Bot.)* Base rocket, reseda.

gualdrapa [goo-al-drah'-pah], *f.* 1. Horse-cloth, housing, foot-cloth. 2. Tatter rag hanging from clothes.

gualdrapazo [goo-al-drah-pah'-tho], *m. (Naut.)* Flap of the sails against the masts.

gualdrapear [goo-al-drah-pay-ar'], *va.* To put one thing upon another.-*vn. (Naut.)* To flap against the masts (vela).

gualdrapeo [goo-al-drah-pay'-o], *m.* Flapping of the sails.

gualdrapero [goo-al-drah-pay'-ro], *m.* Ragamuffin, a ragged fellow.

gualdrín [goo-al-dreen'], *m.* Weather-strip.

gualputra [goo-al-poo'-trah], *f. (Amer.)* Name given to the creeping clover.

guama [goo-ah'-mah], *f.* Fruit of the *guamo*.

guamo [goo-ah'-mo], *m.* A tall, branching tree of narrow leaves, planted to shade the coffee-tree.

guambra [goo-ahm'-brah], *f. (S. Amer.)* A child-servant.

guanábana [goo-ah-nah'-ba-nah], *f.* 1. Fruit of the *guanábano* tree, very sweet and white. 2. A beverage common in Havana made from same.

guanábano [goo-ah-nah'-ba-no], *m.* A fruit-tree of America, a variety of chirimoya.

guanaco [goo-ah-nah'-co], *m. (Zool.)* Guanaco, S. American mammal related to the llama.

guanajo [goo-ah-nah'-ho], *m. (Cuba)* A turkey.

guano [goo-ah'-no], *m.* 1. Kind of American palm tree (árbol). 2. Guano, sea birds' dung, an excellent fertilizing material from the Peruvian Islands.

guantada [goo-an-tah'-dah], *f.* Slap or blow with the palm or inner part of the hand.

guante [goo-ahn'-tay], *m.* 1. Glove, a cover of the hands. **Guantes de ante**, buff gloves. **Guante de goma**, rubber glove. **Se ajusta como un guante**, it fits like a glove. 2. Gauntlet, an iron glove used for defence, and thrown down in challenges. 3. Familiarly, the hand. **Echar el guante**, *(coll.)* to catch or lay hold on with the hand. **Echar el guante a otro**, to grasp, to seize, to imprison. **Echar** or **arrojar el guante**, to challenge or to send a challenge.

guantelete [goo-an-tay-lay'-tay], *m.* 1. Gauntlet. 2. A bandage for the hand.

guantera [goo-ahn-tay-rah], *f. (Aut.)* Glove compartment.

guantería [goo-an-tay-ree'-ah], *f.* A glover's shop and the art of a glover (tienda, fabricación); glove factory (fábrica).

guantero [goo-an-tay'-ro], *m.* Glover, one who makes gloves.

guañín [goo-ah-nyeen'], *a.* Applied to gold under legal standard.

guao [goo-ah'-o], *m.* A tree of the island of Santo Domingo whose smell is fatal.

guapamente [goo-ah-pah-men'-tay], *adv. (coll.)* Bravely, courageously.

guapear [goo-ah-pay-ar'], *vn. (coll.)* 1. To boast of courage (fanfarronear). 2. To take pride in fine dress (ostentarse).

guaperas [goo-ah-pay'-ras], *a.* Excessively good-looking. -*m.* Excessively good-looking youth.

guapeza [goo-ah-pay'-thah], *f. (coll.)* 1. Bravery, courage. 2. Ostentation in dress (ostentación). 3. Good looks (atractivo). 4. Smartness (elegancia), elegance.

guapinal [goo-ah-pe-nahl'], *m.* A resin-yielding tree of Central America.

guapo, pa [goo-ah'-po, pah], *a. (coll.)* 1. Stout, courageous, valiant, bold (valiente), enterprising, good, clever. 2. Spruce, neat, elegant (elegante), ostentatious, vain. 3. Gay, sprightly, fond of courting women. 4. Good-looking, handsome (hombre). **Va de guapo por la vida**, he goes through life with every confidence in his good looks. **¡Hombre, qué guapo estás!**, how smart you're looking!

guaquero [goo-ah-key'-ro], *m.* Earthenware. Vessel for drinking *chicha* found in ancient Peruvian tombs.

guaracha [goo-ah-rah'-chah], *f.* 1. A kind of dance (baile). 2. *(Mex.)* A sandal (alboroto).

guarana [goo-ah-rah'-nah], *f. (Bot.)* Paullinia; and the agreeable drink made in Brazil from its seeds.

guarango [go-ah-rahn'-go], *m.* A shrub used for dyeing; a species of prosopis. (Ecuador.)

guarapo [goo-ah-rah'-po], *m.* Sub-acid drink made in sugar-mills with the fermented cane-liquor. *(Cuba)* **Menear el guarapo**, to chastise.

guarda [goo-ar'-dah], *com.* Guard (persona), keeper (cuidador); anything that preserves others from injury. -*f.* 1. Custody, wardship, guard, keeping (acto). 2. Observance of a law or ordinance. 3. Nun who accompanies men through convents. 4. Each of the outside ribs or guards of a fan. 5. Sheet of paper placed at the beginning and end of volumes to guard the printed sheets in binding. 6. The ward of a lock or of a key. **Guarda de la aduana**, an officer of the custom-house. **Guardacosta**, *(Naut.)* custom-house cutter, a vessel employed to clear the coast of smugglers. **Guarda de coto**, gamekeeper. **Guardafuego**, 1. Screen for a chimney-fire. 2. Fender. **Guardajoyas**, place where jewels or other precious things are kept. **Guardamayor**, chief-guard. **Guarda jurado**, security guard. **Guarda nocturno**, night watchman.

¡guarda! [goo-ar'-dah], *int.* Take care! beware!

guardaaguja [goo-ar-dah-ah-goo'-hah], *m.* A railway switchman.

guardaalmacén [goo-ar-dah-ahl-mah-then'], *m.* Store-keeper.

guardabosque [goo-ar-dah-bos'-kay], *m.* Keeper of a forest, gamekeeper.

guardabrazo [goo-ar-dah-brah'-tho], *m.* A part of the armor to defend the arm.

guardabrisa [goo-ar-dah-bree'-sah], *m.* Windshield.

guardacabras [goo-ar-dah-cah'-bras], *m.* Goatherd.

guardacantón [goo-ar-dah-can-tone'], *m.* A spur-stone, a check-stone.

guardacostas [goo-ar-dah-cos'-tahs], *m.* Coast-defense ship

guardadamente [goo-ar-dah-dah-men'-tay], *adv.* Guardedly.

guardador, ra [goo-ar-dah-dor', rah], *m. & f.* 1. A very careful, watchful, and provident man, one who keeps his property with great care, protective (protector). 2. Keeper. 3. One who observes a law. 4. Miser. 5. Mean, stingy.

guardaespaldas [goo-ar-dah-ays-pahl'-das], *m.* Bodyguard.

guardafango [goo-ar-dah-fahn'-go], *m.* Fender (vehículo).

guardafrenos [goo-ar-dah-fray'-nos], *m.* A brakeman.

guardafuego [goo-ar-dah-foo-ay'-go], *(Naut.)* Breaming board.

guardainfante [goo-ar-dahin-fahn'-tay], *m.* Farthingale, ladies' hoop.

guardaja [goo-ar-dah'-hah], *f. V.* GUEDEJA.

guardalado [goo-ar-dah-lah'-do], *m.* Battlement of a bridge.

guardamangel [goo-ar-dah-man-hel'], *m.* Pantry, buttery.

guardamano [goo-ar-dah-mah'-no], *f.* Guard of a sword.

guardamateriales [goo-ar-dah-mah-tay-re-ah'-les], *m.* Person appointed to purchase bullion and other necessaries for a mint.

guardameta [goo-ar-dah-may'-tah], *m.* Goalkeeper, goalie.

guardamonte [goo-ar-dah-mon'-tay], *m.* 1. Guard of a gun-lock, sword, etc. 2. Forester, keeper of a forest.

guardamozo, or **guardamancebo** [goo-ar-dah-mo'-tho, goo-ar-dah-man-thay'-bo], *m. (Naut.)* Man-rope, entering rope.

guardamuebles [goo-ar-dah-moo-ay'-blays], *m.* 1. Store-room for furniture in great houses. 2. Guard over the furniture of a palace.

guardamujer [goo-ar-dah-moo-herr'], *f.* Servant of the queen, next to the ladies of honor.

guardapapo [goo-ar-dah-pah'-po], *m.* Ancient piece of armor for the face.

guardapelo [goo-ar-dah-pay'-lo], *m.* A locket.

guardapiés [goo-ar-dah-pe-ays'], *m.* 1. A petticoat commonly used under the upper garment. 2. *V.* BRIAL.

guardapolvo [goo-ar-dah-pol'-vo], *m.* 1. A piece of cloth or leather to guard against dust (ropa). 2. The inner lid of a watch (reloj). 3. The dust-guard of a carriage or railway car (cubierta).

guardapuerta [goo-ar-dah-poo-err'-tah], *f.* Storm door (puerta), door curtain (cortina).

guardar [goo-ar-dar'], *va.* 1. To keep, to preserve in a state of security (preservar), to keep from, to look to, to guard (cuidar), to protect. 2. To keep, to take care of, to watch (proteger), to guard, to preserve from damage. 3. To lay up, to store, to deposit for future use. 4. To lay by, to reserve for some future time, to conserve, to keep back, to maintain. 5. To keep, to hold for another. 6. To observe, to respect (mandamiento) 7. To fulfil one's duty. 8. To be on one's guard, to avoid (evitar), to abstain from, to guard against, to fence. **Guardársela a alguno**, to delay vengeance for a favorable opportunity. **Lo guardó en el bolsillo**, he put it away in his pocket. **Guardo los mejores recuerdos**, I have the nicest memories. -*vr.* 1. To be on one's guard (precaverse). 2. **Guardarse de algo**, to avoid something (evitar); to look out for something (cuidarse); to refrain from something (abstenerse); to protect oneself against something. **Guárdate de no ofenderle**, take care not to upset him.

guardarraya [goo-ar-dar-rah'-yah], *f. (Cuba)* 1. An avenue of trees or shrubs upon a plantation of sugar-cane or coffee. 2. Boundary which marks the end of a drill-hole in mines, after it has been measured.

guardarrío [goo-ar-dar-ree'-o], *m. (Orn.)* Kingfisher.

guardarropa [goo-ar-dar-ro'-pah], *f.* Wardroom, checkroom (habitación). -*m.* Checkroom attendant, wardrobe (ropero).

guardarruedas [goo-ar-dar-roo-ay'-das], *m. V.* GUARDACANTÓN.

guardasol [goo-ar-dah-sol'], *m. V.* QUITASOL.

guardavajilla [goo-ar-day-vah-heel'-yah], *f.* A room for keeping the (royal) plate or table-service.

guardaventana [goo-ar-dah-ven-tah'-nah], *f.* Storm window.

guardería [goo-ar-day-ree'-ah], *f.* 1. Occupation of a guard. 2. Day nursery.

guardia [goo-ar'-de-ah], *f.* 1. Guard, a body of soldiers or armed men to watch by way of defence (defensa). **Cuerpo de guardia**, guard-room. 2. *(Naut.)* Watch. *(Mil.)* **Estar de guardia**, to be on duty. **Montar la guardia**, to mount guard. **Salir de guardia**, to come off guard. -*m & f.* 1. Soldier belonging to the guards. **Guardia marina**, midshipman. **Guardia de circulacion**, traffic policeman. **Guardia forestal**, game warden.

guardián, na [goo-ar-de-ahn', nah], *m. & f.* 1. Keeper, one who has charge of something, caretaker (edificio). 2. Guardian, watchman. -*m.* 1. The local superior of convents (franciscanos). 2. *(Naut.)* Keeper of the arms and store-room. **Guardián de parque**, park keeper. **Guardián de prisiones**, warder.

guardianía [goo-ar-de-ah-nee'-ah], *f.* Guardianship.

guardilla [goo-ar-deel'-lya], *f.* 1. Garret, skylight. 2. With seamstresses, ornament and guard of a seam.

guardín de la caña [goo-ar-deen' day lah cah'-nyah], *m.* *(Naut.)* Tiller-rope.

guardoso, sa [goo-ar-do'-so, sah], *a.* 1. Frugal, parsimonious. 2. Mean, stingy.

guare [goo-ah'-ray], *m.* *(Ec.)* Raft made of great rushes, with a square sail.

guarecer [goo-ah-ray-therr'], *va.* 1. To aid, to succour, to assist. 2. To guard, to preserve; to cure.-*vr.* To take refuge, to escape from danger.

guarentigio, gia [goo-ah-ren-tee´-he-o, ah], *a.* *(Law.)* Applied to a contract, writing, or clause, which empowers the justices to cause it to be executed.

guarida [goo-ah-ree'-dah], *f.* 1. Den, the cave or couch of a wild beast. 2. Haunt, the place where one is frequently found (de persona). 3. Protection, aid, shelter, a lurking-place, a cover.

guarín [goo-ah-reen'], *m.* Young pig, last born of a litter.

guarir [goo-ah-reer'], *va. & vn.* To subsist.

guarismo [goo-ah-rees'-mo], *m.* Figure, cipher, an arithmetical character.

guarismo, ma [goo-ah-rees'-mo, mah], *a.* Arithmetical.

guarne [goo-ar'-nay], *m.* *(Naut.)* Each turn of a cable or tackle.

guarnecedor [goo-ar-nay-thay-dor'], *m.* 1. Hatter who cocks hats. 2. One who garnishes or surrounds a thing with ornamental appendages.

guarnecer, guarnescer [goo-ar-nay-therr'], *va.* 1. To garnish, to surround with ornamental appendages. 2. To set a diamond or stone in gold, silver, etc. 3. To trim, to adorn (adornar). 4. To harness horses or mules. 5. To garrison a town or other place. 6. To line (frenos), to plaster (pared). *(Yo guarnezco, yo guarnezca,* from *Guarnecer.* V. CONOCER.)

guarnés [goo-ar-ness'], **m.** Harness-room (para arneses). V. GUADARNÉS.

guarnición [goo-ar-ne-the-on'], *f.* 1. Flounce, furbelow, trimming. 2. Setting of anything in gold or silver (joyas). 3. Guard of a sword (espada). 4. Garrison, a body of soldiers in a fortified town to defend it. 5. Garniture, garnish, any ornamental hem, lace or border. 6. Marines, naval troops. 7. **Guarnición de la bomba,** *(Naut.)* the upper or spear-box of a pump.-*pl.* 1. Ancient steel armor of defence. 2. Gears or traces of mules and horses; harness (de caballo). 3. Gear (equipo); fittings (de casa). **Guarniciones de alumbrado,** light fittings.

guarnicionería [goo-ar-ne-the-o-nay-ree'-ah], *f.* Shop of a harness-maker.

guarnicionero [goo-ar-ne-the-o-nay´-ro], *m.* Harness-maker.

guarniel [goo-ar-ne-el´], *m.* 1. Leather purse used by carriers, with divisions for paper, money, and other things. 2. *(Mex.)* A powder-flask.

guarnir [goo-ar-neer'], *va.* To reeve, to pass a rope through the eyes of blocks, to form a tackle. **Guarnir el cabrestante,** to rig the capstan.

guaro [goo-ah'-ro], *m.* A small, very talkative parrot. *(Acad.)*

guarra [goo-ar'-rah], *f.* A sow.

guarrada [goo-ahr-rah'-dah], *f.* Dirty trick (trampa); rotten thing (dicho); indecent act (indecencia), vulgar thing.

guarrillo [goo-ar-reel'-lyo], *m. dim.* A small pig.

guarro [goo-ar'-ro], *m.* Hog, pig, whether large or small, dirty person. -*a.* Dirty, filthy.

guaruba [goo-ah-roo´-bah], *f.* 1. An American parrot with a red neck. 2. A howling ape.

guasa [goo-ah'-sah], *f. (coll.)* 1. Jest, satire, irony, joke (broma). 2. Insipidity, dullness (sosería).

guasanga [goo-ah-sahn'-gah], *(Cuba)* Noisy mirth.

guasanguero, ra [goo-ah-san'-gay-ro, rah], *a. (Cuba)* Jolly, merry, noisy.

guasca [goo-ahs'-cah], *f. (Peru)* Cord, thong, whip (látigo). **Dar guasca,** to whip, to scourge.

guaso [goo-ah'-so], *m.* 1. V. GAUCHO. 2. Lasso.

guasón, na [goo-ah-sone', nah], *a. (Coll. Andal.)* Jocose, witty (gracioso), satirical, joking (burlón). **Dijo burlón,** he said jokingly.

guasquear [goo-as-kay-ar'], *va. (Amer.)* To whip (azotar), to scourge.

guata [goo-ah'-tah], *f.* Raw cotton (algodón); padding (relleno); twine, cord.

guataca [goo-ah-tah'-cah], *f. (Cuba)* 1. Spade. 2. Applied ironically to a large ear.

guataquear [goo-ah-tah-kay-ar'], *va. (Cuba)* To spade, to clear sowed ground with the spade.

guatemalteco, ca [goo-ah-tay-mal-tay'-co, cah], *a.* Guatemalan, of Guatemala.

guateque [goo-ah-tay'-kay], *m.* Party, celebration, binge.

guatuse [goo-ah-too'-say], *m.* A Nicaraguan animal with reddish-brown fur.

¡guay! [goo-ah'-e], *int.* Oh! an exclamation of pain or grief. V. AY. **Tener muchos guayes,** to labor under many afflictions.

guaya [goo-ah'-yah], *f.* Grief, sorrow, affliction.

guayaba [goo-ah-yah'-bah], *f.* Fruit of the guava tree. **Guayaba blanca,** white guava. **Guayaba roja,** red guava.

guayabal [goo-ah-yah-bahl'], *m.* An orchard of guava trees.

guayabo [goo-ah-yah'-bo], *m. (Bot.)* Guava-tree.

guayacán [goo-ah-yah-cahn'], *m. (Bot.)* V. GUAYACO.

guayacana [goo-ah-yah-cah'-nah], *f. (Bot.)* Dateplum.

guayaco [goo-ah-yah´-co], *m. (Bot.)* Lignumvitae tree, guaiacum. **Guayaco oficinal,** officinal guaiacum, or lignumvitae tree.

guayapil, guayapín [goo-ah-yah-peel´, goo-ah-yah-peen´], *m.* A loose Indian dress for women.

guayusa [goo-ah-yoo'-sah], *f.* A tall shrub of the Napo River, Ecuador; an ilex. The leaves are used for tea.

gubán [goo-bahn'], *m.* Kind of large boat used in the Philippines. It is made without nails, clinker-built, rowed rapidly and easily taken on land.

gubernamental [goo-ber-nah-men-tahl'], *a.* Gubernamental; loyalist (de facción). -*m & f.* Loyalist, government supporter; government soldier.

gubernativo, va [goo-ber-nah-tee´-vo, vah], *a.* Administrative, relating to government; gubernative.

gubia [goo'-be-ah], *f.* Gouge, a round hollow chisel.

gubiadura [goo-be-ah-doo'-rah], *f. (Naut.)* Notch, channel.

gubilete [goo-be-lay'-tay], *m. (Prov.)* Kind of vase. V. CUBILETE.

guedeja [gay-day'-hah], *f.* 1. Lock of hair falling on the temple, forelock. 2. Lion's mane.

guedejilla [gay-day-heel'-lyah], *f. dim.* A small lock of hair.

guedejón, na, guedejoso, sa [gay-day-hone', nah], *a.* V. GUEDEJUDO.

guedejudo, da [gay-day-hoo'-do, dah], *a.* Bushy, clotted (pelo).

guelde [gayl'-day], *m. (Bot.)* Water-elder, guelder-rose, viburnum.

güelfo, fa [goo-el'-fo, fah], *a.* Guelph, partisan of the popes, and opponents of the Ghibellines.

gueltre [gayl'-tray], *m.* A cant word for money or cash.

güembé [goo-em-bay´], *m.* Manila-hemp. V. ABACÁ.

guerindola [gay-rin-do'-lah], *f.* V. GUIRINDOLA.

güermeces [goo-ayr'-may-thes], *m.* A morbid swelling in the throat of hawks, and other birds of prey.

güero, ra [goo-ay'-roh, rah], *a. & m. & f. (Men.)* Blond, blonde (pelo).

guerra [gayr'-rah], *f.* 1. War. 2. Art of war, military science. 3. War, profession of arms. 4. War, hostility, conflict of passions. **Guerra fría,** cold war. **Estado de guerra,** state of war. **Hacer guerra,** to wage war. **Guerra mundial,** world war. **Guerra nuclear,** nuclear war. **Guerra química,** chemical warfare. **Guerra de guerrillas,** guerilla warfare. **Dar guerra,** to be troublesome, to annoy (niño). **Guerra de la Independencia,** War of independence. **Segunda Guerra Mundial,** Second World War.

guerreador, ra [gayr-ray-ah-dor', rah], *m. & f.* Warrior, one passionately fond of military fame.

guerreante [gayr-ray-ahn'-tay], *pa. & m. & f.* Warrior, warring.

guerrear [gayr-ray-ar'], *va. 1.* To war, to wage war, to fight. 2. To oppose, to be in a state of hostility.

guerrera [gayr-ray'-rah], *f.* Military jacket.

guerreramente [gayr-ray-rah-men'-tay], *adv.* Warlikely.

guerrero [gayr-ray'-ro], *m. 1.* Warrior. *V.* GUERREADOR. 2. A soldier, a military man.

guerrero, ra [gayr-ray'-ro, rah], *a. 1.* Martial, warlike (carácter). 2. Warring (contrario). 3. Fighting (belicoso).

guerrilla [gayr-reel'-lyah], *f. dim. 1.* Band of guerrillas (grupo). **Guerra de guerrillas**, guerrilla warfare. 2. Game of cards between two persons, each with twenty cards.

guerrillear [gayr-reel-lyay-ar'], *vn.* To take part in guerrilla warfare.

guerrillero, ra [gayr-reel-lay'-ro], *m & f. 1.* The commander of a skirmish force. 2. A civilian who serves in guerilla warfare.

guía [gee'-a], *m. & f. 1.* Guide, one who directs another in his way (persona). 2. Guide, conductor, leader, director, regulator, one who directs another in his conduct. *-f. 3.* Permit, docket; a writing or letter of safe conduct, proving that the customs and duty are paid at the custom house. 4. A young shoot or sucker of a vine. 5. A certain timber in the water-wheels called norias. 6. An instrument of jewellers for guiding drills. 7. *(Naut.)* Guy, a small rope, to keep weighty things in their places. 8. Earth which indicates the vein of a mine. 9. Guard of a fan. 10. *m.* Sergeant or corporal who attends to dressing the line. 11. Guidance, guiding (acto). **Para que te sirva de guía**, for your guidance. 12. Guide book; hand book (manual). **Guía oficial de ferrocarriles**, official railway guide. **Guía telefónica**, telephone directory. *-pl. 1.* Trains of powder in rockets or fireworks. 2. Horses or mules which go before flee wheel horses or mules; leaders. 3. Guide-lines, reins for controlling the leader horses.

guiadera [gee-ah-day'-rah], *f.* Guide or conductor in mills. **Guiaderas**, two upright pieces of wood in oilmills.

guiado, da [gee-ah'-do, dah], *a. & pp.* of GUIAR. Guided.

guiador, ra [gee-ah-dor', rah], *m. & f.* Guide, director.

guiamiento [gee-ah-meen'-to], *m.* Guidance, the act of guiding, security.

guiar [gee-ar'], *va 1.* To guide, to conduct. to show the way. 2. To guide, to govern by counsel, to lead (dirigir), to teach, to direct, to manage (controlar). 3. To lead a dance. *-vr.* **Guiarse por**, to be guided by.

guija [gee'-hah], *f. 1.* Pebble (piedra), pebble-stone, cobble (camino), coarse gravel. *(Bot.) V.* ALMORTA.*-pl. (coll.)* Strength, force, vigor.

guijarral [gee-har-rahl'], *m.* Heap of pebble-stones, a place abounding in pebbles.

guijarrazo [gee-har-rah'-tho], *m.* Blow with a pebble-stone.

guijarreño, ña [gee-har-ray'-nyo, nyah], *a 1.* Pebbly, gravelly. 2. Hardy, strong and rude.

guijarro [gee-hahr'-ro], *m.* Pebble; cobble (camino), cobblestone.

guijarrillo, ito [gee-har-reel'-lyo, ee'-to], *m. dim.* A small pebble.

guijarro [gee-har'-ro], *m.* Pebble or smooth stone, cobble-stone.

guijarroso, sa [gee-har-roso, sah], *a.* Pebbly.

guijeño, ña [gee-hay'-nyo, nyah], *a. 1.* Full of pebbles or coarse gravel. 2. Hard, sour, difficult.

guijo [gee'-ho], *m.* Small pebbles or gravel for roads (grava).

guijón [gee-hone'], *m. V.* NEGUIJÓN.

guijoso, sa [gee-ho'-so, sah], *a. 1.* Gravelly. 2. *V.* GUIJEÑO.

guilalo [gee-lah'-lo], *m.* A Philippine bark, intended for the postal service.

guilla [geel'-lyah], *f.* A plentiful harvest.

guillame [geel-lyah'-may], *m.* Rabbet plane, a carpenter's tool.

guilledín [geel-lyay-deen'], *m.* Gelding.

guillemote [geel-lyay-mo'-tay], *m. (Zool.)* A puffin.

guillote [geel-lyo'-tay], *m. 1.* Husbandman who enjoys the produce of a farm. 2. Tree-nail or iron pin. 3. Vagrant, sponger, an idle fellow. 4. *(coll.)* A simpleton.

guillotina [geel-lyo-tee'-nah], *f.* Guillotine, a machine for decapitating.

guillotinar [geel-lyo-te-nar'], *va.* To guillotine.

guimbalete [geem-bah-lay'-tay], *m. (Naut.)* Brake or handle of a pump.

guimbarda [geem-bar'-dah], *f. 1.* An ancient dance. 2. A plane like a rabbet plane. 3. A jew's harp.

guinchar [geen-char'], *a.* To prick; to stimulate.

guincho [geen'-cho], *m. 1.* Goad, pike. 2. *(Cuba)* Seagull.

guinda [geen'-dah], *f. 1.* Cherry (fruta). 2. Height of the masts and topmasts. **guindado, da** [geen-dah'-do, dah], *a.* Hoisted, set up.

guindajos [geen-dah'-hos], *m. pl.* Fringe or small tassels for ornament.

guindal [geen-dahl'], *m. (Bot.)* Cherry-tree. *V.* GUINDO.

guindalera [geen-dah-lay'-rah], *f.* Cherry orchard, a plantation of cherry-trees.

guindaleta [geen-dah-lay'-tah], *f. 1.* Crank-rope a rope, used to raise materials to the top of a building. 2. Fulcrum of a balance.

guindaleza [geen-dah-lay'-thah], *f. (Naut.)* Hawser.

guindamaina [geen-dah-mah'-e-nah], *f. (Naut.)* Salute between ships or squadrons.

guindar [geen-dar'], *va. 1.* To lift, to elevate, to raise, to hoist. 2. To procure in concurrence with others. 3. *(coll.)* To hang. *V.* AHORCAR.*-vr.* To be suspended, to hang by or on something.

guindastes [geen-dahs'-tes], *m. pl. (Naut.)* Gears or jeers, an assemblage of tackles.

guindilla [geen-deel'-lyah], *f. 1.* Small kind of red pepper. 2. *(Dim.)* A small cherry.

guindillo [geen-deel'-lyo], *m.* Indian cherry-tree.

guindo [geen'-do], *m. (Bot.)* Cherry-tree. **Guindo griego**, large cherry-tree.

guíndola [geen'-do-lah], *f. (Naut.)* A triangular hanging stage.

guinea [gee-nay'-ah], *f.* Guinea, an English gold coin (moneda). **Cochino de Guinea**, Guinea pig.

guineo [gee-nay'-o], *m.* Dance used amongst negroes. **Plátano guineo**, a short kind of banana. *-a.* Native of or belonging to Guinea

guinga [geen'-gah], or **guingans** [geen-gahns'], *f.* Ginghams.

guinja, *f.* **guinjo**, *m.* [geen'-hah, ho], *V.* AZUFAIFA and AZUFAIFO.

guinjolero [geen-ho-lay'-ro], *m. V.* AZUFAIFO.

guiñada, guiñadura [gee-nyah'-dah, gee-nyah-doo'-rah], *f. 1.* Wink, a hint given by the eye. 2. *(Naut.)* Yaw, the deviation of a ship from her course.

guiñador, ra [gee-nyah-dor', rah], *m. & f.* Winker.

guiñapo [gee-nyah'-po], *m. 1.* Tatter, rag (andrajo). **Poner a uno como un giñapo**, to shower insults on somebody. 2. Ragamuffin, tatterdemalion; a ragged fellow (persona).

guiñaposo, sa, guiñapiento, ta [gee-nyah-po'-so, sah, gee-nyah-pe-en'-to, tah], *a.* Ragged, tattered, torn.

guiñar [gee-nyar'], *va. 1.* To wink (parpadear), to hint or direct by a motion of the eyelids. 2. *(Naut.)* To yaw or make yaws; not to steer in a steady manner.

guiño [gee'-nyo], *m. 1.* Wink (parpadeo); grimace (mueca), wry face. **Hacer giños**, to wink at; to make eyes at (amantes).

guión [gee-on'], *m. 1.* Hyphen, division in writing. 2. Cross, the standard carried before prelates and corporations or communities. 3. Repeat, in music. 4. Scenario of a play, etc. 5. Leader (persona). 6. Script (Cine: texto); subtitle (Cine: traducción).

guionista [gee-o-ness'-tah], *m & f.* (Cine) Screenwriter; writer of subtitles.

guipar [gee-par'], *va.* (*coll.* and vulgar) 1. To see (ver). 2. To spot (observar).

guirigay [gee-re-gah'-e], *m.* Gibberish; meaningless words, jargon.

guirindola [gee-rin-do'-lah], *f.* Bosom of a shirt, frill.

guirlache [geer-lah'-chay], *m.* Roast almond caramel (turrón).

guirnalda [geer-nahl'-dah], or **guirlanda,** *f.* 1. Garland, a wreath or open crown interwoven with flowers (funeral). 2. (*Naut.*) Puddening, a wreath of cordage put around a variety of things on board of ships.

guirnaldar [geer-nal-dar'], *va.* (*Prov.*) To surround a thrashing place with trees.

güiro [goo-ee'-ro], *m.* (*Cuba*) Fruit of disagreeable odor and harsh taste, much like a gourd. *Cf.* GUAJE.

guirre [geer'-ray], *m.* Vulture (islas Canarias).

guisado [gee-sah'-do], *m.* 1. A stew, or made dish; ragout, fricassee. 2. (*Met. Coll.*) Action or deed performed under very remarkable circumstances.

guisador, ra [gee-sah-dor', rah], *m. & f. V.* GUISANDERO.

guisandero, ra [gee-san-day'-ro, rah], *m. & f.* A cook.

guisantal [gee-san-tahl'], *m.* A pea patch; ground planted with peas.

guisante [gee-sahn'-tay], *m.* (*Bot.*) Pea. **Guisante de olor** or **oloroso,** sweet pea, lathyrus.

guisar [gee-sar'], *va.* 1. To cook or dress victuals; to cure meat. 2. (*Met.*) To arrange, to adjust.

guiso [gee'-so], *m.* The seasoning of a dish (aliño); sauce of meat, or any other victuals; condiment.

guisopillo [gee-so-peel'lyo], *m. V.* HISOPILLO.

guisote [gee-so'-tay], *m.* Dish of meat dressed country fashion.

guita [gee'-tah], *f.* Pack-thread, a small hempen cord.

guitar [gee-tar'], *va.* To sew with pack-thread.

guitarra [gee-tar'-rah], *f.* 1. Guitar, a stringed musical instrument played with the fingers (instrumento). 2. Pounder, a pestle for pounding gypsum or whiting. **Ser buena guitarra,** (*Met. Coll.*) to be very artful and cunning.

guitarrear [gee-tar-ray-ar'], *vn.* To play the guitar.

guitarrero, ra [gee-tar-ray'-ro, rah], *m. & f.* 1. Guitar maker. 2. Player of the guitar.

guitarresco, ca [gee-tar-res'-co, cah], *a.* (*Joc.*) Belonging to the guitar.

guitarrista [gee-tar-rees'-tah], *m.* Player of the guitar, guitarist.

guitarrón [gee-tar-rone'], *m.* 1. (*aug.*) A large guitar. 2. (*coll.*) An acute knave.

guito, ta [gee'-to, tah], *a.* Treacherous, vicious (mula).

guitón, na [gee-tone', nah], *m. & f.* Mendicant, vagrant, vagabond.

guitonazo [gee-to-nah'-tho], *m. aug.* A great vagabond.

guitonear [gee-to-nay-ar'], *vn.* To loiter or idle about, to lead a vagabond life; to tramp it.

guitonería [gee-to-nay-ree'-ah], *f.* Idleness; a vagrant or vagabond life.

guizgar [geeth-gar'], *va.* To excite, to invite.

guizque [geeth'-kay], *m.* 1. (*Prov.*) Hook of a hanging lamp. 2. (*Prov.*) Sting of a wasp.

guja [goo'-hah], *f.* Arm used by archers.

gula [goo'-lah], *f.* Gluttony, inordinate desire of eating, and drinking.

gulchenita [gool-chay-nee'-tah], *a. & n.* A member of one of the Muslim monastic orders.

gules [goo'-les], *m. pl.* (*Her.*) Gules, red.

guloso, sa [goo-lo'-so, sah], *a.* Gluttonous, greedy.

gulusmear [gool-loos-may-ar'], *vn.* (*coll.*) *V.* GOLOSINEAR.

gullería [gool-lyay-ree'-ah], *f.* Dainty.

gulloría [gool-lyo-ree'-ah], *f.* 1. (*Orn.*) A kind of lark. 2. *V.* GOLLERÍA.

gúmena [goo'-may-nah], *f.* Cable.

gumeneta [goo-may-nay'-tah], *f. dim.* A small cable.

gumía [goo-mee'-ah], *f.* Kind of dagger or poniard.

gumífero, ra [goo-mee'-fay-ro, rah], *a.* Gum-producing, gummiferous.

gur [goor], *m.* A white cotton fabric which comes from India.

gurbión [goor-be-on'], *m.* 1. Twisted silk, of a coarse quality. 2. Silk stuff resembling grogram. 3. Gumresin extracted from the officinal spurge.

gurbionado, da [goor-be-o-nah'-do, dah], *a.* Made of twisted coarse silk.

gurrar [goor-rar'], *vn.* 1. (*Naut.*) To get clear of another ship. 2. To retrograde, to fall back.

gurrufero [goor-roo-fay'-ro], *m.* A deformed nag or horse.

gurrumina [goor-roo-mee'-nah], *f.* (*coll.*) Uxoriousness, unbecoming submission to a wife.

gurrumino [goor-roo-mee'-no], *m.* (*coll.*) Indulgent husband.

gurullada [goo-rool-lyah'-dah], *f.* 1. A crowd of people (multitud). 2. Crowd of constables or police officers.

gurullo [goo-rool'-lyo], *m.* Lump or knot. *V.* BURUJO.

gurullón [goo-rool-lyone'], *m.* A knot of wool in cloths.

gurumete [goo-roo-may'-tay], *m.* Ship's boy. *V.* GRUMETE.

gurupa [goo-roo'-pah], *f.* Croup of horse. *V.* GRUPA.

gurupera [goo-roo-pay'-rah], *f.* Crupper. *V.* GRUPERA.

gurupetín [goo-roo-pay-teen'], *m. dim.* A small crupper.

gurvio, a [goor'-ve-o, ah], *a.* Curved, arched, incurvated.

gusanear [goo-sah-nay-ar'], *vn.* To itch. *V.* HORMIGUEAR.

gusanera [goo-sah-nay'-rah], *f.* 1. Place or spot where maggots or vermin are bred. 2. (*Met.*) The passion which reigns most in the mind.

gusanico, ito [goo-sah-nee'-co, ee'-to], *m. dim.* A small worm or maggot.

gusaniento, ta [goo-sah-ne-en'-to, tah], *a.* Troubled with maggots or vermin, maggoty, worm-eaten.

gusanillo [goo-sah-neel'-lyo], *m.* 1. (*Dim.*) A small worm or maggot. 2. A kind of embroidery. 3. Bit of a gimlet or auger. **Me anda el gusanillo,** I feel peckish. **Matar el gusanillo,** to have a snack.

gusano [goo-sah'-no], *m.* Maggot, worm, grub, caterpillar (mariposa, polilla). 2. A meek person. 3. Distemper among sheep. **Gusano de seda,** silkworm. **Gusano de luz,** *V.* LUCIÉRNAGA. **Matar el gusano,** to have a drink (beber).

gusanoso, sa [goo-sah-no'-so], *a. V.* GUSANIENTO.

gusarapa [goo-sah-rah'-pah], . (*Prov.*) *V.* GUSARAPO.

gusarapiento, ta [goo-sah-rah-peen'-to, tah], *a.* Wormy, corrupted.

gusarapillo, ito [goo-sah-rah-peel'-lyo, ee'-to], *m. dim.* A small water-worm.

gusarapo [goo-sah-rah'-po], *m.* Water-worm, an aquatic insect.

gusil [goo-seel'], *m.* A kind of harp of horizontal strings in use among the Russians.

gustable [goos-tah'-blay], *a.* 1. Tastable, capable of being tasted or relished. 2. *V.* GUSTOSO.

gustadura [goos-tah-doo'-rah], *f.* Gustation, tasting.

gustar [goos-tar'], *va.* 1. To taste. 2. To perceive by the taste. -*vn.* 3. To like, to love. 4. To enjoy a thing. **Gustar de,** to like to. 5. To experience, to examine. 6. To take pleasure or delight in a thing, to be pleased with. **La comedia no gustó,** the play was not a success. 7. **Me gusta el té,** I like tea. **No le gusta que le llamen Pepe,** he doesn´t like to be called Joe. **Me gusta como anda,** I like the way she walks.

gustativo [goos-tah-tee'-vo], *a.* Lingual: applied to a branch of the inferior maxillary nerve.

gustazo [goos-tah'-tho], *m. aug.* A great pleasure; unhealthy pleasure (malsano), nasty pleasure.

gustillo [goos-teel'-lyo], *m.* 1. Relish. 2. (*Dim.*) Agreeable, delicate taste.

gusto [goos'-to], *m.* 1. Taste, the sense of tasting (sentido). 2. The sensation of tasting (sabor). 3. Pleasure (placer), delight, gratification, complacence, contentment. 4. Liking (agrado). 5. One's own will and determination. 6. Election, choice. 7. Taste, intellectual relish or discernment. 8. Caprice, fancy (antojo), diversion. **Por dar gusto a,** for the sake or gratification of, to please. **Gustos**, sensual pleasures; evil habits; vices. **Dar gusto**, to gratify. **Tiene un gusto amargo**, it has a bitter taste. **Mal gusto**, bad taste. **Para mi gusto**, to my taste. **Tiene gusto para vestir**, she dresses elegantly. **Con mucho gusto**, with pleasure. **Estar a gusto**, to be at ease. **Tener gusto en**, to be glad to. **El gusto es mío**, how do you do? **Tengo mucho gusto en conocerle**, I´m pleased to meet you. **Tomar gusto a**, to take a liking to.

gustosamente [goos-to'-sah-men-tay], *adv.* Tastefully, gladly, acceptably.

gustoso, sa [goos-to´-so, sah], *a.* 1. Gustable, dainty, pleasing to the taste. 2. Tasty (sabroso). 3. Cheerful, merry, content, joyful. 4. Pleasing, pleasant (agradable), entertaining. **Lo hizo gustoso**, he did it gladly.

gutagamba, gutiámbar [goo-tah-gahm'-bah, goo-te-ahm'-bar], *m.* Gamboge. *(Malay.)*

gutapercha [goo-tah-perr'-chah], *f.* 1. Guttapercha. 2. Caoutchouc, Indian-rubber.

gutífero, ra [goo-tee'-fay-ro, rah], *a.* Guttiferous, gum-yielding.

gutiforme [goo-te-for'-may], *a.* In the shape of a drop.

gutural [goo-too-rahl'], *a.* 1. Guttural, pronounced in the throat. 2. Guttural, belonging to the throat.

guturalmente [goo-too-ral-men'-tay], *adv.* Gutturally.

guturoso, sa [goo-too-ro'-so, sah], *a.* 1. *(Bot.)* Throated (musgo). 2. *(Zool.)* Throaty, having a large or capacious throat. 3. Pouter pigeon, vulgarly called *buchona.*

guzla [gooth'-lah], *f.* 1. A soft, harmonious musical instrument among the Greeks and the Asiatics. 2. A fiddle with a single string.

guzmán [gooth-mahn'], *m.* Nobleman who formerly served as midshipman in the navy or cadet in the army.

H

h [ah'-chay], *f.* eighth letter of the Castilian alphabet, is now treated as a mere aspiration. The moderns use *h* to soften the pronunciation of many words, as *facer, fijo,* are now written **hacer, hijo**. For the same purpose it is placed before *u*, followed by *e*, in many words derived from the Latin; as **huevo**, from ovum, an egg; **hueso**, from *os*. The *h* is never sounded in the Spanish language except by the people in Andalusia, Extremadura, and the former Spanish possessions in America. The words in which *h* was preceded by a *p*, and took the sound of *f*, are now written as pronounced, thus: *fenómeno*, phenomenon. After *r* and *t* the *h* is entirely omitted, as in, *reuma*, rheum, *teatro*, theater; but it is retained, but not aspirated, in all words which originally began with *h*, or between two vowels, as **honor, almohaza**. Symbol of hydrogen.

¡ha! [ah], *int.* 1. Ha! 2. Ah, alas! 3. *(Naut.)* Haul away!

haba [ah'-bah], *f.* 1. *(Bot.)* Bean, a kind of pulse, bean (de café) **Haba común**, garden beach vetch. **Haba de soja**, soy bean. **En todas partes cuecen habas**, it´s the same the whole world over.

habanero, ra [ah-bah-nay'-ro, rah], *a.* Havanese, of Havana.

habano, na [ah-bah -no, nah], *a.* Applied to Havana tobacco.

habar [ah-bar'], *m.* Bean field.

habascón [ah-bas-cone'], *m.* A kind of root, like parsnip, in use as a food in most South American towns.

Habeas corpus [ah'-bay-as cor'-poo], *m. (for.)* Habeas corpus.

habenaria [ah-bay-nah´-re-ah], *f.* Habenaria, rein-orchid, a large genus of American orchids.

haber [ah-berr'], *va.* 1. To possess (tener). 2. To have, an auxiliary verb (tiempos compuestos). 3. To take, to recover. 4. To happen, to fall out, to befall. 5. To exist. *-v. impers.* V.

ACAECER. Tomará lo que haya, he´ll take whatever there is. *-vr.* To behave, to act, to conduct oneself; to become, to pretend, to feign. **Hay**, there is, there are. **Había, hubo**, there was, there were. So also with other tenses. **Ha**, it is, since, ago. **Ha más de que**, it is more than since. **Haber que**, to be to. **Hay que**, it is necessary. **No hay de que**, you are welcome; don't mention it. **No haber más que pedir**, it leaves nothing to be desired. **Lo hubiéramos hecho**, we would have done it. **Ha de haberse perdido**, it must have got lost. **No hay plátanos**, there are no bananas. **Hay que trabajar**, one has to work. **Hay que hacerlo**, it has to be done. **Hay que ser fuertes**, we must be strong. **Habérselas con uno**, to be up against somebody.

haber [ah-berr'], *m.* Property, income (ingresos), fortune, assets, credit side (balance). **Pasar algo al haber de uno**, to credit something to somebody. **Haberes**, assets.

habichuela [ah-be-choo-ay'-lah], *f. (Bot.)* French bean or kidney bean. **Habichuela común**, common kidney bean. **Habichuela multiflora**, scarlet bean. **Ganarse las habichuelas**, to earn one´s living.

hábil [ah'-beel], *a.* 1. Clever (listo), skillful (diestro), dexterous, expert, knowing, cunning. 2. Capable, intelligent, learned, able to understand. 3. Agile, active, ready. 4. Apt, fit, handy, able (capaz), qualified for.

habilidad [ah-be-le-dahd'], *f.* 1. Ability (capacidad), skill, dexterity in performing. **Hombre de gran habilidad política**, a man of great political skill. 2. Cleverness, expertness (destreza), mastery, knowledge, talent; cunning. 3. Nimbleness, quickness, speed. 4. Instinct. *-pl.* Accomplishments.

habilidoso, sa [ah-be-le-do'-so, sah], *a. (Andal. and Amer. coll.)* Accomplished.

habilitación [ah-be-le-tah-the-on'], *f.* 1. Habilitation, qualification (título). 2. Fitting out, equipment (de casa).

habilitado, da [ah-be-le-tah'-do, dah], *a. & pp.* of HABILITAR. Habilitate, qualified.

habilitado [ah-be-le-tah'-do], *m.* An officer in every Spanish regiment charged with the agency of his regiment, a paymaster.

habilitador, ra [ah-be-le-tah-dor', rah], *m. & f.* Qualifier, one who makes fit or able.

habilitar [ah-be-le-tar'], *va.* 1. To qualify, to enable (permitir). 2. To provide, to supply. 3. To fit out, to equip (casa), to furnish means. 4. To finance.

hábilmente [ah'-beel-men-tay], *adv.* Dexterously, ably, knowingly, cleverly.

habitable [ah-be-tah'-blay], *a.* Habitable, lodgeable.

habitación [ah-be-tah-the-on'], *f.* 1. Habitation (vivienda), abode, lodging (alquilado). 2. Set of rooms (cuartos), that part of a house intended to be inhabited. **Habitación de matrimonio**, double room. **Habitación individual**, single room.

habitáculo [ah-be-tah'-coo-lo], *m. (coll.)* A cramped, inconvenient dwelling.

habitado [ah-be-tah-do], *a.* Inhabited; live-in; manned (satélite), carrying a crew.

habitador, ra [ah-be-tah-dor', rah], *m & f.* Inhabitant, resident, dweller; abider.

habitante [ah-be-tahn'-tay], *pa.* Inhabiting. *-m. & f.* Inhabitant or habitant, dweller, resident (vecino), occupant (inquilino). **Una ciudad de 10.000 habitantes**, a town of 10.000 inhabitants.

habitar [ah-be-tar'], *va.* To inhabit, to live, to reside, to lodge or lie in a place.

habitico, illo, ito [ah-be-tee'-co], *m. dim.* A small dress or habit.

hábito [ah'-be-to], *m.* 1. Dress, habit, habiliment, garment. **Hábitos**, dress of ecclesiastics. 2. Habit, habitude, custom, customariness. **Tener el hábito de**, to be in the habit of. 3. The robes of the military orders. **Colgar los hábitos**, *(coll.)* To throw off the cowl.

habituación [ah-be-too-ah-the-on'], *f.* Habitude, custom.

habitual [ah-be-too-ahl'], *a.* Habitual, accustomed, inveterate, customary, common, frequent, regular (cliente, lector), incorrigible (mentiroso), besetting (pecado). **Su restaurante habitual,** one´s usual restaurant.

habitualmente [ah-be-too-al-men'-tay], *adv.* Habitually, customarily, by habit.

habituar [ah-be-too-ar'], *va.* To accustom, to habituate, to inure. -*vr.* To become accustomed, to accustom oneself.

habitud [ah-be-tood'], *f.* Habitude, the respect or relation which one thing bears to another.

habla [ah'-blah], *f.* 1. Speech (facultad), idiom, language (nacional) 2. Discourse, argument. 3. Talk (acto), conversation. **Estar sin habla** or **perder el habla,** to be speechless. **Negar** or **quitar el habla,** to refuse to speak to a person. **Ponerse al habla,** 1. To come within speaking distance (entre barcos). 2. *(coll.)* To talk with anyone by means of the telephone.

hablado [ah-blah'-do], *ptp.* de **hablar,** spoken. **El lenguaje hablado,** the spoken language. -*a.* **Bien hablado,** nicely-spoken.

hablador, ra [ah-blah-dor', rah], *m.* & *f.* An impudent prattler, a trifling talker, a gabbler, a prattler, a chattering fellow (parlanchín).

habladorcillo, lla [ah-blah-dor-theel'-lyo, lyah], *m.* & *f. dim.* A babbling dandiprat.

habladuría [ah-blah-doo-ree'-ah], *f.* An impertinent speech, rumor (rumor); nasty remark (injuria), sarcastic remark, idle chatter (chisme), piece of gossip.

hablantín, na, hablanchín, na [ah-blan-teen', nah, ah-blan-cheen', nah], *a. (coll.)* A talkative person.

hablar [ah-blar'], *va.* 1. To speak (lengua), to express thoughts by words. 2. To talk, to answer, to speak in conversation, to commune, to reason, to converse. 3. To harangue, to address, to make a speech. 4. To advise, to admonish. **Hablar disparates** or **necedades,** to talk nonsense. **Hablar alto,** to talk loud. **Hablar en plata,** to speak clearly, without ambiguity. **Hablar por hablar,** to talk for the sake of talking. **Hablar entre dientes,** to mutter, to mumble. **Hablar de la mar,** to talk on an endless subject. **Hablar de memoria,** to talk without reflection, without knowledge of the matter. **No dejar que hablar,** to convince anyone, to impose silence. **Hablar de veras,** to speak in earnest. **No hablarse,** not to speak to each other, from enmity or aversion. **Habla bien el portugués,** he speaks good Portuguese. **Y no hay más que hablar,** so there´s no more to be said about it. **Hablar claro,** to speak plainly. **Dar que hablar a la gente,** to make people talk. **Se habla de que van a comprarlo,** there is talk of their buying it. **No se hablan,** they are not on speaking terms.

hablatista [ah-blah-tees'-tah], *m. (Joc.)* A trifling prattler, an idle talker.

hablilla [ah-bleel'-lyah], *f.* 1. Rumor, report, little tale. 2. Bubbling, a foolish talk.

hablista [ah-blees'-tah], *m.* A person who speaks or writes with great correctness.

habón [ah-bone'], *m. aug.* Large kind of bean.

habrotamno [ah-bro-tahm'-no], *m.* Habrothamnus, a solanaceous shrub, native of Mexico.

haca [ah'-cah], *f.* Pony, pad, a small horse. **¿Qué haca?** or **¿qué haca morena?,** for what good? to what purpose?

hacán [ah-cahn'], *m.* A learned man among the Jews.

hacanea [ah-cah-nay'-ah], *f.* Nag, a small horse somewhat bigger than a pony.

hacecico, illo, ito [ah-thay-thee'-co], *m. dim.* A small sheaf.

hacedero, ra [ah-thay-day'-ro, rah], *a.* Feasible, practicable; easily effected.

hacedor, ra [ah-thay-dor', rah], *m.* & *f.* 1. Maker, author; factor. 2. Steward, one who manages the estate of another. 3. A good workman, an able performer.

hacendado [ah-then-dah-do], *m.* A land-holder, a farmer.

hacendado, da [ah-then-dah'-do, dah], *a.* & *pp.* of HACENDAR. 1. Acred, landed, having a fortune in land, having a real property. 2. Rich.

hacendar [ah-then-dar'], *va.* To transfer or make over the property of an estate.-*vr.* To make a purchase of land in order to settle in a place.

hacendeja [ah-then-day'-hah], *f. dim.* A small farm.

hacendera [ah-then-day'-rah], *f.* Public work, at which all the neighborhood assists.

hacendero, ra [ah-then-day'-ro, rah], *a.* Industrious, laborious.

hacendilla, hacenduela [ah-then-deel'-lyah, ah-then-doo-ay'-lah], *f. dim.* 1. A small farm. 2. A trifling work.

hacendoso, sa [ah-then-do'-so, sah], *a.* Assiduous, diligent, industrious (trabajador), busy (ocupado).

hacer [ah-therr'], *va.* & *vn.* 1. To make, to form, to produce. 2. To do, to practice, to act something good or bad, to make, to perform (realizar). 3. To put in execution, to carry into effect; to effect. 4. To make, to cause to have any quality, to bring into any new state or condition, to prepare (preparar), to dispose, to compose. 5. To make up a number, to complete. 6. To make, to raise as profit from something, to gain (ganar). 7. To make, to turn to some use. 8. To habituate, to accustom (acostumbrar). 9. To give, to grant. 10. To include, to contain (incluir). 11. To cause (causar), to occasion. 12. To resolve, to determine, to judge, to consider. 13. To assemble, to convoke: to correspond. 14. To make, to compel, to force, to constrain, to oblige (obligar): in this sense it is followed by an infinitive verb. **Hacer venir,** to oblige to come. 15. To dress: applied to hawks or cocks for fighting. -*vn.* 16. To grow, to increase or receive anything. 17. To matter, to import (importar). 18. To be, to exist. **Hace frío,** it is cold. 19. To accord, to agree, to fit, to answer, to suit. 20. Joined with the particle *a,* it signifies to be ready or disposed. **Hacer a todo,** to be ready or disposed to do anything. 21. Joined with the particle *de,* and the names of offices or professions, it signifies to perform their duties. **Hacer de escribano,** to act as scrivener or notary. **Hacer de portero,** to act as a porter. 22. Joined with *de, se, el, la, lo,* it signifies to represent, to counterfeit, or to show what is not in reality. **Hacer de bobo,** to counterfeit an idiot. 23. With *por* or *para,* joined to an infinitive verb, it signifies taking pains and care in executing the import of such verb. **Hacer por llegar,** to endeavor to arrive. **Hacer para** or **por salvarse,** to strive to save oneself. 24. Followed by substantives it gives them a verbal signification. **Hacer estimación,** to esteem. **Hacer pensar,** to put in mind, to give cause to suspect. **Hacer avergonzar,** to put one to the blush, to frown anyone down. **Hacer bajar los ojos,** to make one abashed. **Hacer bajar las orejas,** to humble anyone. **Hacer de capitán,** to personate or act the captain. **Haz por venir,** try to come. **Hacer cuerpo presente,** to attend a meeting without taking part in it. **Hacer a uno con alguna cosa,** *(coll.)* to procure a thing for anyone. **No hacer alto,** to overlook, not to mind. **No hagas caso,** never mind. **Hacer el papel,** to personate or act the part of another person. **Hacer la vista gorda,** to wink at, to connive at. **Hacer alarde,** to muster; to boast of. **Hacer aire,** to blow: speaking of the wind. **Hacer alguna cosa a la moda,** to fashion. **Hacer a uno perder los estribos,** to make anyone lose his temper: literally, to make a man lose his stirrups. **Hacer bancarrota,** to fail, to break, to become bankrupt. **Hacer caso de,** to pay attention to, to mind, to care. **Hacer cara,** to make head against, to face, to resist. **Hacer de tripas corazón,** to pluck up courage, to bluster and show much boldness when one is afraid, to pluck up heart. **Hacer de figura** or **hacer figura,** to make a figure or cut a figure. **Hacer fermentar,** to heat. **Hacer frente a,** to make head against, to face, to resist. **Hacer fiesta,** to take a day off. **Hacer fiestas,** to fondle, to endear, to flatter, to cajole, to fawn. **Hacer gasto,** to spend. **Hacer humo,** 1. To smoke. 2. *(Met.)* To continue long in a place. **Hacer opinión,** to form an opinion, to be an authority. **Hace ocho días,** eight days ago. So with other phrases of time. **Hacer juego**, to be well matched. **Hacer la comida**, to dress the dinner. **Hacer limosna**, to give alms. **Hacer las amistades**, to make it up. **Hacer mal de ojo**, *(coll.)* to fascinate. **Hacer memoria**, to recollect, to remember. **Hacer milagros**, to do wonders. **Hacer niebla**, to haze. **Hacer un papel**, to act a part; to make or to cut a figure; to acquit oneself well. **Hacer por**, to try, to do one's best. **Hacer progresos**, to gain ground, to improve. **Hacer pedazos**, to pull to pieces. **Hacer pucheros**, to make wry faces, as children do before they begin to cry. **Hacer pie**, to find the bottom of water without swimming; to be firm and secure in anything; to stop, to reside in a place. **Hacer que hacemos**, to act officially, to affect doing some business, to fidget about for no purpose. **Hacer saber**, to acquaint, to make known. **Hacer sombra**, *(Met.)* to protect, to support; to impede, to obscure. **Hacer su agosto**, to make hay while the sun shines: literally, to make one's harvest. **Hacer ventaja**, to exceed, to surpass. **No hay que hacer** or **eso no tiene que hacer**, it is only to act, it is easily done. **Hacer que**, to feign, to pretend, to affect. **Hágame Vd. el favor**, pray. **Haga buen o mal tiempo**, rain or shine. **Hacer el pelo a una**, to do somebody´s hair. **El árbol hace sombra**, the tree gives shade. **No sé que hacer**, I don´t know what to do. **La ha hecho buena**, a fine mess he´s made of it. **Él protestó y yo hice lo mismo**, he protested and I did the same. **Hacer el cuerpo al frío**, to inure the body to cold. **Les hice venir**, I made them come. **Me lo hizo saber**, he told me it. **Éste hace 100**, this one makes 100. **Hacer el tonto**, to act the fool. **Dar que hacer**, to cause trouble. **Está perdido desde hace 15 días**, it´s been lost for a fortnight. **Hace poco**, a short while back. **Hacer "clic"**, *(Inform.)* to clic.

hacerse [ah-therr´-say], *vr.* 1. To recede, to separate. 2. To become, to enter into some new state or condition (llegar a scr). 3. To accustom oneself (acostumbrarse). **Hacerse de miel**, to treat one gently, not to be very severe. **Hacerse con algo** or **de algo**, to acquire, to attain; to purchase anything which is wanting. **Hacerse lugar**, to gain a name or reputation. **Hacerse memorable**, to become memorable, famous, notorious, etc. **Hacerse añicos**, to take great pains in doing anything. **Hacerse chiquito**, to pretend to be modest; to conceal one's knowledge. **Se hace de noche**, night falls. **Hacerse con una cosa**, to obtain a thing rightly or wrongly. **Se hará de ladrillos**, it will be built of brick. **Todavía no se ha hecho**, it still has not been done. **Hacer cortesías** (mutuamente), to exchange courtesies. **Hacerse un retrato**, to have one´s portrait painted. **Hacerse enfermera**, to become a nurse. **Hacerse el sueco**, to pretend not to hear. **Esto se hace pesado**, this is becoming tedious. **Hacerse grande**, to grow tall, to get tall. **Se me hace imposible trabajar**, it´s becoming impossible for me to work. **Hacerse a una idea**, to get used to an idea. **Hacerse con algo**, to get hold of something. **Logró hacerse con una copia**, he managed to get hold of a copy. **Hacerse a un lado**, to stand aside.

hacia [ah´-the-ah], *adv.* 1. Towards (lugar), in a direction to, near to, about (cerca). **Hacia adelante**, forward. **Hacia acá or hacia esta parte**, hitherward, hitherwards. **Hacia dónde**, whither, toward which, to what place, to where. **Hacia casa, hacia su país**, homeward, homewards. 2. About (tiempo). **Hacia mediodía**, about noon. 3. Towards (actitud). **Su hostilidad hacia la idea**, his hostility towards the idea.

hacienda [ah-the-en´-dah], *f.* 1. Landed property (finca), lands, tenements. 2. Estate, fortune, wealth (fortuna). 3. Farm. 4. Domestic work done by the servants of the house. **Ministro de hacienda** (en España), and **Secretario de hacienda** (en S. América), the Secretary of the Treasury, or Chancellor of the Exchequer. **Hacienda pública**, public treasury, finances.

hacina [ah-thee´-nah], *f.* 1. Stack or rick of corn piled up in sheaves. 2. Any collection of things placed one over another.

hacinador, ra [ah-the-nah-dor´, rah], *m. & f.* Stack-maker, one who piles up the sheaves of corn. **Hacinador de riquezas**, hoarder of riches.

hacinamiento [ah-the-nah-me-en´-to], *m.* 1. Accumulation, act of heaping or hoarding up. 2. Acervation, coacervation, heaping together.

hacinar [ah-the-nar´], *va.* 1. To stack or pile up sheaves of corn. 2. To hoard (ahorrar), to make hoards. 3. To accumulate (acumular); to coacervate.

hacino, na [ah-thee´-no, nah], *a.* V. AVARO and TRISTE.

hacha [ah´-chah], *f.* 1. A large taper with four wicks. 2. An axe or hatchet. **Hacha de armas**, battleaxe. 3. Ancient Spanish dance. 4. *(Fig.)* Genius. **Es un hacha para el bridge**, he´s a genius at bridge.

hachazo [ah-chah´-tho], *m.* Blow or stroke with an axe (golpe).

hache [ah´-chay], *f.* Name of the letter H.

hachear [ah-chay-ar´], *va.* To cut with an axe; to hew. *-vn.* To strike with an axe.

hachero [ah-chay´-ro], *m.* 1. Torch stand, a large candle-stick for tapers or torches. 2. *(Mil.)* V. GASTADOR. 3. Wood-cleaver or wood-cutter; a laborer employed to fell wood and cut timber. 4. *(Prov.)* Carpenter.

hacheta [ah-chay´-tah], *f. dim.* 1. A small hatchet. 2. A small torch or link.

hachis [ah-chees´], *m.* Hashish.

hacho [ah´-cho], *m.* Fagot, or bundle of straw or feather grass, covered with pitch or resin.

hachón [ah-chone´], *m.* 1. A large torch made of bass and pitch. 2. Kind of altar, on which bonfires are lighted for illuminations.

hachuela [ah-choo-ay´-lah], *f. dim.* A small hatchet or axe. **Hachuela de abordar**, *(Naut.)* boarding axe.

hada [ah´-dah], *f.* Fairy. **Cuento de hadas**, fairy tale. **Hada encantada**, enchanted fairy.

hadado, da [ah-dah´-do, dah], *a. & pp.* of HADAR. Fortunate, lucky.

hado [ah´-do], *m.* Fate, destiny, inevitable doom.

hagiógrafo [ah-he-o´-grah-fo], *m.* Hagiographer, a writer of lives of the saints.

haitiano, na [ah-e-te-ah´-no, nah], *a.* Haitian (de Haiti).

haje [ah´-hay], *f.* The African cobra or asp: it has the power of inflating the neck.

halacabullas, halacuerdas [ah-lah-cah-bool´-lyas, ah-lah-coo-err´-das], *m.* *(coll.)* Fresh-water sailors.

halagador, ra [ah-lah-gah-dor´, rah], *m. & f.* Cajoler, flatterer.

halagar [ah-lah-gar´], *va.* To cajole, to flatter (lisonjear); to caress, to dandle, coax, to coy, to allure, to make much of, to wheedle, to hug, to fondle, to treat with tenderness (mostrar afecto).

halago [ah-lah´-go], *m.* Cajolery, flattery, caress, adulation, cooing, pleasure, delight.

halagüeñamente [ah-lah-goo-ay´-nyah-men´-tay], *adv.* Endearingly, fatteringly.

halagüeño, ña [ah-lah-goo-ay´-nyo, nyah], *a.* Endearing, attractive, alluring (atrayente), fawning, flattering (opinión, observación), meek, gentle.

halar [ah-lar´], *va.* *(Naut.)* To haul, to pull by a rope. **Halar al viento**, to haul the wind.

halcón [al-cone´], *m.* *(Orn.)* Falcon, a hawk trained for sport. **Halcón común**, peregrine. **Los halcones y las palomas**, the hawks and the doves.

halconado, da [al-co-nah´-do, dah], *a.* Falcon or hawk-like.

halconcico, illo, ito [al-con-thee´-co, eel´-lyo, ee´-to], *m. dim.* Jashawk, a young falcon or hawk.

halconear [al-co-nay-ar´], *va.* *(coll.)* To look and inveigle (mujeres de ciudad).

halconera [al-co-nay´-rah], *f.* Place where falcons are kept.

halconería [al-co-nay-ree´-ah], *f.* Falconry.

halconero [al-co-nay´-ro], *m.* Falconer, one who rears or trains hawks for sport.

halda [ahl'-dah], *f.* 1. Bag or sack made of sack-cloth (arpillera). 2. Skirt of a garment (falda). **Haldas en cinta**, *(coll.)* disposed and ready for anything.

haldear [al-day-ar'], *vn.* To run along with the skirts flying loose.

haldica, illa, ita [al-dee'-cah], *f. dim.* A small skirt.

haldudo, da [al-doo'-do, dah], *a.* Having flying skirts.

haleche [ah-lay'-chay], *m.* Horse-mackerel, a kind of mackerel. *V.* ESCOMBRO.

halía [ah-lee'-ah], *f.* 1. *(Bot.)* A papilionaceous plant of the Cape of Good Hope. 2. *(Ent.)* An European moth. 3. A nereid, a sea-nymph.

haliéntica [ah-le-en'-te-cah], *f.* Angling, the art of fishing.

haliéntico, ca [ah-le-en'-te-co, cah], *a.* Angling, belonging to the art of angling.

halieto [ah-le-ay'-to], *m.* Sea-eagle.

halinatrón [ah-le-nah-tron'], *m.* Native soda.

haliquedón [ah-le-kay-don'], *a.* Like the sea-swallows.

hálito [ah'-le-to], *m..* 1. The breath (aliento). 2. Vapor (vapor). 3. *(Poet.)* Soft air.

hall [hall], *m.* Hall (teatro) foyer, lounge (hotel).

hallado, da [ah-lyah'-do, dah], *a.* Found. **Bien hallado**, very familiar, welcome, easy, contented. **Mal hallado**, uneasy, not at ease, conetrained.-*pp.* of HALLAR.

hallador, ra [al-lyah-dor', rah], *m. & f.* Finder, discoverer.

hallar [ahl-lyar'], *va.* 1. To find, to obtain by searching or seeking, to locate (localizar). 2. To find, to hit on, to hit upon by chance, to perceive by accident. 3. To find, to meet with, to fall upon. 4. To find out (averiguar), to discover (descubrir). 5. To find, to gain by any mental endeavor, to invent, to excogitate. 6. To find, to remark, to observe, to note, to compare, to verify. 7. To find, to discover something hidden. 8. To find, to detect, to catch, to understand, to comprehend . 9. To manifest, to show anything unexpected.-*vr.* 1. To meet occasionally in any place, to light, to happen to find, to fall upon by chance. 2. To be content or pleased in any place. 3. To be somewhere. 4. To find oneself, to be, to fare with regard to ease or pain. **Se hallaba fuera**, he was away at the time. **Se halla sin dinero**, he has no money. **Hallarse enfermo**, to be ill. **Hallarse con un nuevo obstáculo**, to encounter an obstacle.

hallazgo [al-lyath'-go], *m.* 1. The act of finding or recovering anything lost. 2. Reward given for finding anything lost (premio). 3. Thing found (cosa).

hallulla [al-lyool'-lyah], *f.* 1. A kind of paste made and used to feed fowls. 2. *V.* HALLULLO.

hallullo [al-lyool'-lyo], *m.* Cake baked on or under cinders.

halo, halón [ah'-lo, ah-lone'], *m. (Ast.)* Halo, a red circle round the sun or moon.

halodendro, dra [ah-lo-den'-dro, drah], *a. (Bot.)* Growing in earth impregnated with salts.

halógeno, na [ah-lo'-hay-no, nah], *a. (Chem.)* Halogen, producing saline compounds.

halografía [ah-lo-grah-fee'-ah], *f. (Chem.)* The section of chemistry which deals with salts, halography.

halomancia [ah-lo-mahn'-the-ah], *f.* Halomancy, divination with salt.

haloquimia [ah-lo-kee'-me-ah], *f.* The branch of chemistry which treats of salts and their properties.

haloza [ah-loh'-thah], *f.* Wooden shoe.

haltera [al-tay'-rah], *f.* Barbell, dumbbell.

halterofilia [al-tay-ro-fee'-lyah], *f.* Weight lifting.

halurgia [ah-loor'-he-ah], *f.* Preparation of salts and the art of preparing them.

hamaca [ah-mah'-cah], *f.* Hammock, a kind of suspended bed.

hamaquero [ah-mah-kay'-ro], *m.* Person who carries a hammock.

hamano [ah-mah'-no], *m.* A kind of pink cotton stuff from the Levant.

hambre [ahm'-bray], *f.* 1. Hunger, appetite; the pain felt from fasting. **Tener hambre**, to be hungry, to have an appetite. 2. Scarcity of provisions, famine (de población entera). 3. Greediness, eagerness of appetite or desire. **Muerto de hambre**, starved with hunger. **Vengo con mucha hambre**, I'm terribly hungry. **Hambre canina**, ravenous hunger.

hambrear [am-bray-ar'], *vn.* To hunger, to be hungry. *-va.* 1. To hunger, to cause hunger. 2. To starve, to famish, to kill with hunger, to subdue by famine.

hambrientamente [am-bre-en-tah-men'-tay], *adv.* Hungrily.

hambriento, ta [am-bre-en'-to, tah], *a.* 1. Hungry, starved, greedy, ravenous. 2. Greedy, eager, vehemently desirous.

hambrón, na [am-brone', nah], *m. & f. (coll.)* A hungry person, one who is often hungry.

hamburguesa [am-boor-gay'-sah], *f.* Hamburger.

hampa [ahm'-pah], *f.* 1. Underworld. **El hampa de Chicago**, the Chicago underworld.

hampesco, ca [am-pes'-co, cah], *a.* Vagabond, villainous, vainglorious.

hampo, hampón [ahm'-po, am-pone'], *a.* Bold, valiant, licentious.

hanega [ah-nay'-gah], *f.* A dry measure. *V.* FANEGA.

hanegada [ah'-nay-gah'-dah], *f.* Quantity of land sown with a *fanega* of corn.

hangar [an-gar'], *m. (Aer.)* Hangar.

hanguilla [an-keel'-lyah], *f.* A kind of boat.

hao [ah'-o], *m.* Noise.

haquilla, ita [ah-keel'-lyah, ee'-tah], *f. dim.* Very little pony.

haragán, na [ah-rah-gahn', nah], *m. & f. & a.* 1. Idler, loiterer, lingerer, lounger, lubbard, an idle, lazy person. 2. Idle, slothful, inactive, indolent.

haraganamente [ah-rah-gah-nah-men'-tay], *adv.* Idly, lazily, slothfully, indolently.

haraganazo, za [ah-rah-gah-nah'-tho, thah], *a. aug.* Very idle.

haraganear [ah-rah-gah-nay-ar'], *vn.* To lead an idle life, to be lazy, to act the truant, to lounge, to idle, to loiter.

haraganería [ah-rah-gah-nay-ree'-ah], *f.* Idleness, laziness, sluggishness, inactivity, slothfulness.

harapiento [ah-rah-pe-ayn'-to], *a.* Ragged, tattered, in rags, in tatters.

harapo [ah-rah'-po], *m.* Rag, tatter; fringe. **Estar hecho un harapo**, to go about in rags.

haraposo, sa [ah-rah-po'-so, sah], *a.* Ragged, tattered.

harem, harén [ah-rem', ahren'], *m.* Harem.

harija [ah-ree'-hah], *f.* Mill-dust, the flour which flies about in a corn-mill.

harina [ah-ree'-nah], *f.* 1. Flour, the edible part of corn and meal. **Harina de avena**, oatmeal. **Harina de patata**, potato flour. **Harina de pescado**, fish meal. 2. *(Met.)* Powder, dust.

harinado [ah-re-nah'-do], *m.* Flour dissolved in water.

harinero [ah-re-nay'-ro], *m.* 1. Flour merchant (persona). 2. Place where meal or flour is kept (recipiente).

harinero, ra [ah-re-nay'-ro, rah], *a.* Made of flour, belonging to flour.

harinoso, sa [ah-re-no'-so, sah], *a.* Mealy, containing meal, floury.

harkisa [ar-kee'-sah], *f.* Nickel sulphide.

harma [ar'-mah], *f. (Ant. Bot.)* Wild rue. *V.* GAMARZA.

harmaga [ar-mah'-gah], *f. (Bot.)* *V.* GAMARZA and ALHÁRGAMA.

harmonía [ar-mo-nee'-ah], *f.* Harmony. *V.* ARMONÍA and its adjuncts.

harmonista [ar-mo-nees'-tah], *m.* Musician.

harnerico, illo, ito [ar-nay-ree'-co], *m. dim.* A small sieve.

harnero [ar-nay'-ro], *m.* Sieve; properly, of fine meshes and small diameter. *V.* CRIBA. **Estar hecho un harnero**, to be covered with wounds.

harón, na [ah-ron', nah], *a.* 1. Slow, inactive, sluggish. 2. Balky.

haronear [ah-ro-nay-ar'], *vn.* 1. To dawdle, to move sluggishly; to be tardy or slow. 2. To balk, to stop short (caballo).

haronía [ah-ro-nee'-ah], *f.* Sluggishness, laziness, idleness.

harpado, da [ar-pah'-do, dah], *a.* V. ARPADO.

harpía [ar-pee'-ah], *f.* Harpy. V. ARPÍA.

harpillera [ar-peel'-lyay'rah], *f.* Sacking, sack cloth.

harria [ar'-re-ah], *f.* *(Amer.)* Drove of beasts of burden.

hartada [ar-tah'-dah], *f.* V. HARTAZGO.

hartar [ar-tar'], *va.* 1. To stuff with eating and drinking, to glut. 2. To satiate, to gratify desire. 3. To satiate (calmar el hambre), to satisfy (un deseo), to tire (cansar), to annoy (fastidiar) to cloy, to fill to uneasiness, to fill beyond natural desire. **Hartar de palos,** to shower with blows. *-vr.* 1. To eat one´s fill, to gorge, to be satiated. **Comer hasta hartarse,** to eat to repletion. 2. *(Fig.)* To weary, to get weary. **Hartarse de reír,** to laugh, fit to burst. **Hartarse de esperar,** to get tired of waiting.

hartazgo [ar-tath'-go], *m.* Satiety, the act of glutting or filling beyond natural desire.

harto [ar'-to], *adv.* Enough.

harto, ta [ar'-to, tah], *a. & pp. irr.* of HARTAR. 1. Satiate, satiated, glutted. 2. Sufficient, full, complete. **Estar harto de,** to be fed up with.

hartura [tar-too'-rah], *f.* 1. Satiety, fullness beyond desire or pleasure, glut. 2. Plenty, abundance (abundancia).

hasiz [ah-seeth'], *m.* Guard or keeper of silk.

hasta [ahs'-tah], *prep.* Until, as far as (lugar); also, even, until (tiempo). **Hasta no más,** to the highest pitch. **Hasta ahora, hasta aquí,** hitherto. **Hasta el fin de la calle,** down to the end of the street. **No me levanto hasta las 9,** I don´t get up until 9 o´clock. **No iré hasta después de la reunión,** I shan´t go till after the meeting.

hastial [as-te-ahl'], *m.* 1. A gable end. 2. *(Fig.)* A coarse, rude man. 3. Lateral face of an excavation, in mining.

hastiar [as-te-ar'], *va.* To loathe, to create disgust, to weary (fastidiar), to sicken (asquear).

hastío [as-tee'-o], *m.* Loathing, want of appetite; disgust, abhorring.

hataca [ah-tah'-cah], *f.* 1. A large kind of wooden ladle. 2. Rolling pin, with which paste is moulded.

hatajar [ah-tah-har'], *va.* To divide cattle into flocks or herds.

hatajo [ah-tah'-ho], *m.* 1. A small herd of cattle. 2. Assemblage, collection; abundance.

hatear [ah-tay-ar'], *vn.* To collect one's clothes necessary for traveling, when on a journey.

hatería [ah-tay-ree'-ah], *f.* Allowance of provisions and clothes for shepherds, when traveling with their flocks.

hatero [ah-tay'-ro], *m.* 1. Shepherd or other person who carries provisions to those who attend a flock of sheep. 2. *(Cuba)* Cow-boy, breeder of cattle, or keeper of a cattle-farm.

hatero, ra [ah-tay'-ro, rah], *a.* Applied to the animals that carry the shepherd's baggage.

hatijo [ah-tee'-ho], *m.* Covering of straw or feather-grass over beehives.

hatillo [ah-teel'-lyo], *m. dim.* A small bundle; a few clothes. **Echar el hatillo al mar,** to irritate, to vex oneself.

hato [ah'-to], *m.* 1. A large herd of cattle (animales). **Un hato de carneros,** a flock or fold of sheep. *(Amer.)* A farm for rearing cattle. 2. Fold, place chosen by shepherds to eat and sleep near their flocks (choza). 3. Provisions for shepherds, for some days' consumption (víveres). 4. Clothes, wearing apparel (ropa). 5. Heap, cluster, number driven together. 6. Herd, in contempt, a company of men; a crowd, multitude, or meeting of suspicious people. 7. Assemblage, collection, abundance. 8. *(coll.)* V. CORRILLO.

hay [ah'-ee]. Impersonal form, from **haber,** there is, there are.

haya [ah'-yah], *f. (Bot.)* Beech tree. **Haya común or silvática,** common beech.

hayal, hayedo [ah-yahl'], *m.* Plantation of beech trees.

hayo [ah'-yo], *m. (Cuba)* Coca, the shrub and its leaves.

hayucal [ah-yoo-cahl'], *m. (Prov.)* Grove of beech trees.

hayuco [ah-yoo'-co], *m.* Beech-mast, fruit of the beech.

haz [ahth'], *m.* Fagot, fascine, a bundle (lío) of brushwood or sticks a bundle of hay or grass; a sheaf of corn.

haz [ahth], *f.* 1. Face, visage. 2. Right side or outside of cloth (tela). 3. *(Arch.)* Facing. V. PARAMENTO. **Sobre la haz de la tierra,** upon the face of the earth.

haza [ah'-thah], *f.* Piece of cultivable land.

hazada [ah-thah'-dah], *f.* V. AZADA.

hazadón [ah-thah-done'], *m.* V. AZADÓN.

hazaleja [ah-thah-lay'-hah], *f. (Prov.)* A towel.

hazán [ah-thahn'], *m.* The cantor of a synagogue.

hazaña [ah-thah'-nyah], *f.* 1. Exploit, achievement, an heroic feat. **Las hazañas del héroe,** the hero´s exploits. 2. *(Iron.)* Ignoble action.

hazañería [ah-thah-nyay-ree'-ah], *f.* Show or affectation of scrupulosity.

hazañero, ra [ah-thah-nyay'-ro, rah], *a.* Prudish, affectedly grave and scrupulous, dramatic (persona), histrionic (acción), exaggerated.

hazañero, ra [ah-thah-nyay'-ro, rah], *m. & f.* Affected, prudish person.

hazañosamente [ah-thah-nyo-sah-men'-tay], *adv.* Valorously.

hazañoso, sa [ah-thah-nyo'-so, sah], *a.* Valiant, courageous, heroic (persona, acción).

hazcona [ath-co'-nah], *f.* Dart. V. DARDO.

hazmerreír [ath-may-ray-eer'], *m.* Ridiculous person, laughing-stock, gazing-stock, or jesting-stock.

¡he! [ay], *int.* 1. Ho! hey! a sudden exclamation to give notice of something. 2. Hark! list! hear! listen! Behold! look here. 3. What? Eh? It is used with pronouns, as *te, lo, los,* etc., and *aquí* or *allí.*

hebdómada [eb-do'-mah-dah], *f.* 1. Hebdomad, a week, seven days. 2. Seven years.

hebdomadario, ria [eb-do-mah-dah'-re-o, ah], *m. & f.* Hebdomadary, a member of a chapter or convent. *-a.* Weekly.

hebe [ay'bay], *f.* 1. The down which grows upon the pubis. 2. The age of puberty. 3. An asteroid of this name. 4. A moth.

hebén, [ay-ben'], *a.* Applied to white grapes, like muscatels.

hebepétalo, la [ay-bay-pay'-tah-lo, lah], *a.* Downy-petaled.

hebetina [ay-bay-teeh'-nah], *f.* Willemite, silicate of zinc.

hebilla [ay-beel'-lyah], *f.* A buckle, a clasp.

hebillaje [ay-beehl-lyah'-hay], *m.* Collection of buckles, or mounting of horses, accoutrements.

hebillita [ay-beel-lyee'-tah], *f. dim.* Small buckle.

hebillar [ay-beel-lyar'], *va.* To buckle.

hebillón [ay-beehl-lyone'], *m. aug.* A large buckle.

hebillona, ota [ay-beel-lyo'-nah, oh'-tah], *f. aug.* V. HEBILLÓN.

hebra [ay'-brah], *f.* 1. A needleful of thread of linen, yarn, worsted, or silk. 2. Pistil of the flower or blossom of saffron and other plants. 3. Fiber, filament, thread (de gusano). 4. Vein, layer, stratum. 5. *pl. (Poet.)* Hair. **Tabaco de hebra,** loose tobacco.

hebraico, ca [ay-brah'-eco, cah], *a.* Belonging to the Hebrews.

hebraísta [ay-brah-ees'-tah], *f.* Hebraist, one who is proficient in Hebrew.

hebreo [ay-bray'-o], *m.* 1. A Hebrew. 2. *(coll.)* A merchant, a tradesman.

hebreo, ea [ay-bray'-o, ah], *a.* Hebraic, Judaical. **A la hebrea,** in the Hebrew manner.*-m.* 1. Hebrew language (idioma). 2. *(coll.)* Trader. 3. *(coll.)* Usurer.

hebroso, sa [ay-bro'-so, sah], *a.* Fibrous; consisting of many fibers and threads, stringy (carne).

hecatombe [ay-cah-tom'-bay], *f.* 1. Hecatomb. 2. Massacre, slaughter.

hechiceresco, ca [ay-che-thay-res'-co, cah], *a.* Relating to witchcraft.

hechicería [ay-che-thay-ree'-ah], *f.* 1. Witchcraft, the practices of witches. 2. Witchery, enchantment. 3. Charmingness, the power of pleasing.

hechicero, ra [ay-che-thay'-ro, rah], *m. & f. & a.* 1. Witch, wizard; hag. 2. Charmer, enchanter, bewitcher. 3. Charming, bewitching, attractive in the highest degree.

hechizar [ay-che-thar'], *va.* 1. To bewitch, to enchant, to injure by witchcraft. 2. To charm, to fascinate.

hechizo [ay-chee'-tho], *m.* 1. Bewitchment, fascination. 2. Enchantment, irresistible power of pleasing, enchanter, charmer (de mujer) 3. Entertainment, amusement.

hechizo, za [ay-chee'-tho, thah], *a.* Made or done on purpose, artificial, factitious, imitated, well-adapted (falso).

hecho, cha [ay'-cho, chah], *pp. irr.* of HACER. 1. Made, done. 2. Accustomed, inured, used (acostumbrado). **Hecho al trabajo**, inured to labor and hardship. **Hecho un león**, like a lion, furiously angry. **A lo hecho pecho**, *(Prov.)* we must make the best of what we have done. **Hombre hecho**, a man of experience. *-a.* 1. Complete, finished (acabado); Mature (hombre, queso, vino); perfect; ready-made. **Hecho y derecho**, complete, right and true. **Un hombre hecho y derecho**, a real man.

hecho [ay'-cho], *m.* 1. Action, well or ill performed. 2. Act, feat. 3. Event, incident (suceso). 4. Subject or matter discussed (asunto). 5. *(Law.)* Point litigated. **De hecho**, in fact, actually, effectually. **Hecho consumado**, fait accompli, accomplished fact. **Esto es un hecho**, this is a fact. **Volvamos al hecho**, let´s get back to the facts. **Hechos de los Apóstoles**, facts of the Apostles.

Hecho a la medida [ay'-cho ah lah may-dee'-dah], *a.* Tailor-made, custom-made, custom-built.

hechura [ay-choo'-rah], *f.* 1. Act of performing or doing something (acto). 2. The work done or made, and the price of making it. 3. Form, cut (traje), shape, fashion, make, figure or form given to a thing (forma). 4. Workmanship. 6. Creature, client, a person who owes his rise or fortune to another. **De exquisita hechura**, of exquisite workmanship.

hectárea [ec-tha´-ray-ah], *f.* Hectare, a measure of surface.

héctico, ca [ec'-te-co, cah], *a.* Hectic. *Cf.* HÉTICO.

hecto [ec'-to], *m.* Greek prefix, signifying one hundred.

hectógrafo [ac-to'-grah-fo], *m.* Hectograph.

hectogramo [ec-to-grah'-mo], *m.* Hectogram, the weight of 100 grams.

hectolitro [ec-to-lee'-tro], *m.* Hectoliter, 100 liters.

hectómetro [ec-to´-may-tro], *m.* Hectometer, 100 meters.

hectóreo, ea [ec-to'-ray-o, ah], *a.* Belonging to Hector.

hedentina [ay-den-tee'-nah], *f.* Stench, stink.

heder [ay-derr'], *vn.* 1. To stink, to emit an offensive smell. 2. *(Met.)* To vex, to fatigue, to be intolerable.

hederáceo, cea [ay-day-rah-thay-o, ah], *a.* Hederaceus, relating to ivy.

hediondamente [ay-de-on-dah-men'-tay], *adv.* Stinkingly.

hediondez [ay-de-on-deth'], *f.* A strong stench or stink (olor); thing stinking; fetidness (cosa).

hediondo, da [ay-de-on'-do, dah], *a.* 1 Fetid, mephitical, stinking (maloliente). 2. Irascible, pettish, unpleasant. **Este es un hediondo**, he is a stinkard.

hediondo [ay-de-on'-do], *m. (Bot.)* V. GAMARZA.

hedonismo [ay-do-nees'-mo], *m.* Hedonism, theory of living for pleasure.

hedor [ay-dor'], *m.* Stench, stink, fetor, smell.

hedrar [ay-drar'], *va. (Prov.)* To dig a second time about the vines.

hegemonía [ay-hay-mo-nee'-ah], *f.* Hegemony, pre-eminence, leadership.

hégira [ay'-ge-rah], *f.* Hegira, the Mohammedan epoch.

hejotes, or **eotes** [ay-ho'-tes], *m. pl. (Mex.)* String-beans.

helable [ay-lah'-blay], *a.* Congealable.

helada [ay-lah'-dah], *f.* Frost (escarcha); freeze (fenómeno atmosférico). **Helada blanca**, hoarfrost.

heladería [ay-lah-day-ree'-ah], *f.* Ice-cream parlor, ice-cream stall.

heladero [ay-lah-day-ro], *m.* Ice-cream man.

heladizo, za [ay-lah-dee'-tho, thah], *a.* Easily congealed.

helado, da [ay-lah'-do, dah], *a. & pp.* of HELAR. 1. Gelid, frigid. 2. Frozen, congealed, frost-bitten, glacial, icy. 3. Frozen, chill in affection, indifferent. 4. Astonished, astounded. **Dejar helado a uno**, to dumbfound somebody. **Quedarse helado**, to be scared stiff.

helado [ay-lah'-do], *m.* 1. Ice-cream, frozen custard. 2. In Andalusia, pink sugar.

helamiento [ay-lah-meen'-to], *m.* Congelation, frostiness.

helar [ay-lar'], *va. & vn.* 1. To congeal (líquido), to ice (bebida), or to turn to ice. 2. To freeze, to congeal or be congealed with cold. 3. To freeze, to chill by the loss of power or motion. 4. To astound, to astonish, to amaze (pasmar). 5. To dispirit, to discourage (desalentar).*-vr.* 1. To freeze, to be congealed with cold (líquido), to be frozen. 2. To glaciate, to turn into ice. 3. To congeal, to concrete, to gather into a mass by cold; to be coagulated. 4. To grow motionless, to remain without action; to be stupefied to be dispirited. **Se me heló la sangre o se me heló la sangre en las venas**, *(Met.)* my blood curdled.

héle, hétele, aquí [ay´-lay, ay'-tay-lay, ah-kee'], *int.* Behold it, look here. *V.* HE.

helear [ay-lay-ar'], *va. (Prov.)* To point with the finger.

helechal [ay-lay-chahl'], *m.* A fernery.

helecho [ay-lay'-cho], *m. (Bot.)* Fern. **Helecho macho**, male fern. **Helecho hembra**, female fern.

helena [ay-lay'-nah], *f. (Naut.)* Castor and Pollux, a meteor, called also night-fire, or jack-o'-lantern.

helénico, ca [ay-lay'-ne-co, cah], *a.* Hellenic, Greek.

helanismo [ay-lay-nees'-mo], *m.* 1. Hellenism, Greek idiom. 2. Imitation, or study of Greek civilization.

helenista [ay-lay-nees'-tah], *m.* Hellenist, a name given to the Jews of Alexandria, who spoke Greek, or to the Greeks who embraced Judaism.

helenístico, ca [ay-le-nees'-te-co, cah], *a.* 1. Hellenistic, pertaining to the Hellenists. 2. The Alexandrine Greek dialect, and particularly that of the Septuagint.

helera [ay-lay´-rah], *f.* Pip, disease in fowls.

helgado, da [el-gah'-do, dah], *a.* Jag-toothed.

helgadura [el-gah-doo'-rah], *f.* Irregularity of the teeth.

heliaco, ca [ay-le-ah'-co, cah], *a.* Heliacal, rising or setting of a star.

helianto [ay-le-ahn'-to], *m. (Bot.)* Sun-flower.

hélice [ay'-le-thay], *f.* 1. Propeller (barcos, aviones). 2. *(Ast.)* Northern constellation of Ursa Major. 3. *(Geom.)* Helix, spiral.

helicóptero [ay-le-cop'-tay-ro], *m.* Helicopter.

helio [ay'-le-o], *m.* Helium.

heliocéntrico, ca [ay-le-o-then´-tre-co, cah], *a. (Ast.)* Heliocentric, appearing from the center of the sun.

heliograbado [ay-le-o-grah-bah'-do], *m.* Photogravure.

heliografía [ay-le-o-grah-fee'-ah], *f.* Blueprint.

heliómetro [ay-le-oh'-may-tro], *m.* Heliometer.

helioscopio [ay-le-os-co'-pe-o], *m.* Helioscope, telescope fitted for viewing the sun.

helioterapia [ay-le-o-tay-rah'-pe-ah], *f.* Heliotherapy, treating of disease by sunbaths.

heliotropio, heliotropo [ayle-o-tro, pe-o], *m.* 1. *(Bot.)* Turnsole, heliotrope. 2. Heliotrope, bloodstone, a precious stone. 3. Heliotrope, an instrument for reflecting solar light to an observer at a long distance.

helmíntico, ca [el-meen´-te-co, cah], *a.* Helminthic: applied to medicines against worms.

helota [ay-lo'-tah], *a. & n.* Helot, a bondman of Sparta.

helote [ay-lo'-tay], *m. (Mex.)* Green maize.

helvecio, cia [el-vay'-the-o, ah], *a.* Helvetian, Swiss.

helvético, ca [el-vay'-te-co, cah], *a.* Helvetic, Swiss (persona).

hemacrimo, ma [ay-mah-cree'-mo, mah], *a.* Cold-blooded.

hemafobia [ay-mah-fo´-be-ah], *f.* Dread of blood.

hematemesis [ay-mah-tay-may'-sis], *f.* Hematemesis, vomiting of blood.

hematoma [ay-mah-to-mah], *m.* Bruise.

hemefóbico, ca [ay-mah-fo'-be-co, cah], *a.* Hemaphobic, having an aversion to blood.

hematina [ay-mah-tee'-nah],*f.* 1. Hematoxylin, the coloring matter of logwood. 2. Hematine, the coloring matter of the blood.

hematites [ay-mah-tee'-tes], *f.* Hematites, ore of iron.

hematosis [ay-mah-to'-sis], *f.* Haematosis, conversion of venous blood into arterial.

hematuria [ay-mah-too'-re-ah], *f.* Hematuria, blood in the urine.

hembra [em'-brah],*f.* 1. Female, she (de animales). **El pájaro hembra**, the female bird. **El elefante hembra**, the female elephant, the she-elephant. Nut of a screw. 3. Eye of a hook. 4. *V.* MUJER.

hembrear [em-bray-ar'], *vn.* 1. To be inclined to females (machos). 2. To generate or produce females only, or chiefly.

hembrilla [em-breel'-lyah],*f.* 1. A sort of wheat of very fine grain. 2. *(Mech.)* Any piece into which another is fitted. 3. *(Prov.)* Leather trace of horses for ploughing.

hemeroteca [ay-may-ro-tay'-kah], *f.* Newspaper archive.

hemicarpo [ay-me-car'-po], *m.* The half of a fruit divided naturally, as seen in the umbelliferae.

hemiciclo [ay-me-thee'-clo], *m. V.* SEMICÍRCULO.

hemicilíndrico, ca [ay-me-the-leen'-dre-co, cah], *a.* Semicylindrical.

hemicránea [ay-me-crah'-nay-ah],*f.* Hemicrania, migraine, headache of one side of the head.

hemina [ay-mee'-nah], *f.* 1. A measure containing the third part of a fanega. 2. Hemina, a Greek liquid measure.

hemiope [ay-me-o'-pay], *a. & n.* Hemiope, one who is affected with hemiopia.

hemiopía [ay-me-o-pee'-ah],*f.* Hemiopia, partial obliteration of the field of vision.

hemiplejia [ay-me-play'-he-ah], *f. (Med.)* Hemiplegia, paralysis of one side of the body.

hemíptero, ra [ay-meep'-tay-ro, rah], *a.* Hemipterous. *-m. pl.* The hemiptera; true bugs.

hemisférico, ca [ay-mis-fay'-re-co, cah], *a.* Hemispheric, hemispherical, half-round.

hemisferio [ay-mis-fey'-re-o], *m.* Hemisphere.

hemisferoidal [ay-mis-fay-ro-e-dahl'], *a.* Hemispheroidal.

hemistiquio [ay-mis-tee'-ke-o], *m.* Hemistich, half a verse.

hemofilia [ay-mo-fee'-le-ah],*f. (Med.)* Haemophilia.

hemoglobina [ay-mo-glo-bee'-nah],*f.* Haemoglobin.

hemómetro [ay-mo'-may-tro], *m.* Hemometer, an instrument for measuring the tension of a blood vessel.

hemopatía [ay-mo-pah-tee'-ah], *f. (Med.)* Disease of the blood.

hemoptisis [ay-mop-tee'-sis], *f.* Haemoptysis; spitting of blood.

hemorragia [ay-mor-rah'-he-ah], *f.* Hemorrhage, flux of blood. **Morir por hemorragia**, to bleed to death.

hemorrágico [ay-mor-rah'-he-co], *a.* Hemorrhagic, relating to bleeding.

hemorroide [ay-mor-ro'-e-day],*f. (Med.)* Piles, hemorrhoids.

hemorroidal [ay-mor-ro-e-dahl'], *a.* Hemorroidal.

hemostático, ca [ay-mos-tah'-te-co, cah], *a.* Hemostatic, serving to staunch bleeding.

henal [ay-nahl'], *m.* Hayloft.

henar [ay-nar'], *m.* Meadow of hay.

henchidor, ra [en-chee-dor', rah], *m. & f.* Filler, satiator, one who fills.

henchidura [en-chee-doo'-rah],*f.* Repletion, act of filling.

henchimiento [en-chee-me-en'-to], *m.* Abundance, repletion.

henchir [en-cheer'], *va.* 1. To fill up. 2. To stuff or fill with mingled ingredients, to farce. 3. To sow discord, to produce mischief. *-vr.* To fill oneself (persona). **Henchirse de orgullo**, to swell with pride.

hendedor, ra [en-day-dor', rah], *m. & f.* Divider, one who divides or splits something.

hendedura [en-day-doo'-rah],*f.* Fissure, crack, rent, chink, cleft, cranny, crevice, cut.

hender [en-derr'], *va.* 1. To chink, to break into apertures or chinks, to crack, to flaw, to break, to fissure, to cleave (cortar), to split. 2. To go through: to open a passage (abrirse paso). 2. To break into pieces. *-vr.* To gape, to open in fissures or holes.

hendible [en-dee'-blay], *a.* Fissile, capable of being split.

hendido, da [en-dee'-do, dah], *a. & pp.* of HENDER. Crannied, full of chinks, cleft.

hendrija [en-dree'-hah], *f. (Prov.)* A small fissure or crack.

henequén [ay-nay-ken'], *m. (Mex.)* 1. Maguey, American agave (planta). 2. Fiber of this plant, used for making hammocks, etc (fibra).

henil [ay-neel'], *m.* Hayloft.

heno [ay'-no], *m.* 1. Hay. 2. *(Amer.)* Moss, used for filling mattresses.

heñir [ay-nyeer'], *va.* To knead dough. **Hay mucho que heñir**, *(coll.)* there is much to do.

heparina [ay-pah-ree'-nah], *f.* Heparin.

hepática [ay-pah'-te-cah], *f. (Bot.)* Liverwort.

hepático, ca [ay-pah'-te-co, cah], *a.* Hepatic, hepatical, belonging to the liver.

hepatitis [ay-pah-tee'-tis], *f. (Med.)* Hepatitis, inflammation of the liver.

hepatizacion [ay-pah-te-thah-the-on'], *f.* Hepatization.

hepatizarse [ay-pah-te-thar'-say], *vr.* To become hepatized; to be transformed into a liver-like substance.

heptacordo [ep-tah-cor'-do], *m.* Heptachord, a musical instrument.

heptagonal [ep-tah-go-nahl'], *a. (Math.)* Heptagonal. *V.* HEPTAGONO, which is more used.

heptágono, na [ep-tah'-gono, nah], *a.* Heptagonal, having seven angles or sides.

heptágono [ep-tah'-go-no], *m.* Heptagon, a figure of seven sides and angles.

heptamerón [ep-tah-may-ron'], *m.* A literary work divided into seven parts.

heptámetro [ep-tah'-may-tro], *m.* Heptameter, verse of seven feet.

heptanemo [ep-tah-nay'-mo], *a.* Having seven tentacles.

heptangular [cp-tan-goo-lar'], *a.* Having seven angles.

heptapétalo, la [ep-tah-pay'-tah-lo], *a.* Seven petaled, heptapetalous.

heptarquía [ep-tar-kee'-ah], *f.* Heptarchy, a seven-fold government.

heráldica [ay-rahl'-de-cah],*f.* Heraldry, the art and office of a herald.

heráldico, ca [ay-rahl'-de-co, cah], *a.* Heraldic, relating to a herald.

heraldo [ay-rahl'-do], *m.* Herald, an officer who registers genealogies and adjusts armorial ensigns.

heraprica [ay-rah-pree'-cah],*f. (Pharm.)* Hierapicra, a bitter purgative medicine.

herbáceo, cea [er-bah'-thay-o, ah], *a.* 1. Herby, having the nature of herbs. 2. Herbaceous, belonging to herbs.

herbajar [er-bah-har'], *va.* To put flocks to graze, to pasture. *-vn.* To graze, to browse.

herbaje [er-bah'-hay], *m.* 1. Herbage, grass, pasture, feeding. 2. Payment for pasturage. 3. *(Prov.)* Tribute for cattle. 4. Kind of ancient coarse cloth made of herbs.

herbajero [er-bah-hay'-ro], *m.* One who rents meadows or pastures; one who lets pasturage.

herbar [er-bar'], *va.* To dress skins with herbs.

herbario [er-bah'-re-o], *m.* 1. *V.* BOTÁNICO. 2. Herbarium, a hortus siccus, collection of dried plants (colección). 3. Herbalist's (tienda).

herbario, ria [er-bah'-re-o, ah], *a.* Herbaceous, of or belonging to herbs.

herbazal [er-bah-thahl'], *m.* A place herbaged or covered with herbs or grass; a pasture ground for cattle.

herbecer [er-bay-therr'], *vn.* To begin to grow (hierba).

herbítero, ra [er-bee'-tay-ro, rah], *a.* Herbiferous, bending herbs.

herbívoro, ra [er-bee'-vo-ro, rah], *a.* Herbivorous, herbaceous, feeding on herbs.

herbolado, da [er-bo-lah'-do, dah], *a.* Applied to things poisoned with the juice of plants, as daggers, darts.

herbolario [er-bo-lah'-re-o], *m.* 1. Herbalist, herbarist, herbist, a person skilled in herbs (persona). 2. Herbman, a person who sells herbs. 3. A ridiculous, extravagant man.

herborización [er-bo-re-thah-the-on'], *f.* Herborization, botanizing.

herborizador, herborizante [er-bo-re-thah-dor'], *m.* Herbalist, herbarist, one who herborizes.

herborizar [er-bo-re-thar'], *vn.* To herborize, to go in search of herbs and plants (como coleccionista).

herboso, sa [er-bo'-so, sah'], *a.* Herbous, herby, grassy, abounding in herbs.

hercúleo, ea [er-coo'-lay-o, ah], *a.* Herculean.

hércules [err'-coo-les], *m.* 1. A man of great strength. 2. *(Ast.)* A northern constellation. 3. Name of a gigantic beetle.

heredad [ay-ray-dahd'], *f.* 1. Piece of ground which is cultivated and bears fruit. 2. Hereditament.

heredado, da [ay-ray-dah'-do, dah], *a. V.* HACENDADO. **Estar heredado**, to be in possession of one's family property.-*pp.* of HEREDAR.

heredamiento [ay-ray-dah-me-en'-to], *m.* Landed property, lands, tenements.

heredar [ay-ray-dar'], *va.* 1. To inherit, to heir (propiedad). 2. To make over property to another, to be possessed by himself and his heirs or successors. 3. To possess the disposition or temperament of their parents (niños).

heredero, ra [ay-ray-day'-ro, rah], *m. & f.* 1. Heir, heiress, inheritor to something left by a deceased person. 2. Heir, one possessing the same propensities as his predecessors. 3. *(Prov.)* Vintager, one who gathers the vintage. **Heredero forzoso**, general heir. **Heredero presuntivo**, heir apparent.

heredípeta [ay-ray-dee'-pay-tah], *com.* Legacy-seeker; one who artfully plots to procure legacies or inheritances. *(Acad.)*

hereditario, ria [ay-ray-de-tah'-re-o, ah], *a.* Hereditary, derived from ancestors; entailed on a family.

hereje [ay-ray'-hay], *com.* A heretic. **Cara de hereje**, hideous or deformed aspect.

herejía [ay-ray-hee'-ah], *f.* 1. Heresy. 2. Literary error, contrary to the principles of a science. 3. Injurious expression against anyone (injuria). 3. Dirty trick (trampa).

herejote, ta [ay-ray-ho'-tay, tah], *m. & f.* l. *(coll.)* A great heretic.

herén [ay-ren'], *m. (Bot.)* Vetch. *V.* YERO.

herencia [ay-ren'-the-ah], *f.* Inheritance, hereditament, heritage, heirship, heirdom.

heresiarca [ay-ray-se-ar'-cah], *m.* Heresiarch, a leader in heresy.

heretical [ay-ray-te-cahl'], *a.* Heretical, containing heresy.

herético, ca [ay-ray'-te-co, cah], *a.* Heretical.

hergoma [er-go'-mah], *f.* An Irish linen made with threads of a spider's web.

heria [ay'-re-ah], *f.* 1. Strolling vagrant. *V.* HAMPA.

herida [ay-ree'-dah], *f.* 1. Wound. 2. Affliction, anything which afflicts the mind. 3. Injury, outrage, mischief. 4. Place where the game perches when pursued by the hawk.

herido, da [ay-ree'-do, dah], *a. & pp.* of HERIR. 1. Wounded, injured, hurt. **Mal herido**, badly wounded. 2. Bloody, cruel. **A grito herido**, with loud cries. -*m.* Injured man; wounded man. **Los heridos**, the wounded (guerra), the injured (accidente). **El número de los heridos en el accidente**, the number of people hurt in the accident.

heridor, ra [ay-re-dor', rah], *m. & f.* Wounder, striker.

herimiento [ay-re-me-en'-to], *m.* 1. Act of wounding. 2. Conjunction of vowels in a syllable; elision.

herir [ay-reer'], *va.* 1. To wound, to break the continuity of any part of the body. 2. To wound, to hurt by violence, to cause either bodily or mental pain, to harm, to mischief (dañar). 3. To shine upon, to cast his beams upon, to irradiate (sol). 4. To knock, to dash together, to strike (golpear), to collide. 5. To strike, or to make an impression upon the mind or upon the senses, to affect, to touch, to move (corazón etc.) 6. To play on a stringed instrument. 7. To offend (ofender), to pique, to irritate.-*vr. V.* AGRAVIARSE. **Un sonido me hirió el oído**, a sound reached my ear. **Es un color que hiere la vista**, it's a color which offends the eye. *(Yo hiero, él hirió, hiriera,* from *Herir. V.* ASENTIR.)

hermafrodita, hermafrodito [er-mah-fro-dee'-tah, to], *m.* Hermaphrodite, androgyne, an animal or plant uniting two sexes.

hermana [er-mah'-nah], *f.* 1. Sister. **Media hermana**, half-sister. **Hermana gemela**, twin sister. 2. Sister-in-law. 3. *(Ecl.)* Sister. **Hermana lega**, lay sister. *V.* HERMANO.

hermanable [er-mah-nah'-blay], *a.* Fraternal (hermano), brotherly.

hermanablemente [er-mah-nah-blay-men'-tay], *adv.* Fraternally.

hermanamiento [er-mah-naha-me-ayn'-to], *m.* **Hermanamiento de ciudades**, town-twinning.

hermanar [er-mah-nar'], *va.* 1. To match (para formar par), to suit, to proportion, to fellow, to pair, to harmonize (armonizar). 2. To combine (combinar).-*vn.* To join (unir), to unite.-*vr.* To love one another as brothers.

hermanastro, tra [er-mah-nahs'-tro-trah], *m. & f.* Step-brother, step-sister.

hermanazgo [er-mah-nath'-go], *m.* Fraternity, brotherhood.

hermandad [er-man-dahd'], *f.* 1. Fraternity, the state or quality of a brother. 2. Conformity, resemblance. 3. Amity, friendship. 4. Brotherhood (cofradía, grupo), confraternity, an association of men, fraternity. **La Santa Hermandad**, Spanish militia, formed in the XVIIth century to mantain public order. **Hermandad de ganaderos,** association of cattlemen.

hermanear [er-mah-nay-ar'], *va.* To treat as a brother.

hermanita [er-mah-nee'-tah], *f. dim.* A little sister.

hermanito [er-mah-nee'-to], *m. dim.* A little brother.

hermano, na [er-mah'-no, nah], *a.* Matched, suitable, having resemblance.

hermano [er-mah'-no], *m.* 1. Brother, born of the same parents. 2. Brother-in-law. 3. Similarity: as among the members of a religious community. **Hermano carnal**, brother by the same father and mother. **Hermano de leche**, foster-brother. **Hermano político**, brother-in-law. **Primo hermano**, first cousin. **Medio hermano**, half-brother. -*pl.* 1. Members of the same religious confraternity. 2. Lay-brothers of a religious order.

hermanuco [er-mah-noo'-co], *m.* Name given in contempt to lay-brothers of some religious orders.

herméticamente [er-may'-te-cah-men-tay], *adv.* Hermetically.

hermético, ca [er-may'-te-co, cah], *a.* Hermetical; airtight, watertight; self-contained; reserved (persona), secretive; watertight (teoría); impenetrable (misterio).

hermodátiles [er-mo-dah'-te-les], *m. pl.* Hermodactyl, a bulbous root formerly used as a cathartic.

hermosamente [er-mo-sah-men'-tay], *adv.* Beautifully, handsomely, lovely; perfectly, properly.

hermoseador, ra [er-mo-say-ah-dor', rah], *m. & f.* Beautifier.

hermosear [er-mo-say-ar'], *va.* 1. To beautify, to embellish, to adorn. 2. To glamorize, to add glamor or luster.

hermoso, sa [er-mo'-so, sah], *a.* Beautiful (bello), handsome (hombre), graceful, lovely, comely, neat, goodly, fine (espléndido), beauteous, fair. **Un día hermoso**, a fine day. **Seis hermosos toros**, six magnificent bulls.

hermosura [er-mo-soo'-rah], *f.* 1. Beauty, that assemblage of graces which pleases the eye. 2. Handsomeness (de un hombre), goodliness, fineness, fairness, freshness. 3. Symmetry, agreement of one part with another. 4. Beauty (persona), a beautiful person. **¡Qué hermosura!**, what a beauty!

hernia [ayr'-ne-ah], *f.* Hernia, rupture.

herniario [er-ne-ah'-re-o], *a.* Hernial, relating to hernia. **Saco herniario**, hernial sac.

herniarse [er-ne-ahr'-say], *vr.* To rupture oneself.

hernista [er-nees'-tah], *m.* Surgeon who applies himself to the cure of ruptures.

héroe [ay'-ro-ay], *m.* 1. Hero, a man eminent for bravery and valor. 2. Hero, the principal person in a poem. 3. Among the ancient pagans, one whom they believed to be born of a god or goddess and a human being.

heroicamente [ay-ro-e-cah-men'-tay], *adv.* Heroically.

heroicidad [ay-ro-e-the-dahd'], *f.* Quality or character which constitutes an heroic action (cualidad). *V.* HEROÍSMO.

heroico, a [ay-ro'-e-co, cah], *a.* 1. Heroic, eminent for bravery. 2. Heroical, befitting a hero. 3. Reciting the feats of heroes.

heroína [ay-ro-ee'-nah], *f.* A heroine.

heroína [ay-ro-ee'-nah], *f.* Heroin, a narcotic.

heroinómano, na [ay-ro-ee-no'-mah-no], *m & f.* Heroin addict.

heroísmo [ay-ro-ees'-mo], *m.* Heroism.

herpe [err'-pay], *m.* or *f.* Herpes, tetter, a cutaneous disease: commonly used in the plural.

herpético, ca [er-pay'-te-co, cah], *a.* Herpetic.

herpil [er-peel'], *m.* Sack of esparto netting with wide meshes, made for carrying straw, melons, etc.

herrada [er-rah'-dah], *f.* A pail.

herrada [er-rah'-dah], *a.* Applied to water in which red-hot iron has been cooled.

herradero [er-rah-day'-ro], *m.* 1. Place destined for marking cattle with a hot iron. 2. Marking cattle with a hot iron.

herrador [er-rah-dor'], *m.* Farrier, a shoer of horses.

herradura [er-rah-doo'-rah], *f.* 1. Shoe (animales). **Herradura de caballo**, horse-shoe. 2. Collar or necklace in the form of a horse-shoe. 3. The horse-shoe shape commonly given to the galleries of a theatre, or like audience-chamber.

herraj [er-rah'], *m.* Stones of olives after extracting the oil. *V.* ERRAX.

herraje [er-rah'-hay], *m.* 1. Ironwork, pieces of iron used for ornament and strength. **Herraje de un navío**, ironwork of a ship. 2. Horse-shoe. 3. *V.* HERRAJ.

herramental [er-rah-men-tahl'], *m. & a.* Bag with instruments for shoeing horses.

herramienta [er-rah-me-en'-tah], *f.* 1. Tool, set of tools, tool kit (equipo). **Herramienta mecánica**, power tool. 2. Ironwork. 3. Horns of a beast (de toro). 4. *(coll.)* Teeth (dientes), grinders. 5. Weapon (arma). 6. *(Inform.)* **Herramienta de ayuda en la toma de decisiones**, decision support tool.

herrar [er-rar'], *va.* 1. To garnish with iron. 2. To shoe horses (caballo). 3. To brand cattle with a hot iron (ganado). *(Yo hierro, yo hierre, from Herrar. V.* ACRECENTAR.*)*

herrén [er-ren'], *m.* 1. Maslin, mixed corn for feeding horses. 2. *V.* HERRENAL.

herrenal, or **herreñal** [er-ray-nahl', er-ray-nyahl'], *m.* Piece of ground in which maslin is sown.

herrería [er-ray-ree'-ah], *f.* 1. Ironworks, where iron is manufactured and moulded into pigs or bars (fábrica). 2. Forge (taller). 3. Clamor, confused noise.

herrerico, herrerillo [er-ray-ree'-co, eel'lyo], *m.* Small bird.

herrero [er-ray'-ro], *m.* Smith, one who forges iron.

herrerón [er-ray-rone'], *m.* A bad smith.

herreruelo [er-ray-roo-ay'-lo], *m.* 1. *(Orn.)* Wagtail, a bird whose note resembles the sound of hammering and betokens rain. 2. *V.* FERRERUELO. 3. *(Dim.) V.* HERRERICO.

herrete [er-ray'-tay], *m.* Tag, point of metal at the end of a cord.

herretear [er-ray-tay-ar'], *va.* To tag a cord, to string, or to ribbon.

herretero, ra [er-ray-tay'-ro, rah], *m. & f.* Tag-maker.

herrezuelo [er-ray-thoo-ay'-lo], *m.* Light piece of iron.

herrial [er-re-ahl'], *a.* Applied to a kind of large black grapes, and to the vines which bear them.

herrín [er-reen'], *m.* Rust of iron.

herrón [er-rone'], *m.* 1. A ring, in the middle of which is a hole, which boys pitch at a stake; a quoit. 2. A washer.

herronada [er-ro-nah'-dah], *f.* 1. A violent blow or stroke. 2. *(Met.)* Blow with a bird's beak.

herrugiento, ta [er-roo-he-en'-to, tah], *a.* Rusty.

herrumbre [er-room'-bray], *f.* Rust of iron; irony taste.

herrumbroso, sa [er-room-bro'-so, sah], *a.* 1. Rusty, drossy, scaly. 2. Participating of the qualities of iron.

herventar [er-ven-tar'], *va.* To boil something.

hervidero [er-ve-day'-ro], *m.* 1. Ebullition, the agitation of a boiling fluid (acto). 2. Kind of water-clock or small spring, from which water bubbles out (manantial). 3. Rattling in the throat. 4. Multitude, great quantity or number. **Un hervidero de gente**, a swarm of people.

hervir [er-veer'], *vn.* 1. To boil; to bubble (burbujear); to seethe (mar) **Hervir a fuego lento**, to simmer. *(Yo hiervo, el hirvió, hirviera; from Hervir. V.* ASENTIR.*)* **Empezar a hervir**, to begin to boil. 2. *(Met.)* To swarm with vermin, to be crowded with people. 3. To be fervent, vehement.

hervor [er-vor'], *m.* 1. Ebullition, the agitation of boiling fluids (acto). 2. Fervor, heat, vigor, fret. 3. *(Met.)* Noise and movement of waters. **Alzar or levantar el hervor**, to begin to boil.

hervoroso, sa [er-vo-ro'-so, sah], *a. V.* FOGOSO.

hespéride, hespérido, da [es-pay'-re-day, es-pay'-re-do, dah], *a.* 1. Relating to the Pleiades. 2. *(Poet.)* Western.

hespérides [es-pay'-re-des], *f. pl. V.* PLÉYADES.

héspero [ays'-pay-ro], *m.* The planet Venus, as evening star.

heteróclito, ta [ay-tay-ro'-cle-to, tah], *a.* 1. *(Gram.)* Heteroclite, inflected irregularly. 2. Irregular, abnormal.

heterodino, na [ay-tay-ro-dee'-no, nah], *a.* Heterodyne.

heterodoxia [ay-tay-ro-doc'-se-ah], *f.* Heterodoxy, misbelief.

heterodoxo, xa [ay-tay-ro-doc'-so, sah], *a.* Heterodox, not orthodox.

heterodromo [ay-tay-ro-dro'-mo], *m.* A lever whose fulcrum is between the power and the weight.

heterogamia [ay-tay-ro-gah'-me-ah], *f.* Heterogamy.

heterógamo, mah [ay-tay-ro'-gah-mo, mah], *a.* Heterogamous, bearing flowers of two sexual kinds.

heterogeneidad [ay-tay-ro-hay-nay-ee dahd'], *f.* Heterogeneousness, heterogeneity.

heterogéneo, nea [ay-tay-ro-hay'-nay-o, ah], *a.* Heterogeneous, dissimilar in nature, heterogene, heterogeneal.

heteromorfo, fa [ay-tay-ro-mor'-fo, fah], *a.* Heteromorphic, or morphous; of diverse form in several of its parts.

heterónomo, ma [ay-tay-ro'-no-mo, mah], *a.* Heteronymous, differing from the common type.

heterópsido, da [ay-tay-rop'-se-do, dah], *a.* (Metals) in a state of alkaline earth.

heterosexual [ay-tay-ro-sec-soo-al'], *a. m & f.* Heterosexual.

heterosexualidad [ay-tay-ro-sec-soo-ah-le-dahd'], *f.* Heterosexuality.

hética, hetiques [ay'-te-cah, ay-te-keth'], *f.* Phthisis, consumption, hectic (tísico).

hético, ca [ay'-te-co, cah], *a.* 1. Pertaining or related to tuberculosis. 2. Weak, emaciated (flaco).

heu [ay'-oo], *m.* Sloop, with one sail, of 300 tons, used in northern seas.

heurística [ay-oo-rees-te-cah]. *(Inform.)* Heuristics.

hexacordo [ec-sah-cor'-do], *m. (Mus.)* Hexachord.

hexaedro [ec-sah-ay'-dro], *m.* Hexahedron a cube.

hexagonal [ec-sah-go-nahl'], *a.* Hexagonal.

hexágono [ec-sah'-gono], *m.* Hexagon, a figure of six sides.

hexágono, na [ec-sah'-gono, nah], *a.* Hexagonal, having six sides.

hexámetro [ec-sah'-may-tro], *m.* Hexameter, a verse of six feet.

hexápeda [ec-sah'-pay-dah], *f. V.* TOESA.
hexástilo [ec-sahs´-te-lo], *m. (Arch.)* Hexastyle, a building with six columns in front.
hez [eth], *f.* 1. Scum, lee, the dregs of liquors. 2. Dross of metals. 3. Grains of malt. **La hez del pueblo**, the scum of the people. **Heces**, faeces, excrements.
híadas, híades [ee'-ah-das, ee'-ah-des], *f. pl. V.* PLÉYADES.
hialino, na [e-ah-lee'-no, nah], *a.* Hyaline, transparent.
hialitis [e-ah-lee'-tis], *f.* Hyalitis, inflammation of the vitreous body.
hialóideo, dea [e-ah-lo'-e-day-o, ah], *a.* Vitreous, glass-like.
hialoides [e-ah-lo'-e-des], *f.* Hyaloid membrane, inclosing the vitreous body of the eye.
hialosomo, ma [e-ah-lo-so'-mo, mah], *a. (Zool.)* Transparent in body; hyaline.
hialurgia [e-ah-loor'-hee-ah], *f.* The art of making glass.
hialúrgico, ca [e-ah-loor'-he-co, cah], *a.* Glass working, belonging to glass making.
hiante [e-ahn'-tay], *a.* Applied to a verse with a hiatus.
hiato [e-ah´-to], *m.* Hiatus, panes or cacophony, by the succession of an initial to a final vowel.
hibernación [e-bayr-nah-the-on'], *f.* Hibernation.
hibernal, hibernizo, za [e-ber-nahl´, e-ber-nee'-tho, thah], *a.* Hibernal, wintry.
hibernar [e-ber-nar'], *vn. (Prov.)* To winter, to live in a place during winter.
hibernés, sa [e-ber-nays', sah], *a.* Hibernian, Irish.
hibierno [e-be-err'-no], *m.* Winter. *V.* INVIERNO.
hibisco [e-bees'-co], *m. (Bot.)* Syrian mallow.
híbrido, da [ee'-bre-do, dah], *m. & f.* Hybridous animal, as a mule; hybridous words.-*a.* Hybridous, hybrid.
hibridación [e-bre-dah-the-on'], *f.* Hybridization, hybridism.
hicocervo [e-co-therr'-vo], *m.* Fabulous animal; chimera, a wild fancy.
hidalgamente [e-dal-gah-men´-tay], *adv.* Nobly, in a gentleman-like manner.
hidalgarse [e-dal-gar´-say], *vr. (coll.)* To assume the nobleman, to affect the gentleman.
hidalgo, ga [e-dahl'-go, gah], *a.* Noble, illustrious, excellent, exalted.
hidalgo, ga [e-dahl'-go, gah], *m. & f.* Hidalgo, a noble man or woman, a person of noble descent, one who is ennobled.
hidalgón, na, hidalgote, ta [e-dal-gone´, nah], *m. & f. aug.* An old noble man or woman, proud of the rights and privileges of their class.
hidalguejo, ja, hidalguete, ta, hidalguillo, lla [e-dal-gay'-ho, hah], *m. & f. dim.* A petty country squire, a poor gentleman or lady.
hidalguía [e-dal-gee'-ah], *f.* 1. Nobility, the rights and privileges of noble men. 2. Nobleness of mind, liberality of sentiments.
hidátide [e-dah'-te-day], *f.* 1. Hydatid, a cyst containing a larval tapeworm. 2. *(Min.)* A stone esteemed as precious by the ancients: used also as an adjective.
hidatidiforme [e-dah-te-de-for´-may], *a.* Hydatidiform, bladder-shaped.
hidra [ee'-drah], *f.* 1. Hydra, a fabulous monster. 2. A poisonous serpent. 3. *(Met.)* Seditions, plots. 4. Hydra, a fresh-water polyp.
hidragogo [e-drah-go´-go], *m. & a. (Med.)* Hydragogue.
hidrargírido, da [e-drar-hee'-re-do, dah], *a.* Resembling mercury.
hidrargirio [e-drar-hee'-re-o], *m.* An amalgam of mercury with another metal.
hidrárgiro [e-drar'-he-ro], *m.* Ancient name of mercury (hydrargyrum); entering into composition.
hidratado, da [e-drah-tah´-do, dah], *a.* Hydrate(d), containing water in composition.
hidratar [e-drah-tar'], *va.* To hydrate, to combine with water.
hidrato [e-drah'-to], *m.* Hydrate, a compound with water or hydrogen peroxide. **Hidrato de carbono,** carbohydrate.

hidráulica [e-drah'-oo-le-cah], *f.* Hydraulics, a branch of hydrodynamics.
hidráulico, ca [e-drah'-oo-le-co, cah], *a.* Hydraulical, hydraulic. **Fuerza hidráulica**, water power.
hidráulico [e-drah'-oo-le-co], *m.* Professor of hydraulics.
hidrazina [e-drah-thee'-nah], *f.* Hydrazine (combustible).
hidremia [e-dray'-me-ah], *f.* Hydramia, an excess of water in the blood.
hidria [ee'-dre-ah], *f.* Jar or pitcher for water.
hidro [ee'-dro], *m.* Water in Greek.
hidroavión [e-dro-ah-ve-on´], *m.* Hydroplane, sea-plane.
hidrocarburo [e-dro-car-boo'-ro], *m. (Chem.)* Hydrocarbon.
hidrocéfalo [e-dro-thay'-fah-lo], *m. (Med.)* Hydrocephalus, dropsy in the head.
hidrocerámico, ca [e-dro-thay-rah'-me-co, cah], *a.* Hydroceramic, porous.
hidroclórico, ca [e-dro-clo'-re-co, cah], *a.* Hydrochloric.
hidrodinámica [e-dro-de-nah'-me-cah], *f.* Hydrodynamics, science which relates to the motion of fluids.
hidroeléctrico, ca [e-dro-ay-lec´-tre-co, cah], *a.* Hydroelectric.
hidrofilacio [e-dro-fe-lah'-the-o], *m.* Great cavern full of water.
hidrófilo, la [e-dro'-fe-lo, lah], *a.* Water loving.
hidrofobia [e-dro-fo'-be-ah], *f.* Hydrophobia, a disease; rabies.
hidrófobo [e-dro'-ho-bo], *m.* Person suffering hydrophobia.
hidrófugo, ga [e-dro'-foo-go, gah], *a. (Zool.)* Hydrofuge, shedding water.
hidrogenar [e-dro-hay-nar´], *va.* To hydrogenate.
hidrógeno [e-dro'-hay-no], *m. (Chem.)* Hydrogen. **Hidrógeno líquido**, liquid hydrogen.
hidrogogía [e-dro-go-hee'-ah], *f.* The art or science of canalizing water.
hidrografía [e-dro-grah-fee'-ah], *f.* Hydrography, the description of the watery part of the globe.
hidrográfico, ca [e-dro-grah'-fe-co, cah], *a.* Hydrographical.
hidrógrafo [e-dro'-grah-fo], *m.* Hydrographer.
hidrólisis [e-dro´-le-sis], *f.* Hydrolysis.
hidrolizar [e-dro-le-thar'], *va.* To hydrolyze.
hidrología [e-dro-lo-hee'-ah], *f.* Hydrology, description of the nature and properties of water.
hidromático, ca [e-dro-mah'-te-co, cah], *a.* Hydromatic.
hidromel, hidromiel [e-dro-mel', me-el'], *m.* Hydromel, mead, metheglin.
hidrómetra [e-dro'-may-trah], *m.* Professor of hydrometry.
hidrometría [e-dro-may-tree´-ah], *f.* Hydrometry.
hidrometro [e-dro'-may-tro], *m.* Hydrometer, instrument for measuring the weight of fluids.
hidrónica [e-dro'-ne-cah], *f.* Hydronics.
hidrópata [e-dro'-pah-tah], *m.* Hydropath, follower of hydropathy.
hidropatía [e-dro-pah-tee'-ah], *f.* Hydropathy, hydrotherapy.
hidropático, ca [e-dro-pah'-te-co, cah], *a.* Hydropathic.
hidropesía [e-dro-pay-see'-ah], *f.* Dropsy.
hidrópico, ca [e-dro'-peco, cah], *a.* Hydropic, hydropical, dropsical.
hidroplano [e-dro-plah'-no], *f.* Hydroplane.
hidrópota [e-dro´-po-tah], *a. & n.* A person who drinks only water: a water-drinker.
hidróscopo [e-dros´-co-po], *m.* One who detects the presence of water under ground.
hidrosita [e-dro-see'-tah], *f.* A geode of chalcedony which contains water.
hidrostática [e-dros-tah´-te-cah], *f.* Hydrostatics.
hidrostáticamente [e-dros-tah'-te-cah-men-tay], *adv.* Hydrostatically.
hidrostático, ca [e-dros-tah'-te-co, cah], *a.* Hydrostatical.
hidrosulfúrico, ca [e-dro-sool-foo'-re-co, cah], *a.* Hydrosulphuric, or sulphhydric.
hidrotecnia [e-dro-tec'-ne-ah], *f.* Hydraulics, hydraulic engineering.
hidroterapia [e-dro-tay-rah'-pe-ah], *f.* Hydrotherapeutics.

hidrotórax [e-dro-to'-rax], *f.* Hydrothorax, dropsy of the chest.

hidróxido [e-droc'-se-do], *m.* Hydroxide.

hiedra [e-ay'-drah], *f.* 1. *(Bot.)* Ivy. 2. (Local) Poison-vine. **Hiedra terrestre**, ground ivy. *(Yo hiedro, yo hiedre*, from *Hedrar.* V. ACRECENTAR.)

hiel [eel'], *f.* 1. Gall, bile, an animal juice. 2. *(Met.)* Bitterness, asperity. **No tener hiel**, to be meek, simple, and gentle. **Hieles**, calamities, misfortunes, toils.

hiel de la tierra [e-el' day lah te-ay'-rah], *f.* 1. *(Bot.)* Common fumitory or earth-smoke. 2. Common erythraea centaurium.

hielo [e-ay'-lo], *m.* 1. Ice. 2. Frost. 3. Congealment. **Hielo seco**, dry ice. **Hielo movedizo**, drift ice. 4. *(Fig.)* Coolness, indifference. **Ser más frío que el hielo**, to be as cold as ice.

hiena [e-ay'-nah], *f.* Hyena, a fierce animal.

hierarca [e-ay-rar'-cah], *m.* Hierarch, among the Greeks, the chief of a sacred order.

hierático, ca [e-ay-rah'-te-co, cah], *a.* Hieratic, sacerdotal.

hierba [e-err'-bah], *f.* 1. Herb, a plant not possessing a woody stem, but dying down to the ground after flowering. 2. Green food for cattle, herbage, grass (chiefly in plural). 3. Flaw in the emerald which tarnishes its lustre. *-pl.* 1. Poison given in food; a poisonous plant. 2. Among the clergy, greens, garden-stuff. 3. Grass, pasturage. **Crecer como la mala hierba**, to grow like weeds. **Hierbas**, grass. **Hierba cana**, groundsel. **Y otras hierbas**, *(Fig.)* and so forth.

hierbabuena [e-ayr-bah-boo-ay'-nah], *f.* *(Acad.)* Peppermint, mint. V. YERBABUENA.

hierbajo [e-ayr-bah'-ho], *m.* Weed.

herogenia [e-ay-ro-hay'-ne-ah], *f.* Origin of different religions and the science which treats of such origin.

hieroglífico, ca [e-ay-ro-glee'-fe-co, cah], *a.* Hieroglyphic, hieroglyphical, emblematical. *-m. (Acad.)* V. JEROGLÍFICO.

hieroscopia [e-ay-ros-co'-pe-ah], *f.* V. ARUSPICINA.

hicrro [e-ayı'-ro], *m.* 1. Iron, a malleable metal (metal). 2. Any iron tool (herramienta). 3. Brund, a mark made by burning with a hot iron. 4. An iron instrument to wound with. **Hierro colado or fundido**, cast-iron. **Hierro forjado**, forged iron. **Es de hierro**, he is indefatigable, or as hardy as steel. **Hierros**, irons, fetters, jail. **Como el hierro**, like iron. **Hierro en lingotes**, pig iron.

hietómetro [e-ay-to'-may-tro], *m.* Hyetometer, rain-gauge, or pluviometer.

hi-fi [e'-fe], *m.* Hi fi.

higa [ee-gah], *f.* 1. A fist-shaped, amulet, charm, hung about the neck for preventing or curing disease. 2. An obscene gesture. 3. Ridicule, derision. **Dar higas**, to despise a thing.

higadillo [e-gah-deel'-lyo], *m. dim.* A small liver; the liver of birds, fishes, and other small animals.

hígado [ee'-gah-do], *m.* 1. Liver, one of the entrails. 2. *(Met. Coll.)* Courage, valor, bravery. **Tener malos hígados**, 1. To be white-livered, to be ill-disposed. 2. *(Met.)* To hate. **Echar los hígados**, to be very tired or fatigued. **Hasta los hígados**, *(coll.)* to the heart. **¡Qué hígados tiene!**, what guts he has!

higate [e-gah'-tay], *m.* Pottage, formerly made of figs, pork, and fowl, boiled together, and seasoned with sugar, ginger, cinnamon, pimento, and other spices.

higiene [e-he-ay'-nay], *f. (Med.)* Hygiene.

higiénicamente [e-he-ay'-ne-cah-men-tay], *adv.* Hygienically.

higiénico, ca [e-he-ay'-ne-co, cah], *a.* Hygienic,

higo [ee'go], *m.* 1. Fig, the fruit of the fig-tree. **Higo chumbo** or **de pala**, fruit of the nopal or Indian fig-tree. **Pan de higos**, cake made of figs. 2. A kind of piles.

higrometría [e-gro-my-tree'-ah], *m.* Hygrometry.

higrométrico, ca [e-gro-may'-tre-co, cah], *a.* Hygrometric, measuring moisture.

higrómetro [e-gro'-may-tro], *m.* Hygrometer, an instrument for measuring the degrees of moisture.

higroscopia [e-gros-co'-pe-ah], *f.* Hygroscopy, hygrometry.

higroscopio [e-gros-co'-pe-o], *m.* Hygroscope, a device for indicating the humidity of the air.

higuera [e-gay'-rah], *f. (Bot.)* Fig-tree. **Higuera infernal**, castor-oil plant. **Higuera de Indias** or **de las Indias**, Indian fig-tree, prickly-pear cactus. **Caer de la higuera**, to come down to earth with a bump. **Estar en la higuera**, to be miles away, to be in the clouds.

higueral [e-gay-rahl'], *m.* Plantation of fig-trees.

higuerón [e-gay-rone'], *m.* Large tree in America.

higuito [e-gee'-to], *m. dim.* A small fig.

hija [ee'-hah], *f.* 1. Daughter. 2. Daughter-in-law. V. HIJO, JA.

hijar [e-har'], *m.* V. IJAR.

hijastro, tra [e-hahs'-tro, trah], *m. & f.* Step-child.

hijezna [e-heth'-nah], *m.* The young of any bird.

hijito, ita [e-hee'-to, tah], *m. & f. dim.* Little child, little dear.

hijo [ee'-ho], *m.* 1. Son. 2. Son-in-law.

hijo, ja [ee'-ho, hah], *m. & f.* 1. Child. 2. Young of all animals. 3. Son or native of a place. 4. Child, son, daughter, anything which is the product or effect of another. **Hijo de familia**, 1. A minor. 2. A son of noble parents. 5. Bud or root of the horns of animals. **Hijo de leche**, foster child. **Hijo bastardo, hijo de su madre**, *(coll.)* bastard. **Hijo natural**, illegitimate child. **Como cada hijo de vecino**, everyone. **Ser hijo de papá**, to be daddy's boy. **Nombrar a uno hijo predilecto de la ciudad**, to give the freedom of the city. **Hijo único**, only child. **Hacerle a una un hijo**, to get someone pregnant. **Hijo adoptivo**, adopted child. **Hijo político**, son-in-law. **El Hijo de Dios**, the Son of God.

hijodalgo, hijadalgo [e-ho-dahl'-go, e-hah-dahl'-go], *m. & f.* V. HIDALGO.

hijuela [e-hoo-ay'-lah], *f.* 1. Piece of cloth or linen joined to another which is too short or narrow. 2. A small mattress, put between others, to make the bed even. 3. Pall, a square bit of linen or pasteboard put over the chalice. 4. A small drain for drawing off water from an estate. 5. Schedule or inventory delivered in Spain to parties entitled in distribution to the estate of a person deceased, containing an exact account of their distributive share. 6. An inventory, a catalogue of the articles which belong to the estate of a deceased person. 7. Crossroad. 8. Postman who delivers letters from the office. 9. Palm-seed. 10. Fascine of wood. 11. Cord made of the gut of silkworms.

hijuelo, la [e-hoo-ay'-lo, lah], *m. & f. dim.* 1. A young child (niño). 2. *(Bot.)* Sucker.

hila [ee'-lah], *f.* 1. Row (fila), line. V.HILERA. 2. Thin gut (cuerda). 3. Act of spinning. 4. Lint to lay on sores. 5. Small trench for dividing the water destined for the irrigation of different pieces of ground.

hilacha [e-lah'-chah], *f.* Filament or thread ravelled out of cloth.

hilachoso, sa [e-lah-cho'-so, sah], *a.* Filamentous.

hilada [e-lah'-dah], *f.* 1. Row or line of bricks or stones in a building. 2. V. HILERA.

hiladillo [e-lah-deel'-ly-o], *m.* 1. Ferret silk. 2. Narrow ribbon or tape.

hilado [e-lah'-do], *m.* Spun flax, hemp, wool, silk, or cotton. **Hilado, da**, *pp.* Of HILAR.

hilador, ra [e-lah-dor', rah], *m. & f.* Spinner, spinster.

hilandera [e-lan-day'-rah], *f.* Spinster, woman who spins.

hilandería [e-lan-day-ree'-ah], *f.* Place where hemp is spun.

hilandero [e-lan-day'-ro], *m.* 1. Spinner. 2. Spinning room, a rope walk.

hilanderilla [e-lan-day-reel'-lyah], *f. dim.* A little spinster.

hilanza [e-lahn'-thah], *f. (Prov.)* Thread, line, mode of spinning.

hilar [e-lar'], *va.* 1. To spin, to draw silk, cotton, etc., into thread. 2. To argue, to discuss. **Hilar delgado**, to split hairs. 3. To spin a cocoon (gusanos de seda). **Máquina de hilar**, spinning machine.

hilaracha [e-lah-rah'-chah], *f.* Filament. V. HILACHA.

hilarante [e-lah-rahn'-tay], *a.* Nitrous oxide gas; so called laughing gas.

hilaridad [e-lah-re-dahd'], *f.* Hilarity, laughter, jollity.

hilaza [e-lah'-thah], *f.* 1. Anything spun or drawn out into thread. *V.* HILADO. 2. Yarn. **Hilazas**, filaments of plants.

hilera [e-lay'-rah], *f.* 1. Row, line. 2. *(Mech.)* Wiredrawer. 3. Fine thread. 4. *(Mil.)* File, single file. 5. *(Arch.)* Ridge-pole. 6. *(Zool.)* Spinneret. 7. *(Mas.)* Course. 8. Fine yarn.

hilero [e-lay'-ro], *m.* 1. Sign of currents in the sea. 2. Thread-seller.

hilete [e-lay'-tay], *m. dim.* of HILO.

hilo [ee'-lo], *m.* 1. Thead, a small line of cotton, silk, etc (tela). 2. Wire, metal drawn into threads (metal). 3. A slender thread, formed by liquids falling in drops (líquido) 4. *(Met.)* Continuation, series. 5. Fine thread of spider or silkworms. 6. *V.* FILO. 7. *(Fig.)* Thread, theme (conversación, discurso), curse (vida), train (pensamiento). **Hilo a hilo,** drop by drop. **Hilo de zapatero,** shoemaker's thread. **Hilo de oro** or **de plata,** gold or silver thread. **Hilo para sastre,** tailors' thread. **Hilo en ovillos,** thread in balls. **Hilo de torzal** or **de pelos,** cotton yarn. **Hilo de zurcir,** darning wool. **Hilo de humo,** thin line of smoke. **Traje de hilo,** linen dress. **Coger el hilo,** to pick up the thread. **Perder el hilo,** to lose the thread.

hilván [eel-vahn'], *m.* Basting, long stitches set in clothes to keep them in order for sewing.

hilvanar [eel-vah-nar'], *va.* 1. To baste, to sew slightly. 2. To act or perform in a hurry (trabajo).

himen [ee'-men], *m.* Hymen, the virginal membrane.

himeneo [e-may-nay'-o], *m.* 1. *(Poet.)* Marriage, matrimony. 2. Epithalamium, hymeneal, hymenean. 3. Hymen, the god of marriage.

himenocarpo, pa [e-may-no-car'-po, pah], *a. (Bot.)* Bearing a membranous fruit.

himenófilo [e-may-no'-fe-lo], *m.* Hymenophyllum, filmy fern, lace fern.

himenópteros [e-may-nop'tay-ros], *m. pl.* The hymenoptera: the order of insects which contains those of the highest intelligence, as bees and ants, and others which are indirectly beneficial to husbandmen.

himnario [im-nah'-re-o], *m.* Hymnal, hymnary.

hímnico, ca [eem'-ne-co, cah], *a.* Hymnic, pertaining to hymns; lyric.

himnista [im-nees'-tah], *m. (coll.)* Composer of hymns.

himno [eem'-no], *m.* Hymn.

himnología [im-no-lo-hee'-ah], *f.* Hymnology, the study of hymns; a treatise on hymns.

himplar [im-plar'], *vn.* To roar or bellow.

himpón [im-pon'], *m.* Name of one of the tribunals of the Chinese empire.

hin [een or heen], *m.* Sound emitted by mules or horses; whinny.

hincadura [in-cah-doo'-rah], *f.* Act of fixing something.

hincapié [in-cah-pe-ay'], *m.* An effort made with the foot by fixing it firmly on the ground. **Hacer hincapié,** to make a strenuous attempt.

hincar [in-car'], *va.* 1. To thrust in (meter), to drive into, to nail one thing to another. **Hincar la rodilla,** to kneel down. 2. *(Prov.)* To plant. **Hincar el diente,** to appropriate property to oneself; to censure, to calumniate. **Hincó la mirada en ella,** he fixed his gaze on her. **Hincó el bastón en el suelo,** he stuck his stick in the ground.

hincha [een'-chah], *f. (coll.)* Hatred, displeasure, emnity. **Tener hincha a uno,** to have a grudge against somebody.

hinchable [in-chah'-blay], *a.* Inflatable.

hinchadamente [in-chah-dah-men'-tay], *adv.* Haughtily, loftily.

hinchado, da [in-chah'-do, dah], *a. & pp.* of HINCHAR. 1. Swollen, tumefied swelled. 2. Vain, arrogant (persona), presumptuous. 3. Inflated, turgid, tumid, pompous (estilo).

hinchante [in-chan'-tay], *a.* 1. Annoying (molesto), tiresome. 2. Funny (gracioso).

hinchar [in-char'], *va.* 1. To inflate, to swell with wind. 2. To fill a musical instrument with air. 3. To swell, to raise to arrogance. 3. To blow up (neumático). *-vr.* 1. To swell, to grow turgid, to be tumefied. 2. To be elated with arrogance

or anger. 3. To make a pile (enriquecerse). 4. **Hincharse a correr,** to run hard. **Hincharse a reír,** to laugh a lot.

hinchazón [in-chah-thone'], *m.* 1. Swelling, tumefaction, a tumid inflammation. 2. Ostentation, vanity, pride; inflation, pomposity (estilo)

hincón [in-cone'], *m.* Post to which cables are fastened on the banks of rivers.

hindú [in-doo'], *a. m & f.* Hindu.

hinduismo [in-doo-ees'-mo], *m.* Hinduism.

hiniesta [he-nees'-tah], *f. (Bot.)* Spanish broom.

hiniestra [e-ne-es'-trah], *f. (Prov.)* Window. *V.* VENTANA.

hinnible [in-nee'-blay], *a.* Capable of neighing.

hinojal [e-no-hah'], *m.* Bed or place full of fennel.

hinojo [e-no'-ho], *m.* 1. Knee. *V.* RODILLA. 2. *(Bot.)* Fennel. 3. **Hinojo marino,** *(Bot.)* samphire.

hintero [in-tay'-ro], *m.* Table on which bakers knead their dough.

hiñir [e-nyeer'], *va. (Prov.)* V. HEMIR. *(Yo hiño, yo hiña; él hiñó, hiñera; from Heñir V.* PEDIR.)

hióideo, dea [e-o'-e-day-o, ah], *a.* Hyoid, like a Y in shape.

hipar [e-par'], *vn.* 1. To hiccup. 2. To be harassed with anxiety and grief. 3. To pant (perro), to desire eagerly, to be anxious. 4. To follow the chase by the smell (perros).

hiparca [e-par'-cah], *m.* Name given by the Greeks to the satraps and their lieutenants.

hipear [e-pay-ar'], *vn.* To hiccup. *V.* HIPAR.

hipecoo [e-pay-co'-o], *m. (Bot.)* Horned cumin.

hiperactividad [e-per-ac-te-ve-dahd'], *f.* Hyperactivity.

hiperactivo [e-per-ac-tee'-vo], *a.* Hyperactive.

hipérbola [e-per'-boh-lah], *f. (Geom.)* Hyperbola, section of a cone.

hipérbole [e-per'-boh-lay], *f.* Hyperbole, a figure in rhetoric.

hiperbólicamente [e-per-bo'-ly-cah-men-tay], *adv.* Hyperbolically.

hiperbólico, ca [e-per-bo'-le-co, cah], *a.* Hyperbolical.

hiperbolizar [e-per-bo-le-thar'], *m.* To use hyperboles.

hiperboloide [e-per-bo-lo'-e-day], *f.* Hyperboloid.

hiperbóreo, rea [e-per-bo'-ray-o, ah], *a.* Hyperborean.

hiperconversación [e-per-con-ver-sah-the-on']. *(Inform.)* Hypertalk.

hipercrítico, ca, [e-per-cree'-te-co, cah], *a.* Hypercritical, censorious.

hiperdrulía [e-per-droo-lee'-ah], *f.* Hyperdulia, worship of the Virgin Mary.

hiperemesia or **hiperemesis** [e-per-ay-may'-se-ah], *f.* Hyperemesis, excessive vomiting.

hipergólico, ca [e-per-go'-le-co, cah], *a.* Hypergolic.

hipérico, hipericón [e-pay'-re-co, e-pay-re-cone'], *m. (Bot.)* St. John´s wort. **hiperinflación** [e-per-in-fla-the-on'], *f.* Runaway inflation.

hipermercado [e-per-mer-cah'-do], *m.* Hypermarket.

hipersensibilidad [e-per-sen-se-be-le-dahd'], *f.* Hypersensitivity.

hipersensible [e-per-sen-se-blay], *a.* Hypersensitive.

hipersónico, ca [e-per-so'-ne-co, cah], *a.* Hypersonic.

hipertensión [e-per-ten-se-on'], *f.* Hypertension, high blood pressure.

hipertrofia [e-per-tro'-fe-ah], *f.* Hypertrophy, undue growth.

hipertrofiarse [e-per-tro-fe-ar'-say], *m.* To hypertrophy, to become hypertrophied.

hipertrófico, ca [e-per-tro'-fe-co, cah], *a.* Hypertrophic, relating to hypertrophy.

hípico, ca [ee'-pe-co, cah], *a.* Relating to horses.

hipio [ee'-pe-o], *m.* Surname of Mars and Neptune, meaning *equestrian.*

hipnal [ip-nahl'-], *m.* Kind of serpent said to produce sleep.

hipnosis [ip-no'-sis], *f.* Hypnosis.

hipnótico, ca [ip-no'-te-co, cah], *a. & m. (Med.)* Hypnotic.

hipnotismo [ip-no-tees'-mo], *m.* Hypnotism, mesmerism, hypnotic suggestion.

hipnotizador [ip-no-te-thah-dor'], *a.* Hypnotizing.

hipnotizar [ip-no-te-thar'], *va.* To hypnotize.

hipo [ee'-po], *m.* 1. Hiccough. **Quitar el hipo a uno**, to cure somebody's hiccups. 2. Wish, desire, anxiety (deseo). 3. Anger, displeasure, fury. 4. Disgust (asco); grudge (rencor).

hipocampo [e-po-cahm'-po], *m.* Hippocampus, sea horse.

hipocentauro [e-po-then-tah'-oo-ro], *m.* Hippocentaur, a fabulous monster.

hipocondría [e-po-con-dree'-ah], *f.* Hypochondria, melancholy, hypochondriasis, hypochondriac affection or passion.

hipocondríaco, ca [e-po-con-dre-ah'-co, cah], *a.* Hypochondriasis, hypochondriacal, melancholy, fanciful.

hipocóndrico [e-po-con'-dre-co], **ca,** *m. & f.* Hypochondriac, melancholist.

hipocóndrico, ca [e-po-con'-dre-co, cah], *a.* Hypochondriac, hypochondriacal.

hipocondrio [epo-con'-dre-oh], *m. (Anat.)* Hypochondrium, that part of the body which lies under the cartilages of the false ribs: more generally used in its plural, hypocondres.

hipocras [e-po-crahs'], *m.* Hippocras, medicated wine.

hipocrático, ca [e-po-cra'-te-co, cah], *a.* 1. Hippocratic, relating to Hippocrates. 2. Cadaveric countenance.

hipocrenides [e-po-cray-nee'-des], *f. pl. (Poet.)* Epithet applied to the muses of Parrassus.

hipocresía [e-po-cray-see'-a], *f.* Hypocrisy, dissimulation.

hipócrita [e-po'-cre-tah], *a.* Hypocritical, dissembling, insincere.

hipócrita [e-po'-cre-tah], *com.* Hypocrite, a dissembler.

hipócritamente [e-po'-cre-tah-men-tay], *adv.* Hypocritically.

hipocritilla [e-po-cre-teel'-lyah], *f. dim.* A sly hypocrite.

hipócrito, ta [e-po'-cre-to, tah], *a.* Feigned, dissembled, hypocritical.

hipocritón, na [e-po-cre-tone', nah], *a. aug.* Extremely hypocritical or dissembling.

hipodérmico, ca [e-po-der'-me-co, cah], *a.* Hypodermic.

hipódromo [e-po'-droh-mo], *m.* Hippodrome, race track, arena.

hipofosfito [e-po-fos-fee'-to], *m.* Hypophosphite, a salt of hypophosrous acid.

hipofosforoso, sa [c-po-fos-fo-ro'-so, sah], *a.* Hypophosphorous (acido). -H3 PO2.

hipogástrico, ca [e-po-gahs'-tre-co, cah], *a.* Hypogastric.

hipogastro [e-po-gahs'-tro], *m.* Hypogastrium, the lower part of the belly.

hipogeo [epo-hay'-o], *m.* 1 Subterranean vault where the ancient Greeks kept their dead without cremating them. 2. Hypogeum, an underground chapel or structure.

hipogloso, sa [e-po-glo'-so, sah], *a.* Hypoglossal.

hipogrifo [e-po-gree'-fo], *m.* Hippogriff, a winged horse.

hipohema [e-po-ay'-mah], *m.* Hyphaemia, effusion of blood in the eye.

hipomanes [e-po-mah'-nes], *m.* A vaginal discharge from the mare when in heat.

hipomoclio, hipomoclión [e-po-mo'-cle-o, epo-mo-cle-on'], *m.* Fulcrum of a lever; part on which the beam of a balance revolves.

hiponitrato [e-po-ne-trah'-to], *m.* Subnitrate.

hipopión [e-po-pe-on'], *m. (Med.)* Hypopyon, a collection of pus in the chambers of the eye.

hipopo, pa [e-po'-po, pah], *a.* Hoofed like a horse.

hipopótamo [e-po-po'-tah-mo], *m.* Hippopotamus, a river-horse.

hipóstasis [e-pos' tah ois], *f. (Theol.)* Hypostasis, anyone of the persons of the Holy Trinity.

hipostático, ca [e-pos-tah'-te-co, cah], *a.* Hypostatical.

hiposulfato, furo, fito [e-po-sool-fah'-to, foo'-ro, fee'-to], *m. (Chem.)* Hyposulphite. Hyposulphite of soda, so called (properly thiosulphate), is important in photography.

hipoteca [e-po-tay'-cah], *f.* Mortgage, pledge; security given for the performance of an engagement. **Levantar una hipoteca**, to raise a mortgage.

hipotecable [e-po-tay-cah'-blay], *a.* Capable of being pledged.

hipotecar [e-po-tay-car'], *va.* To hypothecate, to pledge, to mortgage.

hipotecario, ria [e-po-tay-cah'-re-o, ah], *a.* Belonging to a mortgage.

hipotensión [e-po-ten-se-on'], *f. (Med.)* Hypotension.

hipotenusa [e-po-tay-noo'-sah], *f.* Hypotenuse.

hipótesis [e-po'-tay-sis], *f.* Hypothesis, a supposition.

hipotético, ca [e-po-tay'-te-co, cah], *a.* Hypothetic, hypothetical, conditional.

hipsómetro [ep-so'-may-tro], *m.* Hypsometer, an instrument for measuring altitude by determining the boiling point of water at a given altitude.

hipúrico [e-poo'-re-co], *a. (Chem.)* Hippuric (ácido).

hirma [eer'-mah], *f.* Edge of cloth.

hirsuto, ta [ir-soo'-to, tah], *a.* 1. Hirsute, covered with rough hairs. 2. *(Poet.)* Rough, rugged (brusco).

hirundinaria [e-roon-de-nah'-re-ah], *f. (Bot.)* V. CELIDONIA and GOLONDRINERA.

hirviente [ir-ve-en'-tay], *pa.* Boiling.

hisca [ees'-cah], *f.* Bird-lime, a glutinous substance by which the feet of birds are entangled.

hiscal [is-cahl'], *m.* A rope of three strands made of esparto.

hisopada [e-so-pah'-dah], *f.* Water sprinkled with a water-sprinkler.

hisopear [e-so-pay-ar'], *va.* To sprinkle water with a sprinkler.

hisopillo [e-so-peel'-lyo], *m.* 1. A small water-sprinkler. 2. Bit of soft linen at the end of a stick, used to wash and refresh the mouth of a sick person. 3. *(Bot.)* winter-savory.

hisopo [e-so'-po], *m.* 1. *(Bot.)* Hyssop. 2. Water-sprinkler, with which holy water is sprinkled made of a lock of horse-hair fastened to the end of a stick. **Hisopo húmedo**, *(Pharm.)* grease collected in washing fleeces of wool.

hispalense [is-pah-len'-say], *a.* Native of or belonging to Seville.

hispánico, ca [is-pah'-ne-co, cah], *a.* Spanish.

hispanidad [is-pah-ne-dahd'], *f.* 1. Spanish culture, Spanish spirit. 2. Spanish speaking world.

hispanismo [is-pah-nees'-mo], *m.* A Spanish idiom.

hispanizado, da [is-pah-ne-thah-do, dah], *a. & pp.* of HISPANIZAR. V. ESPAÑOLIZADO.

hispanizar [is-pah-ne'-thar], *va.* V. ESPAÑOLIZAR.

hispano, na [is-pah'-no, nah], *a.* Spanish, Hispanic. *-m. & f. (Poet.)* A Spaniard.

hispanoamericano, na [is-pah-no-ah-may-re-cah'-no, nah], *m. & f. & a.* Spanish American, Latin American.

hispanohablante [is-pah-no-ha-blahn'-tay], *a. m & f.* Spanish-speaking, Spanish speaker.

híspido, da [ees'-pe-do, dah], *a.* Bristly like hogs.

histerectomía [is-tay-rec-to-mee'-ah], *f. (Med.)* Hysterectomy, surgical removal of the uterus.

histeria [is-tay'-re-ah], *f.* Hysteria, hysterics.

histéricamente [is-tay'-re-cah-men-tay], *adv.* Hysterically.

histérico [is-tay'-re-co], *m.* Hysterics. V. HISTERISMO.

histérico, ca [is-tay'-re-co, cah], *a.* Hysteric, hysterical; relating to the womb, or to hysteria.

histerismo [is-tay-rees'-mo], *m.* Histeria.

histología [is-to-lo-hee'-ah], *f.* Histology, the science of the tissues, or a treatise upon them.

histológico, ca [is-to-lo'-he-co, cah], *a.* Histological.

histólogo [is-to'-lo-go], *m.* Histologist.

historia [is-to'-re-ah], *f.* 1. History, a narration of events (narración). 2. *(coll.)* Tale (cuento), story, table. 3. History-piece, an historical painting. **Meterse en historias**, to meddle in things without possessing sufficient knowledge thereof, or being concerned in them. **No me vengas con historias**, don't give me that. 4. History (humana) **En toda la historia humana**, in the whole of human history. **Historia universal**, world history.

historiado, da [is-to-re-ah'-do, dah], *a.* Applied to a painting consisting of various parts harmoniously united. *-pp.* of HISTORIAR.

historiador, ra [is-to-re-ah-dor', rah], *m. & f.* Historian, historiographer, chronicler, a writer of history or of facts and events.

historial [es-to-re-ahl'], *a.* Historical, historic. *-m.* 1. Background, history. 2. Employment record.

historialmente [is-to-re-al-men'-tay], *adv.* Historically.

historiar [is-to-re-ar'], *va.* 1. To historify, to record in history. 2. To represent historical events in paintings or tapestry (arte).

históricamente [is-to'-re-cah-men-tay], *adv.* Historically.

histórico, ca [is-to'-re-co, cah], *a.* Historical, historic.

historieta [is-to-re-ay'-tah], *f. dim.* Short story or tale, short novel or anecdote, mixed with fact and fable. **Historieta cómica**, comic strip.

historiografía [is-to-re-o-grah-fee'-ah], *f.* Historiography.

historiógrafo [is-to-re-oh'-grah-fo], *m.* Historigrapher, historian.

historión [is-to-re'-on'], *m.* A tedious, long-winded story.

histrión [is-tre-on'], *m.* 1. Actor, player; used only in contempt. 2. Buffoon, juggler.

histriónico, ca [is-tre-o'-ne-co, cah], *a.* Histrionic, histrionical.

histrionisa [is-tre-oh-nee'-sah], *f.* An actress.

histrionismo [is-tre-o-nees'-mo], *m.* In contempt, histrionism, the art and profession of an actor or player.

hita [ee'-tah], *f.* A sort of nail without a head; stub-nail.

hito, ta [ee'-to, tah], *a.* Fixed, firm; importunate. **Dar en el hito**, to hit the nail on the head.

hito [ee'-to], *m.* 1. Landmark, anything set up to mark boundaries. 2. Guide-post, milestone. 3. Pin, or mark at which quoits are cast; mark to shoot at. **A hito**, fixedly, firmly. **Dar en el hito** or **dar en el hito de la dificultad**, to hit the nail on the head, to come to the point. **Mirar de hito en hito**, to view with close attention.

hitón [e-ton'], *m.* A large square nail without a head. *(Acad.)*

hobachón, na [o-bah-chone', nah], *a.* Sluggish, fat, and lazy.

hobby [ho'-be], *m.* Hobby.

hobechos [o-bay'-chos], *m. pl.* Soldiers armed with pikes: pikemen.

hoblonera [o-blo-nay'-rah], *f.* Hop-ground, hop-yard, hop-garden, any place where hops are cultivated.

hocicada [o-the-cah'-dah], *f.* 1. A blow given with the snout of a beast and sometimes also with the mouth. 2. Fall upon the face, or headlong on the ground. 3. *(coll.)* A smart reprimand.

hocicar [o-the-car'], *va.* To break up the ground with the snout (cerdo), to nuzzle (persona). *-vn.* 1. To fall headlong with the face to the ground (cerdo), to nuzzle (persona), to pet (amantes). 2. To stumble or slide into errors.

hocico [o-thee'-co], *m.* 1. Snout, the nose of a beast. 2. Mouth of a man who has very prominent lips (persona). 3. Anything disproportionably big or prominent. 4. Gesture of thrusting out the lips, pouting. 6. *(Met.)* The face (cara). **Meter el hocico en todo**, to meddle in everything. **Estar de hocico**, to be at variance.

hocicudo, da, or **hocicón, na** [o-the-coo'-do, dah, o-the-cone', nah], *a.* 1. Long-snouted. 2. Blubber-lipped, flap-mouthed. 3. Looking sullen by thrusting out the lips.

hocino [o-thee'-no], *m.* 1. Bill, a sort of hatchet with a hooked point. 2. The narrow bed of a river which flows between mountains.

hociquillo, ito [o-the-keel'lyo, ee'to], *m. dim.* A little snout.

hockey [ho'-kay-e], *m.* Hockey. **Hockey sobre hielo**, ice hockey.

hodometría [o-do-may-tree'-ah], *f.* Odometry, mechanical measurement of distance.

hodómetro [o-do'-may-tro], *m.* Odometer, an instrument for measuring distance traveled.

hogañazo [o-gah-nyah'-tho], *adv. (coll.)* V. HOGAÑO.

hogaño [o-gah'-nyo], *adv. (coll.)* This present year; in this epoch.

hogar [o-gar'], *m.* 1. Hearth, fire-place; the pavement of a room where fire is kindled. 2. *(Met.)* House, residence, home. **No tienen hogar**, they have no home. **Los que han quedado sin hogar**, the homeless.

hogareño [o-gar'], *a.* Home, family; fireside, home-loving (persona), stay-at-home.

hogaza [o-gah'-thah], *f.* 1. A large loaf of household bread. 2. Any large loaf.

hoguera [o-gay'-rah], *f.* 1. Bonfire. 2. Any blaze produced by burning things heaped together.

hoja [o'-hah], *f.* 1. Leaf of trees and plants. 2. Leaf, anything foliated or thinly beaten; scales (metal). 3. **Hoja de puerta**, leaf, one side of a double door. **Hoja de ventana**, shutter. 4. Blade of a sword or knife. 5. Ground cultivated one year, and lying at rest for another. 6. Half of each of the principal parts of a coat, etc. **Hoja de servicios**, *(Mil.)* a certificate setting forth the rank and services of a military officer. **Hoja de papel**, leaf of paper. **Hoja de un libro**, leaf of a book. **Hoja de estaño**, sheet of bismuth, tin, and quicksilver, laid on the back of a looking glass. **Volver la hoja**, to turn over a new leaf to alter one´s sentiments and proceedings. **Hoja de afeitar**, razor blade. **Hoja de cálculo**, *(Inform.)* electronic spreadsheet. **Hoja de trabajo**, *(Inform.)* worksheet. *-pl.* 1. Leaves, greens. 2. Lamina, thin plates, one coat laid over another. **Hoja de ruta**, flight plan (avión). **Hoja de trebol**, cloverleaf, clover leaf, highway intersection.

hojalata or **hoja de lata** [o-hah-lah'-tah, o'-hah day lah'-tah], *f.* Tin plate.

hojalatería [o-ha-lah-tay-ree'-ah]. 1. The art of making tin-plate, or utensils of it. 2. A tin-shop.

hojalatero [o-hah-lah-tay'-ro], *m.* Tin-man, a manufacturer of tin.

hojaldrado [o-hal-drah'-do], *a.* Laminated, foliate, resembling thin cakes. —**Hojaldrado, da**, *pp.* of HOJALDRAR.

hojaldrar [o-hal-drar'], *va.* To make something of puff paste.

hojaldre [o-hahl'-dray], *m.* or *f.* A sort of pancake or paste.

hojaldrista [o-hal-drees'-tah], *m.* Maker of buttered cakes.

hojarasca [o-hah-rahs'-cah], *f.* 1. Withered leaves; redundancy of leaves; foliage. 2. Useless trifles (palabras), rubbish (basura).

hojear [o-hay-ar'], *va.* To turn the leaves of a book. *-vn.* 1. To form metal into sheets; to foliate.

hojica, illa, ita [o-hee'-cah, eel'-lyah, ee'-tah], *f. dim.* A small leaf.

hojoso, sa, hojudo, da [o-ho'-so, sah, o-hoo'-do, dah], *a.* Leafy, full of leaves.

hojuela [o-hoo-ay'-lah], *f.* 1. *(Dim.)* A small leaf, a leaflet. 2. Puff paste, composed of thin flakes lying one on another (hojas delgadas). 3. Flat gold or silver thread in spools for embroidery. 4. Skins of olives after pressing.

¡hola! [oh'-lah], *int.* 1. Hello!, hallo! (saludo, sorpresa), hullo! (por teléfono). 2. A word used in calling to someone at a distance. 2. Ho! ho! a sudden exclamation of wonder or astonishment (sorpresa). 3. *(Naut.)* Hoy! Ahoy!

holán, holán batista [o-lahn'], *m. (coll.)* Cambric: the finest cambric, batiste.

Holanda [o-lahn'-dah], *f.* Holland, fine Dutch linen.

holandés, sa [o-lan-days´, sah], *a.* Dutchman.

holandilla, holandeta [o-lan-deel-lyah, o-lan-day´-tah], *f.* 1. A lead-colored glazed linen, used for lining. 2. Tobacco of inferior quality. *(Acad.)*

holgachón, na [ol-gah-chone', nah], *a.* Fond of ease and little work.

holgadamente [ol-gah-dah-men´-tay], *adv.* 1. Widely, amply, fully, loosely. **Caben holgadamente**, they fit easily. 2. Quietly, carelessly.

holgado, da [ol-gah-do, dah], *a. pp.* of HOLGAR. 1. Loose (ropa), lax, disproportionately wide or broad. 2. Loose, disengaged, at leisure (sin trabajo). 3. Well off, in easy circumstances, free from want. **Andar** or **estar holgado**, to be well off.

holganza [ol-gahn´-thah], *f*. 1. Repose, ease, tranquility of mind, quiet. 2. Diversion, recreation, amusement (diversión), entertainment. 3. *V.* ASUETO.

holgar [ol-gar´], *vn*. 1. To rest (descansar), to cease from labor (obrero etc.), to lie at rest. 2. To spend one's time free from business. 3. *(Acad.)* To take pleasure or satisfaction in. To be unnecessary, to be superfluous. *-vr*. To sport, to dally, to trifle, to idle, to toy, to play the fool.

holgazán, na [ol-gah-thahn´, nah], *m. & f.* Idler, loiterer, vagabond, lounger.*-a.* Idle, lazy, slothful, inactive, indolent.

holgazanear [ol-gah-thah-nay-ar´], *vn*. To idle or to be idle, to lead an idle life, to be lazy, to loiter, to lounge.

holgazanería [ol-gah-thah-nay-ree´-ah], *f*. Idleness, laziness, sluggishness, slothfulness, inactivity, indolence.

holgín, na [ol-heen´, nah], *a. V.* HECHICERO.

holgorio [ol-go´-re-o], *m. (coll.)* Mirth, jollity, noisy merriment.

holgueta [ol-gay´-tah], *f. (coll.)* A feast, a merry-making.

holgura [ol-goo´-rah], *f*. 1. Country, feast, an entertainment in the country. 2. Width, breadth. 3. Ease (confort), repose. 4. Freedom (ocío). 5. Enjoyment (goce), merriment (alegría).

holladura [oh-lyah-doo´-rah], *f*. 1. Act of trampling. 2. Duty paid for the run of cattle.

hollar [ol-lyar´], *va*. 1. To tread upon, to trample under foot. 2. To trample on or to tread in contempt, to pull down, to humble, to depress.

holleca [ol-lyay´-cah], *f. (Orn.) V.* HERRERILLO.

hollecico, illo, ito, uelo [ol-lyay-thee´-co], *m. dim.* A small pellicle or peel of grapes and some other fruits.

hollejo [ol-lyay´-ho], *m*. Pellicle, peel, the thin skill which covers grapes and other fruit.

hollí [ol-lyee´], *m*. Balsam or resinous liquor distilled from a tree of Mexico and which is used mixed with chocolate.

hollín [ol-lyeen´], *m*. Soot, condensed smoke.

holliniento, ta [ol-lye-ne-en´-to, tah], *a*. Fuliginous, sooty.

holocausto [o-lo-cah´-oos-to], *m*. 1. Holocaust (desastre), a burnt sacrifice. 2. *V.* SACRIFICIO.

hológrafo, fa [o-lo´-grah-fo, fah], *a*. Holographic, holograph, written entirely by the testator.

holómetro [o-lo´-may-tro], *m*. Holometer, an instrument for making all kinds of angular measurements.

holoturias [o-lo-too´-re-as], *a. f. pl.* Holothurian(s), belonging to the Holothuridea; a division of echinoderms, including sea-cucumbers, etc.

homarrache [o-mar-rah´-chay], *m*. Buffoon, jack-pudding, a merry-andrew.

hombracho [om-brah´-cho], *m*. A squat and square thick man.

hombrachón [om-brah-chone´], *m. aug.* A very tall, square, thick man.

hombrada [om-brah´-dah], *f*. 1. A manly action. 2. It is used also in an ironical sense for a ridiculous action.

hombrazo [om-brah´-tho], *m. aug.* A large man.

hombre [om´-bray], *m*. 1. Man, mankind. 2. Man, a male human being as distinguished from woman. 3. Man not a boy: one who has reached adult age. 4. Man, one of uncommon qualifications, qualified in a particular manner. 5. Man, a word of familiarity bordering on contempt. 6. Husband, among the populace. 7. Ombre, game at cards. **Hombre de bien,** an honest man. **Hombre de corazón** or **de gran corazón,** a courageous man. **Hombre de pro** or **de provecho,** a worthy, useful man. **Hombre hecho,** a grown man. **Hombre honrado,** an honest, worthy man. **Hombre de negocios,** businessman. **Hombre de su palabra,** a man of his word. **Ser muy hombre,** to be a man of spirit and courage. **Hombre de cabeza,** a talented man. **¡Hombre!** an exclamation of surprise (sorpresa). **¡Hombre al agua!** man overboard! **Una charla de hombre a hombre,** a man-to-man talk. **El hombre del montón,** the average man. **Hombre blanco,** white man. **El hombre de la calle,** the

man in the street. 8. Dear me! (compasión). 9. Come now! (protesta).

hombrear [om-bray-ar´], *vn*. To assume the man before the time (joven).*-vn. & vr.* To vie with another; to put oneself upon a level with.

hombrecillo [om-bray-theel´-lyo], *m. dim.* Manikin, manling, a pitiful little fellow. **Hombrecillos,** *(Bot.)* hops.

hombrecito [om-bray-thee´-to], *m*. Youth, a young man.

hombrera [om-bray´-rah], *f*. Piece of ancient armor for the shoulders (almohadilla).

hombre rana [om´-bray rah´-nah], *m*. Frogman.

hombría de bien [om-bree´-ah day been´], 1. Probity, honesty.

hombrillo [om-breel´-lyo], *m*. Gusset, an angular piece of cloth.

hombro [om´-bro], *m*. Shoulder. **Encogerse de hombros,** to shrug up the shoulders. **A hombro** or **sobre los hombros,** on the shoulders. **Llevar en hombros,** to support, to protect. **Arrimar el hombro,** to work with a will; to lend a hand. **Echar al hombro,** to shoulder, to become responsible for. **Mirar sobre el hombro,** to cast a contemptuous look. **Sacar a uno en hombros,** to carry somebody out on shoulders.

hombrón [om-brone´], *m*. 1. *(aug.)* A big, lusty man. 2. A man distinguished for talents, knowledge, and valor.

hombronazo [om-bro-nah´-tho], *m. aug.* A huge, vulgar man.

hombruno, na [om-broo´-no, nah], *a*. 1. Manlike, virile; belonging to man. 2. Relating to the shoulders.

homecillo [o-may-thee´-lyo], *m. (Bot.)* Hops.

homenaje [o-may-nah´-hay], *m*. Homage, service to a superior lord, obeisance. **Rendir homenaje,** to pay homage, to profess fealty. **Partido homenaje,** benefit match.

homenajeado, ada [o-may-nah-hay-ah´-do], *m & f.* El homenajeado, the person being honored.

homenajear [o-may-nah-hay-ar´], *va*. To honor.

homeópata [o-may-o´-pah-tah], *m*. Homoeopath(ist).

homeopatía [o-may-o-pah-tee´-ah], *f*. Homoeopathy, the medical system of Hahnemann.

homeopático, ca [o-may-o-pah´-te-co, cah], *a*. Homoeopathic, relating to homoeopathy.

homérico, ca [o-may´-re-co, cah], *a*. Homeric.

homicida [o-me-thee´-dah], *com*. Murderer, homicide. **El arma homicida,** the murder weapon.

homicida [o-me-thee´-dah], *a*. Homicidal, murderous.

homicidio [o-me-thee´-de-o], *m*. 1. Murder, homicide. 2. Ancient tribute.

homilía [o-me-lee´-ah], *f*. Homily, a discourse read in a congregation.

homilista [o-me-lees´-tah], *m*. Author or writer of homilies.

homocéntrico, ca [o-mo-then´-tre-co, cah], *a*. Homocentric, having a common center.

homófono, na [o-mo´-fo-no, nah], *a*. Of like sound, homophonous.

homógamo, ma [o-mo´-gah-mo, mah], *a*. Homogamous, having flowers of one sex only.

homogeneidad [o-mo-hay-nay-e-dahd´], *f*. Homogeneity, homogeneousness.

homogeneizar [o-mo-hay-nay-thar´], *va*. To homogenize (leche).

homogéneo, nea [o-mo-hay´-nay-o, ah], *a*. Homogeneous.

homógrafo, fa [o-mo´-grah-fo, fah], *a*. Homonymous, written alike. *Cf.* HOMÓFONO.

homologación [o-mo-lo-gah-the-on´], *f*. Homologation, publication, or confirmation of a judicial act, to render it more valid.

homologado [o-mo-lo-gah´-do], *a*. Officially approved, authorized.

homologar [o-mo-lo-gar´], *va*. 1. To coordinate (coordinar), to bring into line (estandarizar). 2. To compare (comparar). 3. To check and approve (aprobar).

homólogo, ga [o-mo´-lo-go, gah], *a*. Homologous, having the same ratio; synonymous.

homonimia [o-me-nee'-me-ah], *f.* Homonymy, sameness of name where there is difference of meaning; ambiguity, equivocation.

homónimo, ma [o-mo'-ne-mo, mah], *a.* Homonymous, equivocal.

homosexual [o-mo-sek-soo-ahl'], *a. & m.f.* Homosexual.

homosexualidad [o-mo-sec-soo-ah-le-dahd'], *f.* Homosexuality.

honda [on'-dah], *f.* 1. Sling, a stringed instrument for casting stones.

hondable [on-dah'-blay], *a. (Naut.)* Soundable.

hondamente [on-dah-men'-tay], *adv.* 1. Deeply, profoundly, to a great depth. 2. Deeply profoundly, with deep concern; with deep insight.

hondarras [on-dar'-ras], *f. pl. (Prov.)* Dread or lees or any liquor remaining in the vessel which contained it.

hondazo [on-dah'-tho], *m.* Cast or throw with a sling.

hondear [on-day-ar'], *va.* To unload a vessel (descargar).

hondero [on-day'-ro], *m.* Slinger, a soldier armed with a sling.

hondica, illa, ita [on-dee'-cah], *f. dim.* A small sling to cast stones.

hondijo [on-dee'-ho], *m.* V. HONDA.

hondillos [on-deel'-lyo], *m. pl.* The crotch (de los calzones).

hondo, da [on'-do, dah], *a.* 1. Profound, deep, far below the surface. 2. Profound, low with respect to neighboring places. 3. *(Met.)* V. PROFUNDO. **Con hondo pesar**, with deep regret.

hondo [on'-do], *m. (Prov.)* V. FONDO for bottom.

hondón [on-done'], *m.* 1. Bottom of a vessel or jar where the dregs of liquor settle (taza) 2. Any deep or broken ground. 3. A deep hole. 4. Eye of a needle (aguja).

hondonada [on-do-nah'-dah], *f.* 1. Dale, raving, bottom of a steep place (barranco) 2. Comb, a valley surrounded by hills.

hondura [on-doo'-rah], *f.* Depth (medida, lugar), profundity.

honestamente [o-nes-tah-men'-tay], *adv.* Honestly, modestly.

honestar [o-nes-tar'], *va.* 1. To honor, to dignify. 2. To excuse, to palliate.

honestidad [o-nes-te-dahd'], *f.* 1. Honesty, composure, modesty, moderation. 2. Honesty, purity of sentiments and principles, honorableness; urbanity.

honesto, ta [o-nes'-to, tah], *a.* 1. Honest, decent (decente), honorable (honrado), creditable, handsome, hrave. 2. Honest, comely, pure (casto), chaste, virtuous. 3. Honest, reasonable, just.

hongo [on'-go], *m.* 1. *(Bot.)* Mushroom (comestible). 2. Fungus, an excrescence which grows upon the bark of trees, and serves for tinder. 3. A fleshy excrescence growing on the lips of wounds. **Crecen como hongos**, they grow like mushrooms.

honor [o-nor'], *m.* 1. Honor, a public mark of respect to virtue or merit. 2. Honor, reputation, fame, celebrity. 3. Honor (de mujer). 4. Honor, dignity rank, employment: more commonly used an the plural. **Palabra de honor,** word of honor. **Señoras de honor**, maids of honor. **Honores**, 1. Honors, privileges of rank or birth. 2. Honors, or privileges conferred without gain. 3. Public marks of respect to a person of rank. **En honor de uno**, in somebody's honor. **Hacer los honores de la casa**, to do the honors of the house.

honorable [o-no-rah'-blay], *a.* Honorable, illustrious, noble.

honorablemente [o-no-rah-blay-men-tay], *adv.* Honorably, creditably.

honorario, ria [o-no-rah'-re-o, ah], *a.* 1. Honorary, bestowing honor without gain. **Consejero honorario,** honorary counsellor, one who has the rank and title of a counsellor without the pay.

honorario [o-no-rah'-re-o], *m.* 1. Salary or stipend given for labor (profesional). 2. Fees of counsellors, notaries, or physicians.

honorcillo [o-nor-theel'-lyo], *m. dim.* V. HONRILLA.

honoríficamente [o-no-ree'-fe-cah-men'-tay], *adv.* Honorably.

honorificencia [o-no-re-fe-then'-the-ah], *f.* The act of honoring or doing honor.

honorífico, ca [o-no-ree'-fe-co, cah], *a.* Creditable, honorable, liberal, that which gives honor.

honra [on'-rah], *f.* 1. Honor, reverence, respect. 2. Honor, reputation, celebrity, fame, glory. 3. Honor, chastity (mujer). 4. Honor, mark of respect, favor conferred or received. **Honras**, funeral honors. **Tener algo a mucha honra**, to be proud of something.

honradamente [on-rah-dah-men'-tay], *adv.* Honorably, reputably, honestly.

honradez [on-rah-deth'], *f.* Honesty, probity, integrity, fairness, faithfulness.

honrado, da [on-ra'-do, dah], *a.* 1. Honest, honorable, reputable, just, fair. 2. Honest, exact in the performance of engagements. 3. In an ironical sense, refined in point of roguery and fraud.

honrador, ra [on-rah-dor', rah], *m. & f.* Honorer, one that honors.

honramiento [on-rah-me-en'-to], *m.* Act of honoring.

honrar [on-rar'], *va.* 1. To honor, to reverence, to respect (respetar). 2. To cajole, to caress, to fondle. 3. To dignify, to illustrate, to exalt, to glorify. 4. To praise, to applaud. 5. To credit, to grace to adorn. *-vr.* **Me honro con su amistad**, I am honored by his friendship.

honrilla [on-ree'-lah], *f. dim.* Concern for one's reputation; almost always used with the adjective *negra*, black. **Por la negra honrilla he omitido hacerlo**, I have left it undone from some little point of honor or bashfulness.

honrosamente [on-ro-sah-men'-tay], *adv.* Honorably, honestly, creditably.

honroso, sa [on-ro'-so, sah], *a.* 1. Honorable, decent, decorous, creditable. 2. Just, equitable, honest. 3. Jealous of one's honor.

honrudo, da [on-roo'-do, dah], *a.* Firm in maintaining one's honor, and acting conformably to it.

hontanal [on-tah-nahl'], *m.* V. ONTANAR. **Hontanales**, feasts of the ancients held at fountains.

hontanar [on-tah-nar'], *m.* Place in which water rises, source of springs and rivers.

hopa [oh'-pah], *f.* 1. A long cassock with sleeves. 2. The sack of those who are executed for crime.

hopalanda [o-pah-lahn'-dah], *f.* Tail or train of a gown worn by students.

hopear [o-pay-ar'], *vn.* To wag the tail (animales).

hopeo [o-pay'-o], *m. (coll.)* Volatile, coxcomb.

hopo [o'-po], *m.* Tail with a tuft of hair, similar to that of a fox or squirrel. **Seguir el hopo**, to dog, to pursue closely.

hoque [oh-kay], *m.* Treat given to celebrate the completion of a bargain or contract.

hora [o'-rah], *f.* 1. Hour, the twenty-fourth part of a day. 2. Hour, particular time for doing something (tiempo). 3. Hour, the time as marked by the clock. 4. *(Prov.)* Way made in an hour, a league. 6. Time between twelve and one o'clock on the day of the ascension, during which that mystery is celebrated in Catholic churches. **A la hora de esta** or **a la hora de ahora**, *(coll.)* at this moment. **Cada hora**, every hour, continually. **A buena hora**, at a seasonable time. **A la hora**, at the nick of time, then. **En hora buena**, it is well. **Por horas**, by instants. **En la hora de su muerte**, at the moment of his death. **Es hora de irnos**, it's time we went. **A una hora avanzada**, at a late hour. **Hora del cierre**, closing time. **A la hora de comer**, at lunch-time. **Hora de recreo**, play-time. **A última hora**, at the last moment. **Dar la hora**, to strike. **No ver la hora de algo**, to be scarcely able to wait for something. *-pl.* 1. Hours or canonical hours, the stated times of devotion of the Catholic church. 2. Book which contains the office of the blessed Virgin and other devotions.

hora [o´-rah], *adv.* Now, at this time, at present.-*conj. V.* ORA.

horadable [o-rah-dah´-blay], *a.* Capable of being pierced.

horadación [o-rah-dah-the-on´], *f.* Act of boring or piercing.

horadado [o-rah-dah´-do], *m.* Silkworm's cocoon bored through.—**Horadado, da**, *pp.* of HORADAR.

horadar [o-rah-dar´], *va.* To bore or pierce from side to side.

horado [o-rah´-do], *m.* 1. Hole bored from side to side. 2. Cavern, grotto; niche or cavity in a wall.

horambre [o-ram´-bray], *m.* Hole in the cheeks of mills.

horario, ria [o-rah´-re-o, ah], *a.* Horary, horal, relating to an hour, continuing for an hour.

horario [o-rah´-re-o], *m.* Hour hand of a clock or watch (del reloj). **Puesto de horario partido**, part-time job.

horca [or´-cah], *f.* 1. Gallows, gibbet (ejecución). 2. Sort of yoke for dogs or hogs, to prevent them from doing mischief; also used formerly as a punishment. 3. Fork with two wooden prongs, used by farmers for lifting straw, corn, hay, etc. 4. Rope or string of onions or garlic (ajos).

horcado, da [or-cah´-do, dah], *a.* Forked into different branches; forky.

horcadura [or-cah-doo´-rah], *f.* Fork (árbol).

horcajadas (a), or **a horcajadillas** [ah or-cah-hah´-das], *adv.* Astride on horseback.

horcajadura [or-cah-hah-doo´-rah], *f.* Fork formed by the two thighs.

horcajo [or-cah´-ho], *m.* 1. Yoke or collar put on the neck of mules, when employed in drawing. 2. In oil-mills, the Y-shaped division of the beam. 3. Confluence of two streams (de árbol, de río).

horcate [or-cah´-tay], *m.* 1. A yoke or collar of a horse. 2. Hame, collar of a draught-horse.

horco [or´-co], *m.* Rope or string of onions or garlic.

horcón [o-cone´], *m.* A forked pole set upright, to support the branches of fruit-trees (frutales).

horchata [or-chah´-tah], *f.* An emulsion, usually made of melon or pumpkin seeds, or of almonds.

horchatero, ra [or-chah-tay´-ro, rah], *m. & f.* One who makes or sells almond emulsion.

horda [or´-dah], *f.* Horde, clan, tribe. *V.* ADUAR.

hordeáceas [or-day-ah´-thay-as], *f. pl. (Bot.)* Pertaining to barley, hordeaceous.

hordeína [or-day-ee´-nah], *f.* 1. The finest bran of barley. 2. Hordein, a proximate principle from barley.

hordeolo [or-day-o´-lo], *m.* Hordeolum, stye.

hordiate [or-de-ah´-tay], *m.* 1. Beverage of barley water. 2. *f. (Bot.)* Barley without awns or beard. 3. *(Bot.)* Spring naked barley.

horizontal [o-re-thon-tahl´], *a.* Horizontal, parallel to the horizon; on a level.

horizontalmente [o-re-thon-tal-men´-tay], *adv.* Horizontally, flatly.

horizonte [o-re-thon´-tay], *m.* 1. Horizon, the line which terminates the view. 2. *(Geog.)* Horizon, the largest circle of the sphere, which divides it into two equal parts.

horma [or´-mah], *f.* Mould, model in which anything is cast, formed or modeled. **Horma de zapatero** shoemaker's last. **Hallar la horma de su zapato**, 1. *(coll.)* to meet one's wishes, to accommodate or satisfy anyone. 2. To meet with his match, someone who understands his artifices and can oppose his designs. **Horma de sombrero**, hat block.

hormazo [or-mah´-tho], *m. (Prov.)* House and garden.

hormero [or-may´-ro], *m.* Last-maker.

hormiga [or-mee´-gah], *f.* 1. Ant, pismire, or emmet. **Hormiga blanca**, white ant. 2. A cutaneous eruption, producing an itching which resembles the biting of an ant. 3. **Ser una hormiga**, to be hard (trabajador).

hormigón [or-me-gone´], *m.* Concrete. **Hormigón armado**, reinforced concrete. **Hormigón para bloques**, block concrete.

hormigonera [or-me-go-nay´-rah], *f.* Concrete mixer.

hormigos [or-mee´-gos], *m. pl.* 1. Dessert of hazelnuts and honey. 2 Coarse remains of sifted wheat.

hormigoso, sa [or-me-go´-so, sah], *a.* Relating to ants.

hormigueamiento [or-me-gay-ah-me´-en-to], *m.* Formication, act of itching or moving like ants.

hormiguear [or-me-gay-ar´], *vn.* 1. To itch (piel). 2. To run about like ants.

hormigueo [or-me-gay´-o], *m.* Formication, a sensation like that of the creeping or stinging of ants.

hormiguero [or-me-gay´-ro], *m.* 1. Ant hill or hillock, formicarium. 2. Place where there are a crowd of people moving. 3. *pl.* Pile of weeds covered with earth in which ants breed, and after being burned serve as manure. 4. An anteater.

hormiguero, ra [or-me-gay´-ro, rah], *a.* Relating to the cutaneous eruption called *hormiga*.

hormiguita [or-me-gee´-tah], *f. dim.* A small ant.

hormiguillo [or-me-geel´-lyo], *m.* 1. Distemper which affects the hoofs of horses. 2. People ranged in a line who pass from hand to hand the materials for a work to be raised. 3. In Mexico, a beverage made of pounded cookies, sugar, and spice, boiled together. 4. Mixture of salts with silver. 5. *(Prov.) V.* HORMIGUEO.

hormilla [or-meel´-lyah], *f.* 1. *(Dim.)* A small last.

hormona [or-moh´-nah], *f.* Hormone.

hornabeque [or-nah-bay´-kay], *m. (Fort.)* Hornwork, an outwork, composed of a front and two demi-bastions, joined by a curtain.

hornacero [or-nah-thay´-ro], *m.* Person who watches crucible with silver and gold in the furnace.

hornacina [or-nah-thee´-nah], *f.* Vaulted niche in the wall of an altar.

hornacho [or-nah´-cho], *m.* 1. Shaft of a mine, an excavation formed in a hill. 2. Furnace in which metal is melted for casting statues.

hornachuela [or-nah-choo-ay´-lah], *f.* Hole made in a wall.

hornada [or-nah´-dah], *f.* Batch, the bread balled at one time.

hornaguear [or-nah-gay-ar´], *va.* To open the ground in search of pitcoals.

hornaguera [or-nah-gay´-rah], *f.* Pit-coal, hard coal.

hornaguero, ra [or-nah-gay´-ro, rah], *a.* 1. Wide, spacious. 2. Coaly: applied to ground containing coals.

hornaje [or-nah´-hay], *m. (Prov.)* Money paid to a baker for baking bread.

hornaza [or-nah´-thah], *f.* 1. A small furnace, used by gold and silver-smiths, and other founders, to melt and cast metal. 2. A light yellow color, in painting: a yellow glazing.

hornazo [or-nah´-tho], *m.* Cake made with a batter of eggs and butter (pastel).

hornblenda [orn-blen´-dah], *f.* Horn-blende, a greenish-black variety of amphibole.

hornear [or-nay-ar´], *va.* To carry on the trade of a baker.

hornería [or-nay-ree´-ah], *f.* Trade of a baker.

hornero, ra [or-nay´-ro, rah], *m. & f.* Baker.

hornija [or-nee´-hah], *f.* Brush wood burnt in an oven, to heat it for baking bread.

hornijero [or-ne-hay´-ro], *m.* Person who supplies the oven with fuel.

hornilla [or-neel´-lyah], *f.* 1. Small furnace, stew-hole, a small stove in a kitchen-hearth on which something is put to boil or stew. 2. Pigeon-hole, a hole for pigeons to make their nests and breed in.

hornillo [or-neel´-lyo], *m.* 1. *(Dim.)* A small stove. 2. *(Mil.)* Chamber of a mine. 3. A portable furnace. 4. *(Mil.)* Fougade, a small mine dug under some work or fortification, in order to blow it up.

hornito [or-nee´-to], *m. (Mex.)* A mud-volcano.

horno [or´-no], *m.* 1. Oven. 2. Kiln (alfarero). 3. *(Fig.)* Furnace. **Alto horno**, blast furnace. **No estar el horno para bollos**, not to be the right moment.

horología [o-ro-lo-hee´-ah], *f.* Horology.

horón [o-rone´], *m. (Prov.)* Large round hamper or frail.

horópter, horóptero [o-rop´-tayr, tay´-ro], *m.* A straight line through the point where the optical axes meet.

horóscopo [o-ros´-co-po], *m.* Horoscope, the configuration of the planets at the hour of birth.

horqueta [or-kay´-tah], *f.* 1. (*dim.* of HORCÓN.) A little fork. 2. *(Naut.)* V. HORQUILLAS .

horquilla [or-keel´-lyah], *f.* 1. Forked stick, for hanging up and taking down things from an elevated place. 2. Disease which causes the hair of the head to split. 3. A hair-pin (pelo). 4. A pitchfork. 5. The upper extremity of the sternum. 6. *(Anat.)* The fourchette, inferior commissure of the labia majora. 7. Instrument for operating on tongue-tie. 8. *(Mil.)* An instrument with arquebusiers used to sustain the weapon and fix the aim. 9. *(Vet.)* The frog of a horse's foot. 10. Fork (de bicicleta). 11. Footrest (zanco). **Horquilla de cavar**, garden fork.

horquilladura [or-kee´-lyah-doo´-rah], *f. (Prov.)* Forkedness.

horra [or'-rah], *a.* Among graziere, applied to females not with young; also to the head of cattle given to herds to keep at the expense of their owners.

horrendamente [or-ren-dah-men'-tay], *adv.* Dreadfully.

horrendo, da [or-ren´-do, dah], *a.* 1. Vast, enormous; dreadful, hideous, monstrous, fearful, horrible, grim. 2. Extraordinary, uncommon.

hórreo [or'-ray-o], *m.* A kind of granary built upon pilasters, to prevent rats and mice from injuring the grain.

horrero [or-ray´-ro], *m.* One who has the care of a granary; store-keeper.

horribilidad [or-re-be-le-dahd'], *f.* Horribleness, dreadfulness.

horrible [or-ree´-blay], *a.* Horrid, dreadful, hideous, horrible, heinous. **La película es horrible**, the film is dreadful.

horriblemente [or-re-blay-men'-tay], *adv.* Horribly, heinously, horridly, formidably, damnably.

hórrido, da [or'-re-do, dah], *a.* Horrid, vast, enormous, hideous.

horrífico, ca [or-ree´-fe-co, cah], *a. (Poet.)* Horrific, causing horror.

horripilación [or-re-pe-lah-the-on'], *f. (Med.)* Horripilation, a symptom of the approach of fever.

horripilante [or-re-pe-lahn'-tay], *pa.* Horrifying, harrowing, hair-raising.

horripilar [or-re-pe-lar'], *va.* 1. To cause bristling of the hair. 2. To inspire horror. **Horripilar a uno**, to make somebody's hair stand on. *-vr.* To feel horripilation. **Era para horripilarse**, it was enough to make your hair stand on end.

horripilativo, era [or-re-pe-lah-tee'-vo, vah], *a. (Med.)* Causing horripilation, or belonging to it.

horrísono, na [or-ree´-so-no, nah], *a. (Poet.)* Horrisonous, sounding dreadfully.

horro, ra [or'-ro, rah], *a.* 1. Enfranchised, set at liberty. 2. Free (exento), disengaged.

horror [or-ror'], *m.* 1. Horror, consternation, fright. 2. Horror, hate, abhorrence. 3. Horridness, enormity, hideousness, grimness, frightfulness, the cause of fright or astonishment. **¡Es un horror!** *(coll.)* it is a wonder; that is to say, a great deal of something. **Tener horror a algo**, to have a horror of something. **Hoy he trabajado un horror**, today I worked awfully. **Se divirtieron horrores**, they had a tremendous time.

horrorizar [or-ro-re-thar'], *va.* To cause horror, to terrify. *-vr.* To be terrified.

horrorosamente [or-ro-ro-sah-men'-tay], *adv.* Horribly, frightfully.

horroroso, sa [or-ro-ro'-so, sah], *a.* 1. *(coll.)* Horrid, hideous, frightful. 2. Horrid, dreadful, shocking, offensive, awful (feo).

horrura [or-roo'-rah], *f.* 1. Scoria dross, recrement. 2. Dreariness of a thicket or close wood. 3. Filth, dirt, obscenity.

hortaliza [or-tah-lee'-thah], *f.* Garden stuff, pot-herbs, all sort of esculent plants produced in a garden.

hortatorio, ria [or-tah-to'-re-o], *a. V.* EXHORTATORIO.

hortelanear [or-tay-lah-nay-ar'], *vn. (Prov.)* To cultivate an orchard.

hortelana [or-tay-lah'-nah], *f.* A gardener's wife.

hortelano [or-tay-lah'-no], *m.* Gardener, horticulturist. **Hortelano,** (Orn.) ortolan.

hortense [or-ten´-say], *a.* Hortensial, hortulan, relating to gardens.

hortensia [or-ten'-se-ah], *f. (Bot.)* Hydrant.

hortera [or-tay'-rah], *f.* A wooden bowl.-*m.* 1. Shop assistant, grocer's boy. 2. *(Fig.)* Rough type (inculto), coarse person, fraud (fingido). -*a.* Common (ordinario), vulgar; crude, tasteless; flashy (ostentoso).

horterada [or-tay-rah'-dah], *f.* Crude thing; coarse remark; vulgarity. **Ese vestido es una horterada**, that dress is a disgrace.

hortícola [or-tee'-co-lah], *a.* Horticultural.

horticultor, ra [or-te-cool-tor'], *m & f.* Horticulturist.

horticultura [or-te-cool-too'-rah], *f.* Horticulture, culture of orchards.

hosco, ca [os´-co, cah], *a.* 1. Dark brown (oscuro), liver-colored. 2. Sullen (persona), gloomy. 3. Boastful, ostentatious, vainglorious, arrogant.

hoscoso, sa [os-co'-so, sah], *a.* Crisp, rough.

hospedado, da [os-pay-dah'-do, dah], *a.* Applied to a house receiving guests. *-pp.* of HOSPEDAR.

hospedaje [os-pay-dah'-hay], *m.* 1. Kind reception of guests and strangers. 2. Price paid for lodging.

hospedamiento [os-pay-dah-me-en'-to], *m.* Reception of guests.

hospedar [os-pay-dar'], *va.* To receive, to lodge and entertain strangers and travelers, to harbor. *-vr.* To host, to take up entertainment; to lodge or take a temporary residence. *-vn.* To lodge collegians who have finished their studies, though they live in the college, but at their own expense.

hospedería [os-pay-day-ree'-ah], *f.* 1. Hospice, a house close to a monastery, a convent or a college, for the reception and accommodation of travelers and strangers. 2. Hospitium, a house kept in some places, at the expense of communities, to lodge their members. 3. V. HOSPEDAJE.

hospedero [os-pay-day'ro], *m.* 1. One who kindly receives guests and strangers. 2. Hospitaller, he whose trade is to receive and accommodate travelers and strangers.

hospiciano, na [os-pe-the-ah'-no, nah], *m. & f.* Poor person who lives in a house of charity.

hospicio [os-pee'-the-o], *m.* 1. Hospitium, charitable institution, house of charity. 2. Work-house. 3. *(Prov.)* House of correction. 4. Kind reception to guests and strangers. 5. In monasteries, the same as *hospedería.*

hospital [os-pe-tahl'], *a.* Hospitable, affable. **Hospital de aislamiento**, isolation hospital.

hospital [os-pe-tahl'], *m.* Hospital, infirmary, a place for the reception of the sick or support of the poor. **Hospital de sangre**, a field hospital for first aid to the wounded.

hospitalario, ria [os-pe-tah-lah'-re-o, ah], *a.* Applied to the religious communities which keep hospitals.

hospitalero, ra [os-pe-tah-lay'-ro, rah], *m. & f.* 1. Person entrusted with the care and direction of a hospital. 2. Any hospitable person.

hospitalidad [os-pe-tah-le-dahd'], *f.* 1. Hospitality, hospitage, the practice of kindly entertaining travelers and strangers. 2. Hospitableness, kindness to strangers. 3. The days which a person remains in an hospital.

hospitalización [os-pe-tah-le-thah-the-on'], *f.* Hospitalization.

hospitalizar [os-pe-tah-le-thar'], *va.* To hospitalize.

hospitalmente [os-pe-tal-men'-tay], *adv.* Hospitably.

hosquillo, lla [os-keel'-lyo, lyah], *a. dim.* Darkish, somewhat gloomy.

hostal [os-tahl'], *m.* Boarding house, cheap hotel.

hostelero, ra [os-tay-lay'-ro, rah], *m. & f.* An inn-keeper, tavern-keeper.

hostería [os-tay-ree-ah], *f.* Inn, tavern, hostelry.

hostia [os'-te-ah], *f.* 1. Host, victim, sacrifice offered on the altar. 2. Host, the wafer prepared for the sacrifice of the mass.

hostiario [os-te-ah'-re-o], *m.* Waferbox, in which the bread is preserved that is to be consecrated.

hostiero [os-te-ay'-ro], *m.* Person who prepares the host.

hostigamiento [os-te-gah-me-en'-to], *m.* Chastisement, vexation, molestation.

hostigar [os-te-gar'], *va.* To vex, to trouble, to harass, to molest, to gall, to tire.

hostigo [os-tee'-go], *m.* 1. That part of a wall which the rain and winds beat on. 2. The beating of rain and winds against a wall.

hostil [os-teel'], *a.* Hostile, adverse.

hostilidad [os-te-le-dahd'], *f.* Hostility, opposition in war.

hostilizar [os-te-le-thar'], *va.* To commit hostilities; to hostilize.

hostilmente [os-teel-men'-tay], *adv.* Hostilely.

hotel [o-tel'], *m.* 1. *(Neol.)* Hotel. **Hospedarse en un hotel,** to put up at a hotel. 2. Detached house, suburban house.

hotelero [o-tay-lay-ro], *a.* Hotel. **La industria hotelera,** the hotel trade.

hotentote, ta [o-ten-to'-tay], *m. & f. & a.* Hottentot.

hoy [oh'-e], *adv.* 1. Today, this present day. 2. The present time, the time we live in. **Hoy día, hoy en el día** or **hoy en día,** nowadays. **Hoy por hoy,** this very day. **De hoy en adelante** or **de hoy más,** henceforward in future. **Antes hoy que mañana,** rather today than tomorrow, the sooner the better. **De hoy a mañana,** any time now. **De hoy en ocho días,** a week today.

hoya [oh'-yah], *f.* 1. Hole, cavity, pit in the earth (agujero). 2. *V.* SEPULTURA. 3. *(Amer. Peru.)* Bed of a river.

hoyada [o-yah'-dah], *f.* The lowest part of a field.

hoyito [o-yee'-to], *m. dim.* A small hole, cavity, pit, or excavation.

hoyo [o'-yo], *m.* 1. Hole (agujero), pit, excavation. 2. *V.* SEPULTURA. 3. Inequality or unevenness of a surface. 4. (Golf) Hole. **En el hoyo 18,** at the 18th hole.

hoyoso, sa [oh-yo-so, sah], *a.* Pitted, full of holes.

hoyuelo [oh-yoo-ay'-lo], *m.* 1. *(Dim.)* A little hole, a dimple in the chin or cheek. 2. A boy's play.

hoz [oth], *f.* 1. Sickle, a reaping hook, with which corn is cut. 2. Defile, ravine: a narrow pass. 3. *(Anat.)* Every membranous fold of a sickle shape. **De hoz y de coz,** headlong.

hozadero [o-thah-day'-ro], *m.* Place where hogs turn up the ground.

hozadura [o-thah-doo'-rah], *f.* Rooting, turning up the ground, as hogs do with their snouts.

hozar [o-thar'], *va.* To root, to turn up the ground, as hogs (cerdos).

huaca [oo-ah'-cah], *f. (Peru)* Burial place, ruins, etc., of the ancient Indians of Peru. *V.* GUACA.

huacal [oo-ah-cahl'], *m. (Amer.)* 1. Crate for crockery or fruit. 2. *(Mex.)* A small hen-coop, carried on the back. *V.* GUACAL.

huaquero [oo-ah-kay'-ro], *m. (Peru)* A pitcher of fine earthenware found in the huacas.

huasicama [oo-ah-se-cah'-mah], *m. (S. Amer. Indian)* A door keeper.

huasipongo [oo-ah-se-pon'-go], *m. (Ec.)* An Indian hut.

huaso [oo-ah'-so], *m. V.* GUASO. (Vulgar.)

hucha [oo'-chah], *f.* 1. A large chest, trunk (arca). 2. Money-box (alcancía), piggy bank. 3. Money kept and saved, savings (ahorros). **Tener una buena hucha,** to have money laid by.

húchoho [oo'-cho-o], *m.* Word used to call birds.

huebra [oo-ay'-brah], *f.* 1. Extent of ground which a yoke of oxen can plough every day. 2. Pair of mules with a ploughman hired or let out for a day's work. 3. *(Prov.) V.* BARBECHO.

hueca [oo-ay'-cah], *f.* Notch at the small end of a spindle.

hueco, ca [oo-ay'-co, cah], *a.* 1. Hollow (vacío), empty, concave. 2. Empty, vain, ostentatious. 3. Tumid, resonant, inflated (sonido, voz). **Voz hueca,** sonorous and hollow voice. 4. Soft, spongy: applied to ground, or to short wool fit only for carding. **Se ha puesto muy hueco,** he has become very vain or ostentatious.

hueco [oo-ay'-co], *m.* 1. Notch or nick of a wheel, into which the leaves of a pinion or the teeth of a wheel hitch and set it in motion. 2. Interval of time or place. 3. Hollowness. 4. Hollow, gap (brecha), hole. 5. Any vacant space or aperture in a house or other building (de escalera, de ascensor) 6. *V.* MUESCA. 7. *(Met.)* Office or post vacant (vacante). **Deja un hueco que será difícil llenar,** he leaves a gap which will be hard to fill.

huélfago [oo-el'-fah-go], *m.* Difficulty of breathing in beasts and hawks, or other birds.

huelga [oo-el'-gah], *f.* 1. Strike, go on strike. 2. Rest (descanso), repose; relaxation from work; recreation (recreo), merry-making. 3. Fallow, ground lying at rest. 4. The quitting of work by a body of laborers to enforce compliance with some demand. **Huelga de brazos caídos,** sit-down strike. **Huelga de hambre,** hunger strike. **Huelga patronal,** lock out. **Los obreros en huelga,** the workers on strike.

huelgo [oo-el'-go], *m.* 1. Breath (aliento), respiration. **Tomar huelgo,** to breathe, to respire. 2. *V.* HOLGURA. *(Yo huelgo, yo huelgue, from Holgar. V.* ACORDAR.)

huelguista [oo-ayl-gees'-tah], *m & f.* Striker.

huella [oo-el'-lyah], *f.* 1. Track, footstep; the print of the foot of a man or beast (de pie). 2. The horizontal width of the steps of a staircase (escalera). 3. Act and effect of treading or trampling (acto). 4. Impression of a plate or other thing on paper. 5. An impression morally or physically speaking. **Sin dejar huella,** without leaving a trace. **Seguir las huellas de uno,** to follow in somebody's footsteps.

huellas digitales [oo-el'-lyahs de-he-tah'-less], *f. pl.* Fingerprints.

huello [oo-el'-lyo], *m.* 1. Ground, the floor or level of a place. 2. Step, pace. 3. Lower part of an animal's hoof. *(Yo huello, yo huelle, from Hollar. V.* ACORDAR.)

huembe [oo-em'-bay], *m. (Amer.)* A liana so tough as to sustain great weights. *Cf.* GÜEMBÉ.

huequecito [oo-ay-kay-thee'-to], *m. dim.* A small cavity or space.

huérfago [oo-er'-fah-no], *m. V.* HUÉLFAGO.

huerfanito, ita [oo-er-fah-nee'-to, tah], *m. & f. dim.* A little orphan.

huérfano, na [oo-err'-fah-no, nah], *m. & f.* Orphan, a child who has lost a father or mother or both. **Huérfano de padre,** Fatherless.*-a.* Orphan, bereft of parents.

huero, ra [oo-ay'-ro, rah], *a.* 1. Empty, addle (huevo). 2. *(Met.)* Addle, empty, void.*-m. (Mex.)* A person with light-colored hair.

huerta [oo-err'-tah], *f.* 1. A large orchard, fruit garden, or kitchen garden. 2. *(Prov.)* Land which can be irrigated.

huerto [oo-err'-to], *m.* A small orchard or kitchen garden (de verduras), generally near the house; orchard (de frutales); back garden (de casa pequeña).

huesa [oo-ay'-sah], *f.* Grave, sepulture.

huesarrón [oo-ay-sar-rone'], *m. aug.* A large bone.

huesecico, illo, ito [oo-ay-say-thee'-co], *m. dim.* A little bone.

hueso [oo-ay'-so], *m.* 1. Bone. **Hueso de la alegría,** funny bone. **Sin hueso,** boneless. **Estar en los huesos,** to be nothing but skin and bones. 2. Stone, core, the case which contains the seeds and kernels of fruit. 3. The part of a limestone which remains unburnt in the kiln. 4. Anything which produces more pain than profit. 5. Any useless or unprofitable thing. 6. Piece of ground of little value and bad quality. 7. Hard work (trabajo); stumbling block (obstáculo). 8. Very strict person (persona). **Su profesor es un hueso,** his teacher is terribly strict.

huesoso, sa [oo-ay-so'-so, sah], *a.* Bony, osseous.

huésped, da [oo-ays'-ped, dah], *m. & f.* 1. Guest (invitado), lodger (pensión), one entertained in the house of another. 2. Host (anfitrión), hostess, he who entertains others in his house. 3. Inn-keeper, tavern-keeper. 4. Stranger.

hueste

hueste [oo-ays'-tay], *f.* Host, army to campaign. **Huestes,** hosts, armies.

huesudo, da [oo-ay-soo'-do, dah], *a.* Bony, having large bones.

hueva [oo-ay'-vah], *f.* Egg or spawn of fishes.

huevar [oo-ay-var'], *vn.* To lay eggs.

huevecico, illo, ito, zuelo [oo-ay-vay-thee'co], *f. dim.* A small egg.

huevera [oo-ay-vay'-rah], *f.* 1. Ovarium of birds. 2. Egg stand.

huevero, ra [oo-ay-vay'-ro, rah], *m. & f.* Dealer in eggs.

huevo [oo-ay'-vo], *m.* 1. Egg. 2. Spawn, sperm. 3. Hollow piece of wood used by shoemakers for shaping shoes. 4. Small waxen vessel filled with scented drops. 5. Ball (testículo), testicle. **A huevo,** for a trifle, at a low price. **Huevos estrellados,** fried eggs. **Huevos pasados por agua,** soft-boiled eggs. **Huevos escalfados,** poached eggs. **Huevos revueltos,** buttered eggs. **Nos lo han puesto a huevo,** they've made it easy for us. **Me costó un huevo,** it cost me an arm and a leg (precio).

huevón [oo-ay-vone'], *(LAm.) a.* 1. Idle (vago), lazy; dim (tonto); slow (lento); chicken-livered (cobarde). 2. Brave (valiente).

hugonote, ta [oo-gono'-tay, tah], *m. & f. & a.* Huguenot, a French Protestant.

huída [oo-ee'-dah], *f.* 1. Flight, escape, outleap. *V.* FUGA. 2. Hole made to put in or draw out something with facility. *-pl.* Evasions, subterfuges.

huidero [oo-ee-day'-ro], *m.* 1. Place of retreat, where game retires. 2. Laborer in quicksilver mines, who opens the holes in which the beams of the mine are fixed.

huidizo, za [oo-e-dee'-tho, thah], *a.* Fugitive, fleeing (impresión), shy (persona)

huido [oo-cc'-do], *a.* 1. Fugitive, on the run (que ha huido).

huiñapu [oo-e-nyah'-poo], *m. (Amer.)* Maize moistened and spread upon a bed of straw until it begins to germinate for making chicha.

huir [oo-eer'], *vn.* 1. To flee, to escape; to pack, to go, to flinch or get away, to get off. 2. To give the slip, to slip away; with words denoting time, to pass rapidly, to fly (tiempo). 3. To shun, to avoid doing a bad thing, to flee from. *-vr.* To run away, to escape, to take to one's heels, to make one's escape.

huito [oo-e'-to], *m. (Ec.)* A vegetable dye used for skin diseases.

hulanos [oo-lah'-nos], *m. pl.* Uhlans, name of a light Asiatic cavalry introduced into Europe.

hule [oo'-lay], *m.* 1. Rubber (goma). 2. Oil cloth (tela). **Zapatos de hule,** rubber shoes.

hulero [oo-lay'-ro], *m.* A collector of rubber or caoutchouc.

hulla [ool'-lyah], *f.* Pit-coal, hard goal.

hullera [ool-lyay'-rah], *f.* A coal-mine.

humada [oo-mah'-dah], *f. V.* AHUMADA.

humanado, da [oo-mah-nah'-do, dah], *a. & pp.* of HUMANAR. Humanate, invested with humanity (hijo de Dios).

humanamente [oo-mah-nah-men'-tay], *adv.* 1. Humanely (humanidad), kindly, mercifully. 2. Humanly (en términos humanos) , in the power of men. **Eso humanamente no se puede hacer,** that cannot possibly be done.

humanar [oo-mah-nar'], *va.* 1. To humanize, to soften. 2. *(Poet.)* To transform or convert into man. *-vr.* 1. To become man (hijo de Dios). 2. To become humane or meek: to grow familiar; to be humbled, to be lowered.

humanidad [oo-mah-ne-dahd'], *f.* 1. Humanity, the nature of man (género humano). 2. Humanity (cualidad), human kind, the collective body of mankind. 3. Humanity, benevolence, tenderness, kindness, benignity. 4. *(coll.)* Corpulence (gordura), bulkiness of body, fleshiness. 5. Human weakness. *-pl.* Philology, grammatical studies.

humanista [oo-mah-nees'-tah], *m.* Humanist, philologer, grammarian.

humanitario, ria [oo-mah-ne-tah'-re-o, ah], *a.* 1. Humanitarian, philanthropic. 2. Interesting to the generality of mankind, or tending toward their well-being.

humanizar [oo-mah-ne-thar'], *va. & vr. V.* HUMANAR.

humano, na [oo-mah'-no, nah], *a.* 1. Human, peculiar to man (humano). 2. Humane, kind, merciful, benevolent (benévolo), gracious. **En lo humano,** as regards human power or agency.

humareda [oo-mah-ray'-dah], *f.* 1. A great deal of smoke. 2. Confusion, perplexity.

humazga [oo-math'-gah], *f.* Hearth-money, fumage, tax paid on fireplaces.

humazo [oo-mah'-tho], *m.* Smoke; fume proceeding from burning paper which is doubled and twisted.

humeante [oo-may-ahn'-tay], *va.* Fuming, fumant.

humear [oo-may-ar'], *vn.* 1. To smoke (humo), to emit smoke. 2. To vapor, to emit or exhale fumes or vapors (vapor). 3. *(Met.)* To inflame, to fire (pasiones). 4. *(Met.)* To kindle or stir up a tumult, quarrel, or lawsuit.

humectación [oo-mec-tah-the-on'], *f.* 1. Preparation of a medicine by moistening with water. 2. Dampness of the surface. 3. *(Med.)* Action of fomentations.

humectante [oo-mec-tahn'-tay], *pa. (Med.)* Moistening.

humectar [oo-mec-tar'], *va. (Med.)* To moisten, to wet.

humectativo, va [oo-mec-tah-tee'-vo, vah], *a.* Humective, causing moisture.

humedad [oo-may-dahd'], *f.* Humidity, moisture, dampness, moistness. **A prueba de humedad,** damp-proof.

humedal [oo-may-dahl'], *m.* Humid soil, a marsh.

humedecer [oo-may-day-therr'], *va.* To moisten, to wet (mojar), to soak, to steep, to dampen. *(Yo humedezco, yo humedezca,* from *Humedecer. V.* CONOCER.)

humedecido, da [oo-may-day-thee'-do, dah], *a.* Dampened, moistened, humidified.

húmedo, da [oo'-may-do, dah], *a.* Humid, wet, mist, watery, damp.

humeral [oo-may-rahl'], *a. (Anat.)* Humeral, belonging to the humerus.

húmero [oo'-may-ro], *m.* Humerus, a bone situated between the scapula and forearm.

humero [oo-may'-ro], *m.* Tunnel, funnel, the shaft of a chimney; the passage for the smoke.

humildad [oo-meel-dahd'], *f.* 1. Humility, modesty, meekness. 2. Lowliness, meanness, lowness of mind or birth, submission.

humilde [oo-meel'-day], *a.* 1. Humble (carácter), modest, submissive, meek. 2. Humble, low (clase), not high, not great, not tall. 3. Base, ignoble, of little worth or account. **Son gente humilde,** they are humble people.

humildemente [oo-meel-day-men'-tay], *adv.* Humbly, submissively; modestly, meekly.

humildito, ita [oo-meel-dee'-to, tah], *a. dim.* Very humble or modest.

humillación [oo-meel-lyah-the-on'], *f.* 1. Humiliation, submission, abatement of pride. 2. Humiliation, act of humility, abjectness, humbling: obsequiousness. 3. Humiliation, mortification, self-contempt.

humillador, ra [oo-meel-lyah-dor', rah], *m. & f.* Humiliator.

humillante [oo-meel-lyahn'-tay], *pa. & a.* Humbling, indecorous, unbecoming, degrading.

humillar [oo-meel-lyar'], *va.* 1. To humble, to lower; to bend, to bow (cabeza). 2. To humiliate, to crush (enemigos), to subdue, to bring down from loftiness and pride, to degrade, to depreciate. **Humillar a alguno,** to humiliate someone. *-vr.* To humble oneself, to become humble or submissive.

humillo [oo-meel'-lyo], *m.* 1. *(Dim.)* Smoke or vapor which is not dense. 2. Vanity, petty pride: commonly used in the plural. 3. Disease of sucking pigs.

humita [oo-mee'-tah], *f. (Amer. Peru.)* 1. A small cake made of tender maize and sugar. It is wrapped in maize leaves and cooked in an oven or a water-bath. 2. A rocky substance found in small crystals.

humo [oo'-mo], *m.* 1. Smoke, the visible effluvium from something burning. 2. Vapor (vapor), steam, fumes (gases). 3. Thin, clear, black silk stuff. **Hacer humo,** to smoke. *-pl.* 1. Families or houses in a town or village (hogares). 2. *(Met.)* Vanity, petty pride, haughtiness, presumption (presunción). **Bajar los humos a uno,** to take somebody down a peg. **Tener humos para,** to have the nerve to. **Cortina de humo,** smoke screen. **¡Cuántos humos tiene!,** how presumptuous he is! **Hacerse humo,** to vanish into thin air. **Se le bajaron los humos,** he was put in his place. **Se le han subido los humos a la cabeza,** he's got on his high horse. **Tener muchos humos,** to put on airs.

humor [oo-mor'], *m.* 1. Humor, a general name for any fluid of the body. 2. Humor, the disposition of a person to act in any way. 3. Humor, general turn or temper of mind, mood. **Buen humor,** good-nature, pleasant disposition. **Mal humor,** ill-temper. **Hombre de buen humor,** a good-humored man. **Estar de buen humor,** to be in good humor, to be gay. **Tener sentido del humor,** to have a sense of humor. **Humor de todos los diablos,** very bad temper. **Seguirle el humor a uno,** to humor someone, to go along with somebody. **Si estás de humor,** if you feel like it.

humorada [oo-mo-rah'-dah], *f.* 1. Graceful sprightliness 2. A witty saying, stroke of wit.

humorado, da [oo-mo-rah'-do, dah], *a.* 1. Full of humors. 2. Well or ill disposed.

humoral [oo-mo-rahl'], *a.* Humoral, proceeding from the humors.

humorcico, illo, ito [oo-mor-thee'-co], *m. dim.* of HUMOR. Generally used to denote a bad-tempered person.

humorismo [oo-mo-rees'-mo], *m.* Humor, humorousness.

humorista [oo-mo-rees' tah], *m. f.* Humorist.

humoroso, sa [oo-mo-ro'-so, sah], *a.* Watery, containing fluid.

humoso, sa [oo-mo'-so,sah], *a.* Smoky, fumy.

humus [oo'-moos], *m.* Vegetable mould, humus.

hundible [oon-dee'-blay], *a.* Sinkable, capable of submersion or destruction.

hundido [oon-dee-do], *a.* Sunken; deep-set (ojos), hollow.

hundimiento [oon-de-me-en'-to], *m.* 1. Submersion, immersion, the act of sinking. 2. Downfall, destruction of fabrics (edificio). 3. Cave-in (tierra).

hundir [oon-deer'], *va.* 1. To submerge (sumergir), to immerge, to put under water. 2. To sink, to crush, to overwhelm, to beat down. 3. To refute, to confound. 4. To sink, to make to fall, to pull or bear down, to destroy, to ruin, (edificio). *-vr.* 1. To sink, to fall down, to fall to a level. 2. To sink (arena, lodo), to go to the bottom. 3. *(coll.)* To hide, to lie hidden: applied to things which cannot be found. 4. To have dissensions and quarrels. **Se hundió la economía,** the economy collapsed. **Se hundió en la meditación,** he became lost in meditation.

húngaro, ra [oon'-gah-ro, rah], *a.* Hungarian, pertaining to Hungary.

huno, na [oo'-no, nah], *a.* Hun, one of an obscure Asiatic warlike race. *-m.* The Huns.

hupe [oo'-pay], *f.* A white spongy substance which results from the decomposition of certain woods, and serves as tinder.

hura [oo'-rah], *f.* 1. Furuncle, an angry pustule on the head. 2. A tree of the Antilles, known as the American walnut. 3. A carbuncle.

huracán [oo-rah-cahn'], *m.* Hurricane, a violent storm. *(Carib.)*

huracanado [oo-rah-cah-nah-do], *a.* **Viento huracanado,** hurricane wind.

hurañamente [oo-rah-nyah-men´-tay], *adv.* 1. Wildly, in a savage and intractable manner. 2. Diffidently, disdainfully.

huraño, ña [oo-rah'-nyo, nyah], *a.* 1. Shy (tímido), diffident; intractable. 2. Disdainful. 3. Cold-hearted, loveless. 4. Wild (salvaje).

hurción [oor-the-on'], *f.* V. INFURCIÓN.

hurgar [oor-gar'], *va.* 1. To stir, to move with a stick or iron. 2. To stir up disturbances, to excite quarrels.

hurgón [oor-gone'], *m.* 1. Poker for stirring the fire (fuego); a fire-fork. 2. Thrust in fencing (con arma).

hurgonada [oor-go-nah'-dah], *f.* V. ESTOCADA.

hurgonazo [oor-go-nah´-tho], *m.* A violent thrust.

hurgonear [oor-go-nay-ar´], *va.* 1. To stir the fire with a poker (fuego). 2. To make a thrust in fencing (adversario).

hurgonero [oor-go-nay'-ro], *m.* Poker. V. HURGÓN.

hurí [oo-ree'], *f.* Houri, a Mohammedan nymph of paradise.

hurón, na [oo-ro-ne', nah], *m. & f.* 1. Ferret. 2. Ferreter, one who pries into others' secrets. *-a.* Cold-hearted, loveless, shy, intractable, disdainful.

huronear [oo-ro-nay-ar'], *va.* 1. To ferret, to hunt with a ferret. 2. To pry, snoop, ferret (escudriñar).

huronera [oo-ro-nay'-rah],*f.* 1. Ferret hole. 2. Lurking place.

huronero [oo-ro-nay'-ro], *m.* Ferret keeper.

¡hurra! [oor'-rah], *int.* Hurrah!

hurraca [oor-rah'-cah], *f. (Orn.)* Magpie.

hurtable [oor-tah'-blay], *a.* Capable of being stolen.

hurtadillas (a) [oor-tah-deel'-lyas], *adv.* By stealth, slyly, artfully, privately, in a hidden manner.

hurtadineros [oor-tah-de-nay'-ros], *m. (Prov.) V.* ALCANCÍA.

hurtador, ra [oor-tah-dor', rah], *m. & f.* Robber, thief.

hurtagua [oor-tah'-goo-ah], *f. (Prov.) V.* REGADERA.

hurtamano (de) [oor-tah-mah'-no], *adverbial phrase.* Without consideration or pity.

hurtar [oor-tar'], *va.* 1. To steal (robar), to rob, to make way with. 2. To cheat in weight or measure. 3. To recover a piece of ground from the sea or a river (mar) 4. To separate, to part. **Hurtar el cuerpo,** to flee, to avoid a difficulty. 5. To commit plagiarism. *-vr.* To remove or withdraw (retirarse), to abscond.

hurtarropa [oor-tar-ro'-pah], *f.* Boy's play.

hurto [oor'-to], *m.* 1. Theft (acto), robbery, stealing. 2. Theft, the thing stolen (cosa robada). 3. In mines, passage between the principal apartments. **A hurto,** by stealth.

husada [oo-sah'-dah], *f.* A spindleful of thread or worsted.

husaño [oo-sah'-nyo], *m.* A large spindle.

húsar [oo'-sar], *m.* Hussar, originally a Hungarian horse soldier.

husillero [oo-see´-lyay'-ro], *m.* One who attends the spindle in oil-mills.

husillo [oo-seel'-lyo], *m.* 1. *(Dim.)* A small spindle. 2. A hollow cylinder running round in a spiral nut; a screw-pin. *-pl.* Drains, small channels for draining fens.

husita [oo-see'-tah], *m.* Hussite, a follower of John Huss.

husma [oos'-mah]. *f.* **Andar a la husma,** *(coll.)* to peep narrowly in order to discover secrets.

husmeador, ra [oos-may-ah-dor', rah], *m. & f.* Scenter, smeller.

husmeadorcillo, lla [oos-may-ah-dor-theel'-lyo, lyah], *m. & f. dim.* Little smeller.

husmear [oos-may-ar´], *va.* 1. To scent, to find out by smelling. 2. To pry, to peep, or inspect curiously, officiously, or impertinently.*-vn.* To begin to smell bad (carne).

husmo [oos'-mo], *m.* Smell of meat somewhat tainted. **Estar al husmo,** to be on the scent; to watch for a favorable opportunity to do something.

huso [oo'-so], *m.* Spindle, the pin by which the thread is formed, and on which it is wound.

huta [oo'-tah], *f.* Hut, kind of shed in which huntsmen hide, in order to start their dogs at the chase.

hutía [oo-tee'-ah], *f.* Cuban rat.

¡huy! [oo'-e]. Interjection of surprise (sorpresa), astonishment, grief (dolor), on seeing or hearing something.

huyuyo, ye [oo-yoo'-yo, yah], *a. (Cuba)* Untractable, shy, diffident.

I

i [ee], the third of the Spanish vowels called the Latin *i*, to distinguish it from the *y* called Greek. *I* in Spanish is sounded like the English *e* in *even,* or *i* in *idiotism.* As a numeral, it stands for one. In chemistry, it is the symbol for iodine. (I.)

Iberia [e-bay'-re-ah], *f.* 1. An ancient region of Asia, now transcaucasian Georgia. 2. Name given by the ancient Greeks to Spain and Portugal.

ibérico, ca [e-bay'-re-co, cah], *a.* or **íbero** [ebay'-ro], *m.* Spaniard.-*a.* Spanish, Iberian.

iberoaméricano [e-bay-ro-ah-may-re-cah'-no], *a. m & f.* Latin-American.

íbice [ee'-be-thay], *m.* Ibex, kind of goat.

ibidem [e-bee'-dem]. Ibidem. Latin word, meaning *in the same place.* In the same writing of an author.

ibis [ee'-bes], *f. (Orn.)* Ibis, a kind of bird.

icaco [e-cah'-co], *m. (Bot.)* West Indian cocoaplum.

iceberg [e-thay-ber'], *m.* Iceberg.

icneumón [ic-nay-oo-mon'], *m.* 1. Ichneumon, a small animal; a mongoose. The Egyptian ichneumon devours the eggs of the crocodile, and was held sacred by the ancient Eygptians. 2. The ichneumonfly, a hymenopterous insect predatory upon other insects.

icnografía [ec-no-grah-fee'-ah], *f.* 1. Ichnography, ground plan, a delineation of the length, breadth, angles, and lines of a fortification or building. 2. Ground-plot, the ichnography of building.

icnográfico, ca [ec-no-grah'-fe-co, cah], *a.* Ichnographical.

icónico, ca [e-co'-ne-co, cah], *a.* Exactly conformable to the model; a perfect image.

icono [e-co-no], *m.* Ikon, icon.

iconoclasta, iconómaco [e-co-no-clahs'-tah, e-co-no'-mah-co], *m.* Iconoclast, image breaker, heretic who denies the worship due to holy images.

iconografía [e-co-no-grah-fee'-ah], *f.* Iconography, the art of describing by pictures.

iconográfico, ca [e-co-no-grah'-fe-co, cah], *a.* Relating to iconography.

iconólatra [e-co-no'lah-trah], *m.* Iconolater, a worshipper of images.

iconología [e-co-no-lo-hee'-ah], *f.* Iconology, representation by figures.

iconoscopio [e-co-nos-co'-pe-o], *m.* Iconoscope.

icoroso, sa [e-co-ro'-so, sah], *a.* Ichorous, serous.

icosaedro [e-co-sah-ay'-dro], *m.* Icosahedron, a solid bounded by twenty plane faces.

ictericia [ic-tay-ree'-the-ah], *f.* Jaundice, a disease.

ictericiado, da, icotérico, ca [ic-tay-re-the-ah'-do, dah, ec-tay'-re-co, cah], *a.* Icterical, jaundiced.

ictiofagia [ic-te-o-fah'-he-ah], *f.* Ichthyophagy, diet of fish.

ictiófago, ga [ec-te-o'-fah-go, gah], *a.* Fish-eating, relating to the ichthyophagists.-*m. & f.* Ichthyophagist.

ictiología [ic-te-o-lo-he'-ah],*f.* Ichthyology, the science of the nature of fishes.

ictiopetra [ic-te-o-pay'-trah], *f.* A petrified fish.

ictiosauro [ic-te-o-sah'-oo-ro], *m.* Ichthyosaurus.

ictiosis [ic-te-o'-sis],*f.* Ichthyosis, a scaly disease of the skin.

ictita [ic-tee'-tah],*f.* A stone which preserves the impression of a fish.

icho, or **ichu** [ee'-cho, ee'-choo], *m.* Grass in the Andes. *(Peru)*

ida [ee'-dah], *f.* 1. Departure, act of going from one place to another (partida). 2. *(Met.)* Impetuosity, rash, inconsiderate, or violent proceeding, silly. 3. Act of driving a ball out of the truck-table. 4. Mark or impression of the foot or game on the ground. **Ida y vuelta**, out and home, round-trip, excursion. **Dejar las idas por las venidas**, to miss the boat. **Viaje de ida**, outward journey.

idea [e-day'-ah], *f.* 1. Idea, a mental image. 2. Notion (noción), conception. **Idea genial**, bright idea. **Meterse una idea en la cabeza**, to get an idea into one's head. 3. Contrivance, design, intention (propósito), plan, project, scheme. **Con la idea de**, with the idea of. **Cambiar de idea**, to change one's mind. 4. Thread of a discourse. 5. Model, example. 6. Genius, talent. 7. Fancy. conceit, extravagant notion, impression: in this sense it is used commonly in the plural.

ideal [e-day-ahl'], *a.* Ideal, mental, intellectual, imaginary, notional: not physical.

idealidad [e-day-ah-le-dahd'],*f.* 1. Ideality, the ideal. 2. Ideality, the sentiment of the beautiful, the poetic, the eloquent.

idealismo [e-day-ah-lees'-mo], *m.* 1. Idealism, generic name of the philosophic systems which consider the idea as the essence of things. 2. Aptitude of the artist, poet, orator, etc., to raise above reality the objects which he describes.

idealista [e-day-ah-lees'-tah], *a.* Idealistic, striving after the ideal. -*m.* Idealist, believer in idealism.

idealizar [e-day-ah-le-thar'], *va.* To idealize.

idealmente [e-day-al-men'-tay], *adv.* Ideally, intellectually.

idear [e-day-ar'], *va.* 1. To form or conceive an idea. 2. To think, to contrive, to invent, to imagine, to plan, to scheme, to meditate. 2. To discuss a subject on futile grounds, to indulge in airy conceptions.

idem [ee'-dem], *prom. (Lat.)* Idem, the same.

idénticamente [e-den'-te-cah-men'-tay], *adv.* Identically.

idéntico, ca [e-den'-te-co, cah], *a.* Identic, identical, congenerous, the same, implying the same thing.

identidad [e-den-te-dahd'], *f.* Identity, sameness, identicalness.

identificación [e-den-te-fe-cah-the-on'], *f.* Identification. **Identificación errónea**, mistaken identity.

identificar [e-den-te-fe-car'], *va.* To identify; to ascertain the sameness of two objects.-*vr.* To become the same.

ideográfico, ca [e-day-o-grah'-fe-co, cah], *a.* Ideographic, presenting ideas by symbolic characters.

ideografía [e-day-o-gra-fee'-ah], *f.* Ideography, representation of thought by signs especially phonetic.

ideología [e-day-o-lo-hee'-ah], *f.* Ideology, ideas.

ideológico, ca [e-day-o-lo'-he-co, cah], *a.* Ideological.

idílico, ca [e-dee'-le-co, cah], *a.* Idyllic, having the qualities of an idyl.

idilio [e-dee'-le-o], *m. (Poet.)* Idyl, a pastoral poem, romance (amor).

idioma [e-de-o'-mah], *m.* 1. Language, tongue, idiom, the language peculiar to a nation or country. 2. Idiom, mode of speaking peculiar to a dialect or language. **No hablamos el mismo idioma**, we just don't speak the same language.

idiomático, ca [e-de-o-mah'-te-co, cah], *a.* Idiomatic, proper to a language.

idiopatía [e-de-o-pah-tee'-ah],*f.* Idiopathy, a primary disease distinctive in character.

idiopático, ca [e-de-o-pah'-te-co, cah], *a.* Idiopathic, primary, independent (enfermedades).

idiosincrasia [e-de-o-sin-crah'-se-ah],*f.* Idiosyncrasy, a peculiar disposition.

idiota [e-de-o'-tah], *m.* Idiot, a fool, an ignorant person.

idiotez [e-de-o-teth'], *f.* Idiotism, silliness, ignorance, idiocy.

idiotismo [e-de-o-tees, mo], *m.* l. Idiom (gramática), idiotism, peculiarity of expression. 2. Idiocy, folly, natural imbecility of mind.

ido, da [ee'-do, dah], *pp.* of IR. Gone. 1. *(LAm.)* Absent-minded (despistado). 2. *(LAm.)* Nuts, crazy (chiflado). 3. *(CAm. Mex.)* **Estar ido**, to be drunk.

idólatra [e-do'-lah-trah], *a.* Idolatrous, heathen, paganish.

idolatra [e-do'-lah-trah], *m.* 1. Idolater, a worshipper of idols. 2. One who idolizes a woman, or loves her with excessive fondness.

idolatradamente [e-do-lah-trah-dah-men'-tay], *adv.* Idolatrously.

idolatrar [e-do-lah-trar'], *va.* 1. To idolatrize. 2. To idolize, to love excessively.

idolatría [e-do-lah-tree'-ah], *f.* 1. Idolatry. 2. Inordinate love, excessive fondness.

idolito, illo [e-do-lee'-to], *m. (Dim.)* 1. A little idol. 2. Darling, favorite, the object of fondness.

idolo [ee'-do-lo], *m.* 1. Idol, an image worshipped as God. 2. *(Col.)* Idol, a person or thing loved with the utmost affection.

idoneidad [e-do-nay-e-dahd'], *f.* Aptitude (capacidad), fitness, capacity.

idóneo, nea [e-doh'-nay-o, ah], *a.* Fit, convenient, proper, neat, suitable (apropiado); *(Mex.)* genuine (genuino).

idus [ee'-doos], *m.* Ides, last of the three parts into which the Romans divided the month.

iglesario [e-glay-sah'-re-o], *m.* The total of the lands which used to belong to the churches.

iglesia [e-glay'-se-ah], *f.* 1. Church, the collective body of Christians. 2. Church, body of Christians adhering to some particular form of worship. 3. Church, place which Christians consecrate to the worship of God. 4. Temple, place where Christian worship. 5. Ecclesiastical state; chapter; diocese. 6. Right of immunity enjoyed in churches. **Iglesia Anglicana**, Church of England. **Iglesia Católica**, Catholic Church. **Casarse por la iglesia**, to get married in church.

iglú [e-gloo'], *m.* Igloo.

ignaro, ra [ig-nah'-ro, rah], *a.* Ignorant, unlearned, uninstructed.

ignavia [ig-nah'-ve-ah], *f.* Idleness, laziness, carelessness.

igneo, ea [eeg'-nay-o, ah], *a.* Igneous, fiery.

ignescente [ig-nes-then'-tay], *a.* Scintillating, burning, ignescent.

ignición [ig-ne-the-on'], *f.* Ignition, the act of kindling or setting on fire.

ignícola [ig-nee'-co-lah], *m.* Fire-worshipper.

ignífero, ra [ig-nee'-fay-ro, rah], *a. (Poet.)* Igniferous, ignifluous, containing or emitting fire.

ignipotente [ig-ne-po-ten'-tay], *a. (Poet.)* Ignipotent, having power over fire.

igniscencia [ig-nis-then'-the-ah], *f.* Incandescence.

igniscente [ig-nis-then'-tay], *a.* Incandescent, glowing with heat.

ignoble [ig-no'-blay], *a. (Ant.)* V. INNOBLE.

ignografía [ig-no-grah-fe'-ah], *f.* V. ICNOGRAFÍA.

ignominia [ig-no-mee'-ne-ah], *f.* Ignominy, infamy, public disgrace, opprobrium.

ignominiosamente [ig-no-me-neo-sah-men'-tay], *adv.* Ignominiously, opprobriously.

ignominioso, sa [ig-no-me-ne-o'-so, sah], *a.* Ignominious, opprobrious, reproachful, disgraceful.

ignorado, da [ig-no-rah'-do, dah]. *a. & pp.* of IGNORAR. Unknown, occult, fameless.

ignorancia [ig-no-rahn'-the-ah], *f.* Ignorance, unlearnedness, want of knowledge, illiterateness; idiotism; folly; darkness.

ignorante [ig-no-rahn'-tay], *pa. & a.* 1. Ignorant, stupid, unlearned, uninstructed. 2. Ignorant, without knowledge of some particular. -*m.* Ignorant.

ignorantemente [ig-no-ran-tay-men'-tay], *adv.* Ignorantly.

ignorantón, na [ig-no-ran-tone', nah], *a. aug.* Grossly ignorant.

ignorar [ig-no-rar'], *va.* To be ignorant of, not to know (desconocer). **Lo ignoro en absoluto**, I don´t know at all. **Ignoramos su paradero**, we don´t know his whereabouts.

ignoto, ta [ig-no'-to, tah], *a.* Unknown, undiscovered.

igorrote [e-go-rro'-tay], *m.* Name of a tribe of savage Indians of the island of Luzón (Philippines), and of their language.

igual [e-goo-ahl'], *a.* 1. Equal, similar, the same, alike (semejante), coequal, like another in any quality that admits comparison. **No vi nunca cosa igual**, I never saw the like. **Me es igual**, it´s all the same to me. 2. Level, even (llano), flat. **Ir iguales**, to be level. 3. Like, resembling, similar, uniform,

equable. 4. Constant (constante), firm, determined, equanimous, consistent. -*m.* The sign of equality, *viz.=*. **En igual de**, instead of. **Al igual**, equally. **No tiene igual**, he has not his like; it is matchless. **Por igual** or **por un igual**, equally, with equality. **Sin igual**, not to be equalled. -*m & f.* Equal. **Al igual**, equally. **Ser el igual de**, to be the equal of. **No tener igual**, to be unrivalled.

iguala [e-goo-ah'-lah], *f.* 1. Agreement, convention, stipulation, contract, commutation. 2. Equalizing, equalling, the act of equalling. 3. Level, an instrument with which masons adjust their work. 4. Stipend or gratuity given in settlement, and especially a yearly or monthly stipend given in rural districts to doctors and apothecaries for the right to services and medicines.

igualación [e-goo-ah-lah-the-on'], *f.* 1. Equalling, equalizing, equalization, levelling, the act and effect of making equal or even. 2. Agreement, stipulation, contract. 3. *(Alg.)* Equation. 4. Counter-gauge, a trimming of one piece of wood into another.

igualado, da [e-goo-ah-lah'-do, dah], *pp.* of IGUALAR. Equalled. Said of some birds which have shed their down and have even plumage. **Dejar a uno igualado,** *(coll.)* to give one a severe drubbing. -*a. (CAm. Mex.)* Cheeky (irrespetuoso); sly (astuto).

igualador, ra [e-goo-ah-lah-dor', rah], *m. & f.* 1. Equalizer, leveller. 2. A kind of sieve of fine skin for refining the grain of powder.

igualamiento [e-goo-ah-lah-me-en'-to], *m.* Equalizing, equalization, act of equalling.

igualar [e-goo-ah-lar'], *va.* 1. To equalize (hacer igual), to match, to mate. 2. To judge without partiality, to hold in equal estimation. 3. To flatten, to make even or level, to level the ground (allanar). 4. To rake the ground. 5. To adjust differences, to agree upon.-*vn.* To be equal. -*vr.* To level, to efface distinction or superiority, to place oneself upon a level with others. 2. *(Met.)* To give a second blow. 3. *(CAm. Mex.)* To be familiar, to be cheeky (faltar al respeto).

igualdad [e-goo-al-dahd'], *f.* 1. Equality, similitude. 2. Conformity, consimilitude, likeness. 3. Levelness, evenness (superficie), equality of surface. 4. Equality, uniformity. **Igualdad de ánimo**, evenness of mind; constancy, equability.

Igualmente [e-goo-al-men'-tay], *adv.* Equally, uniformly, equably, evenly (modo uniforme); likewise (también); constantly.

iguana [e-goo-ah'-nah], *f.* Iguana, a kind of lizard, a native of America.

iguarandi [e-goo-ah-rahn'-de], *m. (Amer.)* Pellitory.

igüedo [e-goo-ay'-do], *m.* V. CABRÓN.

ijada [e-hah-dah], *f.* 1. Flank, the lateral part of the lower belly. 2. Pain in the side, colic (dolor). **Tener su ijada,** *(Met.)* to have a weak side.

ijadear [e-hah-day-ar'], *vn.* To pant, to palpitate.

ijal [e-hahl'], *m. (Cuba)* V. IJADA.

ijar [e-har'], *m.* Flank. V. IJADA.

ilación [e-lah-the-on'], *f.* Inference, illation, conclusion drawn.

ilativo, va [e-lah-tee'-vo, vah], *a.* Illative, that which denotes illation or conclusion.

ilegal [e-lay-gahl'], *a.* Illegal, unlawful.

ilegalidad [e-lay-gah-le-dahd'], *f.* Illegality, unlawfulness.

ilegalizar [e-lay-gah-le-thar'], *va.* To outlaw, to declare illegal.

ilegalmente [e-lay-gal-men'-tay], *adv.* Illegally, lawlessly, unlawfully.

ilegible [e-lay-hee'-blay], *a.* Illegible.

ilegítimamente [e-lay-hee'-te-mah-men-tay], *adv.* Illegitimately, foully.

ilegitimar [e-lay-he-te-mar'], *va.* To illegitimate, to render or prove a person illegitimate.

ilegitimidad [e-lay-he-te-me-dahd'], *f.* Illegitimacy.

ilegítimo, ma [e-lay-hee'-te-mo, mah], *a*. 1. Illegal, contrary to law. 2. Illegitimate, unlawfully begotten. 3. False (falso).

ileo [e'-lay-o], *m*. Ileus, severe colic due to intestinal obstruction.

ileon [ee'-la-yon], *m*. Ileum, the third division of the small intestines.

ileosía [e-la-yo-see'-ah], *f*. V. ILEO.

ileso, sa [e-lay'-so, sah], *a*. Unhurt, free from damage, harmless. **Salió ileso del accidente**, he came out of the accident unharmed. **Los pasajeros resultaron ilesos**, the passengers were unhurt.

ilíaco, ca [e-lee'-ah-co, cah], *a*. Belonging or relating to Ilium or Troy.

iliberal [e-le-bay-rahl'], *a*. Illiberal.

ilícitamente [e-lee'-the-tah-men'-tay], *adv*. Illicitly, forbiddenly.

ilícito, ta [e-lee'-the-to, tah], *a*. Illicit, unlawful.

ilimitado, da [e-le-me-tah'-do, dah], *a*. Unlimited, boundless, limitless, unconditional.

ilion [ee'-le-on], *m*. Ilium, the upper part of the innominate bone.

ilíquido, da [e-lee'-ke-do, dah], *a*. Unliquidated (cuentas, deudas).

iliterato [e-le-tay-rah'-to], *a*. Illiterate, unlearned.

illutar [ee-llyoo-tar'], *va*. To cover a part of the body with mud or mineral sediment; to illutate; to take a mud bath.

ilógico, ca [e-lo'-he-co, cah], *a*. Illogical.

ilota [e-lo'-tah], *m*. 1. A slave of Lacedemonia; a Helot. 2. One deprived of the rights and privileges of a citizen.

iludir [e-loo-deer'], *va*. V. BURLAR.

iluminación [e-loo-me-nah-the-on'], *f*. 1. Illumination, the act of supplying with light. **Iluminación indirecta**, indirect lighting. 2. Illumination, festive lights, hung out as a token of joy. 3. Illumination, infusion of intellectual light, knowledge, or grace.

iluminado, da [e-loo-me-nah'-do, dah], *a*. & *pp*. of ILUMINAR. Illuminate, enlightened (en mal sentido).

iluminado, da [e-loo-me-nah'-do], *m* & *f*. Illuminate, visionary; illuminist.

iluminador [e-loo-me-nah-dor'], *m*. Illuminator, one who illumines; one who adorns with colors. -*a*. Illuminating.

iluminar [e-loo-me-nar'], *va*. 1. To illumine or illuminate (alumbrar), to light, to fill with light, to supply with light. 2. To illuminate, to adorn with festal lamps or bonfires. 3. To illuminate, to enlighten intellectually, to infuse knowledge or grace. 4. To give light and shade to a painting; to color, to illumine books. 5. To render transparent.

iluminativo, va [e-loo-me-nah-tee'-vo, vah], *a*. Illuminative.

ilusión [e-loo-se-on'], *f*. 1. Illusion (noción falsa), false show, counterfeit appearance; fallaciousness. **Todo es Ilusión**, it´s all an illusion. 2. A sort of smart and lively irony. 3. (*coll*.) Apprehension. 4. Hope, dream (esperanza, suello). **Con ilusión**, hopefully. **No te hagas ilusiones**, don´t get any false ideas. 5. Excitement (emoción), thrill; eagerness; hopeful anticipation (expectación). **Trabajar con ilusión**, to work with will.

ilusionado [e-loo-se-o-nah'-do], *a*. *m* & *f*. Hopeful; excited, eager. **El viaje me trae muy ilusionado**, I am so looking forward to the trip.

ilusionar [e-loo-se-o-nar'], *va*. 1. To cause illusion (alentar). 2. To fascinate. -*vr*. To suffer illusions.

ilusivo, va [e-loo-see'-vo, vah], *a*. Delusive, illusive, false, deceitful.

iluso, sa [e-loo'-so, sah], *a*. 1. Deluded, deceived, ridiculed. 2. Bigoted. -*m* & *f*. Dreamer, visionary.

ilusoriamente [e-loo-so-re-ah-men'-tay], *adv*. Illusively.

ilusorio, ria [e-loo-so'-re-o, ah], *a*. 1. Delusive, illusory, deceptive. 2. (*Law*.) Null, void of effect, of no value.

ilustración [e-loos-trah-the-on'], *f*. 1. Illustration, explanation, elucidation, exposition, explication. 2. *pl*. The engravings of a book or periodical.

ilustrado, da [e-loos-trah'-do, dah], *a*. Wise, intelligent, of abundant knowledge.

ilustrador, ra [e-loos-trah-dor´, rah], *m*. & *f*. Illustrator, explicator.

ilustrar [e-loos-trar'], *va*. 1. To illustrate, to clear up, to explain (aclarar), to enlighten, to elucidate. 2. To inspire, to infuse supernatural light. 3. To aggrandize, to ennoble, to illustrate, to heighten. 4. To provide printed matter with plates or engravings. 5. To make famous (hacer famoso). -*vr*. 1. To acquire knowledge (instruirse). 2. To become celebrated (hacerse famoso).

ilustre [e-loos´-tray], *a*. Illustrious, noble, celebrated, conspicuous, glorious, honorable, magnificent.

ilustremente [e-loos-tray-men´-tay], *adv*. Illustriously, greatly.

ilustrísimo, ma [e-loos-tree'-se-mo, mah], *a*. Appellation of honor given to bishops and other persons of a certain dignity. **Su ilustrísima**, His Grace.

imadas [e-mah'-das], *f*. *pl*. (*Naut*.) Ways, sliding planks used in launching ships.

imagen [e-mah'-hen], *f*. 1. Image, figure, any corporeal representation, imagery, statue, effigy. 2. Image, show appearance, fancy, conception. 3. (*Rhet*.) Picture or lively description. **Ser la viva imagen de**, to be the living image of. **Imagen fantasma**, ghost image.

imagencita, illa [e-mah-hen-thee'-tah, thee-llyah], *f*. *dim*. A little image.

imaginable [e-mah-he-nah'-blay], *a*. Imaginable, contrivable, conceivable.

imaginación [e-mah-he-nah-the-on'], *f*. 1. Imagination, fancy; the power of forming ideal, pictures. 2. Imagination, conception, image of the mind. 3. Conceit, fantasy; any unsolid or fanciful opinion or idea. **Ni por imaginación**, on no account. **Ella se deja llevar por la imaginación**, she lets her imagination run away with her.

imaginar [e-mah-he-nar'], *va*. 1. To imagine, to fancy, to image, to paint in the mind (visualizar). 2. To imagine, to scheme, to contrive, to excogitate, to conceive; to find out. 3. To form erroneous suppositions. **Cosas que nadie imagina**, things that no-one imagines. -*vn*. V. FIGURARSE.

imaginaria [e-mah-he-nah'-re-ah], *f*. (*Mil*.) Reserve guard.

imaginariamente [e-mah-he-nah-reah-men'-tay], *adv*. In a visionary manner.

imaginario [e-mah-he-nah'-re-o], *m*. Painter or sculptor of images.

imaginario, ria [e-mah-he-nah'-re-o], *a*. Imaginary, fancied, visionary.

imaginativa [e-mah-he-nah-tee'-vah], *f*. Imagination, fancy.

imaginativo, va [e-mah-he-nah-tee'-vo, vah], *a*. Imaginative, fantastic, fanciful.

imaginería [e-mah-he-nay-ree'-ah], *f*. Imagery, an embroidery representing flowers, birds, or fishes.

imán [e-mahn'], *m*. 1. Loadstone, the magnet. 2. The mariner's compass. 3. Charm, attraction. 4. Electromagnet.

imanación [e-ma-nah-the-on'], *f*. V. IMANTACIÓN.

imanar [e-mah-nar'], *va*. To magnetize, to communicate the property of a loadstone.

imantación [e-man-tah-the-on'], *f*. Magnetization. V. MAGNETIZACION.

imantar [e-man-tar'], *va*. 1. To touch the mariner's compass needle with loadstone. 2. To magnetize.

imbatible [em-bah-te-blay], *a*. Unbeatable.

imbécil [im-bay'-theel], *a*. 1. Weak, feeble, imbecile. 2. Simple, silly, stupid.

imbecilidad [im-bay-the-le-dahd'], *f*. 1. Imbecility, weakness, debility. 2. Simplicity, silliness. **Decir imbecilidades**, to say silly things.

imbele [im-bay'-lay], *a*. (*Poet*.) Feeble, weak: unfit for war.

imberbe [im-bayr'-bay], *m*. Beardless youth.

imbibición [im-be-be-the-on'], *f*. Imbibition.

imbornal [im-bor-nahl'], *m*. (*Naut*.) Scupper-hole. **Irse por los imbornales**, (*LAm*. *Fig*.) to go off on a tangent.

imborrable [im-bor-rah'-blay], *a.* Indelible, unforgettable (recuerdo).

imbricación [im-bre-cah-the-on'], *f.* Imbrication, overlapping of scales.

imbricado, da [im-bre-cah'-do, dah], *a.* Imbricated, indented with concavities.

imbricativo, va [im-bre-cah-tee'-vo, vah], *a. (Bot.)* Imbricate, overlapping in the bud.

imbuir [im-boo-eer'], *va.* To imbue, to admit into the mind, to infuse into the mind, to instruct.

imbursación [im-boor-sah-the-on'], *f. (Prov.)* Act of putting into a sack.

imbursar [im-boor-sar'], *va. (Prov.)* To put into a sack or bag.

imilla [e-meel'-lyah], *f. (S. Amer.)* The girl sent by each settlement of Indians to the curate, to serve him for a week.

imitable [e-me-tah'-blay], *a.* Imitable.

imitación [e-me-tah-the-on'], *f.* 1. Imitation (copiar); mimicry (parodía). 2. Imitation, that which is offered as copy. **A imitación**, after the example, in imitation of. **Desconfíe de las imitaciones**, beware of imitations.

imitado, da [e-me-tah'-do, dah], *a. & pp.* Of IMITAR. Copied, imitated, imitative.

imitador, ra [e-me-tah-dor', rah], *m. & f.* Imitator, follower.

imitante [e-me-tahn'-tay], *pa.* of IMITAR. Imitator.

imitar [e-me-tar'], *va.* To imitate, to copy, to follow (copiar); to counterfeit (falsificar).

imitativo, va [e-me-tah-tee'-vo, vah], *a.* Imitative, aiming at resemblance.

imóscapo [e-mos'-cah-po], *m. (Arch.)* Apophyge, a concave curve in a column where the shaft rises from the base.

impaciencia [im-pah-the-en'-the-ah], *f.* 1. Impatience, inability to suffer pain; rage under suffering. 2. Impatience, inability to suffer delay, eagerness, hastiness. 3. Impatience, peevishness, vehemence of temper, heat of passion.

impacientar [im-pah-the-en-tar'], *va.* To vex, to irritate, to make one lose all patience. *-vr.* To become impatient, to lose all patience.

impaciente [im-pah-the-en'-tay], *a.* Impatient, fidgety, restless, peevish, not able to endure delay. **Impaciente por empezar**, impatient to start.

impacientemente [im-pah-the-en-tay-men'-tay], *adv.* Impatiently, longingly, peevishly, eagerly, ardently, with great desire.

impactante [im-pahc-tahn'-tay], *a.* Impressive; shattering; crushing, overwhelming.

impactar [im-pahc-tar'], *va.* To impress (impresionar), to have an impact on; to please (gustar).

impacto, ta [im-pahc'-to, tah], *a.* Impacted, thrust into, packed tight, incidence (repercusión); hit; *(LAm.)* punch, blow (boxeo).

impagado [im-pah-gah-do], *a.* Unpaid, still to be paid.

impago [im-pah-go], *(LAm.)* *-a.* Unpaid, still to be paid. *-m.* Non-payment.

impalpabilidad [im-pal-pa-be-le-dahd'], *f.* Impalpability.

impalpable [im-pal-pah'-blay], *a.* Impalpable, not to be perceived by the touch.

impar [im-par'], *a.* 1. Unequal, dissimilar, odd. 2. Uneven, not divisible into equal numbers. **Los números impares**, the odd numbers.

imparable [im-pah-rah'-blay], *a.* Unstoppable.

imparcial [im-par-the-ahl'], *a.* 1. Impartial, equitable. 2. Impartial, indifferent, disinterested, just. 3. Unprejudiced, imprejudicate.

imparcialidad [im-par-the-ah-le-dahd'], *f.* Impartiality, equitableness, justice; indifference.

imparcialmente [im-par-the-al-men'-tay], *adv.* Impartially, equitably, justly, honestly.

imparidad [im-pa-re-dahd'], *f.* Inequality, imparity, dissimilarity.

impartible [im-par-tee'-blay], *a.* 1. Indivisible. 2. *(Law.)* Impartible, communicable, what can be bestowed or conferred.

impartir [im-par-teer'], *va.* 1. To demand or require assistance; chiefly applied to courts of judicature, which demand one another's assistance for the effectual administration of justice. 2. To grant, to impart (instrucción).

impasable [im-pah-sah'-blay], *a.* Impassable.

impasibilidad [im-pah-se-be-le-dahd'], *f.* Impassibility, impassiveness, insusceptibility of suffering, exemption from pain.

impasible [im-pah-see'-blay], *a.* 1. Impassible, incapable of suffering. 2. Impassible, exempt from external impression, insensible to pain.

impastar [im-pas-tar'], *va.* To reduce ground material to paste.

impávidamente [im-pah'-ve-dah-men-tay], *adv.* 1. Intrepidity, undauntedly. 2. *(LAm.)* Cheekily.

impavidez [im-pah-ve-deth'], *f.* 1. Intrepidity, courage, boldness. 2. *(LAm.)* Cheek, cheekiness.

impávido, da [im-pah'-ve-do, dah], *a.* 1. Dauntless, intrepid (valiente), undaunted (impasible). 2. *(LAm.)* Cheeky (insolente).

impecabilidad [im-pay-cah-bele-dahd'], *f.* Impeccability, impeccancy, incapacity for sin.

impecable [im-pay-cah'-blay], *a.* Impeccable, exempt from possibility of sin.

impecablemente [im-pay-cah-blay-men-tay], *adv.* Impeccably, faultlessly.

impedido, da [im-pay-dee'-do, dah], *a.* Invalid, handicapped, impeded, sick, valetudinarian, crippled; having lost the use of the limbs. *-pp.* of IMPEDIR.

impedidor, ra [im-pay-de-dor', rah], *m. & f.* Obstructer, one who impedes.

impediente [im-pay-de-en'-tay], *pa.* Hindering, that which impedes.

impedimento [im-pay-de-men'-to], *m.* Impediment (obstáculo), obstacle, hindrance, obstruction, let, clog, cumbrance, cumbersomeness, impeachment. *(Met.)* Shackles.

impedir [im-pay-deer'], *va.* 1. To impede (dificultar), to hinder, to obstruct, to prevent, to clog, to keep back from, to forbid. 2. To constrain, to restrain, to cohibit; to counteract, to preclude. 3. *(Poet.)* To suspend. 4. To stop (prohibir), to prevent; to thwart (frustrar). **Impedir a uno hacer algo**, to stop somebody from doing something. **Me veo impedido para ayudar**, I find it impossible for me to help.

impeditivo, va [im-pay-de-tee'-vo, vah], *a.* Impeding, hindering, impeditive.

impeler [im-pay-lerr'], *va.* 1. To impel, to give an impulse. 2. To incite, to stimulate, to move. 3. To impel, to press on, to urge forward, to propel.

impenetrabilidad [im-pay-nay-trah-be-le-dahd'], *f.* Impenetrability, impenetrableness.

impenetrable [im-pay-nay-trah'-blay], *a.* 1. Impenetrable, impervious, that cannot be pierced or penetrated. 2. Impenetrable, incomprehensible, not to be conceived by the mind; fathomless.

impenetrablemente [im-pay-nay-trah'-blay-men-tay], *adv.* Impenetrably, imperviously.

impenitencia [im-pay-ne-ten'-the-ah], *f.* Impenitence.

impenitente [im-pay-ne-ten'-tay], *a.* Impenitent, obdurate, hard-hearted.

impensa [im-pen'-sah], *f. (for.)* Expense.

impensable [im-payn-sah'-blay], *a.* Unthinkable.

impensadamente [im-pen-sah-dah-men'-tay], *adv.* 1. Unexpectedly. 2. At random, by chance. 3. Inadvertently (sin querer).

impensado, da [im-pen-sah'-do, dah], *a.* 1. Unexpected (imprevisto), unforeseen, fortuitous. 2. Random (casual).

imperante [im-pay-rahn'-tay], *pa.* Commanding *(Astrol.)* Ruling: applied to a star. Formerly it was used as a substantive.

imperar [im-pay-rar'], *vn.* To command (mandar), to reign (prevalecer). *-va.* To command a person, to direct his actions.

imperativamente [im-pay-rah-te-vah-men´-tay], *adv.* Imperatively, authoritatively.

imperativo, va [im-pay-rah-tee´-vo, vah], *a.* Imperative (necesidad), commanding, expressive of command; a mood in grammar. *-f.* The tone or gesture of command (tono).

imperatoria [im-pay-rah-to´-re-ah], *f. (Bot.)* Masterwort.

imperatorio, ria [im-pay-rah-to´-re-o, ah], *a.* 1. Imperial, royal, belonging to an emperor or monarch. 2. Eminent, possessed of superior qualities.

imperceptible [im-per-thep-tee´-blay], *a.* Imperceptible.

imperceptiblemente [im-per-thep-te-blay-men´-tay], *adv.* Imperceptibly.

impercuso, sa [im-per-coo´-so, sah], *a.* Unstruck: used of coins where a side remains blank.

imperdible [im-per-dee´-blay], *a.* Safety pin.

imperdonable [im-per-do-nay´-blay], *a. (coll.)* Unpardonable, irremissible.

imperecedero, ra [im-pay-ray-thay-day´-ro, rah], *a.* Imperishable, unforgettable.

imperfección [im-per-fec-the-on´], *f.* Imperfection, fault, slight failure or defect.

imperfectamente [im-per-fec-tah-men´-tay], *adv.* Imperfectly, faultily, lamely, inadequately.

imperfecto, ta [im-per-fec´-to, tah], *a.* 1. Imperfect (objeto), not complete (tarea); defective, faulty, crippled, broken. 2. Imperfect, in grammar: referring to past time.

imperforación [im-per-fo-rah-the-on´], *f. (Med.)* Imperforation, the state of being closed.

imperforado, da [im-per-fo-rah´-do, dah], *a. (Med.)* Imperforate, closed up.

imperial [im-pay-re-ahl´], *f.* 1. Roof (autobús). 2. *(Naut.)* Poop-royal, a platform which serves as a covering of the poop-gallery of a ship.

imperial [im-pay-re-ahl´], *a.* 1. Imperial, belonging to an emperor or monarch. 2. Applied to a kind of small black plum.

imperialismo [im-pay-re-ah-lees´-mo], *m.* Imperialism, government by empire.

imperialista [im-pay-re-ah-lees´-tah], *m.* Imperialist.

impericia [im-pay-ree´-the-ah], *f.* Unskilfulness, want of knowledge or experience.

imperio [im-pay´-re-o], *m.* 1. Empire, dominion, command. 2. Dignity of an emperor. 3. Empire, the dominions of an emperor. 4. Kind of linen made in Germany. **Imperio Británico**, British Empire. **Vale un imperio**, it´s worth a fortune.

imperiosamente [im-pay-re-o´-sah-men´-tay], *adv.* Imperiously, lordly, masterly.

imperiosidad [im-pay-re-ose-dahd´], *f* Imperiousness.

imperioso, sa [im-pay-re-o´-so, sah], *a.* 1. Imperious (porte, tono), commanding arrogant, haughty. 2. Powerful, overbearing, magisterial.

imperitamente [im-pay-re-tah-men´-tay], *adv.* Unskillfully, ignorantly.

imperito, ta [im-pay-ree´-to, tah], *a.* Unlearned, unskilled (inhábil); deficient in the knowledge of art and science, inexperienced (inexperto).

impermeabilidad [im-per-may-ah-be-le-dahd´], *f.* Impermeability.

impermeable [im-per-may-ah´-blay], *a.* Waterproof. *-m.* Raincoat (prenda de vestir).

impermutable [im-per-moo-tah´-blay], *a.* Immutable.

impersonal [im-per-so-nahl´], *a.* 1. Impersonal (verbos). 2. Mode of speaking impersonally. **En** or **por impersonal**, impersonally.

impersonalmente [im-per-so-nal-men´-tay], *adv.* Impersonally.

impersuasible [im-per-soo-ah-se´-blay], *a.* Not to be moved by persuasion.

impertérrito, ta [im-per-tayr´-re-to, tah], *a.* Intrepid, unterrified, dauntless.

impertinencia [im-per-te-nen´-the-ah], *f.* 1. Impertinence (insolencia), folly, nonsense. 2. Peevishness, humorousness. 3. Impertinence, troublesomeness, intrusion. 4. Minute accuracy in the perfomance of a thing.

impertinente [im-per-te-nen´-tay], *a.* 1. Impertinent, intrusive (intruso), importunate, meddling. 2. Impertinent (insolente), nonsensical, trifling. 3. Peevish, fretful, cross, froward, ill-humored (malhumorado).

impertinentemente [im-per-te-nen´-tay-men-tay], *adv.* Impertinently.

imperturbable [im-per-toor-bah´-blay], *a.* Imperturbable, not to be disturbed.

imperturbablemente [im-per-toor-bah´-blay-men-tay], *adv.* Imperturbably.

imperturbar [im-per-toor-bar´], *va. (Ven.)* To disturb.

impervio, via [im-payr´-ve-o, ah], *a.* Impervious, impassable, impenetrable.

impetra [im-pay´-trah], *f.* 1. Diploma, license, permission. 2. Bull by which dubious benefices are granted.

impetrable [im-pay-trah´-blay], *a. (Law.)* Impetrable, possible to be obtained.

impetración [im-pay-trah-the-on´], *f.* Impetration, the act of obtaining by prayer or entreaty.

impetrado, da [im-pay-trah´-do, dah], *a. & pp.* of IMPETRAR. Impetrate, impetrated, granted.

impetrador, ra [im-pay-trah-dor´], rah], *m. & f.* One who impetrates.

impetrante [im-pay-trahn´-tay], *pa.* Impetrating. *-m. (Law.)* Grantee; impetrator.

impetrar [im-pay-trar´], *va.* To impetrate, to obtain by entreaty (obtener).

ímpetu [eem´-pay-too], *m.* 1. Impetus, a violent tendency to any point: a violent effort. 2. Impetuosity (impetuosidad), fit, impulse, sally, start, violence or vehemence of passion (violencia).

impetuosamente [im-pay-too-o´-sah-men-tay], *adv.* Impetuosly, vehemently, violently.

impetuosidad [im-pay-too-o-se-dahd´], *f.* Impetuosity, vehemence.

impetuoso, sa [im-pay-too-o´-so, sah], *a.* 1. Impetuous (persona), violent, forcible, fierce. 2. Impetuous, vehement, passionate, heady, hasty (acto).

impía or **flor impía** [im-pee´-ah], *f.* Scarlet-flowered pentapetes, an herb like rosemary.

impiedad [im-pe-ay-dahd´], *f.* 1. Impiety; irreligion, contempt of religion. 2. Impiety, any act of wickedness, impiousness; cruelty.

impío, pía [im-pee´-o, ah], *a.* Impious, irreligious, wicked, profane, godless.

impla [ee´-plah], *f.* Woman´s veil anciently used, and the fabric of which it was made.

implacabilidad [im-plah-cah-be-le-dahd´], *f.* Implacability.

implacable [im-plah-cah´-blay], *a.* Implacable, not to be pacified: inexorable.

implacablemente [im-plah-cah´-blay-men-tay], *adv.* Implacably, relentlessly.

implantación [im-plan-tah-the-on´], *f.* Implantation, act of implanting.Implementation *(Comput.)*

implantar [im-plan-tar´], *va.* To implant, to set for growth; to inculcate, to introduce (costumbre).

implaticable [im-plah-te-cah´-blay], *a.* Intractable, unmanageable.

implexo, a [im-plec-so, sah], *a.* Said of epic or dramatic poems which present vicissitudes in the fortune of the heroes.

implicación [im-ple-cah-the-on´], *f.* 1. Implication; contradiction (contradicción); implicitness. 2. Complicity (complicidad). 3. *(LAm.)* Implication (significado).

implicado, da [im-ple-cah´-do, dah], *a. & pp.* of IMPLICAR. Implicit, entangled, implicated.

implicar [im-ple-car´], *vn.* To oppose, to contradict one another: applied to terms and propositions. *-va.* To implicate (involucrar), to imply (significar), to involve; to entangle, to embarrass. **Esto no implica que...**, this does not imply that...

implicatorio, ria [im-ple-cah-to'-re-o, ah], *a.* Implicative.

implícitamente [im-plee'-the-tah-men-tay], *adv.* Implicitly.

implícito, ta [im-plee'-the-to, tah], *a.* Implicit, inferred; tacitly comprised, not expressed.

imploración [im-plo-rah-the-on'], *f.* Entreaty, imploration, the act of imploring.

implorar [im-plo-rar'], *va.* 1. To implore, to call upon in supplication, to solicit. 2. To implore, to ask with eagerness, to crave, to entreat, to beg.

impolítica [im-po-lee'-te-cah], *f.* 1. Incivility, lack of courtesy, clownishness, rudeness, coarseness. 2. Impolicy.

impolíticamente [im-po-le'-te-cah-men-tay], *adv.* (*coll.*) Impolitically, impoliticly.

impolítico, ca [im-po-lee'-te-co, cah], *a.* 1. Impolitic or impolitical (imprudente), indiscreet, imprudent. 2. Impolite (descortés), rude, coarse, unpolished.

impoluto, ta [im-po-loo'-to, tah], *a.* Unpolluted, pure, free from stain, clean.

imponderabilidad [im-pon-day-rah-be-le-dahd'], *f.* Imponderability (calor).

imponderable [im-pon-day-rah'-blay], *a.* Inexpressible, unutterable, imponderable.

imponedor [im-po-nay-dor'], *m.* He who imposes or charges.

imponente [im-po-nen'-tay], *a.* 1. Imposing (impresionante), awe-inspiring. 2. Terrific (estupendo), tremendous, smashing.

imponer [im-po-nerr'], *va.* 1. To lay, to put, or set in or upon (carga). 2. To impose or lay a tax, a duty, etc. (tarea, impuesto). 3. To impose, to lay on as a burden or penalty. 4. To charge upon or impute falsely (achacar). 5. To advise, to give notice, to acquaint, to instruct someone (instruir). 6. To infuse respect or fear. 7. (*Print.*) To impose, to arrange pages of types for the press. -*vr.* 1. **Imponerse un deber**, to assume a duty. 2. To assert oneself (hacerse obedecer), to get one´s way. 3. To prevail (prevalecer); to grow up (costumbre). **Se impondrá el buen sentido**, good sense will prevail. 4. To be necessary (ser inevitable), to impose itself. **La conclusión se impone**, the conclusion is inescapable. 5. (*Mex.*) To get accustomed (acostumbrarse).

impopular [im-po-poo-lar'], *a.* Unpopular.

impopularidad [im-po-poo-lah-re-dahd'], *f.* Unpopularity.

imporosidad [im-po-ro-see-dahd'], *f.* Imporosity, state of being without pores.

imporoso, sa [im-po-ro'-so, sah], *a.* Imporous, without pores, solid.

importable [im-por-tah'-blay], *a.* What can be imported from abroad: importable.

importación [im-por-tah-the-on'], *f.* Importation (acto), importing. **Artículo de importación**, imported article. **Comercio de importación**, import trade.

importador [im-por-tah-dor'], *m & f.* Importer.

importancia [im-por-tahn'-the-ah], *f.* 1. Importance, import, consequence, moment, concern. 2. Importance, considerableness, a claim to notice; claim to respect. **De cierta importancia**, of some importance. **Carecer de importancia**, to be unimportant. **Restar importancia a**, to diminish the importance of.

importante [im-por-tahn'-tay], *a.* Important, momentous, weighty, material, considerable. **Lo más importante es...**, the main thing is...

importantemente [im-por-tahn'-tay-men-tay], *adv.* Importantly, usefully, materially, essentially.

importar [im-por-tar'], *v. imp.* 1. To import, to be important or convenient, to concern, to matter. **Esto importa mucho**, this is very important. **No le importa**, he doesn´t care. **No le importa conducir todo el día**, he doesn´t mind driving all day. 2. To amount, or amount to. **No importa**, no matter, it is no matter, it matters not. **¿Qué importa? or ¿qué importa eso?** what does it matter? what of that? what does it signify? **Importa mucho**, it matters much. -*va.* 1. To import, to carry

into any country from abroad. **Este país importa carne**, this country imports meat. 2. To carry along with, to be a consequence of.

importe [im-por'-tay], *m.* Amount or gross amount, value (coste); total (total). **Importe total**, final total. **Hasta el importe de**, up to the amount of. **El importe de la factura**, the amount of this bill.

importunación [im-por-too-nah-the-on'], *f.* Importunity, incessant solicitation.

importunadamente [im-por-too-nah-dah'-men-tay], *adv.* Importunately.

importunador, ra [im-por-too-nah-dor', rah], *m. & f.* Importunator, importuner.

importunamente [im-por-too'-nah-men-tay], *adv.* 1. Importunely, with importunity. 2. Importunely, unseasonably.

importunar [im-por-too-nar'], *va.* 1. To importune, to disturb by reiteration of the same request; to crave. 2. To vex, to molest, to harass, to tease, to disturb by reiteration of the same request.

importunidad [im-por-too-ne-dahd'], *f.* Importunity (acto), importunacy, importunateness.

importuno, na [im-por-too'-no, nah], *a.* 1. Importune (molesto), importunate, unseasonable, happening at the wrong time. 2. Importune (inoportuno), troublesome, vexatious, heavy.

imposibilidad [im-po-se-be-le-dahd'], *f.* Impossibility, impracticability, impracticableness.

imposibilitado [im-po-se-be-le-tah'-do], *a. & pp.* of IMPOSIBILITAR. 1. Helpless, without means, poor. 2. Disabled, weakened, unfit for service. **Estar imposibilitado para**, to be unable to.

imposibilitar [im-po-se-be-le-tar'], *va.* To disable, to render impossible (impedir), to weaken, to make unfit for service (incapacitar). **Esto me imposibilita hacerlo**, this makes it impossible for me to do it.

imposible [im-po-see'-blay], *a.* 1. Impossible, impracticable, unfeasible. 2. Extremely difficult. 3. Impossible; intolerable (inaguantable), unbearable. **Es imposible**, it´s impossible. **Es imposible de predecir**, it´s impossible to forecast. 4. Difficult, awkward, impossible (persona). 5. (*LAm.*) Slovenly (descuidado). -*m.* The impossible.

imposiblemente [im-po-se'-blay-men-tay], *adv.* Impossibly.

imposición [im-po-se-the-on'], *f.* 1. Imposition, the act of laying anything on another. 2. Imposition, the act of laying, putting, or setting in or upon. 3. Imposition, the act of imposing taxes or duties, and the tax, charge, or duty imposed. 4. Injunction of anything as a law or duty. 5. Among printers, imposition, the arrangement of pages for the press.

imposta [im-pos'-tah], *f.* (*Arch.*) Impost, that part of a pillar in vaults and arches on which the weight of the whole building lies.

impostor, ra [im-pos-tor', ah], *m. & f.* Impostor (charlatán), juggler, slanderer (calumniador).

impostura [im-pos-too'-rah], *f.* 1. A false imputation or charge. 2. Imposture (fraude), fiction, deceit, cheat, fraud.

impotable [im-po-tah'-blay], *a.* Not drinkable, unpotable.

impotencia [im-po-ten'-the-ah], *f.* 1. Impotence or impotency, inability, weakness. 2. Impotence, frigidity, incapacity of propagation.

impotente [im-po-ten'-tay], *a.* 1. Impotent, weak, feeble, wanting force. 2. Impotent, frigid, without power of propagation.

impracticable [im-prac-te-cah'-blay], *a.* 1. Impracticable, impossible, unfeasible. 2. Impassable (carreteras).

imprecación [im-pray-cah-the-on'], *f.* Imprecation, curse.

imprecar [im-pray-car'], *va.* To imprecate, to curse.

imprecatorio, ria [im-pray-cah-to'-re-o, ah], *a.* Imprecatory.

imprecaución [im-pray-ca-hoo-the-on'], *f.* Imprevision, want of foresight.

imprecisión [im-pray-the-se-on'], *f.* Lack of precision, vagueness.

impreciso [im-pray-the'-so], *a.* Imprecise, vague.

impredecible

impredecible [im-pray-day-the'-blay], *a. (LAm.)* Unpredictable.

impregnación [im-preg-nah-the-on'], *f.* Impregnation.

impregnar [im-preg-nar'], *va.* To impregnate, to saturate with any matter or quality. *-vr.* To be impregnated.

impremeditación [im-pray-may-de-tah-the-on'], *f.* Unpremeditation, absence of plan.

impremeditado, da [im-pray-may-de-tah'-do, dah], *a.* Unpremeditated, unforeseen.

imprenta [im-pren'-tah], *f.* 1. Printing, the art of printing (arte). 2. Printing office, press (aparato). 3. Print, the form, size, etc., of the types used in printing books.

imprescindible [im-pres-thin-de'-blay], *a.* That which cannot be prescinded or put aside. **Cosas imprescindibles**, essential things.

imprescriptible [im-pres-crip-tee'-blay], *a.* Imprescriptible, without the compass of prescription.

impresentable [im-pray-sen-tah'-blay], *a.* Unpresentable.

impresión [im-pray-se-on'], *f.* 1. Impression, the act of pressing one body upon another. 2. Impression, impress, mark made by pressure, stamp. 3. Print, the form, size, etc., of the types used in printing books. 4. Impression, edition, number printed at one time (tirada). 5. Impression, efficacious agency, influence, or operation of one body upon another. 6. Impression (desagradable), impress, image fixed in the mind. **Cambiar impresiones**, to exchange impressions. **Hacer buena impresión**, to make a good impression. **Su muerte me causó una gran impresión**, her death was a great shock to me. 7. *(Astrol.)* Influence of the stars; impression or effect. 8. *(Inform.)* **Impresión en modo gráfico**, dot bit, image mode, graphic mode.

impresionable [im-pray-se-o-nah'-blay], *a.* Emotional, impressionable.

impresionado [im-pray-se-o-nah'-do] *a.* 1. Impressed. 2. Exposed.

impresionante [im-pray-se-o-nahn'-tay], *a.* Impressive, awe-inspiring, striking (espectacular), moving (commovedor).

impresionar [im-pray-se-o-nar'], *va.* 1. To imprint or fix on the mind or memory. **Me impresionó mucho**, it greatly impressed me. 2. To cut (disco); to expose. *-vn.* To impress, to make an impression. **Lo hace sólo para impresionar**, he just does it to impress. *-vr.* To be impressed; to be moved.

impresionismo [im-pray-se-o-nees'-mo], *m. (Lit. & Art)* Impressionism.

impreso [im-pray'-so], *m.* 1. Pamphlet, a short treatise. 2. Form (formulario). **Formulario de solicitud**, application form.

impreso, sa [im-pray'-so, sah], *pp. irr. of* IMPRIMIR. Printed.

impresor [im-pray-sor'], *m.* Printer.

impresora [im-pray-so'-rah], *f. (Inform.)* Printer. **Impresora de línea**, line-printer. **Impresora de margarita**, daisy-wheel printer. **Impresora calidad pseudo-courrier**, near letter quality printer. **Impresora de cadena**, chain printer. **Impresora de impacto**, impact printer. **Impresora de inyección de tinta**, ink jet printer. **Impresora de matriz de puntos**, dot matrix printer. **Impresora de procesador de textos**, wordprocessing printer. **Impresora de puntos**, dot printer. **Impresora láser**, laser printer. **Impresora térmica**, thermal printer. **Impresora trazadora**, printer plotter.

imprestable [im-pres-tah'-blay], *a.* That cannot be lent.

imprevisible [im-pray-ve-se'-blay], *a.* Unforeseeable.

imprevisión [im-pray-ve-se-on'], *f.* Imprevision, improvidence.

imprevisto, ta [im-pray-vees'-to, tah], *a.* Unforeseen, unexpected, unprovided against.

imprimación [im-pre-mah-the-on'], *f.* Priming, the act of laying on the first colors on canvas or boards to be painted; stuff for priming.

imprimadera [im-pre-mah-day'-rah], *f.* The instrument used in priming, or laying on the first colors in painting.

imprimador [im-pre-mah-dor'], *m.* One who lays the first colors on a piece of linen or board to be painted.

imprimar [im-pre-mar'], *va.* To prime, to lay the first colors on in painting.

imprimir [im-pre-meer'], *va.* 1. To print, to stamp. 2. To imprint, to fix an idea on the mind or memory. 3. To put a work to press, to get it printed.

improbabilidad [im-pro-bah-be-le-dahd'], *f.* Improbability, unlikelihood, difficulty to be believed.

improbable [im-pro-bah'-blay], *a.* Improbable, unlikely, difficult to be proved.

improbablemente [im-pro-bah'-blay-men-tay], *adv.* Improbably.

improbar [im-pro-bar'], *va.* To disapprove, to dislike, to censure.

improbidad [im-pro-be-dahd'], *f.* Improbity, dishonesty.

ímprobo, ba [eem'-pro-bo, bay], *a.* 1. Corrupt (poco honrado), wicked. 2. Laborious (tarea), painful.

improcedencia [eem-pro-thay-den'-the-ah], *f.* 1. Wrongness, inapplicability. 2. *(Jur.)* Inadmissibility.

improcedente [eem-pro-thay-dayn'-tay], *a.* 1. Wrong (incorrecto), not right; inappropriate (inadecuado). 2. Unfounded, inadmissible; out of order.

improductivo, va [im-pro-dooc-tee'-vo, vah], *a.* 1. Unproductive, unfruitful. 2. Useless.

impronta [im-pron'-tah], *f.* Cast, or reproduction in any soft substance, like wax, papier-maché, etc., of images in relief or intaglio.

improperar [im-pro-pay-rar'], *va.* To upbraid, to gibe, to taunt.

improperio [im-pro-pay'-re-o], *m.* Contemptuous reproach, injurious censure.

impropiamente [en-pro-pe-ah-men'-tay], *adv.* Improperly.

impropiedad [im pro-pe-ay-dahd'], *f.* Impropriety, unfitness, want of justness.

impropio, pia [im-pro'-pe-o, ah], *a.* 1. Improper, unfit; not conducive to the right end; unqualified. 2. Improper, unbecoming. **Impropio para**, inappropriate for.

improporción [im-pro-por-the-on'], *f.* Disproportion.

improporcionado, da [im-pro-por-the-o-nah'-do, dah], *a.* Disproportionate, unsymmetrical, unsuitable in terms of quality or quantity.

impropriedad [im-pro-pre-ay-dahd'], *f.* Impropriety.

improrrogable [im-pror-ro-gah'-blay], *a.* That which cannot be prorogued.

impróspero, ra [im-pros'-pay-ro, rah], *a.* Unfortunate, unprosperous, unhappy.

imprévidamente [im-pro'-ve-dah-men-tay], *adv.* Improvidently.

imprévido, da [im-pro'-ve-do, dah], *a.* Improvident, wanting forecast or care to provide, thoughtless.

improvisación [im-pro-ve-sah-the-on'], *f.* Improvisation; extemporization; *(Mus.)* Imprompty; *(Teat.)* Ad-lib.

improvisado [im-pro-ve-sah'-do], *a.* Improvised; makeshift (reparación); *(Mus.)* extempore, impromptu.

improvisamente [im-pro-ve-sah-men'-tay], *adv.* Unexpectedly, improvidently.

improvisar [im-pro-ve-sar'], *va.* To extemporize, to speak extempore, *(Teat.)* to ad-lib. **Improvisar una comedia**, to rustle up a meal.

improviso, sa [im-pro-vee'-so, sah], **Improvisto, ta**, *a.* Unexpected (imprevisto), unforeseen, not provided against. **De improviso**, unexpectedly, all of a sudden. **Hablar de improviso**, to play impromptu.

imprudencia [im-proo-den'-the-ah], *f.* Imprudence, indiscretion, heedlessness; impolicy; improvidence. **Imprudencia temeraria**, criminal negligence. **Ser acusado de conducir con imprudencia temeraria**, to be charged with dangerous driving.

imprudente [im-proo-den'-tay], *a.* Imprudent, indiscreet (indiscreto), improvident, unwise (precipitado).

imprudentemente [im-proo-den-tay-men-tay], *adv.* Imprudently.

impúber [im-poo´-ber], *a. V.* IMPÚBERO.

impúbero, ra [im-poo-bay´-ro, rah], *a.* Impuberal, not having reached puberty.

impudencia [im-poo-den´-the-ah], *f.* Impudence, shamelessness, immodesty.

impudente [im-poo-den´-tay], *a.* Impudent, shameless.

impúdicamente [im-poo´-de-cah-men-tay], *adv.* Lewdly (obscenamente), impudently.

impudicicia [im-poo-de-thee´-the-ah], *f.* Unchastity, lewdness (obscenidad), incontinence, lustfulness, impudicity.

impúdico, ca [im-poo´-de-co, cah], *a.* 1. Unchaste, lewd (obsceno), lustful, obscene. 2. Impudent, shameless.

impuesto [im-poo-ays´-to], *m.* 1. Tax. 2. Duty, impost. **Impuesto sobre la renta**, income tax. **Sujeto a impuesto**, taxable. **Impuesto de plusvalía**, capital gains tax. **Impuesto de venta**, sales tax.

impuesto, ta [im-poo-ays´-to, tah], *a. & pp. irr.* of IMPONER. Imposed. **Estar or quedar impuesto de alguna cosa**, to have full knowledge of some business or command.

impugnable [im-poog-nah´-blay], *a.* Impugnable.

impugnación [im-poog-nah-the-on´], *f.* Opposition, contradiction, refutation, impugnation.

impugnador, ra [im-poog-nah-dor´, rah], *m. & f.* One who refutes, attacks or contradicts; impugner, objector.

impugnar [im-poog-nar´], *va.* To impugn (teoría), to contradict, to oppose, to confute.

impugnativo, va [im-poog-nah-tee´-vo, vah], *a.* Impugning.

impulsar [im-pool-sar´], *va.* To impel, to give an impulse, to urge on.

impulsión [im-pool-se-on´], *f.* 1. Impulsion, impulse, momentum (fuerza existente), drive (empuje), communicated force, the effect of one body acting upon another. 2. Impulsion, impulse, influence acting upon the mind, motive.

impulsivo, va [im-pool-see´-vo, vah], *a.* Impulsive.

impulso [im-pool´-so], *m.* Impulsion; impulse. *V.* IMPULSIÓN. **Los impulsos del corazón**, the promptings of the heart. **No resisto al impulso de decir que...**, I can´t resist saying that...

impulsor, ra [im-pool-sor´, rah], *m. & f.* Impeller, *(Mec.)* drive, *(Aer.)* booster.

impune [im-poo´-nay], *a.* Exempt from punishment, unpunished.

impunemente [im-poo-nay-men´-tay], *adv.* With impunity.

impunidad [im-poo-ne-dahd´], *f.* Impunity, freedom from punishment.

impuramente [im-poo-rah-men´-tay], *adv.* Obscenely, impurely.

impureza [im-poo-ray´-thah], *f.* 1. Impurity, foul with extraneous mixtures. 2. Impurity, dishonesty, unchastity. 3. Obscenity, obsceneness, foulness.

impuro, ra [im-poo´-ro, rah], *a.* Impure, foul.

imputable [im-poo-tah´-blay], *a.* Imputable, chargeable.

imputabilidad [im-poo-tah-be-le-dahd´], *f.* Imputableness.

imputación [im-poo-tah-the-on´], *f.* Imputation, attribution of anything, generally of ill.

imputador, ra [im-poo-tah-dor´, rah], *m. & f.* Imputer.

imputar [im-poo-tar´], *m.* To impute, to charge upon, to attribute, to father.

in [een], *prep. Lat.* Used only in composition, where it has generally a negative signification, as **incapaz**, incapable.

inabarcable [in-ah-bar-cah´-blay], *a.* Not capable of being embraced.

inacabable [in-ah-cah-bah´-blay], *a.* Interminable, inconsumptible, that cannot be brought to an end.

inacabado [in-ah-cah-bah´-do], *a.* Unfinished.

inaccesibilidad [in-ac-thay-see´-be-le-dahd´], *f.* Inaccessibility.

inaccesible [in-ac-thay-see´-blay], *a.* inaccessible, not to be approached.

inaccesiblemente [in-ac-thay-se´-blay-men-tay], *adv.* Inaccessibly.

inacción [in-ac-the-on´], *f.* Inaction, cessation from labor.

inaceptable [in-ah-thayp-tah´-blay], *a.* Unacceptable.

inactividad [in-ac-te-ve-dahd´], *f.* Inactivity, laziness, idleness.

inactivo, va [in-ac-tee´-vo, vah], *a.* Inactive, lazy, iddle.

inadaptable [in-ah-dap-tah´-blay], *a.* Not adaptable.

inadaptación [in-ah-dap-tah-the-on´], *f.* Inadequacy; unsuitability, inappropriateness.

inadaptado [in-ah-dap-tah-do], *a.* Maladjusted, who fails to adjust. *-m & f.* Misfit; person who fails to adjust.

inadecuado, da [in-ah-day-coo-ah´-do, dah], *a.* Inadequate, unsuitable.

inadherente [in-a-day-ren´-tay], Unadherent.

inadmisible [in-ad-me-see´-blay], *a.* Inadmissible, unacceptable.

inadvertencia [in-ad-ver-ten´-the-ah], *f.* Inadvertence, carelessness, inattention, heedlessness.

inadvertidamente [in-ad-ver-te-dah´-men-tay], *adv.* Inadvertently.

inadvertido, da [in-ad-ver-tee´-do, dah], *a.* 1. Inadvertent, inconsiderate, careless (descuidado). 2. Unseen, unnoticed (no visto).

inafectado, da [in-ah-fec-tah´-do, dah], *a.* Natural, free from affectation.

inagotable [in-ah-go-tah´-blay], *a.* 1. Inexhaustible, exhaustless. 2. Unexhausted: applied to the powers of the mind. 3. Never-failing.

inaguantable [in-ah-goo-an-tah´-blay], *a.* Insupportable.

inajenable [in-ah-hay-nah´-blay], *a.* Inalienable, that cannot be alienated.

inalámbrico, ca [in-ah-lahm´-bre-co, cah], *a.* Wireless. **Telegrafía inalámbrica**, wireless telegraphy.

inalcanzable [in-ahl-can-thah´-blay], *a.* Unattainable.

inalienable [in-ah-le-ay-nah´-blay], *a.* Inalienable.

inalterable [in-al-tay-rah´-blay], *a.* Unalterable, unchanging; immature, impassive (cara); fast (color); permanent (lustre).

inalterablemente [in-al-tay-rah´-blay-men-tay], *adv.* Unalterably.

inalterado, da [in-al-tay-rah´-do, dah], *a.* Unchanged, stable.

inamisible [in-ah-me-see´-blay], *a.* Which cannot be lost.

inamovible [in-ah-mo-vee´-blay], *a.* Immovable, fixed.

inamovibilidad [in-ah-mo-ve-be-le-dahd´], *f.* Immovability.

inanición [in-ah-ne-the-on´], *f. (Med.)* Inanition, extreme weakness from want of nourishment.

inanidad [in-ah-ne-dahd´], *f.* 1. Emptiness. 2. Vanity, uselessness.

inanimado, da [in-ah-ne-mah´-do, dah], *a.* Inanimate, lifeless.

inánime [in-ah´-ne-may], *a. V.* INANIMADO.

inapagable [in-ah-pah-gah´-blay], *a.* Inextinguishable, unquenchable.

inapeable [in-ah-pay-ah´-blay], *a.* 1. That cannot be lowered or levelled. 2. Incomprehensible (oscuro), inconceivable. 3. Obstinate (terco), stubborn.

inapelable [in-ah-pay-lah´-blay], *a.* Without appeal, not admitting appeal.

inapetencia [in-ah-pay-ten´-the-ah], *f.* Inappetence or inappetency, want of appetite or desire of food.

inapetente [in-ah-pay-ten´-tay], *a.* 1. Having no appetite or desire of food. 2. Disgusted.

inaplacable [in-ah-plah-cah´-blay], *a.* Implacable, unappeasable.

inaplicable [in-ah-ple-cah´-blay], *a.* Inapplicable.

inaplicación [in-ah-ple-ca-the-on´], *f.* Indolence, inapplication.

inaplicado, da [in-ah-ple-cah´-do, dah], *a.* Indolent, careless, inactive.

inapreciable [in-ah-pray-the-ah'-blay], *a.* Inestimable, invaluable (valor), inappreciable.

inaptitud [in-ap-te-tood'], *f. (Prov.) V.* INEPTITUD.

inarticulado, da [in-ar-te-coo-lah'-do, dah], *a.* Inarticulate, not uttered with distinctness.

inasequible [in-ah-say-kee'-blay], *a.* That which cannot be followed, out of reach.

inasimilable [in-ah-se-me-lah'-blay], *a.* Unassimilable.

inastillable [in-as-te-lyah'-blay], *a.* Shatter-proof.

inatacable [in-ah-tah-cah'-blay], *a. (coll.)* That which cannot be attacked.

inaudito, ta [in-ah-oo-dee'-to, tah], *a.* Unheard of, strange, most extraordinary.

inauguración [in-ah-oo-goo-rah-the-on´], *f.* 1. Inauguration, investiture by solemnities. 2. Exaltation or elevation to royal dignity. 3. Auguration, the practice of augury.

inaugural [in-ah-oo-goo-rahl'], *a.* Inaugural, opening, maiden (viaje).

inaugurar [in-ah-oo-goo-rar'], *va.* 1. To divine by the flight of birds. 2. To inaugurate, to invest with a new office by solemnities, to open (canal, puente, exposición).

inaveriguable [in-ah-vay-re-goo-ah'-blay], *a.* That cannot be ascertained, that cannot be easily proved.

inca [een'-cah], *m.* Inca.

incalculable [in-cal-coo-lah'-blay], *a.* Incalculable.

incalificable [in-cah-le-fe-cah'-blay], *a.* Unqualifiable, downright.

incamerar [in-cah-may-rar'], *va.* To unite to the Apostolic Chamber, or ecclesiastical dominion.

incandescencia [in-can-des-then'-the-ah], *f.* Incandescence, white heat.

incandescente [in-can-des-then'-tay], *a.* 1. Incandescent, glowing with heat. 2. Burning (mirada).

incansable [in-can-sah'-blay], *a.* Indefatigable, unwearied.

incansablemente [in-can-sah'-blay-men-tay], *adv.* Indefatigably, tirelessly.

incantable [in-can-tah'-blay], *a.* That which cannot be sung.

incapacidad [in-cah-pah-the-dahd'], *f.* 1. Incapacity, inability, want of power or strength. 2. Incapability, incapableness, natural inability, want of comprehensiveness of mind. 3. Incapability, legal disqualification. **Su incapacidad para**, his inability to.

incapacitado [in-cah-pah-the-tah-do], *a.* 1. Incapacitated; unfitted. 2. *(Mex.)* Disabled, handicapped (minusválido).

incapacitar [in-cah-pah-the-tar'], *va.* To incapacitate, to render incapable.

incapaz [in-cah-path'], *a.* 1. Incapable, unable, not equal to anything, unfit (no apto), inadequate (inadecuado). 2. Incapable, wanting power to do anything. 3. Incapable, wanting understanding, wanting talent. **Incapaz de**, unable to.

incardinación [in-car-de-nah-the-on'], *f. (Law.)* Administration of church revenues without ownership.

incasable [in-cah-sah'-blay], *a.* 1. Unmarriageable. 2. Averse or opposed to marriage.

incautación [in-cah-oo-tah-the-on'], *f.* Seizure, confiscation.

incautamente [in-cah-oo-tah-men'-tay], *adv.* Unwarily, incautiously.

incauto, ta [in-cah'-oo-to, tah], *a.* Incautious, unwary, heedless.

incendiar [in-then-de-ar'], *va.* To kindle, to set on fire, to inflame. **El acto de incendiar maliciosamente una casa**, *(Law.)* arson. *-vr.* To catch fire.

incendiario, ria [in-then-de-ah'-re-o, ah], *m. & f.* 1. Firebug, incendiary, one who sets fires compulsively. 2. Firebrand, agitator, one who inflames factions or promotes quarrels.

incendio [in-then'-de-o], *m.* 1. Fire, conflagration, burning. **Incendio intencionado**, arson. **Echar incendios a uno**, *(And. Cono Sur)* to sling or throw mud at somebody. 2. Inflammation, the act of setting on flame; the state of being in flame.

incensación [in-then-sah-the-on'], *f.* The act of perfuming with incense.

incensar [in-then-sar'], *va.* 1. To perfume, to incense, to offer incense on the altar. 2. To bestow fulsome praise or adulation.

incensario [in-then-sah'-re-o], *m.* Incensory, thurible, the vessel in which incense is burnt.

incensurable [in-then-soo-rah'-blay], *a.* Unblamable, not culpable.

incentivo [in-then-tee'-vo], *m.* Incentive, incitement, spur; encouragement.

inceración [in-thay-rah-the-on'], *f.* Inceration, the act of covering with or mixing with wax.

incertidumbre [in-ther-te-doom'-bray], *f.* Incertitude, uncertainty, doubtfulness, hesitancy, fluctuation.

incesable [in-thay-sah'-blay], *a.* Incessant, unceasing.

incesablemente [in-thay--sah-blay-men-tay], *adv.* Incessantly, without intermission.

incesante [in-thay-sahn´-tay], *a.* Incessant, unceasing, continual, uninterrupted.

incesantemente [in-thay-sahn'-tay-men-tay], *adv.* Incessantly, continually.

incesto [in-thes'-to], *m.* Incest.

incestuosamente [in-thes-too-o-sah-men'-tay], *adv.* Incestuously.

incestuoso, sa [in-thes-too-o'-so, sah], *a.* Incestuous.

incidencia [in-the-den'-the-ah], *f.* 1. Incidence or incidency, an accident, hap, casualty, incident (suceso). 2. Incidence, the direction with which one body strikes upon another. 3. **La huelga tuvo escasa incidencia**, the strike was not widely supported.

incidental [in-the-den-tahl'], *a.* Incidental, dependent, subsidiary.

incidente [in-the-den'-tay], *a.* Incident, casual, incidental, happening by chance.

incidente [in-the-den-'tay], *m.* Incident (suceso), hap, accident, casualty, occurrence, accidental event (suceso accidental) *.-pl. (Com.)* Appurtenances.

incidentemente [in-the-den-tahl'-men-tay], *adv.* Incidentally.

incidir [in-the-deer'], *vn.* To fall in or upon, to meet with, to influence, to affect. **Incidir en un error**, to fall into error. **El impuesto incide más en ellos**, the tax falls most heavily on them.

incienso [in-the-en´-so], *m.* 1. Incense, an aromatic gum used to perfume the altar. 2. Peculiar reverence and veneration paid to a person. 3. Court paid to a person out of flattery or interested views.

inciertamente [in-the-ayr'-tah-men-tay], *adv.* Uncertainly.

incierto, ta [in-the-ayr'-to, tah], *a.* 1. Untrue, false, contrary to reality. 2. Uncertain, doubtful. 3. Unstable, inconstant; unknown (desconocido).

incineración [in-the-nay-rah-the-on´], *f.* Incineration, the act of burning a thing to ashes.

incinerar [in-the-nay-rar´], *va.* To incinerate, to burn to ashes, to cremate (cadáver).

incipiente [in-the-pe-en'-tay], *a.* Beginning, incipient, inceptive, inchoative.

incircunciso, sa [in-theer-coon-thee'-so, sah], *a.* Incircumcised.

incircunscripto, ta [in-theer-coons-creep´-to, tah], *a.* Uncircumscribed.

incisión [in-the-se-on´], *f.* 1. Incision, a cut; a wound with a sharp instrument. 2. *V.* CESURA.

incisivo, va [in-the-see'-vo, vah], *a.* Incisive. **Dientes incisivos**, incisors, cutting teeth.

inciso [in-the-´so], *m.* 1. Comma. *V.* COMA. 2. Partial meaning of a clause. 3. Parenthetical (observación). 4. Interjection (conversación).

inciso, sa [in-thee'-so, sah], *a.* Incised. *V.* CORTADO.

incisorio, ria [in-the-so'-re-o, ah], *a.* Incisory, that which cuts.

incitación [in-the-tah-the-on´], *f.* Incitation, incitement.

incitador, ra [in-the-tah-dor', rah], *m. & f.* Instigator, inciter, exciter.

incitamento, incitamiento [in-the-tah-men'-to], *m.* Incitement, impulse, inciting power, incentive.

incitar [in-the-tar'], *va.* To incite, to excite, to spur, to stimulate. **Incitar a uno a hacer algo**, to urge somebody to do something.

incitativa [in-the-tah-tee'-vah], *f. (Law.)* Writ from a superior tribunal to the common judges, that justice may be administered.

incitativo, va [in-the-tah-tee'-vo, vah], *a.* 1. Incentive, inciting, incensive. 2. *(Law.)* V. AGUIJATORIO.

incitativo [in-the-tah-te-vo], *m.* Incitement.

incivil [in-the-veel'], *a.* Uncivil, unpolished, incivil.

incivilidad [in-the-ve-le-dahd'], *f.* Incivility, rudeness, coarseness, grossness.

incivilmente [in-the-veel-men'-tay], *adv.* Uncivilly, rudely, incivilly.

inclasificable [in-clah-se-fe-cah'-blay], *a.* Unclassifiable, difficult to classify.

inclemencia [in-clay-mcn'-the-ah], *f.* 1. Inclemency, severity, harshness, rigor, unmercifulness. 2. Inclemency of the weather. **La inclemencia del tiempo**, the inclemency of the weather.

inclemente [in-clay-men'-tay], *a.* Inclement, cruel, severe.

inclinación [in-cle-nah-the-on'], *f.* 1. Inclination, the act of inclining and the state of being inclined, slope (pendiente); stoop (cuerpo). **Inclinación lateral,** *(Aer.)* bank. 2. Inclination, propension of mind, favorable disposition, love, affection, liking, fancy. **Tener inclinación hacia la poesía,** to have a penchant for poetry. 3. Inclination, tendency toward any point. 4. A bow, an act of reverence (reverencia). 5. *(Math.)* Inclination, the angle between two lines or planes; in gunnery, the angle between the axis of the piece and the horizon. **Inclinación magnética,** the angle of magnetic dip.

inclinado, da [in-cle-nah'-do, dah], *a. & pp.* of INCLINAR. 1. Inclined to any part (ángulo). 2. *(Met.)* Inclined, disposed, affected, minded.

inclinador, ra [in-cle-nah-dor', rah], *m. & f.* One who inclines.

inclinante [in-cle-nahn'-tay], *pa.* Inclining, bending, drawing to.

inclinar [in-cle-nar'], *va.* 1. To incline, to slope (sesgar), to bow (bajar), to bend; to give a tendency or direction to any place or state. 2. To incline, to influence, to turn the desire toward anything. **Inclinar a uno a hacer algo,** to induce somebody to do something. -*vn.* To resemble, to be alike. -*vr.* 1. To incline (estar inclinado), to lean, to bend to, to tend toward any part. 2. To incline, to lean, to be favorably disposed to. 3. To bend the body (encorvarse), to bow (hacer reverencia). 4. To have a particular reason to follow some opinion or do something. **Inclinarse a hacer algo,** to be inclined to do something. 5. *(Naut.)* To heel.

Inclinativo, va [in-cle-nah-tee'-vo, vah], *a.* Inclinatory.

inclito, ta [een'-cle-to, tah], *a.* Famous, renowned, conspicuous, illustrious.

incluir [in-cloo-eer'], *va.* 1. To include, to comprise, to enclose (carta); to comprehend, to contain. 2. To allow one a share in a business.

inclusa [in-cloo'-sah], *f.* Foundling hospital.

inclusero, ra [in-cloo-say'-ro, rah], *m. & f. & a.* Foundling.

inclusión [in-cloo-se-on'], *f.* 1. Inclusion, the act of inclosing or containing a thing. 2. Easy access, familiar intercourse.

inclusivamente, inclusive [in-cloo-se-vah-men-tay], *adv.* Inclusively.

inclusivo, va [in-cloo-see'-vo, vah], *a.* Inclusive.

incluso, sa [in-cloo'-so, sah], *a & pp. irr.* of INCLUIR. Inclosed. -*adv.* Even, actually. **Incluso la pegó,** he even hit her.

incluyente [in-cloo-yen'-tay], *pa.* Including.

incoado, da [in-co-ah'-do, dah], *a. & pp.* of INCOAR. Inchoate, begun, commenced.

incoagulable [in-co-ah-goo-lah'-blay], *a.* Incoagulable, uncoagulable.

incoar [in-co-ar'], *va.* To commence, to begin, to inchoate.

incoativo, va [in-co-ah-tee'-vo, vah], *a.* Inchoative, inceptive, noting inchoation or beginning.

incobrable [in-co-brah'-blay], *a.* Irrecoverable, irretrievable.

incoercible [in-co-er-thee'-blay], *a.* 1. Incoercible, which cannot be forced or restrained. 2. Incoercible, used of imponderable agents, as light, heat, electricity, magnetism.

incógnito, ta [in-cog'-ne-to, tah], *a.* Unknown. **De incógnito,** 1. Incog or incognito. 2. Hiddenly, or clandestinely. -*f. (Math.)* An unknown quantity, the quantity sought. **Despejar la incógnita,** to clear the unknown quantity of coefficients, exponents, or divisor.

incognoscible [in-cog-nos-thee-blay], *a.* Imperceptible.

incoherencia [in-co-ay-ren'-the-ah], *f.* Incoherence.

incoherente [in-co-ay-ren-tay], *a.* Incoherent, inconsistent.

íncola [een'-co-lah], *m.* Inhabitant.

incoloro, ra [in-co-lo'-ro, rah], *a.* Free of color, colorless.

incólume [in-co'-loo-may], *a.* Sound, safe, unharmed.

incolumidad [in-co-loo-me-dahd'], *f.* Security, safety.

incombinable [in-com-be-nah'-blay], *a.* Uncombinable, which cannot be combined.

incombustibilidad [in-com-boos-te-be-le-dahd'], *f.* Incombustibility.

incombustible [in-com-boos-tee'-blay], *a.* Incombustible.

incomerciable [in-co-mer-the-ah'-blay], *a.* Contraband, unlawful, prohibited. (artículos de comercio).

incomible [in-co-me'-blay], *a.* Uneatable, inedible.

incómodamente [in-co'-mo-dah-men-tay], *adv.* Incommodiously.

incomodar [in-co-mo-dar'], *va.* To incommode, to trouble, to put out. -*vr.* 1. To put oneself out (tomarse molestia). 2. To get cross (enfadarse), to get annoyed. **Estar incomodado con,** to be cross with.

incomodidad [in-co-mo-de-dahd'], *f.* 1. Incommodiousness, inconvenience (inoportunidad) 2. Weariness: annoyance (fastidio). *(Acad.)*

incómodo, da [in-co'-mo-do, dah], *a.* Incommodious, inconvenient (inoportuno), uncomfortable (nada cómodo), tiresome (molesto), annoying. **Un bulto incómodo,** an awkward package. **Sentirse incómodo,** to feel uncomfortable.

incomparable [in-com-pa-rah'-blay], *a.* Incomparable, matchless.

incomparablemente [in-com-pah-rah'-blay-men-tay], *adv.* Incomparably.

incomparado, da [in-com-pa-rah'-do, dah], *a.* V. INCOMPARABLE.

incompartible [in-com-par-tee'-blay], *a.* Indivisible.

incompasible [in-com-pa-see'-blay], *a.* V. INCOMPASIVO.

incompasivo, va [in-com-pa-see'-vo, vah], *a.* Uncompassionate, void of pity.

incompatibilidad [in-com-pah-te-be-le-dahd'], *f.* Incompatibility, contrariety. **Incompatibilidad de intereses,** conflict of interests.

incompatible [in-com-pah-tee'-blay], *a.* Incompatible, inconsistent.

incompensable [in-com-pen-sah'-blay], *a.* Incompensable, that cannot be compensated.

incompetencia [in-com-pay-ten'-the-ah], *f.* Incompetency, inability.

incompetente [in-com-pay-ten'-tay], *a.* 1. Incompetent, not proportionate, not adequate. 2. *(Law.)* Unqualified 3. Unsuitable.

incompetentemente [in-com-pay-ten'-tay-men-tay], Incompetently, unduly, unsuitably.

incomplejo, ja [im-com-play'-ho, hah], *a.* Incomplex, simple.

incompletamente [in-com-play-tah-men-tay], *adv.* Incompletely.

incompleto, ta [in-com-play'-to, tah], *a.* Incomplete, inconsummate.

incomplexo, xa [in-com-plec'-so, sah], *a.* Disunited, without connection, non-adherent.

incomponible [in-com-po-nee'-blay], *a.* Incompoundable.

incomportable

incomportable [in-com-por-tah'-blay], *a.* Intolerable, unbearable.

incomposibilidad [in-com-po-se-be-le-dahd'], *f.* Incompossibility, quality of being not possible, but by the negation or destruction of something.

incomposible [in-com-po-see'-blay], *a.* Incompossible, not possible together.

incomposición [in-com-po-se-the-on'], *f.* 1. Want of proportion, or defective comparison. 2. *V.* DESCOMPOSTURA.

incomprehensible [in-com-pray-en-see'-blay], *a. (Acad.) V.* INCOMPRENSIBLE.

incomprendido [in-com-pren-de'-do], *a.* Misunderstood (persona); not appreciated. *-m & f.* Misunderstood person.

incomprensibilidad [in-com-pren-se-be-le-dahd'], *f.* Incomprehensibility.

incomprensible [in-com-pren-see'-blay], *a.* 1. Incomprehensible, that cannot be comprehended. 2. Incomprehensible, expressing thoughts in an obscure or confused manner.

incomprensiblemente [in-com-pren-see'-blay-men-tay], *adv.* Inconceivably, incomprehensibly.

incomprensión [in-com-pren-se-on'], *f.* Incomprehension, lack of understanding; lack of appreciation.

incomprimible [in-com-pre-mee'-blay], *a.* Incompressible.

incomunicabilidad [in-co-moo-ne-cah-be-le-dahd'], *f.* Incommunicability.

incomunicable [in-co-moo-ne-cah'-blay], *a.* Incommunicable.

incomunicación [in-co-moo-ne-cah-the-on'], *f.* Isolation; lack of communication; *(Jur.)* solitary confinement. **Ello permite la incomunicación de los detenidos**, it allows those detained to be held incommunicado.

incomunicado, da [in-co-moo-ne-cah'-do, dah], *a.* Incommunicated, incommunicating; having no intercourse. *-m.* A prisoner deprived of intercourse with anyone.

incomunicar [in-co-moo-ne-car'], *va.* To deprive a prisoner of intercourse with anyone, to leave without communications; to cut off, to isolate. **Incomunicar un detenido**, to refuse a prisoner access to a lawyer. *-vr.* To isolate oneself.

inconcebible [in-con-thay-bee'-blay], *a.* Inconceivable, unthinkable.

inconciliable [in-con-the-leah'-blay], *a. V.* IRRECONCILIABLE.

inconcino, na [in-con-thee'-no, nah], *a.* Disordered, disarranged.

inconcusamente [in-con-coo'-sah-men-tay], *adv.* Certainly, indubitably.

inconcuso, sa [in-con-coo'-so, sah], *a.* Incontrovertible, incontestable.

incondicional [in-con-de-the-o-nahl'], *a.* 1. Unconditional, absolute, without restriction. 2. *(LAm.)* Servile, fawning. *-m & f.* 1. Staunch (partidario, adepto), staunch supporter; die-hard, hardliner. 2. *(LAm.)* Toady, yes-man.

incondicionalmente [in-con-de-theo-nal-men'-tay], *adv.* Unconditionally, unreservedly.

inconducente [in-con-doo-then'-tay], *a.* Incongruous.

inconexión [in-co-nec-se-on'], *f.* 1. Incoherency, incongruity, want of dependence of one part upon another. 2. Lack of connection, self-contradiction.

inconexo, xa [in-co-nec'-so, sah], *a.* 1. Unconnected, disconnected (desarticulado), unrelated (no relacionado), incoherent, inconsequential, having no dependence of one part upon another. 2. Independent, not supported by any other.

inconfesable [in-con-fay-sah'-blay], *a.* Which cannot be told, unconfessable; shameful, disgraceful.

inconfeso, sa [in-con-fay'-so, sah], *a.* Unconfessed, applied to a criminal who does not confess his guilt.

inconfidencia [in-con-fe-den'-the-ah], *f.* 1. Distrust, mistrust, want of confidence. 2. Disloyalty, want of fidelity to the sovereign.

inconforme [in-con-for'-may], *a.* Non-conformist. **Estar inconforme con algo**, *(CAm.)* to disagree with somebody.

inconformista [in-con-for-mees'-tah], *a. m & f.* Non-conformist.

inconfundible [in-con-foon-de'-blay], *a.* Unmistakable.

incongruamente [in-con-groo-ah-men'-tay], *adv.* Incongruously.

incongruencia [in-con-groo-en-the-ah], *f.* Incongruence, want of symmetry or proportion; unsuitableness, want of adaptation.

incongruente [in-con-groo-en'-tay], *a.* Incongruous, incongruent.

incongruentemente [in-con-groo-ayn'-tay-men-tay], *adv.* Incongruously, incompatibly.

incongruo, grua [in-con'-groo-o, ah], *a.* 1. Incongruous, disproportionate, unsuitable. 2. Applied to ecclesiastical livings which do not yield a competent income, and to the priests who perform the duties of those livings.

inconjugable [in-con-hoo-gah'-blay], *a.* Inconjugable, that cannot be conjugated.

inconmensurable [in-con-men-soo-rah'-blay], *a.* Incommensurable, not to be reduced to any measure.

inconmovible [in-con-mo-vee'-blay], *a.* Unshakable, inflexible, relentless.

inconmutabilidad [in-con-moo-tah-be-le-dahd'], *f. V.* INMUTABILIDAD.

inconmutable [in-con-moo-tah'-blay], *a.* 1. Incommutable, that cannot be exchanged, commuted, or bartered. 2. *V.* INMUTABLE.

inconquistable [in-con-kis-tah'-blay], *a.* 1. Unconquerable, impregnable, inexpugnable, invincible. 2. Incorruptible (persona).

inconsciencia [in-cons-the-en-the-ah], *f.* 1. Unconsciousness. 2. Irresponsibility, unawareness (ignorancia), thoughtlessness (irreflexión).

inconsciente [in-cons-the-en'-tay], *a.* 1. *(Med.)* Unconscious. **Le encontraron inconsciente**, they found him unconscious. 2. Irresponsible, thoughtless (irreflexivo), carefree. **Son gente inconsciente**, they´re thoughtless people. 3. Unconscious (ignorante), unaware.

inconsecuencia [in-con-say-coo-en-the-ah], *f.* Inconsequence, inconclusiveness, want of just inference; unsteadiness, changeableness.

inconsecuente [in-con-say-coo-en'-tay], *a.* Inconsequent, changeable.

inconservable [in-con-ser-vah-blay], *a.* Unpreservable.

inconsiderable [in-con-se-day-rah'-blay], *a.* Valueless, worthless.

inconsideración [in-con-se-day-rah-the-on'], *f.* Inconsideration, want of thought, inattention, inadvertency, abruptness.

inconsideradamente [in-con-se-day-rah'-dah-men-tay], *adv.* Inconsiderately, thoughtlessly.

inconsiderado, da [in-con-se-day-rah'-do, dah], *a.* Inconsiderate, thoughtless, inattentive.

inconsiguiente [in-con-se-gee-en'-tay], *a.* Inconsequent, without just conclusion, without regular inference, contradictory.

inconsistencia [in-con-sis-ten'-the-ah], *f.* 1. Inconsistency, self-contradiction, incongruity, contrariety (contrariedad). 2. Inconsistence, unsteadiness, changeableness.

inconsistente [in-con-sis-ten'-tay], *a.* Inconsistent, incongruous, absurd, lacking firmness (poco sólido), uneven (irregular), loose (tierra); flimsy (tela).

inconsolable [in-con-so-lah'-blay], *a.* Inconsolable.

inconsolablemente [in-con-so-lah'-blay-men-tay], *adv.* Inconsolably.

inconstancia [in-cons-tahn'-the-ah], *f.* Inconstancy, fickleness, unsteadiness, levity, lightness, frailty.

inconstante [in-cons-tahn'-tay], *a.* Inconstant, changeable, mutable, variable, fickle (caprichoso), unsteady (poco firme).

inconstantemente [in-cons-tan'-tay-men-tay], *adv.* Inconstantly, fickly, giddily.

inconstitucional [in-cons-te-too-the-o-nahl'], *a.* Unconstitutional.

inconstitucionalidad [in-cons-te-too-the-o-nah-le-dahd'], *f.* Unconstitutionality.

inconstitucionalismo [in-cons-te-too-the-o-nah-lees'-mo], *m.* Disobedience to the principles of the constitution.

inconstruible [in-cons-troo-ee'-blay], *a.* 1. *(coll.)* Whimsical, fantastical, fanciful, variable, fickle. 2. *(Gram.)* Obscure, unintelligible, difficult to be construed.

inconsútil [in-con-soo'-teel], *a.* Seamless, having no seam.

incontable [in-con-tah'-blay], *a.* Innumerable, countless.

incontaminado, da [in-con-tah-me-nah'-do, dah], *a.* Undefiled, uncontaminated.

incontenible [in-con-tay-ne'-blay], *a.* Uncontrollable, unstoppable, uncontainable.

incontestable [in-con-tes-tah'-blay], *a.* Incontestable, indisputable, incontrovertible.

incontestablemente [in-con-tays-tah-blay-men-tay], *adv.* Incontestably.

incontinencia [in-con-te-nen'-the-ah], *f.* Incontinence or incontinency; unchastity, lewdness. **Incontinencia de orina** *(Med.)* Incontinence of urine, a disease.

incontinente [in-con-te-nen'-tay], *a.* 1. Incontinent: applied to one who has no command of his passions. 2. Incontinent, unchaste.

incontinente [in-con-te-nen'-tay], *adv.* Instantly, immediately, incontinently.

incontinentemente [in-con-te-nayn'-tay-men-tay], *adv.* Incontinently, unchastely.

incontinenti [in-con-te-nen'-te], *adv.* Incontinently, instantly, immediately.

incontrastable [in-con-tras-tah'-blay], *a.* 1. Insurmountable, irresistible, incontrollable, insuperable (dificultad). 2. Inexpugnable, unconquerable. 3. Inconvincible.

incontratable [in-con-trah-tah'-blay], *a.* V. INTRATABLE.

incontrolado [in-con-tro-lah'-do], *a.* Uncontrolled; violent, wild. *-m & f.* Violent person.

incontrovertible [in-con-tro-ver-tee'-blay], *a.* Incontrovertible, indisputable.

inconvencible [in-con-ven-thee'-blay], *a.* 1. Inconvincible, not capable of conviction. 2. V. INVENCIBLE.

inconvenible [in-con-vay-nee'-blay], *a.* 1. Discordant, inconsistent, opposite. 2. Inconvenient.

inconveniencia [in-con-vay-ne-en'-the-ah], *f.* 1. Inconvenience, incommodity, unfitness. 2. Incongruence, unsuitableness. 3. Impoliteness (descortesía). 4. Impropriety (incorrección), wrongness. 5. Silly remark (disparate).

inconveniente [in-con-vay-ne-en'-tay], *a.* 1. Inconvenient (inoportuno), incommodious, troublesome, unsuitable (impropio). 2. Impolite (descortés). 3. Improper (incorrecto).

inconveniente [in-con-vay-ne-en'-tay], *m.* Difficulty, obstacle (dificultad), obstruction, impediment, disadvantage (desventaja). **El inconveniente es que...**, the trouble is that... **No hay inconveniente en**, there is no objection to.

inconversable [in-con-ver-sah'-blay], *a.* Unsociable, incommunicative.

inconvertible [in-con-ver-tee'-blay], *a.* Inconvertible, that which cannot be converted or changed.

incordiar [in-cor-de-ar'], *va.* To bother, to annoy.

incordio [in-cor'-de-o], *m.* Nuisance. *-a. (Vul.)* Wearisome, vexing.

incorporación [in-cor-po-rah-the-on'], *f.* Incorporation, the act of uniting in one mass.

incorporadero [in-cor-po-rah-day'-ro], *m.* The spot where mercury is mixed with metals.

incorporado [in-cor-po-rah'-do], *a. (Tec.)* Built-in. **Con antena incorporada**, with built-in antenna.

incorporal [in-cor-po-rahl'], *a.* Incorporeal.

incorporalmente [in-cor-po-rahl'-men-tay], *adv.* Incorporeally, incorporally.

incorporamiento [in-cor-po-rah-me-en'-to], *m.* V. INCORPORACIÓN.

incorporar [in-cor-po-rar'], *va.* 1. To incorporate, to unite in one mass, to embody, to include (incluir), to involve (involucrar). 2. To incorporate, to form into a corporation. 3. To raise or to make a patient sit up in his bed. *-vr.* 1. To incorporate, to mingle. 2. To become incorporated or united in one mass or body. **Incorporarse en la cama**, to sit up in bed. 3. *(Naut.)* To sail in company, to join the convoy. 4. To join (sociedad, regimiento). **Incorporarse al trabajo**, to go to work.

incorporeidad [in-cor-po-ray-e-dahd'], *f.* Incorporeity, incorporality, immateriality.

incorpóreo, rea [in-cor-po'-ray-o, ah], *a.* Incorporeal, immaterial, unbodied.

incórporo [in-cor'-po-ro], *m.* V. INCORPORACIÓN.

incorrección [in-cor-rec-the-on'], *f.* 1. Incorrectness (datos), inaccurately. 2. Irregularity (irregularidad). 3. Discourtesy (descortesía). **Cometer una incorrección**, to do something improperly.

incorrectamente [in-cor-rec'-tah-men-tay], *adv.* Inaccurately.

incorrecto, ta [in-cor-rec'-to, tah], *a.* 1. Incorrect (cálculo, dato), inaccurate. 2. Irregular (facciones). 3. Discourteous (conducta), bad-mannered. **Ser incorrecto con una**, to take liberties with somebody.

incorregibilidad [in-cor-ray-he-be-le-dahd'], *f.* Incorrigibleness, hopeless depravity.

incorregible [in-cor-ray-hee'-blay], *a.* Incorrigible, forward.

incorregiblemente [in-cor-ray-he'blay-men-tay], *adv. (coll.)* Incorrigibly, obstinately.

incorrupción [in-cor-roop-the-on'], *f.* 1. Incorruption, incapacity of corruption. 2. Incorruptness, purity of manners, integrity, honesty.

incorruptamente [in-cor-roop-tah-men'-tay], *adv.* Incorruptly.

incorruptible [in-cor-roop-tee'-blay], *a.* Incorruptible.

incorrupto, ta [in-cor-roop'-to, tah], *a.* 1. Incorrupt, free from depravation. 2. Uncorrupt or uncorrupted, pure of manners, honest, good, incorruptible. **Incorrupta**, applied to a virgin.

incrasar [in-crah-sar'], *va.* To inspissate, to thicken.

increado da [in-cray-ah'-do, dah], *a.* Uncreated, increate: a divine attribute.

incredibilidad [in-cray-de-be-le-dahd'], *f.* Incredibility, incredibleness, the quality of surpassing belief.

incredulidad [in-cray-doo-le-dahd'], *f.* Incredulity, incredulousness.

incrédulo, la [in-cray'-doo-lo, lah], *a.* Incredulous, hard to believe, refusing credit. *-m. & f.* A miscreant.

increíble [in-cray-ee'-blay], *a.* Incredible, not to be credited. **Es increíble que...**, it is unbelievable that...

increíblemente [in-cray-ee'-blay-men-tay], *adv.* Incredibly.

incrementar [in-cray-men-tar'], *va.* To increase, to intensify. *-vr.* To increase.

incremento [in-cray-men'-to], *m.* Increment, increase, act of growing greater, cause of growing more. **Incremento de temperatura**, rise in temperature.

increpación [in-cray-pah-the-on'], *f.* Severe, reprimand, reproach.

increpador, ra [in-cray-pah-dor', rah], *m. & f.* Chider, rebuker, scolder.

increpar [in-cray-par'], *va.* To chide, to reprehend, to scold, to reproach, to rebuke.

incriminar [in-cre-me-nar'], *va.* 1. To incriminate, to accuse (persona). 2. To exaggerate a fault or defect. 3. To magnify (falta). V. ACRIMINAR.

incristalizable [in-cris-tah-le-thah'-blay], *a.* Uncrystallizable.

incruento, ta [in-croo-en´-to, tah], *a.* Unstained with blood, bloodless.

incrustación [in-croos-tah-the-on´], *f.* Incrustation.

incrustar [in-croos-tar´], *va.* To incrust or incrustate, to cover with an additional coat, to inlay (joyas). *-vr.* **Incrustarse en,** to lodge in (bomba).

incuartación [in-coo-ar-tah-the-on´], *f.* Inquartation, or quartation, the adding of silver to a button of gold (usually in the proportion of three-fourths to one-fourth) in the process of refining gold.

incubación [in-coo-bah-the-on´], *f.* 1. Incubation, the process of hatching eggs. 2. Incubation, the time intervening between exposure and the outbreak of a disease. 3. *(Met.)* Secret preparation of a design.

incubadora [in-coo-bah-do´-rah], *f.* 1. Incubator. 2. Brooder.

incubar [in-coo-bar´], *va.* To incubate, to hatch eggs. *V.* ENCOBAR.

incubo [een´-coo-bo], *m.* 1. Incubus, nightmare. 2. Incubus, a pretended fairy or demon.

incuestionable [in-coo-ays-te-o-nah-blay], *a.* Blameless, guiltless.

inculcación [in-cool-ca-the-on´], *f.* 1. Inculcation, enforcing. 2. *(Print.)* Act of binding or wedging in a form.

inculcar [in-cool-car´], *va.* l. To inculcate, to impress by frequent admonitions. 2. To make one thing tight against another. 3. *(Print.)* To lock up types.*-vr.* To be obstinate, to conform oneself in an opinion or sentiment.

inculpabilidad [in-cool-pah-be-le-dahd´], *f.* Inculpableness, unblamableness.

inculpable [in-cool-pah´-blay], *a.* Inculpable, unblamable.

inculpablemente [in-cool-pah´-blay-men-tay], *adv.* Inculpably.

inculpación [in-cool-pah-the-on´], *f.* Charge, accusation.

inculpadamente [in-cool-pah´-dah-men-tay], *adv.* Faultlessly.

inculpado, da [in-cool-pah´-do, dah], *a.* Faultless.*-pp.* of INCULPAR.

inculpar [in-cool-par´], *va.* To accuse, to blame. **Los crímenes que se le inculpan,** the crimes with which he is charged.

incultamente [in-cool-tah-men´-tay], *adv.* Rudely, without culture.

incultivable [in-cool-te-va´-blay], *a.* Incapable of cultivation, uncultivable.

inculto, ta [in-cool´-to, tah], *a.* 1. Incult, uncultivated, untilled. 2. Uncivilized, unpolished, unrefined, clownish, clumsy.

incultura [in-cool-too´-rah], *f.* Inculture, want or neglect of culture.

incumbencia [in-coom-ben´-the-ah], *f.* 1. Incumbency. 2. Duty imposed upon a person; ministry. **Eso no es de la incumbencia de usted,** that does not concern you; it is not your business.

incumbir [in-coom-beer´], *vn.* To be incumbent upon someone, to have anything imposed as a duty. **No me incumbe a mí,** it is not my job.

incumplido [in-coom-ple-do], *a.* Unfulfilled.

incumplimiento [in-coom-ple-me-ayn-to], *m.* Non-fulfilment; non-completion. **Incumplimiento de contrato,** breach of contract.

incumplir [in-coom-pler´], *va.* To break (regla), to disobey, to fail to observe; to break a promise (promesa).

incunable [in-coo-nah´-blay], *m.* Incunable, incunabulum.

incurable [in-coo-rah´-blay], *a.* Incurable, immedicable; irremediable, hopeless.

incuria [in-coo-re-ah], *f.* Negligence, indolence, inaccuracy.

incurioso, sa [in-coo-re-o´-so, sah], *a.* Negligent, indolent, incurious, inattentive.

incurrimiento [in-coo-rre-me-en´-to], *m.* Act of incurring.

incurrir [in-coo-rreer´], *vn.* To incur (deuda, ira, odio), to become liable to punishment or reprehension: to deserve.

incursión [in-coor-se-on´], *f.* 1. Incurring. 2. Incursion, raid, overrunning an enemy's country. **Incursión aérea or ataque aéreo,** air raid, air attack.

incurso, sa [in-coor´-so, sah], *pp. irr.* of INCURRIR.

incurvación [in-coor-vah-the-on´], *f. V.* ENCORVADURA.

indagación [in-dah-gah-the-on´], *f.* Search, inquiry, examination, inquest.

indagador, ra [in-dah-gah-dor´, rah], *m. & f.* Investigator, inquirer, an examiner.

indagar [in-dah-gar´], *va.* To search, to inquire, to examine into; to investigate (examinar).

índar [een´-dar], *m.* A kind of mattock for clearing out shrubs, grubbing of the ground and like uses.

indebidamente [in-day-be´-dah-men-tay], *adv.* Unjustly, illegally, wrongfully.

indebido, da [in-day-bee´-do, dah], *a.* Undue, illegal, unlawful, void of equity and moderation.

indecencia [in-day-then´-the-ah], *f.* 1. Indecency, indecorum, obscenity (obscenidad). 2. Nuisance. 3. Filth (porquería); wretchedness. 4. Indecent act; indecent thing (palabra).

indecente [in-day-then´-tay], *a.* 1. Indecent, dishonest, unbecoming. 2. Filthy (asqueroso); miserable (despreciable), wretched; low (vil), mean. **Un cuchitril indecente,** a miserable pigsty of a place. **Es una persona indecente,** he´s a low sort, he´s a mean character.

indecentemente [in-day-then´-tay-men-tay], *adv.* Indecently, fulsomely.

indecible [in-day-thee´-blay], *a.* Inexpressible, unutterable. **Sufrir lo indecible,** to suffer terribly.

indeciblemente [in-day-the´-blay-men-tay], *adv.* Inexpressibly, unspeakably.

indecisamente [in-day-the´-sah-men-tay], *adv.* Irresolutely.

indecisión [in-day-the-se-on´], *f.* Irresolution, indecision, want of firmness of mind.

indeciso, sa [in-day-thee´-so, sah], *a.* 1. Irresolute, indecisive (resultado), not constant in purpose. 2. Undecided (persona), not settled.

indeclinable [in-day-cle-nah´-blay], *m.* 1. Incapable of decline or decay, firm, unshaken. 2. *(Gram.)* Indeclinable, not varied by terminations.

indecoro [in-day-co´-ro], *m.* Indecorum, indecorousness, indecency.

indecorosamente [in-day-co-ro´-sah-men-tay], *adv.* Indecorously, indecently.

indecoroso, sa [in-day-co-ro´-so, sah], *a.* Indecorous, indecent, unbecoming.

indefectibilidad [in-day-fec-te-be-le-dahd´], *f.* Indefectibility, quality of suffering no decay or defect.

indefectible [in-day-fec-tee´-blay], *a.* Indefectible, unfailing.

indefectiblemente [in-day-fec-tee´-blay-men-tay], *adv.* Indefectibly.

indefendible [in-day-fen-dee´-blay], *a.* Indefensible, that cannot be defended.

indefensible [in-day-fen-see´-blay], *a.* Indefensible.

indefenso, sa [in-day-fen´-so, sah], *a.* Defenceless, indefensive.

indeficiente [in-day-fee-the-en´-tay], *a.* Indefectible, unfailing.

indefinible [in-day-fe-nee´-blay], *a.* Indefinable.

indefinidamente [in-day-fe-ne-dah-men-tay], *adv.* Indefinitely.

indefinido, da [in-day-fe-nee´-do, dah], *a.* 1. Indefinite, not defined. 2. Indefinite not determined. 3. Indefinite, large beyond the comprehension of man. 4. Indefinite, not limited. **Por tiempo indefinido,** for an indefinite time.

indefinito, ta [in-day-fe-nee´-to, tah], *a.* Indefinite, without limits.

indehescencia [in-day-es-then´-the-ah], *f. (Bot.)* Indehiscence, lack of the power to open spontaneously.

indehiscente [in-day-es-then´-tay], *a.* Indehiscent, not splitting spontaneously.

indeleble [in-day-lay´-blay], *a.* Indelible, not to be blotted out.

indeleblemente [in-day-lay-blay-men-tay], *adv.* Indelibly.

indeliberación [in-day-le-bay-rah-the-on´], *f.* 1. Indetermination, irresolution. 2. Inadvertency.

indeliberadamente [in-day-le-bay-rah´-dah-men-tay], *adv.* Inadvertently, indeliberately.

indeliberado, da [in-day-le-bay-rah´-do, dah], *a.* Indeliberate or indeliberated, unpremeditated; done without sufficient consideration.

indemne [in-dem´-nay], *a.* Undamaged, unhurt, unharmed (persona).

indemnidad [in-dem-ne-dahd´], *f.* Indemnity, exemption from damage.

indemnizable [in-dem-ne-thah´-blay], *a.* What can be made good, or indemnified.

indemnización [in-dem-ne-thah-the-on´], *f.* 1. Indemnification (acto), reimbursement. 2. Indemnity (pago), compensation. **Indemnización de despido**, severance pay. **Indemnización por enfermedad**, sick pay.

indemnizar [in-dem-nee-thar´], *va.* To indemnify, to secure against loss; to maintain unhurt, to make amends; to compensate, to make good to one.

indemostrable [in-day-mos-trah´-blay], *a.* Indemonstrable, incapable of demonstration.

independencia [in-day-pen-den´-the-ah], *f.* Independence, freedom from reliance or control.

independiente [in-day-pen-de-ayn´-tay], *a.* Independent, free: it is sometimes used as a substantive. **Independiente de eso**, Independent of that, besides that. *-m & f.* Independent.

independientemente [in-day-pen-de-ayn´-tay-men-tay], *adv.* Independently.

independizar [in-day-pen-de-thar´], *va.* To emancipate, to free; to make independent. *-vr.* To become free, to become independent.

indescifrable [in-des-the-frah´-blay], *a.* Undecipherable, impenetrable (misterio).

indescribible [in-des-cre-bee´-blay], or **Indescriptible**, *a.* Indescribable.

indeseable [in-day-say-ah´-blay], *a.* Undesirable. *m & f.* Undesirable (persona). **Es un indeseable**, he´s an unsavory sort.

indesignable [in-day-sig-nah´-blay], *a.* That which cannot be designed.

indestructibilidad [in-des-trooc-te-be-le-dahd´], *f.* Indestructibility.

indestructible [in-des-trooc-tee´-blay], *a.* Indestructible, imperishable.

indeterminable [in-day-ter-me-nah´-blay], *a.* 1. Indeterminable. 2. Irresolute, undecided.

indeterminación [in-day-ter-me-nah-the-on´], *f.* Indetermination or indeterminateness, irresolution.

indeterminadamente [in-day-ter-me-nah´-dah-men-tay], *adv.* Indeterminately.

indeterminado, da [in-day-ter-me-nah´-do, dah], *a.* 1. Indeterminate, not defined. 2. Indetermined, irresolute (persona), doubtful. 3. Pusillanimous, chicken-hearted. 4. Indefinite, general; loose.

indevoción [in-day-vo-the-on´], *f.* Indevotion, want of devotion.

indevoto, ta [in-day-vo´-to, tah], *a.* Indevout, irreligious.

India [een´-de-ah], *f. (Met. Coll.)* 1. Great wealth, abundance of money and other precious things. 2. India (País).

indiana [in-de-ah´-nah], *f.* Chintz.

indianismo [in-de-ah-nees´-mo], *m.* 1. Interest in or knowledge of West Indian culture. 2. East Indian idiom.

indianista [in-de-ah-nees´-tah], *m. & f.* 1. Indianist. 2. Person versed in West Indian cultures.

indiano, na [in-de-ah´-no, nah], *a. & m. & f.* 1. East Indian. 2. West Indian. 3. Spanish emigrant who returns rich from Latin America.

indicación [in-de-ca-the-on´], *f.* 1. Indication (señal), any mark, token, sign or note. 2. *(Med.)* Indication, the sign or

symptom which indicates what is to be done (síntoma). 3. Hint, suggestion (sugerencia). **Por indicación de**, at the suggestion of. **Seguiré sus indicaciones**, I will follow your suggestion.

indicado [in-de-cah´-do], *a.* Right, suitable, proper; obvious; likely. **El sitio más indicado**, the most obvious place. **Es el más indicado para el puesto**, he is the most suitable man for the job.

indicador [in-de-ca-dor´], *m.* 1. Indicator, pointer, hand (aguja). 2. The forefinger. 3. Electrical indicator. **Indicador de dirección**, *(Aer.)* direction indicator. **Indicador de velocidades**, speedometer.

indicante [in-de-cahn´-tay], *pa.* Indicating. *-m. (Med.)* Indicant, anything from which an indication is drawn in a disease.

indicar [in-de-car´], *va.* 1. To indicate, to show (mostrar), to point out (señalar). 2. *(Med.)* To indicate, to point out a remedy, to read (termómetro).

indicativo, va [in-de-cah-tee´-vo, vah], *a.* Indicative, pointing.

indicativo [in-de-cah-tee´-vo], *m. (Gram.)* Indicative, one of the modes of verbs.

indicción [in-dic-the-on´], *f.* Indiction, the convening of a synod, council, etc.

índice [een´-de-thay], *m.* 1. Mark, sign, index. 2. Hand of a watch or clock. 3. Pin that casts the shade on a sundial. 4. Index, table of contents to a book. 5. Index, forefinger. **Índice del coste de vida**, cost-of-living index. **Índice de mortalidad**, death rate.

indicación [in-de-cah-the-on´], *f.* Indexing.

indiciado, da [in-de-the-ah´-do, dah], *a.* Suspected of a crime or vice. *-pp.* of INDICIAR. Suspicious, liable to be suspected.

indiciador, ra [in-de-the-ah-dor, rah], *m. & f.* 1. One who entertains suspicions. 2. Informer, one who discovers offenders to the magistrates.

indiciar [in-de-the-ar´], *va. (Law.)* 1. To give reasons, to suspect or surmise. 2. To discover offenders to the magistrates. 3. *V.* INDICAR.

indicio [in-dee´-the-o], *m.* Indication, mark, sign, token, trace (vestigio). **Dar indicios de sorpresa**, to show surprise. **Es indicio de**, it is an indication of.

Índico, ca [een´-de-co, cah], *a.* Indian.

indicolita [in-de-co-lee´-tah], *f.* A variety of tourmaline of indigo-blue color, found in Sweden.

indiferencia [in-de-fay-ren´-the-ah], *f.* 1. Indifference, incuriosity. 2. Neglect, unconcern, coldness, lukewarmness, listlessness. 3. Neutrality, suspension.

indiferente [in-de-fay-ren´-tay], *a.* 1. Indifferent, neutral, apathetic (apático), uninterested. 2. Unconcerned, inattentive, regardless. 3. Lukewarm, cool, frigid, listless. **Eso es indiferente**, *(coll.)* that is immaterial, that makes no difference.

indiferentemente [in-de-fay-ren´-tay-men-tay], *adv.* Indifferently, impartially, coolly.

indígena [in-dee´-hay-nah], *a.* Indigenous, native; *(LAm.)* Indian. *-m. & f.* An Indian.

indigencia [in-de-hen´-the-ah], *f.* Indigence, want, penury, poverty, need.

indigenismo [in-de-hay-nees´-mo], *m.* Study of or interest in West Indian culture.

indigenista [in-de-hay-nees´-tah], *a.* Treating of or defending West Indian culture. *-m. & f.* Supporter of West Indians and their culture.

indigente [in-de-hen´-tay], *a.* Indigent, necessitous, poor, needy.

indigerible [in-de-hay-ree´-blay], *a.* Not possible of digestion.

indigestar [in-de-hays-tar´], *va.* To cause indigestion to. *-vr.* To get indigestible (persona). 2. To cause indigestion (comida). **Esa carne se me indigestó**, that meat gave me indigestion. 3. *(Fig.)* To be insufferable. 4. *(LAm.)* To get worried (inquietarse).

indigestible [in-de-hes-tee´-blay], *a.* Indigestible, hard to digest.

indigestión [in-de-hes-te-on´], *f.* 1. Indigestion. 2. Rudeness of temper, ill-nature.

indigesto, ta [in-de-hes´-to, tah], *a.* 1. Hard to digest, indigestible. 2. Indigest, confused, not separated into distinct parts, not methodized, not well considered. 3. *(coll.)* Rude, ill-natured.

indignación [in-dig-nah-the-on´], *f.* Indignation, anger.

indignado, da [in-dig-nah´-do, dah], *a. & pp.* of INDIGNAR. Provoked, teased, indignant, angry.

indignamente, *adv.* Unworthily (no merecedor), unsuitably.

indignante [in-dig-nahn´-tay], *pa.* Indignant, irritating, infuriating.

indignar [in-dig-nar´], *va.* To irritate, to provoke, to tease. *-vr.* To be inflamed with anger and disdain, to become angry or indignant. **Indignarse con uno**, to get indignant with somebody.

indignidad [in-dig-ne-dahd´], *f.* 1. Indignity (ofensa), want of merit. 2. An unworthy action (acto), meanness. 3. Indignation, passion.

indigno, na [in-deeg´-no, nah], *a.* 1. Unworthy (sin mérito), undeserving. 2. Unbecoming, incongruous, unsuitable. 3. Unworthy, bringing indignity, disgraceful, vile (vil), mean, despicable.

índigo [een´-de-go], *m. (Bot.) V.* AÑIL.

indiligencia [in-de-le-hen´-the-a], *f.* Lack of diligence, carelessness.

indio, ia [een´-de-o, ah], *a.* 1. East or West Indian. 2. Blue, azure (azul). *-m. & f.* East or West Indian. *-m.* 1. *(Chem.)* Indium. 2. **Hacer el indio**, to play the fool. 3. **Indio viejo,** *(CAm. Mex.)* stewed meat with maize and herbs.

indirecta [in-de-rec´-tah], *f.* Innuendo, an oblique hint, a cue, a surmise. **Soltar una indirecta**, to drop a hint.

indirectamente [in-de-rec´-tah-men-tay], *adv.* 1. Indirectly, obliquely. 2. Indirectly, not in express terms.

indirecto, ta [in-de-rec´-to, tah], *a.* Indirect, not direct: oblique.

indisciplina [in-dis-the-plee´-nah], *f.* Want of discipline, insubordination.

indisciplinable [in-dis-the-ple-nah´-blay], *a.* Indisciplinable, incapable of discipline.

indisciplinado, da [in-dis-the-ple-nah´-do, dah], *a.* Untaught, undisciplined.

indiscreción [in-dis-cray-the-on´], *f.* Indiscretion, imprudence, rashness, in consideration, folly, tactless thing (falta social). **Si no es indiscreción...**, if you don´t mind my saying...

indiscretamente [in-dis-cray-tah-men´-tay], *adv.* Indiscreetly.

indiscreto, ta [in-dis-cray´-to, tah], *a.* Indiscreet, imprudent, incautious, foolish; injudicious, inconsiderate.

indiscriminado [in-dis-cre-me-nah´-do], *a.* Indiscriminate.

indisculpable [in-dis-cool-pah´-blay], *a.* Inexcusable.

indiscutible [in-dis-coo-tee´-blay], *a.* Unquestionable, beyond discussion.

indisolubilidad [in-de-so-loo-be-le-dahd], *f.* Indissolubility, indissolubleness.

indisoluble [in-de-so-loo´-blay], *a.* Indissoluble, indissolvable.

indisolublemente [in-de-so-loo´-blay-men-tay], *adv.* Indissolubly.

indispensable [in-dis-pen-sah´-blay], *a.* Indispensable, needful.

indispensablemente [in-dis-pen-sah´-blay-men-tay], *adv.* Indispensably, necessarily.

indisponer [in-dis-po-nerr´], *va.* 1. To disable, to indispose, to render unfit. 2. To indispose, to disincline, to make verse or unfavorable. 3. To indispose or disorder slightly with regard to health: commonly used in its reciprocal sense. *-vr.* 1. To be indisposed, to grow ill. 2. To become peevish or fretful.

indisponible [in-dis-po-nee´-blay], *a.* Not available.

indisposición [in-dis-po-se-the-on´], *f.* 1. Indisposition, disinclination, dislike. 2. Indisposition, slight disorder.

indisposicioncilla [in-dis-po-se-the-on-theel´-lyah], *f. dim.* Slight indisposition.

indispuesto, ta [in-dis-poo-ays´-to, tah], *a. & pp. irr.* of INDISPONER. 1. Indisposed, disordered in health. 2. Indisposed, at variance.

indisputable [in-dis-poo-tah´-blay], *a.* Indisputable, incontrovertible.

indisputablemente [in-dis-poo-tah´-blay-men-tay], *adv.* Indisputably.

indistinción [in-dis-tin-the-on´], *f.* 1. Indistinction, indiscrimination (falta de discriminación). 2. Lack of distinction (igualdad).

indistinguible [in-dis-tin-gee´-blay], *a.* Undistinguishable, indistinguishable.

indistintamente [in-dis-tin-tah-men´-tay], *adv.* Indistinctly, indiscriminately.

indistinto, ta [in-des-teen´-to, tah], *a.* Indistinct (poco claro), indiscriminate (indiscriminado), faint (borroso).

individuación [in-de-ve-doo-ah-the-on´], *f. V.* INDIVIDUALIDAD.

individual [in-de-ve-doo-ahl´], *a.* 1. Individual; peculiar (particular), special; single (cama, habitación). 2. *(And. Cono Sur)* Identical (idéntico). *-m. (Dep.)* Singles, match.

individualidad [in-de-ve-doo-ah-le-dahd´], *f.* Individuality.

individualismo [in-de-ve-doo-ah-lees´-mo], *m.* Individualism.

individualista [in-de-ve-doo-ah-lees´-tah], *a.* Individualistic. *-m. & f.* Individualist.

individualizar [in-de-ve-doo-ah-le-thar´], *va.* To individualize.

individualmente [in-de-ve-doo-ahl-men-tay], *adv.* 1. Individually, numerically. 2. Individually, not separably.

individuar [in-de-ve-doo-ar´], *va.* To individuate, to distinguish; to particularize, to specify individually.

individuo [in-de-vee´-doo-o], *m.* Individual, a single person or thing. **El individuo en cuestión**, the person in question.

individuo, dua [in-de-vee´-doo-o, ah], *a.* Individual, indivisible, inseparable.

indivisamente [in-de-ve-sah-men´-tay], *adv.* Indivisibly.

indivisibilidad [in-de-ve-se-be-le-dahd´], *f.* Indivisibility.

indivisible [in-de-ve-see´-blay], *a.* Indivisible.

indivisiblemente [in-de-ve-see´-blay-men-tay], *adv.* Inseparably, indivisibly.

indiviso, sa [in-de-vee´-so, sah], *a.* Undivided, individuate, not separated into parts.

indo, da [een´-do, dah], *a.* Indian. *(Acad.) V.* INDIO.*-m.* The river Indus, now the Sind.

indócil [in-do´-theel], *a.* 1. Indocile, unteachable. 2. Inflexible, not to be prevailed upon; headstrong, forward.

indocilidad [in-do-the-le-dahd´], *f.* 1. Indocility, refusal of instruction. 2. Inflexibility, stubbornness of mind.

indócilmente [in-do´-theel-men-tay], *adv.* Inflexibly.

indocto, ta [in-doc´-to, tah], *a.* Ignorant, uninstructed, unlearned.

indocumentado [in-do-coo-men-tah´-do], *a.* Without identifying documents, who carries no identity papers. *-m & f.* Person who carries no identity papers; *(Mex.)* illegal immigrant.

indoeuropeo, a [in-do-ay-oo-ro-pay´-o, ah], *a.* Indo-European.

indogermánico, ca [in-do-her-mah´-ne-co, cah], *a.* Indo-Germanic.

índole [een´-do-lay], *f.* Disposition, temper, inclination, peculiar genius, idiosyncrasy, humor, nature (naturaleza).

indolencia [in-do-len'-the-ah], *f.* Indolence, indifference, laziness; insensibility to grief or pain.

indolente [in-do-len'-tay], *a.* Indolent, indifferent.

indolentemente [in-do-len'-tay-men-tay], *adv.* Indolently, inertly.

indoloro [in-do-lo'-ro], *a.* Painless.

indomable [in-do-mah'-blay], *a.* 1. Untamable, indomitable (espíritu), unmanageable (animales salvajes). 2. Inflexible, unconquerable (pasiones).

indomado, da [in-do-mah'-do, dah], *a.* Untamed.

indomesticable [in-do-mes-te-cah'-blay], *a.* Untamable.

indoméstico, ca [in-do-mays'-te-co, cah], *a.* Untamed, fierce, intractable.

indómito, ta [in-do'-me-to, tah], *a.* Untamed, ungoverned, wild.

indostánico, ca [in-dos-tah'-ne-co, cah], *a.* Hindu or Hindoo, belonging to Hindustan

indostano, na [in-dos-tah'-no, nah], *m. & f.* Hindu, a native of Hindustan.

indotación [in-do-tah-the-on'], *f.* (*Law.*) Want of a wife's portion.

indotado, da [in-do-tah'-do, dah], *a.* 1. Unendowed, wanting endowments or talents. 2. Portionless (mujeres).

indrí [in-dree'], *m.* (*Zool.*) A mammal of the lemur family, greatly resembling an anthropoid ape.

indubitable [in-doo-be-tah'-blay], *a.* Indubitable, unquestioned, irrefutable, unquestionable.

indubitablemente [in-doo-be-tah'-blay-men-tay], *adv.* Undoubtedly, indubitably, unquestionably.

indubitado, da [in-doo-be-tah'-do, dah], *a.* Undoubted, indubitate.

inducción [in-dooc-the-on'], *f.* 1. Induction, inducement (persuasión), persuasion. 2. Induction, the act of inferring a general proposition from several particular ones. **Por inducción**, inductively.

inducidor, ra [in-doo-the-dor', rah], *m. & f.* Inducer, persuader.

inducimiento [in-doo-the-me en'-to], *m.* Inducement, motive to anything.

inducir [in-doo-theer'], *va.* To induce (persuadir), to persuade, to influence, to attract. **Inducir a uno a hacer algo**, to induce somebody to do something.

inductancia [in-dooc-tahn'-the-ah], *f.* (*Elec.*) Inductance.

inductil [in-dooc'-teel], *a.* Not ductile.

inductivo, va [in-dooc-tee'-vo, vah], *a.* Inductive.

indudable [in-doo-dah'-blay], *a.* Undoubted, indubitable.

indulgencia [in-dool-hen'-the-ah], *f.* 1. Indulgence, forbearance, tenderness, clemency, forgiveness. 2. Fond kindness. 3. Indulgence, release of the penalty due to sin.

indulgente [in-dool-hen'-tay], *a.* Indulgent, kind, mild, gentle.

indulgentemente [in-dool-hen'-tay-men-tay], *adv.* Indulgently.

indultar [in-dool-tar'], *va.* 1. To pardon, to forgive. 2. To free, to exempt (eximir). -vr. 1. (*And.*) To meddle, to pry (entrometerse). 2. (*Carib.*) To get oneself out of a jam.

indultario [in-dool-tah'-re-o], *m.* He who in virtue of a pontifical privilege can dispense eclesiastical benefices.

indulto [in-dool'-to], *m.* 1. Pardon, forgiveness, amnesty. 2. Indult, privilege, exemption (exención). 3. Impost, tax or duty on merchandise imported into Spain.

indumentaria [in-doo-men-tah'-re-ah], *f.* 1. Clothing (ropa), apparel, dress. 2. Costume (estudio).

induración [in-doo-rah-the-on'], *f.* (*Med.*) Induration, a morbid hardness of any part.

industria [in-doos'-tre-ah], *f.* 1. Industry, diligence, assiduity (dedicación). 2. Ingenuity (maña), subtility, acuteness. **Industria algodonera**, cotton industry. **Industria pesada**, heavy industry. **Industria siderúrgica**, iron and steel industry.

industrial [in-doos-tre-al'], *a.* Industrial.

industrialismo [in-doos-tre-ah-lees'-mo], *m.* Industrialism, a social system which considers industry as the principal and most important of the objects of mankind.

industrialista [in-doos-tre-ah-lees'-tah], *a.* (*LAm.*) Industrialist.

industrialización [in-doos-tre-ah-le-thah-the-on'], *f.* Industrialization.

industrializar [in-doos-tre-ah-le-thar'], *va.* To industrialize. *-vr.* To become industrialized.

industriar [in-doos-tre-ar'], *va.* To teach, to instruct.

industriosamente [in-doos-tre-o-sah-men'-tay], *adv.* Industriously.

industrioso, sa [in-doos-tre-o'-so, sah], *a.* 1. Industrious (trabajador), skillful (mañoso), dexterous; painstaking, laborious, assiduous. 2. Made with ingenuity, skillfully or finely done.

inebriativo, va [in-ay-bre-ah-tee'-vo, vah], *a.* Inebriating.

inedia [in-ay'-de-ah], *f.* Fast, abstinence from food.

inédito, ta [in-ay'-de-to, tah], *a.* Not published, unedited, inedited.

ineducado [in-ay-doo-cah'-do], *a.* 1. Uneducated (sin instrucción). 2. Ill-bred (maleducado).

inefabilidad [in-ay-fah-be-le-dahd'], *f.* Ineffability, unspeakableness; impossibility of being explained.

inefable [in-ay-fah'-blay], *a.* Ineffable, unspeakable.

inefablemente [in-ay-fah-blay-men'-tay], *adv.* Ineffably.

ineficacia [in-ay-fe-cah'-the-ah], *f.* Inefficacy, want of effect, ineffectualness, inefficiency (proceso).

ineficaz [in-ay-fe-cath'], *a.* Inefficacious, ineffectual, ineffective, inefficient.

ineficazmente [in-ay-fe-cath'-men-tay], *adv.* Inefficaciously.

ineficiencia [in-ay-fe-the-ayn'-the-ah], *f.* Inefficiency.

ineficiente [in ay-fc-the-ayn'-tay], *a.* Inefficient.

inelegancia [in-ay-lay-gahn'-the-ah], *f.* Inelegance.

inelegante [in-ay-lay-gahn'-tay], *a.* Inelegant.

ineluctable [in-ay-looc-tah'-blay], *a.* Inevitable, irresistible.

inenarrable [in-ay-nar-rah'-blay], *a.* Inexplicable, inexpressible.

inepcia [in-ep'-the-ah], *f.* (*Rare*) V. NECEDAD. *-a.* 1. Idiocy, incompetence; stupidity. 2. Unsuitability (impropiedad). 3. Silly thing (necedad).

ineptamente [in-ep-tah-men'-tay], *adv.* Unfitly, ineptly.

ineptitud [in-ep-te-tood'], *f.* Ineptitude, inability, unfitness.

inepto, ta [in-ep'-to, tah], *a.* Inept (incompetente), unfit, useless; foolish.

inequívoco, ca [in-ay-kee'-vo-co, cah], *a.* Unequivocal, unmistakable.

inercia [in-ayr'-the-ah], *f.* 1. Inertia, the passive principle in matter; inertness, want of motion. 2. Inactivity, inertia, dulness, indolence.

inerme [in-ayr'-may], *a.* Disarmed, without arms, defenceless.

inerrable [in-er-rah'-blay], *a.* Inerrable, exempt from error.

inerrante [in-er-rahn'-tay], *a.* (*Ast.*) Fixed (estrellas).

inerte [in-ayr'-tay], *a.* 1. Inert, dull, sluggish. 2. Unskilful. 3. (*Med.*) Paralytic paralyzed.

inerudito, ta [in-ay-roo-dee'-to, tah], *a.* Inerudite, unlearned.

inervación [in-er-vah-the-on'], *f.* Innervation, the act of giving nervous stimulus and control to an organ.

inescrutable [in-es-croo-tah'-blay], *a.* Inscrutable, unsearchable.

inescudriñable [in-es-coo-dree-nyah'-blay], *a.* Inscrutable.

inesperadamente [in-es-pay-rah-dah-men'-tay], *adv.* Unexpectedly, suddenly.

inesperado, da [in-es-pay-rah'-do, dah], *a.* Unexpected, unforeseen.

inestabilidad [in-es-tah-be-le-dahd'], *f.* Instability, inconstancy, fickleness, mutability, giddiness.

inestable [in-es-tah'-blay], *a.* Unstable, unsteady.

inestimabilidad [in-es-te-mah-be-le-dahd'], *f.* Inestimableness.

inestimable [in-es-te-mah'-blay], *a.* Inestimable, invaluable.

inestimado, da [in-es-te-mah'-do, dah], *a. (Law.)* That which has not been rated or valued.

inevitable [in-ay-ve-tah'-blay], *a.* Inevitable, unavoidable, fatal.

inevitablemente [in-ay-ve-tah'-blay]. *adv.* Inevitably.

inexactitud [in-ec-sahc-te-tood'], *f.* Inaccuracy, want of exactness.

inexacto, ta [in-ec-sac'-to, tah], *a.* Inexact, inaccurate.

inexcusable [in-ex-coo-sah'-blay], *a.* 1. Inexcusable (imperdonable). 2. Inevitable, indispensable 3. Excuseless.

inexcusablemente [in-ex-coo-sah-blay-men'-tay], *adv.* Inexcusably.

inexhausto, ta [in-ec-sah'-oos-to, tah], *a.* 1. Unexhausted, unemptied, unspent. 2. Full, abundant, plentiful.

inexistencia [in-ec-sis-ten'-the-ah], *f.* Non-existence.

inexistente [in-ec-sis-ten'-tay], *a.* Inexistent, non-existent.

inexorable [in-ec-so-rah'-blay], *a.* Inexorable, relentless, hard-hearted.

inexperiencia [in-ex-pay-re-en'-the-ah], *f.* Inexperience.

inexperto, ta [in-ex-per'-to, tah], *a.* Inexpert, unskillful, inexperienced.

inexpiable [in-ex-pe-ah'-blay], *a.* Inexpiable.

inexplicable [in-ex-ple-cah'-blay], *a.* Inexplicable, inexplainable.

inexplicablemente [in-ex-ple-cah'-blay-men-tay], *adv.* Inexplicably, unaccountably.

inexplorado, da [in-ex-plo-rah'-do, dah], *a.* Unexplored.

inexpresivo [in-ex-pray-see'-vo], *a.* Inexpressive; dull, flat, wooden.

inexpugnable [in-ex-poog-nah'-blay], *a.* 1. Inexpugnable, impregnable. 2. Firm, constant; obstinate, stubborn.

inextinguible [in-ex-tin-gee'-blay], *a.* Inextinguishable, unquenchable; perpetual.

inextricable [in-ex-tre-cah'-blay], *a.* Inextricable.

infacundo, da [in-fah-coon'-do, dah], *a.* Ineloquent, not persuasive, not oratorical.

infalibilidad [in-fah-le-be-le-dahd'], *f.* Infallibility.

infalible [in-fah-lee'-blay], *a.* Infallible; certain, sure; unerring (puntería).

infaliblemente [in-fah-le-blay-men-tay], *adv.* Infallibly.

infamable [in-fah-mah'-blay], *a.* Capable of infamy, calumnious.

infamación [in-fah-mah-the-on'], *f.* Slander, calumny, defamation, the defaming of another.

infamador, ra [in-fah-mah-dor', rah], *m. & f.* Defamer, libeller.

infamante [in-fah-mahn'-tay], *pa. & a.* Defaming; opprobrious, offensive (injurioso), slanderous (difamatorio).

infamar [in-fah-mar],*va.* To defame, to make infamous, to dishonor by reports.

infamativo, va [in-fah-mah-tee'-vo, vah], *a.* That which defames.

infamatorio, ria [in-fah-mah-to'-re-o, ah], *a.* Defamatory, libellous, foul-spoken.

infame [in-fah'-may], *a.* Infamous, vile, despicable, damnable.

infamemente [in-fah-may-men'-tay], *adv.* Infamously, vilely.

infamia [in-fah'-me-ah], *f.* Infamy, dishonor, public reproach or opprobrium: meanness, baseness.

infancia [in-fahn'-the-ah], *f.* 1. Infancy, the first part of life. 2. Infancy, the first age of anything: beginning, commencement (edad).

infando, da [in-fahn'-do, dah], *a.* So abominable as not to be expressed, too bad to be mentioned.

infanta [in-fahn'-tah], *f.* 1. Infant, a female child under seven years of age (niña). 2. Infanta, a princess (princesa). 3. Wife of a prince royal.

infante [in-fahn'-tay], *m.* 1. Infant, a male child under seven years of age (niño). 2. Infante, prince (principe). 3. A foot-soldier.-*pl.* Choristers, boys brought up to sing in cathedral churches.

intantería [in-fan-tay-ree'-ah], *f.* Infantry, foot-soldiers.

infanticida [in-fan-te-thee'-dah], *com.* Infanticide, the murderer of an infant.

infanticidio [in-fan-te-thee'-de-o], *m.* Infanticide (acto), the murder of a child or infant.

infantil [in-fan-teel'], *a.* 1. Infantile, infantine (niño). 2. Child-like (inocente).

infanzón [in-fan-thone'], *m.* Nobleman.

infanzonado, da [in-fan-tho-nah'-do, dah], *a.* Pertaining to a noble.

infanzonazgo [in-fah-tho-nath'-go], *m.* Territory of a nobleman.

infanzonía [in-fah-tho-nee'-ah], *f.* Nobility.

infartación [in-far-tah-the-on'], *f.* Infarction, the stoppage of a channel.

infarto [In-far'-to], *m.* Infarct, that which composes an infarction, heart attack.

infatigable [in-fah-te-gah'-blay], *a.* Indefatigable, unwearied.

infatigablemente [in-fah-te-gah'-blay-men-tay], *adv.* Indefatigably.

infatuado, da [in-fah-too-ah'-do, dah], *a. & pp.* of INFATUAR. Infatuate, infatuated, stupefied; infatuating.

infatuar [in-fah-too-ar'], *va.* To infatuate, to deprive of understanding. -*vr.* 1. To become stupefied. 2. In religious matters, to be or become a bigot.

infaustamente [in-fah-oos-tah-men'-tay], *adv.* Unluckily.

infausto, ta [in-fah'-oos-to, tah], *a.* Unlucky, unhappy, unfortunate, accursed.

infección [in-fec-the-on'], *f.* Infection.

infeccioso [in-fec-the-o'-so], *a.* Infectious.

infectar [in-fec-tar'], *va.* 1. To infect, to hurt by infection. 2. To corrupt, to vitiate, to pervert. -*vr.* To catch, to take by infection.

infectivo, va [in-fec-tee'-vo, vah], *a.* Infective, infectious.

infecto, ta [in-fec'-to, tah], *a. & pp. irr* of INFECIR. Infected, tainted.

infecundidad [in-fay-coon-de-dahd'], *f.* Infecundity, sterility, infertility.

infecundo, da [in-fay-coon'-do, dah], *a.* Infecund, barren, unfruitful, infertile. **La época infecunda de la mujer,** the woman´s infertile period.

infelice [in-fay-lee'-thay], *a. (Poet.)* V. INFELIZ.

infelicidad [in-fay-lee-the-dahd'], *f.* Misfortune, calamity, disgrace, misery, unhappiness, infelicity.

infeliz [in-fay-leeth'], *a.* 1. Unhappy (desgraciado), unfortunate (desdichado), luckless, miserable. 2. *(coll.)* Applied to a man of excessive softness and goodnature (mujer). 3. *(Cono Sur, Mex.)* Trifling, insignificant (nimio). -*m & f.* 1. Wretch, poor devil. 2. Simpleton (inocentón).

infelizmente [in-fay-leeth'-men-tay], *adv.* Unhappily, unluckily, unfortunately.

inferaxilar [in-fay-rac-se-lar'], *a. (Bot.)* Infraaxillary, situated below the axil.

inferencia [in-fay-ren'-the-ah], *f.* Inference, illusion.

inferior [in-fay-re-or'], *a.* 1. Inferior lower in place (situación). 2. Inferior, lower in value or excellency (calidad). **De calidad inferior,** of inferior quality. **No ser inferior a nadie,** to be inferior to none. 3. Inferior, lower in station or rank (rango). 4. Inferior, subordinate, subject. 5. *(Mat.)* Lower. **Cualquier número inferior a 9,** any number under 9.

inferioridad [in-fay-re-o-re-dahd'], *f.* Inferiority, subjection.

inferir [in-fay-reer'], *va.* To infer (deducir), to deduce, to draw conclusions, to collect, to gather. *-vr.* To follow, to be consequential, as inference to premises.

infernáculo [in-fer-nah'-coo-lo], *m.* Kind of boyish play, called in America *rayuela;* hop scotch.

infernal [in-fer-nahl'], *a.* 1. Infernal, hellish. 2. Extremely hurtful. **Máquina infernal**, a machine arranged to throw many projectiles at once.

infernalmente [in-fer-nahl'-men-tay], *adv. (coll.)* Hellishly, infernally.

infernar [in-fer-nahr'], *va.* 1. To damn, to doom to eternal torments. 2. To tease, to vex, to provoke.

inferno, na [in-fer'-no, nah], *a. (Poet.),* Infernal.

ínfero, ra [een'-fay-ro, rah], *a.* Combining form of inferior; and in botany and poetry for inferior.

infértil [in-fer'-teel], *a.* Infertile.

infestación [in-fes-tah-the-on'], *f.* Act of harassing, infestation, annoyance.

infestar [in-fes-tar'], *va.* 1. To infest (infectar), to overrun (invadir), to harass an enemy by incursions. 2. V. INFICIONAR. 3. V. APESTAR.

infeudar [in-fay-oo-dar'], *va.* V. ENFEUDAR.

infición [in-fe-the-on'], *f.* Infection. V. INFECCIÓN.

inficionar [in-fe-the-o-nar'], *va.* 1. To infect, to hurt by infection. 2. To corrupt, to defile, to pervert by bad maxims or bad example. 3. To defile the honors of a noble descent, to taint the purity of noble blood; to vitiate.

infidelidad [in-fe-day-le-dahd'], *f.* 1. Infidelity (adulterio), treachery, deceit, faithlessness. 2. Miscreance, unbelief, want of faith, disbelief of Christianity. 3. The whole body of infidels.

infidelísimo, ma [in-fe-day-lee'-se-mo, mah], *a. super.* of INFIEL.

infidencia [in-fe-den'-the-ah], *f.* 1. Unfaithfulness, faithlessness (cualidad); treason. 2. *(Law.)* Misfeasance.

infidente [in-fe-den'-tay], *a.* Unfaithful.

infiel [in-feel'], *a.* Unfaithful (desleal), infidel; faithless, disloyal; godless; pagan: it is also used as a substantive. **Fue infiel a su mujer**, he was unfaithful to his wife.

infielmente [in-fe-el'-men-tay], *adv.* Unfaithfully.

infiernillo, infernillo [en-fe-er-neel'-lyo, en-fer-neel'-lyo], *m.* Chafing dish.

infierno [in-fe-err'-no], *m.* 1. Hell, the place of the devil and wicked souls; torment of the wicked. 2. Limbo. 3. Anything which causes confusion, pain, or trouble; discord, dispute. **Mandar a uno al quinto infierno**, to tell somebody to go to hell. 4. Refectory or eating room in some convents. 5. A large retort or other chemical vessel.

infigurable [in-fe-goo-rah'-blay], *a.* That which cannot be represented by any figure.

infiltración [in-feel-trah-the-on'], *f. (Med.)* Infiltration.

infiltrar [in-feel-trar'], *va.* To infiltrate; to inculcate.

infiltrarse [in-feel-trar'-say], *vr.* To infiltrate, to insinuate by filtration.

ínfimo, ma [een'-fe-mo, mah], *a.* 1. Lowest, lowermost, most inferior, the least. 2. Abject, vile, low-bred.

infinidad [in-fe-ne-dahd'], *f.* 1. Infinity, infiniteness, immensity, boundlessness. 2. Infinity, endless number. **Durante una infinidad de días**, for days on end.

infinitamente [in-fe-ne-tah-men'-tay], *adv.* Infinitely, immensely.

infinitesimal [in-fe-ne-tay-se-mahl'], *a. (Mat.)* Infinitesimal (fracciones).

infinitésimo, ma [in-fe-ne-tay'-se-mo, mah], *a. (coll.)* Infinitely small.

infinitivo [in-fe-ne-tee'-vo], *m. (Gram.)* Infinitive, one of the modes of verbs.

infinito, ta [in-fe-nee'-to, tah], *a.* Infinite, unbounded, unlimited, immense. 2. Infinite, very numerous, excessive. **Hasta lo infinito**, ad infinitum.

infinito [in-fe-nee'-to], *adv.* Infinitely, immensely.

inflación [in-flah-the-on'], *f.* 1. Inflation, the state of being swelled with wind; flatulence. 2. Inflation, conceit, vanity, haughtiness, vaingloriousness.

inflamabilidad [in-flah-mah-be-le-dahd'], *f.* Inflammability.

inflamable [in-flah-mah'-blay], *a.* Inflammable, easy to be set on flame.

inflamación [in-flah-mah-the-on'], *f.* 1. Inflammation, setting on flame, the state of being in flame. 2. *(Med.)* Inflammation, a morbid state characterized by heat, pain, etc. 3. Inflammation, excitement of passions or of fervor of mind.

inflamar [in-flah-mar'], *va.* 1. To inflame, to kindle, to set on fire. 2. To inflame, to kindle desire. *-vr.* To become red, to become inflamed or heated. **Se inflama fácilmente**, it is highly inflammable.

inflamatorio, ria [in-flah-mah-to'-re-o, ah], *a.* Inflammatory.

inflar [in-flar'], *va.* 1. To inflate (inchar), to swell with wind. 2. *(Met.)* To elate, to inflate, to puff up with pride.*-vr.* To jet, to strut. *-vn. (Mex.)* To booze (beber).

inflexibilidad [in-flec-se-be-le-dahd'], *f.* 1. Inflexibility, stiffnes, rigidity. 2. Inflexibility, inflexibleness, obstinacy, tenacity.

inflexible [in-flec-see'-blay], *a.* 1. Inflexible, not to be bent. 2. Inflexible, not to be prevailed upon, immovable; contumacious. **Inflexible a los ruegos**, unmoved by appeals.

inflexiblemente [in-flec-see'-blay-men-tay], *adv.* Inflexibly, inexorable; invariably.

inflexión [in-flec-se-on'], *f.* 1. Inflection, the act of bending or turning. 2. *(Gram.)* Inflection, variation of a noun or verb. 3. Inflection, modulation of the voice.

inflictivo, va [in-flic-tee'-vo, vah], *a. (Law.)* Inflictive, used as punishment.

infligir [in-fle-heer'], *va.* To inflict, to condemn.

inflorescencia [in-flo-res-then'-the-ah], *f.* Inflorescence; habit or axis of flowering.

influencia [in-floo-en'-the-ah], *f.* 1. *(Ant.)* Influence, the power of the celestial bodies upon terrestrial bodies and affairs. 2. *(Met.)* Influence, influx, influencing, credit, consequence, holding ascendent power, power of directing or satisfying. **Bajo la influencia de**, under the influence of. 3. *(Met.)* Inspiration of divine grace.

influenciar [in-floo-en-the-ar'], *va.* To influence.

influente [in-floo-en'-tay], *pa. & a.* Influencing, influential.

influenza [in-floo-en'-thah], *f.* Flu, influenza.

influir [in-floo-eer'], *va.* 1. To influence, to modify; to prevail upon, to guide. 2 To interfere; to inspire with grace. *-vn.* 1. To have influence, to carry weight. **Es hombre que influye**, he´s a man of influence. 2. **Influir en**, to influence.

influjo [in-floo'-ho], *m.* Influx, influence, power, credit.

influyente [in-floo-yen'-tay], *a.* Influential, effective.

infolio [in-fo'-le-o], *m.* A book in folio form. *(Acad.)*

información [in-for-mah-the-on'], *f.* 1. Information, news (noticias), data (informática), report (informe), account, intelligence given, instruction: hint. **Información secreta**, secret information. **Información deportiva**, sports section. 2. Information, charge or accusation exhibited. 3. Judicial inquiry and process. 4. Brief, the writing given to the pleaders, containing the case. 5. Inquiry, investigation.

informado [in-for-mah-do], *a.* Informed.

informador, dora [in-for-mah-dor'], *m & f.* Informant. **Informador gráfico**, reporter. **Los informadores de la prensa**, the representatives of the media.

informal [in-for-mahl'], *a.* 1. Informal, irregular (incorrecto). 2. Applied to persons who do not keep their word, or who have no regard for the established forms of society (conducta), unreliable (poco fiable), offhand (maleducado), frivolous (frívolo).

informalidad [in-for-ma-le-dahd´], *f.* Informality, want of attention to established forms.

informalmente [in-for-mahl'-men-tay], *adv.* 1. Irregularity; badly; unconventionally. 2. Unreliable; shiftily. 3. Informally, unofficially.

informante [in-for-mahn'-tay], *pa.* Informing, instructing. -*m.* 1. Informant, informer, one who gives information. 2. Informant, one who is peculiarly charged to collect information respecting the descent and quality of a person.

informar [in-for-mar´], *va.* 1. To inform (enterar), to instruct, to supply with intelligence or knowledge, to acquaint, to report. 2. To inform, to animate, to actuate by vital powers. 3. To state a case to a counsellor or judge. -*vn.* 1. To report (acerca de). **El profesor informará de su descubrimiento**, the professor will report on his discovery. 2. *(Jur.)* To plead (abogado). -*vr.* To take cognizance, to make an inquiry, to ask for information. **Informarse de**, to find out about. **Informarse sobre algo**, to gather information about something.

informática [in-for-mah'-te-cah], *f.* Information science, computer science. **Informática en grupo**, workgroup computing, shareware, groupware.

informativo, va [in-for-mah-tee'-vo, vah], *a.* 1. Instructive, that which informs. 2. Animative, informative, having power to animate.

informatización [in-for-mah-te-tha-the-on'], *f.* Computerization.

informatizar [in-for-mah-te-thar'], *va.* To computerize.

informe [in-for'-may], *m.* 1. Information, the act of communicating intelligence or imparting knowledge; a report (declaración). 2. Brief. 3. Piece of information. **Según mis informes**, according to my information. **Dar informes sobre**, to give information about. 4. *(Jur.)* Plea, pleading.

informe [in-for'-may], *a.* 1. Informous, shapeless, formless. 2. Not performed in a regular manner. 3. **Informe de inventario (existencias)**, inventory stock status report.

infortificable [in-for-te-fe-cah'-blay], *a.* That which cannot be fortified.

infortuna [in-for-too'-nah], *f.* *(Astrol.)* Sinistrous influence of the stars.

infortunado, da [in-for-too-nah'-do, dah], *a.* Unfortunate, unlucky, unhappy.

infortunio [in-for-too'-ne-oh], *m.* Infortune, ill luck, calamity, mischance; misery; fatality.

infosura [in-fo-soo´-rah], *f.* Surfeit in cattle and other animals.

infracción [in-frac-the-on'], *f.* 1. Infraction, the act of breaking. 2. Infraction, breach, contravention, infringement, violation of a compact; misdemeanor, trespass.

infracto, ta [in-frahc´-to, tah], *a.* Steady, not easily moved.

infractor, ra [in-frac-tor', rah], *m. & f.* Violator.-*a.* Violating.

infraestructura [in-frah-es-trooc-too'-rah], *f.* 1. Substructure, foundation. 2. *(Aer.)* Ground installations. 3. (R.W.) Roadbed and installations. 4. *(Mil.)* Infrastructure. 5. Groundwork, base, underpinnings.

in fraganti [in frah-gahn'-tee], *adv. V.* EN FLAGRANTE.

infrahumano [in-frah-oo-mah'-no], *a.* Subhuman.

infrangible [in-fran-hee'-blay], *a.* Infrangible, not to be broken; inviolable.

infranqueable [in-fran-kay-ah´-blay], *a.* Unsurmountable, inextricable.

infraoctava [in-frah-oc-tah´-vah], *f.* Six days comprehended in any church festival of eight days, not counting the first and the last.

infrarrojo, ja [in-fra-rro'-ho, hah], *a.* Infrared.

infrascripto, ta [in-fras-creep´-to, tah], or **Infrascrito, ta** [in-fras-cree'-to, tah], *a.* Underwritten, undersigned (nombres).

infravalorar [in-frah-vah-lo-rar'], *va.* To under value.

infrecuencia [in-fray-coo-en'-the-ah], *f.* Infrequency.

infrecuente [in-fray-coo-en'-tay], *a.* Infrequent.

infringir [in-frin-heer´], *va.* To infringe, to violate or break: to infract.

infrucción [in-frooc-the-on´], *f. V.* INFURCIÓN.

infructífero, ra, infrugífero, ra [in-frooc-tee'-fay-ro, rah], *a.* Unfruitful, not producing fruit: useless.

infructuosamente [in-frooc-too-o-sah-men-tay], *adv.* Unfruitfully, fruitlessly.

infructuoso, sa [in-frooc-too-oh'-so, sah], *a.* Fruitless, unproductive, unprofitable, gainless, abortive; unsuccessful.

ínfulas [een'-foo-las], *f. pl.* 1. Ornaments or marks of a sacerdotal or pontifical dignity. 2. Presumption, ostentation, conceit (vanidad).

infundadamente [in-foon-dah'-dah-men-tay], *adv.* Groundlessly, without reason or cause.

infundado, da [in-foon-dah'-do, dah], *a.* Groundless, void of reason, unfounded.

infundible [in-foon-dee'-blay], *a.* Infusible, incapable of fusion.

infundibuliforme [in-foon-de-boo-le-for'-may], *a.* Infundibuliform, funnel-shaped. *(Bot.)*

infundíbulo [in-foon-dee´-boo-lo], *m.* 1. Infundibulum, a funnel shaped prolongation from the base of the brain to the pituitary body. 2. The expanded end of the ureter, of the Fallopian tube, etc.

infundir [in-foon-deer'], *va.* 1. To infuse, to pour liquor into a vessel. 2. To infuse, to make an infusion with any ingredient. 3. To infuse, to inspire with. 4. To infuse, to pour into the mind, to instil. **Infundir ánimo a uno**, to encourage somebody. **Infundir miedo a uno**, to scare somebody.

infurtir [in-foor-teer'], *va. V.* ENFURTIR.

infusibilidad [in-foo-se-be-le-dahd'], *f.* Infusibility, resistance to melting.

infusible [in-foo-see'-blay], *a.* Infusible, incapable of being melted.

infusión [in-foo-se-on´], *f.* 1. Infusion, the act and effect of infusing. 2. *(Med.)* Infusion, the act of pouring water of any required degree of temperature on substances of a loose texture and suffering it to stand a certain time; and the liquor obtained by the above process. 3. The act of sprinkling water on the person baptized. 4. Infusion, influxion, inspiration; the act of pouring into the mind.

infuso, sa [in-foo´-so, sah], *a. & pp.* of INFUNDIR. Infused, introduced: applied solely to the grace of God in the soul.

infusorio, ria [in-foo-so´-re-o, ah], *a.* *(Zool.)* Infusorian. -*pl.* The infusoria, protozoans occurring in infusions.

ingenerable [in-hay-nay-rah'-blay], *a.* Ingenerable, not to be produced or brought into being.

ingeniador, ra [in-hay-ne-ah-dor', rah], *m. & f.* Inventor, contriver.

ingeniar [in-hay-ne-ar'], *va.* To conceive, to contrive, to strike out. -*vr.* To work in the mind, to endeavor to find out, to try by all means to obtain or do something; to manage skillfully. **Ingeniarse con algo**, to manage with something.

ingeniatura [in-hay-ne-ah-too'-rah], *f. (coll.)* 1. Ingenuity, subtility, acuteness; skillful management. 2. *(Amer.)* Engineering.

ingeniería [in-hay-ne-ay-ree'-ah], *f.* Engineering. **Ingeniería eléctrica**, electrical engineering. **Ingeniería mecánica**, mechanical engineering.

ingeniero [in-hay-ne-ay'-ro], *m.* 1. Engineer, one versed in engineering, the science and art of making or using machines and public works. Civil, military, mining, electrical, hydraulic, engineers. **Ingeniero agrónomo**, agronomist. **Ingeniero forestal**, forestry expert. **Ingeniero de aplicaciones**, *(Comput.)* application engineer. **Ingeniero de campo / de mantenimiento**, *(Comput.)* maintenance / field engineer. **Ingeniero de equipos**, *(Comput.)* hardware engineer. **Ingeniero de instalaciones**, *(Comput.)* site application engineer. **Ingeniero de programas**, *(Comput.)* software engineer. **Ingeniero de sistemas**, *(Comput.)* systems engineer. **Ingeniero de telecomunicaciones**, *(Comput.)* computer engineer. **Ingeniero informático**, *(Comput.)* computer engineer. 2. *(LAm. Univ.)* Graduate.

ingenio [in-hay'-ne-o], *m.* 1. Genius, talent (talento), skill, cleverness, creative ability. 2. Ingenuity (inventiva). 3. Engine, any mechanical complication in which various movements and parts concur to one effect. 4. Clever person, talented person (persona). **Aguzar el ingenio**, to sharpen one's wits. **Ingenio nuclear**, nuclear device.

ingeniosidad [in-hay-ne-o'-se-dahd'], *f.* Ingenuity (maña), ingeniousness, invention, wittiness (agudeza).

ingenioso, sa [in-hay-ne-o'-so, sah], *a.* 1. Ingenious (mañoso), inventive. 2. Made with ingenuity.

ingénito, ta [in-hay'-ne-to, tah], *a.* 1. Unbegotten, not generated. 2. Innate, inborn, ingenerate.

ingente [in-hen'-tay], *a.* Very large, huge, prodigious.

ingenuamente [in-hay'-noo-ah-men-tay], *adv.* Ingenuously, fairly, simply.

ingenuidad [in-hay-noo-e-dahd'], *f.* Ingenuousness, candor, frankness, openness, open heartedness.

ingenuo, nua [in-hay'-noo-o, ah], *a.* 1. Ingenuous, open, candid, fair, open-hearted. 2. *(Law.)* Ingenuous, freeborn, not of servile extraction.

ingerencia [in-hay-ren'-the-ah], *f.* Interference, intermeddling.

ingeridor [in-hay-re-dor'], *m.* A grafting knife.

ingeridura [in-hay-re-doo'-rah], *f.* 1. Grafting. 2. The place where a tree is grafted.

ingerir [in-hay-reer'], *va.* 1. To insert, to place in or among other things. 2. To introduce, to inclose within another. 3. To graft. **El automovilista había ingerido 3 litros de alcohol**, the motorist had drunk 3 liters of alcohol. *-vr.* To interfere officiously, to intermeddle.

ingerto, ta [in-her'-to, tah], *a. & pa. irr.* of INGERIR. Grafted, ingrafted.

ingestión [in-hes-te-on'], *f. (Med.)* Ingestion, taking in or introducing into the stomach.

ingina [in-hee'-nah], *f.* V. QUIJADA.

ingle [een'-glay], *f.* Groin, the part next to the thigh.

inglés, sa [in-glays', sah], *a.* English, belonging to or native of England. **A la inglesa**, in the English fashion.

inglés, sa [in-glays'], *m.* English language.

inglesar [in-glay-sar'], 1. *va. & vr.* To anglicize, to acquire English tastes. 2. *va.* To dock a horse's tail.

inglete [in-glay'-tay], *m.* Diagonal, oblique line which divides a square into two triangles.

inglosable [in-glo-sah'-blay], *a.* That admits no gloss or comment.

ingobernable [in-go-ber-nah'-blay], *a.* Ungovernable, uncontrollable.

ingraduable [in-grah-doo-ah'-blay], *a. (coll.)* That cannot be graduated.

ingramatical [in-grah-mah-te-cahl'], *a.* Ungrammatical. **-mente**, *adv.*

ingratamente [in-grah'-tah-men-tay], *adv.* Ungratefully.

ingratitud [in-grah-te-tood'], *f.* Ingratitude.

ingrato, ta [in-grah'-to, tah], *a.* 1. Ungrateful (persona). 2. Unpleasant (sabor), disagreeable. 3. Unproductive, harsh.

ingravidez [in-grah-ve-deth'], *f.* Weightlessness.

ingrávido, da [in-grah'-ve-do, dah], *a.* Weightless.

ingrediente [in-gray-de-en'-tay], *m.* Ingredient.

ingresar [in-gray-sar'], *vn.* To enter, to come in. **Ingresar en una sociedad**, to join a club. **Ingresar en el hospital**, to be admitted to hospital. *-vr.* 1. To deposit, to place. 2. *(Mex.)* To become a member. *-va.* 1. To deposit (dinero); to receive (ganancias). **Ingresar dinero en una cuenta**, to pay money to an account.

ingreso [in-gray'-so], *m.* 1. Ingress, entrance. **Examen de ingreso**, entrance examination. 2. Commencement of a work. 3. Entry, any sum of money received which is to be charged in accounts. **Ingresos anuales**, annual income. **Ingresos brutos**, gross receipts. 4. Surplice fees.

inguinal [in-gee-nahl'], *a. (Med.)* V. INGUINARIO.

inguinario, ria [in-gee-nah'-re-o, ah], *a.* Inguinal, belonging to the groin.

ingurgitación [in-goor-he-tah-the-on'], *f.* 1. Ingurgitation. 2. Introduction of fluids by a tube or syringe.

inhábil [in-ah'-beel], *a.* 1. Unable, incapable, unqualified; disqualified, unfit (no apto). 2. Unskillful (torpe), clumsy, awkward.

inhabilidad [in-ah-be-le-dahd'], *f.* Inability, unskillfullness, incapacity, unfitness.

inhabilitación [in-ah-be-le-tah-the-on'], *f.* 1. Act of disabling or disqualifying. 2. Disqualification; disability.

inhabilitar [in-ah-be-le-tar'], *va.* 1. To disqualify, to make unfit, to disable by some natural or legal impediment. 2. To disqualify, to deprive of a right or claim. *-vr.* To lose a right or claim.

inhábilmente [in-ah'-beel-men-tay], *adv.* Unskillfully.

inhabitable [in-ah-be-tah'-blay], *a.* Uninhabitable.

inhabitado, da [in-ah-be-tah'-do, dah], *a.* Uninhabited.

inhabituado, da [in-ah-be-too-ah'-do, dah], *a.* Unhabituated, unaccustomed.

inhalación [in-ah-lah-the-on'], *f. (Med.)* Inhalation.

inhalador [in-ah-lah-dor'], *m. (Med.)* Inhaler.

inhalar [in-ah-lar'], *va.* To inhale, to absorb.

inhartable [in-ar-tah'-blay], *a.* Insatiable.

inherencia [in-ay-ren'-the-ah], *f.* Inherence or inherency.

inherente [in-ay-ren'-tay], *a.* Inherent.

inhestar [in-es-tar], *va.* V. ENHESTAR.

inhibición [in-e-be-the-on'], *f.* Inhibition, prohibition. **Orden de inhibición**, writ to forbid a judge from further proceeding in the cause before him.

inhibir [in-e-beer'], *va.* 1. To inhibit, to prohibit. 2. *(Law.)* To prohibit an infector court from proceeding further in a cause depending before them.

inhibitorio, ria [in-e-be-to'-re-o, ah], *a.* Prohibitory.

inhiesto, ta [in-e-ays'-to, tah], *a.* Entangled, perplexed. V. ENHIESTO.

inhonestamente [in-o-nes-tah-men'-tay], *adv.* Dishonestly.

inhonestidad [in-o-nes-te-dahd'], *f.* Dishonesty; indecency.

inhonesto, ta [in-o-nays'-to, tah], *a.* 1. Dishonest. 2. Indecent, immodest.

inhonorar [in-o-no-rar'], *va.* V. DESHONRAR.

inhospedable, inhospitable [in-os-pay-dah'-blay], *a.* Inhospitable, repulsive.

inhospital [in-os-pe-tahl']. *a.* V. INHOSPITALARIO.

inhospitalario, ria [in-os-pe-tah-lah'-re-o, ah], *a.* Unhospitable, reluctant to entertain guests.

inhospitalidad [in-os-pe-tah-le-dahd'], *f.* Inhospitality, inhospitableness, want of courtesy to strangers.

inhumación [in-oo-mah-nah-the-on'], *f.* Burial, inhumation.

inhumanamente [in-oo-ma-nah-men'-tay], *adv.* Inhumanly.

inhumanidad [in-oo-mah-ne-dahd'], *f.* Inhumanity, cruelty.

inhumano, na [in-oo-mah'-no, nah], *a.* Inhuman, savage, cruel, *(Cono Sur)* dirty.

inhumar [in-oo-mar'], *va.* To bury, to inter.

iniciación [e-ne-the-ah-the-on'], *f.* Initiation, introduction. beginning.

inicial [e-ne-the-ahl'], *a.* Initial, placed at the beginning. **Letras iniciales or las iniciales,** initials.

iniciar [e-ne-the-ar'], *va.* To initiate, to instruct in the rudiments of an art, to put into a new society. -*vr.* To be initiated, to receive the first orders. **Iniciar sesión, conectarse,** *(Comput.)* to sign-in; to log-in.

iniciativo, va [e-ne-the-ah-tee'-vo, vah], *a.* Initiating or producing initiation, initiatory.-*f.* Initiative, the right of proposing laws, etc., lead (liderazgo), plans (propósitos). **Tomar la iniciativa,** to be first in doing or saying something.

inicio [e-ne'-the-o], *m.* Start, beginning. **Inicio del juego,** book opening.

inicuamente [in-e-coo-ah-men'-tay], *adv.* Iniquitously.

inicuo, cua [in-ee'-coo-o, ah], *a.* Iniquitous, wicked, unjust.

inigualable [in-ee-goo-ah-lah'-blay], *a.* Unsurpassable.

inimaginable [in-e-mah-he-nah'-blay], *a.* Unimaginable, inconceivable.

inimitable [in-e-me-tah'-blay], *a.* Inimitable, above imitation; not to be copied.

inimitablemente [in-e-me-tah'-blay-men-tay], *adv.* Inimitably.

ininteligible [in-in-tay-le-hee'-blay], *a.* Unintelligible, that cannot be understood.

ininterrumpidamente [in-in-tayr-room-pee'-dah-men-tay], *adv.* Uninterruptedly; continuously.

ininterrumpido [in-in-tayr-room-pee'-do], *a.* Uninterrupted; continuous, without a break.

iniquidad [in-e-ke-dahd'], *f.* Iniquity, injustice, unrighteousness.

iniquísimo, ma [en-e-kee'-se-mo, mah], *a.* Superlative of INICUO.

injeridura [in-hay-re-doo'-rah], *f. V.* INGERIDURA.

injerir [in-hay-reer'], *va. V.* INGERIR.

injertar [in-her-tar'], *va.* To ingraft a tree, to graft, to inoculate.

injerto [in-her'-to], *m.* 1. Grafting, the action of transplanting a section of one plant to another. 2. Graft, the part transplanted. **Injerto de órganos,** *(Med.)* medical transplant.

injuria [in-hoo'-re-ah], *f.* 1. Injury, offence, wrong, insult (insulto), outrage. 2. Injury, annoyance, hardship, contumely, mischief. 3. Injury, contumelious language, reproachful appellation. **Llenar a uno de injurias,** to heap abuse on somebody.

injuriado, da [in-hoo-re-ah'-do, dah], *a. & pp.* of INJURIAR. Injured, wronged.

injuriador, ra [in-hoo-re-ah-dor', rah], *m. & f.* Aggressor, injurer, wrongdoer.

injuriante [in-hoo-re-ahn'-tay], *pa.* Injuring, injurer.

injuriar [in-hoo-re-ar'], *va.* To injure, to wrong, to annoy, to harm or hurt unjustly (dañar), to offend.

injuriosamente [in-hoo-re-o'-sah-men-tay], *adv.* Injuriously, offensively, hurtfully.

injurioso, sa [in-hoo-re-oh'-so, sah], *a.* Injurious, contumelious, reproachful, hurtful, opprobrious, offensive, insulting (ofensivo), harmful (dañoso).

injustamente [in-hoos-tah-men'-tay], *adv.* Unjustly.

injusticia [in-hoos-tee'-the-ah], *f.* Injustice, iniquity, wrong. **Una gran injusticia,** a terrible injustice.

injustificable [in-hoos-te-fe-cah'-blay], *a.* Unjustifiable.

injustificadamente [in-hoos-te-fe-cah'-dah-men-tay], *adv.* Unjustifiably.

injustificado [in-hoos-te-fe-cah'-do], *a.* Unjustified, unwarranted.

injusto, ta [in-hoos'-to, tah], *a.* Unjust, wrongful, unfair. **Ser injusto con uno,** to be unjust to somebody.

inlegible [in-lay-hee'-blay], *a.* Illegible.

inllevable [in-lya-vah'-blay], *a.* Insupportable.

inmaculadamente [in-mah-coo-lah'-dah-men-tay], *adv.* Immaculately.

inmaculado, da [in-mah-coo-lah'-do, dah], *a.* Immaculate, holy, pure, spotless.

inmadurez [in-mah-doo-reth'], *f.* Immaturity.

inmaduro, ra [in-mah-doo'-ro, rah], *a.* Immature (individuo), unripe, unripened (fruta).

inmaleable [in-mah-lay-ah'-blay], *a.* Unmalleable.

inmanejable [in-mah-nay-hah'-blay], *a.* Unmanageable; intractable.

inmanente [in-mah-nan'-tay], *a.* Immanent, inherent.

inmarcesible [in-mar-thay-see'-blay], *a.* Unfading, unwithering, imperishable.

inmaterial [in-mah-tay-re-ahl'], *a.* Immaterial, incorporeal.

inmaterialidad [in-mah-tay-re-ah-le-dahd'], *f.* Immateriality.

inmaturo, ra [in-mah-too'-ro, rah], *a.* Immature.

inmediación [in-may-de-ah-the-on'], *f.* Contiguity, contact.

inmediatamente [in-may-de-ah'-tah-men-tay], *adv.* Immediately, forthwith, at once.

inmediatez [in-may-de-ah-teth'], *f.* Immediacy.

inmediato, ta [in-may-de-ah'-to, tah], *a.* Contiguous, meeting so as to touch, close, hard by, next. **De inmediato,** immediately, at once. **Inmediato a,** close to, next to.

inmedicable [in-may-de-cah'-blay], *a.* Incurable.

inmejorable [in-may-ho-rah'-blay], *a.* Unimprovable, not capable of improvement, unsurpassable. **Inmejorables recomendaciones,** excellent references. *adv.* **-mente.**

inmemorable [in-may-mo-rah'-blay], *a.* Immemorable.

inmemorablemente [in-may-mo-rah'-blay-men-tay], *adv.* Immemorably.

inmemorial [in-may-mo-re-ahl'], *a.* Immemorial, past time, out of memory; so ancient that the beginning cannot be traced.

inmensamente [in-men-sah-men'-tay], *adv.* Immensely, infinitely, hugely.

inmensidad [in-men-se-dahd'], *f.* Immensity, unbounded greatness.

inmenso, sa [in-men'-so, sah], *a.* Immense, unlimited, unbounded, infinite. **Sentir una tristeza inmensa,** to be terribly sad.

inmensurable [in-men-soo-rah'-blay], *a.* Immensurable, measureless; not to be counted.

inmergir [in-mer-heer'], *va.* To submerge, to souse (implying immediate withdrawal of the body acted on).

inméritamente [in-may'-re-tah-men-tay], *adv.* Immeritedly.

inmeritorio, ria [in-may-re-to'-re-o, ah], *a.* Immeritorious, undeserving.

inmersión [in-mer-se-on'], *f.* 1. Immersion, dive (buzo). 2. The entry of a planet into the shadow of another during an eclipse.

inmigración [in-me-grah-the-on'], *f.* Immigration.

inmigrado, da [in-me-grah'-do], *m & f.* Immigrant.

inmigrante [in-me-grahn'-tay], *a. m & f.* Immigrant.

inmigrar [in-me-grar'], *vn.* To immigrate.

inminencia [in-me-nayn'-the-ah], *f.* Imminence.

inminente [in-me-nen'-tay], *a.* Imminent, impending, at hand.

inmiscible [in-mis-thee'-blay], *a.* Immiscible, incapable of being mixed.

inmiscuir [in-mis-coo-eer'], *va.* To mix.-*vr.* To interfere in, to intermeddle.

inmobiliaria [in-mo-be-le-ah'-re-ah], *f.* Construction company, builder; property company.

inmoble [in-mo'-blay], *a.* 1. Unmovable, immovable (inmóvil), motionless. 2. Unmovable, immovable, unshaken, unaffected, constant.

inmoderación [in-mo-day-rah-the-on'], *f.* Immoderation, immoderateness; *(Cono Sur)* excess.

inmoderadamente [in-mo-day-rah-dah-men'-tay], *adv.* Immoderately.

inmoderado, da [in-mo-day-rah'-do, dah], *a.* Immoderate, excessive.

inmodestamente [in-mo-des-tah-men-tay], *adv.* Immodestly.

inmodestia [in-mo-days'-te-ah], *f.* Immodesty, indecency, indelicacy.

inmodesto, ta [in-mo-days'-to, tah], *a.* Immodest.

inmodificable [in-mo-de-fe-cah'-blay], *a.* Unmodifiable.

inmolación [in-mo-lah-the-on'], *f.* Immolation, the act of sacrificing, a sacrifice offered.

inmolador, ra [in-mo-lah-dor', rah], *m. & f.* Immolator.

inmolar [in-mo-lar'], *va.* To immolate, to sacrifice.

inmoral [in-mo-rahl'], *a.* Immoral.

inmoralidad [in-mo-rah-le-dahd'], *f.* Immorality; unethical nature.

inmorigerado, da [in-mo-re-hay-rah'-do, dah], *a.* Of bad habits: not self-controlled.

inmortal [in-mor-tahl'], *a.* 1. Immortal, exempt from death. 2. Immortal, endless.

inmortalidad [in-mor-tah-le-dahd'], *f.* Immortality, exemption from death and oblivion.

inmortalizar [in-mor-tah-le-thar'], *va.* 1. To immortalize, to make immortal. 2. To exempt from oblivion, to perpetuate.

inmortalmente [in-mor-tal-men'-tay], *adv.* Immortally.

inmortificación [in-mor-te-fe-cah-the-on'], *f.* Immortification, want of subjection of the passions, licentiousness.

inmortificado, da [in-mor-te-fe-cah'-do, dah], *a.* Unmortified, free from mortification.

inmotivado, da [in-mo-te-vah'-do, dah], *a.* Without reason or cause.

inmoto, ta [in-mo'-to, tah], *a.* Unmoved.

inmovible, inmóvil [in-mo-vee'-blay, in-mo'-veel], *a.* Immovable. **Quedar inmóvil**, to remain motionless. *V.* INMOBLE.

inmovilidad [in-mo-vele-dahd'], *f.* 1. Immobility, unmovableness, resistance to motion. 2. Immovability, incapacity of being removed. 3. Immovableness, the state or quality of being immovable; firmness, constancy.

inmovilizar [in-mo-ve-le-thar'], *vr.* To immobilize; to stop, to paralyze, to bring to a standstill; to tie up (capital).

inmudable [in-moo-dah'-blay], *a.* Inmutable. *V.* INMUTABLE.

inmueble [in-moo-ay'-blay], *a.* Immovables or immovable estate: applied to lands. **Bienes inmuebles**, real estate.

inmundicia [in-moon-dee'-the-ah], *f.* 1. Uncleanliness, nastiness, dirtiness, filthiness. 2. Uncleaness, impurity.

inmundo, da [in-moon'-do, dah], *a.* 1. Unclean, filthy, dirty. 2. Obscene, unchaste.

inmune [in-moo'-nay], *a.* 1. Free, exempt. 2. Enjoying immunity.

inmunidad [in-moo-ne-dahd'], *f.* Immunity, privilege, exception, franchise, freedom; liberty. **Inmunidad parlamentaria**, parliamentary immunity.

inmunizar [in-moo-ne-thar'], *va.* To immunize, to render immune.

inmunología [in-moo-no-lo-hee'-ah], *f.* Immunology.

inmutabilidad [in-moo-tah-be-le-dahd'], *f.* Immutability, immutableness.

inmutable [in-moo-tah'-blay], *a.* Immutable, invariable, unalterable.

inmutación [in-moo-tah-the-on'], *f.* Change, alteration.

inmutar [in-moo-tar'], *va.* To change, to alter.-*vr.* To change one´s appearance, turn pale. **Se inmutó**, his face fell. **Siguió sin inmutarse**, he carried on unperturbed.

inmutativo, va [in-moo-tah-tee'-vo, vah], *a.* That which changes or causes alterations.

innatismo [in-nah-tees'-mo], *m.* Philosophical system of those who claim ideas are innate.

innato, ta [in-nah'-to, tah], *a.* Innate, inborn, natural.

innatural [in-nah-too-rahl'], *a.* Unnatural.

innavegable [in-nah-bay-gah'-blay], *a.* 1. Innavigable, not to be passed by sailing. 2. Unfit for sea, unseaworthy (barcos).

innecesariamente [in-nay-thay-sah-re-ah-men-tay], *adv.* Unnecessarily.

innecesario, ria [in-nay-thay-sah'-re-o, ah], *a.* Unnecessary.

innegable [in-nay-gah'-blay], *a.* Incontestable, incontrovertible, undeniable.

innervación [in-ner-vah-the-on'], *f.* Innervation, the nervous control of an organ.

innoble [i-no'-blay], *a.* Ignoble, mean of birth; not of noble descent.

innocivo, va [in-no-thee'-vo, vah], *a.* Innoxious.

innocuo, ua [in-no-coo-o, ah], *a.* Innocuous, harmless.

innominado, da [in-no-me-nah'-do, dah], *a.* Nameless. **Hueso innominado**, innominate bone.

innovación [in-no-vah-the-on'], *f.* Innovation (acto), innovation (novedad), novelty.

innovador, ra [in-no-vah-dor', rah], *m. & f.* Innovator.

innovar [in-no-var'], *va.* 1. To innovate, to bring in something not known before. 2. To pursue a cause while an appeal or decree of inhibition is pending.

innumerabilidad [in-noo-may-rah-be-le-dahd'], *f.* Innumerability, innumerableness.

innumerable [in-noo-may-rah'-blay], *a.* Innumerable, numberless, countless.

innumerablemente [in-noo-may-rah-blay-men-tay], *adv.* Innumerably.

innutrición [in-noo-tre-the-on´,], *f.* Innutrition, failure of nourishment.

innutritivo, va [in-noo-tre-tee'-vo, vah], *a.* Innutritious, not nourishing.

inobediencia [in-o-bay-de-en'-the-ah], *f.* Disobedience.

inobediente [in-obay-de-en'-tay], *a.* 1. Disobedient. 2. Inflexible (cosas inanimadas).

inobservable [in-ob-ser-vah'-blay], *a.* Unobservable, inobservable.

inobservado [in-ob-ser-vah-do], *a.* Unobserved.

inobservancia [in-ob-ser-vahn´-the-ah], *f.* Inadvertency, neglect, inobservance.

inobservante [in-ob-ser-vahn´-tay], *f.* Inobservant.

inocencia [e-no-then'-the-ah], *f.* 1. Innocence, untainted integrity. 2. Innocence, harmlessness, guilelessness, innocuousness. 5. Innocence, freedom from guilt imputed. 4. Innocence, sincerity, simplicity.

inocentada [e-no-then-tah'-dah], *f. (coll.)* 1. A simple or silly speech or action. 2. Practical joke (trastada).

inocente [e-no-then'-tay], *a.* 1. Innocent (sin culpa), pure, candid, harmless (sin malicia), lamb-like, just. 2. Innocent, free from particular guilt. 3. Innocent, simple (ingenuo), easily imposed upon.

inocentemente [e-no-then-tah-dah-men-tay], *adv.* Innocently, guiltlessly, harmlessly, innocuously, innoxiously.

inocentón, na [e-no-then-tone', nah], *a. aug.* Very simple and credulous.

inoculación [e-no-coo-lah-the-on'], *f.* 1. Inoculation. 2. Vaccination.

inoculador [e-no-coo-lah-dor'], *m.* Inoculator.

inocular [e-no-coo-lar'], *va.* 1. To inoculate, to propagate by incisions or insertions. 2. To contaminate, to pervert by bad examples or doctrines.

inodoro, ra [in-o-do'-ro, rah], *a.* Odorless.-*m.* 1. Deodorizer. 2. Toilet, water-closet.

inofensivo, va [in-o-fen-see'-vo, vah], *a.* Inoffensive.

inoficioso, sa [in-o-fe-the-oh'-so, sah], *a. (Law.)* Done at an improper time, and not in the manner prescribed by the law; irregular; inofficious.

inojeta [in-o-hay'-tah], *f.* Top of a boot.

inolvidable [in-ol-ve-dah'-blay], *a.* Unforgettable, not to be forgotten.

inoperable [in-o-pay-rah'-blay], *a. (Med.) (CAm. Cono Sur, Mex.)* Inoperable, not admitting on oration.

inopia [in-o'-pe-ah], *f.* Indigence, poverty, penury. **Estar en la inopia**, to be in the dark, to have no idea.

inopinable [in-o-pe-nah'-blay], *a.* 1. Unthought of, not to be foreseen or expected. 2. Indisputable, incontrovertible.

inopinadamente [in-o-pe-nah-dah-men'-tay], *adv.* Unexpectedly.

inopinado, da [in-o-pe-nah'-do, dah], *a.* Inopinate, unexpected, unforeseen.

inoportunamente [in-o-por-too-nah-men-tay], *adv.* Inopportunely.

inoportuno, na [in-o-por-too'-no, nah], *a.* 1. Inopportune (intempestivo), untimely. 2. Inconvenient (molesto); inexpedient (imprudente); inappropriate (no apto).

inordenadamente [in-or-day-nah-dah-men-tay], *adv.* Inordinately.

inordenado, da [in-or-day-nah'-do, dah], *a.* Inordinate, irregular, disorderly.

inorgánico, ca [in-or-gah'-ne-co, cah], *a. (Med.)* Inorganic.

inoxidable [in-oc-se-dah'-blay], *a.* 1. Stainless. 2. Rustproof. **Acero inoxidable**, stainless steel.

in promptu [in promp'-too], *adv.* Off hand, impromptu, extempore.

inquebrantable [in-kay-bran-tah'-blay], *a.* 1. Inviolable, irrevocable, unbreakable. 2. Unswerving. **Fe inquebrantable**, unswerving faith.

inquietador, ra [in-ke-ay-tah-dor', rah], *m. & f.* Disturber.

inquietamente [in-ke-ay-tah-men'-tay], *adv.* Disquietly, uneasily, anxiously (con ansiedad), restlessly (agitadamente).

inquietante [in-ke-ay-tahn'-tay], *a.* Worrying, disturbing.

inquietar [in-ke-ay-tar'], *va.* 1. To disquiet, to trouble, to disturb. 2. To molest, to vex, to pain. 3. To stir up or excite disturbances. *-vr.* To become uneasy or restless.

inquieto, ta [in-ke-ay'-to, tah], *a.* 1. Restless, turbulent. 2. Noisy, troublesome, clamorous. 3. Anxious (preocupado), solicitous, uneasy, fidgety, disquiet. **Estar inquieto por**, to be anxious about.

inquietud [in-ke-ay-tood'], *f.* Inquietude, restlessness, uneasiness, vexation, anxiety.

inquilinato [in-ke-le-nah'-to], *m.* 1. *(Law.)* Right acquired by the tenant of a house. 2. Rent (alquiler). 3. *(Cono Sur)* Tenement house (casa pobre).

inquilino, na [in-ke-lee'-no, nah], *m. & f.* 1. Tenant (arrendatario), the inhabitant of a house that is hired from another. 2. One that has temporary possession and use of the property of another; an innate, a lodger. 3. *(Cono Sur. Agr.)* Tenant farmer.

inquina [in-kee'-nah], *f. (coll.)* Aversion, hatred, dislike.

inquiridor, ra [in-ke-re-dor', rah], *m. & I.* Inquirer, inquisitor.

inquirir [in-kee-reer'], *va.* 1. To inquire, to look for carefully or anxiously, to look after. 2. To ascertain by research and inquiry.

inquisición [in-ke-se-the-on'], *f.* 1. Inquisition, examination, judicial inquiry. 2. Inquisition, a court for the detection of heresy. 3. Building where the Inquisition held its sittings.

inquisidor, ra [in-ke-se-dor', rah], *m. & f.* 1. Inquirer, examiner. 2. Inquisitor, a member of the tribunal of Inquisition.

inquisitivo, va [in-ke-se-tee'-vo, vah], *a.* Inquisitive, curious; busy in search.

inquisitorial [in-ke-se-to-re-ahl'], *a.* Inquisitorial, inquisitorious.

insaciabilidad [in-sah-the-ah-be'-le-dahd'], *f.* Insatiableness, greediness.

insaciable [in-sah-the-ah'-blay], *a.* Insatiable, greedy beyond measure, craving.

insaciablemente [in-sah-the-ah'-blay-men-tay], *adv.* Insatiably.

insaculación [in-sah-coo-lah-the-on'], *f. (Law.)* Act of casting lots or balloting for names.

insaculador [in-sah-coo-lah-dor'], *m. (Law.)* Balloter.

insacular [in-sah-coo-lar'], *va.* To ballot, to vote by ballot.

insalivación [in-sah-le-vah-the-on'], *f.* Insalivation, the mixing of saliva with food.

insalivar [in-sah-le-vahr'], *f.* To mix with saliva in the mouth.

insalubre [in-sah-loo'-bray], *a.* Insalubrious, unhealthy.

insalubridad [in-sah-loo-bre-dahd'], *f.* Insalubrity, unhealthfulness.

insalvable [in-sahl-vah'-blay], *a.* Insuperable (obstáculo).

insanable [in-sah-nah'-blay], *a.* Incurable, irremediable.

insania [in-sah'-ne-ah], *f.* Insanity. *V.* LOCURA.

insano, na [in-sah'-no, nah], *a.* 1. Insane (loco), mad. 2. Unhealthy (malsano).

insatisfacción [in-sah-tees-fac-the-on'], *f.* Dissatisfaction.

insatisfactorio [in-sah-tees-fac-to'-re-o], *a.* Unsatisfactory.

insatisfecho [in-sah-tees-fay'-cho], *a.* Unsatisfied.

inscribir [ins-cre-beer'], *va.* 1. To inscribe (grabar), to mark with writing. 2. *(Geom.)* To inscribe, to draw a figure within another. 3. To enrol (matricular), to register (registrar).

inscripción [ins-crip-the-on'], *f.* 1. Inscription (acto); enrolment, registering. *-vr.* To enrol, to register.

inscrito, ta [ins-cree'-to, tah], *pp. irr.* of INSCRIBIR.

inscrutable [ins-croo-tah'-blay], *a. V.* INESCRUTABLE.

insculpir [ins-cool-peer'], *va.* To insculp, to engrave, to cut.

insecable [in-say-cah'-blay], *a. (Prov.)* Not to be dried, that cannot be dried.

insecticida [in-sec-te-thee'-dah], *m.* Insecticide, insect-killer.

insectil [in-sec-teel'], *a.* Insectile.

insectívoro [in-sec-tee'-vo-ro], *a. (Nat. Hist.)* Insectivorous.

insecto [in-sec'-to], *m.* Insect.

insectólogo, ga [in-sec-to'-lo-go, gah], *m. & f.* Entomologist.

insectología [in-sec-to-lo-he'-ah], *f.* Entomology.

inseguridad [in-say-goo-re-dahd'], *f.* Insecurity, uncertainty, unsafeness. **Inseguridad ciudadana**, lack of safety in the streets.

inseguro, ra [in-say-goo'-ro, rah], *a.* Insecure, uncertain, unsafe (peligroso); unsteady (paso).

insembrado, da [in-sem-brah'-do, dah], *a.* Unsowed or unsown.

inseminación [in-say-me-nah-the-on'], *f.* Insemination. **Inseminación artificial**, artificial insemination.

inseminar [in-say-me-nar'], *va.* To inseminate.

insenescencia [in-say-nes-then'-the-ah], *f.* Quality of not becoming old.

insensatamente [in-sen-sah-tah-men'-tay], *adv.* Madly, stupidly.

insensatez [in-sen-sah-teth'], *f.* Insensateness, stupidity, folly.

insensato, ta [in-sen-sah'-to, tah], *a.* Insensate, stupid, mad, fatuous, out of one's wits.

insensibilidad [in-sen-se-be-le-dahd'], *f.* 1. Insensibility, inability to perceive, dulness of mind. 2. Insensibility, want of feeling, hard-heartedness.

insensible [in-sen-see'-blay], *a.* 1. Insensitive (persona), void of feeling, either mental or corporeal; callous, stupid. 2. Imperceptible (imperceptible), not discoverable by the senses. 3. Hard, stupid, unfeeling, obdurate, cold, cold-hearted, loveless.

insensiblemente [in-sen-se-blay-men-tay], *adv.* Insensitively; unfeelingly.

inseparabilidad [in-say-pa-rah-be-le-dahd'], *f.* Inseparableness, inseparability.

inseparable [in-say-pa-rah'-blay], *a.* Inseparable, not easily separated or disjoined.

inseparablemente [in-say-pah-rah'-blay-men-tay], *adv.* Inseparably.

insepulto, to [in-say-pool'-to, tah], *a.* Unburied, uninterred, graveless.

inserción [in-ser-the-on], *f.* Insertion.

insertar [in-ser-tar'], *va.* To insert, to introduce.

inserto, ta [in-ser'-to, ta], *a. & pp. irr.* of INSERTAR. Inserted. V.INGERTO.

inservible [in-ser-vee'-blay], *a.* Unserviceable, useless.

insidia [in-see'-de-ah], *f.* Ambush, snare (trampa), contrivance, maliciousness (cualidad).

insidiador, ra [in-se-de-a-dor', rah], *m. & f.* Plotter, conspirator, intriguer.

insidiar [in-se-de-ar'], *va.* To plot, to waylay.

insidiosamente [in-se-de-oh'-sah-men-tay], *adv.* Insidiously, guilefully.

insidioso, sa [in-se-de oh'-so, sah], *a.* Insidious, sly, circumventive, guileful.

insigne [in-seeg'-nay], *a.* Notable, remarkable, flagrant, noted.

insignemente [in-seeg'-nay-men-tay], *adv.* Notably, signally, conspicuously.

insignia [in-seeg'-ne-ah], *f.* A distinctive mark of honor, a badge (señal). **Insignias**, insignia, distinguishing marks of office or honor.

insignificación [in-sig-ne-fe-cah-the-on'], *f.* Insignificance.

insignificancia [in-sig-ne-fe-cahn'-the-ah], *f.* Insignificance.

insignificante [in-sig-ne-fe-cahn'-tay], *a.* Insignificant, unimportant.

insignificativo, va [in-sig-ne-fe-cah-tee'-vo, vah], *a.* Insignificant; insignificativo.

insincero [in-seen-thay'-ro], *a.* Insincere.

insinuación [in-se-noo-ah-the-on'], *f.* 1. Insinuation, innuendo. 2. Insinuation, power of pleasing, or stealing upon the affections. 3. (*Law.*) Exhibition of a public instrument before a judge. 4. (*Met.*) Kind of exordium.

insinuador [in-se-noo-ah-dor'], *a.* Insinuating.

insinuante [in-se-noo-ahn'-tay], *pa. & a.* Insinuant, insinuating (que insinúa), having the power to gain favor.

insinuar [in-se-noo-ar'], *va.* 1. To insinuate, to hint. 2. To touch slightly on a subject. *-vr.* 1. To insinuate, to ingratiate, to wheedle, to gain on the affections by gentle degrees; to gain another's favor by artful means. 2. To insinuate, to get in, to creep in, to steal into imperceptibly: speaking of the insinuation of a virtue or vice into the mind. **Insinuarse con uno**, to ingratiate oneself. **Insinuarse en**, to worm one's way into.

insípidamente [in-see'-pe-dah-men-tay], *adv.* Insipidly, without taste; without spirit.

insipidez [in-se-pe-deth'], *f.* Insipidity, insipidness, tasteless.

insípido, da [in-see'-pe-do, dah], *a.* Insipid, tasteless, unpleasant; spiritless, flat.

insipiencia [in-se-pe-en'-the-ah], *f.* Ignorance, want of knowledge or taste.

insipiente [in-se-pe-en'-tay], *a.* Ignorant, tasteless, uninformed.

insistencia [in-sis-ten'-the-ah], *f.* Persistence, steadiness, constancy, obstinacy,

insistente [in-sis-ten'-tay], *a.* Insistent; persistent.

insistentemente [in-sis-ten'-tay-men-tay], *adv.* Insistently.

insistir [in-sis-teer'], *vn.* 1. To insist, to persist. 2. To insist, to dwell upon in discourse. **Insistir en algo**, to insist on something. **Insistir en hacer algo**, to insist on doing something.

ínsito, ta [een'-se-to, tah], *a.* Ingrafted, natural.

insociabilidad [in-so-the-ah-be-le-dahd'], *f.* Unsociability, unsociableness.

insociable [in-so-the-ah'-blay], *a.* Unsociable, averse to conversation and society.

insocial [in-so-the-ahl'], *a. V.* INSOCIABLE.

insolación [in-so-lah-the-on'], *f.* 1. Sunshine, sunlight. 2. (*Med.*) Sun-stroke, heat-stroke. **Horas de insolación**, hours of sunshine.

insolar [in-so-lar'], *va.* To insolate, to dry in the sun; to expose to the action of the sun. *-vr.* To fall ill by the heat of the sun.

insoldable [in-sol-dah'-blay], *a.* 1. That cannot be soldered. 2. Irreparable, irretrievable.

insolencia [in-so-len'-the-ah], *f.* 1. Insolence (descaro), impudence, effrontery, malapertness, haughtiness. 2. Effrontery, barefacedness. 3. Insulting.

insolentar [in-so-len-tar'], *va.* To make bold. *-vr.* To become insolent.

insolente [in-so-len'-tay], *a.* 1. Insolent (descarado), impudent, froward, haughty (altivo). 2. Performing uncommon things. 3. Unusual, uncommon; unaccustomed: it is also used as a substantive, for a bare-faced or shameless man.

insolentemente [in-so-len'-tay-men-tay], *adv.* Insolently, haughtily, insultingly.

insolidario [in-so-le-dah'-re-o], *a.* Unsupportive, uncooperative.

in sólidum [in so'-le-doom], *adv.* (*Law.*) Jointly, so as to be answerable for the whole.

insólito, ta [in-so'-le-to, tah], *a.* Unusual, unaccustomed, insolite.

insolubilidad [in-so-loo-be-le-dahd'], *f.* Insolubility.

insoluble [in-so-loo'-blay], *a.* 1. Indissoluble, insoluble. 2. Insolvable, that cannot be paid.

insolutundación [in-so-loo-toon-dah-the-on'], *f.* (*Law.*) Assignment of goods or effects in payment of a debt.

insolvencia [in-sol-ven'-the-ah], *f.* Insolvency.

insolvente [in-sol-ven'-tay], *a.* Insolvent.

insomne [in-som'-nay], *a.* Insomnious, sleepless.

insomnio [in-som'-ne-o], *m.* Insomnia, sleeplessness.

insondable [in-son-dah'-blay], *a.* 1. Unfathomable, not to be sounded, fathomless. 2. Inscrutable, unsearchable. 3. Abysmal.

insonorización [in-so-no-re-thah-the-on'], *f.* Sound-proofing.

insonorizado [in-so-no-re-thah'-do], *a.* Sound-proof.

insonorizar [in-so-no-re-thar'], *va.* To sound-proof.

insonoro, ra [in-so no' ro, rah], *a.* Insonorous, not clear, soundless.

insoportable [in-so-por-tah'-blay], *a.* Insupportable, intolerable.

insoportablemente [in-so-por-tah'-blay-men-tay], *adv.* Insupportably.

insospechable [in-sos-pay-chah'-blay], *a.* Beyond suspicion.

insospechado [in-sos-pay-chah'-do], *a.* Unsuspected.

insostenible [in-sos-tay-nee'-blay], *a.* (*coll.*) Indefensible.

inspección [ins-pec-the-on'], *f.* 1. Inspection, survey, superintendence: control. 2. The house or office of an inspector. 3. Union of five consistorial churches forming an ecclesiastical district in the French organization of the Protestant worship.

inspeccionar [ins-pec-the-o-nar'], *va.* To inspect (examinar), to examine, to oversee, to supervise (supervisar).

inspector, ra [ins-pec-tor', rah], *m. & f.* Inspector, a careful examiner; superintendent, controller, (*Cono Sur*) Conductor (autobús).

inspiración [ins-pe-rah-the-on'], *f.* 1. Inspiration, the act of drawing in the breath. 2. (*Met.*) Inspiration, infusion of ideas into the mind by a superior power.

inspirador, ra [ins-pe-rah-dor', rah], *m. & f.* Inspirer, one who inspires.

inspirante [ins-pe-rahn'-tay], *pa.* Inspiring.

inspirar [ins-pe-rar'], *va.* 1. To inspire, to draw air into the lungs, to inhale. 2. To infuse with fortitude, courage, etc. 3. To inspire, to infuse into the mind, to instill, to induce. 4. To inspire, to animate by supernatural infusion. *-vn.* (*Poet.*) To blow. *-vr.* To be inspired by.

inspirativo, va [ins-pe-rah-tee'-vo, vah], *a.* Inspiratory, producing inspiration.

instabilidad [ins-tah-be-le-dahd'], *f.* V. INESTABILIDAD.

instable [ins-tah'-blay], *a.* Unstable, inconstant, changing, mutable, fickle.

instalación [ins-tah-lah-the-on'], *f.* Installation (acto, equipo), installment; induction. **Instalaciones deportivas**, sports facilities.

instalador [ins-tah-lah-dor'], *m.* Installer; fitter.

instalar [ins-tah-lar'], *va. (Law.)* 1. To install, to give possession of a rank or employment. 2. To induct, to put into actual possession of a benefice. 3. To install; to set up.

instancia [ins-tahn'-the-ah], *f.* 1. Instance or instancy, importunity, persistency, urgency. 2. Instance, prosecution or process of a suit. 3. Instance, pressing argument. **De primera instancia**, instantly, on the first impulse; first, in the first place. **A instancia de**, at the request of. V. JUEZ and JUZGADO.

instantánea [ins-tan-tah'-nay-ah], *f.* Snapshot.

instantáneamente [ins-tan-tah'-nay-ah-men-tay], *adv.* Instantly, instantaneously.

instantáneo, nea [ins-tan-tah'-nay-o, ah], *a.* Instantaneous, instant.

instante [ins-tahn'-tay], *m.* Instant, a point in duration, a moment. **Al instante**, immediately. **Por instantes**, incessantly, continually. **En un instante**, in a flash.

instante [ins-tan'-tay], *pa. & a.* Instant, pressing, urgent.

instantemente [ins-tahn'-tay-men-tay], *adv.* Instantly, with urgent importunity.

instar [ins-tar'], *va.* 1. To press or urge a request or petition. 2. In schools, to impugn the solution of a question. **Instar a uno a hacer algo**, to urge somebody to do something. *-vn.* To urge the prompt execution of something.

instauración [ins-ta-hoo-rah-the-on'], *f.* 1. Instauration, restoration. 2. Establishment.

instaurar [ins-ta-hoo-rar'], *va.* To renew, to re-establish, to rebuild, to restore (renovar).

instaurativo, va [ins-tah-oo-rah-tee'-vo, vah], *a.* Restorative.

instigación [ins-tee-gah-the-on'], *f.* Instigation, incitement, impulse, encouragement.

instigador, ra [ins-te-gah-dor', rah], *m. & f.* Instigator, abetter.

instigar [ins-te-gar'], *va.* To instigate, to incite, to provoke, to urge to ill.

instilación [ins-te-lah-the-on'], *f.* Instillation, pouring in by drops.

instilar [ins-te-lar'], *va.* 1. To instill, to infuse by drops. 2. To instill, to insinuate imperceptibly into the mind.

instintivo, va [ins-tin-tee'-vo, vah], *a.* Instinctive, determined by natural impulse. **-amente**, *adv.*

instinto [ins-teen'-to], *m.* 1. Instinct, natural desire or aversion, natural tendency. 2. Instinct, the power determining the will of brutes. 3. Divine inspiration. 4. Encouragement, incitement, impulse. **Por instinto**, instinctively.

institución [ins-te-too-the-on'], *f.* 1. Institution (organismo), establishment, settlement. 2. Institution (acto), education, instruction. 3. Collation or bestowing of a benefice. **Instituciones**, institutes of any science. **Institución pública**, public institution.

institucional [ins-te-too-the-o-nahl'], *a.* Institutional.

institucionalizar [ins-te-too-the-o-nah-le-thar'], *va.* To institutionalize.

instituente [ins-te-too-en'-tay], *pa.* Instituting: founder.

instituidor, ra [ins-te-too-e-dor', rah], *m. & f.* Institutor, founder.

instituir [ins-te-too-eer'], *va.* 1. To institute, to establish, to found. 2. To institute, to teach, to instruct. 3. To nominate, to appoint; to determine or resolve.

instituta [ins-te-too'-tah], *f.* Institute, a part or section of the Roman law.

instituto [ins-te-too'-to], *m.* Institute, established law; settled order; design, object, end. **Instituto de belleza**, beauty parlor. **Instituto laboral**, technical school.

institutor, ra [ins-te-too-tor', rah], *m. & f.* V. INSTITUIDOR.

institutriz [ins-te-too-treeth'], *f.* Governess, child's private instructress.

instituyente [ins-te-too-yen'-tay], *pa.* Institutor; foundling.

instrucción [ins-trooc-the-on'], *f.* 1. Instruction, the art of teaching; lesson. 2. Precepts conveying knowledge (conocimientos); knowledge. 3. *(Comput.)* Statement, instruction. **Instrucción memoria a memoria**, memory to memory instruction. **Instrucción registro a memoria**, register to memory instruction. **Instrucción registro a registro**, register to register instruction. **Instrucción única, flujo de datos individual**, single instruction, single data stream. **Instrucción única, flujo de datos múltiples**, single instruction, multiple data stream. **Instrucción oculta**, concealed instruction. 4. **Instrucciones** (órdenes), instructions, orders, drill, training (ejército). **De acuerdo con sus instrucciones**, in accordance with your instructions. **Instrucciones para el uso**, directions for use.

instructivamente [ins-trooc-te-vah-men'-tay], *adv.* Instructively.

instructivo, va [Ins-trooc-tee'-vo, vah], *a.* Instructive; educational (película).

instructor [ins-trooc-tor'], *m & f.* 1. Instructor, teacher, lecturer, monitor. 2. *(Comput.)* Trainer

instructora [ins-trooc-to'-rah], *f.* Instructress.

instruir [ins-troo-eer'], *va.* 1. To instruct, to teach, to lecture, to acquaint. 2. To civilize. 3. To inform authoritatively. 4. *(Law.)* To instruct, to model a cause according to established rules.

instrumentación [ins-troo-men-tah-the-on'], *f.* Instrumentation.

instrumental [ins-troo-men-tahl'], *a.* 1. Instrumental, produced by instruments, not vocal. 2. *(Law.)* Belonging to legal instruments.

instrumentalmente [ins-troo-men-tahl'-men-tay], *adv.* Instrumentally.

instrumentista [ins-troo-men-tees'-tah], *m.* Player on an instrument of music (músico).

instrumento [ins-troo-men'-to], *m.* 1. Instrument, a tool, an engine or machine (herramienta). 2. Instrument, the agent or means of something. 3. *(Law.)* Instrument, a writing containing a contract, or serving as proof or evidence. 4. *(Mus.)* Instrument, any musical instrument. 5. *(coll.)* Instrument, one who acts merely for another. **Instrumento de viento**, a wind instrument. **Instrumento de cuerda**, a stringed instrument. **Tablero de instrumentos**, instrument panel. **Instrumento de precisión**, precision instrument. **Instrumentos científicos**, surgical instruments.

insuave [in-soo-ah'-vay], *a.* Unpleasant, disagreeable.

insubordinación [in-soo-bor-de-nah-the-on'], *f.* Insubordination, disorder, want of obedience.

insubordinado, da [in-soo-bor-de-nah'-do, dah], *a. & pp.* of INSUBORDINARSE. Insubordinate, rebellious, resisting authority.

insubordinar [in-soo-bor-de-nar'], *va.* To incite, to resist authority. *-vr.* To rebel against authority (militares).

insubsistencia [in-soob-sis-ten'-the-ah], *f.* Instability, inconstancy.

insubsistente [in-soo-sis-ten'-tay], *a.* 1. Unable to subsist, incapable of duration. 2. Instable, inconstant, changing.

insubstancial [in-soobs-tan-the-ahl'], *a.* Unsubstantial, of little substance or worth, or of none.

insuficiencia [in-soo-fe-the-en'-the-ah], *f.* 1. Insufficiency, inadequateness. **Debido a la insuficiencia de personal**, through shortage of staff. 2. Incompetence. 3. *(Med.)* **Insuficiencia cardíaca**, heart failure.

insuficiente [in-soo-fe-the-en'-tay], *a.* Insufficient (inadecuado), inadequate; wanting abilities.

insuficientemente [in-soo-fe-the-en'-tay-men-tay], *adv.* Insufficiently.

insuflación [in-soo-flah-the-on'], *f.* Insufflation, the blowing into the air-passages of air, a powder, etc.

insuflar [in-soo-flar'], *va.* 1. To blow. V. SOPLAR. 2. To suggest, to prompt. 3. *(Med.)* To insufflate, to blow or breathe into.

insufrible [in-soo-free'-blay], *a.* Intolerable, insufferable, overbearing, insupportable.

insufriblemente [in-soo-fre-blay-men'-tay], *adv.* Insufferably.

ínsula [een'-soo-lah], *f. (Archaic.)* 1. Isle. V. ISLA. 2. *(Joo.)* A petty state or government.

insular, insulano, na [in-soo-lar', in-soo-lah'-no, nah], *a.* Insular V. ISLEÑO.

insulina [in-soo-lee'-nah], *f.* Insulin.

insulsamente [in-sool-sah-men'-tay], *adv.* Insipidly.

insulsez [in-sool-seth'], *f.* Insipidity, flatness, want of taste (insipidez).

insulso, sa [in-sool'-so, sah], *a.* 1. Insipid, tasteless (insípido). 2. *(Met.)* Dull, heavy; flat cold.

insultador, ra [in-sool-tah-dor', rah], *m. & f.* Insulter.

insultante [in-sool-tahn'-tay], *pa.* Insulting, insulter.

insultar [in-sool-tar'], *va.* To insult, to treat with insolence or contempt. *-vr (coll.)* To meet with an accident, to be suddenly attacked with disease.

insulto [in-sool'-to], *m.* 1. Insult (ofensa), act of insulting. 2. A sudden and violent attack. 3. A sudden fit of illness. 4. *(Mex.)* Belly-ache (indigestión).

insumable [in-soo-mah'-blay], *a.* Incalculable, unnumberable.

insumergible [in-soo-mer-hee'-blay], *a.* Not submersible, incapable of being submerged.

insumiso [in-soo-me'-so], *a.* Unsubmissive, rebellious.

insuperable [in-soo-pay-rah'-blay], *a.* Insuperable, insurmountable, overbearing, not to be overcome, unsurpassable (calidad).

insupurable [in-soo-poo-rah'-blay], *a.* That which cannot suppurate or form pus.

insurgente [in-soor-hen'-tay], *m.* Insurgent, one who rises in rebellion against the goverment of his country: it is also used as an adjective.

insurrección [in-soor-rec-the-on'], *f.* Insurrection, a seditious rising, a rebellious commotion.

insurrecionar [in-soor-rec-the-o-nar'], *va.* To promote an insurrection. *-vr.* To rebel against the constituted authorities.

insurrecto, ta [in-soor-rec'-to, tah], *a.* Rebellious. *-m. & f.* Rebel, insurgent.

insustancial [in-soos-tan-the-ahl'], *a.* V. INSUBSTANCIAL.

insustituible [in-soos-te-too-ee'-blay], *a.* Irreplaceable.

intáctil [in-tahc'-teel], *a.* Intangible, intactible, not perceptible to touch.

intacto, ta [in-tahc'-to, tah], *a.* 1. Untouched not touched. 2. Untouched, not meddled with, not spoken of. 3. Pure, unmingled; entire; intact.

intachable [in-tah-chah'-blay], *a.* Irreproachable.

intangible [in-tan-hee'-blay], *a.* Intangible, not to be touched.

integérrimo, ma [in-tay-her'-re-mo, mah], *a. super.* Very sincere.

integración [in-tay-grah-the-on'], *f.* Integration.

integrado [in-tay-grah'-do], *a.* 1. Integrated (entero); in one piece; integrated (sociedad). 2. **Un grupo integrado por,** a group made up of. 3. *(Comput.)* Encapsulated, built-in.

integral [in-tay-grahl'], *a.* Integral, whole, complete, total.

integralmente [in-tay-grahl'-men-tay], *adv.* Integrally.

íntegramente [een'-tay-grah-men-tay], *adv.* V. ENTERAMENTE.

integrante [in-tay-grahn'-tay], *a.* Integral, integrant. **Los integrantes del conjunto,** the members of the group.

integrar [in-tay-grar'], *va.* 1. To integrate, to make up a whole (formar). 2. To find the integral of a differential quantity. 3.

(Fin.) To repay, to reimburse; *(And. Cono Sur, Mex.)* To hang over, to pay up (pagar).

integridad [in-tay-gre-dahd'], *f.* 1. Integrality, wholeness (entereza), completeness. 2. Integrity, honesty, purity of manners, uprightness (honradez). 3. Virginity (virginidad), maidenhead. 4. Confidence, honor.

integrista [in-tay-gres'-tah], *a.* Reactionary; traditionalist. *-m & f.* Reactionary.

íntegro, gra [een'-tay-gro, grah], *a.* 1. Integral, entire, complete, not fractional. **La cantidad íntegra,** the whole sum. 2. Candid, upright, honest, disinterested, just.

intelección [in-tay-lec-the-on'], *f.* Intellection, the act of understanding.

intelectiva [in-tay-lec-tee'-vah], *f.* Intellect, the power of understanding.

intelectivo, va [in-tay-lec-tee'-vo, vah], *a.* Intellective, having power to understand.

intelecto [in-tay-lec'-to], *m. (Ant.)* Intellect, understanding.

intelectual [in-tay-lec-too-ahl'], *a.* Intellectual, relating to the understanding: mental, ideal, belonging to the mind.

intelectualmente [in-tay-lec-too-ahl'-men-tay], *adv.* Intellectually, mentally, ideally.

inteligencia [in-tay-le-hen'-the-ah], *f.* 1. Intelligence (intelecto), commerce of information: mutual communication, comprehension, knowledge, knowing. 2. Intelligence, direction or government understanding, skill, ability, experience. 3. Intelligence, friendly intercourse. 4. Sense, signification of a passage. 5. Intelligence, spirit. **En inteligencia,** in the understanding, suppositively. **La buena inteligencia entre los pueblos,** good understanding between peoples. 6. *(LAm. Mil.)* Intelligence. 7. *(Imform.)* **Inteligencia incorporada,** built-in intelligence. **Inteligencia integrada,** built-in intelligence.

inteligenciado, da [in-tay-le-hen-the-ah'-do, dah], *a. (coll.)* Instructed, informed.

inteligente [in-tay-le-hen'-tay], *a.* Intelligent, skillful (hábil), clever (listo), learned, knowing. **-mente.** *adv.*

inteligibilidad [in-tay-le-he-be-le dahd], *f.* Intelligibility, capacity of being understood.

inteligible [in-tay-le-hee'-blay], *a.* Intelligible, conceivable, perspicuous, to be perceived by the senses.

inteligiblemente [in-tay-le-hee'-blay-men-tay], *adv.* Intelligibly.

intemperancia [in-tem-pay-rahn'-the-ah], *f.* Intemperance, want of moderation; excess.

intemperante [in-tem-pay-rahn'-tay], *a.* Intemperate. V. DESTEMPLADO.

intemperie [in-tem-pay'-re-ay], *f.* Intemperateness, unseasonableness of weather: inclemency. **Estar a la intemperie,** to be out in the open. **Aguantar la intemperie,** to put up with wind and weather.

intempesta [in-tem-pays'-tah], *a. (Poet.)* Excessively dark, dreary: applied to the dead of night.

intempestivamente [in-tem-pays-tee'-vah-men-tay], *adv.* Unseasonably, abortively, intempestively.

intempestivo, va [in-tem-pes-tee'-vo, vah], *a.* Unseasonable, not suited to the time or occasion: abortive.

intención [in-ten-the-on'], *f.* 1 Intention, design, meaning, mind, view. 2. Instinct of brutes. **Segunda intención,** duplicity. **Con intención,** deliberately. **Tener la intención de,** to intend to.

intencionadamente [in-ten-the-o-nah-dah-nen'-tay], *adv.* Designedly.

intencionado, da [in-ten-the-o-nah'-do, dah], *a.* Inclined, disposed, meaningful (significativo).

intencional [in-ten-the-o-nahl'], *a.* Intentional, designed.

intencionalmente [in-ten-the-o-nahl'-men-tay], *adv.* Intentionally.

intendencia [in-ten-den'-the-ah], *f.* 1. Administration, management (dirección). 2. Place, employment, or district of an intendant. 3. Manager's office (oficina). 4. *(Cono Sur)* Mayoralty (alcaldía); governorship (gobernador).

intendenta [in-ten-den'-tah], *f.* Lady of an intendant.

intendente [in-ten-den'-tay], *m.* 1. Manager (gerente). 2. *(Cono Sur)* Mayor (alcalde); governor (gobernador). **Intendente de provincia**, the governor of a province under a viceroy or captain general. **Intendente del ejército**, quarter-master general. **Intendente de marina**, the commandant of a navy-yard.

intensamente [in-ten-sah-men'-tay], *adv.* Intensely, strongly, powerfully.

intensidad [in-ten-se-dahd'], *f.* Intensity; vehemence, power, strength.

intensificar [in-ten-se-fe-car'], *va.* To intensify, to heighten, to deepen.

intensión [in-ten-se-on'], *f.* Intenseness, vehemence, ardency; earnestness, great attention.

intensivo, va, intenso, sa [in-ten'-see-vo, vah, in-ten'-so, sah], *a.* Intense (emoción, sentimiento), intensive, vehement, ardent, lively.

intentar [in-ten-tar'], *va.* l. To try (probar), to attempt, to endeavor. 2. To intend, to mean (proponerse), to design. 3. To enter an action, to commence a lawsuit.

intento [in-ten'-to], *m.* 1. Intention (propósito), intent, object. 2. Attempt (tentativa). **Intento golpista**, attempted coup. **Intento de suicidio**, attempted rape.

intentona [in-ten-to'-nah], *f.* Foolhardy attempt.

interacción [in-ter-ac-the-on'], *f.* Interaction.

interactivo [in-ter-ac-tee'-vo], *a. (Comput.)* Interactive.

interamericano, na [in-ter-ah-may-re-cah'-no, nah], *a.* Inter-American.

interarticular [in-ter-ar-te-col-lar'], *a.* Interarticular, between joints.

interbranquial [in-ter-bran-ke-ahl'], *a. (Zool.)* Interbranchial, between the branchiae or gills.

intercadencia [in-ter-cah-den'-the-ah], *f.* 1. Interruption, interposition. 2. Inconstancy. 3. *(Med.)* Intermission or inequality of the pulse.

intercadente [in-ter-cah-den'-tay], *a.* Changeable, variable.

intercadentemente [in-ter-cah-den'-tay-men-tay], *adv.* Changeably.

intercalación [in-ter-cah-lah-the-on'], *f.* Intercalation, the act of inserting amongst other things.

intercalar [in-ter-cah-lar'], *va.* To intercalate, to insert among other things.

intercalar [in-ter-cah-lar'], *a.* Intercalary.

intercambiable [in-ter-cam-be-ah-blay], *a.* Interchangeable.

intercambiar [in-ter-cam-be-ahr'], *va.* To change over, to interchange; to exchange (prisioneros, revistas); to exchange (sellos).

intercambio [in-ter-cahm'-be-o], *m.* Interchange, mutual exchange, reciprocity.

interceder [in-ter-thay-derr'], *vn.* 1. To intercede, to mediate, to entreat for another. 2. To intercede, to interpose, to place between.

intercelular [in-ter-thay-loo-lar'], *a.* Intercellular.

interceptación [in-ter-thep-tah-the-on'], *f.* Interception, stoppage, the act of intercepting. *(Acad.)*

interceptar [in-ter-thep-tar'], *va.* To intercept, to cut off, to obstruct.

intercesión [in-ter-thay-se-on'], *f.* Intercession, mediation, interposition, interceding.

intercesor, ra [in-ter-thay-sor', rah], *m. & f.* Intercessor, interceder, mediator, excuser, solicitor.

intercesorio, ria [in-ter-thay-so'-re-o, ah], *a.* Intercessory, intervening between two parties; entreating for another.

intercolumnio [in-ter-co-loom'-ne-o], *m.* Intercolumniation, the space between pillars or columns.

intercomunicación [in-ter-co-moo-ne-cah-the-on'], *f.* Intercommunication.

interconectar [in-ter-co-nec-tar'], *va.* To interconnect.

intercostal [in-ter-cos-tahl'], *a.* Intercostal, between the ribs.

intercurrente [in-ter-coor-rayn'-tay], *a.* Intercurrent, intervening.

intercutáneo, nea [in-ter-coo-tah'-nay-o, ah], *a.* Intercutaneous, between the skin and flesh.

interdecir [in-ter-day-theer'], *va.* To interdict, to prohibit.

interdentario, ria [in-ter-den-tah'-re-o, ah], *a.* Interdental, between the teeth.

interdicción [in-ter-dec-the-on'], *f.* Interdiction, prohibition; interdict.

interdicto [in-ter-deec'-to], *m.* 1. A judgment of summary possession. 2. Prohibition, interdiction.

interés [in-tay-res'], *m.* 1. Interest, concern, advantage, concernment. 2. Interest, share or participation in any profit (participación). 3. Interest, any surplus of advantage. 4. Interest, money paid for the use of money. 5. Interest, part taken for or against any person. 6. *(Poet.)* Pathos or interest of dramatic incidents. **Dar a interés**, to put on interest. **Llevar cinco por ciento de interés**, to bear five per cent interest. **De gran interés**, of great interest. **Sentir interés por**, to be interested in. **Intereses creados**, vested interests. **Interés compuesto**, compound interest. **Intereses por pagar**, interest payable.

interesable [in-tay-ray-sah-blay], *a.* Avaricious, mercenary.

interesadamente [in-tay-re-sah'-dah-men-tay], *adv.* Selfishly.

interesado, da [in-tay-ray-sah'-do, dah], *a. & pp.* of INTERESAR. 1. Interested, concerned. **Estar interesado en**, to be interested in. 2. Interested, selfish (egoísta), sordid, mercenary, avaricious. 3. Blessed, prejudiced (parcial). **Actuar de una manera interesada**, to act in a biased way.

interesado, da [in-tay-ray-sah'-do, dah], *m. & f.* A person concerned in any undertaking or business, a partner. **Los interesados**, the concern, persons connected in business, or their affairs in general.

interesante [in-tay-ray-sahn'-tay], *a.* Interesting (de interés), useful (útil), convenient, profitable (provechoso).

interesar [in-tay-ray-sar'], *vn. & vr.* To be concerned or interested in (tener interés en), to have a share in or to take a part in any concern. **La idea no interesó**, the idea was of no interest. *-va.* 1. To interest, to concern, to give a share in. 2. To interest, to concern, to engage by feeling or sentiment (afectar). 3. *(Poet.)* To interest, to affect or touch with pardon: speaking of a poem. **No me interesan los toros**, I´m not interested in bullfighting. **El asunto interesa a todos**, the matter concerns everybody.

interescolar [in-ter-es-co-lar'], *a.* Inter-scholastic, interschool.

interesillo [in-tay-ray-seel'-lyo], *m. dim.* A slight interest.

interestelar [in-ter-ays-tay-lar'], *a.* Interstellar.

interfaz *(Comput.)* Interfacing.

interferencia [in-ter-fay-ren'-the-ah], *f.* 1. *(Opt.)* Interference of rays of light; crossing. 2. *(Fis. Rad.)* Interference, jamming (con intención).

interferir [in-ter-fay-reer'], *va.* 1. *(Fis. Rad.)* To interfere with, to jam (con intención). 2. To interfere with (injerirse en), to upset, to affect. **Su acción ha interferido en nuestras operaciones**, his action has interfered with our operations. *-vn.* To interfere. *-vr.* To interfere.

interfoliar [in-ter-fo-le-ar'], *va.* To interleave a book.

ínterin [een'-tay-rin], *m V.* INTERINIDAD.

ínterin, or **en al ínterin** [een'-tay-rin], *adv.* In the interim, in the meantime. *V.* INTERINAMENTE.

interinamente [in-tay-re-nah-men'-tay], *adv.* In the intervening time (entretanto), in the interim, meantime, provisionally.

interinidad [in-tay-re-ne-dahd'], *f.* Quality of holding temporary charge or office.

interino, na [in-tay-ree'-no, nah], *a.* Provisional, appointed provisionally, having the temporary charge of an employ or office.

interior [in-tay-re-or'], *a.* Interior, internal, inward (pensamiento), inner, domestic (comercio, política). **Habitación interior**, room without a view.

interior, *m.* 1. The interior, the inside, the inner part. 2. Mind, soul. 3. That which is only felt in the soul. 4. In coaches with three compartments, the middle one. 5. *(Geog.)* Interior. **Política interior,** domestic policy.

interioridad [in-tay-re-o-re-dahd'], *f.* 1. Inside, interior part. 2. The act of concealing something, and the thing hidden. **En su interioridad, sabe que**..., in his heart he knows that... **Desconocen las interioridades del mercado,** they don't know all the ins and outs of the market.

interiorizar [in-tay-re-o-re-thar'], *va.* 1. *(Psic.)* To internalize. 2. *(LAm.)* To look into, to investigate closely.

interiormente [in-tay-re-or'-men-tay], *adv.* In the interior, internally, inwardly, interiorly. **Lo que pasa interiormente,** what goes on inside.

interjección [in-ter-hec-the-on'], *f. (Gram.)* Interjection, a part of speech.

interlineación [in-ter-le-nay-ah-the-on'], *f.* Interlineation.

interlineal [in-ter-le-nay-ahl'], *a.* Interlineal

interlinear [in-ter-le-nay-ar'], *va.* V. ENTRERRENGLONAR.

interlocución [in-ter-lo-coo-the-on'], *f.* Interlocution, dialogue, interchange of speech.

interlocutor, ra [in-ter-lo-coo-tor', rah], *m. & f.* 1. Interlocutor, one who speaks in the name of another. 2. Collocutor, colloquist, one of the speakers in a dialogue.

interlocutorio, ria [in-ter-lo-coo-to'-re-o, ah], *a.* Interlocutory, preparatory to a definitive decision.

intérlope [in-ter'-lo-pay], *a.* 1. Interloping, defrauding in commerce between a nation and the colonies of another. 2. *(Mex.)* Fraudulent (fraudulento).

interlunio [in-ter-loo'-ne-o], *m.* Time when the moon, being about to change, is invisible.

intermediar [in-ter-may-de-ar'], *va.* To interpose, to be in the middle.

intermediario [in-ter-may-de-ah'-re-o], *a.* 1. Intermediary. 2. Mediating (mediador). *-m.* 1. Intermediary, go-between. 2. Mediator (árbitro).

intermedio, dia [in-ter-may'-de-o, ah], *a.* Intermediate (etapa), intervening, interposed, intermedial.

intermedio [in-ter-may'-de-o], *m.* 1. Interval, intermedium, time passing between (tiempo); interim. **El período intermedio,** the intervening period. 2. Interlude, an entertainment between the acts of a play; farce interval; middle.

interminable [in-ter-me-nah'-blay], *a.* Interminable, endless.

intermisión [in-ter-me-se-on'], *f.* Intermission, interruption, forbearance.

intermitencia [in-ter-me-ten'-the-ah], *f.* Discontinuance of an intermittent fever; the interval between the fits.

intermitente [in-ter-me-ten'-tay], *a.* Intermittent, intermissive, coming by fits. *-m. (Aut.)* Directional light.

intermitir [in-ter-me-teer'], *va.* To intermit, to discontinue.

intermundo [in-ter-moon'-do], *m.* Space between the worlds.

intermuscular [in-ter-moos-coo-lar'], *a.* Intermuscular, between the muscles.

internación [in-ter-nah-the-on'], *f.* Importation.

internacional [in-er-nah-the-o-nahl'], *a.* International.

internacionalizar [in-ter-nah-the-o-nah-le-thar'], *pa.* To internationalize.

internado, da [in-ter-nah'-do, dah], *a.* Interned.*-m.* Boarding school (colegio), boarding pupils (alumnos).

internamente [in-ter-nah-men'-tay], *adv.* Internally. *V.* INTERIORMENTE.

internar [in ter-nar'], *va.* To pierce, to penetrate beyond the surface, to penetrate into the interior of a country. *-vr.* 1. To insinuate, to gain upon the affections by degrees; to wheedle. 2. To advance (avanzar); to penetrate. 2. **Internarse en,** to go into (avanzar). 3. **Internarse en un estudio,** to go deeply into a subject.

interno, na [in-ter'-no, nah], *a.* Interior, internal, inward, intern. **La política interna,** internal politics. *-m & f.* 1. Boarder (alumno). 2. Prisoner (preso). *-m. (Cono Sur, Telec.)* Extension.

internuncio [in-ter-noon'-the-o], *m.* Internuncio, an agent of the court of Rome; interlocutor.

interpolación [in-ter-po-lah-the-on'], *f.* 1. *(Law.)* Interpellation, summons. 2. Interpellation, an earnest address, a demand for an official statement.

interpelar [in-ter-pay-lar'], *va.* 1. To appeal to, to implore the aid of. 2. *(Law.)* To summon, to cite (citar). 3. To interrogate as to the truth or falsity of an act. 4. To interpellate, to officially interrogate a member of a government, as in continental legislatures. 5. To address (dirigirse).

interplanetario, ria [in-ter-plah-nay-tah'-re-o, ah], *a.* Interplanetary.

interpolación [in-ter-po-lah-the-on'], *f.* 1. Interpolation, something added to the original. 2. Act of adding something to the original.

interpoladamente [in-ter-po-lah'-dah-men-tay], *adv.* In an interpolating manner.

interpolar [in-ter-po-lar'], *va.* 1. To interpolate, to foist in. 2. To interpose, to intermix, to intermit. 3. To interpose, to interrupt.

interponer [in-ter-po-nerr'], *va.* 1. To interpose (insertar), to place between. 2. To thrust in as an interruption or obstruction. 3. **Interponer la autoridad,** *(Law.)* to sanction, to approve, or confirm by the authority of the law. *-vr.* To go between, to interpose.

interposición [in-ter-po-se-the-on'], *f.* 1. Interposition (inserción), the state of being placed between other things or persons. 2. Interposition, intervenient agency, interference, mediation, meddling. 3. Interval, time passing between.

interpósita persona [in-ter-po'-se-ta per-so'-nah]. *(Lat. exp. Law)* Intermediary, agent, one who acts for another.

interpresa [in-ter-pray'-sah], *f.* Military enterprise, a sudden undertaking or attempt.

interpretable [in-ter-pray-tah'-blay], *a. (coll.)* Interpretable.

interpretación [in-ter-pray-tah-the-on'], *f.* 1. Interpretation, the act of interpreting (teatro). 2. Interpretation, elucidation, explanation, exposition, construction, commentary; the sense given by an interpreter. **Mala interpretación,** misinterpretation.

interpretador, ra [in-ter-pray-tah-dor', rah], *m. & f.* Interpreter, translator.

interpretante [in-ter-pray-tahn'-tay], *pa. & m. & f.* Interpreting, translator.

interpretar [in-ter-pray-tar'], *va.* 1. To interpret, to explain, to expound. **Interpretar mal,** to misinterpret. 2. To translate, to interpret, to construe. **Interpretar del chino al ruso,** to translate from Chinese into Russian. 3. To interpret, to take or understand the meaning in a particular sense or manner. 4. To attribute. 5. *(Mus.)* To render, to perform; *(Teat.)* to perform; to play (papel).

interpretativamente [in-ter-pre-tah-tee'-vah-men-tay], *adv.* Interpretatively.

interpretativo, va [in-ter-pray-tah-tee'-vo, vah], *a.* Interpretative.

intérprete [in-ter-pray'-tay], *com.* Interpreter, expounder, translator; indication, sign.

interpuesto, ta [in-ter-poo-ays'-to, tah], *a. & pp. irr.* of INTERPONER. Interposed, intervening, placed between, mediate.

interregno [in-ter-reg'-no], *m.* Interreign, interregnum, the time in which the throne is vacant, vacancy of the throne.

interrogación [in-ter-ro-gah-the-on'], *f.* 1. Question (pregunta). 2. Questioning. 3. Question marks (signo). 4. Interrogation (policía).

interrogador, ra [in-ter-ro-gah-dor'], *m & f.* Interrogator; questioner.

interrogante [in-ter-ro-gahn'-tay], *a.* Questioning.*-m. & f.* Questioner (persona). **La gran interrogante,** the real issue. **Punto interrogante,** question marks.

interrogar [in-ter-ro-gar'], *va.* To question, to interrogate.

interrogativamente [in-ter-ro-gah-tee'-vah-men-tay], *adv.* Interrogatively.

interrogativo, va [in-ter-ro-gah-tee´-vo, vah], *a.* Interrogative.

interrogatorio [in-ter-ro-gah-to´-re-o], *m.* Interrogatory, questionnaire, questioning.

interrumpidamente [in-ter-room-pee'-dah-men-tay], *adv.* Interruptedly.

interrumpido, da [in-ter-room-pee'-do, dah], *a. & pp.* of INTERRUMPIR. Interrupted, broken.

interrumpir [in-ter-room-peer´], *va.* 1. To interrupt, to hinder or obstruct the continuance of a thing. 2. To interrupt, to hinder from proceeding, to cut off (electricidad, servicio), to cut short.

interrupción [in-ter-roop-the-on'], *f.* Interruption, interpellation, discontinuance. *(Comput.)* Interrupt.

interruptor [in-ter-roop-tor'], *m. (Elec.)* Switch. **Interruptor DIP** *(Comput.)*, DIP switch.

intersecarse [in-ter-say-car´], *-vr. (Geom.)* To intersect each other.

intersección [in-ter-sec-the-on´], *f.* 1. Intersection, the point where lines cross each other. 2. A line common to two surfaces which cut one another.

intersectario, ria [in-ter-sec-tah´-re-o, ah], *a.* Interdenominational.

intersticio [in-ters-tee´-the-o], *m.* Interstice, interval (intervalo).

intertropical [in-ter-tro-pe-cahl´], *a.* Intertropical, placed or produced between the tropics.

interuniversitario, ria [in-ter-oo-ne-ver-se-tah'-re-o, ah], *a.* Intercollegiate.

intervalo [in-ter-vah´-lo], *m.* 1. Interval (espacio), space between places. 2. Interval (tiempo), time passing between two assignable points, interlapse.

intervención [in-ter-ven-the-on'], *f.* 1. Intervention (participación), supervision (control), *(LAm.)* government takeover (sindicato), assistance, mediation, interposition; knowledge, consent. 2. *(Med.)* Operation. **Intervención quirúrgica**, surgical operation. 3. *(Telec.)* Taping.

intervenir [in-ter-ve-neer´], *vn.* 1. To intervene, to come between things or persons, to mediate; to intercur, to intermediate. 2. To assist, to attend, to supervise (controlar); *(LAm.)* to install government appointees in (sindicato), to superintend. *-vn.* 1. To intervene (tomar parte); to take part, to participate; to contribute. **No intervino en el debate**, he did not take part in the debate. 2. To intercede (interceder); to mediate (mediar).

interventor, ra [in-ter-ven-tor', rah], *m. & f.* Comptroller, supervisor, inspector, superintendent.

intervertebral [in-ter-ver-tay-brahl'], *a.* Invertebral, between the vertebrae.

interyacente [in-ter-yah-then'-tay], *a.* Interjacent, intervening, lying between.

intestable [in-tes-tah´-blay], *a.* 1. Intestable, legally disqualified to make a will. 2. Legally disqualified to testify.

intestedo, da [in-tes-tah'-do, dah], *a.* Intestate, dying without a will.

intestinal [in-tes-te-nahl'], *a.* Intestinal.

intestino, na [in-tes-te´-no, nah], *a.* Intestine, internal; civil, domestic.

intestino [in-tes-tee´-no], *m.* Intestine, the gut; the bowels.

intimación [in-te-mah-the-on´], *f.* Intimation, hint, notification.

íntimamente [en´-temah-men-tay], *adv.* Intimately.

intimar [in-te-mar´], *va.* To intimate (notificar), to hint, to make known, to order (ordenar).*-vr.* 1. To pierce, to penetrate. 2. To gain on the affections, to insinuate. **Ahora intiman mucho**, they´re very friendly with somebody.

intimidación [in-te-me-dah-the-on´], *f.* Intimidation.

intimidad [in-te-me-dahd'], *f.* 1. Intimacy (amistad), close familiarity or connection, friendship, consociation, inwardness. 2. Privacy, private life (vida privada). **La ceremonia se celebró en la intimidad**, the wedding took place privately.

intimidar [in-te-me-dar'], *va.* To intimidate, to daunt, to fright. *-vr.* To be intimidated, to be overawed.

íntimo, ma [een'-te-mo, mah], *a.* 1. Internal, innermost. 2. Intimate (relación), familiar, conversant, near, closely acquainted. **Una boda íntima**, a quiet wedding. **Es íntimo amigo mío**, he is a close friend of mine.

intitular [in-te-too-lar'], *va.* 1. To entitle, to prefix a title to a book or writing. 2. To entitle, to grace, or dignify with a title or honorable appellation. *-vr.* To use a title or honorable appellation.

intolerabilidad [in-to-lay-rah-be-le-dahd´], *f.* Intolerableness.

intolerable [in-to-lay-rah'-blay], *a.* Intolerable, insufferable.

intolerancia [in-to-lay-rahn´-the-ah], *f.* Intolerance, narrowmindeness.

intolerante [in-to-lay-rahn´-tay], *a.* Intolerant, not favorable to toleration, narrow-minded.

intonso, sa [in-tone'-so, sah], *a. (Poet.)* 1. Unshorn, having the hair uncut. 2. Ignorant, unpolished. 3. A book bound with uncut leaves.

intorsión [in-tor-se-on´], *f. (Bot.)* Intorsion, turning of a plant out of the vertical position.

intoxicación [in-toc-se-cah-the-on'], *f. (Med.)* Intoxication, poisoning caused voluntarily or involuntarily.

intoxicar [in-toc-se-car'], *va. (Med.)* To poison.

intradós [in-trah-dos´], *m.* The concave face of an arch or vault; intrados.

intraducible [in-trah-doo-thee´-blay], *a.* Untranslatable.

intramitable [in-trah-me-tah'-blay], *a. (Law.)* Not capable of advancement upon the calendar.

intramuros [in-trah-moo´-ros], *adv.* Within the walls.

intranquilidad [in-tran-ke-le-dahd'], *f.* Worry, uneasiness, disquiet.

intranquilizar [in-tran-ke-le-thar'], *va.* To disquiet, to make uneasy. *-vr.*To worry.

intranquilo, la [in-tran-kee'-lo, lah], *a.* 1. Uneasy, restless. 2. Worried, discomfited.

intransferible [in-trans-fay-re'-blay], *a.* Untransferable, not transferable.

intransigencia [in-tran-se-hayn'-the-ah], *f.* Intransigence; uncompromising attitude.

intransigente [in-tran-se-hayn'-tay], *a.* Intransigent; uncompromising, intolerant.

intransitable [in-tran-se-tah-blay], *a.* Impassable, impenetrable.

intransitivo, va [in-tran-se-tee´-vo, vah], *a. (Gram.)* Intransitive.

intrasmutabilidad [in-tras-moo-tah-be-le-dahd'], *f.* Immutability.

intrasmutable [in-tras-moo-tah´-blay], *a.* Intransmutable.

intratable [in-trah-tah'-blay], *a.* 1. Intractable (problema), ungovernable, stubborn, obstinate, unmanageable. 2. Intractable, unsociable (persona), rude, hard to deal with.3. Impassable.

intrauterino, na [in-trah-oo-tay-ree'-no, nah], *a.* Intrauterine, existing or occurring in the uterus.

intravenoso [in-trah-vay-noh'-so], *a.* Intravenous.

intrépidamente [in-tray´-pe-dah-men-tay], *adv.* Intrepidly, fearlessly.

intrepidez [in-tray-pe-deth'], *f.* 1. Intrepidity, courage, boldness, fearlessness, dauntlessness, hardiness. 2. Temerity.

intrépido, da [in-tray´-pe-do, dah], *a.* Intrepid, daring, fearless, courageous, dauntless, gallant, hardy.

intriga [in-tree'-gah], *f.* 1. Intrigue, a (complicated) plot or scheme. 2. Entanglement, embroilment.

intrigante [in-tre-gahn´-tay], *m.* Intriguer, cunning meddler. *-a.* 1. Intriguing, scheming. 2. Intriguing (interesante).

intrigar [in-tre-gar'], *vn.* To intrigue, to form plots. *-va.* 1. To intrigue, to interest, to puzzle. 2. *(LAm.)* To conduct in a surprising way (asunto). *-vr. (LAm.)* To be intrigued.

intrincable [in-trin-cah´-blay], *a.* Intricate, perplexed, easily entangled.

intrincación [in-trin-cah-the-on'], *f.* Intricacy, intricateness.

intrincadamente [in-trin-cah-dah-men'-tay], *adv.* Intricately.

intrincado, da [in-trin-cah'-do, dah], *a. & pp.* of INTRINCAR. Intricate (complicado), entangled, perplexed, knotty, obscure, impenetrable.

intrincamiento [in-trin-cah-me-en'-to], *m.* Intricateness, intrication.

intrincar [in-trin-car'], *va.* To perplex, to intricate, to entangle, to knot, to involve, to confound, to obscure.

intríngulis [in-treen'-goo-lis], *m.* 1. *(coll.)* Crafty intention, hidden motive (motivo). 2. *(Peru)* Mystery, enigma, puzzle (misterio).

intrínsecamente [in-treen'-say-cah-men-tay], *adv.* Intrinsically, essentially.

intrínseco, ca [in-treen'-say-co, cah], *a.* 1. Intrinsic, intrinsical, internal, hidden. 2. Close, habitually silent *V.* ÍNTIMO. 3. *(Law.) V.* JUDICIAL.

introducción [in-tro-dooc-the-on'], *f.* Introduction, the art of conducting or ushering to any place or person, intromission. 2. Access, intercourse. 3. Introduction, the act of bringing any new thing into notice or practice. 4. Introduction, the preface of a book.

introducir [in-tro-doo-theer'], *va.* 1. To introduce, to conduct or usher into a place, to lead in. 2. To introduce, to bring into notice or practice. 3. To induce, to facilitate, to conciliate. -*vr.* To insinuate, to gain on the affections: to interfere, to find one's way, to get into (meterse).

introductor, ra [in-tro-dooc-tor', rah], *m. & f.* 1. Introducer, anyone who brings a thing into notice. 2. Introductor, introducer, one who introduces another to a person or place.

introductivo, va [in-tro-dooc-tee'-vo, vah], *a.* Introductory, introductive.

introductorio, ria [in-tro-dooc-to'-re-o, rah], *a. (for.)* Introductory.

introito [in-tro'-e-to], *m.* 1. Entrance, entry. 2. Introit, the beginning of the mass; the commencement of public devotions.

intromisión [in-tro-me-se-on'], *f.* Introduction (inserción), inserting, intromission.

introspección [in-tros-pec-the-on'], *f.* Introspection, examination of the interior.

introspectivo, va [in-tros-pec-tee'-vo, vah], *a.* Introspective.

introversión [in-tro-ver-se-on'], *f.* Introversion.

introverso, sa [in-tro-vayr'-so, sah], *a.* Introverted, self-contemplating.

introvertido [in-tro-vayr-tee'-do], *a.* Introvert, introverted; inward-looking. -*m & f.* Introvert.

intrusamente [in-troo'-sah-men-tay], *adv.* Intrusively.

intrusarse [in-troo-sar'-say], *vr.* To obtrude oneself in a place or office.

intrusión [in-troo-se-on'], *f.* Intrusion, obtrusion, the act of intruding or obtruding oneself into any place, state, or office, without right or welcome.

intruso [in-troo'-so], *m.* Intruder, obtruder, one who forces himself into any place, office, company, etc., without right or welcome; squatter.

intruso, sa [in-troo'-so, sah], *a.* Intruded, intrusive, obtrusive.

intuición [in-too-e-the-on'], *f.* Intuition, knowledge not obtained by deduction of reason.

intuitivamente [in-too-e-te-vah-men'-tay], *adv.* Intuitively.

intuir [in-too-eer'], *va.* To know by intuition; to intuit; to sense, to feel, to have an intuition of. -*vr.* **Eso se intuye,** that can be guessed.

intuitivamente [in-too-e-tee'-vah-men-tay], *adv.* Intuitively.

intuitivo, va [in-too-e-tee'-vo, vah], *a.* Intuitive, evident; perceived without ratiocination.

intumescencia [in-too-mes-then'-the-ah], *f. V.* HINCHAZÓN.

intumescente [in-too-mes-then'-tay], *a.* Intumescent, swollen.

intususcepción [in-too-soos-thep-the-on'], *f. (Med.)* Introsusception, intussusception.

inulina [in-oo-lee'-nah], *f.* Inulin, a substance like starch.

inulto, to [in-ool'-to, tah], *a. (Poet.)* Unrevenged, unpunished.

inundación [in-oon-dah-the-on'], *f.* 1. Food, inundation, overflow of waters, deluges 2. Confluence of any kind.

inundante [in-noon-dhan'-tay], *pa.* Inundating; inundant, that which inundates.

inundar [in-oon-dar'], *va.* 1. To inundate, to overflow, to deluge, to flood. 2. To overrun with numbers. **Se le inundaron los ojos en lágrimas,** a flood of tears fell from her eyes. **Inundar el mercado de un producto,** to flood the market with a product. **La lluvia inundó la campiña,** the rain flooded the countryside.

inurbanamente [in-oor-bah-nah-men'-tay], *adv.* Incivilly, uncivilly.

inurbanidad [in-oor-bah-ne-dahd'], *f.* Incivility, want of education, inurbanity.

inurbano, na [in-oor-bah'-no, nah], *a.* Uncivil, want, unpolished, inurbane.

inusitadamente [in-oo-se-tah-dah-men'-tay], *adv.* Unusually.

inusitado, da [in-oo-se-tah'-do, dah], *a.* Unusual, not in use, not accustomed.

inusual [in-oo-soo-ahl'], *a.* Unusual.

inútil [in-oo'-teel], *a.* Useless, unprofitable, inutile, fruitless, needless, frivolous, idle, vain (esfuerzo, tentativa).

inutilidad [in-oo-te-le-dahd'], *f.* Inutility, uselessness, unprofitableness, needlessness.

inutilizar [in-oo-te-lc-thar'], *va.* To render useless, to disable (barco); to spoil (estropear); to nullify (esfuerzo). -*vr.* To become useless.

inútilmente [in-oo'-teel-men-tay], *adv.* Uselessly, idly.

invadeable [in-vah-day-ah'-blay], *a.* Not fordable, impassable without swimming.

invadir [in-vah-deer'], *va.* To invade, to attack a country.

invaginación [in-vah-he-nah-the-on'], *f.* Invagination.

invalidación [in-vah-le-dah-the-on'], *f.* Invalidation, invalidity.

inválidamente [in-vah'-le-dah-men'-tay], *adv.* Invalidly.

invalidar [in-vah-le-dar'], *va.* To invalidate, to deprive of force or efficacy, to irritate, to nullify.

invalidez [in-vah-le-dayth'], *f.* 1. *(Med.)* Disablement; unfitness; disability. **Invalidez permanente,** permanent disability.

inválido, da [in-vah'-le-do, dah], *a.* Invalid, without force; feeble, weak, null. **Declarar inválida una elección,** to declare an election invalid.

inválido [in-vah'-le-do], *m.* 1. *(Mil.)* Invalid, a soldier who has retired from the service in consequence of age or disability. 2. *(coll.)* Invalid, any person weakened by sickness.

invariabilidad [in-vah-re-ah-be-le-dahd'], *f.* Invariability.

invariable [in-vah-rc-ah'-blay], *a.* Invariable, constant.

invariablemente [in-vah-re-ah-blay-men'-tay], *adv.* Invariably.

invariación [in-vah-re-ah-the-on'], *f.* Immutability, invariableness.

invariado, da [in-vah-re-ah'-do, dah], *a.* Unvaried, constant, invaried.

invasión [in-vah-se-on'], *f.* Invasion, hostile entrance, attack.

invasor, ra [in-vah-sor', rah], *m. & f.* Invader. -*a.* Invading.

invectiva [in-vec-tee'-vah], *f.* Invective, harsh censure.

invencible [in-ven-thee'-blay], *a.* Invincible, insuperable, unconquerable.

invenciblemente [in-ven-the-blay-men'-tay], *adv.* Invincibly.

invención [in-ven-the-on'], *f.* 1. Invention (invento), excogitation, the act or power of inventing (descubrimiento). 2. Invention, discoverer, the thing invented. 3. Invention, contrivance, fiction, artifice.

invencionero, ra [in-ven-the-o-nay'-ro, rah], *m. & f.* 1. Inventor. 2. Plotter. 3. Boaster, decider. 4. *(coll.)* Gesticulator, mimic.

invendible [in-ven-dee'-blay], *a.* Unmerchantable; not marketable, unsaleable.

inventar [in-ven-tar'], *va.* 1. To invent, to discover, to find out, to excogitate, to device (idear). 2. To invent, to forge, to frame, to contrive falsely.

inventariar [in-ven-tah-re-ar'], *va.* 1. To make an inventory, to inventory, to register. 2. *(coll.)* To commemorate the doings of a person.

inventario [in-ven-tah'-re-o], *m.* Inventory, catalogue, stock. **Hacer inventario de**, to make an inventory of.

inventiva [in-ven-tee'-vah], *f.* The faculty of invention.

inventivo, va [in-ven-tee'-vo, vah], *a.* Inventive, quick at contrivance, ready at expedients: inventful.

invento [in-ven'-to], *m.* Invention, discovery.

inventor, ra [in-ven-tor', rah], *m. & f.* Inventor, contriver, framer.

inverecundo, da [in-vay-ray-coon'-do, dah], *a.* Shameless, impudent.

inverísimil [in-vay-re-see'-meel], *a.* V. INVEROSÍMIL.

invernáculo [in-ver-nah'-coo-lo], *m.* Green-house, hothouse, conservatory.

invernada [in-ver-nah'-dah], *f.* 1. Winter Season (estación). 2. Wintering (etapa invernal); hibernation (hibernación). 3. *(And. Cono Sur)* Winter pasture (pasto). 4. *(Carib.)* Heavy rainstorm (tempestad).

invernadero [in-ver-nah-day'-ro], *m.* 1. Winter-quarters: applied generally to wintering places for sheep. 2. V. INVERNÁCULO.

invernal [in-ver-nahl'], *a.* Hibernal, wintry.

invernar [in-ver'-nar'], *vn.* To winter, to pass the winter; to be in the winter season, to hibernate.

invernizo, za [in-ver-nee'-tho, thah], *a.* 1. Winterly suited to the winter: hibernal. 2 Winter-beaten, harassed by frost and severe weather.

inverosímil [in-vay-ro-see'-meel], *a.* Unlikely, improbable.

inverosimilitud [in-vay-ro-se-me-le-tood'], *f.* Improbability, unlikelihood.

inversamente [in-ver-sah-men'-tay], *adv.* Inversely: contrariwise.

inversión [in-ver-se-on'], *f.* 1. Inversion; change of order, time, or place. 2. Investment, the act of employing or spending a sum of money. **Inversión de capital**, capital investment.

inversionista [in-ver-se-o-nees'-tah], *m. & f.* Investor.

inverso, sa [in-ver'-so, sah], *a. & pp. irr.* of INVERTIR. Inverse, inverted, reciprocal. **A la inversa**, on the contrary.

invertebrado, da [in-ver-tay-brah'-do, dah], *a.* Invertebrate, without a backbone.

invertido [in-ver-tee'-do], *a.* Inverted (volcado); reversed (al revés). *-m & f.* Homosexual.

invertir [in-ver-teer'], *va.* 1. To invert (volcar), to turn upside down; to change the order of time or place (cambiar el orden). 2. To employ, to spend (esfuerzo, tiempo), or lay out money, to invest (dinero). **Invirtieron 5 días en el viaje**, they spent 5 days on the journey.

investidura [in-ves-te-doo'-rah], *f.* Investiture, the act of giving possession of a manor office, or benefice.

investigable [in-ves-te-gah'-blay], *a.* Investigable.

investigación [in-ves-te-gah-the-on'], *f.* Investigation (indigación), research; inquest. **Investigación policíaca**, police investigation.

investigador, ra [in-ves-te-gah-dor', rah], *m. & f.* Investigator.

investigar [in-ves-te-gar'], *va.* To investigate (indagar), to search out; to look after.

investir [in-ves-teer'], *va.* To invest, to confer some dignity.

inveterado, da [in-vay-tay-rah'-do, dah], *a. & pp.* of INVETERARSE. Inveterate, old, chronic, obstinate.

inveteradamente [in-vay-tay-rah-dah-men'-tay], *adv.* Inveterately.

inveterarse [in-vay-tay-rar'-say], *vr.* To become antiquated, to grow old, to become chronic: it has been used, though seldom, as an active verb.

invictamente [in-vic-tah-men'-tay], *adv.* Unconquerably, valiantly.

invicto, ta [in-veec'-to, tah], *a.* Unconquerable, unconquered.

invidente [in-ve-den'-tay-men-tay], *a.* Sightless, blind. *-m & f.* Sightless person, blind person.

invierno [in-ve-er'-no], *m.* 1. Winter. 2. *(And. CAm. Carib.)* Rainy season (meses de lluvia). 3. *(Carib.)* Heavy shower (aguacero).

invigilancia [in-ve-he-lahn'-the-ah], *f.* 1. Want of vigilance. 2. Watching, observant attention.

invigilar [in-ve-he-lar'], *vn.* To watch, to be observant, to be attentive.

inviolabilidad [in-ve-o-lah-be-le-dahd'], *f.* Inviolability, inviolableness.

inviolable [in-ve-o-lah'-blay], *a.* Inviolable.

inviolablemente [in-ve-o-lah-blay-men-tay], *adv.* Inviolably, holily: infallibly.

inviolado, da [in-ve-o-lah'-do, dah], *a.* Inviolate, unhurt, uninjured.

invisibilidad [in-ve-se-be-le-dahd'], *f.* Invisibility.

invisible [in-ve-see'-blay], *a.* Invisible, not perceptible. **En un invisible,** *(coll.)* in an instant. *-m. (And. Cono Sur)* Hairpin.

invisiblemente [in-ve-see'-blay-men-tay], *adv.* Invisibly.

invitación [in-ve-tah-the-on'], *f.* Invitation.

invitado, da [in-ve-tah'do, dah], *m. & f.* Guest.*-a.* Invited.

invitador, ra [in-ve-tah-dor', rah], *m. & f.* One who invites, an inviter.

invitar [in-ve-tar'], *va.* 1. To invite. 2. To excite, to stimulate, to execute a thing. **Invitar a uno a hacer algo,** to invite somebody to do something. **Nos invitó a cenar fuera,** he took us out for a meal.

invitatorio [in-ve-tah-to'-re-o], *m.* Invitatory, psalm or anthem sung at the beginning of matins or morning worship.

invocación [in-vo-cah-the-on'], *f.* 1. Invocation, the act of calling upon in prayer. 2. *(Poet.)* Invocation, the form of calling for the assistance or presence of any being.

invocador,ra [in-vo-cah-dor', rah], *m. & f.* One who invokes.

invocar [in-vo-car'], *va.* To invoke (llamar en ayuda), to implore, to cry into. **Invocar la ley,** to invoke the law.

invocatorio, ria [in-vo-cah-to'-re-o, ah], *a.* That which invocates.

involucela [in-vo-loo-thay'-lah], *f. (Bot.)* Involucel.

involución [in-vo-loo-the-on'], *f. (Bot.)* State of being rolled in; involution.

involucral [in-vo-loo-crahl'], *a. (Bot.)* Involucral, relating to an involucre.

involucrar [in-vo-loo-crar'], *va.* 1. To wrap up, to cover. 2. To mingle, to confuse, to upset. 3. To insert in writings questions or subjects foreign to their principal object. 4. To involve (implicar). **Involucrar uno en algo,** to involve somebody in something. 5. To jumble up, to mix up. *-vr.* To meddle, to interfere; to get involved. **Las personas involucradas en el caso,** the people involved in the affair.

involucro [in-vo-loo'-cro], *m. (Bot.)* Involucre. **Involucro partial,** V. INVOLUCELA.

involuntariamente [in-vo-loon-tah'-re-ah-men-tay], *adv.* Involuntarily.

involuntariedad [in-vo-loon-tah-re-ay-dahd'], *f.* Involuntariness.

involuntario, ria [in-vo-loon-tah'-re-o, ah], *a.* Involuntary.

involute [in-vo-loo'-tah], *f. (Arch.)* Volute. V. VOLUTA.

invulnerabilidad [in-vool-nay-rah-be-le-dahd'], *f.* Invulnerability.

invulnerable [in-vool-nay-rah'-blay], *a.* Invulnerable.

inyección [in-yec-the-on´], *f.* 1. Injection, the art of injecting. 2. The liquid injected, shot. **Inyección estimulante,** *(Med.)* booster shot.

inyectador, ra [in-yec-tah-dor´, rah], *m. & f.* 1. One who injects. 2. *(Med.)* Any instrument which serves for making injections.

inyectar [in-yec-tar´], *va.* **To inject**.

inyector [in-yec-tor´], *m. (Mech.)* Injector. **Inyector del combustible,** *(Aer.)* afterburner.

ion [e-on´], *m. (Chem. & Phy.)* Ion.

iónico, ca [e-o´-ne-co, cah] *a.* Ionic.

ionización [e-o-ne-thah-the-on´], *f.* Ionization.

ionizar [e-o-ne-thar´], *va.* To ionize.

ionosfera [e-o-nos-fay´-rah], *f.* Ionosphere.

iota [e-o´-tah], *f.* Ninth letter of the Greek alphabet. *(Cf. Jot.)*

ipso facto [eep´-so fahc´-to], *(Law.)* An adverbial phrase; immediately, without delay; also, by the very fact.

ipso juro [eep´-so yoo´-ray], *(Law.)* An adverbial phrase used in courts of law, to denote that a thing does not require the declaration of the judge, as it constitutes the law itself.

ir [eer], *vn.* 1. To go, to move, not to stand still. 2. To go, to walk (a pie), to move step by step. 3. To be, to exist. 4. To bet, to lay a wager. 5. To consist, to depend on. 6. To import (importar), to concern. **Nada se me va en ello,** I have no concern in it, I do not care for it. 7. To differ, to be different (diferencia), to be distant. 8. To lead (carretera). 9. To devote oneself to a calling, to follow a profession: in this last sense it is used with *por* **Ir por letras,** to study letters. 10. To proceed, to act. 11. To decline a noun or conjugate a verb for another. *Ir* joined to present participles implies the existence or actual execution of the action designated; joined with past participles it signifies to suffer their action; with the preposition *a* and infinitive mode, it implies disposition toward, as **ir a misa,** to go to mass; followed by *con,* it gives the noun an adverbial import, and accompanied by the preposition *contra* or *fuera de,* it signifies to persevere, or act contrary to. -*vr.* 1. To go, to go off or go away (marcharse), to depart or remove from a place. 2. To be dying. 3. To go off, to go out of life, to be gone (morir). 4. To leak (recipiente), to ooze. 5. To exhale, to evaporate. 6. To discharge wind. 7. To break: to grow old. **Ir a caballo,** to ride. **Ir agua arriba,** to work up stream. **Ir a una,** to act with one accord, harmoniously. **Ir y venir,** to turn something in one's mind. **Írsele a uno el alma por alguna cosa,** to long for. **Irse de boca,** to speak without reflection. **Ir (or andar) de capa caída,** to be crestfallen, to decline in fortune or credit. **Ni va, ni viene,** indecision, want of resolution. **Ir de campo,** to go on a picnic. **Ir or irse a pique or por ojo,** *(Naut.)* to founder, to go to the bottom. **Ir adelante,** to go on. **Ir a pie,** to walk. **Ir de una parte a otra,** to go up and down. **Ir en contra de,** to go against. **Ir en decadencia or empobreciendo,** to go down the wind. **Ir en busca de or ir por algo,** to go for. **Ir otra vez,** to go back or to go again. **Ir separadamente,** to go asunder. **Ir sobre seguro,** to go upon sure grounds. **Ir tras la corriente,** to go down the stream. **Ir bien or mal,** speaking of a business, it means that it is going prosperously or unprosperously. **Ir con alguno,** 1. To be of the same opinion as another. 2. To be of the same party as another. 3. To accompany. **Írsele a alguno la cabeza,** to perturb the mind, to confuse the reason. **¿Quién va? or ¿quién va allá?,** who is there?, or who goes there? **Vaya usted con Dios,** farewell; God be with you. **Ir pagando,** *(coll.)* to pay by degrees. **Ir pasando or mejorando,** to be recovering by degrees. **Él se mete en lo que no le va, ni le viene,** he meddles in what does not concern him at all. **Ir delante or por delante,** to go ahead. **No hay que irse atrás,** flinch not. *(Met.)* To treat or discuss, to look for. **Mucho va de Pedro a Pedro,** *(Prov.)* there is a wide difference between man and man. **A donde fueres, haz lo que vieres,** when you are in Rome, do as the Romans do. **Irse los ojos tras de una persona o cosa,** to have an admiring eye, or longing after a person or thing; to look after it with anxiety. **Me voy de con usted,** *(CAm.)* I´m leaving you.

Ir hasta Córdoba, to go as far as Cordoba. **Va para viejo,** he´s getting old. **El enfermo va mejor,** the patient is better. **Eso no va por ti,** (intención) I wasn´t referring to you. **Va mucho en esto,** a lot depends on it. **Va para ingeniero,** (carrera) he´s going to become an engineer. **Vamos, no es difícil,** come now. **Iban fumando,** they were smoking. **Iba cansado,** he was tired. **Vamos a hacerlo,** we are going to do it. **Es hora de irnos,** it´s time we went. **Se nos fue hace 3 años,** he departed from us 3 years ago, he passed away 3 years ago.

ira [ee´-rah], *f.* 1. Ire, anger, passion, indignation, wrath, fury (viento), choler, rage. 2. Ire, desire of vengeance, chastisement. 3. *(Met.)* Violence of the elements or weather. **La ira es mala consejera,** wrath is a bad advisor. **¡Ira de Dios!,** by thunder!

iracundia [e-rah-coon´-de-ah], *f.* Irascibility, ire, irascibleness.

iracundo, da [e-rah-coon´-do, dah], *a.* 1. Passionate, ireful. 2. *(Poet.)* Enraged, furious (viento).

iranio, nia [e-rah´-ne-o, ah], *a.* Iranian, relating to Persia or Iran.

irascible [e-ras-thee´-blay], *a.* Irascible, impetuous, determined.

irenarca [e-ray-nar´-cah], *m.* Irenarch, an officer of the Greek empire, employed to preserve public tranquility.

iridáceo, cea [e-re-dah´-thay-o, thay-ah], *a.* Iridaceous, iris-like.

íride [ee´-re-day], *f. (Bot.)* V. EFÉMERO.

iridectomía [e-re-dec-to-mee´-ah], *f.* Iridectomy, excision of a portion of iris.

irídeo dea [e-ree´-day-o, ah], *a.* Irideous, like the iris or flower-deluce.

iridescente [e-re-des-then´-tay], *a.* Iridescent, rainbow-hued.

iridio [e-ree´-deo], *m. (Min.)* Iridium, a metallic element.

iris [ee´-ris], *m.* 1. Iris, the rainbow. 2. Iris, the circle round the pupil of the eye. 3. Mediator, peace-maker. 4. *(Bot.)* V. LIRIO PAJIZO or ESPADANAL. 5. Prim. 6. *(LAm.)* To wink (guiñar el ojo).

irisado, da [e-re-sah´-do, dah], *a.* Rainbow-hued.

irisar [e-re-sar´], *va.* To throw out rainbow-hued scintillations.

irlanda [ir-lahn´-dah], *f.* 1. Cloth made of cotton and woollen yarn. 2. Fine Irish linen.

irlandés, esa [ir-lan-days´, sah], *a.* Irish, relating to Ireland. -*m.* The Irish language. -*f.* Irish woman.

ironía [e-ro-nee´-ah], *f.* Irony, the use of words designed to convey a meaning opposite to the literal sense. A rhetorical figure.

irónicamente [e-ro´-ne-cah-men-tay], *adv.* Ironically.

irónico, ca [e-ro´-ne-co, cah], *a.* Ironical.

irracional [i-rrah-the-o-nahl´], *a.* Irrational, void of reason, absurd: sometimes used as a substantive for an irrational animal.

irracionalilad [ir-rah-the-o-nah-le-dahd´], *f.* Irrationality, absurdness.

irracionalmente [ir-rah-the-o-nahl´-men-tay], *adv.* Irrationally, absurdly.

irradiación [ir-rah-de-ah-the-on´], *f.* 1. Irradiation, the act of emitting light; irradiance. 2. Illumination, intellectual light.

irradiar [ir-rah-de-ar´], *va.* To irradiate, to emit beams of light.

irrazonable [ir-rah-the-nah´-blay], *a.* Unreasonable.

irreal [ir-ray-ahl´], *a.* Unreal.

irrealista [ir-ray-ah-lees´-tah], *a.* Unrealistic.

irrealizable [ir-ray-ah-le-thah-blay], *a.* Unrealizable, unworkable (trabajo), impossible to carry out, unattainable (meta).

irrebatible [ir-ray-bah-tee´-blay], *a.* Indisputable.

irreconciliable [ir-ray-con-the-le-ah´-blay], *a.* Irreconciliable, unappeasable.

irreconciliablemente [ir-ray-con-the-le-ah´-blay-men-tay], *adv.* Irreconcilably.

irreconocible [ir-ray-co-no-thee´-blay], *a.* Unrecognizable.

irrecuperable [ir-ray-coo-pay-rah´-blay], *a.* Irrecoverable, irretrievable.

irrecusable [ir-ray-coo-sah'-blay], *a.* 1. Not to be refused or declined, unimpeachable. 2. Inevitable.

irredimible [ir-ray-de-mee'-blay], *a.* Irredeemable, irretrievable, irreparable.

irreducible [ir-ray-doo-thee´-blay], *a.* 1. Irreducible (mínimo). 2. Stubborn, obstinate.

ireemplazable, irremplazable [ir-ray-em-plah-thah'-blay, ir-rem-plah-thah'-blay], *a.* Irreplaceable.

irreflexión [ir-ray-flec-se-on'], *f.* Rashness, indiscretion, inconsideration.

irreflexivo, va [ir-ray-flec-see'-vo, vah], *a.* Inconsiderate, indiscreet, unreflecting.

irreformable [ir-ray-for-mah-blay], *a.* Not to be reformed or reclaimed.

irrefragable [ir-ray-frah-gah'-blay], *a.* Irrefragable, irrefutable.

irregular [ir-ray-goo-lar'], *a.* 1. Irregular, disorderly, abnormal. 2. Irregular, immethodical.

irregularidad [ir-ray-goo-lah-re-dahd'], *f.* Irregularity, deviation from rule, disorder, misgovernance, abnormity.

irregularmente [ir-ray-goo-lar'-men-tay], *adv.* Irregularly, loosely.

irrelevante [ir-ray-lay-vahn'-tay], *a.* Irrelevant.

irreligión [ir-ray-le-he-on'], *f.* Irreligion, impiety, unbelief.

irreligiosidad [ir-ray-le-he-o-se-dahd'], *f.* Irreligiousness, impiety.

irreligioso, sa [ir-ray-le-he-o´-so, sah], *a.* Irreligious, impious.

irremediable [ir-ray-may-de-ah´-blay], *a.* Irremediable, incurable: helpless.

irremediablemente [ir-ray-may-de-ah'-blay-men-tay], *adv.* Irremediably, helplessly, irrecoverably.

irremisible [ir-ray-me-see'-blay], *a.* Irremissible, unpardonable.

irremisiblemente [ir-ray-me-see'-blay-men-tay], *adv.* Unpardonably, irremissibly.

irremunerado, da [ir-ray-moo-nay-rah´-do, dah], *a.* Unremunerated.

irreparable [ir-ray-pah-rah´-blay], *a.* Irreparable, irretrievable.

irreparablemente [ir-ray-pah-rah'-blay-men-tay], *adv.* Irreparably, irretrievably, irrecoverably.

irrepetible [ir-ray-pay-tee'-blay], *a.* One-and-only, unique.

irreprensible [ir-ray-pren-see'-blay], *a.* Irreprehensible, irreproachable, irreprovable.

irreprensiblemente [ir-ray-pren-see'-blay-men-tay], *adv.* Irreprehensibly, irreproachably.

irreprochable [ir-ray-pro-chah'-blay], *a.* Irreproachable.

irresistibilidad [ir-ray-sis-te-be-le-dahd'], *f.* Irresistibility.

irresistible [ir-ray-sis-tee´-blay], *a.* Irresistible; impossibly strong (demasiado fuerte).

irresistiblemente [ir-ray-sis-tee-'blay-men-tay], *adv.* Irresistibly.

irresoluble [ir-ray-so-loo'-blay], *a.* 1. Indeterminable, not to be defined; not to be resolved, irresoluble. 2. Irresolute, not constant in purpose.

irresolución [ir-ray-so-loo-the-on'], *f.* Irresolution, want of firmness, irresoluteness, hesitation.

irresoluto, ta, irresuelto, ta [ir-ray-so-loo'-to, tah, ir-ray-soo-el'-to, tah], *a.* Irresolute (carácter), unsteady, unresolved (problema).

irrespetuoso, sa [ir-res-pay-too-o'-so, sah], *a.* Unrespectful, wanting in respect.

irrespirable [ir-res-pe-rah´-blay], *a.* Irrespirable, not fit to be breathed.

irresponsabilidad [ir-res-pon-sah-be-le-dahd'], *f.* Irresponsibility.

irresponsable [ir-res-pon-sah'-blay], *a.* Irresponsible.

irreverencia [ir-ray-vay-ren´-the-ah], *f.* Irreverence, want of respect or veneration.

irreverente [ir-ray-vay-ren´-tay], *a.* Irreverent.

irreverentemente [ir-ray-vay-ren-tay-men-tay], *adv.* Irreverently.

irreversible [ir-ray-ver-see'-blay], *a.* Irreversible.

irrevocabilidad [ir-ray-vo-cah-be-le-dahd'], *f.* Irrevocability.

irrevocable [ir-ray-vo-cah´-blay], *a.* Irrevocable, irreversible.

irrevocablemente [ir-ray-vo-cah'-blay-men-tay], *adv.* Irrevocably.

irrisible [ir-re-see´-blay], *a.* Risible, laughable.

irrisión [ir-re-se-on'], *f.* Irrision, the art of laughing at another, mockery.

irrisoriamente [ir-re-so-re-ah-men´-tay], *adv.* Laughingly, derisively.

irrisorio, ria [ir-re-so'-re-o, ah], *a.* Derisive, risible, ridiculous, absurd; absurdly low, bargain (precio).

irritatilidad [ir-re-tah-be-le-dahd'], *f.* Irritability.

irritable [ir-re-tah´-blay], *a.* 1. That can be rendered void or annulled. 2. Irritable, easily provoked. 3. Irritable, easily irritated.

irritación [ir-re-tah-the-on´], *f.* 1. Irritation, commotion, agitation. 2. Invalidation, abrogation. 3. *(Med.)* Irritation, morbid action of the organs.

irritador, ra [ir-re-tah-dor', rah], *m. & f.* Irritator, stimulator. *-a.* Irritating.

irritamiento [ir-re-tah-me-en´-to], *m.* Irritation; abrogation.

irritante [ir-re-tahn´-tay], *a. & pa.* 1. Annulling or making void. 2. Irritative, irritant, stimulating.

irritante [ir-re-tahn'Tay], *m. (Med.)* Stimulant, irritant.

irritar [ir-re-tar'], *va.* 1. To annul, to render void. 2. To irritate, to exasperate, to agitate violently, to nettle, to offend, to make angry. 3. To alter, to produce a change.

írrito, ta [eer´-re-to, tah], *a.* Null, void.

irrogar [ir-ro-gar'], *va.* To cause, to occasion.

irrompible [ir-rom-pee´-blay], *a.* Unbreakable.

irrupción [ir-roop-the-on'], *f.* Irruption, inroad, invasion.

isagoge [e-sah-go'-hay], *f.* Introduction, preliminary remarks.

isagógico, ca [e-sah-go'-he-co, cah], *a.* Isagogical, introductive, introductory.

iságono [e-sah´-go-no], *m. (Geom.)* Isagon.

isanto, ta [e-sahn´-to, tah], *a. (Bot.)* Having floral envelopes just alike.

isatina [e-sah-tee´-nah], *f.* Isatin, a crystalline compound obtained by oxydizing indigo.

iscofonía [is-co-fo-ne'-ah], *(Med.)* A defect of the voice, difficulty in pronouncing certain consonants.

isla [ees'-lah], *f.* 1. Isle, island. 2. A remote or retired spot. 3. Square, an area of four sides, with houses on each side. 4. *(Mex.)* Isolated dump of trees (árboles). **En isla,** insulated. **Islas de barlovento,** windward islands. **Islas de sotavento,** leeward islands.

islam [is-lahm'], *m.* Islamism, the religion of Muslims.

islámico, ca [es-lah'-me-co, cah], *a.* Islamic.

islamismo [is-lah-mees'-mo], *m.* Mohammedanism.

islamita [is-lah-mee'-tah], *a. & f.* Islamite.

islán [is-lahn'], *m.* A kind of veil anciently worn by women.

islandés, sa [is-lan-day´-sah], *a.* Icelandic, relating to Iceland.

isleño, ña [is-lay´-nyo, nyah], *m. & f.* Islander.

isleo [is-lay'-o], *m.* Island formed by rocks.

isleta [is-lay´-tah], *f. dim.* A small isle, islet.

islilla [is-leel´-lyah], *f.* Flank, part of the body from the hip to the armpit.

islote [es-lo'-tay], *m.* A small barren island.

ismaelita [is-mah-ay-lee´-tah], *a.* Ishmaelite, Mohammedan, Arab.

isobárico, ca [e-so-bah´-re-co, cah], *a. (Phy.)* Isobaric.

isócrono, na [e-so'-cro-no, nah], *a.* Isochronal, having equal times.

isoglos [e-so'-glos], *m.* Isoglos.

isógono, na [e-so´-go-no, nah], *a*. Having two equal angles.

isomérico, ca [e-so-may-re-co, cah], *a*. Isomeric, relating to isomerism.

isomerismo [e-so-may-rees´-mo], *m*. *(Chem.)* Isomerism, the condition of having different properties, but the same molecular composition, or same atomic weight.

isómero, ra [e-so´-may-ro, rah], *a*. 1. Isomerous, equal in number. 2. Isomeric.

isometría [e-so-may-tree´-ah], *f*. Isometrics.

isométrico, ca [e-so-may´-tre-co, cah], *a*. Isometric.

isomorfismo [e-so-mor-fees´-mo], *m*. Isomorphism, identical crystallization.

isomorfo, fa [e-so-mor´-fo, fah], *a*. Isomorphous, isomorphic, of the same construction.

isonomía [e-so-no-mee´-ah], *f*. Equality of civil rights, isonomy.

isónomo, ma [e-so´-no-mo, mah], *a*. Governed by the same law.

isoperimétrico, ca [e-so-pay-re-may-tre-co, cah], *a*. Isoperimetrical.

isósceles [e-sos´-thay-les], *a*. *(Geom.)* Isosceles, a triangle having two sides equal.

isotermo, ma [e-so-ter´-mo, mah], *a* Isothermal, of equal temperature.

isótopo [e-so´-to-po], *m*. *(Phy. & Chem.)* Isotope.

israelí [is-rah-ay-lee´], *a*. & *m*. & *f*. Israeli.

israelita [is-ra-hay-lee´-tah], *m*. Israelite, Jew.

israelítico, ca [is-rah-ay-lee´-te-co, cah], *a*. Israelitish, Jewish.

ístmico, ca [eest´-me-co, cah], *a*. Isthmian, belonging to the isthmus.

istmo [eest´-mo], *m*. Isthmus.

italianismo [e-tah-le-ah-nees´-mo], *m*. Italianism, an Italian idiom or expression.

italianizar [e-tah-le-ah-ne-thar´], *va*. To Italianize.

italiano [e-tah-le-ah´-no], *a*. Italian.-*m*. The Italian language.

itálico, ca [e-tah´-le-co, cah], *a*. Italic.-*f*. Italic type.

ítem [ee´-tem], *m*. Item, near article.-*adv*. Also, moreover.

iterar [e-tay-rar´], *va*. To iterate, to repeat. V. REPETIR.

iterativo, va [e-tay-rah-tee´-vo, vah], *a*. Iterative, repeating, redoubling

itinerario [e-te-nay-rah´-re-o], *m*. Itinerary, book of travels; guide for traveling; march, route.

itinerario, ria [e-te-nay-rah´-re-o, ah], *a*. Itinerary.

itria [ee´-tre-ah], *f*. *(Min.)* Yttria, a white insoluble earth.

itrio [ee´-tre-o], *m*. Yttrium, a rare element belonging to the cerium group.

iza [ee´-thah], *f*. *(Naut.)* Hoisting, hauling up.

izaga [e-thah´-gah], *f*. Place abounding in rushes and reeds.

izamiento [e-thah-me-en´-to], *m*. Hoisting, raising (bandera).

izar [e-thar´], *va*. *(Naut.)* To hoist, to raise up on high. **La bandera está izada**, the flag is flying.

izquierdear [ith-ke-er-day-ar´], *vn*. To degenerate, to fall from its kind; to grow wild.

izquierdista [ith-ke-er-dees´-tah], *a*. & *m*. & *f*. Leftist, left-wing.

izquierdo, da [ith-keer´-do, dah], *a*. 1. Left-handed (zurdo), left; sinister. **A la izquierda**, to the left. 2. Crooked, not right or straight.

izquierdo, da [ith-keer´-do, dah], *m*. & *f*. A left-handed (persona).

J

j [ho´-tah], It is always a consonant in Spanish, and its pronunciation is guttural, or like the sound of *h* strongly

aspirated, as in *ham, her, him, home, who*. **J** is used in some cases in preference to **G** to represent the guttural sound before *e*, thus: *mujer, tejer*.

jaba [hah´-bah], *f*. 1. *(Cuba)* A basket made of the leaves of *yarey*. **Llevar or tener la jaba**, *(coll.)* to be unpolished, uneducated. 2. *(Carib.)* Poverty. 3. *(Carib.)* Beggar´s bag. **Llevar algo en la jaba**, to have something up one´s sleeve.

jabalcón [hah-bal-co-ne´], *m*. Bracket, purlin.

jabalconar [hah-bal-co-nar´], *va*. To support the roof of a house with brackets.

jabalí [hah-bah-lee´], *m*. Wild boar.

jabalina [hah-bah-lee´-nah], *f*. 1. Sow of a wild boar. 2. Javelin, a kind of spear.

jabalonar [hah-bah-lo-nar´], *va*. V. JABALCONAR.

jabardear [hah-bar-day-ar´], *va*. To swarm, to rise as bees in a body.

jabardillo [hah-bar-deel´-lyo], *m*. V. JABARDO for a crowd.

jabardo [hah-bar´-do], *m*. 1. A small swarm of bees. 2. Any crowd or assembly of low people; mob, rabble.

jabato [hah-bah´-to], *m*. A young wild boar. -*a*. 1. Brave, bold. 2. *(Carib. Mex.)* Rude (grosero), gruff; ill-tempered (malhumorado).

jabeca [hah´-bay-cah], *f*. 1. Sweep-net, a large net for fishing. 2. V. JÁBEGA.

jabega [hah´-bay-gah], *f*. A Moorish wind instrument, somewhat like a flute.

jabeguero [hah-bay-gay´-ro], *m*. Fisher-man who fishes with a sweep-net.

jabeque [hah-bay´-kay], *m*. *(Naut.)* 1. Xebec, a small Mediterranean three-masted vessel. 2. A wound made in the face with a knife or other cutting weapon.

jabí [hah-bee´], *m*. 1. Small wild apple or crab. 2. Small kind of grapes. 3. A hard-wood tree of Yucatan.

jabladera [hah-blah-day´-rah], *f*. Crozer, a cooper's tool.

jable [hah´-blay], *m*. Croze, the groove in the staves of casks which receives the heads.

jabón [hah-bo-ne´], *m*. 1. Soap, bar of soap (pastilla de jabón). **Jabón de afeitar**, shaving soap. **Jabón en polvo**, soap powder. 2. *(Met.)* Any saponaceous mass or matter. 3. *(coll.)* Smart stroke with a batlet. 4. Soft soap (adulación). 5. *(Carib. Cono Sur, Mex.)* Fright, scare. **Dar un jabón**, to reprimand severely.

jabonado, da [hah-bo-nah´-do, dah], *a*. & *pp*. of JABONAR. Soaped, cleansed with soap.

jabonado [hah-bo-nah´-do], *m*. 1. Wash, the act of washing with soap. 2. Parcel of linen washed with soap (ropa).

jabonadura [hah-bo-nah-doo´-rah], *f*. The act of washing (acto). **Jabonaduras**, 1. Suds or soapsuds. 2. Lather. **Echarle or darle a uno una jabonadura**, *(coll.)* to reprimand somebody.

jabonamiento [hah-bo-nah-me-en´-to], *m*. V. JABONADURA.

jabonar [hah bo-nar´], *va*. 1. To soap, to cleanse with soap. 2. *(coll.)* To reprimand severely.

jaboncillo, jabonete, or **jabonete de olor** [hah-bon-theel´-lyo, hah-bo-nay´-tay], *m*. 1. Bar of soap; shaving soap. 2. Soap-stone or French chalk used by tailors. 3. Mixture of oils and alkali, especially ammonia, hardly saponified.

jabonera [hah-bo-nay´-rah], *f*. 1. Box or case for a bar of soap. 2. *(Bot.)* Soapwort.

jabonería [hah-bo-nay-ree´-ah], *f*. Soap-manufactory, soap-house.

jabonero [hah-bo-nay´-ro], *m*. Soap maker or seller.

jabonoso, sa [hah-bo-no´-so, sah], *a*. Soapy.

jabuco [hah-boo´-co], *m*. *(Cuba)* A round basket in the form of a very large decanter with a narrow neck.

jaca [hah´-cah], *f*. 1. Nag, pony, mare (jegua). V. HACA. 2. A name of the bread-fruit tree.

jacal [hah-cahl´], *m*. *(Max.)* 1. An Indian hut, a wigwam. 2. *(Zool.)* Jackal. V. CHACAL.

jacamar [hah-cah-mar'], *m.* Jacamar, an insectivorous bird of South America, notable for its beauty.

jacana [hah-cah'-nah], *f.* A tropical South American wading bird.

jácara [hah'-cah-rah], *f.* 1. A sort of romance. 2. A kind of rustic tune for singing or dancing; a kind of dance. 3. Company of young men who walk about at night time singing *jácaras* (personas). 4. Molestation, vexation (molestia). 5. Idle talk or prattle, story, tale (cuento); fable, lie, vainglorious fiction.

jacarandina, jacarandana [hah-cah-ran-dee'-nah, hah-cah-ran-dah´-nah], *f.* 1. Low, foul language, slang, the language of ruffians and prostitutes' bullies. 2. Singing of *jácaras* or boastings. 3. *(Low.)* Assembly of ruffians and thieves.

jacarear [hah-cah-ray-ar´], *vn.* 1. To sing *jácaras.* 2. To go about the streets with singing and noise. 3. To be troublesome and vexatious (armar un lío); to be rude (insultar).

jacarero [hah-cah-ray'-ro], *m.* 1. Ballad-singer. 2. Wag or merry droll, a facetious person.

jacarilla [hah-cah-reel'-ly-ah], *f. dim.* of JÁCARA.

jácaro [hah'-cah-ro], *m.* Boaster, bully.

jácaro, ra [hah´-cah-ro, rah], *a.* Belonging to boasters or noisy singers. **A lo jácaro.** in a boastful or bragging manner.

jacena [hah-thay´-nah], *f.* Girder, a beam on which joists rest.

jacerina [hah-thay-ree'-nah], *f.* Mail, a coat of steel network for defence.

jacilla [hah-theel'-lyah], *f.* Mark which a thing leaves upon the ground where it has been for some time.

jacinto [hah-theen'-to], *m.* 1. Hyacinth (planta). 2. Hyacinth (piedra preciosa).

jacio [hah'-the-o], *m. (Naut.)* A dead calm.

jaco [hah'-co], *m.* 1. Nag, pony. 2. A short jacket, formerly used by soldiers. 3. *V.* JAQUE.

jacobínico, ca [hah-co-bee'-ne-co, cah], *a.* Jacobin, Jacobinical, belonging to Jacobins.

jacobinismo [hah-co-be-nees'-mo], *m.* Jacobinism, the principles of a Jacobin.

jacobino [hah-co-bee'-no], *m.* Jacobin, one of a faction in the French revolution, a downright democrat; an infidel.

jacra, or **jagra** [hah'-crah], *f.* A kind of sugar obtained from the wine of the palm-tree or the cocoanut.

jactancia [hac-tahn'-the-ah], *f.* Jactation, boasting, arrogance, ostentation.

jactanciosamente [hac-tan-the-o-sah-ment´-tay], *adv.* Boastingly.

jactancioso, sa [hac-tan-the-o'-so, sah], *a.* Boastful, vainglorious; arrogant, glorious, ostentatious.

jactarse [hac-tar'-say], *vr.* To vaunt, to boast, to display with ostentation, to glory, to flourish, to brag, to gasconade.

jaculatoria [hah-coo-lah-to'-re-ah], *f.* Ejaculation, a short prayer.

jaculatorio, ria [hah-coo-lah-to'-re-o, ah], *a.* Jaculatory.

jachalí [hah-chah-lee'], *m.* The custard apple, a tropical shrub or low tree valued for its hard wood.

jada [hah'-dah], *f. (Prov.) V.* AZADA.

jade [hah'-day], *m.* Jade (mineral).

jadeante [hah-day-ahn'-tay], *a.* Panting, breathless, gasping.

jadear [hah-day-ar'], *vn.* To pant, to palpitate, to have the breast heaving as for want of breath; to jade.

jadeo [hah-day'-o], *m.* Pant; palpitation, gasping.

jadiar [hah-de-ar'], *va. (Prov.)* To dig up with a spade.

jaecero, ra [hah-ay-thay'-ro, rah], *m. & f.* Harness-maker.

jaén [hah-en´], *m.* A kind of large white grape, with thick rind.

jaez [hah'-eth], *m.* 1. Harness, the traces of draught-horses. 2. Manner or quality in which several things resemble

each other. **Jaeces,** ornaments or harness of horses in processions.

jafético, ca [hah-fay'-te-co, cah], *a.* Japhetic, Indo-Germanic, descended from Japhet.

jagua [hah'-goo-ah], *f.* Fruit of the custard-apple, of a sweet, agreeable taste. *(Cuba)*

jaguar, or **jaguarete** [hah-goo-ar', or hah-goo-ah-ray'-tay], *m.* The Jaguar, a ferocious beast resembling the leopard.

jagüey [hah-goo-ay'-e], *m.* 1. In Peru and Mexico, a large pool or lake. Also, a reservoir for rain-water, when no spring water is at hand. 2. *(Cuba)* The matador liana, a climbing plant which kills the tree which it clasps.

jaharrar [ha-har-rar'], *va.* To plaster, to overlay or make even with plaster.

jaharro [ha-har'-ro], *m.* Plaster, the act of plastering.

jai alai [hah-e ah-lah'-e], *m.* Jai alai, Basque ball game.

jaiba [hah'-e-bah], *f. (Cuba & Mex.)* Certain type of crab (cangrejo). 2. *(And.)* Mouth (boca). *-m & f. (Carib. Mex.)* Sharp customer. *-f. (Mex. Zool.)* Crab; *(CAm.)* fresh-water or river crab (de río).

jabol [hah-e-bol'], *m. (Mex.)* High-ball.

jaire [hah'-e-ray], *m.* 1. The curved line made in a timber which is joined to another for greater solidity. 2. Among shoemakers, the outward inclination of the knife in splitting leather.

¡ja, ja, ja! [hah, hah, hah], *int.* Exclamation, denoting laughter.

jalapa [hah-lah'-pah], *f. (Bot.)* 1. Jalapa. 2. Jalap, the root of the jalap, plant frequently used in medicine.

jalar [hah-lahr'], *va.* 1. *(LAm.)* To pull (tirar de). 2. *(LAm.)* to work hard. 3. *(And. Carib.)* To make, to do (hacer). 4. To guzzle. 5. *(LAm.)* To pull (conquistar). *-vn.* 1. *(LAm.)* To pull (tirar). 2. *(LAm.)* To work hard. 3. *(LAm.)* To go off, to go (irse). 4. *(CAm. Mex.)* To be courting (amantes). 5. *(Mex.)* To exaggerate (exagerar). *-vr.* 1. *(CAm.)* To be courting (amantes). 2. *(LAm.)* To get drunk.

jalbegar [hal-bay-gar´], *va.* 1. To whiten, to whitewash. 2. To paint excessively, to lay too much white on the face.

jalbegue [hal-bay'-gay], *m.* 1. Whitewash. 2. Whitewashing, whitening a wall with lime. 3. Whitewash, a paint or wash to make the skin seem fair.

jaldado, da, jaldo, da [hal-dah'-do, dah, hahl'-do, dah], Of a bright yellow color.

jalde [hahl'-day], *a.* Bright yellow, crocus-colored.

jaldre [hahl'-dray], *m.* A bright yellow color, peculiar to birds.

jalea [hah-lay'-ah], *f.* Jelly, the inspissated juice of fruit, boiled with sugar. **Hacerse una jalea,** *(Met.)* to love with excessive fondness.

jalear [hah-lay-ar'], *va.* 1. To encourage hounds to follow the chase (perro). 2. To animate dancers, by clapping hands (bailarines). 3. To quaver the voice, to use the vibrato. *-vn. (Mex.)* To have a high old time.

jaleo [hah-lay'-o], *m.* 1. Spree, binge (juerga). **Estar de jaleo,** to make merry. 2. Row, uproar (ruido); hassle (confusión). **Armar un jaleo,** to kick up a row. 3. Hallooing (caza). 4. *(Mus.)* Shouting and clapping.

jaletina [hah-lay-tee'-nah], *f.* 1. Calf's foot jelly. 2. Gelatine.

jalma [hahl'-mah], *f.* A kind of packsaddle.

jalmero [hal-may'-ro], *m.* One whose trade is to make packsaddles and harness for mules.

jaloque [hah-lo'-kay], *m.* South-east wind. *V.* SIROCO.

jamaicano, na [hah-mah-e-cah'-no, nah], *a.* Jamaican, pertaining to Jamaica.

jamaiquense, jamaiqués, sa [hah-mah-e-ken'-say, keys', sah], *a. & m. & f.* Jamaican.

jamar [hah-mar'], *vn.* To eat, to stuff oneself. *-vr.* **Se lo jamó todo,** he scoffed the lot.

jamás [hah-mahs'], *adv.* Never, at no time. **Para siempre jamás,** forever. *(Vulg.)*For ever and a day. **Jamás, por jamás or nunca jamás,** never, nevermore.

jamba [hahm´-bah], *f.* *(birch.)* Door-jamb, window-post, which supports the lintel or head-piece.

jambaje [ham-bah´-hay], *m.* *(Arch.)* Collection of jambs.

jámbico, ca [hahm´-be-co, cah], *a.* Iambic. *V.* YÁMBICO.

jamerdana [hah-mer-dah´-nah], *f.* Sewer which runs from a slaughterhouse.

jamerdar [hah-mer-dar´], *va.* 1. To clean the guts of animals. 2. To wash hastily.

jamete [hah-may´-tay], *m.* A sort of stuff formerly worn in Spain.

jametería [hah-may-tay-ree´-ah], *f.* *(Prov.)* *V.* ZALAMERÍA.

jamilla [hah-meel´-lyah], *f.* *V.* ALPECHÍN.

jamón [hah-mone´], *m.* 1. Ham, the salted thigh of a hog. **Jamón York**, boiled ham. **Jamón serrano**, cured ham. 2. *(Carib.)* Bargain (ganga). 3. *(Carib.)* Difficulty (conflicto).

jamona [hah-mo´-nah], *a.* A stout middle-aged woman.

jamuga, or **jamugas** [hah-moo´-gah], *f.* A kind of side saddle for women.

jándalo, la [hahn´-dah-lo, lah], *a.* Having the gait and dialect of an Andalusian; particularly in giving the *h* a strong guttural sound.

jangada [han-gah´-dah], *f.* Raft, a frame or float.

jantio [hahn´-te-o], *m.* *(Bot.)* Lesser burdock.

japonés, sa [hah-po-nays´, sah], *a.* Japanese, relating to Japan.

jaque [hah´-kay], *m.* 1. Braggart, boaster. 2. Check, in the game of chess (ajedrez). **Jaque mate**, checkmate. 3. Saddlebag. 4. Sort of smooth combing of the hair. **Dar jaque a**, to check.

jaquear [hah-kay-ar´], *va.* To give or make check at chess.

jaqueca [hah-kay´-cah], *f.* Migrain headache, a severe headache; *(Cono Sur)* hangover (resaca).

jaquel [hah-kayl´], *m.* Chessboard.

jaquelado, da [hah-kay-lah´-do, dah], *a.* Checkered: applied to cut diamonds or precious stones.

jaquero [hah-kay´-ro], *m.* Fine-toothed comb.

jaquetón [hah-kay-tone´], *m.* *aug.* 1. A large, wide coat. 2. Great swaggerer, boaster.

jáquima [hah´-ke-mah], *f.* Headstall of a halter.

jaquimazo [hah-ke-mah´-tho], *m.* 1. Stroke with the headstall of a halter. 2. Displeasure; an unfair trick, ill turn.

jara [hah´-rah], *f.* 1. *(Bot.)* Cistus or rock-rose, labdanum-tree. 2. A kind of dart or arrow (dardo). *Java cerval*, *(Bot.)* round-leaved cistus.

jarabe [hah-rah´-bay], *m.* 1. Sirup, vegetable juice with sugar. 2. Any very sweet mixed drink, especially if not very cool. **Jarabe de palo**, beating. **Jarabe de arce**, maple syrup. 3. *(Mex.)* Popular dance.

jarabear [hah-rah-bay-ar´], *va.* To prescribe sirups very often. -*vr.* To take sirups or sweet beverages frequently.

jaraiz [hah-rah´-eeth], *m.* Pit for pressing grapes.

jaral [hah-rahl´], *m.* 1. Place planted with the cistus or labdanum shrub (maleza). 2. A very intricate or puzzling point.

jaramago [hah-rah-mah´-go], *m.* *(Bot.)* All the species of cruciferous plants bearing yellow flowers; mustards.

jarameño, ña [hah-rah-may´-nyo, nyah], *a.* Applied to bulls reared on the banks of the Jarama, a river in Spain.

jaramugo [hah-rah-moo´-go], *m.* Small fish used as bait for others.

jarana [hah-rah´-nah], *f.* 1. Carousel, revelry, romping. 2. *(coll.)* Scuffle, contest. 3. Outcry, row, spree (juerga). **No querer meterse en jaranas**, not to like to get into scrapes. 4. Trick, deceit (trampa); *(LAm.)* joke, practical joke. 5. *(And. Carib. Mex.)* Folk dance (baile); *(Carib.)* dance band (banda). 6. *(Mex.)* Small guitar. 7. *(CAm. Fin.)* debt.

jarano [hah-rah´-no], *m.* Mexican wide-brimmed felt hat.

jarapastroso, sa [hah-rah-pas-tro´-so, sah], *a.* Dialectic for *zarrapastroso* ragged.

jarapote [hah-rah-po´-tay], *m.* *(Prov.)* *V.* JAROPEO.

jarapotear [hah-rah-po-tay-ar´], *va.* *(Prov.)* To stuff or fill with medicinal drugs.

jarazo [hah-rah´-tho], *m.* Blow or wound with a dart.

jarcia [har´-the-ah], *f.* 1. Parcel or bundle of a variety of things laid by for use. 2. A multitude of things without order (montón). 3. *(Naut.)* Tackle (pesca), rigging and cordage belonging to a ship, the shrouds. 4. A complete fishing-tackle. 5. *(Carib. Mex.)* Rope (cuerda). 6. *(CAm. Mex.)* Agave; rope (cuerda). **Almacén de jarcias**, rigging-house, store-house for rigging. **Tablas de jarcia**, suit or set of rigging. **Jarcia mayor**, the main shrouds.

jardín [har-deen´], *m.* 1. A garden. 2. Spot which disfigures an emerald. 3. Privy on board of ships. 4. *(LAm.)* Kindergarten, nursery school.

jardincito, jardinito [har-din-thee´-to, har-de-nee´-to], *m.* *dim.* A small garden.

jardinería [har-de-nay-ree´-ah], *f.* Gardening, the art of cultivating gardens.

jardinero, ra [har-de-nay´-ro, rah], *m.* *& f.* Gardener. -*f.* 1. Flower stand, jardiniere. 2. A basket carriage. 3. *(Cono Sur)* Handcart (carrito). 4. *(And.)* Jacket (saco).

jareta [hah-ray´-tah], *f.* 1. Seam made by doubling the edge of cloth, through which a string or lace may be drawn. 2. *(Naut.)* Netting, harpings. 3. *(CAm. Cono Sur)* Pants flies (de pantalón). 4. *(Carib.)* Snag, setback (contratiempo).

jaretera [hah-ray-tay´-rah], *f.* *V.* JARRETERA.

jarife [hah-ree´-fay], *m.* *V.* JERIFE.

jarifo, fa [hah-ree´-fo, fah], *a.* Showy, full-dressed, adorned, elegant.

jaripeo [ha-re-pay´-o], *m.* Rodeo, horse show.

jaro, ra [hah´-ro, rah], *a.* Resembling a wild boar (cerdos).

jarocho [hah-ro´cho], *m.* 1. *(Mex.Coll.)* A rough, stout countryman. 2. Mulatto or negro.

jaropar, jaropear, or **jaropotear** [hah-ro-par´, hah-ro-po-tay-ar´], *va.* To stuff or fill with medicinal drugs; to give any liquor as a medical draught, to medicine.

jarope [hah-ro´-pay], *m.* 1. Medical draught or potion. 2. Any kind of bitter beverage. 3. Sirup.

jaropeo [hah-ro-pay´-o], *m.* The excessive and frequent use of bitters or medical potions; the drug habit.

jarra [har´-rah], *f.* 1. Jug, jar, pitcher, mug (cerveza), churn (leche), of earthenware. 2. *(Prov.)* Ancient equestrian order. **En jarra** or **de jarras**, akimbo.

jarrear [har-ray-ar´], *vn.* *(coll.)* To take out often water or wine with a jug; to drink often.

jarrero [har-ray´-ro], *m.* Vender or maker of jugs or jars.

jarreta, illa, ita [har-ray-tah, eel´-lya, ee´-tah], *f.* *dim.* 1. A small jar. 2. *(Naut.)* Gratings.

jarrete [har-ray´-tay], *m.* Ham, the upper part of the leg, hock (caballo).

jarretera [har-ray-tay´-rah], *f.* 1. Garter. 2. Garter, the highest order of English knighthood.

jarrito [har-ree´-to], *m.* *dim.* A small jug or pot with one handle.

jarro [har´-ro], *m.* 1. Jug or pot with one handle only, pitcher. **Caer como un jarro de agua fría**, to come as a complete shock. 2. *(Prov.)* A chatterer.

jarrón [har-rone´], *m.* *aug.* A large jug or pitcher, an urn.

jaspe [hahs´-pay], *m.* Jasper, a precious stone

jaspeado, da [has-pay-ah´-do, dah], *a.* *& pp.* of JASPEAR. Spotted, like jasper; marbled, mottled; variegated.

jaspeadura [has-pay-ah-doo´-rah], *f.* Marbling, the act of marbling.

jaspear [has-pay-ar´], *va.* To marble, to paint, to vein or speckle with variegated colors in imitation of jasper. -*vr.* *(Carib.)* To get cross.

jasteo, tea [has-tay´-o, ah], *a.* Chasing the fox (perros).

jastial [has-te-ahl´], *m.* Facade of an edifice.

jato, ta [hah´-to, tah], *m.* *& f.* 1. *V.* BECERRO. 2. *(Carib.)* Stray dog (perros). 3. *(Mex.)* Load (carga). 4. *(Mex.)* Stopping place (parada). 5. *(And.)* Saddle (silla de montar).

¡jau! [hah´-oo], *int.* Exclamation to incite animals, especially bulls. Repeated signifies noisy applause.

jauja [hah'-oo-hah], *pr. n.* ¿Estamos aquí, o en Jauja?, a rebuke or caution: take care!

jaula [hah'-oo-lah], *f.* 1. Cage, an inclosure for birds. 2. Cell for insane persons (locos). 3. Lock-up (tienda, garaje). 4. *(Mex. Ferro.)* Cattle truck.

jaulón [hah-oo-lone'], *m. aug.* A large cage for birds.

jauría [hah-oo-ree'-ah], *f.* Pack of hounds.

jauto, ta [hah'-oo-to, tah], *a. (Prov.) V.* SOSO.

javanés, sa [hah-vah-nays', sah], *a.* Javanese, relating to Java.

javia, or **javio aronillero** [hah-ve-ah, or hah'-ve-o ah-ray-neel-lyay'-ro], *m.* The sandbox tree.

jayán, na [hah-yahn', nah], *m. & f.* A tall, strong, and robust person.

jayanazo [hah-ya-nah'-tho], *m. aug.* A huge, big fellow

jazilla [hah-theel'-lyah], *f.* Vestige mark, trace. *V.* JACILLA.

jazmín [hath-meen'], *m. (Bot.)* Jessamine or jasmine, a fragrant flower. **Jazmín real**, catalonian jessamine. **Jazmín amarillo**, Italian jessamine. **Jazmín de Virginia**, ash-leaved trumpet flower.

jazminorro [hath-me-nor'-ro], *m. (Bot.)* Common yellow jessamine.

jazz [yath], *m. (Mus.)* Jazz. **Jazz progresivo**, progressive jazz.

jebe [hay'-bay], *m.* 1. *(Prov.)* Rockalum. *(Acad.)* 2. *(Peru)* Caoutchouc, Indianrubber. 3. Arse (trasero).

jeep [jeep], *m.* Jeep.

jeera [hay-ay'-rah], *f.* Piece of drained marshy ground.

jefatura [hay-fah-too'-rah], *f.* 1. The dignity of a chief, or governor of a province (liderato). 2. The place where the different offices of that government are kept (sede). **Bajo la jefatura**, under the leadership of.

jefe, fa [hay'-fay, fah], *m. & f.* Chief, boss (de un empleado), head superior, lender (líder), manager (gerente). **Jefe de escuadra,** *(Naut.)* Rear admiral. **Jefe de bomberos**, fire officer. **Jefe de estación**, station master. **Jefe de estudios**, deputy head. **Jefe de obras**, project manager. **Jefe supremo**, commander-in-chief.

Jehová [hay-o-vah']. Hebrew word for God. Properly Yahweh.

¡je, je, je! [hay], *int.* Denoting laughter.

jema [hay'-mah], *f.* The part of a beam which is badly squared.

jemal [hay-mahl'], *a.* Of the length of a *jeme.*

jeme [hay'-may], 1. The distance from the end of the thumb to the end of the forefinger (both extended). 2. *(coll.)* A woman's face.

jenabe, jenable [hay-nah'-bay, hay-nah'-blay], *m.* Mustard. *V.* MOSTAZA.

jengibre [hen-hee'-bray], *m.* Ginger, the pungent, spicy rootstock of Zingiber officinale. Used as medicine and as a spice.

jeniquén [hay-ne-ken'], *m.* Sisal hemp. *V.* HENEQUÉN.

jeque [hay'-kay], *m.* 1. An old man; a governor or chief among the Moors. 2. Portmanteau.

jera [hay'-rah], *f. (Prov.)* Extent of ground which can be ploughed in a day with a pair of oxen.

jerapellina [hay-rah-pel-lyee'-nah], *f.* An old ragged suit of clothes.

jerarca [hay-rar'-cah], *m.* Hierarch.

jerarquía [hay-rar-kee'-ah], *f.* 1. Hierarchy, order among the various choirs of angels and ranks of the church. 2. By extension, a rank or grade of importance.

jerárquico, ca [hay-rar'-ke-co, cah], *a.* Hierarchical, belonging to a hierarchy.

jerez [hay-rayth'], *m.* Sherry.

jerezano, na [hay-ray-thah'-no, nah], *a. & m. & f.* Native of or belonging to Jerez de la Frontera.

jerga [herr'-gah], *f.* 1. Course frieze, any coarse cloth. 2. Jargon, gibberish, unintelligible talk, slang. **Jerga informática**, computer jargon. *V.* JERIGONZA. 3. Large sack.

jergón [her-gone'], *m.* 1. Large course mattress or sack, filled with straw or paper cuttings. 2. Suit of clothes ill made. 3. An illshaped person (persona). 4. Kidderminster carpeting. 5. *(coll.)* Paunch, belly.

jerguilla [her-geel'-lyah], *f.* A sort of serge made of silk or worsted.

jerigonza [hay-re-gon'-thah], *f.* 1. Jargon, gibberish, especially of gipsies. 2. Language difficult to understand. 3. Strange and ridiculous action (estupidez).

jeringa [hay-reen'-gah], *f.* 1. Syringe, an instrument for injecting liquids into animal bodies, wounds, etc. 2. *(LAm.)* Pest, nuisance (persona).

jeringación [hay-rin-gah-the-on'], *f.* Syringing, the action and effect of the syringe; the liquid injected by this action.

jeringar [hay-rin-gar'], *va.* To syringe, to inject by means, of a syringe; to wash and cleanse by injections from a syringe.

jeringazo [hay-rin-gah'-tho], *m.* 1. The act of injecting a liquid with the syringe. 2. Clyster, injection, the liquid substance injected with a syringe.

jeringuilla [hay-rin-geel'-lyah], *f.* 1. *dim.* A little syringe. 2. Mock orange, syringa.

jeroglífico [hay-ro-glee'-fe-co], *m.* Hieroglyph, the symbol for a word; an ideograph, especially the sacred writing of the Egyptians.

jeroglífico, ca [hay-ro-glee'-fe-co], *a.* Hieroglyphic, hieroglyphical.

jerpa [herr'-pah], *f.* Sterile shoot of a vine.

jerricote [her-re-co'-tay], *m.* A pottage of almonds, sugar, sage and ginger, in chicken broth.

Jesucristo [hay-soo-crees'-to], *m.* Jesus Christ.

jesuita [hay-soo-ee'-tah], *m.* Jesuit.

Jesús [hay-soos'], *m.* Jesus. Bless you! (al estornudar).

jet [jet], *m.* Jet, jet plane. -f. Jet-set.

jeta [hey'-tah], *f.* 1. Thick, heavy lips; blobber-lip. 2. A hog's snout; *(Cono Sur)* To kick the bucket (morir). 3. Frown (ceño). 4. Cheek (descaro), nerve. **Lo hace por la jeta**, he gets away with it by sheer cheek.

jeto [hay'-to], *m. (Prov.)* An empty beehive rubbed with honey to attract the bees.

jetudo, da [hay-too'-do, dah], *a.* Thick-lipped.

jiba [hee'-bah], *f.* 1. A hump. 2. Bother, tiresomeness.

jibado, da [he-bah'-do, dah], *a.* Hump-backed, crooked.

jibar [he-bar'], *va. (coll.)* To vex, to molest, to annoy.

jíbaro, ra [hee'-bah-ro, rah], *a. (Cuba)* 1. Run wild. 2. Rustic (rústico), rude.-*m.* Countryman.

jibia [hee'-be-ah], *f. (Zool.)* Cuttle-fish.

jibión [he-be-on'], *m.* Cuttle-fish bone used by gold and silversmiths.

jiboso, sa [he-bo'-so, sah], *a.* Gibbous, hump-backed.

jícama [hee'-ca-mah], *f. (Amer.)* A farinaceous root.

jícara [hee'-ca-rah], *f.* 1. Chocolate-cup (tacita). 2. Gourd-tree (calabaza).

jicarazo [he-ca-rah'-tho], *m. aug.* A large chocolate cup. *(Amer. Coll.)* **Dar un jicarazo**, to give poison to a person.

jicotea [he-co-tay'-ah], *f. (Amer.)* A mud-turtle.

jifa [hee'-fah], *f.* Refuse of slaughtered beasts.

jiferada [he-fay-rah'-dah], *f.* Stroke with a butcher's knife.

jifería [he-fah-ree'-ah], *f.* Slaughtering.

jifero, ra [he-fay'-ro, rah], *a.* Belonging to the slaughter-house.

jifero [he-fay'-ro], *m.* 1. Butcher's knife. 2. Butcher.

jifia [hee-fe-ah], *f. (Zool.)* Xiphias, the swordfish.

jiga [hee'-gah], *f.* Jig, a lively dance and tune.

jigote [he-go'-tay], *m.* 1. Minced meat, stewed and dressed with butter; a hash. 2. Any other dish minced.

jijallo [he-hahl'-lo], *m. (Bot.)* Prickly broom, hairy cytisus.

jijene [he-hay'-nay], *m. (S. Amer.)* Sandfly.

jijona [he-ho'-nah], *f.* A variety of flinty wheat. -*m.* Soft nougat.

jilguero [heel-gay´-ro], *m*. Gold-finch.

jilocopo [he-lo-co´-po], *m*. The carpenter bee, xylocopa.

jilote [he-lo´-tay], *V*. HILOTE.

jimagua [he-nah´-goo-ah], *m. & f. (Cuba)* Twin.

jimelga [he-mel´-gah], *f. (Naut.)* The fish of a mast.

jimenzar [he-men-thar´], *va. (Prov.)* To ripple flax or hemp.

jinestada [he-nes-tah´-dah], *f*. Sauce made from milk, rice-flour, dates, spices and other things.

jineta [he-nay´-tah], *f*. 1. A kind of short lance. 2. Art of horsemanship. 3. The office of a sergeant. 4. Ancient tribute imported upon cattle. *Andar a la jineta,* to go at a short trot. **Cabalgar a la jineta,** to ride with very short stirrups.

jinete [he-nay´-tay], *m*. 1. Trooper, cavalryman. 2. One mounted on horseback, a horseman, cavalier.

jinetear [he-nay-tay-ar´], *va. (Mex.)* To tame wild horses by riding them (domar). 2. To ride on horseback (montar), publicly, with ostentation. 3. *(Mex.)* To misappropriate (fondos). -*vr*. 1. *(And. Mex.)* To stay in the saddle (no caer). 2. *(And.)* To be vain (ser presumido).

jinglar [hin-glar´], *vn*. To move from one side to another as if hung in a swing.

jingoísmo [hin-go-ees´-mo], *m*. Jingoism, exaggerated patriotism.

jingoísta [hin-go-ees´-tah], *a*. Jingoistic.-*m. & f*. Jingoist, ardent patriot.

jinjol [heen-hole´], *m*. Jujube. *V*. AZUFAIFA.

jipar [he-par´], *va*. **Le tengo jipado,** I´ve got him taped.

jipato, ta [he-pah´-to, tah], *a. (Cuba)* 1. Pale, of sickly countenance. 2. Full, replete with eating.

jipi [he´-pe], *m & f*. Hippy.

jipijapa [he-pe-hah´-pah], *f*. 1. Fine straw (paja), flexible and durable, used in weaving hats, cigar cases, dippers, etc. 2. Panama hat (sombrero). **Sombrero de jipijapa,** panama hat.

jira [hee´-rah], *f*. 1. Strip of cloth (de tela). 2. Shred, tatter, scrap. 3. Picnic, outing. 4. Tour, excursion.

jirafa [he-rah´-fah], *f*. 1. Giraffe. 2. Boom (micrófono).

jirapliega [he-rah-ple-ay´-gah], *f*. A purgative confection.

jirasal [he-rah-sahl´], *f*. Fruit of the lactree.

jirofina [he-ro-fee´-nah], *f*. A kind of sauce or gravy.

jiroflé [he-ro-flay´], *m*. The clove-tree.

jirón [he-rone´], *m*. 1. Facing of a skirt. 2. Piece torn from a gown or other clothing (andrajo). 3. Banner, pennant. 4. Small part of any whole. 5. *(Peru)* A long street, a row of houses (calle).

jironado, da [he-ro-nah´-do, dah], *a*. 1. Torn into strips or fragments. 2. Garnished with triangular pieces of cloth.

jirpear [heer-pay-ar´], *va*. To dig about vines.

jisca [hees´-cah], *f. (Bot.)* Cylindrical sugar-cane. *V*. CARRIZO.

jiste [hees´-tay], *m*. Yeast, barm, leaven. Froth of beer. *(Acad.)*

jitar [he-tar´], *va. (Prov.)* To emit, to turn out.

jito [hee´-to], *m*. The channel by which melted metal runs, and the hole where it enters the mould.

¡jo! [ho], *int*. Whoa!

jocosamente [ho-co-sah-me´-tay], *adv*. Jocosely, jocularly, waggishly, humorously, good humoredly.

jocoserio, ria [ho-co-say´-reo, ah], *a*. Jocoserious, partaking of mirth and seriousness

jocosidad [ho-co-se-dahd´], *f*. Jocularity, Jocoseness, jocosity, humor.

jocoso, sa [ho-co´-so, sah], *a*. Jocose, jocular, waggish, facetious, ludicrous, good-humored.

jocoyote [ho-co-yo´-tay], *m. (Amer.)* The youngest child, best loved by the parents.

joder [ho-dayr´], *va*. 1. *(Esp.)* To fuck; damn it! (enfadado). 2. *(Fig.)* To annoy (fastidiar), to upset; to harm (dañar); to pester (acosar); to mess up (estropear). **Esto me jode,** I´m fed up with this. **Son ganas de joder,** they´re just trying

to be awkward. 3. To pinch, to steal (robar). -*vr*. 1. To flop (fracasar); to get spoiled (estropearse). **Se jodió todo,** everything was spoiled.

jodido [ho-dee´-do], *a*. 1. Awkward, difficult (difícil). **Es un libro jodido,** it´s a very difficult book. 2. Bloody (condenado). **Ni un jodida peso,** not a dime. 3. *(LAm.)* Selfish (egoísta); evil (malo), wicked (quisquilloso).

jofaina [ho-fah´-e-nah], *f*. A china bowl. *V*. ALJOFAINA.

jogging [jo-ggin], *m*. 1. Jogging. **Hacer jogging,** to jog. 2. *(Cono Sur)* Jogging suit (ropa).

jojoto [ho-ho´-to], *m. (Ven.)* Corn in milk.

jolgorio [hol-go´-re-o], *m. (coll.)* 1. Recreation, relaxation. 2. Mirth, jollity, fun (juerga).

jolito [ho-lee´-to], *m*. Rest, leisure, calm.

jónico, ca, jonio nia [ho´-ne-co, cah, ho´-ne-o, ah], *a*. Ionic (arquitectura). -*m*. A foot in poetry.

jonuco [ho-noo´-co], *m. (Mex.)* A dark, damp corner under a staircase.

jordán [hor-dahn´], *m. (Prov.)* Anything which revives, or gives a fresh bloom.

jorfe [hor´-fay], *m*. 1. A wall made of dry stones only. 2. A high, solitary rock; a tor.

jorfear [hor-fay-ar´], *va*. To form a floor without arches.

jorguín [hor-geen´], *m. (Prov.)* Soot, condensed smoke.

jorjina [hor-hee´-nah], *f*. Witch, sorceress, whose charms consist in soporiferous draughts.

jornada [hor-nah´-dah], *f*. 1. March or journey performed in one day (viaje). 2. Journey, travel by land. 3. A military expedition. 4. Opportunity, occasion, circumstance. 5. Passage through life (etapa). 6. Act, one of the parts into which Spanish plays are divided. 7. Number of sheets printed off in a day. **Al fin de la jornada,** *(Met.)* at the end, at last. **Jornada de 8 horas,** 8 hour day. **Trabajar en jornadas reducidas,** to work short-time. **Hay jornada limitada en la industria,** there is short-time working in the industry.

jornal [hor-nahl´], *m*. 1. Day-work (trabajo), day-labor, the work done by a workman hired by the day. 2. Day-wages (sueldo), or wages paid to day-laborers for one day's work. **Mujer que trabaja a jornal,** charwoman. **A jornal,** by the day. 3. *(Com.)* Journal, diary, a book used by merchants.

jornalero [hor-nah-lay´-ro], *m*. Day-laborer.

joroba [ho-ro´-bah], *f*. 1. Hump, a prominence on the back. 2. *(coll.)* Importunity, incessant, troublesome solicitation. -*m. & f*. A worry, a bore.

jorobado, da [ho-ro-bah´-do, dah], *a*. Crooked, gibbous, humpbacked or crook-backed.-*pp*. of JOROBAR.

jorobar [ho-ro-bar´], *va*. 1. *(coll.)* To importune, to worry, to tease or harass by frequent repetition of the same request (fastidiar). **Esto me joroba,** I´m fed up with this. 2. To break (estropear). -*vr*. 1. To get cross (enfadarse), to get worked up; to get fed up (cansarse). 2. To put up with (aguantar). 3. To fail (fracasar), to go down the drain. 4. To break, to smash (romperse).

jorro [hor´-ro], *m. (Cuba)* Bad tobacco.

josa [ho´-sah], *f*. Piece of ground planted with vines and fruit-trees.

jostrado, da [hos-trah´-do, dah], *a*. Round-headed (dardo, flecha).

jota [ho´-tah], *f*. 1. Name of the letter J. 2. Jot, little. 3. Spanish dance. **No saber una jota,** to be very ignorant. **No entendió ni jota,** he didn´t understand a word of it. 4. *(And. Cono Sur)* Vulture.

jovada [ho-vah´-dah], *f. (Prov.)* Ground which may be tilled by a pair of mules in one day.

joven [ho´-ven], *a*. Young, youthful (aspecto), juvenile.- *m. & f*. Youth, a stripling, a young man; a young woman; a young person. **Los jovenes,** young people. 2. *(Cono Sur)* Waiter.

jovenado [ho-vay-nah´-do], *m*. The time or place in which young persons, after taking the vows, are under the direction of a master in convents.

jovencillo, illa [ho-ven-thee-llyo, eel´-lya], *m. & f. dim.* Youngster.

jovial [ho-ve-ahl´], *a.* 1. Jovial, under the influence of Jupiter. 2. Jovial, gay, airy, merry, cheerful.

jovialidad [ho-ve-ah-le-dahd´], *f.* Joviality, jollity, mirth, merriment, gaiety, good-humor, festivity.

joya [ho'-yah], *f.* 1. Jewel, a precious stone set in gold or silver. 2. Anything well polished and finished. 3. Present, gift. 4. Astragal, a convex architectural moulding. *-pl.* Jewels, trinkets: all the wearing apparel and ornaments of women, especially of brides. **Joyas de imitación**, imitation jewellery.

joyante [ho-yahn'-tay], *a.* Extremely glossy (sedas).

joyel [ho-yel'], *m.* A small jewel.

joyera [ho-yay'-rah], *f.* Woman who keeps a jeweller's shop.

joyería [ho-yay-ree'-ah], *f.* Jeweller's shop (tienda).

joyero [ho-yay'-ro], *m.* 1. Jeweller (persona). 2. Jewel case (estuche).

joyita [ho-yee'-tah], *f. dim.* V. JOYUELA.

joyo [ho'-yo], *m. (Bot.)* Bearded darnel, darnelgrass.

joyuela [ho-yoo-ay'-lah], *f. dim.* Jewel of small value.

juaguarzo [hoo-ah-goo-ar'-tho], *m. (Bot.)* Montpellier rock-rose.

Juan [hoo-ahn'], *m.* John. **San Juan Bautista**, St John the Baptist. **El Papa Juan Pablo II**, Pope John Paul II.

juanete [hoo-ah-nay'-tay], *m.* 1. The knuckle-bone of the great toes, especially when it sticks out more than usual (pie). A bunion. 2. Prominent cheek-bones (pómulo). 3. *(Naut.)* A gallant sail. 4. *(And. CAm.)* Hip (cadera).

juanetero [hoo-ah-nay-tay'-ro], *m.* A young marine apprentice who is occupied in furling and loosening the top-gallant sails.

juanetudo, da [hoo-ah-nay-too'-do, dah], *a.* Applied to persons who have the knuckle-bone of the great toes very protuberant.

juarda [hoo-ar'-dah], *f.* Stain in cloth, occasioned by the wool having imbibed too much oil before it was carded and spun.

juardoso, sa [hoo-ar-do´-so, sah], *a.* Stained, spotted (ropa de lana).

jubarba [hoo-bar´-bah], *f.* Houseleek.

jubertar [hoo-ber-tar'], *va. (Naut.)* To hoist the boat on board.

jubetería [hoo-bay-tay-ree'-ah], *f.* Shop where jackets and doublets are sold; a slop-shop.

jubetero [hoo-bay-tay'-ro], *m.* One who makes and sells jackets and doublets.

jubilación [hoo-be-lah-the-on'], *f.* 1. Retirement (acto, estado). **Jubilación anticipada**, early retirement. 2. Pension (pago), retirement pension.

jubilado [hoo-be-lah'-do], *a.* 1. Retired. 2. *(And. Carib.)* Wise (sagaz). 3. *(And.)* Thick, slow witted. *-m & f.* Retired person.

jubilar [hoo-be-lar'], *va.* 1. To pension off; to superannuate; to exempt anyone from the duties of a charge (persona). 2. To exempt from toil and labor. 3. To lay aside as useless (persona).*-vn.* To become a pensioner in consequence of having been exempted from the labor or burden of a charge, office, or ministry. *-vr.* 1. To retire. 2. *(CAm.)* To play truant (hacer novillos). 3. *(Carib.)* To gain experience (ponerse listo). 4. *(And.)* To deteriorate (deteriorar).

jubileo [hoo-be-lay'-o], *m.* Jubilee, a public festivity; concession of plenary indulgence; an ecclesiastical solemnity, celebrated by the Jews every fifty years. **por jubileo**, rarely, happening seldom.

júbilo [hoo´-be-lo], *m.* Glee, joy, merriment, rejoicing, festivity, hilarity, mirth.

jubiloso, sa [hoo-be-lo´-so, sah], *a.* Gleeful, joyful.

jubón [hoo-bone'], *m.* 1. Doublet (de hombre), jacket. 2. The waist in female dress.

juboncito [hoo-bon-thee'-to], *m. dim.* A small jupon or jacket, a doublet of little value.

jubonero [hoo-bo-nay'-ro], *m.* Maker of jackets, doublets, or jupons.

jucla [hoo'-clah], *f.* A sign which the Arabs place over consonants to replace the vowels which they lack.

judaico, ca [hoo-dah'-e-co, cah], *a.* Judaical, Jewish, relating to the Jews.

judaísmo [hoo-dah-ees'-mo], *m.* Judaism, religion of the Jews.

jadaizante [hoo-dah-e-thahn'-tay], *pa. & m.* Judaizing, Judaizer, one who Judaizes.

judaizar [hoo-dah-e-thar'], *va.* To Judaize, to observe the rites of the Jews.

Judas [hoo'-das], *m.* 1. Judas. 2. One that treacherously deceives his friend, an impostor, traitor. 3. Silkworm that does not spin. 4. *(LAm.)* Peephole (en puerta). 5. *(Cono Sur)* Snooper.

judería [hoo-day-ree'-ah], *f.* 1. Jewry (judíos); a quarter of the town where the Jews live (barrio); tax on Jews. 2. *(CAm. Mex.)* Prank (travesura).

judía [hoo-dee'-ah], *f.* 1. *(Bot.)* French bean, kidney-bean. **Judía colorada**, runner bean. **Judía verde**, French bean. 2. Jewess, a Hebrew woman.

judiada [hoo-de-ah'-ah], *f.* 1. An inhuman action (acto cruel). 2. Excessive and scandalous profit.

judicante [hoo-de-cahn'-tay], *m. (Prov.)* Judge appointed to inquire into the conduct and proceedings of officers of justice.

judicatura [hoo-de-cah-too´-rah], *f.* 1. Judicature, the power and act of administering justice (cargo). 2. Dignity of a judge.

judicial [hoo-de-the-ahl'], *a.* Judicial, juridical, practised in the distribution of justice or used in courts of justice.

judicialmente [hoo-de-the-al-men'-tay], *adv.* Judicially.

judiciaria [hoo-de-the-ah´-re-ah], *f.* Judiciary astrology.

judiciario, ria [hoo-de-the-ah'-re-o, ah], *a.* Astrological, professing the art of foretelling future events.

judiega [hoo-de-ay'-gah], *f.* Kind of olives, good for making oil, but not for eating.

judihuelo, la [hoo-de-oo-ay'-lo, lah], *m. & f.* 1. A young Jew or Jewess. 2. French bean.

judío, día [hoo-dee'-o, ah], *a.* Judaical, Jewish.

judío [hoo-dee'-o], *m.* 1. Jew. 2. Appellation given by boys to the trumpeters who attend the processions in the holy week.

judión [hoo-de-on'], *m.* A large sort of French beans. Dutch kidney-beans.

judo [joo-do], *m.* Judo.

juego [hoo-ay'-go], *m.* 1 Play (acto), amusement, diversion, sport. **Los niños en el juego**, children at play. **Juego duro**, rough play. **Juego de bolos**, nine pins. **Juego de destreza**, game of skill. **Juego de palabras**, a pun, a quibble. **Juegos de palabras**, word games. 2. Game, gaming, gambling (apuestas). **Juego de suerte y ventura**, game of hazard or chance. 3. A set of good cards. 4. Manner of acting of an engine. 5. Set, a number of things suited to each other; or a number of things of which one cannot conveniently be separated from the rest (conjunto). **Juego de mesa**, dinner service. **Juego de café**, coffee set. 6. Disposition, ability, or artfulness to obtain or prevent any end or object. 7. Method, convenient order. 8. Running gear of a vehicle. 9. Play (luces). 10. *(Fig.)* Game. **Le conozco el juego**, I know his little game. **Juego de manos**, juggling feat, legerdemain. **Juego de pelota**, pelota game. **Juego de niños**, play-game. **Entrar en juego**, to come into play. **Hacer juego**, to match, to suit, to fit. **El juego es un vicio**, gambling is a vice. **Seguirle el juego a alguien**, to play along with somebody. **El juego de los colores**, the interplay of the colors. **Juego de caracteres**, *(Comput.)* character set. **Juegos**, *(Comput.)* recreational software. *(Yo juego, yo juegue,* from *Jugar.* V. JUGAR.)

jueguecico, illo, ito [hoo-ay-gay-thee'-co, eel'-lyo, ee'to], *m.* A little game, a bit of play.

juerga [hoo-er'-gah], *f.* *(coll.)* Carousal, revel, spree. **Correr las grandes juergas**, to live it up. **Ir de juerga**, to go on a spree.

juerguista [hoo-er-gees-tah], *m & f.* Reveller.

jueves [hoo-ay'-ves], *m.* Thursday. **Jueves Santo**, Maundy Thursday.

juez [hoo-eth'], *m & f.* 1. Judge, one invested with power and authority to decide and determine causes and law-suits. 2. Judge, one who has sufficient skill to form a correct opinion or judgment of the merit of anything. **Juez árbitro**, arbitrator, umpire. **Juez de letras** or **juez letrado**, a justice of the peace of a small district, who, being a counsellor at law, has more authority in certain cases than other justices. **Juez de primera instancia**, judge of the primary court of claims. **Juez de línea**, linesman. **Juez de salida**, starter.

jugada [hoo-gah'-dah], *f.* 1. Play, the act of playing, a throw (echada). 2. The act of playing a card. 3. Ill turn, dirty trick. **Una bonita jugada**, a pretty piece. **Hacer una jugada**, to make a move.

jugadera [hoo-gah-day'-rah], *f.* Shuttle used to make network. V. LANZADERA.

jugador, ra [hoo-gah-dor', rah], *m. & f.* 1. Player, one who plays. 2. Gamester, gambler (de apuestas). **Jugador de manos**, juggler, one who practices sleight of hand, or plays tricks by legerdemain. **Jugador de bolsa**, speculator, gambler on the stock exchange. **Jugador de fútbol**, footballer.

jugano [hoo-gah'-no], *m. (Ec.)* A solid wood of Guayaquil employed in ship-building.

jugar [hoo-gar'], *va. & vn.* 1. To play, to sport, to frolic, to trifle, to toy. 2. To play, to game, to contend at some game. 3. To gamble (apostar), to game, to play extravagantly for money, to lose at play. 4. To put in action or motion; speaking of a part of the body. 5. To make use of weapons (armas). 6. To move on joints or hinges. 7. To intervene; to take an active part in an affair, to exercise. 8. To mock, to make gone of. **Jugar 5 dólares a una carta**, to stake 5 dollars on a card. **Jugar al tenis**, to play tennis. **La niña juega a ser madre**, the little girl plays at being mother. **Solamente está jugando contigo**, he's just trifling with you. *-vr.* 1. To gamble, to risk. **Se jugó 200 dólares**, he staked 200 dollars. 2. **Jugársela**, to be unfaithful.

jugarreta [hoo-gar-ray'-tah], *f.* 1. *(coll.)* Bad play, unskillful manner of playing. 2. Bad trick (trampa). **Hacer una jugarreta a uno**, to play a dirty trick on somebody.

juglándeo, dea [hoo-glahn'-day-o, ah], *a.* Belonging to the walnut family.

juglar [hoo-goo-lar'], *m.* Buffoon, mimic, juggler, mountebank.

juglar [hoo-glar'], *m.* Minstreel, jongleur; juggler, tumbler, entertainer.

juglara, juglaresa [hoo-glah'-rah, hoo-glah-ray'-sah], *f.* A female buffoon or mimic.

jugo [hoo'-go], *m.* 1. Sap, juice of plants. 2. Juice, moisture. 3. *(Met.)* Marrow, pith, substance of anything. **Jugo de naranja**, orange juice. **Jugos digestivos**, digestive juices.

jugosidad [hoo-go-se-dahd'], *f.* Sappiness, succulence, juiciness (suculencia).

jugoso, sa [hoo-go'-so, sah], *a.* 1. Sappy, juicy (suculento), succulent. 2. *(Fig.)* Substantial, pithy; meaty, full of good stuff, full of solid sense; profitable (rentable).

juguete [hoo-gay'-tay], *m.* 1. Toy (de niño), plaything, gewgaw, trinket. **Un coche de juguete**, a toy car. 2. Jest, joke (chiste). 3. Carol, a song of joy and exultation.

juguetear [hoo-gay-tay-ar'], *vn.* To trifle, to fool, to toy, to frolic, to sport, to dally, to wanton, to play childish tricks.

juguetón, na [hoo-gay-tone', nah], *a.* Playful, acting the buffoon, wanton, playsome.

juicio [hoo-ee'-the-o], *m.* 1. Judgment (facultad), the power of judging; the act of judging. 2. Sense (sentido), soundness of faculties, strength of natural reason. 3. Judgement, notion, opinion (opinión). 4. Prudence, wisdom (práctica). 5. Judgment, the act of exercising judicature (veredicto). 6. Forecast of the events of a year made by astrologers. **Pedir en juicio**, to sue at law. **No estar en su juicio**, to be out of one's senses. **Tener mucho juicio**, to be sedate, steady, well-behaved. **No tener juicio**, to be wild; to be a harum-scarum fellow. **Sano de juicio**, *(Law.)* perfectly sound in mind. **Lo dejo a su juicio**, I leave it to your discretion. **Estar fuera de juicio**, to be out of one's mind.

juiciosamente [hoo-e-the-o-sah-men'-tay], *adv.* Judiciously, considerately.

juicioso, sa [hoo-e-the-o'-so, sah], *a.* Judicious, prudent, mature, clear-sighted.

julepe [hoo-lay'-pay], *m.* 1. Julep, a sirup-like medical potion. 2. *(Fig. and Boll.)* Reprimand, punishment. 2. *(LAm.)* Scare, fright (susto). 4. *(Carib. Mex.)* Bind (trabajo).

juliano, na [hoo-le-ah'-no, nah], *a.* Julian, relating to Julius Caesar, or instituted by him.

julio [hoo'-lee-o], *m.* July, the seventh month of the year.

julo [hoo'-lo], *m.* 1. Bell-mule, that takes the lead of a sumpter's or carrier's mules. 2. Male which guides the flocks of goats, sheep, or cattle. 3. Iulus, a myriapod.

jumá [hoo-mah'], *m.* Mohammedan name of Friday (*i. e.*, day of assembly).

jumenta [hoo-men'-tah], *f.* Female ass.

jumental, or jumentil [hoo-men-tahl', teel'], *a.* Belonging to the ass.

jumentillo, illa, ito, ita [hoo-men-teel'-lyo, lyah, ee'-to, tah], *m. & f. dim.* A little ass or beast of burden.

jumento [hoo-men'-to], *m.* 1. Beast of burden. 2. Ass, jument. 3. A stupid person. V. ASNO.

juncada [hoon-cah'-dah], *f.* 1. Kind of fritters. 2. A horse medicine against the glanders.

juncago [hoon-cah'-go], *m.* *(Bot.)* Bastard rush.

juncal, juncar [hoon-cahl'], *m.* Marshy ground full of rushes.

júnceo, a [hoon'-thay-o, ah], *a.* Rush-like.*-f. pl.* The rush family.

juncia [hoon'-the-ah], *f.* *(Bot.)* Cyperus, a sedge, the root of which serves for fumigation. **Juncia olorosa**, sweet cyperus, English galangal. **Juncia avellanada or redonda**, round-rooted cyperus, the round cyperus. **Juncia comestible**. V. CHUFAS.

junciana [hoon-the-ah'-nah], *f.* Brag, boast.

junciera [hoon-the-ay'-rah], *f.* An earthen vessel with a perforated lid, in which aromatics are kept.

juncino, na [hoon-thee'-no, nah], *a.* Rushy, consisting of rushes.

junco [hoon'-co], *m.* 1. *(Bot.)* Rush. **Junco de esteras**, soft rush. **Junco de flor or florido**, umbelled flowering rush. 2. Junk, Chinese ship.

juncoso, sa [hoon-co'-so, sah], *a.* 1. Full of rushes, resembling rushes; juncous. 2. Covered in rushes (lugar).

jungla [hoon'-glah], *f.* Jungle.

junio [hoo'-ne-o], *m.* June, the sixth month of the year.

junior [hoo'-ne-or], *m.* Novice (monje). -*m & f. (Dep.)* Junior (el más joven).

junípero [hoo-ne'-pay-ro], *m. V.* ENEBRO.

junquera [hoon-kay'-rah], *f. (Bot.)* Rush.

junqueral [hoon-kay-rahl'], *m. V.* JUNCAL.

junquillo [hoon-keel'-lyo], *m.* 1. *(Bot.)* Jonquil. 2. A small round moulding.

junta [hoon'-tah], *f.* 1. Junta or junto, a congress, an assembly, a council (consejo), a convention, tribunal. 2. Any meeting of persons to speak about business (asamblea). 3. Conjunction, union, junction (punto de unión), concession, fraternity. 4. Each lateral surface of a square hewed stone. 5. Joint; coupling (acoplamiento). **Junta de médicos**, a consultation. **Junta de comercio**, board of trade. **Junta de sanidad**, board of health. **Junta directiva**, board of management. **Junta de portavoces**, *(Parl.)* House business committee.

juntador, ra [hoon-tah-dor', rah], *pl. & f.* Joiner, one who joins.

juntamente [hoon-tah-men-tay], *adv.* Jointly; at, the same time, conjunctively.

juntar [hoon-tar'], *va.* 1. To join (unir), to conjoin, to combine, to coalesce, to connect, to unite. 2. To join, to convoke to couple; to associate, to consociate, to congregate. 3. To amass, to collect, to heap, to gather, to lay up.-*vr.* 1. To join, to meet, to assemble (montar), to concur. 2. To be closely united. 3. To copulate. -*vr.* 1. To join (unirse), to come together; to meet (gente), to assemble, to gather. 2. *(Zool.)* To mate, to copulate. 3. To live together (personas).

juntera [hoon-tay'-rah], *f.* Carpenter's plane, jointer.

junterilla [hoon-tay-reel'-lyah], *f. dim.* Small plane.

junto, ta [hoon'-to, tah], *a. & pp. irr.* Of JUNTAR. United, conjoined, anexed. **Fuimos juntos**, we went together. **Vivir juntos**, to live together.

junto [hoon'-to], *adv.* Near, close to, at hand, near at hand, at the same time. **Por junto** or **de por junto**, in the bulk, by the lump, wholesale. **En junto**, together, in all. **Demasiado junto**, too close.

juntura [hoon-too'-rah], *f.* 1. Juncture, the part at which two things are joined together, joining. 2. Joint, articulation of limbs, juncture of movable bones in animal bodies. 3. *(Naut.)* Scarf.

Júpiter [hoo'-pe-ter], *m.* 1. Jupiter, a planet. 2. Among chemists, tin.

jura [hoo'-rah], *f.* 1. Oath, an affirmation, negation, or promise, corroborated by the attestation of the Divine Being. 2. Oath of allegiance. **Jura de bandera**, oath of loyalty. -*m. (CAm. Carib.)* Cop.

jurado [hoo-rah'-do], *m.* 1. Jury (cuerpo), a certain number of persons sworn to declare the truth upon such evidence as shall be given before them. 2. Juror (persona), juryman, one serving in a jury. 3. Jurat, a magistrate in some corporations.

jurador, ra [hoo-rah-dor', rah], *m. & f.* Swearer, profane swearer.

juraduría [hoo-rah-doo-ree'-ah], *f.* Office of a jurat.

juramentar [hoo-rah-men-tar'], *va.* To swear, to put to an oath. -*vr.* To bind oneself by an oath, to obtest by an oath.

juramento [hoo-rah-men'-to], *m.* 1. Oath, an affirmation, negation, or promise, corroborated by the attestation of the Divine Being. 2. Oath, curse, imprecation: commonly used in the plural in this last sense. **Bajo juramento**, on oath. **Prestar juramento**, to take the oath. **Decir juramentos a uno**, to swear at somebody.

jurar [hoo-rar'], *va.* To obtest some superior power; to attest the great name; to promise upon oath; to swear,

to make oath. **Jurar decir la verdad**, to swear to tell the truth. **Jurar como un carretero**, to swear like a trooper.

jurásico, ca [hoo-rah'-se-co, cah], *a.* Jurassic, relating to the mountains of Jura.

juratoria [hoo-rah-to'-re-ah], *f. (Prov.)* Plate of silver containing the holy evangelists, on which magistrates lay their hands in taking an oath.

jurdía [hoor-dee'-ah], *f.* Kind of fishing net.

jurel [hoo-rel'], *m.* A spiny sea-fish of the mackerel family.

jurguina, or **jurgina** [hoor-gee'-nah, hoor-hee'-nah], *f.* Witch, sorceress.

jurídicamente [hoo-ree'-de-cah-men'-tay], *adv.* Lawfully, legally, juridically.

jurídico, ca [hoo-ree'-de-co, cah], *a.* Lawful, legal, juridical; done according to law.

jurisconsulto [hoo-ris-con-sool'-to], *m.* 1. Jurisconsult, one who gives his opinion in law. 2. Civilian, civilist. 3. Jurist, a lawyer.

jurisdicción [hoo-ris-dic-the-on'], *f.* 1. Jurisdiction, legal authority, extent of judicial power, power, authority. 2. Jurisdiction, district to which any judicial authority extends (distrito). 3. Boundary of some place or province.

jurisdiccional [hoo-ris-dic-the-o-nahl'], *a.* Jurisdictional, relating to jurisdiction.

jurisperito, ta [hoo-ris-pay-ree'-to], *m.* A professor of jurisprudence.

jurisprudencia [hoo-ris-proo-den'-the-ah], *f.* Jurisprudence, law, or the science of law.

jurisprudente [hoo-ris-proo-den'-tay], *m. V.* JURISCONSULTO.

jurista [hoo-rees'-tah], *m.* 1. Jurist, lawyer, a man who professes the science of law. 2. Pensioner, one who has an annuity assigned to him upon the revenue of the crown.

juro [hoo'-ro], *m.* 1. Right of perpetual property (derecho). 2. Annuity assigned upon the revenue of the crown. **De juro**, certainly.

jusbarba [hoos-bar'-bah], *f. (Bot.)* Field myrtle.

jusello [hoo-sel'-lyo], *m.* Pottage made of broth, parsley, grated cheese, egg, and toast.

jusi [hog'-se], *m.* A delicate vegetable fiber of the Philippine Islands used for dresses.

justa [hoos'-tah], *f.* 1. Joust, tilt, tournament. 2. Literary contest in poetry or prose.

justador [hoos-tah-dor'], *m.* Titter, one who pays at jousts.

justamente [hoos-tah-men'-tay], *adv.* Justly (con justicia), just (precisamente), exactly; precisely, fairly. **De eso se trata justamente**, that's just the point. **Son justamente las que no están en venta**, they are precisely the ones which are not for sale.

justar [hoos-tar'], *vn.* To joust, to tilt.

justicia [hoos-tee'-the-ah], *f.* 1. Justice, giving to every man his due. 2. Justice, the attribute of God according to which he arranges all things. 3. Reason, honesty; equity; right (derecho). 4. Retribution, punishment.-*m.* Justice, magistrate or tribunal. **Hacer justicia a**, to do justice to. **Tomarse la justicia por su mano**, to take the law into one's own hands.

justiciero, ra [hoos-te-the-ay'-ro, rah], *a.* One who rigorously observes justice; one who chastises crimes with rigid justice.

justificable [hoos-te-fe-cah'-blay], *a.* Justifiable.

justificación [hoos-te-fe-cah-the-on'], *f.* 1. Justification, defence, maintenance, support. 2. Production of the documents or instruments tending to establish a claim or right. 3. Equity, conformity with justice. 4.

Sanctification by grace. 5. *(Print.)* Adjustment of lines in a page of types.

justificadamente [hoos-te-fe-cah-dah-men'-tay], *adv.* Justly, correctly, justifiably.

justificado, da [hoos-te-fe-cah'-do, dah], *a.* Equal, justified, conformable to justice.-*pp.* of JUSTIFICAR.

justificador [hoos-te-fe-cah-dor'], *m.* Justifier, justificator. *V.* SANTIFICADOR.

justificante [hoos-te-fe-cahn'-tay], *pa.* Justifying; justifier.

justificar [hoos-te-fe-car'], *va.* 1. To justify, to free from past sin, to render just. 2. To justify, to clear from imputed guilt (sospechoso); to absolve from an accusation; to exculpate. 3. To prove or establish a claim in a court of judicature. 4. To prove or show by argument or testimony. 5. To justify, to rectify, to adjust, to arrange, to regulate exactly. 6. *(Print.)* To justify or equalize the spaces between the words in a line of types. -*vr.* To vindicate one's character, to clear oneself from imputed guilt.

justificativo, va [hoos-te-fe-cah-tee'-vo, vah], *a.* Justificative, justifying, justificatory.

justillo [hoos-teel'-lyo], *m.* Jacket without sleeves; inner waist of a dress; corset-cover.

justipreciar [hoos-te-pray-the-ar'], *va.* To estimate anything.

justipreciador [hoos-te-pray-the-ah-dor'], *m.* A praiser, a person appointed to set a price upon things.

justiprecio [hoos-te-pray'-the-o], *m.* Appraisement, just valuation.

justo, ta [hoos'-to, tah], *a.* 1. Just (correcto), conformable to justice, rightful, lawful; fair. **Una decisión justa**, a just decision. 2. Just, upright. 3. Just, honest, honorable, good, faithful. 4. Just, exact (exacto), strict, punctual. 5. Just, fit, tight (ropa), close, exactly proportioned. **El traje me viene muy justo**, the suit is rather tight for me. 6. Just, good, pious.

justo [hoos'-to], *m.* A just and pious man.

justo [hoos'-to], *adv.* 1. Tightly (con dificultad), straitly. **Vivir muy justo**, to be hard up. 2. Right, just (exactamente). **Vino justo a tiempo**, he came just in time.

juta [hoo'-tah], *f. (Orn.)* A kind of American goose.

jutía [hoo-tee'-ah], *f. V.* HUTÍA.

juvenil [hoo-vay-neel'], *a.* Juvenile, young, youthful; girlish. **Equipo juvenil**, youth team. **En los años juveniles**, in one's early years.

juventud [hoo-ven-tood'], *f.* Youthfulness, youth (época), juvenility, young people (jóvenes). **La juventud de hoy**, young people today.

juzgado [hooth-gah'-do], *m.* Tribunal, court of justice; judicature.

juzgador, ra [hooth-gah-dor', rah], *m. & f.* Judge, one who judges.

juzgamundo [hooth-gah-moon'-do.], *m. & f.* One who censures the actions of everyone but himself.

juzgante [hooth-gahn'-tay], *pa.* Judging; judge.

juzgar [hooth'-gar'], *va & vn.* 1. To judge, to pass sentence upon, to give judgment. 2. To judge, to apprehend, to form or give an opinion, to opine, to hold. **Juzgar mal**, to misjudge. **A juzgar según lo que hemos visto**, to judge by what we have seen.

K

k The eleventh letter of the alphabet, and eighth of the consonants. It has little use in Spanish except in words taken from other languages. It has the same sound as in English. **K** in chemistry is the symbol of potassium. *(Kalium.)*

ka [kah], *f.* Name of the letter K.

kabila [kah-bee'-lah], *f.* A tribe of Barbary, living in the Atlas region.

kahué [ka-hoo-ay'], *m.* Arabic name of coffee.

Káiser [kah'-e-ser], *m.* Kaiser.

kaki or **caqui** [kah'-ke], *a.* Khaki.

kaleidoscopio [ka-lay-e-dos-co'-pay-o], *m. V.* CALIDOSCOPIO.

kalenda [ka-len'-dah], *f.* Kalends. *V.* CALENDA.

kalmuco, ca [kal-moo'-co, cah], *a. & n.* Kalmuck, a race of Western Mongols. *V.* CALMUCO.

kamikaze [ka-me-kah'-they], *m.* Kamikaze.

kan [kahn], or **khan**, *m.* Khan, chief or prince among the Tartars.

kanna [kahn'-nah], *f.* Canna, a root very esteemed by the Hottentots as the best of stomachics. It resembles ginseng.

kantiano, na [kan-te-ah'-no, nah], *a.* Kantian, relating to the philosophy of Kant.

kantismo [kan-tees'-mo], *m.* Kantism, the philosophic system of Kant.

kárate [kah'-rah-tay], *m.* Karate.

keralila [kay-rah-lee'-lah], *f. (Mex.)* Horny flint.

kermes [kerr'-mes], *m.* 1. *V.* QUÉRMES. Kermes mineral, an impure antimony sulphide.

kg. abr de **Kilogramo**.

kilo [kee'-lo], *m.* A prefix from the Greek signifying a thousandfold. -*m. (Com.)* Kilogram, an abbreviation.

kilociclo [ke-lo-thee'-clo], *m.* Kilocycle.

kilográmetro [ke-lo-grah'-may-tro], *m.* Kilogrammeter, the unit of force required to raise a kilogram one meter in one second (7.2 foot-pounds).

kilogramo [ke-lo-grah'-mo], *m.* Kilogram, a metric unit of weight, 1,000 gram (2 1/5 lbs.).

kilolitro [ke-lo-lee'-tro], *m.* Kiloliter, the measure of 1,000 liters.

kilometraje [ke-lo-may-trah'-hay], *m.* Length or distance in kilometers, mileage.

kilométrico, ca [ke-lo-may'-tre-co, cah], *a.* Kilometric. **Discurso kilométrico**, long-winded speech.

kilómetro [ke-lo'-may-tro], *m.* Kilometer, the distance of 1,000 meters chief unit of long distance in the metric system; about five-eighths of a mile. A Spanish league slightly exceeds five and a half kilometers.

kilotón [ke-lo-ton'], *m.* or **Kilotonelada** [ke-lo-to-nay-lah'-da], *f.* Kiloton.

kilovatio [ke-lo-vah'-te-o], Kilowatt.

kilovoltamperio [ke-lo-vol-tam-pay'-re-o], *m.* Kilovoltampere.

kilovoltio [ke-lo-vol'-te-o], *m.* Kilovolt.

kinoscopio [ke-nos-co'-pe-o], *m.* Kinescope.

kiosco [ke-os'-co], *m.* 1. Kiosk, an open, small pavilion, designed, according to the custom of Orientals; for taking refreshment in the middle of the day. 2. Kiosk, a news-stand, etc., in imitation of the foregoing.

kirie [kee'-re-ay], *m.* Kyrie, the first movement in the mass, after the introit.

kirieleisón [ke-re-ay-lay-e-sone'], *m.* 1. *V.* KIRIE. 2. *(coll.)* Funeral chant.

kiwi [kee'-wee], *m.* Kiwi (fruta).

kirsch [keerch], *m.* Kirschwasser, a cordial distilled from the European wild cherry.

kopú [ko-poo'], *m.* A Chinese fabric.

krausismo [kra-hoo-sees'-mo], *m.* Krausism, the philosophic system of Krause.

Kremlin [krem'-leen], *m.* A Slavic word which signifies fortress. In particular the citadel of this name in Moscow.

kurdo, da [coor'-do, dah], *a.* Kurdish, or Kurd; native of or belonging to Kurdistan.

l

L

l [ay'-lay], L (letra). The *l* always keeps the same sound as in English. **L** as a numeral stands for fifty.

la [lah], *def. art. fem. sing.* The. **La cabeza,** the head. **La casa,** the house.

la [lah], *pron. pers. acc. f. sing.* Her (persona). **Yo la vi ayer,** I saw her yesterday. It (objeto). **La leí el domingo,** I read it on Sunday.

la [lah], *pron. dem.* **Mi casa y la de Vd,** my house and yours. **La de Pedro es mejor,** Peter´s is better. **La de Juan,** John's. **Ir a la de Pepe,** to go to Pepe´s place.

La [lah], *m. (Mus.)* La, the sixth, sound of the hexachord.

L.A.B., Abbreviation of **Libre a bordo.** F.O.B. free on board.

laberinto [lah-bay-reen'-to], *m.* 1. Labyrinth, maze. 2. An intricate and obscure matter, hard to be understood; maze, uncertainty, perplexity. 3. *(Anat.)* Labyrinth of the ear. 4. *(LAm.)* Row, racket (griterío).

labia [lah'-be-ah], *f. (coll.)* Sweet, winning eloquence. **Tener mucha labia,** to have the gift of the gab.

labiado, da [lah-be-ah'-do, dah], *a. (Bot.)* Labiate.

labial [lah-be-ahl'], *a.* Labial, uttered by the lips.

labiérnago [lah-be-ayr'-nah-go], *m.* A shrub with lanceolate, shining leaves.

labihendido, da [lah-be-en-dee'-do, dah], *a.* Harelipped.

labio [lah'-be-o], *m.* I. The lip. 2. Lip, the edge of anything. **Labio hendido,** hare-lip. **Labio inferior,** lower lip. **No morderse los labios,** to be outspoken. **Sin despegar los labios,** without uttering a word.

labiodental [lah-be-o-den-tahl'], *a.* Labiodental.

labionasal [lah-be-o-nah-sahl'], *a.* Labionasal.

labor [lah-bor'], *f.* 1. Labor (trabajo), task, the act of doing what requires an exertion of strength. 2. Labor, work to be done, work done. 3. Symmetry, adaptation of parts to each other; design. 4. A seamstress´s work, any kind of needlework, embroidery (bordado). 5. A thousand tiles or bricks. 6. Cultivation, husbandry, tillage, ploughing (arada). V. LABRANZA. 7. *(Prov.)* Egg of a silkworm. 8. *(Amer.)* The works of a mine. **Campo de labor,** a cultivated field. **Sus labores,** housewife. **Labor de equipo,** teamwork. **Una labor,** a piece of needlework. **Labor de ganchillo,** crochet.

laborable [lah-bo-rah'-blay], *a.* Tillable (cultivable), working (día), work. **Día laborable,** working day.

laborador [lah-bo-rah-dor'], *m.* V. TRABAJADOR and LABRADOR.

laboral [lah-bo-rahl'], *a.* Labor; technical.

laborar [lah-bo-rar'], *pa.* To work, to till.-*vn.* To scheme, to plot.

laborativo, va [lah-bo-rah-tee'-vo, vah]. **Día laborativo,** *(Com.)* clear day.

laboratorio [lah-bo-rah-to'-re-o], *m.* Laboratory, a chemist's work-room.

laborcica, illa, ita [lah-bor-thee'-cah], *f. dim.* 1. An insignificant work or task. 2. Pretty needle-work.

laborear [lab-bo-ray-ar'], *va.* 1. To cultivate, to till the ground. 2. *(Naut.)* To work a ship, to direct her movements. V. MANIOBRAR.

laboreo [lah-bo-ray'-o], *m.* 1. *(Prov.)* Culture, labor. 2. The working of mines. 3. *(And. Cono Sur)* Foreman (capataz).

laboriosamente [lah-bo-re-o-sah-men'-tay], *adv.* Laboriously, painfully.

laboriosidad [lah-bo-re-o-se-dahd'], *f.* Laboriousness (pesadez), industry (trabajo), assiduity.

laborioso, sa [lah-bo-re-o´-so, sah], *a.* 1. Laborious, assiduous, industrious. 2. Laborious, requiring much toil and labor; tiresome, painful.

labra [lah'-brah], *f.* 1. The action of working or chiselling stone. 2. Carving, or other work given to materials before placing them, especially if rough stone.

labrada [lah-brah'-dah], *f.* Land ploughed and fallowed to be sown.

labradero, ra [lah-brah-day'-ro, rah], *a.* Suited to labor, capable of labor.

labradío, día [lah-brah-dee'-o, ah], *a.* V. LABRANTÍO.

labrado, da [lah-brah'-do, dah], *a.* Worked (tela), wrought (metal), carved (madera). *-pp.* of LABRAR.

labrado [lah-brah'-do], *m.* Land cultivated: commonly used in the plural.

labrador, ra [lah-brah-dor', rah], *a.* Industrious, laborious, fit for work.-*m. & f.* 1. Laborer, one who works at the plough or spade. 2. Cultivator, farmer (granjero), a husbandman or woman. 3. Rustic, peasant (campesino).

labradoresco, ca [lah-brah-do-ress'-co, cah], *a.* Belonging or relating to a laborer: rustic, clownish.

labradorita [lah-brah-do-ree'-tah], *f. (Min.)* Labradorite.

labrandera [lah-bran-day´-rah], *f.* Seamstress, embroiderer.

labrante [lah-brahn'-tay], *m.* Stone-cutter, sculptor.

labrantín [lah-bran-teen'], *m.* A petty farmer, who cultivates a small farm.

labrantío, tía [lah-bran-tee'-o, ah], *a.* Producing grain: applied to arable land fit for the culture of grain.

labranza [lah-brahn'-thah], *f.* 1. Tillage, the cultivation of the ground, ploughing, farming (cultivo). 2. Husbandry, the employment of a cultivator or farmer. 3. Farm (granja), land let to a tenant; tilled land; an estate applied to the purposes and pursuits of agriculture.

labrar [lah-brar'], *va.* 1. To work (metales), to labor. 2. To till, to cultivate (tierra). V. ARAR. 3. To build, to construct buildings. 4. To do needlework, to embroider (tela). 5. To inform, to instruct. 6. To finish, to polish to the degree of excellence intended or required. 7. To make designs in fabrics, stones, arms, etc. 8. To carve (madera). 9. To plow (tierras). *-vn.* To make a strong impression on the mind.

labrero, ra [lah-bray'-ro, rah], *a.* Applied to a kind of fishing net.

labriego, ga [lah-bre-ay'-go], *m & f.* Peasant.

labro [lah'-bro], *m.* The upper lip, labrum, of the mouth of animals.

labrusca [lah-broos'-cah], *f.* A wild grape-vine.

laburno [lah-boor'-no], *m. (Bot.)* Laburnum.

laca [lah'-cah], *f.* 1. Lac, or gumlac, a red, brittle, resinous substance, brought from India, and used for dyeing and making sealing wax. 2. Red color, lake (color), a pigment; *e.g.* madder lake. 3. Lacquer (barniz), a kind of varnish. *(Per.)* **Laca de uñas,** nail polish. **Laca para el pelo,** hair spray.

lacar [lah-car'], *va.* To lacquer.

lacayo [lah-cah'-yo], *m.* 1. Lackey, footman, servant, foot boy. 2. Knot of ribbons worn by women.

lacayuelo [lah-cah-yoo-ay´-lo], *m. dim.* Foot-boy.

lacayuno, na [lah-cah-yoo'-no, nah], *a.* Belonging to a lackey or foot-boy.

lacear [lah-thay-ar´], *va.* 1. To adorn with ribbons tied in bows (adornar); to lace. 2. To pin up the game or drive it into an appointed place. 3. (Cono Sur) To whip (zurrar). 4. To snare, to trap (coger); to beat (ojear), to drive.

lacedemónico, ca [lah-thay-day-mo'-ne-co, cah], or **lacedemonio, a** [lah-thay-day-mo'-ne-o, ah], *a.* Lacedemonian, relating to Lacedemonia.

laceración [lah-thay-rah-the-on'], *f.* Laceration, lancination, tearing.

lacerado, da [lah-thay-rah'-do, dah], *a.* 1. Unfortunate, unhappy. 2. Leprous.-*pp.* of LACERAR.

lacerar [lah-thay-rar'], *va.* To mangle, to tear to pieces, to lacerate.

lacería [lah-thay'-re-ah], *f.* 1. Misery, poverty (pobreza), wretchedness. 2. Labor, fatigue, trouble, distress (sufrimiento).

lacería [la-thay-ree´-ah], *f.* A set of nets.

lacerioso, sa [lah-thay-re-o´-so, sah], *a.* Miserable: scrofulous.

lacha [lah´-chah], *f. V.* HALECHE.

lacinia [lah-thee´-ne-ah], *f. (Bot.)* 1. Lacinia, a narrow, deep, slender lobe. 2. The fringe of a Roman toga.

laciniado, da [lah-the-ne-ah´-do, dah], *a. (Bot.)* Laciniate, slashed irregularly.

lacio, cia [lah´-the-o, ah], *a.* Faded, withered, dried up; flaccid, languid.

lacónicamente [lah-co´-ne-cah-men´-tay], *adv.* Laconically, concisely.

lacónico, ca [lah-co´-ne-co, cah], *a.* Laconic, brief, concise.

laconismo [lah-co-nees´-mo], *m.* Laconism, conciseness, brevity, concise expression or style.

lacra [lah´-crah], *f.* 1. Mark left by some wound or disorder; *(LAm.)* sore (llaga). 2. Fault, vice, wickedness. **La prostitución es una lacra social**, prostitution is a blot on society.

lacrar [lah-crar´], *va.* 1. To injure or impair the health. 2. To hurt or injure in point of property or money. 3. To seal with sealing wax.

lacre [lah´-cray], *m.* Sealing wax.

lacrimal [lah-cre-mahl´], *a.* Lachrymal.

lacrimatorio, ria [lah-cre-mah-to´-re-o-ah], *a. & m. & f.* Lachrymatory.

lacrimógeno [lah-cre-mo´-hay-no], *a.* Tear-producing. **Bomba lacrimógena**, tear bomb.

lacrimoso, sa [lah-cre-mo´-so, sah], *a.* Weeping, shedding tears, lachrymose.

lacris [lah´-cris], *m.* Fruit of rose-mary.

lactación [lac-tah-the-on´], *f.* Lactation, the act of suckling.

lactancia [lac-tahn´-the-ah], *f.* Lactation, the act or time of giving suck.

lactante [lac-tahn´-tay], *m.* Sucker, one who sucks milk.

lactar [lac-tar´], *va.* To suckle, to give suck, to feed on milk.

lactario, ria [lac-tah´-re-o, ah], *a.* Lactary, lacteous, lactescent.

lactato [lac-tah´-to], *m. (Chem.)* Lactate.

lácteo, tea [lac´-tay-o, ah], *a.* Lacteous, milky, lacteal, lactean, lactescent. **Vía láctea**, *(Ast.)* galaxy, the milky way.

lactescente [lac-tes-then´-tay], *a.* Lactescent, having a milky juice.

lacticinio [lac-te-thee´-ne-o], *m.* Milk-pottage, and, in general, all sorts of food prepared with milk.

lacticinoso, sa [lac-te-the-no´-so, sah], *a. V.* LÁCTEO.

láctico, ca [lahc´-te-co, cah], *a.* Lactic, relating to milk.

lactífago, ga [lac-tee´-fah-go, gah], *a.* Feeding upon milk, galactophagous.

lactífico, ca [lac-tee´-fe-co, cah], *a.* Lactific, yielding milk.

lactífero, ra [lac-tee´-fay-ro, rah], *a.* Lactiforous, lacteal, milky.

lactómetro [lac-to´-may-tro], *m.* Lactometer, a hydrometer for determining the density of milk.

lactosa [lac-to´-sah], *f.* Lactose, milk sugar.

lactumen [lac-too´-men], *m.* Scab breaking out on the head of sucking children.

lacustre [lah-coos´-tray], *a.* Marshy, belonging to lakes.

lada [lah´-dah], *f. V.* JARA.

ládano [lah´-da-no], *m.* Labdanun, a resin which exudes from a shrub.

ladeado, da [lah-day-ah´-do, dah], *a. & pp.* of LADEAR. 1. Turned to one side, inclined, lopsided (inclinado). 2. *(Cono Sur)* Slovenly (descuidado). 3. *(Cono Sur)* **Andar ladeado**, to be in a bad temper.

ladeamiento [lah-day-ah-me-en´-to], *m. V.* LADEO.

ladear [lah-day-ar´], *va.* To move or turn to one side; to go side by side; to go along rails.-*vn.* 1. *(Naut.)* To incline: applied to the needle of the mariner's compass. 2. To go by the side, to incline to one side. 3. To tilt (inclinarse). 4. To turn aside (apartarse). -*vr.* 1. To incline toward an opinion or party. 2. To lean, to incline (inclinarse). 3. *(Cono Sur)* To fall in love (enamorarse).

ladeo [lah-day´-o], *m.* Inclination or motion to one side.

ladera [lah-day´-rah], *f.* Declivity, gradual descent. -*pl.* 1. Rails or staves of a common cart. 2. Cheeks of a gun-carriage.

laderica, illa, ita [lah-day-ree´-cah, eel´-lyah, ee´tah], *f. dim.* A small declivity of the ground.

ladierno [lah-de-err´-no], *m. (Bot.)* Buckthorn.

ladilla [lah-deel´-lyah], *f.* 1. Crab-louse. 2. *(Bot.)* Common barley.

ladinamente [lah-de-nah-men´-tay], *adv.* Sidewise, artfully, sagaciously.

ladino, na [lah-dee´-no, nah], *a.* 1. Sagacious, cunning (taimado), crafty. 2. *(LAm.)* Smooth-tongued (adulador). 3. *(Mex.)* High-pitched (voz).

lado [lah´-do], *m.* 1. Side, that part of the human body which extends from the armpit to the hipbone. 2. Side or half of an animal. 3. Side, the right or left. 4. Side, part of any body opposed to another part. 5. Side, any part placed in contradistinction or opposition to another. 6. Side, the margin, edge, or verge of anything. 7. *(Met.)* Side, party, faction, interest. 8. *(Met.)* Companion, comrade. 9. Mat used to cover carts, etc. 10. *(Met.)* Patron, protector. 11. Course, manner; mode of proceeding. 12. Side: it is used to note consanguinity. **Al lado**, just by, at hand, or near at hand. **Lado débil**, weak spot. **Al lado**, near. **Estuvo a mi lado**, she was at my side. **Viven al lado de nosotros**, they live next door to us. **Estar de un lado para otro**, to be up and down. **Por todos lados**, on all sides. **Dejar a un lado**, to skip. **Me da de lado**, I don´t care. **Por el lado de la madre**, on the mother´s side.

ladón [lah-don´], *m. V.* LADA.

ladra [lah´-drah], *f.* 1. Barking. 2. Cry of hounds after the game.

ladrador, ra [lah-drah-dor´, rah], *m. & f.* 1. Barker, one that barks. 2. *(coll.)* Talker, one who talks much and to no purpose.

ladrante [lah-drahn´-tay], *pa.* Barking, latrant; barker.

ladrar [lah-drar´], *vn.* 1. To bark, to howl (perro). 2. To use empty threats. 3. To clamor, to vociferate, to make outcries.

ladrear [lah-dray-ar´], *vn.* To bark often and without object.

ladrería [lah-dray-ree´-ah], *f.* 1. Lazaretto, a hospital for the treatment of lepers. 2. Elephantiasis, or leprosy of the Arabs. 3. *(Vet.)* A certain disease of swine and another of horses. 4. *(And. Carib. Mex.)* Brickworks.

ladrido [lah-dree´-do], *m.* 1. Barking or howling of a dog. 2. Vociferation, outcry; calumny; incitement.

ladrillado [lah-dreel-lyah´-do], *m.* Floor made with bricks, tile floor (azulejos).

ladrillador [lah-dreel-lyah-dor´], *m. V.* ENLADRILLADOR.

ladrillal, ladrillar [lah-dreel-lyahl´, lah-dreellyar´], *m.* Brick-field, brick kiln, a place where bricks are made.

latrillazo [lah-dreel-lyah´-tho], *m.* Blow with a brickbat.

ladrillera [lah-dreel-lyay´-rah], *f.* Brick kiln.

ladrillero [lah-dreel-lyay´-ro], *m.* Brick-maker.

ladrillo [lah-dreel´-lyo], *m.* A brick, tile (azulejo), block (chocolate). **Ladrillo de chocolate**, chocolate cake. **ladrillo de fuego**, fire brick.

ladrilloso, sa [lah-dreel-lyo´-so, sah], *a.* Made of brick.

ladrón, na [lah-drone´, nah], *m. & f.* 1. Thief, robber, highwayman, cut-purse. **Ladrona de corazones**, lady killer. 2. Lock, sluice-gate. 3. Snuff of a candle that makes it melt.

ladronamento [lah-dro-nah-men´-to], *adv.* Thievishly, dissemblingly.

ladroncillo [lah-dron-theel´-lyo], *m. dim.* Of LADRÓN. Petty thief, filcher.

ladronera [lah-dro-nay´-rah], *f.* 1. Nest of rogues, den of robbers. 2. Filching, stealing; defrauding, extortion. 3. Sluice-gate in a mill. 4. Money-box. *V.* ALCANCÍA.

ladronería [lah-dro-nay-ree´-ah], *f. V.* LADRONICIO.

ladronesco, ca [lah-dro-nes´-co, cah], *a. (coll.)* Belonging to thieves.

ladronicio [lah-dro-nee'-the-o], *m.* Larceny, theft, robbery. V. LATROCINIO.

lafría [lah-free'-ah], *f.* A robber-fly.

laga [lah'-gah], *f.* A large black bean of the Orient which serves for weighing gold.

lagaña [lah-gah'-nyah], *f.* A slimy fluid running from the eyes.

lagañoso, ha [lah-gah-nyo'-so, sah], *a.* Bleary-eyed, troubled with running of the eyes.

lagar [lah-gar'], *m.* 1. Place where grapes are pressed. 2. Wine-press (de vino), an engine for squeezing the juice from grapes.

lagarada [lah-gah-rah'-dah], *f.* A wine-pressful; each filling of a winepress.

lagarejo [lah-gah-ray'-ho], *m.* A small wine-press.

lagarero [lah-gah-ray'-ro], *m.* 1. Wine presser, one employed in pressing grapes. 2. One employed in pressing the juice of olives.

lagareta [lah-gah-ray'-tah], *f.* Small wine-press.

lagarta [lah-gar'-tah], *f.* 1. Female lizard. 2. Sly woman (mujer).

lagartado, da [lah-gar-tah'-do, dah], *a.* V. ALAGARTADO.

lagartera [lah-gar-tay'-rah], *f.* Lizard hole, a place under ground where lizards breed.

lagartija [lah-gar-tee'-hah], *f.* Small lizard, eft. **Se mueve más que el rabo de una lagartija,** he has ants in his pants, he's very fidgety.

lagartijero, ra [lah-gar-te-hay'-ro, rah], *a.* Catching efts (animales).

lagartillo [lah-gar-teel'-lyo], *m. dim.* A small lizard.

lagarto [lah-gar'-to], *m.* 1. Lizard; *(LAm.)* Alligator (caimán). 2. A large muscle of the arm. 3. A sly crafty person. 4. *(CAm. Mex.)* Get-rich-quick (codicioso). 5. *(Mex.)* Sharp customer (astuto).

lago [lah'-go], *m.* A lake; a large quantity of any liquid. **Los Grandes Lagos,** the Great Leaks.

lagostín [lah-gos-teen'], *m.* V. LANGOSTÍN.

lagotear [lah-go-tay-ar'], *vn. (coll.)* To flatter, to wheedle, to cajole.

lagotería [lah-go-tay-ree'-ah], *f. (coll.)* Flattery, adulation.

lagotero, ra [lah-go-tay'-ro, rah], *a. (coll.)* Flattering, soothing.

lágrima [lah'-gre-mah], *f.* 1. A tear. 2. Any moisture trickling in drops; a drop or small quantity (gota). 3. *(Hot.)* Graymill, gromwell. 4. Wine extracted from the grape by very slight pressure, in order to have the purest juice. **Lágrimas de S. Pedro,** pebbles, stones thrown at any person. **Lágrimas de cocodrilo,** crocodile tears. **Llorar a lágrima viva,** to sob one's heart out.

lagrimable [lah-gre-mah'-blay], *a.* Lachrymable, lamentable; worthy of tears.

lagrimal [lah-gre-mahl'], *m.* Corner of the eye near the nose.

lagrimar, lagrimear [lah-gre-mar'], *vn.* To weep, to shed tears.

lagrimeo [lah-gre-may'-o], *m.* The act of shedding tears.

lagrimón [lah-gre-mone'], *m. jug.* A large tear.

lagrimoso, sa [lah-gre-mo'-so, sah], *a.* 1. Weeping, shedding tears. 2. Watery; lachrymary.

laguna [lah-goo'-nah], *f.* 1. Pond, lake, a large diffusion of stagnant water marsh, lagoon (de atolón). 2. An uneven country, full of marshes. 3. Blanks in a book or writing (en escritos).

lagunajo [lah-goo-nah'-ho], *m.* Small pool of water in a field after rain.

lagunar [lah-goo-nar'], *m.* Timber-roof.

lagunero, ra [lah-goo-nay'-ro, rah], *a.* Belonging to marshes or lakes.

lagunoso, sa [lah-goo-no'-so, sah], *a.* Marshy, fanny, abounding in lakes; laky.

laical [lah-e-cahl'], *a.* Laical, belonging to the laity or people, as distinct from the clergy.

laicismo [la-he-thees'-mo], *m.* Laicism, exclusion of the clergy from teaching and all positions of the state.

laico, ca [lah'-e-co, cah], *a.* V. LEGO.

lairén [la-he-ren'], *a.* Applied to a kind of grapes, and to the vines which produce them.

laja [lah'-hah], *f.* A shill flat stone.

lama [lah'-mah], *f.* 1. Mud, slime, ooze. 2. *(Prov.)* A flat even country. 3. *(Prov.)* Fine sand used for mortar. 4. Foam on the surface of water. 5. Dust of ores in mines. 6. *(Mex.)* Moss (musgo).

lambel [lam-mel'], *m. (Her.)* Lambel, label, a bar with three pendants.

lambrequines [lam-bray-kee'-nes], *m. pl. (Her.)* Ornaments which hang from helmets.

lambrija [lam-bree'-hah], *f.* 1. Worm bred in the human body. V. LOMBRIZ. 2. *(coll.)* Meager, slender person.

lamedal [lah-may-dahl'], *m.* A musty, miry place.

lamedero [lah-may-day'-ro], *m.* A salt-lick.

lamedor, ra [lah-may-dor', rah], *m. & f.* 1. Licker, one that laps and licks. 2. *(Pharm.)* A kind of syrup. 3. *(Mets.)* Enticement, allurement, wheedling.

lamedura [lah-may-doo'-rah], *f.* Act of licking.

lamelar [lah-may-lar'], *va.* To roll copper into sheets.

lamelibranquio [lah-may-le-brahn'-ke-oh], *a.* Lamellibranchiate, having lamellate gills.

lamelicornios [lah-may-le-cor'-ne-os], *a. & m. pl.* Lamellicorn beetles.

lameliforme [lah-may-le-for'-may], *a.* Lamelliform, in thin layers or plates.

lamentable [lah-men-tah'-blay], *a.* Lamentable, deplorable.

lamentablemente [lah-men-tah-blay-men'-tay], *adv.* Lamentably.

lamentación [lah-men-tah-the-on'], *f.* Lamentation, lamenting, groaning.

lamentador, ra [lah-men-tah-dor', rah], *m. & f.* Lamenter, weeper, mourner, complainer.

lamentar [lah-men-tar'], *va.* To lament (pérdida), to mourn (muerte), to bewail, to moan, to complain (quejarse). *-vn. & vr.* To lament, to grieve, to wail, to complain (quejarse), to cry.

lamento [lah-men'-to], *m.* Lamentation, lament, moan, groaning, mourning, cry.

lamentoso, sah [lah-men-to'-so, sah], *a.* Lamentable, mournful, to be lamented.

lameplatos [lah-may-plah'-tos], *m & f.* 1. Lick-plate, nickname given to the servants who attend at table. 2. *(Mex.)* Toady (adulón); scrounger (parásito); disaster (inútil).

lamer [lah-merr'], *va.* 1. To lick, to pass over with the tongue. 2. To lick, to lap, to take in by the tongue. 3. To touch slightly (rozando).

lamerón, na [lah-may-ro-ne', nah], *m. & f. (coll.)* A person very fond of dainties or delicacies.

lameronazo, za [lah-may-ro-nah'-tho, thah], *m. & f. aug. (coll.)* A person extremely fond of dainties.

lamia [lah'-me-ah], *f.* 1. Lamia, a fabulous monster. 2. Kind of shark. 3. A longicorn beetle of Europe.

lamido, da [lah-mee'-do, dah], *a.* 1. Deformed, worn out with use. 2. Very thin (delgado); pale (pálido). 3. Prim (afectado). *-pp.* of LAMER.

lamiente [lah-me-en'-tay], . 1. Licking. 2. Lapping.

lámina [lah'-me-nah], *f.* 1. Thin sheet (metal, vidrio). 2. Plate, engraving (gravado). 3. Print, illustration. 4. Thin layer. 5. *(Bot. & Zool.)* Lamina. **Láminas de acero,** steel in sheets.

laminable [lah-me-nah'-blay], *a.* Capable of lamination, laminable.

laminación [lah-me-nah-the-on'], *f.* 1. Rolling. 2. Lamination.

laminado, da [lah-me-nah'-do, dah], *a.* Laminated, laminate. *-m.* 1. Rolling. 2. Lamination.

laminador, ra [lah-me-nah-dor', rah], *a.* 1. Laminating. 2. Rolling. *-m.* 1. Rolling mill. 2. Laminator.

laminar [lah-me-nar'], *va.* 1. To roll (metales). 2. To laminate. *-a.* Laminar, laminal.

laminaria [lah-me-nah'-re-ah], *f. (Bot.)* Laminaria.

laminería [lah-me-nay-ree'-ah], *f.* Tidbit, choice morsel.

laminero, ra [lah-me-nay'-ro, rah], *m. & f.* 1. Laminator. 2. Decorator of containers for religious objects. *-a.* Fond of sweets.

laminoso, sa [lah-me-no'-so, sah], *a.* Laminose, laminous.

lamiscar [lah-mes-car], *va. (coll.)* To lick up greedily.

lamoso, sa [lah-mo'-so, sah], *a.* Muddy, slimy.

lampa [lahm'-pah], *f. (Per.)* Shovel for grain (agricultura).

lampacear [lam-pa-thay-ar'], *va. (Naut.)* To swab, to clean the decks with a swab.

lampar [lam-par'], *vn. & vr. V.* ALAMPA. To be eager for something.

lámpara [lahm'-pa-rah], *f.* 1. Light, aluminous body. 2. An oil lamp. 3. An electric light or lamp. 4. A spot of grease or oil. **Lámpara de arco,** arc light. **Lámpara de intermitencia,** flashlight. **Lámpara portátil,** emergency light. **Lámpara de radio,** radio tube. **Lámpara de rayos ultravioletas,** sunlamp. **Lámpara de seguridad,** miner's safety lamp. **Lámpara de soldar,** blowtorch. *-m & f. (Carib.)* Thief (ladrón).

lamparero, ra [lam-pa-ray'-ro, rah], *m. & f.* Lamp lighter.

lamparilla [lam-pa-reel'-lyah], *f.* 1. *(Dim.)* A small lamp (lámpara). 2. A night-taper. 3. A sort of coarse camlet.

lamparín [lam-pa-reen'], *m.* Case into which a glass lamp is put.

lamparista [lam-pah-rees'-tah], *n. com* Lamp-lighter.

lamparón [lam-pah-rone'], *m.* 1. *(aug.)* A large grease-spot. 2. King's evil, a scrofulous tumor in the neck.

lamparonoso, sa [lamp-pah-ro-no'-so, sah], *a.* Scrofulous.

lampazo [lam-pah'-tho], *m.* 1. *(Bot.)* Burdock. *V.* BARDANA. 2. *(Naut.)* Swab, a mop used to clean the decks and cabin of a ship. 3. *(LAm.)* Floor mop (estropajo). 4. *(And. Carib.)* Whiping (azotamiento).

lampiño [lam-pee'-nyo], *a.* Beardless; having little hair.

lampión [lam-pe-on'], *m,* A large lantern.

lampíride, lampiro [lam-pee'-re-day, lam-pee'-ro], *m. (Zool.)* Lampyris, the glow-worm, a sorricorn beetle. Also the firefly.

lampote [lam-po'-tay], *m.* Cotton cloth made in the Philippine Islands.

lamprea [lam-pray'-ah], *f. (Zool.)* Lamprey.

lamprear [lam-pray-ar'], *va.* 1. To marinate, to prepare a stew. 2. *(Mex.)* To dip in flour and beaten egg (antes de cocinar).

lamprehuela, lampreilla [lam-pray-oo-ay'-lah, lam-pray-eel'-lya], *f.* Kind of small lamprey.

lana [lah'-nah], *f.* 1. Wool, the fleece of sheep. 2. Short curled hair of some animal 3. Woollen manufacture in general. 4. *(coll.)* Cash, money. **Lana fieltrada,** felt wool. **Lana de camello,** camel's hair. **Hecho de lana,** woollen.

lanada [lah-nah'-dah], *f.* Sponge for cleaning cannons.

lanado, da [lah-nah'-do, dah], *a. V.* LANUGISO.

lanar [lah-nar'], *a.* Woolly, clothed with wool (oveja).

lanaria [lah-nah'-re-ah], *f. (Bot.)* Cud-weed, used in cleaning wool.

lance [lanh'-thay], *m.* 1. Cast, throw (red). 2. Casting of a net to catch fish (peces). 3. Favorable opportunity, critical moment (momento). 4. Chance, casualty, accident, fortuitous event, occurrence (suceso) *(Met.)* Transaction. 5. Sudden quarrel or dispute (riña). 6. Skill and industry of a player. 7. *(Cono Sur)* Duck, dodge (agachada). 8. *(Cono Sur, Arquit.)* Section, range. **Lance de honor,** affair of honor. **Lance de fortuna,** stroke of luck. *-pl.* 1. Missile weapons. 2. Blot or intrigues of a play.

lancear [lan-thay-ar'], *va.* To wound with a lance.

lancéola [lan-thay'-o-lah], *f. (Bot.)* Rib-grass plantain.

lanceolado, da [lan-thay-o-lah'-do, dah], *a.* Lance-shaped, lanceolate.

lancera [lan-thay'-rah], *f.* Hooks in an armory, on which arms are placed.

lancero [lan-thay'-ro], *m.* 1. Pikeman, lancer. 2. Maker of pikes.*-pl.* Type of square dance.

lanceta [lan-thay'-tah], *f.* 1. Lancet. 2. Potter's knife.

lancetada, *f.* **lancetazo,** *m.* [lan-thay-tah'-dah, lan-thay-tah'-tho]. Act of opening or wounding with a lancet.

lancetera [lan-thay-tay'-ro], **m.** A case for carrying lancets.

lancha [lahn'-chah], *f.* 1. Boat, barge, launch, lighter. **Lancha de motor,** motorboat. **Lancha de socorro,** lifeboat. **Lancha patrullera,** patrol boat. **Lancha de pesca,** fishing boat. 2. A thin and flat piece of stone. 3. Snare for partridges.

lanchaje [lan-chah'-hay], *m.* 1. Lighterage. 2.*(Mex.)* Ferry changes.

lanchar [lan-char'], *m.* A quarry from which flat stones are procured.

lanchero [lan-chay'-ro], *m.* 1. Boatman; lighterman. 2. *(Carib.)* Cuban refugee.

lanchón [lan-chone'], *m. (Naut.)* Lighter.

lanchonero [lan-cho-nay'-ro], *m.* Lighterman.

lancurdia [lan-coor'-de-ah], *f.* Small trout.

landre [lahn'-dray], *f.* 1. A morbid swelling of the glands. 2. A purse concealed in the clothes. 3. Acorn.

landrilla [lan-dreel'-lyah], *f.* Small grain which grows under the tongues of hogs.

lanería [lah-nay-ree'-ah], *f.* Shop where washed wool is sold (tienda).

lanero [lah-nay'-ro], *m.* 1. Dealer in wool. 2. Warehouse for wool (almacén).

langaruto, ta [lan-gah-roo'-to, tah], *a. (coll.)* Tall, lank, ill-shaped.

langosta [lan-gos'-tah], *f.* 1. Locust, a devouring insect (saltamonte). 2. Lobster, a marine crustacean (de mar). 3. One who extorts money.

langostera [lan-gos-tay'-rah], *f.* Name of a fishing-net.

langostín [lan-gos-teen'], *m.* Prawn, a shrimp-like crustacean.

langostino [lan-gos-tee'-no], *m.* Prawn *V.* LANGOSTÍN.

langüente [lan-goo-en'-tay], *a.* Infirm, weak.

lánguidamente [lahn'-gee-dah-men-tay], *adv.* Languidly, languishingly.

languidecer [lan-gee-day-ther'], *vn.* To languish, to pine, to wither.

languidez, languideza [lan-gee-deth'], *f.* 1. Languishment, languidness, languishing, heaviness, languor, weariness, faintness. 2. Decay of spirits, melancholy.

lánguido, da [lahn'-gee-do, dah], *a.* 1. Languid, faint, weak, languishing, feeble. 2. Dull, heartless.

lanífero, ra [lah-nee'-fay-ro, rah], *(Poet.)* Laniferous, woolly.

lanificio [lah-ne-fee'-the-o], *m.* Woollen manufacture, the art of manufacturing wool.

lanilla [lah-neel'-lyah], *f.* 1. Nap of cloth, down, villous substance. 2. Swan skin, a very fine flannel (tela). 3. *(Naut.)* Bunting, a thin woollen stuff of which flags are made. 4. *(Bot.)* Down.

lanosidad [lah-no-se-dahd'], *f.* Down of the leaves of plank.

lanoso, sa [lah-no'-so, sah], *a. V.* LANUDO.

lanteja [lan-tay'-hah], *f.* Lentil. *V.* LENTEJA.

lantajuela [lan-tay-hoo-ay'-lah], *f.* 1. Spangle, a small plate of shining metal. 2. Scurf left on the skin after a sore.

lanudo, da [lah-noo'-do, dah], *a.* Woolly (lanoso), consisting of wool, clothed with wool, lanigerous, fleecy. 2. *(And. Carib.)* Rustic, uncouth (maleducado). 3. *(Carib. Mex.)* Well off (rico).

lanuginoso, sa [lah-noo-he-no'-so, sah], *a.* Lanuginous, lanicerous, downy; covered with soft hair.

lanza [lahn'-thah], *f.* 1. Lance, spear, javelin. 2. Pole of a coach or wagon (carro). 3. Pikeman, soldier armed with a pike. **A punta de lanza,** strenuously, with all one's might.

lanzabombas [lan-thah-bom'-bahs], *m.* Bomber, bomb thrower, bomb release.

lanzacohetes [lan-thah-co-ay'-tes], *m.* Rocket launcher.

lanzada [lan-thah'-dah], *f.* Stroke with a lance, thrust with a spear.

lanzadera [lan-thah-day'-rah], *f.* Shuttle, a weaver's instrument.

lanzado, da [lan-thah'-do, dah], *a.* 1. *(Naut.)* Raking, overhanging. 2. Forward, brazen (ser). 3. Randy, in the mood. *-pp.* of LANZAR.

lanzador, ra [lan-thah-dor', rah], *m. & f.* 1. Thrower, ejecter, pitcher (béisbol). 2. Promoter. 3. *(Mil.)* Launcher (de cohetes).

lanzafuego [lan-thah-foo-ay'-go], *m. V.* BOTAFUEGO.

lanzallamas [lan-thahl-lyah'-mas], *m.* Flame thrower.

lanzamiento [lan-thah-me-en'-to], *m.* 1. Launch, launching. 2. Cast, throw. 3. Flinging, hurling. 4. Throwing off. 5. Publication. 6. *(for.)* Eviction. 7. Promotion. **Lanzamiento del disco**, discus throw. **Lanzamiento del martillo**, hammer throw. **Lanzamiento del peso**, shot put. **Lanzamiento de la jabalina**, javelin throw. **Oferta de lanzamiento**, promotional offer.

lanzaminas [lan-thah-mee'-nas], *m.* Mine layer, mine thrower.

lanzar [lan-thar'], *va.* 1. To lance, to throw, to dart, to launch, to fling (con violencia), to pitch (pelota), to throw over (desafío), to hurl (crítica). 2. To cast up, to vomit. 3. *(Law.)* To eject, to dispossess. 4. To let loose. *-vr.* 1. To rush or dart upon; to launch. 2. *(Com.)* To engage or embark on. **Lanzarse en paracaídas**, *(Aer.)* to bail out. **Se lanzó al río**, he jumped into the river. **Lanzar una bomba**, to drop a bomb.

lanzatorpedos [lan-thah-tor-pay'-dos], *m.* Torpedo boat.

lanzón [lan-thone'], *m. aug.* A short and thick lance.

laña [lah'-nyah], *f.* 1. Cramp or crampiron. 2. Green cocoanut.

lañar [lah-nyar'], *va.* 1. To vamp, to fasten two things together with a crampiron. *(Prov.)* To open and gut fish.

lapa [lah'-pah], *f.* 1. Scum or pellicle raised on the surface of some liquors. 2. *(Zool.)* A kind of shell-fish. Lepas. 3. *(Bot.)* Goose-grass, cleavers. 4. *(And. Cono Sur)* Half gourd. 5. *(And.)* Large flat-topped hat (sombrero).

lapachar [lah-pah-char'], *m.* Hole full of mud and mire.

lápade [lah'-pah-day], *f. (Zool.)* Acorn shell-fish.

lapaza [lah-pah'-thah], *f. (Prov.)* Rough panic-grass.

lapicero [lah-pe-thay'-ro], *m.* 1. A metal pencil case. 2. Pencil holder. 3. Mechanical pencil. 4. *(LAm.)* Fountain pen (pluma fuente).

lápida [lah'-pe-dah], *f.* A flat stone, on which inscriptions are engraved. **Lápida mortuoria**, head-stone. **Lapida mural**, tablet let into a wall.

lapidación [lah-pe-dah-the-on'], *f.* Lapidation, stoning to death.

lapidar [lah-pe-dar'], *va.* 1. To throw stones. 2. To stone to death.

lapidaria [lah-pe-dah'-re-ah], *f.* The art or profession of a lapidary, who deals in stones and gems.

lapidario [lah-pe-dah'-re-o], *m.* Lapidary, lapidist, one who deals in stones and gems.

lapidario, ria [lah-pe-dah'-re-o, ah], *a.* Lapidary.

lapideo, dea [lah-pee'-day-o, ah], *a.* Lapideous, stony of the nature of.

lapidificación [lah-pe-de-fe-ca-the-on'], *f.* Petrification, lapidification.

lapidífico, ca [lah-pe-dee'-fe-co, cah], *a.* Lapidescent, lapidific, growing or turning to stone.

lapidoso, sa [lah-pe-do'-so, sah], *a.* Lapideous, stony.

lapilla [lah-peel'-lyah], *f. (Bot.)* Hound's tongue.

lapislázuli [lah-pis-lah'-thoo-le], *m.* Lapis lazuli, an azure stone, of which the ultra-marine color is prepared by calcination.

lápiz [lah'-pith], *m.* Pencil, lead pencil, crayon. **Lápiz de labios** or **lápiz labial**, lipstick. **Lápiz de ojos**, eyeliner. **Escribir algo a lápiz**, to write something in pencil.

lapizar [lah-pe-thar'], *m.* Black-lead mine.

lapizar [lah-pe-thar'], *va.* To draw or delineate with black chalk or black lead.

lapo [lah'-po], *m.* 1. *(coll.)* Blow with the flat side of a sword. 2. *(And. Carib.)* Swig (trago). 3. *(Carib.)* Simple soul (inocente). 4. Spit (escupitajo).

lapón, na [lah-pone', nah], *a. & m. & f.* Laplander, relating to Lapland, Laplandish.

lapso [lahp'-so], *m. (Law.)* Lapse or course of time.

lapsus [lahp-soos], *m.* Lapse, mistake.

lapsus linguae [lap'-soos leen'-goo-ay], *m.* Slip of the tongue.

lar [lahr], *m.* A household god. *V.* LARES.

larario [lah-rah'-re-o], *m.* Place where the pagans worshipped their house-gods.

lardar, lardear [lar-dar', lar-day-ar'], *va.* 1. To lard, to baste meat on the spit (carne). 2. To beat with a stick.

lardero [lar-day'-ro], *a.* Applied to the Thursday before Lent.

lardo [lar'-do], *m.* Lard, the fat of swine and other animals.

lardón [lar-done'], *m.* A marginal note, observation, or addition, in a book or in a proof. Also a piece of paper clinging to the frisket and preventing the impression of some part of a sheet.

lardosico, ica, illo, illa, ito, ita [lar-do-see'-co, ee'-cah], *a. dim.* Greasy, dirty with grease.

lardoso, sa [lar-do'-so, sah], *a.* Greasy, fatty.

lares [lah'-res], *m. pl.* 1. House-gods of the ancient Romans. 2. Home.

larga [lar'-gah], *f.* 1. An added piece which shoemakers put on last, in order to lengthen a shoe. 2. Delay, procrastination: commonly used in the plural.

largamente [lar-gah-men'-tay], *adv.* Largely, copiously; completely; liberally, frankly; for a long time (de tiempo). 2. Generously (compensar, tratar). 3. Comfortably, at ease (vivir).

largar [lar-gar'], *va.* 1. To loosen, to slacken (aflojar). 2. To let go (soltar), to set at liberty. 3. *(Naut.)* To loosen a sail, to ease a rope. 4. To give, to fetch, to deal (vivir). 5. **Nos largó ese rollo de...**, he gave us the usual boring tale about... 6. *(And.)* To throw, to hurl (lanzar). 7. *(And.)* To hand over (entregar). **¡Vaya rollo!**, what a bore! *-vr.* 1. To beat it, to hop it; to quit. **¡Lárgate!**, clear off. 2. *(Naut.)* To set sail. 3. *(LAm.)* To start, to begin (empezar).

largo, ga [lar'-go, gah], *a.* 1. Long, of a certain measure in length (largo, medida). 2. Long, not short (espacio, tiempo). 3. Long, protracted, not soon ceasing or at an end. 4. Large, generous (generoso), free, liberal. 5. Copious (copioso). 6. Prompt, expeditious. 7. Sharp, shrewd; quick (astuto). **Largo de lengua**, too free and unguarded with the tongue, to be mordacious. **De largo a largo**, from one end to the other, length-wise. **Navegar a lo largo de la costa**, *(Naut.)* to navigate along the coast. **Pasar de largo**, to walk by without stopping. **A la corta o a la larga**, sooner or later. **A lo largo**, at length, slowly; in the long run; in course of time. **A lo largo**, 1. At a distance. 2. The long way, lengthwise. **Pasar de largo**, to pass by a person without taking notice of him. **Ese es cuento largo**, that is a long story. **A lo largo de**, along. **Dar largas a un asunto**, to delay a matter. *-m.* 1. Length. **El largo de las faldas**, the length of the skirts. 2. *(Mus.)* Largo. *-adv.* Largely, profusely.

largometraje [lar-go-may-trah'-hay], *m.* Full-length film, feature film.

largomira [lar-go-mee'-rah], *f.* Telescope.

largón, na [lar-gone', nah], *a. aug.* 1. Very long. 2. *(And. Cono Sur)* Delay (demora). 3. **Darse una largona**, *(Cono Sur)* to take a rest.

largor [lar-gor'], *m.* Length, the extent of something from end to end.

largueado, da [lar-gay-ah'-do, dah], *a.* Striped. *V.* LISTADO.

larguero [lar-gay'-ro], *m.* Jamb-post of a door or window. *V.* CABEZAL. *-a.* 1. *(Cono Sur)* Long (largo), lengthly; wordy (discurso); slow (persona). 2. *(Cono Sur)* Generous (generoso), lavish; abundant, copious (copioso).

largueza [lar-gay'-thah], *f.* 1. Length, extent, largeness, width. 2. Liberality, generosity, munificence, frankness.

larguito, ita [lar-gee'-to, tah], *a.* Not very long.
largura [lar-goo´-rah], *f.* Length, longness, stretch, extent.
lárice [lah'-re-thay], *m. (Bot.)* Larch-tree.
laricino, na [lah-re-thee'-no, nah], *a.* Belonging to the larch-tree.
larige [lah-ree'-hay], *a.* Applied to a kind of very red grapes.
laringa [lah-reen'-gah], *f.* Turpentine extracted from the larch-tree; Venice turpentine.
laringe [lah-reen'-hay], *f. (Anat.)* Larynx, the upper part of the trachea, where the voice is formed.
laríngeo, gea [lah-reen´-hay-o, ah], *a.* Laringeal, relating to the larynx.
laringitis [lah-ren-hee-tis], *f.* Laryngitis, inflammation of the larynx.
laringología [lah-rin-go-lo-hee´-ah], *f.* Laryngology, scientific knowledge of the larynx.
laringoscopia [lah-rin-gos-co-pe-ah], *f.* Laryngoscopy, use of the laryngoscope; inspection of the larynx.
laringoscopio [lah-rin-gos-co'-pe-o], *m.* Laryngoscope, a reflecting mirror for examining the larynx.
laringotomía [lah-rin-go-to-mee´-ah], *f. (Surg.)* Laringotomy.
laro [lah'-ro], *m. (Orn.)* Gull, seagull.
larva [lar'-vah], *f.* 1. Mask. *V.* MASCARA and FANTASMA. 2. *(Ent.)* Larva, grub-state of an insect. **Larvas**, hobgoblins; lemures.
larvado, da [lar-vah'-do, dah], *a.* 1. *(Med.)* Larvate, masked. 2. Hidden, latent.
larval [lar-vahl'], *a.* 1. Frightful, ghastly. 2. Larvated, like a mask.
las [lahs], *pron.* of third person plural feminine. It does not admit a preposition, and should not be used for the dative. **Las de Méjico son las mejores,** those of Mexico are the best. **Éstas son las de usted,** these are yours. **Son ellas las que me lo dijeron,** they were the ones who told me. **Esas cortinas son las que quiero,** those curtains are the ones that I want.
las [lahs] *art. def.* The. **Las casas son muy bonitas,** the houses are very nice. **Son las nueve,** it is nine o'clock. **Me gustan las patatas fritas,** I like fritters.
lasaña [lah-sah'-nyah], *f.* A sort of paste fried in a pan.
láscar [lahs'-car], *m.* Lascar, a native seaman or gunner in India.
lascar [las-car'], *va.* 1. *(Naut.)* To ease off; to slacken. 2. *(Mex.)* To graze (piel); to chip (piedra).
lascivamente [las-the-vah-men'-tay], *adv.* Lasciviously, lustfully, libidinously.
lascivia [las-thee'-ve-ah], *f.* 1. Luxuriance, luxury; excess in delicious fare. 2. Lasciviousness, lewdness, lust.
lascivo, va [las-thee'-vo, vah], *a.* 1. Lascivious, lewd, lustful, libidinous. 2. Luxuriant, exuberant.
láser [lah'-ser], *m.* 1. *(Bot.)* Benzoin. 2. Laser.
laserpicio [lah-ser-pee'-the-o], *m. (Bot.)* Laserwort.
lasitud [lah-se-tood'], *f.* Lassitude, weariness, faintness.
laso, sa [lah'-so, sah], *a.* 1. Weary (cansado), tired with labor, subdued by fatigue. 2. Lax, flaccid.
lastar [las-tar'], *va.* To pay, to answer, or suffer for another.
lástima [lahs'-te-mah], *f.* 1. Grief, compassion, pity (sentimiento), condolence. **Es una lástima,** it´s a shame. **Eso me da mucha lástima,** I feel very sorry about that. **Todos me dan lástima,** I feel sorry for them all. 2. Object of compassion or pity (objeto).
lastimar [las-te-mar'], *va.* 1. To hurt (lesionar), to wound (herir), to offend (ofender). 2. To move to compassion, to excite pity (apiadarse de). *-vr.* 1. To be moved to compassion, to grieve, to be sorry for (apiadarse); to complain (quejarse). 2. To hurt oneself. **Se lastimó el brazo,** he hurt his arm.
lastimeramente [las-te-may-rah-men'-tay], *adv.* Sadly, sorrowfully.
lastimero, ra [las-te-may'-ro, rah], *a.* Sad, doleful, mournful, miserable, moving, lamentable, grievous.

lastimosamente [las-te-mo-sah-men´-tay], *adv.* Miserably, pitifully, grievously, lamentably.
lastimoso, sa [las-te-mo'-so, sah], *a.* Doleful, sad, pathetic. *V.* LASTIMERO.
lasto [lahs'-to], *m.* Receipt given or belonging to him who has paid for another.
lastra [lahs'-trah], *f. (Naut.)* Boat, lighter. *V.* LANCHA.
lastrar [las-trar'], *va.* 1. *(Naut.)* To ballast a ship. 2. To keep something steady by means of a weight.
lastre [lahs'-tray], *m.* 1. Rough stones used to ballast ships or build walls. 2. Ballast, a freight put at the bottom of ships to keep them steady, lastage. **Lastre grueso,** heavy ballast. **Lastre lavado,** washed ballast. **Ir en lastre,** to go in ballast. 3. Weight, motive, judgment.
lata [lah'-tah], *f.* 1. Tin, can (envase), tinplate (metal). **Sardinas en lata,** canned sardines. 2. *(coll.)* Annoyance, boredom. **Dar la lata,** to annoy, to bother, to bore. **Dar la lata a uno,** to annoy somebody. 3. Lath (madera). 4. **Estar sin latas,** *(And. CAm.)* to be penniless. 5. *(LAm.)* Drag (persona).
latamente [lah-tah-men'-tay], *adv.* Largely, amply.
latazo [lah-tah-tho], *m.* Nuisance, bore, bind.
latente [lah-ten'-tay], *a.* 1. Latent, obscure, hidden. 2. *(LAm.)* Alive, intense, vigorous.
lateral [lah-tay-rahl'], *a.* Lateral, belonging to the side.
látex [lah'-teks], *m. (Bot.)* Latex.
latido [lah-tee´-do], *m.* 1. Pant, palpitation; motion of the heart. 2. Howling or barking of a dog after game. *-pp.* of LATIR.
latiente [lah-teen´-tay], *pa.* Palpitating, fluttering.
latigadera [lah-te-gah-day´-rah], *f. (Prov.)* Strap or thong by which the yoke is fastened to the pole of a cart.
latigazo [la-te-gah'-tho], *m.* 1. Lash (golpe), crack of a whip (chasquido); a jerk. 2. Reprimand (reprimenda). 3. Drink, swig (beber). **Dar latigazos,** to lash, to whip.
látigo [lah'-te-go], *m.* 1. Whip; thong, or point of a whip. 2. Rope with which something to be weighed is fastened to the steel-yard. 3. The end of every strap which must be passed through a buckle. 4. Mast of a boat when it is extremely tall.
latiguear [lah-te-gay-ar'], *vn.* To smack or crack with the lash of a whip, to lash or ply the whip.
latiguera [lah-te-gay´-rah], *f.* Cord with which a girth is fastened.
latiguero [lah-te-gay'-ro], *m.* Maker or seller of whip thongs or lashes.
latiguillo [lah-te-geel'-lyo], *m. dim.* A small whip.
latín [lah-teen'], *m.* 1. Latin, the Latin tongue. 2. A Latin word or clause interposed in a Romance text. **Saber mucho latín,** to be full of wit and cunning. **Latín vulgar,** vulgar Latin.
latinajo [lah-te-nah'-ho], *m. (coll.)* Latin jargon.
latinamente [lah-te-nah-men'-tay], *adv.* In pure Latin.
latinidad [lah-te-ne-dahd'], *f.* Latinity, the Latin tongue.
latinismo [lah-te-nees´-mo], *m.* Latinism, a mode of speech peculiar to the Latin language.
latinizar [lah-te-ne-thar'], *va.* To Latinize, to give names a Latin termination. *-vn.* To use words borrowed from the Latin.
latino, na [lah-tee´-no, nah], *a.* 1. Latin, written or spoken in the language of the old Romans. 2. Belonging to the Latin language or to the country of Latium. 3. Applied to the Western church, opposed to the Greek. **A la latina,** in a lateen or triangular fashion.
latino, na [lah-tee´-no, nah], *m. & f.* 1. Latinist, one who knows the Latin language. 2. A native of Latium.
latinoamericano, na [lah-te-no-ah-may-re-cah'-no, nah], *a. & m. & f.* Latin American, South American.
latir [lah-teer'], *m.* 1. To palpitate, to beat the heart (corazón); to flutter. 2. To yelp, to bark as a hound in pursuit of game.
latitud [lah-te-tood'], *f.* 1. Breadth (extensión), width, latitude, extent. 2. *(Geog.)* Latitude, the distance of any point from the equator.

latitudinal [lah-te-too-de-nahl'], *a.* Relating to the latitude.

lato, ta [lah'-to, tah], *a.* Large, diffuse, extensive.

latón [lah-tone'], *m.* 1. Brass (metal), latten. **Latón en hojas or planchas**, latten brass; sheet brass. 2. *(Cono Sur)* Big tin, large tin.

latonería [lah-to-nay-ree'-ah], *f.* 1. The art of working in brass. 2. A brass-worker's shop.

latonero [lah-to-nay'-ro], *m.* Brazier, a manufacturer who works in brass.

latones [lah-to'-nes], *m. pl. (Naut.)* Laths or ledges, used on board ships.

latoso, sa [lah-to'-so, sah], *a. (coll.)* Boring, annoying.

latría [lah-tree'-ah], *f.* Latria, worship, adoration due to God only.

latrina [lah-tree'-nah], *f.* Privy house. *V.* LETRINA.

latrocinio [lah-tro-thee'-ne-o], *m.* Robbery, frequent and repeated theft.

laúd [lah-ood'], *m.* 1. Lute, a stringed musical instrument. 2. Merchant vessel, craft.

laudable [lah-oo-dah'-blay], *a.* Laudable, praiseworthy.

laudablemente [lah-oo-dah-blay-men'-tay], *adv.* Laudably.

láudano [lah'-oo-dah-no], *m.* Laudanum, a tincture from opium.

laudar [lah-oo-dar'], *va.* To render a decision as an arbitrator or umpire.

laudatorio, ria [lah-oo-dah-to'-re-o, ah], *a.* Laudatory, acclamatory.

laude [lah'-oo-day], *f.* 1. A tombstone with an epitaph engraved on it. 2. *pl.* Lauds, that part of the divine service which is said after matins, and consists in praise of the Almighty. **A laudes**, at all hours, frequently.

laudemio [lah-oo-day'-me-o], *m. (Law.)* Dues paid to the lord of the manor on all transfers of landed property, within the manor.

launa [lah'-oo-nah], *f.* 1. Lamina, a thin plate of metal. 2. Schistose clay for covering houses.

laura [lah'-oo-rah], *f.* Solitary situation where the ancient monks had their detached cells.

lauráceo, cea [lah-oo-rah'-thay-o, ah], *a.* Laurel-like.

láurea [lah'-oo-ray-ah], *f.* A laurel leaf or crown.

laureado, da [lah-oo-ray-ah'-do, dah], *a. & pp.* of LAUREAR. Laureate, laurelled.

laureando [lah-oo-ray-ahn'-do], *m.* He who is soon to receive a degree in a university.

laurear [lah-oo-ray-ar'], *pa.* 1. To crown with laurel. 2. To graduate, to dignify with a degree at universities.

lauredal [lah-oo-ray-dahl'], *m.* Plantation of laurel-trees.

laurel [lah-oo-rel'], *m.* 1. *(Bot.)* Laurel. 2. A crown of bays as a reward.

lauréola [lah-oo-ray'-o-lah], *f.* 1. A crown of laurel. **Lauréola macho**, spurge laurel. 2. Diadem.

laurífero, ra [lah-oo-ree'-fay-ro, rah], *a. (Poet.)* Lauriferous, producing or carrying laurel.

lauríneo, nea [lah-oo-ree'-nay-o, ah], *a. (Bot.)* Laurel-like.

laurino, na [lah-oo-ree'-no, nah], *a.* Belonging to laurel.

lauro [lah'-oo-ro], *m.* 1. Glory, honor, fame, triumph. 2. *(Bot.) V.* LAUROCERASO.

lauroceraso, lauroreal [lah-oo-ro-thay-rah'-so, lah-oo-ro-ray-ahl], *m. (Bot.)* Cherry-laurel or laurel plum-tree.

lautamente [lah-oo-tah-men'-tay], *adv.* Splendidly.

lauto, ta [lah'-oo-to, tah], *a.* Rich, wealthy.

lava [lah'-vah], *f.* 1. Washing of metals in mines. 2. Lava, a volcanic production.

lavable [lah-vah'-blay], *a.* Washable.

lavabo [lah-vah'-bo], *m.* 1. A washbasin (lavamanos); washstand (con soporte); washroom (cuarto de aseo). 2. *(Rel.)* Lavabo (lavatorio). 3. The napkin on which the priest dries his hands after washing. 4. Lavatory, toilet (retrete).

lavacaras [lah-vah-cah'-ras], *m. (Met.)* A flatterer.

lavación [lah-vah-the-on'], *f.* Lotion, wash.

lavada [lah-vah'-dah], *f.* 1. A large drawnet for fishing. 2. *(LAm.)* Washing.

lavadero [lah-vah-day'-ro], *m.* 1. Washing-place (público, al aire libre); wash house (edificio). 2. Vat or pit in which tanners clean their skins. 3. Laundry, the room in which clothes are washed. 4. Place where gold-bearing sands are washed.

lavado [lah-vah'-do], *m.* Wash (acto), washing. **Lavado bucal**, mouth wash. **Lavado intestinal**, enema. **Lavado en seco**, dry cleaning.

lavador, ra [lah-vah-dor', rah], *m. & f.* 1. Washer, one who washes wool. 2. Burnisher, an instrument which serves to clean and brighten fire arms. 3. *(Cono Sur)* Washbasin (fregadero).

lavadora [lah-vah-do'-rah], *f.* Washing machine, washer (para la ropa).

lavadura [lah-vah-doo'-rah], *f.* 1. Wash, washing, lavation, the act of washing anything. 2. Composition of water, oil, and eggs, beaten together, in which glove-leather is prepared. 3. *V.* LAVAZAS.

lavaje [lah-vah'-hay], *m.* Washing of wools.

lavajo [lah-vah'-ho], *m.* Pool where cattle go to drink; morass.

lavamanos [lah-vah-mah'-nos], *m.* A washing-stand, lavatory.

lavanco [lah-vahn'-coh], *m.* A kind of wild duck.

lavanda [lah-vahn'-dah], *f.* Lavender; lavander water (agua).

lavandera [lah-van-day'-rah], *f.* 1. Laundress, a washer-woman. 2. *(Zool.)* Wagtail. *V.* AGUZANIEVE.

lavandería [lah-van-day-ree'-ah], *f.* 1. Laundry, laundering establishment. 2. Washing, laundering. **Lavandería automática**, laundromat.

lavandero [lah-van-day'-ro], *m.* 1. Washer, he who washes, launderer. 2. One who carries and brings foul linen to be washed.

lavaojos [lah-vah-o'-hose], *m.* Eye-cup.

lavaplatos [lah-vah-plah'-tose], *m.* 1. Dishwasher (aparato). 2. *(Cono Sur)* Dishwasher (persona). 3. *(Cono Sur, Mex.)* Sink (fregadero).

lavar [lah-var'], *va.* 1. To wash, to cleanse by ablution, to rave, to launder. 2. To clear from an imputation or charge of guilt. 3. To white-wash a wall with lime or chalk. **Lavar y marcar**, to shampoo and set. **Lavar la cabeza**, to wash one's hair. *-vr.* To wash, to have a wash. **Lavarse las manos**, to wash one's hands.

lavativa [lah-lya-tee'-vah], *f.* 1. Enema, clyster, a medicinal injection. 2. A clyster-pipe; a syringe. 3. *(Met.)* Vexation, annoyance (molestia).

lavatorio [lah-vah-to'-re-o], *m.* 1. Lavation, the act of washing. 2. Medicinal lotion with which diseased parts are washed. 3. Ceremony of washing the feet on Holy Thursday. 4. Lavatory. *V.* LAVAMANOS.

lavavajilla [lah-vah-vah-heel'-lyahs], *m.* Dishwasher.

lavazas [lah-vah'-thas], *f. .pl.* Foul water running from a washing-place.

lave [lah'-vay], *m.* Washing of metals in mines.

lavotear [lah-vo-tay-ar'], *va. & vr. (coll.)* To wash hurriedly and poorly. *(Acad.)*

lavoteo [lah-vo-tay'-o], *m.* Washing hurriedly and poorly performed.

laxación [lac-sah-the-on'], *f.* Loosening, laxation, slackening.

laxamiento [lac-sah-me-en'-to], *m.* Laxation, laxity, laxness, loosening.

laxante [lac-sahn'-tay], *pa.* Loosening, softening. *-m. & a. (Med.)* Laxative.

laxar [lac-sar'], *va.* To loosen (vientre), to soften.

laxativo, va [lac-sah-tee'-vo, vah], *a. & f.* Laxative, lenitive.

laxidad [lac-se-dahd'], *f. V.* LAXITUD.

laxitud [lac-se-tood'], *f.* 1. Lassitude, weariness. 2. Laxity, laxness.

laxo, xa [lac'-so, sah], *a.* 1. Lax, slack, not tense, feeble. 2. *(Met.)* Lax, vague; loose in opinions or morals.

laya [lah'-yah], *f.* 1. Quality, nature. 2. *(Prov.)* A two-pronged instrument, with which the ground is turned up.

layador [lah-yah-dor´], *m*. He who cultivates the soil with a two-pronged instrument.

layar [lah-yar´], *va*. To turn up the ground with a *laya*.

lazada [lah-thah´-dah], *f*. 1. Slip-knot formed with a ribbon, cord, thread, etc. 2. Any ornament made in the form of a knot. (*Amer.*) The knot or slip made with a *lazo* on an animal's horns or neck, to keep him fast.

lazador [lah-thah-dor´], *a*. He who catches with the lasso.

lazar [lah-thar´], *va*. (*Mex.*) To catch with a lasso.

lazareto [lah-thah-ray´-to], *m*. Lazaretto, lazaret, a public building for the reception of persons coming from places suspected of being infected with the plague, to perform quarantine.

lazarillo [lah-thah-reel´-lyo], *a*. Boy who guides a blind man; a blind person's guide.

lazarino, na [lah-thah-ree´-no, nah], *a*. Leprous, lazar-like, lazarly.

lázaro [lah'-tha-hro], *m*. Lazar, a person deformed and nauseous with filthy and pestilential diseases.

lazo [lah'-tho], *m*. 1. Bow, a slip knot. 2. Any knot or complication of thread, ribbon, string, etc. 3. Ornament in the shape of a knot. 4. Snare, trick, scheme. 5. Tie, bond, chain (vínculo). 6. The act of decoying or driving the game to a certain spot. 7. (*Arch.*) Interlaced lines and flower-work. 8. Pattern made with box and other plants in a garden bed. 9. Cord with which a load is fastened. 10. (*Amer.*) Lasso, a line or rope for catching wild animals (caza). **Lazo de zapato**, bootlace. **Los lazos familiares**, the family bond. *-pl.* Figures in dancing.

lazulita [lah-thoo-lee´-tah], *f*. Lazulite.

le [lay], *pron*. Him or her, to him, to her, dat. and accus. sing. of the personal pronoun *él*, he or it; and of its feminine, *ella*, she. **No le veo**, I don't see him. **Le hablé**, I spoke to him. **Le he comprado esto**, I bought this for him. **No se le conoce otra obra**, no other work of his is known. **Yo le dije**, I told him/her.

leal [lay-ahl], *a*. 1. Loyal, true to government. 2. Faithful, gentle, tame (animales).

leal [lay-ahl´], *m*. Loyalist.

lealmente [lay-al-men'-tay], *adv*. Loyally, faithfully.

lealtad [lay-al-tahd'], *f*. 1. Loyalty, fidelity, attachment to the laws and government, fealty. 2. Gentleness toward a master (bestias).

lebrada [lay-brah´-dah], *f*. Fricassee made of hare.

lebratico, illo, its [lay-brah-tee´-co, eel'-lyo, ee´-to], *m. dim*. A young hare, a leveret.

lebrato [lay-brah'-to], or **lebratón** [lay-brah-tone'], *m*. Young hare.

lebrel [lay-brel'], *m*. Greyhound.

lebrela [lay-bray'-lah], *f*. Greyhound bitch.

lebrero, ra [lay-bray´-ro, rah], *a*. Applied to dogs for hunting hares.

lebrillo [lay-breel'-lyo], *m*. A glazed earthenware tub or pan.

lebrón [lay-bro-ne'], *m*. 1. A large hare. 2. Coward, poltroon. 3. Sharp (listo). 4. Boastful, insolent (arrogante).

lebroncillo [lay-bron-theel'-lyo], *m. V*. LEBRATO.

lebruno, na [lay-broo´-no, nah], *a*. Leporine, of the hare kind.

lección [lec-the-on'], *f*. 1. Art of reading; reading. 2. Lesson, anything read or repeated to a teacher. 3. Lecture, a discourse upon any subject. 4. Lection, the letter or text of a work. 5. Warning, admonition, example. **Lección particular**, private lesson. **Dar una lección a uno**, to teach somebody a lesson.

leccionario [lec-the-o-nah´-re-o], *m*. Lesson book of the matins.

leccioncita [lec-the-on-thee´-tah], *dim*. A short lecture or lesson.

leccionista [lec-the-o-nees´-tah], *m*. One who gives lessons in private houses; a private tutor.

lecha, lechaza [lay´-chah, lay-chah´-thah], *f*. 1. Seminal fluid of fishes. 2. Each of the two sacs which contain it.

lechada [lay-chah´-dah], *f*. 1. Lime slaked in water, whitewash. 2. Pulp for making paper (pulpa). 3. Lime water. 4. (*LAm.*) Milking.

lechal [lay-chahl'], *a*. 1. Sucking (mamífero). **Cordero lechal**, baby lamb. 2. Lactiferous, milky.

lechar [lay-char'], *a*. 1. *V*. LECHAL. 2. Nursing: applied to a woman who has milk in her breasts. 3. Promoting the secretion of milk in female mammals. 4. (*LAm.*) To milk (ordeñar). 5. (*CAm. Mex.*) To whitewash (blanquear).

lechaza [lay-chah´-thah], *f*. *V*. LECHA.

lechazo [lay-chah´-tho], *m*. 1. A suckling, an unweaned mammal. 2. A weaned lamb.

leche [lay´-chay], *f*. 1. Milk. 2. Milk or white fluid in plants. 3. Good luck (suerte). 4. Bash (golpe); bash, bang (choque). 5. Bore, pain (molestia). 6. Hell!, get away! **Cochinillo de leche**, sucking pig. **Vaca de leche**, milch cow. **Leche de canela**, oil of cinnamon dissolved in wine. **Hermano de leche**, foster brother. **Leche crema or quemada**, custard. **Leche en polvo**, powdered milk. **Un tío de mala leche**, a nasty sort. **Hay mucha mala leche entre ellos**, there's a lot of bad blood between them. **No entiende ni leches**, he doesn't understand a bloody thing. **Ir a toda leche**, to scorch along.

lechecillas [lay-chay-theel'-lyas], *f. pl*. 1. Sweetbread of calves, lambs, and kids. 2. Livers and lights.

lechera [lay-chay´-rah], *f*. 1. Milk-woman, milk-maid (persona), dairy-maid. 2. Milk pan, or vessel for serving milk (recipiente). 3. (*LAm.*) Cow. 4. Police can. 5. Milch cow (vaca de leche).

lechería [lay-chay-ree´-ah], *f*. 1. Cow-house, dairy (edificio), lactary. 2. (*Cono Sur*) Cows, herd (vacas). 3. (*And, Mex.*) Meanness (tacañería).

lechero, ra [lay-chay´-ro, rah], *a*. 1. (*coll.*) Milky; containing milk. 2. (*LAm.*) Lucky (con suerte). 3. (*Mex.*) Mean, stingy (tacaño). 4. (*Carib.*) Greedy, grasping (codicioso).

lechero [lay-chay'-ro], *m*. 1. Milkman. 2. Tanpit, where the ooze of bark is prepared.

lecherón [lay-chay-rone'], *m*. (*Prov.*) 1. Milk-pail, milk-vessel. 2. Flannel in which new-born infants are rolled.

lechetrezna [lay-chay-treth'-nah], *f*. (*Bot.*) Spurge.

lechigada [lay-che-gah´-dah], *f*. 1. Litter, a number of animals produced at a single birth. 2. A company of persons of the same kind of life or the same calling.

lechín [lay-cheen'], *m*. 1. Tent, pledget. 2. (*Prov.*) Olives rich in oil.

lechino [lay-chee'-no], *m*. 1. Tent, a roll of lint put into a sore. 2. Small tumor in horses.

lecho [lay´-cho], *m*. 1 Bed (cama), a couch. 2. Litter, straw laid under animals. **Lecho de lobo**, haunt of a wolf. 3. Bed of a river; horizontal surface of a seat. 4. Layer, a stratum or row.

lechón [lay-chone'], *m*. 1. A sucking pig; pig of any size. 2. A dirty fellow as regards dress or manner of living.

lechona [lay-cho'-nah], *f*. 1. Sucking female pig. 2. (*coll.*) A dirty woman.

lechoncico, illo, ito [lay-chon-thee'-co], *m. dim*. A very young pig.

lechoso, sa [lay-cho'-so, sah], *a*. (*Bot.*) Having a milky juice. *-m*. (*S. Amer.*) The papaw-tree; the juice has remarkable digestive properties.

lechuga [lay-choo'-gah], *f*. 1. (*Bot.*) Lettuce. 2. *V*. LECHUGUILLA for a frill. 3. (*Carib.*) Bank note.

lechugado, da [lay-choo-gah'-do, dah], *a*. Having leaves like lettuce.

lechuguero, ra [lay-choo-gay´-ro, rah], *m. & f*. Retailer of lettuce.

lechuguilla [lay-choo-geel'-lyah], *f*. 1. (*Dim.*) Small lettuce. 2. Frill formerly worn around the neck.

lechuguino [lay-choo-gee'-no], *m*. Plot of small lettuces. (*coll.*) *-m. & f*. Dandy, dandizette.

lechuza [lay-choo'-thah], *f.* Owl, barn owl. **Lechuza común**, barn owl. 2. *(Cono Sur, Mex.)* Albino, light blond. 3. *(Carib. Mex.)* Whore (prostituta).

lechuzo, za [lay-choo'-tho, thah], *a.* 1. Suckling: applied to mule colts less than a year old. 2. Collecting debts in trust for another. 3. Owlish; a nickname applied to persons.

lechuzo [lay-choo'-tho], *m.* 1. Nickname of an agent, collector, or commissioner who collects money or debts. 2. Nickname of persons resembling owls in any of their qualities.

lectisternio [lec-tis-terr'-ne-o], *m.* Banquet of the heathen gods.

lectivo, va [lec-tee'-vo, vah], *a.* Applied to the time of lecture in universities.

lector, ra [lec-tor', rah], *m. & f.* 1. Reader. 2. In monastic orders, a lecturer, teacher, or professor. 3. In the Roman Catholic church, the second of the four minor orders.

lectorado [lec-to-rah'-do], *m.* Institution of lecturer.

lectoral [lec-to-rahl'], *f.* 1. A prebendary, dignity in cathedral churches of Spain. 2. *m.* The person who enjoys the prebend called *lectoral.*

lectoral [lec-to-rahl'], *a.* Applied to the prebend or canonry celled *lectoral* in Spain, and to the prebendary who enjoys it.

lectoría [lec-to-ree'-ah], *f.* Lectureship, in monastic orders; the place and office of a lecturer.

lectura [lec-too'-rah], *f.* 1. Reading, lecture, the act of reading. 2. The act of teaching by way of lectures. 3. Among printers, small pica, 11-point. **Una persona de mucha lectura**, a well-read person. **Dar lectura a**, to read.

ledamente [lay-dah-men'-tay], *adv. (Poet.)* Merrily, cheerfully.

ledo, da [lay'-do, dah], *a. (Poet.)* Gay, merry, cheerful, glad, joyful.

leer [lay-err'] *va.* 1. To read. 2. To lecture, to instruct publicly. 3. To read one's thoughts. **Leer entre líneas**, to read between the lines. **Leer la mano a uno**, to read somebody's palm.

lega [lay'-gah], *f.* A lay sister who serves the community.

legacía, legación [lay-gah-thee'-ah, lay-gah-the-on'], *f.* 1. Embassy, legation, deputation. 2. Legateship, office of a legate. 3. Message sent by an ambassador or deputy. 4. Province of the ecclesiastical states governed by a legate. 5. Duration of a legate's embassy or government.

legado [lay-gah'-do], *m.* 1. Legacy, a particular thing given by last will and testament. 2. Deputy, ambassador, legate (enviado). 5. Commander of a Roman legion.

legador [lay-gah-dor'], *m. (Prov.)* Day laborer, who ties the feet of sheep, for shearing them.

legadura [lay-gah-doo'-rah], *f. (Ant.)* Ligature, cord, or strap for tying or binding.

legajico, illo, ito [lay-gah-hee'-co], *m. dim.* A small bundle of loose papers tied together.

legajo [lay-gah'-ho], *m.* Bundle of loose papers tied together.

legal [lay-gahl'], *a.* 1. Legal, lawful, constitutional. 2. Loyal (persona), true, faithful in the performance of duty, punctual. 3. *(And.)* Fine, marvellous.

legalidad [lay-gah-le-dahd'], *f.* Legality, fidelity, punctuality; lawfulness, legitimateness.

legalización [lay-gah-le-thah-the-on'], *f.* 1. Attestation of a signature or subscription by which an instrument or writing is legalized. 2. Notarial certificate.

legalizar [lay-gah-le-thar'], *va.* To legalize, to authorize, to make lawful.

legalmente [lay-gal-men'-tay], *adv.* Legally, lawfully; faithfully.

legamente [lay-gah-men'-tay], *adv.* Ignorantly, in an illiterate manner.

légamo [lay'-gah-mo], *m.* Slime, mud, or clay left by water (arcilla).

legamoso, sa [lay-gah-mo'-so, sah], *a.* Slimy, greasy.

legaña [lay-gah'-nyah], *f.* Lippitude, blearedness of eyes.

legar [lay-gar'], *va.* 1. To depute, to send on an embassy. 2. To bequeath, to leave by last will or testament.

legatario, ria [lay-gah-tah'-re-o, ah], *m. & f.* Legatee, a person to whom a legacy is left, legatory.

legatina [lay-gah-tee'-nah], *f.* A stuff made of silk and wool.

legenda [lay-hen'-dah], *f.* Legend, traditionary history of saints. *(Acad.)*

legendario [lay-hen-dah'-re-o], *m.* 1. Legend, a chronicle or register of the lives of saints. 2. Legendary, author of a legend.

legible [lay-hee'-blay], *a.* Legible, such as may be read.

legión [lay-he-on'], *f.* 1. Legion. **Legión Extranjera**, foreign Legion. 2. Legion, an indefinite number.

legionario, ria [lay-he-o-nah'-re-oh, ah], *a.* Legionary, belonging to a legion.

legislación [lay-hes-lah-the-on'], *f.* 1. Legislation, collection of the laws of a country. 2. Enactment of laws.

legislador, ra [lay-his-lah-dor', rah], *m. & f.* 1. Legislator, law-giver, law-maker. 2. Censor, censurer, he that blames or censures.

legislar [lay-his-lar'], *va.* 1. To legislate, to enact laws. 2. To censure, to criticise.

legislativo, va [lay-his-lah-tee'-vo, vah], *a.* Legislative, law-giving: constitutive.

legislatura [lay-his-lah-too'-rah], *f.* Legislature, the power that makes laws.

legisperito [lay-his-pay-ree'-to], *m. V.* JURISPERITO.

legista [lay-hees'-tah], *m.* Legist, one skilled in law; a professor of laws; a student of jurisprudence.

legítima [lay-hee'-te-mah], *f.* Portion or share of the paternal or maternal estate, which belongs to the children, according to law.

legitimación [lay-he-te-mah-the-on'], *f.* Legitimation, the act of investing with the privileges of lawful birth.

legítimamente [lay-he-te-may-men-tay], *adv.* Legitimately, lawfully.

legitimar [lay-he-te-mar'], *va.* 1. To prove, to establish in evidence. 2. To legitimate, to procure to any the rights of legitimate birth. 3. To make legitimate or adequate; to legalize.

legitimidad [lay-he-te-me-dahd'], *f.* Legitimacy, legitimateness; legality; lawfulness.

legitimista [lay-he-te-mees'-tah], *a. & m. & f.* Legitimist, upholding the divine right of kings, and of succession to the crown by rigorous order of primogeniture.

legítimo, ma [lay-hee'-te-mo, mah], *a.* 1. Legitimate, legal, lawful, authentic. 2. True, certain.

lego [lay'-go], *m.* 1. Layman, laic, one of the people distinct from the clergy. 2. Lay-brother or lay-friar, a person admitted for the service of a religious body. *-a.* 1. Laical, lay, laic. 2. Ignorant, illiterate.

legón [lay-gone'], *m.* Spade.

legra [lay'-grah], *f.* Trepan, surgeon's instrument; a cylindrical saw, trephine.

legración, legradura [lay-grah-the-on', lay-grah-doo'rah], *f.* Act of trepanning.

legrar [lay-grar'], *va.* To trepan, to perforate the skull with a trepan; to trephine.

legua [lay'-goo-ah], *f.* League. **A legua, a la legua, a leguas, de cien lenguas, de muchas or desde media legua**, very far, at a great distance. **Legua marítima**, marine league. **Se ve a la legua**, it stands out a mile, you can see it a mile away.

leguilla [lay-geel'-lyah], *f. V.* LIGUILLA.

legumbre [lay-goom'-bray], *f.* 1. Pulse, leguminous plants. 2. Vegetables, garden-stuff, legume or legumen.

legúmina [lay-goo'-me-nah], *f.* Legumin, a proteid compound called also vegetable casein.

leguminoso, sa [lay-goo-me-no'-so, sah], *a. (Bot.)* Leguminous: applied to plants which bear legumes or pods.

leíble [lay-ee'-blay], *a.* Legible, readable.

leído, da [lay-ee'-do, dah], *a.* Having read much, book-learned. *-pp.* of LEER.

leila [lay'e-lah], *f.* A Moorish dance.

leima [lay'-e-mah], *m.* Interval of music.

lejanía [lay-hah-nee'-ah], *f.* Distance (distancia), remoteness in place.

lejano, na [lay-hah'-no, nah], *a.* Distant, remote, far.

lejía [lay-hee'-ah], *f.* 1. Lye, water boiled with ashes. 2. *(Met.)* Severe reprehension.

lejío [lay-hee'-o], *m.* Among dyers, lye.

lejivial [lay-he-ve-ahl'], *a.* Lixivial.

lejos [lay'-hos], *adv.* At a great distance, far off. **Desde lejos,** from afar. **Está muy lejos,** it´s a long way. **Eso viene de lejos,** *(Fig.)* that´s been going on for a long time.

lejos [lay'-hos], *m.* 1. Perspective, distant, prospect, background. 2. *(Met.)* Similarity, appearance, resemblance. **A lo lejos, de lejos, de muy lejos** or **desde lejos**, at a great distance.

lejos, jas [lay'-hos, has], *a.* Distant, very remote: generally used in the feminine.

lejuelos [lay-hoo-ay'-los], *adv. dim.* At a little distance.

lelilí [lay-le-lee'], *m.* War-whoop of the Moors.

lelo, la [lay'-lo, lah], *a.* Stupid, ignorant, crazy.

lema [lay'-mah], *m.* 1. Argument of a poem explained in the title; motto. 2. Lemma, a proposition previously assumed.

lemosín, na [lay-mo-seen', nah], *a.* Relating to the Lemosin language, or that of the troubadors.

lemosín [lay-mo-seen'], *m.* The Lemosin language.

len [len], *a.* Applied to soft, untwisted silk.

lena [lay'-nah], *f.* Spirit, vigor.

lencera [len-thay'-rah], *f.* A woman who deals in linen; the wife of a linen-draper.

lencería [len'-thay-ree'-ah], *f.* 1. An assortment of linen; plenty of linen (telas). 2. Linen draper's shop (tienda); linen hall, where linen is sold. 3. Linen trade. 4. Lingerie (ropa interior).

lencero, ra [len-thay'-ro, rah], *m. & f.* Linen-draper, linen merchant.

lendel [len-del'], *m.* Circle described by a horse turning a wheel to raise water out of a well.

lendrera [len-dray'-rah], *f.* A close toothed comb for taking out nits.

lendrero [len-dray'-ro], *m.* Place full of nits.

lendroso, sa [len-dro'-so, sah], *a.* Nitty, full of nits.

lene [lay'-nay], *a.* 1. Mild, soft, bland. 2. Mild, pleasant, benevolent. 3. Light, of small weight or consideration.

lengua [len'-goo-ah], *f.* 1. The tongue. 2. Language (idioma), idiom. 3. Information, advice. 4. Speech. 5. Tongue or needle of a balance. 6. Clapper of a bell. **Lengua de tierra**, neck of land running out into the sea. **Tener algo en la punta de la lengua,** to have something on the tip of one's tongue. **Lengua sabia,** learned language. **Lengua de vaca,** cow´s tongue. **De lengua en lengua,** from mouth to mouth. **Irse de la lengua,** to give loose rein to one's tongue. 7. *(Antiq.)* Interpreter. **Andar en lenguas,** to be much talked of. **Morderse la lengua,** *(Met.)* to curb one's speech sharply. **Dar a la lengua,** to chatter. **No morderse la lengua,** not to mince one´s words. **Sacar la lengua a uno,** to poke one´s tongue out at somebody.

lenguado [len-goo-ah'-do], *m.* *(Zool.)* Sole, flounder.

lenguaje [len-goo-ah'-hay], *m.* 1. Language, idiom (forma de hablar), speech. 2. Language, style, manner of speaking or writing. **Lenguaje comercial,** business language. **Lenguaje del cuerpo,** body language. 3. *(Comput..)* **Lenguaje natural,** natural language. **Lenguaje de alto nivel,** high-level language. **Lenguaje de bajo nivel,** low-level language. **Lenguaje de cuarta generación (4GLs),** fourth-generation language (4GLs). **Lenguaje de inteligencia artificial,** artificial-intelligence language. **Lenguaje de máquina,** machine language. **Lenguaje de muy alto nivel,** very-high-level language. **Lenguaje de programación orientado al objeto,** object-oriented programming language. **Lenguaje de recuperación y actualización,** retrieval and update language. **Lenguaje de**

tercera generación, third-generation language. **Lenguaje ensamblador,** assembly language. **Lenguaje para procedimientos,** procedural language. **Lenguaje no procesal,** nonprocedural language. **Lenguaje de control de la impresora,** printer control language. **Lenguaje postcript,** postcript language.

lenguaraz [len-goo-ah-rath'], *a.* 1. Languaged, having various languages. Fluent, voluble. 3. Forward, petulant. 4. Talkative, free-tongued. It is sometimes used as a substantive for a linguist.

lenguaz [len-goo-ath'], *a.* Loquacious, garrulous.

lengüecica, illa, ita [len-goo-ay-thee'-cah, eel'-lyah], *f. dim.* A small tongue.

lengüeta [len-goo-ay-tah], *f.* 1. *(Dim.)* A small tongue. 2. Languet, anything cut in the form of a tongue; a free reed in wind instruments. 3. *(Anat.)* Epiglottis. 4. Needle of a balance. 5. Book-binder´s cutting-knife (cortapapeles). 6. *(Mech.)* Feather, a thin wedge. 7. *(Arch.)* Buttress; moulding. 8. Borer used by saddlers and chair makers. 9. *(LAm.)* Chatterbox (hablador).

lengüetada [len-goo-ay-tah'-dah], *f.* The act of licking.

lengüetería [len-goo-ay-tay-ree'-ah], *f.* The reedwork of an organ. *-f. pl.* *(LAm.)* Gossip, tittle-tattle.

lengüezuela [len-goo-ay-thoo-ay'-lah], *f. dim.* A small tongue.

lenidad [lay-ne-dahd'], *f.* Lenity, mildness, favor.

lenificar [lay-ne-fe-car'], *va.* To lenify, to soften. *V.* SUAVIZAR.

lenificativo, va [lay-ne-fe-cah-tee'-vo, vah], *a.* Mollifying, softening.

lenitivo, va [lay-ne-tee'-vo, vah], *a.* Lenitive, lenient, mitigant.

lenitivo [lay-ne-tee'vo], *m.* Emollient, mitigator, lenient.

lenocinio [lay-no-thee'-ne-o], *m.* Pimping, pandering. *V.* ALCAHUETERÍA.

lentamente [len-tah-men'-tay], *adv.* Slowly, heavily, lazily, lingeringly.

lente [len'-tay], *com.* 1. Lens. 2. Eyeglass. **Lente angular,** wide-angle lens. **Lente telefotográfico,** telephoto lens. **Lentes bifocales,** bifocals, bifocal glasses. **Lentes de contacto,** contact lenses.

lentecer [len-tay-therr'], *vn. & vr.* To grow soft or tender.

lenteja [len-tay'-hah], *f.* *(Bot.)* Lentil. **Lenteja de agua,** gibbous duckweed. **lentejuela** [len-tay-hoo-ay'-lah], *f.* Spangle, a small plate of shining metal.

lenticular [len-te-coo-lar'], *a.* Lenticular, in the form of a lentil. **Hueso lenticular,** the smallest bone of the ear; stapes.

lentiforme [len-te-for'-may], *a.* *(Anat.)* Lens-shaped, lentiform.

lentillas [len-teel'-lyahs], *f. pl.* Contact lenses.

lentisco [len-tees'-co], *m.* *(Bot.)* Mastich-tree.

lentitud [len-te-tood'], *f.* Slowness, sluggishness, coldness.

lento, ta [len'-to, tah], *a.* 1. Slow, sluggish, tardy, heavy, long, lingering. 2. *(Met.)* Glutinous. 3. *(Mus.)* Largo. 4. *(Med.)* Slow.

lentor [len-tor'], *m.* Lentor, sluggishness.

leña [lay'-nyah], *f.* 1. Wood, fire-wood. 2. *(coll.)* Stick, beating. **Echar leña al fuego,** *(Met.)* to foment discord. **Llevar leña al monte,** to carry coals to Newcastle.

leñador, ra [lay-nyah dor', rah], *m. & f.* Woodman, wood-cutter, dealer in wood.

leñar [lay-nyar'], *va.* To cut wood.

leñera [lay-nyay'-rah], *f.* Place for fire-wood.

leñazgo [lay-nyath'-go], *m.* Pile of wood or timber.

leñero [lay-nyay'-ro], *m.* 1. Dealer in wood, timber-merchant. 2. Timber-yard. 3. A logman.

leño [lay'-nyo], *m.* 1. Block, a heavy piece of timber (madera), a log (tronco); the trunk of a tree cut down. 2. *(Poet.)* Ship, vessel. 3. *(Met.)* Person of little talent or ability. 4. *(Bot.)* Woody fibre. **Hacer leño del árbol caído,** to kick somebody when he´s down.

leñoso, sa [lay-nyo'-so, sah], *a.* Woody, ligneous.

león [lay-on´], *m.* 1. Lion. Felis leo. **León marino**, sea lion. **Estar hecho un león**, to be furious. **León pardo**, *V.* LEOPARDO. 2. *(Ast.)* Leo, the fifth sign of the zodiac. 3. *(Met.)* An irritable and cruel person. 4. A neuropterous insect, dragonfly.

leona [lay-o´-nah], *f.* Lioness.

leonado, da [lay-o-nah´-do, dah], *a.* Lion colored, tawny.

leonera [lay-o-nay´-rah], *f.* 1. Cage (jaula) or place where lions are shut up; a menagerie 2. Gambling den (de juego); *(And. Cono Sur)* communal prison cell (celda); *(And.)* noisy gathering.

leonero [lay-o-nay´-ro], *m.* 1. Keeper of lions. 2. Master of a gambling house.

leónica [lay-o´-ne-cah], *f.* Vein or gland under the tongue (caballos).

leonino, na [lay-o-nee´-no, nah], *a.* 1. Leonine, belonging to lions. 2. Leonine verses, the end of which rhymes to the middle.

leonina [lay-o-nee´-nah], *f.* Elephantiasis, a kind of leprosy.

leopardo [lay-o-par´-do], *m.* Leopard, panther.

leotardo [lay-tar´-do], *m.* Leotard, tights.

lépero, ra [lay´-pay-ro, rah], *a. (Mex.)* Of the lowest kind of people, ragged and wretched.

lepidio [lay-pee´-de-o], *m. (Bot.)* Pepper-grass.

lepidóptero, ra [lay-pe-dop´-tay-ro, rah], *a.* Lepidopterous, belonging to the lepidoptera. *-m. pl.* The lepidoptera, a class of insects having wings covered with dust-like scales. It includes butterflies, moths, and sphinxes.

lepisma [lay-pees´-mah], *f.* Lepisma, the bristle-tail, silver-fish, or sugar louse.

leopoldina [lay-o-pol-dee´-nah], *f.* Watch fob.

leporino, na [lay-po-ree´-no, nah], *a.* Like a hare. **Labio leporino**, harelip.

lepra [lay´-prah], *f.* Leprosy.

leprosería [lay-pro-say-ree´-ah], *f.* A hospital for lepers.

leprosidad [lay-pro-se-dahd´], *f. (Med.)* Leprousness.

leproso, sa [lay-pro´-so, sah], *a.* Leprous, leperous. *-m. & f.* Leper.

lercha [lerr´-chah], *f. (Prov.)* A reed passed through the gills of fishes to hang them up.

lerdamente [ler-dah-men´-tay], *adv.* Slowly, heavily, lumpishly, obtusely.

lerdez [ler-deth´], *f.* Slowness, tardiness, heaviness.

lerdo, da [layr´-do, dah], *a.* Slow (lento), heavy (pesado); dull of comprehension, lumpish, obtuse.

lerdón [ler-done´], *m. (Vet.)* Tumor in a horse's pastern.

les [lays], *pron. pers.* 1. Them, to them (a ellos); you, to you (a usted, a ustedes). 2. Them (dativo); you. **Yo les vi,** I saw them. **Yo les presté (a ellas) dinero,** I lent them some money. **Yo les compré a ustedes una casa,** I bought a house from you.

lesbiano, na, lesbio, bia [les-be-ah´-no, nah, les´-be-o, ah], *a. & f. & m.* Lesbian.

lesbio, bia [les´-be-o, ah], *a.* Lesbian, of Lesbos.

lesión [lay-se-on´], *f.* Hurt, damage, wound; injury, wrong. **Lesión cerebral**, brain-damage.

lesionado [lay-se-o-nah-do], *a.* Hurt, injured; injured (jugador), unfit.

lesionar [lay-se-o-nar´], *va.* To hurt (dañar), to injure; to wound (herir). *-vr.* To get hurt.

lesivo, va [lay-see´-vo, vah], *a.* Prejudicial, injurious.

lesna [les´-nah], *f.* Awl, a pointed instrument to bore holes.

lesnordeste [les-nor-des´-tay], *m. (Naut.)* East-north-east wind.

leso, sa [lay´-so, sah], *a.* 1. Wounded, hurt (herido), damaged; perverted, injured (ofendido). 2. *(Cono Sur. And.)* Simple, stupid.

leste [les´-tay], *m.* East wind, east.

lesueste [lay-soo-es´-tay], *m. (Naut.)* East-south-east wind.

letal [lay-tahl´], *a.* Mortal, deadly destructive, lethal.

letanía [lay-tah-nee´-ah], *f.* 1. Litany, a form of prayer. **Letanías,** supplicatory processions. 2. *(coll.)* List or enumeration of things.

letárgico, ca [lay-tar´-he-co, cah], *a.* Lethargic, lethargical.

letargo [lay-tar´-go], *m.* Lethargy, a morbid drowsiness.

letargoso, sa [lay-tar-go´-so, sah], *a.* Causing lethargy, deadening.

leteo, a [lay-tay´o, ah], *a. (Poet.)* Lethean.

letífero, ra [lay-tee´-fay-ro, rah], *a.* Lethiferous, deadly, that which is the cause or sign of death.

letificante [lay-te-fe-cahn´-tay], *pa.* Exhilarating.

letífico, ca [lay-tee´-fe-co, cah], *a.* Cheering, bringing joy.

letra [lay´-trah], *f.* 1. Letter, a character of the alphabet. 2. Hand character, or peculiar manner of writing (escritura). 3. Type, a printing letter. 4. Motto, inscription. 5. Letter, the verbal expression, the literal meaning, the grammatical sense of a phrase. 6. A kind of Spanish poetical composition. 7. Words of a song. 8. An arithmetical character, a figure. **Letra** or **letra de cambio**, bill of exchange. **A la letra**, literally, punctually, entirely. **Letras,** 1. Letters, learning; the learned professions. 2. Rescript, despatch. 3. *(Prov.)* Certification, testimony. **Letras sagradas**, the Bible, the sacred Scriptures. **Letra gótica**, Gothic script. **Letra negrita**, bold type. **En letras de molde**, in print. **Tiene buena letra**, he writes a good hand.

letrada [lay-trah´-dah], *f. (coll.)* Lawyer´s wife.

letradería, letraduría [lay-trah-day-ree´-ah], *f.* 1. *(Low.)* Body or society of lawyers, inn. 2. A foolish speech pompously uttered.

letrado, da [ly-trah´-do, dah], *a.* 1. Learned, erudite, lettered. 2. *(coll.)* Vain, presumptuous. **A lo letrado**, as a lawyer, like a counsellor.

letrado [lay-trah´-do], *m.* Lawyer, professor of law; advocate, counsellor.

letrero [lay-tray´-ro], *m.* An inscription, a title, sign (anuncio), label; a legend on medals or coins, placard (cartel).

letrilla [lay-treel´-lyah], *f.* 1. *(Dim.)* A small letter. 2. A short poem adapted to music.

letrina [lay-tree´-nah], *f.* Privy, water-closet, latrine.

letrón [lay-trone´], *m. aug.* A large letter.

letrones [lay-tro´-nes], *m. pl.* Capital letters or large characters written at the door of churches.

leucemia [lay-oo-thay´-me-ah], *f.* Leukaemia.

leucocito [lay-oo-co-thee´-to], *m. (Anat.)* Leucocyte.

leucoma [lay-oo-co´-mah], *f. (Med.)* Leucoma, disease of the cornea.

leucorrea [lay-oo-cor-ray´-ah], *f.* Leucorrhoea; colloquially, whites.

leucoris [lay-oo-co´-ris], *f.* Generic name of diseases which attack the lymphatic vessels.

leudar [lay-oo-dar´], *va.* To ferment dough with leaven; to raise bread.

leudo, da [lay´-oo-do, dah], *a.* Fermented, leavened (pan).

leva [lay´-vah], *f.* 1. *(Naut.)* Act of weighing anchor. **Pieza de leva**, shot fired as a signal for weighing anchor. 2. Levy, the act of raising men for military service; press. 3. *(Naut.)* Swell of the sea. **Hay mar de leva**, there is a swell in the offing. 4. Cog, tooth, cam, wiper. 5. Play of a piston.-*pl.* Tricks, artful devices. **Bajar la leva a uno**, *(And. Cono Sur)* To do somebody mischief. **Echar levas**, *(And, Mex.)* to boast.

levada [lay-vah´-dah], *f.* 1. Silkworm which moves from one place to another. 2. Salute or flourish made with the foil by fencers before they set to. *V.* LLEVADA.

levadero, ra [lay-vah-day´-ro, rah], *a.* That which is demanded.

levadizo, za [lay-vah-dee´-tho, thah], *a.* That can be lifted or raised.

levadura [lay-vah-doo´-rah], *f.* 1. Ferment, leaven, yeast. 2. *(Med.)* Ferment, septic matter.

levantada [lay-van-tah´-dah], *f. (coll.)* Rise, the act of rising.

levantadamente [lay-van-tah'-dah-men-tay], *adv.* In an elevated or exalted manner.

levantador, ra [lay-van-tah-dor', rah], *m. & f.* 1. One who raises or lifts up. 2. Disturber, rioter. 3. *(Surg.)* Levator, elevator.

levantamiento [lay-van-tah-me-en´-to], *m.* 1. Elevation, the act of raising; sublimity. **Levantamiento de pesas**, weight lifting. 2. Insurrection, revolt, rebellion, commotion. 3. *(Prov.)* Balance of accounts.

levantar [lay-van-tar'], *va.* 1. To raise, to lift or lift up, to heave, to get up, to hold up, to hang up, to mount, to set upright. 2. To build up, to raise, to erect a building. 3. To raise, to excite to tumult or war, to stir up. 4. To impute or attribute falsely. 5. To rouse, to raise, to excite to action. 6. To elevate, to aggrandize, to promote. 7. To rouse or start a game. 8. To cut the cards 9. To levy, to raise men for military service. 10. To increase, to enlarge. 11. To raise the voice, to utter loudly. 12. To cause, to occasion; to begin. 13. *(And.)* To nick, to arrest. 14. *(Cono Sur)* To pick up (persona). -*vr.* 1. To rise, to change a recumbent for an erect posture, to get up from a fall (incorporarse). 2. To rise, to get up from a bed (de la cama). 3. To stand up. 4. To rise, to have more elevation than some other thing. 5. To rise, to break in commotions or insurrections. 6. To start or to rise suddenly (juego). 7. To conclude, to be concluded (sesión). **Levantar falso testimonio**, to accuse falsely. **Levantar la mesa**, to clear the table. **Levantó la mano**, he raised his hand. **Fue imposible levantarlo**, it was impossible to lift it. **Levantarse con el pie izquierdo**, to get out of bed on the wrong side.

levante [lay-vahn'-tay], *m.* 1. Levant, particularly the coasts of the Mediterranean east of Italy. 2. East, east wind (viento). 3. *(Carib.)* Driving of cattle (arreo). 4. *(And.)* Arrogance, haughtiness. 5. *(Cono Sur)* Pick-up (encuentro). **Hacer un levante a uno**, to pick somebody up. 6. **Hacer un levante**, *(Carib.)* To fall in love.

levantín [lay-van-teen'], *m.* Levantine: generally used in the plural.

levantino, na [lay-van-tee'-no, nah], *a.* Levantine, relating to the Levant.

levantisco, ca [lay-van-tees'-co, cah], *a.* 1. Turbulent, restless. 2. V. LEVANTINO.

levar [lay-var'], *va.* *(Naut.)* To weigh anchor.-*vr.* To set sail.

leve [lay'-vay], *a.* Light, of little weight; trifling, trivial (poco importante). **Una herida leve**, a slight wound.

leveche [lay-vay'-chay], *m.* *(Naut.)* The south-west wind.

levedad [lay-vay-dahd'], *f.* Lightness, levity: inconstancy.

levemente [lay-vay-men'-tay], *adv.* Lightly, gently; venially.

leviatán [lay-ve-ah-tahn'], *m.* Leviathan, a monstrous water animal.

levigación [lay-ve-gah-the-on´], *f.* Levigation, separation by washing of a finer powder from a coarser; elutriation.

levigar [lay-ve-gar'], *va.* To levigate, to free from grit, to elutriate.

levita [lay-vee'-tah], *m.* 1. Levite, one of the tribe of Levi. 2. V. DIÁCONO.

levita [lay-vee'-tah], *f.* Frock-coat, Prince Albert coat. **Gente de levita**, middle classes.

levítico, ca [lay-vee'-te-co], *m.* 1. Book of Leviticus. 2. *(coll.)* Ceremonial used at a festival.

levítico, ca [lay-vee'-te-co, cah], *a.* *(coll.)* Levitical, priestly.

levitón [lay-ve-tone'], *m.* A long overcoat, like a frock-coat.

levulosa [lay-voo-lo'-sah], *f.* Fructose.

léxico, or léxicon [lec'-se-co, or lec-se-cone'], *m.* 1. Lexicon, an abridged or special dictionary, principally Greek or Latin. 2. Glossary, vocabulary.

lexicografía [lec-se-co-grah-fee'-ah], *f.* Lexicography, the art of writing dictionaries.

lexicográfico, ca [lec-se-co-grah'-fe-co, cah], *a.* Lexicographic, relating to compiling a lexicon or dictionary.

lexicógrafo [lec-se-co'-grah-fo], *m.* Lexicographer, author or writer of a dictionary.

lexicología [lec-se-co-lo-hee'-ah], *f.* Lexicology, the systematic study of the words of a language.

lexicólogo, ga [lec-se-co'-lo-go], *m & f.* Lexicologist.

ley [lay'-e], *f.* 1. Law, an ordinance, constitution or statute publicly established. 2. Law, a rule of action. 3. Loyalty, faithful attachment to a superior or master. 4. Religion. 5. A legal standard of quality, weight or measure. 6. A principle, or universal property. **Ley de la trampa**, fraud, deceit. **A la ley**, with propriety and neatness. **A toda ley**, according to rule.-*pl.* 1. Body or collection of laws. 2. Study and profession of the law. **Ley escrita**, statute law, as opposed to custom or unwritten law. **Ley antigua**, the law of Moses. **Ley del embudo**, severity for others, indulgence for ourselves. **Ley orgánica**, constitutional law. **De acuerdo con la ley**, in accordance with the law. **Está fuera de la ley**, he´s outside the law. **Recurrir a la ley**, to go to law.

leyenda [lay-yen'-dah], *f.* 1. Reading, lecture, legend (historia), what is read. 2. Inscription on coins or models.

lezda [leth'-dah], *f.* Ancient tax on merchandise.

lezna [leth'-nah], *f.* V. LESNA.

lía [lee'-ah], *f.* 1. A thin bass-rope. 2. Husk of pressed grapes.

liana [le-ah'-nah], *f.* Liana, a twining or climbing plant of the tropical forest.

liar [le-ar'], *va.* To tie (atar), to bind, to fagot.-*vr.* 1. To contract an alliance. 2. To get tied up. 3. To get involved. 4. To get involved (amantes) **Estar liado con**, to live with.

liaza [le-ah'-thah], *f.* Collection of hoops used by coopers.

libación [le-bah-the-on'], *f.* Libation, pouring out wine for a sacrifice.

libamiento [le-bah-me-en'-to], *m.* The offering in ancient sacrifices.

libar [le-bar'], *va.* 1. To suck, to sip, to extract the juice: to taste. 2. To perform a libation. 3. To sacrifice. -*vn.* *(LAm.)* To booze, to drink.

libelar [le-bay-lar'], *va.* To petition, to sue at law.

libelático, ca [le-bay-lah'-te-co, cah], *a.* Applied to the Christians who renounced the Christian religion in a written declaration, for which the Roman emperors exempted them from persecution.

libelo [le-bay'-lo], *m.* 1. Petition, libel; a declaration of charge in writing against a person in court. 2. A defamatory writing, lampoon (sátira), libel.

libélula [le-bay'-loo-lah], *f.* The dragonfly, a neuropterous insect of the greater part of the globe.

líber [lee'-ber], *m.* Bast, liber, or inner bark of exogenous plants.

liberación [le-bay-rah-the-on'], *f.* 1. Setting at liberty, liberation. 2. *(Law.)* Remission of a debt.

liberado [le-bay-rah'-do], *a.* Paid-up, paid-in. -*m.* *(Pol.)* Agent (de un grupo terrorista).

liberal [le-bay-rahl'], *a.* 1. Liberal (carácter), generous, free, open, large, manificent, open-hearted. 2. Quick in the performance of a thing; brisk, active. 3. Liberal: applied to the arts, as opposed to mechanics.

liberalidad [le-bay-rah-le-dahd'], *f.* Liberality, generosity, largeness, munificence, frankness, open-heartedness; gallantry.

liberalismo [le-bay-rah-lees'-mo], *m.* Liberalism, profession of liberal doctrines favorable to political and religious liberty.

liberalizar [le-bay-rah-lee-thar'], *va.* To liberalize.

liberalmente [le-bay-ral-men'-tay], *adv.* Liberally, expeditiously; largely, munificently, generously, frankly.

liberar [le-bay-rar'], *va.* To free, to liberate. **Liberar a uno de una obligación**, to release somebody from a duty.

libérrimo, ma [le-ber'-re-mo, mah], *a. sup.* Most free.

libertad [le-ber-tahd'], *f.* 1. Liberty, freedom, the power of doing without inconvenience what is not contrary to the laws or established customs. 2. Liberty, freedom, as opposed to slavery. 3. Liberty, freedom, the state of one who is not a prisoner. 4. Liberty, freedom, license, assumed familiarity, relaxation of restraint. 5. Liberty, freedom, exemption, privilege, immunity. 6. Freedom, agility, address;

independence, unconventionality. 7. Ransom. **Libertad académica**, academic freedom. **Libertad de comercio**, free trade. **Libertad de estado**, the unmarried state. **Libertad provisional**, freedom on bail. **Estar en libertad**, to be free. **Tomarse la libertad de**, to take the liberty of. **Poner a uno en libertad**, to set somebody free.

libertadamente [le-ber-tah'-dah-men-tay], *adv.* Freely, impudently.

libertado, da [le-ber-tah'-do, dah], *a.* 1. Libertine, impudent. 2. Free, ungoverned. 3. Idle, disengaged. *-pp.* of LIBERTAR.

libertador, ra [le-ber-tah-dor', rah], *m. & f.* Deliverer, liberator. *-a.* Liberating.

libertar [le-ber-tar'], *va.* l. To free, to set at liberty, to liberate. 2. To exempt (eximir), to free, to excuse, to clear from an obligation or debt, to acquit. 3. To free, to rid from, to clear from anything ill. 4. To preserve.

liberticida [le-ber-te-thee'-dah], *m.* Liberticide, a destroyer of liberty.

libertinaje [le-ber-te-nah'-hay], *m.* Libertinism, licentiousness of opinion or practice; libertinage, license, irreligion.

libertino, na [le-ber-tee-no, nah], *m. & f.* Child of a freed man. *-a.* Libertine (juergista), irreligious, dissolute, impudent, licentious, lewd.

liberto [le-ber'-to], *m.* A freed man, an emancipated slave.

libi [lee'-be], *m.* A kind of linseed of Mindanao (P. I.), from which oil is obtained.

libídine [le-bee'-de-nay], *f.* Lewdness, lust.

libidinosamente [le-be-de-no-sah-men'-tay], *adv.* Libidinously.

libidinoso, sa [le-be-de-no'-so, sah], *a.* Libidinous, lewd, lustful.

libra [lee'-brah], *f.* 1. Pound, a weight of sixteen ounces. **Libra medicinal**, pound troy, of twelve ounces, apothecaries' weight, troy weight. 2. **Libra esterlina**, a pound sterling. 3. *(Ast.)* Libra, sign of the zodiac.

libración [le-brah-the-on'], *f.* Libration, the state of being balanced.

libraco [le-brah'-co], *m. (coll.)* An old worm-eaten book or pamphlet. a bad book.

librado [le-brah'-do], *m. (Com.)* Drawee.

librador, ra [le-brah-dor', rah], *m. & f.* 1. Deliverer. 2. The drawer of a bill of exchange. 3. Store keeper of the king's stables. 4. Metal scoop for handling dry sweetmeats, vegetables, etc.

libramiento [le-brah-me-en'to], *m.* 1. Delivery, the act of delivering. 2. Warrant, order of payment.

librancista [le-bran-thees'-tah], *m.* One who holds a warrant or order of payment.

libranza [le-brahn'-thah], *f.* Bank draft.

librar [le-brar'], *va.* 1. To free, to deliver, to extricate, to exempt, to preserve from ill. 2. To give a warrant or order for paying a certain sum. 3. To despatch, to expedite. 4. To commit, to intrust. 5. To place (confianza, esperanza). 6. To pass (sentencia), to issue (edicto), to reveal (secreto). 7. To make out (cheque). **Librar bien or mal**, to get over a thing well or ill. **Librar a uno de una obligación**, to free somebody from an obligation. *-vn.* 1. To give birth. 2. **Librar bien**, to fare well. 3. **Libro a las 3**, I'm free at 3 (tiempo). *-vr.* To free oneself, to escape. **Librarse de**, to escape from. **De buena nos hemos librado**, we did well to get out of that.

libratorio [le-brah-to'-re-o], *m. V.* LOCUTORIO.

librazo [le-brah'-tho], *m. (aug.)* A large book.

libre [lee'-bray], *a.* 1. Free, uncumbered, unrestrained, independent; unembarrassed. 2. Free, at liberty, not enslaved, not a prisoner. 3. Free, exempt, privileged. 4. Free, innocent, guiltless. 5. Single, unmarried. 6. Free, libertine, loose, unrestrained, frank, licentious, impudent. 7. Rash, bold, forward, thoughtless. 8. Independent. 9. Free, clear from distress. 10. Isolated, alone. **Libre cambio**, free trade. **Esa plaza no está libre**, that seat is not free. **Cada cual es libre**

de hacer lo que quiera, Everyone is free to do as he wishes. **Trabajar por libre**, to freelance.

librea [le-bray'-ah], *f.* Livery, clothes given to servants.

librear [le-bray-ar'], *va.* To weigh, to sell or distribute by pounds.

librecambista [le-bray-cam-bees'-tah], *m.* Freetrader. *-a.* Advocating free trading.

librejo [le-bray'-ho], *m. dim.* A little book, a pamphlet.

libremente [le-bray-men'-tay], *adv.* Freely; boldly; audaciously; impudently.

librería [le-bray-ree'-ah], *f.* 1. Book-store, bookseller's shop (tienda). **Librería anticuaria**, antiquarian bookshop. 2. Bookcase (estante), library (biblioteca).

librero [le-bray'-ro], *m.* Book seller (persona).

libreta [le-bray'-tah], *f.* 1. The troy-weight pound. 2. Loaf of bread which weighs sixteen ounces 3. Small memorandum book. **Libreta de banco**, bank book. **Libreta de ahorro**, savings book.

librete [le-bray'-tay], *m.* 1. *(Dim.)* A small book. 2. Small vessel with coals, used for warming the feet: foot-warmer.

libreto [le-bray'-to], *m. (Mus.)* Libretto (opera).

librico, ito [le-bree'-co, ee'-to], *m. dim.* A small book.

librilla [le-breel'-lyah], *f. dim.* A small pound.

librillo [le-breel'-lyo], *m.* 1. Small book. 2. Cigarette paper. **Librillo de cera**, a wax taper for carrying light.

libro [lee'-bro], *m.* 1. A book. 2. Book, a division or part of a work. 3. *(Met.)* Contribution, impost, tax. **Libro de caja**, a cash-book. **Libro de asiento** or **libro de cuentas**, account-book. **Libro de facturas**, invoice-book. **Libro del diario**, *(Naut.)* journal. **Libro en blanco**, a paper-book. **Libro mayor**, ledger. **Libro de memoria**, memorandum-book. **Libro de cocina**, cookery-book. **Libro de cheques**, check-book. **Libro escolar**, report-book. **Libro de texto**, text-book. **Libro de visitas**, visitors' book.

librote [le-bro'-tay], *m. aug.* Large book (mal libro).

licantropía [le-can-tro-pee'-ah], *f.* Lycanthropy, insanity in which the patient imagines himself transformed into a wolf. *V.* ZOANTROPÍA.

licantrópico, ca [le-can-tro'-pe-co, cah], *a.* Lycanthropic, relating to or affected by lycanthropy.

licencia [le-then-the-ah], *f.* 1. Permission, leave, license (permiso), liberty. *(Mil.)* Furlough. 2. Licentiousness (moral), contempt of just restraint, looseness, wantonness. 3. Degree of licentiate. 4. Licence, permit (documento). **Licencia de armas**, gun licence. **Licencia de conducir**, driving licence. **Licencia de utilización in situ**, site licence.

licenciadillo [le-then-the-ah-deel'-lyo], *m.* Nickname given to a little ridiculous person dressed in clerical habits.

licenciado [le-then-the-ah'-do], *m.* 1. Licentiate, a degree in Spanish universities, and the person who has taken that degree. 2. *(coll.)* Any scholar in the Spanish universities. 3. A title given to lawyers. **Licenciado en Filosofía y Letras**, Bachelor of Arts.

licenciado; da [le-then-the-ah'-do, dah], *a. & pp.* of LICENCIAR. Licensed; vainglorious.

licenciamiento [le-then-the-ah-me-en'-to], *m.* 1. The act of taking the degree of licentiate. 2. The disbandment of troops.

licenciar [le-then-the-ar'], *va.* 1. To permit (permitir), to allow, to license (dar permiso); to licentiate. 2. To license, to dismiss, to send away. 3. To make a licentiate. *(Mil.)* To break off, to disband. *-vr.* 1. To become dissolute. 2. To graduate, to take one's degree. **Licenciarse en Derecho**, to take a degree in Law.

licenciatura [le-then-the-ah-too'-rah], *f.* 1. The degree of licentiate (título), and the act of receiving it. 2. Degree course (estudios).

licenciosamente [le-then-se-o-sah-men'-tay], *adv.* Licentiously.

licencioso, sa [le-then-the-o'-so, sah], *a.* Licentious, dissolute, free, loose.

liceo [le-thay´-o], *m.* 1. Lyceum, a public school. 2. Name of certain literary societies. 3. *(Cono Sur, Mex.)* Secondary school.

licio [lee´-the-o], *m. (Bot.)* Boxthorn.

licitación [le-the-tah-the-on´], *f.* Selling by auction.

lícitamente [lee´-the-tah-men-tay], *adv.* Lawfully, justly, licitly.

licitante [le-the-tahn´-tay], *m.* Bidder or buyer at auction.

licitar [le-the-tar´], *va.* To sell at auction.

lícito, ta [lee´-the-to, tah], *a.* Licit, lawful; just, fair (justo); permissible (permisible).

licnomancia [lic-no-mahn´-the-ah], *f.* Superstitious divination by means of flames.

licor [le-cor´], *m.* 1. Liquor, something liquid. 2. Liquor, strong drink, spirits (alcohol); liqueur (frutas).

licorera [le-co-ray´-rah], *f.* Liqueur bottle.

licorista [le-co-rees´-tah], *m. (Com.)* A manufacturer or dealer in spirituous liquors (fabricante, comerciante).

licoroso, sa [le-co-ro´-so, sah], *a.* Applied to generous wine.

lictor [lic-tor´], *m.* Lictor, a minister of justice in ancient Rome.

licuable [le-coo-ah´-blay], *a.* Liquable, that may be melted.

licuación [le-coo-ah-the-on´], *f.* Liquation, liquefaction, the act of melting.

licuadora [le-coo-ah-do´-rah], *f. (Culin.)* Blender, liquidizer.

licuante [le-coo-ahn´-tay], *pa.* of LICUAR. Liquefying, dissolving, melting.

licuar [le-coo-ar´], *va.* To liquefy, to dissolve, to melt (nieve).

licuefacción [le-coo-ay-fac-the-on´], *f.* Liquefaction, conversion into the liquid state.

licuefacer [le-coo-ay-fah-therr´], *va. & vr.* V. LICUAR. *(Acad.)*

licuefactible [le-coo-ay-fac-tee´-blay], *a.* Liquefiable.

licuescencia [le-coo-es-then´-the-ah], *f.* Liquescence, aptness to melt.

licuescente [le-coo-es-then´-tay], *f.* Liquescent, melting.

lichera [le-chay´-rah], *f. (Prov.)* Woollen cover of a bed.

lid [leed], *f.* Conflict, contest, fight; dispute, argument.

líder [lee´-der], *m.* Leader.

liderar [lee-day-rar´], *va.* To lead, to head.

lidia [lee´-de-ah], *f.* 1. *(Taur.)* Bullfight; bullfighting. **Toro de lidia**, fighting bull. 2. *(Mex.)* Trouble, nuisance (molestia).

lidiador [le-de-ah-dor´], *m.* Combatant; one who publicly disputes or argues; *(Taur.)* bullfighter.

lidiar [le-de-ar´], *vn.* 1. To fight, to oppose, to contend. 2. *(Met.)* To deal with annoying, vexing persons. 3. *(Archaic.)* To plead before a court.-*va.* To run or prefight bulls.

lidio [lee´-de-o], *a. (Mus.)* Lydian, a species of ancient music.

liebrastón [le-ay-bras-tone´], *m.* Leveret, a small or young hare.

liebratico [le-ay-brah-tee´-co], *m.* Young hare.

liebre [le-ay´-bray], *f.* 1. Hare. 2. Coward, poltroon. **Coger una liebre**, to fall into mud or mire. 3. *(And. Cono Sur)* Minibus. -*pl.* 1. *(Naut.)* Racks or ribs. 2. *(Naut.)* Dead-eyes.

liebrecica, illa, ita [le-ay-bray-thee´-cah, el´-lyah, ee´-tah], *f. dim.* A young or small hare.

liebrecilla [le-ay-bray-theel´-lyah], *f. (Bot.)* V. AZULEJO.

liebrezuela [le-ay-bray-thoo-ay´-lah], *f. dim.* V. LIEBRECICA.

liencecico, illo, ito [leen-thay-thee´-oo, eel´lyo, ee´-to], *m. dim.* Little linen cloth.

liendre [le-en´-dray], *f.* Nit, the egg of a louse.

lientera, lientería [le-en-tay´-rah, le-an-tay-ree´-ah], *f.* Lientery, diarrhoea which carries off the food undigested.

lientérico, ca [le-en-tay´-re-co, cah], *a.* Lienteric.

liento, ta [le-en´-to, tah], *a.* Damp, moist.

lienza [le-en´-thah], *f.* A narrow strip of any cloth.

lienzo [le-en´-tho], *m.* 1. Linen (tela), cloth made of flax or hemp; canvas. **Lienzo encerado**, glazed linen. **Lienzo curado**, bleached linen. 2. Handkerchief (pañuelo). 3. Painting on linen. 4. *(Fort.)* Curtain, part of a wall lying between the two bastions. 5. Face or front of a building (fachada).

liga [lee´-gah], *f.* 1. A garter. 2. Bird-lime (trampa viscosa). 3. League, coalition, confederacy, combination, alliance. 4. Alloy for gold and silver (metal). 5. *(And.)* Bosom friend (amigo).

ligación [le-gah-the-on´], *f.* 1. Ligation, act of tying. 2. Union, mixture.

ligada [le-gah´-dah], *f. (Print.)* Ligature, logotype.

ligado, da [le-gah´-do, dah], *a. & pp.* of LIGAR. Tied, bound, leagued, confederate.

ligado [le-gah´-do], *m. (Mus.)* Slur.

ligadura [le-gah-doo´-rah], *f.* 1. Ligature, anything tied round another. 2 Ligation, ligature, flee act of binding. 3. Subjection. 4. *(Mus.)* A tie, a slur. 5. *(Arch.)* All the arcs made by cross-timbers in arches. 6. *(Mech.)* An iron wire which binds the strands of a wire cable. 7. *(Naut.)* Seizing, the fastening of two ropes with a thin line; lashing.

ligamaza [le-gah-mah´-thah], *f.* Viscous or glutinous matter around fruits.

ligamento [le-gah-men´-to],*m.* 1. *(Anat.)* Ligament; a cord. 2. Ligament, bond, chain, entanglement.

ligamentoso, sa [le-gah-men-to´-so, sah], *a.* Ligamentous, Ligamental.

ligamiento [le-gah-me-en´to], *m.* 1. Union, act of tying or uniting. 2. Union, concord. 3. Ligament.

ligar [le-gar´], *va.* 1. To tie, to bind, to fasten, to knit, to mix (bebidas). 2. To alloy gold or silver for coinage (metal). 3. To league, to coalesce, to confederate. 4. To render impotent by charms or spells. 5. To exorcise, to purify from the influence of malignant spirits. 6. To pick up, to get off with (chica). 7. To get (conseguir). 8. *(Carib.) (Agr.)* To contract in advance for. -*vn.* 1. To mix (ir juntos); to blend, to go well together. 2. *(Carib. Mex.)* To have a bit of luck (tener un poco de suerte). 3. *(Carib. Mex.)* To look, to stare (mirar). 4. **Ligar con una**, to flirt with somebody (flirtear), to pick a girl up (conocer). -*vr.* 1. To league, to conspire to conjoin, to be leagued, to be allied. 2. To bind oneself to the performance of a contract.

ligazón [le-gah-thone´], *f.* 1. Union, contexture, confixture, connection, ligament, bond. 2. *(Naut.)* Futtock-timbers.

ligeramente [le-hay-rah-men´-tay], *adv.* Swiftly, lightly, easily; giddily, slightly (conocer), hastily (juzgar).

ligereza [le-hay-ray´-thah], *f.* 1. Lightness, celerity, fleetness, agility, nimbleness. 2. Levity, unsteadiness, inconstancy, fickleness, flippancy, flirtation. 3. Lightness, want of weight. **Ligereza de espíritu**, light-heartedness. **Obrar con ligereza**, to act rashly.

ligero, ra [le-hay´-ro, rah], *a.* 1. Light, of little weight (de poco peso). 2. Light, thin (tela, ropa). 3. Swift (rápido), light, active, nimble, fleet. 4. Light, gay, airy, unsteady, giddy. 5. Light, trifling. 6. Easily digestible (comida). 7. Unsound, not calm (sueño). 8. Slight (modesto). 9. Superficial (carácter), shallow, flippant; frivolous, flighty. **A la ligera**, lightly, expeditiously. **Ligero de ropa**, lightly clad. **Un ligero conocimiento**, a slight acquaintance. **Ligero de cascos**, scatter-brained. **Juzgar a la ligera**, to judge hastily.

ligeruela [le-hay-roo-ay´-lah], *a.* Applied to early grapes.

ligio, a [lee´-he-o, ah], *a.* Liege, bound by some feudal tenure.

lignito [lig-nee´-to], *m.* Lignite, brown coal.

lignívoro, ra [lig-nee´-vo-ro, rah], *a.* Wood-eating.-*m. pl.* The longicorn beetles.

lignum crucis [lig-noom croo´-this], *m.* Relic of the cross of Christ.

ligomela [le-go-may´-lah], *a.* V. LIGERUELA.

ligón [le-gon´], *a.* 1. Flirtatious (persona). **Es muy ligón**, he´s a great one for the girls. 2. Attractive; provocative, sexy (prenda). 3. Posh (distinguido). -*m.* Womanizer, wolf.

ligue [lee´-gay], *m.* 1. **Se dedica mucho al ligue**, he´s always after the women (acto). 2. Pick-up (acto). 3. Pick-up (persona); boyfriend (chico), girlfriend (chica).

liguero [le-gay´-ro], *m.* Suspender belt, garter belt.

liguilla [le-geel'-lyah], *f.* Kind of narrow ribbon.

lígula [lee'-goo-lah], *f.* 1. *(Anat.)* Epiglottis, the cartilage which covers the larynx. 2. *(Bot.)* Ligule.

ligulado, da [le-goo-lah'-do, dah], *a. (Bot.)* Ligulate, strap-shaped.

ligurino, na [le-goo-ree'-no, nah], or **Ligústico, ca** [le-goos'-te-co, cah], *a.* Ligurian.

ligústico [le-goos'-te-co], *m. (Bot.)* Lovage.

ligustro [le-goos'-tro], *m. (Bot.)* Privet. *V.* ALHEÑA.

lija [lee´-hah], *f.* 1. Dog-fish, a small variety of shark. 2. Skin of the dog-fish used, dry, for polishing wood, lining boxes, etc. **Papel de lija**, sandpaper.

lijar [le-har'], *va.* 1. To smooth, to polish. 2. *(Prov.) V.* LASTIMAR.

lila [lee'-lah], *f.* 1. *(Bot.)* Lilac-tree. 2. Lilac flower. 3. A kind of light woollen stuff of various colors.

lilaila [le-lah-ee'-lah], *f.* 1. Thin woollen stuff. 2. Artifice, trick, wile.

liliáceo, cea [le-le-ah'-thay-o, ah], *a.* Liliaceous, of the lily family.

lililí [le-le-lee'], *m.* War-whoop of the Moors.

lima [lee'-mah], *f.* 1. *(Bot.)* Lime-tree. 2. Lime, the fruit of the lime-tree, also, the sweet lime, another variety of small lemon. 3. File (herramienta), an instrument for smoothing metals. 4. *(Met.)* Correction, finish, polish. 5. Channel in the roof of a house for the water to pass to the eaves. **Lima de uñas**, nail file. **Dar la última lima a una obra**, to give a work its final polish.

limación [le-mah-the-on'], *f.* The process of filing roughnesses of the teeth.

limadura [le-mah-doo'-rah], *f.* 1. Act of filing. 2. Filing, limature, metallic fragment rubbed off by the file.

limalla [le-mahl'-lyah], *f.* Filings.

limar [le-mar'], *va.* 1. To file, to cut with a file. 2. To file, to polish; to give the finishing stroke to literary productions.

limatón [le-mah-tone'], *m.* Coarse round file.

limaza [le-mah'-thah], *f.* 1. Snail. 2. Archimedes' screw. 3. A disease of the feet of cattle.

limazo [le-mah'-tho], *m.* Viscosity, sliminess.

limazón [le-mah-thone'], *m.* Slug, a snail or slimy animal without a shell.

limbo [leem'-bo], *m.* 1. Limbo, a region assigned to the souls of unbaptized children. 2. *(Ast.)* Limb, edge or border of the sun or moon. 3. Limb, exterior graduated border of a quadrant. 4. *(Zool.)* Circumference, or edge of a bivalve shell. **Estar en el limbo**, to be in limbo.

limen [lee'-men], *m. (Poet.) V.* UMBRAL.

limeño, ña [le-may'-nyo, nyah], *a.* Belonging to or native of the city Lima.

limera [le-may'-rah], *f.* 1. Shopwoman who sells files or limes. 2. *(Naut.)* Helmport, where the tiller is fastened to the rudder of the ship.

limero [le-may'-ro], *m.* 1. Shopkeeper who sells files or limes. 2. *(Bot.)* Lime-tree.

limeta [le-may'-tah], *f.* 1. Vial, a small bottle (botella). 2. *(Amer.)* Medium sized wine bottle. 3. *(Cono Sur)* Broad brow (frente).

limiste [le-mees'-tay], *m.* Cloth made of Segovia wool; cloth of the first quality.

limitación [le-me-tah-the-on'], *f.* 1. Limitation, restriction, modification, circumscription, corrective; conditionality. 2. Limit, district. **Limitación de velocidad**, speed restriction.

limitadamente [le-me-tah-dah-men'-tay], *adv.* Limitedly, finitely.

limitado, da [le-me-tah'-do, dah], *a.* Limited, possessed of little talent. *-f. (Com.)* Of limited liability.*-pp.* of LIMITER.

limitador, ra [le-me tah-dor', rah], *m. & f.* One who limits, circumscriber.

limitáneo, nea [le-me-tah'-nay-o, ah], *a.* 1. Limitary, placed on the boundaries. 2. Limitaneous, belonging to limits.

limitar [le-me-tar'], *va.* 1. To limit (restringir), to confine within bounds, to narrow. 2. To form boundaries, to establish

limits. 3. To restrain, to circumscribe; to reduce expense. *-vr.* To limit oneself, to restrict oneself. **Limitarse a**, to limit oneself to.

límite [lee'-me-tay], *m.* Limit, boundary, bound, border, confine. **Límite forestal**, timber line. **Límite de velocidad**, speed limit. **Poner un límite a**, to set a limit to. **No tener límites**, to have no limits. *-adv.* **Caso límite**, extreme case. **Situaciones límites**, extreme situations.

limítrofe [le-mee'-tro-fay], *a.* Limiting, bounding, conterminous, limitary applied to frontier provinces.

limnea [lim-nay'-ah], *f.* Limnaea, the common pond-snail.

limo [lee'-mo], *m.* Slime (barro), mud.

limón [le-mone'], *m.* 1. Lemon, the fruit of the lemon-tree. 2. *(Bot.)* Lemon-tree. 3. *V.* LIMONERO. *(Per.)*

limonada [le-mo-nah'-dah], *f.* Lemonade. **Limonada de vino**, lemonade mixed with wine.

limonado, da [le-mo-nah'-do, dah], *a.* Lemon colored.

limonar [le-mo-nar'], *m.* Plantation of lemon-trees.

limoncillo [le-mon-theel'-lyo],*m. dim.* A small lemon.

limonera [le-mo-nay'-rah], *f.* Shaft of a cart.

limonero [le-mo-nay'-ro], *m. (Bot.)* Lemon-tree. *m. & f.* Dealer in lemons.*-a.* Applied to the shaft horses in carriages.

limonza [le-mon'-thah], *f.* The citron, or the bitter lemon.

limoscapo [le-mos-cah'-po], *m. (Arch.)* The part of the shaft of a column nearest the base, apophyge.

limosidad [le-mo-se-dahd'], *f.* 1. Sliminess. 2. Foul matter between teeth.

limosna [le-mos'-nah], *f.* Alms, charity. **Pedir limosna**, to beg. **Vivir de limosna**, to live by begging.

limosnero [le-mos-nay'ro], *m.* Almoner.*-a.* Charitable.

limoso, sa [le-mo'-so, sah], *a.* Slimy, muddy, limose.

limpia [leem'-pe-ah], *f.* 1. Cleansing, freeing from dirt. 2. Dredging of harbors. 3. A certain tax paid by ships in harbors where dredging is required. 4. *(CAm. Mex. Agr.)* Weeding, cleaning. *-m.* Boot-black.

limpiabotas [lim-pe-ah-bo'-tas], *m.* A shoe-cleaner.

limpiachimeneas [leem´-pe-ah-che-may-nay'-as], *m.* Chimney-sweeper.

limpiacristales [leem-pe-ah-cres-tah'-lays], *m.* Window-cleaner.

limpiadera [lim-pe-ah-day'-rah], *f.* 1. A clothes-brush. 2. Comb-brush; a plough-cleaner.

limpiadientes [lim-pe-ah-de-en'-tes], *m.* Toothpick.

limpiador, ra [lim-pe-ah-dor', rah], *m. & f.* Cleanser, scourer.

limpiadura [lim-pe-ah-doo'-rah],*f.* Cleaning.*-pl.* Dirt thrown away in cleaning anything.

limpiamente [lim-pe-ah-men'-tay], *adv.* Cleanly, neatly; purely; sincerely, faithfully.

limpiametales [lim-pe-ah-may-tah'-lays], *m.* Metal polish.

limpiamiento [lim-pe-ah-me-en'-to], *m.* Act of cleaning.

limpiaoídos [lim-pe-ah-o-ee'-dos], *m.* Earspoon, earpick.

limpiaojos [lim-pe-ah-o'-hos], *m.* An eyestone.

limpiaparabrisas [lim-pe-ah-pah-rah-bree'-sahs], *m.* Windscreen wiper.

limpiaplumas [lim-pe-ah-ploo'-mas], *m.* A penwiper.

limpiar [lim-pe-ar'], *va.* 1. To clean, to scour, to cleanse. **Limpiar en seco**, to dry-clean. 2. To purify, to clear from guilt. 3. To pursue, to persecute. 4. *(coll.)* To steal (robar). 5. To clean out (en el juego). 6. *(Mex.)* To hit, to bash (pegar). *-vr.* 1. To clear oneself from imputed guilt. 2. To clean oneself. **Limpiarse las narices**, to wipe one´s nose.

limpiauñas [lim-pe-ah-oo'-nyas], *m.* Fingernail cleaner.

limpidez [lim-pe-deth'], *f.* Transparency, limpidity.

límpido, da [leem'-pe-do, dah], *a.* Limpid, crystal-clear, transparent.

limpieza [lim-pe-ay'-thah], *f.* 1. Cleanness (estado), cleanliness, neatness, purity, limpidness. 2. Chastity, purity of morals. 3. Integrity, rectitude; disinterestedness (cualidad). 4. Purity of blood. **Limpieza de bolsa**, emptiness of the purse. **Limpieza en seco**, dry-cleaning.

limpio, pia [leem'-pe-o, ah], *a.* 1. Clean, free from stain; cleanly, limpid. 2. Neat (ordenado), elegant. 3. Pure: applied to families unconnected with Moors or Jews. 4. Pure, unmingled (maíz). 5. Pure (agua), free, clear (despejado). 6. Clear of all charges, net. 7. Pure (moralmente); honest (honrado); fair (juego). 8. Alone (solo). 9. **Estar limpio**, Not to know a single thing. **Jugar limpio**, to deal fair, to act uprightly. **Poner en limpio**, to make a fair copy. **Tierra limpia**, even, flat country. **Costa limpia**, *(Naut.)* clear coast, without shoals, sand-banks, or shallows. **En limpio**, in substance; net price; clearly. **Más limpio que el oro**, as clean as can be. **50 dólares de ganancia limpia**, 50 dollars of clear profit. **Luchar a puñetazo limpio**, to fight with bare fists. *-adv.* Fair, clean. *-m.* En limpio, clearly. **No pude sacar nada en limpio**, I couldn´t make anything of it.

limpión [lim-pe-on'], *m.* A hasty cleaning. **Date un limpión**, *(coll.)* ironical phrase telling someone he will not get what he wishes.

límulo [lee'-moo-lo], *m.* Limulus, king-crab.

limusina [lee-moo-see'-nah], *f.* Limousine.

lináceas [le-nah'-thay-as], *a. & f.* Linaceous, of the flax family.

linaje [le-nah'-hay], *m.* 1. Lineage (familia), race, progeny, offspring, family, house, kin, extraction, generation. 2. Class (clase), condition. 3. *(Prov.)* Nobless, nobility.

linajista [le-nah-hees'-tah], *m.* Genealogist, a writer of pedigrees.

linajudo, da [le-nah-hoo'-do, dah], *m. & f. & a.* 1. One who boasts of his origin or family. 2. *m.* Genealogist.

lináloe [le-nah'-lo-ay], *m.* Aloes. V. ÁLOE.

linar [le-nar'], *m.* Flax field, land on which flax is grown.

linaria [le-nah'-re-ah], *f. (Bot.)* Wild flax, yellow toad flax.

linaza [le-nah'-thah], *f.* Linseed, the seed of flax. **Aceite de linaza**, linseed oil.

lince [leen'-thay], *m.* 1. Lynx; *(C'Am. Mex.)* wild cat. 2. Person of great acuteness and perspicacity. 3. *(LAm.)* Sharpness, intelligence.

lince [leen'-thay], *a.* 1. Sharp-sighted, quick-sighted. **Ojos de lince**, sharp eyes. 2. Acute, penetrating.

lincear [lin-thay-ar'], *va. (coll.)* To discover, to note what may be seen with difficulty.

linchamiento [lin-chah-me-ayn'-to], *m.* Lynching.

linchar [lin-char'], *va.* To lynch.

linches [leen'-chays], *m. pl. (Mex.)* Saddle-bags made from the fiber of the maguey (alforjas).

lindamente [lin-dah-men'-tay], *adv* Neatly, elegantly (con elegancia).

lindar [lin-dar'], *vn.* To be contiguous, to be adjacent. **Lindar con**, to border on.

linde [leen'-day], *m. & f.* Landmark, boundary, limit.

linde [leen'-day], *a.* Contiguous, bordering upon.

lindero, ra [lin-day'-ro, rah], *a.* Contiguous, bordering upon.

lindero [lin-day'-ro], *m.* V. LINDE.

lindeza [lin-day'-thah], *f.* 1. Neatness, elegance (elegancia), prettiness (atractivo). 2. *pl. (Iron.)* Improprieties, insults. 3. Witticism (ocurrencia).

lindo, da [leen'-do, dah], *a.* 1. Neat, handsome (hombre), pretty (bonito), fine, genteel. 2. Complete, perfect. 3. Nice (precioso), lovely; fine (excelente). **De lo lindo**, perfectly, wonderfully. **Un lindo carro**, a lovely car. *-adv. (LAm.)* Nicely, well, marvellously. **Baila lindo**, she dances beautifully. *-m.* Beau, coxcomb, minion.

lindón [lin-done'], *m.* Ridge, ground thrown up between asparagus beds.

lindura [lin-doo'-rah], *f.* V. LINDEZA.

línea [lee'-nay-ah], *f.* 1. Line, longitudinal extension. 2. V. RAYA. 3. V. RENGLÓN. 4. Line (genealogía), lineage, progeny, family ascending or descending. 5. Line, equator, equinoctial line. 6. Line, boundary, limit. 7. Class, order. 8. *(Mil.)* Trench or intrenchment. 9. *(Mil.)* Rank of soldiers. 10. Line, twelfth part of an inch. **Línea aérea**, airline. **Línea de batalla**, line of battle. **Línea de fuego**, firing line. **Primera línea**, front line. **En línea**, in line. **Leer entre líneas**, to read between the lines. **Guardar la línea**, to keep one´s figure. 11. *(Inform.)* **Línea de bloqueo**,

locking line. **"Línea caliente"**, "hot line". **Línea de fuego**, line of fire.

lineal [le-nay-ahl'], *a.* Lineal, composed of lines. **Lineal de partido**, party line.

lineamento [le-nay-ah-men'-to], *m.* Lineament, exterior feature of a body.

lineamiento [le-nay-ah-me-en'-to], *m.* Lineament, feature.

linear [le-nay-ar'], *va.* To draw lines, to form with lines.

linfa [leen'-fah], *f.* 1. Lymph, a fluid of the body. 2. *(Poet.)* Water.

linfático, ca [lin-fah'-te-co, cah], *a.* Lymphatic, pertaining to lymph (vasos y glándulas).

linfoquicia [lin-fo-kee'-the-ah], *f. (Med.)* Serous diarrhoea.

lingotazo [lin-go-tah'-tho], *m.* Swig, shot.

lingote [lin-go'-tay], *m. (Min.)* Ingot, a mass of gold or silver, lingot, a pig of metal.

lingual [lin-goo-ahl'], *a.* Lingual, relating to the tongue.

linguete [lin-gay'-tay], *m.* A pawl; a ratchet.

lingüista [lin-goo-ees'-tah], *m & f.* Linguist, one versed in languages.

lingüística [lin-goo-ees'-te-cah], *f.* Linguistics, the science of languages, comparative philology.

lingüístico, ca [lin-goo-ees'-te-co, cah], *a.* Linguistic, relating to language or linguistics.

linier [le-ne-ayr'], *m. (Dep.)* Linesman.

linimento [le-ne-men'-to], *m. (Med.)* Liniment.

linio [lee'-ne-o], *m.* V. LIÑO.

lino [lee'-no], *m.* 1. *(Bot.)* Flax. 2. Linen (tela fina). 3. Sailcloth, canvas (lona). 4. *(Carib. Cono Sur)* Linseed. **Géneros de lino**, linen goods.

linóleo [le-no'-layo], *m.* Linoleum.

linón [le-non'], *m.* Lawn.

linotipia [le-no-tee'-pe-ah], *f.* Linotype machine.

linotípico, ca [le-no-tee'-pe-co, cah], *a.* Linotype.

linotipista [le-no-te-pees'-tah], *m. & f.* Linotype operator.

linotipo [le-no-tee'-po], *m.* Linotype.

lintel [lin-tel], *m.* Lintel,

linterna [lin-terr'-nah], *f.* 1. Lantern. 2. *(Arch.)* Small tower, cupola. 3. *(Mech.)* Lantern pinion. 4. *(Arg.)* Firefly. **Linterna de proyección**, slide projector. **Linterna eléctrica**, flashlight. **Linterna mágica**, magic lantern. **Linterna de bolsillo**, torch.

linternazo [lin-ter-nah'-tho], *m.* 1. Blow with a lantern. 2. *(coll.)* Wallop, crack.

linternero [lin-ter-nay'-ro], *m.* Lantern maker.

linternilla [lin-ter-neel'-lyah], *f dim.* A small lantern.

linueso [le-noo-ay'-so], *m.* V. LINAZA.

liño [lee'-nyo], *m.* 1. Row of trees or plants. 2. Ridge between furrows in ploughed land.

liñuelo [len-yoo-ay'-lo], *m.* Rope, cord.

lío [lee'-o], *m.* 1. Bundle, parcel, package (paquete). 2. *(coll.)* Entanglement, row (jaleo), mess (confusión), jam (aprieto). 3. Affair (amorío), liaison. 4. Tale (chisme), piece of gossip. **Armar un lío**, to start a fight. **Hacerse uno un lío**, to become entangled, to get all confused. **Ese lío de los pasaportes**, that fuss about the passports. **Se armó un tremendo lío**, there was an almighty row.

liorna [le-or-nah], *f. (coll.)* Uproar, hullabaloo, confusion.

lioso [le-o'-so], *a.* Gossipy.

lipia [lee'-pe-ah], *f.* Lippia, a plant of the verbena family. Lipia citriodora is the lemonscented verbena.

lipis [lee'-pis], *f.* Blue vitriol, copper sulphate.

lipitud [le-pe-tood'], *f. (Med.)* Lippitude, blearedness of the eyes.

lipotimia [le-po-te'-me-ah], *f.* Faint, black-out.

liquen [lee'-ken], *m.* Lichen, a low cryptogamic plant.

líquida [le'-ke-dah], *f. (Ling.)* liquid.

liquidable [le-kee-dah'-blay], *a.* Liquefiable.

liquidación [le-kee-dah-the-on'], *f.* 1 Liquidation, settlement. 2. Balance. 3. Sale, clearance sale. **Vender en liquidación**, to sell out. 4. *(Pol.)* To liquidate, to eliminate.

líquidamente [lee'-ke-dah-men-tay], *adv.* In a liquid manner.

liquidar [le-kee-dar'], *va.* 1. To liquefy, to melt, to dissolve. **Liquidar cuentas**, to clear accounts, to liquidate debts. 2. *(Pol.)* To liquidate, to eliminate; *(LAm.)* to bump up (matar). 3. *(LAm.)* To destroy, to ruin (destrozar). *-vr.* 1. To liquefy, to liquate, to grow liquid. 2. To become liquid: used of letters.

liquidez [le-kee-deth'], *f.* Liquidness, fluidity.

liquidificar [le-ke-de-fe-car'], *va.* To dissolve, to liquify.

líquido, da [lee'-ke-do, dah], *a.* 1. Liquid, fluid, fluent. 2. Evident, clear. 3. Net, neat. **Ganancia líquida**, net profit. 4. *(LAm.)* Exact; accurate, right, correctly measured. *-m.* 1. Liquid, fluid. 2. *(Fin.)* Cash, ready money (efectivo).

lira [lee'-rah], *f.* 1. Lyre, a harp; a lyric poem. 2. Lyra, a northern constellation. 3. *(Fin.)* Lira.

liria [lee'-re-ah], *f.* V. LIGA, bird-lime.

lírico, ca [lee'-re-co, cah], *a.* Lyric, lyrical.

lirio [lee'-re-o], *m.* The lily. **Lirio blanco**, V. AZUCENA. **Lirio florentino**, Florentine iris.

lirón [le-rone'], *m.* 1. Dormouse; *(Fig.)* sleepy head. **Dormir como un lirón**, to sleep like a log. 2. *(Bot.)* V. ALISMA. 3. *(Naut.)* Jackscrew.

lirondo, da [le-ron'-do, dah], *a.* Pure, clean, neat.

lis [lees], *f.* Flor de lis, flower-deluce, iris.

lisa [lee'-sah], *f.* 1. A smooth stone for polishing paper. 2. A mixture for moulding the letters of a bell

lisamente [le-sah-men'-tay], *adv.* Smoothly, plainly. **Lisa y llanamente**, openly and frankly; without dispute or contention.

lisbonense [lis-bo-nen'-say], or **lisbonés, sa** [lis-bo-nays', sah], *a.* Belonging to or native of Lisbon.

lisera [le-say'-rah], *f.* Large cane used in silkworm sheds.

lisiado, da [le-se-ah'-do, dah], *a.* *(Met.)* Lamed (cojo), injured, hurt. *(Prov.)* Anxiously, desirous.*-pp.* of LISIAR.

lisiar [le-se-ar'], *va.* To lame; to hurt a limb, to injure (herir).

lisimaquia [le-se-mah'-ke-ah], *f.* *(Bot.)* Loose strife.

lisis [lee'-sis], *f.* Lysis, the gradual abatement of disease, opposed to crisis.

liso, sa [lee'-so, sah], *a.* 1. Plain, even, flat (carrera), glib, smooth, straight (liso). **Liso como la palma de la mano**, as smooth as glass. 2. Clear, evident. 3. *(And, Mex.)* Fresh, cheeky. **Liso y llano**, straightforward. *-m. (Cono Sur)* Tall beer glass.

lisonja [le-son'-hah], *f.* 1. Adulation. flattery, fawning, coaxing. 2. *(Her.)* Lozenge. 3. *(Geom.)* Rhomb or rhombus. *-m.* Lysol.

lisonjado, da [le-son-hah'-do, dah], *a.* *(Her.)* Lozenged; rhombic.

lisonjeador, ra [le-son-hay-ah-dor', rah], *m. & f.* Flatterer.

lisonjear [le-son-hay-ar'], *va.* 1. To flatter (halagar), to praise deceitfully, to coax, to wheedle, to fawn. 2. To delight, to please (agradar).

lisonjeramente [le-son-hay-rah-men'-tay], *adv.* Flatteringly, fawningly.

lisonjero, ra [le-son-hay'-ro, rah], *m. & f.* A flatterer, a fawner, a parasite. *-a.* 1. Parasitical, wheedling, fawning. 2. Flattering (halagüeño), pleasing (agradable), agreeable.

LISP [leesp], *(Inform.)* LISP (LISt Processor).

lista [lees'-tah], *f.* 1. Slip of paper, shred of linen, a list or strip of cloth (de tela). 2. Selvage, the edge of cloth. 3. List, catalogue (catálogo). *(Law.)* Docket. 4. Stripe (raya). **Pasar lista**, to call over; to muster, to review troops, to call the roll. **Lista de gastos**, bill of expense and charges. **Lista de direcciones**, mailing list. **Lista de premios**, prize or honors list. **Tela a listas**, striped material.

listadillo [lis-tah-deel'-lyo], *m. (Amer.)* 1. Cotton cloth striped white and blue. 2. Striped gingham.

listado, da [lis-tah'-do, dah], *a.* Striped, listed.*-pp.* of LISTAR.*-m. pl.* **Listados**, striped checks, plaid.

listadura [lis-tah-doo'-rah], *f.* 1. The action of listing or applying strips. 2. The thing so listed.

listar [lis-tar'], *va.* 1. To list, to cover with srips of sloth. 2. V. ALISTAR.

listeado, da [lis-tay-ah'-do, dah], *a.* V. LISTADO.

listel, listelo [lis-tel', lis-tay'-lo], *m. (Arch.)* V. FILETE.

listero, ra [lis-tay'-ro], *m & f.* Time keeper, wages clerk.

listillo, lla [lis-teel'-lyo], *m & f.* Know-all.

listín [lis-teen'], *m. (Telec.)* List of numbers, *(Carib.)* newspaper.

listo, ta [lees'-to, tah], *a.* Ready, diligent, prompt, active, clever (carácter). **Todo está listo**, everything is ready. **Ser más listo que el hambre**, to be as smart as they come. **Van listos si piensan eso**, if they think that they've got another thing coming.

listón [lis-tone'], *m.* 1. Ribbon. 2. Ferret, tape. 3. Lath, cleat, strip (madera). 4. *(Arch.)* Fillet. *5. (Dep.)* Bar (salto de altura).

listonado, da [lis-to-nah'-do, dah], *a.* *(Arch.)* Barred, striped, filleted.

listonar [lis-to-nar'], *va.* To batten, to lath.

listonería [lis-to-nay-ree'-ah], *f.* 1. Parcel of ribbons, tapes, and inkles. 2. A ribbon-store; ribbon-manufactory.

listonero, ra [lis-to-nay'-ro, rah], *m. & f.* Ribbon-maker.

lisura [le-soo'-rah], *f.* 1. Smoothness (superficie), evenness, flatness. 2. Sincerity, candor, plainness (sinceridad). 3. *(LAm.)* Shamelessness (descaro), brazenness.

lita [lee'-tah], *f.* Larva of an insect which fixes itself under the tongue of certain quadrupeds.

litación [le-tah-the-on'], *f.* Sacrificing.

litagogo, ga [le-tah-go'-go, gah], *a.* Lithagogue, solvent of urinary calculi; also, lithontriptic, destroying calculi (instrumentos médicos).

litar [le-tar'], *va.* To sacrifice to the divinity.

litarge, litargirio [le-tar'-hay, le-tar-hee'-re-o], *m.* Litharge. V. ALMÁRTAGA.

lite [lee'-tay], *f.* Lawsuit, process. V. PLEITO.

litera [le-tay'-rah], *f.* Litter, stretcher, bed, bunk (cama). **Litera alta**, upper berth (en coche). **Litera baja**, lower berth.

literal [le-tay-rahl'], *a.* Literal.

literalmente [le-tay-rahl'-men-tay], *adv.* Literally.

literario, ria [le-tay-rah'-re-o, ah], *a.* Literary.

literatillo [le-tay-rah-teel'-lyo], *m. dim.* of LITERATO: commonly used in contempt.

literato, ta [le-tay-rah'-to, tah], *a.* Learned, lettered, literate, versed in sciences and letters.

literato [le-tay-rah'-to], *m.* A learned man, a literary man.*-pl.* Literati, the learned.

literatura [le-tay-rah-too'-rah], *f.* Literature, learning; skill in sciences and letters.

literero [le-tay-ray'-ro], *m.* One who drives a litter.

litiasis [le-te-ah'-sis], *f. (Med.)* Lithiasis, the formation of stones or gravel in the human body, especially in the urinary passages.

litigación [le-te-gah-the-on'], *f.* Litigation.

litigante [le-te-gahn'-tay], *pa. & n.* Litigating; litigant; a party concerned in a lawsuit.

litigar [le-te-gar'], *va.* 1. To litigate, to manage a suit at law. 2. To contend, to dispute. *-vn.* To go to law; to argue.

litigio [le-tee'-he-o], *m.* 1. Litigation, lawsuit. 2. Dispute, contest.

litigioso, sa [le-te-he-o'-so, sah], *a.* Litigious, contentious.

litina [le-tee'-nah], *f.* Lithia, lithium oxide.

litio [lee'-te-o], *m.* Lithium, an alkaline metal, the lightest solid element.

litis [lee'-tis], *f.* V. LITE.

litisconsorte [le-tis-con-sor'-tay], *com.* Associate in a lawsuit.

litiscontestación [le-tis-con-tes-tah-the-on'], *f. (Law.)* Answer to a juridical command.

litisexpensas [le-ti-sex-pen'-sas], *f. pl. (Law.)* Costs of suit.

litispendencia [le-tis-pen-den'-the-ah], *f.* The state of a lawsuit which is under judgment or pending.

litocálamo [le-to-ca'-lah-mo], *m.* Petrified or fossil reed.

litoclasto [le-to-clahs'-to], *m.* Lithoclast, an instrument for crushing stone in the bladder.

litocola [le-to-co'-lah], *f.* Lithocolla, lapidary's cement, composed of marble dust, glue, and white of egg.

litófago, ga [le-to'-fah-go, gah], *a*. Rock consuming.

litófilo, la [le-to'-fe-lo, lah], *a*. *(Bot.)* Growing on or attached to rocks.

litófito [le-to'-fe-to], *m*. Lithophyte, a stone plant, coral.

litofotografía [le-to-fo-to-grah-fee'-ah],*f. V.* FOTOLITOGRAFÍA.

litografía [le-to-grah-fee'-ah], *f*. Lithography, printing from prepared stone. Inv. 1799, by Senefelder.

litografiar [le-to-grah-fe-ar'], *va*. To lithograph.

litográfico, ca [le-to-grah'-fe-co, cah], *a*. Lithographic.

litógrafo [le-to'-grah-fo], *m*. Lithologist.

litoídeo, dea [le-to-ee'-day-o, ah], *a*. Lithoid, having the appearance of stone.

litolapaxia [li-to-lah-pahc'-se-ah], *f*. Litholapaxy, crushing of a stone and washing out at one operation.

litología [le-to-lo-hee'-ah], *f*. Lithology, natural history of stones.

litológico, ca [le-to-lo'-he-co, cah], *a*. Lithological, mineralogical.

litólogo [le-to'-lo-go], *m* Lithologist.

litoral [le-to-rahl'], *a*. Littoral, seaboard, pertaining to the shore.*-m*. Coast line, littoral, seaboard.

litoscopio [le-tos-co'-pe-o], *m*. Lithoscope.

litosfera [le-tos-fay'-rah], *f*. Lithosphere.

litote [le-to'-tay], *f*. Litotes, a rhetorical figure: denial of the opposite.

litotricia [le-to-tree'-the-ah], *f*. Lithotrity, the crushing of a stone within the bladder.

litotritor [le-to-tre-tor'], *m*. Lithotrite, instrument for crushing vesical calculi.

litoxilo [le-toc-see'-lo], *m*. Petrified wood.

litrámetro [le-trah'-may-tro], *m*. Litrameter, an instrument for measuring the specific gravity of liquids.

litro [lee'-tro], *m*. Liter, a unit of capacity in the decimal system. One cubic decimeter.

lituano, no [le-too-ah'-no, nah], *a*. Lithuanian.

lituo [lee'-too-o], *m*. 1. Ancient military instrument of music. 2. Lituus, augur's staff.

liturgia [le-toor' he-ah], *f*. Liturgy, form of prayers, manner of celebrating the mass.

litúrgico, ca [le-toor'-he-co, cah], *a*. Liturgical, liturgic, belonging to the liturgy.

livianamente [le-ve-ah-nah-men'-tay], *adv*. Licentiously; with levity; lightly.

liviandad [le-ve-an-dahd'], *f*. 1. Lightness, want of weight. 2. Levity, imprudence. 3. Incontinence, libidinousness.

liviano, na [le-ve-ah'-no, nah], *a*. 1. Light, of little weight. 2. Imprudent, light, unsteady. 3. Incontinent, unchaste, libidinous.

livianos [le-ve-ah'-nos], *m. pl*. Lungs. *V.* BOFES.

lividez [le-ve-deth'], *f*. 1. Lividity, lividness. 2. The black and blue color of a bruise. 3. *(LAm.)* Paleness, pallor.

lívido, da [lee'-ve-do, dah], *a*. 1. Livid (morado). *V.* AMORATADO. 2. Pale (pálido).

lixiviación [lec-se-ve-ah-the-on'], *f*. Leaching, or lixiviation of an alkali.

liza [lee'-thah], *f*. 1. Skate, a sea fish. 2. Arena for tournaments, prize ring.

lizo [lee'-tho], *m*. Skein of silk.

lizón [le-thone'], *m*. *(Bot.)* Water plantain.

ll [el'-lyay], *f.,* It was formerly a letter of the Spanish alphabet. Though double in figure, it is considered simple in its sound. It should not, therefore, be divided at the end of a line, but added to the succeeding vowel with which it forms a complete syllable: as *hallar, seguidi-lla*. It has the liquid sound of *lli* in halliard.

llábana [lyah'-bah-nah], *f*. *(Prov.)* A natural flagstone, smooth and commonly slippery from the action of water.

llaga [lyah'-gah], *f*. 1. An ulcer (úlcera). 2. Wound (herida), sore. 3. Prick, thorn, tormenting thought. 4. Crack between the bricks of a wall.

llagar [lyah-gar'], *va*. To wound, to hurt, to injure.

llama [lyah'-mah],*f*. 1. Flame, light emitted from fire. 2. Flame, force and violence of passion. 3. *V.* ALPACA. In this sense (*lama*), though feminine in America, it is masculine according to the Spanish Academy. 4. *(Prov.)* Marshy ground. **Arder sin llama**, to smoulder. **Estallar en llamas**, to burst into flames. *-f. (Zool.)* Llama (animal).

llamada [lyah-mah'-dah], *f*. 1. Call, the act of calling (a la puerta). 2. Marginal note. 3. Any motion or sign to call attention (ademán). 4. *(Mil.)* A call by drum or trumpet; chamade. 5. *(Com.)* Notice, entry. 6. *(Mex.)* Cowardliness (cobardía). **La última llamada**, the last call. **Llamada a larga distancia**, long-distance call. **Llamada gratuita**, toll free number.

llamador, ra [lyah-mah-dor', rah], *m. & f*. 1. Caller, he who calls (persona). 2 Beadle, messenger. 3. Knocker of a door (aldaba). 4. Servant of a salesman, vulgarly called barker, clicker, or drummer.

llamamiento [lyah-mah-me-en'-to], *m*. 1. Calling, call, the act of calling. 2. Convocation, the act of convening the members of an assembly or corporation. 3. Calling, call, inspiration, divine vocation.

llamar [lyah-mar'], *va*. 1. To call to one (nombrar). 2. To call, to summon (convocar), to cite. 3. To call, or call upon, to invoke, to appeal to. 4. To call, to invoke with ardor of piety 5. To call, to name, to denominate. 6. To incline. 7. To call, to attract. 8. To excite thirst. 9. To knock (puerta). **Llamar a la puerta**, to knock or rap at the door. **Llaman**, someone is knocking. **Llamar por los nombres**, to call roll. **Llamar** or **dar voces para que se haga alguna cosa**, to call out orders to have something done. **¿Cómo le van a llamar?**, what are they going to call him? **Que me llamen a las 7**, please have them call me at 7. **Llamar al departamento de asistencia técnica**, *(Comput.)* service call.*-vn*. 1. To call. **Llamar por ayuda**, to call for help. 2. To knock (a la puerta). *-vr*. To be called, to be named. **Me llamo Mimi**, my name is Mimi. **¡Eso se llama cantar !**, that's what you really call singing.

llamarada [lyah-mah-rah'-dah], *f*. 1. A sudden blaze of fire, a flash. 2. Flash, a sudden burst of wit. 3. Sudden flush of the face.

llamativo, va [lyah-mah-tee'-vo, vah], *a*. 1. Exciting thirst. 2. Showy. **De modo llamativo**, in such a way as to draw attention.

llamazar [lyah-mah-thar'], *m*. Swamp.

llambria [lyahm'-bre-ah], *f*. Steep face of a rock difficult to pass. *(Acad.)*

llamear [lyah-may-ar'], *vn*. To blaze.

llana [lyah'-nah], *f*. 1. Trowel, a tool for spreading mortar. 2. Page of a book or writing. 3. Plain.

llanada [lyah-nah'-dah], *f*. A plain, a tract of level ground.

llanamente [lyah'-nah-men-tay], *adv*. Ingenuously, simply, sincerely; simply; plainly.

llanero, ra [lyah-nay'-ro, rah], *m. & f*. Plainsman or plainswoman, inhabitant of the plains.

llaneza [lyah-nay'-thah], *f*. 1. Plainness, sincerity, simplicity. 2. Want of attention and respect, familiarity. 3. Uncultivated style.

llano, na [lyah'-no, nah], *a*. 1. Plain, even, level (superficie), smooth, flat. 2. Meek, homely, affable. 3. Unmannerly, uncivil. 4 Plain (sencillo), open (franco), honestly rough. 5. Plain, simple, void of ornament. 6. Plain, clear, evident, discernible. 7. Plain, simple, not varied by art (estilo). 8. *V.* PECHERO. **En lenguaje llano**, in plain language. **De llano**, openly.

llano [lyah'-no], *m*. A level field, an even ground.

llanta [lyahn'-tah], *f*. 1. *(Bot.)* V. BERZA LLANTA. 2. Tire, the iron hoop or band of a wheel; *(Carib.)* large finger-ring (anillo).

llantén [lyan-ten'], *m*. *(Bot.)* Plantain. **Llantén de agua**, *V.* LIZÓN.

llantina [lyan-tee'-nah], *f*. A violent fit of crying, especially in children.

llanto [lyahn´-to], *m.* Flood of tears, crying, weeping.

llanura [lyah-noo'-rah], *f.* 1. Evenness, equality; flatness (superficie), level. 3. A vast tract of level ground, a prairie.

llapa [lyah-pah], *f.* 1. An additional portion of mercury added to metal for working in a smelting furnace. 2. *(Peru)* A gratuity given to the buyer.

llapar [lyah-par'], *va.* To add an additional portion of quicksilver in extracting metals.

llares [lyah'-res], *m. pl.* Pot-hanger, an iron chain, on which pots are hung over the fire.

llave [lyah'-vay], *f.* 1. Key (de puerta). 2. Wrench. 3. Spigot, faucet, tap (grifo). 4. Lock, gunlock (de escopeta). 5. Bracket. 6. Hold (lucha). 7. *(Mus.)* Stop, key. **Bajo llave**, under lock and key. **Echar la llave a**, 1. To lock. 2. *(Fig.)* To put the finishing touches on. **Llave de percusión**, percussion lock. **Llave inglesa**, monkey wrench. **Llave maestra**, master key. **Llave de cambio**, shift key. **Cerrar una puerta con llave**, to lock a door. **Llave de paso**, stopcock.

llavero, ra [lyah-vay'-ro, rah], *m. & f.* 1. Keeper of the keys. 2. Ring in which keys are kept. 3. *(Prov.)* Housekeeper.

lle, *pron. obs.* V. LE.

llegada [lyay-gah'-dah], *f.* Arrival, coming.

llegar [lyay-gar'], *vn.* 1. To arrive, to come to any place. 2. To reach (alcanzar), to arrive at, to go as far as, to fetch. 3. To last, to continue. 4. To attain a purpose. 5. To suffice, to be enough (bastar). 6. To ascend; to amount to (sumar).-*va.* 1. To approach, to bring near to. 2. To join. -*vr.* 1. To approach, to draw near. 2. To proceed to some neighboring place. 3. To unite. **Llegar a**, to come to, to get to be, to succeed in. **Llegar a ser**, to come to be. **Llegar y besar**, no sooner said than done. **No llegar a uno la camisa al cuerpo**, to be terrified and anxious. **Llegar a las manos**, to come to blows, to fight. **Llegar a oír**, to hear. **Llegar a saber**, to find out, to be informed of. **No llegar**, to fall short, not to reach. *(Met.)* To be inferior. **Hacer llegar una carta a**, to send a letter to. **Cuando llegue eso**, when that happens. **El importe llega a 50 pesos**, the total is 50 pesos. **Por fin llegó a hacerlo**, he managed to do it eventually. **Si llego a saberlo**, if I had known it.

lleira [lyay'-e-rah], *f. (Prov.)* Place full of pebbles or gravel.

llena [lyay'-nah], *f.* Alluvion, overflow of rivers.

llenamente [lyay'-nah-men-tay], *adv.* Fully, copiously.

llenar [lyay-nar'], *va.* 1. To fill, to stuff. 2. To occupy a public place. 3. To fill, to satisfy (deseo), to content. 4 To make up a number. 5. To beget young. 6. To fill in (formulario), to cover (superficie). -*vr.* 1. To feed gluttonously. 2. To be irritated after having suffered long. **Llenar completamente**, to fill up. *(Fig.)* **Llenar a uno de elogios**, to heap praises on somebody.

llenero, ra [lyay-nay´-ro, rah], *a. (Law.)* Full, complete, absolute.

lleno [lyay'-no], *m.* 1. Glut, plenty, abundance (abundancia), full. 2. Perfection (perfección), completeness. 3. Full moon. 4. An organ-stop.

lleno, na [lyay'-no, nah], *a.* Full, replete, complete. **Lleno hasta el borde**, brimful. **Estar lleno a reventar**, to be full to bursting. **Estar lleno de polvo**, to be covered in dust. **De lleno**, fully.

llenura [lyay-noo'-rah], *f.* Fulness, plenty, copiousness, abundance.

lleta [lyay'-tah], *f.* Stalk of plants bearing fruit.

lleudar [lyay-oo-dar'], *va.* To ferment bread with leaven.

llevada [lyay-vah'-dah], *f.* or **Lleva**. Carriage, transport, act of carrying.

llevadero, ra [lyay-vah-day'-ro, rah], *a.* Tolerable, light.

llevador, ra [lyay-vah-dor', rah], *m. & f.* Carrier, conductor.

llevar [lyay'-var], *va.* 1. To carry, to convey, to transport. 2. To carry, to bear (nombre, título), to wear (ropa), to have about one. 3. To carry, to take, to have with one. 4. To exact, to demand, to ask a price for a thing. 5. To bear, to produce. 6. To excel, to exceed (exceder). 7. To bear, to suffer, to endure. 8. To lead, to guide. 9. To manage a horse. 10. To cut off, to carry off (apartar). 11. To induce, to bring to any opinion (inducir). 12. To introduce. 13. To gain, to obtain. 14. To obtain possession. 15. To fetch away or fetch off. 16 To carry in accounts. 17. With the preposition *por,* it signifies to exercise whatever may be the import of the following noun. **Llevár(se)lo de calle**, to overpower another in argument. **Llevar mosca**, to go away offended and angry. **Llevar en peso**, to carry in the air. **Llevar consigo**, to carry along with, to be attached to, to be a consequence of. **Llevar una caída, golpe, porrazo, chasco, etc.** *(coll.)* to suffer a fall or blow; to be disappointed. **Llevar y conllevar**, to bear and forbear. **Llevar de conformidad**, *(Com.)* to find correct. **Llevar a uno adelante**, To carry forward (plan). **Llevaba puesto un sombrero raro**, she had an odd hat on. **El avión no llevaba paracaídas**, the plane had no parachutes. **Le llevamos al teatro**, we took him to the theater. **Llevar una vida tranquila**, to live a quiet life. **Llevar las desgracias con paciencia**, to bear misfortunes patiently. **El tren lleva una hora de retraso**, the train is an hour late. **Llevo estudiados 3 capítulos**, I have studied 3 chapters. **Ella me lleva dos años**, she´s 2 years older than I am. **Esto me lleva a pensar que...**, this leads me to think that... -*vn.* To be reprimanded, to suffer chastisement. **Llevar a cuestas**, 1. To carry on one´s shoulders or back. 2. *(coll.)* To burden oneself with others´ affairs. -*vr.* To suffer oneself to be led away by passion. **Llevarse bien or mal**, to be on good or bad terms. **No llevarlas todas consigo**, to be suspicious, to be afraid. **Se lo llevaron al cine**, they took him off to the cinema. **Los ladrones se llevaron la caja**, the thieves took the safe away. **Se llevó el primer premio**, she carried off the first prize.

lloíca [lyo-ee'-cah], *f. V.* PECHICOLORADO. Robin redbreast.

lloradera [lyo-rah-day'-rah], *f.* Weeping from slight motives.

llorador, ra [lyo-rah-dor', rah], *m. & f.* Weeper, one who sheds tears.

lloraduelos [lyo-rah-doo-ay'-los], *m. (coll.)* Weeper, mourner.

llorar [lyo-rar'], *vn.* 1. To weep, to cry (persona). 2. To mourn (muerte, pérdida), to lament, to bewail. 3. To affect poverty and distress. 4. *(Met.)* To fall drop by drop. 5. *(Cono Sur)* To suit, to be becoming (quedar bien). 6. *(And. Carib. Cono Sur)* To be very unbecoming (quedar muy mal). **Llorar a moco tendido**, to sob one´s heart out. **El que no llora no mama**, if you don´t ask you don´t get.

lloriquear [lyo-re-kay-ar'], *vn.* To be constantly crying.

lloro [lyo´-ro], *m.* Act of weeping or crying.

llorón [lyo-rone'], *m.* 1. Weeper, one apt to shed tears, mourner. 2. A weeping willow. -*a.* Crying with little cause.

lloronas [lyo-ro'-nas], *f. pl.* Weepers, mourners.

llorosamente [lyo-ro'-sah-men-tay], *adv.* Weepingly.

lloroso, sa [lyo-ro'-so, sah], *a.* Mournful, sorrowful, tearful.

llovediza (Agua) [lyo-vay-dee'-thah], *a.* Rainwater.

llover [lyo-verr'], *vn.* 1. To rain. 2. To pour down rain. 3. To shower, to abound, to come in abundance, as troubles. -*vr.* To penetrate the roof with rain. **Llover a cántaros** or **a chorros**, to rain bucketfuls. **Como llovido del cielo**, unexpectedly. **Llueva o no**, rain or shine. **Siempre que llueve escampa**, *(Carib.)* every cloud has a silver lining. (*Llueve, llueva,* from *Llover* V. ABSOLVER.)

llovida [lyo-vee'-dah], *f.* Rain.

llovioso, sa [lyo-ve-o'-so], *a. V.* LLUVIOSO.

llovizna [lyo-veeth'-nah], *f.* Mist, a fine rain.

lloviznar [lyo-veeth-nar'], *vn.* To drizzle.

llueco, ca [lyoo-ey-co, cah], *a. V.* CLUECO.

lluvia [lyoo´-ve-ah], *f.* 1. Rain, shower, water from the clouds. 2. Shower, abundance, copiousness. 3. Shower, storm. 4. Rainfall (cantidad), spray (insecticida), rose (regadera). **Lluvia artificial**, cloud seeding. **Lluvia ácida**, acid rain. **Lluvia torrencial**, torrential rain.

lluvioso, sa [lyoo-ve-o'-so, sah], *a.* Rainy, wet, showery.

lo, *indef. pron.* It: placed before or after verbs. It is used before adjectives, when by an ellipsis they are used in a general sense, referring to a thing either masculine or feminine, singular or plural. It is used also with reference to whole sentences. **Lo tengo aquí,** I have it here. **Lo veo,** I see it. **Guapa sí que lo es,** she's certainly very pretty.

lo. *pron. rel.* **Lo que,** what. **Lo que digo es...,** what I say is... **Con lo que él gana,** with what he earns. **Lo que se dice un hombre,** a real man.

lo, *art* "neutro". **Lo bello,** the beautiful. **Lo difícil,** what is difficult. **Defiendo lo mío,** I defend what is mine. **Lo mejor de la película,** the best part of the film. **No saben lo aburrido que es,** they don't know how boring it is. *-pron. pers. neut.* It. **No lo creo,** I don't believe it. **No lo he visto nunca,** I've never seen it. *-pron. pers. m.* him. **No lo conozco,** I don't know him.

loa [lo'-ah], *f.* 1. Prologue of a play. 2. Praise (elogio).

loable [lo-ah'-blay], *a.* Laudable, praiseworthy.

loablemente [lo-ah'-blay-men-tay], *adv.* Laudably, commendably.

loador, ra [lo-ah-dor', rah], *m. & f.* Praiser, lauder.

loán [lo-ahn'], *m.* A land measure of the Philippine Islands, equal to 3,600 square feet.

loanda [lo-ahn'-dah], *f.* Kind of scurvy.

loar [lo-ar'], *va.* To praise; to approve.

loasa [lo-ah'-sah], *f.* Loasa, a genus of South American climbing plants of elegant flowers.

loba [lo'-bah], *f.* 1. Ridge between furrows. 2. Long gown worn by clergymen and students. 3. She-wolf.

lóbado [lo'-bah-do], *m.* Morbid swelling incident to horses.

lobanillo [lo-bah-neel'-lyo], *m.* Wen, a callous excrescence.

lobato [lo-bah'-to], *m.* Young wolf.

lobelia [lo-bay'-le-ah], *f. (Bot.)* Lobelia.

lobera [lo-bay'-rah], *f.* Thicket where wolves make their lair.

lobero, ra [lo-bay'-ro, rah], *a.* Relating to wolves.

lobero [lo-bay'-ro], *m.* V. ESPANTANUBLADOS.

lobezno [lo-beth'-no], *m.* A young wolf.

lobina [lo bee'-nah], *f.* Striped bass.

lobo [lo'-bo], *m.* 1. Wolf. **Lobo de mar,** sea dog. 2. Lobe, a division of the lungs, liver, etc. 3. *(Joc.)* Intoxication, inebriation. 4. Iron instrument for defending or scaling walls. **Ver las orejas del lobo,** *(Met.)* to find oneself in the greatest danger. **Son lobos de una camada,** they're birds of a feather. 5. *(Mex.)* Traffic cop. 6. *(LAm.)* Half-breed.

lobo marino [lo'-bo mah-ree'-no], *m.* Seal, sea-calf.

loboso, sa [lo-bo'-so, sah], *a.* Full of wolves (montes, bosques).

lóbrego, ga [lo'-bray-go, gah], *a.* Murky, obscure, sad, mirk.

lobreguecer [lo-bray-gay-therr'], *vn.* To grow dark, to be dark.-*va.* To make dark.

lobreguez [lo-bray-geth'], *f.* Obscurity, darkness.

lóbulo [lo'-boo-lo], *m.* Lobe or lobule, a division or distinct part of the lungs, liver, etc.

lobuno, na [lo-boo'-no, nah], *a.* Wolfish, resembling a wolf.

locación y conducción [lo-ca-the-on' ee con-dooc-the-on'], *f. (Law.)* Contract of letting on lease.

local [lo-cahl'], *a.* Local, relating to a particular place (sitio).

localidad [lo-cah-le-dahd'], *f.* 1. Locality, existence in place; location, place, town (pueblo). 2. Ticket, seat. **Sacar localidades,** to get tickets.

localizable [lo cah le thah'-blay], *a.* Fácilmente localizable, easy to find. **El director no estaba localizable,** the director was not available.

localización [lo-cah-le-thah-the-on'], *f.* Localization, fixing in a definite place.

localizar [lo-cah-le-thar'], *va.* 1. To localize, to fix in a determined place, to locate (ubicar), to place (colocar), to find (encontrar). 2. *(Med.)* To localize. *-vr.* 1. *(Mex.)* To be located (situarse). 2. *(Med.)* To be localized (dolor).

localmente [lo-cahl'-men-tay], *adv.* Locally.

locamente [lo'-cah-men-tay], *adv.* Madly: immoderately, extravagantly; fondly.

locarias [lo-cah'-re-as], *m. (coll.)* A madcap, a wild, hot-brained fellow.

loción [lo-the-on'], *f.* 1. Lotion, a medicine used to wash any part with. 2. Wash, lavation, the act of washing. **loción capilar,** hair restorer.

loco, ca [lo'-co, cah], *a.* 1. Mad, crack-brained. 2. Fool. 3. Abundant, fertile, huge, tremendous (enorme). **A tontas y a locas,** inconsiderately, without reflection. **Estar loco de contento,** *(coll.)* to be mad with joy. **A palabras, locas, orejas sordas,** a silly question deserves no answer. **Loco de atar,** raving mad. **Más loco que una cabra,** as mad as a hatter. **Estar loco por hacer algo,** to be mad keen to do something. **Volverse loco,** to go mad. **He tenido una suerte loca,** I've been fantastically lucky.

loco [lo'-co], *m.* A madman, crazyman.

locomoción [lo-co-mo-the-on'], *f.* 1. *(Phys.)* Locomotion, power of moving. 2. *(LAm.)* Transport.

locomotivo, va [lo-co-mo-tee'-vo, vah], *a.* Locomotive, possessed of the power of moving.

locomotor, ra [lo-co-mo-tor', rah], *a.* Locomotor, having the power of producing motion.

locomotora [lo-co-mo-to'-rah], *f.* A locomotive engine. **Locomotora de maniobras,** shunting engine.

locomotriz [lo-co-mo-treeth'], *a.* Locomotive.

locomóvil [lo-co-mo'-veel], *a.* Locomotive.-*f.* Traction engine.

locro [lo'-cro], *m. (Peru. Ec.)* A stew composed chiefly of winter squash, potatoes, tender corn, meat or fish, etc.

locuacidad [lo-coo-ah-the-dahd'], *f.* Loquacity, talkativeness, garrulity, flippancy.

locuaz [lo-coo-ath'], *a.* Loquacious, talkative, garrulous, flippant.

locución [lo-coo-the-on'], *f.* Locution, manner of speech; phrase, expression.

locuela [lo-coo-ay'-lah], *f.* 1. Each one's particular mode of speaking. 2. Name commonly given to a giddy and conceited young girl.

locura [lo-coo'-rah], *f.* 1. Madness (cualidad, estado), frenzy, lunacy, craziness. 2. Fury; folly, absurdity. **Hacer locuras,** to act in an absurd, foolish manner. **Me gusta con locura,** I'm crazy about it. **Es capaz de cometer cualquier locura,** he is capable of any madness.

locutor [lo-coo-tor'], *m.* Speaker, announcer, commentator (comentarista), presenter (desfile de modelos). **Locutor de radio,** radio announcer, radio commentator. **Locutor de televisión,** television announcer or commentator.

locutorio [lo-coo-to'-re-o], *m.* Parlor, place in monasteries for receiving visits, visiting room (cárcel), telephone box.

locha, *f.* **loche,** *m.* [lo'-chah, lo'-chay], *(Zool.)* Loach, groundling, a small fish.

locho, cha [lo'-cho, chah], *a. (Amer. coll.)* Red-bearded, bright red.

lodazal, lodazar [lo-dah-thahl', lo-dah-thar'], *m.* A muddy place.

lodo [lo'-do], *m.* Mud, mire.

lodoñero [lo-do-nyay'-ro], *m. (Bot.)* Guaiac, lignumvitae tree.

lodoso, sa [lo-do'-so, sah], *a.* Muddy, miry.

logarítmico, ca [lo-gah-reet'-me-co, cah], *a.* Logarithmic, logarithmical.

logaritmo [lo-gah-reet'-mo], *m.* Logarithm.

logia [lo'-he-ah], *f.* Lodge assembly of Freemasons and the place where they meet.

lógica [lo'-he-cah], *f.* Logic, dialectics. **Ser de una lógica aplastante,** to be as clear as day.

lógicamente [lo'-he-caa-men-tay], *adv.* Logically.

lógico, ca [lo'-he-co, cah], *a.* Logical; natural, right, reasonable. **Es lógico que...,** it is natural that...

lógico [lo'-he-co], *m.* Logician, dialectician, a professor of logic.

logístico, ca [lo-hees'-te-co, cah], *a.* Logistic. -*f.* Logistics.

logo [lo-go]. *(Comput.)* Logo.

logografía [lo-go-grah-fee'-ah], *f.* Shorthand.

logogrifo [lo-go-gree'-fo], *m.* Logogriph, an enigma in which the different parts of a word are taken in divers meanings.

logomaquia [lo-go-mah'-ke-ah], *f.* Logomachy, dispute about words.

logoterapeuta [lo-go-tay-rah-pey'-oo-tah], *m & f.* Speech therapist.

logotipo [lo-go-tee'-po], *m.* Logo.

logrado [lo-grah'-do], *a.* Successful.

lograr [lo-grar'], *va.* 1. To gain (obtener), to obtain, to succeed, to procure, to compass. 2. To possess, to enjoy. 3. To avail oneself of. 4. To hit upon, to manage, to do well. **Lograr hacer algo**, to manage to do something. **Lograr que uno haga algo**, to get somebody to do something. *-vr.* To reap the benefit of one's labor and exertions.

logrear [lo-gray-ar'], *vn.* To borrow or lend on interest.

logrería [lo-gray-ree'-ah], *f.* Dealing in interest, usury.

logrero, ra [lo-gray'-ro, rah], *m. & f.* Lender at interest, usurer.

logro [lo'-gro], *m.* 1. Gain, benefit. 2. Attainment of some purpose (éxito). **Uno de sus mayores logros**, one of his greatest successes. 3. Interest; usury.

loma [lo'-mah], *f.* 1. Rising ground in the midst of a plain, a little hill or hillock. 2. Slope. 3. *(Cono Sur)* **En la loma del diablo**, at the back of beyond.

lombarda [lom-bar'-dah], *f.* 1. Lombardy gun. 2. *(Bot.)* Red cabbage.

lombardada [lom-bar-dah-dah], *f.* Shot from a Lombardy gun.

lombardear [lom-bar-day-ar'], *va.* To discharge Lombardy guns.

lombardería [lom-bar-day-ree'-ah], *f.* Park of Lombardy guns.

lombardero [lom-bar-day'-ro], *m.* Soldier appointed to Lombardy guns.

lombárdico, ca [lom-bar'-de-co, cah], *a.* Lombard, belonging to Lombardy.

lombardo, da [lom-bar'-do, dah], *a.* Lombard, belonging to Lombardy.

lombriguera [lom-bre-gay'-rah], *f.* Hole made by worms. 2. *(Bot.)* Southern-wood wormwood.

lombriz [lom-breeth'], *f.* Worm bred in the body, or in the earth. **Lombriz intestinal**, tapeworm.

lombrizal [lom-bre-thahl'], *a. (Anat.)* Vermiform.

lomear [lo-may-ar'], *vn.* To jerk or move the loins of horses in a circular manner.

lomento [lo-men'-to], *m. (Bot.)* Loment, a kind of legume falling in pieces when ripe.

lomera [lo-may'-rah], *f.* 1. Strap of harness which crosses the loins. 2. *(Prov.)* Ridge of a house.

lomiancho, a [lo-me-ahn'-cho, chah], *a.* Strong or broad-backed.

lomica, illa, ita [lo-mee'-cah], *f. dim.* A very little hill or hillock.

lomillo [lo-meel'-lyo], *m.* 1. *(Dim.)* A small loin. 2. A kind of needle work. 3. *(LAm.)* Pads.

lominhiesto, ta [lo-min-e-es'-to, tah], *a.* 1. High-cropped. 2. Presumptuous, arrogant.

lomo [lo'-mo], *m.* 1. Loin (carne). 2. Chine, a piece of the back of an animal. 3. Back of a book or cutting tool: double of any cloth, fold. 4. Ridge between furrows. **Llevar or traer a lomo**, to carry on the back. *-pl.* Ribs; loins.

lomudo, da [lo-moo'-do, dah], *a.* Large in the loins, broad-backed.

lona [lo'-nah], *f.* Canvas. **Lona para hacer velas**, duck-canvas, sail-cloth.

loncha [lone'-chah], *f.* 1. Thin flat stone. 2. Thin slice of meat.

lóndiga [lon'-de-gah], *f.* ALHÓNDIGA.

londinense [lon-de-nen'-say], *a.* Of London, Londonese.

londó [lon-do'], *m. (Com.)* A fabric made in Brittany.

londrina [lon-dree'-nah], *f.* A sort of woollen cloth from London.

loneta [lo-nay'-tah], *f.* Ravens' duck sail-cloth.

longa [lone'-gah], *f.* Long musical note.

longanimidad [lon-gah-ne-me-dahd'], *f.* Longanimity, forbearance.

longánimo, ma [lon-gah'-ne-mo, mah], *a.* Forbearing, generous, magnanimous.

longaniza [lon-gah-nee'-thah], *f.* 1. A kind of long sausage (salchicha). 2. *(Cono Sur)* String, series (serie).

longar [lon-gar'], *a.* Applied to long piece of honey-comb in the hive.

longazo, za [lon-gah'-tho, thah], *a. aug.* Very long.

longevidad [lon-hay-ve-dahd'], *f.* Longevity.

longevo [lon-hay'-vo], *a.* Longeval, long-lived.

longicornios [lon-he-cor'-ne-ose], *a. & m. pl.* Longicorn, the longicorn beetles have very long antennae, sometimes surpassing the entire length of the body. The larvae burrow in the hardest woods.

longifloro, ra [lon-he-flo'-ro, rah], *a.* Long-flowered, longiflorous.

longimetría [lon-he-may-tree'-ah], *f. (Geom.)* Longimetry, the art of measuring distances.

longincuo, cua [lon-heen'-coo-o, ah], *a.* Distant, remote.

longípedo, da [lon-hee'-pay-do, dah], *a.* Long-footed.

longirrostros [lon-hi-rros'-tro-se], *m. pl. a.* Longirostres, a family of birds including snipes, etc. As adjective, longirostral, long-billed.

longísimo, ma [lon-hee'-se-mo, mah], *a. sup.* of LUENGO. Longest. So, too, V. LONGUÍSIMO.

longitud [lon-he-tood'], *f.* 1. Length, longness. 2. Longitude.

longitudinal [lon-he-too-de-nahl'], *a.* Longitudinal.

longitudinalmente [lon-he-too-de-nahl'-men-tay], *adv.* Longitudinally, lengthwise.

longuera [lon-gay'-rah], *f.* Long and narrow strip of land.

longura [lon-goo'-rah], *f.* 1. Length. 2. Long lapse of time. 3. Delay.

lonja [lone'-hah], *f.* 1. Exchange, a public place where merchants meet. **Lonja de pescado**, fish market. 2. Slice or steak of ham, or any other eatable. 3. Grocer's shop (abacería), warehouse, sale-room. **Lonja cerrada** or **abierta**, shut or open shop or exchange. 4. Entrance hall of an edifice. 5. Leather strap, used in falconry.

lonjero [lon-hay'-ro], *m.* Grocer.

lonjista [lon-hees'-tah], *com.* Shopkeeper who deals in groceries.

lontananza [lon-tah-nahn'-thah], *f. (Art.)* Distance, background.

loor [loor'], *m. (Poet.)* Praise.

lopigia [lo-pee'-he-ah], *f.* Disease which makes the hair fall off. V. ALOPECIA.

loquear [lo-kay-ar'], *vn.* 1. To act the fool, to talk nonsense. 2. To rejoice, to exult, to revel, to frolic.

loquero, ra [lo-kay'-ro, rah], *m. & f.* 1. Keeper of a madhouse (manicomio). 2. Physician to a madhouse (persona). 3. *(Cono Sur)* **Esta oficina es un loquero**, this office is a madhouse.

loquesca [lo-kes'-cah], *f.* The frantic demeanor of mad people.

loquillo, illa, ito, ita [lo-keel'-lyo], *a dim.* Wild, almost mad.

loquios [lo'-ke-ose], *m. pl.* Lochia, the evacuations following childbirth for two to three weeks.

loran [lo'-rahn], *m.* Loran, contraction of Long Range Navigation

lord, *m.* (*pl.* **Lores**). Lord, a title of honor given to the highest nobility in England.

lorenzana [lo-ren-thah'-nah], *f.* A sort of coarse linen.

loriga [lo-ree'-gah], *f.* 1. Coat of mail, cuirass. 2. Naveband, the hoop which surrounds the nave of a coach wheel.

lorigado, da [lo-re-gahh'-do, dah], *a.* Armed with a coat of mail, loricate.

loriguillo [lo-re-geel'-lyo], *m.* Shrub used by dyers.

loro, ra [lo'ro, rah], *a.* Tawny, dark brown.

loro [lo'-ro], *m.* 1. Parrot. 2. *(Bot.)* Portugal laurel. 3. Old bat (arpía). 4. *(Cono Sur)* Thieves' look-out man. 5. *(Cono Sur.*

Med.) Bedpan. 6. *(Cono Sur)* **Sacar los loros**, to pick one´s nose. 7. **Estar al loro**, to be on the alert.

los art def *m.pl.* **las** *f. pl.* The. V. EL. **Los árboles**, the trees. **Los niños**, the children.

los, las *pron.* Them. **Los hay**, there are some. **Dámelos**, give them to me. **¿Los libros?, ¡tómalos!**, the books?, take them!

los, las *pron. dem.* **Nuestros cines y los de París**, our cinemas and those of Paris. **Los de Juan son verdes**, John´s are green. **Éstos son los nuestros y ésos los de Pedro**, these are ours, and those are Peter's.

losa [lo'-sah], *f.* 1. Flag, a square stone used for pavements. 2. Painter's block of marble on which colors are ground. 3. Trap for catching birds or rats.

losado [lo-sah'-do], *m. V.* ENLOSADO. **-Losado, da**, *pp.* of LOSAR.

losanje [lo-sahn'-hay], *m. (Her.)* Lozenge; rhomb.

losar [lo-sar´], *va. V.* ENLOSAR.

losica, ita [lo-see'-cah, ee'-tah], *f. dim.* A small flag or stone.

loseta, losilla [lo-say'-tah, lo-seel'-lyah], *f.* 1. A small trap or snare. 2. *V.* LOSICA.

lote [lo'-tay], *m.* 1. Lot, fortune, chance, portion (porción); *(LAm.)* Building site (solar). 2. *(Mex.)* About 100 hectares (medida). 3. *(Cono Sur)* Any old how. 4. Affair. **Darse el lote con**, to have it off with.

lotería [lo-tay-ree'-ah], *f.* 1. Lottery. 2. The game lotto. **Le tocó la lotería**, he won a big prize in the lottery.

loto [lo'-to], *m. (Bot.)* 1. Lotus, the Egyptian and Indian waterlily. 2. The loto-tree, or nettle-tree. *V.* ALMEZ. 3. Jujube-tree.

loza [lo'-thah], *f.* China, fine earthenware. **Loza refractaria**, pyrex ware.

lozanamente [lo-thah-nah-men´-tay], *adv.* 1. Luxuriantly. 2. In a self-assured way.

lozanear [lo-thah-nay-ar'], *vn.* To affect pomp and ostentation in words and actions.

lozanía [lo-thah-nee'-ah], *f.* 1. Luxuriance of verdure, exuberant growth of plants. 2. Elegance; lustiness.

lozano, na [lo-thah'-no, nah], *a.* 1. Luxuriant. 2. Sprightly. 3. Self-assured (seguro); arrogant (arrogante).

lúa [loo´-ah], *f.* 1. Esparto glove (sin separación de los dedos) for cleaning horses. 2. *(Prov.)* A sort of crane for raising weights. 3. *(Naut.)* Lee. 4. *(Prov.)* Saffron-bag.

lubricación [loo-bre-cah-the-on´], *f.* Lubrication.

lubricador, ra [loo-bre-cah-dor', rah], *a.* Lubricating.

lubricante [loo-bre-cahn'-tay], *a.* 1. *(Tec.)* Lubricant, lubricating. 2. Oily (persona). *-m.* Lubricant.

lubricar, lubrificar [loo-bre-car', loo-bre-fe-car´], *va.* To lubricate.

lubricativo, va [loo-bre-cah-tee'-vo, vah], *a.* Lubricant, lubricative.

lubricidad [loo-bre-the-dahd'], *f.* 1. Lubricity, slipperiness. 2. Lewdness.

lúbrico, ca [loo'-bre-co, cah], *a.* 1. Slippery (resbaladizo): lubricous; lewd.

lubrificación [loo-bre-fe-cah-the-on'], *f.* Lubrication.

lubrificador, ra [loo-bre-fe-cah-dor', rah], *a.* Lubricating.

lubrificante [loo-bre-fe-cahn'-tay], *a.* Lubricating.

lucano [loo-cah'-no], *m.* The stag-beetle, commonly called *cometa*.

lucas [loo'-cas], *m. pl.* 1. *(Cant.)* Playing-cards. 2. *(Mex.)* Crazy.

lucerna [loo-ther´-nah], *f.* 1. Glow-worm. 2. Lamp.

lucérnula [loo-therr'-noo-lah], *f. (Bot.)* Lucern, lucerne, alfalfa.

lucero [loo-thay'-ro], *m.* 1. Morning star, Venus, day star, Lucifer. 2. Splendor. 3. Part of a window where light enters. 4. White spot on the forehead of certain quadrupeds. *(Acad.)* **Lucero de la tarde**, evening star. *-pl. (Poet.)* Eyes.

lucha [loo'-chah], *f.* 1. Struggle, strife, contest, wrestle. 2. Dispute, argument. **Lucha de clases**, class war.

luchador, ra [loo-chah-dor', rah], *m. & f.* Wrestler, fighter.

luchar [loo-char'], *va.* 1. To wrestle, to contend, to struggle. **Luchaba con los mandos**, he was struggling with the controls. 2. To discuss, to debate.

lucharniego, ga [loo-char-ne-ay´-go, gah], *a.* Applied to dogs used for catching hares at night.

luchillo [loo-cheel'-lyo], *m. (Naut.)* Gering, goring cloth.

lucidamente [loo-the-dah-men´-tay], *adv.* Lucidly, brightly.

lucidar [loo-the-dar'], *va.* To copy a picture on transparent paper.

lucidez [loo-the-deth'], *f.* 1. Brilliancy, brightness, lucidity (claridad). 2. *(CAm. Cono Sur)* Brilliance (brillantez).

lucido, da [loo-thee'-do, dah], *a.* Magnificent, splendid (brillante), brilliant in performance, elegant (elegante); successful (exitoso). *-pp.* of LUCIR.

lúcido, da [loo'-the-do, dah], *a.* 1. Lucid, clear in reason. 2. Brilliant, shining.

lucidura [loo-the-doo'-rah], *f. (coll.)* Whiteness of white-washed walls.

luciente [loo-the-en'-tay], *pa.* Shining, lucid, luminous, bright.

luciérnaga [loo-the-err'-nah-gah], *f.* Glow-worm, firefly.

Lucifer [loo-the-ferr'], *m.* 1. Lucifer. Satan. 2. A very proud and wicked man. 3. *V.* LUCERO for the morning star.

luciferino, na [loo-the-fay-ree'-no, nah], *a.* Luciferian, devilish.

lucífero, ra [loo-thee'-fay-ro, rah], *a. (Poet.)* Resplendent, shining, luciferous.

lucífugo, ga [loo-thee'-foo-go, gah], *a.* Avoiding the light, lucifugous.

lucillo [loo-theel'-lyo], *m.* Tomb; sarcophagus.

lucimiento [loo-the-me-en'-to], *m.* 1. Lucidity, brightness. 2. Splendor, luster, applause.

lucio, cia [loo'-the-o, ah], *a.* Lucid, bright.

lucio [loo'-the-o], *m. (Zool.)* Common pike, luce.

lucir [loo-theer'], *va.* 1. To emit light, to glitter, to gleam, to glow. 2. To illuminate (iluminar), to enlighten. 3. To outshine, to exceed. 4. To show off, to display. **Lucía traje nuevo**, he was sporting a new suit. *-vn. & vr.* 1. To shine, to be brilliant. **Le luce el trabajo**, he enjoys the fruits of his labor. 2. To dress to advantage. **Lucirlo**, *(coll.)* to dash away, to sport. *(Yo luzco, yo luzca, from Lucir. V.* DESLUCIR.)

lucrarse [loo-crar'-say], *vr.* To get gain or profit from a business or charge.

lucrativamente [loo-crah-te'-vah-men-tay], *adv.* Profitably, lucratively.

lucrativo, va [loo-crah-tee´-vo, vah], *a.* Lucrative, productive of gain.

lucro [loo'-cro], *m.* Gain, profit, lucre.

lucroso, sa [loo-cro'-so, sah], *a.* Lucrific, gainful, profitable.

luctuosa [looc-too-o'-sah], *f.* Ancient tax paid to lords and bishops for the dead.

luctuosamente [looc-too-o'-sah-men-tay], *adv.* Mournfully, sorrowfully.

luctuoso, sa [looc-too-o´-so, sah], *a.* Sad, mournful.

lucubración [loo-coo brah-thc-on'], *f.* Lucubration, nocturnal study.

lucubrar [loo-coo-brar'], *va.* To lucubrate, to study by night.

lúcuma [loo'-coo-mah], *f.* Fruit of the *lúcumo*, a tree of Peru and tropical America.

ludia [loo'-de-ah], *f. (Prov.)* Ferment, yeast.

ludiar [loo-de-ar'], *va. & vr. (Prov.)* To ferment.

ludibrio [loo-dee'-bre-o], *m.* Mockery, derision, scorn.

ludimiento [loo-de-me-en'-to], *m. (Prov.) V.* COLISIÓN.

ludir [loo-deer'], *va.* To rub, to waste by friction, to collide.

ludria [loo'-dre-ah], *f. V.* NUTRIA.

lúe [loo'-ay], *f.* Infection. *(Acad.)*

luego [loo-ay'-go], *adv.* 1. Presently (pronto), immediately, outright, out of hand, *(CAm.)* later (después), *(And. Carib. Cono Sur, Mex.)* sometimes (de vez en cuando). **Luego vuelvo**, I'll be back at once. 2. Soon afterward. *-conj.* Then, therefore. **Pienso, luego existo**, I think, therefore, I am. *(LAm.)* **Luego que llegues avísame**, let me know the moment you arrive. **Desde luego**, of course.

lugano [loo-gah'-no], *m.* A linnet. *V.* JILGUERO.

lugar [loo-gar'], *m.* 1. Place, spot, situation, position (posición). 2. City, town, village (pueblo): properly speaking, it is applied to a village or a very small town. 3. Employment, office, dignity. 4. Time, opportunity (oportunidad), occasion. 5. Leisure, convenience of time. 6. Cause, motive, reason (razón). 7. Text, authority or sentiment of an author. **En lugar de**, instead of, in lieu of. **Lugar seguro**, safe place. **En primer lugar**, in the first place. **Estar fuera de lugar**, to be out of place. **Ocupar el lugar de**, to take the place of. **Tener lugar**, to take place. **Hacer lugar para**, to make room for. **Dar lugar a**, to give rise to.

lugarcico, illo, ito [loo-gar-thee'-co], *m. dim. V.* LUGARILLO.

lugarillo, lugarejo [loo-gah-reel'-lyo, loo-gah-ray'-ho], *m. dim.* Hamlet, a small village.

lugareño, ña [loo-gah-ray'-nyo, nyah], *m. & f. & a.* 1. Belonging to a village. 2. Inhabitant of a village.

lugarete [loo-gah-ray'-tay], *m. dim. V.* LUGARILLO.

lugarón [loo-gah-rone'], *m. aug. V.* LUGARAZO.

lugarote [loo-gah-ro'-tay], *m. aug. V.* LUGARAZO.

lugartenencia [loo-gar-tay-nen'-the-ah], *f.* Lieutenancy.

lugarteniente [loo-gar-tay-ne-en'-tay], *m.* 1. Deputy, substitute, delegate. 2. Lieutenant.

lugre [loo'-gray], *m.* Lugger, a small two or three masted vessel.

lugo [loo'-go], *m.* Kind of linen.

lúgubre [loo'-goo-bray], *a.* Sad, mournful, gloomy, melancholy, lugubrious, dismal.

luir [loo-eer'], *m. (Naut.)* To gall, or be galled or fretted, to wear away by friction.-*va. (Prov.) V.* REDIMIR CENSOS.

lujación [loo-hah-the-on'], *f. V.* LUXACIÓN.

lujar [loo-har'], *va. (Cuba)* 1. To rub. *V.* LUDIR. 2. To smooth the sole of a shoe. 3. *(Med.)* To luxate, to dislocate.

lujo [loo'-ho], *m.* Profuseness, extravagance or excess in pomp, dresses, fare, etc.; superfluity, luxury, finery. **Vivir en el lujo**, to live in luxury.

lujoso, sa [loo-ho'-so, sah], *a.* Showy (vestidos), sumptuous, luxurious: profuse, lavish.

lujuria [loo-hoo'-re-ah], *f.* 1. Lechery, lubricity, lust, carnal pleasure. 2. Excess, profuseness, lavishness.

lujuriante [loo-hoo-re-ahn'-tay], *pa.* Lusting.-*a.* Luxuriant, exuberant.

lujuriar [loo-hoo-re-ar'], *vn.* 1. To be lecherous or libidinous, to lust. 2. To couple together: speaking of animals.

lujuriosamente [loo-hoo-re-o'-sah-men-tay], *adv.* Lecherously, lustfully, voluptuously.

lujurioso, sa [loo-hoo-re-o'-so, sah], *a.* Lecherous, lustful, voluptuous, lewd, libidinous.

lumbago [loom-bah'-go], *m. (Med.)* Lumbago, lumbar rheumatism.

lumbar [loom-bar'], *a.* Lumbar, lumbary.

lumbrada, lumbrarada [loom-brah'-dah, loom-brah-rah'-dah], *f.* A great fire, a fierce conflagration.

lumbre [loom'-bray], *f.* 1. Fire (fuego), anything burning. 2. Spark from a flint. 3. Splendor, brightness (brillo); lucidity, clearness. 4. Light (para cigarrillo). **Cerca de la lumbre**, near the fire. -*pl.* 1. Tinderbox, with the materials for striking fire. 2. Hammer, that part of a gun-lock which strikes fire from the flint. 3. Forepart of horse-shoes.

lumbrera [loom-bray'-rah], *f.* 1. Luminary, anybody which emits light. 2. Skylight. 3. Genius, whizz kid (persona). 4. *(Mex. Taur. Teat.)* Box.

luminar [loo-me-nar'], *m.* 1. Luminary, anybody which emits light. 2. Among painters, light, as opposed to shade. 3. Luminary, a man eminent in science.

luminaria [loo-me-nah'-re-ah], *f.* 1. Illumination, festival lights. 2. Lamp which is kept burning in Roman Catholic churches before the sacrament.-*pl.* Money paid for illuminations.

lumínico, ca [loo-mee'-ne-co, cah], *a. V.* LUMINOSO. -*m.* Light.

luminosamente [loo-me-no'-sah-men-tay], *adv.* Luminously.

luminosidad [loo-me-no-se-dahd'], *f.* 1. Brightness (brillantez), luminosity. 2. *(Fig.)* Brightness, brilliance.

luminoso, sa [loo-me-no'-so, sah], *a.* Luminous, shining, bright (brillante).

luna [loo'-nah], *f.* 1. The moon. 2. Glass plate for mirrors (espejo), glass for optical instruments. 3. Effect of the moon upon lunatic people. 4. **Media luna**, *(Mil.)* half-moon, a ravelin built before the angle or curtain of a bastion. 5. *(Prov.)* Open, uncovered court or hall. **Luna llena or menguante**, full or waning moon. **Estar en la luna**, to have one's head in the clouds.

lunación [loo-nah-the-on'], *f.* Lunation, the period of revolution of the moon.

lunado, da [loo-nah'-do, dah], *a.* Lunated, formed like a half-moon.

lunanco, ca [loo-nahn'-co, cah], *a.* Applied to animals with one quarter higher than another.

lunar [loo-nar'], *m.* 1. Mole, a natural spot or discoloration of the body. **Lunar postizo**, patch which ladies wear on the face as an ornament. 2. Note or stain of infamy (moral). -*a.* Lunar, lunary.

lunaria [loo-nah'-re-ah], *f. (Bot.)* Moonwort, honesty.

lunario [loo-nah'-re-o], *m. V.* CALENDARIO.

lunático, ca [loo-nah'-te-co, cah], *a.* Lunatic, moonstruck, mad.

lunecilla [loo-nay-theel'-lyah], *f.* Crescent worn by women.

lunes [loo'-nes], *m.* Monday. **No ocurre cada lunes y cada martes**, it doesn't happen every day of the week.

luneta [loo-nay'-tah], *f.* 1. The two or three rows of cushioned seats in the pit of a play-house, immediately behind the orchestra. 2. The spot where olives are pressed. 3. A saddler's knife, leather knife. 4. *(Ant.)* A spectacle lens (gafas). 5. Ornament in the shape of a half moon which women used to wear on the head and children on the shoes. 6. *(Arch.) V.* BOCATEJA and LUNETO.

luneto [loo-nay'-to], *m.* A skylight, of half-moon shape, in an arch, lunette.

lúnula [loo'-noo-lah], *f.* 1. A crescent, a figure formed by two arcs of a circle. 2. *(Opt.)* Meniscus, a lens or glass convex on one side and concave on the other.

lupa [loo'-pah], *f.* Magnifying glass.

lupanar [loo-pah-nar'], *m.* Brothel, a bawdy-house.

lupanario, ia [loo-pah-nah'-re-o, ah], *a.* Belonging to a brothel.

lupia [loo'-pe-ah], *f.* 1. Encysted tumor. 2. Wen (lobanillo). 3. *(And.)* Small amount of money.

lupino [loo-pee'-no], *m. (Bot.)* Lupine or lupin. *V.* ALTRAMUZ.

lupulina [loo-poo-lee'-nah], *f.* Lupulin the active principle of hops.

lúpulo [loo'-poo-lo], *m. (Bot.)* Hops.

luquete [loo-kay'-tay], *m.* 1. Zest, a slice of orange with the peel thrown into wine. 2. Match, a card, rope, or small chip dipped in melted sulphur. 3. Grease spot (mancha). 4. Bald patch (calva).

lusitano, na [loo-se-tah'-no, nah], *a.* Lusitanian, Portuguese.

lustración [loos-trah-the-on'], *f.* Lustration, purification by water.

lustrador [loos-trah-dor'], *m.* 1. Hot-press, mangler, a machine which gives a gloss to clothes. 2. Hot-presser. 3. Mirror-polisher.

lustral [loos-trahl'], *a.* Lustral: applied to water used in purifications.

lustramiento [loos-trah-me-en'-to], *m.* Action of decorating or honoring someone. *(Acad.)*

lustrar [loos-trar'], *va.* 1. To expiate, to purify. 2. To illustrate, to make brilliant. 3. To mangle, to fine. 4. To wander.

lustre [loos'-tray], *m.* 1. Gloss, luster, fineness. 2. Clearness, nobleness, splendor, glory. 3. Shoe-polish (sustancia).

lústrico, ca [loos'-tre-co, cah], *a. (Poet.)* Belonging to a lustrum, or to lustration.

lustro [loos'-tro], *m.* 1. Lustrum, the space of five years. 2. Lamp or chandelier for illumination.

lustrosamente [loos-tro'-sah-men-tay], *adv.* Brilliantly, splendidly, glitteringly.

lustroso, sa [loos-tro´-so, sah], *a.* Bright, brilliant, lustrous, shining, glossy, golden.

luten [loo´-ten], *m. (Chem.)* Lute, a kind of paste to make vessels airtight.

lúteo, tea [loo'-tay-o, ah], *a.* Miry, muddy.

luteranismo [loo-tay-rah-nees'-mo], *m.* Lutheranism.

luterano, na [loo-tay-rah´-no, nah], *a. & m. & f.* Lutheran.

luto [loo´-to], *m.* 1. Mourning, the dress of sorrow (ropa). **Medio luto**, half mourning. 2. Mourning, sorrow, condolement, grief (duelo).

lutria [loo'-tre-ah], *f. V.* NUTRIA.

luxación [looc-sah-the-on'], *f.* Luxation, dislocation of a joint.

luz [looth], *f.* 1. Light. 2. Daylight (de día). 3. Guiding light, inspiration. **Dar a luz**, 1. To give birth. 2. To bring out, to publish. **Luz blanca para marcha atrás**, backup light. **Luz intermitente**, 1. Directional signal. 2. Blinker. **Luz negra**, black light. **Luz roja**, stop light. **Luz trasera**, tail-light. **Salir a luz**, a) to come out, to be published. b) to come to light. **Ver la luz**, to see the light of day. **Luces**, 1. Windows, openings. 2. Cultural attainments. **A todas luces**, obviously. **Luces de carretera**, high beams, brights. **Luces de cruce**, low beams, dims. **Luces de población**, parking lights. **Luces de posición**, *(Aer.)* navigation lights. **Traje de luces**, bullfighter's costume. **Como la luz del día**, as clear as daylight. **Quitar la luz a uno**, to stand in somebody´s light. **A la luz de**, in the light of. **Dar luz verde a un proyecto**, to give a plan the go ahead. **Luces de aterrizaje**, landing lights. **Luces de tráfico**, traffic lights.

Luzbel [looth-bel'], *m.* Lucifer, Satan.

M

m [ay'-may], *f.,* It has in the Spanish language the same sound as in English. *M* is never doubled in Spanish. M. 1. Sign for one thousand. 2. Abbr. for midday, noon. 3. Abbr. for misce, mix. 4. Abbr. for majesty, *merced* (grace), *metro*, (meter).

mabre [mah´-bray], *f.* Marver, a plate of iron used to shape a ball of glass upon.

maca [mah´-cah], *f.* 1. Bruise in fruit (fruta). 2. Spot, Stain. 3. Deceit, fraud, trick (defecto).

macabro, bra [mah-cah´-bro, brah], *a.* Macabre, gruesome.

macaco, ca [mah-cah´-co, cah], *m. & f.* 1. Macaque, or macaco, a flat-headed monkey. 2. *(Mex.)* Hobgoblin, bogie for frightening children.-*a.* 1. Ugly (feo), ill-shaped, squat. 2. *(CAm. Carib.)* Silly (tonto). 3. *(Cono Sur)* Brazilian. 3. *(Carib.)* Big shot (persona importante). 4. *(Mex.)* Bogey.

macádam [mah-cah'-dam], *m.* Macadam, macadam paving.

macadamizar [mah-cah-dah-me-thar´], *va.* To macadamize (carretera).

macagua [mah-cah'-goo-ah], *f.* An American bird of prey whose hoarse cry resembles a laugh.

macaisa [mah-cah'-e-sah], *f. (Bot.)* A tree of the Philippine Islands, of very light wood.

macana [mah-cah'-nah], *f.* 1. A wooden weapon in use among the ancient Indians of Mexico and Peru, generally edged with sharp flint. 2. *(And. Cono Sur)* Stupid comment (disparate). 3. *(Cono Sur)* Bad job (chapuza).

macanudo, da [mah-cah-noo´-do, dah], *a. (Sp. Am. coll.)* 1. Extraordinary, terrific. 2. Glaring, conspicuous.

macareno, na [mah-cah-ray´-no nah], *a. (coll.)* Applied to a bragging, boasting person.

macarra [mah-cahr'-rah], *m.* Thug (gamberro). Queer (marica); pimp; lout (bruto).

macarrón [mah-car-rone'], *m.* 1. Macaroni, a kind of paste. 2. *(Naut.)* Awning stanchions. *V.* CANDELEROS.

macarrónico, ca [mah-car-ro´-ne-co, cah], *a.* Macaronic.

macarronismo [mah-car-ro-nees'-mo], *m.* The macaronic style of poetry.

macarse [mah-car'-say], *vr.* To rot, to be spoiled in consequence of a bruise or hurt (macear).

macayo [mah-cah'-yo], *m. (Centr. Amer.)* Macaw.

maceador [mah-thay-ah-dor'], *m.* Beater, hammerer.

macear [mah-thay-ar'], *va.* To beat or drive with a mallet, to knock, to hammer down.-*vn.* To repeat frequently the same demand.

macedonia [mah-thay-do'-ne-ah], *f.* **Macedonia de frutas**, fruit salad.

maceración [mah-thay-rah-the-on'], *f.* 1. Maceration, steeping, infusion. 2. Mortification, maceration, corporeal severity.

macerar [mah-thay-rar'], *va.* 1. To macerate, to soften by steeping or by blows. 2. To mortify, to macerate, to harass with corporeal hardships. 3. *(Chem.)* To bruise plants, to extract their juice.

macero [mah-thay'-ro], *m.* Mace-bearer, mace, macer.

maceta [mah-thay'-tah], *f.* 1. Flower-pot (tiesto). 2. Handle of a stick used at Spanish truck-tables. 3. Handle of many kinds of tools. 4. Haunch of mutton. 5. Two-clawed hammer (martillo). 6. *(Naut.)* Maul, mallet. **Maceta de ajustar**, A driving mallet. **Macetas**, mallets or beetles, with which rope-ends are beaten to make oakum.-*a.* 1. *(And. Cono Sur)* Slow, thick. 2. *(Carib.)* Miserly (tacaño).

macetón [mah-thay-tone´], *m. aug.* of MACETA.

machaca [mah-chah'-cah], *com. (coll.)* A bore, tiresome person.

machacadera [mah-chah-cah-day'-rah], *f.* Instrument for pounding or breaking.

machacador, ra [mah-chah-cah-dor', rah], *m. & f.* Pounder, beetler, bruiser.

machacar [mah-chah-car'], *va.* To pound or break anything into small pieces, to crush (hacer polvo), to contuse. -*vn.* To importune, to harass, to molest, to go on (insistir). **Machacar en hierro frío**, to hammer cold iron; phrase indicating inutility. *(coll.)* To brood upon a thing.

machacón, na [mah-chah-cone´, nah], *a.* Heavy, monotonous (monótono), importunate, tiresome (pesado). **Con insistencia machacona**, with wearisome insistence.

machada [mah-chah'-dah], *f. 1.* Flock of he-goats. 2. *(coll.)* *V.* NECEDAD.

machado [mah-chah'-do], *m.* A hatchet. —**Machado, da**, *pp.* of MACHAR.

machaque [mah-chah'-kay], *m.* The act of pounding or breaking.

machaquería [mah-chah-kay-ree'-ah], *f. (coll.)* Importunity, insistence.

machar [mah-char'], *va.* To pound. *V* MACHACAR. **A macha martillo**, firmly, strongly; in a solid manner. -*vr.* *(Cono Sur)* To get drunk.

machear [mah-chay-ar'], *vn.* To beget more males than females.

machetazo [mah-chay-tah'-tho], *m.* 1. Blow or stroke with a cutlass. 2. *(LAm.)* Large *machete* (instrumento)

machete [mah-chay´-tay], *m.* Cutlass chopping-knife, cane-knife.

machetear [mah-chay-tay-ar'], *va.* 1. To wound or cut with a machete. 2. *(Naut.)* To make slow headway against a heavy sea. -*vn.* 1. *(And. Mex.)* To dig one´s heels in (obstinarse). 2. *(Mex.)* To hammer away (trabajar).

machetero [mah-chay-tay´-ro], *m.* 1. One who clears away bushes with a cutlass. 2. *(Mex.)* Porter (cargador). 3. *(Carib.)* Revolutionary. 4. *(Mex. Univ.)* Plodder.

machial [mah-che-ahl'], *m.* A wooded hill availed of for pasturing goats.

machiega [mah-che-ay'-gah], *a. V.* ABEJA MACHIEGA.

machihembrar [mah-che-em-brar'], *va.* To join or dovetail pieces of wood in a box with grooves.

machina [mah-chee'-nah], *f.* 1. Sheers, a machine for masting or unmasting a vessel. 2. A cutting compass for cutting out the brims of hats.

machismo [mah-chees'-mo], *m.* Manliness, male chauvinism, male pride (orgullo), virility (virilidad).

machista [mah-chees'-tah], *a.* 1. Full of machismo, full of male pride, very masculine.

macho [mah'-cho], *m.* 1. A male animal, in particular, a he-mule or a he-goat. 2. A masculine plant. 3. A piece of some instrument which enters into another. 4. Hook to catch hold in an eye. 5. Screwpin. 6. An ignorant fellow (persona). 7. *(And.)* Splendid, terrific (fantástico). 8. *(CAm.)* U.S. marine (marino). **Macho cabrío**, he-goat. **Es muy macho**, he´s very tough. 9. Pillar of masonry to support a building. 10. Sledge hammer. 11. Block on which a smith's anvil is fixed. 12. A square anvil.

macho [mah'-cho], *a.* Masculine, vigorous, robust; male.

machón [mah-chone'], *m. (Arch.)* Buttress, an arched pillar to support a wall or building.

machorra [mah-chor'-rah], *f.* 1. A barren ewe. 2. A barren woman.

machota, *f.* **machute**, *m.* [mah-cho'-tah, mah-choo'-tay], 1. A kind of beetle or mallet. 2. Mannish woman (mujer). 3. *(And, Carib.)* Carelessly.

machote [mah-cho'-tay], 1. Tough guy, he-man. 2. *(LAm.)* Rough draft (borrador); model (modelo); pattern (pauta). 3. *(Mex.)* Blank form.

machucadura [mah-choo-cah-doo'-rah], *f.* The act of pounding or bruising.

machucamiento [mah-choo-cah-me-en'-to], *m. V.* MACHUCADURA.

machucar [mah-choo-car'], *va.* To pound (hacer polvo), to bruise. *V.* MACHACAR.

machucho, cha [mah-choo´-cho, chah], *a.* 1. Mature, ripe of age and understanding; judicious (juicioso). 2. *(And. Mex.)* Cunning (taimado), sly, shrewd.

machuelo [mah-choo-ay'-lo], *m.* 1. *(dim.)* A small he-mule. 2. Heart of an onion.

macicez [mah-the-theth´], *f. (Prov.)* Solidity, compactness.

macilento, ta [mah-the-len´-to, ta], *a.* Lean, extenuated; withered, decayed.

macis [mah'-this], *f.* Mace, a kind of spice.

macizamente [mah-the-tha'-men-tay], *adv.* In a firm and solid manner.

macizar [mah-the-thar´], *va.* 1. To close an opening or passage, to form into a compact body. 2. To support a proposition by argument.

macizo, za [mah-thee'-ho, thah], *a.* 1. Compact, close, solid (neumático, oro, puerta), massive (grande) certain. **De roble macizo**, of solid oak.

macizo [mah-thee'-tho], *m.* 1. Massiveness, bulk. 2. *(Geog.)* Massif. 3. *(Hort.)* Bed, plot. 4. *(Aut.)* Solid tire. 5. *(Arch.)* Stretch, section.

macla [mah'-clah], *f.* 1. *(Bot.)* Water-caltrops. 2. Wooden instrument to scotch flax or hemp.

macle [mah'-clay], *m. (Her.)* Mascle, a perforated lozenge.

macoca [mah-co´-cah], *f.* A large sort of early figs.

macolla [mah-col'-lyah], *f.* Bunch of flowers, etc., growing on one stalk.

macona, [mah-co'-nah], *f. (Prov.)* Basket without handles.

macrocéfalo, la [mah-cro-thay-fah´-lo, lah], *a.* Macrocephalous, of a large head.

macrocomo, ma [mah-cro-co'-mo, mah], *a. (Biol.)* Long-haired.

macrocosmo [mah-cro-cos'-mo], *m.* Macrocosm, the whole world, or visible system in opposition to the microcosm, or little world of man.

macrogloso, sa [mah-cro-glo'-so, sah], *a.* Macroglossate, having a long tongue.

macruros [mah-croo'-rose], *m. pl.* Macrura, a division of the decapods, including lobsters and shrimps.

macuache [mah-coo-ah´-chay], *m.* 1. An impoverished Mexican Indian. 2. *(Fig.)* A brute, an animal.

macuba [mah-coo´-bah], *f.* Tobacco from the north of Martinique. (*m.* in America.)

macuca [mah-coo'-cah], *f. (Bot.)* Kind of wild pear or pear-tree.

mácula [mah´-coo-lah], *f.* 1. Stain, spot, blemish, macula. 2. Trick, fraud (trampa).

macular [mah-coo-lar'], *va.* To mackle or make a double impression in printing, with types or copper plates.

maculatura [mah-coo-lah-too'-rah], *f. (Print.)* Sheet which has received a double impression in printing.

macuteno [mah-coo-tay'-no], *m. (Mex.)* An infamous man, a petty thief.

macuto [mah-coo'-to], *m.* 1. Knapsack (mochila); satchel. 2. *(Carib.)* Begging basket.

madama [mah-dah'-mah], *f.* Madam. *V.* SEÑORA.

madeja [mah-day'-hah], *f.* 1. Hank or skein of thread (lana), worsted, silk, or cotton. 2. Lock of hair. 3. A weak, lazy person. **Se está enredando la madeja**, the affair is getting complicated.

madejeta, ica, illa, ita [mah-day-hay'-tah], *f. dim.* A small skein.

madera [mah-day'-rah], *f.* 1. Wood, timber, lumber. **Madera de construcción**, timber for building. **Madera dura**, hard wood. **Madera laminada**, plywood. 2. Hoof of a horse or other beast. 3. Said of green or unripe fruit. 4. *(Fig.)* Nature, temperament; aptitude. **Tiene buena madera**, there´s a lot in him. **Tiene madera de futbolista**, he´ll make a soccer player. -*m.* Madeira wine.

maderable [mah-day-rah'-blay], *a.* Bearing timber, timber producing.

maderada [mah-day-rah'-dah], *f.* Raft, a wooden frame or float.

maderaje, maderamen [mah-day-rah'-hay, mah-day-rah'-men], *m.* The timber necessary for a building; a house in frame.

maderamen [mah-day-rah'-men], *m.* Lumber for construction.

madera terciada [mah-day'-rah ter-the-ah'-dah], *f.* Plywood.

maderería [mah-day-ray-ree'-ah], *f.* Timberyard.

maderero [mah-day-ray'-ro], *m.* 1. Timber merchant, lumber dealer. 2. Carpenter.

maderero, ra [mah-day-ray'-ro, rah], *a.* Pertaining to the lumber industry. **Industria maderera**, lumber industry.

maderista [mah-day-rees´-tah], *m. (Prov.)* Conductor of a raft or float.

madero [mah-day'-ro], *m.* 1. Beam (viga), any large piece of timber: sometimes applied to any piece of timber, log (tronco). **Maderos de cuenta**, the main timbers of a vessel. 2. Oaf (idiota). 3. *(Esp.)* cop (policía).

madia [mah'de-ah], *f.* A plant of Chili, from the seed of which an edible oil is extracted.

madona [mah-do'-nah], *f.* Madonna.

madraza [mah-drah'-thah], *f. aug.* A very fond mother.

madrastra [mah-drahs'-trah], *f.* 1. Stepmother. 2. *(Met.)* Anything disagreeable.

madre [mah'-dray], *f.* 1. A mother. 2. Mother superior (convento). 3. Expectant mother (embarazada). 4. Mother, a title given to religious women. 5. Matron (hospital). 6. Basis, foundation, origin. 7. Matrix womb. 8. Bed of a river (de río). 9. Sewer sink. 10. Mother, a substance concreted in liquors, or the lees or scum concreted. 11. Mother, a familiar term of address to an old woman. 12. The principal irrigating ditch whence small branches issue. **Madre de leche**, a wet-nurse. **Mal de madre**, 1. Mother or hysterical passion. 2. The state of children spoiled by their mother. **Madre política**, mother-in-law. **Su señora madre**, your mother. **Sin madre** motherless. **Ciento y la madre**, hundreds of people. -*a.* 1. *(Lit.)* Mother. **Buque**

madre, mother ship. **Lengua madre**, parent language. 2. **La cuestión madre**, the chief problem. 3. *(LAm.)* Tremendous, terrific.

madrear [mah-dray-ar'], *va*. To construct sewers.

madrecilla [mah-dray-theel'-lyah], *f*. 1. Ovary of birds. 2. *(dim.)* V. MADRECITA.

madrecita [mah-dray-thee'-tah], *m. dim.* Of MADRE. Used as an endearing expression instead of mother.

madreclavo [mah-dray-clah'-vo], *m*. Clove, a spice which has remained on the tree two years.

madreperla [mah-dray-perr'-lah], *f*. Mother-of-pearl; pearl-oyster.

madrépora [mah-dray'-po-rah], *f*. Madrepore, white coral.

madrero, ra [mah-dray'-ro, rah], *a. (Prov. Coll.)* Fondling, caressing a mother.

madreselva [mah-dray-sel'-vah], *f. (Bot.)* Honeysuckle.

madrigada [mah-dre-gah'-dah], *a*. Applied formerly to a woman twice married.

madrigado, da [mah-dre-gah'-do, dah], *a*. 1. Practical, experienced. 2. Applied to a bull that has been a sire.

madrigal [mah-dre-gahl'], *m*. Madrigal, a light airy song.

madrigaleja, madrigalete [mah-dre-gah-lay'-hah, mah-dre-gah-lay'-tay], *m. dim.* A short madrigal.

madriguera [mah-dre-gay'-rah], *f*. 1 Burrow, the holes made in the ground by rabbits or conies. 2. Den, lurking-place.

madrileño, ña [mah-dre-lay'-nyo, nyah], *a*. Native of or belonging to Madrid.

madrilla [mah-dreel'-lyah], *f. (Prov.)* A small river fish. V. BOGA.

madrillera [mah-dreel-lyay'-rah], *f. (Prov.)* Instrument for catching small fish.

madrina [mah-dree'-nah], *f*. 1. A godmother (bautizo). 2. Bridesmaid. 3. Protectress. 4. Prop, stanchion. 5. Straps or cords which yoke two horses. 6. *(Mex.)* Police informer.

madriz [mah-dreeth'], *f*. Place where quails nest or sea-urchins grow.

madrona [mah-dro'-nah], *f*. 1. Mother overfond of her children, who spoils them by excessive tenderness. 2. *(Bot.)* Clandestine toothwort.

madroncillo [mah-dron-theel'-lyo], *m*. Strawberry.

madroñal [mah-dron-yahl'], *m*. A grove of madrone-trees.

madroñero, ra [mah-dro-nyay'-ro, rah], *m. & f.* One who sells silk tassels; also a seller of madrones. -*f.* V. MADROÑAL.-*m. (Bot.)* Madrone-tree.

madroño [mah-dro'-nyo], *m*. 1. The madrone, or strawberry-tree. 2. Fruit of the strawberry-tree. 3. Silk tassel.

madrugada [mah-droo-gah'-dah], *f*. 1. Dawn, the first appearance of light. 2. The act of rising early in the morning. **De madrugada**, at break of day. **A las 4 de la madrugada**, at 4 o'clock in the morning.

madrugador, ra [mah-droo-gah-dor, rah], *m. & f.* Early riser.

madrugar [mah-droo-gar'], *vn*. 1. To rise early (levantarse). 2. To contrive, to premeditate. 3. To anticipate, to get there first. -*va*. **Madrugar a uno**, to forestall somebody (adelantarse a).

madrugón [mah-droo-gone'], *m*. 1. Act of rising early in the morning. 2. Early riser.

maduración [mah-doo-rah-the-on'], *f*. Ripeness, maturity.

maduradero [mah-doo-rah-day'-ro], *m*. Place for ripening fruits.

madurador, ra [mah-doo-rah-dor', rah], *a*. That which matures or ripens.

maduramente [mash-doo'-rah-men-tay], *adv*. Maturely, prudently, considerately.

madurante [mah-doo-rahn'-tay], *va*. Maturing, ripening.

madurar [mah-doo-rar'], *va*. To ripen (frutos), to mature (plan), to mellow. *(Med.)* To maturate.-*vn*. 1. To ripen, to grow ripe. 2. To attain the age of maturity. -*vr*. To ripen, to grow ripe.

madurativo, va [mah-doo-rah-tee'-vo, vah], *a*. Maturative.

madurativo [mah-doo-rah-tee'-vo], *m*. 1. Anything that matures. 2. Means employed to induce a person to yield to a request.

madurez [mah-doo-reth'], *f*. 1. Maturity, mellowness, ripeness. 2. Prudence, wisdom.

madurillo, lla [mah-doo-reel'-lyo', yah], *a*. Beginning to ripen.

maduro, ra [mah-doo'-ro, rah], *a*. 1. Ripe, mature, perfect, mellow, full-grown. 2. Prudent, judicious. **Poco maduro**, unripe. **De edad madura**, of mature years. **La cosa está madura para la reforma**, the business is ripe for reform.

maelstrom [mah'-els-trom], *m*. Maelstrom, Norwegian whirlpool.

maesa [mah-ay'-sah], *f*. V. ABEJA MAESTRA.

maese [mah-ay'-say], *m*. V. MAESTRO. **Maestro coral**, a kind of game played with balls.

maesil [mah-ay-seel'], *m*. V. MAESTRIL.

maesillas [mah-ay-seel'-lyas], *f. pl.* Cords which serve in making trimmings to raise or lower the skeins.

maestra [mah-es'-trah], *f*. 1. Mistress, school-mistress, teacher. 2. Master's wife in all trades and professions. 3. Queen bee. 4. Whatever instructs. **La historia es maestra de la vida**, history is the instructress of life. 5. Among masons, a guide line for evening the surface. **Maestra de escuela**, school-teacher.

maestral [mah-es-trahl'], *a*. 1. Suiting or relating to a grand-master of a military order, or to his dignity or jurisdiction. 2. Northwest: applied to the wind. **Mesa maestral**, the sheep-walk board.-*m*. Cell of the queen-bee.

maestralizar [mah-es-trah-le-thar'], *vn. (Naut.)* To vary or decline to west or northwest: applied to the compass needle (in the Mediterranean).

maestrante [mah-es-trahn'-tay], *m*. Any of the members of one of the societies called *maestranzas*.

maestranza [mah-es-trahn'-thah], *f*. 1. Society of noblemen in Spain for practicing equestrian exercises. 2. All the workmen of a navy-yard. 3. Workshop of naval furniture. 4. Factory or workshops for making weapons of war. 5. Spot which the workshops occupy; navy-yard, arsenal.

maestrazgo [mah-es-trath'-go], *m*. Dignity or jurisdiction of a grand-master of a military order.

maestrazo [mah-es-trah'-tho], *m. aug.* A great master.-*a*. Masterly, skilled, highly intelligent.

maestre [mah-es'-tray], *m*. 1. Grand-master of a military order: also called *gran maestro*. 2. *(Naut.)* Mate of a merchant-ship.

maestrear [mah-es-tray-ar'], *vn. (coll.)* To domineer, to act the master.-*va*. 1. To lop vines. 2. *(Prov.)* To adulterate, to falsify. 3. To level the surface of a wall. 4. To direct (dirigir).

maestresala [mah-es-tray-sah'-lah], *m*. The chief waiter, headwaiter, maître d'hôtel.

maestrescuela [mah-es-tres-coo-ay'-lah], *m*. 1. Cathedral dignitary who teaches divinity. 2. Chancellor in some universities.

maestría [mah-es-tree'-ah], *f*. 1. Mastery (dominio), mastership, complete knowledge, skill (habilidad). **Lo hizo con maestría**, he did it very skillfully. 2. In regular orders, the dignity or degree of a master.

maestril [mah-es-treel'], *m*. Cell in which the queen bee is bred; a queen-cell.

maestrillo [mah-es-treel'-lyo], *m. dim.* A little master. **Cada maestrillo tiene su librillo**, *(Prov.)* every one has his hobby.

maestro [mah-es'-tro], *m*. 1. Master, teacher (profesor), professor. 2. Master (aposición), a man eminently skillful in practice or science. 3. A title of respect in monastic orders. 4. Master, a title of dignity in some universities. 5. The main-mast of a vessel. 6. **Maestro de capilla**, a choir-master, one who composes and directs church music. **Maestro de obras**, a contractor, or builder superintendent of construction. **Maestro de armas** or **de esgrima**, fencing master. **Maestro de maquillaje**, make-up expert.

maestro

maestro, tra [mah-es´-tro, trah], *a.* Masterly (genial), principal, first, main. **Llave maestra**, skeleton key. **Obra maestra**, masterpiece.

maestro de ceremonias [mah-es´-tro day thay-ray-mo´-ne-ahs], *m.* Master of ceremonies.

mafia [mah´-fe-ah], *f.* Mafia, criminal gang.

mafioso [mah-fe-o´-so], *m.* **Mafioso**, member of the Mafia.

magallánico, ca [mah-gah-lyah´-ne-co, cah], *a.* Magellanic, relating to the Straits of Magellan.

maganto, ta [mah-gahn´-to, tah], *a.* Spiritless, dull, faint, languid.

magaña [mah-gah´-nyah], *f.* 1. Honeycomb, a flaw in the bore of a gun. 2 *(coll.)* Cunning artifice, stratagem.

magarzuela [mah-gar-thoo-ay´-lah], *f.* Stinking chamomile.

Magdalena [mag-dah-lay´-nah], *f.* 1. A paste composed of sugar, lemon-juice flour, eggs, almonds, and other ingredients. 2. Magdalen, a repentant woman.

magdaleón [mag-dah-layon´], *m.* Sticks of plaster, made up in small cylindrical rolls for use.

magia [mah´-he-ah], *f.* 1. Magic, the art of producing effects by the secret agency of natural powers: in this sense it is also called **magia blanca** or **magia natural**. 2. Magic, the pretended science of putting in action the power of spirits: in this sense it is generally called **magia negra**.

magiar, or **magyar** [mah-he-ar´], *a. & n.* 1. Magyar, of the race predominant in Hungary and Transylvania. 2. Their language.

mágicamente [mah´-he-cah-men-tay], *adv.* Magically.

mágico, ca [mah´-he-co, cah], *a.* Magic, magical, necromantic. *-m. & f.* Magician, one who professes magic.

magín [mah-heen´], *m. (coll.)* Fancy, idea. *V.* IMAGINACIÓN. **Se le ha metido en el magín**, he has gotten it into his head.

magisterial [mah-his-tay-re-al´], *a.* Magisterial.

magisterio [mah-his-tay´-re-o], *m.* 1. Magistery, rule of a master. 2. Mastership, the title and rank of a master in universities (enseñanza). 3. Teaching profession (profesión), body of teachers in a nation, city, etc. (personas). 4. *(fig.)* Affected gravity.

magistrado, da [mah-his-trah´-do], *m & f.* 1. A magistrate. 2. Magistracy, the office or dignity of a magistrate. 3. Court, tribunal.

magistral [mah-his-trahl´], *a.* 1. Magisterial, masterly (genial), oracular. 2. Applied to a prebend in Catholic cathedrals, called **magistral**, and to the person who enjoys it. 3. *(Mod.)* Magistral or magistralia: applied to such medicines as are extemporaneous or in common use.-*f.* Title of a prebendary, in the Roman Catholic church, whose functions consist in teaching and preaching.

magistralmente [mah-hes-trahl´-men-tay], *adv.* Magisterially, masterly.

magistratura [mah-his-trah-too´-rah], *f.* Magistracy, judicature, judgeship.

magnánimamente [mag-nah´-ne-mah-men´-tay], *adv.* Magnanimously, bravely; generously.

magnanimidad [mag-nah-ne-me-dahd´], *f.* Magnanimity, fortitude, greatness.

magnánimo, ma [mag-nah´-ne-mo, mah], *a.* Magnanimous, heroic, generous; honorable.

magnate [mag-nah´-tay], *m.* Magnate, a person of rank, opulence, etc. **Los magnates de la industria**, the top people in industry.

magnesia [mag-nay´-se-ah], *f.* Magnesia, a medicinal powder: magnesium oxide.

magnesiano, na [mag-nay-se-ah´-no, nah], *a.* Magnesian, containing magnesia.

magnesio [mag-nay´-se-o], *m.* Magnesium, a light, grayish-white metal.

magnesita [mag-nay-see´-tah], *f.* Magnesite.

magnéticamente [mag-nay´-te-cah-le], *adv.* Magnetically.

magnético, ca [mag-nay´-te-co, cah], *a.* Magnetic, magnetical, attractive.

magnetismo [mag-nay-tees´-mo], *m.* Magnetism.

magnetizable [mag-nay-te-thah´-blay], *a.* Magnetizable.

magnetización [mag-nay-te-thah-the-on´], *f.* Magnetizing.

magnetizar [mag-nay-te-thar´], *va.* To magnetize.

magneto [mag-nay´-to], *m.* Magneto.

magnetoeléctrico, ca [mag-nay-to-ay-lec´-tre-co, cah], *a.* Magnetoelectric.

magnetofónico, ca [mag-nay-to-fo´-ne-co, cah], *a.* Tape recording.

magnetófono, magnetofón [mag-nay-to´-fo-no, mag-nay-to-fon´], *m.* Tape recorder.

magnetohidrodinámica [mag-nay-to-e-dro-de-nah´-me-cah], *f.* Magneto-hydrodynamics.

magnetómetro [mag-nay-to´-may-tro], *m.* Magnetometer.

magnetrón [mag-nay-tron´], *m.* Magnetron.

magníficamente [mag-nee´-fe-cah-men´-tay], *adv.* Magnificently, loftily, nobly.

magnificar [mag-ne-fe-car´], *va.* To magnify, to extol, to exalt.

magníficat [mag-nee´-fe-cat], *m.* The solid of the blessed Virgin.

magnificiencia [mag-ne-fe-then´-the-ah], *f.* Magnificence, grandeur, splendor (esplendor); gorgeousness.

magnífico, ca [mag-nee´-fe-co, cah], *a.* 1. Magnificent, splendid, grand, costly; gaudy. 2. A title of honor. **Es un muchacho magnífico**, he´s a fine boy.

magnitud [mag-ne-tood´], *f.* 1. Magnitude, comparative bulk. 2. Magnitude, greatness, grandeur.

magno, na [mahg´-no, nah], *a.* Great: used as an epithet in the Spanish language; *e. g.* **Alejandro Magno**, Alexander the Great.

magnolia [mag-no´-le-ah], *f. (Bot.)* Magnolia.

mago, ga [mah´-go, gah], *m. & f.* 1. A title formerly given in the east to philosophers, kings, or wise men, called magi. 2. Magician, one skilled in magic; a necromancer.

magra [mah´-grah], *f.* Rasher, slice of pork (lonja), bacon, or ham with eggs.

magro, gra [mah´-gro, grah], *a.* 1. Meagre, lean (persona). 2. Lean (carne). 3. Poor, thin (tierra).

magrura [mah-groo´-rah], *f.* Leanness, thinness.

magua [mah´-goo-ah], *f. (Cuba)* Jest, joke.

magüeto, ta [mah-goo-ay´-to, tah], *m. & f.* Young steer or heifer.

maguey [mah-gay´-e], *m. (Bot.)* American agave, the century plant. Agave Americana.

maguillo [mah-geel´-lyo], *m.* Wild apple-tree, used as grafting-stock in southern Spain.

magujo [mah-goo´-ho], *m. (Naut.)* Ravehook, an instrument with a crooked point, which serves to pick old oakum out of the seams of the ship's sides and decks.

magulladura [mah-goo-llyah-doo´-rah], *f.* Bruise, contusion; an injury with something blunt and heavy.

magullamiento [mah-goo-lyah-me-en´-to], *m.* Act of bruising: contusion.

magullar [mah-gool-lyar´], *va.* To bruise (amoratar), to mangle, to hurt (dañar), to batter (golpear); *(And, Carib.)* To crumple.

maharrana [ma-ha-rrah´-nah], *f. (Prov. Andal.)* Fresh bacon.

mahometano [mah-o-may-tah´-no], *a. m & a.* Mohammedan.

mahometismo [mah-o-may-tees´-mo], *m.* Mohammedanism.

mahometizar [mah-o-may-te-thar´], *vn.* To profess Mohammedanism.

mahón [mah-on´], *m.* Nankeen or nankin, a kind of light cotton. (Name derived from Port Mahón, in the Balearic Islands.)

mahona [mah-o´-nah], *f.* Turkish transport vessel.

mahonesa [mah-oh-nay´-sah], *f.* Mayonnaise.

maicena [mah-e-thay´-nah], *f. (LAm.)* Cornflor, corn starch.

maído [mah-ee´-do], *m.* Mewing. *V.* MAULLIDO.

maimona [ma-he-mo´-nah], *f.* Beam of a horse-mill in which the spindle runs.

maimonetes [ma-he-mo-nay'-tes], *m. pl. (Naut.)* Pins, placed near the main and foremast, to which ropes are fastened; belaying-pins.

maitinante [ma-he-te-nahn'-tay], *m.* Priest whose duty is to celebrate or attend matins.

maitinario [ma-he-te-nah'-re-o], *m.* Book containing the matins.

maitines [ma-he-tee'-nes], *m. pl.* Matins, earliest of the canonical hours in the Catholic church.

maíz [mah-eeth'], *m. (Bot.)* Maize, Indian corn. **Maíz machacado,** hominy.

maizal [ma-he-thahl'], *m.* Indian cornfield.

maizena [mah-e-thay'-nah], *f. (LAm.) V.*MAICENA.

maja [mah'-hah], *f.* Pestle of a mortar.

majá [mah-hah'], *m.* A thick-bodied snake of Cuba.

majada [mah-hah'-dah], *m.* 1. Sheep-cot, sheep-fold (corral). 2. Dung of animals (estiércol). *(Acad.)* 3. *(Cono Sur)* Flock of sheep (de ovejas); herd of goats (de chivos).

majadal [mah-hah-dahl'], *m.* Land which has been used for a sheep-fold and has been improved by the manure of the flock.

majadear [mah-hah-day-ar'], *m.* To take shelter in the night (ovejas).

majadería [mah-hah-day-ree'-ah], *f.* 1. Absurd speech, nonsense; lumpishness.

majaderico, ca, majaderillo, lla [mah-hah-day-ree'-co, cah, eel'-lyo, lyah], *a. dim.* Rather dull, somewhat silly, gawkish.

majaderillo [mah-hah-day-reel'-lyo], *m.* Bobbin for lace.

majadero, ra [mah-hah-day'-ro, rah], *a.* Dull, foolish, doltish, silly, sottish.

majadero [mah-hah-day'-ro], *m.* 1. Gawk, a foolish, troublesome fellow, a bore. 2. Pestle, an instrument with which something is broken in a mortar.

majaderón [mah-hah-day-rone'], *m. aug.* A great gawk, a great fool, a great bore.

majador, ra [mah-hah-dor', rah], *f.* Pounder, bruiser.

majadura [mah-hah-doo'-rah], *f.* The act of pounding or bruising.

majagranzas [mah-hah-grahn'-thas], *m. (coll.)* A stupid brute: nickname for an ignorant, troublesome fellow.

majagua [mah-hah'-goo-ah], *f.* A tree of Cuba and parts of South America, from the bark of which the strongest and most durable cordage is made.

maja martillo (Á) *adv. exp.* Hammer and tongs; strongly.

majamiento [mah-hay-me-en'to], *m. V.* MAJADURA.

majano [mah-hah'-no], *m.* A small heap of stones serving as a landmark.

majar [mah-har'], *va.* 1. To pound (aplastar), to break in a mortar. 2. To importune, to vex, to molest.

majara [mah-hah'-rah], *a. V.* MAJARETA.

majarete [mah-hah-ray´-tay], *m. (Cuba)* Corn-pudding, a dessert made from grated maize, milk, and sugar.

majarrana [mah-har-rah'-nah], *f. (Prov.)* Fresh pork.

majenca [mah-hen'-cah], *f. (Prov.)* Digging of vines. (Murcia.)

majencar [mah-hen-car'], *va. (Prov.)* To dig the earth about vines, and clear them of weeds.

majencia [mah-hen'-the-ah], *f. (Prov. Coll.)* Spruceness or fineness in one's dress.

majestad [mah-hes-tahd'], *f.* 1. Majesty, dignity; grandeur of appearance, loftiness; gravity. 2. Majesty, royalty, the title of emperors, kings, empresses, and queens. 3. Power, kingship, sovereignty, elevation. **Vuestra majestad,** your Majesty.

majestuosamente [mah-hes-too-o-sah-men'-tay], *adv.* Majestically, kingly.

majestuosidad [mah-hes-too-o-se-dahd'], *f.* Majesty, dignity.

majestuoso, sa [mah-hes-too-o´-so, sah], *a.* 1. Majestic, majestical, august, grand. 2. Stately, pompous, lofty. 3. Grave, solemn.

majeza [mah-hay'-thah], *f. (coll.)* 1. Spruceness, fineness in dress (elegancia). 2. Good looks (atractivo).

majo, ja [mah'-ho, hah], *m. & f.* Boaster, bragger. *-a.* Gallant, gay, spruce, fine, nice (agradable), pretty (guapa), attractive, good-looking (guapo).

majojo [mah-ho'-ho], *m.* Dry, half-thrashed straw and trodden stubble used as fodder.

majolar [mah-ho-lar'], *va.* To put straps to the shoes, to tie them tight.

majorca [mah-hor'-cah], *f. V.* MAZORCA.

majuela [mah-hoo-ay'-lah], *f.* 1. Fruit of the white hawthorn. 2. Strap with which shoes are tied, shoe lacing.

majuelo [mah-hoo-ay'-lo], *m.* 1. Vine newly planted. 2. The white hawthorn.

mal [mahl], *m.* 1. Evil, harm, hurt (daño), injury, mischief. 2. Illness, disease, complaint. 3. Imperfection. 4. Fault, trespass. *-a.* Evil (malvado), bad, wrong (equivocado). **Mal hombre,** an evil man. **El problema está mal,** the problem is wrong. **Es un chico malo,** he's a bad boy. *-adv.* Badly (de mala manera), injuriously, ill, wrongly (equivocadamente), hardly (apenas). **Anda mal,** he is a bad walker. **Mal hecho,** 1. Badly done, ill finished. 2. Unjust, contrary to equity and justice. **Mal que bien,** with good or ill will. **Mal por mal,** for want of something better. **De mal en peor,** worse and worse. **Mal de ojo,** evil eye. **Mal de ojos,** eyesore. **Mal de ánimo,** heart-sore. **Mal que le pese,** in spite of him. **Lo hace muy mal,** he does it very badly. **Oigo mal,** I don´t hear well. **Me entendió mal,** he misunderstood me. **Menos mal que...,** it´s just as well that... **El bien y el mal,** good and evil. **Caer en el mal,** to fall into evil ways. **Estar a mal con uno,** to be on bad terms with somebody. **El mal ya está hecho,** the harm is done now.

mala [mah'-lah], *f.* 1. Deuce of spades. 2. *(Amer.)* A mail-steamer. 3. *(And.)* Bad luck. 4. Mailbag (correo).

malabar [mah-lah-bar'], *a.* **Juegos malabares,** juggling.

malabarismo [mah-lah-bah-rees'-mo], *m.* 1. Juggling, conjuring. 2. **Malabarismos,** *(fig.)* Juggling; balancing act.

malabarista [mah-lah-bah-rees'-tah], *m & f.* Juggler, conjurer.

malacate [mah-lah-cah'-tay], *m.* Hoisting machine in mines.

malacología [mah-lah-co-lo-hee'-ah], *f.* Malacology, the science which treats of mollusks, especially their soft parts.

malaconsejado, da [mal-ah-con-say-hah'-do, dah], *a.* Ill-advised.

malaconsejar [mal-ah-con-say har'], *va.* 1. To advise badly. 2. To incline to evil.

malacostumbrado, da [mah-lah-cos-toom-brah'-do, dah], *a.* Having bad habits or customs (vicioso).

malacostumbrar [mal-ah-cos-toom-brahr'], *va.* **Malacostumbrar a uno,** to get somebody into bad habits.

malacuenda [mah-lah-coo-en'-dah], *f.* Coarse cloth made of tow.

malagaña [mah-lah-gah'-nyah], *f. (Prov.)* Pole set up with dry furze to catch bees swarming.

malagradecido, da [ma-lah-grah-day-thee'-do, dah], *a.* Unappreciative, ungrateful.

malagradecimiento [ma-lah-grah-day-the-me-en'-to], *m.* Ungratefulness, lack of appreciation.

malagueño, ña [mah-lah-gay'-nyo, nyah], *a.* Native of or belonging to Malaga. *-f.* A song popular in the province of Malaga.

malagueta [mah-lah-gay'-tah], *f.* Tabasco pepper.

malamente [mah-lah-men'-tay], *adv.* Badly, wickedly, wrongly. **Estar malamente de dinero,** to be badly off for money.

malandante [mah-lan-dahn'-tay], *a.* Calamitous, unfortunate.

malandanza [mah-lan-dahn´-thah], *f.* Misfortune, calamity.

malandar [mah-lan-dar'], *m. (Prov.)* Wild hog.

malandrín [mah-lan-dreen'], *m.* High-wayman. *-a.* Malign, perverse.

malanga [mah-lahn'-gah], *f.* A farinaceous root of great consumption in Cuba.

malapata [mah-lah-pah'-tah], *m & f.* Pest, nuisance, tedious individual; clumsy sort.

malaquita [mah-lah-kee'-tah], *f. (Min.)* Malachite, precious stone: green copper carbonate.

malar [mah-lar'], *a.* Malar, relating to the cheek.

malaria [mah-lah'-re-ah], *f.* Malaria.

malatía [mah-lah-tee'-ah], *f.* 1. Leprosy. 2. Disease in general.

malato, ta [mah-lah'-to, tah], *a.* 1. Leprous. 2. Sick, diseased. Also noun.

malato [mah-lah'-to], *m. (Chem.)* Malate.

malavenido, da [mah-lah-vay-nee'-do, dah], *a. & f.* Quarrelsome person, a sower of discord; curst, mischievous.

malaventura [mah-lah-ven-too´-rah], *f.* Calamity, misfortune.

malaventurado, da [mah-lah-ven-too-rah´-do, dah], *a.* Unfortunate, ill-fated, luckless.

malaventuranza [mah-lah-ven-too-rahn'-thah], *f.* Infelicity, unhappiness.

malayo, a [mah-lah'-yo, yah], *a.* 1. Malay, belonging to Malacca. 2. The Malay tongue.

malbaratador, ra [mal-bah-rah-tah-dor', rah], *m. & f.* Spendthrift, prodigal.

malbaratar [mal-bah-rah-tar´], *va.* 1. To misspend, to lavish. 2. To disorder.

malbaratero, ra [mal-bah-rah-tay´-ro, rah], *a. V.* MALBARATADOR.

malbaratijo [mal-bah-rah-tee'-ho], *m.* Bad sale, sale in a second-hand shop.

malbaratillo [mal-bah-rah-teel'-lyo], *m.* A cheap, second-hand shop.

malcarado, da [mal-cah-rah'-do, dah], *a.* Grim-faced, foul-faced.

malcasado, da [mal-cah-sah'-do, dah], *a. & pp.* of MALCASAR. Not well married.

malcasar [mal-cah-sar'], *va.* To make someone marry against his or her will: applied to parents, guardians, etc. *-vr.* To contract an improper or unfortunate marriage.

malcaso [mal-cah'so], *m.* Treason, turpitude, crime.

malcocinado [mal-co-the-nah'do], *m.* 1. Tripes, liver, and lights of a quadruped. 2. Place where tripes are sold.

malcomer [mal-coh'-mar], *vn.* To have a poor meal, to eat badly.

malcomido, da [mal-co-mee'-do, dah], *a.* Hungry, destitute of wholesome food.

malcontento, [mal-con-ten'-to], *m.* 1. Malcontent; grumbler. 2. A game at cards.

malcontento, ta [mal-con-ten'-to, tah], *a.* Discontented, malcontent.

malcorte [mal-cor'-tay], *m.* Transgression of the mountain laws in cutting wood or making charcoal.

malcriado, da [mal-cre-ah'-do, dah], *a.* Ill-bred, unmannerly, impolite, clownish; spoiled (niños).

malcriar [mal-cre-ar'], *va.* To spoil (niño).

maldad [mal-dahd'], *f.* 1. Wickedness, iniquity, corruption, abomination. 2. Guiltiness, criminality, mischievousness.

maldecidor, ra [mal-day-the-dor', rah], *m. & f.* Detractor; swearer.

maldecir [mal-day-theer'], *va.* 1. To curse (con maldición), to accurse, to execrate. 2. To detract. *-vn.* **Maldecir de,** to speak ill of, to slander (difamar); to disparage (denigrar). *(Yo maldigo, yo maldiga,* from *Maldecir. V.* BENDECIR.)

maldicho, cha [mal-dee'-cho, chah], *pp. irr. obs.* of MALDECIR. Accursed; calumniated.

maldiciente [mal-de-the-en'-tay], *pa. & m. & f.* Cursing; curser; grumbler, complainer, malcontent.

maldición [mal-de-the-on'], *f.* 1. Malediction, curse, execration; imprecation. 2. Divine chastisement. **Parece que ha caído una maldición sobre este programa,** there seems to be a curse on this programme.

maldita [mal-dee'-tah], *f.* 1. *(coll.)* The tongue (lengua). **Soltar la maldita,** *(coll.)* to give a loose rein to one's tongue, to tell one's mind very freely. 2. *(Carib.)* Sore (llaga).

maldito, ta [mal-dee'-to, tah], *a.* 1. Perverse, wicked (maligno). 2. Chastised by Divine justice. 3. Damned (condenado), cursed, confounded. 4. *(coll.)* None, not one. *-pp. irr.* of MALDECIR, accursed. **Ese maldito libro,** that damned book. **No le encuentro maldita la gracia,** I don´t find it in the least amusing. 5. *(Mex.)* Crafty (taimado). *-m.* 1. **El maldito,** the devil. 2. *(Teat.)* Extra.

maleabilidad [mah-lay-ah-be-le-dahd'], *f.* Malleability, malleableness.

maleable [mah-lay-ah'-blay], *a.* Malleable.

maleante [mah-lay-ahn'-tay], *m.* Corrupter, injurer, malefactor (malhechor), vragant (vago). *-pa.* Corrupting.

malear [mah-lay-ar'], *va.* To pervert, to corrupt, to injure, to damnify. *-vr.* To spoil, to be harmed; to be corrupted.

malecón [mah-lay-cone'], *m.* Dike, embankment, levee, jetty.

maledicencia [mah-lay-de-then'-the-ah], *f.* Slander, calumny.

maleducar [mahl-ay-doo-car'], *va.* To spoil (niños).

maleficencia [mah-lay-fe-then'-the-ah], *f.* Mischievousness, the habit of doing mischief.

maleficiador, ra [mah-lay-fe-the-ah-dor´, rah], *m. & f.* Adulterator, corrupter. **maleficiar** [mah-lay-fe-the-ar'], *va.* 1. To adulterate, to corrupt, to vitiate. 2. To bewitch (hechizar), to injure by witchcraft.

maleficio [mah-lay-fee'-the-o], *m.* Witchcraft (brujería), charm, enchantment.

maléfico, ca [mah-lay´-fe-co, cah], *a.* Mischievous, malicious, injurious to others, especially by witchcraft.

malentendido [mah-layn-ten-dee'-do], *m.* Misunderstanding.

maleolar [mah-lay-o-lar'], *a.* Malleolar, relating to the ankle.

maleólo [mah-lay'-o-lo], *m.* Malleolus, each bony prominence of the ankles.

malestar [mah-les-tar'], *m.* 1. Discomfort, uneasiness. 2. Indisposition, physical disorder.

maleta [mah-lay'-tah], *f.* 1. Portmanteau, valise, gripsack. 2. **Hacer la maleta,** to make preparations for a journey. 3. *(Aut.)* Boot, trunk. 3. *(CAm. Cono Sur)* Saddle-bag. 4. *(And. CAm. Cono Sur)* Bundle of clothes. 5. *(And, Carib.)* Hump (joroba).

maletero [mah-lay-tay'-ro], *m.* Harness-maker, saddler, portmanteau-maker. 2. *(Aut.)* Boot, trunk.

maletilla [mah-lay-teel'-lyah], *f.* Satchel, small handbag. *-m. (Taur.)* Itinerant aspiring bullfighter.

maletín [mah-le-teen'], *m. dim.* A satchel, small case.

maletón [mah-lay-tone'], *m. aug.* A large leather bag, portmanteau.

malevolencia [mah-lay-vo-len'-the-ah], *f.* Malevolence, ill-nature, ill-will, malignancy.

malévolo, la [mah-lay'-vo-lo, lah], *a.* Malevolent, malignant, mischievous, hateful.

maleza [mah-lay'-thah], *f.* 1. Piece of ground, rendered unfruitful by brambles and briers. 2. Undergrowth, thicket, coppice, scrub (arbustos), weeds (hierbas).

malformación [mahl-for-mah-the-on'], *f.* Malformation.

malformado [mahl-for-mah'-do], *a.* Malformed.

malgama [mahl-gah'-mah], *m. (Chem.) V.* AMALGAMA.

malgastador, ra [mal-gas-tah-dor', rah], *m. & f.* Spendthrift, squanderer.

malgastar [mal-gas-tar´], *va.* To misspend, to waste (tiempo, esfuerzo), to lavish, to lose, to throw away.

malhablado, da [mal-hah-blah'-do, dah], *a.* Bold, impudent in speaking, foul-mouthed.

malhadado, da [mal-ah-dah-do, dah], *a.* Wretched, unfortunate.

malhecho [mal-hay'-cho], *m.* Flagitious action: an evil deed.

malhecho, cha [mal-ay´-cho, chah], *a.* Ill-shaped: applied to persons who are humpbacked or otherwise deformed.

malhechor, ra [mal-ay-chor', rah], *m. & f.* Malefactor, offender, misdoer.

malherido, da [mal-ay-ree´-do, dah], *a. & pp.* Of MALHERIR. Badly wounded.

malherir [mal-ay-reer´], *va.* To wound badly.

malhojo [mal-o´-ho], *m (Naut.)* Vegetable refuse.

malhumorado, da [mal-oo-mo-rah'-do, dah], *a.* Ill-humored, peevish; bad-tempered. **Estar malhumorado,** to be in a bad mood.

malicia [mah-lee'-the-ah], *f.* 1. Malice, perversity, wickedness (maldad), malignity. 2. Malice, maliciousness, mischievousness, intention of mischief to another (intención). 3. Suspicion, apprehension. 4. Cunning, artifice. 5. Dissimulation, hypocrisy. 6. Gall, rancor, animosity. 7. Viciousness (carácter). 8. Roguishness (mirada, chiste), naughtiness. **Contó un chiste con mucha malicia,** he told a very naughty story.

maliciar [mah-le-the-ar'], *va.* To corrupt, to adulterate.-*vn.* To put a malicious construction on a thing; to discourse in a malicious manner; to suspect maliciously.

maliciosamente [mah-le-the-o-sah-men'-tay], *adv.* 1. Maliciously. 2. Wickedly. 3. Roguishly. 4. Viciously; mischievously.

maliciosico, ica, illo, illa, ito, ita [mah-le-the-o-see'co], *a.* *dim.* A little malicious.

malicioso, sa [mah-le-the-o'-so, sah], *a.* Malicious, suspicious, wicked (malo), knavish, mischievous (travieso), vicious (vicioso), ill-intentioned (malintencionado).

málico, ca [mah'-le-co, cah], *a.* Malic, belonging to or derived from apples.

malignamente [mah-lig-nah-men'-tay], *adv.* Malignantly, mischievously, hatefully, malevolently.

malignar [mah-lig-nar'], *va.* To vitiate, to corrupt, to deprave. -*vr.* 1. To become sore. 2. To grow worse.

malignidad [mah-lig-ne-dahd'], *f.* Malignity, malice (rencor); perverseness; mischievousness, hatred.

maligno, na [mah-leeg'-no, nah], *a.* Malignant, perverse, malicious (actitud, observación), ill-disposed, hateful.

malilla [mah-leel'-lyah], *f.* 1. Manille, the deuce of spades or clubs, or the seven of hearts or diamonds, in some games. A game of cards like whist. 3. *(coll.)* Person full of wickedness and malice.

malinformar [mahl-en-for-mar'], *va.* To misinform.

malintencionado, da [mal-in-ten-the-o-nah'-do, dah], *a.* Bearing ill-will, ill disposed, with bad intentions.

malinterpretar [mahl-in-ter-pray-tar'], *va.* To misinterpret.

malísimo [mah-lee'-se-mo], *a.* Very bad, dreadful, appalling.

malla [mahl'-lyah], *f.* 1. Mesh, space between the threads of a net. **Hacer malla,** to knit. 2. *(Naut.)* Net-work of a ship. 3. Coat of mail.

mallar [mah-llyar'], *va.* To make net-work.

mallero [mah-lyay'-ro], *m.* Armorer, maker of coats of mail.

malletes [mal-lyay'-tes], *m. pl.* Partners, strong pieces of timber bolted to the beams, encircling the masts, to keep them steady in their steps.

mallo [mahl'-lyo], *m.* 1. Pallmall, game of bowls, skittles, or ninepins. 2. Mall, bowling-green, skittle-ground. 3. Mallet.

malmandado, da [mal-man-dah'-do, dah], *a. (coll.)* Disobedient, obstinate.

malmeter [mal-may-terr'], *vn. (coll.)* To incline, to induce to evil; to make one differ with another; to breed quarrels.

malmirado, da [mal-me-rah'-do, dah], *a.* 1. Impolite, inconsiderate. 2. Indiscreet, imprudent.

malnacido [mal-nah-the'-do], *a.* Rotten, awful.

malnutrido [mal-noo-tre'-do], *a.* Undernourished.

malo, la [mah'-lo, lah], *a.* 1. Bad, evil, not good. 2. Bad, vicious, wicked, mean, nasty, perverse, naughty (niño). 3. Imperfect, defective. 4. Artful, cunning, crafty, mischievous. 5. Sickly, disordered, ill. **Estar malo,** to be ill, to be sick. **Ser malo,** to be wicked. 6. Unhealthy, prejudicial to health. 7. Difficult (difícil), inquiet. 8. Wrong. **Ésta es una mala respuesta,** this is the wrong answer. **Andar a malas,** to go in enmity. **Este papel es malo para escribir,** this paper is bad for writing. **Es un animal malo de domesticar,** it is a difficult animal to tame. **Estar de malas,** to be in a bad mood. -*m.* **El malo,** the Evil. 2. *(Teat.)* Villain; (Cine) Bad guy.

malo [mah'-lo], *int.* Bad; so much the worse.

malogramiento [mah-lo-grah-me-en'-to], *m.* Disappointment.

malograr [mah-lo-grar'], *va.* 1. To disappoint, to disconcert. 2. *(Com.)* To waste or spoil goods (desperdiciar).-*vr.* 1. To be disappointed (decepcionar), to fail. 2. To die before one's time (persona). 3. *(And. Aut.)* To break down.

malogro [mah-lo'-gro], *m.* Disappointment, miscarriage, failure (fracaso), waste (desperdicio).

maloja [mah-lo'-hah], *f.* *(Cuba)* The leaves and stalks of Indian corn, used only for fodder.

maloler [mah-lo-lerr'], *vr.* To stink.

maloliente [mah-lo-le-en'-tay], *pa.* Stinking, foul-smelling.

malolor [mah-lo-lor'], *m.* Stench, stink, pestiferous smell.

malón [mah-lone'], *m.* (Chili) A hostile, predatory incursion of Indians.

maloquear [ma-lo-kay-ar'], *m. (Mex.)* 1. To make a predatory raid (by Indians). 2. To trade with Indians for stolen goods.

maloquero, ra [mah-lo-kay'-ro, rah], *a. & n. (Amer.)* 1. An Indian thief. 2. One who trades with Indian thieves.

malordenado, da [mah-lor-day-nah'-do, dah], *a.* Badly contrived, ill arranged.

malparado, da [mal-pah-rah'-do, dah], *a & pp.* of MALPARAR. Ill-conditioned, impaired, useless.

malparar [mal-pah-rar'], *va.* To ill-treat (maltratar), to impair, to damage (dañar), to hurt, to blemish.

malparecido, da [mal-pah-ray-thee'-do, dah], *a.* Of evil aspect or countenance, ugly.

malparida [mal-pah-ree'-dah], *f.* Woman who has miscarried.

malparir [mal-pah-reer'], *vn.* To miscarry.

malparto [mal-par'-to], *m.* Abortion, miscarriage.

malpaso [mal-pah'-so], *m.* 1. Exigency, tight place, grievous difficulty. 2. Reprehensible fault.

malpensado [mal-pen-sah'-do], *a.* Nasty, evil-minded.

malponer [mal-po-nerr'], *va.* 1. To indispose. 2. To excite quarrels.

malquerencia [mal-kay-ren'-the-ah], *f.* Ill-will, hatred.

malquerer [mal-kay-rerr'], *va.* To abhor, to hate, to bear ill-will.

malquistar [mal-kis-tar'], *va.* To excite disputes and quarrels among friends and others.-*vr.* To incur hatred and displeasure.

malquisto, ta [mal-kees'-to, tah], *a.* Hated, detested, abhorred.

malrotador, ra [mal-ro-tah-dor', rah], *m. & f.* Squanderer, spendthrift.

malrotar [mal-ro-tar'], *va.* To misspend, to lavish, to waste one's fortune.

malsano, na [mal-sah'-no, nah], *a.* 1. Unhealthy (clima, atmósfera), sickly, infirm. 2. Unwholesome, insalubrious, injurious to health.

malsín [mal-seen'], *m.* Tale-bearer, mischief-maker.

malsonante [mal-so-nahn'-tay], *a.* Ill-sounding, offensive, nasty (palabra).

malsufrido, da [mal-soo-free'-do, dah], *a.* Impatient of suffering, weak (débil).

Malta [mahl'-tah], *f.* 1. A bandage in the shape of a Maltese cross. 2. Asphalt, mineral pitch.

maltés, sa [mal-tays', sah], *a.* Maltese, of Malta.

maltosa [mal-to'-sah], *f.* Maltose.

maltrabaja [mal-trah-bah'-hah], *com. (coll.)* Idler, lounger.

maltraer [mal-trah-err'], *va.* 1. To treat ill (maltratar). 2. To insult (insultar). V. MALTRATAR.

maltratadamente [mal-trah-tah-dah-men-tay], *adv.* Ill-used, in an abused manner.

maltratamiento [mal-trah-tah-me-en'-to], *m.* Ill treatment, bad usage; affliction.

maltratar [mal-trah-tar'], *va.* 1. To treat ill (persona), to abuse, to maltreat, to misuse. 2. To spoil, to destroy.

maltrato [mal-trah'-to], *m.* 1. Ill treatment (persona). 2. Abuse (abuso).

maltrecho [malñ-tray'-cho], *a.* Battered, damaged; injured. **Dejar maltrecho a uno,** to leave somebody in a bad way.

malucho, cha [mah-loo'-cho, chah], *a.* 1. *(coll.)* A sickly person. 2. Naughty, wayward.

malva [mahl'-vah], *f. (Bot.)* Mallows. **Malva blanca**, walteria hibiscus. **Malva rosa**, hibiscus mutabilis. **De color malva**, mauve.

malvadamente [mal-vah-dah-men'-tay], *adv.* Wickedly, naughtily, mischievously, hellishly; lewdly.

malvado, da [mal-vah'-do, dah], *a.* Malicious, wicked, insolent, vicious, nefarious.

malvar [mal-var'], *m.* Place covered with mallows.

malvasía [mal-vah-see'-ah], *f.* Malmsey or Malvoisie grape; malmsey wine.

malvavisco [mal-vah-vees'-co], *m. (Bot.)* Marshmallows.

malvender [mal-ven-der'], *va.* To sell off cheap.

malversación [mal-ver-sah-the-on'], *f.* Mis-application or mal-administration of money, malversation.

malversador, ra [mal-ver-sah-dor', rah], *m. & f.* Person who misapplies property.

malversar [mal-ver-sar'], *va.* To misapply, to apply money to wrong purposes.

malvis, malviz [mal-vees', mal-veeth'], *m.* Bird resembling a thrush; redwing.

mallorquín, na [mal-lyor-keen', nah], *a.* Majorcan.

mamá [mah-mah'], *f.* Ma, mamma, mum, mummy: a fond word for mother.

mama [mah'-ma], *f.* 1. The mammary gland, breast. 2. *(Prov. Andal.)* Mamma, mother.

mamacallos [mah-mah-cahl'-lyos], *m. (coll.)* Dolt, simpleton.

mamada [mah-mah'-dah], *f.* 1. *(coll.)* Time which a child takes in sucking (chupada). 2. *(LAm.)* Cinch (cosa fácil). 3. *(Cono Sur)* Drunkenness (borrachera).

mamadera [mah-mah-day'-rah], *f.* Breast-pump.

mamador, ra [mah-mah-dor', rah], *m. & f.* Sucker, suckling, one who sucks.-*n.* Feeding-bottle, nursing-bottle for artificial lactation.

mamahigos [mah-mah-ee'-gose], *a.* Silly, booby.

mamalón [mah-mah-lon'], *m. (Cuba)* Idler who tries constantly to live at another's expense; parasite.

mamante [mah-mahn'-tay], *a.* Sucking.

mamantón, na [mah-man-to-ne', nah], *a.* Sucking (animales).

mamar [mah-mar'], *va.* 1. To suck, to draw milk from the breast (pecho). 2. *(coll.)* To cram and devour victuals. 3. To acquire in infancy. 4. *(coll.)* To get, to obtain. 5. *(Mex.)* To suck off.-*vn.* 1. To suck. 2. *(Fig.)* To get something free. 3. To booze (beber). -*vr.* 1. To wangle (puesto, ventaja). 2. *(And.)* To go back on one's word.

mamario, ria [mah-mah'-re-o, ah], *a.* Mammary: relating to the breast.

mamarrachada [mah-mar-rah-chah'-dah], *f.* 1. A collection of rude or ridiculous figures. 2. A foolish action or speech.

mamarracho [mah-mar-rah'-cho], *m.* An ill-drawn figure of a man; a grotesque ornament.

mamayuca [mah-mah-yoo'-cah], *f.* Crust of bread put into a frying-pan or dish where many eat, to set bounds to or suspend a meal.

mambla [mahm'-blah], *f.* Isolated rounded hillock.

mamelón [mah-may-lon'], *m. (Anat.)* 1. Teat, nipple. 2. Any teat-shaped tubercle.

mameluco [mah-may-loo'-co], *m.* 1. Mameluke, Egyptian soldier. 2. Leotard, practice costume for dancing. 3. Child's rompers. 4. A fool, an idiot (idiota).

mamella [mah-mayl'-lyah], *f.* 1. Small teat, nipple. 2. A small teat-shaped appendage on the neck of goats, etc. V. MARMELLA.

mamellado, da [mah-mel-lyah'-do, dah], *a.* Mammellated: applied to animals having loose skins on their necks.

mamífero, ra [ma-mee'-fay-ro, rah], *a.* Mammiferous, having mammary glands: mammalian. -*pl.* Mammals.

mamiforme [mah-me-for'-may], *a.* Having the shape of a mammary gland. V. MASTÓIDEO.

mamila [mah-mee'-lah], *f.* 1. The chief part of a woman's breast round the nipple. 2. The nipple in men. *(Acad.)*

mamilar [mah-me-lar'], *a.* Mamillary.

mamografía [mah-mo-grah-fe'-ah], *f.* Mammography.

mamola [mah-mo'-lah], *f.* Chuck under the chin.

mamón, na [mah-mone', nah], *m. & f.* 1. A sucking animal. 2. A child that sucks too much, or for too long a time. 3. Sucker, young twig.

mamoso, sa [mah-mo'-so, sah], *a.* 1. Sucking. 2. Applied to panic grass.

mamotreto [mah-mo-tray'-to], *m.* 1. Memorandum-book, hefty tome (libro). 2. *(LAm.)* Contraption (aparato). 3. *(Mex.)* Dead loss (inútil).

mampara [mam-pah'-rah], *f.* Screen before a door or any other place.

mamparo [mam-pah'-ro], *m. (Naut.)* Bulkhead, partition in a ship. **Mamparos de quita y pon**, *(Naut.)* ship and unship bulkheads.

mamporro [mam-por'-ro], *m.* Bash, punch, clout; bump (al caer). **Atizar un mamporro a uno**, to give somebody a swipe.

mampostear [mam-pos-tay-ar'], *va.* To raise mason-work, to cement with mortar.

mampostería [mam-pos-tay-ree'-ah], *f.* 1. Rubble-work (sin labrar), masonry. 2. The employment of collecting alms or tithes.

mampostero [mam-pos-tay'-ro], *m.* 1. Mason, stone mason. 2. Collector of alms or tithes.

mampresar [mam-pray-sar'], *va. (Prov.)* To begin to break horses.

mampuesta [mam-poo-es'-tah], *f.* Row of bricks.

mampuesto [mam-poo-es'-to], *m.* Rubble, rough stone.

mamullar [mah-mool-lyar'], *va.* To eat or chew as if sucking; to mutter; to mumble.

mamut [mah-moot'], *m.* Mammoth, primitive elephant now extinct.

maná [mah-nah'], *m.* 1. Manna, food of the Israelites. 2. Manna, a gum obtained from ash-trees. 3. Tart made of blanched almonds, sugar, spice, etc. 4. Hired of small sugar-plums.

manada [mah-nah'-dah], *f.* 1. Flock, herd, drove of cattle. 2. Handful of corn, etc.; tuft, cluster. 3. Crowd, fry, multitude. **A manadas**, in troops or crowds.

manadera [mah-nah-day'-rah], *f.* Strainer, an instrument for filtration.

manadero [mah-nah-day'-ro], *m.* 1. Source, spring. 2. Shepherd, herdsman.

manadero, ra [mah-nah-day'-ro, rah], *a.* Springing, that which issues.

manadilla [mah-nah-deel'-lyah], *f. dim.* A small flock.

manante [mah-nahn'-tay], *pa.* Proceeding, issuing.

manantial [mah-nan-te-ahl'], *m.* 1. Source, spring. 2. Source, origin, principle, head. -*a.* Flowing, running (agua).

manar [mah-nar'], *va.* 1. To spring from; to distil from, as a liquor. 2. To drop or distil from. 3. To proceed, to issue, to arise. 4. To bound. **Manar sangre**, to run with blood. -*vn.* 1. To run, to flow (líquido). 2. To abound, to be plentiful.

manatí, manato [mah-nah-tee', mah-nah'-to], *m.* 1. Manati, manatee, sea-cow. 2. A whip made of the manati's hide.

manaza [mah-nah'-thah], *f. aug.* A large hand (mano), a mutton-fist.

manca [mahn'-cah], *f.* V. MANCO.

mancamiento [man-cah-me-en'-to], *m.* Want, defect, privation, deficiency, maimedness.

mancar [man-car'], *va.* 1. To maim (mutilar), to render useless an arm or hand. 2. To disable a man for business. 3. *(Cono Sur)* **Mancar el tiro**, to miss. -*vn. (And. Escol.)* To fail; to blow it (fracasar).

manceba [man-thay'-bah], *f.* Mistress, concubine.

mancebía [man-thay-bee'-ah], *f.* Brothel, bawdy-house.

mancebico, illo, ito [man-thay-bee'-co], *m. dim.* A little young man.

mancebo, ba [man-thay'-bo, bah], *m. & f.* 1. Young person, under forty years of age (joven). 2. Journeyman, a hired workman. 3. Bachelor (soltero).

mancera [man-thay'-rah], *f.* Ploughtail, handle of a plough.

mancerina [man-thay-ree'-nah], *f.* (*Prov.*) Saucer. *V.* MACERINA.

mancha [mahn'-chah], *f.* 1. Stain, spot, discoloration; blot, macula. 2. Stigma, mark of infamy. 3. Piece of ground distinct from those which adjoin it. 4. (*Met.*) Stigma, blemish, dishonor, either from mean birth or an ignominious act. 5. A spot on the sun or other heavenly body. **Mancha solar**, sunspot. 6. (*And, Carib.*) Cloud, swarm.

manchado, da [man-chah'-do, dah], *a.* Spotted (animal), speckled (ave), Smudged (papel). **Un abrigo manchado de barro**, a coat stained with mud. *-pp.* of MANCHAR.

manchar [man-char'], *va.* 1. To stain, to corrupt, to soil (persona), to contaminate; to daub; to darken, to cloud. 2. To defile one's character, to tarnish one's name and reputation (persona). **Manchar papel**, to scribble, to write much, and nothing to the purpose. 3. (*Pict.*) To lay in spots of light color before defining the figure. *-vr.* 1. To get dirty (ensuciarse). 2. (*Fig.*) To stain one´s reputation.

manchega [man-chay´-gah], *f.* Garter of different colors, made of worsted, especially in La Mancha.

manchego, ga [man-chay'-go, gah], *a.* Native of or belonging to La Mancha, a province of Spain.

manchica, illa, ita [man-chee'-cah], *f. dim.* A small stain, spot, or macula.

manchón [man-chone'], *m.* 1. Spot where grain grows rank or thick. 2. (*Aug.*) A large stain or spot.

manchú [man-choo'], *a.* Belonging to Manchuria or its inhabitants; Manchurian.

mancilla [man-theel'-lyah], *f.* Spot, blemish.

mancillar [man-theel'-lyar], *va.* To spot, to stain. *V.* AMANCILLAR.

mancipar [man-the-par'], *va.* To subject, to enslave, to mancipate.

manco, ca [mahn'-co, cah], *a.* 1. Handless, one-handed (una mano), lacking one or both hands, or without the use of them. 2. Maimed, defective, faulty, imperfect. 3. (*Fig.*) **No ser manco**, to be useful (útil).

manco, ca [mahn'-co, cah], *m. & f.* 1. A handlers or a one-handed person (una mano). 2. (*Cono Sur*) Old horse, nag (caballo).

mancomún [man-co-moon'], *m.* Concurrence of two or more persons in the execution of a thing; it is now used only in the adverbial phrase, **de mancomún**, jointly, by common consent.

mancomunadamente [man-co-moo-nah'-dah-men-tay], *adv.* Conjointly, by common consent.

mancomunar [man-co-moo-nar'], *va.* 1. To associate, to unite (personas). 2. (*Law.*) To make two or more persons pay jointly the costs of a lawsuit. *-vr.* To act together, to join in the execution of a thing.

mancomunidad [man-co-moo-ne-dahd'], *f.* Union, conjunction, fellowship.

mancornar [man-co-moo-nar'], *va.* 1. To throw a young steer with its horns fixed in the ground, leaving it motionless. 2. To tie a pair of animals by the horns, so as to make them go together.

mancuerna [man-coo-err'-nah], *f.* 1. Pair of animals or things. 2. Thong for throwing a steer. 3. (*Cuba*) Stem with two or three leaves, which is cut from the plant in collecting tobacco.

manda [mahn'-dah], *f.* 1. Offer, proposal. 2. Legacy or donation left by virtue of last will.

mandadera [man-dahday'rah], *f. V.* DEMANDADERA.

mandadero, ra [man-dah-day'-ro, rah], *m. & f.* 1. Porter, messenger; one engaged to run errands. 2. *V.* DEMANDADERO.

mandado [man-dah'-do], *m.* 1. Mandate, precept, command. 2. Errand, message, advertisement, notice. **Muchacho de mandados**, errand-boy. **Mandado, da**, *pp.* of MANDAR.

mandamiento [man-dah-me-en'-to], *m.* 1. Mandate, precept, order (orden), command. 2. Commandment, one of the ten precepts of the Decalogue. 3. Peremptory order issued by a judge, respecting the execution of his sentence. *-pl.* (*coll.*) The five fingers of the hand. **Mandamientos de la ley de Dios**, the ten commandments. **Mandamientos de la Iglesia or de la Santa Madre Iglesia**, commandments of the church.

mandante [man-dahn'-tay], *pa.* Commanding.

mandar [man-dar'], *va.* 1. To command, to give orders, to order (ordenar), to ordain, to enact. 2. To lead, to head (grupo). 3. To leave or bequeath in a last will or testament (legar). 4. (*Prov.*) To send (enviar), to transmit. 5. To offer, to promise. 6. To ask for. 7. (*LAm.*) To throw (echar). 8. (*LAm.*) To give, to strike (golpe). 9. (*LAm.*) To break in (caballo). **Mandar hacer**, (*coll.*) to have made, to order or cause to be made, to bespeak.*-vr.* 1. In buildings, to communicate with. 2. To have free use of one's limbs, to manage oneself without the aid of others. 3. (*Carib. Cono Sur*) To go away (irse). 4. (*LAm.*) **Mándese entrar**, please come in. **Mandar a alguno a puntapiés, a puntillazos** or **a zapatazos**, to have complete ascendancy over anyone. **Mandar hacer un traje**, to order a suit. **Mandar salir a uno**, to order somebody out.

mandarín [man-dah-reen'], *m.* Mandarin, a Chinese magistrate.

mandarina [man-dah-ree'-nah], *f.* 1. (*Bot.*) Tangerine (fruta). 2. Mandarin language, Chinese dialect.

mandarria [man-dar'-re-ah], *f.* (*Naut.*) Iron maul, a large hammer or sledge.

mandatario [man-dah-tah'-re-o], *m.* 1. Attorney, agent. 2. Mandatory; mandatary. 3. (*Mex.*) Collector of religious confraternities.

mandato [man-dah'-to], *m.* 1. Mandate, precept, injunction, order (orden), ordinance 2. Charge, trust, commission. 3 Ecclesiastical ceremony of washing the feet of twelve persons on Maundy Thursday. 4. Mandate (gobierno). 5. Term (período). **Mandato judicial**, warrant. **Territorio bajo mandato**, mandated territory.

¡mande! [mahn'-day], *int.* (*Naut.*) Holla! a word of command on shipboard, enjoining attention.

mandíbula [man-dee´-boo-lah], *f.* Jawbone, mandible.

mandibular [man-dee-boo-lar'], *a.* Mandibular, belonging to the jaw.

mandil [man-deel´], *m.* 1. Coarse apron used by men or women. 2. (*Low.*) Servant to a pimp or prostitute. 3. (*Cono Sur*) Horse blanket (de caballo).

mandilada [man-de-lah'-dah], *f.* 1. An apronful. 2. (*Low.*) A number of ruffians.

mandilar [man-de-lar'], *va.* To wipe a horse with a course apron or cloth.

mandilejo [man-de-lay'-ho], *m.* 1. (*dim.*) A small apron, a ragged apron. 2. (*Low.*) Servant of a rogue or prostitute, pimp, pander.

mandilete [man-de-lay'-tay], *m.* (*Mil.*) Door of the porthole of a battery.

mandilón [man-de-lone'], *m.* (*coll.*) Coward, a mean, dastardly fellow.

mandioca [man-de-o'-cah], *f.* The Brazilian name of the yucca (manioc) or cassava, yielding tapioca.

mando [mahn´-do], *m.* 1. Command, authority, power, dominion, rule (de país), leadership (liderazgo). **Alto mando**, high command. **Ejercer el mando**, to be in command. **Entregar el mando**, to hand over command. 2. Lead (en carretera). **Tomar el mando**, to take the lead. 3. Leaders (personas). 4. (*Mec.*) Control. **Mando a distancia**, remote control. 5. (*Rad. Téc.*) Controls.

mandoble [man-do'-blay], *m.* 1. A two-handed blow (golpe). 2. A severe reprimand. 3. Large sword (espada).

mandolina [man-do-lee'-nah], *f.* Mandolin, a stringed instrument played with a plectrum.

mandón, na [man-done', nah], *a.* Imperious, domineering. *-m.* An imperious, haughty person.

mandrachero [man-drah-chay'-ro], *m.* Proprietor of a gaming-table.

mandracho [man-drah'-cho], *m. (Prov.)* Gambling-house.

mandrágora [man-drah'-go-rah], *f. (Bot.)* Mandrake.

mandria [mahn'-dre-ah], *m.* Coward, poltroon. *-a.* Worthless.

mandril [man-dreel'], *m.* 1. *(Zool.)* Mandril, a West African baboon. 2. Mandrel, chuck, spindle of a lathe.

mandrín [man-dreen'], *m.* 1. Mandrel. 2. A hollow iron instrument which serves to join the ends of a metallic rod or to support the arms of a wheel.

manducación [man-doo-cah-the-on'], *f. (coll.)* Manducation, act of chewing or eating.

manducar [man-doo-car'], *va. (coll.)* To manducate, to cut, to chew.

manducatoria [man-doo-cah-to'-re'-ah], *f.* Dining-room, refectory.

manea [mah-nay'-ah], *f.* Shackles, fetters, hopple. *V.* MANIOTA.

manear [mah-nay-ar'], *va.* To hobble, to fasten with fetters or shackles (caballos, asnos).

manecica, ita [mah-nay-thee'-cah, ee'-tah], *f. dim.* A small hand (reloj).

manecilla [mah-nay-theel'-lyah], *f.* 1. *(dim.)* A small hand. 2. A mark or index, in grammar. 3. Book clasp. 4. Hand of a clock or watch (reloj).

manejable [mah-nay-hah'-blay], *a.* Manageable, tractable, handy (herramienta).

manejado [mah-nay-hah'-do], *a. (Pict.)* Handled.-*pp.* of MANEJAR.

manejar [mah-nay-har'], *va.* 1. To manage, to wield, to move with the hand. 2. To manage, to train a horse to graceful action. 3. To manage, to conduct, to govern, to contrive. 4. To handle (herramienta, lengua), to hand, to palm. 5. To manage (persona), to carry on. **Ella maneja a su marido,** she manages her husband. *-vr.* 1. To know how to conduct oneself (comportarse). 2. To be able to move after having been deprived of motion. 3. To manage (arreglárselas). **Se maneja bien con los chiquillos,** she manages all right with the kids.

manejo [mah-nay'-ho], *m.* 1. Employment of the hands to any purpose, handling (acto). **Manejo doméstico,** housekeeping. 2. Management, conduct, administration. 3. Horsemanship, manage. 4. Handling, cunning, trick; intrigue, device. **Hay que ver el manejo que tiene la chica,** you should see how quick the girl is.

maneota [mah-nay-o'-tah], *f.* Shackles, hobbles, fetters. *V.* MANIOTA.

manera [mah-nay'-rah], *f.* 1. Manner, form, figure; method, mode, kind, guise: manner of style. 2. Manner, or style, in painting, or carving in stone. 3. Ceremonious behavior, deportment. 4. Fore part or fall of breeches. 5. *(Ant.)* Quality, class of persons. 6. Manners (modales). **Manera de ser,** way of life. **No hay manera,** there's no solution. **De esta manera,** in this way. **De otra manera,** otherwise. **De tal manera que,** in such a way that. **De maneras muy groseras,** with very bad manners. **De manera** or **por manera,** so as, in such a manner.

manero, ra [mah-nay'-ro, rah], *a.* Tame: applied to hawks in falconry.

manes [mah'-nes], *m. pl.* Manes, ghost of the dead.

manezuela [mah-nay-thoo-ay'-lah], *f.* 1. *(dim.)* A small hand. 2. A clasp, a buckle.

manfla [mahn'-flah], *f. (coll.)* 1. A concubine. 2. *(Prov.)* Old sow.

manga [mahn'-gah], *f.* 1. Sleeve, part of a garment. 2. Arm of an axle-tree, on which the nave turns. 3. Kind of cloak-bag or portmanteau (bolso). 4. Stripe of cloth hanging from the shoulder of clerical cloaks. 5. Hose for water, firehose. *(Acad.)* 6. Body of troops in a line. 7. Fishing-net. 8. Bug made of woollen, linen, or paper, in the form of a sleeve, used to strain and clarify liquors; Hippocrates' sleeve. 9. **Manga** or **manga marina,** hurricane whirl-wind, water-spout. 10. *(Mex.)* Blanket or oblong piece of cloth, round at the ends, with a slit in the middle to put the head through, used as a covering when traveling on horseback. *V.* PONCHO. 11. *(LAm.)* Crowd (multitud). 12. *(LAm. Agr.)* Corral entrance. 13. *(CAm.)* Poncho, coarse blanket. 14. *(Mex.)* Condom (preservativo). 15. A variety of mango (árbol y fruta). **Manga de camisa,** shirtsleeve. **Estar en mangas de camisa,** to be in one's shirt-sleeves. **Ser de manga ancha,** to be easy-going. **Manga de agua,** rain cape.

manga de aire [mahn'-gah day ah'-e-ray], *f. (Aer.)* Jet stream.

mangana [man-gah'-nah], *f.* Lasso, lariat.

manganear [man-gah-nay-ar'], *va. (Amer. Mex.)* To throw a lasso at a running animal.

manganeo [man-gah-nay'-o], *m.* Sport in which lassoing is the chief diversion.

manganato [man-gah-nah'-to], *m.* Manganate, a salt of manganic acid.

manganesa, or **manganesia** [man-gah-nay'-sah], *f.* Peroxide of manganese, used in the manufacture of glass and paints, and in medicine.

manganeso [man-gah-nay'-so], *m.* Manganese, a hard, brittle, grayish-white metallic element.

mangánico, ca [man-gah'-ne-co, cah], *a.* Manganic, relative to manganese.

manganilla [man-gah-neel'-lyah], *f.* 1. Sleight of hand, a juggling trick. 2. *(Prov.)* Pole for gathering acorns.

manganoso [man-gah-no'-so], *a.* Manganous.

mangante [man-gahn'-tay], *a.* Brazen. *-m.* Beggar (mendigo); scrounger (gorrón); thief (ladrón); shoplifter (ratero); loafer (vago); rotter (caradura), villain.

mangar [man-gahr'], *va.* 1. To pinch (robar). 2. To beg (mendigar), to scrounge. *-vn.* To pilfer (robar); *(Cono Sur)* to scrounge.

mangla [mahn'-glah], *f.* Gum which exudes from the rock-rose or dwarf sunflower.

manglar [man-glar'], *m.* Plantation of mangrove trees.

mangle [mahn'-glay], *m. (Bot.)* Mangrove tree.

mango [mahn'-go], *m.* 1. Handle, haft, heft; helve, the handle of an axe. 2. *(Bot.)* Indian mango-tree.

mangonada [man-go-nah'-dah], *f.* Push with the arm.

mangonear [man-go-nay-ar'], *vn. (coll.)* 1. To wander about; to rove idly. 2. To intermeddle: to pry. 3. *(LAm.)* To pillage, to plunder (saquear). *-vn.* 1. To meddle (entrometerse). 2. To boss people about (ser mandón). 3. *(LAm.)* To graft, to be on the fiddle; to fix things.

mangoneo [man-go-nay'-o], *m.* 1. Meddling (entrometido), interference. 2. Bossing people about (con personas). 3. *(LAm.)* Graft, fiddling; *(Pol.)* fixing, fiddling of results.

mangorrero, ra [man-gor-ray'-ro, rah], *a.* 1. Wandering, roving, rumbling. 2. Hafted (cuchillo).

mangosta [man-gos'-tah], *f.* Mongoose, a quadruped noted for its ability to kill the most venomous snakes.

mangote [man-go'-tay], *m. (coll.)* A large and wide sleeve.

mangual [man-goo-ahl'], *m.* Weapon consisting of a pole with iron chains terminated by balls attached to it.

manguardia [man-goo-ar'-de-ah], *f.* Buttress of a bridge.

manguera [man-gay'-rah], *f.* 1. Hose, a tube for conveying liquids. 2. *(Naut.)* Piece of canvas tarred for various uses. 3. *(And.)* Bicycle tyre inner tube. 4. *(Met.)* Water-spout. 5. *(Cono Sur)* Corral, yard.

mangueta [man-gay'-tah], *f.* 1. Bladder and pipe for administering clystere. 2. Jamb of a glass-door. 3. Lever.

manguilla [man-geel'-lyah], *f. dim.* A small sleeve.

manguita [man-gee'-tah], *f.* 1. Sheath. *V.* FONDA. 2. *(dim.)* *V.* MAGUILLA.

manguitero [man-gee-tay'-ro], *m.* 1. Muff-maker, muff-seller. 2. Leather dresser, one who dresses fine skins or white leather.

manguito [man-gee'-to], *m.* 1. Muff, a cover for the hands. 2. Sleeve which is tight from the elbow to the wrist.

maní [mah-nee'], *m. (Cuba, Peru, Chili)* Peanut. *V.* CACAHUATE.

manía [mah-nee´-ah], *f.* 1. Mania, frenzy, madness. 2. Extravagance, whimsical obstinacy. 3. Inordinate desires. **Tiene manías,** he´s rather odd. **Tener manía a uno,** to dislike somebody.

maniaco, ca [mah-ne-ah´-co, cah], *a.* Maniac, magical, mad, frantic.*m & f.* Maniac, a mad person.

manialbo [mah-ne-ahl´-bo], *a.* White-footed (caballo).

maniatar [mah-ne-ah-tar´], *va.* To manacle, to handcuff.

maniático, ca [mah-ne-ah´-te-co, cah], *a. 1.* Maniacal; *(hum.)* fanatical. 2. *(Fig.)* Crazy (chiflado); odd (excéntrico), eccentric, peculiar; fussy (delicado). *-m. f.* 1. Maniac; *(hum.)* fanatic. 2. *(Fig.)* Maniac; odd individual.

manicero [mah-ne-thay´-ro], *m. (Cuba)* Peanut vendor.

manicomio [mah-ne-co´-me-o], *m.* Asylum or hospital for the mentally ill. *(Acad.)*

manicordio [mah-ne-cor´-de-o], *m.* Manichord, a musical instrument: a clavichord.

manicorto, ta [mah-ne-cor´-to, tah], *a.* Illiberal, parsimonious.

manicurista [mah-ne-coo-rees´-tah], *m. & f.* Manicurist.

manicuro, ra [mah-ne-coo´-ro, rah], *m. & f.* Manicurist.

manida [mah-nee´-dah], *f.* Resort, abode, nest, any place where persons or animals take shelter. **Manida de pícaros,** nest of thieves.

manido, da [mah-nee´-do, dah], *a.* 1. Hidden, concealed. 2. (Peru) Said of meats which smell bad; *-pp.* Of MANIR.

manifacero, ra [mah-ne-fah-thay´-ro, rah], *a. (Prov.)* Intriguing, meddlesome, intrusive.

manifestación [mah-ne-fes-tah-the-on´], *f.* 1. Manifestation (emoción), declaration, explication, statement (declaración). 2. A writ resembling the English habeas corpus. 3. Demonstration; mass meeting.

manifestador, ra [mah-ne-fes-tah-dor´, rah], *m. & f.* Discoverer, publisher.

manifestante [mah-ne-fes-tahn´-tay], *com.* Demonstrator.

manifestar [mah-ne-fes-tar´], *va.* 1. To manifest, to make known, to show (emoción). 2. To state, to declare (política). *-vr.* 1. To show (emoción), to become apparent. 2. To demonstrate, to hold a mass meeting. *(Yo manifiesto, yo manifieste,* from *Manifestar.* V. ACRECEMNTAR.)

manifiestamente [mah-ne-fe-ays´-tah-men-tay], *adv.* Clearly.

manifiesto, ta [mah-ne-fe-es´-to, tah], *a.* Manifest (verdad), plain, open, obvious, clear (claro), overt, evident (patente).-*pp. irr.* of MANIFESTAR.

manifiesto [mah-ne-fe-es´-to], *m.* 1. Act of exposing the Holy Sacrament to public adoration. 2. Manifest or manifesto, public protestation or declaration. **Poner de manifiesto,** to manifest, to make public, to expose, to lay open.

manigua [mah-nee´-goo-ah], *f. (Cuba)*1. Thicket, jungle (selva). 2. Monte played for diversion.

manigueta [mah-ne-gay´-tah], *f.* Handle (mango), clasp.

manija [mah-nee´-hah], *f.* 1. Handle of an instrument or working tool. 2. Shackles, handcuffs. 3. Ring, brace. 4. *(And. Mex.)* Door handle (puerta). 5. *(Agr.)* Hobble. 6. *(Cono Sur)* Mug (vaso). 7. *(Cono Sur, aut.)* Starting handle.

manilargo, ga [mah-ne-lar´-go, gah], *a.* 1. Large-handed, that is, having long hands. 2. Prone to fisticuffs, pugilistic.

maniluvio [mah-ne-loo´-ve-o], *m.* Bath for the hands used as a remedy.

manilla [mah-neel´-lyah], *f.* 1. *(dim.)* Small hand. 2. Bracelet for the arm or wrist (pulsera). 3. Manacle, handcuff (de hierro). 3. Hand (de reloj). 4. *(And. Mex.)* Door handle.

maniobra [mah-ne-o´-brah], *f.* 1. Work with the hand, handiwork. 2. Handling, artifice for obtaining a thing (acto). 3. *(Mil.)* Maneuver, evolution, movement of troops. 4. *(Naut.)* Working of a ship. 5. *(Naut.)* Gear, rigging (aparejo). **Maniobras de combate,** preventer rigging. **Hacer maniobras,** to maneuver. **Estar de maniobras,** to be on maneuver.

maniobrar [mah-ne-o-brar´], *va..* 1. To work with the hands. 2. *(Naut.)* To work a ship. 3. *(Met.)* To seek the means of effecting anything. 4. *(Mil.)* To maneuver troops. Also, *vn.*

maniobrista [mah-ne-o-brees´-tah], *m. (Naut.)* A skillful naval tactician.

maniota [mah-ne-o´-tah], *f.* Hobble or cord tied about the feet of beasts to prevent running away.

manipodio [mah-ne-po´-de-o], *m. (coll.)* Bawdry, pollution.

manipulación [mah-ne-poo-lah-the-on´], *f.* Manipulation: used in speaking of minerals. **Manipulación defectuosa,** *(Comput.)* mishandling. **Manipulación simbólica,** *(Inform.)* symbolic manipulation.

manipulador, ra [mah-ne-poo-lah-dor´], *m & f.* Manipulator; handler. *-m. (Elec. Telec.)* Key, tapper.

manipulante [mah-ne-poo-lahn´-tay], *m. (coll.)* Administrator, negotiator.

manipular [mah-ne-poo-lar´], *va. (coll.)* To manipulate, to handle, to manage business in a peculiar manner; to meddle with everything.

manípulo [mah-nee´-poo-lo], *m.* 1. Maniple, a fanon worn by the officiating priests of the Roman Catholic church. 2. Maniple, a division of the Roman army. 3. A handful, expressed in recipes by an M.

maniqueismo [mah-ne-kay-ees´-mo], *m.* Manicheism.

maniqueo, a [mah-ne-kay´-o, ah], *a.* Manichean.

maniquí [mah-ne-kee´], *m.* 1. Puppet, one governed by another´s caprice. 2. Manikin, a movable figure, which can be put in different postures, for the study of drapery.

manir [mah-neer´], *va.* To keep meat until it grows tender; to mellow.*-vr.* To become tender or mellow (carne).

manirroto, ta [mah-nir-ro´-to, tah], *a.* Extravagant, wasteful.

manita [mah-nee´-tah], *f.* 1. The hour-hand of a watch or clock. 2. Small hand. **Manita de cerdo,** trotters. **Echar una manita a uno,** to lend somebody a hand.

manivacío, cía [mah-ne-vah-thee´-o, ah], *a. (coll.)* Empty-handed, idle, lazy.

manivela [mah-ne-vay´-lah], *f.* Winch, handle, crank.

manjar [man-har´], *m.* 1. Food, victuals. 2. *(Met.)* Refection or entertainment which recruits the spirits. 3. Any of the four suits of a pack of cards. **Manjar exquisito,** tasty morse. **Manjar espiritual,** food for the mind.

manjarria [man-har´-re-ah], *f. (Cuba)* The driving beam of a canemill.

manjelín [man-hay-leen´], *m.* Weight used for diamonds: carat.

manjolar [man-ho-lar´], *va.* To carry a hawk in the hand, in a basket or a cage.

manjorrada [man-hor-rah´-dah], *f.* Abundance of ordinary victuals.

mano [mah´-no], *f.* 1. The hand. 2. Fore foot of a quadruped. 3. Among butchers, the feet of cattle after being cut off. 4. Proboscis, the snout or trunk of an elephant. 5. Hand, side, right or left. 6. Hand of a clock or watch (reloj). 7. Pestle. 8. A long cylindrical stone, with which cocoa is ground, to make chocolate. 9. Quire of paper. 10. Command, power. 11. Reprimand, censure. 12. The musical scale. 13. First hand at play (cartas). 14. Workmanship; power or means of making or attaining something. 15. Hand, time or turn in correcting something. 16. Cover, or varnish, colors, coat, laid over a thing (pintura). 17. Industry. 18. V. PATROCINIO. 19. V. SOCORRO. *-pl.* 1. Handicraft, handiwork. 2. Works of the hand considered by themselves. 20. Lot, series (grupo). 21. Skill, dexterity (destreza). 22. *(LAm.)* Misfortune (desgracia), mishap; unexpected event (imprevisto). 23. *(LAm. Aut.)* One-way street. **Mano en el juego,** deal, in a game. **A la mano,** at hand, near at hand. **A mano,** at hand; with the hand, studiously. **Manos de carnero,** sheep's trotters. **Manos de vaca,** cow-heels. **¡Manos a la obra!** *(Naut.)* bar a hand! to work! **Manos libres,** emoluments annexed to an office or place. **A dos manos;** willingly, readily. **A manos llenas,** liberally, abundantly, copiously. **Ser sus pies y sus manos,** to be one's chief support and consolation in distress. **Venir con sus manos lavadas,** to usurp the fruit of another's labor. **Bajo mano** or **de mano,** underhandedly, secretly. **Estar a mano,** to be square, to be quits. **Alzar la mano,** *(Met.)* (1) to lift the hand, threatening to strike. (2) To cease protecting an individual. (3) To leave off attending to a business which one had begun to care for. **Mano de santo,** sure remedy. **Bordado a mano,** hand-embroidered. **Llegó a mis manos,** it reached me. **Coger a uno con las manos en la masa,** to catch somebody red-handed. **De segunda mano,** second-hand. **Ha hecho cuanto ha estado en su mano,** he has done all in his power. **Darse la mano,** to shake hands. **Se le fue la mano,** his hand slipped. **Llevarse las manos a la cabeza,** to throw one's hands in the air. **No hay quien le meta mano,** there's nobody to touch him. **Tener mano para,** to be clever at. **Mano de obra,** labor.

manobra [mah-no'-brah], *f. (Prov.)* Raw material.

manobre [mah-no'-bray], *m. (Prov.)* A hodman, hod-carrier.

manojico, illo, ito [mah-no-hee'-co], *m. dim.* A small bundle, a small fagot.

manojo [mah-no'-ho], *m.* 1. A bundle of herbs or other things which may be held in the hand. 2. A fuzot or bundle of twigs bound together for the fire. **Manojo de llaves,** hunch of keys. **Un manojo de apio,** a bunch of celery. **A manojos,** abundantly.

manómetro [mah-no'-may-tro], *m. (Phys.)* Manometer, an instrument for ascertaining the tension of gases; pressure gauge.

manopla [mah-no'-plah], *f.* 1. Gauntlet, a glove for defense. 2. Coachman's whip. *3. (Carib. Cono Sur)* knuckle duster (puño de hierro). 4. *(Cono Sur)* Spanner (llave inglesa).

manosear [mah-no-say-ar'], *va.* 1. To handle (tocar), to touch, to feel. 2. To rumple clothes (ajar).

manoseo [mah-no-say'-o], *m.* Handling, fingering, touching; rumpling; pawing; *(LAm.)* feeling up, touching up.

manotada, *f.* **manotazo,** *m.* [mah-no-tah'-dah, mah-no-tah'-tho]. Blow with the hand, a cuff (golpe).

manotear [mah-no-tay-ar'], *va.* To strike with the hand. *-vn.* To wring the hands from emotion, to gesticulate.

manoteo [mah-no-tay'-o], *m.* 1. A blow with the hand. 2. Manual gesticulation (gestos). *3. (Mex.)* Theft, robbery (robo).

manquear [man-kay-ar'], *vn.* To affect the cripple, to pretend to be maimed.

manquedad [man-kay-dahd'], *f.* or **Manquera,** *f.* 1. Lameness, an injury which prevents the use of the hands or arms. 2. Defect, imperfection.

mansalva, A [ah man-sahl'-vah], *adv.* Unsportsmanly, cowardly. **Tiro a mansalva,** pot shot.

mansamente [man'-sah-men-tay], *adv.* Meekly, gently, quietly.

mansedumbre [man-say-doom'-bray], *f.* Meekness, gentleness (persona), peacefulness, mildness, manageableness.

mansejón, na [man-say-hone', nah], *a.* Tame (animales).

mansera [man-say'-rah], *f. (Cuba)* A vat placed below the hammers of a sugar-mill, which receives the cane-juice.

mansión [man-se-on'], *f.* 1. Mansion (casa suntuosa). 2. **Mansión señorial,** stately home.

manso, sa [mahn'-so, sah], *a.* 1. Tame (animales). 2. Meek, gentle (persona), tractable; soft, quiet, mild, gentle, lamb-like.

manso [mahn'-so], *m.* Male, which guides the flocks of goats, sheep, or cattle; bellwether.

manta [mahn'-tah], *f.* 1. A woollen blanket (de cama); in some parts of America, domestic cotton skirting. **Manta blanca,** bleached cotton. **Manta eléctrica,** electric blanket. **Liarse la manta a la cabeza,** to decide to go the whole hog. 2. A horse-blanket. *3. (Mil.)* Mantelet, a movable parapet. 4. Thrashing, drubbing. *5. (Min.)* A bag of agave for loading ore in clearings. 6. The devilfish octopus. 7. *(S. Amer.)* A mantle. 8. A game of cards resembling *tresillo* or *ombre.*

manteador, ra [man-tay-ah-dor', rah], *m. & f.* Tosser, one who tosses in a blanket.

manteamiento [man-tay-ah-me-en'-to], *m.* Tossing in a blanket.

mantear [man-tay-ar'], *va.* To toss in a blanket. *-vn. (Prov.)* To gad frequently abroad in a mantle (mujeres).

manteca [man-tay'-cah], *f.* 1. Lard, fat. 2. Butter. 3. Pulpy and oily parts of fruits. 4. A name given to certain metallic chlorides, as of antimony, bismuth, and zinc. 5. Dough (dinero); goods (género). 6. *(LAm.)* Hash, marijuana. 7. *(And.)* Servant, girl.

mantecada [man-tay-cah'-dah], *f.* Buttered toast and sugar.

mantecado [man-tay-cah'-do], *m.* 1. Butter-cake. 2. Ice-cream (helado).

mantecón [man-tay-cone'], *m.* Milk-sop; sweet-tooth, a dainty person.

mantecoso, sa [man-tay-co'-so, sah], *a.* Buttery (como la mantequilla), consisting of butter, mellow.

mantel [man-tel'], *m.* 1. Table-cloth: commonly used in the plural. 2. Altar cloth. **Levantar los manteles,** to clear the table. **Poner los manteles,** to lay the table.

mantelería [man-tay-lay-ree'-ah], *f.* Table linen.

manteleta [man-tay-lay'-tah], *f.* Mantelet, a small mantle, cloak, or scarf (prenda de señora).

mantelete [man-tay-lay'-tay], *m.* 1. Mantelet, a short mantle worn by bishops. 2. Mantelet, a movable parapet. *3. (Her.)* Mantling, the representation of a mantle or any drapery drawn about a coat of arms.

mantellina [man-te-lyee'-nah], *f.* A short cloak worn by women.

mantenedor [man-tay-nay-dor'], *m.* The principal in a tournament.

mantener [man-tay-nerr'], *va.* 1. To maintain, to support (idea, opinión), to keep up with the hand; to hold up. 2. To maintain, to support life, to nourish, to keep, to feed (alimentar). 3. To maintain, to continue, to keep up (costumbre, disciplina). 4. To be the first challenges at a tournament. 5. To persevere, to persist in a design. 6. To support a weight. 7. To pursue, to continue. 8. To maintain, to hold out, to defend or sustain an opinion. 9. To support anyone in the possession of a thing. **Mantener correspondencia,** to keep up a correspondence. **Mantener algo en equilibrio,** to keep something balanced. **Le mantiene la esperanza,** he is sustained by hope. **Mantener la comida caliente,** to keep the food hot. *-vr.* 1. To continue residing in a place. 2. To continue in the same condition without alteration. 3. To nourish or gain nourishment, to maintain oneself. **Mantenerse firme,** to stand one's ground. **Mantenerse en lo dicho,** to abide by.

manteniente [man-tay-ne-en'-tay], *m.* A violent blow with both hands.

mantenimiento [man-tay-ne-me-en'-to], *m.* Maintenance, sustenance, upkeep.

manteo [man-tay'-o], *m.* 1. A long cloak or mantle worn by priests and formerly by students. 2. Sort of woollen petticoat.

mantequera [man-tay-kay'-rah], *f* 1. A churn (para batir). 2. A butter dish or bowl (de mesa).

mantequero, ra [man-tay-kay'-ro, rah], *m. & f.* One who sells butter, dairy-man, dairy-maid.

mantequilla [man-tay-keel'-lyah], *f.* Butter (manteca de vaca). **Mantequilla fresca,** fresh butter. **Mantequilla derretida,** melted butter.

mantequillera [man-tay-keel-lyay'-rah], *f.* Butter dish.

mantera [man-tay'-rah], *f.* Mantle-maker, one who makes or sells mantles.

mantero, ra [man-tay'-ro, rah], *m. & f.* One who sells or manufactures blankets.

mántide [mahn'-te-day], *f. (Zool.)* The praying mantis, an orthopterous insect.

mantilla [man-teel'-lyah], *f.* 1. Mantilla, or veil (de mujer). **Mantilla de encajes,** lace mantilla. 2. Housing, saddle-cloth.

-pl. The outer (long) clothes of little children (de bebé). 3. (typ.) A blanket. **Estar en mantillas**, to be in a state of infancy.

mantillo [man-teel'-lyo], m. Humus, dung, organic portion of soil.

mantillón, na [man-teel-lyone', nah], a. (Prov.) Dirty, slovenly.

manto [mahn'-to], m. 1. Silken veil for ladies, a mantle, a kirtle. 2. Cloak (capa), robe; a mantle of state. 3. Mantelpiece of a chimney. 4. In mines, a horizontal vein. 5. Veil, cover.

mantón [man-tone'], m. 1. (Aug.) A large cloak or mantle. 2. A kind of shawl; in Cuba, a woman's mantilla.

manuable [mah-noo-ah'-blay], a. Tractable, manageable.

manual [mah-noo-ahl'], a. 1. Manual, handy, performed by hand. 2. Easily handled or performed with the hand. 3. Tractable, pliant; light, prompt. **Tener habilidad manual**, to be clever with one's hands. **Trabajo manual**, manual labor.

manual [mah-noo-ahl'], m. 1. Manual, a portable book. 2. Book in which the heads of matters are set down; note-book, account-book. 3. Ritual, a book of rites. 4. Old name of the journal, a book of accounts recorded so as to be easily posted in the ledger. (Acad.) 5. pl. Extra fees given to the priests for being present in the choir. **Manual de instrucciones**, instruction book, servicing manual.

manualidad [mah-noo-ah-le-dahd'], f. Manual craft.

manualmente [mah-noo-al'-men-tay], adv. Manually, by hand.

manubrio [mah-noo'-bre-o], m. 1. Handlebar (de una bicicleta). 2. Handle (manivela). 3. (Mus.) Barrel organ.

manucodiata [mah-noo-co-de-ah'-tah], f. Bird of paradise.

manuella [mah-noo-el'-lyah], f. Hand-spike.

manufactura [mah-noo-fac-too'-rah], f. Manufacture, any mechanical work.

manufacturar [mah-noo-fac-too-rar'], va. To manufacture.

manufacturero, ra [mah-noo-fac-too-ray'-ro, rah], a. Belonging to manufacture.

manumisión [mah-noo-me-se-on'], f. Manumission.

manumiso, sa [mah-noo-mee'-so, sah], pp. irr. of MANUMITIR. Emancipated. -a. Free, disengaged.

manumisor [mah-noo-me-sor'], m. (Law.) Liberator.

manumitir [mah-noo-me-teer'], va. To manumit, to emancipate.

manuscrito, ta [mah-noos-cree'-to, tah], a. Manuscript, not printed.

manuscrito [mah-noos-cree'-to], m. Manuscript, a book written and not printed.

manutención [mah-noo-ten-the-on'], f. 1. Maintaining. 2. Maintenance, supply of the necessaries of life (sustento). 3. Maintenance, support, protection. 4. Conservation.

manutener [mah-noo-tay-nerr'], va. (Law.) To maintain, to support.

manzana [man-thah'-nah], f. 1. An apple. 2. Block of houses bounded on every side by a street; square. 3. (Ant.) Knob of a sword. **La manzana de la discordia**, (fig.) apple of discord. **Manzana silvestre**, wild apple.

manzanal [man-thah-nahl'], m. 1. V. MANZANAR. 2. V. MANZANO.

manzanar [man-thah-nar'], m. Orchard, a garden of apple-trees.

manzanil [man-thah-neel'], a. Like an apple.

manzanilla [man-thah-neel'-lyah], f. 1. (Bot.) Common chamomile. **Manzanilla fina**, golden cotula. 2. Small ball or knob at the top of coaches, bedsteads, etc. 3. Kind of small olive. 4. Lower part of the chin. 5. The pad, or cushion, of the feet of animals having claws. 6. (dim.) A small apple. 7. Manzanilla (jerez).

manzanillo, ito [man-thah-nee'-lyo, ee-to], m. (Bot.) Little apple-tree. **Olivo manzanillo**, a kind of olive-tree. -m. Manchineel, a tropical American tree, having an apple-like fruit reputed to be poisonous.

manzanita [man-thah-nee'-tah], f. 1. (dim.) Little apple. 2. Tame of a California shrub, or small tree, related to the madroño. Named from its fruit.

manzano [man-thah'-no], m. (Bot.) Apple-tree.

maña [mah'-nyah], f. 1. Handiness, skill, contrivance, dexterity, cleverness, expertness, ability, faculty. 2. Cunning, craftiness, artifice, craft. 3. An evil habit or custom. 4. Bundle of hemp or flax when reaped. **Darse maña**, to contrive, to bring about, to manage. **Tiene maña para hacerlo**, he's got the knack of doing it.

mañana [mah-nyah'-nah], f. 1. Morning. 2. The part of the day from twelve o'clock at night to twelve o'clock at noon. **Por la mañana**, in the morning. **Pasado mañana**, the day after tomorrow. **Esta mañana**, this morning. **A la mañana siguiente**, the following morning. **A las tres de la mañana**, at three o'clock in the morning. -adv. 1. Tomorrow. 2. Soon. 3. Expression of negation. 4. In time to come. **Tomar la mañana** (1) To rise very early. (2) (coll.) To drink liquor before breakfast. **Muy de mañana**, very early. **A partir de mañana**, as from tomorrow. **Pasado mañana**, the day after tomorrow. **Hasta mañana**, see you tomorrow. **Muy de mañana**, very early. **No dejes para mañana lo que puedas hacer hoy**, do not put off till tomorrow what you can do today.

mañanear [mah-nyah-nay-ar'], vn. To rise early habitually.

mañanica, ita [mah-nyah-nee'-cah], f. Break of day, early morning (madrugada).

mañear [mah-nyay-ar'], va. To act with craft and address to attain one's end.

mañería [mah-nyay-ree'-ah], f. 1. Sterility. 2. Right of succeeding to the possessions of those who die without legitimate succession.

mañero [mah-nyay'-ro, rah], a. 1. Dexterous, skillful, artful. 2. Meek, tractable. 3. (Cono Sur) Vicious (animal).

mañosamente [mah-nyo-sah-men'-tay], adv. Dexterously, neatly, handily, cleverly; subtly; maliciously, graftly.

mañoso, sa [mah-nyo'-so, sah], a. 1. Dexterous, skillful, handy, clever (hábil). 2. (And.) Lazy (perezoso). 3. (And. CAm. Cono Sur, Mex.) Vicious (animal); obstinate (terco).

mañuela [mah-nyoo-ay'-lah], f. Low cunning, mean trick.

maoísmo [mah-o-ees'-mo], m. Maoism.

maoísta [mah-o-ees'-tah], a. Maoist. -m & f. Maoist.

mapa [mah'-pah], m. Map, a geographical picture. **Mapa mural**, wall map. **El mapa político**, the political scene. **Mapamundi**, a map of the world.-f. Anything excellent and prominent in its line.

mapache [mah-pah'-chay], m. (Zool.) Racoon.

mápula [mah'-poo-lah], f. (Min.) A precious stone mined near Popayan in Colombia.

mapurite [mah-poo-ree'-tay], m. (Amer. Ven.) A skunk.

maque [mah'-kay], m. (Mex.) A certain varnish or lacquer.

maqueta [mah-kay'-tah], f. 1. Model; scale model. 2. Dummy (libro).

maquí [mah-kee'], m. 1. Kind of ginger. 2. A lemur of Madagascar.

maquiavélico, ca [mah-ke-ah-vay'-le-co, cah], a. Machiavelian.

maquiavelismo [mah-ke-ah-vay-lees'-mo], m. Machiavelism.

maquievelista [mah-ke-ah-vay-lees'-tah], m. Machievelian.

maquila [mah-kee'-lah], f. 1. Multure (tributo), toll-corn, corn which the miller takes for grinding. 2. Toll in general. 3. Corn measure, the 24th part of a fanega.

maquilar [mah-ke-lar'], va. 1. To measure and take the miller's dues for grinding corn. 2. To clip, to retrench, to cut off.

maquilero, maquilón [mah-ke-lay'-ro, mah-ke-lone'], m. One who measures or takes the miller's dues for grinding corn.

maquillaje [mah-keel-lyah'-hay], m. Make-up, cosmetics.

maquillar [mah-kel-lyahr'], va. To make up. -vr. to make up.

máquina [mah'-ke-nah], f. 1. Machine. 2. Engine. 3. A vast structure. 4. Project, imaginative scheme (projecto). 5. (Cuba) An automobile. **Máquina calculadora digital**, digital computer. **Máquina de coser**, sewing machine. **Máquina tragaperras**, fruit machine. **Máquina para hacer punto**, knitting machine. **Coser a máquina**, to machine. **Máquina de escribir**, typewriter. **Escribir a máquina**, to type. **Máquina de vapor**, steam engine. **Máquina de encauzamiento**, *(Comput.)* pipeline machine. **Máquina vectorial**, *(Comput.)* vector machine.

maquinación [mah-ke-nah-the-on´], *f.* Machination, artifice, contrivance.

maquinador, ra [mah-ke-nah-dor', rah], *m. & f.* Contriver, schemer, machinator; plotter.

maquinal [mah-ke-nahl'], *a.* Machinal, relating to machines, mechanical.

maquinalmente [mah-ke-nahl'-men-tay], *adv.* Mechanically; undesignedly.

maquinar [mah-ke-nar'], *va.* To machinate, to plan, to contrive, to hatch, to conspire, to compass.

maquinaria [mah-ke-nah'-re-ah], *f.* 1. Applied mechanics, the art of contriving and building machines. 2. Machinery. 3. Mechanics.

maquinista [mah-ke-nees'-tah], *m.* Machinist, mechanician, mechanist.

mar [mar], *m. y f.* 1. The sea 2. Sea (océano), some large lakes. 3. Sea, proverbially for any large quantity. 4. Swell (marejada). **Alta mar** or **mar ancha**, the main sea, the high seas. **Baja mar**, low water, ebbtide. **Mar llena, pleamar**, high water. **Correr los mares**, to follow the seas. **Salir a la mar**, to put to sea. **La mar está muy crecida**, the sea runs very high. **Un mar de confusiones**, a sea of confusion. **Estar hecho un mar de lágrimas**, to weep floods. **Está la mar de contento**, he´s terribly happy.

marabú [mah-rah-boo'], *m.* Marabou, an African bird of the stork family and the white plumes from it.

maraca [mah-rah'-kah], *f.* 1. *(Mus.)* Maraca, rattle. 2. *(Cono Sur)* Whore (prostituta).

maranata [mah-rah-nah'-tah], *f.* Maranatha, a form of anathematizing.

maraña [mah-rah'-nyah], *f.* 1. Place rendered impassable by brambles or briers. 2. Entanglement of a skein of silk, thread, cotton, etc. 3. Silk waste and stuff made from it. 4. Perplexity, puzzle. 5. Fraud, imposition. 6. Intrigue, plot.

marañado, da [mah-rah-nyah'-do, dah], *a.* Entangled, perplexed.

marañero, ra [mah-rah-nyay'-ro, rah], **Marañoso, sa**. *a.* Entangling, insnaring, perplexing.

marañón [mah-rah-nyone'], *m. (Cuba)* The common cashew; also its fruit, the cashew-nut.

marasmo [mah-rahs'-mo], *m. (Med.)* Consumption, marasmus, wasting.

maratón [mah-rah-tone'], *f.* Marathon.

maravedí [mah-rah-vay-dee'], *m. (pl.* Maravedíes.) Maravedi, an old Spanish coin.

maravilla [mah-rah-veel'-lyah], *f.* 1. Wonder, an uncommon event; a marvel (objeto, asunto), admiration. 2. *(Bot.)* Common marigold. **A las (mil) maravillas**, uncommonly well; wonderfully. **Hacer maravillas**, to work wonders.

maravillar [mah-rah-vil-lyar´], *va.* To admire, to regard with wonder.-*vr.* To wonder, to marvel, to be astonished, to be struck with admiration.

maravillosamente [mah-rah-vel-lyo'-sah-men-tay], *adv.* Wonderfully, marvellously, miraculously.

maravilloso, sa [mah-rah-vil-lyo´-o-so sah], *a.* Wonderful, marvellous, monstrous, astonishing, admirable, miraculous; strange.

marbete [mar-bay'-tay], *m.* 1. Stamp, the manufacturers mark on cloth. 2. Label (etiqueta).

marca [mar'-cah], *f.* 1. A frontier province. 2. The due measure or weight of anything. 3. Marker, stamp, an instrument used for marking (herramienta). 4. Landmark, light-house. 5. A mark made upon a person or thing to distinguish it from another. 6. The act of marking. **De marca**, excellent of its kind. **Marca registrada**, registered

trademark. **Coches de 3 marcas distintas**, cars of 3 different makes.

marcadamente [mar-cah-dah-men'-tay], *adv.* Markedly, notably.

marca de fábrica [mar'-cah day fah'-bre-cah], *f.* Trade mark.

marcado [mar-cah'-do], *a.* Marked, strong, pronounced; distinct. **Con marcado acento argentino**, with a marked Argentinian accent. -*m.* Set (pelo).

marcador [mar-cah-dor'], *m.* Marker, assay-master, book-mark (de libro); high-lighter (para escribir). **Marcador de caminos**, road-sign. **Inaugurar el marcador**, to open the scoring.

marcapasos [mar-cah-pah'-sos], *m. (Med.)* Pacemaker.

marcar [mar-car'], *va* 1. To mark, to brand; to embroider initials; to mark off (tierra). **Marcar el campo**, to mark the ground for a camp. 2. To mark (indicar), to observe, to note; to designate. **Las agujas marcan las 2**, the hands point to 2 o´clock. 3. To keep a tally of (números). 4. *(Mus.)* To mark (paso); to beat (compás). 5. *(Telec.)* To dial. 6. *(Dep.)* To score (gol, tanto). **Marcar un tanto en la discusión**. to score a point in the argument. 7. To put a price.

marcasita [mar-cah-se'-tah], *f.* Marcasite, a dimorphous iron sulphide.

marcear [mar-thay-ar´], *va.* To shear the wool, hair, or fur of animals.

marceo [mar-thay-o], *m.* Trimming away of the lower soiled parts of honey-combs in spring by beekeepers.

marcha [mar'-chah], *f.* 1. March, a solemn movement of troops: a journey of soldiers. **Marchas forzadas**, forced marches. **Abrir la marcha**, to come first. **Estar en marcha**, to be in motion. 2. March, signal to move. 3. Marching tune. **Marcha fúnebre**, funeral march. 4. *(Prov.)* Bonfire. 5. The movement of a watch. 6. Regularity, working order of a machine. **Tocar la marcha**, to strike up a march. 7. *(Dep.)* Walk; walk (excursión), hike. 8. Speed (velocidad). **A toda marcha**, at full speed. 9. Progress (progreso), march (avance); trend (rumbo); path (de huracán). **La marcha de los acontecimientos**, the march of events. **No le va la marcha**, he´s not with it. 10. Charm (duende), magic, appeal, mystery (misterio); inpiration (inspiración); style (estilo). 11. *(Carib.)* Slow trot (caballo). 12. *(Mex. Aut.)* Self-starter.

marchamar [mar-chah-mar'], *va.* To mark goods at the custom-house.

marchamero [mar-chah-may'-ro], *m.* Custom-house officer who marks goods.

marchamo [mar-chah'-mo], *m.* Mark put on goods at the custom-house.

marchante [mar-chahn'-tay], *m.* 1. Shop-keeper, dealer (tratante). 2. *(Prov. Andal.)* Customer (cliente), buyer. 3. *(Cuba)* Sharper, trickster. -*a.* 1. V. MERCANTIL 2. Merchantable.

marchantear [mar-chan-tay-ar], *va.* To trade, especially in live-stock.

marchar [mar-char'], *vn. & vr.* 1. To go, to go away, to go off, to depart from a place, to move (viajar). 2. To march, to walk gravely. 3. *(Mil.)* To march, in military form. 4. *(Naut.)* To have much headway, to sail fast. 5. *(Mec.)* To go; to run, to function, to work; to run (tren). **El motor no marcha**, the engine isn´t working. 6. To go, to proceed. **Todo marcha bien**. Everything is going well. 7. To go away, to leave. **Marcharse a otro sitio**, to go somewhere else.

marchazo [mar-chah'-tho], *m.* Braggadocio, boaster, braggart.

marchitable [mar-che-tah'-blay], *a.* Perishable, liable to wither.

marchitamiento [mar-che-tah-me-en'-to], *m.* The act of withering or fading.

marchitar [mar-che-tar'], *va.* 1. To wither, to make fade. 2. To fade, to wear away, to deprive of vigor. -*vr.* 1. To wither, to fade, to fall away; to dry up. 2. To pine away, to grow lean.

marchitez [mar-che-teth'], *f.* Withering, fading, marcidity.

marchito, ta [mar-chee'-to, tah], *a*. Faded, withered, decayed, marcid.

marchoso [mar-cho'-so], *a*. 1. Ultramoderm (moderno); trendy. 2. Lively (animado), fast-living. 3. Fun-loving (amigo de placeres).

marcial [mar-the-ahl'], *m*. Aromatic powder used anciently for dressing gloves.

marcial [mar-the-ahl'], *a*. 1. Martial, war-like. 2. *(Pharm.)* Martial, having iron. 3. Frank, unceremonious.

marcialidad [mar-the-ah-le-dahd'], *f*. 1. Martialness. 2. Freedom, assumed familiarity or liberty.

marciano [mar-the-ahl'-no], *a*. Martian. *-m & f*. Martian.

marco [mar'-co], *m*. 1. Door-case, window-case. 2. Picture-frame. 3. Mark, a weight of eight ounces. 4. An instrument for measuring the length of shoes, etc. 5. A measure for liquids. 6. The necessary size of timber for being foiled. 7. Model, archetype. 8. Measure of ground which should have a *fanega* of grain. 9. Mark, the unit of German money-values. **Marco para cuadro**, picture frame. **Cuadro de ventana**, window frame. **márcola** [mar'-co-lah], *f*. Pruning hook for trimming trees.

marea [mah-ray'-ah], *f*. 1. The tide. 2. Sea shore; tidal area. 3. Soft wind. 4. Collection of street dirt. 5. Drizzle (llovizna); *(Cono Sur)* sea mist. **Marea creciente**, flood-tide. **Marea menguante**, ebb-tide. **Dirección de las mareas**, setting of the tide. **Ir contra marea**, to sail against the tide. **Navegar con la marea**, to tide it up or down. **Mareas vivas**, spring-tides. **La marea crece**, the tide flows.

mareado [mah-ray-ah'-do], *a*. **Estar mareado** 1. To fell sick (nauseado); to feel dizzy (aturdido); to be seasick. 2. To be a bit drunk (bebido).

mareaje [mah-ray-ah'-hay], *m*. Art of navigating a ship.

mareamiento [mah-ray-ah-me-en'-to], *m*. Sea-sickness.

mareante [mah-ray-ahn'-tay], *a*. Skilled in navigating a ship.

marear [mah-ray-ar'], *va*. 1. To work a ship. 2. To molest and harass by impertinent questions (irritar). 3. To sell goods at auction. 4. *(Med.)* To make somebody feel sick (causar náuseas). 5. *(Carib. Mex.)* To cheat. *-vr*. 1. To be sea sick. 2. To be damaged at sea; to be averaged (mercancía). 3. *(Carib. Cono Sur)* To fade (paño).

marecanita [mah-ray-cah-nee'-tah], *f*. *(Min.)* Marekanite, a variety of obsidian occurring in rounded globules.

marejada [mah-ray-hah'-dah], *f*. Swell of the sea, head sea, surf. **Tuvimos una marejada del noroeste**, we had a great sea from the north-west.

mare magnum [mah'-ray mahg'-noom], *m*. *(Let.)* Expressing the abundance or magnitude of anything; also confusion, disorder.

maremoto [mah-ray-mo'-to], *m*. Tidal wave.

mareo [mah-ray'-o], *m*. 1. Sea-sickness (en mar); sick feeling (náuseas); dizziness (aturdimiento). 2. *(coll.)* Molestation, vexation. 3. Nuisance, bore (lata). **Es un mareo que...**, it is a nuisance having to...

mareógrafo [mah-ray-o'-grah-fo], *m*. Stereograph, a recording tide-gauge.

marero [mah-ray'-ro], *a*. Sea-breeze, wind coming from the sea.

mareta [mah-ray'-tah], *f*. *(Naut.)* Slight commotion of the sea.

maretazo [mah-ray-tah'-tho], *m*. Surge of the sea.

márfega, or **múrfega** [mar' fah-gah], *f*. 1. A coarse woollen frieze, or sack-cloth, anciently used for mourning. 3. *(Prov.)* Rug, a bed coverlet.

marfil [mar-feel'], *m*. Ivory. **Marfil vegetal**, vegetable ivory, the fruit of a palm-tree of equatorial America.

marfileño, ña [mar-fe-lay'-nyo, nyah], *a*. *(Poet.)* Belonging to ivory.

marfuz [mar-footh'], *a*. 1. Repudiated, rejected. 2. Fallacious, deceitful.

marga, marea [mar'-gah, mah-ray'-ah], *f*. 1. Marl, loam, clay-marl. 2. A coarse cloth, formerly used for mourning.

margaíta [mar-gah-e'-tah], *f*. Marl in which either the limestone or clay exceeds eighty parts.

margajita [mar-gah-hee'-tah], *f*. Iron pyrites.

margal [mar-gahl'], *m*. Soil chiefly clayey.

margallón [mar-gal-lyone'], *m*. V. PALMITO.

margar [mar-gar'], *va*. To manure with marl.

margarato [mar-gah-rah'-to], *m*. *(Chem.)* Margarate.

margárico, ca [mar-gah'-re-co, cah], *a*. **Acido margárico**, margaric acid.

margarina [mar-gah-ree'-nah], *f*. Margarine.

margarita [mar-gah-ree'-tah], *f*. 1. Daisy. **Criar margaritas**, to be pushing up the daisies. 2. Pearl. 3. Periwinkle.

margen [mar'-hen], *com*. 1. Edge, border (borde). 2. Margin (de papel). 3. Marginal notation. 4. *(Fig.)* Latitude. 5. *(Fig.)* Chance. 6. *(Fig.)* Margin; gap (intervalo), space; leeway (libertad de acción). **A media margen**, with a center margin. **Dar margen para**, to bring about. **Margen de beneficio**, profit margin. **Dejar a uno al margen**, to leave somebody out. **Mantenerse al margen**, to keep out.

margenar [mar-hay-nar'], *va*. 1. V. MARGINAR. 2. To leave a margin on paper.

marginación [mar-he-nah-the-on'], *f*. 1. Exclusion (acto). 2. Isolation (estado).

marginado, da [mar-he-nah'-do, dah], *a. & pp*. of MARGINAR. Marginated, having a margin. **Quedar marginado**, to be excluded. **Sentirse marginado**, to feel rejected.

marginal [mar-he-nahl'], *a*. Marginal, belonging to the margin.

marginar [mar-he-nar'], *va*. 1. To make annotations on the margin (página). 2. To exclude (persona), to leave out.

margoso, sa [mar-go'-so, sah], *a*. Marly, loamy.

margrave [mar-grah'-vay], *m*. Margrave, a German title of sovereignty.

marguera [mar-gay'-rah], *f*. Marlpit.

María [mah-ree'-ah], *f*. 1. *(coll.)* A white waxtaper, placed in the middle of eight shorter yellow wax-candles, in Roman Catholic churches. 2. An old silver coin worth twelve reals vellon. 3. Mary, a proper name. **María Antonieta**, Marie Antoinette.

mariachi [mah-re-ah'-che], *m*. 1. Mariachi, Mexican street band (conjunto). 2. Member of a mariachi. 3. Mariachi music (música).

marial [mah-re-ahl'], *a*. Praising the Virgin Mary.

marianismo [mah-re-ah-nees'-mo], *m*. Mariolatry.

mariano, na [mah-re-ah'-no, nah], *a*. Marian. **Año mariano**, Marian Year.

marica [mah-ree'-cah], *f*. 1. Magpie. 2. Jack of diamonds. *-m*. 1. Sissy. 2. V. MARICÓN.

maricastaña [mah-re-cas-tah'-nyah], *f*. **En tiempo de Maricastaña**, ages ago, in days of yore.

maricón [mah-re-con'], *m*. 1. Sissy. 2. *(coll.)* Fairy, queer, puff (sodomita).

mariconada [mah-re-co-nah'-dah], *f*. Dirty trick.

maridable [mah-re-dah'-blay], *a*. Conjugal, matrimonial, connubial, marital.

maridaje [mah-re-dah'-hay], *m*. 1. Marriage (unión), conjugal union. 2. Intimate connection or union.

maridanza [mah-re-dahn'-thah], *f*. *(Prov.)* Treatment of a wife.

maridar [mah-re-dar'], *vn*. To marry. *-va*. To unite, to join.

maridazo [mah-re-dah'-tho], *m*. V. GURRUMINO.

maridillo [mah-re-deel'-lyo], *m*. 1. A sorry, pitiful husband. 2. A brazier, used by women to warm the feet.

marido [mah-ree'-do], *m*. Husband, a married man.

mariguana or **marihuana** [mah-re-goo-ah'-nah, mah-re-oo-ah'-nah], *f*. Marihuana or marijuana.

marimacho [mah-re-mah'-cho], *m*. Virago, a robust, masculine woman.

marimanta [mah-re-mahn'-tah], *f*. Bug bear, a phantom.

marimba [mah-reem'-bah], *f.* 1. (*Mus.*) Marimba; (*Carib. Cono Sur*) out-of-tune instrument. 2. (*Cono Sur*) Beating (paliza). 3. (*And. Med.*) Large goitre.

marímbula [mah-reem'-boo-lah], *f.* The jew's-harp. *V.* BIRIMBAO.

marimorena [mah-re-mo-ray'-nah], *f.* (*coll.*) Dispute, difference, quarrel.

marina [mah-ree'-nah], *f.* 1. Shore, sea-coast. 2. (*Pict.*) Sea-piece. 3. Sea-manship (marinería), nautical art, marine, sea affairs. 4. The navy. **Soldados de marina**, marines. **Departamento de marina**, naval department.

marinada [mah-re-nah'-dah], *f.* 1. A stew much in favor among sailors. 2. A ship's provisions and the brine (marinade) with which it is prepared.

marinaje [mah-re-nah´-hay], *m.* 1. Sea-manship, the art of working a ship. 2. Sailors, considered as a body.

marinar [mah-re-nar'], *va.* 1. To marinate, to salt fish. 2. To man a ship taken from the enemy.

marinear [mah-re-nay-ar'], *va.* To be a mariner.

marinerado, da [mah-re-nay-rah´-do, dah], *a.* Manned, equipped. *V.* TRIPULADO.

marinería [mah-re-nay-ree´-ah], *f.* 1. Seamanship (arte). 2. Profession of sea-faring men. 3. The body of seamen.

marinero [mah-re-nay´-ro], *m.* Mariner, seaman, sailor. **A lo marinero**, in a seaman-like manner.

marinero [mah-re-nay´-ro], **ra**, *a.* Ready to sail.

marinesco, ca [mah-re-nes´-co, cah], *a.* Nautical. **A la marinesca**, in a seaman-like manner, ship-shape.

marino, na [mah-ree´-no, nah], *a.* Marine, belonging to the sea. **Fauna marina**, marine life.

marino [mah-ree´-no], *m.* Mariner, seaman, seafaring man.

marión, marón [mah-re-on', mah-rone'], *m.* Sturgeon.

marioneta [mah-re-o-nay'-tah], *f.* Marionette, puppet.

mariposa [mah-re-po'-sah], *f.* 1. Butterfly. **Mariposa de la col**, cabbage-white. 2. A night-taper. 3. Butterfly stroke (natación). 4. (*And. CAm.*) Toy windmill (juguete). 5. (*And.*) Blindman's buff.

mariposear [mah-re-po-say-ar'], *vn.* To flit like a butterfly (revolotear); to be fickle and capricious (ser inconstante); to flirt (coquetear).

mariquita [mah-re-kee'-tah], *f.* Lady-bird, lady-cow, or lady-fly, a hemispherical beetle.

marisabidilla [mah-re-sah-be-deel'-lyah], *f.* Blue stocking, a woman who presumes on being learned.

mariscal [mah-ris-cahl'], *m.* 1. Marshal, a general officer of high rank in some armies. 2. Farrier, blacksmith. **Mariscal de campo**, field-marshal, major-general, a rank inferior to lieutenant-general.

mariscalato [mah-ris-cah-lah'-to], *m.* *V.* MARISCALÍA.

mariscalía [mah-ris-cah-lee´-ah], *f.* Marshalship, the dignity or office of a marshal.

mariscar [mah-ris-car'], *va.* To gather shellfish or the strand.

mariscos [mah-rees'-cos], *m. pl.* Seafood.

marisma [mah-rees'-mah], *f.* Lake formed by the overflow of the tide.

marismo [mah-rees'-mo], *m.* (*Bot.*) *V.* ORZAGA.

marisquería [mah-rees-kay-ree'-ah], *f.* Shellfish bar, seafood restaurant.

marital [mah-re-tahl'], *a.* Marital, pertaining to a husband.

marítimo, ma [mah-ree'-te-mo, mah], *a.* Maritime, maritimal, marine, shipping (agente). **Ciudad marítima**, seaside town. **Seguro marítimo**, marine insurance.

maritornes [mah-re-tor'-nes], *f.* (*coll.*) An ill-shaped, awkward woman.

marjal [mar-hahl'], *m.* Fen, marsh, moor, moorland, marshy ground.

marjoleta [mar-ho-lay'-tah], *f.* (*Prov.*) *V.* MAJUELA.

marjoleto [mar-ho-lay'-to], *m.* *V.* MAJUELO or ESPINO MAJUELO.

márketing [mar'-kay-teen], *m.* Marketing; marketing technique.

marlo [mar'-lo], *m.* (*Amer.*) An ear of Indian corn.

marlota [mar-lo'-tah], *f.* Robe, a kind of Moorish gown.

marmatita [mar-mah-tee´-tah], *f.* (*Min.*) Marmatite, a ferriferous variety of sphalerite.

marmella [mar-mel'-lyah], *f.* Each of two long oval warts which some goats have under the neck.

marmellado, da [mar-mel-lyah'-do, dah], *a.* Having warts (*marmellas*) under the throat.

marmita [mar-mee'-tah], *f.* Kettle, flesh-pot, porridge-pot, a small copper.

marmitón [mar-me-tone'], *m.* Scullion, one who is engaged to wash the dishes and plates in the kitchen.

mármol [mahr'-mol], *m.* 1. Marble. **Mármol pintado**, spotted marble. **Mármol rayado**, streaked marble. 2. Pillar, column. 3. Marver, flatting-table. 4. (*typ.*) Imposing-stone.

marmolejo [mar-mo-lay´-ho], *m.* A small pillar or column of marble.

marmoleño, ña [mar-mo-lay'-nyo, nyah], *a.* Made of marble, resembling marble.

marmolería [mar-mo-lay-ree'-ah], *f.* Any work made of marble.

marmolista [mar-mo-lees'-tah], *m.* Worker in marble, sculptor.

marmóreo, ea, marmoroso, sa [mar-mo'-ray-o, ah, mar-mo-ro'-so, sah], *a.* Marbled, marble, marmorean, made of marble.

marmosete [mar-mo-say'-tay], *m.* Among printers; a vignette, or ornamental cut, at the end of a chapter, or of a volume.

marmota [mar-mo'-tah], *f.* 1. (*Zool.*) Marmot, ground-hog, wood-chuck. 2. (*fig.*) Sleepy-head. **Dormir como una marmota**, to sleep like a log.

maroma [mah-ro´-mah], *f.* 1. Rope (cuerda), a thick cord made of bass or hemp. **Andar en la maroma**, 1. To dance on a rope. 2. (*Met.*) To engage in a perilous undertaking. 2. (*LAm.*) Tight rope (cuerda floja); acrobatic performance (actuación); (*Carib.*) Circus.

marota [mah-ro´-tah], *f.* (*Amer. Mex.*) *V.* MARIMACHO.

marqués [mar-kess'], *m.* Marquis, marquess.

marquesa [mar-kay´-sah], *f.* 1. Marchioness, the lady of a marquis. 2. *V.* MARQUESINA.

marquesado [mar-kay-sah´-do], *m.* Marquisate.

marquesica, illa,ita [mar-kay-see'-cah], *f. dim.* A little marchioness, a young marchioness.

marquesina [mar-key-see'-nah], *f.* Marquee, tilt over an officer's tent, serving more effectually to keep out the rain.

marquesita [mar-kay-see'-tah], *f.* Marcasite, pyrite, mundic, a metallic sulphide.

marquesote [mar-kay-so´-tay], *m.* (*Mex.*) Caramel, burnt sugar.

marqueta [mar-kay'-tah], *f.* Crude cake of wax.

marquetería [mar-kay-tay-ree'-ah], *f.* 1. Cabinet-manufactory. 2. Marquetry, checkered or inlaid work.

marquida, marquisa [mar-kee'-dah], *f.* Cant; low Prostitute.

marquito [mar-kee'-to], *m. dim.* A photographic kit; holder for a smaller plate.

marra [mar'-rah], *f.* 1. Want, deficiency, defect. 2. Club, knobbed stick.

márraga [mar'-ah-gah], *f.* *V.* MARGA.

marrajo [mar-rah'-ho], *m.* White shark.

marrajo, ja [mar-rha´-ho, hah], *a.* Sly cunning, crafty, artful, wily.

marrana [mar-rah'-nah], *f.* Sow, a female pig.

marranada [mar-rah-nah'-dah], *f.* 1. Hoggish action. 2. Swinishness, brutishness, filthiness; dirty, low act.

marranada [mar-rah-nah'-dah], *f.* *V.* CANALLA.

marranamente [mar-rah-nah-men'-tay], *adv.* Piggishly, swinishly.

marranchón, na [mar-ran-chon'], *a.* *V.* MARRANO.

marranería [mar-rah-nay-ree'-ah], *f.* 1. *V.* MARRANADA. 2. Trade in hogs.

marraneta [mar-rah-nay´-tah], *f.* (*Prov.*) A young sow.

marrano [mar-rah'-no], *m.* 1. Pig, hog. 2. Rafter or woodwork which supports a floor or cistern.

marrano, na [mar-rah'-no], *a.* Dirty, indecent.

marrar [mar-rar'], *vn.* 1. To deviate from truth or justice. 2. V. ERRAR. *-va.* **Marrar el tiro,** to miss; to miss the mark.

marras [mar'-ras], *adv. (coll.)* Long ago, long since. **Es un problema de marras,** it´s the same old problem. **Hace marras que no le veo,** *(And.)* it´s ages since I saw him.

marrasquino [mar-ras-kee'-no], *m.* Maraschino, a cordial.

marregón [mar-ray-gone'], *m. (Prov.)* Strawsack. V. JERGÓN.

marrilla [mar-reel'-lyah], *f.* A rather slender club.

marrillo [mar-reel'-lyo], *m. (Prov.)* Thick, short stick.

marro [mar'-ro], *m.* 1. Kind of game, quoits. 2. Slip given by a deer or hare in the course of the chase. 3. Disappointed, failure. 4. Crooked bat for striking a ball.

marrojar [mar-ro-har'], *va.* To lop off the useless branches of trees.

marrón [mar-rone'], *m.* 1. Quoit, pitcher. 2. *(Cuba)* A runaway slave. 3. Chestnut (color); brown. 4. *(Culin.)* Marron glacé. 5. *(And.)* Curipaper. 6. *(Carib.)* Coffee with milk. 7. *(Jur.)* Charge (acusación); sentence (condena). **Comerse un marrón,** to cough up. **Le pillaron de marrón,** they gave him 5 years´ bird. *-a.* Chestnut, brown; brown (zapatos).

marroquí [mar-ro-kee'], **marroquín, na** [mar-ro-keen', nah], *a.* Morocco, belonging to Morocco.

marrubio [mar-roo'-be-o], *m. (Bot.)* Common white horehound.

marrueco, ca [mar-roo-ay'-oo, cah], *a.* Moroccan, belonging to Morocco.

marrullería [mar-rool-lyay-ree'-ah], *f.* Cunning, craft; artful tricks.

marrullero, ra [mar-rool-lyay'-ro, rah], *a.* Crafty, cunning.

marsellés [mar-sel-lyess'], *m.* A kind of short jacket.

marsellés, sa [mar-sel-lyess', sah], *a.* Relating to Marseilles. *-f.* Marseillaise, the French national hymn.

marsopa, or **marsopla** [mar-so'-plah], *f.* Blunt-headed cachalot, porpoise.

marsupiales [mar-soo-pe-ah'-less], *a. m. pl.* The marsupial animals, such as opossums and kangaroos.

marta [mar'-tah], *f.* Pine marten. **Martas,** martens, creased marten-skins.

martagón, na [mar-tah-gone', nah], **m.** & *f.* 1. *(coll.)* Cumling, artful person. 2. *m. (Bot.)* Wild lily, Turk's-cap lily.

Marte [mar'-tay], *m.* Mars; iron.

martellina [mar-tel-lyee'-nah], *f.* Marteline, a marble-worker's hammer having a surface presenting rows of teeth.

martes [mar'-tes], *m.* Tuesday. **Martes de carnaval,** Shrove Tuesday. **El martes pasado,** last Tuesday, **El martes que viene,** next Tuesday. **Vendrá el martes,** he will come on Tuesday.

martillada [mar-til-lyah'-dah], *f.* Stroke with the hammer.

martillador, ra [mar-til-lyah-dor', rah], *m.* & *f.* Hammerer.

martillar [mar-til-lyar'], *va.* To hammer (golpear con martillo), to malleate, to pound (machacar).

martillego [mar-til-lyay'-ho], *m. dim.* A small hammer.

martilleo [mar-til-lyay'-o], *m.* Noise caused by hammering.

martillo [mar-teel'-lyo], *m.* 1. A hammer; claw-hammer. 2. Person who perseveres in something. 3. Tuning hammer. 4. Malleus (hammer) the largest of the ossicles of the ear. **A martillo,** with strokes of a hammer. **Martillo mecánico,** power hammer.

martinete [mar-te-nay'-tay], *m.* 1. A swift or martin. 2. The crest of the king-fisher. 3. Jack in a harpsichord; hammer of a pianoforte. 4. Hammer in copper-works. 5. A pile-driver, drop-hammer.

martingala [mar-tin-gah'-lah], *f.* 1. Martingale, a strap fastened to the girth and noseband of a horse. 2. Ancient kind of breeches.

martini [mar-tee'-ne], *m.* Martini, mixed alcoholic drink.

mártir [mar'-teer], *com.* A martyr.

martirio [mar-tee'-re-o], *m.* Martyrdom.

martirizador, ra [mar-te-re-thah-dor', rah], *m.* & *f.* One who commits martyrdom.

martirizar [mar-te-re-thar'], *va.* 1. To martyr, to put to death as a martyr. 2. To inflict great sufferings; to martyrize.

martirologio [mar-te-ro-lo'-he-o], *m.* Martyrology, a register of martyrs.

marxismo [Mark-sees'-mo], *m.* Marxism, marxianism.

marxista [mark-sees'-tah], *a.* & *m.* & *f.* Marxist.

marzo [mar'-tho], *m.* March, the third month of the year.

mas [mahs], *conj.* But, yet. **Mas que,** although, even if. **Mas si,** perhaps if.

más [mahs], *adv.* 1. More, to a greater degree. 2. Plus; the sign +. 3. Besides moreover. **A más correr,** with the utmost speed. **A más tardar,** at latest. **A más y mejor,** greatly, highly, at best; excellently. **De más a más,** still more and more. **Por lo más,** at most. **Por más que,** However much. **Más que** or **de,** more than, but. **Más de tres años,** more than three years. **Sin más ni más,** without further ado; heedlessly. **Más bien,** rather. **Los más,** the largest number. **Lo más antes,** as soon as possible. **Más vale** or **más valiera si. . .** It is better or would be better if . . . **Sin más acá ni más allá,** without ifs or ands. **Él es el más inteligente,** he is the most intelligent. **Un libro de lo más divertido,** a most amusing book. **Trabajar más,** to work harder. **Más o menos,** more or less. **Como el que más,** as well as anyone. **Nada más,** nothing else. **Nada más llegar te llamo,** I´ll call you as soon as I arrive. **Cada vez viene más tarde,** he comes later and later. **Es más pobre que las ratas,** he is as poor as a church mouse. **Hay más de cien personas,** there are over a hundred people. **Más tarde o más temprano,** sooner or later. **¿Qué más da?,** What difference does it make? **Más vale hacerlo enseguida,** it's better to do it straight away. **Dame dos paquetes más,** give two more packets.

mas [mahs], *m.* 1. *(Prov.)* Farm-house and stock. 2. A weight for gold and silver used in the Philippines equal to 3.768 gm. or 58 grains. 3. The sign + (matemáticas).

masa [mah' sah], *f.* 1. Dough. 2. Mortar. 3. Mass of gold, silver, or other metal. 4. The whole mass of a thing; the lump. 5. Mass, congeries, the union or concurrence of many things. 6. A gentle disposition. 7. *(Prov.)* Farm-house. 8. Estate of a bankrupt. 9. *(And. Cono Sur)* As a whole, altogether.

masacrar [mah-sah-crar'], *va.* To massacre.

masacre [mah-sah'-cray], *f.* Massacre.

masaje [mah-sah'-hay], *m.* Massage. **Dar masaje a,** to massage.

masajista [mah-sah-hees'-tah], *m.* or *f.* Masseur, masseuse.

masar [mah-sar'], *va.* V. AMASAR.

masato [mah-sah'-to], *m.* A fermented liquor made from the yucca or plantain-tree by Indians bordering on the branches of the Amazon river.

mascabado, da [mas-cah-bah'-do, dah], *a.* Applied to inferior sugar; raw, unrefined, muscovado.

mascada [mas-cah'-dah], *f. (Mex.)* 1. A silk neckerchief (pañuelo de cuello). 2. The iron ring by which the neck of criminals condemned to death by the *garrote* is broken. 3. *(LAm.)* Quid (tabaco de mascar). 4. *(And. CAm.)* Buried treasure (tesoro). 5. *(CAm.)* Rebuke (reprimenda).

mascador, ra [mas-cah-dor', rah], *m.* & *f.* Chewer, masticator.

mascadura [mas-cah-doo-rah], *f.* Mastication, manducation, chewing.

mascar [mas-car'], *va.* 1. To chew (comida), to masticate. 2. To pronounce or talk with difficulty (palabras).

máscara [mahs'-cah-rah], *f.* 1. Mask, a cover to disguise the face. **Quitar la máscara a uno,** to unmask somebody. 2. Masquerade. 3. Mask, any pretence or subterfuge. 4. A face-mask used by beekeepers. 5. Mascara (rimel). *com.* Masker, masquerader, mummer; a person in a mask.

mascarada [mas-cah-rah'-dah], *f.* Masquerade, mummery.

mascarero [mas-cah-ray'-ro], *m.* Dealer in masks.

mascarilla [mas-cah-reel'-lyah], *f.* 1. *(dim.)* A small mask which covers only the forehead and eyes. **Quitarse la mascarilla,** to take off the mask, to declare one's sentiments boldly. 2. Mould taken from the face of a dead person; death-mask. 3. Face pack (maquillaje).

mascarón [mas-cah-rone'], *m. (Aug.)* 1. A large hideous mask. 2. Hideous or grotesque forms: *e. g.,* satyrs' faces, used to adorn fountains and buildings. 3. Person ridiculously grave and solemn. **Mascarón de proa,** figure-head of a vessel.

mascota [mas-co'-tah], *f.* Mascot.

masculinidad [mas-coo-le-ne-dahd'], *f.* Masculinity, manhood.

masculino, na [mas-coo-lee'-no, nah], *a.* 1. Masculine, male, virile. 2. *(Gram.)* Masculine (género).

mascullar [mas-cool-lyar'], *va.* To falter in speaking.

masecoral, masejicomar [mah-say-co-rahl', mah-say-he-co-mar'], *m.* Sleight of hand, legerdemain.

masera [mah-say'-rah], *f.* A kneading trough.

masería, masía [mah-say-ree'-ah, mah-see´-ah], *f.* Farmhouse. *V.* MASADA.

masetero [mah-say-tay'-ro], *m.* Masseter, a muscle of the lower jaw.

masica [mah-see'-cah], *f.* The breadnut tree of Central America.

masicote [mah-se-co´-tay], *m.* Massicot, oxide of lead prepared without fusion by the dry method.

masificación [mah-se-fe-cah-the-on'], *f.* Growth, extension.

masilla [mah-seel'-lyah], *f.* 1. Glaziers' putty (ventanas). 2. *(dim.)* A little mass.

masivamente [mah-se'-vah-men-tay], *adv.* Massively; on a large scale.

masivo [mah-see'-vo], *a.* Massive (ataque, dosis); large-scale (evacuación); mass (ejecución).

maslo [mahs'-lo], *m.* 1. Root of the tail of quadrupeds. 2. Shaft or stem of some plants.

masón [mah-sone'], *m.* 1. Mess of dough given to fowls. 2. *(Aug.)* A large mass. 3. *V.* FRANCMASÓN.

masonería [mah-so-nay-ree'-ah], *f.* Free masonry.

masónico, ca [mah-so´-ne-co, cah], *a.* Masonic.

masoquismo [mah-so-kees'-mo], *m.* Masochism.

masoquista [mah-so-kees'-tah], *a. m & f.* Masochistic, masochist.

masora [mah-so'-rah], *f.* Masorah, a Hebrew, work on the Bible. The tradition relied on by the Jews to preserve the text of the Old Testament from corruption.

masorético, ca [mah-so-ray'-te-co, cah], *a.* Masoretic.

masque [mahs'-kay], *adv. (Mex.)* No matter, let it be so. (*mas* and *que.*)

massbus [mahs-boos]. *(Inform.)* Massbus.

mastelero [mas-tay-lay'-ro], *m. (Naut.)* Top-mast. **Mastelero mayor** or **de gavia,** main top-mast. **Mastelero de proa,** fore top-gallant-mast.

masticación [mas-te-cah-the-on´], *f.* Mastication.

masticar [mas-te-car'], *va.* 1. To masticate, to chew. 2. To ruminate or meditate.

masticatorio, ria [mas-te-cah-to'-re-o, ah], *a.* Masticatory.

mastigador [mas-te-gah-dor'], *m.* Instrument put into horses' mouths to prevent their chewing.

mástil [mahs'-teel], *m.* 1. *V.* MASTELERO. 2. Upright post of a bed or loom. **Mástil de barrena,** shank of an auger. 3. Trunk or stem of a tree. 4. Wide breeches worn by Indians. 5. The handle of some musical instruments. 6. Support (sostén). 7. Flag-pole (bandera).

mastín, na [mas-teen', nah], *m. & f.* 1. Mastiff, a dog of the largest size: bulldog. 2. A clumsy fellow; clown.

mastodonte [mas-to-don'-tay], *m.* The mastodon, a fossil mammal like the elephant.

mastoideo, dea [mas-to-e-day'-o, ah], *a.* Mastoid, nipple-shaped.

mastoides [mas-to'-e-days], *m.* The mastoid prominence of the temporal bone.

mastoiditis [mas-toy-dee'-tis], *f. (Med.)* Mastoiditis, mastoid inflammation.

mastranto, mastranzo [mas-trahn'-to, mas-trahn'-tho], *m. (Bot.)* Round-leaved mint.

mastuerzo [mas-too-err'-tho], *m. (Bot.)* Common cress.

masturbación [mas-toor-bah-the-on´], *f.* Masturbation.

masturbarse [mas-toor-bar'-say], *vr.* To masturbate.

mata [mah'-tah], *f.* 1. Small bush (arbusto), shrub, undershrub. 2. Sprig (ramita), blade. 3. Grove, a cluster of trees of one species, copse. 4. The mastic-tree. 5. Lock of matted hair. 6. Piece of ore only partly fused. 7. *(Agr.)* Field, plot. **Mata de olivos,** field of olive trees. 8. **Mata de pelo,** head of hair. **Mata rubia,** kermes oak.

mata, *f.* 1. Game at cards. *V.* MATARRATA. 2. Slaughter. (From MATAR.)

matacán [mah-tah-cahn'], *m.* 1. A poisonous composition for killing dogs. 2. *(Bot.) V.* NUEZ VÓMICA. 3. A hare previously hunted. 4. Stone which may be grasped in the hand and thrown. 5. *(And, Carib.)* Fawn, young deer.

matacandelas [mah-tah-can-day'-las], *f.* Extinguisher.

matacandil [mah-tah-can-deel'], *m. (Prov. Murcia)* Lobster.

matachín [mah-tah-cheen'], *m.* 1. Merry andrew, jack-pudding. 2. Dance performed by grotesque figures. 3. Slaughterman, butcher.

matadero [mah-tah-day'-ro], *m.* 1. Slaughterhouse; severe labor. 2. *(Mex. Cono Sur)* Brothel.

matador [mah-tah-dor'], *m.* 1. Murderer. 2. A card in the game of ombre.-*a.* Mortal; murderous, homicidal.

matadora [mah-tah-do´-rah], *f.* Murderess.

matadura [mah-tah-doo'-rah], *f.* Wound on a horse's back made by the harness; gall.

matafuego [mah-tah-foo-ay'-go], *m.* 1. Fire-engine, fire-extinguisher. 2. Fire-man.

matahambre [mah-tah-ahm'-bray], *m. (Cuba)* Marchpane, dainty made of yucca flour, sugar, etc.

matahormigas [mah-tah-or-mee'-gas], *a. & m. & f. (coll.)* Half-witted, doltish.

matalobos [mah-tah-lo'-bos], *m. (Bot.)* Wolf´s-bane, aconite.

matalón, matalote [mah-tah-lone', mah-tah-lo'tay], *m.* An old worn-out horse.

matamoros [mah-tah-mo'-ros], *m.* Braggart, boaster. *V.* MATASIETE.

matamoscas [mah-tah-mos'-cahs], *m.* Flyswat; flypaper.

matanza [mah-tahn'-thah], *f.* 1. The action of slaughtering. 2. Cattle to be slaughtered. 3. Massacre, butchery; slaughter in the field of battle. 4. Obstinacy, eagerness of pursuit. 5. *(Carib.)* Slaughterhouse (matadero); *(And.)* tienda; *(CAm.)* meat market.

mataperros [mah-tah-per'-ros], *m. (Met. and coll.)* A mischievous, street-lounging boy.

matapolvo [mah-tah-pol'-vo], *m.* Light rain which scarcely settles the dust.

matar [mah-tar'], *va.* 1. To kill, to put to death (persona); to make away with; to execute. 2. To murder, to assassinate. 3. To put out a light, to extinguish the fire. 4. To slake lime. 5. To worry, to vex, to molest (fastidiar). 6. To make a horse's back sore by the rubbing of the harness. **Matar de un golpe,** to knock on the head. **Matar de hambre,** to famish, to starve, to kill with hunger. **A mata caballo,** in the utmost hurry. -*vn.* 1. To kill. 2. To mate (ajedrez). -*vr.* 1. To commit suicide (suicidarse). 2. To make the utmost exertions to obtain a thing. **Matarse por,** to struggle to. 3. To be extremely concerned at a failure or disappointment. **Mátalas callando,** *(coll.)* by crafty silence, or underhand means, he obtains his end.

matarife [mah-tah-re'-fay], *m. (Prov.)* Slaughterman. *V.* MATACHÍN.

matarrata [mah-tar-rah'-tah], *f.* Game at cards.

matasanos [mah-tah-sah'-nos], *m.* Quack, charlatan: empiric.

matasellos [mah-tah-sayl'-lyos], *m.* Postmark.

matasiete [mah-tah-se-ay'-tay], *m.* Bully, braggadocio.

matasuegras [mah-tah-soo-ay'-gras], *m.* Streamer, blower (juguete).

mate [mah'-tay], *m.* 1. Checkmate in chess. **Dar mate,** to scoff at anyone. 2. Size, used by painters and gilders; gold or silver-sizing. 3. The leaves of a shrub of that name, used in South America as a substitute for tea. 4. Unpolished ore. 5. *(Amer.)* A gray gourd. **Entrar a mate,** *(Prov. Mex.)* to correspond or understand each other by signs (amor). 6. *(LAm.)* Maté (bebida). 7. *(CAm.)* To go crazy. -*a.* Unpolished, rough, matt; faded.

matear [mah-tay-ar'], *vn.* l. *(Prov.)* To grow up into stalks (trigo, cebada). 2. *(Amer.)* To take mate-tea.

matemáticamente [mah-tay-mah'-te-cah-men-tay], *adv.* Mathematically.

matemáticas [mah-tay-mah'-te-cas], *f.* Mathematics. **Matemáticas puras,** pure mathematics.

matemático, ca [mah-tay-mah'-te-co, cah], *a.* Mathematical.

matemático [mah-tay-mah'-teh-co], *m.* Mathematician.

materia [mah-tay'-re-ah], *f.* 1. Matter, substance. 2. Material of which something is made. **Prima** or **primera materia,** raw material. 3. Matter, subject, thing treated; cause, occasion. **En materia de,** in the matter of. 4. Matter, question considered, point discussed. **Será materia de muchas discusiones,** it will be the subject of a lot of arguments. 5. Matter, pus. 6. Matter, corporeal substance; opposed to spirit.

material [mah-tay-re-ahl'], *a.* 1. Material, not spiritual. 2. Rude, uncouth, ungenteel. 3. Real, true; literal (literal); physical. **El autor material del hecho,** the actual perpetrator of the deed. -*m.* 1. Ingredient, component, portion of which something is made. **Hecho de mal material,** made of bad material. 2. *(Tec.)* Equipment, plant; materials. **Material escolar,** teaching materials. **Material de oficina,** stationery. 3. *(Tip.)* Copy. 4. Leather (zapatos). 5. *(LAm.)* Made of bricks. **Material defectuoso,** *(Inform.)* faulty equipment.

materialidad [mah-tay-re-ah-le-dahd'], *f.* 1. Materiality, corporeity. 2. Surface or appearance of things; sound of words. 3. *(Theol.)* Materiality, physical fact of actions done in ignorance of right and wrong.

materialismo [mah-tay-re-ah-lees'-mo], *m.* Materialism.

materialista [mah-tay-re-ah-lees'-tah], *com.* Materialist.

materialmente [mah-tay-re-al-men-tay], *adv.* Materially, corporeally.

maternal [mah ter nahl'], *a.* Maternal. V. MATERNO.

maternalmente [mah-ter-nahl'-men-tay], *adv.* Maternally.

maternidad [mah-ter-ne-dahd'], *f.* 1. Maternity, the condition of being a mother. 2. *(Amer.)* Maternity, a hospital for women lying-in.

materno, na [mah-terr'-no, nah], *a.* Maternal (parentesco), motherly, mother (lengua).

mático [mah'-te-co], *m.* *(Acad.)* Matico, a shrub of the pepper family, native of Peru and Bolivia, the leaves containing an astringent, aromatic oil.

matinal [mah-te-nahl'], *a.* *(Pont.)* V. MATUTINAL.

matiné [mah-te-nay´], *f.* *(Th.)* Matinee, morning or afternoon performance.

matiz [mah-teeth'], *m.* 1. Shade of colors; mixture of a variety of colors. 2. Shade (de significado); touch (de ironía).

matizado, da [mah-te-thah'-do, dah], *a. & pp.* of MATIZAR. Variegated.

matizar [mah-te-thar'], *va.* 1. To mix colors agreeably. 2. To embellish, to adorn, to beautify. 3. To make more precise (aclarar); to go into fine detail over (sutilizar). **Se matizarán los cursos con deportes,** classes will be interspersed with sports.

mato [mah'-to], *m.* V. MATORRAL.

matojo [mah-toh'-ho], *m.* 1. A barrilla-producing bush about two feet high which grows in Spain. 2. *(Cuba)* Shoot which trees put out after being cut.

matón [mah-tone'], *m.* Bully, a noisy, quarrelsome fellow.

matorral [mah-tor-rahl'], *m.* 1. Field full of brambles and briers, a bushy place. 2. A thicket, copse.

matoso, sa [mah-to'-so, sah], *a.* Bushy, covered with bushes.

matraca [mah-trah'-cah], *f.* 1. A wooden rattle (objeto). 2. Jest, contemptuous joke (guasa). 3. *(And.)* Hash, pot. 4. *(Mex.)* Machine gun (metralleta). **Dar matraca,** to banter.

matraquear [mah-trah-kay-ar'], *va.* To jest, to scoff, to mock, to ridicule.

matraquista [mah-trah-kees'-tah], *com.* Wag, jester, punster.

matraz [mah-trath'], *f.* Matrass, vessel used by apothecaries.

matrería [mah-tray-ree'-ah], *f.* *(Mex. Cuba)* Penetration, shrewdness, suspiciousness.

matrero, ra [mah-tray'-ro, rah], *a.* Cunning (astuto), sagacious, knowing. -*m.* Artful knave; cunning, knavish soldier; fugitive from justice (fugitivo); trickster (tramposo).

matriarcado [mah-tre-ar-cah'-do], *m.* Matriarchy.

matricida [mah-tre-thee'-dah], *com.* Matricide, murderer of one's mother.

matricidio [mah-tre-thee'-de-o], *m.* Matricide, slaughter of a mother.

matrícula [mah-tree'-coo-lah], *f.* 1 Register (registro), list. 2. Matriculation. **Un barco con matrícula de Bilbao,** a boat registered in Bilbao. **Matrícula de honor,** prize (universidad). **Derechos de matrícula,** registration fees. 3. License plate (coches).

matriculación [mah-tre-coo-lah-the-on'], *f.* Matriculation, registration (coche, barco).

matriculador [mah-tre-coo-lah-dor'], *m.* He who matriculates.

matricular [mah-tre-coo-lar'], *va.* To matriculate, to register, to enroll, to enter a list.

matrimonial [mah-tre-mo-ne-ahl'], *a.* Matrimonial, connubial, nuptial. **Enlace matrimonial,** link by marriage.

matrimonialmente [mah-tre-mo-ne-ahl'-men-tay], *adv.* Matrimonially.

matrimonio [mah-tre-mo'-ne-o], *m.* 1. Marriage, matrimony. 2. *(coll.)* Husband and wife, couple (personas). **Matrimonio de conveniencia,** marriage of convenience. **Matrimonio por la iglesia,** church marriage.

matriz [mah-treeth'], *f.* 1. Mother church, metropolitan church. 2. Matrix, womb. 3. Mould, form, matrice. 4. The original draft of a writing. 5. A female screw. -*a.* First, principal, chief. 6. *(Inform.)* **Matriz lógica de campo programable,** programmable logic array, programmed logic array.

matrona [mah tro' nah], *f.* 1. A matron. 2. A midwife.

matronaza [mah-tro-nah'-thah], *f. aug.* A corpulent respectable matron.

maturrango, ga [mah-too-rahn'-go, gah], *m. & f.* Appellation given to a European in Buenos Aires. It means a bad horseman or bad horse.

Matusalén [mah-too-sah-layn'], *a. (coll.)* Old as Methuselah.

matute [ma-tooh'-tay], *m.* l. Smuggling (acto). 2. Smuggled goods (géneros), a prohibited commodity.

matutear [mah-too-tay-ar'], *va.* To smuggle goods.

matutero, ra [mah-too-tay'-ro, rah], *m. & f.* Smuggler, contrabandist.

matutinal [mah-too-te-nahl'], *a.* Belonging to the morning; morning.

matutino, na [mah-too-tee'-no, nah], *a.* Matutinal, belonging to the morning.

maula [mah'-oo-lah], *f.* l. Anything worthless (objeto); rubbish trumpery, trash. 2. Cunning, craft, deceitful tricks, imposition. -*com. (coll.)* Cheat, bad paymaster. **Es una buena maula,** *(coll.)* he is a good-for-nothing fellow. **Ella es buena maula,** she is a hussy: used jocularly.

maulería [mah-oo-lay-ree'-ah], *f.* 1. Frippery, old clothes-shop, a piece-broker's shop. 2. Craft, cunning.

maulero [mah-oo-lay'-ro], *m.* 1. Piece-broker, seller of old clothes. 2. Impostor, deceitful type (engañador), cheat (tramposo), swindler.

maullador, ra [mah-oo-llyah-dor', rah], *a.* Applied to a mewing cat.

maullar [ma-hoo-llyar'], *vn.* To mew (gatos).

maullido, maúllo [mah-oo-llyee'-do, mah-ool'-lyo], *m.* Mew, cry of a cat.

mauraca [mah-oo-rah'-cah], *f. (Prov. Andal.)* Act of roasting chestnuts, acorns, or ears of Indian corn over coals in the open air.

mauritano, na [mah-oo-re-tah'-no, nah], *a.* Mauritanian.

mauseolo [mah-oo-say-o'-lo], *m. V.* MAUSOLEO.

mausoleo [mah-oo-so-lay'-o], *m.* Mausoleum.

maxilar [mac-se-lar'], *a.* Maxillary, maxillar.

máxima [mahc'-se-mah'], *f.* 1. A maxim, an axion. 2. Sentence, apothegm. 3. Idea, thought. 4. Musical point.

máximamente and **máxime** [mahc'-se-may], *adv.* Principally.

máximo, ma [mahc'-se-mo, mah], *a. sup.* Chief, principal; very great. **El máximo dirigente,** the top leader. **Su máximo esfuerzo,** their greatest effort.

máximum [mac-se-moom], *m.* Maximum, extreme limit.

maya [mah'-yah], *f.* 1. *(Bot.)* Common daisy. 2. May-queen, a little girl adorned with flowers. 3. Name of the native language of Yucatan and of its ancient civilization.

mayador, ra [mah-yah-dor', rah], *a.* Mewing.

mayal [mah-yahl'], *m.* 1. Flail, a thrashing instrument. 2. Lever in oilmills.

mayar [mah-yar'], *vn.* To mew. *V.* MAULLAR.

mayo [mah'-yo], *m.* 1. May, the fifth month. 2. Maypole.

mayólica [mah-yo'-le-cah], *f.* Majolica ware (loza esmaltada).

mayonesa [mah-yo-nay'-sah], *f.* Mayonnaise dressing; oil and yolks of eggs beaten together.

mayor [mah-yor'], *a.* Greater, larger. **Hombre mayor,** an elderly man, also a man of great age. 2. High (atar, calle; main, principal (plaza). 3. Main, major, larger (parte). 4. Head (en rango). 5. *(Superl.)* Biggest, largest (en tamaño). -*m.* 1. Superior, mayor or chief of a community. 2. Major, a field officer (rango). 3. *(Geog.)* Lake Maggiore, in northern Italy. 4. *(Arch.) V.* SILLAR.-*f. (Log.)* Major, first proposition in a syllogism.-*pl.* 1. Ancestors, forefathers (antepasados). 2. Superiors. 3. *(Naut.)* Three principal sails of a ship. 4. In grammar schools, the higher class. **Mayor or mayor de edad,** person of age. **Hermano mayor,** eldest brother. **Llegar a mayores,** to get out of hand. **Vender al por mayor,** to sell wholesale.

mayora [mah-yo'-rah], *f.* Mayoress.

mayoral [mah-yo-rahl'], *m.* 1. Head shepherd (pastor); leader. 2. Overseer, steward (mayordomo).

mayorana [mah-yo-rah'-nah], *f. V.* MEJORANA.

mayorazga [mah-yo-rath'-gah], *f.* 1. The wife of a person possessing an entailed estate. 2. She who possesses an entailed estate.

mayorazgo [mah-yo-rath'-go], *m.* 1. Primogeniture. 2. Entailed estate, (inherited by primogeniture). 3. Heir to an entailed estate (heredero).

mayorazguista [mah-yo-rath-gees'-tah], *m. (Law.)* Author who treats on entails.

mayordoma [mah-yor-do'-mah], *f.* Steward's wife.

mayordomía [mah-yor-do-mee'-ah], *f.* Administration, stewardship, controllership.

mayordomo [mah-yor-do'-mo], *m.* Steward (de casa), the principal servant of a nobleman or gentleman; majordomo, super intendent; *(Cono Sur)* foreman (capataz); *(And.)* servant (criado).

mayoría [mah-yo-ree'-ah], *f.* 1. Advantage, excellence, superiority. 2. Major's commission. 3. Majority, full age. **En la mayoría de los casos,** in most cases. **Por una mayoría arrolladora,** by an overwhelming majority. **Gobierno de la mayoría,** majority government.

mayoridad [mah-yo-re-dahd'], *f.* Superiority.

mayorista [mah-yo-rees'-tah], *m.* Student of the highest classes in grammar schools. -*m & f.* Wholesaler.

mayormente [mah-yor'-men-tay], *adv.* Principally, chiefly (principalmente), especially (especialmente).

mayúscula [mah-yoos'-coo-lah], *a.* Capital letter (letra).

maza [mah'-thah], *f.* 1. Club, a stick shod with iron. 2. Mace, an ensign of authority. 3. Engine or pile engine. 4. Nave or

hub of a wheel. 5. Rag pinned to men or women's clothes to make a laughing-stock of them. 6. Beetle for flax or hemp. 7. An importunate or troublesome fellow. 8. The thick end of a billiard-cue. 9. Something noisy tied to a dog's tail (carnaval). **Maza de fraga,** hammer.

mazacote [mah-thah-co'-tay], *m.* 1. Kali, barilla. 2. Mortar cement. 3. Dry, tough mass. 4. Injurious nickname for a peevish person. 5. *(Amer.)* Antimony.

mazada [mah-thah'-dah], *f.* Blow with a mallet (golpe), offensive expression.

mazagatos [mah-thah-gah'-tos], *m.* Noise, dispute, contention.

mazamorra [mah-thah-mor'-rah], *f.* 1. Bread-dust; biscuit spoiled and broken in pieces. 2. Anything broken into small bits. 3. Sort of pap, made of the flour of Indian corn, honey, and sugar. 4. *(LAm.)* Blister (ampolla).

mazaneta [mah-thah-nay-tah], *f.* Apple-shaped ornament in jewels.

mazapán [mah-thah-pahn'], *m.* Marchpane, a sweet paste of almonds, sugar, churn milk.

mazar [mah-thar'], *va.* *(Prov.)* To churn milk.

mazarí [mah-thah-ree'], *m.* A tile-shaped brick.

mazmorra [math-mor'-rah], *f.* Moorish dungeon, underground.

mazo [mah'-tho], *m.* 1. Mallet, a wooden hammer (martillo). 2. Bundle, a quantity of ribbons or other things tied together (manojo). **Mazo de llaves,** bunch of keys. 3. An importunate, tiresome person.

mazonería [mah-tho-nay-ree'-ah], *f.* 1. Masonry, brickwork. 2. Relief or relievo-work.

mazorca [mah-thor'-cah], *f.* 1. Spindle full of thread, *spun* from the distaff in the shape of a cone. 2. Ear of corn the spike or cob of corn (de maíz). 3. Spindle-shaped work upon a balustrade.

mazorral [mah-thor-rahl'], *a.* Rude, uncouth, clownish.

mazote [mah-tho'-tay], *m.* 1. A kind of cement or mortar. 2. A block-head.

mazotear [mah-tho-tay-ar'], *va.* To strike with a club or mallet.

mazurca [mah-thoor'-cah], *f.* Mazurka.

me [may], *pron.* Me, the dative and accusative case of the pronoun **I,** placed either before or after a verb. **Me lo compró,** he bought it from me. **Me lavé,** I washed.

meada [may-ah'-dah], *f.* The quantity of urine made at one time (orinar), piss. **Echar una meada,** to have a piss. 2. Spot or mark left by making water (mancha).

meados [may-ah'-dos], *m. pl. V.* ORINES.

meajuela [may-ah-hoo-ayl'-lah], *f.* Small piece attached to the bits of a bridle.

mear [may-ar'], *vn.* 1. To urinate, to piss, to have a piss, to make water. -*va.* To walk all over (humillar).

meato [may-ah'-to], *m.* Passage or channel of the body; meatus.

meauca [may-ah-oo'-cah], *f.* A sea-fowl, so called from its cry; a gull.

meca [may'-cah], *f.* **Casa de meca,** house of noise and confusion. **Andar de Ceca en Meca,** to wander about.

mecánica [may-cah'-ne-cah], *f.* 1. Mechanics. *V.* MAQUINARIA. 2. *(coll.)* A mean, despicable action or thing. 3. *(Mil.)* Management of soldiers' affairs.

mecánicamente [may-cah'-ne-cah-men-tay], *adv.* Meanly, sordidly, mechanically.

mecánico, ca [may-cah'-ne-co, cah], *a.* 1. Mechanical, done by machinery (máquina). 2. Mean, servile; of mean occupation (oficio). **Potencias mecánicas,** mechanical powers.

mecánico [may-cah'-ne-co], *m.* 1. Mechanician, mechanic, manufacturer, handicraftsman.

mecanismo [may-cah-nees'-mo], *m.* Mechanism, action performed according to mechanical laws.

mecanización [may-cah-ne-thah-the-on'], *f.* Mechanization.

mecanizar [may-cah-ne-thar'], *va.* To mechanize.

mecanografía [may-cah-no-grah-fee'-ah], *f.* Typewriting.
mecanografiar [may-cah-no-grah-fe-ar'], *va.* To type.
mecanógrafo, fa [may-cah-no´-grah-fo, fah], *m. & f.* Typist.
mecapal [may-cah-pahl'], *m. (Mes.)* Porter's leather strap, a kind of leather band with two cords attached, serving porters to carry a load more conveniently.
mecate [may-cah´-tay], *m. (Mex.)* Rope or cord made of the maguey or American agave.
mecatito [may-cah-tee´-to], *m.* Small cord, twine.
mecedero [may-thay-day'-ro], *m. V.* MECEDOR.
mecedor, ra [may-thay-dor', rah], *m. & f.* 1. Rocker, one who rocks something to and fro. 2. *m.* Stirrer, a pole with which wine is stirred in a hogshead, wort in a vat, and soap in a boiler. 3. Swing (columpio). 4. *(CAm. Mex.)* Rocking chair (asiento). 5. *(Carib.)* Stirrer (cuchara). **Mecedora**, *f.* Rocking-chair.
mecedura [may-thay-doo'-rah], *f.* Act of rocking something.
mecer [may-therr'], *va.* 1. To stir (líquido), to agitate, to jumble, to mix. 2. To rock (cuna), to shake. 3. To dandle a child (niño).
mecereón [may-thay-ray-on'], *m. (Bot.)* Mezereon.
mecha [may'-chah], *f.* 1. Wick, for candles, tapers, and torches. 2. Roll of lint put into a sore. 3. Match, match-cord, for firing ordnance. 4. Bacon, with which fowls and meat are larded. 5. A lock of hair; a bundle of threads or fibers. 6. *(And, Carib.)* Joke (broma). 7. *(Mex.)* Fear (miedo). 8. Shoplifting (ratería). **Alargar la mecha**, to augment a salary; to protract a business: to allow a debtor time to discharge a debt. **A toda mecha**, at full speed.
mechar [may-char'], *va.* To lard fowls, game, or meat, with bacon; to force or stuff.
mechazo [may-chah'-tho], *m.* Burning of a slow match (fuse) without setting off the blast.
mechera [may-chay'-rah], *f.* Larding-pin.
mechero [may-chay'-ro], *m.* 1. Tube for the wick of a lamp; socket of a candle sticks. 2. Cigarette lighter (encendedor); burner (cocina). **Mechero piloto**, pilot light. **Mechero de gas**, gas burner.
mechificar [may-che-fe-car´], *va. (Peru Ven. coll.)* To annoy, to make fun of.
mechinal [may-che-nahl'], *m.* Square stones left projecting in a wall to be continued.
mechoacán [may-cho ah cahn´], *m. (Bot.)* Mechoacan bindneed, an inferior kind of jalap.
mechón [may-chone'], *m. aug.* 1. Large lock of hair; large match (pelo). 2. A large bundle of threads or fibers separated from the rest (hilos).
mechoso, sa [may-cho´-so, sah], *a.* Full of matches or wicks.
mecida [may-thee'-dah], *f. V.* MECEDURA.
meco, ca [may'-co, cah], *a. (Mex.)* Blackish red; copper-colored: used of animals. *-m. & f. (Mex.)* Savage Indian.
mecónico, ca [may-co'-ne-co, cah], *a.* Meconic acid, a white solid discovered in opium.
medalla [may-dahl'-lyah], *f.* 1. A medal. 2. *(Sculpt.)* A round or oval target on which a figure is carved in relief. 3. *(coll.)* Gold coin weighing an ounce.
medallón [may-dal-lyon'], *m. aug.* 1. Medallion (medalla). 2. *(Arch.)* Round or oval bas-relief placed on buildings. 3. A locket for a portrait or some souvenir.
médano, medaño [may'-dah-no, may-dah'-nyo], *m.* 1. Sand-bank on the sea-shore, dune. 2. A mound of sand covered by shallow water.
media [may'-de-ah], *f.* 1. Stocking, hose. **Medias lisas**, plain hose. **Medias rayadas**, ribbed hose. **Medias-medias**, socks, half-hose. 2. Measure of about half a hundredweight.
mediacaña [may-de-ah-cah´-nyah], *f.* 1. *(Arch.)* A concave mouldings. 2. A strip of wood with mouldings. 3. A gouge, a chisel with a curved cutting edge. 4. A half-round file. 5. Curling-tongs for the hair.
mediación [may-de-ah-the-on´], *f.* Mediation (intercesión), intervention, interposition, intercession.

mediador, ra [may-de-ah-dor', rah], *m. & f.* Mediator, intercessor.
mediana [may-de-ah'-nah], *f.* 1. Flesh of the shoulder near the neck of animals. 2. Household bread. 3. *(Prov.)* Top of a fishing-rod. 4. *V.* BARZÓN. 5. *(Aut.)* Central reservation.
medianamente [may-de-ah-nah-men-tay], *adv.* Middlingly, moderately, meanly. **Un trabajo medianamente bueno**, a moderately good piece of work.
mediados de (A), *adv. (coll.)* About the midst of, in the midst of.
medianejo, ja [may-de-ah-nay'-ho, hah], *a. (coll.)* Barely middling or moderate; hardly mediocre.
medianería [may-de-ah-nay-ree'-ah], *f.* 1. A wall common to two contiguous houses. 2. Half of a piece of land or of a rent.
medianero, ra [may-de-ah-nay'-ro, rah], *a.* 1. Mediating, interceding, mediatory. 2. Intermediate; having the half of something. **Pared medianera**, partition wall.
medianero [may-de-ah-nay'-ro], *m.* 1. Mediator, go-between. 2. Owner of a house which has a common wall (de casa). 3. *(Carib. Mex.)* Partner; *(Agr.)* share-cropper.
medianta, medianidad [may-de-ah-nee'-ah, may-de-ah-ne-dahd'], *f.* 1. Moderation or temperance in the execution of a thing. 2. Mediocrity, mean, middle state; moderate means.
medianil [may-de-ah-neel'], *m. (Agr.)* Middle-piece of ground.
mediano, na [may-de-ah'-no, nah], *a.* Moderate, middling (regular), mediocre, indifferent (indiferente). **De tamaño mediano**, medium-sized.
medianoche [may-de-ah-no-chay], *f.* Midnight.
medianos [may-de-ah'-nos], *m. pl.* In grammar schools, the class in syntax.
mediante [may-de-ahn'-tay], *adv.* By means of, by virtue of.
mediar [may-de-ar'], *vn.* 1. To come to the middle of a thing, to be at the middle (estar en medio). 2. To intercede for another, to mediate (interceder). 3. To intervene (intervenir). 4. To come up (suceder). **Media un abismo entre los dos gobiernos**, there is a wide gap between the two governments. **Median relaciones cordiales entre los dos**, cordial relations exist between the two.
mediastino [may-de-as-tee´-no], *m. (Anat.)* 1. Mediastinum, the intervening space between the lungs. 2. *(Bot.)* Delicate septum of the silique of the mustard family.
mediatamente [may-de-ah-tah-men-tay], *adv.* Mediately.
mediato, ta [may-de-ah´-to, tah], *a.* Mediate.
mediator [may-de-ah tor´], *m.* Ombre, game at cards.
médica [may'-de-cah], *f.* 1. Doctor's wife. 2. Doctress, female physician.
medicable [may-de-cah´-blay], *a.* Curable, medicable.
medicación [may-de-cah-the-on'], *f.* Medication, treatment.
medicamento [may-de-cah-men´-to], *m.* Medicament, medicine, physic.
medicar [may-de-car´], *va. V.* MEDICINAR.
medicastro [may-de-cahs´ tro], *m.* Quack, empiric in physic.
medicina [may-de-thee'-nah], *f.* Medicine, the healing arts. 2. Medicine, a remedy. **Medicina alternativa**, alternative medicine.
medicinal [may-de-the-nahl'], *a.* Medicinal, healing, belonging to physic.
medicinar [may-de-the-nar'], *va.* To medicine, to administer medicines, to apply medicaments.
medición [may-de-the-on'], *f.* Measurement, measuration, measuring.
medicucho [may-de-coo'-cho], *a.* Quackish, quack (used adjectively).
médico [may'-de-co], *m & f.* Physician, doctor, medical practitioner. **Médico de cabecera**, family doctor. **Médico residente**, house physician.
médico, ca [may'-de-co, cah], *a.* Medical, medicinal.
medida [may-dee'-dah], *f.* 1. Measure, that by which something is measured; standard, gauge (sistema, recipiente). 2. Measuring (acto), measurement. 3. Height, length, breadth,

or quantity measured. 4. Proportion, relation, correspondence. 5. *(Arith.)* Root, a number which, repeated various times, exactly produces another. 6. Measure, syllables metrically numbered. 7. Measure, means to an end. 8. Measure, moderation (moderación), prudence. 9. Girdle on the statues of saints bearing their name. 10. Size, fitting (camisa, zapato). **A medida** or **a sabor de su paladar**, to his health's content. **A medida que**, according as, in proportion; at the same time that, whilst. **En gran medida**, to a great extent. **Tomar las medidas a uno**, to measure somebody. **Medida para líquidos**, liquid measure. **Medida preventiva**, preventive measure. **Tomar medidas**, to take steps.

medidamente [may-de-dah-men-tay], *adv.* Moderately.

medidor, ra [mae-de-dor', rah], *m. & f.* Measurer, evaluator. *-m.* Meter, gauge. **Medidor de franqueo**, postage meter. **Medidor del gas**, gas meter.

mediero [may-day'-ro], *m.* 1. Hosier, dealer in stockings. 2. Knitter of stockings. 3. Share-cropper, co-partner in the cultivation of lands, etc.

medieval [may-de-ay-vahl´], *a. & m.* Mediaeval, pertaining to the middle Ages. *(Neol.)*

medio, dia [may'-de-o, ah], *a.* 1. Half, in part (mitad). 2. Mid, midway, middle (punto). 3. Mean, average. 4. *(LAm.)* Big, huge (grande). **Media noche**, midnight, twelve at night. **Medio día**, midday, noon. **Medio hermano**, half-brother or half-blood. **Medio borracho**, halfseas over. **Media naranja**, *V.* CÚPULA. **A medias**, by halves. **Ir a medias**, to go halves with one. **A media mañana**, mid-morning. **A media voz**, in a low voice. **Clase media**, middle class. **Oriente Medio**, Middle East. **Término medio**, average. **Media botella de vino**, half a bottle of wine.

medio [may'-de-o], *m.* 1. Middle (centro). 2. Medium. 3. Step, measure. 4. Means. 5. Surroundings, environment. 6. *(Math.)* Half. 7. Middle finger. 8. *(Sports)* Lineman. *-pl.* 1. Means (método), resources. 2. Center of the bull-ring. *-adv.* Half (término medio). **A medio cocer**, half cooked. **Corto de medios**, short of funds. **De medio a medio**, 1. Right in the middle. 2. Absolutely. **De por medio**, 1. Halfway. 2. In the middle. **En medio de**, 1. In the middle of. 2. Despite. **Estar de por medio**, to mediate. **Por medio de**, by means of, through. **Medios de publicidad**, advertising media. **Medio dormido**, half asleep. **Hablaba a media voz**, she was speaking in a low voice. **En medio de la plaza**, in the middle of the square. **Quitar algo de en medio**, to remove something. **Meterse de por medio**, to intervene. **Los medios de comunicación**, the media.

mediocre [may-de-o'-cray], *a.* Middling, mean, moderate, mediocre.

mediocridad [may-de-o-cre-dahd'], *f.* Mediocrity, small degree, middle rate, middle state.

mediodía [may-de-o-dee'-ah], *m.* 1. Noon, midday, noonday, noontide, meridian. 2. South. 3. South wind.

mediopaño [may-de-o-pah'-nyo], *m.* Thin woollen cloth.

mediquillo [may-de-keel'-lyo], *m.* Indian of the Philippine Islands, having medical experience, but no title.

medir [may-deer'], *va.* 1. To measure, to ascertain the length, magnitude, or quantity of a thing. 2. To measure or examine the number or syllables of a verse. 3. To compare, to measure, to estimate the quality of things. 4. **Medir por millas**, to measure in miles. *-vn.* 1. To measure (objeto, persona). **La tela mide 90 cms**, the cloth measures 90 cms. *-vr.* 1. To be moderate, to act with prudence. **No perder la calma**, to keep one´s head. 2. *(LAm.) (Dep.)* To play each other. 3. *(LAm.)* To try on (ropa).

meditabundo, da [may-de-tah-boon'-do, dah], *a.* Pensive, musing, thoughtful.

meditación [may-de-tah-the-on'], *f.* Meditation, cogitation, deep thought, contemplation. **Meditaciones**, meditations.

meditar [may-de-tar'], *va.* To meditate, to contemplate, to consider.

Mediterráneo, nea [may-de-ter-rah'-nay-o, ah], *a.* Mediterranean, encircled with land, midland.

médium [may'-de-oom], *m.* Medium, a person fit for spiritualistic communications.

medo, da [may'-do, dah], *a.* Mede, belonging to ancient Media.

medra [may'-drah], *f.* Proficiency, progress, amelioration, improvement.

medrar [may-drar'], *vn.* To thrive, to prosper, to grow rich, to improve (mejorar).

medriñaque [may-dre-nyah'-kay], *m.* 1. A Philippine stuff for lining and stiffening women's garments. 2. A short petticoat.

medro [may'-dro], *m. V.* MEDRA. *-pl.* Progress, improvement.

medrosamente [may-dro'-sah-men-tay], *adv.* Timorously, fearfully, faintly.

medroso, sa [may-dro'-so, sah], *a.* 1. Fearful, timorous, faint-hearted, cowardly. 2. Terrible, inspiring fear.

medula, or **médula** [may-doo'-lah, may'-doo-lah], *f.* 1. Marrow, medulla. 2. The substance or essence of anything.

medular [may-doo-lar'], *a.* Medullar, medullary.

meduloso, sa [may-doo-lo'-so, sah], *a.* Full of marrow, marrowish.

medusa [may-doo'-sah], *f.* Jelly-fish.

megabus [may-gah-boos]. *(Inform.)* Megabus.

megabyte [may-gah-bite], *m. (Inform.)* Megabyte.

megaciclo [may-gah-thee'-clo], *m.* Megacycle.

megáfono [may-gah'-fo-no], *m.* Megaphone.

magalomanía [meh-gah-lo-mah-nee'-ah], *f.* Megalomania, delusions of grandeur.

megalómano, na [me-gah-lo´-mah-no, nah], *a.* Megalomaniacal.-*m. & f.* Megalomaniac.

mego, ga [may'-go, gah], *a.* Gentle, mild, meek, peaceful.

mejana [may-hah'-nah], *f.* Islet in the middle of a river.

mejicano, na [may-he-cah'-no, nah], *a.* Mexican, native of or belonging to Mexico.-*m.* The Mexican language, Aztec.

mejido, da [may-hee'-do, dah], *a.* Beaten with sugar and water (huevos).

mejilla [may-heel'-lyah], *f.* The cheek.

mejillón, mijillón [may-hil-lyone'], *m.* A kind of cockle.

mejor [may-hor'], *a.* Better, *comp.* of BUENO. *-adv.* Better, more exactly. **A lo mejor**, when least expected. **El mejor día**, some fine day. **A cual mejor**, as well as could be wished. **Llevar lo mejor**, to come off victorious. **Mejor que mejor**, much better. **Lo mejor será**, the better way will be. **Tanto mejor**, so much the better. **Lo mejor de la novela**, the best part of the novel. **Está mucho mejor**, he´s much better.

mejora [may-ho'-rah], *f.* 1. Improvement, amelioration, addition, growth. 2. Appeal to a superior court. 3. The act of leaving by will a larger share than the legatee by law had a right to. 4. Outbidding at a public sale (en subasta). **Mejora de la resolución en pantalla**, *(Comput.)* display enhancement.

mejorable [may-ho-rah'-blay], *a.* Improvable.

mejoramiento [may-ho-rah-me-en'-to], *m.* Improvement, amelioration.

mejorana [may-ho-rah'-nah], *f. (Bot.)* Sweet marjoram.

mejorar [may-ho-rar'], *va.* 1. To improve, to ameliorate, to heighten, to cultivate, to mend. 2. To outbid, or bid over. 3. To leave, by will, to a son or grandson an increased share beyond his legal right. 3. To enhance (realzar); to raise (postura); to improve (oferta). *-vn.* To recover from a disease or calamity. *-vr.* To improve, to grow better.

mejoría [may-ho-ree'-ah], *f.* 1. Improvement, amelioration, mending. 2. Repairs. 3. The state of growing better in health. 4. Advantage, superiority.

mejunje [may-hoon'-hay], *m. (coll.) V.* MENJURJE.

melada [may-lah'-dah], *f.* A slice of toasted bread soaked in honey.

melado, da [may-lah'-do, dah], *a.* Of the color of honey.-*pp.* of MELAR.

meladucha [may-lah-doo'-chah], *f.* A course, mealy apple.

meladura [may-lah-doo'-rah], *f. (Cuba)* Purified sap of the sugar-cane; sirup, treacle.

meláfiro [may-lah'-fe-ro], *m.* Melaphyre, a pre-tertiary basalt.

melaína [may-lah-ee'-nah], *f.* 1. Black coloring matter of cephalopod mollusks. 2. Pigment of the skin of colored people.

melancolía [may-lan-co-lee'-ah], *f.* Melancholy, gloomy madness, gloom, gloominess.

melancólico, ca [may-lan-co'-le-co, cah], *a.* Melancholy (triste), sad, gloomy, fanciful, cloudy, mournful, hypochondriacal, dreamy (soñador).

melancolizar [may-lan-co-le-thar'], *va.* To affect with melancholy, to render gloomy and dejected, to dispirit.

melandro [may-lahn'-dro], *m. (Prov. Ast.)* Badger.

melanesiano, na [may-lah-nay-se-ah'-no, nah], *a.* Melanesian, relating to the islands between New Guinea and the Fijis, called collectively Melanesia.

melanuro, ra [may-lah-noo'-ro, rah], *a.* Black-tailed.

melapia [may-lah'-pe-ah], *f.* Kind of apple, related to the pippin.

melar [may-lar'], *vn.* 1. In sugar-works to boil down the juice of the sugar-cane a second time until it obtains the consistency of honey. 2. To deposit honey as bees.

melaza [may-lah'-thah], *f.* 1. Molasses 2. *(Prov.)* Dregs of honey.

melca [layl-cah], *f. V.* ZAHINA.

melcocha [mel-co'-chah], *f.* Paste made with honey, flour, and spice; molasses candy (melaza).

melcochero [mel-co-chay'-ro], *m.* Molasses-candy maker or seller, ginger breed baker.

melele [may-lay'-lay], *a.* Foolish, silly *V.* MELILOTO.

melena [may-lay'-nah], *f.* 1. Dishevelled hair hanging loose over the eyes. 2. Foretop hair or mane that falls on a horse's face; also a lion's mane. 3. A soft, fleecy skin put on the forehead of working oxen to prevent their being hurt by the yoke. **Estar en melena,** to have one's hair down.

melena [may-lay'-nah], *f.* Black stools from intestinal hemorrhage.

melenudo, da [may-lay-noo'-do, dah], *a.* Hairy, having bushy hair.

melero [may lay' ro], *m.* 1. Dealer in honey. 2. Place destined to preserve honey.

melgacho [mel-gah'-cho], *m.* Dog-fish.

melgar [mel-gar'], *m.* Patch of wild alfalfa.

melgarejo [mel-gah-ray'-ho], *m.* The helmsman's post. *V.* TIMONERA.

mélico, ca [may'le-co, cah], *a.* Lyrical, belonging to song, or to lyric poetry. *(Acad.)*

melífero, ra [may-lee'-fay-ro, rah], *a.* Melliferous, productive of honey.

melificado, da [may-le-fe-cah'-do, dah], *a.* Mellifluous, mellificent. *-pp.* of MELIFICAR.

melificar [may-le-fe-car'], *va. & vn.* To make honey as bees.

melifluamente [may-le'-floo-ah-men-tay], *adv.* Mellifluently.

melifluidad [may-le-floo-e-dahd'], *f.* Mellifluence, suavity, delicacy.

melifluo, flua [may-lee'-floo-o, ah], *a.* Mellifluous, mellifluent, honey mouthed; flowing with honey.

meliloto [may-le-lo'-to], *m. (Bot.)* Bird's foot trefoil; melilot, a sweet clover.

meliloto [may-le-lo-to], **ta,** *a.* Silly, stupid.

melindre [may-leen'-dray], *m.* 1 Fritters made with honey and flour (bollo). 2. Prudery, affectation (mojigatería). 3. Fastidiousness.

melindrear [may-lin-dray-ar'], *vn.* To act the prude; indulge in affectation; to be squeamish.

melindrero, ra [may-lin-dray'-ro, rah]. *V.* MELINDROSO.

melindrillo [May-lin-dreel'-lyo], *m. (Prov.)* Ferret, narrow tape.

melindrizar [may-lin-dre-thar'], *vn. (coll.) V.* MELINDREAR.

melindroso, sa [may-lin-dro'-so, sah], *a.* Prudish, precise, finical, too nice, too formal, fastidious, dainty, very particular.

melisa [may-lee'-sah], *f.* Balm. **Agua de melisa,** balm-water distilled from the fresh leaves. *V.* TORONJIL.

mella [mel'-lyah], *f.* 1. A hollow or crack made in something by a blow which it has received. Notch, nick (rotura), in edged tools. 2. Gap (en dientes), empty space. **Hacer mella,** to make an impression upon the mind by reproach or advice.

mellado, da [mel-lyah-do, dah], *a. & pp.* Of MELLAR. 1. Notched, hacked. 2. Toothless, wanting teeth.

mellar [mel-lyar'], *va.* 1. To notch, to hack, to nick (hacer muecas), to cut in small hollows. 2. To deprive of luster and splendor. **Mellar la honra,** to wound one's character and honor.

mellica [mel-lyee'-cah], *f. (Prov.) V.* MELLIZA.

melliza [mel-lyee'-thah], *f.* Kind of sausage made of lean pork, almonds, pineapple kernels, and honey.

mellizo, za [mel-lyee'-tho, thah], *a. V.* GEMELO.

mellón [mel-lyone'], *m.* A handful of straw lighted as a torch.

melocotón [may-lo-co-tone'], *m.* 1. *(Bot.)* Common peach-tree (árbol). 2. Peach, fruit of that tree (fruto).

melocotonero [may-lo-co-to-nay'-ro], *m.* 1. Peach-tree. 2. Vender of peaches.

melodía [may-lo-dee'-ah], *f.* 1. Melody, harmony, melodiousness. 2. Melody, sweetness of sound.

melódico [may-lo'-de-co], *a.* Melodic.

melodiosamente [may-lo-de-o-sah-men-tay], *adv.* Melodiously, harmoniously.

melodioso, sa [may-lo-de-o'-so, sah], *a.* Melodious, musical, harmonious.

melodrama [may-lo-drah'-mah], *m.* Melodrama.

melodramático [may-lo-drah-mah-te-co], **ca,** *a.* Melodramatic.

meloe [may-lo'-ay], *m.* Meloe, oil-beetle, blister-beetle. *V.* also CANTÁRIDA.

melografía [may-lo-grah-fee'-ah], *f.* The art of writing music.

meloja [may-lo'-hah], *f.* Metheglin, honey boiled with water and fermented; mead.

melojo [may-lo'-ho], *m.* Plant like the white oak.

melomanía [may-lo-mah-nee'-ah], *f.* Melomania, a mania for music.

melómano, na [may-lo'-mah-no, nah], *a.* Music-mad, excessively fond of music.

melón [may-lone'], *m. (Bot.)* 1. Melon (fruit). *(Col.)* Nut (cabeza). **Melón de agua,** water melon.

melonar [may-lo-nar'], *m.* Field or bed of melons.

melonero, ra [may-lo-nay'-ro, rah], *m. & f.* One who raises or deals in melons.

melonífero, ra [may-lo-nee'-fay-ro, rah], *a.* 1. Melon-bearing. 2. Melon-shaped.

melosidad [may-lo-se-dahd'], *f.* 1. Sweetness arising from honey, lusciousness. 2. Meekness, gentleness of behavior.

meloso, sa [may-lo'-so, sah], *a.* 1. Having the taste or qualities of honey mellow (dulce). 2. Gentle, mild, pleasing.

melote [may-lo'-tay], *m.* 1. Molasses, treacle. 2. *(Prov.)* Conserve of honey.

melsa [mel'-sah], *f.* 1. *(Prov.) V.* BAZO. 2. Phlegm, lentor, slowness.

melusa [may-loo'-sah], *f. (Cuba)* Portion of honey, or of fruit-juice which sticks to clothing or to the fingers.

membrado, da [mem-brah'-do, dah], *a. (Her.)* Membered: applied to the beak and legs of a bird, when of a different tincture from the body.

membrana [mem-brah'-nah], *f.* 1. Membrane, a thin skin; a caul. 2. *(Anat.)* Membrane. **Membrana mucosa,** mucous membrane.

membranáceo, cea [mem-brah-nah'-thay-o, ah], *a.* Membranaceous, membrane-like.

membranoso, sa [mem-brah-no'-so, sah], *a.* Membranous, filmy.

membrete [mem-bray'-tay], *m.* 1. Short annotation or note written to remember a thing. 2. In letters or notes, a line in which the person's name is inserted to whom it is written. 3. A note or small bit of paper given as a memorandum to a person in office, to put him in mind of any one's pretentions. 4. A card of invitation.

membrilla [mem-breel'-lyah], *f.* (*Prov.*) The tender bud of a quince-tree.

membrillar [mem-bril-lyar'], *m.* Plantation of quince-trees.

membrillero, membrillo [mem-bril-yay'-ro, mem-breel'-lyo], *m.* 1. (*Bot.*) Quince-tree. 2. Quince, the fruit of the quince-tree.

membrudamente [mem-broo'-dah-men-tay], *adv.* Robustly, strongly.

membrudo, da [mem-broo'-do, dah], *a.* Strong, robust, corpulent; membered.

memo, ma [may'-mo, mah], *a.* Silly, foolish. **Hacerse memo**, to pretend not to understand.

memorable, memorando, da [may-mo-rah'-blay, may-mo-rahn'-do, dah], *a.* Memorable, commemorable, notable, filmous.

memorablemente [may-mo-rah'-blay-men-tay], *adv.* Memorably.

memorándum [may-mo-rahn'-doom], *m.* 1. Memorandum, notebook (libreta). 2. Memorandum, diplomatic note of informal character, often not signed, set down for reference or explanation.

memorar [may-mo-rar'], *va.* To remember, to record, to mention.

memoratísimo, ma [may-mo-rah-tee'-se-mo, mah], *a. sup.* Worthy of eternal memory.

memoria [may-mo'-re-ah], *f.* 1. Memory, reminiscence, recollection. 2. Fame, glory. 3. Memory, memorial, monumental record. 4. An anniversary or pious work which anyone founds to preserve his memory. 5. Memoir, an account of transactions familiarly written: commonly used in the plural (personales). 6. Bill, account. 7. Memorandum, a note to help the memory (memorándum). 8. Codicil. 9. (*Inform.*) Memory. **Memoria de acceso aleatorio**, random access memory. **Memoria de acceso aleatorio estable**, non volatile random access memory. **Memoria de sólo lectura**, read only memory. **Memoria de sólo lectura alterable eléctricamente**, electrically alterable read only memory. **Memoria de sólo lectura programable borrable electrónicamente**, electrically erasable programmable read only memory. **Memoria intermedia**, buffer. **Memoria intermedia de interrupción**, interrupt buffer. **Memoria primaria**, primary storage. **Memoria principal**, main memory. **Hacer memoria**, to remember, to put in mind. **Saber de memoria**, to know by heart. **Hablar de memoria**, to speak from memory. **Ser flaco de memoria**, to have a short memory, forgetful. **En memoria de**, in memory of. **Tener mala memoria**, to have a bad memory. **Traer algo a la memoria**, to recall something. **Memoria programable**, programmable memory. **Aprender de memoria**, to learn by heart. **Memoria del teclado**, key-board memory. *-pl.* 1. Compliments, expression of kindness and civility. 2. Memorandum-book. 3. Two or more rings put on the finger as a memorandum.

memorial [may-mo-re-ahl'], *m.* 1. Memorandum-book. 2. Memorial (petición), brief. 3. Bulletin (publicación).

memorialista [may-mo-re-ah-lees'-tah], *m.* An amanuensis; a person who writes petitions for others.

memorión [may-mo-re-on'], *m. aug.* A strong memory.

memorioso, sa [may-mo-re-o'-so, sah], *a.* Mindful, retentive (memoria).

memorizar [may-mo-re-thar'], *va.* To memorize.

mena [may'-nah], *f.* 1. Small sea-fish, kind of anchovy. 2. A mineral vein ore. 3. *V.* VITOLA. Ball gauge. 4. (*Naut.*) Size of cordage.

ménade [may'-nah-day], *f.* 1. Bacchante, priestess of Bacchus. 2. A woman beside herself, in a frenzy.

menador, ra [may-nah-dor', rah], *m. &f.* (*Prov.*) Winder, one who turns a wheel to wind silk.

menaje [may-nah'-hay], *m.* 1. Furniture, movables, house-stuff, furnishing (de una casa). 2. Furniture, fittings (escuela). 3. House keeping (economía doméstica). **Sección de menaje**, hardware and kitchen department (en almacenes).

menar [may-nar'], *va.* (*Prov. Murcia.*) To wind silk on a reel or spinning-jenny.

mención [men-the-on'], *f.* Mention, oral or written recital of something. **Hacer mención de**, to mention.

mencionar [men-the-o-nar'], *va.* To mention, to name. **Dejar de mencionar**, to fail to mention.

mendicación [men-de-cah-the-on'], *f. V.* MENDIGUEZ.

mendicante [men-de-cahn'-tay], *a.* Mendicant, begging. *m.* Mendicant, one of a begging fraternity.

mendicidad [men-de-the-dad'], *f.* Mendicity, mendicancy, beggary.

mendigante, ta [men-de-gahn'-tay, tah], *m. & f.* Mendicant, beggar.

mendigar [men-de-gar'], *va.* To ask charity, to live upon alms, to beg, to mendicate; to crave, to entreat.

mendigo [men-dee'-go], *m.* Beggar. *-a.* (*Mex.*) Yellow (cobarde).

mendiguez [men-de-gheth'], *f.* Beggary, indigence, mendicancy.

mendosamente [men-do'-sah-men-tay], *adv.* Falsely, erroneously, equivocally.

mendoso, sa [men-do'-so, sah], *a.* False, mendacious.

mendrugo [men-droo'-go], *m.* Crust (pan).

mendruguillo [men-droo-geel'-lyo], *m. dim.* A small bit of bread.

meneador, ra [may-nay-ah-dor', rah], *m. & f.* Mover, manager, director.

menear [may-nay-ar'], *va.* 1. To move from place to place. 2. To manage, to direct. 3. To shake (cabeza); to wag (cola); to sway (caderas). **Sin menear el dedo**, without lifting a finger. 4. To get on with (asunto). *-vr.* 1. To be brisk and active, to stir about. 2. To wriggle, to waddle; to move from side to side; to shake (agitarse); to way (caderas).

meneo [may-nay'-o], *m.* 1. A wriggling or waddling motion of the body (movimiento). 2. Trade, business. **Dar un meneo a**, to jerk.

menester [may-nes-terr'], *m.* 1. Necessity, need, want. **Ser menester**, to be necessary, to be wanting. 2. Employment, business, occupation (trabajo), office; function (función). **Salir para un menester**, to go out on an errand. *-pl.* (*coll.*) 1. Natural or corporal necessities. 2. Implements, necessary tools of a workman.

menesteroso, sa [may-nes-tay-ro'-so, sah], *a.* Needy, necessitous.

menestra [may-nes'-trah], *f.* 1. Pottage made of different pulse and roots. 2. Vegetable soup.

menestral [may-nes-trahl'], *m.* Mechanic, handicraftsman, workman.

mengano, na [men-gah'-no, nah], *m. & f* Such a one; so and so (the second of two).

mengua [men'-goo-ah], *f.* 1. Decay (decadencia), decline. 2. Poverty (pobreza), indigence. 3. Disgrace arising from cowardly conduct (persona). 4. Discredit (descrédito).

menguadamente [men-goo-ah-dah-men-tay], *adv.* 1. Ignominiously. 2. Meanly (tacañería). 3. Foolishly (estúpidamente).

menguado [men-goo-ah'-do], *m.* 1. Coward, a silly, mean-spirited fellow. 2. An avaricious, miserable wretch. 3. Decrease, narrowing of stockings, etc.

menguado, da [men-goo-ah'-do, dah], *a.* 1. Diminished (disminuido), impaired, stunted. 2. Cowardly (cobarde), pusillanimous; foolish (tonto). **Hora menguada**, fatal moment. *-pp.* Of MENGUAR.

menguante [men-goo-ahn'-tay], *m.* 1. Ebb-tide, low-water, neap-tide. 2. Decline, decay. 3. Decrease of the moon. *-a.*

Decreasing (que disminuye); dwindling; decaying (decadente), waning (luna); ebb (marea).

menguar [men-goo-ar'], *va.* 1. To decay, to decline, to fall off. 2. To fail to be deficient. 3. To narrow stockings. *-vn.* To diminish (disminuir), to get less, to dwindle, to decrease; to go down (marea, número).

mengue [men'-gay], *m. (coll.)* To deuce, the devil.

menhir [men-neer'], *m.* Menhir, a great megalithic vertical stone.

menina [may-nee'-nah], *f.* Maid of honor.

meninge [may-neen'-hay], *f.* Meninges, membranes enveloping the brain and spinal cord.

meningitis [may-neen-hee'-tis], *f.* Meningitis, inflammation of the membranes of the brain.

menino [may-nee'-no], *m.* 1. Page of the queen and infants. 2. *(Prov.)* An affected, spruce little fellow.

menipea [may-ne-pay'-ah], *f.* Kind of satire in prose and verse.

menisco [may-nees'-co], *m.* 1. Meniscus (anatomía). 2. Glass concave on one side and convex on the other.

menjuí [men-hoo-ee'], *m.* V. BENJUÍ.

menjunje, menjurje [men-hoon'-hay, men-hoor'-hay], *m. (coll.)* Beverage composed of different ingredients, and of an unpleasant taste.

menologio [may-no-lo'-he-o], *m.* Menology, the martyrology of the Greeks divided into the months of the year.

menopausia [may-no-pah'-oo-se-ah], *f.* Menopause, cessation of menstruation, the change of life in women.

menor [may-nor'], *m. & f.* 1. Minor, one under age. 2. Minor premise, the second proposition in a syllogism. 3. Minor, minorite, a Franciscan friar or nun. **Los menores de edad,** those who are under age. *-pl.* 1. The third class in a grammar-school. 2. Minor orders.

menor [may-nor'], *a. comp.* 1. Less, smaller (en tamaño), minor. 2. Minor, in music. **Menor edad,** minority, under age. **Hermano menor,** younger brother. **Por menor,** by retail, in small parts; minutely.

menorete [may-no-ray'-tay], *a. dim. coll.* **Al menorete or por el menorete,** at least.

menoría [may-no-ree'-ah], *f.* Inferiority (inferioridad), subordination (subordinación).

menorista [may-no-rees'-tah], *m.* Student of grammar in the third class. *-m & f,* Retailer.

menorquín, na [may-nor-keen', nah], *a.* Native of or belonging to the island Minorca.

menorragia [may-nor-rah'-he-ah], *f. (Med.)* Menorrhagia, excessive menstrual flow.

menos [may'-nos], *adv.* 1. Less, in a lower degree. 2. Except, with the exception of. **A lo menos or por lo menos,** at least, however. **Mucho menos,** much less. **Poco más o menos.** A little more or less. **Venir a menos,** to decay, to grow worse; to become poor. **Ni más, ni menos,** neither more nor less, just equal. **Lo menos 10,** 10 at least. **Ir a menos,** to come down in the world. **Cada vez menos,** less and less. **Poco menos de una libra,** a little less than a pound. **Tener en menos,** to look down on. **Tanto menos,** so much the less. **Ha venido a menos,** he has come down in the world. **Hacer de menos a uno,** to be unfaithful to somebody. *-prep.* Except. **Todos menos él,** everybody except him. **Cualquier cosa menos eso,** anything but that. **Todo incluido menos el transporte,** everything included but the transport. **Cuatro menos uno son tres,** four minus one is three. **Son las cuatro menos diez,** it is ten to four.

menoscabador, ra [may-nos-cah-bah-dor', rah], *m. & f.* Detracter, lessener. **menoscabar** [may-nos-cah-bar'], *va.* 1 To impair, to lessen (disminuir), to make worse. 2. To reduce, to deteriorate.

menoscabo [may-nos-cah'-bo], *m.* Diminution, deterioration, loss.

menoscuenta [may-nos-coo-en'-tah], *f.* Discount.

menospreciable [may-nos-pray-the-ah-blay], *a.* Despicable, contemptible.

menospreciablemente [may-nos-pray-the-ah-blay], *adv.* Comtemptuously.

menospreciador, ra [may-nos-pray-the-ah-dor', rah], *m. & f.* Contemner, despiser.

menospreciar [may-nos-pray-the-ar'], *va.* To underrate (subestimar), to undervalue, to despise (despreciar), to contemn, to neglect, to overlook, to make light of.

menosprecio [may-nos-pray'-the-o], *m.* Contempt, scorn (desdén); the act of undervaluing a thing, neglect, contumely.

mensaje [men-sah'-hay], *m.* 1. Message, despatch, errand. 2. Petition or congratulation which the Cortes addressed to the king. 3. An official communication between the legislative and the executive power. *(Acad.)* **Mensaje de buenos augurios,** goodwill message. **Mensaje de la corona,** King's speech.

mensajero, ra [men-sah-hay'-ro, rah], *m. & f.* 1. Messenger. 2. The secretary bird. 3. *(Naut.)* Bull's eye traveler. A wooden thimble. **Mensajero de buenas noticias,** bearer of good news.

ménsola [men'-so-lah], *f. (Arch.)* V. MENSULA.

menstruación [mens-troo-ah-the-on'], *f.* Menstruation.

menstrual [mens-troo-ahl'], *a.* Menstrual.

menstrualmente [mens-troo-ahl'-men-tay], *adv.* Monthly, menstrually.

menstruante [mens-troo-ahn'-tay], *a.* Menstruating.

menstruar [mens-troo-ar'], *vn.* To menstruate.

menstruo [mens'-troo-o], *m.* 1. Menses (producto), catamenia, courses. 2. *(Chem.)* Menstruous, any liquor used as a solvent. 3. Menstruation. *-a.* Menstruous, monthly, menstrual.

mensual [men-soo-ahl'], *a.* Monthly, menstrual.

mensualidad [men-soo-ah-le-dahd'], *f.* A month's pay; monthly salary.

mensualmente [men-soo-ahl-men-tay], *adv.* Monthly.

ménsula [men'-soo-lah], *f. (Arch.)* Cantilever, bracket.

mensura [men-soo'-rah], *f.* Measure.

mensurabilidad [men-soo-rah-be-le-dahd'], *f.* Mensurability.

mensurable [men-soo-rah'-blay], *a.* Mensurable.

mensurador, ra [men-soo-rah-dor', rah], *m. & f.* Measurer, meter.

mensural [men-soo-rahl'], *a.* Applied to something used to measure.

mensurar [men-soo-rar'], *va.* V. MEDIR and JUZGAR.

menta [men'-tah], *f. (Bot.)* Mint.

mentado, da [men-tah'-do, dah], *a.* Famous, celebrated, renowned.-*pp.* of MENTAR.

mental [men-tahl'], *a.* Mental, intellectual (capacidad, trabajo), ideal.

mentalidad [men-tah-le-dahd'], *f.* Mentality, mind.

mentalizar [men-tah-le-thar'], *va.* To prepare, condition; to sensitize, to make aware; to persuade (convencer). *-vr.* To prepare oneself (mentalmente).

mentalmente [men-tahl'-men-tay], *adv.* Mentally, intellectually, ideally.

mentar [men-tar'], *va.* To mention, to record.

mente [men'-tay], *f.* 1. Mind, understanding; intellectual power. 2. Sense, meaning; will, disposition. **Mente consciente,** concious mind. **No tengo mente,** it is not in my mind.

mentecatería [men-tay-cah-tay-ree'-ah], *f.* Folly, absurdity, nonsense.

mentecato, to [men-tay-cah'-to, tah], *a.* Silly, foolish, stupid, crack-brained.-*a.* Fool.

mentecatón [men-tay-cah-tone', nah], *a. aug.* Very silly.

mentidero [men-te-day'-ro], *m.* Talking corners, where idlers meet to tattle.

mentir [men-teer'], *va.* 1. To lie, to utter falsehoods. 2. To disappoint, to frustrate, to deceive (engañar), to feign. 3. To gainsay, to retract; to equivocate, to falsify.

mentira [men-tee'-rah], *f.* 1. Lie, falsehood, mendacity. 2. Error, mistake in writing. 3. White mark (señal). 4. **Sacar**

mentiras, *(And. Cono Sur)* to crack one's knuckles. 5. **De mentira**, *(LAm.)* Pretend, sham (artificial). **Una mentira como una casa**, a whopping great lie. **Aunque parezca mentira**, however incredible it seems.

mentirilla, ita [men-te-reel'-lyah, ee, tah], *f. dim.* Falsehood told in jest. **De mentirillas**, in jest.

mentirón [men-te-rone'], *m. aug.* Great lie.

mentirosamente [men-te-ro-sah-men-tay], *adv.* Falsely, deceitfully, lyingly.

mentirosito, ta [men-te-ro-see'-to, tah], *a. dim.* A little false, deceitful.

mentiroso, sa [men-te-ro'-so, sah], *a.* 1. Lying (que miente), mendacious. 2. Erroneous, equivocal, incorrect. *-m. y f.* Liar.

mentís [men-tees'], *m.* You lie, or thou liest. Term of insult.

mentol [men-tole'], *m.* Menthol.

mentolado, da [men-to-lah'-do, dah], *a.* Mentholated.

mentón [men-tone'], *m.* Chin.

mentor [men-tor'], *m.* Mentor, counsellor, guide.

menú [may-noo'], *m.* Menu (lista), bill of fare.

menudear [may-noo-day-ar'], *va.* To repeat (repetir), to detail minutely (narración).*-vn.* 1. To relate or describe little things (al explicarse). *(Com.)* To sell by retail. 2. *(Cono Sur, Mex.)* To abound (abundar).

menudencia [may-noo-den'-the-ah], *f.* Trifle (bagatela), littleness; minuteness (minuciosidad), minute, accuracy.

menudeo [may-noo-day'-o], *m.* Act of repeating minutely; retail.

menudero, ra [may-noo-day'-ro, rah], *m. & f.* Dealer in tripes, giblets, sausages, etc.

menudico, ica, ito, ita [may-noo-dee'-co, cah], *a.* Somewhat small.

menudillo [may-noo-deel'-lyo], *m.* Extremities of animals. **Menudillos**, giblets of fowls.

menudo, da [may-noo'-do, dah], *a.* 1. Small (pequeño), slender of body; minute. 2. Of no moment or value, worthless. 3. Common, vulgar. 4. Examining minutely into things. 5. Small money, change. 6. Exact, scrupulous (persona). **Hombre menudo**, a mean, miserable fellow. **A menudo**, repeatedly, frequently, continually, often.

menudo [may-noo'-do], *m.* 1. Intestines, viscera. 2. Tithe of fruits.

menura, or menura-lira [may-noo'-rah-lee'-rah], *f.* Lyre-bird.

meñique [may-nyee'-kay], *a.* Very small, tiny, diminute. **Dedo meñique**, little finger. *-m.* Little finger (dedo auricular).

meollar [may-ol-lyar'], *m. (Naut.)* Thin line of spun-yarn made of oakum or untwisted ropes.

meollo [may-ol-lyo], *m.* 1. Marrow. 2. Judgment, understanding. 3. Soft part of bread, crumb (pan). 4. The substance or essential part of something (asunto).

meón, na [may-on', nah], *a. (coll.)* Continually making water.

meona [may-o'-nah], *f. (coll.)* New-born female infant, in distinction from the male.

mequetrefe [may-kay-tray'-fay], *m.* Insignificant, noisy fellow, jackanapes, coxcomb.

meramente [may-rah-men'-tay], *adv.* Merely, solely, nakedly.

merar [may-rar'], *va.* To mix liquors: generally applied to the mixture of wine and water.

merca [merr'-cah], *f. (coll.)* A purchase. V. COMPRA.

mercachifle [mer-cah-chee'-flay], *m.* 1. Peddler, hawker (vendedor ambulante). 2. *(Fig.)* Money grubber.

mercadantesco, ca [mer-cah-dan-tes'-co, cah], *a.* Mercantile.

mercadear [mer-cah-day-ar'], *vn.* To trade, to traffic. *-va.* To market (vender); to haggle over (regatear).

mercader [mer-cah-der'], *m.* Dealer, trader, shop-keeper.

mercadera [mer-cah-day'-rah], *f.* Shop keeper's wife, tradeswoman.

mercadería [mer-cah-day-ree'-ah], *f.* 1. Commodity, merchandise. Trace, the business of a trader. *-pl.* Goods.

mercadillo [mer-cah-deel'-lo], *m.* Bazaar (caridad).

mercado [mer-cah'-do], *m.* 1. Market, marketing. 2. Market, market place, mart. **Mercado negro**, black market. **Mercado**

mundial, world market. **Mercado de valores**, stock market. **Mercado de vendedores**, seller's market.

mercadotecnia [mer-cah-do-tec'-ne-ah], *f.* Marketing, marketing techniques.

mercaduría [mer-cah-doo-ree'-ah], *f.* Merchandise, trade.

mercancía [mer-can-thee'-ah], *f.* 1. Trade, traffic. 2. Merchandise, salable goods.

mercante [mer-cahn'-tay], *m. & a.* Dealer, trader; mercantile, commercial. **Buque mercante**, a trading vessel.

mercantil [mer-can-teel'], *a.* Commercial, mercantile, merchant-like.

mercantilizar [mer-can-te-le-thar'], *va.* To commercialize.

mercantilmente [mer-can-teel'-men-tay], *adv.* Merchantly, in a commercial or mercantile manner.

mercar [mer-car'], *va. V.* COMPRAR.

merced [mer-thed'], *f.* 1. Gift, favor (favor), grace, mercy. 2. Wages, pay for services especially to day-laborers. 3. Will, pleasure. 4. Appellation of civility, with which untitled persons are addressed. **Vuestra or vuesa merced**, your honor, your worship, sir. 5. A religious military order, whose chief object is to redeem captives. **Estar a merced**, to live at another's expense. **Hágame usted la merced**, do me the favor.

mercenario [mer-thay-nah'-re-o], *m.* 1. Day-laborer. 2. Mercenary, hireling. 3. A friar of the religious order *la Merced.*

mercenario, ria [mer-thay-nah'-re-o, ah], *a.* Mercenary, hired, hireling.

mercería [mer-thay-ree'-ah], *f.* 1. Trade of a haberdasher (géneros), who deals in small wares, mercery. 2. *(Amer.)* Fine hardware store (tienda). 3. *(Cono Sur)* Ironmonger's (ferretería).

mercerizado, da [mer-thay-re-thah'-do, dah], *a.* Mercerized.

mercero, a [mer-thay'ro], *m & f.* 1. Haberdasher. 2. The keeper of a fine hardware store.

mercurial [mer-coo-re-ahl'], *m. & a.* 1. *(Bot.)* All good, mercury. 2. Mercurial.

mercúrico [mer-coo'-re-co], *a.* Mercuric, of the higher combining equivalence of mercury.

mercurio [mer-coo'-re-o], *m.* 1. Mercury, quicksilver. 2. Planet Mercury.

mercurioso, sa [mer-coo-re-o'-so, sah], *a.* Mercurous, relative to mercury, especially in its lower valence.

mercurocromo [mer-coo-ro-cro'-mo], *m. (Med.)* Mercurochrome.

merchante [mer-chahn'-tay], *m.* Merchant, who buys and sells goods without keeping an open shop. *-a.* Merchant. V. MERCANTE.

merdellón, na [mer-del-lyone', nah], *a. (Low.)* Slovenly, unclean, dirty.

merdoso, sa [mer-do'-so, sah], *a.* Nasty, filthy.

merecedor, ra [may-ray-thay-dor', rah], *m. & f.* One who deserves reward or punishment. **Merecedor de confianza**, trustworthy.

merecer [may-ray-therr'], *vn.* 1. To deserve, to merit. 2. V. LOGRAR. 3. To owe, to be indebted for. **Merecer mucho**, to be very deserving.*-va.* 1. To do anything deserving reward or censure. **Merecer el trabajo**, to be worth the while. **Te lo tienes merecido**, it serves you right. 2. *(And.)* To catch (atrapar); to snatch (robar).

merecidamente [may-ray-the-dah-men-tay], *adv.* Worthily, meritoriously, condignly.

merecido, da [may-ray-thee'-do, dah], *a.* Meritorious, condign.*-pp.* of MERECER.

merecido [may-ray-thee'-do], *m.* Deserts, due, condign punishment. **Llevar su merecido**, to get one's deserts.

merecimiento [may-ray-the-me-en'-to], *m.* Condignity, merit (cualidad), deserts (lo merecido).

merendar [may-ren-dar'], *vn.* 1. To take a collation between dinner and supper. 2. *(Prov.)* To eat the principal meal at noon. *-va.* 1. To pry into another's writings or actions. 2. To anticipate, to be in advance of another. **Merendar lo que**

escribe otro, to peep at somebody else´s cards. -*vr.*
Merendarse algo, to wangle something. *(Yo meriendo, yo meriende,* from *Merendar. V.* ACERTAR.)
merendero, ra [may-ren-day´-ro, rah], *a.* Picking up the seeds in cornfields (cuervos). -*m.* Open-air café.
merendilla [may-ren-deel´-lyah], *f. dim.* of MERIENDA. A light lunch.
merendona [may-ren-do´-nah], *f. aug.* A plentiful or splendid collation.
merengue [may-ren´-gay], *m.* 1. Kiss sugar-plum, a confection of sugar and white of eggs; meringue. 2. *(And. Carib. Cono Sur)* Sickly person (enclenque). 3. *(Cono Sur)* Row (alboroto).
meretricio, cia [may-ray-tree´-the-o, ah], *a.* Meretricious, harlot, lustful.
meretricio [may-ray-tree´-the-o], *m.* Carnal sin.
meretriz [may-ray-treeth´], *f. V.* RAMERA.
merey [may-ray´-e], *f. (Bot.)* Cashew-tree.
mergánsar [mer-gahn´-sar], *m. (Orn.)* Goosander, merganser.
mergo [merr´-go], *m. (Orn.)* Diver.
merián [may-re-ahn´], *com. (Zool.)* Merianopossum of South America, a marsupial without a pouch.
meridiana [may-re-de-ah´-nah], *f.* Meridional line. **A la meridiana**, at midday, noon.
meridiano [may-re-de-ah´-no], *m.* Meridian, a large circle of the celestial sphere. -*a.* Meridional, noon.
meridional [may-re-de-o-nahl´], *a.* Southern, southerly, meridional.
merienda [may-re-en´-dah], *f.* 1. Luncheon, collation between dinner and supper, afternoon snack. 2. *(Prov.)* Principal meal eaten at noon. 3. *(coll.)* Hump-back. **Hacer merienda de negros**, free-for-all, bedlam. **Ir de merienda**, to go for a picnic.
merino [may-ree´-no], *m.* 1. Shepherd of merino sheep. 2. Merino (carnero, lana, tela). -*a.* 1. Moving from pasture to pasture (ovejas). 2. Applied to thick, curled hair.
méritamente [may´-re-tah-men-tay], *adv. V.* MERECIDAMENTE.
mérito [may´-re-to], *m.* Merit (valor), worth, excellence (excelencia), virtue. **Hacer mérito de**, to mention. **Restar méritos de**, to detract from.
meritoriamente [may-re-to´-re-ah-men-tay], *adv.* Meritoriously.
meritorio, ria [may-re-to´-re-o, ah], *a.* 1. Meritorious. 2. Employed in an office, without salary; emeritus.
merla [merr´-lah], *f. (Orn.)* Blackbird, merle.
merlán [merr-lahn´], *m.* The European whiting, a small fish of the cod family.
merlín [mer-leen´], *m. (Naut.)* Marline, a loosely twisted hempen line.
Merlín, *m.* Merlin, name of a famous enchanter. **Saber mas que Merlín**, to be very shrewd or keen.
merlo [merr´-lo], *m. (Zool.)* Black wrasse, a sea-fish very frequent in the Mediterranean.
merlón [mer-lone´], *m. (Mil.)* Merlon the solid part of a parapet between the embrasures.
merluza [mer-loo´-thah], *f.* Hake, a fish of the cod family.
merma [merr´-mah], *f.* Waste, leakage, soakage, decrease (disminución).
mermar [mer-mar´], *vn. vr.* To waste, to diminish, to dwindle, to lessen. -*va.* To reduce, to lessen; to cut down (pago, raciones).
mermelada [mer-may-lah´-dah], *f.* Marmalade, a conserve.
mero [may´-ro], *m.* Polluck, a Mediterranean foodfish of delicate flavor.
mero, ra [may´-ro, rah], *a.* 1. Mere, pure, simple, naked. 2. *(Mex.)* Precise, exact (preciso). 3. *(Mex.)* Right (justo). 4. *(Mex.)* **El mero centro**, the very center.
merodeador [may-ro-day-ah-dor´], *m.* Marauder, pillager.
merodear [may-ro-day-ar´], *vn.* To pillage, to maraud.
merodeo [may-ro-day´-o], *m.* The act of pillaging or marauding.

merodista [may-ro-dees´-tah], *m.* Pillager, marauder.
mes [mess], *m.* 1. Month. **Mes lunar**, lunar month. **El mes que viene**, next month. 2. Catamenia, menses, courses. **Al mes**, in a month's time, by the month, at the expiration of a month. **Dentro de un mes**, in a months' time. **El mes corriente**, the current month. **Pagar por meses**, to pay by the month.
mesa [may´-sah], *f.* 1. Table, an article of furniture. 2. Table, the fare or viands put on a table. 3. Table, a flat surface on the top of hills or mountains. 4. Landing place of a staircase. 3. In printing offices, a case for types. 4. The table of accounts of the rents of cathedral churches, prelates, or dignitaries in Spain. 7. Set or rubber, anyone of the games played at a truck-table. 8. Spanish truck-table or the hire of it. 9. The flat of a sword, of a shoe-maker's awl, etc. l0. Communion table. **Levantar la mesa**, to take away the cloth. **Sentarse a mesa puesta**, to live at other people's expense. **Mesa redonda**, (a) round table conference. (b) Table d'hote (en restaurantes). **Mesa de billar**, billiard table. **Bendecir la mesa**, to say grace. **Vino de mesa**, table wine.
mesada [may-sah´-dah], *f.* Monthly pay, wages, or allowance; stipend.
mesana [may-sah´-nah], *f. (Naut.)* Mizzenmast or sail.
mesar [may-sar´], *va.* To pluck off the hair with the hands.
meseguero [may-say-gay-ro], *m.* 1. Keeper of the fruits of the harvest. 2 *(Prov.)* The guard of the vineyard. -*a.* Relating to the harvest fruits.
mesentérico, ca [may-sen-tay´-re-co, cah], *a.* Mesenteric, relating to the mesentery.
mesenterio [may-sen-tay´-reo], *m.* Mesentery, a fold of the peritoneum enveloping the small intestine and connecting it to the abdominal wall posteriorly.
meseraica [may-say-rah´-e-cah], *a.* Mesenteric (vein). The portal vein with its branches.
meseta [may-say´-tah], *f* 1. Landing place of a staircase. 2. Plateau, tableland, meseta (llanura).
Mesías [may-see´-as], *m.* Messiah, Jesus Christ.
mesilla [may-seel´-lyah], *f.* 1. *(dim.)* Small table; sideboard. 2. Screw. 3. Board-wages. 4. Censure by way of a jest. **Mesilla de chimenea**, mantelpiece. **Mesilla de noche**, bedside table.
mesita [may-see´-tah], *f. dim.* 1. A small table. 2. **Mesita de un pie**, stand.
mesmedad [mes-may-dahd´], *f.* Nature, actuality, used only in the pleonastic phrase: **Por su misma mesmedad**, by the very fact.
mesmerismo [mes-may-rees´-mo], *m.* Mesmerism, hypnotism.
mesocracia [may-so-crah´-the-ah], *f.* Mesocracy, government by the middle class.
mesón [may-sone´], *m.* 1. Inn, hostelry. 2. *(Phy. & Chem.)* Meson. 3. *(CAm.)* Lodging house.
mesonaje [may-so-nah´-hay], *m.* Street or place which contains numerous inns and public-houses.
mesoncillo [may-son-theel´-lyo], *m. dim.* A little inn.
mesonero, ra [may-so-nay´-ro, rah], *m. & f.* Inn-keeper, publican, landlord of an inn (dueño), host, hostess. -*a.* Waiting, serving in an inn.
mesonista [may-so-nees´-tah], *com.* Waiter in an inn or public-house.
mesopotámico, ca [may-so-po-tah´-me-co, cah], *a.* Mesopotamian, relating to Mesopotamia.
mesta [mes´-tah], *f.* 1. The proprietors of cattle and sheep, considered as a body. 2. Annual meeting of shepherds and owners of flocks, which bears the title of **El honrado concejo de la mesta**, the honorable board of **Mesta**.
mesteño, ña [mes-tay´-nyo, yah], *a.* 1. Belonging to the *mesta* or graziers. 2. *V.* MOSTRENCO.
mestizaje [mes-te-tha-hay], *m.* 1. Cross-breeding (acto). 2. Half-castes (personas).
mestizar [mees-te-thar´], *va.* To cross breeds or races of animals. *(Acad.)*

mestizo

mestizo, za [mes-tee'-tho, thah], *a.* 1. Of a mongrel breed, hybrid, hybridous. 2. *(Amer.)* Mestee or mustee, the offspring of a white man and an Indian woman, or vice versa.

mesto [mes'-to], *m. (Bot.)* 1. Large, prickly oak. 2 Turkey oak. *V.* REBOLLO.

mestura [mes-too'-rah], *f. (Prov.)* Mashlin, mixed wheat and rye.

mesura [may-soo'-rah], *f.* 1. A grave deportment, a serious countenance. 2. Civility, politeness (cortesía). 3. Moderation (moderación); measure.

mesuradamente [may-soo-rah'-dah-men-tay], *adv.* Gently, prudently, measurably.

mesurado, da [may-soo-rah'-do, dah], *a.* Moderate (moderado), circumspect, modest; regular, temperate, regulated. *-pp.* of ·MESURAR.

mesurar [may-soo-rar'], *va.* To assume a serious countenance, to act with solemn reserve. *-vr.* To behave with modesty and prudence.

meta [may'-tah], *f.* 1. Boundary, limit. 2. *(Dep.)* Goal; winning post (de carrera), finishing line. -m. Goal-keeper.

metábola [may-tah'-bo-lah], *f.* 1. *(Med.)* Transformation of one disease into another. 2. Metabolism, the sum of the assimilative and destructive processes in the body. 3. *(Rhet.)* Pleonasm, bringing together several synonymous expressions to set forth a single idea.

metabolismo [may-tah-bo-lees'-mo], *m.* Metabolism.

metacarpiano, na [may-tah-car-pe-ah'-no, nah], *a.* Metacarpal, relating to the Metacarpus.

metacarpo [may-tah-car'-po], *m. (Anat.)* Metacarpus, the part of the hand between the wrist and the fingers.

metacronismo [may-tah-cro-nees'-mo], *m.* Metachronism, anachronism.

metafísica [may-tah-fee'-se-cah], *f.* 1. Metaphysic, metaphysics, ontology. 2. The art of subtilizing in any matter.

metafísicamente [may-tah-fe'-se-cah-men-tay], *adv.* Metaphysically.

metafísico, ca [may-tah-fee'-se-co, cah], *a.* Metaphysical, abstract, obscure.

metafísico [may-tah-fee'-se-co], *m.* Metaphysician, ontologist.

metáfora [may-tah'-fo-rah], *f.* Metaphor, a rhetorical figure.

metafóricamente [may-tah-fo'-re-cah-men-tay], *adv.* Metaphorically, figuratively.

metafórico, ca [may-tah-fo'-re-co, cah], *a.* Metaphorical.

metaforizar [may-tah-fo-re-thar'], *va.* To use metaphors.

metal [may-tahl'], *m.* 1. Metal. 2. Brass, latten. 3. The sound or tone (tono-color) of the voice. 4. Quality, nature or condition of a thing.

metalario, metálico, metalista [may-tah-lah'-re-o, may-tah'-le-co, may-tah-lees'-tah], *m.* Workman or dealer in metal, metallist, metallurgist.

metalescente [may-tah-les-then'-tay], *a.* Metallic in lustre.

metálica [may-tah'-le-cah], *f. V.* METALURGIA.

metálico, ca [may-tah'-le-co, cah], *a.* 1. Metallic. 2. Medallic, pertaining to medals.-*m.* Bullion. **Metálico en caja**, *(Com.)* cash on hand.

metalífero, ra [may-tah-lee'-fay-ro, rah], *a. (Poet.)* Metalliferous.

metalistería [may-tah-lis-tay-ree'-ah], *f.* Metal-working.

metalizado [may-tah-te-tha'-do], *a.* 1. Metallic (pintura). 2. *(Fig.)* Mercenary, dedicated to making money.

metalizar [may-tah-le-thar'], *va.* To make a body acquire metallic properties.-*vr.* 1. To be converted into or impregnated with metal. 2. *(Met.)* To be controlled by love of money.

metalografía [may-tah-lo-grah-fee'-ah], *f.* Metallography.

metaloide [may-tah-lo'-e-day], *m.* Metalloid, a simple body resembling the metals in some of its properties, such as sulphur carbon, phosphorus.

metalurgia [may-tah-loor'-he-ah], *f.* Metallurgy.

metalúrgico, ca [may-tah-loor'-he-co, cah], *a.* Relating to metallurgy.

metalúrgico [may-tah-loor'-he-co], *m.* Metallurgist.

metalla [may-tahl'-lyah], *f.* Small piece of gold leaf used to cover parts imperfectly gilt.

metamorfosear [may-tah-mor-fo-say-ar'], *va.* To metamorphose, to transform.

metamórfico, ca [may-tah-mor'-fe-co, cah], *a. (Geol.)* Metamorphic, igneous (rocas).

metamorfosis, metamorfosis [may-tah-mor-fo'-sis], *f.* Metamorphosis, transformation.

metaplasmo [may-tah-plahs'-mo], *m. (Gram.)* The changing, taking away, or adding to the letters of a word; metaplasm.

metástasis [may-tahs'-tah-sis], *f. (Med.)* Metastasis, translation or removal of a disease from one place to another.

metasticizar [may-tahs-te-the-thar'], *vn.* To metastasize.

metatarsiano, na [may-tah-tar-se-ah'-no, nah], *a. (Anat.)* Metatarsal.

metatarso [may-tah-tar'-so], *m. (Anat.)* Metatarsus, the part of the foot or limb between the ankle and the toes; it consists of five bones in man.

metate [may-tah'-tay], *m. (Mex.)* A curved stone in the shape of an inclined plane resting on three feet, used for grinding maize for *tortillas*, or cocoa for chocolate.

metátesis [may-tah-tay'-sis], *f. (Rhet.)* Metathesis, a transposition.

metedor, ra [may-tay-dor', rah], *m. & f.* 1. He who puts one thing into another. 2. Smuggler. 3. Clout of now-born children.

metedura [may-tay-doo'-rah], *f.* 1. Putting, placing (acto de meter). 2. **Metedura de pata**, bloomer.

meteduría [may-tay-doo-ree'-ah], *f.* Smuggling.

metemuertos [may-tay-moo-err'-tose], *m.* 1. Attendant in a play-house. 2. Busybody, a vain, meddling person.

meteórico, ca [may-tay-o'-re-co, cah], *a.* Meteoric, meteorous.

meteorismo [may-tay-o-rees'-mo], *m. (Med.)* Meteorism, distension of the abdomen by gases.

meteorita [may-tay-o-ree'-tah], *f.* Meteorite.

meteorizar [may-tay-o-re-thar'], *va.* To cause meteorism or tympanites.-*vr.* To suffer from this disorder.

meteoro [may-tay-o'-ro], *m.* An atmospheric phenomenon.

meteorología [may-tay-o-ro-lo-hee'-ah], *f.* Meteorology.

meteorológico, ca [may-tay-o-ro-lo'-he-co, cah], *a.* Meteorological. **Informe or boletín meteorológico**, weather report.

meteorologista [may-tay-o-ro-lo-hees'-tah], *m.* Meteorologist.

meter [may-terr'], *va.* 1. To place or to put in, to include one thing within another, to get on. 2. To smuggle goods into a country (géneros). 3. To make, to cause (causar), to occasion, to urge, to move. 4. To engage, to prevail upon, to induce. 5. To stake (dinero), to put to hazard. 6. To cram down victuals. 7. To put things close together, to cram or heap them together. 8. To impose upon, to deceive. 9. To compress, to straighten, to reduce. 10. *(coll.)* To eat. *V.* COMER. 11. To score (tanto). **Meter bulla**, to make a noise. **Meter cizaña**, to sow discord, to breed disturbances. **Meter prisa**, to urge, to hasten. **A todo meter**, full-speed. **Meter un susto a uno**, to put the wind up somebody. **Meter a uno a trabajar**, to put somebody to work. **Le metieron 5 años de cárcel**, they put him away for 5 years. *-vr.* 1. To meddle, to intermeddle, to interfere. 2. To be on terms of familiarity with a person. 3. To choose a profession or trade. 4. To be led astray, to plunge into vice. 5. To empty into the sea (ríos). 6. To attack sword in hand. 7. To go into, to get into (introducirse). 8. To extend, to project. 9. To provoke somebody (provocar). **Meterse con alguno**, to pick a quarrel. **Meterse donde no le llaman**, to thrust oneself where he is not called. **Meterse en vidas ajenas**, to dive into other people's affairs. **Meterse en todo**, to be jack of all trades. **Meterse soldado**, to become a soldier. **Meterse en un agujero**, to get into a hole. **Se metió en la cama**, she got into bed. **Meterse en peligro**, to get into danger. **El río se mete en el mar**, the river flows into the sea. **Meterse a escritor**, to become a writer.

metesillas [may-tay-seel'-lyas], *m. V.* METEMUERTOS.
meticulosamente [may-te-coo-lo'-sah-men-tay], *adv.* Meticulously, scrupulously.
meticuloso, sa [may-te-coo-lo'-so, sah], *a.* Meticulous, scrupulous, finicky.
metido, da [may-tee'-do, dah], *a. & pp.* of METER. 1. Placed or put in or into; engaged: deceived. **Estar muy metido en algún negocio,** to be deeply engaged in an affair. 2. *(LAm.)* Meddling, meddlesome (entrometido). 3. *(Carib. Cono Sur)* Half tight (bebido).
metileno [may-te-lay'-no], *m. (Chem.)* Methylene, an organic radical known only in combination.
metilo [may-tee'-lo], *m. (Chem.)* Methyl.
metimiento [may-te-me-en'-to], *m.* Inclusion, the act and effect of putting one thing into another.
metódicamente [may-to'-de-cah-men-tay], *adv.* Methodically, orderly.
metódico, ca [may-to'-de-co, cah], *a.* Methodical, formal.
metodismo [may-to-dees'-mo], *m.* 1. Systematic method. 2. Methodism, the system and practices of the Methodist church, developed by John Wesley and his followers.
metodista [may-to-dees'-tah], *n. com.* 1. Methodist, a religious sectary, follower of John Wesley. 2. *a. V.* METÓDICO.
método [may'-to-do], *m.* Method, manner, mode, custom, order, form.
metonimia [may-to-nee'-me-ah], *f.* Metonymy, a rhetorical figure.
metonímico, ca [may-to-nee'-me-co, cah], *a.* Metonymical, relating to metonymy.
metopa [may-to'-pah], *f. (Arch.)* Metope, the space between the triglyphs in the Doric order.
metraje [may-trah'-hay], *m.* Length in meters. **Película de largo metraje,** full length film.
metralla [may-trahl'-lyah], *f.* Grape-shot, case-shot, canister-shot.
metrallar [may-trahl-lyar'], *va.* To canister, to attack with grape-shot.
metralleta [may-trahl-lyay'-tah], *f.* Submachine gun, tommy gun.
metreta [may-tray'-tah], *f.* A Greek and Roman measure of liquids.
métrica [may'-tre-cah], *f.* Metrical art, poetry.
métricamente [may'-tre-cah-men-tay], *adv.* Metrically.
métrico, ca [may'-tre-co, cah], *a.* Metrical, composed in verse.
metrificar [may-tre-fe-car'], *va. V.* VERSIFICAR.
metritis [may-tree'-tis], *f. (Med.)* Metritis, inflammation of the womb.
metro [may'-tro], *m.* 1. Meter, unit of measure in the decimal system (medida). 2. Metre, verse. 3. Subway train. **Metro cúbico,** cubic meter. **Metro cuadrado,** square meter.
metrología [may-tro-lo-hee'-ah], *f.* A treatise on weights and measures.
metrónomo [may-tro'-no-mo], *m.* Metronome.
metrópoli [may-tro'-po-le], *f.* 1. Metropolis, the chief city of a country. 2. Archiepiscopal church.
metropolitano [may-tro-po-le-tah'-no], *m.* 1. Metropolitan, archbishop. 3. Subway train.
México [may'-he-co], Mexico.
mezcal [meth-cahl]', *m. (Mex.)* 1. A species of maguey, or American agave. 2. An intoxicating liquor prepared from this plant.
mezcla [meth'-clah], *f.* 1. Mixture (sustancia), commixture, compound, composition, medley. 2. Mortar. 3. Mixed cloth.
mezcladamente [mayth-clah'-dah-men-tay], *adv.* In a mixed or promiscuous manner.
mezcladillos [meth-clah-deel'-lyos], *m. pl.* A kind of paste made by confectioners.
mezclador, ra [mezh-clah-dor', rah], *m. & f.* One who mixes, mingler, compounder.
mezclar [meth-clar'], *va.* 1. To mix, to mingle, to unite, to commix, to blend (armonizar), to merge (combinar). 2. To

spread false reports, to sow discord, to excite disturbances. **Mezclar a la iglesia en el debate,** to drag the Church into the debate. *-vr.* 1. To mix, to be united into a mass. 2. To marry a person of inferior rank. 3. To introduce oneself into anything. **Mezclarse con cierta gente,** to mix with certain people.
mezclilla [meth-clee'-lyah], *f.* Denim, coarse cotton drill.
mezcolanza [meth-co-lahn'-thah], *f. (coll.)* Bad mixture of colors, mishmash.
mezquinamente [meth-ke'-nah-men-tay], *adv.* Miserably, avariciously.
mezquindad [meth-keen-dahd'], *f.* 1. Penury, poverty, indigence. 2. Avarice, covetousness, paltriness, currishness, meanness (cualidad).
mezquino, na [meth-kee'-no, nah], *a.* 1. Poor, indigent, penurious; diminutive. 2. Avaricious, covetous, mean (tacaño), paltry; miserable (cualidad), lean. 3. Petty, minute, puny. *-m.* 1. Mean person (avaro); petty individual (miserable). 2. *(And. CAm. Mex.)* Wart (verruga).
mezquita [meth-kee'-tah], *f.* Mosque, a Mohammedan temple or place of worship.
mezquite [meth-kee'-tay], *m.* The mezquite shrubs of Mexico. 1. The honey-mezquite. 2. The screw bean.
mí [mee], *pro.* Me; the oblique case of the pronoun *yo* when it is governed by any preposition other than *con*: as, *de mí,* from me. **Para mí no hay duda,** so far as I'm concerned there's no doubt. **Por mí mismo,** by myself.
mi [mee], *adj. pos.* My; placed before nouns. **Mi amor,** my love. **Ésta es mi casa,** this is my house. *-pl.* **mis,** my. **Éstos son mis padres,** these are my parents. **Ésos son mis libros,** those are my books.
mi. *m.* Mi, the third note of the scale.
miaja [me-ah'-hah], *f.* Crumb, minute portion.
miar [me-ar'], *m.* To mew, as a cat.
miasma [me-ahs'-mah], *m. (Med.)* Miasm or miasma. *-pl.* Miasmata.
miasmático, ca [me-as-mah'-te-co, cah], *a.* Miasmatic producing miasm.
miau [me-ah'-oo], *m.* Mew of a cat.
mica [mee'-cah], *f.* 1. Mica, a mineral cleaving in thin scales, transparent to translucent. Called also isinglass. 2. Female long-tailed monkey. *(Ame.)* **Agarrar una mica,** to get sloshed (emborracharse).
micáceo, cea [me-cah'-the-o, ah], *a.* Micaceous, mica-like.
micasquisto [me-cas-kees'-to], *m.* Micaschist.
micción [mic-the-on'], *f.* Micturition, the act of urinating.
mico [mee'-co], *m.* 1. Monkey, an ape with a long tail. 2. *(coll.)* Libidinist. 3. An ugly (feo), ill-shaped man; conceited person (engreído); flirt (mariposón); hot man (cachondo). 4. *(CAm.)* Cunt (vajina).
micología [me-co-lo-hee'-ah], *f.* 1. Mycology, the science of fungi.
micra [mee'-crah], *f.* Micron (unit of length).
micro [me-cro], *a.* A Greek word, signifying small, much used in combination.
micro [mee'-cro], *m. (coll.)* Mike.
microamperio [me-cro-am-pay'-re-o], *m.* Microampere.
microbiano, na [me-cro-be-ah'-no, nah], *a.* Microbial, microbic.
microbicida [me-cro-be-thee'-dah], *m.* Microbicide *-a* Microbicidal.
microbilanza [me-cro-be-lahn'-thah], *f.* Microbalance.
microbio [me-cro'-be-o], *m.* Microbe.
microbiología [me-cro-be-o-lo-hee'-ah], *f.* Microbiology.
microbiológico, ca [me-cro-be-o-lo'-he-co, cah], *a.* Microbiological.
microbiólogo [me-cro-be-o'-lo-go], *m.* Microbiologist.
microbús [me-cro-boos'], *m.* Minibus.
microcanal [me-cro-cah-nahl']. *(Inform.)* Microchannel.
microcéfalo, la [me-cro-thay'-fah-lo, lah], *a.* Microcephalous, microcephalic, having an unusually small skull.
microcircuito [me-cro-ther-coo-ee'-to], *m.* Microcircuit.

micrococo

micrococo [me-cro-co'-co], *m.* Micrococcus.
micocosmo [me-cro-cos'-mo], *m.* Microcosm.
microchip [me-cro-cheep'], *m.* Microchip.
microfilm [me-cro-feelm'], *m.* Microfilm.
microfísica [me-cro-fee'-se-cah], *f.* Microphysics.
micrófono [me-cro'-fo-no], *m.* Microphone.
microfotografía [me-cro-fo-to-grah-fee'-ah], *f.* 1. Microphotography. 2. Microphotograph.
micrografía [me-cro-grah-fee'-ah], *f.* Micrography.
microinstrucciones [me-cro-ins-trooc-the-o-nays]. *(Inform.)* Firmware.
micrómetro [me-cro'-may-tro], *m.* Micrometer.
microómnibus, microbús [me-cro-om'-ne-boos, me-cro-boos'], *m.* Microbus.
microonda [mi-cro-on'-dah], *f.* Microwave.
microorganismo [me-cro-or-gah-nees'-mos], *m. pl.* Microorganisms.
microprocesador [me-cro-pro-thay-sah-dor'], *m.* Microprocesor. **Microprocesador modular de bits**, *(Comput.)* bit slice microprocessor.
microscópico [me-cros-co'-pe-co], **ca**, *a.* Microscopic, microscopical.
microscopio [me-cros-co'-pe-o], *m.* Microscope. **Microscopio electrónico**, electron microscope.
microsurco [me-cro-soor'-co], *m.* Microgroove.
michelín [me-chay-leen'], *m.* Spare tire, roll of fat.
michito [me-chee'-to], *m. dim.* Kitten, a young cat.
micho, cha [mee'-cho, chah], *m. & f.* Puss, name of a cat.
mida [mee'-dah], *m.* Mida, bean-fly, worm that breeds in vegetables. *(Yo mido, yo mida; el midió, midiera; from Medir.* V. PEDIR.)
miedo [me-ay'-do], *m.* Fear, dread, apprehension. **Morirse de miedo**, to die for fear. **No haya miedo**, there is nothing to be apprehended. **Por miedo a**, for fear of. **Hace un frío de miedo**, it´s terribly cold.
miedoso, sa [me-ay-do'-so, sah], *a.* Fearful, timorous, easily afraid.
miel [me-el'], *f.* Honey. **Miel de caña**, Molasses. **Dejar a uno con la miel en los labios**, to deprive one of what he was just beginning to enjoy. **Las mieles del triunfo**, the sweets of success. **Hacerse de miel**, to snatch something away from somebody.
mielga [me-el'-gah], *f.* 1. *(Bot.)* Lucerne, when it grows wild. 2. A kind of dog-fish. 3. Rake, an instrument for raking hay, etc. 4. Stripe of ground.
melitis [me-ay-lee'-tis], *f.* Myelitis, in flammation of the spinal cord.
miembro [me-em'-bro], *m.* 1. Member, a limb of the body. 2. Member, one of a community or corporation. 3. Member, any branch or part of an integral. 4. Member, a head, a clause of a discourse or period. **Hacerse miembro de**, to become member of.
mienta [me-en'-tah], *f.* *(Bot.)* Mint. V. HIERBABUENA.
mientras [me-en'-tras], *adv.* In the meantime, in the meanwhile; when. **Mientras que**, whilst, during the time that, as long as, so long as.
miera [me-ay'-rah], *f.* 1. Juniper oil. 2. Resin.
miércoles [me-err'-co-les], *m.* Wednesday. **Miércoles de ceniza**, Ash Wednesday.
mierda [me-err'-dah], *f.* *(coll.)* 1. Excrement, faeces, ordure, shit. 2. Dirt, muck. **Es una mierda**, it´s shit. **El libro es una mierda**, the book is crap. **Es una mierda de coche**, it´s an awful car.
mierdacruz [me-er-dah-crooth'], *f.* *(Bot. Prov.)* Ciliate sparrow-wort.
mierla [me-err'-lah], *f.* *(Orn.)* Blackbird. V. MERLA.
mies [me-ess'], *f.* 1. Wheat and other grain of which bread is made, corn (grano). 2. Harvest, the time of reaping (temporada). 3. *(Met.)* Multitude converted or ready for conversion.
miga [mee'-gah], *f.* 1. Crumb, the soft part of bread. 2. A small fragment of anything. 3. Marrow, substance, or

principal part. **Migas**, crumbs of bread fried with oil, salt, and pepper. **Hacer buenas, or malas migas**, *(coll.)* to agree or disagree readily with one.
migaja [me-gah'-hah], *f.* 1. A small particle, scrap, or bit of bread. 2. Scrap, crumb, small particles of bread, meat, etc., left at the table. 3. A small bit of anything, ace. 4. *(coll.)* Nothing, little or nothing. *-pl.* Offals, leavings; broken victuals.
migajada [me-gah-hah'-dah], *f.* A small particle.
migajica, illa, ita, uela [me-gah-hee'-cah], *f. dim.* A very small particle of bread.
migajón [me-gah-hone'], *m.* Crumb, without crust; marrow core.
mígala [mee'-gah-lah], *f.* Mygale, bird-spider, a very huge species of spider.
migar [me-gar'], *va.* To crumble, to break into small bits.
migración [me-grah-the-on'], *f.* Migration.
migratorio, ria [me-grah-to'-re-o, ah], *a.* Migrating, migratory.
miguero, ra [me-gay'-ro, rah], *a.* Crummy, relating to crumbs fried in a pan.
mijar [me-har'], *m.* A millet-field.
mijero [me-hay'-ro], *m.* Milestone.
mijo [mee'-ho], *m.* 1. *(Bot.)* Millet or millet panic-grass. **Mijo alemán**, german panic-grass. 2. *(Bot.)* Turkey-millet. 3. (LOCAL) Maize.
mikado [me-kah-do], *m.* Mikado, the sovereign of Japan.
mil [meel], *m.* One thousand or ten hundred. **Perdió muchos miles de pesos**, he lost several thousand dollars. **Tres mil coches**, three thousand cars. **Lo ha hecho mil veces**, he´s done it hundreds of times.
milagrero, ra [me-lah-gray'-ro, rah], *m. & f.* Person fond of considering natural events as miracles, and publishing them as such; a miracle-monger.
milagro [me-lah'-gro], *m.* 1. Miracle, wonder, something above human power. 2. Offering of wax or any other substance, hung up in churches in commemoration of a miracle. **Vida y milagros**, *(coll.)* life, character, and behavior. **Hacer milagros**, *(fig.)* to work wonders.
milagrón [me-lah-grone'], *m.* *(coll.)* Dread, astonishment; extreme.
milagrosamente [me-lah-gro'-sah-men-tay], *adv.* Miraculously, marvellously.
milagroso, sa [me-lah-gro'-so, sah], *a.* Miraculous, done by miracle; marvellous, admirable.
milamores [meel-lah-mo'-res], *f.* Perennial plant, a species of valerian.
Milán [me-lahn'], *m.* 1. The city Milan. 2. Kind of linch cloth, so called from being made in Milan.
milanés, sa [me-la-nays', sah], *a.* Native of or belonging to Milan, Milanese.
milano [me-lah'-no], *m.* 1. Kite (ave), a bird of prey. **Mesa de milanos**, keen hunger and little to eat. 2. Flying gurnard (pez). **Cola de milano**, dovetail.
milenario, ria [me-lay-nah'-re-o, ah], *a.* Millenary, consisting of a thousand.
milenario [me-lay-nah'-re-o], *m.* 1. Millenary, the space of a thousand years. 2. Millennium. 3. Millenary, one who expects the millennium.
milenio [me-lay'-ne-o], *m.* Millennium.
mileno, na [me-lay'-no, nah], *a.* Applied to cloth, the warp of which contains a thousand threads.
milenrama [me-len-rah'-mah], *f.* *(Bot.)* Common milfoil or yarrow.
milésimo, ma [me-lay'-se-mo, mah], *a.* 1. Thousandth, millesimal, the ordinal of a thousand. 2. The thousandth part of anything. —**Milésima**, *f.,* mill, the thousandth part of the monetary unit.
milhojas [mil-o'-has], *f.* *(Bot.)* Yarrow, milfoil. V. MILENRAMA.
mili [me'-le], *f.* Military service. **Estar en la mili**, to do one´s military service.

miliar [me-le-ar'], *a.* Miliary, having the size or form of a millet-seed.

miliárea [me-le-ah'-ray-ah], *f.* Milliare, one-thousandth of an acre.

milicia [me-lee'-the-ah], *f.* 1. Art and science of war, warfare (arte). 2. Military men in general, the militia or soldiery (soldados). 3. Militia, the trained bands of the inhabitants of a country: in this last sense it is almost always used in the plural.

miliciano [me-le-the-ah'-no], *m.* Militiaman (soldado). *-a.* Military, militar.

miligramo[me-le-grah'-mo], *m.* Milligram, the thousandth part of a gram.

mililitro [me-le-lee'-tro], *m.* Milliliter, the thousandth part of a liter.

milímetro [me-lee'-may-tro], *m.* Millimetre, the thousandth part of a meter, 25,4 to the inch.

militante [me-le-tahn'-tay], *a.* Militant; military.

militar [me-le-tar'], *m.* Soldier, a military man (soldado). *-pl.* Military, the soldiery.*-a.* Militar, military, soldierly, warlike (espíritu), martial.

militar [me-le-tar'], *vn.* 1. To serve in the army, to follow the profession of arms. 2. To hold, to militate, to stand good, to go against (razones, argumentos). **Militar en un partido**, to belong to a party. **Militar en favor de**, to speak for.

militarismo [me-le-tah-rees'-mo], *m.* Militarism, predominance in the goverment of state of the military spirit.

militarización [me-le-tah-re-thah-the-on'], *f.* Militarization.

militarizar [me-le-tah-re-thar'], *va.* To militarize.

militarmente [me-le-tar'-men-tay], *adv.* Militarily, in a military stile.

milla [meel'-lyah], *f.* 1. Mile, a linear measure, eight stadia, or one thousand geometric steps. 2. *(Naut.)* Knot.

millar [mil-lyar'], *m.* 1. Number of a thousand. 2. Thousand, proverbially a great number: in this last sense it is almost always used in the plural. 3. A certain quantity of cocoa, which in some parts is three pounds and a half, and in others more.

millarada [mil-lyah-rah'-dah], *f.* Several thousands. **Echar millaradas**, to brag of wealth and riches. **A millaradas**, Innumerable times.

millo [meel'-lyo], *m. (Prov.)* In the Canary Islands, and in Galicia, maize.

millón [mil-yone'], *m.* 1. Million, ten hundred thousand. 2. Million, any very great number. **Un millón de sellos**, a million stamps. **Mil millones**, a billion. (GB, a thousand millions).

millonario [mil-lyo-nah'-re-o], *m.* Millionaire, a person very rich in money.

millonésimo, ma [mil-lyo-nay'-se-mo, mah], *a.* Millionth.

milmillonésimo, ma [mil-meel-lyo-nay'-se-mo, mah], *a.* Thousand millionth, billionth.

milo [mee'-lo], *m. (Prov. Ast.)* Earth-worm.

milocha [me-lo'-chah], *f.* (Local) Kite, a toy.

milpa [meel'-pah], *f. (Mex.)* A maize-field (plantación).

milpiés [mil-pe-ays'], *m.* Centipede, millipede.

milréis [mil-rays'], *m.* Milreis, Brazilian and Portuguese coin.

mimado, da [me-mah'-do, dah], *a.* Spoiled, humored.

mimar [me-mar'], *va.* To coax, to wheedle, to flatter, to fondle, to caress, to indulge, to humor, to pet.

mimbral [mim-brahl'], *m.* Plantation of osiers.

mimbre [meem'-bray], *m. (Bot.)* 1. Twig of an osier. 2. Osier, willow.

mimbrear [mim-bray-ar'], *vn.* V. CIMBRAR.

mimbrera [mim-bray'-rah], *f. (Bot.)* Osier.

mimbreral [mim-bray-rahl'], *m.* Plantation of osiers.

mimbroso, sa [mim-broh'-so, sah], *a.* Made of osiers.

mimeografiar [me-may-o-grah-fe-ar'], *va.* To mimeograph.

mimeógrafo [me-may-o'-grah-fo], *m.* Mimeograph.

mimetismo [me-may-tees'-mo], *m.* mimetism, protective coloring.

mímica [mee'-me-cah], *f.* Pantomime, sign-language (señas).

mímico, ca [mee'-me-co, cah], *a.* Mimic.

mimo [mee'-mo], *m.* 1. Mime, mimic. 2. Endearingness, fondness, indulgence. 3. Prudery, delicacy. 4. Ancient mimes or farcical representations. **Dar mimos a un niño**, to spoil a child.

mimología [me-mo-lo-hee'-ah], *f.* Act of imitating the voice and actions of others.

mimosa [me-mo'-sah], *f. (Bot.)* Mimosa, the sensitive-plant.

mimoso, sa [me-mo'-so, sah], *a.* Delicate, endearingly soft (blandengue), fond, foolishly nice or tender.

mina [mee'-nah], *f.* 1. Conduit, mine, a subterraneous canal or cavity in the ground. 2. Mine, a place which contains metals or minerals. 3. Spring, source of water. 4. Business which yields great profit and demands but little exertion. 5. *(coll.)* A large quantity of money. 6. *(Mil.)* Mine under a fortress. 7. Lead; refill (de lapicero).

minador, ra [me-nah-dor', rah], *m. & f.* Miner, one who works in mines; one who makes military mines; engineer.

minal [me-nahl'], *a.* Belonging to a mine.

minar [me-nar'], *va.* 1. To mine, to dig mines and burrows. 2. To mine, to sap, to ruin by mines. 3. To make uncommon exertions to attain some end or collect information.

minarete [me-nah-ray'-tay], *m.* Minaret, a spire in Saracen architecture.

mineraje [me-nay-rah'-hay], *m.* Labor of mining.

mineral [me-nay-rahl'], *a.* Mineral, consisting of inorganic bodies.

mineral [me-nay-rahl'], *m.* 1. Mineral, an inorganic substance, matter dug out of the earth, ore. 2. A spring of water, the mineral source or origin of fountains. 3. A source or origin which produces a plenty of something. 4. Mine which contains metals, minerals, or precious stones.

mineralización [me-nay-rah-le-thah-the-on'], *f. (Phys.)* Mineralization, the state of a metal in combination with another body.

mineralogía [me-nay-rah-lo-hee'-ah], *f.* Mineralogy.

mineralógico, ca [me-nay-rah-lo'-he-co, cah], *a.* Belonging to mineralogy, mineralogical.

mineralogista [me-nay-rah-lo-hees'-tah], *m.* Mineralogist.

mineralurgia [me-nay-rah-loor'-he-ah], *f.* Metallurgy.

mineralurgista [me-nay-rah-loor-hees'-tah], *m.* Metallurgist.

minería [me-nay-ree'-ah], *f.* 1. The art of mining. 2. Force of miners; the whole body of workers in a mine. 3. Body of mine-operators.

minero [me-nay'-ro], *m.* 1. Mine, place in the earth which contains metals or minerals. 2. Miner, one who digs for metals, or makes military mines. 3. Source, origin.

mingo [meen'-go], *m.* One of the three balls in the game of billiards, which is never struck by a cue, but by another ball: the red ball. **Poner el mingo**, to excel (sobresalir), to attract attention (llamar la atención).

minguito [min-gee'-to], *m.* Piece of bread, one-quarter of a loaf.

mini....*pref.* mini.... **Minibikini**, microscopic bikini.

miniar [me-ne-ar'], *va.* To paint in miniature.

miniatura [me-ne-ah-too'-rah], *f.* Miniature, a painting on vellum, ivory, or paper.

miniaturista [me-ne-ah-too-rees'-tah], *com.* Painter of miniatures.

miniaturización [me-ne-ah-too-re-thay-the-on'], *f.* Miniaturization.

mínima [mee'-ne-mah], *f. (Mus.)* Minim; half-note.

minimista [me-ne-mees'-tah], *m.* Student of the second class in grammar.

mínimo, ma [mee'-ne-mo, mah], *a.* Least, smallest (más pequeño). **Cifra mínima**, minimun number. *-m.* Minimum. **Como mínimo**, as a minimum.

minino, mino [me-nee'-no, mee'-no], *m.* Word used for calling a cat.

minio [mee'-ne-o], *m.* Minium, red-lead, an oxide of lead.

ministerial [me-nis-tay-re-ahl'], *a*. Ministerial.
ministerialmente [me-nis-tay-re-ahl'-men-tay], *adv*. Ministerially.
ministerio [me-nis-tay´-re-o], *m*. 1. Ministry, office, public place, employment. 2. Manual labor. 3. Ministry, administration, the principal officers of government. 4. Ministry, the charge or office of a minister or secretary of state, and the time which he is in office.
ministra [me-nees'-trah], *f*. 1. Ministress, she who serves. 2. Wife of a cabinet minister.
ministrador, ra [me-nis-trah-dor', rah], *m.& f*. One who ministers.
ministrante [me-nis-trahn'-tay], *pa*. Serving, ministrating.
ministrar [me-nis-trar'], *va. & vn*. 1. To minister, to serve an office or employment, to perform the functions of a public place. 2. To minister, to supply, to furnish.
ministril [me-nis-treel'], *m*. 1. Apparitor, tipstaff; a petty officer of justice. 2. Minstrel, one who plays the flute and other musical wind-instruments. **Ministriles**, musical wind-instruments.
ministro [me-nees'-tro], *m*. 1. Minister, agent. 2. Minister employed in the administration of justice. 3. Secretary of state. **Ministro de Estado**, or **de relaciones exteriores**, the secretary of state or minister of foreign affairs. **Ministro de la Gobernación**, or **de relaciones interiores**, minister of the interior. **Ministro de Hacienda**, secretary of the treasury. 4. Minister or agent of a foreign power. 5. A petty officer of justice. 6. One of the heads of some religious communities.
minoración [me-no-rah-the-on'], *f*. Minoration.
minorar [me-no-rar'], *va*. To lessen, to reduce to a smaller compass, to diminish, to clip.-*vr*. To lower, to fall.
minorativo, va [me-no-rah-tee'-voh, vah], *a*. Lessening, that decreases or lessens.
minoría [me-no-ree'-ah], *f*. Minority, the smaller number.
minoridad [me-no-re-dahd'], *f*. Minority, nonage.
minoritario [me-no-re-tah'-re-o], *a*. Minority.
minotauro [me-no-tah'-oo-ro], *m*. Minotaur, fabulous monster.
minucia [me-noo'-the-ah], *f*. 1. Minuteness, smallness; mite, atom, anything of very little value. 2. Small tithes paid of wool, lambs, etc. -*pl*. Minutiae.
minuciosamente [me-noo-the-o'-sah-men-tay], *adv*. Thoroughly, meticulously; in a very detailed way.
minuciosidad [me-noo-the-o-se-dahd'], *f*. 1. Minute explanation of a thing. 2. A trifle.
minucioso, sa [me-noo-the-o'-so, sah], *a*. Superfluously exact, nice, scrupulously and minutely cautious, thorough (meticuloso), very detailed (detallado).
minué, minuete [me-noo-ay´, me-noo-ay'-tay], *m*. Minuet, a kind of grave and stately dance.
minuendo [me-noo-en'-do], *m*. (*Arith.*) Minuend.
minúscula [me-noos´-coo-lah], *a*. Small, lower-case letters.
minúsculo [me-noos'-coo-lo], *a*. Tiny, minute, minuscule; *(Tip.)* small.
minusvalía [me-noos-vah-le'-ah], *f*. 1. Handicap (physical). 2. (*Com.*) Depreciation, capital loss.
minusvalidez [me-noos-vah-le-dayth'], *f*. State of being handicapped, disablement.
minusválido [me-noos-vah'-le-do], *a*. Handicapped, disabled. -*m & f*. Handicapped person.
minuta [me-noo'-tah], *f*. 1. Minute, first draft of an agreement in writing (borrador); an enumeration of the principal heads of a contract. 2. Papers containing brief notes or memorandums (apuntes). **Libro de minutas**, minute-book, memorandum-book, a common-place book. 3. *(Culin.)* Menu. 4. *(Cono Sur)* Junk (basura). 5. *(CAm.)* Flavored ice drink (bebida).
minutar [me-noo-tar'], *va*. To take down the principal heads of an agreement; to make the first draft of a contract, to minute.

minutario [me-noo-tah´-re-o], *m*. The book in which public notaries keep a memorandum of the documents they authorize.
minutero [me-noo-tay'-ro], *m*. Minute hand of a watch or clock.
minutisa [me-noo-tee'-sah], *f. (Bot.)* Sweet-william pink.
minuto [me-noo´-to], *m*. 1. Minute, the sixtieth part of an hour; the sixtieth part of a degree; sixty seconds. 2. Minute, moment, any small space of time.
miñón [me-nyone'], *m*. 1. Name given to some troops of light infantry in Spain. 2. Minion, scoriae of iron ore.
miñona [me-nyo'-nah], *f. (typ.)* Minion, 7-point type.
mío, mía [mee'-o, mee'-ah], *pron. poss.* My, mine. **Es muy mío**, he is much my friend. **Los míos**, my people. **Es mío**, it is mine. **Éste es el mío**, this is mine.
miocardio [me-o-car´-de-o], *m*. Myocardium.
mioceno, na [me-o-thay'-no, nah], *a. (Geol.)* Miocene.
miografía [me-o-grah-fee´-ah], *f*. Myography. *V.* MIOLOGÍA.
miología [me-o-lo-hee´-ah], *f*. Myology, part of anatomy which treats of the muscles; a treatise on muscles.
miope [me-o'-pay], *a*. Myopic, near sighted.
miopía [me-o-pe'-ah], *f*. Myopia, near sightedness.
miosota [me-o-so'-tah], *f. (Bot.)* Myosotis, forget-me-not, a plant of the borage family.
miquelete [me-kay-lay´-tay], *m*. Miquelet, mountain soldier belonging to the militia of Catalonia and the Pyrenees.
mira [mee'-rah], *f*. 1. The sight of a gun. 2. A point of mathematical instruments to direct the sight. 3. Care: vigilance; expectation, design. **Estar a la mira**, to be on the lookout, to be on the watch. **Mira de bombardero**, bombsight. **Tener miras sobre**, to have designs on. **De miras estrechas**, narrow-minded.
¡mira! [mee'-rah], *int*. Look! behold! take care! see!
mirabel [me-rah-bel'], *m*. 1. *(Bot.)* Summer cypress goose-foot. 2. *(Prov.)* Sun flower.
mirabolano [me-rah-bo-lah´-no], *m*. *(Bot.)* Myrobalan, a dried astringent prune-like fruit of India, used as a cathartic.
mirada [me-rah'-dah], *f*. 1. Glance, a transient view. 2. Gaze, steadfast look. **Mirada fija**, stare. **Apartar la mirada**, to look away. **Clavar la mirada en**, to fix one´s eyes on.
miradero [me-rah-day'-ro], *m*. Place exposed to view on all sides; watchtower, or any elevated spot which commands an extensive prospect.
mirado, da [me-rah'-do, dah], *a*. Considerate (considerado), circumspect, prudent, moderate, sensible (juicioso), cautious (cauto). **Ser mirado en los gastos**, to be sensible about what one spends. 2. **Bien mirado**, well thought of. 3. Finicky, fussy. -*pp*. of MIRAR.
mirador, ra [me-rah-dor', rah], *m. & f*. 1. Spectator, looker-on. 2. *m*. Mirador, gallery which commands an extensive view. 3. *m*. A kind of balcony (balcón). 4. A boat used in the tunny-fishery.
miradura [me-rah-doo´-rah], *f*. Act of looking. *V.* MIRADA.
miraje [me-rah'-hay], *m*. Mirage, looming.
miramiento [me-rah-me-en'-to], *m*. 1. Awe, reverence, dread. 2. Consideration (consideración), reflection; expectation. 3. Circumspection (circunspección), prudence. 4. Reverential civility, attentions. **Sin miramientos**, unceremoniously. **Tratar sin miramientos a uno**, to treat somebody without consideration.
mirar [me-rar'], *va*. 1. To look or look at, to look upon or toward, to give a look, to watch (observar). 2. To respect, to have regard for, to esteem, to appreciate, to look on (considerar). 3. To have some private end, to aim at, to have in view. 4. To look, to be directed with regard to any object. 5. To observe, to watch, to spy (vigilar). 6. To take notice, to notice. 7. To fool, to consider, to reflect, to meditate. 8. To inquire, to collect information. 9. To look, to take care, to attend, to protect. -*vn*. 1. To look; to glance. 2. *(Arch.)* To look on to, to face. 3. *(Fig.)* To have in mind. -*vr*. 1. To look at oneself. 2. To look at one another. **Mirar a uno con**

malos ojos, to look at one with an evil eye. **Mirar alrededor**, to look about. **Mirar por uno**, to take care of, to look after. **Mirar de reojo**, to squint. **Mirar por encima**, to examine slightly. **Mirar sobre el hombro**, to cast a contemptuous look or frown. **Lo hago mirando el porvenir**, I do it bearing the future in mind. **No mira las dificultades**, he doesn´t take into account the difficulties. **Mirar a uno como**, to look on somebody as. **Mirar hacia otro lado**, to look the other way. **Mirar atrás**, to look back. **Mirarse al espejo**, to look at oneself in the mirror.

mirasol [me-rah-sole´], *m. (Bot.)* Turnsol, sunflower. V. GIRASOL.

miriagramo [me-re-ah-grah´-mo], *m.* Myriagram, ten thousand grams.

miriámetro [me-re-ah´-may-tro], *m.* Myriameter, ten thousand meters.

miriápodos [me-re-ah´-po-dos], *a. & m. pl.* Myriapods, centipedes, articulates which have a great number of feet.

mirífico, ca [me-ree´-fe-co, cah], *a.* Marvellous, wonderful.

mirilla [me-reel´-lyah], *f.* Peep-hole; spy-hole; *(Fot.)* viewer.

miriñaque [me-re-nyah´-kay], *m.* 1. Bauble, gewgaw, trifling articles. 2. Manila grass-cloth. 3. Hoop-skirt.

mirística [me-rees´-te-cah], *f.* The nutmeg-tree.

mirla [meer´-lah], *f. (Orn.)* Blackbird. V. MIRLO.

mirlamiento [meer-lah-me-en´-to], *m.* Air of importance, affected gravity.

mirlarse [meer-lar´-say], *vr.* To assume an air of importance, to affect gravity.

mirlo [meer´-lo], *m.* 1. *(Orn.)* Blackbird. 2. Air of importance, affected gravity. 3. Tongue (lengua).

mirmego, ga [meer-may´-go, gah], *a.* Like an ant.

mirón, na [me-rone´, nah], *m. & f.* 1. Spectator, looker-on (espectador), bystander. 2. Prier, busybody, gazer. **Ir de mirón**, to go along just to see.

mirra [meer´-rah], *f.* Myrra, a resinous gum.

mirrado, da [mir-rah´-do, dah], *a.* Composed of myrrh, perfumed with myrrh; myrrhine.

mirrauste [mir-rah´-oos-tay], *m.* Pigeon sauce, made of bread, almonds, and other ingredients.

mirrino, no [mir-ree´-no, nah], *a.* Myrrhine, of or like myrrh. *(Acad.)*

mirtáceo, cea [meer-tah´-thay-o, ah], *a.* Myrtaceous, pertaining to the myrtle family.

mirtidano [meer-te-dah´-no], *m.* Sprout which springs at the foot of a myrtle.

mirtiforme [meer-te-for´-may], *a.* Myrtiforal, having the shape of myrtle.

mirtino, na [meer-tee´-no, nah], *a.* Resembling myrtle.

mirto [meer´-to], *m. (Bot.)* Myrtle. V. ARRAYÁN.

misa [mee´-sah], *f.* 1. Mass, the service of the Roman Catholic Church. 2. Music composed for a solemn mass. **Misa del gallo**, Midnight mass. **Misa mayor**, high mass. **Oír misa**, to go to mass. **No saben de la misa la media**, they don´t know the half of it.

misacantano [me-sah-can-tanh´-no], *m.* 1. Priest who is ordained and says the mass. 2. Priest who celebrates the first mass.

misal [me-sahl´], *m.* 1. Missal, the mass-book. 2. *(typ.)* Two-line pica.

misantropía [me-san-tro-pee´-ah], *f.* Misanthropy.

misantrópico, ca [me-san-tro´-pe-co, cah], *a.* Misanthropic, misanthropical, hating mankind.

misántropo, pa [me-sahn´-tro-po], *m & f.* Misanthropist.

misar [me-sar´], *vn. (doll.)* To say mass; to hear mass.

misario [me-sah´-re-o], *m.* Acolyte, one who attends on the priest during mass.

miscelánea [mis-thay-lah´-ne-ah], *f.* Miscellany, mixture, medley.

miscibilidad [mis-the-be-le-dahd´], *f.* Miscibility, capacity for being mixed.

miscible [mis-thee´-blay], *a.* Miscible, such as can be mixed.

miserable [me-say-rah´-blay], *a.* 1. Miserable, wretched, hapless, unhappy, lamentable. 2. Exhausted, dejected. 3. Covetous, avaricious, niggard; hard. 4. Mean, stingy (persona). 5. Squalid, sordid (cuarto, lugar). 6. Rotten, vile (moralmente).

miserablemente [me-say-rah´-blay-men-tay], *adv.* Miserably, unhappily, covetously, sordidly.

míseramente [mee´-say-rah-men-tay], *adv.* Meanly. V. MISERABLEMENTE.

miserear [me-say-ray-ar´], *vn.* To act penuriously.

miserere [me-say-ray´-ray], *m.* 1. The psalm **miserere**. 2. A solemn Lenten service in which this psalm is sung. 3. *(Med.)* **Cólico miserere**, ileus.

miseria [me-say´-re-ah], *f.* 1. Misery, miserableness, calamity, wretchedness, forlornness, need; oppression. 2. Covetousness, avariciousness, narrowness, hardness, stinginess, meanness (tacañría). 3. Trifle, a very small matter. 4. Poverty (pobreza), want (carencia). 5. Squalor, squalid conditions (condiciones). **Caer en la miseria**, to fall into abject poverty.

misericordia [me-say-re-cor´-de-ah], *f.* Mercy, mercifulness, clemency, loving-kindness.

misericordiosamente [me-say-re-cor-de-o´-sah-men-tay], *adv.* Piously, clemently, mercifully.

misericordioso, sa [me-say-re-cor-de-oh´-so, sah], *a.* Pious, humane, compassionate, merciful.

misero, ra [me-say´-ro, rah], *a.* 1. Mass loving. 2. Applied to a priest who says mass very often.

mísero, ra [mee´-say-ro, rah], *a.* V. MISERABLE.

misérrimo, ma [me-ser´-re-mo, mah], *a. sup.* Very miserable.

misil [me-seel´], **m.** Missile. **Misil tierra-aire**, ground-to-air missile. **Misil de crucero**, cruise missile.**Misil de ataque**, attack missile. **"Misiles"** (Juego), "missile command".

misión [me-se-on´], *f.* 1. Mission, the act of sending. 2. Mission, travel undertaken by priests and other religious persons to propagate religion. 3. Country or province where missionaries preach the gospel among infidels. 4. Missionary sermon. 5. Charges, cost, expense. 6. Money and victuals allowed to reapers during the harvest.

misionar [me-se-o-nar´], *va. & vn.* To preach as a missionary. *(coll.)* To reprimand.

misionero, misionario [me-se-o-nay´-ro], *m* Missionary, one sent to propagate religion.

misivo, va [me-see´-vo, vah], *a.* Missive: applied to a letter or small note sent to any person.

mismamente [mes´-mah-men-tay], *adv.* Only (sólo) just; literally (literalmente); even (hasta); really (en realidad).

mismísimo, ma [mis-mee´-se-mo, mah], *a. sup.* Very same.

mismo, ma [mees´-mo, mah], *a.* Same, equal, equal, self-same, like. **Yo mismo lo hago**, I myself do it. **Viven en la misma calle**, they live in the same street. **Es lo mismo**, it´s the same thing. **Lo mismo no vienen**, they may not come. **En ese mismo momento**, at that very moment. *-adv.* Right. **Aquí mismo**, right here. *-conj.* **Lo mismo que**, just like.

misoginia [me-so-hee´-ne-ah], *f.* Misogyny, hatred of women.

misógino, na [me-so´-he-no, nah], *a.* Misogynous, hating women.

miss [mees], *f.* Beauty queen.

mistar [mis-tar´], *vn.* To speak or make a noise with the mouth: used generally with a negative.

mistela [mis-tay´-lah], *f.* Drink made of wine, water, sugar, and cinnamon.

míster [mees´-tayr], *m.* 1. Briton. 2. *(Dep.)* Trainer, coach.

misterio [mis-tay´-re-o], *m.* 1. Mystery, something above human intelligence. 2. Mystery, anything artfully made difficult; abstruseness, abstrusity. **No hay misterio**, there is no mystery about it.

misteriosamente [mis-tay-re-o´-sah-men-tay], *adv.* Mysteriously, secretly.

misterioso, sa [mis-tay-re-o´-so, sah], *a.* Mysterious, dark, obscure, mysterial, mystic, mystical.

mística [mees'-te-cah], *f.* Mysticalness, mystical theology.

místicamente [mees'-te-cah-men-tay], *adv.* Mystically; spiritually; emblematically.

misticismo [mis-te-thees'-mo], *m.* Mysticism, the doctrine of a sect of philosophers: a modern word.

místico, ca [mees'-te-co, ah], *a.* 1. Mystic, mystical, sacredly obscure. 2. Mystical, emblematical. 3. Mystical, spiritual, belonging to mystical divinity, or to the contemplation of spiritual things.

místico [mees'-te-co], *m.* 1. A mystic, a person devoted to religious contemplation; a writer in mystical divinity. 2. Small coasting vessel in the Mediterranean.

misticón [mis-te-cone'], *m. aug.* A great mystic man; a person who affects a mystical or holy life in a high degree.

mistificar [mis-te-fe-cahr'], *va.* 1. To hoax (embromar), to play a practical joke on; to hoodwink (engañar). 2. To mix up (confundir). 3. To falsify (falsificar).

mistilíneo, nea [mis-te-lee'-nay-o, ah], *a. (Geom.) V.* MIXTILÍNEO.

mistión, misto, mistura, misturar. *V.* MIXTIÓN, MIXTO, MIXTURA, and MIXTURAR.

misturera [mis-too-ray'-rah], *f. (Mex. Peru)* Flower-girl who sells bouquets or mixed flowers.

mita [mee'-tah], *f.* Mita, ancient tribute. The number of Indians subjected to compulsory labor by terms, in conformity with the law of that name.

mitad [me-tahd], *f.* 1. Half. **Por mitades,** by halves. **Mitad y mitad,** by equal parts. 2. Middle (centro). **A mitad de,** halfway along. **Estar a mitad de camino,** to be halfway there. 3. *(Dep.)* Half. **La primera mitad,** the first half.

mitayo [me-tah'-yo], *m.* Indian serving his turn of compulsory labor.

mítico, ca [mee'-te-co, cah], *a.* Mythical.

mitigación [me-te-gah-the-on'], *f.* Mitigation, moderation, extenuation.

mitigador, ra [me-te-gah-dor', rah], *m & f.* Mitigator, mollifier.

mitigar [me-te-gar'], *va.* 1. To mitigate, to soften, to mollify (ira), to lull. 2. To quench (sed), to assuage.

mitigativo, va, mitigatorio, ria [me-te-gah-tee'-vo, vah], *a.* Lenitive, mitigant, mitigative.

mitin [mee'-tin], *m.* Political or labor meeting.

mito [mee'-to], *m.* Myth, allegorical fiction, chiefly about a religious subject.

mitocondrio [me-to-con'-dre-o], *m.* Mitochondrion.

mitología [me-to-lo-hee'-ah], *f.* Mythology, the history of the fabulous gods of antiquity.

mitológico, ca [me-to-lo'-he-co, cah], *a.* Mythological. -*m.* Mythologist.

mitologista, mitólogo [me-to-lo'-he-co], *m.* Mythologist.

mitón [me-tone'], *m.* Mitt, a sort of ladies' glove without fingers.

mitosis [me-to'-sis], *f. (Biol.)* Mitosis.

mitote [me-to'-tay], *m.* 1. An Indian dance. 2. *(Amer.)* Household festival. 3. *(Amer.)* Fastidiousness, affectedness. 4. *(Mex. Coll.)* Riot, uproar, disturbance, confusion.

mitotero, ra [me-to-tay'-ro, rah], *a. & n. (Mex. Amer.)* 1. Precise, finical, dainty, fastidious. 2. Jolly, fond of diversion.

mitra [mee'-trah], *f.* Miter, an ornament for the head, worn by bishops; the dignity of a bishop.

mitrado [me-trah'-do], *a.* Mitered: applied to a person bearing a miter at festivals.-*pp.* of MITRAR.

mitrar [me-trar'], *vn. (coll.)* To be mitered or wear a miter.

mitridato [me-tre-dah'-to], *m.* Mithridate, antidote.

mixtamente [mix'-tah-men-tay], *adv.* Belonging to both ecclesiastical and civil courts.

mixtilíneo, nea [mix-te-lee'-nay-o, ah], *a. (Geom.)* Mixtilinear.

mixtión [mix-te-on'], *f.* Mixtion, mixture, commixture.

mixtiori [mix-te-fo'-re], *a. (Lat. Law.)* Applied to a crime that may be tried either in ecclesiastical or secular courts.

mixto, ta [mix'-to, tah], *a.* 1. Mixed, mingled. 2. Mixed, composed of various simples. 3. Half-breed, of a crossbreed: of mixed breed, mongrel.-*m. V.* MIXTURA.

mixtura [mix-too'-rah], *f.* Mixture, a mass formed by mingling ingredients. 2. Meslin, mixed corn, as rye and wheat.

mixturar [mix-too-rar'], *va.* To mix, to mingle.

mixturero, ra [mix-too-ray'-ro, rah], *a.* 1. Mixing, which mixes.

miz [meeth], *m.* Puss, the common appellation of cats.

mizo, za [mee'-tho, thah], *m. & f. V.* MICHO, CHA.

mnemónico [nay-mo-en-co]. *(Inform.)* Mnemonic.

moaré [mo-ah-ray'], *m.* Moiré, watered silk.

mobiliario, ria [mo-be-le-ah'-re-o, ria], *a.* House-furnishing, relating to furniture.-*m.* Furniture (muebles), fitment, household goods (artículos domésticos).

moca [mo'-cah], *f.* Mocha coffee.

mocadero, mocador [mo-cah-day'-ro, mo-cah-dor'], *m. (Prov.)* Pocket-handkerchief.

mocarro [mo-car'-ro], *m.* Mucus of the nose, not cleaned away (vulgarly, snot).

mocasín [mo-ca-seen'], *m.* 1. Moccasin, an Indian shoe of soft leather: 2. The moccasin snake.

mocear [mo-thay-ar'], *va.* To act as a boy; to revel, to rake.

mocedad [mo-thay-dahd'], *f.* 1. Juvenility, youthfulness (juventud). 2. Light and careless kind of living (vida).

mocetón, na [mo-thay-tone', nah], *m. & f.* A young, robust person.

mochada [mo-chah'-dah], *f.* Butt, a stroke with the head of a horned animal.

mochar [mo-char'], *va.* 1. To cut, to lop off. *V.* DESMOCHAR. 2. *(Cono Sur)* To pinch. 3. *(And.)* To fire, to sack.

mochazo [mo-chah'-tho], *m.* Blow with the butt-end of a musket.

mochil [mo-cheel'], *m.* Farmer's boy.

mochila [mo-chee'-lah], *f.* Knapsack, a bag in which soldiers carry their linen and provisions. **Hacer mochila,** to provide provisions for a journey.

mochilera [mo-che-lay'-rah], *a.* Pouched.

mochilero [mo-che-lay'-ro], *m.* One who carries the baggage of soldiers.

mochín [mo-cheen'], *m.* Young shoot of a tree. *V.* VERDUGO.

mocho, cha [mo'-cho, chah], *a.* 1. Dishonored. 2. Cropped, shorn. 3. Lopped, having the branches cut off. 4. Maimed, mutilated. 5. *(Mex. Coll.)* Hypocritical.

mochuelo [mo-choo-ay'-lo], *m. (Orn.)* Red owl. **Tocar el mochuelo,** to get always the worst part of something.

moción [mo-the-on], *f.* 1. Motion (movimiento), movement. 2. Leaning, inclination of mind. 3. Divine inspiration. 4. *(Neol.)* Motion, a proposal to be voted on in an assembly. **Moción de censura,** motion of censure.

mocito, ta [moth-ee'-to, tah], *a. dim.* Juvenile, youthful.-*m. & f.* A very young person.

moco [mo'-co], *m.* 1. Mucus, a viscid fluid secreted by mucous membranes. 2. Any viscid, glutinous matter. 3. Snuff of a lamp or candle (mecha). 4. Candle drippings. 5. Slag of iron. **Moco de pavo,** 1. Crest which hangs over the forehead of a turkey. 2. Any worthless thing. **¿Es moco de pavo?** do you call that nothing? **No sabe quitarse los mocos,** the fellow does not know how to blow his nose. **Quitar a uno los mocos,** to knock off one's nose with a blow. **Llorar a moco tendido,** to sob one's heart out. **Tirarse el moco,** to hesitate (vacilar).

mocora [mo-co'-rah], *f.* A tree of Ecuador from which hats are sometimes made.

mocosidad [mo-co-se-dahd'], *f.* Mucosity, mucousness, viscosity.

mocoso, sa [mo-co'-so, sah], *a.* 1. Snively: running from the nose. 2. Despicable, worthless. 3. Ignorant, thoughtless.

mocoso, sa [mo-co'-so, sah], *m. & f.* An ignorant, thoughtless person; an inexperienced youth.

mocosuelo, la [mo-co-soo-ay'-lo, lah], *m. & f. dim.* A thoughtless, inexperienced youth.

moda [mo'-dah], *f.* Fashion, form, mode, custom; especially in dress. **Un sombrero a la moda,** a fashionable hat. **Pasado de moda,** old fashioned. **Ponerse de moda,** to become fashionable.

modales [mo-dah'-les], *m. pl.* Manners, breeding, education.

modalidad [mo-dah-le-dahd'], *f.* 1. Modality, method. 2. Character nature. 3. *(Mus.)* Mode and tone. 4. Form (clase), way (manera). **Una nueva modalidad teatral,** a new dramatic form.

modelar [mo-day-lar'], *va.* To model, to form (formar).

modelismo [mo-day-lees'-mo], *m.* Modelling (hobby).

modelo [mo-day'-lo], *m.* 1. Model, pattern (patrón), standard (norma), copy, exemplar, paragon, rule. 2. *(Mex.)* Blank form (forma). **Servir de modelo,** to serve as a model. **Modelo de tecla,** *(Inform.)* keystroke pattern. *-m & f.* Model (alta Costura).

módem [mo'-daym], *m. (Inform.)* Modem. **No hay módem instalado,** nul modem.

moderación [mo-day-rah-the-on'], *f.* Moderation, temperance, frugality; abstemiousness, circumspection, continence. **Con moderación,** in moderation.

moderadamente [mo-day-rah'-dah-men-tay], *adv.* Moderately, temperately, reasonably, measurably.

moderado, da [mo-day-rah'-do, dah], *a.* 1. Moderate, temperate, abstemious, abstinent, considerate; gentle, 2. In politics, conservative.

moderador [mo-day-rah-dor'], *m.* Moderator. *-m & f.* (TV) Presenter.

moderadora [mo-day-rah-do'-rah], *f.* Moderatrix.

moderante [mo-day-rahn'-tay], *m.* Moderator, in some colleges, he who presides over the studies of pupils.

moderantismo [mo-day-ran-tees'-mo], *m.* Conservatism in politics.

moderar [mo-day-rar'], *va.* To moderate, to regulate, to adjust, to restrain (violencia), to curb, to repress.-*vr.* To become moderate, to refrain from excesses.

moderativo, va [mo-day-rah-tee'-vo, vah], *a.* Moderating.

moderatorio, ria [mo-day-rah-to'-re-o, ah], *a.* That which moderates.

modernamente [mo-dayr'-nah-men-tay], *adv.* Recently (recientemente), lately, newly, freshly.

modernismo [mo-der-nees'-mo], *m.* Modernism.

modernización [mo-der-ne-thah-the-on'], *f.* Modernization.

modernizar [mo-der-ne-thar'], *va.* To modernize.

moderno, na [mo-derr'-no, nah], *a.* Late, recent, modern, new, novel.

modestamente [mo-days'-tah-men-tay], *adv.* Modestly, comelily, meekly, maidenly, honestly.

modestia [mo-des'-te-ah], *f.* Modesty, decency, chastity, meekness, maidenliness; coyness; humility.

modesto, ta [mo-des'-to, tah], *a.* Modest, decent, pure, chaste, maidenly, unpretending, unassuming.

módico, ca [mo'-de-co, cah], *a.* Moderate in price.

modificación [mo-de-fe-cah-the-on'], *f.* Modification, the act of modifying.

modificador, ra [mo-de-fe-cah-dor', rah], *m. & f.* Modifier.

modificar [mo-de-fe-car'], *va.* To modify, to moderate.

modificativo, va [mo-de-fe-cah-tee'-vo, vah], *a.* Modificative, that which modifies.

modillón [mo-dil-lyone'], *m. (Arch.)* Modillion, bracket.

modio [mo'-de-o], *m.* Roman dry measure.

modiolo [mo-de-o'-lo], *m. (Arch.)* Intermodillion, the quadrangular space between the modillions of a column.

modismo [mo-dees'-mo], *m.* Particular phraseology in a language deviating from the rules of grammar; mannerism.

modista [mo-dees'-tah], *f.* Milliner, dressmaker, modiste.

modisto [mo-dees'-to], *m & f.* Fashion designer.

modo [mo'-do], *m.* 1. Mode (método), method, manner, form. 2. Moderation, temperance. 3. Civility, urbanity. 4. Mode or mood in grammar. 5. *(Mus.)* A system of dividing the intervals of an octave; a Greek or Gregorian mode. **Del modo, del mismo modo que** or **al modo que,** in the same manner as. **A modo,** after a similar manner. **De modo,** so that. **Modo de gobierno,** form of government. **De este modo,** this way. **Del mismo modo,** in the same way. **De diversos modos,** in various ways. **De un modo o de otro,** one way or another. **Modo de programa,** *(Inform.)* program mode. **Modo de programación conversacional,** *(Inform.)* conversational programming mode. **Modo ampliado,** *(Inform.)* emphasized mode. **Modo de doble impresión,** *(Inform.)* double strike printing mode. **Modo de espaciado proporcional,** *(Inform.)* proportional spacing mode. **Modo de impresión super / subscript,** *(Inform.)* super / subscript printing mode.

modorra [mo-dor'-rah], *f.* 1. Drowsiness (sueño), heaviness. 2. Dawn or approach of day. 3. Flabby softness of the pulp of fruit. 4. A disease in sheep arising from plethora: sturdy.

modorrar [mo-dor-rar'], *va.* To drowse, to render heavy with sleep. *-vr.* To become flabby: applied to the pulp of fruit.

modorrilla [mo-dor-reel'-lyah], *f.* The third night-watch.

modorro, ra [mo-dor'-ro, rah], *a.* 1. Drowsy (soñoliento), sleepy, heavy. 2. Drowsy, dull (tonto), stupid.

modoso, sa [mo-doh'-so, sah], *a.* Temperate, sedate, in manner and gestures.

modrego [mo-dray'-go], *m.* Dunce, dolt, thick-skull.

modulación [mo-doo-lah-the-on'], *f.* Modulation, agreeable harmony. **Modulación de frecuencia,** *(Inform.)* frequency modulation.

modulador, ra [mo-doo-lah-dor', rah], *m. & f.* Modulator.

modulante [mo-doo-lahn'-tay], *a.* Modulating.

modular [mo-doo-lar'], *vn.* To modulate, to sing with harmony and variety of sound.

módulo [mo'-doo-lo], *m.* 1. *(Arch.)* Module, measure of columns. 2. Modulation of voice. 3. Unit of measure of running water for household use, irrigation, and manufacturing application. 4. Size of coins and medals. 5. *(Cono Sur)* Shelf unit (estantería).

mofa [mo'-fah], *f.* Mockery, jeer, scoff, ridicule, sneer.

mofador, ra [mo-fah-dor', rah], *m. & f.* Scoffer, scorner, jeerer, jester, mocker.

mofadura [mo-fah-doo'-rah], *f.* Jeer, scoff; scorn, jesting.

mofar [mo-far'], *va.* To deride, to jeer, to scoff; to mock, to ridicule, to flout. *-vr.* To sneer, to scoff, to behave with contempt.

mofeta [mo-fay'-tah], *f.* 1. Mephitis, a pestilential exhalation in mines or other deep places. 2. Skunk or polecat (animal).

moflete [mo-flay'-tay], *m.* Chub-cheek (mejilla).

mofletudo, da [mo-flay-too'-do, dah], *a.* Chub-cheeked.

mogate [mo-gah'-tay], *m.* Varnish, glazing which covers anything. **A medio mogate,** carelessly, heedlessly.

mogato, ta [mo-gah'-to, tah], *a.* V. MOJIGATO .

mogol, la [mo'-gol, go'-lah] *(Acad.)*, or **Mongol, la,** *a.* Mongolian. **Gran Mongol,** Grand Mogul, title of the ancient Emperor of the Mongolians.

mogólico, ca [mo-go'-le-co, cah], *a.* Relating to Mongolia.

mogollón, na [mo-gol-lyone'], *m & f.* 1. A hanger-on, a trencher friend, a parasite. **Comer de mogollón,** to sponge upon others. 2. Fuss, row (lío). 3. Large amount (cantidad). **Un mogollón de gente,** a mass of people.

mogote [mo-go'-tay], *m.* 1. An insulated rock or cliff with a flat crown, appearing at sea. 2. Pointed stack of corn.

mogrollo [mo-grol'-lyo], *m.* 1. Parasite, sponger. 2. Clown, rustic.

moharra [mo-ar'-rah], *f.* The point in which an ensign or flag-staff terminates.

moharrache, moharracho [mo-ar-rah'-chay, mo-ar-rah'-cho], *m.* Jack-pudding; a low jester.

mohatra [mo-ah'-trah], *f.* The act of selling for high prices and buying on the lowest terms, in order to overreach the buyer or seller.

mohatrar [mo-ah-trar'], *va.* To buy under price and sell above it; to make a deceitful sale.

mohatrero, ra [mo-ah-tray'-ro, rah], *m. & f.* Extortioner.

mohatrón [mo-ah-trone'], *m.* Extorter.

mohecer [mo-ay-therr'], *va.* To moss, to cover with moss.

mohiento, ta [mo-e-en'-to, tah], *a. V.* MOHOSO.

mohín [mo-een'], *m.* Grimace. **Hacer un mohín,** to make a face.

mohina [mo-ee'-nah], *f.* Animosity, desire of revenge (rencor).

mohino, na [mo-ee'-no, nah], *a.* 1. Fretful, peevish (disciplente). 2. Begotten by a stallion and she-ass (mulas). 3. Black (caballos, mulas). 4. Sad (triste), mournful. --*m.* One who plays alone against several others.

moho [mo'-o], *m.* 1. *(Bot.)* Moss. 2. Mould, concreted matter; rust (en metal); mouldiness. 3. Bluntness occasioned for want of application. 4. Lazy feeling (pereza).

mohoso, sa [mo-o'-so, sah], *a.* Mouldy, musty, rusty (metal), mossy.

mojada [mo-hah'-dah], *f.* 1. The act of wetting or moistening; dampening (al mojarse). 2. Sop, a piece of bread steeped in liquor. 3. *(coll.)* Stab, a wound with a pointed weapon (herida).

mojado, da [mo-hah'-do, dah], *a.* Wet; drenched, soaked. **Llover sobre mojado,** to be quite unnecessary.

mojador, ra [mo-hah-dor', rah], *m. & f.* Wetter, moistener.

mojadura [mo-hah-doo'-rah], *f.* Act of moistening or wetting.

mojama [mo-hah'-mah], *f.* Salt tuna-fish, dried or smoked.

mojar [mo-har'], *va.* 1. To wet, to moisten, to damp (humedecer), to drench (empapar). 2. To meddle, to interfere. 3. To stab (apuñalar). 4. To celebrate (triunfo). 5. *(Carib.)* To tip; *(Carib.)* to bribe (sobornar). **La lluvia mojó a todos,** the rain soaked everybody. **Mojar la ropa en un líquido,** to soak clothes in a liquid. **Mojar en mi business.** -*vn.* To be immersed in my business. -*vr.* To get wet.

mojarra [mo-har'-rah], *f.* 1. Sea-fish, small and very broad. 2. *(Amer.)* A heart-shaped, or short and broad dagger.

mojarrilla [mo-har-reel'-lyah], *m. (coll.)* Punster, jester.

moje [mo'-hay], *m. (coll.)* Sauce of fricassee, ragout, or any other dressed meat.

mojeles [mo-hay'-less], *m. pl. (Naut.)* Blocks, pulleys.

mojicón [mo-he-cone'], *m.* 1. Blow in the face with a clinched fist (bofetada). 2. Kind of biscuit.

mojiganga [mo-he-gahn'-gah], *f.* A morrice or morris dance; masquerade, mask, mummery.

mojigatería [mo-he-gah-tay-ree'-ah], *f.* Hypocrisy, religious fanaticism.

mojigatez [mo-he-gah-teth'], *f.* Bigotry. *V.* MOJIGATERÍA.

mojigato, ta [mo-he-gah'-to, tah], *m. & f.* Dissembler, hypocrite (hipócrita), a person who affects humility and servile submission to obtain his end.-*a.* Deceitful, hypocritical, hypocritic.

mojí, mojil [mo-hee', mo-heel'], *a. V.* CAZUELA.

mojón [mo-hone'], *m.* 1. Landmark (hito). 2. Heap, pile (montón). 3. Kind of game, like pitching. 4. Solid excrement. -*m & f. (Carib.)* Idiot (bruto); shortie (chaparro).

mojona [mo-ho'-nah], *f.* 1. Duty on wine sold by retails 2. Survey of land; the setting up of landmarks.

mojonación [mo-ho-nah-the-on'], *f. V.* AMOJONAMIENTO.

mojonar [mo-ho-nar'], *va. V.* AMOJONAR.

mojonera [mo-ho-nay'-rah], *f.* Landmark.

mojonero [mo-ho-nay'-ro], *m.* Gauger, a person appointed by government to measure wine.

mola [mo'-lah], *f.* 1. Mole, a formless concretion in the uterus, false conception commonly called **mola-matriz.** 2. Barley or flour mixed with salt and used in sacrifices.

molada [mo-lah'-dah], *f.* Quantity of colors ground at once.

molar [mo-lahr'], *a.* Molar, belonging to a mill-stone, or any other thing for grinding, as the teeth.

molar [mo-lahr'], *va.* **Lo que más me mola es...,** what I´m really into is...(gustar). **No me mola,** I don´t go for that. -*vn.*

1. To be in, to be fashionable. 2. To be classy (dar tono). 3. To swank (darse tono). 4. To be OK (valer).

molcajete, or **morcajete** [mol-cah-hay'-tay], *m. (Mex.)* A mortar, either of burnished clay or stone, used to pound spices and smell seeds.

moldar [mol-dar'], *va.* To mould. *V.* AMOLDAR.

molde [mol'-day], *m.* 1. Mould, the matrix in which anything is cast or receives its form: pattern (patrón), mould, block. 2. A form ready for printing. 3. A person who has reached the highest grade in anything; example, model. **De molde,** in print, printed or published; fitting, to the purpose.

moldeador [mol-day-ah-dor'], *m. (Prov.)* Moulder.

moldear [mol-day-ar'], *va.* To mould, to make moulds.

moldura [mol-doo'-rah], *f.* Moulding, an ornamental cavity in wood or stone.

moldurar [mol-doo-rar'], *va.* To make a moulding or ornament of something.

mole [mo'-lay] *a.* Soft, mild.-*f.* Vast size or quantity; massiness. **Se sentó con todo su mole,** he sat down with his full weight.

mole [mo'-lay], *m.* Mexican stew of meat or fowl with a special hot sauce.

molécula [mo-lay'-coo-lah], *f.* Molecule, invisible particle of bodies.

molecular [mo-lay-coo-lar'], *a.* Molecular, relating to molecules.

moledera [mo-lay-day'-rah], *f. (coll.)* Bother, annoyance. *V.* CANSERA.

moledero, ra [mo-lay-day'-ro, rah], *a.* That which is to be ground.

moledor, ra [mo-lay-dor', rah], *m. & f.* 1. Grinder, one who grinds and prepares colors. 2. Bore, a tiresome fellow (aburrido). 3. A tool employed by powder-makers for reducing powder to small grains. 4. Each of the crushing cylinders in a sugar-mill.

moledura [mo-lay-doo'-rah], *f.* The act of grinding. *V.* MOLIENDA.

molendero [mo-len-day'-ro], *m.* 1. Miller, grinder. 2. Chocolate manufacturer, one who grinds the cocoa and beats it with sugar and flavoring.

moler [mo-lerr'], *va.* 1. To grind, to pound (pulverizar), to pulverize, to mill (trigo). 2. To vex, to molest; to fatigue (cansar). 3. To waste, to consume by use. 4. To masticate, to chew. **Moler a azotes,** to lash, to whip.

molero [mo-lay'-ro], *m.* Maker or seller of mill-stones.

molestador, ra [mo-les-tah-dor', rah], *m. & f.* Disturber, vexer, molester.

molestamente [mo-lays'-tah-men-tay], *adv.* Troublesomely, vexatiously, grievously.

molestar [mo-les-tar'], *va.* To vex, to disturb, to molest, to trouble (dolor), to hurry, to tease, to grate, to cut to the heart, to annoy (fastidiar), to upset (incordiar). **Me molesta ese ruido,** that noise upsets me. **Me molesta tener que repetirlo,** I hate having to repeat it. -*vn.* To be a nuisance (fastidiar); to get in the way (estorbar). **No quiero molestar,** I don´t want to intrude. -*vr.* To bother (darse trabajo); to go to trouble (incomodarse). **Molestarse en,** to bother to.

molestia [mo-les'-te-ah], *f.* Injury, molestation, hardship, grievance, nuisance, excruciation. **Es una molestia,** it´s a nuisance.

molesto, ta [mo-les'-to, tah], *a.* Grievous, vexatious, oppressive, molestful, heavy, troublesome (que molesta), inconvenient (incómodo), discontented (descontento); restless (inquieto); ill-at-ease (incómodo). **Estar molesto con uno,** to be cross with somebody.

moleta [mo-lay'-tah], *f.* 1. Muller, a stone flat at the bottom and round at the top, used by painters to grind colors on marble. 2. An apparatus for smoothing and polishing flint glass. 3. Muller, grinder for printing-ink on the ink-table.

moletón [mo-lay-tone'], *m.* Milled flannel, canton or cotton flannel, swan's-down.

molibdato [mo-lib-dah'-to], *m.* Molibdate.

molibdeno [mo-lib-day'-no], *m.* Molybdenum, a white, brittle, lustreless metal.

molíbdico [mo-leeb'-de-co], *a.* Molybdic, relating to, derived from, or compounded with molybdenum.

molicie [mo-lee'-the-ay], *f.* 1. Tenderness, softness (blandura), effeminacy. 2. An unnatural crime.

molido, da [mo-lee'-do, dah], *a. & pp.* of MOLER. Ground (machacado); fatigued; flogged.

molienda [mo-le-en'-dah], *f.* 1. The act of grinding or pounding. 2. Quantity pounded or ground at once, grist. 3. Weariness (cansancio), fatigue, lassitude. 4. Season of grinding sugar-cane or olives (temporada).

moliente [mo-le-en'-tay], *pa.* Grinder, grinding. **Moliente y corriente**, *(coll.)* right, justly, exactly.

molificación [mo-le-fe-cah-the-on'], *f.* Mollification.

molificar [mo-le-fe-car'], *va.* To mollify, to soften, to mitigate.

molificativo, va [mo-le-fe-cah-tee'-vo, vah], *a.* That which mollifies, lenitive.

molimiento [mo-le-me-en'-to], *m.* 1. The act of grinding, pounding, or beating up. 2. Fatigue, weariness, lassitude.

molina [mo-lee'-nah], *f.* Oil-mill of large capacity. *(Recent.)*

molinar [mo-le-nar'], *m.* Place where there are mills; milling-plant.

molinejo [mo-le-nay'-ho], *m. dim.* A small mill.

molinera [mo-le-nay'-rah], *f.* 1. Miller's wife. 2. Woman who tends or works in a mill.

molinero [mo-le-nay'-ro], *m.* Miller, grinder.

molinero, ra [mo-le-nay'-ro, rah], *a.* Anything which is to be ground or pounded; anything belonging to a mill.

molinete [mo-le-nay'-tay], *m.* 1. *(Naut.)* Windlass. 2. Turnstile. 3. *(dim.)* A little mill. 5 Brandish, twirl about the head in fencing. 5. *(Mech.)* Friction roller; sway-plate of a vehicle; smoke dispeller.

molinillo [mo-le-neel'-lyo], *m.* 1. *(dim.)* A little mill; a hand-mill. 2. Churn-staff, chocolate-mill, a stick with which chocolate is beat up in a chocolate-pot. **Molinillo de café**, coffee mill.

molinismo [mo-le-nees'-mo], *m.* Molinism or quietism, principles of a sect.

molinista [mo-le-nees'-tah], *m.* Molinist, a follower of the doctrines of Molinism.

molinito [mo-le-nee'-to], *m. dim.* A small mill.

molino [mo-lee'-no], *m.* 1. Mill, an apparatus in which corn is ground; corn-mill (trituradora). **Molino de viento**, wind-mill. **Molino de agua**, water-mill. **Molino de mano**, hand-mill. **Molino de papel**, paper-mill. 2. A restless (inquieto), noisy fellow. 3. *(coll.)* Mouth.

molitivo, va [mo-le-tee'-vo, vah], *a.* Mollient.

molla [mol'-lyah], *f.* 1. Lean meat without bone. 2. *(Prov.)* Crumb of bread.

mollar [mol-lyar'], *a.* 1. Soft (fruta), tender, pappy, pulpous. 2. Fleshy, lean, without bone (carne). 3. Gullible (crédulo). 4. Cushy (trabajo). 5. Super (bueno).

mollear [mol-lyay-ar'], *vn.* To grow soft and pliable, to soften or to grow less hard, to yield easily.

molledo [mol-lyay'-do], *m.* 1.The fleshy part of a limb. 2. Crumb of bread.

molleja [mol-lyay'-hah], *f.* 1. Gland, particularly that which is seated at the root of the tongue. 2. Gizzard, the strong muscular stomach of a fowl; maw.

mollejón [mol-lyay-hone'], *m.* 1. *(Aug.)* A large gland. 2. A big, corpulent person.

mollejuela [mol-lyay-hoo-ay'-lah], *f. dim.* A small gland.

mollera [mol-lyay'-rah], *f.* Crown or top of the head. **Ser duro de mollera**, to be obstinate. **Cerrado de mollera**, rude, ignorant.

mollero [mol-lyay'-ro], *m. (Prov.)* Fleshy part of the arm.

molleta [mol-lyay'-tah], *f.* 1. Snuffers. 2. Bread made of the finest flour.

mollete [mol-lyay'-tay], *m.* Manchet, a small loaf made of the finest flour. **Molletes**, plump or round cheeks.

mollina, mollizna [mol-lyee'-nah, mol-lyeeth'-nah], *f* Mist, small rain.

molliznar, molliznear [mol-lyeeth-nar'], *vn.* To drizzle, to mizzle, to fall in small, slow drops.

molón [mo-lon'], *a.* 1. Super (bueno), smashing. 2. Posh (elegante).

molondro, molondrón [mo-lon'-dro, mo-lon-drone'], *m.* A sluggish, mean-spirited and ignorant fellow, poltroon.

moloquita [mo-lo-kee'-tah], *f. (Min.)* A variety of agate of dull-green hue.

molotov [mo-lo-tov], *m.* **Cóctel molotov**, Molotov cocktail.

moltura [mol-too'-rah], *f. V.* MOLIENDA.

molusco [mo-loos'-co], *m.* Mollusk, one of the mollusca, invertebrates having an unsegmented body, and usually a calcareous shell.

moma [mo'-mah], *f. (Mex.)* Blindman's-buff.

momentáneamente [mo-men-tah-nay-men-tay] *adv.* 1. Instantly. 2. Momentarily.

momentáneo, nea [mo-men-tah´-nay-o, ah], *a.* Momentous, momentary, of short duration.

momento [mo-men'-to], *m.* 1. Moment, the least space of time. 2. Moment, consequence, momentum, weight, importance. 3. *(Math.)* Difference. 4. *(Mech.)* Power, force. **Al momento**, in a moment, immediately. **Por momentos**, successively, continually. **En el momento actual**, at the present time.

momería [mo-may-ree'-ah], *f.* Mummery, a farcical entertainment, in which masked persons play frolics and antic tricks.

momia [mo'-me-ah], *f.* Mummy, a dead body preserved by embalming.

momificar [mo-me-fe-car'], *va.* To mummify, to convert into a mummy.-*vr.* To resemble a mummy.

momio, mia [mo'-me-o, ah], *a.* Meagre, lean (carne).

momo [mo'-mo], *m.* Buffoonery, low jests, scurrile mirth, wry faces (cara), grimaces.

momórdiga [mo-mor'-de-gah], *f. (Bot.) V.* BALSAMINA.

momperada [mom-pay-rah´-dah], *f.* A kind of glazed woollen stuff.

mona [mo'-nah], *f.* 1. Female monkey or ape (especie). 2. *(coll.)* A mimic, a ludicrous imitator. 3. In jocular style, drunkenness and drunkard (borrachera). 4 *(Prov)* Cake made of flour, eggs, and milk. 5. Iron plate worn for protection on the right leg by bull-fighters on horseback. 6. *(And.)* Blonde. 7. *(LAm.)* Colombian golden marijuana. **Aunque la mona se vista de seda, mona se queda**, *(Prov.)* dress a monkey as you will, it remains a monkey still. **Dormir la mona**, to sleep off a hangover.

monacal [mo-nah-cahl'], *a.* Monachal, monastic, monkish, belonging to monks.

monacalmente [mo-nah-cahl'-men-tay], *adv.* Monastically.

monacato [mo-nah-cah´-to], *m.* Monkhood, monachism.

monacillo [mo-nah-theel'-lyo], *m.* Acolyte, acolithe, or acolutist, a boy who serves in a church.

monacordio [mo-nah-cor'-de-o], *m.* Spinet, an old-fashioned stringed musical instrument with keys.

monada [mo-nah'-dah], *f.* 1. Grimace (mueca), a ludicrous or ridiculous distortion of the countenance. 2. Monkeyism, monkey-shine, behavior characteristic of a monkey (comportamiento). 3. Fawning, flattery. 4. Lovely thing. **La casa es una monada**, the house is lovely.

mónada [mo'-nah-dah], *f.* 1. Monad, an indivisible thing. 2. A microscopic infusorian, monad.

monadelfo, fa [mo-nah-del'-fo, fah], *a.* Monadelphous, (stamens) united into one cluster.

monago, monaguillo [mo-nah´-go, mo-nah-geel'-lyo], *m. V.* MONACILLO.

monaguismo [mo-nah-gees´-mo], *m.* Monachism, monasticness.

monarca [mo-nar'-cah], *m.* Monarch, king, sovereign, lord.

monarquía [mo-nar-kee'-ah], *f.* Monarchy, the government of a single person, kingdom, empire, kingship.

monárquico, ca [mo-nar'-ke-co, cah], *a.* Monarchical, monarchal, kingly, king-like.

monasterial [mo-nas-tay-re-ahl'], *a.* Monastic.

monasterillo [mo-nas-tay-reel'-lyo], *m. dim.* A small monastery.

monasterio [mo-nas-tay'-re-o], *m.* Monastery, a house of religious retirement; convent, minster; cloister.

monásticamente [mo-nahs'-te-cah-men-tay], *adv.* Monastically.

monástico, ca [mo-nahs'-te-co, cah], *a.* Monastic, monastical, monachal, monkish.

monazo, za [mo-nah'-tho, thah], *m. & f. aug.* Large monkey or ape.

monda [mon'-dah], *f.* 1. Pruning of trees (acto); the pruning season (temporada). 2. Peel (piel), peelings, skin. 3. *(And. Carib. Mex.)* Beating. 4. *(Fig.)* **Fue la monda,** it was a scream. **Este nuevo baile es la monda,** this new dance is awful.

mondadientes [mon-dah-de-en'-tays], *m.* Toothpick.

mondador, ra [mon-dah-dor', rah], *m. & f.* Cleaner, purifier.

mondadura [mon-dah-doo'-rah], *f.* Cleaning (limpieza), cleansing, the act of freeing from filth. **Mondaduras,** parings, peelings, anything which comes off by cleaning.

mondaoídos [mon-dah-o-ee'-dose], or **Mondaorejas** [mon-dah-o-ray'-has], *m.* Ear-spoon.

mondar [mon-dar'], *va.* 1. To clean (limpiar), to cleanse, to free from filth. 2. To husk, to strip off the husks of fruit, to peel (pelar), to decorticate; to deprive of money. 3. To cut the hair. 4. *(And, Carib.)* To beat (dar una paliza). **Mondar los huesos,** to pick bones quite clean.

mondejo [mon-day'-ho], *m.* Paunch or belly of a pig or sheep stuffed with minced meat.

mondo, da [mon'-do, dah], *a.* Neat, clean (limpio), pure (puro), unadulterated. **Mondo y lirondo,** *(coll.)* pure, without any admixture.

mondonga [mon-don'-gah], *f.* In contempt, a kitchen-wench or a maid-servant.

mondongo [mon-don'-go], *m.* Paunch, tripes, black pudding. **Hacer el mondongo,** *V.* MONDONGONIZAR.

mondongonizar [mon-don-go-ne-thar'], *va.* To dress tripe, to make black puddings.

mondonguero, ra [mon-don-gay'-ro, rah], *m. & f.* One who makes black puddings or deals in them.

mondonguil [mon-don-geel'], *a. (coll.)* Relating to tripes or puddings.

monear [mo-nay-ar'], *vn.* 1. To act in an affected, ridiculous, or preposterous manner (comportarse); to monkey (hacer muecas). 2. *(Cono Sur, Mex.)* To boast, to swank (jactarse).

moneda [mo-nay'-dah], *f.* Money, pieces of gold, silver, or copper, coined for the purpose of trade; coinage. **Moneda corriente,** current coin. **Pagar a uno con la misma moneda,** to pay somebody back with his own coin. **Una moneda de 5 dólares,** a 5-dollar piece.

monedaje [mo-nay-dah'-hay], *m.* Coinage, the charges paid for coining money.

monedar, monedear [mo-nay-dar'], *va.* To coin.

monedería [mo-nay-day-ree'-ah], *f.* Mint, factory of money.

monedero [mo-nay-day'-ro], *m.* 1. Officer of the mint who coins money, coiner, moneyer. **Monedero falso,** coiner or maker of base money. 2. Purse (portamonedas).

monedilla, ita [mo-nay-deel'-lyah], *f. dim.* A small piece of money.

monería [mo-nay-ree'-ah], *f.* 1. Grimace, a ludicrous or ridiculous distortion of the countenance; mimicry (imitación). 2. Trifle, gewgaw, bauble.

monesco, ca [mo-nes'-co, cah], *a.* Apish, having the qualities of a monkey.

monetario [mo-nay-tah'-re-o], *m.* 1. Cabinet of ancient coins and models. 2. Collection of coins and medals; the whole number of cases, tables or drawers which contain them. 3.

Treasury-chamber, museum or place which holds such a collection.

monetario [mo-nay-tah-re-o] *a.* Monetary, pertaining to money or finance.

monotización [mo-nay-te-thah-the-on'], *f* Monetization, the act of legally declaring to be money.

monetizar [mo-nay-te-thar'], *va.* To monetize, to legalize as money.

mongol, la [mon-gol'], *a. V.* MOGOL.

moniato [mo-ne-ah'-to], *m.* A farinaceous root of which a kind of bread is made in some parts of South America.

monicaco, monicongo [mo-ne-cah'-co], *m.* A conceited, thoughtless person. *V.* CHUCHUMECO.

monición [mo-ne-the-on'], *f.* Admonition, publication of the bans of marriage.

monigote [mo-ne-go'-tay], *m. (coll.)* 1. Lay-brother of religious orders. 2. A person who is considered without knowledge or skill in his own profession. 3. *(Met. and coll.)* A poorly made painting or statue.

moniliforme [mo-ne-le-for'-may], *a.* Moniliform, like a string of beads.

monillo [mo-neel'-lyo], *m.* Waist, bodice, a jacket without sleeves, worn by women.

monipodio [mo-ne-poh'-de-o], *m.* Any combination or agreement among several persons with an unlawful object.

monismo [mo-nees'-mo], *m. (Phil.)* Monism.

mónita [mo'-ne-tah], *f.* 1. Artifice, artfulness, affected flattery. 2. *(Peru. Coll.)* Severs reproof.

monitor [mo-ne-tor'], *m.* 1. Monitor (profesor). 2. An armor-clad vessel. 3. *(Inform. Tec.)* Monitor, display. **Monitor en color,** color monitor.

monitoria [mo-ne-to'-re-ah], *f.* Summons issued by an ecclesiastical judge to command the personal appearance and deposition of a witness.

monitorio, ria [mo-ne-to'-re-o, ah], *a.* Monitory, admonitory.

monja [mon'-hah], *f.* Nun, a religious woman confined in a cloister.-*pl.* Appellation given to sparks in burned papers.

monje [mon'-hay], *m.* 1. Monk: also, recluse, anchorite. 2. Brown peacock.

monjía [mon-hee'-ah], *f.* Proband, enjoyed by a monk in his convent.

monjil [mon-heel'], *m.* 1. Habit or dress of a nun (hábito). 2. Mourning dress or weeds of a widow.

monjío [mon-hee'-o], *m.* The day and ceremony of a lady's taking the veil.

mono, na [mo'-no, nah], *a. (coll.)* Cute, pretty. **Una chica muy mona,** a very attractive girl. -*m.* 1. Monkey. 2. *(Fig.)* Mimic (imitador). 3. Coveralls (de obrero). 4. Cocky youngster (engreído). 5. Joker (naipes). 6. Ugly devil (feo). 7. Pansy (maricón). 8. Cop (policía). 9. *(Carib.)* Debt (deuda). 10. Sign (señal). **Meter los monos a,** to scare the daylights out of someone. **Mono de imitación,** copycat (niño).

monoceronte, monocerote [mo-no-thay-ro'-tay], *m.* Unicorn.

monocordio [mo-no-cor-de-o], *m.* Monochord, an instrument of one string anciently used.

monocotiledóneo, ea [mo-no-co-te-lay-do'-nay-o, ah], *a. (Bot.)* Monocotyledonous.

monocromático, ca [mo-no-cro-mah'-te-co, cah], *a.* Monochromatic, of one color: applied to yellow light, and also to a painting done in one color.

monócromo [mo-no'-cro-mo], *m. y a.* Monochrome, a painting done in one color.

monóculo, la [mo-no'-coo-lo, lah], *a.* Monoculous, monocular, one-eyed.

monóculo [mo-no'-coo-lo], *m.* 1. Monocle. 2. Bandage for only one eye.

monodonte [mo-no-don'-tay], *m. (Zool.)* Narwhal, sea-unicorn.

monogamia [mo-no-gah'-me-ah], *f.* Monogamy, marriage of one wife only.

monógamo [mo-no'-gah-mo], *m.* He who marries only one woman.

monogástrico, ca [mo-no-gahs'-tre-co, cah], *a. (Zool.)* Monogastric, having a single stomach.

monografía [mo-no-grah-fee'-ah], *f.* Monograph, a description of one genus, one species, etc.; an extended essay upon a single topic.

monográfico, ca [mo-no-grah'-fe-co, cah], *a.* Monographic, drawn in plain lines. **Programa monográfico**, program devoted to a single subject.

monograma [mo-no-grah'-mah], *m.* Monogram, a cipher or character compounded of several letters and standing for some name.

monoico, ca [mo-no'-e-co, cah], *a.* Monoecious, bearing distinct male and female flowers upon one stem.

monolito [mo-no-lee'-to], *m.* Monolith, a stone monument in a single piece.

monólogo [mo-no'-lo-go], *m.* Monologue, soliloquy.

monomanía [mo-no-mah-nee'-ah], *f.* Monomania, insanity upon one subject.

monomaníaco, ca [mo-no-mah-nee'-ah-co, cah], *a.* Monomaniac.

monomio [mo-no'-me-o], *m. (Alg.)* Monomial; expression consisting of a single term.

monona [mo-no'-nah], *a. (coll.)* Graceful and pretty, especially if very young (mujer).

monopastos [mo-no-pahs'-tose], *m.* Pulley with one wheel.

monopatín [mo-no-pah-teen'], *m.* Skateboard.

monopétalo, la [mo-no-pay'-tah-lo, lah], *a.* Monopetalous, having only one flower-leaf; gamopetalous.

monoplano [mo-no-plah'-no], *m.* Monoplane.

monópodo, da [mo-no'-po-do, dah], *a.* Monopode, having but one foot.

monopolio [mo-no-po'-le-o], *m.* Monopoly, the exclusive privilege of selling anything, and the combination or agreement among tradesmen for selling a thing at a certain price.

monopolista [mo-no-po-lees'-tah], Monopolist, forestaller, monopolizer.

monopolizar [mo-no-po-le-thar'], *va.* To monopolize, to forestall.

monosilábico, ca [mo-no-se-lah'-be-co, cah], *a.* Monosyllabic, consisting of one syllable.

monosílabo, ba [mo-no-see'-lah-bo, bah], *m. & f.* Monosyllable.

monospermo, ma [mo-nos-perr'-mo, mah], *a. (Bot.)* Monospermous, single seeded.

monóstrofe [mo-nos'-tro-fay], *f.* A poetical composition of a single strophe; monostrophe.

monoteísmo [mo-no-tay-ees'-mo], *m.* Monotheism, belief in only one God.

monoteísta [mo-no-tay-ees'-tah], *a.* Monotheistic, holding or relating to monotheism.-*m.* Monotheist.

monotipia [mo-no-tee'-pe-ah], *f (typ.)* Monotyping.

monotipo [mo-no-tee'-po], *m.* Monotype.

monotonía [mo-no-to-ne'-ah], *f.* Monotony, uniformity of sound.

monótono, na [mo-no'-to-no, nah], *a.* Monotonous, monotonic.

monóxido [mo-noc'-see-do], *m.* Monoxide.

monseñor [mon-say-nyor'], *m.* Monsignor.

monserga [mon-ser'-gah], *f.* 1. *(coll.)* Gabble, confused language. 2. Drivel (disparates), tedious. **Dar la monserga**, to get on somebody's nerves.

monstruo [mons'-troo-o], *m.* 1. Monster, a production contrary to the order of nature, idol (del mundo pop), wonder boy. 2. *(Bio.)* Freak, monster. -*a.* Fantastic, fabulous.

monstruosamente [mons-troo-o'-sah-men-tay], *adv.* Monstruously.

monstruosidad [mons-troo-o-se-dahd'], *f.* Monstruosity, monstrosity, excessive ugliness, monstrousness.

monstruoso, sa [mons-troo-o'-so, sah], *a.* 1. Monstrous, contrary to or deviating from the stated order of nature. 2. Monstrous, too irregular, enormous: shocking.

monta [mon'-tah], *f.* 1. Amount, sum total. 2. Value, worth, price. 3. Signal given with a trumpet for the cavalry to mount their horses.

montacargas [mon-tah-car'-gas], *m.* Elevator hoist, freight elevator.

montada [mon-tah'-dah], *f.* The elevation given to the bit of a bridle.

montadero [mon-ta-day'-ro], *m.* One who mounts; mounting-stone.

montado [Mon-tah'-do], *a.* 1. Applied to a horse ready for being mounted (caballo). 2. Applied to a trooper or horseman.-*pp* of MONTAR.

montador [mon-tah-dor'], *m.* 1. Mounter (persona). 2. Mounting block (objeto). 3. Film editor (que hace el montaje).

montadura [mon-tah-doo'-rah], *f.* 1. Mounting (acto). 2. Setting (of a gem). 3. Harness, trappings.

montaescaleras [mon-tah-cah-lay'-ras], *m.* Chair lift.

montaje [mon-tah'-hay], *m.* 1. Assembly. 2. Editing (película). 3. Set-up (arreglo de antemano). 4. Fiddle (estafa). 5. *(Teat.)* Stage design.

montanera [mon-tah-nay'-rah], *m.* The feeding of hogs with acorns, driven for that purpose into groves of oak.

montanero [mon-tah-nay'-ro], *m.* Forester, keeper of a forest.

montano, na [mon-tah'-no, nah], *a.* Mountainous.

montantada [mon-tan-tah-dah], *f.* 1. Ostentation, boasting. 2. Multitude.

montante [mon-tahn'-tay], *m.* 1. A broadsword used by fencing-masters. 2. A kind of fireworks which, when lighted, forms this figure. 3. *(Naut.)* Flood tide. 4. *(Arch.)* Upright, standard, a piece of wood, stone, or metal which divides a window into various parts (de ventana). 5. *(Mil.)* Stempel, an upright timber used for support in a mine (poste).

montantear [mon-tan-tay-ar'], *vn.* 1. To wield the broadsword in a fencing-school. 2. To vaunt, to brag.

montantero [mon-tan-tay'-ro], *m.* He who fights with a broadsword.

montaña [mon-tah'-nyah], *f.* 1. Mountain, mount. V. MONTE. 2. *(And, Carib.)* Forest (selva). 3. *(CAm.)* Virgin jungle (selva virgen). -*pl.* Highlands; a ridge of mountains. **Montaña rusa**, roller coaster.

montañés, sa [mon-tah-nyes', sah], *a.* 1. Mountain, pertaining to the mountains. 2. Mountainous, inhabiting mountains, highlander. -*m. & f.* Mountaineer, mountainer, an inhabitant of the mountains, a highlander.

montañeta, montañuela [mon-tah-nyay'-tah, nyoo-ay'-lah], *f. dim.* A small mountain.

montañoso, sa [mon-tah-nyo'-so, sah], *a.* Mountainous, hilly.

montar [mon-tar'], *vn.* 1. To mount or go on horseback (en caballo). 2. To amount to, to be worth. 3. To cock a gun. 4. To be of importance. **Montar a caballo**, to ride, **Me ayudó a montar**, he helped me up. **Monta a**, to amount to. -*va.* 1. To impose a penalty for cattle entering a forest. 2. To mount (bicicleta, caballo), to set, to provide with a setting. 3. To mount, to set up, to put in place the parts of a machine or apparatus. 4. To cover, to copulate with: said of a horse or ass. 5. To mount, to carry, or be equipped with. 6. *(Mar.)* To double a cape or headland. 7. To edit (película). **Tanto monta**, it's all the same. **Vestido or traje de montar**, riding habit. **Montar un reloj**, to wind a watch or clock. **Montar a uno sobre un tronco**, to lift somebody on to a log. **Montar un color sobre otro**, to overlap one color with another. **Montar una tienda**, to open a shop. **Montar un número**, to make a scene.

montaraz [mon-tah-rath'], *m.* Forester, guard of woods or farms.

montaraz [mon-tah-rath'], *a.* 1. Mountain (de montaña), mountainous. 2. Wild (salvaje), untamed, haggard.

montazgar [mon-tath-gar'], *va.* To levy or collect the toll for cattle passing from one province into another.

montazgo [mon-tath'-go], *m.* 1. Toll to be paid for cattle passing from one province into another. 2. Place through which the cattle pass.

monte [mon´-tay], *m.* 1. Mountain (montaña), mount, a large hill, a vast protuberance of the earth. 2. Wood (bosque), forest, a woody place. 3. Difficulty, obstruction, obstacle (obstáculo). 4. A bushy head of hair much entangled. 5. Stock of cards which remain after each player has received his share. 6. (*Amer.*) A game at cards. 7. (*CAm. Carib.*) Outskirts (alrededores). 8. (*Mex.*) Grass (pasto). 9. (*LAm.*) Hash (droga). **Monte alto** or **de árboles,** a lofty grove or wood. **Creer que todo el monte es orégano,** to think everything in the garden is lovely.

montea [mon-tay'-ah], *f.* 1. Art or trade of cutting or hewing stone. 2. Plan or profile of a building. 3. (*Arch.*) Convexity of an arch.

montear [mon-tay-ar'], *va.* 1. To beat a wood in pursuit of game, to hunt. 2. To draw the plan or profile of a building. 3. To vault, to form arches.

montecillo [mon-tay-theel´-lyo], *m. dim.* 1. A small wood or forest. 2. Hillock, hummock, a small mount.

montepío or **monte de piedad,** *m.* Charitable pawnshop.

montera [mon-tay'-rah], *f.* 1. A kind of cap glade of cloth (sombrero). 2. Skylight, covering of glass over a gallery, court. etc. 3. Receiver, condenser of a still or alembic. 4. (*Naut.*) Skysail, skyscraper. 5. Hunter's wife.

monterería [mom-tay-ray-ree´-ah], *f.* Shop or place where caps are made or sold.

montería [mon-tay-ree´-ah], *f.* 1. Hunting (arte), hunt (cacería), chase. 2. Place where hunting-caps are made or sold. 3. Hunting party (personas). 4. (*And.*) Canoe. 5. (*CAm.*) Concession. 6. (*CAm. Mex.*) Timber camp (maderería).

montero [mon-tay'-ro], *m.* Huntsman, hunter.

monteruca [mon-tay-roo'-cah], *f.* An ugly cap.

monterrey [mon-ter-ray'-e], *m.* A kind of thin paste rolled up into spiral tubes.

montés, sa [mon-tes', sah], *a.* Montigenous, mountain, bred or found in a forest or mountain.

montesa [mon-tay'-sah], *f.* One of the military orders of Spain.

montescos [mon-tes'-cos], *m. pl.* **Haber Montescos y Capeletes,** to have great disputes and contentions (to be Montagues and Capulets).

montesino, na [mon-tay-see'-no, nah], *a.* Montigenous, bred or found in a forest or mountain.

monto [mon'-to], *m.* Amount, sum.

montón [mon-tone'], *m.* 1. Heap, pile. **Montón de gente,** crowd, multitude. 2. Congeries, mass, cluster. 3. A dirty, lazy fellow. **A montones,** abundantly, by heaps.

montuosidad [mon-too-o-see-dahd'], *f. (Prov.)* Mountainousness.

montuoso, sa [mon-too-o'-so, sah], *a.* Full of woods and thickets, mountainous, hilly.

montura [mon-too'-rah], *f.* 1. Horses and mules intended for the saddle. 2. Saddle (silla), trappings and accoutrements of horses (arreos). **Cabalgar sin montura,** to ride bareback.

monuelo [mo-noo-ay'-lo], *m. dim.* A coxcomb, a fop.

monumental [mo-noo-men-tahl'], *a.* Monumental (enorme), belonging to monuments.

monumento [mo-noo-men'-to], *m.* 1. Monument, anything by which the memory of persons or things is preserved, such as a statue, a tomb, a cenotaph, etc. 2. Altar raised in churches on Holy Thursday to resemble a sepulchre. **Monumentos,** monuments or remains of antiquity. 3. Pretty girl (chica).

monzón [mon-thone'], *m.* Monsoon, a periodical wind in the East Indian Ocean.

moñá [mo'-nyah], *f.* 1. Lay-figure of a woman to show a style of dress. 2. Peevishness, fretfulness. 3. An ornament of ribbons used on the head by bullfighters. 4. (*coll.*) Drunkenness (borracho). 5. Very elaborate cap for nursing infants. 6. Hair ribbon (cinta). 7. Sash, prize ribbon (premio). 8. Doll (muñeca).

moño [mo'-nyo], *m.* 1. Hair on the crown of the head tied together; tuft. 2. Tuft of feathers on the heads of birds. 3. A bow of ribbons. 4. (*LAm.*) Pride, haughtiness (altivez). 5. (*Cono Sur*) To give in. **Estar hasta el moño,** to be fed up.

moñudo, da [mo-nyoo'-do, dah], *a.* Crested, topped.

moquear [mo-kay-ar'], *vn.* To snivel, to run at the nose; to blow the nose.

moqueo [mo-kay'-o], *m.* Runny nose.

moquero [mo-kay'-ro], *m. (coll.)* Pocket handkerchief.

moqueta [mo-kay'-tah], *f.* Moquette (alfombra), a woollen stuff, with a wool of hemp, from which carpets and rugs are made.

moquete [mo-kay´-tay], *m.* Blow on the face or nose.

moquetear [mo-kay-tay-ar'], *vn.* To discharge much mucus from the nose.-*va.* To give blows in the face.

moquillo [mo-keel'-lyo], *m.* 1. (*dim.*) A little mucus. 2. Pip, a disease in fowls.

moquita [mo-kee'-tah], *f.* Snivel, running from the nose in cold weather.

mora [mo'-rah], *f.* 1. (*Law.*) Delay, procrastination. 2. Mulberry (del moral), the fruit of the mulberry-tree.

morabita [mo-rah-bee´-tah], *m.* Member of a sect formed by a son-in-law of Mohammed.

morabito [mo-rah-bee'-to], *m.* 1. A Mohammedan hermit. 2. V. MORABITA.

moracho, cha [mo-rah'-cho, chah], *a.* Dark purple.

morada [mo-rah'-dah], *f.* Habitation, abode, residence, mansion, lodging, home, continuance (casa). **La eterna morada,** the great beyond. **Última morada,** resting place.

morado, da [mo-rah'-do, dah], *a.* Violet, mulberry-colored. **Ojo morado,** black eye. **Ponerse morado,** to do oneself well, to eat a lot.

morador, ra [mo-rah-dor', rah], *m. & f.* Inhabitant, lodger.

moraga [mo-rah'-gah], *f.* Handful or bundle formed by female gleaners.

morago [mo-rah'-go], *m.* V. MORAGA.

moral [mo-rahl´], *m.* (*Bot.*) Mulberry tree. -*f.* 1. Morale, buoyant spirits despite danger. 2. Moral ethics, morality (moralidad).-*a.* Moral. **Apoyo moral,** moral support.

moraleja [mo-rah-lay'-hah], *f.* A brief moral observation.

moralidad [mo-rah-le-dahd'], *f.* 1. Morality, the doctrine of the duties of life. 2. Morality, form of an action, which makes it the subject of reward or punishment.

moralista [mo-rah-lees´-tah], *m & f.* Moralist, one who teaches the duties of life.

moralizador, ra [mo-rah-le-thah-dor', rah], *m. & f.* Commentator, critic, moralizer.

moralizar [mo-rah-le-thar'], *va. & vn.* 1. To moralize, to apply to moral purposes; to explain in a moral sense. 2. To moralize, to speak or write on moral subjects.

moralmente [mo-rahl'-men-tay], *adv.* Morally, in the ethical sense; according to the rules of virtue; popularly, by common sense.

morar [mo-rar'], *vn.* To inhabit, to dwell, to reside, to lodge, to live; to continue.

moratón [mo-rah-tone'], *m.* Bruise.

moratoria [mo-rah-to'-re-ah], *f.* 1. Letters of license granted to a debtor. 2. (*Com.*) Delay (para pagar).

moravo, va [mo-rah´-vo, vah], *a.* Moravian.

morbidez [mor-be-deth´], *f.* Softness, delicacy.

mórbido, da [mor'-be-do, dah], *a.* 1. Morbid (enfermo). 2. Soft, delicate (arte).

morbilidad, morbididad [mor-be-le-dahd', mor-be-de-dahd'], *f.* 1. Morbidity. 2. Sickness rate.

morbo [mor'-bo], *m.* 1. Disease. 2. (*Fig.*) Unhealthy curiosity.

morboso, sa [mor-bo'-so, sah], *a.* 1. Diseased, morbid (enfermo). 2. (*Fig.*) Diseased, morbid.

morcajo [mor-cah'-ho], *m.* A low grade wheat cultivated in Old Castile.

morcella [mor-thel'-lyah], *f.* Spark from a lamp.

morcilla [mor-theel'-lyah], *f.* 1. Black pudding, hog's pudding; *(Mex.)* Tripe (callos). 2. *(Teat.)* Gag, unscriped lines. 3. Prick (pene). 4. *(Carib.)* Lie (mentira).

morcillero, ra [mor-theel-lyay'-ro, rah], *m. & f.* One who makes or deals in black puddings.

morcillo, lla [mor-theel´-lyo, lyah], *a.* Entirely black (caballos).

morcillo [mor-theel´-lyo], *m.* The fleshy part of the arm from the shoulder to the elbow.

morcón [mor-cone'], *m.* 1. A large black pudding made of the blind gut; a large sausage. 2. *(coll.)* A short, plumpy fellow (rechoncho). 3. Sloppy individual (descuidado).

mordacidad [mor-dah-the-dahd'], *f.* 1. Mordacity, biting quality. 2. Roughness, asperity, acrimony in unripe fruit. 3. Mordacity, a nipping, sarcastic language.

mordante [mor-dahn'-tay], *m.* *(Print.)* Guide, container: a frame used by compositors to keep their copy secure, and mark the place up to which their work is completed.

mordaz [mor-dath'], *a.* Corrosive, biting (crítica), nipping; sarcastic; acrimonious, 3. satirical, keen.

mordaza [mor-dah'-thah], *f.* 1. Gag, to prevent speaking or crying (de boca). 2. Sort of nippers or pincers.

mordazmente [mor--dath'-men-tay], *adv.* Acrimoniously, nippingly.

mordedor, ra [mor-day-dor', rah], *m. & f.* 1. Biter, one who bites. 2. One who satirizes.

mordedura [mor-day-doo'-rah], *f.* Bite, wound made by biting; mordication.

mordente [mor-den'-tay], *m.* 1. Mordant, a substance used in dyeing for fixing the colors. 2. *(Mus.)* Mordent, or double appoggiatura, a musical embellishment. 3. *(Bus.)* Turn.

morder [mor-derr'], *va.* 1. To bite, to seize with the teeth, to nip (pinchar). 2. To be sharp or pungent to the taste; to make rough to the touch. 3. To seize or stick fast one thing in another. 4. To bite, to gnaw, to wear away gradually. 5. *(Met.)* To nip, to carp at, to taunt, to nibble (mordisquear), to find fault with, to satirize. 6. To gossip (denigrar). 7. To recognize (reconocer). **No morderse los labios**, *(coll.)* to speak one's opinions frankly and openly. **Morderse la lengua**, to refrain from saying what one is tempted to say. - *vn.* To bite. **Estoy que muerdo**, I'm simply furious. *(Yo muerdo, yo muerda,* from *Morder. V.* MOVER.)

mordicante [mor-de-cahn'-tay], *pa. & a.* Biting, pungent, acrid.

mordicar [mor-de-car'], *va.* To gnaw, to nibble; to smart, to sting.

mordicativo, va [mor-de-cah-tee'-voh, vah], *a.* Biting, gnawing, mordicant.

mordida [mor-dee'-dah], *f.* 1. Bite. 2. *(Mex. Coll.)* Bribe (soborno).

mordido, da [mor-dee'-do, dah], *a.* Diminished, wasted away.-*pp.* of MORDER.

mordido [mor-dee'-do], *m.* Bit, mouthful of meat.

mordiente [mor-de-en'-tay], *m.* 1. Gold size, mordant, used by painters. 2. Mordant. *V.* MORDENTE. 3. Mordant, the acid or other corrosive by which etching is done.

mordihuí [mor-de-oo-ee'], *m.* Weevil, a grub bred in wheat.

mordimiento [mor-de-me-en'-tol, *m.* Bite, mordication, biting.

mordiscar [mor-dis-car'], *va.* 1. To nibble. 2. *V.* MORDER.

mordisco, mordiscón [mor-dees'-co], *m.* Bite, the act of seizing with the teeth; the piece bitten off. **Deshacer algo a mordiscos**, to bite something to pieces.

morel de sal [mo-rel´ day sahl], *m.* *(Met.)* Purple red used for painting in fresco.

morena [mo-ray'-nah], *f.* 1. Brown bread. 2. Moray, a muraenoid eel.

morenilla, morenita [mo-ray-neel´-lyah], *f.* A brunette.

morenill [mo-ray-neel´-lyo], *m.* A black powder, used by sheep-shearers for the wounds of sheep.

morenillo, illa, ito, ita [mo-ray-neel'-lyo], *a. dim.* of MORENO, brunette: used always as endearing.

moreno, na [mo-ray'-no, nah], *a.* 1. Brown, inclining to black. 2. Swarthy (persona). 3. Tanned (bronceado). 4. *(And, Carib.)* Mulatto. **Ponerse moreno**, to become sunburned.

morera [mo-ray'-rah], *f.* *(Bot.)* White mulberry-tree. -*pl. V.* MORERAL.

moreral [mo-ray-rahl'], *m.* Plantation of white mulberry-trees.

morería [mo-ray-ree'-ah], *f.* 1. Suburb or quarter where Moors reside (barrio). 2. A Moorish province or lands.

moretón [mo-ray-tone'], *m.* *(coll.)* Bruise, ecchymosis.

morfa [mor'-fah], *f.* Scale, disease produced by scale-insects on orange and lemon-trees.

morfema [mor-fay'-mah], *m.* Morpheme.

morfeo [mor-fay'-o], *m.* *(Myth.)* Morpheus.

morfina [mor-fee´-nah], *f.* Morphine, the chief alkaloid of opium.

morfología [mor-fo-lo-hee'-ah], *f.* Morphology, the science of organic forms.

morfológico, ca [mor-fo-lo'-he-co, cah], *a.* Morphologic, morphological.

morga [more'-gah], *f.* Indian berries.

morganático [mor-gah-nah'-te-co], *a.* Morganatic. *V.* MATRIMONIO.

moribundo, da [mo-re-boon'-do, dah], *a.* Dying, near death.

moriche [mo-ree'-chay], *m.* An American tree, like the coconut, useful to mankind.

moriego, ga [mo-re-ay´-go, gah], *a.* *(Prov.)* Moorish.

morigeración [mo-re-hay-rah-the-on'], *f.* Morigeration, obedience, obsequiousness, temperance.

morigerar [mo-re-hay-rar'], *va.* To endeavor to curb or restrain one's affections and passions; to moderate.

morillo [mo-reel'-lyo], *m.* 1. *(dim.)* A little Moor. 2. Andiron.

morir [mo-reer'], *vn.* 1. To die, to expire. 2. To die, to perish, to come to nothing. 3. To hanker, to desire excessively. 4. To perish or be lost for want of anything. 5. *(Ferro.)* To end (línea). 6. To die down (fuego). **Morir de sed**, to die with thirst. **Morir de frío**, to perish with cold. **Morir ahogado**, to drown. **Morir de hambre**, to die of starvation. **Moría el día**, the day was almost over. -*vr.* 1. To go out, to be extinguished or quenched (fuego, luz). 2. To go numb. **Morirse por**, to be excessively fond of. **Irse muriendo**, to die away gradually. **Me moría de vergüenza**, I nearly died of shame. **Me moría de miedo**, I was half-dead with fright. **Morirse por algo**, to be dying for something. *(Yo muero, yo muera; él murió, muriera,* from *Morir. V.* DORMIR.)

morisco, ca [mo-rees´-co, cah], *a.* Moorish, belonging to the Moors.-*m. & f.* 1. Name given to the Moors who remained in Spain after its restoration. 2. *(Mex.)* Quadroon.

morisma [mo-rees'-mah], *f.* Mohammedan sect, multitude of Moors.

morisqueta [mo-ris-kay'-tah], *f.* *(coll.)* 1. Moorish trick. 2. Deception, fraud, trick. 3. Rice boiled without salt, the ordinary food of the Indian natives of the Philippines.

morlaco, ca [mor-lah'-co, cah], *a.* Cunning, sly, fox (taimado). *m.* Sly fox, cunning person.

mormones [mor-mo'-nes], *m. pl.* Mormons, a sect founded by Joseph Smith in 1830.

mormullo, mormureo [mor-mool'-lyo, mor-moo-ray´-o], *m.* Mutter, murmur a low noise. *V.* MURMULLO.

mormuración [mor-moo-rah-the-on'], *f. V.* MURMURACIÓN.

mormurador [mor-moo-rah-dor'], *m.* Murmurer, detractor.

mormurar [mor-moo-rar'], *va.* To murmur. *V.* MURMURAR.

moro, ra [mo'-ro, rah], *a.* 1. Moorish, belonging to the Moors. 2. In jocular style, it is applied to wine not mixed with water or christened. 3. Dappled (caballo). -*m. & f.* 1. Moor, a native of Africa. 2. Domineering husband (marido). 3. Drug pusher (vendedor). **Haber moros y cristianos**, to have a great scuffle or dispute.

morocada [mo-ro-cah'-dah], *f.* Blow given by a ram with its horn, butt.

morocho, cha [Mo-ro´-cho, chah], *a.* (*Amer.*) 1. Fresh, vigorous, well preserved (persona). 2. Applied to a hard kind of Indian corn. 3. *V.* GEMELO.

morón [mo-rone'], *m.* Hill, hillock.

moroncho, cha [mo-ron'-cho, chah], *a. V.* MORONDO.

morondanga [mo-ron-dahn'-gah], *f.* (*coll.*) Hodge-podge, medley.

morondo, da [mo-ron'-do, dah], *a.* Bald (calvo), leafless (sin hojas).

moronía [mo-ro-nee'-ah], *f.* A dish made of a variety of vegetables. *V.* ALBORONÍA.

morosamente [mo-ro'-sah-men-tay], *adv.* Slowly, tardily.

morosidad [mo-ro-se-dahd'], *f.* Slowness (lentitud), tardiness, detention, delay, arrears (atrasos).

moroso, sa [mo-ro´-so, sah], *a.* Slow (lento), tardy, heavy. **Deudor moroso**, slow payer.

morquera [mor-kay'-rah], *f.* (*Bot.*) Spanish thyme.

morra [mor'-rah], *f.* 1. Upper part of the head, top, crown. 2. Vulgar game with the fingers; odd or even. **Andar a la morra**, to come to blows.

morrada [mor-rah'-dah], *f.* Butting of the heads by two persons (cabezazo).

morral [mor-rahl´], *m.* 1. A bag hung to the mouths of mules or horses out of which they eat when traveling 2. Game-bag (caza).

morralla [mor-rahl'-lyah], *f.* 1. Small fry (peces), little fish. 2. Heap or medley of useless things. 3. Rabble (personas).

morrear [mor-ray-ahr'], *va. vn.* To kiss.

morreo [mor-ray'-o], *m.* Kiss.

morrillo [mor-reel'-lyo], *m.* 1. Pebble. 2. Fat of the nape of a sheep.

morriña [mor-ree'-nyah], *f.* 1. Murrain, a disease among cattle. 2. Sadness, melancholy.

morrión [mor-re-on'], *m.* 1. Morion, steel helmet. 2. Vertigo, a disease in hawks.

morro [mor'-ro], *m.* 1. Anything that is round like the head. 2. Headland, head, bluff. 3. A prominent, overhanging lip. 3. (*Aer. Aut.*) Nose. 4. Pebble (guijarro). 5. Small rounded hill (cerro). **Beber a morro**, to drink from the bottle. **Estar de morros**, to be in a bad mood. **Poner morro**, to look cross. *-a.* Purring (gato).

morroncho, cha [mor-ron'-cho, chah], *a.* (*Prov.*) Mild, meek, tame.

morrocotudo, da [mor-ro-cotoo'-do, dah], *a.* 1. Strong (fuerte), stout, solid. 2. Of much importance or difficulty (difícil). 3. (*Cono Sur, Mex.*) Big (grande). 4. (*And.*) Rich (rico). 5. (*Cono Sur*) Clumsy (amazacotado).

morrudo, da [mor-roo'-do, dah], *a.* Blobber-lipped, flap-mouthed, having prominent lips.

morsa [mor'-sah], *f.* Walrus, morse, a large marine seal-like mammal.

mortadela [mor-tah-day'-lah], *f.* Bologna sausage.

mortaja [mor-tah´-hah], *f.* 1. Shroud (de muerto), winding-sheet, grave-clothes. 2. Mortise, a hole cut into wood. 3. (*Amer.*) Cigarette paper. (*Acad.*)

mortal [mor-tahl'], *a.* 1. Mortal, subject to death (que muere). 2. Mortal, fatal (herida), deadly (golpe), destructive. 3. Mortal, deadly (distancia, espera), implacable. 4. One who has the appearance or symptoms of death.

mortal [mor-tahl'], *m.* Mortal, human being: commonly used in the plural.

mortalidad [mor-tah-le-dahd'], *f.* Mortality, liability to death.

mortalmente [mor-tahl'-men-tay], *adv.* Mortally.

mortandad [mor-tan-dahd´], *f.* Mortality, frequency of death; massacre, butchery.

mortecino, na [mor-tay-thee'-no, nah], *a.* 1. Dying a natural death, moribund. 2. Dying away or extinguishing; on the point of dying. 3. (*Low.*) Weak (débil), exhausted. **Hacer la mortecina**, to feign death. **Color mortecino**, a pale or deadly color. **La luz mortecina del crepúsculo**, the fading glow of twilight.

morterada [mor-tay-rah'-dah], *f.* 1. Sauce made at once in a mortar. 2. Quantity of stones thrown out at once by a stone mortar.

morterete [mor-tay-ray'-tay], *m.* 1. (*dim.*) A small mortar. 2. Piece of wax in shape of a mortar, with a wick in it, to serve as a lamp: it is placed in a glass with water. 3. (*Met.*) Hollow piece of iron used for firing gunpowder at fireworks.

morterico, illo, ito [mor-tay-ree'-co], *m. dim.* A small mortar.

mortero [mor-tay'-ro], *m.* 1. Mortar, a piece of ordnance. 2. Mortar, a vessel in which materials are pounded with a pestle. 3. Mortar, a building cement. **Mortero de una bomba de agua**, (*Naut.*) pump-box of a ship's pump.

morteruelo [mor-tay-roo-ay'-lo], *m.* 1. (*dim.*) A small mortar. 2. A kind of game of boys. 3. Fricassee of hog's liver.

mortífero, ra [mor-tee´-fay-ro, rah], *a.* Death-dealing, fatal.

mortificación [mor-te-fe-cah-the-on'], *f.* 1. Mortification of the body, by hardships and macerations. 2. Mortification, gangrene. 3. Mortification, vexation, trouble.

mortificar [mor-te-fe-car'], *va.* 1. To mortify, to destroy vital qualities. 2. To mortify, to subdue inordinate passions. 3. To mortify, to afflict, to disgust, to vex. **Estos zapatos me mortifican**, these shoes are killing me. *-vr.* 1. To mortify, to gangrene. 2. To mortify, to practice religious severities; to conquer one's passions.

mortuorio [mor-too-o'-re-o], *m.* Burial, funeral.*-a.* Mortuary, belonging to the dead. **Casa mortuoria**, house of the deceased.

morueca [mo-roo-ay´-cah], *f.* Heap of loose stones.

morueco [mo-roo-ay'-co], *m.* Ram, a male sheep.

moruno, na [mo-roo'-no, nah], *a.* Morish, belonging to the Moors.

morusa [mo-roo'-sah], *f.* (*coll.*) Cash, specie; money in hand.

mosa [mo´-sah], *f.* (*Zool.*) Moose.

mosaico, ca [mo-sah'-e-co, cah], *a.* Mosaic. **Obra mosaica**, mosaic work.

mosaísmo [mo-sah-ees'-mo], *m.* The Mosaic law or civilization.

mosca [mos'-cah], *f.* 1. Fly, a two-winged insect; the house-fly. 2. (*coll.*) Cash, specie; money in hand (dinero). 3. An impertinent intruder. 4. Vexation, trouble. 5. *pl.* Sparks from a light (centellas). 6. *pl.* Exclamation of complaint or surprise. **Mosca de burro**, horse-fly. **Mosca muerta**, hypocrite. **Picarle la mosca**, to spend a bad quarter of an hour, to be disquieted. **Sacudir las moscas**, to shake off an incumbrance. **Tener la mosca detrás de la oreja**, to be wary. **Por si las moscas**, just in case.

moscada [mos-cah'-dah], *a. V.* NUEZ MOSCADA.

moscarda [mos-car'-dah], *f.* 1. Gadfly, horsefly. 2. (*Prov.*) Eggs of bees.

moscardear [mos-car-day-ar´], *vn.* (*Prov.*) To lay eggs as bees in the cells of their combs.

moscardón [mos-car-done´], *m.* 1. Large gadfly or horsefly. 2. A hornet (abejón). 3 An importuning, sly fellow, a cheat.

moscareta [mos-cah-ray'-tah], *f.* (*Orn.*) Fly-catcher.

moscatel [mos-cah-tel'], *a.* 1. Muscat or muscatel; musk-flavored: applied to a kind of grape and to the wine made from them. 2. A tiresome (pesado), ignorant fellow.

moscella [mos-thayl'-lah], *f. V.* MORCELLA.

mosco [mos'-co], *m. V.* MOSQUITO.

moscón [mos-cone'], *m.* 1. A large fly, a blow-fly. 2. A hanger-on, a crafty, deceitful fellow.

moscovita [mos-co-vee'-tah], *a.* Muscovite, Russian.

Moscú [mos-koo], Moscow.

mosqueado, da [mos-kay-ah'-do, dah], *a.* Spotted (moteado), painted.*-pp.* of MOSQUEAR.

mosqueador [mos-kay-ah-dor'], *m.* 1. Fly-trap, flap for killing flies. 2. (*coll.*) Tail of animals.

mosquear [mos-kay-ar'], *va.* 1. To flap, to frighten flies away with a flap, to catch flies. 2. To reply with a witticism.

-vr. (coll.) To become angry or cross (ofenderse); To smell a rat (sospechar)

mosqueo [mos-kay'-o], m. 1. The act of catching flies or driving them away with a flap. 2. Annoyance (enfado). 3. Hassle (lío).

mosquero [mos-kay'-ro], m. Fly-trap.

mosqueruela [mos-kay-roo-ay'-lah], f. Muscadine pear.

mosqueta [mos-kay'-tah], f. White musk-rose.

mosquetazo [mos-kay-tah'-tho], m. Musket-shot.

mosquete [mos-kay'-tay], m. Musket, blunderbuss, an ancient firearm which was jested upon a crotch to fire it.

mosquetería [mos-kay-tay-re´-ah], f. 1. A body of musketeers. 2. The company in the pit of a theater.

mosqueteril [mos-kay-tay-reel'], a. (coll.) 1. Belonging to musketeers. 2. Belonging to the crowd in the pit of a theater.

mosquetero [mos-kay-tay'-ro], m. 1. Musketeer, a foot-soldier. 2. Person who frequents the pit in a playhouse.

mosquil, mosquino, na [mos-keel', mos-kee'-no, nah], a. Belonging to flies.

mosquita [mos-kee'-tah], f. A small bird of Sardinia in whose nest the cuckoo lays an egg. **Mosquita muerta,** hypocrite. **Hacerse la mosquita muerta,** to look as if butter would not melt in one's mouth.

mosquitero, ra [mos-ke-tay'-ro, rah], m. & f. Mosquito bar or net, a gauze cover hung over a bed, to keep off gnats and mosquitoes.

mosquito [mos-kee'-to], m. 1. Gnat, mosquito. 2. Tippler.

mostacera [mos-tah-thay'-rah], f. Mustard-pot.

mostacilla [mos-tah-theel'-lyah], f. 1. Sparrow-shot, the smallest kind of bird-shot. 2. Seed bugle; very small glass, gold, silver, or steel beads.

mostacho [mos-tah'-cho], m. 1. V. BIGOTE. 2. Spot in the face, gloom in the countenance.

mostachón [mos-tah-chone'], m. A kind of ginger-bread.

mostachoso, sa [mos-tah-cho'-so, sah], a. Wearing a mustache.

mostajo [mos-tah'-ho], m. (Bot.) White beam-tree:

mostaza [mos-tah'-thah], f. 1. (Bot.) Mustard. 2. Mustard-seed. 3. Fine shot.

mostazo [mos-tah'-tho], m. (Bot.) Mustard; a plant. 2. (Aug.) Strong, thick must.

mostear [mos-tay-ar'], vn. 1. To yield must (uvas). 2. To put must into vats or earthen jars to ferment. 3. To mix must with old wine, in order to revive it. V. REMOSTAR.

mostela [mos-tay´-lah], f. (Prov.) Sprig or twig of vines.

mostelera [mos-tay-lay'-rah], f. Place where the sprigs or twigs of vines are laid up.

mostellar [mos-tel-lyar'], m. A tree having a white hard wood and a fleshy-red fruit.

mostillo [mos-teel'-lyo], m. 1. Cake made of must and other ingredients. 2. Sauce made of must and mustard.

mosto [mos'-to], m. 1. Must, the pressed juice of the grape not yet fermented. 2. Stum, must, new wine.

mostrable [mos-trah'-blay], a. That which may be shown.

mostrado, da [mos-trah'-do, dah], a. Accustomed, habituated, inured.-pp. Of MOSTRAR.

mostrador, ra [mos-trah-dor´, rah], m. & f. 1. Demonstrator, one who demonstrates, one who shows.-m. 2. Pointer, hand of a clock or watch (reloj). 3. Counter, the table of a shop (tienda).

mostrar [Mos-trar'], va. 1. To show, to exhibit, to view, to point out (señalar), to lay before. 2. To show, to establish, to prove, to explain (explicar), to expound, to demonstrate (demostrar). 3. To show or make a thing appear what it is not, to feign, to dissemble. 4. To show any quality of the mind. **Mostrar en pantalla,** (Comput.) to display. -vr. To appear, to show oneself. **Se mostró muy amable,** he was very kind. **No se muestra muy imaginativa,** she does not seem to be very imaginative. (Yo muestro, yo muestre, from Mostrar. V. ACORDAR.)

mostrenco, ca [mos-tren'-co, cah], a. 1. Strayed, having no owner (sin dueño). 2. Vagabond, vagrant: applied to a stroller

without house or home. 3. Dull, ignorant, stupid. 4. (Prov.) Fat (gordo), bulky. **Bienes mostrencos,** goods which have no known owner.

mota [mo'-tah], f. 1. A small knot on cloth, which is taken off with burling irons or scissors (nudillo en paño). 2. A bit of thread or anything similar sticking to clothes. 3. Mote, small particle of matter.4. A slight defect or fault. 5. Bank or mound of earth. 6. Quota of each sailor to a common fund for subsistence stores, when the crew of a merchant vessel join together in trading. 7. Speck, tiny piece (partícula). 8. Dot (dibujo). 9. (Agr.) Ridge, boundary mark (mojón). 10. (LAm.) Lock of wavy hair (pelo). 11. (And. Carib. Mex.) Powder stuff (borla). 12. (Mex. Bot.) Marijuana plant (droga). **Mota de polvo,** speck of dust. **No hace mota de aire,** there isn´t a breath of air.

motacilla [mo-tah-theel´-lyah], f. V AGUZANIEVE.

mote [mo'-tay], m. 1. Motto or sentence added to a device, or prefixed to anything written. 2. Nickname (apodo). 3. (Peru, Bol.) Popcorn.

motear [mo-tay-ar'], vn. To speckle, to mark with spots.

motejador, ra [mo-tay-hah-dor'], rah], m. & f. Mocker, scoffer, censurer.

motejar [mo-tay-har'], va. To censure, to ridicule, to nickname.

motero [mo-tay'-ro], m. motorcyclist, motorcycle maniac.

motete [mo-tay'-tay], m. Motet or motetto, a short musical composition to be sung in church.

motil [mo-teel´], m. V. MOCHIL.

motilar [mo-te-lar'], va. To cut the hair, to crop.

motilón, na [mo-te-lone', nah], a. Poor, indigent. -m. (coll.) Lay-brother of a religious order.

motín [mo-teen'], m. Mutiny, insurrection, riot (disturbio).

motita [mo-tee'-tah], f. A small bit of thread sticking to cloths.

motivar [mo-te-var'], va. 1. To give a reason for anything, to assign a motive (causar). 2. To explain (explicar).

motivo [mo-tee'-vo], m. 1. Motive, cause, reason, occasion, impulse. 2. Motif, motive, or theme in a musical composition. **Motivo de divorcio,** grounds for divorce. **Por cuyo motivo,** for which reason. **Por motivos de salud,** for reasons of health.

motivo, va, a. Motive, moving, causing motion, having the power to move. **De su motivo,** of one's own accord. **Con motivo de,** owing to, by reason of.

moto [mo'-to], f. Motorbike; scooter (escúter).

motocicleta [mo-to-the-clay´-tah], f. Motorcycle.

motociclismo [mo-to-the-clees'mo], m. Motorcycling.

motociclista [mo-to-the-clees'-tah], m & f. Motorcyclist.

moto-cross [mo'-to-cross], m. Moto-cross.

motolita [mo-to-lee'-tah], f. V. AGUZANIEVE.

motolito, ta [mo-to-lee'-to, tah], **Motolótico, ca,** a. Easily deceived, ignorant.

motón [mo-tone'], m. (Naut.) Block, pulley, tackle for ropes to run in. **Motón sencillo,** single-block. **Motón de gancho,** hook-block. **Motones,** (Naut.) pulleys with sheaves. **Motones herrados,** iron-bound blocks.

motonave [mo-to-nah'-vay], f. Motor ship.

motonería [mo-to-nay-ree'-ah], f. (Naut.) Blocks and pulleys in ships.

motonero [mo-to-nay' ro], m. Block maker.

motor, ra [mot-tor', rah], a. Motor, motive causing motion. -m. Motor, a prime mover, particularly an electrical machine. **Motor de aviación,** aircraft engine. **Motor delantero,** front-mounted engine. **Motor diesel,** diesel engine.

motorismo [mo-to-rees'-mo], m. Motorcycling.

motorista [mo-to-rees'-tah], m. 1. (LAm.) Motorman. 2. Motorcyclist (motociclista).

motorizado [mo-to-re-thah'-do], a. Motorized.

motril [mo-treel'], m. V. MOCHIL.

motriz [mo-treeth'], a. Motor, motive, moving cause. **Fuerza motriz,** moving cause.

movedizo

movedizo, za [mo-vay-dee'-tho, thah], *a.* 1. Movable, easily moved (movible). 2. Variable, unsteady (poco seguro), inconstant, shifting (arenas).

movedor, ra [mo-vay-dor', rah], *m. & f.* Mover, motor, exciter, occasioner.

movedura [mo-vay-doo'-rah], *f. V.* MOVIMIENTO.

mover [mo-verr'], *va.* 1. To move, to put in motion (objeto). 2. To move, to prevail upon, to persuade, to induce. 3. To move, to stir passion, to touch pathetically, to cause or give occasion to. 4. To move, to stir up (descontento), to put into commotion. 5. To move, to excite, to commence a thing. 6. To move, to inspire (inspirar). **El agua mueve la rueda**, the water turns the wheel. **Mover a uno a hacer algo**, to move somebody to do something. *-vn.* 1. *(Arch.)* To spring an arch. 2. To bud, to begin to sprout. 3. To miscarry, to have an abortion.*-vr.* 1. To move, to be in a state of changing place, to walk. 2. To move, to have vital action. 3. To move, to go forward. **Hay que moverse**, we must get a move on. *(Yo muevo, yo mueva. V.* MOVER.)

movible [mo-vee'-blay], *a.* 1. Movable (no fijo), locomotive. 2. Variable.

movida [mo-vee'-dah], *f.* 1. Move (ajedrez). 2. *(Pol.)* Movement. 3. Thing (asunto), affair, business; gathering (concentración); happening (acontenimiento). **La movida cultural**, the cultural scene.

movido [mo-vee'-do], *a.* 1. Blurred (movimiento de camara). 2. Active (persona); restless (inquieto). 3. *(And. CAm. Cono Sur)* Soft-shelled (huevo). 4. *(And. CAm. Cono Sur)* Weak, feeble (débil).

moviente [mo-ve-en'-tay], *pa. & a.* Moving, motory.

móvil [mo'-veel], *a.* Movable, capable of moving or of being moved.*-m.* Mover, motor.

movilidad [mo-ve-le-dahd'], *f.* 1. Mobility, movableness, aptitude to be moved. 2. Mobility, inconstancy, unsteadiness, levity.

movilización [mo-ve-le-thah-the-on'], *f.* Mobilization.

movilizar [mo-ve-le-thar'], *va.* 1. To put in movement. 2. To mobilize (organizar), to make ready for active service.*-vr.* 1. To be set in motion. 2. To be mobilized, to go into active service.

movimiento [mo-ve-me-en'-to], *m.* 1. Movement, motion, moving, shake (negando), nod (asintiendo). **Movimiento continuo**, perpetual motion. **Estar en movimiento**, to be in motion. 2. Commotion, disturbance, sedition, revolt. 3. *(Arch.) V.* ARRANQUE. 4. Movement; activity; bustle (bullicio). **Una tienda de mucho movimiento**, a busy shop. 5. *(Liter. Teat.)* Action. 6. Tempo (compás). 7. Change, alteration (emociones). **Movimiento de ánimo**, perturbation.

moya [mo'-yah], *f. (Amer. Colom.)* A small, unglazed jar for boiling salt.

moyana [mo-yah'-nah], *f.* 1. A small culverin. 2. *(coll.)* Lie, falsehood. 3. Bread made of bran for feeding dogs.

moyo [mo'-yo], *m.* 1. Liquid measure of about 32 gallons or 129 liters. 2. Number of tiles fixed at 110.

moyuelo [mo-yoo-ay'-lo], *m.* Grits, pollard, coarse meal.

moza [mo'-thah], *f.* 1. Girl, a maid-servant engaged to do all kinds of work. **Moza de fortuna**, prostitute. **Moza de servicio**, domestic servant. 2. A clothes-pounder, used to beat linen when it is being washed. 3. Last or conquering game.

mozalbete, mozalbillo [mo-thal-bay'-tay, mo-thal-beel'-lyo], *m.* A lad, a beardless youth.

mozallón [mo-thahl-lyone'], *m.* A young, robust laborer.

mozcorra [moth-cor'-rah], *f. (Vulg.)* A common prostitute.

mozo, za [mo'-tho, thah], *a.* 1. Young, youthful (joven). 2. Applied to any unmarried person (soltero).

mozo [mo'-tho], *m.* 1. Youth, a young man, a lad. 2. Man-servant engaged to do all kinds of work in the house. 3. Bachelor, a man unmarried. 4. *(coll.)* Fellow. 5. Waiter. **Mozo de caballos**, groom, horse-boy. 6. Dumbwaiter. **Mozo de estación**, porter. **Buen mozo**, handsome lad.

mozón [mo-thone'], *m. aug.* A robust young man.

mozuela [mo-thoo-ay'-lah], *f. dim.* 1. A very young lass or woman: sometimes applied in contempt. 2. *(Vulg.)* A prostitute.

mozuelo [mo-thoo-ay'-lo], *m. dim.* A very young man or lad.

mozuelo, la [mo-thoo-ay'-lo, lah], *a. dim.* Young, youthful.

mu [moo], *f.* A child's word for sleep. 2. **No pasó ni mu**, nothing at all happened.

muaré [moo-ah-ray'], *m.* Moiré (tela).

mucamuca [moo-cah-moo'-cah], *f. (Peru.) V.* ZORRA MOCHILERA.

muceta [moo-thay'-tah], *f.* 1. Part of the dress worn by bishops when officiating. 2. A short cape worn by doctors.

mucilaginoso, sa [moo-the-lah-he-no'-so, sah], *a.* Mucilaginous, slimy.

mucílago *(Acad.),* or **mucilago** [moo-thee'-lah-go], *m.* Mucilage, a solution of gum; any viscous or slimy body.

mucina [moo-thee'-nah], *f.* Mucin, an alkaline glutinous fluid.

mucíparo, ra [moo-thee'-pah-ro, rah], *a.* Muciparous, secreting mucus.

mucol [moo-cole'], *m.* Mucilage considered as an excipient.

mucor [moo-cor'], *m.* Mucor, mouldiness.

mucosidad [moo-co-se-dahd'], *f.* Mucosity, mucilaginousness.

mucoso, sa [moo-co'-so, sah], *a.* Mucous, slimy, viscous, mucilaginous.

mucronato, ta [moo-cro-nah'-to, tah], *a.* Mucronate, tipped with a sharp point.

múcura [moo'-coo-rah], *f.* A kind of pitcher or ewer used in Venezuela among Indians.

muchachada [moo-chah-chah'-dah], *f.* A boyish trick, a girlish trick, gaiety.

muchachear [moo-chah-chay-ar'], *vn.* To act in a boyish or childish manner, to fumble or play childishly.

muchachería [moo-chah-chay-ree'-ah], *f.* 1. Boyish trick. 2. Clamorous noise made by a crowd of boys.

muchachez [moo-chah-cheth'], *f.* Childhood; puerility; boyhood.

muchacha [moo-chah'-chah], *f.* Girl; lass, child.

muchacho [moo-chah'-cho], *m.* 1. Boy (chico), lad; servant (criado). 2. *(LAm.)* Clamp (abrazadera), holdfast; *(Cono Sur)* shoeborn (zapato); miner's lamp (lámpara). *-a.* Boyish, girlish, childish.

muchedumbre [moo-chay-doom'-bray], *f.* Multitude, many, a great number; plenty, abundance, much.

muchísimo, ma [moo-chee'-se-mo, mah], *a.* Superlative of MUCHO. Very much, very large; a great deal.

mucho, cha [moo'-cho, chah], *a.* Much, large in quantity, long in time, many in number; abundant, plentiful. **No es mucho**, it is no wonder. **Mucho tiempo**, a long time. **Hace mucho calor**, it's very hot. **Es mucha mujer**, what a woman she is! **Hay muchos conejos**, there are lots of rabbits. **Tengo mucho que hacer**, I have lots to do. *-adv.* Much, in a great degree; excessively, by far, often, long (tiempo): to a certain degree. **Mucho menos**, much less. **Correr mucho**, to run fast. **Con mucho el mejor**, far and away the best. **Es mucho difícil**, *(Mex.)* it's jolly difficult.

muda [moo'-dah], *f.* 1. Change, alteration. 2. Change of linen. 3. The act and time of moulting (temporada) and shedding feathers. 4. A transition of the voice in boys who come to maturity. 5. Roost of birds of prey. 6. A cosmetic. **Estar en muda**, to keep silence in company.

mudable [moo-dah'-blay], *a.* Changeable, variable, mutable, fickle (de carácter), light.

mudamente [moo'-dah-men-tay], *adv.* Silently, tacitly, mutely.

mudanza [moo-dahn'-thah], *f.* 1. Alteration, change; mutation, commutation. 2. Removal from place to place. 3. Inconstancy, levity. 4. Certain number of motions in a dance. **Estar de mudanza**, to be moving.

mudar [moo-dar'], *va.* 1. To change (cambiar), to put one thing in place of another, to remove, to deviate. 2. To change, to cause alteration, to vary, to alter. 3. To change one thing for another, or to quit something for the sake of another. 4. To shed the feathers, to moult. 5. To change the voice: applied to boys who come to maturity. 6. To change, to vary in a moral sense; to mend the disposition. **Me van a mudar la pluma**, they´re going to change the pen for me. **Le mudan las sábanas todos los días**, they change his sheets every day. -vr. 1. To change, to undergo change. 2. To change the sentiments and manners. 3. To shift, to dress in fresh linen or clothes. 4. To move into another house (casa). 5. *(coll.)* To wander from the topic of conversation.

mudéjar [moo-day'-har], *a. & m. pl.* Used of a Mohammedan who, without changing his religion, became a subject of Christian sovereigns.

mudez [moo-deth'], *f.* Dumbness; impediment of speech.

mudo, da [moo'-do, dah], *a.* Dumb, silent (callado), still, mute. **Quedarse mudo de asombro**, to be dumbfounded. **Quedarse mudo de envidia**, to be green with envy.

mué, muer [moo-ay', moo-err'], *m.* Tabby, moiré, watered silk.

mueblaje [moo-ay-blah'-hay], *m.* Fitment, collection of furniture.

mueble [moo-ay'-blay], *m.* 1. Any movable piece of furniture. **Mueble combinado**, piece of unit furniture. -pl. Movable goods, chattels, furniture, household stuff. 2. *(Mex.)* Car (coche).

mueblista [moo-ay-blees'-tah], *m.* Furniture dealer, furniture maker.

mueca [moo-ay'-cah], *f.* Grimace, wry face, grin.

muedín [moo-ay-deen'], *m.* Muezzin, one who calls the Mohammedan faithful to prayer. V. ALMUÉDANO.

muela [moo-ay'-lah], *f.* 1. In cornmills, runner, the upper millstone (de molino). 2. Grindstone (de afilar), whetstone. 3. Water sufficient to set a mill in motion. 4. Hill, hillock; any artificial mound 5. Track or circle made with anything. 6. Grinder, one of the back teeth, molar teeth. **Al que le duele la muela, que se la saque**, it is none of my business. **Dolor de muelas**, toothache.

muellaje [moo-el-yah'-hay], *m.* Wharfage, dockage, a harbor tax.

muelle [moo-el'-lyay], *a.* 1. Tender, delicate (delicado), soft (blando). 2. Licentious luxurious.-m. 1. Spring, an elastic body (elástico). 2. Regulator, a small spring which regulates the movements of a watch. 3. *(Naut.)* Mole, pier; jetty; quay, wharf; a place in a seaport for shipping goods, etc.

muellear [moo-el-yay-ar'], *vn.* To bear against, to prop. A word much used by type-founders.

muellemente [moo-ayl'-lyay-men-tay], *adv.* Tenderly, gently, softly.

muérdago [moo-err'-dah-go], *m.* *(Bot.)* Mistletoe.

muermera [moo-er-may'-rah], *f.* *(Bot.)* Common virgin's-bower; traveler's-joy.

muermo [moo-err'-mo], *m.* Glanders, a contagious disease in horses, affecting the nose and accompanied by a pustular eruption.

muermo [moo-ayr'-mo], *a.* *(Esp.)* Boring (pesado); wet (débil), indecisive; slow (lento). -m & f. Crashing bore (pesado); drip, wet fish (débil); dolt (tonto). -m. Boredom (aburrimiento); blues (depresión).

muermoso, sa [moo-er-mo'-so, sah], *a.* Snoring, breathing with difficulty; glandered.

muerte [moo-err'-tay], *f.* 1. Death, the extinction of life. 2. Death, murder (homicidio), assassination (asessinato), the act of killing unlawfully. 3. Death, image of mortality, represented by a skeleton. 4. A violent affection that cannot be borne, labor, difficulty, severe affliction. **Muerte civil**, (1) *(Law.)* civil death. (2) *(coll.)* A miserable and painful life. **Buena muerte**, a good end, the contrite death of a person. **Bajo pena de muerte**, on pain of death. **Hasta la muerte**, until death. **A muerte o a vida**, kill or cure, at all risks. **Tomarse la muerte por su mano**, to imperil one's life, health, or welfare against good advice. **Muerte súbita**,

sudden death. **Dar muerte a**, to kill. **Luchar a muerte**, to fight to the death. **Un susto de muerte**, a terrible fright.

muerto [moo-err'-to], *m.* 1. Corpse (cadáver), a dead body. 2. *(Naut.)* The standing part of a running rope.-pl. 1. Stripes, strokes, blows. 2. *(Naut.)* Ground-ways.

muerto, ta [moo-err'-to, tah], *a. & pp. irr.* of MORIR. 1. Dead, extinguished, lifeless. 2. Languid, faded (colores). 3. Slaked (cal). **Más muerto que vivo**, half-dead. **No tener donde caerse muerto**, to be utterly destitute. **Estar muerto de cansancio**, to be dead tired. **Estar muerto de hambre**, to be dying of hunger.

muesca [moo-ays'-cah], *f.* 1. Groove cut in the staves of casks and baskets, in which the bottoms and headpieces are fixed; hack, nick, mortise. 2. An empty or void space. V. MELLA. 3. Dove-tail scarf.

muestra [moo-ays'-trah], *f.* 1. A small sample of cloth. 2. Outer piece of cloth where the stamp of the maker is put. 3. A shop sign (de tienda). 4. Any indicative sign or demonstration of a thing (demostración). 5. Specimen, design, model (pauta), copy. 6. Clock which does not strike (reloj). **Es muestra de cariño**, it is a token of affection. **Muestra gratuita**, free sample. **Muestra representativa**, cross-section sample.

muestrario [moo-es-trah'-re-o], *m.* Samples, set of samples.

mufla [moo'-flah], *f.* Muffle, an earthen cover placed over tests and coppels in the assaying of metals. **muflas**, thick winter gloves, which serve instead of a muff.

mufti [moof'-te], *m.* Mufti, the high-priest of the Mohammedans.

mugido [moo-hee'-do], *m.* The lowing of an ox, cow, or bull.

múgil [moo'-heel], *m.* Mullet. V. MÚJOL.

mugir [moo-heer'], *vn.* To low, to moo (vaca), to bellow like an ox.

mugre [moo'-gray], *f.* Grime, dirt, or filth which sticks to clothes and other things.

mugriento, ta [moo-gre-en' to, tah], *a.* Greasy, dirty, filthy, grimy.

mugrón [moo-grone'], *m.* Sprig or shoot of a vine.

muguete [moo-gay'-tay], *m.* Lily of the valley.

mujer [moo-herr'], *f.* 1. Woman, the female of the human race. **Ser mujer**, to be a woman, to have attained the age of puberty. 2. Wife (esposa), mate. **Mujer de su casa** or **mujer de gobierno**, housewife, a woman skilled in female business. **Mujer varonil**, a manly woman. **Ser muy mujer**, to be very feminine. **Mujer fatal**, femme fatale.

mujeracha [moo-hay-rah'-chah], *f.* *(coll.)* A coarse woman of the lowest class.

mujercilla [moo-her-theel'-lyah], *f.* A worthless woman: jade, hussy; a strumpet.-m. Hilding, a sorry, paltry, cowardly fellow.

mujeriego, ga [moo-hay-re-ay'-go, gah], *a.* 1. Feminine, womanly, given to women. 2. Womanish, given to women.-m. Womankind; all the women of a place.

mujeril [moo-hay-reel'], *a.* Womanish, womanly, feminine.

mujerilmente [moo-hay-reel'-men-tay], *adv.* Effeminately.

mujerío [moo-hay-ree´-o], *m.* A gathering of women.

mujerona [moo-hay-ro'-nah], *f. aug.* A stout woman; a matron.

mujerzuela [moo-hayr-thoo ay' lah], *f.* Whore.

mula [moo'-lah], *f.* 1. She-mule. 2. A kind of thick soled shoe. 3. A certain Moorish vessel. 4. *(Mex.)* Trash, junk, unsaleable goods (trastos). 5. *(CAm.)* Shame (vergüenza). 6. *(And.)* Pipe (pipa). 7. *(And.)* Idiot (idiota). 8. *(Mex.)* Tough guy (duro). 9. *(Cono Sur)* Lie (mentira); trick (engaño).

muladar [moo-lah-dar'], *m.* 1. Place where the dirt and sweepings of houses are put. 2. Dung-heap: rubbish heap. 3. Anything very dirty or infectious.

muladí [moo-lah-dee'], *a.* Renegade Spanish Christian who lived among the Moors.

mular [moo-lar'], *a.* Belonging to mules.

mulatero [moo-lah-tay'-ro], *m.* Muleteer, mule-driver; a mule-boy.

mulato, ta [moo-lah'-to, tah], *a.* Mulatto, tawny.-*n.* Mulatto, the offspring of a white person and a black person.

múleo, muléolo [moo'-lay-o, moo-lay'-o-lo], *m.* Name of a pointed, purple-colored footwear used among the Roman patricians.

mulero [moo-lay'-ro], *m.* Mule-boy, who takes care of mules employed in agriculture; a muleteer.-*a.* Applied to a horse fond of mules.

muleta [moo-lay'-tah], *f.* 1. A young she-mule, not yet trained to work. 2. Crutch, prop, support (para andar). 3. An instrument of rope-makers. 4. *V.* MULETILLA.

muletada [moo-lay-tah'-dah], *f.* Herd of mules.

muletero [moo-lay-tay'-ro], *m.* Muleteer, mule-driver.

muletilla [moo-lay-teel'-lyah], *f.* 1. Word or phrase often repeated inadvertently in talking. 2. A wand or rod. 3. A rod with a cape (commonly red) which the bullfighter uses to provoke the bull when he is about to kill it. 4. A passementerie button (botón). 5. A cane (bastón), the head of which forms a kind of crutch.

muleto [moo-lay'-to], *m.* A young he-mule not yet broken.

mulilla [moo-leel'-lyah], *f. dim.* of MULA.

mulla [mool'-lyah], *f.* The act of digging around vines.

mullida [mool-yee'-dah], *f.* Ridge of soil between furrow and furrow.

mullido [mool-yee'-do], *m.* A soft cushion, or pillow.

mullidor, ra [mool-lye-dor', rah], *m. & f..* 1. Bruiser, mollifier. 2. *V.* MUÑIDOR.

mullir [mool-lyeer'], *va.* 1. To beat up anything, in order to make it soft and spongy (ablandar). **Mullir la cama**, to beat up the bed. 2. To call, to convene. *V.* MUÑIR. 3. To adopt proper measures for attaining one's purpose. 4. To dig about the roots of vines and trees.

mulo [moo'-lo], *m.* Mule.

mulso, sa [mool'-so, sah], *a.* Of mixed honey and sugar.

multa [mool'-tah], *f.* 1. Fine, ticket (aparcamiento). 2. A wild fruit-tree of Puerto Rico.

multar [mool-tar'], *va.* To penalize, to fine, or impose a fine.

multicaule [mool-te-cah'-oo-lay], *a. (Bot.)* Multicauline, having many stems.

multicoloro, ra [mool-te-co-lo'-ro, rah], *a.* Many-hued, many-colored.

multifacético, ca [mool-te-fah-thay'-te-co, cah], *a.* With many phases.

multifloro, ra [mool-te-flo'-ro, rah], *a.* Many-flowered.

multiforme [mool-tee-for´-may], *a.* Multiform.

multigrado [mool-te-grah'-do], *a.* Multigrade (aceite).

multígrafo [mool-tee'-grah-fo], *m.* Multigraph.

multilátero, ra [mool-te-lah'-tay-ro, rah], *a.* Multilateral.

multimillonario, ria [mool-te-mil-lyo-nah'-re-o, ah], *m. & f.* Multimillionaire.

multinomio, mia [mool-te-no'-me-o, ah], *a. (Alg.)* Polynomial.

múltiple [mool'-te-play], *a.* Multiple, complex; opposed to simple.

multiplexor [mool-te-plec-sor]. *(Comput.)* Multiplexor.

multiplicable [mool-te-ple-cah'-blay], *a.* Multiplicable, multipliable.

multiplicación [mool-te-ple-cah-the-on'], *f.* Multiplication.

multiplicador, ra [mool-te-ple-cah-dor', rah], *m. & f.* Multiplier; multiplicator.

multiplicando [mool-te-ple-cahn'-do], *m. (Arith.)* Multiplicand.

multiplicar [mool-te-ple-car'], *va. & vr.* To increase, to multiply.

multíplice [mool-tee'-plee-thay], *a.* Multiple; multiplex.

multiplicidad [mool-te-ple-the-dahd'], *f.* Multiplicity.

múltiplo, pla [mool'-te-plo, plah], *a.* Multiple, exactly divided by another quantity. *V.* MULTÍPLICE.

multiprocesador [mool-te-rpo-thay-sah-dor]. *(Comput.)* Multiprocessor.

multitud [mool-te-tood'], *f.* Multitude, a great number, crowd (gente). *V.* MUCHEDUMBRE. **La multitud**, the multitude, the mass.

multitudinario [mool-te-too-de-nah'-re-o], *a.* Massive; big (reunión); mass (manifestación).

multiuso [mool-te-oo'-so], *a.* For many uses.

multivalvo, va [mool-te-vahl'-vo, vah], *a. (Con.)* Multivalve: applied to a class of shell-fish.

mumiforme [moo-me-for'-may], *a.* Mummiform; like a mummy.

mundanalidad [moon-dah-nah-le-dahd'], *f.* Worldliness.

mundano, na [moon-dah'-no, nah], *a.* 1. Mundane, worldly (del mundo). **Mujer mundana**, common prostitute. 2. Society (de alta sociedad). **Son gente muy mundana**, they´re high society people.

mundial [moon-de-ahl'], *a.* Worldwide; universal. **Las comunicaciones mundiales**, world communications.

mundialmente [moon-de-ahl'-men-tay], *adv.* Throughout the world.

mundificar [moon-de-fe-car'], *va.* To cleanse, to make clean.

mundificativo, va [moon-de-fe-cah-tee'-vo, vah], *a.* Mundificant, cleansing.

mundillo [moon-deel'-lyo], *m.* 1. An arched frame put over braziers to dry or air linen. 2. Cushion on which bone-lace is made. 3. Warming-pan. 4. World circle.

mundo [moon'-do], *m.* 1. World, the collective idea of all bodies whatever; terrestrial sphere, globe. 2. *(coll.)* Great multitude, great quantity. 3. *(Met.)* The manners of men; worldly desires and practices. 4. A dissipated life. **El nuevo mundo**, North and South America. **El otro mundo**, the next world, the world to come. **No ser de este mundo**, to live retired from the world, to be very innocent and simple. **Ver mundo**, to travel. **Medio mundo**, many people. **Desde que el mundo es mundo**, from the beginning of time. **Echar al mundo**, to create. **Echarse al mundo**, to plunge into dissipation. **Echar del mundo**, to banish from society, to send to Coventry. **No caber en el mundo**, to be inflated with pride. **Ponerse el mundo por montera**, to care nothing for what people will say. **Tener mundo or mucho mundo**, to be acute, not easily deceived. **En todo el mundo**, everywhere. **El mundo es un pañuelo**, it´s a small world.

munición [moo-ne-the-on'], *f.* 1. Munition or ammunition, materials for war (balas etc.); war-like stores. 2. Charge of fire-arms. **Botas de munición**, army boots.

municionar [moo-ne-the-o-nar'], *va.* To supply with ammunition or war-like stores.

municipal [moo-ne-the-pahl'], *a.* Municipal, corporate.

municipalidad [moo-ne-the-pah-le-dahd'], *f.* Municipality; town council, the governing board of a city.

munícipe [moo-nee'-the-pay], *m.* Citizen, denizen; member of a corporation.

municipio [moo-ne-thee'-pe-o], *m.* 1. Place which enjoys the rights and privileges of a city. 2. Corporation (ayuntamiento).

munificencia [moo-ne-fe-then´-the-ah], *f.* Munificence, liberality.

munificentísimo, ma [moo-ne-fe-then-tee'-se-mo, mah], *a. super.* of MUNÍFICO.

munífico, ca [moo-nee´-fe-co, cah], *a.* Munificent, liberal.

muñeca [moo-nyay'-cah], *f.* 1. The wrist. 2. A doll (de niña). **Muñeca de trapo**, rag doll. 3. A small bundle of medicinal ingredients put into a decoction. 4. *(Cono Sur)* Pull, influence. -*pl.* In the mint, the screws that pinch the coin, and give it the due thickness.

muñeco [moo-nyay'-co], *m.* 1. Puppet (títere), representing a male figure (figura), doll (juguete). 2. A soft, effeminate fellow. 3. Puppet (instrumento). 4. Pretty little boy (niño). 5. Row (lío).

muñeira [moo-nyay'-e-rah], *f.* A popular dance of Galicia.

muñequear [moo-nyay-kay-ar'], *va.* To play with the wrist in fencing.

muñequera [moo-nyay-kay'-rah], *f.* Bracelet, an ornament for the wrist of dolls.

muñequería [moo-nyay-kay-ree'-ah], *f.* Excessive fondness for clothes and ornaments.

muñidor [moo-nye-dor'], *m.* 1. Bandle of a corporation or confraternity; apparitor, messenger. 2. *(Amer.)* Undertaker.

muñir [moo-nyeer'], *va.* To summon (convocar), to call to a meeting.

muñón [moo-nyone'], *m.* 1. Brawn, the fleshy part of the body. 2. Stump of an amputated arm or leg. 3. Trunnion of a cannon; gudgeon, lug, swing-block.

muñonera [moo-nyo-nay'-rah], *f.* Trunnion-plate, trunnion-socket, *(Mech.)* gudgeon-socket.

murajes [moo-rah'-hes], *m.* A medicinal herb of pungent taste.

mural [moo-rahl'], *a.* Mural, belonging to walls.

muralla [moo-rahl'-lyah], *f.* Rampart which surrounds a place; wall.

murar [moo-rar'], *va.* To wall, to surround with a rampart.

murciano, na [moor-the-ah'-no, nah], *a.* Murcian, of Murcia.

murciélago [moor-the-ay'-lah-go], *m.* *(Zool.)* The bat.

murena [moo-ray'-nah], *f.* A kind of eel. V. MORENA.

murga [moor'-gah], *f.* 1. V. ALPECHÍN. 2. Street musicians who play for a gratuity. 3. Bore, nuisance (lata). **Dar la murga**, to be a pain.

muriático, ca [moo-ree-ah'-te-co, cah], *a.* *(Chem.)* Muriatic.

muriato [moo-re-ah'-to], *m.* *(Chem.)* Muriate.

múrice [moo'-re-thay], *m.* 1. Porcelain shell-fish; generic name of sea-shells which end in a straight canal; murex, Tyrian purple. 2. *(Poet.)* Purple.

múrido, da [moo'-re-do, dah], *a.* Mouse like.

murmujear [moor-moo-hay-ar'], *va.* To murmur, to mutter.

murmullar [moor-mool-lyar'], *vn.* *(Prov.)* V. MURMURAR, 2d def.

murmullo [moor-mool'-lyo], *m.* 1. Muttering, mumbling in speaking. 2. Murmuring (susurro), purling.

murmuración [moor-moo-rah-the-on'], *f.* Backbiting, privy calumny, slander, gossiping, obloquy.

murmurador, ra [moor-moo-rah-dor', rah], *m. & f.* Murmurer, detractor, backbiter (criticón). *-a.* Gossip (chismoso); backbiting (criticón).

murmurar [moor-moo-rar'], *va.* 1. To murmur (persona), to purl, to flow gently (corriente). 2. To murmur, to grudge, to grumble, to mutter (quejarse). 3. To backbite, to censure an absent person. 4. To rustle (hojas, viento), to hum (abejas, multitud). **Siempre están murmurando del jefe**, they're always grumbling about the boss.

murmurio [moor-moo'-re-o], *m.* The purling or murmuring of a stream.

muro [moo'-ro], *m.* Wall. V. PARED and MURALLA.

murria [moor'-re-ah], *f.* 1. Heaviness of the head, lowness of spirits, melancholy, mumps, reverie, spleen. 2. A former astringent medicament.

murrino, na [moor-ree'-no, nah], *a.* Applied to a cup or vase much esteemed in old times.

murrio, ria [moor'-re-o, ah], *a.* Sad, melancholy.

murta [moor'-tah], *f.* Myrtle. V. ARRAYÁN and MIRTO.

murtal [moor-tahl'], *m.* Grove of myrtles.

murtilla, murtina [moor-teel'-lyah, moor-tee'-nah], *f.* *(Bot.)* 1. A shrub growing in Chile. 2. The fruit of the same shrub. 3. The fruit of the myrtle.

murtón [moor-tone'], *m.* Myrtle-berry the fruit of myrtle.

murucuya [moo-roo-coo'-yah], *f.* *(Bot.)* Purple passion-flower.

murueco [moo-roo-ay'-co], *m.* V. MORUECO.

mus [moos], *m.* A card game.

musa [moo'-sah], *f.* 1. Muse, the goddess of poetry. 2. Poetic genius. 3. Musa, Latin name of the plantain and banana trees.

musaraña [moo-sah-rah'-nyah], *f.* 1. Fetid shrew-mouse. 2. Spirit, ghost, hobgoblin. 3. Any insect or small animal;

vermin. *(Fig.)* **Pensar en las musarañas**, to go wool-gathering.

muscardina [moos-car-dee'-nah], *f.* Muscurdin(e), a disease of silkworms due to a fungus.

muscaria, or **muscícapa** [moos-cah'-re-ah, moos-thee'-cah-pah], *f.* *(Orn.)* Fly-catcher.

múscido, da [moos'-the-do, dah], *a.* Like a fly.

muscívoro, ra [moos-thee'-vo-ro, rah], *a.* Devouring flies; fly-catching.

musco [moos'-co], *m.* Moss.

musco, ca [moos'-co, cah], *a.* Chestnut color.

muscosidad [moos-co-se-dahd'], *f.* Mossiness.

musculado, da [moos-coo-lah'-do, dah], *a.* *(Met.)* Muscular, brawny.

muscular [moos-coo-lar'], *a.* Muscular.

musculatura [moos-coo-lah-too'-rah], *f.* Musculature, the entire muscular system.

músculo [moos'-coo-lo], *m.* 1. Muscle, a fleshy fibre susceptible of contraction and relaxation. 2. Whale of a prodigious size.

musculoso, sa [moos-coo-lo'-so, sah], *a.* Muscular, full of muscles.

muselina [moo-say-lee'-nah], *f.* Muslin, fine cotton cloth. **Muselina fina estampada**, French jaconet muslin.

museo [moo-say'-o], *m.* 1. Museum, a place set apart for the study of the sciences and arts. 2. Repository of learned curiosities. **Museo de arte**, art gallery.

muserola [moo-say-ro'-lah], *f.* The noseband of a horse's bridle.

musgaño [moos-gah'-nyo], *m.* 1. Shrew-mouse. V. MUSARAÑA. 2. Large field-spider.

musgo [moos'-go], *m.* Moss.

musgoso, sa [moos-go'-so, sah], *a.* 1. Mossy. 2. Moss-covered.

música [moo'-se-cah], *f.* 1. Music, the science of harmonical sounds. 2. Music, instrumental or vocal harmony. 3. Harmony, or melody modulated sound. 4. Company of musicians. 5. A musical composition. 6. Written sheets of music. 7. Music: applied by antiphrasis to a dissonant sound. **Música de campanas**, chimes. **Música celestial**, fine talk. **Música de fondo**, background. **Irse con la música a otra parte**, to take one's troubles elsewhere.

musical [moo-se-cahl'], *a.* Musical.

músico, ca [moo'-see-co, cah], *m. & f.* Musician, one skilled in harmony, harmonist; one who performs upon instruments of music.*-a.* Musical, harmonious, relating to music.

musicómano, na [moo-se-co'-mah-no, nah], *a.* Music-mad. V. MELÓMANO.

musitación [moo-se-tah-the-on'], *f.* Muttering, or whispering of a sick person, generally accompanying delirium.

musitar [moo-se-tar'], *vn.* To mumble, to mutter; also, to whisper.

muslera [moos-lay'-rah], *f.* Cuish, ancient armor for the thigh.

muslime [moos-lee'-may], *a.* Moslem.

muslímico, ca [moos-lee'-me-co, cah], *a.* Moslem, Mohammedan.

muslo [moos'-lo], *m.* 1. Thigh, which includes all between the buttocks and the knee. 2. Leg (pollo). 3. Drumstick.

musmón [moos-mone'], *m.* 1. Mouflon, a wild sheep with very large curved horns, native of Corsica and Sardinia, considered by some as the original type of the domestic sheep.

musquerola [moos-kay-ro'-lah], *f.* Muscadine pear.

mustelino, na [moos-tay-lee'-no, nah], *a.* Weasel-like.

mustelo [moos-tay'-lo], *m.* *(Zool.)* Fish without scales, having a hard rough skin, and of about five feet in length.

mustiamente [moos'-te-ah-men-tay], *adv.* In a sad and melancholic manner.

mustio, tia [moos'-te-o, ah], *a.* 1. Parched, withered; sad (triste), sorrowful. 2. *(Mex.)* Hypocritical.

musulmán [mo-sool-mahn'], *m.* Mussulman, Moslem, Muslim.

muta [moo'-tah], *f.* Pack of hounds.
mutabilidad [moo-tah-be-le-dahd'], *f.* Mutability, inconstancy, fickleness.
mutación [moo-tah-the-on'], *f.* 1. Mutation, change (cambio). *V.* MUDANZA. 2. A change of scene in a theater. 3. Unseasonable weather.
mutante [moo-tahn'-tay], *a. m & f.* Mutant.
mutila [moo-tee'-lah], *f.* Mutilla, a solitary ant.
mutilación [moo-te-lah-the-on'], *f.* Mutilation, maimedness.
mutilado [moo-te-lah'-do], *a.* Crippled, disabled. *-m & f.* Cripple, disabled person.
mutilar [moo-te-lar'], *va.* 1. To mutilate, to maim, to cripple (lisiar), to mangle. 2. *(Fig.)* To mutilate (texto); to deface (objeto, estatua).
mútilo, la [moo'-te-lo, lah], *a.* Maimed. *(Acad.)*
mutis [moo'-tees], *m.* A word used by theatrical prompters to signify that one or all of those in the scene are to go off. **¡Mutis!** *int.* Silence!
mutual [moo-too-ahl'], *a.* Mutual, reciprocal. *V.* MUTUO.
mutualidad [moo-too-ah-le-dahd'], *f.* 1. Mutuality (reciprocidad), state of being mutual. 2. *(Com.)* System of mutual insurance companies or societies (sociedad).
mutuamente [moo'-too-ah-men-tay], *adv.* Mutually, conversely, reciprocally.
mutuante [moo-too-ahn'-tay], *com.* Lender, loaner.
mutuo, tua [moo'-too-o, ah], *a.* Mutual, reciprocal, commutual.
mutuo [moo'-too-o], *m.* Loan.
muy [moo'-e], *adv.* Very; a particle which, being joined to a positive adjective, converts it into a superlative one; greatly, highly; too (demasiado). **Muy bueno**, very good. **Muy de noche**, very late at night. **Eso es muy de él**, that´s just like him. **Es muy mujer**, she´s very feminine.
muz [mooth], *m. (Naut.)* Extremity of the cutwater.
muzárabe [moo-thah'-rah-bay], *a. V.* MOZÁRABE.
muzo [moo'-tho], *m.* Wood of a tree of Columbia, veined black and red, much esteemed for handsome furniture.
my [me], *f.* Mu, twelfth letter of the Greek alphabet, corresponding to M.
mycin [me-theen]. *(Comput.)* Mycin. **Mycin vacía**, emycin (empty mycin).

N

n [ay´-nay], fourteenth letter of the alphabet, has the same pronunciation in Spanish as in the English language. 1. In maritime or geographical charts, *N* stands for north. 2. In medals and inscriptions, for Number or **Número**. 3. N (potencia). **Diez a la potencia n**, ten to the power of n. 4. X (fulano). **La condesa N**, Countess X.
naba [nah'-bah], *f. (Bot.)* 1. Rutabaga, Swedish turnip. 2. The root of this plant.
nabal, nabar [nah-bahl', nah-bar'], *m.* Turnip field.*-a.* Belonging to turnips, made of turnips, pottage made of turnips.
nabería [nal-bay-ree'-ah], *f.* Turnip-pottage or heap of turnips.
nabillo [nah-beel'-lyo], *m. dim.* A small turnip.
nabina [nah-bee'-nah], *f.* Rape and turnip seed.
nabiza [nah-bee'-thah], *f. (Bot.)* 1. The lateral branches of the root of turnips. 2. The young shoots from the root or stem of turnips.
nabla [nah'-blah], *f.* Ancient instrument of music like a psaltery.
nabo, nabo común [nah'-bo], *m.* 1. *(Bot.)* Rape, turnip; the plant and the root. 2. Cylindrical timber, spindle, newel. 3. *(Naut.)* Mast.
naboria [nah-bo'-re-ah], *a. & n.* Free Indian who used to be employed in domestic service.

nácar [nah'-car], *m.* 1. Mother-of-pearl, nacre. 2. Pearl-color. *-a. (Amer.)* Scarlet.
nacarado, da [nah-cah-rah'-do, dah], *a.* Set with mother-of-pearl; of a pearl color.
nacáreo, rea [nah-cah'-ray-o, ah], *a. V.* NACARINO.
nacarino, na [nah-cah-ree'-no, nah], *a.* Like nacre, nacreous.
nacarón [nah-cah-ron'], *m.* Large pearl shell of inferior quality.
nacencia [nah-then'-the-ah], *f. (LAm.)* 1. Birth. 2. Swelling, tumor, outgrowth.
nacer [nah-therr'], *vn.* 1. To be born, to come into the world. 2. To flower, to blossom (flores). 3. To hud, to shoot, to grow (plantas). 4. To rise, to appear on the horizon. 5. To take its rise, to have its beginning from. 6. To spring, to take its rise, to flow from (río). 7. To be reared in some habit. 8. To infer one thing from another. 9. To appear or start up all of a sudden 10. Followed by a preposition, it signifies natural propensity or destiny: as, **Nació para ser gran general**, he was born to be a great general. 11. To spring up (agua), to rise (estrella). **Nacer de pies**, to be born to good luck. **Haber nacido tarde**, to be deficient in experience or intelligence. **Nacer en tal día**, to escape from peril. **Entre ellos ha nacido una fuerte simpatía**, a strong friendship has sprung up between them. *-vr.* To be propagated by nature, not sown, as grass. *(Yo nazco, yo nazca,* from *Nacer. V.* CONOCER.*)*
nacido, da [nah-thee'-do, dah], *a.* Proper, apt, fit, connate.-*pp.* of NACER. **Nacido de padres ricos**, born of wealthy parents. **Recién nacido**, newborn.
nacido [nah-thee'-do], *m.* 1. A living man: generally used in the plural. 2. Pimple, pustule, tumor.
naciente [nah-the-en'-tay], *pa. & a.* 1. Growing (creciente), which grows or springs up; very recent (nuevo). 2. *(Her.)* Naissant. *-m.* 1. East (este). 2. *(Cono Sur)* Spring, source.
nacimiento [nah-the-me-en'-to], *m.* 1. Birth, nativity. 2. Growing of plants. 3. Beginning of a thing (origen). 4. Nativity, the place of birth. 5. Rising of the plants. 6. Nativity, the coming of our Lord into the world. 7. Origin, descent, lineage. 8. The origin or the physical or moral cause of a thing. **Nacimiento de un río**, head of a river. **De nacimiento**, from its birth.
nación [nah-the-on'], *f.* 1. *(coll.)* Birth, issue into life. 2. A nation. 3. *(coll.)* Foreigner. 4. *(Amer.)* A race, or tribe of Indians. **De nación**, native of.
nacional [nah-the-o-nahl'], *a.* National, gentile. **Vuelos nacionales**, domestic flights.
nacionalidad [nah-the-o-nah-le-dahd'], *f.* National manners and customs, nationality.
nacionalismo [nah-the-o-nah-lees'-mo], *m.* Patriotism, love of country.
nacionalista [nah-the-o-nah-lees'-tah], *a. m & f.* Nationalist.
nacionalización [nah-the-o-nah-le-thah-the-on'], *f.* Nationalization.
nacionalizar [nah-the-o-nah-le-thar'], *va., vn., & vr.* To nationalize, to become nationalized, to become a citizen (de un país).
nacionalmente [nah-thei-o-nahl'-men-tay], *adv.* Nationally.
nacionalsocialismo, Partido [nah-the-oh-nahl-so-the-ah-lees'-mo, par-tee'-do], *m.* Nazi party (National Socialist German Workers' Party).
nacrita [nah-cree'-tah], *f.* Variety of tale with a nacreous lustre.
nacho, cha [nah'-cho, chah], *a. V.* ROMO and CHATO.
nada [nah'-dah], *f.* Nothing, nothingness, naught; nonentity; little, or very little. **En menos de nada** or **en una nada**, in an instant. **Enfadarse por nada**, to be vexed by the most insignificant thing. **Más vale algo que nada**, *(Prov.)* half a loaf is better than no bread. **Nada de eso**, nothing of the kind. **Casi nada**, next to nothing. **No reparar en nada**, to stop at nothing. **Hace nada**, just a moment ago. **Por nada del mundo**, not for anything in the world. **No ha sido nada**, it´s nothing.

nada [nah'-dah], *adv.* In no degree, by no means. **Nada menos**, nothing less: a particular negation.

nadaderas [nah-dah-day'-ras], *f. pl.* Corks or bladders used in learning to swim.

nadadero [nah-dah-day'-ro], *m.* Swimming-place.

nadador, ra [nah-dah-dor', rah], *m. & f.* Swimmer.

nadadora [nah-dah-do'-rah], *f.* Dragonfly.

nadante [nah-dahn'-tay], *pa.* 1. *(Poet.)* Natant, swimming. 2. *(Her.)* Naiant.

nadar [nah-dar'], *vn.* 1. To swim. 2. To float on the water, not to sink. 3. To be wide or loose. 4. *(Met.)* To abound, to be plentiful.

nadie [nah'-de-ay], *indef. prom.* Nobody, no-one, no one, none. **Apenas nadie**, hardly anybody. **No había nadie**, there was nobody. **A nadie se le ocurriría hacer tal cosa**, nobody would think of doing such a thing. **Nadie más**, nobody else. **No he hablado con nadie**, I haven't spoken to anyone.

nadir [nah-deer'], *m.* Nadir, the point opposite to the zenith.

nado (A) [nah'-do]. 1. Afloat. **Poner un bajel a nado**, to set a ship afloat. **Pasó el río a nado**, he swam across the river. 2. With difficulty and great toil. **Salir a nado**, to save oneself by swimming; to effect something with great difficulty and labor. **Echarse a nado**, to hazard, to undertake something boldly.

nafta [nahf'-tah], *f.* Naphtha, fluid bitumen; *(Cono Sur)* gasoline.

naftalina [naf-tah-lee'-nah], *f.* Naphthalene, a solid crystalline body obtained from coal-tar by distillation.

naguaclato, naguatate [nah-goo-ah-clah'-to], *m. (Mex.)* Interpreter.

naguas [nah'-goo-as], *f. pl.* Under-petticoat. V. ENAGUAS.

naife [nah'-ee-fay], *m.* A rough, unwrought diamond.

naipe [nah'-ee-pay], *m.* Playing card. **Naipes españoles**, Spanish playing cards.

naire [nah'-e-ray], *m.* Elephant-keeper.

nalga [nahl'-gah], *f.* Buttock, hip, rump.

nalgada [nal-gah'-dah], *f.* 1. Ham, the cured thigh of a hog. 2. Blow on the rump.

nalgado, da [nal-gah'-do, dah], *a.* Having round and fleshy posteriors.

nalgatorio [nal-gah-to'-re-o], *m. (coll.)* Seat, posteriors, nates.

nalguear [nal-gay-ar'], *vn.* To shake the posteriors in walking.

nalguilla [nal-geel'-lyah], *f.* The thick part of the hub of a wheel.

nana [nah'-nah], *f. (Mex. Coll.)* 1. A child's nurse. 2. A slumber song.

nancito [nan-thee'-to], *m.* A yellow berry of Nicaragua.

nandú [nan-doo'], *m.* The American ostrich.

nanquín [nan-keen'], *m.* Nankeen. V. MAHÓN.

nansa [nahn'-sah], *f.* Fish-pond.

nao [nah'-o], *f.* Ship, vessel. V. NAVE.

naonato, ta [nah-o-nah'-to, tah], *a.* Born on board ship.

napa [nah'-pah], *f.* 1. A cord for drawing in the tuna-nets. 2. *(Low.)* Backside.

napea [nah-pay'-ah], *f.* Wood-nymph.

napelo [nah-pay'-lo], *m. (Bot.)* Monk's-hood, wolf's-bane.

napia [nah'-pe-ah], *f.* Snout, nose.

napoleón [nah-po-lay-on'], *m.* A French silver five-franc piece.

Nápoles [nah'-po-lays], Naples.

napolitano, na [nah-po-le-tah'-no, nah], *a.* Neapolitan, relating to Naples.

naque [nah'-kay], *m.* Ancient company of two comedians.

naranja [nah-rahn'-hah], *f.* 1. Orange, the fruit of the orange-tree. **Media naranja**, *(Arch.)* cupola. 2. A cannon-ball of the size of an orange. -*a.* Orange.

naranjada [nah-ran-hah'-dah], *f.* 1. Conserve of oranges. 2. Orange-water, orangeade. 3. A rude saying or deed.

naranjado, da [nah-ran-hah'-do, dah], *a.* Orange-colored.

naranjal [nah-ran-hahl'], *m.* Orangery, grove or plantation of orange trees.

naranjazo [nah-ran-hah'-tho], *m.* Blow with an orange.

naranjero, ra [nah-ran-hay'-ro, rah], *m. & f.* 1. One who sells oranges. 2. *(Prov.)* Orange-tree.

naranjero, ra [nah-ran-hay'-ro, rah], *a.* 1. Applied to pieces of artillery which carry balls of the size of oranges. 2. Applied to a blunderbuss with a mouth of the size of an orange.

naranjilla [nah-ran-heel'-lyah], *f.* Small green orange used in making a conserve.

naranjo [nah-rahn'-ho], *m. (Bot.)* 1. Orange-tree. 2. *(coll.)* A booby, a noodle, an ignorant fellow.

narciso [nar-thee'-so], *m.* 1. *(Bot.)* Daffodil. **Narciso poético**, poet's narcissus. 2. Narcissus flower. 3. A precious stone of the color of daffodil. 4. Fop, coxcomb.

narcosis [nar-co'-sis], *f.* 1. Narcosis. 2. Narcotization.

narcótico, ca [nar-co'-te-co, cah], *a.* Narcotic, narcotical. producing stupor.

narcotina [nar-co-tee'-nah], *f.* Narcotine, an inodorous, insipid alkaloid of opium.

narcotismo [nar-co-tees'-mo], *m.* Narcotism, a state of stupor produced by narcotics.

narcotráfico [nar-co-trah'-fe-co], *m.* Drugs traffic.

nardino [nar-dee'-no], *a.* Made of spikenard.

nardo [nar'-do], *m. (Bot.)* Spikenard, nard, a plant of India, bulbous-rooted; and the ointment or confection prepared from it.

narguile [nar-gee'-lay], *m.* Narghile, hookah, an oriental pipe for smoking tobacco in which the smoke passes through perfumed water.

narigón [nah-re-gone'], *m. aug.* A large nose, a large-nosed person.

narigón, na, narigudo, da [nah-re-gone', nah], *a.* Having a large and long nose.

narigueta, nariguita [nah-re-gay'-tah, nah-re-gee'-tah], *f. dim.* A small nose.

nariz [nah-reeth'], *f.* 1. The nose. 2. The nostril. **Nariz chata**, flat or pugnose. **Dar en las narices**, *(coll.)* to smell or perceive a thing at a distance. *(Met.)* To find out what another person is about. **Meter la nariz en todas partes**, to be a busybody. **En mis propias narices**, under my very nose. **Tocarse las narices**, to be idle. 3. Sense of smell (olfato). 4. The projecting point of a bridge or pier which breaks the violence of the current. 5. The tubs or pipe of an alembic or other similar thing. 6. *(Naut.)* Cut-water, break of a ship's head. **Narices or ventanas de la nariz**, nostrils. **Hinchar las narices**, to be excessively irritated. **No ver (uno) más allá de sus narices**, not to see beyond one's nose, to be half-witted.

narizado, da [nah-re-thah'-do, dah], *a.* Having a large nose.

narra [nar'-rah], *f.* A tree of the Philippines whose wood is employed in boat-building; it tinges water a blue color and exhales an agreeable smell.

narración [nar-rah-the-on'], *f.* Narration, account, relation, legend.

narrador [nar-rah-dor'], *a.* Narrator. Also used as a noun.

narrar [nar-rar'], *va.* To narrate, to relate, to recite, to tell.

narrativa [nar-rah-tee'-vah], *f.* 1. Narrative (narración), relation, history, account. 2. Art or talent of relating things past (arte, talento).

narrativo, va, narratorio, ria [nar-rah-tee'-vo, vah], *a.* Narrative, narratory.

narria [nar'-re-ah], *f.* 1. Sledge, a carriage without wheels. 2. A fat, heavy, bulky woman.

narval [nar-vahl'], *m. (Zool.)* Narwhal, sea-unicorn.

nasa [nah'-sah], *f.* 1. Fyke, a fish-trap (trampa) (used in the Mediterranean) with a conical mouth; a bag-net. 2. Round, narrow-mouthed net; bow-net. 3. A wicker basket for holding fish (cesta); a kipe (provincial name). 4. *(Acad.)* Basket or jar for keeping bread, flour or such things.

nasal [nah-sahl'], *a.* Nasal, relating to the nose.

nasardo [nah-sar'-do], *m.* Nasard, one of the registers of an organ.

nasturcio [nas-toor'-the-o], *m.* (*Bot.*) Nasturtium.

nata [nah'-tah], *f.* 1. Cream. **Nata batida**, whipped cream. 2. The most esteemed or principal part of a thing; the cream. 3. *pl.* Whipped cream with sugar. 4. *V.* NATILLA.

natación [nah-tah-the-on'], *f.* 1. The art of swimming. 2. The act of swimming. **Natación a braza**, breaststroke. **Natación submarina**, underwater swimming.

natal [nah-tahl'], *a.* Natal, native.-*m.* Birth, birthday.

natalicio, cia [nah-tah-lee'-the-o, ah], *a. & m. & f.* Natal; nativity, birthday.

natalidad [nah-tah-le-dahd'], *f.* Birth rate.

natatorio, a [nah-tah-to'-re-o, ah], *a.* Natatory, relating to swimming.

naterón [nah-tay-rone'], *m.* Second curds after the first cheese is made. *V.* REQUESÓN.

natillas [nah-tee'-lyas], *f. pl.* Custard, a composition of milk, eggs, and sugar boiled together; it may be thickened with flour or starch, making a batter.

natío [nah-tee'-o], *m.* (*Prov.*) Birth; sprouting: used of plants.-*a.* Native.

natividad [nah-te-ve-dahd'], *f.* Nativity.

nativo, va [nah-tee'-vo, vah], *a.* 1. Native (país), produced by nature, natal; not artificial. 2. Fit, proper, apt. 3. Vernacular.

nato [nah'-to]. *a.* 1. Born. **Un actor nato**, a born actor. **Un criminal nato**, a hardened criminal. 2. Ex officio (por derecho).

natrón [nah-trone'], *m.* 1. Natron, native carbonate of soda. 2. A saline substance which separates from crucibles in glass-works.

natura [nah-too'-rah], *f.* 1. (*Ant.*) Nature. 2. The genital parts. 3. In music, a major scale.

natural [nah-too-rahl'], *m.* 1. Temper, genius, natural disposition (temperamento). 2. Instinct of brutes. 3. Native of a place or country.-*a.* 1. Natural, according to nature. 2. Natural, native, not artificial. 3. Native, pertaining to the place of birth. 4. Common, usual, regular, resembling nature. 5. Natural, ingenuous, without art or craft, unaffected. 6. Natural, not performed by industry or art. 7. Natural, that which imitates nature, and treats of her secrets and operations. 8. Natural, produced by the sole power of nature. **Al natural**, without art or affectation. **Buen natural**, good nature. **Fruta al natural**, fruit in its own juice. **Está muy guapa al natural**, she is very pretty just as she is.

naturaleza [nah-too-rah-lay'-thah], *f.* 1. Nature, aggregate, order, and disposition of all created beings; often personified. 2. Nature, the native state or property of things. 3. Nature, constitution of an animated body; complexion, constitution. 4. Nature, the property, virtue, or quality of things. 5. Nature, the regular course of things, the quality, order, and disposition of affairs. 6. Nature, instinct, property, or inclination. 7. Sex, genitals, especially the female. 8. Species, kind. 9. The state of a native with respect to the place where he was born. 10. Naturalization. 11. Nature, genius, temperament. **El joven es suizo de naturaleza**, the young man is Swiss by nationality.

naturalidad [nah-too-rah-le-dahd'], *f.* 1. State of being born in a certain place or country; birthright. 2. Naturalness, conformity to nature and truth. Ingenuity, candor. **Con la mayor naturalidad**, as if nothing had happened.

naturalismo [nah-too-rah-lees'-mo], *m.* 1. Naturalism, mere state of nature. 2. Realism, in a literary and artistic sense, strict copying of nature, without concealing its deformities.

naturalista [nah-too-rah-lees'-tah], *m.* Naturalist, one versed in the knowledge of nature, or natural philosophy, more especially of natural history.

naturalización [nah-too-rah-le-thah-the-on'], *f.* Naturalization, the act of investing aliens with the rights of native subjects.

naturalizar [nah-too-rah-le-thar'], *va.* To naturalize, to invest with the rights of native subjects.-*vr.* To be accustomed, to grow fit for any purpose.

naturalmente [nah-too-rahl'-men-tay], *adv.* Naturally (de modo natural), natively, by nature; humanly; plainly, without fiction, ingenuously, frankly.

naufragar [nah-oo-frah-gar'], *vn.* 1. To be stranded or ship-wrecked (persona), to suffer shipwreck (barco). 2. To suffer wreck or ruin in one's affairs, to fail in one's purposes.

naufragio [nah-oo-frah'-he-o], *m.* 1. Shipwreck. 2. Miscarriage, disappointment, calamity, heavy loss.

náufrago, ga [nah'-oo-frah-go, gah], *a.* Relating to shipwreck, wrecked.

naumaquia [nah-oo-mah'-ke-ah], *f.* Naumachy, a mock sea-fight.

náusea [nah'-oo-say-ah], *f.* Nauseousness, squeamishness, nausea, disposition to vomit. (Most used in the plural.) **Tener náuseas**, to feel nauseated.

nauseabundo [nah-oo-say-ah-boon'-do], *a.* Nauseous, loathsome, exciting nausea.

nausear [nah-oo-say-ar'], *vn.* To nauseate, to loathe, to become squeamish: to suffer nausea.

nauseativo, va [nah-oo-say-ah-tee'-vo, vah], *a.* Nauseous.

nauseoso, sa [nah-oo-say-o'-so, sah], *a. V.* NAUSEABUNDO.

nauta [nah'-oo-tah], *m.* Mariner, a seafaring man.

náutica [nah'-oo-te-cah], *f.* Navigation, the art of conducting ships over the ocean.

náutico, ca [nah'-oo-te-co, cah], *a.* Nautical.

nautilo [nah-oo-tee'-lo], *m.* Nautilus, a cephalopod mollusk.

nava [nah'-vah], *f.* A plain or level piece of ground.

navaja [nah-vah'-hah], *f.* 1. Clasp knife (cuchillo), folding-knife. 2. Razor. 3. Tusk of a wild boar. 4. Tongue of backbites. **Navaja de muelle**, flick knife.

navajada [nah-vah-hah'-dah], *f.* A thrust or gash with a knife.

navajazo [nah-vah-hah'-tho], *m. V.* NAVAJADA.

navajero [nah-vah-hay'-ro], *m.* 1. Razor-case. 2. A piece of linen on which a barber cleans his razor. 3. Criminal who carries a knife.

navajita [nah-vah-hee'-tah], *f. dim.* A small clasp-knife.

navajo [nah-vah'-ho], *m. V.* NAVAZO.

navajón [nah-vah-hone'], *m. aug.* A large knife.

navajonazo [nah-vah-ho-nah'-tho], *m.* Gash or wound made with a large knife.

naval [nah-vahl'], *a.* Naval, consisting of ships; belonging to ships. **Armada naval**, royal navy, royal fleet.

navarro, rra [nah-var'-ro, rah], *a.* Belonging to or native of Navarre.

navazo [nah-vah'-tho], *m.* 1. Kitchen-garden in Sanlúcar upon a sandy shore. 2. Level piece of ground where the rains make a pool.

nave [nah'-vay], *f.* 1. Ship, a vessel with decks and sails. 2. Nave, the middle part or body of a church. 3. (*Mex.*) Car (coche). **Nave de San Pedro**, the Roman Catholic Church. **Nave espacial**, spacecraft, space ship.

navecilla [nah-ve-theel'-yah], *f.* A vessel for incense.

navegable [nah-vay-gah, blay], *a.* Navigable (río), seaworthy (barco).

navegación [nah-vay-gah-the-on'], *f.* 1. Navigation, the act or practice of passing by water. 2. Passage, time which a ship takes in going from one place to another (barcos). 3. Navigation, art of navigating.

navegador, ra [nah-vay-gah-dor', rah], *a.* Navigating. -*m.* Navigator.

navegante [nah-vay-gahn'-tay], *pa. & m.* Navigator; navigating.

navegar [nah-vay-gar'], *vn.* 1. To navigate, to sail (barco), to pass by water. 2. To go from place to place for the purpose of trade. 3. (*Ant.*) To carry wares by sea from one part to another for trade.-*va.* To sail, to go, to travel (e. g. ten knots per hour).

naveta [nah-vay'-tah], *f.* 1. Vessel for incense in the church. 2. Small drawer.

navichuelo, la [nah-ve-choo-ay'-lo, lah], *m. & f. (Naut.)* A small vessel.

navicular [nah-ve-coo-lar'], *a.* Applied to the middle bone of the foot; the scaphoid.

navidad [nah-ve-dahd'], *f.* 1. Nativity. 2. Christmas day. **Por Navidades**, at Christmas.

navideño, ña [nah-ve-day'-nyo, nyah], *a.* Belonging to the time of nativity.

naviero, ra [nah-ve-ay'-ro, rah], *a.* Shipping. **Empresa naviera**, steamship concern.

navío [nah-vee'-o], *m.* A ship, especially a large ship, or a ship-of-war. **Navío de guerra**, a ship of war, a man of war. **Navío de línea** or **de alto bordo**, ship of the line. **Navío mercante**, merchant ship. **Navío de transporte**, transport. **Navío guardacosta**, guard-ship. **Navío de carga**, ship of burden. **Navío pesado**, a bad sailor.

náyade [nah'-yah-day], *f.* Naïad, water-nymph.

naylón [nah'-e-lone], *m.* Nylon.

nazareno, na [nah-thah-ray'-no, nah], *a.* 1. Nazarene, native of Nazareth. 2. Nazarite, one who neither shaved the beard, cut the hair, nor drank strong drink. *-m.* He who goes in processions in Passion Week, dressed in a long brown robe.

nazareo, ea [nah-thah-ray'-o, ah], *a.* Nazarite, among the Jews.

nazi [nah'-the], *m. & f. & a.* Nazi. **Partido Nazi**, Nazi Party. *V.* NACIONALSOCIALISMO, PARTIDO

nazismo [nah-thees'-mo], *m.* Nazism.

nébeda [nay'-bah-dah], *f.* Catmint, an aromatic herb.

nebladura [nay-blah-doo'-rah], *f.* Damage which crops receive from mist.

neblí [nay-blee'], *m. (Zool.)* Falcon gentle.

neblina [nay-blee'-nah], *f.* 1. Mist, small rain. 2. Confusion, obscurity.

nebrina [nay-bree'-nah], *f.* Juniper-berry.

nebuloso, sa [nay-boo-lo'-so, sah], *a.* Misty (aire), cloudy (cielo), nebulous, foggy, hazy.

necear [nay-thay-ar'], *vn.* To talk nonsense, to play the fool.

necedad [nay-thay-dahd'], *f.* Gross ignorance, stupidity; imprudence; foolishness (cualidad), folly, foppery, idiocy.

necesaria [nay-thay-sah'-re-ah], *f.* Privy, necessary, water-closet.

necesariamente [may-thay-sah'-re-ah-men-tay], *adv.* Necessarily, indispensably, consequently, needfully.

necesario, ria [nay-thay-sah'-re-o, ah], *a.* Necessary, requisite, needful. **Si fuere necesario**, if need be. **Lo necesario**, what is needful.

neceser [nay-thay-serr'], *m.* A case of necessary articles, as for the dressing-table. **Neceser de costura**, work-box, sewing box. **Bolsa de aseo,** toilet case. **Neceser de afeitar,** shaving kit.

necesidad [nay-they-se-dahd'], *f.* Necessity (apuro), need (miseria), want; cogency, extremity, constraint. **La necesidad carece de ley**, necessity has no law. **Esto es de primera necesidad**, this is absolutely essential. **Encontrarse en una necesidad**, to be in a difficult situation. **Pasar necesidades**, to suffer hardships.

necesitado, da [nay-thay-se-tah'-do, dah], *a.* Necessitous, poor, needy.*-pp.* of NECESITAR .

necesitado, da [nay-thay-se-tah'-do, dah], *m. & f.* A poor person, a needy man or woman.

necesitar [nay-they-se-tar'], *va.* To necessitate, to constrain, to compel. **Necesitamos 2 más**, we need 2 more. *-vn.* To want, to need, to lack. *-vr.* To be needed, to be wanted.

neciamente [nay'-the-ah-men-tay], *adv.* Ignorantly, stupidly, foolishly.

necio, cia [nay'-the-o, ah], *a.* 1. Ignorant, stupid, idiotic foolish (tonto). 2. Imprudent, injudicious. 3. *(And.)* Peevish (displicente). 4. *(And. Carib. Cono Sur)* Touchy, hypersensitive (quisquilloso). 5. *(CAm.)* Stubborn (enfermedad). *-m. & f.* Fool.

nécora [nay'-co-rah], *f.* Small crab.

necróforo [nay-cro'-fo-ro], *m.* Necrophorus, the sexton or burying beetle, noted for its keenness of smell.

necrolatría [nay-cro-lah-tree'-ah], *f.* Worship of the dead.

necrología [nay-cro-lo-hee'-ah], *f.* Necrology, a register of persons deceased.

necrológico, ca [nay-cro-lo'-he-co, cak], *a.* Necrological, belonging to necrology.

necrologio [nay-cro-lo'-he-o], *m.* Necrology, mortuary, register of bishops.

necrópolis [nay-cro'-po-les], *f.* Necropolis.

necropsia, or **necroscopia** [nay-crop'-se-ah], *f.* Necrosis, autopsy, post-mortem examination.

necrosis [nay-cro'-sis], *f.* Necrosis, mortification of the bones.

nectar [nec'-tar], *m.* 1. Nectar, the supposed drink of the gods. 2. Any very pleasant drink. 3. Nectar, the honey of plants.

nectáreo, rea [nec-tah'-ray-o, ah], *a.* Nectareal, noctarean, sweet as nectar.

nectarífero, ra [nec-tah-ree'-fay-ro, rah], *a.* Nectar-bealing.

nectarino, na [nec-tah-ree'-no, nah], *a. V.* NECTÁREO.

nectario [nec-tah'-re-o], *m. (Bot.)* Nectary, the part of a plant which secretes nectar or honey.

neerlandés, sa [nay-er-lan-days', sah], *a.* Netherlandish, Flemish, Dutch.

nefandamente [nay-fahn'-dah-men-tay], *adv.* Basely, nefariously, abominably.

nefando, da [nay-fahn'-do, dah], *a.* Base, nefarious, abominable, heinous.

nefario, ria [nay-fah'-re-o, ah], *a.* Nefarious, abominable, extremely wicked.

nefas [nay'-fas], *adv.* **Por fas o por nefas**, right or wrong.

nefasto [nay-fahs'-to], *a.* Pernicious (influencia); harmful; unlucky (viaje), ill-fated; *(LAm.)* Dreadful (atroz).

nefrítico, ca [nay-free'-te-co, cah], *a.* 1. Nephritic, belonging to the kidneys; troubled with the gravel. 2. Applied to a kind of jasper.

nefritis [nay-free'-tis], *f. (Med.)* Nephritis, Bright's disease.

negable [nay-gah'-blay], *a.* That which may be denied.

negación [nay-gah-the-on'], *f.* 1. Negation, the act of denying, denial (negativa). 2. Want or total privation of anything. 3. Negative particle.

negado, da [nay-gah'-do, dah], *a.* Incapable, inapt, unfit. *-pp.* of NEGAR.

negador, ra [nay-gah-dor', rah], *m. & f.* Denier, disclaimer.

negar [nay-gar'], *va.* 1. To deny (hecho, verdad), to contradict. 2. To deny, to refuse, not to grant, to gainsay. 3. To forbid, to prohibit, to hinder, to oppose. 4. To deny, to contradict an accusation (acusación). 5. To deny, to disown, to disclaim (relación, responsabilidad). 6. To deny, to disregard, to forget what one has previously held in esteem, to withdraw from a company frequented before. 7. To hide, to conceal. 8. To dissemble. 9. To refuse to acknowledge the obligations a person has contracted. **Negar la mano a uno**, to refuse to shake hands with somebody. *-vr.* 1. To decline doing something. 2. To desire to be denied to persons who call to see one. **Negarse con la cabeza**, to shake one's head. **Negarse a una visita**, to refuse to see a visitor. *(Yo niego, yo niegue, from Negar. V. ACERTAR.)*

negativa [nay-gah-tee'-vah], *f.* Negation; repulse; negative, refusal. **Negativa rotunda**, flat refusal.

negativamente [nay-gah-tee'-vah-men-tay], *adv.* Negatively.

negativo, va [nay-gah-tee'-vo, vah], *a.* Negative, implying negation or denial, negatory.*-f.* Negative, a developed photographic plate or film, showing reversed lights and shadows.

negligencia [nay-gle-gen'-the-ah], *f.* Negligence, neglect, heedlessness, forgetfulness, habit of acting carelessly.

negligente [nay-gle-hen'-tay], *a.* Negligent, careless, heedless, absent, thoughtless, listless.

negligentemente [nay-gle-hen'-tay-men-tay], *adv.* Negligently, neglectfully, giddily, loosely, listlessly, heedlessly.

negociabilidad [nay-go-the-ah-be-le-dahd'], *f. (Neol. Com.)* Negotiability, particularly of bills of exchange.

negociable [nay-go-the-ah'-blay], *a.* Negotiable.

negociación [nay-go-the-ah-the-on'], *f.* Negotiation, management; commerce. **Negociación colectiva,** collective bargaining.

negociado [nay-go-the-ah'-do], *m.* 1. Each separate division or section in the official departments (sección). 2. *V.* NEGOCIO. 3. *(Cono Sur)* Shop, store. 4. *(And. Cono Sur)* Illegal transaction. - *pp.* of NEGOCIAR.

negociador [nay-go-the-ah-dor'], *m.* 1. A man of business. 2. Negotiator, one employed to deal with others.

negociante [nay-go-the-ahn'-tay], *pa. & m.* Trader, dealer; negotiating, trading.

negociar [nay-go-the-ar'], *vn.* 1. To trade, to buy and sell goods. 2. To negotiate bills of exchange; to negotiate political affairs.

negocio [nay-go'-the-o], *m.* 1. Occupation, employment, management, business (empresa). 2. Affair (asunto), pretension, treaty, agency, concern. 3. Negotiation, trade, commerce. *4. (And. Cono Sur)* Firm (firma), company. 5. *(And, Carib.)* **El negocio,** the fact. 6. *(And.)* Tale, piece of gossip. **Fingir negocios,** to affect the man of business. 4. Utility or interest in trading. **Eso es negocio tuyo,** that´s your affair. **El negocio del espectáculo,** show business. **Buen negocio,** profitable deal. *-pl.* Business, commercial transactions. **El mundo de los negocios,** the business world.

negocioso, sa [nay-go-the-o'-so, sah], *a.* Diligent, prompt, careful.

negozuelo [nay-go-thoo-ay'-lo], *m. dim.* Any insignificant affair or business.

negra [nay'-grah], *f.* 1. A foil for fencing. 2. Negress, black woman. 3. Black piece (ajedrez). 4. *(CAm.)* Black mark. 5. Bad luck (mala suerte). **Tener la negra,** to be out of luck.

negrada [negrah'-dah], *f.* Black slaves (conjunto de negros).

negrear [nay-gray-ar'], *vn.* To grow black, to appear black (volverse negro).

negrecer [nay-gray-therr'], *vn.* To blacken, to become black. *(Yo negrezco, yo negrezca,* from *Negrecer. V.* CONOCER.)

negrero [nay-gray'-ro], *m.* 1. Trafficker in slaves. **Negrero** or **barco negrero,** a slaver. 2. *(Cuba)* The white man who is fond of Negresses.

negreta [nay-gray'-tah], *f. (Orn.)* Coot, a kind of duck of a blackish color.

negrilla [nay-greel'-lyah], *f.* 1. *(typ.)* Boldface type. 2. *(Zool.)* Conner eel.

negrillera [nay-gril-lyay'-rah], *f.* Plantation of black poplar.

negrillo [nay-greel'-lyo], *m.* 1. *(dim.)* A young Negro. 2. Black silver ore, stephanite. 3. *(Bot.)* V. OLMO.

negrito, ta [nay-gree'-to, tah], *a. (Mex.)* V. NEGRO, 6th def. *-f. (Tip.)* Bold face. **En negrita,** in bold type.

negro, gra [nay'-gro, grah], *a.* 1. Black, dark. **Un coche negro,** a black car. 2. Brown or gray; not well bleached. 3. Blackish; of a dark-brown color (oscuro). 4. Gloomy, black (estado, humor), dismal, melancholy. 5. Unfortunate, wretched. 6. *(Coll. Amer.)* An endearing expression, equivalent to my dove, my dear. 7. Cross, peeved (enfadado). **Más negro que el azabache,** as black as ink. **La cosa se pone negra,** it´s not going well. **Estoy negro con esto,** I´m getting desperate about it.

negro, gra, *m. & f.* Negro, a blackamoor; Negress. **Negro de humo,** lamp-black. **Negro de plomo,** ochre-black. **Negro de carbón,** blue-black. 2. *(Met.* The least of anything. 3. *(Carib.)* Black coffee.

negrura [nay-groo'-rah], *f.* Blackness.

negruzco, ca [nay-grooth'-co, cah], *a.* Blackish, nigrescent, dark brown.

neguijón [nay-gee-hone'], *m.* Caries, rottenness of the teeth.

neguilla [nay-geel'-lyah], *f.* 1. *(Bot.)* Fennel-flower, love-in-a-mist. 2. Obstinate denial.

nema [nay'-mah], *f.* Seal or sealing of a letter.

nematócero, ra [nay-mah-to'-thay-ro, rah], *a.* Nematocerous, nemocerous, of thread-like antennae.

nemeo, mea [nay-may'-o, ah], *a.* Nemaean: applied to some ancient games.

némine discrepante [nay'-me-nay dis-cray-pahn'-tay], *(Lat.)* Unanimously: no one dissenting.

nemoroso, sa [nay-mo-ro'-so, sah], *a.* Woody, nemorous, consisting of wood; relating to wood.

nene, nena [nay'-nay, nay'-nah], *m. & f. (coll.)* An infant, a baby.

nenúfar [nay-noo'-far], *m. (Bot.)* White water-lily.

neoclasicismo [nay-o-clah-se-thees'-mo], *m.* Neoclassicism.

neoclásico [nay-o-clah'-se-co], *a.* Neoclassical.

neofascismo [nay-o-fas-thees'-mo], *m.* Neofascism.

neofascista [nay-o-fas-thees'-tah], *a. m & f.* Neofascist.

neófito [nay-o'-fe-to], *m.* 1. Neophyte, one regenerated; a convert. 2. Novice, beginner.

neografía [nay-o-grah-fee'-ah], *f.* Neography, a new system of writing.

neografismo [nay-o-grah-fees'-mo], *m.* Neography, new method of writing; contrary to the received custom.

neógrafo, fa [nay-o'-grah-fo, fah], *a.* Applied to one who uses a new and peculiar mode of writing.

neolatino, na [nay-o-lah-tee'-no, nah], *a.* Neo-Latin, Romanic: used of the languages derived from Latin.

neología [nay-o-lo-hee'-ah], *f.* Neology, introduction or use of new words and phrases.

neológico, ca [nay-o-lo'-he-co, cah], *a.* Neological, employing new words and phrases.

neologismo [nay-o-lo-hees'-mo], *m.* Neologism, a new and yet unsanctioned expression.

neólogo [nay-o'-lo-go], *m.* Neologist, a coiner of words.

neomenia [nay-o-may'-ne-ah], *f.* Neomenina, first day of new moon.

neón [nay-on'], *m. & a.* Neon. **Luces de Neón,** neon lights.

neoplasma [nay-o-plahs'-mah], *m. (Med.)* Neoplasm, a new growth due to morbid action.

neorama [nay-o-rah'-mah], *m.* Panorama upon a cylindrical surface, the observer being placed at the center.

neoyorquino, na [nay-o-yor-kee'-no, nab], *a.* From New York. *-m. & f.* New Yorker.

nepente [nay-pen'-tay], *m.* Nepenthe, a drug supposed to drive away all pain.

nepote [nay-po'-tay], *m. V.* SOBRINO. A privileged relative of the Pope.

nepotismo [nay-po-tees'-mo], *m.* Nepotism; favoritism exercised towards nephews or other relatives.

Neptuno [nep-too'-no], *m.* 1. The planet Neptune. 2. *(Poet.)* The sea.

nequicia [nay-kee'-the-ah], *f.* Perversity.

nereida [nay-ray'-e-dah], *f.* Nereid, a sea-nymph.

nervado, da [ner-vah'-do, dah], *a. (Bot.)* Nervate, nerved.

nervadura [ner-vah-doo-rah], *f.* Nervation or nervature of leaves; arrangement of nerves.

nervino, na [ner-vee'-no, nah], *a.* Calming and fortifying the nerves; nervine.

nervio [nerr'-ve-o], *m.* 1. A nerve. 2. The main and most powerful part of anything. 3. String of a musical instrument. 4. *(Naut.)* A small rope, the middle of which is fixed to a stay. 5. Nerve, energy, vigor (vigor); moral fiber (moral). 6. In botany, the perfect and unbranched vessels extending from the base towards the tip; nerve. 7. Tendon, or aponeurosis. 8. *(Anat.)* Tendon (tendón). 9. *(Fig.)* Soul, leading light (persona). **Crispar los nervios a uno,** to get on somebody´s nerves. **Tener nervios de acero,** to have nerves of steel. **Un hombre sin nervio,** a weak man.

nerviosidad [ner-ve-o-se-dahd'], *f. V.* NERVOSIDAD.

nervioso, sa [ner-ve-o'-so, sah], *a.* 1. Nervous, relating to the nerves. 2. Nervous (estado temporal), vigorous (palabra, frase). 3. *(Bot.)* Nerved. **Sistema nervioso,** nervous system. **Poner nervioso a uno,** to make somebody nervous.

nervosamente [ner-vo-sah-men-tay], *adv.* Nervously.

nervosidad [ner-vor-se-dahd'], *f.* 1. Strength, nervousness. 2. Efficacy, vigor. 3. Flexibility.

nervoso, sa [ner-vo´-so, sah], *a.* 1 Nervous, relating to the nerves. 2 Nervous, strong, vigorous, robust.

nervudo, da [ner-voo'-do, dah], *a.* Nervous, well strung, strong, vigorous.

nesciencia [nes-the-en'-the-ah],*f.* Ignorance, nescience, want of knowledge.

nesciente [nes-the-en'-tay], *a.* Ignorant, foolish.

nesga [nes'-gah], *f.* Gore, a triangular piece of linen or stuff sewn upon cloth.

nestorianismo [nes-to-re-ah-nees'-mo], *m.* Nestorianism, a heresy of the fifth century.

nestoriano [nes-to-re-ah'-no], *m.* Nestorian, one of the followers of Nestorius.

netezuelo, la [nay-tay-thoo-ay'-lo, lah], *m. & f. dim.* A little grandchild.

neto, ta [nay'-to, tah], *a.* Neat, pure, clean (puro), unadulterated; net, clear, genuine; without foreign mixture. **Producto neto,** net produce. **En neto,** purely. **Peso neto,** net weight.

neto [nay'-to], *m. (Arch.)* Naked pedestal of a column.

neuma [nay-oo'-mah], *m.* Expression by signs of what one wishes or thinks.

neumático, ca [nay-mah´-te-co, cah], *a.* Pneumatic, **Perforación neumática,** Pneumatic drilling.-*m.* Automobile tire. **Neumático de repuesto,** spare tire.

neumococo [nay-oo-mo-co'-co], *m.* Pneumococcus.

neumonía [nay-oo-mo-nee´-ah], *f.* Pneumonia, lung fever, inflammation of the lungs.

neumónico, ca [nay-oo-mo'-ne-co, cah], *a.* Pneumonic, relating to the lungs, or to pneumonia.

neuralgia [nay-oo-rahl'-he-ah], *f.* Neuralgia, pain along a nerve, without fever.

neurálgico, ca [nay-oo-rahl´-he-co, cah], *a.* Neuralgic, relating to neuralgia.

neurastenia [nay-oo-ras-tay'-ne-ah],*f. (Med.)* Neurasthenia.

neurasténico, ca [nay-oo-ras-tay'-ne-co, cah], *a.* Neurasthenic, suffering from nervous exhaustion. *(Neol.)*

neurítico, ca [nay-oo-ree'-te-co, cah], *a. (Med.)* Neurotic. -*pl.* Neurotica: applied to medicines supposed to strengthen the nerves.

neuritis [nay-oo-ree'-tis], . *(Med.)* Neuritis.

neurocirugía [nay-oo-ro-the-roo-he'-ah], *f.* Neurosurgery.

neurología [nay-oo-ro-lo-hee'-ah], *f.* Neurology, a description of the nerves.

neurólogo, ga [nay-oo-ro'-lo-go], *m & f.* Neurologist.

neuroma [nay-oo-ro'-mah], *m.* Neuroma, a tumor of a nerve.

neurona [nay-oo-ro'-nah], *f. (Anat.)* Neuron, neurone.

neuropatía [nay-oo-ro-pah-tee'-ah], *f.* A nervous disorder; neuropathy.

neuróptero, ra [nay-oo-rop'-tay-ro, rah], *a.* Neuropterous.

neurosis [nay-oo-ro'-sis], *f.* Neurosis, functional nervous disease.

neurotomía [nay-oo-ro-to-mee'-ah],*f. (Med.)* 1. Neurotomy, dissection of nerves. 2. Section or division of a nerve.

neutral [nay-oo-trahl'], *a.* Neutral, neuter, indifferent; it has been used.

neutralidad [nay-oo-trah-le-dahd'], *f.* Neutrality.

neutrino [nay-oo-tree'-no], *m. (Phy. & Chem.)* Neutrino, as a substantive, especially in the plural.

neutralidad [nay-oo-trah-le-dahd'], *f.* 1. Neutrality, a state of indifference. 2. Neutrality, state of peace with belligerent nations.

neutralizar [nay-oo-trah-le-thar'], *va. (Chem.)* To neutralize.

neutralmente [nay-oo-trahl'-men-tay], *adv.* Neutrally, indifferently.

neutro, tra [nay'-oo-tro, trah], *a.* 1 Neutral, neuter, not engaged on either side. 2 *(Gram.)* Neuter, a noun that implies no sex; a verb that is neither active nor passive, intransitive. **Verbo neutro,** intransitive verb.

neutrón [nay-oo-trone], *m. (Phy. & Chem.)* Neutron.

nevada [nay-vah'-dah], *f.* 1. Snowfall, descent of snow. 2. Snowfall, the quantity of snow which falls at one time, a heavy fall of snow. 3. *(Bot.)* V. NEVADILLA.

nevadilla [nay-vah-deel'-lyah], *f. (Bot.)* Whitlow-wort, any species of Paronychia with dry silvery stippler and clustered flowers.

nevado, da [nay-vah'-do, dah], *a.* White as snow. -*pp.* of NEVAR.

nevar [nay-var'], *vn.* To snow; to fall in snow. **Nevar mucho,** to snow heavily. -*va.* To make white as snow. *(Nieva, nieve, from Nevar. V.* ACERTAR.)

nevasca [nay-vahs'-cah], *f.* 1. Fall of snow; snow and wind. 2. Snowstorm.

nevatilla [nay-vah-teel'-yah], *f. (Zool.)* Wag-tail. V. AGUZANIEVE.

nevera [nay-vey'-rah], *f.* 1. Ice-house. 2. Applied to any very cold room or place. 3. Icebox, refrigerator.

nevereta [nay-vay-ray'-tah], *f.* V. AGUZANIEVE.

nevería [nay-vay-ree´-ah], *f.* Ice-house, a place where ice is sold.

nevero, ra [nay-vay'-ro, rah], *m. & f.* One who sells ice. -*m.* Place of perpetual snow.

nevisca [nay-vees'-cah], *f.* V. NEVASCA.

neviscar [nay-vis-car'], *vn.* To snow lightly.

nevoso, sa [nay-vo'-so, sah], *a.* 1. Snowy, abounding with snow, nival, niveous. 2. Snowy: applied to weather indicating snow.

nexo [nek'-so], *m.* Knot, string, union.

nexo [nek'-so], *adv.* (Cant or low) No. (*Cf.* nix and Ger. nights.)

ni [nee], *conj.* Neither, nor. **Ni fui, ni tengo intención de ir,** I did not go, nor do I intend to go. **Ni le amo, ni le temo,** I neither love nor fear him. **Ni siquiera,** not even. **Ni usted lo sabe,** even you do not know it. **No dice ni si ni no,** he is neither *pro* nor *con.* **No quiere ni sal ni mostaza,** he doesn´t want either salt or mustard. **Ni a ti te lo dirá,** he won´t tell even you. **Ni que fueses su mujer,** not even if you were his wife. **Ni come ni duerme,** he neither eats, nor sleeps. **Ni más ni menos,** no more, no less. **Ni tú ni yo le podemos ayudar ahora,** neither you nor I can help him now. **Ni siquiera,** not even. **No quiero ni vino ni cerveza,** I don't want either wine or beer. **Se fue sin comer ni beber,** he left without eating or drinking.

niacina [ne-ah-thee'-nah], *f.* Niacine.

nícalo [nee'-cah-lo], *m.* V. NISCALO.

nicaragüense [ne-cah-rah-goo-en'-say], *m. & f. & a.* Nicaraguan.

nicerobino [ne-thay-ro-bee'-no], *a.* Applied to a precious ointment used by the ancients.

nicho [nee´-cho], *m.* 1. Niche, a recess in a wall to place a statue in. 2. Any hole or corner to put something in. 3. Any employment or destination in which a person ought to be placed according to his merits.

nicotina [ne-co-tee'-nah], *f.* Nicotine, a highly poisonous alkaloid of tobacco.

nictálope [nic-tah´-lo-pay], *m.* Nyctalops, one who sees best at night.

nictalopia [nic-tah-lo'-pe-ah], *f.* Nyctalopy, a disease of the eye; day-blindness.

nidada [ne-dah'-dah], *f.* Nestful of eggs, on which a hen sits; brood, covey.

nidal [ne-dahl'], *m.* 1. A nest, place where a hen or other bird lays her eggs. 2. Nest-egg (dinero). 3. Basis, foundation, motive. 4. Haunt.

nidificar [ne-de-fe-car'], *vn.* To nest, to build nests.

nidito [ne-dee'-to], *m. dim.* A small nest.

nido [nee´-do], *m.* 1. Nest, the bed formed by the bird for incubation. 2. Nest, any place where animals are produced (criadero). 3. Nest, habitation, abode, residence. 4. Hiding place (escondite). 5. *(Fig.)* Hiding place (guarida). **Nido de ladrones**, nest of thieves. **Nido de amor**, love nest. **Nido de víboras**, nest of vipers.

niebla [ne-ay'-blah], *f.* 1. Fog (densa), mist (neblina), haze, damp. 2. Disease of the eyes, which dims, the sight. 3. Mildew (hongo parásito). 4. Mental obscurity, confusion of ideas.

niego [ne-ay'-go], *a.* New-born (halcón). V. HALCÓN.

niel [ne-el'], *m.* Embossment, relief; raised work.

nielar [ne-ay-lar'], *va.* To form with a protuberance, to carve in relief, or raised work on plate; to engrave, to enamel.

nieta [ne-ay'-tah], *f.* Grand-daughter, grandchild.

nieto [ne-ay'-to], *m.* 1. Grand-son, grandchild. 2. Descendant.

nieve [ne-ay'-vay], *f.* 1. Snow. 2. Snowy weather: commonly used in the plural. 3. Fall of snow. 4. Extreme whiteness. 5. *(LAm.)* Ice cream (helado). 6. Snow (cocaína). **Las primeras nieves**, the first snows.

nigromancia [ne-gro-mahn'-the-ah], *f.* Necromancy; black art.

nigromante [ne-gro-mahn'-tay], *m.* Necromancer, conjurer, magician.

nigromántico, ca [ne-gro-mahn'-te-co, cah], *a.* Necromantic. -*m.* & *f.* V. NIGROMANTE.

nigua [nee'-goo-ah], *f.* Chigoe, jigger flea, an insect found in tropical America, which burrows under the nails.

nihilismo [ne-he-lees´-mo], *m.* 1. Nihilism, denial of all belief. 2. Russian anarchism, antagonism to religion, society, and government.

nihilista [ne-he-lees'-tah], *m.* Nihilist, anarchist.

niki [nee'-ke], *m.* T-shirt.

nimiamente [nee'-me-ah-men-tay], *adv.* Excessively.

nilad [ne-lahd'], *m.* A shrub of about six feet high which grows in the Philippine archipelago.

nilíaco, ca [ne-lee'-ah-co, cah], *a.* Belonging to the Nile.

nilómetro [ne-lo'-may-tro], *m.* Nilometer, a column or gauge for measuring the height of water in the Nile.

nilón [ne-lone'], *m.* Nylon.

nimiedad [ne-me-ay-dahd'], *f.* 1. Superfluity, excess, nimiety. 2. Niceness, extravagant nicety. 3. *(coll.)* A rediculous sparingness, or frugality.

nimio, mia [nee´-me-o, ah], *a.* Excessive (excesivo), too much, prolix.

ninfa [neen'-fah], *f.* 1. Nymph. 2. Young lady. 3. Pupa, the chrysalis of a caterpillar.

ninfea [nin-fay'-ah], *f. (Bot.)* Water-lily. **Ninfea blanca**, white water-lily.

ninfo [neen'-fo], *m.* A beau, a young effeminate fop, a dude.

ninfómana [nen-fo'-mah-nah], *f.* Nymphomaniac.

ninfomanía [nin-fo-mah-nee'-ah], *f.* Nymphomania, morbid, insane sexual desire in women.

ningún [nin-goon'], *a.* None, not one: used before masculine nouns. **De ningún modo**, in no manner, by no means.

ninguno, na [nin-goo'-no, nah], *a.* None, not one, no, neither. **De ninguna manera**, by no means, in no manner. **Ninguna cosa**, nothing. **Ninguna belleza**, no beauty. -*pron.* Nobody, no-one; none; neither. **No lo sabe ninguno**, nobody knows. **Ninguno de los dos**, neither of them.

niña [nee'-nyah], *f.* 1. Pupil of the eye. 2. Little girl, a female child. 3. Tart, whore (prostituta). 4. *(LAm.)* Miss, mistress. **La niña bonita**, number fifteen. **Ser las niñas de los ojos de uno**, to be the apple of somebody´s eye.

niñada [ne-nyah'-dah], *f.* Puerility, childishness, a childish speech or action.

niñato [ne-nyah'-to], *m.* Calf found in the belly of a cow which has been killed.

niñear [ne-nyay-ar'], *vn.* To act like a child, to behave in a childish manner.

niñera [ne-nyay'-rah], *f.* Nursemaid, servant employed to take care of children. 2. Baby-sitter.

niñería [ne-nyay-ree'-ah], *f.* 1. Puerility, childish action (acto). 2. Bauble, gewgaw, plaything. 3. Trifle, thing of no importance.

niñero, ra [ne-nyay'-ro, rah], *a.* & *m.* & *f.* One who is fond of children, or who delights in childish tricks; a dandler.

niñeta [ne-nyay'-tah], *f.* The small pupil of the eye.

niñez [ne-nyeth'], *f.* 1. Childhood, infancy. 2. Infancy, the first age of anything: beginning, commencement.

niñita [ne-nyee'-tah], *f. dim.* Babe, infant.

niño, ña [nee'-nyo, nyah], *a.* Childish, child-like, puerile (infantil).

niño [nee'-nyo], *m.* 1. Child, infant. 2. Person of little experience or prudence. 3. *(LAm.)* Master, sir. 4. *(Cono Sur)* undesirable. **Desde niño**, from infancy, from a child. **No es niño**, he is no more a child. **Niño prodigio**, child prodigy. **Ser el niño mimado de uno**, to be somebody´s pet. **Cuando nazca el niño**, when the baby is born.

nioto [ne-o'-to], *m.* V. CAZÓN.

nipa [nee'-pah], *f.* A kind of palm-tree in the Philippine Islands; from the leaves thatches for roofs are made, and from the roots a spirituous drink.

nipe, or **nipis** [nee'-pay, nee'-pis], *m. (Com.)* A fabric made from the fibers of the *nipa* in the Philippines and in Madagascar.

nipón, na [ne-pone', nah], *m.* & *f.* & *a.* Nipponese, Japanese.

niquel [nee'-kel], *m.* Nickel, a silvery white metal.

niquelado [ne-kay-lah'-do], *a.* (Ore) Holding nickel; also nickel-plated.

niquelar [ne-kay-lar'], *va.* To nickel-plate.

niqui [nee'-ke], *m.* T-shirt.

niquiscocio [ne-kis-co'-the-o], *m.* Trifle, a thing of little importance.

níscalo [nees´-cah-lo], *m.* A non-poisonous mushroom.

níspera [nees´-pay-rah], *f.* A Nicaraguan timber-tree. V. ZAPOTE.

níspero [nees´-pay-ro], *m. (Bot.)* Medlar-tree.

níspola [nees´-po-lah], *f.* Fruit of the medlar-tree.

nitidez [ne-te-dayth'], *f.* 1. Brightness; spotlessness (limpieza); clarity, sharpness. 2. *(Fig.)* Unblemished nature.

nítido, da [nee´-te-do, dah], *a. (Poet.)* Bright, shining, lustrous, nitid, neat, spotless (limpio).

nito [nee'-to], *m.* A brake found in the Philippine Islands, from the petioles of which is obtained a fiber used in making hats and cigar-cases.

nitos [nee´-tos], *m.* Insignificant word, meaning nothing, in reply to an impertinent question, or to conceal anything.

nitral [ne-trahl'], *m.* Place where niter is formed; nitre-bed.

nitrato [ne-trah'-to], *m. (Chem.)* Nitrate.

nitrería [ne-tray-ree´-ah], *f.* Saltpeter-works, where saltpeter is prepared and refined.

nítrico [nee´-tre-co], *a.* Nitric, applied to an acid; consisting of niter.

nitrito [ne-tree'-to], *m.* Nitrite, a compound of nitrous acid.

nitro [nee´-tro], *m.* Niter, saltpeter; nitrate of potassium.

nitrobencina [ne-tro-ben-thee'-nah], *f. (Chem.)* Nitrobenzene.

nitrocelulosa [ne-tro-thay-loo-lo'-sah], *f.* Nitrocellulose, nitrated cellulose.

nitrógeno [ne-tro'-hay-no], *m. (Chem.)* Nitrogen, azote.

nitroglicerina [ne-tro-gle-thay-ree´-nah], *f.* Nitro-glycerine, a powerful explosive, basis of dynamite.

nitroso, sa [ne-tro´-so, sah], *a.* Nitrous, nitry, impregnated with nitre.

nivel [ne-vel'], *m.* 1. Level, instrument for ascertaining the level of a surface. 2. Level, a plane or surface without inequalities, levelness. 3. Level, standard. **A nivel**, perfectly level, in a line or row. **Nivel del agua**, water level. **Alto nivel de trabajo**, high level of employment. **No está al nivel de los demás**, he is not up to the standard of the others.

nivelación [ne-vay-lah-the-on'], *f.* 1. Act of levelling. 2. Levelling, the operation of obtaining comparative elevations in surveying.

nivelador [ne-vay-lah-dor'], *m.* One who ascertains the level of a surface, leveller.

niveladora [ne-vay-lah-do'-rah], *f. (Mech.)* Bulldozer.

nivelar [ne-vay-lar], *va.* 1. To ascertain the level of a surface. 2. To make even, to level. 3. To observe equality and justice.

níveo, ea [nee'-vay-o, ah], *a. (Poet.)* Snowy, like snow.

nizardo, da [ne-thar'-do, dah], *a.* Native of or belonging to Nice.

no [no], *adv.* No or not, nay. **No importa nada**, it signifies nothing. **No vale nada**, it is worth nothing. **Decir que no**, to give a flat denial. **Pues no**, but no, not so. **No sé qué**, I know not what, an inexplicable something. **Por si o por no**, at any rate. **Sin faltar un sí ni un no**, without an iota wanting. **No sea que**, lest. **No tengo nada**, I have nothing. **Cosa no esencial**, non-essential thing.

nobiliario [no-be-le-ah'-re-o], *m.* A genealogical account of the peerage of a country, nobiliary.

noble [no'-blay], *a.* 1. Noble, of noble extraction, high-born. 2. Illustrious, eminent, conspicuous, magnific, magnifical, generous. 3. Honorable, respectable. **Estado noble**, nobility. *-m.* Nobleman.

noblemente [no-blay-men-tay], *adv.* Nobly, generously, magnanimously.

nobleza [no-blay'-thah], *f.* 1. Nobleness, nobility (cualidad), antiquity of family with luster of pedigree. 2. Nobility, the body of noblemen (personas). 3. Gentility, elegance of behavior. 4. Nobleness, nobility, dignity, greatness, generousness, magnanimity, worth; stateliness. 5. Fine damask silk.

nocedal [no-thay-dahd'], *m.* V. NOGUERAL.

noche [no'-chay], *f.* 1. Night. 2. *(Poet.)* Night, death. 3. Night, state of obscurity, confusion, or ignorance. **Anoche** or **ayer noche**, last night. **Noche y día**, night and day, always, constantly. **De la noche a la mañana**, overnight. **Hasta muy entrada la noche**, until late at night. **Hacer noche en un sitio**, to spend the night in a place.

Nochebuena [no-chay-boo-ay'-nah], *f.* Christmas eve.

nochecita [no-chay-thee'-tah], *f. (Amer.)* Twilight.

nochizo [no-chee'-tho], *m. (Bot.)* Wild common hazel-nut tree.

noción [no-the-on'], *f.* 1. Notion, idea. 2. Acceptation, meaning of a word. **No tener la menor noción de algo**, not to have the faintest idea about something.

nocional [no-the-o-nahl'], *a.* Notional.

nocivamente [no-the-vah-men'-tay], *adv.* Mischievously, hurtfully, harmfully.

nocivo, va [no-thee'-vo, vah], *a.* Noxious, hurtful, mischievous, malignant.

noctambulismo [noc-tam-boo-lees'-mo], *m.* The act of walking in sleep. V. SOMNAMBULISMO.

noctámbulo, la [noc-tahm'-boo-lo, lah], *m. & f.* Somnambulist, one who walks in his sleep; sleep-walker (sonámbulo); night-bird (nocheriego); roister (jaranero).

noctíluca [noc-tee'-loo-cah], *f.* Glow worm, noctiluca.

noctíluco [noc-tee'-loo-co], *m.* Noctiluca, a microscopic infusorian, a usual cause of phosphorescence in the ocean.

noctuinos [noc-too-ee'-nose], *m. pl.* Moths, nocturnal lepidóptera.

nocturlabio [noc-toor-lah'-be-o], *m.* Nocturnal, an antiquated instrument for measuring the altitude of the pole by night.

nocturnal [noc-toor-nahl'], *a.* Nocturned, nightly; done or doing by night.

nocturno, na [noc-toor'-no, nah], *a.* 1. Nocturna, nightly. 2. Lonely, melancholy, mournful. **Ave nocturna**, night-bird, such as owls.

nocturno [noc-toor'-no], *m.* 1. Nocturn, one of the three parts into which matins are divided. 2. *(Mus.)* Nocturn, a serenade; a dreamy sentimental composition appropriate to the evening or night.

nodal [no-dahl'], *a.* Nodal, referring to the nodes of a vibrating surface.

nodo [no'-do], *m.* 1. Node, a morbid shelling on the bone. 2. *(Ast.)* Node, the point where the orbit of a heavenly body intersects the ecliptic.

nodriza [no-dree'-thah], *f.* Nurse, a woman that has the care of another's child.

nódulo [no'-doo-lo], *m.* Nodule, a concretion formed in bodies; a small node.

nogada [no-gah'-dah], *f.* Sauce made of pounded walnuts and spice.

nogal [no-gahl'], *m. (Bot.)* 1. Common walnut-tree (árbol). Juglans. 2. The wood of the common walnut-tree.

noguera [no-gay'-rah], *f. (Bot.)* Walnut-tree.

noguerado, da [no-gay-rah'-do, dah], *a.* Of a walnut color.

nogueral [no-gay-rahl'], *m.* Plantation of walnut-trees.

nolición [no-lae-the-on'], *f.* Nolition, unwillingness; opposed to *volition.* (Theology.)

noli me tángere [no-le may tahn'-hay-ray], *m.* Nolimetangere, a malignant ulcer on the face or nose.

nómada, or **nómade** [no'-mah-dah, day], *a.* Nomad, nomadic, having no fixed abode.

nombradamente [nom-brah'-dah-men-tay], *adv.* Namely, expressly.

nombradía [nom-brah-dee'-ah], *f.* Fame, reputation, conspicuousness, credit.

nombrado [nom-brah'-do], *m.* Nominee, a person nominated to a place or office. *-a.* 1. Afore-mentioned (susodicho). 2. *(Fig.)* Famous, renowned.

nombrador [nom-brah-dor'], *m.* Nominator, appointer.

nombramiento [nom-brah-me-en'-to], *m.* 1. Nomination, naming (denominación), or mentioning by name. 2. Appointment, creation, commission.

nombrar [nom-brar'], *va.* 1. To name (dar nombre a), to mention by name (mencionar). 2. To nominate (para un puesto), to appoint. **Nombrar a uno embajador**, to nominate somebody as ambassador.

nombre [nom'-bray], *m.* 1. Name, the discriminative appellation of an individual; title. **Nombre de pila**, christian name. 2. Fame, reputation, credit. 3. Nickname. **Poner nombres a uno**, to call one names. 4. Power by which someone acts for another. 5. *(Gram.)* Noun. 6. *(Mil.)* Countersign watch-word. **Nombre apelativo**, (a) surname. (b) generic name. **Nombre colectivo**, collective noun. **Poner nombre**, to fix a price. **Nombre propio**, proper name. **Bajo el nombre**, under the name of. **Sin nombre**, nameless. **Su conducta no tiene nombre**, his conduct is unspeakable.

nomenclador [no-men-clah-dor'], *m.* 1. Nomenclature, a list of names; glossary; vocabulary of terms. 2. Nomenclator, one who assigns names in a science.

nomenclátor [no-men-clah'-tor], *m.* Nomenclator.

nomenclatura [no-men-clah-doo'-rah], *f.* 1. A catalogue. 2. Nomenclature, technical glossary.

nomeolvides [no-may-ol-vee'-des], *f. (Bot.)* Forget-me-not.

nómina [no'-me-nah], *f.* 1. Catalogue, an alphabetical list of things or persons. 2. Payroll.

nominación [no-me-nah-the-on'], *f.* 1. Nomination, the act of mentioning by name. 2. Power of presenting to a benefice.

nominador, ra [no-me-nah-dor', rah], *m. & f.* Nominator, appointing power; one who appoints another to a position.

nominal [no-me-nahl'], *a.* Nominal, belonging to a name; relating to names rather than things; titular.

nominal [no-me-nahl'], *m.* Nominal, nominalist, one of a sect of scholastical philosophers.

nominalmente [no-me-nahl'-men-tay], *adv.* Nominally.

nominar [no-me-nar'], *va.* To name. V. NOMBRAR.

nominativo [no-me-nah-tee'-vo], *m. (Gram.)* Nominative: applied to the first case of nouns. *-a.* 1. Nominative. 2. *(Com. Fin.)* Bearing a person´s name. **El cheque será nominativo a favor de X**, the check should be made out to X.

nominilla

nominilla [no-me-neel'-lyah], *f.* A warrant or a certificate enabling a pensioner of an office to draw his dues.

nómino [no'-me-no], *m.* Nominee, a person appointed or nominated to any office or employment.

nomocanon [no-mo-cah'-none], *m.* Nomocanon, collection of imperial constitutions and canons.

nomografía [no-mo-grah-fee'-ah], *f.* Nomography, a treatise on laws.

nomógrafo [no-mo'-grah-fo], *m.* Nomographer, a writer on laws.

nomología [no-mo-lo-hee'-ah], *f.* Nomology, the science of laws and their interpretation.

nomológico, ca [no-mo-lo'-he-co, cah], *a.* Nomological.

nomparell [nom-pah-rayl'], *f. (typ.)* Nonpareil, a size of type; six-point.

non [none], *a.* Odd (número), uneven.

non [none], *m.* An odd number. **Andar de nones**, to be idle, to have nothing to do. **Estar de nones**, to serve for nothing. *(coll.)* **Pares y nones**, even or odd.

nona [no'-nah], *f.* 1. None, last of the minor canonical hours, answering to three o'clock P. M. 2. *(Cono Sur)* Grandma, granny.

nonada [no-nah'-dah], *f.* Trifle, little or nothing, nothingness.

nonadilla [no-nah-deel'-lyah], *f. dim.* of NONADA.

nonagenario, ria [no-nah-hay-nah'-re-oh, ah], *a.* Ninety years old, nonagenarian.

nonagésimo, ma [no-nah-hes'-se-mo, mah], *a.* Ninetieth, nonagesimal.

nonagonal [no-nah-go-nahl'], *a.* Enneagonal, nine-sided.

nonágono [no-nah'-go-no], *m.* Nonagon.

nonato, ta [no-nah'-to, tah], *a.* Not naturally born, but extracted from the mother's womb by Cesarean section.

nono [no-no], *a.* Ninth. V. NOVENO.

No obstante [no obs-tahn'-tay], *conj.* Nevertheless, notwithstanding, however.

nopal [no-pahl'], *m. (Bot.)* Nopal, cochineal fig-tree, prickly Indian pear-tree. It is vulgarly called in Castile, *higuera chumba.*

nopalera [no-pah-lay'-rah], *f. (Amer.)* Cochineal plantation.

noque [no'-kay], *m.* 1. A tan-pit or vat in which the ooze is kept for tanning hides. 2. Heap or basket of bruised olives.

noquero [no-kay'-ro], *m.* Currier, leather-dresser.

norabuena [no-rah-boo-ay'-nah], *f.* Congratulation. V. ENHORABUENA.

noramala [no-rah-mah'-lah], *f.* A term of contempt or displeasure. *Also adv.\ V.* ENHORAMALA.

nord [nord], *m. (Naut.)* North wind.

nordest, nordeste [nor-dest', nor-des'-tay], *m.* North-east. **Nordeste cuarto al norte**, north-east-by-north. *Nordeste cuarto al este*, north-east-by-east.

nordestear [nor-des-tay-ar'], *vn. (Naut.)* To be north easting.

nórdico, ca [nor'-de-co, cah], *m. & f. & a.* Nordic. **Es la ciudad más nórdica de Europa**, it is the most northerly city in Europe.

nordovest [nor-do-vest'], *m.* North-west.

nordovestear [nor-do-ves-tay-ahr'], *vn. (Naut.)* To decline to north-west.

noreste [no-rays'-tay], *m.* North-east.

noria [no'-re-ah], *f.* 1. An irrigating wheel. 2. Wheel for drawing water from a well; a chain-pump. 3. Draw-well, a deep well.

norial [no-re-ahl'], *a.* Relating to the well called *noria.*

norma [nor'-mah], *f.* 1. Square, a rule or instrument by which workmen form or measure their angles. 2. Model, a standard or rule to guide and govern all operations. **Norma de vida**, principle. **Está sujeto a ciertas normas**, it is subject to certain rules.

normal [nor-mahl'], *a.* 1. Normal, according to an established law. 2. Model, serving as a standard. **Escuela normal**, normal school.-*f.* Normal, a perpendicular. **-mente**, *adv.*

normalidad [nor-mah-le-dahd'], *f.* Normality, normally (con normalidad); *(Pol.)* calm, normal conditions. **La situación**

ha vuelto a la normalidad, the situation has returned to normal.

normalización [nor-mah-le-thah-the-on'], *f.* Normalization.

normalizar [nor-mah-le-thar'], *va.* To normalize, to restore to normal; *(Tec.)* to standardize. *-vr.* To return to normal.

normalmente [nor-mahl'-men-tay], *adv.* Normally; usually.

normando, da [nor-mahn'-do, dah], *a.* Norman, relating to Normandy.

normativa [nor-mah-te-vah], *f.* Rules, regulations; guideline.

normativo [nor-mah-tee'-vo], *a.* 1. Normative (prescrito). 2. Regular (regular), standard. **Español normativo**, standard Spanish.

nornodeste [nor-no-des'-tay], *m. (Naut.)* North-north-east.

nornorueste [nor-no-roo-es'-tay], *m.* North-north-west.

noroeste [no-ro-ess'-tay], *m.* North-west.

nortada [nor-tah'-dah], *f.* Strong, continued north wind.

norte [nor'-tay], *m.* 1. North, the arctic pole. 2. North, the northern part of the sphere. 3. North or north wind (viento). 4. Rule, law, guide (guía), clew, direction. 5. *(Carib.)* United States. 6. *(Carib.)* Drizzle (llovizna). **En la parte del norte**, in the northern part. **Pregunta sin norte**, aimless question.

norteamericano, na [nor-tay-ah-may-re-cah'-no, nah], *m. & f. & a.* North American (generally from U.S.)

nortear [nor-tay-ar'], *va. (Naut.)* To steer or stand to the northward.

noruego, ga [no-roo-ay´-go, gah], *m. & f. & a.* Norwegian.

norueste [no-roo-es'-tay], *m.* North-west.

noruestear [no-roo-es-tay-ar'], *vn.* To decline to the north-west.

nos, *pron. pers.* 1. Us. **Nos lo dará**, he will give it to us. 2. Ourselves (reflexivo); to each other (recíproco). **No nos hablamos**, we don´t speak to each other.

nosabo (Hacer el). *(Prov. Coll.)* To make believe, to feign ignorance.

nosografía [no-so-grah-fee'-ah], *f. (Med.)* Nosography, description of diseases.

nosología [no-so-lo-hee'-ah], *f. (Med.)* Noso¹ogy, classification of diseases.

nosotros, tras [no-so os, tras], *pron.* We, ourselves. **No irán sin nosotros**, they won´t go without us.

nostalgia [nos-tahl'-he-ah], *f.* Nostalgia, inordinate homesickness.

nostálgico [nos-tahl'-he-co], *a.* Nostalgic, homesick.

nota [no'-tah], *f.* 1. Note, mark, or token put upon anything to make it known; schedule. 2. Note, explanatory annotation in a book or writing. 3. Censure, notice, remark upon one's actions, critique. **Incurrir en la nota**, to incur the imputation. 4. Style, manner of writing (estilo). 5. Memorandum or note taken down to help the memory; *(Com.)* account, statement. 6. Official communication of a government or a foreign minister. 7. Note, reproach, stigma. **Buena** or **mala nota**, good or bad standing or reputation in society. 8. *(Mus.)* Musical character, a single sound. 9. *(LAm.)* Effects of drugs. **Nota de gastos**, expense account. **Obtener buenas notas**, to get good marks. **Dar la nota**, to set the tone. **Tomar nota**, to take note. *-pl.* The collection of minutes of proceedings taken by a notary.

notabilidad [no-tah-be-le-dahd'], *f.* 1. Notability. *(Neol.)* 2. Notable (persona).

notabilísimo, ma [no-tah-be-lee'-se-mo mah], *a.* Super, of *Notable.*

notable [no-tah'-blay], *a.* 1. Notable, remarkable, noteworthy, conspicuous. 2. Very great.

notable [no-tah'-blay], *m.* Introductory observation.

notablemente [no-tah'-blay-men-tay], *adv.* Notably, observably, notedly.

notación [no-tah-the-on'], *f.* 1. An algebraic sign. 2. Notation, the art of representing the written sign in music. 3. Part of prosody which treats of the accentuation of syllables.

notar [no-tar'], *va.* 1. To note, to mark. 2. To remark, to observe, to note (observar), to heed, to notice, to take notice of, to mind. 3. To take short notes on a subject (apuntar). 4.

To comment, to expound. 5. To annotate a writing or book. 6. To dictate what another may write. 7. To find fault, to censure, to criticize (criticar): to reprehend. **No lo había notado,** I hadn´t noticed it. **Te noto muy cambiado,** I find you very changed. *-vr.* To show, to be apparent, to be obvious. **La combinación no se te nota,** your slip doesn´t show.

notaría [no-tah-ree'-ah], *f.* 1. Employment or profession of a notary (profesión). 2. A notary's office (despacho).

notariado [no-tah-re-ah'-do], *m.* Profession of a notary.

notarial [no-tah-re-ahl'], *a.* Notarial; legal (estilo), lawyer´s.

notariato [no-tah-re-ah'-to], *m.* Title of a notary.

notario [no-tah'-re-o], *m.* 1. Notary, an officer whose business is to take notes of protests and other transactions, to draw and pass public instruments, and to attest and legalize private dealings and writings: it is now commonly applied to those officers who transact ecclesiastical affairs. 2. Amanuensis. **Entre dos amigos un notario y dos testigos,** *(Prov.)* ever among friends legal vouchers and warranties should not be omitted.

notho, tha [no'-to, tah], *a.* Bastard, illegitimate.

noticia [no-tee'-the-ah], *f.* 1. Notice, knowledge (conocimientos), information, note, light. 2. News, intelligence. **Noticias alegres,** glad tidings. **Poner en la noticia de,** to bring to one's knowledge, to advise, inform. **Tener noticias de uno,** to have news of somebody. **No tener la menor noticia de algo,** to know nothing at all about a matter.

noticiar [no-te-the-ar'], *va.* To give notice, to communicate intelligence.

noticiario [no-te-the-ah'-re-oh], *m.* 1. Newsreel. 2. Newscast.

noticiero [no-te-the-ay'-ro], *m. (Mex.)* 1. Newsreel. 2. Newscast. 3. *(Mex.)* News bulletin. *-a.* 1. News (noticias). 2. News-bearing (que da noticias).

noticioso, sa [no te thc-o'-so, sah], *a.* Informed; knowing, learned, instructed.

notificación [no-te-fe-cah-the-on'], *f.* Notification, judicial intimation.

notificado, da [no-te-he-cah'-do, dah], *a. & pp.* of NOTIFICAR. Notified: applied to a person who has received a judicial notification.

notificar [no-te-fe-car'], *va.* To notify, to make known, to intimate; to inform.

notilla, ita [no-teel'-lyah], *f. dim.* A short note, memorandum, etc.

noto, ta [no'-to, tah], *a.* 1. Known, notorious. 2. Illegitimate, not born in wedlock.

noto [no'-to], *m.* South wind, notus.

notoriamente [no-to-re-ah'-men-tay], *adv.* Notoriously, manifestly, glaringly.

notoriedad [no-to-re-ay-dahd'], *f.* Notoriety, notoriousness, public knowledge. **Hechos de amplia notoriedad,** widely-known facts.

notorio, ria [no-to'-re-o, ah], *a.* Notorious, publicly known, glaring, flagrant, famous (famoso), well-known (conocido). **Un hecho notorio,** a well-known fact.

noumeno [no-oo-may'-no], *m. (Phil.)* Being or essence which every phenomenon declares or reveals; noumenon, «the thing in itself.»

novación [no-vah-the-on'], *f. (Law.)* Renovation of an obligation formerly contracted.

noval [no-vahl'], *a.* Applied to land newly broken up and converted into arable ground, and to the fruits it produces.

novar [no-var'], *va. (Law.)* To renew an obligation formerly contracted.

novatada [no-vah-tah'-dah], *f.* 1. Rag (broma), ragging, hazing. 2. Beginner´s mistake (error).

novato, ta [no-vah'-to, tah], *a. (Colt.)* New, commencing in anything. *-m.* Beginner (principiante).

novator [no-vah-tor'], *m.* Innovator, an introducer of novelties; novator.

novecientos, tas [no-vay-the-en'-tos, tas], *s. & a.* Nine hundred.

novedad [no-vay-dahd'], *f.* 1. Novelty, a new state of things, newness (cualidad), modernness. 2. Admiration excited by novelties or any extraordinary thing. 3. *(Coil.)* Remarkable occurrence, danger, trouble. 4. New feature (innovación), new development. **Los negocios continúan sin novedad,** Business goes on as usual. **Sin novedad en el frente,** all quiet on the front. **El enfermo sigue sin novedad,** the patient´s condition is unchanged.

novedoso [no-vay-doh'-so], *a.* 1. Original, novel (idea, método). 2. *(Cono Sur, Mex.)* V. NOVELESCO.

novel [no-vel'], *a.* New (nuevo), inexperienced. *-m.* Beginner (principiante).

novela [no-vay'-lah], *f.* 1. Novel, a fictitious story, a tale. 2. Falsehood, fiction. 3. *(Law.)* Novel, any new law added to the Justinian codes. **Novela de amor,** love story. **Novela por entregas,** serial.

novelador [no-vay-lah-dor'], *m.* Novelist, a writer of novels.

novelar [no-vay-lar], *va.* 1. To compose, to write, or to publish novels. 2. To relate stories.

novelería [no-vay-lay-ree'-ah], *f.* 1. Narration of fictitious stories. 2. Taste for novels and novelties.

novelero, ra [no-vay-lay'-ro, rah], *a.* 1. Fond of novels and fictitious tales (aficionado). 2. Fond of hearing and telling news. **Un novelero,** a newsmonger. 3. Newfangled. 4. Inconstant, wavering, unsteady. 5. Gossipy (chismoso). 6. Romantic (cuento).

novelesco, ca [no-vay-les´-co, cah], *a.* 1. Novelistic, pertaining to novels. 2. Romantic (romántico), fantastic; story-book (aventura).

novelista [no-vay-lees'-tah], *m. & f.* Novelist, a writer of novels.

novena [no-vay'-nah], *f.* 1. Term of nine days appropriated to some special worship. 2. Offering for the dead.

novenario [no-vay-nah'-re-o], *m.* Novenary, nine days' condolence for the deceased, or nine days of public worship offered to some saint.

novendial [no-ven-de-ahl'], *a.* Applied to any day of the novenary, or worship offered for the souls of the faithful.

noveno, na [no-vay'-no, nah], *a.* Ninth, the ordinal number of nine; ninthly.

noveno [no-vay´-no], *m.* One of the nine parts into which tithes are divided.

noventa [no-ven'-tah], *m. & a.* Ninety.

noventón, na [no-ven-tone', nah], *a.* Ninety years old. *-m.* A nonagenarian.

novia [no'-ve-ah], *f.* 1. Bride, a woman newly married (recién casada). 2. Woman betrothed. 3. Sweetheart (amiga); fiancée (prometida); bride (en boda). **Echarse una novia,** to get oneself a girl.

noviaje [no-ve-ah'-hay], *m.* Term of betrothal.

noviazgo [no-ve-ath'-go], *m.* Engagement, betrothal.

noviciado [no-ve-the-ah´-do], *m.* 1. Novitiate, the time spent in a religious house by way of trial before the vow is taken. 2. House or apartment in which novices live. 3. Novitiate, the time in which the rudiments of a science or art are learned; noviceship.

novicio [no-vee´-the-o], *m.* 1. Novice, one who has entered a religious house, but not yet taken the vow; a probationer. 2. Novice, a freshman, one in the rudiments of any knowledge.

novicio, cia [no-vee'-the-o, ah], *a.* Probationary: applied to a novice or probationer.

noviembre [no-ve-em'-bray], *m.* November.

novilunio [no-ve-loo'-ne-o], *m.* New moon conjunction of the moon.

novilla [no-veel'-lyah], *f.* Cow between three and six years of age; heifer.

novillada [no-veel-lyah'-dah], *f.* 1. Drove of young bulls or bullocks. 2. Fight of young bulls or bullocks.

novillejo, eja [no-veel-lyay'-do, dah], *m. & f. dim.* A young bull, a heifer.

novillero [no-veel-lyay'-ro], *m.* 1. Stable in which young cattle are kept 2. Herdsman who attends young cattle. 3. Piece of pasture ground where calves are put, separate from other cattle, to be weaned. 4. Truant, idler. 5. *(Taur.)* Novice, young bullfighter.

novillo [no-veel'-lyo], *m.* 1. A young bull or ox, particularly one not trained to the yoke. 2. *(Low.)* Cuckold. **Hacer novillos,** *(coll.)* to play truant.

novio [no'-ve-o], *m.* 1. Bridegroom (en boda). 2. A man betrothed to a woman. 3. One new to some dignity or state. 4. Sweetheart, boyfriend (amigo). **Los novios,** the engaged couple (prometidos). **Viaje de novios,** honeymoon.

novísimo, ma [no-vee'-se-mo, mah], *a.* Newest, most recent; last in the order of things.-*m.* Each of the four last incidents of mankind: death, judgment, heaven, and hell.

novocaína [no-vo-cah-ee'-nah], *f.* Novocaine.

nubada, nubarrada [noo-bah'-dah], *f.* 1. Shower of rain (chaparrón). 2. Plenty, abundance.

nubado, da, nubarrado, da [noo-bah'-do, dah], *a.* Clouded, figured like clouds.

nubarrón [noo-bar-rone'], *m.* A heavy shower of rain, a large cloud.

nube [noo'-bay], *f.* 1. A cloud. 2. Cloud, a crowd, a multitude, anything that spreads wide so as to interrupt the view (humo, insectos). 3. Film which obstructs the sight (en ojo). 4. Cloud or shade in precious stones. **Andar** or **estar por las nubes,** (1) V. **Subir a las nubes.** (2) To run mountain high: said of waves. (3) To be extremely annoyed. **Subir a las nubes,** to raise or increase prices very much.

nubífero, ra [noo-bee'-fay-ro, rah], *a.* *(Poet.)* Cloud-bringing.

nubiloso [noo-be-lo'-so] *a.* V. NUBLOSO.

núbil [noo'-beel], *a.* Nubile, marriageable.

nublado [noo-blah'-do], *m.* 1. A large cloud. 2. Perturbation of the mind, gloominess. 3. Dread or fear of impending danger. 4. Anger, black mood (enfado).

nublado, da [noo-blah'-do, dah], *a & pp.* of NUBLAR. Cloudy, misty, nebulous.

nublar, nublarse [noo-blar'], *va. & vr.* 1. To darken, to obscure. 2. To cloud, to disturb (vista); to affect (razón).

nubloso, sa [noo-blo'-so, sah], *a.* 1. Cloudy, dark, overcast. 2. Gloomy, ill-fated.

nubosidad [noo-bo-see-dahd'], *f.* Cloudiness, clouds.

nuboso [noo-bo'-so], *a.* Cloudy.

nubus [noo-boos]. *(Inform.)* Nubus.

nuca [noo'-cah], *f.* Nape of the neck, nucha.

nuclear [noo-clay-ar'], *a.* Nuclear. **Energía nuclear,** nuclear energy. **Física nuclear,** nuclear physics.

nucleico, ca [noo-clay'-co, cah], *a.* Nucleic.

núcleo [noo'-clay-o], *m.* 1. Kernel of a nut, nucleus. 2. Nucleus, a center of union or of development.

nudifloro, ra [noo-de-flo'-ro, rah], *a.* Nudiflorous, having naked flowers.

nudifoliado, da [noo-de-fo-le-ah'-do, dah], *a.* Having smooth or bare leaves; nudifolious.

nudillo [noo-deel'-lyo], *m.* 1. Knuckle, the joint of the fingers. 2. *(Arch.)* Wooden abutment to roofing-timbers. 3. Small knot in stockings. 4. Nodule.

nudismo [noo-dees'-mo], *m.* Nudism.

nudista [noo-dees'-tah], *m & f.* Nudist.

nudo [noo'-do], *m.* 1. Knot, complication of a cord or string. 2. Knoll, node, articulation or joint of plants. 3. Joint in animal bodies. 4. The principal difficulty or doubt in certain matters (problema). 5. Tie, union, bond of association (vínculo). 6. Node, a swelling on nerves or bones. 7. Knot, intricacy, difficulty. 8. The crisis of a drama. **Echamos doce nudos por hora,** we ran twelve knots an hour. **Atravesársele a uno un nudo en la garganta,** to have a lump in one's throat, to be speechless on account of violent emotion. **Nudo corredizo,** slipknot.

nudoso, sa [noo-do'-so, sah], *a.* Knotty (madera), nodous, knotted, knaggy.

nuégados [noo-ay'-gah-dose], *m. pl.* A sort of paste of flour, honey, and nuts.

nuera [noo-ay'-rah], *f.* Daughter-in-law.

nuestramo [noo-es-trah'-mo], *f.* Our master, contracted from *nuestro amo.*

nuestro, tra [noo-es'-tro, trah], *a.* Our, pertaining to us. **Los nuestros,** the persons of the same party or profession as the speaker. **Un barco nuestro,** a boat of ours. **Es el nuestro,** it is ours.

nueva [noo-ay'-vah], *f.* News, fresh amount of anything.

nuevamente [noo-ay-vah-men-tay], *adv.* Newly, recently, freshly.

nueve [noo-ay'-vay], *m. & a.* 1. Nine, an arithmetical character by which the number nine is denoted. 2. A card with nine marks. 3. Ninth. **El nueve de Enero,** the ninth of January. **El libro nueve,** the ninth book.

nuevecito [noo-ay-vay-thee'-to], *a. dim.* Quite new, fresh, very lately made.

nuevo, va [noo-ay'-vo, vah], *a.* 1. New, not old; novel, modern, fresh. 2. New, having the effect of novelty, not known before. 3. New, renovated, repaired. 4. New, not being before. 5. Recently arrived in a country or place. 6. Inexperienced, not habituated, not familiar. 7. Beginning. **De nuevo,** again, a new, recently, of late. **¿Qué hay de nuevo?** what is the news? Is there any news? **Es nuevo en el oficio,** he´s new to the trade. **Somos nuevos aquí,** we´re new here. **La casa es nueva,** the house is new.

nuez [noo-eth'], *f.* 1. Walnut, the fruit of the walnut-tree; *(Mex.)* pecan nut. 2. Fruit of some trees in the shape of a nut. 3. Adam's apple, the prominent part of the throat. 4. Plummet. 5. **Nuez moscada** or **de especia,** *(Bot.)* nutmeg. **Nuez del país** or **nuez chiquita,** butter-nut. **Nuez grande,** hickory-nut. **Nuez dura,** hickory-nut.

nueza [noo-ay'-thah], *f. (Bot.)* Briony. **Nueza blanca,** white-berried briony. **Nueza negra,** Common black briony.

núfar [noo'-far], *f.* The spatterdock, or yellow water-lily.

nugatorio, rig [noo-gah-to'-re-o, ah], *a.* Nugatory, futile, deceitful.

nulamente [noo-lah-men'-tay], *adv.* Invalidly, ineffectually.

nulidad [noo-le-dahd'], *f.* 1. Nullity, want of force or efficacy. 2. Defeasance, a condition annexed to an act or deed, which, when performed by the obligee, renders the act or deed void. 3. *(coll.)* Insignificance.

nulo, la [noo'-lo, lah], *a.* 1. Null, void of effect, of no force. 2. Useless (persona). **Es nulo para la música,** he´s useless at music.

numen [noo'-men], *m.* 1. Divinity, deity. 2. Genius, talent: commonly applied to poetical genius.

numerable [noo-may-rah'-blay], *a.* Numerable.

numeración [noo-may-rah-the-on'], *f.* Numeration, the art of numbering: first part of arithmetic.

numerador [noo-may-rah-dor'], *m.* 1. Numerator, numberer, he who numbers. 2. Numerator, the upper term of a common fraction.

numeral [noo-may-rahl'], *a.* Numeral, relating to numbers.

numerar [noo-may-rar'], *va.* 1. To number, to enumerate, to numerate, to calculate, to cipher. 2. To page, to mark the pages of a book. 3. To number, to reckon as one of the same kind. **Páginas sin numerar,** unnumbered pages.

numerario, ria [noo-may-rah'-re-o, ah], *a.* Numerary, belonging to a certain number. -*m.* Hard cash, coin.

numéricamente [noo-may'-re-cah-men-tay], *adv.* Individually, numerically.

numérico, ca [noo-may'-re-co, cah], *a.* Numerical, individual, numeral; denoting number.

número [noo'-may-ro], *m.* 1. Number, an aggregate of units. 2. Character, cipher, or figure which denotes the number. 3. Number, comparative multitude. 4. Number, harmony, proportional measure or cadence in music or poetry. 5. *(Gram.)* Number; singular or plural. 6. Determinate number of persons of any company or society. 7. Verse. 8. Size (de zapato). 9. Number, issue (periódico). 10. Item, number (de programa). *-pl.* Numbers, one of the five books of the Pentateuch. **Número uno,** number one, one's own selfish interests. **Sin número,** numberless, innumerable. **Número entero,** whole number. **Número primo,** prime number. **Número de referencia,** reference number. **Hacer el número,** to go over the top.

número Mach [noo'-may-ro mask], *m.* Mach number, ratio of the velocity of a moving body to the speed of sound.

numerosamente [noo-may-ro'-sah-men-tay], *adv.* Numerously.

numerosidad [noo-may-ro-se-dahd'], *f.* Numerosity, numerousness.

numeroso, sa [noo-may-ro'-so, sah], *a.* 1. Numerous, containing many. 2. Harmonious, melodious; consisting of parts rightly numbered, rhythmical, harmonical.

númida [noo'-me-dah], *a.* Numidian, of Numidia.

numídico, ca [noo-mee'-de-co, cah], *a. V.* NÚMIDA.

numisma [noo-mees'-mah], *m.* Coin.

numismática [noo-mis-mah'-te-cah], *f.* Numismatics, science of medals and coins.

numismático, ca [noo-mis-mah'-te-co, cah], *a.* Numismatical.

numismatografía [noo-mis-mah-to-grah-fee'-ah], *f.* Numismatography, description of ancient medals.

numo [noo'-mo], *m.* Money, coin.

numularia [noo-moo-lah'-re-ah], *f. (Bot.)* Money-wort.

numulario [noo-moo-lah'-re-o], *m.* A banker.

nunca [noon'-cah], *adv.* Never, at no time. **Nunca jamás,** never, never more. **No viene nunca,** he never comes.

nunciatura [noon-the-ah-too'-rah], *f.* Nunciature, the office or house of a nuncio.

nuncio [noon'-the-o], *m.* 1. Messenger. 2. Nuncio, envoy or ambassador from the Pope to Roman Catholic princes. 3. **El Nuncio** or **la casa del Nuncio,** the mad-house in Toledo.

nuncupativo, va [noon-coo-pah-tee'-vo, vah], *a.* 1. Nuncupative, nominal; verbally pronounced. 2. (Of a will) Declared orally by the testator and later written down.

nuncupatorio, ria [noon-coo-pah-to'-re-o, ah], *a.* Nuncupatory.

nupcial [noop-the-ahl'], *a.* Nuptial, pertaining to marriage, hymeneal.

nupcias [noop'-the-as], *f. pl.* Nuptials, wedding, marriage. **Casarse en segundas nupcias,** to marry again.

nutación [noo-tah-the-on'], *f.* 1. Direction of plants towards the sun. 2. *(Ast.)* Nutation, movement of the earth's axis, by which it inclines more or less to the plane of the ecliptic.

nutante [noo-tahn'-tay], *a. (Bot.)* Nodding.

nutra, nutria [noo'-trah, noo'-tre-ah], *f.* 1. Otter. 2. A kind of small sea-otter, the fur of which is so called.

nutricio, cia [noo-tree'-the-o, ah], *a.* Nutritious, nourishing, nutritive.

nutrición [noo-tre-the-on'], *f.* 1. Nutrition, the act or quality of nourishing. 2. *(Pharm.)* A certain preparation of medicines.

nutrido [noo-tree'-do], *a.* 1. Bien nutrido, well-nourished. 2. *(Fig.)* Large (grande), considerable; numerous (numeroso); abundant (abundante). **Abundante de,** full of.

nutrimental [noo-tre-men-tahl'], *a.* Nutrimental, having the quality of food.

nutrimento [noo-tre-men'-to], *m.* 1. Nutriment, food, aliment, nourishment. 2. Nutrition.

nutrir [noo-treer'], *va.* 1. To nourish, to fatten, to feed. 2. To nourish, to encourage, to foment, to support.

nutritivo, va [noo-tre-tee'-vo, vah], *a.* Nutritive, nourishing.

nutriz [noo-treeth'], *f.* Nurse.

nutual [noo-too-ahl'], *a.* Irremovable: said of chaplains and other ministers not removable at pleasure of the grantor.

ny [nee], *f.* Nu, thirteenth letter of the Greek alphabet, corresponding to N.

nylon [ny-lon], *m.* Nylon.

Ñ

ñ [ay'-nyay] is the fifteenth letter in the Spanish alphabet. The ancient Spanish writers used *nn* in words derived from the Latin having *gn*, as from *lignum was* written *lenno,* and now *leño,* the *n* with a *tilde,* or circumflex, being substituted in their place. Ñ has a strong nasal sound, resembling that of *n* in the English word *poniard,* and exactly similar to that of *gn* in the French word *poignard.*

ñagaza [nyah-gah'-thah], *f.* Bird-call, a decoy. *V.* AÑAGAZA.

ñame [nyah'-may], *m.* Yam.

ñandú [nyan-doo'], *m.* An Argentine variety of the American ostrich. *V.* NANDÚ.

ñapa [nyah'-pah], *f. (Amer.)* That which is thrown in for, at the end of a bargain. **Dar de ñapa,** to give a thing free. *V.* CONTRA and PILÓN.

ñaque [nyah'-kay], *m.* Heap of useless trifles.

ñigua [nyee'-goo-ah], *f. V.* NIGUA.

ñiquiñaque [nye-kee-nyah'-kay], *m.* An expression used by the vulgar to depreciate something.

ñoclo [nyo'-clo], *m.* A kind of macaroon, or round sweetmeat.

ñoña [nyo'-nyah], *f. (coll.)* Excrement.

ñoñería [nyo-nyay-ree'-ah], *f.* 1. Decrepitude, second childhood. 2. Insipidness (sosería); spinelessness (falta de carácter). 3. *(Cono Sur)* Senility (vejez). 4. *(Carib.)* Inanity (estupidez). 5. *(Carib.)* Endearment (cariñoso).

ñono, ña [nyo'-nyo, nyah], *a. (coll.)* 1. Delicate, plaintive, timid (tímido). 2. Decrepit, impaired by age (viejo). 3. *(And, Carib.)* Vain, that likes to be flattered (vanidoso). 4. *(Mex.)* Thick (bruto).

ñorbo [nyor'-bo], *m.* A certain flower of Peru.

ñurumé [nyoo-roo-may'], *m. (Zool.)* An ant-eater of Paraguay.

O

o [oh], the sixteenth letter in the Spanish alphabet is pronounced like the English *o* in cone. *O,* in arithmetic, serves for naught or cipher; it is also used as a circle, of which there is no end, and therefore emblematic of eternity. *O,* in sea-charts, signifies west; Oeste. The seven anthema sung in the church, the seven days before the nativity of our Lord, are called *OO,* because they all commence with this letter.

o, *conj.* Or, either. **O rico o pobre,** either rich or poor. When followed by another *o,* the conjunction *u* is used instead of *o,* to avoid cacophony; as, *Siete u ocho,* seven or eight.

¡o! *int. V.* ¡Oh!

O conectado, *x. (Inform.)* Wired OR.

oasis [o-ah'-sis], *m.* Oasis, a fertile spot in a desert.

obcecación [ob-thay-cah-the-on'], *f.* Obduracy, blindness.

obcecado, da [ob-thay-cah'-do, dah], *a.* Blind (ciego); stubborn (terco); disturbed (trastornado).*-pp.* of OBCECAR.

obcecar [ob-thay-car'], *va.* To blind, to darken or obscure.

obduración [ob-doo-rah-the-on], *f.* Hardness of heart, obstinacy, obduracy.

obedecedor, ra [o-bay-dar-thay-dor', rah], *m. ·& f.* Obeyer, one who obeys or submits.

obedecer [o-bay-day-therr'], *va.* To obey, to yield to. **Obedecer a,** to be due to. *(Yo obedezco, yo obedezca,* from *Obedecer. V.* CONOCER.)

obedecimiento [o-bay-day-the-me-en'-to], *m.* Obedience, obsequiousness.

obediencia [o-bay-de-en'-the-ah], *f.* 1. Obedience, submission. 2. Obsequiousness, pliancy, flexibility; docility in animals. **A la obediencia**, at your service, your most obedient.

obediencial [o-bay-de-en-the-ahl'], *a.* Obediential, according to the rules of obedience.

obediente [o-bay-de-en'-tay], *a.* Obedient, obsequious, compliant, submissive.

obedientemente, *adv.* Obediently.

obelisco [o-bay-lees'-co], *m.* Obelisk, a slender stone pyramid. 2. Dagger, mark for reference.

obelo [o-bay'-lo], *m.* Obelisk. V. OBELISCO.

obencadura [o-ben-cah-doo'-rah], *f.* *(Naut.)* A complete set of shrouds in general.

obenques [o-ben'-kes], *m.* *pl* *(Naut.)* Shrouds. **Obenques mayores**, the main shrouds.

obertura [o-ber-too'-rah], *f.* *(Mus.)* Overture.

obesidad [o-bay-se-dahd], *f.* Obesity, corpulence.

obeso, sa [o-bay'-so, sah], *a.* Obese, fat, corpulent.

óbice [o'-be-thay], *m.* Obstacle, impediment, hindrance, opposition.

obispado [o-bis-pah'-do], *m.* 1. Bishopric, the diocese of a bishop. 2. Episcopate, the office and dignity of a bishop.

obispal [o-bis-pahl'], *a.* Episcopal belonging to a bishhop; bishopric, diocese.

obispar [o-bis-par'], *vn.* 1. To be made bishop, to obtain a bishopric. 2. *(coll.)* To die, to expire.

obispillo [o-bis-peel'-lyo], *m. dim.* 1. Boy-bishop, a chorister boy dressed like a bishop, and allowed to imitate a bishop. 2. A large black pudding; a pork or beef sausage. 3. Rump or croup of a fowl.

obispo [o-bees'-po], *m.* 1. Bishop. **Obispo de anillo** or **de título**, bishop in partibus. **Obispo auxiliar**, assistant bishop. 2. A large black pudding.

óbito [o'-be-to], *m.* Death of a person (religión y ley).

obituario [o-be-too-ah'-re-o], *m.* 1. Obituary, a register of burials (necrología). 2. Decease (muerte).

objeción [ob-hay-the-on'], *f.* Objection, opposition, exception. **Objeción de conciencia**, conscientious objection.

objetar [ob-hay-tar'], *va.* To object, to oppose, to remonstrate, to resent (argumento).

objetivamente [ob-hay-tee'-vah-men-tay], *adv.* Objectively.

objetivar [ob-hay-te-var'], *va.* To make objective.

objetividad [ob-hay-te-ve-dahd'], *f.* Objectivity.

objetivismo [ob-hay-te-vees'-mo], *m.* 1. Objectivity. 2. Objectivism.

objetivo, va [ob-hay-tee'-vo, vah], *a.* Objective (no subjetivo). -*m.* 1. Lens. 2. Objective (meta). 3. Objective, target. 4. *(Fot.)* Lens; object lens. **Objetivo del juego**, trick.

objeto [ob-hay'-to], *m.* 1. Object (artículo). 2. Subject (tema). 3. Object, aim, end, purpose (meta). **Al objeto de**, with the object of. **Fue el objeto de un asalto**, he was the target of an attack.

objetor [ob-hay-tor'], *m.* Objector. **Objetor de conciencia**, conscientious objector.

oblación [o-blah-the-on'], *f.* Oblation, offering, gift.

oblada [o-blah'-dah], *f.* Funeral offering of bread for the souls of the deceased.

oblata [o-blah'-tah], *f.* 1. Host and chalice offered before being consecrated in the celebration of the mass. 2. Sum of money given to the church to defray the expense of bread, wine, candles, etc., for celebrating mass.

oblato, ta [o-blah'-to, tah], *a. & n.* 1. One who, on becoming a monk, donated his property to the community. 2. Anciently, a child offered to God to make him embrace the clerical profession. 3. A lay monk of certain orders. 4. A certain tax anciently paid. 5. An invalided soldier; who had a right of receiving a living and clothing from some abbey or priory.

oblea [o-blay'-ah], *f.* 1. Wafer, paste made to close letters. 2. *(Cono Sur)* Stamp (Correos).

obleero [o-blay-ay'-ro], *m.* 1. One who sells wafers about the streets.

oblicuángulo [o-ble-coo-ahn'-goo-lo], *a.* Oblique-angled.

oblicuidad [o-ble-coo-e-dahd'], *f.* Obliquity, deviation from physical rectitude.

oblicuo, cua [o-blee'-coo-o, ah], *a.* Oblique, not direct, not perpendicular, not parallel, crooked.

obligación [o-ble-cah-the-on'], *f.* 1. Obligation, the binding power of an oath, vow or duty; contract. 2. *(For.)* Obligation, bond; written security for the carrying out of something. 3. Obligation, duty of acknowledging a benefit received. 4. Obligation, bond, of a public debt or of a company, bearing interest. 5. *(Acad.)* Provision office, the place where provisions are sold, pursuant to a previous contract. -*pl.* 1. Character and integrity which a man must possess to be worthy of esteem. **Es hombre de obligaciones**, he is a man of integrity and honor. 2. Family which one is obliged to maintain. 3. Engagements. **Faltar a sus obligaciones**, to fall in one´s duty. **Primero es la obligación que la devoción**, business before pleasure.

obligado [o-ble-gah'-do], *m.* 1. Contractor who engages to supply a city with some kind of provisions. 2. *(Law.)* Obligee, one bound by a contract. 3. Obligato, properly obligato, an accompaniment indispensable to the proper performance of a piece of music.

obligante [o-ble-gahn'-tay], *pa.* Obligating, imposing.

obligar [o-ble-gar'], *va.* 1. To oblige, to compel, to bind, to constrain, to necessitate. 2. To oblige, to confer favors, to lay obligations of gratitude. **Obligar a uno a hacer algo**, to force somebody to do something. -*vr.* To oblige or bind oneself.

obligatorio, ria [o-ble-gah-to'-re-o, ah], *a.* Obligatory, binding, coercive, compulsory.

obliteración [o-ble-tay-rah-the-on'], *f.* Obliteration.

obliterar [o-ble-tay-rar'], *va.* 1. *(LAm.)* To blot out, to obliterate, to make disappear. 2. *(Med.)* To obstruct or close some channel of the body.

oblongo, ga [o-blon'-go, gah], *a.* Oblong, greater in length than in breadth.

obnoxio, xia [ob-nok'-se-o, ah], *a.* Obnoxious, hurtful.

oboe [o-bo'-ay], *m.* 1. Oboe or haut-boy, a musical wind-instrument with a double reed. 2. Player on the oboe.

óbolo [o'-bo-lo], *m.* 1. Obolus, Athenian money. 2. Obole, a weight of twelve grains. 3. A small gift for charity.

obra [o'-brah], *f.* 1. Work, anything made. 2. Work, writings of an author. 3. Work, a new building on which men are at work (en construcción). 4. The repairs made in a house. 5. Work, every moral action. 6. Means, virtue, power. 7. Toil, work, labor, employment. 8. Workmanship (hechura). 9. *(Cono Sur)* Brick-works. **Obra de arte mayor**, masterly piece of work. **Obra piadosa**, charity. **Por obra de**, thanks to. **Obra literaria**, literary work. **Cerrado por obras**, closed for repairs.

obrada [o-brah'-dah], *f.* As much ground as two mules or oxen can plough in a day.

obrador, ra [o-brah-dor', rah], *m. & f.* 1. Workman or workwoman, artificer, mechanic. 2. Workshop. **Obradores**, *(Naut.)* workshop or working-places in a dock-yard.

obradura [o-brah-doo'-rah], *f.* That which is expressed at every pressful in oil-mills.

obraje [o-brah'-hay], *m.* 1. Manufacture (fabricación), anything made by art. 2. Manufactory, workshop (taller). *(Amer.)* A manufactory of coarse cloth baize, and other woollen stuffs. 3. *(And. Cono Sur)* Sawmill, timber yard (aserradero). 4. *(And.)* Textile plant (textil).

obrajero [o-brah-bay'-ro], *m.* 1. Foreman (capataz), overseer, superintendent. 2. *(Cono Sur)* Lumberman (maderero). 3. *(And.)* Craftsman (artesano).

obrar [o-brar'], *va.* 1. To work, to manufacture. 2. To operate, to produce effects; to act. 3. To operate, to produce the desired effect (medicinas). 4. To put into practice, to execute; to construct, to build (construir). 5. To ease nature. 6. To work, to bring about (milagro). -*vn. 1.* To act (actuar); to proceed. 2. To work, to have an effect (medicina). 3. To relieve nature. **Su carta obra en mi poder,** I have received your letter.

obrepción [o-brep-the-on´], *f.* Obreption, false narration to obtain some end.

obrepticiamente [o-brep-tee´-the-ah-men-tay], *adv.* Falsely, deceitfully.

obrepticio, cia [o-brep-tee´-the-o, ah], *a.* Obreptitious, obtained by a false statement of matters or fact, by deceit or surprise.

obreria [o-bray-ree´-ah], *f.* 1. Task of a workman. 2. Money destined for the repairs of a church.

obrero, ra [o-bray´-ro, rah], *m. & f.* 1. Worker, workman, day-laborer. 2. Missionary. 3. Prebendary who superintends the repairs of church buildings. 4. Person who collects money for the building of churches. -*a.* Working (clase); labor (sindicato).

obreropatronal [o-bray-ro-pah-tro-nahl´], *a.* Relating to capital and labor. **Relaciones obreropatronales,** capital and labor relations.

obrita [o-bree´-tah], *f. dim.* Small or little work.

obrizo, za [o-bree´-tho, thah], *a.* Pure, refined (oro).

obscenidad [obs-thay-ne-dahd´], *f.* Obscenity, impurity, unchastity, lewdness.

obsceno, na [os-thay´-no, nah], *a.* Obscene, impure, lewd, lustful.

obscuramente, *adv.* 1. Obscurely, darkly, faintly, abstrusely. 2. Obscurely, privately. 3. Obscurely, confusedly, not plainly.

obscurantismo [obs-coo-ran-tees´-mo], *m.* Obscurantism.

obscuras (a) [obs-coo´-ras, ah], *adv.* Obscurely, darkly.

obscurecer [obs-coo-ray-therr´], *va.* V. OSCURECER. 1. To obscure, to darken. 2. To cloud over. 3. To fill with gloom or darkness. 4. To cloud, to confuse the reason. 5. To render a subject less intelligible. 6. *(Pict.)* To use deep shades. -*v. impers.* To grow dark. -*vr.* 1. To cloud over. 2. To disappear.

obscurecimiento [obs-coo-ray-the-me-en´-to], *m.* 1. Obscuration, act of darkening. 2. Blackout (durante la guerra).

obscuridad [obs-coo-re-dahd], *f.* V. OSCURIDAD. 1. Obscurity, darkness. 2. Cloudiness, gloominess, opacity, density. 3. Obscurity, darkness of meaning, abstruseness, confusedness. 4. The humbleness of a stock whence a family or any other thing proceeds. 5. Retired, private life.

obscuro, ra [obs-coo´-ro, rah], *a.* V. OSCURO. 1. Obscure, dark, gloomy. 2. Obscure, unintelligible, confused, abstruse. 3. Obscure, little known, unknown. 4. *(Pict.)* Dark, deep, heavy. **Andar a obscuras** , *(Met.)* to grope in the dark, to proceed in a business without understanding its nature or principles.

obsecración [ob-say-crah-the-on´], *f.* Obsecration, entreaty, supplication.

obsecuente [ob-say-coo-en´-tay], *a.* Obsequious, obedient.

obsequiante [ob-say-ke-ahn´-tay], *pa. & n.* Obsequious; courtier, gallant.

obsequiar [ob-say-ke-ar´], *va.* To court, to wait upon, to serve, to obey. **Le obsequiaron con un reloj,** they presented him with a clock.

obsequio [ob-say´-ke-o], *m.* Obsequiousness, complaisance, civility, desire of pleasing, present (regalo). **Por obsequio de,** for the sake of, out of respect to.

obsequioso, sa [ob-say-ke-o´-so, sah], *a.* 1. Obsequious, obedient, compliant, obliging (servicial), attentive. 2. *(Mex.)* Fond of giving presents.

observación [ob-ser-vah-the-on´], *f.* 1. Observation, the act of observing (acto); remark (comentario), note. **Observaciones sueltas,** desultory remarks. 2. Observance, careful obedience. **Estar en observación,** to be under observation. **Hacer una observación,** to make a remark.

observador, ra [ob-ser-vah-dor´, rah], *m. & f.* 1. Observer, remarker. 2. Observer, one who keeps any law, custom, or practice. -*m.* An astronomer.

observancia [ob-ser-vahn´-the-ah], *f.* 1. Observance, respect, reverence, regard. 2. Attentive practice, obedience, observation, ritual practice. 3. The original state of some religious orders, in contradistinction to their reformed condition. **Poner en observancia,** to execute punctually whatever is ordered.

observante [ob-ser-vahn´-tay], *pa. & a.* Observant, respectfully obedient; observing. -*m.* Monk of certain branches of the order of St. Francis.

observar [ob-ser-var´], *va.* 1. To observe (mirar), to regard attentively. 2. To observe, to notice, to mind, to heed. 3. To observe, to keep religiously or ritually, to follow. 4. To obey, to execute with punctuality and exactness. 5. **Observar algo a uno,** *(LAm.)* to point something out to somebody.

observatorio [ob-ser-vah-to´-re-o], *m.* Observatory, a place for astronomical or meteorological observations.

obsesión [ob-say-se-on´], *f.* Obsession.

obsesionar [ob-say-se-o-nar´], *va. & vr.* To obsess, to be obsessed (idea.) **Estar obsesionado con algo,** to be obsessed by something.

obsesivo [ob-say-see´-vo], *a.* Obsessive.

obseso, sa [ob-say´-so, sah], *a.* Beset, tempted, as with evil spirits.

obsidiana [ob-se-de-ah´-nah], *f.* Obsidian, a glassy, volcanic rock.

obsoleto [ob-so-lay´-to], *a.* Obsolete.

obstáculo [obs-tah´-coo-lo], *m.* Obstacle, impediment, obstruction, clog, hindrance. **No es obstáculo para que yo...,** it is no obstacle to my...

obstante (no) [obs-tahn´-tay], *pa.* Notwithstanding, nevertheless, however.

obstar [ob-star´], *vn.* To oppose, to obstruct, to hinder, to withstand.

obstetrical [obs-tay-tre-cahl´], *a.* Obstetrical.

obstetricia [obs-tay-tre´-the-ah], *f.* Obstetrics, midwifery.

obstétrico, ca [obs-tay´-tre-co, cah], *a.* Obstetrical, relating to childbirth. -*f.*

obstinación [obs-te-nah-the-on´], *f.* Obstinacy, stubbornness, obduracy.

obstinadamente [obs-te-nah´-dah-men-tay], *adv.* Obstinately, stubbornly.

obstinado, da [obs-te-nah´-do, dah], *a.* Obstinate, obdurate, headstrong, opinionated. *pp.* of OBSTINARSE.

obstinarse [obs-te-nar´-say], *vr.* To be obstinate.

obstrucción [obs-trooc-the-on´], *f.* 1. *(Med.)* Obstruction in the vessels of the body. 2. Obstruction, closure of any passage.

obstructivo, va [obs-trooc-tee´-vo, vah], *a.* Obstructive, obstruent.

obstruir [obs-troo-eer´], *va.* To obstruct or block up the natural passages of the body (bloquear). -*vr.* To be obstructed or choked (abertura).

obtemperar [ob-tem-pay-rar´], *va. (Ant.)* To obey, to assent (used with prep. *a*).

obtención [ob-ten-the-on´], *f.* Attainment, obtainment, the act of attaining or obtaining.

obtener [ob-tay-nerr´], *va.* 1. To attain, to obtain, to procure. 2. To preserve, to maintain. *(Yo obtengo, obtenga, obtuve, obtuviera; from Obtener.* V. TENER.)

obtento [ob-ten´-to], *m.* 1. Benefice, prebend, living, 2. Attainment.

obtentor [ob-ten-tor´], *m.* One who obtains a living on being ordained priest.

obtestación [ob-tes-tah-the-on´], *f.* Obtestation, protestation, a rhetorical figure in which the speaker calls to witness God, nature, men, or inanimate things.

obturador, triz [ob-too-rah-dor´, treeth´], *a.* Serving to stop up or plug. -*m.* 1. Plug, stopper; breechblock. 2. Obturator, a surgical plate for closing a fissure. 3. Gas-check, a circular plate of glass placed over the mouth of vessels filled with gas, for carrying them. 4. A photographic shutter.

obturar [ob-too-rar´], *va.* To stop up, to plug, to obturate.

obtusángulo [ob-too-sahn'-goo-lo], *m. & a.* Obtuse angle; obtusangular.

obtuso, sa [ob-too'-so, sah], *a.* 1. Obtuse, blunt, not pointed; not shrill. 2. Obtuse, dull.

obué [o-boo-ay'], *m.* Oboe and oboe-player. *V.* OBOE.

obús [o-boos'], *m.* 1. Howitzer, a kind of mortar used for firing shells and grapeshot (cañón). 2. *(Neol.)* A conical shell.

obusero, ra [o-boo-say'-ro, rah], *a. (Mil.)* Shell-throwing: used of cannons and of a vessel provided with howitzers.

obvención [ob-ven-the-on'], *f.* A casual profit, obvention.

obviamente [ob'-ve-ah-men-tay], *adv.* Obviously.

obviar [ob-ve-ar'], *va.* To obviate (evitar), to prevent. *-vn.* To oppose, to stand in the way (estorbar).

obvio, via [ob'-ve-o, ah], *a.* Obvious, evident.

obyecto, ta [ob-yec'-to, tah], *m. (Met.)* Interposed.

oca [o'-cah], *f.* 1. *(Orn.)* Goose. 2. *(Bot.)* Oca oxalic, with yellow flowers. 3. Kind of game called *Royal goose.*

ocal [o-cahl'], *m.* 1. Cocoon of silk formed by two silkworms together, and the silk made from it.*-a.* Applied to very delicate sweet pears and apples.

ocalear [o-cah-lay-ar'], *vn.* To make *ocals* (gusanos de seda).

ocarina [o-cah-ree'-nah], *f. (Mus.)* Ocarina.

ocasión [o-cah-se-on'], *f.* 1. Occasion (vez), opportunity, chance (oportunidad), juncture, convenience. 2. Occasion, accidental cause or motive (motivo). 3. Danger, risk. 4. Cause (motivo). **Por ocasión,** by chance. **En algunas ocasiones,** sometimes. **Aprovechar la ocasión,** to take one's chance.

ocasionado, da [o-cah-se-o-nah'-do, dah], *a.* Provoking, vexatious, insolent; perilous. *-pp.* of OCASIONAR.

ocasionador, ra [o-cah-se-o-nah-dor', rah], *m. & f.* Occasioner, one that causes or promotes.

ocasional [o-cah-se-o-nahl'], *a.* 1. Occasional (composición), extemporaneous. 2. Chance (fortuito), accidental.

ocasionalmente, *adv.* Occassionally.

ocasionar [o-cah-se-o-nar'], *va.* 1. To cause, to occasion; to move, to excite. 2. To endanger.

ocasioncilla, ita [o-cah-se-on-theel'-lyah, thee'-tah], *f. dim.* of OCASIÓN.

ocaso [o-cah'-so], *m.* 1. The setting of the sun or any heavenly body. 2. Occident, the west. 3. Death.

occidental [oc-the-den-tahl'], *a.* Occidental, western.

occidente [oc-the-den'-tay], *m.* 1. Occident, the west. 2. Europe, in contrast to Asia or the Orient. 3. *(Met.)* Age, decadence.

occiduo, dua [oc-thee'-doo-o, ah], *a.* Occidental.

occipital [oc-the-pe-tahl'], *a.* Occipital, a bone in the hinder part of the head.

occipucio [oc-the-poo'-the-o], *m.* Occiput, the back part of the head, where it joins the spine.

occiso, sa [oc-thee'-so, sah], *a.* Murdered, killed.

oceánico, ca [o-thay-ah'-ne-co, cah], *a.* 1. Oceanic, belonging to the ocean. 2. Living or grooving in the ocean.

océano [o-thay'-ah-no], *m.* 1. The ocean. 2. Any vast expanse. **Océano Ártico,** Artic Ocean.

oceanografía [o-thay-ah-no-grah-fee'-ah], *f.* Oceanography, oceanic geography.

ocelotl (or **ocelote**), *m.* Ocelot, a leopard-like cat of Mexico and South America.

ochava [o-chah'-vah], *f.* The eighth part of something. *Ochavas del molinete, (Naut.)* the whelps of the windlass.

ochavado, da [o-chah-vah'-do, dah], *a.* Octagonal, eight-sided. *-pp.* of OCHAVAR.

ochavar [o-chah-var'], *va.* To forth an octagon.

ochavear [o-chah-vay-ar'], *va.* To be divided into eighths.

ochavo [o-chah'-vo], *m.* 1. An old small Spanish brass coin, valued at two maravedies. 2. Something octagonal.

ochenta [o-chen'-tah], *a. & m.* Eighty.

ochentavo, va [o-chen-tah'-vo, vah], *a.* The one-eightieth part.

ochentón, na [o-chen-tone', nah], *a.* Eighty years old.

ochete [o-chay'-tay], *m.* Bore or empty part of hollow projectiles.

ocho [o'-cho], *a. & m.* 1. Eight. 2. Eight, the figure 8. 3. A card with eight marks. **El ocho de Marzo,** the eighth of March.

ochocientos [o-cho-the-en'-tos], *a. & m.* Eight hundred.

ochosén [o-cho-sen'], *m.* The smallest coin among the ancient Spaniards.

ocio [o'-the-o], *m.* 1. Leisure (tiempo libre), freedom from business; vacancy of mind. 2. Pastime (pasatiempo), diversion. **Ratos de ocio,** leisure.

ociosamente, *adv.* Idly, uselessly.

ociosidad [o-the-o-se-dahd'], *f.* Idleness, laziness, sluggishness, leisure.

ocioso, sa [o-the-o'-so, sah], *a.* Idle (inactivo), lazy, fruitless, unprofitable; foppish, useless (acto, palabras).

oclocracia [o-clo-crah'-the-ah], *f.* Ochlocracy, government by the multitude.

oclusión [o-cloo-se-on'], *f.* Occlusion, obliteration.

ocote [o-co'-tay], *m.* A very resinous pine-tree of Mexico; pitch-pine.

ocozoal [o-co-tho-ahl'], *m.* Mexican serpent, like a viper.

ocre [o'-cray], *m.* Ochre, a brown or yellow earth.

ocropira [o-cro-pee'-rah], *f.* Yellow fever.

ocroso, sa [o-cro'-so, sah], *a.* Ochreous, of the nature or color of ochre.

octaedro [oc-tah-ay'-dro], *m. (Geom.)* Octahedron, a solid bounded by eight plane triangles.

octagonal [oc-tah-go-nahl'], *a.* Octagonal.

octágono, na [oc-tah'-go-no, nah], *a.* Having eight sides and angles.

octágono [oc-tah'-go-no], *m.* An octagon.

octal [oc-tahl], *m.(Comput.)*Octal.

octangular [oc-tan-goo-lar'], *a.* Octangular.

octano [oc-tah'-no], *m. (Chem.)* Octane.

octante [oc-tahn'-tay], *m.* Octant, an instrument containing the eighth part of a circle.

octava [oc-tah'-vah], *f.* 1. Octave, a space of eight days comprising a church festival. 2. A poetical composition of eight lines of eleven syllables, rhyming thus: 1, 3, 5; 2, 4, 6; 7 and 8. 3. *(Mus.)* Octave. 4. *V.* OCTAVARIO.

octavar [oc-tah-var'], *vn.* 1. To form octaves on stringed instruments. 2. To deduct the eighth part.

octavario [oc-tah-vah'-re-o], *m.* 1. Book which contains the office for an octave festival. 2. Festival lasting a week.

octavilla [oc-tah-veel'-lyah], *f.* 1. Half-pint for excise taken on the retail of vinegar, oil, and wine. 2. *(Mus.)* Octave.

octavín [oc-tah-veen'], *m.* 1. A piccolo flutes. 2. Flageolet.

octavo [oc-th'-vo], *m.* 1. An eighth. 2. In America, an octoroon.

octavo, va *a.* 1. Eighth; octave, octonary. 2. Octavos de final, *(Dep.)* quarter-finals.

octeto [oc-tay'-to], *m. (Mus.)* Octet.

octogenario, ria [oc-to-hay-nah'-re-o, ah], *a.* Octogenary, eighty years old.

octogentésimo [oc-to-hen-tay'-se-mo], *a.* Eight hundredth.

octogésimo [oc-to-hay'-se-mo], *a.* Eightieth.

octógono, na [oc-toh'-go-no, nah], *a.* *V.* OCTÁGONO.

octopétala [oc-to-pay'-tah-lah], *a. (Bot.)* Octopetalous, of eight petals.

octosilábico, ca, octosílabo, ba [oc-to-se-lah'-be-co, cah], *a.* Octosyllabic.

octubre [oc-too'-bray], *m.* October.

octuplicar [oc-too-ple-car'], *va.* To multiply by eight, to increase eight-fold.

óctuplo, pla [oc'-too-plo, plah], *a.* Octuple, eight-fold.

ocular [o-coo-lar'], *a.* Ocular. **Testigo ocular,** eyewitness. *-m.* Eyeglass, ocular, eye-piece.

oculista [o-coo-lees'-tah], *m & f.* Oculist; eye specialist.

ocultación [o-cool-tah-the-on'], *f.* 1. Concealment, hiding. 2. *(Ast.)* Occultation of a star or planet. 3. Wrongful silence.

ocultador, ra [o-cool-tah-dor', rah], *m. & f.* Hider, concealer.

ocultamente [o-cool'-tah-men-tay], *adv.* Secretly, hiddenly.

ocultar [o-cool-tar'], *va.* 1. To hide (esconder), to conceal, to disguise (disfrazar), to secrete, to mask, to hoodwink, to cloak. 2. To keep back, to keep secret what ought to be said. *-vr.* To hide oneself. **Ocultarse a la vista,** to keep out of sight. **Ocultarse tras,** to hide behind.

ocultismo [o-cool-tees'-mo], *m.* Occultism.

oculto, ta [o-cool'-to, tah], *a.* Hidden (escondite), concealed, occult (ciencia), secret (pensamiento), clandestine. **De oculto,** incognito. **En oculto,** secretly, in secret.

ocupación [o-coo-pah-the-on'], *f.* 1. Occupation; business, concern; employment, office, pursuit; action. 2. Prolepsis. a rhetorical figure.

ocupado, da [o-coo-pah'-do, dah], *a.* Busy (persona), occupied (plaza), engaged. **La línea está ocupada,** *(Telec.)* the line is engaged. **Estoy muy ocupado,** I'm very busy.

ocupador [o-coo-pah-dor'], *m.* Occupier, possessor, occupant.

ocupante [o-coo-pahn'-tay], *pa. & n.* Occupant; an actual possessor of lands.

ocupar [o-coo-par'], *va.* 1. To occupy, to take possession of (espacio, silla). 2. To hold an employ (puesto), to fill a public station. 3. To occupy, to busy, to employ (obreros), to give employment. 4. To disturb, to interrupt, to obstruct. 5. To inhabit a house. 6. *(Met.)* To occupy or gain the attention. 7. *(Mex.)* To use (emplear). **Ocupa sus ratos libres pintando,** he uses his spare time to paint. **Las obras ocupan más de 1000 hombres,** the work keeps more than 1000 men busy. *-vr.* To occupy, to follow business. **Ocuparse de,** to concern oneself with. **Me ocuparé de ello mañana,** I will deal with it tomorrow.

ocurrencia [o-coor-ren'-the-ah], *f.* 1. Occurrence (suceso), accident, incident, occasion. 2. Bright thought or original idea which occurs to the mind (idea). **Me dio la ocurrencia de,** it occurred to me to.

ocurrente [o-coor-ren'-tay], *a.* Off hand, original, bright (listo), wity (chistoso). *-pa.* of OCURRIR.

ocurrir [o-coor-reer'], *vn.* 1. To meet, to go to meet, to anticipate. 2. To occur, to happen, to fall on the same day: applied to two feasts of different solemnities. 3. To obviate, to make opposition to. 4. To repair to proceed. **Se me ocurre una idea,** *(coll.)* a thought strikes me. *-v. impers.* To occur, to be presented to the memory or attention. **Nunca se me había ocurrido,** it had never crossed my mind.

oda [o'-dah], *f.* 1. Ode, a lyric poem. 2. Ode, a poem written to be set to music.

odalisca [o-dah-lees'-cah], *f.* Odalisk, a woman of the harem of the Sultan of Turkey; a servant of his sisters, daughters, and wives, and often a concubine.

odiar [o-be-ar'], *va.* 1. To hate, to abhor, to detest. 2. *(Cono Sur)* To irk (fastidiar), to bore (aburrir). *-vr.* To hate one another.

odio [o'-de-o], *m.* Hatred, abhorrence, detestation, malevolence. **Tener odios,** to hate.

odiosamente [o-de-o'-sah-men-tay], *adv.* Odiously, hatefully.

odiosidad [o-de-o-se-dahd'], *f.* 1. Hatefulness, odiousness, odium. 2. *(And. Carib. Cono Sur)* Irksome, annoyance.

odioso, sa [o-de-oh'-so, sah], *a.* 1. Odious, hateful, detestable. 2. *(And. Cono Sur)* Irksome (molesto), annoying.

odisea [o-de-say'-ah], *f.* 1. The Odyssey, a poem written by Homer. 2. Adventure, ordeal.

odómetro [o-do'-may-tro], *m.* Instrument for measuring the road passed over; odometer.

odontalgia [o-don-tahl'-he-ah], *f.* Odontalgia, toothache.

odontálgico [o-don-tahl'-he-co], *m.* Odontalgic, remedy for toothache.

odontecnia [o-don-tec'-ne-ah], *f.* Dental surgery.

odontina [o-don-tee'-nah], *f.* 1. A remedy for curing toothache. 2. A dentifrice.

odontología [o-don-to-lo-hee'-ah], *f.* Odontology, the science of dentistry.

odontólogo [o-don-to'-lo-go], *m.* Odontologist, dentist.

odontotecnia [o-don-to-tec'-ne-ah], *f.* Practical art of dentistry.

odorífero, ra [o-do-ree'-fay-ro, rah], *a.* Odoriferous, fragrant, perfumed.

odorífico, ca [o-do-ree'-fe-co, cah], *a.* Odor-producing. **Órgano odorífico,** the organ which, in the hemiptera, secretes the smell which they emit at will.

odre [o'-dray], *m.* 1. Bag generally used for wine, oil, and other liquids, commonly made of a dreseed goatskin; a leather bottle lined with pitch. 2. Drunkard (borracho).

odrería [o-dray-ree'-ah], *f.* Shop where leather bottles are made or sold.

odrero [o-dray'-ro], *m.* One who makes or deals in leather bottles.

odrina [o-dree'-nah], *f.* Ox-skin bag.

oenas [o-ay'-nas], *f.* Stock-dove, wood-pigeon.

oenate [o-ay-nah'-tay], *f. (Orn.)* Fallow-finch, stone-chatter.

oesnorueste [o-es-no-roo-es'-tay], *m.* West-north-west.

oessudueste [o-es-soo-doo-es'-tay], *m.* West-south-west.

oeste [o-es'-tay], *m.* 1. West (región). 2. The west wind (viento). **En la parte del oeste,** in the western part. *-a.* West (parte), western; westerly (dirección); west (viento).

ofendedor, ra [o-fen-day-dor', rah], *m. & f. V.* OFENSOR.

ofender [o-fen-derr'], *va.* 1. To offend, to harm, to indure, to make angry. **Por temor a ofenderle,** for fear of offending him. 2. *(Mex.)* To touch up (mujer). *-vr.* To be vexed or displeased; to take offence.

ofendido [o-fen-dee'-do], *a.* Offended. **Darse por ofendido,** to take offence.

ofensa [o-fen'-sah], *f.* 1. Offence, injury, transgression, crime. 2. Offence; attack. 3. Offence, breaking the law of God.

ofensiva [o-fen-see'-vah], *f.* Offensive. **Ofensiva de paz,** peace offensive.

ofensivamente [o-fen-see'-vah-men-tay], *adv.* Offensively, injuriously.

ofensivo, va [o-fen-see'-vo, vah], *a.* 1. Offensive, displeasing, disgusting (asqueroso). 2. Assailant, not defensive. *-f.* **Tomar la ofensiva,** to take the offensive; to prepare for attack, and to attack in fact.

ofensivo [o-fen-see'-vo], *m.* Anything which serves as a defence or remedy.

ofensor, ra [o-fen-sor', rah], *m. & f.* Offender.

oferente [o-fay-ren'-tay], *m.* Offerer, one who offers.

oferta [o-ferr'-tah], *f.* 1. Offer, promise, offering. 2. Supply. **La ley de la oferta y la demanda,** the law of supply and demand.

ofertorio [o-fer-too'-re-o], *m.* 1. Offertory, the act of offering; the thing offered; the part of the mass where the priest offers up the host and wine. 2. The anthem belonging to this service.

oficial, la [o-fe-the-ahl', lah], *m. & f.* 1. Workman, workwoman, artificer, tradesman; journeyman. **Buen oficial,** a first-rate hand, a good operative. 2. Officer who holds a commission in the army or navy. 3. Clerk in a public office. **Oficial mayor de la secretaría de estado,** first under secretary of the state department. **Oficial mayor,** chief clerk (oficina). 4. Hangman, executioner. 5. *(Prov.)* Butcher, one who cuts up and retails meat. 6. Municipal magistrate. 7. Craftsman (artesano). **Es buen oficial,** he is a clever workman; he is a good officer. **Oficial médico,** medical officer. **Oficial de seguridad,** security officer. **Oficial técnico,** technical officer.

oficial [o-fe-the-ahl'], *a.* Official, pertaining to a public charge.

oficialazo [o-fe-the-ah-lah'-tho], *m. aug.* A skilful workman.

oficialejo [o-fe-the-ah-lay'-ho], *m. dim.* A petty workman.

oficialía [o-fe-the-ah-lee'-ah], *f.* 1. Clerk's place in a public office. **Oficialía mayor,** chief clerkship. 2. Artist's working-room.

oficialidad [o-fe-the-ah-le-dahd'], *f.* Body of officers of an army or regiment.

oficialmente [o-fe-the-al-men'-tay], *adv.* Officially, in an official manner.

oficiar [o-fe-the-ar'], *va.* To officiate, commonly in worship, to minister.

oficina [o-fe-thee'-nah], *f.* 1. Workshop. 2. Office, counting-house. 3. *(Cono Sur)* Nitrate house. **oficinas,** offices, the lower apartments in houses, such as cellars. **Horas de oficina,** business hours.

oficinal [o-fe-the-nahl'], *a.* Officinal: applied to the drugs prepared by apothecaries.

oficinesco, ca [o-fe-the-nes'-co, cah], *a.* Departmental, relating to the offices of state, in a derogatory sense; «redtape.»

oficinista [o-fe-the-nees´-tah], *m.* Anyone employed in a public or a secretary's office.

oficio [o-fee'-the-o], *m.* 1. Office, employ, job (profésion), work, occupation, ministry. 2. Function, operation. 3. Official letter. 4. Trade, business, craft. 5. Notary's office. 6. Benefit, service. 7. *(Ec.)* Service; mass. **Oficio de difuntos,** office for the dead. **De oficio,** officially, by duty, not by request. **Mozo de oficio,** an under-servant in the king's palace. **Tomarlo por oficio,** to do a thing frequently. **Oficios,** solemn church service or divine service. **Los deberes del oficio,** the duties of the post. **Sabe su oficio,** he knows his job. **Estos son los gajes del oficio,** these are the occupational hazards or drawbacks.

oficiosamente [o-fe-the-o'-sah-men-tay], *adv.* Officiously.

oficiosidad [o-fe-the-o-se-dahd'], *f.* 1. Diligence, application to business. 2. Officiousness.

oficioso, sa [o-fe-the-o'-so, sah], *a.* 1. Officious, diligent, attentive to business, compliant, accommodating. 2. Officious, meddling, forward. **De fuente oficiosa,** from a semiofficial source.

oficleido [o-fe-clay'-e-do], *m.* Ophicleide, a brass wind-instrument, deeptoned, of open mouth-piece, and nine (or cleven) keys.

ofidios [o-fee'-de-ose], *m. pl.* Ophidia, the serpents or snakes.

ofiólatra [o-fe-o'-lah-trah], *a.* Ophiolatrous, relating to serpent-worship.

ofita [o-fee´-tah], *f.* Ophite, a kind of greenish porphyry.

ofrecedor [o-fray-thay-dor'], *m.* Offerer.

ofrecer [o-fray-therr'], *va.* 1. To offer, to make an offer, to hold out. 2. To present (presentar). 3. To exhibit, to manifest. 4. To dedicate, to consecrate. *-vr.* To offer (persona), to occur (suceder), to present itself. **Ofrecerse en sacrificio,** to offer oneself in sacrifice. **Ofrecerse de ayudante,** to offer one's services as an assistant. **Ofrecerse con la boca chica,** to make a complimentary offer without intending fulfilment. **¿Se le ofrece a usted algo?** at your service, what can I do for you? *(Yo ofrezco, yo ofrezca,* from *Ofrecer.* V. CONOCER.)

ofrecimiento [o-fray-the-me-en'-to], *m.* 1. Offer, promise, offering. 2. Occurrence, incident. 3. Extemporary discourse.

ofrenda [o-fren'-dah], *f.* Offering, oblation, gift.

ofrendar [o-fren-dar'], *va.* 1. To present offerings to God. 2. To contribute toward some end or purpose.

oftalmía [of-tal-mee'-ah], *f.* Ophthalmia, an inflammation of the eye.

oftálmico [of-tahl'-me-co], *a.* Ophthalmic.

oftalmografía [of-tal'-mo-grah-fee´-ah], *f.* Ophthalmography, a minute description of the eye.

oftalmología [of-tal-mo-lo-hee'-ah], *f.* Ophthalmology, the branch of medicine concerned with the eye and its diseases.

oftalmólogo [of-tal-mo'-lo-go], *m.* Ophthalmologist, oculist.

oftalmómetro [of-tal-mo'-may-tro], *m.* Ophthalmometer, an instrument for examining the refraction of the eye.

oftalmoscopia [of-tal-mos-co'-pe-ah], *f.* Ophthalmoscopy, examination of the eye.

oftalmoscopio [of-tal-mos-co'-pe-o], *m.* Ophthalmoscope, a mirror with a central aperture for viewing the interior of the eye.

ofuscación, *f.* **ofuscamiento,** *m.* [o-foos-cah-the-on', o-foos-cah-me-en'-to]. Obfuscation, dimness of the sight; confused reason.

ofuscar [o-foos-car'], *va.* To obfuscate, to darken, to render obscure. **Ofuscar la razón or el entendimiento,** to disturb the mind, to confuse the judgment. *(Met.)* To dazzle (deslumbrar).

ogro [o'-gro], *m.* Ogre, a fabulous monster.

¡oh! *int.* O! Oh! **¡Oh, quiera Dios!** God grant! **¡Oh, qué hermosa casa!** oh, what a fine house! *(Naut.)* Ho! **¡Oh, el barco!** ho! ship ahoy!

ohmio [o'-me-o], *m. (Elec.)* Ohm.

oíble [o-ee'-blay], *a.* Audible, that can be heard.

oída [o-ee'-dah], *f.* Act and effect of hearing.

oído, da [o-ee'-do, dah], *pp.* of OÍR. Heard. *- m.* 1. The sense of hearing (sentido). 2. Ear, organ of hearing. 3. Ear, power of judging of harmony. 4. Touch-hole of a gun. **Está sordo de un oído,** he is deaf in one ear. **Hablar al oído,** to whisper in one's ear. **Dolor de oídos,** earache. **Tener buen oído,** to have a quick ear. **Llegar a oídos,** or **a sus oídos,** to come to one's ears or knowledge. **Tocar de oído,** to play by ear. **Entra por un oído y sale por otro,** it goes in one ear and out of the other. **Ser todo oídos,** to be all ears.

oidor, ra [o-e-dor', rah], *m. & f.* Hearer, one who hears. *-a.* Hearing.

oidoría [o-e-do-ree'-ah], *f.* Office or dignity of an *oidor.*

oír [o-eer'], *va.* 1. To hear, to listen. **Has oído campanas y no sabes dónde,** you don't really know what you're talking about. 2. To understand, to comprehend. 3. To attend the lectures on some science or art, in order to study it. 4. To go to mass (misa); to hear (consejo). 5. To hear, to heed, to answer (súplica). 6. *(Jur.)* To hear (causa). **Oír misa,** to attend at or hear mass. **No haber oído la campana,** to be unobservant or ignorant of common things. **¿Oyes? or ¿oye Vd.?** I say, do you hear? **Oiga or oigan,** exclamation of surprise. **Oye, oye,** hear! hear! **Oír, ver, y callar,** mind your own business. **Oír hablar de,** to hear it said that. **Le oí abrir la puerta,** I heard him open the door. *(Yo oigo, oiga, oyera; él oyó.* V. OÍR.)

oíslo [o-ees'-lo], *m.* Person beloved, wife (or husband). Very ancient word.

ojal [o-hahl'], *m.* 1. Button-hole. 2. Hole through anything.

ojalá [o-hah-lah'], *int.* Would to God! God grant! I hope so! **¡Ojalá que él viva!** may he live! **Ojalá que vaya,** I wish he may go, I wish he went. *-conj. (LAm.)* Even though.

ojaladera [o-hah-lah-day'-rah], *f.* A woman who works button-holes.

ojaladura [o-hah-lah-doo'-rah], *f.* The set of button-holes in a garment.

ojalar [o-hah-lar'], *va.* To make button holes.

ojazo [o-hah'-tho], *m. aug.* A large eye.

ojeada [o-hay-ah'-dah], *f.* Glance, glimpse, ogle.

ojeador [o-hay-ah-dor'], *m.* One who starts game for the chase.

ojeadura [o-hay-ah-doo'-rah], *f.* Act of glazing clothes.

ojear [o-hay-ar'], *va.* 1. To eye, to view with attention, to glance at (mirar). 2. To start game by hallooing. 3. To startle something. 3. *(Cono Sur)* To put the evil eye on (hechizar).

ojeo [o-hay'-o], *m.* The act of starting game for the chase by hallooing. **Echar un ojeo,** to start and drive game toward the sportsmen.

ojera [o-hay´-rah], *f.* 1. Bluish circle under the lower eye-lid, indicative of indisposition (sombra). 2. An eye-bath or eye-cup, a glass vessel for bathing the eye.

ojeriza [o-hay-ree'-thah], *f.* Spite, grudge, ill-will.

ojeroso, sa, ojerudo, da [o-hay-ro'-so, sah], *a.* Applied to persons with blackish circles under the eyes.

ojete [o-hay'-tay], *m.* 1. Eyelet-hole in clothes. 2. *(coll.)* Anus.

ojetear [o-hay-tay-ar'], *va.* To make eyelet-holes in clothes.

ojetera [o-hay-tay'-rah], *f.* 1. Piece of whalebone sewed near the eyelet-holes in clothes. 2. A woman or a machine which makes eyelet-holes.

ojialegre [o-he-ah-lay'-gray], *a.* Having lively, sparkling eyes.

ojiazul [o-he-ah-thool'], *a.* Blue-eyed. *(Neol. Amer.)*

ojito [o-hee'-to], *m. dim.* A small eye.

ojienjuto, ta [o-he-en-hoo'-to, tah], *a.* Dry-eyed.
ojillos [o-hel'-lyos], *m. pl.* Bright eyes; lovely eyes; roguish eyes.
ojimiel, ojimel [o-he-me-el´, *m.* Oxymel, a mixture of honey and vinegar.
ojimoreno, na [o-he-mo-ray'-no, nah], *a.* Brown-eyed.
ojinegro, gra [o-he-nay'-gro, grah], *a.* Black-eyed.
ojiva [o-hee'-vah], *f.* 1. Diagonal rib of a vaulted arch. 2. Ogive, a pointed arch.
ojival [o-he-vahl'], *a.* Ogival, belonging to an ogive.
ojizaino, na [o-he-thah-ee'-no, nah], *a.* Squint-eyed, moon-eyed.
ojizarco, ca [o-he-thar'-co, cah], *a.* Blue or gray-eyed.
ojo [o'-ho], *m.* 1. The eye. 2. Eye, sight, ocular knowledge. 3. Eye of a needle (aguja). 4. Eye, any small perforation. 5. Head formed on liquors; drop of oil or grease which swims on liquors. 6. Arch of a bridge (puente). 7. Eye or socket, for receiving a handle. 8. Attention, cure, notice. 9. Keyhole. 10. Lather, formed from soap. 11. *(typ.)* Face of a priming type. 13. Mesh of a net. 14. Eye or hollow in bread or cheese (pan, queso). 15. Expression of ardent affection or endearment, or the object of it. 16. **Ojo de pollo,** *(LAm.)* corn, callus. **A cierra ojos** or **a ojos cerrados,** without hesitation; at all events. **En un abrir y cerrar de ojos,** in the twinkling of an eye. **A ojo,** (1) by the bulk or lump. (2) At the discretion of another. **A ojo, a los ojos de alguno** or **a sus ojos,** face to face, in presence of anyone. **Al ojo,** at sight, at hand. **Ojo alerta,** look sharp. **Ojos que no ven, corazón que no siente,** *(Prov.)* out of sight, out of mind. **Mal de ojo,** fascination, enchantment. **Mal de ojos,** sore eyes. **Niñas de los ojos,** apple of one's eye; darling treasure. **Ojo de buey,** (1) *(Bot.)* oxeye. (2) *(coll.)* Doubloon of eight dollars. **Dichosos los ojos que ven a usted,** delighted to scc you again! (expression used on meeting another after a considerable interval). **Entrarle (a uno) una cosa por el ojo** or **por los ojos,** to delight, to charm one. **Ojo eléctrico,** electric eye.
ojoso, sa [o-ho'-so, sah], *a.* Full of eyes.
ojota [o-ho'-tah], *f.* 1. A kind of shoe worn by Indian women. *(Peru.)* 2. *(And. Cono Sur)* Tanned llama leather (piel de llama).
ojuelo [o-hoo-ay'-lo], *m. dim.* A small eye. *-pl.* 1. Sparkling eyes, smiling eyes. 2. *(Prov.)* Spectacles.
ola [o'-lah], *f.* 1. A wave. 2. A sudden, violent commotion. **Ola de calor,** heat wave. **La nueva ola,** the latest fashion.
olaje [o-lah'-hay], *m.* Succession of waves, surge.
olán [o-lahn'], *m.* Holland, Dutch linen, batiste.
olé [o´-lay], *m.* Andalusian dance. **¡Olé!** *int.* Bravo!
oleáceo, cea [o-lay-ah'-thay-o, ah], *a.* Of the olive family (ash, etc.).
oleada [o-lay-ah'-dah], *f.* 1. Surge, swell of the sea. 2. A plentiful produce of oil. 3. Surging of crowded people. **Una gran oleada de gente,** a great surge of people.
oleaginosidad [o-lay-ah-he-no-se-dahd'], *f.* Oleaginousness, oiliness.
oleaginoso, sa [o-lay-ah-he-no´-so, sah], *a.* Oleaginous, oily.
oleaje [o-lay-ah´-hay], *m.* V. OLAJE.
olear [o-lay-ar´], *va.* To administer extreme unction.
oleario, ri [o-lay-ah'-re-o, ah], *a.* Oily.
oleato [o-lay-ah'-to], *m.* Oleate, a compound of oleic acid.
oleaza [o-lay-ah´-thah], *f.* *(Prov.)* The watery dregs which remain in the mill after the oil has been extracted.
oledero, ra [o-lay-day'-ro, rah], *a.* Odorous, fragrant.
oledor, ra [o-lay-dor', rah], *m. & f.* Smeller, one who smells.
oleico, ca [o-lay'-e-co, cah], *a.* Oleic, pertaining to oil.
oleína [o-lay-ee'-nah], *f.* Olein, a colorless oily substance, the base of fatty oils.
óleo [o´-lay-o], *m.* 1. Oil. V. ACEITE. **Al óleo,** in oil colors. 2. Extreme unction, the holy oil; act of anointing.
oleoducto [o-lay-o-dooc'-to], *m.* Pipeline.
oleolato [o-lay-o-lah'-to], *m.* Essential oils.
oleomargarina [o-lay-o-mar-gah-ree'-nah], *f.* Oleomargarine.

oleosidad [o-lay-o-se-dahd'], *f.* Oiliness.
oleoso, sa [o-lay-o'-so, sah], *a.* Oily, oleaginous.
oler [o-lerr'], *va.* 1. To smell, to scent, to snort (cocaína). 2. To smell, to find out, to search, to scent, to discover (descubrir). 3. To pry, to inspect curiously. *-vn.* 1. To smell, to strike the nostrils. 2. To smell, to have a particular tincture or smack of any quality. **Oler a chamusquina,** to come from hot words to hard blows. **No oler bien alguna cosa,** *(Met.)* to be a suspicious thing. *(Yo huelo, huela; olí.* V. OLER.)
olfacción [ol-fac-the-on'], *f. (Med.)* Olfaction, the act or the sense of smell.
olfatear [ol-fah-tay-ar'], *va.* To smell, to scent.
olfato [ol-fah'-to], *m.* Scent, the sense or organ of smell.
olfatorio, ria [ol-fah-to'-re-o, ah], *a.* Olfactory.
olíbano [o-lee'-bah-no], *m. (Bot.)* Incense, a gum-resin produced by the Lycian juniper.
oliente [o-le-en'-tay], *pa.* Smelling, odorous.
oliera [o-le-ay'-rah], *f.* Vessel in which holy oil is kept.
oligarca [o-le-gar'-cah], *m.* Oligarch, a member of an oligarchy.
oligarquía [o-le-gar-kee'-ah], *f.* Oligarchy, a form of government by the few.
oligárquico, ca [o-le-gar'-ke-co, cah], *a.* Oligarchical.
olimpiada [o-lim-pe-ah´-dah], *f.* Olympiad, period of four years, olympic games.
olímpico, ca [o-leem'-pe-co, cah], *a.* Olympic.
olimpo [o-leem'-po], *m.* 1. Height, eminence. 2. *(Poet.)* Heaven.
oliscar [o-lis-car'], *va.* 1. To smell, to scent. 2. To investigate, to ascertain. *-vn.* To stink.
olisquear [o-lis-kay-ar'], *va.* V. OLISCAR.
oliva [o-lee'-vah], *f.* 1. Olive-tree (árbol). V. OLIVO. 2. The olive itself (aceituna).
olivar [o-le-var'], *m.* Plantation of olive-trees, olive-grove, olive-yard.
olivarse [o-le-var'-say], *vr.* To form bubbles (pan).
olivastro de Rodas [o-le-vahs'-tro], *m. (Bot.)* V. LINÁLOE.
olivera [o-le-vay´-rah], *f.* Olive-tree. V. OLIVO.
olivífero, ra [o-le-vee´-fay-ro, rah], *a. (Poet.)* Producing olives, olive-bearing.
olivo [o-lee´-vo], *m. (Bot.)* Olive-tree.
olla [ol-lyal'], *f.* 1. A round earthen pot, or wide-mouthed jar (recipiente). 2. Olla, an olio, a dish made of boiled meat and vegetables. 3. Any gulf in which are whirlpools; a whirlpool (de río). 4. Chimney (alpinismo). 5. *(Cono Sur)* **Olla común,** canteen.
olla a presión [ol'-lyah ah pray-se-on'], *f.* Pressure cooker.
olla express [ol'-lyah ex-press'], *f. (Mex.)* Pressure cooker.
ollao [ol-lyah'-o], *m. (Naut.)* Eyelet-hole, round hole in sails.
ollar [ol-lyar'], *a.* Soft, readily workable (piedra).
ollaza [ol-lyah'-thah], *f. aug.* A large pot or boiler.
ollazo [ol-lyah'-tho], *m.* Blow with an earthen pot or jar.
ollería [ol-lyay-ree'-ah], *f.* Pottery; a shop where earthenware is sold.
ollero [ol-lyay'-ro], *m.* 1. Potter. 2. Dealer in earthenware.
ollita [ol-lyee'-tah], *f. dim.* Pipkin, a small pot.
olluela [ol-lyoo-ay'-lah], *f.* Pit or hollow under the Adam's apple.
olmeda [ol-may'-dah], *f.* **Olmedo,** *m.* Elm-grove.
olmo [ol'-mo], *m. (Bot.)* Elm-tree.
ológrafo [o-lo'-grah-fo], *a.* Holographic, written in the hand of the testator.
olor [o-lor'], *m.* 1. Odor (aroma), scent. 2. Stink, stench. 3. Cause or motive of suspicion. 4. *(Met.)* Fame, reputation. 5. *(Cono Sur, Mex.)* Spices. **Agua de olor,** sweet-scented water. **Buen olor,** nice smell. **Tiene mal olor,** it smells bad.
oloroso, sa [o-lo-ro´-so, sah], *a.* Odoriferous, fragrant, perfumed.
olote [o-lo´-tay], *m. (Amer.)* Corn-cob.
olvidadizo, za [ol-ve-dah-dee´-tho, thah], *a.* Short of memory, forgetful, oblivious.

olvidado, da [ol-ve-dah'-do, dah], *a. & pp.* of OLVIDAR. 1. Forgotten, forsaken, forlorn. 2. Forgetful (persona). 3. Ungrateful (ingrato). 4. *(And. Cono Sur) V.* OLVIDADIZO.

olvidar [ol-ve-dar'], *va.* To forget, to neglect, to omit. **Olvidar hacer algo,** to forget to do something.

olvido [ol-ve'-do], *m.* Forgetfulness (cualidad), carelessness, heedlessness, neglect, oblivion (estado). **Echar al olvido or en olvido,** to forget designedly, to cast in oblivion.

ombligada [om-ble-gah'-dah], *f.* Part corresponding to the navel, in skins of animals.

ombligo [om-blee'-go], *m.* 1. The navel, umbilicus. 2. Navel-string, the umbilical cord. 3. Center or middle of a thing. **Ombligo do Venus,** Venus navelwort, or pennywort.

ombliguero [om-ble-gay'-ro], *f. (Bot.) V.* OREJA DE ABAD, or MONJE.

ombliguero [om-ble-gay'-ro], *m.* Bandage put upon the navel of new-born children.

ombría [om-bree'-ah], *f.* Shade, place secluded from the sun.

ombú [om-boo'], *m. (Argen. Cuba)* Tree with a wood so spongy that it burns at once to ashes.

omega [o-may'-gah], *f.* Omega, last letter in the Greek alphabet: long O.

omental [o-men-tahl'], *a.* Belonging to the omentum; omental.

omento [o-men'-to], *m.* Omentum, the caul or covering of the bowels.

omicron [o'-me-crone], Name of the Greek short O, fifteenth of their alphabet.

ominosamente [o-me-no'-sah-men-tay], *adv.* Ominously, with good or bad omen.

ominoso, sa [o-me-no'-so, sah], *a.* Ominous (de mal agüero), foreboding ill.

omisión [o-me-se-on'], *f.* Omission, carelessness, neglect, negligence, heedlessness.

omiso, sa [o-mee'-so, sah], *a.* Neglectful, remiss, heedless, careless.

omitir [o-me-teer'], *va.* To omit, to neglect.

ómnibus [om'-ne-boos], *m.* Omnibus, a public carriage for a number of persons.

omnímodamente [om-ne'-mo-dah-men-tay], *adv.* Entirely, by all means.

omnímodo, da [om-nee'-mo-do, dah], *a.* Entire, total.

omnipotencia [om-ne-po-ten'-the-ah], *f.* Omnipotence.

omnipotente [om-ne-po-ten'-tay], *a.* Omnipotent, almighty.

omnipotentemente [om-ne-po-ten'-tay-men-tay], *adv.* Omnipotently.

omnipresencia [om-ne-pray-sen'-the-ah], *f.* Omnipresence.

omnisciencia [om-nis-then'-the-ah], *f.* Omniscience.

omniscio, ia [om-nees'-the-o, ah], *a.* Omniscient.

omnívoro, ra [om-nee'-vo-ro, rah], *a.* Omnivorous, living upon foods of all kinds.

omoplato [o-mo-plah'-to], *m. (Anat.)* Omoplate, the shoulder-blade, scapula.

onagra [o-nah'-grah], *f. (Bot.)* A genus of the evening-primrose family, now referred to Enothera.

onagro [o-nah'-gro], *m.* Wild ass.

once [on'-thay], *a. & m.* Eleven; figure eleven. **El once de enero,** the eleventh of January. **El libro once,** the eleventh book.

oncear [on-thay-ar'], *va.* To weigh out by ounces.

oncejera, oncijera [on-thay-hay'-rah], *f.* A small snare for catching birds.

oncejo [on-thay'-ho], *m. (Prov.)* String, band, tie.

onceno, na [on-thay'-no, nah], *a.* Eleventh.

onda [on'-dah], *f.* 1. A wave. 2. Fluctuation, agitation. **Radio de onda corta,** short-wave radio. **Onda de choque,** shock wave. **Onda marina,** ocean wave. **Onda sonora,** sound wave. **Agarrar la onda,** *(LAm.)* to get it (entender). **Estar en la onda,** to be in (moda).

ondeado [on-day-ah'-do], *m. & a.* Anything in waves.

ondear [on-day-ar'], *vn.* 1. To undulate. 2. To fluctuate. 3. To ripple (agua), to fly (bandera); to stream (flotar al viento).

La bandera ondea a media asta, the flag is flying at half mast. *-vr.* To float backward and forward.

ondina [on-dee'-nah], *f.* Undine, water-sprite.

ondulación [on-doo-lah-the-on'], *f.* Waving, undulation.

ondulado, da [on-doo-lah'-do, dah], *a.* Waved, wavy (pelo), Undulations (superficie), undulating (terreno), corrugated (papel). **Ondulado permanente,** permanent wave. **Cabello ondulado,** wavy hair.

ondular [on-doo-lar'], *vn.* To ripple, to wave, to undulate.

oneiromancía [o-nay-ee-ro-mahn'-the-ah], *f.* Oneiromancy, divination by means of dreams.

oneroso, sa [o-nay-ro'-so, sah], *a.* Burdensome, troublesome, onerous (pesado).

onfacino, na [on-fah-thee'-no, nah], *a.* Extracted from green olives (aceite).

onice *f.* ónix, *m.* [o'-ne-thay, o'-ne-kay]. Onyx, a precious stone.

onomatopéyico, ca [o-no-mah-to-pay'-ye-co, cah], *a.* Onomatopeic, imitative in sound.

onomatopeya [o-no-mah-to-pay'-yah], *f.* Onomatopoeia, the selection of words to imitate natural sounds.

onoquiles [o-no-kee'-les], *f. (Bot.)* Dyer's bugloss, alkanet.

ontología [on-to-lo-hee'-ah], *f.* Ontology, metaphysics.

ontologista [on-to-lo-hees'-tah], *m.* Ontologist, metaphysician.

onza [on'-thah], *f.* 1. Ounce, the twelfth part of a pound, troy weight, or nineteenth of a Castilian pound. 2. Ounce, lynx.

onzavo, va [on-thah'-vo, vah], *a.* Eleventh. *-m.* Eleventh part.

opa [o'-pah], *f.* A hole left in a newly-built wall on removing the scaffold.*-a. (Amer.)* 1. Dumb, silent. 2. Silly, foolish.

opacamente [o-pah-cah-men-tay], *adv.* Obscurely, darkly.

opacidad [o-pah-the-dahd'], *f.* 1. Opacity, cloudiness, darkness. 2. *(Fig.)* Dullness, lifelessness (oscuridad). 3. *(Fig.)* Gloominess (melancolía).

opaco, ca [o-pah'-co, cah], *a.* 1. Opacous, opaque. 2. Melancholy, gloomy. 3. *(Fig.)* Dull, lustreless, lifeless (oscuro).

opalino, na [o-pah-lee'-no, nah], *a.* Opaline, opalescent.

ópalo [o'-pah-lo], *m.* Opal, a precious stone.

opción [op-the-on'], *f.* 1. Option, choice (elección). 2. Right to an office or dignity (derecho). 3. Chance, likelihood (posibilidad). **No hay opción,** there is no choice. **Con opción a 8 más,** with an option on 8 more.

opcional [op-the-o-nahl'], *a.* Optional.

ópera [o'-pay-rah], *f.* Opera, a musical drama.

operable [o-pay-rah'-blay], *a.* 1. Capable of operating. 2. Operable, practicable.

operación [o-pay-rah-the-on'], *f.* 1. Operation, the act of exercising some power or faculty. 2. Operation, agency, effect or action produced. 3. *(Surg.)* Operation. *(Com.)* Transaction, venture. **Operaciones de banco,** banking business. **Operaciones marítimas,** shipping trade or business. 4. A chemical process. *-pl.* 1. Operations of an army. 2. Works, deeds, actions. **Operaciones de rescate,** rescue operations. **Operaciones en bolsa,** stock-exchange transactions.

operador, ra [o-pay-rah-dor'], *m & f.* 1. Surgical operator. 2. *(Min.)* Prospector. 3. Cameraman (rodaje); projectionist (proyección). 3. *(Comput.)* Operator. **Operador de equipos informáticos,** computer (equipment) operator. **Operador de introducción de datos,** data-entry operator. **Operador de procesadores de texto,** word processing operator.

operante [o-pay-rahn'-tay], *pa. & n.* Operator; operating.

operar [o-pay-rar'], *va.* 1. To produce, to bring about (cambio, cura). 2. *(Med.)* To operate. 3. *(LAm.)* To use, to operate (máquina); to manage (negocio). **Operar a uno de apendicitis,** to operate on somebody for appendicitis. *-vn.* 1. To operate, to act. 2. *(Com.)* To operate, to deal. *-vr.* 1. To occur (ocurrir). 2. *(Med.)* To have an operation.

operario [o-pay-rah'-re-o], *m.* 1. Operator, laborer. 2. Friar who assists sick or dying persons.

operativo, va [o-pay-rah-tee´-vo, vah], *a.* Operative. *-m.* *(LAm.)* Operation. **Operativo policial**, police operation.

operculado, da [o-per-coo-lah´-do, dah], *a.* Operculate, covered with a lid.

opercular [o-per-coo-lar´], *a.* Opercular, serving as a lid.

opérculo [o-perr´-coo-lo], *m.* Operculum, lid, cover of a pore or cell.

opereta [o-pay-ray´-tah], *f.* Operetta, a light opera.

operista [o-pay-rees´-tah], *com.* Opera singer.

operoso, sa [o-pay-ro´-so, sah], *a.* Laborious, operose.

opiado, da [o-pe-ah´-do, dah], *a.* Opiate, narcotic.

opiata [o-pe-ah´-tah], *f.* Opiate.

opiate, ta [o-pe-ah-to, tah], *a.* & *a.* Opiate narcotic.

opilación [o-pe-lah-the-on´], *f.* 1. Oppilation, obstruction of the vessels of the body. 2. *(coll.)* Amenorrhoea, abnormally scanty or obstructed menstruation.

opilar [o-pe-lar´], *va.* To oppilate, to obstruct.

opilativo, va [o-pe-lah-tee´-vo, vah], *a.* Obstructive, oppilative.

opimo, ma [o-pe´-mo, mah], *a.* Rich, fruitful, abundant.

opinable [o-pe-nah´-blay], *a.* Disputable, problematical.

opinante [o-pe-nahn´-tay], *pa.* & *a.* Arguing; opinionated.

opinante [o-pe-nahn´-tay], *m.* Arguer.

opinar [o-pe-nar´], *vn.* To argue, to judge, to form one opinion, to opine (dar opinión). **Opinar que...**, to think that. **Fueron opinando uno tras otro**, they gave their opinions in turn.

opinativo, va [o-ge-nah-tee´-vo, vah], *a.* Opinionative, opinative.

opinión [o-pe-ne-on´], *f.* 1. Opinion, persuasion of the mind, judgment. 2. Reputation, character. **Hacer opinión**, to form an opinion, to be a man whose opinion is an authority. **Cambiar de opinión**, to change one´s mind.

opinioncilla, ita [o-pe-ne-on-theel´-lyah], *f. dim.* Opinion founded on slight grounds.

opio [o´-pe-o], *m.* Opium.

opíparo, ra [o-pee´-pah-ro, rah], *a.* Opiparous, sumptuous (comida).

oploteca [o-plo-tay´-cah], *f.* Museum of ancient, rare, or valuable weapons.

ópol [o´-pol], *m.* Juice, sap of a plant, in general. *(Gr.)*

oponente [o-po-nayn´-tay], *a.* Opposing (contrario), contrary. *-m* & *f.* Opponent (adversario).

oponer [o-po-nerr´], *va.* 1. To oppose, to go against, to contradict. 2. To oppose, to object in a disputation. *-vr.* 1. To oppose, to be adverse, to act against, to be contrary. 2. To front, to be opposite to. 3. To steed in competition with another. **Oponerse la razón a la pasión**, to use reason against passion. **Yo no me opongo**, I don´t oppose it. *(Yo opongo, oponga; opuse, opusiera; opondré*; from *Oponer.* V. PONER.)

opopónaca, opopónace [o-po-po´-nah-cah, o-po-po´-nah-thay], *f. (Bot.)* Rough parsnip.

opopónaco, opopónax [o-po-po´-nah-co], *m.* Opoponax, a gum resin obtained from the rough parsnip.

oportunamente [o-por-too´-nah-men-tay], *adv.* Opportunely, conveniently.

oportunidad [o-por-too-ne-dahd´], *f.* 1. Opportunity, convenience, appropriateness of time or circumstances. 2. Opportuneness (cualidad); timeliness; appropriateness. **Igualdad de oportunidades**, equality of opportunity. **En dos oportunidades**, on two occasions.

oportunismo [o-por-too-nees´-mo], *m.* Opportunism.

oportunista [o-por-too-nees´-tah], *m.* & *f.* Opportunist.

oportuno, na [o-por-too´-no, nah], *a.* Convenient (adecuado), seasonable, opportune (buena hora), appropriate (apropiado), expedient (aconsejable). **Una respuesta oportuna**, a suitable reply.

oposición [o-po-se-the-on´], *f.* 1. Opposition, situation so as to face something opposed, counterview. 2. Opposition, contrariety of affection, of interest, of party, of measures, of meaning, etc. 3. Opposition, the members of a legislative house who oppose the measures of the ministry. 4. (Fine arts) Contrast. 5. Competition among competitors for a prebend, professorship, etc. 6. *(Ast.)* Opposition between two heavenly bodies. **Hacer oposiciones**, to be a candidate for.

opositar [o-po-se-tar´], *vn.* To go in for a public competition.

opositor, ra [o-po-se-tor´, rah], *m.* & *f.* Opposer, opponent. *-a.* Opposing (contrario). **El líder opositor**, the leader of the opposition.

opresión [o-pray-se-on´], *f.* 1. Oppression, cruelty, severity, coercion, hardship. 2. Oppression, pressure.

opresivamente [o-pray-se-vah-men-tay], *adv.* Oppressively, overwhelmingly.

opresivo, va [o-pray-see´-vo, vah], *a.* 1. Oppressive, cruel. 2. Oppressive, heavy, overwhelming.

opresor [o-pray-sor´], *m.* Oppressor; extortioner. *-a.* Oppressive, tyrannical.

oprimir [o-pre-meer´], *va.* 1. To oppress by hardship or severity. 2. To overpower, to overwhelm, to subdue. 3. To crush, to press, to squeeze (presionar). 4. To be too tight for (ropa).

oprobio [o-pro-be-o], *m.* Opprobrium, ignominy, shame, injury.

oprobioso, sa [o-pro-be-o´-so, sah], *a.* Opprobrious, reproachful.

optar [op-tar´], *va.* To choose, to select. **Optar entre**, to choose between. **Poder optar**, to apply for.

optativo [op-tah-tee´-vo], *m. (Gram.)* Optative, one of the modes of verbs. *-a.* Optional (opcional).

óptica [op´-te-cah], *f.* 1. Optics, the science of light and vision (ciencia). 2. Optician´s (tienda).

óptico, ca [op´-te-co, cah], *a.* Optic, optical, visual. *-m.* Optician.

óptimamente [op´-te-mah-men-tay], *adv.* In the best way, perfectly.

optimismo [op-te-mees´-mo], *m.* Optimism.

optimista [op-te-mees´-tah], *com.* Optimist.

óptimo, ma [op´-te-mo, mah], *a.* Best, the best, optimum, eminently good.

optómetra [op-to´-may-trah], *m.* Optometrist.

optomotría [op-to-may-tree´-ah], *f.* Optometry.

opuestamente [o-poo-ays´-tah-men-tay], *adv.* Oppositely.

opuesto, ta [o-poo-es´-to, tah], *a.* Opposite (ángulo, lado), contrary (opinión), adverse. *-pp. irr.* of OPONER.

opugnación [o-poog-nah-the-on´], *f.* Oppugnancy, opposition.

opugnador [o-poog-nah-dor´], *m.* Oppugner, opposer.

opugnar [o-poog-nar´], *va.* To oppugn; to impugn, to attack, to resist, to contradict.

opulencia [o-poo-len´-the-ah], *f.* Opulence, wealth, affluence.

opulentamente [o-poo-len-tay], *adv.* Opulently.

opulento, ta [o-poo-len´-to, tah], *a.* Opulent, wealthy, rich, affluent.

opuncia [o-poon´-the-ah], *f.* Prickly pear cactus.

opúsculo [o-poos´-coo-lo], *m.* A short, compendious treatise.

oquedal [o-kay-dahl´], *m.* Plantation of lofty trees.

ora [o´-rah], *adv.* At present. V. AHORA. Whether.

oración [o-rah-the-on´], *f.* 1. Oration (discurso), harangue, declamation. 2. Prayer, supplication. 3. Sentence: in grammar, an expression composed of one or more words which makes perfect sense. **Partes de la oración**, the parts of speech. 4. Position, a proposition which denies or affirms a thing. 5. A part of the mass. 6. *(LAm.)* Pagan invocation, magic charm. **Las oraciones**, sun-setting, the Angelus, when the angel's salutation to the Virgin is repeated by the people; also, the bell which calls to this prayer. **Oración compuesta**, complex sentence. **Pronunciar una oración**, to make a speech.

oracional [o-rah-the-o-nahl´], *m.* Prayerbook.

oracionero [o-rah-the-o-nay´-ro], *m.* He who goes praying from door to door.

oráculo [o-rah´-coo-lo], *m.* 1. Oracle, something delivered by supernatural wisdom. 2. Oracle, the place where, the determinations of heaven are inquired. 3. Oracle, person famed for wisdom.

orada [o-rah'-dah], *f V.* DORADA.

orador, ra [o-rah-dor', rah], *m. & f.* 1. Orator, a public speaker. 2. Panegyrist, encomiast, preacher.

oral [o-rahl'], *a.* Oral, delivered by the mouth.

oralmente [o-ral-men'-tay], *adv.* Orally, by mouth.

orangután [o-ran-goo-tahn'], *m.* Orang-utan (orang-outang), an anthropoid ape of Borneo.

orar [o-rar'], *vn. & a.* 1. To harangue. 2. To pray. 3. To ask, to demand.

orate [o-rah'-tay], *com.* Lunatic, madman. **Casa de orates**, a mad-house.

oratoria [o-rah-to'-re-ah], *f.* Oratory, eloquence.

oratoriamente [o-rah-to-re-ah-men-tay], *adv.* Oratorically.

oratorio [o-rah-to'-re-o], *m.* 1. Oratory, a private place for prayer. 2. Oratorio, a dramatic musical composition upon a sacred subject. It receives its name from the Oratory in Rome. 3. A congregation of presbyters.

oratorio, ria [o-rah-to'-re-o, ah], *a.* Oratorial, rhetorical, oratorical.

orbe [or'-bay], *m.* 1. Orb, sphere. 2. Orb, terrestrial sphere, celestial body. 3. Orb, circle described by any of the mundane spheres. 4. Globe-fish.

orbicular [or-be-coo-lar'], *a.* Orbicular, circular.

órbita [or'-be-tah], *f.* 1. Orbit, the path of a planet. 2. Cavity in which the eye is placed, orbit. 3. *(Mex.)* Socket.

orbitales [or-be-tah'-les], *a. & m. pl.* Orbital: used of the bones which form the orbit of the eye.

orca [or'-cah], *f.* Grampus, orca.

orcaneta [or-cah-nay'-tah], *f. (Bot.)* Dyer's bugloss, alkanet.

orchilla [or-cheel'-lyah], *f. (Bot.)* Archil, roccella, true dyer's orchil.

orco [or'-co], *m.* 1. *(Zool.)* Grampus. *V.* ORCA. 2. Hell.

orcotomía [or-co-to-mee'-ah], *f.* Orchotomy, castration.

órdago [or'-dah-go], **De órdago**, first class.

ordalía [or-dah-lee'-ah], *f.* Ordeal, a trial by fire or water.

ordeata [or-day-ah'-tah], *a.* 1. Peeled barley. 2. Ptisan, a medical drink.

orden [or'-den], *com.* 1. Order, regularity, settled mode. 2. Order, method, course, rule, regulation. 3. Order, class. 4. Order, a society of dignified persons. 5. Order a religious fraternity. 6. The sixth sacrament of the Roman Catholic church. 7. Arrangement of chords in a musical instrument. 8. Order, mandate, precept-command. 9. Relation of one thing to another. 10. Order of architecture. 11. *(Mex.)* Order (pedido). 12. *(Mex.)* Portion (porción). **Por su orden**, in its turn, successively. **No haber orden de conseguir algo**, *(coll.)* to have no means or possibility of obtaining a thing. **De primer orden**, first-rate. **Fuera de orden**, out of order. **Orden público**, public order. **Orden del día**, order of the day. **Dar una orden**, to give an order. **Orden religiosa**, religious order.

ordenación [or-day-nah-the-on'], *f.* 1. Methodical arrangement; disposition, ordination. 2. Edict, ordinance. 3. Clerical ordination. 4. Part of architecture which treats of the capacity which every room should have. 5. Part of the composition of a picture.

ordenada [or-day-nah'-dah], *f. (Math.)* Ordinate, a line drawn perpendicular to the axis of a curve.

ordenadamente [or-day-nah'-dah-men-tay], *adv.* Orderly.

ordenado, da [or-day-nah'-do, dah], *a.* Ordained, ordinate, orderly (en orden), just. *-pp.* of ORDENAR.

ordenador, ra [or-day-nah-dor', rah], *m. & f.* One who ordains, ordainer; orderer. *V.* COMISARIO. *-m.* Computer. **Ordenador central**, mainframe computer. **Ordenador de gestión**, business computer. **Ordenador para juegos**, game computer. **Ordenador para jugar al ajedrez**, chess computer.

ordenamiento [or-day-nah-me-en'-to], *m.* 1. The act and effect of ordaining, regulating, or putting in order. 2. Law, edict, ordinance.

ordenando, ordenante [or-day-nahn'-do, or-day-nahn'-tay], *m.* He who is ready to receive holy orders.

ordenanza [or-day-nahn'-thah], *f.* 1. Method, order. 2. Law, statute, ordinance (decreto); command; ordination. 3. *m.* Orderly man, a corporal or soldier who attends a commanding officer. **Estar de ordenanza**, to be on duty, to be in waiting.

ordenar [or-day-nar'], *va.* 1. To arrange (poner en prueba), to put in order, to class, to dispose. 2. To order (mandar), to command, to enact. 3. To ordain, to regulate; to direct. 4. To order, to confer holy orders. **Ordenar sus asuntos**, to put one´s affairs in order. *-vr.* To be ordained, to receive holy orders.

ordeñadero [or-day-nyah-day'-ro], *m.* Milk-pail.

ordeñador, ra [or-day-nyah-dor', rah], *m. & f.* Milker, one who milks animals. *-f.* Milking machine.

ordeñar [or-day-nyar'], *va.* 1. To milk animals. 2. To pick olives by hand.

ordinal [or-de-nahl'], *a.* Ordinal, noting order. *-m.* Ordinal, ritual; a book containing orders.

ordinariamente [or-de-nah'-re-ah-men-tay], *adv.* Frequently; ordinarily; customarily; rudely.

ordinariez [or-de-nah-re-eth'], *f.* 1. *(coll.)* Low rank of a person; common stock. 2. Rough manners, rude behavior.

ordinario, ria [or-de-nah'-re-o, ah], *a.* 1. Ordinary (normal), common, usual, customary, familiar. 2. Coarse, mean, of low rank, vulgar, rude (grosero). **Decreto, provisión** or **auto ordinario**, decree given by a judge at the instance of one of the contending parties. **Son gente muy ordinaria**, they´re very common people.

ordinario [or-de-nah'-re-o], *m.* 1. Ordinary, settled establishment of daily expense: commonly applied to the expenses of the table. 2. Ordinary, established judge of ecclesiastical causes. 3. Ordinary, a bishop. 4. Mail, post, or courier, who goes and arrives at stated times (recadero). 5. The carrier, muleteer, or driver of beasts of burden, who usually goes and comes from one place to another. 6. Ordinary, a book containing the prayers of the mass. **De ordinario**, regularly, commonly.

orear [o-ray-ar'], *va.* 1. To cool, to refresh (viento). 2. To dry, to air, to expose to the air. *-vr.* To take the air, to take an airing, to air (ropa).

orégano [o-ray'-gah-no], *m. (Bot.)* Wild marjoram; *(Mex.)* grass.

oreja [o-ray'-hah], *f.* 1. Auricle, the external ear. 2. Ear, the organ of hearing. 3. Flap of a shoe for adjusting to the instep (zapato). 4. Flatterer, tale-bearer. 5. *(Mech.)* Lug, flange, ear, a projecting piece of certain instruments, as the claw of a hammer, the barb of an arrow, the head of a nail. 6. *(LAm.)* Curiosity. 7. *(LAm.)* Grass (soplón). **Con las orejas caídas**, crestfallen, down in the mouth; dejected. **Bajar las orejas**, to yield; to humble oneself. **Poner las orejas coloradas**, to make one blush to the ears. **Verle las orejas al lobo**, to escape from great danger.

orejano, na [o-ray-hah'-no, nah], *a.* 1. *(Amer.)* Ownerless, unbranded: said of animals. In Spain, motherless: said of a calf. 2. *(Carib.)* Cautious (cauteloso). 3. *(CAm. Carib.)* Peasant, countryman.

orejeado, da [o-ray-hay-ah'-do, dah], *a.* Informed, advised, instructed. *-pp.* of OREJEAR.

orejear [o-ray-hay-ar'], *vn.* 1. To shake the ears (caballos). 2. To act with reluctance. 3. *(Prov.)* To whisper in the ear. 4. *(Cono Sur)* To uncover one´s cards one by one. 5. *(And. Carib. Cono Sur)* To suspect (recelar).

orejera [o-ray-hay'-rah], *f.* Earmuff.

orejeta [o-ray-hay'-tah], *f.* Each of the two wooden languets which the scabbard of a sword carries within.

orejita [o-ray-hee'-tah], *f. dim.* A small auricle or external ear.

orejón [o-ray-hone'], *m.* 1. Slice of dried apple or other fruit as **Orejones de durazno**, dried peaches. 2. Pull by the ear. 3. A young nobleman of Peru, educated for public employments. 4. *(And. Mex.)* Goitre. 5. *(And.)* Herdsman (vaquero); plainsman (llanero). 6. *(Mex.)* Cuckold. *-a.* 1. *(And.)* Absent-minded (distraído). 2. *(And. CAm. Mex.)* Rough, coarse.

orejudo, da [o-ray-hoo´-do, dah], *a.* Flap-eared, long-eared.

orellana [o-rel-lyah'-nah], *f. (Bot.)* Arnatto or arnotto, a drug of dyestuff; prepared from the seeds of the arnotta.

oreo [o-ray'-o], *m.* Breeze, fresh air.

orfandad, orfanidad [or-fan-dahd'], *f.* 1. Orphanage, state of orphans; want of friends or support. 2. *(Fig.)* Forlornness, scarcity (escasez), paucity.

orfebrería [or-fay-bray-ree'-ah], *f.* Gold or silver twist or braid.

orfeón [or-fay-on'], *m.* Glee club, choral society.

órfico, ca [or´-fe-co, cah], *a.* Orphean, relating to Orpheus.

organdí [or-gan-dee'], *m.* Organdy.

organero [or-gah-nay´-ro], *m.* Organ-maker, organ-builder.

orgánicamente [or-gah'-ne-cah-men-tay], *adv.* Organically.

orgánico, ca [or-gah´-ne-co, cah], *a.* 1. Organic, organical, consisting of various parts. 2. Organic, relating to the organs. 3. Harmonious.

organigrama [or-gah-ne-grah'-mah], *m.* Flow chart; organization chart.

organillero [or-gah-nil-lyay´-ro], *m.* Organ grinder.

organillo [or-gah-neel´-lyo], *m. dim.* Barrel-organ, hand-organ.

organismo [or-gah-nes'-mo], *m.* 1. Organism, an organized or living being. 2. Social organization. **Organismos de gobierno,** organs of government.

organista [or-gah-nees'-tah], *com. (Mus.)* Organist.

organizable [or-gah-ne-thah´-blay], *a.* Organizable, capable of organization.

organización [or-gah-ne-thah-the-on'], *f.* 1. Organization, construction. 2. Order, arrangement. **Organización de las Naciones Unidas,** United Nations Organization.

organizador, ra [or-gah-ne-thah-dor', rah] *a.* Organizing. **Comité organizador,** organizing committee. *-m. & f.* Organizer.

organizar [or-gah-ne-thar´], *va.* 1. To tune an organ. 2. To organize, to form organically.

órgano [or´-gah-no], *m.* 1. Organ, a musical wind instrument, a pipe organ. 2. Organ, natural instrument, as the tongue is the organ of speech. 3. Machine for cooling liquors. 4. *(Amer.)* The high round fluted cactus, called so because it resembles an organ-pipe. 5. *(Met.)* Organ or medium by which a thing is communicated.

organografía [or-gah-no-grah-fee´-ah], *f.* Description of organs; organography.

orgasmo [or-gahs'-mo], *m. (Med.)* Orgasm.

orgía [or-hee´-ah], *f.* Frantic revel.

orgullo [or-gool´-lyo], *m.* 1. Pride, haughtiness, loftiness. 2. Activity, briskness.

orgullosamente [or-gool-lyo'-sah-men-tay], *adv.* Haughtily.

orgulloso, sa [or-gool-lyo´-so, sah], *a.* 1. Proud, haughty, lofty, lordly. 2. Brisk, active. **Estar orgulloso de,** to be proud to.

orientación [o-re-en-tah-the-on'], *f.* 1. Orientation, position, exposure. 2. Bearings. 3. Orientation, guidance. **Orientación profesional,** vocational guidance. **Una casa con orientación norte,** a house with a northely orientation. **Lo hizo para mi orientación,** he did it for my guidance.

oriental [o-re-en-tahl'], *a.* 1. Oriental, eastern. 2. *(Cono Sur)* Uruguayan; *(Cuba)* Oriente province. *m.* An oriental.

orientar [o-re-en-tar'], *va.* 1. To turn a thing to the eastward. 2. To orientate, to orient; to find the petition of with regard to the cardinal points. **Orientar una vela,** *(Naut.)* to trim a sail. 3. To guide (guiar), to direct. **Me ha orientado en la materia,** he has guided me through the subject. *-vr.* 1. To know the place which is occupied, to find one's bearings (persona). 2. To confide the course to be taken.

orientativo [o-re-ayn-tah-tee´-vo], *a.* Guiding, illustrative.

oriente [o-re-en´-tay], *m.* 1. Orient, the east; the Levant. 2. Source, origin. 3. Youth, juvenile age. 4. East wind (viento). 5. Orient; Asia, and the contiguous regions of Europe and Africa.

orificación [o-re-fe-cah-the-on'], *f.* Filling of a tooth (con oro, plata.)

orificar [o-re-fe-car'], *va.* To fill a tooth (con oro, plata.)

orífice [o-ree'-fe-thay], *m.* Goldsmith.

orificia [o-re-fee'-the-ah], *f.* Art and profession of a goldsmith.

orificio [o-re-fee'-the-o], *m.* Orifice, mouth, aperture. 2. **Orificio de centrado** *(Comput.),* hub.

origen [o-ree'-hen], *m.* 1. Origin, source, motive, fountain, original. 2. Natal country; family, lineage, extraction. 3. Beginning or moral cause of things. **País de origen,** country of origin.

original [o-re-he-nahl'], *a.* 1. Original, primitive. 2. *(coll.)* Extravagant.

original [o-re-he-nahl'], *m.* 1. Original, first copy, archetype. 2. Source, fountain.

originalidad [o-re-he-nah-le-dahd'], *f. (coll.)* Originality.

originalmente [o-re-he-nahl'-men-tay], *adv.* Originally, radically.

originar [o-re-he-nar'], *va.* To originate, to bring into existence. *-vr.* To originate, to take existence, to descend, to derive existence from, to cause, to occasion.

originariamente [o-re-he-nah'-re-ah-men-tay], *adv.* Radically, originally.

originario, ria [o-re-he-nah'-re-o, ah] *a.* Original (original), primary, primitive. **Ser originario de,** to originate from. **País originario,** country of origin.

originario [o-re-he-nah'-re-o], *m.* Native, descendent.

orilla [o-reel'-lyah], *f.* 1. Limit, extent, border, margin. 2. Edge of stuff or cloth. 3. Bank of a river, shore of the sea. 4. Extent, limit of something not material. 5. *(Ant.)* Footpath in a street, avoiding mud. 6. *(LAm.)* Pavement (acera). **A la orilla,** near a place, on the brink. **Orilla del mar,** seashore.

orilla [o-rel-lyah], *f.* A brisk wind or fresh breeze. **Hacer buena** or **mala orilla,** andalusian expressions for good or bad weather.

orillar [o-reel-lyar'], *va.* 1. To arrange, to conclude, to expedite, to put in order. 2. To leave a selvage on cloth. 3. To adorn the border of some fabric or garment. *-vr. & vn.* To approach or reach the shore.

orillo [o-reel'-lyo], *m.* Selvage or list of cloth.

orín [o-reen'], *m.* 1. Rust, the red oxide of iron. 2. Stain, taint of guilt; defect. 3. *pl.* V. ORINA.

orina [o-ree'-nah], *f.* Urine.

orinal [o-re-nahl'], *m.* Urinal, chamber-vessel, chamber-pot.

orinar [o-re-nar'], *vn.* To urinate, to make water.

oriniento, ta [o-re-ne-en'-to, tah], *a.* Rusty, moldy.

orinque [o-reen'-kay], *m. (Naut.)* Buoyrope.

oriol [o-re-ole'], *m.* Golden oriole or thrush.

orión [o-re-on'], *m. (Ast.)* Orion, a conspicuous constellation.

oriundo, da [o-re-oon'-do, dah], *a.* Originated, derived from.

orla [or'-lah], *f.* 1. List, selvage, border, fringe, trimming. 2. *(Her.)* Orle. 3. *(typ.)* An ornamental border.

orlador, ra [or-lah-dor', rah], *m. & f.* Borderer, one who makes borders.

orladura [or-lah-doo´ rah], *f.* Border, edging, list.

orlar [or-lar'], *va.* To border, to garnish with an edging.

orlo [or'-lo], *m.* An organ-stop, named after an ancient reed-instrument.

orlón [or-lone'], *m.* Orlon.

ormesi [or-may-see'], *m.* A kind of silk stuff.

ornadamente [or-nah'-dah-men-tay], *adv.* Ornamentally.

ornado, da [or-nah'-do, dah], *a. & pp.* of **Ornar.** Ornamented, ornate.

ornamentar [or-nah-men-tar'], *va.* To adorn, to embellish, to ornament, to bedeck.

ornamento [or-nah-men´-to], *m.* Ornament, embellishment, decoration. *-pl.* 1. Sacred vestments. 2. Frets, mouldings, etc., in architectural works. 3. The moral qualities of any person.

ornar [or-nar'], *va*. To adorn, to embellish, to garnish.
ornato [or-nah'-to], *m*. Dress, apparel; ornament, decoration.
ornis [or'-nees], *m*. A sort of muslin from India.
ornitolito [or-ne-to-lee'-to], *m*. Part of a bird petrified.
ornitología [or-ne-to-lo-hee'-ah], *f*. Ornithology.
ornitológico, ca [or-ne-to-lo'-he-co, cah], *a*. Ornithological.
ornitólogo [or-ne-to'-lo-go], *m*. Ornithologist.
ornitomancia [or-ne-to-mahn'-the-ah], *f*., divination by the flight of birds.
ornitorrinco [or-ne-tor-ren'-co], *m*. Platypus.
oro [o'-ro], *m*. 1. Gold. 2. Gold color (pelo de mujer). 3. Ornaments, or trinkets made of gold. 4. Gold, money, wealth, riches. 5. *pl*.—Diamonds, a suit at cards. **A peso de oro,** to succeed by means of money. **Como oro en paño,** we show our values of things by the care we take of them. **Oro en pasta, bruto o virgen,** bullion. **Oro en libritos, libritos de oro fino,** gold-leaf. **Oro en polvo,** gold-dust. **Oro mate,** gold-size. **Como un oro, como mil oros,** as clean and beautiful as gold. **No es oro todo lo que reluce,** *(Prov.)* all is not gold that glitters. **Oro es lo que oro vale,** gold is worth what it will buy; other things than money have value.
orobanquia [o-ro-bahn'-ke-ah], *f*. Broom-rape; a parasitic, gamopetalous plant which sometimes destroys a whole crop, especially of beans.
orografía [o-ro-grah-fee'-ah], *f*. Orography, description of mountains.
orología [o-ro-lo-hee'-ah], *f*. Orology, a treatise on mountains.
orondo, da [o-ron'-do, dah], *a*. 1. Pompous, showy: hollow. 2. *(LAm.)* Calm, serene.
oropel [o-ro-pel'], *m*. 1. A thin plate of brass, latten-brass. 2. Tinsel, anything showy and of little value.
oropelero [o-ro-pay-lay'-ro], *m*. Brass-worker.
oropéndola [o-ro-pen'-do-lah], *f*. Loriot, golden oriole.
oropimente [o-ro-pe-men'-tay], *m*. Orpiment, a sulphide of arsenic.
oroya [o-ro'-yah], *f*. *(Amer. Peru)* Hanging basket or sling for carrying passengers and goods over rope bridges; it is generally made of leather.
orozuz [o-ro-thooth'], *m*. *(Bot.)* Licorice or liquorice.
orquesta [or-kes'-tah], *f*. 1. Orchestra, a body of musicians using stringed and wind-instruments. 2. Orchestra, place in a playhouse for musicians.
orquestación [or-kes-tah-the-on'], *f*. Orchestration.
órquide [or'-ke-day], *f*. *(Bot.)* Orchid.
orquídeo, dea [or-kee'-day-o, ah], *a*. Orchidaceous.
orquitis [or-kee'-tis], *f*. Orchitis, inflammation of the testicle.
orraca [or-rah'-cah], *f*. A kind of spirit distilled from the coconut.
ortega [or-tay'-gah], *f*. Hazel-grouse.
ortiga [or-tee'-gah], *f*. *(Bot.)* Nettle.
ortigaje [or-te-gah'-hay], *m*. A disease of grape-vines marked by the yellow color of the leaves.
ortivo, va [or-tee'-vo, vah], *a*. *(Ast.)* Oriental, eastern, ortive.
orto [or'-to], *m*. Rising of a star.
ortodoncia [o-to-don-the-ah], *f*. Orthodontics.
ortodóntico [or-to-don'-te-co], *m*. *(Med.)* Orthodontist.
ortodoxia [or-to-dok'-se-ah], *f*. Orthodoxy: (Catholicism).
ortodoxo, xa [or-to-dok'-so, sah], Orthodox, not heretical.
ortografía [or-to-grah-fee'-ah], *f*. Orthography.
ortográficamente [or-to-grah'-fe-cah-men-tay], *adv*. Orthographically.
ortográfico, ca [or-to-grah'-fe-co, cah], *a*. Orthographical.
ortógrafo [or-to'-grah-fo], *m*. Orthographer.
ortología [or-to-lo-hee'-ah], *f*. Orthoepy, art of pronunciation.
ortopedia [or-to-pay-de-ah], *f*. Orthopaedia, orthopaedics, art of correcting deformities in the human body, especially in children.
ortopédico, ca [or-to-pay'-de-co, cah], *a*. Orthopaedic, relating to orthopaedia.

ortopedista [or-to-pay-dees'-tah], *m*. *(Med.)* Orthopaedist.
ortóptero [or-top'-tay-ro], *a*. Orthopeterous. -*m. pl*. The orthoptera, an order of insects, having wings folded lengthwise, as the common locust.
oruga [o-roo'-gah], *f*. 1. *(Bot.)* Rocket, an herb of the mustard family. 2. Caterpillar.
orujo [o-roo'-ho], *m*. Skin or peel of pressed grapes.
orvalle [or-vahl'-lyay], *m*. *(Bot.)* V. GALLOCRESTA.
orza [or'-thah], *f*. 1. Gallipot, a jar for sweetmeats, small earthen pot, crock. 2. *(Naut.)* Luff.
orzaderas [or-thah-day'-ras], *f. pl*. *(Naut.)* Lee-boards.
orzaga [or-thah'-gah], *f*. *(Bot.)* Orach.
orzar [or-thar'], *vn*. *(Naut.)* To luff, to steer closer to the wind.
orzuelo [or-thoo-ay'-lo], *m*. 1. Stye, a small inflamed swelling on the eyelid; a hordeolum. 2. Snare to catch birds; a trap for catching wild beasts.
os [ose], *pron*. You or ye. It is placed before and after verbs, and used instead of *vosotros*. **Os digo,** I tell you. **Os bendigo,** I bless you. **Vosotros os vestís,** you dress yourselves. 2. Each other (recíproco). **Os escribís,** you write each other.
osa [o'-sah], *f*. She-bear. **Osa mayor,** ursa major.
osadamente [osah'-dah-men-tay], *adv*. Boldly, daringly.
osadía [o-sah-dee'-ah], *f*. 1. Courage, boldness, intrepidity, hardiness. 2. Zeal, fervor, ardor.
osado, da [o-sah'-do, dah], *a*. Daring, bold, high-spirited, high-mettled. -*pp*. of OSAR.
osambre [o-sahm'-bray], *m*. **Osamenta** [o-sah-men'-tah], *f*. A skeleton.
osar [o-sar'], *vn*. 1. To dare, to venture, to outdare. 2. To imagine, to fancy.
osario [o-sah'-re-o], *m*. 1. Charnel-house. 2. Any place where there are bones.
oscilación [os-the-lah-the-on'], *f*. Oscillation, vibration of a pendulum, swing (vaivén); winding (luz); fluctuation (precios).
oscilador [os-the-lah-dor], *m*. Oscillator.
oscilar [os-the-lar'], *vn*. 1. To oscillate, to vibrate as a pendulum (péndulo), to rock (mecerse). 2. To fluctuate. 3. To hesitate (persona). **Los precios oscilan mucho,** prices are fluctuating a lot.
oscilatorio, ria [os-the-lah-to'-re-o, ah], *a*. Oscillatory, vibratory.
oscitante [os-the-tahn'-tay], *a*. *(Med.)* Oscitant, gaping, yawning.
osco, ca [os'-co, cah], *a*. Oscan, belonging to this ancient region of Italy.
osculación [os-coo-lah-the-on'], *f*. *(Geom.)* Osculation.
osculatorio, ria [os-coo-lah-to'-re-o, ah], *a*. *(Geom.)* Osculatory.
ósculo [os'-coo-lo], *m*. Kiss. V. BESO.
oscuramente [os-coo-rah-men-tay], *adv*. V. OBSCURAMENTE.
oscurantismo [os-coo-ran-tees'-mo], *m*. Antiquated ideas; «old fogyism.»
oscuras (A) [ah os-coo'-ras], *adv*. V. A OBSCURAS.
oscurecer [os-coo-ray-therr'], *va*. V. OBSCURECER.
oscurecimiento [os-coo-ray-the-me-en'-to], *m*. V. OBSCURECIMIENTO.
oscuridad [os-coo-re-dahd'], *f*. V. OBSCURIDAD.
oscuro, ra [os-coo'-ro, rah], *a*. V. OBSCURO.
osecico, illo, osezuelo [o-say-thee'-co], *m. dim*. Small bone.
óseo, a [oh'-say-o, ah], *a*. Osseous, bony.
osera [o-say'-rah], *f*. Den of bears.
osezno [o-seth'-no], *m*. Whelp or cub of a bear.
osfresia [os-fray'-se-ah], *f*. The sense of smell.
osfrésico, ca [os-fray'-se-co, cah], *a*. Olfactory, relating to the sense of smell.
osículo [o-see'-coo-lo], *m. dim*. Ossicle, a diminutive bone.
osificación [o-se-fe-cah-the-on'], *f*. Ossification.
osificarse [o-se-fe-car'-say], *vr*. To ossify.
osífico, ca [o-see'-fe-co, cah], *a*. Ossific.

osmazoma [os-mah-tho'-mah], *f.* or **Osmazomo**, *m.* Osmazome, a substance contained in meat, imparting taste and odor to broths.

ósmico [os'-me-co], *a.* Osmic, relating to osmium.

osmio [os'-me-o], *m. (Min.)* Osmium.

oso [o'-so], *m.* 1. Bear. **Oso hormiguero**, ant-eater. **Oso colmenero**, bear that robs beehives. **Piel de oso**, bear-skin. **Oso de peluche**, teddy bear. 2. *(Carib.)* Braggart; bully.

ososo, sa [o-soh´-so, sah], *f.* Osseous, bony.

ostaga [os-tah'-gah], *f. (Naut.)* Tie, runner.

oste [os'-tay], *int. (Ant.)* V. OXTE.

ostealgia [os-tay-ahl'-he-ah], *f.* Boneache, ostalgia.

osteítis [os-tay-ee'-tis], *f.* Osteitis, inflammation of bone.

ostensible [os-ten-see'-blay], *a.* Ostensible, apparent.

ostensiblemente [os-ten-see'-blay-men-tay], *adv.* Ostensibly.

ostensión [os-ten-se-on'], *f.* Show, manifestation.

ostensivo, va [os-ten-see'-vo, vah], *a.* Ostensive, showing, betokening.

ostentación [os-ten-tah-the-on'], *f.* 1. Ostentation, appearance. 2. Ambitious display, vain show, flourish parade.

ostentador, ra [os-ten-tah-dor', ran], *m & f.* Boaster, ostentator.

ostentar [os-ten-tar'], *va.* 1. To show (mostrar), to demonstrate. 2. To have (tener). 3. To have, to possess (poderes legales). **Ostentar el título en el deporte**, to hold the title in sport. *-vn.* To boast, to brag; to be fond of vain shows.

ostentativo, va [os-ten-tah-tee'-vo, vah], *a.* Ostentatious.

ostento [os-ten'-to], *m.* Portent, prodigy.

ostentosamente [os-ten-to'-sah-men-tay], *adv.* Ostentatiously, boastfully; gaudily.

ostentoso, sa [os-ten-to´-so, sah], *a.* Sumptuous, ostentatious, boastful, jaunty, gaudy, garish.

osteócopo [os-tay-o'-co-po], *a. (Med.)* Osteocopic, bonebreaking (dolor).

osteografía [os-tay-o-grah-fee'-ah], *f.* Osteography, description of the bones.

osteolita [os-tay-o-lee'-tah], *f.* Osteolite, fossil bone.

osteología [os-tay-o-lo-hee'-ah], *f.* Osteology, that part of anatomy which deals with the bones.

osteólogo [os-tay-o'-lo-go], *m.* Osteologer, a describer of the bones.

osteópata [os-tay-o'-pah-tah], *m.* Osteopath.

osteopatía [os-tay-o-pah-tee'-ah], *f.* Osteopathy.

ostiario [os-te-ah´-re-o], *m.* Ostiary, door-keeper, one of the minor orders of the Roman Catholic church.

ostiatim [os-te-ah'-tim], *adv.* From door to door.

ostión [os-te-on'], *m. (Prov. Andal.)* An oyster larger and coarser than the common one.

ostra [os'-trah], *f.* 1. Oyster. 2. *(Fig.)* Dull person (pesado); retiring individual (huraño); regular (permanente).

ostracismo [os-trah-thees'-mo], *m.* Ostracism, a method of banishment practiced by the Athenians.

ostracita [os-trah-thee'-tah], *f.* Ostracite, the common oyster in its fossil state.

ostral [os-trahl'], *m.* Oyster-bed.

ostrera [os-tray'-rah], *f.* 1. V. OSTRAL. 2. Oyster-wench, oyster-woman. 3. Oyster-plover.

ostrero [os-tray'-ro], *m.* Dealer in oysters.

ostrífero, ra [os-tree'-fay-ro, rah], *a.* Producing oysters, ostriferous.

ostro [os'-tro], *m.* 1. Oyster; large oysters are denominated in the masculine gender; they are also called *Ostrones*. 2. South wind. 3. Purple anciently obtained from a mollusk: Tyrian purple.

ostrogodo, da [os-tro-go'-o, dah], *a.* Ostrogothic.

ostugo [os-too'-go], *m.* Piece, part.

osudo, da [o-soo'-do, dah], *a.* Bony.

osuno, na [o-soo'-no, nah], *a.* Bear-like, bearish.

otacústico [o-tah-coos'-te-co], *a.* Otacoustic, assisting the sense of hearing. *-m.* Otacousticon, instrument to assist hearing.

otalgia [o-tahl'-he-ah], *f.* Otalgia, earache.

otálgico, ca [o-tahl'-he-co, cah], *a.* Otalgic, suitable for allaying earache.

otáñez [o-tah'-nyeth], *m. (hum.)* An old squire who courts or attends a lady; an old beau.

oteador, ra [o-tay-ah-dor', rah], *m. & f.* Spy, sly, observer.

otear [o-tay-ar'], *va.* To observe, to examine, to pry into, to discover by artifice; to inspect, to descry (alcanzar a ver), to look down on (mirar desde arriba).

otero [o-tay´-ro], *m.* Hill, eminence, height, in a plain.

ótico, ca [oh'-te-co, cah], *a. (Med.)* Otic, aural, employed in treating the ear.

otitis [o-tee'-tes], *f.* Otitis, inflammation of the ear.

oto [o´-to], *m. (Zool.)* Bustard, otis. V. AVUTARDA.

otología [o-to-lo-hee'-ah], *f. (Med.)* Otology, study of ear diseases.

otólogo, [o-to'-lo-go], *m.* Otologist, ear specialist.

otomana [o-to-mah'-nah], *f.* Ottoman, a cushioned seat, like a sofa.

otomano, na [o-to-mah'-no, nah], *a.* Ottoman, relating to the Turkish empire.

otona [o-to'-nah], *f. (Bot.)* Ragwort.

otoñada [o-to-nyah'-dah], *f.* Fall season, autumn season.

otoñal [o-to-nyahl'], *a.* Fall, autumnal.

otoñar [o-to-nyar'], *vn.* 1. To spend the fall season. 2. To grow in fall (plantas). *-vr.* To be seasoned, to be tempered.

otoño [o-to'-nyo], *m.* 1. Fall, autumn. 2. Aftermath, second crop of grass.

otorgador, ra [o-tor-gah-dor', rah], *m. & f.* Consenter, granter, stipulator.

otorgamiento [o-tor-gah-me-en'-to], *m.* 1. Grant, license. 2. The act of making an instrument in writing (acto).

otorgancia [o-tor-gahn'-the-ah], *f. (Law.)* Authorization. **Auto de otorgancia**, act of empowering or authorizing.

otorgante [o-tor-gahn'-tay], *pa. & m. & f.* 1. Granter; authorizing. 2. The party that signs and executes any public instrument.

otorgar [o-tor-gar'], *va.* 1. To consent, to agree to (consentir en), to condescend. 2. To covenant, to stipulate. 3. *(Law.)* To declare, to execute, to do. **Quien calla otorga**, silence gives consent.

otorrea [o-tor-ray'-ah], *f.* Otorrhoea, a discharge from the ear.

otorrino (laringólogo) [o-tor-ree'-no], *m & f. (Med.)* Ear, nose and throat specialist.

otoscopio [o-tos-co'-pe-oh], *m. (Med.)* Otoscope.

otro, tra [o'-tro, trah], *a.* Another, other. **Otra taza de café**, another cup of coffee. **Otra cosa**, something else. **Con otras 8 personas**, with another 8 people. *-pron.* Another one, others. **El otro**, the other one. **Tomar el sombrero de otro**, to take somebody else´s hat. *-int.* Again! exclamation of disgust.

otrosí [o-tro-see'], *adv.* Besides, moreover. *-m. (Law.)* Every petition made after the principal.

ova [o'-vah], *f. (Bot.)* Sea-lettuce, laver. *-pl. (Prov.)* Eggs. V. HUEVAS.

ovación [o-vah-the-on'], *f.* Ovation, a lesser triumph among the Romans.

ovacionar [o-vah-the-o-nahr'], *va.* To acclaim.

ovado, da [o-vah'-do, dah], *a. & pp.* of OVAR. 1. Oval. 2. Fecundated by the male bird.

oval [o-vahl'], *a.* Oval, oblong; *(Mex. Med.)* pessary.

ovalado, da [o-vah-lah'-do, dah], *a.* Egg-shaped, ovalformed.

óvalo [o'-vah-lo], *m.* Oval, a body or figure in the shape of an egg.

ovar [o-var'], *vn.* To lay eggs.

ovárico, ca [o-vah'-re-co, cah], *a.* Ovarian.

ovario [o-vah'-re-o], *m.* 1. Ovary, the organ in a female by which impregnation is performed. 2. *(Bot.)* Ovarium, ovary, the seed-vessel of plants, the lowest part of the pistil. 3. Ornament in architecture in the form of an egg.

ovecico [o-vay-thee'-co], *m. dim.* A small egg.

oveja [o-vay'-hah], *f.* 1. Ewe, a female sheep. **Cada oveja con su pareja,** like seeks like. **Encomendar las ovejas al lobo,** to set the wolf to guard the sheep. **Oveja negra,** black sheep. 2. *(Cono Sur)* Whore.

ovejero [o-vay-hay'-ro], *m.* Shepherd.

ovejuela [o-vay-hoo-ay'-lah], *f. dim.* A young ewe.

ovejuno, na [o-vay-hoo'-no, nah], *a.* Relating to ewes.

overa [o-vay'-rah], *f.* Ovary of oviparous animals.

overo, ra [o-vay'-ro, rah], *a.* Dappled: applied to animals speckled, or trout-colored. *-pl. (coll.)* Eyes which look quite white, as if without a pupil.

ovezuelo [o-vay-thoo-ay'-lo], *m. dim.* A small egg.

oviforme [o-ve-for'-may], *a.* Egg-shaped.

ovil [o-vel'], *m.* Sheep-cot. V. REDIL.

ovillar [o-vil-lyar'], *vn.* To wind into a clew (lana), to hank. *-vr.* To shrug or contract oneself into a ball or clew.

ovillejo [o-vil-lyay'-ho], *m.* 1. *(dim.)* A small clew or ball. 2. A kind of metrical composition.

ovillo [o-veel'-lyo], *m.* 1. Clew, thread wound upon a bottom. 2. Any confused heap or multitude of things.

ovino, na [o-vee'-no, nah], *a.* Ovine, pertaining to sheep. **Ganado ovino,** sheep.

ovíparo, ra [o-vee'-pah-ro, rah], *a.* Oviparous, bringing forth eggs.

ovoide [o-vo'-e-day], *a.* Ovoid, egg-shaped. *-m.* 1. Ovoid. 2. *(LAm. Dep.)* Rugby ball.

óvolo [o'-vo-lo], *m. (Arch.)* Ovolo, a quarter-round; a convex moulding.

ovoso, sa [o-vo'-so, sah], *a.* Full of sea-weeds.

ovulación [o-voo-lah-the-on'], *f.* Ovulation.

óvulo [o'-voo-lo], *m.* Ovule, germ contained in an ovary before impregnation.

oxalato [ok-sah-lah'-to], *m. (Chem.)* Oxalate, salt formed with oxalic acid.

oxálico [ok-sah'-le-co], *a.* Oxalic: applied to acid made from sorrel.

oxálide [ok-sah'-le-day], *f. (Bot.)* Oxalis.

oxalme [ok-sahl'-may], *m.* Acid brine.

oxear [ok-say-ahr'] *va.* To shoo or scare away fowls.

oxidación [ok-se-dah-the-on'], *f. (Chem.)* Oxidation.

oxidar [ok-se-dar'], *va.* To oxidate, to oxidize, to rust. *-vr.* To absorb oxygen.

óxido [ok'-se-do], *m.* Oxide. **Óxido de zinc,** zinc oxide.

oxigenable [ok-se-hay-nah'-blay], *a. (Chem.)* Oxygenazable.

oxigenación [ok-se-hay-nah-the-on'], *f.* Oxygenation, combining with oxygen.

oxigenado, da [ok-se-hay-nah'-do, dah], *a.* 1. Oxygenated. 2. Peroxided (pelo). **Rubia oxignada,** peroxide blond. *-pp.* of OXIGENAR.

oxigenar [ok-se-hay-nar'], *va.* To oxygenate, to saturate with oxygen. *-vr.* To oxygenate, to be oxygenated.

oxígeno [ok-see'-hay-no], *m. (Chem.)* Oxygen. **Oxígeno líquido,** liquid oxygen.

oxigonio [ok-se-go'-ne-o], *a.* Acute-angled.

oxígono, na [ok-see'-go-no, nah], *a.* Acute-angled; having all the angles acute.

oximaco [ok-se-mah'-co], *m.* A bird of prey with a curved black bill.

¡oxte! [ox'-tay], *int.* Keep off, clear off, begone. **¡Oxte puto!** exclamation on touching anything very hot or burning.

oyamel [o-yah-mel'], *m.* Mexican fir.

oyente [o-yen'-tay], *pa.* Hearing. *m. & f.* Auditor, hearer.

ozena [o-thay'-nah], *f. (Med.)* Ozaena, an ulceration of the nostrils, producing a fetid pus.

ozono [o-tho'-no], *m.* Ozone, considered an allotropic form of oxygen, generally produced by electricity.

ozonómetro [o-tho-no'-may-tro], *m.* Ozonometer, an instrument for measuring the amount of ozone in the air.

P

p [pay], seventeenth letter of the alphabet, is pronounced in the Spanish as in the English language.

pabellón [pah-bel-lyone'], *m.* 1. Pavilion, a kind of tent (tienda); field-bed. 2. Curtain hanging in the form of a tent. 3. **Pabellón de armas,** *(Mil.)* bell tent. 4. *(Naut.)* National colors, flag (bandera). 5. Summer house in the shape of a pavilion (en jardín). 6. Mouth (de trompeta). **Pabellón de música,** bandstand. **Pabellón de convivencia,** flag of convenience.

pábilo [pah'-be-lo], *m.* 1. Wick, as of a torch or candle. 2. Snuff of a candle.

pablar [pah-blar'], *va. (coll.)* Word used for consonance, as **Ni hablar, ni pablar,** not to speak.

pábulo [pah'-boo-lo], *m.* Pabulum, nourishment, food, provender, support, nutriment.

paca [pah'-cah], *f.* 1. The spotted cavy. 2. Bale of goods, bundle, package.

pacal [pah-cahl'], *m.* Bundle, parcel.

pacana [pah-cah'-nah], *f.* Pecan, an American tree like a walnut-tree, with an olive-shaped nut.

pacato, ta [pah-cah'-to, tah], *a.* Pacific, quiet, timid (tímido), tranquil, mild, gentle (modesto).

pacedero, ra [pah-thay-day'-ro, rah], *a.* Pasturable, fit for pasture (tierra).

pacedura [pah-thay-doo'-rah], *f.* Pasture-ground.

pacer [pah-therr'], *vn.* 1. To pasture, to graze. 2. To gnaw, to corrode, to feed. *-va.* 1. To eat, to graze (hierba). 2. To graze, to pasture (ganado).

pachamanca [pah-chah-mahn'-cah], *f.* (Peru) Barbecue, meat roasted out-of-doors, by covering with hot stones; barbecue feast.

pachanga [pah-chan'-gah], *f.* 1. Party (fiesta); binge (juerga), booze-up. 2. *(Carib.)* Mix-up (lío).

pachón [pah-chone'], *m.* 1. A peaceful, phlegmatic man. 2. Pointer, pointer-dog.

pachona [pah-cho'-nah], *f.* Pointer-bitch.

pachorra [pah-chor'-rah], *f.* Sluggishness, a slow and phlegmatic disposition.

pachorrudo, da [pah chor roo' do, dah], *a.* Sluggish, tardy, phlegmatic.

pachulí [pah-choo-lee'], *m.* 1. *(Bot.)* Patchouli (perfume). 2. *(Esp.)* Bloke (tío).

paciencia [pah-the-en'-the-ah], *f.* 1. Patience, endurance. 2. Patience, the quality of expecting long without rage or discontent. 3. Patience, forbearance, long-suffering. 4. Slowness, tardiness in action. 5. Exhortatory exclamation to have patience. **Perder la paciencia,** to loose one´s temper.

paciente [pah-the-en'-tay], *a.* 1. Patient, calm under affliction or pain, forbearing. 2. Consenting, accommodating: spoken of a contented cuckold.

paciente [pah-the-en'-tay], *m & f.* 1. Patient, sufferer, that which receives impressions from external agents. 2. *(coll.)* Patient; a sick person.

pacientemente [pah-the-ayn'-tay-men-tay], *adv.* Patiently, tolerantly.

pacienzudo, da [pah-the-en-thoo'-do, dah], *a. (coll.)* Patient, tolerant.

pacificación [pah-the-fe-cah-the-on'], *f.* Pacification, the act of making peace; quietness, peace of mind.

pacificador, ra [pah-the-fe-cah-dor', rah], *m. & f.* Pacificator, pacifier, peace-maker, reconciler.

pacíficamente [pah-thee'-fe-cah-men-tay], *adv.* Pacifically.

pacificar [pah-the-fe-car'], *va.* To pacify, to appease (apaciguar); to calm (calmar). *-vn.* To treat for peace.

pacífico, ca [pah-thee'-fe-co, cah], *a.* Pacific, peaceful, desirous of peace; tranquil, undisturbed; mild, gentle. -*m.* Pacific (Océano).

pacifista [pah-the-fees'-tah], *m. & f.* Pacifist.

paco [pah'-co], *m.* 1. Paco, a kind of vicuña: alpaca. 2. (Chile) Police force. 3. Diminutive of *Francisco.* 4. *pl.* Silver ores containing chlorides, etc., and iron. 5. *(LAm.)* Cop, policeman.

pacotilla [pah-co-teel´-lyah], *f.* 1. Venture, goods embarked in a ship on the private account of an individual. **Ser de pacotilla,** of poor quality. *(Acad.)* 2. *(And. CAm. Cono Sur)* Rabble, crowd, mob.

pactar [pac-tar'], *va.* To covenant, to contract, to stipulate. -*vn.* To come to an agreement.

pacto [pahc'-to], *m.* Pact, covenant, agreement. **Pacto de caballeros,** gentleman's agreement. **Pacto social,** social contract. **Pacto de Varsovia,** Warsaw Pact.

pácul [pah´-cool], *m.* A wild plantain of the Philippines which yields a textile fiber not so good as the abacá.

padecer [pah-day-therr'], *va.* 1. To suffer corporal affliction. 2. To sustain an injury. 3. To be liable to. 4. To endure (aguantar). -*vn.* **Padecer de,** to suffer from. **Padece del corazón,** he suffers with his heart. *(Yo padezco, yo padezca, from Padecer. V.* CONOCER.)

padecimiento [pah-day-the-me-en'-to], *m.* Suffering, sufferance.

padilla [pah-deel´-lyah], *f.* 1. A small frying-pan. 2. A small oven.

padrastro [pah-drahs´-tro], *m.* 1. Stepfather. 2. Obstacle, impediment. 3. Height, eminence which commands a tower or other place 4. Hangnail.

padrazo [pah-drah'-tho], *m. aug.* of PADRE. An indulgent parent.

padre [pah'-dray], *m.* 1. Father. 2. Father, the appellation of the first person of the Trinity. 3. Male of all animals. 4. Father, ancestor (antepasado). 5. Source, origin, principal author. 6. Father, one who acts with paternal care. 7. Father, an ecclesiastical writer of the first centuries. 8. Father, the appellation of a religious man. 9. Father, the title of a confessor. **Padre de familia,** householder, housekeeper. **Padre Santo,** the Pope. **Padre nuestro,** the Lord's prayer; the large bead in the rosary over which the Lord's prayer is to be said. **Padre espiritual,** confessor. **Padre político,** father-in-law, -*pl.* 1. Parents, the father and mother. 2. Ancestors. 3. The members of a religious congregation taken as a body. **¡Mi padre!** no, indeed! never! **¡Que lo haga su padre!,** get someone else to do it! **Se llevó un susto padre,** he was frightened out of his wits. **Se pega la vida padre,** he lives like a king. **Tiene un éxito padre,** he's a big hit.

padrear [pah-dray-ar'], *vn.* 1. To resemble the father in features or habits. 2. To be kept for procreation (ganado).

padrinazgo [pah-dre-nath'-go], *m.* Compaternity, act of assisting at baptism, title or charge of a god-father.

padrino [pah-dree'-no], *m.* 1. Godfather (de un niño). 2. Second in duel. 3. Protector, assistant. **Padrino de boda,** best man. 4. Sponsor (que patrocina). **El que no tiene padrinos no se bautiza,** you can't get anywhere without connections.

padrón [pah-drone'], *m.* 1. Poll, a register of persons in a place who pay taxes (censo). 2. A kind of public monument among the Romans. 3. Mark or note of infamy. 4. An indulgent parent. 5. *(LAm.)* Stallion (caballo); *(And.)* breeding bull (toro).

paella [pah-el'-lyah], *f.* Rice dish originated in Valencia, Spain.

pafio, fia [pah'-fe-o, ah], *a.* Paphian, of Paphos.

paflón [pa-flone'], *m.* *(Arch.)* Soffit, the under side of a cornice or archway. *Cf.* PLAFÓN.

paga [pah'-gah], *f.* 1. Payment, fee (honorarios), salary. 2. Satisfaction for a fault or error committed. 3. Sum or fine paid. 4. Monthly pay of a soldier. 5. Friendly intercourse, mutual friendship. **Entrega contra paga,** cash on delivery.

pagadero, ra [pah-gah-day'-ro, rah], *a.* Payable, due. **Pagadero a plazos,** payable in instalments.

pagadero [pah-gah-day'-ro], *m.* Time and place of payment.

pagado, da [pah-gah'-do, dah], *a.* Paid. **Pagado por adelantado,** paid in advance. -*pp.* of PAGAR.

pagador, ra [pah-gah-dor', rah], *m. & f.* 1. Payer, one who pays. 2. Paymaster. **Mal pagador,** bad payer.

pagaduría [pab-gah-doo-ree'-ah], *f.* Paymaster's office.

pagamento [pah-gah-men´-to], *m.* Payment.

paganismo [pah-gah-nees'-mo], *m.* Paganism, heathenism.

pagano [pah-gah'-no], *m.* 1. Heathen, pagan. 2. Peasant, rustic. 3. *(coll.)* One who pays his share.

pagano, na [pah-gah´-no, nah], *a.* Heathenish, unchristian, paganish.

pagar [pah-gar'], *va.* 1. To pay, to discharge a debt (deuda), to acquit. 2. To be liable for customs duties; *used* of merchandise. 3. To pay (crimen, ofensa), to atone, to make amends. 4. To please, to give pleasure. 5. To pay, to reward, to requite (amor), to fee. -*vn.* 1. *(LAm.)* To pay. 2. *(Cono Sur)* To take bets (tomar apuestas). -*vr.* To be pleased (with oneself); to be fond of (another). **Pagar la visita,** to return a visit. **Pagar el pato,** *(coll.)* to receive unmerited punishment, or to pay for another man´s misconduct. **Su tío le paga los estudios,** his uncle is paying for his education. **Paga 20 dólares de habitación,** he pays 20 dollars for his room. **Lo pagó con la vida,** he paid for it with his life.

pagaré [pah-gah-ray'], *m.* A note of hand, a promissory note.

pagaya [pa-gah'-yah], *f.* A Philippine oar, tied about with a twining stem.

página [pah'-he-nah], *f.* Page of a book.

paginar [pah-he-nahr'], *va.* To paginate, to number the pages.

pago [pah'-go], *m.* 1. Payment, discharge of a debt. 2. Payment, reward, the thing given in discharge of a debt or promise. **Suspender el pago,** to stop payment. 3. Lot of land; especially of vineyards. **Pronto pago,** prompt payment. **Dar cuenta con pago,** to close or balance an account. **En pago,** in payment, as a recompense, in return. **Pago en especie,** payment in kind. **Efectuar un pago,** to make a payment. **En pago de,** in return for. -*a. (coll.)* Paid.

pagoda [pah-go´-dah], *f.* Pagoda, Chinese temple.

pagodita [pa-go-dee'-tah], *f.* An earth which the Chinese employ in making figures.

pagote [pah-goh´-tay], *m.* *(coll.)* One who is charged with the faults of others, and pays or suffers for them all, scapegoat.

pagua [pah'-goo-ah], *f.* 1. *(Mex.)* Avocado, alligator pear. 2. *(Cono Sur)* Hernia (hernia); large swelling (hinchazón).

paguro [pah-goo'-ro], *m.* Small crab.

paila [pah'-e-lah], *f.* 1. A large pan of copper, brass, or iron. 2. A boiler.

pailón [pah-e-lone'], *m.* A large copper.

pairar [pah-e-rar'], *vn.* *(Taut.)* To bring to, to lie to. *V.* CAPEAR.

pairo [pah'-e-ro], *m.* *(Naut.)* Act of lying to with all sail set.

país [pah-ees'], *m.* 1. Country (nación), land (tierra), region, ground. 2. In painting, landscape (paisaje). 3. *(Met.)* Field, subject: applied to scientific researches. **País natal,** native land. **Vino del país,** local wine.

paisaje [pah-e-sah'-hay], *m.* Landscape, countryside, scenery.

paisana [pah-e-sah'-nah], *f.* 1. Country-woman, a woman of the same country as another person. 2. A kind of country dance.

paisanaje [pah-e-sah-nah'-hay], *m.* 1. The lay inhabitants of a country, in contradistinction to the military men and clergy: the peasantry. 2. Quality of being of the same country.

paisano, na [pah-e-sah´-no, nah], *a.* Of the same country.

paisano [pah-e-sah'-no], *m.* 1. Fellow-countryman, one of the same country as another. 2. Countryman: appellation given by soldiers to those who are not military men; a civilian. 3. Compatriot (compatriota). 4. *(Cono Sur)* Foreigner (extranjero); *(Cono Sur)* Arab (árabe); *(Mex.)* Spaniard; *(And. Cono Sur)* Chinaman, Chinese woman.

paja [pah'-hah], *f.* 1. Straw, the stalk on which corn grows; haum. 2. Straw, the stalk of corn after being thrashed. 3.

Beard of grain, blade of grass. 4. Straw, chaff, anything proverbially worthless, froth. 5. *(CAm.)* Lie (mentira). 6. *(Cono Sur)* Dope (droga). 7. *(And. CAm.)* Tap (grifo); canal (canal). **Paja trigaza,** wheat straw. **Techo de paja,** thatched roof.

pajada [pah-hah'-dah], *f.* Straw boiled with bran.

pajado, da [pah-hah'-do, dah], *a.* Pale, straw-colored.

pajar [pah-har'], *m.* Place where straw is kept.

pájara [pah'-hah-rah], *f.* 1. The female of any bird, hen-bird. 2. *(Prov.)* Paper kite (cometa). 3. Loose woman (putilla); thieving woman (ladrona). **Pájara pinta,** a game of forfeits. **Dar pájara a uno,** *(And. CAm.)* to swindle somebody. **Sufrir una pájara,** to suffer a fainting (en el deporte).

pajarear [pah-hah-ray-ar'], *va.* 1. To go bird-catching. 2. To loiter about. 3. *(Mex.)* To be skittish: speaking of horses.

pajarel [pah-hah-rel'], *m. V.* JILGUERO.

pajarera [pah-hah-ray'-rah], *f.* Aviary.

pajarería [pah-hah-ray-ree'-ah], *f.* 1. Abundance of sparrows or little birds. 2. Place where straw is sold. 3. Pet shop (tienda). 4. *(Carib.)* Vanity (vanidad).

pajarero [pah-hah-ray'-ro], *m.* 1. Bird catcher (cazador). 2. One who idles about. 3. Bird fancier (criador). 4. *(And. CAm.)* Bird-scarer.

pajarero, ra [pah-hah-ray'-ro, rah], *a.* 1. Merry, cheerful, gay. 2. Shy (caballos). 3. Gaudy, ill-matched (colores). 4. *(Carib.)* meddlesome (entrometido).

pajaril [pah-hah-reel'], *m. (Naut.)* Passaree or passarado, a rope fastened to the corner of a sail.

pajarilla [pah-hah-reel'-lyah], *f.* 1. *(dim.)* A small bird, hen or female of a bird. 2. Milt of a hog. 3. *(Prov.) V.* PALOMILLA (as insect). **Se abrasan las pajarillas,** it's intolerably hot.

pajarito, ta [pah-hah-ree'-to, tah], *m. & f.* dim. A small bird. -f. Bow tie; V.CUELLO.

pájaro [pah'-hah-ro], *m.* 1. Bird, a general name for the feathered kind: used generally for the smaller birds. 2. Sparrow. **Adiestrar pájaros,** to teach birds to sing. 3. *(Met.)* A conspicuous person; a sly fellow. 4. *(Carib.)* Queer (homosexual). **Pájaro solitario,** man who shuns company. -pl. The song-birds. **Más vale pájaro en mano que ciento volando,** a bird in the hand is worth two in the bush. **Pájaro carpintero,** woodpecker. **Tener pájaros en la cabeza,** to be featherbrained. -a. 1. *(Cono Sur)* Scatty (atolondrado), feather-brained; shady (sospechoso); loud (chillón). 2. *(Carib.)* Poofy, queer (afeminado). 3. *(Cono Sur)* Vague, distracted. **Es un pájaro de cuidado,** he's a nasty piece of work, a nasty customer.

pajarota [pah-hah-ro'-tah], *f.* A false, idle report, a hoax.

pajarraco [pah-har-rah'-co], *m.* 1. A large bird. 2. *(coll.)* A low, cunning fellow.

pajaza [pah-hah'-thah], *f.* Refuse of straw left by horses in the manger.

pajazo [pah-hah'-tho], *m.* Prick of stubbles received in a horse's face when feeding among them.

paje [pah'-hay], *m.* 1. Page, a young boy attending on a great personage. 2. *(Naut.)* Cabin-boy.

pajear [pah-hay-ar'], *vn. (coll.)* To behave, to conduct oneself.

pajel [pah-hel'], *m. (Zool.)* Red sea bream.

pajera [pah-hay'-rah], *f.* A place where straw is kept.

pajero [pah-hay'-ro], *m.* One who deals in straw, and carries it about for sale.

pajica, pajilla [pah-hee'-cah, pah-heel'-lyah], *f.* Cigar made of a maize-leaf: *(CAm. Carib. Mex.)* Straw hat.

pajita [pah-hee'-tah], *f.* 1. Drinking straw. 2. **Quedarse mascando pajita,** *(Carib.)* to be left feeling foolish.

pajizo, za [pah-hee'-tho, thah], *a.* 1. Made of straw, thatched with straw. 2. Straw-color.

pajón [pah-hone'], *m.* 1. Coarse straw. 2. *(coll.)* An unpolished, ill-bred man. -a. *(Mex.)* Lank (pelo).

pajoso, sa [pah-ho'-so, sah], *a.* Made of straw.

pajote [pah-ho'-tay], *m.* Straw interwoven with a bulrush, with which gardeners cover fruit-trees and plants.

pajuela [pah-hoo-ay'-lah], *f.* 1. Short, light straw. 2. Match for lighting.

pajuelero [pah-hoo-ay-lay'-ro], *m.* Match-maker.

pajujero [pah-hoo-hay'-ro], *m. (Prov.)* Place where straw is deposited to rot and become manure.

pajuncio [pah-hoon'-the-o], *m. (Prov.)* 1. Booby, ninny, fool. 2. In contempt, rush, worthless thing.

pajuz [pah-hooth'], *m. (Prov.)* Refuse of straw in the manger or stable.

pajuzo [pah-hoo'-tho], *m. (Prov.)* Bad straw, designed for manure.

pala [pah'-lah], *f.* 1. A wooden shovel for grain; shovel. **Palas con mango,** shovels with handles. 2. Peel used by bakers. 3. Blade of an oar. 4. Upper-leather of a shoe (zapato). 5. The breadth or flat surface of the teeth. 6. Craft, cunning, artifice. 7. Dexterity, cleverness. 8. *(Bot.)* Common Dante of a spathe. 9. Leaf of the prickly pear. 10. Smooth part of an epaulet from which the fringe hangs. **Pala mecánica,** power shovel. **Pala para el pescado,** fish slice. **Pala matamoscas,** fly swat.

palabra [pah-lah'-brah], *f.* 1. Word (vocablo), a single part of speech. 2. Word, affirmation, confirmation. 3. Word, promise (promesa), offer. 4. *(Div.)* The Word, or only-begotten Son. 5. **Palabra clave,** *(Comput.)* keyword. **Palabra de matrimonio,** promise of marriage. **Se han dado palabra,** they are engaged. **Palabras mayores,** offensive or insulting words; also, things that require great expense. **Soltar la palabra,** not to oblige a person to keep his word. **Dejar a uno con la palabra en la boca,** to turn away without listening to one who is speaking. **Decir a uno cuatro palabritas al oído,** *(coll.)* to intimidate a person by informing him that his character is known; also, to obtain a thing by secret flattery. **De palabra,** by word of mouth. **Pedir la palabra,** to ask for the floor. **Tomar la palabra,** to take a man at his word, to speak first. **A la primera palabra,** at the first word (meaning quick apprehension). **En una palabra,** in a word. **Sin chistar palabra,** without a word. **Ceder la palabra a uno,** to yield to somebody. **Es hombre de palabra,** he is a man of his word. **Palabra de código,** *(Comput.)* code word.

¡palabra! [pah-lah'-brah], *int.* I say, a word with you.

palabrada [pah-lah-brah'-dah], *f* Low, scurrilous language.

palabrería [pah-lah-bray-ree'-ah], *f.* Wordiness, much talk, emptiness of meaning.

palabrero, ra [pah-lah-bray'-ro, rah], *a.* Talkative, loquacious.

palabrista [pah-lah-brees'-tah], *com.* One who is full of idle talk, a loquacious person.

palabrita [pah-lah-bree'-tah], *f.* 1. *(dim.)* A short word: it is commonly used for an endearing expression. 2. Word full of meaning.

palabrota [pah-lah-bro'-tah], *f. aug.* A course expression, rude word.

palaciego, ga [pah-lah-the-ay'-go, gah], *a.* Pertaining to the palace. -m. Courtier (persona).

palacio [pah-lah'-the-o], *m.* 1. Palace, a royal residence; a house eminently splendid. 2. Castle, the mansion of the ancient nobility. **Palacio episcopal,** bishop's palace. **Palacio real,** royal palace.

palacra, palacrana [pah-lah'-crah, pah-lah-crah'-nah], *f.* A piece of native gold: ingot of pure gold.

palada [pah-lah'-dah], *f.* 1. A shovelful. 2. *(Naut.)* Every stroke of an oar.

paladar [pah-lah-dar'], *m.* 1. Palate, the roof of the mouth. 2. Palate, the instrument of taste and the taste itself. 3. Taste, relish; longing desire. **A medida or a sabor de su paladar,** according to the taste of anyone.

paladear [pah-lah-day-ar'], *va.* 1. To rub the palate of a new-born child with any sweet substance. 2. To amuse, to divert. 3. To clean the mouth or palate of animals. -vn. To manifest a desire of sucking (recién nacido). -vr. To get the taste of a thing by little and little; to relish.

paladeo [pah-lah-day'-o], *m.* The act of tasting or relishing.

paladial [pah-lah-de-ahl'], *a.* Palatal, pronounced by the palate, as **y, r.**

paladín [pah-lah-deen'], *m.* Paladin, a knight.

paladinamente [pah-lah-de'-nah-men-tay], *adv.* Publicly, clearly.

paladino, na [pah-lah-dee'-no, nah], *a.* Manifest, clear, apparent, public.

paladio [pah-lah'-de-o], *m. (Min.)* Palladium, a metal.

paladión [pah-lah-de-on'], *m.* Palladium, safeguard.

palafrén [pah-lah-frén], *m.* Palfrey, a small horse for ladies; a servant's horse.

palafrenero [pah-lah-fray-nay'-ro], *m.* Groom, hostler.

palahierro [pah-lah-e-er'-ro], *m.* Bushing for the spindle of the upper millstone.

pala mecánica [pah'-lah may-cah'-ne-cah], *f.* Power shovel, steam shovel.

palamenia [pah-lah-may'-ne-ah], *f.* The oars of a row-galley.

palanca [pah-lahn'-cah], *f.* 1. Lever. 2. A staff or pole by which a burden is supported between two men. 3. Exterior fortification with stakes. 4. *(Fig.)* Lever; pull, influence. 5. *(And. Mex.)* Punting pole (barca). **Palanca de impulsión,** operating lever. **Palanca de mano,** hand lever. **Palanca de retroceso,** return lever. **Mecanisno de palanca,** lever system.

palancada [pah-lan-cah'-dah], *f.* Stroke with a lever.

palancana, palangana [pah-lan-gah'-nah], *f.* 1. A basin. 2. *(And. CAm.)* Platter, serving dish. -*m & f. (Cono Sur)* Intruder (intruso); *(LAm.)* Shallow person (frívolo).

palanganero [pa-lahn'-gah-nay'-ro], *m.* Wash-stand, usually resting on three feet.

palangre [pah-lahn'-gray], *m.* A line from which several fish-hooks are suspended.

palanquera [pah-lan-kay'-rah], *f.* Inclosure with stakes or poles.

palanquero [pa-lahn-kay'-ro], *m.* Driver of stakes, pile-driver.

palanqueta [pah-lan-kay'-tah], *f.* 1. *(Mil.)* Bar-shot or cross-bar-shot, two balls joined by a bar. 2. *(dim.)* A small lever.

palanquín [pah-lan-keen'], *m.* 1. Porter who carries burdens. 2. *(Naut.)* Double-tackle, clew garnet. 3. Palanquin, a covered carriage or litter used in the east.

palastro [pah-lahs'-tro], *m.* Iron plate, sheet of hammered iron.

palatina [pah-lah-tee'-nah], *f.* Tippet, neckcloth for women in winter.

palatinado [pah-lah-te-nah'-do], *m.* 1. Palatinate; dignity of a palatine. 2. A county palatine.

palatino, na [pah-lah-tee'-no, nah], *a.* Palatial, belonging to the palace or the courtiers.

palay [pah-lah'-ee], *m. (Phil. Is.)* Rice with its husk.

palazo [pah-lah'-tho], *m.* Blow with a shovel or stick.

palazón [pah-lah-thone'], *m. (Naut.)* Masting, the masts of vessels.

palco [pahl'-co], *m.* 1. *(Th.)* Box, box seat. 2. Scaffold raised for spectators. **Palco de la presidencia,** *(Taur.)* president's box.

paleador [pah-lay-ah-dor'], *m.* Man who works with a shovel.

palear, ra [pah-lay-ahr']. *V.* APALEAR.

palenque [pah-len'-kay], *m.* 1. Palisade, enclosure made with piles; paling. 2. Passage from the pit to the stage in a play-house. 3. *(And. Cono Sur)* Tethering post (caballos). 4. *(Cono Sur)* Din, racket (alboroto).

paleografía [pah-lay-o-grah-fee'-ah], *f.* Paleography, art of reading ancient MSS.

paleolítico [pah-lay-o-lee'-te-co], *a.* Paleolithic.

paleología [pah-lay-o-lo-hee'-ah], *f.* Paleology, the study of ancient languages.

paleontología [pah-lay-on-to-lo-hee'-ah], *f.* Paleontology, the science which treats of organic fossil remains and of the ancient life of the globe.

paleontólogo, ga [pah-lay-on-to'-lo-go], *m & f.* Paleontologist.

paleozoico [pah-lay-o-tho'-e-co], *a. (Geol.)* Paleozoic.

palería [pah-lay-ree'-ah], *f.* Art and business of draining low wet lands.

palero [pah-lay'-ro], *m.* 1. One who makes or sells shovels. 2. Ditcher, drainer; pioneer. -*a. (And.)* Big-headed (fanfarrón).

palestina [pah-les-tee'-nah], *f.* Two-line small pica; type of 22 points.

palestra [pah-les'-trah], *f.* 1. A place for wrestling and other athletic exercises: a palaestra. 2. A place for disputations or debates. 3. (Poop) Art of wrestling.

paléstrico, ca [pah-lees'-tre-co, cah], *a.* Relating to a place for wrestling or other exercises; palestric, palestrical, belonging to the exercise of wrestling.

palestrita [pah-les-tree'-tah], *m.* One versed in athletic or logical exercises.

paleta [pah-lay'-tah], *f.* 1. Fire-shovel. 2. Palette, a painter's tablet. 3. Iron ladle, used in public kitchens to distribute viands. 4. *(dim.)* A small shovel. 5. Blade-bone of the shoulder. 6. Trowel, a mason's tool. 7. *pl.* Chopsticks to eat with. 8. *(LAm.)* Lollipop (pirulí). 9. *(LAm.)* Topside of beef.

paletada [pah-lay-tah'-dah], *f.* Trowelful of mortar.

paletilla [pah-lay-teel'-lyah], *f.* 1. *(dim.)* A little fire-shovel. 2. A shoulder-blade. 3. *V.* PALMATORIA. 4. A cartilage under the pit of the stomach.

paleto [pah-lay'-to], *m.* 1. Fallow-deer. *V.* GAMO. 2. Clown, rustic (palurdo).

paletón [pah-lay-tone'], *m.* Bit, the part of a key in which the wards are formed.

paletoque [pah-lay-to'-kay], *m.* Kind of dress like a scapulary which hangs to the knees.

pali [pah'-le], *a. & m.* An ancient language of India, derived from the Sanscrit.

palia [pah'-le-ah], *f.* 1. Altar-cloth. 2. Veil which hangs before the tabernacle; square piece of linen put over the chalice.

paliación [pah-le-ah-the-on'], *f.* Palliation, extenuation.

paliadamente [pah-le-ah'-dah-men-tay], *adv.* Dissemblingly, in a palliative manner.

paliar [pah-le-ar'], *va.* 1. To palliate, to extenuate, to excuse, to relieve (dolor), to lessen (efecto); to diminish (importancia). 2. To mitigate, to excuse (ofensa). 3. To conceal, to gloss over (defecto).

paliativo, va [pah-le-ah-tee'-vo, vah], **paliatorio, ria,** *a.* Palliative, mitigating, that may be palliated.

palidecer [pah-le-day-ther'], *m.* To grow pale.

palidez [pah-le-deth'], *f.* Paleness, wanness, pallor, ghastliness.

pálido, da [pah'-le-do, dah], *a.* Pallid, pale, ghastly, sickly (enfermo).

palillero [pah-leel-lyay'-ro], *m.* 1. One who makes or sells toothpicks. 2. Toothpick case.

palillo [pah-leel'-lyo], *m.* 1. *(dim.)* A small stick. 2. Knitting-needle case, a utensil which women carry fastened to the waist by the apron-strings. 3. Toothpick (mondadientes). 4. Bobbin, a wooden implement for making net-work or laces. 5. Drum-stick. 6. Peruvian plant similar to the guava-tree. -*pl.*1. After-dinner table-talk. 2. Small pins put on the billiard table in certain games. 3. *(coll.)* Trifles, things of no moment. **Palillos chinos,** chopsticks. **Estar hecho un palillo,** to be as thin as a rake.

palimpsesto [pa-limp-ses'-to], *m.* Palimpsest, an ancient parchment twice written upon, the first writing more or less erased.

palíndromo [pah-lin-dro'-mo], *m.* Palindrome, a word, line, or sentence, which, read either from left to right, or viceversa, has the same meaning.

palio [pah'-le-o], *m.* 1. Cloak, short mantle (manto). 2. Pallium, a pontifical ornament, worn by patriarchs and archbishops. 3. Anything in the form of a canopy (dosel). 4. Premium or plate given as a reward in racing. **Recibir con palio**, to receive under a pall, as kings, etc.

palique [pah-lee'-kay], *m. (coll.)* Trifling conversation, chit-chat, small talk.

palito [pah-lee'-to], *m. dim.* A little stick.

palitroque, palitoque [pah-le-tro'-kay], *m.* 1. A rough, ill-shaped stick. 2. *(Cono Sur)* Skittles (juego); skittle alley (local), bowling alley.

paliza [pah-lee'-thah], *f.* Cudgelling, caning, cowhiding, beating, thrashing, drubbing. **Dar una paliza a uno**, to give somebody a beating. **El viaje fue una paliza**, the journey was ghastly.

palizada [pah-le-thah'-dah], *f.* 1. Palisade or palisado. 2. Paling, *V.* ESTACADA.

palma [pahl'-mah], *f.* 1. *(Bot.)* Date palm-tree. **Palma indiana**, coconut-tree. 2. Leaf of a palm-tree. 3. Palm of the hand. 4. Quick sole of a horse's hoof. 5. Insignia of victory. 6. Insignia of virginity. 7. *(Fig.)* Clapping, applause. **Llevarse la palma**, to carry the day. **Andar en palmas**, to be universally applauded. **Conocer como la palma de la mano**, to know like the back of one´s hand.

palmacristi [pal-mah-crees'-te], *f.* Palma Christi, the castor-oil plant.

palmada [pal-mah'-dah], *f.* Slap with the palm of the hand. *-pl.* Clapping of hands, applause. **Dar palmadas**, to clap.

palmadilla [pal-mah-deel'-yah], *f.* A kind of dance.

palmar [pal-mar'], *a.* 1. Measuring a palm, or three inches. 2. Relating to palms. 3. Clear, obvious, evident.

palmar [pal-mar'], *m.* 1. Plantation or grove of palm-trees. 2. Fuller's thistle. *-pl. (Amer.)* Woods of dwarf palms, a kind of palmetto.

palmar [pal-mar'], *vn.* 1. To peg out (morir). 2. To loose (en juego). **Hemos palmado**, we've lost.

palmario, ria [pal-mah'-re-o, ah], *a.* Clear, obvious, evident.

palmatoria [pal-mah-to'-re-ah], *f.* 1. A rod with which boys at school were beaten on the hand (castigo). 2. A small candlestick with a handle (de vela).

palmeado, da [pal-may-ah'-do, dah], *a.* 1. Palmiped, web-footed, palmated (aves). 2. *(Bot.)* Palmate: applied to the leaves and roots of plants. *-pp.* of PALMEAR.

palmear [pal-may-ar'], *va.* To slap with the open hand.

palmejar [pal-may-har'], *m. (Naut.)* Thick stuff, thick plank nailed to the inner sides of ships.

palmera [pal-may'-rah], *f.* Palm-tree. *V.* PALMA.

palmero [pal-may'-ro], *m.* Palmer, a pilgrim, a crusader who bore a palm in his hand.

palmeta [pal-may'-tah], *f.* 1. Ferule. *V.* PALMATORIA. 2. Slap on the palm of the hand. **Palmeta matamoscas**, fly swater.

palmífero, ra [pal-mee'-fay-ro, rah], *a. (Poet.)* Palmiferous.

palmípedo, da [pal-mee'-pay-do, dah], *a.* Web-footed, palmiped.

palmitieso [pal-me-te-ay'-so], *a.* Hard-hoofed horse.

palmito [pal-mee'-to], *m.* 1. Dwarf, fan-palm; palmetto. 2. Its root. 3. Little face (cara de mujer). **Buen palmito**, a pretty face. 4. *(Cuba)* Top of a palm-tree containing a bud which is palatable and nutritious.

palmo [pahl'-mo], *m.* 1. Palm, a measure of length from the thumb to the end of the little finger extended; hand, handbreadth. **En un palmo de tierra**, in a short space of ground. 2. Game, commonly called span-farthing. **Palmo a palmo**, inch by inch. **Medir a palmos**, *(Met.)* to have complete knowledge of something. **Dejar a uno con un palmo de narices**, to disappoint one in an affair in which he expected to succeed. **Quedarse con un palmo de narices**, to be out of luck. 3. *(CAm.)* Cunt (vagina). **Con un palmo de lengua fuera**, panting.

palmotear [pal-mo-tay-ar'], *va.* To slap with the hand. *V.* PALMEAR.

palmoteo [pal-mo-tay'-o], *m.* Clapping of hands, clap.

palo [pahl'-lo], *m.* 1. Stick, cudgel. 2. Timber, log. 3. Wood of some American trees which serves for medicine or dyes.

4. Blow given with a stick; whack. 5. Execution on the gallows. 6. Suit at cards (cartas). 7. Stalk of fruit, pedicle. 8. In writing, a line which projects above or below. 9. *(Her.)* Pale, a vertical band one-third the width of the shield. 10. Club (porra), banderilla (banderilla), spear (garrocha). 11. *(LAm.)* Swig, draught of liquor. 12. **Dar un palo**, to do a job (robo). 13. *(LAm.)* **Un palo de casa**, a splendid house. **Dar palo**, to turn out contrary to one's expectations. **Palo de escoba**, broomstick. **Cuchara de palo**, wooden spoon. **Andar a palos**, to be always squabbing. **A palo seco**, bare.

palo dulce [pah´-lo dool'-thay], *m. (Bot.)* Licorice. *V.* OROZUZ.

palo santo [pah´-lo sahn´-to], *m. (Bot.)* Lignum-vitae.

paloma [pah-lo'-mah], *f.* 1. Pigeon, dove. **Paloma mensajera**, homing pigeon. **Paloma torcaz**, ring-dove. 2. A meek, mild, dove-like person. 3. *(Ast.)* Columba, one of the southern constellations. 4. Handstand (ejercicio). 5. *(CAm. Carib. Mex.)* Kite (cometa).

palomaduras [pah-lo-mah-doo´-ras], *f. pl. (Naut.)* Seams of the sails, where the bolt-rope is sewed to them.

palomar [pah-lo-mar'], *a.* Applied to hard-twisted linen or thread. *-m.* Pigeon-house, dove-cot.

palomariego, ga [pah-lo-mah-re-ay'-go, gah], *a.* Applied to domestic pigeons in the fields.

palomear [pah-lo-may-ar'], *vn.* 1. To shoot pigeons. 2. To care for them.

palomera [pah-lo-may'-rah], *f.* 1. A bleak place. 2. Small dove-cot.

palomería [pah-lo-may-ree'-ah], *f.* Pigeon-shooting.

palomero [pah-lo-may´-ro], *m.* One who deals in doves or pigeons.

palomero [pah-lo-may-ro], *a.* Applied to arrows with long iron points.

palomilla [pah-lo-meel'-lyah], *f.* 1. *(dim.)* A young pigeon. 2. A sort of ashy moth reared in barley. 3. Backbone of a horse. 4. Peak of a packsaddle. 5. Horse of a milk-white color. 6. A wall-bracket; a galley-rack. 7. Brass box of the axis of a wheel. 8. Chrysalis or pupa. 9. *(Bot.)* Common fumitory. 10. *(And. Cono Sur)* Urchin (travieso); *(CAm. Cono Sur, Mex.)* Mob of kids (niños).

palomina [pah-lo-mee'-nah], *f.* 1. Pigeon-dung. 2. *(Bot.)* Fumitory. 3. A kind of black grape.

palomino [pah-lo-mee'-no], *m.* 1. A young pigeon. 2. *(coll.)* Stain of excrements upon the shirt. 3. *(And. Cono Sur, Mex.)* Palomino (caballo); white horse (caballo). 4. Pigeon droppings (excremento).

palomita [pah-lo-mee´-tah], *f.* 1. Squab, pigeon. **Palomitas de maíz**, popcorn.

palomo [pah-lo'-mo], *m.* Cock-pigeon.

palón [pah-lone'], *m. (Her.)* Guidon, an ensign resembling a flag.

palotada [pah-lo-tah'-dah], *f.* Stroke with a battledoor. **No dar palotada**, not to have hit on the right thing in all that is said or done; not to have begun a line or title of what was undertaken or ordered; not to answer anything to the purpose.

palote [pah-lo'-tay], *m.* 1. Stick of a middling size, drumstick. 2. Rule or line used by scholars in writing. 3. *(Carib. Cono Sur)* Rolling pin; *(Cono Sur)* beanpole (persona). *-pl.* The first lines formed by boys in writing.

paloteado [pah-lo-tay-ah'-do], *m.* 1. Rustic dance performed with sticks. 2. Noisy scuffle or dispute, in which they come to blows.—**Paloteado, da**, *pp.* of PALOTEAR.

palotear [pah-lo-tay-ar'], *vn.* To scuffle, to clash, to strike sticks against one another; to contend or dispute loudly.

paloteo [pah-lo-tay'-o], *m.* Fight with sticks.

palpable [pal-pah'-blay], *a.* 1. Palpable, perceptible to the touch. 2. Palpable, plain, evident, clear.

palpablemente [pal-pah'-blay-men-tay], *adv.* Palpably, evidently.

palpadura [pal-pah-doo'-rah], *f.* or **palpamiento** [pal-pah-me-en'-to], *m.* Palpation, the act of feeling, touching, palpableness.

palpar [pal-par'], *va.* 1. To feel, to touch. 2. To grope in the dark. 3. To know positively, as if one had felt it. *4.* To appreciate, to understand. *-vr.* To be felt. **Es una enemistad que se palpa**, it´s a hostility which one can feel.

pálpebra [pahl´-pay-brah], *f.* Eyelid. V. PÁRPADO.

palpebral [pal-pay-brabl'], *a.* Palpebral, belonging to the eyelid.

palpitación [pal-pe-tah-the-on'],*f.* Palpitation, as of the heart: panting, heaving.

palpitante [pal-pe-tahn'-tay], *pa.* Vibrating, palpitating, throbbing (corazón).

palpitar [pal-pe-tar'], *vn.* 1. To palpitate, to pant, to flutter, to heave. 2. *(And. Cono Sur)* Me palpita, I have a hunch.

palpo [pahl'-po], *m.* Palpus, an organ of touch in insects, accessory to the mouth.

palta [pahl'-tah], *f. (Bot. Peru.)* Alligator-pear. V. AGUACATE.

palto [pahl'-to], *m. (Bot.)* Alligator-pear tree.

palude [pah-loo'-day],*f.* Lake, pool. V. LAGUNA.

palúdico, ca [pah-loo'-de-co, cah], *a.* 1. Malarial, afflicted with malaria. 2. Paludal, marshy.

paludismo [pah-loo-dees'-mo], *m. (Med.)* Malaria.

paludoso, sa [pah-loo-do'-so, sah], *a.* Marshy, swampy.

palumbario [pah-loom-bah'-re-o], *a.* Dove-hunting (azor).

palurdo [pah-loor'-do], *m.* A clown, a churl, a rustic.

palurdo, da [pah-loor'-do, dah], *a.* Rustic, clownish, rude.

palustre [pah-loos´-tray], *a.* Marshy, fenny, boggy. *-m.* Trowel.

palustrillo [pah-loos-treel'-lyo], *a.* Angle-float, a plasterer's trowel.

pallaco [pal-lyah'-co], *m. (Amer.)* Piece of ore of good quality found in a waste-heap.

pallaquear [pal-lyah-kay-ar'], *va.* (Peru) V. PALLAR.

pallar [pal-lyar'], *va.* To extract the richest metallic part of minerals.

pallete [pal-lyay'-tay], *m. (Naut.)* Fender, paunch-mat.

pallón [pal-lyone'], *m.* 1. The quantity of gold or silver resulting from an assay. 2. Assay of gold when incorporated with silver.

pamandabuán [pah-man-dah-boo-ahn'], *m.* A Philippine craft like a dugout, but larger; it carries oars and sometimes a mast, with a sail of matting.

pamela [pah-may'-lah], *f.* Picture hat, sun hat.

pamema [pa-may'-mah], *f.* 1. Trifle, bagatelle to which it was desired to give importance; folderol (bagatela). 2. Flattery (halagos). 3. Fuss (quejas).

pampa [pahm'-pah], *f.* 1. *(S. Amer.)* An extensive plain. 2. *(Cono Sur)* Region of nitrate deposits; open area on the outskirts of a town (descampado). *m.* A tree of the Philippine Islands. The wood is used for making chests and for sheathing boats.

pámpana [pahm'-pah-nah], *f.* Vine-leaf (hoja). **Tocar or zurrar la pámpana**, *(coll.)* to threaten, to chastise.

pampanada [pam-pah-nah'-dah],*f.* Juice of tendrils or vine-shoots.

pampanaje [pam-pah-nah'-hay], *m.* 1. Abundance of vine-shoots. 2. Vain parade.

pampanilla [pam-pah-neel'-lyah], *f.* A covering of foliage, used by Indians to screen their nakedness.

pámpano [pahm'-pah-no], *m.* 1. Young vine-branch or tendril. 2. *(Zool.)* V. SALPA. 3. *(Amer.)* A delicious steel-blue harvest-fish.

pampanoso, sa [pam-pah-no'-so, sah], *a.* Abounding with foliage, tendrils, and clusters of grapes.

pampero [pam-pay'-ro], *m.* 1. *(Arg.)* A violent wind from the south-west; so called because it blows from the pampas. 2. Inhabitant of the pampas (persona).

pampero, ra [pam-pay'-ro, rah], *m. & f. & a.* A dweller on the pampas.

pampirolada [pam-pe-ro-lah'-dah],*f.* 1. Sauce made of garlic, bread, and water, pounded in a mortar. 2. *(coll.)* A silly thing without substance.

pamplemusa [pam-play-moo'-sah],*f. (Bot.)* The shaddock and its fruit; grape-fruit.

pamplina [pam-plee´-nah], *f.* 1. *(Bot.)* Duck-weed. 2. *(Bot.)* Mouse-ear. 3. A plant yielding food to canary birds. 4. *(coll.)* Futility, trifle, a worthless thing. 5. Soft soap (jabón). 6. Nonsense (disparates). **Sin más pamplinas**, without any more beating about the bush.

pamporcino [pam-por-thee'-no], *m. (Bot.)* Cyclamen.

pamposado, da [pam-po-sah´-do, dah], *a.* Lazy, idle, cowardly.

pampringada [pam-prin-gah´-dah], *f.* 1. *V.* PRINGADA. 2. *(Met. Coll.)* 1. Frivolous, futile thing.

pan [pahn], *m.* 1. Bread, a loaf. 2. Pie-crust. 3. Mass of figs, salt, sugar, etc., in the shape of a loaf. 4. Food in general. 5. Wheat. **Este año hay mucho pan**, this year there is plenty of wheat. 6. A wafer or bread for the Eucharist, baked with baking-irons. 7. Leaf of gold or silver. 8. Greek prefix, signifying «all.» 9. All grains, except wheat, of which bread is made. **Pan casero o bazo**, household bread. **Pan por pan, vino por vino**, the plain unvarnished truth. **Pan de centeno**, rye bread. **Pan moreno**, brown bread. **Es el pan nuestro de cada día**, *(fig.)* our daily bread. **Eso es pan comido**, it´s a cinch. **Contigo pan y cebolla**, with you I´d gladly have love in a cottage. **Estar a pan y agua**, to be on bread and water. **Por un mendrugo de pan**, for a bite to eat. **Es más bueno que el pan**, he is kindness itself. **Se venden como pan bendito**, they sell like hot cakes. **Quitarle a uno el pan de la boca**, to take the bread out of somebody's mouth.

pana [pah´-nah], *f.* 1. Velveteen (paño), corduroy. 2. *pl.* *(Naut.)* Limber-boards, which form part of the lining of the ship's floor. *-m & f. (Carib.)* Pal, buddy.

panacea [pah-nah-thay´-ah],*f.* Panacea, universal medicine.

panada [pah-nah´-dah], *f.* Panada or panado.

panadear [pah-nah-day-ar'], *va.* To make bread for sale.

panadeo [pah-nah-day´-o], *m.* Baking bread.

panadería [pah-nah-day-ree´-ah], *f.* 1. Trade or profession of a baker. 2. Baker's shop (tienda), bake-house.

panadero, ra [pah-nah-day´-ro, rah], *m. & f.* Baker, maker or seller of bread, kneader. *-f.* Baker's wife.

panadizo, panarizo [pah-nah´-dee'-tho], *m.* 1. Whitlow, felon 2. *(coll.)* Pale-faced, sickly person.

panado, da [pah-nah'-do, dah], *a.* Applied to bread macerated in water for sick persons. *-m.* Panada or panado.

panal [pah-nahl´], *m.* 1. Honey-comb. 2. Anything pleasing to the taste.

panameño, ña [pah-nah-may'-nyo, nyah], *m. & f. & a.* Panamanian, from Panama.

panamericanismo [pah-nah-may-re-cah-nees'-mo], *m.* Pan Americanism.

panamericano, na [pahn-ah-may-re-cah'-no, nah], *a.* Pan-American, of both Americas.

panarra [pah-nar'-rah], *m.* Dolt, simpleton.

panática [pah-nah´-te-cah], *f.* Provision of bread.

panca [pahn'-cah], *f.* 1. The husk of an ear of maize. 2. A Philippine fishing-boat. It is provided with outriggers and with paddles, and is steered by a *papaya*.

pancarpia [pan-car'-pe-ah], *f.* A garland.

pancarta [pan-car'-tah], *f.* Placard, banner.

pancera [pan-thay'-rah], *f.* Armor which covers the belly.

páncreas [pahn´-cray-as], *m. (Anat.)* Pancreas, sweetbread.

pancromático, ca [pan-cro-mah'-te-co, cah], *a. (Photog.)* Panchromatic.

panda [pahn'-dah], *m. (Zool.)* Panda.

panda [pahn'-dah],*f.* 1. Gallery in a cloister. 2. *V.* PANDILLA.

pandear [pan-day-ar'], *vn.* To bend, to be inclined, to belly, to bulge out.

pandeo [pan-day'-o], *m.* Bulge, anything that bulges out in the middle.

panderada [pan-day-rah'-dah], *f.* 1. Number of timbrels joined in concert. 2. Stroke with a timbrel. 3. *(coll.)* A silly, untimely, or unreasonable proposition.

panderazo [pan-day-rah'-tho], *m.* Blow with a timbrel.
pandereta [pan-day-ray´-tah], *f.* Tambourine.
panderetear [pan-day-ray-tay-ar'], *vn.* To play on the timbrel.
pandereteo [pan-day-ray-tay'-o], *m.* The act of beating the timbrel.
panderetero, ra [pan-day-ray-tay'-ro, rah], *m. & f.* 1. One who beats the timbrel. 2. A maker or seller of timbrels.
panderillo [pan-day-reel'-lyo], *m. dim.* A small timbrel.
pandero [an-day´-ro], *m.* 1. Timbrel, a musical instrument. 2. *(coll.)* Silly person who talks at random (tonto). 3. *(Prov.)* Paper kite (cometa).
pandilla [pan-deel'-lyah], *f.* 1. Plot, league, party, faction. 2. Party of persons joined together for recreation in the country or for mischief.
pandillador, pandillero, pandillista [pan-dil-lyah-dor', lyay'-ro, lyis'-tah], *m.* Gangster, member of a rowdy gang.
pando, da [pahn'-do, dah], *a.* 1. Bulged. 2. Slow of motion (aguas profundas). 3. Heavy, bulky (personas). 4. *(CAm.)* Oppressed (oprimido); full (saciado). 5. *(CAm. Mex.)* Round-shouldered (de hombros).
pandorga [pan-dor´-gah], *f.* 1. Concert of musical instruments. 2 *(coll.)* Fat, bulky woman (gorda). 3. *(Prov.)* Kite (cometa). 4. *(And.)* Bother (molestia). 5. *(Mex.)* Practical joke (broma).
panecico, illo, ita [pan-nay-thee'-co], *m.* A small loaf of bread, a roll of bread.
panegírico, ca [pah-nay-hee´-re-co, cah], *a.* Panegyrical.
panegírico [pah-nay-hee´-re-co], *m.* Panegyric, eulogy.
panegirista [pah-nay-he-rees´-tah], *m.* Panegyrist, encomiast, eulogist.
panel [pah-nayl'], *m.* 1. Panel (madera). 2. **Paneles de instrumentos**, dashboard. **Panel de control (área de estado)**, *(Comput.)* control panel (status area).
panela [pah-nay'-lah], *f.* 1. *(Col.)* Brown sugar. 2. *(Her.)* A heart-shaped shield.
panera [pah-nay´-rah], *f.* 1. Granary. 2. Pannier, a bread-basket.
panes [pah'-nees], *m. pl.* 1. Corn or grain in the field. 2. Fauns, satyrs.
panetela [pah-nay-tay'-lah], *f.* 1. Panada, soup made by boiling bread and water. 2. *(Amer.)* Sponge-cake. 3. A long and slender cigar of Havana.
panetería [pah-nay-tay-ree´-ah], *f.* Room or office in the palace of the Spanish monarch, where bread and table-linen are kept for use; pantry.
panetero [pah-nay-tay'-ro], *m.* Pantler, the officer in the palace who keeps the bread.
pánfilo [pahn'-fe-lo], *m.* 1. A slow, sluggish, heavy person. 2. A jesting game, extinguishing a small candle in pronouncing this word.
panfleto [pan-flay'-to], *m.* Pamphlet; *(LAm.)* satire, lampoon, scandal sheet.
pangelín [pan-hay-leen'], *m.* Angelin-tree, forty or fifty feet high, with leaves like the walnut and a nut with a bitter and sourish taste.
pangolín [pan-go-leen'], *m.* Pangolin, the scaly ant-eater.
paniaguado [pah-ne-ah-goo-ah'-do], *m.* 1. Table-fellow, one who receives board and lodging from a friend. 2. Comrade, an intimate friend.
pánico, ca [pah'-ne-co, cah], *a.* Panic, struck with groundless fear. Also *m.*
panículo [pah-nee'-coo-lo], *m.* Panicle, pellicle, a membrane.
paniego, ga [pah-ne-ay'-go, gah], *a.* Eating or yielding much bread.
paniego [pah-ne-ay'-go], *m.* Bag of coarse cloth, in which charcoal is carried and sold.
panificar [pan-ne-fe-car'], *va.* To convert pasture-land into arable ground or corn-fields.
panilla [pah-neel'-lyah], *f.* A small measure of oil (1/4 lb.).
panizal [pah-ne-thahl'], *m.* A maize-field.
panizo [pah-nee'-tho], *m.* 1. *(Bot.)* Panic-grass. 2. *(Prov.)* Maize, Indian-corn.

panocha [pah-no'-chah], *f.* 1. Corncob, ear of maize. 2. *(Mex.)* Unrefined brown sugar (azúcar). 3. *(And. CAm. Cono Sur)* Large pancake of maize and cheese. 4. Brass, money (dinero). 5. *(Mex.)* cunt.
panoja [pah-no'-hah], *f.* *(Bot.)* Panicle, a species of inflorescence, consisting of a branched raceme or corymb. Grasses present spikes arranged in panicles.
panorama [pah-no-rah'-mah], *m.* Panorama; vista, view, scene; outlook (perspectiva), prospect.
panorámica [pah-no'-rah-me-cah], *f.* General view.
panorámico [pah-no-rah'-me-co], *a.* Panoramic.
pansofía [pan-so-fee'-ah], *f.* Universal science.
pantaletas [pan-tah-lay´-tahs], *f. pl.* Panties.
pantalla [pan-tahl'-lyah], *f.* 1. Lamp-shade (de lámpara). 2. Any screen or shelter (biombo). **Pantalla de chimenea**, fire-screen. 3. A person who puts himself before a thing to shelter and conceal it. 4. Screen (cine). **Pantalla de televisión**, television screen. **Los personajes de la pantalla**, screen personalities. 5. *(Cono Sur)* Fan (abanico). 6. *(Fig.)* Blind, pretext; decoy. 7. *(LAm.)* Henchman (esbirro). 8. *(CAm.)* Large mirror. 9. *(Comput.)* Display. **Pantalla de cristal líquido**, liquid cristal display. **Pantalla de mapa de bits**, bitmap display. **Pantalla táctil**, touch sensitive screen. **Pantalla de radar**, radar screen.
pantalón [pan-tah-lone'], *m.* V. PANTALONES.
pantalones [pan-tah-lo´-ness], *m. pl.* 1. Pants, slacks. **Ponerse los pantalones**, *(Coll.)* to show who is the boss (generally applied to the man of the house). **Llevar los pantalones**, *(Coll.)* to wear the pants, to be the head of a household. 2. *(And.)* Man, male. 3. *(Carib.)* Guts, courage.
pantano [pan-tah'-no], *m.* 1. Pool of stagnant water, fen, moor, marsh (natural), morass 2. A reservoir or lake for the purpose of irrigation (artificial). 3. Hindrance, obstacle, difficulty.
pantanoso, sa [pan-tah-no'-so, sah], *a.* 1. Marshy, fenny, boggy. 2. Full of difficulties, obstacles, and obstructions.
panteísmo [pan-tay-ees'-mo], *m.* Pantheism, belief that the universe is God.
panteísta [pan-tay-ees'-tah], *com.* Pantheist.
panteología [pan-tay-o-lo-hee'-ah], *f.* Pantheology.
panteón [pan-tay-on'], *m.* Pantheon, a temple of ancient Rome, now consecrated to the Holy Virgin under the title of Our Blessed Lady of the Rotunda. Hence, a splendid mausoleum for kings and other celebrities.
pantera [pan-tay'-rah], *f.* 1. Panther. 2. A mineral crystal enclosing foreign bodies.
panti [pahn'-te], *m.* Tights.
pantógrafo [pan-to´-grah-fo], *m.* Pantograph, a mathematical instrument for copying a drawing.
pantómetro [pan-to'-may-tro], *m.* Pantometer; proportional compasses for measuring heights and angles.
pantomima [pan-to-mee'-mah], *f.* Pantomime, a dumb show.
pantomímico, ca [pan-to-mee'-me-co, cah], *a.* Pantomimic, pantomimical.
pantomimo [pan-to-mee´-mo], *m.* Pantomime, a mimic, one who expresses his meaning by signs.
pantoque [pan-to'-kay], *m.* *(Naut.)* Bilge or fiat of the ship.
pantorrilla [pan-tor-reel'-lyah], *f.* Calf of the leg.
pantorrillera [pan-tor-reel-lyay'-rah], *f.* A stocking used to make the calf look big.
pantorrilludo, da [pan-tor-reel-lyoo'-do, dah], *a.* Having large or thick calves.
pantuflazo [pan-too-flah'-tho], *m.* Blow given with a slipper.
pantuflo [pan-too'-flo], *m.* Slipper.
panza [pahn'-thah], *f.* 1. Belly (abultado), paunch. 2. The projecting part of certain artificial bodies.
panzada [pan-thah´-dah], *f.* 1. Bellyful (hartazgo). 2. Push with the belly.
panzón [pan-thone'], *m.* Large-bellied person.
panzudo, da [pan-thoo'-do, dah], *a.* Big-bellied.
pañal [pah-nyahl'], *m.* 1. Swaddling-clout or cloth. 2. Cloth in which anything is wrapped up. 3. Tail of a shirt. *-pl.* 1.

Swaddling-clothes. 2. *(Met.)* The elements of education and instruction. **Estar en pañales**, to have little knowledge of anything. 3. Childhood, infancy. 4. Diaper. **Criarse en buenos pañales**, to be born with a silver spoon.

pañalico, illo, ito [pah-nyah-lee'-co], *m. dim.* A small swaddling-cloth.

pañalón [pah-nyah-lone'], *m.* One who has part of his clothes always falling off.

pañero [pah-nyay'-ro], *m.* Woollen draper, clothier.

pañete [pah-nyay'-tay], *m.* 1. *dim.* of PAÑO. 2. Cloth of inferior quality or light body (tela). *-pl.* 1. A kind of pants worn by fishermen and tanners. 2. Linen attached to the crucifix below the waist. 3. *(Cono Sur)* Horse blanket.

pañito, pañizuelo [pah-nyee'-to], *m. dim.* A small cloth. *(Mex.)* Small handkerchief; also, a Madras pocket-handkerchief.

paño [pah'-nyo], *m.* 1. Cloth, woollen stuff. 2. Any woven stuff, whether of silk, flax, hemp, wool or cotton. **Paño de seda negro**, strong black silk serge. 3. The breadth of any stuff made of wool, silk, etc. 4. **Paños de corte**, very fine pieces of Flemish tapestry. 5. The red color of a bloodshot eye; livid spot on the face; a ring-worm. 6. Spot in looking glasses, crystals, or precious stones. 7. *(Naut.)* Canvas, sail-cloth. 8. *(Arquit.)* Stretch, length. 9. Mist, cloud, cloudiness (en cristal); flaw (en diamantes). 10. *(Carib.)* Fishing net (red). 11. *(And.)* Plot of land (tierra). **Paños**, clothes, garments. **Paños menores**, small clothes, undergarments; dishabille. **Paño de sol**, *(Mex.)* a large square handkerchief embroidered with colored silk thrown over the head and shoulders as a protection from the sun, when traveling. **Paño de cocina**, dishcloth. **Paño higiénico**, sanitary towel. **Paños de secar**, tea towel.

pañol [pah-nyole'], *m. (Naut.)* Room in a ship where stores are kept. **Pañol de pólvora**, *(Naut.)* magazine. **Pañol del agua**, water store.

pañolero de Santa Bárbara [pah-nyo-lay'-ro], *m. (Naut.)* The gunner's yeoman. **Pañolero del pañol de proa**, *(Naut.)* the boatswain's yeoman.

pañolón [pah-nyo-lone'], *m.* A long square shawl.

pañoso, sa [pah-nyo'-so, sah], *a.* Ragged, dressed in rags.

pañuelo [pah-nyoo-ay'-lo], *m.* Handkerchief, kerchief, hand-cloth, scarf (de cabeza). **Pañuelos estampados**, printed handkerchiefs.

papa [pah'-pah], *m.* 1. The Pope. 2. *f. (Prov. and Amer.)* Potato. 3. *(Peru.)* A piece of silver found where there are no mines of this metal. 4. *(Zool.)* The yellow-bird, American goldfinch or yellow wabbler. 5. *pl.* Pap, a soup for infants; any sort of pap; any kind of food. V. PUCHAS. 6. Not a blind thing. **No entiendo ni papa**, I don't understand a word. 7. *(Cono Sur)* Bash, blow. 8. *(Carib.)* Soft job, plum. 9. *(Mex.)* Porridge (sopa).

papá [pah-pah'], *m. (coll.)* Papa, a fond name for father.

papada [pa'-pah'-dah], *f.* Double-chin; gill. **Papada de buey** or **toro**, dewlap of oxen. **Papada de puerco**, neck of a hog or pig.

papadilla [pah-pah-deel'-lyah], *f.* The fleshy part under the chin.

papado [pah-pah'-do], *m.* Popedom, pontificate, papacy.

papafigo [pah-pah-fee'-go], *m.* The fig-pecker, beccafico, the European garden-warbler.

papagaya [pah-pah-gah'-yah], *f.* Female parrot.

papagayo [pah-pah-gah'-yo], *m.* 1. Parrot. 2. Red fish full of venomous prickles. **Hierba del papagayo**, three-colored amaranth. 3. *(Carib. Mex.)* Large kite (cometa). 4. *(And.)* Bedpan (bacinilla).

papahigo [pah-pah-ee'-go], *m.* 1. Cap, headgear covering the face and neck. 2. V. PAPAFIGO. 3. *(Naut.)* Course, the lower sail.

papahuevos [pah-pah-oo-ay'-vos], *m.* Simpleton, clodpoll.

papal [pah-pahl'], *a.* Papal, papistical.

papalina [pah-pah-lee'-nah], *f.* 1. Cap with flaps which cover the ears (gorra). 2. Binge (juerga). 3. *(CAm.)* Potato chips.

papalote [pah-pah-lo'-tay], *m. (Cuba)* Kite. V. COMETA.

papalmente, *adv.* In a papal manner.

papamoscas [pah-pah-mos'-cas], *m.* 1. *(Orn.)* V. MOSCARETA. 2. Ninny.

papanatas [pah-pah-nah'-tas], *m.* Oaf, simpleton, ninny.

papandujo, ja [pah-pan-doo'-ho, hah], *a. (coll.)* Too soft: applied to over-ripe fruit.

papar [pah-par'], *va.* 1. To swallow soft food without chewing (tragar). 2. *(coll.)* To eat. 3. To pay little attention to things which claim much notice. *-vr.* **Paparse algo**, to eat up, to scoff.

páparo [pah'-pah-ro], *m.* Gawk, gump a rustic who stares stupidly.

paparrabias [pah-par-rah'-be-as], *m. & f. (coll.)* A testy, fretful person.

paparrasolla [pah-par-rah-sol'-lyah], *f.* Hobgoblin, a bugbear for children.

paparrucha [pah-par-roo'-chah], *f. (coll.)* 1. Silliness, folly, impertinence (disparate). 2. Hoax, humbug. 3. V. PATRAÑA. **Contar grandes paparruchas**, to tell incredible tales.

papasal [pah-pah-sahl'], *m.* Game among boys; any trifling amusement.

papaya [pah-pah'-yah], *f.* Papaw, the fruit of the *Papayo.*

papayo [pah-pah'-yo], *m. (Bot.)* Papaw tree.

pápaz [pah'-path], *m.* Christian priest, so called in Africa.

papazgo [pah-path'-go], *m.* Popedom, pontificate.

papear [pah-pay-ahr'], *vn.* To eat, to scoff.

papel [pah-pel'], *m.* 1. Paper. 2. Paper, writing, treatise, discourse. 3. Part acted in a play; actor, actress. 4. Anything written or printed which does not form a book. 5. A figure; a person of importance. 6. *(Com.)* Document; obligation (oficial). 7. *(Fin.)* **Papel moneda**, paper money (billetes). 8. Stocks, shares (valores). 9. *(And.)* One-peso note. 10. *(LAm.)* Bag. *-pl.* 1. Manuscripts. 2. Wry faces, gesticulations. **Hacer papel**, to cut a figure, to play a part, to personate. **Papel jaspeado**, marbled paper. **Papel sellado**, stamped paper, stamp. **Papel pintado**, stained paper. **Papel de seda**, tissue-paper. **Papel viejo**, waste paper. **Papel de lija**, sand-paper. **Hoja de papel**, leaf of paper. **Pliego de papel**, sheet of paper. **Papel de entapizar**, wall-paper, paper-hanging. **Papel de cartas**, notepaper. **Papel de fumar**, cigarette paper. **Papel para máquinas de escribir**, typing paper. **Papel prensa**, newsprint. **Sobre el papel**, on paper. **Los papeles, por favor**, your papers, please. **Desempeñar un papel**, *(fig.)* to play a part. **Hacer el papel de**, to act as.

papeleador [pah-pay-lay-ah-dor'], *m.* Searcher of papers; scribbler.

papelear [pah-pay-lay-ar'], *vn.* 1. To run over papers. 2. *(coll.)* To figure, or make a figure.

papeleo [pah-pay-lay'-o], *m. (Coll.)* Red tape.

papelera [pah-pay-lay'-rah], *f.* 1. A number of written papers placed together. 2. Writing-desk, scrutoire, paper-case (mesa).

papelería [pah-pay-lay-ree'-ah], *f.* 1. Heap of papers without order (montón). 2. A stationery shop (tienda).

papelero [pah-pay-lay'-ro], *m.* Paper maker (fabricante).

papeleta [pah-pay-lay'-tah], *f.* 1. Slip of paper on which something is written (trozo de papel). 2. Case of paper in which money or sweetmeats are kept. 3. *(CAm.)* Visiting card.

papelillo [pah-pay-leel'-lyo], *m. dim.* V. PAPELEJO.

papelina [pah-pay-lee'-nah], *f.* 1. A small wine-glass with a foot. 2. A very thin sort of cloth; poplin.

papelista [pah-pay-lees'-tah], *m.* One who is always employed about papers and writings.

papelito [pah-pay-lee'-to], *m. dim.* A small paper, paper for a hair-curl.

papelón [pah-pay-lone'], *m.* 1. *(Aug.)* A large piece of paper posted up, such as edicts and proclamations; prolix writing. 2. Pamphlet. 3. Boaster. 4. *(And. Carib.)* Sugar loaf. **Escritor de papelones sueltos**, pamphleteer.

papelonear [pah-pay-lo-nay-ar'], *vn.* To be boastful or presumptuous.

papera [pah-pay'-rah], *f.* 1. Wen on the throat. 2. Mumps.

papero [pah-pay'-ro], *m.* 1. Pot in which a child's pap is made. 2. Potato grower; potato dealer.

papialbillo [pah-pe-ahl-beel'-lyo], *m.* Weasel.

papila [pah-pee'-lah], *f. (Med.)* Papilla, the fine termination of nerves in some organs.

papilar [pah-pe-lar'], *a.* Papillary, papillous, very small eminences on the skin.

papilla [pah-peel'-lyah], *f.* 1. Pap, food for infants. 2. Guile, deceit, artifice. **Dar papilla**, to deceive by insidious caresses.

papilonáceo, a [pah-pe-lo-nah'-thay-o, ah], *a.* Papilionaceous, butterfly-like.

papión [pah-pe-on'], *m.* A kind of large monkey. *V.* CEFO.

papiráceo, cea [pah-pe-rah'-thay-o, ah], *a.* Papyraceous, papery, dry and thin.

papiro [pah-pee'-ro], *m. (Bot.)* Egyptian papyrus or paper-tree.

papirolada [pah-pe-ro-lah'-dah], *f.* Sauce made of garlic and bread. *V.* PAMPIROLADA.

papirotada [pah-pe-ro-tah'-dah], *f.* Fillip on the neck or face; rap at the nose.

papirote [pah-pe-ro'-tay], *m. (coll.)* Fillip.

papista [pah-pees'-tah], *a.* Papist, Roman Catholic. **Más papista que el papa**, more papist than the Pope, more royalist than the king.

papo [pah'-po], *m.* 1. The fleshy part which hangs from the chin. 2. Quantity of food given to a bird of prey at once. 3. Down of thistles. **Papos**, furbelow.

papudo, da [pah-poo'-do, dah], *a.* Double-chinned.

papujado, da [pah-poo-hah'-do, dah], *a.* 1. Full gorged (pájaros). 2. Swollen, thick, elevated.

pápula [pah'-poo-lah], *f.* Papula, a scrofulous tumor on the throat.

paquebote [pah-kay-bo'-tay], *m.* Packet or packet-boat, a vessel appointed to carry the mail.

paquete [pah-kay'-tay], *m.* l. A small packet, a little bale, a parcel (correos). 2. Bundle of letters sealed or tied up together. 3. A packet-boat. 4. Dandy (majo). 5. **Meter un paquete a uno**, to put somebody on a charge. 6. *(Comput.)* **Paquete integrado**, integrated package. **Paquete de hojas de cálculo electrónicas**, electronic spreadsheet. **Paquete exclusivo**, dedicated package. **Paquete de aplicaciones**, application package. 7. *(Med.)* Dose. 8. *(LAm.)* Nuisance (cosa pesada). 9. *(Mex.)* Tough job (asunto). 10. *(Cono Sur)* Queer. 11. *(LAm.)* Package holiday (vacaciones).

paquidermo, ma [pah-ke-derr'-mo, mah], *a.* Thick-skinned, pachydermatous. *m. pl. (Zool.)* The pachydermata.

par [pahr], *a.* 1. Equal, alike, on a par, even. **Sin par**, matchless.-*adv.* Near. *V.* CERCA or JUNTO.

par [pahr], *m.* 1. Pair, couple. 2. Peer of the realm. 3. Handle of a bell. 4. Equal (igual). 5. (Golf) Par. **Pares y nones**, odd or even: a play. **A la par**, jointly, equally; at par, without discount. **A pares**, by pairs, two and two. **De par en par**, broad, open (puerta). **Ir a la par**, to go halves, to have an equal share in the business. **A par de**, near, joining, like. **A pares**, by pairs. **Números pares**, round or even numbers. **Caminar al par de**, to walk abreast of. **Estar abierto de par en par**, to be wide open. **Estar por debajo de la par**, to be under par. -*f.* **Las pares**, the placenta or after-birth.

para [pah'-rah], *prep.* For, to, in order to (finalidad), toward, wherefore, to the end that. **Ese hombre es para todo** or **es para nada**, that man is fit for everything or he is fit for nothing. **Para entre los dos**, between us both. **Para evitar**, to avoid. **¿Para qué?** why?, what for? **Leer para sí**, to read to oneself. **Para siempre**, for ever. **Para eso**, for that, for so much: used in contempt. **Lo traje para ti**, I brought it for you. **Ir para casa**, to go home. **Tengo bastante para vivir**, I have enough to live on. **Lo traje para que lo veas**, I brought it so that you could see it. **Para mañana**, for tomorrow. **Tan amable para todos**, so kind to everybody.

parabás [pah-rah-bahs'], *m.* Thick border of a palm mat on the step of an altar.

parabién [pah-rah-be-en'], *m.* Compliment of congratulation, felicitation. **Dar el parabién**, to congratulate, to compliment.

parabienero [pah-rah-be-ay-nay'-ro], *m. (coll.)* One who congratulates; a person full of compliments.

parábola [pah-rah'-bo-lah], *f.* 1. Parable. 2. *(Geom.)* Parabola.

parabólico, ca [pah-rah-bo'-le-co, cah], *a.* Parabolical, parabolic, relating to parables or parabolas.

parabrisas [pah-rah-bree'-sahs], *m.* Windshield.

paracaídas [pah-rah-cah-e'-das], *m.* Parachute. **Paracaídas de frenado**, *(Aer.)* drag chute.

paracaidista [pah-rah-cah-ee-dees'-tah], *m & f.* Parachutist, parachute jumper. *(Mex. Coll.)* Squatter.

paracéntrico, ca [pah-rah-then'-tre-co, cah], *a.* Paracentric, deviating from circularity.

parachoques [pah-rah-cho'-kes], *m.* Bumper, fender; *(Ferro.)* buffer.

paracleto, paráclito [pah-rah-clay'-to, pah-rah'-cle-to], *m.* Paraclete, name given to the Holy Ghost.

paracronismo [pah-rah-cro-nees'-mo], *m.* Parachronism.

parachoques [pah-rah-cho'-kays], *m.* Fender (automóvil.)

parada [pah-rah'-dah], *f.* 1. Halt, halting, the place where one halts. 2. The end of the motion of anything. 3. Stop, suspension, pause. 4. Fold for cattle. 5. Relay of mules or horses. 6. Dam (presa), bank. 7. Stakes (apuestas), set, bet; anything staked. 8. Parade, a place of parade for troops. 9. *(CAm. Mex.)* Clip of cartridges (cartuchos). 10. *(LAm.)* Vanity (vanidad), pride, presumption. 11. *(And.)* Crafty trick. 12. *(And.)* Farmer's market. **Parada de autobús**, bus stop. **Parada de taxis**, taxi stand.

paradera [pah-rah-day'-rah], *f.* 1. Sluice, flood-gate. 2. A kind of fish-net.

paradero [pah-rah-day'-ro], *m.* 1. Halting-place. 2. Term or end of anything. **No saber el paradero de alguno**, not to know the whereabouts of a person; not to know what has become of him.

paradigma [pah-rah-deeg'-mah], *m.* Example, instance, paradigm.

paradisíaco, ca [pah-rah-de-see'-ah-co, cah], *a.* Paradisiacal, relating to paradise.

paradislero [pah-rah-dis-lay'-ro], *m.* 1. Sportsman waiting for his game. 2. Newsmonger.

parado, da [pah-rah'-do, dah], *a.* 1. Stationary, still, stopped, motionless. 2. Remiss, careless, indolent, cold, inactive. 3. Unemployed, without business or employment (obrero). 4. **Estuve parado durante 2 horas**, *(LAm.)* I was standing for 2 hours. 4. *(And. Carib.)* To be unlucky. 5. *(LAm.)* Still (pelo), straight. 6. *(Carib. Cono Sur)* Vain (vanidoso). **Me quedé parado**, I was completely confused. **Salir bien parado**, to come off well.

paradoja [pah-rah-do'-hah], *f.* Paradox.

paradójico, ca [pah-rah-do'-he-co, cah], *a.* Paradoxical.

paradojo, ja [pah-rah-do'-ho, hah], *a.* Paradoxical, extravagant.

parador [pah-rah-dor'], *m.* 1. Sojourner, lodger. 2. Inn, hostelry. **Parador para turistas**, tourist court, motel.

parafernales (Bienes), [pah-rah-fer-nah'-les], *a. & m. pl.* Paraphernalia, goods which a wife brings, independent of her portion, and which are at her disposal.

parafernalia [pah-rah-fer-nah'-le-ah], *f.* Paraphernalia.

parafina [pah-rah-fee'-nah], *f.* Paraffin, a translucent solid mixture of hydrocarbons, used in candles, and in other industrial applications.

parafrasear [pah-rah-frah-say-ar'], *va.* To paraphrase.

paráfrasis [pah-rah'-frah-sis], *f.* Paraphrase, explanation in more intelligible terms.

prafraste [pah-rah-frahs'-tay], *m.* Paraphrast, expounder.

parafrástico, ca [pah-rah-frahs'-te-co, cah], *a.* Paraphrastic, paraphrastical.

paragoge [pah-rah-go´-gay], *f. (Gram.)* Addition of a letter or syllable at the end of a word.

paragonar [pah-rah-go-nar´], *va.* To paragon, to compare, to equal.

paraguas [pah-rah'-goo-as], *m.* 1. Umbrella. 2. *(And. Carib. Mex.)* Mushroom (seta comestible); toadstool (no comestible).

paraguayo [pah-rah-goo-ah'-ee], *m.* A species of parrot.

paraguayano, na [pah-rah-goo-ah-yah´-no, nah], *a.* Of Paraguay.

paraíso [pah-rah-ee´-so], *m.* 1. The garden of Eden. 2. Paradise, any delightful place. 3. Paradise, heaven.

paraje [pah-rah'-hay], *m.* 1. Place, residence. 2. Condition, disposition.

paral [pah-rahl'], *m.* 1. Wooden trough in which the keel of a ship runs in launching. 2. A scaffolding-pole.

paraláctico, ca [pah-rah-lahc´-te-co, cah], *a.* Parallactic.

paralaje [pah-rah-lah´-hay], *f. (Ast.)* Parallax. So, too, **Paralaxi.**

paralelepípedo [pah-rah-lay-lay-pee'-pay-do], *m. (Geom.)* Parallelopiped.

paralelismo [pah-rah-lay-lees'-mo], *m.* Parallelism.

paralelizar [pah-rah-lay-le-thar'], *va.* To parallel, to compare.

paralelo, la [pah-rah-lay'-lo, lah], *a.* Parallel, similar, correspondent.

paralelo [pah-rah-lay'-lo], *m.* Parallel, resemblance, comparison.

paralelogramo, ma [pah-rah-lay-lo-grah'-mo, mah], *a.* Parallelogramical.

paralelogramo [pah-rah-lay-lo-grah'-mo], *m.* Parallelogram.

paralipómenos [pah-rah-le-po'-may-nos], *m.* Two books of the Bible, 1st and 2d Chronicles.

parálisis [pah-rah´-le-sis], *f.* Paralysis. **Parálisis cerebral,** cerebral palsy. **Parálisis infantil,** infantile paralysis, poliomyelitis.

paralítico, ca [pah-rah-lee´-te-co, cah], *a.* V. PERLÁTICO.

paralizar [pah-rah-le-thar'], *ra.* 1. To paralyze, to palsy. 2. To impede moral action. 3. To stop (tráfico). **Estar paralizado de un brazo,** to be paralyzed in one arm. *-vr.* To become paralyzed.

paralogismo [pah-rah-lo-hees'-mo], *m.* Paralogism, false reasoning.

paralogizar [pah-rah-lo-he-thar'], *vn.* To paralogize, to reason sophistically.

paramentar [pah-rah-men-tar'], *va.* To adorn, to embellish.

paramento [pah-rah-men'-to], *m.* 1. Ornament (adorno), embellishment, facing. 2. Cloth, with which anything is covered.

paramera [pah-rah-may´-rah], *f.* A great extent of territory where bleak deserts abound.

paramilitar [pah-rah-me-le-tar], *a.* Paramilitary.

parámetro [pah-rah´-may-tro], *m. (Geom.)* Parameter.

páramo [pah'-rah-mo], *m.* 1. Paramo, an Alpine plain open to the winds. 2. Any place extremely cold. 3. Waste land (descampado). 4. *(And.)* Drizzle (llovizna).

parancero [pah-ran-thay'-ro], *m.* Bird-catcher.

parangón [pah-ran-gone'], *m.* Paragon, model, comparison.

parangona [pah-ran-go´-nah], *f. (Print.)* Paragon type; about 20-point.

parangonar, parangonizar [pah-ran-go-nar'], *va.* To paragon, to match, to compare.

paranínfico [pah-rah-nccn'-fe-co], *a. (Arch.)* Applied to a style of building having statues of nymphs instead of columns.

paraninfo [pah-rah-nen'-fo], *m.* (Archaic.) Paranymph: a bridesmaid or best man.

paranoia [pah-rah-noy´-ah], *f.* Paranoia.

paranoico, ca [pah-rah-noy'-co, cah], *m. & f. & a.* Paranoiac.

paranormal [pah-rah-nor-mal'], *a.* Paranormal.

paranza [pah-rahn'-thah], *f.* Hut in which sportsmen lie in ambush for game (caza).

parao [pah-rah'-o], *m.* Large vessel in the Philippines, carrying a high cabin at the poop.

parapeto [pah-rah-pay'-to], *m.* 1. *(Mil.)* Parapet, breast-work. 2. Rails or battlements on bridges and quays. **Parapetos de combate,** *(Naut.)* netting, parapets in the waist of the ship.

paraplejia [pah-rah-play'-he-ah], *f.* Paraplegia.

parapléjico, ca [pah-rah-play'-he-co, cah], *a.* Paraplegic.

parapoco [pah-rah-po'-co], *com.* A numskull, a blockhead.

parapsicología [pah-rah-pse-co-lo-hee'-ah], *f.* Parapsychology.

parar [pah-rar'], *vn.* 1. To stop, to halt, to desist, to give over. 2. **Parar en,** to end up as (proyecto). 3. To point (caza). **El coche ha parado,** the car has stopped. **Parar en seco,** to stop dead. **No para de quejarse,** he never stops complaining. **Fueron a parar en la comisaría,** they finished up at the police station. *-va.* 1. To stop, to detain, to put an end to the motion or action of a thing (coche, motor, respiración). 2. To get ready, to prepare (arreglar). 3. To end, to bring to a close. 4. To treat or use ill. 5. To stake at cards (naipes). 6. To point out the game. 7. To devolve, to come to the possession of. 8. To happen, to fall out. 9. To come to an end, to finish (acabar). 10. To change one thing into another. 11. **Pararla con uno,** *(And.)* to take it out on somebody (vengarse). **Ir a parar,** to come to, to end this or that way. **No poder parar,** not to rest; to be uneasy. **Sin parar,** non-stop, instantly, without delay. *-vr.* 1. To stop, to halt (proceso). 2. To assume another character. 3. **Pararse en algo,** to pay attention to something. 4. *(LAm.)* To stand up (levantarse), to straighten up (enderezarse); to stand on end (pelo). 5. *(LAm. Fig.)* To prosper, to become wealthy.

pararrayo [pah-rar-rah'-yo], *vn.* A lightning-rod or conductor.

parasca [pah-rahs'-cah], *f.* A portion of the Scriptures assigned to be read in the synagogue.

paraselene [pah-rah-say-lay´-nay], *f. (Met.)* Mock-moon.

parasema [pah-rah-say'-mah], *f.* Figure-head of a vessel.

parasismo [pah-rah-sees´-mo], *m.* Paroxysm, a fit.

parasítico, ca [pah-rah-see´-te-co, cah], *a.* Parasitic, living upon another.

parásito, ta [pah-rah'-se-to, tah], *a.* Parasitic. *-m.* Parasite. **Ruidos parásitos,** interference, static.

parasitología [pah-rah-se-to-lo-hee'-ah], *f.* Parasitology.

parasol [pah-rah-sole'], *m.* Parasol. V. QUITASOL.

paratesis [pah-rah-tay'-sis], *f.* Prayer which the Greek bishop makes at the ceremony of confirmation.

paratifoidea [pah-rah-tee-foy-day'-ah], *f. (Med.)* Paratyphoid, paratyphoid fever.

parauso [pah-rah'-oo-so], *m.* Drill for metals; a mandrel.

parazonio [pah-rah-tho'-ne-o], *m.* Broad-sword without a point.

parca [par'-cah], *f.* Fate, death.

parcamente [par-cah-men'-tay], *adv.* Sparingly, parsimoniously.

parce [par'-thay], *m.* Written excuse or pardon given to grammar scholars.

parcela [par-thay'-lah], *f.* 1. Plot (solar), piece of ground. 2. *(Fig.)* Part, portion; area.

parcero [par-thay'-ro], *m.* Partner, copartner.

parchazo [par-chah'-tho], *m.* 1. *(Augm.)* A large plaster. 2. *(Met. Coll.)* Deception, jest.

parche [par'-chay], *m.* 1. A plaster for a wound or sore. 2. Parchment with which a drum is covered. 3. *(Poet.)* Drum. 4. Patch on the face.

parcial [par-the-ahl'], *a.* 1. Partial, inclined to favor without reason. 2. Partial, partisan (partidista), inclined to favor a party or side of the question. 3. Partial (incompleto), affecting only one part; subsisting only in a part. 4. Partial, friendly, familiar. 5. Sociable, communicable.

parcialidad [par-the-ah-le-dahd'], *f.* 1. Partiality (cualidad), prejudice against or in favor of a person. 2. Friendship, familiar intercourse, sociability. 3. Party (grupo), faction.

parcializar [par-the-ah-le-thar'], *va.* To partialize, to render partial.

parcialmente [par-the-ahl'-men-tay] , *adv.* Partially, familiarly, friendly.

parcidad [par-the-dahd'], *f.* Parsimony, frugality.

parcionero [par-the-o-nay'-ro], *m.* Partner in a business.

parco, ca [par'-co, cah], *a.* 1. Sparing, scanty. 2. Sober, moderate. *-m. (Prov.)* **Muy parco en elogios,** sparing in one's praises. *V.* PARCÉ.

pardal [par-dahl'], *a.* Clownish, rustic; cunning. *-m.* 1. *(Orn.)* A sparrow. 2. A leopard. 3. A crafty fellow. 4. PARDILLO. 5. *(Bot.)* Aconite, wolf's-bane.

pardear [par-day-ar'], *vn.* To grow gray or brownish; to become dusky.

par diez [par de-eth']. Kind of jocular oath. *V.* PAR DIOS.

pardillo [par-deel'-lyo], *m.* 1. Greater redpoll, linnet. 2. Robin-redbreast. 3. A kind of grape, and the wine made from it. 4. Yokel, rustic (persona: rústico). *-a.* Grayish, brown (paño).

pardo, da [par'-do, dah], *a.* 1. Gray, drab, brown; a mixture of black and white containing some yellow or red (color). 2. Cloudy (nube). **Oso pardo,** brown bear. **De noche todos los gatos son pardos,** all cats are gray after dark; dim light favors the concealment of blemishes.

pardo [par'-do], *m.* Leopard.

pardusco, ca [par-doos'-co, cah], *a.* Light brown, grayish, grizzly.

parear [pah-ray-ar'], *va.* To match (formar pares), to pair, to couple. *-vn. (Carib.)* To skive.

parecer [pah-ray-therr'], *m.* 1. Opinion (opinión), advice, counsel. 2. Countenance, air, mien: look (aspecto). **A mi parecer,** in my opinion.

parecer [pah-ray-therr'], *vn.* 1. To appear, to be visible. 2. To seem. 3. To form a judgment of a thing, to seem. 4. To appear, to be found (objeto perdido). 5. To judge, to approve or disapprove. 6. To look like (semejar). **Al parecer,** seemingly, to all appearance. **Parece muy difícil,** it seems very difficult. **Parece que va a llover,** it looks as though it's going to rain. **Me parece bien que vayas,** I think you should go. **Pareció el sol entre las nubes,** the sun showed through the clouds. *-vr.* To present oneself to view; to assimilate or conform to; to be like, to resemble. **Se parecen mucho,** they look very much alike. **Se parece al abuelo,** he takes after his grandfather. *(Yo parezco, yo parezca,* from *Parecer.* *V.* CONOCER.)

pareciente [pah-ray-the-en'-tay], *a.* Similar, apparent.

parecido, da [pah-ray-thee'-do, dah], *a.* & *pp.* of PARECER. 1. Appeared, found. 2. Resembling, like (semejante). 3. Good or ugly-looking, well or ill-favored, with the adverbs *bien* or *mal.* **Son muy parecidos,** they are very similar. **Bien parecido,** good-looking.

pared [pah-red'], *f.* 1. Wall of bricks or stones. 2. Surface of a field of barley which is close and even. **Entre cuatro paredes,** confined, retired: imprisoned. **Darse contra las paredes,** to butt against the wall, to struggle ineffectively. **Las paredes oyen,** walls have ears. **Pegado a la pared,** to be broke. **Se sube por las paredes,** he's hopping mad. **Es como si hablara a una pared,** it's like talking to a brick wall. **Estaba blanco como la pared,** he was as white as a sheet/ghost.

paredaño, ña [pah-ray-dah'-nyo, nyah], *a.* Having a wall between.

paredilla [pah-ray-deel'-lyah], *f. dim.* A slight wall.

paredón [pah-ray-done'], *m. aug.* 1. A thick wall (muro); standing wall (de ruina). 2. Wall of rock (de roca). 3. **Llevar a uno al paredón,** to put somebody up against a wall.

paregórico [pah-ray-go'-re-co], *a.* Paregoric, anodyne.

pareja [pah-ray'-hah], *f.* 1. Pair (par), couple (esposos), brace; match; coupling. 2. Boyfriend (amigo), girlfriend (amiga); lover (amante); other half (cónyuge). 3. *(LAm.)* Pair of horses (caballos); team of draught animals (de tiro). **Pareja de baile,** dancing partner. **No encuentro la pareja de este guante,** I can't find the glove that goes with this one.

parejo, ja [pah-ray'-ho, hah], *a.* Equal (igual), similar (semejante). **Por parejo** or **por un parejo,** on equal terms, on a par.

parejura [pah-ray-hoo'-rah], *f.* Equality, similitude, uniformity.

parénesis [pah-ray'-nay-sis], *f.* Admonition, precept, instruction.

parental [pa-ren-tahl'], *a.* Parental.

parentela [pah-ren-tay'-lah], *f.* Parentage, kindred, kinsfolk, relations.

parentesco [pah-ren-tes'-co], *m.* 1. Cognation, kindred, relationship. 2. Union, chain, link.

paréntesis [pah-ren'-tay-sis], *m.* 1. Parenthesis, a short digression included in a sentence. 2. Interruption or suspension of things. **Entre** or **por paréntesis,** parenthetically, by parenthesis. **Entre paréntesis,** *(coll.)* by-the-bye. 3. Parenthesis, the character ().

pareo [pah-ray'-o], *m.* The act of pairing (unión), couplin, or matching.

parergón [pah-rer-gone'], *m.* Additional ornament.

pares [pah'-res], *f. pl. V.* SECUNDINAS.

paresia [pah-ray'-se-ah], *f. (Med.)* Paresis, slight paralysis.

parhelia [par-ay'-le-ah], *f.* **Parhelio,** *m.* Parhelion, a mock sun.

parhilera [par-e-lay'-rah], *f. (Arch.)* Ridge-pole, ridge-piece.

paria [pah'-re-ah], *m.* Pariah, a Hindu outcast: one of the lowest caste.

parias [pah'-re-as], *f.* 1. Tribute paid by one prince to another. 2. Placenta.

parición [pah-re-the-on'], *f.* Child-bearing, parturition; season of bringing forth young.

parida [pah-ree'-dah], *f.* 1. Woman lately delivered (mujer). *V.* PARIDO. 2. Silly thing, stupid remark (dicho).

paridad [pah-ree-dahd'], *f.* 1. Parity, the act of comparing; equality (igualdad). 2. Comparison (comparación).

paridera [pah-re-day'-rah], *a.* Fruitful, prolific (hembras). *-f.* 1. Place where cattle bring forth their young. 2. Act of bringing forth young.

parido, da [pah-ree'-do, dah], *a.* & *pp.* Of PARIR. *Parida,* 1. Delivered, brought to bed. 2. Lately delivered.

parienta [pah-re-ayn'-tah], *f.* 1. Relative, relation. 2. **La parienta,** the wife.

pariente, ta [pah-re-en'-tay, tah], *m.* & *f.* 1. Relation, by birth or marriage; kinsman, kinswoman. 2. Anything resembling another. 3. *(coll.)* Appellation given by husband and wife to each other. **Pariente político,** relative by marriage. **Los parientes políticos,** the in-laws.

parietal [pah-re-ay-tahl'], *a.* Relating to a wall. *(Anat.)* Parietal (hueso).

parietaria [pah-re-ay-tah'-re-ah], *f. (Bot.)* Pellitory.

parificar [pah-re-fe-car'], *va.* To exemplify.

parihuela [pah-re-oo-ay'-lah], *f.* Handbarrow, litter; **parihuelas,** stretcher.

pario (mármol) [pah'-re-o], *a.* Parian marble.

parir [pah-reer'], *va.* 1. To bring forth a foetus, to give birth. 2. To lay eggs, to spawn. 3. To produce, to cause. 4. To explain, to clear up, to publish. **Poner a parir,** to oblige one to perform a thing against his will; to put one to his trumps.

parisién, siense [pah-re-se-en', se-en'-say], *m.* & *f.* & *a.* Parisian.

parking [pahr'-keen], *m.* Car park.

parla [pahr'-lah], *f.* Easy delivery, loquacity, gossip.

parladillo [par-lah-deel'-lyo], *m.* An affected style.

parlador, ra [par-lah-dor', rah], *m.* & *f.* A chattering person.

parladuría [par-lah-doo-ree'-ah], *f.* An impertinent speech; loquacity.

parlamental [par-lah-men-tahl'], *a.* Parliamentary.

parlamentar, parlamentear [par-lah-men-tar'], *vn.* 1. To talk, to converse. 2. To parley (enemigos), to treat for the surrender of a place.

parlamentario [par-lah-men-tah'-re-o], *m.* 1. Member of parliament. 2. A person who goes to parley with an enemy.

3. A flag of truce, a cartel. 4. Parliamentarian, one who adhered to the English parliament in the time of Charles I.

parlamentario, ria [par-lah-men-tah'-re-o, ah], *a.* Parliamentary, parliamentarian.

parlamento [par-lah-men'-to], *m.* 1. Speech or harangue in a public assembly. 2. Parliament, the legislative assembly of Great Britain. 3. Parley (entre enemigos). 4. A flag of truce.

parlanchín, na [par-lan-cheen', nah], *a. & a.* Chatterer, jabberer.

parlante [par-lahn'-tay], *pa.* Speaking; a talker.

parlar [par-lar'], *va.* 1. To chatter. 2. To disclose what ought to be kept secret. **Parlar en balde,** to talk nonsense.

parlatorio [par-lah-to'-re-o], *m.* 1. Converse, parley. 2. Parlor, the place in convents where nuns are allowed to converse with their friends.

parlera, parlantina [par-lay'-rah, par-lan-tee'-nah], *f (coll.)* A talkative little woman.

parlería [par-lay-ree'-ah], *f.* 1. Loquacity, garrulity, gossip: tale, jest. 2. Singing or chirping of birds: purling of brooks and rivers.

parlerito, ita [par-lay-ree'-to, tah], *a. dim. (coll.)* Talkative, garrulous.

parlero, ra [par-lay'-ro, rah], *a.* 1. Loquacious, talkative (hablador). 2. Talking (pájaro); singing, song; expressive (ojos). -*m.* 1. Tale-bearer, tattler. 2. Bird that chirps and chatters. 3. Purling brook or rill. 4. Interesting conversation.

parleta [par-lay'-tah], *f.* Conversation on the weather, or on trifling subjects.

parlón, na [par-lone', nah], *a.* Loquacious, garrulous.

parlotear [par-lo-tay-ar'], *vn.* To prattle, to prate, to chatter, to gossip.

parloteo [par-lo-tay'-o], *m.* Prattle, talk.

parmesano, na [par-may-sah'-no, nah], *a.* Parmesan, of Parma.

parnaso [par-nah'-so], *m.* 1. *(Poet.)* Parnassus, Helicon. 2. A collection of selected poems. 3. Assemblage of poets.

paro [pah'-ro], *m.* 1. Lockout, suspension of work. **Paro forzoso,** layoff (en una fábrica.), unemployment (desempleo), stoppage, standstill, (suspensión en el trabajo). 2. *(Orn.)* Titmouse. 3. *(And. Carib.)* Throw (de dados).

parodia [pah-ro´-de-ah], *f.* Parody.

parodiar [pah-ro-de-ar'], *va.* To parody.

paródico, ca [pah-ro´-de-co, cah], *a.* Parodical.

parola [pah-ro'-lah], *f.* 1. *(coll.)* Eloquence, fluency (soltura), volubility. 2. Chat (charla), idle talk.

póroli [pah'-ro-lee], *m.* Double of what was laid in stakes at the game of bank.

parolina [pah-ro-lee'-nah], *f. V.* PAROLA.

parón [pah-rone'], *m.* Sudden halt.

parónimo, ma [pah-ro´-ne-mo, mah], *a.* Paronymous; words cognate or alike.

paronomasia [pah-ro-no-mah'-se-ah], *f.* Paronomasia, a rhetorical figure.

parótida [pah-ro'-te-dah], *f.* 1. A parotid gland. 2. Swelling of the parotid glands, mumps.

paroxismal [pah-rok-sis-mahl'], *m.* Paroxysmal.

paroxismo [pah-rok-sees'-mo], *m.* Paroxysm. *V.* PARASISMO.

parpadear [par-pah-day-ar'], *vn.* 1. To wink, to open and shut the eyes by turns. 2. To blink (ojo); to blink (luz).

parpadeo [par pah-day'-o], *m.* Blinking, winking; flickering; twinkling.

párpado [par'-pah-do], *m.* The eyelid.

parpalla [par-pahl'-lyah], *f.* A milled copper piece.

parpar [par-par'], *m.* Quacking, the cry of a duck.

parque [par'-ka], *m.* 1. Park, an enclosed wood or ornamental grounds. 2. Park of artillery, park of provisions. **Parque de automóviles,** car park. **Parque nacional,** national park. 3. *(LAm. Mil.)* Equipment (equipo); ammunition (munición); ammunition dump (depósito).

parquedad [par-kay-dahd'], *f.* Parsimony.

parra [par'-rah], *f.* 1. Vine raised on stakes or nailed to a wall. 2. Earthen jar or pot, broad and low, with handles.

párrafo [par'-rah-fo], *m.* Paragraph, a distinct part of a discourse. **Párrafo aparte,** new paragraph (punto y aparte), to change the subject (cambio de conversación).

parragón [par-rah-gone'], *m.* Standard silver for assayers.

parral [par-rahl'], *m.* 1. Vine abounding with shoots for want of dressing, and the place where there are such vines. 2. A large earthen jar for honey.

parranda [pahr-rhan'-dah], *f.* 1. Spree party (juerga). 2. *(And. Cono Sur, Mex.)* Lot, group, heap.

parrar [par-rar'], *vn.* To extend, to spread out in branches and bowers.

parricida [par-re-thee'-dah], *com.* Parricide, one who kills his father or mother, or any other person to whom he owes reverence.

parricidio [par-re-thee'-de-o], *m.* Parricide, murder of a father or mother, or of any person to whom reverence is due.

parrilla [par-reel'-lyah], *f.* 1. An earthen jug with broad base and narrow neck. -*pl.* Gridiron, broiler, toaster; grate, furnace grating (objeto). 2. *(Aut.)* Radiator grille (de radiador); *(Cono Sur)* roof rack.

parriza [par-ree'-thah], *f.* Wild vine.

párroco [par´-ro-co], *m.* Rector or incumbent of a parish; a parson.

parrón [par-rone'], *m. V.* PARRIZA.

parroquia [par-ro'-ke-ah], *f.* 1. Parish, the parochial church (iglesia). 2. Parish, the precinct or territory of a parochial church (zona). 3. The spiritual jurisdiction of a rector or parson in his parish. 4. The clergy of a parish.

parroquial [par-ro-ke-ahl'], *a.* Parochial. -*f.* Parochial church.

parroquialidad [par-ro-ke-ah-le-dahd'], *f.* Parochial right, the right of a parishioner.

parroquiano, na [par-ro-ke-ah'-no], *m & f.* 1. Parishioner. 2. Customer, an accustomed buyer or patron.

parroquiano, na [par-ro-ke-ah'-no, nah], *a.* Belonging to a parishioner. *V.* PARROQUIAL.

parsi [par'-se], *a. & m.* 1. Parsee, a Zoroastrian. 2. The sacred language of Persia (before being mixed with Arabic).

parsimonia [par-se-mo´-ne-ah], *f.* Economy, frugality (frugalidad), husbandry, temperance.

parte [par'-tay], *f.* 1. Part, a portion of some whole (sección). 2. Part, a determinate quantity of some aggregate number. 3. Part, portion, share (participación, porción), lot. 4. District, territory, place (región). 5. Part, the right or left side. 6. Part, side (lado), every one of two or more things opposite to each other. 7. Part, the sense given to words or acts. 8. Party, a person concerned in a business with others (persona). 9. *(Law.)* Party, one of two litigants. 10. It is used for the time present with reference to the past. **De ocho días a esta parte,** within these last eight days. 11. Part, character in a play. 12. Partes, parts (cualidades), talents. 13. *(Anat.)* Partes, parts. 14. *(Mex. Mec.)* Spare part. **Tercera parte,** third. **Parte del mundo,** part of the world. **En gran parte,** to a large extend. **Formar parte de,** to form a part of. **Llevar la mejor parte,** to come off best. **Mirar a otra parte,** to look the other way. **Por todas partes se va a Roma,** all roads lead to Rome. **Por parte de madre,** on the mother's side. **Parte contraria,** opposing party. -*m.* 1. Royal or official communication. 2. Receiving-house for the post office. 3. Official notice of mails. 4. Dispatch, telegram, urgent message. **Parte por parte,** part by part, distinctly. **A partes** or **en partes,** by parts, or in parts. **De parte a parte,** from side to side, through. **De parte,** by orders, by command. **En parte,** partly, in part. -*f. pl.* 1. Parts, talents, endowments. 2. Privy parts. 3. Party, faction. **Por todas partes,** on all hands, on all sides. -*adv.* In part, partly.

partear [par-tay-ar'], *va.* To deliver or assist women in childbirth.

partenópeo, pea [par-tay-no´-pay-o, ah], *a.* Parthenopean, Neapolitan.

partenueces [par-tay-noo-ay'-thes], *m.* Nut-cracker.

partera [par-tay'-rah], *f.* Midwife.
partería [par-tay-ree'-ah], *f.* Midwifery, obstetrics.
partero [par-tay'-ro], *m.* Obstetrician, man-midwife, accoucheur.
partesana [par-tay-sah'-nah], *f.* Partizan; a kind of halberd.
partesanero [par-tay-sah-nay'-ro], *m.* Pikeman.
partible [par-tee'-blay], *a.* Divisible, separable, partible.
partición [par-te-the-on'], *f.* Partition, division, distribution, lot.
particionero, ra [par-te-the-o-nay'-ro, rah], *a.* Participant, having a part in a business.
participación [par-tee-the-pah-the-on'], *f.* 1. Parcipation, sharing in common. (*Com.*) Copartnership. **Cuenta en participación**, joint account. 2. Participation, communication, conversation. 3. (*Dep.*) Entry. 4. Lottery ticket (de lotería). 5. Notice (aviso).
participante [par-te-the-pahnt'-tay], *pa.* Sharing, participant.
participar [par-te-the-par'], *va. & vn.* 1. To give notice, to inform of, to announce (noticia). 2. To participate, to partake, to share. 3. To partake, to take part, to participate, to have something of the property, nature, claim, right, etc. **Participar en una carrera**, to enter in a race. **Participar de una cualidad**, to share a quality.
partícipe [par-tee'-the-pay], *a.* Participant, sharing.
participial [par-te-the-pe-ahl'], *a.* (*Gram.*) Participial.
participio [par-te-thee'-pe-o], *m.* (*Gram.*) Participle.
partícula [par-tee'-coo-lah], *f.* 1. Particle, small part. 2. (*Gram.*) Particle. 3. Molecule. **Partícula beta**, beta particle.
particular [par-te-coo-lar'], *a.* 1. Particular (especial), peculiar (propio), special. 2. Particular, odd, distinguished from others. 3. Particular, individual, single, not general. private (personal). 4. Applied to a play represented in a private theater. **En particular**, particularly, in particular. **Nada de particular**, nothing special. **Secretario particular**, private secretary.
particular [par-te-coo-lar'], *m.* 1. A private gentleman (persona). 2. A peculiar matter or subject treated upon; topic (asunto). **No dijo mucho sobre el particular**, he didn't say much about the matter.
particularidad [par-te-coo-lah-re-dahd'], *f.* 1. Particularity (propiedad), peculiarity. 2. Friendship, intimacy (amistad).
particulariza [par-te-coo-lah-re-thar'], *va.* To particularize (especificar), to detail (dar detalles), to distinguish (distinguir). -*vr.* To singularize, to be particular.
particularmente [par-te-coo-lar-men-tay], *adv.* Particularly, especially, namely.
partida [par-tee'-dah], *f.* 1. Departure, going away from a place (salida). 2. Death, decease. 3. Party of soldier. 4. Item in an account, charge, entry (entrada), record, annotation. 5. Parcel, lot. 6. Game at play (ajedrez, naipes). 7. (*Naut.*) Crew of a ship, gang. 8. Consignment (envío). 9. Stake (apuesta), wager, bet. **¡Buena partida!**, excellent conduct! **Partida doble**, (*Com.*) double entry. **Partida simple**, single entry (in book-keeping). **Partida de defunción**, death certificate. **Partida de nacimiento**, birth certificate. **Echar una partida**, to have a game. -*pl.* Parts, talents, accomplishments.
partidamente [par-tee'-dah-men-tay], *adv.* Separately, distinctly.
partidario [par-te-dah'-re-o], *m.* 1. Partisan, the commander of a party of troops. 2. Party-man, adherent to a faction.-*a.* 1. Having the care of a certain district. 2. Partisan. **Soy muy partidario de**, I'm in favor of.
partido, da [par-tee'-do, dah], *a.* 1. Divided, split. 2. Free, liberal, munificent. 3. (*Her.*) Party, parted. -*pp.* Of PARTIR.
partido [par-tee'-do], *m.* 1. Party, a number of persons confederated. 2. Advantage, profit, utility (provecho). 3. Favor, protection, interest. 4. A game, a contest, a match (equipo). 5. Odds given to one in a game: party engaged to play a game. 6. Treaty, agreement; terms proposed for adjusting a difference. 7. Proper means for the performance

of what is to be done. 8. Interest or one's own convenience. 9. (*Cono Sur*) Hand (naipes). 12. (*And. Carib.*) **Al partido**, share and share alike. **Tomar partido**, (a) to embrace a resolution, to resolve. (b) to engage or enlist in a party. **Partido político**, political party. **Partido de fútbol**, football match. **Sacar partido de**, to profit from, to take advantage of.
partidor [par-te-dor'], *m.* 1. Parter, divider. **Partidor de leña**, cleaver, the instrument and the workman employed in cleaving wood. 2. Bodkin to divide the hair. 3. (*Arith.*) V. DIVISOR.
partija [par-tee'-hah], *f.* V. PARTICIÓN.
partil [par-teel'], *a.* Applied to the astrological aspects.
partimento, partimiento [par-te-men'-to], *m.* V. PARTICIÓN.
partir [par-teer'], *va.* 1. To part, to divide, to sever, to disunite, to separate, to cut, to cleave. 2. To break by violence (abrir). 3. To part, to share (repartir), to divide, to distribute. 4. To crack the stones of fruit (nuez). 5. To attack in combat or battle. 6. To resolve. 7. (*Arith.*) To divide. 8. To divide a beehive in two, at the proper season. **Partir la cabeza a uno**, to split somebody's head open. -*vn.* 1. To part, to depart, to march, to set out on a journey (ponerse en camino). 2. To start (comenzar). **A partir del lunes**, from Monday. -*vr.* To be divided in opinion. **Partir la diferencia**, to split the difference. **Partir por entero**, to carry off the whole: to divide a number. **Partir mano**, to desist, to abandon. **Partirse el alma**, to make a tremendous effort, to die; to die broken-hearted.
partitivo, va [par-te-tee'-vo, vah], *a.* (*Gram.*) Partitive.
partitura [par-te-too'-rah], *f.* The musical score. **Partitura de una ópera**, the full score of an opera.
parto [par'-to], *m.* 1. Childbirth, parturition. 2. Newborn child. 3. Any natural production. 4. Any literary composition. 5. Any particular thing that may happen, and is hoped to be of importance. **Tener un parto difícil**, to have a difficult labor.
parturiente [par-too-re-en'-tay], *a.* Parturient.
párulis [pah'-roo-lis], *m.* Gumboil, an abscess of the gums.
parva [par'-vah], *f.* 1. Unthrashed corn laid in heaps to be thrashed. 2. Multitude, large quantity. 3. V. PARVEDAD, 2d def.
parvada [par-vah'-dah], *f.* (*Prov.*) Place for unthrashed corn.
parvedad, parvidad [par-vay-dahd'], *f.* 1. Littleness, minuteness. 2. Snack, bite of food taken in the morning of a fast day.
parvo, va [par'-vo, vah], *a.* Small, little.
parvulario [par-voo-lah'-re-o], *m.* Nursery school, kindergarden.
parvulez [par-voo-leth'], *f.* Smallness, small size.
parvulico, ica, illo, illa, ito, ita [par voo-lee'-co], *a. dim.* Very little.
párvulo, la [par'-voo-lo, lah], *a.* Very small; innocent; humble, low.-*n.* A child.
pasa [pah'-sah], *f.* 1. Raisin, dried grape. 2. Passage of birds. -*pl.* The curled hair of negroes.
pasabalas [pah-sah-bah'-las], *m.* (*Mil.*) Ball calibre-gauge.
pasable [pah-sah'-blay], *a.* 1. Passable (tolerable). 2. (*LAm.*) Fordable (arroyo). 3. (*Cono Sur*) Saleable.
pasacalle [pah-sah-cahl'-lyay], *m.* Music played on the guitar and other instruments in the streets. An ancient dance.
pasacampana [pah-sah-cam-pah'-nah], *f.* (*Vet.*) A tumor which forms on the calcaneum of horses.
pasada [pah-sah'-dah], *f.* 1. Passage, the act of passing (acto). 2. Pace, step; measure of five feet. 3. A malicious action to someone's hurt. 4. (*Ant.*) Competency, sufficiency. **De pasada**, on the way, in passing, hastily, cursorily. 5. (*CAm. Cono Sur*) Telling-off (reprimenda). 6. (*And.*) Shame (vergüenza).
pasadera [pah-sah-day'-rah], *f.* 1. A stepping-stone. 2. Sieve, strainer. 3. (*Naut.*) Furling-line of spun-yarn.
pasaderamente [pah-sah-day'-rah-men-tay], *adv.* passably.

pasadero, ra [pah-sah-day'-ro, rah], *a.* 1. Supportable, sufferable. 2. Passable, tolerably good (tolerable). *-m. V.* PASADERA.

pasadillo [pah-sah-deel'-lyo], *m.* A small embroidery on both sides of a piece of stuff.

pasadizo [pah-sah-dee'-tho], *m.* A narrow passage or covered way.

pasado, da [pah-sah'-do, dah], *pp.* of PASAR. **1. Lo pasado pasado**, what is past is forgotten and forgiven. **El mes pasado**, last month. 2. Stale (comida); overripe (fruta); overdone (muy hecho); stale (cuento, noticia); antiquated (idea); old (ropa); faded (belleza). **La carne está pasada**, the meat is off. *-m.* 1. Past time (tiempo). 2. A (military) deserter. *-pl.* Ancestors. *V.* ASCENDIENTES and ANTEPASADOS.

pasador [pah-sah-dor'], *m.* 1. One who carries a thing from one place to another. 2. A smuggler, one who deals in contraband goods (persona). 3. Bolt of a lock (pestillo). 4. A woman's brooch (de pelo). 5. Cylinder which founded use for making tubes without soldering. 6. A clock peg. 7. Bolt-pin, linch-pin, cotter. 8. A shoemaker's tool for smoothing the inside of a shoe. 9. A sieve. 10. A piece of a loom. *-pl.* 11. Irons placed between the tympanum and the brisket. 12. Cord straps. 13. *(Naut.)* Marline-spike.

pasagonzalo [pah-sah-gon-thal'-lo], *vn. (Colt.)* Flip, a slight blow, briskly given.

pasahilo [pah-sah-ee'-lo], *m.* Thread-guide.

pasaje [pah-sah'-hay], *m.* 1. Passage, the act of passing (acto). 2. Road, way, the place of passing. 3. Passage-money. 4. (coll.) Event, accident, a piece of business. 5. Transition or change of voice. 6. Passage of a book or writing. 7. *(Carib. Cono Sur, Mex.)* Cul-de-sac (sin salida). 8. *(Liter. Mus.)* Passage. 9. *(And. Carib.)* Story (cuento). 10. *(And.)* Tenement building (pisos).

pasajeramente [pah-sah-hay'-rah-men-tay], *adv.* Transiently, going along, without detention.

pasajero, ra [pah-sah-hay'-ro, rah], *a.* 1. Applied to a common thoroughfare. 2. Transient, transitory, fugitive. 3. Applied to birds of passage.

pasajero, ra [pah-sah-hay'-ro, rah], *m. & f.* Traveler, passenger. **Pasajero de cámara**, cabin passenger:

pasamanar [pah-sah-mah-nar'], *va.* To make ribbons, trimmings, lace, etc.

pasamanera [pa-sah-mah-nay'-rah], *f.* Lace-woman, lace-maker.

pasamanería [pah-sah-mah-nay-ree'-ah], *f.* The trade of a lace-man; the profession of a fancy-trimming maker, twister; or ribbon-weaver, and the place where those things are sold; passementerie work.

pasamanero [pah-sah-mah-nay'-ro], *m.* Lace-maker, lace-man, a fancy-trimming maker, a twister, a ribbon-maker.

pasamanillo [pah-sah-mah-neel'-lyo], *m. dim.* A narrow lace; a small twist for the edge of a coat.

pasamano [pah-sah-mah'-no], *m.* 1. Balustrade, banister (de escalera), rail (barra). 2. Kind of lace or edging for clothes; passementerie. 3. *(Naut.)* Gangway.

pasamontañas [pah-sah-mon-tah'-nyahs], *m.* Balaclava (casco), ski mask.

pasante [pah-sahn'-tay], *m.* 1. Assistant or student of a physician or lawyer. 2. A student who acts the teacher or lecturer to beginners. 3. *(Her.)* Passant: applied to animals in a shield appearing to walk. 4. Game of cards.

pasantía [pah-san-tee'-ah], *f.* Profession of a student of the law or medicine, who practices under the direction of another.

pasapán [pah-sah-pahn'], *m. (coll.) V* GARGUERO.

pasapasa [pah-sah-pah'-sah], *m.* Legerdemain, slight of hand, hocus-pocus.

pasaporte [pah-sah-por'-tay], *m.* 1. Passport. 2. *(Mil.)* Furlough. 3. A free license to do anything.

pasapuré [pah-sah-pooh'-ray], *m.* Grinder, mincer.

pasar [pah-sar'], *vn.* 1. To pass, to move from place to place. 2. To go or pass in any manner or to any end, to go through.

3. To go to any determinate place. 4. To make way for a person, inviting him to come forward. 5. To be in motion, or to steer from one place to another: speaking of immaterial things. 6. With the preposition *a* and some infinitives, to proceed to. 7. To ascend, to be promoted to a higher post. 8. To pass away, to elapse (tiempo). 9. To travel through a place or country. 10. To die. 11. To pass, to become current, as money. 12. To be marketable (mercancías). 13. To pass, to be in a certain state, speaking of health, conveniences of life, etc. 14. To pass, to be spent, to go away progressively. 15. To be executed before a notary. *-va.* 1. To convey from one place to another. 2. To send or carry a thing from one part to another (enviar). 3. To pierce, to penetrate, to go through (armadura). 4. To pass beyond the limit of the place of destination (frontera, límite). 5. To change for better or worse, from one thing to another. 6. To pass or advance from one class to another. 7. To exceed in number, quantity, quality, or abilities. 8. To depart, to decease. 9. To suffer, to bear, to undergo (penas). 10. To strain or percolate liquor, to clarify it. 11. Not to censure or find fault with anything. 12. To pass over in silence, to omit (omitir). 13. To dissemble, to overlook. 14. To stop, to terminate. 15. To run over one's lesson, to rehearse; to run over a book. 16. To carry one thing above another, so as to touch it lightly. 17. To teach privately; to study privately with some professor. 18. To present an act, charter, or privilege to be confirmed. 19. To handle an affair with judgment and prudence (asunto). 20. To draw up an instrument. 21. To dry by the sun or in an oven. *-v. imp.* To pass, to happen (suceder), to turn out. *-vr.* 1. To pass over to another party. 2. To cease, to finish; to lose its force (efecto). 3. Not to shut well. 4. To be spoiled (fruta). 5. To pass unimproved: applied to a favorable opportunity. 6. To go too far (excederse). 7. To fade (belleza); to go bad (comida). **Pasar de largo**, (a) to pass by without stopping; (b) *(Met.)* not to reflect upon what one reads. **Pasa al frente**, *(coll.)* this sum is carried forward. **Pasar el tiempo**, to loiter, to pass away time. **Pasar por alto**, to overlook, to overpass, not to take notice. **Pasar en claro alguna cosa**, to omit any mention of a thing. **Pasar por encima**, to overcome difficulties. **Ir pasando**, to be about the same, neither better nor worse. **¿Cómo lo pasa Vd.?** how do you do? **Pasarse de bueno**, to be too good. **Pasarse de cortés**, to be over polite. **Nos hicieron pasar a otra habitación**, they showed us into another room. **El médico pasará visita**, the doctor will call. **El túnel pasa la montaña**, the tunnel goes right through the mountain. **Hemos pasado el aniversario**, we are past the anniversary. **Pasarlo bien**, to have a good time. **El hilo pasa por el agujero**, the thread goes through the hole. **El río pasa por la ciudad**, the river flows through the city. **Pasaré por tu casa**, I'll call on you. **Pasar de los límites**, to exceed the limits. **Pasa por buen pintor**, he is considered to be a good painter. **Han pasado 4 años**, 4 years have gone by. **Lo que pasa es que...**, what's happening is that... **Siempre me pasa lo mismo**, I'm always having the same trouble. **Se me pasó el turno**, I missed my turn. **Se ha pasado todo el día leyendo**, he has spent the whole day reading.

pasarela [pah-sah-ray'-lah], *f.* Footbridge (puente); *(Teat. etc.)* Walkway, catwalk.

pasatiempo [pah-sah-te-em'-po], *m.* Pastime, diversion, amusement, game.

pasavante [pah-sah-vahn'-tay], *m.* 1. Safe-conduct furnished to a ship by the commander of the enemy's forces. 2. A permit for articles of commerce.

pasavolante [pah-sah-vo-lahn'-tay], *m.* An inconsiderate speech or action.

pasavoleo [pah-sah-vo-lay'-o], *m.* Ball which passes the line in bowling.

pascua [pahs'-coo-ah], *f.* 1. Passover, a feast among the Jews. 2. Easter, the day on which the Savior's resurrection is commemorated. 3. *(Met.)* Christmas. 4. *(coll.)* Any festival of the church which lasts three days. **Hacer pascua**, to begin to eat meat after Lent. **Santas pascuas**, be it so. **Pascua de Navidad**, Christmas. **Estar como unas pascuas**, to be as happy as a sandboy.

pascual [pas-coo-ahl'], *a.* Paschal, relating to Easter.

pascuilla [pas-coo-eel'-lyah], *f.* The first Sunday after Easter.

pase [pah'-say], *m.* 1. An act of a court of justice which orders a decree to be expedited and carried into effect. 2. A written permission to sell or carry goods freely from place to place. 3. A kind of passport. 4. (Cine) Showing. 5. (LAm.) Dose (drogas). **Pase de impresión**, (Comput.) print pass.

paseadero [pah-say-ah-day'-ro], *m.* Walk, avenue, public walk.

paseador, ra [pah-say-ah-dor', rah], *m. & f.* A walker: applied to one who walks much, or to a horse.

paseante [pah-say-ahn'-tay], *m. & f.* 1. Walker (que pasea), one who goes for a walk. 2. Idler, lazy vagabond.

pasear [pah-say-ar'], *va. & vn.* 1. To walk, to take the air, to exercise. 2. To be at the walk, to be in the field. 3. To move at the slowest pace (caballo). 4. To walk about, to bring out to walk (niño, perro). 5. To take the air or exercise on horseback or in a coach. 6. (CAm.) To squander (dinero). -*vr.* 1. To walk for exercise or amusement. 2. To loiter, to wander idly, to gape about. 3. (Mex.) To take a day off. **Pasearse en bicicleta**, to go for a ride. **Pasearse en coche**, to go for a drive. **Pasearse a caballo**, to ride.

paseata [pah-say-ah'-tah], *f.* (coll.) A walk, airing drive.

paseo [pah-say'-o], *m.* 1. Ride, drive. 2. Walk, outing (excursión). 3. Short walk (distancia). 4. Parade (avenida). **Paseo al aire libre**, outdoor walk. **Paseo campestre**, picnic. **Ir de paseo**, to go walking, to go on an outing. **Paseo marítimo**, promenade. **Enviar a uno a paseo**, to tell somebody to go to blazes.

pasera [pah-say'-rah], *f.* (Prov.) Place where raisins are dried, and the act of drying them.

pasibilidad [pah-se-be-le-dahd'], *f.* Passibleness, susceptibility to impressions from external agents.

pasible [pah-see'-blay], *a.* Able to endure, long-suffering.

pasicorto, ta [pah-se-cor'-to, tah], *a.* Short-stepped (caballos).

pasiego, ga [pah-se-ay'-go, gah], *m. & f* A highlander of Santander, celebrated for his sturdiness, and the women as the best wet-nurses.

pasiflora [pah-se-flo'-rah], *f.* The botanical name of the passion-flower.

pasilargo, ga [pah-se-lar'-go, gah], *a.* Long-stepped (caballos).

pasillo [pah-seel'-lyo], *m.* 1. (dim.) A short step. 2. A small, narrow passage. 3. Basting-stitch.

pasión [pah-se-on'], *f.* 1. Passion, any effect caused by external agency; susceptibility of effect from external action; the act of suffering torments. 2. Passion, the last suffering of the Redeemer. 3. Passion, affection or violent emotion of the mind, anger. 4. Passion, ardent inclination, fondness. **Pasión de ánimo**, a passion or emotion of the soul; a broken heart. **Con pasión**, passionately.

pasionaria [pah-se-o-nah'-re-ah], *f.* (Bot.) Passion-flower: a climbing vine, native of Peru, where it is more often called *ñorbo*.

pasionario [pah-se-o-nah'-re-o], *m. pl.* Passion-book, from which the passion is sung in Holy Week.

pasionero [pah-se-o-nay'-ro], *m.* One who sings the passion.

pasito [pah-see'-to], *adv.* Gently, softly. **Pasito a pasito**, very leisurely or gently.

pasito [pah-see'-to], *m. dim.* A short step.

pasitrote [pah-se-tro'-tay], *m.* Short trot of horses alone.

pasiva [pah-see'-vah], *f.* (dram.) Passive voice of the verb.

pasivamente [pah-see-vah-men-tay], *adv.* Passively.

pasivo, va [pah-see'-vo, vah], *a.* 1. Passive, receiving impression from some external agent. 2. Passive, unresisting, not acting. 3. (Gram.) Passive. **Voz pasiva**, passive voice; capable of being elected.

pasivo [pah-see'-vo], *m.* (Com.) Liabilities.

pasmado [pas-mah-do], *a.* 1. Astonished, amazed. **Dejar pasmado a uno**, to amaze somebody. 2. Bewildered (atontado). **Estar pasmado**, to stand gaping. 3. (LAm.) Infected (herida); unhealthy-looking (persona). 4. (CAm. Mex.) Thick (tonto). 5. (LAm.) Overripe (fruta).

pasmar [pas-mar'], *va.* 1. To cause a spasm, or a suspension or loss of the senses (atontar). 2. To benumb, to make torpid: to stupefy, to stun. 3. To chill (enfriar), to deaden. -*vn.* To marvel, to wonder. -*vr.* 1. To wonder, to be astonished (asombrarse). 2. To suffer from lockjaw. 3. (LAm.) To become infected (infectarse); to fall ill (enfermar); to catch a fever (con fiebre). 4. (Carib. Mec.) To dry up (fruta). 5. To fade (color).

pasmarota, pasmarotada [pas-mah-ro'-tah], *f.* 1. A feigned spasm, often used by beggars. 2. Admiration or astonishment without cause or motive.

pasmazón [pas-mah-thone'], *f.* (Mex.) Swelling upon the loins of horses, caused by the saddle or harness.

pasmo [pahs'-mo], *m.* 1. Spasm, convulsion; violent and involuntary contraction. 2 (Med.) Lockjaw, tetanus. 3. Astonishment, amazement (asombro), admiration. 4. Object of admiration or astonishment. **De pasmo**, V. PASMOSAMENTE. 5. (Med.) Chill (enfriamiento). 6. (LAm.) Fever (fiebre).

pasmosamente [pas-mo'-sah-men-tay], *adv.* Wonderfully, astonishingly.

pasmoso, sa [pas-mo'-so, sah], *a.* Marvellous, wonderful.

paso, sa [pah'-so, sah], *a. & pp. irr.* of PASAR. Dried (fruta).

paso [pah'-so], *m.* 1. Pace, step (de pie), a measure of space. 2. Passage, the act of passing. 3. Pace, gait, manner of walking (modo de andar). 4. Pace, pacing, a motion of mules and horses. 5. Flight of steps. 6. Passage, lobby, passage for a room; pass, a narrow entrance. 7. Step, measure or diligence in the pursuit of an affair: commonly used in the plural. 8. Step, instance of conduct, mode of life. 9. Footstep (sonido). 10. Passport, license, pass. 11. Explanation given by a master or usher. 12. Passage in a book; or writing (episodio). 13. Progress, advance, improvement. 14. Death, decease. 15. Image carried about during Holy Week. 16. (Elec. Tec.) Pitch. 17. Difficulty, awkward situation, crisis (apuro). (LAm.) Ford (vado). -*pl.* 1. Running stitches with which clothes are basted. 2. Conduct, proceedings, steps.-*adv.* Softly, gently. **Paso a paso**, step by step; slowly. **A buen paso**, at a good rate, step, or gait. **A cada paso**, at every step, frequently. **A ese paso**, at that rate. **Al paso**, without delay, instantly; going along; in the manner of, like. **Andar en malos pasos**, to follow evil paths. **Salir del paso** or **del vado**, to get out of a difficulty. **A pocos pasos**, at a short distance; with little care. **Dar paso,** to clear the way; to promote, to facilitate. **De paso**, passing by; lightly, briefly, by the way; at the same time, at once. **Vista de paso**, a cursory view. **Al paso que**, at he same time that, whilst. **Paso de cebra**, zebra crossing. **Paso a nivel**, level crossing. **Abrirse paso**, to make one's way. **Paso atrás**, step backwards. **A paso de tortuga**, at a snail's pace. **Romper el paso**, to break step. **Dar un mal paso**, to take a false step.

paspié [pas-pe-ay'], *m.* A kind of dance.

pasquín [pas-keen'], *m.* Pasquinade, lampoon.

pasquinada [pas-kee-nah'-dah], *f.* Pasquinade.

pasquinar [pas-ke-nar'], *va.* To ridicule, to lampoon, to satirize.

pasta [pahs'-tah], *f.* 1. Paste, any viscous or tenacious mixture. 2. Paste, flour and water boiled; the mass from which vermicelli and other things are made for soup. 3. Pie-crust. 4. Bullion, mass of gold or silver for coining. 5. In book-binding, pasteboard covered with leather burnished or mottled; roan leather (libros). 6. Pulp from which paper or cardboard is made. 7. V. EMPASTE. 8. **Pasta** or **buena pasta**, excessive meekness or mildness. 9. (Culin.) Dough; pastry (para pastel); pastries (pasteles), cakes; noodles (fideos), spaghetti. 10. Dough (dinero), money. **Pasta de carne,** meat paste. **Pasta gansa,** big money.

pasta de dientes [pahs'-tah day de-ayn'-tes], *f.* Toothpaste.

pasta dentífrica [pahs'-tah den-tee'-fre-cah], *f.* Toothpaste.

pastar [pas-tar], *m.* To pasture, to graze. *-va.* To lead cattle to graze, to feed cattle.

pasteca [pas-tay'-cah], *f.* (*Naut.*) Snatch-block.

pastel [pas-tel], *m.* 1. Pie, pastry. **Pastel de carne** or **de picadillo,** mince pie. **Pastel de manzana,** *etc.,* apple pie, etc. 2. (*Bot.*) Woad. 3. Trick in the dealing of cards. 4. Meeting, assembly for some secret design. 5. (*Print.*) Mass of types to be recast; words too black, having too much ink. 6. (*Art.*) Pastel (pintura).

pastelada [pas-tay-lah'-dah], *f.* Plot, snare.

pastelear [pas-tay-lay-ar'], *vn.* To trim politically; to try to secure popularity by time-serving.

pastelera [pas-tay-lay'-rah], *f.* Pastrycook's wife; she who makes and sells pastry.

pastelería [pas-tay-lay-ree'-ah], *f.* 1. Pastrycook's shop (tienda), confectionery (dulces), confectionery's cake shop (tienda). 2. Pastry, pies or baked paste (pasteles).

pastelero [pes-tay-lay'-ro], *m.* 1. Pastrycook. 2. A political trimmer.

pastelillo, ito [pas-tay-leel'-lyo], *m. dim.* A little pie, a patty. **Pastelillo,** Tart: a kind of pastry.

pastelón [pas-tay-lone'], *m. aug.* A large pie.

pasterización [pas-tay-re-tha-the-on'], *f.* Pasteurization.

pasterizar [pas-tay-re-thar'], *va.* Pasteurize.

pasteurizado [pas-tay-oo-re-thah'-do], *a.* Pasteurized.

pasteurizar [pas-tay-oo-re-thar'], *va.* To pasteurize.

pastilla [pas-teel'-lyah], *f.* 1. Tablet, lozenge. 2. Drop, candy. **Pastilla de menta,** peppermint drop. **Pastilla para la tos,** cough drop.

pastinaca [pas-te-sah'-cah], *f.* 1. (*Bot.*) Parsnip. 2. (*Cool.*) Stingray.

pasto [pahs'-to], *m.* 1. Pasture, the act of grazing. 2. Pasture, the grass which serves for the feeding of cattle (hierba). 3. A pasture-ground (campo). 4. Any pabulum, food, aliment, or nourishment (comida). **Pasto espiritual,** Spiritual nourishment. **A pasto,** abundantly, plentifully, at meals, as ordinary meat or drink. **Echar el pasto al ganado,** to put animals out to pasture. **Vino de pasto,** ordinary wine.

pastor, ra [pas-tor', rah], *m. & f.* 1. Shepherd, shepherdess, one who tends sheep (de ovejas). 2. Pastor, shepherd, a clergyman. 3. An American freshwater fish.

pastoral [pas-to-rahl'], *a.* Pastoral, rural, rustic. *-f.* Pastoral, a poem in which the speakers assume the character of shepherds; an idyll.

pastoralmente [pas-to-rahl'-men-tay], *adv.* Pastorally, rustically, shepherd-like.

pastorcico, illo, ito [pastor-thee'-co], *m. dim.* A little shepherd.

pastorear [pas-to-ray-ar'], *va.* 1. To graze, to pasture (rebaño); to bring cattle to pasture. 2. To feed souls with sound doctrine. 3. (*CAm.* Cono Sur) To lie in wait for (acechar). 4. (*CAm.*) To spoil (mimar).

pastorela [pas-to-ray'-lah], *f.* Pastoral, an ample melody in rustic style.

pastoreo [pas-to'-ray-o], *m.* Pasturing, act of tending flocks.

pastoría [pas-to-re'-ah], *f.* A pastoral or rural life, pastors.

pastoril [pas-to-reel'], *a.* Pastoral.

pastorilmente [pas-to-reel-men-tay], *adv.* V. PASTORALMENTE.

pastosidad [pas-to-se-dahd'], *f.* Mellowness, softness.

pastoso, sa [pas-toh'-so, sah], *a.* 1. Soft, mellow, doughy (material), clammy. 2. Painted or drawn with a colored crayon or pencil. 3. (*Cono Sur*) Grassy. 4. (*And.*) Lazy (vago).

pastura [pas-too'-rah], *f.* 1. Pasture, the grass on which animals feed (campo). 2. Fodder, dry food for cattle (comida).

pasturaje [pas-too-rah'-hay], *m.* 1. Pasturage, a common ground on which cattle graze. 2. Duty paid for the right of grazing cattle on a certain ground.

pasudo, da [pah-soo'-do, dah], *a.* (*Amer.*) Kinky, woolly, curly, as a Negro's hair.

pata [pah'-tah], *f.* 1. Foot and leg of beasts. 2. Duck, the female of the drake. 3. A barilla-producing plant of the benches of the Canary Islands. 4. Leg (de mueble). **Pata de cabra,** (a) a crowbar, a nailpuller; (b) a shomaker's heel-burnisher. **Pata de gallina,** a radial crack in trees; the beginning of rot. **Pata de gallo,** (a) a ridiculous saying, a bull (used generally with *salir con*); (b) crow's-foot, a wrinkle near the eye. (3) Stupidity, silliness. **A la pata coja,** hopscotch, a game played by hopping on one foot over a diagram upon the ground. **A pata,** on foot. **Patas arriba,** reversed, topsyturvy, heels-over-head; upside down, in disorder. **Estirar la pata,** to peg out. **Tener mala pata,** to be unlucky.

pataca [pah-tah'-cah], *f.* 1. (*Bot.*) Jerusalem artichoke. 2. Copper coin.

pataco, ca [pah-tah'-co, cah], *a.* V. PATÁN.

patacón [pah-tah-cone'], *m.* Dollar or patacoon, a silver coin weighing an ounce; cut with shears.

patache [pah-tah'-chay], *m.* (*F. Naut.*) Tender, a vessel attending a squadron.

patada [pah-tah'-dah], *f.* 1. Kick (coz), a blow with the foot. 2. (*coll.*) Step, pace. 3. Track, murk left by the foot of an animal. *A* **patadas,** in abundance. **Echar a uno a patadas,** to kick somebody out. **Tratar a uno a patadas,** to push somebody around.

patagalana [pah-ta-ga-lah'-nah], *f.* (*coll.*) Limping; having a short leg.

patagón [pah-tah-gone'], *m* 1. A large clumsy foot. 2. A Patagonian.

patagónico, ca [pah-tah-go'-ne-co, cah], *a.* Patagonian.

patagorcillo, lla [pah-tah-gor-theel'-lyo], *m. & f.* Fricassee made of the livers and lights of animals.

patagua [pah-tah'-goo-ah], *f.* 1. Patagua, a stout tree of America, of the linden family, which grows in miry places and has a white light wood. 2. A nearly cylindrical vessel on which mate is spread,

patalear [pah-tah-lay-ar'], *vn.* 1. To kick about violently. 2. To stamp the foot (en el suelo). 3. To putter.

pataleo [pah-tah-lay'-o], *m.* 1. The act of stamping the foot (en el suelo). 2. Noise made by the feet. 3. (*Fig.*) Protest; scene (lío), fuss.

pataleta [pah-tah-lay'-tah], *f.* 1. (*coll.*) A fainting-fit. 2. A ridiculous speech or action; an absurd enterprise.

pataletilla [pah-tah-lay-teel'-lyah], *f.* A kind of dance.

patán, na [pat-tahn', nah], *a.* Clownish, churlish, rustic. *-m. & f.* Clown, a churl, a countryman or women.

patanería [pah-tah-nay-ree'-ah], *f.* Clownishness, churlishness, rusticity, rudeness.

patarata [pah-ta-rah'-tah], *f.* 1. Fiction, idle story. 2. Affected concern or affectation (afectación), kickshaw.

patarraez [pah-tar-rah-eth'], *m.* (*Naut.*) Preventer shroud. **Patarraez de una máquina de arbolar,** (*Naut.*) the shroud of a sheer-hulk for masting ships.

patata [pah-tah'-tah], *f.* (*Bot.*) Potato. **Patata de siembra,** seed potato. **Patatas fritas,** French fries, chips, crisps. **No entendió una patata,** he didn't understand a word of it.

patatal [pah-tah-tahl'], *m.* Potato field.

patatero, ra [pah-tah-tay'-ro, rah], *m. & f.* 1. A potato-seller. 2. One who is fond of potatoes.

patatús [pah-tah-toos'], *m.* (*coll.*) Swoon, a fainting-fit.

patax [pah-tahx'], *m.* V. PATACHE.

pateadura [pah-tay-ah-doo'-rah], *f.* Kicking, stamping (acto).

patear [pah-tay-ar'], *va. & vn.* 1. To kick (dar patadas). 2. To stamp the foot (pisotear). 3. To drive about to obtain some end. 4. To be extremely irritated or vexed. 5. (*Carib.*) To abuse. **Tuve que patear toda la ciudad,** I had to tramp round the whole town.

patena [pah-tay'-nah], *f.* 1. Paten, a dish for the eucharistic bread. **Limpio como una patena,** as clean as a whistle, as a new pin.

patentado

patentado [pah-ten-tah'-do], *a.* Patent, patented; proprietary. -*m.* patentee.

patentar [pah-ten-tahr'], *va.* To patent.

patente [pah-ten'-tay], *a.* 1. Patent, manifest, evident, clear, palpable. 2. *(Cono Sur)* Superb (excelente). -*f.* 1. Patent, a writ conferring exclusive right or privilege; warrant, commission. 2. Letters of marque. 3. Letter of obedience expedited by prelates and addressed to their religious subjects. 4. Money paid by newcomers to the members of a company or office. 5. *(LAm. Aut.)* Number plate (placa); driving licence (carnet). **Patente de sanidad**, bill ol health. **Patente de invención**, patent.

patentemente [pah-ten'-tay-men-tay], *adv.* Openly, clearly, visibly, obviously.

patentizar [pah-ten-te-thar'], *va.* To make a thing evident.

patera [pah-tay'-rah], *f.* Goblet, patera.

paternal [pah-ter-nahl'], *a.* Paternal, fatherly.

paternalmente [pah-ter-nahl'-men-tay], *adv.* Paternally, fatherly.

paternidad [pah-ter-ne-dahd'], *f.* 1. Paternity (de hijo), fathership. 2. A title of respect given to religious men.

paterno, na [pah-terr'-no, nah], *a.* Paternal, fatherly.

paternóster [pah-ter-nos'-ter], *m.* 1 The Lord's prayer: paternoster. 2. A big tight knot.

patesca [pah-tes'-cah], *f. (Naut.)* A large block.

pateta [pah-tay'-tah], *m.* 1 A nickname given to a lame person. 2. *(coll.)* Devil, old Nick.

patéticamente [ ], *adv.* Pathetically.

patético, ca [pah-tay'-te-co, cah], *a.* 1. Pathetic, passionate, moving. 2. Plaintive. 3. *(Cono Sur)* Clear, evident.

patiabierto, ta [pah-te-ah-be-err'-to, tah], *a.* Straddling, club-footed, crooked-legged.

patialbillo [pah-te-al-beel'-lyo], *m.* Weasel. *V.* PAPIALBILLO.

patiblanco, ca [pah-te-blan'-co, cah], *a.* White-footed.

patibulario, ria [pah-te-boo-lah'-re-o,·ah], *a.* Horror-producing (horroroso), sinister. **Rostro patibulario**, sinister expression.

patíbulo [pah-tee'-boo-lo], *m.* Gibbet, gallows.

patico, ito [pah-tee'-co, ee'-to], *m. dim.* A young goose, a gosling.

paticojo, ja [pah-te-co'-ho, hah], *a. (coll.)* Lame, crippled.

patiestevado, da [pah-te-es-tay-vah'-do, dah], *a.* Bow-legged.

patihendido, da [pah-te-en-dee'-do, dah], *m.* Cloven-footed.

patilla [pah-teel'-lyah], *f.* 1. *(Naut.)* Spike nailed to the stern post, on which the rudder moves. 2. Chape of a buckle. 3. Trigger. 4. *(Cono Sur)* Bench. 5. *(And. Carib.)* Watermelon (sandía). 6. *(Cono Sur. Bot.)* Layer. 7. Sidepiece (de gafas). 8. *(Comput.)* Pin. -*s. pl.* 1. Whiskers, sideburns. 2. *(Coll.)* Demon.

patimuleño, ña [pah-te-moo-lay'-nyo, nyah], *a.* Mule-footed: applied to horses with narrow hoofs.

patín [pah-teen'], *m.* 1. Skate. **Patines de rueda**, roller skates. **Patines de hielo**, ice skates. 2. *(Orn.)* Goosander. 3. Small courtyard.

pátina [pah'-te-nah], *f.* Patina.

patinador, ra [pah-te-nah-dor', rah], *m. & f.* Skater.

patinaje [pah-te-nah'-hay], *m.* 1. Skating. 2. Skidding.

patinar [pah-te-nar'], *vn.* 1. To skate (persona). 2. To skid (coche). 3. To screw-up (meter la pata).

patinazo [pah-te-nah'-tho], *m.* 1. *(Aut.)* Skid. 2. Screw-up (error), blunder. **Dar un patinazo**, to make a boob.

patineta [pah-te-nay'-tah], *f.* or **patinete** [pah-te-nay'-tay], *m.* Skate-board.

patio [pah'-te-o], *m.* 1. Court, an open space in front of a house or behind it. 2. Pit in playhouses. 3. Hall in universities, academies, or colleges. **Patio de recreo**, playground.

patita [pah-tee'-tah], *f.* A small foot or leg of beasts. **Poner de patitas en la calle**, to put a person in the street, to discharge him.

patitieso, sa [pah-te-te-ay'-so, sah], *a.* 1. Deprived by sudden accident of sense and feeling (paralizado). 2. Stiff, stately, starchy: applied to a proud, pesumptuous person of an affected gait. 3. Benumbed, stupefied, surprised.

patito [pah-tee'-to], *m.* Duckling.

patituerto, ta [pah-te-too-err'-to, tah], *a.* 1. Crook-legged, having crooked legs or feet. 2. Ill-disposed, perverse.

patizambo, ba [pah-te-thahm'-bo, bah], *a.* Knock-kneed, bandy-legged.

pato, ta [pah'-to, tah], *a.* Equal, similar.

pato [pah'-to], *m.* 1. Drake, duck. 2. *(Esp.)* Bore, dull person (pesado). 3. Boredom (aburrimiento). 4. To be clumsy (torpe). 5. *(And.)* Sponger (gorrón). 6. *(And.)* Sucker (inocentón). 7. *(Cono Sur)* **Ser un pato**, to be broke. *V.* ÁNADE. **Estar hecho un pato**, to get a ducking. **Pagar el pato**, to suffer undeserved punishment. *V.* PAGAR. **Pato real**, mallard. **Pato de reclamo**, decoy duck.

patochada [pah-to-chah'-dah], *f.* Blunder, nonsense, folly.

patógeno, na [pah-to'-hay-no, nah], *a.* Pathogenic.

patognómico, ca [pah-tog-no'-me-co, cah], *a.* Pathognomonic: applied to those signs of a disease which are characteristic, or inseparable from it.

patojear [pah-to-hay-ar'], *vn. (Cuba)* To waddle in walking.

patojo, ja [pah-to'-ho, hah], *a.* Waddling, like a duck.

patología [pah-to-lo-hee'-ah], *f. (Med.)* Pathology, the branch of medicine concerned with the cause, origin and nature of disease, including the changes occurring as a result of disease.

patológico, ca [pah-to-lo'-he-co, cah], *a.* Pathologic.

patologista [pah-to-lo-hees'-tah], or **Patólogo**, *m. (Med.)* Pathologist.

patón, na [pah-tone', nah], *a.* Large-footed, clumsy-footed.

patón [pah-tone'], *m.* Clumsy foot.

patoso [pah-to'-so], *a.* 1. Boring (aburrido). 2. Troublesome (molesto). 3. Clumsy (torpe). -*m.* Bore (pelmazo). 2. Trouble-maker (agitador).

patraña [pah-trah'-nyah], *f.* A fabulous story (cuento), a fictitious account.

patrañuela [pah-trah-nyoo-ay'-lah], *f. dim.* An insignificant tale.

patria [pah'-tre-ah], *f.* 1. Native country, place of birth, home. 2. The native or proper place for anything. 3. *(Met.)* Heaven. **Madre patria**, mother country. **Luchar por la patria**, to fight for one's country.

patriarca [pah-tre-ar'-cah], *m.* 1. Patriarch, a father and head of a numerous progeny in primitive ages. 2. Founder of a religious order. 3. Patriarch, a bishop of the highest rank. 4. Patriarch, an honorary title conferred by the Pope. **Vive como un patriarca**, he enjoys all the conveniences of life.

patriarcado [pah-tre-ar-cah'-do], *m.* Patriarchate, the dignity and jurisdiction of a patriarch.

patriarcal [pah-tre-ar-cahl'], *a.* Patriarchal.

patriciado [pah-tre-the-ah'-do], *m.* Dignity of a patrician.

patricio, cia [pah-tree'-the-o, ah], *a.* Native, national; patrician.

patricio [pah-tree'-the-o], *m.* Patrician, noble.

patrimonial [pah-tre-mo-ne-ahl'], *a.* 1. Patrimonial, claimed by right of birth. 2. Patrimonial, relating to a patrimony.

patrimonialidad [pah-tre-mo-ne-ah-le-dahd'], *f.* Birthright, privilege conferred by birth of obtaining eclesiastical benefices.

patrimonio [pah-tre-mo'-ne-o], *m.* 1. Patrimony. 2. Possessions acquired by oneself. 3. *(Com.)* Net worth. **El patrimonio artístico de la nación**, our national art heritage. **Patrimonio nacional**, national wealth.

patrio, tria [pah'-tre-o, ah], *a.* 1. Native, belonging to a native place or country. 2. Paternal.

patriota [pah-tre-oh'-tah], *m & f.* Patriot.

patriótico, ca [pah-tre-oh'-te-co, cah], *a.* Patriotic, beneficent.

patriotismo [pah-tre-o-tes'-mo], *m.* Patriotism.

patrocinar [pah-tro-the-nar'], *va.* To favor, to patronize, to protect, to countenance, to sponsor. **Un movimiento patrocindo por...**, a movement under the auspices of...

patrocinio [pa'-tro-thee'-ne-o], *m*. Protection, patronage, favor.

patrón, ona [pah-trone', nah], *m. & f*. 1. Patron (protector), patroness. 2. Master (de esclavo), boss, mistress. *-m.*1. Standard, model. 3. Pattern (costura). 4. *(Agr.)* Prop (puntal). 5. *(Agr.)* Stock (de árbol).

patrona [pah-tro'-nah], *f*. 1. Patroness, a female patron. 2. Patroness; tutelar salut of a church, protectress of a province, town, etc. 3. Galley which follows immediately that of the commodore.

patronado, da [pah-tro-nah'-do, dah], *a*. Having a patron: applied to churches and prebends. *-m. (Prov.)* V. PATRONATO.

patronal [pah-tro-nahl'], *a*. **Organización patronal**, employer's organization. **La clase patronal**, management. **Cierre patronal**, lockout.

patronato, patronazgo [pah-tro-nah'-to], *m*. 1. Patronage, patronship, the right of presenting to a benefice. 2. Foundation of a charitable or pious establishment. **Bajo el patronato de**, under the auspices of.

patronear [pah-tro-nay-ar'], *va*. To be a commander of a trading vessel.

patronía [pah-tro-nee'-ah], *f*. Mastership of a vessel.

patronímico [pah-tro-nee'-me-co], *m. & a* 1. Patronimic, family name. 2. A surname formed from the father's name; as from Sancho, Sánchez, from Pedro, Pérez.

patrono [pah-tro'-no], *m*. 1 Lord of the manor. 2. V. PATRÓN.

patrulla [pah-trool-lyah], *f*. 1. Patrol, a small detachment of soldiers to secure the safety or peace of a place. 2. A crowd of people going about the streets.

patrullar [pah-troo'-lyar'], *va*. To patrol, to go the rounds in a camp or garrison.

patrullera [pah-trool lyay-rah], *f*. Patrol boat.

patudo, da [pah-too'-do, dah], *a. (coll.)* Having large feet or paws.

patulea [pah-too-lay'-ah], *f. (coll.)* Soldiery or disorderly folks.

patullar [pah-tool-lyar'], *vn*. 1. To trample (pisar), to run through thick and thin. 2. To labor hard in the pursuit of something.

paúl [pah-ool'], *m*. A low, damp place, a bog.

paulatinamente [pah-oo-lah-tee' nah men-tay], *adv*. Gently, slowly, by little and little.

paulatino, na [pah-oo-lah-tee'-no, nah], *a*. Slowly, by degrees.

paulina [pah-oo-lee'-nah], *f*. 1. Decree of excommunication, interdict. 2. *(coll.)* Reproof, chiding, objurgation. 3. An anonymous, offensive letter (carta).

paulinia [pah-oo-lee'-ne-ah], *f*. Paullinia, or guarana, a shrub of Brazil. The seeds yield a stimulating beverage, and are used medicinally for headaches.

paulonia [pah-oo-lo'-ne-ah], *f. (Bot.)* Paulownia, a tree of Japan with large heart-shaped leaves and pale-violet flowers.

pauperismo [pah-oo-pay-rees'-mo], *m*. Pauperism, abject poverty.

paupérrimo, ma [pah-oo-perr'-re-mo, mah], *a. sup*. Very poor.

pausa [pah'-oo-sah], *f*. 1. Pause, stop, intermission. 2. Pause, suspense, delay. 3. Rest, repose. 4. *(Mus.)* Pause, rest, a stop in music, and the character which marks it. **A pausas**, at leisure, by pauses.

pausadamente [pah-oo-sah'-dah-men-tay], *adv*. Slowly, deliberately.

pausado, da [pah-oo-sah'-do, dah], *a*. 1. Slow, deliberate. 2. Calm, quiet, paused. *-pp*. of PAUSAR.

pausar [pah-oo-sar'], *vn*. To pause, to cease, to hesitate, to forbear from motion or action.

pauta [pah'-oo-tah], *f*. 1. Ruled paper, and the apparatus by which the lines are ruled upon it (línea). 2. Rule, guide, pattern, example, model. 3. Ruler (regla). **Marcar la pauta**, to set a standard.

pautada [pah-oo-tah'-dah], *f*. The ruled staff on which music is written.

pautador [pah-oo-tah-dor'], *m*. One who marks lines on paper with a ruling-machine.

pautar [pah-oo-tar'], *va*. 1. To rule lines on paper. 2. To give rules, to prescribe the manner of performing an action.

pava [pah'-vah], *f* 1. Turkey-hen, the female of the turkey. **Pelar la pava**, to talk, to court. 2. Peahen, the female of the peacock. 3. *(LAm.)* Kettle (para hervir). 4. *(And. Carib.)* Broad-brimmed straw hat (sombrero). 5. *(And. CAm.)* Fringe (fleco). 6. *(Cono Sur, Mex.)* Chamber pot (orinal). 7. *(And. Cono Sur)* Coarse banter (guasa); tasteless joke (chiste). *-a. (coll.)* Applied to any woman very inactive or indolent.

pavada [pah-vah'-dah], *f*. 1. A flock of turkeys. 2. A childish game.

pavana [pah-vah'-nah], *f*. 1. Pavan (danza). **Pasos de pavana**, a grave, solemn step; a stately gait. 2. Kind of neckcloth, formerly worn by women.

pavería [pah-vay-ree'-ah], *f*. 1. Place for rearing turkeys. 2. *(Cono Sur)* silliness, stupidity.

pavero, ra [pah-vay'-ro, rah], *a*. Rearing or feeding turkeys. *-m. & f*. 1. One who feeds or sells turkeys. 2. *(And. Cono Sur)* Practical joker.

pavés [pah-bes'], *m*. Kind of large, oblong shield.

pavesa [pah-vay'-sah], *f*. 1. Embers, hot cinders; snuff of the candle. 2. Remains, relic. **Estar hecho una pavesa**, *(coll.)* to be very weak or debilitated. **Ser una pavesa**, *(coll.)* to be very mild or gentle.

pavesada [pah-vay-sah'-dah], *f*. V. EMPAVESADA.

pavesear [pah vay-say-ar'], *vn*. To flicker, to flutter.

pavía [pah-vee'-ah], *f*. A clingstone peach.

paviano, na [pah-ve-ah'-no, nah], *a*. Pavian, belonging to Pavia, in Italy.

pávido, da [pah'-ve-do, dah], *a*. Timid, fearful.

pavilla, ita [pah-veel'-lyah, ee'-tah], *f. dim*. A little turkey-hen.

pavillo, ito [pah-veel'-lyo, ee'-to], *m. dim*. A small turkey.

pavimentación [pah-ve-men-tah-theon'], *f*. Paving.

pavimentar [ ], *va*. To pave.

pavimento [pah-ve-men'-to], *m*. Pavement, a floor of stone, tiles, or other materials.

paviota [pah-ve-o'-tah], *f. (Orn.)* Mew, sea-gull. V. GAVIOTA.

pavipollo [pah-ve-pol'-lyo], *m*. A young turkey.

pavito real [pah-vee'-to ray-ahl'], *m*. Pea-chick or pea-chicken.

pavo [pah'-vo], *m*. 1. *(Orn.)* Turkey. 2. Peacock-fish. **Pavo silvestre**, *(Orn.)* wood-grouse. **Pavo real**, *(Orn.)* peacock. V. PAVÓN. 3. Idiot (necio); sucker (víctima). 4. **Ponerse hecho un pavo**, to blush like a lobster. 5. *(And.)* Large kite (cometa). 6. *(And.)* Big shot (espadón); evil-looking person (sospechoso). 7. **Ir de pavo**, *(LAm.)* to travel free. 8. *(Carib.)* youngster (joven).

pavo [pah'-vo], *a. (coll.)* Peacock-like.

pavón [pah-vone'], *m*. 1. *(Orn.)* Peacock. 2. A piece of wood with which gunpowder is glazed. 3. *(Ast.)* A northern constellation.

pavonada [pah-vo-nah'-dah], *f*. 1. Short walk 2. Strut, an affected stateliness in walking.

pavonar [pah-vo-nar'], *va*. To give iron or steel a bluish color.

pavonazo [pah-vo-nah'-tho], *m. (Pict.)* Crimson or purple color.

pavoncillo, ito [pah-von-theel'-lyo], *m. dim*. A little peacock.

pavonear [pah-vo-nay-ar'], *vn*. 1. To strut, to flaunt about the streets, to flutter. 2. *(coll.)* To amuse with false hopes.

pavor [pah-vor'], *m*. Fear, dread, terror.

pavordear [pah-vor-day-ar'], *va*. To swarm (abejas).

pavorido, da [pah-vo-ree'-do, dah], *a*. Intimidated, struck with terror.

pavorosamente [pah-vo-ro-sah-men-tay], *adv.* Awfully, fearfully.

pavoroso, sa [pah-vo-roh´-so, sah], *a.* Awful, formidable, dreadful.

pavura [pah-voo´-rah], *f.* Fear, dread, terror. *V.* PAVOR.

paya [pah´-yah], *f.* Hoyden or hoiden: a wild, boisterous girl; a tomboy.

payasada [pah-yah-sah-dah], *f.* Clownish trick, stunt; ridiculous thing.

payaso [pah-yah´-so], *m.* A clown

payo [pah´-yo], *m.* 1. Clown, churl. 2. Non-gipsy (entre gitanos).

payuelas [pah-yoo-ay´-lahs], *f. pl. (Med.)* Chicken pox.

paz [pat], *f.* 1. Peace, tranquility, ease. 2. Peace, respite from war; truce, armistice, an agreement between belligerents to end a war. 3. Peace, rest from commotions, quiet from disturbances, and reconciliation from differences. 4. Peace, the quiet and good correspondence of one with the others. 5. A pleasant, peaceful disposition. 6. Equality of luck among card-players. 7. Clear or even accounts. 8. A salute or kiss on the meeting of absent friends. 9. A ceremony of the mass. **A la paz de Dios**, God be with you. **Bandera de paz**, a flag of truce. **En paz**, quit, clear. **Gente de paz**, a friend: a familiar way of answering to one who asks, who is there? or, who knocks at the door? **Descansar en paz**, to rest in peace. **Mantener la paz**, to keep the peace. **Hacer las paces**, to make peace.

¡paz! [path], *int.* Peace! hush! **Paz sea en esta casa**, peace be in this house, a salute on entering.

pazán [pah-thahn´], *m.* Egyptian antelope.

pazguato, ta [path-goo-ah´-to, tah], *m. & f.* Dolt, a simple, stupid person.

pazpuerco, ca [path-poo-err´-co, cah], *a.* Dirty, slovenly.

pe [pay], *f.* Name of the letter P. **De pe a pa**, entirely, from beginning to end.

peaje, pedaje [pay-dah´-hay, pay-dah-hay], *m.* Bridge-toll, ferriage.

peajero [pay-ah-hay´-ro], *m.* Toll-gatherer.

peal [pay-ahl´], *m.* 1. Sock. 2. Worthless person. 3. Lasso.

peal [pay-ahl´], *a.* Heavy, dull, sickly.

peana [pay-ah´-nah], *f.* 1. Pedestal, the basis of a statue. 2. Frame at the foot of an altar to tread upon.

peatón, ona [pay-ah-ton´, nah], *m. & f.* Pedestrian. -*m.* Rural postman.

peatonal [pay-ah-to-nahl´], *a.* Pedestrian. **Calle peatonal**, pedestrianized street.

peazgo [pay-ath´-go], *m.* Bridge-toll. *V.* PEAJE.

pebete [pay-bay´-tay], *m.* 1. An aromatic composition used as a perfume. 2. Stench. an unpleasant smell. 3. Tube filled with gunpowder and other ingredients, and used to convey fire to rockets and other artificial fireworks; fuse (de cohete). 4. *(Cono Sur)* Roll (panecillo).

pebetero [pay-bay-tay´-ro], *m.* Censer, a vessel in which perfumes are burnt.

pebrada [pay-brah´-dah], *f. V.* PEBRE.

pebre [pay-bray], *m.* 1. A kind of sauce made of garlic, cloves, and other spices. 2. Pepper. *V.* PIMIENTA.

peca [pay´-cah], *f.* Freckle, a speck, a spot.

pecable [pay-cah´-blay], *a.* Peccable, liable to sin.

pecadazo [pay-cah-dah´-tho], *m. aug.* A heinous or atrocious sin.

pecadillo [pay-cah-deel´-lyo], *m. dim* Peccadillo, a slight fault.

pecado [pay-cah´-do], *m.* 1. Sin. **Pecado mortal**, deadly sin. **Pecado venial**, venial sin. **Pecado original** original sin. 2. Extravagance, excess. 3. *(coll.)* Devil, the instigator of sin. **Por mis pecados**, for my sins. 4. Defect (defecto). **Más feo que un pecado**, as ugly as sin. **Estar en pecado**, to be in sin. **Los siete pecados capitales**, the seven deadly sins. **Pecado, da**, *pp.* of PECAR.

pecador [pay-cah-dor´], *m.* 1. Sinner, a person who has committed a sin. 2. Sinner, any individual capable of sinning.

3. *(Met.)* A sinner, an offender, a delinquent: one who neglects totally that which he ought to do. **Pecador de mí!** poor me, sinner as I am! 4. An ignorant, stupid person.

pecadora [pay-cah-do´-rah], *f* 1. *V.* PECADOR. 2. A prostitute.

pecadorazo, za [pay-cah-do-rah´-tho, thah], *m. & f. aug.* A great sinner.

pecadorcillo, illa, ito, ita [pay-cah-dor-theel´-lyo], *m. & f. dim.* Little sinner.

pecaminosamente [pay-cah-me-no´-sah-men-tay], *adv.* Sinfully, wickedly.

pecaminoso, sa [pay-cah-me-no´-so, sah], *a.* Sinful.

pecante [pay-cahn´-tay], *a.* Peccant, vicious, abundant.

pecar [pay-car´], *vn.* 1. To sin, to violate the laws of God. 2. To sin, to offend against right, to be wanting in what is right and just, or in the rules of art. 3. To commit excesses of any description. 4. To boast, to brag. 5. To have a strong propensity. 6. To occasion or to merit punishment. **Peca de generoso**, he is too generous. **Nunca se peca por demasiado cuidado**, one can´t be too careful.

pecarí [pay-cah-ree´], *m. (Zool.)* Peccary, a wild hog of Mexico and South America.

peccata minuta [pec-cah´-tah me-noo´-tah]. *(coll.)* Slight offense, trivial vice or sin.

pece [pay´-thay], *m.* 1. Clay wetted for making mud walls. 2. Ridge of land between two furrows. 3. *(Obs.)* Fidel. *V.* PEZ.

pececico, illo, ito [pay-thay-thee´-co], *m. dim.* A small fish.

peceño, ña [pay-thay´-nyo, nyah], *a.* 1. Of the color of pitch: applied to the hair of horses. 2. Applied to things which have a pitchy taste.

pecera [pay-thay´-rah], *f.* Glass globe for gold-fish.

pecezuela [pay-thay-thoo-ay´-lah], *f. dim.* A small piece.

pecezuelo [pay-thay-thoo-ay´-lo], *m. dim.* 1. Small foot. 2. Small fish.

pecha [pay´-chah], *f.* Tax, impost, tribute.

pechada [pay-chah´-dah], *f. (Amer.)* A blow upon the chest.

pechar [pay-char´], *m.* To pay taxes.

pechera [pay-chay´-rah], *f.* 1. Stomacher. 2. The bosom of a shirt (camisa). 3. A breast collar for horses and mules. 4. *(Cono Sur. Tec.)* Apron.

pechería [pay-chay-ree´-ah], *f.* Paying tax, toll, or duty.

pechero, ra [pay-chay´-ro, rah], *a.* Liable to pay duty or taxes; commoner, in contraposition to nobleman.

pechero [pay-chay´-ro], *m.* Bib, a piece of linen put on the breast of children.

pechiblanco, ca [pay-che-blahn´-co, cah], *a.* White-breasted.

pechicatería [pay-che-cah-tay-ree´-ah], *f. (Cuba)* Meanness, parsimony.

pechico, illo [pay-chee´-co], *m. dim.* A small breast, teat, etc.

pechicolorado [pay-che-co-lo-rah´-do], *m.* Robin-redbreast, a kind of gold-finch.

pechigonga [pay-che-gon´-gah], *f.* A game at cards.

pechina [pay-chee´-nah], *f.* 1. A kind of shell which pilgrims carry on their hats and shoulders. 2. Curvilineal triangle, formed by the arches, where they meet, to receive the annulet of the cupola.

pechirrojo [pay-cheer-ro´-ho], *m. (Orn.) V.* PECHICOLORADO.

pechisacado, da [pay-che-sah-cah´-do, dah], *a. (Met. Coll.)* Haughty, arrogant.

pechito [pay-chee´-to], *m. dim. V.* PECHITO.

pecho [pay´-cho], *m.* 1. The breast. 2. The internal part of the breast, especially in men; chest. 3. Breast, the mammary gland (de mujer). 4. Bosom, breast, as the seat of the passions, the seat of tenderness, or the receptacle of secrets. 5. Regard, esteem, confidence. 6. Courage, valor, fortitude. 7. Quality and strength of the voice to sing, preach, etc. 8. Breast, heart, conscience. 9. Tax formerly paid to the government by those who did not belong to the nobility. 10. Any contribution paid to anyone besides the king. **Dar el pecho**, to suckle. **Hombre de pelo en pecho**, a brave, daring man. **Tomar a pecho**, to take to heart. **A pecho descubierto**, unarmed, without defence.

pechuelo [pay-choo-ay'-lo], *m. dim.* A small or little breast.

pechuga [pay-choo'-gah], *f.* 1. Breast of a fowl. 2. Bosom of man or woman. 3. *(Geog.)* Slope, hill. 4. *(LAm.)* Nerve, gall, cheek. 5. *(And. CAm.)* Abuse of trust (abuso de confianza). 6. *(CAm.)* Trouble, annoyance (molestia).

pechugón [pay-choo-gone'], *m.* Blow on the breast. -*a.* 1. Busty, big-bosomed (de mucho pecho). 2. *(LAm.)* Forward (descarado); outspoken (franco); sponging, parasitical; on the make (egoísta). 3. *(Cono Sur)* Bold, single-minded (resuelto).

pechuguera [pay-choo-gay'-rah], *f.* Cough, hoarseness (ronquera).

pechuguica, illa [pay-choo-gee´-cah], *f. dim.* A small breast of a fowl.

peciento, ta [pay-the-en'-to, tah], *a.* Of a pitchy color.

peciluengo, ga [pay-the-loo-en'-go, gah], *a.* Long-stalked: applied to fruit with stalks on trees.

pecina [pay-thee'-nah], *f.* 1. Fish-pond. 2. *V.* LODAZAL.

pecinal [pay-ce-nahl'], *m.* Pool of standing or muddy water.

pecio [pay'-the-o], *m.* Fragment of a ship which has been ship-wrecked.

pecíolo [pay-thee'-o-lo], *m. (Bot.)* Petiole, leaf-stalk or flower-stalk.

pécora [pay'-co-rah], *f.* 1. A sheep, head of sheep. 2. A cunning person, knave; a gay, merry person. 3. Bitch (lagarta). 4. Harpy (arpía). 5. Loose woman, whore (puta).

pecorea [pay-co-ray'-ah], *f.* 1. Robbery committed by straggling soldiers; marauding. 2. Idle, strolling and loitering about the streets.

pecoso, sa [pay-co'-so, sah], *a.* Full of freckles, freckled.

pectina [pec-tee´-nah], *f.* Pectin, vegetable jelly, a substance obtained from pears and used in confectionery.

pectoral [pec-to-rahl'], *a.* Pectoral, belonging to the breast. -*m.* Cross worn by bishops on the breast; breast-plate.

peculado [pay-coo-lah'-do], *m.* Peculation, theft, embezzlement of public money.

peculiar [pay-coo-le-ar'], *a.* Peculiar, its own, or one´s own, special.

peculiaridad [pay-coo-le-ah-re-ay-dahd'], *f.* Peculiarity; special feature.

peculiarmente [pay-coo-le-ahr'-men-tay], *adv.* Peculiarly.

peculio [pay-coo'-le-o], *m.* Stock or capital which the father permits a son to hold for his own use and benefit.

pecunia [pay-coo'-ne-ah], *f. (coll.)* Hard cash, specie.

pecuniariamente [pay-coo-ne-ah'-re-ah-men-tay], *adv.* In ready money.

pecuniario, ria [pay-coo-ne-ah'-re-o, ah], *a.* Pecuniary, relating to money.

pedacico, illo ito [pay-dah-thee'-co], *m.* Small piece or bit, a gobbet. **A pedacicos,** piecemeal.

pedagogía [pay-dah-go-hee'-ah], *f.* Pedagogy, the science and art of teaching.

pedagógico, ca [pay-dah-go'-he-co, cah], *a.* Pedagogical.

pedagogo [pay-dah-go'-go], *m.* 1. Pedagogue, schoolmaster, pedant. 2. A prompter, ruler, or director to another.

pedaje [pay-dah'-hay], *m.* Bridge-toll. *V.* PEAJE.

pedal [pe-dahl'], *m.* Pedal (bicicleta). 1. The pedal pipes of an organ, and the keys, played by the feet, which control them. 2. The pedal of a pianoforte or harp. 3. The treadle of a sewing-machine, etc. 4. A pedal-base holding-note.

pedalear [pe-dah-lay-ahr'], *vn.* To pedal.

padáneo [pay-dah'-nay-o], *a.* Petty, puisne, inferior: applied to the members of inferior courts of justice.

pedante [pay-dahn'-tay], *m.* Pedant, a schoolmaster, a vain man of low knowledge.

pedantear [pay-dan-tay-ar'], *m.* To pedantize, to play the pedant, to use pedantical expressions.

pedantería [pay-dan-tay-ree'-ah], *f.* Pedantry, awkward ostentation of needless learning.

pedantesco, ca [pay-dan-tes´-co, cah], *a.* Pedantic, awkwardly ostentatious of learning.

pedantismo [pay-dan-tees'-mo], *m.* Pedantry.

pedazo [pay-dah'-tho], *m.* Piece, bit; a part of a whole, a lump. **Pedazo del alma,** my dear, my love. **A pedazos** or **en pedazos,** in bits, in fragments. **Estar hecho pedazos,** (a) to be broken in pieces; (b) *(Met.)* to be very fatigued.

pedazuelo [pay-dah-thoo-ay'-lo], *m. dim.* A small piece or bit.

pedenial [pay-dey-nahl´], *m.* 1. Flint. 2. Silex.

pedestal [pay-des-tahl´], *m.* 1. Pedestal, the basis of a column or statue. 2. *V.* PEANA. 3. Foundation, the fundamental part of a thing.

pedestre [pay-des'-tray], *a.* Pedestrious, pedaneous, going on foot (viajero).

pediatra [pay-de-ah'-trah], *m. & f.* Pediatrician, child specialist.

pediatría [pay-de-ah-tree'-ah], *f.* Pediatrics.

pedicoj [pay-de-coh'], *m.* Jump on one foot.

pedicular [pay-de-coo'-lar'], *a.* Pedicular, lousy.

pedículo [pay-dee´-coo-lo], *m.* 1. *(Bot.)* Peduncle of a flower. 2. *(Med.)* The pedicle of a tumor.

pedicuro [pay-de-coo'-ro], *m.* Chiropodist.

pedida [pay-dee'-dah], *f.* **Pedida de mano,** engagement.

pedido [pay-dee'-do], *m.* 1. A voluntary contribution, which is called for by government in urgent necessities of the state. 2. *V.* PETICIÓN. 3. *(Com.)* An order of goods or merchandise.— **Pedido, da,** *pp.* of PEDIR. **A pedido de,** at the request of.

pedidor, ra [pay-de-dor', rah], *m. & f.* Petitioner, craver.

pedidura [pay-de-doo'-rah], *f.* Begging, petitioning.

pedigón [pay-de-gone´], *m. (coll.)* Craver, an insatiable asker.

pedigree [pay-de-gree'], *m.* Pedigree.

pedigüeño, ña [pay-de-goo-ay´-nyo, nyah], *a.* Craving, demanding frequently and importunately.

pediluvio [pay-de-loo'-ve-o], *m. (Med.)* Pediluvium, a bath for the feet.

pedimento [pay-de-men'-to], *m.* Petition. *V.* PETICIÓN.

pedir [pay-deer'], *va.* 1. To ask for, to request, to supplicate, to solicit. 2. To ask, to demand or require information. 3. To crave, to manifest a desire of obtaining something from another. 4. To demand and fix a price on goods set for sale (precio). 5. To demand, to inquire after, to wish for. 6. To ask for a woman in marriage (matrimonio). **Pedir limosna,** to beg, to ask alms. **Pedir justicia** or **pedir en juicio,** to claim, to bring an action or claim against a person before a judge. **Pedir cuentas,** to call for the accounts. **Pedir cuenta,** to bring a person to account. **A pedir de boca,** according to desire; adequately. **Pedírselo a uno el cuerpo,** to long anxiously. **Pedir la paz,** to sue for peace. **La casa está pidiendo una mano de pintura,** the house is crying out for a dab of paint. (*Yo pido, pida: el pidió* or *pidiera. V.* PEDIR.)

pedo [pay'-do], *m.* 1. Wind from the bowels; flatulence, fart. **Tirarse un pedo,** to let off a fart. 2. *(Cono Sur)* **Agarrarse un pedo,** to get sloshed. **Andar pedo,** to be sloshed (borracho).

pedorrear [pay-dor-ray-ar'], *va.* 1. To discharge wind. 2. *(Met.)* To sing or play badly.

pedorreras [pay-dor-ray'-ras], *f. pl.* 1. A kind of very tight breeches. 2. Flatulencies.

pedorrero, ra, pedorro, rra [pay-dor-ray'-ro, rah], *a.* Discharging much wind, flatulent.

pedorreta [pay-dor-ray'-tah], *f.* Noise made by children with the mouth.

pedrada [pay-dah' dah], *f.* 1. Throw or cast of a stone; lapidation (acto). **Matar a uno a pedradas,** to stone somebody to death. 2. A blow from a stone or the mark left by it. 3. A smart repartee, taunt, sneer. **Pedrada** or **pedradas,** an exclamation in denouncing a crime, you should be stoned. 2. A sneer at one who shows his teeth.

pedrea [pay-dray'-ah], *f.* 1. Throwing stones (combate). 2. Falling of stones. 3. Conflict of boys fighting with stones: lapidation. 4. Small prizes in the lottery (premios).

pedrecita [pay-dray-thee'-tah], *f. dim.* A small stone.

pedregal [pay-dray-gahl'], *m.* Place full of stones.

pedregoso, sa [pay-dray-go'-so, sah], *a.* 1. Stony, abounding with stones. 2. Afflicted with the gravel.

pedrejón [pay-dray-hone'], *m.* Large loose stone.

pedreñal [pay-dray-nyahl'], *m.* Kind of small firelock.

pedrera [pay-dray'-rah], *f.* Quarry, a stone-pit.

pedrería [pah-dray-ree'-ah], *f.* A collection of precious stones; jewels.

pedrero [pay-dray'-ro], *m.* 1. Stone-cutter (persona). 2. A swivel-gun. 3. Slinger, one who throws with a sling. 4. Lapidary, one who deals in precious stones.

pedrezuela [pay-dray-thoo-ay'-lah], *f. dim.* A small stone.

pedriscal [pay-dres-cahl'], *m. V.* PEDREGAL.

pedrisco [pay-drees'-co], *m.* 1. Hailstone (lluvia de piedras). 2. Heap of stones (montón).

pedrisquero [pay-dris-kay'-ro], *m.* A stone, hailstone.

pedriza [pay-dree'-thah], *f.* l. Quarry. *V.* PEDRERA. 2. Heap of loose stones.

pedrusco [pay-droos'-co], *m.* Rough piece of marble.

pedunculado, da [pay-doon-coo-lah'-do dah], *a. (Bot.)* Peduncled.

pedunculillo [pay-doon-coo-lee'-lyo], *m. dim. (Bot.)* Pedicle or pedicel.

pedúnculo [pay-doon'-coo-lo], *m.* 1. *(Bot.)* Peduncle, flower-stalk. 2. Name of certain cerebral appendages.

peer [pay-err'], *vn.* To break wind.

pega [pay'-gah], *f.* 1. The art of joining or cementing things. 2. Varnish of pitch put on earthen vessels. 3. Act of firing a blast. 4. *(coll.)* A jest, a joke (chasco), a trick, hoax (truco). 5.*(Orn.)* Magpie. 6. Snag, difficulty (dificultad). 7. Searching question (pregunta). 8. *(Carib. Cono Sur, Mex.)* Job (trabajo). 9. *(Carib.)* Birdlime (liga). **Todo son pegas,** there´s nothing but problems. **De pega,** false.

pegadillo [pay-gah-deel'-lyo], *m.* 1. *(dim.)* A little patch; a sticking-plaster. 2. Man who is introduced into a house or conversation, and remains, to the general annoyance.

pegadizo, za [pay-gah-dee'-tho, thah], *a.* 1. Clammy, glutinous, viscous. 2. Catching, contagious. 3. Adhering selfishly: applied to one who sticks to another from base motives. 4. Sticky (pegajoso). 5. Sham, imitation (postizo). 6. Parasitic (persona).

pegado [pay-gah'-do], *m.* Patch, sticking-plaster, cataplasm. **Pegado, da**, *pp.* of PEGAR.

pegador [pay-gah-dor'], *m.* Paper-hanger, one who applies wallpaper. **Pegador de carteles**, bill-poster, bill-sticker.

pegadura [pay-gah-doo'-rah], *f.* 1. Pitching, daubing with pitch. 2. The sticking of one thing to another.

pegajoso, sa [pay-gah-ho'-so, sah], *a.* 1. Sticky, viscous, glutinous, dauby, mucous. 2. Catching, contagious. 3. Attractive, alluring; adhesive.

pegamento [pay-gah-men'-to], *m.* Glue, adhesive; glue (droga). **Pegamento de caucho**, rubber solution.

pegamiento [pay-gah-me-en'-to], *m.* The act and effect of conglutinating or cementing.

pegante [pay-gahn'-tay], *a.* Viscous, glutinous.

pegar [pay-gar'], *va.* 1. To join one thing to another with cement or viscous matter. 2. To join, to unite, to sew one thing with another. 3. To close or apply closely two things. 4. To dash things violently together, to clap. 5. To chastise, to punish, to beat. 6. To infect (enfermedad), to communicate a distemper. 7. To hit (pelota), to give, to hit, to deal (golpe). 8. *(LAm.)* To be lucky; to manage it (lograrlo); to make a hit (caer en gracia). 9. *(Mex.)* To tie, to fasten; to hitch up (caballo). 10. *(Carib.)* To start (trabajo). -*vn.* l. To root or take root (plantas). 2. To make an impression on the mind; to communicate vices, manners, etc. 3. To assault, to attack. 4. To join, to be contiguous, to cleave, to cling. 5. To begin to take effect. 6. To fall asleep. 7. To say or do something disagreeable or displeasing. **Pegarla**, to betray one's confidence. 8. To hit, to beat (dar golpes). 9. To strike hot (sol). 10. *(Carib. Mex.)* To work hard. -*vr.* 1. To intrude, to enter without invitation or permission. 2. To stick, to adhere;

to unite itself by its tenacity or penetrating power, to cohere, to grow. 3. To insinuate itself, to steal upon the mind. 4. To be taken with, to be strongly affected with a passion. 5. To spend one's fortune on things which belong to others. **No pegar ojo**, not to sleep a wink. **Pegársele (a uno),** (a) to stick to one, to derive advantage from something; (b) to be prejudiced in the management of other's interests. **Pegar una silla a una pared**, to move a chair up against a wall. **Dicen que pega a su mujer**, they say he knocks his wife about. **Pegar un grito**, to let out a yell. **El piano pega en la pared,** the piano is touchng the wall. **Pega con**, to match. **La flecha pegó en el blanco**, the arrow hit the target. **A estas horas el sol pega fuerte**, the sun strikes very hot at this time.

pega reborda [pay'-gah-ray-bor'-dah], *f. (Zool.)* Shrike, butcher-bird.

pegaseo, sea [pay-gah'-say-o, ah], *a. (Poet.)* Belonging to Pegasus.

pegásides [pay-gah'-se-days], *f. pl.* The Muses.

pegaso [pay-gah'-so], *m.* 1. Pegasus, a winged horse. 2. A northern constellation west of Andromeda.

pegata [pay-gah'-tah], *f. (coll.)* Trick, fraud, imposition.

pegatina [pay-gah-tee'-nah], *f.* Sticker.

pegatista [pay-gah-tees'-tah], *m.* An indigent wretch, who lives upon the offals of other men's tables; a sponger.

pego [pay-go], *m. (Esp.)* 1. **Dar el pego**, it looks great. 2. **Me ha dado el pego**, he´s done me down.

pegote [pay-go'-tay], *m.* 1. Kind of sticking-plaster. 2. Fricassee with a thick, clammy sauce. 3. A sponger, a toad-eater, a sycophant. 4. Botch (chapuza). 5. **Tirarse el pego**, to show off.

peguera [pay-gay'-rah], *f.* 1. Pile of pine-wood, burnt for the purpose of making pitch. 2. Place where sheep are marked with pitch.

peguero [pay-gay'-ro], *m.* One who makes or deals in pitch.

pegujal, pegujar [pay-goo-hahl'], *m.* 1. Stock or capital which a son holds by permission of his father, for his own use and benefit. 2. A small dead or live stock on a farm.

pegujalero, pegujarero [pay-goo-hah-lay'-ro], *m.* A small farmer, grazier who keeps but a small flock of sheep.

pegujón [pay-goo-hone'], *m.* Pellet or little ball of wool or hair.

pegunta [pay-goon'-tah], *f.* Mark of pitch on wool, cattle, etc.

peguntar [pay-goon-tar'], *va.* To mark cattle, etc., with melted pitch.

peinada [pay-e-nah'-dah], *f.* Combing, the act of combing and dressing hair.

peinado [pay-e-nah'-do], *m.* 1. Hairdressing, coiffure. 2. Hair style.

peinado, da [pay-e-nah'-do, dah], *a. & pp.* of PEINAR. 1. Combed, curled, dressed (pelo). 2. Applied to a man very effeminate in dress.

peinador, ra [pay-e-nah-dor', rah], *m. & f.* 1. One who dresses or combs hair (persona). 2. Hairdresser. -*m.* 3. Cloth put about the neck while the hair is combed. 4. *(LAm.)* Dressing table (tocador).

peinadura [pay-e-nah-doo'-rah], *f.* 1. The act of combing or dressing the hair. 2. Hair pulled out with a comb.

peinar [pay-e-nar'], *va.* 1. To comb or dress the hair (pelo). 2. To comb wool. 3. To touch or rub slightly. 4. To excavate or eat away part of a rock or earth. 5. *(Poet.)* To move or divide anything gently. **Las aves peinan las olas**, the birds skim the waves. **Peinar el estilo**, to correct, to chastise, or to purify the style. -*vr.* To comb one´s hair; to do one´s hair.

peinazo [pay-e-nah'-tho], *m.* Cross-piece of a door or window-frame.

peine [pay'-ee-nay], *m.* 1. Comb, an instrument for the hair. 2. Card, an instrument to card wool. 3. Rack, an engine of torture. 4. Weaver´s reed. 5. Hemp-comb. 6. Instep of the foot; hoof. **¡Se va a enterar lo que vale un peine!,** now he´ll find out what´s what!

peinería [pay-e-nay-ree'-ah], *f.* Shop where combs are made and sold.

peinero, ra [pay-e-nay'-ro, ah], *m. & f.* Comb-maker, comb-seller.

peineta [pay-ee-nay'-tah], *f.* An ornamental convex dressing-comb for the hair which women use.

peje [pay'-hay], *m.* 1. Fish. 2. Cunning, crafty fellow.

pejemuller [pay-hay-mool'-lyerr'], *f.* Mermaid, a sea-woman.

pejepalo [pay-hay-pah'-lo], *m.* An inferior kind of codfish, by reason of being tough and dry.

pejiguera [pay-he-gay'-rah], *f.* Difficulty, embarrassment, disgust.

pel [payl], *f.* Skill, hide, pelt. *V.* PIEL.

pela [pay'-lah], *m.* 1. Peeling (peladura). 2. Peseta. **Doscientas pelas,** two hundred pesetas. 2. *(Mex.)* A whipping in school. 3. *(Met.)* A reprimand.

pelada [pay-lah'-dah], *f.* 1. Pelt, the skin of a sheep stripped of the wool. 2. *(LAm.)* Haircut (corte de pelo). 3. *(Cono Sur)* Bald head (calva). 4. *(And. CAm. Carib.)* Blunder (error).

peladera [pay-lah-day'-rah], *f.* Shedding of the hair, alopecia.

peladero [pay-lah-day'-ro], *m.* Place where birds and hogs are scalded for stripping them.

peladilla [pay-lah-deel'-lyah], *f.* 1. Sugar-almond. 2. Small pebble; round whitish stone.

peladillo [pay-lah-deel'-lyo], *m.* A variety of clingstone peach of smooth purplish skin and firm flesh.

peladillos [pay-lah-deel'-lyos], *m. pl.* The wool stripped from the skin of a sheep.

peladiza [pay-lah-dee'-thah], *f.* In tanneries the wool which is removed from sheep-skins.

pelado, da [pay-lah'-do, dah], *a. & pp.* of PELAR. 1. Plucked; bared, decorticated. 2. Hairless, without hair (cabeza). 3. Applied to fields or mountains without shrubs or plants; bare, bald. 4. *(LAm.)* Broke (sin dinero), penniless. 5. *(Mex.)* Coarse, crude (grosero). 6. *(CAm. Carib.)* Impudent (descarado). **Estar pelado** or **ser un pelado,** *(coll.)* to be penniless, to be nobody. **Cobra el sueldo pelado,** he gets just the bare salary. **El cinco mil pelado,** exactly five thousand.

pelador [pay-lah-dor'], *m.* Plucker, one, who plucks or decorticates.

peladura [pay-lah-doo'-rah], *f.* 1. Plucking, decortication. 2. Peeling (acción). 3. Bare patch (calva).

pelafustán [pay-lah-foos-tahn'], *m.* Ragamuffin, vagabond, vagrant.

pelagallos [pay-lah-gahl-lyos], *m. (coll.)* Nickname applied to persons of the lowest rank who have no known occupation.

pelagatos [pay-lah-gah'-tos], *m.* 1. Vagrant. 2. Ragamuffin.

pelagiano, na [pay-lah-he-ah'-no, nah], *a.* Pelagian, denying original sin.

pelagóscopo [pay-lah-gos'-co-po], *m.* An optical instrument for seeing objects below the water.

pelagra [pay-lah'-grah], *f. (Med.)* An endemic disease of southern Europe, characterized by scaly inflammation of the skin.

pelaire [pay-lah'-e-ray], *m.* Wool-dresser.

pelairía [pay-lah-e-ree'-ah], *f.* Trade of a wool-comber.

pelaje [pay-lah'-hay], *m.* 1. Nature and quality of the hair and of wool. 2. Quality, and external appearance, especially of clothes.

pelambrar [pay-lam-brar'], *va.* To steep hides in lime-pits to take off the hair. *V.* APELAMBRAR.

pelambre [pay-lahm'-bray], *m.* 1. The quantity of hides put into lime-pits. 2. The mixture of lime and water with which tanners strip off hair from hides. 3. Hair of the body in general, particularly that which comes off. 4. Want of hair. 5. Bare patch (calva). 6. *(Cono Sur)* Gossip, slander (murmullos).

pelambrera [pay-lam-bray'-rah], *f.* 1. Quantity of hair in one place. 2. Want or shedding of hair. 3. The place where hides are macerated in limepits.

pelambrero [pay-lan-bray'-ro], *m.* The workman who steeps hides in limepits.

pelambrón, na [pay-lam-brone'], *a. (coll.)* V. POBRETÓN.

pelamen [pay-lah'-men], *m. (coll.)* V. PELAMBRE.

pelamesa [pay-lah-may'-sah], *f.* 1. Scuffle in which the hair is torn off. 2. A bushy head of hair.

pelámide [pay-lah'-me-day], *f.* Young brood of tunny-fish.

pelandusca [pay-lan-doos'-cah], *f. (coll.)* A strumpet.

pelantrín [pay-lan-treen'], *m. (Prov.)* A petty farmer.

pelar [pay-lar'], *va.* 1. To cut or pull out the hair; to pluck the feathers. 2. To divest of the bark or husk, to blanch, to shell (guisantes). 3. To trick, to cheat, to rob. 4. To boil, to scald. 5. To fleece, to clean out (naipes). 6. To do in (matar). 7. *(LAm.)* To beat up. **Esta agua está pelando,** this water is boiling. *-vr.* 1. To cast the hair. 2. **Pelárselas por algo,** to crave. 3. **Corre que se las pela,** he runs like nobody's business.

pelarruecas [pay-lar-roo-ay'-cas], *f.* A poor woman who lives by spinning.

pelaza [pay-lah'-thah], *f.* 1. Quarrel, affray, scuffle. 2. A caterwauling of cats.

pelaza [pay-lah'-thah], *a.* Applied to chopped or beaten straw of the stalks of barley.

pelazga [pay-lahth'-gah], *f. (coll.)* Quarrel, scuffle.

peldaño [pel-dah'-nyo], *m.* Every step of a flight of stairs (de escalera).

pelde [pel-day], *m.* V. APELDE.

peldefebre [pel-day-fay'-bray], *m.* Camlet, barracan, a stuff made of wool and goat's hair mixed; camel's hair.

pelea [pay-lay'-ah], *f.* 1. Battle, action, engagement, combat, fight. 2. Quarrel (riña), dispute, conflict. 3. Struggle, toil, fatigue. **Pelea de gallos,** cock-fight. **Armar una pelea,** to kick up a row.

pelcador [pay-lay-ah-dor'], *m.* Fighter, combatant.

peleante [pay-lay-ahn'-tay], *pa.* Combating, fighting.

pelear [pay-lay-ar'], *va.* 1. To fight, to combat. 2. To quarrel, to contend, to dispute. 3. To toil, to labor hard. **Pelear con todas sus fuerzas,** *(coll.)* to fight tooth and nail, might and main. *-vr.* To scuffle, to come to blows.

pelechar [pay-lay-char'], *va.* 1. To get hair. 2. To change the coat (caballos). 3. To fledge, to shed feathers. 4. *(coll.)* To improve one's fortune (enriquecerse), to recover health (salud)

pelele [par-lay'-lay], *m.* 1. A man of straw; insignificant fellow. 2. Rompers (traje de niño).

pelendengue [pay-len-den'-gay], *m.* Frivolous coppery, extreme nicety in dress.

peleón [pay-lay-on'], *a. & m.* 1. Very ordinary wine. 2. Pugnacious (persona), aggressive; quarrelsome.

peleona [pay-lay-oh'-nah], *f.* Scuffle, quarrel, dispute.

pelete [pay-lay'-tay], *m.* 1. He who punts at certain card games. 2. *(coll.)* A poor man. 3. Rag doll, puppet (muñeco). **Era un pelele en sus manos,** he was a puppet in his hands.

peletería [pay-lay-tay-ree'-ah], *f.* 1. Trade of a furrier or skinner. 2. Fellmonger's shop, where fine skins and furs are sold.

peletero [pay-lay-tay'-ro], *m.* Furrier, one who dresses fine skins or deals in furs.

pelgar [pel-gar'], *m.* A ragamuffin, a blackguard.

peliagudo, da [pay-le-ah-goo'-do, dah], *a.* 1. Downy, furry, having long fine hair or fur (animales). 2. *(coll.)* Arduous, difficult. 3. Ingenious, skilful, dexterous.

peliblanco, ca [pay-le-blahn'-co, cah], *a.* Having white hair.

peliblando, da [pay-le-blahn'-do, dah], *a.* Having fine soft hair.

pelicabra [pay-le-cah'-brah], *f.* Satyr, a fabulous animal.

pelícano [pay-lee'-cah-no], *m. (Orn.)* Pelican.

pelicano, na [pay-le-cah'-no, nah], *a.* Having gray hair; hoary.

pelicorto, ta [pay-le-cor'-to, tah], *a.* Having short hair.

película [pay-lee'-coo-lah], *f.* Film, a thin membrane, thin layer. **Película cinematográfica,** motion-picture film.

Película de largo metraje, full-length film. **Película sonora** or **película hablada,** talking picture. **Rollo de películas,** film roll. **Tira de película,** filmstrip.

peliculero [pay-le-coo-lay'-ro], *m.* Scenario writer.

peligrar [pay-le-grar'], *vn.* To be in danger; to be in peril, to risk, to peril.

peligro [pay-lee'-gro'], *m.* Danger, risk (riesgo), peril, hazard, jeopardy, menace (amenaza). **Correr peligro, tener peligro,** or **estar en peligro,** to be in peril or danger.

peligrosamente [pay-le-gro'-sah-men-tay], *adv.* Perilously, dangerously, hazardously, jeopardously.

peligrosidad [pay-le-gro-se-dahd'], *f.* Danger; riskiness.

peligroso, sa [pay-le-groh'-so, sah], *a.* Dangerous, perilous; hazardous.

pelilargo, ga [pay-le-lar'-go, gah], *a.* Having long hair.

pelillo [pay-leel'-lyo], *m.* 1. *(dim.)* Short, tender hair. 2. Trifle, a slight cause of disgust or displeasure. **Echar pelillos a la mar,** not to bear malice; to become reconciled. **No tener pelillos en la lengua,** to speak one's mind openly. **No reparar en pelillos,** not to bother with details.

pelinegro, gra [pay-le-nay'-gro, grah], *a.* Having black hair.

pelirrojo, ja [pay-leer-ro'-ho, hah], *a.* Red-haired.

pelirrubio, bia [pay-leer-roo'-be-o, ah], *a.* Having fair, light, or flaxen hair.

pelitieso, sa [pay-le-te-ay'-so, sah], *a.* Having strong, bushy hair.

pelito [pay-lee'-to], *m.* Short, tender hair.

pelitre [pay-lee'-tray], *m.* *(Bot.)* Pellitory of Spain.

pelitrique [pay-le-tree'-kay], *m.* Fiddle-faddle, trifle.

pella [pel'-lyah], *f.* 1. Ball, anything in a round form. 2. Mass of metal in its crude state. 3. Lard in the state in which it is taken from hogs. 4. A sum of money borrowed and not paid, or of money taken under false pretences. 5. *(Orn.)* Heron. 6. Head of cauliflower.

pellada [pel-lyah'-dah], *f.* 1. Gentle blow, dab. 2. A trowelful of mortar or slaked lime.

pelleja [pel-lyay'-hah], *f.* 1. Skin or hide stripped from an animal (piel). 2. *(Low.)* A strumpet. 3. Whore (puta).

pellejería [pel-lyay-hay-ree'-ah], *f.* 1. Shop where skins are dressed and sold. 2. *(Cono Sur)* Difficulty, jam.

pellejero [pel-lyay-hay'-ro], *m.* Furrier, he whose trade is to dress and sell skins, leather-dresser, pelt-monger.

pellejina [pel-lyay-hee'-nah], *f.* A small skin.

pellejo [pel-lyay'-ho], *m.* 1. Skin, hide, felt, pelt (de animal). 2. A skin dressed and pitched, in which liquors are carried. 3. Peel, skin (fruta). 4. *(Joc.)* Tippler, drunkard (borracho). **No quisiera estar en su pellejo,** *(coll.)* I would not stand in his shoes. **Arriesgarse el pellejo,** to risk one's neck. **Salvar el pellejo,** to save one's skin.

pellejudo, da [pel-lyay-hoo'-do, dah], *a.* Having a great quantity of skin.

pellejuela [pel-lyay-hoo-ay'-lah], *f. dim.* A small skin or hide, stripped from an animal.

pellejuelo [pel-lyay-hoo-ay'-lo], *m. dim.* A small skin.

pellica [pel-lee'-cah], *f.* 1. Coverlet of fine furs. 2. A robe of fine furs. 3. A small dressed skin.

pellico [pel-lyee'-co], *m.* 1. Dress made of skins or furs. 2. *(Prov.)* Offensive language.

pelliquero [pel-lye-kay'-ro], *m.* A maker of coverlets of fine fur.

pelliza [pel-lyee'-thah], *f.* Pelisse, fur cloak, dregs formed of skins.

pellizcar [pel-lyeeth-car'], *va.* 1. To pinch, to squeeze between the fingers and thumb; to pinch or wound artfully, to gripe. 2. To pilfer. 3. To take but little food; to take only a bit or pinch. *-vr.* *(Met.)* To long for anything.

pellizco [pel-lyeeth'-co], *m.* 1. Pinch, the act of pinching. 2. A nip. 3. A small bit or portion. 4. *(Met.)* Remorse, disquietude. **Un pellizco de sal,** a pinch of salt.

pellón, pellote [pel-lyone', pel-lyo'-tay], *m.* 1. A long robe made of skins or furs. 2. *(Amer.)* A skin, checkered in colors, placed on a riding-saddle.

pelluzgón [pel-lyooth-gone'], *m.* Lock of hair, wool, or tow.

pelma [pel'-mah], *f.* V. PELMAZO.

pelmacería [pel-mah-thay-ree'-ah], *f.* Heaviness, slowness.

pelmazo [pel-mah'-tho], *m.* 1. What is crushed or flattened. 2. Heavy paste or cake: food which lies heavy on the stomach. 3. A slow, heavy person; a procrastinator.

pelo [pay'-lo], *m.* 1. Hair. 2. Down, the tender feathers of birds (pájaros). 3. A down or bloom which grows on the skins or husks of fruit (de fruta). 4. Soft fibers of plants. 5. Any slender thread of wool, silk, etc. 6. Pile, the hair or bur on the right side of cloth. 7. Hair spring in watches (de reloj). 8. Flaw in precious stones or crystals (en joyas); split in metals, horses' hoofs, etc. 9. Abscess in a woman's breast. 10. A hair or splinter; trifle, anything of little value. 11. *(Com.)* Raw silk. 12. Color of animals' skins. V. PELAJE. 13. The grain of wood. **Venir a pelo,** to come to the purpose. **Pelo arriba** or **a contrapelo,** against the grain. **Gente de pelo,** rich people. **No tener pelo de tonto,** to be bright, quick, clever. **En pelo,** bare-backed, naked. **Ha quedado al pelo,** it fits like a glove. **Dar a uno para el pelo,** to knock somebody silly. **No se mueve un pelo de aire,** there isn't a breath of air stirring. **Soltarse el pelo,** to burst out, to drop all restraint. **No tiene pelo de tonto,** he's no fool.

pelón, na [pay-lone', nah], *a. (coll.)* Hairless (calvo), bald. - *m. & f.* 1. Poor, indigent man. 2. In Peru, a caressing term applied to children.

pelona, pelonia [pay-lo'-nah, pay-lo-nee'-ah], *f.* Baldness (calvicie).

pelonería [pay-lo-nay-ree'-ah], *f. (coll.)* Poverty, want, indigence.

pelosilla [pay-lo-seel'-lyah], *f. (Bot.)* Mouse-ear; hawkweed.

peloso, sa [pay-lo'-so, sah], *a.* Hairy.

pelota [pay-lo'-tah], *f.* 1. Ball, a round plaything. 2. Ball of soft material. 3. Cannon or musket ball. 4. Ball game or play performed with balls. 5. Balls (testículos). 6. **En pelotas,** stark naked. 7. *(LAm.)* Bunch, gang (de amigos). 8. *(CAm. Carib. Mex.)* Passion (pasión). 9. *(CAm. Carib. Mex.)* Passion (pasión). **Juego de pelota,** ball-game in general: also tennis and the tennis court. **Devolver la pelota a uno,** to turn the tables on somebody. **Coger a uno en pelotas,** to catch somebody on the hop.

pelotari [pay-lo-tah'-re], *m.* Professional player of jai alai.

pelota vasca [pay-lo'-tah vahs'-cah], *f.* Jai alai, Basque ball game.

pelotazo [pay-lo-tah'-tho], *m.* 1. Blow or stroke with a ball. 2. *(Esp.)* Drink.

pelote [pay-lo'-tay], *m.* Goat's hair.

pelotear [pay-lo-tay-ar'], *vn.* 1. To play at ball. 2. To argue, to dispute (discutir); to contend. 3. To throw from one part to another. *-va.* To examine the items of an account, and compare them with the parcels received. *-vr.* To throw snowballs at each other; to quarrel, to dispute.

pelotera [pay-lo-tay'-rah], *f.* Battle, quarrel, dispute, contention: applied in general to women's quarrels.

pelotería [pay-lo-tay-ree'-ah], *f.* 1. Heap of balls. 2. Heap of goat's hair.

pelotero [pay-lo-tay'-ro], *m.* 1. Ball-maker. 2. *(LAm.)* Ball player, sportsman, footballer, baseball player.

pelotilla [pay-lo-teel'-lyah], *f.* 1. *(dim.)* A small ball. 2. Small bell of wax, stuck with small pieces of glass, and fastened to a cat-o'-nine-tails, with which penitent persons once lashed themselves.

peloto [pay-lo'-to], *a. (Prov.)* V. CHAMORRO.

pelotón [pay-lo-tone'], *m.* 1. *(Aug.)* A large ball (pelota). 2. Bundle or ball of hair closely pressed together. 3. *(Mil.)* Platoon, a small body of foot-soldiers. 4. A crowd of persons close together without order (de personas). **Cabeza de pelotón,** leading group.

peltre [pel'-tray], *m.* Pewter, an alloy of tin and lead.

peltrero pel-tray´-ro], *m.* Pewterer, pewter-worker.

peluca [pay-loo´-cah], *f.* Wig; periwig, peruke. 2. The person who wears a wig. 3. A very severe reproof from a superior to an inferior.

pelucón [pay-loo-cone´], *m.* One who struts about in a large bushy wig; any fantastical fellow.

peludo, da [pay-loo´-do, dah], *a.* Hairy, hirsute, covered with hair.

peludo [pay-loo´-do], *m.* A bass mat of mat oval shape.

peluquera [pay-loo-kay´-rah], *f.* 1. Hairdresser. 2. A haircutter's or peruke-maker's wife.

peluquería [pay-loo-kay-ree´-ah], *f.* 1. Shop where wigs are made and sold. 2. Hairdresser´s, barber´s; barbershop.

peluquero [pay-loo-kay´-ro], *m.* Hairdresser, hair-cutter, wig-maker.

peluquilla, ita [pay-loo-keel´-lyah], *f. dim.* A small wig.

peluquín [pay-loo-keen´], *m.* A small bag-wig, peruke.

pelusa [pay-loo´-sah], *f.* 1. Down which covers plants or fruit. 2. Villous substance falling from clothes. 3. *(Joc.)* Cash, riches.

pelusilla [pay-loo-seel´-lyah], *f. dim.* 1. The down of plants or fruit when it is very short. 2. Envy (envidia).

pelvímetro [pel-vee´-may-tro], *m.* Pelvimeter.

pelvis [pel´-vis], *f. (Anat.)* Pelvis, pelvic cavity.

pena [pay´-nah], *f.* 1. Punishment, pain (dolor), penalty; chastisement, correction. 2. Pain, painfulness, affliction, sorrow, grief (tristeza), uneasiness of mind, anxiety (molestar); a violent emotion of the mind. 3. Pain, labor, hardship, difficulty (dificultad), toil. 4. Necklace. 5. *(LAm.)* Bashfulness (timidez), shyness, timidity; embarrassment (vergüenza). **Pena capital, de muerte** or **ordinaria**, capital punishment or penalty. **A duras penas**, with great difficulty or trouble; scarcely; hardly. **Ni pena ni gloria**, without pain or pleasure. **Da pena verlos así**, it grieves me to see them like that. **Tener una pena**, to have a pain. **Alma en pena**, soul in torment. **Pena de muerte**, death penalty.

pena, *adv.* V. SOPENA.

penachera, *f.* V. PENACHO.

penacho [pay-nah´-cho], *m.* 1. Tuft of feathers on the heads of birds. 2. Plumes, feathers worn as an ornament. 3. Loftiness, haughtiness, presumption. 4. Anything that rises in the form of a tuft or crest of feathers.

penachudo, da [pay-nah-choo´-do, dah], *a.* Crested, tufted, plumed.

penadamente, *adv.* V. PENOSAMENTE.

penadilla [pay-nah-deel´-lyah], *f.* A kind of blister or small pustule.

penado, da [pay-nah´-do, dah], *a. & pp.* Of PENAR. 1. Punished, chastised; suffered. 2. Painful. 3. Narrow-mouthed (vasijas).

penal [pay-nahl´], *a.* Penal, concerning punishment; judicial.

penalidad [pay-nah-le-dahd´], *f.* 1. Act of suffering punishment. 2. Suffering, calamity, trouble (trabajos), hardship; penalty.

penalización [pay-nah-le-thah-the-on´], *f.* Penalty; penalization. **Recorrido sin penalizaciónes**, clear round.

penalizar [pay-nah-le-thar´], *va.* To penalize.

penalti [pay´-nahl-te], *m.* penalty.

penante [pay-nahn´-tay], *pa. & a.* 1. Suffering pain or affliction; love lorn, love-sick. 2. Narrow-mouthed (vasijas). *-m. (Prov.)* Lover, gallant.

penar [pay-nar´], *vn.* 1. To suffer pain, to agonize; to be tormented in a future life (alma). 2. To crave, to desire anxiously. 3. To linger. *-va.* To chastise, to inflict punishment. *-vr.* 1. To grieve, to mourn.

penates [pay-nah´-tes], *m. pl.* Penates, the house-gods of the ancient heathens.

penatígero [pay-nah-tee´-hay-ro], *m. (Poet.)* He who carried the household gods of someone.

penca [pen´-cah], *f.* 1. Pricking leaf of a cactus or other similar plant (hoja). 2. A leather strap with which convicts were whipped by the hangman. 3. *(And.)* **Penca de hombre**,

a fine looking man. 4. **Agarrar una penca**, *(LAm.)* to get drunk.

pencar [pen-cahr´], *vn.* To slog away.

pencazo [pen-cah´-tho], *m.* Lash with the hangman's strap.

penco [pen´co], *m. (Mex. and Cuba)* An raw-boned, hard-trotting horse.

pencudo, da [pen-coo´-do, dah], *a.* Acuminated.

pendanga [pen-dahn´gah], *f. (coll.)* A common prostitute.

pendejo [pen-day´-ho], *m.* 1. Hair over the pubis and groin. 2. Coward (cobarde), poltroon. 3. *(Cono Sur)* Kid (muchacho). *-a.* 1. *(LAm.)* silly (necio), stupid; irresponsible (irresponsable). 2. *(And.)* Smart (listo). 3. *(Carib. Mex.)* Ham-fisted (torpe).

pendencia [pen-den´-the-ah], *f.* Quarrel, affray, dispute, feud, jangling contention.

pendenciar [pen-den-the-ar´], *vn.* To wrangle, to quarrel.

pendenciero, ra [pen-den´-the-ay´-ro, rah], *a.* Quarrelsome.

pender [pen-derr´], *vn.* 1. To impend, to hang over (amenaza). 2. To depend. 3. To be irresolute, to leave a thing undecided. **Cuenta pendiente**, an unsettled account. **Deuda pendiente**, a balance unpaid.

pendiente [pen-de-en´-tay], *a.* 1. Pendant (asunto), hanging (colgado). 2. *(Fig.)* **Estamos pendientes de lo que él decida**, we are dependent on what he may decide. **Tener una asignatura pendiente**, to have an outstanding subject. **Pendiente de**, pending, in abeyance.

pendiente [pen-de-en-tay], *f.* Slope, declivity: grade, gradient, of a road or railway; dip or pitch. *-m.* Earring, a pendant.

pendil [pen-deel´], *m.* A mantle worn by women. **Tomar el pendil**, to elope unexpectedly.

pendingue (tomar el). To take French leave.

péndol [pen´-do-le], *m. (Naut.)* Boot topping.

péndola [pen´-do-lah], *f.* 1. A pen. V. PLUMA. 2. Pendulum.

pendolaje [pen-do-lah´-hay], *m.* The plunder of a captured vessel.

pendolario [pen-do-lah´-re o], *m.* V. PENDOLISTA.

pendolero, ra [pen-do-lay´-ro, rah], *a.* Hanging, pendant.

pendolista [pen-do-lees´-tah], *m.* 1. Penman. 2. *(coll.)* Cheat, swindler, impostor.

pendolita [pen-do-lee´-tah], *f.* The spiral spring of the balance of a watch.

pendón [pen-done´], *m.* 1. Standard, the colors of a country (estandarte). 2. Banner carried in processions. 3. Standard, a shoot or principal branch of a stock, preserved at the felling of woods. 4. *(Her.)* Pennon, a family banner, borne in coats of arms. 5. *(coll.)* Nickname of a tall, awkward woman. 6. *pl.* Reins of the leading mule. 7. Whore (prostituta).

pendona [pen-do´-nah], *f.* Whore.

pendoncito [pen-don-thee´-to], *m. dim.* Pennon, a small flag.

pendonear [pen-do-nay-ahr´], *vn.* To loaf around the streets.

péndulo, la [pen´-doo-lo, lah], *a.* Pendant, hanging, pendulous. *-m.* 1. Pendulum. 2. An instrument for measuring the action of gravity. **Péndulo sideral**, an astronomical clock.

pene [pay´-nay], *m.* Penis, male organ of reproduction.

peneque [pay-nay´-kay], *a. (coll.)* Intoxicated, drunken.

penetrabilidad [pay-nay-trah-be-le-dahd´], *f.* Penetrability.

penetrable [pay-nay-trah´-blay], *a.* 1. Penetrable. 2. That can be understood.

penetración [pay-nay-trah the on´], *f.* 1. Penetration, the act of piercing or penetrating (acto). 2. Penetration, mental discernment, intelligence. 3. Penetration, acuteness, sagacity, clear sightedness (cualidad).

penetrador, ra [pay-nay-trah-dor´, rah], *m. & f.* Discerner, he who penetrates or distinguishes. *-a.* V. PENETRANTE.

penetral [pay-nay-trahl´], *m. (Poet.)* The interior or most retired part.

penetrante [pay-nay-trahn´-tay], *pa. & a.* 1. Penetrating, piercing. 2. Heart-rending. 3. Clear-sighted, keen. 4. Applied to a deep wound.

penetrar [pay-nay-trar´], *va.* To penetrate, to pierce; to pass through; to force in. 2. To penetrate, to affect the mind. 3. To penetrate, to fathom, to comprehend. 4. To permeate; to pervade. -*vn.* 1. To penetrate, to go in. **El cuchillo penetró en la carne,** the knife went into the flesh. 2. To enter (persona). 3. To pierce (emoción). **La ingratitud penetró hondamente en su corazón,** the ingratitude pierced him to the heart. -*vr.* **Penetrarse de.** 1. To become imbued (absorber). 2. To understand fully.

penetrativo, va [pay-nay-trah-tee'-vo, vah], *a.* Penetrative, penetrant.

penicilina [pay-ne-the-lee'-nah], *f. (Med.)* Penicillin.

península [pay-neen'-soo-lah], *f.* Peninsula.

peninsular [pay-neen-soo-lahr'], *a.* Peninsular.

penique [pay-nee'-kay], *m.* Penny, an English copper coin.

penisla [pay-nees'-lah], *f. V.* PENÍNSULA.

penitencia [pay-ne-ten'-the-ah], *f.* 1. Penitence, penance (condición). 2. Repentance. 3. Any act of mortification (acto). 4. Public punishment which the Inquisition inflicted upon some culprits. **Imponer una penitencia a uno,** to give somebody a penance. **Hacer penitencia,** to do penance.

penitenciado, da [pay-ne-ten-the-ah'-do, daha], *a. & n.* One who was punished by the Inquisition. -*pp.* of PENITENCIAR.

penitencial [pay-ne-ten-the-ahl'], *a.* Penitential.

penitenciar [pay-ne-ten-the-ar'], *va.* To impose penance for a fault.

penitenciaría [pay-ne-ten-the-ah-ree'-ah], *f.* 1. An ecclesiastical court at Rome. 2. Office of a penitentiary canon. 3. Penitentiary, a reformatory prison.

penitenciario [pay-ne-ten-the-ah'-re-o], *m.* 1. Penitentiary, a dignitary canon who has the power of absolving in certain cases. 2. Penitentiary, the president of an ecclesiatical court at Rome.

penitente [pay-ne-ten'-tay], *a.* Penitent, repentant, contrite.

penitente [pay-ne-ten'-tay], *com.* 1. Penitent, one who does penance. 2. Penitent, one who confesses to a confessor. 3. Associate in a party of pleasure or debauchery.

pennado, da [pen-nah'-do, dah], *a. (Bot.)* Pinnate.

penol [pay-nol'], *m. (Naut.)* Yard-arm.

penología [pay-no-lo-hee'-ah], *f.* Penology.

penosamente [pay-no-sah-men-tay], *adv.* Painfully (dolorosamente), grievously

penoso, sa [pay-no'-so, sah], *a.* 1. Painful (doloroso), grievous, laborious (difícil), distressing, tormenting. 2. *(And. Carib. Mex.)* Bashful, timid (timido).

penoso [pay-no'-so], *m.* An affected fop, a buck or dude.

pensado, da [pen-sah'-do, dah], *a. & pp.* Of PENSAR. Deliberate, premeditated. **De caso pensado,** on purpose, designedly. **Lo tengo bien pensado,** I have thought it over.

pensador, ra [pen-sah-dor', rah], *a.* Thoughtful, meditative, contemplative.—*m. & f.* Thinker, profound student.

pensamiento [pen-sah-me-en'-to], *m.* 1. Thought (facultad), idea (propósito), meditation, contemplation. 2. Thought, resolution, design. **Ni por pensamiento,** not even the thought of it. **En un pensamiento,** in a jiffy, in a moment. **Venir al pensamiento,** to come to somebody's mind. **Mi pensamiento es,** my idea is to. 3. *(Bot.)* Pansy.

pensar [pen-sar'], *vn.* 1. To think, to consider, to reflect, to cogitate, to meditate. 2. To think, to imagine, to fancy, to muse. 3. To think, to intend, to mean. 4. To take into serious consideration; to weigh maturely. 5. To feed cattle. **Sin pensar,** unexpectedly, thoughtlessly. **Pensar en,** to think of. **Pensar para sí,** to think to oneself. -*va.* 1. To think. 2. To think over (problemas). 3. **Pensar** + infin, to intend to. 4. To think up (idea). **Lo pensó mejor,** she thought better of it. **Esto es para pensarlo,** this needs thinking about.

pensativamente [pen-sah-te-vah-men-tay], *adv.* Moodily, thoughtfully.

pensativo, va [pen-sah-tee'-vo, vah], *a.* Pensive, thoughtful, cogitative.

pensil [pen-seel'], *a.* Pensile, hanging supported. -*m.* A beautiful garden.

pensilvano, na [pen-seel-vah'-no, nah], *a.* Pennsylvanian.

pensión [pen-se-on'], *f.* 1. Pension, an annual charge laid upon anything. 2. Pension, a fixed sum paid annually by government. 3. Toil, labor attending an enterprise or office, trouble, encumbrance, painful duty. 4. Boarding house (casa de huéspedes). 5. Board and lodging (precio). 6. *(Fig.)* Drawback, snag. 7. *(And. Cono Sur)* Worry (preocupado). **Pensión completa,** full board. **Pensión vitalicia,** annuity.

pensionado, da [pen-se-o-nah'-do, dah], *m. & f.* Pensioner, pensionary one who receives a pension. -*pp.* of PENSIONAR.

pensionar [pen-se-o-nar'], *va.* 1. To impose annual charges, pensions, or other burdens. 2. To give a grant (estudiante). 3. *(And. Cono Sur)* To bother (molestar).

pensionario [pen-se-o-nah'-re-o], *m.* 1. One who pays a pension. 2. Pensionary, the recorder of a city.

pensionista [pen-se-o-nees-tah], *com.* 1. Pensioner (jubilado), pensionery, one who receives a pension. 2. Boarder in a boarding-house (huésped). 3. *(LAm.)* Subscriber. 4. Boarder, in a boarding school (interno).

Penta. A Greek word signifying five.

pentacórdeo [pen-tah-cor'-day-o], *m.* Pentachord, five-stringed harp.

pentadáctilo, la [pen-tah-dac-te-lo, lah], *a.* Five fingered or toed; having five finger-like processes or radial arms.

pentaedro [pen-tah-ay'-dro], *m.* Pentahedron, a solid of five faces.

pentagloto [pen-tah-glo'-to], *a.* Pentaglottical, written in five languages.

pentágono [pen-tah'-go-no], *m.* Pentagon.

pentágrafo [pen-tah'-grah-fo], *m.* Pentagraph.

pentagrama [pen-tah-grah'-mah], *m.* The musical staff.

pentámetro [pen-tah'-may-tro], *m.* Petameter.

pentángulo [pen-tahn'-goo-lo], *m.* Pentangle.

pentapétalo, la [pen-tah-pay'-tah-lo, lah], *a. (Bot.)* Pentapetlous.

pentasílabo, ba [pen-tah-see'-lah-bo, bah], *a.* Of five syllables.

pentástilo [pen-tahs'-te-lo], *m. (Arch.)* Pentastyle.

pentateuco [pen-tah-tay'-oo-co], *m.* The Pentateuch.

pentecostés [pen-tay-cos-tays'], *m.* Pentecost, Whitsuntide.

penúltimo, ma [pay-nool'-te-mo, mah], *a.* Penultimate.

penumbra [pay-noom'-brah], *f.* Penumbra.

penuria [pay-noo'-re-ah], *f.* Penury, indigence.

peña [pay'-nyah], *f.* 1. Rock, large stone. 2. Group (grupo), circle. **Peña deportiva,** supporter's club. **Forma parte de la peña,** he's a member of the circle. 3. *(And. CAm. Carib.)* V. SORDO. 4. *(Cono Sur)* Pawnshop (montepío).

peñón [pay-nyah'-do], *m.* V. PEÑASCO.

peñascal [pay-nyas-cahl'], *m.* Rocky hill or mountain.

peñasco, peñedo [pay-nyahs'-co], *m.* 1. A large rock (piedra). 2. A strong silk stuff.

peñascoso, sa [pay-nyas-co'-so, sah], *a.* Rocky, mountainous.

peñol [pay-nyole'], *m.* A large rock, rocky mountain.

péñola [pay'-nyo-lah], *f. (Poet.)* A pen.

peñón [pay-nyone'], *m.* A large rock, rocky mountain.

peón [pay-on'], *m.* 1. Pedestrian. 2. Day-laborer. **Peón de albañil,** hodman. 3. Foot-soldier. 4. Top, spinning-top (peonza), humming-top. 5. In prosody, a foot of four syllables, three short and one long. 6. Pawn in chess (ajedrez); man, in draughts.

peonada [pay-o-nah'-dah], *f.* Day-work of a laborer.

peonaje [pay-o-nah'-hay], *m.* 1. Multitude of people on foot. 2. The body of *peones* who work at once in the same place.

peonería [pay-o-nay-ree'-ah], *f.* As much land as can be ploughed in a day.

peonía [pay-o-nee'-ah], *f.* 1. *(Bot.)* Peony. 2. Quantity of land given to a soldier in a conquered country.

peonza [pay-on'-thah], *f.* 1. Top, whipping top, gig. 2. A noisy, little fellow.

peor [pay-ore'], *a.* Worse (comparativo); worst (superlativo). **Tu ejercicio es peor que el mío,** your exercise is worse than mine. **Tu ejercicio es el peor de todos,** your exercise is the worst of all.-*adv.* Worse. **Peor que nunca**, worse than ever. **Lo peor es que...**, the worst of it is that... **En el peor de los casos**, if the worst comes to the worst.

peoría [pay-o-ree'-ah], *f.* Deterioration, detriment.

peormente [pay-or'-men-tay], *adv.* Worse.

pepián [pay-pe-ahn'], *m.* V. PIPIÁN.

pepinar [pay-pe-nar'], *m.* Cucumber field.

pepinillos [pay-pe-neel'-lyos], *m. pl.* (*dim.*). Gherkins, pickled cucumbers.

pepino [pay-pee'-no], *m.* (*Bot.*) Cucumber.

pepita [pay-pee'-tah], *f.* 1. Seed of some fruits, such as melons, apples, etc: kernel. 2. Pip, a distemper in fowls. 3. Nugget, piece of pure native gold. -*pr.* 4. Josie. See JOSEFA in Appendix.

pepitaña [pay-pe-tah'-nyah], *f.* (*Prov.*) A pipe made of corn-stalk.

pepitoria [pay-pe-to'-re-ah], *f.* 1. Fricassee made of giblets, livers, and lights. 2. Medley of things. 8. (*Mex.*) Peanut or almond candy.

pepitoso, sa [pay-pe-to'-so, sah], *a.* 1. Abounding in grains or seeds. 2. Applied to fowls with the pip.

peplo [pay'-plo], *m.* Peplum, a loose gown of the ancient Greek women.

pepón [pay-pone'], *m.* (*Bot.*) Watermelon. V. SANDÍA. -*a.* (*And.*) Good-looking, dishy.

pepsina [pep-see'-nah], *f.* Pepsin, the digestive ferment.

péptico, ca [pep'-te-co, cah], *a.* Peptic.

peptona [pep-to'-nah], *f.* Peptone.

pequeñamente [pay-kay'-nyah-men-tay], *adv.* Little, in a small degree or quantity, not much.

pequeñez [pay-kay-nyeth'], *f.* 1. Smallness of size (tamaño); littleness, minuteness. 2. Youth, tender age. 3. Lowness of mind, pusillanimity. **Preocuparse por pequeñeces**, to worry about trifles.

pequeñito, ta [pay-kay-nyee'-to, tah], *a. dim.* V. PEQUEÑUELO.

pequeño, ña [pay-kay'-nyo, nyah], *a.* 1. Little or small of size, minute. 2. Young, of a tender age. 3. Low-spirited, humble, abject.

pequín [pay-keen'], *m.* Silk stuff manufactured in Pekin.

per [per], *prep.* Used in Spanish in composition only, as *perdonable*, pardonable.

pera [pay'-rah], *f.* 1 Pear, the fruit of the pear-tree. 2. A small tuft of hair left to grow on the chin (barba, barbilla). 3. (*coll.*) A sinecure. 4. Bulb (bocina). 5. Bulb (bombilla). 6. Cushy job (empleo). 7. (*LAm. Dep.*) Punchball. **Pedir peras al olmo**, to look for pears on elm-trees. **Tocarse la pera**, to sit on one's backside.

perada [pay-rah'-dah], *f.* Conserve made of the juice of pears.

peraile [pay-rah'-e-lay], *m.* Woolcomber. V. PELAIRE.

peral [pay-rahl'], *m.* (*Bot.*) Pear-tree.

peraleda [pay-rah-lay'-dah], *f.* Orchard of pear-trees.

peraltar [pay-ral-tar'], *va.* To raise the arch of a vault or dome above a semicircle to the figure of a parabola.

peralte [pay-rahl'-tay], *m.* Height of an arch above a right angle.

perantón [pay-ran-tone'], *m.* 1. (*Bot.*) Marvel-plant. 2. A very tall person.

peraza [pay-rah'-thah], *f.* Fruit of an ingrafted pear-tree.

perca [perr'-cah], *f.* (*Zool.*) Perch.

percal [per-cahl'], *m.* (*Com.*) Percale, a dress material. (*Per.*)

percalina [per-cah-lee'-nah], *f.* Percaline, a lining material of one color; book muslin.

percance [per-cahn'-thay], *m.* 1. Perquisite, something above the settled salary: generally used in the plural. 2. Mischance, misfortune. **Percance, del oficio**, V. GAJES DEL OFICIO.

percarburo [per-car-boo'-ro], *m.* (*Chem.*) Percarbid(e).

percatar [per-cah-tar'], *vn.* 1. To think, to consider maturely. 2. To take care; to be on one's guard. -*vr.* **Percatarse de**, to notice (observar); to heed (hacer caso de); to guard against (guardarse de).

percebe [per-thay'-bay], *m.* A mollusk having five crusty plates and a fleshy foot. It is common on the coast of Galicia, and eaten cooked without any seasoning.

percibimiento [per-thay-be-me-en'-to], *m.* Prevention, warning. V. APERCIBIMIENTO.

percepción [per-thep-the-on'], *f.* Perception, notion (idea), idea, feeling.

perceptibilidad [per-thep-te-be-le-dahd'], *f.* Perceptibility, faculty of perception.

perceptible [per-thep-tee'-blay], *a.* Perceptible (visible), perceivable.

perceptiblemente [per-thep-tee'-blay-men-tay], *adv.* Perceivably, perceptibly.

perceptivo, va [per-thep-tee'-vo, vah], *a.* Perceptive.

percha [per'-chah], *f.* 1. Perch, a piece of timber to support anything. 2. Clothes-rack (perchero). 3. Snare for catching partridges. 4. String on which fowlers hang their game. 5. (*Zool.*) Perch. 6. (*Cono Sur*) Pile (montón). 7. (*Mex.*) Gang (grupo). 8. Build, physique (tipo); figure (de mujer). **Percha de herramientas**, toolrack. **Tener percha**, to be smart.

perchador, ra [per-chah-dor', rah], *m. & f.* Napper, one who raises the nap on cloth.

perchar [per-char'], *va.* To raise the nap on cloth.

perchero [per-chay'-ro], *m.* Clothes rack, hallstand.

percherón [per-chay-rone'], *m.* Percheron, Percheron Norman horse.

perchonar [per-cho-nar'], *vn.* 1. To leave on a vine-stock several long shoots. 2. To lay snares for catching game.

percibir [per-the-beer'], *va.* 1. To receive, to collect. 2. To perceive (notar), to comprehend.

percibo [per-thee'-bo], *m.* Act of receiving or perceiving.

perclórico [per-clo'-re-co], *a.* Perchloric.

percloruro [per-clo-roo'-ro], *m.* (*Chem.*) Perchloride.

percocería [per-co-thay-ree'-ah], *f.* Small work of silver or spangles; filagree, etc.

percuciente [per-coo-the-en'-tay], *a.* Percutient, striking.

percudir [per-coo-deer'], *va.* To tarnish the lustre of things (deslumbrar).

percusión [per-coo-se-on'], *f.* Percussion, collision.

percusor [per-coo-sor'], *m.* One who strikes.

percutir [per-coo-teer'], *va.* (*Med.*) To percuss.

perdedero [per-day-day'-ro], *m.* Occasion or motive of losing.

perdedor, ra [per-day-dor', rah], *m. & f.* Loser.

perder [per-derr'], *va.* 1. To lose, to be deprived of something. 2. To lose, to forfeit, to suffer diminution of. 3. To lose, to squander away, to lavish, to misspend. 4. To lose, to miss, not to find. 5. To lose, to ruin (arruinar), to send to perdition. 6. To lose, to be disappointed, not to obtain what has been wished (decaer). 7. To spoil, to mar, to damage. 8. To bet, to lay a wager. **Perder la ocasión or el lance**, to let an opportunity slip. **Perder terreno**, to lose ground. **Perder tiempo**, (a) to lose time, or not to profit of it; (b) to labor in vain. **He perdido la costumbre**, I have got out of the habit. **No pierde nada**, he doesn't miss a thing. -*vr.* (1.) To go astray, to miss one's way. 2. To be lost (desaparecer), to be confounded, to be bewildered. 3. To forget or lose the thread of one's subject or discourse. 4. To be spoiled (arruinarse), to be lost or given up to vice. 5. To fall into disuse, to be out of fashion. 6 To cease to be perceived by sight or hearing. 7. To run risk of losing life. 8. To love excessively. 9. (*Naut.*) To be shipwrecked. 10. To sustain a loss. 11. To congeal itself: applied to rivers which disappear under the earth and rise again. 12. (*LAm.*) To go on the streets (prostituirse). **Tener que perder**, to be a person of credit, to have much to lose. **Perder los estribos**, to lose patience. **Salir perdiendo**, to lose. **Ha perdido mucho en mi estimación**, he has gone down a lot in my estimation. **Echar a perder**, to spoil. **Nada se pierde con intentar**, there's no harm in trying.

perdición [per-de-the-on'], *f.* 1. Losing or the act of losing anything. 2. Perdition, destruction, ruin, loss. 3. Unbridled, excessive love. 4. Prodigality, extravagance. 5. Perdition, hell.

pérdida [perr'-de-dah], *f.* 1. Loss, privation of what was possessed. 2. Loss, detriment, damage; waste (de tiempo). 3. Quantity or thing lost. 4. Wastage (de líquido). **Pérdida contable**, book loss. **Vender algo con pérdida**, to sell something at a loss. **Pérdida de datos**, *(Comput.)* data leakage.

perdidamente [per-de'-dah-men-tay], *adv.* Desperately, furiously; uselessly.

perdidizo, za [per-de-dee'-tho, thah], *a.* Lost designedly or on purpose. **Hacerse perdidizo**, to lose designedly at cards, as gamesters do at times.

perdido, da [per-dee'-do, dah], *a. & pp.* Of PERDER. 1. Lost, strayed, misguided; profligate, dissolute. **Gente perdida**, Vagrants, vagabonds. **Mujer perdida**, prostitute. 2. **Estar perdido por**, to be mad about. 3. **Ponerse perdido de barro**, to get covered in mud. 4. *(LAm.)* Idle (vago); down and out (pobre).

perdidoso, sa [per-de-do'-so, sah], *a.* Sustaining loss.

perdigana [per-de-gah'-nah], *f. (Prov.)* A young partridge.

perdigar [per-de-gar'], *va.* 1. To broil partridges slightly before they are roasted. 2. To stew larded meat in an earthen pan. 3. To dispose, to prepare.

perdigón [per-de-gone'], *m.* 1. A young partridge. 2. Partridge trained to decoy others. 3. *(Prov.)* Squanderer, lavisher of money at the gaming-table. **Perdigones**, hail-shot, small shot, bird-shot.

perdiguero, ra [per-de-gay'-ro, rah], *a.* Setter, retriever: applied to a dog used by fowlers who pursue partridges.

perdiguero [per-de-gay'-ro], *m.* Poulterer, dealer in partridges or any other kind of game.

perdimiento [per-de-me-en'-to], *m.* V. PERDICIÓN and PÉRDIDA.

perdiz [per-deeth'], *f. (Orn.)* Partridge. **Perdiz real**, common partridge.

perdón [per-done'], *m.* 1. Pardon, forgiveness, absolution; mercy (indulto), grace remission of a debt. 2. Drop of oil wax, etc., which falls burning. **Con perdón**, under favor; with your leave. **Pedir perdón a uno**, to ask somebody's forgiveness. **¡Perdón!**, sorry!

perdonable [per-do-nah'-blay], *a.* Pardonable, forgivable.

perdonador, ra [per-do-nah-dor', rah], *m. & f.* Pardoner, excuser.

perdonanza [per-do-nahn'-thah], *f. V.* DISIMULO and PERDÓN.

perdonar [per-do-nar'], *va.* 1. To pardon (ofensa, persona), to forgive; to remit a debt. 2. To exempt anyone from doing what he should execute (de obligación); to spare, to excuse. 3. To beg leave or permission: an expression of civil denial or light apology. **¡Perdone!**, *(coll.)* sorry! *-vr.* To decline doing anything; to excuse oneself from doing anything. **Perdónanos nuestras deudas**, forgive us our trespasses. **No perdona nada**, he is wholly unforgiving. **Perdonar la vida a uno**, to spare somebody's life. **No perdonar ocasión**, to miss no chance.

perdonavidas [per-do-nah-vee'-das], *m. (coll.)* Bully, hector.

perdulario, ria [per-doo-lah'-re-o, ah], *a.* Extremely careless of one's own interest or person.

perdurable [per-doo-rah-blay], *a.* Perpetual, everlasting, continual.

perdurablemente [per-doo-rah'-blay-men-tay], *adv.* Eternally, perpetually.

perdurar [per-doo-rahr'], *vn.* To last, to endure, to survive; to stand.

perecear [pay-ray-thay-ar'], *va.* To protract, to delay, to put off.

perecedero, ra [pay-ray-thay-day'-ro, rah], *a.* Perishable, decaying, fading.

perecedero [pay-ray-thay-day'-ro], *m.* Misery, extreme want.

perecer [pay-ray-therr'], *vn.* 1. To perish, to die, to be destroyed. 2. To perish, to suffer or undergo damage, toil,

or fatigue. 3. To be extremely poor, to perish for want of the necessaries of life. *-vr.* 1. To crave, to desire anxiously. 2. To be violently agitated, to die with love. **Perecer de hambre**, to perish with hunger. **Perecer de risa**, to be convulsed with laughter. **Perecer ahogado**, to drown. *(Yo perezco, yo perezca, from Perecer. V.* CONOCER.)

perecido, da [pay-ray-thee'-do, dah], *a & pp.* of PERECER. Dying with anxiety, lost, undone.

pereciente [pay-ray-the-en'-tay], *pa.* Perishing.

perecimiento [pay-ray-the-me-en'-to], *m.* Loss, decay, decline; wreck of a ship.

peregrinación [pay-ray-gre-nah-the-on'], *f.* 1. Peregrination, traveling in foreign countries (viajes). 2. Pilgrimage. 3. The course of this life.

peregrinamente [pay-ray-gree'-nah-men-tay], *adv.* Rarely, curiously.

peregrinante [pay-ray-gre-nahn'-tay], *pa.* Sojourner; traveling; he who peregrinates.

peregrinar [pay-ray-gre-nar'], *m.* 1. To peregrinate, to travel in foreign countries (viajar). 2. To go on a pilgrimage. 3. To exist in this mortal life.

peregrinidad [pay-ray-gre-ne-dahd'], *f.* Strangeness, wonderfulness.

peregrino, na [pay-ray-gree'-no, nah], *a.* 1. Peregrine, foreign (persona). 2. Traveling or sojourning in foreign countries. 3. Going on a pilgrimage; migratory (pájaros). 4. Strange, wonderful, seldom seen (raro). 5. Very handsome or perfect.

peregrino [pay-ray-gree'-no], *a.* A pilgrim, a palmer.

perejil [pay-ray-heel'], *m.* 1. *(Bot.)* Parsley. 2. Showy dress or apparel. *-pl.* Honorary titles attached to offices.

perejilón [pay-ray-he-lone'], *m. (Prov.)* Creeping crow-foot.

perendeca [pay-ren-day'-cah], *f. (coll.)* Whore, hussy, trull.

perendengue [pay-ren-den'-gay], *m.* 1. Pendant of the ears, ear crop. 2. Any cheap or tawdry feminine ornament (adorno). 3. **Perendengues**, snags (pegas). 4. Standing, importance (categoría).

perene [pay-ray'-nay], *a. V.* PERENNE.

perengano, na [pay-ren-gah'-no, nah], *m. & f.* So-and-so: used after other names, as **fulano, mengano, zutano, y perengano**. In America the word *parencejo* is commonly used.

perennal [pay-ren-nahl'], *a.* 1. *V.* PERENNE. 2. Continually mad, without lucid intervals.

perennalmente [pay-ray-nahl'-men-tay], *adv. V.* PERENNEMENTE.

perenne [pay-ren'-nay], *a.* Perennial, perpetual. **De hoja perenne**, evergreen.

perennemente [pay-ray'-nay-men-tay], *adv.* Continually, perpetually.

perennidad [pay-ren-ne-dahd'], *f.* Perennity, continuity.

perentoriamente [pay--ren-to'-re-ah-men-tay], *adv.* Peremptorily.

perentoriedad [pay-ren-to-re-ay-dahd'], *f.* Peremptoriness, great urgency.

perentorio, ria [pay-ren-to'-re-o, ah], *a.* Peremptory (orden), absolute, decisive.

perero [pay-ray'-ro], *m.* Instrument formerly used to pare fruit.

pereza [pay-ray'-thah], *f.* 1. Laziness, tardiness, negligence, idleness, carelessness, sloth. 2. Slowness in movements. 3. Difficulty in rising from bed or from a seat.

perezosamente [pay-ray-tho-sah-men-tay], *adv.* Lazily, slothfully, negligently, idly.

perezoso, sa [pay-ray-tho'-so, sah], *a.* Lazy, careless, indolent, slothful, negligent, idle; sometimes used as a noun, for a lazy person or a lubber. *-m. (Zool.)* The sloth.

perfección [per-fec-the-on'], *f.* Perfection, superior excellence, faultlessness, completeness; beauty, grace; high degree of virtue. *-pl.* Accomplishments .

perfeccionador [per-fec-the-o-nah-dor'], *m.* Perfecter.

perfeccionamiento [per-fec-the-o-nah-me-en'-to], *m.* The act of perfecting, finishing, completion.

perfeccionar [per-fec-the-o-nar´], va. To perfect (hacer perfecto), to complete (proceso), to finish, to heighten.

perfectamente [per-fec´-tah-men-tay], adv. Perfectly, completely.

perfectible [per-fec-tee´-blay], a. Perfectible, capable of being made perfect.

perfectivo, va [per-fec-tee´-vo, vah], a. Perfective.

perfecto, ta [per-fec´-to, tah], a. 1. Perfect, complete (completo), accomplished. 2. Faultless, consumate, accurate. 3. Beautiful, fair, handsome. 4. Excellent, of the highest grade. 5. (Gram.) Perfect (tense). -m. Improvements made in an inheritance.

perficiente [per-fe-the-en´-tay], a. That which perfects.

pérfidamente [perr´-fe-dah-men-tay], adv. Perfidiously.

perfidia [per-fee´-de-ah], f. Perfidy, treachery.

pérfido, da [perr´-fe-do, dah], a. Perfidious, treacherous, disloyal.

perfil [per-feel´], m. 1. Profile, contour, outline. **Tomar perfiles**, to place oiled paper over a painting, in order to draw its outlines. 2. Light architectural ornament; hair. 3. Stroke of certain letters. 4. Profile, side-view. 5. Features (rasgos). 6. Social courtesies (cortesías).

perfilado, da [per-fe-lah´-do, dah], a. Applied to a well-formed face (rostro), nose (rariz, etc. -pp. of PERFILAR.

perfiladura [per-fe-lah-doo´-rah], f. Art of drawing profiles; the sketching of outlines.

perfilar [per-fe-lar´], va. 1. To draw profiles, to sketch outlines. 2. (Fig.) To put the finishing touches (rematar). -vr. 1. To incline, to be bent to one side. 2. To show one´s profile (persona). 3. (Fig.) To take shape. **El proyecto se va perfilando**, the plan is taking shape. 4. (LAm.) To slim. 5. (Cono Sur. Dep.) To dribble and shoot.

perfoliada, or **perfoliata** [per-fo-le-ah´-tah], f. (Bot.) Hare's-ear. V. CORAZONCILLO. St. John's wort.

perfoliado, da [per-fo-le-ah´-do, dah], a. (Bot.) Perfoliate.

perforación [per-fo-rah-the-on´], f. Perforation; piercing (proceso); drilling, boring; punching.

perforador, ra [per-fo-rah-dor´, rah], a. Perforating. -f. 1. Jackhammer. 2. Punch; drill.

perforar [per-fo-rar´], va. To perforate; to puncture (pinchar); to make (agujero); to sink (pozo).

perfumadero [per-foo-mah-day´-ro], m. V. PERFUMADOR, 2d def.

perfumado, da [per-foo-mah´-do, dah], a. & pp. of PERFUMAR. Odoriferous, perfumated.

perfumador [per-foo-mah-dor´], m. 1. Perfumer. 2. Vessel in which perfumes are kept. 3. Perfuming-pan.

perfumar [per-foo-mar´] or **perfumear** [per-foo-may-ar´], va. To perfume, to fumigate.

perfume [per-foo´-may], m. Perfume; odor, fragrance; good or bad smell or flavor.

perfumería [per-foo-may-ree´-ah], f. A perfumer's shop.

perfumero, ra [per-foo-may´-ro, rah], m. & f. Perfumer.

perfumista [per-foo-mees´-tah], m. Perfumer, dealer in perfumes.

perfunctoriamente [per-foonc-to´-re-ah-men-tay], adv. Perfunctorily, superficially.

perfunctorio, ria [per-foonc-to´-re-o, ah], a. Perfunctory.

perfusión [per-foo-se-on´], f. Affusion, sprinkling water on the head.

pergaminero [per-gah-me-nay´-ro], m. Parchment-maker.

pergamino [per-gah-mee´-no], m. 1. Parchment, vellum; skin dressed for writing. 2. Parchment, diploma, a formal writing on parchment.

pergenio [per-hay-ne-o], m. V. PERGEÑO.

pergeño [per-hay´-nyo], m. (coll.) Skill, dexterity.

pérgola [per´-go-lah], f. Pergola.

peri [pay´-re], f. 1. A beautiful and beneficent fairy in Persian mythology. 2. (Gram.) An inseparable prefix derived from the Greek, and meaning around.

periancio, periantio [pay-re-ahn´-the-o], m. (Bot.) Perianth.

períbolo [per-ree´-bo-lo], m. (Arch.) Peribolos, the inclosed court of an edifice.

pericardio [pay-re-ar´-de-o], m. Pericardium.

pericarpio [pay-re-car´-pe-o], m. Pericarp, covering of any fruit.

pericia [pay-ree´-the-ah], f. Skill, knowledge, practical experience.

perico [pay-ree´-co], m. 1. Curls formerly worn by women. 2. A kind ot small parrot, parakeet, indigenous to Cuba and South America. 3. Dim. of PEDRO. 4. Wig, toupé (peluca). 5. Chamberpot (orinal). 6. (And.) Coffee with a dash of milk.

pericón [pay-re-cone´], m. 1. Knave of clubs in the game of Quínolas. 2. A large fan.

pericón, na [pay-re-cone, nah], a. Fit for all things: generally, applied to horses fit for draught or saddle.

pericona [pay-re-co´-nah], f. Shaft mule; a mule fit for the coach as well as the saddle.

pericráneo [pay-re-crah´-nay-o], m. Pericranium.

peridromo [pay-re-dro´-mo], m. (Arch.) Peridrome, a covered gallery around a building.

periecos [pay-re-ay´-cose], m. pl. Perioeci, people on the opposite side of the globe, in the same latitude.

periferia [pay-re-fay´-re-ah], f. Periphery. V. CIRCUNFERENCIA.

periférico [pay-re-fay´-re-co], a. Peripherical; marginal; outlying (barrio).

perifollo [pay-re-fol´-lyo], m. (Bot.) Common chervil. **Perifollos**, ribbons and other ornaments of women, particularly if excessive or tawdry.

perifonear [pay-re-fo-nay-ar´], va. To broadcast by radio.

perifrasear [pay-re-frash-say ar´], va. To periphrase, to use circumlocutions.

perífrasi, perífrasis [pay-ree´-frah-ses], f. (Rhet.) Periphrasis, circumlocution.

perifrástico, ca [pay-re-frahs´-te-co, cah], a. Periphrastic, round about, circumlocutory.

perigallo [pay-re-gahl´-lyo], m. 1. Skin hanging from the chin of lean persons. 2. Kind of glossy ribbon worn by women. 3. (coll.) A tall, lean man. 4. Kind of slender sling. 5. (Naut.) Line, a thin rope; navel-line; topping-lift.

perigeo [pay-re-hay´-o], m. (Astron.) Perigee, perigeum.

perigonio [pay-re-go´-ne-o], m. (Bot.) Perigynium, perianth.

perihelio [pay-re-ay´-le-o], m. (Astron.) Perihelion.

perilla [pay-reel´-lyah], f. 1. (dim.) A small pear. 2. Ornament in form of a pear. 3. Pommel of a saddle-bow, a knob. 4. A small tuft of hair growing on the chin. V. PERA, 2d def. **De perilla**, to the purpose, at a proper time.

perillán, na [pay-reel-lyahn´, nah], a. (coll.) Artful, knavish, vagrant.

perillán, na [pay-reel-lyahn´, nah], m. & f. 1. Huckster, sly, crafty fellow. 2. (coll.) A clever fellow.

perillo [pay-reel´-lyo], m. Ginger-bread nut.

perilustre [per-e-loos´-tray], a. (Ant.) Very illustrious.

perímetro [pay-ree´-may tro], m. Perimeter. V. ÁMBITO.

perínclito, ta [pay-reen´-cle-to, tay], a. Famous, renowned, grand.

perineal [pay-re-nay-ahl´], a. Perineal.

perineo [pay-re-nay´-o], m. (Anat.) Perineum.

perineumonía [pay-re-nay-mo-ne´-ah], f. Pneumonia, inflammation of the lungs. V. PULMONÍA.

perinola [pay-re-no´-lah], f. 1. A handtop with four faces; a teetotum. 2. A neat little woman.

períoca [pay-re´ o-cah], f. Synopsis, plot of a book.

periódicamente [pay-re-o´-de-cah-men-tay], adv. Periodically.

periódico, ca [pay-re-o´-de-co, cah], a. Periodical, periodic.

periódico [pay-re-o´-de-co], m. Newspaper, periodical. **Periódico de la tarde**, evening newspaper.

periodismo [pay-re-o-dees´-mo], m. Journalism.

periodista [pay-re-o-dees´-tah], m & f. 1. Journalist, newspaperman (hombre), newspaperwoman (mujer), reporter, pressman (hombre), presswoman (mujer). 2.

Author or publisher of a periodical. **Periodista de televisión**, television journalist.

periodístico, ca [pay-re-o-dees'-te-co, cah], *a.* Journalistic. **Informe periodístico**, newspaper report.

período [pay-ree'-o-do], *m.* 1. Period, a determinate space of time. 2. Period, clause, a complete sentence. 3. Period, the time of revolution of a planet. 4. *(Mus.)* Period, phase.

periostio [pay-re-os'-te-o], *m.* Periosteum, the nutritive membrane which covers a bone.

peripatético [pay-re-pah-tay'-te-co], *m.* Peripatetic, a follower of Aristotle.

peripatético, ca [pay-re-pah-tay'-te-co, cah], *a.* 1. Belonging to the Peripatetics. 2. Applied colloquially to any person of ridiculous or extravagant opinions.

peripecia [pay-re-pay'-the-ah], *f. (Poet.)* Peripetia, sudden change of condition in the persons of a drama, or in fortune.

periplo [pay-ree'-plo], *m.* Diary of a voyage; voyage around a coast.

peripuesto, ta [pay-re-poo-es'-to, tah], *a.* Very gay, very fine, very spruce in dress. **Tan peripuesto**, all dressed up.

periquete [pay-re-kay'-tay], *m. (coll.)* Jiffy, instant. **En un periquete**, in a jiffy.

periquillo [pay-re-keel'-lyo], *m.* A small sweetmeat made of sugar alone.

periquito [pay-re-kee'-to], *m.* 1. *(Orn.)* Parakeet, small parrot. 2. *(Naut.)* Sky-sail, skyscraper.

periscios [pay-rees'-the-ose], *m. pl.* Periscii, inhabitants of the polar circles.

periscopio [pay-ris-co'-pe-o], *m.* Periscope.

peristáltico, ca [pay-ris-tahl'-te-co, cah], *a.* Peristaltic: applied to the motion of the intestines.

peristilo [pay-ris-tee'-lo], *m (Arch.)* Peristyle, colonnade.

perita [pay-ree'-tah], *f. dim.* A small pear.

peritaje [pay-re-tah'-he], *m.* 1. Expert work (trabajo); expertise (pericia); report of an expert (informe).

perito, ta [pay-ree'-to, tah], *a.* Skillful, able, experienced. -*m.* 1. Connoisseur. 2. Appraiser of goods. 3. A critical person, a skilful workman. **Perito agrónomo**, agronomist. **Perito forense**, legal expert.

peritoneo [pay-re-to-nay-o], *m. (Anat.)* Peritoneum, the serous membrane of the abdomen.

peritonitis [pay-re-to-nee'-tis], *f (Med.)* Peritonitis.

perjudicador, ra [per-hoo-de-cah-dor', rah], *m. & f.* One who prejudices, injures, or causes damage.

perjudicar [per-hoo-de-car'], *va.* 1. To prejudice, to cause damage to another, to injure, to harm (salud, fama). 2. To wrong (en lo moral). 3. To spoil the appearance of, not to suit (desfavorecer). **Perjudicar los intereses de alguien**, to prejudice someone's interests.

perjudicial [per-hoo-de-the-ahl'], *a.* Prejudicial, hurtful, mischievous, pernicious.

perjudicialmente [per-hoo-de-the-ahl'-men-tay], *adv.* Prejudicially, mischievously.

perjuicio [per-hoo-ee'-the-o], *m.* Prejudice, mischief, injury, detriment, damage, grievance, harm. **En perjuicio de**, to the detriment of. **Sufrir grandes perjuicios**, to suffer great damage.

perjurador, ra [per-hoo-rah-dor', rah], *m. & f.* Perjurer, forswearer.

perjurar [per-hoo-rar'], *vn.* To swear falsely; to commit perjury. -*vr.* To perjure oneself.

perjurio [per-hoo'-re-o], *m.* Perjury, false oath.

perjuro, ra [per-hoo'-ro, rah], *a.* Perjured, forsworn.

perjuro, ra [per-hoo'-ro, rah], *m. & f.* 1. Forswearer, perjurer. 2. V. PERJURIO.

perla [perr'-lah], *f.* Pearl, margarite: anything precious, clear, or bright. **Perlas**, fine teeth. **De perlas**, much, to the purpose; excellently, eminently fine. **Ser una perla**, to be a treasure.

perlático, ca [per-lah'-te-co, cah], *a.* Paralytic, palsied.

perlería [per-lay-ree'-ah], *f.* Collection of pearls.

perlesía [per-lay-see'-ah], *f.* Paralysis, palsy.

perlino, na [per-lee'-no, nah], *a.* Pearl-colored.

perlita [per-lee'-tah], *f. dim.* A small pearl.

perlongar [per-lon-gar'], *vn. (Naut.)* To coast, to sail along the coast.

permanecer [per-mah-nay-therr'], *vn.* To persist, to endure, to last. **Permanecer dormido**, to go on sleeping.

permaneciente [per-mah-nay-the-en', tay], *pa. & a.* Permanent; persisting.

permanencia [per-mah-nen'-the-ah], *f.* Duration, permanency, perseverance, constancy, consistency, permanence (cualidad), stay (estancia).

permanente [per-mah-nen'-tay], *a.* Permanent, durable, lasting. -*f.* Permanent, permanent wave.

permanentemente [per-mah-nen'-tay-men-tay], *adv.* Permanently.

permanganato [per-man-gah-nah'-to], *m. (Chem.)* Permanganate.

permeabilidad [per-may-ah-be-le-dahd'], *f.* Permeability, previous nature.

permisible [per-me-see'-blay], *a.* Permissible.

permisión [per-me-se-on'], *f.* 1. Permission, leave. 2. Confession, grant; the thing yielded.

permisivamente [per-me-see'-vah-men-tay], *adv.* Permissively.

permisivo, va [per-me-see'-vo, vah], *a.* Permissive.

permiso [per-mee'-soo], *m.* Permission, leave, licence (documento), allowance, liberty, excuse me (queriendo entrar, pasar). **Dar su permiso**, to give one's permission. **Permiso de entrada**, entry permit.

permisor [per-me-sor'], *m.* Granter. *V.* PERMITIDOR.

permistión [per-mis-te-on'], *f.* Permixtion, the act of mixing.

permitente [per-me-ten'-tay], *pa.* He that grants or permits.

permitidero, ra [per-me-te-day'-ro, rah], *a.* What may be permitted.

permitidor [per-me-te-dor'], *m.* Permitter, granter, he who allows or permits.

permitir [per-me-teer'], *va.* 1. To permit, to consent, to agree to, to give leave. 2. To permit, to suffer without authorizing or approving. 3. To permit, to give time or place to execute a thing. 4. To permit, not to hinder what one could and ought to avoid. To show oneself, to appear benign, generous, and liberal. **Permitir a uno hacer algo**, to allow somebody to do something. -*vr.* To be permitted, to be allowed. **Eso no se permite**, that is not allowed.

permuta [per-moo'-tah], *f.* Exchange of one thing for another, barter.

permutable [per-moo-tah'-blay], *a.* Permutable, capable of being permuted.

permutación [per-moo-tah-the-on'], *f.* 1. *V.* PERMUTA. 2. *(Math.)* Permutation, alteration of the order of elements or numbers.

permutante [per-moo-tahn'-tay], *pa. & a.* Permutant; exchanging.

permutar [per-moo-tar'], *va.* To exchange (cambiar), to barter, to commute, to permute. -*vn.* **Permutar con uno**, to exchange with somebody.

perna [perr'-nah], *f.* Flat shellfish.

pernada [per-nah'-dah], *f.* Blow with the leg; a violent movement of the leg.

pernaza [per-nah'-thah], *f. (Aug.)* A thick or big leg.

pernear [per-nay-ar'], *vn.* 1. To kick, to shake the legs (agitar las piernas). 2. To drive about in pursuit of an affair. 3. To be vexed, to fret. -*va.* To drive pigs to market and sell them by retail.

perneo [per-nay'-o], *m. (Prov.)* Public sale of hogs.

pernería [per-nay-ree'-ah], *f.* Collection of pins or bolts.

pernetas (En) [per-nay'-tas], *adv.* Bare-legged.

pernete [per-nay'-tay], *m. (Naut.)* Small pin, peg, or bolt.

perniabierto, ta [per-ne-ah-be-err'-to, tah], *a.* Bandy-legged.

perniciosamente [per-ne-the-o'-sah-men-tay], *adv.* Perniciously, noxiously, hurtfully.

pernicioso, sa [per-ne-the-oh'-so, sah], *a.* Pernicious, mischievous, destructive.

pernil [per-neel´], *m.* 1. Ham, shoulder of an animal, especially of pork. 2. Thigh of breeches; pantalets.

pernio [perr´-ne-o], *m.* A kind of hinges for doors and windows.

perniquebrar [per-ne-kay-brar'], *va.* To break the legs.

pernituerto, ta [per-ne-too-err'-to, tah], *a.* Crook-legged.

perno [perr'-no], *m.* 1. A round-headed pin; a large nail, a spike. 2. Hook of a hinge for doors and windows. 3. *(Mech.)* Joint pin, crank pin. 4. *(Naut.)* A bolt. **Perno de ojo**, eye-bolt. **Estar hasta el perno,** *(And.)* to be at the end of one's tether.

pernoctar [per-noc-tar'], *vn.* To pass the night: to be awake, to watch, or to sit up the whole night.

pero [pay'-ro], *m.* 1. A kind of apple. 2. Apple-tree.

pero, *conj.* But, except, yet (sin embargo). **Hizo muy mal, pero muy mal,** he was wrong, a thousand times wrong. **Pero vamos a ver,** well, let's see. -*m.* Fault, defect. **He encontrado un pero,** I have found a snag.

perogrullada, or **verdad de perogrullo** [pay-ro-grool-lyah'-dah], *f.* Platitude, truism, truth of no moment and universally known.

perojimenez [pay-ro-he-may'-neth], *m.* A variety of grape and the wine made from it.

perol [pay-role'], *m.* Boiler, kettle, copper, *(Carib.)* Saucepan (cacerola); *(Cono Sur, Mex.)* Metal casserole dish; *(Carib.)* Kitchen utensil (útil).

perón [pay-rone'], *m.* *(Mex. Bot.)* V. PERO.

peroné [pay-ro-nay'], *m.* *(Anat.)* Fibula, perone, the lesser bone of the leg.

peroración [pay-ro-rah-the-on'], *f.* Peroration (discurso), the conclusion of an oration (conclusión).

perorar [pay-ro-rar'], *vn.* 1. To conclude a speech or oration. 2. To make an harangue or speech, to declaim. 3. To solicit effectually.

perorata [pay-ro-rah'-tah], *f. (coll.)* An harangue, a speech.

peróxido [pay-rok'-se-do], *m.* Peroxide, highest grade of oxide.

perpendicular [per-pen-de-coo-lar'], *a.* 1. Perpendicular. 2. At right angles (en ángulo recto). -*f.* Perpendicular; vertical.

perpendicularmente [per-pen-de-coo-lahr'-men-tay], *adv.* Perpendicularly.

perpendículo [per-pen-dee'-coo-lo], *m.* 1. Plumb, plummet: an instrument by which perpendicularity is discerned. 2. Pendulum.

perpetración [per-pay-trah-the-on'], *f.* Perpetration, the act of committing a crime.

perpetrador, ra [per-pay-trah-dor', rah], *m. & f.* Perpetrator, aggressor:

perpetrar [per-pay-trar'], *va.* To perpetrate, to commit a crime.

perpetua [per-pay'-too-ah], *f. (Bot.)* Eternal flower, everlasting, the blossom of goldilocks. **Perpetua encarnada,** *(Bot.)* globe amaranth.

perpetuación [per-pay-too-ah-the-on'], *f.* Perpetuation.

perpetuamente [per-pay'-too-ah-men-tay], *adv.* Perpetually, for ever.

perpetuán [per-pay-too-ahn'], *m.* Everlasting, a kind of woollen stuff.

perpetuar [per-pay-too-ar'], *va.* 1. To perpetuate. 2. To continue without cessation or intermission.

perpetuidad [per-pay-too-e-dahd'], *f.* 1. Perpetuity, duration. 2. Perpetuity, exemption from intermission or cessation. **Condena a perpetuidad,** life sentence.

perpetuo, tua [per-pay'-too-o, ah], *a.* Perpetual; everlasting; ceaseless.

perpiaño [per-po-ah´-nyo], *m.* Perpender, a front binding-stone in a wall.

perplejamente [per-play'-hah-men-tay], *adv.* Perplexedly, confusedly.

perplejidad [per-play-he-dahd'], *f.* Perplexity, irresolution, embarrassment.

perplejo, ja [per-play'-ho, hah], *a.* Doubtful, uncertain, perplexed. **Me miró perplejo,** he looked at me in perplexity.

perpunte [per-poon'-tay], *m.* A quilted under-waistcoat to protect the body from cutting weapons.

perquirir [per-ke-reer'], *va.* To seek diligently.

perra [perr'-rah], *f.* 1. A female dog; bitch, slut. **Perra salida,** a bitch in heat. 2. Drunkenness. 3. Slothfulness, laziness. 4. Tantrum, pet (rabieta). **El niño cogió una perra,** the child had a tantrum. 5. Mania (manía), crazy idea. **Le cogió la perra de ir a Eslobodia,** he got an obsession about going to Slobodia. 6. *(Cono Sur)* Old hat (sombrero); leather water bottle (cantimplora).

perrada [per-rah'-dah], *f.* 1. Pack of dogs (perros). 2. A false compliment. 3. Dirty trick (mala jugada).

perramente [per'-rah-men-tay], *adv.* Very ill; badly.

perrazo [per-rah'-tho], *m. aug.* A large dog.

perrengue [per-ren'-gay], *m. (coll.)* 1. One who is peevish; a snarler. 2. Negro.

perrera [per-ray'-rah], *f.* 1. Kennel, doghouse (de perros). 2. Drag, grind, fag, employment attended with much fatigue and little profit (trabajo). 3. *com.* A bad payer (mal pagador). 4. Mule or horse spent with age and cast off. 5. *(Carib.)* Row, shindy.

perrería [per-ray-ree'-ah], *f.* 1. Pack of dogs (perros). 2. Set or nest of rogues. 2. Expression or demonstration of vexation or wrath.

perrero [per-ray'-ro], *m.* 1. Dog-catcher (que recoge perros vagabundos). 2. Houndman, person whose business is to take care of hounds or dogs used in the chase. 3. One who is very fond of hounds and dogs. 4. Impostor, cheat.

perrezno, na [per-reth'-no, nah], *m. & f.* Whelp, puppy.

perrico [per-ree´-co], *m. dim.* A little dog.

perrillo [per-reel'-lyo], *m.* 1. *(dim.)* A little dog. **¡Perrillo de falda!,** lap-dog. 2. Trigger of a gun. 3. A semi-lunar piece of a hollers bridle.

perrito [per-ree'-to], *m. dim.* A little dog.

perro [per'-ro], *m.* 1. Dog. **Perro de aguas,** water-dog. **Perro de presa,** bull dog. **Perro de ayuda,** newfoundland dog, a large dog kept to defend his master. 2. One who obstinately asserts an opinion or perseveres in an undertaking. 3. Damage, loss, deception. 4. *(Met.)* Dog, name of contempt or ignominy pivot to a person. 5. *(And.)* Drowsiness. 6. *(Cono Sur)* Clothes peg. **Ponerse como un perro** or **hecho un perro,** to get into a vehement passion. **¡A otro perro con ese hueso!** tell that to the marines! **Perro viejo** (an old dog), a clever, experienced man. **Perro esquimal,** husky. **Perro lobo,** alsatian. **Perro del hortelano,** dog in the manger. **Tiempo de perros,** dirty weather. **Se llevan como perros y gatos,** they're always squabling, they fight like cat and dog. **Perro ladrador, poco mordedor,** his bark is worse than his bite. **Llevar una vida de perros,** to lead a dog's life. **Es un perro viejo,** he's an old fox. **A perro flaco todos on pulgas,** misfortunes rain upon the wretched. **A otro perro con ese hueso,** pull the other one. **Morir como un perro,** to die a forgotten man. **Perro sarnoso,** mangy cur. **Allí no atan los perros con longanizas,** money does not grow on trees there.

perroquete [per-ro-kay'-tay], *m. (Naut.)* Top-mast.

perruna [per-roo'-nah], *f.* Dog-bread, coarse bread for dogs.

perruno, na [per-roo'-no, nah], *a.* Doggish, canine; currish.

persa [perr'-sah], *a. & n.* Persian.

persecución [per-say-coo-the-on'], *f.* 1. Persecution. 2. Toils, troubles, fatigue, molestation.

perseguidor, ra [per-say-gee-dor', rah], *m. & f.* Persecutor; one who harasses or molests; a foe.

perseguimiento [per-say-gee-me-en'-to], *m.* Persecution; hunt.

perseguir [per-say-geer'], *va.* 1. To pursue a fugitive (fugitivo). 2. To dun, to importune, to beset. 3. To persecute, to pursue with malignity (propósito). 4. To persecute, to pursue, to importune much. **La persiguió durante 2 años,** he was after her for 2 years. **Le persigue la mala suerte,** he is dogged by ill luck. *(Yo persigo, persiga; él persiguió, persiguiera;* from *Perseguir. V.* PEDIR.

perseo [per-say´-o], *m. (Ast.)* Perscus, a northern constellation.

persevante [per-say-vahn´-tay], *m.* Pursuivant at arms.

perseverancia [per-say-vay-rahn'-the-ah], *f.* Perseverance, constancy.

perseverante [per-say-vay-rahn'-tay], *a.* Perseverant, persistent.

perseverantemente [per-say-vay-rahn'-tay-men-tay], *adv.* Constantly, perseverantly.

perseverar [per-say-vay-rar'], *vn.* To persevere, to persist, to abide.

persiana [per-se-ah'-nah], *f.* 1. Persienne, slatted shutter (postigo). 2. Blind (enrollable). **Persianas,** Venetian blinds.

persiano, na [per-se-ah´-no, nah], *a. & n.* Persian.

pérsico, ca [per´-se-co, cah], *a.* Persianan. Peach-tree and its fruit.

persignarse [per-sig-nar'-say], *vr.* 1. To make the sign of the cross. 2. To admire, to be surprised at a thing. 3. To handsel, to begin to sell; to make the first act of sale.

pérsigo [perr´-se-go], *m. (Bot.)* Peach.

persistencia [per-sis-ten´-the-ah], *f.* Persistence, steadiness, perseverance, obstinacy.

persistente [per-sis-ten'-tay], *pa. & a.* Permanent, firm, persistent.

persistir [per-sis-teer´], *vn.* To persist, to continue firm, to persevere.

persona [per-so´-nah], *f.* 1. Person, individual, or particular man or woman. 2. Person, the exterior appearance. 3. Personage, a distinguished character; a man of merit or talents. 4.*(Gram.)* Person, the quality of the noun that modifies the verb. 5. Person, man or Roman in a fictitious dialogue. **De persona a persona,** from person to person, from man to man. **En persona** or **por su persona,** personally, in person. **Es buena persona,** he´s a good sort. **Tercera persona,** third party. **Pagaron 2 dólares por persona,** they paid 2 dollars a head.

personado [per-so-nah´-do], *m.* Benefice which confers a prerogative on the incumbent, yet without jurisdiction.

personaje [per-so-nah´-hay], *m.* 1. Personage, a man or woman of eminence. 2. Personage, character assumed, a disguised person, a stranger. 3. A kind of ecclesiastical benefice.

personal [per-so-nahl´], *a.* Personal, particular. -*m.* 1. Personnel (plantilla), staff; establishment (total); crew, complement. 2. **El personal,** the people, the public. **Personal de una oficina,** office personnel. **Estar falto de personal,** to be short-handed. **Había exceso de personal en el cine,** there were too many people in the cinema.

personalidad [per-so-nah-le-dahd'], *f.* 1. Personality, the personal existence of anyone. 2. Personality, reflection upon private actions or character. 3. Legal capacity for intervening in some business.

personalizar [per-so-nah-le-thar'], *va.* To fall into personalities in writing or talking. -*vr.* To show oneself a party at law. -*vn.* To make a personal reference.

personalmente [per-so-nahl-men-tay], *adv.* Personally, in person; hypostatically.

personarse [per-so-nar'-say], *vr.* 1. *V.* AVISTARSE. 2. To appear in person, to go personally. **El juez se personó en el lugar del accidente,** the judge went to the scene of the accident.

personaza [per-so-nah'-thah], *f. aug.* Huge personage.

personería [per-so-nay-ree'-ah], *f.* Charge or employment of an agent, deputy, or attorney.

personero, ra [per-so-nay´-ro, rah], *m. & f.* Deputy, agent, attorney, trustee, receiver.

personificación [per-so-ne-fe-cah-the-on'], *f.* Personification.

personificar [per-so-ne-fe-car'], *va.* To personify (encarnar), to personalize.

personilla [per-so-neel´-lyah], *f.* Mannikin, a ridiculous little fellow.

perspectiva [pers-pec-tee'-vah], *f.* 1. *(Art.)* Perspective, the science of perspective. 2. Work executed according to the rules of perspective. 3. View (vista), vista. 4. A deceitful appearance. **Buenas perspectivas de mejora,** good prospects. **Encontrarse ante la perspectiva de,** to be faced with the prospect of.

perspectivo [pers-pec-tee'-vo], *m.* Professor of perspective.

perspicacia, perspicacidad [pers-pe-cah'-the-ah], *f.* 1. Perspicaciousness, perspicacity, quickness of sight. 2. Perspicacity, clear-sightedness (agudeza de vista), keenness.

perspicaz [pers-pe-cath'], *a.* 1. Perspicacious, quick-sighted. 2. Acute, sagacious, clear-sighted.

perspicuamente [pers-pe-coo-ah-men'-tay] *adv.* Perspicuously.

perspicuidad [pers-pe-coo-e-dahd'], *f.* 1. Perspicuity, clearness, transparency. 2. Perspicuity, clearness to the mind, neatness of style.

perspicuo, cua [pers-pee'-coo-o, ah], *a.* 1. Perspicuous, clear, transparent. 2. Perspicuous, clear to the understanding: it is applied to him who writes with clearness and elegance, and to his style.

perspiración [pers-pe-rah-the-on'], *f.* Perspiration (sudor).

perspirar [pers-pe-rar'], *vn.* To perspire (sudar).

perspiratorio, ria [pers-pe-rah-to'-re-o' ah], *a.* Perspiratory.

persuadidor, ra [per-soo-ah-de-dor', rah], *m. & f.* Persuader.

persuadir [per-soo-ah-deer'], *va.* To persuade, to influence by argument or expostulation, to induce. **Dejarse persuadir,** to allow oneself to be persuaded. -*vr.* To be persuaded, to form a judgment or opinion; to be convinced.

persuasible [per-soo-ah-see'-blay], *a.* Persuasible, persuadable.

persuasión [per-soo-ah-se-on'], *f.* Persuasion, the act or state of being persuaded; opinion, judgment.

persuasiva [per-soo-ah-see'-vah], *f.* Persuasiveness, persuasive.

persuasivo, va [per-soo-ah-see´-vo, vah], *a.* Persuasive, moving.

persuasor, ra [per-soo-ah-sor', rah], *m. & f.* Persuader.

pertenecer [per-tay-nay-therr'], *vn.* 1. To belong to, to appertain, to concern. 2. To behoove, to become, to pertain; to relate to. **Pertenecer a,** to concern. *(Yo pertenezco, yo pertenezca,* from *Pertenecer. V.* ABORRECER.)

pertenecido [per-tay-nay-thee'-do], *m. V.* PERTENENCIA. **Pertenecido, da,** *pp.* of PERTENECER.

perteneciente [per-tay-nay-the-en´-tay], *pa. & a.* 1. Belonging, appertaining. 2. Apt, fit, ready.

pertenencia [per-tay-nen'-the-ah], *f.* 1. Right of property; place or territory belonging to anyone. 2. Appurtenance, dependence; an accessory or appendage.

pértica [perr´-te-cah], *f.* Perch, a measure of 10 geometric feet (9.70 feet).

pértiga [perr´-te-gah], *f.* 1. A long pole or rod. 2. A tall, slender woman. 3. Hook on which a door or window is hung. 4. *V.* PÉRTICA.

pertigal [perr-te-gahl'], *m.* Pole. *V.* PÉRTIGA.

pértigo [perr´-te-go], *m.* Pole of a wagon or cart.

pertiguear [per-te-gay-ar'], *va.* To beat a tree with a pole to gather the fruit.

pertiguería [per-te-gah-ree'-ah], *f.* Office or employment of a verger.

pertiguero [per-te-gay´-ro], *m.* Verger, he that carries the mace before the dean.

pertinacia [per-te-nah'-the-ah], *f.* Pertinancy (obstinación), obstinacy, stubbornness, doggedness.

pertinaz [per-te-nath'], *a.* Pertinacious (persona), obstinate, opinionated, persistent (tos), pertinacy (obstinación).

pertinazmente [per-te-nath'-men-tay], *adv.* Pertinaciously, contumaciously.

pertinente [per-te-nen'-tay], *a.* Pertinent, related to the matter at hand; to the purpose. **No es pertinente hacerlo ahora,** this is not the appropriate time to do it.

pertinentemente [per-te-nen'-tay-men-tay], *adv.* Pertinently, opportunely, congruously.

pertrechar [per-tray-char'], *va.* 1. To supply a place with ammunition and warlike stores. 2. To dispose, to arrange, to prepare. *-vr.* To be provided with the necessary stores and tools for defense.

pertrechos [per-tray'-chos], *m. pl.* 1. Ammunition, arms, and other warlike stores. 2. Tools, instruments.

perturbable [per-toor-bah'-blay], *a.* Capable of being perturbed.

perturbación [per-toor-bah-the-on'], *f.* Perturbation (mental), disquiet of mind; confusion.

perturbadamente [per-toor-bah'-dah-men-tay], *adv.* Confusedly.

perturbado [per-toor-b-ah'-do], *a.* Mentally unbalanced. *-m. f.* Mentally unbalanced person.

perturbador, ra [per-toor-bah-dor', rah], *m. & f.* Perturbator, perturber, disturber, perturbatrix. *a.* 1. Perturning (noticia). 2. Unruly (conducta), subversive (movimiento).

perturbar [per-toor-bar'], *va.* 1. To perturb, to disturb (orden, calma); to interrupt, to harrow. 2. *(Med.)* To upset, to disturb; to perturb (mentalmente).

peruano, na [pay-roo-ah'-no, nah], *a.* Peruvian, of Peru.

peruétano [pay-roo-ay'-tah-no], *m.* 1. *(Bot.)* Wild or choke pear-tree. 2. Anything that overtops or rises above the rest. *-a. (And. Carib. Mex.)* Boring, tedious; stupid.

perulero, ra [pay-roo-lay'-ro, rah], *a.* 1. One who has come from Peru to Spain. 2. *m.* A wealthy man. (*Cf.* INDIANO.) 4. A narrow-bottomed and strait-mouthed pitcher.

peruviano [pay-roo-ve-ah'-no], *m.* Peruvian balsam.

perversamente [per-ver'-sah-men-tay], *adv.* Perversely, malevolently.

perversidad [per-ver-se-dahd'], *f.* Perversity (cualidad), obstinate wickedness, malignity.

perversión [per-ver-se-on'], *f.* 1. Perversion, the act of perverting. 2. Perversion, perverseness, depravation, corruption.

perverso, sa [per-verr'-so, sah], *a.* Perverse, extremely wicked, mischievous.

pervertido, da [per-ver-tee'-do], *a. m & f.* Perverted, deviant.

pervertidor, ra [per-ver-te-dor', rah], *m. & f.* Perverter, corrupter.

pervertimiento [per-ver-te-me-en'-to], *m.* Perversion, act of perverting.

pervertir [per-ver-teer'], *va.* 1. To pervert, to distort from the true end (texto). 2. To pervert, to corrupt, to turn from the right. 3. To seduce from the true doctrine and faith. *-vr.* To become corrupted or depraved. *(Yo pervierto, yo pervierta; él pervirtió, pervirtiera,* from *Pervertir. V.* ADHERIR.)

pervigilio [per-ve-lee'-he-o], *m. (Med.)* Vigilance, pervigilium, watching, want of sleep, restlessness.

pervulgar [per-vool-gar'], *va.* 1. To divulge, to make public. 2. *(Acad.)* To promulgate.

peryodato [per-yo-dah'-to], *m. (Chem.)* Periodate.

peryoduro [per-yo-doo'-ro], *m.* Periodide, an iodide containing more iodine than a protoiodide.

pesa [pay'-sah], *f.* 1. Weight, a piece of a determined weight. 2. Piece of metal suspended from clocks. 3. A counterweight. **Pesa de una romana,** weight or drop-ball of a steel yard.

pesada [pay-sah'-dah], *f. (Com.)* Quantity weighed at once.

pesadamente [pay-sah'-dah-men-tay], *adv.* 1. Heavily, weightily, ponderously, cumbrously. 2. Sorrowfully, grievously. 3. Slowly (lentamente), tardily, lazily.

pesadez [pay-sah-deth'], *f.* 1. Heaviness, the quality of being heavy (peso). 2. Gravity, weight tendency to the center. 3. Slowness (lentitud), sluggishness, drowsiness. 4. Peevishness, fretfulness. 5. Excess, abundance. 6. Trouble, pain, fatigue (fatiga). 7. Obesity, corpulence. **Es una pesadez tener que...,** it´s a bore having to...

pesadilla [pay-sah-deel'-lyah], *f.* 1. Nightmare. 2. *(Fig.)* Worry, obsession, bogey. **Ese equipo es nuestra pesadilla,** that is our bogey team.

pesado, da [pay-sah'-do, dah], *a.* 1. Heavy, ponderous, massive. 2. Deep, profound (used of sleep). 3. Peevish, fretful, troublesome, violent; cumbersome, cumbrous. 4. Tedious (persona), wearisome, tiresome, dull, fastidious. 5. Offensive, causing pain, injurious; oppressive. 6. Lazy, clumsy, tardy, sluggish. 7. Fat, gross, corpulent. 8. Hard, insufferable, mischievous. **Día pesado,** a cloudy, gloomy day. **Tener el estómago pesado,** to feel full up. **Esto se hace pesado,** this is becoming tedious. *-pp.* of PESAR. *-m & f.* 1. Boring person (aburrido); bore; loud mouth (fanfarrón). 2. *(Carib. Fig.)* Big shot.

pesador, ra [pay-sah-dor', rah], *m.* 1. Weigher, one who weighs. 2. *(And. CAm. Carib.)* Butcher.

pesadumbre [pay-sah-doom'-bray], *f.* 1. Heaviness, weightiness, gravity. 2. Quarrel, dispute, contest. 3. Grief, trouble, displeasure, affliction, pain, disgust.

pesalicores [pay-sah-le-co'-res], *m.* Hydrometer, areometer.

pésame [pay'-sah-may], *m.* Compliment of condolence.

pesamentero, ra [pay-sah-men-tay'-ro, rah], *m. & f. (Mex.)* One who under pretext of condolence gets into a house to sponge for meals.

pesante [pay-sahn'-tay], *m.* A weight of half a drachm.

pesantez [pay-san-teth'], *f.* Gravity, the force of gravity.

pesar [pay-sar'], *m.* 1. Sorrow, grief (tristeza), concern, repentance. 2. The saying or deed which causes sorrow or displeasure. **Con gran pesar mío,** much to my sorrow.

pesar (A) [ah pay-sar'], *adv.* In spite of, notwithstanding. **A pesar de,** in spite of.

pesar [pay-sar'], *vn.* 1. To weigh, to be of weight (tener peso). 2. To weigh, to be considered as important, to be valuable. 3. To repent, to be sorry for (arrepentirse). 4. To prevail, to preponderate. 5. To weigh heavily (resultar pesado). 6. To count for a lot (opinión). 7. *(And. CAm.)* To sell meat. *-va.* 1. To weigh (peso), to ascertain the weight of a thing. 2. To weigh (examinar), to examine, to consider. 3. *(Naut.)* To use the lead for establishing the exact position which any piece of the ship should have. **Mal que le pese,** *(coll.)* in spite of him. **Me pesa el abrigo,** the coat weighs me down. **Pesar las responsabilidades,** to weigh up one´s chances. **Pese a las dificultades,** in spite of the difficulties. **Pesa 5 kilos,** it weighs 5 kilos. **Ese paquete no pesa,** that parcel isn´t heavy.

pesario [pay-sah'-re-o], *m.* Pessary, an instrument worn in the vagina to correct a displacement of the womb.

pesaroso, sa [pay-sah-ro'-so, sah], *a.* 1. Sorrowful, full of repentance. 2. Restless, uneasy.

pesca [pes'-cah], *f.* 1. Fishing, angling. 2. Fish, in the natural state in the water. **Pesca con arpón,** spear fishing. **Pesca de altura,** deep-sea fishing. **Allí la pesca es muy buena,** the fishing is very good there.

pescadazo [pes-cah-dah'-tho], *m. aug.* Great fish.

pescadera [pes-cah-day'-rah], *f.* Fish woman.

pescadería [pes-cah-day-ree'-ah], *f.* Fish-market (mercado); fish shop (tienda).

pescadero, ra [pes-cah-day'-ro], *m & f.* Fishmonger (by retail).

pescadilla [pes-cah-deel'-lah], *f.* Whiting; small hake.

pescadillo [pes-cah-deel' lyo], *m. dim.* A little flab.

pescado [pes-cah'-do], *m.* 1. Fish, chiefly that which is fit for food. *(Pescado* is a fish when caught; in the water, uncaptured, it is a *pez.)* 2. Codfish when salted. 3. Foodfishes. 4. *(And. Cono Sur)* Secret police. **Día** or **comida de pescado,** a fish-day, or fasting fare, though not of fish. **Pescado, da,** *pp.* of PESCAR.

pescador [pes-cah-dor'], *m.* 1. Fisherman, fisher, angler (de caña). 2. Fish having a pouch under the jaws to catch others. **Pescador, ra,** is used also adjectively.

pescadora [pes-cah-do'-rah], *f.* Fish-wife, fish-woman, a woman that sells fish; the wife of a fisher.

pescante [pes-cahn'-tay], *m.* 1. Crane, an instrument for raising heavy weights. 2. Coach-box (de carruaje). 3. Machine used in shifting the decorations on the stage. **Pescante de bote,** *(Naut.)* a davit. **Pescante de ancla,** fish-davit.

pescar [pes-car'], *va.* 1. To fish, to angle, to catch fish (coger). 2. To pick up anything. 3. To take one at his word, to catch in the act. 4. To obtain one's end. 5. To land, to get (lograr), to manage; to grasp (significado). 6. To catch (persona). -*vn.* 1. To fish, to go fishing. 2. **La chica viene a ver si pesca,** the girl is coming to see if she can get hitched. 3. *(And. Cono Sur)* To nod, to doze. **Viene a pescar un marido,** she´s come to get herself a husband. **Logró pescar unos cuantos datos,** he managed to bring up a few facts.

péscola [pes'-co-lah], *f.* The beginning of a furrow in a ploughed field.

pescozada [pes-co-thah'-dah], *f.* V. PESCOZÓN.

pescozón [pes-co-thone'], *m.* Blow on the neck or head with the hand.

pescozudo, da [pes-co-thoo'-do, dah], *a.* Having a thick neck.

pescuezo [pes-coo-ay'-tho], *m.* 1. The neck. 2. Stiff-necked haughtiness, loftiness, or pride. **Sacar el pescuezo,** to be haughty, to be elated. **Poner a uno el pie sobre el pescuezo,** to humiliate one.

pescuño [pes-coo'-nyo], *m.* Large wedge for fastening the coulter of a plough.

pesebre [pay-say'-bray], *m.* Crib, rack, or manger (cuadra).

pesebrejo [per-say-bray'-ho], *m.* Cavity in which horses' teeth are fixed.

pesebrera [pay-say-bray'-rah], *f.* Range of mangers in a stable.

pesebrón [pay-say-brone'], *m.* Boot of a coach.

peseta [pay-say'-tah], *f.* Peseta (moneda española). **Arrojar la peseta,** to be sick, to vomit.

pesetero [pay-say-tay'-ro], *a.* 1. Money-grubbing (avaro), mercenary. 2. *(Mex.)* Small-time (comerciante). 3. *(Carib.)* Mean (tacaño).

pesga [pes'-gah], *f.* Weight. V. PESA and PESO.

pesiar [pay-se-ar'], *vn.* To utter curses or execrations.

pesillo [pay-seel'-lyo], *m.* Small scales for weighing gold or silver coin.

pésimamente [pay'-se-mah-men-tay], *adv. super.* Very badly.

pesimismo [pay-se-mees'-mo], *m.* 1. Pessimism, condition of a pessimist. 2. A system of German philosophy which considers existence as an evil.

pesimista [pay-se-mees'-tah], *m & f.* Pessimist, one who looks at the dark side of things.

pésimo, ma [pay'-se-mo, mah], *a. super.* Very bad. **Lo hiciste pésimo,** *(Mex.)* you did it terribly.

pesita [pay-see'-tah], *f. dim.* A small.

peso [pay'-so], *m.* 1. Weight, gravity, heaviness. 2. Weight, importance. 3. Weight or power of reason. 4. Peso, monetary currency of many South American countries (moneda). 5. Burden. 6. Judgment, good sense. 7. Weighty object (objeto). 8. Weight (boxeo). 9. Heavy feeling (modorra). 10. Scales, balance, weghing machine. **Caerse de su peso,** to go without saying. **Peso ligero,** lightweight. **Peso medio,** middleweight. **Peso pluma,** featherweight. **El peso de los años,** the weight of the years. **Razones de peso,** good reasons. **Vender a peso,** to sell by weight. **Pesos y medidas,** weights and measures.

pésol [pay'-sole], *m.* French bean. V. FRISOL.

pespuntador, ra [pes-poon-tah-dor', rah], *m. & f.* Back-stitcher.

pespuntar [pes-poon-tar'], *va.* To back-stitch, to sew with a back seam.

pespunte [pes-poon'-tay], *m.* Back-stitching, back seam.

pesquera [pes-kay'-rah], *f.* Fishery, a place for catching fish.

pesquería [pes-kay-ree'-ah], *f.* 1. Trade or calling of a fisherman. 2. Act of fishing. 3. Fishery.

pesquero [pes-kay'-ro], *a.* Fishing. -*m.* Fishing boat.

pesquisa [pes-kee'-sah], *f.* Investigation (indagación), inquiry, examination. -*m.* Policeman.

pesquisante [pes-ke-sahn'-tay], *pa.* Investigating; inquirer.

pesquisar [pes-ke-sar'], *va.* To inquire, to examine, to investigate.

pesquisador, ra [pes-ke-sa-dor', rah], *m. & f.* Examiner, searcher, inquirer. **Juez pesquisador,** a magistrate appointed to inquire into the circumstances of a violent death.

pestaña [pes-tah'-nyah], *f.* 1. Eye-lash (de ojo). 2. Fag-end of a piece of linen. 3. Fringe, edging. **No pegué pestaña,** I didn´t get a wink of sleep. **Pestaña de protección contra grabación,** *(Comput.)* write-protect notch.

pestañear [pes-tah-nyay-ar'], *va.* To wink, to blink. **No pestañear** or **sin pestañear,** to look with the eyes fixed, not to wink.

pestañeo [pes-tah-nyay'-o], *m.* Winking, blinking.

peste [pes'-tay], *f.* 1. Pest, plague, pestilence. 2. Pest, anything troublesome, vexatious or mischievous. 3. Corruption of manners. 4. Foul smell. 5. *(coll.)* Great plenty or abundance. 6. *(And. Carib.)* Bubonic plague. 7. *(Cono Sur)* Smallpox (viruela). 8. *(And.)* Cold (resfrío). 9. *(Cono Sur)* Infectious disease (enfermedad). **Peste negra,** black Death. **Una peste de ratones,** a plague of mice. -*pl.* Words of menace.

pesticida [pes-te-thee'-dah], *m.* Pesticide.

pestíferamente [pes-tee'-fay-rah-men-tay], *adv.* Pestiferously, pestilently.

pestífero, ra [pes-tee'-fay-ro, rah], *a.* 1. Pestiferous (dañino), causing much damage. 2. Applied to anything extremely bad or mischievous. 3. Foul smelling.

pestilencia [pes-te-len'-the-ah], *f.* Pest, plague, pestilence (plaga).

pestilencial [pes-te-len-the-ahl'], *a.* Pestiferous, pestilential, infectious, contagious, destructive.

pestilencioso, sa [pes-te-len-the-o'-so, sah], *a.* Pestilential.

pestilente [pes-te-len'-tay], *a.* Pestilent (dañino), pernicious. V. PESTÍFERO.

pestillo [pes-teel'-lyo], *m.* 1. Bolt, for a door. 2. Bolt of a look.

pestiño [pes-tee'-nyo], *m.* Fritter or pancake.

pestorejazo [pes-to-ray-hah'-tho], *m.* V. PESCOZÓN.

pestorejo [pes-to-ray'-ho], *m.* The posterior fleshy part of the neck.

pestorejón [pes-to-ray-hone'], *m.* Blow on the back of the neck.

pesuña [pes-soo'-nyah], *f.* Solid hoof of graminivorous animals.

pesuño [pes-soo'-nyo], *m.* Hoof of cloven-footed animals.

petaca [pay-tah'-cah], *f.* 1. A trunk or chest covered with hides or leather; a covered hamper. 2. A case for keeping cigars or fine-cut tobacco (de cigarrillos). 3. *(CAm. Mex. Anat.)* Hump. -*m & f.* 1. *(LAm.)* Short squat person (rechoncho). 2. Lazy person (vago).

petaláceo, cea [pay-tah-lah'-thay-o, ah], *a. (Bot.)* Petalaceous, petalous.

petalismo [pay-tah-lees'-mo], *m.* Petalism, banishment in Syracuse, by writing the name on a leaf.

pétalo [pay'-tah-lo], *m. (Bot.)* Petal, flower-leaf.

petaquilla [pay-tah-keel'-lyah], *f.* Hamper covered with hides or leather; a small trunk.

petar [pay-tar'], *va. (coll.)* To please, to gratify, to content.

petardear [pay-tar-day-ar'], *va.* 1. To bend down a gate or door with petards. 2. To cheat (estafar), to deceive, to gull, by borrowing and not paying.

petardero [pay-tar-day'-ro], *m.* 1. A gunner whose duty consists in landing, fixing, and firing petards. 2. Impostor, cheat, swindler.

petardista [pay-tar-dees'-tah], *com.* 1. Deceiver, defrauder, a cheat, an impostor. 2. Swindler.

petardo [pay-tar'-do], *m.* 1. Petard, a warlike engine. 2. Cheat, fraud, imposition, gull, hoax, scurvy trick, disappointment. **Ser un petardo,** to be dead boring.

petate [pay-tah'-tay], *m.* 1. Fine sort of mat made of palm; used for a sleeping-mat by the natives in South America and the Philippines (para dormir). 2. Impostor, swindler, extorter (estafador). 3. *(Prov.)* A good-for-nothing fellow, a despicable person, poor devil (pobre hombre). **Líar el petate,** *(coll.)* to pack up one´s duds, to move away or be dismissed.

petequia [pay-tay-ke´-ah], *f. (Med.)* Petechia, spot on the skin in malignant fevers.

petequial [pay-tay-ke-ahl´], *a.* Petechial, pestilentially spotted.

petición [pay-te-the-on´], *f.* 1. Petition, the act of asking. 2. Petition, single branch or article of a prayer. 3. Demand, claim, request. 4. *(Law.)* Petition, the writing with which one juridically demands before the judge; prayer annexed to a judicial declaration produced in court. **Petición de aumento de salarios,** demand for higher wages. **Petición de divorcio,** petition for divorce. **"Petición de emisión"** (**RTS**), *(Comput.)* "request to send" (RTS).

peticionario, ria [pay-tee-the-on-ah´-re-o, ah], *m. & f.* Petitioner. (Used also as an adjective.)

petillo [pay-teel´-lo], *m. dim.* A small stomacher; a breast jewel.

petimetra [pay-te-may´-trah], *f.* A belle, a smart lady.

petimetre [pay-te-may´-tray], *m.* Fop, coxcomb, beau.

petirrojo [pay-teer-ro´-ho], *m. (Orn.)* Robin-redbreast.

petitoria [pay-te-to´-re-ah], *f. V.* PETICIÓN.

petitorio, ria [pay-te-to´-re-o, ah], *a.* Petitory, petitionary.

petitorio [pay-te-to´-re-o], *a.* Impertinent and repeated petition.

peto [pay´-to], *m.* 1. Breastplate. 2. Plastron used by fencers. 3. Dickey, false shirt or blouse front.

petraria [pay-trah´-re-ah], *f.* Ancient machine for throwing stones.

petrarquista [pay-trar-kees´-tah], *a. & m.* Follower of Petrarch.

pétreo, a [pay´-tray-o, ah], *a.* 1. Rooky. 2. Stony, of stone, hard, inflexible.

petrera [pay-tray´-rah], *f. (Prov.)* Battle fought with stones.

petricación [pay-tre-fe-cah-the-on´], *f.* Petrification.

petrificado [pay-tre-fe-cah'-do], *a.* Petrified.

petrificante [pay-tre-fe-cahn´-tay], *pa.* Petrifying.

petrificar [pay-tre-fe-car´], *va.* To petrify, to change to stone. *-vr.* To petrify, to become stone.

petróleo [pay-tro'-lay-o], *m.* Petrolcum, oil.

petrolero, ra [pay-tro-lay´-ro, rah], *a.* Petroleum. **Flota petrolera,** tanker fleet. *-m.* 1. Arsonist. 2. Oil tanker. *-m. & f.* Dealer in oil.

petrolífero, ra [pay-tro-lee´-fay-ro, rah], *a.* Oil-bearing.

petroquímica [pay-tro-kee´-me-cah], *f.* Petrochemistry.

petroso, sa [pay-tro´-so, sah], *a.* Rocky.

petulancia [pay-too-lahn´-the-ah], *f.* Petulance, insolence, flippancy, pertness.

petulante [pay-too-lahn´-tay], *a.* Petulant, insolent, flippant, pert.

petunia [pay-too´-ne-ah], *f. (Bot.)* Petunia.

peucédano [pay-oo-thay´-dah-no], *m. (Bot.)* Sulphur-wort.

peyorativo, va [pay-yo-rah-tee´-vo, vah], *a.* Depreciatory, disparaging (mostly as regards morals).

pez [peth], *f.* Pitch, tar. **Pez griega,** rosin, colophony. **Pez naval,** a mixture of pitch, rosin, tallow, etc., melted for applying to ships.

pez [peth], *m.* 1. Fish: a generic term; the zoological class of fishes among vertebrate animals. *Cf.* PESCADO. 2. Fish, a name common to all fresh-water fishes when they are small and eatable. **Pez colorado,** or **de color,** the goldfish, golden carp. **Pez espada,** swordfish. **Pez martillo,** the hammer-headed shark. **Pez sapo,** the toad-fish. **Pez sierra,** the sawfish. **Pez volador,** the flying fish. 3. *(Acad.)* Catch, haul; anything advantageous which has cost toil or solicitude.

Picar el pez, to be entrapped or deceived. **Salga pez o salga rana,** hit or miss.

pezolada [pay-tho-lah´-dah], *f.* Threads at the fag-end of cloth.

pezón [pay-thone´], *m.* 1. *(Bot.)* Stem of fruits, leaf-stalk or flower-stalk. 2. Nipple, teat, dug. 3. Arm of an axle-tree; end of a vertical beam in paper mills.

pezonera [pay-tho-nay´-rah], *f.* 1. Nipple-shield. 2. Linch-pin.

pezpita *f.* **pezpítalo,** *m.* [peth-pee´-tah, peth-pee´-tah-lo], *(Orn.)* Wagtail.

pezuelo [pay-thoo-ay´-lo], *m.* The beginning of cloth where the warp is knotted, in order to commence the weaving.

pezuña [pay-thoo´-nyah], *f.* 1. Nose-worm, a disease incident to sheep. 2. *V.* PESUÑA. 3. *(And. Mex.)* Dirt hardened on the feet.

pez vela [peth vay´-lah], *m.* Sailfish.

piache, or **tarde piache** [pe-ah´-chay]. Too late, act of coming or being late.

piada [pe-ah'-dah], *f.* 1. Chirping of birds, puling of chickens. 2. Mimicking of another's voice.

piador, ra [pe-ah-dor', rah], *m. & f.* One who pules like a chicken or chirps like a bird.

piadosamente [pe-ah-do´-sah-men-tay], *adv.* Piously, holily, clemently, mercifully, faithfully.

piadoso, sa [pe-ah-do´-so, sah], *a.* 1. Pious, godly, mild, merciful, clement. 2. Reasonable, moderate.

piafar [pe-ah-far'], *vn.* To paw, to stump (caballos).

piale [pe-ah'-lay], *m. (Amer.)* A cast of the lasso about the legs of the animal to be caught.

piamáter [pe-ah-mah'-ter], *f.* Piamater, membrane covering the brain.

piamente [pee´-ah-men-tay], *adv.* In a mild manner, piously.

pián, pián [pe-ahn´, pe-ahn´], *adv.* One foot after another rising and falling; with precaution.

pian piano [pe-ahn' pe-ah'-no], *adv.* Gently, softly.

pianista [pe-ah-nees´-tah], *com.* Pianist, a performer upon the pianoforte. *-m.* 1. A pianoforte-maker. 2. One who sell pianos.

piano, or **pianoforte** [pe-ah´-no, pe-ah-no-for´-tay], *m.* Piano, pianoforte. **Piano de cola,** a grand piano. **Tocar el piano,** to play the piano. **Piano mécanico,** pianola.

pianola [pe-ah-no´-lah], *f.* Pianola, player piano.

piante [pe-ahn'-tay], *pa.* Peeping.

piar [pe-ar'], *vn.* 1. To peep, to pule, to cry like a chicken, to chirp as a bird. 2. To call, to whine, to cry or wish for anything with anxiety. **Piar por,** to cry for.

piara [pe-ah´-rah], *f.* 1. Herd of swine. 2. Drove of mares or mules. 3. *(Prov.)* Flock of ewes.

piariego, ga [pe-ah-re-ay´-go, gah], *a.* Applied to a person who has a herd of mares, mules, or swine.

pica [pee´-cah], *f.* 1. Pike, a long lance. 2. A bullfighter's javelin. 3. *(Med.)* Pica, a depraved appetite for things unfit for food, as chalk, etc. **A pica seca,** with great labor and without utility. 4. Spades (naipes). *-m.* Inspector (de autobús).

picacero, ra [pe-cah-thay´-ro, rah], *a.* Applied to birds of prey that chase magpies.

picacureba [pa-cah-co-ray´-bah], *f.* Brazilian pigeon.

picacho [pe-cah'—cho], *m.* Top, summit; sharp point of any thing.

picada [pe-cah'-dah], *f.* Puncture, incision made by pricking. *Picadas, (Her.)* birds whose beak is of a different enamelling.

picadero [pe-cah-day´-ro], *m.* 1. Riding-house (escuela), riding-school. 2. Block, boat skid; *(Naut.)* stock-block. 3. Stamping-ground of a buck in rutting time.

picadillo [pe-cah-deel´-lyo], *m.* Minced meat, hash.

picado, da [pe-cah´-do, dah], *a. & pp.* of PICAR. 1. Pricked (material). 2. Minced (carne). 3. Choppy (mar). 4. **Estar picado,** to be offended (enojado).

picado [pe-cah'-do], *m.* Minced meet, hash.

picador [pe-cah-dor'], *m.* 1. Horse-breaker (caballos). 2. "Picador" (toros), horseman armed with a spear to fight the bull. 3. Pricker. 4. Block on which meat is chopped.

picadura [pe-cah-doo'-rah], *f*. 1. The act of pricking. 2. Puncture, a wound made by pricking (pinchazo). 3. Ornamental gusset in clothes. 4. Bite of on animal or bird.

picaflor [pi-cab-flor'], *m*. (*Orn*.) Humming-bird. This bird is known also by the names of *Colibrí*, *Pájaro mosca*, and (in Mexico) *Chupa mirtos*. V. CHUPA FLORES.

picamaderos [pe-cah-mah-day'-ros], *m*. Woodpecker.

picante [pe-cahn'-tay], *pa*. & *a*. Pricking, piercing, stinging, sharp (comentario); piquant, high-seasoned, acrid, hot (comida, sabor).

picante [pe-cahn'-tay], *m*. 1. Piquancy, pungency, acrimony; keen satire. 2. (*Amer*.) Dish with red-pepper sauce.

picantemente [pe-cahn'-tay-men-tay], *adv*. Piquantly.

picapedrero [pe-cah-pay-dray'-ro], *m*. Stone-cutter.

picapleitos [pe-cah-play'-tos], *m*. (*coll*.) A litigious person: a pettifogging lawyer.

picaporte [pe-cah-por'-tay], *m*. A kind of picklock or latch-key (pestillo).

picaposte [pe-cah-pos'-tay], *m*. V. PICAMADEROS.

picapuerco [pe-cah-poo-err'-co], *m*. (*Orn*.) Bird of the woodpecker kind.

picar [pe-car'], *va*. 1. To prick with a pointed instrument (perforar). 2. To prick, to pierce with a small puncture. 3. To sting (insecto), pierce, or wound with a point darted out, as that of wasps or scorpions. 4. To mince or chop anything fine, to break into small pieces. 5. To peck like birds. 6. To nibble, to pick up or bite a little at a time: to eat squeamishly. 7. To nibble at the bait, as fish (pez). 8. To begin to get customers and thrive in business. 9. To pursue or harass an enemy. 10. To itch, to smart. 11. To burn or irritate the palate (paladar). 12. To prick, to spur (caballo), to goad, to incite, to stimulate. 13. To spur a hole. 14. To pique, to vex, to provoke with words or actions (provocar). 15. To tame a horse. 16. Joined with *en*, to begin to operate, or have effect. 17. To burn, to scorch. -*vr*. 1. To be offended or vexed, to be piqued (persona). 2. To be moth-eaten, to be damaged. 3. To begin to rot (fruta). 4. To be elated with pride. 5. (*Met*.) To be deceived. 6. To be in heat (animales). 7. To fret, to be angry, to be peevish. **Picar el anzuelo**, to bite the hook. **Picar la carne**, to chop meat. **El sol pica**, the sun scorches. **Picar muy alto**, to aim too high. **Le pican los celos**, he is feeling pangs of jealousy. **Picar en**, to peck at. **Yo no pico en esas cosas**, I don´t dabble in such things. **Ha picado mucha gente**, lots of people have fallen for it. **Me pican los ojos**, my eyes hurt. **El que se pica, ajos come**, if the cap fits, wear it. **Le pica la conciencia**, his conscience pricks him.

pícaramente [pee-cah-rah-men-tay], *adv*. Knavishly, roguishly.

picarazo, za [pe-cah-rah´-tho, thah], *a*. Great rogue.

picardear [pe-car-day-ar'], *vn*. To play the knave.

picardía [pe-car-dee'-ah], *f*. 1. Knavery, roguery: deceit, malice, foulness, a wanton trick, wantoness. 2. Lewdness. 3. Meeting of rogues. **Le gusta decir picardías a la gente**, he likes saying naughty things to people.

picardihuela [pe-car-de-oo-ay'-lah], *f*. A prank, a roguish trick.

picaresca [pe-cah-res'-cah], *f*. A nest of rogues, meeting of knaves.

picaresco, ca, picaril [pe-cah-res'-co, cah, pe-cah-reel'], *a*. Roguish (travieso), knavish.

picarillo [pe-cah-reel'-lyo], *m*. *dim*. A little rogue.

pícaro, ra [pee'-cah-ro, rah], *a*. 1. Knavish, roguish, vile, low. 2. Mischievous, malicious, crafty, sly (taimado), naughty (travieso). 3. Merry, guy. -*m*. & *f*. Rogue, knave, villain (granuja), loafer.

picaros [pee'-cah-ros], *m*. *pl*. Scullions, kitchen-boys.

picarón [pe-cah-rone'], *a*. & *m*. *aug*. 1. Great rogue (granuja), villain. 2. (*And. Cono Sur, Mex*.) Fritter.

picaronazo, za [pe-cah-ro-nah´-tho, thah], *a*. *aug*. Very roguish, villainous.

picarote [pe-cah-ro'-tay], *a*. *aug*. Subtle, crafty; notorious villain.

picarrelincho [pe-car-ray-leen'-cho], *m*. (*Orn*.) V. AGUZANIEVE.

picatoste [pe-cah-tos'-tay], *m*. Toast of bread fried with slices of ham.

picaza [pe-cah´-thah], *f*. 1. (*Orn*.) Magpie, commonly called *urraca*. 2. (*Prov*.) Hoe for clearing the ground of weeds.

picazo [pe-cah'-tho], *m*. 1. Blow with a pike. 2. Sting of an insect, stroke with the beak of a bird. 3. Young magpie.

picazón [pe-cah-thone´], *m*. 1. Itching, prurience, itch. 2. Peevishness, fretfulness. 3. (*Fig*.) Annoyance (disgusto), pique; uneasy feeling (remordimiento).

pícea [pee'-thay-ah], *f*. (*Bot*.) Silver fir.

pichel [pe-chel'], *m*. Pewter tankard, a mug. (*Mex*.) Pitcher.

pichelería [pe-chay-lay-ree'-ah], *f*. Factory of tankards or tin pots.

pichelero [pe-chay-lay'-ro], *m*. Maker of pewter pots or tankards.

pichelete [pe-chay-lay'-tay], *m*. *dim*. A small tankard or mug.

pichiciago [pe-che-the-ab´-go], *m*. (*Zool*.) A burrowing animal of Chile, having the back covered with curious defensive plates, called also CLAMIFORO.

pichón [pe-chone'], *m*. 1. A young pigeon. 2. (*Coll*.) Darling (hombre). 3. (*Mex. Coll*.) Pushover. 4. (*LAm*.) Novice (novato), greenhorn. **Tiro de pichón**, trapshooting.

picnic [peek'-neek], *m*. 1. Picnic (excursión). 2. Picnic basket (cesta).

picnostilo [pec-nos-tee'-lo], *m*. (*Arch*.) Too little space between columns.

pico [pee'-co], *m*. 1. Beak of a bird, bill, nib. 2. A sharp point of any kind. 3. A pickle. 4. Twibill, an iron tool used by paviers. 5. Dock-spade, a spade with a long crooked bill. 6. Spout of a jar or any similar vessel (de jarra). 7. The beak iron of an anvil. 8. Peak, top, or summit of a hill. 9. Balance of an account, small odds. 10. Mouth. 11. Loquacity, garrulity. 12. (*Orn*.) Woodpecker (especie). 13. A weight of 1371/2 pounds used in the Philippine Islands. 14. Talkativeness (labia). 15. Spade (naipes). 16. (*And. CAm. Mex*.) Kiss (beso). 17. Fix, shot (droga). **Pico de oro**, a man of great eloquence. **Tener mucho pico**, to talk too much and divulge secrets. **Perder por el pico**, to lose by too much chattering. **Lo tengo en el pico de la lengua**, I have it on the tip of my tongue. **Darse el pico**, to kiss (besar). **Son las 3 y pico**, it´s just after 3. **Irse del pico**, to talk too much.

picolete [pe-co-lay'-tay], *m*. Staple for the bolt of a lock.

picón, na [pe-cone', nah], *a*. 1. Applied to animals with the upper teeth projecting over the under ones; or to cattle nipping the grass the contrary way for want of teeth. 2. (*And. Carib*.) Cheeky (respondón). 3. (*And. Carib*.) Touchy (quisquilloso). 4. (*Carib*.) Mocking.

picón [pe-cone´], *m*. 1. Lampoon or nipping jest employed to induce another to do or perform something. 2. A sort of very small charcoal used in braziers. 3. Small fresh-water fish. 4. (*Prov*.) Broken rice.

piconero [pe-co-nay'-ro], *m*. Maker of small charcoal for braziers.

picor [pe-cor´], *m*. 1. The pungent taste left by anything which is hot or piquant. 2. Itching in a part of the body.

picoso, sa [pe-co'-so, sah], *a*. Pitted with the small-pox.

picota [pe-so'-tah], *f*. 1. A kind of pillar or gibbet on which the heads of those who have been hanged are exposed. 2. A kind of pillory. 3. (*Naut*.) Cheek of a pump. 4. Top or peak of a mountain. 5. Point of a turret or steeple.

picotada [pe-co-tah´-dah], *f*. V. PICOTAZA.

picotazo [pe-co-tah´-tho], *m*. Stroke with the beak of a bird.

picote [pe-co'-tay], *m*. 1. Coarse stuff made of goat´s hair. 2. A glossy silk stuff.

picoteado, da [pe-co-tay-ah'-do, dah], *a*. Peaked, having many points or angles. -*pp*. of PICOTEAR.

picotear [pe-co-tay-ar'], *va.* To strike with the beak. -*vn.* l. To gossip. 2. To toss the head (caballo). 3. To nibble, to pick (comer). -*vr.* To wrangle or quarrel (mujeres).

picotería [pe-co-tay-ree'-ah], *f.* Loquacity, volubility, gossip.

picotero, ra [pe-co-tay'-ro, rah], *a.* Wrangling, chattering, prattling.

picotillo [pe-co-teel'-lyo], *m.* Interior cloth of goat's hair.

picrato [pe-crah'-to], *m.* Picrate, a salt of picric acid.

pícrico [pee'-cre-co], *a.* Picric, of an exceedingly bitter taste. **Ácido pícrico,** picric acid, a yellow crystalline body.

pictografía [pic-to-grah-fee'-ah], *f.* Pictography, picture writing.

pictórico, ca [pic-to'-re-co, cah], *a.* 1. Pictorial. 2. Worth painting (escena). 3. Artistic (talento).

picudilla [pe-coo-deel'-lyah], *f.* 1. Kind of pointed olive. 2. An insectivorous bird.

picudo, da [pe-coo'-do, dah], *a.* 1. Beaked, pointed (puntiagudo). 2. Prattling, babbling, chattering. 3. *(Carib.)* Over-the-top (cursi). 4. *(Mex.)* Crafty, clever (astuto). -*m.*Boll weevil.

pido [pee'-do], *m. (coll.)* Demand, request, petition.

pidón, na [pe-done', nah], *a. (coll.)* V. PEDIGÜEÑO.

pie [pe-ay'], *m.* 1. The foot. 2. Foot leg, that by which anything is supported. 3. Foot, the base. 4. Trunk of trees and plants. 5. Lees, sediment. 6. Last hand or player in a game of cards. 7. The last word pronounced by an actor. 8. Foot, a measure of length. 9. Motive (causa), occasion. 10. Footing, basis, foundation, groundwork. 11. Footing, rule, use, custom. 12. Foot, verse, a certain number of syllables. 13. End or conclusion of a writing. 14. First color given in dyeing. 15. Foot of a stocking. 16. Foothold (seguridad). 17. *(Cono Sur)* Deposit (enganche). **No creas a pie juntillas todo lo que te digan,** don't believe all they tell you. **Al pie de la hora,** instantly, without delay. **A sus pies, señora,** at your service, madam. **Pie ante pie,** step by step. **A pie,** on foot. **Al pie,** near, close to, at the foot of. **A pie firme,** without stirring, steadfastly. **En pie,** constantly, firmly; uprightly, erect. **Estar con un pie en la sepultura,** to have one foot in the grave. **De pies a cabeza,** from head to foot. **Echar el pie atrás a alguno,** to outdo someone. **Echar el pie atrás,** to flinch, to desist. **Soldados de a pie,** foot soldiers, infantry. **Pie de atleta,** athlete's foot. **A pie firme,** steadfastly. **Levantarse con el pie izquierdo,** to get up on the wrong side of the bed. **Estar de pie,** to be standing. **Parar los pies a uno,** to curb somebody. **A los pies de la cama,** at the foot of the bed. **Estar al pie del cañón,** to be ready to act. **En pie de guerra,** on a war footing. **Dar pie a,** to give cause for.

piececito [pe-ay-thay-the'-to], *m. dim.* A little foot.

piedad [pe-ay-dahd'], *f.* 1. Piety, godliness: mercy, pity (compasión), compassion. 2. Charity. **Tener piedad de,** to take pity on.

pie de imprenta [pe-ay day im-pren'-tah], *m.* Printer's mark.

piedra [pe-ay'-drah], *f.* 1. A stone. 2. Gravel in the kidneys. 3. Hail. 4. Place where foundlings are exposed. 5. Gun-flint. 6. Hardness of things. **Piedra de amolar** or **afilar,** whetstone, grinding stone. **Piedra imán,** magnet. **Piedra lipis,** copper sulphate. **Piedra sepulcral,** a gravestone, a headstone. **No dejar piedra por mover,** not to leave a stone unturned. **Quedarse de piedra,** to be thunderstruck. **Tener el corazón de piedra,** to be hardhearted.

piedrecita, illa, ita, piedrezuela [pe-ay-dray-thee'-cah], *f. dim.* A little stone.

piel [pe-el'], *f.* 1. The skin. 2. Hide of an animal cured and dressed, pelt. 3. Peel or skin of fruits. **Piel de gallina,** goose-flesh, the skin roughened by cold. **Piel de cabra,** goatskin. **Piel de cerdo,** pigskin. **Abrigo de pieles,** fur coat.

piélago [pe-ay'-lah-go], *m.* 1. The high sea. 2. Great plenty or abundance. *V.* TARQUÍN.

pielecita [pe-ay-lay-thee'-tah], *f. dim.* A small hide.

pienso [pe-en'-so], *m.* Fodder, feed. **Piensos compuestos, mixed feed. Dar un pienso,** to bait or give food to an animal. **¡Ni por pienso!,** I wouldn't dream of it!

pierna [pe-err'-nah], *f.* 1. The leg. 2. Leg of butcher's meat or of fowls. 3. Down stroke of letters. 4. Check of a printing-press. 5. *(Cono Sur)* Player. **En piernas,** bare-legged. **A pierna suelta** or **a pierna tendida,** at one's ease; without care; soundly. **Estirar las piernas,** to take a walk, to stretch one's legs. **Cortar las piernas,** to render a thing impossible.

piernitendido, da [pe-er-ne-ten-dee'-do, dah], *a.* With extended legs.

pieza [pe-ay'-thah], *f.* 1. Piece, part of a whole; a fragment. 2. Coin, piece of money. 3. Piece of cloth woven at one time. 4. Piece of furniture. 5. Room in a house. 6. Piece of ordnance. 7. Buffoon, wag, jester. 8. Any bird or animal of the chase. 9. Any manufactured article and each of the parts which compose it. 10. Piece or man in the games of draughts, chess, etc. 11. *(Her.)* Each of the parts into which the coat of arms or shield is divided. **Quedarse de una pieza** or **hecho una pieza,** *(coll.)* to be stunned, to remain astonished. **Hacer piezas,** to take anything to pieces. **Pieza arqueológica,** object. **Juan es una pieza,** *(LAm.)* Juan is as honest as the day is long. **Pieza de oro,** gold coin. **Buena pieza,** rogue, villain. **Me he quedado de una pieza,** I was speechless. **Pieza de aritllery,** piece of artillery. **Pieza de ajedrez,** chess piece.

piezgo [pe-eth'-go], *m.* 1. Neck of a leather bottle; the hind or fore foot of an animal. 2. A dressed skin for wine or other liquors.

pífano, pífaro [pee'-fah-no, pee'-fah-ro], *m.* 1. Fife, a musical instrument. 2 Fifer.

pifia [pee'-fe-ah], *f.* l. A failure to properly strike the billiard ball with the cue, a miss. 2. Error, blunder (error). 3. *(And. Cono Sur)* Joke (chiste); mockery (burla). 4. *(And.)* Hissing, booing (rechifla).

pifiar [pe-fe-ar'], *vn.* 1. To suffer the breath to be too audible in playing the flute. 2. To miss the billiard ball. 3. *(Cono Sur)* To fail (fracasar), to come to cropper. 4. *(And. CAm.)* To be disappointed, to suffer a setback.

pigargo [pe-gar-go], *m.* Ring-tail hawk.

pigmentación [peeg-men-tah-the-on'], *f.* Pigmentation.

pigmento [pig-men'-to], *m.* Pigment, coloring matter of the skin.

pigmeo, mea [pig-may'-o, ah], *a.* Dwarfish. *m. & f.* A dwarf.

pignorar [pig-no-rar'], *va.* To pledge, to hypothecate.

pigre [pee'-gray], *a.* Slothful, lazy, indolent.

pigricia [pe-gree'-the-ah], *f.* 1. Laziness (pereza), idleness. 2. Place in schools for lazy boys. 3. *(And. Cono Sur)* Trifle, bagatelle; small bit, pinch.

pigro, gra [pee'-gro, grah], *a.* Negligent, careless, lazy.

pihuela [pe-hoo-ay'-lah], *f.* 1. Leash, a leather strap tied to a hawk's leg. 2. Obstruction, hindrance, impediment. **Pihuelas,** fetters, shackles.

pijama [pe-hah'-mah] or **piyama** [pe-yah'-mah], *m.* (Used mostly in the plural.) Pajamas or pyjamas.

pijo [pee'-ho], *a.* 1. Stuck-up (engreído). 2. Fussy (quisquilloso). 3. Thick (tonto). -*m.* Spoiled brat (mimado).

pijota [pe-ho'-tah], *f. (Zool.)* Hake, coaling. V. MERLUZA.

pijote [pe-ho'-tay], *m. (Naut.)* Swivel-gun loaded with small grape-shot

pijotería [pe-ho-tay-ree'-ah], *f.* 1. Nuisance (molestia), small annoyance. 2. *(LAm.)* Insignificant sum (pequeña cantidad). 3. *(LAm.)* Meanness (tacañería).

pila [pee'-lah], *f.* 1. A large (stone) trough containing water for cattle. 2. Baptismal font. 3. Pile, heap of things thrown together (montón). **Una pila de,** a heap of. 4. Pile of shorn wool belonging to one owner. 5. Parish. 6. A holy-water basin. **Nombre de pila,** Christian name. 7. *(Arch.)* Buttress of an arch of a bridge. 8. Galvanic or voltaic pile. **Pila de agua bendita,** holy water stoup. 9. Battery; cell. **Aparato a pilas,** battery-run apparatus.

pilada [pe-lah'-dah], *f.* Quantity of mortar made at once; pile, heap.

pilar [pe-lar'], *m*. 1. The large water basin of a fountain. 2. Pillar, a column of stone; post. 3. Pillar, a person who supports something. 4. Stone or mound for a landmark on roads. **Pilar de una cama,** bed-post.

pilarejo, pilarito [pe-lah-ray'-ho, pe-lah-ree'-to], *m*. *dim*. A small pillar.

pila seca [pe'-lah say'-cah], *f*. Dry cell or dry battery.

pilastra [pe-lahs'-trah], *f*. Pilaster, a square column.

pilatero [pe-lah-tay'-ro], *m*. In woollen factories, fuller who assists at fulling the cloth.

pilche [peel-chay], *m*. (Peru) Cup or bowl of wood. *(Acad.)*

píldora [peel'-do-rah], *f*. 1. Pill, a medicine. 2. Affliction, bad news. **Píldora antifatiga,** anti-fatigue pill.

pildorera [peel-do-ray'-rah], *f*. Pill box.

píleo [pee'-lay-o], *m*. 1. A hat or cap worn by the ancient Romans. 2. Red hat worn by cardinals.

pileta, pilica [pe-lay'-tah, pe-lee'-cah], *f*. *dim*. of PILA.

pillada [pil-lyah'-dah], *f*. A knavish trick (trampa), a sham, an unworthy action.

pillador [pil-lyah-dor'], *m*. Pillager, plunderer, swindler.

pillaje [pil-lyah'-hay], *m*. Pillage, plunder, marauding, foray.

pillar [pil-lyar'], *va*. 1. To pillage, to plunder, to foray. 2. To lay hold of (atrapar), to chop at. 3. To catch (coger); to catch (sorprender). 4. To get (ganga, puesto). 5. To grasp (significación). 6. To knock down (coche). **Quien pilla-pilla,** he who plunders most has most. **Pillar una mona,** to become intoxicated. **Por fin le pilló la policía,** the police nabbed him eventually.

pillastre, pillastrón [pil-lyahs'-tray, pil-lyas-trone'], *m*. A roguish fellow, an impudent man.

pillería [pil-lyay-ree'-ah], *f*. 1. A number of vagabonds or rogues going together (banda). 2. A knavish trick or sham.

pillo, lla [peel'-lyo, lyah], *a*. Applied to a loafer, or blackguard. *-m*. 1. A vagabond, a rascal. 2. A petty thief.

pilluelo [pe-lyoo-ay'-lo], *m*. Rascal, vagabond, hoodlum.

pilocarpo [pe-lo-car'-po], *m*. Jaborandi, a Brazilian plant, which yields the medicinal lkaloid pilocarpin.

pilón [pe-lone'], *m*. 1. A large watering trough for cattle, the basin of a fountain (abrevadero). 2. Drop or ball of a steel-yard. 3. Great stone or counterpoise in an olive-press. 4. Heap of grapes ready to be pressed. 5. Heap of mortar (mortero). 6. *(Mex.)* Drinking fountain. 7. *(Mex.)* Tip (propina). **Pilón de azúcar,** a loaf of refined sugar formed in; mould. **Beber del pilón,** to believe current rumors.

piloncillo [pi-lon-theel'-lyo], *m*. *(Amer.)* The crust of sugar that remains in the boiler.

pilonero, ra [pe-lo-nay'-ro, rah], *m. & f*. Newsmonger.

pilongo, ga [pe-lon'-go, gah], *a*. 1. Peeled and dried (castaño). 2. Thin, lean, meagre.

pilórico, ca [pe-lo'-re-co, cah], *a*. Pyloric, relating to the pyloric orifice.

píloro [pee'-lo-ro], *m*. Musk-rat. 2. *(Anat.)* Pylorus, inferior part of the stomach.

piloso, sa [e-lo'-so, sah], *a*. Pilous, hairy.

pilotaje [pe-lo-tah'-hay], *m*. 1. Piloting. 2. Pilotage, pilot's fee. 3. Pilots. 4. Steering, driving. 5. Piling, piles.

pilotar, pilotear [pe-lo-tar', pe-lo-tay-ar'], *va*. 1. To pilot. 2. To steer, to drive. 3. *(LAm.)* To guide (persona).

pilote [pe-lo'-tay], *m*. Pile.

pilotín [pe-lo-teen'], *m*. Pilot's apprentice, or second pilot.

piloto [pe-lo'-to], *m*. 1. Pilot of a ship or aircraft. 2. The pilot fish. 3. *(Naut.)* First mate. 4. *(Cono Sur)* Raincoat. 5. *(Aut.)* Driver. **Piloto automático,** *(Aer.)* Autopilot. **Piloto de prueba,** test pilot. *-a.* **Casa piloto,** model home.

piltraca, piltrafa [peel-trah'-cah], *f*. Piece of flesh which is almost nothing but skin.

pimentada [pe-men-tah'-dah], *f*. Sauce, the principal ingredient of which is Cayenne paper.

pimental [pe-men-tahl'], *m*. Ground bearing pepper; pepper patch.

pimentero [pe-men-tay'-ro], *m*. 1. Pepper box. 2. *(Bot.)* The plant which produces pepper.

pimentón [pe-men-tone], *m*. Ground red pepper, paprika.

pimienta [pe-me-en'-tah], *f*. *(Bot.)* Pepper (black pepper). **Pimienta de Tabasco or malagueta,** myrtle.

pimiento [pe-me-en'-to], *m*. 1 *(Bot.)* Capsicum, red or Cayenne pepper. 2. The plant of every species of capsicum. 3. The fruit of all the species of capsicum. **Pimiento dulce,** the sweet fruit of the common capsicum. **Pimiento picante,** the fruit of shrubby and bird-pepper capsicum. 4. Mildew, blight in plants, as wheat, barley, etc. 5. Chaste-tree. *V*. SAUZGATILLO.

pímpido [peem'-pe-do], *m*. Kind of dog-fish, resembling the *mielga.*

pimpinela [pim-pe-nay'-lah], *f*. *(Bot.)* Burnet, pimpinel, a rossaceous plant.

pimpleo, a [pim-play'-o, ah], *a*. Belonging to the muses.

pimplón [pim-plone'], *m*. *(Prov. Sant.)* Waterfall, cascade.

pimpollar [pim-pol-lyar'], *m*. Nursery of young plants and trees.

pimpollecer [pim-pol-lyay-therr'], *vn*. To sprout, to bud.

pimpollejo, ico, ito [pim-pol-lyar'-ho], *m*. *dim*. A small sprout, sucker, or shoot.

pimpollo [pim-pol'-lyo], *m*. 1. Sucker, sprout, shoot. 2. Rosebud not yet opened (capullo). 3. A spruce, lively lad. 4. Anything perfect of its kind. 5. To look very smart (elegante).

pimpollón [pim-pol-lyone'], *m*. *aug*. A large sucker, sprout, or shoot.

pimpolludo, da [pim-pol-lyoo'-do, dah], *a*. Full of buds or sprouts.

pina [pee'-nah], *f*. 1. A mound of earth in the form of a cone. 2. Jaunt, felloe, any piece of the circumference of a coach or cart wheel.

pinabete [pe-nah-bay'-tay], *m*. *(Bot.)* Spruce fir-tree.

pinacoteca [pe-nah-co-tay'-cah], *f*. Gallery, or museum, of paintings.

pináculo [pe-nah'-coo-lo], *m*. Pinnacle, the highest part of a magnificent building.

pinado, da [pe-nah-do, dah], *a*. *(Bot.)* Pinnate, pinnate.

pinal, pinar [pe-nahl', pe-nar'], *m*. Grove of pines.

pinariego, ga [pe-nah-re-ay'-go, gah], *a*. Belonging to pines.

pinastro [pe-nahs'-tro], *m*. Wild pine.

pinaza [pe-nah-thah], *f*. *(Naut.)* Pinance, a small vessel.

pincel [pin-thel'], *m*. 1. Pencil, a small brush used by painters. 2. Painter. **Es un gran pincel,** he is a great painter. 3. The work painted. 4. Mode of painting. 5. Second feather in a martin's wing.

pincelada [pin-thay-lah'-dah], *f*. Stroke with a pencil. **Dar la última pincelada,** to give the finishing stroke.

pincelero [pin-thay-lay'-ro], *m*. Pencil-maker, one who makes and sells hair pencils or small brushes.

pincelillo, ito [pin-thay-leel'-lyo], *m. dim* A small pencil.

pincerna [pin-therr'-nah], *com*. One who serves drinks at feasts.

pinchadura [pin-chah-doo'-rah], *f*. *(coll.)* Puncture, act of pricking.

pinchar [pin-char'], *va*. 1. *(coll.)* To prick, to wound. 2. To prod (estimular). **Le pinchan para que se case,** they keep prodding him to get married. *-vr.* To prick oneself (droga).

pinchazo [pin-chah'-tho], *m*. A prick, a stab; jab (de droga).

pinche [peen'-chay], *m*. 1. Scullion, kitchen-boy (de cocina); any ragged boy. 2. *(Cono Sur)* Minor office clerk (oficinista). 3. *(And.)* Bad horse, nag. 4. *(Cono Sur)* Hatpin. *-a.* 1. *(Mex.)* Bloody (maldito). 2. *(CAm.)* Stingy (tacaño).

pincho [peen'-cho], *m*. 1. Thorn, prickle of plants, pointed stick (aguijón); *(Cono Sur)* spike, prickle. 2. *(Culin.)* **Un pincho de tortilla,** a portion of omelette.

pindárico, ca [pin-dah'-re-co, cah], *a*. Pindaric, after the style of Pindar.

pindonga [pin-don'-gah], *f*. A gad-about (mujer).

pindonguear [pin-don-gay-ar'], *vn*. *(coll.)* To gad about (mujeres).

pineda [pe-nah'-dah], *f*. 1. A kind of linen garters. 2. *(Prov.)* *V*. PINAL.

pingajo [pin-gah'-ho], *m.* A rat or patch hanging from clothes.

pinganello [pin-gah-nayl'-lyo], *m. V.* CALAMOCO.

pinganilla [pin-gah-neel´-lyah], *a. (Amer. Peru, coll.)* Bedecked, fashionably attired. **En pinganillas,** *(Mex.)* on tiptoe. *V.* DE PUNTILLLAS.

pinganitos [pin-gah-nee'-tos], *m.* **En pinganitos,** in a prosperous or elevated state.

pingo [peen'-go], *m.* 1. Rag (harapo). 2. *pl.* Worthless clothes (ropa), duds, whether ragged or in good repair. 3. *(Amer.)* A fine saddle horse. **Andar,** or **ir de pingo,** to gad about and neglect home duties (mujer). 4. Slut (marrana). 5. *(Mex.)* Scamp (niño). 6. *(Cono Sur)* Lively child (niño).

pingorote [pin-go-ro´-tay], *m. V.* PERUÉTANO, 2d def.

pingorotudo, da [pin-go-ro-too´-do, dah], *a. (Prov.)* High, lofty, elevated.

ping-pong [ping-pong], *m.* Ping-pong.

pingüe [peen'-goo-ay], *m. (Naut.)* Pink, a vessel with a very narrow stern; a pink-stern.

pingüe [pin-goo-ay], *a.* 1. Fat, greasy, oily, pinguid. 2. Rich, plentiful, abundant.

pingüedinoso, sa [pin-goo-ay-de-noh'-so, sah], *a.* Fatty, oleaginous, pinguid.

pingüino [pin-goo-ee'-no], *m.* Penguin.

pingüísimo, ma [pin-goo-ee'-se-mo, mah], *a. sup.* Excessively fat.

pinguosidad [pin-goo-o-se-dahd'], *f.* Fatness.

pinico [pe-nee'-co], *m. dim.* 1. Small step. 2. Small pine.

pinífero, ra [pe-nee'-fay-ro, rah], *a. (Poet.)* Piniferous.

pinillo [pe-neel'-lyo], *m. (Bot.)* Groundpine, germander.

pinito [pe-nee'-to], *m. dim.* First step. **Hacer pinitos,** to take the first steps (as of a little child or a convalescent).

pinjante [pin-hahn'-tay], *m. (Arch.)* Moulding at the eaves of buildings.

pino, na [pee'-no, nah], *a.* Very perpendicular, as the sides of a mountain. *-m. (coll.)* The first step of a child or of a convalescent beginning to walk. **A pino,** erect, upright: applied to bells turned half-round in ringing.

pino [pee'-no], *m.* 1. *(Bot.)* Pine. **Pino albar,** Scotch pine. **Pino de comer,** stone pine. **Pino real,** clustian pine. **Pino rodeno** or **rodezno,** cluster pine. **Pino uñal,** Siberian pine. 2. Ship constructed of pine. **Hacer el pino,** stand on one's head.

pinocha [pe-no'-chah], *f.* Pine loaf.

pínola [pee´-no-lah], *f.* 1. Detent of a repeating watch. 2. Spindle.

pínole [pee´-no-lay] *(Acad.),* or **Pinole** [pe-no'-lay], *m.* 1. An aromatic powder used in making chocolate. 2. *(Mex.)* Parched corn, ground and mixed with sugar and water for a drink.

pinoso, sa [pe-no'-so, sah], *a.* Producing or belonging to pines.

pinta [peen'-tah], *f.* 1. Spot (punto), blemish, scar. 2. Any mark by which the qualities of a thing are known. 3. Trump (triunfo en cartas). **¿Qué pinta?,** ¿what's trump? 4. Drop (gota). 5. Pint, a liquid measure. 6. Appearance (aspecto), look. 7. Worthless creature (persona inútil). 8. *(And. Carib. Cono Sur)* Coloring, coloration; *(LAm.)* birthmark (señal). **Una tela a pinta azules,** a cloth with blue spots. **Tener buena pinta,** to look good (persona). *-pl.* 1. Spots on the skin in malignant fevers. 2. Basset, a game of cards.

pintacilgo, pintadillo [pin-tah-theel'-go, pin-tah-deel'-lyo], *m. (Orn.)* Goldfinch.

pintada [pin-tah´-dah], *f.* The Guinea fowl.

pintadera [pin-tah-day´-rah], *f.* Instrument for ornamenting bread.

pintado, da [pin-tah´-do, dah], *a. & pp.* of PINTAR. 1. Painted, mottled. **Venir pintado,** to fit exactly. 2. *(LAm.)* Like, identical. **El niño salió pintado al padre,** the boy looked exactly like his father.

pintamonas [pin-tah-mo'-nas], *m. (coll.)* Nickname for a bad painter, a dauber.

pintar [pin-tar'], *va.* 1. To paint, to picture, to represent by delineation and colors. 2. To paint, to describe, to delineate, to represent something by writing or words. 3. To fancy, to imagine, to feign according to fancy. 4. To exaggerate, to heighten by representation. 5. To pay, to discharge, to satisfy. **Pintar algo azul,** to paint something blue. **No pinta nada,** he cuts no ice. *-vn.* 1. To begin to ripen (fruta). 2. To show, to give signs of. *-vr.* 1. To paint one's face (maquillarse). 2. *(LAm.)* To scarper (escaparse).

pintarrajar, pintarrajear [pin-tar-rah-jar'], *va. (coll.) V.* PINTORREAR.

pintarrajo [pin-tar-rah'-ho], *m. (Col.)* A bungling piece of painting.

pintarrojo [pin-tar-ro'-ho], *m. (Prov. Gal.)* Robin. *V.* PARDILLO.

pintarroia, *f. V.* LIJA.

pintica, illa, ita [pin-tee'-cah], *f. dim.* A little spot or dot.

pintiparado, da [pin-te-pah-rah'-do, dah], *a.* Perfectly like, closely resembling; apposite, fit. *-pp.* of PINTIPANAR.

pintiparar [pin-te-pah-rar'], *va.* To compare, to estimate the relative quality.

pintojo, ja [pin-toh'-ho, hah], *a.* Spotted, stained, mottled.

pintor [pin-tor'], *m.* Painter. **Pintor de brocha gorda,** house painter.

pintora [pin-to'-rah], *f.* Paintress; a painter's wife.

pintorcillo [pin-tor-theel'-lyo], *m. dim.* Applied to a wretched painter or dauber.

pintoresco, ca [pin-to-res'-co, cah], *a.* Picturesque.

pintorreador [pin-tor-ray-ah-dor'], *m.* Dauber, miserable painter.

pintorrear [pin-tor-ray-ar´], *va.* To daub, to paint without skill.

pintura [pin-too´-rah], *f.* 1. Painting, the art of representing objects by delineation and colors. 2. Picture, painting, a painted resemblance. **Pintura al temple,** size painting. 3. Forming letters with the pen. 4. *(Met.)* Picture, written description of anything. **Pintura embutida,** painting in mosaic, etc. 5. Paint (material).

pinturero, ra [pin-too-ray´-ro, rah], *a. & n.* Exaggerating, buffoon-like.

pinul, pinullo [pe-nool'-lyo], *m.* An Indian drink made from maize. *Cf.* PINOLE.

pínula [pee'-noo-lah], *f.* 1. Detent of a repeating watch. 2. Sight of an optical instrument.

pinzas [peen´-thas], *f. pl.* 1. Pincers (tenazas). 2. Forceps, tweezers. 3. Clothes pin (de ropa), peg. **Pinza de pelo,** *(Carib.)* hair grip.

pinzón [pin-thone'], *m. (Orn.)* Chaffinch.

pinzote [pin-tho'-tay], *m. (Naut.)* Whip-staff, formerly fastened to the rudder.

piña [pee'-nyah], *f.* 1. Cone or nut (del pino). 2. Pineapple. 3. Virgin silver treated with mercury. 4. A white, matt, transparent, and very fine fabric, made in the Philippines from the leaves of the pineapple, and which serves for handkerchief bands, towels, and garments of women and children. 5. *(Carib. Mex.)* Hub. 6. Punch (golpe). 7. *(Mex.)* Chamber (revólver).

piñata [pe-nayh'-tah], *f.* 1. Pitcher, pot. 2. Jar or pot ornamented with fancy paper and filled with sweetmeats, which is hung from the ceiling so that the merrymakers, one by one and blindfolded, try to break it with a stick. It is very popular at Christmas festivities and at children's parties.

piño [pe-nyo], *m.* Ivory, tooth.

piñón [pe-nyone´], *m.* 1. The pine-nut seed or kernel. 2. Pinion, the joint of the wing remotest from the body. 3. Pinion, the tooth of a wheel. 4. Spring-nut of a gun. **Comer los piñones,** to celebrate Christmas eve.

piñonata [pe-nyoh-nah'-tah], *f.* Conserve of pine-nut kernels.

piñonate [pe-nyoh-nah'-tay], *m.* Paste made of the kernels of pine-nuts and sugar.

piñoncico, illo, ito [pe-nyon-thee'-co], *m. dim.* 1. A small pine-nut kernel. 2. Pinion, the joint of the wing remotest from the body.

piñuela [pe-nyoo-ay'-lah], *f.* 1. Figured silk. 2. Nut or fruit of cypress. 3. (Nicaragua) The American agave, from which the *cabuya* is made.

pío, a [pee'-o, ah], *a.* 1. Pious, devout, religious, holy. 2. Mild, merciful. 3. Pied, piebald (caballo).

pío [pee'-o], *m.* 1. Puling of chickens. 2. Anxious desire. **No decir ni pío**, not to breathe a word.

piocha [pe-o'-chah], *f.* Trinket for women's headdresses.

piojento, ta [pe-o-hen'-to, tah], *a.* Lousy.

piojería [pe-o-hay-ree'-ah], *f.* 1. Lousiness. 2. Misery (miseria), poverty.

piojicida [pe-o-he-thee'-dah], *com.* In jocular style, a louse-killer.

piojillo [pe-o-heel'-lyo], *m.* 1. (*dim.*) A small louse (bichos en plantas, pájaros). 2. A white spot in leather which is not well dressed.

piojo [pe-o'-ho], *m.* 1. A louse. 2. Disease in hawks and other birds of prey. **Piojo pegadizo,** Crablouse; a troublesome hanger-on.

piojoso, sa [pe-o-hoh'-so, sah], *a.* 1. Lousy, mean, contemptible. 2. Miserable, stingy.

piojuelo [pe-o-hoo-ay'-lo], *m. dim.* A small louse.

piola [pe-o'-lah], *f.* 1. (*Naut.*) Housing house-line, a line of three strands. 2. (*LAm.*) Rope (soga), tether. 3. (*And. Carib.*) Cord (cuerda). 4. (*Cono Sur*) Cock (pene).

pionero [pe-o-nay'-ro], *a.* Pioneering. *-m & f.* Pioneer.

pionía [pe-o-nee'-ah], *f.* A hard, red, bean-shaped seed used in Venezuela among the country people for making collars and bracelets. *V.* BUCARE.

piorno [pe-or'-no], *m.* (*Bot.*) Spanish broom.

piorrea [pe-or-ray'-ah], *f.* (*Med.*) Pyorrhea.

pipa [pee'-pah], *f.* 1. A cask for wine and other liquors. 2. Pipe, a liquid measure of two hogsheads. 3. *V.* PEPITA. 4. Pipe (para fumar). **Fumar una pipa**, to smoke a pipe. 5. Pipe which children make of corn-stalks; reed of a clarion. 6. (*LAm.*) Belly (barriga). 7. Rod (pistola). 8. **Pasarlo pipa**, to have a great time.

pipar [pe-par'], *vn.* To smoke a tobacco-pipe.

pipería [po-pay-ree'-ah], *f.* Collection of pipes.

piperina [pe-pay-ree'-nah], *f.* Piperin, an alkaloidal principle obtained from white pepper.

pipero [pe-pay'-ro], *m.* Cooper, pipe or butt maker.

pipí [pe-pee'], *m.* 1. (*Orn.*) Pitpit, a bird known also as honey-creeper. 2. Pee, piss, wee-wee (entre niños).

pipián [pe-pe-ahn'], *m.* A kind of Indian fricassee.

pipiar [pe-pe-ar'], To pule, to chirp, to peep.

pípila [pee'-pe-lah], *f.* (*Mex. Amer.*) Hen-turkey.

pipiolo [pe-pe-o'-lo], *m.* (*coll.*) Novice (novato), raw; hand, beginner; recruit.

pipirigallo [pe-pe-re-gahl'-lyo], *m.* (*Bot.*) Sainfoin, a forage plant.

pipiripao [pe-pe-re-pah'-o], *m.* (*coll.*) A splendid feast.

pipiritaña [pe-pe-re-tah'-nyah], *vr.* **Pipitaña** [pe-pe-tah'-nyah], *f.* Flute made of green cane.

pipo [pee'-po, *m.* 1. Small bird that eats flies. 2. (*Carib.*) Child (niño). 3. (*And. Carib.*) Crooked employee (empleado). 4. (*And.*) Contraband liquor (licor).

pipote [pe-po'-tay], *m.* A keg.

pipotillo [pe-po-teel'-lyo], *m. dim.* A small keg.

pique [pee'-kay], *m.* 1. Pique (resentimiento), offence taken. 2. A beau, gallant, lover. 3. A term in a game. 4. Bottom, ground. 5. (*LAm.*) Bounce (rebote). 6. (*CAm. Cono Sur. Min.*) Mineshaft. 7. (*And.*) Jigger flea (insecto). **Irse a pique**, (*Naut.*) to founder. **A pique**, in danger, on the point of. **Estar a pique**, to be about or on the point of: *Piques* (*Naut.*) crotches. *V.* HORQUILLAS.

pique [pe-kay'], *m.* Pique, a heavy cotton fabric having a corded or lozenge-shaped pattern.

piquera [pe-kay'-rah], *f.* 1. A hole in a hive, through which bees fly in and out (de colmena). 2. Cock-hole in a barrel. 3. (*Mex.*) Dive (taberna).

piquería [pe-kay-ree'-ah], *f.* Body of pikemen.

piquero [pe-kay'-ro], *m.* (*Mil.*) Pikeman.

piqueta [pe-kay'-tah], *f.* Pick-axe, mattock, pitcher.

piquete [pe-kay'-tay], *m.* 1. Sore or wound of little importance. 2. Small hole made in clothes with a pinking iron (agujero). 3. A pointed stake shod with iron. 4. Picket or piquet, a small detachment of soldiers. 5. Picket (de huelguistas). 6. (*Cono Sur*) Yard, small corral. 7. (*Carib.*) Street band. **Piquete avanzado**, picket-guard.

piquetero [pe-kay-tay'-ro], *m.* In mines, the boy who carries the picks or mattocks to the workmen.

piquetilla [pe-kay-teel'-lyah], *f. dim.* A small pick-axe.

piquillo [pe-keel'-lyo], *m. dim.* A small beak or bill.

piquituerto [pe-ke-too-err'-to], *m.* (*Orn.*) Cross-bill, picarin.

pira [pee'-rah], *f.* 1. A funeral pyre, on which the dead are burnt. 2. **Hacer pira**, to clear off; (*Escol.*) to cut class.

pirado [pe-rah'-do], *a.* Crazy (tonto); high (drogado).

piragón [pe-rah-gon'], *m. V.* PIRAUSTA.

piragua [pe-rah'-goo-ah], *f.* (*Naut.*) Pirogue, a small vessel, canoe.

piragüismo [pe-rah'-goo-ah], *m.* Canoeing.

piragüista [pe-rah-goo-ees'-tah], *m & f.* Canoeist.

piramidal [pe-rah-me-dahl'], *a.* Pyramidal.

piramidalmente [pe-rah-me-dahl'-men-tay], *adv.* Pyramidally.

pirámide [pe-rah'-me-day], *f.* Pyramid.

piramista [pe-rah-mees'-tah], *f.* A kind of butterfly.

pirata [pe-rah'-tah], *m.* 1. Pirate, corsair. 2. A cruel wretch. *-a.* **Disco pirata**, bootleg record. **Pirata informático**, (*Comput.*) hacker.

piratear [pe-rah-tay-ar'], *vn.* 1. To pirate; to rob at sea, to cruise, to steal. 2. (*Comput.*) Hacking.

piratería [pe-rah-tay-ree'-ah], *f.* 1. Piracy on the sea 2. Piracy, any robbery; bootlegging (de disco). **Pirateo de software**, software piracy.

pirático, ca [pe-rah'-te-co, cah], *a.* Piratical, piratic.

pirausta [pe-rah-oos'-tah], *f.* Large firefly; an insect formerly fabled to live in fire, and to die apart from it.

pirenaico, ca [pe-ray-nah'-e-co, cah], *a.* Pyrenean, of the Pyrenees.

pirexia [pe-rek'-se-ah], *f.* Pyrexia, essential, fever.

pírico, c [pee'-re-co, cah], *a.* Relating to fire, particularly to fireworks.

pirita [pe-ree'-tah], *f.* 1. Pyrites, an obsolescent name for the sulphurets of iron, copper, and other metals. 2. Marcasite, a fossil. *V.* MARCASITA.

piritoso, sa [pe-re-to'-so, sah], *a.* Pyritous.

pirofilacio [pe-ro-fe-lah'-the-o], *m.* Subterraneous fire.

piróforo [pe-ro'-fo-ro], *m.* 1. Pyrophore, a composition which will ignite in contact with air. 2. A tropical firefly.

piromancia [pe-ro-mahn'-the-ah], *f.* Pyromancy, divination by fire.

piromanía [pe-ro-mah-nee'-ah], *f.* Pyromania, a morbid desire to start fires.

pirómano, na [pe-ro'-mah-no], *m & f.* Arsonist, fire raiser.

piromántico, ca [pe-ro-mahn'-te-co, cah], *a.* Belonging to pyromancy.

pirómetro [pe-ro'-may-tro], *m.* Pyrometer, an instrument for measuring heat and its effects.

pironomia [pe-ro-no'-me-ah], *f.* Pyronomy, the art of regulating fire for chemical processes.

piropear [pe-ro-pay-ar'], *va.* To pay an amorous compliment to.

piropo [pe-ro'-po], *m.* 1. Precious stone. *V.* CARBUNCLO. 2. Compliment, flattery, endearing expression.

piróscapo [pe-ros'-cah-po], *m.* A steam ship.

piróscopo [pe-ros'-co-po], *m.* Pyroscope, an instrument for measuring radiant heat.

piroseno [pe-ro-say'-no], *m.* Pyroxene, a bisilicato mineral.

pirosis [pe-ro´-sis], *f.* Pyrosis, a burning sensation in the stomach.

pirotecnia [pe-ro-tec´-ne-ah], *f.* Pyrotechnics or pyrotechny, the art of making fire-works and of the use of explosive substances.

pirotécnico, ca [pe-ro-tec´-ne-co, cah], *a.* Pyrotechnical.

piroxilina [pee-roc-se-lee´-nah], *f.* Gun cotton.

pirriquio [pir-ree´-ke-o], *m.* Foot of Latin verse.

pirrónico, ca [pir-ro´-ne-co, cah], *a.* V. ESCÉPTICO.

pirueta [pe-roo-ay´-tah], *f.* Pirouette, circumvolution, twirling round on the toe, dancing, gyration.

pis [pees], *m.* V. PIPÍ.

pisa [pee´-sah], *f.* 1. Tread, the act of treading. 2. Kick, a blow with the foot. 3. Portion of olives or grapes pressed at once.

pisada [pee-sah´-dah], *f.* 1. Footstep, footprint (huella). **Seguir las pisadas**, to follow one's example. 2. Kick with the foot.

pisador [pee-sah-dor´], *m.* 1. Treader of grapes. 2. Horse that prances in walking.

pisadura [pe-sah-doo´-rah], *f.* Act of treading.

pisafalto, pisasfalto [pe-sah-fahl´-to], *m.* Mixture of bitumen and pitch.

pisapapeles [pe-sah-pah-pay´-les], *m.* Paper weight.

pisar [pe-sar´], *va* 1. To tread, to trample (atropellar); to stamp on the ground, to step on (casualidad); to flatten (dañando). 2. To beat down stones and earth with a mallet. 3. To touch upon, to be close to. 4. To despise, to abandon. 5. To tread, to copulate (pájaros). 6. To pinch, to steal (robar). 7. *(And.)* To cover (hembra); *(CAm.)* To fuck. **Pisar el acelerador**, to step on the accelerator. **No se deja pisar por nadie**, he doesn´t let anybody trample over him. -*vn.* 1. To tread, to step, to walk (andar). 2. *(Fig.)* **Pisar fuerte,** to act determinedly.

pisaúvas [pe-sah-oo´-vas], *m.* Treader of grapes.

pisaverde [pe-sah-verr´-day], *m. (coll.)* Fop, coxcomb, popinjay.

piscator [pis-cah-tor´], *m.* A universal almanac.

piscatorio, ria [pis-cah-to´-re-o, ah], *a.* Piscatory.

piscicultura [pis-the-cool-too´-rah], *f.* Pisciculture, fish culture.

pisciforme [pis-the-for´-may], *a.* Fish-shaped.

piscina [pis-thee´-nah], *f.* 1. Fish pond (tanque). 2. Swimming pool. 3. Piscina, basin with a drain for water disposal in connection with sacred rites.

piscis [pees´-this], *m. (Ast.)* Pisces, a zodiacal sign.

piso [pee´-so], *m.* 1. Tread, trampling, footing. 2. Floor (suelo), pavement, flooring, surface: foundation of a house. 3. Story or floor, as first floor, second floor, etc.: loft. **Piso bajo**, ground floor. **A un piso**, on the same floor. 4. Money paid for board and lodging in a lodging-house, inn, etc. 5. Sole (de zapato). 6. *(Cono Sur)* Stool (tablero). 7. Mat (estera); *(Cono Sur, Mex.)* Table runner (tapete).

pisón [pe-sone´], *m.* Rammer, an instrument for driving earth, stones, or piles (herramienta). **A pison**, by blows of a rammer.

pisonear [pe-so-nay-ar´], *va.* To ram, to drive down.

pisotear [pe-so-tay-ar´], *va.* To trample, to tread underfoot.

pisoteo [pe-so-tay´-o], *m.* The act of treading underfoot.

pisotón [pe-so-ton´], *m.* 1. Stamp on the foot. 2. Newspaper scoop (periodismo).

pista [pees´-tah], *f.* 1. Trace, track, spoor of an animal. 2. Footprint. 3. Track for foot or horse racing. 4. *(Aer.)* Airstrip. 5. Clue (de indicio). 6. Tack (de cinta). 7. *(Dep.)* Track, course; court (cancha). **Pista de aterrizaje**, landing strip, landing field. **Pista de despegue**, runway. **Seguir la pista de uno**, to be on somebody´s track. **Pista de hielo,** ice rink.

pistacho [pis-tah´-cho], *m.* Pistachio, pistachio nut.

pistadero [pis-tah-day´-ro], *m.* Pestle, for pounding.

pistar [pis-tar´], *va.* To pound with a pestle; to extract the juice of a thing.

pistero [pis-tay´-ro], *m.* A round jug with a spout, used to give broth, medicines, etc.

pistilo [pis-tee´-lo], *m. (Bot.)* Pistil, the central female part of a flower, which contains the ovule.

pisto [pees´-to], *m.* 1. A kind of thick broth given to the sick. 2. *(Prov.)* Dish of tomatoes and red pepper fried with oil. 3. *(And. CAm.)* Dough. 4. *(And.)* Barrel (de revólver). 5. *(Mex.)* Shot of liquor. **A pistos**, by little and little, by driblets.

pistola [pes-to´-lah], *f.* Pistol, small hand-gun. **Un par de pistolas**, a brace of pistols. **Pistola de agua**, water pistol.

pistolera [pis-to-lay´-rah], *f.* Holster.

pistolero [pis-to-lay´-ro], *m.* Gunman.

pistoletazo [pis-to-lay-tah´-tho], *m.* Pistol-shot; the wound of a pistol; the report of a pistol.

pistolete [pis-to-lay´-tay], *m.* Pistolet, pocket pistol.

pistón [pis-tone´], *m.* 1. Piston, embolus, as the sucker of a pump. 2. A percussion-cap, primer. 3. The piston of a brass wind-instrument.

pistonera [pis-to-nay´-rah], *f.* A box or case for carrying percussion-caps.

pistoresa [pis-to-ray´-sah], *f.* Short dagger.

pistraje, pistraque [pis-trah´-hay], *m.* Broth or sauce of an unpleasant taste.

pistura [pis-too´-rah], *f.* Act of pounding.

pita [pee´-tah], *f.* 1. *(Bot.)* American agave or century-plant. 2. Kind of thread made of the agave (fibra). 3. Term used to call hens. 4. Game among boys.

pitaco [pe-tah´-co], *m.* Stem or stalk of the aloe-plant.

Pitágoras [pe-tah´-go-rahs], *m.* Pythagoras.

pitagórico, ca [pe-tah-go´-re-co, cah], *a. & n.* Pythagorean.

pitancería [pe-tan-thay-ree´-ah], *f.* 1. Place where allowances of meat and other things are distributed. 8. Distribution or office of distributor of allowances.

pitancero [pe-tan-thay´-ro], *m.* 1. Person appointed to distribute allowances of meat or other things. 2. Friar who is not ordained, but lives upon charity. 3. Steward or purveyor to a convent. 4. Superintendent of a choir in cathedrals.

pitancica, illa, ita [pe-tan-thee´-cah], *f. dim.* Small pittance.

pitanza [pe-tahn´-thah], *f.* 1. Pittance, daily allowance; alms. 2. *(coll.)* Price of something; salary given for any work. 3. *(Cono Sur)* Bargain.

pitaña [pe-tah´-nyah], *f.* V. LEGAÑA.

pitañoso, sa [pe-tah-nyo´-so, sah], *a.* V. LEGAÑOSO.

pitar [pe-tar´], *vn.* 1. To pipe, to play on a pipe. 2. *(LAm.)* To smoke. 3. To work (funcionar). **Pitó el árbitro**, the referee blew his whistle. **Salir pitando**, to beat it. -*va.* 1. To discharge a debt. 2. To distribute allowances of meat or other things. 3. To blow (silbato); to referee (partido). 4. To whistle at (árbitro).

pitarra [pe-tar´-rah], *f.* Distemper of the eyes. *V.* LEGAÑA.

pitillera [pe-tel-lyay´-rah], *f.* Cigarette case.

pitillo [pe-teel´-lyo], *m.* Cigarette.

pítima [pee´-te-mah], *f.* 1. *(Med.)* Plaster placed over the heart to quiet it. 2. *(coll.)* Drunkenness.

pitío [pe-tee´-o], *m.* Whistling of a pipe or of birds.

pitipié [pe-te-pe-ay´], *m.* V. ESCALA.

pito [pee´-to], *m.* 1. Whistle (instrumento, tren). 2. Hooter (de un coche). 3. Pipe, a small flute; boy's whistle (silbato). 4. *(Orn.)* Magpie, woodpecker (pájaro), tick (insecto). 5. A species of bug in India. 6. *(Prov.)* Cocoon of a silkworm open at one end. 7. Game among boys. 8. *(coll.)* Miembro viril. **No tocar pito**, not to have a share in a thing. **No vale un pito**, it (he) is not worth a straw. **Tener voz de pito,** to have a squeaky voice. **No me importa un pito**, I couldn't care less. **Entre pitos y flautas**, what with one thing and another.

pitoflero, ra [pe-to-flay´-ro, rah], *m. & f. (coll.)* A musician of little skill.

pitométrica [pe-to-may´-tre´-cah], *f.* Gauge, the art of gauging vessels.

pitón [pe-tone´], *m.* 1. Tenderling, the top of an animal´s horn when it begins to shoot forth. 2. Protuberance, prominence. 3. Sprig or shoot of a tree; sprout of the agave. 4. *(Zool.)* Python.

pitonisa [pe-to-ne´-sah], *f.* 1. Pythia, pythoness, the priestess of Apollo. 2. Witch (bruja), sorceress, enchantress.

pitorra [pe-tor´-rah], *f.* *(Orn.)* Woodcock. V. CHOCHAPERDIZ.

pitorreo [pe-tor-ray´-o], *m.* V. CHOTEO.

pitpit [peet´-peet], *m.* Pitpit, guitguit, a small American bird. Cf. PIPI.

pituita [pe-too-ee´-tah], *f.* Pituita, mucus.

pituitario, ria [pe-too-e-tah-re-o, ah], *a.* *(Anat.)* Pituitary. **Glándula pituitaria**, pituitary gland.

pituitoso, sa [pe-too-e-to'-so, sah], *a.* Pituitous, pituitary, mucous.

piulco [pe-ool'-co], *m.* Surgical aspirator, syringe-shaped.

pivote [pe-vo´-tay], *m.* 1. Pivot (gorrón). 2. Pivot (baloncesto).

píxide [peek'-se-day], *f.* 1. A small box of wood or metal. 2. Pyx, box in which the consecrated host is kept.

pizarra [pe-thar´-rah], *f.* 1. Slate, a gray mineral (piedra). 2. Slate, for writing or figuring. 3. Blackboard (en colegios).

pizarral [pe-tha-rahl'], *m.* Slate quarry.

pizarreño, ña [pe-thar-ray´-nyo, nyah], *a.* Slate-colored, slaty, slatey.

pizarrero [pe-thar-ray´-ro], *m.* Slater, one who polishes slates.

pizarrín [pe-that-reen'], *m.* Slate-pencil.

pizarrón [pe-thar-rone'], *m.* Blackboard.

pizca [peeth´-cah], *f.* *(coll.)* Mite, whit, jot, anything proverbially small. **Ni pizca**, nothing at all, not an iota. **Una pizca de sal**, a pinch of salt.

pizcar [peeth-car'], *va.* *(coll.)* 1. To pinch. V. PELLIZCAR. 2. *(Mex.)* To harvest or glean (maiz).

pizpereta, pizpireta [pith-pe-ray´-tah], *a.* Sharp, brisk, lively (mujeres).

pizpita [pith-pee´-tah], *f.* *(Orn.)* Wagtail V. PEZPITA.

placa [plah´-cah], *f.* 1. Star, insignia of an order of knighthood. 2. A photographic plate. 3. *(Mex.)* Check for baggage (para equipaje). 4. *(LAm. Mus.)* Gramophone record. **Placas de transparencias**, transparency (or lantern) plates. **Placa de matrícula**, number plate. **Placa madre**, *(Comput.)* motherboard.

placabilidad [plah-cah-be-le-dahd'], *f.* Placability.

placable [plah-cab'-blay], *a.* Placable.

placear [plah-thay-ar'], *va.* To publish, to proclaim, to post up.

placebo [plah-thay' bo], *m.* *(Med.)* Placebo.

placel [plah-thel'], *m.* *(Naut.)* Banks of sand or rocks in the sea.

pláceme [plah'-thay-may], *m.* Compliment of congratulation.

placenta [plah-then´-tah], *f.* 1. *(Anat.)* Placenta, after-birth. 2. *(Bot.)* Placenta.

placenteramente [plah-then-tay-rah-men-tay], *adv.* Joyfully.

placentero, ra [plah-then-tay'-ro, rah], *a.* Joyful, merry, pleasant, mirthful, humorous.

placer [plah-therr'], *m.* 1. Pleasure (deleite), content, rejoicing, amusement, complacence. 2. Will, consent. 3. The place near the bane of a river where gold-dust is found. 4. V. PLACEL. **A placer**, (a) with the greatest pleasure; (b gently, commodiously. **Por hacer placer**, to oblige or please a person. **Los placeres del ocio**, the pleasures of idleness.

placer [plah-thay'-res], *v. impers.* To please, to gratify, to humor, to content. **Que me place**, it pleases me; I approve of it.

placero, ra [plah-thay'-ro, rah], *a.* 1. Belonging to a market or other public place. 2. Roving idly about.

placeta [plah-thay'-tah], *f. dim.* A small square or public place.

placetilla, placetuela [plah-thay-teel'-lyah], *f. dim.* V. PLACETA.

placible [plah-thee'-blay], *a.* Placid, agreeable.

plácido [plah'-the-do, dah], *a.* Placid, easy, quiet.

placiente [plah-theen'-tay], *a.* Pleasing, mild; acceptable.

placilla, ita [plah-theel'-lyah], *f. dim.* V. PLACETA.

plafón [plah-fone'], *m.* *(Arch.)* Soffit of an architrave.

plaga [plah'-gah], *f.* 1. Plague, pest, any public calamity, as pestilence, scarcity, etc. 2. Scourge (de un pueblo). 3. Disaster, catastrophe, anything vexatious. 4. Plenty, abundance of a harmful thing. 5. Climate, country; zone. 6. *(Naut.)* Each of the cardinal points of the compass. **Plaga del jardín**, garden plague.

plagar [plah-gar'], *va.* To plague, to torment. **Han plagado la ciudad de carteles**, they have covered the town with posters. **Esta sección está plagada de minas**, this part has mines everywhere. *-vr.* To be overrun with.

plagiar [plah-he-ar'], *va.* 1. To plagiarize, or commit literary thefts (libros). 2. Among the ancient Romans, to buy and enslave a free man. 3. *(LAm.)* Kidnapping (secuestro).

plagiario, ria [plah-he-ah´-re-o, ah], *a. & m. & f.* Plagiari, plagiarist, copier.

plagiato [plah-he-ah´-to], *m.* 1. Abduction. 2. V. PLAGIO.

plagio [plah´-he-o], *m.* Plagiarism (copia), a literary theft.

plagoso, sa [plah-goh'-so, sah], *a.* Wounding, making wounds.

plaguear [plah-gay-ar'], *vn.* To beg alms piteously.

plan [plahn], *m.* 1. Plan (proyecto), design, draft of a building, town, etc. 2. Plan, the delineation of the horizontal posture of something. 3. Plan, writing in which a thing is described minutely (idea). 4. Slab, *(Naut.)* floor-timber. 5. Date (aventura); date (persona); boyfriend, girlfriend. 6. Programme (programa). 7. *(Med.)* Régime. 8. Level; height. 9. Set-up, system (sistema). 10. *(Cono Sur, Mex.)* Flat bottom (barco). 11. *(LAm.)* Level ground (llano). 12. *(And. CAm. Carib.)* Flat (de espada). **Plan de combate**, *(Naut.)* quarter-bill. **Plan de vuelo**, *(Aer.)* flight plan. **Plan de desarrollo**, development plan. **Ha sido un plan muy pesado**, it turned out to be a very tedious kind of amusement. **Ponerse en plan**, to get in the mood. **En ese plan**, in that way. **Lo hicieron en plan de broma**, they did it for a laugh.

plana [plah´-nah], *f.* 1. Page of a book or writing. 2. A level, fruitful piece of ground. 3. Trowel, a bricklayer's tool. 4. Copy or page written by scholars during school-hours. **A plana renglón**, copied word for word; arriving or happening at the nick of time. **Plana de anuncios**, advertisement page.

planada [plah-nah´-dah], *f.* Plain, level ground.

plancha [plahn´-chah], *f.* 1. Flatiron. 2. Plate (lámina), a thin piece of metal, slab (losa). 3. Iron (utensilio); ironing (acto); ironed clothes (ropa planchada). 4. Press-up (ejercito). **Plancha de acero**, steel plate. **Plancha de cobre**, copper plate. **Plancha eléctrica**, electric iron.

planchada [plan-chah´-dah], *f.* *(Naut.)* Framing or apron of a gun.

planchador, ra [plan-chah-dor´, rah], *m. & f.* Ironer. **Planchadora eléctrica**, ironer, electric ironer.

planchar [plan-char´], *va.* 1. To iron linen. 2. *(LAm.)* To flatter. 3. *(Mex.)* To stand up (dejar plantado). V. APLANCHAR.

planchear [plan-chay-ar´], *va.* To plate, to sheath, to cover with metal.

plancheta [plan-chay´-tah], *f.* Circumferentor, instrument used to measure distances and take heights.

planchica, illa, ita [plan-chee´-cah], *f. dim.* A small plate.

planchón [plan-chone´], *m. aug.* A large plate.

planeador [plah-nay-ah-dor´], *m.* *(Aer.)* Glider.

planear [plah-nay-ar´], *va.* 1. To plan (proyectar). 2. To organize. *-vn.* *(Aer.)* To glide.

planeo [plah-nay´-o], *m.* *(Aer.)* Gliding.

planeta [plah-nay´-tah], *m.* Planet, a heavenly body.

planetario [plah-nay-tah´-re-o], *m.* 1. Planetarium, orrery, an astronomical instrument. 2. Astronomer.

planetario, ria [plah-nay-tay´-re-o, ah], *a.* Planetary.

planga [plahn´-gah], *f.* Kind of eagle, with black and white feathers.

planicie [plah-nee´-the-ay], *f.* V. LLANO and LLANURA.

planificación [plah-ne-fe-cah-the-on'], *f.* City planning.

planificar [plah-ne-fe-cahr'], *va.* To plan.

planilla [plah-neel'-lyah], *f.* 1. List, blank form. 2. List of candidates for office.

planipedia [plan-ne-pay'-de-ah], *f.* A mean play, acted by strollers.

planisferio [plah-ni-fay'-re-o], *m.* Planisphere, a sphere projected on a plane.

plano, na [plah'-no, nah], *a.* Plain, level, smooth, flat. **Caer de plano**, to fall flat. **Rechazar algo de plano**, to turn something down flat.

plano [plah'-no], *m.* 1. Plan, design, draft, groundplot, delineation. 2. *(Geom.)* Plane, a level surface. 3. *(Cine, Fot.)* Shot. 4. Flat (de espada). **De plano**, openly, clearly. **De distinto plano social**, of a different social level. **Primer plano**, foreground. **Estar en primer plano**, to be in the limelight. **Levantar un plano**, to make a survey (topografía). **Plano inclinado**, chute. **Poner en primer plano**, to bring to the fore. (Cine) **Primer plano**, close-up shot.

planocóncavo, va [plabh-no-con'-cah-vo, vah], *a.* Plano-concave.

planocónico, ca [plah-no-co'-ne-co, cah], *a.* Plano-conical.

planoconvexo, xa [plah-no-con-vec'-so, sah], *a.* Plano-convex.

planometría [plah-no-may-tree'-ah], *f.* Planometry, the mensuration of plane surfaces.

planoplano [plah-no-plah'-no], *m. (Alg.)* Biquadrate.

planta [plahn'-tah], *f.* 1. Sole of the foot. 2. Plant, any vegetable production. 3. Plantation, the act of planting. 4. A planation or nursery of young plants. 5. Plan of a building. 6. Position of the feet in dancing or fencing. 7. Project: disposition; point of view. 8. Plant or site of a building. **Planta baja**, ground floor. **De buena planta**, well-built (hombre). **Planta de embalaje**, assembly plant.

plantación [plan-tah-the-on'], *f.* Plantation, planting, act of planting.

plantado [plan-tah-do], *a.* **Dejar plantado a uno**, to leave somebody suddenly.

plantador, ra [plan-tah-dor', rah], *m. & f.* Planter, one who plants; an instrument used for planting.

plantaje [plan-tah'-hay], *m.* Collection of plants.

plantaminas [plan-tah-mee'-nahs], *m.* Minelayer.

plantar [plan-tar'], *va.* 1. To plant (terreno, plantas). 2. To set up (monumento), to fix upright. 3. To strike a blow (golpe). 4. To put into a place: to place or introduce somewhere. **Plantar en la cárcel**, to throw into jail. 5. To plant, to found, to establish. 6. *(coll.)* To leave in the lurch, to disappoint. 7. To jilt. **Plantar a uno en la calle**, to pitch somebody into the street. **Plantar a uno**, to curb somebody. -*vr.* 1. To stand upright, to stop. 2. To arrive soon. 3. To stop, to halt, to be unwilling to go (animal). 4. In some games not to wish more cards than are held. 5. *(And. CAm. Mex.)* To doll someone up.

plantaria [plan-tah'-re-ah], *f. V.* ESPARGANIO.

plantario [plan-tah'-re-o], *m.* Plot of ground where young plants are grown or reared.

plante [plahn'-tay], *m.* 1. Stoppage, strike (huelga). 2. Mutiny (motín).

planteamiento [plan-tay-ah-me-ayn-to] *m.* 1. Exposition (exposición). 2. Raising (de un problema). 3. Laying out, layout, setting out (enfoque de un problema).

plantear [plan-tay-ar'], *va.* To set forth, to state (exponer), plan (proponer), to trace, to try, to attempt, to create (problema), to raise, to bring up (cuestión, dificultad), to start (pleito). **Nos ha planteado muchos problemas**, it has created a lot of problems for us. -*vr.* To think (pensar).

plantel [plan-tel'], *m.* 1. Nursery or nursery-garden, a plantation of young trees. 2. Seminary or training school.

plantífero, ra [plan-tee'-fay-ro, rah], *a.* Rearing plants.

plantificar [plan-te-fe-car'], *va.* 1. To plant. *V.* PLANTAR. 2. *(coll.)* To beat, to box, or kick.

plantígrado, da [plan-te-grah'-do, dah], *a.* Plantigrade, walking on the sole of the foot. Also PLANTÍOGRADO, DA.

plantilla [plan-teel'-lyah], *f.* 1. *(dim.)* A young plant. 2. The insole, the inner sole of a shoe (de zapato). *(coll.)* Mustard or other draughts applied to the feet. 3. Vamp, a sole of linen, put to the feet of stockings. 4. Model, pattern, foundry pattern. 5. Plate of a gun-lock. 6. Celestial configuration. 7. Establishment (personas), personnel; list, roster; *(Dep.)* team, squad. **Plantilla de personal**, staff. 8. *(Comput.)* Template.

plantillar [plan-teel-lyar'], *va.* To vamp or sole shoes or stocking.

plantío, ia [plan-tee'-o, ah], *a.* Planted, ready to be planted (tierra).

plantío [plan-tee'-o], *m.* 1. Plantation, the act of planting. 2. Nursery, a plantation of young trees.

plantista [plan-tees'-tah], 1. Bully, hector, bravado. 2. In gardens, royal parks, etc., a planter of trees and shrubbery.

plantón [plan-tone'], *m.* 1. Scion, a sprout or shoot from a plant; a shoot ingrafted on a stock. 2. *(Mil.)* Sentry who performs duty as punishment. **Estar de plantón**, to stand waiting for someone for a long time. **Dar plantón a uno**, to stand somebody up.

planudo, da [plah-noo'-do, dah], *a. (Naut.)* Applied to a vessel which draws little water, as being too flat.

plañidera [plah-nye-day'-rah], *f.* Mourner woman paid for weeping at funerals.

plañido [plah-nye'-do], *m.* Moan, lamentation, crying. **Plañido, da,** *pp.* of PLAÑIR.

plañir [plah-nyeer'], *vn.* To lament, to grieve, to bewail, to sob; to whimper and whine.

plaqué [plah-kay'], *m.* Plaque, an object of metal, covered with a thin layer of gold or silver.

plaqueta [plah-kay'-tah], *f.* Small plate, tag. **Plaqueta sanguínea**, blood platelet.

plasma [plash'-mah], *f.* Prase, a precious stone. -*m.* Plasma (sangre).

plasmador, ra [plas-mah-dor', rah], *m. & f.* Moulder, former.

plasmante [plas-mahn'-tay], *pa.* Moulding; moulder.

plasmar [plas-mar'], *va.* To mould, to form of clay, to make moulds.

plasta [plahs'-tah], *f.* 1. Thick paste, soft clay, anything soft. 2. *(Met. Coll.)* Botch (chapuza), something done without rule or order. -*m & f.* Bore (pelmazo).

plaste [plahs'-tay], *m.* Size, of glue and lime.

plastecer [plas-tay-thar'], *va.* To size, to besmear with size.

plastecido [plas-tay-thee'-do], *m.* Act of sizing. —**Plastecido, da,** *pp.* of PLASTECER.

plástica [plahs'-te-cah], *f.* Art of moulding in clay.

plasticidad [plas-te-the-dahd'], *f.* 1. Plasticity. 2. *(Fig.)* Expressiveness, descriptiveness.

plástico, ca [plahs'-te-co, cah], *a.* Plastic.

plastificado [plas-te-fe-cah'-do], *a.* Treated with plastic.

plastografía [plas-to-grah-fee'-ah], *f.* Plastography.

plata [plah'-tah], *f.* 1. Silver (metal). 2. Plate, wrought silver. 3. *(LAm.)* money (dinero). 4. *(Her.)* Plate; white. **Plata virgen or bruta**, crude mass of silver. **Plata labrada**, (a) wrought silver; (b) payment made in articles equivalent to money. **Valer tanto como la plata**, to be worth its weight in gold. **En plata**, briefly, without turnings or windings.

platabanda [plah-tah-bahn'-dah], *f.* Band or bar of flat iron.

plataforma [plah-tah-for'-mah], *f.* 1. *(Mil.)* Platform, an elevation of earth raised on ramparts; temporary platform. 2. A machine for making pieces of watches. 3. The platform of a street-car or tramway. 4. The stage of a microscope. **Plataforma de lanzamiento,** *(Aer.)* launching pad. **Plataforma de seguridad,** safety island. **Plataforma giratoria,** (r.w.) turntable. **Plataforma subterránea de lanzamiento,** *(Aer.)* silo.

platal [plah'-tahl], *(coll.)* Great wealth. *V.* DINERAL.

platanal, platanar [plah-tah-nal', plah-tah-nar'], *m.* Banana grove.

plátano [plah'-tah-no], *m.* 1. Banana. 2. Plantain. 3. Banana tree. 4. Plane tree.

platea [plah-tay'-ah], *f.* Parquet, orchestra.

platear [plah-tay-ar'], *f.* To silver.

plateresco, ca [plah-tay-res'-co, cah], *a.* Applied to fanciful ornaments in architecture; over-florid, plateresque.

platería [plah-tay-ree'-ah], *f.* 1. Silver-smith's shop (tienda). 2. Trade of a silversmith.

platero [plah-tay'-ro, *m.* Silversmith, plate-worker. **Platero de oro**, goldsmith.

plática [plah'-te-cah], *f.* 1. Talk, chat (charla), conversation: colloquy, converse. 2. Sermon (religioso), speech delivered on some public occasion, address, lecture. 3. Pratic or pratique, permission to a ship's crew to come on shore to buy and traffic. 4. V. PRÁCTICA. **Tomar pláctica**, to obtain practice. **Estar de plática**, to be chatting. **Se pasaron la mañana de plática**, they spent the morning chatting.

platicar [plah-te-car'], *va.* 1. To chat, to converse, to talk, to speak, to commune (charlar). 2. To practice a profession.

platija, [plah-tee'-hah], *f.* (Zool.) Plaice, flounder.

platilla [plah-teel'-lya], *f.* Silesian linen.

platillo [plah-teel'-lyo], *m.* 1. (dim.) A small dish, saucer. 2. A side dish, as opposed to the entree or main course. 3. (Mus.) Cymbal, a percussion instrument. 4. Valve of a pump. **Platillo volador,** (Aer.) flying saucer.

platina [plah-tee'-nah], *f.* 1. An ore of platinum. 2. An exterior metallic ornament of carriages. 3. Platen, bedplate; also imposing-table, in printing. 4. Supports of any machine and lids which inclose the works of watches.

platino [plah-tee'-no], *m.* Platinum, the heaviest of metals.

platirrostro, tra [plah-teer-ros'-tro, trah], *a.* Platyrhine, having a broad nose, snout, or beak. -*m.* V. TODI.

plato [plah'-to], *m.* 1. Dish, plate (utensilio), a vessel to eat on. 2. Dish, mess, food served in a dish. 3. Daily fare. 4. Ornament in the frieze of Doric, architecture. 5. Chuck in which are made the teeth of wheels for watches. **Platos lisos, llanos or trincheros**, dining-plates. **Plato de segunda mesa**, makeshift, person or thing which has belonged to another, and whose possession is not flattering. **Plato frutero**, fruit dish. **Pagar los platos rotos**, to pay for the damage. **Un plato de arroz**, a dish of rice. **Plato fuerte**, main course.

platón [plah-tone'], *m.* (Aug.) Platter, a large dish.

platónicamente [plah-to-ne-cah-men-tay], *adv.* Platonically.

platónico, ca [plah-to'-ne-co, cah], *a.* Platonic, relating to Plato. **Amor platónico**, platonic love.

plato tocadiscos [plah'-to to-ca-dees'-cos], *m.* Turntable.

plato volador [plah'-to voh-lah-dor'], *m.* Flying saucer.

platuja [plah-too-hah], *f.* (Prov.) V. PLATIJA.

plausibilidad [plah-oo-se-be-le-dahd'], *f.* Plausibility, speciousness.

plausible [plah-oo-see'-blay], *a.* Plausible, specious.

plausiblemente [plah-oo-see'-blay-men-tay], *adv.* Plausibly, colorably.

plauso [plah'-oo-so], *m.* Applause by the clapping of hands.

plaustro [plah'-oos-tro], *m.* (Poet.) Cart, wagon, carriage. V. CARRO.

playa [plah'-yah], *f.* Beach, shore (orilla), strand, sea coast. **En la playa**, on the beach, at the seaside.

playado, da [plah-yah'-do, dah], *a.* Applied to a river or sea with a shore.

playazo [plah-yah'-ro], *m.* Wide or extended shore.

playeras [plah-yay'-rahs], *f. pl.* Sneakers (zapatillas de lona).

playero [plah-yay'-ro], *a.* Beach (de playa).

playón [plah-yone'], *m. aug.* A large shore or beach.

playuela [plah-yoo-ay'-lah], *f.* Dim. of PLAYA.

plaza [plah'-thah], *f.* 1. Square, place, or market-place (mercado). 2. Place, a fortified town. 3. Room, space (espacio); stall. 4. Place, office, public employment. 5. Enlisting or enrolling of soldiers in the king's service. 6.

Reputation, character, fame. **Plaza de armas**, military department, garrison, military parade-ground. (Naut.) The waist. **De dos plazas**, two-seater.

plazo [plah'-tho], *m.* 1. Time (término), limit. 2. Installment (pago), payment. 3. Terms. 4. Due date. **A plazo**, on time, on credit. **De largo plazo**, long-term. **Nos dan plazo de 8 días**, they allow us a week. **Se ha cumplido el plazo**, time is up.

plazuela [plah-thoo-ay'-lah], *f. dim.* A small square or place.

ple [play], *m.* (Mex.) V. BLE.

pleamar [play-ah-mar'], *f.* (Naut.) High water, high tide.

plebe [play'-bay], *f.* Common people, populace.

plebeyo, ya [play-bay'-yo, yah], *a.* Plebeian. -*m. & f.* Commoner.

plebiscito [play-bes-thee'-to], *m.* 1. Plebiscitum, a Roman law voted by the plebe at the instance of their tribune. 2. Plebiscite, an expression by vote of the will of the people.

pleca [play'-cah], *f.* (Print.) A straight line, a rule.

plectro [plec'-tro], *m.* 1. Plectrum, a small staff or tool for plucking the strings of a lyre, etc. 2. (Poet.) Plectrum, poesy.

plegable [play-gah'-blay], *a.* Pliable, capable of being folded.

plegadamente [play-gah-dah-men-tay], *adv.* Confusedly.

plegadera [play-gah-day'-rah], *f.* Folder, used by book binders.

plegadizo, za [play-gah-dee'-tho, thah], *a.* Pliable, folding.

plegado [play-gah-do], *m.* Folding; bending.

plegador [play-gah-dor'], *m.* 1. An instrument for folding or plaiting. 2. Plaiter, he that plaits. 3. (coll.) Collector of alms for religious communities. 4. Beam of a silk-loom.

plegadura [play-gah-doo'-rah], *f.* 1. Fold, double, complication. 2. Plaiting, folding, doubling. 3. Cream made by doubling.

plegamiento [play-gah-me-ayn-to], *m.* Jacknifing (de camión).

plegar [play-gar'], *va.* 1. To fold, to plait, to double. 2. To corrugate, to crimple, to purse up. 3. To turn the warp on the yarn-beam. 4. Among bookbinders, to fold the sheets of a book that is to be bound.(Yo pliego, yo pliegue, from Plegar. V. ACERTAR.)

plegaria [play-gah'-re-ah], *f.* 1. Public prayer, supplication. 2. Bell rung at noon for prayer.

pleguería [plah-gay-ree'-ah], *f.* Fold, crumple.

pleita [play'-ee-tah], *f.* A piloted strand of bass.

pleiteador, ra [play-e-tay-ah-dor', rah], *m. & f* **Pleader, a litigious person,** a wrangler.

pleiteante [play-c-tay-ahn'-tay], *pa. & n.* Litigating; pleader, litigant.

pleitear [play-e-tay-ar'], *va.* 1. To plead, to litigate, to contend. 2. (LAm.) Brawler.

pleitesía [play-tay-see'-ah], *f.* Tribute. **Rendir pleitesía**, to render tribute, to pay homage (to some one).

pleitista [play-e-tees'-tah], *m.* Pettifogger, an encorager of lawsuits.

pleito [play'-e-to], *m.* 1. Convenant, contract, bargain. 2. Dispute, contest, controversy. 3. Debate, contention, strife. 4. Litigation, judicial contest, lawsuit. 5. (LAm.) Quarrel (discusión). **Pleito de acreedores**, proceedings under a commission of bankruptcy. **Ganar el pleito**, to win one's case.

plenamar [play-ah-mahr'], *f.* V. PLEAMAR.

plenamente [play-nah-men'-tay], *adv.* Fully, completely.

plenariamente [play-nah-re-ah-men'-tay], *adv.* Completely, fully, plenarily.

plenario, ria [play-nah'-re-o, ah], *a.* Complete, full, plenary.

plenilunio [play-ne-loo'-ne-o], *m.* Full moon.

plenipotencia [play-ne-po-ten'-the-ah], *f.* Plenipotence, fulness of power.

plenipotenciario [play-ne-po-ten-the-ah'-re-o], *m.* Plenipotentiary.

plenitud [play-nee-tood'], *f.* Plenitude, fulness, abundance.

pleno, na [play'-no, nah], *a.* Full. *V.* LLENO. **En pleno verano**, at the height of summer. **Le dio en plena cara**, it hit him full in the face.

pleonasmo [play-o-nahs'-mo], *m.* Pleonasm, a figure of speech.

pleonástico, ca [play-o-nahs'-te-co, cah], *a.* Pleonastic, involving pleoneasm.

plepa [play'-pah], *f.* 1. A charge; a person who has many defects, physically or morally. 2. Pain (molesto).

plétora [play'-to-rah], *f.* Plethora (abundancia), fulness of blood.

pletórico, ca [play-to'-re-co, cah], *a.* Plethoric.

pleural [play-oo-rahl'], *a.* Pleural, relating to the pleura.

pleuresía [play-oo-ray-see'-ah], *f.* Pleurisy, a disease. **Pleuresía falsa**, pleurodynia.

pleurítico, ca [play-oo-ree'-te-co, cah], *a.* Pleuritical, pleuritic.

pleuritis [play-oo-ree'-tis], *f.* Inflammation of the pleura, pleurisy.

pleurodinia [play-oo-ro-dee'-ne-ah], *f.* Pleurodynia, stitch in the side; pain in the intercostal muscles.

plexímetro [plec-see'-may-tro], *m.* Pleximeter, a medical instrument for practicing percussion.

plexo [plec'-so], *m. (Anat. and Bot.)* Plexus; network.

pléyadas, pléyades [play'-yah-dahs], *f. pl. (Ast.)* The Pleiades.

plica [plee'-cah], *f.* 1. Sealed parcel containing a will or document to be published in due time; escrow. 2. *(Med.)* Matted hair; plica.

pliego [ple-ay'-go], *m.* 1. Sheet of paper (hoja). 2. Parcel of letters enclosed in one cover. 3. A tender or proposal by persons who wish to contract with the government. 4. *V.* PLEGADURA and PLIEGUE.

pliegue [ple-ay'-gay], *m.* 1. Fold or pleat in clothes, crease; gather. 2 Ruff anciently worn.

plinto pleen'-to], *m. (Arch.)* Plinth of a pillar.

plisado [ple-sah-do], *m.* Pleating.

plomada [plo-mah'-ah], *f.* 1. Artificer's lead-pencil. 2. Plumb, plummet. 3. *(Naut.)* Lead used by seamen for sounding the depth of water. 4. All the weights attached to fishing-nets; sinkers.

plomar [plo-mar'], *va.* To put a leaden seal, hanging by a thread to some instrument, privilege, etc.

plomazón [plo-mah-thone'], *f.* Gilding cushion.

plombagina [plom-bah-hee'-nah], *f.* Plumbago, graphite.

plomería [plo-may-ree'-ah], *f.* 1. Covering of lead on roofs. 2. Storehouse of lead ware (taller).

plomero [plo-may'-ro], *m.* Plumber, a worker in lead.

plomizo, za [plo-mee'-tho, thah], *a.* Leaden, made of lead; having the qualities of lead.

plomo [plo'-mo], *m.* 1. Lead, a very heavy metal (metal). 2. Any piece of lead. **Plomo en plancha**, lead in sheets. 3. Ball of lead. **Andar con pies de plomo**, to proceed with the utmost circumspection. **A plomo**, perpendicularity, plumb. **Caer a plomo**, to fall flat down. 4. Plumb, a plummet. 5. *(LAm.)* Bullet. 6. *(Mex.)* Gunfight.

plomoso [plo-mo'-so], **sa**, *a.* Leaden. *V.* PLOMIZO.

plóter [plo-tayr'], *m. (Comput.)* Printer plotter.

pluma [ploo'-mah], *f.* 1. Feather, the plume of birds. 2. Pen, for writing (de escribir). **Pluma estilográfica**, fountain pen. 3. Art of writing, penmanship (caligrafía), 4, Writer, author. **Buena pluma**, a good penman, a skiful writer. **Golpe de pluma**, dash with the pen. 5. *(coll.)* Wealth, opulence. 6. *(coll.)* Air expelled from the bowels. 7. *(CAm.)* Fib, talc (mentira). 7. *(Cono Sur)* Prostitute (puta). 8. *(Cono Sur)* Crane (grúa).

plumada [ploo-mah'-dah], *f.* 1. Act of writing something short. 2. Dash with a pen, a line with a crayon. 3. Feathers which falcons have eaten, and have still in the crop.

plumado, da [ploo-mah'-do, dah], *a.* Feathered, feathery, plumy.

plumaje [ploo-mah'-hay], *m.* 1. Plumage of a fowl or bird. 2. Plume, an ornament of feathers (adorno).

plumajería [ploo-mah-hay-ree'-ah], *f.* Heap of leathers.

plumajero [ploo-mah-hay'-pro], *m.* One who dresses feathers and makes plumes.

plumazo [ploo-mah'-tho], *m.* 1. A mattress or pillow stuffed with feathers (colchón, almohada). 2. Stroke (de una pluma). **Abolir de un plumazo**, to abolish by a stroke of the pen (denoting rapidity of action).

plumazón [ploo-mah-thone'], *f.* Collection of feathers.

plúmbeo, bea [ploom'-bay-o, ah], *a.* Leaden, made of lead, having the qualities of lead.

plumeado [ploo-may-ah'-do], *m. (Pict.)* Series of lines similar to those made with a pen in a miniature.

plumear [ploo-may-ar'], *va. (Pict.)* To draw lines with a pen or pencil, to shade a drawing.

plúmeo, mea [ploo'-may-o, ah], *a.* Plumigerous, having feathers, plumous.

plumería [ploo-may-ree'-ah], *f. V.* PLUMAJERÍA.

plumero [ploo-may'-ro], *m.* 1. Bunch of feathers, feather-duster (para limpiar). 2. Box in which feathers or plumes are preserved (portaplumas). 3. Plume (adorno). 4. Plumage.

plumífero, ra [ploo-mee'-fay-ro, rah], *a. (Poet.)* Plumigerous.

plumilla [ploo-meel'-lyah], *f.* Script type.

plumión [ploo-me-on'], *m. V.* PLUMÓN.

plumista [ploo-mees'-tah], *m.* 1. One who lives by writing, a petty notary. 2. A worker in feather, plume-maker.

plumita [ploo-mee'-tah], *f. dim.* A small feather of pen.

plumón [ploo-mone'], *m.* 1. Soft, downy feathers. 2. Feather-bed (cama), flock-bed.

plumoso, da [ploo-mo'-so, sah], *a.* Covered with feathers, plumigerous, plumy.

plúmula [ploo'-moo-lah], *f. (Bot.)* Plumule.

plural [ploo-rahl'], *a. (Gram.)* Plural.

pluralidad [ploo-lah-le-dahd'], *f.* Plurality, multitude; majority. **A pluralidad de votos**, by the majority of voices.

pluriempleado [ploo-re-aym-play'-ah-do], *a.* Having more than one job.

pluriempleo [ploo-re-aym-play'-o], *m.* Having more than one job.

plus [ploos], *m.* Extra pay, bonus.

pluscuamperfecto [ploos-kwam-per-fec'-to], *m.* The pluperfect tense or past perfect.

plusmarca [ploos-mahr'-cah], *f.* Record.

plusmarquista [ploos-mahr-kees'-tah], *m & f.* Record holder.

pluspetición [ploos-pay-te-the-on'], *f.* Asking for more than what is due.

plus ultra [ploos ool'-trah]. **Ser el non plus ultra**, *(coll.)* to be transcendent.

plusvalía [ploos-vah-lee'-ah], *f.* Appreciation, added value.

plúteo [ploo'-tay-o], *m.* Each compartment of book-shelves in a library.

plutocracia [ploo-to-crah'-the-ah], *f.* Plutocracy.

plutocrático, ca [ploo-to-crah'-te-co, cah], *a.* Plutocratic.

plutonio [ploo-to'-ne-o], *m.* Plutonium.

pluvial [ploo-ve-ahl'], *m. (Orn.)* Golden plover.

pluvial, pluvioso, sa [ploo-ve-ahl'], *a.* Rainy. **Capa pluvial**, a priest's cope, worn at the celebration of mass.

pluviatil [ploo-ve-ah'-teel], *a.* Softened or mellowed by rain (temperatura).

pluvímetro *(Acad.)* [ploo-vee'-may-tro], or **Pluviómetro**, *m* Rain-gauge

pneumático [nay-oo-mah'-te-co], **ca**, *a. V.* NEUMÁTICO.

poa [po'-ah], *f. (Naut.)* Bow-line, bridle.

pobeda [po-bay'-dah], *f.* Plantation of poplars.

población [po-blah-the-on'], *f.* 1, Population, the act of populating. 2. Population, the state of a city, town, or country with regard to the number of its inhabitants. 3. *V.* POBLADO.

poblacho [po-blah'-cho], *m.* 1. A mean and ugly village. 2. Populace, rabble, mob.

poblachón [po-blah-chone'], *m. aug.* 1. *V.* POBLACHO, 1st def. 2. A large collection of houses, more than a village and less than a town.

poblado [po-blah'-do], *m.* Town, village, or place inhabited (habitado).—**Poblado, da,** *pp.* of POBLAR. **La ciudad más poblada del país,** the most populous city in the country.

poblador, ra [po-blah-dor', rah], *m. & f.* Populator, founder (fundador).

poblar [po-blar'], *va. & vn.* 1. To found a town, to populate a district, to people (habitar). 2. To fill, to occupy. 3. To breed, to procreate fast. 4. To bud, to put forth leaves. **Las estrellas que pueblan el espacio,** the stars that fill space.

poblazo [po-blah'-tho], *m.* V. POPULACHO.

poblezuelo [po-blay-thoo-ay'-lo], *m. dim.* A small village.

pobo [po'-bo], *m. (Bot.)* White poplar. V. ÁLAMO BLANCO.

pobre [po'-bray], *a.* 1. Poor, necessitous, indigent, needy. 2. Poor, barren, dry. 3. Humble, modest. 4. Poor, unhappy, pitiable, wretched. 5. Poor, trifling, paltry, unimportant. **Pobre y soberbio,** proud pauper. **¡Pobre de mí!,** poor old me!

pobre [po'-bray], *m.* 1. A poor person (necesitado), a beggar (mendigo). 2. A man of very pacific and quiet temper.

pobrecico, ica, illo, illa, ito, ita [po-bray-thee'-co], *a. dim.* A poor little thing.

pobremente [po'-bray-men-tay], *adv.* Poorly, miserably, needily.

pobrería [po-bray-ree'-ah], *f.* Poor people, beggars.

pobrero [po-bray'-ro], *m.* One who is appointed by a religious community to distribute charities.

pobreta [po-bray'-tah], *f. (coll.)* Strumpet, prostitute.

pobrete, pobreto [po-bray'-tay], *m.* 1. A poor, unfortunate man. 2. A useless person, of mean abilities and sentiments.

pobretería [po-bray-tay-ree'-ah], *f.* 1. Poor people, beggars. 2. Poverty, indigence.

pobretón, na [po-bray-tone', nah], *a.* Very poor.

pobreza [po-bray'-thah], *f.* 1. Poverty, indigence, necessity, want, need. 2. Poorness, sterility, barrenness. 3. Heap of worthless trifles. 4. Voluntary vow of poverty. 5. Poorness, lowness or littleness of spirit. **Pobreza de espíritu,** poorness of spirit.

pobrezuelo [po-bray-thoo-ay'-lo], *m. dim.* A poor man.

pobrismo [po-brees'-mo], *m.* Poor people, beggars.

pocero [po-thay'-ro], *m.* 1. One who digs pits and wells. 2. Nightman, one who cleanses wells, pits, or common sewer's.

pocho, cha [po'-cho, chah], *a.* 1. *(coll.)* Discolored, that has lost the color. 2. *(Fig.)* Depressed, gloomy. 3. *(Cono Sur)* Chubby (gordito).

pochola [po-cho'-lah], *f.* Nice girl.

pocholada [po-cho-lah'-dah], *f.* Nice thing.

pocico [po-thee'-co], *m. dim.* A small well.

pocilga [po-theel'-gah], *f.* 1. Hogsty, a place for swine. 2. Any nasty, dirty place.

pocillo [po-theel'-lyo], *m.* 1. *(dim.)* Small well. 2. Vessel for collecting any liquor or fluid. 3. *(Prov.)* Chocolate-cup.

pócima [po'-the-mah], *f.* Potion, a draught of physic.

poción [po-the-on'], *f.* Drink, liquor; potion. V. BEBIDA.

poco, ca [po'-co, cah], *a.* Little, scanty (escaso), limited, small in quantity, small in extent (pequeño), not much, few, some. **De poco interés,** of small interest. **Todas las medidas son pocas,** any measure will be inadequate. **-adv.** Little (no mucho), in a small degree or quantity, in a scanty manner, shortly, briefly, in a short time. **Poco antes** or **poco después,** a little before or after. **Poco a poco,** gently, softly; stop! by little and little. **De poco tiempo acá,** latterly. **Tener en poco,** to set little value on a thing. **A poco, por poco, en poco,** to be very near a thing. **Qué poco,** how little: indicating the difficulty or impossibility of anything. **Ahora trabaja muy poco,** he only works a little now. **Poco amable,** unkind. **Por poco,** almost. **-m.** Little, a small part or proportion. **Un poco,** a little.

pocoyán [po-co-yahn'], *m.* A bee of the Philippine Islands, somewhat larger than the European.

póculo [po'-coo-lo], *m.* 1. Drinking cup. 2. *(Obs.)* Drink.

poda [po'-dah], *f.* Pruning of trees, pruning season (temporada).

podadera [po-dah-day'-rah], *f.* Pruning-knife, pruning-hook, hedging-bill.

podador, ra [po-dah-dor', rah], *m. & f.* Pruner of trees or vines.

podadura [po-dah-doo'-rah], *f. (Prov.)* V. PODA.

podagra [po-dah'-grah], *f.* Gout in the feet.

podar [po-dar'], *va.* To prune trees; to head, to lop (mondar).

podazón [po-dah-thone'], *f.* The pruning season.

podenco [po-den'-co], *m.* Hound.

podenquillo [po-den-keel'-lyo], *m. dim.* A young or small bound.

poder [po-derr'], *m.* 1. Power (fuerza), faculty, authority (autoridad), dominion, command, influence, mastery, force. 2. Military strength of a state. 3. Power or letter of attorney. 4. Power, possession (posesión). 5. Power, ability, force, vigor, capacity, possibility. **A poder de,** by force. **Poder esmerado** or **supremo,** supreme power. **El dinero es poder,** money is power. **Tiene poder para arruinarnos,** he has the power to ruin us. **Poder ejecutivo,** executive power.

poder [po-derr'], *va.* 1. To be able, may or can, to possess the power of doing anything (capacidad). 2. To be invested with authority or power. 3. To have force or energy to act or resist. 4. In geometry, to value, to produce. **A más no poder,** able to resist no longer. **No poder más,** not to be able to do more; to be exhausted; not to help to do a thing. *-v. imp.* To be possible or contingent. *-vn.* 1. May (posibilidad). 2. Can (absoluto). 3. **Puede que vaya,** I may go. **Puede no venir,** he may not come. **Los que pueden,** those who can. 4. *(CAm. Mex.)* To annoy, to upset.

poderdante [po-der-dahn'-tay], *com.* The constituent, the person who authorizes another.

poderhabiente [po-der-ah-be-en'-tay], *m.* Attorney, one authorized or empowered to transact another's business.

poderío [po-day-ree'-o], *m.* 1. Power, authority (señorío), dominion, jurisdiction. 2. Wealth, riches.

poderosamente [po-day-ro'-sah-men-tay], *adv.* Powerfully, mightily.

poderoso, sa [po-day-ro'-so, sah], *a.* 1. Powerful, mighty, potent. 2. Rich, wealthy. 3. Eminent, excellent. 4. Powerful, efficacious. 5. Powerful, able, forcible.

podio [po'-de-o], *m.* A long pedestal on which several columns are supported.

podofilina [po-do-fe-lee'-nah], *f.* Podophyllin, a purgative principle obtained from the may-apple or podophyllum.

podologo, ga [po-do'-lo-go], *m & f.* Chiropodist.

podómetro [po-do'-may-tro], *m.* Pedometer, instrument for measuring a person's steps or the circumvolutions of a wheel.

podón [po-done'], *m.* Mattock, hoe, an instrument for pulling up weeds.

podre [po'-dray], *f.* Pus, corrupted blood.

podrecer [po-dray-therr'], *va. & vn.* V. PUDRIR. *-vr.* To be putrid, rotten, or corrupt.

podrecimiento [po-dray-the-me-en'-to], *m.* 1. Rottenness, putrefaction. 2. Pain, grief.

podredumbre [po-dray-doom'-bray], *f.* 1. Pus, putrid matter, corruption (corrupción). 2. Grief, internal pain (tristeza).

podredura [po-dray-doo'-rah], *f.* Putrefaction, corruption.

podrición [po-dre-the-on'], *f.* V. PODREDURA.

podridero [po-dre-day'-ro], *m.* V. PUDRIDERO.

podrido [po-dre'-do], *a.* 1. Rotten, bad; putrid (putrefacto). 2. *(Cono Sur)* Fed-up (harto).

podrimiento [po-dre-me-ayn'-to], *m.* V. PODRIMIENTO.

podrir [po-drer'], *va.* V. PUDRIR.

poema [po-ay'-mah], *m.* Poem, a metrical composition.

poesía [po-ay-see'-ah], *f.* 1. Poetry. **Poesías,** poetical works. 2. Poetical composition.

poeta [po-ay'-tah], *m.* A poet.

poetastro [po-ay-tahs'-tro], *m.* Poetaster.

poética [po-ay'-te-cah], *f.* Poetry; poetics, the art or practice of writing poems.

poéticamente [po-ay'-te-cah-men-tay], *adv.* Poetically.

poético, ca [po-ay'-te-co, cah], *a.* Poetic, poetical.
poetilla [po-ay-teel'-lyah], *m. dim.* Poetaster.
poetisa [po-ay-tee'-sah], *f.* Poetess, a female poet.
poetizar [po-ay-te-thar'], *vn.* To poetize, to write like a poet.
poetón [po-ay-tone'], *m.* Poetaster, a vile poet.
pogrom [po-grom'], *m.* Pogrom, organized massacre of helpless people.
poíno [po-ee'-no], *m.* A wooden frame, on which barrels of wine or beer are laid.
polaca [po-lah'-cah], *f.* Polonaise, a Polish song and dance.
polaco, ca [po-lah'-co, cah], *a.* Polish, relating to Poland. *-m.* The Polish language. *-m. & f.* A native of Poland.
polacra [po-lah'-crah], *f.* *(Naut.)* Polacre, a vessel with three pole-masts, used in the Mediterranean.
polaina [po-lah'-e-nah], *f.* Legging gaiter, puttee. *-pl.* Spats.
polar [po-lar'], *a.* Polar.
polaridad [po-lah-re-dahd'], *f.* Polarity.
polarización [po-lah-re-thah-the-on'], *f.* Polarization, a modification of light by refraction or by reflection at 35°.
polarizar [po-lah-re-thar'], *va.* To polarize.
polca [pol'-cah], *f.* 1. Polka, a well known dance originally from Poland. 2. *(And.)* Blouse; *(And. Cono Sur)* Long jacket.
polcar [pol-car'], *vn.* To dance the polka.
polea [po-lay'-ah], *f.* 1. Pulley. 2. *(Naut.)* Tackle-block, or the double block of a tackle.
poleadas [po-lay-ah'-das], *f. pl.* V. GACHAS or PUCHAS.
poleame [po-lay-ah'-may], *m.* Collection of masts for vessels.
poleita [po-lay-ee'-tah], *f.* *(Naut.)* A small block.
polémica [po-lay'-me-cah], *f.* 1. Polemics, dogmatical divinity. 2. *(Mil.)* The science of fortification. 3. Literary or political controversy.
polémico, ca [po-lay'-me-co, cah], *a.* Polemical, polemic.
polemizar [po-lay-me-thar'], *vn.* To indulge a polemic. **No quiero polemizar**, I don't want to get involved in an argument.
polemonio [po-lay-moh'-ne-o], *m.* *(Bot.)* Jacob's-ladder, Greek valerian.
polemoscopio [po-lay-mos-co'-pe-o], *m.* *(Opt.)* Polemoscope, telescope used by military commanders.
polen [po'-len], *m.* *(Bot.)* Pollen.
polenta [po-len'-ah], *f.* Porridge, a kind of batter or hasty pudding.
polco [po-lay'-o], *m.* 1. *(Bot.)* Penny royal. 2. A strutting gait; a pompous style. 3. Stiff, cold wind.
poleví [po-lay-vee'], *m.* A high wooden heel formerly worn by women.
poliandria [po-le-ahn-dre'-ah], *f.* *(Bot.)* Polyandria.
poliantea [po-le-an-tay'-ah], *f.* Polyanthea, a literary collection.
poliantes tuberosa [po-le-ahn'-tes too-bay-ro'-sah], *f.* *(Bot.)* Common tuberose.
poliarquía [po-le-ar-kee'-ah], *f.* Polygarchy, government of many persons.
poliárquico, ca [po-le-ar'-ke-ko, cah], *a.* Relating to polygarchy.
policán, or **pelicán** [pay-le-cahn'], *m.* Pelican, instrument for drawing teeth.
policarpo [po-le-car'-po], *a.* *(Bot.)* Polycarpous.
pólice [pos'-le-thay], *m.* The thumb.
policía [po-le-thee'-ah], *f.* 1. Police, a branch of the executive government of a country, which watches over the preservation of public order (organización). 2. Politeness, good-breeding (cortesía). 3. Cleanliness, neatness (limpieza). **Policía de barrio**, neighborhood police. **Policía militar**, military police.
policíaco, ca [po-le-thee'-ah-co, cah], *a.* Police, relative to the police. **Novela policíaca**, detective novel, mystery story. **Vigilancia policíaca**, police watch.
policial [po-le-the-ahl'], *a.* Police. *-m.* *(CAm.)* Policeman.
policromo, ma [po-le-cro'-mo, mah], *a.* Polychrome vari-colored.
polideportivo [po-le-day-por-te'-vo], *m.* Sports center.
poliéster [po-le-ays'-tayr], *m.* Polyester.

polietileno [po-le-ay-te-lay'-no], *m.* Polyethylene.
polifacético [po-le-fah-thay'-te-co], *a.* Many-sided, versatile.
polifónico, ca [po-le-fo'-ne-co, cah], *a.* Polyphonic.
polífono, na [po-lee'-fo-no, nah], *a.* V. POLIFÓNICO.
polígala [po-lee'-gah-lah], *f.* *(Bot.)* Milkwort. **Polígala vulgar**, common milkwort.
poligamia [po-le-gah'-me-ah], *f.* 1. Polygamy. 2. *(Bot.)* Polygamia, the name of a class in the Linnaean system.
polígamo, ma [po-lee'-gah-mo, mah], *m. & f.* 1. Polygamist. 2. One who has several wives or husbands.
poligarquía [po-le-gahr'-ke-ah], *f.* V. POLIARQUÍA.
políglota [po-lee'-glo-tah], *f.* A polyglot, or a Bible in many languages.
polígloto, ta [po-le'-glo-to, tah], *a.* Polyglot, written in various languages. *-m. & f.* One who knows many languages.
polígono [po-lee'-go-no], *m.* 1. Polygon, a multilateral figure. 2. *(Bot.)* Polygon, a small evergreen plant, a species of germander. 3. Face of a fortification for instructing pupils how to attack a place. 4. Practical school of artillery. 5. *(Esp.)* Site (solar), building lot, area (zona); housing estate (viviendas).
polígono, na [po-lee'-go-no, nah], *a.* Polygonal, multangular.
poligrafía [po-le-grah-fee'-ah], *f.* Polygraphy, the art of writing in ciphers.
polihedro [po-le-ay'-dro], *m.* *(Geom.)* Polyhedron.
polilla [po-leel'-lyah], *f.* 1. Moth, clothes-moth. 2. Consumer, waster.
polimatía [po-le-mah-tee'-ah], *f.* Polymathy, the knowledge of many arts and sciences.
polimerización [po-le-may-re-tha-the-on'], *f.* Polymerization.
polímero [po-lee'-may-ro], *m.* Polymer.
polimorfismo [po-le-mor-fees' mo], *m.* Polymorphism.
polimorfo, fa [po-le-mor'-fo, fah], *a.* Polymorphous, of several forms.
polín [po-leen'], *m.* *(Naut.)* Wooden roller, for moving great guns or any other heavy object.
polinización [po-le-ne-thah-the-on'], *f.* Pollination.
polinomio [po-le-no'-me-o], *m.* *(Math.)* Polynomial, an expression of more than two terms.
poliomielitis [po-le-o-me-ay-lee'-tis], *f.* Infantile paralysis, poliomyelitis, polio.
polipétalo, la [po-le-pay'-tah-lo, lah], *a.* Polypetalous.
poliorima [po-le-o-rah'-mah], *m.* Polyorama, an apparatus presenting a view of many objects.
pólipo [po'-le-po], *m.* 1. Polypus, a genus of zoophytes. 2. Polypus, a fleshy or gelatinous tumor. 3. V. PULPO.
poliscopio [po-les-co'-pe-o], *m.* *(Opt.)* Polyscope.
polisílabo, ba [po-le-see'-lah-bo, bah], *a.* Polysyllabic, polysyllabical.
polisílabo [po-le-see'-lah-bo], *m.* Polysyllable.
polisón [po-le-sone'], *m.* Bustle, pad formerly worn beneath a woman's skirt.
polispermático, ca [po-lis-per-mah'-te-co, cah], or **polispermo, ma**, *a.* *(Bot.)* Polyspemous, many seeded.
politécnico, ca [po-le-tek'-ne-co, cah], *a.* Polytechnico, embracing many arts.
politeísmo [po-le-tay-ees'-mo], *m.* Polytheism.
politeísta [po-le-tay-ees'-tah], *com. & a* Polytheist.
política [po lee' te-cah], *f.* 1. Policy, politics; the art or science of government. 2. Politeness, civility. **Mezclarse en la política**, to go in for politics. **Política económica**, economic policy.
políticamente [po-lee'-te-cah-men-tay], *adv.* Politically, civilly.
politicastro [po-le-te-cahs'-troh], *m.* Politicaster: used in contempt.
político, ca [po-lee'-te-co, cah], *a.* 1. Political, politic (diplomático). 2. Polite, courteous (cortés). 3. In-law (pariente). **Padre político**, father-in-law.
político [po-lee'-te-co], *m.* Politician.
politiquear [po-le-te-kay-ar'], *vn.* To affect the politician.

politizar

politizar [po-le-te-thar'], *va.* To politicize.

poliuretano [po-le-oo-ray-tah'-no], *m.* Polyurethane.

póliza [po'-le-thah], *f.* 1. Check, draft, an order for the payment of money. 2. **Póliza de seguro**, policy of insurance. 3. A permit of the custom-house. 4. Entrance-ticket for some ceremony. 5. Tax stamp (impuesto). 6. Insurance certificate (de seguro).

polizón [po-le-thone'], *m.* 1. Bum, tramp (vago) 2. Stowaway.

polla [pol'-lyah], *f.* 1. Pullet, young hen, chicken. 2. *(coll.)* A comely young lass. 3. Money staked in games at carafe by all the players; pool. 4. *(Cono Sur)* Lottery. 5. *(Esp.)* Prick (pene).

pollada [po-lyah'-dah], *f.* Flock of young fowls; hatch, covey.

pollagallina [pol-lyah-gal-lyee'-nah], *f.* Hen-chicken.

pollastro, ra [po-lyahs'-tro, trah], *m. & f.* A large chicken. 1. *(coll.)* A cunning fellow: a knowing person. 2. A fine stout lad.

pollazón [pol-lyah-thone'], *m.* Hatching and rearing fowls; hatch.

pollera [po-lyay'-rah], *f.* 1. A narrow-mouthed basket or net (cesto), in which pullets are kept; a hen-coop (criadero). 2. A go-cart, in which children learn to walk. 3. A short, trooped petticoat.

pollería [pol-lyay-ree'-ah], *f.* Shop or market where poultry is sold.

pollero [pol-lyay'-ro], *m.* 1. One who keeps or rears fowls. 2. Place or yard where fowls are kept. 3. One who keeps or feeds fowls for sale; a poulterer. 4. *(LAm.)* Gambler.

pollico, ica, illo, illa, ito, ita [pol-lyee'-co], *n.* A small chicken.

pollina [pol-lyee'-nah], *f.* Young she-ass.

pollino [pol-lyee'-no], *m.* 1. Properly, a young, untamed ass, but now applied to any ass or jument. 2. *(Met.)* Ass, a stupid fellow.

pollito, ta [pol-lyee'-to, tah], *m. & f.* Chickens: applied to boys and girls of tender age.

pollo [pol'-lyo], *m.* 1. Chicken just hatched, nestling. 2. Young bee. 3. *(coll.)* Artful, clever man. 4. A bird which has not yet changed its feathers.

polluelo, la [pol-loo-ay'-lo, lah], *m. & f. dim.* A small chicken.

polo [po'-lo], *m.* 1. Pole, the extremity of the axis of the earth. 2. Pole of the magnetic needle. 3. Support, foundation. 4. Personal service of forty days in the year by the natives of the Philippine Islands. 5. Pole; focus, centre. **Polo de atracción**, focus of interest. **Polo negativo**, negative pole.

polo [po'-lo], *m.* Polo, polo game.

polonés, sa [po-lo-nays', sah], *a.* Polish. *V.* POLACO

polonesa [po-lo-nay'-sah], *f.* 1. Polonaise. *V.* POLACA. 2. A fur-trimmed jacket, girded at the waist.

poltrón, na [pol-trone', nah], *a.* 1. Idle, lazy, lubberly. 2. Commodious, easy. **Silla poltrona**, elbow-chair.

poltrón [pol-trone'], *m. (coll.)* Poltroon.

poltronería [pol-tro-nay-ree'-ah], *f.* Idleness, laziness, indolence, sluggishness.

poltronizarse [pol-tro-ne-thar'-say], *vr.* To become lazy.

polución [po-loo-the-on'], *f.* 1. Pollution, stain; bodily deformity. 2. A voluntary or involuntary emission of semen.

poluto, ta [po-loo'-to, tah], *a.* Polluted, contuminated, defiled; unclean, filthy.

polvareda [pol-vah-ray'-dah], *f.* 1. Cloud of dust (polvo). 2. Altercation, dispute, debate.

polvera [pol-vay'-rah], *f.* Compact, vanity case.

polvificar [pol-ve-fe-car'], *va. (coll.)* To pulverize, to reduce to powder or dust.

polvillo, ito [pol-veel'-lyo], *m. dim.* 1. Fine dust. 2. *(And. Cono Sur. Agr.)* Blight. 3. *(And. Cono Sur)* Tobacco refuse.

polvo [pol'-vo], *m.* 1. Dust, earth reduced to dust. 2. Powder, dust, the state of solid bodies comminuted. 3. Powder for the hair: in the two last senses it is commonly used in the plural. 4. A pinch (porción), so much as can be taken between the ends of the fingers. **Polvo de patata** or **patata en polvo**, a confectioned potato. **Sacudir el polvo**, to bent out the dust with a stick: to whip severely. **Quitar el polvo de un mueble**, to dust a piece of furniture. **Hacer algo polvo**, to smash something. **Ponerse polvos**, to powder one's face.

polvo de hornear [pol'-vo day or-nay-ar'], *m.* Baking powder.

polvo de talco [pol'-vo day tahl'-co], *m.* Talcum powder.

pólvora [pol'-vo-rah], *f.* 1. Powder, gunpowder. 2. Artificial fireworks (fuegos artificiales). 3. Provocation, cause of anger (mal genio). 4. Vivacity (viveza), liveliness, briskness. 5. Powder, dust. **Es una pólvora**, he is as hot as pepper. **Mojar la pólvora**, to appease, to allay the rage of an angry person. **Propagarse como la pólvora**, to spread like wildfire.

polvorear [pol-vo-ray-ar'], *va.* To powder, to sprinkle as with dust.

polvoriento, ta [pol-vo-re-en'-to, tah], *a.* Dusty, full of dust; covered with dust.

polvorín [pol-vo-reen'], *m.* 1. Powder reduced to the finest dust. 2. Powder-flask, priming-horn. 3. Powder-magazine. 4. *(Cono Sur)* Gnat (insecto). 5. *(And. Carib.)* Cloud of dust (polvareda).

polvorista [pol-vo-rees'-tah], *m.* 1. Manufacturer of gunpowder. 2 Maker of fire-works.

polvorizable [pol-vo-re-thah'-blay], *a.* Pulverizable.

polvorización [pol-vo-re-thah-the-on'], *f.* Pulverization.

polvorizar [pol-vo-re-thar'], *va.* 1. To pulverize. 2. *V.* POLVOREAR.

polvorón [pol-vo-rone'], *m. (LAm. Culin.)* Cake.

polvoroso, sa [pol-vo-ro'-so, sah], *a.* Dusty, covered with dust.

poma [po'-mah], *f.* 1. Apple. *V.* MANZANA. 2. Perfume-box, a bottle containing perfumes (frasco). 3. Metallic vessel with different perfumes, having small apertures to admit their escape when set on a fire to perfume rooms.

pomada [po-mah'-dah], *f.* 1. Ointment (medicina). 2. Pomatum, pomade (cosmético). **Pomada para los labios**, lip-salve. 2. **Hacer algo pomada**, *(Cono Sur)* to break something to bits.

pomar [po-mar'], *m.* Orchard, a garden of fruit-trees, particularly of apple-trees.

pomelo [po-may'-lo], *m. (Esp.)* Grapefruit.

pómez [po'-meth], *f.* Pumice-stone.

pomífero, ra [po-mee'-fay-ro, rah], *a. (Poet.)* Pomiferous, having apples.

pomo [po'-mo], *m.* 1. Fruit in general, but in particular the fruit of the apple-tree. 2. Glass bull in the shape of an apple, used to hold perfumes (frasco). 3. Pommel of sword (espada). 4. *(Prov.)* Nosegay, a bunch of flowers. 5. A glass bottle.

pomología [po-mo-lo-hee'-ah], *f.* Pomology, science and practice of fruit-growing.

pompa [pom'-pah], *f.* 1. Pomp, ostentation in feasts or funerals, pageantry. 2. Pomp, splendor, parade, grandeur. 3. Pomp, a procession of splendor and ostentation. 4. Bubble. 5. Fold in clothes raised by the wind. 6. The expanded tail of a turkey or peacock. 7. *(Naut.)* Pump. *V.* BOMBA.

pompas fúnebres [pom'-pahs foo'-nay-brays], *f. pl.* Funeral, burial, funeral services.

pompearse, pompeonearse [pom-pay-ar'-say], *vr.* To appear with pomp and ostentation.

pompeyano, na [pom-pay-yah'-no, nah], *a.* Pompeian, of Pompeii.

pomposamente [pom-po'-sah-men-tay], *adv.* Pompously, magnificently, loftily, flourishingly.

pomposo, sa [pon-po'-so, sah], *a.* Pompous, ostentatious, magnificent, splendid, majestic, inflated, swelled.

pómulo [po'-moo-lo], *m.* Prominence of the cheek-bone (hueso); cheek (mejilla).

ponchada [pon-chah'-dah], *f.* The quantity of punch made at one time.

ponche [pon'-chay], *m.* Punch, a liquor.

ponchera [pon-chay'-rah], *f.* 1. Punch bowl (para ponche). 2. *(And. Carib. Mex.)* Washbasin (palangana); *(And.)* Bath (bañera). 3. *(Cono Sur)* Paunch (barriga).

poncho [pon'-cho], *m.* Poncho (manta), man's jacket; blanket (frazada).

poncho, cha [pon'-cho, chah], *a.* Lazy (vago), indolent, heedless.

ponchón, na [pon-chone´, nah], *a.* Extremely careless, excessively lazy.

ponderable [pon-day-rah'-blay], *a.* 1. Ponderable, capable of being weighed; measurable by scales. 2. Wonderful, important.

ponderación [pon-day-rah-the-on´], *f.* 1. Weighing mentally, pondering or considering. 2. Exaggeration, heightening.

ponderado, ta [pon-day-rah'-do, dah], *a. & pp.* of PONDERAR. 1. Presumptuous, arrogant, insolent. 2. Exaggerated.

ponderador, ra [pon-day-rah-dor', rah], *m. & f.* 1. Ponderer; he who exaggerates. 2. One who weighs or examines.

ponderal [pon-day-rahl'], *a.* Ponderal, relating to weight.

ponderar [pon-day-rar'], *va.* 1. To weigh (estadística). 2. To ponder, to consider, to attend (considerar). 3. To exaggerate, to heighten; to cry up. **Ponderar algo a uno**, to speak warmly of something to somebody.

ponderativo, va [pon-day-ray-tee´-vo, vah], *a.* Exaggerating, hyperbolical.

ponderosamente [pon-day-ro-sah-men-tay], *adv.* Attentively, carefully: with great attention.

ponderosidad [pon-day-ro-se-dahd'], *f.* Ponderousness, ponderosity, weightiness. *V.* PESADEZ.

ponderoso, sa [pon-day-ro´-so, sah], *a.* 1. Heavy, ponderous, weighty. 2. Grave, circumspect, cautious.

ponedero, ra [po-nay-day´-ro, rah], *a.* 1. Laying eggs. 2. Capable of being laid or placed.

ponedero [po-nay-day'-ro], *m.* 1. Nest, hen's nest. 2. Nest-egg.

ponedor, ra [po-nay-dor', rah], *m. & f.* 1. One who puts, sets, or places. 2. Better, wagerer; outbidder. 3. In paper-mills, the maker who delivers the sheet to the coucher. *-a.* Applied to horses trained to rear on their hind legs, and to fowls laying eggs.

ponencia [po-nen'-the-ah], *f.* Charge, post, or office of a chairman of a committee, or of a final judge or arbiter: and the exercise of such office.

ponente [po-nen´-tay], *a.* Who has the casting vote: arbitrator, final judge: said of a judge or the chairman of a committee.

ponentino, na, ponentisco, ca [po-nen-tee'-no, nah], *a.* Occidental, western, belonging to the west.

poner [po-nerr'], *va.* 1. To put, to place (colocar), to set, to lay a thing in a place. 2. To establish and determine distances. 3. To dispose, to arrange (escaparate). 4. To suppose (suponer), to believe. 5. To impose (impuesto, multa), to enjoin. 6. To oblige, to compel. 7. To wager, to bet, to stake (en el juego). 8. To appoint, to invest with office. 9. To bring an example or comparison in confirmation. 10. To leave, to permit without interposition. **Yo lo pongo en Vd.**, I leave it to you. 11. To write, to set down what another dictates. 12. To lay eggs; to bring forth. 13. To employ; to apply one to some employment or office (en colocación). **Poner toda su fuerza**, to act with all one's might. 14. To labor for an end. 15. To add (añadir), to join. 16. To contribute, to bear apart. 17. To enforce; to adduce, to concert, to agree. 18. To treat one badly. 19. To cause (emoción, miedo). 20. To give (nombre). To switch on, to turn on, to put on (radio). **Poner algo a secar al sol**, to put something to dry in the sun. **Ponlo más fuerte**, turn it up. **Al niño le pusieron Luis**, they called the child Louis. **Pongamos 120**, let´s say 120. **La has puesto colorada**, now you´ve made her blush. *-vr.* 1. To apply oneself to, to set about. 2. To object, to oppose. 3. To undergo a change; to become. **Ponerse pálido**, to grow pale. 4. To set: applied to the luminous heavenly bodies. 5. To arrive in a short time at a determined place (lugar). 6. To dress, to deck out, or adorn oneself. 7. Joined with *de, por, cual, como*, to treat as the words express; sometimes in the true sense, sometimes ironically. E. g. **Poner por escrito**,

to put in writing. **Al poner del sol**, at sunset. **Poner al sol**, to expose to the sun, to sun. **Poner a asar**, to spit, to roast. **Eso no quita ni pone**, that neither adds nor diminishes. **Poner en duda**, to question, to doubt. **Poner nombre**, to rate or appraise goods. **Ponerse bien**, to get on in the world; to obtain full information of an affair. **Ponerse colorado**, to flush, to blush. **¿Quién se pone a ello?** who dares to do it? **Ponerse a bien con Dios**, to make one's peace with God. **Ponerse a razones**, to enter into a dispute. **Ponérsele a uno**, to take a whim, a fancy. **Ponerse en ocasión**, to expose oneself to danger. **Ponerse los zapatos, el sombrero**, to put on one's shoes, one's hat. **Ponerse moreno**, to become sunburned. **Póngase Vd. en la razón**, be moderate in your demands. **Ponerse a escribir**, to set about, or devote oneself, to writing. **Poner en relieve**, to carve in relief, to describe graphically. **Nada se pone por delante**, nothing stops him, to inflict public punishment. **Poner como a un Cristo a alguno**, to flog a person severely. **Poner de vuelta y media**, to humiliate a person, by word or action. **Poner delante**, to remind, to suggest. **Poner coto**, to stop an abuse; to put a bound. **Se puso serio**, he became serious. **Se pusieron a gritar**, they started to shout. **Poner una escucha telefónica**, to tap. **Poner una trampa**, to trap. **Poner en funcionamiento**, entry into service. (*Yo pongo, yo puse, pusiera; ponga.* V. PONER.)

pongo [pon´-go], *m.* (*Peru, Ec.*) A narrow and dangerous pass of a river. (*Peru and Bol.*) An Indian servant. (*Zool.*) A kind of anthropomorphous ape.

poni [po'-ne], *m.* Pony.

poniente [po-ne-en´-tay], *m.* 1. The west (oeste). 2. (*Naut.*) West wind (viento).

ponleví [pon-lay-vee'], *m.* High wooden heel, formerly worn by women.

pontazgo, pontaje [pon-tath'-go, pon-tah'-hay], *m.* Bridge-toll, portage.

pontear [pon-tay-ar'], *va.* To erect bridges.

pontezuelo, la [pon-tay-thoo-ay'-lo, lah], *m. & f. dim.* Small bridge.

pontificado [pon-te-fe-cah´-do], *m.* Pontificate, the govermnent of the Pope; papacy, popedom.

pontifical [pon-te-fe-cahl'], *a.* Pontifical, papal, belonging to the Pope, or to an arch-bishop or bishop.

pontifical [pon-te-fe-cahl'], *m.* 1. A pontifical robe worn by bishops when they officiate at the mass. 2. Pontifical, a book containing the rites and ceromonies of the Roman Catholic church. 3. Parochial tithes.

pontificalmente [pon-te-fe-cahl'-men-tay], *adv.* Pontifically.

pontificar [pon-te-fe-car'], *vn.* 1. To govern as high pontiff. 2. To celebrate the solemn mass pontifically.

pontifice [pon-tee'-fe-thay], *m.* 1. Pope, pontiff. 2. Archbishop or bishop of a diocese.

pontificio, cia [pon-te-fee'-the-o, ·ah], *a.* Pontifical.

pontil [pon-teel'], *m.* 1, Pontil or ponty, an iron rod for handling hot bottles in glass-making. 2. Glass over which emery is spread.

pontín [pon-teen'], *m.* A vessel for coasting trade in the Philippines.

ponto [pon'-to], *m.* 1. (*Nat.*) Starting-pole. 2. (*Poet.*) The sea.

pontón [pon-tone'], *m.* 1. Ponton or pontoon (de puente), a floating bridge to cross a river. 2. Hulk, an old ship serving as store-ship, hospital, or prison-ship. 3. (*Naut.*) Mud-scow, a kind of flat-bottomed boat, furnished with pulleys, tackles, etc., to clean harbors. 4. Timber above nineteen feet long. 5. A log bridge.

pony [po'-ne], *m.* Pony.

ponzoña [pon-tho'-nyah], *f.* 1. Poison, venom, toxine. 2. Anything infectious or malignant.

ponzoñosamente [pon-tho-nyo'-sah-men-tay], *adv.* Poisonously.

ponzoñoso, sa [pon-tho-nyo'-so, sah], *a.* 1. Poisonous, venomous, toxic. 2. Prejudicial to sound morals.

popa [po'-pah], *f. (Naut.)* Poop, stern. **Navío de popa llana,** *(Naut.)* A square sterned vessel. **Velas de popa,** *(Naut.)* aftersails. **De popa a proa,** *(Naut.)* from stem to stern. **A popa, en popa, de popa,** *(Naut.)* aft, abaft. **Viento en popa** *(Naut.),* before the wind. *(Met.)* Prosperity.

popamiento [po-pah-me-en'-to], *m.* Act of despising or cajoling.

popar [po-par'], *vn.* 1. To depreciate, to contemn. 2. To cajole, to flatter, to fawn; to caress, to soothe, to wheedle.

popero [po-pay'-ro], *m.* Helmsman, steersman.

popeses [po-pay'-ses], *m. pl. (Naut.)* Stays of the mizzenmast: aftermost, sternmost.

poplíteo, tea [po-plee'-tay-o, ah], *a.* Popliteal, belonging to the space behind the knees.

popote [po-po'-tay], *m.* A kind of Indian straw, of which brooms are made.

populacho [po-poo-lah'-cho], *m.* Populace, mob, rabble, crowd.

populación [po-poo-lah-the-on'], *f.* Population. *V.* POBLACIÓN.

popular [po-poo-lar'], *a.* 1. Popular, relating to the people (del pueblo). 2. Popular, pleasing to the people (ampliamente aceptado). 3. Popular. 4. Vulgar, current. *m. & f.* Plebeian.

popularidad [po-poo-lah-re-dahd'], *f.* Popularity.

popularizar [po-poo-lah-re-thar'], *va.* To popularize, to make popular. *-vr.* To become popular.

popularmente [po-poo-lahr-men-tay], *adv.* Popularly.

populazo [po-poo-lah'-tho], *m.* Populace, mob, rabble.

populeón [po-poo-lay-on'], *m.* White popular ointment.

populoso, sa [po-poo-lo'-so-sah], *a.* Populous, numerous, full of people.

popurrí [po-poor-ree'], *m.* Potpourri.

poquedad [po-kay-dahd'], *f.* 1. Parvity, paucity, littleness. 2. Cowardice, pusillanimity. 3. Trifle, thing of no value. **Poquedad de ánimo,** imbecility. 4. Mite, very small portion of a thing (poca cantidad).

póquer [po'-kayr], *m.* Poker.

poquillo, lla [po-keel'-lyo, lyah], *a. dim.* 1. Small, little. 2. Trifling.

poquillo [po-keel'-lo], *adv. dim.* Very little time.

poquísimo, ma [po-kee'-se-mo, mah], *a. sup.* Very little, excessively small.

poquitico, ica, illo, illa, ito, ita [po-ke-tee'-co], *a. dim.* Almost nothing.

poquito, ta [po-kee'-to, tah], *a.* 1. *(dim.)* Very little. 2. Weak of body and mind, diminutive. **Poquita cosa,** a trifling thing. **A poquitos,** in minute portions. **De poquito,** pusillanimous. **poquito a poco,** gently.

por [por], *prep.* 1. For, on account of. **Por** refers to the source or to the reason or motive for an action. **Por miedo de las consecuencias,** for fear of consequences. 2. By, through: indicating in passive expressions the agent by whom an action is performed. **Esta carta fue escrita por el general al rey,** this letter was written *by* the general to the king. 3. Indicates multiplication or unit of number or measure. **Seis por ocho,** six (multiplied) by eight. **Por docenas,** by the dozen. **Diez por ciento,** ten per cent. 4. For the sake of, in behalf of, in favor of. **Hablo por el señor A.,** I speak for Mr. A. **¡Una limosna por Dios!** an alms for God's sake! *(Cf.* PORDIOSERO.) 5. After the verbs, *to go, to send,* and the like, it shows the immediate object of the errand. **Ir por leña,** to go for fire-wood. **Por ahí,** about that, a little more or less. **Por tanto** or **por ende,** for so much, for that. 6. Through (a través de), between; to. **¿Por qué calle vino Vd?** through what street did you come? 7. As, by, on account of. **Recibir por esposo,** to take as a husband. 8. By means of, indicating the future action of the verb. **Está por venir, por ver, por saber,** that is to come, to be seen, to be known. 9. Indicates exchange or offset of a thing against another. **Quiere vender su casa por $80,000,** he wants to sell his house for $80,000. **Ojo por ojo, y diente por diente,** an eye for an eye and a tooth for a tooth. 10. It is sometimes redundant, as,

Fernando está por alcalde, Ferdinand is Mayor. **Uno vale por muchos,** one is worth many. **La casa está por acabar,** the house is not yet finished. **Por ahora,** for the present. **Por San Juan,** about Saint John's or midsummer. **Por bien o por mal,** well or ill. **Por encima,** slightly, superficially; over, upon. **Por acá o por allá,** here or there. **Por más que** or **por mucho que,** however much; in vain. **Por si acaso,** if by chance. **Sin qué ni por qué** or **sin qué ni para qué,** without rhyme or reason. **¡Sí, por cierto!** yes, indeed. **De por sí,** by itself. **El niño corría por toda la casa,** the child ran all over the house. **Por más que Vd. diga,** you may say what you will, it is in vain. **Por cuanto,** whereas. **Por lo tanto,** therefore. **Por supuesto,** of course. **Hablar por hablar,** to talk just for talking's sake. **Fue por necesidad,** it was from necessity. **Por lo que dicen,** from what they say. **Por centenares,** by the hundred. **Llevar periódicos por las casas,** to deliver papers round the houses. **Por la mañana,** in the morning. **Hablo por todos,** I speak on behalf of everybody. **Por difícil que sea,** however hard it is.

porca [por'-cah], *f.* A ridge of land between two furrows.

porcal [por-cahl'], *a.* Applied to a kind of large plumes.

porcaso [por-cah'-so], *m.* The hogtapir.

porcelana [por-thay-lah'-nah], *f.* 1. Porcelain, chinaware (loza). 2. Enamel, used by goldsmiths and jewellers. 3. Porcelain-color, a mixture of white and blue. 4. Kind of wide china cup.

porcentaje [por-then-tah'-hay], *m.* Percentage; proportion, ratio; rate. **Un elevado porcentaje de,** a high percentage of.

porchada [por-chah'-dah], *f.* Paper holder (stretcher) in paper-factories.

porche [por'-chay], *m.* 1. Porch (de casa), portico. 2. Arcade (de tiendas).

porcino [pr-thee'-no], *m.* 1. A young pig (lechón). **Pan porcino,** *(Bot.)* sow-bread *V.* ARTANITA. 2. Bruise, a swelling caused by a blow on the head.

porcino, na [por-thee'-no, nah], *a.* Hoggish, porcine.

porción [por-the-on'], *f.* 1. Part, portion. 2. Lot, parcel of goods. 3. Pittance, daily allowance of food. **Una porción de,** a number of.

porcionero, ra [por-the-o-nay'-ro, rah], *a.* Apportioning; participant.

porcionista [por-the-o-nees'-tah], *com.* 1. Holder of a share or portion. 2. Boarder in a college, or one who pays for his portion and assistance in a college.

porcipelo [por-the-pay'-lo], *m. (coll.)* Bristle.

porco [por'-co], *m. (Prov.) V.* PUERCO.

porcuno, na [por-coo'-no, nah], *a.* Hoggish.

pordiosear [por-de-o-say-ar'], *va.* To beg, to ask charity.

pordiosería [por-de-o-say-ree'-ah], *f.* Beggary, asking charity.

pordiosero, ra [por-de-o-say'-ro, rah], *m. & f.* Beggar.

porfía [por-fee'-ah], *f.* 1. An obstinate dispute or quarrel (disputa). 2. Obstinacy (terquedad), stubbornness; conceitedness. 3. Repetition; importunity. **A porfía,** in an obstinate manner.

porfiadamente [por-fe-ah-dah-men-tay], *adv.* Obstinately, pertinaciously, contentiously.

porfiado, da [por-fe-ah'-do, dah], *a.* Obstinate (terco), stubborn, opinionated, conceited. *-pp.* of PORFIAR.

porfiador, ra [por-fe-ah-dor', rah], *m. & f.* Contender, wrangler, brawler, pleader.

porfiar [por-fe-ar'], *va.* 1. To contend. 2. To wrangle. 3. To importune by repetition. 4. To persist in a pursuit (persistir).

porfídico, ca [por-fee'-de-co, cah], *a.* Porphyritic, containing porphyry, or like it.

pórfido, pórfiro [por'-fe-do, por'-fe-ro], *m.* Porphyry, jasper.

porisma [po-rees'-mah], *f. (Geom.)* Porism.

pormenor [por-may-nor'], *m.* Detail, minute account.

porno [por'-no], *a.* Porno, pornographic.

pornografía [por-no-grah-fee'-ah], *f.* Pornography, obscenity.

pornográfico, ca [por-no-grah'-fe-co, cah], *a.* Pornographic, obscene.

poro [po'-ro], *m.* 1. Pore, as of the skin. 2. Pore, interstice.

porongo [po-ron'-go], *m. (Peru and Bol.)* An earthenware jug or pitcher.

pororoca [po-ro-ro'-cah], *f.* Brazilian name for the extraordinary collision of the waters of the river Amazons with the ocean at the great equinoctial tides.

porosidad [po-ro-se-dahd'], *f.* 1. Porosity. 2. That which is exhaled through the pores.

poroso, sa [po-ro'-so, sah], *a.* Porous.

porque [por'-kay], *com.* 1. Because, for the reason that, on this or that account. 2. Why, for which or what reason: relatively.

por qué [por-kay'], *conj.* Why? for what reason? interrogatively.

porqué [por-kay'], *m. (coll.)* 1. Cause, reason (motivo), motive. 2. Allowance, pittance, pension. **El porqué de la revolución**, the factors that underlie the revolution.

porquecilla [por-kay-thel-lyah], *f. dim.* A small sow.

porquera [por-kay'-rah], *f.* Lair, the conch of a wild boar.

porquería [por-kay-ree'-ah], *f.* 1. Nastiness, uncleanliness, filth (sustancia). 2. Hoggishness, brutishness, rudeness (cualidad). 3. Trifle thing of little value (objeto). 4. A dirty, ungenteel action. 5. Nuisance, dirty trick (acto). 6. Rubbish (basura). **Porquerías,** *(coll.)* small dishes made of the entrails of swine. **Estar hecho una porquería**, to be covered in muck. **La novela es una porquería**, the novel is just rubbish.

porqueriza [por-kay-ree'-thah], *f.* Hogsty.

porquerizo, porquero [por-kay-ree'-tho], *m.* Swineherd.

porquerón [por-kay-rone'], *m.* Catchpoll, bumbailiff.

porqueta [porkay'-tah], *f. V.* CUCARACHA.

porquezuela [por-kay-thoo-ay'-lah], *f. dim.* 1. A small sow. 2. A slut or dirty woman.

porquezuelo [por-kay-thoo-ay'-lo], *m. dim.* 1. A young pig. 2. A nasty, dirty man.

porra [por'-rah], *f.* 1. Stick with a large head or thick knob at the end (palo); club. 2. The last player in certain games. 3. *(coll.)* Vanity, boast, presumption. 4. *(coll.)* A stupid, heavy, ignorant person. 5. *(And. Cono Sur)* Curl (mechón). 6. *(CAm. Mex.)* Political gang (pandilla). 7. *(Mex.) (Dep.)* Fans. 8. *(CAm.)* Metal cooking pot (olla). **Mandar a uno a la porra**, to chuck somebody out. **¡Vete a la porra!**, go to blazes!

porráceo, cea [por-rah'-thay-o, ah], *a.* Of a dark or leek-green color.

porrada [por-rah'-dah], *f.* 1. Blow with a club-headed stick. 2. *(coll.)* Foolishness, nonsense.

porrazo [por-rah'-tho], *m.* Blow with any instrument, or that occasioned by a fall.

porrear [por-ray-ar'], *vn. (coll.)* To persist importunely, to dwell long upon.

porrería [por-ray-ree'-ah], *f. (coll.)* Obstinacy, stupidity (necedad), folly, silliness, tediousness.

porreta [por-ray'-tah], *f.* The green leaf of leeks, garlic, or onions. **En porreta,***(coll.)* stark naked.

porrilla [por-reel'-lyah], *f.* 1. A small hammer used by smiths. 2. *(dim.)* A small club-headed stick. 3. *(Vet.)* Osseous tumor in horses' joints.

porrillo (A) [por-reel'-lyo], *adv. (coll.)* Copiously, abundantly.

porrina [por-ree'-nah], *f.* State of crops when small and green.

porrino [por-ree'-no], *m.* The tender plant of a leek.

porrizo [por-ree'-tho], *m.* Bed or plot of leeks.

porro, rra [por'-ro, rah], *a.* 1. *(coll.)* Dull, stupid, ignorant. 2. *(Esp.)* Joint. 3. *(And. Carib.)* Folk dance.

porrón [por-rone'], *m.* 1. An earthen pitcher for water. 2. A kind of flask. **Un porrón de**, a lot of.

porrón, na [por-rone', nah], *a.* Heavy, sluggish (torpe); slow (lerdo).

porrudo [por-roo'-do], *m. (Prov.)* Shepherd's crook.

porta [por'-tah], *f.* 1. Door, gate. 2. *(Naut.)* Gun-port, embrasure of a battery. **Portas de las miras de proa,** *(Naut.)*

head chaseports. **Portas de guardatimón**, *(Naut.)* stern-ports.

portaaguja [por-tah-ah-goo'-hah], *f.* A surgical needle-holder.

portaanimálcules [por-tah-ah-ne-mahl'-coo-los], *m.* Live box, animalcule cage. (Microscopy.)

portaaviones [por-tah-ah-ve-o'-nees], *m.* Aircraft carrier.

portabandera [por-tah-ban-day'-rah], *f.* Pocket in the girdle which supports the staff of the colors.

portacaja [por-tah-cah'-hah], *f.* The carrier of a silk loom.

portacarabina [por-tah-ca-rah-bee'-nah], *f.* Leather bag in which the muzzle of a horseman's carabine rests.

portacartas [por-tah-car'-tas], *m.* Mailbag for letters.

portada [por-tah'-dah], *f.* 1. Portal, porch (pórtico). 2. Frontispiece, the principal front of a building; façade (fachada). 3. Title-page of a book. 4. Division of a certain number of threads to form the warp.

portadera [por-tah-day'-rah], *f.* A chest in which provisions are carried on a horse or mule: commonly used in the plural.

portador, ra [por-tah-dor', rah], *m. & f.* 1. Bearer, carrier, porter. 2. Tray or board on which bread or meat is carried. **Páguese al portador**, pay the bearer.

portaestandarte [por-tah-es-tan-dar'-tay], *m. (Mil.)* Standard-bearer cornet.

portafolio [por-tah-fo'-le-o], *m.* Briefcase.

portafusil [por-tah-foo-seel'], *m. (Mil.)* Sling of a musket.

portaguión [por-tah-gee-on'], *m.* Standard-bearer of cavalry.

portaje [por-tah'-hay], *m. V.* PORTAZGO.

portal [por-tahl'], *m.* 1. Porch (pórtico), entry, entrance. 2. Portico, piazza. 3. *(Prov.)* Gate of a town (de ciudad).

portalazo [por-tah-lah'-tho], *m. aug.* A large door or porch.

portalejo [por-tah-lay'-ho], *m. dim.* Little porch or portico.

portaleña [por-tah-lay'-nyah], *f.* 1. Embrasure, for cannon. *V.* CAÑONERA. 2. Planks of which doors are made.

portalero [por-tah-lay'-ro], *m.* An officer who has the charge of preventing smuggling, receiving the duties, etc., at the gates of a town.

portalico, illo, ito [por-tah-lee'-co], *m dim.* A small vestibule or porch.

portalón [por-tah-loone'], *m. (Naut.)* Gangway.

portamanteo [por-tah-man-tay'-o], *m.* Portmanteau, cloak-bag.

portamonedas [por tah-mo-nay'-das], *m.* A small purse, porte-monnaie.

portanario [por-tah-nah'-re-o], *m. (Anat.)* Pylorus.

portante [por-tahn'-tay], *m.* Quick pace of a horse.

portantillo [por-tan-teel'-lyo], *m. dim.* A gentle amble, an easy pace.

portanuevas [por-tah-noo-ay'-vas], *com* Newsmonger.

portañola [por-tah-nyo'-lah], *f. (Naut.)* Port-hole. **Portañolas de la luz de los camarotes,** *(Naut.)* light-ports. **Portañolas de los remos,** *(Naut.)* row-ports.

portañuela [por-tah-nyoo-ay'-lah], *f.* 1. Lining of the fall of breeches. 2. Fly of pantalón (de pantalón).

portaobjetos [por-tah-ob-hay'-tos], *m.* Object-holder of a microscope, stage; glass slip.

portaollas [por-tah-ol'-lyas], *m.* Pot-holder.

portapaz [por-tah-path'], *com.* The plate on which the pax or image is presented to be kissed by the pious at mass.

portaparaguas [por-tah-pah-rah'-goo-as], *m.* Umbrella-stand.

portaplacas, portaplanchas [por-tah-plahn'-chas], *m.* Dark slide, photographic plate-holder.

portar [por-tar'], *va.* To carry, to bring. -*vr.* 1. To behave (conducirse), to comport, to act. 2. To show up well (distinguirse). 3. *(LAm.)* To behave well. **Se ha portado como un cochino**, he has behaved like a pig.

porta-rollo [por-tah-rohl'-lyo], *m.* A photographic roll-holder.

portaronzal [por-tah-ron-thahl'], *m.* A strap fixed at the left holster to which the halter is fastened.

portátil [por-tah'-teel], *a.* Portable, easily carried.

portaventanero

portaventanero [por-tah-ven-tah-nay'-ro], *m*. Carpenter who makes windows and doors.

portaviento [por-tah-ve-en'-to], *m*. Airblast of a furnace.

portavoz [por-tah-voth´], *m*. 1. Loudspeaker, megaphone (altoparlante). 2. Spokesman (persona), mouthpiece.

portaz [por-tath], *m*. *(Zool.)* The nylghau.

portazgo [por-tath'-go], *m*. Toll, turn-pike-duty.

portazguero [por-tah-gay'-ro], *m*. Toll-gatherer, collector.

portazo [por-tah'-tho], *m*. 1. A loud slam with a door. 2. Act of slamming door in one's face. **Dar un portazo**, to slam the door.

porte [por'-tay], *m*. 1. Cost of carriage (gasto); freight, portage, porterage: postage (Correos). 2. Deportment, demeanor, conduct (conducta). 3. Nobility: illustrious descent. 4. Size or capacity of a thing. 5. *(Naut.)* Burden or tonnage of a ship. **Porte franco**, frank, free of postage. **Navío de mil toneladas de porte**, a ship of one thousand tons burden.

porteador, ra [por-tay-ah-dor', rah], *a*. Carrying, transporting.

portear [por-tay-ar'], *va*. To carry or convey for a price. *-vr*. To pass from one place to another.

portento [por-ten'-to], *m*. Prodigy, wonder; portent.

portentosamente [por-ten-to'-sah-men-tay], *adv*. Prodigiously.

portentoso, sa [por-ten-to'-so, sah], *a*. Prodigious, marvelous, portentous.

porteo [por-tay'-o], *m*. Transportation, portage. **Gastos de porteo**, transportation or portage costs.

portería [por-tay-ree´-ah], *f*. 1. The principal door of a large building: a porter's lodge (conserjería). 2. Employment or office of a porter. 3. *(Naut.)* All the ports in a ship.

portero, ra [por-tay'-ro, rah], *m. & f.* Porter (conserje), gate-keeper. **Portero automático**, answering device.

portezuela [por-tay-thoo-ay'-lah], *f*. 1. *(dim.)* A little door. 2. Flap, pocket-flap. 3. *(Mex.)* A pass between hills.

pórtico [por'-te-co], *m*. Portico (portal), piazza; porch; hall: lobby.

portillo [por-teel´-lyo], *m*. 1. Aperture in a wall. 2. Opening, passage, gap (abertura), breach (brecha). 3. Wicket (postigo), gate, a small door in another larger. 4. Means to an end. 5. Cavity in anything broken. 6. Small gate of a town, through which nothing is allowed to pass that is liable to pay duty.

portón [por-tone´], *m*. The inner or second door of a house.

portorriqueño, ña [or-tor-re-kay'-nyo, nya], *a*. Puerto Rican. *V.* PUERTORRIQUEÑO.

portuario, ria [por-too-ah'-re-o, ah], *a*. Relative to a seaport. **Ciudad portuaria**, seaport city.

portugués [por-too-ghes´], *m*. The Portuguese language.

portugués, sa [por-too-ghes´, sah], *a*. Portuguese. **A la Portuguesa**, in the Portuguese fashion.

portuláceas [por-too-lah´-thay-as], *a. & f. pl.* Of the purslane or portulaca family; portulacas.

porvenir [por-vay-neer´], *m*. Future, time to come. **En el porvenir**, in the future. **Un hombre sin porvenir**, a man with no future.

pos (En) [pos], *adv*. After, behind; in pursuit of.

posa [po´-sah], *f*. 1. Passing bell; the ringing of bells for persons deceased. 2. Stops made by the clergy who conduct a funeral, to sing a response. 3. *pl.* *(coll.)* Breech, seat; buttocks.

posada [po-sah´-dah], *f*. 1. Home, dwelling-house. 2. Longing or lodging house (hospedaje). **Posada con asistencia**, board and lodging, inn, tavern, hotel. 3. Pocket-case, containing a knife, spoon, and fork. 4. *(CAm. Mex.)* Typical party held at Christmas.

posadera [po-sah-day'-rah], *f*. Hostess,

posaderas [po-sah-day´-ras], *f. pl.* Buttocks. *V.* ASENTADERAS.

posadería [po-sah-day-ree'-ah], *f*. Inn, tavern, lodging-house.

posadero [po-sah-day'-ro], *m*. 1. Inn-keeper, the keeper of a lodging or boarding-house, or tavern. 2. Seat made of flags or bass-ropes. 3. Breech, seat, buttocks.

posado, da [po-sah'-do, dah], *a. & pp.* of POSAR. Lodged, rested, lined, reclined, landed (avión).

posante [po-sahn'-tay], *pa*. Reposing: used at sea for smooth sailing.

posar [po-sar'], *vn*. 1. To lodge, to board. 2. To sit down, to repose, to rest. 3. To perch, to light or sit upon. *-va*. To lay down a burden (carga). *-vr*. 1. To alight (ave, insecto). 2. To settle (líquido). 3. To land (avión). **El avión se encontraba posado**, the aircraft was on the ground.

posca [pos´-cah], *f*. Mixture of vinegar and water, formerly given by way of refreshment.

posdata [pos-dah'-tah], *f*. Postscript.

pose [po'-say], *m*. A kind of hook for fishing upon sandbanks. *-f*. 1. Pose. 2. Attitude (actitud). 3. Composure (aplomo). 4. Pose (afectación); affectedness; affected posture (postura afectada).

poseedor, ra [po-say-ay-dor', rah], *m. & f.* Possessor, holder, owner.

poseer [po-say-err'], *va*. 1. To hold, to possess, to have, to own (ventaja). 2. To be master of a language or other thing.

poseído, da [po-say-ee'-do, dah], *a. & pp.* of POSEER. 1. Possessed. 2. Applied to one who executes desperate actions (enloquecido).

poseído [po-say-ee'-do], *m.* *(Prov.)* Arable land belonging to a private person, as distinguished from commons.

posesión [po-say-se-on'], *f.* 1. Possession, the act of possessing, dominion. 2. Possession, the thing possessed. 3. Possession by evil spirits. 4. *(Met.)* Reputation, good or bad. *-pl.* Lands, real estates (propiedades). **Las cartas están en posesión de su padre**, the letters are in the possession of his father.

posesional [po-say-se-o-nahl'], *a.* Including or relating to possession.

posesionarse [po-say-se-o-nar'-say], *vr.* To take possession of.

posesionero [po-say-se-o-nay'-ro], *m.* Cattle-keeper who has acquired possession of pasturace.

posesivo, va [po-say-see'-vo, vah], *a.* *(Gram.)* Possessive, denoting possession.

poseso, sa [po-say´-so, sah], *a. & pp. irr.* of POSEER. Possessed; possessed by evil spirits.

posesor, ra [po-say-sor, rah], *m. & f.* V. POSEEDOR.

posesorio, ria [po-say´-re-o, ah], *a.* Possessory.

poseyente [po-say-yen´-tay], *pa.* Possessing, possessive.

posfecha [pos-fay'-chah], *f.* Post-date.

posfechar [pos-fay-char'], *va:* To post-date.

posibilidad [po-si-be-le-dahd'], *f.* 1. Possibility, the state or condition of being possible. 2. Possibility, the state of being possible: feasibility; likelihood. 3. Wealth, riches. **No existe posibilidad alguna de que venga,** there is no possibility of his coming. **Estar en la posibilidad de,** to be in a position to.

posibilitar [po-se-be-le-tar'], *va.* To render possible, to facilitate.

posible [po-see'-blay], *a.* Possible. **Posibles,** wealth, income, capital, means. **Serviré a Vd. con mis posibles,** I will serve you with all my might. **¿Es posible?** is it possible? **Lo antes posible,** as soon as possible. **Hacer posible una cosa,** to make something possible.

posiblemente [po-se'-blay-men-tay], *adv.* Possibly.

posición [po-se-the-on´], *f.* 1. Position, the art of placing. 2. Position, posture, situation. 3. Question and answers of an interrogatory. 4. Position, rule in arithmetic. 5. *(LAm.)* Position, post, job (puesto).

posicionar [po-se-the-o-nar'], *va.* To position. *-vr.* to adopt an attitude.

positivamente [po-se-te-vah-men-tay], *adv.* Positively, absolutely, certainly, by all means.

positividad [po-se-te-ve-dahd'], *f.* State of positive electricity.

positivismo [po-se-te-vees´-mo], *m.* 1. Positiveness, holding to what is positive. 2. Positivism, a system of philosophy receiving only proved facts, rejecting a priori notions. 3. Agnosticism, chiefly in England. 4. Utilitarianism.

positivo, va [po-se-tee´-vo, vah], *a.* 1. Positive, sure, certain, indubitable, true. 2. Positive: applied to laws settled by arbitrary appointment. 3. Positive, absolute, real. 4. *(Gram.)* Positive, a degree of comparison. **De positivo,** certainly, without doubt.

pósito [po´-se-to], *m.* A public granary (granero). **Pósito pío,** granary which lends grain to widows or poor laborers without charging interest.

positón, positrón [po-se-tone´, po-se-trone´], *m.* Positron.

positura [po-se-too´-rah], *f.* 1. Posture, state, disposition. 2. *V.* POSTURA.

posma [pos´-mah], *f. (coll.)* Sluggishness, sloth, dulness. *-com.* A dull, sluggish, dronish person. Also *a.*

poso [po´-so], *m.* 1. Sediment, dregs, lees, feculence. 2. Rest, repose.

posoperativo [pos-o-pay-rah-to-re-o], *a.* Post-operative.

posparto [pos-pahr-to], *m. V.* POSTPARTO.

pospelo (A) [pos-pay´-lo], *adv.* Against the grain; reluctantly.

pospierna [pos-pe-err´-nah], *f.* The thigh of an animal.

posponer [pos-po-ner´], *va.* 1. To place one thing after another. 2. To postpone, to put off, to delay (aplazar). 3. To postpone, to set in value below something else.

pospuesto, ta [pos-poo-es´-to, tah], *pp. irr.* of POSPONER.

posta [pos´-tah], *f.* 1. Post-horses. 2. Post-house, post-office; post stage, where post-horses are stationed. 3. Post, distance from one relay or, post-house to another. 4. Chop of meat or fish. 5. Slug of lead, mould-shot. 6. Night-sentry. 7. Stake in cards. *-m.* Person who travels post. **Correr la posta, or ir en posta,** to post or travel post. **A posta,** designedly, on purpose.

postal [pos-tahl´], *a.* Postal. **Giro postal,** money order. **Paquete postal,** parcel post. **Tarjeta postal,** postal card. *-f.* Postcard.

postdata [pos-dah-tah], *f. V.* POSDATA.

poste [pos´-tay], *m.* 1. Post-pillar (columna). 2. Kind of punishment. **Poste indicador,** signpost. **Poste de llegada,** winning post.

postelero [pos-tay-lay´-ro], *m. (Naut.)* Skid or skeed, knee of the quarterdeck of a ship.

postema [pos-tay´-mah], *f.* 1. An abscess tumor. 2. Dull, troublesome person (pelmazo).

postemero [post-tay-may´-ro], *m.* Large lancet.

póster [pos´-tayr], *m.* Poster.

postergación [pos-ter-gah-the-on´], *f.* Act of leaving behind.

postergar [pos-ter-gar´], *va.* To leave behind.

posteridad [pos-tay-re-dahd´], *f.* Posterity.

posterior [pos-tay-re-or´], *a.* 1. Posterior, following. 2. Later (en orden). 3. Later, subsequent (tiempo). **Ser posterior a,** to be later than.

posterioridad [pos-tay-re-o-re-dahd´], *f.* Posteriority.

posteriormente [pos-tay-re-or´-men-tay], *adv.* Lastly, afterward, hereafter.

posteta [pos-tay´-tah], *f. (Print.)* Number of printed sheets stitched together; a quantity of sheets for packing books.

postgraduado [pos-grah-doo-ah´-do], *a.* Postgraduate. *-m & f.* Postgraduate.

postigo [pos tee´-go], *m.* 1. Wicket (puerta pequeña), small door. 2. Sally-port, postern (portillo). 3. A door of one leaf. 4. Any of the divisions of a door or widow. 5. *V.* PORTILLO for a small gate of a town.

postiguillo [pos-te-geel´-lyo], *m. dim.* A small wicket or back-door.

postila [pos-tee´-lyah], *f.* Postil, marginal notes.

postilación [pos-te-lah-the-on´], *f.* Act of making marginal notes.

postilador [pos-te-lah-dor´], *m.* Annotator, postiler.

postilar [pos-te-lar´], *va.* To write marginal notes upon, to gloss, to comment.

postilla [pos-teel´-lyah], *f.* Scab or crust on wounds.

postillón [pos-teel-lyone´], *m.* 1. Postilion driver. 2. Hack.

postilloso, sa [pos-teel-lyo´-so, sah], *a.* Scabby, pustulous.

postín [pos-teen´], *m.* 1. Elegance (lujo); tone (entono). 2. Side (fachenca), swank.

postitis [pos-tee´-tis], *f.* Posthitis, inflammation of the prepuce.

postiza [pos-tee´-thah], *f.* 1. *(Naut.)* Dead work on galleys for guiding the oar. 2. *V.* CASTAÑUELA.

postizo, za [pos-tee´-tho, thah], *a.* Artificial, not natural; false (dientes); dummy (exterior). **Dientes postizos,** false teeth. **Pelo postizo,** false hair.

postizo [pos-tee´-tho], *m.* With wigmakers, hair to supply the front or back of the head.

postliminio [post-le-mee´-ne-o], *m.* Postliminy, among the Romans, reinstatement of one taken by the enemy to his possessions.

postmeridiano, na [post-may-re-de-ah´-no, nah], *a.* Postmeridian, afternoon.

postor [pos-tor´], *m.* Bidder at a public sale; bettor.

postparto [post-par´-to], *m.* The latest young of animals in the season: applied chiefly to ewes.

postración [pos-trah-the-on´], *f.* 1. Prostration, kneeling. 2. Prostration, dejection, depression.

postrado, da [pos-trah´-do, dah], *a. & pp.* of POSTRAR. Prostrate, prostrated.

postrador, ra [pos-trah-dor´, rah], *m. & f.* 1. One who prostrates himself. 2. Foot-stool in the choir, on which the chorister kneels.

postrar [pos-trar´], *va.* 1. To prostrate, to humble (humillar). 2. To debilitate (debilitar), to exhaust. *-vr.* 1. To prostrate oneself, to kneel to the ground. 2. To be extremely debilitated.

postre [pos´-tray], *a.* Last in order. *V.* POSTRERO.

postre [pos´-tray], *m.* Dessert, the last course at table. **¿Qué hay de postre?,** what is there for dessert?

postremo, ma [pos-tray´-mo, mah], *a. V.* POSTRERO and ÚLTIMO.

postrer [pos-trayr´], *a. V.* POSTRERO. (Used before a noun.)

postreramente [pos-tray-rah-men-tay], *adv.* Ultimately, lastly.

postrero, ra [pos-tray´-ro, rah], *a.* Last in order, hindermost.

postrero [pos-tray´-ro], *m. V.* TRASERO.

postrimeramente [pos-tre-may´-rah-men-tay], *adv.* Finally, at last.

postrimería [pos-tre-may-ree´-ah], *f.* 1. Death. *V.* NOVÍSIMO. 2. The last years of life.

postrimero, ra [pos-tre-may´-ro, rah], *a. V.* POSTRERO and TRASERO.

póstula [pos´-too-lah], *f.* Solicitation, petition.

postulación [pos-too-lah-the-on´], *f.* 1. Postulation (proposición); petition. 2. Nomination for prelate of some church, made by the chapter, of a person who requires dispensation.

postulado [pos-too-lah´-do], *m.* Postulate, position assumed without proof; axiom.

postulador [pos-too-lah-dor´], *m.* 1. Member of a chapter who votes for an unqualified prelate. 2. One who solicits the canonization of a saint.

postulanta [pos-too-lahn´-tah], *f.* Postulant, female candidate for admission to a religious order.

postulante [pos-too-lahn´-tay], *m. f.* Aspirant to a position.

postular [pos-too-lar´], *va.* 1. To seek for (pedir), to solicit, to postulate (proponer). 2. To elect a prelate laboring under a canonical impediment. 3. *(CAm. Mex.)* To nominate (candidato).

póstumo, ma [pos´-too-mo, mah], *a.* Posthumous.

postura [pos-too´-rah], *f.* 1. Posture, position, situation. 2. Posture, collocation of the parts of the body with respect to each other (del cuerpo). 3. Act of planting trees or plants; the tree or plant transplanted. 4. Assize of provisions. 5. Bid (en subasta), price fixed by a bidder or buy-out. 6. Bet, wager. 7. Paint which women put on their faces. 8. Egg of a fowl or bird, and the act of laying it (acto). 9. Agreement, contract.

potable

potable [po-tah'-blay], *a.* 1. Potable, drinkable. 2. Good enough (aceptable).

potador [po-tah-dor'], *m.* He who examines and marks weights and measures.

potaje [po-tah'-hay], *m.* 1. Pottage, boiled food. 2. Vegetables dressed for food in days of abstinence. 3. Drink made of several ingredients. 4. Medley of useless things.

potajería [po-tah-hay-ree'-ah], *f.* 1. Heap of dry pulse. 2. Place where dry pulse or vegetables are preserved for use.

potala [po-tah'-lah], *f.* 1. Stone which serves to moor boats. 2. A small, slow-going vessel.

potanza [po-tahn'-thah], *f.* Cook, in clockwork; a bearing for the pallets.

potar [po-tar'], *va.* To equalize and mark weights and measures.

potasa [po-tah'-sah], *f.* Potash.

potásico [po-tah'-se-co], *a.* 1. *(Chem.)* Potassio, relating to potassium in its higher valence. **Yodo potásico,** potassio or potassium iodide.

potasio [po-tah'-se-o], *m.* Potassium, a metallic element lighter than water, upon which it burns with a violet flame.

pote [po'-tay], *m.* 1. A jug for keeping liquids (jarra). 2. Pot, jar (tarro); flower-pot. 3. Standard measure or weight. 4. Pout, sulky look (puchero).

potecillo, ito [po-tay-theel'-lyo], *m. dim.* A little pot or jar.

potencia [po-ten'-the-ah], *f.* 1. Power, the faculty of performing. 2. Power, authority, dominion. 3. Power, ability, potency. 4. Possibility. 5. Power of generation; productive virtue. 6. Power, kingdom, state. 7. *(Math.)* Power, product of a quantity multiplied by itself. 8. A tool for ironing the brim of a hat. *(Cf.* «potence» in heraldry.)-*pl.* The nine rays of light which encircle the head of the infant Jesus, designed to express his universal power over everything created. **Potencias beligerantes,** belligerent powers. **Potencias del alma,** the memory, understanding, and will. **Potencia muscular,** muscular power. **Las grandes potencias,** the great powers. **Es una guerra civil en potencia,** it is a civil war in the making.

potencial [po-ten-the-ahl'], *a.* 1. Potential, possessing a power. 2. Potential, having the effect, without the external properties. 3. *(Gram.)* Potential mode.

potencialidad [po-ten-the-ah-le-dahd'], *f.* Potentiality, equivalence.

potencialmente [po-ten-the-ahl'-men-tay], *adv.* Potentially: equivalently.

potenciar [po-ten-the-ahr'], *va.* To favor (promover); to develop (desarrollar); to strengthen (fortalecer).

potentado [po-ten-tah'-do], *m.* Potentate, sovereign, monarch.

potente [po-ten'-tay], *a.* 1. Potent, powerful (poderoso), mighty. 2. Potent, strong, vigorous. 3. *(coll.)* Great, bulky.

potentemente [po-ten'-tay-men-tay], *adv.* Powerfully, potently.

potentísimo, ma [po-ten-tee'-se-mo], *a. sup.* Most powerful.

potenza [po-ten'-thah], *f.* A potent cross (heráldica).

poteo [po-tay'-o], *m.* Drinks, drinking.

poterna [po-terr'-nah], *f. (Mil.)* Postern, sally-port.

potestad [po-tes-tahd'], *f.* 1. Pointer, dominion, command, jurisdiction. V. POTENTADO. 2. *(Arith.)* Power, the product of multiplying a number by itself. **Patria potestad,** paternal authority.

potestativo, va [po-tes-tah-tee'-vo, vah], *a. (For.)* That which is in the faculty or power of anyone: facultative.

potista [po-tees'-tah], *com. (Vul.)* Tippler, drunkard.

potito [po-tee'-to], *m.* 1. Small jar. 2. *(LAm.)* Backside.

potra [po'-trah], *f.* 1. *(coll.)* (a) Rupture, scrotal hernia; (b) suerte). 2. Fily. V. POTRO.

potrada [po-trah'-dah], *f.* Troop of young mares at pasture.

potranca [po-trahn'-cah], *f.* Filly, young mare (no más de tres años).

potrear [po-tray-ar'], *va.* 1. *(coll.)* To vex, to molest, to annoy. 2. *(And. CAm.)* To beat. 3. *(Carib. Mex.)* To break, to tame (caballo).

potrera [po-tray'-rah], *a.* Applied to a hempen head-stall for horses.

potrero [po-tray'-ro], *m.* 1. Surgeon who cures ruptures. 2. Herder, herdsman of colts. 3. Pasture ground. 4. *(Amer.)* A farm for rearing horses. 5. *(Cono Sur)* Playground (parque). 6. *(Mex.)* Open grassland (llanura).

potrico, illo [po-tree'-co], *m. dim.* 1. A small colt. 2. *(Cono Sur)* Tall glass (vaso). 3. *(And.)* Small canoe (canoa).

potril [po-treel'], *m. & a.* Pasture for young horses.

potrilla [po-treel'-lyah], *f.* Nickname given to old persons affecting rakish youth.

potro, tra [po'-tro, trah], *m. & f.* 1. Colt, foal, a young horse up to the time when it changes its milk teeth, or about four and a half years of age. -*m.* 2. A wooden horse; rack (de tormento), a kind of torture. 3. A wooden frame for shoeing unruly horses (de herrar). 4. Anything which molests or torments. 5. An earthen chamber-pot. 6. Bubo, a venereal tumor. 7. Pit in the ground in which beekeepers divide a beehive into two portions, giving a queen-bee to each. 8. A kind of stand where they card wool a second time. **Potro de madera,** vaulting horse.

potroso, sa [po-tro'-so], *a.* 1. Afflicted with a rupture. 2. *(coll.)* Fortunate, lucky.

poyal [po-yahl'], *m.* 1. A sort of striped stuff with which benches are covered. 2. V. POYO.

poyata [po-yah'-tah], *f.* Shelf, cupboard.

poyatilla [po-yah-teel'-lyah], *f. dim.* A little shelf.

poyato [po-yah'-to], *m.* Terrace, in landscape gardening.

poyo [po'-yo], *m.* 1. Bench, a seat made of stone and mortar against a wall. 2. Fee given to judges.

poza [po'-thah], *f.* 1. Puddle. 2. *(Agr.)* A pool for macerating hemp. 3. Hole made in children's bread, and filled with must or honey.

pozal [po-thahl'], *m.* 1. Bucket, pail. 2. Coping of a well. 3. Vessel sunk in the earth to catch any fluid.

pozanco [po-thahn'-co], *m.* Pond of stagnant water.

pozero [po-thay'-ro], *m.* Well-digger.

pozo [po'-tho], *m.* 1. Well (de agua). 2. A deep hole in a river; a whirlpool. 3. Anything complete in its line. **Es un pozo de ciencia,** he is deeply learned. **Pozo de petróleo,** oil well. **Pozo de ventilación,** ventilation shaft.

pozol, pozole [po-thohl'], *m.* Boiled barley and beans. (Aztec.)

pozuela [po-thoo-ay'-lah], *f. dim.* A small puddle or pond.

pozuelo [po-thoo-ay'-lo], *m.* 1. *(dim.)* A small well or pit. 2. Vessel sunk in the ground to collect oil, etc., in mills.

práctica [prahc'-te-cah], *f.* 1. Practice, constant habit. 2. Practice, customary use; exercise. 3. Practice, manner, mode, method (método). 4. Practice of any profession. 5. The act of learning a profession under a master. **En la práctica,** in practice. **Prácticas profesionales,** professional training. **Aprender con la práctica,** to learn by practice.

practicable [prac-te-cah'-blay], *a.* Practicable, feasible.

practicador, ra [prac-te-cah-dor', rah], *m. & f.* Practicer, practitioner.

prácticamente [prahc'-te-cah-men-tay], *adv.* Practically. **Está prácticamente terminado,** it´s practically finished.

practicante [prac-te-cahn'-tay], *m.* Practitioner in surgery and medicine under a master. -*pa.* Practising.

practicar [prac-te-car'], *va.* 1. To practise (habilidad, virtud), to perform (ejecutar), to do, to put in execution. 2 To practice, to do habitually. 3. To learn the practice of a profession under a master. **Practicar el francés con su profesor,** to practice one´s French with one´s teacher.

práctico, ca [prahc'-te-co, cah], *a.* 1. Practical (estudio, formación). 2. Skillful, experienced, expert (persona). 3. Practical; handy (herramienta); convenient (casa). -*m.* A skilful pilot.

practicón, na [prac-te-cone', nah], *m. & f.* One of great practical knowledge and experience.

pradal [prah-dahl´], *m.* Extent of country abounding in meadows and pasture-lands.

pradecillo [prah-day-theel´-lyo], *m.* A small meadow

pradeño, ña [prah-day'-nyo, nyah], *a.* Relating to meadows or fields.

pradera, pradería [prah-day'-rah, prah-day-ree'-ah], *f.* 1. Country abounding in meadows and pasture-grounds (prado). 2. Mead, meadow, rich pasture-ground.

praderoso, sa [prah-day-ro´-so, sah], *a.* Relating to meadows.

pradico, illo [prah-dee'-co], *m. dim.* A small meadow.

prado [prah'-do], *m.* 1. Lawn, field, meadow; a piece of pasture-ground. 2. Prado, a public walk in Madrid. **Prado de guadaña**, meadow mowed annually.

pragmática [prag-mah'-te-cah], *f.* 1. Royal ordinance. 2. Rescript of a sovereign to an application made to him in a particular case.

pragmático, ca [prag-mah'-te-co, cah], *a.* Pragmatic, pragmatical. *-m.* Commentator upon national laws.

prasio [prah'-se-o], *m.* Prase, quartz of a leek-green color, usually cryptocrystalline.

prasma [prahs'-mah], *m.* Dark green agate.

prática [prha'-te-cah], *f. V.* PRÁCTICA.

pravedad [prah-vay-dahd'], *f.* Perversity, iniquity, depravity.

pravo, va [prah'-vo, vah], *a.* Depraved, perverse, knavish, lewd.

praxis [prahk'-sis], *f.* Practice. *V.* PRÁCTICA

pre [pray], Daily pay allowed to soldiers.

pre, A preposition used in the composition of nouns and verbs, either to augment the signification or to mark priority of time and rank.

preadamita [pray-ah-dah-mee'-tah], *a. & n.* Preadamite, existing before Adam.

preámbulo [pray-ahm'-boo-lo], *m.* 1. Preamble (de libro, discurso), exordium, preface. 2 *(coll.)* Evasion, circumlocution. **Sin más preámbulos**, without further ado.

prebenda [pray-ben'-dah], *f.* 1. Prebend, the right of enjoying any temporal fruits by reason of employment office, etc. 2. Prebend, ecclesiastical benefice: commonly used to express a canonry. 3. Sinecure. 4. *(Acad.)* Portion, piously given to a woman, to enable her to marry or to become a nun; or to a student as a foundation scholarship. **Prebenda de oficio**, any of the four prebends, doctoral, magisterial, lectural, or penitentiary.

prebendado [pray-ben-dah'-do], *m.* Prebendary, a dignitary who enjoys a prebend in a cathedral or collegiate church. **Prebendado, da**, *pp.* of PREBENDAR.

prebendar [pray-ben-dar'], *va.* To confer an ecclesiastical benefice or prebend.

prebostal [pray-bos-tahl'], *a.* Provostal.

prebostazgo [pray-bos-tath'-go], *m.* Provostship.

preboste [pray-bos'-tay], *m.* 1. Provost, one who governs a college or community. 2. *(Mil.)* Provost marshal, the officer in charge of military police and thus responsible for military discipline.

precariamente [pre-cah'-re-ah-men-tay], *adv. (For.)* Precariously.

precariedad [pre-cah'-re-dahd], *f.* Precariousness.

precario, ria [pray-cah'-re-o, ah], *a.* 1. Precarious, held only as a loan, and at the will of the owner. 2. Precarious, uncertain (dudoso). 3. Unpredictable (impredecible). *-m.* Precarious state. **Dejar a uno en precario**, to leave somebody in a difficult situation.

precaución [pre-cah-oo-the-on'], *f.* Precaution, guard, vigilance. **Tomar precauciones**, to take precautions.

precaucionado, da [pray-cah-oo-the-o-nah'-do, dah], *a.* Sagacious, cautious, clear-sighted.

precaucionarse [pray-cah-oo-the-o-nar'-say], *vr.* To be cautious.

precautelar [pray-cah-oo-tay-lar'], *va.* To caution, to forewarn.

precaver [pray-cah-verr'], *va.* To prevent or obviate, to stave off (evitar); to forestall (anticipar). *-vr.* To guard against, to be on one's guard.

precavido, da [pray-cah-vee'-do, dah], *a.* Cautious, far-sighted, on one's guard. *-pp.* of PRECAVER.

precedencia [pray-thay-den'-the-ah], *f.* 1. Precedence, priority (prioridad). 2. Pre-eminence, preference. 3. Superiority (preeminencia), primacy.

precedente [pray-thay-den'-tay], *a.* Preceding (anterior), foregoing. *-m.* Precedent. **Sin precedente**, all-time; without exception.

preceder [pray-thay-der'], *va.* To precede (anteceder), to go before; to be superior in rank or order, to excel. **Le precedía un coche**, he was preceded by a car.

preceptista [pray-thep-tees´-tah], *m. & a.* Preceptist, theorist.

preceptivamente [pre-thep-tee'-vah-men-tay], *adv.* Preceptively.

preceptivo, va [pray-thep-tee'-vo, vah], *a.* Preceptive, mandatory, directory.

precepto [pray-thep'-to], *m.* Precept, order, injunction, mandate, rule.

preceptor, ra [pray-thep-tor'], *m & f.* Master, teacher, preceptor.

preces [pray'-thes], *f. pl.* 1. Prayers; public or private devotion. 2. Supplication for a bull or commission from the Vatican.

precesión [pray-thay-se-on'], *f.* 1. *V.* RETICENCIA. 2. *(Ast.)* Precession.

preciado, da [pray-the-ah'-do, dah], *a.* 1. Valued, appraised; esteemed (estimado). 2. Valuable, precious, excellent. 3. Proud, elated. presumptuous (presuntuoso). *-pp.* of PRECIAR.

preciador, ra [pray-the-ah-dor', rah], *m. & f.* Appraiser.

preciar [pray-the-ar'], *va.* To value, to appraise. *-vr.* To boast, to brag; to take pride in, to glory. **Preciarse de algo**, to pride oneself on something.

precinta [pray-theen'-tah], *f.* 1. Strap of wood, iron, tin, or leather, to secure the corners of boxes. 2. *(Naut.)* Parcelling, narrow pieces of tarred canvas, with which the seams of ships are covered, and which are also put around cables and ropes.

precintado [pre-thin-tah'-do], *a.* Sealed.

precintar [pray-thin-tar'], *va.* 1. To strap the corners of boxes with leather to prevent their opening. 2. To cross boxes of goods, as a mark that they are not to be opened.

precinto [pray-theen'-to], *m.* 1. The act of strapping. 2. A sealed strap with which trunks, parcels, etc., are bound lengthwise and crosswise, so that they may be opened only by the proper individuals.

precio [pray'-the-o], *m.* 1. Price, cost (costo), value (valor). 2. Price, reward; premium. 3. Price, value; estimation, esteem, consideration; character, credit. **Precio al contado**, cash price. **Precio de coste**, at cost price. **Precio neto**, net price. **Precio de venta**, sale price. **No tener precio**, to be priceless.

preciosamente [pre-the-o'-sah-men-tay], *adv.* Preciously, richly.

preciosidad [pray-the-o-oo-dahd´], *f.* Worth (valor), excellence, preciousness (excelencia), beautiful thing (objeto). **Es una preciosidad**, it´s lovely.

precioso, sa [pray-the-o'-so, sah], *a.* 1. Precious (excelente), valuable (valioso), excellent, 2. Pleasant, gay, merry.

precipicio [pray-the-pee'-the-o], *m.* 1. Precipice. 2. A sudden fall. 3. Ruin, destruction (ruina).

precipitación [pre-the-pe-tah-the-on'], *f.* 1. Precipitation, haste (prisa), precipitancy. 2. *(Chem.)* Precipitation, the fall of solid particles to the bottom of a liquid.

precipitadamente [pre-the-pe-tah'-dah-men-tay], *adv.* Precipitately, hastily, in a hurry.

precipitadero [pray-the-pe-tah-day'-ro], *m. V.* PRECIPICIO.

precipitado

precipitado, da [pray-the-pe-tah'-do, dah], *a. & pp.* of PRECIPITAR. Precipitate, hasty (partida), abrupt, sudden. *-m. (Chem.)* Precipitate.

precipitante [pray-the-pe-tahn'-tay], *m. (Chem.)* Precipitater.

precipitar [pray-the-pe-tar'], *va.* 1. To precipitate, to cast headlong. 2. To expose, to ruin. 3. To perform the chemical process of precipitation. *-vr.* To act in a precipitate manner (lanzarse); to run headlong to destruction; to haste, to hurry (correr). **Precipitarse a hacer algo,** to rush to do something. **Precipitarse sobre uno,** to rush at somebody.

precípite [pray-thee'-pe-tay], *a.* In danger, on the verge of falling.

precipitoso, sa [pray-the-pe-to'-so, sah], *a.* 1. Steep, slippery, precipitous (lugar). 2. Precipitous, rash, inconsiderate.

precipuo, pua [pray-thee'-poo-o, ah], *a.* Chief, principal.

precisamente [pray-the-sah-men'-tay], *adv.* 1. Precisely (con precisión), exactly, nicely. 2. Inevitably, indispensably, necessarily. 3. Just at the moment. **Precisamente por eso,** for that very reason. **Llegó precisamente cuando nos íbamos,** he arrived just as we were leaving.

precisar [pray-the-sar'], *va.* To compel, to oblige, to necessitate (necesitar), to determine exactly (determinar). **No precisa lavado,** it needs no washing. **Hay alguna rareza que no puedo precisar,** there is some oddity which I cannot pin down.

precisión [pray-the-se-on'], *f.* 1. Necessity (necesidad), obligation. 2. Compulsion, the state of being compelled. 3. Preciseness, exactness. 4. Precision (exactitud), exact limitation. **Tener precisión de hacer alguna cosa,** to be obliged or under the necessity of doing a certain thing. 5. *(Mex.)* Urgency.

precisivo, va [pray-the-see'-vo, vah], *a.* That which prescinds or abstracts, precisive.

preciso, sa [pray-thee'-so, sah], *a.* 1. Necessary (necesario), requisite, needful. 2. Precise (exacto), exact, punctual. 3. Distinct, clear. 4. Severed, cut off; abstracted. **Una descripción precisa,** a precise description. **Las cualidades precisas,** the essential qualities. 5. *(Carib.)* Conceited.

precitado, da [pray-the-tah'-do, dah], *a.* Forecited, quoted before.

precito, ta [pray-thee'-to, tah], *a.* Damned, condemned to hell.

preclaramente [pray-clah'-rah-men-tay], *adv.* Illustriously, distinctly.

preclaro, ra [pray-clah'-ro, rah], *a.* Illustrious, famous, eminent.

precocidad [pray-co-the-dahd'], *f.* Precocity, untimely ripeness of fruit, forwardness.

precocinado [pray-co-the-nah'-do], *a.* Precooked.

precocinar [pray-co-the-nahr'], *va.* To precook.

precognición [pray-cog-ne-the-on'], *f.* Precognition.

preconización [pray-co-ne-thah-the-on'], *f.* Preconization.

preconizador [pray-co-ne-thah-dor'], *m.* One who proclaims the elected prelates in the Roman consistory.

preconizar [prey-co-ne-thar'], *va.* To patronize, to proclaim, to publish in the Roman consistory, to praise (elogiar), to recommend (recomendar), to suggest (proponer).

preconocedor, ra [pray-co-no-thay-dor', rah], *m. & f.* One who foresees or anticipates a future event.

preconocer [pray-co-no-therr'], *va.* To foreknow, to foretell.

precordial [pray-cor-de-ahl'], *a.* Praecordial, relating to the diaphragm.

precoz [pray-coth'], *a.* Precocious, ripe before the usual time, forward.

precursor, ra [pray-coor-sor', rah], *a.* Preceding, going before. *-m.* Precursor, harbinger, forerunner, herald.

predecesor, ra [pray-day-thay-sor', rah], *m. & f.* Predecessor, antecessor, forerunner.

predecir [pray-day-theer'], *va.* To foretell, to anticipate, to predict. *(Yo predigo, prediga, predije, from Predecir. V. DECIR.)*

predefinición [pray-day-fe-ne-the-on'], *f.* Predetermination of the Divine Providence.

predefinir [pray-day-fe-ner'], *va.* To predetermine.

predestinación [pray-des-te-nah-the-on'], *f.* Predestination, preordination.

predestinado [pray-des-te-nah'-do], *m.* Foreordained to eternal glory.—**Predestinado, da,** *pp.* of PREDESTINAR.

predestinar [pray-des-te-nar'], *va.* To predestine, to destine beforehand, to foredoom, to predestinate.

predeterminación [pray-day-ter-me-nah-the-on'], *f.* Predetermination, foreordination.

predeterminar [pray-day-ter-me-nar'], *va.* To predetermine, to anticipate a resolution, to foredoom.

predial [pray-de-ahl'], *a.* Predial, consisting of or relating to landed property, or farms.

prédica [pray'-de-cah], *f.* Preachment, sermon, discourse by a non-Catholic preacher.

predicable [pray-de-cah'-blay], *a.* 1. Fit to be preached. 2. Commendable, praiseworthy. 3. Predicable.

predicable [pray-de-cah'-blay], *m.* Predicable, a logical term.

predicación [pray-de-cah-the-on'], *f..* Preaching, sermon.

predicadera [pray-de-cah-day'-rah], *f. (Prov.)* Pulpit. **Predicaderas,** *(coll.)* style of the pulpit, facility of preaching or praying.

predicado [pray-de-cah'-do], *m. (Log.)* Predicate.

predicador, ra [pray-de-cah-dor', rah], *m. & f.* Preacher, orator, homilist, eulogist.

predicamental [pray-de-cah-men-tahl'], *a.* Predicamental.

predicamento [pray-de-cah-men'-to], *m.* 1. Predicament, degree of estimation in which a person is held. 2. Category, class or kind described by any definitive marks.

predicante [pray-de-cahn'-tay], *m.* Sectarian or heretical preacher.

predicar [pray-de-car'], *va.* 1. To render clear and evident, to publish. 2. To preach. 3. To praise to excess. 4. To reprehend vice. *-vr.* To predicate, to comprise an affirmation.

predicatorio [pray-de-cah-to'-re-o], *m.* V. PÚLPITO.

predicción [pray-dic-the-on'], *f.* Prediction. **Predicción del tiempo,** weather forecast.

predicho, cha [pray-dee'-cho, chah], *pp. irr.* of PREDECIR.

predilección [pray-de-lec-the-on'], *f.* Predilection. **Tener predilección por,** to have a predilection for.

predilecto, ta [pray-de-lec'-to, tah], *a.* Beloved in preference to others; darling, favorite.

predio [pray'-de-o], *m.* Landed property, farm, real property. **Predio rústico,** piece of arable ground. **Previo urbano,** dwelling-house in town or country.

prediolo [pray-de-o'-lo], *m.* A small farm.

predisponer [pray-dis-po-nerr'], *va.* 1. To predispose, to prearrange. 2. *(Not Acad.)* To predispose towards, to contract disease readily.

predisposición [pray-dis-po-se-the-on'], *f.* 1. Predisposition. 2. Inclination, propensity.

predispuesto, ta [pray-dis-poo-es'-to, tah], *a. & pp. irr.* of PREDISPONER. Predisponent, predisposed.

predominación [pray-do-me-nah-the-on'], *f.* V. PREDOMINIO.

predominante [pray-do-me-nahn'-tay], *pa.* Predominant, prevailing.

predominar [pray-do-me-nar'], *va.* 1. To predominate, to overrule, to overpower, to control, to compel. 2. To exceed in height, to overlook, to command; to prevail (prevalecer).

predominio [pray-do-mee'-ne-o], *m.* Predominance (dominio), superiority (superioridad).

preelección [pray-ay-lec-the-on'], *f.* Predestination.

preeminencia [pray-ay-me-nen'-the-ah], *f.* Pre-eminence, mastery.

preeminente [pray-ay-me-nen'-tay], *a.* Pre-eminent, superior.

preestablecer [pray-es-tah-blay-therr,], *va.* To pre-establish.

preexcelso, sa [pray-ex-thel'-so, sah], *a.* Illustrious, great, eminent.

preexistencia [pray-ek-sis-ten'-the-ah], *f.* Pre-existence.

preexistente [pray-ek-sis-ten-tay], *pa.* Pre-existent.

preexistir [pray-ek-sis-teer'], *vn.* To pre-exist.

prefabricado, da [pray-fah-bre-cah'-do dah], *a.* Prefabricated.

prefabricar [pre-fah-bre-cahr'], *va.* To prefabricate.

prefacio [pray-fah´-the-o], *m.* 1. Part of the mass which immediately precedes the canon. 2. Preface.

prefación [pray-fah-the-on'], *f.* Preface, introduction.

prefacioncilla [pray-fah-the-on-theel-lyah], *f. dim.* A short preface.

prefecto [pray-fec'-to], *m.* 1. Prefect, head of a county or municipality. 2. Master or principal of a college. 3. Prefect, a magistrate in ancient Rome.

prefectura [pray-fec-too´-rah], *f.* Prefecture.

preferencia [pray-fay-ren´-the-ah], *f.* Preference, choice, preeminence. **Mostrar preferencia por**, to show preference to.

preferente [pray-fay-ren´-tay], *pa. & a.* Pre-eminent: preferring.

preferible [pray-fay-ree'-blay], *a.* Preferable.

preferiblemente [pre-fay-ree'-blay-men-tay], *adv.* Preferably.

preferido [pre-fay-ree'-do], *a.* Favorite. **Es mi cantante preferido**, he is my favorite singer.

preferir [pray-fay-reer'], *va.* To prefer. **Preferir té a café**, to prefer tea to coffee. *-vr.* To proffer, to offer spontaneously to do anything. (*Yo prefiero, prefiera; él prefirió*; from *Preferir* V. ADHERIR.)

prefiguración [pray-fe-goo-rah-the-on'], *f.* Prefiguration.

prefigurar [pray-fe-goo-rar'], *va.* To prefigure, to foretoken, to model a statue, to sketch a painting.

prefijar [pray-fe-har'], *va.* To prefix, to determine.

prefijo, ja [pray-fee'-ho, hah], *pp. irr.* Of PREFIJAR. Prefixed.

prefijo [pray fec'-ho], *m. (Gram.)* Prefix.

prefinición [pray-fe-ne-the-on'], *f.* Act of prefining or fixing a term.

prefinir [pray-fe-neer'], *va.* To determine.

prefoliación [pray-fo-le-ah-the-on'], *f. (Bot.)* Vernation, prefoliation, arrangement of leaves within the bud.

prefulgente [pray-fool-hen'-tay], *a.* Resplendent, lucid, shining.

pregaria [pre-gah'-re-ah], *f. V.* PLEGARIA.

pregón [pray-gone'], *m.* Publication by the common crier, cry.

pregonador, ra [pray-go-na-dor', rah], *m. & f.* Hawker, huckster, street-vender.

pregonar [pray-go-nar'], *va.* 1. To proclaim in public places (proclamar). 2. To cry goods or provisions about the streets (mercancía). 3. To render public, to make known; to applaud publicly.

pregoneo [pray-go-nay'-o], *m.* Hawking, crying goods on the streets.

pregonería [pray-go-nay-ree'-ah], *f.* 1. Office of common crier. 2. A kind of tax or tribute.

pregonero [pray-go-nay´-ro], *m.* 1. Common crier, town crier (municipal). 2. One who renders public or divulges a secret. 3. One who proclaims the biddings at public sales.

pregonero, ra [pray-go-nay'-ro, rah], *a.* Publishing, praising, proclaiming.

preguerra [pray-gayr'-rah], *f.* Prewar.

pregunta [pray-goon'-tah], *f.* Question, query, inquiry. **Absolver las preguntas**, *(For.)* to answer under oath. **Estar a la cuarta pregunta**, *(coll.)* to be hard up or penniless. **Contestar a una pregunta**, to answer a question. **A preguntas necias, oídos sordos**, ask a silly question and you will get a silly answer. **Hacer una pregunta**, to ask a question. *-vn.* To ask, to inquire. *-vr.* To wonder.

preguntador, ra [pray-goon-tah-dor', rah], *m. & f.* Questioner, examiner, interrogator.

preguntante [pray-goon-tahn'-tay], *pa.* Inquiring.

preguntar [pray-goon-tar'], *va.* To ask, to question, to demand, to inquire. **Preguntar algo a uno**, to ask somebody something. *-vr.* To wonder.

preguntón, na [pray-goon-tone', nah], *m. & f.* An inquisitive person, a busy inquirer.

prehistoria [pray-is-to´-re-ah], *f.* Prehistoric or legendary times.

prehistórico, ca [pray-is-to´-re-co, cah], *a.* Prehistoric, legendary; previous to the beginning of history.

preinserto, ta [pray-in-serr'-to, tah], *a.* That which is previously inserted.

prejudicial [pray-hoo-de-the-ahl'], *a. (Law.)* Pre-judicial, requiring a previous judicial decision before the final sentence.

prejuicio [pray-hoo-ee'-the-o], *m.* Prejudice, bias, prejudgment.

prejuzgar [pray-hooth-gar'], *va.* To judge or decide things before the right time, to prejudge.

prelacía [pray-lah-thee'-ah], *f.* Prelacy, prelature.

prelación [pray-lah-the-on'], *f.* Preference, preferment.

prelada [pray-lah'-dah], *f.* A female prelate, the abbess or superior of a convent or nunnery.

prelado [pray-lah'-do], *m.* Prelate, an ecclesiastic of the highest order and dignity; the superior of a convent or religious house.

prelativo, va [pray-lah-tee'-vo, vah], *a.* Deserving preferment.

prelatura [pray-lah-too'-rah], *f.* 1. Prelacy, prelature. 2. The whole body of prelates.

preliminar [pray-le-me-nar'], *a.* Preliminary, proemial, exordial. *-m.* A preliminary sketch; protocol.

prelucir [pray-loo-theer'], *vn.* To sparkle or shine forth.

preludiar [pray-loo-de-a'], *vn.* 1. To attempt, to essay. 2. *(Mus.)* To make a flourish or introduction to the main piece. *-va.* To announce (anunciar), to herald.

preludio [pray-loo'-dee-o], *m.* Prelude; flourish.

prelusión [pray-loo-se-on'], *f.* Prelude, prologue, preface.

premática [pray mah'-te-cah], *f. (Old.)* V. PRAGMÁTICA.

prematrimonial [pray-mah-tre-mo-ne-ahl'], *a.* Premarital.

prematuramente [pray-mah-too-rah-men-tay], *adv.* Prematurely.

prematuro, ra [pray-mah-too'-ro, rah], *a.* Premature, precocious; unseasonable. **Bebé prematuro**, premature baby.

premeditación [pray-may-de-tah-the-on'], *f.* Premeditation, forethought, precogitation.

premeditado, da [pray-may-de-tah´-do, dah], *a. & pp.* of PREMEDITAR. Premeditated, prepense, pre-conceived.

premeditar [pray-may-de-tar'], *va.* 1. To consider or meditate carefully, to weigh maturely. 2. To premeditate.

premiado [pray-me-ah'-do], *a.* Prize (novela); prize winning. *-m & f.* Prizewinner.

premiador, ra [pray-me-ah-dor', rah], *m. & f.* Rewarder.

premiar [pray-me-ar'], *va.* To reward (recompensar), to remunerate, to give or award a prize.

premio [pray'-me-o], *m.* 1. Reward (recompensa), recompense, remuneration. 2. Premium, interest. **Premio de seguro**, rate or premium of insurance. 3. Premium, increase in value of money or securities. 4. Prize, award (en concurso). **Premio de consolación**, consolation prize.

premiosamente [pre-me-o'-sah-men-tay], *adv.* Tightly, compressedly; by force.

premiosidad [pray-mee-o-se-dahd'], *f.* Want of ease and readiness in the manner of speaking or of writing.

premioso, sa [pray-me-o'-so, sah], *a.* 1. Tight (vestido), close, pinching. 2. Troublesome, tiresome, burdensome. 3. Unready in speech (al hablar), expressing oneself with difficulty.

premisa [pray-mee'-sah], *f.* 1. Premise, in logic; an antecedent proposition. 2. Mark, indication.

premiso, sa [pray-mee'-so, sah], *a.* 1. Premised. *V.* PREVENIDO. 2. *(Law.)* Precedent, former, going before.

premoción [pray-mo-the-on'], *f.* Previous movement or motion.

premonición [pray-mo-ne-the-on'], *f.* Premonition.

premonitorio [pray-mo-ne-to'-re-o], *a.* Indicative, warning, premonitory.

premonstratense, premostratense [pray-mons-trah-ten-say], *a.* Premonstratensian: applied to an order of regular canons founded by St. Norbert.

premorir [pray-mo-reer'], *va. (Law.)* To die before another.

premura [pray-moo'-rah], *f. (coll.)* Narrowness, pressure (presión), haste, hurry. **Con premura de tiempo,** under pressure.

prenatal [pray-nah-tahl'], *a.* Antenatal, prenatal.

prenda [pren'-dah], *f.* 1. Pledge (garantía), security for the fulfilment of an obligation. 2. Pledge, any household ornament or furniture, especially when pawned or sold. 3. Pledge, earnest, security. 4. A garment or ornament. 5. Any object dearly loved, as wife or children; jewel (joya), pledge of affection. 6. Talents, gifts (cualidades). 7. Forfeits (juegos). **Dejar algo en prenda,** to pawn something. **No soltar prenda,** to give nothing away.

prendado [pren-dah'-do], *pp.* of PRENDAR.

prendador, ra [pren-dah-dor', rah], *m. & f.* Pledger, pawner; one who redeems a pledge.

prendamiento [pren-dah-me-en'-to], *m.* Act of pledging or pawning.

prendar [pren-dar'], *va.* 1. To take pledges, to lend on pledges. 2. To please, to ingratiate oneself. *-vr.* To take a fancy to something: used with the preposition *de*.

prendedero [pren-day-day'-ro], *m.* 1. Hook, fillet, brooch. 2. Fillet, a band tied round the head, which serves to keep the hair up.

prendedor [pren-day-dor'], *m.* 1. Catcher 2. Breast-pin.

prender [pren-derr'], *va.* 1. To seize, to grasp, to catch (persona), to pin. 2. To imprison. 3. *(coll.)* To detain for the purpose of entertaining in a friendly manner. 1. To take root (plantas). 2. To cover: applied to the act of brutish procreation. 3. To catch or take fire (fuego, horno). 4. To adorn, to embellish (mujeres). *-vn.* 1. To catch, to stick (engancharse). 2. To catch (fuego), to take (inyección); to take, to take root (planta).

prendería [pren-day-ree'-ah], *f.* Shop in which old clothes and furniture are sold; pawnbroker's shop; frippery.

prendero, ra [pren-day'-ro, rah], *m. & f.* 1. Broker, one who sells old furniture and clothes; fripper. 2. Pawnbroker (prestamista).

prendido [pren-dee'-do], *m.* 1. Dress of women. 2. Pattern for bone-lace.—**Prendido, da,** *pp.* of PRENDAR.

prendimiento [pren-de-me-en'-to], *m.* 1. Seizure, capture (captura). 2. *(Cono Sur, Med.)* Constipation.

prenoción [pray-no-the-on'], *f.* Prenotion or first knowledge of things.

prenombre [pray-nom'-bray], *m.* Prenomen, name prefixed to the family name among the Romans.

prenotar [pray-no-tar'], *va.* To note by anticipation.

prensa [pren'-sah], *f.* 1. Press, an instrument with which something is pressed. 2. Press, a machine for printing. 3. Press. *V.* IMPRENTA. **Dar a la prensa,** to publish. **Aprobar un libro para la prensa,** to pass a book for the press. **Tener mala prensa,** to have a bad press.

prensado [pren-sah'-do], *m.* Luster, which remains on stuff. **Prensado, da,** *pp.* of PRENSAR.

prensador, ra [pren-sah-dor', rah], *m. & f.* Presser, one who presses clothes and stuff, pressing machine.

prensadura [pren-sah-doo'-rah], *f.* The act of pressing, pressure.

prensapapeles [pren-sah-pah-pay'-les], *m.* A paper weight.

prensar [pren-sar'], *va.* To press. *V.* APRENSAR.

prensista [pren-sees'-tah], *m.* Pressman in a printing-office.

prenunciar [pray-noon-the-ar'], *va.* To foretell, to prognosticate.

prenuncio [pray-noon'-the-o], *m.* Prediction, prognostication.

preñada [pray-nye-dah'-dah], *a.* Pregnant (animales).

preñadilla [pray-nah-deel'-lyah], *f.* A delicate fish of the rivers of Ecuador, olive-green, with black spots and about four inches long; called **imba** by the Indians.

preñado, da [pray-nyah'-do, dah], *a.* 1. Full, pregnant. 2. Big with child, pregnant. 3. Enclosing within itself something undiscovered. *-m.* Pregnancy (embarazo), gestation. **Palabras preñadas de amenaza,** words charged with menace.

preñar [pray-nyar'], *va.* To get pregnant, to impregnate, to fertilize.

preñez [pray-nyeth'], *f.* 1. Pregnancy, gestation. *V.* PREÑADO. 2. Conception 3. The state of a thing that is impending or hanging over. 4. Confusion, difficulty, obscurity.

preocupación [pray-o-coo-pah-the-on'], *f.* 1. Preoccupation, anticipation in taking possession. 2. Prepossession, bias, prejudice (prejuicio); preconception (ofuscación). **Tiene la preocupación de que su mujer le es infiel,** he has an obsession that his wife is unfaithful to him.

preocupadamente [pray-o-coo-pah'-dah-men-tay], *adv.* Prejudicedly.

preocupado [pray-o-coo-pah'-do], *a.* Worried, anxious, concerned.

preocupar [pray-o-coo-par'], *va.* Preoccupy (inquietar). 2. To prejudice (influir), to prepossess the mind. **Esto me preocupa muchísimo,** this worries me greatly. *-vr.* To worry (inquietarse), to care; to concern (ocuparse). **No te preocupes por eso,** don´t worry about that.

preordinación [pray-or-de-nah-the-on'], *f.* Preordination.

preordinadamente [pray-or-de-nah'-dah-men-tay], *adv.* In a manner preordained.

preordinar [pray-or-de-nar'], *va.* To preordain, to foreordain.

preparación [pray-pah-rah-the-on'], *f.* 1. Preparation (acto). 2. Preparedness (estado), readiness. 3. Training (formación). 4. Competence (competencia). 5. *(Cono Sur)* Appetizer (bocadito). **Estar en preparación,** to be in preparation.

preparado [pray-pah-rah'-do], *a.* 1. Prepared (dispuesto); *(Culin.)* ready to serve. 2. Competent (competente), able. **"Preparado para transmitir",** *(Comput.)* "clear to send" (CTS).

preparamento, preparamiento [pray-pa-rah-men'-to], *m.* Preparation.

preparar [pray-pah-rar'], *va.* To prepare (disponer), to make ready. *-vr.* To be prepared, to be in readiness. **Prepararse para,** to prepare to.

preparativo, va [pray-pah-rah-tee'-vo, vah], *a.* Preparative, qualifying.

preparativo [pray-pah-rah-tee'-vo], *m.* Thing prepared, preparative.

preparatoriamente [pray-pah-rah-to'-re-ah-men-tay], *adv.* Preparatorily.

preparatorio, ria [pray-pah-rah-to'-re-o, ah], *a.* Preparatory, previous, introductory.

preponderancia [pray-pon-day-rahn'-the-ah], *f.* Preponderance, overbalancing.

preponderante [pray-pon-day-rahn'-tay], *a.* Preponderant, that which turns the scale.

preponderar [pray-pon-day-rar'], *vn.* 1 To preponderate, to outweigh, to overbalance. 2. To prevail. 3. To overpower.

preponer [pray-po-nerr'], *va.* To put before, to prefer.

preposición [pray-po-se-the-on'], *f. (Gram.)* Preposition, a part of speech.

prepositivo, va [pray-po-se-tee'-vo, vah], *a.* Prepositive, prefixed.

prepósito [pray-po'-se-to], *m.* 1. President, chairman. 2. Provost.

prepositura [pray-po-se-too'-rah], *f.* Dignity of a provost.

preposteración [pray-pos-tay-rah-the-on'], *f.* Inversion of the regular order of things.

prepósteramente [pray-pos'-tay-rah-men-tay], *adv.* Preposterously.

preposterar [pray-pos-tay-rar'], *va.* To render preposterous, to transpose.

prepóstero, ra [pray-pos'-tay-ro, rah], *a.* Preposterous, absurd.

prepotencia [pray-po-ten'-the-ah], *f.* Preponderance, superiority, prepotency.

prepotente [pray-po-ten'-tay], *a.* 1 Very powerful. 2. Abusive of power over one's inferiors.

prepucial [pray-poo-the-ahl'], *a.* Preputial, relating to the prepuce.

prepucio [pray-poo'-the-o], *m.* Prepuce, foreskin.

prepuesto, ta [pray-poo-es'-to, tah], *pp. irr.* of PREPONER. Preferred.

prerrogativa [pray-ro-gah-tee'-vah], *f.* Prerogative, privilege; liberty.

presa [pray'-sah], *f.* 1. Capture (acto), seizure. 2. Prize (cosa apresada, barco), spoils or booty taken from an enemy. 3. Dike (dique), dam, mole, bank, drain, trench (trinchera), conduit. 4. Slice of meat, a bit of any other kind of eatables. 5. Tusks, fangs (colmillos). 6. Claw (ave de rapiña). 7. Carcass of a fowl or bird killed by a hawk or other bird of prey. 8. Among fishermen, fish weir (represa), stake work. **Hacer presa**, to catch and tie something so that it cannot escape. 9. Clutch (asimiento).

presada [pray-sah'-dah], *f.* Color of a leek; a pale green color.

presagiar [pray-sah-he-ar'], *va.* To presage, to forebode, to foretell.

presagio [pray-sah'-he-o], *m.* Presage, an omen, a token.

presagioso, sa, présago, ga [pray-sah-he-oh'-so, sah, pray'-sah-go, gah], *a.* Ominous, presaging, divining, guessing.

presbicia [pres-bee'-the-ah], *f.* Farsightedness, presbyopia.

présbite, ta [pres'-be-tay, tah], *a. & m. & f* Presbyopic, seeing objects better at a distance; a presbyope.

presbiterado, presbiterato [pres-be-tay-rah'-do, pres-be-tay-rah'-to], *m.* Priesthood, the dignity or order of priest.

presbiteral [pres-be-tay-rahl'], *a.* Sacerdotal, relating to a presbyter.

presbiterianismo [pres-be-tay-re-ah-nees'-mo], *m.* Presbyterianism.

presbiteriano, na [pres-be-tay-re-ah'-no, nah], *a. & m. & f.* Presbyterian

presbiterlato [pres-be-tay-re-ah'-to], *m.* Dignity of a presbyter or elder among the Presbyterians.

presbiterio [pres-be-tay'-re-o], *m.* Presbyterium, chancel, the part in a church where the high altar stands.

presbítero [pres-bee'-tay-ro], *m.* A priest.

presciencia [pres-the-en'-the-ah], *f.* Prescience, foreknowledge, forethought.

prescindible [pres-thin-dee'-blay], *a.* Capable of being prescinded or abstracted.

prescindir [pres-thin-deer'], *va.* 1. To prescind, to cut off to abstract. **Prescindiendo de eso**, laying that aside. 2. To cease from doing something. -*vn.* 1. To do without (pasarse sin). 2. To dispense with (deshacer de); to disregard (desatender). **Han prescindido del coche**, they've given up their car. **No podemos prescindir de él**, we can't manage without him.

prescito, ta [pres-thee'-to, tah], *a.* V PRECITO.

prescribir [pres-cre-beer'], *va.* 1. To prescribe, to determine. 2. To acquire a right by uninterrupted possession 3. To despair of success; to stand in need of. -*vn.* To prescribe, to form a custom which has the force of law.

prescripción [pres-crip-the-on'], *f.* 1 Prescription, the act of prescribing. 2. Introduction, anything proemial. 3. *(Law.)* Prescription, right or title acquired by peaceful possession. **Prescripción médica**, medical prescription.

prescriptible [pres-crip-tee'-blay], *a.* Prescriptible, that may be prescribed

prescripto, ta [pres-creep'-to, tah], *pp. irr.* of PRESCRIBIR. Prescribed, prescript, accurately laid down in a precept.

presea [pray-say'-ah], *f.* Jewel, any ornament of great value.

preselección [pray-leclthe-on'], *f.* Seeding; short listing (de candidatos).

preseleccionar [pray-say-layc-the-o-nahr'], *va.* To seed; to shortlist (candidates).

presencia [pray-sen'-the-ah], *f.* 1. Presence, coexistence. 2. Presence figure, port, air, mien, demeanor. 3. *(Met.)* Memory or representation of a thing. **Presencia de ánimo**, serenity, coolness, presence of mind. **En presencia de**, in the presence of.

presencial [pray-sen-the-ahl'], *a.* Presential, relating to actual presence.

presencialmente [pray-sen-the-ahl'-men-tay], *adv.* Presentially.

presenciar [pray-sen-the-ar'], *vn.* To be present, to witness, to assist at.

presentable [pray-sen-tah'-blay], *a.* Presentable, producible.

presentación [pray-sen-tah-the-on'], *f.* 1. Presentation, presentment, exhibition. 2. A church festival in memory of the Virgin's presentation in the temple, celebrated on the 21st of November. 3. The act of offering or presenting an ecclesiastical benefice. 4. Introduction. **Presentación en sociedad**, coming-out, début.

presentado [pray-sen-tah'-do], *m. & a.* 1. Teacher of divinity, who expects soon to be ranked as master. 2. Presentee, person presented.—**Presentado, da**, *pp.* of PRESENTAR.

presentador, ra [pray-sen-tah-dor'-rah], *m. & f.* Presenter, one that presents, one who offers a benefice.

presentalla [pray-sen-tahl'-lyah], *f.* Gift offered by the faithful to the saints.

presentar [pray-sen-tar'], *va.* 1. To present, to exhibit, to view. 2. To present, to favor with a gift, to offer openly and freely. 3. To present or prefer to ecclesiastical benefices. 4. To perform (obra); to show (película); to present (estrella). 5. To introduce (persona). **El coche presenta ciertas modificaciones**, the car has certain modifications. **Ser presentada en la sociedad**, to come out, to make one's début. -*vr.* 1. To appear in a court of justice; to present oneself before anyone. 2. To run, to stand (candidato). 3. To show (mostrarse). **Presentarse a la policía**, to report to the police. **El día se presenta muy hermoso**, it looks like being a lovely day.

presente [pray-sen' tay], *a.* 1. Present, being face to face (persona). 2. *(Gram.)* Present, one of the tenses of verbs; in this last sense it is also used as a substantive. 3. Present: applied to the time now passing, or what is now in its course. 4. *(LAm.)* By hand (en sobre). **Estar presente en**, to present at. **La presente carta**, this letter. -*m.* Present, gift, keepsake. **Al presente or de presente**, at present, now. **Tener presente**, to bear in mind. **Hacer presente**, (a) to state, to set forth, to inform; (b) to consider one as present (for emoluments, etc.). **La presente**, the present letter.

presentemente [pray-sen-tay-men-tay], *adv.* Presently, at present, now.

presentero [prey-sen-tay'-ro], *m.* Presenter; one who offers a benefice.

presentillo [pray-sen-teel'-lyo], *m. dim.* A small gift.

presentimiento [pray-sen-te-me-en'-to], *m.* Presentiment, foreboding, misgiving.

presentir [pray-sen-teer'], *va.* To have a presentiment of a future event, to foresee, to forebode. *(Yo presiento, yo presienta; él presintió from Presentir. V.* ADHERIR.)

presera [pray-say'-rah], *f. (Bot.)* Goosegrass, cleavers. V. AMOR DE HORTELANO.

presero [pray-say'-ro], *m.* The person who has the care of a dam or dike.

preservación [pray-ser-vah-the-on'], *f.* Preservation, conservation.

preservador, ra [pray-ser-vah-dor', rah], *m. & f.* Preserver.

preservar [pray-ser-var'], *va.* To preserve, to defend from evil; to save.

preservativamente [pray-ser-vah-tee'-vah-men-tay], *adv.* Preservatively.

preservativo [pray-ser-vah-tee'-vo], *m.* Preservative, preventive.

preservativo, va [pray-ser-vah-tee'-vo, vah], *a.* Preservative, having the power of preserving.

presidencia [pray-se-den'-the-ah], *f.* 1. Presidency. 2. Chairmanship.

presidenta [pray-se-den'-tah], *f.* President's wife; moderatrix.

presidente [pray-se-den'-tay], *m.* 1. President, one placed at the head of others; chairman (de comité, de reunión); speaker; judge. 2. President, the chief executive officer of a republic.

presidiar [pray-se-de-ar'], *va.* To garrison a place.

presidiario [pray-se-de-ah'-re-o], *m.* A criminal condemned to hard labor or banishment in a garrison.

presidio [pray-see'-de-o], *m.* 1. Garrison of soldiers. 2. Fortress garrisoned by soldiers. 3. Assistance, aid, help, protection. 4. Place destined for punishing criminals by hard labor; bridewell, house of correction; penitentiary (cárcel). 5. Punishment by hard labor.

presidir [pray-se-deer'], *va.* To preside in an assembly, community, meeting, etc.

presilla [pray-seel'-lyah], *f.* 1. A small string with which something is tied or fastened. 2. Loop in clothes (lazo), which serves as a button-hole. 3. Sort of linen. **Presilla de un sombrero**, loop for a hat.

presión [pray-se-on'], *f.* Pressure. **Presión arterial**, blood pressure. **Hacer presión**, to pressure, to try to influence.

preso, sa [pray-so, sah], *m. & f.* Prisoner. **Preso político**, political prisoner.

preso, sa [pray'-so, sah], *pp. irr.* of PRENDER. Taken. **Estar preso de pánico**, to be panic-stricken.

prespiración [pres-pe-rah-the-on'], *f.* Penetration of water into the earth.

prest [prest], *m.* V. PRE.

presta [pres'-tah], *f.* (*Bot. Prov.*) V. HIERBABUENA or MENTA.

prestación [pres-tah-the-on'], *f.* 1. (*Law.*) Act of lending or granting. 2. (*Aut. Mec.*) Feature, detail. 3. (*Comput.*) Capability. 4. (*Mex. Com.*) Fringe benefit. **Prestación comercial**, obligatory service.

prestadizo, za [pres-tah-dee'-tho, thah], *a.* That may be lent or borrowed.

prestado, da [pres-tah'-do, dah], *a. & pp.* of PRESTAR. Lent. **Tomar prestado**, to borrow. **Dar prestado**, to lend. **De prestado**, for a short time; improperly.

prestador, ra [pres-tah-dor', rah], *m. & f.* Lender; one who lends money at usurious interest.

prestamente [pres'-tah-men-tay], *adv.* Speedily, promptly, quickly.

prestamista [pres-tah-mees'-tah], *com.* Money-lender.

préstamo [pres'-tah-mo], *m.* Loan. V. EMPRÉSTITO. **Préstamo hipotecario**, mortgage.

prestancia [pres-tahn'-the-ah], *f.* Excellence. V. EXCELENCIA.

prestante [pres-tahn'-tay], *a.* V. EXCELENTE.

prestar [pres-tar'], *va.* 1. To lend, to grant the use of something. 2. To credit, to give credit. 3. To aid, to assist. 4. To give, to communicate. 5. (*Prov.*) To extend, to expand. 6. (*Law.*) To pay the interest, duty, etc., which is ordered. **Prestar paciencia**, to bear something with patience. 7. To take, to swear (juramento). 8. (*LAm.*) To borrow (pedir prestado). 9. (*Carib. Cono Sur*) To do good to, to be good for. -*vn.* 1. To be useful, to contribute to the attainment of something. 2. To guard, to preserve: applied to God, who lends all things. -*vr.* To offer oneself, to agree to anything. **La situación se presta a muchas interpretaciones**, the situation lends itself to many interpretations. **Prestar servicio de asistencia** (*Comput.*), to provide assistance.

preste [pres'-tay], *m.* Priest who celebrates the high mass. **Preste Juan**, prester John, title of the Abyssinian monarchs, because anciently the king was a priest.

préster [pres'-ter], *m.* 1. Hurricane. 2. Meteor like lightning.

presteza [pres-tay'-thah], *f.* Quickness, promptitude, haste, speed, nimbleness.

prestidigitación [pres-te-de-he-tah-the-on'], *f.* Legerdemain, sleight of hand, jugglery.

prestidigitador [pres-te-de-he-tah-dor'], *m.* Juggler, prestidigitator.

prestidigitar [pres-te-de-he-tar'], *va.* To juggle, to perform feats of sleight of hand.

prestigiador [pres-te-he-ah-dor'], *m.* Cheat, juggler, impostor.

prestigiar [pres-te-he-ar'], *va.* To give prestige to; to make famous (dar fama); to honor (honrar).

prestigio [pres-tee'-he-o], *m.* 1. Conjuring, juggling, imposture. 2. Sleight of hand, legerdemain. 3. Prestige (fama), fame, favorable reputation (reputación). **Tener buen** or **mal prestigio de una persona**, (*coll.*) to be well or ill inclined to a person. **Tener una cosa buen** or **mal prestigio**, to forebode good or evil from an affair.

prestigioso, sa [pres-te-he-o'-so, sah], *a.* Deceitful, illusory, prestigious.

prestito [pres-tee'-to], *adv.* Quickly, promptly.

presto, ta [pres'-to, tah], *a.* 1. Quick (rápido), prompt, ready (listo), diligent. 2. Ready, prepared, disposed.

presto [pres'-to], *adv.* Soon, quickly (rápidamente), speedily. **De presto**, promptly, swiftly.

presumible [pray-soo-mee'-blay], *a.* Presumable, supposable.

presumidico, ica, illo, illa, ito, ita [pray-soo-me-dee'-co], *a. dim.* Confident, a little presumptuous.

presumido, da [pray-soo-mee'-do, dah], *a.* Presumptuous, arrogant, insolent, forward. -*pp.* of PRESUMIR.

presumir [pray-soo-meer'], *va.* 1. To presume (suponer), to suppose, to suspect, to conjecture. 2. (*And. Cono Sur*) To court (pretender); to flirt with (coquetear con). -*vn.* To show off (chulearse), to presume, to boast, to form confident opinions, to make arrogant attempts. **Para presumir ante las amistades**, in order to show off before one's friends. **Presumir de experto**, to pride oneself on being an expert.

presunción [pray-soon-the-on'], *f.* 1. Presumption, supposition, conjecture (conjetura). 2. Presumptuousness, blind and arrogant confidence; vanity, conceitedness (cualidad). 3. Suspicion (sospecha).

presuntamente [pray-soon-tah-men-tay], *adv.* Presumptively.

presuntivamente [pray-soon-tee'-vah-men-tay], *adv.* Conjecturally.

presuntivo, va [pray-soon-tee'-vo, vah], *a.* 1. Presumptive, taken by previous supposition. 2. Presumptive, supposed.

presunto, ta [pray-soon'-to, tah], *pp. irr.* Of PRESUMIR. Presumed. **El presunto asesino**, the alleged murderer.

presuntuosamente [pray-soon-too-oh'-sah-men-tay], *adv.* Presumptuously, arrogantly.

presuntuoso, sa [pray-soon-too-oh'-so, sah], *a.* Presumptuous, vain, arrogant, insolent.

presuponer [pray-soo-po-nerr'], *va.* To presuppose, to take for granted.

presuposición [pray-soo-po-se-the-on'], *f.* Presupposition, presupposal, pretext.

presupuesto [pray-soo-poo-es'-to], *m.* 1. Motive, pretext, pretence. 2. An estimate, calculation; budget of state (de obras, proyecto). 3. Supposition.

presupuesto, ta [pray-soo-poo-es'-to, tah], *pp. irr.* of PRESUPONER.

presura [pray-soo'-rah], *f.* 1. Hurry, haste, promptitude. 2. Oppression, pressure, anxiety. 3. Eagerness, importunity.

presurosamente [pray-soo-roh'-sah-men-tay], *adv.* Hastily, promptly.

presuroso, sa [pray-soo-ro'-so, sah], *a.* Hasty (apresurado), prompt, quick (rápido); light, nimble.

pretal [pray-tahl'], *m.* Poitrel, breast-plate, or breast-leather of a home.

pretencioso [pray-ten-the-oh'-so], *a.* 1. Pretentious (vanidoso), presumptuous; showy. 2. (*LAm.*) Conceited (presumido).

pretender [pray-ten-derr'], *va.* 1. To pretend, to claim (afirmar), to solicit. 2. To try (aspirar), to attempt. 3. To woo, to court (mujer). **Han pretendido robarme**, they have attempted to rob me. **El libro pretende ser importante**, the book tries to look important. **Pretende llegar a ser médico**, she hopes to become a doctor.

pretendiente, ta [pray-ten-de-en'-tay, tah], *m. & f.* Pretender, candidate, office-hunter, solicitor.

pretensión [pray-ten-se-on'], *f.* 1. Pretension, solicitation for obtaining something. 2. Pretension, claim (reclamación, afirmación). 3. Aim, object (objetivo). **Tener pretensiones de**, to have pretensions to. **Tener pocas pretensiones**, to be undemanding.

pretenso, sa [pray-ten'-so, sah], *pp. irr.* Of PRETENDER.

pretensor, ra [pray-ten-sor', rah], *m. & f.* Pretender, claimant.

pretera [pray-tay'-rah], *f.* Backgammon.

preterición [pray-tay-re-the-on'], *f.* 1. Preterition, the act of going past, the state of being past. 2. (Law.) Preterition, the act of omitting lawful children in a last will.

preterir [pray-tay-reer'], *va.* (Law.) To omit lawful children in a last will.

pretérito, ta [pray-tay'-re-to, tah], *a.* 1. Preterite, past. 2. (Gram.) Preterite: applied to past tenses of verbs.

pretermisión [pray-ter-me-se-on'], *f.* Preterition, pretermission.

pretermitir [pray-ter-me-teer'], *va.* To omit, to pretermit, to pass by.

preternatural [pray-ter-nah-too-rahl'], *a.* Preternatural.

preternaturalizar [pray-ter-nah-to-rah-le-thar'], *va.* To pervert, to render preternatural.

preternaturalmente [pray-ter-nah-too-rahl'-men-tay], *adv.* Preternaturally.

pretexta [pray-tex'-tah], *f.* A long gown worn by magistrates of ancient Rome.

pretextar [pray-tex-tar'], *va.* To make use of a pretext, to feign an excuse.

pretexto [pray-tex'-to], *m.* Pretext, excuse (disculpa), pretence, mask, cover.

pretil [pray-teel'], *m.* Parapet (puente, balcón), battlement, breastwork.

pretina [pray-tee'-nah], *f.* 1. Girdle, waistband; belt. 2. Waist, everything which girds or surrounds. 3. (Carib.) Flies (bragueta).

pretinazo [prey-tee-nah'-tho], *m.* Blow given with a girdle.

pretinero [pray-tee-nay'-ro], *m.* One who makes girdles.

pretinilla [pray-te-neel'-lyah], *f. dim.* A small belt or girdle.

pretor [pray-tor'], *m.* 1. Pretor, a magistrate in ancient Rome. 2. Blackness of the waters where tunny-fish abound.

pretoría [pray-to-re'-ah], *f.* Dignity of a pretor. V. PRETURA.

pretorial, pretoriano, na [pray-to-re-ahl'], *a.* Pretorian.

pretoriense [pray-to-re-en'-say], *a.* Belonging to the pretor's palace.

pretorio [pray-to'-re-o], *m.* Place in ancient Rome where the pretor resided and administered justice.

pretorio, ria [pray-to'-re-o, ah], *a.* V. PRETORIAL.

pretura [pray-too'-rah], *f.* Pretorship.

prevalecer [pray-vah-lay-therr'], *vn.* 1. To prevail (imponerse), to predominate (dominar), to outshine. 2. To take root (plantas). 3. To grow and increase (used of things not material). (*Yo prevalezco, yo prevalezca*, from *Prevalecer.* V. CONOCER.)

prevaleciente [pray-vah-lay-the-en'-tay], *pa. & a.* Prevalent; prevailing.

prevalente [pray-vah-len'-tay], *a.* Prevalent.

prevalerse [pray-vah-lerr'-say], *vr.* To use anything, or to avail oneself of it; to prevail.

prevaricación [pray-vah-re-cah-the-on'], *f.* Prevarication.

prevaricador, ra [pray-vah-re-cah-dor', rah], *m. & f.* 1. Prevaricator. 2. Turn-coat.

prevaricar [pray-vah-re-car'], *vn.* 1. To fail in one's word, duty, or judgment. 2. (coll.) To turn the coat, to change sides.

prevaricato [pray-vah-re-cah'-to], *m.* (Law.) Prevarication in a solicitor or advocate.

prevención [pray-ven-the-on'], *f.* 1. Disposition, preparation (preparativo). 2. Supply of provisions; sustenance, subsistence. 3. Foresight, forecast, forethought (cualidad). 4. Advice, intimation, warning instruction, monition. 5. Prevention, preoccupation. 6. (Mil.) Police guard. **A prevención** or **de prevención**, by way of precaution. (Met.) Prejudice, pro or contra. **Medidas de prevención**, emergency measures.

prevenidamente [pray-v-ay-nee'-dah-men-tay], *adv.* Beforehand, previously.

prevenido, da [pray-vay-nee'-do, dah], *a. & pp.* of PREVENIR. 1. Prepared, provided; plentiful, abundant. 2 Provident, careful, cautious. **Hombre prevenido vale por dos**, forewarned is forearmed.

preveniente [pray-vay-ne-en'-tay], *pa.* Predisposing, prevenient.

prevenir [pray-vay-neer'], *va.* 1. To prepare (disponer), to arrange beforehand. 2. To foresee (preveer), to foreknow. 3. To prevent or anticipate, to forestall (anticipar). 4. To advise, to caution, to give notice. 5. To prevent (impedir), to impede, to hinder. 6. To prevent, to preoccupy. 7. To ingratiate oneself. 8. (Acad.) To come upon, to surprise. **Prevenir a uno de algo**, to provide somebody with something. **Prevenir a uno**, to warn somebody. **Más vale prevenir que curar**, prevention is better than cure. *-vr.* To be prepared; to be predisposed (disponerse); to guard or be in a state of defence. (*Yo prevengo, yo prevenga, previene*, from *Prevenir.* V. VENIR.)

preventivamente [pray-ven-tee'-vah-men-tay], *adv.* Preventively.

preventivo, va [pray-ven-te'-vo, vah], *a.* Preventive; previously prepared or arranged.

prever [pray-verr'], *va.* 1. To foresee (antever), to foreknow. 2. To anticipate, to envisage (anticipar); to plan (proyectar); to make allowances (tener en cuenta). **No teníamos previsto nada para eso**, we had not made any allowance for that. **Ya lo preveía**, I expected as much. (*Yo preveo, yo prevea, él previó*, from *Prever.* V. VER.)

previamente [pray'-ve-ah-men-tay], *adv.* Previously.

previo, via [pray'-ve o, ah], *a.* Previous, antecedent, prior. **Autorización previa**, prior authorization.

previsible [pray-ve-see'-blay], *a.* Foreseeable; predictable.

previsión [pray-ve-se-on'], *f.* Foresight (clarividencia), fore-knowledge, prescience, forecast (pronóstico). **Previsión del tiempo**, weather forecast.

previsor, ra [pray-ve-sor', rah], *m. & f.* One who foresees; prudent (precavido).

previsto, ta [pray-vees'-to, tah], *pp. irr.* Of PREVER.

prez [preth'], *m.* 1. Honor or glory gained by a meritorious act. 2. Notoriety.

priapismo [pre-ah-pees'-mo], *m.* (Med.) Priapism, a disease.

priesa [pre-ay'-sah], *f.* V. PRISA.

prietamente [pre-ay'-tah-men-tay], *adv.* V. APRETADAMENTE.

prieto, ta [pre-ay'-to, tah], *a.* 1. Blackish (oscuro), of a very dark color. 2. Narrow-minded, illiberal. 3. Close-fisted, mean (tacaño). 4. Tight (apretado), compressed.

prima [pree'-mah], *f.* 1. Female cousin (pariente). 2. Morning, the first three hours of the day. 3. Prime, one of the seven canonical hours. 4. Tonsure. 5. (Mil.) The first quarter of the night, from eight to eleven o'clock. 6. Treble, the most slender string of stringed instruments. 7. (Com.) Premium given for insurance. 8. Premium, the price in excess beyond the face value of a paper. 9. The obligation of paying the agreed rate per cent if a paper is not taken up or a purchase completed. 10. Bonus, extra payment (de sueldo). 11. (Cono Sur) **Bajar la prima**, to moderate one's language.

primacía [pre-mah-thee'-ah], *f.* 1. Priority, precedence in time or place (prioridad). 2. Primateship, primacy (primer lugar), mastership.

primacial [pre-mah-the-ahl'], *a.* Relating to primacy.

primada

primada [pre-mah'-dah], *f. (coll.)* Trick, of which someone is the object as being slow-witted.

primado [pre-mah'-do], *m.* 1. Primeness, the state of being first. 2. Primate, the chief ecclesiastic of a country.

primado, da [pre-mah'-do, dah], *a.* Primary, first in intention; first in dignity. **Iglesia primada**, primacial church.

primal, la [pre-mahl', lah], *a.* Yearling.

primal [pre-mahl'], *m.* Lace, a plaited cord of silk.

primariamente [pre-mah'-re-ah-men-tay], *adv.* Principally, chiefly, primarily.

primario, ria [pre-mah'-re-o, ah], *a.* Principal, primary.

primario [pre-mah'-re-o], *m.* Professor who lectures at the hour of prime.

primate [pre-mah'-tay], *f.* Most important. -*m.* 1. *(Zool.)* Primate. 2. Important person (prócer).

primavera [pre-mah-vay'-rah], *f.* 1. The spring season (estación). 2. Kind of flowered silk. 3. *(Bot.)* Primrose. 4. *(Met.)* Season of beauty, health and vigor: prime.

primaveral [pre-mah-vay-rahl'], *a.* Spring-like.

primazgo [pre-math'-go], *m.* Cousinship, relation of consanguinity among cousins.

primearse [pre-may-ar'-say], *vr.* To treat each other as cousins.

primer [pre-merr'], *a.* First; used before nouns. V. PRIMERO.

primera [pre-may'-rah], *f.* 1. Kind of card game. 2. *(Ferr.)* First class. 3. **De primera**, first-class. **Comer de primera**, to eat really well. 4. **A la primera de cambio**, as soon as I turned my back.

primeramente [pre-may'-rah-men-tay], *adv.* First; in the first place, mainly, primely.

primerizo, za [pre-may-ree'-tho, thah], *a.* 1. First, that antecedes or is preferred to other persons or things. 2. Firstling, first produced or brought forth; primiparous.

primeriza [pre-may-ree'-thah], *f.* Woman who has born her first child; primipara.

primero, ra [pre-may'-ro, rah], *a.* 1. First, the ordinal number of one. 2. Chief, principal (principal), leading. 3. Superior, most excellent. 4. Prior, former. 5. Basic (fundamental); urgent (urgente); raw (materia). **De buenas a primeras**, all at once, rashly, without reflection. **A primeros de siglo**, at the start of the century. **Lo primero es que...**, the fundamental thing is that...

primero [pre-may-ro], *adv.* First (primeramente), rather (antes), sooner. **Primero pediría limosna que prestado**, he would rather beg than borrow. **De primero**, at the beginning, before.

primeros auxilios. [pre-may'-ros ah-ooc-see'-lee-os], . *pl.* First aid, assistance.

primevo, va [pre-may'-vo, vah], *a.* Primeval, original.

primichón [pre-me-chone'], *m.* Skein of fine, soft silk, for embroidering.

primicia [pre-mee'-the-ah], *f.* 1. First-fruits of anything. 2. Offering of the first-fruits. 3. **Primicia informativa**, scoop.

primicial [pre-me-the-ahl'], *a.* Primitial, relating to first-fruits.

primigenio, nia [pre-me-hay'-ne-o, ah], *a.* Primogenial, first-born.

primilla [pre-meel'-lyah], *f.* 1. *(coll.)* Pardon of the first fault committed. 2. *(dim.)* A little female cousin.

primísimo, ma [pre-mee'-se-mo, mah], *a. sup.* Uncommonly neat, extremely spruce.

primitivamente [pre-me-tee'-vah-men-tay], *adv.* Originally.

primitivo, va [pre-me-tee'-vo, vah], *a.* 1. Primitive, original (original), primeval. 2. Primary (color). 3. Ordinary (acción). 4. *(Hist.)* Primitive; uncivilized. **Es una obra primitiva**, it is an early work. **En condiciones primitivas**, in primitive conditions.

primo, ma [pree'-mo, mah], *a.* 1. First, the ordinal number of one. 2. Of the first rank, excellent. **Hilo primo**, fine waxed thread, used by shoemakers.

primo [pree'-mo], *m.* 1. Cousin (pariente). **Primo hermano**, first cousin, cousin german. 2. *(coll.)* Simpleton, one easily

deceived. **Hacer el primo**, to be easily taken in.-*adv.* First, in the first place.

primogénito, ta [pre-mo-hay'-ne-to, tah], *a.* First-born, eldest, firstling, primogenitive.

primogenitura [pre-mo-hay-ne-too'-rah], *f.* Primogeniture, seniority, the right of the first-born.

primoprimus [pre-mo-pree'-moos], *m.* The first impulse or emotion of the mind.

primor [pre-mor'], *m.* 1. Beauty (belleza); dexterity, ability, accuracy, exquisiteness, excellence, delicacy (delicadeza). 2. Nicety, neatness of workmanship. 3. Care, skill (maestría). 4. Fine thing, lovely thing (objeto). **Hecho con primor**, done most skillfully. **Hace primores con la aguja**, she makes lovely things with her needlework.

primordial [pre-mor-de-ahl'], *a.* Primordial, original.

primorear [pre-mo-ray-ar'], *vn.* To perform with elegance and neatness.

primorosamente [pre-mo-roh'-sah-men-tay], *adv.* Finely, nicely, neatly, handsomely, excellently.

primoroso, sa [pre-mo-ro'-so, sah], *a.* Neat, elegant, excellent, fine, curious, handsome; graceful, dexterous. **Artesano de manos primorosas**, a neat, able workman.

prímula [pree'-moo-lah], *f. (Bot.)* Primrose, cowslip.

princesa [prin-thay'-sah], *f.* 1. Princess, the consort or daughter of a prince, or the heiress to a principality. 2. Princess; in Spain, the apparent heiress to the crown.

principada [prin-the-pah'-dah], *f.* Act of authority or superiority performed by him who has no right to execute it.

principado [prin-the-pah'-do], *m.* 1. Princedom, the rank, estate, or power of a prince. 2. Principality, the territory of a prince. 3. Pre-eminence, superior excellence.

principal [prin-the-pahl'], *a.* 1. Principal (más importante), chief, capital, essential. 2. Illustrious, renowned, celebrated. 3. Foremost, first, chief: **Casa principal**, capital house, hotel. **Cuarto principal**, apartments on the first floor or story.

principal [prin-the-pahl'], *m.* 1. In a garrison, the main guard. 2. Principal, capital, stock. 3. Principal, head of a commercial establishment (persona).

principalidad [prin-the-pah-le-dahd'], *f.* Principalness, the state of being principal; nobility.

principalmente [prin-the-pahl'-men-tay], *adv.* Principally, mainly, chiefly.

príncipe [preen'-the-pay], *m.* 1. Prince, a sovereign or chief ruler. 2. Prince, a sovereign of rank next to a king. 3. Prince, son of a king, kinsman of a sovereign: popularly, the eldest son of his that reigns under any denomination is called a prince. 4. Prince, the most eminent, chief, or principal of anybody of men. 5. Prince, appellation of honor granted by kings. 6. With bee-masters, the young queen bees not yet in a state to breed. **Como un príncipe**, princely, or in a prince like manner. **Príncipe consorte**, prince consort. **Príncipe heredero**, crown prince.

principela [prin-the-pay'-lah], *f.* A sort of light camlet.

principiador, ra [prin-the-pe-ah-dor', rah], *m. & f.* Beginner.

principiante [prin-the-pe-ahn'-tay], *m.* Beginner, a learner.

principiar [prin-the-pe-ar'], *va.* To commence, to begin.

principiera [prin-the-pe-ay'-rah], *f. (Prov.)* A small metal saucepan in which broth is warmed.

principillo, principito [prin-the-peel'-lyo], *m. dim.* A petty prince.

principio [prin-thee'-pe-o], *m.* 1. Beginning (comienzo), commencement. 2. Principle, element, constituent part. 3. Principle, original cause; ground of action, motive; origin (origen), fountain. 4. Principle, first position, fundamental truth. 5. Principle, first on which morality is founded (moral). 6. Any of the courses served up at table besides the boiled meat. 7. *(Chem.)* An element or body not decomposable by means now at command. **Principios**, the preliminaries to a volume, as license, approbation, dedication, etc. **Al principio** or **a los principios**, at the beginning. **Del principio al fin**, from beginning to end. **Bajo el mismo principio**, on the same ground. **A principios del mes**, early in the month.

principote [prin-the-po´-tay], *m. (coll.)* He who assumes a lofty air and importance; a petty prince.

pringada [prin-gah´-dah], *f.* Toasted bread steeped in gravy.

pringar [prin-gar´], *va.* 1. To baste meat which is roasting. 2. To stain with grease, to scald with boiling fat; to tar a person: this formerly was the punishment of slaves. 3. To wound (herir), to ill-treat. 4. To meddle, to interfere; to take a share in. 5. *(Cono Sur)* To give (enfermedad). 6. *(Cono Sur)* To put in the family way (mujer). 7. To drop a brick (meter la pata). **Pringar el pan en la sopa,** to dip one´s bread in the soup. **Pringar a uno en un asunto,** to involve somebody in a matter. *-vn.* 1. To take a beating (perder). 2. *(Mil.)* To sweat one´s guts out (trabajar). 3. To peg out (morir). 4. *(CAm. Carib. Mex.)* To drizzle (lloviznar). *-vr.* To draw unlawful advantage from a thing intrusted to one´s care. **O nos pringamos todos, o ninguno,** either we all carry the can or none of us do.

pringón, na [prin-gone´, nah], *a.* Nasty, dirty (sucio), greasy (mancha). *-m.* 1. The act of begreasing oneself. 2. Stain of grease.

pringoso, sa [prin-go´-so, sah], *a.* Greasy, fat.

pringue [preen´-gay], *com.* 1. Grease, lard. 2. Greasiness, oiliness, fatness. 3. The act of begreasing or staining with grease.

pringuera [preen-gay´-rah], Dripping.

prior [pre-or´], **m.** 1. Prior, the superior of convents or religious houses. 2. *(Prov.)* Rector, curate. 3. Prior in some cathedrals. 4. President of the *Consulado* in Andalusia, a court appointed to try and decide causes concerning trade and navigation.*-a.* Prior, precedent.

priora [pre-o´-rah], *f.* Prioress.

prioral [pre-o-rahl´], *a.* Belonging to a prior or prioress.

priorato [pre-o-rah´-to], *m.* 1. Priorship, dignity of a prior or prioress. 2. District of the jurisdiction of a prior. 3. Priory of Benedictines.

priorazgo [pre-o-rath´-go], *m.* Priorship. *V.* PRIORATO.

prioridad [pre-o-re-dahd´], *f.* Priority (precedencia); precedence in time or place; seniority (antigüedad), greater age. **Tener prioridad,** to have priority.

prioste [pre-os´-tay], *m.* Steward of a brotherhood or confraternity.

prisa [pree´-sah], *f.* 1. Urgency, celerity, promptness in executing. 2. Haste, hurry (apresuramiento). 3. Speed (velocidad). **A toda prisa,** with the greatest promptitude. **Darse prisa,** To hurry up. **Estar de prisa,** to be in a hurry. **Andar de prisa,** to be very busy, to be driven for time. **Vivir de prisa,** to live fast, to abuse body and mind. **Voy con mucha prisa,** I´m in a great hurry. **Tener prisa,** to be in a hurry.

prisco [prees´-co], *m.* A kind of peach.

prisión [pre-se-on´], *f.* 1. Seizure, capture, apprehension. 2. Prison (cárcel), jail. 3. Anything which binds or holds physically. 4. Bond, union; cement or cause of union. *-pl.* Chains, shackles, fetters.

prisioncilla, ita [pre-se-on-theel´-lyah], *f. dim.* A small prison or jail.

prisionero, ra [pre-se-o-nay´-ro], *m & f.* 1. Prisoner, a soldier taken by an enemy. 2. Captivated by affection or passion.

prisma [prees´-mah], *m.* 1. *(Geom.)* Prism. 2. A triangular prism of glass.

prismático, ca [pris-mah´-te-co, cah], *a.* Prismatic.

prismatizar [pris-mah-te thar´], *va.* To decompose light by a prism.

priste [prees´-tay], *m.* Saw-fish.

prístino, na [prees´-te-no, nah], *a.* Pristine, first, original.

prisuelo [pre-soo-ay´-lo], *m.* Muzzle, which serves to keep the mouths of ferrets shut.

pritaneo [pre-tah-nay´-o], *m.* Prytaneum, senate-house in Athens.

privación [pre-vah-the-on´], *f.* 1. Privation (acto), want. 2. Privation the act of degrading from rank or office. 3. *(Met.)* Deprivation of anything desired, loss. **Sufrir privación de libertad,** to suffer loss of liberty.

privada [pre-vah´-dah], *f.* 1. Privy, water-closet. 2. Filth thrown into the street.

privadamente [pre-vah-dah-men-tay], *adv.* Privately, privily; separately.

privadero [pre-vah-day´-ro], *m.* One who cleans wells or cesspools.

privado, da [pre-vah´-do, dah], *a. & pp.* of PRIVAR. 1. Privy, private (particular), performed in presence of a few. 2. Private, particular, personal, not relating to the public.

privado [pre-vah´-do], *m.* Favorite, minion, court minion.

privanza [pre-vahn´-thah], *f.* Favor, protection; familiar intercourse between a prince or great personage and a person of inferior rank.

privar [pre-var´], *va.* 1. To deprive, to despoil; to dispossess of a public place or employment. 2. To prohibit (prohibir), to interdict. 3. To suspend sensation. 4. To delight (extasiar). 5. To drink (beber). **Privar a uno de algo,** to deprive somebody of something. **No me prives de verte,** don´t keep me from seeing you. *-vn.* 1. To enjoy the peculiar protection of a prince or great personage. 2. To obtain (existir), to be present; to prevail (predominar). **En ese período privaba la minifalda,** at that time miniskirts were in. *-vr.* 1. To deprive oneself (abstenerse de). 2. To get tanked up (emborracharse).

privativamente [pre-vah-tee´-vah-men-tay], *adv.* Conclusively, solely, privatively.

privativo, va [pre-vah-tee´-vo, vah], *a.* 1. Privative, causing privation. 2. Special, singular, particular, peculiar; exclusive.

privatización [pre-vah-te-thah-the-on´], *f.* Privatization.

privatizar [pre-vah-te-thar´], *va.* To privatize.

privilegiadamente [pre-ve-lay-he-ah´-dah-men-tay], *adv.* In a privileged manner.

privilegiar [pre-ve-lay-he-ar´], *va.* To privilege, to grant a privilege.

privilegiativo [pre-ve-lay-he-ah-tee´-vo], **va,** *a.* Containing a privilege.

privilegio [pre-ve-lay´-he-o], *m.* 1. Privilege, immunity; grant, concession, grace: liberty, franchise, faculty. 2. Patent, copyright. **Privilegio del fuero,** exemption from secular jurisdiction, enjoyed by ecclesiastics.

pro [pro], *com.* Profit (provecho), benefit, advantage. *V.* PROVECHO. **Buena pro,** much good may it do you. **En pro,** in favor of, for the benefit of: **Hombre de pro,** a worthy men.

proa [pro´-ah], *f.* Prow of a ship, foreship, bow. **Por nuestra proa,** *(Naut.)* ahead of us. **Llevar la proa hacia la mar,** *(Naut.)* to stand off, to stand out to sea. **Poner la proa al rumbo,** *(Naut.)* to stand on the course.

proal [pro-ahl´], *a.* Relating to the prow; forward.

probabilidad [pro-bah-be-le-dahd´], *f.* Probability, likelihood, credibility, chance (perspectiva), prospect. **Probabilidades de vida,** expectation of life.

probabilísimo, ma [pro-bah-be-lee´-se-mo, mah], *a. sup.* Most probable.

probabilismo [pro-bah-be-lees´-mo], *m.* Probability, doctrine of probable opinions.

probabilista [pro-bah-be-lees´-tah], *m.* Probabilist, one who acts upon probabilities.

probable [pro-bah´-blay], *a.* Probable, likely, credible, capable of proof. **Es probable que,** it is probable that...

probablemente [pro-bah´-blay-men-tay], *adv.* Probably, credibly, likely.

probación [pro-bah-the-on´], *f.* Proof, probation, trial, examination.

probado, da [pro-bah´-do, dah], *a.* Proved, tried. *-pp.* of PROBAR.

probador, ra [pro-bah-dor´, rah], *m. & f.* 1. Taster (persona), one who tries or proves anything. 2. Defender, advocate. 3. Fitting-room (tienda).

probadura [pro-bah-doo'-rah], *f*. Trial, the act of tasting or trying anything.

probanza [pro-bahn'-thah], *f*. Proof, evidence.

probar [pro-bar'], *va*. 1. To try, to examine the quality of a thing. 2. To prove (hecho, teoría), to give evidence, to justify, to make good. 3. To taste, to try by the mouth (comida). 4. With the preposition **a** and an infinitive mode, it signifies to attempt, to endeavor. **Probó a levantarse y no pudo,** he attempted to rise and could not. **Prueba un poco de esto,** try a bit of this. *-vn*. To suit (sentar), to fit, to agree. *(Yo pruebo, yo prueba, from Probar. V. ACORDAR.)*

probativo, va, probatorio, ria [pro bah-tee'-vo, vah], *a*. Probatory, probationary.

probatoria [pro-bah-toh'-re-ah], *f*. Legal investigation: preliminary examination.

probatura [pro-bah-too'-rah], *f. (coll.)* V. PROBADURA.

probeta [pro-bay'-tah], *f*. 1. A kind of barometer. 2. Powder-prover, a device for testing the explosive force of powder. 3. *(Chem.)* A test tube.

probidad [pro-be-dahd'], *f*. Probity, honesty, sincerity, veracity.

problema [pro-blay'-mah], *m*. 1. Problem, a doubtful question proposed. 2. *(Geom.)* Problem, practical proposition.

problematicamente [pro-blay-mah'-te-cah-men-tay], *adv*. Problematically.

problemático, ca [pro-blay-mah'-te-co, cah], *a*. Problematical, disputable, unsettled.

probo, ba [pro'-bo, bah], *a*. Upright, honest.

probóscide [pro-bos'-the-day], *f*. (Non-Acad.) 1. Proboscis, the trunk of an elephant. 2. Proboscis, the projecting sucking mouth-parts of certain insects. V. TROMPA.

procacidad [pro-cah-the-dahd'], *f*. Procacity, petulance, insolence (desvergüenza), forwardness, brazenness (descaro), indecency (indecoro).

procaína [pro-cah-ee'-nah], *f*. Novocaine.

procaz [pro-cath'], *a*. Procacious, petulant, forward, insolent (atrevido), indecent (indecoro).

procedencia [pro-thay-den'-the-ah], *f*. 1. Derivation: the act of proceeding. 2. The place from which persons or articles come.

procedente [pro-thay-den'-tay], *pa*. 1. Coming from, proceeding from. 2. According to legal rules, according to law.

proceder [pro-thay-derr'], *m*. Procedure, manner of proceeding, conduct, demeanor, management.

proceder [pro-thay-derr'], *vn*. 1. To proceed (pasar), to go on. 2. To issue, to proceed from (conducirse). 3. To behave, to conduct oneself. 4. To proceed, to prosecute a design. 5. *(Law.)* To proceed against, to carry on a judicial process. 6. To proceed by generation. **Todo esto procede de su negativa,** all this springs from his refusal. **Conviene proceder con cuidado,** it is best to go carefully.

procedimiento [pro-thay-de-me-en'-to], *m*. 1. Procceding, procedure, transaction. 2. Proceeding or legal procedure. **Por un procedimiento deductivo,** by a deductive process. 3. Link control protocol, procedure.

procela [pro-thay'-lah], *a*. *(Poet.)* Storm, tempest.

proceloso, sa [pro-thay-lo'-so, sah], *a*. Tempestuous, stormy.

prócer [pro'-ther], *a*. Tall, lofty, elevated. *-m*. Person who occupies an exalted station or is high in office; the grandees and high-titled nobility of Spain.

procerato [pro-thay-rah'-to], *m*. Exalted station.

proceridad [pro-thay-re-dahd'], *f*. 1 Procerity, tallness, height or stature. 2. Elevation, eminence.

procero, prócero [pro-thay'-ro], *a*. V. PRÓCER.

procesado [pro-thay-sah'-do], *a*. 1. Applied to the writings in a process. 2. Comprised in a criminal suit. *-pp*. of PROCESAR.

procesador [pro-thay-sah-dor'], *m*. Processor. **Procesador de textos,** word processor. **Procesador de equipos,** hardware processor. **Procesador de matrices,** array processor.

procesal [pro-thay-sahl'], *a*. Belonging to a process or lawsuit.

procesamiento [pro-thay-saha-me-ayn'-to], *m*. 1. Processing. 2. *(Comput.)* **Procesamiento de datos,** data processing. **Procesamiento de textos,** word processing.

procesar [pro-thay-sar'], *va*. *(Law.)* 1. To indict, to accuse, to inform against, to sue criminally (demandar). 2. To institute a suit.

procesión [pro-thay-se-on'], *f*. 1. Procession, proceeding from another. 2. Procession, train marching in ceremonious solemnity; parade. **La procesión va por dentro,** still waters run deep.

procesional [pro-thay-se-o-nahl'], *a*. Processional or processionary; relating to processions.

procesionalmente [pro-thay-se-o-nahl'-men-tay], *adv*. Processionally.

procesionario [pro-thay-se-o-nah'-re-o], *m*. Book carried about in processions.

proceso [pro-thay'-so], *m*. 1. Process, lawsuit. 2. Judicial records concerning a lawsuit. **Error de proceso,** *(Law. Prov.)* one who by ability, although convicted, evades the fine. 3. Progress. V. PROGRESO. 4. *(Comput.)* **Proceso prioritario,** foreground processing. **Proceso algorítmico,** algorithmic process.

procidencia [pro-the-den'-the-ah], *f*. *(Med.)* Procidence.

procinto [pro-theen'-to], *m*. Procinct, complete preparation.

proción [pro-the-on'], *m*. *(Ast.)* Procyon, a star, the most conspicuous in the constellation Canis minor, famous for its variable proper motion.

proclama [pro-clah'-mah], *f*. Proclamation, publication, banns of marriage.

proclamación [pro-clah-mah-the-on'], *f*. 1. Proclamation, the publication of a decree by superior order. 2. Acclamation, public applause.

proclamar [pro-clah-mar'], *va*. 1. To proclaim (publicar), to give public notice. 2. To bestow public praise, to shout. *-vr*. **Proclamarse campeón,** to become champion.

proclítico, ca [pro-clee'-te-co, cah], *a*. *(Gram.)* Proclitic, attached to a following word.

proclive [pro-clee'-vay], *a*. Proclivous, inclining; disposed.

proclividad [pro-cle-ve-dahd'], *f*. Proclivity, propensity to evil.

procomún, procomunal [pro-co-moon'], *m*. A public utility.

procónsul [pro-con'-sool], *m*. Proconsul.

proconsulado [pro-con-soo-lah' do], *m*. Proconsulship, office of proconsul or vice-consul.

proconsular [pro-con-soo-lar'], *a*. Proconsular, vice-consular.

procreación [pro-cray-ah-the-on'], *f*. Procreation, generation.

procreador, ra [pro-cray-ah-dor', rah], *m. & f*. Procreator, generator, getter.

procreante [pro-cray-ahn'-tay], *pa*. Procreating.

procrear [pro-cray-ar'], *va*. To procreate, to generate, to produce.

procronismo [pro-cro-nees'-mo], *m*. Prochronism, anachronism.

procumbente [pro-coom-ben'-tay], *a*. *(Bot.)* Procumbent.

procura [pro-coo'-rah], *f*. 1. Power of attorney. V. PROCURACIÓN. 2. *(Prov.)* V. PROCURADURÍA.

procuración [pro-coo-rah-the-on'], *f*. 1. Care, diligence, careful management. 2. Power or letter of attorney. 3. Procurement, the act of procuring. 4. Place and office of an attorney or administrator. 5. V. PROCURADURÍA.

procurador, ra [pro-coo-rah-dor', rah], *m. & f*. Procurer, obtainer, one that solicits.

procurador [pro-coo-rah-dor'], *m & f*. 1. Attorney, procurator, lawyer (abogado), one who takes upon himself the charge of other people's business. 2. Proctor, attorney at law.

procuradora [pro-coo-rah-do´-rah], *f.* She who manages the affairs of a nunnery.

procuraduría [pro-coo-rah-do-ree'-ah], *f.* Attorney's office; the employment of an attorney; procurement; proctorship.

procurante [pro-coo-rahn´-tay], *pa.* Solicitor, intendant.

procurar [pro-coo-rar'], *va.* 1. To solicit, to adopt measures for attaining an end, to try (intentar). 2. To procure, to manage (lograr), to transact for another. 3. To act as an attorney. 4. To get, to obtain (conseguir). **Procura conservar la calma**, try to keep calm. **Por fin procuró dominarse**, eventually he managed to control himself.

procurrente [pro-coor-ren´-tay], *m.* Peninsula, a great mass of earth reaching into the sea: as all Italy.

prodición [pro-de-the-on'], *f.* Treason, treachery.

prodigalidad [pro-de-gah-le-dahd'], *f.* 1. Prodigality (derroche), profusion, waste, extravagance (despilfarro), lavishness (liberalidad). 2. Plenty, abundance.

pródigamente [pro'-de-gah-men-tay], *adv.* Prodigally (con prodigalidad), lavishly (generosamente), wastefully, profusely.

prodigar [pro-de-gar'], *va.* To waste, to lavish (disipar), to misspend, to fling away. *-vr.* To be generous with what one has; to show off (dejarse ver).

prodigiador [pro-de-he-ah-dor'], *m.* Prognosticator, foreteller.

prodigio [pro-dee'-he-o], *m.* Prodigy, portent, monster; marvel.

prodigiosamente, *adv.* Prodigiously, miraculously, marvellously, amazingly; monstrously, enormously, beautifully. **Ella cantó prodigiosamente**, she sung charmingly.

prodigiosidad [pro-de-he-o-se-dahd'], *f.* Prodigiousness, portentousness.

prodigioso, sa [pro-de-he-oh'-so, sah], *a.* 1. Prodigious, marvellous, extraordinary; monstrous. 2. Fine, exquisite, excellent.

pródigo, ga [pro'-de-go, gah], *a.* Prodigal (derrochador), wasteful, lavish (liberal); liberal, generous, munificent. **La pródiga naturaleza**, bountiful nature. **Ser pródigo de sus talentos**, to be generous in offering one's talents.

prodrómico, ca [pro-dro'-me-co, cah], *a. (Med.)* Prodromic, relating to a prodrome.

pródromo [pro'-dro-mo], *m. (Ned.)* Prodrome, a sign of approaching disease.

producción [pro-dooc-the-on'], *f.* 1. Production, growth, product (objeto). 2. Enunciation, mode of expressing oneself, enouncement.

producibilidad [pro-doo-the-be-le-dahd'], *f.* Producibleness, productiveness.

producible [pro-doo-thee'-blay], *a.* Producible.

producidor, ra [pro-doo-the-dor', rah], *m. & f.* Producer, procreator.

producir [pro-doo-theer'], *va.* 1. To produce, to bring forth, to engender, to generate (motivar). 2. *(Law.)* To produce, to bring as evidence, to allege, to maintain, to exhibit. 3. To produce, to bear (vegetal). 4. To produce (países). 5. To produce, to cause, to occasion. 6. To yield revenue. 7. To quote, to cite. **Le produjo gran tristeza**, it caused her much sadness. **Producir en serie**, to mass-produce. *-vr.* 1. To enounce or explain oneself. 2. To become manifest, to be published. 3. To come about (cambio); to arise (dificultad, crisis); to happen (accidente); to break out (disturbio). **En ese momento se produjo una explosión**, at that moment there was an explosion. *(Yo produzco, yo produzca; produje; from* PRODUCIR. *V.* CONDUCIR.)

productible [pro-dooc-tee'-blay], *a.* Capable of yielding some product; productible.

productivo, va [pro-dooc-tee'-vo, vah], *a.* Productive, constitutive, originary.

producto [pro-dooc'-to], *m.* 1. Product, something produced, as grain, fruit, metals; production. 2. Proceed (ingreso), produce, fruit, growth. 3. *(Math.)* Product, quantity produced by multiplication. 4. Product, the final result of a chemical operation.—**Producto, ta**, *pp. irr.* of PRODUCIR. **Productos agrícolas**, agricultural produce. **Productos de consumo**, consumer goods.

productor [pro-dooc-tor'], *a.* 1. Productive, producing. **Clase productora**, those who produce. *-m.* **productora**. 1. Producer. 2. Workman (obrero). 3. (Cine, Tv.) Producer.

proejar [pro-ay-har'], *vn.* 1. To row against the wind or current. 2. To resist, to bear up under misfortunes.

proel [pro-el], *m. (Naut.)* Seaman stationed at the prow.

proemial [pro-ay-me-ahl'], *a.* Proemial, preliminary, introductory.

proemio [pro-ay'-me-o], *m.* Proem, preface, introduction.

proeza [pro-ay'-thah], *f.* Prowess, valor, bravery.

profanación [pro-fah-nah-the-on'], *f.* Profanation, profaneness, irreverence.

profanador, ra [pro-fah-nah-dor´, rah], *m. & f.* Profaner, polluter, violator.

profanamente [pro-fah'-nah-men-tay], *adv.* Profanely.

profanamiento [pro-fah-nah-me-en'-to], *m. V.* PROFANACIÓN.

profanar [pro-fah-nar'], *va.* 1. To profane, to violate, to desecrate (violar). 2. To defile, to disgrace, to dishonor, to abuse.

profanidad [pro-fah-ne-dahd'], *f.* 1. Indecency, immodesty, or excess in dress and outward show. 2. Want of competence or knowledge for handling a matter.

profano, na [pro-fah'-no, nah], *a.* 1. Profane, irreverent (irrespetuoso). 2. Worldly, irreligious. 3. Extravagant, flashy, loud, immodest or unchaste in dress and outward show. 4. Wanting in knowledge or authority upon a subject.

profecía [pro-fay-thee´-ah], *f.* 1. Prophecy, supernatural knowledge and prediction of future events. 2. Conjecture, surmise.

profecticio [pro-fec-tee´-the-o], *a.* Acquired by a son who lives under his father's direction; derived from one's fathers.

proferir [pro-fay-rer'], *va.* To pronounce, to utter (palabra, sonido), to express, to name. *(Yo profiero, yo profiera; él profirió; from Proferir. V.* ADHERIR.)

profesante [pro-fay-san´-tay], *pa. & m. & f.* Professor; professing.

profesar [pro-fay-sar´], *va.* 1. To profess (admiración, creencia), to declare openly, to teach publicly (materia). 2. To be admitted into a religious order by making the vows. 3. To profess, to exercise, to evince.

profesión [pro-fay-se-on'], *f.* 1. Profession, calling, vocation, occupation (en formulario). 2. Declaration, assurance. 3. Custom, habit. **Abogado de profesión**, a lawyer by profession.

profesional [pro-fay-se-o-nahl´], *a.* Professional; relating to or in accordance with a protection.

profesionalmente [pro-fay-se-o-nahl'-men-tay], *adv.* Professionally.

profeso, sa [pro-fay´-so, sah], *a.* Professed: applied to those who have taken vows.

profesor, ra [pro-fay-sor', rah], *m. & f.* Professor, teacher. **Profesor de gimnasia**, gym instructor. **Es profesora de griego**, she is professor of Greek.

profesorado [Pro-fay-so-rah'-do], *m.* 1. Faculty, body of teachers. 2. Teaching profession (profesión).

profeta [pro-fay'-tah], *m.* 1. Prophet, foreteller. 2. Title given to Mohammed by the Moslems.

profetal [pro-fay-tahl'], *a.* Relating to prophecy.

proféticamente [pro-fay'-te-cah-men-tay], *adv.* Prophetically.

profético, ca [pro-fay´-te-co, cah], *a.* Prophetic, prophetical.

profetisa [pro-fay-tee´-sah], *f.* Prophetess.

profetizar [pro-fay-te-thar'], *va.* 1. To prophesy; to predict. 2. To conjecture, to surmise.

proficiente [pro-fe-the-en'-tay], *a.* Proficient, making progress in any business.

proficuo, cua [pro-fee'-coo-o, ah], *a.* Profitable, useful, advantageous.

profiláctica [pro-fe-lahc'-te-cah], *f.* *(Med.)* Hygiene, prophylactia medicine.

profiláctico [pro-fe-lahc'-te-co], *a.* Prophylactic, preventive, preservative.

profilaxis [pro-fe-lahk'-sis], *f.* Prophylaxis, preventive treatment of disease in an individual.

prófugo, ga [pro'-foo-go, gah], *a.* Fugitive, vagabond.

profundamente [pro-foon-dah-men-tay], *adv.* Profoundly, deeply, highly, acutely, high.

profundidad [pro-foon-de-dahd'], *f.* 1. Profundity, depth (hondura), concavity. 2. Height, excellence, grandeur; impenetrability; intensity. Tener una profundidad de 30 cm, to be 30 cm deep.

profundizar [pro-foon-de-thar'], *va.* 1. To make deep (ahondar), to dig deep, to deepen. 2. To penetrate, to dive into a matter; to fathom, to explore.

profundo, da [pro-foon'-do, dah], *a.* 1. Profound, deep (hondo); descending far below the surface; low with respect to the neighboring places. 2. Profound (misterio, pensador), intellectually deep, recondite. 3. Intense, dense; at full extents. Tener 20 cm de profundo, to be 20 cm deep.

profundo [pro-foon'-do], *m.* 1. *(Poet.)* Profound, the sea, the deep. 2. *(Poet.)* Hell.

profusamente [pro-foo'-sah-men-tay], *adv.* Profusely, lavishly, prodigally, extravagantly.

profusión [pro-foo-se-on'], *f.* Profusion, lavishness, profuseness, extravagance, prodigality.

prufuso, sa [pro-foo'-so, sah], *a.* 1. Profuse (abundante), plentiful. 2. Lavish (extravagante), prodigal: extravagant.

progenie [pro-hay'-ne-ay], *f.* Progeny (hijos), race, offspring, issue.

progenitor [pro-hay-ne-tor'], *m.* Progenitor (antepasado), ancestor, forefather.

progenitura [pro-hay-ne-too'-rah], *f. V.* PROGENIE and PRIMOGENITURA.

progimnasma [pro-him-nahs'-mah], *m.* Essay, attempt; a preparatory exercise.

progne [prog-nay], *f. (Poet.)* The swallow.

programa [pro-grah'-mah], *m.* 1. Proclamation, public notice. 2. Theme, subject of a discourse, design, or picture. 3. Prospectus, program, prearranged plan or course of proceedings; scheme of lectures by a professor, or order of exercises. 4. Specification according to which a certain procedure must be carried out, program. Programa de estudios, curriculum. 5. *(Cono Sur)* Love affair (amorío). 6. *(Comput.)* Programas de aprendizaje, training software. Programas de ayuda, help software. Programas de comunicaciones, communication software. Programas de contabilidad, accounting software. Programas de dominio público, public domain software. Programas de entretenimiento, entertainment software. Programas de redes, networking software. Programas de utilidades, utility software. Programas educativos, educational software. Programas gratuitos, freeware. Programas para diagramas, flowcharting software. Programas para estadísticas, statistical software. Programas para gráficos, graphics software. Programas para la recuperación de datos, data recovery software. Programas para la empresa, business software. Programa de ajuste, retrofit software.

programación [pro-grah-mah-the-on'], *f.* Programing. Programación fija, *(Comput.)* firmware.

programado [pro-grah-mah'-do], *a.* Programed; planned (visita).

programador, ra [pro-grah-mah-dor'], *m & f.* Programer. *(Comput.)* Programador de aplicaciones, applications programer. Programador de sistemas, systems programmer.

programar [pro-grah-mar'], *va.* To plan; to draw up a program for (detalladamente); *(Comput.)* to program.

progresar [pro-gray-sar'], *vn.* To progress, make progress; to improve, better.

progresión [pro-gray-se-on'], *f.* Progression, process; progressiveness.

progresista [pro-gray-sees'-tah], *a. & com.* Progressive.

progresivamente [pro-gray-see'-vah-men-tay], *adv.* Progressively, onward, forward.

progresivo, va [pro-gray-see'-vo, vah], *a.* Progressive (que avanza), advancing.

progreso [pro-gray'-so], *m.* Progress, advancement, growth; forwardness. Hacer progresos, to progress.

prohibente [pro-e-ben'-te], *pa.* Prohibiting.

prohibición [pro-e-be-the-on'], *f.* Prohibition, interdict. Levantar la prohibición de, to remove the ban on.

prohibicionista [pro-e-be-the-o-nes'-tah] *m & f.* Prohibitionist.

prohibir [pro-e-beer'], *va.* To prohibit, to forbid, to restrain. Prohibir una droga, to prohibit a drug. Queda terminantemente prohibido, it is strictly forbidden to.

prohibitivo, va [pro-e-be-tee'-vo, vah], *a.* Prohibitory, forbidding.

prohibitorio, ria [pro-e-be-to'-re-o, ah], *a.* Prohibitory.

prohijador, ra [pro-e-ha-dor', rah], *m. & f.* Adopter, he that adopts a son.

prohijamiento [pro-e-hah-me-en'-to], *m.* Adoption.

prohijar [pro-e-har'], *va.* 1. To adopt, to make him a son who is not so by birth. 2. To ascribe, to attribute, to impute.

prohombre [pro-om'-bray], *m.* 1. In trades-unions the officer who governs the union. 2. One who enjoys special consideration among those of his class.

pro indiviso [pro in-de-vee'-so], *adv. (For.)* Undivided, undistributed: sold of legacies.

prójimo [pro'-he-mo], *m.* Fellow creature (semejante); neighbor (vecino). No tener prójimo, to be unfeeling or cruel, to be hard-hearted.

prolabio [pro-lah'-be-o], *m. (Med.)* Prolabium, the red external part of a lip.

prolapso [pro-lahp'-so], *m. (Med.)* Prolapse, descent of a viscus.

prole [pro'-lay], *f.* Issue, offspring, progeny, race; fruit.

prolegómeno [pro-lay-go'-may-no], *m.* Prolegomena, introductory discourse.

prolepsis [pro-lep'-sis], *f. (Rhet.)* Prolepsis, anticipation and answering of objections or counter-arguments.

proletariado [pro-lay-tah-re-ah'-do], *m.* 1. Proletarianism, the condition of the poorest classes. 2. The class of proletarians, the proletariat.

proletario, ria [pro-lay-tah'-re-o, ah], *a.* Proletarian, without property, very poor; plebeian.

prolífero, ra [pro-lee'-fay-ro, rah], *a. (Biol.)* Proliferous, reproducing freely; in botany, marked by excessive development of parts.

proliferar [pro-le-fay-rahr'], *vn.* To proliferate.

prolífico, ca [pro-lee'-fe-co, cah], *a.* Prolific, fruitful, productive.

prolijamente [pro-lee'-hah-men-tay], *adv.* Prolixly, tediously.

prolijidad [pro-la-he-dahd'], *f.* 1. Prolixity, tediousness. 2. Minute attention to trifles: trifling nicety.

prolijo, ja [pro-lee'-ho, hah], *a.* 1. Prolix (extenso), tedious (pesado), particular. 2. Over careful, triflingly nice. 3. Troublesome, impertinent, long-winded.

prólogo [pro'-lo-go], *m.* 1. Prologue, preface (preámbulo); introduction. 2. Prologue to a play.

prologuista [pro-lo-gees'-tah], *m.* Writer of prologues.

prolonga [pro-lon'-gah], *f. (Mil.)* Rope which ties the carriage of a cannon when passing difficult places.

prolongación [pro-lon-gah-the-on'], *f.* Prolongation (acto), lengthening, lingering, extension (de carretera).

prolongadamente [pro-lon-gah'-dah-men-tay], *adv.* Tardily.

prolongado, da [pro-lon-gah'-do, dah], *a.* Prolonged, extended. -*pp.* of PROLONGAR.

prolongador, ra [pro-lon-gah-dor', rah], *m. & f.* One who prolongs or delays anything.

prolongamiento [pro-lon-gah-me-en'-to] *m.* Delay. V. PROLONGACIÓN.

prolongar [pro-lon-gar'], *va.* 1. To prolong (alargar), to protract, to lengthen out, to continue. 2. *(Com.)* To allow to stand over. **Prolongar un plazo**, To grant an extension of time. *-vr. (Naut.)* To go alongside. **Prolongarse a la costa**, *(Naut.)* to range along the shore. **La sesión se prolongó bastante**, the meeting went on long enough.

proloquio [pro-lo'-ke-o], *m.* Maxim, moral, apothegm.

prolusión [pro-loo-se-on'], *f.* Prolusion, prelude. V. PRELUSIÓN.

promediar [pro-may-de-ar'], *va.* To divide into two equal parts (objeto), to shank equally. *-vn.* To mediate (mediar), to form by mediation; to interpose in a friendly manner.

promedio [pro-may'-de-o], *m.* 1. Middle, the part equally distant from the two extremities (de distancia). 2. An average. **El promedio de asistencia diaria**, the average daily attendance.

promesa [pro-may'-sah], *f.* Promise (ofrecimiento), offer; pious offering. **Simple promesa**, a promise not confirmed by a vow or oath. **Faltar a una promesa**, to break a promise.

prometedor, ra [pro-may-tay-dor', rah], *a.* Promising, full of promise.

prometer [pro-may-terr'], *va.* 1. To promise (ofrecer), to bid fair. 2. To assever, to assure, to insure: often used menacingly. **Prometer hacer algo**, to promise to do something. **Esto promete ser interesante**, this promises to be interesting. *-vr.* 1. To flatter oneself, to expect with confidence (esperar). 2. To devote oneself to the service or worship of God. 3. To give a promise of marriage. **Prometerse algo bueno**, to promise oneself a treat. *-vn.* To promise, to show signs of forwardness (tener porvenir). **Es un jugador que promete**, he´s a promising player.

prometida [pro-may-tee'-dah], *f.* Fiancée.

prometido [pro-may-tee'-do], *m.* 1. Promise (promesa), offer. 2. Outbidding, overbidding. 3. Fiancé (persona). **Prometido, da**, *pp.* of PROMETER.

prometimiento [pro-may-te-me-en'-to], *m.* Promise, offer.

prominencia [pro-me-nen'-the-ah], *f.* Prominence, protuberance (elevación), process, knob, elevation of a thing, above its surroundings.

prominente [pro-me-nen'-tay], *a.* Prominent (protuberante), protubcrant; jutting out.

promiscuamente [pro-mes'-coo-ah-men-tay], *adv.* Promiscuously.

promiscuo, cua [pro-mees'-coo-o, ah], *a.* Promiscuous, confusedly mingled (revuelto); ambiguous (sentido).

promisorio, ria [pro-me-so'-re-o, ah], *a.* Promissory.

promoción [pro-mo-the-on'], *f.* Promotion (ascenso), advancement, encouragement, preferment. **Promoción de ventas**, sales promotion. **Fue de mi promoción**, he belonged to the same class/regiment as I did.

promocionar [pro-mo-the-o-nahr'], *va.* To promote; to give rapid promotion (persona). *-vr.* To improve oneself.

promontorio [pro-mon-to'-re-o], *m.* 1. A considerable elevation of ground. 2. Anything bulky and unwieldy; an impediment, obstruction. 3. Promontory, headland, forehand, cape.

promotor, ra [pro-mo-tor'], *m & f.* 1. Promoter, advancer, forwarder, furtherer. 2. **Promotor fiscal**, *(Law.)* a secular or ecclesiastical attorney-general. **Promotor de ventas**, sales promoter.

promovedor, ra [pro-mo-vay-dor', rah], *m. & f.* Promotor.

promovendo [pro-mo-ven'-do], *m.* A person who aspires to promotion.

promover [pro-mo-verr'], *va.* 1. To promote (proceso), to advance, to further, to forward, to help. 2. To promote (intereses), to raise to a higher dignity or employment (ascender).

promulgación [pro-mool-ga-the-on'], *f.* Promulgation.

promulgador, ra [pro-mool-gah-dor', rah], *m. & f.* Publisher, promulgator.

promulgar [pro-mool-gar'], *va.* To promulgate, to publish.

pronación [pro-nah-the-on'], *f.* Pronation, the act of turning the hand (or fore limb) downward; also the position of a limb so turned.

proneidad [pro-nay-dahd'], *f.* Proneness, inclination, propensity.

prono, na [pro'-no, nah], *a.* 1. Prone, bending downward. 2. Prone, inclined, disposed.

pronombre [pro-nom'-bray], *m. (Gram.).* Pronoun. **Pronombre personal**, personal pronoun.

pronominal [pro-no-me-nahl'], *a.* Pronominal.

pronosticación [pro-nos-te-cah-the-on'], *f.* Prognostication, foreboding, forecasting.

pronosticador, ra [pro-nos-te-cah-dor', rah], *m. & f.* 1. Foreteller, prognosticator, foreboder, forecaster.

pronosticar [pro-nos-te-car'], *va.* To prognosticate, to predict, to foretell, to conjecture, to augur.

pronóstico, ca [pro-nos'-te-co, cah], *a.* Prognostic, foreshowing.

pronóstico [pro-nos'-te-co], *m.* 1. Prognostic, prediction, divination, omen (presagio), forerunner. 2. Almanac or calendar published by astrologers. **Pronóstico del tiempo**, weather forecast. 3. *(Med.)* Prognosis. **De pronóstico reservado**, of uncertain gravity.

prontamente [pron'-tah-men-tay], *adv.* Promptly, lightly, nimbly.

prontitud [pron-te-tood'], *f.* 1. Promptitude, promptness. 2. Readiness or liveliness of, with quickness of fancy; activity.

pronto, ta [pron'-to, tah], *a.* 1. Prompt (respuesta), quick (servicio), rapid, ready, hasty, fast, forward, expedient. **De pronto**, without premeditation, unintentionally; for the present; to suit the occasion. 2. *(Cono Sur)* Ready (dispuesto); tight (borracho).

pronto [pron'-to], *adv.* 1. Promptly, quickly (rápidamente), expeditiously; at once (enseguida); soon (dentro de poco). 2. Early (temprano). **Lo más pronto posible**, as soon as possible. **Por lo pronto**, meanwhile. **Levantarse pronto**, to get up early. **Iremos a comer un poco pronto**, we´ll go and have lunch a bit early.

pronto [pron'-to], *m.* A sudden emotion of the mind, a quick motion. **Por el pronto**, provisionally, temporarily. **Primer pronto**, first movement. **Un pronto**, a sally.

prontuario [pron-too-ah'-re-o], *m.* 1. Memorandum-book. 2. Compendium of rules of some science or art.

prónuba [pro'-noo-bah], *f. (Poet.)* Bridesmaid; goddess of wedlock.

pronunciación [pro-noon-the-ah-the-on'], *f.* 1. Pronunciation, utterance; enunciation; articulation. 2. *(Law.)* Publication.

pronunciador, ra [pro-noon-the-ah-dor', rah], *m. & f.* Publisher, pronouncer.

pronunciamiento [pro-noon-the-ah-me-en'-to], *m.* 1. *(Law.)* Publication. 2. Insurrection, uprising.

pronunciar [pro-noon-the-ar'], *va.* 1. To pronounce, to utter, to articulate (articular), to enunciate. 2. To pronounce judgment, to issue by authority. 3. To pass upon, to deliberate on, while the principal point is decided. *(Acad.)* **Pronunció unas palabras en las que...**, she said that.... *-vr.* 1. To rise in insurrection, to declare oneself (declararse). **Pronunciarse a favor de**, to pronounce in favor of. 2. *(Pol.)* To revolt, to rise, to rebel. 3. *(Fig.)* To become pronounced (hacerse más marcado). 4. To cough up (soltar la pasta).

propagación [pro-pah-gah-the-on'], *f.* Propagation, successive production, offspring; extension.

propagador, ra [pro-pah-gah-dor', rah], *m. & f.* Propagator.

propaganda [pro-pah-gahn'-dah], *f.* 1. Propaganda. 2. Advertising.

propagantista [pro-pah-gahn-dees'-tah], *m. & f. & a.* Propagandist.

propagar [pro-pah-gar'], *va.* 1. To propagate, to generate, to multiply the species. 2. To propagate, to diffuse, to extend. 3. To propagate, to enlarge, to increase, to promote.

propagativo, va [pro-pah-gah-tee'-vo, vah], *a.* That which propagates.

propaladia [pro-pah-lah´-de-a], *f.* Title of a play.

propalar [pro-pah-lar'], *va.* To publish, to divulge (divulgar), to disseminate (diseminar).

propano [pro-pah'-no], *m.* Propane.

propao [pro-pah'-o], *m.* (*Naut.*) Breast work, bulkhead

propartida [pro-par-tee'-dah], *f.* Time approaching that of departing.

propasar [pro-pah-sar'], *va.* To go beyond, to transgress, to exceed. *-vr.* To be deficient in good-breeding.

propender [pro-pen-derr'], *vn.* To tend towards, to incline to by nature.

propensamente [pro-pen'-sah-men-tay], *adv.* In a propense manner, with inclination or propension.

propensión [pro-pen-se-on'], *f.* Propension, propensity, tendency, inclination, liability.

propenso, sa [pro-pen'-so, sah], *a.* Inclined, disposed, minded, apt to, prone, open to. **Propenso a accidentes**, accident-prone.

propiamente [pro'-pe-ah-men-tay], *adv.* Properly, with propriety; fittingly.

propiciación [pro-pe-the-ah-the-on'], *f.* 1. Propitiation, atonement. 2. Act of making propitious.

propiciador, ra [pro-pe-the-ah-dor', rah], *m. & f.* Propitiator.

propiciamente [pro-pee'-the-ah-men-tay], *adv.* Propitiously.

propiciar [pro-pe-the-ar'], *va.* 1. To propitiate (atraer), to conciliate. 2. To favor (favorecer); to create a favorable atmosphere for; to cause (provocar); to aid (ayudar).

propiciatorio, ria [pro-pe-the-ah-to'-re-o, ah], *a.* Propitiatory.

propiciatorio [pro-pe-the-ah-to'-re-o], *m.* Propitiatory, mercy-seat; the covering of the ark of the covenant.

propicio, cia [pro-pee'-the-o, ah], *a.* Propitious, kind, favorable (momento).

propiedad [pro-pe-ay-dahd'], *f.* 1. (*For.*) Dominion, possession (pertenencia), eminent domain; exclusive right of possession. *V.* DOMINIO. 2. Landed estate or property (objeto, tierras). 3. Property, particular quality which is peculiar to a thing. 4. Propriety (lo apropiado), appropriateness, aptness, expedience. 5. (*Gram.*) Exact signification of a term. 6. Propensity, inclination. 7. Close imitation. 8. (*Phil.*) *V.* PROPIO. **Ser de la propiedad de**, to be the property of. **Propiedad particular**, private property. **Propiedad industrial**, patent rights.

propienda [pro-pe-en'-dah], *f.* Listing nailed to the sides of a quilting or embroidering frame.

propietaria [pro-pe-ay-tah´-re-ah], *f.* Proprietress, a temple possessor in her own right.

propietariamente [pro-pe-ay-tah'-re-ah-men-tay], *adv.* With the right of property.

propietario, ria [pro-pe-ay-tah'-re-o, ah], *a.* Proprietary, invested with the right of property; belonging with full right of property.

propietario [pro-pe-ay-tah'-re-o], *m.* 1. Proprietary, proprietor, owner, landlord. 2. **Propietario de una finca**, freeholder. 3. Proprietary, a religious who sins against the vow of poverty.

propíleo [pro-pee'-lay-o], *m.* Propyleum, vestibule of a temple; a peristyle of columns.

propina [pro-pee'-nah], *f.* Present, pay beyond the agreed price, gratuity, tip. **Dar algo de propina**, to give something extra.

propinación [pro-pe-nah-the-on'], *f.* Treat, invitation to drink.

propinar [pro-pe-nar'], *va.* 1. To invite, to drink, to present a glass of wine or liquor. 2. (*coll.*) To prescribe medicines. 3. To deal (golpe), to hit; to give (paliza).

propincuidad [pro-pin-coo-e-dahd'], *f.* Propinquity, proximity, nearness.

propincuo, cua [pro-peen'-coo-o, ah], *a.* Near, contiguous.

propio, pia [pro'-pe-o, ah], *a.* 1. Proper, one's own, belonging to anyone. 2. Proper, suitable, becoming accommodated, adapted, fit, convenient. 3. Proper (apro-

piado), peculiar (particular) to anyone. 4. Proper (sentido), natural, original, genuine. 5. Exact, precise in speaking or writing. 6. *V.* MISMO. 7. Resembling, like, similar. **Con su propia mano**, with his own hand. **Tienen casa propia**, they have a house of their own. **Una bebida propia del país**, a typical drink of the country.

propio [pro'-pe-o], *m.* 1. (*Phil.*) Proper, peculiar or distinctive quality: characteristic property of a class, genus, or species. 2. Special delivery for letters of importance: messenger. *-pl.* Lands, estates, etc., belonging to a city or civic corporation.

propóleos [pro-po´-lay-os], *m.* Propolis, bee-glue.

proponedor, ra [pro-po-nay-dor', rah], *m. & f.* Proposer, offerer, proponent.

proponer [pro-po-nerr'], *va.* 1. To propose (idea, proyecto), to offer for consideration, to hold out, to represent. 2. To resolve, to determine, to mean. 3. To resent; to propose the means. **Le propuse que fuéramos juntos**, I proposed to him that we should go together. *-vr.* 1. **Proponerse hacer algo**, to propose to do something. 2. **Te has propuesto hacerme perder el tren**, you set out deliberately to make me miss the train.

proporción [pro-por-the-on'], *f.* 1. Proportion, portion, comparative relation of one thing to another. 2. Symmetry, adaptation of one thing to another: aptitude, fitness. 3. Similarity of arguments and reasons. 4. Opportunity, occasion, chance (oportunidad). 5. Relationship (relación); rate (porcentaje). 6. (*Mex.*) **Proporciones**, wealth. **A proporción**, conformably, proportionally; as fast as. **Estar fuera de proporción**, to be out of proportion. **Esto no guarda proporción con lo otro**, this is out of proportion with the rest.

proporcionable [pro-por-the-o-nah'-blay], *a.* Proportionable. *V.* PROPORCIONADO.

proporcionablemente, proporcionadamente, *adv.* Proportionably, proportionally.

proporcionado, da [pro-por-the-o-nah´-do, dah], *a.* Proportionate, regular, competent, commensurate, conformable, harmonious. *-pp.* of PROPORCIONAR.

proporcional [pro-por-the-o-nahl'], *a.* Proportional.

proporcionalidad [pro-por-the-onah-le-dahd´], *f.* Proportionableness, proportionality.

proporcionalmente [pro-por-the-o-nahl'-men-tay], *adv.* Proportionally, commensurately.

proporcionar [pro-por-the-o-nar'], *va.* 1. To proportion, to form symmetrically. 2. To adjust (adaptar), to adapt. 3. To afford, to furnish. **Proporcionar dinero a uno**, to give somebody money. *-vr.* To prepare oneself for any design.

proposición [pro-po-se-the-on'], *f.* 1. Proposition, the act of proposing. 2. Proposal, scheme, overture. 3. Proposition, assertion of affirmation or denial. 4. (*Math.*) Proposition, an established truth required to be demonstrated.

propósito [pro-poh'-se-to], *m.* 1. Purpose, aim, object, design, intention (intención). 2. Subject matter (tema). **A propósito**, for the purpose; fit for; apropos; by-the-bye. **De propósito**, on purpose, purposely. **Fuera de propósito**, untimely, not to the purpose, foreign to the subject, out of the question. **Volvamos al propósito**, let us return to the point in question.

propretor [pro-pray-tor'], *m.* Roman magistrate.

proptosis [prop-to'-ses], *f.* (*Med.*) Ptosis, falling of an organ.

popuesta [pro-poo-es'-tah], *f.* 1. Proposal, proposition, offer, overture. 2. Representation, declaration. 3. Proposal for employment.

propuesto, ta [pro-poo-es'-to, tah], *pp. irr.* of PROPONER. Proposed.

propugnación [pro-poog-nah-the-on'], *f.* Advocacy.

propugnáculo [pro-poog-nah'-coo´-lo], *m.* 1. A fortress. 2. (*Met.*) Bulwark, defence, support.

propugnar [pro-poog-nahr'], *va.* To advocate (proponer), to propose; to defend (apoyar).

propulsión [pro-pool-see-ohn´], *f.* Propulsion. **Propulsión a chorro**, jet propulsion. **Avión de propulsión**, jet plane.

propulsar [pro-pool-sar´], *va.* To repel *V.* REPULSAR.

propulsiva [pro-pool-see'-vah], *f.* PROPULSA.

propulsor [pro-pool-sor'], *m.* Propeller, propellant: a mechanism driven by a motive power within a vessel, and which acts upon the water, as oars, wheels, screw.

prora [pro'-rah], *f.* *(Poet.)* Prow of a ship.

prorrata [pror-rah'-tah], *f.* 1. Quota, a portion assigned to each contribuent. 2. Apportionment.

prorratear [pror-rah-tay-ar'], *va.* 1. To divide a quantity into certain shares. -*vn.* 2. To apportion.

prorrateo [pror-rah-tay'-o], *m.* Division into shares, distribution, average.

prórroga, prorrogación [pror'-ro-gah], *f.* 1. Prorogation, lengthening out to a distant time; prolongation. 2. *(For.)* Amplification of powers to cases and persons which they did not comprise.

prorrogable [pror-ro-gah'-blay], *a.* Capable of being prorogued.

prorrogación [pror-ro-gah-the-on'], *f.* Deferment, prorogation.

prorrogar [pror-ro-gar'], *va.* To prorogue (sesión), to put off, to adjourn.

prorrumpir [pror-room-peer'], *vn.* 1. To break forth, to burst out with violence, to issue. 2. To burst forth, to burst out into cries and lamentations.

prosa [pro'-sah], *f.* 1. Prose. 2. Tedious conversation, dull, absurd speech. 3. Prose chanted after mass. 4. *(Cono Sur)* Vanity (vanidad). 5. *(And. CAm.)* Pomposity.

prosador [pro-sah-dor'], *m.* *(coll.)* A sarcastic speaker, a malicious babbler.

prosaico, ca [pro-sah'-e-co, cah], *a.* 1. Prosaic, written in prose; belonging to prose. 2. Prosy, dull, tedious (monótono).

prosaísmo [pro-sah-ees'-mo], *m.* 1. Defect of verses which lack rhythm. 2. Prosiness, dulness.

prosapia [pro-sah'-pe-ah], *f.* Race, ancestry, lineage (linaje), a generation of people.

proscenio [pros-thay'-ne-o], *m.* Proscenium, place on the stage.

proscribir [pros-cre-beer'], *va.* To proscribe (partido), to outlaw (criminal), to censure capitally; to doom to destruction.

proscripción [pros-crip-the-on'], *f.* Prescription, banishment, outlawry.

proscripto [pros-creep'-to], *m.* Outlaw (bandido).

proscripto, ta, proscrito, to [pros-creep'-to, pros-cree'-to, tah], *pp. rr.* of PROSCRIBIR. Proscribed.

prosecución [pro-say-coo-the-on'], *f.* 1. Prosecution, pursuit, endeavor to carry on anything. 2. Pursuit, the act of following another.

proseguible [pro-say-gee'-blay], *a.* Pursuable.

proseguimiento [pro-say-gee-me-en'-to], *m.* V. PROSECUCIÓN.

proseguir [pro-say-geer'], *va.* To pursue (estudio), to prosecute, to follow, to continue anything already begun (continuar). -*vn.* 1. **Continuar en una actitud,** to continue in one's attitude. 2. To continue (condición). **Prosiguió con el cuento,** he went on with the story.

proselitismo [pro-say-le-tees'-mo], *m.* Proselytism, zeal for making proselytes.

prosélito [pro-say'-le-to], *m.* Proselyte, convert.

prosista [pro-sees'-tah], *m & f.* 1. Author who writes in prose. 2. *(coll.)* Prattler, babbler, idle talker, proper.

prosita [pro-see'-tah], *f. dim.* A short discourse in prose.

prosodia [pro-so'-de-ah], *f.* 1. Orthoepy, the science or art of correct pronunciation. 2. Loquacity, idle talk. 3. Prosody, the science of metrical forms; formerly a division of grammar. 4. Regular mode of pronouncing each syllable of a word when singing.

prosódico, ca [pro-so'-de-co, cah], *a.* Orthoepic, relating to pronunciation; or prosodic.

prosopografía [pro-so-po-grah-fee'-ah], *f.* Prosopography, description of the physiognomy of a person or animal

prosopopeya [pro-so-po-pay'-yah], *f.* 1. Prosopopoeia, personification, a figure of speech. 2. *(coll.)* Splendor, pageantry.

prospecto [pros-pec'-to], *m.* Prospectus; leaflet, sheet of instructions.

prósperamente [pros'-pay-rah-men-tay], *adv.* Prosperously, luckily.

prosperar [pros-pay-rar'], *va.* To prosper, to make happy; to favor. -*vn.* To prosper, to be prosperous, to thrive.

prosperidad [pros-pay-re-dahd'], *f.* Prosperity, good fortune, success.

próspero, ra [pros'-pay-ro, rah], *a.* Prosperous (rico), successful (venturoso), fortunate, fair.

prostaféresis [pros-tah-fay'-ray-sis], *f.* *(Ast.)* Prosthaphaeresis, correction to be applied to the mean place of a heavenly body to obtain the true place or movement.

próstata [pros'-ta-tah], *f.* The prostate gland.

prostático, ca [pros-tah'-te-co, cah], *a.* Prostatic, pertaining to the prostate.

prostatitis [pros-ta-tee'-tis], *f.* Prostatitis, inflammation of the prostate.

prosternación [pros-ter-nah-the-on'], *f.* Profound reverence and humiliation, falling down.

prosternarse [pros-ter-nar'-say], *vr.* To fall down, to prostrate oneself in adoration (postrarse), to bend as a suppliant.

prostíbulo [pros-tee'-boo-lo], *m.* House of prostitution, disorderly place.

prostilo [pros-tee'-lo], *a.* *(Arch.)* Prostyle, having only pillars in front.

prostitución [pros-te-too-the-on'], *f.* 1. Prostitution, the act of setting or being set to sale for vile purposes. 2. Prostitution, the life of a strumpet.

prostituir [pros-te-too-eer'], *va.* To prostitute (mujer), to expose to crimes for a reward; to expose on vile terms. -*vr.* To hack, to turn hackney or prostitute.

prostituta [pros-te-too'-tah], *f.* Prostitute, woman of the town, whore.

prostituto, ta [pros-te-too'-to, tah], *pp. irr.* of PROSTITUIR. Prostituted.

protagonismo [pro-tah-go-nees'-mo], *m.* Defense (defensa); support (apoyo); initiative (iniciativa); leadership (liderazgo); leading role (papel).

protagonista [pro-tah-go-nees'-tah], *m & f.* Protagonist, principal personage of a dramatic story.

protagonizar [pro-tah-go-ne-thahr'], *va.* 1. To take the chief role in, to play the leading part. 2. To lead (rebelión, proceso); to stage (manifestación); to figure in (accidente). **Una entrevista protagonizada por X,** an interview whose subject was X.

prótasis [pro'-tah-sis], *f.* 1. Protasis, the first piece of a dramatic poem. 2. *(Gram.)* Protasis, the first part of a compound period.

protección [pro-tec-the-on'], *f.* Protection, support, favor, countenance.

proteccionismo [pro-tec-the-o-nees'-mo], *m.* The economic doctrine of protection or protectionism: opposite of free trade.

proteccionista [pro-tec-the-o-nees'-tah], *m.* Protectionist, a partisan of protectionism.

protector [pro-tec-tor'], *m.* 1. Protector, defender, guardian, conservator. 2. Steward of a community, charged with maintaining its interest.

protectora [pro-tec-to'-rah], *f.* Protectress, a woman who protects.

protectorado [pro-tec-to-rah'-do], *m.* Protectorate, the dignity of a protector and the time during which it lasts.

protectoría [pro-tec-to-ree'-ah], *f.* Protectorship, protectorate.

protectorio, ria [pro-tec-to'-re-o, ah], *a.* Relating to a protector.

protectriz [pro-tec-treeth'], *f.* Protectress.

proteger [pro-tay-herr'], *va.* To protect (resguardar), to defend (defender), to favor, to countenance.

protegido

protegido da [pro-tay-hee'-do, dah], *m. & f.* Protege, protegee, favorite.-*a. & pp.* of PROTEGER. Protected, sheltered.

proteína [pro-tay-ee'-nah], *f.* Protein.

protervamente [pro-tayr'-vah-men-tay], *adv.* Frowardly, stubbornly, perversely.

protervia, protervidad [pro-terr'-ve-ah], *f.* Obstinacy, protervity, peevishness, stubbornness.

protervo, va [pro-terr'-vo, vah], *a.* Stubborn, peevish, obstinate, perverse.

prótesis [pro'-tay-sis], *f. (Gram.)* Prosthesis or prothesis, addition of letters at the beginning of a word, for the sake of euphony; as *aqueste* for *este.*

protesta [pro-tes'-tah], *f.* 1. *(Law.)* Protest (queja), a solemn declaration. 2. A solemn promise, asservation, or assurance. **Hacer protestas de lealtad**, to protest one's loyalty.

protestación [pro-tes-tah-the-on'], *f.* 1. Protestation, profession, a solemn declaration 2. Threat, menace.

protestante [pro-tes-tahn'-tay], *com.* A Protestant.

protestante [pro-tes-tahn'-tay], *a.* Protestant, belonging to protestants. *-pa.* Protesting.

protestantismo [pro-tes-tan-tees'-mo], *m.* Protestantism.

protestar [pro-tes-tar'], *va.* 1. To protest, to give a solemn declaration. 2. To assure, to assever. 3. To threaten, to menace. 4. To make a public declaration of faith and belief. 5. *(Law.)* To make a solemn declaration for the purpose of preserving one's right. **Protestar una letra**, to protest a bill of exchange. *-vn.* 1. To protest (quejarse); to object (objetar); to remonstrate. 2. To protest (inocencia). **Protestar contra una demora**, to protest about a delay.

protestativo, va [pro-tes-tah-tee'-vo, vah], *a.* That which protests.

protesto [pro-tes'-to], *m.* 1. *(Com.)* Protest of a bill. 2. *V.* PROTESTA.

protético, ca [pro-tay'-te-co, cah], *a.* Prothetic, prefixed.

protocolar, protocolizar [pro-to-co-lar'], *va.* To place in the protocol, to record, to register.

protocolario [pro-to-co-lah-re-o], *a.* 1. Established by protocol (exigido por el protocolo). 2. *(Fig.)* Formal (ceremonial).

protocolo [pro-to-co'-lo], *m.* Protocol, registry, a judicial record. **Protocolo de control de enlace**, link control protocol, procedure.

protomedicato [pro-to-may-de-cah'-to], *m.* 1. Tribunal or college of king's physicians, where student of medicine are examined and licensed. 2. Office of a first or royal physician.

protomédico [pro-to-may'-de-co], *m.* First physician, one of the three physicians to the king.

protón [pro-tone'], *m. (Phy.)* Proton.

protonotario [pro-to-no-tah'-re-o], *m.* Prothonotary, chief clerk or chief notary.

protoplasma [pro-to-plahs'-mah], *m.* Protoplasm.

protosulfuro [pro-to-sool-foo'-ro], *m.* Protosulphide.

prototípico, ca [pro-to-tee -pe-co, cah], *a.* Prototypal, belonging to a prototype.

prototipo [pro-to-tee'-po], *m.* Prototype, origins.

protóxido [pro-tok'-se-do], *m.* Protoxide.

protozoario, ria [pro-to-tho-ah'-re-o, ah], *a.* Protozoic.

protozoo [pro-to-tho'-o], *m.* Protozoan, protozoon, one-celled organism.

protuberancia [pro-too-bar-rahn'-the-ah], *f.* Protuberance, prominence.

provecto, ta [pro-vec'-to, tah], *a.* Advanced in years, learning, or experience.

provecho [pro-vay'-cho], *m.* 1. Profit, benefit, advantage, utility, gain. 2. Profit, improvement, proficiency, progress; advancement. **Hombre de provecho**, a useful man. **Ser de provecho**, to be useful or profitable. **Buen provecho**, good appetite. **En provecho propio**, to one's own advantage.

provechosamente [pro-vay-cho'-sah-men-tay], *adv.* Profitably, gainfully, advantageously, usefully.

provechoso, sa [pro-vay-cho'-so, sah], *a.* Profitable, beneficial, gainful, lucrative, useful, advantgeous.

proveedor, ra [pro-vay-ay-dor', rah], *m. & f.* Purveyor, contractor, furnisher.

proveeduría [pro-vay-ay-doo-ree'-ah], *f.* 1. Store-house for provisions. 2. Employment and office of purveyor.

proveer [pro-vay-err'], *va.* 1. To provide (disponer), to procure beforehand, to get ready, to furnish, to fit, to accommodate. 2. To supply with provisions to provide provisions for an army (suministrar). 3. To dispose, to adjust. 4. To confer a dignity or employment. 5. To decree, to doom by a decree, to despatch a suit at law. 6. To minister, to supply with the necessaries of life, to maintain. *-vr. (coll.)* To ease the body.

proveído [pro-vey-ee'-do], *m.* Judgment, sentence, decree. **Proveído, da**, *pp.* of PROVEER.

proveimiento [pro-vay-e-me-en'-to], *m.* Supply, the act of providing or supplying with provisions.

proveniente [pro-vay-ne-en'-tay], *pa.* Proceeding, originating in.

provenir [pro-vay-neer'], *vn.* To arise, to proceed; to take rise or origin from, to originate in. **Provenir de**, to come from.

provenzal [pro-ven-thahl'], *a.* Provençal, relating to Provence, and its language; Languedocian.

proverbiador [pro-ver-be-ah-dor'], *m.* Collection of proverbs.

proverbial [pro-ver-be-ahl'], *a.* Proverbial.

proverbialmente [pro-ver-be-ahl-men-tay], *adv.* Proverbially.

proverbiar [pro-ver-be-ar'], *vn. (coll.)* To use proverbs.

proverbio [pro-vayr'-be-o], *m.* 1. A proverb. 2. Prophecy, prediction from certain words. **Proverbios**, Book of Proverbs, a canonical book of the Old Testament.

proverbista [pro-ver-bees'-tah], *m. (coll.)* One attached to the use of proverbs.

próvidamente [pro'-ve-dah-men-tay], *adv.* Providently, carefully.

providencia [pro-ve-den'-the-ah], *f.* 1. Providence, foresight (cualidad), forecast, forethought (prevención). 2. Providence, the act of providing disposition or measures taken to obtain some end. 3. Divine Providence. 4. State or order of things. **Dictar providencia**, to take steps to.

providencial [pro-ve-den-the-ahl'], *a.* Providential.

providencialmente [pro-ve-den-the-ahl'-men-tay], *adv.* Providentially, provisionally.

providenciar [pro-ve-den-the-ar'], *va.* To ordain, to command.

providente [pro-ve-den-tay], *a.* Provident, prudent, careful.

próvido, da [pro'-ve-do, dah], *a.* Provident, careful, diligent.

provincia [pro-veen'-the-ah], *f.* 1. Province, one of the divisions of a kingdom. 2. A certain number of convents under the direction of a provincial. 3. Provincial court appointed to try and decide civil causes. 4. Province, an important business which is to be treated upon.

provincial [pro-vin-the-ahl'], *a.* Provincial.

provincialismo [pro-vin-the-ah-lees'-mo], *m.* Provincialism.

provinciano, na [pro-vin-the-ah'-no, nah], *a. m & f.* Provincial; country (rural).

provisión [pro-ve-se-on'], *f.* 1. Store of provisions collected for use (suministro); provender. 2. Writ, decree, or sentence issued by Spanish tribunals in the king's name. 3. Title or instrument, by virtue whereof an incumbent holds his benefice. 4. Act of conferring an employment or office (acto). 5. *(Com.)* A remittance of funds by the drawer of a bill of exchange to the drawee so that he may accept it.

provisional [pro-ve-se-o-nahl'], *a.* Provisional.

provisionalmente [pro-ve-se-o-nahl'-men-tay], *adv.* Provisionally.

proviso, or **al proviso** [pro-vee'-so], *adv.* Upon the spot, immediately, instantly.

provisor, ra [pro-ve-sor', rah], *m. & f.* 1. Provider. *V.* PROVEEDOR. 2. Vicar-general, an ecclesiastical judge.

provisoría [pro-ve-so-ree´-ah], *f.* 1. In some convents and colleges, the store-room, where provisions are kept; pantry. 2. Place or office of a provisor or vicar-general.

provisorio, ria [pro-ve-so´-re-o, ah], *a. (LAm.)* Provisional, temporarily established.

provisto, ta [pro-vees´-to, tah], *a.* 1. Provided with a benefice. 2. *(Cono Sur)* Provisions, supplies. *-pp. irr.* of PROVEER.

provocación [pro-vo-cah-the-on´], *f.* 1. Provocation, displeasure, irritation. 2. Cause or motive of anger.

provocador, ra [pro-vo-cah-dor´, rah], *m. & f.* Provoker; causer, promoter.

provocar [pro-vo-car´], *va.* 1. To provoke (persona), to rouse (enojar), to excite, to nettle. 2. To anger, to enrage, to offend. 3. To vomit. 4. To facilitate, to promote. 5. To move, to excite. 6. To bring about (cambio); to promote (proceso); to cause (explosión, protesta, guerra). 7. *(LAm.)* **¿Te provoca un café?,** would you like some coffee? (gustar, apetecer).

provocativo, va [pro-vo-cah-tee´-vo, vah], *a.* 1. Provocative, exciting, inducing. 2. Quarrelsome, provoking.

próximamente [proc´-se-mah-men-tay], *adv.* Soon, nearly, immediately, proximately, in the near future.

proximidad [proc-se-me-dahd´], *f.* 1. Proximity, nearness, vicinity. 2. Relation, kindred by birth.

próximo, ma [proc´-se-mo, mah], *a.* Next (anterior, siguiente), nearest (cercano), neighbor, proximate. **En fecha próxima,** soon. **El mes próximo,** next month.

proyección [pro-yec-the-on´], *f.* 1. Projection, shooting forward (acto). 2. *(Arch.)* Corbel, jetty, projecture. 3. *(Math.)* Apparent representation of an object upon a plane; graphic representation. 4. Movement impressed upon a projectile. **La proyección de los periódicos sobre la sociedad,** the hold of newspapers over society.

proyectar [pro-yec-tar´], *va.* 1. To project, to scheme, to contrive. 2. To throw into the air, to project. 3. To draw a figure in the vertical and horizontal planes of projection. *-vr.* 1. To strike against a bottom. 2. To throw itself forward, as a shadow. 3. *(Naut.)* To be ranged along the same line. **Está proyectado para,** it is designed to.

proyectil [pro-yec-teel´], *m.* Missile, projectile. **Proyectil balístico,** ballistic missile. **Proyectil cohete,** rocket missile; space rocket. **Proyectil de alcance intermedio,** intermediate range ballistic missile. **Proyectil de sondeo,** probe rocket. **Proyectil dirigido,** guided missile. **Proyectil interceptor,** interceptor missile. **Proyectil antiproyectil,** anti-missile missile.

proyectista [pro-yec-tees´-tah], *m.* Projector, schemer.

proyecto [pro-yec´-to], *m.* Project, scheme, plan, design. **Cambiar de proyecto,** to change one´s plans. **Tener proyectos para,** to have plans for.

proyecto, ta [pro-yec´-to, tah], *a.* Projected, expanded, dilated.

proyector [pro-yec-tor´], *m.* 1. Projector. 2. Searchlight. 3. Spotlight.

proyectura [pro-yec-too´-rah], *f.* Projecture, part of a building which juts beyond the wall. *V.* VUELO.

prudencia [proo-den´-the-ah], *f.* 1. Prudence, counsel, management, circumspection. 2. Temperance, moderation.

prudencial [proo-den-the-ahl´], *a.* Prudential (adecuado); sensible (razonable). **Tras un intervalo prudencial,** after a decent interval.

prudencialmente [proo-den-the-ahl´-men-tay], *adv.* Prudentially.

prudente [proo-den´-tay], *a.* Prudent, circumspect, judicious (decisión), considerate,

prudentemente [proo-den-tay-men-tay], *adv.* Prudently,

prueba [proo-ay´-bah], *f.* 1. Proof, reason, argument, evidence. 2. Sign, token (indicio), indication, mark. 3. Experiment, essay, attempt; a test-portion, a test, trial. 4. *(Print.)* Proof, proof-sheet. 5. In photography, proof, the first print from a negative. 6. *(Dep.)* Event; race. 7. *(LAm.)* Circus act. **A prueba de** with a noun is to be rendered by «proof» connected by hyphen with the equivalent of the

noun. Thus; **A prueba de luz,** light-proof. **A prueba de bomba,** bomb-proof; satisfactorily. **Tomar una cosa a prueba,** to take a thing on trial. **Prueba de acceso,** entrance test. **A prueba de balas,** bullet-proof. **Sala de pruebas,** fitting room. **Prueba de Turing,** *(Comput.)* Turing test.

prurito [proo-ree´-to], *m.* 1. Prurience, itching. 2 Great desire or appetite.

prusiato [proo-se-ah´-to], *m. (Chem.)* Prussiate,

prúsico [proo´-se-co], *a.* Prussic, hydrocyanic. **Ácido prúsico,** Prussic, hydrocyanic acid.

psicoanálisis [se-co-ah-nah´-le-sis], *f.* Psychoanalysis.

psicoanalista [se-co-ah-nah-lees´-tah], *m & f.* Psychoanalyst.

psicodélico [se-co-day´-le-co], *a.* Phychedelic. *-m.* Light show.

psicofísica [se-co-fee´-se-ca], *f.* Psychophysics.

psicología [se-co-lo-hee´-ah], *f.* Psychology, study of the subconscious. **Psicología industrial,** industrial psychology.

psicológico, ca [se-co-lo´-he-co, cah], *a.* Psychological.

psicólogo, ga [se-co´-lo-go, gah], *m. & f.* Psychologist.

psiconeurótico, ca [se-co-nay-oo-roh´-te-co, cah], *a.* Psychoneurotic.

psicópata [se-co´-pah-tah],*m.* Psychopath.

psicopatía [se-co-pah-tee´-ah], *f.* Psychopathy.

psicopático, ca [se-co-pah´-te-co, cah], *a.* Psychopathic.

psicopatología [se-co-pah-to-lo-hee´-ah], *f.* Psychopathology.

psicosis [se-co´-sis], *f.* Psychosis.

psicosomático, ca [se-co-so-mah´-te-co-cah], *a.* Psychosomatic, referring to illnesses not organic in origin.

psicotecnia [se-co-tec´-ne-ah], *f.* Psychological testing.

psicotécnico, ca [se-co-tec´-ne-co, cah], *a.* Psychotechnological.

psicoterapia [se-co-tay-rah´-pe-ah], *f.* Psychotherapy.

psique [see´-kay], *f.* Psyche.

psiquiatra [se-ke-ah´-trah], *m.* Psychiatrist.

psiquiatría [se-ke-ah-tree´-ah], *f.* Psychiatry.

psíquico, ca [see´-ke-co, cah], *a.* Psychic.

púa [poo´-ah], *f.* 1. Sharp point (punta), barb (de gancho, alambre). 2. *(Bot.)* Graft. 3. Tooth (de un peine). 4. Prick. 5. *(Zool.)* Spine. 6. *(Mus.)* Plectrum. 7. *(coll.)* Sharpie. **Alambre de púas,** barbed wire.

púber [poo´-ber], *a.* Pubescent.

púbero, ra [poo´-bay-ro, rah], *a.* Pubescent, arrived at puberty.

pubertad [poo-ber-tahd´], *f.* Puberty, pubescence.

pubes [poo´-bes], *m. (Anat.)* Pubes, the pubic region.

pubescencia [poo-bes-then´-the-ah], *f.* Pubescence, puberty.

pubescer [poo-bes-therr´], *vn.* To attain the age of puberty.

púbico [poo´-be-co], *a.* Pubic.

pubis [poo´-bes], *m.* Pubis.

pública [poo´-ble-cah], *f.* In universities, a lecture before the examination for the degree of licentiate.

publicación [poo-ble-cah-the-on´], *f.* Publication, proclamation.

publicador, ra [poo-ble-cah-dor´, rah], *m.& f.* Publisher, proclaimer.

públicamento [poo-ble-cah-men-tay], *adv.* Publicly, openly.

publicano [poo-ble-cah´-no], *m.* Publican, toll-gatherer.

publicar [po-ble-car´], *va.* 1. To publish, to proclaim, to make known. 2. To publish, to print a book.

publicata [poo-ble-cah´-tah], *f.* 1. Certificate of publication. 2. Each of the three announcements of the banns of marriage.

publicidad [poo-ble-the-dahd´], *f.* 1. Publicity, notoriety. **En publicidad,** publicily. 2. *(Com.)* Advertising. **Publicidad de lanzamiento,** advance publicity.

publicista [poo-ble-thees´-tah], *m.* Publicist, a writer on public law or on topics of public interest.

publicitario [poo-ble-the-tah´-re-o], *a.* Advertising; publicity. *-m.* Advertising man.

público, ca [poo´-ble-co, cah], *a.* 1. Public, notorious, known by all. 2. Vulgar, common, general. **En público,** publicly.

público [poo´-ble-co], *m.* Public, the general body of a nation. **Hay poco público,** there aren´t many people.

pucha [poo'-chah], *f. (Cuba)* A small bouquet of flowers, nosegay.

puchada [poo-chah'-dah], *f.* 1. A cataplasm, chiefly of flour. 2. Watered mortar, used by stone masons.

puchecilla [poo-chay-theel'-lyah], *f.* A thin batter of flour and water.

pucherito [poo-chay-ree'-to], *m. (coll.)* Crying grimaces of children.

puchero [poo-chay'-ro], *m.* 1. A glazed earthen pot (olla). 2. Olla, a dish composed of beef or lamb, ham or bacon, Spanish peas, and vegetables: a standing dish in Spanish countries. 3. Daily food, regular aliment. 4. Grimace or distortion of the face which precedes crying (mueca). **Hacer pucheros,** *(coll.)* to snivel.

puches [poo'-ches], *com. pl.* Sort of pap. *V.* GACHAS.

pucho [poo'-cho], *m. (Amer.)* 1. Tip or end of a cigar (colilla). 2. A small quantity or sum; driblet. 3. *(LAm.)* Scrap (resto); *(fig.)* trifle (minimedad).

pucuna [poo-coo'-nah], *f.* A blow-gun in Peru. *(Indian.)*

pudendas [poo-dayn-dahs] *a. & f. pl.* The pudenda.

pudendo, da [poo-den'-do, dah], *a.* Shameful, obscene, immodest.

pudendo [poo-dayn-do], *m.* The male organ.

pudibundo, da [poo-de-boon'-do, dah], *a.* Shamefaced, modest.

pudicicia [poo-de-thee'-the-ah], *f.* Pudicity, chastity, modesty.

púdico, ca [poo'-de-co, cah], *a.* Chaste, modest, maidenly.

pudiente [poo-de-en'-tay], *a. & m.* Powerful (poderoso), rich, opulent.

pudín [poo-deen'], *m.* Pudding.

pudor [poo-dor'], *m.* Bashfulness, modesty (recato), shyness (timidez), shamefacedness.

pudoroso, sa [poo-do-ro'-so, sah], *a.* Modest (recatado), shamefaced, bashful, shy.

pudrición [poo-dre-the-on'], *f.* Rottenness, the act of rotting (proceso).

pudridero [poo-dre-day'-ro], *m.* 1. Rotting-place, where something is put to rot, fermenting pit. 2. Royal vault in the monastery at Escorial.

pudridor [poo-dre-dor'], *m.* Vessel in which rags are steeped for making paper.

pudrimiento [poo-dre-me-en'-to], *m.* Rottenness, putrefaction. *V.* PUDRICIÓN.

pudrir [poo-dreer'], *va.* 1. To rot (descomponer), to make putrid, to bring to corruption. 2. To molest, to consume, to cause extreme impatience. *-vn.* To have died (haber muerto), to be buried, to rot. *-vr.* 1. To corrupt, to become rotten, to decay. 2. To be broken-hearted, to die of grief. **Mientras se pudría en la cárcel,** while he was languishing in jail.

puebla [poo-ay'-blah], *f.* Seed which a gardener sows.

pueblecico, ito [poo-ay-blay-thee'-co], *m. dim.* Any small town.

pueblerino [poo-ay-blay-ree'-no], *a.* Rustic, countrified (lugareño), small-town, village. *-f.* Villager (aldeano).

pueblo [poo-ay'-blo], *m.* 1. Town, village (aldea); any inhabited place. 2. Population, inhabitants of a place. 3. Common people (plebe), populace. 4. Nation, people. **Pueblo elegido,** chosen people. **Pueblo de mala muerte,** dregs of society.

puente [poo-en'-tay], *com.* 1. A bridge. **Puente volante,** flying-bridge. **Puente levadizo,** draw-bridge. 2. *(Naut.)* Deck of a ship. 3. *(Mus.)* Bridge, in stringed instruments. 4. Transom, lintel, crossbeam. **Hacer puente,** to take a long weekend. **Puente aéreo,** airlift. **Cabeza de puente,** bridgehead. **Puente colgante,** suspension bridge. **Puente de mando,** bridge. **A enemigo que huye puente de plata,** let the enemy escape.

puentecico, illo, ito [poo-en-tay-thee'-co], *m. dim.* A small bridge.

puentecilla [poo-en-tay-theel'-lyah], *f. dim.* A small bridge of a stringed instrument.

puerca [poo-err'-cah], *f.* 1. A sow (cerda). 2. Sow-bug, slater, woodlouse (cochinilla), a crustacean commonly found in damp spots. 3. Scrofulous swelling, glandulous tumor. 4. Slut, slatternly woman.

puercamente [poo-err'-cah-men-tay], *adv.* 1. Dirtily, filthily, hoggishly, nastily. 2. Rudely, coarsely, vulgarly, meanly.

puerco, ca [poo-err'-co, cah], *a.* 1. Nasty (asqueroso), filthy, dirty, foul, abominable, coarse (grosero). 2. Rude, coarse, mean.

puerco [poo-err'-co], *m.* 1. Hog (cerdo). 2. Wild-boar (jabalí). **Puerco montés,** *V.* JABALÍ. 3. A brutish, ill-bred man.

puericia [poo-ay-ree'-the-ah], *f.* Boyhood.

puericultor, ora [poo-ay-re-cool-tor'], *m & f.* Specialist in puericulture.

puericultura [poo-ay-re-cool-too'-rah], *f.* Puericulture, child care, prenatal and infant welfare.

pueril [poo-ay-reel'], *a.* 1. Boyish, childish, puerile. 2. Belonging to the first quadrant of the celestial map.

puerilidad [poo-ay-re-le-dahd'], *f.* Puerility, boyishness, childishness, silliness; trifle.

puerilmente [poo-ay-reel'-men-tay], *adv.* Puerilely, childishly, boyishly.

puérpera [poo-err'-pay-rah], *f.* A lying-in woman.

puerperal [poo-er-pay-rahl'], *a.* Puerperal, relating to childbirth.

puerperio [poo-er-pay'-re-o], *m.* 1. Child birth, travail, labor. 2. The puerperal condition; the time immediately following labor.

puerquezuela [poo-er-kay-thoo-ay'-lo], *m. dim.* Little pig.

puerro [poo-err'-ro], *m. (Bot.)* Leek.

puerta [poo-err'-tah], *f.* 1. Door or doorway, gateway. 2. Beginning of an undertaking. 3. Door, gate, that which serves to stop any passage. 4. Duty paid at the entrance of the gates in towns. 5. The Turkish government, the Porte. **Puerta de dos hojas,** folding-door. **Puerta trasera,** back door. **Llamar a la puerta,** to knock at the door. **A puerta cerrada,** secretly. **Dar con la puerta en los hocicos,** to slam the door in one's face. **Puerta corredera,** sliding door. **A las puertas de la muerte,** at death's door. **Estar en puertas,** to be imminent. **De puerta en puerta,** from door to door. **Puerta O,** *(Comput.)* OR gate. **Puerta Y,** *(Comput.)* AND gate.

puertaventana [poo-er-tah-ven-tah'-nah], *f.* Door with a window in it.

puertecita [poo-er-tay-thee'-tah], *f. dim.* A small door.

puertecillo [poo-er-tay-theel'-lyo], *dim.* A small port.

puertezuela [poo-er-toy-thoo-ay'-lah], *f. dim. V.* PUERTECITA.

puertezuelo [poo-er-tay-thoo-ay'-lo], *m. dim. V.* PERTECILLO.

puerto [poo-err'-to], *m.* 1. Port, harbor, haven for ships. **Puerto habilitado,** a port of entry. **Puerto franco,** free port. 2. Pass, through mountains. 3. Asylum, shelter, refuge (refugio). **Llegar a puerto,** to solve a problem. 4. *(Prov.)* Dam in a river.

puerto aéreo or **aeropuerto** [poo-err'-to ah-ay'-ray-o, ah-ay-ro-poo-err'-to], *m.* Airport.

puertorriqueño, ña [poo-err-tor-re-kay'-nyo, nyah], *a. & m. & f.* Puerto Rican, from Puerto Rico.

pues [poo-es'], *adv., conj.* 1. Then (entonces), therefore. 2. Inasmuch as; since. 3. Sure, surely; certainly. **¡Pues no faltaba más!** surely, of course.

Pues, *int.* Well, then; therefore. **¿Y pues?** well, and what of that? **Pues sí,** *(Iron.)* Yes, indeed! **¿Pues y qué?** why not? what else? what then? **Pues no le tenía yo por rico,** indeed I did not think him rich. **Pues ese es mi rival,** well, that is my rival.

puesta [poo-es'-tah], *f.* 1. Putting, placing (acto). 2. *(Astron.)* Setting. 3. Egg-laying. 4. Resigning a hand of cards. **Puesta del sol,** sunset. **A puesta** or **puestas de sol,** at sunset. **Puesta en libertad,** freeing. **Puesta a punto,** final preparation, setup.

puesto [poo-es´-to], *m.* l. Place or space occupied (lugar); particular spot, an assigned post. 2. Shop or place where anything is sold by retail; stall, booth. 3. Post (trabajo), employment, dignity, office. 4. House in which stallions are kept and let to mares. 5. *(Mil.)* Barrack for soldiers. 6. Place covered with bushes to conceal sportsmen. 7. *(Cono Sur)* Small farm. **Puesto de trabajo**, work station. **Puesto de control**, checkpoint. **Puesto de socorro**, first-aid post.

puesto, ta [poo-es´-to, tah], *pp. irr.* of PONER. Put. **Con el sombrero puesto**, with one´s hat on. **Tenerlos bien puestos**, to be a real man.

puesto [poo-es´-to], *adv.* Because, for this reason that, on this account that. **Puesto que**, although. *V.* AUNQUE.

¡puf! [poof], *int.* A word expressive of the unpleasant sensation of a bad smell.

pufo [poo´-fo], *m.* 1. Trick (trampa). 2. Debt (deuda).

púgil [poo´-heel], *m.* Prize-fighter, boxer, bruiser, pugilist.

pugilar [poo-he-lar´], *m.* Hebrew manual of the Scriptures used in synagogues.

pugilato [poo-he-lah´-to], *m.* Pugilism, boxing or fighting.

pugna [poog´-nah], *f.* Combat, conflict, battle. **Estar en pugna con**, to clash with.

pugnacidad [poog-nah-the-dahd´], *f.* Pugnacity, quarrelsomeness.

pugnante [poog-nahn´-tay], *pa.* Fighting, opposing.

pugnar [poog-nar´], *vn.* To fight (luchar), to combat, to contend; to rival; to solicit; to importune. **Pugnar por**, to fight for.

pugnaz [poog-nath´], *a.* Pugnacious, quarrelsome.

puja [poo´-hah], *f.* 1. Outbidding or overbidding at a public sale (en subasta). 2. *(And.)* Ticking-off.

pujadero, ra [poo-hah-day´-ro, rah], *a.* That which might be outbid, or enhanced.

pujador, ra [poo-hah-dor´, rah], *m. & f.* Outbidder, overbidder, highest bidder.

pujame, pujamen [pooh-hah´-may], *m. (Naut.)* Under part of the sails.

pujamiento [poo-hah-me-en´-to], *m.* Flow or violent agitation of the blood.

pujante [poo-hahn´-tay], *a.* Powerful (potente), puissant, strong (fuerte), predominant, forcible.

pujanza [poo-hahn´-thah], *f.* Power, might, strength, puissance.

pujar [poo-har´], *va.* 1. To outbid. 2. To labor under an impediment of speech, to falter. 3. To be eager in the pursuit of a thing, to endevor earnestly. 4. *(coll.)* To make a face as if to cry. -*vn.* 1. To bid (en subasta) 2. To struggle (esforzarse). **Pujar para hacer algo**, to struggle to do something. 3. To falter (vacilar). 4. To struggle for words (no encontrar palabras). 5. To be on the verge of tears (hacer pucheros). 6. *(CAm.)* To moan (quejarse).

pujavante [poo-hah-vahn´-tay], *m.* Butteris, an instrument for paring a horse's foot.

pujo [poo´-ho], *m.* 1. Tenesmus (medicina). 2. Violent desire, eagerness, longing (ansia); anxiety. **Sentir pujo de llorar**, to be on the verge of tears.

pulcritud [pool-cre-tood´], *f.* Pulchritude, beauty, grace, gentility.

pulcro, cra [pool´-cro, crah], *a.* l. Beautiful, graceful. 2. Affectedly nice in dress (elegante). 3. Exquisite (exquisito); dainty (delicado).

pulga [pool´-gah], *f.* 1. Flea. 2. Playing tops for children (de juego). 3. *(LAm. Comput.)* Bug. **Tener malas pulgas**, to be easily piqued or fretted, to be ill-tempered. **Buscar las pulgas a uno**, to tease somebody.

pulgada [pool-gah´-dah], *f.* Inch, the twelfth part of a foot.

pulgar [pool-gar´], *m.* 1. The thumb. **Dedo pulgar del pie**, the great toe. 2. Shoots left on vines.

pulgarada [pool-gah-rah´-dah], *f.* 1. Fillip, flick (papirote). 2. Pinch, quantity taken between the thumb and forefinger. 3. *V.* PULGADA.

pulgón [pool-gone´], *m.* Vine-fretter, plant louse, aphis.

pulgoso, sa [pool-goh´-so, sah], *a.* Pulicose, abounding with fleas.

pulguera [pool-gay´-rah], *f.* 1. Place abounding with fleas. 2. *(Bot.)* Pulic, flea-wort.

pulguita [pool-gee´-tah], *f. dim.* A little flea.

pulguilla [pool-geel´-lya], *f. dim.* A little flea.

pulicán [poo-le-cahn´], *m.* Pelican, instrument for drawing teeth.

pulicaria [poo-le-cah´-re-ah], *f.* Flea-wort. *V.* ZARAGATONA.

pulidamente [poo-lee´-dah-men-tay], *adv.* Neatly (con pulcritud), sprucely, cleancy, nicely, compactly.

pulidero [poo-le-day´-ro], *m.* 3. Polisher, glosser. 2. Polisher, an instrument for polishing or burnishing.

pulidez, pulideza [poo-le-deth´], *f.* Neatness, cleanliness.

pulido, da [poo-lee´-do, dah], *a.* Neat (pulcro), cleanly (limpio), nice. -*pp.* of PULIR.

pulidor, ra [poo-le-dor´], *m & f.* 1. Polisher, furbisher. 2. Instrument for polishing and burnishing.

pulimentable [poo-le-men-tah´-blay], *a.* Susceptible of polish.

pulimentar [poo-le-men-tar´], *va.* 1. To gloss (dar lustre), to polish very bright (pulir). 2. *(coll.)* To finish.

pulimento [poo-le-men´-to], *m.* 3. Polish, glossiness, artificial gloss (brillo). 2. *(coll.)* Finishing.

pulir [poo-leer´], *va.* 1. To polish, to burnish, to furbish. 2. To adorn, to beautify. 3. To pinch (robar); to sell (vender). -*vr.* 1. To be polished: to adorn, beautify, embellish, or deck oneself. 2. To become polished or elegant in dress or manners.

pulmón [pool-mone´], *m.* Lung. **Pulmón de hierro**, *(Med.)* iron lung.

pulmonaria [pool-mo-nah´-re-ah], *f. (Pot.)* Lungwort. **Pulmonaria oficinal**, common lungwort.

pulmonía [pool-mo-nee´-ah], *f.* Pneumonia, lung fever.

pulmoníaco ca, pulmonario, ria [pool-mo-nee´-ah-co, cah], *a.* Affected with inflammation of the lungs; pulmonary, pulmonic.

pulpa [pool´-pah], *f.* 1. Pulp, the most solid part of the flesh. 2. Pulp of fruit (de fruta). 3. *(Cono Sur)* Boneless meat.

pulpejo [pool-pay´-ho], *m.* The fleshy prominence of some organs of the body, especially the bell of the thumb or lobe of the ear.

pulpería [pool-pay-ree´-ah], *f.* In America, a grocery store (tienda), where all sorts of provisions and liquors are retailed. In Cuba, and some parts of South America, it is called *Bodega*.

pulpero [pool-pay´-ro], *m.* 1. In America, grocer. 2. Catcher of cuttle-fish.

pulpeta [pool-pay´-tah], *f.* Slice of stuffed meat.

pulpetón [pool-pay-tone´], *m. aug.* Large slice of stuffed meat.

púlpito [pool´-pe-to], *m.* 1. Pulpit. 2. The dignity or office of a preacher. **Paño de púlpito**, pulpit-cloth.

pulpo [pool´-po], *m.* Cuttle-fish, poulp, octopus.

pulposo, sa [pool-po´-so, sah], *a.* Pulpous, fleshy.

pulque [pool´-kay], *m.* Liquor prepared in America from the maguey or Agave Americana. **Pulque curado**, *(Coll. Mex.)* the same liquor, prepared with pineapple and sugar; a common beverage in that country.

pulquería [pool-kay-ree´-ah], *f.* The Place where the liquor pulque is sold.

pulsación [pool-sah-the-on´], *f.* 1. Pulsation. 2. Pulse, the beating of an artery (latido). 3. Tap (en máquina de escribir). 4. *(Comput.)* **Pulsación doble**, strike over.

pulsada [pool-sah´-dah], *f.* Any pulse beat.

pulsador, ra [pool-sah-dor´, rah], *m. & f.* One who examines the pulse.

pulsar [pool-sar´], *va.* 1. To touch. *V.* TOCAR. 2. To feel the pulse. 3. To explore, to try, to sound or examine an affair. -*vn.* 1. To pulsate, to beat as the pulse.

pulsátil [pool-sah´-teel], *a.* 1. Sounding when struck, as bells. 2. *V.* PULSATIVO.

pulsativo, va [pool-sah-tee´-vo, vah], *a.* Pulsing, beating.

pulsatorio, ria [pool-sah-to´-re-o, ah], *a.* Relating to the pulse.

pulsear [pool-say-ar'], *vn.* To test who has most strength in the wrists by grasping hands and resting the elbows on a table (entre dos personas).

pulsera [pool-say'-rah], *f.* 1. Bandage-applied to a vein or artery. 2. Bracelet for the wrists. **Pulsera para reloj**, watch strap.

pulsímetro [poo-see´-may-tro], *m.* 1. Pulsimeter, an instrument for learning the readiness with which evaporation is effected in a vacuum. 2. Pulsimeter, an instrument for measuring the rapidity of the pulse.

pulsión [pool-se-on'], *f.* Propulsion, propagation of undulatory motion in an elastic fluid.

pulsista [pool-sees'-tah], *m. & a.* Applied to a medical man well skilled in the doctrine of the pulse.

pulso [pool´-so], *m.* 1. Pulse, the beating of an artery, perceived by the touch. 2. Part of the wrist where the pulse is felt (muñeca). **Echar un pulso a**, to have a trial of strengh with. **Levantar una silla a pulso**, to lift a chair with one hand. 3. Steadiness of the hand (firmeza). **A pulso**, with the strength of the hand. 4. Attention, care, circumspection. **Obra con gran pulso**, he acts with a great deal of circumspection. **Tomar el pulso**, (1) to feel the pulse. (2) To feel one's pulse, to try or know one's mind artfully. 5. *(And.)* V. PULSERA.

pultáceo, cea [pool-tah'-thay-o, ah], *a.* Pultaceous, semifluid.

pululante [poo-loo-lahn´-tay], *pa.* Pullulating.

pulular [poo-loo-lar'], *vn.* 1. To pullulate, to germ, to bud. 2. To multiply with great rapidity, as bacteria or insects. 3. To swarm (estar plagado), to be lively.

pulverizable [pool-vay-re-thah'-blay], *a.* Reducible to powder; pulverable, pulverizable.

pulverización [pool-vay-re-thah-the-on'], *f.* Pulverization (de sólidos), comminution, spray (de perfume, insecticida).

pulverizador de átomos [pool-vah-ree-thah-dore' day ah'-to-mos], *m.* Atom smasher.

pulverizar [pool-vay-re-thar'], *va.* To pulverize (sustancia), to grind, to comminute, to powder (reducir a polvo), to spray (plantas).

pulverulento, ta [pool-vay-roo-len'-to, tah], *a.* Pulverulent, dusty (superficie), in the storm of powder.

pulzol, puzol, punzó [pool-thole', poon-the'], *m. & a.* A bright scarlet color.

pulla [pool´-lyah], *f.* 1. Loose, obscene expression. 2. Repartee, witty saying. 3. Eagle that dwells in the trunks of trees.

pullista [pool-lyees'-tah], *com.* One fond of witty sayings, or who says loose expressions.

pum! [poom], *int.* Bang! exclamation expressing a noise, explosion, or knock.

puma [poo'-mah], *m. (Zool.)* Puma, the American panther or cougar.

pumarada [poo-ma-rah'-dah], *f.* An Asturian name for an apple-orchard.

puna [poo'-nah], *f. (Peru and Bol.)* 1. A lofty, bleak region, uninhabitable through cold. 2. Difficulty of breathing from rarefied air. Cf. VETA.

punción [poon-the-on'], *f.* Puncture of a swelling to evacuate it.

puncha [poon'-chah], *f.* Thorn, prick, anything that pricks the flesh.

pundonor [poon-do-nor'], *m.* Point of honor (honra); punctiliousness.

pundonorcillo [poon-do-nor-theel'-lyo], *m.* Punctilio.

pundonorosamente [poon-do-no-ro-sah-men-tay], *adv.* Punctiliously.

pundonoroso, sa [poon-do-no-ro'-so, sah], *a.* Having a nice sense of honor (honrado), punctilious (escrupuloso).

punganos [poon-gah'-nos], *m. pl.* Instruments to open cockles, oysters, etc.

pungente [poon-gen'-tay], *pa.* Pungent.

pungimiento [poon-he-me-en'-to], *m.* Act of punching or pricking.

pungir [poon-heer'], *va.* 1. To punch, to prick (punzar). 2. To stimulate the passions, the spirit, the heart.

pungitivo, va [poon-he-tee'-vo, vah], *a.* Punching, pricking.

punible [poo-nee'-blay], *a. (Law.)* Punishable, actionable.

punición [poo-ne-the-on'], *f.* Punishment, chastisement.

púnico, ca [poo'-ne-co, cah], *a.* Punic, relating to the Carthaginians.

punki [poon'-ke], *a.* Punk. *-m & f.* Punk.

punta [poon´-tah], *f.* 1. Point, the sharp end of an instrument (extremo puntiagudo). 2. Extremity of anything which terminates in an angle; top, head, summit; point, prong, nib, tip. 3. Point, headland, promontory. 4. Prong of an antler. 5. Tartness, sour taste. 6. Point-lace. 7. *(typ.)* A bodkin for picking type from a form. 8. Somewhat, some good points: implying a high grade of intellectual or moral qualities (used with *tener*.) 9. Tracing-point, style, graver. 10. The end of a log, after beams, etc., have been sawed from it. 11. The pointing out of game by a dog. **De puntas**, on tiptoe, softly. **Puntas**, scallops (vestido). **Tener algo en la punta de la lengua**, to have something on the tip of one's tongue. **Se le pusieron los pelos de punta**, her hair stood on end. **Horas punta**, rush hours. **Sacar punta a**, to sharpen, to find fault with. **Ir de punta en blanco**, to get all dressed up. 12. Small nail (clavo). 13. *(Carib.)* Best quality tobacco (tabaco). 14. *(LAm.)* Group (grupo). 15. **En punta**, *(CAm.)* wholesome.

puntación [poon-tah-the-on´], *f.* Punctuation. *V.* PUNTUACIÓN.

puntada [poon-tah'-dah], *f.* 1. Stitch with a needle and thread. **Puntada cruzada**, cross-stitch. 2. Word carelessly dropped in conversation (indirecta). 3. *(LAm. Med.)* Stitch; sharp pain (dolor agudo). 4. *(Mex.)* Witty remark, witticism.

punta de combate [poon'-tah day com-bah'-tay], *f. (Mil.)* Warhead.

puntal [poon-tahl'], *m.* 1. Prop to support a wall or building; fulcrum. 2. The stay in the bed of a plough-share. 3. *(Naut.)* Stanchion. **Puntal de la bodega**, *(Naut.)* depth of the hold.

puntapié [poon-tah-pe-ay'], *m.* A kick. **Mandar (a alguno) a puntapié**, to have complete ascendency over one.

puntar [poon-tar'], *va.* To mark with small dots or points.

punteado [poon-tay-ah-do], *a.* Dotted (moteado), covered with dots; stippled (grabado con puntos). -m. Series of dots; stippling.

punteadura [poon-tay-ah-doo'-rah], *f.* Teeth of a wheel.

puntear [poon-tay-ar'], *va.* 1. To play upon the guitar. 2. To punctuate, to mark, to point out. 3. To sew, to stitch. 4. *(Cono Sur)* To fork over (tierra). 5. *(Cono Sur)* To head (marcha). *-vn. (Naut.)* To go obliquely, catching the wind when it is slack.

puntel [poon-tel´], *m.* Pontil or pontee, a glass-blower´s iron rod.

puntera [poon-tay'-rah], *f.* 1. *(Bot.)* Common houseleek. 2. A patch over the tip of a shoe (de zapato). 3. Tip, a reenforcing piece put over the toe of a shoe. 4. *(coll.)* A kick (puntapié).

puntería [poon-tay-ree'-ah], *f.* 1. The act of levelling or pointing firearms. 2. Aim, the direction of a weapon (el apuntar). 3. Teeth of a wheel. **Tener mala puntería**, to be a bad shot.

punterico, illo, ito [poon-tay-ree'-co], *m. dim.* A little fescue.

puntero [poon-tay'-ro], *m.* 1. Fescue, a pointer to point out letters to children (palo). 2. A pointed instrument for marking anything, puncheon (herrero). 3. Chisel used by stone-cutters. 4. Graver, style. 5. *(LAm. Dep.)* Leading team, team which is ahead. 5. *(LAm.)* Hand (de reloj). **Puntero de celda (resaltar)**, cell pointer (highlight).

puntero, ra [poon-tay'-ro, rah], *a.* Taking good aim with firearms.

punterola [poon-tay-ro'-lah], *f. (Min.)* Poll-pick, a bar of iron with a steel point.

puntiagudo, da [poon-te-ah-goo'-do, dah], *a.* Sharp-pointed, mucronated.

puntica, ita [poon-tee'-cah], *f. dim.* A small point or sharp end of an instrument.

puntico, ito [poon-tee'-co], *m. dim.* of PUNTO.

puntilla [poon-teel'-lyah], *f.* 1. A small point. 2. A narrow lace edging. **De puntillas,** softly, gently; on tiptoe. **Ponerse de puntillas,** to persist obstinately in one's opinion. 3. *(Mech.)* Brad, joiner'snail; a carpenter's tracing-point. 4. *V.* CACHETE.

puntillazo [poon-til-lyah'-tho], *m.* Kick.

puntillo [poon-teel'-lyo], *m.* 1. Punctilio, trifling, despicable thing, in which a punctilious person places honor. 2. *(dim.)* A small point.

puntillón [poon-til-lyone'], *m.* Kick. *V.* PUNTILLAZO.

puntilloso, sa [poon-til-lyo'-so, sah], *a.* Ticklish, difficult, litigious, punctilious.

puntizón [poon-te-thone'], *m.* Holes pricked in the paper sheet by the frisket.

punto [poon'-to], *m.* 1. Dot, point (señal). 2. Point, subject under consideration (en discusión). 3. End or design. 4. Degree, state. 5. Nice point of ceremony: point of honor; punctilio. 6. Opportunity, fit place or time (lugar, tiempo). **Al punto,** instantly. 7. Point, period in writing. 8. Aim, sight. 9. Stitch, in sewing or surgery. 10. Point, gist, substance of a matter. 11. Actual state of any business matter. 12. Turn, finished state of something prepared by the fire. 13. Part or question of a science. 14. The smallest part of a thing. 15. Tumbler of a gun-lock. 16. Hole in stockings; mesh of a net; vacancy in lace. 17. Right sound of musical instruments. 18. Part of the bell where the clapper strikes. 19. Weight used in passementerie to keep the narrow linens stretched. 20. In straps, a hole for receiving the tongue of a buckle. 21. Speckle, dot upon the face of a silk fabric which bears no special design. 22. Each nib of a pen. 23. A fine cloth of thread cotton, or silk (material). 24. In schools, each mistake of a scholar in reciting a lesson from memory. 25. Dot, spot, on dice or cords. 26. End of the course in universities, recess, intermission in business in courts, when the time of vacation arrives. 27. Highest point or pitch. 28. Cab-stand, fixed place for public vehicles for hire. 29. Point object of destination or action. 30. Twelfth part of a line. 31. *(Comput.)* Spot. **Poner los puntos muy altos,** to soar very high; to make extravagant pretensions. **Punto de malla,** mesh of a net. **Punto de media,** stocking-net. **Punto de tul,** tulle. **En su último punto,** in the highest pitch. **Punto crudo,** the moment in which something happens. **A punto fijo,** exactly, with certainty. **Punto de apoyo,** point of support, fulcrum. **Bajar de punto,** to decay, to decline. **Punto,** or **punto final,** period. **Punto y coma,** semicolon. **Dos puntos,** Colon. **Vencer por puntos,** to win on points. **Punto del revés,** purl. **Punto de parada,** breakpoint. **Punto de arranque,** starting point. **Hemos llegado a un punto muerto,** we have reached deadlock. **Llegar a punto,** to come just at the right moment. **Estar en su punto,** *(Culin.)* to be done to a turn.

puntoso, sa [poon-to'-so, sah], *a.* 1 Acuminated, having many points. 2. Spirited, lively, courageous. 3. Too punctilious in etiquette.

puntuación [poon-too-ah-the-on'], *f.* 1. Punctuation 2 Marking (escuela).

puntual [poon-too-ahl'], *a.* 1. Punctual (llegada), exact (cálculo), accurate. 2. Certain, sure. 3. Convenient, adequate.

puntualidad [poon-too-ah-le-dahd'], *f.* 1. Punctuality (exactitud), exactness (precisión). 2. Certitude, preciseness.

puntualizar [poon-too-ah-le-thar'], *va.* 1. To imprint on the mind or memory (recordar). 2. To finish, to accomplish, to complete. 3. To give a detailed account (precisar).

puntualmente [poon-too-ahl'-men-tay] *adv.* Punctually, exactly, faithfully, accurately.

puntuar [poon-too-ar'], *va.* To punctuate, to point, to evaluate (valorar); to mark (examen).

puntuoso, sa [poon-too-o'-so, sah], *adv. V.* PUNTOSO and PUNDOROSO.

puntura [poon-too'-rah], *f.* 1. Puncture. 2. Point which holds the sheet in a printing-press.

punzada [poon-thah'-dah], *f.* 1. Prick, push. 2. Sting, pain; compunction.

punzador, ra [poon-thah-dor', rah], *m. & f.* Pricker, wounder.

punzadura [poon-thah-doo'-rah], *f.* Puncture, prick.

punzante [poon-than'-tay], *a.* 1. Shooting (dolor). 2. Sharp (herramienta). 3. *(Fig.)* Biting (comentario).

punzar [poon-thar'], *va.* 1. To punch, to bore or perforate. 2. To prick (pinchar), to wound. 3. To sting, to cause pain (dolor). 4. To sting or afflict the mind.

punzó, or **punzón** [poon-tho'], *a.* Deep scarlet red.

punzón [poon-thone'], *m.* 1. Punch, an instrument used by artists and workmen; puncheon, puncher; typefounder's punch. 2. Young horn of a deer.

punzonar [poon-tho-nar'], *va.* To punch.

punzoncico, illo, ito [poon-thon-thee'-co], *m. dim.* A small punch.

punzonería [poon-tho-nay-ree'-ah], *f.* Collection of moulds for making a fount of types.

puñada [pooh-nyah'-dah], *f.* Cuff, blow with the fist. *-pl.* Fisticuffs.

puñado [pooh-nyah'-do], *m.* Handful; a few. **A puñados,** plentifully, abundantly. **¡Gran puñado!** or; **¡qué puñado!** *(coll.)* expression of contempt for the quantity or the quality of a thing offered.

puñal [pooh-nyahl'], *m.* Poniard, dagger.

puñalada [pooh-nyay-lah'-dah], *f.* 1. Stab with a dagger, knife. 2. A sudden blow or shock of grief or pain. **Dar** or **tirar una puñalada a uno,** to make a pass at a person. **Murió de una puñalada,** he was stabbed to death.

puñalejo [pooh-nyah-lay'-ho], *m. dim.* Small poniard.

puñalero [pooh-nyah-lay'-ro], *m.* Maker or seller of poniards.

puñeta [pooh-nyay'-tah], *f.* 1. Silly thing (bobada); silly complaint (queja); stupid remark (dicho). 2. **Hacer la puñeta a uno,** to muck somebody around. **Tengo un catarro de la puñeta,** I've got a bloody awful cold.

puñetazo [pooh-nyay-tah'-tho], *m.* Punch, blow with the fist shut. **Dar puñetazos en,** to hammer on.

puñete [pooh-nyay'-tay], *m.* Blow with the fist. **Puñetes,** bracelets for the wrists.

puño [pooh'-nyo], *m.* 1. The fist. 2. Handful (cantidad), grasp. 3. Scantiness, narrowness. 4. Wristband. 5. Handruffle; cuff, mittens. 6. Hilt (de espada), guard of a sword; handle (de herramienta); head of a staff or cane. 7. *(Naut.)* Each of the lower points of a sail in which the tacks are fastened. **Apretar los puños,** to exert the utmost efforts. **Pegar a puño cerrado,** to strike with might and main. **Hombre de puños,** a strong, valiant man. **Ser como un puño,** to be miserable; close-fisted. **De propio puño,** in one's own handwriting.

puones [poo-oh'-nes], *m. pl.* The large, uneven teeth of cards.

pupa [poo'-pah], *f.* 1. Pustule, pimple, blister (ampolla); lip sore (úlcera). 2. The plaintive sound of children to express uneasiness.

pupila [poo-pee'-lah], *f.* 1. Pupil of the eye. 2. Orphan girl, ward.

pupilaje [poo-pe-lah'-hay], *m.* 1. Pupilage, wardship. 2. Board, the state of one who boards with another. 3. Boarding-house.

pupilar [poo-pe-lar'], *a.* Pupillary, belonging to a pupil or ward, or to the pupil of the eye.

pupilero, ra [poo-pe-lay'-ro, rah], *m. & f.* Master or mistress of a boarding house or boarding-school.

pupilo [poo-pee'-lo], *m.* 1. Pupil, ward. 2. Pupil, scholar; student.

pupitre [poo-pee'-tray], *m.* A writing-desk.

puposo, sa [poo-po'-so, sah], *a.* Pustulous, pustulate.

puramente [poo-rah-men'-tay], *adv.* Purely, chastely; entirely, merely: genuinely.

puré [poo-ray'], *m*. Puree, thick soup. **Puré de patatas**, mashed potatoes. **Puré de manzanas**, apple sauce.

pureza [poo-ray'-thah], *f*. Purity, innocence, integrity; chastity; purity of diction; fineness, genuineness; cleanness, excellence.

purga [poor'-gah], *f*. 1. Purge, a cathartic medicine. 2. *(Amer.)* Refining, especially of sugar.

purgable [poor-gah'-blay], *a*. That may be purged.

purgación [poor-gah-the-on'], *f*. 1. Purgation. 2. Catamenia. 3. Gonorrhoea, gleet: commonly used in the plural. 4. Act of clearing from imputation of guilt.

purgador, ra [poor-gah-dor', rah], *m. & f*. One who purges, purger.

purgante [poor-gahn'-tay], *a. & m*. Purgative, laxative, cleanser.

purgar [poor-gar'], *va*. 1. To purge, to purify, to cleanse. 2. To atone, to expiate (pecado). 3. To purify (purificar), to refine. 4. To suffer the penalties of purgatory. 5. To purge, to evacuate the body. 6. To clear from guilt or imputation of guilt. -*vr*. To rid or clear oneself from guilt.

purgativo, va [poor-gah-tee'-vo, vah], *a*. Purgative, cathartic, purging.

purgatorio [poor-gah-to'-re-o], *m*. 1. Purgatory. 2. Any place where life is imbittered by painful drudgery and troubles.

purificación [poo-re-fe-cah-the-on'], *f*. 1. Purification, making pure, cleansing, expurgation. 2. Purification, a festival of the Christian church, on 2nd February. 3. The ancient act of churching women. 4. Cleansing the chalice after the wine is drunk at mass.

purificadero, ra [poo-re-fe-cah-day'-ro, rah], *a*. Cleansing, purifying.

purificador, ra [poo-re-fe-cah-dor', rah], *m. & f*. 1. Purifier, purger. 2. Purificator, the cloth with which the priest wipes the chalice.

purificar [poo-re-fe-car'], *va*. To purify, to clean, to cleanse, to clear, to fine. -*vr*. 1. To be purified, to be cleansed. 2. To be churched.

purificatorio, ria [poo-re-fe-cah-to'-re-o, ah], *a*. Purificatory, purificative.

puriforme [poo-re-for-may], *a*. Puriform, presenting the appearance of pus.

purísima (La) [lah poo-ree'-se-mah], *f*. Epithet of the Virgin Mary in the mystery of her immaculate conception.

purismo [poo-rees'-mo], *m*. The act of affecting too much purity of diction, purism.

purista [poo-rees'-tah], *m*. 1. Purist, one over-particular as to purity of literary style. 2. One who writes or speaks in a pure style.

puritanismo [poo-re-tah-nees'-mo], *m*. Puritanism.

puritano, na [poo-re-tah'-no, nah], *a*. Puritan (iglesia, tradición), puritanical (actitud), puritanic.

puritano, na [ ], *m. dim*. A Puritan.

puro, ra [poo'-ro, rah], *a*. 1. Pure (color, lengua, sustancia), free, unmingled. 2. Pure, clear (cielo), clean, neat, genuine, net, fine. 3. Pure (moralmente), chaste, modest. 4. Pure, guiltless, innocent, just. 5. Pure, incorrupt, not vitiated, exempt from imperfections. 6. *(Mex.)* Only, just. 7. *(And. Carib. Mex.)* Identical. -*m*. Cigar, a little roll of tobacco for smoking, to distinguish it from *cigarro* and *cigarrillo*, a small roll of paper filled with fine-chopped tobacco. **De puro aburrimiento**, out of sheer boredom. **Por pura casualidad**, by sheer chance.

púrpura [poor'-poo-rah], *f*. 1. Rockshell, purple-shell, royal purple. 2. Cloth dyed with purple. 3. Dignity of a king or cardinal. 4. *(Poet.)* Blood.

purpurante [poor-poo-rahn'-tay], *pa*. Giving a purple color.

purpurar [poor-poo-rar'], *va*. 1. To purple, to make red. 2. To dress in purple. 3. To take or show a purple color.

purpúreo, rea [poor-poo'-ray-o, ah], *a*. 1. Purple. 2. Belonging to a cardinal or to the cardinalate.

purpúrico [poor-poo'-re-co], *a*. **Ácido purpúrico**, purpuric acid, obtained by treating uric acid with nitric acid; murexide.

purpurina [poor-poo-ree'-nah], *f*. 1. Bronze ground for painting. 2. Purpurin, a coloring matter obtained from madder.

purpurino, na [poor-poo-re'-no, nah], *a*. Purple.

purrela [poor-ray'-lah], *f*. Wine of the most inferior quality.

purriela [poor-re-ay'-lah], *f*. Anything despicable or of little value.

purulencia [poo-roo-len'-the-ah], *f*. Purulence, purulency.

purulento, ta [poo-roo-len'-to, tah], *a*. Purulent.

pus [poos], *m*. Pus.

pusilánime [poo-se-lah'-ne-may], *a*. Pusillanimous, mean-spirited, dastardly, timorous, faint-hearted.

pusilanimemente [poo-se-lah'-ne-may-men-tay], *adv*. Heartlessly.

pusilanimidad [poo-se-lah-ne-me-dahd'], *f*. Pusillanimity, cowardliness, timorousness.

pústula [poos'-too-lah], *f*. Pustule, pimple.

pustoloso, sa [poos-to-lo'-so, sah], *a*. Pustulous, pustular.

puta [poo'-tah], *f*. Whore, prostitute, harlot. **Casa de putas**, brothel. -*a*. Bloody; bloody awful. **De puta madre**, terrific.

putada [poo-tah'-dah], *f*. Dirty trick.

putaísmo, putanismo [poo-tah-ees'-mo], *m*. Whoredom, harlotry.

putañear [poo-tah-nyay-ar'], *vn*. *(Low.)* To whore, to go whoring.

putañero [poo-tah-nyay'-ro], *a*. *(Low.)* Whorish, given to lewdness. -*m*. Whoremaster, whoremonger.

putativo, va [poo-tah-tee'-vo, vah], *a*. Putative, reputed.

puteado [poo-tay-ah'-do], *a*. 1. Corrupted (maleado), perverted. 2. Fed up (harto).

puteal [poo-tay-ahl'], *m*. Stone used as the cover of a well on which soothsayers prophesied.

putear [poo-tay-ar'], *va*. 1. To corrupt malear), to pervert. 2. To mess around (fastidiar). 3. To kick around (maltratar). 4. To upset (enfadar). 4. *(LAm.)* To swear at (insultar). -*vn*. 1. To go whoring (ir de putas). 2. To have a rough time of it (padecer).

putería [poo-tay-ree'-ah], *f*. *(Low.)* 1. The manner of living and trade of a prostitute. 2. Brothel. 3. Meretricious arts of lewd women.

putero [poo-tay'-ro], *m*. *(Low.)* Whoremaster, whoremonger.

putesco, ca [poo-tes'-co, cah], *a*. *(coll.)* Relating to whores.

putilla, ita [poo-teel'-lyah], *f. dim. (coll.)* Young prostitute.

puto [poo'-to], *m*. *(Low.)* Catamite, sodomite. -*a*. Bloody, bloody awful.

putput [poot'-poot], *m*. *(Orn.)* Hoopoe. V. ABUBILLA.

putredinal [poo-tray-de-nahl'], *a*. Putrefying, corrupting.

putrefacción [poo-tray-fac-the-on'], *f*. Putrefaction, corruptness.

putrefactivo, va [poo-tray-fac-tee'-vo, vah], *a*. Putrefactive.

putrefacto [poo-tray-fahc'-to], *a*. Rotten, putrid; decayed.

putridez [poo-tre-deth'], *f*. Putridity.

pútrido, da [poo'-tre-do, dah], *a*. Putrid, rotten.

puya [poo'-yah], *f*. Pointed rod.

puyero, ra [poo-yay'-ro, rah], *m. & f. (Cuba)* 1. V. PULLISTA. 2. One who is knock-kneed.

puzol, *m*. **puzolana**, *f*. [poo-thole', pool-tho-lah'-nah]. Puzzolana, a porous volcanic production.

Q

q [koo], eighteenth letter of the Spanish alphabet, which is always followed by *u*; it sounds as the English *k*.

Qbus [o-boos]. *(Inform.)* Qbus.

que [kay], *pron. rel.* 1. That. 2. Who (persona, sujeto), speaking of persons. 3. Which (cosa), speaking of things. 4. What, a particle expressive of admiration. **¡Qué desgracia!** what a misfortune! 5. What as an interrogative. **¿Qué es eso?** or **¿qué cosa es esa?** what is that? **¿Qué es eso?** or **¿qué hay?** what is the matter, or what is the matter there? 6. Than, as, a comparative particle: **más qué** or **más de,** more than, **tanto que,** as much as. **Algo que** something that. 7. Whether. **Que venga o que no venga,** whether he comes or not. **Más bien tarde que temprano,** rather sooner than later. 8. Because, why. 9. *conj.* Used after a verb it is a particle, which governs and determines another verb. **Le mandó que viniese,** he ordered him to come. 10. Where, in what place? **¿Qué es del libro?** Where is the book? 11. **Lo que,** that which. **Sea lo que fuere,** let it be what it may. **Hay en eso algo más de lo que se presume.** There is in that affair more than what is imagined. **No hay para qué,** there is no occasion for it. **No hay de qué,** don't mention it; you are welcome. **Sin qué ni para qué,** without cause or motive. Note.—*Que* in interrogatory or exclamatory use receives the accent to distinguish it from the relative and the conjunction. See the examples.

-*Conj.* Not translated. **Quiero que vayas,** I want you to go. **Te dije que lo hicieras,** I told you to do it. **me apuesto a que no lo haces,** I bet you don't do it. **¡Que te diviertas!,** enjoy yourself!

-*Adj. interr.* What. **¿Qué hora es?,** What time is it? **¿Qué quieres?,** what do you want? **¡Qué de gente!,** what a lot of people! **¿Qué te parece?,** what do you think of it?

quebrable [kay-brah´-blay], *a.* Breakable.

quebrada [kay-brah´-dah], *f.* 1. Ravine. 2. A deep pass (puerto). 3. A commercial failure.

quebradero [kay-brah-day´-ro], *m.* Breaker. **Quebradero de cabeza,** 1. That which molests, importunes, or occupies the mind. 2. Object of amorous care.

quebradillo [kay-brah-deel´-lyo], *m.* 1. Wooden shoe-heel. 2. Flexure of the body in dancing.

quebradizo, za [kay-brah-dee´-tho, thah], *a.* 1. Brittle, fragile. 2. Infirm, sickly. 3. Flexible (voz). 4. (*Met.*) V. FRÁGIL.

quebrado, da [kay-brah´-do, dah], *a.* Broken (terreno); debilitated, enervated. -*pp.* of QUEBRAR.

quebrado [kay-brah´-do], *m.* 1. (*Arith.*) Fraction, broken number. 2. (*Poet.*) Verse consisting of two, three, or four syllables, left so on purpose after a stanza of verses of eight or more syllables. 3. Bankrupt. 4. (*coll.*) A ruptured person.

quebrador, ra [kay-brah-dor´, rah], *m. & f.* 1. Breaker. 2. One who violates a law.

quebradura [kay-brah-doo´-rah], *f.* 1. The act of breaking or splitting. 2. A cleaving or chopping, a gap, a fissure, a slit, a fracture. 3. Rupture, hernia.

quebraja [kay-brah´-hah], *f.* Crack, flaw, split in wood or iron.

quebrajar [kay-brah-har´], *va.* V. RESQUEBRAJAR.

quebrajoso, sa [kay-brah-ho´-so, sah], *a.* Brittle, fragile.

quebramiento [kay-brah-me-en´-to], *m.* V. QUEBRANTAMIENTO.

quebrantable [kay-bran-tah´-blay], *a.* Frangible, brittle.

quebrantador, ra [kay-bran-tah-dor´, rah], *m. & f.* 1. Breaker; debilitator. 2. (*Met.*) Violator, transgressor of any law.

quebrantadura [kay-bran-tah-doo´-rah], *f.* Fracture, rupture, a bursting.

quebrantahuesos [kay-bran-tah-oo-ay´-sos], *m.* 1. (*Orn.*) Osprey. 2. A troublesome person, bore (pesado).

quebrantamiento [kay-bran-tah-me-en´-to], *m.* 1. Fracture, rupture; breaking a prison. 2. Weariness, fatigue. 3. Violation of the law; e. g. (a) (*Law.*) Act of breaking a will. (b) **Quebrantamiento** or **robo de una casa,** burglary. (c) **Quebrantamiento de sepultura,** desecration of a grave.

quebrantanueces [kay-bran-tah-noo-ay´-thes], *m.* (*Orn.*) Nutcracker.

quebrantaolas [key-bran-tah-o´-las], *m.* Breakwater.

quebrantar [kay-bran-tar´], *va.* 1. To break (romper), to crack, to burst open, to crash. 2. To pound, to grind. 3. To persuade, to induce. 4. To move to pity. 5. To transgress a law, to violate a contract. 6. To vex, to molest, to fatigue. 7. To weaken, to debilitate (resistencia). 8. To diminish, to temper the excess of anything. 9. To annul, to revoke; to break a will. 10. To shatter (posición). 11. To tone down (color). 12. (*LAm.*) To break in (caballo). -*vr.* To be shattered (persona).

quebrantaterrones [kay-brahn-tah-ter ro´-nes], *m.* (*coll.*) Clodhopper, rustic.

quebranto [kay-brahn´-to], *m.* 1. The act of breaking. 2. Weakness, debility, lassitude. 3. Commiseration, pity, compassion. 4. Object worthy of pity. 5. Great loss (pérdida), severe damage (daño). 6. (*Naut.*) Cambering of a ship's deck or keel. 7. Depression (depresión). 8. Sorrow (aflicción).

quebrar [kay-brar´], *va.* 1. To break (romper), to burst open; to cast asunder. 2. To double, to twist (torcer). 3. To interrupt, to intercept. 4. To transgress a law, to violate a contract. 5. To temper, to moderate. 6. To spoil the bloom of the countenance. 7. To overcome, to conquer. 8. To diminish friendship, to dissolve a connection, or abandon a correspondence. 9. To tone down. -*vn.* To fail, to be insolvent, to become bankrupt.-*vr.* l. To be ruptured, to labor under a rupture. 2. To interrupt the continuity of hills or banks. **Quebrar amistad,** to cut acquaintance. **Quebrar el corazón,** to break one's heart. **Quebrarse la cabeza,** to be oversolicitous in the pursuit of anything. (*Yo quiebro, quiebre, from Quebrar. V.* ALENTAR.)

queche [kay´-chay], *f.* (*Naut.*) Smack, a Dutch-built vessel; ketch.

quechemarín [kay-chay-mah reen´], *m.* Coasting lugger.

quechua [kay´-choo-ah], *a. & m.* Kechuan, the official language of the Peruvian empire at the time of the conquest.

queda [kay´-dah], *f.* The time of retirement marked by the sound of a bell or the beat of a drum; curfew.

quedada [kay-dah´-dah], *f.* Stay, residence, sojourn.

quedar [kay-dar´], *vn.* 1. To stay, to stop in a place. 2. To continue, to tarry, to remain (en un estado). 3. To be wanting. 4. To hold, to last, to subsist. 5. To knock down a thing to the last bidder. 6. To behave, to conduct oneself, to acquire a reputation or to be reputed. **Quedar por andar,** to have to walk farther. **Quedar por cobarde,** to shrink back as a coward. **Quedar por valiente,** to enjoy the reputation of a brave man. **Quedar limpio,** (*coll.*) to remain with an empty purse, to be square. **Quedar con uno,** to agree, to arrange or compound with anyone. 7. With a past participle it is often employed in place of *estar,* to be. **Quedar armado,** to be armed. **Quedar bien** or **mal,** to behave or come off well or ill in an affair: to fail or succeed in an attempt. **Quedar ciego,** to go blind. **Ha quedado como un canalla,** he showed himself a swine. **Nos queda poco dinero,** we haven´t much money left. **Quedan pocos días para la fiesta,** only a few days remain till the party. **Quedar en,** to turn out to be. -*va.* (*Prov.*) To leave. -*vr.* 1. To remain, to continue; to retain, to possess, to keep. 2. To falter, to lose the thread of a speech or argument; to stop short. 3. (*Cono Sur*) To become paralysed (miembro). **Quedarse helado,** to be astonished, to be thunderstruck. **Quedarse en ayunas de alguna cosa,** not to understand a word of the matter. **Quedarse a obscuras** or **en blanco,** to be left in the dark (literally or figuratively); to be left in the lurch. **Quedársele a uno en el tintero,** to forget a thing entirely. **Quedarse con unos amigos,** to stay with some friends. **Se quedó con mi pluma,** he kept my pen. **Quedarse con uno,** to bore the pants off somebody (aburrir).

quedito, ta [kay-dee´-to, tah], *a. dim.* Soft, gentle; easy. This diminutive is more energetic than its primitive, *quedo.*

quedito [kay-dee´-to], *adv.* V. QUEDO.

quedo [kay´-do], *adv.* Softly, gently; in a low voice.

quedo, da [kay'-do, dah], *a*. Quiet (voz), still (inmóvil), noiseless; easy, gentle.

quehacer [kay-ah-therr '] *m*. Occupation, domestic business (chore). **Cada uno tiene sus quehaceres**. Every one has his own affairs. **Tener mucho que hacer**, to have a lot to do.

queirópteros [kay-rop'-tay-ros], *a. & m. pl.* Cheiropterous; the cheiroptera, the bats.

queja [kay'-hah], *f*. 1. Complaint, expostulation, murmur, grumbling, moan (quejido). 2. Resentment of an injury or insult. 3. Quarrel, dispute. **Tener una queja de alguno**, *(coll.)* to have a bone to pick with one. **Presentar queja de uno**, to make a complaint about somebody.

quejarse [kay-har'-say], *vr*. To complain of, to expostulate, to murmur, to grumble (refunfuñar). **quejarse de**, to clamor against; to mention with sorrow, to lament. **Quejarse de vicio**, to complain without cause. *V*. QUERELLARSE.

quejicoso, sa [kay-he-co'-so, sah], *a*. Plaintful, querulous, always complaining.

quejidito [kay-he-dee'-to], *m. dim*. Slight complaint, a low moan.

quejido [kay-hee'-do], *m*. Groan, moan, lament.

quejigal [kay-he-gahl'], *m*. Plantation of muricated oaks.

quejigo [kay-hee'-go], *m. (Bot.)* Muricated oak.

quejita [kay-hee'-tah], *f. dim*. Murmur; resenting; slight complaint.

quejosamente [kay-ho-sah-men-tay], *adv*. Querulously.

quejoso, sa [kay-ho'-so, sah], *a*. Plaintful, querulous (tono).

quejumbre [key-hoom'-bray], *f. (Prov.)* V. QUEJA.

quejumbroso, sa [kay-hoom-bro'-so, sah]. *a*. Complaining, plaintive.

quelidón [kay-le-done'], *m*. Martin, a bird of the swallow family.

quelidonia [kay-le-do'-ne-ah], *f. (Bot.)* Celandine, an herb of the poppy family.

quelónidos [kay-lo'-ne-dos], or **quelonios**, *a. & m. pl.* Chelonieus: turtles and tortoises.

quema [kay'-mah], *m*. 1. Burn, the act of burning (acto), combustion, fire, conflagration. 2. *(Met.)* Oven, furnace.

quemado [kay-mah-do], *a*. 1. Burned, burnt. **Aquí huele a quemado**, I smell something burning in here. 2. Burned out (agotado). 3. Discredited (moralmente).

quemador, ra [kay-mah-dor', rah], *m. & f.* Incendiary; burner.

quemadura [kay-ma-doo'-rah], *f*. 1. Mark or hurt by fire, burn. 2. *(Agr.)* Brand, smut upon plants.

quemajoso, sa [kay-mah-ho'-so, sah], *a*. Smarting, burning.

quemar [kay-mar'], *va*. 1. To burn, to consume by fire. 2. To fire, to set on fire, to kindle. 3. To burn, to parch, to dry, or scorch. 4. To dispose of a tiling at a low price. 5. To scorch (líquido). 6. To cut (plantas). 7. To burn up (fortuna). 8. *(Fig.)* To annoy, to upset (molestar). 9. *(CAm. Mex.)* To denounce (denunciar). 10. *(Carib. Mex.)* To swindle (estafar). 11. *(Carib.)* To shoot (con arma de fuego). **Estar quemado con algo**, to be sick and tired of something. -*vn*. To be too hot. **Esto está que quema**, it´s burning hot. -*vr*. 1. To be very hot, to be parched with heat; to heat oneself. 2. To fret, to be impatient, to be offended. 3. *(coll.)* To be near, to almost attain or touch a thing desired. 4. To burn oneself out (agotarse). 5. To fret (inquietarse). 6. *(Carib. Cono Sur)* To get depressed (deprimirse). 7. To be discredited (moralmente, políticamente). Quemaropa, (1) immediate, very near, quite close, contiguous. (2) *(Met.)* Unawares, unexpectedly: applied to an unanswerable argument, or to an action unobjectionable either from its promptitude or justice. **Quemarse la sangre**, to be subject to constant vexations. **¡Que te quemas!**, you´re getting warm.

quemazón [kay-mah-thone'], *f*. 1. Burn, hurt by fire; combustion, conflagration. 2. The act of burning. 3. Excessive heat (calor). 4. Eagerness, covetousness. 5. *(coll.)* Pert language, smart repartee. 6. *(Cuba)* Auction where goods are sold very cheap.

quencho [ken'-cho], *m. (Orn.)* Gull.

quequisque [kay-kees'-kay], *m. (Bot.)* An arum.

queratitis [kay-rah-tee'-tis], *f*. Keratitis, inflammation of the cornea.

querella [kay-rayl'-lyah], *f*. 1. Complaint (queja), expression of pain or grief. 2. A complaint before a judge against anyone. 3. Petition or libel exhibited to a court of justice by children, praying that the last will of their parents be set aside.

querellador, ra [kay-rayl-lyah-dor', rah], *m. & f.* Lamenter; complainant.

querellante [kay-rayl-lyahn'-tay], *pa*. Murmuring, complaining.-*m. & f.* Complainant.

querellarse [kar-rayl-lyar'-say], *vr*. 1. To lament, to bewail one's own sorrow; to complain of another (quejarse), to be querulous. 2. To complain or prefer a complaint in a court of justice.

querellosamente [kay-rayl-lyo'-sah-men-tay], *adv*. Plaintively, querulously.

querelloso, sa [key-rayl-lyo'-so, sah], *a*. Querulous.

querencia [kay-ren'-the-ah], *f*. 1. Haunt of wild hearts. 2. Favorite and frequent place of resort.

querencioso, sa [kay-ren-the-o´-so, sah], *a*. Frequented by wild beasts.

querer [kay-rerr'], *va*. 1. To wish, to desire (desear), to list. **Quiero comer**, I have an appetite. 2. To love (amar), to cherish, to like. 3. To will, to resolve, to determine. 4. To attempt, to procure, to require (requerir). 5. To conform, to agree. 6. To accept a challenge at a game of hazard. 7. To suit, to fit. 8. To cause, to occasion.-*vn*. To be near being, to verify anything. **Sin querer**, unwillingly. **Querer más**, to have rather. **¿Qué quiere decir eso?** what does that mean? **¿Qué más quiere?** what more does he wish? what more is necessary? **Como Vd. quiera**, as you will it, let it be so. **Como quiera**, anyhow, in anyway. **Quien todo lo quiere, todo lo pierde**, *(Prov.)* all covet, all lose. **No quiero más**, I don´t want any more. **Querer es poder**, where there´s a will there´s a way. **Pero no quiso**, but he refused. **Querer bien a uno**, to be fond of somebody. -*m*. Will, desire, study.

queresa [kay-ray'-sah], *f. V.* CRESA.

querido, da [kay-ree'-do, dah], *a. & pp* of QUERER. Wished, desired, dear, beloved (persona amada).-*m. & f.* Darling, fondling lover, sweetheart. **Querido, querida** or **querido mío**, my dear, my love, honey, my pet, my darling.

quermes [kayr'-mes], *m*. Kermes, an insect used as a scarlet dye. **Quermes mineral**, kermes mineral, a preparation of antimony.

querocha [kay-roh'-chah], *f. V.* CRESA.

querochar [kay-ro-char'], *m*. To emit the semen of bees.

querosina [kay-ro-see'-nah], *f*. Kerosene, coal oil.

querub, querube [kay'-roob]. *(Poet.)* V. QUERBÍN. *(Heb.)*

querúbico, ca [kay-roo'-be-co, cah], *a*. Cherubic, relating to cherubs.

querubín [kay-roo-been'], *m*. Cherub, a celestial spirit.

quesadilla [kay-sah-deel'-lyah], *f*. 1. A sort of cheese-cake (tarta). 2. A sweetmeat; a fritter.

quesear [kay-say-ar'], *vn*. To make cheese.

quesera [kay-say'-rah], *f*. 1. Dairy. 2. Cheese-board, cheese-mould, cheese-vat.

quesería [kay-say-ree'-ah], *f*. 1. Season for making cheese. 2. Dairy (tienda).

quesero [kay-say'-ro], *m*. Cheesemonger, cheesemaker.

quesero, ra [kay-say'-ro, rah], *a*. Caseous, cheesy.

quesillo, ito [kay-seel'-lyo], *m. dim*. A small cheese.

queso [kay'-so], *m*. 1. Cheese. 2. **Quesos** (pies), plates. **Queso de bola**, Dutch cheese.

quetzal [kee-thahl'], *m*. 1. *(Orn.)* Quetzal. 2. Quetzal, Guatemalan monetary unit.

¡quiá! [ke-ah']. Interjection denoting incredulity or denial. Come now! No, indeed!

quiasmo [ke-ahs'-mo], *m*. 1. Chiasm, junction of two things which form a cross. 2. *(Anat.)* Decussation of the optic nerves.

quibey [ke-bay'-e], *m. (Bot.)* Dog's bane, an herb which grows in the island of Puerto Rico, very poisonous to animals which eat it. The flower resembles a violet, but is white.

quiquicial, *m.* **quicialera,** *f* [ke-the-ahl'] [ke-the-ah-lay'-rah]. 1. Sidepost, or jamb of a door or window; a jamb. 2. *V.* QUICIO.

quicio [kee'-the-o], *m.* 1. Hinge of a door; a but-hinge. 2. Prop, support. **Fuera de quicio,** violently, unnaturally. **Sacar una cosa de quicio,** to unhinge, to overturn, to violate or pervert.

quid [kid], *m.* Essence, gist. **El quid del asunto,** the gist of the matter.

quídam [kee'-dam], *m. (coll.)* A certain person.

quiebra [ke-ay'-brah], *f.* 1. Crack (grieta), fracture. 2. Gaping or opening of the ground. 3. Loss, damage. 4. Failure, bankruptcy. 5. **Quiebras del terreno** or **de la tierra,** undulations of the ground or surface.

quiebrahacha [ke-ay-brah-ah'-chah], *m. (Cuba)* A tree much esteemed for the solidity and firmness of its wood; a kind of fir.

quiebro [ke-ay'-bro], *m.* 1. *(Mus.)* Trill. 2. Movement or inclination of the body.

quien [ke-en'], *prom. rel.* 1. Who, which. 2. One or the other. *V.* CUAL and QUE. When interrogative it is accented; as, **¿Quién ha venido?** who has come? **La señorita con quien hablaba,** the young lady to whom I was talking. **No hay quien lo aguante,** nobody can stand him.

quienquiera [ke-en-ke-ay'-rah], *pron.* Whosoever, whatever.

quietador, ra [ke-ay-tah-dor', rah], *m. & f.* Quieter.

quietamente [ke-ay'-tah-men-tay], *adv.* Quietly, calmly.

quietar [ke-ay-tar'], *va.* To appease. *V.* AQUIETAR.

quiete [ke-ay'-tay], *f.* Rest, repose, quiet.

quietismo [ke-ay-tees'-mo], *m.* Quietism, sect of mystics.

quietista [ke-ay-tees'-tah], *a. & m.* Quietist.

quieto, ta [ke-ay'-to, tah], *a.* 1. Quiet, still (inmóvil); undisturbed. 2. Quiet, peaceable, pacific (carácter). 3. Orderly, virtuous, moderate. **Estar quieto como un poste,** to stand stock-still.

quietud [ke-ay-tood'], *f.* Quietude, quietness, quiet, want of motion, rest, repose; tranquility.

quijada [ke-hah'-dah], *f.* Jaw or jawbone.

quijal, quijar [ke-hahl', ke-har'], *m.* Grinder, a back tooth; jaw.

quijarudo, da [ke-hah-roo'-do, dah], *a.* Large-jawed.

quijera [ke-hay'-rah], *f.* 1. Cheeks of a cross-bow. 2. Piece of leather on the headstall of a horse. 3. Among carpenters, a strengthening piece put on each side.

quijo [kee'-ho], *m.* A hard rock found in several mines as the matrix of ore.

quijones [ke-ho'-nes], *m. pl.* Dill, an aromatic herb resembling anise.

quijotada [ke-ho-tah'-dah], *f.* A quijotic enterprise, an action ridiculously extravagant.

quijote [ke-hoh'-tay], *m.* 1. Armor for the thigh. 2. A man who engages in quixotic enterprises. 3. Fleshy part over the hoofs of horses or asses.

quijotería [ke-ho-tay-ree'-ah], *f.* Quixotry, quixotism.

quijotesco, ca [ke-ho-tes'-co, cah], *a.* Quixotic.

quilatador [ke-lah-tah-dor'], *m.* Assayer of gold and silver.

quilatar [ke-lah-tar'], *va.* To assay gold and silver.

quilate [ke-lah'-tay], *m.* 1. Degree of purity of gold or precious stones. 2. A carat, the twenty-fourth part in weight and value of gold. 3. Weight of four grams. 4. An ancient coin. 5. Decree of perfection.

quilatera [ke-lah-tay'-rah], *f.* Instrument for ascertaining the carats of pearls.

quilo [ke-lo], *V.* KILO.

quilómetro [ke-loh'-may-tro], *m. V.* KILÓMETRO.

quiloso, sa [ke-lo'-so, sah], *a.* Chylous, chylaceous.

quilla [keel'-lyah], *f. (Naut.)* Keel of a ship. **Descubrir la quilla,** to heave down a ship. **Dar de quilla** or **tumbar a la quilla,** to careen, to overhaul a vessel.

quillaje [keel-lyah'-hay], *m.* Harbor dues which used to be paid in France.

quillotro, tra [kil-lyo'-tro, trah], *a. (coll.)* This or that other.

quimbámbulas [kim-bam'-boo-las], *f. pl. (Cuba)* Rough, craggy spots.

quimera [ke-may'-rah], *f.* 1. Dispute, quarrel (riña), scuffle, feud. 2. Chimera, wild fancy. 3. Hallucination (alucinación). 4. Unfounded suspicion (sospecha).

quimérico, ca, quimerino, na [ke-may'-re co, cah], *a.* Chimerical, fantastic, unreal.

quimerista [ke-may-rees'-tah], *m.* 1. Wrangler, brawler. 2. One who indulges in chimeras.

quimerizar [ke-may-re-thar'], *vn.* To fill the head with fantastic ideas.

química [kee'-me-cah], *f.* Chemistry. **Química de polímeros,** polymer chemistry.

químicamente [kee'-me-cah-men-tay], *adv.* Chemically.

químico [kee'-me-co], *m.* Chemist.

químico, ca [kee'-me-co, cah], *a.* Chemical.

quimificar [ke-me-fe-car'], *va.* To convert into chyme.

quimista [ke-mees'-tah], *m. V.* ALQUIMISTA.

quimo [kee'-mo], *m. (Med.)* Chyme.

quimón [ke-mone'], *m.* Fine printed cotton, chintz.

quimono [ke-mo'-no], *m.* Kimono, Japanese garb.

quimosina [ke-mo-see'-nah], *f.* Rennin.

quina, quinaquina [kee'-nah], *f.* Peruvian or Jesuits' bark.

quinal [ke-nahl'], *m.* (Peru) The cinchona-tree and a group of such trees.

quinario, ria [ke-nah'-re-o, ah], *a.* Consisting of five.

quinario [ke-nah'-re-o], *m.* A Roman coin of five units.

quinas [kee'-nas], *f. pi.* 1. Arms of Portugal, consisting of five scutcheons, in memory of the five wounds of Christ. 2. Fives, on dice.

quincalla [kin-cahl'-lyah], *f.* Hardware, notions, trinkets.

quincallería [kin-cal-lyay-ree'-ah], *f.* 1. Notions store. 2. Hardware store. 3. Trinket manufacturing.

quince [keen'-thay], *a. & m* 1. Fifteen. 2. Fifteenth (fecha). 3. A game at cards. **Quince días,** fortnight.

quincena [kin-thay'-nah], *f.* 1. Fortnight, two weeks (quince días). 2. Semi-monthly pay (pago). 3. *(Mus.)* Interval comprising fifteen successive notes of two octaves. 4. Fifteenth, a register in the pipes of an organ.

quincenal [kin-thay-nahl'], *a.* Biweekly, fortnightly.

quincenalmente [kin-thay-nahl-men'-tay] *adv.* Every two weeks, fortnightly.

quinceno, na [kin-thay'-no, nah], *a.* Fifteenth.

quincha [keen'-chah], *f.* (Peru) A wall of clay and canes.

quincuagenario, ria [kin-coo-ah-hay-nah'-re-o, ah], *a.* Fiftieth.

quincuagésima [kin-coo-ah-hay'-se-mah], *f.* Quinquagesima Sunday.

quincuagésimo, ma [kin-coo-ah-hay'-see-mo, mah], *a.* Fiftieth.

quincuatro [kin-coo-ah'-tro], *m.* Roman festival of five days in honor of Minerva.

quincunce [kin-coon'-thay], *m.* Quincunx.

quincurión [kin-coo-re-on'], *m.* A chief or corporal of five soldiers.

quindecágono, na [kin-day-cah'-go-no, nah], *a.* Quindecagon.

quindécima [kin-day'-the-mah], *f.* The fifteenth part.

quindejas [kin-day'-has], *f. (Prov.)* Rope of three strands, made of bass or *esparto.*

quindenio [kin-day'-ne-o], *m.* Space or period of fifteen years.

quinete [ke-nay'-tay], *m.* Kind of camlet.

quingentésimo, ma [kin-hen-tay'-se-mo, mah], *a.* The five hundredth.

quiniela [ke-ne-ay'-lah], *f.* Pools coupon.

quinientos, tas [ke-ne-en'-tos, tas], *a.* Five hundred.

quinina [ke-nee'-nah], *f.* Quinine, the principal alkaloid of cinchona.

quino [kee'-no], *m.* 1. The cinchona-tree, an evergreen of the madder family. 2. A juice like opium extracted from various African vegetables in the banks of the Gambia.

quinoidina [ke-noi-dee'-nah], *f.* Quinoidine, a resinous substance of yellow and red cinchona barks.

quínolas, quinolillas [kee'-no-las], *f. pl.* Reversis, a game at cards.

quinque [keen-kay'], *m.* An Argand lamp (lámpara).

quinquefolio [kin-kay-fo'-le-o], *m. (Bot.)* Common cinquefoil.

quinquenio [kin-kay'-ne-o], *m.* Space or period of five years; lustrum.

quinquercio [kin-kerr'-the-o], *m.* Five Grecian games of wrestling, jumping, rumling, quoits, etc.

quinquenal [kin-kay-nahl'], *a.* Quinquennial.

quinqui [kin'-ke], *m.* Bandit (bandido); delinquent (delincuente); small-time dealer (vendedor).

quinquillería [kin-keel-lyay-ree'-ah], *f.* Hardware. V. QUINCALLERÍA and BUHONERÍA.

quinquillero [kin-keel-lyay'-ro], *m.* Hawker, peddler, hardwareman. V. BUHONERO.

quinta [keen'-tah], *f.* 1. Country-seat, a country-house (casa). 2. The act of choosing one out of five. 3. The act of drawing lots for men to serve in the army. 4. Quint, the sequence at five cards in the game of piques. 5. *(Mus.)* Fifth, an interval of three tones and a semitone major.

quinta columna [keen'-tah co-loom'-nah], *f.* Fifth column.

quintacolumnista [kin-tah-co-loom-nees'-tah], *m. & f.* Fifth columnist.

quintador, ra [kin-tah-dor', rah], *m.* 1. One who draws lots in fives.

quintaesencia [kin-tah-ay-sen'-the-ah], *f.* Quintessence.

quintal [kin-tahl'], *m.* 1. Quintal, a hundred-weight. 2. Fifth part of one hundred. **Quintal métrico,** weight of one hundred kilograms, ton.

quintalada [kin-tah-lah'-dah], *f.* The sum of 2,5 per cent on the freights paid to masters of vessels.

quintaleño, ña, quintalero, ra [kin-tah-lay'-nyo, nyah], *a.* Capable of containing a quintal.

quintana [kin-tah'-nah], *f.* A country house.

quintanar [kin-tah-nar'], *m.* Quintain, ancient tilting-post.

quintante [kin-tahn'-tay], *m.* An astronomical instrument larger than the sextant.

quintañón, na [kin-tah-nyone', nah], *a.* A hundred years old; much advanced in years.

quintar [kin-tar'], *va.* 1. To draw one out of five. 2. To draw lots for soldiers. 3. To come to the number of five. 4. To pay to govermnent the duty of 20 per cent on gold or silver. 5. To plough ground the fifth time.-*vn.* To attain the fifth: applied to the moon on the fifth day.

quintería [kin-tay-ree'-ah], *f.* Farm; grange.

quinterillo [kin-tay-reel'-lyo], *m. dim.* A farmer who rents a small farm.

quinterno [kin-terr'-no], *m.* 1. Number of five sheets of paper. 2. Lot, or row, of five numbers in the ancient lottery.

quintero [kin-tay'-ro], *m.* 1. Farmer, one who rents a farm (dueño). 2. Overseer of a farm; servant who takes care of a farm.

quinteto [kin-tay'-to], *m.* Quintet, a musical composition for five performers.

quintil [kin-teel'], *m.* The month of July, according to the ancient Roman calendar.

quintilla [kin-teel'-lyah], *f.* A metrical composition of five verses.

quintillizos [kin-tel-lye-thos], *m & pl.* Quintuplets.

quintillón [kin-teel-lyon'], *m.* Quintillon.

quintín [kin-teen'], *m.* Sort of fine cloth of a loose texture.

quinto [keen'-to], *m.* 1. One-fifth. 2. Fifth, a duty of 20 per cent on prizes, etc., paid to the Spanish government. 3. Share of pasture land. 4. One called up for military service, draft, conscription, draftee.

quinto, ta [keen'-to, tah], *a.* Fifth, the ordinal number of five.

quintuplicar [kin-too-ple-car'], *va.* To multiply by five.

quíntuplo, pla [keen'-too-plo, plah], *a.* Quintuple, five-fold.

quiñón [ke-nyone'], *m.* Share of profit arising from an enterprise undertaken with another person.

quiosco [ke-os'-co], *m.* Kiosk, pavilion, stand. **Quiosco de periódicos,** newstand.

quipos [kee'-pos], *m. pl.* Ropes of various colors, and with different knots, used by the ancient inhabitant of Peru to record memorable events and keep accounts.

quiquiriquí [ke-ke-re-kee'], *m.* Imitation of cock-crowing; cock-a-doodle-doo.

quiragra [ke-rah'-grah], *f.* Gout in the hand.

quirieleisón [ke-re-ay-lay-re-sone'], *m.* Lord, have mercy upon us! the responses chanted in the funeral service. V. KIRIELEISÓN.

quirinal [ke-re-nahl'], *a.* Relating to the feast of Romulus, and to one of the seven hills of Rome.

quirite [ke-ree'-tay], *m.* Roman citizen or knight.

quirivel [ke-re-vel'], *m. (Bot.)* V. PERDIGUERA.

quirófano [ke-ro'-fah-no], *m.* Operating room.

quirografía [ke-ro-grah-fee'-ah], *f.* Chirography, the art of writing.

quiromancia [ke-ro-mahn'-the-ah], *f.* Chiromancy, palmistry.

quiromántico [ke-ro-mahn'-te-co], *m.* Palmister, chiromancer.

quirópteros [ke-rop'-tay-ros], *m. pl.* Bats: the cheiroptera.

quiroteca [ke-ro-tay'-kah], *f. (coll.)* Glove.

quirúrgico, ca [ke-roor'-he-co, cah], *a.* Surgical.

quirurgo [ke-roor'-go], *m. (coll.)* Surgeon.

quisicosa [ke-se-co'-sah], *f. (coll.)* Enigma, riddle, obscure question.

quisling [kees'-lin], *m.* Quisling, traitor of his country.

quisquilla [kis-keel'-lyah], *f.* 1. A ridiculous nicety; bickering, trifling dispute (bagatela). 2. *(Zool.)* Shrimp.

quisquilloso, sa [kis-kil-lyo'-so, sah], *a.* Fastidious, precise, morose; touchy (sensible), quibbling (sofístico).

quiste [kees'-tay], *m. (Acad.)* Cyst, a tumor with fluid contents.

quita [kee'-tah], *f.* Acquittance, or discharge from a debt, or a part of it (deuda); *(LAm.)* rebate (descuento).

¡quita! *int.* God forbid! **¡Quita de ahí!** away with you! out of my sight!

quitación [ke-tah-the-on'], *f.* 1. Salary, wages, pay, income. 2. V. QUITA.

quitador, ra [ke-tah-dor', rah], *m. & f.* One who takes away, remover.

quitaguas [ke-tah'-goo-ahs], *m.* V. PARAGUAS.

quitaipón [ke-tah-e-pone'], *m.* V. QUITAPÓN. **De quita y pon,** adjustable, removable: used of mechanical contrivances.

quitamanchas [ke-tah-mahn'-chas], *m.* A clothes-cleaner.

quitameriendas [ke-tah-may-re-en'-das], *f. (Bot.)* Common meadow saffron.

quitamiento [ke-tah-me-en'-to], *m.* V. QUITA.

quitamotas [ke-tah-mo'-tas], *m. & f.* A servile flatterer.

quitante [ke-tahn'-tay], *pa.* Taking away, removing.

quitanza [ke-tahn'-thah], *f. (Com.)* Receipt, discharge.

quitapelillos [ke-tah-pay-leel'-lyos], *com. (coll.)* Flatterer, fawner, wheedler.

quitapenas [ke-tah-pay'-nahs], *m.* Pistol (pistola); knife (navaja).

quitapesares [ke-tah-pay-sah'-res], *com. (coll.)* Comfort, consolation.

quitapón [ke-tah-pone'], *m.* Ornament of the headstall of draught horses and mules.

quitar [ke-tar'], *va.* 1. To take away, to remove; to separate, to extract. 2. To release or redeem a pledge. 3. To hinder, to disturb. 4. To forbid, to prohibit. 5. To abrogate, to annul. 6. To free from an obligation. 7. To usurp, to rob (robar). 8. To strip or deprive of anything. 9. To suppress an office. 10. To parry a thrust. **No quita nada de su valor,** it does not detract at all from its value. **Le van a quitar ese privilegio,** they are going to take that privilege away from him. **Quitar a uno de hacer algo,** to stop somebody from doing something. *-vr.* 1. To abstain, to refrain. 2. To retire, or withdraw. 3. To get rid of. **Quitarse de la vista de uno,** to remove oneself from somebody´s side. **Quitarse la ropa,** to take off one´s clothing.

quitasol [ke-tah-sole´], *m.* Parasol, sunshade.

quitasueño [ke-tah-soo-ay´-nyo], *m. (Coll.)* Anxiety or worry causing sleeplessness.

quite [kee´-tay], *m.* 1. Obstacle, impediment, hindrance; the act of taking away. 2. Parade, parry, in fencing. **No tiene quite,** it is unavoidable, there is no help for it.

quiteño, ña [ke-tay´-nyo, nyah], *a.* Native of or belonging to Quito.

quito, ta [kee´-to, tah], *a. & pp. irr. obs.* of QUITAR. Free from an obligation, clear from a charge, quite. *-m.* A dyewood (yielding black) of the Napo region in South America.

quitrín [ke-treen´], *m. (Cuba)* Gig, a light chaise.

quiyá [kee-yah´], *f.* Name of an otter of the Argentine Republic.

quizá, quizás [ke-thah´, ke-thahs´], *adv.* Perhaps. *V.* ACASO.

quórum [kwo´-room], *m.* Quorum (de una asamblea), a term from Latin.

R

r [er´-ray, er´-ay], *f.* This letter at the beginning of a word, after *l, n, s,* and in compound words, the primitive of which begins with *r,* has a hard and rough sound, as, *rata, malrotar, enriquecer, cariredondo.* When *ab* and *ob* are not prepositions, as in *abrogar, obrepción,* the *r* becomes liquid; as in *abrojo, obrero.—R* in the middle of a word, or between two vowels, has a very smooth sound; as in *morosidad, peregrinar.* The harsh and rough sound of *r* between two vowels, in the middle of simple words, is always expressed by double *rr;* thus, *barraca, correcto. R* is used as a contraction of *reprobar,* like *A* for *aprobar,* in voting for degrees in universities; it is also used as a contraction for **real,** royal, and for *reverendo,* reverend.

raba [rah´-bah], *f.* Bait used in the pilchard-fishery.

rabada [rah-bah´-dah], *f.* Hind quarter of mutton.

rabadán [rah-bah-dahn´], *m.* The principal shepherd of a sheep-walk.

rabadilla [rah-bah-deel´-lyah], *f.* Rump, croup, the extremity of the backbone.

rabanal [rah-bah-nahl´], *m.* Ground sown with radishes.

rabanero, ra [rah-bah-nay´-ro, rah], *a.* 1. Very short: applied to the garments of women. 2. *f. (Coll.)* A shameless and insolent woman.*-m. & f.* Seller of radishes.

rabanete [rah-bah-nay´-tay], *m dim.* A small radish.

rabanillo [rah-bah-neely o], *m.* 1. *(dim.)* Small radish. 2. The tart sharp taste of wine which is on the turn. 3. *(Coll.)* Ardent desire, longing. 4. Acrimony, asperity, rudeness.

rabaniza [rah-bah-nee´-thah], *f.* Radish seed.

rábano [rah´-bah-no], *m. (Bot.)* Radish. **Rábano picante or rusticano,** horse radish. **Tomar el rábano por las hojas,** to get hold of the wrong end of the stick.

rabazuz [rah-ba-thooth´], *m.* Inspissated juice of licorice.

rabear [rah-bay-ar´], *vn.* To wag the tail.

rabel [rah-bel´], *m.* 1. Rebeck, an ancient musical instrument with three strings, played with a bow. 3. *(Coll.)* Breech, backside.

rabelejo, ico, illo, ito [rah-bay-lay´-ho], *m. dim.* of RABEL.

rabera [rah-bay´-rah], *f.* 1. Tail, the hind or back part of anything. 2. Handle of a cross-bow. 3. Remains of uncleaned grain or seeds.

raberón [rah-bay-rone´], *m.* The tops of a felled tree, cut for fire wood.

rabí [rah-bee´], *m.* Rabbi, rabbin.

rabia [rah´-be-ah], *f.* 1. Hydrophobia, rabies. 2. Rage, fury. **Me da rabia,** it maddens me. **Tomar rabia a,** to take a dislike to. 3. *(LAm.)* **Con rabia,** extremely, terribly.

rabiar [rah-be-ar´], *vn.* 1. To labor under hydrophobia. 2. To rage (enfadarse), to be furious. 3. To labor under racking pain. 4. To flush, to be agitated and hurried to excess. **Rabiar por,** to wish or long for a thing with itching desire or anxiety. **Rabiar de hambre,** to be furiously hungry. **Quema que rabia,** it is as hot as hell.

rabiatar [rah-be-ah-tar´], *va.* To tie by the tail.

rabiazorras [rah-be-ah-thor´-ras], *m. (Prov.)* Among shepherds, the east wind.

rabicán, rabicano [rah-be-cahn´], *a.* White-tailed, having white hairs in the tail (caballos).

rabicorto, ta [rah-be-cor´-to, tah], *a.* Short-tailed.

rábido, da [rah´-be-do, dah], *a. (Poet.)* V. RABIOSO.

rabieta [ra-be-ay´-tah], *f. (Coll.)* Violent, fretting impatience.

rabihorcado [rah-be-or-cah´-do], *m. (Orn.)* Frigate bird, or frigate pelican.

rabilargo, ga [rah-be-lar´-go, gah], *a.* Long-tailed; having a long train.

rabilargo [rah-be-lar´-go], *m. (Orn.)* Blue crow.

rabillo [rah-beel´-lyo], *m.* 1. Mildew on the stalk of corn. 2. *(dim.)* Little tail. 3. Tip (punta); corner (ángulo); thin part (parte delgada). **Mirar con el rabillo del ojo,** to look out of the corner of one´s eyes.

rabinegro, gra [rah-be-nay´-gro, grah], *a.* Black-tailed.

rabínico, ca [rah-bee´-ne-co, cah], *a.* Rabbinical.

rabinismo [rah-be-nees´-mo], *m.* Rabbinism.

rabinista [rah-be-nees´-tah], *com* Rabbinist.

rabino [rah-bee´-no], *m.* Rabbi, a teacher of the Hebrew law. **Gran rabino,** the chief of a synagogue.

rabiosamente [rah-be-o-sah-men-tay], *adv.* Furiously, outrageously, madly, ragingly.

rabioso, sa [rah-be-o´-so, sah], *a.* 1. Rabid, mad: applied to dogs and other brutes. 2. Furious (enfado), outrageous, choleric, raging, fierce. **Poner rabioso a uno,** to enrage somebody.

rabisalsera [rah-be-sal-say´-rah], *m. (Coll.)* Pert, smart, forward, saucy, impudent (mujeres).

rabiseco, ca [rah-be-say´-co, cah], *a.* 1. Dry-tailed, poor, lean, starving. *(Met.)* Snappish, peevish.

rabito [rah-bee´-to], *m. (dim.)* A small tail.

rabiza [rah-bee´-thah], *f.* 1. Point of a fishing-rod, to which the line is fastened. 2. *(Naut.)* End, tip of anything, particularly the tapering end of a rope.

rabizar [rah-be-thar´], *m.* To point the end of a rope.

rable [rah´-blay], *m.* Ferret, an instrument to skim melted glass.

rabo [rah´-bo], *m.* 1. Tail of animals: applied to certain animals, as pigs, etc. instead of *cola.* 2. Tail, the lower, back, or hind part of anything; train. 3. All instruments to cut velvet in the loom. 4. In paper-mills, the tail which supports the hammer that beats the pulp. **Rabo de puerco,** *(Bot.)* hog's fennel, sea-sulphur wort. **Rabo de junco,** *(Orn.)* tropic bird. **Rabo entre piernas,** *(Coll.)* crestfallen, dejected. *V.* RABERA. **Mirar con el rabo del ojo,** to look askance.

rabón, na [rah-bohn´, nah], *a.* 1. Docked, bob-tailed, short-tailed. 2. *(LAm.)* Short (pequeño). 3. *(Cono Sur)* Stark naked (desnudo). 3. *(Carib. Cono Sur)* Damaged (cuchillo). 4. *(Mex.)* Down on one´s luck (desgraciado).

rabona [rah-bo´-nah], *f. (Peru)* A canteen woman, or wife of a soldier.

rabosear [rah-bo-say-ar´], *va.* To spatter with dirt.

raboso, sa [rah-bo´-so, sah], *a.* Ragged, tattered.

rabotada [bah-bo-tah´-dah], *f.* 1. A gruff and insolent reply with rude gestures. *(Acad.)* 2. A hit with a tail.

rabotear [rah-bo-tay-ar'], *va.* To crop the tail.

rabudo, da [rah-boo'-do, dah], *a.* Long-tailed.

rábula [rah'-boo-lah], *m.* An ignorant, vociferous lawyer.

racahut [rah-cah-oot'], *m.* Raccahout, a farinaceous preparation from potatoes, edible acorns, etc.

rácano [rah'-cah-no], *a.* 1. Bone-idle. 2. Stingy (tacaño). 3. Sly (artero).

racha [rah'-chah], *f.* 1. Gust of wind. 2. Short period of good luck. **Buena racha**, piece of luck.

racial [rah-the-ahl'], *a.* Racial, race.

racimado, da [rah-the-mah'-do, dah], *a.* Clustered, in racemes.

racimar [rah-the-mar'], *va.* *(Prov.)* V. REBUSCAR. *-vr.* V. ARRACIMARSE.

racimo [rah-thee'-mo], *m.* 1. Bunch of grapes. 2. Cluster of small things disposed in order; raceme. 3. *(Coll.)* Criminal hanging on the gallows.

racimoso, sa [rah-the-mo'-so, sah], *a.* Full of grapes, racemose, racemiferous.

racimudo, da [rah-the-moo'-do, dah], *a.* In large bunches or racemes.

raciocinación [rah-the-o-the-nah-the-on'], *f.* Ratiocination, the art of reasoning.

raciocinar [rah-the-o-the-nar'], *va.* To reason, to argue, to ratiocinate.

raciocinio [rah-the-o-thee'-ne-o], *m.* Reasoning, argument.

ración [rah-the-on'], *f.* 1. Ration, food for one meal. 2. Board-wages; allowance for soldiers or sailors, pittance. **Ración de hambre**, scanty allowance. **Raciones**, rations. 3. A prebend in Spanish cathedrals.

racionabilidad [rah-the-o-nah-be-le-ahd'], *f.* Rationality, the power of reasoning.

racional [rah-the-o-nahl'], *a.* 1. Rational, reasonable. 2. *(Ast.)* Rational: applied to the horizon where plane is conceived to pass through the center of the earth. 3. Rational, the essential predicate that constitutes the difference between man and beast. 4. *(Math.)* Rational. *-m.* Rational, pectoral, or breast plate, one of the sacred vestments of the chief priest among the Jews.

racionalidad [rah-the-o-nah-le-dahd'], *f.* 1. Rationality, reasonableness. 2. Fitness, agreement with right. 3. Faculty of reasoning.

racionalizar [rah-the-o-nah-le-thar'], *va.* To rationalize.

racionalmente [rah-the-o-nahl'-men-tay], *adv.* Rationally.

racionamiento [rah-the-o-nah-me-en'-to], *m.* Rationing.

racionar [rah-the-o-nar'], *va.* To ration.

racionista [rah-the-o-nees'-tah], *va.* 1. Person on an allowance. 2. Second-rate actor.

racismo [rah-thees'-mo], *m.* Racism.

racista [rah-thees'-tah], *com.* Racist.

rada [rah'-dah], *f.* Road, roadstead, anchoring-ground for ships.

radar [rah'-dahr], *m.* (Radio) Radar.

radiación [rah-de-ah-the-on'], *f.* Radiation.

radiactividad [rah-de-o-ahc-te-ve-dahd'], *f.* Radioactivity.

radiactivo [rah-de-o-ahc-tee'-vo], *a.* Radioactive.

radiado, da [rab-de-ah'-do, dah], *a.* *pp.* of RADIAR. Radiated.

radiador [rah-de-ah-dor'], *m.* 1. Radiator. 2. Radiator, steam heater.

radial [rah-de-ahl'], *a.* Radial.

radiante [rah-de-ahn'-tay], *a.* Radiant.

radiar [rah-de-ar'], *va.* 1. To radiate. 2. To broadcast, to radio.

radicación [rah-de-ca-the-on'], *f.* Taking root.

radical [rah-de-cahl'], *a.* Radical.-*com.* Radical. -*m.* Radical.

radicalmente [rah-de-cahl'-men-tay], *adv.* Radically.

radicar [rah-de-car'], *vn.* 1. To take root. 2. To be located. *-vr.* To establish oneself, to take up residence.

radícula [rah-dee'-coo-lah], *f.* *(Bot.)* Radicle, radicule.

radio [rah'-de-o], *m.* 1. Radius. 2. Spoke (de rueda). 3. Radium. **Radio de acción**, sphere of jurisdiction. *-f.* Radio.

radioactividad [rah-de-o-ac-te-ve-dahd'], *f.* Radioactivity. **Radioactividad atmosférica**, *(Mil.)* fallout.

radioactivo, va [rah-de-o-ac-tee'-vo, vah], *a.* Radioactive.

radioaficionado, da [rah-de-o-ah-fe-the-o-nah'-do, dah], *m.* & *f.* Radio amateur.

radioastronomía [rah-de-o-as-tro-no-mee'-ah], *f.* Radio astronomy.

radioaviación [rah-de-o-ah-ve-ah-the-on'], *f.* *(Aer.)* Radio navigation.

radiobaliza [rah-de-o-bah-lee'-tha], *f.* Radio beacon.

radiobiología [rah-de-o-be-o-lo-hee'-ah], *f.* Radiobiology.

radiocompás [rah-de-o-com-pahs'], *m.* Radio compass, radio direction finder.

radiocomunicación [rah-de-o-co-moo-ne-cah-the-on'], *f.* Radio communication.

radiodifundir [rah-de-o-de-foon-deer'], *va.* To broadcast via radio.

radiodifusora [rah-de-o-de-foo-so'-rah], *f.* Broadcasting station, radio station.

radioelemento [rah-de-o-ay-lay-men'-to], *m.* Radioelement.

radioemisora [rah-de-o-ay-me-so'-rah], *f.* Radio station.

radioescucha [rah-de-o-es-coo'-chah], *com.* Radio listener.

radiofaro [rah-de-o-fah'-ro], *m.* Radio beacon.

radiofoto [rah-de-o-fo'-to], *f.* Radiophoto.

radiofrecuencia [rah-de-o-fray-coo-en'-the-ah], *f.* Radio frequency.

radiografía [rah-de-o-grah-fee'-ah], *f.* 1. Radiograph, X-ray film. 2. Radiography.

radiógrafo [rah-de-o'-grah-fo], *m.* Radiographer, X-ray specialist.

radiograma [rah-de-o-grah'-ma], *m.* Radiogram.

radioisótopo [rah-de-o-so'-to-po], *m.* Radioisotope.

radiología [rah-de-o-lo-hee'-ah], *f.* Radiology.

radiólogo [rah-de-o'-lo-go], *m.* Radiologist.

radiómetro [rah-de-o'-may-tro], *m.* Radiometer.

radionavegación [rah-de-o-nah-vay-gah-the-on'], *f.* Radio navigation.

radionavegante [rah-de-o-nah-vay-gahn'-tay], *m.* Radio navigator.

radioquímica [rah-de-o-kee'-me-cah], *f.* Radiochemistry.

radiorreceptor [rah-de-or-ray-thep-tor'], *m.* Radio receiver.

radioscopia [rah-de-os-co'-pe-ah], *f.* Radioscopy.

radiosensitivo, va [rah-de-o-sen-se-tee'-vo, vah], *a.* Radiosensitive.

radioso, sa [rah-de-o'-so, sah], *a.* Radiant.

radiosonda [rah-de-o-son'-dah], *f.* Radiosonde.

radiotecnia [rah-de-o-tec'-ne-ah], *f.* Radiotechnology.

radiotelefonía [rah-de-o-tay-lay-fo-nee'-ah], *f.* Wireless, radiotelephony.

radioteléfono [rah-de-o-tay-lay'-fo-no], *m.* Radiotelephone. **Radio teléfono, emisor-receptor portátil**, walkie-talkie.

radiotelegrafista [rah-de-o-tay-lay-grah-fees'-tah], *com.* Wireless operator.

radiotelégrafo [rah-de-o-tay-lay'-grah-fo], *m.* Radiotelegraph.

radiotelegrama [rah-de-o-tay-lay-grah'-mah], *m.* Radiotelegram.

radiotelescopio [rah-de-o-tay-les-co'-pe-o], *m.* Radio telescope.

radioterapia [rah-de-o-tay-rah'-pe-ah], *f.* Radiotherapy.

radiotransmisor [rah-de-o-trans-me-sor'], *m.* Radio transmitter.

radioyente [rah-de-o-yen'-tay], *m.* & *f.* V. RADIOESCUCHA.

raedera [rah-ay-day'-rah], *f.* 1. Scraper, raker. 2. Roller or cylinder for reducing lead into sheets.

raedor, ra [rah-ay-dor', rah], *a.* Scraper, eraser. V. RASERO.

raedura [rah-ay-doo'-rah], *f.* 1. Rasure, crasure. 2. Scrapings, filings, parings.

raer [rah-err'], *va.* 1. To scrape, to grate: to rub off, to abrade, to fret. 2. To rase or blot out, to erase. 3. To lay aside entirely, to efface (vicio, mala costumbre).

rafa [rah'-fah], *f.* 1. Buttress to support mud walls. 2. A small cut or opening in a canal.

ráfaga [rah'-fah-gah], *f.* 1. A violent gust of wind. 2. Any cloud of small density which appears at a distance. 3. Instantaneous flash or gleam of light.

raído, da [rah-ee'-do, dah], *a. & pp.* of RAER. 1. Scraped. 2. Worn out. 3. Impudent, shameless: free, undisguised.

raigal [rah-e-gahl'], *a.* Relating to the root.

raigambre [rah-e-grahm'-bray], *f.* Collection of roots of different trees united.

raigón [rah-e-gon'], *m.* 1. Large root. 2. Root (de un diente).

raimiento [rah-e-me-en'-to], *m.* 1. Scraping. 2. Effrontery.

raíz [rah-eeth'], *f.* 1. Root. 2. Foundation. **Raíz cuadrada**, square root. **Raíz cúbica**, cube root. **A raíz de**, (a) level with; (b) right after. 3. As a result of. **De raíz**, completely, from the ground up.

raja [rah'-hah], *f.* 1. Splinter, chip. 2. Slice. 3. Crack (grieta), fissure. 4. Sliver (pedacito). 5. Cunt (vajina).

rajá [rah-hah'], *m.* Rajah.

rajable [rah-hah'-blay], **rajadizo, za** [rah-hah-dee'-tho, tha], *a.* Easily split, easily splintered.

rajadura [rah-hah-doo'-rah], *f.* Crack, cleft.

rajar [rah-har'], *va.* 1. To split (hender); to crack; to cleave; to slit; to slice (fruta). 2. *(LAm.)* To slander (difamar). 3. *(LAm.)* To flunk. 4. *(And. Carib.)* To crush (aplastar). 5. *(Cono Sur.)* To fire (obrero). 6. *(Carib.)* To pester (fastidiar). *-vn.* To chatter (hablar); to brag (jactarse). *-vr.* 1. To split (henderse). 2. To back out (desistir). 3. *(And. Carib. Cono Sur)* To run away (huir). 4. *(And. Cono Sur)* To be mistaken (equivocarse). To break off or break open, to chip, to break into chinks, to cleave. 5. To split*(Coll.)* To crack, to boast, to tell falsehoods.

rajeta [rah-hay'-tah], *f.* Sort of coarse cloth of mixed colors.

rajica, illa, ita [rah-hee'-cah], *f. dim.* 1. A small chink, crack, or fissure. 2. A small splinter or chip of wood.

rajuela [rah-hoo-ay'-lah], *f. dim.* V. RAJICA.

ralea [rah-lay'-ah], *f.* 1. Race, breed, stock. 2. Genus, species, quality.

ralear [rah-lay-ar'], *vn.* 1. To thin, to make thin, or rare. 2. *(Prov.)* To manifest or discover the bad inclination of breed or anything. 3. *(Agr.)* To make thin racemes or bunches of grapes.

ralentí [rah-len-tee'], *m.* 1. Slow motion (cine). 2. Neutral. **Funcionar al ralentí**, to be ticking over.

raleón, na [rah-lay-on', nah], *a.* Applied to a bird of prey which takes the game pursued by another.

raleza [rah-lay'-thah], *f.* Thinness, want of compactness; rarity; liquidity.

ralillo, illa, ito, ita [rah-leel'-lyo], *a.* Somewhat thin or rare.

ralladera [ral-lyah-day'-rah], *f.* Grater, an instrument for grating.

rallado [rahl-lyah'-do], *a.* Grated (queso).

ralladura [ral-lyah-doo'-rah], *f.* Mark left by the grater; the small particles taken off by grating.

rallar [ral-yar'], *va.* 1. To grate, to reduce to powder. 2. To vex, to molest.

rallo [rahl'-lyo], *m.* Grater, an instrument for grating.

rallón [ral-lyone'], *m.* Arrow or dart.

rallye [rah-le], *m.* Rally.

ralo, la [rah'-lo, lah] *a.* 1. Thin (pelo), rare, not compact. 2. V. RARO.

rama [rah'-mah], *f.* 1. Shoot or sprig of a plant, bough, limb, of a tree. 2. Branch of a family. 3. Rack used in manufactories, to bring cloth to its proper length and breadth. 4. *(Print.)* Chase for enclosing types. **En rama**, raw material, crude stuff. **Tabaco en rama**, leaf tobacco. **Seda en rama**, raw silk. **Andarse por las ramas**, to go about the bush, not to come to the point.

ramada [rah-mah'-dah], *f. (Prov.)* V. ENRAMADA.

ramadán [rah-mah-dahn'], *m.* Ramadan, the Mohammedan month of fasting, their ninth lunar month.

ramaje [rah-mah'-hay], *m.* 1. Branch age, collection of branches. 2. Flowering branchs designed in cloth.

ramal [rah-mahl'], *m.* 1. A strand of a rope. 2. Anything springing from another, as a staircase. 3. Halter, of a horse or mule. 4. Principal passage in mines; branch, division. 5. A thin, dependent upon something else; offset, branch, etc.

ramalazo [rah-mah-lah'-tho], *m.* 1. Lash (azote), a stroke with a cord or rope. 2. Marks left by lasher. 3. A sudden and acute pain or grief (dolor). Spot in the face. 5. Result or consequence of injuring another.

ramalito [rah-mah-lee'-to], *m. dim.* A small halter, small brands, a lash or cord of a cat-o'-nine-tails.

rambla [rahm'-blah], *f.* 1. A sandy place, ground covered with sand after a flood. 2. A ravine or water-course which carries off the water of heavy rains (arroyo).

ramblazo [ram-blah'-tho], *m.* Gravelly bed of a current or rivulet.

ramblizo [ram-blee'-tho], *m. (Prov.)* V. RAMBLAZO.

ramera [rah-may'-rah], *f.* Whore, prostitute.

ramería [rah-may-ree'-ah], *f.* Brothel, bawdy-house, formerly the residence of licensed prostitutes in Spanish towns.

ramerita, rameruela [rah-may-ree'-tah], *f. dim.* A little whore.

ramero [rah-may'-ro], *m.* A young hawk hopping from branch to branch.

ramial [rah-me-ahl'], *m.* Ramie-patch, ground planted in ramie.

ramificación [rah-me-fe-cah-the-on'], *f.* 1. Ramification, the production of branches. 2. Ramification, division or separation into branches.

ramificarse [rah-me-fe-car'-say], *vr.* To ramify, to be divided into branches.

ramilla, ita [rah-meel'-lyah], *f. dim.* 1. Small shoot or sprig, twig. 2. *(Met.)* Any light trifling thing.

ramillete [rah-mel-lay'-tay], *m.* 1. Bouquet (flores), bunch of flowers. 2. *(Fig.)* Collection.

ramilleto [rah-meel-lyay'-to], *m.* 1. Nosegay, tuft. 2. Cluster of single-pedicelled flowers, umbel. 3. Pyramid of sweetmeats and fruits served at table. 4. Collection of flowers or beauties of literature.

ramilletero, ra [rah-mil-lyay-tay´-ro, rah], *m. & f.* One who makes and sells nosegays.

ramilletero [rah-mil-lyay-tay'-ro], *m.* Vase with artificial flowers put on altars.

ramillo, ito [rah-meel'-lyo], *m.* 1. *(dim.)* A small branch. 2. *(Prov.)* V. DINERILLO.

ramina [rah-mee'-nah], *f.* Ramie yarn.

ramio [rah'-me-o], *m.* Ramie, a plant belonging to the nettle family yielding a fine textile fibre.

ramiza [rah-mee'-thah], *f.* Collection of lopped branches.

rámneo, nea [rahm'-nay-o, ah], *a. (Bot.)* Rhamnaceous, of the buckthorn family.

ramo [rah'-mo], *m.* 1. Branch of a bough or limb (de árbol); branchlet; also a limb cut off from a tree. 2. Any part separated from a whole. 3. A string of onions. 4. Branch of trade. 5. Concern, business. 6. Branch or special part of an art or science. 7. Branch, outgrowth of something not material. **Domingo de Ramos**, Palm Sunday.

ramojo [rah-mo'-ho], *m.* Small branch lopped from a tree, small wood.

ramón [rah-mone'], *m.* Top of branches cut off for the feed of sheep in snowy weather.

ramonear [rah-mo-nay-ar'], *vn.* 1. To cut off the branches of trees. 2. To nibble the tops of branches (ganado).

ramoneo [rah-mo-nay´-o], *m.* Act of cutting or lopping branches.

ramoso, sa [rah-mo'-so, sah], *a.* Branchy, ramous.

rampa [rahm'-pah], *f.* 1. *(Prov.)* Cramp. 2. *(Mil.)* Slope of a glacis. 3. Activity.

rampante [ram-pahn'-tay], *a. (Her.)* Rampant.

rampiñete [ram-pe-nyay'-tay], *m.* Bar of iron with a curved point used by artillery men.

ramplón, na [ram-plone', nah], *a.* Applied to a large coarse shoe, rude, unpolished. *-m. (Vet.)* The calk of a shoe.

ramplón [ram-plone'], *m.* Calk of horses, shoes.

rampojo [ram-po'-ho], *m.* 1. Rape, the stalk of a cluster of crepes when freed from the fruit. 2. *(Mil.)* Caltrop, an iron with three spikes, thrown into the rond, to annoy the enemy's horse. *V.* ABROJO.

rampollo [ram-poy-lyo], *m.* Branch cut from a tree to be planted.

ramujos [rah-moo'-hose], *m. pl.* Twin, small wood.

rana [rah'-nah], *f.* 1. A frog. 2. *(Vet.)* Ranula. *V.* ALEVOSA. **Rana marina** or **pescadora**, *(Zool.)* frogfish, fishing-frog, or angler. **Pero salió rana**, but he turned out badly.

ranacuajo [rah-nah-coo-ah'-ho], *m.* 1. Spawn of frogs. *V.* RENACUAJO. 2. A little, insignificant man.

rancajada [ran-cah-hah'-dah], *f.* Wound in plants or sprouts.

rancajado, da [ran-cah-hah'-do, dah], *a.* Wounded with a splinter of wood.

rancajo [ran-cah'-ho], *m.* Splinter in the flesh.

rancanca [ran-cahn'-cah], *m.* South American bird of prey: its plumage is chiefly black, but the cheeks and throat are bare and of a bright carmine color.

ranciadura [ran-the-ah-doo'-rah], *f. V.* RANCIDEZ.

ranciarse [ran-the-ar'-say], *vr. V.* ENRANCIARSE.

rancidez [ran-the-deth'], *f.* Rancidity, rancidness, rankness.

rancio, cia [rahn'-the-o, ah], *a.* Rank (comestible), rancid, stale, strong-scented, long kept, old (vino).

rancio [rahn-the-o], *m.* Rancidity, rankness, fulsomeness.

rancioso, sa [ran-the-o'-so, sah], *a.* 1. *V.* RANCIO. 2. Having the taste of oil.

rancheadero [ran-chay-ah-day'-ro], *m.* Place containing huts.

ranchear [ran-chay-ar'], *va.* To build huts, to form a mess.

ranchera [ran-chay'-rah], *f. (Mex.)* Typical Mexican song.

ranchería [ran-chay-ree'-ah], *f.* 1. Hut or cottage where laborers meet to mess together: horde. 2. *(Amer.)* A collection of huts, like a hamlet.

ranchero [ran-chay'-ro], *m.* 1. Steward of a mess. 2. An owner of a small farm. 3. *(Mex.)* Countryman, farm-dweller, rancher.

rancho [rahn'-cho], *m.* 1. Food given dully to a set of persons, as soldiers or convicts. 2. Mess, a set of persons who eat and drink together. 3. A free clear passage. **Hacer rancho**, to make room. 4. A friendly meeting of persons to discuss a question. 5. *(Naut.)* Restroom; mess. **Rancho de enfermería**, mess-room for the sick. 6. Each of the divisions of the crew. 7. Provision of food for a voyage. 8. Hut in which peasants are sheltered overnight (cobertizo). 9. *(Mex.)* A stock-farm; a small farm (granja), a ranch. 10. *(Amer.)* A place consisting of a few huts, where travelers may find provisions.

randa [rahn'-dah], *f.* Lace, trimming, netting, network.

randado, da [ran-dah-do, dah], *a.* Laced, adorned with lace.

randaje [ran-dah'-hay], *m.* Network, lace-work.

randal [ran-dahl'], *m.* Sort of stuff made into lace or net fashion.

randera [ran-day'-rah], *f.* Lace-worker.

ranear [rah-nay-ar'], *vn* To croak as frogs.

raneta [rah-nay'-tah], *f.* Rennet, a kind of apple.

rangífero [ran-hee'-fay-ro], *m.* Reindeer.

rango [rahn'-go], *m.* Rank (categoría), quality.

rangua [rahn'-goo-ah], *f.* An iron box in which the spindles of machines move, pivot collar, shaft socket.

ranilla [rah-neel'-lyah], *f.* 1. *(dim.)* A small frog. 2. Frog of the hoof of horse or mule. 3. Cracks in the hood of horses. 4. Disease in the bowels of cattle.

raninas [rah-nee'-nas], *f. pl.* Ranulary veins, two veins under the tongue.

raniz [rah-neeth'], *m. & f.* A kind of linen.

ránula [rah'-noo-lah], *f.* Tumor under the tongue of a horse.

ranunculáceo, cea [rah-noon-coo-lah'-thay-o, ah], *a.* Ranunculaceous, of the crowfoot or buttercup family.

ranúnculo [rah-noon'-coo-lo], *m. (Bot.)* Crow-foot, buttercup.

ranura [rah-noo'-rah], *f.* 1. Groove, rabbet. 2. *(Comput.)* Slot

raña [rah'-nyah], *f.* A device which fishermen use for catching cuttle-fishes on rocky bottoms.

rapa [rah'-pah], *f. (Prov.)* Flower of the olive-tree.

rapacejo [rah-pah-thay'-ho], *m.* Border, edging.

rapacería [rah-pah-thay-ree'-ah], *f.* Puerility; a childish, boyish speech or action.

rapacidad [rah-pah-the-dahd'], *f.* Rapacity, robbery.

rapecillo, lla [rah-pah-theel'-lyo, lyah], *m. & f. dim.* A little boy or girl.

rapador, ra [rah-pah-dor', rah], *m. & f.* 1. One who scrapes or plunders. 2. *(Coll.)* Barber.

rapadura [rah-pah-doo'-rah], *f.* 1. Shaving, the act of shaving; the state of being shaved; rasure; plundering. 2. *(LAm.)* Brown sugar (azúcar). *V.* RASPADURA.

rapagón [rah-pah-gone'], *m.* A beardless young man.

rapamiento [rah-pah-me-en'-to], *m.* Act of shaving or erasing.

rapante [rah-pahn'-tay], *a.* 1. Snatching, robbing, or tearing off. 2. *(Her.)* Rampant.

rapapiés [rah-pah-pe-ays'], *m.* Squib that runs along the ground; chaser.

rapapolvo [rah-pah-pol'-vo], *m. (Coll.)* A sharp reproof.

rapar [rah-par'], *va.* 1. To shave (barba), as with a razor. 2. *(Coll.) V.* AFEITAR. 3. To plunder, to carry off with violence; to skin, to peel. *-vr. (Mex.)* To pass, bring, or hold.

rapasa [rah-pah'-sah], *f. (Min.)* A stone very soft and easy to work.

rapaz [rah-path'], *a.* Rapacious (ávido); ferocious, thieving (ladrón); predatory.

rapaz, za [rah-path', thah], *m. & f.* A young boy or girl.

rapazada [rah-pah-thah'-dah], *f.* Childish action or speech.

rapazuela [rah-pah-thoo-ay'-lah], *f. dim. V.* RAPACILLO.

rapazuelo, la, *m. & f. dim. V.* RAPACILLO.

rapazuelo, ela [rah-pah-thoo-ay'-lo, lah], *a. dim.* Rapacious, greedy.

rape [rah'-pay], *m. (Coll.)* Shaving, cutting off hair or beard carelessly (afeitado).

rapé [rah-pay'], *m.* Rappee, a kind of snuff. **Rapé francés**, French snuff.

rapeta [rah-pay'-tah], *f.* **rapetón** [rah-pay-tone'], *m. (Prov.)* A net for sardine-fishing on the Cantabrian coast.

rápidamente [rah'-pe-dah-men-tay], *adv.* Rapidly.

rapidez [rah-pe-deth'], *f.* Rapidity, velocity, celerity.

rápido, da [rah'-pe-do, dah], *a.* 1. Rapid, quick, swift. 2. *(And. Carib. Cono Sur)* Fallow (campo). 3. *(Carib.)* Clear (tiempo).

rapidura [ray-pe-doo'-rah], *f.* Crude sugar. *V.* RASPADURA, 3d def.

rapiego, ga [rah-pe-ay'-go, gah], *a.* Ravenous (pájaros).

rapiña [rah-pee'-nyah], *f.* Rapine, robbery. **Ave de rapiña**, bird of prey. **Vivir de rapiña**, to live off the catch.

rapiñador, ra [rah-pe-nyah-dor', rah], *m. & f.* Plunderer, robber.

rapiñar [rah-pe-nyar'], *va. (Coll.)* To plunder, to rob.

rapista [rah-pees'-tah], *m. (Coll.)* Barber, shaver.

rapo [rah'-po], *m.* A round-rooted turnip.

rapónchigo [rah-pon'-che-go], *m. (Bot.)* Esculent bellflower, rampion.

rapóntico [rah-pon'-te-co], *m. (Bot.) V.* RUIBARBO RAPÓNTICO.

raposa [rah-po'-sah], *f.* 1. Female fox. *V.* ZORRA. Canis vulpes. 2. *(Met.)* Cunning, deceitful person.

raposear [rah-po-say-ar'], *m.* To use artifices like a fox, to be foxy.

raposera [rah-po-say'-rah], *f.* Fox-hole, fox-den.

raposería [rah-po-say-ree'-ah], *f.* Cunning of a fox; artful kindness.

raposilla, ita [rah-po-seel'-lyah], *f. dim.* Artful wench.

raposino, na [rah-po-see'-no, nah], *a.* Foxy. *V.* RAPOSUNO.

raposo [rah-po'-so], *m.* Male fox. **Raposo ferrero**, iron-colored fox, whose skin is used for furs.

raposuno, no [rah-po-soo'-no, nah], *a.* Vulpine, foxy.

rapsoda [rap-so'-dah], *a.* Rhapsodic, rapt.

rapsodia [rap-so'-de-ah], *f.* Rhapsody, incoherent composition.

rapta [rahp'-tah], *a.* Applied to a woman who is snatched by a man by force or artifice; abducted.

rapto [rahp'-to], *m.* 1. Rapine, robbery, kipnapping (secuestro). 2. Ecstasy (éxtasis), rapture, exultance. 3. Abduction of a woman by force or deceit. 4. Outburst, fit. 5. *(Ast.) V.* MOVIMIENTO.

raptor, ra [rap-tor'], *m & f.* Abductor, kipnapper.

raque [rah'-kay], *m. (Naut.)* Salvage, beach-combing.

raquear [rah-kay-ar'], *vn.* To beach-comb, to salvage shipwrecks.

raqueta [rah-kay'-tah], *f.* 1. Racket. 2. *(Bot.)* Wall rocket. 3. Croupier's rake. **Raqueta de nieve**, snowshoe.

raquetero [rah-kay-tay'-ro], *m.* Racket-maker, racket-seller.

raquialgia [rah-ke-ahl'-he-ah], *f.* 1. Rachialgia, pain in the spinal column. 2. Progressive decay of the spinal column.

raquis [rah'-kees], *m.* Backbone.

raquítico, ca [rah-kee'-te-co, cah], *a.* Rickety, diseased with the rickets.

raquitis [rah-kee'-tis], *f.* Rickets, a disease.

raramente [rah-rah-men'-tay], *adv.* Rarely, seldom: ridiculously, oddly.

rarefacción [rah-ray-fac-the-one'], *f.* Rarefaction (aire).

rarefacer [rah-ray-fah-therr'], *va. V.* RARIFICAR. *-vn.* To rarefy.

rarefacto, ta [rah-ray-fac'-to, tah], *pp. irr.* of RAREFACER.

rareza [rah-ray'-thah], *f.* 1. Rarity (cualidad), rareness, uncommonness, infrequency. 2. Rarity, a thing valued for its scarcity; a curiosity, oddity.

raridad [rah-re-dahd'], *f.* 1. Rarity, uncommonness, infrequency. 2. Rarity, thinness, subtility. 3. Oddity.

rarificar [rah-re-fe-car'], *va.* To rarefy, to make thin, to dilate. *-vr.* To rarefy, to become thin.

rarificativo, va [rah-re-fe-cah-tee'-vo, vah], *a.* That which has the power of rarefying.

raro, ra [rah'-ro, rah], *a.* 1. Rare (poco frecuente), porous, having little density. 2. Rare, scarce, uncommon, odd (extraño). 3. Renowned, famous, excellent. 4. Extravagant, odd. **Rara vez**, seldom. **Son raros los que saben hacerlo**, very few people know how to do it. **De rara perfección**, of rare perfection.*-adv.* Rarely.

ras [rahs], *m.* Level, an even surface. **Ras en ras, ras con ras**, on an equal footing upon a par.

rasadura [rah-sah-doo'-rah], *f.* The act of measuring salt, and other dry articles, with a strickle.

rasamente [rah-sah-men-tay], *adv.* Publicly, openly, clearly.

rasante [rah-sahn'-tay], *a.* Low. **Tiro rasante**, low shot. *-m.* Slope. **Cambio de rasante**, brow of a hill.

rasar [rah-sar'], *va.* 1. To strike, to level corn with a strickle. 2. To graze, to skim (casi tocar), to touch lightly.

rascacielos [ras-cah-the-ay'-los], *m.* Skyscraper.

rascadera [ras-cah-day'-rah], *f. V.* RASCADOR and ALMOHAZA.

rascador [ras-cah-dor'], *m.* 1. Scraper, to scrape and clean bones, metal. etc.; scratcher; rasp. 2. Hat-pin, bodkin.

rascadura [ras-cah-doo'-rah], *f.* 1. The act of scratching, scraping, or rasping. 2. Scratch, made by scraping.

rascalino [rash-cah-lee'-no], *m. V.* TIÑUELA.

rascamiento [ras-cah-me-en'-to], *m.* Act of scraping or scratching.

rascamoño [ras-cah-mo'-nyo], *m.* Women's hat-pin, bodkin.

rascar [ras-car'], *va.* 1. To scratch (cabeza), to scrape (raer). 2. To sniff out (descubrir), to smell out. *-vr.* 1. To scratch. 2. *(LAm.)* To get drunk (emborracharse).

rascazón [ras-cah-thone'], *f.* Pricking, tickling, or itching sensation which induces scratching.

rasclo [rahs'-clo], *m.* An instrument used in coral-fishing.

rasco [rahs'-co], *m. V.* RASCADURA.

rascón, na [ras-cone', nah], *a.* Sour, sharp (amargo), acrid. *-m. (Orn.)* Rail, a wading bird; marsh-hen, mud-hen, sora.

rascuñar [ras-coo-nyar'], *va. V.* RASGUÑAR.

rascuño [ras-coo'-nyo], *m. V.* RASGUNO.

rasel [rah-sel'], *m. (Naut.)* Narrow part of a ship towards the head and stern.

rasero [rah-say'-ro], *m.* Strickle, strike, an instrument for levelling the contents of a dry measure. **Medir por un rasero**, to apply the same measure or standard to everything.

rasete [rah-say'-tay], *m.* Satinet, a sort of light fabric with a satiny gloss; sixteen for lining.

rasgado, da [ras-gah'-do, dah], *a, & pp.* of RASGAR. 1. Rent, open. 2. Applied to a wide balcony or large window (balcón, ventana). **Ojos rasgados**, large or full eyes. **Boca rasgada**, wide mouth.

rasgado [ras-gah'-do], *m. V.* RASGÓN.

rasgador, ra [ras-gah-dor', rah], *m. & f.* Tearer, cleaver, one who scratches, tears, or lacerates.

rasgadura [ras-gah-doo'-rah], *f.* Rent, tatter, strip torn from a fabric.

rasgar [ras-gar'], *va.* 1. To tear or cut asunder, to rend, to claw, to lacerate. 2. *V.* RASGUEAR.

rasgo [rahs'-go], *m.* 1. Dash (raya), stroke, line elegantly drawn (de pluma). **Rasgo de pluma**, dash of a pen. 2. A grand, magnanimous action. **Rasgo de generosidad**, stroke of generosity. 3. Feature (característica), trait. **Rasgo fisonómico**, facial feature.

rasgón [ras-gone'], *m.* Rent, rag, tatter, laceration.

rasgueado [ras-gay-ah'-do], *m.* Act of making flourishes. —**Rasgueado, da**, *pp.* of RASGUEAR.

rasguear [ras-gay-ar'], *vn.* To flourish, to form figures by lines. *-va.* To play a dash or arpeggio on the guitar.

rasguillo [ras-geel'-lyo], *m. dim.* A small dash of a pen.

rasgueo [ras-gay'-o], *m.* 1. The act of forming into fine strokes by a pen. 2. Lines elegantly drawn.

rasgueta [ras-gay'-tah], *f. (Mex.)* A currycomb.

rasguñar [ras-goon-nyar'], *va.* 1. To scratch, to scrape. 2. To sketch the outlines of a drawing or picture.

rasguñito, ñuelo [ras-goon-nyee'-to], *m. dim.* Slight scratch or sketch.

rasguño [ras-goo'-nyo], *m.* 1. Scratch, scar; nip. 2. Sketch, the dotted outlines of a drawing or picture.

rasilla [rah-seel'-lyah], *f.* 1. Serge, a kind of woollen stuff. 2. A fine tile for flooring.

raso [rah'-so], *m.* Satin. **Rasos franceses dobles lisos**, double French plain satin. **Rasos franceses labrados**, French figured silk. *-a.* 1. Clear of obstructions or impediments. 2. Clear (despejado). 3. Plain: flat (llano). 4. Having no title or mark of distinction. **Tiempo raso**, fine weather. **Cielo raso**, clear sky. **Soldado raso**, a private, a common soldier. **Al raso**, by the open air.

raspa [rahs'-pah], *f.* 1. Board of an ear of corn. 2. Spine, fin-ray of fish. 3. Grape stalk (de uva). 4. Rasp, a coarse file. 5. Rind of certain fruits. 6. *(LAm.)* Scolding (reprimenda). 7. *(Carib. Mex.)* Brown sugar. 8. *(Cono Sur)* Rasp (herramienta).

raspadera [ras-pah-day'-rah], *f. (Prov.)* Raker.

raspadillo [ras-pah-deel'-lyo], *m.* Fraud or imposition practiced by gamblers.

raspador [ras-pah-dor'], *m.* Rasp, coarse file.

raspadura [ras-pah-doo'-rah], *f.* 1. The act of filing, rasping, or scraping; erasure (borradura). 2. Filings, raspings, scrapings, shavings. 3. (Cuba) Pan sugar, crude sugar. *V.* CHANCACA. 4. Certain cakes made with crude sugar.

raspajo [ras-pah'-ho], *m. (Prov.)* Stalk of a bunch of grapes.

raspamiento [ras-pah-me-en'-to], *m.* Act of rasping or filing.

raspante [ras-pahn'-tay], *pa. & a.* Rasping, rough: applied to wine which grates the palate.

raspar [ras-par'], *va.* 1. To scrape, to rasp (limar), to pure off. 2. To prick, to have a sourish taste (vino). 3. To steal, carry off. 4. *(Mex.)* To scold (regañar). 5. *(Mex.)* To say unkind things to (maltratar).

raspear [ras-pay-ar'], *vn.* To have a hair in the pen, which occasions blots.

raspinegro, gra [ras-pe-nay'-gro, grah], *a. (Prov.)* V. ARISPRIETO.

raspón (De) [ras-pone', day], *adv.* Scrapingly, thievishly. -*m.* 1. Scratch (rasguño), graze. 2. *(LAm.)* Scolding (regaño). 3. *(Mex.)* Cutting remark (dicho). 4. *(And.)* Straw hat (sombrero).

rasqueta [ras-kay'-tah], *f. (Naut.)* Scraper, an instrument for scraping the planks of a ship.

rastel [ras-tel'], *m.* Bar or lattice of wood or iron.

rastillador, ra [ras-tel-lyah-dor'], *m. dim. f.* V. RASTRILLADOR.

rastillar [ras-til-lyar'], *va.* To hackle flax. V. RASTRILLAR.

rastillero [ras-til-lyay'-ro], *m. (Low.)* Shoplifter, robber who steals and flies.

rastra [rahs'-trah], *f.* 1. Sled or sledge (de transporte), a carriage without wheels. 2. The act of dragging along. 3. Anything hanging and dragging about a person. 4. A track or mark left on the ground. V. RASTRO. 5. String of dried fruit. 6. Train, the result of some action which brings damage or inconvenience (consecuencia). 7. Trawl (de pesca). 8. *(Mex.)* Prostitute (puta). **Andar a rastras**, to have a difficult time of it.

rastrallar [ras-tral-lyar'], *vn.* To crack with a whip.

rastrallido [ras-tral-lyee'-do], *m.* The crack of a whip.

rastreador, ra [ras-tray-a-dor', rah], *m. & f.* Tracker, smeller, follower.

rastrear [ras-tray-ar'], *va.* 1. To trace, to follow by the footsteps (seguir). 2. To harrow or rake on the farm, or drag in fishing (sacar a la superficie). 3. To inquire into, to investigate, to fathom. 4. To sell carcasses by wholesale in a slaughterhouse. -*vn.* To skim the ground, to fly very low.

rastreo [ras-tray'-o], *m. (Prov.)* Fringe or small pieces of stuff hanging round.

rastrero, ra [ras-tray'-ro, rah], *a.* 1. Creeping, dragging. 2. Applied to a dog that runs by a trail. 3. Low, humble (disculpa), cringing. 4. Applied to things floating in the air or to birds flying near the ground. -*m.* Inspector of a slaughterhouse; a workman employed there.

rastrillada [ras-tree'-lyah'-dah], *f.* A rakeful.

rastrillador, ra [ras-treel-lyah-dor', rah], *m. & f.* Heckler; flax-dresser, hatcheller; raker.

rastrillaje [ras-treel-lyah'-hay], *m.* Raking; batchelling; handling with a rake or hatchel.

rastrillar [ras-treel-lyar'], *va.* 1. To hackle, to dress flax, to comb, to hatcher. 2. To separate the straw from the corn with a rake; to rake (recoger).

rastrilleo [ras-treel-lyay'-o], *m.* The act of hackling or raking.

rastrillo [ras-treel'-lyo], *m.* 1. Hackle, an instrument to dress flax and hemp; flax-comb. 2. Portcullis. 3. Hammer of a gun-lock. 4. Ward of a key (de cerradura, llave). 5. Ward of a lock. 6. Gateway of a palisade.

rastro [rahs'-tro], *m.* 1. Track on the ground; trail (huella). 2. Rake, harrow (grada). 3. Slaughterhouse (matadero); place where meat is sold by the carcass. 4. Sign, token, vestige, relic. 5. Grapple for gathering oysters. **Seguir el rastro de uno**, to follow somebody's trail. **Desaparecer sin dejar rastro**, to vanish without trace.

rastrojera [ras-tro-hay'-rah], *f.* Stubble ground and the time which the stubble lasts.

rastrojo [ras-tro'-ho], *m.* Stubble (de campo). **Sacar (a uno) de los rastrojos**, to raise one from a humble position.

rasura [rah-soo'-rah], *f.* 1. Shaving as with a razor (afeitado). 2. Scraping, filing. -*pl.* Boiled lees of wine, which serve to clean plate, etc.

rasurada [rah-soo-rah'-dah], *f.* Shave.

rasurar [rah-soo-rar'], *va.* To shave with a razor (afeitar).

rata [rah'-tah], *f.* 1. Rat. 2. She-mouse. -*m.* Mean devil (tacaño).

rata almizclada or **almizclera** [rah'-tah al-mith-clah'-dah, al-mith-clay'-rah], *f. (Zool.)* Muskrat.

ratafía [ra-tah-fee'-ah], *f.* Ratafia, a spirituous liquor. V. ROSOLI.

ratania [ra-tah'-ne-ah], *f. (Bot.)* Ratany or ratanhy, a Peruvian shrub of astringent properties.

ratear [rah-tay-ar'], *va.* 1. To lessen or abate in proportion. 2. To distribute or divide proportionally. 3. To filch, to commit petty thefts. -*vn.* To trail along the ground, to creep.

rateo [rah-tay'-o], *m.* Distribution made at a certain rate or proportion.

rateramente [rah-tay-rah-men-tay], *adv.* Meanly, vilely.

ratería [rah-tay-ree'-ah], *f.* 1. Larceny, petty theft. 2. Vile conduct in things of little value.

ratero, ra [rah-tay'-ro, rah], *a.* 1. Creeping on the ground. 2. Skimming the ground, flying low; spoken of birds. 3. Committing petty thefts (ladrón); pilfering. 4. Mean, vile.

rateruelo, ela [rah-tay-roo-ay'-lo, lah], *m. & f. dim.* Little pilferer.

ratificación [rah-te-fe-cah-the-on'], *f.* Ratification, the act of ratifying; confirmation, approbation.

ratificar [rah-te-fe-car'], *va.* To ratify (tratado), to approve.

ratificatorio, ria [rah-te-fe-cah-to'-re-o, ah], *a.* Ratificatory, confirming.

ratigar [rah-te-gahr'], *va. (Prov.)* To secure any loads on carts with a rope.

rátigo [rah'-te-go], *m. (Prov.)* Articles carried in carts.

ratihabición [rah-te-ah-be-the-on'], *f. (Law.)* Ratification, making valid.

ratina [rah-tee'-nah], *f.* Petersham, ratteen, woollen cloth woven like serge.

ratito [rah-tee'-to], *m. dim.* A little while, a short time.

rato [rah'-to], *m.* 1. *(Prov.)* He-mouse. V. RATÓN. 2. Short space of time. **Al cabo de rato**, it turned out ill after thinking so long about it. **Buen rato**, a pretty time, a good while; many: a great quantity. **A ratos perdidos**, in leisure hours. **De rato en rato, a ratos**, from time to time occasionally. **Hace rato que se fue**, he's been gone a while. **Pasar el rato**, to kill time. **Hay para rato**, there's still a long way to go.

rato, ta [rah'-to, tah], *a. (For.)* Firm, valid, conclusive.

ratón [rah-tone'], *m.* 1. He-mouse. 2. *(Naut.)* Hidden rock which frets cables. 3. *(Mil.)* Mechanism serving to fire off mines. 4. *(Carib.)* Hangover (resaca). 5. *(Carib.)* Squib, cracker (petardo).

ratona [rah-toh'-nah], *f.* Female mouse or rat.

ratonar [rah-to-nar'], *va.* To gnaw like mice or rats. -*vr.* 1. To become sick as cats from eating rats. 2. (For hidden rocks) To fret or wear any cables.

ratoncito [rah-ton-thee'-to], *m. dim.* A little mouse.

ratonera [rah-to-nay'-rah], *f.* 1. Mouse trap (trampa). **Caer en la ratonera**, to fall into a snare. **Ratonera, gato de agua**. Rat-trap, placed on water. 2. Hole where rats breed. 3. *(And. Cono Sur)* Hovel (barrio bajo).

ratonero, ra [rah-to-nay'-ro, rah], **Ratonesco, ca** [rah-to-nes'-co, cah], *a.* Belonging to mice, mousy.

raudal [rah-oo-dahl'], *m.* 1. Torrent (torrente), rapid stream. 2. Plenty, abundance. **Entrar a raudales**, to pour in.

raudamente [rah'-oo-dah-men-tay], *adv.* Rapidly.

raudo, da [rah'-oo-do, dah], *a.* Rapid, precipitate.

rauta [rah'-oo-tah], *f (Coll.)* Road, way, route.

raya [rah'-yah], *f.* 1. Stroke, dash, or line drawn with a pen. 2. A line or limit between two provinces or countries (límite); frontier. 3. The term line or boundary put to anything. 4. Stripe, streak. **Tener a raya**, to keep within bounds. **Tener a uno a raya**, to keep one at bay. 5. Part in the hair. 6. Strip of ground cleared of combustible matter. *(Acad.)* **Tres en raya**, a boyish play. **A raya**, correctly, within just limits. 7. *m. (Zool.)* Ray.

rayado, da [rah-yah'-do, dah], *a.* 1. Striped (tela, diseño). 2. Ruled (papel), fined. 3. Streaked, variegated. 4. *(And. Cono Sur)* Cracked (loco). 5. *(Carib.)* No parking area.

rayano, na [rah-yah'-no, nah], *a.* Neighboring, contiguous.

rayar [rah-yar'], *va.* 1. To form strokes, to draw lines (papel). 2. To mark with lines or strokes, to streak (como diseño), to variegate in hues. 3. To rifle or striate the interior of firearms. 4. To expunge. 5. *(LAm.)* To spur on (caballo). *-vn.* 1. To excel, to surpass. 2. *(Met.)* To approximate, to touch. *-vr.* 1. To get scratched (objeto). 2. *(And.)* To see one's wishes fulfilled. 3. *(And. Cono Sur)* To get angry (enojarse).

rayo [rah'-yo], *m.* 1. A right line. 2. Ray of light (de luz). 3. Radius of a circle; spoke of a wheel. 4. Thunderbolt; flash of lightning. 5. Firearms, *(Met.)* Sudden havoc, misfortune (desgracia), or chastisement. 6. A lively, ready genius; great power or efficacy of action (persona). **Rayo directo, incidente, reflejo,** and **refracto,** direct, incidental, reflected, and refracted light. **Rayo equis,** X ray. **Rayo visual,** field of vision. **Echar rayos,** to show great anger or wrath. **La noticia cayó como un rayo,** the news was a bombshell. **Pasar como un rayo,** to rush past. **Sabe a rayos,** it tastes awful.

rayón [rah-yone'], *m.* Rayon.

rayoso, sa [rah-yo'-so, sah], *a.* Full of lines.

rayuela [rah-yoo-ay'-lah], *f.* l. *(dim.)* A small line. 2. Game of drawing lines.

rayuelo [rah-yoo-ay'-lo], *m. (Orn.)* Small kind of snipe.

raza [rah'-thah], *f.* 1. Race, generation, lineage, family, clan: branch of a family. 2. Quality of cloth and other things. 3. Each of the races of mankind. 4. Ray of light. 5. Cleft in a horse's hoof. **Raza blanca,** white race.

razado [rah-thah'-do], *a.* Applied to coarse woollen cloth of unequal color.

rázago [rah'-thah go], *m.* Coarse cloth made of tow.

razón [rah-thone'], *f.* 1. Reason (facultad), the rational faculty. 2. Ratiocination. Reason (motivo), clearness of faculty. 4. Reasonableness, moderation. **Póngase Vd. en la razón,** be moderate in your demand. 5. Reason, cause, motive, principle. 6. Reason, argument, ground of persuasion; consideration, occasion. 7. Account, calculation. 8. Order, mode, method. 9. Reason, reasonableness, right, justice. 10. Expression or word which explains the idea; term. 11. Ratio, a relation between two mathematical quantities. 12. Firm, partnership, name of a commercial establishment. **A razón de,** at the rate of. **En razón,** with regard to. **Tener razón,** to be right. **Dar la razón a uno,** to agree that somebody is right. **Razón de más,** all the more reason. **Dar razón de sí,** to give an account of oneself.

razonable [rah-tho-nah'-blay], *a.* Reasonable; moderate; fair; just.

razonablejo, ja [rah-tho-nah-blay'-ho, hah], *a. (Coll.)* Moderate, rational.

razonablemente [rah-tho-nah'-blay-men-tay], *adv.* Reasonably; moderately.

razonado, da [rah-tho-nah'-do, dah], *a.* Rational, prudent, judicious. *-pp.* of RAZONAR.

razonador, ra [rah-tho-nah-dor', rah], *m. & f.* Reasoner.

razonamiento [rah-tho-nah-me-en'-to], *m.* Reasoning, argument, discourse, oration.

razonante [rah-tho-nahn'-tay], *pa.* Reasoning; reasoner.

razonar [rah-tho-nar'], *va.* 1. To reason, to discourse. 2. To talk (hablar), to converse. *-va.* 1. To name, to call. 2. To advocate, to allege. 3. To take a memorandum of things, to place to account. 4. To compute, to regulate.

razoncita [rah-thon-thee'-tah], *f. dim.* A short memorandum or account.

re [ray], *prep.* Always used in composition, signifying repetition. Also as an intensive, signifying *very*; as, *rebueno,* very good. *-m. (Mus.)* Re, the second note of the musical scale.

reacción [ray-ac-the-on'], *f.* 1. Reaction, revulsion. 2. Rebound. 3. *(Met.)* Resistance, opposition. 4. An alliance of efforts to overthrow a political power or to replace it by another. 5. *(Med.)* Reaction, a period of feverishness succeeding a chill.

reaccionar [ray-ac-the-o-nar'], *va.* To react, to respond.

reaccionario, ria [ray-ac-the-o-nah'-re-o, ah], *a.* 1. Reactionary; revulsive. 2. Reactionary, revolutionary. 3. Conservative, absolutist.

reacción en cadena [ray-ac-the-on' en cah-day'-nah], *f.* Chain reaction.

reacio, cia [ray-ah'-the-o, ah], *a.* Obstinate, intractable, reluctant.

reactividad [ray-ac-te-ve-dahd'], *f.* Reactivity.

reactivo [ray-ac-tee'-vo], *m.* Reagent, an agent employed to determine the composition of other bodies. Used also as adjective.

reactor [ray-ac-tor'], *m.* Reactor. **Reactor nuclear,** nuclear reactor.

readmisión [ray-ad-me-se-on'], *f.* Readmission.

readmitir [ray-ad-me-teer'], *va.* To readmit.

reafirmación [ray-ah-feer-mah-the-on'], *f.* Reaffirmation.

reafirmar [ray-ah-feer-mahr'], *va.* To reaffirm.

reagradecer [ray-ah-grah-day-therr'], *va.* To estimate highly.

reagradecimiento [ray-ah-grah-day-the-me-en'-to], *m.* Act of esteeming, estimation.

reagravación [ray-ah-grah-vah-the-on'], *f.* Reaggravation.

reagravar [ray-ah-grah-var'], *va.* To aggravate anew.

reagrupación [ray-ah-groo-pah-the-on], *f.* Regrouping.

reagrupar [raygroo-pahr'], *va.* To regroup.

reagudo, da [ray-ah-goo'-do, dah], *a.* Very acute.

reajustar [ray-ah-hoos-tahr'], *va.* To readjust.

reajuste [ray-ah-hoos'-tay], *m.* Readjustment.

real [ray-ahl'], *a.* 1. Real (verdadero), actual. 2. Royal, kingly, king-like. 3. Grand, magnificent, splendid. 4. Real, true, certain. 5. Open, fair, ingenuous, candid; generous, noble. *-m.* 1. Camp, the king's tent. 2. Main body of an army. **Real de plata,** silver real, or two reals vellón. **Está sin un real,** he hasn't a bean.

reala [ray-ah'-lah], *f.* Herd which a shepherd forms of his own flock, and of other owners.

realce [ray-ahl'-thay], *m.* 1. Raised work, embossment. 2. Brightness of colors, reflection of light; high light. 3. Lustre, splendor (esplendor).

realdad [ray-al-dahd'], *f.* Royal power, and its exercise; sovereignty.

realegrarse [ray-ah-lay-grar'-say], *vr.* To be very joyful.

realeza [ray-ah-lay'-thah], *f.* Royalty, regal dignity.

realidad [ray-ah-le-dahd'], *f.* Reality, fact; truth and sincerity (verdad). **En realidad, en realidad de verdad,** truly, really, effectually.

realimentación [ray-ah-le-men-tah-the-on'], *f. (Elec.)* Feedback.

realismo [ray-ah-lees'-mo], *m.* 1. Royalism, support of a monarchy. 2. Absolutism in political government. 3. *(Neol.)* Realism in art, or literature.

realista [ray-ah-lees'-tah], *m.* 1. Royalist, loyalist, one who supports a monarch or monarchy: used as an adjective. 2. Realist, a partisan of realism in art or literature.

realizable [ray-ah-le-thah'-blay], *a.* Realizable.

realización [ray-ah-le-thah-the-on'], *f.* 1. Realization, accomplishment, fulfillment. 2. Sale, reduction of merchandise for sale.

realizar [ray-ah-le-thar'], *va.* 1. To realize (bienes), to bring into being or action. 2. *(Com.)* To realize upon, to convert into money. 3. To make (viaje). 4. To fulfil (promesa). *-vr.* 1. To come true (sueño). 2. To fulfil oneself (persona).

realmente [ray-ahl'-men-tay], *adv.* Really (en efecto), effectually; formally, actually; royally.

realzar [ray-al-thar'], *va.* 1. To raise, to elevate; to emboss. 2. To heighten the colors in a painting, to emboss. 3. To illustrate, to aggrandize.

reamar [ray-ah-mar'], *pa.* To love in return; to love much.

reanimar [ray-ah-ne-mar'], *va.* To cheer, to reanimate.

reanudar [ray-ah-noo-dar'], *va* To renew, to resume. **Reanudar las esperanzas**, to renew one's hopes. **Reanudar el trabajo**, to resume work.

reañejo, ja [ray-ah-nyay'-ho, hah], *a.* Oldish, growing old.

reaparecer [ray-ah-pah-ray-therr'], *vn.* To reappear.

reaparición [ray-ah-pah-re-the-on'], *f.* Reappearing, reappearance.

reapertura [ray-ah-per-too'-rah], *f.* Reopening.

reapreciar [ray-ah-pray-the-ar'], *va.* To revalue, to re-estimate.

reapretar [ray-ah-pray-tar'], *va.* To press again, to squeeze.

rearar [ray-ah-rar'], *va.* To plough again.

reasegurar [ray-ah-say-goo-rar'], *va.* (*Com.*) To reinsure.

reaseguro [ray-ah-say-goo'-ro], *m.* (*Com.*) Reinsurance.

reasignar [ray-ah-sig-nar'], *va.* To assign anew.

reasumir [ray-ah-soo-meer'], *va.* To retake, to resume, to reassume.

reasunción [ray-ah-soon-the-on'], *f.* The act of resuming, reassumption.

reata [ray-ah'-tah], *f.* 1. Rope which ties one horse or mule to another, to make them go in a straight line (caballos). 2. (*Met.*) Blind submission to the opinion of others. **Reatas,** (*Naut.*) Woolding, ropes tied round a mast to strengthen it. 3. (*And. Carib. Mex.*) Flowerbed, border (de flores). 4. (*Mex.*) Bamboo screen (enrejado).

reatadura [ray-ah-tah-doo'-rah], *f.* The act of tying one beast after another with a rope.

reatar [ray-ah-tar'], *va.* 1. To tie one beast to another with a rope; to retie or tie tightly. 2. (*Naut.*) To woold, to tie ropes round masts or yards in order to strengthen them.

reato [ray-ah'-to], *m.* The obligation of atonement for a sin after absolution.

reaventar [ray-ah-ven-tar'], *va.* To winnow corn a second time.

rebaba [ray-bah'-bah], *f.* 1. Seam of a cussing in plaster or metal; burr or flash. 2. Projecting piece of stone in a wall, etc. 3. Mortar crowded out between stones and bricks. 4. The chipped edge of sawed timbers and planks.

rebaja [ray-bah'-hah], *f.* 1. Abatement, deduction, diminution. 2. (*Com.*) Drawback, a return of duties on exportation, rebate.

rebajamiento [ray-bah-hah-me-en'-to], *m.* 1. Curtailment, abatement. 2. Abasement.

rebajar [ray-bah-har'], *va.* 1. To abate, to lessen, to diminish (intensidad). 2. To lower the price (precio), to dock a bill or account, to allow a discount, to curtail the quantity. 3. To weaken the light and give a deeper shade to the tints of a painting. 4. (*Mil.*) To dismiss from service, to muster out. **Rebajar el precio a uno en un 5 por 100**, to give somebody a discount of 5 %. *-vr.* 1. To humble oneself, to be humbled. 2. To commit low actions.

rebajo [ray-bah'-ho], *m.* Groove in timber or stone.

rebalaje [ray-bah-lah'-hay], *m.* Crooks or windings in a river.

rebalsa [ray-bahl'-sah], *f.* Stagnant water, a pool or puddle.

rebalsar [ray-bal-sar'], *va.* 1. To dam water to form a pool. 2. To stop, to detain.

rebanada [ray-bah-nah'-dah], *f.* Slice of bread and other things.

rebanadilla [ray-bah-nah-deel'-lyah], *f. dim.* A small slice.

rebanador, ra [ray-bah-nah-dor', rah], *a.* Slicing. *-m. & f.* Slicer. *-f.* Slicing machine.

rebanar [ray-bah-nar', *va.* 1. To slice, to cut into slices. 2. To slice, to cut, to divide.

rebanco [ray-bahn'-co], *m.* (*Arch.*) The second bench or seat.

rebanadera [ray-bah-nyah-day'-rah], *f.* Drag, a hooked instrument for taking things out of a well.

rebanadura [ray-bah-nyah-doo'-rah], *f.* V. ARREBAÑADURA.

rebañar [ray-bah-nyar'], *va.* V. ARREBAÑAR.

rebañego, ga [ray-bah-nyay'-go, gah], *a.* Gregarious.

rebaño [ray-bah'-nyo], *m.* 1. Flocks or flocks of sheep, herd of cattle. 2. Crowd, heap. 3. Flock, assembly of the faithful.

rebañuelo [ray-bah-nyoo-ay'-lo], *m. dim.* Small flock or heap.

rebaptizando, da [ray-bap-te-thahn'-do, dah], *a.*A person who is to be rebaptized.

rebaptizar [ray-bap-te-thar'], *va.* V. REBAUTIZAR.

rebasadero [ray-bah-sah-day'-ro], *m.* (*Naut.*) Difficult place to pass.

rebasar [ray-bah-sar'], *va.* 1. (*Naut.*) To sail past any point or difficult place. 2. (*Met.*) To exceed (en calidad, número), to go beyond, to pass from a line or given point. **Han rebasado ya los límites razonables**, they have already gone beyond all reasonable limits.

rebastar [ray-bas-tar'], *vn.* To be more than enough.

rebatar [ray-bah-tar'], *va.* V. ARREBATAR.

rebate [ray-bah'-tay], *m.* Dispute, disagreement.

rebatible [ray-bah-tee'-blay], *a.* That can be refuted or rebutted.

rebatimiento [ray-bah-te-me-en'-to], *m.* Repulsion, refutation.

rebatir [ray-hah-teer'], *va.* 1. To rebate, to curb, to resist (tentación); to repel (ataque). 2. To parry, to ward off (golpe). 3. To object, to refute; to rebut. 4. (*Arith.*) To allow from a sum a quantity which ought not to have been comprised in it. 5. To repress the passions of the soul.

rebato [ray-bah'-to], *m.* 1. An unexpected attack (ataque), a surprise; an unexpected event; alarm, a fit, a transport. 2. A sudden fit of passion. **De rebato**, suddenly. 3. Summons of the people by a bell in case of danger.

rebautizar [ray-bah-oo-te-thar'], *va.* To rebaptize.

rebeber [ray-bay-berr'], *va.* 1. To drink often. 2. V. EMBEBER.

rebeca [ray-bay'-kah], *f.* Cardigan.

rebeco, ca [ray-bay'-co, cah], *a.* Cross-grained, intractable, harsh.

rebelar [ray-bay-lar'], *va.* To excite rebellion. *-vr.* 1. To revolt, to rebel, to mutiny. 2. To get at variance, to break off friendly intercourse. 3. To resist, to oppose; to excite the passions irrationally.

rebelde [ray-bel'-day], *m.* Rebel. *-a.* 1. Rebellious. 2. Stubborn, ill-tractable, perverse. 3. (*Law.*) Not attending the summons of a judge, non-appearance in court. 4. Rebellious (pasiones, afecciones).

rebeldía [ray-bel-dee'-ah], *f.* 1. Rebelliousness, contumacy, disobedience. 2. Obstinacy, stubbornness. 3. (*Law.*) Default, non-appearance in court. **En rebeldía**, by default.

rebelión [ray-bay-le-on'], *f.* Rebellion, revolt, insurrection.

rebelón, na [ray-bay-lone', nah], *a.* Restive (caballo).

rebellín [ray-bayl-lyeen'], *m.* (*Mil.*) Ravelin.

rebencazo [ray-ben-cah'-tho], *m.* Blow with a port-rope.

rebendecir [ray-ben-day-theer'], *va.* To bless or consecrate anew.

rebenque [ray-ben'-kay], *m.* 1. Rope for flogging galley slaves. 2. (*Naut.*) Ratline, or ratlin, a short cross-rope.

rebeza [ray-bay'-thah], *f.* (*Naut.*) Change in the course of tides or currents.

rebién [ray-be-en'], *adv.* (*Coll.*) Very well.

rebina [ray-bee'-nah], or **rebinadura** [ray-be-nah-doo'-rah], *f.* (*Agr.*) Ploughing a third time.

rebinar [ray-be-nar'], *va.* (*Agr.*) V. TERCIAR.

rebisabuela [ray-be-sah-boo-ay'-lah], *f.* The great-great-grandmother.

rebisabuelo [ray-be-sah-boo-ay'-lo], *m.* The great-great-grandfather.

rebisnieta, rebiznieta [ray-beeth-ne-ay'-tah], *f.* The great-great-granddaughter.

rebisnieto, rebiznieto [ray-beeth-ne-ay'-to], *m.* The great-great-grandson.

reblandecer [ray-blan-day-therr'], *va.* To make tender.

reblandecimiento [ray-blan-day-the-me-en'-to], *m.* (*Med.*) Softening of organic tissues. **Reblandecimiento cerebral**, softening of the brain.

rebobinar [ray-bo-be-nahr'], *va.* To rewind.

rebociño [ray-bo-thee'-nyo], *m. (Prov.)* A short cloak or mantle for women.

rebolisco [ray-bo-lees'-co], *m.* (Cuba) Tumult of people without a real occasion.

rebolla [ray-bol'-lyah], *f.* Local name of a kind of oak-tree.

rebollar [ray-bol-lyar'], *m.* Thicket of oak saplings.

rebollidura [ray-bol-lye-doo'-rah], *f. (Mil.)* Honey-comb, a flaw in the bore of ordnance.

rebollo [ray-bol'-lyoh], *m.* 1. *(Bot.)* The Turkey oak. 2 *(Prov.)* Boll or trunk of a tree.

rebolludo, da [ray-bol-lyoo'-do, dah], *a.* 1. *V.* REHECHO and DOBLE. 2. Applied to a rude, hard diamond.

reboñar [ray-bo-nyar'], *vn. (Prov.)* To stop on account of too much water (molino de agua).

reborda [ray-bor'-dah], *f.* A certain mode of fishing along the Levant coasts.

reborde [ray-bor'-day], *m.* Ledge.

rebosadero [ray-bo-sah-day'-ro], *m.* Place where anything overflows.

rebosadura [ray-bo-sah-doo'-rah], *f.* **rebosamiento,** *m.* Overflow, as of liquor in a vessel.

rebosante [ray-bo-sahn'-tay], *a.* Brimming with, overflowing with.

rebosar [ray-bo-sar'], *vn.* 1. To run over, to overflow (líquido, recipiente). 2. To abound (abundar), to be plenty. 3. To evince, to display, to be unable to hide an affection or passion of the spirit.

rebotadera [ray-bo-tah-day'-rah], *f.* Iron plate which raises the nap on cloth to be shorn.

rebotador, ra [ray-bo-tah-dor', rah], *m. & f.* One who rebounds; clincher.

rebotadura [ray-bo-tah-doo'-rah], *f.* The act of rebounding.

rebotallero, ra [ray-bo-tah-lyay'-ro, rah], *a. (Min.)* Searcher, working on a percentage.

rebotar [ray-bo-tar'], *va.* 1. To rebound (pelota). 2. To change color, to turn (vino, licores). *-va* 1. To clinch a spike or nail (clavo), to turn the point of something sharp. 2. To raise the nap of cloth to be shorn. 3. To repel. *-vr.* To change one's opinion, to retract.

rebote [ray-bo'-tay], *m.* Rebound, rebounding, resilience. **De rebote,** on a second mission.

rebotica [ray-bo-tee'-cah], *f.* Back room behind an apothecary's shop.

rebotiga [ray-bo-tee'-gah], *f. (Prov.) V.* TRASTIENDA.

rebotín [ray-bo-teen'], *m.* The second growth of mulberry leaves.

rebozado [ray-bo-thah'-do], *a.* Fried in batter.

rebozar [ray-bo-thar'], *va.* 1. To overlay or baste meat. 2. *V.* EMBOZAR. *-vr.* To be muffled up in a cloak.

rebozo [ray-bo'-tho], *m.* 1. The act of muffling oneself up. *V.* EMBOZO. 2. Muffler for the face. *V.* REBOCIÑO. **De rebozo,** secretly, hiddenly.

rebramar [ray-brah-mar'], *vn.* To low and bellow repeatedly; to answer one noise by another.

rebramo [ray-brah'-mo], *m.* Noise with which deer respond to each other.

rebrote [ray-bro'-tay], *m.* New outbreak.

rebrotín [ray-bro-teen'], *m.* The second growth of clover which has been cut.

rebudiar [ray-boo-de-ar'], *vn.* To snuffle and grunt.

rebueno, na [ray-boo-ay'-no, nah], *a. (Coll.)* Very good, excellent.

rebufar [ray-boo-far'], *vn.* To blow or snort repeatedly, like animals.

rebufo [ray-boo'-fo], *m.* The recoil of a fire-arm; expansion of air at the muzzle on firing a shot. (Literally, snorting.)

rebujal [ray-boo-hahl'], *m.* 1. Number of cattle in a flock below even fifties. (For instance, in a flock of 430 sheep the 30 are *rebujal.*) 2. A small piece of amble label.

rebujalero [ray-boo-hah-lay'-ro], *m.* A petty farmer.

rebujar [ray-boo-har'], *va.* To wrap up linen and other cloth in an awkward manner.

rebujo [ray-boo'-ho], *m.* 1. Muffler, a part of female dress. 2. *(Prov.)* A portion of tithe paid in money. 3. Wrapper for any common article.

rebullicio [ray-bool-lyee'-the-o], *m.* Great clamor or tumult.

rebullir [ray-bool-lyeer'], *vn.* To stir, to begin to move.

reburujar [ray-boo-roo-har'], *va. (Coll.)* To wrap up, to pack in bundles.

reburujón [ray-boo-roo-hone'], *m.* Bundle wrapped up carelessly.

rebusca [ray-boos'-cah], *f.* 1. Research, searching. 2. Gleaning fruit and grain. 3. Refuse, remains (restos), relic. *4. (And. Cono Sur)* Small business (negocio).

rebuscador, ra [ray-boos-cah-dor', rah], *m. & f.* Gleaner, researcher.

rebuscar [ray-boos-car'], *va.* 1. To glean grapes left by the vintagers. 2. To search (objeto), to inquire with great curiosity and attention. *-vn.* To search carefully.

rebusco [ray-boos'-co], *m.* Research; gleaning. *V.* REBUSCA.

rebutir [ray-boo-teer'], *va. (Prov.)* To stud; to fill up.

rebuznador, ra [ray-booth-nah-dor', rah], *m. & f.* One who brays like an ass.

rebuznar [ray-booth-nar'], *va.* To bray, as an ass.

rebuzno [ray-booth'-no], *m.* Braying of an ass.

recabar [ray-cah-bar'], *va.* 1. To obtain by entreaty. 2. To claim as a right (reclamar). 3. *(LAm.)* To ask for (solicitar).

recadero [ray-cah-day'-ro], *m. (Prov.)* Porter, messenger (mensajero).

recado [ray-cah'-do], *m.* 1. Message (mensaje), errand. 2. Present, gift sent to an absent person (regalo). 3. Compliments sent to the absent. 4. Provision of things necessary for some purpose (compras). 5. Outfit, all needed implements for doing certain things. 6. Precaution, security. 7. Instrument, record. 8. *(Amer.)* Saddle and trappings of a horse (montura). 9. *(Carib.)* Greetings (saludos). **Recado de escribir,** escritoire, writing-desk. **A recado, a buen recado,** with great care and attention. **Hacer un recado,** to go out on an errand.

recaer [ray-cah-err'], *vn.* 1. To fall back, to relapse. 2. To devolve. 3. To fall under another's power. **Las sospechas recayeron sobre el conserje,** suspicion fell on the porter. *(Yo recaigo, yo recaiga, from Recaer. V.* CAER.)

recaída [ray-cah-ee'-dah], *f.* 1. Relapse, in sickness. 2. A second fall, a second offence.

recalada [ray-cah-lah'-dah], *f. (Naut.)* The act of descrying the land; landfall.

recalar [ray-cah-lar'], *va.* 1. To soak, to impregnate with liquor. 2. *(Naut.)* To descry a known point, after a cruise. 3. To bring another vessel to port. 4. To penetrate a calm (corriente de aire).

recalcadamente [ray-cahl-cah'-dah-men-tay], *adv.* Closely, contiguously; vehemently.

recalcar [ray-cal-car'], *va.* 1. To squeeze. 2. To accent words or phrased with marked design. **Recalcar algo a uno,** to insist on something to somebody. *-vr.* To inculcate, to repeat often.

recalcitrante [ray-cal-the-trahn'-tay], *a.* Recalcitrant, perverse, obstinate.

recalcitrar [ray-cal-the-trar'], *vn.* 1. To kick or strike with the heel. 2. To wince, to kick as unwilling of the rider (caballos). 3. To oppose, to make resistance where obedience is due (resistir).

recalentamiento [ray-cah-len-tah-me-en'-to], *m.* Rekindling: heat.

recalentar [ray-cah-len-tar'], *va.* 1. To heat again, to rekindle. 2. To excite (apetito sexual). *-vr.* To become scorched or injured through heat: applied to farm products.

recalmón [ray-cal-mohn'], *m.* A sudden decrease in the force of the wind.

recalvastro, tra [ray-cal-vahs'-tro, trah], *a.* Bald from forehead to crown.

recalzar [ray-cal-thar'], *va.* 1. To prick the outlines of a design on paper. 2. To mould up plants; to prepare mortar or cement.

recalzo [ray-cahl'-tho], *m.* 1. The act of repairing a decayed wall. 2. Outside felloe of a cart-wheel.

recalzón [ray-cal-thone'], *m.* Outer felloe of a wheel.

recamado [ray-cah-mah'-do], *m. (Com.)* Embroidery of raised work.

recamador, ra [ray-cah-mah-dor', rah], *m. & f.* Embroiderer.

recamar [ray-cah-mar'], *va.* To embroider with raised work, to fret.

recámara [ray-cah'-mah-rah], *f.* 1. Bedroom (dormitorio). 2. Chamber, breech (de cañón).

recamarera [ray-cah-mah-ray'-rah], *f. (Mex.)* Upstairs maid.

recamarilla [ray-cah-mah-reel'-lyah], *f.* **dim.** A small wardrobe; a small chamber of a firearm.

recambiar [ray-cam-be-ar'], *va.* 1. To recharge, to cleanse a second time. 2. To add the re-exchange on a protested bill. 3 *(Com.)* To draw again upon the drawer or indorser of a bill of exchange not paid when mature.

recambio [ray-cahm'-be-o], *m.* 1. A new exchange or barter. 2. Re-exchange. 3. Retribution, reward. **Recambio de piezas,** *(Comput.)* parts replacement.

recamo [ray-cah'-mo], *m.* 1. Embroidery of raised work. 2. Button hole, bordered with lace, and garnished at the end with a tassel.

recanación [ray-cah-nah-the-on'], *f.* Act of measuring by canal, a measure of about two ells.

recancanilla [ray-can-cah-neel'-lyah], *f.* 1. Affectation of limping, by boys, for amusement. 2. Tergiversation; an affected tone of talking.

recantación [ray-can-tah-the-on'], *f.* Recantation, public retractation.

recantón [ray-can-tone'], *m.* Cornerstone, set upright at the corners of houses and streets.

recapacitar [ray-cah-pah-the-tar'], *vn.* To recall, to recollect, to think over (sobre).

recapitulación [ray-cah-pe-too-lah-the-on'], *f.* Recapitulation, summary.

recapitular [ray-cah-pe-too-lar'], *va.* To recapitulate, to sum up a charge or discourse; to draw to a head.

recarga [ray-car'-gah], *f.* 1. Additional tax or duty. 2. Second charge of firearms.

recargado, da [ray-car-gah'-do, dah], *a.* Overdone, excessive. **Recargado de adornos,** overly ornamented.

recargar [ray-car-gar'], *va.* 1. To reload, to load again. 2. To remand to prison on a new charge. 3. To make a new charge or accusation (sentencia); to recharge. 4. *(For.)* To increase the sentence of a culprit. **Recargar el café de azúcar,** to put too much sugar in the coffee.

recargo [ray-car'-go], *m.* 1. A new charge or accusation. 2. Increase of a fever. 3. A new burden (nueva carga). 4. Extra charge.

recata [ray-cah'-tah], *f.* The act of tasting or trying again.

recatadamente [ray-kah-tah'-dah-men-tay], *adv.* Cautiously, prudently; modestly; cunningly.

recatado, da [ray-cah-tah'-do, dah], *a.* 1. Prudent, circumspect; shy, coy. 2. Honest, candid, modest. *-pp.* of RECATAR.

recatamiento [ray-cah-tah-me-en'-to], *m.* V. RECATO.

recatar [ray-cah-tar'], *va.* 1. To secrete. 2. To try or taste again. *-vr.* To take care, to proceed with prudence (ser prudente); to be cautious. **Recatarse de algo,** to fight shy of something.

recatear [ray-cah-tay-ar'], *vn.* 1. To give sparingly, to hold back. 2. V. RECATEAR.

recatería [ray-cah-tay-ree'-ah], *f.* V. RECATONERÍA.

recato [ray-cah'-to], *m.* 1. Prudence, circumspection, caution. 2. Modesty (modestia), honor; bashfulness, coyness.

recatón [ray-cah-tone'], *m.* Metal socket of a lance or pike. V. REGATÓN.

recatonazo [ray-cah-to-nah'-tho], *m.* Stroke with a pike or lance.

recatonear [ray-cah-to-nay-ar'], *va.* To buy by wholesale, in order to retail again.

recatonería, recatonía [ray-cah-to-nay-ree'-ah], *f. V.* REGATONERÍA.

recaudación [ray-cah-oo-dah-the-on'], *f.* 1. The act of collecting rents or taxes; recovery of debts. 2. Collector's office.

recaudador [ray-cah-oo-dah-dor'], *m.* Tax-gatherer, collector of rents.

recaudamiento [ray-cah-oo-dah-me-en'-to], *m.* 1. Collection of rents or taxes. 2. Office or district of a collector.

recaudar [ray-cah-oo-dar'], *va.* 1. To gather, to collect rents or taxes (impuestos). 2. To put or hold in custody.

recaudo [ray-cah'-oo-do], *m* 1. Collection of rents or taxes. 2. Provision, supply. 3. Caution, security for or against.4. V. RECADO. 5. *(CAm. Cono Sur, Mex.)* Spices (especias). 6. *(CAm. Cono Sur, Mex.)* Daily supply of fresh vegetables.

recavar [ray-cah-var'], *va.* To dig the ground a second time.

recazar [ray-cah-thar'], *va.* To seize prey in the air or on the ground, like a hawk.

recazo [ray-cah'-tho], *m.* 1. Guard, part of the hilt of a sword. 2. Back part of the blade of a knife.

recebar [ray-thay-bar'], *va* To spread gravel.

recebo [ray-thay'-bo], *m.* Sand or fine gravel spread over the bed of a highway to even it and make it firm.

recel [ray-thel'], *m.* A sort of striped tapestry.

recelar [ray-thay-lar'], *va. & vr.* 1. To fear, to distrust, to suspect. 2. To excite a mare sexually towards receiving the jackass (caballos).

recelo [ray-thay'-lo], *m.* Misgiving, imagination of something ill without proof, suspicion (suspicacia).

receloso, sa [ray-thay-lo'-so, sah], *a.* Distrustful, suspicious.

recentadura [ray-then-tah-doo'-rah], *f.* Leaven preserved for raising bread.

recental [ray-then-tahl'], *a.* Applied to a sucking lamb.

recentar [ray-then-tar'], *va.* To put sufficient leaven into dough to raise it. *-vr.* V. RENOVARSE.

receñir [ray-thay-nyeer'], *va.* To regird, to gird tight.

recepción [ray-thep-the-on'], *f.* 1. Reception, receiving, acceptation. 2. Reception (ceremonia). 3. Drawing room (cuarto).

recepcionista [ray-thep-the-o-nees'-tah], *m & f.* Receptionist (hotel), desk clerk.

receptación [ray-thep-tah-the-on'], *f.* Reception of stolen goods.

receptacular [ray-thep-tah-coo-lar'], *a. (Bot.)* Contained in the receptacle.

receptáculo [ray-thep-tah'-coo-lo], *m.* l. Receptacle, vessel for liquids. 2. Refuge, asylum. 3. Gutter for the eaves of buildings.

receptador [ray-thep-tah-dor'], *m.* Receiver of stolen goods; abettor of crimes.

receptar [ray-thep-tar'], *va.* To receive stolen goods, to abet any crime. *-vr.* To take refuge.

recepticios, as [ray-thep-tee'-the-os, as], *a. (For.)* Property under the sole control of a married woman.

receptividad [ray-thep-te-ve-dahd'], *f.* Receptivity, receptiveness.

receptivo, va [ray-thep-tee'-vo, vah], *a.* Receptive.

recepto [ray-thep'-to], *m.* Asylum, place of refuge.

receptor, ra [ray-thep-tor', rah], *a.* Applied to one who receives anything, especially stolen goods.

receptor [ray-thep'-tor], *m.* 1. Receiver, treasurer. 2. Investigating official. 3. Radio receiver. **Receptor de control,** monitor. **Descolgar el receptor,** television receiver.

receptoría [ray-thep-to-ree'-ah], *f.* 1. Receiver's or treasurer's office. 2. Place of a receiver or treasurer. 3. Power of a delegate judge.

recercador, ra [ray-ther-cah-dor', rah], *a.* Girding, hemming in, investing.

recésit [ray-thay'-sit], *m.* Vacation. V. RECLE.

receso [ray-thay'-so], *m.* 1. Recess, remote apartment; recession. 2. *(Mex.)* Recess, the time when the legislature is not in session. **Receso del sol,** the apparent motion of the sun away from the equator.

receta [ray-thay'-tah], *f.* 1. Prescription, recipe of a physician or surgeon. 2. *(Coll.)* Memorandum of orders received; order for goods. 3. Account of parcels sent from one office to another.

recetador [ray-thay-tah-dor'], *m.* Prescriber of medicines.

recetar [ray-thay-tar'], *va.* 1. To prescribe, medicines. 2. *(Met.)* To make extravagant charges or unreasonable demands.

recetario [ray-thay-tah'-re-o], *m.* 1. Memorandum or register of the prescriptions made by a physician. 2. Apothecary's file of prescriptions not paid for by his customers. 3. Pharmacopoeia.

recetor [ray-thay-tor'], *m.* Receiver, treasurer. *V.* RECEPTOR.

recetoria [ray-thay-to-ree'-ah],*f.* Treasury, place for keeping money.

rechazador, ra [ray-chah-thah-dor', rah], *m. & f.* Repelled contradictor.

rechazamiento [ray-chah-thah-me-en'-to], *m.* 1. Repulsion. 2. Repelling (ataque).

rechazar [ray-chah-thar'], *va.* 1. To repel (ataque), to repulse, to drive back (enemigo), to impel in an opposite direction, to force back. 2. To contradict, to impugn.

rechazo [ray-chah'-tho], *m.* 1. Rejection. 2. Recoil (de cañón), rebound. **De rechazo,** incidentally, casually, by rebounds.

rechifla [ray-chee'-flah], *f.* Whistle (silbido), whistling of the winds.

rechiflar [ray-che-flar'], *va.* 1. To mock, to make fun of, to ridicule. 2. To whistle insistently, to make cat-call. 3. *(Cono Sur)* To get cross (enojarse).

rechinador, ra [ray-che-nah-dor', rah], *a.* Creaking, grating.

rechinamiento [ray-che-nah-me-en'-to], *m.* Creaking of a machine, gnashing of teeth.

rechinante [ray-che-nahn'-tay], *pa.* Creaking; gnashing.

rechinar [ray-che-nar'], *vn.* 1. To creak (madera, puerta), to clash; to hurtle; to grate (piezas sin lubricar, dientes). **Rechinar los dientes,** to gnash the teeth. 2. To engage in anything with reluctance. 3. *(And. Cono Sur, Mex.)* To rage (rabiar).

rechinido [ray-che-nee'-do], *m. V.* RECHINO.

rechino [ray-chee'-no], *m.* Creaking, clang, clangor, clash.

rechoncho, cha [ray-chon'-cho, chah], *a. (Coll.)* Chubby (persona).

rechupete (De) [ray-choo-pay'-tay], *(Coll.)* Exquisite, highly agreeable. **Me ha salido de rechupete,** it turned out marvelously for me.

recial [ray-the-ahl'], *m.* Rapid, rapids in rivers.

reciamente [ray'-the-ah-men-tay], *adv.* Strongly, forcibly, stoutly.

recibí [ray-the-bee'], *m.* Received payment.

recibidero, ra [ray-the-be-day'-ro, rah], *a.* Receivable.

recibidor [ray-the-be-dor'], *m.* 1. Receiver 2. Entrance hall.

recibimiento [ray-the-be-me-en'-to], *m.* 1. Reception, receipt. 2. Entertainment to one from abroad. 3. Antechamber (antecámara). 4. General reception of company.

recibir [ray-the-beer'], *va.* 1. To accept, to receive, to let in 2. To take charge of. 3. To sustain, to support. 4. To imbibe, to drink in, to draw in. 5. To super, to receive, to admit. 6. To receive company or visits. 7. To receive, to go and meet a person. 8. To fasten, to secure with mortar. 9. To experience an injury; to receive an attack. *-vr.* To be admitted to practice a profession **Recibir a cuenta,** to receive on account. **Recibir a prueba,** to receive on trial. **Recibir a uno con los brazos abiertos,** to welcome somebody with open arms. **La oferta fue mal recibida,** the offer was badly received.

recibo [ray-thee'-bo], *m.* 1. Reception. 2. Receipt, discharge, acquittance. **Acusar recibo,** *(Com.)* to acknowledge receipt. 3. Visit, entertainment or reception of friends.

reciclado [ray-the-clah'-do], *a.* Recycled. *-m.* Recycling.

reciclaje [ray-the-clah'-hay], *m.* Recycling; retraining.

reciclar [ray-the-clahr'], *va.* To recycle; to retrain (persona); to modify (plan).

recidiva [ray-the-dee'-vah], *f.* 1. Relapse of a disease when convalescence was progressing. 2. *(For.)* V. REINCIDENCIA.

recién [ray-the-en'], *adv.* Recently, lately (used before participles instead of *reciente*). **Recién casado,** newly-wed. **Recién muerto,** recently deceased. **Recién hecho,** newly-made.

reciente [ray-the-en'-tay], *adv.* Recent, new, fresh; just made, modern.

recientemente [ray-the-en'-tay-men-tay], *adv.* Recently, newly, freshly, just now, latterly, lately.

recinchar [ray-thin-char'], *va.* To bind round one thing to another with a girdle.

recinto [ray-theen'-to], *m.* Precinct, district. **Recinto amurallado,** walled enclosure.

recio, cia [ray'-the-o, ah], *a.* 1. Stout, strong, robust, vigorous. 2. Coarse, thick (grueso), clumsy. 3. Rude, uncouth, intractable. 4. Arduous, grievous, hard to bear. 5. Severe, rigorous (tiempo). 6. Swift, impetuous. **Recio de complexión,** of a strong constitution. **En lo más recio del invierno,** in the depths of winter.

recio, *adv.* Strongly, stoutly: rapidly; vehemently, vigorously. **Hablar recio,** to talk loud. **De recio,** strongly, violently, precipitately, rapidly.

récipe [ray'-the-pay], *m. (Coll.)* 1. Prescription of a physician. 2. Displeasure, disgust; ungenteel or bad usage.

recipiente [ray-the-pe-en'-tay], *m. (Chem.)* 1. Recipient (persona), receiver. 2. Receiver, bell-glass, of an air-pump. 3. Bowl, pot (utensilio de cocina).

reciprocación [ray-the-pro-cah-he-on'], *f.* Reciprocation, mutuality.

recíprocamente [ray-the'-pro-cah-men-tay], *adv.* Reciprocally, mutually, conversely.

reciprocar [ray-the-pro-car'], *va.* To reciprocate. *-vr.* To correspond mutually.

recíproco, ca [ray-thee'-pro-co, cah], *a.* Reciprocal, mutual (mutuo). **Verbo recíproco,** reciprocal verb, as **reciprocarse.**

recisión [ray-the-se-on'], *f.* Recision, abrogation.

recísimo, ma [ray-thee'-se-mo, mah], *a. sup.* Most vehement.

recitación [ray-the-tah-the-on'], *f.* Recitation, reciting.

recitado [ray-the-tah'-do], *m. (Mus.)* Recitative, tuneful pronunciation.— **Recitado, da,** *pp.* of RECITAR.

recitador, ra [ray-the-tah-dor', rah], *m. & f.* Reciter.

recital [ray-the-tahl'], *m. (Mus.)* Recital; *(Liter.)* reading.

recitar [ray-the-tar'], *va.* To recite, to rehearse.

recitativo, va [ray-the-tah-tee'-vo, vah], *a.* Recitative.

recizalla [ray-the-thahl'-lyah], *f.* Second filings or fragments.

reclamación [ray-clah-mah-te-on'], *f.* 1. Reclamation. 2. Objection (objeción), remonstrance. 3. *(Com.)* Complaint, claim (reivindicación). **Reclamación salarial,** wage claim.

reclamante [ray-clah-mahn'-tay], *m. & f.* Claimant.

reclamar [ray-clah-mar'], *va.* 1. To decoy birds with a call or whistle. 2. To reclaim, to demand; to cry unto. 3. *(Naut.)* To hoist or lower a yard by means of a block. *-vn.* To contradict, to oppose.

reclamo [ray-clah'-may], *m. (Naut.)* Sheave-hole in a top-mast-head.

reclamo [ray-clah'-mo], *m.* 1. Decoy-bird (caza). 2. Call, an instrument to call birds. 3. Allurement, inducement (aliciente), enticement. 4. *(Naut.)* Tie-block. 5. Reclamation. 6. *(Print.)* Catch-word. **Acudir al reclamo,** *(Coll.)* to answer, to go where there is a thing suitable to one's purpose.

reclinable [ray-cle-nah'-blay], *a.* Capable of being reclined.

reclinación [ray-cle-nah-the-on'], *f.* Reclining.

reclinado, da [ray-cle-nah'-do, dah], *a. pp.* of RECLINAR. Reclined, recumbent.

reclinar [ray-cle-nar'], *va. & vn.* To recline, to lean back. **Reclinarse en, sobre,** to lean on or upon.

reclinatorio [ray-cle-nah-to'-re-o], *m.* 1. Couch, thing to lean on. 2. A stool for kneeling on at prayers.

recluir [ray-cloo-eer´], *va.* To shut up, to seclude.

reclusión [ray-cloo-se-on´], *f.* 1. Reclusion, shutting up. 2. Recess, place of retirement; closeness. **Reclusión mayor,** imprisonment in condition of maximum security.

recluso, sa [ray-cloo´-so, sah], *a. & m. & f.* Recluse. -*pp. irr.* of RECLUIR.

reclusorio [ray-cloo-so´-re-o], *m.* Recess, place of retirement.

recluta [ray-cloo'-tah], *f.* Recruiting (ejército): supply. -*m.* Recruit, a new soldier who enlists voluntarily.

reclutador [ray-cloo-tah-dor'], *m.* Any person employed in recruiting or raising new soldiers.

reclutamiento [ray-cloo-tah-me-en'-to], *m.* Recruiting of soldiers.

reclutar [rar-cloo-tar'], *va.* 1. To recruit, to supply an army with new men. 2. To repair anything wasted by new supplies. 3. *(Cono Sur)* To round up (ganado). 4. *(Cono Sur)* To contract (obrero).

recobrar [ray-co-brar'], *va.* 1. To recover, to get back what was lost. 2. *(Naut.)* To rouse in, to take up the end of a rope which hangs loose. -*vr.* To recover from sickness, to regain vigor of body or mind; to recollect.

recobro [ray-co'-bro], *m.* Recovery, restoration of thing lost.

recocer [ray-co-therr'], *va.* To boil again, to boil too much. -*vr.* To consume oneself with rage and indignation.

recocho, cha [ray-co'-cho, chah], *a.* Boiled too much, over-done.

recocido, da [ray-co-thee'-do, dath], *a.* 1. Over boiled. 2. Skilful, clever. 3. Over-ripe, dried up. -*m.* The operation of annealing metals. -*f.* The act of boiling again. -*pp.* of RECODER.

recodadero [ray-co-dah-day'-ro], *m.* Place for leaning on one's elbow.

recodar [ray-co-dar'], *vn. & vr.* To lean with the elbow upon anything.

rocodo [ray-co'-do], *m.* 1. A turn in a road or street; the bend of a river. 2. A corner or angle jutting out.

recogedero [ray-co-hay-day'-ro], *m.* 1. Place where things are gathered or collected. 2. Instrument with which things are gathered.

recogedor [ray-co-hay-dor'], *m.* 1. One who shelters or harbors. 2. Gatherer, gleaner.

recoger [ray-co-herr'], *va.* 1. To retake, to take back. 2. To gather (objetos), to collect, to hoard; to pick out; to contract. 3. To gather the fruits. 4. To receive, to protect, to shelter (necesitado). 5. To lock up in a mad-house. 6. To suspend the use, or stop the course of anything. 7. To extract intelligence from books. **Recoger un vale,** to take up a note. **Van a recoger las monedas antiguas,** they are going to call in the old coins. **Te vendremos a recoger a las 8,** we´ll come for you at 8 o´clock. -*vr.* 1. To take shelter (refugiarse); to withdraw into retirement (retirarse). 2. To reform, or retrench one's expenses. 3. To go home, to retire, to rest. 4. To abstract oneself from worldly thoughts.

recogida [ray-co-hee'-dah], *f.* 1. The act of taking back anything which circulates. 2. A woman shut up in a house of correction. 3. *(Agr.)* Harvest. 4. *(Mex. Agr.)* Roundup.

recogidamente [ray-co-he-dah-men-tay], *adv.* Retiredly.

recogido, da [ray-co-hee'-do, dah], *a.* Retired, secluded (lugar); contracted. -*pp.* of RECOGER.

recogimiento [ray-co-he-me-en'-to], *m.* 1. Collection, assemblage. 2. Retreat, shelter. V. RECLUSIÓN. 3. House where women are confined, or live in retirement. 4. Abstraction from worldly concerns; preparation for spiritual exercises. 5. Absorption (estado); seclusion. 6. Devotion (cualidad).

recolar [ray-co-lar'], *va.* To strain a second time.

recolección [ray-co-lec-the-on'], *f.* 1. Summary, abridgment. 2. Harvest of grain or fruit. 3. Collection of money or taxes. 4. Convent where a strict observance of the rules prevails. 5. Retirement, abstruction from worldly affairs.

recolectar [ray-co-lec-tar'], *pa.* 1. To gather the harvest. 2. To collect many things, to hoard. 3. To collect from different litigants.

recoleto, ta [ray-co-lay'-to, tah], *a.* Belonging to a convent where strict order is maintained. -*m. & f.* Devotee who lives retired; a recollect.

recolorado, da [ray-co-lo-rah'-do, dah], *a.* Copper-nosed, red-faced, red-nosed.

recombinar [ray-com-be-nar'], *va.* To recombine.

recomendable [ray-co-men-dah'-blay], *a.* Commendable, laudable.

recomendablemente [ray-co-men-dah-blay-men-tay], *adv.* Laudably.

recomendación [ray-co-men-dah-the-on'], *f.* 1. Recommendation (indicación). 2. Injunction, application. 3. Praise, eulogy (elogio). 4. Dignity, authority. **Carta de recomendación,** letter of introduction. **Recomendación del alma,** prayers for the dying.

recomendar [ray-co-men-dar'], *va.* 1. To charge, to enjoin. 2. To recommend (indicar), to commend. 3. To entrust (confiar). 4. To advise (aconsejar). **Recomendar a uno que haga algo,** to recommend somebody to do something. *(Yo recomiendo, yo recomiende,* from *Recomendar.* V. ACRECENTAR.)

recomendaticio, cia [ray-co-men-dah-tee'-the-o, ah], *a.* Commendatory.

recomendatorio, ria [ray-co-me-dah-to'-re-o, ah], *a.* Recommendatory.

recompensa [ray-com-pen'-sah], *f.* 1. Compensation, satisfaction. 2. Recompense, reward, remuneration, fee, gratuity. **En recompensa,** in return.

recompensable [ray-com-pen-sah'-blay], *a.* Capable of being rewarded.

recompensación [ray-com-pen-sah-the-on'], *f.* Compensation, reward, recompense.

recompensar [ray-com-pen-sar´], *va.* To recompense, to reward, to gratify, to fee.

recomponer [ray-com-po-nerr'], *va.* To recompose, to mend, to repair.

recomposición [ray-com-po-se-the-on'], *f.* *(Chem.)* Recomposition.

recompostura [ray-com-pos-too-rah], *f.* V. RECOMPOSICIÓN.

recomprar [ray-com-prar'], *va.* To buy again, to buy back.

recompuesto, ta [ray-com-poo-es'-to, tah], *pp. irr.* from RECOMPONER.

reconcentramiento [ray-con-then-trah-me-en´-to], *m.* Act of introducing or establishing in the center.

reconcentrar [ray-con-then-trar'], *va.* 1. To introduce, to enter into something else, to concentre (atención). 2. To dissemble. 3. To make more concentrated (solución). -*vr.* To root, to take root: applied to sentiments and affections.

reconciliable [ray-con-the-le-ah'-blay], *a.* Reconcilable.

reconciliación [ray-con-the-le-ah-the-on'], *f.* 1. Reconciliation, reconcilement, renewal of friendship; agreement of things seemingly opposite. 2. Short confession detailing things previously omitted.

reconciliador, ra [ray-con-the-le-ah-dor', rah], *m. & f.* Reconciliator, reconciler.

reconciliar [ray-con-the-le-ar'], *va.* 1. To reconcile; to make friends with one; to accommodate. 2. To hear a short confession. 3. To consecrate anew any sacred place which has been polluted or defiled. -*vr.* 1. To confess offences. 2. To renew friendship.

reconciliatorio, ria [ray-con-the-le-ah-to'-re-o, ah], *a.* Conciliatory.

reconcomerse [ray-con-com-err'-say], *vr.* To scratch frequently from continual itching.

reconcomio [ray-con-co'-me-o], *m.* *(Coll.)* 1. Shrugging the shoulders with satisfaction or resignation, or from itching or stinging. 2. Fear, apprehension. 3. Craving, violent desire.

recóndito, ta [ray-con'-de-to, tah], *a.* Recondite, secret, hidden, concealed, latent, abstruse. **En lo más recóndito de,** in the depths of.

reconducción [ray-con-dooc-the-on'], *f.* Renewal of a lease.

reconducir [ray-con-doo-theer'], *va.* 1. To conduct back. 2. *(For.)* To renew a lease or contract.

reconfesar [ray-con-fay-sar'], *va.* To confess again.

reconfortante [ray-con-for-tahn-tay], *a.* Comforting; cheering; heart-warming. *-m. (LAm.)* Tonic.

reconfortar [ray-con-for-tahr'], *va.* To confort (confortar); to cheer (animar).

reconocedor, ra [ray-co-no-thay-dor', rah], *m. & f.* Examiner; one who recognizes.

reconocer [ray-con-no-therr'], *va.* 1. To try, to examine closely, to find out, to ascertain. 2. To summit to the command or jurisdiction of others. 3. To own, to confess. 4. To acknowledge favors received. 5. To consider, to contemplate. 6. To comprehend, to conceive. 7. To acknowledge the right of property of others; to recognize (aceptar). 8. To reconnoitre, to scout. 9. To recognize the official existence of a country, or to sanction acts done in another land. *-vr.* 1. To repent. 2. To confess oneself culpable (admitir). 3. To judge justly of one's own self. **Se le reconoce por el pelo,** you can recognize him by his hair. **Le reconocen por inteligente,** they agree that he is intelligent. **Por fin reconocieron abiertamente que era falso,** eventually they openly admitted that it was untrue. *(Yo reconozco, yo reconozca,* from *Reconocer.* V. CONOCER.)

reconocidamente [ray-co-no-the'-dah-men-tay], *adv.* Gratefully, confessedly.

reconocido, da [ray-co-no-thee'-do, dah], *a.* 1. Acknowledged, confessed. 2. Grateful, obliged. 3. *n.* Recognizee; one in whose favor a bond is given. *-pp.* of RECONOCER.

reconociente [ray-co-no-the-en'-tay], *pa.* Recognizing.

reconocimiento [ray-co-no-the-me-en'-to], *m.* 1. Recognition. 2. Acknowledgment, gratitude; owning, confession. 3. Recognizance, subjection, submission. 4. Examination, inquiry. 5. Recognizance, acknowledgment of a bond or other writing in court. 6. Survey, inspection.

reconquista [ray-con-kees'-tah], *f.* Reconquest, a place reconquered.

reconquistar [ray-con-kis-tar'], *pa.* To reconquer (territorio).

reconsideración [ray-con-se-day-rah-the-on'],*f.* Reconsideration.

reconsiderar [ray-con-se-day-rahr'], *va.* To reconsider.

reconstituir [ray-cons-te-too-eer'], *va. & vr.* To reconstitute, to reconstruct.

reconstituyente [ray-cons-te-too-yen'-tay], *m. (Med.)* Tonic.

reconstrucción [ray-cons-trooc-the-on'], *f.* V. REEDIFICACIÓN.

reconstruir [ray-cons-troo-eer'], *va.* To reconstruct.

recontar [ray-con-tar'], *va.* To recount (cantidad), to relate distinctly.

recontento [ray-con-ten'-to], *m.* Contentment, deep satisfaction.

recontento, ta [ray-con-ten'-to, tah], *a.* Very content.

reconvalecer [ray-con-vah-lay-therr'], *vn.* To recover from sickness. *(Yo reconvalezco, yo reconvalezca,* from *Reconvalecer.* V. CONOCER.)

reconvención [ray-con-ven-the-on'], *f.* Charge, accusation; recrimination, expostulation; reproach (reproches).

reconvenir [ray-con-vay-neer'], *va.* 1. To charge, to accuse. 2. To retort, to recriminate, to accuse the prosecutor; to convert the plaintiff into the defendant; to expostulate. 3. To call to saccount, to reproach, to reprimand (reprender), to remonstrate.

reconvertir [re-con-ver-teer'], *va.* To reconvert; to rationalize (industria).

recopilación [ray-co-pe-lah-the-on'], *f.* 1. Summary, abridgment. 2. Collection of things taken from books. **Recopilación de las leyes,** abridgment or collection of the statutes.

recopilador [ray-co-pe-lah-dor'], *m.* Compiler, collector, abridger.

recopilar [ray-co-pe-lar'], *va.* To abridge, to collect.

record, récord [ray'-cord], *a.* Record. **En un tiempo record,** in a record time.

recordable [ray-cor-dah'-blay], *a.* Worthy of being recorded.

recordación [ray-cor-dah-the-on'], *f.* 1. Remembrance, calling to recollection. 2. V. RECUERDO.

recordador, ra [ray-cor-dah-dor', rah], *m. & f.* One who remembers; or that which serves to remind one of something.

recordar [ray-cor-dar'], *va.* To remind; to call to recollection (traer a la memoria). **Recordar algo a uno,** to remind somebody of something. *-vn.* 1. To awaken from sleep. 2. To remember. **No recuerdo,** I don't remember. *-vr.* To hit upon, to remember. *(Yo recuerdo, yo recuerde,* from *Recordar.* V. ACORDAR.)

recordativo, va [ray-cor-dah-tee'-vo, vah], *a.* That which reminds or may be reminded.

recordatorio, ria [ray-cor-dah-to'-re-o, ah], *a. (For.)* 1. Said of the official writing or order by which the fulfilment of a requisition or obligation is recalled. 2. Recollection.

recorrer [ray-cor-rerr'], *va.* 1. To run over, to examine, to survey (registrar). 2. To read over, to peruse. 3. To mend, to repair. *-vn.* 1. To recur, to have recourse to. 2. To rearrange a paragraph or page in printing. **Recorrer la memoria,** to call to recollection. **Recorrer una provincia a pie,** to go over a province on foot. **Recorrer un escrito,** to run one's eye over a document.

recorrido [ray-cor-ree'-do], *m.* 1. Route (ruta.) 2. Distance traveled (distancia). 3. Repair. 4. Scolding. **El recorrido del primer día fue de 450 km,** the first day's run was 450 kms. **Tren de largo recorrido,** long-distance train.

recortada [ray-cor-tah'-dah], *f.* In painting, a shadow as strong at the beginning as at the end.

recortado [ray-cor-tah'-do], *m.* Figure cut out of paper.

recortado, da [ray-cor-tah'-do], *a. (Bot.)* Notched, incised, cut irregularly. *p.p.* of RECORTAR.

recortadura [ray-cor-tah-doo'-rah],*f.* V. RECORTE.

recortar [ray-cor-tar'], *va.* 1. To cut away (exceso), to shorten, to pare off. 2. To cut figures in paper. 3. To delineate a figure in profile. *-vr.* To stand out, to be outlined.

recorte [ray-cor'-tay], *m.* Outline, profile. *-pl.* Cuttings, trimmings, projecting pieces trimmed away by a cutting instrument; clippings. **Recortes de periódico,** newspaper cuttings. **El libro está hecho de recortes,** the book is a scissors-and-paste job.

recorvar [ray-cor-var'], *va.* V. ENCORVAR.

recorvo, va [ray-cor'-vo, vah], *a.* V. CORVO.

recoser [ray-co-serr'], *va.* To sew again a rip or rent.

recostadero [ray-cos-tah-day'-ro], *m.* Reclining or resting-place.

recostado, da [ray-cos-tah'-do, dah], *a. & pp.* of RECOSTAR. Recumbent, reclined.

recostar [ray-cos-tar'], *va.* To lean against, to recline. *-vr.* To go to rest; to repose or recline (reclinar). *(Yo me recuesto, yo me recueste,* from *Recostarse.* V. ACORDAR.)

recova [ray-co'-vah], *f.* 1. Purchasing eggs in the country (negocio), butter, or poultry, to retail in town. 2. A poultry market (mercado). 3. (Peru, Chile) Market-place. 4. Pack of hounds.

recovar [ray-co-var'], *va.* To buy fowls, eggs, etc., to sell again.

recoveco [ray-co-vay'-co], *m.* 1. Turning, winding. 2. Simulation, artifice.

recovero [ray-co-vay'-ro], *m.* Huckster, in eggs, butter, or poultry.

recre [ray'-cray], *m.* Vacation of choristers V. RECLE.

recreación [ray-cray-ah-the-on'], *f.* Recreation, relief, diversion, amusement.

recrear [ray-cray-ar'], *va.* To amuse, to delight, to gratify, to glad or gladden, to recreate (crear de nuevo). *-vr.* To divert oneself.

recreativo, va [ray-cray-ah-tee'-vo, vah], *a.* Recreative, diverting.

recrecer [ray-cray-therr'], *va. & vn.* 1. To grow again. 2. To augment, to increase (crecer). 8. To occur, to happen. *-vr.* To grow big, to be overgrown. 2. To recover one's spirits.

recrecimiento [ray-cray-the-me-en'-to], *m.* Growth, increase, augmentation.

recreído, da [ray-cray-ee'-do, dah], *a.* Intractable, returned to liberty (halcón).

recremento [ray-cray-men'-to], *m.* Recrement, spume, dregs, dross, scoria, residuum.

recreo [ray-cray'-o], *m.* 1. Recreation, amusement (diversión). 2. Recess. **Hora de recreo,** recess hour. **Sala de recreo,** recreation room. **Patio de recreo,** play-ground. **Viaje de recreo,** pleasure trip.

recría [ray-cree'-ah], *f.* Repasturing of colts.

recriar [ray-cre-ar'], *va.* To favor by good feeding and care, the development of colts and mules reared in another region.

recriminación [ray-cre-me-nah-the-on'], *f.* Recrimination, counter-charge.

recriminar [ray-cre-me-nar'], *va.* To recriminate, to make a counter-charge.

recrudecer [ray-croo-day-ther'], *vn, vr.* To recrudesce.

recrudecimiento [ray-croo-day-the-me-ayn'-to], *m.* Recrudescence.

recta [rec-tah], *f.* Straight line. **Recta de llegada,** home straight.

rectamente [rec-tah-men-tay], *adv.* Rightly, justly, justifiably, honestly, fairly, good.

rectangular [rec-tan-goo-lar'], *a.* Right-angled.

rectángulo, la [rec-tahn'-goo-lo, lah], *a.* Rectangular: rectangled. *-m.* Rectangle.

rectificable [rec-te-fe-cah'-blay], *a.* Rectifiable, which may be rectified.

rectificación [rec-te-fe-cah-the-on'], *f.* Rectification.

rectificador, ra [rec-te-fe-cah-dor', rah], *a.* Rectifying, verifying. *-m. & f.* Rectifier, verifier.

rectificar [rec-te-fe-car'], *va.* 1. To rectify, to make right. 2. To verify, to confirm. 3. To rectify (cálculo), to clarify, to redistil.

rectificativo, va [rec-te-fe-cah-tee'-vo, vah], *a.* That which rectifies or corrects.

rectilíneo, nea [rec-te-lee'-nay-o, ah], *a.* Rectilinear, rectilineous, rectilineal.

rectitud [rec-te-tood'], *f.* l. Straightness, the shortest distance between two points. 2. Rectitude, uprightness, honor, honesty; exactitude.

recto, ta [rec'-to, tah], *a.* 1. Straight (línea), erect; right (ángulo). 2. Just (juez), upright, honest (persona), faithful, fair. **La flecha fue recta al blanco,** the arrow went straight to the target. 1. (*Anat.*) Rectum. 2. Superior of a community or establishment. **Rector de una universidad,** rector of a university. 3. Curate, rector.

rectorado [rec-to-rah'-do], *m.* Rectorship.

rectoral [rec-to-rahl'], *a.* Rectorial. *-f.* Rectory, a rector's dwelling.

rectorar [rec-to-rar'], *vn.* To attain the office of rector.

rectoría [rec-to-ree'-ah], *f.* 1. Rectory, curacy. 2. Office and dignity of a rector.

recua [ray'-coo-ah], *f.* l. Drove of beasts of burden. 2. Multitude of things in succession.

recuadrar [ray-coo-ah-drahr'], *va.* V. CUADRICULAR.

recuadro [ray-coo-ah'-dro], *m.* (*Arch.*) Square compartment.

recuarta [ray-coo-ar'-tah], *f.* One of the chords of a guitar: the second string put in the place of the fourth when the strings are doubled.

recudimiento, recudimiento [ray-coo-de-men'-to], *m.* Power vested in a person to gather rents or taxes.

recudir [ray-coo-deer'], *va.* To pay money in part of wages or other dues. *-vn.* To rebound, to redound, to set out again to revert to the original place or state.

recuelo [ray-coo-ay'-lo], *m.* The lye which is caught in a vat after passing through a strainer.

recuenco [ray-coo-en'-co], *m.* Ground which forms an inclosed space or corner.

recuento [ray-coo-en'-to], *m.* l. Inventory (inventario). V. INVENTARIO. 2. Recension, muster.

recuentro [ray-coo-en'-tro], *m.* V. RENCUENTRO.

recuerdo [ray-coo-err'-do], *m.* 1. Remembrance, hint given of what has passed, memento, memory; recognition (memoria). 2. Souvenir (regalo). 3. Jewel (joya). 4. Regards (saludos). **Guardar un feliz recuerdo de uno,** to have happy memories of somebody.

recuero [ray-coo-ay'-ro], *m.* Muleteer, mule-driver.

recuesta [ray-coo-es'-tah], *f.* 1. Request, intimation. V. REQUERIMIENTO. 2. Duel.

recuesto [ray-coo-es'-to], *m.* Declivity, a gradual descent.

recula [ray-coo'-lah], *f.* (*Prov.*) Recoil, retrocession.

reculada [ray-coo-lah'-dah], *f.* 1. (*Naut.*) The falling of a ship astern. 2. The action of falling back or retrograding; recoil.

recular [ray-coo-lar'], *vn.* 1. To fall back, to retrograde, to recoil. 2. (*Coll.*) To give up, to yield.

reculo, la [ray-coo'-lo, lah], *a.* Having no tail (pollos, gallinas). *-m.* V. RECULADA.

reculones (A) [ray-coo-lo'-nes], *adv.* (*Coll.*) Retrogradely.

recuperable [ray-coo-pay-rah'-blay], *a.* Recoverable.

recuperación [ray-coo-pay-rah-the-on'], *f.* Recovery, the act of recovering or rescuing, recuperative. **Recuperación de datos,** data retrieval.

recuperador, ra [ray-coo-pay-rah-dor', rah], *m. & f.* Rescuer, redeemer.

recuperar [ray-coo-pay-rar'], *va.* To recover (recobrar), to rescue, to regain. *-vr.* To recover from sickness, to gather strength.

recuperativo, va [ray-coo-pay-rah-tee'-vo, vah], *a.* That which recovers or has the power of recovering.

recura [ray-coo'-rah], *f.* Comb-saw, used by comb-makers.

recurar [ray-coo-rar'], *va.* To make or open the teeth of combs.

recurrente [ray-coor-ren'-tay], *a.* (*Anat.*) Recurrent: used of certain arteries which turn back towards their origin. *-pa.* of RECURRIR.

recurrir [ray-coo-reer'], *va.* To recur, to have recourse to. *-vn.* To revert.

recurso [ray-coor'-so], *m.* 1. Recourse, application for help or protection. 2. Recourse, return to the same place. 3. Appeal, recourse to a higher court of justice. **Sin recurso,** definitively, without appeal. 4. (*Comput.*) **Recurso de distribución de datos,** data distribution facility. **Recurso de gestión de datos,** data management facility.

recusable [ray-coo-sah'-blay], *a.* Refusable, exceptionable.

recusación [ray-coo-sah-the-on'], *f.* Refusal, exception; recusation.

recusante [ray-coo-sahn'-tay], *pa.* Refusing, recusant.

recusar [ray-coo-sar'], *va.* 1. To refuse (rechazar), to admit, to decline admission. 2. To recuse or challenge a judge. **Recular los testigos,** to object to, to challenge, witnesses.

red [red], *f.* 1. Net (pesca), particularly for fishing and fowling. 2. Grate of the parlour in nunneries. 3. Grate through which fish or bread is sold. 4. Prison with a strong grate (cerca). 5. Snare, trap, fraud (trampa). 6. Silk coif or headdress. 6. (*Fig.*) Network, system; mains supply system. **Red barrederal,** drag net. **Red de araña,** cobweb. **Red de combate,** (*Naut.*) netting. **Red de pájaros,** a thin, clear stuff. **Caer en la red,** to fall into the snare. **Red de espionaje,** spy network. **Red vascular,** vascular system. **Red de ventas,** (*Comput.*) dealers network.

redacción [ray-dac-the-on'], *f.* 1. Compilement: the act of editing a newspaper or other publication. 2. The office where it is published (oficina). 3. The editorial staff. 4. Composition (escuela).

redactar [ray-dac-tar'], *va*. To compile, to write (escribir), to compose, to edit a work or a periodical.

redactor [ray-dac-tor'], *m*. Compiler, editor (director).

redada [ray-dah'-dah], *f*. 1. Casting a net, a netful of fish. 2. Multitude, crowd.

redaño [ray-dah'-nyo], *m*. (*Anat.*) Caul, kell, the omentum.

redar [ray-dar'], *va*. To cast a net.

redargución [ray-dar-goo-the-on'], *f*. Retort, refutation.

redargüir [ray-dar-goo-eer'], *va*. 1. To retort, to reply. 2. (*For.*) To impugn a writing as suffering from some defect.

redaza [ray-dah'-thah], *f*. A certain fishing-net.

redazo [ray-dah'-tho], *m*. In artillery, a kind of fire-pillow.

redear [ray-day-ar'], *va*. V. MAJADEAR.

redecilla [ray-day-theel'-lyah], *f*. 1. A head-dress formerly used in Spain. 2. (*dim.*) V. REDECICA.

redecita [ray-day-thee'-tah], *f. dim*. A small net.

rededor [ray-day-dor'], *m*. Environs. V. CONTORNO. **Alrededor**, round about, thereabout, little more or less.

redel [ray-del'], *m*. (*Naut.*) Loof-frame.

redención [ray-den-the-on'], *f*. 1. Redemption, the act of redeeming. 2. Recovery of lost liberty, ransom. 3. Salvation, refuge.

redentor, ra [ray-den-tor', rah], *m. & f*. Redeemer, one who rescues, redeems, or ransoms. **Nuestro redentor**, our Redeemer, Jesus Christ.

redero [ray-day'-ro], *m*. Net-maker; one who catches birds or fish with nets.

redero, ra [ray-day'-ro, rah], *a*. Reticular, retiform, reticulated.

redhibición [red-e-be-the-on'], *f*. Redhibition, the rescinding of a sale through hiding a defect in the thing sold.

redhibir [red-e-beer'], *va*. To rescind a sale (by the buyer), on account of the concealment by the seller of some defect or vice in the thing sold.

redhibitorio, ria [red-e-be-to'-re-o, ah], *a*. Redhibitory, relating to redhibition; giving the right to redhibition.

redición [rayt-de-the-on'], *f*. Repetition of what had been said.

redicho, cha [ray-dee'-cho, chah], *a*. Speaking with affected precision.

rediezmar [ray-de-eth-mar'], *va*. To decimate again, to tithe a second time.

rediezmo [ray-de-eth'-mo], *m*. The ninth part of crops already tithed.

redil [ray-deel'], *m*. Sheep-fold, sheep cot, fold-coop.

redimible [ray-de-mee'-blay], *a*. Redeemable.

redimir [ray-de-meer'], *va*. 1. To redeem, to rescue, to ransom (cautivo). 2. To redeem a pledge. 3. To succor, to relieve, to extricate or liberate. **Redimirse de algún trabajo**, to extricate oneself from trouble and difficulties.

redina [ray-dee'-nah], *f*. Weigh wheel, a wheel of velvet looms.

redingote [ray-din-go'-tay], *m*. Riding-coat, a kind of great-coat.

redistribución [ray-dis-tre-boo-the-on'], *f*. A new or second distribution.

rédito [ray'-de-to], *m*. Revenue, rent, proceeds.

redituable, reditual [ray-de-too-ah'-blay], *a*. Producing rent, benefit, or profit; rentable.

redituar [ray-de-too-ar'], *va*. To yield or produce any benefit or profit; to rent.

redivivo, va [ray-de-vee'-vo, vah], *a*. Redivivus, revived, restored.

redoblado, da [ray-do-blah'-do, dah], *a. & pp*. of REDOBLAR. 1. Redoubled (celo). 2. Stout and thick. 3. (*Mil.*) Quick step.

redoblamiento [ray-do-blah-me-en'-to], *m*. Reduplication.

redoblar [ray-do-blar'], *va*. 1. To double (esfuerzo, celo), to increase by as much again. 2. To clinch (clavo), to rivet. 3. To touch the same chord twice. (*Mil.*) To play double beats on the drum.

redoble [ray-do'-blay], *m*. 1. Repeated touching of the same chord; double beat on the drum. 2. Amplification of a discourse by putting forward new arguments.

redoblegar [ray-do-blay-gar'], *va*. V. REDOBLAR and DOBLEGAR.

redoblón [ray-do-blone'], *m*. Rivet, clinch-nail.

redoler [ray-do-lerr'], *vn*. (*Coll.*) To suffer pain silently and continually.

redolino [ray-do-lee'-no], *m*. (*Prov.*) Wheel for drawing lots.

redolor [ray-do-lor'], *m*. A dull ache remaining after some acute suffering.

redoma [ray-do'-mah], *f*. 1. A broad-bottomed bottle; a flask (frasco). 2. (*Cono Sur*) Fishbowl (pez).

redomadazo, za [ray-do-ma-dah'-tho, thah], *a. aug*. Very artful or sly.

redomado, da [ray-do-mah'-do, dah], *a*. Artful, sly, crafty, cunning.

redomazo [ray-do-mah'-tho], *m*. Stroke or blow in the face with a bottle.

redonda [ray-don'-dah], *a*. Applied to a round ball or capsule of silk. -*f*. 1. Circle, neighborhood. V. COMARCA. 2. Pasture-ground. 3. (*Mus.*) Semibreve, whole note. **A la redonda**, round about. **En muchas millas a la redonda**, for many miles round or about.

redondamente [ray-don-dah-men-tay], *adv*. 1. In circumference, in a circle, around. 2. Roundly, clearly, plainly.

redondeador [ray-don-day-ah-dor'], *m*. Rounding-tool, used for trimming the brims of hats.

redondear [ray-don-day-ar'], *va*. 1. To round, to make round. 2. To give to soles of shoes the same form as the last has on its sole. . -*vr*. 1. To extricate oneself from difficulties; to clear oneself of debts. 2. To acquire property or revenues so as to live in comfortable circumstances. (*Coll.*)

redondel [ray-don-del'], *m*. 1. (*Coll.*) A circle. 2. A round cloak, a capote.

redondela [ray-dn-day'-lah], *f*. Table stand.

redondeo [ray-don-day'-o], *m*. (*Com.*) One free of all indebtedness.

redondete [ray-don-day'-tay], *a. dim*. Roundish, circular.

redondez [ray-don-deth'], *f*. Roundness, circular form, globosity.

redondilla [ray-don-deel'-lyah], *f*. Roundel or roundelay a stanza of four verses, of eight syllables each.

redondo, da [ray-don'-do, dah], *a*. 1. Round (forma), circular, spherical; orbed, orbicular. 2. Round. 3. Free from debts; unencumbered, in easy circumstances (negocio). 4. Applied to land turned to pasture. 5. Applied to persons whose grandparents were of equal rank by birth. 6. Clear, manifest, straight. 7. Just; exact, entire. **Girar en redondo**, to turn right round. **En números redondos**, in round numbers. **Será un negocio redondo**, it will be a really good deal. 8. (*Mex.*) Dense, thick (lerdo).

redondo [ray-don'-do], *m*. 1. Specie, hard cash. 2. Globe, orb, anything found.

redondón [ray-don-done'], *m*. A large circle or orbicular figure.

redopelo [ray-do-pay'-lo], *m*. 1. Rubbing cloth against the grain. 2. Scuffle, affray. **Al redopelo**, against the natural lay of the hair: hence, against all rule and reason. **Traer al redopelo**, to vex, to drag about contemptuously.

redor [ray-dor'], *m*. 1. A round mat. 2. (*Poet.*) V. REDEDOR.

redro [ray'-dro], *adv*. (*Coll.*) Behind, backwards. *m*. Each of the rings upon the horns of goats.

redrojo, redruejo [ray-dro'-ho], *m*. 1. A small bunch of grapes remaining after the vintage. 2. After-fruit or blossom. 3. A puny child, slow of growth. 4. (*Cono Sur*) Rest (exceso). 5. (*Mex.*) Rags (harapos).

redrojuelo [ray-dro-hoo-ay'-lo], *m*. (*Coll.*) Languid boy who does not thrive.

redruña [ray-droo'-nyah], *f*. Left-hand or side in hunting.

reducción [ray-dooc-the-on'], *f*. 1. Reduction, the act of reducing. 2. Mutation, alteration, exchange for an equivalent.

3. Reduction of a place or country by force of arms. 4. Conversion of infidels to the true religion; Indian people converted. 5. *(Chem.)* Resolution of compounds. 6. Reduction, an operation in algebra. 7. Solution, liquefaction.

reducible [ray-do-the'-blay], *a.* Reducible, convertible.

reducidamente [ray-doo-the-dah-men´-tay], *adv.* Sparingly.

reducido, da [ray-doo-thee'-do, dah], *a & pp.* of REDUCIR. Reduced, diminished, narrow, close, limited (limitado), confined (espacio).

reducimiento [ray-doo-the-me-en'-to], *m.* Reduction, reducement.

reducir [ray-doo-theer'], *va.* 1. To reduce a thing to its former state (tamaño). 2. To exchange, to barter; to convert, to commute; to resolve. 3. To diminish, to lessen (número); to contract, to abridge. 4. To divide into small parts. 5. To convert a solid body into a liquid. 6. To comprehend, to contain, to include, to confine. 7. To reclaim, to bring back to obedience. 8. To persuade, to convert. 9. *(Pict.)* To reduce a figure or picture to smaller dimensions. 10. *(Chem.)* To decompose a body. **Reducir algo al absurdo,** to make something seem ridiculous. **Reducir una cosa a escombros,** to reduce a house to rubble. *-vr.* To confine oneself to a moderate way of life; to resolve on punctuality. *(Yo reduzco, yo reduzca,* from *Reducir. V.* CONDUCIR.)

reductillo [ray-dooc-teel'-lyo], *m. dim.* A small redoubt.

reductivo, va [rar-dooc-tee'-vo, va], *a.* Reductive.

reducto [ray-dooc'-to], *m. (Mil.)* Redoubt.

redundancia [ray-doon-dahn'-the-ah], *f.* Superfluity, redundance, overflowing; excess, copiousness.

redundante [ray-doon-dahn´-tay], *pa. & a.* Redundant, superfluous.

redundantemente [ray-doon-dahn'-tay], *adv.* Redundantly.

redundar [ray-doon-dar'], *vn.* 1. To overflow, to be redundant. 2. To redound, to conduce, to contribute.

reduplicación [ray-doo-ple-cah-the-on'], *f.* Reduplication.

reduplicado, da [ray-doo-ple-cah'-do], *a. & pp.* of REDUPLICAR. Reduplicate, reduplicative.

reduplicar [ray-doo-ple-car'], *va.* To reduplicate, to double, to redouble; to repeat the same thing.

reedificable [ray-ay-de-fe-cah'-blay], *a.* Capable of being rebuilt.

reedificación [ray-ay-de-fe-cah-the-on'], *f.* Rebuilding.

reedificador, ra [ray-ay-de-fe-cah-dor', rah], *m. & f.* Rebuilder, re-edifier.

reedificar [ray-ay-de-fe-car'], *va.* To rebuild; to restore, to re-edify.

reelección [ray-ay-lec-the-on'], *f.* Re-election.

reelecto, ta [ray-ay-lec'-to, tah], *pp. irr.* Of REELEGIR.

reelegir [ray-ay-lay-heer'], *va.* To re-elect.

reembarcar [ray-em-bar-car'], *va.* To reship, to re-embark. *-vr.* To re-embark, to take shipping again.

reembarco [ray-em-bar'-co], *m.* Reembarkation, reshipment.

reembargar [ray-em-bar-gar'], *va* To seize or to embargo a second time.

reembolsable [ray-em-bol-sah'-blay], *a.* Capable of reimbursing; payable.

reembolsar [ray-em-bol-sar'], *va.* To recover money advanced; to reimburse (persona), to repay (dinero).

reembolso [ray-em-bol'-so], *m.* Recovery, of money advanced.

reempacar [ray-an-pah-car'], *va.* To repack, to pack anew.

reemplazable [ray-em-plah-thah'-blay], *a.* Replaceable.

reemplazar [ray-em-pla-thar'], *va.* To substitute, to replace.

reemplazo [ray-em-plah'-tho], *m.* Replacement, substitution, substitute.

reemplear [ray-em-play-ar'], *va.* To re-employ; to repurchase.

reencargar [ray-en-car-gar'], *va.* To recommend again; to recharge.

reencarnación [ray-en-car-nah-the-on´], *f.* Reincarnation.

reencarnar [ray-en-car-nar'], *vn. & vr.* To reincarnate.

reencomendar [ray-en-co-men-dar´], *To* commend again, to recommend eagerly.

reencuentro [ray-en-coo-en'-tro], *m.* 1. Reencounter, collision a slight combat, a skirmish. 2. Affray.

reenganchar [ray-en-gan-char'], *va.* 1. *(Mech.)* To couple again. 2. *(Mil.)* To re-enlist. *-vr.* To enlist oneself again, to be crimped or drafted.

reenganchamiento, reenganche [ray-en-gan-chah-me-en'-to], *m. (Mil.)* Act of re-enlisting or being crimped or drafted again into the army: money given to a soldier who enlists again.

reengendrador [rar-en-han-drah-dor'], *m.* One who regenerates or restores; regenerator.

reengendramiento [ray-en-hen-drah-me-en´-to], *m.* Regeneration.

reengendrante [ray-en-hen-drahn'-tay], *pa.* Regenerating; one who regenerates or restores.

reengendrar [ray-en-hen-drar'], *va.* 1. To regenerate, to reproduce, to produce anew. 2. To renew, to revive.

reenrumbar [ray-en-room-bar´], *va.* To re-route, to redirect.

reensayar [ray-en-sah-yar'], *va.* To re-examine, to prove again.

reensaye [ray-en-sah'-yay], *m.* Re-examination; second assay.

reensayo [ray-en-sah´-yo], *m.* Second essay, or rehearsal, of a comedy or other thing.

reestrenar [ray-ays-tray-nahr'], *va.* To revive, to put on again.

reestreno [ray-ays-tray-no], *m. (Teat.)* Revival; (Cine) Reissue.

reestructuración [ray-ays-trooc-too-rah-the-on'], *f.* Restructuring, reorganizing.

reestructurar [ray-ays-trooc-too-rahr'], *va.* To restructure.

reexaminación [ray-ek-sah-me-nah-the-on'], *f.* Re-examination.

reexaminar [ray-ek-sah-me-nar'], *va.* To re-examine.

reexportación [ray-ex-por-tah-the-on'], *f. (Com.)* Re-exportation.

reexportar [ray-ex-por-tar'], *va.* To re-export, to export imported commodities.

refacción [ray-fac-the-on'], *f.* 1. Refection, refreshment. 2. Restitution, reparation.

refajo [ray-fah´-ho], *m.* 1. A kind of short petticoat used by mountaineers or highlanders; kilt. 2. An inner petticoat of baize or other strong material.

refalsado, da [ray-fal-sah'-do, dah], *a.* False, deceitful.

refección [ray-fec-the-on'], *f.* Refection, refreshment; reparation.

refectolero [ray-fec-to-lay-ro], *m. V.* REFITOLERO.

refectorio [ray-fec-to´-re-o], *m.* Refectory, the eating-room in convents.

referencia [ray-fay-ren'-the-ah], *f.* Reference, relation to narration. **Con referencia a,** with reference to.

referente [ray-fay-ren´-tay], *pa.* Referring, relating. **Referente a,** relating to, referring to.

referendo [ray-fay-ren'-do], *m.* Referendum.

referéndum [ray-fay-ren-doom], *m.* Referendum.

referible [ray-fay-ree´-blay], *a.* Referrible.

referir [ray-fay-reer'], *va.* 1. To refer (relacionar), to relate, to report. 2. To direct, to mark out a certain course. 3. To mark weights and measures. **Referir que,** to say that... **Todo lo refiere a su teoría favorita,** he refers everything to his favorite theory. *-vr.* 1. To refer, to have relation to; to respect. 2. To refer to some former remark. **Referirse al parecer de otro,** to refer to another's opinion. *(Yo refiero, yo refiera,* from *Referir. V.* ADHERIR.)

refigurar [ray-fe-goo-rar'], *va.* To retrace an image formerly seen or conceived.

refilón (De) [ray-fe-lone', day], *adv.* Obliquely. *V.* DE SOSLAYO. **Mirar a uno de refilón,** to take a sideways glance at.

refina [ray-fee'-nah], *f.* A kind of superfine wool.

refinación [ray-fe-nah-the-on'], *f.* Purification, the act of refining.

refinadera [ray-fe-nah-day'-rah], *f.* Refiner, a long cylindrical stone used to work chocolate.

refinado, da [ray-fe-nah'-do, dah], *a.* Refined: subtle, artful; fine, nice. *-pp.* of REFINAR.

refinador [ray-fe-nah-dor'], *f.* Refiner.

refinadura [ray-fe-nah-doo'-rah], *f.* Refining, purifying liquors or metals; refinement.

refinamiento [ray-fe-nah-me-en'-to], *m.* 1. Refining. 2. Nicety, exactness. 3. *(Neol.)* Exaggeration in drawing distinctions.

refinar [ray-fe-nar'], *va.* 1. To refine (sistema), to purify, to fine. 2. To refine, to make elegant; to bring to perfection; to render more dexterous or useful.

refinería [ray-fe-nay-ree'-ah], *f.* Refinery.

refino, na [ray-fee'-no, nah], *a.* Extra fine, refined.

refirmar [ray-feer-mar'], *va.* To strengthen, to secure, to ratify.

refitolero, ra [ray-fe-to-lay'-ro, rah], *m. & f.* 1. One who has the care of the refectory. 2. *(Coll.)* Busybody, intermeddler. 3. (Cuba) *a.* Obsequious, with affectation.

refitor [ray-fe-tor'], *m.* In bishoprics, the portion of tithe received by the cathedral chapter.

refitorio [ray-fe-to'-re-o], *m.* Refectory. V. REFECTORIO.

reflectar [ray-flec-tar'], *vn. (Opt.)* To reflect, to cast back.

reflector [ray-flec-tor'], *m.* 1. Reflector of light, heat, or sound. 2. Searchlight. 3. Spotlight.

refleja [ray-flay'-hah], *f.* Reflection, observation, remark.

reflejar [ray-flay-har'], *vn.* 1. To reflect the rays of light. 2. To reflect, to meditate upon. V. REFLEXIONAR.

reflejo [ray-flay'-ho], *m.* 1. Reflex. 2. Reflection (imagen), glare. 3. Streaks (de pelo). **Mirar su reflejo en el agua,** to look at one´s reflection in the water.

reflejo, ja [ray-flay-ho], *a.* 1. Reflected, reflective, reflex (movimiento). 2. Meditative.

reflexibilidad [ray-flek-se-be-le-dahd'], *f.* Reflexibility.

reflexible [ray-flek-see'-blay], *a.* Reflective, reflexible.

reflexión [ray-flek-se-on'], *f.* 1. Reflection: applied to the reflection of light. 2. *(Art.)* A reflected or secondary light. 3. Meditation, attentive consideration, reflection, cogitation. **Con reflexión,** on reflection. **Hacer reflexiones,** to meditate.

reflexionar [ray-flek-se-o-nar'], *vn.* To reflect, to meditate, to consider.

reflexivamente [ray-flek-see'-vah-men-tay], *adv.* Reflexively.

reflexivo, va [ray-flek-see'-vo, vah], *a.* Reflexive, reflective (persona): considerate, cogitative. **Verbo reflexivo,** a reflexive verb.

reflorecer [ray-flor-ray-therr'], *vn.* 1. To reflourish, to blossom again. 2. To return to former splendor. *(Yo reflorezco, yo reflorezca,* from *Reflorecer.* V. CONOCER.)

refluente [ray-floo-en'-tay], *pa. & a.* Refluent; flowing back.

refluir [ray-floo-eer'], *vn.* To flow back, to reflow.

reflujo [ray-floo'-ho], *m.* Reflux, ebb. **Reflujo de la marea,** *(Naut.)* ebb or ebb-tide.

refocilación [ray-fo-the-lah-the-on'], *f.* Reinvigoration, restoration of strength by refreshment: refection.

refocilar [ray-fo-the-lar'], *va.* To strengthen, to revive, to reinvigorate, to refect, to amuse (divertir), to cheer up (alegrar). *-vr.* 1. To be strengthened or revived. 2. To cheer up no end (alegrarse).

refocilo [ray-fo-thee'-lo], *m.* Reinvigoration, pleasure.

reforestación [ray-fo-res-ah-the-on'], *f.* Reforestation.

reforjar [ray-for-har'], *va.* To reforge, to execute again.

reforma [ray-for'-mah], *f.* 1. Reform, correction, amendment. 2. Dismissal from an office or employment. 3. Reformation, the act of reforming. 4. Reformation, change from worse to better reform. 5. Renovated discipline in religious houses.

reformable [ray-for-mah'-blay], *a.* Reformable.

reformación [ray-for-mah-the-on'], *f.* Reformation, reform. V. REFORMA.

reformado [ray-for-mah'-do], *m.* A reformed officer, an officer on halfpay; disbanded. *-pp.* of REFORMAR.

reformador, ra [ray-for-mah-dor', rah], *m. & f.* Reformer, corrector, mender.

reformar [ray-for-mar'], *va.* 1. To reform, to restore a thing to its primitive form (modificar). 2. To reform, to correct, to mend. 3. To lessen, to reduce, to diminish. 4. To dispossess of a place or employment, to discharge, to dismiss. 5. To clear up, to explain: speaking of the meaning of words or phrases. *-vr.* 1. To reform, to change from worse to better, to mend, to have one's manners reformed. 2. To use prudence and moderation in speech and conduct.

reformativo, va [ray-for-mah-tee'-vo, vah], *a.* That which reforms.

reformatorio, ria [ray-for-mah-to'-re-ah], *a.* Corrective. *-m.* House of correction, reformatory.

reformista [ray-for-mees'-tah], *com.* Reformer, reformist.

reforzada [ray-for-thah'-dah], *f.* 1. Sort of narrow tape, list, or fillet. 2. A small sausage. 3. The bass string of a stringed instrument.

reforzado, da [ray-for-thah'-do, dah], *a. & pp.* of REFORZAR. 1. Strengthened. 2. Applied to a re-enforced gun, which has more metal than usual at the breech, to make it stronger.

reforzado [ray-for-thah'-do], *m.* V. REFORZADA for a kind of tape.

reforzamiento [ray-for-thah-me-ayn-to], *m.* Reinforcement.

reforzar [ray-for-thar'], *va.* To strengthen, to fortify: to animate. *-vr.* To be strengthened and recovered. *(Yo refuerzo, yo refuerce,* from *Reforzar.* V. ACORDAR.)

refoseto [ray-fo-say'-to], *m. (Mil.)* Cuvette in a fosse.

refracción [ray-frac-the-on'], *f.* Refraction, as of light.

refractar [ray-frac-tar'], *va.* To refract, to change the direction of a ray of light. *-vr.* To be refracted.

refractario, ria [ray-frac-tah'-re-o, ah], *a.* 1. Refractory, disobedient, rebellious, obstinate. 2. Not fulfilling one's promise. 3. Refractory, resisting fusion.

refracto, ta [ray-frahc'-to, tah], *a.* Refracted (rayos de luz).

refrán [ray-frahn'], *m.* Proverb, idiom, saying of common use. **Tener refranes,** *(Coll.)* to be versed in tricks and villainies.

refranero [ray-frah-nay'-ro], *m.* Collection of proverbs.

refrangibilidad [ray-fran-he-be-le-dahd'], *f.* Refrangibility, refrangibleness.

refrangible [ray-fran-hee'-blay], *a.* Refrangible.

refregadura [ray-fray-gah-doo-rah], *f.* V. REFREGÓN.

refregamiento [ray-fray-gah-me-en'-to], *m.* Rubbing, friction.

refregar [ray-fray-gar'], *va.* 1. To rub one thing against another (frotar), to fray. 2. *(Coll.)* To upbraid, to censure, to reprove, to be stained all over.

refregón [ray-fray-gone'], *m.* 1. Rubbing, friction. 2. Mark (senal) made or left by rubbing. 3. A brief conversation.

refreír [ray-fray-eer'], *va.* To fry well or excessively.

refrenamiento, *m.* **refrenación,** *f.* [ray-fray-nah-me-en'-to], *f.* Curb, the act of curbing or refraining; refrenation.

refrenar [ray-fray-nar'], *va.* 1. To curb a horse with a bridle (caballo). 2. To refrain, to coerce, to hold back, to rein.

refrendación [ray-fren-dah-the-on'], *f.* Legalizing by subscription

refrendar [ray-fren-dar'], *va.* 1. To legalize a public act, to countersign (firmar); to mark weights, etc. 2. To vise passports and countersign them. 3. *(Coll.)* To repeat what had been done (repetir).

refrendario [ray-fren-dah'-re-o], *m.* Officer appointed to countersign edicts, ordinances, or other public acts.

refrendata [ray-fren-dah'-tah], *f.* Counter-signature, the act of countersigning; countersign.

refrescador, ra [ray-fres-cah-dor', rah], *a.* Refreshing, refrigerating.

refrescadura [ray-fres-cah-doo'-rah], *f.* Refreshing (act and effect).

refrescamiento [ray-fres-cah-me-ayn-to], *m.* V. REFRESCO.

refrescante

refrescante [ray-fres-cahn'-tay], *pa.* Cooling, refreshing, refreshful.

refrescar [ray-fres-car'], *va.* 1. To refresh, to moderate the heat of anything, to cool (enfriar), to refrigerate. 2. To drink iced drinks. 3. To renew, to refresh; to awaken feeling. 4. To recover strength and vigor. 5. To rest after fatigue. *-vn.* To cool, to take the air. Used frequently also as a reflexive verb. *-vr.* 1. *-vn.* 2. *(And. Colombia)* To have a tea.

refrescativo, va [ray-fres-cah-tee´-vo, vah], *a.* Refrigerative, refreshing.

refresco [ray-fres'-co], *m.* 1. Refreshment: moderate food for gathering strength. 2. A cold beverage. 3. Entertainment of cool beverages, sweetmeats, and chocolate. **De refresco**, anew, once more.

refriega [ray-fre-ay´-gah], *f.* Affray, skirmish, encounter, scuffle, strife, fray.

refrigeración [ray-fre-hay-rah-the-on´], *f.* Refrigeration, cooling, refrigerating.

refrigerador [ray-fre-hay-rah-dor´], *m.* Refrigerator.

refrigerante [ray-fre-hay-rahn'-tay], *a.* Refrigerant, cooling, refrigerative. *-m.* 1. *(Chem.)* Refrigerator, cooling chamber. 2. *(Med.)* Cooler.

refrigerar [ray-fre-hay-rar´], *va.* To cool, to refresh, to comfort, to refrigerate.

refrigerativo, va [ray-fre-hay-rah-tee'-vo vah], *a.* Refrigerative, cooling, refrigerant.

refrigeratorio [ray-fre-hay-rah-to´-re-o], *m.* Refrigerator, part of a still employed to cool the condensing vapors.

refrigerio [ray-fre-hay´-re-o], *m.* 1. Refrigeration, comfort experienced through coolness. 2. Refreshment, refection, a light repast. 3. Consolation, comfort.

refringente [ray-frin-hen´-tay], *pa. & a.* Refracting; refractivo.

refringir [ray-frin-heer'], *va.* To refract, break, or intercept the rays of light. Also *vr.*

refrito [ray-free'-to], *pp. irr.* of REFREÍR.

refrotar [ray-fro-tar´], *va.* To rub.

refuelle [ray-foo-ayl´-lyay], *m.* A kind of net for catching fish.

refuerzo [ray-foo-err´-tho], *m.* 1. Reinforcement, increase of strength. 2. Backing, bracing, strengthening piece; welt of a shoe. 3. Succor, help, aid.

refugiado, da [ray-foo-he-ah'-do, dah], *a. & pp.* of REFUGIAR. Sheltered. It has been used as a substantive for a refugee or emigrant.

refugiar [ray-foo-he-ar'], *va.* To shelter, to refuge, to afford protection. *-vr.* To take refuge, to fly for shelter.

refugio [ray-foo'-he-o], *m.* 1. Refuge, retreat, shelter, asylum, safe harbor. 2. In Madrid, a brotherhood formed to alleviate the suffering of the poor. **Refugio antiaéreo**, bomb shelter. **Refugio de montaña**, mountain hut.

refulgencia [ray-fool-hen´-the-ah], *f.* Refulgence, splendor.

refulgente [ray-fool-hen'-tay], *a.* Refulgent.

refulgir [ray-fool-heer'], *vn.* To shine with splendor, to be resplendent.

refundición [ray-foon-de-the-on'], *f.* The act of casting metals anew.

refundir [ray-foon-deer'], *va.* 1. To melt or cast metals anew. 2. To contain, to include. 3. *(And. CAm. Mex.)* To lose (perder). 4. *(Cono Sur)* To ruin (arruinar). *-vn.* To redound. **Refundir infamia**, to defame, to dishonor.

refunfuñador, ra [ray-foon-foo-nyah-dor', rah], *m. & f.* Grumbler, growler, snarler.

refunfuñadura [ray-foon-foo-nyah-doo´-rah], *f.* Growling, grumbling. *V.* REFUNFUÑO.

refunfuñar [ray-foon-foo-nyar´], *va.* To snarl, to growl (gruñir), to snort; to grumble (quejarse), to mutter.

refunfuño [ray-foon-foo'-nyo], *m.* Grumbling, murmuring, growl, short.

refutación [ray-foo-tah-the-on´], *f.* Refutation, confutation.

refutable [ray-foo-tah´-blay], *a.* Refutable.

refutador, ra [ray-foo-ta-dor´, rah], *m. & f.* Refuter.

refutar [ray-foo-tar´], *va.* To refute, to confute, to convict; to control. *V.* REHUSAR.

refutatorio, ria [ray-foo-tah-too´-re-o, ah], *a.* That which refutes.

regadera [ray-gah-day'-rah], *f.* 1. Shower. 3. Canal for irrigation.

regadío [ray-gah-dee'-o], *m.* Irrigated fund.

regadío, ía [ray-gah-dee'-o], *a.* Irrigated.

regadizo, za [ray-gah-de'-tho, thah], *a.* That which can be irrigated or watered.

regador [ray-gah-dor´], *m.* 1. One who waters or irrigates. 2. Instrument used by comb-makers.

regadura [ray-gah-doo'-rah], *f.* Irrigation.

regaifa [ray-gah'-e-fah], *f.* A stone in an oil-mill with a grooved channel along which the oil runs into the vat.

regajal, regajo [ray-gah-hahl', ray-gah'-ho], *m.* Puddle or pool of stagnant water; rill which makes it.

regala [ray-gah'-lah], *f. (Naut.)* Gunwale or gunnel.

ragalada [ray-ga-lah'-dah], *f.* 1. King's stables. 2. The number of horses belonging to the king's stables.

regaladamente [ray-gah-lah-dah-men-tay], *adv.* Delicately, pleasantly, daintily.

regalado, da [ray-gah-lah'-do, dah], *a.* Delicate (delicado), dainty, suave, lickerish. *-pp.* of REGALAR. **Me lo dio medio regalado**, he gave it to me for a song.

regalador, ra [ray-gah-lah-dor', rah], *m. & f.* 1. One fond of entertaining his friends; a person of a generous disposition. 2. Sort of stick used by wing-bag makers for cleaning the skins.

regalar [ray-gah-lar'], *va.* 1. To present, to favor with a gift. 2 To regale, to refresh, to entertain. 3. To caress, to cajole, to make much of. 4. To regale, to gratify, to make merry, to delight, to cherish. **Regalar algo a uno**, to give somebody something. *-vr.* 1. To regale, to feast; to fare sumptuously. 2. To entertain oneself, to take pleasure.

regalejo [ray-gah-lay'-ho], *m. dim.* A small gift.

regalía [ray-gah-lee'-ah], *f.* 1. The rights or prerogatives of the crown (del rey). 2. Privilege (privilegio), exemption. 3. *(And. CAm. Carib.)* Gift (regalo). 4. *(LAm.)* Royalty (derechos); advance payment (avance). *-pl.* Perquisites.

regalillo [ray-gah-leel'-lyo], *m.* 1. *(dim.)* A small present. 2. Muff, for the hands.

regaliolo [ray-gah-le-o'-lo], *m. (Orn.)* Golden-crested wren.

regalito [ray-gah-lee'-to], *m. dim.* A small present.

regaliz [ray-gah-leeth'], *m. (Bot.)* Licorice.

regalo [ray-gah'-lo], *m.* 1. Present, gift, largess. 2. Pleasure (placer), gratification. 3. Dainty, something nice and delicate; regalement. 4. Convenience, repose, comfort, luxury (comodidad). 5. Affliction dispensed by Providence. **Regalo de boda**, wedding present.

regalón, na [ray-gah-lone', nah], *a.* 1. Delicate, fond of convenience and ease. 2. Spoiled, pampered (niños). 3. *(LAm.)* **Es el regalón de su padre**, he´s the apple of his father´s eyes.

regantío, ía [ray-gan-tee'-o, ah], *a.* Applied to the land or its fruits, that are usually watered. *V.* REGADÍO.

reagañada [ray-gah-nyah'-dah], *f.* A kind of delicate cake.

regañado, da [ray-gah-nyah'-do, dah], *a.* 1. Given reluctantly, or with repugnance. 2. Applied to a kind of plum or bread which splits. 3. Frowning. *-pp.* of REGANAR.

regañador, ra [ray-gah-nyah-dor', rah], *m. & f.* Grumbler.

regañamiento [ray-gah-nyah-me-en'-to], *m.* Grumbling, snarling, growl.

regañar [ray-gah-nyar'], *vn.* 1. To snarl (perro), to growl, to murmur, to grumble (persona), to claw off. 2. To be peevish, to quarrel (2 personas). 3. To crack or open like ripe fruit. 4. To dispute familiarly at home, to have domestic broils. *-va.* *(Coll.)* To reprehend, to chide. **A regañadientes**, reluctantly, with reluctance.

regañir [ray-gah-nyeer'], *vn.* To yelp, to howl repeatedly.

regaño [ray-gah'-nyo], *m.* 1. A gesture of annoyance; sternness of look. 2. Threat, warning. 3. Scorched bread. 4. *(Coll.)* Reprimand.

regañón, na [ray-gah-nyone', nah], *a.* 1. Snarling, growling; a grumbler, murmurer, snarler. 2. Troublesome: generally applied to the north-east wind.

regar [ray-gar'], *va.* 1. To water (planta), to irrigate (tierra). 2. To sprinkle with water: to rain heavily. 3. To wash or water countries (ríos, nubes). 4. *(Fig.)* To sprinkle (esparcir). 5. *(And. CAm.)* To spill (derramar). 6. *(Carib.)* To hit (pegar). **Una costa regada por un mar tranquilo,** a coast washed by a calm sea. *-vn.* 1. *(Carib.)* To joke (bromear). 2. *(Carib.)* To act rashly (actuar sin pensar).

regata [ray-gah'-tah], *f.* 1. A small channel or conduit, through which water is conveyed to gardens. 2. Regatta, a race of boats or light craft.

regatar [ray-gah-tar'], *va. (Naut.)* To put a ferrule to a boat-hook. *-vn. V.* REGATEAR.

regate [ray-gah'-tay], *m.* 1. A quick motion of the body to avoid a blow. 2. Escape, evasion.

regatear [ray-gah-tay-ar'], *va.* 1. To haggle (objeto), to be tedious in a bargain. 2. To retail provisions bought by wholesale. 3. To refuse or decline the execution of a thing (negar); to avoid. **Aquí regatean el vino,** they are mean with their wine here. *-vn.* 1. To wriggle, to move sidewise; to use evasions. 2. *(Naut.)* To rival in sailing.

regateo [ray-gah-tay'-o], *m.* The act of haggling or bartering.

regatería [ray-gah-tay-ree'-ah], *f.* Huckste´s shop. *V.* REGATONERÍA.

regatero, ra [ray-gah-tay´-ro, rah], *a. & m. & f.* Haggling; hawker. *V.* REGATÓN.

regatista [ray-gah-tees'-tah], *m & f.* Competitor (sailing).

regato [ray-gah'-to], *m.* A small rivulet.

regatón, na [ray-gah-tone', nah], *m. & f.* 1. Huckster, regrater. 2. Haggler. 3. Socket, ferrule.*-a.* Retailing.

regatonear [ray-gah-to-nay-ar'], *vn.* To huckster, to buy by wholesale and sell by retail.

regatonería [ray-gah-to-nay-ree'-ah], *f.* 1. Sale by retail. 2. Huckster's shop.

regazar [ray-gah-thar'], *pa.* To tuck up. *V.* ARREGAZAR.

regazo [ray-gah'-tho], *m.* 1. Lap of a woman; part of the dress. 2. Lap, part of the body from the waist to the knees. 3. Fond and endearing reception.

regencia [ray-hen'-the-ah], *f.* 1. Regency, ruling or governing. 2. Regency, administration of a regent; vicarious govermnent. 3. Regency, the district governed by a regent. 4. Regency, those collectively to whom vicarious regality is entrusted. 5. Regentship.

regeneración [ray-hay-nay-rah-the-on'], *f.* 1. Regeneration. 2. *(Surg.)* Granulation in a wound.

regenerado, da [ray-hay-nay-rah'-do, dah], *a. & pp.* of REGENERAR. Regenerate, regenerated.

regenerar [ray-hay-nay-rar'], *va.* To regenerate, to reproduce.

regenerativo, va [ray-hay-nay-rah-tee'-vo, vah], *a.* That which regenerates.

regenta [ray-hen'-tah], *f.* Wife of a regent, regentess.

regentar [ray-hen-tar'], *va.* To rule; to govern; to exercise any business affecting superiority.

regente [ray-hen'-tay], *m.* 1. Regent, one invested with vicarious royalty (príncipe). 2. Regent, the president of a court of justice. 3. Master of a school in religious orders. 4. In Spanish universities, some supernumerary professors. 5. Manager, director: in printing-office. *-pa.* Ruling.

regentear [ray-hen-tay-ar'], *va.* 1. To domineer, to rule as master. 2. To be a pedant.

regera [ray-hay´-rah], *f. (Naut.)* Sternfast, stern-moorings.

regiamente [ray'-he-ah-men-tay], *adv.* Royally, in a kingly manner.

regibado, da [ray-he-bah'-do, dah], *a.* Hump-backed, crook-backed, gibbous.

regicida [ray-he-thee'-dah], *com. & a.* Regicide, murderer of a king.

regicidio [ray-he-thee'-de-o], *m.* Murder of a king, regicide.

regidor [ray-he-dor'], *m.* 1. Alderman, a magistrate of a city. 2. Governor, director, prefect.*-a. V.* REGITIVO.

regidora [ray-he-do'-rah], *f.* An alderman's or governor's wife.

regidoría, regiduría [ray-he-do-ree'-ah], *f.* Governorship; the place, employment, or office of an alderman.

regilera [ray-he-lay'-rah], *f.* Windmill of paper, a child's plaything.

régimen [ray'-he-men], *m.* 1. Regimen, management, rule (regla), conduct, system. 2. *(Gram.)* Government of parts of speech. 3. *(Med.)* Regimen, a prescribed manner of living. **Bajo el régimen del dictador,** under the dictator´s régime. **Estar a régimen,** to be on a diet. **Prisión de régimen abierto,** open prison.

regimentar [ray-he-men-tar'], *va.* To organize a regiment.

regimiento [ray-he-me-en´-to], *m.* 1. Administration, government. 2. Magistracy of a city; office or employment of an alderman or a city magistrate; municipality. 3. Regiment of soldiers; a corps.

regio, gia [ray'-he-o, ah], *a.* 1. Royal, regal, kingly. 2. Stately, sumptuous, magnificent. **Agua regia,** aqua regia, nitro-hydrochloric acid.

regiomontano, na [ray-he-o-mon-tah'-no, nah], *a. & m. & f.* Name applied to persons and things from Monterrey, Mexico.

región [ray-he-on'], *f.* 1. Region, kingdom, tract of land, ground. 2. Space occupied by an element. 3. Region, a cavity of the body.

regional [ray-he-o-nahl'], *a.* 1. Belonging to a region or district. 2. *(Mex.)* Peculiar to the country, native.

regionalismo [ray-he-o-nah-lees'-mo], *m.* 1. Regionalism, localism. 2. Local idiom.

regir [ray-heer'], *va.* 1. To rule (país), to govern, to direct. 2. To rule, to conduct, to manage (empresa), to lead, to command. 3. To govern as verbs or prepositions. 4. To have the bowels in good order. **Los factores que rigen los cambios de mercado,** the factors which govern changes in the market. *-vn.* 1. *(Naut.)* To obey the helm. 2. To be in force. **Regirse por,** to be ruled by.

registrado, da [ray-his-trah'-do, dah], *a.* Registered. *-pp.* of REGISTRAR.

registrador [ray-his-trah-dor'], *m.* 1. Register, registrar, recorder (persona), master or clerk of records. 2. Searcher. 3. Toll gatherer, who enters all imported goods in the toll-register. 4. Controller.

registrador, ra [ray-his-trah-dor', rah], *a.* Registering, recording. **Registradora or Caja registradora,** cash register.

registrar [ray-his-trar'], *va.* 1. To inspect, to search (equipaje, lugar, persona). 2. To investigate, to examine, to control. 3. To register (anotar), to record. 4. To put slips of paper between the leaves of a book. *-vr.* To be registered or matriculated. **No se ha registrado nunca nada parecido,** nothing of the kind has ever been recorded.

registro [ray-hees'-tro], *m.* 1. The act of searching or examining. 2. Place or spot where anything can be surveyed. 3. Entry of goods or merchandise (entrada). 4. Enrolling office, where registers or records are kept; census. *V.* PROTOCOLO. 5. Register (libro), in which entries are made; a certificate of entry. 6. Register of a stove or grate. 7. *(Print.)* Catchword; register or correspondence of the pages. 8. Prier, one who inquires too closely. 9. Regulator of a watch or clock. 10. Mark put in breviaries or missals at certain places. 11. Register in an organ or harpsichord. 12. Direction to book-binders at the end of a volume. 13. Search (búsqueda). **Registro de defunciones,** register of deaths. **Registro mercantil,** business register. **Firmar el registro,** to sign the register. 14. Bookmark (de libro). 15. *(And. Cono Sur)* Wholesale textiles store (tienda). 16. *(Comput.)* Record.

regitivo, va [ray-he-tee´-vo, vah], *a.* Ruling, governing.

regizgar [ray-heeth-gar'], *vn. (Prov.)* To shudder with cold.

regla [ray'-glah], *f.* 1. Rule (instrumento), ruler, for drawing a straight line; rule in arithmetic, 2. Rule of religious orders. 3. Rule, maxim, precept; law, statute, precept, canon, fundamental principle. 4. Instrument by which paper is ruled for musical compositions. 5. Manner of making or casting up accounts. 6. Moderation (moderación), measure, order, rule, management. 7. Order of nature. 8. Menstruation. **A regla**, regularly, prudently. **Regla fija**, standard. **Reglas del juego**, rules of the game. **Todo está en regla**, everything is in order.

regladamente [ray-glah'-dah-men-tay], *adv.* Regularly, orderly.

reglado, da [ray-glah'-do, dah], *a.* Regulated, temperate. *-pp.* of REGLAR.

reglamentación [ray-glah-men-tah-the-on'], *f.* 1. Regulation (acto). 2. Rules (reglas).

reglamentar [ray-glah-men-tahr'], *va.* To regulate; to make rules for; to establish regulations for.

reglamentario [ray-glah-men-tah-re-o], *a.* Regulation, obligatory, set; statutory (estatuario); proper (apropiado), due. **En el traje reglamentario**, in the regulation dress.

reglamento [ray-glah-men'-to], *m.* Regulation (reglas), order, ordinance, by-law. **Reglamento de aduana**, customs regulations.

reglar [ray-glar'], *a.* Regular. **Puerta reglar**, the regular door for entering nunneries.

reglar [ray-glar'], *va.* 1. To rule (línea, papel), to draw lines with a rule. 2. To rule, to regulate, to measure. *-vr.* To mend, to reform. **Reglarse a lo justo**, to be right.

reglero [ray-glay'-ro], *m.* Ruler, for drawing lines.

regleta [ray-glay'-tah], *f.* *(Print.)* Lead, piece of metal put between lines of types. Reglet.

reglón [ray-glone'], *m.* Level, used by masons.

regnícola [reg-nee'-co-lah], *a. & m. & f.* Native of a kingdom.

regocijadamente [ray-go-the-hah'-dah-men-tay], *adv.* Merrily, joyfully.

regocijado, da [ray-go-the-hah'-do, dah], *a.* Merry, joyful, rejoicing, festive. *-pp.* of REGOCIJAR.

regocijador, ra [ray-go-the-hah-dor', rah], *m. & f.* Rejoicer, cheerer, gladder.

regocijar [ray-go-the-har'], *va.* To gladden, to cheer, to delight, to exult, to rejoice, to exhilarate. **La noticia regocijó a la familia**, the news delighted the family. *-vr.* To rejoice (alegrarse), to be merry (pasarlo bien).

regocijo [ray-go-thee'-ho], *m.* 1. Joy (alegría), pleasure, satisfaction, mirth, merriment, hilarity, exhilaration. 2. Rejoicing, demonstration of joy. 3. Bull-feast in the morning.

regodearse [ray-go-day-ar'-say], *vr.* *(Coll.)* 1. To be merry, to rejoice; to be delighted. 2. To dally, to trifle, to play the fool. 3. To assume an air of reluctance, to cloak some ardent desire. 4. To joke, to jest. 5. *(LAm.)* To be fussy (ser exigente).

regodeo [ray-go-day'-o], *m.* 1. Joy, mirth, merriment. 2. A feigned refusal of a thing earnestly desired. 3. Joke, jest, diversion, dalliance.

regojo [ray-go'-ho], *m.* 1. Crumb or piece of bread left on the table after meals. 2. A puny boy.

regojuelo [ray-go-hoo-ay'-lo], *(dim.)* A very small morsel of bread.

regolar [ray-go-lar'], *m.* *(Prov.)* Scholar, student.

rogoldano, na [ray-gol-dah'-no, nah], *a.* Applied to the wild chestnut.

regoldar [ray-gol-dar'], *vn.* 1. To belch, to cruet. 2. To boast, to brag.

regolfar [ray-gol-far'], *va. & vr.* To flow back.

regolfo [ray-gol'-fo], *m.* 1. Reflux, the act of flowing back against the current; whirlpool. 2. Gulf, bay; an arm of the sea.

regomello [ray-go-mayl'-lyo], *m.* *(Prov.)* Remorse, compunction.

regona [ray-go'-nah], *f.* Large canal for irrigating lands.

regordete, ta [ray-gor-day'-tay, tah], *a.* Chubby (persona), plump, short and stout.

regostarse [ray-gos-tar'-say], *vr.* To delight, to take pleasure, to dally.

regosto [ray-gos'-to], *m.* Delight, pleasure.

regraciación [ray-grah-the-ah-the-on'], *f.* Act of thanking, gratitude.

regraciar [ray-grah-the-ar'], *va.* To testify gratitude, to thank.

regresar [ray-gray-sar'], *vn.* 1. To return to a place, to regress. 2. To retain or recover possession of an ecclesiastical benefice. *-va.* To resign a benefice in favor of another.

regresión [ray-gray-se-on'], *f.* Regression, return, regress.

regreso [ray-gray'-so], *m.* 1. Return, regression, regress. 2. Reversion, devolution. 3. The act of resigning a benefice in favor of another. 4. The act of retaking possession of a benefice or property resigned or ceded.

regruñir [ray-groo-nyeer'], *vn.* To snarl, to growl.

reguardarse [ray-goo-ar-dar'-say], *vr.* To take care of oneself.

regüeldo [ray-goo-el'-do], *m.* 1. Eructation, belch. 2. Boast, brag.

reguera [ray-gay'-rah], *f.* 1. Canal for watering lands or plank. 2. Stern of a ship or tail of a greyhound.

reguero [ray-gay'-ro], *m.* 1. A small rivulet. 2. Mark, spot left from any liquid being spilt (señal). 3. *V.* REGUERA.

reguerón [ray-gay-rone'], *m.* The principal canal of irrigation.

reguilete [ray-gee-lay'-tay], *m. V.* REHILETE.

regulable [ray-goo-lah-blay], *a.* Adjustable.

regulación [ray-goo-lah-the-on'], *f.* Regulation, adjustment; comparison, computation. **Regulación del tráfico**, traffic control.

regulado, da [ray-goo-lah'-do, dah], *a. & pp.* of REGULAR. Regulated; orderly, regular.

regulador, ra [ray-goo-lah-dor', rah], *m. & f.* 1. Regulator, governor, as of a machine, particularly a steam engine. 2. A standard clock for the regulation of others.

regulador de humedad [ray-goo-lah-dor' day oo-may-dahd'], *m.* *(Mech.)* Humidistat.

regular [ray-goo-lar'], *pa.* To regulate, to adjust; to put in order, to methodize, to compare.*-a.* 1. Regular, orderly. 2. Moderate sober, formal. 3. Common, ordinary, frequent; likely, probable, convenient. 4. Regular: applied to a religious order. **Por lo regular**, commonly. **Tiene un latido regular**, it has a regular beat.

regular [ray-goo-lar'], *m.* Regular, in the Catholic church; person who belongs to a religious order.

regularidad [ray-goo-lah-re-dahd'], *f.* 1. Regularity, order, orderliness. 2. Common usage, custom. 3. Exact discipline.

regularizar [ray-goo-lah-re-thar'], *va.* To systemize, to subject to rules.

regularmente [ray-goo-lahr'-men-tay], *adv.* Orderly in manner: ordinarily, generally, naturally.

régulo [ray'-goo-lo], *m.* 1. Chief of a petty state. 2. Basilisk. 3. *(Chem.)* Regulus, the purest part of metals. 4. *(Ast.)* Regulus, a star of the first magnitude in the constellation Leo. 5. *(Orn.)* Golden-crested kinglet. *V.* ABADEJO.

regurgitación [ray-goor-ge-tah-the-on'], *f.* *(Med.)* Regurgitation.

regurgitar [ray-goor-he-tar'], *vn.* To regurgitate, to overflow.

rehabilitación [ray-ah-be-le-tah-the-on'], *f.* Rehabilitation.

rehabilitar [ray-ah-be-le-tar'], *va.* 1. To rehabilitate; to reinstate one in his rights and privileges. 2. To refit, to repair, to restore.

rehabituarse [ray-ah-be-too-ar'-say], *vr.* To return to vicious habits.

rehacer [ray-ah-therr'], *va.* 1. To mend, to repair, to make again. 2. To add new strength and vigor. 3. To increase the weight or quantity of something. *-vr.* 1. To regain strength and vigor (reponerse). 2. *(Mil.)* To rally, to form anew; to resume the former position. *(Yo rehago, yo rehaga, yo rehice, from Rehacer. V. HACER.)*

rehacimiento [ray-ah-the-me-en'-to], *m.* Renovation, renewal; recuperation.

rehacio, cia [ray-ah'-the-o, ah], *a.* Obstinate, stubborn.

reharto, ta [ray-ar'-to, tah], *pp. irr.* of REHARTAR. Supersaturated.

rehartar [ray-ar-tar'], *va.* To satiate again.

rehecho, cha [ray-ay'-cho, chah], *a. & pp. irr.* of REHACER. 1. Renewed, renovated; done over again. 2. Squat, broad shouldered.

rehelear [ray-hay-lay-ar'], *vn.* To be bitter. Note.—The h is aspirated in this word. *(Acad.)*

reheleo [ay-hay-lay'-o], *m.* Bitterness.

rehén [ray-en'], *m.* Hostage: generally used in the plural.

rehenchimiento [ray-en-che-me-en'-to], *m.* Act of stuffing or refilling.

rehenchir [ray-en´-cheer´], *va.* To fill again, to stuff anew.

rehendija, rehendrija [ray-en-dee'-hah], *f.* Crevice, cleft.

reherimiento [ray-ay-re-me-en'-to], *m.* Repulsion.

reherir [ray-ay-reer'], *va.* To repel, to repulse.

reherrar [ray-er-rar'], *va.* To reshoe a horse.

rehenrir [ray-en-reer'], *vn.* 1. To boil again. 2. To be inflamed with love, to be blinded by passion. -*vr.* To ferment, to grow sour.

rehiladillo [ray-e-lah-deel'-lyo], *m.* Ribbon. V. HILADILLO.

rehilandera [ray-e-lan-day'-rah], *f.* Wind-mill made of paper. V. REGILERA.

rehilar [ray-e-lar'], *va.* To twist or contract too much. -*vn.* 1. To stagger, to reel. 2. To whiz, to whir, as a missile in flight.

rehilete, rehilero [ray-e-lay'-tay], *m.* 1. A kind of shuttlecock played with battledores. 2. A small arrow bearded with paper or feathers. 3. A malicious saying, smart speech.

rehilo [ray-ee'-lo], *m.* Shaking, shivering.

rehinchimiento [ray-in-che-me-en´-to], *m.* The act of filling or stuffing again.

rehogar [ray-o-gar'], *va.* To dress meat with a slow fire, basting it with butter or oil.

rehollar [ray-ol-lyar'], *va.* **To trample under foot, to tread upon.** V. PISOTEAR.

rehoya [ray-o'-yah], *f.* V. REHOYO.

rehoyar [ray-o-yar'], *va.* To dig holes again for planting trees.

rehoyo [ray-o'-yo], *m.* A deep hole or pit.

rehuída [ray-oo-ee'-dah], *f.* A second flight, running away again; rapid turn of hunted game.

rehuir [ray-oo-eer'], *vn.* 1. To withdraw, to retire. 2. To return to the place where it was roused. 3. To reject, to condemn. -*va.* To deny or reduce.

rehumedecer [ray-oo-may-day-therr'], *va. & vr.* To dampen well.

rehundido [ray-oon-dee'-do], *m. (Arch.)* Part which serves as a seat for a projection. V. VACIADO.

rehundir [ray-oon-deer'], *va.* 1. To sink. 2. To melt metals. 3. To waste, to dissipate, to lavish. -*vn.* To increase perceptibly.

rehurtado, da [ray-oor-tah'-do, dah], *a.* 1. Making windings to make dogs lose the scent (caza). 2. Artfully evasive, delusive, furtive. -*pp.* of REHURTARSE.

rehurtar [ray-oor-tar'], *va.* To steal or cheat again. -*vr.* To take a different route whence it rose (caza).

rehurto [ray-oor'-to], *m.* A movement of the body to avoid impending danger; a shrug.

rehusar [ray-oo-sar'], *va.* To refuse, to decline, to deny what is solicited or required, to abnegate.

reidero [ray-e-day'-ro], *m.* Immoderate laughter.-*a.* Ready to laugh.

reidor, ra [ray-e-dor', rah], *m. & f.* Laugher.

reimpresión [ray-im-pray-se-on'], *f.* . Reimpression of a book, etc., reprint. 2. Number of copies reprinted at once.

reimpreso, sa [ray-im-pray'-so, sah], *pp. irr.* of REIMPRIMIR.

reimprimir [ray-im-pre-meer'], *va.* To reprint, to print a new edition.

reina [ray'-e-nah], *f.* 1. Queen. 2. *(Coll.)* Any woman admired and loved. 3. Queen-bee. 4. Queen at chess. **Reina mora,** *V.* INFERNÁCULO. **Reina de la fiesta,** carnival queen.

reinado [ray-e-nah'-do], *m.* Reign, time of a sovereign's rule.

reinante [ray-nahn'-tay], *pa.* Reigning, excelling; prevailing.

reinar [rar-e-nar'], *va.* 1. To reign, to govern, to command. 2. To reign (prevalecer), to prevail, to predominate. 3. To reign, to obtain power or dominion. **Reina una confusión total,** total confusion reigns.

reincidencia [ray-in-the-den'-the-ah], *f.* Backsliding, falling in again, relapse into vice or error.

reincidente [ray-in-the-den'-tay], *pa.* Relapsing, falling away.

reincidir [ray-in-the-deer'], *m.* To relapse back into vice or error; to backslide.

reincorporación [ray-in-cor-po-rah-the-on´], *f.* Reincorporation, renewing.

reincorporar [ray-in-cor-po-rar'], *va.* To re-incorporate a second time. -*vr.* To re-embody.

reino [ray'-e-no], *m.* 1. Kingdom, reign, dominion of a king. 2. Kingdom, name given to districts which, although only a part of the territories subject to a monarch, had before a king. 3. Kingdom, a class or order of beings, as vegetable or animal kingdom. 4. Kingdom of heaven.

reinserción [ray-en-ser-the-on'], *f.* **Reinserción social,** social rehabilitation.

reintegración [ray-in-tay-grah-the-on'], *f.* Reintegration or redintegration; the act of restoring

reintegrar [ray-in-tay-grar'], *va.* 1. To reintegrate (completar), to restore. 2. To be reinstated or restored. 3. To pay back (suma). 4. To attach a fiscal stamp to (documento). **Reintegrar una cantidad,** to refund. -*vr.* To return to.

reintegro [ray-in-tay´-gro], *m.* 1. Reimbursement, refund, repayment. 2. Return of one's stake (lotería).

reír [ray-eer'], *vn.* 1. To laugh; to smile. **Reír a carcajadas,** to laugh excessively and loudly. 2. To laugh at or sneer. 3. *(Med.)* To have convulsions resembling laughter. 4. To smile: applied to agreeable landscapes, arbors, lakes, and meads. **Sólo para hacer reír,** just to make people laugh. -*vr.* 1. To begin to tear or rend. 2. To scoff, to make jest of. **Reírse de nada,** to giggle or titter idly, to laugh at a feather. **Reírse de,** to laugh at.

reiteración [ray-e-tay-rah-the-on'], *f.* 1. Repetition, reiteration. 2. *(Comput.)* Replication. **Reiteración absoluta,** absolute replication. **Reiteración mixta,** mixed replication. **Reiteración relativa,** relative replication.

reiteradamente [ray-e-tay-rah-dah-men-tay], *adv.* Repeatedly.

reiterar [ray-e-tay-rar'], *va.* To reiterate, to repeat, to reaffirm.

reiterativo, va [ray-e-tay-rah-tee'-vo, vah], *a.* Reiterative, expressing repeated action.

reivindicación [ray-e-vin-de-cah-the-on'], *f. (For.)* Recovery, claim (reclamación), grievance (queja). **Reivindicación salarial,** wage claim.

reivindicar [ray-e-vin-de-car'], *va.* 1. To recover, to claim (reclamar); to assert one´s claim to. 2. To vindicate (reputación). 3. *(Jur.)* To recover (derecho). 4. *(LAm.)* To demand (exigir).

reja [ray'-hah], *f.* 1. Plough sharer, cotter or courter. 2. Ploughing, turning over ground with a plough; tillage. 3. Iron grate of a window or fence. 4. *(LAm.)* Prison (cárcel). 5. *(Cono Sur)* Cattle truck. **Estar entre rejas,** to be behind bars.

rejado [ray-hah'-do], *m.* Grate of a door or window.

rejalcar [ray-hal-car´], *va.* To plough.

rejalgar [ray-hal-gar'], *m.* Realgar, red sulphide of arsenic. *(Arab.)*

rejazo [ray-hah'-tho], *m.* Stroke or blow with a plough share.

rejería [ray-hay-ree'-ah], *f.* Manufactory of the iron-work of grates, doors, or windows.

rejero [ray-hay-ro], *m.* Maker of bars, lattices, and grates.

rejilla [ray-heel'-lyah], *f.* 1. A small lattice in confessionals, to hear women's confessions; or a grating in a door in order to see who knocks. 2. Cane, for the backs and seats of chairs. etc. 3. *V.* REJUELA, 2d def. 4. Small stove (brasero). 5. *(Cono Sur)* Meat (fresquera). 6. *(Mex.)* Luggage ruck.

rejo [ray'-ho], *m.* 1. A pointed iron bar or spike (punta). 2. Sting of a bee or other insect. 3. Nail or round iron with which quoits are played. 4. Rim of iron put around the frame of a door to strengthen it. 5. Strength, vigor. 6. In seeds, the radicle, the organ from which the root is formed. 7. *(LAm.)* Whip (látigo). 8. *(Carib.)* Stick (porra). 9. *(Carib.)* Stick (porra). 10. *(And.)* Milking (ordeño).

rejón [ray-hone'], *m.* 1. Dagger, poniard. 2. A kind of lance or spear used by bullfighters. 3. A short broad knife with a sharp point.

rejonazo [ray-ho-nah'-tho], *m.* Thrust with a dagger.

rejoneador [ray-ho-nay-ah-dor'], *m.* Bull-fighter who throws the spear called *rejón.*

rejonear [ray-ho-nay-ar'], *va.* To wound bulls with the spear used by bullfighters.

rejoneo [ray-ho-nay'-o], *m.* The act of fighting bulls with a spear.

rejuela [ray-hoo-ay'-lah], *f.* 1. *(dim.)* A small grate. 2. A small brasier of wood covered with brass used for a stove.

rejurar [ray-hoo-rar'], *vn.* To swear again.

rejuvenecer [ray-hoo-vay-nay-therr'], *vn.* To grow young again.

relación [ray-lah-the-on'], *f.* 1. Relation, report, narration, memoir, account (narración). 2. A brief report to a judge, of the state and merits of a cause. 3. Prologue, a long piece in a dramatic poem which an individual recites. 4. Relation, correspondence, analogy, coherence, concurrence. **Relación jurada**, deposition upon oath. **Entrar en relaciones**, *(Com.)* to connect oneself. **Buenas relaciones**, good relations. **Relaciones amorosas**, courting. **Llevan varios meses de relaciones**, they've been going out for some months.

relacionado, da [ray-lah-the-o-nah'-do, dah], *a.* Relative, related, connected. **Relacionado con**, related to, in connection with.

relacionar [ray-lah-the-o-nar'], *va.* To relate, to report, to narrate. -*vr.* 1. **Es hombre que se relaciona**, he's a man with connections. 2. To make contacts (formar amistades).

relacionero [ray-lah-the-o-nay'-ro], *m.* Reporter, narrator; ballad-singer.

relajación [ray-lah-hah-the-on'], *f.* 1. Relaxation (sosiego), extension, dilatation: relenting. 2. *(For.)* Remission or diminution of a penalty imposed upon a delinquent. 3. Commutation of a vow, release from an oath. 4. Delivery of an offender by the ecclesiastical judge to a criminal court of justice, in cases of murder. 5. *V.* QUEBRADURA. 6. Relaxation of discipline or good order, laxity of conduct; relaxation, intermission from a task or work.

relajadamente [ray-lah-hah'-dah-men-tay], *adv.* Dissolutely, licentiously.

relajado [ray-lah-hah'-do], *a. (Coll.)* Dissolute, dissipated. -*pp.* of RELAJAR.

relajador, ra [ray-lah-hah-dor', rah], *a.* Relaxing, remitting.

relajamiento [ray-lah-hah-me-en'-to], *m.* Relaxation, laxity, slackness.

relajante [ray-lah-hahn'-tay], *a.* 1. Relaxing (ejercicio). 2. *(Cono Sur)* Sickly (comida). 3. Revolting (repugnante).

relajar [ray-lah-har'], *va. 1.* To relax (sosegar), to slacken (aflojar), to make less tense. 2. To relax, to remit, to render less rigorous. 3. To annul a vow, to release from an oath or obligation. 4. To deliver a capital offender from an ecclesiastical to the criminal tribunal. 5. To relax, to ease, to amuse, to divert. 6. *(For.)* To lighten a penalty. 7. *(LAm.)* To cloy (comida). 8. *(Carib.)* To mock (hacer mofa). -*vr.* 1. To be relaxed, loosened, or diluted: applied to a member of the animal body. 2. To grow vicious; to be corrupted by evil customs. 3. *V.* QUEBRARSE. 4. To become dissolute (moralmente).

relamer [ray-lah-merr'], *va.* To relick, to lick again. -*vr.* 1. To lick one's lips (persona); to relish. 2. To be extravagantly fond of dress; to paint (maquillarse). 3. To boast, to rag.

relamido, da [ray-lah-mee'-do, dah], *a.* Affected, too fine or nice in dress. -*pp.* of RELAMER.

relámpago [ray-lahm'-pah-go], *m.* 1. Flash of lightning, meteor. 2. Anything passing as suddenly as a flash of lightning. 3. Thought or idea flashing upon the mind; ingenious witticism. 4. Blemish in the eyes of horses.

relampagueante [ray-lam-pah-gay-ahn'-tay], *pa.* Lightening.

relampaguear [ray-lam-pah-gay-ar'], *vn.* 1. To lighten, to emit flashes of lightning. 2. To flash, to sparkle, to gleam. 3. *(Carib.)* To twinkle (parpadear).

relampagueo [ray-lam-pah-gay'-o], *m.* Lightening, flashing or darting light.

relance [ray-lahn'-thay], *m.* 1. Repeated casting of a net, a second chance or lot. 2. A fortuitous event. 3. A repeated attempt. 4. Series of lucky or unlucky chances. **De relance**, fortuitously, by chance.

relanzar [ray-lan-thar'], *va.* 1. To repel, to repulse. 2. To cast in again the tickets or lots to be drawn.

relapso, sa [ray-lahp'-so, sah], *a.* Relapsed, falling back into criminal conduct.

relatador, ra [ray-lah-tah-dor', rah], *m & f.* Relater, narrator.

relatante [ray-lah-tahn'-tay], *pa.* Reporting, narrating.

relatar [ray-lah-tar'], *va.* 1. To relate, to report, to narrate, to give out. 2. *(For.)* To make a report of a lawsuit.

relativamente [ray-lah-tee'-vah-men-tay], *adv.* Relatively, comparatively.

relatividad [ray-lah-te-ve-dahd'], *f.* Relativity.

relativo, va [ray-lah-tee'-vo, vah], *a.* 1. Relative, comparative. 2. *(Gram.)* Relative, relating to an antecedent. 3. *(Music.)* Relative major or minor key.

relato [ray-lah'-to], *m.* Statement, narration.

relator, ra [ray-lah-tor'], *m & f.* 1. Relater, teller, narrator. 2. Reporter, a counsellor at law appointed by the supreme courts to make the briefs of the causes that are to be tried: he reads them before the court, they having first been examined and approved by both the parties concerned.

relatora [ray-lah-to'-rah], *f.* The wife of the reporter of a court of justice.

relatoría [ray-lah-to-ree'-ah], *f.* Office of a reporter of judicial causes in a court of justice.

relevadura [ray-lay-vah-doo'-rah], *f.* A second washing.

relavajo [ray-lah-vah'-hay], *m.* Washing-place for things or clothes.

relavar [ray-lah-var'], *va.* To wash again.

relave [ray-lah'-vay], *m.* Second washing of metals.

relavillo [ray-lah-veel'-lyo], *m. dim.* Slight rewashing.

relax [ray-lacs], *m.* 1. Relaxation (sosiego); rest (descanso). **Hacer relax**, to relax.

releer [ray-lay-err'], *va.* To read over again, to revise.

relegación [ray-lay-gah-the-on'], *f.* Relegation, judicial banishment; exile.

relegar [ray-lay-gar'], *va.* To relegate, to banish; to exile.

relejar [ray-lay-har'], *vn.* To diminish in thickness in proportion to the height (muro).

releje [ray-lay'-hay], or **relej** [ray-lay'], *m.* 1. *(Mil.)* Raised work in the chamber of a piece of ordinance where the powder is placed, in order to economize. 2. Tapering of a wall or talus from below upward. 3. A clammy moisture sticking to the lips or mouth.

relente [ray-len'-tay], *m.* 1. Night dew, softness occasioned by the falling of dew. 2. *(Coll. and met.)* Slowness, deliberation in speech or action.

relentecer [ray-len-tay-therr'], *vn. & vr.* To be softened, to relent and soften by the falling of dew.

relevación [ray-lay-vah-the-on'], *f.* 1. Relevation, the act of raising or lifting up, liberation. 2. Alleviation, relief from a burden or obligation. 3. Remission, forgiveness, pardon.

relevante [ray-lay-vahn'-tay], *a.* Excellent, great, eminent.

relevar [ray-lay-var'], va.1. To emboss. 2. To exonerate, to disburden; to relieve from a burden or charge. 3. To forgive, to pardon. 4. To exalt, to aggrandize. 5. To relieve or substitute a sentinel or body of troops by another. **Relevar a uno de una obligación**, to relieve somebody of a duty. **Relevar a uno de un cargo**, to relieve somebody of his post. -vn. (*Art.*) To raise an object so as to appear like raised work.

relevo [ray-lay'-vo], m. (*Mil.*) Relief. **Relevo de la guardia**, changing of the guard.

reliar [ray-le-ahr'], va. To roll (cigarrillo).

relicario [ray-le-cah'-re-o], m. 1. Shrine, a place where relics are collected and guarded. 2. Reliquary, a casket in which relics are kept.

relictos [ray-leek'-tos], m. pl. (*For.*) Possessions which one leaves at his death.

relief [ray-le-ef'], m. (*Mil.*) Warrant for an officer to receive either rank or pay that fell to him during his absence.

relieve [ray-le-ay'-vay], m. 1. Relief, relievo, raised work, embossment. **Alto relieve, todo relieve**, alto-relievo. **Bajo relieve**, bas-relief. **Medio relieve**, demi-relief. 2. Offals, scrapes, or remnants on the table after meals; leavings; broken victuals. 3. The thread of the arbor of a screw.

religa [ray-lee'-gah], f. The second portion of alloy put to a metal to fit it for working.

religación [ray-le-gah-the-on'], f. Binding, tying.

religar [ray-le-gar'], va. To bind, to solder.

religión [ray-le-he-on'], f. 1. Religion; piety, worship. 2. A community with regulations approved by the Church. 3. Belief in any divinity. **Entrar en religión**, (*Coll.*) to take the habit of a religious order.

religionario, religionista [ray-le-he-o-nah'-re-o], com. Religionist; sectary: Protestant.

religiosamente [ray-le-he-o-sah men tay], adv. 1. Religiously, piously. 2. Religiously, exactly, punctually. 3. Moderately.

religiosidad [ray-le-he-o-se-dahd'], f. Religiousness; piety, sanctity; punctuality.

religioso, sa [ray-le-he-o' so, sah], a. 1. Religious, godly, pious. 2. Religious, teaching or professing religion. 3. Religious, exact, strict in observance of holy duties. 4. Moderate.

relimar [ray-le-mar'], va. To file again.

relimpiar [ray-lim-pe-ar'], va. To clean a second time.

relimpio, ia [ray-leem'-pe-o, ah], a. (*Coll.*) Very neat, clean.

relinchador, ra [ray-lin-chah-dor', rah], a. Neighing or whinnying often.

relinchante [ray-lin-chahn'-tay], pa. Neighing, whinnying.

relinchar [ray-lin-char'], vn. To whinny, to neigh, as a horse.

relincho, relinchido [ray-leen'-cho], m. Neigh, neighing, whinny of a horse.

relindo, da [ray-leen'-do, dah], a. Very neat and fine.

relinga [ray-leen'-gah], f. (*Naut.*) Bolt-rope.

relingar [ray-lin-gar'], va. (*Naut.*) To sew bolt-ropes to sails. -vn. To rustle: said of bolt-ropes and sails moved by the wind.

reliquia [ray-lee'-ke-ah], f. 1. Relic (tesoro), residue, remains. 2. Relics of saints. 3. Footstep, tract, vestige (vestigio). 4. Habitual complaint. **Reliquia de familia**, heirloom.

reliz [ray-leeth'], m. (*Mex.*) A landslide.

rellanar [rayl-lyah-nar'], va. To relevel. -vr. To stretch oneself at full length.

rellano [rayl-lyah'-no], m. Landing-place of a stair.

rellenar [rayl-lyay-nar'], va. 1. To fill again. 2. To stuff with victuals, to feed plentifully. 3. (*Coll.*) To stuff a fowl or gut with forced meat. -vr. To stuff oneself.

relleno [ray-lyay'-no], m. 1. Stuffing. 2. Repletion, act of refilling. **Relleno de pavo**, turkey stuffing.

relleno, na [rayl-lyay'-no, nah], a. & pp. of RELLENAR. 1. Cropful, crop-sick, satiated. 2. Packed, stuffed.

reloco, ca [ray-lo'-co, cah], a. (*Coll.*) Raving and, furiously insane.

reloj ray-lo'], m. Clock (de pared), watch (de muñeca). **Reloj de agua**, clepsydra. **Reloj de arena**, sand-glass, hour-glass.

Reloj de bolsillo, pocket-watch. **Reloj de sol** or **reloj solar**, sun-dial. **Reloj lunar**, lunar dial. **Reloj de longitudes**, chronometer. **Reloj de despertador**, alarm-clock. **Estar como un reloj**, (*Coll.*) to be regular and well-disposed.

relojera [ray-lo-hay'-rah], f. 1. Clockcase. 2. Watchmaker's wife.

relojería [ray-lo-hay-ree'-ah], f. 1. The art of making clocks and watches. 2. Watchmaker's shop.

relojero [ray-lo-hay'-ro], m. Watchmaker, clockmaker.

reluciente [ray-loo-the-en'-tay], a. Resplendent, glittering, brilliant, shining (brillante).

relucir [ray-loo-theer'], vn. To shine (brillar), to glow, to glisten, to glitter; to excel, to be brilliant.

reluchar [ray-loo-char'], m. To struggle, to wrestle, to strive, to labor, to debate.

relumbrante [ray-loom-brahn'-tay], pa. Resplendent.

relumbrar [ray-loom-brar'], vn. To sparkle, to shine, to glisten, to glitter, to glare.

relumbrera [ray-loom-bray'-rah], f. V. LUMBRERA.

relumbrón [ray-loom-brone'], m. 1. Luster, dazzling brightness; fleeting idea or sound. 2. Tinsel: any expression or phrase striking but of false showiness.

remachado, da [ray-mah-chah'-do, dah], a. 1. Clinched, riveted. 2. Flat-nosed. -pp. of REMACHAR.

remachador [ray-mah-chah-dor'], m. Riveter, rivet gun. **Remachador de tipo pistola**, zipgun.

remachar [ray-mah-char'], va. To flatten; to clinch (clavo), to rivet (metales); to secure, to affirm.

remache [ray-mah'-chay], m. Flattening, clinching, securing; rivet.

remachón [ray-mah-chone'], m. Buttress. V. MACHÓN.

remador, ra [ray-mah-dor'], m & f. Rower. V. REMERO.

remadura [ray-mah-doo'-rah], f. Rowing.

remaldecir [ray-mal-day-theer'], f. To curse the cursers.

remallar [ray-mal-lyar'], va. To mend the meshes of a net or coat of mail.

remanadera [ray-mah-nah-day'-rah], f. In tanneries, graining-board, on which hides are pounded.

remandar [ray-man-dar'], va. To order several times.

remanecer [ray-mah-nay-therr'], vn. 1. To appear, to occur. 2. To remain, to be left. (*Yo remanezco, yo ramanezca,* from *Remanecer.* V. ABORRECER.)

remaneciente [ray-mah-nay-the-en'-tay], pa. & a. Remaining, remanent, left out.

remanente [ray-mah-nen'-tay], m. Remainder, residue; remanent, remnant.

remangadura [ray-man-gah-doo'-rah], f. (*Prov.*) The act of tucking up.

remangar [ray-man-gar'], va. To tuck up. V. ARREMANGAR.

remango [ray-mahn'-go], m. Plaits of the petticoat at the waist.

remansarse [ray-man-sar'-say], vr. To obstruct the course of a fluid.

remanso [ray-mahn'-so], m. 1. Smooth, stagnant water. 2. Tardiness, sluggishness (pachorra).

remante [ray-mahn'-tay], m. Rower.

remar [ray-mar'], m. 1. To row, to paddle. 2. To toil, to struggle.

remarcar [ray-mar-car'], va. To mark again.

rematadamente [ray-mah-tah'-dah-men-tay], adv. Entirely, totally.

rematado, da [ray-mah-tah'-do, dah], a. 1. Ended, terminated. 2. Totally lost, utterly ruined. **Es loco rematado**, he is stark mad. -pp. of REMATAR.

rematamiento [ray-mah-tah-me-en'-to], m. V. REMATE.

rematar [ray-mah-tar'], va. 1. To close, to terminate, to finish (proceso), to abut, to end at. 2. To adjudge to the best bidder. 3. To kill game with one shot (animal). 4. To finish a seam. 5. (*Arquit.*) To top, to be at the very top of. 6. (*Com.*) To sell off cheaply (vender). 7. (*LAm.*) To buy at an auction (en subasta, comprar). -vn. To terminate, to be at an end (terminar). **Rematar al mejor postor**, to knock down to the highest bidder. **Fue una situation que remató en tragedia,** it was a situation which ended in tragedy. -vr. To be utterly ruined or destroyed.

remate [ray-mah´-tay], m. 1. End, conclusion, expiration. **Remate de cuentas,** closing of accounts. 2. An edge, a border, a limb. 3. The last or best bidding. 4. Artificial flowers put at the corners of altars. 5. Vignette, in a book. 6. (Arch.) Finial, the top or finishing of a pinnacle or gable; also, the entire pinnacle; abutment. **De remate,** utterly, irremediably, without hope. 7. (Com.) Sale (venta); (LAm.) auction (subasta).

rembalso [rem-bahl´-so], m. Rabbeting of a window-shutter, which makes it close with the frame.

remecedor [ray-may-thay-dor´], m. A persons who knocks down olives with a pole or long rod.

remecer [ray-may-therr´], va. To rock; to swing, to move to and fro.

remedable [ray-may-dah´-blay], a. Imitable.

remedador, ra [ray-may-dah-dor´, rah], m. & f. Imitator, mimic.

remedar [ray-may-dar´], va. 1. To copy, to imitate, to mimic: to gesticulate, to mock. 2. To follow the track and footsteps of others. 3. To adopt the dress and manners of another.

remediable [ray-may-de-ah´-blay], a. Remediable.

remediador, ra [ray-may-de-ah-dor´, rah], m. & f. Protector, comforter, helper, curer.

remediar [ray-may-de-ar´], va. 1. To remedy (poner remedio a), to mend, to repair. 2. To assist, to support, to help (necesitado). 3. To free from danger, to liberate, to repair mischief. 4. To avoid executing anything that may cause damage (evitar), or to do it contrary to the will of another. **Lo que no se puede remediar, se ha de aguantar,** what cannot be cured must be endured.

remedición [ray-may-de-the-on´], f. Act of measuring a second time.

remedio [ray-may´-de-o], m. 1. Remedy, reparation, help. **No tener remedio,** to be irremediable or unavoidable. **Como último remedio,** as a last resort. **No hay más remedio que,** the only thing is to. **Esto no tiene remedio,** it is unavoidable. **No tener remedio,** there is no help for it. **Sin remedio,** without fail. 2. Amendment, correction. 3. Remedy, curative medicine. 4. Resource, refuge. 5. Action at law. **No tener un remedio,** to be destitute of aid or assistance.

remedión [ray-may-de-on´], m. aug. A performance at a theater in place of one previously announced, when the last cannot be presented for some unlooked-for reason.

remedir [ray-may-deer´], va. To remeasure.

remedo [ray-may´-do], m. Imitation, copy; mockery.

remellado, remellón [ray-mel-lyah´-do, ray-mel-lyone´], a. Unnaturally everted, ectropic.

remellar [ray-mel-lyar´], va. To unhair hides in a tannery.

rememorar [ray-may-mo-rar´], va. To remember, to recall.

rememorativo, va [ray-may-mo-ray-tee´-vo, vah], a. That which remembers or recalls.

remendado, da [ray-men-dah´-do, dah], a. 1. Patched: mended. 2. Spotted, tabby (caballos, perros). -pp. of REMENDAR.

remendar [ray-men-dar´], va. 1. To patch, to mend; to correct. 2. To adjust one thing to another. (Yo remiendo, yo remiende, from Remendar. V. ACERTAR.)

remendón [ray-men-done´], m. Botcher, patcher, one who mends old clothes; a cobbler, a fripper.

rementir [ray-men-teer´], vn. To lie frequently.

remera [ray-may´-rah], f. Flight-feather, each of the large feathers with which the wings of birds terminate.

remero [ray-may´-ro], m. Rower, paddler. V. RIMERO.

remesa [ray-may´-sah], f. Sending of goods; remittance of money.

remesar [ray-may-sar´], va. 1. To pluck out the hair. 2. (Com.) To remit (dinero), to send money or goods.

remesón [ray-may-sone´], m. 1. Plucking out of hair; hair plucked out. 2. Stopping a horse in full gallop. 3. A skillful thrust in fencing.

remeter [ray-may-terr´], va. To put back, to put in; to put a clean cloth on children.

remiel [ray-me-el´], m. The second extract of soft sugar taken from cane.

remiendo [ray-me-en´-do], m. 1. Batch, clout. 2. Amendment, addition. 3. Reparation, repair. 4. Brindle, the state of being spotted or tabby. 5. (Coll.) Badge of military orders worn by the knights. 6. (Print.) Short work of which few copies are printed. **A remiendos,** by patchwork, by piecemeal. **Echar un remiendo a,** to patch.

remilgadamente [ray-meel-gah´-dah-men-tay], adv. With affected nicety or gravity; with prudery, squeamishly.

remilgado, da [ray-meel-gah´-do, dah], a. & pp. of REMILGARSE. Applied to persons affectedly nice, grave, or prudish: used as a substantive, especially in the feminine.

remilgarse [ray-meel-gar´-say], vr. To be affectedly nice or grave.

remilgo [ray-meel´-go], m. 1. Affected nicety or gravity; prudery (gazmoñería), squeamishness (sensibilidad). 2. Prim look (mueca). **Hacer remilgos a,** to react in a prudish way to.

reminiscencia [ray-me-nis-then´-the-ah], f. Reminiscence, recollection, memory.

remirado, da [ray-me-rah´-do, dah], a. Prudent (prudente), cautious. -pp. of REMIRAR.

remirar [ray-me-rar´], va. To revise; to review. -vr. 1. To do or finish a thing with great care. 2. To inspect or consider with pleasure. 3. To reflect on or examine oneself.

remisamente [ray-me´-sah-men-tay], adv. Remissly, carelessly.

remisible [ray-me-see´-blay], a. Remissible.

remisión [ray-me-se-on´], f. 1. The act of sending (envío). 2. Remission, sending back, remitting, remitment. 3. Remission, forgiveness, grace. 4. Remissness, indolence. 5. Remission, abatement, cessation of intenseness. 6. The act of referring to another book or work (referencia).

remisivamente [ray-me-see´-vah-men-tay], adv. With remision.

remisivo, va [ray-me-see´-vo, vah], a. Remitting, serving to remit.

remiso, sa [ray-mee´-so, sah], a. 1. Remiss, careless, indolent. 2. Remiss, not rigorous.

remisoria [ray-me-so´-re-ah], f. Order of a superior judge to refer a cause to another tribunal: generally used in the plural.

remisorio, ria [ray-me-so´-re-o, ah], a. Having power to forgive or pardon. **Letras remisorias,** judge's orders, transferring a cause to another court.

remite [ray-me-tay], m. Name and address of sender.

remitente [ray-me-ten´-tay], m. & f. Remitter, sender. **Devuélvase al remitente,** return to sender.

remitir [ray-me-teer´], va. 1. To remit, to transmit. 2. To remit, to pardon, to forgive. 3. To remit, to give up, to suspend, to defer, to put off. 4. To return a cause to an inferior court. 5. To remit, to relax, to make less tense. 6. To refer (usuario). 7. To postpone (aplazar). **Remitir una dirección a uno,** to leave a decision to somebody. -vn. To remit, to slacken (disminuir), to grow less tense. -vr. 1. To refer or submit to the judgment and opinion of another. 2. To quote, to cite.

remo [ray´-mo], m. 1. (Naut.) An oar. **Pala de un remo,** (Naut.) blade or wash of an oar. **Manual de un remo,** (Naut.) handle of an oar. 2. Long and hard labor. 3. Rowing. **Practicar el remo,** to row. -pl. (Coll.) 1. The arms and legs of a person; the hind and fore legs of a horse. 2. The wings of a bird.

remoción [ray-mo-the-on´], f. Removal, act of removing.

remodelación [ray-mo-day-lah-the-on´], f. Remodelling; (Aut.) Restyling.

remodelar [ray-mo-day-lalr´], va. To remodel; (Aut.) to restyle.

remojadero [ray-mo-hah-day´-ro], *m*. Steeping-tub.
remojar [ray-mo-har´], *va*. 1. To steep, to imbrue, to wet much or long, to soak again (sin querer). 2. To celebrate with a drink (suceso). 3. *(Mex.)* To bribe (sobornar).
remojo [ray-mo´-ho], *m*. The act of steeping or soaking. **Dejar la ropa en remojo**, to leave clothes to soak.
remojón [ray-mo-hon´], *m*. 1. Soaking, drenching. **Darse un remojón**, to go in for a dip. 2. *(Culin.)* Piece of bread soaked in milk.
remolacha [ray-mo-lah´-chah], *f*. *(Bot.)* Beetroot. The red beet.
remolar [ray-mo-lar´], *m*. The master carpenter who makes oars, or the shop where oars are made.
remolcador [ray-mol-cah-dor´], *m*. 1. Towboat, tug. 2. Towcar.
remolcar [ray-mol-car´], *va*. To tow, to take in tow (coche, bote.)
remoler [ray-mo-lerr´], *va*. 1. To regrind, to grind excessively (moler). 2. *(And. CAm.)* To annoy (fastidiar). *-vn*. *(Cono Sur, And.)* To live it up.
remolimiento [ray-mo-le-me-en´-to], *m*. Act of regrinding.
remolinante [ray-mo-le-nahn´-tay], *pa*. Whirling, making gyrations.
remolinar [ray-mo-le-nar´], *vn*. To make gyrations. *-vr*. 1. To whirl oneself round. 2. To be surrounded by a multitude; to be confounded with the crowd.
remolinear [ray-mo-le-nay-ar´], *va*. To whirl anything about. *-vn*. *V*. REMOLINAR.
remolino [ray-mo-lee´-no], *m*. 1. Whirlwind (viento). 2. Whirlpool (en río). 3. Cow-lick, or twisted tuft of hair upon some part of an animal (pelo). 4. Crowd (de gente), throng. 5. Disturbance, commotion.
remolón, na [ray-mo-lone´, nah], *a*. 1. Soft, indolent, lazy: applied to those who shun labor with art and study. 2. Applied to the upper tusk of a wild boar.
remolón [ray-mo-lon´], *m*. The upper tusk of a wild boar: sharp tooth in horses.
remolonear [ray-mo-lo-nay-ar´], *vn*. To lag, to loiter in doing what ought to be done. *-vr*. To be idle, to refuse stirring, from sloth and indolence.
remolque [ray-mol´-kay], *m*. 1. Towing (de un coche, bote.) 2. Towrope (cable). **Llevar un coche a remolque, to tow** a car.
remondar [Ray-mon-dar´], *va*. To clean a second time; to take away what is useless.
remono, na [ray-mo´-no, nah], *a*. Very neat, very pretty.
remonta [ray-mone´-tah], *f*. 1. Repair of the feet of shoes or boots. 2. The act of supplying the cavalry with fresh horses; collection of cavalry horses; remounting cavalry.
remontamiento [ray-mon-tah-me-en´-to], *m*. Act of soaring or towering.
remontar [ray-mon-tar´], *va*. 1. To frighten away (animales), to oblige one to withdraw. 2. To remount the cavalry; to supply them with fresh horses. 3. To repair the saddles of mules and horses. 4. To put new soles or feet to boots. *-vr*. 1. To tower (edificio), to soar (pájaros). 2. To conceive great and sublime ideas; to form sublime conceptions. 3. To go back (recuerdos), go up stream (río). **Sus recuerdos se remontan en el siglo pasado**, her memories go back to the last century. **Remontaron el río**, they went up the stream.
remonte [ray-mon´-tay], *m*. Soar, a towering flight; elevation or sublimity of ideas.
remontista [ray-mon-tees´-tah], *m*. Commissioner for the purchase of cavalry horses.
remoquete [ray-mo-kay´-tay], *m*. 1. Thump with the fist. 2. A witty expression (comentario). 3. Gallantry, courtship.
rémora [ray´-mo-rah], *f*. 1. Sucking fish, remora. 2. Hindrance, obstacle; cause of delay.
remordedor, ra [ray-mor-day-dor´, rah], *a*. Causing remorse.
remorder [ray-mor-derr´], *va*. 1. To bite repeatedly. 2. To cause remorse, to sting, to make uneasy. *-vr*. To manifest concern, to suffer remorse.

remordimiento [ray-mor-de-me-en´-to], *m*. Remorse, uneasiness, compunction.
remosquear [ray-mos-kay-ar´], *va*. *& vr*. To blur: said of ink in printing when it spreads beyond the face of the types.
remostar [ray-mos-tar´], *va*. To put must into old wine. *-vr*. To grow sweet and assume the flavor of must (vino).
remostecerse [ray-mos-tay-ther´-say], *vr*. *V*. REMOSTARSE.
remosto [ray-mos´-to], *m*. The act of putting must into old wine.
remotamente [ray-mo´-tah-men-tay], *adv*. 1. Remotely, at a distance. 2. Without chance of happening or of succeeding. 3. Confusedly. 4. Unlikely.
remoto, ta [ray-mo´-to, tah], *a*. Remote, distant, far off; foreign, alien; unlike.
removedor [ray-mo-vay-dor´], *m*. A mover.
remover [ray-mo-verr´], *va*. 1. To remove (objetos), to shift from place to place. 2. To remove an obstacle (quitar). 3. To alter. 4. To dismiss. **Remover el pasado**, to stir up the past. *(Yo remuevo, yo remueva*, from *Remover*. *V*. MOVER.)
removimiento [ray-mo-ve-me-en´-to], *m*. 1. Removal. 2. Revulsion.
remozadura, *f*. **remozamiento**, *m*. [ray-mo-thah-doo´-rah]. Act of appearing or becoming young.
remozar [ray-mo-thar´], *va*. To endeavor, to appear young; to make one appear younger than he is (persona); to give a new look (organización). *-vr*. To be rejuvenated.
remplazar [rem-pla-thar´], *va*. *V*. REEMPLAZAR.
remplazo [rem-plah´-tho], *m*. *V*. REEMPLAZO.
rempujar [rem-poo-har´], *va*. 1. To push a person out of his place. 2. To jostle. 3. To impel, to carry away. 4. To beat game, so as to drive it to a determined place.
rempujo [rem-poo´-ho], *m*. 1. Impulse, push, thrust. 2. Pressure of an arch upon its supporters. *V*. EMPUJE.
rempujón [rem-poo-hone´], *m*. Impulse, push, thrust.
remuda [ray-moo´-dah], *f*. 1. Exchange, re-exchange. 2. **Remuda de caballos**, relay of horses.
remudamiento [ray-moo dah-me-en´-to], *m*. 1. Removal, exchange. 2. Change of clothing.
remudar [ray-moo-dar´], *va*. 1. To move or change again. 2. To exchange one thing for another.
remugar [ray-moo-gar´], *va*. *(Prov.)* *V*. RUMIAR.
remullir [ray-mool-lyeer´], *va*. To beat up again, to mollify.
remunerable [ray-moo-nay-rah´-blay], *a*. Remunerable, rewardable.
remuneración [ray-moo-nay-rah-the-on´], *f*. Remuneration, recompense, reward: gratuity, consideration.
remunerador, ra [ray-moo-nay-rah-dor´, rah], *m*. *& f*. Remunerator.
remunerar [ray-moo-nay-rar´], *va*. To reward, to remunerate.
remuneratorio, ria [ray-moo-nay-rah-to´-re-o, ah], *a*. Remunerative.
remusgo [ray-moos´-go], *m*. Too cool an atmosphere or situation.
remusguillo [ray-moos-geel´-lyo], *m*. *dim*. Coolish place, chilly situation.
renacentista [ray-nah-then-tees´-tah], *a*. Renaissance.
renacer [ray-nah-therr´], *vn*. 1. To be born again, to spring up again, to grow again. 2. To acquire grace by baptism. **Hoy me siento como renacido**, today I feel renewed. *(Yo renazco, yo renazca*, from *Renacer*. *V*. CONOCER.)
renaciente [ray-nah-the-en´-tay], *pa*. *& a*. Renascent, springing anew.
renacimiento [ray-nah-the-men-en´-to], *m*. 1. Regeneration: new birth. 2. The Renaissance in architecture and literature.
renacuajo [ray-nah-coo-ah´-ho], *m*. 1. Spawn of frogs or young tadpoles. 2. Little, shapeless man.
renadío [ray-nah-dee´-o], *m*. Crop which, after having been reaped in the blade, sprouts again.
renal [ray-nahl´], *a*. Renal, belonging to the kidneys.
rencilla [ren-theel´-lyah], *f*. A grudge remaining after a quarrel.
rencilloso, sa [ren-theel-lyo´-so, sah], *a*. Peevish, quarrelsome, touchy.

renco, ca [ren'-co, cah], *a.* Hipshot, having the hip dislocated, lame.

rencor [ren-cor'], *m.* Rancor, animosity, grudge. **Guardar rencor**, to bear malice.

rencorosamente [ren-co-ro'-sah-men-tay], *adv.* Rancorously.

rencoroso, sa [ren-co-ro´-so, sah], *a.* 1. Rancorous, spiteful (malicioso). 2. Resentful (resentido); bitter (amargado).

rencoso [ren-co'-so], *a.* Applied to a ram with one testicle concealed.

renda [ren'-dah], *f. (Prov.)* The second dressing of vines.

rendaje [ren-dah´-hay], *m.* Reins of the bridle of horses or mules.

rendejo [ren-dah'-ho], *m.* Mimic. *V.* ARRENDAJO.

rendar [ren-dar'], *va. (Prov.)* To dress vines a second time.

rendición [ren-de-the-on'], *f.* 1. Rendition, surrendering, yielding. 2. Product, profit accruing. 3. *(Cono Sur)* Trading balance; *(Fin.)* balance.

rendidamente [ren-dee'-dah-men-tay], *adv.* Humbly, submissively, compliantly.

rendido, da [ren-dee'-do, dah], *a.* Tired out, fatigued, submissive (sumiso), humble (admirador).

rendija [ren-dee'-hah], *f.* Crevice, crack, cleft.

rendimiento [ren-de-me-en'-to], *m.* 1. Rendition, delivery into the hands of another. 2. Weariness, faintness. 3. Humiliation, submission; obsequiousness (servilismo), humbling, compliance. 4. Rent, income; yearly produce. **El rendimiento del motor**, the performance of the engine. **Rendimiento del capital**, return on capital.

rendir [ren-deer'], *va.* 1. To subject (voluntad), to subdue (país), to conquer (vencer), to overcome. 2. To render, to surrender, to yield, to give up, to deliver up. **Rendir el puesto**, *(Mil.)* to give up a post, to commit it to another. 3. To render, to give back (devolver), to return, to restore, to produce. 4. To vomit, to throw up from the stomach. **Rendir gracias** *V.* AGRADECER. **Rendir obsequios**. *V.* OBSEQUIAR. *-vn.* 1. To yield (producir). **El negocio no rinde**, the business doesn't give good results. **Este año he rendido poco**, it has done poorly this year. *-vr.* l. To be tired, to be worn out with fatigue (cansarse). 2. To yield (ceder), to submit to another, to give way. 3. *(Naut.)* To spring (mástil). **Rendir la guardia**, to set the watch.

renegado [ray-nay-gah'-do], *m.* 1. Renegade, apostate. 2. A malicious, wicked person. 3. Ombre, a sort of card game. **Renegado, da**, *pp.* of RENEGAR.

renegador, ra [ray-nay-gah-dor', rah], *m. & f.* Shearer, blasphemer; apostate.

renegar [ray-nay-gar'], *va.* 1. To deny (negar), to disown, to abnegate. 2. To detest (odiar), to abhor. *-vn.* 1. To apostatize. 2. To blaspheme, to curse. 3. To abhor, to detest (odiar). 4. To curse, to swear (jurar). 5. To grumble (quejarse). 6. *(And. Mex.)* To get angry (enojarse). 7. *(And. Cono Sur, Mex.)* To protest (protestar). **Renegar de su familia**, to disown one's family. **Renegar de**, to detest.

rengífero [ren-hee'-fay-ro], *m.* The reindeer.

renglón [ran-glone'], *m.* 1. Line written or printed from one margin to another (línea). **A renglón seguido**, in the very next line. 2. Part of one's revenue or income. 3. *(LAm.)* Line of goods (género). 4. *(LAm.)* Area, department.

renglonadura [ren-glo-nah-doo'-rah], *f.* Ruling of paper: ruled lines.

rengo, ga [ren'-go, gah], *a.* Hurt in the reins, back, or hip.

rengue [ren'-gay], *m.* Train.

reniego [ray-ne-ay´-go], *m.* 1. A kind of execration or blasphemy. 2. Curse (juramento). 3. grumble (queja). *(Yo reniego, yo reniegue*, from *Renegar*. *V.* ACRECENTAR.)

reniforme [ray-ne-for'-may], *a.* Reniform, kidney-shaped.

renil [ray-neel'], *a.* Barren, a barren ewe.

renitencia [ray-ne-ten'-the-ah], *f.* Resistance, opposition.

renitente [ray-ne-ten'-tay], *a.* Renitent, repugnant.

reno [ray´-no], *m.* Reindeer.

renombrado, da [ray-nom-brah'-do, dah], *a.* Renowned, celebrated, famous. *-pp.* of RENOMBRAR.

renombre [ray-nom'-bray], *m.* 1. Surname (apellido), family name. 2. Renown, glory, fame.

renovable [ray-no-vah'-blay], *a.* Renewable, replaceable.

renovación [ray-no-vah-the-on'], *f.* 1. Renovation, renewal. 2. Change, reform. 3. Act of consuming old bread designed for the host, and of consecrating new. **Renovación de la suscripción**, renewal of one's subscription.

renovador, ra [ray-no-vah-dor', rah], *m. & f.* Renovator, reformer.

renovante [ray-no-vahn'-tay], *va.* Renovating, renewing.

renovar [ray-no-var'], *va.* 1. To renew (aviso), to renovate. 2. To change, to reform. 3. To polish. 4. To barter. 5. To reiterate, to republish. 6. To consume old wafers designed for the host, and consecrate new bread. **Renovar la memoria**, to bring to recollection. *-vr.* To recollect oneself, to reform. *(Yo renuevo, yo renueve*, from *Renovar. V.* ACORDAR.

renquear [ren-kay-ar'], *m.* To limp (cojear), to halt, to claudicate.

renta [ren'-tah], *f.* 1. Rent, profit, income (ingresos). 2. Rent, money paid for anything held of another. 3. Tax, contribution; revenue. 4. Public debt (deuda). 5. *(LAm.)* Rent. **A renta**, let at a rent. **Renta nacional**, national income. **Vivir de sus rentas**, to live on one's private income.

rentabilidad [ren-tah-be-le-dahd'], *f.* Return, yield, profitability.

rentable [ren-tah'-blay], *a.* Profitable, income-yielding. **La línea ya no es rentable**, the line is no longer economic.

renter [ren-tar'], *va.* To yield.

rentería [ren-tay-ree'-ah], *f.* Productive land or property.

rentero, ra [ren-tay´-ro], *m & f.* 1. Renter, farmer. 2. One who farms out land.

rentilla [ren-teel'-lyah], *f.* 1. *(dim.)* A small rent. 2. A card game. 3. A dice game.

rentista [ren-tees'-tah], *m.* 1. Financier: a modern word. 2. One who possess an income irrespective of its source. 3. Bondholder, one who lives upon interest paid from the public treasury.

rentístico, ca [ren-tees'-te-co, cah], *a.* Belonging to public revenues.

rento [ren'-to], *m. (Prov.)* 1. Country residence with farm-yard. 2. Annual rent paid by a laborer or colonist.

rentoso, sa [ren-to'-so, sah], *a.* Yielding income, rent-producing.

renuencia [ray-noo-en'-the-ah], *f.* Contradiction, reluctance.

renuente [ray-noo-en'-tay], *a.* Indocile, intractable, remiss.

renuevo [ray-noo-ay'-vo], *m.* 1. Sprout, shoot; a young plant to be transplanted. 2. Nursery of young trees and plants. 3. Renovation, renewal. *V.* REMUDA.

renuncia [ray-noon'-the-ah], *f.* Renunciation, resignation, renouncement, abjurement.

renunciable [ray-noon-the-ah'-blay], *a.* That can be renounced or resigned: transferable.

renunciación [ray-noon-the-ah-the-on'], *f.* Renunciation. *V.* RENUNCIA.

renunciamiento [ray-noon-the-ah-me-en'-to], *m.* Renouncement. *V.* RENUNCIA.

renunciante [ray-noon-the-ah'-tay], *pa. & m. & f.* Renouncer, renouncing, abjurer.

renunciar [ray-noon-the-ar'], *va.* 1. To renounce (derecho), to resign (puesto, responsabilidad). 2. To renounce, to disown; to abnegate. 3. To renounce, to leave, to forego, to give up (hábito, proyecto), to lay to; to fall from; to refuse, to reject; to depreciate, to abandon. *-vn.* To revoke, to renege at cards.

renunciatario [ray-noon-the-ah-tah'-re-o], *m.* A person to whom something has relinquished.

renuncio [ray-noon'-the-o], *m.* 1. Revoke, the fault committed in playing cards, by not furnishing a card of the same suit which was played by another. 2. *(Met. Coll.)* Error, mistake.

renvalsar [ren-val-sar'], *va.* To shave off doors or windows so that they may fit well.

reñidamente [ray-nyee-dah-men'-tay], *adv.* Quarrelsomely, in a wrangling manner.

reñidero [ray-nyee-day'-ro], *m.* Cockpit; fighting-pit; a place for fighting animals.

reñido, da [ray-nyee'-do, dah], *a.*At variance with another. *-pp.* of REÑIR. **Un partido reñido**, a hard-fought game. **Está reñida con su familia**, she has fallen out with his family.

reñidor, ra [ray-nye-dor', rah], *m. & f.* Quarreler, wrangler.

reñir [ray-nyeer'], *va. & vn.* 1. To wrangle, to quarrel (disputar), to dispute, to fight (pelear), to fall out. 2. To scold (regañar), to reprimand, to chide, to reproach. 3. To argue, to discuss. **Ha reñido con su novio**, she´s fallen out with her boyfriend. **Se pasan la vida riñendo**, they spend their whole time quarrelling. *(Yo riño, yo riña; el riñó, riñera;* from *Reñir.* V. PEDIR.)

reo [ray'-o], *com.* 1. Offender, criminal, culprit (delincuente). 2. Defendant in a suit at law. 3. Series, continuity. 4. *(Cono Sur)* Tramp (vagabundo).

reoctava [ray-oc-tah'-vah], *f.* V. OCTAVILLA.

reojar [ray-o-har'], *va.* To bleach wax.

reojo [ray-o'-ho], *m.* **Mirar de reojo**, to look obliquely, to dissemble the looks by directing the view above a person; to look contemptuously or angrily.

reordenar [ray-ro-day-nahr'], *va.* To realign.

reorganización [ray-or-gah-ne-thah-the-on'], *f.* Reorganization.

reorganizar [ray-or-gah-ne-thar'], *va.* To reorganize, to organize anew.

reóstato [ray-os'-tah-to], *m.* Rheostat.

repacer [ray-pah-therr'], *va.* To consume the entire grass of pasture-ground.

repadecer [ray-pah-day-therr'], *va. & vn.* To suffer extremely.

repagar [ray-pah-gar'], *va.* To pay a high or excessive price.

repajo [ray-pah'-ho], *m.* Inclosure for the pasture of cattle.

repantingarse [ray-pan-te-gar'-say], **repanchingarse**, *vr.* To lean back in a chair with the legs stretched out.

repapilarse [ray-pah-pe-lar'-say], *vn.* To eat to excess, to lick one's lips, to smack with relish.

reparable [ray-pah-rah'-blay], *a.* 1. Reparable, remediable: objectionable. 2. Worthy of attention.

reparación [ray-pah-rah-the-on´], *f.* 1. Reparation (acto), repair. 2. Repeating a lesson among scholars. 3. Compensation, pay. **Efectuar reparaciones en**, to carry out repairs to.

reparada [ray-pah-rah-dah], *f.* Sudden bound of a horse.

reparador, ra [ray-pah-rah-dor', ah], *m. & f.* 1. Repairer. 2. Observer, one who makes remarks.

reparamiento [ray-pah-rah-me-en´-to], *m.* V. REPARO and REPARACIÓN.

reparar [ray-pah-rar'], *va.* 1. To repair, to restore. 2. To observe with careful attention (observar). 3. To consider (considerar), to reflect, to give heed. 4. To repair, to amend an injury by an equivalent (ofensa), to make up, to compensate, to expiate, to make amends, to correct. 5. To suspend, to detain. 6. To guard, to defend, to protect, to help. 7. To give the final touch to moulds. *-vn* 1 To regain strength, to recover from illness. 2. To stop or halt in any part. 3. *(CAm. Mex.)* To rear (caballo). **Reparar en**, to observe. **Sin reparar en los gastos**, heedless of expense. *-vr.* 1. To refrain, to forbear. 2. *(Mex.)* To rear on the hind legs, as a horse.

reparativo, va [ray-pah-rah-tee'-vo, vah], *a.* Reparative.

reparo [ray-pah'-ro], *m.* 1. Repair, reparation, supply of loss, restoration. 2. Restoration, repair of an edifice. 3. Careful inspection and investigation, notice. 4. Inconveniency, difficulty, doubt (duda), objection (objeción). 5. Strengthening cataplasm for the stomach. 6. Anything to support, assist, or defend. 7. Provisional anchorage for repairing damages. 8. Parry or guard, in fencing. 9. *(CAm. Mex.)* Bucking, rearing (caballo).

reparón [ray-pah-ron'], *m. (Coll.)* Great doubt or difficulty.

reparón, na [ray-pah-ron', nah], *a.* Too cautious, too circumspect.

repartible [ray-par-tee'-blay], *a.* Distributable.

repartición [ray-par-te-the-on'], *f.* 1. Partition, distribution (distribución). 2. *(Cono Sur)* Government department, administrative section. 3. *(LAm. Pol.)* Redistribution (de tierras).

repartidamente [ray-par-tee'-dah-men-tay], *adv.* In several portions or partitions.

repartidero, ra [ray-par-te-day'-ro, rah], *a.* Distributing, parting.

repartidor, ra [ray-par-te-dor', rah], *m. & f.* 1. Distributer; delivery man. 2. Assessor of taxes.

repartimiento [ray-par-te-me-en'-to], *m.* 1. Partition, division, distribution,apportionment. 2. Portion of territory which was given as a fief to the conquerors of Spanish America. 3. Assessment of taxes.

repartir [ray-par-teer'], *va.* 1. To divide, to distribute (distribuir), to apportion, to share out. 2. To scatter, to sow. 3. To assess taxes. 4. To allot (trabajos), to give out (premios), to serve out (comida), to deliver (cartas, leche, pan). **Las guarniciones están repartidas por toda la costa**, the garrisons are distributed all round the coast. *-vr.* To be distributed.

reparto [ray-par'-to], *m.* 1. Distribution (distribución). 2. (Correos) Delivery. 3. *(Teat.)* Casting; cast (lista), cast list. 4. *(CAm. Carib. Mex.)* Building site (solar).

repasadera [ray-pah-sah-day'-rah], *f.* Planes, a carpenter's tool.

repasadora [ray-pah-sah-do'-rah], *f.* Woman occupied in carding wool.

repasar [ray-pah-sar'], *va.* 1. To repass, to pursue the same course (used also intransitively). 2. To re-examine, to revise (texto), to review and correct or polish work already done (notas). 3. To glance rapidly over something written. 4. To explain again, to run over the results of one's former studies. 5. To clean dyed wool for carding. 6. To sew again, to mend clothes. 7. To air clothes at the fire. 8. To remix mercury with metal to purify it.

repasata [ray-pah-sah'-tah], *f. (Coll.)* Reprehension, censure, chiding.

repas agent on the patient.

repaso [ray-pah'-so], *m.* 1. The act and effect of running over a thing that one has already studied. 2. Revision, the act of re-examining and revising: examining a thing after it is finished. 3. The act and effect of repealing or remixing quicksilver with metal. 4. Reprimand, chastisement. *-pl.* A number of flaws or porosities in the body of an organ. **Repaso general**, general overhaul. **Dar un repaso a una lección**, to revise a lesson.

repastar [ray-pas-tar'], *va.* To feed a second time.

repasto [ray-pahs'-to], *m.* Increase of food; an additional meal.

repatriación [ray-pah-tre-ah-the-on'], *f.* Repatriation.

repatriar [ray-pah-tre-ar'], *vn. (mer.)* To return to one's country, to repatriate. *-va.* To repatriate; to deport (criminal); to send home, to send back to one´s country of origin.

repechar [ray-pay-char'], *va. & vn.* To mount a declivity or slope.

repecho [ray-pay'-cho], *m.* Declivity, slope (vertiente). *a.* To repel (enemigo); to refute, to reject (idea, oferta). **Este material repele el agua**, this material is water-repellent.

repeliente [ray-pay-le-en'-tay], *pa.* Repellent.

repellar [ray-pel-lyar'], *va.* To run a trowel over the plaster thrown on a wall.

repelo [ray-pay'-lo], *m.* 1. A small part or share of anything that rises against the grain, or has transverse fibres. 2. Anything which goes against the grain, crooked grain. 3. A

repelón

slight scuffle or dispute (riña). 4. Repugnance, aversion. 5. *(And. Mex.)* Junk (baratijas).

repelón [ray-pay-lone'], *m.* 1. The action of pulling out the hair. 2. A small part torn from anything; a thread loose in stockings. 3. A short gallop. **A repelones**, by degrees, by little and little.

repeloso, sa [ray-pay-lo'-so, sah], *a.* 1. Of a bad grain, having transverse timbres (madera). 2. Touchy, peevish.

repelús [ray-pay-loos'], *m.* Inexplicable fear. **Me da repelús**, it gives me the willies.

repensar [ray-pen-sar'], *va.* To consider, to reflect, to contemplate; to think deeply.

repente [ray-pen'-tay], *m.* A sudden movement (movimiento), an unexpected event. **De repente**, suddenly, all of a sudden.

repentinamente [ray-pen-tee'-nah-men-tay], *adv.* Suddenly.

repentino, na [ray-pen-tee'-no, nah], *a.* Sudden (súbito), unforeseen, unexpected (imprevisto), abrupt, extemporaneous, unpremeditated.

repentirse [ray-pen-tee'-no], *vr.* V. ARREPENTIRSE.

repentista [ray-pen-tees'-tah], *m.* Maker of extempory verses.

repentizar [ray-pen-te-thar'], *va.* To improvise (en discurso), to compose verses off hand.

repentón [ray-pen-tone'], *m.* 1. An unexpected event or incident. 2. A sudden movement.

repeor [ray-pay-or'], *a.* Much worse.

repercudida [ray-per-coo-dee'-dah], *f.* Repercussion, rebound.

repercudir [ray-per-coo-deer'], *vn.* To rebound. V. REPERCUTIR.

repercusión [ray-per-coo-se-on'], *f.* Repercussion (sonido), reverberation (reverberación), Repercussion (consecuencia). **Repercusiones**, repercussions.

repercusivo, va [ray-per-coo-see'-vo, vah], *a.* Repercussive; repellent.

repercutir [ray-per-coo-teer'], *vn.* 1. To cause repercussion, to repercuss, to drive back, to rebound (objeto); to retrograde, to reverberate. 2. *(Mex.)* To smell bad (oler mal). -*va.* To repel.

repertorio [ray-per-to'-re-o], *m.* 1 Repertory, index of noteworthy matters (lista). 2. Repertory, repertoire, a list of plays, especially such as are presented in a theater by a stock company.

repesar [ray-pay-sar'], *va.* To reweigh, to weigh again.

repeso [ray-pay'-so], *m.* 1. Weighing a second time. 2. Weight-office, whither articles may be carried to be weighed a second time. 3. Charge of reweighing. **De repeso**, with the whole weight of a body; with the whole force of authority and persuasion.

repetición [ray-pay-te-the-on'], *f.* 1. Repetition, reiteration; iteration. 2. Repeater, a repeating clock or watch. 3. Collegial dissertation or discourse; a thesis. 4. *(For.)* An action for an accounting.

repetidamente [ray-pay-tee'-dah-men-tay], *adv.* Repeatedly.

repetidor, ra [ray-pay-te-dor', rah], *m. & f.* Repeater, a teacher or student who repeats with another his lessons, and explains them.

repetir [ray-pay-teer'], *va.* 1. To demand or claim repeatedly and urgently. 2. To repeat, to reiterate, to use again, to do again, to try again (volver a hacer). 3. To repeat, to recite, to rehearse. **Le repito que es imposible**, I repeat that it is impossible. -*vn.* 1. To have the taste of what was eaten or drunk in the mouth. 2. To deliver a public discourse previous to the examination for the higher degrees in the universities. -*vr.* 1. To repeat oneself (artista). 2. To recur (suceso). *(Yo repito, yo repita; él repitió;* from REPETIR. V. PEDIR.)

repetitivo, va [ray-pay-te-tee'-vo, vah], *a.* That which contains a repetition.

repicado, da [ray-pe-cah´-do, dah], *a.* 1. Chopped. 2. Starched, stiff; affectedly nice. -*pp.* of REPICAR.

repicapunto [ray-pe-cah-poon'-to], *adv.* **De repicapunto**, nicely, delicately, excellently.

repicar [ray-pe-car'], *va.* 1. To chop (carne). 2. To chime, to ring a merry peal. 3 To reprick (picar otra vez). 4. In the game of piquet; to count ninety before the adverse party counts one. -*vr.* To glory, to boast, to pique oneself on.

repilogar [ray-pe-lo-gar'], *va.* To recapitulate, to epitomize, to repeat the sum of a former discourse.

repinarse [ray-pe-nar'-say], *va.* To soar, to elevate.

repintar [ray-pin-tar'], *va.* To repaint (volver a pintar), to paint again. -*vr.* 1. To paint oneself. 2. *(Print.)* To set off, to make a double impression.

repique [ray-pee'-kay], *m.* 1. Act of chopping or cutting. 2. Chime, a merry peal on festive occasions; the peal of bells. **El último repique** or **llamada**, the last peal. 3. Dispute, altercation, a slight scuffle. 4. In piquet, counting ninety before the other player can count one.

repiquete [ray-pe-kay'-tay], *m.* 1. A merry peal rung on festive occasions. 2. Chance, opportunity. 3. *(Cono Sur)* Trill, song. 4. *(And.)* Pique, resentment (resentimiento).

repiquetear [ray-pe-kay-tay-ar'], *va.* 1. To ring a merry peal on festive occasions. 2. To tap, to beat (mesa, tambor). -*vr.* To bicker, to wrangle, to quarrel.

repiqueteo [ray-pe-kay-tay'-o], *m.* A continued peal of bells.

repisa [ray-pee'-sah], *f.* 1. Pedestal or abutment for a bust or vase. 2. A bracket.

repiso [ray-pee'-so], *m.* Weak, vapid wine.

repiso, sa [ray-pee'-so, sah], *a.* Sorrowful, repentant. *(Acad.)*

repitiente [ray-pe-te-en'-tay], *pa.* Repeating, he who repeats and defends a thesis.

repizcar [ray-peeth-car'], *va.* To pinch. V. PELLIZCAR.

repizco [ray-peeth'-co], *m.* The act of pinching. V. PELLIZCO.

replantar [ray-plan-tar'], *va.* To replant ground.

replantear [ray-plan-tay-ar'], *va.* 1. To mark out the ground plan of an edifice again. 2. To raise again (cuestión).

replanteo [ray-plan-tay'-o], *m.* 1. The act of replanting. 2. Second description of the ground plan of a building.

repleción [ray-play-the-on'], *f.* 1. Fullness due to overeating. 2. Satisfaction of a need or desire.

replegable [ray-play-gah'-blay], *a.* Capable of being folded back.

replegar [ray-play-gar'], *va.* 1. To redouble, to fold often (doblar). 2. *(Mil.)* To fall back or to double the wing of an army, regiment, etc., upon its center or any other part, as the evolution may be necessary. -*vr.* To withdraw, to fall back.

repleto, ta [ray-play'-to, tah], *a.* Replete (lleno), very full. **Repleto de**, fillled with. **La plaza estaba repleta de gente**, the square was solid with people.

réplica [ray'-ple-cah], *f.* 1. Reply, answer (respuesta); repartee; objection. 2. *(Art.)* Replica, copy.

replicación [ray-ple-cah-the-on'], *f.* *(Law.)* V. RÉPLICA.

replicador, ra [ray-ple-cah-dor', rah], *m. & f.* Replier, disputant.

replicante [ray-ple-cahn'-tay], *pa. & n* Replier, respondent; replying.

replicar [ray-ple-car'], *vn.* 1. To reply, to make return to an answer. 2. To reply, to impugn the arguments of the adverse party; to contradict. -*va.* *(Law.)* To respond; to repeat.

replicón, na [ray-ple-cone', nah], *a.* *(Coll.)* Replica, frequent disputer.

repliegue [ray-ple-ay'-gay], *m.* 1. The act of doubling or folding often (pliegue). 2. A fold, crease, convolution.

repoblación [ray-po-blah-the-on'], *f.* Repopulation (gente), act of repeopling.

repoblar [ray-po-blar'], *va.* To repeople; to repopulate (zona, país); to afforest.

repoda [ray-poh'-dah], *f.* The act of pruning a second time.

repodar [ray-po-dar'], *va.* To prune again.

repodrir [ray-po-dreer'], *va. & vr.* V. REPUDRIR.

repollar [ray-pol-lyar'], *vn.* To form round heads of leaves, like cabbage.

repollo [ray-pol'-lyo], *m.* 1. *(Bot.)* White cabbage. 2. Round head formed by the leaves of plants.

repolludo, da [ray-pol-lyoo'-do, dah], *a.* Cabbage-headed; round-head.

reponche [ray-pon'-chay], *m. V.* RUIPONCE.

reponer [ray-po-nerr'], *va.* 1. To replace (devolver a su lugar); to collocate. 2. To restore a suit at law to its primitive state. 3 To oppose anew, to reply. *-vr.* To recover lost health or property. **Reponerse de,** to recover from. (*Yo repongo, yo reponga; yo repuse, repondré;* from *Reponer. V.* PONER.)

reportación [ray-por-tah-the-on'], *f.* Moderation, forbearance.

reportado, da [ray-por-tah'-do, dah], *a.* Moderate, temperate, forbearing. *-pp.* of REPORTAR.

reportaje [ray-por-tah'-hay], *m.* Report, article, news item. **Reportaje gráfico,** illustrated report.

reportamiento [ray-por-tah-me-en'-to], *m.* Forbearance.

reportar [ray-por-tar'], *va.* 1. To moderate or repress one's passions, to refrain, to forbear: 2. To obtain (beneficio), to reach; to attain. 3. To carry or bring (traer). 4. To return an instrument with the certificate of its execution. 5. (*Fig.*) To check (moderar). 6. (*LAm.*) To report (informar); to denounce (denunciar). **Esto le habrá reportado algún beneficio,** this will have brought him some benefit. *-vr.* 1. To forbear. 2. (*CAm. Mex.*) To present oneself.

reporteril [ray-por-tay-reel'], *a.* (*Neol.*) Reportorial, relating to reporters. (Note.—The noun is *Reporter,* taken from the English.)

reportorio [ray-por-to'-re-o], *m.* Almanac, calendar.

reposadamente [ray-po-sah'-dah-men-tay], *adv.* Peaceably, quietly.

reposadero [ray-po-sah-day'-ro], *m.* 1. A vat in which indigo is prepared. 2. A trough for receiving melted metal.

reposado, da [ray-po-sah'-do, dah], *a.* Quiet (tranquilo), peaceful, gentle (descansado). *-pp.* of REPOSAR.

reposar [ray-po-sar'], *vn.* 1. To rest (descansar), to repose; to take a nap (dormir), to lie by, to lie to. 2. To rest in the grave; to rest in peace. *-va.* **Reposar la comida,** to let one's meal go down. *-vr.* To settle (líquido).

reposición [ray-po-se-the-on'], *f.* 1. The act of restoring a suit at law to its primitive state. 2. (*Chem.*) Preservation of liquids in proper vessels. 3. Reposition.

reposo [ray-poh'-so], *m.* Rest, repose, tranquility.

repostar [ray-pos-tar'], *va.* To restock, to resupply with. *-vr.* To lay in a fresh supply. **Repostar combustible,** to refuel.

repostería [ray-pos-tay-ree'-ah], *f.* 1. Office or shop for preparing confectionery and beverages (tienda). 2. All the provisions, instruments, and persons employed in this office.

repostero, ra [ray-pos-tay'-ro], *m & f.* 1. Pastrycook (pastelero). 2. Covering ornamented with a coat of arms. 3. (*And.*) Kitchen shelf unit. 4. Butler to the king (palaciego).

repregunta [ray-pray-goon'-tah], *f.* 1. A second demand or question on the same subject. 2. (*Law.*) A cross-examination.

repreguntar [ray-pray-goon-tar'], *va.* To question repeatedly about the same subject.

reprenda [ray-pren'-dah], *f.* Pledge taken a second time.

reprender [ray-pren-derr'], *va.* To reprehend, to reprimand, to blame, to censure, to reprove, to chide; to correct.

reprendiente [ray-pren-de-en'-tay], *pa.* Censuring, reprimanding.

reprensible [ray-pren-see'-blay], *a.* Reprehensible.

reprensión [ray-pren-se-on'], *f.* Reprehension, blame, censure, reprimand, reproof, lesson. **Sujeto sin reprensión,** an irreprehensible person.

reprensor, ra [ray-pren-sor', rah], *m. & f.* Reprehender, censurer, reprover.

represa [ray-pray'-sah], *f.* 1. Water collected for working a mill; dam (presa). 2. The act of stopping or retaining; restriction. 3. Pool, lake (estanque).

represalia, represaria [ray-pray-sah'-le-ah, ray-pray-sah'-re-ah], *f.* Reprisal, reprise.

represar [ray-pray-sar'], *va.* 1. To recapture or retake from the enemy. 2 To stop (parar), to detain, to retain. 3. To repress, to moderate one's passions.

representable [ray-pray-sen-tah'-blay], *a.* That which may be represented.

representación [ray-pray-sen-tah-the-on'], *f.* 1. Representation, the act of representing. 2. Power, authority. 3. Dramatic poem. 4. Figure, image, idea. 5. Remonstrance, memorial, address. 6. Authority, dignity, character of a person. 7. (*Law.*) Right of succession to an inheritance in the person of another. **Hacer representaciones a,** to make representations to. **Representación visual,** (*Comput.*) visual display. **Representación simbólica,** (*Comput.*) symbolic representation.

representador, ra [ray-pray-sen-tah-dor', rah], *m. & f.* 1. Representative. 2. Player, actor.

representante [ray-pray-sen-tahn'-tay], *pa.* Representing another.

representante, ta [ray-pray-sen-tahn'-tay, tah], *m. & f.* 1. Player, comedian. 2. Representer, representative.

representar [ray-pray-sen-tar'], *va.* 1. To represent, to make appear, to set forth; to manifest; to refer; to express (expresar). 2. To play on the stage, to perform, to act (papel). 3. To represent another, as his agent, deputy, or attorney. 4. To be the symbol or image of anything. 5. To look (edad). 6. To mean (significar). **Representa unos 55 años,** he looks about 55. **Representar una dificultad a uno,** to represent a difficulty to somebody. *-vr.* To offer, to occur; to present itself. **Representarse una escena,** to imagine a scene.

representativo, va [ray-pray-sen-tah-tee'-vo, vah], *a.* Representative.

represión [ray-pray-se-on'], *f.* Repression.

represivo, va [ray-pray-see'-vo, vah], *a.* Repressive, restrictive.

reprimenda [ray-pre-men'-dah], *f.* Reprimand.

reprimido [raypre-mee'-do], *a.* Repressed.

reprimir [ray-pre-meer'], *va.* 1. To repress, to refrain, to contain, to control, to curb (refrenar); to suppress (bostezo, risa). *-vr.* **Reprimirse de,** to stop oneself from.

reprobable [ray-pro-bah'-blay], *a.* Reprehensible.

reprobación [ray-pro-bah-the-on'], *f.* Reprobation, reproof.

reprobado, da [ray-pro-bah'-do, dah], *a.* 1. Flunked, not passed (en un examen). 2. *V.* RÉPROBO.

reprobador, ra [ray-pro-bah-dor', rah], *m. & f.* Reprover, condemner.

reprobar [ray-pro-bar'], *va.* To reject, to condemn (censurar), to contradict, to exclude, to upbraid, to reprobate, to damn (condenar). (*Yo repruebo, yo repruebe,* from *Reprobar. V.* ACORDAR.)

reprobatorio, ria [ray-pro-bah-to'-re-o, ah], *a.* That which reprobates or reproves; objurgatory.

réprobo, ba [ray'-pro-bo, bah], *m. & f. & a.* Reprobate, graceless, wicked.

reprochar [rayprochar'], *va.* 1. To reproach, to impute blame to. 2. To reject, to dismiss, to exclude.

reproche [ray-pro'-chay], *m.* 1. Reproach, reproof. 2. Fault which may be reproved. 3. Repulse, rebuff, displeasure.

reproducción [ray-pro-dooc-the-on'], *f.* 1. Reproduction. 2. Reproduction of a summons, or any other judicial precept or decree.

reproducir [ray-pro-doo-theer'], *va.* To reproduce.

reproductible [ray-pro-dooc-tee'-blay], *a.* That can be reproduced or reproduced anew.

reproductividad [ray-pro-dooc-tee-ve-dahd'], *f.* Reproductiveness.

reproductivo [ray-pro-dooc-tee'-vo], *a.* Reproductive, producing anew.

reproductor, ra [ray-pro-dooc-tor'], *a. & n.* Serving for reproduction.

repromisión [ray-pro-me-se-on'], *f.* Repeated promise.

repropiarse [ray-pro-pe-ahr'-say], *vr.* To be unwilling to obey, to be restive (caballos).

repropio [ray-pro-pe-o], *a.* Restive (caballos).

reprueba [ray-proo-ay-bah], *f.* New proof in addition to a preceding one.

reptil [rep-teel'], *a. & m.* Reptile; crawler, creeper.

reptilívoro, ra [rep-te-lee'-vo-ro, rah], *a.* Devouring reptiles, reptilivorous.

república [ray-poo'-ble-cah], *f.* 1. Republic, commonwealth. 2. Republic, public welfare; political goverment. **República bananera**, banana republic. **Segunda República**, Second Spanish Republic.

republicanismo [ray-poo-ble-cah-nees´-mo], *m.* Republicanism.

republicano, na [ray-poo-ble-cah'-no, nah], *a.* 1. Republican, inhabitant of a republic. 2. Republican, approving republican government, democratic.

republicano, na [ray-poo-ble-cah'-no, nah], *m. & f.* Republican, democrat, common-wealthsman. *V.* REPÚBLICA.

repúblico [ray-poo'-ble-co], *m.* A man greatly attached to the welfare of the public, a patriot; a man capable of holding public offices, a statesman.

repudiación [ray-poo-de-ah-the-on'], *f.* Repudiation, divorce.

repudiar [ray-poo-de-ar'], *va.* 1 To repudiate (mujer, violencia), to divorce a wife. 2. To renounce (herencia), to relinquish.

repudio [ray-poo'-de-o], *m.* Repudiation, divorce.

repudrir [ray-poo-dreer'], *va.* To rot (pudrir). *-vr.* To pine away.

repuesta [ray-poo-es'-tah], *f.* Money staked in the game of ombre.

repuesto [ray-poo-ess´-to], *m.* 1. Refill (de pluma). 2. Extra, spare. 3. Replacement (reemplazo). 4. Stock (provisión). **De repuesto**, as a substitute, extra, as a spare. **Rueda de repuesto**, spare wheel.

repuesto, ta [ray-poo-es'-to, tah], *p. irr.* of REPONER.

repugnancia [ray-poog-nahn'-the-ah], *f.* 1. Reluctance (desgana), repugnance, resistance. 2. Repugnance, aversion, loathing (asco). 3. Opposition, contradiction, contrariety. **Con repugnancia**, in a reluctant manner.

repugnante [ray-poog-nahn'-tay], *a.* Repugnant, repulsive, loathsome.

repugnar [ray-poog-nar'], *va.* 1. To oppose, to contradict (contradecir), to repugn, to withstand. 2. To act with reluctance, to implicate. 3. To disgust, to revolt (dar asco a). *-vr.* To conflict, to be in opposition.

repujado, da [ray-poo-ha'-do, dah], *a.* Repoussé, formed in relief.

repulgado, da [ray-pool-gah'-do], *a. V.* AFECTADO. *-pp.* of REPULGAR.

repulgar [ray-pool-gar'], *va.* 1. To hem, to double in the border of cloth with a seam; to border, to double the edge. 2. To put an edging upon pastry.

repulgo [ray-pool'-go], *m.* 1. Hem, the border of cloth doubled in with a seam. 2. The external ornament of a pie. 3. Vain and ridiculous scruple. **Detenerse en repulgos de empanada**, to waste time over trifles.

repulido, da [ray-poo-lee'-do, dah], *a.* Prim, neat, spruce. *-pp.* of REPULIR.

repulir [ray-poo-leer'], *va.* 1. To repolish (objeto). 2. To dress affectedly (persona). Used also as reflexive.

repulsa [ray-pool'-sah], *f.* 1. Refusal, counter-check, repulse. 2. *(Fig.)* Strong condemnation (censura); severe reprimand (reprimenda).

repulsar [ray-pool-sar'], *va.* To reject, to decline, to refuse.

repulsión [ray-pool-se-on'], *f.* 1. *V.* REPULSA. 2. Repulsion.

repulsivo, va [ray-pool-see'-vo, vah], *a.* Repulsive, repulsory.

repulso, sa [ray-pool'-so, sah], *pp.* ·*rr.* of REPELER.

repulular [ray-poo-loo-lar'], *va.* To repullulate.

repullo [ray-pool'-lyo], *m.* 1. Jerk, leap; a sudden violent motion of the body. 2. A small arrow or dart. 3. An external mark of pain or grief.

repunta [ray-poon'-tah], *f.* 1. Point, headland. 2. Sign of displeasure (indicio); disagreement, dispute, scuffle. 3. Very short thing, very small portion.

repuntar [ray-poon-tar'], *vn. (Naut.)* To begin to ebb. 2. *(LAm.)* To make itself felt (manifestarse). 3. *(Cono Sur)* To rise to previous levels. *-vr.* 1. To be on the turn (vino). 2. To be soured, to be displeased with one another.

repurgar [ray-poor-gar'], *va.* 1. To glean or purify again. 2. To administer a second purging draught.

reputación [ray-poo-tah-the-on'], *f.* Reputation, repute, character, credit, fame, renown.

reputante [ray-poo-tahn'-tay], *pa.* One who estimates.

reputar [ray-poo-tar'], *va.* To repute, to estimate (estimar), to appreciate, to deem (considerar). **Reputar a uno de inteligente**, to consider somebody intelligent.

requebrado, da [ray-kay-brah'-do, dah], *a. & pp.* of REQUEBRAR. Enamored, using tender expressions. *-m. & f.* Lover, loving expression.

requebrador [ray-kay-brah-dor'], *m.* Wooer, suitor.

requebrar [ray-kay-brar'], *va.* To woo, to court, to make love, to dally. *(Yo requiebro, yo requiebre,* from *Requebrar. V.* ACRECENTAR.)

requejada, *f.* **requejal,** *m.* [ray-kay- hah'-dah, ray-kay-hahl'], *(Prov.) V.* REQUEJO.

requejo [ray-kay'-ho], *m. (Prov.)* Ground ending in a hill before entering upon a plain.

requemado, da [ray-kay-mah'-do, dah], *a.* 1. Brown-colored, sun-burnt (piel). 2. Thin silk for veils, black and lustreless. *-pp.* of REQUEMAR.

requemadura [ray-kay-mah-doo'-rah], *f.* A burn upon a burn.

requemamiento [ray-kay-mah-me-ayn'-to], *m. V.* RESQUEMO.

requemar [ray-kay-mar'], *va.* 1. To burn a second time. 2. To roast to excess (comida). 3. To extract the juice of plants. 4. To inflame the blood. 5. To scorch (fuego). 6. *(Fig.)* To inflame (sangre). *V.* RESQUEMAR. *-vr.* 1. To burn with passion, to be deeply in love. 2. To scorch; to parch, to get parched.

requemazón [ray-kay-mah-thone'], *f. V.* RESQUEMO.

requeridor [ray-kay-re-dor'], *f.* A person who requests, advises, or intimates.

requerimiento [ray-kay-re-me-en'-to], *m.* 1. Request (petición), requisition. 2. Intimation. injunction, summons (llamada).

requerir [ray-kay-reer'], *va.* 1. To require, to need (necesitar). 2. To summon. 3. To intimate, to notify. 4. To investigate. 5. To request (pedir). 6. To court, to woo a woman. 7. To induce, to persuade. **Esto requiere cierto cuidado**, this requires some care. **El ministro requirió sus gafas**, the minister sent for his glasses. *(Yo requiero, yo requiera; él requirió, requiriera;* from *Requerir. V.* ASENTIR.)

requesón [ray-kay-sone'], *m.* Cottage cheese.

requesonarse [ray-kay-so-nar'-say], *vr.* To become curds a second time.

requiebro [ray-ke-ay'-bro], *m.* 1. Endearing expressions, the language of love; love-tale. 2. Quiver, trill of the voice.

requiebro [ray-ke-ay'-bro]. *m.* Crushed ore.

réquiem [ray'-ke-aym], *m.* Requiem.

requilorio [ray-ke-lo'-re-o], *m. & pl. (Coll.)* Useless ceremony, or circumlocution, before doing a simple thing.

requintador, ra [ray-kin-tah-dor', rah], *m. & f.* Outbidder, in the letting of lands or tenements.

requintar [ray-kin-tar'], *va.* 1. To outbid a fifth part, in tenements, after an agreement is made. 2. To exceed, to surpass, to superadd. 3. *(Mus.)* To raise or lower the tone five points. 4. *(And.)* To abuse (insultar). *-vn. (Carib.)* To resemble each other (parecerse).

requinto [ray-keen'-to], *m.* 1. The second fifth taken from a quantity from which one-fifth had before been taken. 2. An advance of a fifth in rent. 3. Extraordinary impost levied on the Peruvians in the time of Philip II. 4. A very small and high-pitched flute, and the one who plays it.

requirir [ray-ke-reer'], *va. V.* REQUERIR.

requisa [ray-kee'-sah], *f.* 1. Night and morning visit of a jailer to his prisoners. 2. Survey, inspection (inspección). 3. *(LAm.)* Seizure (confiscación).

requisar [ray-ke-sar'], *va.* 1. To inspect, to review. 2. To make a levy of horses for army use. 3. *(LAm.)* To seize, to confiscate (confiscar).

requisición [ray-ke-se-the-on'], *f.* 1. A levy of horses for military service. 2. *(Cono Sur, Mex.)* Search (registrar).

requisito [ray-ke-see'-to], *m.* Requisite, necessary condition.

requisito, ta [ray-ke-see'-to, tah], *pp. irr.* of REQUERIR. **Requisito previo,** pre-requisite.

requisitorio, ria [ray-ke-se-to'-re-o, ah], *a.* Requisitory: applied to a warrant from one judge to another, requiring compliance with his orders: used as a substantive in the feminine termination.

requive [ray-kee'-vay], *m.* V. ARREQUIVE.

res [res], *f.* Head of cattle or sheep; an animal (doméstico, salvaje); a creature.

resaber [ray-sah-berr'], *va.* To know very well. *-vn.* To affect too much the learned man.

resabiar [ray-sah-be-ar'], *va.* To cause one to become vicious or contract evil habits. *-vr.* 1. To get vices, to become vicious. 2. To be discontented or dissatisfied, to fall into a pit. 3. *V.* SABOREARSE.

resabido, da [ray-sah-bee'-do, dah], *a.* Very learned; affecting learning. *-pp.* of RESABER.

resabio [ray-sah'-be-o], *m.* 1. An unpleasant taste left on the palate. 2. Vicious habit, bad custom.

resabioso, sa [ray-sah-be-oh'-so, sah], *a.* (Peru) Crafty, artful.

resaca [ray-sah'-cah], *f.* 1. *(Naut.)* Surge, surf, the undertow. 2. *(Com.)* A redraw, a draft against the indorser of a protested bill. 3. Hangover (después de beber). 4. *(And. CAm. Mex.)* Strong liquor (aguardiente). 5. *(Cono Sur)* The dregs of society (personas). 6. *(Carib.)* Beating (paliza).

resacar [ray-sah-car'], *va. (Com.)* To redraw.

resalado, da [ray-sah-lah'-do, dah], *a.* Very graceful, charming: commonly said of women only.

resalir [ray-sah-leer'], *vn.* To jut out, to project.

resaltar [ray-sal-tar'], *vn.* 1. To rebound (rebotar), to fly back. 2. To crack, to burst in pieces. 3. To jut out (salir), to project. 4. To appear, to be evident. **Hacer resaltar algo,** to throw something into relief.

resalte [ray-sahl'-tay], *m.* Prominence, protuberance; any striking point.

resalto [ray-sahl'-to], *m.* Rebound (rebote), resilience, prominence; act of shooting boars when rising from their bed.

resaludar [ray-sah-loo-dar'], *vn.* To return a salute, to salute again.

resalutación [ray-sah-loo-tah-the-on'], *f.* Return of a salute, act of resaluting.

resalvia [ray-sahl'-ve-ah], *f. (Agr.)* A count of the staddles which must be left in felling trees.

resalvo [ray-sahl'-vo], *m.* Staddle, sapling, or branch of a tree left for new growth in forestry.

resallar [ray-sal-lyar'], *va.* To weed again.

resallo [ray-sahl'-lyo], *m.* A re-weeding.

resanar [ray-sah-nar'], *va.* To regild defective spots.

resangría [ray-san-gree'-ah] *f* Bleeding again.

resarcible [ray-sar-thee'-blay], *a.* Indemnifiable.

resarcidor, ra [ray-sar-the-dor', rah], *m. & f.* Indemnifier.

resarcimiento [ray-sar-the-me-en'-to], *m.* Compensation, reparation of damage, indemnity.

resarcir [ray-sar-theer'], *va* To compensate (compensar), to recompense, to reward, to make amends, to repair, to indemnify. **Resarcirse de lo perdido,** to make up one's loss.

resbaladero [res-bah-lah-day'-ro], *m.* A slippery place or road; anything dangerous.

resbaladero, ra [res-bah-lah-day'-ro, rah], *a.* Applied to a slippery place or road.

resbaladizo, za [res-bah-lah-dee'-tho, thah], *a.* 1. Slippery, glib. 2. *V.* RESBALADERO. 3. Exposed to temptation.

resbalador, ra [res-bah-lah-dor', rah], *m. & f.* Slider; backslider.

resbaladura [res-bah-lah-doo'-rah], *f.* Slippery track; backsliding.

resbalante [res-bah-lahn'-tay], *pa.* Slider; slipping.

resbalar [res-bah-lar'], *vn. & vr.* 1. To slip (sin querer), to slide; not to tread firm. 2. To tail in the performance of engagements. 3. To slide (deslizarse). 4. To slip up (fallar). **El embrague resbala,** the clutch is slipping. **Me resbala,** it leaves me cold.

resbalo [res-bah'-lo], *m. (Anger. Ec.)* A very precipitous hill.

resbalón [res-bah-lone'], *m.* 1. Slip, the act of slipping. 2. Slip, fault, error, offence. **De resbalón,** erroneously; unsteadily.

resbaloso, sa [res-bah-lo'-so, sah], *a.* Slippery. *V.* RESBALADIZO.

rescaldar [res-cal-dar'], *va.* To heat, to scorch.

rescatador, ra [res-cah-tah-dor', rah], *m. & f.* Redeemer, ransomer.

rescatar [res-cah-tar'], *va.* 1. To ransom (cautivo), to redeem (delitos), to extricate. 2. To exchange, to barter, to commute. 3. *(Amer.)* To buy ore in mines. 4. To save, to rescue (salvar). 5. To get back (dinero).

rescate [res-cah'-tay], *m.* 1. Ransom, redemption by purchase. 2. Ransom money paid for the redemption of slaves. 3. Exchange, permutation, barter. **Operaciones de rescate,** rescue operations.

rescatín [res-cah-teen'], *m. (Amer.)* One who buys from Indians their small collections of ore.

rescaza [res-cah'-thah], *f. V.* ESCORPINA.

rescindente [res-the-den'-tay], *pa. & a.* Rescinding.

rescindir [res-thin-deer'], *va.* To rescind (contrato), to annul, to cut back (puestos de trabajo).

rescisión [res-the-se-on'], *f.* Rescission.

rescisorio, ria [res-the-so'-re-o, ah], *a.* Rescissory.

rescoldera [res-col-day'-rah], *f.* Pyrosis, heartburn.

rescoldo [res-col'-do], *m.* 1. Embers, hot ashes, cinders. 2. *(Met.)* Scruple, doubt, apprehension.

rescontrar [res con-trar'], *va.* To balance in accounts, to compensate.

rescribir [res-cre-beer'], *va.* To reply, to write an answer to a letter.

rescripto [res-creep'-to], *m.* Rescript order, mandate.

rescriptorio, ria [res-crip-to'-re-o, ah], *a.* Belonging to a rescript. *(Yo rescuentro, yo rescuentre, from Rescontrar. V.* ACORDAR.)

rescuentro [res-coo-en'-tro], *m.* Balance of accounts, compensation.

resecación [rar-say-cah-the-on'], *f.* Drying up, drying out, thoroughly drying.

resecar [ray-say-car'], *vn.* To dry again, to dry thoroughly.

reseco, ca [ray-say'-co, cah], *a.* Too dry; very lean.

reseco [ray-say'-co], *m.* Drying out of trees or shrubs; dry part of a honeycomb.

reseda [ray-say'-dah], *f. (Bot.)* 1. Mignonette. 2. Woad. *V.* GUALDA.

resegar [ray-say-gar'], *va.* To reap again, to cut or mow a second time.

resellante [ray-sel-lyahn'-tay], *pa.* Recoining, restamping.

resellar [ray-sel-lyar'], *va.* 1. To recoin, to coin again. 2. To limp in one's ideas, so as to accept others less advanced.

resello [ray-sel'-lyo], *m.* Recoinage.

resembrar [ray-sem-brar'], *va.* To resow.

resentido, da [ray-sen-tee'-do, dah], *a.* Angry, resentful, displeased. *-pp.* of RESENTIRSE.

resentimiento [ray-sen-te-me-en'-to], *m.* 1. Flaw, crack, cleft. 2. Resentment, grudge.

resentirse [ray-sen-teer'-say], *vr.* 1. To begin to give way, to fail, to be out of order. 2. To resent, to express displeasure.

3. To remain weak (debilitarse). **Resentirse por algo**, to resent something. **Me resiento todavía del golpe**, I can still feel the effects of the injury.

reseña [ray-say'-nyah], *f.* 1. A distinguishing mark on the human or animal body. 2. Signal. 3. Description (descripción), succinct narration, or review of historical events. 4. *(Mil.)* Review of soldiers; muster. 5. (Cono Sur: esp Chile) Procession held on Passion Sunday.

reseñar [ray-say-nyar'], *va.* 1. To summarize, to review, to outline 2. To review (tropas). 3. To describe (describir); to write up (narrar). 4. To book (delincuente).

resequido, da [ray-say-kee'-do], *a.* V. RESECO.

reserva [ray-serr'-vah], *f.* 1. Reserve (provisión, surtido), something kept in store. 2. Reserve, secret (secreto). 3. Discretion, caution (cualidad). **Andar con reservas**, to proceed cautiously. **Llanta** or **neumático de reserva**, spare tire. **Reserva natural**, nature reserve. **Con ciertas reservas**, with certain reservations.

reservación [ray-ser-vah-the-on'], *f.* Reservation.

reservadamente [ray-ser-vah-dah-men-tay], *adv.* Secretly, reservedly.

reservado, da [ray-ser-vah'-do, dah], *a. & pp.* of RESERVAR. Reserved, cautious (actitud), circumspect, close, reserved (asiento), private (asunto). **Caso reservado**, a great crime, which none but a superior can absolve. *(Coll.)* Confidential.

reservado [ray-ser-vah'-do], *m.* 2. The Host kept in the ciborium. 2. Reserved or private room (restaurante). 3. Reserved compartment (tren).

reservar [ray-ser-var'], *va.* 1. To reserve, to keep in store (guardar). 2. To defer, to postpone. 3. To privilege, to exempt. 4. To separate, to set aside, to lay aside, to keep back. 5. To restrain, to limit, to confine. 6. To conceal (ocultar), to hide; to shut up (callar). 7. *V.* JUBILAR.- . **Lo reserva para el final**, he´s keeping it till last. **Prefiero reservar los detalles**, I prefer to keep the details to myself. *vr.* 1. To preserve oneself. 2. To act with circumspection or caution.

resfriado [res-fre-ah'-do], *m.* Cold, a disease caused by cold; the obstruction of respiration.—**Resfriado, da**, *pp.* of RESFRIAR.

resfriador [res-fre-ah-dor'], *m.* Refrigerator.

resfriadura [res-fre-ah-doo'-rah], *f.* Cold in horses.

resfriamiento [res-fre-ah-me-en'-to], *m.* Refrigeration, V. ENFRIAMIENTO.

resfriar [res-fre-ar'], *va.* 1. To cool, to make cold. 2. To moderate ardor or fervor. *-vn.* To begin to be cold. *-vr.* 1. To catch a cold. 2. To proceed with coolness, not to pursue a business with the activity it requires.

resfriecer [res-fre-ay-ther'], *vn. (Brov.)* To begin to grow cold (tiempo).

resfrío [res-free'-o], *m.* Cold. V. RESFRIADO.

resguardar [res-goo-ar-dar'], *va.* To preserve, to defend; to protect, to harbor. *-vr.* To be guarded against, to be on one's guard (cautela).

resguardo [res-goo-ar'-do], *m.* 1. Guard, preservation, security, safety. 2. Defence (protección), shelter, protection. 3. Security for the performance of a contract or agreement. 4. Watchfulness to prevent smuggling. 5. Body of custom house officers. 6. Preventive-service. 6. Voucher (vale), certificate; guarantee (garantía); slip (recibo). **Resguardo de consigna**, cloakroom check.

residencia [ray-se-den'-the-ah], *f.* 1. Residence, mansion, lodging, home. 2. Residence, the time appointed for clergymen to reside at a benefice. 3. Account demanded of a person who holds a public station; instrument or account rendered. 4. Place and function of a resident at foreign courts. 5. Among the Jesuits, a house of residence not yet formed into a college. **Residencia para ancianos**, old people´s home.

residencial [ray-se-den-the-ahl'], *a.* Residentiary.

residenciar [ray-se-den-the-ar'], *va.* To call a public officer to account for his administration.

residenciado, da [ray-se-den-the-ah'-do, dah], *a. & pp.* of RESIDENCIAR. Resident, residentiary.

residente [ray-se-den'-tay], *pa. & a.* Residing or resident in a place, residentiary.

residente [ray-se-den'-tay], *m.* Resident, a minister at foreign courts, of lower rank than a plenipotentiary.

residentemente [ ], *adv.* Constantly, assiduously,

residir [ray-se-deer'], *vn.* 1. To reside, to dwell, to lodge. 2. To be present, to assist personally by reason of one's position. 3. To be lodged or inherent in, as a faculty or right. **Residir en**, to reside in. **La dificultad reside en que...**, the difficulty lies in the fact that...

residuo [ray-see'-doo-o], *m.* 1. Residue, remainder. **Residuos de una mesa**, leavings, fragments. 2. *(Chem.)* Residuum. 3. Refuse (basura), waste; left-overs (sobras). **Residuos nucleares**, nuclear waste.

resiembra [ray-se-em'-brah], *f.* Seed thrown on ground without letting it remain.

resigna [ray-seeg'-nah], *f.* Resignation of a benefice.

resignación [ray-sig-nah-the-on'], *f.* 1. Resignation, submission to the will of another, abnegation. 2. Resignation of a public place or employment.

resignadamente [ray-sig-nah'-dah-men-tay], *adv.* Resignedly.

resignante [ray-sig-nahn'-tay], *pa. & m.* Resigner; resigning.

resignar [ray-sig-nar'], *va.* To resign, to give up, to yield up, to abrogate. *-vr.* To resign, to submit to the will of another.

resignatorio [ray-sig-nah-to'-re-o], *m.* Resignee.

resina [ray-see'-nah], *f.* Resin, rosin.

resinero, ra [ray-se-nay'-ro, rah], *a.* Relating to resins.

resinífero, ra [ray-se-nee'-fay-ro, rah], *a.* Resin-boaring, resiniferous.

resinita [ray-se-nee'-tah], *f.* Mineral resin, a stone looking like pitch.

resinócero [ray-se-no'-thay-ro], *m.* A compound of rosin and wax; resinointment.

resinoso, sa [ray-se-no'-so, sah], *a.* Resinous.

resina [ray-see'-sah], *f.* The eighth part formerly taken as duty on wine vinegar, or oil.

resisar [ray-se-sar'], *va.* To diminish any measures or things which have already been taxed.

resistencia [ray-sis-ten'-the-ah], *f.* Resistance, opposition (oposición), defense, endurance (del cuerpo), strength (fuerza); toughness (dureza). **Oponer resistencia a**, to resist. **El maratón es una prueba de resistencia**, the marathon is a test of endurance.

resistente [ray-sis-ten'-tay], *pa.* Resisting, repelling.

resistero [ray-sis-tay'-ro], *m.* 1. The hottest part of the day, from twelve to two o'clock in the summer season. 2. Heat produced by the reflection of the sun's rays and the place where it is perceived.

resistible [ray-sis-tee'-blay], *a.* Resistible, endurable, supportable.

resistidero [ray-sis-te-day'-ro], *m.* The hottest part of the day. *V.* RESISTERO.

resistidor, ra [ray-sis-te-dor', rah], *m & f.* Resister, opponent.

resistir [ray-sis-teer'], *vn. & va.* 1. To resist (enemigo), to oppose. 2. To contradict, to repel. 3. To endure (durar), to tolerate. 4. To reject, to oppugn. 5. To put up with (agotamiento, decepción). 6. To resist; to struggle (luchar); to put up a fight (combatir). **No puedo resistir este frío**, I can´t bear this cold. **El coche resiste todavía**, the car is still going. *-vr.* To struggle, to contend. **Me resisto a creerlo**, I refuse to believe it.

resma [res'-mah], *f.* Ream of paper; *i. e.* long ream of 500 sheets.

resmilla [res-meel'-lyah], *f.* Parcel of one hundred sheets of letter-paper.

resobado, da [ray-so-bah'-do, dah], *a.* Hackneyed, commonplace.

resobrar [ray-so-brar'], *vn.* To be much over and above.

resobrino, na [ray-so-bree'-no, nah], *m. & f.* Son or daughter of a nephew or niece.

resol [ray-sole'], *m.* Reverberation of the sun´s rays.

resolana [ray-so-lah´-nah], *f. (Prov.) V.* RESOLANO.

resolano [ray-so-lah'-no], *m.* Place sheltered from the wind for taking the sun.

resolar [ray-so-lar'], *va.* To repave (pavimento); to resole (zapatos).

resoluble [ray-so-loo'-blay], *a.* Resolvable, resoluble.

resolución [ray-so-loo-the-on'], *f.* 1. Resolution, deliberation; resoluteness. 2. Determination, courage boldness, firmness. 3. Decision (decisión); solution of a doubt (respuesta); conclusiveness; determination of a difference. **Tomar una resolución**, to take a decision. 4. Easiness of address, freedom from constraint. **En resolución**, in short, in a word. 5. Dissolution; analysis or resolution. 6. Activity, promptitude; mind. 7. *(Med.)* Resolution, ordinary termination of an inflammation. 8. *(Cono Sur)* Finishing (terminación).

resolutivamente [ray-so-loo-tee'-vah-men-tay], *adv.* Resolutely, determinately.

resolutivo, va [ray-so-loo-tee'-vo, vah], *a.* 1. *(Med.)* Resolutive, having the power to dissolve: in this sense it used as a substantive. 2. Analytical.

resoluto, ta [ray-so-loo'-to, tah], *a. & pp. irr.* 1. Resolute, bold, audacious. 2. Compendious, brief. 3. Prompt, dexterous.

resolutoriamente [ray-so-loo-to'-re-ah-men-tay], *adv.* Resolutely.

resolutorio ria [ray-so-loo-to'-re-o, ah], *a.* Resolute, prompt.

resolvente [ray-sol-ven'-tay], *pa. & a.* Resolvent, resolving.

resolver [ray-sol-ver'], *va.* 1. To resolve (problema), to determine, to decide (asunto). 2. To sum up, to reduce to a small compass. 3 To decide, to decree. 4. To solve a difficulty, to unriddle; to find out. 5. To dissolve, to analyze (cuerpo de materiales); to dissipate. 6. To undo, to destroy. 7. To divide a whole into its parts. *-vr.* 1. To resolve (problema), to determine. 2. To be included or comprised. **Todo se resolvió en una riña más,** in the end it came down to one more quarrel.

resolladero [ray-so-lyah-day'-ro], *m.* Vent, air-hole; breathing-hole.

resollar [ray-sol-lyar'], *vn.* 1. To respire, to breathe audibly (respirar). 2. To talk; commonly used with a negative. **No resolló,** he did not utter a word. 3. To rest, to take breath. **Hace tiempo que no resuella,** he has given no sign of life for some time. *(Yo resuello, yo resuelle,* from *Resollar. V.* ACORDAR.)

resonación [ray-so-nah-the-on'], *f.* Resounding, noise of repercussion.

resonancia [ray-so-nahn'-the-ah], *f.* 1. Resonance (repercusión), repercussion of sound. 2. *(Poet.)* Consonance, harmony.

resonante [ray-so-nahn'-tay], *pa. & a.* Resonant, resounding.

resonar [ray-so-nar'], *vn.* To resound, to be echoed back, to chink, to clatter.

resoplar [ray-so-plar'], *vn.* 1. To breathe audibly and with force. 2. To snort, as a high-mettled horse or a bull.

resoplido, resoplo [ray-so-plee'-do], *m.* 1. Continued audible breathing; a continual blowing through the nose (respiración). 2. Snorting as of a horse or bull. **Dar resoplidos,** to breath heavily.

resorber [ray-sor-berr'], *va.* To sip again, to reabsorb.

resorte [ray-sor'-tay], *m.* 1. Spring (muelle), an elastic body; an elastic piece of tempered steel. 2. Cause, medium, means (medio). 3. *(LAm.)* Elastic band (gomita). 4. *(LAm.)* Responsibility (responsabilidad).

respailar [res-pah-e-lar'], *va. (Coll.)* To show by gestures vexation over doing something.

respaldar [res-pal-dar'], *m.* Leaning-stock. *V.* RESPALDO.

respaldar [res-pal-dar'], *va.* 1. To endorse (documento), as on the back of a writing. 2. *(Fig.)* To back, to support. 3. *(LAm.)* To ensure (asegurar); to guarantee. *-vr.* 1. To lean, as against a chair or bench. 2. To dislocate the backbone (caballo).

respaldo [res-pahl'-do], *m.* 1. Back or fore part of anything. 2. Endorsement (firma). 3. Leaning-stock, back of a seat (silla).

respectivamente, respective, *adv.* Respectively, proportionally.

respectivo, va [res-pec-tee'-vo, vah], *a.* Respective, relative, comparative. **En lo respectivo a,** as regards.

respecto [res-pec'-to], *m.* Relation, proportion; relativeness; respect. **Respecto a** or **respecto de,** in consideration of. *-adv.* With respect to, with regard to. **Al respecto,** relatively, respectively.

respetable [res-pay-tah'-blay], *a.* Respectable, considerable.

respetador, ra [res-pay-tah-dor', rah], *m. & f.* Respector, venerator.

respetar [res-pay-tar'], *va.* To respect, to venerate, to revere, to honor. **Hacerse respetar,** to win respect.

respeto [res-pay'-to], *m.* Respect (consideración), regard, consideration, veneration; attention; observance. **Respeto a** or **respeto de,** with regard to. **Respeto de sí mismo,** self-respect. **Faltar al respeto,** to be disrespectful.

respetuosamente [res-pec-too-o'-sah-men-tay], *adv.* Respectfully.

respetuoso, sa [res-pay-too-o´-so, sah], *a.* 1. Respectable. 2. Respectful, ceremonious; obsequious, dutiful.

réspice [res'-pe-thay], *m.* 1. *(Coll.)* Short, brusque reply (respuesta). 2. A short, but sharp reproof.

respigador, ra [res-pe-gah-dor', rah], *m. & f.* Gleaner.

respigar [res-pe gar'], *m.* To glean, as after reapers.

respigón [res-pe-gone'], *m.* 1. Hangnail. 2. Sore upon the fleshy part of the hoof of horses.

respingar [res-pin-gar'], *vn.* 1. To kick, to wince. 2. To obey reluctantly.

respingo [res-peen´-go], *m.* 1. Kick, jerk. 2. Reluctance, unwillingness, peevishness.

respingoso, sa [res-pin-go'-so, sah], *a.* 1. Kicking, wincing (animales). 2. Growing, tetchy.

respirable [res-pe-rah'-blay], *a.* Respirable, capable of respiration.

respiración [res-pe-rah-the-on'], *f.* Respiration, breathing; expiration; vent. **Quedarse sin respiración,** to be out of breath.

respiradero [res-pe-rah-day'-ro], *m.* 1. Vent, breathing-hole. 2. *(Arch.)* Air-passage, louver. 3. Cupping-glass. 4. Rest, repose. 5. An organ of respiration.

respirante [res-pe-rahn'-tay], *pa.* Respiring, breathing, exhaling.

respirar [res-pe-rar'], *vn.* 1. To respire, to breathe. (Sometimes used as transitive.) 2. To rest, to respire, to take rest from toil. 3. To exhale scents or odors. 4. To speak: in this sense it is frequently used with a negative. **No respiró,** he did not open his lips. 5. To get breath. 6. To exhale; to animate. **Sin respirar,** without drawing breath. **No tener por donde respirar,** *(Coll.)* to have no valid answer to a charge.

respiratorio, ria [res-pe-rah-to -re-o, ah], *a.* Respiratory, serving for breathing or related to it.

respiro [res-pee'-ro], *m.* 1. Act of breathing. 2. Moment of rest (descanso). 3. *(Met.)* Longer time for making payment.

resplandecencia [res-plan-day-then'-the-ah], *f.* Resplendency, splendor, lustre; fame, glory.

resplandecer [res-plan-day-therr'], *vn.* 1. To emit rays of light. 2. To glitter, to glisten, to gleam, to be brilliant, to glow. 3. To shine (relucir), to outshine, to be eminent or conspicuous.

resplandeciente [res-plan-day-the-en'-tay], *pa. & a.* Resplendent, shining (brillante), glittering; luminous, light.

resplandina

resplandina [res-plan-dee'-nah], V. (Coll.) Sternness of countenance, sharp reproof.

resplandor [res-plan-dor'], m. 1. Splendor, brightness, brilliancy (brillantez), luminousness. 2. A kind of shining paint for women. 3. (Mex.) Sunlight (luz del sol). 4. Glare (brillo).

responder [res-pon-derr'], va. & vn. 1. To answer; to resolve a doubt, to respond. 2. To re-echo. 3. To acknowledge, to own as a benefit received; to be grateful. 4. To yield, to produce. 5. To answer, to have the desired effect. 6. To correspond (corresponder); to be situated; to answer to. 7. To show oneself pleased. 8. To be, or to make oneself responsible for something. 9. To reply to a letter (contestar). 10. To answer back (replicar). 11. To obey (mandos), to respond to (situación, tratamiento). **Responder a una pregunta,** to answer a question. **Responder a una descripción,** to fit a description. **Responder de,** to be responsible for. **Responder al nombre de,** to be called, to go by the name of.

respondiente [res-pon-de-en'-tay], pa. & a. Respondent; answering.

respondón, na [res-pon-done', nah], a. Giving answers constantly; ever ready to reply.

responsabilidad [res-pon-sah-be-le-dahd'], f. Responsibility, liability, accountableness. **Responsabilidad solidaria,** joint responsibility.

responsabilizar [res-pon-sah-be-le-thar'], va. **Responsabilizar a uno,** to make somebody responsible. -vr. To make oneself responsible.

responsable [res-pon-sah'-blay], a. Responsible, liable, accountable, answerable. **Hacerse responsable de algo,** to assume responsibility for something.

responsar, responsear [res-pon-sar'], vn. To repeat the responses.

responsión[res-pon-se-on'], f. Sum which the members of the Order of St. John, who enjoy an income, contribute to the treasury of the order.

responsivo, va [res-pon-see'-vo, vah], a. (For.) Responsive, pertinent to the question, relevant in reply.

responso [res-pon'-so], m. Responsary, separate from the divine office for the dead.

responsorio [res-pon-so'-re-o], m. Response.

respuesta [res-poo-es'-tah], f. 1. Answer, reply; response. 2. Report of firearms. 3. Sound echoed back 4. Refutation.

resquebradura, resquebrajadura [res-kay-brah-ha-doo'-rah], f. Crack, cleft, flaw, split.

resquebrajar [res-kay-brah-har'], vn. To crack, to split. -vr. To crack, to split.

resquebrajo [res-kay-brah'-ho], m. Crack, cleft.

resquebrajoso, sa [res-kay-brah-ho'-so, sah], a. Brittle, fragile.

resquebrar [res-kay-brar'], vn. To crack, to begin to open; to burst.

resquemar [res-kay-mar'], va. & vn. To burn or sting the tongue (comida).

resquemo [res-kay'-mo], m. **resquemazón** [res-kay-mah-thone'], f. 1. Pungency of any food. 2. A disagreeable taste and odor which eatables acquire from being burned by too much fire.

resquicio [res-kee'-the-o], m. 1. Chink between the jamb and leaf of a door (abertura); crack, cleft. 2. Subterfuge, evasion. 3. (Met.) Faint hope. 4. Chance (posibilidad). 5. (And. Carib.) Vestige (vestigio). 6. (Carib.) Little bit (pedacito).

resta [res'-tah], f. Rest, residue, remainder (residuo). V. RESTO.

restablecer [res-tah-blay-therr'], va. To restore, to re-establish, to reinstate. -vr. To recover from a disease, to mend.

restablecimiento [res-tah-blay-the-me-en'-to], m. Re-establishment, restoration, resettlement.

restador [res-tah-dor'], m. (Arith.) Remainder.

restallar [res-tal-lyar'], vn. 1. To crack, as a whip. 2. To crackle, to creak.

restante [res-tahn'-tay], pa. & m. Remainder, residue; remaining. **Lo restante,** the rest.

restañadura [res-tah-nyah-doo'-rah], f. The act of recovering with tin; retinning.

restañar [res-tah-nyar'], va. 1. To retin, to cover with tin a second time. 2. To stanch, to stop blood. 3. V. RESTALLAR. -vr. To restagnate, to stand without flow.

restaño [res-tah'-nyo], m. 1. Kind of glazed silk, interwoven with gold or silver. 2. V. ESTANCACIÓN.

restar [res-tar'], va. 1. To subtract, to find the residue of anything. 2. In tennis, to return a ball, to strike it back (pelota). **Restar autoridad a uno,** to take away authority. -vn. To be left, to remain due.

restauración [res-tah-oo-rah-the-on'], f. 1. Restoration, redintegration, restoring. 2. Restoration, liberty recovered by an oppressed or subjugated people.

restaurador, ra [res-tah-oo-rah-dor', rah], m. & f. Restorer.

restaurante [res-tah-oo-rahn'-tay], m. 1. Restorer, re-establisher. 2. (Gallicism) Restaurant. V. FONDA. -pa. Restoring.

restaurar [res-tah-oo-rar'], va. To restore, to retrieve; to repair, to renew.

restaurativo, va [res-tah-oo-rah-tee'-vo, vah], a. Restorative.

restinga [res-teen'-gah], f. Ridge of rocks in the sea; sand-bank.

restingar [res-teen-gar'], m. Place containing ridges of rocks or sand banks.

restitución [res-te-too-the-on'], f. Restitution, restoring.

restituible [res-te-too-ee'-blay], a. That which may be restored.

restituidor, ra [res-te-too-e-dor', rah], m. & f. Restorer, re-establisher.

restituir [res-te-too-eer'], vn. 1. To restore, to give up, to give back, to lay down. 2. To re-establish. 3. To reanimate. -vr. To return to the place of departure.

restitutivo, va [res-te-too-tee'-vo, vah], **Restitutorio, ria** [res-te-too-to'-re-o, ah], a. Relating to restitution.

resto [res'-to], m. 1. Remainder, residue, balance, rest (lo que queda). 2. Sum staked at play. 3. Rebound of the ball in the game of tennis. 4. Stake (apuesta). 5. (Fig.) Without limit. 6. Arrest, attachment. **Restos humanos,** human remains.

restregar [res-tray-gar'], va. 1. To rub (frotar), to scrub (fregar). 2. (Coll.) To rub it in, to rub sarcastically.

restregón [res-tray-gone'], m. Scrubbing.

restreñimiento [res-tray-nye-me-ayn'-to], m. (Prov.) V. RESTRIÑIMIENTO.

restribar [res-tre-bar'], vn. To lean upon strongly,

restricción [res-trec-the-on'], f. Restriction, limitation, modification. **Restricciones eléctricas,** electricity cuts. **Sin restricción de,** without restrictions as to.

restrictivamente [res-trec-tee'-vah-men-tay], adv. Restrictively.

restrictivo, va [res-trec-tee'-vo, vah], a. Restrictive, restringent.

restricto, ta [res-treec'-to, tah], a. Limited, confined, restrictive.

restringa [res-treen'-gah], f. V. RESTINGA.

restringente [res-trin-hen'-tay], m. Restrainer; restringent. -pa. Restraining.

restringible [res-trin-hee'-blay], a. Restrainable, limitable.

restringido [res-trin-hee'-do], a. Restricted, limited.

restringir [res-trin-heer'], va. To restrain, to restrict, to restringe, to confine, to control, to constrain, to limit.

restriñente [res-tre-nyen'-tay], pa. & a. Restringent; binding.

restriñidor, ra [res-tre-nye-dor', rah], m. & f. Restrainer, binder.

restriñimiento [res-tre-nye-me-en'-to], m. Restriction, making costive.

restriñir [res-tre-nyeer´], *va.* To bind, to make costive, to restrain.

restrojera [res-tro-hay´-rah], *f.* *(Prov.)* Female servant taken to attend reapers at harvest-time.

restrojo [res-tro´-ho], *m.* V. RASTROJO.

resucitado, da [ray-soo-the-tah´-do, dah], *a.* & *pp.* of RESUCITAR. **Pájaro resucitado**, little humming-bird; it is dormant in winter, hence its name.

resucitador, ra [ray-soo-the-tah-dor´, rah], *m.* & *f.* Restorer, reviver.

resucitar [ray-soo-the-tar´], *va.* 1. To resuscitate, to revive. 2. To renew, to renovate, to modernize. -*vn.* 1. To revive, to return to life. 2. To recover from a dangerous disease.

resucha [ray-soo´-chah], *f.* A worthless animal (vaca, buey).

resudación [ray-soo-dah-the-on´], *f.* Perspiration, transudation.

resudar [ray-soo-dar´], *m.* To transude, to perspire, to transpire.

resudor [ray-soo-dor´], *m.* Slight perspiration.

resuello [ray-soo-ay´-lyo], *m.* 1. Breath (aliento), breathing (respiración), respiration. 2. Pursiness, shortness of breath.

resueltamente [ray-soo-el-tah-men´-tay], *adv.* Resolutely, resolvedly, confidently, boldly.

resuelto, ta [ray-soo-el´-to, tah], *a* & *pp. irr.* of RESOLVER. 1. Resolute (decidido), audacious, bold, determined, steady, constant, confident. 2. Prompt, quick, diligent. **Estar resuelto a algo**, to be set on something.

resulta [ray-sool´-tah], *f.* 1. Rebound, resilience. 2. Result, effect, consequence. 3. Vacancy, a post or employment unoccupied. 4. Success. **De resultas**, in consequence.

resultado [ray-sool-tah´-do], *m.* Result, issue, consequence.—**Resultado, da**, *pp.* of RESULTAR.

resultancia [ray-sool-tahn´ the ah], *f.* Result, resultance.

resultante [ray-sool-tahn´-tay], *pa.* Resulting, following, proceeding from.

resultar [ray-sool-tar´], *vn.* 1. To rebound. 2. To result, as a consequence or effect, to follow; to proceed from. 3. To remain, to be done or provided for. 4. To prove (llegar a ser). 5. To stem from (derivarse de). 6. To ensue (seguir). 7. To turn out well (salir bien). 8. To look well (parecer bien). **El conductor resultó muerto**, the driver was killed. **Ahora resulta que no vamos**, now it turns out that we´re not going. **Resultó de lo mejor**, it worked out very well. **Esa corbata no resulta con ese traje**, that tie doesn´t go with the suit.

resumbruno, na [ray-soom-broo´-no, nah], *a.* Brown, of the color of a hawk's feathers, between red and black.

resumen [ray-soo´-men], *m.* 1. Abridgment, summary, extract, compendium. 2. Recapitulation, detail repeated. 3. *(Law.)* Brief. **En resumen**, briefly, in short; lastly.

resumidamente ray-soo-mee´-dah-men-tay], *adv.* Briefly, compendiously, summarily.

resumido, da [ray-soo-mee´-do, dah], *a.* & *pp.* of RESUMIR. Abridged. **En resumidas cuentas**, in short, briefly.

resumir [ray-soo-meer´], *va.* 1. To abridge (reducir). 2. To reassume, to resume; to repeat, as the propounder of a thesis, the syllogism of an opponent. 3. To summarize (condensar). *vr.* To include; to convert. **Resumirse en**, to be reduced to.

resunción [ray-soon-the-on´], *f.* Summary, abridgment. 2. Repetition of several words inserted in a speech.

resuntivo, va [ray-soon-tee´-vo, vah], *a.* That which restores or resumes.

resupinado, da [ray-soo-pe-nah-do, dah], *a.* *(Cabot.)* Resupinate, inverse in position.

resurgir [ray-soor-her´], *vn.* 1. To reappear (reaparecer), to revive; to be resurrected (resucitar). 2. *(Fig.)* To acquire a new spirit.

resurrección [ray-soor-rec-the-on´], *f.* Resurrection, revival, resuscitation.

resurtida [ray-soor-tee´-dah], *f.* Rebound, repercussion.

resurtir [ray-soor-teer´], *vn.* To rebound, to fly back.

retablo [ray-tah´-blo], *m.* 1. Picture drawn on a board. 2. Splendid ornament of altars.

retacar [ray-tah-car´], *va.* To hit the ball twice on a truck-table. -*vr.* *(Cono Sur)* To dig one´s heels in.

retacería [ray-tah-thay-ree´-ah], *f.* Collection of remnants.

retaco [ray-tah´-co], *m.* 1. A short, light fowling-piece. 2. A short tack or stick of a truck-table. 3. A short thick person.

retador [ray-tah-dor´], *m.* Challenger.

retaguardia [ray-tah-goo-ar´-de-ah], *f.* Rear-guard. **A retaguardia**, in the rear.

retahíla [ray-tah-ee´-lah], *f.* File, range, or series of many things following one another.

retajar [ray-tah-har´], *va.* 1. To cut round (cortar). 2. To cut again and again the nib of a pen. 3. To circumcise. 4. *(LAm.)* To castrate (castrar).

retal [ray-tahl´], *m.* Remnant of cloth or lace; clipping.

retallar [ray-tal-lyar´], *vn.* To shoot or sprout anew. -*va.* To regrave, to retouch a graving. V. RETALECER.

retallecer [ray-tal-lyay-therr´], *vn.* To resprout, to put forth new shoots from the root-stock.

retallo [ray-tah´-lyo], *m.* A new sprout of a plant sprung from the root-stock.

retama [ray-tah´-mah], *f.* *(Bot.)* 1. Broom. **Retama de flor blanca**, white single seed broom. **Retama blanca**, Spanish genista, furze, green-weed.

retamal, retamar [ray-tah-mahr´], *m.* **Retamera,** *f.* Place where furze or broom grows, and is gathered.

retamilla [ray-tah-meel´-lyah], *f.* *(Bot.)* Jointed genista or furze.

retamón [ray-tah-mone´], *m.* *(Bot.)* 1. Purging broom. 2. V. RETAMA DE ESCOBAS.

retapar [ray-tah-par´], *va.* To cover again.

retar [ray-tar´], *va.* 1. To impeach or charge one with a criminal offense before the king. 2. To challenge (desafiar), to combat; to reprehend. 3. *(Cono Sur)* To insult (insultar).

retardación [ray-tar-dah-the-on´], *f.* Retardation, delay, detention, loitering.

retardar [ray-tar-dar´], *va.* To retard, to defer, to delay, to obstruct.

retardilla [ray-tar-deel-lyah], *f.* A slight difference or dispute.

retardo [ray-tar´-do], *m.* Cunctation, delay, procrastination, retardment.

retasa [ray-tah´-sah], *f.* Second valuation or assessment.

retasar [ray-tah-sar´], *va.* To value or assess a second time.

retazar [ray-tah-thar´], *va.* To tear in pieces; to divide up (dividir); to chop (leña).

retazo [ray-tah´-tho], *m.* 1. Remaining piece, remnant, cuttings. 2. Fragment or portion of some discourse or reasoning.

retejador [ray-tay-hah-dor´], *m.* & *a.* Repairer of a tile-roof; mending, reparative.

retejar [ray-tay-har´], *va.* 1. To repair the roof of a building, to tile anew. 2. To mend, to patch; to risk.

retejer [ray-tay-herr´], *va.* To weave closely.

retejo [ray-tay´-ho], *m.* Repairing of a roof, retiling.

retemblar [ray-tem-blar´], *vn.* To tremble or shake repeatedly: to vibrate. *(Yo retiemblo, yo retiemble,* from *Retemblar.* V. ACRECENTAR.)

retemblor [ray-tem-blor´], *m.* A second vibration, repeated shaking.

retén [ray-tayn´], *m.* 1. Store, stock, reserve. 2. Military reserve corps. 3. Detent, ratchet, catch.

retención [ray-ten-the-on´], *f.* 1. Retention, keeping back. 2. Retention of an office which was held before advancing to another. 3. Stagnation, retention within the body of an excretion which ought to be expelled.

retenedor, ra [ray-tay-nay-dor´, rah], *m.* & *f.* Retainer.

retener [ray-tay-nerr´], *va.* 1. To retain, to withhold; to keep back from its owner. 2. To guard, to preserve. 3. To maintain and enjoy a position after being advanced to another. 4. To suspend, as by a king, the use of an ecclesiastical rescript. **Retener a uno preso**, to keep somebody in detention. *(Yo* *retengo, yo retenga; él retuvo, retuviera;* from *Retener. V.* TENER.)

retenida [ray-tay-nee'-dah], *f. (Naut.)* Guy. **Retenida de proa**, *(Naut.)* headfast, a rope to fasten the head of a ship.

retenidamente [ray-tay-nee'-dah-men-tay], *adv.* Retentively.

retentar [ray-ten-tar'], *va.* To threaten with a relapse of a former disorder.

retentiva [ray-ten-tee'-vah], *f.* 1. Retentiveness. 2. Memory.

retentivo, va [ray-ten-tee'-vo, vah], *a.* Retentive, retaining.

retentriz [ray-ten-treeth'], *a. (Med.)* Retentive.

reteñir [ray-tay-nyeer'], *va.* To dye over again, to tinge a second time. -*vn.* To tingle, to sound, to resound. *V.* RETINIR.

retesamiento [ray-tay-sah-me-en'-to], *m.* Coagulation, hardness.

retesarse [ray-tay-sar'-say], *vr.* To become hard, to be stiff, as teats with milk.

reteso [ray-tay'-so], *m.* 1. Stiffness or distention of teats with milk. 2. *V.* TESO.

reticencia [ray-te-then'-the-ah], *f.* 1. Reticence (reserva), concealment by silence. 2. Insinuation (sugerencia), suggestion; implication (transcendencia).

reticulado, da [ray-te-coo-lah'-do, dah], *a. V.* RETICULAR.

reticular [ray-te-coo-lar'], *a.* Reticular, resembling network.

retículo [ray-tee'-coo-lo], *m.* 1. Network, reticular tissue: used generally of plant structure. 2. Cobweb, micrometer of a telescope or microscope.

retín [ray-teen'], *m. V.* RETINTÍN.

retina [ray-tee'-nah], *f.* Retina of the eye.

retinte [ray-teen'-tay], *m.* 1. Second dye given to anything. 2. *V.* RETINTÍN.

retintín [ray-tin-teen'], *m.* 1. A tinkling sound (tilín); jingle (tintineo); clink. 2. An affected tone of voice usually satirical. **Decir algo con retintín**, to say something sarcastically.

retinto [ray-teen'-to], *a.* Dark, obscure, almost black. -*pp. irr.* of RETEÑIR.

retiñir [ray-te-nyeer'], *vn.* To tinkle, to resound, to click.

retiración [ray-te-rah-the-on'], *f. (Typ.)* Second form put in a press in order to print the back of a sheet.

retirada [ray-te-rah'-dah], *f.* 1. *(Mil.)* Retreat. **Tocar retirada**, to sound a retreat. 2. Retreat, retirement, place of security. 3. Place of retirement, closet.

retiradamente [ray-te-rah'-dah-men-tay], *adv.* Secretly, retiredly.

retirado, da [ray-te-rah'-do, dah], *a. & pp.* of RETIRAR. Retired, solitary, cloistered; close; remote (lugar), distant; retired (oficial), pensioned. **Hombre retirado**, a man fond of retirement. **Oficial retirado**, half pay officer.

retiramiento [ray-te-rah-me-en'-to], *m.* Retirement. *V.* RETIRO.

retirar [ray-te-rar'], *va.* 1. To withdraw, to retire, to lay aside (mover), to reserve, to hide away (quitar). 2. To repel, to force the enemy to retire or retreat. 3. To print the back of a sheet. 4. To revoke; to retreat. 5. To take out (pieza). 6. To withdraw (moneda, sello). 7. To retire, to pension off (jubilar). 8. To withdraw (acusación, palabras). -*vr.* 1. To retire, to retreat, to cease to pursue; to recede, to go back. 2. To retire from intercourse with the world; to retire from trade. 3. To retire from a public station. 4. To retire from company. 5. To take refuge; to retire to one's house or department. 6. *(Mil.)* To raise a siege or blockade; to abandon a post (jubilarse). 7. To retire or retreat from danger. 8. To retire (después de cenar). **Retirarse ante un peligro**, to retreat. **Cuando me retire de los negocios**, when I retire from business.

retiro [ray-tee'-ro], *m.* 1. Retreat, the act of retiring (acto); recess: act of declining any business. 2. Retreat, retirement, place of retirement (lugar). 3. Concealedness, privacy, obscurity, retirement, private life. **Retiro prematuro**, early retirement.

retirona [ray-te-ro'-nah], *f. (Coll.) V.* RETIRADA.

reto [ray'-to], *m.* 1. Challenge to combat (desafío). 2. Threat (amenaza), menace. 3. *(Cono Sur)* Telling off (reprimenda).

retobado, da [ray-to-bah'-do, dah], *a.* 1. *(Peru. Met. and coll.)* Artful, crafty. 2. *(LAm.)* Wild (animal); wild (persona), unruly; rebellious (rebelde). 3. *(And. CAm. Mex.)* Grumbling (gruñón). 4. *(And. Cono Sur)* Cunning (taimado).

retobar [ray-to-bar'], *va. (Amer. Com.)* To cover parcels of goods with hides for transportation.

retobo [ray-to'-bo], *m.* 1. A covering of hides. 2. *(LAm.)* Stubbornness (terquedad); grumble (protesta). 3. *(LAm.)* Aftertaste (resabio).

retocamiento [ray-to-cah-me-en'-to], *m.* Action of retouching.

retocar [ray-to-car'], *va.* 1. To uptouch a painting, to mend. 2. To finish any work completely. 3. To play back (grabación).

retomar [ray-to-mar'], *va.* To take up again.

retoñar, retoñecer [ray-to-nyar', ray-to-nyay-therr'], *vn.* 1. To sprout or shoot again: applied to a plant which has been cut. 2. To appear again: applied to cutaneous distempers.

retoño [ray-toh'-nyo], *m.* Sprout or shoot from a plant which has been cut above the neck of the root.

retoque [ray-toh'-kay], *m.* 1. Repeated and frequent pulsation. 2. Finishing stroke, to render a work perfect. 3. Symptom, threatening, of some disease.

retorcedura [ray-tor-thay-doo'-rah], *f.* Twisting, wreathing.

retorcer [ray-tor-therr'], *va.* 1. To twist (brazo), to contort, to convolve. 2. To retort, to convince by returning an argument. 3. *(Met.)* To interpret perversely. -*vr.* 1. To get into knots (cuerda). 2. To writhe (persona); to squirm. **Retorcerse de dolor**, to writhe in pain. (*Yo retuerzo, yo retuerza*, from *Retorcer. V.* COCER.)

retorcido [ray-tor-thee'-do], *m.* A kind of twisted sweetmeat. **Retorcido, da**, *pp.* of RETORCER.

retorcijo [ray-tor-thee'-ho], *m. V.* RETORCIMIENTO.

retorcimiento [ray-tor-the-me-en'-to], *m.* Twisting (brazo), wreathing (cuerpo entero), contortion.

retórica [ray-to'-re-cah], *f.* Rhetoric. *pl. (Coll.)* Sophistries or reasons not fitted to the case.

retóricamente [ray-to-ree'-cah-men-tay], *adv.* Rhetorically.

retórico, ca [ray-toh'-re-co, cah], *a.* Rhetorical, oratorical. -*m.* Rhetorician, one who speaks with eloquence; one who teaches rhetoric.

retornable [ray-tor-nah-blay], *a.* **Envase no retornable**, non-returnable empty.

retornamiento [ray-tor-nah-me-en'-to], *m.* Return.

retornante [ray-tor-nahn'-tay], *pa.* Returning.

retornar [ray-tor-nar'], *vn.* To return, to come back, to retrocede or retrograde. -*va.* 1. To return (devolver), to restore, to give back. 2. To turn, to twist, to contort, to cause to go back. 3. To replace (devolver a su lugar).

retornelo [ray-tor-nay'-lo], *m.* 1. Ritornello, the burden of a song. 2. *(Poet.)* The final strophe of a song.

retorno [ray-tor'-no], *m.* 1. Return (vuelta), coming back; return chaise or horse. 2. Repayment (pago), return of a favor. 3. Barter, exchange (cambio), traffic. 4. *(Mex. Aut.)* Turning place.

retorsión [ray-tor-se-on'], *f.* 1. Retortion, bending back. 2. Retortion, retorsion, act of replying sharply.

retorsivo, va [ray-tor-see'-vo, vah], *a.* That which retorts.

retorta [ray-tor'-tah], *f.* 1. Retort, a chemical vessel. 2. A sort of linen of medium fineness.

retortero [ray-tor-tay´-ro], *m.* Twirl, rotation. **Andar al retortero**, To hover about. **Traer al retortero**, (1) *(Coll.)* To bring one from one side almost to the other. (2) *(Met. and coll.)* To keep one on the go (with peremptory occupations). (3) *(Met. and coll.)* To twist one around, to deceive with false promises and dissembled flatteries.

retortijar [ray-tor-te-har'], *va.* To twist, to form into a ring. *V.* ENSORTIJAR.

retortijón [ray-tor-te-hone'], *m.* The act of twisting, contortion. **Retortijón de tripas**, griping.

retostado, da [ray-tos-tah'-d, dah], *a. & pp.* of RETOSTAR. Brown-colored.

retostar [ray-tos-tar'], *va.* To toast again, to toast brown.

retozador, ra [ray-to-thah-dor', rah], *m. & f.* Frisker, one not constant, a wanton.

retozadura [ray-to-thah-doo'-rah], *f. V.* RETOZO.

retozar [ray-to-thar'], *vn.* 1. To frisk and skip about, to romp, to frolic, to dally with, to sport, to play. 2. To hoiden, to romp immodestly. 3. Of passions, to sport within us. *-va.* To tickle, to invite laughter and merriment; to titillate amorously. **Retozar la risa,** to be moved to laughter.

retozo [ray-to'-tho], *m.* Friskiness, romping (holgorio), wantonness, lascivious gaiety, frisk, a frolic, dalliance. **Retozo de la risa,** suppressed laugh.

retozón, na [ray-to-thone', nah], *a.* Wanton, rompish, frolicsome, playful (juguetón), gamesome, coltish.

retozona [ray-to-tho'-nah], *f.* Romp, a rude, noisy girl.

retrabar [ray-trah-bar'], *pa.* To revive a quarrel.

retracción [ray-trac-the-on'], *f.* Retraction, drawing back.

retractable [ray trac-tah'-blay], *a.* Retractable, which may be or should be retracted or recanted.

retractación [ray-trac-tah-the-on'], *f.* Retractation, recantation.

retractar [ray-trac-tar'], *va.* To retract. *-vr.* To go back on one's word. **Me retracto de la acusación hecha,** I withdraw the accusation.

retráctil [ray-trahc'-teel], *a. (Zool.)* Retractile, hidden in repose.

retractilidad [ray-trac-te-le-dahd'], *f.* Retractility.

retracto [ray-trahc'-to], *m. (Law.)* Retrieval, the act or right of retrieving or recovering a thing sold to another.

retractor [ray-trac-tor'], *m.* Retractor, a surgical instrument for holding apart the edges of an incision.

retraer [ray-trah-err'], *va.* 1. To reclaim, to dissuade. 2. To retrieve, to recover a thing sold. *-vr.* 1. To take refuge, to flee. 2. To withdraw from (retirarse de), to retire, to live a retired life. 3. In politics, to retire, to abandon all participation in public matters. *(Yo retraigo, yo retraiga, retraje , from Retraer. V.* TRAER.)

retraído [ray-trah-ee´-do], *m.* 1. Fugitive, one who has taken sanctuary in a sacred place. 2. A lover of solitude. **Retraído, da,** *pp.* of RETRAER.

retraimiento [ray-trah-e-me-en'-to], *m.* 1. Retreat, refuge (lugar), asylum. 2. Inner apartment or room. 3. Retirement from public political life.

retranca [ray-trahn'-cah], *f.* 1. A kind of large cropper for mules and lethal beasts of burden. 2. *(Amer.)* Brake of a wagon or railway car.

retranquear [ray-tran-kay-ar'], *va. (Arch.)* To model pillars.

retranqueo [ray-tran-kay'-o], *m. (Arch.)* Position given to bodies outside of their square.

retransmisión [ray-trans-me-se-on'], *f.* Repeat, rebroadcast.

retransmitir [ray-trans-me-teer'], *va.* To relay (mensaje), to pass on; to repeat; to broadcast live (en vivo).

retrasado, da [ray-trah-sah'-do, dah], *a.* 1. Late, retarded. **Retrasado mental,** moron, person mentally retarded. 2. To be slow (reloj). **Tengo el reloj retrasado 8 minutos,** my watch is 8 minutes slow. 3. Backward, underdeveloped (país). 4. Unused (comida).

retrasar [ray-trah-sar'], *va.* To defer, to put off, to dally, to delay. *-vn & vr.* To retrograde, to decline (producción), to be slow (reloj), to be late (persona, tren).

retraso [ray-trah'-so], *m.* 1. Delay (demora), putting off, time lag (intervalo), slowness (tardanza). **Llegar con retraso,** to be late. 2. Backwardness (de país). 3. **Retraso mental,** mental deficiency.

retratable [ray-trah-tah´-blay], *a.* Retractable, retractible.

retratación [ray-trah-tah-the-on'], *f.* Retractation, recantation.

retratador, ra [ray-trah-tah-dor', rah], *m. & f.* Limner, portrait-painter.

retratar [ray-trah-tar'], *va.* 1. To portray, to draw portraits, to limn. 2. To imitate, to copy. 3. To paint, to describe. 4. To photograph. 5. To retract, to gainsay, to disavow. 6. To retrieve, to get back a thing sold. *-vr.* 1. To recant; see 5th def. (with these significations the spelling *retractar* is quite to be preferred.) 2. To have one's picture painted. 3. To pay (dinero).

retratillo [ray-trah-teel'-lyo], *m. dim.* A small portrait.

retratista [ray-trah-tees'-tah], *m.* 1. Portrait-painter, limner. 2. *(Amer.)* Portrait photographer.

retrato [ray-trah'-to], *m.* 1. Portrait, effigy. 2. Copy, resemblance, imitation. 3. Metrical description, poetical portrait. 4. *(Law.) V.* RETRACTO. 5. *(Fig.)* Portrayal (descripción), depiction. 6. *(Fig.)* Likeness (semejanza). **Ser el vivo retrato de,** to be the very image of.

retrayente [ray-trah-yen'-tay], *pa. & m. & f.* Retractor, recanter; retrieving.

retrechería [ray-tray-chay-ree'-ah], *f.* 1. Cunning or craft for eluding the confession of the truth or the fulfilment of what was offered. 2. *(Coll.)* Flattery, sycophancy.

retrechero, ra [ray-tray-chay'-ro, rah], *a. & n. (Coll.)* 1. Flattering; a flatterer. 2. dissimulating, concealing the truth; eluding the fulfiment of what was offered. 3. *(LAm.)* Mean (tacaño); unreliable (tramposo), deceitful; suspicious (sospechoso).

retrepado, da [ray-tray-pah'-do, dah], *a.* Leaning backward in a natural or affected manner (orgullo); reclining (silla).

retreparse [ray-tray-par'-say], *vr.* To lean back, to recline in a chair.

retreta [ray-tray'-tah], *f. (Mil.)* 1. Retreat, to withdraw, or go back to their quarters for the night (soldados). 2. Open-air band concert.

retrete [ray-tray'-tay], *m.* 1. Closet, a small room for privacy. 2. Water-closet.

retretico, illo, ito [ray-tray-tee'-co], *m. dim.* Little water-closet, close-stool.

retribución [ray-tre-boo-the-on'], *f.* Retribution, recompense, reward (recompensa); damage.

retribuir [rar-tre-boo-eer'], *m.* To pay back (pagar), to recompense (compensar).

retribuyente [ray-tray-boo-yen'-tay], *pa. & a.* Retributive, retributory; retributing.

retroacción [ray-tro-ac-the-on'], *f.* Retroaction.

retroactivo, va [ray-tro-ac-te´-vo, vah], *a.* Retroactive: spoken of a law which is applied to past transactions. **Ley de efecto retroactivo,** retrospective law.

retrocarga [ray-tro-car'-gah], (used in the expression **De retrocarga**), breech loading.

retroceder [ray-tro-they-derr'], *vn.* 1. To retrograde, to go backward (volver atrás), to retrocede, to fail back: to grow worse. 2. To recede from, to draw back from an opinion or judgment. **Retrocedió unos pasos,** he went back a few steps.

retrocesión [ray-tro-thay-se-on'], *f.* Retrocession, returning or receding.

retroceso [ray-tro-thay´-so], *m.* 1. Retrocession. 2. *(Fig.)* Backing down. 3. *(Med.)* Renewed attack.

retrocohete [ray-tro-co-ay'-tay], *m (Aer.)* Retro-rocket.

retrogradación [re-tro-grah-dah-the-one´], *f.* Retrogradation, retrogression.

retrogradar [ray-tro-grah-dar'], *vn.* 1. To retrograde. 2. To incline to reaction, to oppose progress (política) *V.* RETROCEDER.

retrógrado, da [ray-tro'-gah-do, dah], *a.* Retrograde.

retronar [ray-tro-nar'], *vn.* To thunder again, to continue thundering after a storm is nearly over.

retropilastra [ray-tro-pe-lahs'-trah], *f.* Pilaster behind column.

retropropulsión [ray-tro-pro-pool-se-on´], *f.* Jet propulsion.

retrospectiva [ray-tros-payc-tee´-vah], *f.* 1. Retrospective (exhibición). 2. **En retrospectiva,** with hindsight.

retrospectivamente [ray-tros-payc-tee´-vah-men-tay], *adv.* Retrospectively; in retrospect.

retrotracción [ray-tro-trac-the-on'], *f. (Law.)* Antedating anything.

retrotraer [ray-tro-trah-err'], *va.* To apply to the present time what happened before. *(Yo retrotraigo, yo retrotraiga, yo retrotraje,* from *Retrotraer. V.* TRAER.)

retrovender [ray-tro-ven-derr'], *va (Law.)* To sell back to the first vender for the same price.

retroversión [ray-tro-ver-se-on'], *f. (Med.)* Retroversion, backward displacement.

retrovisión [ray-tro-ve-se-on'], *f.* Rear view. **Espejo de retrovisión,** rear-view mirror.

retrovisor [ray-tro-ve-sor'], *a.* **Espejo retrovisor,** driving mirror.

retrucar [ray-troo-car'], *vn.* To hit again, like a ball rebounding; to kiss (billar).

retruco [ray-troo'-co], *vn.* Repercussion of a ball.

retruécano [ray-troo-ay'-cah-no], *m.* A pun, a quibble, a play upon words.

retruque [ray-troo'-kay], *m.* 1. Betting, a higher wager on a card. 2. A kiss (billar). 3. *(And. Cono Sur)* Sharp retort (réplica). 4. *(Cono Sur, Mex.)* On the rebound; as a consequence.

retuerto, ta [ray-too-err'-to, tah], *pp. irr.* of RETORCER. Retwisted. *-a.* Very bad, sterile.

retumbante [ray-toom-bahn'-tay], *pa. & a.* Resonant, pompous, sonorous, bombastic, ridiculously tumid.

retumbar [ray-toom-bar'], *vn.* To resound, to make a great noise, to jingle, to boom, to clink. **La cascada retumbaba a lo lejos,** the waterfall boomed in the distance.

retumbo [ray-toom'-bo], *m.* Resonance, echo.

retundir [ray-toon-deer'], *va.* 1. To equal or hew stones in a building. 2. *(Met.)* To repel, to discuss.

reuma [ray'-oo-mah]. 1. *f.* Rheum defluxion. 2. *m.* Rheumatism.

reumático, ca [ray-oo-mah'-te-co, cah], *a.* Rheumatic.

reumatismo [ray-oo-mah-tees'-mo], *m.* Rheumatism.

reunión [ray-oo-ne-on'], *f.* 1. Meeting (asamblea), conference. 2. Gathering. 3. Joining, reuniting (reunión). 4. Bringing together. **Reunión en la cima,** Summit, conference.

reunir [ray-oo-neer'], *va.* 1. To join, to reunite (juntar). 2. To bring together, to assemble (datos), to pool (recursos), to save (ahorrar). 3. To combine (cualidades), to have, to possess (condiciones). **Los 4 reunidos no valen lo que él,** the 4 of them together are not as good as he is. **Reunió a sus amigos para discutirlo,** he assembled his friends to talk it over. *-vr.* 1. To meet (personas). 2. To gather. **Reunirse para,** to get together to.

revacunar [ray-vah-coo-nar'], *va.* To revaccinate.

reválida [ray-vah'-le-dah], *f.* 1. Passing one's final exams. 2. Final exams (para un título).

revalidar [ray-vah-le-dar'], *va.* To revalidate. *-vr.* To pass one's final exams (para un título).

revalorar [ray-vah-lo-rahr'], *va.* To revalue.

revalorizar [ray-vah-lo-re-thar'], *m.* To reevaluate.

revancha [ray-vahn'-chah], *f.* 1. Revenge, compensation for loss in gaming; return match. (A Gallicism used instead of **desquite**) 2. *V.* DESQUITE. **Tomarse la revancha,** to take revenge.

revecero ra [ray-vay-thay'-ro, rah], *a.* Changeable, mutable.

reveedor [ray-vay-ay-dor'], *m. V.* REVISOR.

revejecer [ray-vay-hay-therr'], *vn.* To grow prematurely old.

revejecido, da [ray-vay-hay-thee'-do, dah], *a. & pp.* of REVEJECER. Prematurely old, antiquated.

revejido, da [ray-vay-hee'-do, dah], *a.* Become old prematurely.

revelación [ray-vay-lah-the-on'], *f.* 1. Revelation, the act and effect of revealing. 2. Revelation from heaven; revealed religion. **Fue una revelación para mí,** it was a revelation to me.

revelado [ray-vay-lah'-do], *m.* Developing.

revelador, ra [ray-vay-la-dor', rah], *m. & f.* 1. Revealer. 2. Developer, in photography.

revelamiento [ray-vay-lah-me-en'-to], *m.* 1. *V.* REVELACIÓN. 2. Photographic development.

revelante [ray-vay-lahn'-tay], *pa.* Revealing.

revelar [ray-vay-lar'], *va.* 1. To reveal, to manifest, to communicate, to disclose (secreto). 2. To impart from heaven, to show the future. 3. To develop a photographic plate. 4. To betray (mostrar); to give away (delatar).

reveler [ray-vey-lerr'], *va. (Med.)* To redirect the cause of on illness in any important organ towards a less important organ.

revellín [ray-vel-lyeen'], *m. (Mil.)* Ravelin.

revendedera [ray-ven-day-day'-dah], *f. V.* REVENDEDORA.

revendedor [ray-ven-day-dor'], *m.* Retailer (al por menor), hawker (de calle), huckster, peddler.

revendedora [ray-ven-day-do'-rah], *f.* Huckstress, a female peddler.

revender [ray-ven-derr'], *va.* To retail (al por menor), to sell by retail, to peddle, to hawk (por la calle).

revenirse [ray-vay-neer'-say], *vr.* 1. To be consumed by degrees. 2. To be pricked, to grow sore, to ferment (vino, conservas). 3. To relinquish a preconceived opinion, to give up a point obstinately contested. 4. To discharge moisture. *(Yo me revengo, yo me revenga; él se revino, revendrá* from *Revenirse. V.* VENIR.)

reventa [ray-ven'-tah], *f.* Retail; second sale. **Precio de reventa,** resale price.

reventación [ray-ven-tah-the-on'], *m.* Disruption, rupture; vanishing in spray.

reventadero [ray-ven-tah-day'-ro], *m.* 1. A rough, uneven ground, of difficult access (terreno áspero). 2. Any painful and laborious work (trabajo). 3. *(And. Cono Sur, Mex.)* Bubbling spring (hervidero).

reventar [ray-ven-tar'], *vn.* 1. To burst, to break in pieces, to crack; of waves, to break into foam. 2. To toil, to drudge. 3. To burst forth, to break loose; applied to a violent passion. 4. To sprout, to shoot; to grow. 5. To long for, to crave. **Casi reventaba de ira,** he almost exploded with anger. *-va.* 1. To molest, to harass, to violate. 2. To burst (globo), to brake (barrera). 3. To flog (caballo), to work to death (persona). 4. To sink, to ruin (proyecto). 5. To do down (perjudicar). **Reventar de risa,** to burst into laughter. **Tengo una cubierta reventada,** I have a puncture. *(Yo reviento, yo reviente,* from *Reventar. V.* ACRECENTAR.)

reventazón [ray-ven-tah-thone'], *f.* 1. Disruption, rupture. 2. *(Naut.)* Breaker, the breaking of waves into foam.

reventón [ray-ven-tone'], *m.* 1. Bursting or cracking. **Reventón de neumático** or **de llanta,** tire blowout. 2. Great difficulty and distress (apuro). 3. Steep, declivity. 4. Toil, drudgery, severe labor and fatigue. 5. Death (muerte). 6. *(Cono Sur)* Outcrop of ore. 7. *(Cono Sur. Fig.)* Explosion (estallido).

rever [ray-verr'], *va.* To review (sentencia), to revise, to overlook, to resurvey.

reverberación [ray-ver-bay-rah-the-on'], *f.* Reverberation, the reflection of light. 2. Calcination in a reverberatory furnace.

reverberar [ray-ver-bay-rar'], *vn.* To reverberate (sonido), to reflect upon a polished surface (superficie), to play (luz).

reverbero [ray-ver-bay'-ro], *m.* 1. *V.* REVERBERACIÓN. 2. Reflector for the light of a light-house. 3. Reflector of polished glass or metal. **Horno de reverbero,** a reverberatory furnace, a smelting furnace.

reverdecer [ray-ver-day-therr'], *vn.* 1. To grow green again (tierra, planta). 2. To sprout again, to acquire new vigor and strength. *(Yo reverdezco, yo reverdezca,* from *Reverdecer. V.* CONOCER.)

reverencia [ray-vay-ren'-the-ah], *f.* 1. Reverence, respect, veneration, homage, honor, observance. 2. Bow of reverence (inclinación); obeisance. 3. Reverence, title given in Spain to members of religious orders. **Hacer una reverencia,** to bow.

reverenciable [ray-vay-ren-the-ah'-blay], *a.* Reverend.

reverenciador, ra [ray-vey-ren-the-ah-dor', rah], *m. & f.* Reverencer.

reverencial [ray-vay-ren-the-ahl'], *a.* Reverential.

reverencialmente [ray-vay-ren-the-al'-men-tay], *adv.* Reverentially, reverently.

reverenciar [ray-vay-ren-the-ar'], *va.* To venerate, to revere, to respect; to hallow; to reverence.

reverendamente [ray-vay-ren-dah-men'-tay], *adv.* Repectfully, reverentially.

reverendísimo, ma [ray-vay-ren-dee'-se-mo, mah], *a. sup.* Most reverend, right reverend.

reverendo, da [ray-vay-ren'-do, dah], *a.* 1. Reverend, the honorary epithet of prelates and distinguished members of religious orders; worthy of reverence. 2. Extremely circumspect and cautious. 3. Solemn (solemne). 4. *(LAm.)* Big (inmenso).

reverente [ray-vey-ren'-tay], *a.* Respectful, reverent; low.

reversible [ray-ver-see'-blay], *a. (Law.)* Returnable, revertible.

reversión [ray-ver-se-on'], *f.* Reversion, return.

reverse [ray-verr'-se], *m.* 1. Reverse side of coins. 2. Back part of anything.

reverso [ray-ver'-so], *m.* Back, other side; wrong side; reverse (de moneda). **El reverso de la medalla**, the other side of the coin.

reverter [ray-ver-terr'], *vn.* To overflow. *V.* REBOSAR. (*Yo reviento, yo revierta,* from *Reverter. V.* ATENDER.)

revés [ray-ves'], *m.* 1. Back part (dorso), back side, wrong side, underside (lado inferior). 2. Stroke with the back of the hand (golpe). 3. Disappointment, cross, misadventure. 4. Change of temper and disposition. 5. Reverse. *V.* REVERSO. **De revés**, diagonally, from left to right. **Al revés or del revés**, on the contrary, contrariwise (in slang. Over the left). **Todo nos salió al revés**, it all turned out wrong for us. **Llevar algo del revés**, to wear something the wrong way round.

revesado, da [ray-vay-sah'-do, dah], *a.* 1. Intractable, stubborn, obstinate. 2. Difficult entangled, perplexed, obscure. *-pp.* of REVESAR.

revesar [ray-vay-sar'], *va.* To vomit.

revestimiento [ray-ves-te-me-en'-to], *m.* Revestment, a coating or covering of a surface for strengthening or beautifying it.

revestir [ray-ves-teer'], *va.* 1. To dress, to put on clerical robes, to revest, to wear (vestir). 2. To repair or fortify a wall; to line (forrar); to crust. 3. *(Fig.)* To cloak (encubrir). 4. To have, to possess (cualidad). *-vr.* 1. To be swayed or carried along by some power or other to be invested with. 2. To be haughty, lofty, or elated with pride. **Los árboles se revisten de hojas**, the trees put on their leaves again.

revezar [ray-vay-thar'], *vn.* To alternate, to come in by turn, to relieve one after another, to work in rotation.

revezero [ray-vay-thay'-ro], *m.* One who alternates.

revezo [ray-vay'-tho], *m.* Alternacy, the act of relieving one another; reciprocal succession.

revidar [ray-ve-dar'], *va. (Prov.)* To reinvite.

reviejo, ja [ray-ve-ay'-ho, hah], *a.* Very old. *-m.* Withered branch of a tree.

reviernes [ray-ve-err'-nes], *m.* Each of the first seven Fridays after Easter.

revindicar [ray-van-de-car'], *va.* To claim.

revirado, da [ray-ve-rah'-do, dah], *a. (Bot.)* Twisted: applied to fibers of trees.

revirar [ray-ve-rar'], *va. (Naut.)* To veer again, to tuck again.

reviro [ray-vee'-ro], *m. (Naut.)* Canting or flaring, the curvature given to a timber in a ship.

revirón [ray-ve-rone'], *m.* Piece of sole leather put between the solepieces to make then even. *-a.* 1. *(CAm. Carib.)* Disobedient, rebellious.

revisar [ray-ve-sar'], *va.* To revise (texto, apuntes), to review, to examine (teoría), to review (tropas), to check. **Revisar las cuentas**, to audit accounts.

revisión [ray-ve-se-on'], *f.* Revision (repaso), reviewing, re-examination (reexaminación).

revisita [ray-ve-see'-tah], *f.* Revision, second examination.

revisor, ra [ray-ve-sor'], *m & f.* Reviser, censor. corrector, reviewer.

revisoria [ray-ve-so-ree'-ah], *f.* Office of censor or reviser.

revista [ray-vees'-tah], *f.* 1. Review (examen), revision. 2. *(Mil.)* Review (de tropas). 3. Magazine, review (periódico), publication. 4. Section (sección), page. 5. *(Teat.)* Revue; variety show. 6. *(And.)* Trim (de pelo). **Revista musical**, musical comedy, musical review. **Revista del corazón**, magazine of real life romance stories. **Revista de modas**, fashion paper.

revistar [ray-vis-tar'], *va.* To revise a suit at law, to try a cause a second time: to review troops.

revisto, ta [ray-vees'-to, tah], *pp. irr.* of REVER.

revitalizar [ray-ve-tah-le-thar'], *va.* To revitalize.

revite [ray-vee'-tay], *m.* Invitation to play in games.

revividero [ray-ve-ve-day'-ro], *m.* Place for rearing silkworms.

revivificar [ray-ve-ve-fe-car'], *va.* To revivificate, to vivify.

revivir [ray-ve-veer'], *vn.* To revive (suceso), to return to life, to acquire new life: to resuscitate (vivir de nuevo).

revocable [ray-vo-cah'-blay], *a.* Revocable, reversible.

revocablemente [ray-vo-cah'-blay-men-tay], *adv.* In a revocable manner.

revocación [ray-vo-cah-the-on'], *f.* Revocation: abrogation; act of recalling. **Revocación de una sentencia**, *(Law.)* reversal.

revocador, ra [ray-vo-cah-dor', rah], *m. & f.* 1. One who revokes abrogates or recalls. 2. Plasterer, white washer.

revocadura [ray-vo-cah-doo'-rah], *f.* 1. *V.* REVOQUE. 2. *(Pict.)* Painted borders of canvas.

revocante [ray-vo-cahn'-tay], *pa.* Revoker, recalling, abrogating.

revocar [ray-vo-car'], *va.* 1. To revoke (decisión), to repeal, to annul, to abrogate, to abolish; to countermand. *(Law.)* To reverse. 2. To dissuade from (persona), to induce one to desist. 3. To plaster (enlucir), to whitewash (enlacar), or to freshen paintings. 4. To yield to an impulse, to retrocede. 5. To recall, to call one from one place to another.

revocatorio, ria [ray-vo-cah-to'-re-o, ah], *a.* That which revokes or annulls; reversal.

revoco [ray-vo'-co], *m.* 1. Plaster, Whitewash. *V.* REVOQUE. 2. Cover of broom or furze laid on charcoal baskets.

revolar [ray-vo-lar'], *vn.* To fly again, to take a second flight. *V.* REVOLOTEAR.

revolcadero [ray-vol-cah-day'-ro], *m.* A weltering or wallowing place for wild boars and other beasts.

revolcadura [ray-vol-cah-doo'-rah], *f.* Action of wallowing.

revolcar [ray-vol-car'], *va.* 1. To knock down (derribar), to tread upon. 2. To overcome, to outshine in a controversy. 3. To floor (adversario). *-vr.* 1. To wallow in mire or anything filthy (animal). 2. To be obstinately bent upon an idea or design. (*Yo revuelco, yo revuelque,* from *Revolcar. V.* ACORDAR.)

revolcón [ray-vol-cone'], *m. (Coll.) V.* REVUELCO.

revolear [ray-vo-lay-ar'], *vn.* To flutter, to take short flights; to fly precipitately. *-va. (Cono Sur, Mex.)* To whirl (lazo).

revolotear [ray-vo-lo-tay-ar'], *vn.* To flutter, to fly round, to hover.

revoloteo [ray-vo-lo-tay'-o], *m.* Fluttering; a short flight; a quick motion with the wings. *V.* REVOLTILLO.

revoltijo [ray-vol-tee' ho], *m. V.* REVOLTILLO.

revoltillo [ray-vol-teel'-lyo], *m.* 1. Parcel of things jumbled together. 2. Tripes of a sheep. 3. Medley, confusion, disorder; mash; jumble (confusión). 4. Fricassee. 5. *(CAm. Cono Sur, Mex.)* Bundle.

revoltón [ray-vol-tone'], *m.* Vine-fretter, vine-grub. (used also adjectively.)

revoltoso, sa [ray-vol-toh'-so, sah], *a.* Turbulent, seditious, naughty (niño).

revoltura [ray-vol-too'-rah], *f. (Mex.)*, A mixture of fluxes added to silver one.

revolución [ray-vo-loo-the-on'], *f.* 1. Revolution, the act of revolving. 2. Revolution of a planet. 3. Revolution, change in the state of a government; disturbance, sedition, commotion.

revolucionador, ra [ray-vo-loo-the-o-nah-dor, rah], *n. & a.* Revolutionist; revolutionary.

revolucionar [ray-vo-loo-the-o-nar'], *va.* To disturb or agitate a country, to produce a revolution. *-vr.* To rise or break into a commotion: it is a neologism.

revolucionario, ria [ray-vo-loo-the-o-nah'-re-o, ah], *a.* Revolutionary. *-m. & f.* Revolutionist, revolutioner, socialist.

revolvedero [ray-vol-vay-day'-ro], *m.* Coursing-place.

revolvedor, ra [ray-vol-vay-dor', rah], *m. & f.* Revolter, disturber; a turbulent, seditious, or rebellious person.

revólver [ray-vol'-ver], *m.* Revolver, a pistol containing five or more revolving chambers.

revolver [ray-vol-verr'], *va.* 1. To move a thing up and down (mover); to stir (líquido), to shift, to return; to revert; to retrace or go back again. 2. To revolve, to wrap up (envolver); to convolve. 3. To stir up disturbances, to excite commotions. 4. To revolve in the mind, to hesitate. 5. To face an enemy in order to attack him. 6. To evolve, to separate. 7. To turn short swiftly (caballos). 8. To go into, to investigate (indagar). **Han revuelto toda la casa,** they've messed up the whole house. *-vn.* **Revolver en una maleta,** to rummage in a case. *-vr.* 1. To move to and fro. 2. To change, as the weather. 3. To turn round (volverse); to writhe (con dolor). 4. To be stirred up (sedimento). 5. *(And.)* To get a lucky break (prosperar). **Se revolvía en su silla,** he was fidgeting about on his chair.

revolvimiento [ray-vol-ve-me-en'-to], *m.* Commotion, perturbation, revolution.

revoque [ray-vo'-kay], *m.* 1. Act of whitewashing (acto). 2. Plaster, whitewash (cal), rough-cast laid on houses or walls.

revotarse [ray-vo-tar'-say], *vr.* To vote contrary to a previous vote; to reconsider a ballot.

revuelco [ray-voo-el'-co], *m.* Wallowing, rolling.

revuelo [ray-voo-ay'-lo], *m.* 1. Flying to and fro of a bird. 2. Irregular motion; disturbance. **De revuelo,** by the way, speedily, promptly. **Armar un gran revuelo,** to cause a great stir. (*Yo revuelo, yo revuele,* from *Revolar.* V. ACORDAR.)

revuelta [ray-voo-el'-tah], *f.* 1. Second turn (vuelta), return. **Dar vueltas y revueltas a algo,** to go on turning something over and over. 2. Revolution, revolt (motín), sedition; contention, dissension, commotion (commoción), fuss (jaleo). 3. Delay, tardiness. 4. Meditation, reflection. 5. Commutation, change. 6. Point from which a thing commences a tortuous or oblique direction.

revuelto, ta [ray-voo-ell'-to, tah], *a. &: pp. irr.* of REVOLVER. 1. Mixed up (objetos), in a turmoil, in confusion. 2. Perverse, dissatisfied. 3. Unruly (revoltoso), restless (inquieto), mischievous (niño); rebellious (población). **Huevos revueltos,** scrambled eggs. **Todo estaba revuelto,** everything was in disorder.

revulsión [ray-vool-se-on'], *f.* Revulsion.

revulsivo, va, revulsorio, ria [ray vool-see'-vo, vah], *a.* Revulsory, revulsive.

rey [ray'-e], *m.* 1. King. **Rey de armas,** *(Her.)* the king at arms. **Los reyes,** epiphany, twelfth-night. **Dios guarde al rey** God save the king. 2. A Spanish dance. 3. Queen-bee; chief among animals. 4. King in cards or chess. **Rey de bastos** or **de copas,** (a) king of clubs or hearts. (b) A wooden king, a king without authority.

reyecico, illo, ito [ray-yay-thee'-co], *m. dim.* A petty king, the king of a small kingdom.

reyerta [ray-yerr'-tah], *f.* Dispute, difference, quarrel.

reyezuelo [ray-yay-thoo-ay'-lo], *m.* 1. A petty king. 2. *(Orn.)* Kinglet.

rezadero, ra [ray-thah-day'-ro, rah], *a.* Praying often.

rezado [ray-thah'-do], *m.* Prayer, divine service. V. REZO. **Rezado, da,** *pp.* of REZAR.

rezador, ra [ray-thah-dor', rah], *m. & f.* One who prays often.

rezagado [ray-thah-gah'-do], *m.* Straggler, one who is left behind on a march; tramp, one too indolent to work.

rezagante [ray-thah-gahn'-tay], *pa.* Delayer; leaving behind.

rezagar [ray-thah-gar'], *va.* 1. To leave behind (dejar atrás); to outstrip; more commonly reflexive. 2. To suspend action, to put off, to defer, to postpone (aplazar). *-vr.* To stay behind (quedar atrás); to loiter (ir despacio).

rezago [ray-thah'-go], *m.* 1. Remainder, residue. 2. Group of straggling cattle (ganado). 3. *(And. Mex.)* Unclaimed letters (Correos).

rezar [ray-thar'], *va.* 1. To pray, to say or rend prayers (oración). 2. To quote, to recite. 3. *(Vulg.)* To announce, to say in writing. *-vn.* To growl, to mutter, to pray, to read (texto), to grumble (quejarse). **Eso no reza conmigo,** that has nothing to do with me.

rezelar, va. rezelo, *m.* (and derivatives). V. RECELAR, REZELO.

rezno [reth'-no], *m.* 1. Tick, bot, bott (larva), sheep-tick, dog-tick. 2. V. RICINO.

rezo [ray'-tho], *m.* 1. Prayer, the act of praying. 2. Divine office, formulary of devotion.

rezón [ray-thone'], *m.* *(Naut.)* Grappling.

rezongador, ra [ray-thon-gah-dor', rah], *m. & f.* Grumbler, growler, mutterer.

rezongar [ray-tho-gar'], *vn.* To grumble, to mutter, to murmur, to growl.

rezonglón, na, rezongón, na [ray-thon-glon', nah], *a. & m.* Grumbler; grumbling.

rezumadero [ray-thoo-mah-day'-ro], *m.* Dripping-place; dripping.

rezumarse [ray-thoo-mar'-say], *vr.* 1. To ooze, to flow by stealth; to run gently, to leak. 2. To transpire, to escape from secrecy, to notice.

rho [ro], *f.* Rho (*r*), seventeenth letter of the Greek alphabet, corresponding to *r.*

ría [ree'-ah], *f.* Mouth of a river.

riachuelo, riatillo [re-ah-choo-ay'-lo, re-ah-teel'-lyo], *m.* Rivulet, streamlet; small river.

riada [re-ah'-dah], *f.* Freshet, overflow, flood.

riba [ree'-bah], *f.* *(Prov.)* Bank between a higher and lower field.

ribadoquín [re-bah-do-keen'], *m.* Small gun now disused.

ribaldería [re-bal-day-ree'-ah], *f.* Ribaldry; wickedness; coarse abuse.

ribaldo, da [re-bahl'-do, dah], *a. & n.* Ribaldous; ribald; wicked, obscene. V. RUFIÁN.

ribazo [re-bah'-tho], *m.* A sloping bank; mound, hillock.

ribecillo [re-bay-theel'-lyo], *m.* Narrow silk or worsted galloon.

ribera [re-bay'-rah], *f.* 1. Shore of the sea, bank of a river; strand, verge of any water. 2. Irrigated plain. 3. *(Cono Sur, Mex.)* Riverside community (de campo); shanty town (chabolas). **Ser de monte y ribera,** to be fit for everything.

ribereño, ña [re-bay-ray'-nyo, nyah], *a.* Belonging to the seashore or bank of a river.

riberiego, ga [re-bay-re-ay'-go, gah], *a.* Grazing on the banks of rivers: applied to such flocks as are not removed to other sheep-walks, or are not *trashumantes,* as opposed to *estantes.* Grazier of sheep on the banks of rivers.

ribero [re-bay'-ro], *m.* Bank or parapet of a dam of water.

ribes [ree'-bes], *f.* *(Bot.)* Currant-bush.

ribete [re-bay'-tay], *m.* 1. Ribbon or tape sewed to the edge of cloth; seam, border, fringe, binding. 2. Cantle, the small quantity given above the precise measure or weight. 3. Additions to a tale, for embellishment.

ribetear [re-bay-tay-ar'], *va.* To edge, to border.

riboflavina [re-bo-flah-vee'-nah], *f.* Riboflavin.

ricacho, cha [re-cah'-cho, chah], *a.* *(Coll.)* Very rich.

ricadueña [re-cah-doo-ay'-nyah], *f.* Lady, daughter or wife of a noble.

ricafembra, ricahembra [re-cah-fem´-brah], *f.* Lady, daughter or wife of a noble.

ricahombría [re-cah-om-bree'-ah], *f.* Dignity of the *ricos hombres,* ancient nobility of Castile.

ricamente [re'-cah-men-tay], *adv.* 1. Richly, opulently. 2. Excellently, splendidly. **Muy ricamente**, very well. **He dormido tan ricamente**, I´ve slept splendidly.

ricazo, za [re-cah'-tho, thah], *a. aug.* Very rich, opulent.

ricial [re-the-ahl'], *a.* Growing again: applied to the after-crop of corn, cut green for the feed of cattle.

ricino [re-thee'-no], *m. (Bot.)* PalmaChristi, the castor-oil plant.

rico, ca [ree'-co, cah], *a.* 1. Noble, of an ancient and illustrious family. 2. Rich, wealthy, opulent. 3. Pleasing to the taste, delicious (sabroso). **Estos pasteles son riquísimos**, these cakes are very good. 4. Choice, select, able. 5. Valuable (joya), precious; luxurious (muebles). 6. Bonny (niño); cute, lovely. ¡**Oye, rico!**, hey, man!

ricohombre, ricohome [re-co-om'-bray, re-co-o'-may], *m.* Grandee, a peer of the flint rank in Spain, a nobleman of the ancient nobility of Castile.

rictus [reek'-toos], *m.* Rictus, gaping of the mouth, grimace, grin (de burla), sneer (de desprecio).

ricura [re-koo'-rah], *f.* 1. Tastiness (lo sabroso), delicious quality. 2. Smashing girl (chica).

ridículamente [re-dee'-coo-lah-men-tay], *adv.* Ridiculously, contemptibly.

ridiculez [re-de-coo-leth'], *f.* 1. A ridiculous speech or action. 2. Ridicule, folly, extravagance, oddity, eccentricity. 3. Extreme nicety or sensibility.

ridiculizar [re-de-coo-le-thar'], *va.* To ridicule, to burlesque, to laugh at.

ridículo, la [re-dee'-coo-lo, lah], *a.* 1. Ridiculous, odd, eccentric, laughable, ludicrous. 2. Strange, contemptible; despicable; absurd. 3. Excessively nice and sentimental. **Hacer el ridículo**, to make oneself ridiculous.

ridículo [re-dee'-coo-lo], *m.* 1. Ridicule, mockery. 2. Handbag, reticule.

ridiculoso, sa [re-de-coo-lo'-so, sah], *a.* Ridiculous, extravagant.

rIego [re-ay'-go], *m.* Irrigation; watering (aspersión). **Riego por aspersión**, watering by spray.

riel [re-el'], *m.* 1. A small ingot of unrefined gold or silver, lingot. 2. Rail of a railway whether for locomotives or for street use. In this sense it is also spelled **rail**, as in English.

rielado, da [re-ay-lah'-do, dah], *a.* Reduced to ingots (oro, plata).

rielar [re-ay-lar'], *vn. (Poet.)* 1. To glisten, to be reflected upon the waters: used of moonlight. 2. To shine with a tremulous light.

rielera [re-ay-lay'-rah], *f.* Mould in which ingots of gold or silver are cast.

rienda [re-en'-dah], *f.* 1. Rein of a bridle. 2. Moderation, restraint in speech and action. -*pl.* 1. *(Met.)* Government, direction. 2. Reins of the feuding horse. **A rienda suelta**, loose-reined, violently, swiftly. **Soltar la rienda**, to give way to vices or passions. **Tener las riendas**, to bolt the reins, to hold back a horse. **Tirar las riendas**, to draw back, to restrain.

riente [re-en'-tay], *pa.* Smiling, laughing (risueño).

riesgo [re-es'-go], *m.* Danger, risk, hazard, peril, jeopardy. **Con riesgo de**, at the risk of.

riesgoso, sa [re-es-go'-so, sah], *a.* Risk.

rifa [ree´-fah], *f.* 1. Scuffle, dispute, contest. 2. Raffle, a species of gums or lottery.

rifador [re-fah-dor'], *m.* Raffler; disputer.

rifadura [re-fah-doo'-rah], *f. (Naut.)* Act of splitting a sail.

rifar [re-far'], *va.* 1. To raffle, to cast dice for a prize. 2. *(Naut.)* To split a sail, in a storm. -*vn.* To quarrel, to dispute.

-*vr.* 1. **Rifarse algo**, to quarrel over something. 2. *(CAm.)* To take a risk (arriesgarse).

rifirrafe [re-fe-rah'-fay], *m. (Coll.)* A short quarrel, hasty words.

rígidamente [ree'-he-dah-men-tay], *adv.* Rigidly.

rigidez [re-he-deth'], *f.* Rigidity, asperity.

rígido, da [ree'-he-do, dah], *a.* Rigid (tieso), rigorous, severe, inflexible, harsh, to get stiff (aterirse), strict (moralmente). **Quedarse rígido**, to go rigid.

rigodón [re-go-done'], *m.* Rigadoon, a country dance.

rigor [re-gor'], *m.* 1. Rigor, a convulsive shuddering with a sense of cold. 2. Rigidity of the nerves. 3. Rigor (severidad), sternness, severity, harshness of temper. 4. Rigour, strictness, exactness, precision (precisión). 5. Power, intensity, keenness, hardness, vehemence. 6. Cruelty or excess of chastisement. 7. The last push or extremity. **A todo rigor**, if the worst comes to the worst. **En rigor**, at most **Una edición hecha con el mayor rigor crítico**, an edition produced with absolute meticulousness.

rigorismo [re-go-rees'-mo], *m.* Rigorousness, severity.

rigorista [re-go-rees'-tah], *a. & com.* Applied to one very rigid, severe, or inflexible in moral opinions.

rigorosamente, rigurosamente [re-go-ro-sah-men´-tay], *adv.* Rigorously (con precisión); severely (severamente), scrupulously. **Eso no es rigurosamente exacto**, that is not strictly accurate.

riguroso, sa [re-goo-ro'-so, sah], *a.* Rigorous (estudio, método), strict (aplicación), austere, rigid, severe (medida), harsh; scrupulously nice. **Su tratamiento riguroso de los empleados**, his harsh treatment of the employees.

rija [ree'-hah], *f.* 1. A kind of lachrymal fistula. 2. Quarrel, scuffle, dispute.

rijador, ra [re-hah-dor', rah], *a.* Quarrelsome, litigious.

rijente [re-hen'-tay], *a.* Rough, cruel, horrid.

rijo [ree'-ho], *m.* Concupiscence, lust, sensuality.

rijoso, sa [re-ho'-so, sah], *a.* 1. Quarrelsome (peleador). 2. Restless at the sight of the female (caballos). 3. Lustful (cachondo), sensual.

rima [ree'-mah], *f.* 1. Rhyme, complete or incomplete, known as assonance. 2. Arrangement of things in a regular series. **Octava rima**, ottava rima.

rimado, da [re-mah'-do, dah], *a. & pp.* Of RIMAR. Versified.

rimar [re-mar´], *va. & vn.* 1. To inquire after, to investigate. 2. To rhyme, to make verses.

rimbombante [rim-bom-bahn'-tay], *pa.* 1. Resounding (resonante). 2. Pompous, bombastic. 3. *(Fig.)* Showiness (ostentación).

rimbombar [rim-bom-bar'], *vn.* To resound, to echo.

rimbombe, rimbombo [rim-bom'-bay], *m.* Repercussion of sound.

rimel [ree'-mayl], *m.* Eye shadow.

rimero [re-may'-ro], *m.* Collection of things placed regularly one over another in a pile.

rincón [rin-cone], *m.* 1. Inside corner, an angle formed by the meeting of two walls; a coin. 2. Place of privacy, a lurking-place. 3. House, dwelling. 4. Small district or country. *Cf.* ESQUINA.

rinconada [rin-co-nah'-dah], *f.* Corner, formed by two houses, streets, or roads.

rinconcillo [rin-con-theel'-lyo], *m. dim.* A small corner.

rinconera [rin-co-nay'-rah], *f.* 1. Small triangular table in a corner. 2. *(Arquit.)* Wall between corner and window.

rinconero, ra [rin-co-nay'-ro, rah], *a.* Transverse, athwart.

ringle [reen'-glay], *m.* **Ringla** [reen'-glah], *f.* V. RINGLERA.

ringlera [rin-glay'-rah], *f. (Coll.)* Row, file.

ringlero [rin-glay'-ro], *m.* Line drawn with a pencil, for writing straight.

ringorrango [rin-go-rahn'-go], *m. (Coll.)* 1. Flourish with a pen (en escritura). 2. Extravagant nicety in dress.

rinoceronte [re-no-thay-ron´-tay], *m.* Rhinoceros.

rinoscopia [re-nos-co´-pe-ah], *f. (Med.)* Rhinoscopy, examination of the nasal cavities.

riña [ree'-nyah], *f.* Quarrel (disputa), scuffle, dispute, fray, brawl, fight.

riñón [ree-nyohn'], *m.* 1. Kidney. **Tener cubierto el riñón**, to be rich. 2. Central point of a country.

riñonada [ree-nyo-nah'-dah], *f.* 1. Coat of fat about the kidneys. 2. Dish of kidneys.

río [re'-o], *m.* 1. River, stream. 2. Any large quantity of fluids. **Río de lágrimas**, flood of tears. **Río abajo**, downstream. **Cuando el río suena, agua lleva**, there's no smoke without fire.

riolada [re-o-lah'-dah], *f.* The assemblage of many things at one time.

riostra [re-os'-trah], *f.* Post placed obliquely to strengthen an upright post, spur, strut.

riostrar [re-os-trar'], *va.* To strengthen by means of oblique posts.

ripia [ree'-pe-ah], *f.* Shingle, for roofing houses.

ripiar [re-pe-ar'], *va.* To fill up the chinks of a wall with small stones and mortar.

ripio [ree'-pe-o], *m.* 1. Remainder, residue, rubble (basura). 2. Word used to fill up a verse. **No perder ripio**, not to miss the least occasion.

riponce [re-pon'-thay], *m. (Bot.)* V. RAPÓNCHIGO.

riqueza [re-kay'-thah], *f.* 1. Riches, wealth (bienes), opulence. 2. Fertility, fruitfulness. 3. Ornament, embellishment. **Vivir en la riqueza**, to live in luxury.

risa [ree'-sah], *f.* 1. Laugh, laughter. 2. Cause or object of laughter; pleasing emotion. 3. Derisory smile or laugh. **Caerse de risa**, to shake with laughter: **Comerse de risa**, to suppress a desire to laugh (through respect). **Destornillarse de risa**, to laugh excessively. **Tentado a**, or **de, la risa**, (1) prone to laugh immoderately. (2) Amorous, lascivious. **Tomar algo a risa**, to take something as a joke. **Ser la risa (el hazmerreír) de todos,** to be the laughing stock of everyone. **Llorar de risa**, to cry laughing. **Tener un ataque de risa**, to have a fit of laughter.

risada [re-sah'-dah], *f.* Horse-laugh; immoderate laughter.

risco [rees'-co], *m .* A steep rock (inclinado), crag.

riscoso, sa [ris-co'-so, sah], *a.* Steep and rocky.

risibilidad [re-se-be-le-dahd'], *f.* Risibility.

risible [re-see'-blay], *a.* Risible, laughable, ludicrous.

risica, ita [re-see'-cah, ee'-tah], *f. dim.* 1. Feigned laugh. 2. Smile.

risotada [re-so-tah'-dah], *f.* Loud laugh, horse-laugh.

ríspido, da [rees'-pe-do, dah], *a.* V. ÁSPERO.

ristra [rees'-trah], *f.* 1. String of onions or garlic. 2. Row, file, series of things.

ristre [rees'-tray], *m.* Rest or socket for a lance, used to couch the lance in the posture of attack.

risueño, ña [re-soo-ay'-nyo, nyah], *a.* Smiling; pleasing, agreeable.

rítmico, ca [reet'-me-co, cah], *a.* Rhythmical.

ritmo [reet'-mo], *m.* Rhyme, rhythm. V. RIMA. **Ritmo de crecimiento**, rate of growth. **Trabajar a ritmo lento**, to go slow (lento).

rito [ree'-to], *m.* Rite, ceremony.

ritual [re-too-ahl'], *m.* Ritual, a book of religious rites and observances; ceremonial.-*a.* Ritual, according to some religious institution.

rival [re-vahl'], *m.* Rival, competitor.

rivalidad [re-vah-le-dahd'], *f.* 1. Rivalry. 2. Competition, emulation.

rivalizar [re-vah-le-thar'], *va.* To corrival, to vie with.

rivera [re-vay'-rah], *f. (Prov.)* Brook, river, stream.

riza [ree'-thah], *f.* 1. Green stubble of grain cut for food. 2. Desolation, ravage, destruction.

rizado [re-thah'-do], *m.* Fluting, crimp, frizzle. -*a.* Curly (pelo); ridged (superficie); undulating (terreno).

rizador [re-thah-dor'], *m.* 1. Curling iron, for hair. 2. Hairdresser's frizzler.

rizagra [re-thah'-grah], *f.* An instrument for extracting the roots of teeth.

rizal [re-thahl'], *a.* V. RICIAL.

rizar [re-thar'], *va.* 1. To curl hair. 2. To crimple craps with a crimping iron; to plait.

rizo, za [ree'-tho, thah], *a.* Naturally curled or frizzled.

rizo [ree'-tho], *m.* 1. Curling or frizzling the hair; curl, frizzle, ringlet: crimpling of cloth. 2. Cut velvet. **Rizos**, *(Naut.)* points, used to reef the courses and top-sails of a ship. **Rizar el rizo**, to loop the loop.

ro [ro], *int.* Word used to lull children.

roa [ro'-ah], *f. (Naut.)* Stem. V. RODA.

roano, na [ro-ah'-no, nah], *a.* Sorrel, roan (caballo).

rob [rob], *m.* Rob, the inspissated juice of ripe fruit, mixed with honey or sugar to the consistency of a conserve; fruit jelly.

roba [ro'-bah], *f. (Prov.)* V. ARROBA.

robada [ro-bah'-dah], *f. (Prov.)* Space of ground of 400 square yards in extent.

robado, da [ro-bah'-do, dah], *a. & pp.* of ROBAR. Robbed, stolen; naked, without ornament.

robador, ra [ro-bah-dor', rah], *m. & f.* Robber.

robaliza [ro-bah-lee'-thah], *f.* Kind of fish, perch.

róbalo [ro'-bah-lo], *m.* Sea-bass, labrax; a fish like bream.

robamiento [ro-bah-me-en'-to], *m.* V. ARROBAMIENTO.

robar [ro-bar'], *va.* 1. To rob (dueño), to plunder, to steal (objeto). 2. To abduct, to kidnap (persona). 3. To sweep away part of its banks (río). 4. To overcharge, to overreach in the sale of goods. 5. To gain another's affections, to ingratiate oneself. 6. To diminish the color, to weaken or lower the coloring. 7. With bee-masters, to take the heed from a divided hive and put them into an empty one, by removing the honey-comb. **Robar algo a uno**, to steal something from somebody. **Robar el corazón a uno**, to steal somebody's heart.

robda [rob'-dah], *f.* Kind of ancient tribute.

robezo [ro-bay'-tho], *m.* A wild-goat. V. BICERRA.

robí [ro-been'], *m.* Rust of metal.

robinia [ro-bee'-ne-ah], *f.* The locust tree.

robladero, ra [ro-blah-day'-ro, rah], *a.* Clinched; recurvate, recurvous.

robladura [ro-blah-doo'-rah], *f.* Riveting, clinching.

roblar [ro-blar'], *va.* 1. To strengthen, to make strong. 2. To clinch a nail, to rivet.

roble [ro'-blay], *m.* Oak, oak-tree. *(Fam.)* Robust, strong person (persona). *(Met.)* Anything very strong and hard. **Más fuerte que un roble**, as strong as an ox.

roblecillo, ito [ro-blay-theel'-lyo], *m. dim.* A small oak-tree.

robleda [ro-blay'-dah], *f.* Oak-grove.

robledal, robledo [ro-blay-dahl', ro-blay'-do], *m.* Plantation of oak-trees, oak-grove.

roblizo, za [ro-blee'-tho, thah], *a.* Oaken, strong, hard.

roblón [ro-blone'], *m.* A rivet.

robo [ro'-bo], *m.* Robbery, theft; the thing robbed or stolen. **Robo en la vía pública**, highway robbery. **Robo a mano armada,** armed robbery. **Robo de ciclo**, *(Comput.)* cycle stealing.

roboración [ro-bo-rah-the-on'], *f.* Corroboration, strengthening.

roborante [ro-bo-rahn'-tay], *pa. & a.* Corroborant: applied to strengthening medicines; corroborating.

roborar [ro-bo-rar'], *va.* To confirm, to corroborate, to give strength.

roborativo, va [ro-bo-rah-tee'-vo, vah], *a.* Corroborative.

robot [ro'-bot], *m.* Robot.

robótica [ro-boh'-te-cah], *f.* Robotics.

robradura [ro-brah-doo'-rah], *f.* Clinching, riveting.

robrecillo, ito [ro-bray-thel'-lyo], *m. dim.* V. ROBLECILLO.

robredo [ro-bray'-do], *m.* V. ROBLEDAL.

robustamente [ro-boos'-tah-men-tay], *adv.* Robustly.

robustez [ro-boos-teth'], *f.* Robustness, hardiness, lustiness, force.

robusto, ta [ro-boos'-to, tah], *a.* Strong, robust, vigorous, hale.

roca [ro'-cah], *f.* 1. Rock, precipice; vein or bed of hard stone. 2. Cliff, rocky height on land or in the sea. 3. *(Geol.)* Rock, a simple or compound mineral mess, which, by its extent, forms an important part of the earthy crust. 4. Anything very firm and hard. 5. Stone. **Corazón de roca,** heart of stone. **Firme como una roca,** as solid as a rock.

rocada [ro-cah'-dah], *f.* Portion of wool or flax for the distaff.

rocadero [ro-cah-day'-ro], *m.* 1. Knob or head of a distaff. 2. Piece of paper formed like a cone, and put round the flux or wool on a distaff. 3. Rock of a distaff or spinning-wheel.

rocador [ro-cah-dor'], *m.* Head of a rock or distaff.

rocalla [ro-cahl'-lyah], *f.* 1. Drift of pebbles washed together by floods or torrents; talus of rocks. 2. Chippings of stone made in working it. 3. Flint glass, of which beads and rosaries are made.

rocambolesco [ro-cahm-bo-les'-co], *a.* Odd (raro), bizarre; ornate (estilo), baroque.

roce [ro'-thay], *m.* 1. Friction, rub (acto), attrition. 2. Familiarity (familiaridad), frequent conversation. **Tener roce con,** to be in close contact with.

rocha [ro'-chah], *f. V.* ROZA, 2d def.

rocho [ro'-cho], *m.* Roc, a fabulous bird of extraordinary size and strength.

rociada [ro-the-ah'-dah], *f.* 1. The act of sprinkling or irrigating gently; aspersion (aspersión); a sprinkling. 2. *(Naut.)* Spray. 3. Drops of dew on plants; herbs with dew on them, given to animals as medicine. 4. Shower of stones or balls: scattering (de insultos). 5. Slander, aspersion. 6. Roughness, asperity used with a person in discharging him.

rociadera [ro-the-ah-day'-rah], *f. V.* REGADERA.

rociado [ro-the-ah'-do], **da,** *a.* Dewy; bedewed. *-pp.* of ROCIAR.

rociador [ro-the-ah-dor'], *m.* Sprinkler. **Rociador de aire,** airbrush.

rociamiento [ro-the-ah-me-en'-to], *m.* Sprinkling or bedewing.

rociar [ro-the-ar'], *vn.* To be bedewed or sprinkled with dew; to fall in dew. *-va.* 1. To sprinkle with wine, water, or other fluids. 2. To strew about. 3. To plunder several persons at the same time.

rocín [ro-theen'], *m.* 1. Hack (caballo), jade working horse; a horse of little value. 2. A heavy, ignorant clown.

rocinal [ro-the-nahl'], *a.* Belonging to a hack horse.

rocinante [ro-the-nahn'-tay], *m. V.* ROCÍN: applied to a miserable hack.

rocinazo [ro-the-nah'-tho], *m. aug.* 1. A large hack. 2. A very ignorant person.

rocinillo [ro-the-neel'-lyoh], *m. dim.* A very small truck.

rocío [ro-thee'-o], *m.* 1. Dew (de noche). 2. Slight shower of rain (llovizna), sprinkling. 3. Divine inspiration, holy thoughts. **Rocío de la mar,** *(Naut.)* spoon-drift, the foam of the sea in a storm.

rockero [ro-kay'-ro], *a.* Rock; **música rockera,** rock music. **Es muy rockero,** (aficionado) he´s a real rock fan.

rococó [ro-ko-ko'], *a.* Rococo.

rocoso, sa [ro-co'-so, sah], *a.* Rocky, craggy.

roda [ro'-dah], *f.* 1. *(Naut.)* Stem. 2. Duty or impost on sheep-flocks.

rodaballo [ro-dah-bahl'-lyo], *m.* Turbot, flounder.

rodada [ro-dah'-dah], *f.* Rut (de rueda), the track of a wheel.

rodadero, ra [ro-dah-day'-ro, rah], *a.* Rolling or wheeling easily.

rodadizo, za [ro-dah-dee'-tho, thah], *a.* Easily rolled round.

rodado, da [ro-dah'-do, dah], *a.* 1. Dapple, dappled, roan (caballos). 2. *V.* PRIVILEGIO. 3. Round, fluent (frases). 4. Experienced (experimentado). 5. Rounded (piedra). **Venir rodado,** to attain an object accidentally. *-pp.* of RODAR.

rodado [ro-dah'-do], *m. (Min.) V.* SUELTO.

rodador [ro-dah-dor'], *m.* 1. Roller, anything that rolls or falls rolling down. 2. Vagabond, vagrant. 3. A kind of mosquito.

rodadura [ro-dah-doo'-rah], *f.* 1. Rolling, the act of rolling. 2. Rut (rodada), the truck of a wheel.

rodaja [ro-day'-hah], *f.* 1. A small wheel (ruedecilla). 2. Rowel of a spur. 3. Jagging-iron used by pastry-cooks: bookbinder's tool. 4. *(And.)* Vehicle tax (impuesto).

rodaje [ro-dah'-hay], *m.* 1. Wheel-works, as of a watch. 2. *(And.)* Vehicle tax (impuesto).

rodajilla [ro-dah-heel'-lyah], *f. dim.* A very small wheel or circular body.

rodal [ro-dahl'], *m.* Place, spot, seat.

rodamiento [ro-dah-me-ayn'-to], *m.* **Rodamiento a bolas,** ball bearing.

rodante [ro-dahn'-tay], *pa.* Rolling.

rodapelo [ro-dah-pay'-lo], *m.* Rubbing against the grain. *V.* REDOPELO.

rodapié [ro-dah-pe-ay'], *m.* 1. Fringe of silk or other stuff found at the feet of a bedstead, table, or balcony, to hide the feet. 2. The stained or painted lower part of white-washed walls, about from the ground, a socle. 3. A board or low shutter put on balconies.

rodaplancha [ro-dah-plahn'-chah], *f.* The main ward of a key.

rodar [ro-dar'], *vn.* 1. To roll, to revolve on an axis. 2. To roll, to run on wheels (sobre ruedas). 3. To roll, to move along on the surface, to roll down a hill. 4. *V.* RODEAR. 5. To abound, to be in great plenty. 6. To wander about in vain in quest of business; to be tossed about; to go about, to go up and down. 7. To lose an employment, station, dignity, or esteem. 8. To happen accidentally. **Rodar por la escalera,** to fall downstairs. **Ir rodando,** to move about. *-va.* 1. To drive, to impel, to give an impulse. 2. To travel (viajar). 3. To race, to drive (en carreteras). 3. To shoot, to film (cine). 4. *(Carib.)* To seize (agarrar); to imprison (encarcelar). 5. *(LAm.)* To round up (ganado). **Ha rodado medio mundo,** he´s been over half the world.

rodeado, da [ro-day-ah'-do, dah], *a. & pp.* of RODEAR. Surrounded. **Rodeado de negocios,** overwhelmed with business.

rodeador, ra [ro-day-ah-dor', rah], *m. & f.* Roller, wrapper.

rodear [ro-day-ar'], *vn.* 1. To go round a place or object; to encompass. 2. To go a round-about way, to come about. 3. To make use of circumlocutions; to use circuitous language or indirect expressions. *-va.* 1. To wrap up, to put one thing around another; to circle, to compass, to girdle. 2. To whirl about. 3. To dispose, to arrange. **Los soldados rodearon el edificio,** the soldiers surrounded the building. *-vr.* 1. **Rodearse de,** to surround oneself with. 2. To turn round (volverse).

rodela [ro-day'-lah], *f.* Shield, a round buckler or target.

rodelero [ro-day-lay'-ro], *m.* Soldier armed with a shield or target.

rodenal [ro-day-nahl'], *m.* A clump of rodello pines.

rodeno [ro-day'-no], *m.* A kind of pine.

rodeno, na [ro-day'-no, nah], *a.* Red (rocas, pines).

rodeo [ro-day'-o], *m.* 1. Detour, the act of going round; a circuitous way or road; turn to elude another (desvío). 2. Place in a fair or market where horned cattle are exposed to sale. 3. Delay, protraction, tedious method. 4. Evasion (evasión), subterfuge. 5. *(Coll. Mex.)* Enclosing cattle for the purpose of counting and marking them. 6. *(LAm.)* Roundup, rodeo. **Dar un rodeo,** to make a detour. **Dejarse de rodeos,** to talk straight.

rodeón [ro-day-on'], *m.* A complete rolling or winding round.

rodera [ro-day'-rah], *f.* Rut, cart track.

rodero, ra [ro-day'-ro, rah], *a.* Relating to wheels.

rodero [ro-day'-ro], *m.* Collector of the duty on sheep.

rodete [ro-day'-tay], *m.* 1. A small wooden wheel for moving a millwheel. 2. Bolster, a horizontal circle at the fore axle-tree of a carriage for turning it. 3. A kind of ward in a lock. 4. A rower of platted hair which women tie on the top of their heads for ornament. 5. A kind of pad or bolster put on the head of women (de pelo), to carry vessels with greater ease, or for ornament. 6. Border round the sleeves of gowns. 7. Roll (de grasa). 8. Pad (para llevar carga). 9. Ward (de cerradura).

rodezno [ro-deth'-no], *m.* 1. A large wheel, consisting of many pieces. 2. A toothed wheel in grist-mills.

ródico, ca [ro'-de-co, cah], *a.* Relating to rhodium.

rodilla [ro-deel'-lyah], *f.* 1. The knee. 2. Shoulder in a lock to fit the lizard of a key. *V.* RODETE, 3d def. 3. Dusting cloth, cloth for cleaning (paño). **De rodillas,** on one's knees. **Doblar las rodillas,** to bend the knees; to kneel down. **Pedir algo de rodillas,** to ask for something on bended knees.

rodillada [ro-dil-lyah'-dah], *f.* Push with the knee, a kneeling position.

rodillazo [rod-dil-lyah'-zo], *m.* Push with the knee.

rodillera [ro-dil-lyay'-rah], *f.* 1. Anything put for comfort or protection over the knees (protección). 2. Patch, or re-enforcing piece, added to the knees of pants or long underwear; knee cap. 3. Damage upon the knees of horses from kneeling. 4. Bulging of pantaloons over the knee. 5. Pad (para llevar carga).

rodillero, ra [ro-dil-lyay'-ro, rah], *a.* Belonging to the knees.

rodillo [ro-deel'-lyo], *m.* 1. Roller, a cylinder of wood for moving heavy things. 2. Roller or rolling-stone, to level walks or roads. 3. Roller for distributing printing ink; brass roller, used to form plate-glass. 4. Rolling-pin used by pastry-cooks. **Rodillo pintor,** paint roller.

rodilludo, da [ro-dil-lyoo'-do, dah], *a.* Having large knees.

rodio [roh'-de-o], *m.* Rhodium, a metal.

rodio, dia, rodiota [roh'-de-o, ah, ro-de-o'-tah], *a.* Rhodian, belonging to Rhodes or its inhabitants.

rododendro [bo-do-den'-dro], *m.* Rhododendron, a shrub of the heath family.

rodomiel [ro-do-me-el'], *m.* The juice of roses mixed with honey.

rodrigar [ro-dre-gar'], *va.* To prop up vines.

rodrigazón [ro-dre-gah-thone'], *f.* Time for putting props to vines.

rodrigón [ro-dre-gone'], *m.* 1. Stay or prop for vines. 2. *(Coll.)* Page or servant who waits upon women.

roedero [ro-ay-day'-ro], *m.* Place frequently gnawed.

roedor, ra [ro-ay-dor', rah], *m. & f.* Gnawer; detractor. **Gusano roedor,** a gnawing worm: remorse.

roedores [ro-ay-do'-rays], *m. pl. (Zool.)* The rodents.

roedura [ro-ay-doo'-rah], *f.* 1. Gnawing, corroding. 2. The part gnawed off and the mark left behind.

roel [ro-el'], *m. (Her.)* Bezant, a roundel or upon a shied.

roela [ro-ay'-lah], *f.* Round piece of crude silver or gold.

roer [ro-err'], *va.* 1. To gnaw (comida), to corrode, to consume by degrees (metal); to destroy gradually. 2. To molest, to harass. **Roer el anzuelo,** to free oneself from peril. 3. To gnaw bones.

roete [ro-ay'-tay], *m.* A medicinal wine prepared from pomegranates.

rogación [ro-gah-the-on'], *f.* Request, petition, supplication. -*pl.* Rogation.

rogador, ra [ro-gah-dor', rah], *m. & f.* Supplicant, petitioner.

rogar [ro-gar'], *va.* 1. To implore, to entreat; to crave, to court: to obtest. 2. To pray, to say prayers. **Rogar a uno,** to ask somebody to. **Rogar que,** to ask that. -*vn.* 1. To beg (pedir). **Hacerse de rogar,** to play hard to get, to have to be coaxed. 2. To pray. -*vr.* **"Se ruega la mayor puntualidad",** "Please be punctual".

rogativa [ro-gah-tee'-vah], *f.* Supplication, prayer.

rogativo, va [ro-gah-tee'-vo, vah], *a.* Supplicatory.

rogatorio, ria [ro-gah-toh'-re-o, re-ah], *a.* Rogatory, pertaining to investigation.

rogo [ro'-go], *m. (Poet.)* Fire, funeral pyre.

roído [ro-ee'-do], *a. & pp.* of ROER. 1. Gnawed, corroded. 2. Penurious, despicable.

rojeante [ro-hay-an'-tay], *pa.* Rubific, rubifying.

rojear [ro-hay-ar'], *vn.* 1. To redden (volverse rojo), to be ruddy; to blush. 2. To be reddish (tirar a rojo); to show red (mostrarse rojo).

rojete [ro-hay'-tay], *m.* Rouge for the face.

rojez, rojeza [ro-heth'], *f.* Reddish.

rojizo, za [ro-hee'-tho, thah], *a.* Reddish.

rojo, ja [roh'-ho, hah], *a.* 1. Red, ruby. 2. Ruddy, reddish, of high gold color. **Poner rojo a uno,** to make somebody blush. -*m.* 1. Red, red color. 2. **Rojo de labios,** rouge, lipstick. 3. Red, Republican.

rojura [ro-hoo'-rah], *f.* Redness.

rol [rol], *m.* 1. List (lista), roll, catalogue (catálogo). 2. Muster-roll of a merchant ship.

roldana [rol-dah'-nah], *f. (Naut.)* Sheave, pulley-wheel.

rolde [rol'-day], *m.* Circle formed by persons or things.

roleo [ro-lay'-o], *m.* Volute. *V.* VOLUTA.

rolla [rol'-lyah], *f.* Collar of a draught-horse.

rollar [rol-lyar'], *va. V.* ARROLLAR.

rollete [rol-lyay'-tay], *m. dim.* A small roll.

rollizo, za [rol-lyee'-tho, thah], *a.* Plump (persona), round (objeto), robust, strapping.

rollo [rol'-lyo], *m.* 1. A roll, anything of a cylindrical form; roll of cloth (paño): rouleau. 2. *V.* ROLLA. 3. A column of cloth, an insignia of jurisdiction. 4. Gallows erected in a cylindrical form. 5. Acts or records rolled up, that they may be carried with greater case. 6. Long round stone. 7. *(Culin.)* Rolling pin. 8. *(Culin.)* Roll (empanada). 9. *(Esp.)* Bore (cosa pesada); boring speech (discurso); tedious explanation (explicación); lecture (conferencia); tale (cuento). **La conferencia fue un rollo,** the lecture was an awful bore. **Cortar el rollo,** to stop the flow. 10. *(Esp.)* Alternative culture (contracultura), alternative life-style. **Montarse el rollo,** to organize one's life-style. 11. *(Esp.)* Ambience (ambiente), atmosphere. **Me va el rollo,** I like this scene. 12. **Largar el rollo,** *(And. Cono Sur)* to be sick (vomitar).

rollón [rol-lyone'], *m. V.* ACEMITE.

rollona [rol-lyo'-nah], *a. (Coll.)* Fat, plump, and robust: applied to a short, lusty woman.

romadizarse [ro-mah-de-thar'-say], *vr. V.* ARROMADIZARSE.

romadizo [ro-mah-dee'-tho], *m.* Nasal catarrh (permanente), cold in the head (resfriado).

romaico, ca [ro-mah'-e-co, cah], *a. & n.* Romaic, belonging to modern Greece.

romana [ro-mah'-nah], *f.* Steelyard, a balance or lever. **Hacer romana,** to balance, to equipoise.

romanador [ro-mah-nah-dor'], *m.* Weighmaster in a slaughterhouse.

romanar [ro-mah-nar'], *va.* To weigh with a steel-yard.

romance [ro-mahn'-thay], *m.* 1. The common or vernacular Spanish language (castellano), as derived from the Roman or Latín. 2. Romance (amorío), a species of poetry, a tale of wild adventures in war or love, a ballad. **Hablar en romance,** to speak out, to speak plainly. -*pl. (Coll.)* Wiles, stratagems, deceitful tricks.

romancear [ro-man-thay-ar'], *va.* 1. To translate into Spanish or into the vulgar language. 2. *(Gram.)* To periphrase, to express by circumlocution.

romancero, ra [ro-man-thay'-ro, rah], *a.* 1. Singing or composing romances or ballads. 2. Using evasions and subterfuges.

romancero [ro-man-thay'-ro], *m.* 1. Collection of romances or ballads; legendary tales. 2. Romancer.

romancesco [ro-man-thes'-co], *a.* Proper to a novel or romance; novelistic, romantic.

romancista [ro-man-thees'-tah], *m.* Author who writes in the vulgar or native language, on subjects generally discussed in the Latin tongue.-*a.* A surgeon who did not study Latin; (a charlatan).

romancito [ro-man-thee'-to], *m. dim.* A short romance.

romanear [ro-mah-nay-ar'], *va.* To weigh with a steelyard. -*vn.* To outweigh, to preponderate.

romaneo [ro-mah-nay'-o], *m.* Weighing with a steelyard.

romanesco [ro-mah-nes´-co], *a.* 1. Roman, belonging to the Roman arts and customs. 2. *V.* ROMANCESCO.

romanía (De), *adv.* Crestfallen.

románico [ro-mah'-ne-co], *a.* Romanic, Romanesquo (en arquitectura).

romanilla, ita [ro-mah-neel'-lyah], *f. dim.* A small steelyard.

romanista [ro-mah-nees'-tah], *a. & n.* Romanist, versed in Roman law or Romance philology.

romanizar [ro-mah-ne-thar'], *va.* To Romanize, to follow the manners, customs, and fashions of Rome.

romano, na [ro-mah'-no, nah], *a.* 1. Roman relating to Rome. 2. Tubby, variegated with gray and black (gato). 3. *(Typ.)* A type of about great primer size, 16-point. Bourgeois or 9-point. **A la Romana,** in the Roman fashion.

romanticismo [ro-man-te-thees'-mo], *m.* 1. The spirit of Christian civilization in literature, as contrasted with that of Greco-Roman paganism. 2. Romanticism, romantic literary style as opposed to the classic.

romántico, ca [ro-man-tee-co'-cah], *a.* 1. Not bound by the literary rules of classic authors. 2. Romantic, proper to novels. 3. Romantic, sentimental in excess.

romanza [ro-mahn'-thah], *f. (Music.)* Romance, romanza, a simple rhythmical melody.

romanzado, da [ro-man-thah'-do, dah], *a.* Turned or translated into Spanish. *-pp.* of ROMANZAR.

romanzar [ro-man-thar'], *va. V.* ROMANCEAR.

romanzón [ro-man-thone'], *m.* A long and tedious romance.

romaza [ro-mah'-thah], *f. (Bot.)* Dock. **Romaza aguda,** sharp-pointed dock.

rombo [rom'-bo], *m.* Rhomb, a quadrangular figure, having its four sides equal, with unequal angles.

romboidal [rom-bo-e-dahl'], *a.* Rhomboidal, like a rhomb.

romboide [rom-bo'-e-day], *m. (Geom.)* Rhomboid.

romera [ro-may'-rah], *f. (Bot.)* Rosemary-leaved sun-rose.

romeraje [ro-may-rah'-hay], *m. V.* ROMERÍA.

romeral [ro-may-rahl'], *m.* Place abounding with rosemary.

romería [ro-may-ree'-ah], *f.* 1. Pilgrimage. **Ir de romería,** to go on a pilgrimage. 2. Trip, excursion.

romero [ro-may'-ro], *m.* 1. *(Bot.)* Rosemary. 2. Pilgrim, palmer.

romero, ra [ro-may'-ro, rah], *a.* Traveling on religious account.

romí, romín [ro-mee', ro-meen'], *m.* Bastard saffron. *V.* AZAFRÁN ROMIN.

romo, ma [roh'-mo, mah], *a.* 1. Obtuse, blunt. 2. Flat-nosed: in this sense it is used as a substantive.*-n.* Hinny, mule begotten by a horse and a she-ass.

rompecabezas [rom-pay-cah-bay'-thas], *m.* 1. Puzzle, riddle (acertijo), jigsaw (juego), puzzle. 2. An offensive weapon, a slingshot.

rompecoches [rom-pay-co'-ches], *m.* Everlasting, a strong cloth.

rompedera [rom-pay-day'-rah], *f.* Chisel for cutting hot iron.

rompedero, ra [rom-pay-day'-ro, rah], *a.* Brittle, fit to be broken.

rompedor, ra [rom-pay-dor', rah], *m. & f.* Breaker, destroyer, crusher; one who wears out his clothes very soon.

rompedura [rom-pay-doo'-rah], *f. V.* ROTURA.

rompeesquinas [rom-pay-es-kee'-nas], *m.* A hector or braggart who hangs about street corners.

rompehuelgas [rom-pay-oo-ell'-gahs], *m.* Strike-breaker.

rompeolas [rom-pay-oh'-lahs], *m.* Breakwater.

romper [rom-perr'], *va. & vn.* 1. To break, to force asunder; to break in pieces, to dash, to fracture, to crash; to cut asunder. 2. To wear out clothes soon (gastar). 3. To defeat, to rout. 4. To break up land, to plough it for the first time. 5. To pierce, to penetrate. 6. To break off; to fall out, to quarrel. 7. To dawn, to begin. 8. To interrupt; a speech or conversation. 9. To deliberate, to resolve. 10. To break out (guerra), to spring up, to dissipate clouds. 11. To violate, to infringe; to transgress. 12. To exceed, to go beyond the limits. 13. To prune vine-stalks of their useless green branches. 14. To

snap (cuerda), to tear (papel). 15. To break (ayuno, continuidad, silencio). 16. To break (contrato, pacto). 17. To break (olas). 18. **Romper en llanto,** to burst into tears. 19. **Quien rompe paga,** one must pay the consequences. *-vr.* 1. To become free and easy in one's deportment. 2. To break, to smash; to tear, to rip. **No te vayas a romper,** don´t be so fussy.

rompiente [rom-pe-en'-tay], *m.* Surf breakers; shoreline or submerged rock on which the sea breaks.

rompimiento [rom-pe-me-en'-to], *m.* 1. Rupture, the act of breaking (acto). 2. Aperture in a solid body (abertura), crack (grieta); cleft, fracture. 3. Funeral dues paid by such as have their own tomb. 4. An apparent depth of a piece of painting which seems to break its superficies. 5. First ploughing of land. 6. *(Met.)* Rupture, dispute among persons.

rompope [rom-po'-pay], *m. (Mex. & C. A.)* Kind of eggnog.

ron [ron], *m.* Rum, spirit made from molasses or cane-juice.

ronca [ron'-cah], *f.* 1. Threat, menace; boast, brag. 2. Cry of a buck in rutting-time. 3. A kind of halberd. **Echar roncas,** *(Coll.)* (1) to threaten, to menace. (2) To be hoarse.

roncador, ra [ron-cah-dor', rah], *m. & f.* Snorer. *-m.* 1. Snoring-fish. 2. The little buss, roncador, a food-fish of California. 3. *V.* SOBRESTANTE. *-f. (Peru, Eg.)* A large spur which makes noise.

roncamente [ron-cah-men-tay], *adv.* Hoarsely, with a harsh voice; in a coarse, vulgar manner.

roncar [ron-car'], *vn.* 1. To snore (estando dormido), to make a harsh noise; to roar (ciervo, mar, tiempo). 2. *(Coll.)* To threaten (amenazar), to boast, to brag. 3. To cry like a buck in rutting-time. 4. *(And. Cono Sur)* To be bossy.

ronce [ron'-thay], *m.* Flattery.

roncear [ron-thay-ar'], *vn.* 1. To defer, to protract, to use evasions, to lag. 2. To wheedle. 3. *(Naut.)* To sail badly or slowly.

roncería [ron-thay-ree'-ah], *f.* 1. Sloth, laziness, tardiness. 2. Flattery, soothing expressions. 3. *(Naut.)* Bad sailing.

roncero, ra [ron-thay'-ro, rah], *a.* 1. Slothful, tardy. 2. Snarling, growling. 3. Flattering, wheedling, melliloquent. 4. Slow, tardy. 5. Unwilling (desganado); slack (gandul), slow. 6. Grumpy (gruñón). 7. *(And. CAm. Cono Sur)* Sly (taimado), sharp; nosey (entrometido).

roncha [ron'-chah], *f.* l. Weal, hives; a bean-like swelling. 2. Bruise (cardenal), ecchymosis. 3. Loss of money by fraud or imposition. 4. *(Prov. Ar.)* Slice of anything cut round.

ronchar [ron-char'], *va.* To chow anything crisp or hard. *V.* RONZAR. *-vn.* To make wheals.

ronchón [ron-chone'], *m. aug.* A large swelling.

ronco, ca [ron'-co, cah], *a.* Hoarse (persona), husky, having a rough voice.

ronco [ron'-co], *m. (Coll.)* Snore. *V.* RONQUIDO.

roncón [ron-cone'], *m.* Drone of a bagpipe.

ronda [ron'-dah], *f.* 1. Rounds, the act of going about at night. 2. Night;. patrol; rounds performed by a night watch; a beat. **Ir de ronda,** to go the rounds. 3. Space between the houses and the inside of the wall of a fortress. 4. Three first cards in a hand to play (naipes). 5. Round (bebidas, negociaciones). 6. *(Cono Sur)* Ring-a-ring-a-roses.

rondador [ron-dah-dor'], *m.* 1. Watchman, night guard. 2. One who is going about at night, one who is hovering about one place.

rondalla [ron-dahl'-lyah], *f.* Fable, story.

rondar [ron-dar'], *va. & vn.* 1. To go round by night in order to prevent disorders (inspeccionar). 2 To take walks by night about the streets, to serenade. 3. To go round, to follow anything continually, to haunt, to harass (acosar). 4. To hover about one place, to move round a thing. 5. To threaten to relapse, to impend. 6. To flutter (mariposa). **Me está rondando un catarro,** I´ve got a cold hanging about.

rondel [ron-del'], *m.* Roundelay, kind of poetry little used.

rondeña [ron-day'-nyah], *f.* Music or song peculiar to Ronda and like that of the fandango.

rondín [ron-deen'], *m.* 1. Rounds of a corporal on the walls to visit the sentinels. 2. Watchmen in naval arsenals.

rondí, or **rondiz** [ron-dee', ron-deeth'], *m.* Base or fierce of a precious stone.

rondó [ron-doh'], *m. (Mus.)* Rondeau, a kind of jig or lively tune, which ends with the first strain repeated.

rondón [ron-done']. A word merely used adverbially. **De rondón,** rashly, abruptly, intrepidly.

ronfeo [ron-fay'-o], *f.* A long, broad sword.

rongigata [ron-ge-hah'-tah], *f. V.* REHILANDERA.

ronquear [ron-kay-ar'], *vn.* To be hoarse with cold.

ronquedad [ron-kay-dahd'], *f.* Hoarseness, roughness of voice.

ronquera [ron-kay'-rah], *f.* Hoarseness, occasioned by catching cold.

ronquido [ron-kee'-do], *m.* 1. Snore. 2. Any rough, harsh sound.

ronquillo, illa, ito, ita [ron-keel'-lyo], *a. dim.* of RONCO. Slightly hoarse.

ronronear [ron-ro-nay-ar'], *vn.* To purr.

ronza [ron'-thah], *f. (Naut.)* The state of a vessel adrift.

ronzal [ron-thahl'], *m.* 1. Halter, a fastening for a beast. 2. *(Naut.) V.* PALANCA.

ronzar [ron-thar'], *va.* 1. *(Naut.)* To rouse, to haul without the aid of a tackle. 2. To chew hard things.

roña [ro'-nyah], *f.* 1. Scab (de oveja), mange in sheep, manginess. 2. *(Coll.)* Craft, fraud, cunning. 3. *(Met.)* Nastiness, dirt, filth (mugre). 4. *(Met.)* Moral infection or hurt. 5. Moral danger (peligro moral). 6. Meanness (tacañería). 7. *(Carib. Mex.)* Envy (envidia); grudge (inquina), ill will. 8. *(And. Med.)* Feigned illness. 9. Rust (óxido).

roñada [ro-nyah'-dah], *f. (Naut.)* Garland.

roñería [ro-nyay-ree'-ah], *f.* 1. Craft, cunning, deceitfulness. 2. Sordid parsimony.

roñoso, sa [ro-nyo'-so, sah], *a.* 1. Scabby, diseased with a scab, leprous. 2. Dirty (sucio), nasty, filthy. 3. Wily, sly, crafty. 4. Mean, sordidly parsimonious. 5. *(And.)* Unpolished, coarse (tosco). 6. *(And.)* Tricky (tramposo). 7. *(Carib. Mex.)* Bitter (rencoroso).

ropa [ro'-pah], *f.* 1. Cloth; all kinds of silk, woollen, or linen, used for domestic purposes. 2. Wearing apparel, clothes. 3. Robe, gown (vestiduras). **Ropa blanca,** linen. **Poca ropa,** ill-clothed: poor. 4. Dress of particular authority for the bar, senate, etc. 5. Anything put between or under others for a seat. **Ropa usada or ropa vieja,** cast-off wearing apparel. **A quemaropa,** (1) point blank. (2) Off one's guard.

ropaje [ro-pah'-hay], *m.* 1. Wearing apparel. 2. Drapery in pictures and statues. 3. Apparel, generally elegant, proper to some authority. 4. Odd garb (raro); heavy clothing (excesivo).

ropálico, ca [ro-pah'-le-co, cah], *a.* Applied to verses with the first word a monosyllable, and all the others increasing progressively.

ropavejería [ro-pah-vay-hay-ree'-ah], *f.* Frippery, old-clothes shop.

ropaverejero [ro-pah-vay-ray-hay'-ro], *m.* Flipper, old-clothes man.

ropería [ro-pay-ree'-ah], *f.* 1. Trade of dealers in old clothes (negocio). 2. Store for ready-made clothing (tienda). 3. Wardrobe of a community or clothes-room of a hospital. 4. Office or keeper of a wardrobe.

ropero [ro-pay'-ro], *m.* 1. Salesman who deals in clothes. 2. Sleeper of the wardrobe or vestiary in a religious community. 3. Head shepherd, who superintends the making of cheeses, and has the care of them. 4. Boy who guards the clothes of herdsman.

ropeta [ro-pay'-tah], *f. dim.* A short garment.

ropetilla [ro-pay-teel'-lyah], *f.* 1. A wretched, short garment. 2. Jacket with loose hanging sleeves.

ropilla [ro-peel'-lyah], *f.* 1. Kind of short jacket with double sleeves, the outer ones hanging loose. 2. *(dim.)* A short garment.

ropita [ro-pee'-tah], *f. dim. V.* ROPETA.

ropón [ro-pone'], *m.* A wide, loose gown, worn over the clothes (bata).

roque [ro'-kay], *m.* Rook, castle, a man at Chess. *V.* TORRE.

roqueda [ro-kay'-dah], *f.* Rocky place.

roquedo [ro-kay'-do], *m.* Rock, stony precipice.

roqueño, ña [ro-kay'-nyo, nyah], *a.* Rocky, full of rocks (rocoso). **Montañas Roqueñas,** the Rocky Mountains.

roquero, ra [ro-kay'-ro, rah], *a.* 1. Rocky, abounding with rocks; situated on rocks. 2. *V.* Rockero. 3. Person who sings Rock & Roll.

roqués [ro-kes'], *a.* Applied to a kind of falcon.

roqueta [ro-kay'-tah], *f.* Ancient kind of tower in a fortress.

roquete [ro-kay'-tay], *m.* 1. A garment worn by bishops and abbots. 2 Rocket. *V.* ATACADOR.

rorro [ror'-ro], *m.* A sucking child.

rosa [ro'-sah], *f.* 1. *(Bot.)* Rose. 2. Red spot in any part of the body. 3. Rose diamond. 4. Bunch of ribbons or like things in the form of a rose: rosette. 5. Rosy or florid aspect; rose-color. 6. Flower of saffron; artificial rose. **Rosas,** flowers, delights, pleasures; amenity. **Agua de rosas,** rose water. **Palo de rosa,** rosewood. **Estar como una rosa,** to be fresh and clean. **Color de rosa,** pink.

rosáceo, cea [ro-sah'-thay-o, ah], *a.* Rosaceous, rose colored. *-f. pi.* The rose family of plants.

rosacruz [ro-sah-crooth'], *m.* Rosicrucian, a name given to a sect of philosophers.

rosada [ro-sah', dah], *f. V.* ESCARCHA.

rosado, da [ro-sah'-do, dah], *a. & pp.* of ROSARSE. 1. Rose, crimsoned, flushed. 2. Rosy, relating to roses. 3. Made up with roses. **Agua rosada,** rosewater. *-m.* Rosé (vino).

rosal [ro-sahl'], *m. (Bot.)* Rose-bush (planta). **Rosal amarillo,** single yellow rose. **Rosal blanco,** single white rose. **Rosal japonés,** japanese rose.

rosariero [ro-sah-re-ay'-ro], *m.* Maker and seller of rosaries.

rosario [ro-sah'-re-o], *m.* 1. Rosary, a string of beads for praying. 2. The collection of *avemarías* and *padrenuestros* said at once, and counted by the beads of a rosary. 3. An assemblage of people who sing the prayers of the rosary in procession. 4. Chain-pump. 5. *(Coll.)* Backbone. 6. Feminine proper name.

rosarse [ro-sahr'-say], *vr. V.* SONROSEARSE.

rosbif [ros-beef'], *m.* Roast beef. *(Eng.)*

rosca [ros'-cah], *f.* 1. Screw, a mechanical power. 2. Anything round and spiral; spiral motion. 3. A distinctive badge of the scholars in some colleges in Spain. 4. *(Cono Sur)* Pad (para llevar carga). 5. *(Cono Sur)* Card players (naipes). 6. *(Cono Sur)* Noisy argument (discusión). **Rosca de pan,** a round twisted loaf of bread. **Comerse una rosca,** to make it. **Hacer la rosca a uno,** to suck up to somebody.

rosco [ros'-co], *m. (Culin.)* Doughnut.

roscón [ros-cone'], *m. aug.* 1. A large screw. 2. A twisted loaf of bread.

rosega [ro-say'-gah], *f. (Naut.)* Creeper, grapnel, to recover things fallen into the water.

róseo, sea [ro'-so-o, ah], *a.* Rosy, roseate.

roséola [ro-say'-o-lah], *f.* Roseola, an exanthem commonly without fever, of small rosy spots; false measles, rötheln.

rosero, ra [ro-say'-ro, rah], *m. & f.* Collector of saffron flowers.

roseta [ro-say'-tah], *f.* 1. *V.* COROLA. Small rose (rosa pequeña). 2. Rowel (de espuela). 3. Rosette (cinta de colores).

rosetón [ro-say-tone'], *m.* 1. A large rose on pieces of architecture and sculpture. 3. *(Aug.)* A large rose. *(Mex.)* Free, gratis.

rosicler [ro-se-clerr'], *m.* 1. Roset, a bright rose color. 2. Rich silver ore, ruby silver.

rosillo, illa [ro-seel'-lyo], *a.* Clear red.

rosita [ro-see'-tah], *f. 1. dim.* A small rose. 2. *(Cono Sur)* earring (pendiente).

rosmaro [ros-mah'-ro], *m.* Walrus, morse, rosmarine.

roso, sa [ro'-so, sah], *a.* Red, rosy. *V.* ROJO.

rosoli [ro-so'-le], *m.* Rossolis, sundew, a pleasant, sweet spirituous liquor, composed of brandy, sugar, cinnamon, anise, etc.

rosquete [ros-kay'-tay], *m.* *(Prov.)* A small cake made in a spiral shape.

rosquilla [ros-keel'-lyah], *f.* 1. A kind of very sweet cake made in a spiral shape. 2. Vine fretter.

rostral [ros-trahl'], *a.* 1. *V.* ROSTRATA. 2. *(Arch.)* Rostral column.

rostrado, da [ros-trah'-do, dah], *a.* Rostral, resembling the beak of a ship.

rostrico, rostrillo [ros-tree'-co, ros-treel'-lyo], *m.* 1. Veil or headdress on images. 2. Small seed pearl.

rostrituerto, ta [ros-tre-too-err'-to, tah], *a.* Showing anger or displeasure in the countenance.

rostro [ros'-tro], *m.* 1. Rostrum, the beak of a ship, and the bill or beak of a bird. 2. Countenance, human face. 3. Aspect of affairs. **A rostro firme,** resolutely, in front of. **Rostro a rostro,** face to face.

rota [ro'-tah], *f.* 1. Rout, defeat. 2. *(Naut.)* Course. 3. Rota, an ecclesiastical court in Catholic countries. 4. *V.* NUNCIATURA. 5. Rattan, a kind of Indian cane.

rotación [ro-tah-the-on'], *f.* 1. Rotation, circular motion; circumrotation. 2. Revolution of planets.

rotador, ra [ro-tah-dor', rah], *a.* Serving for rotation. *-m. pl.* The rotifera or so-called wheel-animalcules.

rotamente [ro-tah-men-tay], *adv.* Impudently, barefacedly.

rotante [ro-tahn'-tay], *pa.* Rolling, vagrant.

rotar [ro-tar'], *vn.* *V.* RODAR.

rotativo, va [ro-tah-te'-vo, vah], *a.* Rotating. *-m.* 1. Rotary press. 2. Newspaper (periódico). 3. Revolving light.

roto, ta [ro'-to, tah], *a. & pp. irr.* of ROMPER. 1. Broken, destroyed. 2. Leaky, battered, or pierced. 3. Debauched, lewd, intemperate, ragged. *-m.* Hole (en vestido), torn piece, worn part. **Nunca falta un roto para un descosido,** you can always find a companion in misfortune.

rotograbado [ro-to-grah-bah'-do], *m.* Rotogravure.

rotonda [ro-ton'-dah], *f.* 1. The hindmost of the three parts of a diligence. 2. Rotunda, a circular temple or meeting-room.

rotor [ro-tor], *m.* Rotor.

rótula [ro'-too-lah], *f.* 1. Kneecap. 2. Lozenge. 3. *(Mech.)* Swivel.

rotulación [ro-too-lah-the-on'], *f.* Labeling.

rotulado [ro-too-lah'-do], *m.* 1. Label. 2. Poster, sign.

rotulador, ra [ro-too-lah-dor', rah], *a.* Labeling, lettering. *-m. & f.* Labeler, letterer.

rotular [ro-too-lar'], *va.* 1. To label (objeto). 2. To self-address.

rotulista [ro-too-lees'-tah], *m.* 1. Poster artist. 2. Sign painter.

rótulo [ro'-too-lo], *m.* 1. Inscription on books and papers, title. 2. Printed bill posted up; show-bill, poster. 3. Certificate of the virtues of one for beatification. 4. List, manifest, of the contents of a chest, of a boat, etc.

rotunda [ro-toon'-dah], *f.* 1. Rotunda, a round building. 2. Round-house for locomotives.

rotundamente [ro-toon-dah-men'-tay], *adv.* 1. Spherically. 2. Explicitly.

rotundidad [ro-toon-de-dahd'], *f.* Roundness, rotundity, sphericity.

rotundo, da [ro-toon'-do, dah], *a.* 1. Round (redondo), circular, round, spherical. 2. Flat (negativa); clear (victoria), convincing.

rotura [ro-too'-rah], *f.* 1. Rupture, fracture, crack (grieta), breakage. 2. *(Agr.)* Breaking up of ground which has never been tilled. 3. Hernia in beasts. 4. Dissoluteness, libertinism.

roturación [ro-too-rah-the-on'], *f.* Plowing of new ground, breaking up ground for tilling.

roya [ro'-yah], *f.* Rust, a disease of corn; mildew red blight.

royal [ro-yahl'], *m.* Kind of French linen.

royo, ya [ro'-yo, yah], *a.* *(Prov.)* Red. *V.* ROJO.

roza [ro'-thah], *f.* 1. Stubbing, clearing the ground of brambles and bushes. 2. Ground cleared of brambles and bushes.

rozadero [ro-thah-day'-ro], *m.* Stubbing-place; ground cleared of trees.

rozado, da [ro-thah'-do, dah], *a. & pp.* of ROZAR. 1. Stubbed, cleared of brambles and bushes. 2. *(Naut.)* Fretted, galled.

rozador, ra [ro-thah-dor', rah], *m. & f.* Stubber, weeder.

rozadura [ro-thah-doo'-rah], *f.* 1. Friction; rubbing. 2. Gall, a slight wound by fretting off the skin. 3. Clashing, clash.

rozagante [ro-thah-gahn'-tay], *a.* 1. Pompous, showy, trailing on the ground (túnica, vestido). 2. Haughty, lofty, arrogant.

rozamiento [ro-thh-me-en'-to], *m.* Friction; rubbing.

rozar [ro-thar'], *va.* 1. To stub up, to clear the ground of brambles and bushes. 2. To nibble the grabs (ganado). 3. To scrape. 4. To graze (hierba), to touch slightly. 5. To remove the bulging or curvature of a wall. 6. To gall, to hurt by fretting the skin. **Rozar a uno al pasar,** to brush past somebody. *-vn.* To touch slightly against each other. *-vr.* 1. To strike or cut each other (pies). 2. To treat or discourse familiarly. 3. To falter, to stammer. 4. *(Naut.)* To fret, to gall: applied to cables or things which rub against one another. 5. To have a resemblance or connection with something else.

roznar [roth-nar'], *m.* 1. To grind hard things with the teeth (animales). 2. To bray, as an ass.

roznido [roth-nee'-do], *m.* 1. Noise made by the teeth in eating hard things. 2. Braying of an ass.

rozno [roth'-no], *m.* A little ass.

rozo [ro'-tho], *m.* 1. Chip of wood. 2. Stubbing, wooding; rubbing; fretting.

rua [roo'-ah], *f.* 1. Village street. 2. High road.

ruán [roo-ahn'], *m.* 1. *V.* RUANO. 2. Sort of linen manufactured at Rouen.

ruana [roo-ah'-nah], *f.* *(Amer. Col.)* *V.* PONCHO.

ruanete [roo-ah-nay'-tah], *m.* Kind of foreign linen.

ruano, na [roo-ah'-no, nah], *a.* 1. Prancing about the streets (caballos). 2. Sorrel-colored, roan (caballos). 3. Round, of a circular form.

ruante [roo-an'-tay], *a.* 1. Prancing or strutting through the streets; rider. 2. *(Her.)* Spreading the tail (pavos).

ruar [roo-ar'], *m.* 1. To roll through the streets (coche). 2. To strut about the streets, to court the ladies. 3. To ride.

rúbeo, oa [roo'-bay-o, ah], *a.* Ruby, reddish.

rubéola [roo-bay'-o-lah], *f.* Measles.

rubeta [roo-bay'-tah], *f.* Toad.

rubí [roo-bee'], *m.* 1. Ruby, a precious stone of a red color. 2. Red color, redness of the lips. **Rubí de Bohemia,** rosy quartz. **Rubí del Brasil,** red topaz. **Rubí espinela,** spinel ruby, tinged with chromium oxide.

rubia [roo'-be-ah], *f.* 1. *(Bot.)* Madder, a root used by dyers and in medicine. 2. Small red-colored river fish. 3. Blonde. **Rubia de bote,** peroxide blonde. **Rubia platino,** platinum blonde.

rubiáceas [roo-be-ah'-thay-as], *f. pl.* The madder family of plants; rubiceae.

rubial [roo-be-ahl'], *m.* 1. Field planted with madder. 2. District or soil having a red color.

rubicán [roo-be-cahn'], *a.* Rubican, of a bay or sorrel color with white hairs (caballo).

rubicela [roo-be-thay'-lah], *f.* Rubicelle, a red dish-yellow topaz.

rubicundez [roo-be-coon-deth'], *f.* 1. Flush, red color. 2. Ruby color.

rubicundo, da [roo-be-coon'-do, dah], *a.* 1. Golden-red; blonde. 2. Rosy with health. 3. Reddish, rubicund (cara).

rubificar [roo-be-fe-car'], *vn.* To rubify, to make red.

rubín [roo-been'], *m.* Ruby. *V.* RUBÍ.

rubio, bia [roo'-be-o, ah], *a.* Golden, fair, ruddy.

rubio [roo'-be-o], *m.* Red gurnard.

rubión [roo-be-on'], *a.* Of a slight reddish color: applied to a kind of wheat.

rublo [roo'-blo], *m* Rouble, a Russian coin.

rubor [roo-bor'], *m*. 1. Blush, red color of the cheeks, flush. 2. Shame, bashfulness. **Causar rubor a una,** to make somebody blush.

ruborizarse [roo-bo-re-thar'-say], *vr*. To blush, to flush with embarrassment.

ruboroso, sa [roo-bo-roo´-so, sah], *a*. Shameful. V. VERGONZOSO.

rúbrica [roo'-bre-cah], *f*. 1. Red mark (señal). 2. Rubric, a peculiar mark or flourish added to one's signature. 3. Rubric, in law and prayer books. 4. (*Met.*) Blood used to attest a truth. **Bajo la rúbrica de,** under the heading of.

rubricante [roo-bre-cahn'-tay], *pa. & a*. Rubifying; rubific.

rubricante [roo-bre-cahn'-tay], *m*. Junior counsel appointed to sign the divisions of the acts or proceedings of the council.

rubricar [roo-bre-car'], *va*. 1. To mark with a red color. 2. To sign with one's peculiar mark or flourish without writing the name. 3. To subscribe, sign, and seal a writing. 4. (*Met.*) To sign anything with one's blood.

rubriquista [roo-bre-kees'-tah], *m*. A person versed in the ceremonies of the church.

rubro, bra [roo'-bro, brah], *a*. Red, reddish; rubric. -*m*. 1. (*LAm.*) Heading title. 2. (*LAm.*) Book-keeping (de cuenta). 3. (*LAm.*) Section, department (sección).

ruc [rooc], *m*. Very large fabulous bird. V. ROCHO.

rucio, cia [roo'-the-o, ah], *a*. 1. Bright silver gray (caballos, asnos). 2. (*Coll.*) Light gray (pelo).

ruda [roo'-dah], *f*. (*Bot.*) Rue.

rudamente [roo'-dah-men-tay], *adv*. Rudely, roughly, churlishly, loutishly, abruptly, ruggedly.

rudera [roo-day´-rah], *f*. Rubbish, ruins of demolished buildings.

rudeza [roo-day'-thah], *f*. 1. Roughness, asperity or unevenness of surface. 2. Roughness of temper, rudeness, coarseness of behavior and address, churlishness, grossness. 3. Stupidity, dullness.

rudimentario, ria [roo-de-men-tah'-re-o, ah], *a*. (*Biol.*) Rudimentary, undeveloped.

rudimento [roo-de-men'-to], *m*. 1. V. PRINCIPIO. 2. Rudiment, first trace of an organ. -*pl*. Rudiments of a science or art.

rudo, da [roo´-do, dah], *a*. 1. Rude, rough, unpolished (sin labrar), coarse, churlish, clownish. 2. Hard, rigorous, severe. 3. Stupid (estúpido), dull. 4. Simple (sencillo), uncultured; plain (llano).

rueca [roo-ay'-cah], *f*. 1. Distaff for flax. 2. Winding, twisting. 3. (*Naut.*) Fish of a mast or yard.

rueda [roo-ay'-dah], *f*. 1. A wheel. 2. Circle formed by a number of persons (círculo); crown. 3. A round slice of eatables. 4. Short sun-fish. 5. (*For.*) The placing of one prisoner among others in order to obtain recognition. 6. Breaking on the wheel, a torture anciently used. 7. A kind of hoops for feminine attire. 8. The semicircular spread of a peacock's tail (pavo). 9. Turn, time, succession. **Rueda de prensa,** press conference.

ruedecica [roo-ay-day-thee'-cah], **cilla, zuela,** *f*. *dim.* A small wheel.

ruedo [roo-ay'-do], *m*. 1. Rotation, turning or going around; circuit. 2. Border (borde), selvage, fringe. 3. Plat, mat (esterilla), or rug made of base, and formed into round or square mats. 4. A plush mat. 5. Circumference of anything (contorno). 6. (*Cono Sur*) Luck (suerte). 7. Arena, bullfighting ring.

ruego [roo-ay'-go], *m*. Request, prayer, petition, entreaty, supplication. **A ruego de,** at the request of.

ruejo de Molina [roo-ay'-ho], *m*. (*Prov.*) Mill-wheel.

ruequecilla [roo-ay-kay-theel'-lyah], *f*. A small distaff.

rufalandaina [roo-fah-lan-dah'-e-nah], *f*. Noisy mirth.

rufalandario, ria [roo-fah-lan-dah'-re-o, ah], *a*. Slovenly, negligent in dress; not clean.

rufián [roo-fe-ahn'], *m*. Ruffian, pimp (chulo), pander, the bully of a brothel.

rufiana [roo-fe-ah'-nah], *f*. Bawd, procuress.

rufianar [roo-fe-ah-nar'], *va*. To pimp, to pander.

rufiancete, cillo [roo-fe-an-thay'-tay], *m*. *dim.* Little ruffian or pimp.

rufianejo [roo-fe-ah-nay'-ho], *m*. *dim.* V. RUFIANCETE.

rufianería [roo-fe-ah-nay-ree'-ah], *f*. Pimping. V. ALCAHUETERÍA.

rufianesco, ca [roo-fe-ah-nes´-co, cah], *a*. Pimp-like, relating to bawds and pimps.

rufo, fa [roo'-fo, fah], *a*. 1. Carroty, red-haired (pelirrojo). 2. Frizzed, curled.

ruga [roo'-hah], *f*. 1. Wrinkle, corrugation. V. ARRUGA. 2. A slight furrow.

rugar [roo-gar'], *va*. To wrinkle, to corrugate. V. ARRUGAR.

rugby [roog'-be], *m*. Rugby.

rugible [roo-hee´-blay], *a*. Capable of bellowing or roaring.

rugido [roo-hee'-do], *m*. 1. Reprint of a lion. 2. Rumbling in the bowels. **Rugido de tripas,** intestinal rumblings.

rugiente [roo-he-en´-tay], *a*. Bellowing, roaring.

rugimiento [roo-he-me-ayn'-to], *m*. V. RUGIDO.

ruginoso, sa [roo-he-no'-so, sah], *a*. Covered with rust, rusty.

rugir [roo-heer'], *vn*. 1. To roar (león), to bellow (toro); to halloo. 2. To make a noise, to creek, to rustle. -*vr*. To be whispered about.

rugosidad [roo-go-se-dahd'], *f*. The state of being wrinkled or corrugated, rugosity.

rugoso, sa [roo-go'-so, sah], *a*. Rugose, full of wrinkles (arrugado); ridged (desigual).

ruibarbo [roo-e-bar'-bo], *m*. (*Bot.*) Rhubarb. **Ruibarbo compacto,** thick leaved rhubarb. **Ruibarbo mutante,** nodding rhubarb.

ruido [roo-ee'-do], *m*. 1. Noise, clamor, din (alboroto), clatter; murmur, outcry (grito). 2. Dispute, difference, lawsuit. 3. Rumor, report, empty sound or show. 4. Sound made purposely and for some individual end. **Ser más el ruido que las nueces,** great cry and little wool (more noise than nuts). **Ruido de fondo,** background noise. **No hagas tanto ruido,** don´t make so much noise.

ruidosamente [roo-e-do'-sah-men-tay], *adv*. Noisily, loudly.

ruidoso, sa [roo-e-do'-so, sah], *a*. Noisy (estrepitoso), clamorous, obstreperous.

ruin [roo-een'], *a*. 1. Mean (vil), vile, low, despicable, churlish, forlorn; little. 2. Humble, decayed; wicked, malicious. 3. Covetous, avaricious, insidious, treacherous, infamous. 4. Applied to a vicious animal. -*m*. A wicked, infamous person. -*f*. Small nerve in the tail of cats. -*pl*. (*Coll.*) Braid.

ruina [roo-ee'-nah], *f*. 1. Ruin, decline, downfall, destruction (de esperanzas), confusion, overthrow, fall (del imperio). **Será mi ruina,** it will be the ruin of me. -*pl*. Ruins of an edifice. **Ir en ruina,** to be destroyed, to go to ruin. 2. Cause of ruin, decadence.

ruinar [roo-e-nar'], *va*. To ruin, to destroy. V. ARRUINAR.

ruindad [roo-in-dahd'], *f*. 1. Meanness (cualidad), baseness, malice. 2. Humility, poverty. 3. Covetousness, avariciousness.

ruinmente [roo-in'-men-tay], *adv*. Basely, meanly.

ruinoso, sa [roo-e-no'-so, sah], *a*. Worthless, ruinous, baneful, destructive.

ruiponce [roo-e-pon'-thay], *m*. (*Bot.*) V. RAPÓNCHIGO.

ruipóntico [roo-e-pon'-te-co], *m*. (*Bot.*) Rhubarb, pie-plant, an herb the leaf stalks of which are used in cooking.

ruiseñor [roo-e-say-nyor´], *m*. (*Orn.*) Nightingale.

rujada [roo-hah'-dah], *f*. (*Prov. Ar.*) Heavy shower of rain.

rujar [roo-har'], *va*. (*Prov.*) To irrigate, to bath.

rular [roo-lar'], *vn*. (*Vulg.*) To roll. V. RODAR.

ruleta [roo-lay'-tah], *f*. Roulette, a game of chance.

rulo [roo'-lo], *m*. 1. Ball (pelota), bowl. 2. A conical stone which turns in oil-mills. 3. Roller (rodillo). 4. Hair-curler (del pelo).

ruló [roo-lo´], *m*. A printer's ink-roller.

rumano, na [roo-mah'-no, nah], *a.* Rumanian, belonging to Rumania. *-m.* Rumanian, the Romance tongue of this country.

rumba [room'-bah], *f.* Rumba or rhumba.

rumbadas [room-bah'-dahs], *f. pl. V.* ARRUMBADAS.

rumbo [room'-bo], *m.* 1. Rhumb, a point of the compass. 2. Road (camino), route, way. 3. Course of a ship. 4. Pomp, ostentation, pageantry. 5. Course of events (tendencia); line of conduct (conducta). 6. Generosity (liberalidad); lavish display (boato). 7. *(CAm.)* Party (fiesta). 8. *(Cono Sur)* Cut (herida). **Ir con rumbo a,** to be heading for. **Viajar con rumbo,** to travel in style.

rumbosamente [room-bo'-sah-men-tay], *adv.* Pompously, magnificently, liberally.

rumboso, sa [room-bo'-so, sah], *a.* Pompous, magnificent, splendid, liberal.

rumia [roo'-me-ah], *f.* Rumination, chewing the cud.

rumiador, ra [roo-me-ah-dor', rah], *m. & f. & a.* Ruminator; mediator; ruminant.

rumiadura [roo-me-ah-doo'-rah], *f.* Rumination.

rumiante [roo-me-ahn'-tay], *pa. & a.* Ruminant; musing.

rumiar [roo-me-ar'], *va.* 1. To ruminate, to chew the cud. 2. To brood upon a subject (asunto); to muse, to meditate.

rumión, na [roo-me-on', nah], *a.* Ruminating much.

rumo [roo'-mo], *m.* The first hoop of the head of a cask.

rumor [roo-mor'], *m.* 1. Rumor, report, hearsay. 2. A gentle sound, murmur (murmullo).

rumorcico, illo, ito [roo-mor-thee'-co], *m. dim.* A flying report.

rumorearse [roo-mo-ray-ar'-say], *vr.* **Se rumorea que...,** it is rumored that...

rumoreo [roo-mo-ray'-o], *m.* Murmuring, rumoring.

rumoroso, sa [roo-mo-ro'-so, sah], *a.* Causing rumor.

runas [roo'-nas], *f. pl.* Runes, alphabetical characters employed by the ancient Scandinavians.

runcho [roon'-cho], *m. (Ec. Colom.)* Opossum.

runfla [roon'-flah], *f.* Series, multitude (multitud), number of things, gang (pandilla).

rúnico, ca [roo'-ne-co, cah], *a.* Runic, relating to the Goths, Scandinavians, and other nations of ancient Europe, or their language.

runrún [roon-roon'], *m. (Coll.)* Rumor (rumor), report. *V.* RUMOR.

ruñar [roo-nyar'], *va.* To groove the ends of staves for the heads and bottoms of burrels, to fit.

rupia [roo'-pe-ah], *f.* 1. Rupee, the standard monetary unit of India, Pakistan, Bhutan, Sri Lanka, the Maldive, the Seychelles and Nepal. 2. A skin disease characterized by the formation of large crusts.

rupicabra [roo-pe-cah'-brah], *f.* Chamois-goat.

ruptil [roop-teel'], *a. (Bot.)* Ruptile.

ruptura [roop-too'-rah], *f.* Rupture. *V.* ROTURA.

ruqueta [roo-kay'-tah], *f. (Bot.) V.* JARAMAGO.

rural [roo-rahl'], *a.* Rural, country. *-m. (Cono Sur)* Estate car, station wagon.

ruralmente [roo-rahl'-men-tay], *adv.* Rurally.

rus [roos], *m. V.* ZUMAQUE.

rusco, ca [roos'-co, cah], *a.* Rude, peevish, forward. *V.* BRUSCO.

rusiente [roo-se-en'-tay], *a.* Turning red by the action of fire.

ruso, sa [roo'-so, sah], *a.* Russian. *-m.* The Slavic tongue spoken in Russia.

rustical [roos-te-cahl'], *a.* Rustical, rural, wild.

rústicamente [roos'-te-cah-men-tay], *adv.* Rustically, rudely, boisterously.

rusticano, na [roos-te-cah'-no, nah], *a.* 1. Wild: said of the radish and other plants. 2. Rural.

rusticar [roos-te-car'], *vn.* To go to the country, to pass time there; to rusticate.

rusticidad [roos-te-the-dahd'], *f.* Rusticity, simplicity; rudeness, clownishness, clumsiness, crudity (grosería), coarseness (ordinariez).

rústico, ca [roos'-te-co, cah], *a.* 1. Rustic belonging to the country (del campo). 2. Rustic, unmannerly (sin educación), clownish. **En rústica,** in paper covers, unbound.

rústico [roos'-te-co], *m.* Rustic, peasant, country clown.

rustiquez, rustiqueza [roos-te-keth'], *f.* Rusticity. *V.* RUSTICIDAD.

rustro [roos'-tro], *m. V.* RUMBO.

ruta [roo'-tah], *f.* Route, itinerary.

rutilante [roo-te-lahn'-tay], *a.* Brilliant, fleshing.

rutilar [roo-te-lar'], *vn. (Poet.)* To radiate, to shine, to be splendid.

rútilo, la [roo'-te-lo, lah], *a.* Of a bright yellow or orange color.

rutina [roo-tee'-nah], *f.* Routine, custom, habit.

rutinario, ria [roo-te-nah'-re-o, ah], *a.* Done by routine, routinary.

rutinero, ra [roo-te-nay'-ro, rate], *a.* Fond of routine, routinist.

ruzafa [roo-thah'-tah], *f.* Garden, park.

S

s [sy'-say] is the twentieth letter in the order of the Spanish alphabet. It has always a harsh, hissing sound, like *ss* in English as *dispossess.* No Spanish word begins with *s* followed by a consonant: in all words derived from other languages, the *s* is either omitted or preceded by *e,* as, **ciencia,** science; **espíritu,** spirit; **Escipión,** Scipio. *S* is never doubled.-**S.** is a contraction for **Señor,** Mr. or Sir; **Santo.** Saint, **Su, sus,** his, her, their, or your; **Sud** or **Sur,** south; **S. O.,** south-west, **S. E.** south-east; **S. M., Su Majestad, SS. AA., sus Altezas**; S. S. S.; **Smo.** stands for **santísimo,** very holy. In commerce s/c stands for **Su cuenta** (your account).

sábado [sah'-bah-do], *m.* 1. Saturday. 2. Sabbath, among the Jews. **Sábado de Gloria,** Easter Saturday.

sabalera [sah-bah-lay' rah], *f.* Kind of fire-grate in furnaces.

sabalero [sah-bah-lay'-ro], *m.* Shad-fisher.

sábalo [sah'-bah-lo], *m.* Shad.

sábana [sah'-bah-nah], *f.* 1. Sheet for a bed (de cama). 2. Altar-cloth. **Pegársele a uno las sábanas,** to rise late (to lie abed) from laziness.

sabana [sah'-bah-nah], *f. (Amer. Cuba)* Savannah, an extended plain.

sabandija [sah-ban-dee'-hah], *f.* Any disgusting insect or reptile (insecto, reptil).

sabanear [sah-bah-nay-ar'], *va.* 1. To scour the savannah in order to find an animal or to collect the herd. 2. *(CAm.)* To flatter (halagar). 3. *(CAm. Carib.)* To pursue, to chase (perseguir).

sabanero, ra [sah-bah-nay'-ro, rah], *a.* 1. Dwelling in a savannah. 2. Relative to a savannah.

sabanero [sah-bah-nay'-ro], *m.* The man on horseback who takes care of the cattle grazing on the plains.

sabanilla [sah-bah-neel'-lyah], *f.* 1. *(Dim.)* A small sheet. 2. A short piece of linen. 3. Altar-cloth; napkin.

sabañón [sah-bah-nyone'], *m.* Chilblain.

sabatario [sah-bah-tah'-re-o], *a.* Applied to the Jews who keep Saturday for their Sabbath; Sabbatarian.

sabático, ca [sah-bah'-te-co, cah], *a.* 1. Sabbatical, belonging to Saturday, or the Jewish Sabbath. 2. Every seventh year among the Jews.

sabatina [sah-bah-tee'-nah], *f.* 1. Divine service performed on Saturday. 2. A literary exercise performed by students on Saturday evening.

sabatino, na [sah-bah-tee'-no, nah], *a.* Performed on Saturday or belonging to it.

sabedor, ra [sah-bay-dor', rah], *m. & f.* One who knows or is informed of something.

sabeísmo [sah-bay-ees'-mo], *m.* Ancient fire-worship.

sabeliano, na [sah-bay-le-ah'-no, nah], *a. & n.* Sabellian, relating to Sabellius or Sabellianism.**sabeo, bea** [sah-bay'-o, ah], *a.* Sabaean, Arabian, of Sheba.

saber [sah-berr'], *va.* 1. To know, to have knowledge of. 2. To experience, to know by experience. 3. To be able, to be possessed of talents or abilities: to be learned or knowing. **Saber mucho latín,** to be very sagacious and prudent. 4. To subject, to submit. 5. To fit, to suit, 6. To relish, to savor, to taste. 7. To use, to practice customarily; to be in the habit. 8. To resemble, to appear like. 9. *V.* PODER. **El dice que no sabe escribir,** he says that he cannot write. *-v. imp.* To have a taste of. **Hacer saber,** to make known, to communicate. **Sabérselo todo,** in an ironical sense, to know everything: applied to assuming, intolerant persons. **No se sabe,** it is not known. **No sabe en dónde tiene la cara,** he does not know his duty. **No saber de sí,** to be overwhelmed with occupation. **No sé que,** I don't know what; an indefinable something. **Sabe que rabia,** it has a sharp taste. **Cuando lo supe,** when I heard about it. **Vete a saber,** your guess is as good as mine. **Tiene que saber contenerse,** he must control himself. *-vn.* **Saber a,** to taste of. **Esto sabe a queso,** this tastes of cheese. *-vr.* **Se sabe que...,** it is known that... **Por fin se supo el secreto,** finally the secret was revealed.

saber [sah-berr'], *m.* 1. Learning, knowledge, lore. *V.* SABIDURÍA. 2. Science, faculty.

sabiamente [sah'-be-ah-men-tay], *adv.* Wisely (prudentemente), knowingly, learnedly, sagely.

sabicú [sah-be-coo'], *m. (Amer. Cuba)* A handsome tree of Cuba, belonging to the pulse family, having white fragrant flowers and a hard wood.

sabidillo, lla [sah-be-deel'-lyo, lyah], *a. dim.* of SABIDO. Commonly applied to persons who have pretensions to learning and wisdom.

sabido, da [sah-bee'-do, dah], *a. & pp.* Of SABER. Learned, well-informed.

sabiduría [sah-be-doo-ree'-ah], *f.* 1. Learning, knowledge, wisdom, sapience. 2. *V.* NOTICIA.

sabiendas (A) [sah sah-be-en'-das], *adv.* Knowingly (sabiendo) and prudently, consciously (con intención). **A sabiendas de que...,** knowing full well that....

sabiente [sah-be-en'-tay], *pa.* Sapient, knowing.

sabihondez [sah-be-on-deth'], *f.* Assumption of being wise, without being really so.

sabihondo, da [sah-be-on'-do, dah], *a.* Presuming to decide difficult questions without sufficient knowledge.

sabina [sah-bee'-nah], *f. (Bot.)* Savin or sabine.

sabinar [sa-be-nar'], *m.* A clump of sabines.

sabino, na [sah-bee'-no, nah], *a.* 1. Applied to horses or mules of a mixed white and chestnut color. 2. Sabine, of the Sabines, neighbors of the ancient Romans.

sabio, bia [sah'-be-o, ah], *a.* Sage, wise (juicioso), learned (docto), sapient, knowing; cunning.

sabio, bia [sah'-be-o], *m. & f.* A sage, a wise person.

sablazo [sah-blah'-tho], *m.* 1. Stroke with a sabre. 2. Sponging (gorronería). **Dar un sablazo a uno,** to touch somebody for a loan.

sable [sah'-blay], *m.* 1. Sabre, cutlass. 2. *(Her.)* Sable, black.

sablear [sah-blay-ahr'], *va.* **Sablear algo a uno,** to scrounge something from somebody.

sablón [sah-blone'], *m.* Coarse sand, gravel.

saboca, *f. (Prov.) V.* SABOGA.

saboga [sah-bo'-gah], *f.* A species of shad.

sabogal [sah-bo-gahl], *a.* Applied to the net for catching shad.

saboneta [sah-bo-nay'-tah], *f.* A hunting-case watch.

sabor [sah-bor'], *m.* 1. Relish, taste, savor. 2. Pleasure; desire. **A sabor,** at pleasure; to the taste; according to one's wish. **Sin sabor,** tasteless.

saborear [sah-bo-ray-ar'], *va.* 1. To give a relish: to give a zest. 2. To engage one's affections; to make one embrace our opinion. 3. To flavor, to add a flavor to. **Saborear el triunfo,** to enjoy one's triumph. *-vr.* 1. To enjoy eating and drinking with peculiar pleasure. 2. To be pleased or delighted.

saboreo [sah-bo-ray'-o], *m. V.* PALADERO.

sabotaje [sah-bo-tah'-hay], *m.* Sabotage.

sabotear [sah-bo-tay-ar'], *va.* To sabotage.

saboyana [sah-bo-yah'-nah], *f.* 1. A kind of wide petticoat. 2. A delicious paste of a particular composition.

saboyano, na [sah-bo-yah'-no, nah], *a.* Of Savoy, Savoyard.

sabrosamente [sah-bro-sah-men'-tay], *adv.* Pleasantly, tastefully.

sabrosico, ica, illo, illa, ito, ita [sah-bro-see'-co], *a. dim.* A little savory.

sabroso, sa [sah-bro'-so, sah], *a.* 1. Savory, palatable, salted, saltish. 2. Delightful, pleasurable to the mind. 3. Solid (libro). 4. Salty, daring (cuento, chiste). 5. *(And. Carib.)* Lovely, nice, pleasant (agradable). 6. *(And. Carib. Mex.)* Talkative (parlanchín). 7. *(Mex.)* Big-headed (fanfarrón).

sabucal [sah-boo-cahl'], *m.* Clump of willows.

sabuco [sah-boo'-co], *m. V.* SAÚCO.

sabuesa [sah-boo-ay'-sah], *f.* Bitch of a hound or bangle.

sabueso [sah-boo-ay'-so], *m.* Hound, bloodhound, beagle, harehound, foxhound.

sábula [sah'-boo-la], *m.* Gravel, coarse sand.

sabuloso, sa [sah-boo-lo'-so, sah], *a.* Sabulous, gritty, sandy, gravelly.

saburra [sah-boor'-rah], *f.* Accumulation of matters in the stomach, in consequence of bad digestion, saburra.

saburral [sah-boor-rahl'], *a.* Saburral, relating to foulness of the stomach.

saca [sah'-cah], *f.* 1. Exportation, extraction; the net of extracting or exporting. 2. Suck, a large bag made of coarse stuff. 3. First authorized register of a sale. 4. *(Prov.)* Valuation, computation; agreement. **Estar de saca,** (a) to be on sale; (b) to be marriageable: spoken of women.

sacabala [sah-ca-bah'-lah], *f. (Surg.)* A kind of bullet-extracting forceps.

sacabalas [sah-cah-bah'-las], *m.* A kind of forceps for drawing a ball from a great gun.

sacabocado, sacabocados [sah-ca-bo-cah'-do], *m.* 1. A hollow punch. 2. Anything that cuts out a round piece. 3. Anything that effects one's purpose.

sacabotas [sah-cah-bo'-tas], *m.* Bootjack.

sacabrocas [sah-cah-bro'-cas], *m.* Pincers used by shoemakers.

sacabuche [sah-cah-boo'-chas], *m.* 1. *(Naut.)* A tube or pipe which scribes as a pump. 2. Sackbut, a musical wind-instrument. 3. Player on the sackbut. 4. Nickname of a despicable person.

sacacorchos [sah-cah-cor'-chos], *m.* Corkscrew.

sacacuartos [sah-cah-coo-ahr'-tos], *m. V.* SACADINERO.

sacada [sah-cah'-dah], *f.* District separated from a province.

sacadilla [sah-cah-deel'-lyah], *f.* Noise made to rouse game.

sacadinero, sacadineros [sah-cah-de-nay'-ro], *m. (Coll.)* Catchpenny; expensive toys or baubles.

sacador, ra [sah-cah-do', rah], *m. & f.* Extracter, exporter.

sacadura [sah-cah-doo'-rah], *f.* 1. A sloping cut, by which tailors make clothes fit better. 2. *(And. Cono Sur)* Extraction.

sacafilásticas [sah-cah-fe-lahs'-te-cas], *f.* A kind of iron used by artillery-men to take the spikes out of guns.

sacafondo [sah-cah-fon'-do], *m.* A cooper's auger.

sacaliña [sah-cah-lee'-nyah], *f.* 1. An ancient kind of dart. 2. A knack of tricking a person out of something; a wheedle to get one's money. *V.* SOCALIÑA.

sacamanchas [sah-cah-mahn'-chas], *m.* 1. He who takes out spots or stains from clothes. 2. *(Coll.)* He who publishes another's faults. 3. Cleaning material.

sacamiento [sah-cah-me-en'-to], *m.* Taking a thing from the place where it is; taking or drawing out.

sacamolero [sah-cah-mo-lay-ro], *m. V.* SACAMUELAS.

sacamuelas [sah-cah-moo-ay´-las], *m.* 1. Tooth-drawer, dentist (dentista). 2. Anything which causes a shedding of teeth. 3. Chatterer (parlanchín).

sacanabo [sah-cah-nah'-bo], *m. (Naut.)* Pump-hook.

sacanete [sah-cah-nay´-tay], *m.* Lansquenet, a game at cards.

sacapelotas [sah-cah-pay-lo'-tas], *m.* 1. Nickname given to common people. 2. Ancient instrument for extracting balls.

sacapotras [sah-cah-po'-tras], *m.* Nickname of a bad surgeon.

sacapuntas [sah-cah-poon'-tahs], *m.* Pencil sharpener.

sacar [sah-car´], *va.* 1. To extract, to get out, to draw out, to remove, to take out, to put out of place. 2. To dispossess of an employment or office, to except or exclude. 3. To manufacture (producto), to produce. 4. To imitate, to copy (copia). 5. To clear, to free; to place in safety. 6. To find out, to resolve, to know; to dissolve; to discover, to insert. 7. To pull out, to eradicate, to take, to extort, to sack. 8. To brood, to hatch eggs (huevos). 9. To compel to bring forth what was hidden; to show (cualidad), to manifest. 10. To excite passion or anger. **Esa pasión lo saca de sí,** this passion carries him beside himself. 11. To deduce, to infer; to deride (deducir). 12. To ballot, to draw lots. 13. To procure, to obtain (conseguir); to gain at play. 14. To throw a ball, making it bounce on the ground. 15. To produce (obra), to create, to invent. 16. To extend, to enlarge. 17. To buy in a shop. 18. To transcribe, to copy. 19. To appear or go out with anything new. 20. To carry corn to be thrashed. 21. To draw a sword, bayonet, etc. 22. It is used instead of *salir con;* as, **Hemos sacado buen tiempo,** we set out with fine weather. *V.* TRAER. 23. To cite, to name, to quote. **Sacar a bailar** *(Coll.)* to name or cite unnecessarily any person or thing not alluded to in conversation. 24. To injure, to impair: applied to things which affect the beauty, health, etc. 25. To obtain by cunning and craft. 26. To put on (lustre). 27. To mention (en periódico). 28. *(And. CAm.)* To flatter (lisonjear). 29. *(And. Mex.)* **Sacar algo a uno,** to reproach somebody for something. **Sacar agua,** to draw water. **Sacar a bailar a una señora,** to invite a lady to dance. **Sacar en claro** or **en limpio,** to clear up all doubts, to come to a conclusion. **Sacar fruto,** to reap the fruit of one's labor. **Sacar a luz,** to print, to publish; to develop, to exhibit. **Sacar apodos,** to call nicknames. **Sacar el pecho,** to come up to the breast. *(Met.)* To stand up in defence of a person. **Sacar la cara,** to present oneself by proxy. **Sacar la espina,** to eradicate an evil. **Sacar mal la cuenta,** to turn out unfavorably. **Sacar las uñas,** to avail oneself of every means in an emergency. **Sacar una información a uno,** to get information out of somebody. **Sacar la lengua,** to stick one´s tongue out. **Sacan 200 coches diarios,** they make 200 cars a day. **Nos quiso sacar una foto,** he wanted to take a photo of us. **Han sacado 35 diputados,** they have got 35 members. **Sacar faltas a uno,** to point out somebody´s defects. **Sacar adelante,** to bring up (niño).

sacarífero, ra [sah-cah-ree´-fay-ro, rah], *a.* Sugar-producing.

sacarificación [sah-cah-re-fe-cah-the-on'], *f.* Conversion into sugar.

sacarinaMexah-cah-ree'-nah], *f.* Saccharin, artificial sweetener.

sacarino, na [sah-cah-ree'-no, nah], *a.* Saccharine.

sacaroideo, ea [sah-cah-roi-day'-o, ah], *a.* Like sugar.

sacarol [sah-cah-rohl'], *m.* Sugar as an excipient.

sacarímetro, sacarómetro [sah-cah-ree'-mah-tro], *m.* Saccharimeter.

sacatapón [sah-cah-tah-pone'], m. Corkscrew; bung-drawer.

sacate [sah-cah'-tay], *m. (Mex.)* Grass, herb; hay.

sacatrapos [sah-cah-trah'-pos], *m.* 1. Worm for drawing the wad of a firelock. 2. One who obtains what he wants by artifice.

sacelación [sah-thay-lah-the-on'], f. *(Med.)* Application of small bags of heating materials to a diseased part.

sacelo [sah-thay'-lo], *m.* Chapel or hermitage among the Romans.

sacerdocio [sah-ther-do'-the-o], *m.* Priesthood, ministry.

sacerdotal [sah-ther-do-tahl'], *a.* Sacerdotal, ministerial.

sacerdote [sah-ther-do'-tay], *m.* Priest, clergyman, minister.

sacerdotisa [sah-ther-do-tee'-sah], *f.* Priestess.

saciable [sah-the-ah'-blay], *a.* Satiable, that may be satiated.

saciar [sah-the-ar'], *va.* 1. To satiate, to cloy. 2. To gratify desire (deseo). 3. To satisfy (anhelo). *-vr.* To satiate oneself.

saciedad [sah-the-ay-dahd'], *f.* Satiety. **Demostrar algo hasta la saciedad,** to prove something up to the hilt.

saciña [sah-thee'-nyah], *f. (Bot.)* A kind of willow.

saco [sah'-co], *m.* 1. Sack, bag (bolso). **Sacos vacíos,** ready-made bags. 2. A coarse stuff worn by country people. 3. Coarse cloth worn as penance. 4. Anything which includes within itself many other things. 5. Pillage, sack, plunder; heap. *V.* SAQUEO. 6. Long coat (prenda). 7. Nick (cárcel). **A saco,** sacking, plundering. **No echar una cosa en saco roto,** not to be heedless of advice, not to waste an opportunity. 6. Sagum, short, round jacket worn by Roman soldiers. (Note. —The fourth acceptation is commonly taken in an unfavorable sense.) **Saco de arena,** sandbag. **Saco de viaje,** traveling bag.

sacra [sah'-crah], *f.* Each of the three tablets on the altar, which the priest, in saying mass, may read without opening the missal.

sacramental [sah-crah-men-tahl'], *a.* Sacramental. *-m. & f.* Individual or confraternity destined to the worship of the sacrament of the altar.

sacramentalmente [sah-crah-men-tahl'-men-tay], *adv.* Sacramentally; in confession.

sacramentar [sah-crah-men-tar'], *va.* To administer the sacraments. *-vn. V.* JURAMENTAR. *-vr.* To transubstantiate Christ into the eucharist.

sacramentario [sah-crah-men-tah´-re-o], *a.* Applied to heretics who deny the real presence in the eucharist.

sacramente [sah'-crah-men-tay], *adv. V.* SAGRADAMENTE.

sacramento [sah-crah-men'-to], *m.* 1. Sacrament. 2. *V.* MISTERIO. 3. Sacrament, Christ transubstantiated in the host. **Sacramento del altar,** the eucharist.

sacratísimo, ma [sah-crah-tee'-se-mo, mah], *a. sup.* of SAGRADO.

sacre [sah'-cray], *m.* 1. *(Orn.)* Saker, a large lanner falcon. 2. Small cannon.

sacrificadero [sah-cre-fe-cah-day'-ro], *m.* Place where a sacrifice is performed.

sacrificador [sah-cre-fe-cah-dor'], *m.* Sacrificer, sacrificator.

sacrificante [sah-cre-fe-cahn'-tay], *pa. & a.* Sacrificing, hazarding, sacrificial, sacrificatory.

sacrificar [sah-cre-fe-car'], *va.* 1. To sacrifice, to offer or perform a sacrifice. 2. To pay homage. 3. To sacrifice, to destroy or give up for the sake of something else. 4. To sacrifice, to expose to hazard and danger. *-vr.* 1. To devote oneself to God. 2. To submit, to conform oneself to.

sacrificio [sah-cre-fee´-the-o], *m.* 1. Sacrifice, the act of offering to heaven; offering. 2. Sacrifice, submission, obsequiousness; obedience, compliance. 3. Sacrifice, anything destroyed or quitted for the sake of something else. **Sacrificio del altar,** sacrifice of the mass. 4. Any dangerous surgical operation.

sacrílegamente [sah-cree'-lay-gah-men-tay], *m.* Sacrilegiously.

sacrilegio [sah-cre-lay'-he-o], *m.* Sacrilege; church-robbing, pecuniary punishment for sacrilege.

sacrílego, ga [sah-cree'-lay-go, gah], *a.* Sacrilegious.

sacrismoche, cho [sah-cris-mo'-chay, cho], *m.* In jocular style, a man in a ragged black coat.

sacristán [sah-cris-tahn'], *m.* 1. Sacristan, sexton, clerk. 2. Hoop formerly worn by women.

sacristana [sah-cris-tah'-nah], *f.* 1. Sacristan or sexton's wife. 2. Nun, or lay woman who provides things necessary for church service.

sacristancillo, ito [sah-cris-tahn-thel'-lyo], *m. dim.* A little sexton or clerk.

sacristanía [sah-cris-tah-nee'-ah], *f.* Office of a sexton.

sacristía [sah-cris-tee'-ah], *f.* 1. Sacristy, vestry. 2. Office and employment of a sacristan or sexton. 3. *(Coll.)* Stomach.

sacro, cra [sah'-cro, crah], *a.* Holy, sacred. *V.* SAGRADO.
   Fuego sacro, St. Anthony's fire. **Hueso sacro,** the sacrum.

sacrosanto, ta [sah-cro-sahn'-to, tah], *a.* Sacred, consecrated, very holy.

sacudida [sah-coo-dee'-dah], *f.* 1. The act of shaking off or rejecting anything, jerk (tirón), shock (de terremoto), blast (de explosión), jolt (choque). **Sacudida eléctrica,** electric shock. **Dar una sacudida a una alfombra,** to beat a carpet. 2. *(Fig.)* Violent change; sudden jolt.

sacudidamente [sah-coo-dee'-dah-men-tay], *adv.* Rejectingly.

sacudido, da [sah-coo-dee'-do, dah], *a. & pp.* of SACUDIR. 1. Harsh, indocile, intractable. 2. Unembarrassed, resolved.

sacudido [sah-coo-dee'-do], *m.* Spanish step in dancing.

sacudidor [sah-coo-de-dor'], *m.* 1. Shaker, one who shakes off. 2. Instrument for beating or cleansing.

sacudidura [sah-coo-de-doo'-rah], *f.* Dusting, cleansing.

sacudimiento [sah-coo-de-me-en'-to], *m.* Act of shaking off or rejecting.

sacudir [sah-coo-deer'], *va.* 1. To shake (árbol, edificio, persona, tierra), to jerk (cuerda), to hustle. 2. To dart, to throw, to discharge; to beat (como castigo), to chastise with blows. 3. To remove, to separate. 4. *(Naut.)* To flap in the wind. 5. To shake (conmover). **Una tremenda emoción sacudió a la multitud,** a great wave of excitement ran through the crowd. **Sacudir a uno,** to beat somebody up. *-vr.* To reject with disdain, to turn away in a harsh and violent manner.

sacha [sah'-chah], *f.* A garden hoe.

sachadura [sah-chah-doo'-rah], *f.* Hoeing or turning up the ground with a hoe or dibble.

sachar [sah-char'], *va.* To turn the ground with a hoe or dibble.

sacho [sah'-cho], *m.* A hoe.

sadismo [sah-dees'-mo], *m.* Sadism.

saduceísmo [sah-doo-thay-ees'-mo], *m.* Sadduceeism, Sadducism.

saduceo, ea [sah-doo-thay'-o, ah], *a.* Saducean.

saeta [sah-ay'-tah], *f.* 1. Arrow, dart. 2. Cock of a sundial, gnomon; hand of a watch or clock (de reloj). 3. Magnetic needle. 4. Bud of a vine. 5. *(Ast.)* A northern constellation. 6. *pl.* Moral sentence or couplet of missionaries; pious ejaculations. 7. *(Mus.)* Sacred song in flamenco style sung during Holy Week processions.

saetada [sah-ay-tah'-dah], *f.* **saetazo** [sah-ay-tah'-tho], *m.* Arrow-wound.

saetear [sah-ay-tay-ahr'], *va.* *V.* ASAETEAR.

saetera [sah-ay-tay'-rah], *f.* 1. Loop-hole in turrets and old walls, through which fire-arms are discharged. 2. A small grated window in prisons.

saetero, ra [sah-ay-tay'-ro, rah], *a.* 1. Relating to arrows. 2. Applied to a honey-comb made in a right line.

saetero [sah-ay-tay'-ro], *m.* Archer, bowman.

saetía [sah-ay-tee'-ah], *f.* 1. *(Naut.)* Settee, a vessel with lateen sails, used in the Mediterranean. 2. Loophole. *V.* SAETERA.

saetilla [sah-ay-teel'-lyah], *f. dim.* 1. Small arrow or dart. 2. Small magnetic needle. 3. Hand of a watch. 4. Moral sentence.

saetín [sah-ay-teen'], *m.* 1. Mill-race through which water runs from the dam to the wheel of a mill (molino). 2. Peg, pin, tack. 3. *(Com.)* Sateen, a variety of plain satin.

saetón [sah-ay-tone'], *m.* Dart, a sharp-pointed weapon from a crossbow.

sáfico, ca [sah'-fe-co, cah], *a.* Sapphic: applied to a kind of verse of five feet.

safio [sah'-fe-o], *m.* *(Prov.)* *V.* CONGRIO.

safra [sah'-frah], *f.* *(Cuba)* The season for cutting the sugar-cane, and boiling its juice for sugar. *V.* ZAFRA.

safre [sah'-fray], *m.* Saffre, cobalt blue. *V.* ZAFRE.

saga [sah'-gah], *f.* 1. Witch. 2. Saga, a primitive mythological tradition or legend of Scandinavia.

sagacidad [sah-gah-the-dahd'], *f.* 1. Sagacity, quickness of scent in dogs. 2. Sagaciousness, penetration.

sagapeno [sah-gah-pay'-no], *m.* Sagapenum or gum sagapen, a resinous juice.

sagatí [sah-gah-tee'], **saetí,** *m.* Sagathee, a kind of woollen cloth like serge.

sagaz [sah-gath'], *a.* 1. Sagacious, quick of scent (perros). 2. Sagacious, discerning, far-sighted, farseeing, prescient, keen-witted.

sagazmente [sah-gath-men-tay], *adv.* Sagaciously.

sagita [sah-hee'-tah], *f.* 1. The versed sine of an arc, sagitta. 2. The height of an arch.

sagital [sah-he-tahl'], *a.* 1. Sagittal belonging to an arrow, sagittated. 2. *(Anat.)* Sagittal: applied to a suture of the skull.

sagitario [sah-he-tah'-re-o], *m.* 1. Archer. 2. Sagittarius, sign in the zodiac.

sagma [sahg'-mah], *f.* *(Arch.)* Measure taken of many members, as of a cornice.

sago [sah'-go], *m.* A loose, wide greatcoat. *V.* SAYO.

sagradamente [sah-grah-dah'-men-tay], *adv.* Sacredly, inviolably, religiously.

sagrado, da [sah-grah'-do, dah], *a.* 1. Sacred, consecrated; venerable, holy. 2. Cursed, execrable.

sagrado [sah-grah'-do], *m.* 1. Asylum, a sacred place where debtors or malefactors take refuge. 2. Asylum, haven or refuge, even though not sacred.

sagrariero [sah-grah-re-ay'-ro], *m.* Keeper of relics.

sagrario [sah-grah'-re-o], *m.* 1. Place in a church wherein consecrated things are deposited. 2. Cibary, the place where the consecrated host is kept.

sagú, or **sagui** [sah-goo', sah'-gee], *m.* Sago, a farinaceous food obtained from various Asiatic palms.

ságula [sah'-goo-lah], *f.* *(Prov.)* A small frock. *V.* SAYUELO.

saguntino, na [sah-goon-tee'-no, nah], *a.* Native of or belonging to Saguntum.

sahina [sah-ee'-nah], *f.* *V.* ZAHINA.

sahornarse [sah-or-nar'-say], *vr.* To be excoriated.

sahorno [sah-or'-no], *m.* Excoriation.

sahumado, da [sah-oo-mah'-do, dah], *a. & pp.* of SAHUMAR. Fumigated; select apposite, proper.

sahumador [sah-oo-mah-dor'], *m.* 1. Perfumer. 2. A perfuming-pot, used to impregnate something with a sweet scent.

sahumadura [sah-oo-mah-doo'-rah], *f.* 1. The act of perfuming with a sweet scent. 2. *(Naut.)* Fumigation in ships.

sahumar [sah-oo-mar'], *va.* 1. To perfume (incensar). 2. To fumigate, to smoke (fumigar), to fume.

sahumerio [sah-oo-may'-re-o], *m.* 1. Smoke, vapor, steam, fumigation. 2. The medical application of fumes to parts of the body. 3. Aromatics burnt for perfumes.

sahumo [sah-oo'-mo], *m.* Smoke, steam, vapor. *V.* SAHUMERIO.

saíca [sah-ee'-cah], *f.* Saick, a kind of Turkish vessel.

saín [sah-een'], *m.* Grease or fat of an animal; dirt on clothes.

saína [sah-ee'-nah], *f.* *V.* ALCANDÍA.

sainar [sah-e-nar'], *va.* To fatten animals.

sainete [sah-e-nay'-tay], *m.* 1. A kind of farce or short dramatic composition. 2. Flavor, relish, zest. 3. A high-flavored sauce. 4. Any delicate bit of a fine taste. 5. Anything pleasing or engaging. 6. Taste or elegance in dress.

sainetear [sah-e-nay-tay-ar'], *vn.* To act farces.

sainetillo [sah-e-nay-teel'-lyo], *m. dim.* A slight relish or flavor.

saíno [sah-ee'-no], *m.* A kind of West Indian hog.

saja, sajadura [sah'-hah, sah-hah-doo'-rah], *f.* Scarification.

sajar [sah-har'], *va.* To scarify.

sajelar [sah-hay-lar'], *va.* Among potters, to sift and to clean the clay.

sajón, na [sah-hone', nah], *a.* Saxon.

sal [sahl], *f.* 1. Salt, common salt. 2. *(Chem.)* Salt, a compound of a base and an acid. 3. Wit, facetiousness. 4. Grace, charm, pep. 5. *(Fig. LAm.)* Misfortune, piece of bad luck. **Sal gema**, rock salt. **Sal y pimienta**, salt and pepper. **Sal gorda**, kitchen salt. **Sal de fruta**, fruit salts.

sala [sah´-lah], *f.* 1. Hall, the first large room in a house (cuarto grande). 2. Hall where judges meet to try and decide causes (de edificio público). 3. Board of commissioners. 4. A public meeting, a public entertainment. **Sala de muestras**, showroom. **Sala de estrados**, hall or court of justice. **Sala de espectáculos**, concert room. **Sala de fiestas**, dance hall. **Sala de pruebas**, fitting room.

salacidad [sah-lah-the-dadh´], *f.* Salacity, lechery.

salacot [sah-lah-cot´], *m.* A Philippine hat in the shape of a parasol, and with many trimmings.

saladamente [sah-lah-dah-men-tay], *adv.* Wittily, facetiously; saltly.

saladar [sah-lah-dar´], *m.* Salt-marsh.

saladero [sah-lah-day´-ro], *m.* Salting-place, salting-tub.

saladillo [sah-lah-deel´-lyo], *m. dim.* of SALADO. Fresh bacon half-salted.

salado, da [sal´-lah´-do, dah], *a. & pp.* of SALAR. 1. Salted, salty. 2. Witty (gracioso), facetious. 3. *(Bot.)* Applied to plants growing on the seashore from which soda is obtained by burning. 4. *(LAm.)* Unlucky (desgraciado). 5. *(Cono Sur)* Dear (artículo). **Es un tipo muy salado**, he´s a very amusing chap. -*m.* 1. Sea. 2. Land rendered barren by too large a portion of saline particles.

salador, ra [sah-lah-dor´, rah], *m. & f.* Salter; salting-place for meat.

saladura [sah-lah-doo´-rah], *f.* Salting, seasoning with salt.

salamandra [sah-lah-mahn´-drah], *f.* 1. Salamander, a kind of lizard. 2. *(Met.)* That which exists in the ardor of love or affection.

salamanqués, sa [sah-lah-man-kays´, key-sah], *a.* V. SALAMANTINO.

salamanquesa [sah-lah-man-kay´-sah], *f.* Star-lizard.

salamí [sah-lah-me´], *m.* Salami.

salángana [sah-lahn´-gah-nah], *f.* An Asiatic swift which makes the edible nests of which the Chinese are fond.

salar [sah-lar´], *va.* 1. To salt (plato), to season with salt; to preserve with salt, to cure, to corn. 2. *(And.)* To feed salt to (para conservar). 3. *(LAm.)* To ruin (arruinar), to spoil.

salariar [sah-lah-re-ar´], *va.* To give a salary or wages.

salario [sah-lah´-re-o], *m.* Wages, salary, hire; a temporary stipend; military pay.

salaz [sah-lath´], *a.* 1. Salty. 2. Salacious, lustful.

salazón [sah-lah-thon´], *f.* Seasoning, salting.

salce [sahl´-thay], *m. (Bot.)* Willow. Salix. V. SAUCE.

salceda [sal-thay´-dah], *f.* Plantation of willows.

salcedo [sal-thay´-do], *m.* A damp spot naturally overgrown with trees.

salcereta [sal-thay-ray´-tah], *f.* Dicebox.

salcochar [sal-co-char´], *va.* To dress meat, leaving it half raw and without salt.

salchicha [sal-chee´-chah], *f.* 1. Kind of small sausage. 2. *(Mil.)* Saucisse a long narrow bag of pitched cloth filled with powder, serving to set fire to mines.

salchichería [sal-che-chay-ree´-ah], *f.* Shop in which sausages are sold.

salchichero, ra [sal-che-chay´-ro, rah], *m. & f.* Maker or seller of sausages.

salchichón [sal-che-chone´], *m. aug.* A large sausage.

saldar [sal-dar´], *va.* To liquidate a debt (deuda), to settle an account, to sell off (existencias).

saldo [sahl´-do], *m.* 1. Balance (balance). 2. Amount left. 3. Clearance sale (liquidación). 4. Remnants (restos). **Saldo acreedor**, credit balance. **Saldo deudor**, debit balance.

salebrosidad [sah-lay-bro-se-dahd´], *f.* Saltness.

saledizo [sah-lay-dee´-tho], *m.* Jutting; corbel, jetty, coving.

saledizo, za [sah-lay-dee´-tho], *a.* Salient.

salegar [sah-lay-gar´], *m.* Salt-lick, a spot where salt is fed to cattle.

salera [sah-lay´-rah], *f.* One of the stones of which the salt-lick (*salegar*) is composed.

salero [sah-lay´-ro], *m.* 1. Salt-cellar, for the table (de mesa). 2. Salt-pan: magazine of salt. 3. *(Coll.)* Witty saying; gracefulness, wit.

saleroso, sa [sah-lay-ro´-so, sah], *a.* Facetious, witty, humorous; graceful.

saleta [sah-lay´-tah], *f. dim.* A small hall.

salgada, salgadera [sal-gah´-dah, sal-gah-day´-rah], *f. (Bot.)* V. ORZAGA.

salguera [sal-gay´-rah], *f. V.* MIMBRERA.

salguero [sal-gay´-ro], *m.* Osier, willow.

salicilato [sah-le-the-lah´-to], *m. (Chem.)* Salicylate.

sálico, ca [sah´-le-co, cah], *a.* Salic, of the Salian Franks.

salicor [sah-le-cor´], *f. (Bot.)* Long, fleshy-leaved salwort.

salicornia [sah-le-cor´-ne-ah], *f.* Glasswort.

salida [sah-lee´-dah], *f.* 1. Start, setting or going out, departure, exit (lugar). 2. Outlet, outgate. 3. Environs of a town. 4. Issue, result (resultado), conclusion. 5. Projection, prominence (saliente). 6. Salableness. 7. Expenditure, outlay. 8. *(Mil.)* Sally, sortie. **Puerta de salida**, sally-port. 9. Subterfuge, pretext. 10. Means or reasons by which an argument, difficulty or peril is overcome 11. *(Naut.)* Headway. **Estar de salida**, to be ready for sailing. **La salida fue triste**, leaving was sad. **Salida de emergencia**, emergency exit. **Es sólo una salida**, it´s only a pretext.

salidizo, za [sa-le-dee´-tho, thah], *f. & a. V.* SALEDIZO.

salido, da [sah-lee´-do, dah], *a. & pp.* of SALAR. Gone out, departed. **salido**, projecting, prominent. **Salida**, in heat, eager for the male.

saliente [sah-le-en´-tay], *a. & pa.* 1. Outjutting, salient, projecting. 2. *(Fig.)* Salient; outstanding. 3. Outgoing (miembro).

salífero, ra [sah-lee´-fay-ro, rah], *a.* Salt-bearing.

salificable [sah-le-fe-cah´-blay], *a.* Salifiable.

salín [sah-leen´], *m.* Salt magazine. V. SALERO.

salina [sah-lee´-nah], *f.* Salt-pit, salt-pan (depresión), salt-work, salt-mine (mina).

salinero [sah-le-nay´-ro], *m.* Salter, dealer in salt; salt-man, salt-maker.

salino, na [sah-lee´-no, nah], *a.* Saline.

salir [sah-leer´], *vn. irr.* 1. To go out of a place, to leave (persona). 2. To depart (autobús, tren), to set out, to march out, to come out, to go forth, to go away or to go abroad, to come forth. 3. To get out of a narrow place or crowd. 4. To appear to show itself. **Salió entonces una nueva moda**, at that time a new fashion appeared. 5. To shoot, to spring; to grow. 6. To proceed, to issue from. 7. To get over difficulties, to escape from danger; to extricate oneself from errors or doubts. 8. *(Naut.)* To exceed, to excel, to pass another vessel in sailing. 9. To happen, to occur (succder). 10. To cost (costar). **El caballo me salió en sesenta guineas**, the horse stood me in sixty guineas. **Salen caros en Méjico los géneros ingleses**, English goods are dear in Mexico. 11. To finish well or ill; to correspond or imply; to complete a calculation. 12. *(Mil.)* To sally, to issue out. 13. To acquire; to become; to grow common or vulgar. 14. To dismiss, to dispose of. 15. To say or do a thing unexpectedly or unseasonably. 16. To resemble, to appear like (parecerse). 17. To separate, to retire, to desist; to be chosen or elected. **Salir al cabo or salir con**, to go through. **Salir a luz**, to leave the press, to be published or printed; to be produced; to be developed. **Salir con algo**, to obtain something. **Salir de sus casillas**, to step out of one's line or usual way of acting; to be off the hinges; to be out of oneself; to lose one's temper. **El salió herido**, he came out wounded. **Salir de la dificultad**, to extricate oneself from a difficulty. **Salir los colores al rostro**, to blush. -*vr.* 1. To violate a contract; not to fulfil one's engagements. 2. To drop, to leak (líquido). 3. To support or maintain an opinion. **Salirse de la religión**, to quit a religious order. **Salirse con**

la suya, to accomplish one's end, to have one's way. **Salir a nado,** to save oneself by swimming, to do something very difficult. **Salir a su padre,** to resemble one's father. **Salir de una empresa,** to relinquish an enterprise. **Salir del vado, del paso,** to get out of a difficulty. **Salir calabazas,** to be plucked, to fail in an examination. **Salir pitando,** (1) to run away hastily and in confusion. (2) *(Coll.)* To get hot quickly in debate. **Salir del coma,** to emerge from a coma.

salitrado, da [sah-le-trah´-do, dah], *a.* Impregnated with or composed of saltpetre.

salitral [sah-le-trahl´], *a.* Nitrous. *-m.* Saltpetre bed or works.

salitre [sah-lee´-tray], *m.* Saltpetre, nitre.

salitrería [sah-le-tray-ree´-ah], *f.* Saltpetre-work.

salitrero, ra [sah-le-tray´-ro, rah], *a.* Saltpetre refiner, dealer in saltpetre.

salitroso, sa [sah-le-tro´-so, sah], *a.* Nitrous, salinitrous.

saliva [sah-lee´-vah], *f.* Saliva. **Gastar saliva,** to waste one´s breath.

salivación [sah-le-vah-the-on´], *f.* Salivation, spitting out.

salival [sah-le-vahl´], *a.* Salivous, salivary.

salivar [sah-le-var´], *vn.* To spit, to salivate.*-a.* Salivary.

salivera [sah-le-vay´-rah], *f.* Round knob on the bits of a bridle.

salivoso, sa [sah-le-vo´-so, sah], *a.* Salivous. *V.* SALIVAL.

sallador [sal-lyah-dor´], *m.* Weeder, weeding-hook, hoe.

sallar [sal-lyar´], *va.* To weed.

sallo [sah´-lyo], *m. (Prov.)* Hoe.

salma [sahl´-mah], *f.* Ton, twenty hundred-weight.

salmantino, na [sal-man-tee´-no, nah], *a.* Salamancan, relating to Salamanca.

salmear, salmodiar [sal-may-ar´], *va.* To sing psalms.

salmer [sal-merr´], *m. (Arch.)* Plane or impost from which an arch springs.

salmerón [sal-may-rone´], *a.* Which has a large ear (trigo).

salmista [sal-mees´-tah], *m* Psalmist; chanter of psalms.

salmo [sahl´-mo], *m.* Psalm.

salmodia [sal-mo´-de-ah], *f.* l. Psalmody. 2. The Psalter.

salmógrafo [sal-mo´-grah-fo], *m.* Writer of psalms.

salmón [sal-mone´], *m. (Zool.)* Salmon. **Salmón pequeño,** salmonet.

salmonado, da [sal-mo-nah´-do, dah], *a.* Tasting like salmon.

salmoncillo, ito [sal-mon-theel´-lyo], *m. dim.* A small salmon.

salmonera [sal-mo-nay´-rah], *f.* A net for fishing salmon.

salmonete [sal-mo-nay´-tay], *m.* Redmullet, or surmullet.

salmorejo [sal-mo-ray´-ho], *m.* Sauce for rabbits.

salmuera [sal-moo-ay´-rah], *f.* l. Brine. 2. Pickle made of salt and water.

salmuerarse [sal-moo-ay-rar´-say], *vr.* To be diseased by eating too much salt (ganado).

salobral [sah-lo-brahl´], *a.* Salty, briny. *-m.* Brine.

salobre [sah-lo´-bray], *a.* Brackish, saltish.

salobreño, ña [sah-lo-bray´-nyo, nyah], *a.* Saltish, containing salt (tierra).

saloma [sah-lo´-mah], *f. (Naut.)* Singing out of sailors, chantey.

salomar [sah-lo-mar´], *vn. (Naut.)* To sing out.

salón [sah-lone´], *m.* 1. *(Aug.)* Saloon, a large hall (sala). 2. Meat salted and smoked. **Salón de actos,** assembly room. **Salón de belleza,** beauty parlor. **Salón de sesiones,** assembly hall.

salpa [sahl´-pah], *f. (Zool.)* Gilt-head, salon, bighead.

salpicadera [sahl-pe-cah-day´-rah], *f.* Fender.

salpicadero [sahl-pe-cah-d-ay-ro], *m. (Aut.)* Dashboard.

salpicadura [sal-pe-cah-doo´-rah], *f.* The act of spattering, and the stain made by it; dab, dash of dirt.

salpicar [sal-pe-car´], *va.* 1. To splatter, to splash, to dab, to dash. 2. To work without continuity or order, to fly from one subject to another. 3. To sprinkle (conversación, oración). 4. *(And. Cono Sur)* Raw vegetable salad. **Salpicar un coche de barro,** to splash a car with mud. **Este asunto salpica al gobierno,** the government has got egg on its face over this affair.

salpicón [sal-pe-cone´], *m.* 1. Salmagundi, a mixed dish. 2. Anything else in small pieces. 3. Bespattering.

salpimentar [sal-pe-men-tar´], *va.* To season with pepper and salt.

salpimentón [sal-pe-men-tone´], *m.* Salmagundi. *V.* SALPICÓN.

salpimienta [sal-pe-me-en´-tah], *f.* Mixture of salt and pepper.

salpinga [sal-peen´-gah], *f.* African serpent.

salpresar [sal-pray-sar´], *va.* To season with salt.

salpreso, sa [ ], *pp. irr.* of SALPRESAR.

salpuga [sal-poo´-ah], *f.* A poisonous kind of ant.

salpullido or **sarpullido** [sal-pool-lyee´-do, sar-pool-lyee´-do], *m.* Prickly heat, skin rash.

salpullir [sal-pool-lyeer´], *va.* To break out in pustules or pimples.

salsa [sahl´-sah], *f.* 1. Sauce, condiment. 2. Ornaments, decorations. 3. Seasoning, spice. 4. Scene (ambiente). **Salsa mayonesa,** mayonnaise. **salsa de tomate,** tomato sauce. **Estar en su salsa,** to be in one´s element.

salsedumbre [sal-say-doom´-bray], *f.* Salineness, saltness.

salsera [sal-say´-rah], *f.* 1. Saucer, a pan for sauce. 2. *V.* SASERILLA.

salsereta [sal-say-ray´-tah], *f. dim.* A small saucer; a dice-box.

salserilla [sal-say-reel´-lyah], *f. dim.* A small saucer, in which colors are mixed.

salsero [sal-say´-ro], *m. (Bot.)* Spanish thyme.

salserón [sal-say-rone´], *m. (Prov.)* Measure of grain, containing about a peck.

salseruelo [sal-say-roo-ay´-lo], *m. V.* SALSERILLA.

salsifí [sal-se-fee´], *m.* Salsify, oysterplant.

salsilla, ita [sal-seel´-lyah], *f. dim.* Sauce of little flavor or taste.

saltabanco, saltabancos, saltaembanco or **saltaembancos** [sal-tah-bahn´-co], *m.* Saltimbanco, mountebank, quack.

saltabardales [sal-tah-bar-dah´-les], *m.* Romp, a wild youth.

saltabarrancos [sal-tah-bar-rahn´-cos], *m. (Coll.)* A noisy, turbulent fellow.

saltación [sal-tah-the-on´], *f.* 1. Saltation, leaping or hopping. 2. Dancing, dance.

saltadero [sal-tah-day´-ro], *m.* 1. Leaping-place, high ground from which leaps can be taken. 2. An artificial fountain, a jet.

saltado, da [sal-tah´-do, dah], *a.* Prominent, jutting over. *-pp.* of SALTAR.

saltador, ra [sal-tah-dor´, rah], *m. & f.* Jumper, leaper; hopper.

saltadura [sal-tah-doo´-rah], *f.* Hollow made in the surface of a stone when heaving it.

saltambarca [sal-tam-bar´-cah], *f.* A rustic dress, open behind.

saltamontes [sal-tah-mon´-tes], *m.* Locust, grasshopper.

saltante [sal-tahn´-tay], *pa.* Salient, leaping, jumping.

saltaojos [sal-tah-oh´-hos], *m.* Kind of peony.

saltaperico [sal-tah-pay-ree´-co], *m. (Prov.) V.* SALTAMONTES.

saltar [sal-tar´], *vn.* 1. To leap, to jump (muro, obstáculo), to hop; to frisk, to skip (omitir); to rebound, to dash. **Saltar a tierra,** to land, to disembark. 2. To burst (explosivo), to break in pieces; to fly asunder, to crack (madera), to flash. 3. To be clear and obvious, to occur to the memory; to excel, to surpass. 4. To be irritated, to be agitated, to betray emotion. 5. To speak incoherently and irrelevantly. 6. *(Naut.)* To chop about, to change suddenly (viento). **Saltar de gozo,** to be highly delighted. **Andar a la que salta,** to give oneself up to a vagabond life. **Saltar en paracaídas,** to jump. **Saltar por una ventana,** to jump out of a window. **Hacer saltar un edificio,** to blow a building up. *-va.* 1. To leap, to pass over or into by leaping. 2. To cover the female (animales). *-vr.* 1. **Saltarse un párrafo,** to skip a paragraph. 2. **Saltarse todas las reglas,** to break all the rules.

saltarelo [sal-tah-ray´-lo], *m.* Ancient Spanish dance.

saltarén [sal-tah-ren'], *m.* 1. Certain tune on the guitar. 2. Grasshopper.

saltarín, na [sal-tah-reen', nah], *m. & f.* 1. Dancer, dancing master. 2. A restless young rake.

saltarregla [sal-tar-ray'-glah], *f.* Bevelsquare, sliding-rule.

saltaterandate [sal-tah-tay-ran-dah'-tay], *m.* A kind of embroidery.

saltatriz [sal-tah-treeth'], *f.* A female rope-dancer: ballet-girl; danseuse, a professional dancing woman.

salteador [sal-tay-ah-dor'], *m.* Highway man, footpad.

salteamiento [sal-tay-ah-me-en'-to], *m.* Assault, highway robbery.

saltear [sal-tay-ar'], *va.* 1. To assault, to attack, to invade; to rob on the highway (robar); to hold up (atracar). 2. To fly from one work to another without continuity. 3. To anticipate maliciously in the purchase of anything; to surprise, to take by surprise (sorprender). 4. To circumvent or gain ascendency over another's feelings.

salteo [sal-tay'-o], *m.* Assault on the high road; highway robbery.

salterio [sal-tay'-re-o], *m.* 1. Psalter psalm-book. 2. Psalitery, a kind of harp. 3. Rosary, made of 150 Hail Marys. 4. A kind of flute.

saltero, ra [sal-tay'-ro, rah], *a.* Living on mountains, highlander.

saltico, ito [sal-tee'-co, ee'-to], *m. dim.* A little hop or leap.

saltillo [sal-teel'-lyo], *m.* 1. A little hop or leap. **A saltillos**, leaping, hopping. 2. (*Naut.*) Beak, bulk-head.

saltimbanco, saltimbanqui [sal-tim-bahn'-co], *m.* V. SALTABANCO.

salto [sahl'-to], *m.* 1. Leap, bound; distance leaped; leaping, jerk, jump (al agua). 2. Leaping-place, ground from which leaps can be taken. 3. Irregular transition from one thing to another. 4. Assault, plunder, robbery. 5. Skip, omission of clauses, lines, or leaves in reading or writing. 6. Ascent to a higher post without passing through the intervening. 7. (*Amer. Colom. Argen.*) Cataract, falls. **Salto mortal**, somerset. **Salto de viento**, (*Naut.*) the sudden shifting of the wind. **A saltos**, leaping by hops. **De un salto**, at one jump. **Salto en el vacío**, leap in the dark. **Dar un salto**, to jump. **Salto de altura**, high jump. **Triple salto**, hop. **Aquí hay un salto de 50 versos**, there is a gap here of 50 lines. **Salto de agua**, waterfall.

saltón [sal-tohn'], *m.* Grasshopper.

saltón, na [sal-tohn', nah], *a.* Hopping or leaping much. **Ojos saltones**, goggle-eyes.

salubérrimo, ma [sah-loo-ber'-re-mo, mah], *a. sup.* Most salubrious.

salubre [sah-loo'-bray], *a.* Healthful. V. SALUDABLE.

salubridad [sah-loo-bre-dahd'], *f.* Healthfulness (sanidad), salubrity, salutariness, wholesomeness.

salud [sah-lood'], *f.* 1. Health. 2. Welfare, prosperity. 3. Salvation. 4. (*LAm.*) Bless you! (al estornudar). **En sana salud**, in good health. **Estar bien de salud,** to be in good health. **Devolver la salud a uno,** to give somebody back his health.

saludable [sah-loo-dah'-blay], *a.* Salutary, healthful, salubrious, wholesome for soul or body.

saludablemente [sah-loo-dah-blay-men-tay], *adv.* Salubriously, healthfully, healthily.

saludación [sah-loo-dah-the-on'], *f.* V. SALUTACIÓN.

saludador [sah-loo-dah-dor'], *m.* 1. Greeter, saluter. 2. Quack, who cures distempers by the breath, the saliva, etc.

saludar [sah-loo-dar'], *va.* 1. To greet, to salute, to hail, to accost. 2. To express content or joy by words or actions. 3. To proclaim a king or emperor. 4. To fire a salute. 5. To apply delusive remedies to cure diseases, like quacks. **Saludar a uno**, to go and say hello to somebody. **Le saluda atentamente** yours faithfully.

saludo [sah-loo'-do], *m.* 1. Salute with a volley of firearms. 2. Salute, salutation, greeting. **Volver el saludo**, to return the

salute or bow. **Atentos saludos**, best wishes. **Saludo completo**, full handshake.

salumbre [sah-loom'-bray], *f.* Flower of salt, red spume which forms on salt.

salutación [sah-loo-tah-the-on'], *f.* 1. Salutation, greeting, salute. 2. Exordium of a sermon.

salutíferamente [sah-loo-tee'-fay-rah-men-tay], *adv.* Salubriously.

salutífero, ra [sah-loo-tee'-fay-ro, rah], *a.* Salutiferous, healthful, salubrious.

salva [sahl'-vah], *f.* 1. Pregustation, the tasting of viands before they are served up to royalty. 2. Salute of firearms, salvo. **Hacer la salva**, to drink to one's health, to beg leave to speak. 3. Rash proof of innocence, given by running a great risk. 4. Oath, solemn promise (promesa), assurance.

salvación [sal-vah-the-on'], *f.* 1. Salvation. 2. Preservation from great danger. **Ejército de Salvación**, the Salvation Army.

salvachía [sal-vah-chee'-ah], *f.* (*Naut.*) Salvage, a strap formed by braided cords, used to fasten shrouds and stays.

salvadera [sal-vah-day'-rah], *f.* Sandbox for writing.

salvado [sal-vah'-do], *m.* Bran. **Salvado, da,** *pp.* of SALVAR.

salvador, ra [sal-vah-dor', rah], *m. & f.* Saviour, rescuer, redeemer. **El Salvador, el Salvador del mundo**, our Savior, our Redeemer.

salvaguardar [sal-vah-goo-ahr-dar'], *va.* To safeguard; (*Comput.*) to backup.

salvaguardia [sal-vah-goo-ar'-de-ah], *m.* 1. Safeguard, security, protection, shield of friendship, palladium. 2. Guard, watchman. *-f.* Safe conduct, a kind of passport.

salvajada [sal-va-hah'-dah], *f.* Rude, unmannerly behavior.

salvaje [sal-vah'-hay], *a.* 1. Savage, wild, barbarous, ferocious, ignorant, foolish, undomesticated. 2. Wild, rough, mountainous.

salvaje [sal-vah'-hay], *m.* A savage, born and brought up in the wilderness.

salvajemente [sal-vah'-hay-men-tay], *adv.* Savagely, wildly.

salvajería [sal-vah-hay-ree'-ah], *f.* Rusticity; clownish, uncouth conduct, savageness.

salvajez [sal-vah-heth'], *f.* Savageness, rustic indocility.

salvajina [sal-vah-hee'-nah], *f.* 1. A wild beast. 2. A multitude of wild animals. 3. Collection of skins of wild beasts.

salvajino, na [sal-vah-hee'-no, nah], *a.* 1. Savage, wild, untamed. 2. Having the taste of game (carne).

salvajismo [sal-vah-hees'-mo], *m.* Barbarism, savagery.

salvamente [sal-vah-hees'-mo], *adv.* Securely, safely.

salvamento, salvamiento [sal-vah-men'-to], *m.* Safety, the act of saving, place of safety; salvation. **Operaciones de salvamento**, rescue operations.

salvante [sal-vahn'-tay], *pa.* Saving, excepting. *-adv.* (*Coll.*) Save.

salvar [sal-var'], *va.* 1. To save (persona), to free from danger; to receive into eternal happiness. 2. To save, to help or save by an excuse or reservation. 3. To remove impediments or difficulties. 4. To mention and correct errors of the pen in a notarial instrument, at the foot thereof. 5. To pass over or near a thing. 6. To taste, to prove the food or drink of nobles. 7. To prove judicially the innocence of a person. 8. To except, to exclude (excluir). 9. To rise above (árbol, edificio). 10. (*Cono Sur*) To pass (exam). *-vr.* To escape from danger, to get over difficulties, to attain salvation. **Me salvó la vida**, he saved my life. **El agua salvaba el peldaño más alto**, the water came up to the top-most step.

salvavidas [sal-vah-vee'-das], *m.* 1. Life-preserver. 2. Life-boat made unsinkable by the help of cork.

¡salve! [sahl'-vay], *v. defective.* God bless *you!—f.* Salutation or prayer to the Virgin Mary.

salvedad [sal-vay-dahd'], *f.* License, security, safe-conduct, excuse.

salvia [sahl'-ve-ah], *f.* (*Bot.*) Sage Salvia. **Salvia oficinal**, garden sage.

salviado, da [sal-ve-ah'-do, dah], *a.* Containing sage.

salvilla [sal-veel'-lyah], *f.* 1. Salver (bandeja), a glass stand. 2. A tray, a waiter, a plate on which something is presented.

salvo, va [sahl'-vo, vah], *pp. irr.* of SALVAR. Saved, proved, corrected.

salvo [sahl'-vo], *adv.* Saving, excepting, barring. **Poner algo a salvo,** to put something in a safe place. **A salvo,** without injury or diminution. **Dejar algo a salvo,** to make an exception of something.

salvoconducto [sal-vo-con-dooc'-to], *m.* Pass, safe-conduct or letters of safeconduct; passport; license or permission.

salvohonor [sal-vo-o-nor'], *m. (Coll.)* Breech posteriors.

salz [salth'], *m. V.* SAUCE.

salza [salh'-thah], *f.* A mud-volcano.

sama [sah'-mah], *f.* A kind of seabream.

sámago [sah'-mah-go], *m.* A defective, useless piece of building wood.

samaritano, na [sah-mah-re-tah'-no, nah], *a.* Samaritan.

samba [sam'-ba], *f.* Samba, popular dance and musical rhythm of Brazil.

sambenitar [san-bay-ne-tar'], *va.* To make infamous, to dishonor publicly.

sambenito [sam-bay-nee'-to], *m.* 1. Garment worn by a penitent convict of the Inquisition. 2. An inscription in churches, contain the name, punishment, and signs of the chastisement of those doing penance; note of infamy. 3. Evil report due to an act. **Echar el sambenito a otro,** to pin the blame on somebody else.

sambeque [sam-bay'-kay], *m. (Cuba) V.* ZAMBRA.

samblaje [sam-blah'-ha], *m..* Joinery. *V.* ENSAMBLADURA.

sambuca [sam-boo'-cah], *f.* 1. Ancient triangular musical stringed instrument. 2. Ancient warlike machine, a sort of huge bridge for storming walls.

sambumbia [sam-boom'-be-ah], *f.* 1. *(Cuba)* A fermented drink made from cane-juice, water, and peppers. 2. *(Peru)* Hubbub, confusion.

samnítico, ca [sam-nee'-te-co, cah], *a.* Belonging to the Samnites or to the ancient gladiators.

san [sahn], *a.* Saint: used always in the masculine gender, and before the noun. *V.* SANTO.

sanable [sah-nah'-blay], *a.* Curable, healable.

sanador, ra [sah-nah-dor', rah], *m. & f.* Curer, healer.

sanalotodo [sah-nah-lo-to'-do], *m.* Panacea, remedy or plaster for all distempers and sores, a general remedy.

sanamente [sah-nah-men-tay], *adv.* Naturally, agreeably.

sanar [sah-nar'], *va.* 1. To heal, to cure, to restore to health. 2. To reclaim from vice. *-vn.* To heal (herida), to recover from sickness (persona).

sanate [sa-nah'-tay], *m.* A Nicaragua bird like the magpie.

sanativo, va [sah-nah-tee'-vo, vah], *a.* Sanative, curative.

sanatorio [sah-nah-to'-re-o], *m.* Sanatorium, sanitarium.

sanción [san-the-on'], *f.* 1. Sanction, law. 2. Solemn authorization. **Imponer sanciones,** to impose sanctions.

sancionar [san-the-o-nar'], *va.* To sanction (castigar), to authorize.

sancochar [san-co-char'], *f.* To parboil.

sancocho [san-co'-cho], *m. (Amer. Ec.)* A dish composed of yucca, meat, plantains, cocoa, the chief breakfast dish through all South America.

sanctasanctórum [sanc-tah-sanc-to'-room], *m.* Sanctuary.

sanctus [sahnc'-toos], *m.* A part of the mass. **Tocan a sanctus** or **santus,** they ring the bell at mass before the canon.

sandalia [san-dah'-le-ah], *f.* Sandal, a kind of slippers.

sandalina [san-dah-lee'-nah], *f.* A stuff manufactured in Venice.

sandalino, na [san-dah-lee'-no, nah], *a.* Tinctured with sanders.

sándalo [sahn'-dah-lo], *m. (Bot.)* 1. Bergamot mint. 2. True sandal-wood or sanders. 3. *(Bot.)* Sanders, sandal-wood.

sandáraca [san-dah'-ra-cah], *f.* 1. Sandarach, a red sulphuret of arsenic. 2. Sandarac, a white resin exuded by the juniper-tree.

sandez [san-deth'], *f.* Folly, simplicity: want of understanding. **Decir sandeces,** to talk nonsense.

sandía [san-dee'-ah], *f. (Bot.)* Water melon.

sandiar [san-de-ar'], *m.* Water melon-patch.

sandio, dia [sahn'-de-o, ah], *a.* Foolish, nonsensical.

sandix [san-dix'], *m.* Minium, red lead.

sandunga [san-doon'-gah], *f. (Coll.)* Gracefulness, elegance; cajoling, wheedling; flattering, allurement, fascination.

sandunguero, ra [san-doon-gay'-ro, rah], *a.* Alluring, wheedling, fascinating; elegant.

sandwich [sand-wich], *m.* Sandwich.

saneable [sah-nay-ah'-blay], *a.* Reparable.

saneado, da [sah-nay-ah'-do, dah], *a.* 1. Drained. 2. Beat of its kind.

saneamiento [sah-nay-ah-me-en'-to], *m.* 1. Surety, bail, guarantee; indemnification (compensación), reparation. 2. Drainage (alcantarillado).

sanear [sah-nay-ar'], *va.* 1. To give security, to give bail. 2. To indemnify, to repair (daño). 3. To clean, disinfect (edificio). 4. To drain. 5. To compensate (comprador). 6. To restructure (capital, compañía).

sanedrín [sah-nay-dreen'], *m.* Sanhedrim, the supreme council of the Jewish nation.

sanes [sah'-nes]. **Por vida de sanes,** a minced oath.

sangley [san-glay'-e], *m.* Chinese trader in the Philippine Islands.

sangradera [san-grah-day'-rah], *f.* 1. Lancet for blood-letting. 2. An earthen basin. 3. Lock, sluice (desagüe), drain.

sangrador [san-grah-dor'], *m.* 1. Phlebotomist, blood-letter. 2. Fissure, opening.

sangradura [san-grah-doo'-rah], *f.* 1 *(Surg.)* Bleeding; part of the arm usually bled. 2. Draining of a canal or river. 3. *(Cono Sur)* Outlet.

sangrante [san-grahn'-tay], *a.* 1. Bleeding (herida, persona). 2. *(Fig.)* Crying (injusticia).

sangrar [san-grar'], *vn.* 1. To bleed, to let blood; to open a vein. 2. To drain, to draw water from a canal or river. 3. *(Print.)* To indent the first line of a paragraph. *-va.* To bleed. *-vr.* To be bled.

sangraza [san-grah'-thah], *f.* Corrupt or filthy blood.

sangre [sahn'-gray], *f.* 1. Blood; gore. 2. Blood, race, family, kindred. **Ser de la sangre azul,** *(Coll.)* to belong to the nobility. 3. Substance, fortune. 4. Wound from which blood issues. **A sangre fría,** in cold blood. **La sangre se me hiela en las venas,** my blood curdles in my veins. **Bullir la sangre,** to be vigorous and healthy as in youth. **querer beber la sangre a otro,** to hate a person mortally. **No creo que llegue la sangre al río,** I don't think it will be too disastrous.

sangría [san-gree'-ah], *f.* 1. *(Surg.)* Bleeding, blood-letting. 2. Any incision which emits blood. 3. Present made to a person who bleeds. 4. An extraction or stealing of something to small parcels. 5. *(Print.)* Indenting a line. 6. Inside of the arm, where a vein is usually opened. 7. *V.* SANGRADURA. 8. A beverage of red wine, lemon, and water; sangaree. 9. Irrigation (acequía). 10. *(Culin.)* Fruit cup.

sangrientamente [san-gre-en-tah-men'-tay], *adv.* Bloodily, cruelly.

sangriento, ta [san-gre-en'-to, tah], *a.* 1. Bloody (batalla), bloodstained, gory. 2. Bloody, cruel (chiste), sanguinary, bloodthirsty.

sangual [san-goo-ahl'], *m. (Orn.)* Osprey.

sanguaza [san-goo-ah'-thah], *f.* 1. Serpous blood. 2. Reddish fluid of vegetables.

sangüeso [san-goo-ay'-so], *m. (Bot.)* Raspberry-bush.

sanguífero, ra [san-gee'-fay-ro, rah], *a.* Sanguiferous.

sanguificación [san-gee-fe-cah-the-on'], *f. (Med.)* Sanguification.

sanguificar [san-gee-fe-car'], *va.* To sanguify, to make blood.

sanguificativo, va [san-gee-fe-cah-tee´-vo, vah], *a.* Producing blood.

sanguijuela [san-gee-hoo-ay'-lah], *f.* 1. Leech. 2. Sharper, a cheat. **Sanguijuelas del Estado**, sinecure officials (drawing pay, but doing nothing for it).

sanguinaria [san-gee-nah´-re-ah], *f.* 1. (*Bot.*) Blood-root, a medicinal herb. 2. Bloodstone, of a dark green color, variegated by red spots; hematite; an amulet to prevent bleeding from the nose.

sanguinariamente [san-gee-nah'-re-ah-men-tay], *adv.* Sanguinarily.

sanguinario, ria [san-gee-nah'-re-o, ah], *a.* Sanguinary, cruel, bloody.

sanguíneo, nea, sanguino, na [san-gee'-nay-o, ah], *a.* 1. Sanguine, red, the color of blood. 2. Sanguineous.

sanguinolencia [san-gee-no-len'-the-ah], *f.* Bloodiness, blood-thirstiness.

sanguinolento [san-gee-no-len'-to], **ta**, *a. V.* SANGRIENTO.

sanguinoso, sa [san-gee-no'-so, sah], *a.* 1. Sanguine, sanguinous. 2. Bloody, sanguinary, cruel.

sanguiñol [san-gee-nyol'], *m.* (*Bot.*) *V.* SANGUEÑO.

sanícula [sah-nee'-coo-lah], *f.* (*Bot.*) Sanicle. **Sanicula europea**, Wood sanicle.

sanidad [sah-ne-dahd'], *f.* 1. Soundness, health, vigor, sanity. **En sanidad**, in health. **Carta de sanidad**, bill of health. **Casa de sanidad**, health-office. **Juez de sanidad**, commissioner of the board of health. 2. Candor, ingenuousness.

sanie, sanies [sah'-ne-ay, sah'-ne-es], *f.* (*Med.*) Sanies.

sanioso, sa [sah-ne-o'-so, sah], *a.* (*Med.*) Sanious.

sanitario, ria [sah-ne-tah'-re-o, ah], *a.* Sanitary, promotive of health.

sanjuanero, ra [san-hoo-ah-nay'-ro, rah], *a.* Applied to fruits ripe on St. John´s day.

sanjuanista [san-hoo-ah-nees'-tah], *a. & m.* A knight of St. John of Jerusalem.

sanmiguelada [san-me-gay-lah'-dah], *f.* (*Prov.*) Michaelmas.

sanmigueleño [san-me-gay-lay-nyo], **ña**, *a.* Applied to fruits ripe at Michaelmas.

sano, na [sah´-no, nah], *a.* 1. Sound (madera, órgano), healthy (clima), wholesome, hale, hearty; salutary; sane; secure. 2. Sincere, well-disposed, discreet, wise, steady. 3. Safe, free from fault, harmless. 4. Entire, complete: **Sano y salvo**, safe and sound. **No ha quedado plato sano en toda la casa**, there wasn´t a plate left whole in the house.

sánscrito [sahns´-cre-to], *m.* Sanskrit, the sacred language of Hindustan.

santa [sahn'-tah], *f.* Female saint. *-m. V.* SANTUARIO.

Santa Bárbara [sahn´-tah bar'-ba-rah], *f.* 1. (*Naut.*) Magazine, powder-room. 2. St. Barbara.

santamente [san'-tah-men-tay], *adv.* 1. Reverently, piously, religiously; simply. 2. Briskly, freely.

santasantórum [san-tah-san-to'-room], *m.* 1. Sanctuary, sanctum-sanctorum, holy of holies. 2. Sanctum: something especially valued by anyone. 3. The mysterious or occult.

santazo, za [san-tah'-tho, thah], *a. aug.* A great saint.

santelmo [san-tel'-mo], *m.* (*Naut.*) St. Elmo's light, a fiery meteor on the masts of ships in stormy weather.

santero, ra [san-tay'-ro, rah], *m. & f.* Caretaker of a sanctuary.

santiago [san-te-ah'-go], *m.* 1. St. James, the war-whoop of the Spaniards on engaging with Moors and other infidels. 2. A middling sort of linen manufactured in Santiago.

santiagués, sa [san-te-ah-ghes´, sah], *a.* Belonging to Santiago de Galicia.

santiaguiño, ña [san-te-ah-gee'-no, nah], *a.* Belonging to Santiago de Chile.

santiaguista [san-te-ah-gees'-tah], *a.* Belonging to the order of Santiago. *-m.* A knight of Santiago or St. James.

santiamén [san-te-ah-men'], *m.* (*Coll.*) Moment, twinkling of an eye.

santico, ca [san-tee'-co, cah], *m. & f.* 1. (*Dim.*) Little image of a saint. 2. In familiar language, a good child.

santidad [san-te-dahd'], *f.* 1. Sanctity, sanctitude, piety, holiness, godliness. 2. Holiness, a title given to the Pope.

santificable [san-te-fe-cah'-blay], *a.* Sanctifiable.

santificación [san-te-fe-cah-the-on'], *f.* Sanctification, making holy. **Santificación de las fiestas**, Keeping holidays.

santificador [san-te-fe-cah-dor'], *m.* Sanctifier.

santificante [san-te-fe-cahn'-tay], *pa.* Blessing, sanctifying.

santificar [san-te-fe-car'], *pa.* 1. To sanctify, to hallow. 2. To dedicate to God. 3. To bless, to praise. 4. To honor and serve as a saint. 5. (*Met.*) To justify, to exculpate. *-vr.* 1. To employ oneself in pious works. 2. To justify, to clear from guilt.

santiguada [san-te-goo-ah'-dah], *f.* Blessing, the act of making the sign of the cross.

santiguador, ra [san-te-goo-ah-dor', rah], *m. & f.* One who cures by the sign of the cross.

santiguamiento [san-te-goo-ah-me-en'-to], *m.* Act of crossing or curing with the sign of the cross.

santiguar [san-te-goo-ar'], *va.* 1. To bless (persignar), to make the sign of the cross over a sick person. 2. To chastise, to punish. *-vr. 1.* To make the sign of the cross over oneself; to cross oneself. 2. To make a great fuss (exagerar).

santiguo [san-tee'-goo-o], *m.* The act of making the cross over oneself.

santimonia [san-te-mo'-ne-ah], *f.* 1. Sanctity, sanctimony, holiness. 2 (*Bot.*) Corn marigold, garden chrysanthemum.

santiscario [san-tis-cah'-re-o], *m.* (*Coll.*) Caprice, whim: used only in the colloquial and rather uncommon phrase. **De mi santiscario.**

santísimo, ma [san-tee'-se-mo, mah], *a. sup.* Most holy. **El Santísimo**, the holy sacrament.

santo, ta [sahn'-to, tah], *a. & n.* 1. Saintly, holy, virtuous, ghostly. 2. Saint, a person eminent for piety (persona). 3. (*Coll.*) Simple, plain, artless. 4. Sacred, dedicated to God; inviolable. 5. Grateful, delightful, pleasant. 6. Just, upright, pious. 7. Holy: applied to the Roman Catholic and apostolic church. **Santo y bueno**, well and good. **Santo día**, the whole day. **Todos los Santos**, all Saints' day. **Santo varón**, a holy man: a harmless idiot or simpleton; a great hypocrite.

santo [sahn'-to], *m.* 1. Saint, the image of a saint. 2. (*Mil.*) Watchword. **Santo Tomás**, St. Thomas. **Llegar y besar el santo**, to pull it off at the first attempt. **Se le fue el santo al cielo**, he forgot what he was about to say. **Santo y seña**, password. **No es santo de mi devoción**, I'm not very keen on him. **Desnudar a un santo para vestir a otro**, to rob Peter to pay Paul.

santolina [san-to-lee'-nah], *f.* (*Bot.*) Lavender-cotton.

santón [san-tone'], *m.* 1. (*Aug.*) A pretended saint, a hypocrite. 2. A kind of recluse among the Moors.

santoral [san-to-rahl'], *m.* A collection of sermons or lives of the saints; church-choir book.

santuario [san-too-ah'-re-o], *m. 1.* Sanctuary; temples and sacred things. 2. (*And. Carib.*) Native idol (ídolo).

santucho, cha [san-too'-cho, chah], *m. & f.* (*Coll.*) Hypocrite.

santurrón, na [san-toor-rohn', nah], *m. & f. & a.* (*Coll.*) Hypocrite, canter, zealot.

santurronería [san-toor-ro-nay-ree'-ah], *f.* Hypocrisy. *V.* BEATERÍA.

santus [san-toos], *m. V.* SANCTUS.

saña [sah'-nyah], *f.* Anger (furor), passion, rage and its effects.

sañosamente [sah-nyo-sah-men-tay], *adv.* Furiously.

sañoso, sa [sah-nyo'-so, sah], *a.* Furious.

sañudo, da [sah-nyoo'-do, dah], *a.* Furious, enraged.

sapa [sah'-pah], *f.* Woody residue left after chewing *buyo*, a compound of areca and betel-nuts with lime. *Cf.* BUYO, 3d def.

sapajú [sah-pa-hoo'], *m.* Sapajou, ospuchin, a South American monkey, often seen in captivity.

sapán [sah-pahn'], *m.* (*Bot.*) Sapan wood, a brownish-red dye-wood; sapan-tree.

sapera [sah-pay´-rah], *f.* (*Bot.*) Sea-heath.

sápido, da [sah'-pe-do, dah], *a.* High-flavored, of an exquisite taste.

sapiencia [sah-pe-en'-the-ah], *f.* Wisdom.

sapienciales [sah-pe-en-the-ah'-les], *m. pl.* Books of wisdom, works on morals: used in the singular as an adjective.

sapiente [sah-pe-en'-tay], *a.* Wise. V. SABIO.

sapientísimamente [aah-pe-en-tee'-se-mah-men-tay], *adv.* Most wisely.

sapillo [sah-peel'-lyo], *m.* 1. *(Dim.)* A little toad. 2. A small tumor under the tongue.

sapina [sah-pee'-nah], *f.* A glasswort, or plant yielding barilla, which grows in the Levant and in southern Spain.

sapino [sah-pee'-no], *m. (Bot.)* Savin, sabin, a small tree of the pine family.

sapo [sah'-po], *m.* 1. A large toad. V. ESCUERZO. **Echar sapos y culebras**, *(Coll.)* to be beside oneself; to be extremely angry. 2. *(LAm.)* Game of throwing coins into the mouth of an iron toad. 3. *(CAm. Carib.)* Informer (soplón).

saponáceo, cea [sah-po-nah'-thay-o, ah], *a.* Saponaceous, soapy.

saponaria [sah-po-nah'-re-ah], *f. (Bot.)* Common soapwort.

saponificable [sah-po-ne-fe-cah'-blay], *a.* Saponifiable.

saponificación [sah-po-ne-fe-cah-the-on'], *f.* Saponification, the process or result of making soap.

saponificar [sah-po-ne-fe-car'], *va.* To saponify, to convert fat or oil into soap by the action of an alkali. *-vr.* To become saponified.

saporífero, ra [sah-po-ree'-fay-ro, rah], *a.* Imparting savor.

saprino [sah-pree'-no], *m. (Ent.)* A diminutive beetle of the silpha family, about one-tenth of an inch in length; of most brilliant coloring, punctated with black. Found all over the world.

saque [sah'-kay], *m.* 1. The act of tossing a ball. 2. He that tosses the ball. 3. A line or base from which a ball is tossed. **Saque inicial**, kick-off. **Saque de portería**, goal-kick.

saqueador, ra [sah-kay-ah-dor', rah], *m. & f.* Depopulator, ransacker, free hooter.

saquear [sah-kay-ar'], *va.* 1. To ransack, to plunder, to foray, to pillage. 2. To take away unlawfully.

saqueo [sah-kay'-o], *m.* Pillage, plunder, foray.

saquera [sah-kay'-rah], *f. (Prov.)* Needle for sewing sacks, a packing needle.

saquería [sah-kay-ree'-ah], *f.* Place for or collection of sacks.

saquete, saqueto [sah-kay'-tay], *m. dim.* Little sack.

saquilada [sah-ke-lah'-dah], *f.* A small quantity of grain put into a sack to be ground.

saquillo, ito [sah-keel'-lyo, ee'-to], *m. dim.* A small bag.

saraguete [sah-rah-gay'-tay], *m.* Hop, a family dance.

sarampión [sah-ram-pe-on'], *m.* Measles, an eruptive disease.

sarangosti [sa-ran-gos'-te], *m. (Naut.)* Saragosti, a gum used in the East Indies, instead of pitch and tar, to caulk ships.

sarao [sah-rah'-o], *m.* Ball, an entertaiment of dancing.

sarape [sa-rah'-pay], *m.* Serape, Mexican blanket.

sarcasmo [sar-cahs'-mo], *m.* Sarcasm, keen and bitter irony.

sarcástico, ca [sar-cahs'-te-co, cah], *a.* Sarcastic, taunting.

sarcia [sar'-the-ah], *f.* Load, burden. V. CARGA.

sarcillo [sar-theel'-lyo], *m. (Prov.)* Hoe.

sarcócola [sar-co'-co-lah], *f.* Sarcocolla, a resinous gum from Ethiopia.

sarcófago [sar-co'-fah-go], *m.* 1. Tomb, grave. 2. Sarcophagus.

sarcología [sar-co-lo'-he-ah], *f. (Anat.)* Sarcology, that part of anatomy which treats the fleshy parts of the body.

sarcótico, ca [sar-co'-te-co, cah], *a.* Sarcotic, promotive of healing wounds by generating new flesh.

sarda [sar'-dah], *f.* A kind of mackerel.

sardesco, ca [sar-des'-co, cah], *a.* 1. Belonging to a small ass or horse. 2. *(Coll.)* Rude; stubborn.

sardesco [sar-des'-co], *m.* A small ass.

sardina [sar-dee'-nah], *f.* Sardine; anchovy.

sardinel [sar-de-nel'], *m.* Work of bricks placed on edge.

sardinero, ra [sar-de-nay'-ro, rah], *a.* Belonging to anchovies. *-m. & f.* Dealer in anchovies or pilchards.

sardineta [sar-de-nay'-tah], *f.* 1. A small anchovy or pilchard. 2. Part of cheese which overtops the cheesevat. 3. *(Naut.)* Knittle, a small line for various purposes on shipboard. 4. *pl.* Loops of galloon ending in a point placed on certain military uniforms.

sardio, sardo [sar'-de-o], *m.* Sard, sardine, a precious stone.

sardo, da [sar'-do, dah], *a.* Sardinian.

sardonia [sar-do'-ne-ah], *f. (Bot.)* Crow-foot, spearwort.

sardónice [sar-do'-ne-thay], *f.* Sardonyx, a precious stone.

sardónico, ca [sar-do'-ne-co, cah], *a.* 1. Sardonic, relating to the herb sardonia. 2. Insincere, affected (risa).

sardonio, sardónique, sardónix [sar-do'-ne-o]. *m.* V. SARDÓNICE.

sarga [sar'-gah], *f.* 1. Serge, a silk stuff; also, a kind of woollens. 2. *(Art.)* Fabric painted in distemper or oil, like tapestry, used for decorating rooms. 3. A kind of osier or willow.

sargadilla [sar-gah-deel'-lyah], *f.* A soda-ash plant common in Spain and in the south of France.

sargado, da [sar-gah'-do, dah], *a.* Sergelike. V. ASARGADO.

sargal [sar-gahl'], *m.* A clump of osiers.

sargatillo [sar-gah-teel'-lyo], *m.* A kind of willow of Spain.

sargazo [sar-gah'-tho], *m. (Bot.)* Sealentils, gulf-weed, sargasso. Sargassum.

sargenta [sar-hen'-tah], *f.* 1. Sergeant's halberd. 2. Sergeant's wife.

sargentear [sar-hen-tay-ar'], *va.* 1. To perform the duty of a sergeant. 2. To take the command. 3. To act in an overbearing manner.

sargentería [sar-hen-tay-ree'-ah], *f.* Place or duty of a sergeant.

sargentía [sar-hen-tee'-ah], *f.* Office of a sergeant.

sargento [sar-hen'-to], *m.* Sergeant. **Sargento primero**. Sergeant-major. **Sargento mayor de un regimiento**, *(Mil.)* a mayor.

sargentón [sar-hen-tone'], *m.* 1. *(Aug.)* A tall sergeant. 1. *(Coll.)* A strong, masculine woman.

sargo [sar'-go], *m. (Zool.)* A kind of sea-roach or sea-bream.

sarguero [sar-gay'-ro], *m.* Painter of sarga.

sargueta [sar-gay'-tah], *f.* A thin, light serge.

sarilla [sah-reel-lyah], *f. (Bot.)* Marjoram.

sarjía [sar-hee'-ah], *f.* Scarification. V. SAJA.

sármata [sar'-ma-tah], *a.* V. SARMÁTICO.

sarmático, ca [sar-mah'-te-co, cah], *a.* Sarmatian.

sarmentador, ra [sar-men-tah-dor', rah], *m. & f.* One who gathers pruned vine-shoots.

sarmentar [sar-men-tar'], *va.* To gather pruned vine-shoots.

sarmenticio, cia [sar-men-tee'-the-o, ah], *a.* Applied to Christians in derision, because they suffered themselves to be burned with the slow fire of vine-shoots.

sarmentillo [sar-men-teel'-lyo], *m. dim.* Of SARMIENTO.

sarmentoso, sa [sar-men-to'-so, sah], *a.* 1. Full of vine-shoots. 2. Creeping, twining, leaning on other bodies for support; used of plants.

sarmiento [sar-me-en'-to], *m.* Vine-shoot, the branch on which grapes grow.

sarna [sar'-nah], *f.* 1. Itch, a cutaneous disease. 2. Mange, the itch or scab in cattle.

sarnazo [sar-nah'-tho], *m.* A malignant itch.

sarnoso, sa [sar-no'-so, sah], *a.* Itchy, affected with itch, scabbed, scaly; mangy. *-m.* Scab, a nickname for a paltry fellow.

sarpullido or **salpullido** [sar-pool-lyee'-do, sal-pool-lyee'-do], *m.* Prickly heat, skin rash.

sarpullir, *vn.* To be flea-bitten. *-vn.* To be full of flea-bites.

sarracénico, ca [sar-rah-thay'-ne-co, cah], *a.* Saracenic, belonging to the Saracens.

sarraceno, na [sar-rah-thay'-no, nah], *m. & f.* Saracen, Moor: a name of the middle ages for the Arabs and their descendants.

sarracín [sahr-rah'-theen'] *a.* V. SARRACENO.

sarracina [sar-rah-thee´-nah], *f.* A tumultuous contest between a number of persons.

sarria [sar'-re-ah], *f.* 1. A wide net made of ropes. 2. *(Prov.)* Large basket.

sarrillo [sar-reel'-lyo], *m.* 1. A rattling in the throat of a dying person. 2. *(Bot.)* V. YARO.

sarrio [sar'-re-o], *a.* A kind of wild goat, with the horns bent forward.

sarro [sar'-ro], *m.* 1. A hard, strong bitumen. 2. Sediment which adheres to vessels. 3. Incrustation of the tongue in fevers; sordes: tartar of the teeth. 4. A tumor which grows in the tongue and roughens it.

sarroso, sa [sa-rro'-so, sah], *a.* Incrusted, covered with sediment.

sarta [sar'-tah], *f.* String of bends or pearls; any set of things filed on a line: series. **Una sarta de mentiras,** a pack of lies.

sartal [sar-tahl'], *a.* Stringed. *-m.* String of breads, etc.

sartalejo [sar-tah-lay'-ho], *m. dim.* A small string of pearls or precious stones.

sartén [sar-tayn´], *f.* Frying-pan. **Tener la sartén por el mango,** to have the command or advantage in a situation. **Saltar de la sartén y caer en las brasas,** to jump out of the frying-pan into the fire.

sartenada [sar-tay-nab'-dah], *f.* As much meat or fish as a frying-pan can hold.

sartenazo [sar-tay-nah´-tho], *m.* 1. Blow with a frying-pan. 2. *(Coll.)* A weighty blow with something. 3. *(Met. Coll.)* Trick played off: jest, joke.

sarteneja [sar-tay-nay´-hah], *f. dim.* A small frying-pan. *(Mex.)* Dried out pool, parched soil, cracked soil.

sartenica, illa, ita [sar-tay-nee´-cah], *f. dim.* A small frying-pan.

sartorio [sar-to'-re-o], *m.* Sartorius, the tailor's muscle.

sasafrás [sah-sa-frahs´], *m. (Bot.)* Sassafras.

sastra [sahs'-trah], *f.* Wife of a tailor, tailoress.

sastre [sahs'-tray], *m.* Tailor. **Es un cajón de sastre,** he is a superficial scribbler **Es un buen sastre,** *(Coll.)* he is a cunning blade.

sastrecillo [sas-tray-theel'-lyo], *m. dim.* A petty tailor.

sastrería [sas-tray-ree´-ah], *f.* 1. Tailor's trade; tailoring. 2. A tailor's shop (tienda).

Satán, Satanás [sah-tahn', sah-tah-nahs'], *m.* Satan.

satánicamente [sah-tah-ne-cah-men-tay], *adv.* Satanically.

satánico, ca [sah-tah´-ne-co, cah], *a.* Satanic, devilish.

satélite [sah-tay'-le-tay], *m.* 1. *(Ast.)* Satellite. **Satélite artificial,** artificial satellite, man-made satellite. 2. Satellite, obsequious follower, subordinate associate. 3. *(Coll.)* Bailiff, constable.

saterión [sah-tay-re-on'], *m. (Bot.)* V. SATIRIÓN.

satín [sah-teen'], *m. (Neol.)* Satin. V. RASO.

satinador, ra [sah-te-nah-dor', rah], *m. & f.* Glazing apparatus, rolling press (aparato); one who glosses (persona).

satinar [sah-te-nar'], *va.* To gloss, to make glossy, to calender, to glaze.

sátira [sah'-te-rah], *f.* 1. Satire, a poem in which wickedness or folly is censured. 2. A lively, bitter, and witty woman. 3. A biting joke.

satíricamente [sah-tee'-re-cah-men-tay], *adv.* Satirically.

satírico [sah-tee'-re-co], *m.* Satirist, one who writes satires.

satírico, ca [sah-tee'-re-co, cah], *a.* Satirical, censorious.

satirilla [sah-te-reel'-lyah], *f. dim.* A sharp, sneering insinuation.

satirillo [sah-te-reel'-lyo], *m. dim.* A little satyr.

satirio [sah-tee'-re-o], *m.* Kind of water rat.

satirión [sah-te-re-on'], *m. (Bot.)* The orchis which yields salep.

satirizante [sah-te-re-thahn'-tay], *pa.* Satirizing, writing satires.

satirizar [sah-te-re-thar'], *va.* To satirize, to write satires, to lampoon, to libel.

sátiro [sah'-te-ro], *m.* Satyr, a sylvan god.

satisdación [sah-tis-dah-the-on'], *f. (Law.)* V. FIANZA.

satisfacción [sah-tis-fac-the-on'], *f.* 1 Satisfaction, amends, atonement, recompense, apology (disculpa), excuse. 2. Gratification (de ofensa), the act of pleasing, content, complacence, satisfaction, the state of being pleased. 3. Presumption; confidence, security. 4. Satisfaction, one of the three parts of the sacrament of penance. **A satisfacción,** fully, according to one's wishes. **Con satisfacción,** *(Coll.)* without ceremony, in a friendly manner. **Tomar satisfacción,** to satisfy oneself, to vindicate oneself, to revenge.

satisfacer [sah-tis-fah-therr'], *va.* 1. To satisfy, to pay fully what is due (deuda, paga). 2. To satisfy, to content, to gratify (éxito), to humor. 3. To satisfy, to expiate, to atone; to reward. 4. To satisfy, to give a solution. 5. To allay the passions; to indulge; to satiate. 6. To free from debt, perplexity, or suspense. *-vr.* 1. To satisfy oneself; to take satisfaction; to be revenged (vengarse). 2. To be satisfied, to vindicate oneself. 3. To be convinced, to be undeceived or disabused. **Satisfacer una letra,** to honor a draft. **Satisfacerse con muy poco,** to be content with very little. *(Yo satisfago, yo satisfice, yo satisfaga,* from *Satisfacer.* V. HACER.

satisfactoriamente [sah-tes-fac-to'-re-ah-men-tay], *adv.* Satisfactorily.

satisfactorio, ria [sah-tis-fac-to´-re-o, ah], *a.* Satisfactory.

satisfecho, cha [sah-tis-fay'-cho, chah], *a. & pp. irr.* of SATISFACER. Satisfied, confident, content; arrogant. **Satisfecho consigo mismo,** self-satisfied.

sativo, va [sah-tee'-vo, vah], *a.* Sown, that which is cultivated, as opposed to what grows wild.

sátrapa [sah'-trah-pah], *m.* 1. Satrap, a Persian governor. 2. *(Met. Coll.)* A sly, crafty fellow.

satrapía [sah-trah-pee´-ah], *f.* Dignity of a Persian satrap.

saturable [sah-too-rah'-blay], *a.* Saturable.

saturación [sah-too-rah-the-on'], *f.* 1. Saturity, filling one thing with another. 2. Saturation; the solution in a liquid of all the solid which it can hold; the impregnation of an acid with alkali.

saturar [sah-too-rar'], *va.* 1. To saturate, to imbibe, to impregnate. 2. To fill, to glut.

saturativo, va [sah-too-rah-tee´-vo, vah], *a.* Possessing the power of saturating, saturant.

saturnal [sah-toor-nahl´], *a.* Saturnalian. **Saturnales,** saturnalia.

saturnino, na [sah-toor-nee´-no, nah], *a.* Saturnine, melancholy, grave, gloomy.

saturno [sah-toor'-no], *m.* 1. *(Ast.)* Saturn. 2. Lead.

sauce [sah'-oo-thay], *m.* (Boy) Willow.

saucedal, *m.* **saucera,** *f.* [sah-oo-thar-dahl', sah-oo-thay'-rah], Plantation of willows, V. SALCEDA.

saúco [sah-oo´-co], *f.* 1. *(Bot.)* Elder or alder-tree. 2. Second hoof of horses.

sauna [sah-oo-nah], *f.* Sauna.

sauquillo [sah-oo-keel'-lyo], *m. (Bot.)* Dwarf elder.

saurios [sah'-oo-re-os], *m. pl.* Saurians, a division of reptiles; lizards.

sausería [sah-oo-say-re´-ah], *f.* Larder in a palace.

sasier [sah-oo-se-err'], *m.* Chief of the larder in a palace.

sauz [sah'-ooth], *m. (Bot.)* V. SUCE.

sauzal [sau-oo-thahl'], *m.* V. SAUCEDAL and SALCEDA.

sauzgatillo [sah-ooth-gah-teel'-lyo], *m. (Bot.)* Agnus castus tree, chase tree.

savia [sah'-ve-ah], *f.* The sap of plants, the nutrient fluid.

saxafrax [sah-sah-frahx'], *f. (Bot.)* V. SAXIFRAGA.

saxátil [sak-sah'-teel], *a.* Growing among or adhering to rocks: said of animals and plants; saxicolous.

sáxeo, ea [sak'-say-o, ah], *a.* Stony.

saxícola [sak-see'-co-lah], *f. (Zool.)* A genus of birds of the family Turdidae.

saxífraga, saxifragua [sak-see'-frah-gah, sak-se-frah'-goo-ah], *f. (Bot.)* The saxifrage plant; mountain saxifrage.

saxo [sak-so], *m. (Mus.)* Sax.

saxofón, saxófono [sax-o-fone', sax-o'-fo-no], *m.* Saxophone.

saya [sah'-yah], *f.* 1. Dress skirt (falda), outer skirt, of a woman; petticoat (enaguas) 2. Ancient tunic or gown worn by men.

sayal [sah-yahl'], *m.* A coarse woollen stuff, sackcloth.

sayalería [sah-yah-lay-ree'-ah], *f.* Shop for weaving coarse cloth.

sayalero [sah-yah-lay'-ro], *m.* Weaver of coarse stuff.

sayalesco, ca [sah-yah-les'-co, cah], *a.* Made of sackcloth or other coarse stuff.

sayalete [sah-yah-lay'-tay], *m. dim.* A thin or light stuff used for undergarments.

sayaza [sah-yah'-thah], *f. aug.* A coarse petticoat.

sayete, sayito [sah-yay'-tay], *m. dim.* A small frock, a short dress.

sayo [sah'-yo], *m.* A large wide coat without buttons, any loose coat or dress; small frock. **Sayo vaquero**, a loose jacket worn by cowboys. **A su sayo**, of one's own accord, in one's own mind. **Cortar (a uno) un sayo**, to blame or censure anyone in his absence.

sayón [sa-yon'], *m.* 1. A corpulent, ill-looking fellow. 2. Aug. of SAYO.

sayonazo [sah-yo-nah'-tho], *m. aug.* of SAYÓN.

sayuela [sah-yoo-ay'-lah], *f.* l. Woollen shift worn by some religious. 2. Kind of fig-tree.

sayuelo [sah-yoo-ay'-lo], *m. dim.* Little frock, small kind of jacket.

sazón [sah-thone'], *f.* 1. Maturity, state of perfection. 2. Season, taste, relish, flavor, seasoning. 3. Occasion, opportunity, season, conjunction. **A la sazón**, then, at that time. **En sazón**, seasonably, opportunely.

sazonadamente [sah-tho-nah'-dah-men-tay], *adv.* Maturely, seasonably.

sazonado, da [sah-tho-nah'-do, dah], *a. & pp.* of SAZONAR. 1. Seasoned, mature, mellow. 2. Applied to a witty saying, or to a word to the purpose.

sazonador, ra [sah-tho-nah-dor', rah], *m. &.f.* Seasoner.

sazonar [sah-tho-nar'], *va.* l. To season, to give a relish. 2. To mature, to bring to maturity. *-vr.* To ripen, to mature.

scooter [scoo'-tayr], *m.* Motor scooter.

se [say]. *The reflexive pronoun,* himself, herself, itself. **Él se lava,** he washes himself. **Ella se peina,** she combs herself. **Él se cortó,** he cut himself. Possessive to the person or thing that governs the verb used before the pronouns *me, te, le,* it reflects the action of the verb on the object which they represent. *Se* is used instead of the other cases of the pronouns of the third person, as **¿Le entregó Vd. la carta?** did you deliver him or her the letter? **Sí, se la entregué,** yes, I delivered it *to him,* or *to her.*

Passive voice. Se represents frequently the passive form of a verb, as **Se dice,** it is said. **Se cree,** it is thought. **Se hace,** it is done.

Reciprocal. Each other, one another. **Se ayudan mutuamente,** they help each other. **Los jugadores se pasan el balón,** the players pass the ball to one another.

sea que [say'-ah kay], *adv.* Whether.

sebáceo, cea [say-bah'-thay-o, ah], Sebaceous, tallowy.

sebastiano [say-bas-te-ah'-no], *m. V.* SEBESTÉN.

sebato [say-bah'-to], *m. (Chem.)* Sebate.

sebe [say'-bay], *f.* Stockade, wattle of high pales interwoven with long branches.

sebesta [say-bes'-tah], *f.* Sebesten-fruit, sebestine.

sebestén [say-bes-ten'], *m. (Bot.)* Sebesten-tree, a tree of India and western Asia resembling the sloe.

sebillo [say-beel'-lyo], *m.* Paste made with suet, to soften the bands; kind of soap.

sebo [say'-bo], *m.* 1. Tallow (para velas), candlegrease, suet; any kind of grease or fat. **Sebo en rama** or **en bruto**, rough tallow. 2. *(Met. Coll.)* A large capital, a great fortune. 3. *(Naut.)* Animal grease, with which the bottoms of ships, the masts, etc., are besmeared.

seboso, sa [say-bo'-so, sah], *a.* Tallowy (de vela), fat, greasy (mugriento), unctuous; greased.

seca [say'-cah], *f.* 1. Drought, dry weather. 2. Inflammation and swelling in the glands. 3. *V.* SECANO, 3d def. **A secas**, alone, singly.

secacul [say-cah-cool'], *m. (Bot.)* A plant like a parsnip, and having a very aromatic root.

secadal [say-cah-dahl'], *m.* A dry, barren ground.

secadero [say-cah-day'-ro], *m.* Place where something is dried (lugar); drying shed, room, or floor; drier; fruit drier.

secadero, ra, *a.* Capable of being dried (fruta).

secadillo [say-cah-deel'-lyo], *m.* A sort of dry, round biscuit: commonly used in the plural.

secador [say-cah-dor'], *m.* 1. Place where clothes are hung to dry. 2. **Secador de cabello**, hair-drier.

secadora [say-cah-do-rah], *f.* Drier, clothes drier.

secamente [say-cah-men-tay], *adv.* 1. Dryly, morosely; crabbedly, peevishly. 2. Coldly, frigidly.

secano [say-cah'-no], *m.* 1. Dry, unirrigated, arable land. 2. Dryness. 3. Sandbank uncovered by water (banco de arena).

secante [say-cahn'-tay], *m.* Drier, a drying oil used for painting. *-f. (Geom.)* Secant.

secar [say-car'], *va.* To dry out, to dry off, to dry (lágrimas), to wipe (superficie), to blot (tinta). *-vr.* 1. To dry (ropa lavada), to be dried up (planta), to grow dry. 2. To become lank, lean, or meager, to decay. 3. To grow cool in intercourse with a friend. 4. To be extremely thirsty. 5. To feel repugnance to do anything, however necessary.

secaral [say-cah-rahl'], *m.* Dryness, drought. *V.* SEQUERAL.

secatura [say-cah-too'-rah], *f.* 1. Insipidity; want of spirit or life, flatness, want of understanding. 2. Coolness, indifference.

sección [sec-the-on'], *f.* 1. Act of cutting. 2. Section, a division of a book. 3. *(Geom.)* Section, the cutting of lines, figures, and solid bodies. 4. *(Arch.)* Section of a building; delineation of its height and depth. 5. Topographical division, section: in hydraulics, section, capacity of the bed of a river, its width and depth.

seccionar [sec-the-o-nar'], *va.* To section, to divide into sections (dividir).

seccionario, ria [sec-the-o-nah'-re-o, ah], *a.* Sectional, relating to a section.

secesión [say-thay-se-on'], *f.* Secession.

seceso [say-thay'-so], *m.* Excrement, stool.

seco, ca [say'-co, cah], *a.* 1. Dry, not wet, not moist. 2. Dry, not rainy (clima). 3. Dry, not succulent. 4. Barren, arid, sapless, withered. 5. Lean, lank, meager. 6. Bare (estilo), only, mere. **A secas**, solely. 7. Barren, without ornament or embellishment. 8. Rude, dry, ill-mannered. **Es un hombre seco**, he is a man of few words, he is not sociable. 9. Lukewarm, cold, without affection. **Pan seco**, stale, dry bread. **En seco**, (1) without cause or motive. (2) In a dry place. 10. *(LAm.)* Slap, smack (golpe).

secor [say-cor'], *m. V.* SEQUEDAD.

secreción [say-cray-the-on'], *f.* 1. *(Med.)* Secretion, act of separating the fluids of the body. 2. *V.* APARTAMIENTO.

secreta [say-cray'-tah], *f.* 1. Secret police, plain-clothes police. 2. Secret policeman, plain-clothes policeman. 3. Privy, water-closet. 4. Secret inquiry or verbal investigation.

secretamante [say-cray-tah-men-tay], *adv.* Secretly, clandestinely.

secretar [say-cray-tar'], *va.* 1. *(Med.)* To secrete, to secern, to separate. 2. To prepare skins, the hair of which is to be taken off and prepared for making felt hats.

secretaría [say-cray-tah-ree'-ah], *f.* 1. Secretary's office. 2. Secretaryship.

secretario, a [say-cray-tah'-re-ah], *a, f.* 1. Secretary. **Secretario general,** general secretary. **Secretaria particular,** personal secretary. 2. Minister of State *(Mex.)*; Secretary of State (USA). 3. A scribe, a notary. 4. Clerk, amanuensis, one who writes for another. **Secretario de Estado,** etc., *V.* MINISTRO. **Secretario general,** general secretary. **Secretario de prensa,** press secretary.

secretear [say-cray-tay-ar'], *vn. (Coll.)* To speak in private (conversar), to whisper (cuchichear).

secretico, illo, ito [say-cray-tee'-co], *m. dim.* A trifling secret. **Secretillos,** private conversation between friends.

secretista [say-cray-tes'-tah], *m.* 1. Author who writes on the secrets of nature: naturalist. 2. Secretist, a dealer in secrets.

secreto, ta [say-cray'-to, tah], *a.* 1. Secret, hidden (escondido), obscure, occult; dark; clandestine. 2. *(Coll.)* Confidential.

secreto [say-cray'-to], *m.* 1. Secrecy, careful silence. 2. Secret, the thing hidden or concealed, arcanum (escondido); nostrum. 2. Caution, silence, dissimulation, concealment; darkness. 4. Scrutoire, a case or hidden drawer for papers; a secret drawer in a desk or trunk. **Secreto a voces,** open secret. **Observar el secreto,** to maintain secrecy. **Secreto de Estado,** state secret. **Secreto profesional,** professional confidence. **De secreto,** secretly. **De secreto inviolable,** top secret. **En secreto,** in secret, in private, informally. **Tener una cosa secreta,** to keep something to oneself. 5. Secrecy (cualidad). 6. Secret drawer (cajón). 7. Combination (de cerradura).

secretón [say-cray-tone'], *m.* Fine dimity.

secretorio, ria [say-cray-to´-re-o, ah], *a. (Med.)* Secretory.

secta [sec'-tah], *f.* 1. A sect. 2. Doctrine or opinion of a sect.

sectador, ra [sec-tah-dor', rah], *m. & f.* Sectarist.

sectario, ria [sec-tah'-re-o, ah], *a. & n.* Sectarian; sectary.

sector [sec-tor'], *m. (Geom.)* Sector. **Sectores simples / de doble cara,** *(Comput.)* single / double side sectors.

secuaz [say-coo-ath´], *a. & m. & f.* Following the opinions of others, sectary of the school of; sequacious; attendant.

secuela [say-coo-ay'-lah], *f.* 1. Sequel, continuation. 2. Sequence, the act of following a party or doctrine. 3. Consequence (consecuencia), induction.

secuencia [say-coo-en'-the-ah], *f.* Sequence (cine).

secuestrable [say-coo-es-trah'-blay], *a.* Sequestrable, legally forfeitable.

secuestración [say-coo-es-trah-the-on'], *f.* Sequestration, the setting aside of property from the possession and control of persons, pending judicial proceedings. *V.* SECUESTRO.

secuestrador, ra [say-coo-es-trah-dor'], *m.* Sequestrator.

secuestrar [say-coo-es-trar'], *va.* To sequestrate, to sequester, to distress, to kidnap, to abduct (persona); to confiscate, to seize (artículos); to hijack (avión).

secuestrario, ria [say-coo-es-trah´-re-o, ah], *a.* Belonging to sequestration.

secuestro [say-coo-es'-tro], *m.* 1. Sequestration. 2. The person in whose hands sequestered property is trusted as a deposit. 3. Seizure of a person by robbers, demanding money for ransom. 4. Sequestrum, a piece of dead bone separated from the living. **Depositario de un secuestro,** garnishee, he in whose hands money is attached.

secular [say-coo-lar'], *a.* 1. Secular, happening or coming once in a century. 2. Secular, not spiritual or ecclesiastical. 3. Not bound by monastic rules. 4. Lay, laical.

secularidad [say-coo-lah-re-dahd'], *f.* Secularity.

secularizable [say-coo-la-re-thah'-blay], *a.* Secularizable, capable of being secularized.

secularización [say-coo-lah-re-thah-the-on´], *f.* Secularization.

secularizar [say-coo-lah-re-thar'], *va.* To secularize.

secundar [say-coon-dar'], *va.* 1. To aid another in some toil. 2. To favor the purposes of another, to second. 3. To repeat a second time.

secundariamente [say-coon-dah'-re-ah-men-tay], *adv.* Secondarily.

secundario, ria [say-coon-dah'-re-o, ah], *a.* 1. Secondary, second in order; subordinate. 2. Accessory.

secundinas [say-coon-dee'-nas], *f. pl.* After-birth and secundines.

secura [say-coo'-rah], *f.* 1. Dryness, droughtiness. 2. Coolness, indifference.

sed [sayd], *f.* 1. Thirst. 2. Drought. 3. Eagerness, anxiety, violent desire. **Tener mucha sed,** to be very thirsty.

seda [say'-dah], *f.* 1. Silk, the thread of the silkworm. 2. Stuff formed of silken threads. 3. Sewing-silk. **Seda en rama** or **cruda,** raw silk. **Seda de coser,** sewing-silk. 4. Wild boar's bristles. **Ser una seda, como una seda,** to be of a sweet temper. **Tejedor de seda,** silk-weaver.

sedadera [say-dah-day'-rah], *f.* Hackle for dressing flax.

sedal [say-dahl'], *m.* 1. Angling-line fixed to a fishing-hook. 2. Seton, an artificial ulcer: by farriers it is called a rowel. 3. **Sedal de zapatero,** shoemaker's thread

sedante [say-dahn'-tay], *a. (Med.)* Sedative. *-m.* Sedative.

sedar [say-dar'], *va.* To allay, to quiet.

sedativo, va [say-dah-tee'-vo, vah], *a. (Med.)* Sedative.

sede [say'-day], *f.* See, seat (de gobierno). **La Santa Sede,** the holy see, or the papal dignity. **Sede plena,** actual occupation of a chair or dignity. **Sede vacante,** vacant bishopric.

sedear [say-day-ar'], *va.* To clean jewels, gold, or silver with a brush.

sedentario, ria [say-den-tah'-re-o, ah], *a.* Sedentary.

sedeña [say-day'-nyah], *f.* Fine tow of flax, produced by the second hackling; cloth made of such tow.

sedeño, ña [say-day'-nyo, nyah], *a.* 1. Silky, silken (sedoso); silk-like. 2. Made or consisting of hair.

sedera [say-day'-rah], *f.* 1. A brush made of bristles. 2. *(Prov.)* Weaver´s seat.

sedería [say-day-ree'-ah], *f.* 1. Silks, silk stuff. 2. Shop of a silk-mercer (tienda).

sedero [say-day'-ro], *m.* Silk-mercer

sedición [say-de-the-on'], *f.* Sedition, popular commotion; an insurrection, mutiny.

sediciosamente [say-de-the-o-sah-men-tay], *adv.* Seditiously, factiously, mutinously.

sedicioso, sa [say-de-the-o´-so, sah], *a.* Seditious, factious, mutinous.

sediento, ta [say-de-en'-to, tah], *a.* 1. Thirsty, dry. ·2. Eagerly, desirous, anxious.

sedimentación [say-de-men-tah-the-on'], *f.* Sedimentation.

sedimentar [say-de-men-tar'], *va. & vr.* To settle, deposit (depositar).

sedimento [say-de-men'-to], *m.* Sediment, feculence, lees.

sedoso, sa [say-do'-so, sah], *a.* Silky, like silk, silk-like, silken.

seducción [say-dooc-the-on'], *f.* Seduction (acto), deceiving; abuse.

seducir [say-doo-theer'], *va.* To seduce (mujer), to corrupt, to abuse, to lead on (moralmente), to charm (cautivar). **Seduce a todos con su simpatía,** she captivates everyone with her charm.

seductivo, va [say-dooc-tee'-vo, vah], *a.* Seductive, apt to mislead; corruptful.

seductor, ra [say-dooc-tor', rah], *a.* Seductive, fascinating, charming (encantador). *-m. & f.* 1. Seducer, corrupter, deceiver. 2. Seducer, charmer.

segable [say-gah´-blay], *a.* Fit to be reaped.

segadera [sah-gah-day´-rah], *f.* Reaping hook, sickle.

segadero, ra [say-gah-day'-ro, rah], *a.* Fit to be reaped.

segador ra [say-gah-dor', rah], *m. & f.* Reaper, harvester: sickle man. *-f.* A reaping or harvesting-machine.

segar [say-gar´], *va.* 1. To reap (trigo), to cut down with a reaping-hook, to crop; to moor. 2. To cut off, to abscind anything grown higher than the rest. *(Yo siego, yo siegue, from Segar. V.* ACRECENTAR.)

segazón [say-gah-thone'], *f.* Harvest season, reaping.

seglar [say-glar'], *a*. 1. Worldly. 2. Secular, laical, lay: in this last sense it is used as a substantive.

seglarmente [say-glar'-men-tay], *adv*. Secularly.

segmento [seg-men'-to], *m*. 1. Segment, part cut off. 2. *(Geom.)* Segment, the part of a circle comprised between an arc and its chord. 3. Segment, each ring or articulation of articulated animals.

segregación [say-gray-gah-the-on'], *f*. Segregation, separation.

segregar [say-gray-gar'], *va*. 1. To segregate, to set apart. 2. To disunite, to unfasten. 3. *(Med.)* To secrete. 4. To excommunicate.

segregativo, va [say-gray-gah-tee'-vo, vah], *a*. That which separates.

segueta [say-gay'-tah], *f*. A very slender fine saw for jewellers or marquetry.

seguida [say-gee'-dah], *f*. The act of following or state of being followed; procession: continuation. **De seguida,** successively, without interruption. **En seguida,** forthwith, immediately.

seguidero [say-gee-day'-ro], *m*. Guide rule, ruled lines to follow in writing.

seguidilla [say-gee-deel'-lyah], *f*. A merry Spanish tune and dance.

seguidillera [say-gee-deeh-lyay'-rah], *f*. Person fond of singing and dancing *seguidillas*.

seguido, da [say-gee'-do, dah], *a*. Continued, successive, straight, directed. *-pp*. of SEGUIR. **5 días seguidos,** 5 days running. **Una enfermedad muy seguida,** a very lengthy illness.

seguido [say-gee'-do], *m*. Narrowing a stocking at the foot.

seguidor, ra [say-gee-dor', rah], *m*. & *f*. 1. Follower 2. A leaf of ruled paper to guide boys in writing straight.

seguimiento [say-gee-me-en'-to], *m*. Pursuit, the act of following another, hunt: continuation of a lawsuit.

seguir [say-geer'], *va*. 1. To follow, to pursue (carrera, rumbo). 2. To follow, to prosecute, to be in pursuit of one. 3. To follow, to accompany, to attend; to come after; to make at; to march in. 4. To follow, to profess, or exercise any science or art. 5. To manage a suit at law or any other business. 6. To agree or conform to. 7. To copy, to imitate. 8. To direct to the proper road or method. **Seguir los acontecimientos de cerca,** to monitor events closely. *-vn*. 1. To follow (venir después). 2. To continue (continuar). **Y los que siguen,** and the next ones. *-vr*. 1. To ensue, to follow as a consequence (venir después). 2. To succeed, to follow in order. 3. To issue, to spring from. 4. To go on.

segullo [say-gool'-lyo], *m*. The first stratum of a gold-mine.

según [say-goon'], *prep*. According to. **Según Vd. me dice,** according to what you tell me. **Según y como,** just as. **Vuelvo la caja, según y como la recibí,** I return the box just as I received it.

segunda [say-goon'-dah], *f*. 1. Second in music. 2. Double wards of a lock or key. 3. *V*. INTENCIÓN. *V*. SEGUNDO DA.

segundar [say-goon-dar'], *vn*. 1. To repeat over again (repetir). 2. To be second.

segundero, ra [say-goon-day'-ro, rah], *a*. *(Agr.)* Second crop from some plants in the same year. *-m*. *(Naut.)* Second hand upon a chronometer and other time-pieces.

segundilla [say-goon-deel'-lyah], *f*. 1. Small bell used for certain acts of devotion. 2. *(Peru)* The end of some ceremony which may be seen without paying.

segundillo [say-goon-deel'-lyo], *m*. *(Mus.)* Semitone, one of them which are called accidentals.

segundo, da [say-goon'-do, dah], *a*. Second, immediately following the first; favorable. **De segunda mano, por segunda mano,** at second hand. **En segundo lugar,** secondly. **Segunda intención,** duplicity, falsity.

segundo [say-goon'-do], *m*. Second of time or of a degree.

segundogénito, ta [say-goon-do-hay'-ne-to, tah], *a*. Second-born (niños).

segundón [say-goon-don'], *m*. The second son of a family or any of the brothers after the eldest.

segur [say-goor'], *f*. 1. Axe (hacha). 2. Axe or emblem of the law. 3. Sickle, a reaping-hook.

segurador [say-goo-rah-dor'], *a*. Securer, asserter, security, bondsman.

seguramente [say-goo-rah-men-tay], *adv*. Securely, probably, certainly; fastly; safely. **Seguramente tendrá otro,** they'll probably have another.

segurar [say-goo-rar'], *va*. *V*. ASEGURAR.

segureja [say-goo-ray'-hah], *f. dim*. A small hatchet, a hollow drawing-knife for cleaning the inside of staves.

seguridad [say-goo-re-dahd'], *f*. 1. Security, surety, certainty, safety (lo salvo), confidence. 2. Fastness; custody; corroboration. 3. Pledge-bail. **Seguridad en carretera,** road safety. **Para mayor seguridad,** to be on the safe side. **En la seguridad de su victoria,** in the certainty of winning.

seguro, ra [say-goo'-ro, rah], *a*. 1. Secure, free from danger; easy, assured, confident, confiding. 2. Secure, sure, certain. 3. Firm, constant. **Estar seguro de una cosa,** *(Coll.)* to depend upon a thing. **A segura le llevan preso,** that which is most secure is not beyond danger. **Está más seguro en el banco,** it's safer in the bank. **Es seguro que...,** it is certain that.....

seguro [say-goo-ro], *m*. 1. Permission, leave, license. 2. Insurance of goods on sea or land. 3. *(Mech.)* Click, stop, detent, pawl, ratchet; tumbler of a lock. **Compañía de seguros,** insurance company. **Cámara u oficina de seguros,** insurance office. **Póliza de seguro,** policy of insurance. **Premio de seguro,** premium of insurance. **A buen seguro,** certainly, indubitably. **De seguro,** assuredly. **Sobre seguro,** confidently. **Hacer el seguro,** to insure.

seguro colectivo [say-goo'-ro co-lec-tee'-vo], *m*. Group insurance.

seguro de enfermedad [say-goo'-ro day en-fer-may-dahd'], *m*. Health insurance.

seguro sobre la vida [say-goo'-ro so'-bray lah vee'-dah], *m*. Life insurance.

seguro social [say-goo'-ro so-the-ahl'], *m*. Social security.

seis [say-ees], *a*. Six, sixth. *V*. SEXTO. *-m*. 1. The figure 6. 2. Six, upon cards or dice. **Seis por ocho,** *(Mus.)* 6/8, six-eight measure; six eighth notes to a measure.

seisavado, da [say-sah-vah'-do, dah], *a*. That which has six sides and six angles.

seisavo [say-sah'-vo], *m*. 1. *V*. HEXÁGONO. 2. The sixth part of a number.

seiscientos, tas [say-ces-the-en'-tos, tas], *a*. Six hundred.

seiseno, na [say-e-say-no, nah], *a*. Sixth. *V*. SEXTO.

seisillo [say-e-seel'-lyo], *m*. *(Mus.)* Union of six equal notes.

seísmo [say-ee'-mo], *m*. Tremor, shock, earthquake.

seismógrafo [say-ees-mo-grah-fo], *m*. Seismograph, an instrument for recording the direction and force of earthquakes.

seismología [say-ees-mo-lo-hee'-ah], *f*. Seismology, the study of earthquakes.

seismológico, ca [say-ees-mo-lo'-he-co, cah], *a*. Seismological.

seismómetro [say-ees-mo'-may-tro], *m*. Seismometer. *V*. SEISMÓGRAFO.

selección [say-lec-the-on'], *f*. Selection, choice, exception. **Selección múltiple,** multiple choice.

seleccionar [say-lec-the-o-nar'], *va*. To pick, to choose, to select.

selectividad [say-lec-te-ve-dahd'], *f*. Selectivity, selectiveness.

selecto, ta [say-lec'-to, tah], *a*. Select (en calidad), choice, excellent.

selene [say-lay'-nay], *f*. The moon.

selenio [say-lay'-ne-o], *m*. Selenium, a chemical element, related to sulphur.

selenita [say-lay-nee'-tah], *com*. Inhabitant of the moon.

selenites [say-lay-nee'-tes], *f*. Selenite, crystallized gypsum.

selenografía [say-lay-no-grah-fee'-ah], f. Selenography, description of the moon.

sellado [sayl-lyah'-do], a. Sealed; stamped, franked. -m. 1. Sealing (acto). 2. (Cono Sur) Stamps, stamp duty.

sellador [sel-lya-dor'], m. Sealer.

selladura [sel-lyah-doo'-rah], f. Sealing.

sellar [sel-lyar'], va. 1. To seal (documento, carta), to put on a seal. 2. To seal, to stamp (pasaporte). 3. To conclude, to finish a thing. 4. To cover, to close up. 5. To obligate as by benefits. Sellar los labios, to silence.

sello [sel'-lyo], m. 1. Stamp. 2. Signet. 3. Seal. 4. (Fig.) Seal stamp, impression. Sello fiscal, revenue stamp. Sello postal, Sello de correo, postage stamp. Sellos de premio, trading stamps. Sello aéreo, airmail stamp.

selva [sel'-vah], f. Forest (bosque), jungle (jungla). Selva espesa, thicket.

selvático, ca [sel-vah'-te-co, cah], a. Forest-born, reared in a forest, belonging to a forest.

selvatiquez [sel-vah-te-keth'], f. Rusticity, savageness, wildness.

selvicultura [sel-ve-cool-too'-rah], f. Forest culture, forestry.

selvoso, sa [sel-vo'-so, sah], a. 1. Belonging to forests. 2. Well-wooded.

semafórico, ca [say-ma-fo'-re-co, cah], a. Semaphoric, telegraphic.

semáforo [say-mah'-fo-ro], m. 1. Traffic light, stoplight. 2. Semaphore, marine signal telegraph, railroad traffic sign.

semana [say-mah'-nah], f. 1. A week. Semana Santa, Passion-week, Holy week, Easter. Día entre semana, working day. 2. Any septenary period of time; hebdomad.

semanal [say-mah-nahl'], a. Hebdomadal, weekly.

semanalmente [say-mah-nahl'-men-tay], adv. Weekly.

semanario, ria [say-mah-nah'-re-o, ah], a. & m. & f. Weekly publication.

semanería [say-mah-nay-ree'-ah], f. Functions performed, or work done in the course of a week.

semanero [say-mah-nay'-ro], m. One who enters upon weekly functions in his turn.

semanero, ra [say-mah-nay'-ro, rah], a. Applied to persons engaged by the week.

semántica [say-man'-te-cah], f. Semantics.

semblante [sem-blahn'-tay], m. 1. Expression in the face of some emotion; look, mien, feature. 2. Face, countenance. 3. Aspect, looks, phase of things, on which we base a contempt of them; feature. Las cosas han tomado otro semblante or cambiado de semblante, (Coll.) things have taken a different aspect. Tener buen semblante, to look well (salud).

semblanza [sem-blahn'-thah], f. In literature, biographical sketch.

sembradera [sem-brah-day'-rah], f. Anything used for sowing seed; seeder.

sembradío, día [sem-brah-dee'-o, ah], a. Fit or prepared for sowing of seed.

sembrado [sem-brah'-do], m. Corn-field; ground sown with grain.

sembrador, ra [sem-brah-dor', rah], a. Sowing seed. -m. & f. Sower (persona). -f. (Amer.) Seeder, a machine for sowing seeds.

sembradura [sem-brah-doo'-rah], f. Insemination, sowing or scattering seed.

sembrar [sem-brar'], va. 1. To sow, to scatter seed. 2. To scatter (objetos), to spread, to propagate, to divulge. 3. To give a cause or beginning. 4. To perform a useful undertaking. 5. To collect without order. Sembrar de sal, to sow the land with salt (a punishment for treason). El que siembra recoge, one reaps what one has sown.

semeja [say-may'-hah], f. 1. Resemblance, likeness. 2. Mark, sign. No es él, ni su semeja, it is not he, nor anything like him.

semejable [say-may-hah'-blay], a. Like, resembling, similar.

semejablemente [say-may-hah'-blah-men-tay], adv. Likely.

semejado, da [say-may-hah'-do, dah], a. Like. V. PARECIDO. -pp of SEMEJAR.

semejante [say-may-hahn'-tay], a. Similar (parecido), like, conformable. -m. V. SEMEJANZA. Nuestros semejantes, our fellow-creatures. Son muy semejantes, they are very much alike.

semejantemente [say-men-han'-tay-men-tay], adv. Likewise, in the same manner, similarly.

semejanza [say-may-hahn'-thah], f. Resemblance, conformity, semblance, similitude; likeness, likelihood. Tener semejanza con, to look like.

semejar [say-may-har'], vn. To be like, to resemble; to liken. -vr. To resemble.

semen [say'-men], m. 1. Semen, sperm, the fertilizing fluid of animals. 2. (Bot.) Seed.

semencera [say-men-thay'-rah], f. Sowing scattering seed for growth. V. SEMENTERA.

semental [say-men-tahl'], a. Seminal.

sementar [say-men-tar'], va. To sow, to scatter seed.

sementera [say-men-tay'-rah], f. 1. Sowing seed. 2. Land sown with seed (tierra). 3. The seed sown. 4. Seedtime. 5. Origin, cause, beginning.

sementero [say-men-tay'-ro], m. 1. Seedlip or seedlop, a vessel in which the sower carries his seed; hopper. 2. Sowing, scattering seed.

sementilla [say-men-teel'-lyah], f. dim. of SIMIENTE.

sementino, na [say-men-tee'-no, nah], a. Belonging to seed or seed-time.

semestral [say-mes-trahl'], a. Semi-yearly, semi-annually. Informe semestral, semiannual report. Cuota semestral, semiannual fee.

semestre [say-mes'-tray], a. Lasting six months. -m. Space of six months, semester; leave of absence for six months.

semi [say'-me], prefix. Semi, a word which, in composition, signifies half; sometimes it is equivalent to casi, almost.

semianual [say-me-ah-noo-ahl'], a. Semi-annual, half-yearly.

semibreve [say-me-bray'-vay], f. (Mus.) Semibreve, whole note (0).

semicabrón, semicapro [say-me-car-brone'], m. Satyr.

semicircular [say-me-theer-coo-lar'], a. Semicircular, semiangular.

semicírculo [say-me-theer'-coo-lo], m. Semicircle.

semiconsciente [say-me-cons-the-ayn'-tay], a. Semiconscious.

semicorchea [say-me-cor-chay'-ah], f. (Mus.) Semiquaver; sixteenth note.

semicircunferencia [say-me-theer-coon-fay-ren'-the-ah], f. Semicircumference.

semicopado [say-me-co-pah'-do], m. A note which joins the second part of a measure with the first of that which follows it; a syncopated note.

semicromático, ca [say-me-cro-mah'-te-co, cah], a. (Mus.) Semichromatic.

semidea [say-me-day'-ah], f. (Poet.) Demigoddess.

semidiáfano, na [say-me-de-ah'-fah-no, nah], a. Semidiaphanous.

semidiametro [say-me-de-ah'-may-tro], m. Semidiameter, radius.

semidiapasón [say-me-de-ah-pah-sone'], m. (Mus.) Semidiapason, defective octave.

semidiapente [say-me-de-ah-pen'-tay], m. (Mus.) Semidiapente, defective fifth.

semidiatesarón [say-me-de-ah-tay-sah-rone'], m. (Mus.) Semidiatessaron, defective fourth.

semidifunto, ta [say-me-de-foon'-to, tah], a. Half-dead, almost dead.

semidiós [say-me-de-os'], m. Semidiosa [say-me-de-oh'-sah], f. Demi-god; demi-goddess.

semidítono [say-me-dee'-to-no], m. (Mus.) Semiditone, minor third.

semidoble [say-me-do'-blay], a. Semidouble: applied in the Catholic church to feasts.

semidocto [say-me-doc'-to], _m._ Sciolist, a half-learned man, half scholar. -_a._ Half-learned.

semidormido, da [say-me-dor-mee'-do, dah], _a._ Half asleep, sleepy.

semidragón [say-me-drah-gone'], _m._ Semidragon.

semiesfera [say-me-es-fay'-rah], _f._ Hemisphere.

semiesférico, ca [say-me-es-fay'-re-co, ah], _a._ Semiglobular, hemispherical.

semifinal [say-me-fe-nahl'], _a._ Semifinal. **Semifinales,** semifinals.

semiflósculo [say-me-flos'-coo-lo], _m. (Bot.)_ Semifloret.

semiflosculoso, sa [ay-me-flos-coo-lo'-so, sah], _a. (Bot.)_ Semifloscular, semiflosculous.

semifluido, da [say-me-floo'-e-do, dah], _a._ Semi-fluid.

semifusa [say-me-foo'-sah], _f. (Mus.)_ Double demisemiquaver, a sixtyfourth note.

semigola [say-me-go'-lah], _f. (Mil.)_ Demigorge, half the entrance into a bastion.

semihombre [say-me-om'-bray], _m._ Half-man.

semilla [say-meel'-lyah], _f._ 1. Seed, from which plants are produced. 2. Origin, abuse. **Semillas,** all sorts of seed and grain, wheat and barley excepted; quantity of seed sown.

semillatero [say-mee-lyah-tay'-ro], _m. (Prov.)_ V. SEMILLERO.

semillero [say-meel-lyay'-ro], _m._ 1. Seedplot, ground on which plants are sown to be afterwards transplanted; nursery. 2. _(Fig.)_ Hotbed; breeding ground. **Un semillero de delincuencia,** a hotbed of crime.

semilunar [say-me-loo-nar'], _a._ Semilunar, semilunery.

semilunio [say-me-loo'-ne-o], _m._ Half the time in which the moon performs its course; half-moon.

semimetal [say-me-may-tahl'], _m._ Semimetal, imperfect metal.

seminal [say-me-nahl'], _a._ 1. Seminal, radical. 2. Spermatic.

seminario [say-me-nah'-re-o], _m._ 1. Seed-plot, nursery, ground in which plants are sown to be afterwards transplanted. 2. Seminary, a school. 3. Musical school for children. 4. Beginning, root, origin, source.

seminarista [say-me-nah-rees'-tah], _m._ A scholar who boards and is instructed in a seminary.

semínima [say-mee'-ne-mah], _f._ 1. _(Mus.)_ Crotchet, quarter note. 2. Trifle, thing of no moment.

semioctava [say-me-oc-tah'-vah], _f._ Poetical composition of four verses in alternate rhymes.

semiordenada [say-me-or-day-nah'-dah], _f. (Math.)_ Semiordinate.

semipedal [say-me-pay-dahl'], _a._ Measuring half a foot in length.

semipelagiano, na [say-me-pay-lah-he-ah'-no, nah], _m. & f._ Semi-Pelagian, one who adopts part of the errors of Pelagius.

semiplena [say-me-play'-nah], _f. (For.)_ Imperfect proof, half proof.

semiplenamente [say-me-play'-nah-men-tay], _adv._ Half proved.

semipoeta [say-me-po-ay'-tah], _m._ Poetaster.

semiprobanza [say-me-pro-bahn'-thah], _f._ A half proof; imperfect evidence.

semiprueba [say-me-proo-ay'-bah], _f. (Law.)_ Semiproof.

semipútrido, da [say-me-poo'-tre-do, dah], _a._ Half putrid.

semiracional [say-me-rah-the-o-nahl'], _a._ Stupid, ignorant.

semirrecto [say-mir-rec'-to], _a._ Of forty-five degrees: half a right angle.

semirrubio, bia [say-mir-roo'-be-o, ah], _a._ Nearly blonde.

semisalvaje [say-me-sal-vah'-hay], _m._ Semisavage, half savage.

semisestil [say-me-ses-teel'], _m. (Ast.)_ Semisextile.

semisumador [say-me-soo-mah-dor], . _(Comput.)_ Half-adder.

semita [say-mee'-tah], _m._ Semite, a descendant of Shem.

semiterciana [say-me-ter-the-ah'-nah], _f._ Semitertian.

semítico, ca [say-mee'-te-co, cah], _a._ Semitic, relating to Shem. **Lengua semítica,** semitic tongue, one of a great family of languages, of which hebrew, Arabic, Ethiopic, and Assyrian are types.

semitono [say-me-toh'-no], _m._ (plus.) Semitone.

semitransparente [say-me-trans-pah-ren'-tay], _a._ Almost transparent.

semivibración [say-me-ve-brah-the-on'], _f._ Vibration of the pendulum that ascends or descends.

semivivo, va [say-me-vee'-vo, vah], _a._ Half alive.

semivocal [say-me-vo-cahl'], _a._ Semivowel, as _f, l, m, n, r, s._

semivulpa [say-me-vool'-pah], _f._ Animal like a wolf.

sémola [say'-mo-lah], _f._ 1. Groats or grits, made of decorticated wheat; wheat ground coarse. 2. An Italian paste of the quality of vermicelli, in the form of very small grain, for the use of the sick.

semoviente [say-mo-ve-en'-tay], _a._ Moving of itself.

sempiterna [sem-pe-terr'-nah], _f._ Sort of serge, everlasting.

sempiternamente [sem-pe-ter'-nah-men-tay], _adv._ Eternally.

sempiterno, na [sem-pe-terr'-no, nah], _a._ Eternal, everlasting, sempiternal.

sen, _m._ **sena** _f._ [sen, say'-nah], 1. _(Bot.)_ Senna, a purgative shrub. 2. _f._ Six marks on dice. -_pl._ **Senas,** double sixes.

Sena [say'-nah], _m._ The river Seine. See Appendix.

senado [say-nah'-do], _m._ 1. Senate, a council of senators. 2. Any meeting of grave persons. 3. Senate-house, town-hall.

senadoconsulto [say-nah-do-con-sool'-to], _m._ Senatus-consultum, degree of a senate.

senador [say-nah-dor'], _m._ Senator.

senaduría [say-nah-doo-ree'-ah], _f._ Senatorship, a senator's dignity.

senara [say-nah'-rah], _f._ A piece of sown ground, assigned to servants as part of their wages.

senarero [say-nah-ray'-ro], _m._ Servant who enjoys a piece of sown ground as part of his wages.

senario [say-nah'-re-o], _m._ A senary number; a verse consisting of six iambic feet.

senatorio, ria [say-nah-to'-re-o, ah], _a._ Senatorial.

senciente [sen-the-en'-tay], _pa. & a._ Sentient, perceiving.

sencillamente [sen-thel'-lya-men-tay], _adv._ Ingenuously, plainly, abstractedly.

sencillez [sen-theel-lyeth'], _f._ 1. Slightness, slenderness. 2. Simplicity, plainness, artlessness, harmlessness. 3. Silliness, weakness, ignorance.

sencillo, lla [sen-theel'-lyo, lyah], _a._ 1. Simple, unmixed, uncompounded. 2. Light, slight, thin, of light body (fabrics). 3. Silly, weak, easily imposed upon. 4. Ingenuous, plain, artless, harmless. 5. Simple, not ornate in style, expressing ideas naturally. 6. Single: applied to coin of less value than another of the same name. **Es muy sencillo,** it's very simple.

senda [sen'-dah], _f._ 1. Path, foot-path. 2. Means for attaining an end.

senderar [sen-day-rar'], _va._ To make a path. -_vn._ To walk on a path or footpath.

senderear [sen-day-ray-ar'], _va._ 1. To guide or conduct on a footpath. 2. To adopt extraordinary means to obtain an end. 3. To make a path.

sendero [sen-day'-ro], _m._ Path, footpath. V. SENDA.

sendica, illa, ita [sen-dee'-cah], _f. dim._ Little pathway.

sendos, das [sen'-dos, das], _a._ 1. Each of two, either, one each, each. 2. Great; abundant. **Les dio sendos libros,** she gave them a book each. **Con sendas peculiaridades,** each with its own peculiarity.

senectud [say-nec-tood'], _f._ Old age, senescence.

senescal [say-nees-cahl'], _m._ 1. Seneschal, lord high chamberlain or high steward. 2. Chief commander of a town, especially in time of war. 3. Chief chief of justice. It is used only in speaking of foreign countries.

senescalía [say-nes-cah-lee'-ah], _f._ Place, dignity, or employment of a seneschal.

senil [say-neel'], _a._ 1. Senile. 2. _(Ast.)_ Fourth quadrant of the celestial map.

seno [say'-no], *m.* 1. Chest, thoracic cavity; bosom. 2. Womb. **Seno materno**, womb. 3. Lap of a woman. 4. Circular space formed by moving round. 5. Hole, cavity, sinus. 6. Gulf, bay. 7. Any cavity in the interior of the human body. 8. Security, support; asylum, refuge. 9. *(Geom.)* The sine of an arc. 10. Sinus, cavity of a wound. 11. Center, middle part. 12. *(Naut.)* Curvature of a sail. **Seno recto**, sine. **Seno segundo**, cosine. **Seno todo** or **total,** total sine or radius. **Seno verso**, versed sine.

sensación [sen-sah-the-on'], *f.* Sensation, feeling. **Una sensación de placer**, a feeling of pleasure.

sensacional [sen-sah-the-o-nahl'], *a.* Sensational.

sensacionalismo [sen-sah-the-o-nah-lees'-mo], *m.* Sensationalism.

sensatez [sen-sah-teth'], *f.* Judiciousness, reasonableness, prudence, good sense.

sensato, ta [sen-sah'-to, tah], *a.* Sensible, judicious, prudent, reasonable, wise.

sensibilidad [sen-se-be-le-dahd'], *f.* Sensibility, quickness of perception, sensitiveness.

sensible [sen-see'-blay], *a.* 1. Sensitive. 2. Sensible, having the power of perceiving by the senses (que siente). 3. Sensitive, having sense or perception, but not reason. 4. Perceived by the mind. 5. Causing grief or pain. 6. Sensible, having quick intellectual feeling, easily moved or affected. 7. Regrettable (lamentable). 8. Perceptible (cambio), tangible (diferencia); heavy (golpe). **Un aparato muy sensible**, a very sensitive device. **Una sensible mejoría**, a noticeable improvement.

sensiblemente [sen-see'-blay-men-tay], *adv.* Sensibly, with grief or pain.

sensitiva [sen-se-tee'-vah], *f.* *(Bot.)* Sensitive plant.

sensitivo, va [sen-se-tee'-vo, vah], *a.* Sensitive; sensual; sensible.

sensorio [son-so'-re-o], *m.* Sensorium or sensory, the seat of sensation.

sensorio, ria [sen-so'-re-o, ah], *a.* Belonging to the sensorium.

sensual [sen-soo-ahl'], *a.* 1. Sensitive, having sense or perception. 2. Sensual (sexual), lewd, lustful. 3. Belonging to the carnal appetites.

sensualidad [sen-soo ah le-dahd'], *f.* Sensuality, lust, lewdness.

sensualismo [sen-soo-ah-lees'-mo], *m.* 1. Sensationalism, a doctrine opposed to idealism, which places the origin of ideas in the senses. 2. Sensuality.

sensualista [sen-soo-ah-lees'-tah], *a.* Sensualistic.

sensualmente [sen-soo-ahl'-men-tay], *adv.* Sensually, carnally.

sentada [sen-tah'-dah], *f.* Stone put in its proper place. *V.* ASENTADA.

sentadillas (A) [sen-tah-deel'-lyas], *adv.* With both legs on one side; side-saddlewise; as women ride horseback.

sentado, da [sn-tah'-do, dah], *a.* Sedate, judicious, grave, prudent. **Estar sentado**, to sit. **Dar algo por sentado**, to take something for granted.

sentamiento [sen-tah-me-ayn'-to], *m.* *(Arch.)* *V.* ASIENTO.

sentar [sen-tar'], *vn.* 1. To fit, to become, to suit (ropa). **Esta chaqueta no me sienta bien**, this coat does not fit me well. **Ese color le sienta bien a su cara**, that color suits her complexion well. **Sentar bien**, to down well. **A mí me sienta como un tiro**, it suits me like a hole in the head. *-va.* 2. To set up, to establish (cimientos). To seat (persona). *V.* ASENTAR. 4. To press down the seams of clothes, as tailors, with a goose. 5. To please, to be agreeable. 6. *(And. Carib.)* To crush (persona). 7. *(And.)* To rein in (caballo). **No le sentó bien la conversación**, the conversation did not please him. **Sentar las bases**, to lay the fundations. *-vr.* 1. To sink, to subside. *V.* ASENTARSE. 2. To sit down (persona), to squat, to seat oneself. 3. *(Coll.)* To fall plump upon one's breech. 4. To occupy the seat which belongs to one's plans or employment, to seat oneself in an office or dignity.

sentencia [sen-ten'-the-ah], *f.* 1. Sentence, the judicial decision of a suit at law, judgment; the penalty in a criminal case. 2. Opinion, persuasion of the mind. 3. Sentence, a maxim. 4. Sentence, a period in writing. **Decir sentencias a alguno**, to scold, to abuse one. **Fulminar la sentencia**, to pass judgment. **Sentencia de muerte**, death sentence.

sentenciar [sen-ten-the-ar'], *va.* 1. To sentence, to pass judgment; to condemn. 2. To oppress one's opinion. 3. To determine, to decide.

sentenciario [sen-ten-the-ah'-re-o], *m.* Collection of sentences.

sentención [sen-ten-the-on'], *f.* A severe, rigorous sentence.

sentenciosamente [sen-ten-the-o-sah'-men-tay], *adv.* Sententiously.

sentencioso, sa [sen-ten-the-o'-so, sah], *a.* Sententious (personas), pithy (dicho), axiomatic.

sentenzuela [sen-ten-thoo-ay' lah], *f. dim.* Slight sentence.

sentidamente [sen-tee'-dah-men-tay], *adv.* Feelingly, painfully.

sentido, da [sen-tee'-do, dah], *a.* 1. Sensible, fooling, expressive of sensibility. 2. Split, cloven, relaxed. 3. Putrefying. 4. *(Mex.)* Having good hearing (de buen oído). **Darse por sentido**, to show resentment. *-pp.* of SENTIR.

sentido [sen-tee'-do], *m.* 1. Sense (del cuerpo), the faculty of perceiving objects: any of the five senses. 2. Sense (juicio), understanding, reason. 3. Acceptation, signification, import, sense, meaning, construction. 4. Mode of understanding something, or the judgment made of it. 5. Intelligence or knowledge by which certain things are executed. 6. *(Mex.)* Ear (oreja). **Sentido común**, common sense. **Estar sentido**, *(Coll.)* to be miffed, to be a little offended. **Los cinco sentidos**, the five senses. **Perder el sentido**, to lose consciousness. **Sentido común**, common sense. **Iban en sentido inverso al nuestro**, they were traveling in the opposite direction to us.

sentimental [sen-te-men-tahl'], *a.* 1. Sentimental, affecting, pathetic. 2. Emotional, easily affected. 3. Sentimental, ridiculously affected.

sentimentalismo [sen-te-men-tah-lees'-mo], Sentimentalism, sentimentality.

sentir [sen-teer'], *va.* 1. To feel, to perceive by the senses (percibir). 2. To hear (oír). **Sin sentir**, without being seen, felt, or known. 3. To endure, to suffer (enfermedad). 4. To grieve, to regret (lamentar), to mourn, to be sorry for. **Sentir el ruido de un coche**, to hear the noise of a car. **Sin sentir frío**, without feeling the cold. *-vn.* 1. To judge, to form an opinion. 2. To foresee, to foreknow. 3. To accommodate the action to the expression, to exhibit a suitable feeling. *-vr.* 1. To be moved, to be affected, to complain. 2. To crack or flaw (vasos, campanas). 3. To be in a ruinous state. 4. To be sensible of, to feel pain in any part of the body; to acknowledge the obligation or necessity. 5. To resent. 6. *(Naut.)* To spring (mástil). **Sentirse como en su casa**, to feel at home. **Sentirse actor**, to feel oneself to be an actor. 7. *(LAm.)* To get cross (enfadarse).

sentir [sen-teer'], *m.* 1. Feeling, opinion, judgment. 2. *V.* SENTIMIENTO.

seña [say'-nyah], *f.* 1. Sign, mark (del cuerpo), token or note given without words, nod, dumb motion. 2. Signal, notice given by a sign. 3. Sign, a token of something. 4. *(Mil.)* Password, watchword. **Por señas, por más señas**, as a stronger proof of it. **Señas particulares**, identifying marks. **Hacer señas a uno**, to make a sign to somebody. **Hablar por señas**, to talk by signs.

señal [say-nyahl'], *f.* 1. Sign, mark, signature, token (indicio); mark or note of distinction. 2. Landmark to mark a boundary. 3. Sign, indication, symptom. **Señales claras o evidentes**, open marks. 4. Vestige, stamp, impression, footstep; scar. 5. Representation, image. 6. Earnest, handsel, pledge; earnest money given in token that a bargain is ratified. 7. *(Mil.)* Standard, banner. 8. Sign, wonder, prodigy, prognostic. 9. Signal, a sign to give notice. 10. A diagnostic or prognostic symptom. *-pl. (Naut.)* Signals. 11. *(LAm.)* Earmark. **Señales de bruma**, fog-signals. **Señales de peligro**, signals of distress. **En señal**, in proof of. **Ni señal**, not a trace. **Es buena señal**, it´s a good sign. **Hacer una señal grosera**, to make a rude sign. **Señal de peligro**, danger signal. **Señal de ocupado**, danger signal.

señaladamente [say-nyah-lah-dah'-men-tay]. *Adv.* Especially (especialmente), remarkably, namely; signally.

señalado, da [say-nyah-lah´-dah], *a. & pp.* of SEÑALAR. Famous, celebrated, noble. **Dejar señalado a uno**, to scar somebody permanently.

señalamiento [say-nyah-lah-me-en'-to], *m.* Assignation, determining or appointing a certain time or place.

señalar [say-nyah-lar'], *va.* 1. To stamp, to mark out (significar). 2. To sign decrees or despatches. 3. To signalize, to point out, to make known. 4. To speak positively, to say expressly. 5. To name, to nominate, to constitute; to fix; to determine. 6. To mark with a wound, especially in the face. 7. To make signals, to indicate. **Señalar con el dedo**, to point with the finger. **Señalan la llegada de la primavera**, they announce the arrival of spring. **Tuve que señalarle varios errores**, I had to point out several mistakes to him. *-vr.* 1. To distinguish oneself, to excel. 2. To mark the game at piquet. **Señalar los motivos de,** to account for.

señaleja [say-nyah-lay'-hah], *f. dim.* A little sign or mark.

señalero [say-nayh-lay'-ro], *m.* A person who formerly bore the royal ensign; king's ensign.

señas [say'-nyahs], *f. pl.* Address, residence of someone.

señolear [say-nyo-lay-ar'], *m.* To catch birds with a lure.

señor [say-nyor'], *m.* 1. Lord, master, or owner of a thing (de bienes). 2. Sir, a title given to an equal or inferior; mister. 3. God, the lord and master of all things. 4. Master; governor. **Quiere parecer un señor**, he tries to look like a gentleman. **El señor de la casa**, the master of the household. **El señor presidente**, the president. **Señor director**, the manager, the headmaster. **Muy señor mío**, Dear Sir.

señora [say-nyo'-rah], *f.* 1. Lady, a word of complaisance used of women. 2. Lady, mistress or owner of a thing (de bienes). 3. Madam: used in address to ladies of every degree. 4. Dame, gentlewoman. 5. Mother-in-law. 6. Mistress of a house or school. **Nuestra señora**, the Virgin Mary. **Muy señora mía**, Dear Madam.

señoreaje [say-nyo-ray-ah´-hay], *m.* 1. Seigniorage, acknowledgment of power. 2. Duty belonging to the king for the coining of money.

señoreante [say-nyo-ray-ahn´-tay], *pa.* Dominccring.

señorear [say-nyo-ray-ar'], *va.* 1. To master, to domineer (dominar), to lord, to rule despotically. 2. To excel, to occupy a higher station. 3. To treat another repeatedly with the title of lord. 4. To govern one´s passions. *-vr.* To affect peculiar gravity in one's deportment; to assume an air of importance (darse humos).

señoría [say-nyo-ree'-ah], *f.* 1. Lordship, a title given to persons of a certain rank and distinction (título). 2. Person to whom this title is given. 3. Government of a particular state; senate; prince. 4. Seigniory, a lordship.

señorial [say-nyo-re-ahl'], *a.* Manorial, manerial.

señoril [say-nyo-reel´], *a.* Lordly, belonging to a lord, genteel.

señorilmente [say-nyo-ril'-men-tay], *adv.* Nobly, grandly, majestically, lordly.

señorío [say-nyo-ree'-o], *m.* 1. Seigniory, dominion, command. 2. Imperiousness, arrogance of command. 3. Lordship, manor or territory belonging to a lord. 4. Gravity or stateliness of deportment. 5. Freedom and selfcontrol in action.

señorita [say-nyo-ree´-tah], *f. dim.* 1. Miss: a title of honor given to young ladies; a little, pretty, or amiable young lady. 2. Madam, a term of compliment used in addressing young ladies. 3. *(LAm.)* Schoolteacher (profesora).

señorito [say-nyo-ree'-to], *m. dim.* 1. Master: a title of honor given to young gentlemen, a little, pretty, or amiable young

lord. 2. Lordling, one who assumes an air of dignity and importance.

señorón, na [say-nyo-rone', nah], *m. & f. aug.* Great seignior or lady.

señuelo [say-nyoo-ay´-lo], *m.* Lure, enticement, attachment.

sépalo [say´-pah-lo], *(Both.)* Sepal, each division of the calyx.

separable [se-pah-rah'-blay], *a.* Separable.

separación [say-pah-rah-the-on´], *f.* 1. Separation. 2. Resignation, withdrawal. 3. Parting. **Separación de poderes**, separation of powers. **Separación racial**, racial segregation. **Separación entre registros**, *(Comput.)* interrecord gap, record gap. **Separación entre los caracteres (puntos)**, character pitch.

separadamente [say-pah-rah'-dah-men-tay], *adv.* Separately, severally.

separado, da [say-pah-rah'-do, data], *a. & pp.* of SEPARAR. Separate, separated. **Vive separado de su mujer**, he is separated from his wife.

separador, ra [say-pah-rah-dor', rah], *m. & f.* Separator, divider.

separar [say-pah-rar'], *va.* 1. To separate (objeto), to part, to divide, to cut, to chop, to hackle. 2. To separate, to set sports, to lay aside; to repose; to divorce. 3. To anatomize; to dissect in order to show or study the structure of animal bodies . **Los negocios le separan de su familia**, business keeps him away from his family. *-vr.* To separate, to part (componentes), to be disunited; to come off, to go off, to fly off; to withdraw, to drop all communication and intercourse to retire, to sequester. **Separarse de un grupo**, to leave a group. **Se ha separado de su mujer**, he has left his wife.

separatista [say-pah-rah-tees´-tah], *a. & n.* Separatist, laboring to part a territory or colony from the capital.

separativo, va, **separatorio, ria** [say pa-rah-tee´-vo, vah], *a.* That which separates, separators.

sepedón [say-pay-done'], *m.* Seps, a kind of serpent.

sepelio [say-pay'-le-o], *m.* Burial by the church of the faithful.

sepia [say'-pe-ah], *f.* 1. *(Zool.)* Cuttlefish. *V.* JIBIA. 2. Sepia, a coloring matter obtained from the cuttle-fish, and used in water-colors.

sepsis [sep´-sis], *f. (Med.)* Sepsis.

septenario [sep-tay-nah´-re-o], *m.* 1. Septenary, septenarious, of seven figures. 2. Of seven elements. *-m.* Space of seven days, seven years, etc.

septenio [sep-tay´-ne-o], *m.* Space of seven years.

septentrión [sep-ten-tre-on'], *m.* 1. Septentrion, the north; that part of the sphere which extends from the equator to the arctic pole. 2. *(Naut.)* North wind. 3. *(Ast.)* The Great Bear.

septentrional [sep-ten-tre-o-nahl´], *a.* Septentrional, northern, north, northerly.

septicemia [sep-te-thay´-me-ah], *f. (Med.)* Septicemia, blood poisoning.

séptico, ca [sep'-te-co, cah], *a.* Septic, septical, productive of putrefaction.

septiembre [sep-te-em'-bray], *m.* September.

séptima [sep'-te-mah], *f.* 1. Sequence of seven cards, in the game of piquet. 2. *(Mus.)* The interval of a seventh.

séptimo, ma [sep'-te-mo, mah], *a.* Seventh, the ordinal number of seven; one of the seven parts into which a whole is divided.

septo [sep'-to], *m. (Anat.)* Septum.

septuagenario, ria [sep-tooth-hay-nah´-re-o, ah], *a.* Septuagenary, seventy years old.

septuagésima [sep-too-ah-hay´-se-mah], *f.* The third Sunday before the first Sunday in Lent.

septuagésimo, ma [sep-too-ah-hay´-se-mo, mah], *a.* 1. Seventieth, the ordinal number of seventy. 2. Septuagesimal, consisting or seventy.

septuplicación [sep-too-ple-cah-the-on'], *f* Multiplying by seven.

septuplicar [sep-too-ple-car'], *va.* To make seven-fold; to multiply by seven.

séptuplo, pla [sep'-too-plo, plah], *a.* Septuple, seven-fold.

sepulcral [say-pool-crahl'], *a.* Sepulchral, monumental.

sepulcro [say-pool'-cro], *m.* 1. Sepulcher, grave, tomb. 2. A small chest in which the sacred host is preserved in Roman Catholic churches. 3. *(Met.)* An unhealthy country.

sepultación [say-pool-tah-the-on'], *f.* Sepulture: Interment.

sepultador [say-pool-tah-dor'], *m.* Burier, grave-digger.

sepultar [say-pol-tar'], *va* 1. To bury (enterrar), to inter, to entomb. 2. To hide (esconder), to conceal.

sepultura [say-pool-too´-rah], *f.* 1. Sepulture, interment. 2. Tomb, grave (tumba).

sepulturero [say-pool-too-ray'-ro], *m.* Grave-digger, sexton.

sequedad [say-kay-dahd'], *f.* 1. Aridity, dryness. 2. Barrenness, sterility, scarcity of provisions in a country. 3. Defect in nutrition of a member. 4. Asperity of intercourse, sourness of temper, abruptness: dryness of style. 5. Want of devotion and fervor in spiritual matters.

sequedad, sequeral [say-kay-dahd', say-kay-rahl'], *m.* A dry, barren soil.

sequero [say-kay'-ro], *m.* 1. Dry, unirrigated arable ground. 2. *V.* SECADERO.

sequeroso, sa [say-kay-ro'-so, sah], *a.* Dry, wanting moisture.

sequete [say-kay'-tay], *m.* 1. Piece of hard, dry bread. 2. Harshness and asperity of address or intercourse. 3. A violent shock.

sequía [say-kee'-ah], *f.* Dryness; thirst, drought (falta de lluvias). *V.* SEQUEDAD.

sequillo [say-keel'-lyo], *m.* Biscuit made of flour and sugar.

sequío [say-kee'-o], *m.* Dry, unirrigated arable ground.

séquito [say-ke-to], *m.* 1. Retinue (comitiva), suite. 2. Popularity, public applause.

sequizo, za [say-kee'-tho, thah], *a.* Dry: applied to fruits and other eatables that are not juicy.

ser [serr], *vn.* 1. To be: an auxiliary verb, by which the passive is formed. 2. To be in some place or situation. 3. To be or to exist really. 4. To be, to happen, to occur, to fall out. **¿Cómo fue eso?** how did that happen? 5. To be worth. **¿A cómo es eso?** what is the price of that? 6. To be born in a place; to originate in (origen). **¿De dónde es usted? - Soy de Sevilla,** where are you from? - I am from Seville. 7. To affirm or deny. 8. To be the property of one, to belong to, to pertain (posesión). 9. To be useful, to serve, to contribute to anything. 10. Joined to nouns which signify employment or occupation, it means to be occupied in them. **Ya sea de este modo o de otro,** whether it be this way or the other. **Sea lo que fuere,** be that as it may. **En ser,** in being, in existence. **Ser uno de tantos,** to be one of the number. **Es quien es,** or **se porta como quien es,** he is what he ought to be, or he behaves as he should. **Ser cómplice de,** to have a hand in. **Ser para todo,** to be fit for everything; to be up to everything. **¿Qué es del libro?** where is the book? **Mañana será otro día,** tomorrow may bring better luck. **Ser uña y carne,** to be hand and glove, to be close friends. **Eso no es de la incumbencia de Vd.,** that does not concern you; it is none of your business. **Es difícil,** it´s difficult. **Ese coche no es para correr mucho,** that car isn´t made to go very fast. **Somos seis,** there are six of us. **Fue construido,** it was built. **Ser o no ser,** to be or not to be. **Es de desear que,** it is to be wished that...**Está siendo estudiado, it's being examined.**

ser [serr], *m.* Being, the entity, essense, or nature of things; vague; point or burden of a piece.

sera [say'-rah], *f.* A large pannier or basket.

serado [say-rah´-do], *m.* A parcel of panniers or baskets.

seráfico, ca [say-rah´-fe-co, cah], *a.* Seraphic, angelic (angélico): applied especially to St. Francis and his religionists.

serafín [say-rah-feen'], *m.* 1. Seraph, seraphim, angel. 2. An extreme beauty.

serafina [say-rah-fee'-nah], *f.* A Port of swan-skill, resembling fine baize.

seraje [say-rah´-hay], *m.* Panniers or baskets, especially of charcoal.

serape [say-ra´-pay], *m.* *(Mex.)* A narrow blanket, worn by men, or thrown over the saddle. *V.* MANGA.

serapino [say-rah-pee´-no], *m.* A sort of gum, obtained by incision from the fennel-giant.

serasa [say-rah'-sah], *f.* Chintz. *V.* ZARAZA.

serasquier [say-ras-ke-err'], *m.* Seraskier, a Turkish generalissimo.

serba [serr´-bah], *f.* Service, a kind of wild pear, the fruit of the service-tree.

serbal, serbo [ser-bahl', serr'-boh], *m.* *(Bot.)* Service-tree. **Serbal de cazadores,** mountain-ash service-tree.

serena [say-ray´-nah], *f.* Evening dew. **A la serena,** *V.* AL SERENO.

serenamente [say-ray'-nah-men-tay], *adv.* Serenely, composedly, coolly, quietly.

serenar [say-ray-nar'], *va. & vn.* 1. To clear up, to grow fair, to become serene (tiempo). 2. To settle, to grow clear. 3. To pacify, to tranquilize (tranquilizar), to moderate, to compose; to be serene.

serenata [say-ray-nah'-tah], *f.* Serenade, concert, night-music.

serenero [say-ray-nay'-ro], *m.* Night-wrap, a loose cover which ladies used to throw over the head at night.

serení [say-ray-nee'], *m.* 1. A light boat on board large vessels, used for greater despatch. 2. A yawl.

serenidad [say-ray-ne-dahd'], *f.* 1. Serenity, the clearness of mild and temperate weather. 2. Serene highness, a title given to princes. 3. Serenity, meekness, mildness, sereneness, serenitude. 4. *V.* DESVERGÜENZA.

serenísimo, ma [say-ray-nee'-se-mo, mah], *a. sup.* 1. Most serene, honorary title of princes, or kings' children. 2. Extremely serene, calm, or quiet.

sereno [say-ray'-no], *m.* 1. Evening dew, night dew (rocío). 2. Night-watch, watchman (persona). 3. Settled (tiempo); cloudless (cielo). **Estar sereno,** to be sober. **Dormir al sereno,** to sleep out in the open.

serial [say-re-ahl'], *m.* Serial.

seriamente [say'-re-ah-men-tay]. *adv.* Seriously, gravely, solemnly, in earnest, for good and all.

sericícola [say-re-thee´-co-lah], *a.* Sero-cultural, relating to silk culture.

sericicultura [say-re-the-cool-too'-rah], *f.* Silk-culture, sericiculture.

sérico, ca [say´-re-co, cah], *a.* Silken.

serie [say´-re-ay], *f.* Series, order, gradation, sequence, suite. **Fabricar en serie,** to mass-produce. **Artículos fuera de serie,** goods left over.

seriedad [say-re-ay-dahd'], *f.* 1. Seriousness, gravity (gravedad). 2. Sternness of mien, rudeness of address. 3. Simplicity, plainness, sincerity. 4. Dignity (dignidad). **Falta de seriedad,** frivolity.

serigrafía [say-re-gah-fee'-ah], *f.* Silk-screen process.

serijo, serillo [say-ree'-ho, say reel'-lyo], *m.* A small basket made of palm-leaves.

serio, ria [say´-re-o, ah], *a.* 1. Serious (actitud, expresión), grave, dignified. 2. Serious, important, weighty. 3. Grand, majestic, solemn. 4. Uncouth, rude, severe, gold. 5. Plain, true, sincere. **Ponerse serio,** to look serious. **Un traje serio,** a formal suit. **Es una persona poco seria,** he's a very irresponsible sort.

sermocinal [ser-mo-the-nahl'], *a.* Oratorical, relating to a public speech.

sermón [ser-mon'], *m.* 1. Sermon, homily. 2. Censure, reprehension.

sermonario, ria [ser-mo-nah'-re-o, ah], *a.* Relating to a sermon.

sermonario [ser-mo-nah'-re-o], *m.* Collection of sermons.

sermonear [ser-mo-nay-ar´], *va.* *(Coll.)* To lecture, to censure, to reprimand; to sermonize.

sermonización [ser-mo-ne-thah-the-on´], *f.* Speaking in public; colloquy, conversation.

seroja. *f.* **serojo,** *m.* [say-ro´-hah, ho]. A withered leaf, fallen from a tree. **serojas,** small trees left on a piece of woodland, after the large trees have been cut down.

serón [say-rone´], *m.* 1. A large frail or pannier used to carry figs, raisins, etc.; seroon. 2. Hamper, crate.

seronero [say-ro-nay´-ro], *m.* The maker of trails or panniers called *serones.*

serosidad [say-ro-se-dahd´], *f.* Serosity, serousness, thin or watery blood.

seroso, sa [say-ro´-so, sah], *a.* Serous, thin, watery.

serotino, na [say-ro-tee´-no, nah], *a.* Serotinous, produced late in the season.

serpa [serr´-pah], *f.* Layer, a long twig or spray of vine planted in the ground, without being separated from the mother plant, in order to rage another stock.

serpear [ser-pay-ar´], *vn.* To wind like a serpent, to move in undulations, to crawl, to creep; to meander, to serpentize.

serpentaria [ser-pen-tah´-re-ah], *vn.* (*Bot.*) Snake-root, a medicine root.

serpentario [ser-pen-tah´-re-o], *m.* A northern constellation: the constellation Ophiuchus.

serpentear [ser-pen-tay-ar´], *vn.* To move like a serpent, to serpentine.

serpenticida [ser-pen-te-thee´-dah], *com.* Serpent-killer.

serpentígero, ra [ser-pen-tee´-hay-ro, rah], *a.* (*Poet.*) Serpentigerous, bearing serpents.

serpentín [ser-pen-ten´], *m.* 1. (*Min.*) Serpentine, a speckled green stone resembling the serpent's skin. 2. Cock, hammer of a gun or musketlock. 3. (*Chem.*) Worm for distilling liquors. 4. Serpent, a musical instrument; a wind-instrument of low pitch, now disused. 5. Ancient piece of ordnance.

serpentina [ser-pen-tee´-nah], *f.* 1. Cock, hammer of a gun-rock. 2. Culverin, missile weapon. 3. (*Chem.*) Serpentine, or worm for distilling liquors.

serpentinamente [ser-pen-tee´-nah-men-tay], *adv.* In a serpentine manner.

serpentino, na [ser-pen-tee´-no, nah], *a.* 1. Serpentine, winding like a serpent; resembling a serpent; belonging to the oil of serpents. 2. Applied to a slanderous tongue. 3. Serpentine: applied to a kind of marble.

serpentón [ser-pen-tohn´], *m.* 1. (*Aug.*) A large serpent. 2. A musical instrument. *V.* SERPENTÍN.

serpia [serr´-pe-ah], *f.* (*Prov.*) Gummy or viscous matter of a vine-stock.

serpiente [ser-pe-en´-tay], *f.* 1. Serpent (culebra). **Serpiente de cascabel,** rattle-snake. 2. Serpent, devil, Satan.

serpiginoso, sa [ser-pe-he-no´-so, sah], *a.* (*Med.*) Serpiginous.

serpigo [ser-pee´-go], *m.* (*Med.*) Tetter, ring-worm, serpigo.

serpol [ser-pole´], *m.* (*Bot.*) Wild thyme.

serpollo [ser-pol´-lyo], *m.* Shoot, sprout especially of a tree which has been pruned.

serradizo, za [ser-rah-dee´-tho, thah], *a.* Fit to be sawed.

serrado, da [ser-rah´-do, dah], *a.* Serrate, toothed like a saw, laciniate. *-pp.* of SERRAR.

serrador [ser-rah-dor´], *m.* Sawer or sawyer. *V.* ASERRADOR.

serradoras [ser-rah-do´-ras], *f. pl.* Sawdust. *V.* SERRÍN.

serrallo [ser-rahl´-lyo], *m.* 1. Seraglio, the palace of the grand signior. 2. Place of obscenity. (*Per.*)

serranía [ser-ah-nee´-ah], *f.* Ridge of mountains, a mountainous country.

serraniego, ga [ser-rah-ne-ar´-go, gah], *a.* *V.* SERRANO.

serranil [ser-rah-neel´], *m.* Kind of knife.

serrano, na [ser-rah´-no, nah], *a. & m. & f.* Mountaineer, highlander, inhabiting mountains.

serrar [ser-rar´], *va.* To saw. *V.* ASERRAR. (*Yo sierro, yo sierre,* from *Serrar.* *V.* ACERTAR.)

serreta [ser-ray´-tah], *f.* 1. Dim. of SIERRA. 2. Piece of a cavesson or nose-band, used in breaking a horse.

serrato, ta [ser-rah´-to, tah], *a.* (*Anat.*) Denticulated, serrated.

serrezuela [ser-ray-thoo-ay´-lah], *f. dim.* A small saw.

serrijón [ser-re-hone´], *m.* Short chain of mountains.

serrín [ser-reen´], *m.* Sawdust. *V.* ASERRADURAS.

serrino, na [ser-ree´-no, nah], *a.* 1. Belonging to chains of mountains. 2. Applied to a quick, irregular pulse.

serrucho [ser-roo´-cho], *m.* Hand-saw with a small handle. **Serrucho braguero,** pit-saw.

servador [ser-vah-dor´], *m.* Preserver: applied by poets to Jupiter..

serventesio [ser-ven-tay´-se-o], *m.* (*Poet.*) Quartetto, like the first four verses of an octave.

servible [ser-vee´-blay], *a.* Fit for service, serviceable, adaptable.

servicial [ser-ve-the-ahl´], *a.* Obsequious, diligent, obliging, compliant, friendly, accommodating, serviceable. *m.* (*Coll.*) Clyster.

servicialmente [ser-ve-the-ahl´-men-tay], *adv.* Obsequiously, serviceably.

serviciar [ser-ve-the-ar´], *va.* To collect the sheep-walk dues, donations to the state, etc.

servicio [ser-vee´-the-o], *m.* 1. Service, the act of serving; the state of a servant. 2. Service, favor, kind office; good turn. 3. Divine service. 4. Utility, benefit, advantage. 5. Close-stool, privy-chair. 6. Service, cover, course. **Servicio de mesa,** service for the table. 7. Personal service or residence of beneficed clergy. 8. Toilet. 9. Service (en hotel). 12. Serve, service (tenis). 13. Job, case (de policía). **Estar al servicio de,** to be in the service of. **Hacer un servicio para uno,** to do somebody a service. **Servicio a domicilio,** delivery service. **Servicio incluido,** service charge included. 14. (*Comput.*) **Servicio de asistencia en materia de software,** software support service. **Servicio de asistencia telefónica,** phone assistance. **Servicio y apoyo,** service and support.

servidero, ra [ser-ve-day´-ro, rah], *a.* 1. Fit for service, utilizable. 2. Requiring personal attendance.

servido, da [ser-vee´-do, dah], *a. & pp.* of SERVIR. 1. Served, pleased. 2. Second-hand, used.

servidor [ser-ve-dor´], *m.* 1. Servant (criado), waiter. 2. One who politely tenders his services to another. **Servidor de Vd.,** your servant; at your service. 4. Pan of a close-stool.

servidora [ser-ve-do´-rah], *f.* 1. Maid, female servant. 2. A term of courtesy used by women.

servidumbre [ser-ve-doom´-bray], *f.* 1 Attendance, servitude (estado); whole establishment of servants. 2. Slavery, mancipation, state of a slave. 3. Mighty or inevitable obligation to do anything. 4. Servitude, service, the act of serving or attending at command. 5. (*Law.*) Right which one has over another person or thing, as the liberty of passing through a house or garden; right of way. 6. Subjection of the passions.

servil [ser-veel´], *a. & m.* 1. Servile (actitud), slavish (imitación), fawning; sneaking. 2. Servile, peculiar to servants, dependent, menial. 3. Servile, low, mean, abject; mechanical.

servilidad [ser-ve-le-dahd´], *f.* (*Prov.*) Servility, meanness, baseness, submision from fear.

servilismo [ser-ve-lees´-mo], *m.* Servilism, blind adhesion to authority.

servilmente [ser-veel´-men-tay], *adv.* Servilely, slavishly; basely; indecently.

servilla [ser-veel´-lyah], *f.* A kind of thin-soled shoe.

servilleta [ser-veel-lyay´-tah], *f.* Napkin used at table.

servilletero, ra [ser-veel-lyay-tah´-ro, rah], *a.* Relating to table-linen.

servio, via [serr´-ve-o, ah], *a.* Servian, native of or relating to Servia.

serviola [ser-ve-o´-lah], *f.* (*Naut.*) Cathead, anchor beam.

servir [ser-veer´], *va.* 1. To serve, to perform menial services. **Servir de mayordomo,** to serve as steward. 2. To serve, to do a favor or kind office. To serve (en restaurante), to hold an employment, to occupy a public station. 4. To court a lady. 5. To serve, to perform somebody else's functions; to act as a substitute. 6. To serve (comida), to wait at table. 9. To heat the oven. l0. To dress victuals for the table. 11. To administer. **Para servir a Vd.**, at your service. **Servir de,** to serve for. **Servir a la patria,** to serve one´s country. **Servir patatas a uno,** to serve somebody with potatoes. *-vn.* 1. To serve, to be in the services of another (criado), to be subject to another. 2. To correspond, to agree. 3. To serve, to answer the purpose; to conduce; to be useful or convenient (ser útil). 4. To serve, to be a soldier. 5. To be employed at anything by another's orders. **Sirvió 10 años,** he served 10 years. **No sirve para nada,** it´s no use at all. *-vr.* 1. To deign, to vouchsafe, to condescend, to please. **Sirva de aviso,** let this be a warning. 2. To make use of; to employ for some purpose. **Sírvase usted darme su dirección,** please give me your address. **Yo no serviría para futbolista,** I'd be no good as a footballer. **Si el señor se sirve pasar por aquí,** if the gentleman would care to come this way.

servo [ser-vo], *m.* Servo.

servoasistido [ser-vo-ah-sees-tee'-do], *m.* Servo-assisted.

servodirección [ser-vo de-rayc-the-on'], *m. f.* Power steering.

servofreno [ser-vo-fray'-no], *m.* Power brake.

servomotor [ser-vo-mo-tor'], *m.* Servomotor.

sesada [say-sah'-dah], *f.* Fried brains.

sésamo [say'-sah-mo], *m.* Sesame, gingili, an annual herb the seeds of which yield a bland oil.

sesalpil [say-sah-peel'], *m.* Sex-appeal.

sesear [say-say-ar´], *vn.* To pronounce the *c* (before *e* and *i*) and *z* as *s*, (a feature of the Andalusian and South American countries).

seseli [say-say'-le], *m.* (*Bot.*) Wild spicknel, seseli.

sesenta [say-scn'-tah], *m.* Sixty, figures of 60.-*a.* Sixty, sixtieth.

sesentavo, va [say-sen-tah'-vo, vah], *a. &: n.* One-sixtieth; a sixtieth part.

sesentón, na [say-sen-tone´, nah], *m. & f. & a.* One turned of sixty, sexagenalian, sixty years old.

sesera [sary-say´-rah], *f.* 1. Brain-pan. 2. The entire brain.

sesga [ses'-gah], *f.* Gore or goring.

sesgadamente [ses-gah-dah-men-tay], *adv.* Slantwise, slopwise, slopingly. *V.* SESGAMENTE.

sesgado, da [ses-gah'-do, dah], *a. & pp.* of SESGAR. Sloped, oblique, slanting.

sesgadura [ses-gah-doo´-rah], *f.* Slope, the act of sloping.

sesgamente [ses'-gah-men-tay], *adv.* Obliquely, slopingly; mildly.

sesgar [ses-gar'], *va.* To slope (inclinar), to cut slantwise, to take or give an oblique direction.

sesgo, ga [ses´-go, gah], *a.* 1. Sloped, oblique, turned or twisted obliquely. 2. Serene, tranquil, unruffled. 3. Severe of aspect, grave, uncouth. **Al sesgo,** slopingly, obliquely.

sesgo [ses-go], *m.* 1. Slope, obliqueness, oblique direction. 2. Mean medium.

sesil [say-seel´], *a.* (*Bot.*) Sessile, joined to the stem without any stalk.

sesión [say-se-on'], *f.* 1. Session, sitting, meeting of a council or congress. 2. Conference, consultation. **Abrir la sesión,** to open the meeting. **Celebrar una sesión,** to hold a meeting.

sesma [ses'-mah], *f.* 1. The sixth part of a yard or any other thing. 2. A division of territory. 3. *V.* SEXMA.

sesmero [ses-may´-ro], *m.* A person appointed to manage the public affairs, belonging to the district called *sesma* or *sesmo. V.* SEXMERO.

sesmo [ses´-mo], *m.* 1. A division of territory in some Spanish provinces. 2. *V.* LINDE.

seso [say'-so], *m.* 1. The brain: generally used in the plural. 2. Brain. understanding, prudence, wisdom. 3. Stone put under a pot to keep it steady on the fire. **No tener seso,** not to have common sense. **Tener los sesos de un mosquito, de un chorlito,** not to have the brains of a sparrow.

sesqui [ses'-ke]. (*Lat.*) Used in composition, and implying one and a half, as *sesquihora,* an hour and a half.

sesquiáltero, ra [ses-ke-ahl'-tay-ro, rah], *a.* Sesquialter, one and a half.

sesquidoble [ses-ke-do'-blay], *a.* Two and a half times.

sesquimodio [ses-ke-mo'-de-o], *m.* A bucket and a half.

sesquióxido [ses-ke-ok'-se-do], *m.* Sesquioxide.

sesquipedal [ses-ke-pay-dahl'], *a.* Sesquipedal, sesquipedalian, a foot and a half in length.

sesquiplicado, da [ses-ke-ple-cah'-do, dah], *a.* Sesquiplicate.

sesteadero [ses-tay-ah-day'-ro], *m.* A proper place for taking a nap after dinner; resting-place for cattle.

sestear [ses-tay-ar´], *vn.* To take a nap or rest after dinner.

sestero [ses-tay´-ro], *m. V.* SESTEADERO.

sesudamente [say-soo'-dah-men-tay], *adv.* Maturely, wisely, prudently

sesudo, da [say-soo'-do, dah], *a.* Judicious, discreet, prudent, wise.

seta [say'-tah], *f.* 1. Bristle, the stiff hair of swine. 2. (*Bot.*) A general name for all the species of mushroom (hongo): it is given particularly to the field agaric, agaricus campestris: called also in Spanish *seta de cardo.* 3. Blobber-lip. *V.* JETA. 4. Snuff of a candle.

sete [say'-tay], *m.* Mint, or office where money is struck with a die.

setecientos, tas [say-tay-the-en'-tos, tas], *a. & n.* Seven hundred.

setena [say-tay'-nah], *f.* Seven things of a kind. *-pl.* A punishment by which, anciently, seven-fold payment was obligated.

setenta [say-ten'-tah], *a.* Seventy.

setentavo, va [say-ten-tah'-vo, vah], *a. & n.* One-seventieth; a seventieth part.

setentón, na [say-ten-tone', nah], *a. & n.* Seventy years old; turned of seventy.

setentrión [say-ten-tre-on'], *m.* Septentrion, the north; the north wind.

setentrional [say-ten-tre-o-nahl'], *a.* Septentrional, northern, northerly.

setero, ra [say-tay'-ro, rah], *a.* Bristly, hairy.

setiembre [say-te-em'-bray], *m. V.* SEPTIEMBRE.

sétima [say'-te-mah], *f. V.* SÉPTIMA.

sétimo, ma [say'-te-mo, mah], *a.* Seventh. *V.* SÉPTIMO, MA.

seto [say'-to], *m.* Fence (cercado), defence, inclosure. **Seto vivo,** hedge, quickset.

setuagenario, ria [say-too-ah-hay-nah'-re-o]. *V.* SEPTUAGENARIO.

setuagésimo, ma [say-too-ah-hay'-se-mo], *a. V.* SEPTUAGÉSIMO.

setuplicar [say-too-ple-car'], *va. V.* SETUPLICAR.

sétuplo, pla [say-too-plo], *a. V.* SÉPTUPLO.

seudo [say-oo'-do], *a.* Pseudo, false.

seudomédico [say-oo-do-may'-do-co], *m.* Charlatan, quack.

seudomorfo, fa [say-oo-do-mor'-fo, fah], *a.* Pseudomorphous.

seudónimo, ma [say-oo-do'-ne-mo, mah], *a.* Pseudonymous, fictitious. *-m.* Pseudonym, pen name.

severamente [say-vay'-rah men tay], *adv.* Severely.

severidad [say-vay-re-dahd'], *f.* 1. Severity, rigor, harshness, austerity, acerbity. 2. Severity, strictness, punctuality, exactness. 3. Gravity, seriousness.

severizarse [say-vay-re-thar'-say], *vr.* To become serious or grave.

severo ra [say-vay'-ro, rah], *a.* 1. Severe (carácter), rigorous, rigid, harsh (invierno). 2. Grave, serious. 3. Severe, punctual, exact, strict.

sevillano, na [say-veel-lyah'-no, nah], *a.* Of Seville, Sevillan.

sexagenario, ria [sek-sah-hay-nah'-re-o, ah], *a.* Sexagenary, sixty years old.

sesagésima [sek-sah-hay'-se-mah], *f.* Sexagesima, second Sunday before Lent.

sexagésimo, ma [sek-sah-hay'-se-mo, mah], *a*. Sexagesimal, sixtieth.

sexagonal [sek-sah-go-nahl'], *a*. Sexagonal.

sexángulo, la [sek-sahn'-goo-lo, lah], *a*. Sexangular. *-m*. Sexangle.

sexenio [sek-say'-ne-o], *m*. Space of six years.

sexo [sek'-so], *m*. 1. Sex, the organic difference between male and female. 2. Womankind, by way of emphasis. **El sexo débil**, the gentle sex. **El sexo masculino**, the male sex.

sexología [sek-so-lo-hee'-ah], *f*. Sexology.

sexólogo, ga [sek-so'-lo-go], *m & f*. Sexologist.

sexta [sex'-tah], *f*. 1. One of the hours into which the Hebrews, and Romans divided the artificial day, and including three of the hours now used. 2. A sequence of six cards at the game of piquet. 3. Sixth, one of the minor canonical hours after tierce.

sextante [sex-tahn'-tay], *m*. 1. Coin weighing two ounces. 2. Sextant, an astronomical instrument.

sextario [sex-tah'-re-o], *m*. Ancient measure.

sextercio [sex-ter'-the-o], *m*. *V*. SESTERCIO.

sextil [sex-teel'], *a*. *(Astro.)* Sextile.

sextilla [sex-teel'-lyah], *f*. Sextain, a Spanish metrical composition of six feet.

sextina [sex-tee'-nah], *f*. A kind of Spanish metrical composition.

sexto, ta [sex'-to, tah], *a*. Sixth, the ordinal number of six. *-m*. Book containing canonical decrees.

sexual [sex-soo-ahl'], *a*. Sexual.

sexualidad [sec-soo-ah-le-dahd'], *f*. 1. Sexuality. 2. Sex (sexo). **Determinar la sexualidad**, to determine the sex of.

si [see], *conj*. If, although; in case that, provided that, unless, when. **Si bien**, although. *V*. AUNQUE. **Si acaso, por si acaso**, if by chance. **Si no**, if not, otherwise.

sí [see], *adv*. Yes, yea; without doubt indeed. *-m*. 1. Assent, consent, permission. 2. *(Mus.)* Si, the seventh note of the scale. **Dar el sí**, to say yes: to promise to marry. **Creo que sí**, I think so. **Porque sí**, because that's the way it is.

sí, *pronoun*. Reflexive form of the personal pronoun of the third person, in both genders and numbers; employed in oblique cases and always with a preposition. Himself, herself themselves. **De por sí**, apart, separately. **De sí**, of itself; spontaneously. **Lo quieren todo para sí**, they want the whole lot for themselves. **No lo tiene en sí misma**, she doesn't have it in her. **Ella lo quiere para sí**, she wants it for herself.

siampán [se-am-pam'], *m*. Dye-stuff produced in the province of this name.

sibarita [se-bah-ree'-tah], *com*. Sybarite, a native of Sybaris. *-a*. Given to pleasures, luxurious, sensuous.

sibarítico, ca [se-ba-ree'-te-co, cah], *a*. 1. Sybaritical, luxurious. 2. Sensual.

sibil [se-beel'], *m*. A small cellar under ground (sótano), where wine, water, or other things are kept fresh.

sibila [se-bee'-lah], *f*. Prophetess; sibyl.

sibilante [se-be-lahn'-tay], *a*. *(Poet.)* Sibilant, hissing.

sibilino, na [se-be-lee'-no, nah], *a*. Sibylline.

sibucao [se-boo-cah'-o], *m*. Sapan-tree which furnishes a dye-wood: it belongs to the leguminosae. *Cf*. SAPÁN.

sicamor [se-cah-mor'], *m*. *(Bot.)* European Judas-tree.

sicario [se-cah'-re-o], *m*. A paid assassin. *Cf*. SEIDE.

siciliano, na [se-the-le-ah'-no, nah], Sicilian, relating to Sicily.

siclo [see'-clo], *m*. Shekel, an ancient Jewish coin.

sicoanálisis [se-co-ah-nah'-le-sis], *f*. *V*. PSICOANÁLISIS.

sicofanta [se-co-fahn'-tay], *m*. Sycophant, flatterer, parasite.

sicología [se-co-lo-hee'-ah], *f*. *V*. PSICOLOGÍA.

sicológico, ca [se-co-lo'-he-co, cah], *a*. *V*. PSICOLÓGICO.

sicólogo, ga [se-co'-lo-go, gah], *m. & f*. *V*. PSICÓLOGO.

sicomoro [se-co'-mo-ro], *m*. *(Bot.)* Sycamore, the mulberry-leaved fig-tree.

siconeurótico, ca [se-coh-nay-oo-roh'-te-co, cah], *a*. *V*. PSICONEURÓTICO.

sicópata [se-co'-pah-tah], *m*. *V*. PSICÓPATA.

sicopático, ca [se-co-pah'-te-co, cah], *a*. *V*. PSICOPÁTICO.

sicosis [se-co'-sis], *f*. *V*. PSICOSIS.

sicoterapia [se-co-tay-rah'-pe-ah], *f*. *V*. PSICOTERAPIA.

SIDA [see'-dah], *m*. abr. de **síndrome de inmuno-deficiencia adquirida** (acquired immuno-deficiency syndrome, AIDS).

sideral [see-day-rahl'], *a*. Sidereal, astral, space. **Viajes siderales**, space travel.

sidéreo, rea [se-day'-ray-o, ah], *a*. Sidereal, starry.

siderismo [se-day-rees'-mo], *m*. *(Neol.)* Worship of the stars. *V*. SABEÍSMO.

sideritis [se-day-ree'-tis], *f*. Siderites, a mineral. **Sideritis** or **Sideritide**, *(Bot.)* iron-wort.

siderografía [se-day-ro-grah-fee'-ah], *f*. The art of engraving on steel.

siderotecnia [se-day-ro-tek'-ne-ah], Siderotechny, the art of working iron.

siderurgia [se-day-roor'-he-ah], *f*. Siderurgy.

siderúrgico, ca [se-day-roor'-he-co'-cah], *a*. Pertaining to iron and steel. **Industria siderúrgica**, iron and steel industry.

sidra [see'-drah], *f*. Cider.

sidrería [se-dray-ree'-ah], *f*. Cider bar.

siega [se-ay'-gah], *f*. Harvest (época), reaping time, mowing, fruits gathered.

siembra [se-em'-brah], *f*. 1. Seed-time. 2. Corn-field.

siempre [se-em'-pray], *adv*. 1. Always, at all times. 2. *(LAm.)* Certainly (seguramente). **Siempre jamás**, for ever and ever. **Como siempre**, as usual.

siempreviva [se-em-pray-vee'-vah], *f*. *(Bot.)* House-leek.

sien [se-ayn'], *f*. Temple, the upper part of the side of the head.

sierpe [se-err'-pay], *f*. 1. Serpent. *V*. SERPIENTE. 2. A shrew, peevish, clamorous, spiteful woman. 3. Anything which moves by undulation in a serpentine shape. 4. A peevish, fretful person. 5. *(Bot.)* Sucker.

sierra [se-er'-rah], *f*. 1. Saw. **Sierra de mano**, a panel-saw or hand-saw. **Sierra para metales**, hacksaw. **Sierra circular**, circular saw. **Sierra mecánica**, power saw. 2. Ridge of mountains and craggy rocks. 3. Waves rising mountain high in a storm. 4. *(Zool.)* Saw-fish. **Van a la sierra a pasar el fin de semana**, they're off to the mountains for the weekend.

sierrecilla [se-er-ray-theel'-lyah], *f*. *dim*. Small saw.

siervo, va [se-err'-vo, vah], *m. & f*. 1. Serf, slave, servant. 2. Servant by courtesy.

sieso [se-ay'-so], *m*. Fundament, anus.

siesta [se-es'-tah], *f*. 1. The hottest part of the day; the time for a nap after lunch; siesta, nap (sueñecito). 2. Sleep taken after lunch. **Echarse una siesta**, to have a siesta, nap, doze.

siete [se-ay'-tay], *a. & m*. 1. Seven. 2. Seventh. 3. Seven, the figure 7. 4. Card with seven figures. **De siete en siete**, by seven and seven. **Más que siete**, *(Coll.)* very much, in excess, too much. **Hablar más que siete**, to talk too much.

sieteañal [se-ay-tay-ah-nyahl'], *a*. Septennial.

sietedurmientes [se-ay-tay-door-me-en'-tes], *m. pl*. Seven sleepers, great sleeper.

sieteenrama [se-ay'-tay-en-rah'-mah], *f*. *(Bot.)* *V*. TORMENTILLA.

sietemesino, na [se-ay-tay-may-see'-no, nah], *a*. Born seven months after conception.

sietenal [se-ay-tay-nyahl'], *a*. Seven years old, septennial.

sífilis [see-fe-lis], *f*. Syphilis, a specific venereal disease; vulgarly, the pox.

sifilítico, ca [se-fe-lee'-te-co, cah], *a*. Syphilitic, relating to syphilis or affected by it.

sifón [se-fone'], *m*. 1. Siphon, a bent tube with unequal arms, for drawing liquids over the side of a cask or other vessel. 2. *(And.)* Beer (cerveza).

sigilación [se-he-lah-the-on'], *f*. Impression, mark.

sigilado, da [se-he-lah'-do, dah], *a*. Marked with some defect or affected by some disease. *-pp*. of SIGILAR.

sigilar [se-he-lar'], *va*. 1. To keep a thing secret. 2. To seal.

sigilo [se-hee'-lo], *m.* 1. Seal. *V.* SELLO. 2. Secret, secrecy, discretion. **Sigilo sacramental**, inviolable secrecy of the confession.

sigilosamente [se-he-lo'-sah-men-tay], *adv.* Silently, secretly.

sigiloso, sa [se-he-lo'-so, sah], *a.* Silent, reserved; keeping a secret.

sigla [see'-glah], *f.* Initial letter, employed as an abbreviation (in inscriptions, etc.).

siglo [see'-glo], *m.* 1. Century, a hundred years. 2. Age (época), duration of anything. 3. A very long time (largo tiempo). **Un siglo que no te veo,** I have not seen you for ages. **Por los siglos de los siglos,** for ever and ever. **Siglo de cobre,** the brazen age. **Siglo de hierro,** the iron age. **Siglo de plata,** the silver age. **Siglo de oro,** the golden age (Spain, about 1492-1660).

sigma [seeg'-mah], *f.* Sigma, eighteenth letter of the Greek alphabet, corresponding to *s*.

signáculo [sig-nah' coo-lo], *m.* Seal, signet.

signar [sig-nar'], *va.* To sign (firmar), to mark with a signet. -*vr.* To make the sign of the cross.

signatario, ria [sig-nah-tah'-re-o, ah], *a.* Signatory, signing. **Poderes signatarios,** authority to sign. -*m. & f.* Signatory, signer.

signatura [sig-nah-too'-rah], *f.* Sign, mark; signature in printing; a Roman tribunal.

significación [sig-ne-fe-cah-the-on'], *f.* 1. Signification, meaning expressed by a sign or word. 2. Signification, the act of making known by signs; significance. 3. *V.* SIGNIFICATIVO.

significado [sig-ne-fe-cah'-do], *m.* Signification, object signified by means of words.—**Significado, da,** *pp.* of SIGNIFICAR.

significador, ra [sig-ne-fe-cah-dor', rah], *m. & f.* One who signifies.

significante [sig-ne-fe-cahn'-tay], *a.* Significant, expressive.

significantemente [sig-ne-fe-cahn'-tay-men-tay], *adv. V.* SIGNIFICATIVAMENTE.

significar [sig-ne-fe-car'], *va.* 1. To signify, to denote, to mean (palabra). 2. To declare, to make known (expresar). 3. To import, to be worth. -*vr.* To become known (distinguirse).

significativamente [sig-ne-fe-cah-tee'-vah-men-tay], *adv.* Significatively.

significativo, va [sig-ne-fe-cah-tee'-vo, vah], *a.* Significative, expressive.

signo [seeg'-no], *m.* 1. Sign, mark. 2. *(Coll.)* Fate, destiny. 3. Benediction with the sign of the cross. 4. *(Ast.)* Sign of the zodiac. 5. Type, emblem. 6. Any of the characters in which music is written. **Signo de admiración,** exclamation mark. **Signo del zodíaco,** sign of the zodiac.

siguiente [se-gee-en'-tay], *a.* Following, successive, sequent.

sílaba [see'-lah-bah], *f.* 1. Syllable. 2. *(Mus.)* Two or three sounds which correspond with every letter of the gamut.

silabar [se-la-bar'], *vn. V* SILABEAR.

silabario [se-la-bah'-re-o], *m.* A book which contains and explains syllables; syllabary.

silabear [se-lah-bay-ar'], *an.* To pronounce by syllables.

silabeo [se-la-bay'-o], *m.* Syllabication, the act of forming syllables.

silábico, ca [se-lah' be oo, cah], *a.* Syllabical, syllabic.

silba [seel'-bah], *f.* Whistling, catcall, hissing (in public derision).

sílabus, or **silabo,** *m.* Syllabus, a brief statement by the Pope of errors condemned (in 1864).

silbador, ra [sil-bah-dor', rah], *m. & f.* Whistler; exploder, a hisser.

silbar [sil-bar'], *vn.* 1. To whistle. 2. To whiz (bullets) -*va.* To hiss, to express disapprobation (en público), to catcall.

silbático, illo, ito [sil-bah-tee'-co], *m. dim.* A small whistle.

silbato [sil-bah'-to], *m.* 1. Whistle, a wind instrument. 2. A small chink or crack, through which passes any liquid or air that whizzes.

silbido [sil-bee'-do], *m.* Whistle, whistling hiss; sibilation. **Silbido de oídos,** whizzing or humming in the ear.

silbo [seel'-bo], *m.* Whistle, hiss, whistling.

silboso, sa [sil-bo'-so, sah], *a. (Poet.)* Whistling, hissing.

silenciario, ria [se-len-the-ah'-re-o, ah], *a.* Observing profound silence.

silenciario [se-len-the-ah'-re-o], *m.* Silentiary, officer appointed to preserve silence in a place or assembly; silent place.

silenciero, ra [se-len-the-ay'-ro, rah], *a.* Charged with preserving silence; which preserves peace.

silencio [se-len'-the-o], *m.* 1. Silence; habitual taciturnity; secrecy. 2. State of holding the peace. 3. Reservedness, prudence. 4. Stillness, repose. -*int.* Silence! hush. **En silencio,** in silence. **Reducir al silencio,** to silence.

silenciosamente [se-len-the-o'-sah-men-tay], *adv.* Silently, softly, gently.

silencioso, sa [se-len-the-oh'-so, sah], *a.* Silent; solitary, mute.

sileno [se-lay'-no], *m.* Silenus, a demigod.

siler montano [se-lerr' mon-tah'-no], *m. (Bot.)* Mountain lasserwort.

silería [se-lay-ree'-ah], *f.* Place where subterranean granaries are made.

silero [se-lay'-ro], *m.* A subterraneous granary for wheat, a silo.

sílex [se'-lex], *m.* Silex.

sílfide [sil-fe-day], *f.* **Silfo,** *m.* Sylph.

silguero [sil-gay'-ro], *m. (Orn. Prov.)* Linnet. *V.* JILGUERO.

silibo [se-lee'-bo], *m. (Bot.)* Silybum, a genus of plants.

silicato [se-le-cah'-to], *m.* Silicate, a compound of silicic acid.

sílice [see'-le-thay], *m.* Silica, silicon dioxide (occurring as quartz or as opal).

silíceo, ea [se-lee'-thay-o, ah], *a.* Siliceous, flinty.

silicio [se-lee'-the-o], *m.* 1. Silicon, a non-metallic element, next in abundance to oxygen. 2. *V.* CILICIO.

silicona [se-le-co'-nah], *f.* Silicone.

silicua [se-lee'-coo-ah], *f.* 1. Siliqua carat, a former weight of four grains. 2. Silique, a seed-vessel, husk, pod; or shell of leguminous plants.

silícula [se-lee'-coo-lah], *f. (Bot.)* Silicle, a short silique.

silicuoso, sa [se-le-coo-o'-so]. *a.* Siliquose, having a pod or capsule.

siligo [se-lee'-go], *m. V.* NEGUILLA.

silla [seel'-lyah], *f.* 1. Chair, movable seat (asiento). 2. See, the seat of episcopal power, the diocese of a bishop. 3. **Silla** or **silla de montar.** Saddle. 4. Seat. 5. Seat, anus. **Silla de rejilla, de junco,** cane or bamboo-bottomed chair. **Silla de columpio,** rocking-chair. **Silla giratoria,** pivot chair. **Silla plegadiza,** folding-chair, camp-stool. **Pegársele (a uno) la silla,** to make a very long call, to be a stayer. **Silla de cubierta,** deck chair. **Silla eléctrica** electric chair. **Le movieron la silla para que se cayese,** they pulled the rug out from under him.

sillar [sil-lyar'], *m.* 1. A square hewn stone. 2. Back of a horse where the saddle is placed.

sillarejo [sil-lyah-ray'-ho], *m.* A small hewn stone.

sillera [sil-lyay'-rah], *f.* Place where sedan-chairs are shut up.

sillería [sil-lyay-ree'-ah], *f.* 1. Sent, set or parcel of chairs. 2. Shop where chairs are made or sold. 3. Stalls about the choir of a church. 4. Building of hewn stone.

sillero [sil-lyay'-ro], *m.* Saddler, chairmaker (artesano).

silleta [sil-lyay'-tah], *f.* 1. *(Dim.)* A small chair. 2. Hollow stone on which chocolate is ground. 3. Close stool (taburete). 4. Side-saddle.

silletero [sil-lyay-tay'-ro], *m.* 1. Chair man, one employed in carrying sedan-chairs. 2. Chair-maker, one who makes or sells chairs.

sillico [sil-lyee'-co], *m.* Basin of close-stool.

sillín [sil-lyeen'], *m.* 1. A seat, saddle. 2. A small saddle for a driving-horse or a bicycle.

sillita [sil-lyee'-tah], *f. dim.* A small chair.

sillón [sil-lyone'], *m.* 1. A large armchair. 2. Side-saddle for ladies (de montar).

silo [see'-lo], *m.* 1. A subterraneous granary for wheat, a silo. 2. Any cavern or dark place.

silogismo [se-lo-hees'-mo], *m.* Syllogism.

silogístico, ca [se-lo-hees'-te-co, cah], *a.* Syllogistic, syllogistical.

silogizar [se-lo-he-thar'], *vn.* To syllogize, to reason, to argue.

silueta [se-loo-ay'-tah], *f.* Silhouette, a profile in shadow, outline (de edificio), skyline (de ciudad).

siluro [se-loo'-ro], *m.* Catfish, sheatfish, silurus.

silva [seel'-vah], *f.* 1. A miscellany 2. A kind of Spanish metrical composition.

silvamar [sil-vah-nar'], *m.* Sarsaparilla.

silvano [sil-vah'-no], *m.* 1. Sylvan, a wood-god or satyr. 2. Tellurium.

silvático, ca [sil-vah'-te-co, cah], *a. V.* SELVÁTICO.

silvestre [sil-ves'-tray], *a.* Wild, uncultivated; rustic, savage.

silvoso, sa [sil-vo'-so, sah], *a. V.* SELVOSO.

sima [see'-mah], *f.* 1. Deep and dark cavern; abyss; chasm; pit; deep fissure, pothole.

simarruba [se-mar-roo'-bah], *f. (Bot.)* Bitter-wood, quassia.

simbólicamente [sem-bo'-le-cah-men-tay], *adv.* Symbolically, typically, hieroglyphically.

simbólico, ca [sim-bo'-le-co, cah], *a.* 1. Symbolical, representative, expressing by signs. 2. Analogous, resembling.

simbolización [sim-bo-le-thah-the-on'], *f.* Symbolization.

simbolizar [sim-bo-le-thar'], *vn.* To symbolize, to resemble, to figure.

símbolo [seem'-bo-lo], *m.* 1. Symbol mark, sign, device. 2. *(Mil.)* Watch word. 3. Symbol, a badge to know one by. 4. Symbol, type, representation, figure. 5. Creed, belief, articles of faith.

símbolo, la [seem'-bo-lo], *a. V.* SIMBÓLICO.

simetría [se-may-tree'-ah], *f.* Symmetry, proportion, shapeliness, harmony.

simétricamente [se-may'-tre-cah-men-tay], *adv.* Symmetrically.

simétrico, ca [se-may'-tre-co, cah], *a.* Symmetrical, proportionate.

simia [see'-me-ah], *f.* A female ape. *V.* MONA.

simiente [se-me-en'-tay], *f.* 1. Seed. *V.* SEMILLA. 2. *V.* SEMEN. 3. Source origin.

simienza [se-me-en'-thah], *f. (Prov.)* Seed-time. *V.* SEMENTERA.

simil [see'-mil], *m.* 1. Resemblance, similarity. *V.* SEMEJANZA. 2. Simile, comparison, similitude.-*a.* Similar; like. *V.* SEMEJANTE.

similar [se-me-lar'], *a.* 1. Similar, homogeneous. 2. Resembling.

similitud [se-me-le-tood'], *f.* Similitude, resemblance.

similitudinariamente [se-me-le-too-de-nah'-re-ah-men-tay], *adv.* Similarly.

similitudinario, ria [se-me-le-too-de-nah'-re-o, ah], *a.* Similar, similitudinary.

simio [see'-me-o], *m..* Male ape. *V.* MONO.

simonía [se-mo-nee'-ah], *f.* Simony.

simoniaco, ca, simoniático, ca [se-mo-nee'-ah-co, cah], *a.* Simoniac or simoniacal.

simpatía [sim-pah-tee'-ah], *f.* 1. Sympathy (compasión), fellow-feeling (solidaridad), congeniality. 2. Charm (de lugar, persona), personality. **Tener simpatía por alguien,** to find someone charming and congenial. **Ganarse la simpatía de todos,** to win everybody's affection. **Mostrar su simpatía por,** to show one's support for.

simpáticamente [sim-pah-te-cah-men-tay], *adv.* Sympathetically. *V.* CONFORMEMENTE.

simpático, ca [sim-pah'-te-co, cah], *a.* Sympathetic, sympathetical, analogous, nice (persona), kind (bondadoso),

charming (encantador). **No le hemos caído muy simpáticos,** she didn't much take to us.

simpatizar [sim-pah-te-thar'], *vn.* (used with the prep. *con*). To be congenial, to have a liking for someone. **Simpatizo mucho con él,** I like him, he and I get along well.

simplazo, za [sim-plah'-tho, thah], *aug.* A great simpleton, a stupid person.

simple [seem'-play], *a.* 1. Single, simple, pure, mere, naked, unsigned; unconditional. 2. Silly, foolish, simple, crazy, idiotical. 3. Simple, undesigning, artless. 4. Simple, plain, mild, gentle, ingenuous (persona). 5. Insipid, tasteless. 6. Single, brief. 7. Informal, extra-judicial. **Es cosa de una simple plumada,** it's a matter of a mere stroke of the pen. **Somos simples aficionados,** we are just amateurs. **Un simple abogado,** a solicitor of little importance. **Es un simple soldado** he's just an ordinary soldier. -*m.* 1. Simple, an herb or plant which alone serves for medicine. 2. Simpleton (persona).

simplecillo, illa, ito ita [sim-play-theel'-lyo], *m. & f.* A little simpleton.

simplemente, *adv.* Simply, with simplicity and plainness, sillily; absolutely, merely.

simpleza [sim-play'-thah], *f.* 1. Simpleness (cualidad), silliness, fatuity. 2. Rusticity, rudeness. 3. Simplicity, sincerity. **Se enojó por una simpleza,** he got annoyed over nothing.

simplicidad [sim-ple-the-dahd'], *f.* l. Simplicity, plainness, artlessness, homeliness. 2. Simpleness, silliness, fatuity.

simplicista [sim-ple-thees'-tah], *m.* Simplist, simpler, herbalist.

simplificar [sim-ple-fe-car'], *va.* To simplify, to make simple.

simplísimo, ma [im-plee'-se-mo, mah], *a. sup.* Extremely silly or foolish.

simplista [sim-plees'-tah], *m.* Simplist, herbalist.

simplón, na [sim-plone', nah], *m. & f. aug.* of SIMPLE. Great simpleton.

simplonazo, za [sim-plo-nah'-tho, thah], *a. aug.* of SIMPLÓN. Extremely simple or silly.

simulación [se-moo-lah-the-on'], *f.* 1. Simulation, feigning, hollowness. 2. Subterfuge, evasion.

simulacro [se-moo-lah'-cro], *m.* 1. Simulachre, image, idol. 2. Ghost, phantom. **Un simulacro de ataque,** a mock attack.

simuladamente [se-moo-lah'-dah-men-tay]. *adv.* In a dissembling or hypocritical manner.

simulador, ra [se-moo-lah-dor', rah], *m. & f.* Simulator, dissembler.

simular [se-moo-lar'], *va.* To simulate, to practise simulation.

simulcadencia [se-mool-cah-den'-the-ah], *f. (Rhet.)* Figure of rhetoric repeating a consonant in a word forming a cadence.

simulcadente [se-mool-cah-den'-tay], *a.* Applied to words or sentences having a cadence.

simultáneamente [se-mool-tah'-ne-ah-men-tay], *adv.* Simultaneously.

simultaneidad [se-mool-tah-nay-dahd'], *f.* Simultaneity.

simultáneo, nea [se-mool-tah'-nay-o, ah], *a.* Simultaneous.

simún [se-moon'], *m.* Simoom (viento), a hot wind of the desert in Africa and Arabia.

sin [seen], *prep.* Without, besides. Joined to a verb it is a negative or privative. **Sin embargo,** notwithstanding, nevertheless, however. **Sin pies ni cabeza,** without head or tail, without order. **Almendras sin cáscara,** shelled almonds. **Salió sin abrigo,** he went out without a coat. **Sin qué ni por qué,** without cause or motive. **Sin afeitar,** unshaven. **Sin lavar,** unwashed. **Sin saberlo ella,** without her knowing it.

sinabafa [se-nah-bah'-fah], *f.* Cloth or stuff of the natural color of wool.

sinagoga [se-nah-go'-gah], *f.* Synagogue, a Jewish congregation, and the place where they meet for worship and religious instruction.

sinalefa [se-nah-lay'-fah], *f. (Gram.)* Synalepha, the union or blending into a single syllable of two successive vowels of different syllables.

sinamay [se-nah-mah'-e], *m.* A very light fabric made in the Philippines from the filaments of *abacá.*

sinantéreas [se-nan-tay'-ray-ahs], *a. & f. pl. (Bot.)* Synantherge, a former order of plants now called *Compositae.*

sinapismo [se-nah-pees'-mo], *m.* Sinapism, mustard-poultice.

sincategoremático, ca [sin-cah-tay-go-ray-mah'-te-co, cah], *a.* Syncategorematic.

sincerador, ra [sin-thay-rah-dor', rah], *m. & f.* Exculpator, excuser.

sinceramente [sin-thay'-rah-men-tay], *adv.* Sinecerely, frankly, heartily, cordially.

sincerar [sin-thay-rar'], *va.* To exculpate. *-vr.* To excuse, justify, or vindicate oneself. **Sincerarse ante el juez,** to justify one's conduct to the judge.

sinceridad [sin-thay-re-dahd'], *f.* Sincerity, purity of mind, frankness, cordiality, good-will.

sincero, ra [sin-thay'-ro, rah], *a.* Sincere, ingenuous, honest; pure.

sincipucio [sin-the-poo'-the-o], *m.* Sinciput.

sincondrosis [sin-con-dro'-sees], . *(Anat.)* Synchondrosis, union of two bones by means of a cartilage.

síncopa [seen'-coo-pah], *f.* 1. Syncopa, a contraction of words, by cutting off a part. 2. *(Mus.)* Syncopation, the beginning of a tone upon an unaccented beat, and its continuation through the following accented beat.

sincopado, da [sin-co-pah'-do, dah], *a.* Syncopated.

sincopal [sin-co-pahl'], *m. V.* SÍNCOPE.

sincopal [sin-co-pahl'], *a.* Applied to malignant fevers.

sincopar [sin-co-par'], *m.* 1. To syncopate, to contract, words. 2. To abridge.

síncope [seen'-co-pay], *f. (Med.)* Syncope, a fainting-fit.

sincopizar [sin-co-pe-thar'], *va. & vr.* To swoon, to faint.

sincresis [sin-cray'-sis], *f.* Fusion, mixture.

sincretismo [sin-cray-tees'-mo], *m.* 1. Syncretism, a philosophical system allied to electicism. 2. Conciliation of different religious doctrines.

sincrónico [sin-cro'-ne-co], *a.* Synchronous; synchronized.

sincronismo [sin-cro-nees'-mo], *m.* Synchronism, coincidence in time of different events; simultaneousness.

sincronizar [sin-cro-ne-thar'], *va.* To synchronize.

sindéresis [sin-day'-ray-sis], *f.* Discretion, natural capacity for judging rightly.

sindicación [sin-de-cah-the-on'], *f.* The act of informing against.

sindicado [sin-de-cah'-do], *m.* A body of trustees; a syndicate. **-Sindicado. da,** *pp.* of SINDICAR.

sindicador, ra [sin-de-cah-dor', rah], *m. & f.* Informer, prosecutor.

sindicadura [sin-de-cah-doo'-rah], *f.* Office and dignity of a syndic.

sindical [sin-de-cahl'], *m.* Syndical, relating to a syndic or syndicate.

sindicalismo [sin-de-cah-lees'-mo], *m.* Unionism.

sindicar [sin-de-car'], *va.* To inform, to lodge an information; to accuse.

sindicatura [sin-de-ca-too'-rah], *f.* Trusteeship.

síndico [sin'-de-co], *m.* 1. Syndic; recorder. 2. One whose office is to collect the fines imposed by a court. 3. Treasurer of the alms of religious houses. **Síndico or procurador general,** the attorney-general of a town or corporation.

síndrome [sin'-dro-may], *m.* Syndrome. **Síndrome tóxico,** poisoning.

sinécdoque, sinédoque [se-nec'-do-kay], *f. (Rhet.)* Synecdoche, a trope which puts a part for the whole, or the whole for a part.

sinecura [se-nay-coo'-rah], *f.* Sinecure, an office having emoluments with few or no duties.

sinedra [se-nay'-drah], *f.* Seats for the audience in a public hall.

sinedrio [se-nay'-dre-o], *m. V.* SANEDRÍN.

sinéresis [se-nay'-ray-sis], *f.* Syneresis, a figure whereby two syllables are united into one.

sínfisis [seen'-fe-sis], *f. (Anat.)* Symphysis, union of bones by means of an intervening body.

sínfito [seen'-fe-to], *m. (Bot.)* Comfrey.

sinfonía [sin-fo-nee'-ah], *f.* 1. Symphony, concert of concordant sounds; composition of instrumental music. 2. Symphony, a concerted instrumental piece for many instruments. 3. *V.* GAITA.

sinfonista [sin-fo-nees'-tah], *com.* 1. Symphonist, one who composes a symphony. 2. A player in an orchestra.

sinfonola [sin-fo-no'-lah], *f.* Jukebox.

singladura [sin-glah-doo'-rah], *f. (Naut.)* A day's run (recorrido); the distance traversed by a ship in 24 hours.

singlar [sin-glar'], *vn. (Naut.)* To sail daily with a favorable wind on a direct course.

singlón [sin-glone'], *m. (Naut.)* Any of the timbers placed over the keel.

singular [sin-goo-lar'], *a.* 1. Singular, single, not common to others; unique. 2. Singular, individual, particular. 3. Singular, extraordinary, extravagant, strange. 4. Singular, excellent. 5. *(Gram.)* Singular. **En singular,** in the singular. **Se refiere a él en singular,** it refers to him in particular.

singularidad [sin-goo-lah-re-dahd'], *f.* Singularity, notability, oddity.

singularizar [sin-goo-lah-re-thar'], *va.* To distinguish (distinguir), to particularize, to singularize. *-vr.* To distinguish oneself (distinguirse); to be singular.

singularmente [sin-goo-lahr'-men-tay]. *adv.* Singularly.

singulto [sin-gool'-to], *m.* Hiccough, singultus.

siniestra [se-nes-es'-trah], *f.* The left hand. *V.* IZQUIERDA.

siniestramente [se-ne-es'-trah-men-tay], *adv.* Sinistrously, perversely.

siniestro, tra [se-ne-es'-tro, trah], *a.* 1. Sinister, left, on the left side. 2. Sinistrous, vicious. 3. Sinister, unhappy, unlucky.

siniestro [se-ne-es-tro], *m.* 1. Perverseness, depravity, evil habit. 2. *(Com.)* Shipwreck, or great damage.

Sinnúmero [sin-noo'-may-ro], *m.* A numberless quantity. **Un sinnúmero de personas,** an endless number of persons.

sino [see'-no], *conj.* But: used in contrasting an affirmative idea with a negative. **No es blanco, sino negro,** it is not white, but black. 2. Except, besides (salvo). **Nadie lo sabe sino Juan,** nobody knows it except John. 3. Solely, only: always proceded by a negative proposition. **No sino,** not only so.

sino [see'-no]. *m.* Fate, destiny.

sinoble [se-no'-blay] *a (Her.) V.* SINOPLE.

sinoca [se-no'-cah], *f. (Med.)* Synocha, inflammatory continued fever.

sinocal [se-no-cahl'], *a.* Synochal, pertaining to the synocha fever.

sinodal [se-no-dahl'], *a.* Synodic, synodical. *-m.* Examiner of curates and confessors.

sinodático [se-no-dah'-te-co], *m.* Pecuniary contribution paid by the clergy to the bishops.

sinódico, ca [se-no'-de-co, cah], *a.* 1. Synodal, synodical. 2. Synodic, reckoned from one conjunction of the moon with the sun until another.

sínodo [see'-no-do], *m.* 1. Synod, an ecclesiastical assembly. 2. Conjunction of the heavenly bodies. 3. Stipend allowed to missionaries in America.

sinólogo, ga [se-no'-lo-go, gah], *m. & f.* Sinologue, versed in the Chinese language and literature.

sinónimo, ma [se-no'-ne-mo, mah], *a.* Synonymous. *-pl.* Synonima.

sinónimo [se-no'-ne-mo], *m.* Synonym.

sinónomo, ma [se-no'-no-mo, mah], *a. V.* SINÓNIMO.

sinople [se-no'-play], *a. (Her.)* Sinople, green.

sinopsis [se-nop'-sis], *f.* Synopsis, compendium, epitome.

sinóptico, ca [se-nop'-te-co, cah], *a.* Synoptic, synoptical, compendious.

sinovia [se-noo´-ve-ah], *f.* Synovia, the fluid of the joints.

sinovial [se-no-ve-ahl'], *a.* Synovial, secreting synovia.

sinrazón [sin-rah-thone'], *f.* Wrong, injury, injustice.

sinsabor [sin-sah-bor'], *m.* Displeasure, disgust, pain, uneasiness (inquietud), offensiveness.

sinsonte [sin-son'-tay], *m.* The mocking-bird.

sintáctico, ca [sin-tahc´-te-co, cah], *a. (Gram.)* Syntactic, belonging to syntax.

sintagma [sin-tahg´-mah], *m.* Orderly method, system.

sintaxis [sin-tahk'-ses], *f.* 1. *(Gram.)* Syntax. 2. Co-ordination of things among themselves.

síntesis [seen'-tay-ses], *f.* Synthesis opposed to analysis.

sintético, ca [sin-tay'-te-co, cah], *a.* Synthetical.

sintetizador [sin-tay-te-thah-dor'], *m.* Synthesizer. **Sintetizador de la voz,** voice synthesizer.

sintetizar [sin-tay-te-thar'], *va.* To synthesize or synthetize: to unite by synthesis.

síntoma [sin´-to-mah], *m.* 1. Med. Symptom. 2. Sign. token.

sintomáticamente [sin-to-mah'-te-cah-men-tay], *adv.* Symptomatically.

sintomático, ca [sin-to-mah´-te-co, cah], *a.* Symptomatic, symptomatical.

sintomatología [sin-to-mah-to-lo-hee´-ah], *f. (Med.)* Symptomatology, a part of pathology.

sintonía [sin-to-nee'-ah], *f.* Syntony (acto); tunning.

sintonizar [sin-to-ne-thar'], *va.* (Radio) To syntonize.

sinuosidad [se-noo-o-se-dahd'], *f.* Sinuosity, sinuousness.

sinuoso, sa [se-noo-oh´-so, sah], *a.* Sinuous (camino), wavy (línea).

sinusitis [se-noo-see'-tees], *f.* Sinusitis.

sinvergüenza [sin-ver-goo-ayn'-thah], *m & f.* 1. Scoundrel (pillo), villain, rascal; rotter (canalla). 2. Shameless person (descarado).

sipia [see'-pe-ah], *f.* Refuse of olives, which remains in oil-mills.

siquiatra [se-ke-ah'-trah], *m. & f.* V. PSIQUIATRA.

siquiatría [se-ke-ah-tree'-ah], *f.* V. PSIQUIATRÍA.

síquico, ca [see'-ke-co, cah], *a.* V PSÍQUICO.

siquier, siquiera [se-ke-err´, se-ke-ay-rah], *conj.* At least (por lo menos): though, although; or; scarcely; otherwise. **Dame siquiera un poquito,** give me at least a little of it. **Ni siquiera quiso escucharlo,** he would not even listen to him. **Dame un abrazo siquiera,** at least give me a hug. **Come un poco siquiera,** at least eat a little bit.

sirena [se-ray´-nah], *f.* 1. Syren, a sea-nymph. 2. A woman who sings charmingly. 3. *(Zool.)* Siren, a batrachian.

sirga [seer´-gah], *f.* 1. *(Naut.)* Towrope, tow-line. 2. Line used in draging nets. **A la sirga,** sailing with a dragging line.

sirgadura [seer-gah-doo´-rah], *f. (Naut.)* Towing or hauling a barge or vessel along a canal, or by the banks of a river.

sirgar [seer-gar'], *va. (Naut.)* To tow a vessel with a line.

sirgo [seer'-go], *m.* Twisted silk; stuff made of silk.

siriaco, ca [se-re-ah'-co, cah], *a.* Syrian, of Syria. -*m.* Syriac, the language of ancient Syria.

sirio [see'-re-o], *m. (Ast.)* Sirius or dog-star.

sirle [seer'-lay], *m.* Sheep-dung or goat's dung.

siro, ra [see'-ro, rah], *a.* V. SIRIACO.

siroco [se-ro'-co], *m.* Sirocco, a south-east wind on the Mediterranean.

sirte [seer´-tay], *f.* 1. Syrte, hidden rock, quicksand, moving sandbunk. 2. Peril, danger.

sirvienta [seer-ve-en´-tah], *f.* Female servant, serving-maid.

sirviente [seer-ve-en'-tay], *pa. & com.* Serving, being a servant, menial, serving-man. V. SIRVIENTA.

sisa [see´-sah], *f.* 1. Petty theft (robo). 2. Any pilfering trifle clipped from the whole. 3. Clippings, tailors´ cabbage. 4. Size, linseed oil boiled with ochre used by gilders. 5. Assize. 6. Excise on eatables or liquors.

sisador, ra [se-sah-dor', rah], *m. & f.* Filcher, petty thief; one that exacts more than is due; sizer; cutter.

sisar [se-sar´], *va.* 1. To pilfer, to filch; to steal small quantities of a thing (artículos); to curtail, to lessen. 2. To cut clothes. 3. To size, to prepare with size, for gilding.

sisca [sees'-cah], *f. (Bot. Prov.)* Cylindrical sugar-cane.

sisear [se-say-ar'], *vn.* To hiss, to sound *s* inarticulately, in order to express disapproval.

siseo [se-say'-o], *m.* Hissing.

sisero [se-say'-ro], *m.* Excise collector.

sisimbrio [se-seem'-bre-o], *m. (Bot.)* Water-radish, radish water-cress.

sísmico, ca [sees'-me-co, cah], *a. a.* Seismic. **Movimiento sísmico,** earthquake.

sismógrafo [sis-mo'-grah-fo], *m.* Seismograph, apparatus to register the motions of an earthquake.

sisón [se-sone´], *m.* 1. Filcher, pilferer, petty thief. 2. *(Orn.)* Godart or moor-cock.

sistema [sis-tay'-mah], *m.* 1. System, a combination of things acting together. 2. System, a scheme which reduces many things to a regular dependence or corporation. 3. Hypothesis, supposition. 4. Gold or silver lace of one pattern. **Sistema de calefacción,** heating system. **Sistema montaño,** mountain range. 5. **Sistema de apoyo ejecutivo,** executive support system. **Sistema de ayuda en la toma de decisiones,** decision support system. **Sistema de control del inventario,** inventory control system. **Sistema de correo oral,** voice mail system. **Sistema de diseño y fabricación,** design and manufacturing system. **Sistema de gestión de nóminas,** payroll system. **Sistema de información de gestión,** management information system (MIS). **Sistema de informes informáticos,** information reporting system. **Sistema de procesamiento de transacciones,** transaction processing system. **Sistema de registro de las cuentas por pagar,** accounts payable system. **Sistema de registro de pedidos,** order-entry system. **Sistema de registro de las cuentas por cobrar,** accounts receivable system. **Sistema integrado para la oficina,** integrated office system. **Sistema "libro mayor",** general ledger system.**Sistema de fabricación asistida por ordenador,** computer-aided manufacturing system. **Sistema de inteligencia artificial,** artificial intelligence system. **Sistema experto,** expert sistem, knowledge processing system. **Sistema de gestor de datos,** expert system, knowledge processing system. **Sistema visual,** vision system.

sistemar [sis-tay-mar'], *va. (Amer.)* To systematize, to order.

sistemáticamente [sis-tay-mah'-te-cah-men-te], *adv.* Systematically.

sistemático, ca [sis-tay-mah´-te-co, cah], *a.* Systematic.

sistematizar [sis-tay-mah-te-thar'], *va.* To reduce to system, to systematize.

sistilo [sis-tee'-lo], *m. (Arch.)* Systyle.

sístole [sees'-to-lay], *f.* 1. *(Anat.)* Systole, contraction of the heart. 2. *(Rhet.)* Shortening of a long syllable.

sistro [sees'-tro], *m.* Sistrum, an ancient musical stringed instrument; a curved metal band crossed by many wires or rods.

sitácidos [si-tah'-the-dos], *m. pl.* The psittacid birds, the gray parrots.

sitiador [se-te-ah-dor'], *m.* Besieger.

sitial [se-te-ahl'], *m.* 1. Seat of honor for princes and prelates in a public assembly. 2. Stool, form, seat without a back.

sitiar [se-te-ar'], *va.* 1. To besiege, to lay siege to a place. 2. To surround, to hem in, to compass. 3. To deprive of the means of effecting something. **Sitiar por hambre,** *(Met.)* to compel one by necessity to submit.

sitibundo, da [se-te-boon'-do, dah], *a. (Poet.)* V. SEDIENTO.

sitio [see´-te-o], *m.* 1. Room (espacio), place (lugar, space taken up by a body or object. 2. Situation, location of a town, city, or building. 3. *(Mil.)* Siege, blockade. 4. Country house, country residence. 5. *(CAm. Cono Sur)* Building site (solar). 6. *(Carib. Mex.)* Small farm. 7. *(LAm.)* Taxi rank (parada). **Sitio de inspección**, checkpoint. **En cualquier sitio**, anywhere. **Dejar a uno en el sitio**, to kill somebody.

sito, ta [see'-to, tah], *a.* Situated, placed, located, lying, assigned. *V.* SITUADO.

sitófago, ga [se-toh'-fah-go, gah], *a.* Living upon wheat.

situación [se-too-ah-the-on'], *f.* 1. Situation, position. 2. Situation, condition of affairs. 3. Assignation, appointment, assignment. **Situación económica**, financial position.

situado [se-too-ah'-do], *m.* 1. Allowance, pay, or salary assigned upon certain goods or effects. 2. Post, position.

situado, da [se-too-ah'-do], *a. & pp.* of SITUAR. Situate, situated, placed, located, lying.

situar [se-too-ar'], *va.* 1. To put a thing in a certain place, to situate. 2. To assign a fund, out of which a salary, rent, or interest is to be paid. -*vn.* To be established in any place or business: to station oneself. **Esto se sitúa entre los dos mejores**, this places him among the best.

slalom [slah-lom], *m.* Slalom.

slogan [slo'-gan], *m.* Slogan.

smoking [smo'-kin], *m.* Tuxedo, dinner-jacket.

snob or **esnob** [es-nob'], *m.* Snob.

snobismo [sno-bees'-mo], *m. V.* ESNOBISMO.

so [so], *prep.* Under; below. Used in composition, it occasionally diminishes the import of the verb, as in *soasar*, to underdo meat; in other cases it augments it, as *sojuzgar*, to subjugate; and it sometimes retains its signification, as in *soterrar*, to put underground, to inter. **So color**, under color; on pretence. **¡So burro!** you, idiot!

soasar [so-ah-sar'], *va.* To half roast, to parboil, to underdo meat.

soata [so-ah'-tah], *f. (Amer.)* Dish composed of maize and uyama, a kind of squash, served for breakfast in Guayana, Venezuela.

soba [so'-bah], *f.* 1. The act and effect of making something soft and limber; rumpling, contusion; beating. 2. Kneading (amasado).

sobacal [so-bah-cahl'], *a.* Axillary, relating to the armpit or to an axil.

sobaco [so-bah'-co], *m.* 1. Armpit, armhole, axilla. 2. *(Bot.)* Axil.

sobadero, ra [so-bah-day'-ro, rah], *a.* That may be handled.

sobado [so-bah'-do], *m.* 1. The repeated and violent handling of something. 2. *V.* SOBADURA. **Sobados**, loaves of bread made in La Mancha. 3. *a.* worn, shabby (desgastado), dog-eared (manoseado). —**Sobado, da** *pp.* of SOBAR.

sobadura [so-bah-doo'-rah], *f.* Kneading, rubbing.

sobajadura [so-bah-hah-doo'-rah], *f.* Scrubbing, rubbing.

sobajamiento [so-bah-hah-me-en'-to], *m.* Friction, rubbing, scrubbing.

sobajanero [so-bah-hah-nay'-ro], *m. (Coll.)* Errand-boy.

sobajar [so-bah-har'], *va.* To scrub, to rub hard.

sobanda [so-bahn'-dah], *f.* Bottom or end of a cask.

sobaquera [so-bah-kay'-rah], *f.* 1. Opening left in clothes under the armpit; arm-hole. 2. *(CAm. Carib.)* Underarm odor. **Coger a alguien las sobaqueras**, to gain ascendency over a person. **Funda sobaquera**, shoulder holster.

sobaquina [so-bah-kee'-nah], *f.* Small of the armpit

sobar [so-bar'], *va.* 1. To handle (tela), to soften. 2. To pummel, to chastise with blows. 3. To handle with too much familiarity and frequency. 4. To fondle, to feel (personas); to finger, to paw, to lay hands on. (persona). 5. *(LAm.)* To set (hueso). 6. *(And.)* To skin (despellejar). 7. To pester (molestar). 8. *(And. Carib. Mex.)* To flatter (lisonjear).

sobarba [so-bar'-bah], *f.* Nose-band of a bridle.

sobarbada [so-bar-bah'-dah], *f.* 1. A check given a horse by pulling the reins with violence. 2. Chuck under the chin; jerk. 3. *(Met.)* Reprimand, scolding.

sobarbo [so-bar'-bo], *m.* Lever or pallet for raising the pestles in a fulling-mill.

sobarcar [so-bar-car'], *va.* 1. To carry something heavy under the arm. 2. To draw clothes up to the armholes.

sobeo [so-bay'-o], *m.* Caresses, love-play, fondling.

soberanamente [so-bay-rah'-nah-men-tay], *adv.* Sovereignly, supremely.

soberanear [so-bay-rah-nay-ar'], *vn.* To lord it, to domineer like a sovereign.

soberanía [so-bay-rah-nee'-ah], *f.* 1. Sovereignity, supreme power over others, majesty. 2. Pride, haughtiness, arrogance, loftiness.

soberano, na [so-bay-rah'-no, nah], *a.* 1. Sovereign, supreme, kingly. 2. Sovereign, superior, predominant. **Una soberana paliza**, a real walloping.

soberano [so-bay-rah'-no], *m.* Sovereign; lord, paramount; king; liege.

soberbia [so-berr'-be-ah], *f.* 1. Pride (orgullo), haughtiness (altanería); an inordinate desire to be preferred to others; presumption; arrogance; loftiness. 2. Pomp, pageantry. 3. Anger, passion. 4. Insulting word or action.

soberbiamente [so-ber-be-ah-men-tay], *adv.* Haughtily, arrogantly, proudly, superbly.

soberbio, bia [so-berr'-be-o, ah], *a.* 1. Proud (orgulloso), arrogant, elated, haughty, passionate. 2. Losty, sublime, eminent, superb. 3. Fiery, mettlesome (caballos).

sobina [so-bee'-nah], *f.* A wooden pin or peg.

sobo [so'-bo], *m.* Frequent working of a thing to make it soft and limber.

sobón, na [so-bone', nah], *a.* 1. One who makes himself too familiar by half; too free with his hands. 2. A sly, lazy fellow (gandul). 3. *(And.)* Soapy (adulón). **¡No seas sobón!**, get your hands off me!

sobordo [so-bor'-do], *m.* Manifest, freight-list; the statement of a cargo taken on board of a vessel; a memorandum of the articles daily received while a vessel is lading.

sobornación [so-bor-nah-the-on'], *f. V.* SOBORNO.

sobornado [so-bor-nah'-do], *m.* Mishaped loaf of bread in the oven.—**Sobornado, da**, *pp.* of SOBORNAR.

sobornador, ra [so-bor-na-dor', rah], *m. & f.* Suborner, corrupter, one who is guilty of subornation.

sobornal [so-bor-nahl'], *a.* Added to the load which a vessel carries. -*m.* A small bale; a seroon.

sobornar [so-bor-nar'], *va.* To suborn, to bribe, to procure by secret collusion, to corrupt, to buy off.

soborno [so-bor'-no], *m.* 1. Subornation. 2. Bribe, gift or money offered for doing a bad action; the act of buying someone off. 3. Incitement, inducement. 4. In Peru, used for *Sobornal*.

sobra [so'-brah], *f.* 1. Overplus, surplus (excedente), excess. **Sobras de la comida**, offals, leaving, broken victuals. 2. Grievous offence, injury. **De sobra**, over and above; superfluously. **Estar de sobra**, *(Coll.)* to be one too many.

sobradamente [so-brah-dah-men-tay], *adv.* Abundantly: superabundantly; excessively.

sobradar [so-brah-dar'], *va.* To erect edifices with lofts or granaries.

sobradillo [so-brah-deel'-lyo], *m.* 1. *(Dim.)* A cock-loft. 2. Penthouse; a shelter over a balcony or window.

sobrado [so-brah'-do], *m.* 1. *V.* DESVÁN and GUARDILLA. 2. *(Prov.)* Granary.

sobrado, da [so-brah'-do, dah], *a.* 1. Hold, audacious, licentious. 2. Rich, wealthy (rico). 3. Bold (atrevido). 4. *(Cono Sur)* Colossal (enorme). -*adv. V.* SOBRADAMENTE.

sobrancero, ra [so-bran-thay'-ro, rah], *a.* 1. Disengaged, unemployed. 2. A supernumerary ploughman, who supplies the place of another.

sobrante [so-brahn'-tay], *m.* 1. Residue, superfluity, overplus. 2. Rich, wealthy. -*pa.* of SOBRAR.

sobrar [so-brar'], *vn.* 1. To have more than is necessary or required. 2. To be over and above: to be more than enough (ser más que suficiente), to be intrusive. 3. To remain (quedar de más), to be left. **Más vale que sobre que no que falte,**

(Prov.) it is better to have too much of a thing than to be in want of it.

sobrasada [so-brah-sah'-dah], *f. V.* SOBREASADA.

sobrasar [so-brah-sar'], *va.* To add fire under a pot to make it boil sooner or better; to surround with coals.

sobre [so'-bray], *prep.* 1. Above (encima de), over (cantidad). *V.* ENCIMA. 2. Super, over: used in composition, as *sobrecargar,* to overcharge or overload. **Tiene mucha ventaja sobre todos los demás,** he possesses great advantages over the rest. 3. Moreover, besides. 4. A little more; a few more. 5. Above, higher; with power or superiority. 6. *(Naut.)* Off. 7. To, towards, near. 8. On, upon. 9. After, since. 10. Before or around. **Está sobre la mesa,** it's on the table. **Estar sobre uno,** to keep on at somebody. **Un préstamo sobre una propiedad,** a loan on a property.

sobre [so'-bray], *m.* 1. Envelope of a letter. 2. Address, superscription.

sobreabundancia [so-bray-ahn-boon-dahn'-the-ah], *f.* Superabundance.

sobreabundante [so-bray-ah-boon-dahn'-tay], *a.* Superabundant, more than enough; luxuriant.

sobreabundantemente [so-bray-ah-bon-dahn'-tay-men-tay], *adv.* Superabundantly.

sobreabundar [so-bray-ah-boon-dar'], *vn.* To superabound; to be exuberant.

sobreaguar [so-bray-ah-goo-ar'], *vn.* To be on the surface of water, to float on water.

sobreaguda [so-bray-ah-goo'-dah], *f.* One of the seven small letters in music.

sobreagudo [so-bray-ah-goo'-do], *m. (Mus.)* Highest treble in music.

sobrealiento [so-bray-ah-le-en'-to], *m.* Difficult respiration.

sobrealimentar [so-bray-ah-le-men-tar'], *va.* 1. Supercharge. 2. To give extra nourishment.

sobrealzar [so-bray-al-thar'], *va.* To praise, to extol.

sobreañadir [so-bray-ah-nyah-deer'], *va.* To superadd, to superinduce.

sobrañal [so-brey-ah-nyahl'], *a.* Applied to animals more than a year old.

sobreasada [so-bray-ah-sah'-dah], *f.* In Mallorca, a kind of sausage half roasted, and done over again when it is to be eaten.

sobreasar [so-bray-ah-sar'], *va.* To roast again what was half roasted before.

sobrebásico, ca [ro-bray-bah'-se-co, cah], *a. (Chem.)* Having an excess of base; a basic salt.

sobreboya [so-bray-bo'-yah], *f. (Naut.)* Marking buoy, a small buoy fastened to a large one in the water, to show its position.

sobrebrazal [so-bray-brah-thahl'], *m. (Naut.)* False rail.

sobrecaja [so-bray-cah'-hah], *f.* Outer case.

sobrecalza [so-bray-cahl'-thah], *f. V.* POLAINA.

sobrecama [so-bray-cah'-mah], *f.* Coverlet, quilt.

sobrecaña [so-bray-cah'-nyah], *f. (Vet.)* Tumor on a horse's leg.

sobrecarga [so-bray-car'-gah], *f.* 1. An additional bundle thrown over a load. 2. Additional trouble or vexation. 3. Surcharge (correos), overburden. 4. Rope thrown over a load to make it fast (cuerda). **Sobrecarga de importación,** import surcharge.

sobrecargado, da [so-bray-car-gah'-do, dah], *a. & pp.* of SOBRECARGAR. Overloaded.

sobrecargar [so-bray-car-gar'], *va.* 1. To overload (camión), to surcharge, to overburden. 2. To make one seam over another.

sobrecargo [so-bray-car'-go], *m.* 1. Ship's purser (barco). 2. Plane stewardess (avión).

sobrecarta [so-bray-car'-tah], *f.* 1. Cover, envelope, of a letter. 2. The second injunction; decree or warrant, repenting a former order.

sobrecartar [so-bray-car-tar'], *va.* To repeat a former injunction.

sobrecebadera [so-bray-thay-bah-day'-rah], *f. (Naut.)* Sprit top-sail.

sobrecédula [so-bray-thay'-doo-lah], *f.* Second royal order or despatch.

sobreceja [so-bray-thay'-hah], *f.* The part of the forehead over the eyebrows.

sobrecejo [so-bray-thay'-ho], *m.* Frown (ceño); supercilious aspect, cloudiness of look.

sobrecelestial [so-bray-thay-les-te-ahl'], *a.* Supercelestial.

sobreceño [so-bray-thay'-nyo], *m.* Frown. *V.* SOBRECEJO.

sobrecerco [so-bray-therr'-co], *m.* Ornament or fringe placed round another to strengthen it.

sobrecincha [so-bray-theen'-chah], *f.* One of the girths of a saddle; a surcingle.

sobrecincho [so-bray-theen'-cho], *m.* Surcingle, an additional girth, put over the common girth.

sobreclaustro [so-bray-clah'-oos-tro], *m.* Apartment over a cloister.

sobrecoger [so-bray-co-herr'], *vn.* To surprise, to overtake. -*m.* To become apprehensive.

sobrecogimiento [so-bray-co-he-me-en'-to], *m.* Fearfulness, apprehension.

sobrecomida [so-bray-co-mee'-dah], *f.* Dessert. *V.* POSTRE.

sobrecomprimir [so-bray-com-pre-meer'], *va. (Aer.)* To pressurize.

sobrecopa [so-bray-co'-pah], *f.* Cover or lid of a cup.

sobrecrecer [so-bray-cray-therr'], *vn.* To outgrow, to overgrow.

sobrecreciente [so-bray-cray-the-en'-tay], *pa.* Outgrowing, overgrowing.

sobrecruces [so-bray-croo'-thes], *m. pl.* Cross-joints to strengthen a wheel.

sobrecubierta [so-bray-coo-be-err'-tah], *f.* 1. Double cover. 2. Coverlet, quilt. 3. *(Naut.)* Upper deck.

sobredezmero [so-bray-deth-may'-ro], *m.* Assistant in collecting duties.

sobredicho, cha [so-bray-dee'-cho, chah], *a.* Above-mentioned.

sobrediente [so-bray-de-en'-tay], *m.* Gag-tooth which grows over another.

sobredorar [so-bray-do-rar'], *va.* 1. To gild anew, to over-gild. 2 To palliate, to extenuate, to exculpate.

sobredosis [so-bray-do'-sees], *f.* Overdose.

sobreedificar [so-bray-ay-de-fe-car'], *va.* To build over something.

sobreempeine [so-bray-em-pay'-e-nayh], *m.* That part of spatterdashes or gaiters which covers the instep.

sobreentender [so-bray-en-ten-derr'], *va. & va. V.* SOBRENTENDER.

sobreescrito [so-bray-es-cree'-to], *m.* 1. Superscription, inscription, direction, address. 2. Mien, aspect; pretext.

sobreesdrújulo, la [so-bray-es-droo'-hoo-lo, lah], *a. V.* SOBRESDRÚJULO.

sobreestadía [so-bray-es'-tah-dee'-ah], *f. (Com.)* One of the extra lay days: an allowance of time made in loading and unloading a vessel and the sum paid.

sobreexceder [so-bray-ex-thay-derr'], *va. V.* SOBREXCEDER.

sobrefaz [so-bray-fath'], *f.* 1. Superficies, surface, outside. 2. *(Mil.)* Face prolonged, the distance between the angle of the shoulder of a bastion and the curtain.

sobrefino, na [so-bray-fee'-no, nah], *a.* Superfine, overfine.

sobreguarda [so-bray-goo-ar'-dah], *m.* Second guard placed for greater security.

sobreguardilla [so-bray-goo-ar-deel'-lyah], *f.* Penthouse, shelter, shed.

sobrehaz [so-bray-ath'], *f.* 1. Surface, outside. 2. Outside cover of something.

sobrehueso [so-bray-oo-ay'-so], *m.* 1. Morbid swelling on the bones or joints. 2. Trouble, encumbrance, burden.

sobrehumano, na [so-bray-oo-mah'-no, nah], *a.* Superhuman.

sobrehusa [so-bray-oo'-sah], *f.* A stew made in Andalusia from fried fish.

sobreimpresión [so-bray-em-pray-se-on'], *f.* Overprint (correos).

sobreimprimir [so-bray-em-pre-meer'], *va.* To overprint.

sobrejalma [so-bray-hahl'-mah], *f.* Woollen cover for a packsaddle.

sobrelecho [so-bray-lay'-cho], *m.* That side of a stone which lies on a bed of mortar.

sobrellave [so-brel-lyah'-vay], *f.* Double key, a large key. -*m.* In royal palaces, an officer who keeps a second key of every door.

sobrellenar [so-bray-lyay-nar'], *va.* To overfill, to overflow, to glut.

sobrelleno, na [so-brel-lyay'-no, nah], *a.* Overfull, superabundant.

sobrellevar [so-brel-lyay-var'], *adv.* 1. To ease another's burden; to carry (peso). 2. To inure to hardships by degrees, to undergo. 3. To overlook the failings of interiors or subjects.

sobremallero [so-bray-mal-lyay'-ro], *m.* One of the four kinds of net used in the sardine-fishery off the Cantabrian coast.

sobremanera [so-bray-mah-nay'-rah], *adv.* Beyond measure; excessively.

sobremano [so-bray-mah'-no], *f.* (*Vet.*) Osseous tumor on the hoofs of horses' fore feet.

sobremesa [so-bray-may'-sah], *f.* 1. Table-carpet, tablecloth (mantel). 2. Dessert (del postre). 3. Sitting on after a meal. **Charla de sobremesa**, after-dinner talk, table talk. **Un cigarro de sobremesa**, an after dinner cigar. *V.* POSTRE. **De sobremesa**, immediately after dinner.

sobremesana [so-bray-may-sah'-nah], *f.* (*Naut.*) Mizzen top-sail.

sobrenadar [so-bray-nah-dar'], *va.* To swim on the surface of any fluid, to overfloat.

sobrenatural [so-bray-nah-too-rahl'], *a.* Supernatural, preternatural, metaphysical.

sobrenombre [so-bray-nom'-bray], *m.* 1. Surname, the family name. 2. Nickname; a name given in contempt.

sobrentender [so-bren-ten-derr'], *va. & vr.* To understand something not expressed, but which must be supposed from what has gone before; to be understood.

sobreojo [so-bray-o'-ho], *m.* A supercilious aspect; a look of envy, hatred, or contempt.

sobrepaga [so-bray-pah'-gah], *f.* Increase of pay; extra pay.

sobrepaño [so-bray-pah'-nyo], *m.* Upper cloth, put over others; wrapper.

sobreparto [so-bray-par'-to], *m.* 1. Time of lying-in, which follows the delivery. 2. Delicate state of health which follows confinement.

sobrepasar [so-bray-pah-sar'], *va.* 1. To excel, to surpass. 2. To exceed (límite).

sobrepeine [so-bray-pay'-nay], *m.* The act of cutting the hair but slightly.-*adv.* (*Coll.*) Slightly, briefly.

sobrepelliz [so-bray-pel-lyeth'], *f.* Surplice.

sobrepeso [so-bray-pay'-so], *m.* Over-weight.

sobrepié [so-bray-pee-ay'], *m.* (*Vet.*) Osseous tumor at the top of horses' hoofs.

sobreplán [so-bray-plahn'], *m.* (*Naut.*) Rider.

sobreponer [so-bray-po-nerr'], *va.* To add one thing to another; to put one over another. -*vr.* To exalt oneself above other things; to wise oneself, to overcome, to overpower. **Sobreponerse a una enfermedad**, to pull through an illness. (*Yo sobrepongo, yo sobreponga; yo sobrepuse; from Sobreponer. V.* PONER.)

sobreprecio [so-bray-pray'-the-o], *m.* 1. Surcharge. 2. Markup.

sobreprima [so-bray-pree'-ma], *f.* Increased premium (en seguros).

sobreproducción [so-bray-pro-dooc-the-on'], *f.* Overproduction.

sobrepuerta [so-bray-poo-err'-tah], *f.* 1. Cornice, a kind of louver-board put over interior doors, from which curtains are hung. 2. In a general sense, any painting, woven stuff, carved work, etc., put over doors for ornament.

sobrepuesto, ta [so-bray-poo-es'-to, tah], *a. & pp. irr.* of SOBREPONER. Counterfeit, fictitious.

sobrepuesto [so-bray-poo-es'-to], *m.* 1. Honeycomb formed by bees after the hive is full. 2. Earthen vessel added to beehives when they are too full.

sobrepuja [so-bray-poo'-hah], *f.* Outbidding, bidding more than another.

sobrepujamiento [so-bray-poo-hah-me-en'-to], *m.* The act and effect of surpassing, excelling.

sobrepujante [so-bray-poo-hahn'-tay], *pa.* Surpassing, excelling.

sobrepujanza [so-bray-poo-hahn'-thah], *f.* Great strength and vigor.

sobrepujar [so-bray-poo-har'], *va.* To exceed, to surpass, to excel, to foil, to overturn.

sobrequilla [so-bray-keel'-lyah], *f.* (*Naut.*) Keelson.

sobrerronda [so-brer-ron'-dah], *f.* (*Mil.*) Counter-round.

sobrerropa [so-brer-ro'-pah], *f.* A sort of long robe worn over other clothes.

sobresal [so-bry-sahl'], *f.* (*Chem.*) An acid salt.

sobresalario [so-bray-sah-lah'-re-o], *m.* Perquisites: what is added to a salary.

sobresalido, da [ro-bray-sah-lee'-do, dah], *a. & pp.* of SOBRESALIR. Elated, inflated, haughty.

sobresaliente [so-bray-sah-le-en-tay], *a.* Excelling, surpassing, excellent.

sobresaliente [so-bray-sah-le-en'-tay], *m.* 1. (*Mil.*) Officer who commands a small body of troops always ready for an emergency. 2. Substitute. 3. An actor or actress (*sobresaliente*), ready to perform the part of one absent or sick.

sobresalir [so-bray-sah-leer'], *vn.* To exceed in height, to overtop, to overreach, to surpass, to outvie. (*Yo sobresalgo, yo sobresalga, from Sobresalir. V.* SALIR.)

sobresaltadamente [so-bray-sal-tah'-dah-men-tay], *adv.* Suddenly, unexpectedly.

sobresaltado, da [so-bray-sal-tah'-do, dah], *a.* Startled, frightened.

sobresaltar [so-bray-sal-tar'], *va.* 1. To rush violently upon, to assail, to surprise or to fall upon unexpectedly. 2. To frighten, to terrify, to startle. -*vn.* To fly in one's face, to be striking (cuadros). -*vr.* To be startled at, to be surprised, confused, or perplexed.

sobresalto [so-bray-sahl'-to], *m.* A sudden assault, a surprise (sorpresa); a sudden dread or fear. **De sobresalto**, unexpectedly, unawares.

sobresanar [so-bray-sah-nar'], *va.* 1. To heal superficially. 2. To screen, to palliate.

sobresanos [so-bray-sah-'nos], *m. pl.* (*Naut.*) Tabling, a broad hem on sails, to strengthen that part which is fastened to the bolt-rope.

sobrescribir [so-bres-cre-berr'], *va.* To superscribe, to inscribe, to address or direct a letter.

sobrescrito [so-bres-cree'-to], *m.* Superscription, address or direction of a letter.—**Sobrescrito, ta**, *pp.* of SOBRESCRIBIR.

sobresdrújulo, la [so-bres-droo'-hoo-lo, lah], *a.* Accented upon the syllable preceding the antepenult; as, *devuélvemelo*.

sobreseer [so-bray-say-err'], *vn.* 1. To desist from a design; to supersede; to relinquish a claim or pretension; to overrule. 2. (*Law.*) To discontinue an action.

sobreseguro [so-bray-say-goo'-ro], *adv.* In a safe manner, without risk.

sobreseimiento [so-bray-say-e-me-en'-to], *m.* Omission; suspension; discontinuance.

sobresello [so-bray-sel'-lyo], *m.* A double seal.

sobresembrar [so-bray-sem-brar'], *va.* 1. To sow over again. 2. To diffuse erroneous doctrines; to sow discord.

sobreseñal [so-bray-say-nyahl'], *f.* Ensign or standard arbitrarily adopted by the ancient knights.

sobresolar [so-bray-so-lar'], *va.* 1. To pave anew. 2. To new-sole boots or shoes.

sobrestadías [so-brays-tah-dee'-ahs], *f.* V. SOBREESTADÍA.

sobrestante [so-bres-tahn'-tay], *m.* Overseer; foreman; comptroller; overlooker.

sobrestante [so-bres-tahn´-tay], *a.* Immediate, near.

sobresueldo [so-bray-soo-el´-do], *m.* Addition to one's pay or allowance.

sobresuelo [so-bray-soo-ay'-lo], *m.* A second floor or pavement laid over another.

sobretarde [so-bray-tar'-day], *f.* Close of the evening.

sobretejer [so-bray-tay-herr'], *va..* To work a stuff on both sides.

sobretodo [so-bray-to'-do], *m.* Overcoat, surtout, a great-coat.

sobretodo [so-bray-to'-do], *adv.* Above all; before all things.

sobreedor [so-bray-ah-dor'], *m.* Supervisor, overseer.

sobrevalorar [so-bray-va-lo-rahr'], *va.* To overvalue.

sobrevenda [so-bray-ven'-dah], *f. (Med.)* Surband, bandage placed over others.

sobrevenida, [so-bray-vay-nee'-dah], *f.* Supervention.

sobrevenir [so-bray-vay-neer'], *m.* To happen (ocurrir); to fall out, to come unexpectedly; to come between; to come in the way; to supervene.

sobreventar [so-bray-ven-tar'], *m. (Naut.)* To gain the weather-gauge of another ship.

sobreverterse [so-bray-ver-terr'-say], *vr.* To run over, to overflow.

sobrevestir [so-bray-ves-teer´], *va.* To put on a great coat.

sobrevidriera [so-bray-ve-dre-ay´-rah], *f.* Wire net before a glass window.

sobreviento [so-bray-ve-en'-to], *m.* Gust of wind; impetuous fury, surprise.

sobreviniente [so-bray-ve-ne-en'-tay], *pa.* Happening, falling out, coming in the way.

sobreviviente [so-bray-ve-ve-en'-tay], *va. pa. & m. & f.* Survivor, surviving. V. SUPERVIVIENTE.

sobrevivir [so-bray-ve-veer'], *vn.* To survive (accidente, desastre), to outlive. **Sobrevivir a alguno,** to outlive or survive a person.

sobrevolar [so-bray-vo-lahr'], *va.* To fly over.

sobrexceder [so-brex-thay-derr'], *va.* To surpass, to excel another, to exceed.

sobrexcitación [so-brex-the-tah-the-on´], *f.* Over-stimulation of vital organs.

sobriamente [so-bre-ah-men-tay], *adv.* Soberly, frugally, abstemiously.

sobriedad [so-bre-ay-dahd'], *f.* Sobriety, abstemiousness, abstinence.

sobrina [so-bree'-nah], *f.* Niece.

sobrinazgo [so-bre-nath'-go]. 1. The relationship of a nephew or niece. 2. Nepotism.

sobrino [so-bree'-no], *m.* Nephew.

sobrio, ria [so'-bre-o, ah], *a.* Sober (templado), temperate, frugal, abstemious.

soca, or **soca de planta** [so'-cah], *f. (Amer.)* The sugar-cane which is cut down to be planted for the new crop.

socaire [so-cah'-e-ray], *m.* 1. *(Naut.)* Slatch, slack of a rope or cable. 2. Shelter, lee, lee gauge.

socairero [so-cah-e-ray'-ro], *m.* Skulker, lurker, one who hides himself from his business or duty.

socaliña [so-cah-lee'-nyah], *f.* Cunning or artifice to gain a thing from one who is not obliged to give it.

socaliñar [so-ca-lee-nyar'], *va.* To extort by cunning or stratagem.

socaliñero, ra [so-cah-le-nyay´-ro, rah], *m. & f.* Artful exacter, a cheat.

socalzar [so-cal-thar'], *va.* To strengthen the lower part of a building or wall which threatens ruin.

socamarero [so-cah-may-ray'-ro], *m.* 1. The second steward, or man-servant of a great house. 2. The second lord chamberlain.

socapa [so-cah'-pah], *f.* Pretext, pretence. **A socapa,** on presence, under color.

socaspicol [so-cah-pis-cole'], *m.* V. SOCHANTRE.

socar [so-car'], *va. (Naut.)* To set taut a rope, shroud, or stay.

socarra [so-car'-rah], *f.* 1. The act of half roasting meat, or leaving it half rare. 2. Craft, cunning.

socarrar [so-car-rar'], *va.* To half roast or dress meat.

socarrén [so-car-rayn´], *m.* Eave, the edge of the roof, gable end.

socarrena [so-car-ray'-nah], *f.* Hollow, cavity, interval.

socarrina [so-car-ree'-nah], *f. (Coll.)* Scorching, singeing.

socarrón, na [so-car-rone', nah], *a.* Cunning (taimado), sly (humor), crafty.

socarronería [so-car-ro-nay-ree´-ah], *f.* Craft (astucia), cunning, artfulness.

socava [so-cah'-vah], *f.* 1. The act of mining or undermining. 2. The act of opening the ground around trees.

socavar [so-cah-var'], *va.* To excavate, to undermine (excavar). **Socavar la tierra,** to turn up the ground.

socavón [so-cah-vone'], *m.* 1. Cave, cavern (cueva); a passage under ground. 2. Adit, the entrance to a mine. **Socavones,** pits or shafts in mines.

sociabilidad [so-the-ah-be-le-dahd'], *f.* Sociableness, sociability, civility.

sociable [so-the-ah'-blay], *a.* 1. Sociable (persona), ready to unite in a general interest. 2. Sociable, inclined to company, companionable. 3. Sociable, familiar, friendly, courteous.

sociablemente [so-the-ah'-blay-men-tay], *adv.* Sociably, companionably.

social [so-the-ahl'], *a.* 1. Social, relating to society, or to a general or public interest. 2. Social, companionable, relating to company or friendly intercourse.

socialismo [so-the-ah-lees'-mo], *m.* Socialism, a political doctrine proposing a reconstruction of society.

socialista [so-the-ah-lees'-tah], *m & f.* Socialist, one professing socialism.

socialmente [so-the-ahl'-men-tay], *adv.* Socially.

sociedad [so-the-ai-dahd´], *f.* 1. Society, the company and converse of persons of sense and information. 2. Friendship, familiar intercourse. 3. Society, union of many in one general interest; corporation, consociation, fraternity, fellowship. 4. Society (asociación), partnership. **Sociedad inmobiliaria,** building society. **Notas de sociedad,** gossip column.

sociedad anónima [ah-no'-ne-mah], *f.* (Abbreviated S.A.) Incorporated company *(Inc.)*

socio [so'-the-o], *m.* 1. Partner, associate. 2. Member (de un club). **Se ruega a los señores socios....,** members are asked to...

sociología [so-the-o-lo-hee´-ah], *f.* Sociology, the study of the evolution and organization of society.

sociológico, ca [so-the-o-lo'-he-co, cah], *a.* Sociological.

sociólogo, ga [so-the-o'-lo-go, gah], *m. & f.* Sociologist.

socolor [so-co-lor'], *m.* Pretext, pretence, color.

socollada [so-col-lyah'-dah], *f. (Naut.)* Jerk, the violent straining of the ropes, cables, and shrouds, caused by the rolling and pitching of a ship.

soconusco [so-co-noos'-co], *m.* The cocoa from the province of that name in Chiapas (Mexico) and in N. W. Guatemala, considered to be of the best quality.

socorredor, ra [so-cor-ray-dor', rah], *m. & f.* Succourer, assister; administering relief, helper.

socorrer [so-cor-rerr'], *pa.* 1. To succour, to aid, to help (persona), to favor. 2. To pay a part of what is due.

socorrido, da [so-cor-ree'-do, dah], *a & pp.* of SOCORRER. Furnished, well supplied. **La plaza de Acapulco es muy socorrida,** the market of Acapulco is well supplied. *(Coll.)* Handy, useful.

socorrismo [so-cor-rees'-mo], *m.* Life-saving.

socorrista [so-cor-rees'-tah], *m & f.* Lifeguard, life-saver.

socorro [so-cor'-ro], *m.* 1. Succor, support, assistance, help (ayuda). 2. Part of a salary or allowance paid beforehand. 3. Succor, a fresh supply of men or provisions thrown into a besieged place. **Trabajos de socorro,** relief work.

socrático, ca [so-crah'-te-co, cah], *a.* Socratic, relating to the doctrines of Socrates.

socucho [so-coo'-cho], *m. (Mex.)* 1. A large and narrow room in the lower story of a house. 3. Hiding-place, cave.

socrocio [so-cro'-the-o], *m.* 1. Poultice or cataplasm of a saffron color. 2. Pleasure, delight, satisfaction.

sochantre [so-chahn'-tray], *m.* Subchanter, the deputy of the preceptor in a cathedral.

soda [so'-dah], *f.* 1. *(Bot.)* V. SOSA. 2. Soda water (bebida).

sodio [so'-de-o], *m. (Chem.)* Sodium, a silver-white, alkaline, metallic element.

sodomía [so-do-mee'-ah], *f.* Sodomy, an unnatural crime.

sodomita [so-do-mee'-tah], *m. & a.* Sodomite, one who commits sodomy

sodomítico, ca [so-do-mee'-te-co, cah], *a.* Belonging to sodomy.

soez [so-eth'], *a.* Mean, vile, base, worthless, shameful.

soezmonte [so-eth'-men-tay], *adv.* Meanly, basely, vilely, shamefuly.

sofá [so-fah'], *m.* Sofa.

sofá cama [so-fah' cah'-mah], *m.* Studio couch.

sofaldar [so-fal-dar'], *va.* To truss up; to raise up; to tuck up; to lift up anything in order to discover it.

sofaldo so-fahl'-do], *m.* The act of trussing or tucking up clothes.

sofí [so-fee'], *m.* 1. Sufi, sofi, the Emperor or Shah of Persia. 2. A sect of mystics of that country. V. SUFÍ.

sofión [so-fe-one'], *m.* Hoot, shout in scorn or contempt; reprimand (reprimenda), censure.

sofisma [so-fees'-mah], *m.* Sophism, a fallacious argument.

sofismo [so-fees'-mo], *m.* V. SUFISMO.

sofista [so-fees'-tah], *m.* Sophister, a disputant; an artful but insidious logician; a caviller, a sophist.

sofistería [so-fis-tay-ree'-ah], *f.* Sophistry, fallacy.

sofisticación [so-fis-te-cah-the-on'], *f.* Sophistication, adulteration.

sofisticado [so-fis-te-cah'-do], *a.* Sophisticated; affected, over-refined.

sofísticamente [so-fees'-te-cah-men-tay], *adv.* Sophistically, fallaciously.

sofisticar [so-fis-te-car'], *va.* To cavil, to falsify; to sophisticate.

sofístico, ca [so-fees'-te-co, cah], *a.* Sophistical, fallacious.

sófito [so'-fee-to], *m. (Arch.)* Soffit, under side of the cornice ornamented with panels, etc.

soflama [so-flah'-mah], *f.* 1. A subtile flame; the reverberation of fire (fuego). 2. Glow, blush. 3. Deceitful language.

soflamar [so-flah-mar'], *va.* 1. To use deceitful language, to impose upon, to deceive (engañar). 2. To rise a blush.

soflanero [so-flah-nay'-ro], *m.* Sophister, one that makes use of captious or deceitful language.

sofocación [so-fo-cah-the-on'], *f.* 1. Suffocation, strangling. 2. *(Med.)* Suffocation, apnea, loss of breath.

sofocado [so-fo-cah'-do], *a.* **Estar sofocado,** to be out of breath.

sofocante [so-fo-cahn'-tay], *m.* Ribbon with a tassel, worn by ladies round the neck. -pa. of SOFOCAR.

sofocar [so-fo-car'], *va.* 1. To choke, to impede respiration, to suffocate (persona). 2. To quench, to smother (incendio). 3. To oppress, to harass. 4. To importune, to molest. 5. To provoke by abusive language. -vr. 1. To suffocate (ahogarse). 2. *(Fig.)* To blush. **No vale la pena de que te sofoques,** it's not worth upsetting yourself about it.

sofoco [so-fo'-co], *m.* 1. Suffocation. 2. Great aversion given or received, loathing.

sofocón [so-fo-cone'], *m.* Displeasure, provocation. **Llevarse un sofocón,** to have a sudden shock.

sófora [so'-fo-rah], *f. (Bot.)* A tree of Japan cultivated for ornament in European gardens.

sofreír [so-fray-eer'], *vn.* To fry slightly.

sofrenada [so-fray-nah'-dah], *f.* 1. A sudden check given to a horse with the bridle (caballo). 2. A rude reprehension; a severe reprimand (bronca). 3. A fit of sickness, or any other accident that forewarns us of our frailties.

sofrenar [so-fray-nar'], *va.* 1. To check a horse by a violent pull of the bridle. 2. To reprehend rudely; to reprimand severely (bronca).

sofrenazo [so-fray-nah-tho], *m.* A violent pull of the bridle.

sofrito, ta [so-free'-to, tah], *pp. irr.* of SOFREIR.

software [soft-oo-ah-ray], *m. (Comput.)* Software. **Software del ratón,** mouse software. **Software para presentaciones gráficas,** presentation graphics software.

soga [so'-gah], *f.* 1. Rope; halter (de animal), cord. 2. *(Coll.)* A sly, cunning fellow. 3. Measure of land which varies in different provinces; measure of rope. **Sopa de un pozo,** bucket-rope for a a well. -int. A term expressing astonishment and aversion. **Siempre se rompe la soga por lo más delgado,** the rope always breaks at the thinnest part. **Estar con la soga al cuello la garganta,** *(Met.)* to be in imminent danger.

soguear [so-gay-ar'], *va. 1.* To measure with a rope. 2. *(And. CAm. Cono Sur)* To tie with a rope (atar). 3. *(Carib.)* To tame (domesticar).

soguería [so-gay-ree'-ah], *f.* Ropewalk, rope-yard; collection of ropes.

soguero [so-gay'-ro], *m.* A rope-maker, a cord-maker.

soguica, illa, ita [so-gee'-cah], *f. dim.* A small rope.

soguilla [so-geel'-lyah], *f. (Prov.)* A small band of braid or plaited hair.

soja [so-hah], *f.* Soya.

sojuzgador [so-hooth-gah-dor'], *m.* Conqueror, subduer.

sojuzgar [so-hooth-gar'], *va.* To conquer, to subjugate.

sol [sole], *m.* 1. Sun, sunshine, sunlight. 2. *(Met.)* The light, warmth or influence of the sun. 3. A kind of face of ancient make. 4. *(Mus.)* G, sol, the fifth note of the scale. **Sol mayor,** G major. 5. Sol, a Peruvian currency." **Rayo del sol,** sunbeam. **Quemadura del sol,** sunburn. **Reloj del sol,** sundial. **La luz del sol,** sunlight. **El sol sale,** the sun rises. **El sol se pone,** the sun sets. **Al sol puesto,** at nightfall. **A la puesta del sol,** at sunset. **Al salir del sol,** at sunrise. **El sol pica,** the sun scorches. **No dejar ni a sol ni a sombra,** to molest or pursue a person constantly. **Tomar el sol,** to bask in the sun. **Soles,** sparkling, dazzling eyes. **Este niño es un sol,** this is a lovely child.

solada [so-lah'-dah], *f.* Floor, site; seat.

solado [so-lah'-do], *m.* Floor, covered with tiles or flags: pavement.—Solado, da, *pp.* of SOLAR.

solador [so-la-dor'], *m.* Tiler, pavier.

soladura [so-lah-doo'-rah], *f.* Act of paving; materials used for paving or pavement.

solamente [so-lah-men-tay], *adv.* Only, solely.

solana [so-lah'-nah], *f.* Sunparlor, sunporch, a place warmed by the sun, open gallery for taking the sun, solarium, sunroom.

solanáceas [so-lah-nah' thay as], *f. pl.* The solanaceae, the nightshade family.

solanar [so-lah-nar'], *m. (Prov.)* V. SOLANA for a gallery.

solanazo [so-lah-nah'-tho], *m. aug.* A violent, hot, and troublesome easterly wind.

solano [so-lah'-no], *m.* 1. Easterly winds. 2. *(Bot.)* Nightshade.

solapa [so-lah'-pah], *f.* 1. Lapel (de chaqueta), a double breast on clothes. 2. Color, presence, pretext. 3. *(Vet.)* Cavity of a small wound in animals.

solapadamente [so-lah-pah'-dah-men-tay], *adv.* In a dissembling manner; deceitfully.

solapado, da [so-lah-pah'-do, dah], *a.* Cunning, crafty, artful, evasive (evasivo). -pp. of SOLAPAR.

solapadura

solapadura (Obra de) [so-lah-pah-doo´-rah], *f. (Naut.)* Clincher-work, clinching.

solapamiento [so-lah-pah-me-en´-to], *m. (Vet.)* Cavity of a wound in animals.

solapar [so-lah-par´], *va.*. 1. To button one breast-part of clothes over another. 2. To cloak, to hide under a false pretence.

solape, solapo [so-lah´-pay], *m.* Lapel; pretense. *V.* SOLAPA. **A solapo,** in a hidden or furtive manner.

solar [so-lar´], *m.* 1. Ground on which a house is built, ground-plot. 2. Spot on which stands the original mansion of a noble family. 3. *(CAm. Carib.)* Patio (corral). 4. *(And. Carib.)* Tenement house (tugurio). -*a.* Solar, solary, belonging to the sun.

solar [so-lahr´], *va.* 1. To floor a room; to pave a stable or coach-yard. 2. To sole shoes or boots.

solariego, ga [so-lah-re-ay´-go, gah], *a.* 1. Belonging to the ancient mansion of a noble family. 2. Relating to free hold and other estates, which appertain with full and unlimited right of property to the owner. 3. Descending from an ancient noble family.

solas (A) [so´-lahs], *adv.* All alone by myself, yourself, himself, herself, themselves. *V.* SOLO. **Ella estaba a solas,** she was alone. **Los niños estaban a solas,** the children were by themselves.

solaz [so-lath´], *m.* Solace (consuelo), consolation, relaxation, comfort. **A solaz,** pleasantly, agreeably.

solazar [so-lah-thar´], *va.* To solace, to comfort (alegrar), to cheer, to amuse. -*vr.* To be comforted, to be joyful, to relax.

solazo [so-lah´-tho], *m. aug. (Coll.)* A scorching sun.

solazoso, sa [so-lah-tho´-so, sah], *a.* Comfortable, delectable.

soldada [sol-dah´-dah], *f.* Wages, pay given for service.

soldadero, ra [sol-dah-day´-ro, rah], *a.* Stipendiary, receiving wages or hire.

soldadesca [sol-dah-des´-cah], *f.* 1. Soldiery, the profession of a soldier (profesión); military art or science, soldiership (used in a depreciative sense). 2. Sham-fight. **A la soldadesca,** in a soldierly manner, for the use of soldiers.

soldadesco, ca [sol-dah-des´-co, cah], *a.* Soldierly, soldier-like, military.

soldado [sol-dah´-do], *m.* 1. Soldier. **Soldado raso,** a common soldier, a private. **Soldado de infantería,** infantryman. **Soldado de a caballo,** trooper, horse-soldier, cavalryman. 2. **Soldado, da,** *pp.* of SOLDAR.

soldador [sol-dah-dor´], *m.* 1. Solderer. 2. Soldering-iron.

soldadura [sol-dah-doo´-rah], *f.* 1. The act of soldering by means of a metallic cement, welding. 2. Solder (sustancia). 3. Correction or mending of something. **Soldadura autógena,** welding.

soldán [sol-dahn´], *m.* Sultan, Mohammedan title. *V.* SULTÁN.

soldar [sol-dar´], *va.* To solder (estañar), to weld (autógena), to mend, to correct, to join (unir), to cement (cementar); to patch up (disputa). -*vr.* To knit (huesos).

soleado [so-lay-ah´-do], *a.* Sunny.

solear [so-lay-ahr´], *va.* To put in the sun (dejar al sol), to bleach (blanquear).

solecismo [so-lay-thees´-mo], *m. (Coll.)* A scorching sun.

solecito [so-lay-thee´-to], *m. (Coll.)* A scorching sun.

soledad [so-lay-dahd´], *f.* 1. Solitude (estado), loneliness (aislamiento), solitariness. 2. Solitude, a lonely place, a desert (lugar). 3. The state of an orphan, orphanage. 4. Grieving, mourning.

soledoso, sa [so-lay´-do-so, sah], *a.* Solitary.

solejar [so-lay-har´], *m.* A place exposed to the sun.

solemne [so-lem´-nay], *a.* 1. Yearly, anniversary, performed once a year at the revolution of the sun. 2. Celebrated, famous. 3. Grand, solemn, high. 4. Festive, joyous, gay, cheerful. **Es un solemne bobo,** *(Coll.)* he is a downright booby.

solemnemente [so-lem´-nay-men-tay], *adv.* Solemnly, in a festive manner.

solemnidad [so-lem-ne-dahd´], *f.* 1. Solemnity (cualidad), solemnness. 2. Solemnity, a religious festival, and the pomp or magnificence of a feast or festival. 3. *pl.* Formalities prescribed by law. **Pobre de solemnidad,** a poor man in real distress.

solemnizador, ra [so-lem-ne-thah-dor´, rah], *m. & f.* One who solemnizes; a panegyrist.

solemnizar [so-lem-ne-thar´], *va.* 1. To solemnize, to praise, to applaud. 2. To solemnize, to perform in a festive manner; to keep or cerebrate joyously.

sóleo [so´-lay-o], *m.* Soleus, a muscle of the calf of the leg.

soler [so-lerr´], *vn. irr. & defect. 1.* To accustom or be accustomed; to be used to; to be apt to, to be wont; to keep. 2. *(Cono Sur)* To occur (ocurrir). **Suele pasar por aquí,** he usually comes this way. **Suele ocurrir,** it sometimes happens. **Suele dar buenas propinas,** he usually gives good tips. **Solíamos venir todos los años,** we used to come every year. -*m. (Naut.)* Under flooring of a ship.

solera [so-lay´-rah], *f.* 1. Entablature, the uppermost row of stones of a wall, on which the beams rest; stringpiece, cross-beam, rib. 2. A flat stone, which serves as a foundation to the base of a pillar; a plinth (plinto). 3. Lower millstone (piedra de molino). 4. *(Prov.)* Lees (del vino). 5. *(Mex.)* Flagstone (baldosa). 6. *(Cono Sur)* Kerb (de acera).

solercia [so-lerr´-the-ah], *f.* Industry; abilities, talents; artfulness.

solería [so-lay-ree´-ah], *f.* 1. Floor or pavement of a room. 2. Parcel of skins used for soles. *V.* SOLADO.

solero [so-lay´-ro], *m. (Prov.)* Lower millstone.

solerte [so-lerr´-tay], *a.* Cunning, sagacious.

soleta [so-lay´-tah], *f.* 1. A linen sole put into stockings. 2. *(Mex.)* A biscuit covered with sugar icing. 3. Ladies' fingers; a cake.

soletar, soletear [so-lay-tar´, so-lay-tay ar´] *va.* To vamp a pair of stockings with a linen sole.

soletoro, ra [so-lay-tay´-ro, rah], *m. & f.* Vamper, one who soles and pieces old things with something new.

solevantado, da [so-lay-van-tah´-do, dah], *a. & pp.* of SOLEVANTAR. In quiet, agitated, perturbed.

solevantamiento [so-lay-van-tah-me-en´-to], *m.* The act of rising in rebellion. *V.* SUBLEVACIÓN.

solevantar [so-lay-van-tar´], *va.* 1. To raise something and put something else under it (objeto). 2. To induce one to leave his habitation, home, or employment. 3. To agitate, to excite commotion.

solevar [so-lay-var´], *va.* To raise, to lift up. *V.* SOLEVANTAR.

solfa [sol´-fah], *f.* 1. The art of uniting the various sounds of music, solfa, musical notations (signos). 2. Accordance, harmony; concord. 3. *(Coll.)* A sound beating or flogging. **Estar en solfa,** to be arranged (or to arrange) with art and judgment. **Poner a uno en solfa,** to make someone look ridiculous

solfatara [sol-ta-tah´-rah], *f. (Geol.)* Solfatara, a volcanic area emitting vapors and sublimates.

solfeador [sol-fay-ah-dor´], *m.* 1. Songster, one who sings according to the rules of melody and measure. 2. Music-master. 3. *(Coll.)* One who deals out blows.

solfear [sol-fay-ar´], *m.* 1. To sing according to the rules of melody and measure. 2. *(Coll.)* To cudgel, to flog. 3. *(Cono Sur)* To nick, to swipe (hurtar).

solfeo [sol-fay´-o], *m.* 1. Solfa (música), singing of scales, voice practice, melodious song. 2. *(Coll.)* Beating, flogging, drubbing (paliza).

solfista [sol-fes´-tah], *com.* Musician.

solicitación [so-le-the-tah-the-on´], *f.* Solicitation, importunity, temptation. inducement.

solicitado, da [so-le-the-tah´-do, dah], *a. (Com.)* In good request or demand.

solicitador, ra [so-le-the-tah-dor´, rah], *m. & f.* Solicitor, agent; one who solicits for another.

solícitamente [so-lee'-the-tah-men-tay], *adv.* Solicitiously, diligently.

solicitante [so-le-the-tahn'-tay], *pa.* V. SOLICITADOR.

solicitar [so-le-the-tar'], *va.* To solicit, to importune, to entreat; to urge; to court, to ask for (permiso), to attract (atención, interés), to pursue (persona).

solícito, ta [so-lee'-the-to, tah], *a.* Solicitous, anxious, careful, nice.

solicitud [so-le-the-tood'], *f.* Solicitude, anxiety, importunity. **Solicitud de bus,** *(Comput.)* bus request.

sólidamente [so'-le-dah-men-tay], *adv.* Solidly, anally, with true reasons.

solidar [so-le-dar'], *va.* 1. To harden, to render firm and solid. 2. To consolidate, to establish.

solidariamente [so-le-dah'-re-ah-men-tay], *adv.* Jointly, mutually.

solidaridad [so-le-dah-re-dahd'], *f.* Solidarity, community, equal participation.

solidario, ria [so-le-dah'-re-o, ah], *a.* 1. Solidary, equal in participation, one in interests. 2. Individually and collectively responsible. **Hacerse solidario de una opinión,** to echo an opinion.

solidez [so-le-deth'], *f.* 1. Solidity, firmness, strength. 2. Integrity, firmness of mind.

solidificar [so-le-de-fe-cahr'], *va.* To solidify, to harden.

sólido, da [so'-le-do, dah], *a.* 1. Solid, firm, compact, consistent. 2. Built on sound reasons. -*m.* 1. A solid, compact body. 2. *(Med.)* Solid, the part containing the fluids of the animal body.

soliloquiar [so-le-lo-ke-ar'], *vn.* To discourse or reason with oneself; to talk to oneself, to soliloquize.

soliloquio [so-le-lo'-ke-o], *m.* Soliloquy, monologue.

solimán [so-le-mahn'], *m.* *(Chem.)* Corrosive sublimate.

solio [so'-le-o], *m.* Throne with a canopy.

solípedo, da [so-lee'-pay-do, dah], *a.* Solipede, solidungulous, whole-hoofed.

solitaria [so-le-tah-re-ah], *f.* Tapeworm. V. TENIA.

solitariamente [so-le-tah'-re-ah-men-tay], *adv.* Solitarily, lonesomely.

solitario, ria [so-le-tah'-re-o, ah], *a.* 1. Solitary, lonely (vida, persona); lonely, bleak, lonesome, isolated (lugar). 2. Cloistered, retired. -*m.* 1. Solitary, lonely, recluse, a hermit. **Vivir solitario,** to live alone. 2. Solitaire, a card game played by one person alone. 3. Solitaire, a single rich diamond.

sólito, ta [so'-le-to, tah], *a.* Accustomed.

soliviadura [so-le-ve-ah-doo'-rah], *f.* The act of raising a little.

soliviantar [so-le-ve-an-tar'], *va.* To induce to novelties or changes.

soliviar [so-le-ve-ar'], *va.* 1. To raise or lift up in order to take anything from underneath. 2. To rob, to steal. -*vr.* To rise, to get up a little.

solivio [so-lee'-ve-o], *m.* The act of rising or raising a little.

solivión [so-le-ve-on'], *m. aug.* A sudden and violent lifting up.

solla [sol'-lyah], *f.* Plaice.

sollado [sol-lyah'-do], *m.* *(Naut.)* Orlop.

sollamar [sol-lyah-mar'], *va.* To scorch, to singe, to burn slightly.

sollar [sol-lyar'], *va.* *(Met.)* To blow, to blow with bellows.

sollastre [sol-lyahs'-tray], *m.* 1. Scullion, kitchen-boy. 2. *(Coll.)* A skillful rogue.

sollastría [sol-lyas-tree'-ah], *f.* Scullery; the business of a scullion.

sollastrón [sol-lyas-trone'], *m. aug.* 1. A very crafty, subtle, sly fellow. 2. A loafer. 3. A designing, low fellow.

sollo [sol'-lyo], *m.* Common pike.

sollozar [sol-lyo-thar'], *vn.* To sob.

sollozo [sol-lyo'-tho], *m.* 1. Sob. 2. *(Cal. and Mex.)* Huckleberry.

solo [so'-lo], *m.* 1. Solo, musical composition for one voice; a tune played by a single instrument. 2. A game at cards. 3.

A play in certain games of cards, a lone hand. 3. *(Cono Sur)* Tedious conversation (lata).

solo, la [so'-lo], *a.* 1. Alone, single, solitary. 2. Alone, only, lonely, without company, bereft of favor and protection. **A solas,** alone, unaided. **Venir solo,** to come alone. **Tendremos que comer pan solo,** we shall have to eat plain bread.

sólo [so'-lo], *adv.* Only. V. SOLAMENTE.

solomillo, solomo [so-lo-meel'-lyo, so-lo'-mo], *vn.* Loin, the fleshy and boneless part on the spine; chine.

solsticial [sols-te-the-ahl'], *a.* Solstitial.

solsticio [sols-tee'-the-o], *m.* Solstice, the tropical point.

soltar [sol-tar'], *va.* 1. To untie, to loosen. 2. To set at liberty, to discharge. 3. To burst out into laughter or crying (risa). 4. To explain, to decipher, to solve. 5. To drop (dejar caer), to cast off (amarra), to release (freno), to set free (animales), to let go of (riendas). **Soltar la carga,** to throw down a burden. **Soltar la palabra,** to absolve one from an obligation or promise; to pledge one's word for anything. **Soltó una par de palabrotas,** he came out with a couple of rude words. -*vr.* 1. To get loose. 2. To grow expeditious and handy in the performance of a thing. 3. To forego all decency and modesty. 4. To lose control (perder el control). 5. To become expert (adquirir pericia). **No se vaya a soltar el perro,** don't let the dog get out. **Soltarse de las manos de uno,** to escape from somebody's clutches. **Soltarse del estómago,** to have diarrhoea.

soltera [sol-tay'-rah], *f.* A spinster, an unmarried woman. V. SOLTERO, RA.

soltería [sol-tay-ree'-ah], *f.* Celibacy.

soltero [sol-tay'-ro], *m.* Bachelor, an unmarried man.

soltero, ra [sol-tay'-ro, rah], *a.* Single (persona no casada), unmarried. **Madre soltera,** unmarried mother.

solterón [sol-tay-rone'], *m.* An old bachelor.

solterona [sol-tay-ro'-nah], *f.* An old maid.

soltura [sol-too'-rah], *f.* 1. The act of discharging or setting at liberty. 2. Release from confinement. 3. Agility, activity. 4. Laxity, looseness, licentiousness.

solubilidad [so-loo-be-le-dahd'], *f.* Solubility, solubleness.

soluble [so-loo'-blay], *a.* 1. Soluble, that can be loosened or untied. 2. Resoluble, that may be resolved (problema). 3. Solvable.

solución [so-loo-the-on'], *f.* 1. Solution, the act of loosening or untying. 2. Resolution of a doubt, removal of an intellectual difficulty. 3. Solution, the reduction of a solid body into a fluid state. 4. The climax or catastrophe in a drama or epic poem. 5. Lean, satisfaction. **Dar solución a una duda,** to solve or explain a doubt.

solucionar [so-loo-the-o-nahr'], *va.* To solve.

solutivo, va [so-loo-tee'-vo, vah], *a.* Solutive, having the power of loosening, untying, or dissolving.

solvabilidad [sol-vah-be-le-dahd'], *f.* *(Com.)* Solvency, abilit to pay one's debts.

solvencia [sol-ven'-the-ah], *f.* 1. Solvency, ability to pay debts contracted. 2. Solid reputation (reputación). 3. *(Cono Sur)* Ability (aptitud). **Fuentes de toda solvencia,** completely reliable sources.

solventar [sol-ven-tar'], *va.* To pay debts (cuenta, deuda).

solvente [sol-ven'-tay], *pa. & a.* 1. Solvent, unbinding, dissolvent, having power to cause dissolution. 2. Solvent, able to pay debts contracted.

solver [sol-verr'], *va.* To loosen, to untie; to solve, to find out.

solviente [sol-ve-en'-tay], *va.* Solving, loosening, having power to cause solution.

soma [so'-mah], *f.* 1. The coarse sort of flour. 2. *(Prov.)* Load, burdensomeness. **Bestia de soma,** a beast of burden.

somanta [so-mahn'-tah], *f.* *(Coll.)* Beating, severe chastisement.

somatén [so-mah-ten'], *m.* 1. Alarm (alarma), uproar, confusion (jaleo). **Tocar a somatén,** sonar la alarma. 2. Mob, an unexpected attack.

somatología [so-mah-to-lo-hee'-ah], *f.* Somatology, the doctrine of organic bodies, especially of the human body; embracing anatomy and physiology.

sombra [som'-brah], *f.* 1. Shade (protección), interception of light. 2. Shadow (proyectora por objeto), shade, the representation of a body by which the light is intercepted. 3. Shade, shadow, spirit, ghost (fantasma), manes. 4. *(Met.)* Shade, shadow, shelter, favor, protection. 5. Resemblance, appearance. 6. Sign, vestige. 7. Shadow, dark part of a picture. 8. Shade, parts of a picture not brightly colored. 9. Umber, a brown color. 8. *(CAm. Cono Sur)* Parasol (quitasol). 9. *(CAm. Cono Sur)* Guide lines (para escribir). **Andar a sombra de tejado,** to abscond. **Hacer sombra,** to protect; to impede; to obscure, to outshine. **No ser ni su sombra,** to be but the shadow of one's former self. **No se fía ni de su sombra,** he doesn't even trust his own shadow. **Tener buena sombra,** to be likeable. **Hacer sombra a uno,** to put someone in the shade. **Gobierno en la sombra,** shadow cabinet. **Sombras chinescas,** shadow play, shadow pantomime. **Dirigente en la sombra,** shadow leader.

sombras *(Coll.)* darkness, obscurity (oscuridad); ignorance (ignorancia).

sombraje [som-brah'-hay], *m.* Hut covered with branches.

sombrajo [som-brah'-ho], *m.* 1. Shadow or figure corresponding to the body by which the light is intercepted. 2. A shed or hut in vineyards.

sombrar [som-brar'], *va.* To frighten to astonish. *V.* ASOMBRAR.

sombreado [som-bray-ah'-do], *m.* Shading, the act of marking with different gradations of colors. —**Sombreado, da,** *pp.* of SOMBREAR.

sombrear [som-bray-ar'], *va.* To shade, to mark with different gradations of colors; to paint in obscure colors.

sombrerazo [som-bray-rah'-tho], *m.* 1. *(Aug.)* A large hat. 2. A flap or blow with a hat.

sombrerera [som-bray-ray'-rah], *f.* 1. Hat-box, hat-case. 2. Hatter's wife, milliner. 3. *(Cono Sur)* Hatstand.

sombrerería [som-bray-ray-ree'-ah], *f.* 1. Manufactory of hats. 2. Shop where hats are sold.

sombrerero [som-bray-ray'-ro], *m.* Hatter, hat-maker.

sobrerete [som-bray-ray'-tay], *m. dim.* 1. A small hat. 2. Bonnet, cap (cubo, hongo). 3. Spark-arrester, spark-catcher (locomotora); cowl (chimenea)

sombrerillo, ito [som-bray-reel'-lyo, ee'-to], *m.* 1. *(Dim.)* A small or little hat. **Sombrerillo de señora,** lady's hat. 2. *(Bot.)* Navelwort.

sombrero [som-bray'-ro], *m.* Hat. **Sombrero apuntado** or **de tres picos,** a cocked hat. **Sombrero jarano,** broad brimmed Mexican hat. **Sombrero de copa,** top hat. **Sombrero de paja,** straw hat. **Sombrero safari,** safari hat. **Sombrero tejano,** stetson. **Sombrero apuntado,** cocked hat. **Sombrero hongo,** bowler hat. **Sombrero de jipijapa,** Panama hat.

sombría [som-bree'-ah], *f.* Shady place.

sombrilla [som-breel'-lyah], *f.* 1. Parasol. 2. Slight shade.

sombrita [som-bree'-tah], *f. dim.* A slight shade.

sombrío, bría [som-bree'-o, ah], *a.* 1. Shady, gloomy (persona), sombre (lugar). 2. Hazy, murky, thick (del tiempo). 3. Taciturn.

sombrío [som-bree'-o], *m.* 1. Part of a piece of painting, which is to be shaded or painted in darker colors than the rest. 2. A dull, heavy color. 3. A shady place.

sombroso, sa [som-bro'-so, sah], *a.* Shady.

someramente [so-may-rah-men-tay], *adv.* Superficially.

somero, ra [so-may'-ro, rah], *a.* Superficial, shallow; making but a slight impression on the mind.

someter [so-may-terr'], *va.* 1. To subject (persona), to submit; to subdue, to reduce to submission. *-vr.* To humble oneself; to submit, to acquiesce, to comply. **Someterse a una operación,** to undergo an operation.

sometimiento [so-may-te-me-en'-to], *m.* Submission (estado), subjection, subduing.

somnambulismo [som-nam-boo-lees'-mo], *m.* Somnanbulism, walking in sleep. **Somnambulismo artificial,** hypnotism.

somnámbulo, la [som-nahm'-boo-lo, lah], *m. & f. & a.* 1. Sonmambule, somnambulist. 2. Medium, a person habitually submitted to the influence of hypnotism.

somnífero, ra [som-nee'-fay-ro, rah], *a.* Somniferous, soporiferous.

somnílocuo, cua [som-nee'-lo-cwo, cwah], *a.* Somniloquous, given to talking in sleep.

somnolencia [som-no-len'-the-ah], *f.* Sleepiness, drowsiness, somnolency.

somonte [so-mon'-tay], *a.* Coarse, rough, shaggy.

somorgujador [so-mor-goo-hah-dor'], *m.* Diver, one that goes under water to search for anything.

somorgujar [so-mor-goo-har'], *va & vr.* o dip, to plunge, to duck.

somorgujo, somorgujón, somormujo [so-mor-moo'-ho], *m.* *(Orn.)* Dun-diver, diver, merganser, grebe. **A lo somurjo, a lo lomormujo,** under water.

sompesar [som-pay-sar'], *va.* To take up a thing in order to guess its weight; to heft.

son [sohn], *m.* 1. Sound, noise, report, tale, reason, mode. **En son,** in such a manner, apparently. **Sin ton ni son,** without rhyme or reason. **A son de qué,** for what reason. **A son,** at or to the sound of. **Bailar a cualquier son,** to be easily moved by affection or passion. **Al son de la marcha nupcial,** to the sounds of the wedding march. **Bailar uno al son que le tocan,** to adapt oneself to circumstances. **Bailar sin son,** to be exceedingly eager. **¿A qué son?** with what motive? 2. *(Carib.)* Cuban folk song and dance. 3. Style, manner.

sonable [so-nah'-blay], *a.* 1. Sonorous, loud, sounding. 2. Celebrated, famous.

sosada [so-sah'-dah], *f. V.* SONATA.

sonadera [so-nah-day'-rah], *f.* The act of blowing the nose.

sonado, da [so-nah'-do, dah], *a.* 1. Celebrated, famous (famoso). 2. Generally reported. 3. **Estar sonado,** to be crazy. *-pp.* of SONAR.

sonador, ra [se-nah-dor'-rah], *m. & f.* 1. One who makes a noise. 2. Handkerchief.

sonaja [so-nah'-hah], *f.* Timbrel, a musical instrument.

sonajero [so-nah-hay'-ro], *m.* 1. A small timbrel. 2. A rattle.

sonajica, illa, ita, uela [so-nah-hee'-cah], *f. dim.* Small timbrel.

sonambulismo [so-nahm-boo-lees'-mo], *m. V.* SONAMBULISM. *(Acad.)*

sonámbulo, la [so-nahm'-boo-lo', lah], *m. & f. & a.* Somnambule, somnambulist.

sonante [so-nahn'-tay], *a.* Sounding, sonorous. **Dinero contante y sonante,** ready cash.

sonar [so-nar'], *va.* 1. To sound, to play upon a musical instrument. 2. To like or dislike. **Bien me sonó lo que dijo,** I was much pleased with what he said. 3. To sound, to pronounce. 4. To allude, to refer to a thing without any direct mention. *-vn.* 1. To sound or make a noise. 2. To be pronounced. 3. To be talked of (ser mencionado). 4. To sound familiar (ser conocido). 5. *(Cono Sur)* To come a cropper (fracasar). **Han sonado las 10,** it has struck 10. **Esas palabras suenan extrañas,** those words sound strange. **No me suena el nombre,** the name doesn't ring a bell with me. *-v. imp.* To raise or propagate rumours, to be reported, to be whispered. *-vr.* To blow one's nose.

sonata [so-nah'-tah], *f.* Sonata, a musical composition in three or four movements.

sonda [son'-dah], *f.* 1. *(Naut.)* Sounding, heaving the lead. 2. Sound, load, a cord with a heavy weight attached for sounding. 3. Borer, any instrument for examining the strata of the earth. 4. *(Med.)* Sound; probe. 5. In artillery, searcher, proof stick.

sondable [son-dah'-blay], *a.* That may be sounded.

sondalesa [son-dah-lay´-sah], *f. (Naut.)* Lead-line, the log sounding-line. **Sondalesa de mano,** *(Naut.)* hand-lead. **Sondalesa de la bomba,** *(Naut.)* gauge-rod of the pump.

sondar, sondear [son-dar´, son-day-ar´], *va.* 1. *(Naut.)* To sound, to heave the lead. **Sondar la bomba,** *(Naut.)* to sound the pump. 2. To try, to sift, to sound another's intentions; to explore, to fathom.

sondeo [son-day´-o], *m.* The act and effect of sounding; exploring, fathoming.

sonecillo [so-nay-theel´-lyo], *m dim.* 1. A sound scarcely perceptible. 2. A short little tune.

sonetico [so-nay-tee´-co], *m.* 1. *(Dim.)* V. SONTÍN. 2. A merry little song.

sonetín [so-nay-teen´], *m.* An insignificant sonnet.

sonetista [so-nay-tees´-tah], *m.* One who writes sonnets.

soneto [so-nay´-to], *m.* Sonnet.

songuita [son-gee´-tah], *f. (Cuba)* Jest, irony.

sónico, ca [soh´-ne-co, cah], *a.* Sonic. **Barrera sónica,** sonic barrier.

sonido [so-nee´-do], *m.* 1. Sound, noise. 2. Fame, report, rumor. 3. Sound, pronunciation. 4. Literal signification. **Sonido agudo,** acute sound.

sonochada [so-no-chah´-dah], *f.* 1. The beginning of night. 2. Watching in the early hours of night.

sonochar [so-no-char´], *vn.* To watch the first hours of the night.

sonómetro [so-no´-may-tro], *m.* Sonometer, an instrument for testing the vibration of strings.

sonora [so-no´-rah], *f.* Cithern, a musical instrument.

sonoramente [so-no´-rah-men-tay], *adv.* Sonorously; harmoniously.

sonoridad [so-no-re-dahd´], *f.* Sonorousness.

sonoro, ra, sonoroso, sa [so-no´-ro, rah], *a.* 1. Sonorous, soniferous. 2. Pleasing, agreeable, harmonious. **Efectos sonoros,** sound effects.

sonreír, sonreírse [son-ray-eer´, eer-say], *vn. & vr.* To smile. *(Yo sonrío, yo sonría; él sonrió, sonriera; from Sonreír. V. REIR.)*

sonrisa [son-ree´-sah], *f.* **Sonriso,** *m.* Smile.

sonrodadura [son-ro-dah-doo´-rah], *f.* The act of sticking in the mud.

sonrodarse [son-ro-dar´-say], *vn.* To stick in the mud.

sonrojar, sonrojear [son-ro-har´], *va.* To make one blush with shame, to flush.

sonrojo [son-ro´-ho], *m.* 1. Blush (rubor). 2. Offensive word which causes a blush (dicho).

sonrosado, da [son-ro-sah´-do, dah], *a.* Pink, blushing pink.

sonrosar, sonrosear [son-ro-sar´], *va.* To dye a rose color. **Sonrosearse**-*vr.* To blush.

sonroseo [son-ro-say´-o], *m.* Blush.

sonsaca [son-sah´-cah], *f.* Wheedling; petty theft.

sonsacador, ra [son-sah-cah-dor´, rah], *m. & f.* 1. Wheedler, prier, shooter, coaxer. 2. A petty thief.

sonsacamiento [son-sah-cah-me-en´-to], *m.* Wheedling, extortion, petty theft.

sonsacar [son-sah-car´], *va.* 1. To steal privately out of a bag (obtener). 2. To obtain by gunning and craft. *(Met.)* To entice, to allure. 3. To pump a secret out of a person (engatusar).

sonsaque [son-sah´-kay], *m.* Wheedling; petty theft.

sonsonete [son-so-nay´-tay], *m* 1. Noise arising from repeated gentle beats imitating some musical sound. 2. Sing-song voice. 3. Tap (golpecitos). 4. Monotonous delivery (voz). 5. Jingle (copla).

soñador, ra [so-nyah-dor´, rah], *m. & f.* Dreamer; one who relates dreams and idle stories.

soñante [so-nyahn´-tay], *pa.* Dreaming.

soñar [so-nyar´], *va.* 1. To dream, to have dreams. 2. To dream, to think idly, to entertain fantastical ideas. **Ni soñarlo,** not even dreamed of. **Soñar con algo,** to dream of something. **Soñar en voz alta,** to talk in one's sleep. **Soñé contigo ayer noche,** I dreamt about you last night. *(Yo sueño, yo sueñe, from Soñar. V. ACORDAR.)*

soñarrera [so-nyar-ray´-rah], *f.* 1. *(Prov.)* Dreaming, heavy sleep. 2. Drowsiness, propensity to sleep long.

soñera [so-nyay´-rah], *f.* Sleepiness, wish to sleep.

soñolencia [so-nyo-len´-the-ah], *f.* Sleepiness, drowsiness, somnolence.

soñolientamente [so-nyo-le-ayn´-tay], *adv.* Sleepily, heavily.

soñoliento, ta [so-nyo-le-en´-to, tah], *a.* 1. Heavy, sleepy, drowsy. 2. Sleepy, soporiferous, causing sleep. 3. Sleepy, dull, lazy.

sopa [so´-pah], *f.* 1. Soup (caldo, pan mojado). 2. Soup, broth. 3. Bread cut or broken to be thrown into soup; generally in plural. **Sopa de ajo, de gato,** meager soup, made of bread, oil, salt, garlic and water. **Sopa de leche,** milk porridge or milk soup. **Sopa de guisantes,** pea-soup. **Sopa borracha,** soup made with wine, biscuit, sugar and cinnamon. **Sopa de fideos,** noodle soup. **Los encontramos hasta en la sopa,** they´re everywhere. **Estoy hecho una sopa,** I'm soaking wet. **Estar como una sopa,** to be tight. **Dar sopas con honda a uno,** to be streets ahead of one.

sopaipa [so-pah´-ee-pah], *f.* A sort of fritter steeped in honey.

sopalancar [so-pah-lan-car´], *va.* To put a lever under something to lift it.

sopanda [so-pahn´-dah], *f.* 1. Brace, any of the leather thongs which support the body of a coach. 2. Joist, crossbeam, a stout timber placed horizontally.

sopapeadura [so-pah-pay-ah-doo´-rah], *f.* 1. Buffet or slap with the hand under the chin; a chuck. 2. *(Coll.)* A number of slaps or chucks.

sopapear [so-pah-pay-ar´], *va.* 1. *(Coll.)* To chuck under the chin, to slap. 2. *(Coll. Met.)* To vilify, to abuse.

sopapo [so-pah´-po], *m.* 1. Box, blow, or slap with the hand. 2. Sucker, a movable valve in hydraulic vessels or pumps.

sopar [so-par´], *va.* To sop bread. V. ENSOPAR.

sopear [so-pay-ar´], *va.* 1. To sop, to steep breed. V. ENSOPAR. 2. TO tread, to trample, to domineer. 3. To maltreat.

sopeña [so-pay´-nyah], *f.* Cavity formed by a rock at its foot.

sopera [so-pay´-rah], *f.* Tureen.

sopero [so-pay´-ro], *m.* 1. Soup-plate (plato sopero); lover of soups (persona). 2. *(And.)* Nosey (curioso).

sopesar [so-pay-sar´], *va.* 1. To try the weight of, try to lift (levantar) 2. To weigh, to consider (palabras). 3. To weigh up (situación).

sopetear [so-pay-tay-ar´], *va.* 1. To sop, to steep bread in sauce, broth, or other liquors. 2. To abuse with foul language.

sopeteo [s-pay-tay´-o], *m.* The act of dipping breed in broth, etc.

sopetón [so-pay-tone´], *m.* 1. Plentiful soup. 2. A heavy box or slap with the hand (golpe). **De sopetón,** suddenly.

sopica, illa, ita [so-pee´-cah], *f. dim.* Sippet, a light soup.

sopilote [so-pe-lo´-tay], *m. (Mex.)* A vulture.

sopista [so-pees´-tah], *m.* Person living upon charity.

¡sopla! [so´-plah], *int.* An expression of admiration.

sopladero [so-plah-day´-ro], *m.* Draught or air-hole to subterraneous passages.

soplado, da [so-plah´-do, dah], *a. & pp.* of SOPLAR. Blown; overnice and spruce.

soplador, ra [so-plah-dor´, rah], *m. & f.* 1. Blower, that which blows. 2. That which excites or inflames. 3. *(Fig.)* Troublemaker. 4. *(And. CAm.)* Prompter.

soplamocos [so-plah-mo´-cos], *m. (Coll.)* Box or slap on the nose (puñetazo).

soplar [so-plar´], *vn. & va.* 1. To blow, to emit wind at the mouth. 2. To blow with bellows. 3. To blow, to make a current of air. 4. To be blown away by the wind (vela). 5. To blow, to drive by the wind, to separate with wind. 6. To rob or steal in an artful manner (robar). 7. To suggest notions or ideas, to inspire. 8. In the game of draughts to huff a man. 9. To tipple, to drink much. 10. To split on (delatar). 11. To charge (cobrar). **Soplar a uno,** to whisper to somebody. -*vr.* To eat or drink a great deal. **Soplarse una docena de pasteles,** to wolf a dozen cakes.

soplete [so-play'-tay], *m*. In glasshouses, a blow pipe; a soldering pipe.

soplico [so-plee'-co], *m. dim*. A slight puff or blast.

soplido [so-plee'-do], *m. V.* SOPLO.

soplillo [so-pleel'-lyo], *m*. 1. Crape, a thin stuff. 2. Anything extremely thin and light. 3. *(Dim.) V.* SOPLICO.

soplo [so'-plo], *m*. 1. Blow, puff, gust (viento), blowing, act of blowing (con la boca). 2. Instant, moment, short space of time. 3. Blast. 4. Tip, tip off, advice given secretly, and with caution; generally malicious advice or information (chismoso). **La semana pasó como un soplo**, the week sped by.

soplón, na [so-plone', nah], *a. & n. 1.* Informer. 2. *(Mex.)* Cop. 3. *(CAm.)* Prompter (teatro).

soploncillo, illa [so-plon-theel'-lyo, lyah], *m. & f. & a. dim*. Little tattler.

sopón [so-pone'], *m*. Person living upon charity soup. Aug. of SOPA.

soponcio [so-pon'-the-o], *m*. Grief or fit arising from disappointment.

sopor [so-por'], *m*. Heaviness, drowsiness, sleepiness.

soporífero, ra [so-po-ree'-fay-ro, rah], *a*. Soporific, soporiferous. *V.* SOPORÍFICO.

soporífico, ca [so-po-ree'-fe-co, cah], *a*. Opiate, narcotical, soporific, somniferous.

soporoso, sa [so-po-ro'-so, sah], *a*. Soporiferous.

soportable [so-por-tah'-blay], *a*. Tolerable, supportable.

soportador, ra [so-por-tah-dor', rah], *m. & f.* Supporter.

soportal [so-por-tahl'], *m*. Portico.

soportar [so-por-tar'], *va*. To suffer, to tolerate, to support, to abide.

soprano [so-prah'-no], *m. V.* TIPLE.

so protesta [so pro-tes'-tah], *adv. (Com.)* Under protest.

sopuntar [so-poon-tar'], *va*. To place marks under a superfluous or erroneous word.

sor [sore], *f*. Sister. *V.* HERMANA. **Sor María**, sister Mary (monjas).

sora [so'-rah], *f*. Peruvian drink made of a decoction of maize.

sorba [sor'-bah], *f*. Sorb-apple. *V.* SERBA.

sorbedor [sor-bay-dor'], *m*. Sipper, one who sips.

sorber [sor-berr'], *va*. 1. To sip (con los labios), to suck (mar); to sup. 2. To imbibe, to soak as a sponge, to absorb. **Sorber por una paja**, to drink through a straw. **Sorber por las narices**, to sniff.

sorbete [sor-bay'-tay], *m*. 1. Sherbet, a beverage of fruit-juice, sugar, etc., chilled; water ice. 2. *(Carib. Cono Sur)* Drinking straw (pajita). 3. *(Mex.)* Top hat (sombrero de copa). 4. *(CAm.)* Ice-cream (helado).

sorbetón [sor-bay-tone'], *m. aug*. A large draught of liquor.

sorbible [sor-bee'-blay], *a*. Which may be sipped.

sorbición [sor-be-the-on'], *f. (Men.)* Absorption.

sorbillo, ito [sor-beel'-lyo], *m. dim*. Sup, a small draught.

sorbo [sor'-bo], *m*. 1. Imbibition, drinking or sipping; absorption. 2. Sup, draught. 3. Anything comparatively small. **Beber a sorbos**, to sip.

sorce [sor'-thay], *m*. Field-mouse.

sorda [sor'-dah], *f*. 1. Woodcock. *V.* CHOCHA. 2. *(Naut.)* Stream-cable employed in launching a ship.

sordamente [sor-dah-men-tay], *adv*. Secretly, silently.

sordastro, tra [sor-dahs'-tro, trah], *a*. Deaf.

sordera, sordez [sor-day'-rah, sor-deth'], *f*. Deafness.

sórdidamente [sor-de-dah-men-tay], *adv*. Sordidly, dirtily.

sordidez [sor-de-deth'], *f*. 1. Sordidness, nastiness. 2. Covetousness, avarice.

sórdido, da [sor'-de-do, dah], *a*. 1. Sordid, dirty (sucio), filthy. 2. Licentious, impure, indecent, scandalous.

sordina [sor-dee'-nah], *f*. 1. Kit, a small fiddle. 2. Mute, a piece put on the bridge of a fiddle, to weaken the sound. 3. Muffler, damper,, a mute for a trumpet.

sordo, da [sor'-do, dah], *a*. 1. Deaf, unable to hear. 2. Silent, still, quiet (máquina). 3. Deafening. **Quedarse sordo**, to go

deaf. **Permanecer sordo a**, to remain deaf to. **Sordo como una tapia**, deaf as a stone.

sordomudo, da [sor-do-moo'-do], *a. m & f.* Deaf and dumb.

sorgo [sor'-go], *m. V.* ZAHINA.

soriasis [so-re-ah'-sis], *f*. Psoriasis, a squamous disease of the skin, of remarkable chronicity.

sórico [so'-re-co], *a*. Belonging to psoriasis.

sorites [so-ree'-tes], *m. (Log.)* Sorites, proposition or argument accumulated on another.

sorna [sor'-nah], *f*. 1. Sluggishness, laziness, slowness (lentitud). 2. A feigned sloth in doing or saying anything.

sornavirón [sor-nah-ve-rone'], *m. (Coll.)* Sudden stroke with the back of the open hand.

soro [so'-ro], *m*. Year-old hawk.

soroche [so-ro'-chay], *m. (Peru and Ec.)* 1. Disease caused by rarefaction of the air at great altitudes in men and beasts. 2. A friable, shining silver ore.

soroque [so-ro'-kay], *f. (Min.)* Matrix of ores.

sóror, *f*. Sister. *V.* SOR.

sorprendente [sor-pren-den'-tay], *a*. 1. Surprising. 2. Rare, extraordinary, Strange. *-pa*. of SORPRENDER.

sorprender [sor-pren-derr'], *va*. 1. To surprise, to fall upon unexpectedly, to take by surprise; to come upon; to overtake. 2. To execute something silently and with caution. 3. To surprise, to astonish by something wonderful or sudden. - *vr*. To be surprised, to be amazed. **No me sorprendería de que fuera así**, I wouldn't be surprised if it were like that.

sorpresa [sor-pray'-sah], *f*. 1. Surprise (emoción); taking by surprise; deceit, imposition. 2. Surprise, sudden confusion or perplexity. 3. Amazement, astonishment, consternation. **Tomar por sorpresa**, to surprise, to take unawares. **Con gran sorpresa**, much to my surprise.

sorra [sor'-rah], *f*. 1. *(Naut.)* Ballast of stones or coarse gravel. 2. Side of a tunny-fish.

sorregar [sor-ray-gar'], *va*. To water in another course: applied to rivulets which casually change their channels.

sorrero, ra [sor-ray'-ro, rah], *a. (Prov.) V.* ZORRERO.

sorriego [sor-re-ay'-go], *m*. Water which passes occasionally from one channel to another.

sorrostrada [sor-ros-trah'-dah], *f*. Great face or beak.

sorteador [sor-tay-ah-dor'], *m*. One who casts lots.

sorteamiento [sor-tay-ah-me-en'-to], *m. V.* SORTEO.

sortear [sor-tay-ar'], *va*. 1. To draw or cast lots. 2. To fight bulls with skill and dexterity. 3. To cleverly elude or shun a conflict, risk, or difficulty. 4. To dodge (obstáculo). **El torero sorteó al toro**, the bullfighter eluded the bull. **Sorteamos el tráfico**, we dodged the traffic.

sorteo [sor-tay'-o], *m*. Act of casting or drawing lots.

sortero [sor-tay'-ro], *m*. Fortune-teller. *V.* AGORERO.

sortiaria [sor-te-ah'-re-ah], *f*. Superstitious divination by letters, schedules, or playing-cards.

sortija [sor-tee'-hah], *f*. 1. Ring (anillo), finger-ring. 2. Ring, a circle of metal, used for a variety of purposes: hoop. 3. A curl of hair, naturally or artificially made.

sortijita, sortijuela [sor-te-hee'-lah], *f. dim*. Little ring, ringlet.

sortijón [sor-te-hone'], *m. aug*. A large ring.

sortilegio [sor-te-lay'-he-o], *m*. Sortilege, sorcery (brujería), magical prediction (vaticinio).

sortílego, ga [sor-tee'-lay-go, gah], *m. & f. & a*. Sorcerer, conjurer, fortune-teller.

sos *(Arg.)* Sois.

sosa [so'-sah], *f*. 1. *(Bot.)* A name given to various marine plants which, on being burned, afford soda or miller or mineral alkali; glasswort, kelp. 2. Soda-ash, barilla; sal soda. 3. Soda, sodium oxide, a strong alkali.

sosacar [so-sah-cahr'], *va. V.* SONSACAR.

sosamente [so-sah-men'-tay], *adv*. Insipidly, tastelessly.

sosaño [so-sah'-nyo], *m*. Derision, mockery.

sosegadamente [so-say-gah-dah-men-tay], *adv*. Quietly, calmly.

sosegado, da [so-say-gah'-do, dah], *a.* Quiet (tranquilo), peaceful, pacific, calm (persona). *-pp.* of SOSEGAR.

sosegador, ra [so-say-gah-dor´, rah], *m. & f.* Pacifier, appeaser.

sosegar [so-say-gar'], *va.* 1. To appease, to calm (calmar), to pacify, to silence, to quiet. 2. To lull (arrullar), to put to sleep. *-vn.* 1. To rest, to repose. 2. To be calm or composed. **Soségese Vd.,** compose yourself.

sosería [so-say-ree'-ah], *f.* Insipidity (insipidez), tastelessness; insipid expression.

sosez [so-seth'], *f. (Prov.)* Insipidness, silliness. **Decir soseces,** to use silly jokes.

sosiego [so-se-ay'-go], *m.* Tranquillity, calmness.

sosio [so'-se-o], *m. (Chem.)* V. SODIO.

soslayar [sos-lah-yar'], *va.* To do or place a thing obliquely (ladear).

soslayo [sos-lah´-yo], *m.* Slant, obliquity. **Al soslayo** or **de soslayo,** askew, sidewise.

soso, sa [soh'-so, sah], *a.* 1. Insipid, unsalted, tasteless (insípido). 2. Cold, coy, silly, senseless.

sospecha [sos-pay'-chah], *f.* Suspicion, mistrust, jealousy.

sospechar [sos-pay-char'], *va.* To suspect; to mistrust; to conjecture.

sospechilla [sos-pay-cheel'-lyah], *f. dim.* Slight suspicion.

sospechosamente [sos-pay-cho'-sah-men-tay], *adv.* Suspiciously, doubtfully, jealously.

sospechoso, sa [sos-pay-cho´-so, sah], *a.* Suspicious, liable to suspicion; inclined to suspect: suspected, mistrustful. **Todos son sospechosos,** everybody is under suspicion. **Tiene amistades sospechosas,** some of his acquaintances are suspect.

sospesar [sos-pay-sar'], *va.* To suspend, to raise above the ground.

sosquín [sos-keen'], *m.* Slap or blow treacherously given.

sostén [sos-ten'], *m.* 1. Support, the act of sustaining or supporting. 2. *(Naut.)* Firmness or steadiness of a ship in pursuing her course. 3. Brassière, bra (prenda). 4. Sustenance (alimento). **El principal sostén del gobierno,** the mainstay of the government.

sostenedor, ra [sos-tay-nay-dor', rah], *m. & f.* Supporter.

sostener [sos-tay-nerr'], *va.* 1. To sustain, to support, to maintain, to hold out, to countenance. 2. To sustain, to bear, to endure, to suffer, to tolerate. 3. To sustain, to maintain, to supply with the necessaries of life (con alimentos). 4. To maintain (acusación); to stand by (opinión); to stand by (promesa); to keep up (presión). **Los dos sosteníamos la cuerda,** we were both holding the rope. **Su partido le sostiene en el poder,** his party keeps him in power. *-vr.* 1. To support or maintain oneself. 2. *(Naut.)* To bear up. 3. To continue (continuar). **Apenas podía sostenerse de puro cansancio,** he was so utterly tired he could hardly stand. **El mercado se sostiene firme,** the market remains firm. *(Yo sostengo, sostenga, sostuve. sostendré,* from *Sostener.* V. TENER.)

sostenido, da [sos-tay-nee'-do, dah], *a. & pp.* of SOSTENER. Supported, supportful, sustained. *-m. (Music.)* Sharp, a note raised a semitone; also the character which denotes it.

sostenimiento [sos-tay-ne-me-en'-to], *m.* Sustenance, the act of sustaining; support

sostituir [sos-te-too-eer'], *va.* To substitute. V. SUBSTITUIR.

sostituto [sos-te-too'-to], *m.* Substitute. V. SUBSTITUTO.

sota [so'-tah], *f.* 1. Knave, at cards 2. Deputy, substitute: used in composition to express the same meaning. 3. Helper.

sotabanco [so-tah-bahn'-co], *m. (Arch.)* Pediment of an arch over a cornice.

sotabraga [so-tah-brah´-gah], *f. (Mil.)* Axle-tree band, yoke hoop.

sotacaballerizo [so-tah-cah-bal-lyay-ree'-tho], *m.* Deputy equerry.

sotacochero [so-tah-co-chay'-ro], *m.* Postilion.

sotacola [so-tah-co'-lah], *f.* Crupper. *V.* ATAHARRE.

sotacómitre [so-tah-co´-me-tray], *m. (Naut.)* Boatswain's mate.

sotacoro [so-tah-co'-ro], *m.* Place under the upper choir.

sotalcaide [so-tal-cah'-e-day], *m.* Subwarden.

sotamaestro [so-tah-mah-es´-tro], *m.* Usher at a school.

sotaministro [so-tah-me-nees'-tro], *m. V.* SOTOMINISTRO.

sotamontero [so-tah-mon-tay´-ro], *m.* Under-huntsman, deputy forester.

sotana [so-tah´-nah], *f.* 1. Cassock, of a priest or scholar. 2. *(Coll.)* Flogging, drubbing.

sotanado, da [so-tah-nah'-do, dah], *a.* Vaulted, arched, groined.

sotanear [so-tah-nay-ar'], *va. (Coll.)* To boat, to chastise or reprehend severely.

sotaní [so-tah-nee'], *m.* Short round under petticoat without plaits.

sotanilla [so-tah-neel'-lyah], *f.* 1 *(Dim.)* A small cassock. 2. The dress of collegians.

sótano [so'-tah-no], *m.* Cellar under ground (bodega).

sotaventado, da [so-tah-ven-tah'-do, dah], *a. (Naut.)* Driven to leeward, lee. *-pp.* of SOTAVENTAR.

sotaventar [so-tah-ven-tahr'], *va. (Naut.)* To fall to leeward, to lose the weather-gauge.

sotavento [so-tah-ven´-to], *m.* Leeward, lee. **Tener buen sotavento,** *(Naut.)* to have sea-room. **Costa de sotavento,** *(Naut.)* lee-shore. **A sotavento,** under the lee.

sotayuda [so-tah-yoo'-dah], *m.* Under-assistant to officers at court.

sotechado [so-tay-chah'-do], *m.* A roofed or covered place.

soteño, ña [so-tay'-nyo, nyah], *a.* Produced in groves or forests.

soterráneo, nea [so-ter-rah'-nay-o, ah], *a.* Subterraneous.

soterrar [so-ter-rar'], *va.* 1. To bury, to put under ground. 2. To hide, to conceal, to overwhelm. *(Yo sotierro, yo sotierre,* from *Soterrar.* V. ACRECENTAR.)

sotillo [so-teel'-lyo], *f. dim.* Little grove.

soto [so'-to], *m.* Grove (arboleda), thicket (matorral), forest.

sotrozo [so-tro'-tho], *m.* Linch-pin, axlepin. *(Mech.)*, key.

soviet [so-ve-et´], *m.* Soviet.

soviético, ca [so-ve-ay'-te-co, cah], *a.* Soviet.

soy V. ser. I am.

soya [so'-yah], *f.* Soya bean.

sprinter [es-prin'-teyr], *m & f.* Sprinter.

sputnik [es-poot'-nik], *m.* Sputnik, Russian satellite.

standard [es-tand'-ard], *m.* Standard. **Standard de vida,** standard of living.

status [es-tah-toos], *m.* Status.

stress [es-trays'], *m.* Stress.

stressante [es-tray-sahn'-tay], *a.* Stressful.

su [soo], *pron. poss.* His, her, its, their, one's. **Se alaba a un soldado por su valor, una mujer por su hermosura, a una casa por su situación y a los libros por su mérito,** a soldier is praised by *his* courage, a woman by *her* beauty, a house by *its* situation and books by *their* merit. **Fui en su busca,** I went in search of him, of her, or of them.

suarda [soo-ar´-dah], *f.* 1. Grease which clings to the clothes. 2. The greasy matter which sweat brings on the skin of animals.

suasivo, va [soo-ah-see´-vo, vah], *a.* V. PERSUASIVO.

suasorio, ria [soo-ah-so'-re-o, ah], *a.* Suasory, suasive.

suave [soo-ah'-vay], *a.* 1. Smooth (superficie), soft (aire), delicate, mellow. 2. Easy, tranquil, quiet. 3. Gentle (movimiento, reprimenda, curva, color), tractable, docile (persona), mild, meek. 4. *(Cono Sur, Mex.)* Vast, huge (enorme). 5. *(Mex.)* Good-looking (atractivo). **Tabaco suave,** mild tobacco.

suavecico, illo, ito [soo-ah-vay-thee'-co], *a. dim.* of SUAVE.

suavemente [soo-ah-vay-men-tay], *adv.* Gently, sweetly, softly, mildly, kindly.

suavidad

suavidad [soo-ah-ve-dahd'], *f.* 1. Softness, delicacy, sweetness. 2. Suavity, meekness; tranquillity, gentleness, lenity, forbearance.

suavizador [soo-ah-ve-thah-dor'], *m.* Softner.

suavizar [soo-ah-ve-thar'], *va.* 1. To soften. 2. To mollify (persona), to mitigate. 3. To render metals pliable or ductile.

sub [soob], A Latin preposition signifying *under, below.*—It is used only in composition, and then it means under, less, or in a subordinate degree; also a deputy; as, **Sub-lunar**, under the moon. **Sub-inspector**, the deputy inspector.

subacetato [soob-ah-thay-tah'-to], *m. (Chem.)* Subacetate.

subácido, da [soob-ah'-the-do, dah], Subacid.

subalcaide [soob-al-cah'-e-day], *m.* Deputy or sub-governor or jailer.

subalternar [soob-al-ter-nar'], *va.* To subject, to subdue.

subalterno, na [soob-al-terr'-no, nah], *a.* Subaltern, inferior, subject. *-m.* Subaltern, a subaltern officer.

subarrendador, ra [soob-ar-ren-dah-dor', rah], *m. & f.* Undertenant, sub-renter.

subarrendamiento [soob-ar-ren-dah-me-en'-to], *m.* Farming or renting under another renter.

subarrendar [soob-ar-ren-dar'], *va.* To sublet, to sublease. *(Yo subarriendo, yo subarriende,* from *Subarrendar. V.* ACRECENTAR.)

subarrendatario, ria [soob-ar-ren-dah-tah'-re-o, ah], *m. & f.* One who takes a sub-lease: a sub-renter.

subasta, subastación [soo-bahs'-tah], *f* Auction, juridical sale of goods by public auction.

subastar [soo-bas-tar'], *m.* To sell by auction.

subcampeón, ona [soob-cam-pay-on'], *m & f.* Runner-up.

subcarbonato [soob-car-bo-nah'-to], *m. (Chem.)* Subcarbonate, a salt in which the base is in excess of the carbonic acid.

subcolector [soob-co-lec-tor'], *m.* Subcollector.

subcomendador [soob-co-men-dah-dor'], *m.* Deputy-commander of a military order.

subconsciencia [soob-cons-the-en'-the-ah], *f.* Subconsciousness.

subconsciente [soob-cons-the-en'-tay], *a.* Subconscious.

subcutáneo, nea [soob-coo-tah'-nayo, ah], *a.* Subcutaneous; below the skin.

subdecano [soob-day-cah'-no], *m.* Subdean.

subdécuplo, pla [soob-day'-coo-plo, plah], *a.* Subdecuple, containing one part of ten.

subdelegable [soob-day-lay-gah'-blay], *a.* That which may be subdelegated.

subdelegación [soob-day-lay-gah-the-on'], *f.* Subdelegation, substitution.

subdelegado [soob-day-lay-gah'-do], *m.* Subdelegate.

subdelegar [soob-day-lay-gar'], *va.* To subdelegate, to commit to another one's jurisdiction or power.

subdesarrollado, da [soob-day-sah-rol-lyah'-do, dah], *a.* Under-developed.

subdesarrollo [soob-day-sah-rol'-lyo], *m.* Underdevelopment.

subdiaconado, subdiaconato [soob-de-ah-co-nah'-do], *m.* Subdeaconship.

subdiácono [soob-de-ah'-co-no], *m.* Subdeacon.

subdirección [soob-de-rayc-the-on'], *f.* Section, subdepartment.

subdirector, ra [soob-de-rayc-tor'], *m & f.* Subdirector, assistant manager.

subdirectorio [soob-de-rayc-to'-re-o], *m. (Comput.)* Subdirectory.

subdistinción [soob-dis-tin-the-on'], *f.* Subdistinction.

subdistinguir [soob-dis-tin-geer'], *va.* To distinguish that which has already been distinguished.

súbdito, ta [soob'-de-to, tah], *a.* Subject, inferior.

subdividir [soob-de-ve-deer'], *va.* To subdivide.

subdivisible [soob-de-ve-see'-blay], *a.* Subdivisible.

suubdivisión [soob-de-ve-se-on'], *f.* Subdivision, subsection.

subduplo, pla [soob-doo'-plo, plah], *a.* Subduple, containing one part of two.

subejecutor [soob-ay-hay-coo-tor'], *m.* Deputy executor.

subentender [soob-en-ten-derr'], *va.* To understand what is tacitly meant.

subérico [soo-bay'-re-co], *a.* Suberic, extracted from cork.

suberina [soo-bay-ree'-nah], *f.* Suberine, a modification of cellulose found in cork.

suberoso, sa [soo-bay-ro'-so, sah], *a.* Suberose, corky.

subestimación [soo-bays-te-mah-the-on'], *f.* Substation.

subestimar [soo-bays-te-mahr'], *va.* To underestimate (capacidad, enemigo), to undervalue (objeto, propiedad).

subfletar [soob-flay-tar'], *va. (Naut.)* To hire a ship of another freighter.

subgerente [soob-hay-ren'-tay], *m.* Assistant manager.

subida [soo-bee'-dah], *f.* 1. Ascension, going up; mounting. 2. Ascent, acclivity, rise (cantidad, precio). 3. Attack of a disease. 4. Enhancement, rise, augmentation of value or price; amelioration of things. **En la subida había muchas flores,** there were a lot of flowers on the way up.

subidero, ra [soo-be-day'-ro, rah], *a.* Mounting, rising.

subidero [soo-be-day-ro]. *m.* Ladder, mounting-block.

subido, da [soo-bee'-do, dah], *a. & pp.* of SUBIR. 1. Raised on high, mounted. 2. Strong, having a deep tinge of color: strong-scented. 3. Finest, most excellent.

subidor [soo-be-dor'], *m.* Porter, one who carries things from lower to higher places.

subiente [soo-be-en'-tay], *m. (Arch.)* Ornaments of foliage ascending on columns or pilasters.

subilla [soo-beel'-lyah], *f. Awl. V.* ALESNA.

subíndice [soo-een'-de-thay], *m. (Comput.)* subscript.

subinquilino [soo-in-ke-lee'-no], *m.* Undertenant, one who rents a house of another tenant.

subintración [soob-in-trah-the-on'], *f.* 1. Immediate succession of things. 2. *(Med.)* Subingression.

subintrar [soob-in-trar'], *va.* To enter successively one after another.

subir [soo-beer'], *vr.* 1. To mount, to ascend, to come up, to go up (calle, cuesta), to climb. 2. To increase (precio, sueldo), to swell, as rivers, etc. 3. Of numbers, to amount to. 4. To enter leaves, as silkworms on commencing their cocoons. 5. To rise in dignity, fortune, etc. 6. *(Mus.)* To raise the voice gradually. *-va.* 1. To enhance, to increase the value. **Subir el color,** to raise a color, to render it brighter. 2. To raise, to lift up: to build up, to erect. 3. To set up, to straighten from an inclined position. **Subir a caballo,** to mount a horse. **Subirse el vino, licor a la cabeza,** to become tipsy. **Subir una pared,** to build a wall. **Le subieron los colores a la cara,** she blushed. **Seguíamos subiendo,** we went on climbing. **Sigue subiendo la bolsa,** the market is still rising. **Subirse al tren,** to get on the train.

súbitamente [soo'-be-tah-men-tay], *adv.* Suddenly, on a sudden.

súbito, ta [soo'-be-to, tah], *a.* Sudden (repentino), hasty (precipitado), unforeseen, unexpected (imprevisto). **Súbito, de súbito,** *adv.* Suddenly, unexpectdly.

subjección [soob-hay-the-on'], *f. (Rhet.)* A figure used in debating and answering within ourselves.

subjetivo, va [soob-hay-tee'-vo, vah], *a.* Subjective.

subjuntivo [soob-hoon-tee'-vo], *m. (Gram.)* Subjunctive.

sublevación [soo-blay-vah-the-on'], *f.* **Sublevamiento.** *m.* Insurrection, sedition, revolt.

sublevar [soo-blay-var'], *va.* To excite a rebellion. *-vr.* To rise in rebellion.

sublimación [soo-ble-mah-the-on'], *f.* Sublimation, act of sublimating.

sublimado [soo-ble-mah'-do] **Sublimado corrosivo.** *m. (Chem.)* Corrosive sublimate.—**Sublimado, da**, *pp.* of SUBLIMAR.

sublimar [soo-ble-mar'], *m.* 1. To heighten, to elevate, to sublime, to exalt. 2. *(Chem.)* To sublimate.

sublimatorio, ria [soo-ble-mah-too'-re-o, ah], *a.* Sublimatory.

sublime [soo-blee´-may], *a.* Sublime, exalted, eminent, heroic, majestic.

sublimemente [soo-blee'-may-men-tay], *adv.* Sublimely, loftily.

sublimidad [soo-ble-me-dahd'], *f.* Sublimity, loftiness, grandeur.

sublujación [soo-bloo-hah-the-on'],*f.* An imperfect luxation of a joint.

sublunar [soob-loo-nar'], *a.* Sublunar, sublunary: terrestial, earthly.

submarinista [soob-mah-re-nees-tah], *a.* **Exploración submarinista,** underwater exploration. *-m & f.* Underwater fisherman.

submarino, na [soob-mah-ree'-no, nah], *a.* Submarine. *-m.* Submarine torpedo boat.

subministrar [soob-me-nes-trahr'], *m. V.* SUMINISTRAR.

subnormal [soob-nor-mahl'], *a.* Subnormal. *-m & f.* Subnormal person.

subordinación [soob-or-de-nah-the-on´], *f.* Subordination, subjection, subordinacy.

subordinadamente [soo-bor-de-nah-dah-men-tay], *adv.* Subordinately, subserviently.

subordinado, da [soob-or-de-nah´-do, dah], *a. & pp.* of SUBORDINAR. Subordinate, subservient; subordinated.

subordinar [soob-or-de-nar'], *m.* To subordinate, to subject.

subpolar [soob-po-lar'], *a.* Under the pole.

subprecio [soob-pray'-the-o], *m. (Com.)* Mark-down.

subprefecto [soob-pray-fec´-to], *m.* Subprefect, deputy prefect.

subprefectura [soob-pray-fec-too´-rah], *f.* 1. In France and America, subprefecture, a division of a prefecture. 2. The office of subprefect, and time of its duration. 3. Town in which the subprefect lives and the place where he has his offices.

subproducto [soob-pro-dooc'-to], *m.* By-product.

subrayar [soob-rah-yar'], *va.* To underscore, to underline.

subrepción [soob-rep the-on'], *f.* 1. A hidden action, an underhand business. 2. Subreption, obtaining a favor by false representation; surreption.

subrepticiamente [soob-rayc-tee'-the-ah-men-tay], *adv.* Surreptitiously.

subrepticio, cia [soob-rep-tee'-the-o, ah], *a* 1. Surreptitious, fraudulently obtained. 2. Surreptitious, done in a clandestine manner.

subrigadier [soo-bre-gah-de-err'], *m.* Sub-brigadier, an officer who discharged the duties of second sergeant in the Royal Guards.

subrogación [soob-ro-gah-the-on'], *f.* Surrogation or subrogation, the act of putting in another's place.

subrogar [soob-ro-gar´], *m.* To surrogate or to subrogate, to substitute.

subsanar [soob-sah-nar'], *m.* 1. To exculpate, to excuse (falta). 2. To mend, to repair.

subscribir [soobs-cre-beer'], *m.* 1. To subscribe, to put a signature at the end of a writing. 2. To subscribe to, to accede, to agree to. *-vr.* To subscribe, to promise to pay a stipulated sum for the aid of some undertaking.

subscripción,*f.* 1. Subscription, signature. 2. Subscription, contribution to an enterprise.

subscripto, ta, subscrito, ta [soobs-creep'-to, tah], *pp. irr.* of SUBSCRIBIR,

subscriptor, ra [soobs-creep-tor'], *m. & f.* Subscriber.

subsecretario [soob-say-cray-tah´-re-o], *m.* The assistant secretary.

subsecuencia [soob-say-coo-en'-the-ah], *f.* Subsequence.

subsecuente [soob-say-coo-en'-tay], *a.* Subsequent. *V.* SUBSIGUIENTE.

subsecuentemente [soob-say-coo-ayn-tay-men-tay], *adv. V.* SUBSIGUIENTEMENTE.

subseguirse [soob-say-geer´-say], *vr.* To follow next.

subséxtuplo, pla [soob-sex´-too-plo, plah], *a.* Subsextuple, containing one part of sex.

subsidiariamente [soob-se-de-ah'-re-ah-men-tay], *adv.* In a subsidiary manner.

subsidiario, ria [soob-se-de-ah'-re-o, ah], *a.* Subsidiary, auxiliary.

subsidio [soob-see'-de-o], *m.* 1. Subsidy (subvención), aid (ayuda): commonly of money. 2. Subsidy war-tax. **Subsidio de enfermedad,** sick benefit. **Subsidio de paro,** unemployment benefit. *(And.)* Anxiety (inquietud).

subsiguiente [soob-se-gee-en´-tay], *a.* Subsequent, succeeding.

subsiguientemente [soob-se-ge-ayn'-tay-men-tay], *adv.* Subsequenty.

subsistencia [soob-sis-ten-the-ah], *f.* 1. Subsistence, permanence, stability. 2. Subsistence, competence, livelihood, living.

subsistente [soob-sis-ten´-tay], *pa. & a.* Subsistent, subsisting.

subsistir [soob-sis-teer'], *vn.* 1. To subsist (malvivir), to last. 2. To subsist, to have the means of living. 3. *(And.)* To live together (vivir juntos). **Todavía subsiste el edificio,** the building still stands.

subsolano [soob-so-lah'-no], *m.* Northeast wind.

substancia [soobs-tahn'-the-ah],*f.* 1. Nutriment, sustenance, aliment, pabulum; whatever nourishes. 2. Sap which nourishes. 3. Substance, essence, being, nature of things. 4. Substance, property, wealth. **En substancia,** (1) *(Med.)* in substance. (2) *V.* SUBTANCIA.

substancial [soobs-tan-the-ahl'], *a.* 1. Substantial, real, material. 2. Nutritive, nutritious. 3. Essential, of prime importance.

substancialmente [soobs-tan-the-ahl'-men-tay], *adv.* Substantially.

substanciar [soobs-tan-the-ar'], *va.* 1. To extract the substance, to abridge. 2. To substantiate, to prove fully. 3. To pursue the proceedings in a cause until its final determination.

substancioso [soobs-tan-the-o'-so], *a.* 1. Nutritive, nutritious. 2. Substantial.

substantivar [soobs-tan-te-var'], *va.* To use adjectives as substantives. *V.* SUSTANTIVAR.

substantivo [soobs-tan-tee'-vo], *m. (Gram.)* V SUSTANTIVO.

substitución [soobs-te-too-the-on´], *f.* Substitution. *V.* SUBTITUCIÓN.

substituir [soobs-te too-cer'], *va.* To substitute. *V.* SUSTITUIR.

substituyente [soobs-te-too-yen'-tay], *pa.* Substituting. *V.* SUSTITUYENTE.

substituto [soobs-te-too'-to], *m.* Substitute. *V.* SUSTITUTO.

substracción [soobs-trac-the-on'], *f.* 1. Subtraction, taking part from a whole. 2. Privation, concealment.

substraendo [soobs-trah-en'-do], *m.* The subtrahend.

substraer [soob's-trah-err'], *va.* To subtract, to remove. *-vr.* To withdraw oneself, to elude.

subtangente [soob-tan-hen'-tay], *f. (Geom.)* Subtangent.

subtender [soob-ten-derr'], *va.* 1. To sustain, to bear up. 2. *(Geom.)* To subtend.

subteniente [soob-tay-ne-en'-tay], *m. V.* ALFÉREZ.

subtensa [soob-ten'-sah], *f. (Geom.)* Subtense; chord.

subtenso, sa [soob-ten´-so, sah], *pp. irr.* of SUBTENDER.

subterfugio [soob-ter-foo'-he-o], *m.* Subterfuge, evasion, trick.

subterráneamente [soob-tayr-rah'-nay-ah-men-tay] , *adv.* Subterraneously.

subterráneo, nea [soob-ter-rah´-nay-o, ah], *a.* Subterraneous, subterranean. *-m.* 1. Subway. 2. Subterraneous structure. 3. Underground cave or vault.

subtitulado [soob-te-too-lah-do], *m.* Subtitling.

subtitular [soob-te-too-lahr'], *va.* To subtitle.

subtítulo [soob-tee'-too-lo], *m.* Subtitle.

subtropical [soob-tro-pe-cahl'], *a.* Subtropical.

suburbano

suburbano, na [soo-boor-bah'-no, nah], *a.* Suburban, relating to a suburb.-*a.* Suburban resident.

suburbio [soo-boor'-be-o], *m.* Suburb (afueras), outskirt.

subvención [soob-ven-the-on'], *f.* Help, assistance, grant, subsidy.

subvencionar [soob-vayn-the-o-nar'], *va.* To subsidize, to aid.

subvenir [soob-vay-neer'], *va.* 1. To aid, to assist, to succor. 2. To provide (necesidades), to supply, to furnish, to defray (gastos).

subversión [soob-ver-se-on'], *f.* Subversion.

subversivo, va [soob-ver-see'-vo, vah], *a.* Subversive, destructive.

subversor [soob-ver-sor'], *m.* Subverter, overturner.

subvertir [soob-ver-teer'], *va.* To subvert (minar), to destroy, to ruin.

subyugar [soob-yoo-gar'], *va.* To subdue (país), to subjugate, to overcome.

succino [sooc-thee'-no], *m.* Succinite, amber.

succión [sooc-the-on'], *f.* 1. Suction, drawing in with the breath. 2. Suck.

suceder [soo-thay-derr'], *vn.* 1. To succeed, to come after one, to follow in order. 2. To inherit, to succeed by inheritance, to come into an estate. 3. *(For.)* To come into the place of one who has quitted or died.-*a. impers.* To happen (pasar), to come to pass, to come about, to fall out. **Sucedió así**, it happened so. **Suceda lo que suceda**, happen what may. **Lo que sucede es que....**, the fact is that..... **Suceder a una fortuna**, to inherit a fortune.

sucesible [soo-thay-see'-blay], *a.* Capable of success.

sucesión [soo-thay-se-on'], *f.* 1. Succession, series, concatenation. 2. Issue (hijos), offspring, children. 3. Inheritance (herencia).

sucesivamente [soo-thay-see'-vah-men-tay], *adv.* Successively.

sucesivo, va [soo-thay-see'-vo, vah], *a.* Successive, following in order, consecutive (consecutivo). **En lo sucesivo**, in time, in process of time; hereafter.

suceso [soo-thay'-so], *m.* 1. Event (acontecimiento), incident. 2. Issue, result, outcome; sucess. 3. *V.* TRANSCURSO.

sucesor, ra [soo-thay-sor', rah], *m.* Successor, succeeder.

suche [soo'-chay], *m.* 1. A fragrant yellow flower esteemed in Peru. 2. A fish of Lake Titicaca, held in high esteem.

suchicopal [soo-che-co-pahl'], *m.* kind of copol or styrax.

suciamente [soo'-the-ah-men-tay], *adv.* Nastily, filthily, foully.

suciedad [soo-the-ay-dahd'], *f.* Nastiness, filthiness (cualidad), obscenity.

sucino [soo-thee'-no], *m.* Amber. *V.* SUCCINO.

sucintamente [soo-then-tah-men-tay], *adv.* Succinctly, briefly

sucintarse [soo-then-tahr'-say], *vr.* *V.* CEÑIRSE.

sucinto, ta [soo-theen'-to, tah], *a.* 1. Girded, tucked up. 2. Brief, succinct, compendious, concise (declaración).

sucio, cia [soo'-the-o, ah], *a.* 1. Dirty, nasty, filthy (mugriento). 2. Stained with sin, tainted with guilt and imperfections. 3. Obscene (palabra), unchaste, smutty. 4. Uncivil, unpolished. 5. *(Naut.)* Foul; applied to a ship's bottom, to the sky or weather; to rowing out of rhythm; and to a rocky shore, or a bottom where there are reefs.

suco [soo'-co], *m.* Juice; sap.-*a.* *(Amer.)* Orange-colored.

sucoso, sa [soo-co'-so, sah], *a.* Juicy, succulent. *V.* JUGOSO.

sucotrino [soo-co-tree'-no], *a.* Socotrine.

súcubo [soo'-coo-bo], *m.* Succubus, a pretended demon, which, in intercourse with men, took the form of a woman.

sucucho [soo-coo'-cho], *m.* Storeroom of a ship.

súcula [soo'-coo-lah], *f.* Cylinder. *V.* CABRIA.

suculencia [soo-coo-len'-the-ah], *f.* Juiciness, succulence.

suculento, ta [soo-coo-len'-to, tah], *a.* Succulent (jugoso), juicy. *V.* JUGOSO.

sucumbir [soo-coom-beer'], *vn.* 1. *(Law.)* To lose a suit at law. 2. To succumb, to yield, to sink under a difficulty. 3. *(Met.)* To die.

sucursal [soo-coor-sahl'], *a.* & *f.* Branch, subsidiary (filial), succursal used primarily of a minor church, thence of other establishments; branch of a commercial house.

sud [good], *m.* 1. The south. 2. South, the south wind.

sudadero [soo-dah-day'-ro], *m.* 1. Handkerchief, for wiping off the sweat. 2. Bath, sweating-room, sudatory. 3. Moist ground, a place where water oozes out by drops. 4. Sweating-place for sheep previous to their being shorn.

sudamericano, na [soo-dah-may-re-cah'- no, nah], *a.* South American.

sudador, ra [soo-dah-dor', rah], *a.* & *n.* That which sweats or exudes.

sudante [soo-dahn'-tay], *pa.* Sweating.

sudar [soo-dar'], *va.* 1. To sweat, to perspire, to exude. Sometimes used transitively. 2. To give with repugnance. 3. To toil, to labor. 4. To ooze (recipiente), to distil. 5. To cough up (dinero). **Hacer sudar la prensa**, to print much. **Sudar la gota gorda**, to sweat blood.

sudario [soo-dah'-re-o], *m.* 1. Handkerchief or cloth for wiping off the sweat. 2. Cloth put on the face of the dead.

sudatorio, ria [soo-dah-to'-re-o, ah], *a.* Sudorific, causing sweat.

sudeste [soo-des'-tay], *m.* South east.

sudoeste [soo-do-es'-tay], *m.* 1. Southwest. **Sudoeste cuarto al oeste**, south-west by west. **Sudoeste cuarto al sur**, south-west by south. 2. South-west wind; *(Naut.)* south-wester.

sudor [soo-dor'], *m.* 1. Sweat, perspiration. 2. Sweat, labor, toil drudgery. 3. Viscous matter or gum that distils from trees. **Cubrirse de sudor**, to sweat profusely.

sudoriento, ta [soo-do-re-en'-to, tah], *a.* Sweated, moistened with sweat.

sudorífero, ra [soo-do-ree'-fay-ro, rah], *a.* Sudorific, causing sweat.

sudorífico, ca [soo-do-ree'-fe-co, cah], *a.* Sudorific, promoting sweat.

sudorífico [soo-do-ree'-fe-co], *m.* Sudorific, a medicine promoting sweat.

sudoso, sa [soo-do'-so, sah], *a.* Sweaty, moist with sweat.

sudsudeste [sood-soo-des'-tay], *m.* South-south-east.

sudsudoeste [sood-soo-do-es'-tay], *m.* South-south-west.

sudueste [soo-doo-es'-tay], *m.* South west. *V.* ÁFRICO and SUDOESTE.

sueco, ca [soo-ay'-co, cah], *a.* Swedish. **Hacerse uno el sueco**, *(Coll.)* to wink at a thing, to pretend not to have taken notice.

suegra [soo-ay'-grah], *f.* 1. Mother in-law. 2. A hard crust of bread.

suegrecita [soo-ay-gray-thee'-tah], *f. dim.* *(Coll.)* Little mother-in-law.

suegro [soo-ay'-gro], *m.* Father-in-law.

suela [soo-ay'-lah], *f.* 1. Sole of the shoe (zapato). 2. Sole-leather (trozo de cuero). 3. *(Zool.)* Sole. 4. A horizontal rafter, laid as the foundation for partition-walls. 5. Leather tip of a billiard cue. **Media suela**, half sole. **Duro como la suela de un zapato**, tough as leather, tough as old boots.

sueldo [soo-el'-do], *m.* 1. Old Spanish coin. 2. An ancient Roman coin. 3. Sou or sol, a French penny. 4. Pay given to soldiers. 5. Wages, salary, stipend (mensual). **Sueldo atrasado**, back pay. **Asesino a sueldo**, hired assasin.

suelo [soo-ay'-lo], *m.* 1. Ground (tierra), soil, surface of the earth (superficie). 2. Earth, terra firma, the principal part of the world; hence the earth. 3. Pavement, ground-floor. 4. Floor (de cuarto), flooring, story. 5. The bottom or lower part of various things, as of a well, a vase, of a jar of wine; sole of anything that touches the ground. 6. Dregs, legs, settlings of any liquid. 7. Ground-plot, ground on which a building stands. 8. End; bottom. -*pl.* 1. *(Vulg. Vet.)* Sole, planter files of a horse's hoof. 2. Scatterings or leavings of grain. **Echarse por los suelos**, (a) to stretch oneself on the ground, (b) to humble oneself too much. **Venirse al suelo**, to fall to the ground. **Dar consigo en el suelo**, to fall down. **Por los suelos**, cast down, in a state of depreciation; prostrate.

suelta [soo-el'-tah], *f.* 1. Act of loosening or letting loose; solution. 2. Fetters, with which the feet of a beast are tied when grazing. **Dar suelta a las palomas**, to release pigeons.

sueltamente [soo-el-tah-men-tay], *adv.* Loosely, lightly, expeditiously; licentiously; spontaneously; laxly.

suelto, ta [soo-el'-to, tah], *a. & pp. irr.* Of SOLTAR. 1. Loose (no envasado), light (ágil), expeditious, swift, able. 2. Free (en movimiento), bold, afaring. 3. Easy, disengaged. 4. Voluble, fluent. 5. Blank (versos sin rima). 6. *(Coll.) V.* SOLTERO. 7. Small change (dinero). **Suelto de lengua**, audacious, shameless, ill-tongued, free to speak. **Arena suelta**, loose sand. **Comprar cosas sueltas, al suelto**, to buy things by the lump or bulk. **El libro tiene dos hojas sueltas**, the book has two pages loose. **Lo dejamos suelto**, we leave it untied. **Son tres poesías sueltas**, these are 3 separate poems.

suelto [soo-el'-to], *m.* Loose piece of metal or mineral found near mines.

sueño [soo-ay'-nyo], *m.* 1. Sleep (dormir), the act of sleeping. 2. Vision, dream, the fancies of a sleeping person. 3. Drowsiness, heaviness, inclination to sleep (somnolencia). **Tengo sueño**, I am sleepy. 4. Any fantastical idea without foundation. 5. Shortness, lightness, or swiftness with which something appears or passes. **Caerse de sueño**, to be overcome with drowsiness. **Conciliar el sueño**, to woo sleep. **Espantar el sueño**, to scare away sleep, to prevent sleeping. **En sueños**, or **entre sueños**, dreaming, sleeping. **A sueño pesado**, in a profound sleep; deep sleep; difficult to dispel. **Tener el sueño ligero**, to be a light sleeper. **Se me ha quitado el sueño**, I´m not sleepy any more.

suero [soo-ay'-ro], *m.* 1. Whey. 2. Serum.

sueroso, sa [soo-ay-ro'-so, sah], *a. V.* SEROSO.

suerte [soo-er'-tay], *f.* 1. Chance (azar), fortuitous event; lot (elección), fortune, luck (fortuna), fate (destino), doom, good-luck, haphazard. 2. Rind, sort: species. 3. Manner, mode, way. 4. Skillful movements of a bullfighter. 5. Piece of ground separated from the rest by bounds or landmarks. 6. Original, stock, lineage. 7. Sort, kind (especie). **La suerte está echada**, the die is cast. **De suerte que no debe nada**, so that he owes nothing. **Echar suertes**, to cast or draw lots. **Dejar a uno a su suerte**, to abandon somebody. **Lo echaron a suertes**, they drew lots for it. **Estar de suerte**, to be in luck. **Tuvo la suerte de que hacía buen tiempo**, he was lucky that it was fine. *-pl.* **Suertes**, feats, tricks; legerdemain.

suestar [soo-es-tar'], *vn. (Naut.)* To veer towards the south east.

sueste [soo-es'-tay], *m.* South east. **Sueste cuarto al este**, *(Naut.)* south east by east. **Sueste cuarto al sur**, *(Naut.)* south east by south.

suficiencia [so-fe-the-en'-the-a], *f.* Sufficiency. **A suficiencia**, sufficiently, enough.

suficiente [soo-fe-the-en'-tay], *a.* 1. Sufficient, enough (bastante). 2. Qualified, apt, fit (idóneo), capable (capaz), competent.

suficientemente [soo-fe-the-ayn'-tay-men-tay], *adv.* Sufficiently, competently.

sufijo, ja [soo-fee'-ho, hah], *a.* Suffixed, affixed. *-m.* Suffix, affix.

sufismo [soo-fees'-mo], *m.* Sufism, A mystical doctrine among Mohammedans, chiefly in Persia.

sufocación [soo-fo-cah-the-on'], *f.* Suffocation. *V.* SOFOCACIÓN.

sufocador, ra [soo-fo-cah-dor', rah], *m. & f.* Suffocator, choker.

sufocante [soo-fo-cahn'-tay], *pa. & a.* Suffocating, suffocative.

sufocar [soo-fo-car'], *va.* 1. To suffocate, to choke, to smother. 2. To quench or put out fire. 3. To molest, to harass, to oppress. *V.* SOFOCAR.

sufoco [soo-fo'-co], *m. (Prov.)* Suffocation, fumigation.

sufra [soo'-frah], *f.* A stout strap which receives the shafts of a carriages; ridge-band.

sufragáneo, sufragano [soo-frah-gah'-nay-o], *m.* Suffragan, a bishop subject to a metropolitan. *-a.* Belonging to a suffragan.

sufragar [soo-frah-gar'], *va.* 1. To favor, to aid (ayudar), to assist. 2. To suffice, to be sufficient. 3. To defray (proyecto); to make up.

sufragio [soo-frah'-he-o], *m.* 1. Vote suffrage (voto), voice. 2. Favor, support, aid (apoyo), assistance. 3. Suffrage, any work appropriated to the souls of the deceased in purgatory.

sufragista [soo-frah-hees'-tah], *f.* Suffragist.

sufrible [soo-free'-blay], *a.* Sufferable, tolerable, bearable.

sufridera [soo-fhe-day'-rah], *f.* Smith's tool for punching holes on an anvil.

sufridero, ra [soo-fre-day'-ro, rah], *a.* Supportable, tolerable.

sufrido, da [soo-free'-do, dah], *a. & pp.* of SUFRIR. 1. Bearing up under adversities, long-suffering (paciente). 2. Consenting, accommodating: spoken of a contented cuckold. **Mal sufrido**, impatient, rude, severe.

sufridor, ra [soo-fre-dor', rah], *m. & f.* Sufferer (persona), one who suffers patiently.

sufriente [soo-fre-en'-tay], *pa.* Tolerating, bearing.

sufrimiento [soo-fre-me-en'-to], *m.* Sufferance, patience, tolerance.

sufrir [soo-freer'], *va.* 1. To suffer, to bear with patience, to undergo. 2. To bear or carry a load; to sustain an attack. 3. To clinch a nail. 4. To permit, to tolerate. 5. To bear and suffer. 6. To abide; to comport; to go under. **No sufre la menor descortesía**, he won´t tolerate the slightest rudeness. *-vn.* To suffer. **Sufrir de**, to suffer from. **Sufre de reumatismo**, he suffers from rheumatism. **Es menester sufrir y consufrir**, we must bear and forbear.

sufumigación [soo-foo-me-gah-the-on'], *f.* Suffumigation, operation of fumes, administered as a remedy or cure.

sufusión [soo-foo-se on'], *f.* Suffusion, kind of cataract in the eyes.

sugerencia [soo-hay-ren'-the-ah], *f.* Suggestion.

sugerente [soo-hay-ren'-tay], *pa.* Suggesting.

sugerir [soo-hay-reer'], *va.* 1. To hint (insinuar), to suggest, to intimate. 2. To suggest, to prompt.

sugestión [soo-hes-te-on'], *f.* 1. Suggestion (sugerencia), intimation, hint (insinuación). 2. Temptation by the devil. 3. **Sugestión magnética, hipnótica**, hypnotic suggestion, control of the will of the person hypnotized.

sugestionar [soo-hes-te-o-nar'], *va. & vr.* To influence by suggestion.

sugestivo [soo-hays-tee'-vo], *a.* 1. Stimulating (estimulante), evocative (evocador). 2. Attractive (atractivo).

sugo [soo'-go], *m. (Prov.) V.* JUGO.

suicida [soo-e-thee'-dah], *com.* Suicide, a self-murderer.

suicidarse [soo-e-the-dar'-say], *vr.* To commit suicide.

suicidio [soo-e-thee'-de-o], *m.* Suicide, self-murder.

suite [soo-ee'-tay], *m.* A Central American dwarf palm used for thatching. Geonoma (species).

Suiza [soo-ee'-thah], *f.* Switzerland.

suizo, za [soo-ee'-tho, thah], *a.* Swiss.

sujeción [soo-hay-the-on'], *f.* 1. Subjection, the act of subduing; coercion, control, obedience; the act of submitting or surrendering; connection. 2. Objection, argument.

sujetador [soo-hay-tah-dor'], *m.* Fastener; clip (para pelo), clip (para papeles), bra (prenda).

sujetar [soo-hay-tar'], *va.* 1. To subdue (dominar), to reduce to submission. 2. To subject, to put under, to keep down (persona), to overcome, to conquer, to make liable, to nail down (clavo), to fasten together (papeles). *-vr.* To be inherent, to adhere.

sujeto, ta [soo-hay'-to, tah], *a. & pp. irr.* of SUJETAR. 1. Subject, liable (propenso a), exposed, chargeable. 2. Amenable before a court of justice. **Estar sujeto a cambios inesperados**, to be liable to sudden changes.

sujeto

sujeto [soo-hay´-to], *m*. 1. Subject, topic, theme, matter in discussion. 2. *(Gram.)* Subject, that of which something is affirmed (or denied). 3. A person: commonly used to express any undefined person or individual. **Es un buen sujeto**, *(Coll.)* he is a clever fellow also, he is an honest man. **Un sujeto sospechoso**, a suspicious character. **Buen sujeto**, good chap.

sulfanilamida [sool-fah-ne-lah-mee´-dah], *f*. Sulfanilamide, sulfa.

sulfapiridina [sool-fah-pe-re-dee´-nah], *f*. Sulfapyridine.

sulfatiazol [sool-fah-te-ah-thole´], *m*. Sulfathiazole.

sulfato [sool-fah´-to], *m*. Sulphate. **Sulfato de cobre**, copper sulphate.

solfido [sool-fee´-do], *m*. Sulphid, sulfid or sulphide.

sulfhídrico [soolf-ee´-dre-co], *a*. Sulphydric, hydrosulphuric (acid).

sulfito [sool-fee´-to], *m*. Sulphite, a salt of sulphurous acid.

sulfonamida [sool-fo-nah-mee´-dah], *f*. Sulfonamide.

sulfonamidas [sool-fo-nah-me´-dahs], *f. pl.* Sulfa drugs.

súlfur [sool´-foor], *m*. Brimstone, sulphur. V. AZUFRE.

sulfurar [sool-foo-rar´], *va*. To irritate, to anger, to enrage.

sulfúreo, rea [sool-foo´-ray-o, ah], *a*. Sulphureous, sulphurous.

sulfúrico [sool-foo´-re-co], *a*. 1. Sulphuric (ácido). 2. Sulphuric, consisting of sulphur.

sulfuro [sool-foo´-ro], *m*. Sulphid, sulphide, sulfid: a combination of sulphur with a metal.

sulfuroso, sa [sool-foo-ro´-so, sah], *a*. 1. Sulphurous, containing sulphur. 2. Sulphurous acid, containing one molecule of sulphur to two of oxygen.

sultán [sool-tahn´], *m*. 1. Sultan, an appellation which the Turks give to their emperor. 2. Mohammedan prince or governor.

sultana [sool-tah´-nah], *f*. Sultana or sultaness, the queen of a Turkish emperor.

suma [soo´-mah], *f*. 1. Sum, the whole of anything. 2. Sum, many particulars aggregated to a total; a sum of money. 3. Substance, heads of anything. 4. Sum, amount or result of reasoning or computation, act of summing up, conclusion. 5. Sum, compendium, abridgment. **En suma**, in short; finally. **Hacer sumas**, to add up. **Suma global**, lump sum.

sumaca [soo-mah´-cah], *f*. A small schooner used in the coasting trade along the Atlantic coast of South America.

sumador [soo-mah-dor], . *(Comput.)* Adder. **Sumador de un dígito**, one digit-adder.

sumadora mecánica [soo-mah-do´-rah may-cah´-ne-cah], *f*. Adding machine.

sumamente [soo´-mah-men-tay], *adv*. Chiefly; extremely, mightily, highly.

sumando [soo-mahn´-do], *m. (Math.)* Each of the quantities which are added together.

sumar [soo-mar´], *va..* 1. To sum, to collect particulars into a total; to add. 2. To collect into a narrow compass (recoger); to sum up, to recapitulate. **La cuenta suma 6 dólares**, the bill adds up to $6. -*vn*. To cast up accounts; to result.

sumaria [soo-mah´-re-ah], *f*. The preparatory proceeding in a suit at law; verbal process.

sumariamente [soo-mah´-re-ah-men-tay], *adv*. Summarily; in a plain manner.

sumario, ria [soo-mah´-re-o, ah], *a*. Summary, compendious; plain, without formalities.

sumario [soo-mah´-re-o], *m*. Compendium, abridgment, summary; abstract, compend; result of computation.

sumergible [soo-mer-hee´-blay], *a*. Submergible, submersible, sinkable. -*m*. Submersible, submarine.

sumergimiento [soo-mer-he-me-en´-to], *m*. V. SUMERSIÓN.

sumergir [soo-mer-heer´], *va*. 1. To submerge, to drown, to immerse (bañar). 2. To embarrass, to involve in difficulties.

sumersión [soo-mer-se-on´], *f*. Submersion, immersion.

sumidad [soo-me-dahd´], *f*. Top, summit.

sumidero [soo-me-day´-ro], *m*. 1. Sewer, drain (cloaca), sink (fregadero). 2. *(Carib.)* Quagmire (tremedal). 3. *(Fig.)* Drain.

sumido, da [soo-mee´-do, dah], *a. & pp* of SUMIR. Drowned; overflowed, plunged into vice.

sumillería [soo-mil-lyay-ree´-ah], *f*. Lord chamberlain's office.

suministración [soo-me-nis-trah-the-on´], *f*. Supply, the act of furnishing or supplying, subministration.

suministrador, ra [soo-me-nis-trah-dor´, rah], *m. & f*. Provider, one who subministers.

suministrar [soo-mee-nis-trar´], *va*. To subminister, to supply (artículos, información), to furnish, to minister.

sumir [soo-meer´], *va*. To take; to receive. in this sense it is confined to the receiving of the chalice in the celebration of the mass. -*vr*. 1. To sink under ground (objeto), to be swallowed up. 2. To be sunk (boca, pecho). **Sumir un barco**, *(Naut.)* to stave a vessel. **El desastre le sumió en la tristeza**, the disaster plunged him into sadness. 3. *(LAm.)* To cower (encogerse).

sumisamente [soo-mee´-sah-men-tay], *adv*. Submissively low.

sumisión [soo-me-se-on´], *f*. 1. Submission, obsequiousness, compliance, acquiescence, obedience. 2. *(Law.)* Renunciation.

sumiso, sa [soo-mee´-so, sah], *a*. Submissive, humble, resigned, compliant, meek.

sumista [soo-mees´-tah], *m*. Abridger writer of compendiums or summaries computer; young student in morality.

sumo, ma [soo´-mo, mah], *a*. Highest, loftiest, greatest; most elevated; excessive. **A lo sumo**, at most; to the highest pitch.

suncho [soon´-cho], *m. (Naut.)* Clamp. **Sunchos de la bomba**, Pump-clamps.

sunción [soon-the-on´], *f*. Receiving the chalice at mass.

sunsún [soon-soon´], *m*. (Cuban) A humming-bird.

suntuario, ria [soon-too-ah´-re-o, ah], *a*. Sumptuary: applied to laws relating to expense or regulating the cost of living.

suntuosamente [soon-too-o´-sah-men-tay], *adv*. Sumptuous.

suntuosidad [soon-too-o-se-dahd´], *f*. Sumptuosity, costliness, sumptuousness.

suntuoso, sa [soon-too-oh´-so, sah], *a*. Sumptuous, expensive; new-fangled.

supedáneo [soo-pay-dah´-nay-o], *m*. Species of pedestal to a crucifix.

supeditación [soo-pay-de-tah-the-on´], *f*. The act of subduing or trampling under foot.

supeditado, da [soo-pay-de-tah´-do, dah], *pp*. of SUPEDITAR. Trampled under foot. **Supeditado de los contrarios**, suppressed by enemies.

supeditar [soo-pay-de-tar´], *adv*. To subdue, to trample under foot, to overpower.

súper. A Latin preposition, used in composition, denoting (a) over, above: (b) pre-eminence.

superable [soo-pay-rah´-blay], *a*. Surmountable, conquerable.

superabundancia [soo-per-ah-boon-dahn´-the-ah], *f*. Superabundance, overflow.

superabundante [soo-per-ah-boon-dahn´-tay], *pa. & a*. Superabundant, luxuriant.

superabundantemente [soo-per-ah-boon-dahn-tay], *adv*. Superabundantly, overflowingly.

superabundar [soo-per-ah-boon-dar´], *vn*. To superabound.

superación [soo-pay-rah-the-on´], *f*. 1. Overcoming (acto). 2. Improvement (mejora).

superano [soo-pay-rah´-no], *m. (Mus.)* V. TIPLE.

superante [soo-pay-rahn´-tay], *pa*. Surpassing, surmounting.

superar [soo-pay-rar´], *va*. To overcome (adversario), to conquer, to surpass (rival), to excel, to overpower, to exceed (esperanzas). **Las escenas superan a toda imaginación**, the scenes are more extraordinary than anyone could imagine.

superavit [soo-pay-rah´-vit], *m*. Overplus, residue.

supercarburante [soo-per-car-boo-rahn´-tay], *m*. High-grade fuel.

superchería [soo-per-chay-ree´-ah], *f.* Artful fallacy, fraud, deceit, or cozenage; foul dealing.

superchero, ra [soo-per-chay´-ro, rah], *a.* Wily, deceitful, insidious.

superciliar [soo-per-the-le-ar´], *a.* Superciliary, above the eyebrows.

supereminencia [soo-per-ay-me-nen´-the-ah], *f.* Supereminence.

supereminente [soo-per-ay-me-nen´-tay], *a.* Supereminent.

supererogación [soo-per-ay-ro-gah-the-on´], *f.* Supererogation.

supererogatorio, ria [soo-per-ay-ro-gah-to´-re-o, ah], *a.* Supererogatory.

superestructura [soo-per-es-trooc-too´-rah], *f.* Superstructure.

superfetación [soo-per-fay-tah-the-on´], *f.* Superfetation, superimpregnation.

superficial [soo-per-fe-the-ahl´], *a.* 1. Superficial, on the surface. 2. Superficial, shallow, smattering.

superficialidad [soo-per-fe-the-ah-le-dahd´], *f.* Superficiality.

superficialmente [soo-per-fe-the-al´-men-tay], *adv.* Superficially, flashily, on the surface.

superficiario, ria [soo-per-fe-the-ah´-re-o, ah], *a.* V. SUPERFICIONARIO.

superficie [soo-per-fee´-the-ay], *f.* Superficies, surface, area. **Superficie inferior**, lower surface. **El submarino salió a la superficie**, the submarine surfaced.

superficionario, ria [soo-per-fe-the-o-nah´-re-o, rah], *a.* (*Law.*) Applied to those who occupy the property of others by paying rent.

superfino, na [soo-per-fee´-no, nah], *a.* Superfine.

superfluamente [soo-per-floo-ah-men´-tay], *adv.* Superfluously.

superfluidad [soo-per-floo-e-dahd´], *f.* Superfluity.

superfluo, ua [soo-per´-floo-o, ah], *a.* Superfluous, exuberant.

superfosfato [soo-per-fos-fah´-to], *m.* Superphosphate.

superhombre [su-per-om´-bray], *m.* Superman.

superhumeral [soo-per-oo-may-rahl´], *m.* Ephod, scapulary: band for the cover of a reliquary.

superíndice [soo-per-een´-de-thay], *m.* (*Comput.*) Superscript.

superintendencia [soo-per-in-ten-den´-the-ah], *f.* 1. Superintendence, supervision. 2. Charge and jurisdiction of superintendent; superintendency.

superintendente [soo-per-in-ten-den´-tay], *com.* 1. Superintendent, intendent; an officer of high rank, who oversees any allotment of public business. **Superintendente de la casa de moneda**, warden of the mint. 2. Comptroller, overseer, supervisor.

superior [soo-pay-re-or´], *a.* Superior, paramount, higher, greater. **Ser superior**, to be superior to. **Vive en el piso superior**, he lives on the upper floor. **Un estudio de nivel superior a los existentes**, a study on a higher plane than the present ones.

superior, ra [soo-pay-re-or´, rah], *m.& f.* Superior

superiorato [soo-pay-re-o-rah´-to], *m.* Office of a superior and the term of such office.

superioridad [soo-pay-re-o-re-dahd´], *f.* Superiority, pre-eminence.

superiormente [soo-pay-re-or-men´-tay], *adv.* Masterly, in a superior manner.

superlativar [soo-per-lah-te-var´], *va.* To make a term superlative.

superlativo, va [soo-per-lah-tee´-vo, vah], *a.* Superlative. **En grado superlativo**, superlatively.

supermercado [soo-per-mer-cah´-do], *m.* Supermarket.

superno, na [soo-per´-no, nah], *a.* Supreme, highest, supernal.

supernumerario, ria [soo-per-noo-may-rah´-re-o, ah], *a.* Supernumerary.

superpoblado, da [soo-per-po-blah´-do, dah], *a.* Overpopulated (país, región).

superposición [soo-per-po-se-the-on´], *f.* 1. Addition. 2. Placing above. 3. Superposition.

superpotencia [soo-per-po-ten´-the-ah], *f.* (*Pol.*) Superpower.

superproducción [soo-per-pro-dooc-the-on´], *f.* Overproduction.

supersaturar [soo-per-sah-too-rar´], *va.* To supersaturate.

supersónico, ca [soo-per-so´-ne-co, cah], *a.* Supersonic.

superstición [soo-pers-te-the-on´], *f.* Superstition.

supersticiosamente [soo-pers-te-the-o´-sah-men-tay], *adv.* Superstitiously.

supersticioso, sa [soo-pers-te-the-o´-so, sah], *a.* Superstitious; scrupulous beyond need.

supersubstancial [soo-per-soobs-tahn-the-ahl´], *a.* Supersubstantial (eucaristía).

supervalente [soo-per-vah-len´-tay], *a.* Prevalent, exceeding in value.

supervalorar [soo-per-va-lo-rahr´], *va.* To overvalue, to overstate.

supervención [soo-per-ven-the-on´], *f.* (*For.*) The taking effect of a new law.

superveniencia [soo-per-vay-ne-en´-the-ah], *f.* Supervention, the act of supervening.

superveniente [soo-per-ve-ne-en´-tay], *pa. & a.* Supervenient, supervening.

supervenir [soo-per-ve-neer´], *m.* To supervene; to come as an extraneous addition. V. SOBREVENIR.

supervisor, ra [soo-per-ve-sor´], *m & f.* Supervisor.

supervivencia [soo-per-ve-ven´-the-ah], *f.* 1. Survivorship. 2. Money or annuity, stipulated in marriage settlements in favor of the surviving consort.

superviviente [soo-per-ve-ve-ayn´-tay], *a.* Surviving. -*m & f.* Survivor.

supinación [soo-pe-nah-the-on´], *f.* Supination, lying with the face upward.

supinador [soo-pe-nah-dor´], *a.* Supinator, a muscle turning the hand palm upward.

supino, na [soo-pee´-no, nah], *a.* 1. Supine, indolent, lying with the face upward. 2. Ignorant from negligence.

supino [soo-pe-no], *m.* (*Gram.*) Supine.

suplantación [soo-plan-tah-the-on´], *f.* Supplanting, the act of supplanting.

suplantador, ra [soo-plan-tah-dor´, rah], *m. & f.* Supplanter.

suplantar [soo-plan-tar´], *va.* 1. To falsify a writing by blotting out words, and putting others in their place. 2. (*Coll.*) To supplant, to displace by stratagem.

suplefaltas [soo-play-fahl´-tas], *m.* (*Coll.*) Substitute.

suplemento [soo-play-men´-to], *m.* 1. Supply, the act of supplying. Supplement.

supletorio, ria [soo-play-to´-re-o, ah], *a.* Suppletory, supplemental, that which fills up deficiencies.

súplica [soo´-ple-cah], *f.* Petition, request, supplication, memorial. (*Coll.*) A favor asked.

suplicación [soo-ple-cah-the-on´], *f.* 1. Request, petition, supplication. 2. (*For.*) Appeal from the decision of a court. 3. Conical tube of thin and light paste; a kind of pastry. V. BARQUILLO. **A suplicación**, by petition, memorializing.

suplicante [soo-ple-cahn´-tay], *pa. & f.* Supplicant, petitioning; memorialist, petitioner, suitor; suitress.

suplicar [soo-ple-car´], *va.* 1. To entreat, to implore, to supplicate, to crave. 2. To make a humble reply to a superior. **Suplicar de la sentencia**, to petition against the sentence; to appeal to a higher court.

suplicatorio [soo-ple-cah-to´-re-oh], *f.* (*Law.*) Letter supplicatory, rogatory, a writ or any legal instrument sent in by a tribunal or judge to another of equal authority, that they may attend to what is solicited (inmunidad parlamentaria).

suplicio [soo-plee´-the-o], *m.* 1. Punishment (castigo), torture (tortura). **Es un suplico tener que escuchar eso**, it's torture to have to listen to that. 2. Place of execution. 3. *(Met.)* Bodily or mental suffering, anguish.

suplidor, ra [soo-ple-dor', rah], *m. & f.* Substitute, deputy.

supliente [soo-ple-en'-tay], *pa. & a.* Substitute, supplying.

suplimiento [soo-ple-me-en'-to], *m.* V. SUPLEMENTE.

suplir [soo-pleer'], *va.* 1. To supply (necesidad), to fill up as deficiencies happen, to furnish. 2. To supply, to serve instead of. 3. To excuse, to overlook, to disguise.

suponedor, ra [soo-po-ne-dor', ra], *m. & f.* Supposer.

suponer [soo-po-nerr'], *va.* 1. To suppose, to surmise. **Supongamos, supóngase,** let us suppose. 2. To suppose, to fancy, to imagine (imaginar). 3. To attribute (atribuir). *-vn.* To possess weight or authority. **Con las dificultades que son de suponer,** with all the difficulties that one might expect. **Es un suponer,** I was only thinking about. **El traslado le supone grandes gastos,** the move involves a lot of expense for him. *(Yo supongo, suponga, supuse, supondré,* from *Suponer.* V. PONER.)

suportar [soo-por-tar'], *va.* V. SOBRELLEVAR.

suposición [soo-po-se-the-on'], *f.* 1. Supposition (supuesto), surmise. 2. Authority (autoridad), distinction (distinción), eminence in point of talents. 3. Imposition, falsehood. 4. (Logic) Acceptance of one term in piece of another.

supositar [soo-po-se-tar'], *va. (Divin.)* To exist under both divine and human nature in one person.

supositicio, cia [soo-po-se-tee'-the-o, ah], *a.* Suppositious. V. FINGIDO.

supositivo, va [soo-po-se-tee'-vo, vah], *a.* Suppositive, implying supposition.

supositorio [soo-po-se-to'-re-o], *m. (Med.)* Suppository. V. CALA.

suprarrenal [soo-pra-ray-nahl'], *a.* Suprarenal. **Glándula suprarrenal,** suprarenal gland.

supraspina [soo-pras-pee'-nah], *f. (Anat.)* Cavity at the top of the shoulder, the supra-spinal fosea of the scapula.

supraspinato [soo-pras-pe-nah'-to], *m. (Anat.)* Supraspinatus, muscle which raises the arm.

suprema [soo-pray'-mah], *f.* The supreme council of the Inquisition.

supremacía [soo-pray-mah-thee'-ah], *f.* Supremacy.

supremamente [soo-pray-mah-men-tay], *adv.* Ultimately, supremely.

supremo, ma [soo-pray'-mo, mah], *a.* Supreme; highest, most excellent, paramount; excessive.

supresión [soo-pray-se-on'], *f.* Suppression: obstruction; extinction.

supresivo, va [soo-pray-see'-vo, vah], *a.* Suppressive, tending to suppress.

supreso, sa [soo-pray'-so, sah], *pp. irr.* of SUPRIMIR. Suppressed.

suprimir [soo-pre-meer'], *va.* 1. To suppress (rebelión, crítica), to impede, to obstruct. 2. To abolish a place or employment, to extinguish (derecho, institución). 3. To suppress (libro), to keep in, to omit, to conceal.

suprior, ra [soo-pre-or', rah], *m. & f.* Sub-prior, sub-prioress.

supriorato [soo-pre-o-rah'-to], *m.* Office of sub-prior or prioress.

supuesto [soo-poo-es'-to], *m.* 1. Supposition. 2. *(Phil.)* Individuality of a complete and incommunicable substance.

supuesto, ta, *a. & pp. irr.* of SUPONER. Supposititious, suppositive, supposed. **Por supuesto,** of course. **Supuesto que,** allowing that; granting that; since.

supuración [soo-poo-rah-the-on'], *f.* Suppuration.

supurante [soo-poo-rahn'-tay], *pa.* Suppurating, generating pus.

supurar [soo-poo-rar'], *va.* To waste or consume moisture by heat. *-m. (Med.)* To suppurate, to form pus.

supurativo, va [soo-poo-rah-tee'-vo, vah], *a.* Suppurative.

supuratorio, ria [soo-poo-rah-to'-re-o, ah], *a.* That which suppurates.

suputación [soo-poo-tah-the-on'], *f.* Computation, calculation, supputation.

suputar [soo-poo-tar'], *va.* To compute, to calculate, to suppute.

sur [soor], *m.* South: south wind. **Navegar al sur,** *(Naut.)* to steer a southerly course; to stand to the southward.

sura [soo'-rah], **surata** [soo-rah'-tah], *f.* A chapter or section of the Koran.

surada [soo-rah'-dah], *f. (Naut.)* A strong south wind.

sural [soo-rahl'], *a.* Sural: applied to the veins that run down the leg.

surcador, ra [soor-cah-dor', ra], *m. & f.* Ploughman, plowman, plougher.

surcar [soor-car'], *va.* 1. To furrow, to make furrows with a plough (tierra). 2. *(Met.)* To furrow, to flute (agua, olas). 3. To pass through a liquid. **Surcar los mares,** *(Naut.)* to plough the seas.

surco [soor'-co], *m.* 1. Furrow, hollow track. 2. Line, wrinkle. **A surco,** applied to pieces of ground furrowed in the middle.

surculado, da [soor-coo-lah'-do, dah], *a.* Applied to plants of one stem without branches.

súrculo [soor'-coo-lo], *m.* Single stem of a tree or plant without branches.

surculoso, sa [soor-coo-lo'-so, sah], *a.* Applied to a plant which has only one stem.

sureste [soo-rays'-tay], *m.* South-east.

surf [soorf], *m.* **Surf a vela,** windsurfing; surfboarding.

surgente [soor-hen'-tay], *pa.* Surging, salient.

surgidero [soor-he-day'-ro], *m.* Road, port, anchoring-place.

surgidor [soor-he-dor'], *m.* A person who anchors.

surgir [soor-heer'], *vn.* 1. To spout (líquido), to spurt (agua). V. SURTIR. 2. To appear, to present itself, to sprout. **Han surgido varios problemas,** several problems have arisen. 3. *(Naut.)* To anchor.

surirela [soo-re-ray'-lah], *f.* Surirella, a genus of diatoms, mostly freshwater.

suroeste [soo-ro-ess'-tay], *m.* South-west.

surrealismo [soor-re-ah-lees'-mo], *m.* Surrealism.

surrealista [soor-ray-ah-lees'-tah], *a.* Surrealist(ic).

sursueste [soor-soo-es'-tay], *m.* South-south-east.

surtida [soor-tee'-dah], *f.* 1. *(Mil.)* Sallyport. 2. Sally, sortie. 3. Backdoor.

surtidero [soor-te-day'-ro], *m.* Conduit. V. BUZÓN. **Surtidero de agua,** reservoir, basin.

surtido [soor-tee'-do], *m.* 1. Assortment, supply (existencias). **De surtido,** in common use. 2. Selection (selección), range. —**Surtido, da,** *pp.* of SURTIR.

surtidor, ra [soor-tee-dor', rah], *m. & f.* Purveyor, caterer. **Surtidor,** jet, spout, or shoot of water.

surtimiento [soor-te-me-en'-to], *m.* Supply, the act of supplying; assortment.

surtir [soor-teer'], *vn.* To spout, to spurt with violence (agua). *-va.* To supply (suministrar), to furnish, to provide, to accommodate, to fit out. **Surtir efecto,** to have the desired effect. **Surtir un pedido,** to fill an order.

surto, ta [soor'-to, tah], *pp.* Anchored: it is the old irregular participle of *Surgir.*

susamiel [soo-sah-me-el'], *f.* Paste, made of almonds, sugars and spice.

suscepción [soos-thep-the-on'], *f.* The act of receiving sacred orders.

susceptibilidad [soos-thep-te-be-le-dahd'], *f.* 1. Susceptibility to influences, aptitude for receiving an action. 2. Delicacy, susceptibility of emotions; sensibility.

susceptible [soos-thep-tee'-blay], *a.* Susceptible. **Susceptible de sufrir daño,** liable to suffer damage.

susceptivo, va [soos-thep-tee'-vo, vah], *a.* Susceptible, susceptive.

suscitación [soos-the-tah-the-on'], *f.* Excitation; an excited state.

suscitar [soos-the-tar'], *va.* 1. To excite, to stir up (rebelión). 2. To rouse, to promote vigor, to suscitate, to provoke (conflicto, escándalo), to arouse (sospecha).

suscribir [soos-cre-beer'], *va. V.* SUBSCRIBIR. Still a popular spelling.

suscripción [soos-crip-the-on'], *f. V.* SUBSCRIPCIÓN.

suscriptor, ra [soos-creep-tor', rah], *m. & f.* Subscriber. *V.* SUBSCRIPTOR.

suscrito, ta [soos-cree'-to, tah], *a. & pp. irr.* of SUSCRIBIR.

suscritor, ra [soos-cre-tor', rah], *m. & f. V.* SUSCRIPTOR.

susidio [soo-see'-de-o], *m. (Amer.)* Inquietude, restlessness, sudden dread.

susodicho, cha [soo-so-dee'-cho, chah], *a.* Forementioned, aforesaid.

suspendedor, ra [soos-pen-day-dor', rah], *m. & f.* Suspender.

suspender [soos-pen-derr'], *va.* 1. To suspend, to keep suspended (objeto); to hang. 2. To suspend, to stop (trabajo, pago), to delay, to dally. 3. To surprise, to amaze (pasmar). **Suspender los pagos,** to stop payment. **Suspender hasta más tarde,** to put off till later.

suspensión [soos-pen-se-on'], *f.* 1. Suspension, detention, pause. 2. Hesitation, suspense, uncertainty, indetermination. 3. Admiration, amazement. 4. Suspension, privation, an ecclesiastical censure. **Suspensión de hostilidades,** cessation of hostilities.

suspensivo, va [soos-pen-see'-vo, vah], *a.* That which has the power of suspending. *-pl. (Gram.)* Dotted lines showing that something has been omitted; thus ...

suspenso, sa [soos-pen'-so, sah], *pp. irr.* of SUSPENDER. Hung; suspended, suspense (colgado). *-m.* 1. *(Univ.)* Fail, failure. 2. *(LAm.)* Suspense. **Estar en suspenso,** to be in suspense.

suspensorio, ria [soos-pen-so'-re-o, ah], *a.* Suspensory.

suspensorio [soos-pen-so'-re-o], *m.* Suspensory bandage.

suspicacia [soos-pe-cah'-the-ah], *f.* Suspiciousness, jealousy.

suspicaz [soos-pe-cath'], *a.* Suspicious, jealous.

suspicazmente [soos-pe-cath'-men-tay], *adv.* Suspiciously.

suspirador, ra [soos-pee-rah-dor', rah], *m. & f.* One who continually sighs or suspires; one who breathes with difficulty.

suspirar [soos-pe-rar'], *vn.* 1. To sigh, to suspire, to groan. 2. To crave, to desire anxiously. **Suspirar por el mando,** to aspire after command.

suspiro [soos-pee'-ro], *m.* 1. Sigh, suspiration: breath. 2. Hissing of the wind, sharp sound of a piece of glass. 3. *pl.* Lady's-fingers, a variety of cake. 4. *(Bot.)* V. TRINITARIA. **El último suspiro,** the end of a thing; the last gasp or breath.

sustancia [soos-tahn'-the-ah], *f. V.* SUBSTANCIA. **Sustancia** is the more conversational form. **En sustancia,** briefly, summarily. **Sin sustancia,** lacking in substance.

sustancial [soos-tan-the-ahl'], *a. V.* SUBSTANCIAL.

sustancialmente [soos-tan-the-ahl'-men-tay], *adv. V.* SUBSTANCIALMENTE.

sustanciar [soos-tan-the-ahr'], *va. V.* SUBSTANCIAR.

sustancioso, sa [soos-tan-the-oh'-so, sah], *a. V.* SUBSTANCIOSO.

sustantivadamente [soos-tan-te-vah'-dah-men-tay], *adv.* Substantively, as a substantive.

sustantivar [soos-tan-te-var'], *va.* To use adjectives or any other part of speech as substantives.

sustantivo [soos-tan-tee'-vo], *m. (Gram.)* Substantive, noun.

sustantivo, va [soos-tan-tee'-vo], *a.* Substantive, betokening existence.

sustenido [soos-tay-nee'-do], *m.* 1. Spanish step in dancing. 2. *(Mus.)* Sharp. V. SOSTENIDO.

sustenido, da [soos-tay-nee'-do], *a. (Mus.)* Sharp, a semitone higher.

sustentable [soos-ten-tah'-blay], *a.* Defensible, sustainable.

sustentación [soos-ten-tah-the-on'], *f.* Sustentation, support.

sustentáculo [soos-ten-tah'-coo-lo], *f.* Prop, stay, support.

sustentador, ra [soos-ten-tah-dor', rah], *m. & f.* Sustainer.

sustentamiento [soos-ten-tah-me-en', to], *m.* Sustenance, necessaries of life.

sustentante [soos-ten-tahn'-tay], *pa.* Sustaining.

sustentante [soos-ten-tahn'-tay], *m.* Defender, supporter; he who sustains conclusions in a faculty.

sustentar [soos-ten-tar'], *va.* 1. To sustain, to bear up: to feed or support, to nourish (alimento). 2. To sustain, to assert, to maintain. **Sustentarse del aire,** to live on vain hopes; to live upon the air; to be extravagant.

sustento [sus-ten'-to], *m.* 1. Food, sustenance; maintenance (mantenimiento). 2. Support, the act of supporting, sustaining, or maintaining.

sustillo [soos-teel'-lyo], *m. dim.* A slight fright.

sustitución [soos-te-too-the-on'], *f.* Substitution, surrogation.

sustituidor, ra [soos-te-too-e-dor', rah], *m. & f.* One that substitutes.

sustituir [soos-te-too-eer'], *va.* 1. To substitute, to surrogate. 2. To substitute, to put one thing instead of another. **Tendremos que sustituir al profesor enfermo,** we'll have to substitute the teacher who is ill. *-vn.* To substitute; to deputize. **Sustituir a,** to replace.

sustituto [soos-te-too'-to], *m.* Substitute, one acting with delegated power.

sustituto, ta [soos-te-too'-to], *a. & pp. irr.* of SUSTITUIR. Substitute, surrogate, delegate.

sustituyente [soos-te-too-yen'-tay], *pa.* Substituting.

susto [soos'-to], *m.* Fright, sudden terror. **Caerse del susto,** to be frightened to death.

sustracción [soos-trac-the-on'], *f. V.* SUBSTRACCIÓN.

sustraendo [soos-trac-en'-do], *m.* Subtrahend. *V.* SUBSTRAENDO.

sustraer [soos-trah-err'], *va. V.* SUSTRAER. *(Yo sustraigo, yo sustraiga, sustraje,* from *Sustraer. V.* TRAER.)

sustrato [soos-trah'-to], *m.* Substratum.

susurración [soo-soor-rah-the-on'], *f.* Susurration, a whisper.

susurrador, ra [soo-soor-rah-dor', rahl, *m. & f.* Whisperer.

susurrante [soo-soor-rahn'-tay], *a.* Whispering (viento), murmuring (arroyo), rustling (follaje).

susurrar [soo-soor-rar'], *vn.* 1. To whisper (persona), to divulge a secret. 2. To purl, as a stream: to hum gently, as the air, to murmur (arroyo). *-vr.* To be whispered about, to begin to be divulged.

susurro [soo-soor'-ro], *m.* Whisper (cuchicheo), humming, murmur.

susurrón, na [soo-soor-rone', nah], *a.* Murmuring or whispering secretly. *-m..* Grumbler, malcontent.

sutil [soo-teel'], *a.* 1. Subtle, thin (aire), slender. 2. Subtle (observación), acute, cunning, keen (persona, mente). 3. Light, volatile.

sutileza [soo-te-lay'-thah], *f.* 1. Subtility, thinness, slenderness, fineness (cualidad). 2. Subtlety, cunning, artifice, sagacity: acumen, perspicacity; nicety. 3. One of the four qualities of the glorified body. **Sutileza de manos,** address in handling or operating, sleight of hand: light-fingeredness or nimbleness of a thief.

sutilidad [soo-te-le-dahd'], *f. V.* SUTILEZA.

sutilización [soo-te-le-tha-the-on'], *f.* Subtilization, the act of subtilizing; subtilation.

sutilizador, ra [soo-te-le-thah-dor', rah], *m. & f.* One who subtilizes or attenuates.

sutilizar [soo-te-le-thar'], *va.* 1. To subtilize, to make thin and subtile (reducir). 2. To subtilize, to file, to polish (pulir). 3. To subtilize, to discuss in a profound and ingenious manner.

sutilmente [soo-teel'-men-tay], *adv.* Subtlely, pointedly; nicely, finely, delicately.

sutorio, ria [soo-to'-re-o, ah], *a.* Belonging to the shoemakers trade; sutorial.

sutura [soo-too'-rah], *f.* 1. Seam, suture. V. COSTURA. 2. *(Anat.)* Sutura, the close connection of two bones.

suversión [soo-ver-se-on'], *f.* Subversion, ruin, destruction. *V.* SUBVERSIÓN.

suversivo, va [soo-ver-see'-vo, vah], *a.* Subversive. *V.* SUBVERSIVO.

suvertir [soo-ver-teer], *va. V.* SUBVERTIR.

suyo, ya [soo'-yo, yah], *pron. poss.* His (de él), hers (de ella), theirs (de ellos, de ellas), one's; his, her, or its own, one's own or their own. **Es el suyo**, it is his. **Lo suyo**, his. **No es amigo suyo**, he is no friend of hers. *-a & pron.* **Eso es muy suyo**, that's just like him. **Aguantar lo suyo**, to shoulder one's burden. **Cada cual a lo suyo**, it's best to mind one's own business.

suya [soo'-yah], *f.* View, intention, design. **Salirse con la suya**, to put one's wished for end in execution. **Él hizo una de las suyas**, he played one of his pranks.

suyos [soo'-yos], *m. pl.* Their own, near friends, relations, acquaintances, servants.

svástica [es-vahs'-te-cah], *f.* Swastika or swastica.

T

t [tay], twenty-first letter of the alphabet, is pronounced in Spanish as in the English words *tap, true.* It never undergoes the variations it does in English, in *creature, nation,* etc.; consequently, **criatura, patio, tía,** etc., must be pronounced *cre-ah-too'-rah, pah'-te-o, tee'-ah.* **T** is never written double.

taba [tah'-bah], *f.* 1. Ankle-bone, astragalus. 2. Knuckle-bones, a vulgar game with sheep's shanks (juego). **Menear las tabas**, to move about nimbly.

tabacal [tah-bah-cahl'], *m.* Tobacco-field (plantación).

tabacalero, ra [tah-bah-ca-lay'-ro, rah], *a. (Phil. Islands)* Relating to the culture, manufacture, or sale of tobacco; tobacco, as adjective.-*m.* Tobacconist (en tienda), tobacco grower (cultivador), tobacco merchant (comerciante).

tabaco [tah-bah'-co], *m.* 1. *(Bot.)* Tobacco. **Tabaco en polvo,** snuff. **Tabaco en rama** or **de hoja,** Leaf-tobacco. **Tabaco fruticoso,** shrubby tobacco. **Tabaco de pipa,** pipe tobacco. **Tabaco negro,** dark tobacco. 2. Mildew on plants, as wheat, barley, etc. *V.* ROYA. 3. Cigar. 4. *(LAm.)* Reefer, joint (droga). 5. *(Carib.)* Slap (golpe).

tabacoso, sa [tah-bah-coo'-so, sah], *a. (Coll.)* Using much tobacco, snuffy.

tabalada [tah-bah-lah'-dah], *f.* 1. A heavy fall upon the breech. 2. *(Coll.) V.* TABANAZO.

tabalario [tah-bah-lah'-re-o], *m. (Coll.)* The breech, posteriors.

tabalear [tah-bay-lay-ar'], *va.* To rock to and fro. *-vn.* To drum with the finger on a table.

tabaleo [tah-bah-lay'-o], *m.* 1. Drumming of the fingers on the table. 2. *(Coll.)* A spanking.

tabalete [tah-bah-lay'-tay], *m.* A kind of woollen stuff finer than drugget.

tabanazo [ta-bah-nah'-tho], *m. (Coll.)* Blow with the hand.

tabanco [tah-bahn'-co], *m.* 1. Stall for selling eatables to the poor. 2. *(Mex.)* A floor dividing a room into upper and lower apartments. *V.* TAPANCO.

tabanera [tah-bah-nay'-rah], *f.* A place where there are many horse-flies.

tábano [tah'-bah-no], *m. (Ent.)* Gadfly, horse-fly, breeze-fly.

tabanque [tah-bahn'-kay], *m.* Treadle, which serves for putting a potter's wheel in motion.

tabaola [tab-bah-o'-lah], *f.* Confused noise of a crowd. *V.* BATAHOLA.

tabaque [tah-bah'-kay], *m.* 1. A small work-basket. 2. A kind of nail somewhat larger than tacks.

tabaquera [tah-bah-kay'-rah], *f.* 1. A kind of round snuff-box used by common people (para tabaco). 2. Case for a tobacco-pipe (de pipa). 3. Bowl of a tobacco-pipe.

tabaquería [tah-bah-kay-ree'-ah], *f.* 1. Tobacco and snuff shop (tienda). 2. *(Carib.)* Cigar factory (fábrica).

tabaquero [tah-bay-kay'-ro], *m.* Tobacconist (en tienda), tobacco grower (cultivador), tobacco merchant (comerciante).

tabaquillo [tah-bah-keel'-lyo], *m. (Dim.)* 1. A weak sort of tobacco. 2. A small work-basket.

tabaquista [tah-bah-kees'-tah], *com.* One who takes much snuff, or professes to be a judge of tobacco.

tabardete [tah-bar-day'-tay], *m. V.* TABARDILLO.

tabardillo [tah-bar-deel'-lyo], *m.* A burning fever.

tabardina [tah-bar-dee'-nah], *f.* A coarse coat like the *tabardo,* but shorter.

tabardo [tah-bar'-do], *m.* Wide, loose coat of coarse cloth with hanging sleeves, worn by laborers in bad weather, tabard.

tabarra [tah-bahr'-rah], *f.* Nuisance, bore. **Dar la tabarra,** to be a nuisance.

tabasco [tah-bahs'-co], *m.* Tabasco pepper or sauce.

tabaxir [tah-bak-seer'], *m. (Bot.)* Tabasheer, a silicious concretion formed in the joints of the bamboo, opal-like, and used in the East Indies as a medicine.

tábega [tah'-bay-gah], *f.* A small kind of sailing craft.

tabelario, ria [tah-bay-lah'-re-o, ah], *a.* Tabellary, relating to secret balloting by tablets, among the ancient Romans.

tabelión [tah-bay-le-on'], *m.* (Roman history.) *V.* ESCRIBANO.

tabellar [tah-bel-lyar'], *va.* 1. To fold cloth in woollen manufactories, leaving the ends free so that the purchaser may easily mark them. 2. To mark with the maker's name or seal.

taberna [tah-berr'-nah], *f.* 1. A tavern, always applied to a house where wine is retailed. 2. *(Cuba)* Trading on the highways.

tabernáculo [tah-ber-nah'-coo-lo], *m.* 1. Tabernacle; a movable chapel, where the Jews kept the ark of the Testament. 2. Tabernacle, the place where the host is kept.

tabernario, ria [tah-ber-nah'-re-o, ah], *a. (Coll.)* Relating to a tavern.

tabernera [tah-ber-nay'-rah], *f.* Tavern-keeper's wife: woman who keeps a tavern.

tabernería [tah-ber-nay-ree'-ah], *f.* Business of a tavern-keeper.

tabernero [tah-ber-nay'-ro], *m.* Tavern-keeper, one who keeps a liquor shop.

tabernil [tah-ber-neel'], *a. (Coll.)* TABERNARIO.

tabernilla [tah-ber-neel'-lyah], *f. dim.* A small tavern: very often applied to the house where the best wine is retailed.

tabes [tah'-bes], *f. (Med.)* Consumption, tabes.

tabí [tah-bee'], *m.* Tabby, an ancient kind of silken stuff like a heavy taffeta.

tabica [tah-bee'-cah], *f. (Arch.)* Lintel or cross-board put over a vacancy in a wall.

tabicar [tah-be-car'], *va.* 1. To shut up with a wall; to wall up (puerta). 2. To close, to shut up something which ought to be open or free.

tabicón [tah-be-cone'], *m.* A thick wall. *V.* TABIQUE MAESTRO.

tábido, da [tah'-be-do, dah], *a. (Med.)* 1. Tabid, wasted by disease, consumptive. 2. Putrid, corrupted.

tabífico, ca [tah-bee'-fe-co, cah], *a.* Wasting, causing consumption.

tabillas [tah-beel'-lyas], *f. pl.* Husks of clover-seed; husks of radish-seed.

tabinete [tah-bay-nay'-tay], *m.* A silk and cotton stuff much used for making women's footwear.

tabique [tah-bee'-kay], *m.* A thin wall (pared), a partition-wall made of bricks or tiles placed on edge. **Tabique colgado,** a partition raised on a beam. **Tabique maestro,** the chief partition-wall.

tabiteña [tah-be-tay'-nyah], *f.* (*Prov.*) A kind of pipe or small flute, made of a stalk of wheat.

tabla [tah´-blah], *f.* 1. A board (madera). 2. A similar piece of other material, as of marble or copper. 3. Plain space on clothes. 4. Table, for eating and other purposes. 5. *V.* ARANCEL. 6. *V.* TABLILLA, 4th def. 7. Table of contents prefixed to a book. 8. List, catalogue. 9. A piece of painting on boards or stones. 10. The broadest and most fleshy part of any of the members of the body. 11. Bed or plot of earth in a garden. 12. House where merchandise is registered as sold at market, in order to collect the duty. 13. Plank or board of a ship to escape drowning in shipwreck. 14. Place where meat is weighed and sold: butcher's block. *-pl.* 1. Stages on which actors perform. 2. An equal or drawn game at chess or drafts. 3. Astronomical tables. 4. Tables containing the decalogue. **Tabla de juego**, gambling-house. **Tabla de dibujo**, drawing board. **Tabla de planchar**, ironing board. **Tabla de multiplicar**, multiplication table. **Tabla de tiempos**, (*Comput.*) timing chart.

tablachina [tah-blah-chee´-nah], *f.* Kind of wooden shield or buckler.

tablacho [tah-blah´-cho], *m.* Sluice or flood-gate.

tabladillo [tah-blah-deel´-lyo], *m. dim.* A small stage.

tablado [tah-blah´-do], *m.* 1. Stage, flooring (plataforma). 2. Stage of a theater. 3. Boards or bottom of a bedstead. 4. (*Met.*) Scaffold.

tablaje [tah-blah´-hay], 1. Pile of boards. 2. Gambling or gaming-house; perquisites of the keeper of a gaming-table.

tablajear [tah-blah-hay-ar'], **vn.** To gamble; to be a gambler by profession.

tablajería [tah-blah-hay-ree´-ah], *f.* Gaming, gambling; hire of the gaming-table.

tablajero [tah-blah-hay´-ro], *m.* 1. Scaffold-maker; a carpenter, who builds scaffolds and stages. 2. Keeper of a gaming-house; gambler. 3. Butcher. *V.* CORTADOR. 4. (*Prov.*) Young surgeon walking the hospital.

tablar [tah-blar'], *m.* Division of gardens into plots or beds.

tablazo [tah-blah´-tho], *m.* 1. Blow or stroke with a board. 2. Arm of the sea or of a river.

tablazón [tah-blah-thone'], *f.* 1. Boards or planks put together, so as to form a platform or other piece of construction; lumber. 2. Decks and sheathing of a ship. **Tablazón exterior**, (*Naut.*) outside planks or planking.

tablear [tah-blay-ar'], *va.* 1. To divide a garden into beds or plots (tierra). 2. To make the ground even with a thick board. 3. To hammer bars of iron into plates.

tablero [tah-blay'-ro], *m.* 1. Board planed and fashioned for some purpose. 2. Timber fit for sawing into boards. 3. Dog-nail, a sort of nails used in flooring houses. 4. Stock of a crossbow. 5. **Tablero de ajedrez** or **de damas**, chess or checker-board, draft-board. **Tablero de chaquete** or **tablas reales** or **pretera**, (*Mex.*) backgammon-board, tables. 6. Gambling-house, gaming-table. 7. (*Arch.*) Any plane level part of a building surrounded with a moulding. *V.* ÁBACO. 8. Shop counter; money-table. **Tablero de conmutadores**, a switch-board.

tableta [tah-blay'-tah], *f.* 1. (*Dim.*) Tablet, a small piece of board (de madera). 2. A tablet or memorandum. 3. Cracknel, a kind of paste hard baked, a sweet mass. 4. (*Med.*) Tablet, pill. 5. Bar (de chocolate), stick. **Tableta para escribir**, tablet, writing-pad.

tableteado [tah-blay-tay-ah´-do], *m.* The crackling sound of boards trod upon.—**Tableteado, da**, *pp.* of TABLETEAR.

tabletear [tah-blay-tay-ar'], *vn.* To move tables or boards, making a noise with them.

tabletera [tah-blay-tay'-rah], *f. & a. V.* TABLERA.

tabletica, [tah-blay-tee´-cah], *f. dim.* 1. A small tablet. 2. Kind of hard pastry cakes.

tablica, ita [tah-blee´-cah, ee´-tah], *f. dim.* A small board or table.

tablilla [tah-bleel´-lyah], *f.* 1. (*Dim.*) *V.* TABLICA. 2. Kind of sweet cakes; in pharmacy, a tablet or troche. 3. Bands on a billiard or truck table.

tablón [tah-blone'], *m. aug. 1.* Plank, a thick board; beam; stroke. **Tablón de anuncios**, notice board. 2. (*LAm.*) Plot, bed.

tabloncillo [tah-blon-theel'-lyo], *m.* Flooring-board; in some bull-rings, a row of seats at the foot of the guardrail.

tabloza [tah-blo´-thah], *f.* Painter's palette. *V.* PALETA.

tabú [tah-boo'], *a.* Taboo. **Varias palabras tabús**, several taboo words.

tabuco [tah-boo´-co], *m.* Hut, small apartment.

tabuquillo, tabuquito [tah-boo-keel´-lyo], *m. dim.* A small, miserable hut or cottage.

tabulación [tah-boo-lah-the-on'], *f.* Tabbing.

tabulador [tah-boo-lah-dor'], *m.* Tab.

tabular [tah-boo-lar'], *va.* To tabulate.

taburacura [tah-boo-rah-coo´-rah], *f.* A kind of yellow rosin.

taburete [tah-boo-ray'-tay], *m.* Chair without arms. **Taburetes**, forms with backs in the pit of a playhouse.

taburetillo [tah-boo-ray-teel'-lyo], *m. dim.* Drawing room chair for ladies.

taca [tah-cah], *f.* 1. Cupboard, small closet. 2. Each plate of the crucible of a forge.

tacada [tah-cah'-dah], *f.* 1. Act of striking the ball with the cue. 2. (*Prov.*) *V.* MANCHA.

tacamaca, tacamahaca [tah-cah-ma-ha cah], *f.* 1. Tacamahac, kind of medicinal gum resin from various tropical trees. 2. The balsam-poplar of the United States.

tacañamente [tah-cah-nyah-men'-tay], *a.* Sordidly, meanly.

tacañear [tah-cah-nyay-ar'], *m.* To act the miser; to behave in a wicked or malicious manner.

tacañería [tah-cah-nyay-ree´-ah], *f.* 1. Malicious cunning; low craft. 2. Narrowness of mind; sordid parsimony, closeness, meanness.

tacaño, ña [tah-cah´-nyo, nyah], *a.* 1. Malicious, artful, knavish. 2. Stingy, sordid, close, mean.

tacazo [tah-cah´-tho], *m.* A smart stroke with a cue.

taceta [ta-thay´-tah], *f.* A copper basin or bowl, used in oil-mills.

tacha [tah´-chah], *f.* 1. Fault, defect, imperfection, macula. 2. Crack, fissure, flaw. 3. A sort of small nails, somewhat larger than tasks. **Sano y sin tacha**, sound and without blemish. *V.* TACHO. **Poner tacha**, to make objections.

tachable [tah-chah´-blay], *a.* Exceptionable, liable to objection, censurable.

tachar [tah-char'], *va.* 1. To censure, to tax, to find fault with (criticar); to charge with a fault; to reprehend. **Tachar a alguno de ligero**, to accuse one of levity. 2. To blot, to efface, to scratch out, to dash. 3. To blame, to reprehend. (*Law.*) To impeach. **Tachar testigos**, to object, to refuse, or challenge a witness. 4. To cross out (borrar).

tachero [tah-chay'-ro], *m.* (*Cuba*) One who works at molasses boilers.

tacho [tah'-cho], *m.* 1. (*Cuba*) A boiler in which molasses is brought to the consistency necessary to convert it into sugar (para azúcar). 2. (*Peru, Bol.*) A narrow-mouthed earthen jar used for heating water.

tachón [tah-chone'], *m.* 1. Stroke or line drawn through a writing to blot it out. 2. Tacks used as an ornament for chairs; lace trimming. 3. A sort of large tacks with gilt or plated heads.

tachonar [tah-cho-nar'], *va.* 1. To adorn with lace trimming. 2. To garnish with tacks or nails with gilt heads. 3. To spot, to sprinkle.

tachonería [tah-cho-nay-ree´-ah], *f.* Ornamental work with gilt-headed tacks.

tachoso, sa [tah-cho´-so, sah], *a.* Faulty, defective, blemished.

tachuela [tah-choo-ay´-lah], *f.* 1. Tack (clavito), a small nail. 2. (*And. Carib.*) Metal pan (recipiente); (*Carib. Mex.*) metal cup. 3. (*CAm. Cono Sur, Mex.*) Short stocky person.

tacica, illa, ita [tah-thee´-cah], *f. dim.* A small cup.

tácitamente [tah'-the-tah-men-tay], *adv.* Silently, secretly; tacitly, informally.

tácito, ta [tah'-the-to, tah], *a.* 1. Tacit, silent. 2. Implied, inferred.

taciturnidad [tah-the-toor-ne-dahd'], *f.* 1. Taciturnity, silence. 2. Melancholy, deep sadness.

taciturno, na [tah-the-toor'-no, nah], *a.* Tacit, silent, reserved; melancholy.

taco [tah'-co], *m.* 1. Stopper (tapón), stopple. 2. Wad (de fusil), wedding. 3. Rammer. 4. Pop-gun (fusil de juguete). 5. *(Coll.)* Volley of oaths. 6. Cue (billar). **Echar tacos**, *(Coll.)* to swear or speak in a great rage. 7. **Tener 16 tacos**, to be 16 (years old). 8. *(Cono Sur, Mex.)* Obstruction, blockage (obstáculo). 9. *(Mex.)* Rolled tortilla, taco. 10. (Cono Sur) Short stocky person (chaparro). 11. *(CAm. Carib.)* Worry (preocupación).

tacómetro [tah-co'-may-tro], *m.* Tachometer.

tacón [tah-cone'], *m.* Heel-piece of a shoe, heel. **Tacones altos**, high heels.

taconazo [tah-co-nah'-tho], *m.* Blow with a shoe-heel.

taconear [tah-co-nay-ar'], *vn.* *(Coll.)* To make a noise with the heel-piece, to heel; to walk or strut loftily on the heels.

taconeo [tah-co-nay'-o], *m.* Noise made with the heels in dancing steps or in walking.

taconero [tah-co-nay'-ro], *m.* Heelmaker, one who makes wooden heels.

táctica [tahc'-te-cah], *f.* 1. The art of orderly array. 2. *(Mil.)* Tactics. **Táctica naval**, naval tactics.

táctico [tahc'-te-co], *m.* Tactician.

táctil [tak'-till], *a.* Tactual.

tacto [tahc'-to], *m.* 1. Touch, the sense of feeling (sentido). 2. The act of touching or feeling (acto). 3. Handiness, dexterity, certainty, tact. **Ser áspero al tacto**, to feel rough.

tacuacha [tah-coo-ah'-chah], *f.* *(Cuba)* A trick skillfully done. **Ocular una tacuacha**, to play a very pretty trick.

tadorno [tah-dor'-no], *m.* *(Orn.)* Shell-drake.

tafallo [ta-fahl'-lyo], *m.* *(Prov.)* V. CHAFALLO.

tafanario [tah-fa-nah'-re-o], *m.* *(Coll.)* Breech, notes.

tafetán [tah-fay-tahn'], *m.* Taffeta, a thin silk. **Tafetanes**, flags, colors, standard, ensign. **Tafetán inglés**, court-plaster; sticking plaster.

tafetanillo [tah-fay-ta-neel'-lyo], *m. dim.* A very thin taffeta.

tafia [tah'-fe-ah], *f.* *(Van.)* Rum.

tafilete [tah-fe-lay'-tay], *m.* Morocco leather.

tafiletear [tah-fe-lay-tay-ar'], *va.* To adorn with morocco leather.

tafiletería [tah-fe-lay-tay-ree'-ah], *f.* Art of dressing morocco leather, and the place where it is dressed.

tafurea [tah-foo-ray'-ah], *f.* *(Naut.)* A flat-bottomed boat for carrying horses.

tagalo, la [tah-gah'-lo, lah], *a.* Tagal, belonging to the Tagala, the aboriginal Malay race of the Philippine Islands. *-m.* Their language, which has a written form. *-pl.* The Tagala.

tagarino [tay-ga-ree'-no], *m.* Moor who lived among the Christians, and by speaking their language well could scarcely be known.

tagarnillera [tah-gar-neel-lyay'-rah], *f.* An artful, deceitful person.

tagarnina [tah-gar-nee'-nah], *f.* 1. V. CARDILLO. 2. *(Coll.)* A bad cigar. 3. *(And. CAm. Mex.)* Drunkenness.

tagarote [tah-ga-ro'-tay], *m.* 1. *(Orn.)* Hobby. 2. Scribe, clerk, pen-pusher, a writer in an office. 3. A gentleman sponger (hidalgo que vive a expensas de los demás). 4. A tall, ill-shaped person.

tagarotear [tah-ga-ro-tay-ar'], *va.* *(Coll.)* To write a bold, free, and running hand.

tahalí [tah-ah-lee'], *m.* Shoulder-belt.

taharal [tah-ah-rahl'], *m.* Plantation of tamarisk-trees.

taheño [tah-ay'-nyo], *a.* Having a red beard.

tahona [tah-oh'-nah], *f.* 1. Horse-mill; a corn-mill, worked by mules or horses; crushing-mill. 2. Baker's shop

(panadería), where bread is baked and sold: generally applied to places where fine bread is baked.

tahonero [tah-o-nay'-ro], *m.* Miller who directs or manages a horse-mill.

tahulla [tah-ool'-lyah], *m.* *(Prov.)* A piece of ground, near forty square yards, sown with about two pecks of grain.

tahur [tah-oor'] *m.* Gambler, gamester, cogger.

tahur, ra [tah-oor', rah], *a.* Belonging to gambling or to gamblers.

tahurería [tah-oo-ray-ree'-ah], *f.* Gambling; gaming-house; fraudulent gambling.

taifa [tah'-e-fah], *f.* 1. Faction, party. 2. *(Coll.)* Assemblage of evil life or little sense.

taimado, da [tah-e-mah'-do, dah], *a.* Sly (astuto), cunning, crafty, lazy (perezoso).

taimería [tah-e-may-ree'-ah], *f.* Rascality, viciousness, shameless craftiness.

taita [tah'-e-tah], *f.* A fondling name with which a child calls its father. *-m.* 1. *(Cono Sur)* In direct address, term of respect used before a name. 2. *(Cono Sur)* Tough (matón), bully; quarrelsome person (pendenciero). 3. Pimp (coime).

taja [tah'-hah], *f.* 1. *(Prov.)* A kind of saddle-tree put over packsaddles for carrying burdens. 2. Cut, incision; dissection. 3. Tally, a stick notched in conformity with another stick.

tajada [tah-hah'-dah], *f.* 1. Slice, a cut, a fritter. 2. *(Coll.)* Hoarseness. 3. **Coger una tajada**, to get tight (emborracharse).

tajadera [tah-hah-day'-rah], *f.* 1. Chopping-knife (hacha), chopping-block (tajadero). 2. *(Prov.)* Sluice of a mill-dam. 3. V. CORTAFRÍO. 4. *(Mech.)* Round chisel (cincel), gouge.

tajadero [tah-hah-day'-ro], *m.* Chopping-block for meat; trencher.

tajadilla [tah-hah-deel'-lyah], *f.* 1. A small slice of anything. 2. A small slice of liver, etc., in low chop-houses. 3. *(Prov.)* Bit of confected orange or lemon, sold as a relish by retailers of brandy.

tajado, da [tah-hah'-do, dah], *pp.* of TAJAR. 1. Cut, notched. 2. *(Her.)* Applied to a diagonal bar of a shield.

tajador, ra [tah-hah-dor', rah], *m. &. f.* One who cuts or chops. V. TAJADERO.

tajadura [tah-hah-doo'-rah], *f.* 1. Cut, notch; section. 2. Act and effect of cutting.

tajalápices [tah-ha-lah'-pe-thess], *m.* Pencil sharpener.

tajamanil [tah-hah-mah-neel'], *m. & f.* V. TEJAMANIL.

tajamar [tah-hah-mar'], *m.* 1. *(Naut.)* Cutwater (de puente), stem. 2. Cutwater, edge on the up-stream side of a bridge-pier. **Escoras del tajamar**, props of the cutwater.

tajamiento [ta-hah-me-en'-to], *m.* V. TAJADURA.

tajamoco [tah-hah-mo'-co], *m.* *(Ent.)* Goatchafer.

tajante [tah-hahn'-tay], *m.* *(Prov.)* Butcher. *-pa.* 1. Cutting. 2. *(Fig.)* Incisive, sharp, emphatic; sharp (distinción). **Es una persona tajante**, he's an incisive person.

tajantemente [tah-han'-tay-men-tay], *adv.* *(Fig.)* Incisively, sharply, emphatically.

tajaplumas [tah-hah-ploo'-mas], *m.* Penknife. V. CORTAPLUMAS.

tajar [tah-har'], *va.* 1. To cut, to chop, to cut off, to cut out, to hew. 2. To cut a pen.

tajea [tah-hay'-ah], *f.* 1. Furrow or small channel for the irrigation of lands. V. ATARJEA. 2. Culvert, drain under a road.

tajero [tah-hay'-ro], *m.* V. TARJERO.

tajo [tah'-ho], *m.* 1. Cut (acto herida), incision. 2. Cutting of a quill with a penknife. 3. Chopping-block or board. 4. Cutting, reaping, or digging of laborers in a line; cut or opening in a mountain. 5. Cutting edge (filo). 6. As name of a river, see Appendix. **Darse un tajo en el brazo**, to cut one's arm. **Largarse al tajo**, to get off to work.

tajón [tah-hone'], *m.* 1. *(Aug.)* A large block. 2. Chopping-block. 3. A vein of earth or soft stone in a lime-stone quarry.

tajoncillo [tah-hon-theel'-lyo], *m. dim.* A small block.

tajuela, *f.* **tajuelo,** *m.* [tah-hoo-ay'-lah]. A low stool with four feet.

tal [tahl'], *a.* l. Such, so, as. 2. Equal, similar, of the same form or figure. 3. As much, so great. 4. Used before the names of persons not known, and to determine what is not specified. **Estaba allí un tal Ramirez,** one Ramirez was there. **Tal cual,** middling, so-so; so as it is. **El tal** or **la tal,** that person, such a one: generally used contemptuously. **Tal para cual,** every one with his like; also, tit for tat: a Roland for an Oliver. **Tal por cual,** worthless, of no importance; good and bad. **No hay tal,** there is no such thing. **A tal,** with such a condition, under the circumstances. **Con tal que,** provided that. **Otro que tal,** similar, very like, equally worthless. **¿Qué tal?** how's that? how goes it? what do you say? what do you think? **Tal cosa,** such a thing. **Y como tal,** and as such. **Como tal,** just as. **Ella sigue tal cual,** she's so-so.

tala [tah'-lah], *f.* 1. Felling of trees (acto). 2. Destruction, ruin, desolation, havoc. 3. *(Carib.)* Axe (hacha). 4. *(Carib.)* Vegetable garden (huerto). 5. *(Cono Sur)* Grazing (pasto).

talabartero [tah-lah-bar-tay'-ro], *m.* Belt-maker.

talabarto [tah-lah-bar'-to], *m.* Sword-belt.

talabricense [tah-lah-bre-then'-say], *a.* Of Talavera. *-n.* A Talaveran.

talador, ra [tah-lah-dor', rah], *m & f.* Destroyer, one who lays waste.

taladrador, ra [tah-lah-drah-dor', rah], *m. & f.* Borer, piercer, penetrater. *-f.* Drill.

taladrar [tah-lah-drar'], *va.* 1. To bore, to perforate. 2. To pierce, to penetrate the ear. 3. To penetrate into or comprehend a difficult point. **Un ruido que taladra los oídos,** an ear-splitting noise.

taladrillo [tah-lah-dreel'-lyo], *m. dim.* A small borer, little bore.

taladro [tah-lah'-dro], *m.* 1. Drill (herramienta). 2. Auger. 3. Drill hole (agujero).

talaje [tah-lah'-hay], *m.* *(Sp. Am.)* 1. Pasturage. 2. Grazing.

talamera [tah-lah-may'-rah], *f.* Tree used for ensnaring birds.

talamite [tah-lah-mee'-tay], *m.* A galley rower.

tálamo [tah'-lah-mo], *m.* 1. Pre-eminent place where brides celebrated their weddings and received congratulations. 2. Bride-chamber, bridal bed.

talanquera [tah-lan-kay'-rah], *f.* 1. Parapet, breast-work of pales. 2. Defence, a spot which defends from danger.

talante [tah-lahn'-tay], *m.* 1. Mode or manner of performing anything. 2. Appearance, aspect (aspecto). 3. Will (humor), pleasure, disposition. **Estar de buen talante,** to be ready or in a good disposition to do anything. **Hacer algo de buen talante,** to do something willingly.

talar [tah-lar'], *va.* 1. To fell trees (árboles). 2. To desolate, to lay waste a country.

talar [tah-lar'], *a.* Applied to long robes reaching to the heels.

talares [tah-lah-rays]. *m. pl.* The wings on the heels of Mercury; talaria.

talavera [tah-lah-vay'-rah], *f.* Earthenware manufactured in Talavera.

talaveran, na [tah-lah-vay-rah'-no, nah], *a.* Of Talavera.

talco [tahl'-co], *m.* 1. Mica, a laminated translucent mineral. 2. A class of silicates. 3. Talcum powder.

talcualillo, lla [tal-coo-ah-leel'-lyo, lyah], *a. (Coll.)* 1. Somewhat beyond mediocrity. 2. Somewhat improved in health: said of the sick.

tálea [tah'-lay-ah], *f.* Stockade or palisade which the Romans made use of in their camps.

taled [tah-led'], *m.* A kind of woollen amice with which the Jews cover their heads and necks in their religious ceremonies.

talega [tah-lay'-gah], *f.* 1. Bag, a wide short sack (bolsa). 2. Sack containing 1,000 dollars in silver. **Una** or **dos talegas,** *(Met.)* one or two thousand dollars. 3. A bagful. 4. *(Coll.)* Sins which a penitent sinner is going to confess. 5. Bag for the hair. 6. *(Coll.)* Knowledge which one has acquired

previous to attending a public school. **talegazo** [tah-lay-gah'-tho], *m.* Stroke or blow with a full bag.

talego [tah-lay'-go], *m.* 1. Bag or sack made of coarse sackcloth (bolsa grande). **Tener talego,** to have money. 2. A clumsy, awkward fellow.

talegón [tah-lay-gone'], *m. aug.* of TALEGA or TALEGO.

taleguilla [tah-lay-geel'-lyah], *f.* 1. A small bag. **Taleguilla de la sal,** *(Coll.)* daily expenditure, money spent each day. 2. The breeches that bullfighters wear.

taleguito [tah-lay-gee'-to], *m. dim.* of TALEGO.

talentada [tah-len-tah'-dah], *f. (Prov.)* Will, propensity, inclination.

talento [tah-len'-to], *m.* 1. Talent, ancient weight or money of different value. 3. Talent, abilities, endowments, or gifts of nature; ingenuity, genius, accomplishments: in the sense of abilities it is commonly used in the plural.

talentoso, sa [tah-len-to'-so, sah], *a.* Able, ingenious, talented.

talero [tah-lay'-ro], *m.* Short whip.

talidad [tah-le-dahd'], *f.* That which determines a thing to be included generically or specifically in another.

talión [tah-le-on'], *m.* Retaliation, requital.

talionar [tah-le-o-nar'], *va.* To retaliate, to requite.

talismán [tah-lis-mahn'], *m.* 1. Talisman, a magical character. 2. Doctor of the Mohammedan law.

talla [tahl'-lyah], *f.* 1. Raised work, cut in wood or stone, sculpture (escultura). **Obra de talla,** carved work. 2. Dues paid by vessels to the lord of the manor. 3. Hansom, or reward for the capture of some noted criminal. 4. *(Prov.)* Jug with water put into the air to cool, or suspended in a draught. 5. Stature, size. 6. Operation of cutting for the stone. 7. *(Mil.)* A wooden instrument for measuring a man's height. **Poner talla,** to offer a reward for the apprehension of a criminal. **Camisas de todas las tallas,** shirts in all sizes. **No dio la talla,** he didn't measure up, he wasn't up to it.

tallado, da [tal-lyah'-do, dah], *a. & pp.* of TALLAR. Cut, chopped, carved, engraved. **Bien** or **mal tallado,** of a good or bad figure. *-m.* Carving; sculpting; engraving. **Tallado en madera,** woodcarving.

tallador [tal-lyah-dor'], *m.* 1. Engraver. 2. Carver. 3. Die-sinker.

talladura [tal-lyah-doo'-rah], *f.* Engraving.

tallar [tal-lyar'], *m.* Grove or forest of fire-wood fit for cutting.

tallar [tal-lyar'], *a.* Applied to wood fit for cutting or for fuel.

tallar [tal-lyar'], *va.* 1. To cut, to chop. 2. To carve in wood, to engrave on copper-plate. 3. To charge with dues or imposts. 4. To show all the cards in one's hand at basset. *-vn. (Cono Sur)* To chat (chismear); to gossip.

tallarín [tal-lyah-reen'], *m.* A kind of thin paste.

tallarola [tal-lyah-ro'-lah], *f.* Iron plate used for cutting the silk in velvet looms.

tallazo [tal-lyah'-tho], *m. aug.* of TALLE and TALLO.

talle [tahl'-lyay], *m.* 1. Shape, form, figure, proportion of the human body. 2. Waist, the middle of the body. 3. Mode or manner of performing a thing. 4. Fit of clothes (número). 5. Genus, species, class. **Largo de talle,** *(Coll.)* long drawn out. 6. Look, appearance (aspecto).

tallecer [tal-lyay-therr'], *vn.* To shoot, to sprout.

taller [tal-lyerr'], *m.* 1. Workshop, office, laboratory. 2. School, academy, a seminary of arts and sciences. 3. Ancient coin. **Taller de máquinas,** machine shop. **Taller de reparaciones,** repair shop.

talleta [tal-lyay'-tah], *f. (Amer.)* A paste of almonds, nuts, and honey. V. ALFAJOR.

tallista [tah-lyees'-tah], *m.* Carver in wood, engraver.

tallo [tahl'-lyo], *m.* 1. Shoot, sprout, stem which bears leaves, etc. 2. *(And.)* Cabbage (repollo). 3. *(LAm.)* Vegetables, greens. 4. *(Culin.)* Crystallized fruit.

talludo, da [tal-lyoo'-do, dah], *a.* 1. Grown into long stalks. 2. Tall, slender. 3. Callous, hardened in vicious habits. 4.

Overgrown, grown to seed. 5. (*CAm. Mex.*) **Es un viejo talludo**, he's old but there's life in him yet.

talluelo [tal-lyoo-ay´-lo], *m. dim.* of TALLO.

talmente [tahl'-men-tay], *adv.* (*Coll.*) In the same manner.

talmud [tal-mood'], *m.* Talmud, a book which contains the doctrines and ceremonies of the law of Moses.

talmúdico, ca [tal-moo'-de-co, cah], *a.* Talmudic, relating to the Talmud.

talmudista [tal-moo-dees'-tah], *m.* Professor or interpreter of the Talmud.

talo [tah'-lo], *m.* A kind of cake of maize flour.

talón [tah-lone'], *m.* 1. The heel. 2. Heel-piece of a shoe (de zapato). 3. (*Arch.*) Cymatium, ogee fluting. 4. (*Com.*) Check (cheque), sight draft, voucher. 5. The stub of such a draft. 7. A coupon or check for baggage (en Amér. **contraseña**). **Levantar los talones**, to take to one's heels. **Dar con el talón en el fondo**, (*Naut.*) to touch ground with the stern-post.

talonario [tah-lo-nah'-re-o], *m.* Stubs, coupons. **Talonario de cheques**, check book.

talonear [tah-lo-nay-ar'], *vn.* To be nimble, to walk fast. *-va.* (*LAm.*) To dig one's heels into (caballo).

talonesco [tah-lo-nes'-co], *a.* (*Coll.*) Relating to the heels.

talpa, talparia [tahl'-pah], *f.* (*Coll.*) Abscess in the pericranium, tumor in the head.

talque [tahl'-kay], *m.* A kind of argillaceous earth, of which crucibles are made.

talus, talud [tah'-loos, tah-lood'], *m.* Talus, a slope on the outside part of a wall or rampart.

talvina [tal-vee'-nah], *f.* A kind of milk, extracted from several seeds, of which porridge and dumplings are made.

tamal [tah-mahl'], *m.* 1. (*Amer.*) A kind of small dumpling, made of Indian meal, stuffed with minced meat or other eatables, and boiled in the husk of the Indian corn. 2. (Honduras) A bundle of sarsaparilla. 3. (*LAm.*) Fraud (trampa), trick, set a trap.

tamalero, ra [tah-mah-lay'-ro, rah], *m. & f.* (*Mex.*) Tamal-seller.

tamándoa [tah-mahn'-do-ah], *f.* Ant-eater of Peru.

tamañamente [ta-mah-nyah-men'-tay], *adv.* As great as, tantamount.

tamañico, ica, illo, illa, ito, ita [tah mah-nyee'-co], *a.* Very small.

tamañito, ta [tah-mah-nyee'-to, tah], *m.* 1. Fearful, intimidated. 2. Abashed, ashamed.

tamaño [tah-mah'-nyo], *m.* Size, shape, bulk, stature, magnitude. **Tamaño de bolsillo**, pocket-size. **Tener el mismo tamaño**, to be the same size.

tamaño, ña [tah-mah'-nyo, nyah], *a.* 1. Showing the size, shape, or bulk or anything. 2. Very little.

tamañuelo, la [tah-mah-nyoo-ay'-lo, lah], *a. dim.* Small, slender, little.

támaras [tah'-ma-ras], *f. pl.* 1. Clusters of dates. 2. Chips, faggots of brush-wood.

tamarindo [tah-ma-reen'-do], *m.* (*Bot.*) Tamarind-tree and fruit.

tamarisco, tamariz [tah-ma-rees'-co, tah-mah-reeth'], *m.* (*Bot.*) Tamarisk-shrub.

tamarizquito, tamarrusquito, ta [tah-ma-rith-kee'-to, tah-mar-roos-kee'-to, tah], *a.* (*Coll.*) Very small.

tamba [tahm'-bah], *f.* (*Low.*) Blanket of a bed.

tambalear, tambalearse [tam-bah-lay-ar'], *vn. & vr.* To stagger, to waver.

tambaleo [tam-bah-lay'-o], *m.* Reeling, staggering.

tambanillo [tam-bah-neel'-lyo], *m.* A raised ornament on the angles of buildings.

tambarillo [tam-bah-reel'-lyo], *m.* Chest or trunk with an arched cover.

tambero, ra [tam-bay'-ro, rah], *m. & f.* (*Peru*) Inn-keeper (fondista); dairy farmer (granjero).

también [tam-be-en'], *conj. & adv.* Also, too, likewise; as well, moreover. **Y bebe también**, and he drinks as well.

tambo [tahm'-bo], *m.* (*Peru, Amer.*) Inn.

tambor [tam-bor'], *m.* 1. A drum. 2. Drummer (persona). **Baquetas del tambor**, drumsticks. **Tambor mayor**, drum-major. 3. (*Mil.*) Small inclosure as a screen to the gates of a fortress. 4. A small room, made in another room by partition-walls, tambor or wooden screen at the doors of churches. 5. (*Arch.*) Tambor, tholus, keystone of a vaulted roof or cupola. 6. Barrel, arbor, of a watch or clock any cylindrical part of machinery. Hence further: rolling-pin, band-pulley, tumbler, wheel-house, paddle-box. 7. Tambor-frame for embroidering silk, muslin, or linen. **Tambor del oído**, ear drum. 8. (*Carib. Mex.*) Burlap (tela).

tambora [tam-bo'-rah], *f.* Bass drum.

tamborete [tam-bo-ray´-tay], *m. dim.* 1. Timbrel. 2. (*Naut.*) Cap of the mast-head, moorshead.

tamboril [tam-bo-reel'], *m.* Tambourine, tabor, tabret, a kind of drum beaten in villages on festive occasions.

tamborilada [tam-bo-re-lah'-dah], *f.* (*Coll.*) Fall on the breech; a slap on the face or shoulders (espaldarazo).

tamborilazo [tam-bo-re-lah'-tho], *m.* Blow or fall on the breech.

tamborilear [tam-bo-re-lay-ar'], *vn.* 1. To drum (con los dedos); to beat (el tamboril). 2. To cry up, to be loud in one's praise. 3. (*Print.*) To plane or level types.

tamborilero [tam-bo-re-lay'-ro], *m.* Drummer.

tamborilete [tam-bo-re-lay´-tay], *m.* (*Typ.*) Planer, a smooth wooden block used for levelling a form of type.

tamborilillo [tam-bo-re-leel'-lyo], *m.* A small tambourine.

tamborinero [tam-bo-re-nay'-ro], *m.* V. TAMBORILERO.

tamboritear [tam-bo-re-tay-ar'], *pa.* V. TAMBORILEAR.

tamboritero [tam-bo-re-tay'-ro], *m.* V. TAMBORILERO.

tamborito [tam-bo-ree'-to], *m.* National dance and musical rhythm of Panama.

tamborón [tam-bo-rone'], *m.* A large drum.

tamén, tamene [tah-mayn', tah-may'-nay], *m.* (*Mex.*) Indian porter or carrier.

tamerlán [tah-mer-lahn'], *m.* Emperor of the Tartars.

tamiz [tah-meeth'], *m.* A fine sieve, made of silk or hair.

tamo [tah'-mo], *m.* 1. Down which falls from woollen or linen in weaving. 2. Dust in corn. 3. Mould under beds on dusty floors.

tamojo [tah-mo´-ho], *m.* (*Bot.*) V. BARBILLA TAMOJO.

tampoco [tam-po'-co], *adv.* Neither, nor, not either. **Yo tampoco lo compré**, I didn't buy one either. **Ni yo tampoco**, nor did I. **'Yo no fui' 'Yo tampoco'**, 'I didn't go', 'neither did I'.

tamujo [tah-moo'-ho], *m.* (*Bot.*) Buckthorn, box-thorn.

tan [tahn'], *m.* Sound of the tamborine, or of anything like that.

tan [tahn'], *adv.* So, so much, as well, as much. **Tan grande**, so great, very much. **Tan rápido**, so fast. **A es tan feo como B**, A is as ugly as B. **No te esperaba tan pronto**, I wasn't expecting you so soon. V. TANTO.

tanate [tah-nah´-tay], *m.* (*Mex.*) A seroon made of hide, to transport articles; in some parts a basket of particular form, and also a *pita* bag.

tanatero [tah-nah-tay'-ro], *m.* (*Mex.*) The miner who takes out the ore, and carries it in the *tanate*.

tanato [tah-nah'-to], *m.* (*Chem.*) Tannate, a salt of tannic acid.

tanca [tahn'-cah], *f.* A viscous matter with which bees daub their hives before they begin to work at the honey-comb; bee-glue.

tanda [tanh'-dah], *f.* 1. Turn, rotation. 2. Task, something to be done imposed by another. 3. Certain number of persons or cattle employed in a work (turno). 4. Any undetermined number or quantity: generally applied to a number of stripes and lashes. 5. Series (serie). 6. Game (billar); innings (béisbol). 7. (*LAm. Teat.*) Show, performance; (*Cono Sur*) farce (farsa); (*Cono Sur*) musical (comedia musical).

tanga [tahn'-gah], *f.* Tanga, G-string.

tanganillas (En) [tan-gah-neel'-lyas], *adv.* Waveringly, in danger of falling.

tanganillo [tan-gah-neel'-lyo], *m. dim.* A small prop or stay.

tángano [tahn'-gah-noo], *m.* Hob, a boys game; bone or stone used in this game.

tangencia [tan-hen'-the-ah], *f.* Tangency, the state of touching

tangente [tan-hen'-tay], *a. (Geom.)* Tangent. **Salirse por la tangente**, to go off at a tangent.

tangerina [tan-hay-ree'-nah], *f.* Tangerine.

tangibilidad [tan-he-be-le-dahd'], *f.* Tangibility.

tangible [tan-hee'-blay], *a.* Tactile, susceptible of touch.

tangidera [tan-he-day'-rah], *f. (Naut.)* Cable.

tango [tahn'-go], *m.* Tango, Argentine musical rhythm and dance.

tanino [tah-nee'-no], *m. (Chem.)* Tannin, tannic acid, gallotannic acid.

tanor, ra [tah-nor', rah], *a.* A Philippine Malay who served as domestic to the Spaniards.

tanoría [tah-no-ree'-ah], *f.* Domestic service by the Philippines to the Spaniards.

tanque [tahn'-kay], *m.* 1. Vat, large trough, tank. 2. A small pool, a pond. 3. *(Mil.)* Tank. 4. Beeswax.

tanqueta [tan-kee'-tah], *f.* Small tank.

tanquía [tan-kee'-ah], *f.* An ointment for making hair fall off.

tantalato [tan-ta-lah'-to], *m. (Chem.)* Tantalate, a salt of tantalic acid.

tantálico [tan-tah'-le-co], *a.* Tantalic, an acid from tantalium.

tantalita, *f.* tantalito, *m.* [tan-ta-lee'-tah, to], *f.* Tantalite, a mineral composed chiefly of ferrous tantalate.

tántalo [tahn'-tah-lo], *m. (Min.)* Tantalum, a metal.

tantarantán [tan-tah-rah-tahn'], *m.* 1. Rub-a-dub-dub, redoubled beat of a drum (tambor).

tanteador [tan-tay-ah-dor'], *m.* Measurer, calculator, marker.

tantear [tan-tay-ar'], *va.* 1. To measure, to proportion. 2. To mark the game with counters. 3. To consider carefully, to scrutinize. 4. *(Art.)* To sketch the outlines of a design. 5. To keep the score of. 6. *(CAm. Mex.)* To lie in wait for (acechar). 7. *(Mex.)* To swindle (estafar); to make a fool of (burlarse). **Tantear si la superficie está bien segura**, to test the surface to see if it is safe.

tanteo [tan-tay'-o], *m.* 1. Computation, calculation, average. 2. Number of counters for marking a game. 3. Prudent judgment of an affair. 4. Outlines of a picture.

tantico, tantillo [tan-tee'-co, tan-teel'-lyo], *m.* Small sum or quantity.

tanto [tahn'-to], *m.* 1. A certain sum or quantity. 2. Copy of a writing. 3. Counter, mark of a game. **Tanto por ciento**, percentage. **Por un tanto alzado**, for a lump sum.

tanto, ta [tahn'-to], *a.* 1. So much, as much; very great. 2. Odd, something over a determined number. **Veinte y tantos**, twenty and upwards. **Tiene tanto dinero como yo**, he has as much money as I have. **Es uno de tantos**, it´s one of many.

tanto [tahn'-to], *adv.* 1. So, in such a manner. 2. A long time. **Tanto más o menos**, so much more or less. **Tanto que**, as much as. **Tanto mejor**, so much the better. **Tanto peor**, so much the worse. **Tanto monta**, it is as good as the other; it is all the same. **Tanto más cuanto**, thereabouts, more or less. **En tanto** or **entre tanto**, in the mean time. **Tanto por tanto**, at the same price; upon a par. **Tantos a tantos**, equal numbers. **Por el tanto** or **por lo tanto**, (1) for that same reason; on that ground. (2) For the same price. **Por tanto** or **por lo tanto**, therefore, for the reasons expressed. **La mitad y otro tanto**, the half and as much more. **Tanto uno como otro**, both one and the other; both of them.

tañedor, ra [tah-nyay-dor', rah], *m. & f.* Player on a musical instrument.

tañer [tah-nyerr'], *va.* To play an instrument harmoniously.

tañido, da [tah-nyee'-do, dah], *pp.* of TAÑER. Played; touched.

tañido [tah-nyee'-do], *m.* Tune: sound: clink.

tao [tah'-o], *m.* Badge worn by officers of the orders of St. Anthony and St. John.

tapa [tah'-pah], *f.* 1. Lid (de caja, olla), cover, cap (de botella). 2. Horny part of a hoof. 3. Heel-piece of a shoe (de zapato). 4. Sluicegate (de canal). 5. *(Mex. Aut.)* Hubcap. 6. *(Carib.)* Commission (comisión). **Tapa de los sesos**, top of the skull. **Tapa de bomba**, *(Naut.)* the hood of the pump.

tapaagujeros [tah-pa-ah-goo-hay'-ros], *m. (Coll.)* 1. A clumsy mason. 2. One who supplants another in any matter; a makeshift.

tapabalazo [tah-pah-bah-lah'-tho], *m. (Naut.)* Shot-plug.

tapaboca [tah-pah-bo'-cah], *m. (Coll.)* 1. Slap on the mouth (manotada). 2. Any action or observation which interrupts the conversation, and cuts one short. 3. Choke-pear; any sarcasm by which another is put to silence. 4. *(Mil.)* Tampion, tamkin.

tapacubos [tah-pah-coo'-bos], *m.* Hubcap (de automovil.)

tapaculo [tah-pah-coo'-lo], *m.* Fruit of the dog-rose.

tapada [tah-pah'-dah], *f.* A woman concealing her face under a thick veil or Spanish mantilla to avoid being known.

tapadera [tah-pah-day'-rah], *f.* 1. A loose lid or movable cover of a pot or other vessel (tapa); covercle. 2. The leather cover of the stirrup of a Mexican saddle.

tapadero [tah-pah-day'-ro], *m.* A large stopper or stopple.

tapadijo [tah-pah-dee'-ho], *m.* Evasion, subterfuge, blind term. *(Neol.)*

tapadillo [tah-pah-deel'-lyo], *m.* 1. The act of a woman's covering herself with her veil or mantle, that she may not be seen. 2. *(Prov.)* V. COBERTIZO. 3. A certain flute-stop of an organ.

tapadizo [tah-pah-dee'-tho], *m.* 1. Action of women hiding the face with a mantle. 2. *(Prov.)* V. COBERTIZO.

tapado [tah-pah'-do], *m. (Arg., Ch.)* 1. Spotless horse or mare. 2. *(Col. & Hond.)* Indian barbecue. 3. Ladies' wrap or cape. 4. *(And. Cono Sur)* Buried treasure (tesoro). *-a.* 1. *(Cono Sur)* Animal of one color. 2. *(And.)* Lazy (vago).

tapador, ra [tah-pah-dor', rah], *m. & f.* 1. One who stops or shuts up, coverer. 2. Plug, stopper, stopple.

tapadura [tah-pah-doo'-rah], *f.* Act of stopping, covering, or hiding.

tapafogón [tah-pah-fo-gone'], *m.* Cap of a gun, which covers the venthole.

tapafunda [tah-pah-foon'-dah], *f.* Holster-cover of pistols.

tapajuntas [tah-pah-hoon'-tahs], *m.* 1. Flashing joint (en construcción). 2. Molding on window or doorframe.

tápalo [tah'-pah-lo], *m. (Mex.)* Shawl. V. CHAL.

tapamiento [tah-pah-me-en'-to], *m.* Act of stopping or covering.

tapaojos [tah-pah-o'-hos], *m. (Amer.)* A bandage for the eyes of horses or mules (venda).

tapar [tah-par'], *va.* 1. To stop up, to cover, to put under cover, to choke up, to obstruct, to occlude. 2. To conceal (derrota), to hide, to cover up (cara), to mantle, to hoodwink, to dissemble. 3. *(And.)* To crush (aplastar); to rumple (chafar). 4. *(And.)* To abuse (insultar). **Tapar la boca**, to stop one's mouth. **Tapar una abertura de agua**, *(Naut.)* to stop or fother a leak. **El árbol tapa el sol a la ventana**, the tree keeps the sunlight off the window.

tapara [tah-pah'-rah], *f. (Sp. Am.)* Calabash.

tapara [tah-pah'-rah], *f.* Caper.

taparo [tah-pah'-ro], *m.* 1. *(Sp. Am.)* Calabash tree. 2. One-eyed person (tuerto).

taparrabo [tah-par-rah'-bo], *m.* 1. Breechclout, loincloth. 2. Swim trunks.

tapatío, tía [tah-pah-tee'-o, ah], *a. & m. & f* Name applied to persons and things from Guadalajara, Mexico.

tapeo [tah-pay'-o], *m.* **Ir de tapeo**, *(Esp.)* to go round the bars.

tapetado, da [tah-pay-tah'-do, dah], *a.* Of a dark-brown or blackish color.

tapete [tah-pay'-tay], *m*. 1. A small floor-carpet or rug. 2. A cover for a table or chest. **Estar sobre el tapete**, to be on the tapis (discusión).

tapia [tah'-pe-ah], *f*. 1. Mud-wall. 2. Massive wall. **Sordo como una tapia**, stone-deaf.

tapiador [tah-pe-ah-dor'], *m*. Builder of mud-walls.

tapial [tah-pe-ahl'], *m*. Mould for making mud-walls.

tapiar [tah-pe-ar'], *va*. 1. To stop up with a mud-wall. 2. To stop a passage, to obstruct a view.

tapicería [tah-pe-thay-ree'-ah], *f*. 1. Tapestry (arte). 2. Office in the royal palace where the tapestry and carpets are kept. 3. Shop where tapestries are sold (tienda).

tapicero [tah-pe-thay'-ro], *m*. One who makes tapestry. **Tapicero mayor**, Tapestry-keeper in a palace.

tapiería [tah-pe-ay-ree'-ah], *f*. Series of mud-walls.

tapines, tapinos [tah-pee'-nes, tah-pee'-nos], *m. pl. (Naut.)* Stoppers for ventholes.

tapinosis [tah-pe-no'-sis], *f. (Rhet.)* Figure where, with words and low phrases, any great thing is explained.

tapioca [tah-pe-o'-cah], *f*. Tapioca, the prepared starch of the cassava.

tapir [tah-peer'], *m*. Tapir, a pachydermatous mammal, having a sort of proboscis. It lives in forests and by rivers. Found in Malaysia and in South America. Syn. DANTA, ANTA, GRAN BESTIA.

tapirujarse [tah-pe-roo-har'-say], *vr*. V. TAPERUJARSE.

tapisote [tah-pe-so'-tay], *m. (Bot.)* Yellow-flowered pea.

tapiz [tah-peeth'], *m*. 1. Tapestry (de pared). 2. Grass-plot adorned with flowers.

tapizar [tah-pe-thar'], *va*. To hang with tapestry (pared); to upholster (mueble), to cover; to upholster (coche); to carpet (suelo).

tapizar [tah-pe-thar'], *m*. Cork, plug, bung.

tapón [tah-pon'], *a. (CAm. Cono Sur)* Tailless. -*m*. 1. Stopper (de botella), cap, top; cork (corcho); plug, bung, wad; *(Med.)* tampon; *(Mex. Elec.)* Fuse. 2. Chubby person (persona). 3. Obstacle (estorbo). 4. Traffic jam.

taponar [tah-po-nahr'], *va*. To stopper (botella), to put the cup on; to plug (tubo); to block; *(Med.)* to tampon.

tapsia [tap'-se-ah], *f. (Bot.)* Deadly carrot.

tapujarse [tah-poo-har'-say], *vr*. To muffle oneself in a cloak or veil.

tapujo [tah-poo'-ho], *m*. 1. Muffle, a cover for the face. 2. False pretext, subterfuge (subterfugio), feigned excuse, secrecy (secreto). **Andar con tapujos**, to behave deceitfully.

taque [tah'-kay], *m*. 1. Noise made by a door on being locked.2. Bang or rap given to it in order to call someone.

taquera [tah-kay'-rah], *f*. Rack or stand for billiard-cues

taquigrafía [tah-ke-grah-fee'-ah], *f*. Tachygraphy, shorthand, the art of quick writing. Syn. ESTENOGRAFÍA.

taquigráfico, ca [tah-ke-grah'-fe-co, cah], *a*. Tachygraphic, shorthand.

taquígrafo [tah-keeh-grah'-fo], *m*. Short-hand writer.

taquilla [tah-keel'-lyah], *f*. 1. Ticket office, box office. **Éxito de taquilla**, box-office hit, dramatic success. 2. Letter file or cabinet for documents in offices. 3. *(CAm.)* Bar; liquor store (tienda). 4. *(And. CAm. Cono Sur)* Tack (clavo).

taquillero, ra [tah-keel-lyay'-ro, rah], *a. (Th.)* Relating to box office. **Éxito taquillero**, box-office hit. -*m. & f*. Ticket seller.

taquímetro [tah-kee'-may-tro], *m*. Tachymeter, kind of theodolite for surveying.

taquín [tah-keen'], *m*. V. CARNICOL.

taquinero [tah-ke-nay'-ro], *m. (Prov.)* A person who plays a game of knuckle-bones.

tara [tah'-rah], *f*. 1. *(Com.)* Tare, an allowance made to a purchaser of the weight of the box, cask, sack, etc., in which goods are packed. 2. Tally, a stick on which the weight is marked.

tarabita [tah-rah-bee'-tah], *f*. (S. A.) Rope bridge. V. PUENTE DE CIMBRIA. Called *oroya* in Peru.

taracea [tah-rah-thay'-ah], *f*. 1. Marquetry, checkered work, inlaid work. 2. *(Coll.)* Patchwork of cloth or linen.

taracear [tah-rah-thay-ar'], *va*. To inlay, to make inlaid work.

tarado [tah-rah'-do], *a*. 1. Damaged, defective, imperfect; maimed (animal). 2. *(Cono Sur)* Physically impaired (mutilado), crippled; odd (raro), eccentric. 3. *(LAm.)* Stupid (idiota); crazy (loco).

tarafes [tah-rah'-fes], *m. pl. (Cant.)* Dice.

taragallo [tah-rah-gahl'-lyo], *m*. Clog, suspended from the necks of beasts, to prevent them from running away.

taraja [tah-rah'-hah], *f*. (S. A.) Screw plate.

tarambana [tah-ram-bah'-nah], *com*. Giddy, unstable person; madcap.

tarando [tah-rahn'-do], *m*. Reindeer.

tarángana [tah-rahn'-gah-nah], *f*. V. MORCILLA.

tarantela [tah-ran-tay'-lah], *f*. A powerful, impressive tune, such as is played for the bite of the tarantula.

tarántula [ta-rahn'-too-lah], *f*. Tarantula, a kind of venomous spider.

tarantulado, da [tah-ran-too-lah'-do, dah], *a*. V. ATARANTADO.

tarará [tah-ra-rah'], *f*. Sound of a trumpet, as a signal for action.

tararear [tah-rah-ray-ar'], *va. & vn*. 1. To sound the trumpet. 2. To chuck under the chin. 3. *(Coll.)* To sing a song using the word *tarara* instead of the proper words.

tararira [tah-rah-ree'-rah], *f. (Coll.)* Noisy mirth. -*com*. Noisy person.

tarasca [tah-rahs'-cah], *f*. 1. Figure of a serpent formerly borne in the procession of Corpus Christi day, indicating the triumph of Christ over the devil. 2. Crooked, ugly, ill-natured, licentious, and impudent woman. 3. Carnival dragon (monstruo). 4. *(And. CAm. Cono Sur)* Big mouth (boca).

tarascada [tah-ras-cah'-dah], *f*. 1. Bite (mordisco), a wound with the teeth. 2. *(Coll.)* A pert, harsh answer (réplica).

tarascar [tah-ras-car'], *va*. To bite.

tarascón [tah-ras-cone'], *m. aug*. of TARASCA.

taratántara [tah-ra-tahn'-tah-rah], *f*. A word imitative of the sound of a trumpet. *(Latin.)*

taravilla [tah-ra-veel'-lyah], *f*. 1. A mill-clack. 2. A kind of wooden latch for doors or windows; sneck. 3. A person who prattles much and fast.

taray [tah-rah'-e], *m. (Bot.)* Tamarisk, an evergreen shrub.

tarazar [tah-ra-thar'], *va*. 1. To bite. 2. To molest, to harass, to mortify.

tarazón [tah-ra-thone'], *m*. A large slice, especially of fish.

tarazoncillo [tah-ra-thon-theel'-lyo], *m. dim*. A small slice.

tarbea [tar-bay'-ah], *f*. A large hall.

tardador, ra [tar-dah-dor', rah], *m. & f*. Delayer, deferrer, tarrier.

tardanza [tar-dahn'-thah], *f*. Slowness (lentitud), delay (demora), tardiness, detention; dalliance, lingering.

tardar [tar-dar'], *vn. & vr*. To delay (retardarse), to put off, to take, to dally, **A más tardar**, at the latest, no later than. **Aquí tardan mucho**, they are very slow here. **Escribiré sin tardar**, I'll write without delay. **Tardará dos horas**, he'll take two hours.

tarde [tar'-day], *f*. 1. Afternoon; the time from noon till night. 2. Evening, the close of the day. **A la tarde**, in the evening. **Por la tarde**, in the afternoon. -*adv*. Late; past the time. **De tarde en tarde**, now and then, occasionally; seldom. **Tarde, mal y nunca**, slow and unpunctual. **Hacerse tarde**, to grow late. **Más vale tarde que nunca**, better late than never. **Para luego es tarde**, by-and-bye is too late; don't put off. **Algo tarde**, backward, latish. **Tarde o temprano**, sooner or later.

tardecer [tar-day-therr'], *vn*. To verge upon evening; to grow late.

tardecica, ita [tar-day-thee'-cah], *f. dim*. The close of the evening.

tardecillo [tar-day-theel'-lyo], *adv*. A little late; slowly.

tarde piache [tar-day pe-ah'-chay], *a. (Coll.)* Very late, the opportune time past.

tardíamente [tar-dee'-ah-men-tay], *adv.* Too late, out of time.

tardío, día [tar-dee'-o, ah], *a.* 1. Late, too late. 2. Slow, tardy, dilatory.

tardo, da [tar'-do, dah], *a.* 1. Slow (lento), sluggish, tardy. 2. Dull, inactive, lazy.

tardón, na [tar-don', nah], *a. aug.* Very tardy, phlegmatic.

tarea [ta-ray'-ah], *f.* 1. Task, work imposed by another (trabajo asignado); shift, 2. Care, toil, drudgery; exercise. **Ahora disfruta sus tareas**, he now enjoys the fruits of his labor. **Tarea del colegio**, schoolwork, homework. **Es una tarea poco grata**, it´s not a very satisfying job.

targum [tar-goom'], *m.* Targum, Chaldaic version of the Bible.

tarida [tah-ree'-dah], *f.* Ancient vessel used in the Mediterranean for carrying implements of war.

tarifa [tah-ree'-fah], *f.* Tariff (precio), a list of the prices of goods or merchandise, book of rates or duties; rate (tasa); price list (lista de precios); fare (en vehículos). **Tarifa de suscripción**, subscription rate.

tarima [tah-ree'-mah], *f.* 1. A movable platform on a floor or pavement (plataforma); low bench (banquillo), table, footstool. 2. Bedstead.

tarimilla [tah-re-meel'-lyah], *f. dim.* A small bedstead.

tarimón [tah-re-mone'], *m. aug.* A large bedstead; a foot-stool.

tarina [tah-ree'-nah], *f.* Middle-sized dish for meat.

tarja [tar'-hah], *f.* 1. An ancient Spanish copper coin worth about one-fourth of a real. 2. Tally. 3. Target, shield, buckler. 4. Sign-board. **Beber sobre tarja,** *(Coll.)* to get drink on tick.

tarjador, ra [tar-hah-dor', rah], *m. & f.* One who keeps a tally.

tarjar [tar-har'], *va.* 1. To tally, to mark on a tally what has been sold on credit. 2. *(And. Cono Sur)* To cross out (tachar).

tarjea [tar-hay'-ah], *f.* 1. A canal for watering lands or plants. 2. Sewer.

tarjero [tar-hay'-ro], *m.* Tally-keeper. *V.* TARJADOR.

tarjeta [tar-hay'-tah], *f. dim.* of TARJA. 1. Sign-board, sign. 2. Card, used in messages of civility or business. **Tarjeta de visita**, a visiting card. **Tarjeta de correos** or **postal**, postal card. **Tarjeta de negocios**, business card. **Tarjeta de gráficos**, graphics card. **Tarjeta de visita**, visiting card. **Tarjeta procesador**, *(Inform.)* processor card. **Tarjeta de vídeo**, *(Inform.)* video card.

tarjeta de crédito [tar-hay'-tah day cray'-de-to], *f.* Credit card. **Tarjeta Visa**, Visa card.

tarjeteo [tar-hay-tay'-o], *m.* Exchange of cards.

tarjetero [tar-hay-tay'-ro], *m.* 1. Cardcase. 2. Card index.

tarjetón [tar-hay-tone'], *m. aug.* A large buckler or target.

tarlatana [tar-lah-tah'-nah], *f.* A sort of thin linen or thread crape.

tarpón [tar-pon'], *m.* Tarpon.

tarquín [tar-keen'], *m.* Mire, mud.

tarquinada [tar-kee'-nah-dah], *f. (Coll.)* Rape.

tarraja [tar-rah'-hah], *f. (Arch.)* Metal instrument for cutting ornamental mouldings in gypsum.

tarro [tar'-ro], *m.* 1. Earthenware or glass vessel. 2. *(And. Cono Sur)* Tin (lata), can 3. *(Carib. Cono Sur, Mex.)* Horn (cuerno). 4. *(Cono Sur)* Stroke of luck (chiripa). 4. *(Carib.)* Cuckolding (del marido). 5. *(Carib.)* Difficult matter (asunto).

tarso [tar'-so], *m. (Anat.)* Tarsus, the ankle.

tarta [tar'-tah], *f.* 1. Tart (torta), a delicate pastry. 2. Pan for baking tarts. **Tarta nupcial**, wedding cake.

tártago [tar'-tah-go], *m.* 1. *(Bot.)* Spurge. 2. Misfortune (desgracia), unfortunate event. 3. A severe jest, galling satire or lash.

tartajear [tar-tah-hay-ar'], *m.* To stutter, to stammer.

tartajoso, sa [tar-tah-ho'-so, sah], *a.* Stammering, stuttering.

tartalear [tar-tah-lay-ar'], *vn. (Coll.)* 1. To reel, to stagger. 2. To be perplexed; not to be able to talk (al hablar).

tartaleta [tar-tah-lay'-tah], *f.* A kind of light paste for covering tarts. **tartaletas,** fruit-pies.

tartamudear [tar-tah-moo-day-ar'], *vn.* To stutter, to stammer, to falter, to lisp, to fumble, to halt.

tartamudeo, *m.* **tartamudez,** *f.* [tar-tah-moo-day'-o, tar-tah-moo-deth'], Lisp, stuttering, stammering.

tartamudo, da [tar-tah-moo'-do, dah], *a. & m.* Stuttering, stammering; stutterer.

tartán [tar-tahn'], *m. (Com.)* Tartan, a Scotch plaid.

tartana [tar-tah´-nah], *f.* 1. *(Naut.)* Tartan, a small coasting vessel in the Mediterranean. 2. Long covered wagon for passengers with two wheels.

tartanero [tar-tah-nay'-ro], *m.* The driver of a *tartana*.

tartáreo rea [tar-tah'-ray-o, ah], *a. (Poet.)* Tartarean, hellish.

tartárico [tar-tah'-re-co], *a.* Tartaric, relating to tartar of wine. *V.* TÁRTRICO.

tartarizar [tar-tah-re-thar'], *va.* To tartarize, to impregnate with tartar, to refine with the salt of tartar.

tártaro [tar´-tah-ro], *m.* 1. Argol, tartar, the lees of wine. 2. Dental tartar.

tártaro, ra [tar'-tah-ro, rah], *a.* Tartarian, of Tartary.

tartera [tar-tay'-rah], *f.* 1. Baking-pan for tarts and other pastry. 2. Dripping-pan.

tartrato [tar-trah'-to], *m. (Chem.)* Tartrate, a salt of tartaric acid.

tártrico [tar´-tre-co], *a.* Tartaric. **Ácido tártrico,** tartaric acid.

tarugo [tah-roo'-go], *m.* 1. A wooden peg or pin; stopper, plug (tapón), bung. 2. *(Carib.)* Fright (susto). 3. *(LAm.)* Chump (imbécil). 4. *(Mex.)* Fear (miedo).

taruguillo [tah-roo-geel'-lyo], *m. dim.* Of TARUGO.

tarumba [tah-room'-bah], *a.* **Volver a uno tarumba,** *(Coll.* phrase) to confuse one, to get him mixed. **Volverse tarumba,** to become rattled. *(Amer. Turumba.)*

tas [tahs], *m.* Kind of anvil used by silversmiths.

tasa [tah'-sah], *f.* 1. Rate, price of provisions fixed by magistrates, assize. 2. Measure, rule (medida, norma). 3. Valuation or appraisement of valuables. **Tasa de crecimiento,** growth-rate. **Tasa de nacimiento,** birth rate.

tasación [tah-sah-the-on'], *f.* Valuation, appraisement. *V.* TASA.

tasadamente [tah-sah-dah-men'-tay], *adv.* Barely, scantily, scarcely.

tasado, da [tah-sah'-do, dah], *a.* Limited, restricted. **Tiempo tasado,** limited amount of time.

tasador [tah-sah-dor'], *m.* 1. Appraiser, valuator, valuer. 2. *(Law.)* Taxing judge.

tasajear [tah-sah-hay-ar'], *va. (Amer.)* To cut meat for making jerked beef, to jerk (carne).

tasajo [tah-sah'-ho], *m.* Jerked beef, hung-beef.

tasar [tah-sar'], *va.* 1. To appraise, to value, to estimate. 2. To observe method and rule; to regulate. 3. **Tasar judicialmente,** to tax, to rate at. 4. To give scantily of what one is obliged to give.

tascador [tas-cah-dor'], *m.* Brake, for dressing flax or hemp.

tascar [tas-car'], *va.* 1. To brake, to scutch or dress flax or hemp. 2. To nibble the grass (animales). 3. To swingle (lino), to beat.

tascina [tas-thee'-nah], *f. (Min.)* Silver selenide.

tasco [tahs'-co], *m.* 1. Refuse of flax or hemp. 2. *(Naut.)* Toppings of hemp.

tasconio [tas-co'-ne-o], *m. V.* TALQUE.

tasquera [tas-kay'-rah], *f.* Dispute, scuffle, contest.

tasquil [tas-keel'], Chip which flies from a stone on working it.

tástara [tas-tar´-rah], **f.** *(Prov.)* Coarse bran.

tastaz [tas-tath], *m.* Polishing powder made of old crucibles.

tata [tah'-tah], *m.* Word by which little children begin to call their parents. Used in Mexico vulgarly at all ages. *-a.* 1. Nanny (niñera); nursemaid; maid (chacha). 2. *(LAm.)* Younger sister (hermana menor).

tatarabuela [tah-tah-ra-boo-ay'-lah], *f.* The great-great grandmother.

tatarabuelo [tah-tah-rah-boo-ay'-lo], *m.* The great-great-grandfather.

tataradeudo, da [tah-tah-rah-day'-oo-do, dah], *m. & f.* Very old and distant relation.

tataranieta [tah-tah-rah-ne-ay'-tah], *f.* A great-great-granddaughter.

tataranieto [tah-tah-rah-nee-ay'-to], *m.* A great-great-grandson.

tatas [tah'-tas], *adv. (Prov.)* **Andar a tatas**, to walk timidly; to go on all fours.

¡tate! [tah'-tay], *int.* Take care, beware; stay, so it is. **Tate, tate,** little by little.

tato [tah'-to], *m.* 1. *(Coll. Prov.)* A younger brother. 2. Hog-headed armadillo.

tato, ta [tah'-to, tah], *a. & n.* Stammering; stutterer who converts *c* and *s* into *t*.

tatuaje [tah-too-ah'-hay], *m.* Tattooing (acto), tattoo (dibujo).

tatuar [tah-too-ar'], *a.* To tattoo.

tau [tah'-oo], *m.* V. TAO. -*f.* 1. The Greek t, nineteenth letter of the Greek alphabet. 2. Tau cross, tau (cruz).

taumaturgo [tah-oo-mah-toor'-go], *m.* The author of great and stupendous things, miracle worker; thaumaturge.

taurina [tah-oo-ree'-nah], *f.* Taurin, a crystallizable substance found in the bile of various animals.

taurino, na [tah-oo-ree'-no, nah], *a.* Relating to a bull; taurine. **El negocio taurino**, the bullfighting business.

tauro [tah'-oo-ro], *m. (Ast.)* Taurus, a sign of the zodiac.

taurómaco [tah-oo-ro'-mah-co], *m.* One fond of bullfighting.

tauromaquia [tah-oo-ro-mah'-ke-ah], *f.* The art of bullfighting.

tautología [tah-oo-to-lo-hee'-ah], *f.* Tautology.

tautológico, ca [tah-oo-to-lo'-he-co, cah], *a.* Tautological.

tautologista [tah-oo-to-lo-hees'-tah], *com.* Tautologist.

tautometría [tah-oo-to-may-tree'-ah], *f.* Repetition of the same measure.

tauxia [tah'-ooc-se'-ah], *f.* V. ATAUXIA.

taxativamente [tac-sah-tee'-vah-men-tay], *adv.* Limitedly.

taxativo, va [tak-sah-tee'-vo, vah], *a. (Law.)* Limited to circumstances (restringido).

taxi [tak'-se], *m.* Taxi, taxicab.

taxidermia [tak-se-derr'-me-ah], *f.* Taxidermy, the art of preserving dead animals so as to present a life-like appearance.

taxidermista [tak-se-dayr-mees'-tah], *m & f.* Taxidermist.

taxímetro [tak-see'-may-tro], *m.* 1. Taximeter. 2. Taxi, taxicab.

taxista [tak sees'-tah], *m & f* Taxidriver, cabby.

taz a taz, or **taz por taz** [tath ah tath], *adv. (Coll.)* This for that; tit for tat.

taza [tah'-thah], *f.* 1. Cup. 2. Cup, the liquor contained in a cup (contenido). 3. Basin of a fountain (de fuente). 4. A large wooden bowl. 5. *(Coll.)* Buttocks, breech. 6. Bowl (de retrete). 7. *(Cono Sur)* Washbasin (palangana). 8. **Taza de noche,** *(Cono Sur)* Chamberpot.

tazaña [tah-thah'-nyah], *f.* Serpent. V. TARASCA.

tazmía [tath-mee'-ah], *f.* Share of tithes.

tazón [tah-thone'], *m. aug.* A large bowl or basin; pitcher.

te [tay], *pron.pers.* 1. You; thee (a Dios). 2. You (dativo). **Te he traído esto,** I've brought you this. 3. Yourself (reflexivo). **Te vas a caer,** You'll fall.

té [tay], *m.* 1. *(Bot.)* Tea; a plant (planta). 2. Tea, decoction of tea leaves-*f.*Name of the letter T. -*pron.* Thee, the oblique case of Thou.

tea [tay'-ah], *f.* Candlewood, a piece of resinous wood, which burns like a torch.

teame, teamide [tay-ah'-may, tay-ah-mee'-day], *f.* A stone repelling iron.

teatino [tay-ah-tee'-no], *m.* 1. A delicate sort of paste. 2. Theatin, one of a religious order founded by Pope Paul IV.

teatral [tay-ah-trahl'], *a.* Theatrical, belonging to a theater.

teatralmente [tay-ah-tral-men'-tay], *adv.* Theatrically.

teatro [tay-ah'-tro], *m.* 1. Stage, on which any show is exhibited. 2. Theater, stage, playhouse. 3. The people attending at a playhouse. 4. Theater, collection of plays belonging to a nation. 5. The profession or practice of dramatic art. 6. Stage, place where anything is exposed to the applause or censure of the world. **Teatro de aficionados,** amateur theater. **Escribir para el teatro,** to write for the stage. **El teatro de Cervantes,** Cervantes' plays. **Hacer teatro,** to exaggerate.

tebaico, ca [tay-bah'-e-co, cah], *a.* Thebaic, belonging to Egyptian Thebes.

tebano, na [tay-bah'-no, nah], *a.* Theban, of Thebes.

teca [tay'-cah], *f.* Teak, a large East-Indian tree, and its hard, elastic wood valued for ship-building.

tecale, tecali [tay-cah'-lay], *m. (Mex.)* A very white, transparent marble: in many of the windows of convents it is used instead of glass.

techado [tay-chah'-do], *m.* V. TECHO. **Techado, da,** *pp.* of TECHAR.

techar [tay-char'], *va.* To roof; to cover with a roof.

techo [tay'-cho], *m.* 1. Roof (exterior), ceiling (interior), the inner roof of a building. 2. *(Met.)* Dwelling-house, habitation, place of abode: native soil; cover. **Bajo techo,** under cover. **Ha tocado techo,** it has reached its ceiling.

techumbre [tay-choom'-bray], *f.* Upper roof, ceiling; a lofty roof; as of a church.

tecla [tay'-clah], *f.* 1. Key (máquina de escribir). 2 *(Fig.)* Touchy subject. **Dar en la tecla,** *(Coll.)* 1. To catch on, to get the knack. 2. To get into the habit. **Techa de borrado,** delete key. **Tecla del cursor,** cursor key. **Tecla de edición,** edit key.

teclado [tay-clah'-do], *m.* Keyboard (Mús, máquina de escribir); manual (de órgano).

teclear [tay-clay-ar'], *vn.* 1. To finger. 2. *(Fig.)* To drum, to rap one's fingers (con dedos). 3. *(Cono Sur)* To be weak (estar enfermo). 4. *(Cono Sur)* To be very poor (ser pobre). 5. *(And. Cono Sur)* To be going very badly (negocio). -*va.* To feel out, to try out, to experiment with.

tecleo [tay-clay'-o], *m.* 1. Fingering. 2. Drumming (con dedos), tapping.

tecnecio [tec-nay'-the-o], *m.* Technetium.

técnica [tec'-ne-cah], *f.* Technique; method (método); craft (destreza), skill. **Técnica de E/S,** *(Inform.)* I/O technique.

técnicamente [tec'-ne-cah-men-tay], *adv.* Technically.

tecnicidad [tec-ne-the-dahd'], *f.* Technicality.

tecnicismo [tec-ne-thees'-mo], *m.* 1. Technical vocabulary. 2. Technical term.

técnico, ca [tec'-ne-co, cah], *a.* Technical. -*m.* Technician. -*f.* Technique. **Es un técnico en la materia,** he's an expert on the subject.

tecnicolor [tec-ne-co-lor'], *m.* Technicolor.

tecnocracia [tec-no-crah'-the-ah], *f.* Technocracy.

tecnología [tec-no-lo-hee'-ah], *f.* Technology, language proper and exclusive to the arts and sciences. **Tecnología de la Información,** Information Technology. **Tecnología magneto-óptica,** *(Inform.)* magneto-optical technology.

tecnológico, ca [tec-no-lo'-he-co, cah], *a.* Technological, technical.

tecomate [tay-co-mah'-tay], *m. (Mex.)* A cup made of a gourd.

tedero [tay-day'-ro], *m.* Iron candlestick for holding burning fir or a torch.

tedéum [tay-day'-oom], *m.* Te Deum, a hymn of the church.

tediar [tay-de-ar'], *va.* To loathe, to hate, to abhor.

tedio [tay'-de-o], *m.* Disgust, dislike, abhorrence, tediousness.

tedioso, sa [tay-de-oh'-so, sah], *a.* Tedious, loathful, fastidious, tiresome, disgusting, nauseous to the taste or mind.

tegual [tay-goo-ahl'], *m.* Tax or duty paid to the king.

tegumento [tay-goo-men'-to], *m.* Tegument, covering.

teína [tay-ee'-nah], *f. (Chem.)* Thein the alkaloid of the tea-plant.

teinada [tay-e-nah'-dah], *f.* V. TINADA.

teísmo [tay-ees'-mo], *m.* Theism, deism.

teísta [tay-ees'-tah], *com.* Theist, deist.

teja [tay´-hah], *f.* Roof-tile, for covering buildings. **De tejas abajo**, in a natural order, without supernatural interference; in this world.

tejadillo [tay-hah-deel´-lyo], *m.* Roof of a coach.

tejado [tay-hah´-do], *m.* Roof covered with tiles; shed. **Tiene el tejado de vidrio**, he himself is open to the same charge. —**Tejado, da**, *pp.* of TEJAR.

tejamanil [tay-hah-mah-neel´], *m.* (*Mex.*) Shingles. V. TAJAMANIL.

tejano, na [tay-hah´-no, nah], *m. & f. & a.* Texan.

tejar [tay-har´], *m.* Tile-works, tile-kiln.

tejar [tay-har´], *va.* To tile, to cover with tiles.

tejaroz [tay-hah-roth´], *m.* Penthouse, a shed covered with tiles.

tejavana [tay-hah-vah´-nah], *f.* Shed (covertizo); shed roof (tejado).

tejazo [tay-hah´-tho], *m.* Blow with a tile.

tejedera [tay-hay-day´-rah], *f.* 1. V. TEJEDORA. 2. Water-spider.

tejedor [tay-hay-dor´], *m.* 1. Weaver (artesano). 2. Cloth manufacturer. 3. (*Orn.*) Weaver-bird.

tejedora [tay-hay-do´-rah], *f.* Female weaver.

tejedura [tay-hay-doo´-rah], *f.* 1. Texture (textura), weaving, the act of weaving (acto). 2. Anything woven.

tejeduría [tay-hay-doo-ree´-ah], *f.* 1. The art of weaving (arte). 2. Mill, a factory for weaving (fábrica).

tejemaneje [tay´-hay-mah-nay´-hay], *m.* (*Coll.*) Doing things in an artful way. **Se trae un tremendo tejemaneje con sus papeles**, he´s making a tremendous to-do with his papers.

tejer [tay-herr´], *va.* 1. To weave cloth. 2. To regulate, to adjust. 3. To discuss; to devise; to entangle. 4. To cross and mix according to rule, as in dancing.

tejera, tejería [tay-hay´-rah, tay-hay-ree´-ah], *f.* Tile-kiln. V. TEJAR.

tejero [tay-hay´-ro], *m.* Tile-maker.

tejido [tay-hee´-do], *m.* 1. Texture (textura), weaving, the act of weaving. 2. Texture, fabric, web, a thing woven. V. TELA. 3. Tissue of an organized body. **Tejido celular**, cellular tissue (*Bot.*), connective tissue (*Anat.*). **Tejido de punto**, knitting; knitted fabric. -**Tejido, da**. *pp.* of TEJER.

tejillo [tay-heel´-lyo], *m.* 1. A band used by women as a girdle. 2. (*Dim.*) A small quoit.

tejo [tay´-ho], *m.* 1. Quoit, round tile with which boys play; also the game. 2. (*Bot.*) Yew-tree. 3. A round metal plate.

tejocote [tay-ho-co´-tay], *m.* (*Bot. Mex.*) A fruit resembling a sloe.

tejoleta [tay-ho-lay´-tah], *f.* 1. Piece of burnt clay; tile. 2. A shuffle-board.

tejolote [tay-ho-lo´-tay], *m.* (*Mex.*) Stone pestle for a culinary mortar.

tejón [tay-hone´], *m.* 1. A wedge or plate of gold. 2. (*Zool.*) Badger.

tejuelo [tay-hoo-ay´-lo], *m.* 1. Space between the bands on the back of a book for the title. 2. (*Mech.*) Bush, pillow block, socket, sole-plate.

tela [tay´-lah], *f.* 1. Cloth, fabric, any stuff woven in a loom. **Tela de cebolla**, onion skin. **Tela de saco**, sackcloth. 2. Gold or silver lace. 3. Chain or warp of cloth which is put at one time in a loom. 4. Pellicle, the thin interior skin of the animal body or of fruits; membrane. 5. Film or pellicle on the surface of liquors. 6. Quibble, quirk. 7. Cobweb of a spider, web of some other insects. **Tela de araña**, spider´s web. 8. Argument; matter (materia); thread of a discourse. **El asunto trae mucha tela**, it´s a complicated matter. 9. Membrane or opacity in the eye. 10. (*And.*) Thin maize pancake (tortilla).

telabrejo [tay-lah-bray´-ho], *m.* (*Mex.*) 1. A thing of small account. 2. A person of small account.

telamón [tay-lah-mon´], *m.* (*Arch.*) V. ATLANTE.

telar [tay-lar´], *m.* 1. Loom, in which cloth is woven; a frame in which other things are made. 2. Upper part of the scene-work in a theater, out of sight of the public, where the curtains are raised and lowered.

telaraña [tay-lah-rah´-nyah], *f.* 1. Cobweb. 2. A small cloud. 3. Anything trifling and of little weight. **Mirar las telarañas**, (*Coll.*) To be absentminded.

telecomunicación [tay-lay-co-moo-ne-cah-the-on´], *f.* 1. Telecommunication. 2. (*Comput.*) Telecommuting

telecopiadora [tay-lay-co-pe-ah-do´-rah], *f.* Fax copier.

telediario [tay-lay-de-ah´-re-o], *m.* Television news bulletin.

teledirección [tay-lay-de-rec-the-on´], *f.* Remote control.

teledirigido, da [tay-lay-de-re-hee´-do, dah], *a.* Remote-control.

teledirigir [tay-lay-de-re-heer´], *va.* To operate by remote control.

teleférico [tay-lay-fay´-re-co], *m.* Cable car

telefio [tay-lay´-fe-o], *m.* Orpine.

telefonazo [tay-lay-fo-nah´-tho], (*Coll.*) Phone call.

telefonear [tay-lay-fo-nay-ar´], *va. vn.* To telephone, to phone.

telefonema [tay-lay-fo-nay´-mah], *m.* Telephone message.

telefonía [tay-lay-fo-nee´-ah], *f.* Telephony.

telefónico, ca [tay-lay-fo´-ne-co, cah], *a.* Telephonic, telephone.

telefonista [tay-lay-fo-nees´-tah], *f.* Telephone operator. -*m.* Telephone service man.

teléfono [tay-lay´-fo-no], *m.* Telephone, phone. **Teléfono automático**, dial phone. **Teléfono rojo**, the hot line. **Está hablando por teléfono**, he´s on the phone.

telefoto, *m.* **telefotografía**, *f.* [tay-lay-fo´-to, tay-lay-fo-to-grah-fee´-ah]. Telephotography.

telegrafía [tay-lay-grah-fee´-ah], *f.* Telegraphy.

telegrafiar [tay-lay-grah-fe-ar´], *va. vn.* To telegraph.

telegráficamente [tay-lay-grah´-fe-cah-men-tay], *adv.* Telegraphically.

telegráfico, ca [tay-lay-grah´-fe-co, cah], *a.* Telegraphic, telegraph.

telegrafista [tay-lay-grah-fees´-tah], *com.* Telegrapher, telegraphist.

telégrafo [tay-lay´-grah-fo], *m.* Telegraph.

telegrama [tay-lay-grah´-mah], *m.* Telegram.

teleguiar [tay-lay-gee-ar´], *va.* To operate by remote control.

teleimpresor [tay-lay-im-pray-sor´], *m.* Teleprinter.

telemando [tay-lay-mahn´-do], *m.* Remote control.

telemecánico, ca [tay-lay-may-cah´-ne-co, cah], *a.* Telemechanic. -*f.* Telemechanics.

telemedición [tay-lay-may-de-the-on´], *f.* Telemetering.

telemetría [tay-lay-may-tree´-ah], *f.* Telemetry.

telemétrico, ca [tay-lay-may´-tre-co, cah], *a.* Telemetric.

telémetro [tay-lay´-may-tro], *m.* 1. Range finder. 2. Telemeter.

telenovela [tay-lay-no-vay´-lah], *f.* Soap opera.

teleobjetivo [tay-lay-ob-hay-tee´-vo], *m.* Telephoto lens.

teleología [tay-lay-o-lo-hee´-ah], *f.* Teleology.

telepatía [tay-lay-pah-tee´-ah], *f.* Telepathy.

telepático, ca [tay-lay-pah´-te-co, cah], *a.* Telepathic.

telequinesia [tay-lay-ke-nay´-se-ah], *f.* Telekinesis.

telera [tay-lay´-rah], *f.* 1. Plough pin. 2. Pen (para ganado). 3. Jaw (of a vice).

telerán [tay-lay-ran], *m.* Teleran.

telerreceptor [tay-ler-ray-thep-tor´], *m.* Television set.

telescópico, ca [tay-les-co´-pe-co, cah], *a.* Telescopic

telescopio [tay-les-co´-pe-o], *m.* Telescope.

telesilla [tay-lay-seel´-lya], *m.* Chair lift.

telespectador, ra [tay-les-pec-tah-dor´, rah], *m. & f.* Televiewer.

telesquí [tay-les-kee´], *m.* Ski lift.

telestesia [tay-les-tay´-se-ah], *f.* Telesthesia.

telestudio [tay-les-too´-de-o], *m.* Television studio.

teleta [tay-lay´-tah], *f.* Blotting paper.

teletipo [ta-lay-tee´-po], *m.* Teletype.

teletubo [tay-lay-too´-bo], *m.* Television picture tube.

televidente [tay-lay-ve-den´-tay], *m.* Television viewer, televiewer.

televisar [tay-lay-ve-sar´], *m.* To televise.

televisión [tay-lay-ve-se-on´], *f.* Television. **Televisión por cable**, cable television. **Mirar la televisión**, to watch television.

televisivo [tay-lay-ve-see´-vo], *a.* Television. **Serie televisiva**, television series.

televisor [tay-lay-ve-sor´], *m.* Television set.

tellina [tel-lyee´-nah], *f.* Bivalve shellfish: mussel.

telliz [tel-lyeeth´], *m.* Cloth thrown over the saddle of a horse for ornament.

telliza [tel-lyee´-thah], *f.* Coverlet of a bed.

telón [tay-lon´], *m.* (*Theat.*) Drop curtain. **Telón de boca**, front curtain. **Telón de hierro**, iron curtain.

telúrico, ca [tay-loo´-re-co, cah], *a.* Telluric.

telurio [tay-loo´-re-o], **Teluro**, *m.* (*Min.*) Tellulium, a metallic element.

tema [tay´-mah], *m.* Text, proposition, theme, subject, composition. **Tema de actualidad**, current issue. **Pasar del tema**, to dodge the issue. *-f.* 1. Topic of madmen's discourses. 2. Dispute, contention; obstinacy in asserting a controverted point. 3. Animosity, passionate malignity, capricious opposition. **A tema**, emulously, obstinately. **Cada uno tiene su tema**, (*Coll.*) every man has his hobby. **Tener tema**, to be stubborn.

temario [tay-mah´-re-o], *m.* 1. Schedule. 2. List of topics. 3. Program (programa). 4. Agenda (de junta).

temático, ca [tay-mah´-te-co, cah], *a.* 1. Relating to a theme or subject, thematic. 2. *V.* TEMOSO.

tembladal [tem-blah´-dah], *m. V.* TREMEDAL.

tembladera [tem-blah-day´-rah], *f.* 1. Tankard, a wide-mouthed vessel with two handles. 2. Diamond-pin, or other similar ornament of the headdress of ladies. 3. (*Zool.*) Torpedo electric ray.

tembladero [tem-blah-day´-ro], *m. V.* TREMEDAL.

temblador, ra [tem-blah-dor', rah], *m. & f.* Quaker, shaker, trembler.

temblante [tem-blahn´-tay], *m.* Kind of loose bracelet worn by women. *-pa.* Trembling quavering.

temblar [tem-blar'], *vn.* To tremble (persona), to shake with fear, to move with violent agitation; to quake, to shiver (de frío). **Temblar las carnes**, (*Coll.*) to have a horror of a thing. **Temblar de miedo**, to tremble with fright. **Tiemblo de pensar en lo que pueda ocurrir**, I tremble to think what may happen.

tembleque [tem-blay´-kay], *m.* 1. Diamond-pin or plume or other similar ornament of the headdress of ladies. 2. *V.* LENTEJUELA. 3. Violent shaking. 4. (*LAm.*) Weakling (persona). **Le entró un tembleque**, he began to shake violently.

temblequear, tembletear [tem-blay-kay-ar'], *vn.* To tremble, to shake with fear; to move with violent agitation.

temblón, na [tem-blone', nah], *a.* Tremulous. **Hacer la temblona**, to affect timidity.

temblón [tem-blone'], *m.* (*Bot.*) Aspen or asp tree.

temblor [tem-blor'], *m.* Trembling, involuntary motion proceeding from fear or weakness. **Temblor de tierra**, earthquake. **Le entró un temblor violento**, he began to shake volently.

temblorcillo [tem-blor-theel'-lyo], *m. dim.* A slight shivering.

tembloroso, sa [tem-blo-ro´-so, sah], *a.* Trembling, trembly, tremulous, quivering, shaking. **Con voz temblorosa**, in a shaky voice.

tembloso, so [tem-blo´-so, sah], *a.* Tremulous.

temedero, ra [tay-may-day'-ro, rah], *a.* Awful, dreadful.

temedor, ra [tay-may-dor', rah], *a.* 1. Applied to a trembler. 2. Awful, dreadful.

temedor, ra [tay-may-dor'], *m. & f.* Trembler.

temer [tay-merr'], *va.* 1. To apprehend, to fear, to dread; to reverence, to respect. 2. To suspect, to misdoubt. **Temo que lo ha perdido**, I´m afraid he has lost it. *-vn.* To be afraid. **No temas**, don´t be afraid.

temerariamente [tay-may-rah'-re-ah-men-tay], *adv.* Rashly, hastily, inconsiderately.

temerario, ria [tay-may-rah'-re-o, ah], *a.* Rash (persona), inconsiderate, imprudent, daring, overbold, hasty (juicio); headlong.

temeridad [tay-may-re-dahd'], *f.* Temerity, rashness (cualidad), imprudence; fool-hardiness. **Ser una temeridad**, (1) said of imprudence or rashness. (2) (*Coll.*) To be excessive.

temerón, na [tay-may-rone', nah], *a.* Affecting noise, authority, or bullying.

temerosamente [tay-may-ro'-sah-men-tay], *adv.* Timorously.

temeroso, sa [tay-may-ro'-so, sah], *a.* 1. Awe-inspiring; exciting fear or suspicion, dreadful (espantoso). 2. Timid, timorous; fearful (miedoso); cowardly.

temible [tay-mee'-blay], *a.* Dreadful, terrible, awful.

temiente [tay-me-en'-tay], *pa.* One who dreads or apprehends.

temor [tay-mor'], *m.* Dread, fear (miedo), apprehension, suspicion (recelo). **Sin temor a**, fearless of.

temoso, sa [tay-mo´-so, sah], *a.* Obstinate, stubborn.

tempanador [tem-pa-nah-dor'], *m.* Instrument for cutting off the tops of beehives.

tempanar [tem-pa-nar'], *pa.* To furnish staves; to cover the tops of beehives.

témpano [tem'-pah-no], *m.* 1. Floe (de hielo). 2. *V.* TÍMPANO. 3. Tympan, stretched skin or other thing: open, plain space. 4. Large cork put in the top of beehives. 5. (*Arch.*) Tympan of an arch. **Témpano de hielo**, a piece of ice.

temperación [tem-pay-rah-the-on'], *f. V.* TEMPERAMENTO.

temperadamente [tem-pay-ra-dah-men´-tay], *adv. V.* TEMPLADAMENTE.

temperamental [tem-pay-rah-men-tahl'], *a.* 1. Temperamental. 2. Vigorous, forceful (fuerte).

temperamento [tem-pay-rah-men'-to], *m.* 1. Temperature, climate (clima). 2. Arbitration, compromise, means for ending disputes or dissensions. 3. Temperament (genio), constitution (constitución); as nervous, lymphatic, etc. 4. (*LAm.*) Climate (clima), summer (verano).

temperancia, temperanza [tem-pay-rahn´-the-ah], *f. V.* TEMPLANZA.

temperante [tem-pay-rahn'-tay], *pa.* (*Med.*) That which tempers.

temperar [tem-pay-rar'], *va.* 1. *V.* ATEMPERAR. 2. (*Amer.*) *V.* VERANEAR.

temperatura [tem-pay-rah-too'-rah], *f.* Temperature, the degree of cold or warmth, measured by the thermometer.

temperie [tem-pay´-re-ay], *f.* Temperature of the air; its constitution as produced by different degrees of heat and cold, dryness and dampness.

tempero [tem-pay'-ro], *m.* Seasonableness, fitness of the soil for the growth of seeds.

tempestad [tem-pes-tahd'], *f.* 1. Tempest, storm. 2. Violent perturbation of the mind. **Tempestades**, violent, abusive language.

tempestar [tem-pes-tar'], *vn.* To be a tempest, to screech out.

tempestivamente [tem-pes-tee'-vah-men-tay], *adv.* Seasonably, opportunely.

tempestivo, va [tem-pes-tee´-vo, vah], *a.* Seasonable, opportune.

tempestuosamente [tem-pes-too-oh'-sah-men-tay], *adv.* Tempestuously, turbulently.

tempestuoso, sa [tem-pes-too-oh'-so, sah], *a.* Tempestuous, stormy, turbulent.

templa [tem'-plah], *f.* (*Art.*) Distemper, size for painting.

templadamente [tem-plah-dah-men´-tay], *adv.* Temperately, moderately, abstemiously, freshly; calmly.

templadera [tem-plah-day'-rah], *J.* (*Prov.*) Sluice put into a channel to let a certain quantity of water pass.

templadico, ca [tem-plah-dee'-co, cah], *a. dim.* Somewhat temperate.

templado, da [tem-plah'-do, dah], *a.* 1. Temperate, tempered, moderate (moderado), abstemious (en beber), frugal, lukewarm. 2. Well-tuned. 3. Bold, forthright (franco); courageous (valiente). 4. Bright (listo); *(CAm. Mex.)* able (hábil), competent. 5. *(And.)* Severe (severo). 6. *(And. Carib.)* Tipsy (borracho). *-pp.* of TEMPLAR.

templador, ra [tem-plah-dor', rah], *m. & f.* Tuner; one who tempers. *-m.* 1. Tuning key for musical instruments. 2. *(Peru)* Circular stockade in the midst of the arena for refuge of bullfighters.

templadura [tem-plah-doo'-rah], *f.* Temper, the act of tempering.

templanza [tem-plahn'-thah], *f.* 1. Temperance, moderation (cualidad), abstinence, abstemiousness. 2. Sobriety. 3. Disposition of the air or climate of a country: degree of heat or cold. 4. *(Art.)* Due proportion and good disposition of colors.

templar [tem-plar'], *va.* 1. To temper, to soften, to moderate, to cool. 2. To temper steel; to anneal glass. 3. To tune musical instruments. 4. To observe a due proportion of parts in a painting. 5. *(Naut.)* To trim the sails to the wind. 6. To mix, to assuage, to soften. 7. To prepare, to dispose. 8. To train a hawk. 9. *(And.)* To knock down (derribar); *(CAm.)* to hit (golpear); to beat (pegar). *-vr.* 1. To be moderate (persona); to refrain from excess. 2. To warm up (agua). 3. *(And. CAm.)* To die (morir). 4. *(Carib.)* To flee (huir). 5. *(And. Carib.)* To get drunk (emborracharse). 6. *(Cono Sur)* To fall in love (enamorarse). 7. *(Cono Sur)* To go too far (excederse).

templario [tem-plah'-re-o], *m.* Templar, one of the order of Templars.

temple [tem'-play], *m.* 1. Temperature of the season or climate. 2. Temper given to metals. 3. Temperament, medium, due mixture of opposites. 4. Frame or disposition of the mind (espíritu). 5. The concordance of musical instruments. 6. Religion of the Templars; a temple or church. **Al temple,** painted in distemper. 7. *(LAm.)* Infatuation (enamoramiento).

templecillo [tem-play-theel'-lyo], *m. dim.* A small temple.

templete [tem-play'-tay], *m. dim.* V. TEMPLECILLO. Applied to architectural ornaments in form of a temple.

templista [tem-plees'-tah], *m.* Painter in distemper.

templo [tem'-plo], *m.* 1. Temple, church for the worship of God. 2. Blessed soul. 3. Temple dedicated to the false gods of the Gentiles. **Templo metodista,** Methodist chapel. **Como un templo,** huge (grande).

témpora [tem'-po-rah], *f.* Ember week, days of fast prescribed by the Roman Catholic church, in the four seasons of the year: generally used in the plural.

temporada [tem-po-rah'-dah], *f.* A certain space of time. **La temporada de la ópera** or **del teatro,** the opera or play season. **Temporada alta,** high season. **En plena temporada,** at the height of the season.

temporal [tem-po-rahl'], *a.* 1. Temporary, temporal. 2. Secular, temporal, pertaining to the civil power. 3. Temporal, belonging to the temples of the head. *-m.* 1. Season, whether good or bad. 2. Tempest, storm (tormenta). 3. *(Prov.)* Temporary laborer. 4. *(Carib.)* Shady character (persona).

temporalidad [tem-po-rah-le-dahd'], *f.* 1. Temporality, the secular revenues of the clergy. 2. Temporal concerns, affairs of this life.

temporalizar [tem-po-rah-le-thar'], *va.* To make temporary what might or should be everlasting.

temporalmente [tem-po-ral-men'-tay], *adv.* Temporarily, with respect to this life; for some time, or for a certain time.

temporáneo, nea [tem-po-rah'-nay-o, ah], *a.* Temporary, unstable.

temporario, ria [tem-po-rah'-re-o, ah], *a.* Temporary, not lasting.

temporero, temporil [tem-po-ray'-ro], *m.* Temporary laborer, one who works only for a season.

temporizador, ra [tem-po-re-thah-dor', rah], *m. & f.* Temporizer, trimmer.

temporizar [tem-po-re-thar'], *vn.* 1. To pass the time in any place or thing. 2. To comply with the times, to temporize. V. CONTEMPORIZAR.

tempranal [tem-prah-nahl'], *a.* Producing early fruits (tierra).

tempranamente [tem-prah-nah-men'-tay], *adv.* Early, prematurely.

tempranero, ra [tem-prah-nay'-ro, rah], *a. V.* TEMPRANO.

tempranilla [tem-prah-neel'-lyah], *f. (Prov.)* Sort of early grape.

temprano, na [tem-prah'-no, nah], *a.* Early, soon, anticipated, forehanded.

temprano [tem-prah'-no], *adv.* Very early, prematurely, soon.

temulento, ta [tay-moo-len'-to, tah], *a.* Intoxicated, inebriated.

tena [tay'-nah], *f. (Agr.)* A flock of sheep or goats, not over sixty head.

tenacear [tay-nah-thay-ar'], *va.* To tear with pincers. *-vn.* To insist obstinately and pertinaciously.

tenacero [tay-nah-thay'-ro], *m.* He who makes or uses pincers.

tenacicas [tay-nah-thee'-cas], *f. pl.* 1. *(Dim.)* Small tongs. 2. Pincers; snuffers.

tenacidad [tay-nah-the-dahd'], *f.* 1. Toughness. 2. Tenacity. 3. Ingrained nature; persistence; stubbornness.

tenacilla [tay-nah-teel'-lyah], *f. pl. dim.* Small tongs. **Tenacillas de boca,** flat-pointed pliers. **Tenacillas de punta,** sharp-pointed pliers.

tenáculo [tay-nah'-coo'-lo], *m. (Med.)* Tenaculum, a curved sharp hook for holding an artery which is to be tied.

tenada [tay-nah'-dah], *f. (Prov.)* Sheep-fold, sheep-cot.

tenallón [tay-nal-lyone'], *m. (Mil.)* Tenaillon, outwork on the flanks of a fortification: commonly used in the plural in both languages.

tenante [tay-nahn'-tay], *m. (Her.)* Supporter; figure of a man, angel, etc. supporting a shield.

tenate [tay-nah'-tay], *m (Mex.)* V. TANATE.

tenaz [tay-nath'], *a.* 1. Tenacious, sticking. 2. Firm, stubborn, obstinate, persevering (persona). 3. Avaricious, covetous. 4. Hard to remove, (mancha).

tenaza [tay-nah'-thah], *f.* 1. Tenaille, a kind of outwork of a fortress. 2. Claws or talons of animals. *-pl.* 3. Tongs. 4. Pincers, forceps. **Unas tenazas,** a pair of pliers.

tenazada [tay-nah-thah'-dah], *f.* 1. The act of griping with pincers or tongs. 2. The act of biting strongly.

tenazmente [tay-nath-men'-tay], *adv.* Tenaciously.

tenazón [tay-nah-thone'], *f.* A tenazón, point-blank, without taking aim. **Parar de tenazón,** to stop a horse short in his course.

tenazuelas [tay-nah-thoo-ay'-las], *f. pl. dim.* Tweezers.

tenca [ten'-cah], *f. (Zool.)* Tench.

tención [ten-the-on'], *f.* Holding, retaining.

tencón [ten-cone'], *f. (Zool.)* A large tench.

ten con ten [ten con ten'], *m.* Moderation, temperance.

tendajo [ten-dah'-ho], *m. V.* TENDEJÓN.

tendal [ten-dahl'], *m.* 1. Tilt, canvas cover (toldo). 2. A long and broad piece of canvas placed under olive-trees when picking the fruit. 3. *V.* TENDEDERO. 4. *(LAm.)* Heap (montón). 5. *(Cono Sur)* Shearing shed; *(And. Carib.)* Brickworks (fábrica).

tendalera [ten-dah-lay'-rah], *f. (Coll.)* Confusion and disorder of things lying about on the floor.

tendaloro [ten-dah-lay'-ro], *m.* Place where washed wool is dried.

tendedero [tan-day-day'-ro], *m.* 1 Clothes-line. 2. Place for hanging clothes.

tendedura [ten-day-doo'-rah], *f.* Tension, stretching or extending.

tendejón [ten-day-hone'], *m.* Sutler's tent in a camp.

tendel [ten-del'], *m.* Line by which masons raise a wall; plumb-line.

tendencia [ten-den'-the-ah], *f.* Tendency, inclination, direction towards a place, inference or result. **Tendencia del mercado,** run of the market. **Tener tendencia a,** to have a tendency to.

tendencioso, sa [ten-den-the-o'-so, sah], *a.* Tendentious. **Literatura tendenciosa**, Propaganda literature.

tendente [ten-den'-tay], *a.* Tending, lending, directing.

tender [ten-derr'], *va.* To stretch or stretch out (estirar), to unfold, to expand, to spread out (extender, desplegar); to distend. *-vn.* To direct, to tend, to refer a thing to some end or object. **Las plantas tienden a la luz,** plants grow towards the light. **Ella tiende al pesimismo,** she has a tendency to be pessimistic. *-vr.* 1. To stretch oneself at full length (echarse). 2. In card-playing, to throw all the cards upon the table (naipes).

tenderete [ten-day-ray´-tay], *m.* 1. Kind of game at cards. 2. *V.* TENDALERA. 3. *(Mex.)* A second-hand clothing, shop. 4. *V.* TENDEDERO. 5. Stall (puesto mercado).

tendería [ten-day-ree'-ah], *f.* Place full of shops.

tendero, ra [ten-day´-ro, rah], *m.* & *f.* Shopkeeper; haberdasher; grocer.

tendezuela [ten-day-thoo-ay'-lah], *f. dim.* of TIENDA.

tendidamente [ten-dee'-dah-men-tay], *adv.* Diffusely, diffusively.

tendido [ten-dee'-do], *m.* 1. A row of seats for spectators at a bullfight. 2. Quantity of clothes dried by a laundress at once. 3. Roof of a house from the ridge to the eaves. 4. *(Amer.)* Riffle, among miners. 5. *(And. Mex.)* Stall (puesto mercado). 6. *(CAm. Carib.)* Long tether. 7. *(And. Mex.)* Bedclothes (ropa de cama). —**Tendido, da,** *pp.* of TENDER.

tendiente [ten-de-en'-tay], *pa.* Tending, expanding.

tendón [ten-done'], *m.* Tendon. **Tendón de Aquiles,** *(Anat.)* Achilles' tendon.

tenducha, tenducho [ten-doo-chah, cho], *f.* & *m.* A wretched shop.

tenebrario [tay-nay-brah'-re-o], *m.* A large candlestick or girandole, used in Roman Catholic churches in Holy week.

tenebrosidad [tay nay-bro-se-dahd'], *f.* Darkness, obscurity, gloom.

tenebroso, sa [tay-nay-bro´-so, sah], *a.* Tenebrous, dark (oscuro), gloomy (sombrío); obscure in style, horrid.

tenedero [tay-nay-day'-ro], *m. (Naut.)* Bottom of the sea where the anchor catches. Gripe of an anchor. **Fondo de buen tenedero,** good anchoring ground.

tenedor [tay-nay-dor'], *m.* 1. Holder, keeper, tenant; guardian. **Tenedor de libros,** book-keeper. **Tenedor de póliza,** policy-holder. 2. Fork to eat with. 3. He who detains balls at play.

teneduría [tay-nay-doo-ree'-ah], *f.* 1. The position of book-keeper. 2. The art of book-keeping.

tenencia [tay-nen'-the-ah], *f.* 1. Possession (de propiedad), holding, the act of holding or possessing. 2. Lieutenancy, lieutenantship. **Tenencia ilícita de armas,** illegal possession of weapons.

tener [tay-nerr'], *va.* 1. To have, to contain, to comprise, to comprehend, to have within. 2. To take, to gripe, to hold last (agarrar). 3. To hold, to possess, to enjoy, to have (sentimiento). 4. To be rich and opulent in ready money. 5. To hold, to maintain, to support. 6. To subject, to domineer, to hold in subjection. 7. To hold an opinion, to keep (promesa), to retain. 8. To hold, to estimate, to judge, to take, to set a value upon. In this sense it is followed by the preposition **en** and the adjectives **poco, mucho,** etc. 9. To lodge, to receive in one's house. 10. To be obliged, to have to do; to be at the expense of anything. 11. To be adorned or favored with anything. 12. To detain, to stop. 13. To keep or fulfil. 14. With nouns of time, it signifies duration or age; when united with **que** and followed by an infinitive verb, it implies necessity or obligation. **Tener que hacer,** to have something to do. **Tener que ir,** to be obliged to go. 15. To have: used as an auxiliary verb. l6. With some nouns it means to suffer what the noun signifies. **Tener hambre,** to be hungry. **Tener sueño,** to be sleepy. **Tener miedo,** to be afraid. **Tener verguenza,** to be ashamed. **Tener celos de uno,** to be jealous of one. **Tener para sí,** to maintain a particular or singular opinion, liable to objections. **Hemos**

tenido muchas dificultades, we have had a lot of difficulties. **Lo tenía en la mano,** he was holding it in his hand. **Tener gran admiración a uno,** to have a great admiration for somebody. **Lo tengo por poco honrado,** I consider him to be rather dishonest. *-vr.* 1. To take care not to fall (estar de pie). 2. To stop, to halt. 3. To resist, to oppose. 4. To adhere, to stand to. **Tenerse en pie,** to keep on foot; to stand. **Tenga Vd. la bondad de decirme,** please tell me. **Tener razón,** to be right. **Tener consigo,** to have with or about one. **No tenerlas todas consigo,** to be not easy in mind, to be suspicious. **Tener correa para rato,** to have stamina. **Tener** forms numerous other phrases, many of which will be found under the respective nouns or adjectives with which it is associated. *(Yo tengo, tuve, tenga, tendré. V.* TENER.)

tenería [tay-nay-ree´-ah], *f.* Tan-yard, tannery.

tenesmo [tay-nes´-mo], *m.* Tenesmus.

tengua [ten'-goo-ah], *a.* & *n. (Amer. Mex.)* Hare-lipped.

tenia [tay'-ne-ah], *f.* Tape-worm.

teniente [tay-ne-en'-tay], *a.* 1. Immature, unripe. 2. Deaf. 3. Miserly, mean.

teniente [tay-ne-en'-tay], *m.* 1. Deputy, substitute. 2 Lieutenant. **Teniente de una compañía,** lieutenant of a company. **Teniente general,** lieutenant-general. 3. Miser.

tenis [tay'-nis], *m.* Tennis. **Cancha de tenis,** tennis court.

tenista [tay-nees'-tah], *m.* & *f.* Tennis player.

tenor [tay-nor'], *m.* 1. Permanent establishment or order of something; continuity of state. 2. Tenor, contents, sense contained. 3. Tenor, one of the four voices in music; tenorist; who sings tenor. 4. Tenor, a nautical instrument of this pitch. **A tenor de,** on the lines of. **El tenor de esta declaración,** the sense of this statement.

tenorio [tay-no-re-o], *m.* Ladykiller, Don Juan.

tensar [ten-sahr'], *va.* To tauten; to draw (arco).

tensión [ten-se-on'], *f.* 1. Tension, the act of stretching. 2. Tension, the state of being extended. 3. *(Elec.)* Voltage; tension. *(Anat.)* **Tensión arterial,** blood presure. 4. *(Med.)* Tension; strain (estrés). **Tensión nerviosa,** nervous strain.

tenso, sa [ten'-so, sah], *a.* Tense (estirado), tight, extended, stiff. **Es una situación muy tensa,** it is a very tense situation.

tentación [ten-tah-the-on'], *f.* 1. Temptation, enticement. 2. That which is offered to the mind. **Resistir la tentación,** to resist temptation.

tentacioncilla [ten-tah-the-on-theel'-lyah], *f. dim.* A slight temptation.

tentaculado, da [ten-tah-coo-lah'-do, dah], *a. (Zool.)* Tentaculate, having tentacles.

tentáculo [ten-tah'-coo-lo], *m.* Tentacle, a flexible process generally about the head.

tentadero [ten-tah-day'-ro], *m.* Corral or enclosed place for fuming calves.

tentador, ra [ten-tah-dor', rah], *m.* & *f* Tempter.

tentadura [ten-tah-doo´-rah], *f. (Min.)* Test for finding out the metal incorporated with mercury.

tentalear [ten-tah-lay-ar'], *va. (Prov.)* To try, to feel to examine.

tentar [ten-tar'], *va.* 1. To touch (tocar); to try (probar), to examine or prove by touch, to feel. 2. To grope. 3. To tempt (atraer), to instigate, to incite, to stimulate. 4. To attempt, to procure. 5. To hesitate. 6. To probe a wound; to tent. 7. To experiment; to try; to prove. **Andar tentando,** to make essays or trials; to grope or feel where one cannot see. **Me tentó con una copita de anís,** she tempted me with a glass of anise. **Tentar a uno a hacer algo,** to tempt somebody to do something. *(Yo tiento, yo tiente, from Tentar. V.* ACRECENTAR.)

tentativa [ten-tah-tee'-vah], *f.* Attempt (intento), trial, first examination, effort (esfuerzo).

tentativo, va [ten-tah-tee'-vo, vah], *a.* Tentative.

tente bonete [ten'-tay bo-nay'-tay], *adv.* Abundantly, excessively. **Tente en el aire,** *(com.)* the child of a quadroon and a mulatto, on either nice. **Tente en pie,** *m. (Coll.)* a light repast taken between meals.

tentemozo [ten-tay-mo´-tho], *m.* Prop to a house, to prevent its falling.

tentempié [ten-tem-pe-ay´], *m.* Snack, hasty repast.

tentón [ten-tone´], *m. (Coll.)* Touch, act of touching: especially applied to touching anything suddenly.

tenudo, da [tay-noo´-do, dah], *pp. irr. obs.* of TENER. Held. It was generally joined with the verb *ser,* when it signified, to be obliged, to be necessitated.

tenue [tay´-noo-e], *a.* 1. Thin (palo), tenuous, delicate. 2. Worthless, of little value or importance. 3. Applied to soft consonants (sonido).

tenuemente [tay-noo-ay-men´-tay], *adv.* Slightly.

tenuidad [tay-noo-e-dahd´], *f.* 1. Tenuity, weakness. 2. Trifle, thing of little value or importance.

tenuta [tay-noo´-tah], *f.* Provisional possession of an estate during a lawsuit.

tenutario, ria [tay-noo-tah´-re-o, ah], *a.* Provisional tenant.

teñidura [tay-nye-doo´-rah], *f.* Art of dyeing or tingeing.

teñir [tay-nyeer´], *va.* 1. To tinge (colorar), to dye (con tinte); to stain: to paint the trace. 2. *(Met.)* To give another color to things, to dissemble or misrepresent. 3. *(Pict.)* To darken, to sadden a color. **Teñir una prenda de azul,** to dye a garment blue. *(Yo tiño, él tiñó, yo tiña,* from *Teñir.* V. PEDIR.)

teocalli [tay-o-cahl´-lyee], *m. (Mex.)* Teocalli, a pyramidal mound on which the Aztecs celebrated their sacrifices.

teocracia [tay-o-crah´-the-ah], *f.* Theocracy, govermnent by priests.

teocrático, ca [tay-o-crah´-te-co, cah], *a.* Theocratic, theocratical.

teodolito [tay-o-do-lee´-to], *m.* Theodolite.

teologal [tay o lo-gahl´], *a.* Theological.

teología [tay o lo-hee´-ah], *f.* Theology, divinity. **Teología moral,** casuistry. **No meterse en teologías,** *(Coll.)* not to involve oneself in subtleties.

teológicamente [tay-o-loh´-he-cah-men-tay], *adv.* Theologically.

teológico, ca [tay-o-loh´-he-co, cah], *a. V.* TEOLOGAL.

teologizar [tay-o-lo-he-thar´], *vn.* To treat or discourse upon the principles of theology, to theologize.

teólogo [tay-o´-lo-go], *m.* 1. A divine, a clergyman. 2. A professor or student of theology.

teólogo [tay-oh´-lo-go], **ga.** *a.* Theological.

teorema [tay-o-ray´-mah], *m.* Theorem.

teorético, ca [tay-o-ray´-te-co, cah], *a.* Theoretic.

teoría, teórioca [tay-o-ree´-ah, tay-o´-re-cah], *f.* Theory, speculation. **Teoría atómica,** atomic theory.

teóricamente [tay-oh´-re-cah-men-tay], *adv.* Theoretically.

teórico, ca [tay-oh´-re-co, cah], *a.* Theoretical, speculative.

teoso, sa [tay-oh´-so, sah], *a.* Resinous.

teosofía [tay-o-so-fee´-ah], *f.* Theosophy, a philosophy of the universe, universal religion, a mystical speculation.

teosófico, ca [tay-o-so´-fe-co, cah], *a.* Theosophical, pertaining to theosophy.

teósofo [tay-oh´-so-fo], *m.* Theosophist.

teotl, teutl [tay-otl´], *m.* The supreme being among the Aztecs.

tepalcate [tay-pal-cah´-tay], *m. (Mex.)* Small pieces of broken earthenware (vasija).

tope [tay´-pay], *m.* Green sod.

tepeguaje [tay-pay-goo-ah´-hay], *m.* A very hard and compact Mexican wood. *-a. (Met. Mex.)* Set, obstinate.

tepeizquinte [tay-pay-eeth-keen´-tay], *m.* South American animal, resembling a sucking pig.

tepetate [tay-pay-tah´-tay], *m.* 1. A layer of soil used for building houses in Mexico. 2. All mining ground which holds no ore.

tequila [tay-kee´-lah], *m.* Tequila, Mexican liquor distilled from the century plant.

tequío [tay-kee´-o], *m.* In Mexico, charm, tax. *V.* CARGA CONCEJIL.

terapéutica [tay-rah-pay´-oo-te-cah], *f.* Therapeutics, the branch of medicine, which treats of remedies.

terapéutico, ca [tay-rah-pay´-oo-te-co, cah], *a.* Therapeutic, remedial, curative.

terapia [tay´-rah-pe], *f.* Therapy. **Terapia de grupo,** group therapy.

tercamente [ter-cah-men´-tay], *adv.* Opinionately, opinionatively, obstinately.

tercena [ter-thay´-nah], *f.* 1. Wholesale tobacco warehouse. 2. *(And.)* Butcher´s (tienda).

tercenal [ter-thay-nahl´], *m. (Prov.)* Heap containing thirty sheaves of corn.

tercenista [ter-thay-nees´-tah], *m.* Keeper of a wholesale tobacco warehouse.

tercer [ter-therr´], *m.* Third.-a. Third: used before a substantive.

tercera [ter-thay´-rah], *f.* 1. *(Mus.)* Third, a consonance comprehending an interval of two tones. 2. One of the strings of a guitar. 3. Series of three cords in order at play. 4. Procuress, bawd.

terceramente [ter-thay´-rah-men-tay], *adv.* Thirdly.

tercería [ter-thay-ree´-ah], *f.* 1. Mediation (arbitración), arbitration. 2. Arbitration dues or fees. 2. Depository. 4. Temporary occupation of a castle, fortress, etc.

tercerilla [ter-thay-reel´-lyah], *f.* Triplet, metrical composition.

tercermundista [ter-thayr-moon-dees´-tah], *a.* Third-world.

tercero, ra [ter-thay´-ro, rah], *a.* Third.

tercero [ter-thay´-ro], *m.* 1. Third (persona, piso). 2. Mediator (árbitro), arbitrator. 3. Collector of tithes. 4. Religious of the third order of St. Francis. 5. Pimp, procurer, bawd.

tercerol [ter-thay-role´], *m. (Naut.)* Main-sail; third pair of oars.

tercerola [ter-thay-ro´-lah], *f.* 1. Short kind of carbine. 2. Tierce, small cask.

tercerón, na [ter-thay-rone´, nah], *m. & f. (Amer.)* A yellow man or woman, the offspring of a white and a mulatto woman.

terceto [ter-thay´-to], *m.* 1. A kind of metrical composition; a tiercet, terzet, or terza-rima. 2. *(Mus.)* Terzetto, trio, a composition for three voices. 3. *V.* TERCERILLA.

tercia [terr´-the-ah], *f.* 1. Third, the third part. 2. Store-house or barn, where tithes are deposited. 3. One of the hours into which the Romans divided the day. 4. Canonical hour which follows immediately the first so called from falling at three o´clock.

terciación [ter-the-ah-the-on´], *f.* Act of ploughing a third time.

terciado [ter-the-ah´-do], *m.* 1. Cutlass, a short and broad sword. 2. Kind of ribbon somewhat broader than tape. *-a.* **Azúcar terciado,** brown sugar. **terciado, da** [ter-the-ah-do], *-pp.* of TERCIAR.

terciana [ter-the-ah´-nah], *f.* Tertian. **Fiebre terciana,** tertian fever.

tercianario, ria [ter-the-ah-nah´-re-o, ah], *m. & f.* 1. A person suffering from malaria. 2. A country where malaria is common.

tercianela [ter-the-ah-nay´-lah], *f.* Sort of silk, resembling taffeta.

tercianiento, ta [ter-the-ah-ne-en´-to, tah], *a. (Amer. Peru) V.* TERCIANARIO.

terciano, na [ter-the-ah´-no, nah], *a.* Tertian, occurring with a regular intermission between two or more things.

terciar [ter-the-ar´], *va.* 1. To sling anything diagonally. 2. To divide a thing into three parts. 3. To tertiate, to plough the third time. 4. To slant, to slope (inclinar). 5. *(And. Cono Sur, Mex.)* To hoist on to one´s shoulder. 6. *(LAm.)* To water down (vino). *-vn.* 1. To make up the number of three. 2. To mediate, to arbitrate, to go between. 3. To join, to share, to make one of a party. **Terciar la carga,** to divide a burden into three equal parts. **Terciar entre dos rivales,** to mediate between two rivals. *-vr.* 1. **Si se tercia una buena oportunidad,** if a good chance presents itself. 2. **Si se tercia**

alguna vez que yo pase por allí, if I should happen to go that way.

terciario, ria [ter-the-ah'-re-o, ah], *a.* 1. Third in order or degree. 2. Tertiary, belonging to a geological period following the Mesozoic. *-m. (Arch.)* Rib in the vaulting of Gothic arches.

terciazón [ter-the-ah-thone'], *m.* Third ploughing.

tercio, cia [terr'-the-o, ah], *a.* Third.

tercio [terr'-the-o], *m.* 1. The third part (tercera parte). 2. Half a load. 3. Regiment of infantry in ancient Spanish warfare. 4. Third part of a horse-course. 5. Third part of the rosary; third part of a sword. 6. *(LAm.)* Pack, package, bale. 7. *(Carib.)* Fellow (hombre). **Hacer buen tercio,** to do good to a person. **Hacer tercio,** to join an association. **Hacer mal tercio,** to do a bad turn, to serve ill. *-pl.* 1. Height of horses, measured by hands. 2. Robust or strong limbs of a man.

terciodécuplo, pla [ter-the-o-day'-coo-plo, plah], *a.* Product of any quantity multiplied by thirteen.

terciopelado [ter-the-o-pay-lah'-do], *m.* Stuff resembling velvet.

terciopelado, da [ter-the-o-pay-lah'-do, dah], *a.* Velvet-like.

terciopelero [ter-the-o-pay-lay'-ro], *m.* Velvet-weaver.

terciopelo [ter-the-o-pay'-lo], *m.* Velvet.

terco, ca [terr'-co, cah], *a.* 1. Pertinacious, obstinate (obstinado), opinionative, contumacious. 2. Firm or hard as marble (material). **Terco como una mula,** as stubborn as a mule.

terebinto [tay-ray-been'-to], *m. (Bot.)* Turpentine or mastich-tree.

terebrante [tay-ray-brahn'-tay], *a. (Med.)* Boring, piercing (dolor).

tereniabín [tay-ray-ne-ah-been], *m.* White, sweetish, purgative matter, resembling mastich, which adheres to the leaves of plants; liquid manna.

térete [tay'-ray-tay], *a.* Round, plump, robust.

tergiversación [ter-he-ver-sah-the-on'], *f.* Tergiversation, evasion, subterfuge.

tergiversar [ter-he-ver-sar'], *va.* To distort (torcer), to boggle, to shift. *-vn.* To prevaricate (no resolverse); to chop and change (vacilar).

terliz [ter-leeth'], *m.* Tick, ticking, bed-ticking; tent-cloth.

termal [ter-mahl'], *a.* Thermal.

termas [ter-mas], *f. pl.* Hot baths.

térmico [ter'-me-co], *a.* Thermic, heat.

terminable [ter-me-nah'-blay], *a.* Terminable.

terminacho [ter-me-nah'-cho], *m. (Coll.)* Rude word or phrase (de palabra) (fea).

terminación [ter-me-nah-the-on'], *f.* 1. Termination, conclusion. 2. *(Gram.)* Termination, or last syllable of a word.

terminado [ter-me-nah'-do], *m.* Story, door, or flight of rooms.—**Terminado, da**, *pp.* of TERMINAR.

terminador, ra [ter-me-nah-dor', rah], *m. & f.* One who terminates.

terminal [ter-me-nahl'], *a.* Final, ultimate, terminal. *-m. (Elec. Comput.)* Terminal. *-f. (Aer. Ferro.)* Terminal; *(LAm. Ferro.)* Terminus.

terminante [ter-me-nahn'-tay], *pa.* Ending, closing, terminating.*-a.* Conclusive or decisive with regard to a point in question; definite. **En términos terminantes,** in definite terms, with propriety or punctuality, in point.

terminantemente [ter-me-nan-tay-men'-tay], *adv.* Absolutely, conclusively, by all means. **Queda terminantemente prohibido,** it is strictly forbidden to.

terminar [ter-me-nar'], *va. & vn.* 1. To end (forma, objeto), to close, to terminate. 2. To finish (acabar), to consummate; to end at, to abut. 3. *(Med.)* To come to a crisis. 4. *(Gram.)* To end a word. **Esto va a terminar en tragedia,** this will end in tragedy. **Cuando termine de hablar,** when he finishes speaking. *-vr.* To end, to come to an end.

terminativo, va [ter-me-nah-tee'-vo, vah], *a.* Terminative, respective, relative to a term.

término [terr'-me-no], *m.* 1. The end of anything. 2. Term, boundary, landmark (de tierra); limit, goal. 3. Manner, behavior, conduct. 4. District of a town or city. 5. Aim, object. 6. Term, the word by which a thing is expressed. 7. Term, the appointed time or determined place (plazo). 8. Crisis of a disease. 9. Determinate object of an operation. 10. Period including the beginning and end of something. 11. The precise moment to do anything. 12. Term or word of any language, a technical word, diction; conception. 13. Condition, constitution, state. 14. *(Arch.)* Stay, resembling the support which the ancients gave the head of their god Terminus. 15. Compartment in a painting. 16. *(Mus.)* Tone, pitch. **Primer término,** foreground of a picture. **En términos hábiles,** on reasonable terms, so as not to prejudice another. **Términos,** terms of an argument, syllogism, or arithmetical question. **¿En qué términos?** upon what terms? **Poner término a,** to put an end to. **Término medio** middle term. **Según los términos del contrato,** according to the terms of the contract. **En otros términos,** in other words.

terminología [ter-me-no-lo-hee'-ah], *f. (Neol.)* Terminology, the technical terms of a science or an art.

terminote [ter-me-no'-tay], *m. aug.* of TÉRMINO. A vulgar or affected expression.

termite [ter-mee'-tay], *m.* Termite, a white ant.

termodinámica [ter-mo-de-nah'-me-cah], *f.* Thermodynamics. **termodinámica aérea,** aerothermodynamics.

termoeléctrico, ca [ter-mo-ay-lec'-tre-co, cah], *a.* Thermoelectric.

termófilo, la [ter-mo'-fe-lo, lah], *a.* Fond of living in warm countries.

termología [ter-mo-lo-hee'-ah], *f.* A treatise on heat.

termómetro [ter-mo'-may-tro], *m.* Thermometer.

termos [ter'-mos], *m.* Thermos or vacuum bottle.

termostato [ter-mos-tah'-to], *m.* Thermostat.

terna [terr' nah], *f.* 1. A ternary number. 2. A kind of stuff of a fine appearance after the fur or pile is fallen off. 3. Game at dice.

ternario, ria [ter-nah'-re-o, ah], *a.* Ternary, ternarious, containing three unities.

ternario [ter-nah'-re-o], *m.* 1. Three days' devotion or religious offices. 2. *(Mus.)* A measure of three equal parts.

terne [terr'-nay], *a. (Coll.)* V. VALENTÓN.

ternecico, ica, ito, ita [ter-nay-thee'-co], *a.* Very tender.

ternejal [ter-nay-hahl'], *a.* V. TERNE.

ternejón, na [ter-nay-hone', nah], *a.* V. TERNEJÓN.

ternerico, ica, illo, illa, ito, ita [ter-nay-ree'-co, cah, el'-lyo, eel'-lyah, ce' to, ee'-tah], *m. & f.* A young calf.

ternero, ra [ter-nay'-ro, rah], *m. & f.* Calf; veal; heifer.

ternerón, na [ter-nay-rone', nah], *a.* 1. Easily moved, weeping at will. 2. *(Cono Sur, Mex.)* Overgrown, big (mozo).

terneruela [ter-nay-roo-ay'-lah], *f. & m.* A sucking calf.

terneza [ter-nay'-thah], *f.* 1. Softness, delicacy, pliantness. 2. Tenderness (cualidad), affection, endearment, fondness. 3. Suavity. 4. Readiness to shed tears.

ternilla [ter-neel'-lyah], *f.* Gristle, the cartilaginous part of the body.

ternilloso, sa [ter-neel-lyo'-so, sah], *a.* Gristly, cartilaginous, webbed, finfooted.

ternísimo, ma [ter-nee'-se-mo, mah], *a. super.* of TIERNO.

terno [terr'-no], *m.* 1. Ternary number (grupo de tres). 2. *(Coll.)* Wearing apparel, dress, rich clothes (traje). **Un terno de diamantes,** a set of diamonds. 3. Ornaments for celebrating high-mass. 4. Oath. *V.* VOTO. **Echar ternos or tacos,** to swear excessively, to speak in a great rage. 5. *(Print.)* Union of three sheets one within another. 6. In the game of lotto, the lot of obtaining three numbers in the row of five.

ternura [ter-noo'-rah], *f.* Tenderness (cualidad), delicacy, humanity, fondness. *V.* TERNEZA.

terquedad [ter-kay-dahd'], *f.* Stubbornness, obstinacy (obstinación), pertinacity, contumacy, inflexibility.

terracota [ter-rah-co'-tah], *f.* Terracotta.

terrácueo, cuea [ter-rah'-coo-ay-o, ah], *a.* Terraqueous.

terrada [ter-rah'-dah], *f.* Kind of bitumen made with ochre and glue.

terradillo [ter-rah-deel'-lyo], *m. dim.* A small terrace.

terrado [ter-rah'-do], *m.* Terrace, flat roof of a house. *V.* AZOTEA.

terraja [ter-rah'-hah], *f.* 1. A screwplate, screw-stock, or die-stock. 2. *V.* TARRAJA.

terraje [ter-rah'-hay], *m.* Rent paid to the owner of land.

terrajero [ter-rah-hay'-ro], *m. V.* TERRAZGUERO.

terral [ter-rahl'], *m. & a.* Applied to a land breeze.

terrapene [ter-rah-pay'-nay], *m.* (*Zool.*) Terrapin.

terraplén, terrapleno [ter-rah-playn'], *m.* (*Mil.*) The horizontal surface of a rampart terrace, mound; hence the graded road-bed of a railway.

terraplenar [ter-rah-play-nar'], *va.* To raise a rampart; to make a platform or terrace.

terraplenador [ter-rah-play-nah-dor'], *m.* One who makes a terrace or platform.

terráqueo, quea [ter-rah'-kay-o, ah], *a.* Terraqueous, containing both land and water.

terrateniente [ter-rah-tay-ne-en'-tay], *m.* Master or possessor of land or property.

terraza [ter-rah'-thah], *f.* 1. A glazed jar with two handles. 2. Terrace, a space somewhat raised and separated from the surface which is prolonged along the wall of a garden or courtyard (terraza). 3. Pavement café (café). 4. Nut (cabeza).

terrazgo [ter-rath'-go], *m.* 1. Arable land. 2. Land-tax or rent of arable land paid to the landlord.

terrazguero [ter-rath-gay'-ro], *m.* Laborer who pays rent to the lord of the manor for the land which he occupies.

terrazo [ter-rah'-tho], *m.* (*Art.*) Ground of a painting.

terrazuel [ter-rah-thoo-ay'-lah], *f. dim.* of TERRAZA.

terrear [ter-ray-ar'], *m.* To show the ground: speaking of crops which stand very thin.

terregoso, sa [ter-ray-go'-so, sah], *a.* Cloddy, full of clods.

terremoto [ter-ray-mo'-to], *m.* Earthquake.

terrenal [ter-ray-nahl'], *a.* Terrestrial, earthly, mundane.

terrenidad [ter-ray-ne-dahd'], *f.* Quality of the soil or ground.

terreno, na [ter-ray'-no, nah], *a.* 1. Terrene, earthly, terrestrial. 2. Worldly, terrestrial, perishable.

terreno [ter-ray'-no], *m.* 1. Land, ground (tierra, suelo), a field. 2. Field, sphere of action. 3. (*Geol.*) A group of several formations which have a certain analogy by their antiquity, form, or composition. **Terreno abierto**, (*Mil.*) open ground: that is, free of rocks, mountains, or other formidable obstacles and of fortified posts. **Los accidentes del terreno**, the characteristics of the terrain. **Ganar terreno**, to gain ground. **Terreno de fútbol**, football ground. **Eso no es mi terreno**, that's not my field.

térreo, rea [ter'-ray-o, ah], *a.* Terreous, earthy.

terrera [ter-ray'-rah], *f.* 1. A steep piece of ground. 2. (*Orn.*) Kind of lark.

terrero [ter-ray'-ro], *m.* 1. Terrace, platform. 2. Heap of earth. 3. Mark, to shoot at. 4. Terrace, or other part of the palace, where court is paid to the ladies. **Hacer terrero**, to court a lady. 5. In the Canary Islands, an open, clear spot where an athletic contest, common in the country, takes place. 6. (*Mil.*) An artificial wall of earth.

terrero, ra [ter-ray'-ro, rah], *a.* 1. Earthly (de la tierra), terreous. 2. Abject, humble. 3. Skimming the ground (pájaros).

terrestre [ter-res'-tray], *a.* Terrestrial; earthly (de la tierra), land; land (ruta), overland; (*Mil.*) ground (fuerzas).

terrestridad [ter-res-tre-dahd'], *f.* Earthiness.

terrezuela [ter-ray-thoo-ay'-lah], *f.* 1. (*Dim.*) A small piece of ground. 2. Light and poor soil.

terribilidad [ter-re-be-le-dahd'], *f.* Terribleness, roughness, asperity, ferocity.

terrible [ter-ree'-blay], *a.* 1. Terrible, dreadful, ferocious, horrible. 2. Rude, unmannerly. 3. Immense, very large.

terriblemente [ter-ree'-blay-men-tay], *adv.* Terribly, frightfully.

terrícola [tar-ree'-co-lah], *com.* Inhabitant of the earth.

terrífico, ca [ter-ree'-fe-co, cah], *a.* Terrific, frightful.

terrígeno, na [ter-ree'-hay-no, nah], *a.* Terrigenous, earth-born.

terrino, na [ter-ree'-no, nah], *a.* Terrene, earthy.

territorial [ter-re-to-re-ahl'], *a.* Territorial.

territorio [ter-re-toh'-re-o], *m.* 1. Territory, district; ground; land. 2. Territory, a district still under provisional or colonial government.

terrizo, za [ter-ree'-tho, thah], *a.* 1. Earthy, earthen. 2. Unglazed.

terrojo [ter-ro'-ho], *m.* 1. Red earth. 2. *V.* TERRAZGO.

terromontero [ter-ro-mon-tay'-ro], *m.* Hill, hillock.

terrón [ter-rone'], *m.* 1. A flat clod of earth, globe. 2. Lump of anything. **Terrón de azúcar**, lump sugar. 3. Heap, collection of things. 4. Dregs of olives which remain in the mill. *-pl.* Landed property.

terronazo [ter-ro-nah'-tho], *m.* 1. (*Aug.*) A large clod of earth. 2. Blow with a clod.

terroncillo [ter-ron-theel'-lyo], *m. dim.* A small clod.

terrontera [ter-ron-tay'-rah], *f.* Break in a mountain.

terror [ter-ror'], *m.* Terror, dread, consternation.

terrorífico, ca [ter-ro-ree'-fe-co, cah], *a.* *V.* TERRÍFICO.

terrorismo [ter-ro-rees'-mo], *m.* The act of terrifying: applied to unlawful violence.

terrorista [ter-ro-rees'-tah], *m.* A person who employs authority to commit unlawful violence.

terrosidad [ter-ro-se-dahd'], *f.* Earthiness.

terroso, sa [ter-ro'-so, sah], *a.* Terreous, earthy.

terruca [ter-roo'-cah], *f.* 1. (*Dim.*) *V.* TERREZUELA. 2. (*Neol. Coll.*) Native country.

terruño [te-roo'-nyo], *m.* 1. A piece of land (parcela). 2. One's native soil.

tersar [ter-sar'], *va.* To smooth, to polish, to clean, to make smooth and clean.

tersícore [ter-se'-co-ray], *f.* Terpsichore, the muse of the dance.

tersidad [ter-se-dahd'], *f.* Smoothness, terseness.

terso, sa [terr'-so, sah], *a.* 1. Smooth (liso), polished, glossy (brillante). 2. Pure, elegant, correct, terse (estilo). **Piel tersa**, smooth skin.

tersura [ter-soo'-rah], *f.* Smoothness, cleanliness, purity; elegance, terseness.

tertulia [ter-too'-le-ah], *f.* 1. Club, assembly, circle, coterie, evening party (reunión informal). 2. Part of the boxes in a play-house reserved for women only. **Estar de tertulia**, to talk, to sit around talking.

tertuliano, na [ter-too-te-ah'-no, nah], *a.* Member of a club, assembly, or circle of friends.

tertulio, a, [ter-too'-le-o, ah], *a.* Relating to a meeting of friends or party.

teruelo [tay-roo-ay'-lo], *m.* (*Prov.*) Bowl or box in which lots are put to be cast.

teruncio [ter-roo'-the-o], *m.* A Roman coin, the fourth part of an as.

terutero [tay-roo-tay'-ro], *m.* A bird which lives by the banks of rivers and whose note resembles the sound of its name.

terzón, na [ter-thone', nah], *a. & n.* Heifer, a three-year-old ox.

terzuelo, la [ter-thoo-ay'-lo, lah], *a.* Applied to the third bird which leaves the nest.

terzuelo [ter-thoo-ay'-lo], *m.* Third part of anything.

tesaliense, tesalio, lia, tésalo, la [tay-sah-le-en'-say, tay-sah'-le-o, ah, tay'-sah-lo, lah], *a.* Thessalian, of Thessaly.

tesalónico, ca [tay-sah-lo'-ne-co, cah], *a.* Thessalonian, of Thessalonica.

tesar [tay-sar'], *va.* 1. (*Naut.*) To haul (cuerda) taut, to tauten. 2. (*Prov.*) As applied to yoked oxen, to back, to pull back.

tesauro [tay-sah'-oo-ro], *m.* Dictionary, vocabulary, index.

tesela

tesela [tay-say'-lah], *f.* Tessella, each of the small cubes or squares for making mosaic pavements.

teselato, tao [tay-say-lah´-to, tah], *a.* Tessellate, tessellated, inlaid, mosaic.

tésera [tay'-say-rah], *f.* Sign or counter sign; a cubical piece of wood or bone used by the Romans as a pledge of hospitality, etc.

tesis [tay'-sis], *f.* 1. Thesis. 2. *V.* CONCLUSIÓN.

teso, sa [tay'-so, sah], *a. V.* TIESO.

teso [tay'-so], *m.* Brow of a hill.

tesón [tay-sone´], *m.* Tenacity, firmness, inflexibility.

tesorería [tay-so-ray-ree'-ah], *f.* Treasury, treasurers office, exchequer: treasurership, office or dignity of a treasurer.

tesorero, ra [tay-so-ray'-ro, rah], *m. & f.* 1. Treasurer. 2. Canon who keeps the relics.

tesoro [tay-so'-ro], *m.* l. Treasure (dineral), wealth, riches. 2. Treasury exchequer. 3. Anything valuable and precious. 4. Treasure, a complete abridgment of useful knowledge. **Tesoro escondido**, buried treasure. **El libro es un tesoro de datos**, the book is a mine of memories.

test [test], *m.* Test.

testa [tes'-tah], *f.* 1. Forehead, front, face. 2. Front, face, of material things.

testáceo, cea [tes-tah'-thay´-o, ah], *a.* Testaceous, provided with a hard constinuous shell, as a mollusk. *-m.* Testacean, a shell-bearing invertebrate especially a mollusk.

testación [tes-tah-the-on´], *f.* 1. Leaving by will. 2. Obliteration.

testada [tes-tah'-dah], *f. V.* TESTARADA.

testado, da [tes-tah'-do, dah], *a. & pp.* of TESTAR. Dying testate.

testador [tes-tah-dor'], *m.* Testator.

testadora [tes-tah-do'-rah], *f.* Testatrix.

testadura [tes-tah-doo'-rah], *f.* Obliteration, lineal erasure of written letters.

testaférrea [tes-tah-fayr'-ray-ah], *m. V.* TESTAFERRO.

testaferro [tes-tah-fer'-ro], *m.* One who lends his name on a contract or business belonging to another; used in a depreciative sense.

testamentaria [tes-tah-men-tah-ree'-ah], *f.* Testamentary, execution.

testamentaria [tes-tah-men-tah'-re-ah], *f.* Executrix.

testamentario [tes-tah-men-tah'-re-o], *m.* Executor.

testamentario, ria [tes-tah-men-tah´-re-o, ah], *a.* Testamentary.

testamento [tes-tah-men'-to], *m.* 1. Last will, testament. **Testamento cerrado**, a sealed testament. **Testamento abierto**, a will made viva voce before three witnesses and a notary, before five witnesses, citizens of the place in which it is executed. Or before seven, even though nonresident, and without a notary. 2. Part of the Holy Scriptures.

testar [tes-tar'], *va. & n.* 1. To will, to make a last will or testament, to leave, to bequeath. 2. To blot, to scratch out.

testarada [tes-tah-rah'-dah], *f.* 1. A stroke or blow with the head. 2. Stubbornness, obstinacy.

testarrón, na [tes-tar-rone´], *a. V.* TESTARUDO.

testarronería [tes-tar-ro-nay-ree'-ah], *f.* Stubborness, obstinacy, tenacity.

testarudo, da [tes-tah-roo'-do, dah], *a.* Obstinate, stubborn.

teste [tes'-tay], *m.* Testis, testicle.

testera [tes-tay'-rah], *f.* 1. Front or fore part of anything; forehead of an animal. 2. Head-stall of the bridle of a horse, or head-piece of a bridle.

testerada [tes-tay-rah'-dah], *f. V.* TESTARADA.

testero [tes-tay'-ro], *m. V.* TESTERA.

testicular [tes-te-coo-lar', *a.* Testicular, pertaining to the testicles.

testículo [tes-tee'-coo-lo], *m.* A testicle.

testificación [tes-te-fe-cah-the-on'], *f.* Attestation, testification.

testificante [tes-te-fe-cahn'-tay], *pa.* witnessing, attesting.

testificar [tes-te-fe-car'], *va.* To attest (atestiguar), to witness, to certify, to testify (dar testimonio).

testificata [tes-te-fe-cah´-tah], *f. (Law.)* Legal testimony.

testificativo, va [tes-te-fe-cah-tee'-vo, vah], *a.* That which testifies.

testigo [tes-tee'-go], *m & f.* 1. Witness, one who gives testimony. 2. Inanimate witness, evidence. **Testigo de vista** or **ocular**, an eye-witness. **Testigo de cargo**, witness for the prosecution.

testimonial [tes-te-mo-ne-ahl'], *a.* That which bears a true testimony: applied to a testimonial or writing produced as an evidence.

testimoniales [tes-te-mo-ne-ah'-les], *f. pl.* Testimonials, an authentic writing verifying what is contained in it; a certificate: in particular, a certificate of good character given by a bishop to a parishioner who moves to another diocese.

testimoniar [tes-te-mo-ne-ar'], *va.* To testify, to attest, to bear witness, to aver; to avouch.

testimoniero, ra [tes-te-mo-ne-ay'-ro, rah], *a.* 1. Bearing false witness. 2. Dissembling, hypocritical.

testimonio [tes-te-mo'-ne-o], *m.* 1. Testimony, deposition of a witness, proof by witness. 2. Testimony, open attestation, attestation. 3. An instrument legalized by notary. **Testimonio** or **falso testimonio**, false accusation or testimony; imposture.

testimoñero, ra [tes-te-mo-nyay'-ro, rah], *a.* Hypocritical. *V.* TESTIMONIERO.

testón [tes-tone'], *m.* A coin having a head.

testudo [tes-too'-do], *m.* Machine for covering soldiers in an attack on a fortification.

testuz, testuzo [tes-tooth´, tes-too´-tho], *m. (Vet.)* Hind part of the head, nape; in some animals, crown of the head. *(Acad.)*

tesura [tay-soo'-rah], *f.* 1. Stiffness, firmness. 2. Starched and affected gravity.

teta [tay'-tah], *f.* 1. Mammary gland, breast. 2. Nipple (pezón), teat (de biberón); dug of animals. **Teta de vaca**, teat or dug of a cow; kind of large grapes. **Niño de teta**, a child at the breast; a suckling.

tetánico, ca [tay-tah'-ne-co, cah], *a.* Tetanic, tetanical.

tétano [tay´-tah-no], **tétanos**, *m. (Med.)* Tetanus, lockjaw; tonic spasm.

tetar [tay-tar'], *va.* To suckle, to give suck. *V.* ATETAR.

tetaza [tay-tah'-thah], *f. aug.* Flabby, ugly dugs.

tetera [tay-tay'-rah], *f.* Tea-pot, tea kettle, with strainer.

tetero [tay-tay'-ro], *m. (Amer.)* Nursing bottle. *V.* BIBERÓN.

tetica, ita [tay-tee'-cah], *f. dim.* A small dug or teat.

tetilla [tay-tee'-lyah], *f.* 1. *(Dim.)* A small nipple or teat (de hombre). 2. Kind of paste in the figure of a teat.

tetina [tay-tee'-nah], *f.* Teat (de biberón).

tetona [tay-to'-nah], *a.* Having large teats.

tetracordio [tay-trah-cor'-de-o], *m. (Mus.)* Tetrachord, fourth.

tetraédrico, ca [tay-trah-ay'-dre-co, cah], *a.* Tetrahedral.

tetraedro [tay-trah-ay'-dro], *m. (Geom.)* Tetrahedron.

tetragínico, ca [tay-trah-hee'-ne-co, cah], *a. (Bot.)* Having four pistils.

tetrágono [tay-trah'-go-no], *m. (Geom.)* Tetragon.

tetrágono, na [ ], *a. (Geom.)* Tetragonal.

tetragrámatron [tay-trah-grah'-mah-trone], *m.* Word composed of four letters, particularly the name of *Dios*.

tetrámetro [tay-trah'-may-tro], *m.* Iambic verse of eight feet or four measures. *-pl. (Zool.)* A section of coleoptera, having four joints upon the tarsi.

tetrapétalo [tay-trah-pay'-tah-lo] *(Bot.)* Tetrapetalous: four-petalled.

tetrarca [tay-trar'-cah], *vn.* Tetrarch.

tetrarquía [tay-trar-kee'-ah], *f* Tetrarchate, tetrarchy.

tetrástilo [tay-trahs'-te-lo], *m.* Building sustained by four columns or pilasters.

tetrasílabo, ba [tay-trah-see'-lah-bo, bah], *a. V.* CUATRISÍLABO.

tétricamente [tay'-tre-cah-men-tay], *adv.* Gloomily.

tétrico, ca [tay´-tre-co, cah], *a.* Crabbed, grave, gloomy (pensamiento, humor), sullen.

tetuda [tay-too´-dah], *a.* 1. Having large nipples. 2. *(Prov.)* Applied to a kind of oblong olives.

teucalí [tay-oo-cah-lee´], *m.* V. TEOCALLA.

teucrio [tay´-oo-cre-o], *m. (Bot.)* Germander.

teucro, cra [tay´-oo-cro, crah], *a. & a.* Trojan.

teurgia [tay-oor´-he-ah], *f.* Theurgy, black magic, superstitious art of calling on beneficent genii.

teutón [tay-oo-tone´], *m. (& pl.).* Teuton, especially the ancient Germanic tribes or language.

teutónico, ca [tay-oo-toh´-ne-co, cah], *a.* 1. Teutonic, of a German military order. 2. German, Teutonic.

textil [tex-teel´], *a.* Textile, capable of being made into threads and woven.

texto [tex´-to], *m.* 1. Text, the original words of an author. 2. Text of Scripture. 3. *(Print.)* Name of a size of types: great primer.

textorio, ria [tex-to´-re-o, ah], *a.* Textrine, textorial, belonging to weaving.

textual [tex-too-ahl´], *a. 1.* Textual (de texto), agreeing with the text. 2. *(Fig.)* Exact; literal. **Son sus palabras textuales,** those are his exact words.

textualista [tex-too-ah-lees´-tah], *m.* 1. Textualist, he who adheres to the text. 2. Texturist, one ready in quotation of texts.

textualmente [tex-too-ahl´-men-tay], *adv. 1.* According to the text; textually. 2. *(Fig.)* Exactly; literally.

textura [tex-too´-rah], *f.* 1. Texture, as of stuff or cloth. 2. Succession and order of things.

tez [teth], *f.* 1. Grain; shining surface. 2. Bloom of the complexion, hue.

tezado, da [tay-thah´-do, dah], *a.* Very black. V. ATEZADO.

tezcucano, na [teth-coo-cah´-no, nah], *a.* Tezcucan, belonging to Tezcuco, a city of Mexico.

tezontle [tay-thon´-tlay], *m. (Mex.)* A porous stone esteemed for building in Mexico.

theta [thay´-tah], *f.* Eighth letter of the Greek alphabet, represented in Latin by *th,* in modern Spanish by *t* alone.

ti [tee]. The oblique case of **tú,** thou. When preceded by the preposition **con,** it takes the termination **go,** as **contigo,** with you. **Ti mismo,** yourself, thyself.

ti [tee], *pron.* You; yourself. **Esto no se refiere a ti,** this doesn´t refer to you.

tía [tee´-ah], *f.* 1. Aunt (pariente). 2. *(Coll.)* A good old woman (mujer). 3. *(Coll.)* Used in Spain to express colloquially a common woman. **Cuéntaselo a tu tía,** *(Coll.)* tell it to your grandmother. **Tía,** a name given to decent old persons in low condition, in stead of *Doña;* as, **da esto a la tía Isabel,** give this to aunt Elizabeth. **Tía buena,** smashing girl.

tialismo [te-ah-lees´-mo], *m.* Ptyalism, abnormal discharge of saliva.

tiangui [te-ahn´-gee], **Tiangue** [te-ahn´-gay] (in the Philippine Islands), *m.* The market, and market-days, in the small towns of the Mexican republic and in the Philippine Islands.

tiara [te-ah´-rah], *f.* 1. Tiara, miter worn by the Pope. 2. Pontificate, papal dignity. 3. Diadem of the ancient kings of Persia.

tibetano, na [te-bay-tah´-no], *a. m. & f.* Tibetan.

tibia [tee´-be-ah], *f.* 1. Shinbone. 2. A flute.

tibial [te-be-ahl´], *a. (Anat.)* Tibial, relating to the tibia.

tibiamente [tee´-be-ah-men-tay], *adv.* Tepidly, carelessly, lukewarmly.

tibieza [te-be-ay´-thah], *f.* 1. Tepidity, lukewarmness (de sustancia); coldness. 2. Coolness, frigidity, jejuneness. 3. Carelessness, negligence.

tibio, bia [tee´-be-o, ah], *a. 1.* Tepid, lukewarm (agua), careless, remiss. 2. *(CAm. Carib.)* Cross, angry.

tibir [te-beer´], *m.* Name of gold-dust on the African coast.

tibor [te-bor´], *m.* 1. A large china jar. 2. *(Amer. Cuba)* A chamber pot.

tiburón [te-boo-ron´], *m.* 1. Shark. 2. *(Fig.)* Gogetter, unscrupulous person; *(Cono Sur)* wolf, Don Juan.

tictac [tic-tac´], *m.* Tick tock (de reloj); beat (de corazón); tapping (de máquina de escribir).

tiempecillo, tiempecito [te-em-pay-theel´-lyo, thee´-to], *m. dim.* A little time.

tiempo [te-em´-po], *m.* 1. Time. 2. Term, a limited space of time (específico, limitado). 3. Any of the four seasons. 4. Time, opportunity, occasion; tide, season; leisure. 5. Weather, temperature, climate. 6. State, condition. 7. Draft, portion. 8. *(Gram.)* Time, tense. 9. Age. 10. Time, space, duration of an action. 11. Time, musical measure. **Tiempo borrascoso,** stormy weather. **Tiempo variable,** unsettled weather. **Tiempo apacible,** moderate weather. **Haga buen o mal tiempo,** rain or shine. **A tiempo,** timely, in time, just in time (en el momento oportuno); on time. **Nunca llega a la oficina a tiempo,** he never arrives at the office on time. **A un tiempo,** at once; at the same time. **Con tiempo,** timely, beforehand. **De tiempo en tiempo,** from time to time. **Por tiempo,** for some time, undetermined time. **La carta llegó a su tiempo,** the letter was duly received. **A tiempo que,** just as. **Abrir el tiempo,** the weather clears up. **Dar tiempo al tiempo,** to await the right occasion to do something. **Tomarse tiempo,** to take time, to defer. **En tiempo hábil,** in the appointed time. **Cada cierto tiempo,** every so often. **Todo el tiempo,** all the time. **El tiempo apremia,** time presses. **El tiempo dirá,** time will tell. **Ganar tiempo,** to save time. **En los tiempos que corremos,** in these dreadful times. **Primer tiempo,** first half. **En mis tiempos,** in my time, when I was young. **Malgastar el tiempo,** to waste time. **¿Qué tiempo tiene ese niño?,** how old is that child? **Tiempo de declinación,** *(Comput.)* decay time. **Tiempo de desplazamiento de caracteres,** *(Comput.)* skew time. **Tiempo de formación,** *(Comput.)* rise time. **Tiempo de subida,** *(Comput.)* rise time.

tienda [te-en´-dah], *f.* 1. *(Mil.)* Tent. 2. *(Naut.)* Awning over vessels. 3. Tilt for carts or wagons. 4. Shop or stall. **Poner or abrir tienda,** to open a shop. **Tienda de informática,** *(Comput.)* computer store.

tienta [te-en´-tah], *f.* 1. *(Med.)* Probe. 2. Craft, cunning, artful industry. **A tientas,** doubtfully uncertainly in the dark, at random. **Andar a tientas,** to grope in the dark, to fumble.

tientaaguja [te-en-tah-ah-goo´-hah], *f.* An auger for testing the ground on which it is proposed to build.

tiento [te-en´-to], *m.* 1. Touch, the act of feeling (sensación física). 2. A blind man's stick. 3. Circumspection, prudent consideration (prudencia). 4. Poy, a rope-dancer's pole. 5. Sureness of the hand, a steady band. 6. Stroke. V. GOLPE. 7. Mahlstick, maulstick, a painter's staff. 8. *(Mus.)* Prelude, flourish. 9. *(Zool.)* Tentacle. **Dar un tiento,** to make a trial. **Por el tiento,** by the touch. **Al tiento,** obscurely, doubtfully.

tiernamente [te-er-nah-men´-tay], *adv.* Tenderly, compassionately.

tiernecico, ica, illo, illa, ito, ita [tee-er-nay-thee´-co], *a. dim.* of TIERNO.

tierno, na [te-err´-no, nah], *a.* 1. Tender, soft, docile: delicate; lady-like. 2. Affectionate, fond, amiable, mild, easily moved to tears. 3. Recent, modern, young; tender: applied to age.

tierra [te-er´-rah], *f.* 1. Earth, the solid part of our globe, land (superficie), soil, ground, mould. 2. Native country. 3. Earth, the terraqueous globe. 4. Arable land. 5. Land, country, region, a distinct part of the globe: as **Tierra Santa,** the Holy Land. 6. *(LAm.)* Dust (polvo). **Tierra de los duendes,** fairy-land. **Tierra adentro,** *(Naut.)* in land. **Correr hacia la tierra,** *(Naut.)* to stand inshore. **Tomar tierra,** *(Naut.)* to anchor in a port. **Tierra firme,** continent. **Besar la tierra,** *(Coll.)* to fall with one's mouth against the ground. **Besar la tierra que otro pisa,** to kiss the ground another treads on (excessive respect). **Echar tierra a alguna cosa,** to bury an affair in oblivion. **Echarse por tierra,** to be humiliated. **Poner tierra en,** or **por medio,** to absent oneself.

tiesamente [te-ay´-sah-men-tay], *adv.* Firmly, stiffly, strongly.

tieso, sa [te-ay'-so, sah], *a.* 1. Stiff (rígido), hard, firm, solid. 2. Robust, strong; valiant, animated. 3. Stubborn (terco), obstinate, inflexible. 4. Tight, rigid (rígido): too grave or circumspect. **Con las orejas tiesas,** with its ears pricked. **Me recibió muy tieso,** he received me very stiffly. **Ponerse tieso con uno,** to stand one's ground. **Estar tieso,** to be broke.

tieso [te-ay'-so], *adv. V.* TIESAMENTE.

tieso [te-ay'-so], *m.* Firmness, inflexibility: hardness.

tiesta [te-es´-tah], *f.* Edge of the staves which serve for the ends of casks.

tiesto [te-es´-to], *m.* 1. Potsherd. 2. A large earthen pot.

tiesura [te-ay-soo´-rah], *f.* 1. Stiffness (rigidez), rigidity. 2. Stiffness, harshness in behavior.

tifo [tee´-fo], *m. (Med.)* Typhus, a malignant fever. **Tifo de América,** yellow fever. **Tifo asiático,** asiatic cholera. **Tifo de Oriente,** the plague.

tifoideo, dea [te-foi-day'-o, ah], *a.* Typhoid, typhus-like.—*f.* Typhoid fever.

tifón [te-fone'], *m.* 1. Whirlwind. *V.* TORBELLINO. 2. Typhoon (huracán). 3. *(Mex. Min.)* Outcrop of ore.

tifus [tee´-foos], *m.* Typhus fever. **Tifus icteroides,** yellow fever.

tignaria [tig-nah´-re-ah], *f.* Knowledge of the fittest timber for building.

tigre [tee´-gray], *m.* 1. Tiger. 2. *(And.)* Black coffee with a dash of milk; *(And.)* Cocktail (combinado).

tigresa [te-gray-sah], *f.* Tigress.

tigridia [te-gree´-de-ah], *f. (Bot.)* Tigridia, tiger-flower, a plant of the iris family, native of Mexico, cultivated for the beauty of its flowers.

tija [tee´-hah], *f.* The shaft of a key.

tijera, or **tijeras** [te-hay'-rah], *f.* 1. Scissors. 2. Carpenter's horse, cooper's mare, for holding the wood while dressing, any instrument in the form of an X. 3. Sheep-shearer. 4. A small channel or drain. 5. Detractor, murmurer. **Meter la tijera en,** to cut into. **Silla de tijera,** folding chair.

tijerada [te-hay-rah´-dah], *f. V.* TIJERETADA.

tijereta [te-hay-ray'-tah], *f.* 1. *(Dim.)* Small scissors. 2. Small tendril of vines. 3. A common insect, the earwig. 4. A South American bird.

tijeretada [te-hay-ray-tah´-dah], *f.* A cut with scissors, a clip.

tijeretazo [te-hay-ray-tah´-tho], *m.* A cut with scissors.

tijeretear [te-hay-ray-tay-ar´], *va.* 1. To cut with scissors. 2. To dispose of other people's affairs at one's pleasure. 3. *(CAm. Cono Sur, Mex.)* To gossip (chismear).

tijerica, ita [te-hay-ree´-cah], *f. dim.* A small pair of scissors.

tijerilla [te-hay-reel´-lyah] *f. dim. V.* TIJERETA.

tijeruela [te-hay-roo-ay'-lah], *f.* Small tendril of vines.

tila [tee´-lah], *f. (Bot.)* 1. Lime-tree, linden-tree. 2. The flower of this tree. 3. Infusion, tea, of linden flowers.

tilar [te-lar'], *m.* Grove or plantation of lime or linden trees.

tildar [tel-dar'], *va.* 1. To blot, to scratch out. 2. To brand, to stigmatize. 3. To mark letters with a dash, as the ñ, to put an accent.

tilde [teel'-day], *f.* 1. Tilde (sobre la ñ). 2. Accent (acento). 3. Dot or dash over a letter. 3. Iota, a tittle (cosa insignificante).

tildón [til-done'], *m. (Aug.)* A long dash or stroke.

tilia [tee´-le-ah], *f. (Bot.) V.* TILO.

tilichero [te-le-chay´-ro], *m. (Amer.)* Peddler, a vender of small articles.

tiliches [te-lee´-ches], *m. pl. (Amer.)* Small fancy articles.

tilín [te-leen'], *m.* A word imitating the sound of a bell. **Hacer tilín,** to please, to become a favorite.

tilla [teel'-lyah], *f. (Naut.)* Midship, gangway.

tillado [teel-lyah´-do], *m.* A wooden floor.

tillar [teel-lyar'], *va.* To floor. *V.* ENTARIMAR.

tilma [teel'-mah], *f. (Mex.)* A cloak fastened at the shoulder by a knot.

tilo [tee´-lo], *m.* 1. *(Bot.)* Linden-tree, lime-tree. 2. *(Cono Sur) V.* TILA.

tilosis [te-lo'-sis], *f.* Falling out of the eyelashes.

timador, ra [te-mah-dor'],*m & f.* Swindler, trickster.

tímalo [tee'-mah-lo], *m.* Grayling (pez).

timar [te-mar'], *va.* 1. To steal (propiedad); to swindle somebody out of. 2. To swindle (persona). *-vr.* To make eyes at each other.

timba [teem'-bah], *f.* 1. *(Coll.)* Hand in a game of chance; also a low gambling-house (en juego de azar). 2. *(Phil. Is.)* bucket for water. 3. *(CAm. Carib. Mex.)* Pot-belly.

timbal [tim-bahl'], *m.* Kettle drum. *V.* ATABAL.

timbalear [tim-bah-lay-ar'], *vn.* To beat the kettle-drum.

timbaleo [tim-bah-lay'-o], *m.* Beat of the kettle-drum.

timbalero [tim-bah-lay'-ro], *m.* Kettle drummer.

timbirimba [tim-bah-reem'-bah], *f. (Coll.) V.* TIMBA.

timbra [teem'-brah], *f. (Bot.)* Mountain hyssop.

timbrar [tim-brar'], *va.* 1. To put the crest to the shield in a coat of arms. 2. To stamp a seal or device upon paper (estampillar).

timbre [teem'-bray], *m.* 1. *(Her.)* Timbre or simmer, crest of a coat of arms. 2. Seal, device, stamped upon paper, indicating a person's name, etc. 3. A bell provided with a spring. 4. Tone color, clang-tint, peculiar harmonious sound of the voice or instruments. 5. Any glorious deed or achievement. **Timbre de alarma,** alarm bell. **Tocar el timbre,** to ring the bell. **Timbre nasal,** nasal timbre.

timiama [te-me-ah'-mah], *f.* Sweet perfume. *V.* ALMEA.

tímidamente [tee'-me-dah-men-tay], *adv.* Timidly, fearfully, timorously.

timidez [te-me-deth'], *f.* Timidity, fear, cowardice.

tímido, da [tee'-me-do, dah], *a.* Timid, cowardly, dastardly.

timo [tee´-mo], *m.* Swindle (estafa), confidence trick, confidence game; gag (broma). **Dar un timo a uno,** to swindle somebody.

timón [te-mone'], *m.* 1. Beam of a plough (arado); pole of a coach (carruaje). 2. *(Naut.)* Helm, rudder. 3. Part which governs the movement of various machines. **Timón de dirección,** rudder. **Coger el timón,** to take the helm.

timonear [te-mo-nay-ar'], *va. (Naut.)* To govern the helm; to steer.

timonel [te-mo-nel'], *m. (Naut.)* Timoneer, helmsman.

timonera [te-mo-nay´-rah], *f.* l.*(Naut.)* The helmsman's post before the bittacle. 2. Each of the large tail-feathers of a bird.

timonero [te-mo-nay'-ro], *m.* Timoneer, helmsman.

timorato, to [te-mo-rah'-to, tah], *a.* 1. Full of the fear of God. 2. Timorous (tímido). 3. Prudish (mojigato).

timpa [teem'-pah], *f.* Bar of iron in a furnace hearth.

timpánico, ca [tim-pah'-ne-co, cah], *a. (Anat.)* Tympanic, relating to the eardrum.

timpanillo [tim-pah-neel'-lyo], *m. dim.* 1. A small kettle drum, a small tympanum or tympan. 2. *(Print.)* Inner tympan of a printing-press. 3.*(Arch.)* Gablet, a small ornamental gable or gabled canopy.

timpanítico, ca [tim-pah-nee'-te-so, cah], *a.* Affected with tympanites or wind-dropsy.

timpanitis [tim-pah-nee´-tis], *f. (Med.)* 1. Tympanites, distension of the abdomen by gases. 2. Myringitis, inflammation of the eardrum.

tímpano [teem'-pah-no], *m.* 1. Kettledrum. 2. *(Anat.)* Tympanum, the drum of the ear. 3. Tympan of a printing-press. 4. Cylinder. 5. *(Arch.)* Tympanum.

tina [tee´-nah], *f.* 1. A large earthen jar. 2. Vat, dyer's cooper (recipiente). 3. Bathing-tub.

tinaco [te-nah´-co], *m.* 1. Wooden trough, tub, or vat. 2. *(Mex.)* Water tank (cisterna).

tinada [te-nah'-dah], *f.* 1. Pile of wood or timber. 2. Shed for cattle.

tinado, tinador [te-nah´-do, te-nah-dor'], *m.* Shed for sheltering cattle.

tinaja [te-nah´-hah], *f.* A large earthen jar.

tinajería [te-nah-hay-ree´-ah],*f. (Prov.)* The place where large earthen jars are kept.

tinajero [te-nah-hay'-ro], *m.* 1. One who makes or sells water-jars. 2. *(Mex.)* Kitchen dresser. 3. *V.* TINAJERÍA.

tinajica, illa, ita [te-nah-hee'-cah], *f. dim.* A small earthen wide-mouthed jar.

tinajón [te-nah-hone'], *m.* 1. A large wide-mouthed jar for catching rain. 2. A fat and lusty person.

tinero [te-nay'-ro], *m.* Dyer who takes care of the copper in woollen manufactories.

tineta [te-nay'-tah], *f. dim.* of TINA. Kit, small tub.

tinge [teen'-hay], *m. (Orn.)* Kind of black owl.

tingladillo [tin-glah-deel'-lyo], *m. (Naut.)* Clinker-work, lap-pointed work having the edges overlapping and riveted together.

tinglato [tin-glah'-to], *m.* 1. A small roof jutting out from the wall to shelter people from the rain. 2. A hovel, a covered passage. 3. Workshop, shed.

tinglar [tin-glar'], *vn. (Naut.)* To make lap-jointed work.

tingle [teen'-glay], *f.* Instrument used by glaziers for opening the lead and flatting it on the glass.

tinica, illa, ita [te-nee'-cah], *m. dim.* A small vat.

tinicla [te-nee'-clah], *f. (Mil. Antiq.)* Large coat of arms.

tiniebla [te-ne-ay'-blah], *f.* Darkness (oscuridad), obscurity, privation of light. **Estamos en tinieblas sobre sus proyectos**, we are in the dark about his plans. *-pl.* l. Utter darkness, hell; the night; gross ignorance; matins sung the last three days of Holy week.

tinillo [te-neel'-lyo], *m.* A tank for collecting must as it flows from the wine-press.

tino [tee'-no], *m.* 1. Skill in discovering things by the act of feeling (habilidad). 2. A steady hand to hit the mark. 3. Judgment, prudence, circumspection. 4. Knack, dexterity. 5. *(Zool.)* A wood-boring beetle. 6. Tact (tacto), good judgement (juicio). 7. Moderation (moderación). **Salir de tino**, to be out of one's senses. **Sacar de tino**, (a) to astound, to confound. (b) to make one angry; to act inconsiderately.

tinta [teen'-tah], *f.* 1. Tint, hue, color. 2. Ink. 3. Dye (de pulpo), ink. 3. Act, process of dyeing. 4. *pl.* Colors prepared for pointing. **De buena tinta**, *(Coll.)* Efficaciously, ably. **Saber algo de buena tinta**, to know from good authority. **Tinta de imprenta**, printing-ink. **Con tinta**, in ink. **Medias tintas**, half measures (medidas).

tintar [tin-tar'], *va.* To tinge, to dye. *V.* TEÑIR.

tinte [teen'-tay], *m.* 1. Act and effect of dyeing or staining (acto). 2. Tint, paint, color, stain: dye. 3. A dyer's shop. 4. Palliation, cloak, color.

tintero [tin-tay'-ro], *m.* 1. Ink-well, inkstand. 2. A printer's ink-fountain or ink-table. **Dejar or dejarse en el tintero**, *(Coll.)* to forget or omit designedly. **Quedársele a uno en el tintero**, *(Coll.)* to forget a thing entirely.

tintillo [tin-teel'-lyo], *m. (Dim.)* A light-colored wine.

tintín [tin-teen'], *m.* Clink, a sharp sound of metals, or of glasses striking together.

tintinear [tin-te-nay-ar'], *vn.* To tinkle (de campanilla), to jingle (de cadena).

tintineo [tin-te-nay'-o], *m.* Tinkling (de una campanilla)

tintirintín [tin-te-ren-teen'], *m.* Echo or sound of a trumpet, or other sharp-sounding instrument.

tinto, ta [teen'-to, tah], *a. 1.* Deep-colored. 2. Dyed (teñido); stained (manchado). *V.* TEÑIDO. **Vino tinto**, red wine.

tintóreo, rea [tin-toh'-ray-o, ah], *a.* Tinctoreal, affording color, or pertaining to hues.

tintorera [tin-to-ray'-rah], *f. (Zool. Amer.)* The female of the shark.

tintorería [tin-to-ray-ree'-ah], *f.* 1. Dry cleaning and dyeing. 2. Dry cleaning shop (tienda). 3. *(Tec.)* Dye-works (fábrica).

tintorero, ra [tin-to-ray'-ro, rah], *m. & f.* Dyer.

tintura [tin-too'-rah], *f.* 1. Dyeing or staining (acto). 2. Tincture, color or taste superadded by something. 3. Tint, color, stain, spot. 4. Paint for ladies. 5. Superficial knowledge, smattering. 6. Tincture, extract of drugs. **Tintura de yodo**, iodine.

tinturar [tin-too-rar'], *va.* 1. To tingle, to dye, to imbue or impregnate with color or taste. 2. To tincture, to imbue the mind, to teach superficially.

tiña [tee'-nyah], *f.* 1. Scalled-head, ring-worm of the scalp, favus. It forms yellow crusts. 2. *(Coll.)* Want, indigence, wretchedness. 3. Meanness (tacañería), close-fistedness. 4. Small spider which injures beehives.

tiñería [te-nyay-ree'-ah], *f.* Poverty, indigence, misery. *(Vulg.)* Meanness.

tiñoso, sa [te-nyo'-so, sah], *m.* 1. Scabby, scurvy. 2. Penurious, niggardly, miserable (miserable); sordid, mean.

tiñuela [te-nyoo-ay'-lah], *f. V.* CUSCUTA.

tío [tee'-o], *m.* 1. Uncle. 2. *(Coll.)* Good old man: used colloquially for a peasant. *V.* TÍA. **Tío abuelo**, great-uncle. **Ese tío del sombrero alto**, that guy with the tall hat. **Es un tío grande**, he's a great guy.

tiorba [te-or'-bah], *f.* Theorbo, a large lute.

tiovivo [tee-oh-vee'-vo], *m.* Merry-go-round, carrousel.

tipa [tee'-pah], *f. (Amer.)* 1. A basket made of hide. 2. A great tree of Peru the wood of which is prized for the cubing of ships.

tipazo [te-pah'-tho], *m.* Tall guy (hombre grande), big guy; arrogant fellow (arrogante); *(And.)* Big wig (persona importante).

típico, ca [tee'-pe-co, cah], *a.* 1. Typical (característico), characteristic. 2. Quaint (pintoresco); picturesque; full of local color (lleno de color local); rich in folklore (folklórico); traditional (tradicional). **Baile típico**, regional dance. **Unas jóvenes con su típico peinado**, some girls with their hair done in the traditional fashion.

tiple [tee'-play], *m.* 1. Treble, the highest musical register of instruments or voices; soprano (voz). 2. *(com.)* One who sings treble. 3. A small guitar. 4. *m.* (Slang) Tipple, wine. 5. *(Naut.)* Mast of a single piece.

tiplisonante [te-ple-so-nahn'-tay], *a. (Coll.)* Treble-toned.

tipo [tee'-po], *m.* 1. Type (clase), sort, kind, pattern, model, figure. 2. Printing type. 3. Rate. 4. Fellow, chap (hombre). 5. Build, physique (de hombre). **Tipo de cambio,** rate of exchange. **Tipo de interés**, rate of interest. **Tipo nuevo de bicicleta**, a new kind of bicycle. **Dos tipos sospechosos**, two suspicious characters. **Tipo gótico**, Gothic type.

tipografía [te-po-grah-fee'-ah], *f.* 1. Printing. *V.* IMPRENTA. 2. Typography, type-setting.

tipográfico, ca [te-po-grah'-fe-co, cah], *a.* Typographical.

tipógrafo [te-po'-grah-fo], *m.* Printer.

tipolita, [te-po-lee'-tah], *f.* Typolite, a stone or fossil which preserves the impression of an animal or plant.

típula [tee'-poo-lah], *f.* Tipula, crane fly, daddy-long-legs; an insect looking like a huge mosquito.

tiquín [te-keen'], *m.* A long cane used in place of oars by Philippine Indians.

tira [tee'-rah], *f.* 1. A long narrow stripe; list. 2. A light dart or arrow. 3. *(Naut.)* Fall. 4. Strip; slip of paper. **Tira de un aparejo**, fall of a tackle. **Tira de películas**, film strip.

tirabala [te-rah-bah'-lah], *m.* Pop-gun.

tirabeque [te-rah-bay'-kay], *m. (Agr.)* Tender peas.

tirabotas [te-rah-bo'-tas], *f.* Boot-hook for pulling on boots.

tirabraguero [te-rah-brah-gay'-ro], *m. (Surg.)* Truss.

tirabuzón [te-rah-boo-thone'], *a* 1 Cork screw (sacacorchos). 2. *(Met.)* Curl (rizo), ringlet of hair.

tiracabeza [te-rah-cah-bay'-thah], *f.* Obstetric forceps.

tirachinas [te-rah-che'-nahs], *m.* Catapult.

tiracol [te-rah-cole'], *m. V.* TIRACUELLO.

tiracuello [te-rah-coo-ay'-lyo], *m.* A sword-belt worn by officers.

tirada [te-rah'-dah], *f.* 1. Cast, throw, the act of throwing (acto). 2. Distance of one place from another (distancia). 3. Process, or space of time. 4. *(LAm.)* Boring speech (discurso). 5. *(Cono Sur)* Hint (indirecta). 6. *(Carib.)* Dirty trick (mala pasada). **De una tirada** or **en una tirada**, at one stretch. 7. Act of printing or stamping. 8. Edition, total number of copies printed. **Tirada aparte**, offprint, reprint.

tiradera [te-rah-day'-rah], *f.* 1. Strap. 2. Indian arrow. 3. *(CAm. Carib. Cono Sur)* Sash (faja); belt (correa); *(Carib.)* harness, strap (de caballo).

tiradero [te-rah-day'-ro], *m.* 1. Post, where a hunter stations himself to shoot game. 2. *(Mex.)* Mess.

tirado, da [te-rah'-do, dah], *a.* As applied to a ship, long and low. *-m.* 1. Wire-drawing. 2. Act of printing press-work.

tirador, ra [te-rah-dor', rah], *m. & f.* 1. Thrower (persona); drawer (cajón). 2. Sharp-shooter, good marksman (persona). 3. An iron button fixed to a door, window, etc., whereby it is opened or shut. 4. *(Print.)* Pressman. 5. Catapult (tirachinas). 6. *(And. Cono Sur)* Wide gaucho belt (cinturón). **Tirador de oro**, gold-wire drawer. *(Prov.)* Rifleman.

tirafondo [te-rah-fon'-do], *m. (Med.)* A ball extractor; extractor for foreign bodies in a wound.

tiralíneas [te-rah-lee'-nay-as], *m.* Instrument for drawing lines; ruling pen, ruler.

tiramiento [te-rabh-me-en'-to], *m.* Tension, act of stretching or making tense.

tiramira [te-rah-mee'-rah], *f.* A long narrow path; a long ridge of mountains.

tiramollar [te-rah-mol-lyar'], *va. (Naut.)* To ease off, to slacken. **Tiramollar un aparejo**, to overhaul a tackle.

tiranamente [te-rah-nah-men'-tay], *adv* Tyrannically. *V.* TIRÁNICAMENTE.

tiranía [te-rah-nee'-ah], *f.* 1. Tyranny, despotic government. 2. Tyranny, severity, inclemency, rigorous command. 3. Exorbitant price of merchandise. 4. Ascendency of some passion.

tiránicamente [te-rah'-ne-cah-men-tay], *adv.* Tyrannically, violently, imperiously.

tiranicida [te-rah-ne-thee'-dah], *a. & m* Tyrannicide, one who kills a tyrant.

tiranicidio [te-rah-ne-thee'-de-o], *m.* Tyrannicide, the killing of a tyrant.

tiránico, ca [te-rah'-ne-co, cah], *a.* Tyrannical, despotic, imperious.

tiranización [te-rah-ne-thah-the-on'], *f.* Tyranny, despotism.

tiranizadamente [te-rah-ne-thah-dah-men'-tah], *adv.* Tyrannically.

tiranizar [te-rah-ne-thar'], *va.* 1. To tyrannize, to domineer, to oppress. 2. To usurp. 3. To extort high prices.

tirano, na [te-rah'-no, nah], *a. & n.* 1. Tyrannical, despotic, arbitrary. 2. Applied to a merchant who sells goods at an exorbitant price. 3. Tyrannical (pasiones).

tirano [te-rah'-no], *m.* 1. Tyrant, a despotic ruler, severe master. 2. Merchant who sells goods at an exorbitant price. 3. Ruling passion. 4. *(Zool.)* Tyrant fly-catcher.

tirante [te-rahn'-tay], *m.* 1. Joist which runs across a beam. 2. Trace part of a harness; gear. 3. *(Mech.)* Brace, collar-piece, beam; stay rod, tie rod. 4. Suspenders, braces. 5. *(Arch.)* Anchor, truss-rod, a special apparatus employed in certain constructions. *-a.* 1. Tight (cuerda), extended, drawn; tightly bound. 2. Tense, strained (relaciones, situación). **Traer or tener la cuerda tirante**, to use too much rigor. **Las cosas andan algo tirantes**, things are rather strained.

tirantez [te-ran-teth'], *f.* 1. Length of a thing which runs in a straight line. 2. Tenseness, tightness (tensión). **Ha disminuido la tirantez**, the tension has lessened.

tirapié [te-rah-pay'], *m.* Stirrups or strap, with which shoemakers make their work fast.

tirar [te-rar'], *va. & vn.* 1. To throw (lanzar), to cast, to dart, to fling; to toss. 2. To imitate, to resemble. 3. To attract (imán); to draw towards one. 4. To incline to, to tend (tender). 5. To hurt, to injure, to thwart. 6. To tug, to pull (objeto); to draw. 7. To discharge firearms, to fire, to let off. 8. To persuade, to induce, or lend by compulsion. 9. To earn, to acquire, to gain, or become entitled to it. 10. To continue in the same state without declining from it. **El enfermo va tirando**, the invalid is pulling through. 11. To enlarge, to extend. 12. To lavish. 13. *(Print.)* To print sheets. 14. To draw metal into slender threads. 15. *V.* QUITAR. 16. To receive or take an

allotted part. 17. To direct one's course, to take the road. **Tire Vd. por este camino**, take this way. **Tire Vd. a la derecha**, turn to the right. 18. To tend, to aim at (proponerse); to make use of means and direct them to some end. **Tirar a la mar**, *(Naut.)* To throw overboard; to stand out to sent. **A todo tirar**, to the utmost, to the greatest extent. **Tira y afloja**, (1) a boyish game. (2) *(Met.)* last and loose, blowing hot and cold, ordering and counter-ordering. **Tirarlas de guapo or de rico**, to claim (presume on being) to be pretty, or rich. **El viento ha tirado la valla**, the wind has knocked the fence down. **Has tirado el dinero comprando eso**, you´ve thrown your money away buying that. **Este vestido tira un poco de aquí**, this dress is a bit tight here. **No le tira el estudio**, study does not attract him. **Tirar a su padre**, to take after one´s father. **Tira tú ahora**, it´s your go now. *-vr.* To throw oneself (lanzarse). **Tirarse por la ventana**, to throw oneself out of the window.

tirela [te-ray'-lah], *f.* A striped stuff.

tireta [te-ray'-tah], *f. (Prov.)* Ribbon or thong of leather.

tirica, ita [te-ree'-cah], *f. dim.* A small stripe of linen.

tiricia [te-ree'-the-ah], *f.* Jaundice. *V.* ICTERICIA.

tirilla [te-reel'-lyah], *f.* 1. A piece of backstitched linen used for a neck-band of a shirt. 2. *(Cono Sur)* Shabby dress.

tirio, ria [tee'-re-o, ah], *a.* Tyrian, of Tyre.

tirita [te-ree'-tah], *f. (Cos.)* Tag, tape; *(Med.)* plaster.

tiritaña [te-re-tah'-nyah], *f.* 1. A sort of thin silk; thin woollen cloth. 2. A thing of little value.

tiritar [te-re-tar'], *vn.* To shiver, to shake from cold. **Tiritar de risa**, to titter. **Dejaron el pastel tiritanto**, they almost finished the cake off.

tiritón [te-re-tone'], *m. (Coll.)* Shivering, shaking from cold.

tiritona [te-re-to´-nah], *f. (Coll.)* Shivering, especially affected.

tiro [tee'-ro], *m.* 1. Cast, throw (lanzamiento), shot, fling. 2. Shot, range, the distance traversed by a projectile. 3. Mark made by a throw (señal). 4. Charge, shot; gun which is discharged. 5. Theft. 6. Prank, imposition. 7. Serious physical or moral injury. 8. Set of coach-horses or mules. 9. Trace of coach-harness. 10. Rope which pulls up the materials used in building. 11. Landing-place of a stairway. 12. The report of firearms. 13. **Tiro de una mina**, the shaft of a mine. 14. *(Arquit.)* Flight of stairs. 15. Draught (de chimenea). 16. Veiled attack (ataque). 17. *(And. Cono Sur, Mex.)* Marble (canica). 18. *(Cono Sur)* Distance, course (carreras). 19. *(Mex.)* Issue (número). 20. *(Cono Sur)* Hint (indirecta). 21. *(Carib.)* Craftiness (astucia). **Una pistola de tres o cuatro tiros**, a three or four barrelled pistol or revolver. **Tiro al blanco**, target practice. **Le pegó un tiro a su amante**, she shot her lover. **Matar a uno a tiros**, to shoot somebody. **Estar a tiro**, to be within range.

tirocinio [te-ro-thee'-ne-o], *m.* 1. First attempt, essay, or trial. 2. Novitiate, in the religious sense.

tiroideo, dea [te-ro'-e-day-o, ah], *a.* Thyroid.

tiroides [te-ro'-e-des], *f.* Thyroid, thyroid gland.

tirolés, sa [te-ro-les´, sah], *a.* Tyrolian, of the Tyrol. *-m.* Peddler, trader in toys and tinware.

tirón [te-ron'], *m.* 1. Tyro, beginner, novice, apprentice. 2. Pull (acción brusca), haul, tug. 3. *V.* ETIRÓN. 4. Time. *V.* VEZ. **De un tirón**, at once, at a stroke. **Le dieron un tirón a su bolso**, they snatched her bag. **Se lo bebió de un tirón**, he drank it down in one go.

tiroriro [te-ro-ree'-ro], *m. (Coll.)* Sound of a musical wind-instrument; the instrument itself.

tirotear [te-ro-tay-ar'], *vn.* To shoot at random.

tiroteo [te-ro-tay'-o], *m.* Shooting at random (tiros), sharp-shooting; irregular discharge of musketry; gunfight (batalla); skirmish (escaramuza).

tirreno, na [tir-ray'-no, nah], *a.* Tyrrhene, relating to ancient Tuscany.

tirria [teer´-re-ah], *f. (Coll.)* Aversion, antipathy, dislike. **Tener tirria a**, to dislike.

tirso [teer'-so], *m.* Wand, used in sacrifices to Bacchus. *V.* TALLO.

tisana [te-sah'-nah], *f.* A medical drink.

tisanuro, ra [te-sah-noo'-ro, rah], *m.* Thysanuran: applied to a division of wingless insects; spring-tails, bristletails.

tísica [tee'-se-cah], *f.* Phthisis. *V.* TISIS.

tísico, ca [tee'-se-co, cah], *a. & n.* 1. Phthisical. 2. Applied to a person troubled with phthisis or consumption. **Estar tísico**, to be phthisical, consumptive.

tisis [tee'-sis], *f.* Phthisis, phthisie, pulmonary consumption.

tisú [te-soo'], *m.* Tissue, a silk stuff interwoven with gold and silver.

titanato [te-tah-nah'-to], *m. (Chem.)* Titanate, a salt of titanic acid.

titánico, ca [te-tah'-ne-co, cah], *a.* 1. Titanic, relating to the Titans. 2. Huge, colossal. 3. *(Chem.)* Pertaining to the metal titanium.

titanio [te-tah'-ne-o], *m.* Titanium.

titano [te-tah'-no], *m. (Chem.)* Titanium, a dark-gray metallic element.

títere [tee'-tay-ray], *m.* 1. Puppet marionette. 2. Dwarf, a ridiculous little fellow. **No dejar títere con cabeza**, to turn everything upside down.

titerero, ra [te-tay-ray'-ro, rah], *a. V.* TITIRITERO.

tití [te-tee'], *m.* A very small monkey.

titicana [te-te-cah'-nah], *f. (Bot.)* A sour cane of America.

titilación [te-te-lah-the-on'], *f.* Titillation, tickling slight pleasure.

titilar [te-te-lar'], *va.* l. To titillate, to tickle. 2. To please by slight gratification.

titímalo [te-tee'-mah-lo], *m. (Bot.)* Spurge, a plant with a milky acrid juice. *V.* LECHETREZNA.

titiritaina [te-te-re-tah'-e-nah], *f. (Coll.)* Confused noise of flutes or festive amusements.

titiritero [te-te-re-tay'-ro], *f & m.* Puppet player, a puppet-show man.

tlto [tee'-to], *m. (Bot.)* A land of chick-peas.

titubear [te-too-bay-ar'], *vn.* 1. To totter (al andar), to stagger. 2. To stutter, to stammer. 3. To waver, to hesitate (vacilar). **Titubear en**, to hesitate to.

titubeo [te-too-bay'-o], *m.* Vacillation, wavering; making trials or essays.

titulado [te-too-lah'-do], *m.* Person having a title of nobility. *-a* To be entitled (libro). 3. *(Univ.)* Having a degree (persona). **—Titulado, da,** *pp.* of TITULAR.

titular [te-too-lar'], *a.* Titular, distinguished by a title; titulary.

titular [te-too-lahr'], *va.* To title, to give a title or name. *-vn.* To obtain a title from a sovereign. *-vr.* 1. To be given some title. 2. To hold such and such a title, to be entitled (llamarse).

titulillo [te-too-leel'-lyo], *m. dim.* 1. A petty title. 2. In typography, the caption or motto put at the top of the page above the text.

titulizado, da [te-too-le-thah'-do, dah], *a.* Titled, distinguished.

título [tee'-too-lo], *m.* 1. Title, an inscription on the exterior of something. 2. Title, heading, a division of the contents of a literary work. 3. Title, an appellation of honor: in Spain it designates the dignity of duke, marquis, count, viscount, or baron (noble). 4. Title, foundation of a claim or right: legal title to property. 5. A diploma, a patent, a title, given to empower anyone to exercise a profession (cualificación profesional). 6. Cause, reason, pretext. 7. *(Com.)* Claim, a name given to diverse documents which represent public debt. **A título**, on presence, under pretext. **A título de**, by way of title. **Título universitario**, university degree. **Título de propiedad**, title deed. **Le sobran títulos para hacerlo**, he has every right to do it.

tiza [tee'-thah], *f.* 1. Calcined stag's horn. 2. Whiting, a kind of chalk or pipeclay, used by silversmiths. 3. Chalk for blackboards or for billiard cues.

tizna [teeth'-nah], *f.* Matter for staining or blackening.

tiznajo [teeth-nah'-ho], *m. (Coll.) V.* TIZNÓN.

tiznar [teeth-nar'], *va.* 1. To smut, to stain (manchar). 2. To tarnish, to blot. *-vr.* 1. To get smudged, to get soiled (mancharse). 2. *(CAm. Cono Sur, Mex.)* To get drunk (emborracharse).

tizne [teeth'-nay], *com.* Soot which sticks to frying-pans or kettles (mugre); the smut of coal.

tiznón [teeth-none'], *m.* A large spot, soil, or stain.

tizo [tee'-tho], *m.* Half-burnt charcoal.

tizón [tee-thon'], *m.* 1. Half-burnt wood. 2. Smut in wheat and other grains. 3. *(Met.)* Spot, stain (mancha), disgrace. 4. That part of a hewn stone which is concealed in the wall.

tizona [tee-tho'-nah], *f. (Coll.)* Name of El Cid's famous sword.

tizonada [te-tho-nah'-dah], *f.* Stroke with a half-burnt stick.

tizonazo [te-tho-nah'-tho], *m.* 1. Stroke with burning charred wood. 2. In Jocular style, hell fire.

tizoncillo [te-thon-theel'-lyo], *m.* 1. *(Dim.)* A small burning coal. 2. Mildew, a little smut in corn.

tizonear [te-tho-nay-ar'], *vn.* To stir up a fire; to arrange wood or coals for lighting a fire.

tizonera [te-tho-nay´-rah], *f.* Heap of ill-burnt charcoal.

tizonero [te-tho-nay´-ro], *m.* Poker, for stirring the fire.

tlascalteca [tlas-cal-tay'-cah], *a.* Of Tlascala, a state in Mexico.

tlazole [tlah-tho'-lay], *m. (Mex.)* Maize tops serving as forage to beasts.

tmesis [may-sis], *f. (Gram.)* Figure in poetry which divides a compound word into two.

TNT, Abbreviation of **Trinitrotolueno**, *m.* TNT, Trinitrotoluene.

toa [to´-ah], *f.* In some parts of America rope, hawser.

toalla [to-ah-lyah], *f.* 1. Towel. 2. Pillow-sham. **Toalla afelpada**, turkish towel.

toallero [to-ahl-lyay'-ro], *m.* Towel rail.

toalleta [to-al-lyay'-tah], *f. dim.* Napkin; small towel.

toba [to'-bah], *f.* 1. *(Bot.)* Cotton thistle. 2. *(Prov.)* Stalk of a thistle given to asset. 3. Calcareous matter on the teeth. 4. Tophus, a spongy stone; a calcareous tufa; sinter.

tobera [to-bay'-rah], *f.* Towel, tubers, an iron pipe, through which the nozzle of bellows is thrust in a forge.

tobillera [to-be-lyay'-rah], *f.* 1. Anklet. 2. *(Coll.)* Bobby-soxer, adolescent girl (adolescente).

tobillo [to-beel-lyo], *m.* The ankle.

tobogán [to-bo-gahn'], *m.* 1. Toboggan (trineo). 2. Switchback (de feria). 3. Children slide (para niños).

toca [to'-cah], *f.* A hood; a thin stuff: toque, a kind of headdress (sombrero).

tocadiscos [to-cah-dees'-cos], *m. (Coll.)* Phonograph, record player.

tocado [to-cah'-do], *m.* Ornament, dress; coiffure, headdress (sombrero), head-gear a set of ribbons for garnishing a dress. **Tocado de mujer,** commode, the head-dress.

tocado, da [to-cah'-do], *a. & pp.* of TOCAR. Touched, felt; contaminated; infected. **Estar tocada alguna cosa,** to have begun to rot or putrefy.

tocador, ra [to-cah-dor', rah], *m. & f.* 1. One who beats or touches. *-m.* 2. Handkerchief round the head. 3. Toilet, a lady´s dressing-case or table (neceser, mueble). 4. Dressing room (cuarto). 5. *(Prov.)* Key for tuning musical instruments.

tocadorcito [to-cah-dor-thee'-to], *m. dim.* of TOCADOR.

tocamiento [to-cah-me-en'-to], *m.* 1. Touch, contact. 2. Supernatural inspiration.

tocante [to-cahn'-tay], *a.* Respecting, relative.

tocante, or **tocante a,** *prep.* Concerning, relating to; in order to.

tocar [to-car'], *va.* 1. To touch. 2. Touch a thing lightly; to reach with the hand. 3. To play on a musical instrument. 4. To toll or ring a bell. 5. To try metals on a touch stone, to touch, to magnetize; to examine, to prove. 6. To touch, to bent of, to discuss a matter lightly (tema). 7. To know a thing certainly. 8. To touch (conmover), to inspire, to move, to persuade. 9. To strike slightly, to sound anything. 10. To hit, to strike (obstáculo). 11. To suffer, to undergo (consecuencias). 12. To touch, to communicate or infect; to chastise. 13. To comb and dress the hair with ribbons. -vn. 1. To appertain, to belong. 2. To interest, to concern; to be a duty or obligation; to import. 3. To fall to one's share or lot. 4. To touch, to be contiguous to; to arrive in passing. 5. To be allied or related. **Tocar de cerca alguna cosa,** to have an interest, to be concerned. **Tocar de cerca algún asunto,** to have complete knowledge of a subject or matter. **Tocar a la puerta,** to rap at the door. **Tocar la diana,** (All.) to bent the reveille. **A toca teja,** (Coll.) ready money. **Tocarle a uno,** to fall to somebody. **Te toca jugar,** it´s your turn. **Ahora toca torcer a la derecha,** now you have to turn right. -vr. 1. (Coll.) To be covered, to put on the hat. 2. To comb and arrange the hair.

tocasalva [to-cah-sahl'-vah], f. V. SALVILLA.

tocata [to-cah'-tah], f. A musical composition of brief extend for some instrument: toccata.

tocayo, ya [to-cah'-yo, yah], a. Having the same name, namesake.

tochedad [to-chey-dahd'], f. Clownishness, rusticity, ignorance.

tocho [toh'-cho], m. 1. (Prov.) Pole. 2. Bar of iron.

tocho, cha [toh'-cho, chah], a. Clownish, unpolished, homespun.

tochura [to-choo'-rah], f. (Prov.) Waggishness, sarcastic gaiety.

tocinero, ra [to-the-nay'-ro, rah], m. & f. Porkman, one who sells pork or bacon.

tocino [to-thee'-no], m. 1. Bacon, salt pork. 2. Hog's lard. **Tocino rancio,** rank pork.

tocología [to-co-lo-hee'-ah], f. Tocology, the art of obstetrics.

tocólogo [to-co'-lo-go], m. Tocologist, obstetrician.

tocón [to-cone'], m. Stump of a tree; stump of an arm or leg.

toconal [to-co-nahl'], m. An olive-yard plumed with stumps.

tocororo [to-co-ro'-ro], m. (Zool.) A Cuban trogon, with lively colors.

tocuyo [to-coo'-yo], m. (Ven. Peru) A plain home-spun cotton stuff.

todabuena, todasana [to-dah-boo-ay´-nah, to-dah-sah'-nah], f. (Bot.) A medicinal species of St. John´s-wort.

todavía [to-dah-vee'-ah], adv. 1. Notwithstanding, nevertheless. 2. Yet, still. **Todavía no,** not yet. **Todavía no lo ha encontrado,** he still has not found it.

todi [to'-de], m. (Zool.) Tody, a West Indian insectivorous bird, having the head and neck of brilliant green.

todo, da [toh'-do, dah], a. y pron. All, whole (entero), entire, every. **Me gusta todo,** I like everything. **Toda la casa ardió,** the whole house burnt. **Con todo eso,** not withstanding, nevertheless, however. **A todo,** at most. **Del todo,** entirely, quite. **En todo y por todo,** wholly, absolutely. **Ser el todo,** to be the principal or chief. **Hacer a todo,** to be fit for anything. **Me gusta todo,** I like everything. **Todos los días,** every day.-adv. Entirely, totally, completely, all. **A todo riesgo,** fully comprehensive. **Con todas mis fuerzas,** with all my might. **Todo el mundo,** everybody, everyone. **Todo lo que sé,** all that I know. **En todo el día no lo he visto,** I haven't seen him all day. **Todos ustedes,** all of you. **Todo eran quejas,** it was all complaints.

todo [toh'-do], m. 1. Whole composition of integral parts. 2. (Geom.) A greater quantity compared with a less. 3. All, everything. **Todos,** everybody. **Lo han vendido todo,** they´ve sold it all. **Tienen un coche nuevo y todo,** they have a new car and everything. **Ir a todo,** to go forward resolutely. **A pesar de todo,** even so. **Para todo,** all-purpose.

todopoderoso, sa [to-do-po-day-ro'-so, sah], a. All-powerful, almighty; properly applied to God only. -m. The Almighty.

toesa [to-ay'-sah], f. Toise, fathom; a French measure.

tofana [to-fah'-nah], f. & a. A very active poison.

tofo [to'-fo], m. Tumor in the belly of cattle.

toga [to'-gah], f. 1. Toga, loose cloak (worn by professors, judges graduates, etc.). 2. Dignity of a superior judge. **Tomar la toga,** to qualify as a lawyer.

togado, da [to-gah'-do, dah], a. Gowned: applied to those who have a right to wear a toga.

toisón [to-e-sone'], m. The name of the highest order of Spanish knighthood; the Golden Fleece. V. TUSÓN.

tojal [to-hahl'], m. Clump of furze or whin.

tojines [to-hee'-nes], m. pl. (Naut.) Belaying cleats.

tojino [to-hee´-no], m. (Naut.) Notch or knob to secure anything from moving in a ship; pieces of wood on the sides of a vessel used as steps.

tojo [to'-ho], m. (Bot.) Whin, furze.

tola [to'-lah], f. An Indian mound (S. America.)

tolano [to-lah´-no], m. Tumor in horses' gums. -pl. (Coll.) Short hair on the neck.

tolda [tol´-dah], f. 1. (Naut.) Awning. 2. (Carib.) Large sack (bolsa grande). 3. (And.) Tent (tienda).

toldadura [tol-dah-doo´-rah], f. Hanging of stuff to moderate the light or heat.

toldar [tol-dar'], va. V. ENTOLDAR.

toldero [tol-day'-ro], m. (Prov.) Retailer of salt.

toldilla [tol-deel'-lyah], f. (Naut.) Bound-house.

toldillo [tol-deel'-lyo], m. 1. Covered sedan-chair. 2. (Dim.) Small awning.

toldo [tol'-do], m. 1. Awning (de playa). 2. (Prov.) Shop where salt is retailed. 3. Ostentation, pomp. 4. (And. Cono Sur) Indian hut. 5. (Mex.) Hood, top. 6. (Fig.) pride.

tole tole [to´-lay to´-lay], m. Confused noise of the populace. (Coll.) **Tomar el tole,** to run off, to flee.

toledano, na [to-lay-dah'-no, nah], a. Toledan, of Toledo.

toledo [to-lay'-do], m. A song-bird of Central America.

tolerable [to-lay-rah´-blay], a. Tolerable, supportable.

tolerablemente [to-lay-rah'-blay-men-tay], adv. Tolerably, middlingly.

tolerancia [to-lay-rahn'-the-ah], f. Toleration, permission; tolerance, indulgence.

tolerante [to-lay-rahn´-tay], a. Tolerant: applied to a government which tolerates freedom of worship, and to persons who tolerate what they cannot approve.

tolerantismo [to-lay-ran-tees'-mo], m. Free exercise of all worship and religious opinions.

tolerar [to-lay-rar´], va. To tolerate, to suffer, to permit; to indulge, to overlook, to comport. **No se puede tolerar esto,** this cannot be tolerated. **Su madre le tolera demasiado,** his mother spoils him.

tolete [to-ray´-tay], m. 1. (Naut.) Thole, thole-pin. 2. (Amer.) A small club for catching alligators. 3. (Cuba) A stick.

tolla [tol´-lyah], f. 1. Bog, commonly covered with moss. V. TOLLADAR. 2. (Cuba) A canoe-shaped trough for watering horses.

tolladar [tol-lyah-dar'], m. V. ATOLLADERO.

tollina [tol-lyee´-nah], f. (Coll.) Cudgelling, cowhiding.

tollo [tol'-lyo], m. 1. (Zool.) Spotted dog-fish. 2. Cave or hollow for concealing sportsmen in wait for game. 3. Bog. V. ATOLLADERO.

tolondro, tolondrón [to-lon´-dro], m. 1. Contusion on the head arising from a blow 2. A giddy, hare-brained fellow.

tolondrón, na [to-lon-drone', nah], a. Giddy, hare-brained; foolish. **A tolondrones,** precipitately, giddily, inconsiderately, interruptedly; with contusions or bruises.

tolú [to-loo'], m. A balsam which owes its name to a town in Colombia.

tolva [tol´-vah], f. Hopper (recipiente), in a mill.

tolvanera [tol-vah-nay'-rah], f. Cloud of dust raised by whirlwinds.

toma [to'-mah], f. 1. Taking, receiving, hold, gripe, grasp. 2. Capture, conquest, seizure. 3. Portion of anything taken at once (cantidad). 4. Opening into a canal or drain. 5. Inlet (entrada); outlet (salida); plug (enchufe). 6. (Cine, TV) Take, shot. 7. (LAm.) Irrigation channel (acequia). **Toma de conciencia,** awareness. **Toma de antena,** aerial socket.

Toma directa, live shot. *-int.* There, well, what. **Toma de circuito integrado,** *(Comput.)* IC socket.

tomada [to-mah´-dah], *f.* 1. Conquest, capture, seizure. 2. Take, the quantity of copy taken at one time by a compositor for setting up; the same in type.

tomadero [to-mah-day´-ro], *m.* 1. Handle (asidero), haft. 2. Opening into a drain.

tomado [to-mah´-do], *m.* Ornamental plait in cloths. **-Tomado, da,** *pp.* of TOMAR.

tomador, ra [to-mah-dor´, rah], *m. & f.* 1. Taker, receiver. 2. Retriever, a dog that finds or fetches the game. 3. *(Coll.)* Pickpocket, pilferer.

tomadura [to-mah-doo´-rah], *f.* Catch, seizure, gripe, hold, grasp, capture: commonly, the portion of a thing taken at once.

tomajón, na [to-mah-hone', nah], *a.* Taking or accepting easily or frequently.

tomar [to-mar'], *va.* 1. To take (aire, baño, curva, decisión, medida, paso, ruta), to catch, to seize, to grasp (agarrar), to recover. 2. To receive in any mode; to get. 3. To occupy, to capture, to take possession of. 4. To eat or drink. 5. To understand, to apprehend; to interpret, to perceive. 6. To contract, to acquire (afecto, asco). 7. To take into service, to employ. 8. To intercept or block roads or paths. 9. To take by stealth, to rob. 10. To buy, to purchase. 11. To undertake, to apply oneself to a business. 12. To imitate, to copy. 13. To take, to choose, to select. 14. To surprise, to overtake. 15. To surprise, to overwhelm. 16. To cover the female. 17. To take a trick in cards. 18. *(Naut.)* To arrive in port or at an anchoring-place. 19. To take into one's company. 20. With names of instruments, to set about, or execute the action implied. **Tomar la pluma,** to write. 21. In playing ball, to call a halt, because the players are not in their proper places, or some, other reason. *-vn.* 1. To take, to take root. 2. *(LAm.)* To drink (beber). 3. **Toma y daca,** give and take. *-vr.* To get covered with rust (metales). **Tomar calor,** to get warm, to push an affair warmly. **Tomar frío,** to catch cold. **Tomar el fresco,** to take the air. **Tomar el sol,** to take the sun, or expose oneself to the sun. **Tomar fuerzas,** to gather strength. **Tomar resolución,** to resolve. **Tomar por su cuenta,** to take upon one's acount. **Tomar puerto,** *(Naut.)* to get into a port. **Tomarse con alguno** or **tomarla con alguno,** to pick a quarrel with one. **Tomar la puerta,** to go out of the house, to be off. **Tomar a pecho,** to take to heart; to undertake a thing with too much zeal. **Tomar a uno entre cejas** or **entre dientes,** to take a dislike to a person. **Tomar el trabajo** (or **tanto trabajo),** to take trouble for the sake of helping another. **Tomar la delantera,** to excel another. **Tomar el rábano por las hojas,** to put the cart before the horse. **Tomamos unas cervezas,** we had a few beers. **Tomarse la venganza por su mano,** to take vengeance with one´s own hands. **Se lo sabe tomar bien,** he knows how to take it.

tomate [to-mah´-tay], *m. (Bot.)* Tomato, a nutritious vegetable, the fruit of the tomato-plant.

tomatera [to-mah-tay´-rah], *f.* 1. Tomato plant (planta). 2. *(Cono Sur)* Drunk spree (juerga).

tomavistas [to-mah-vees´-tas], *m.* 1 Motion picture camera. 2. Television camera.

tómbola [tom'-bo-lah], *f.* Raffle.

tomento, tomionto [to may'-to], *m.* Coarse tow.

tomentoso, sa [to-men-to'-so, sah], *m. (Bot.)* Tomentose, tomentous; coated with downy wool-like hairs.

tomillar [to-mil-lyar´], *m.* Bed of thyme.

tomillo [to-meel'-lyo], *m. (Bot.)* Thyme.

tominejo, ja [to-me-nay´-ho, hah], *m. & f.* Genus of small bright-plumaged birds, of which the humming-bird is the smallest.

tomiza [to-mee'-thah], *f.* Bass rope.

tomo [to'-mo], *m.* Bulk or body of a thing (bulto). 2. Importance, value, consequence. **Es cosa de mucho tomo,** it is a matter of great consequence. 3. Tome, volume. **De tomo y lomo,** of weight and bulk; of importance.

tomón, na [to-mon'], *a.* Accepting. *V.* TOMAJÓN.

ton [ton], *m. V.* TONO. Used only in the phrase, **sin ton ni son,** without motive or cause, without rhyme or reason; unreasonably, inordinately.

tona [to'-nah], *f. (Prov.)* Surface of a liquid.

tonada [to-nah´-dah], *f.* 1. Tune, a metrical composition suited for singing and the music set to it. 2. *(LAm.)* Accent (acento). 3. *(Carib.)* Fib (embuste); pun (juego de palabras).

tonadica [to-nah-dee´-cah], *f. dim.* A short tune or song.

tonadilla [to-nah-deel'-lyah], *f.* 1. *(Dim.) V.* TONADICA. 2. An interlude of music formerly used in comedies; now seldom employed, and then only at the end.

tonalidad [to-nah-le-dahd'], *f.* 1. *(Mus.)* Key; tonality; tone. 2. (Arte) Shade; color scheme. **Una bella tonalidad de verde,** a beautiful shade of green.

tonante [to-nahn'-tay], *pa. (Poet.)* Thundering (Jupiter).

tonar [to-nar'], *vn. (Post.)* To thunder, to emit a thundering noise.

tonca, tonga [ton'-cah], *f. (Bot.)* The tonka bean, employed in flavoring tobacco (vainilla adulterada.). In Peru called *Pucherí.*

tondino [ton-dee'-no], *m. (Arch.)* Moulding on the astragal of a column.

tonel [to-nel´], *m.* 1. Cask, barrel. 2. *(Naut.)* An ancient measure of ships; ten **toneles** make twelve **toneladas.**

tonelada [to-nay-lah´-dah], *f.* 1. Ton (medida), a measure or weight of twenty hundred-weight. 2. Ton, tonnage (capacidad de un barco). 3. Collection of casks in a ship. **Bajel de quinientas toneladas,** *(Naut.)* a ship of five hundred tons burden. 4. Tonnage duty.

tonelaje [to-nay-lah´-hay], *m.* Tonnage.

tonelería [to-nay-lay-ree´-ah], *f.* 1. Trade of a cooper; workshop of a cooper. 2. Quantity of wafer casks for a ship.

tonelero [to-nay-lay´-ro], *m.* Cooper, trooper.

tonelete [to-nay-lay´-tay], *m.* 1. Ancient armor pasting from the waist to the knees. 2. *(Dim.)* Little butt or barrel.

tonga, tongada [ton'-gah], *f.* 1. Couch; a layer or stratum; lay, row, ledge, flake. 2. *(And. Cono Sur)* Job, task (tarea). 3. *(And.)* Nap (siesta).

tónica [toh'-ne-cah], *f. (Mus.)* Keynote, tonic.

tónico, ca [toh'-ne-co, cah], *a.* Tonic, strengthening.

tónico [toh'-ne-co], *m. (Med.)* Tonic, a medicine.

tonificar [to-ne-fe-cahr'], *va.* To tone up; to invigorate.

tonillo [to-neel'-lyo], *m.* Disagreeable, monotonous tone in reading or speaking.

tonina [to-nee'-nah], *f. (Com.)* Fresh tunny.

tonismo [to-nees'-mo], *m.* Tetanus, according to some writers.

tono [toh'-no], *m.* 1. Tone, modulation of the voice. 2. The manner of doing a thing. 3. Tune. 4. *(Med.)* Tone. 5. A small spiral of horns or metal, which, placed in horns or trumpets, modifies their tone. 6. Tuning-fork (diapason). 7. Deportment, manner, social address. 8. Shade (de color). **Estar a tono,** to be in key. **Bajar el tono,** to lower one´s voice. **Fuera de tono,** inappropriate.

tonsila [ton-see'-lah], *f.* Tonsil.

tonsilar [ton-se-lar'], *a.* Tonsillar, belonging to the tonsils.

tonsilitis [ton-se-le'-tis], *f. (Med.)* Tonsilitis.

tonsura [ton-soo'-rah], *f.* 1. Tonsure, the first clerical degree of the Roman Catholic church. 2. The act of cutting hair or wool.

tonsurar [ton-soo-rar´], *va.* 1. To tonsure (un clérigo) to give the first clerical degree. 2. To cut the hair, to cut off wool.

tontada [ton-tah´-dah], *f.* Nonsense; a foolish speech or action.

tontaina [ton-tah´-e-nah], *com. & a.* Stupid, fool; foolish.

tontamente [ton-tah-men-tay], *adv.* Foolishly, stupidly.

tontazo, za [ton-tah'-tho, thah], *a. aug.* Doltish, very stupid.

tontear [ton-tay-ar'], *vn.* To talk nonsense (hacer el tonto), to act foolishly; to fool.

tontedad, tontera [ton-tay-dhd', ton-tay'-rah], *f. V.* TONTERÍA.

tontería [ton-tay-ree'-ah], *f. 1.* Foolishness (cualidad), foolery, folly, foppery, ignorance; nonsense. 2. Silly thing (cosa); foolish act (acto). 3. Triviality (bagatela). 4. Silly scruple (escrúpulo). **Hacer una tontería**, to do a silly thing. **Lo vendió por una tontería**, he sold it for a song.

tontico [ton-tee'-co], *m. dim.* A little dolt.

tontillo [ton-teel'-lyo], *m. 1. (Dim.) V.* TONTICO. 2. Hoop skirt, a part of a lady's dress.

tontina [ton-tee'-nah], *f.* Tontine, a division of a sum of money among various persons, to be divided at a fixed epoch, with the interest, among the survivors.

tonto, ta [ton'-to, tah], *a.* Stupid, foolish, ignorant, fatuous. **Hacerse el tonto**, to play the fool. **Tonto de capirote**, great fool, idiot. **A tontas y a locas**, sillily and madly, without rhyme or reason, inordinately. *-m. 1.* Clown, funny man. 2. *(And. CAm. Cono Sur)* Jemmy (palanca).

¡top! *(Naut.)* Hold! stop! a word of command.

topacio [to-pah'-the-o], *m.* Topaz, a precious stone.

topada [to-pah'-dah], *f. V.* TOPETADA.

topadizo, za [to-pah-dee'-tho, thah], *a. (Coll.) V.* ENCONTRADIZO.

topador [to-pah-dor'], *m.* Encounterer, one who butts or strikes against another. Said properly of rams and other horned animals.

topar [to-par'], *va. 1.* To run or strike against. 2. To meet with by chance (persona). 3. To depend upon, to consist in. **La dificultad topa en esto**, *(Coll.)* the difficulty consists in this. 4. To accept a bet at cards. *-vn. 1.* To butt or strike with the head. 2. *(Met.)* To abut or lean against. *3. (Mex.)* To quarrel (reñir).

toparca [to-par'-cah], *m.* Toparch, a ruler of a small state, composed of very few places.

toparquía [toh'-par-kee'-ah], *f.* Toparchy, seigniory, jurisdiction or lordship.

tope [toh'-pay], *m. 1.* Top, the highest point or part. 2. Butt (con cabeza), the striking of one thing against another. 3. Rub, the point of difficulty. 4. Obstacle, impediment (pega). 5. Scuffle (pelea), quarrel (riña). 6. The highest point of a mast. **A tope o al tope**, juncture, union, or incorporation of the extremities of things. **Al tope**, conjointly, contiguously. **Hasta el tope**, up to the top, or the brim.

tope [toh'-pay], *a.* Maximum. **Edad tope para un puesto**, maximum age for a job.

topera [to-pay'-rah], *f.* Mole-hole.

topetada [to-pay-tah'-dah], *f.* Butt, by a horned animal.

topetar [to-pay-tar'], *va.* To butt (golpear); to offend, to encounter.

topetón [to-pay-ton'], *m.* Collision, encounter, blow.

topetudo, da [to-pay-too'-do, dah], *a.* Applied to animals accustomed to butt.

tópico, ca [toh'-pe-co, cah], *a.* Topical, belonging to a particular place. *-m. (Med.)* Topical application.

topil [to-peel'], *m. (Mex.) V.* ALGUACIL.

topinaria [to-pe-nah'-re-ah], *f. V.* TARPARIA.

topinera [to-pe-nay'-rah], *f. V.* TOPERA.

topo [toh'-po], *m. 1. (Zool.)* Mole. 2. Stumbler. 3. *(Coll.)* A numbskull, a dolt. 4. A league and a half among the Indians.

topografía [to-po-grah-fee'-ah], *f.* Topography.

topográficamente [to-po-grah'-fe-cah-men-tay], *adv.* Topographically.

topográfico, ca [to-po-grah'-fe-co, cah], *a.* Topographical.

topógrafo [to-pó-grah-fo], *m.* Topographer.

toque [toh'-kay], *m. 1.* Touch (acto), the act of touching. 2. Ringing of bells. 3. A military call by drum or bugle. 4. Essay, trial, test. 5. Touch-stone. 6. Experience, proof. 7. Aid, assistance, or inspiration by God. 8. *(Coll.)* Blow given to anything. **Toque de luz**, light in a picture. **Dar un toque**, to give one a trial in any business. **El primero** or **el segundo toque (de un tambor)**, the first or second beat of a drum.

El último toque (de una campana), the last peal of a bell. 9. *(And.)* Turn (vuelta).

toqueado [to-kay-ah'-do], *m.* Sound of a stroke with the hands or feet.

toquería [to-kay-ree'-ah], *f. 1.* Collection of women's headdresses. 2. Business of making women's veils.

toquero [to-kay'-ro], *m.* Veil-maker for nuns, headdress maker.

toquetear [to-kay-tay-ar'], *va. 1.* To touch repeatedly (manosear). 2. *(Mus.)* To mess about on.

toquilla [to-kee'-lyah], *f. 1. (Dim.)* Small headdress of gauze, small veil. 2. Ribbon or lace round the crown of a hat. 3. A small triangular kerchief used by women for the neck or on the head. 4. The plant from which Panama hats are made.

tora [toh'-rah], *f. 1.* Tribute paid by Jewish families. 2. Book of the Jewish law; Pentateuch, torah (or thorah). *(Heb.)* 3. A herb.

tora [toh'-rah], *f.* Frame or figure of a bull in artificial fireworks.

torácico, ca [to-rah'-the-co, cah], *a. (Anat.)* Thoracic.

torada [to-rah'-dah], *f.* Drove of bulls.

toral [to-rahl'], *a: 1.* Main, principal. 2. Mold (molde).

tórax [to'-rax], *m.* Chest, breast, thorax.

torazo [to-rah'-tho], *m. aug.* Large bull.

torbellino [tor-bel-lyee'-no], *m. 1.* Whirlwind (viento), cyclone. 2. A lively, boisterous, restless person. 3. A concurrence or multitude of things that present themselves at the same time.

torca [tor'-cah], *f.* Cavern in mountains.

torcal [tor-cahl'], *m.* Place where there are caves.

torcaz [tor-cath'], *a.* Applied to gray wild pigeons with white necks.

torce [tor'-thay], *f.* Link of a chain or collar.

torcecuello [tor-thay-coo-ayl'-lyo], *m. (Orn.)* Wry-neck.

torcedero [tor-thay-day'-ro], *m.* Twisting-mill, an engine for twisting.

torcedero, ra [tor-thay-day'-ro, rah], *a. V.* TORCIDO.

torcedor, ra [tor-thay-dor', rah], *m. & f. 1.* Twister, a spindle for twisting thread. 2. Anything which causes displeasure or grief.

torcedura [tor-thay-doo'-rah], *f. 1.* Twisting. 2. A light, paltry wine.

torcer [tor-therr'], *va. 1.* To twist (miembro), to double, to curve, to distort (sentido), to warp (madera). 3. To turn, to deviate from the right road, to deflect, to turn aside. 3. To crook, to pervert from rectitude; to leave the paths of virtue. (Used intransitively in this sense.) 4. To put a wrong construction on anything. 5. To pervert (justicia), as judges do justice. 6. To dissuade, to induce to change an opinion. 7. To impugn, to retort, to refute an argument. *-vn. 1.* To turn (camino, vehículo, viajero). 2. To spin (pelota). **El coche torció a la izquierda**, the car turned left. *-vr. 1.* To be dislocated, to be spruced; to go crooked. 2. To turn sour (vino). 3. To deceive at gaming. **Torcerse un pie**, to twist one's foot.

torcho [tor'-cho], *a.* Said of iron forged into very thin wire.

torcida [tor-thee'-dah], *f.* Wick for lamps and candles.

torcidamente [tor-the'-dah-men-tay], *adv.* Obliquely, tortuously, crookedly.

torcidillo [tor-the-deel'-lyo], *m.* A kind of twisted silk.

torcido, da [tor-thee'-do, dah], *a. & pp.* of TORCER. 1. Oblique, tortuous, crooked (camino). 2. *(And. CAm. Carib.)* Unlucky (desgraciado).

torcido [tor-thee'-do], *m. 1.* A kind of twisted sweetmeat. 2. *(Prov.)* Light, bad wine.

torcijón [tor-the-hone'], *m. 1.* Gripes, pains in the bowels. 2. *V.* TOROZÓN.

torcimiento [tor-the-me-en'-to], *m. 1.* Turning or bending of what was straight. 2. Deflection, deviation from the paths of virtue. 3. Circumlocution or periphrasis.

torculado [tor-coo-lah'-do], *m.* Female screw.

tórculo [tor´-coo-lo], *m.* A small press; a rolling press for prime.

tordella [tor-day´-lyah], *f.* Large kind of thrush.

tórdiga [tor´-de-gah], *f.* Neat's leather for coarse shoes.

tordillo, lla [tor-deel´-lyo, lyah], *a.* Of a thrush-color, grayish, grizzled.

tordo [tor´-do], *m.* (*Orn.*) Thrush.

tordo, da [tor´-do, dah], *a.* Speckled black and white (caballos).

toreador [to-ray-ah-dor´], *m.* Bullfighter: commonly applied to bullfighters on foot.

torear [to-ray-ar´], *va.* 1. To fight in the ring (toro). 2. To let a bull to cows. 3. To dodge (esquivar). 4. (*Fig.*) To keep at bay (mantener a raya). 5. (*Fig.*) To plague (acosar). 6. (*CAm. Cono Sur*) To provoke (animal), to enrage. 7. (*And. Cono Sur*) To bark furiously at (perro). -*vn.* 1. (*Taur.*) To fight, to be a bullfighter. **No volverá a torear**, he will never fight again. 2. (*And. Cono Sur*) To bark furiously.

toreo [to-ray´-o], *m.* Art or practice of fighting bulls.

torería [to-ray-ree´-ah], *f.* (*Cuba, Peru, etc.*) 1. Pranks of young folks. 2. The office of bullfighter.

torero, ra [to-ray´-ro], *m & f.* Bullfighter.

torés [to-res´], *m.* (*Arch.*) Torus, large ring or round moulding at the base of a column.

torete [to-ray-tay], *m.* 1. (*Dim.*) A small bull (animal). 2. (*Colt.*) A difficult point, an intricate business.

torga [tor´-gah], *f.* Yoke put on the necks of hogs.

toril [to-reel´], *m.* Place where bulls are shut up until they are brought out.

torillo [to-ray´-lyo], *m.* 1. (*Dim.*) Little bull. 2. Dowel, a pin for fastening timber. 3. (*Anat.*) Peritoneum.

torio [to´-ree-o], *m.* (*Chem.*) Thorium.

toriondez [to-re-on-deth´], *f.* (*Prov.*) The cow's desire for the bull.

toriondo, da [to-re-on´-do, dh], *a.* Applied to cattle rutting.

torloroto [tor-lo-ro´-to], *m.* A shepherd's pipe or flute.

tormellera [tor-may-lyay´-rah], *f.* Craggy, covered with high rocks.

tormenta [tor-men´-tah], *f.* 1. Perturbation of the waters of the ocean through the violence of winds. 2. Storm (tempestad), tempest; hurricane. 3. Storm, adversity, misfortune (desgracia). **Sufrió una tormenta de celos,** she suffered a great pang of jealousy.

tormentador, ra [tor-men-tah-dor´, rah], *m. & f.* V. ATORMENTADOR.

tormentar [tor-men-tar´], *vn.* To be violently agitated; to suffer a storm.

tormentario, ria [tor-men-tah´-re-o, ah], *a.* Projectile (artillería).

tormentila [tor-men-tee´-lah], *f.* (*Bot.*) Tormentil, septfoil, a slender trailing Old World herb with yellow flowers; its root is a powerful astringent, and has been used in diarrhoea.

tormentín [tor-men-teen´], *m.* (*Naut.*) A small mast on the bowsprit.

tormento [tor-men´-to], *m.* 1. Torment, pain, anguish, torture, pang, affliction. 2. Rack, torture. 3. (*Mil.*) Battering ordnance. **Dar tormento**, to torture, to put to the rack. **Estos zapatos son un tormento**, these shoes are agony.

tormentoso, sa [tor-men-to´-so, sah], *a.* 1. Stormy, boisterous, turbulent. 2. (*Naut.*) Easily dismasted (barco).

tormo [tor´-mo], *m.* Tor, a high, pointed, isolated rock.

torna [tor´-nah], *f.* 1. Restitution. 2. Return (vuelta). V. TORNADA. 3. Drain of water for irrigation. -*pl.* 1. Return, recompense, restitution.

tornaboda [tor-nah-bo´-dah], *f.* Day after a wedding.

tornachile [tor-nah-chee´-lay], *m.* (*Mex.*) A thick pepper.

tornada [tor-nah´-dah], *f.* Return from a journey.

tornadera [tor-nay-day´-rah], *f.* A two-pronged winnowing fork used in Castile.

tornadizo, za [tor-nah-dee´-tho, thah], *a. & m.* Turncoat, deserter.

tornado [tor-nah´-do], *m.* Hurricane in the Gulf of Guinea off western Africa: tornado.

tornadura [tor-nah-doo´-rah], *f.* 1. Return: recompense. 2. Land measure of ten feet.

tornaguía [tor-nah-gee´-ah], *f.* Return of a receipt issued by the custom-house, showing that the goods have arrived at their destination.

tornajo [tor-nah´-ho], *m.* Trough.

tornapunta [tor-nah-poon´-tah], *f.* (*Arch.*) Stay, prop. V. PUNTUAL.

tornar [tor-nar´], *va. & vn.* 1. To return, to restore, to make restitution. 2. To return, to come back again (volver). 3. To repeat, to do again. 4. To change (transformar). **Tornar cabeza a alguna cosa,** (*Coll.*) to attend to anything, to consider, to be attentive.

tornasol [tor-nah-sole´], *m.* l. (*Bot.*) Turnsole, sunflower. V. GIRASOL. 2. Changeable color of stuff.

tornasolar [tor-nah-so-lar´], *va.* To cause changes in color.

tornátil [tor-nah´-teel], *a.* Turned, made by a turner or with a wheel.

tornaviaje [tor-nah-ve-ah´-hay], *m.* Return-trip.

tornavirada [tor-nah-ve-rah´-dah], *f.* A roundabout way; a round trip.

tornavoz [tor-nah-voth´], *m.* Sound-board (de púlpito), or sounding-board.

torneador [tor-nay-ah-dor´], *m.* 1. Turner, one who works on a lathe. V. TORNERO, 1st def. 2. Tilter at tournaments.

torneante [tor-nay-ahn´-tay], *pa.* Tilting at tournaments, turning, revolving.

tornear [tor-nay-ar´], *va. & vn.* 1. To shape by turning on a lathe. 2. To turn, to wind round about, to put into a circular motion. 3. To tilt at tournaments. 4. To meditate.

torneo [tor-nay´-o], *m.* 1. Tournament; public festival of knights. 2. Dance in imitation of tournaments. **Torneo por equipos**, team tournament.

tornera [tor-nay´-rah], *f.* Doorkeeper of a nunnery.

tornería [tor-nay-ree´-ash], *f.* Turning, the act of forming on a lathe.

tornero, ra [tor-nay´-ro], *m & f.* l. Turner, one who turns on a lathe. 2. The maker of lathes. 3. (*Prov.*) Messenger or servant of a nunnery.

tornillero [tor-nil-lyay´-ro], *m.* (*Coll.*) Deserter.

tornillo [tor-neel´-lyo], *m.* 1. Bolt (perno, pasador). 2. Screw. 3. (*Mil.*) Desertion. 4. Small vise. **Faltar un tornillo,** (*Coll.*) to have a screw loose. **Apretar los tornillos a,** (*Coll.*) to put the screws on.

torniquete [tor-ne-kay´-tay], *m.* 1. Turnstile. 2. Tourniquet.

torniscón [tor-nis-con´], *m.* (*Coll.*) 1. Crack on the head. 2. Slap in the face (manotada). 3. (*Sp. Am.*) Sharp pinch (apretón).

torno [tor´-no], *m.* 1. Winch. 2. Lathe (de tornear). 3. Potter's wheel. 4. Vise. 5. Revolution, turn. 6. Turn, bend (en un río). **Torno de hilar**, spinning wheel. **Torno de mano**, clomp. **En torno a**, around. 7. Brake (freno). **En torno a este tema**, on this theme.

toro [toh´-ro], *m.* 1. Bull. **Toro mejicano**, bison. V. BISONTE. **Correr toros**, to fight bulls. 2. (*Arch.*) Ogee moulding. 3. Moulding of the breech of a cannon. **Pillar el toro a uno**, to get somebody into a corner. **Este año no habrá toros**, there will be no bullfight this year.

torondo, torondón [to-ron´-do, done´], *m.* V. TOLONDRO.

toronja [to-ron´-hah], *f.* (*Bot.*) Grapefruit, shaddock.

toronjil [to-ron-heel´], *m.* **Toronjina,** *f.* [tor-ron-heel´]. (*Bot.*) Balm-gentle.

toronjo [to-ron´-ho], *m.* (*Bot.*) Grapefruit tree.

toroso, sa [to-ro´-so, sah], *a.* Strong, robust.

torozón [to-ro-thone´], *m.* Gripes, pains in the bowels (animales).

torpe [tor´-pay], *a.* 1. Awkward, clumsy, slow (poco ágil), dull, heavy, torpid, having a slow motion. 2. Dull, stupid, rude. 3. Lascivious, unchaste, obscene. 4. Indecorous, disgraceful, infamous. 5. Dull, slow of comprehension.

torpedero [tor-pay-day'-ro], *m.* Torpedo-boat, a small fighting craft, very swift, designed for discharging torpedoes.

torpedo [tor-pay´-do], *m.* 1. *(Zool.)* Torpedo, electric ray, camp-fish, numbfish. 2. Torpedo, an explosive weapon of naval warfare.

torpemente [tor'-pay-mentay], *adv.* 1. Awkwardly, clumsily. 2. Obscenely, basely; slowly. 3. Stiffly. 4. Slow-wittedly. 5. *(Fig.)* Vilely, dishonestly. 6. *(Fig.)* Crudely.

torpeza [tor-pay'-thah], *f.* 1. Heaviness, dulness, rudeness. 2. Torpidness, torpor; slowness. 3. Impurity, unchastity, lewdness, obscenity. 4. Want of ornament or culture. 5. Rudeness, ugliness. **Fue una torpeza mía**, it was tactless of me.

torpor [tor-por'], *m.* Torpor, numbness, want of motion.

torrar [tor-rar'], *va. V.* TOSTAR.

torre [tor'-rah], *f.* 1. A tower; turret, embattled tower. 2. Steeple of a church, in which bells are hung. 3. *(Prov.)* Country-house with a garden. 4. Castle, rook (en ajedrez). 5. *(Naut.)* Turret. **Torre de control, torre de mando**, *(Aer.)* control tower. **Torre de perforación**, derrick. **Torre de conducción eléctrica**, electricity pylon. 6. *(Carib. Mex.)* Factory chimney.

torrear [tor-ray-ar'], *va.* To fortify with towers or turrets.

torrecilla [tor-ray-theel'-lyah], *f.* Turret.

torrefacción [tor-ray-fac-the-on'], *f.* Torrefaction, roasting.

torrefacto [tor-ray-fahc'-to], *a.* High roast.

torreja [tor-ray'-hah], *f. (Mex.)* Fritter.

torrejón [tor-ray-hone'], *m.* Ill-shaped turret.

torrencial [tor-ren-the-ahl'], *a.* Torrential; overpowering.

torrentada [tor-ren-tah'-dah], *f.* Sweep of a torrent, impetuous current.

torrente [tor-ren´-tay], *m.* 1. Torrent (de río), a rapid stream; an impetuous current. 2. Abundance, plenty. 3. Strong, coarse voice.

torrentera [tor-ren-tay'-rah], *f.* Gully washed out by a freshet.

torreón [tor-ray-one'], *m.* A great tower in fortresses for defense.

torrero [tor-ray'-ro], *m.* 1. Bailiff or steward of a country-house and garden. 2. A lighthouse-keeper.

torreta [tor-ray'-tah], *f.* 1. *(Aer., Mil., Naut.)* Turret; conning tower (de submarino). 2. *(Elec.)* Pylon, mast.

torreznada [tor-reth-nah'-dah], *f.* Plentiful dish of rashers.

torreznero [tor-reth-nay´-ro], *a. (Coll.)* A lazy fellow, who sits over the fire.

torrezno [tor-reth'-no], *m.* 1. Rasher of bacon. 2. A voluminous book.

tórrido, da [tor´-re-do, dah], *a.* Torrid, parched, hot.

torrija [tor-ree'-hah], *f.* Slice of bread, fried in white wine, eggs, and butter or oil.

torrontés [tor-ron-tes'], *a.* Applied to a kind of white grapes.

torsión [tor-se-on'], *f.* 1. Torsion, act and effect of twisting. 2. State of being twisted.

torso [tor´-so], *m.* Trunk or body of a statue.

torta [tor'-tah], *f.* 1. A round cake made of various ingredients (pastel). 2. *(Coll.)* **Torta** or **torta de pan**, a loaf of bread. 3. Font, or portion of type fresh from the casting. 4. *(CAm. Mex.)* Omelette. 5. *(Tip.)* Fount. 6. Punch (puñetazo). **Agarrar una torta**, to get pissed.

tortada [tor-tah´-dah], *f.* A kind of large pie.

tortedad [tor-tay-dahd´], *f.* Condition of twist *(Acad.)*

tortera [tor-tay'-rah], *f.* 1. Pan for baking tarts or pies. 2. Knob at the end of a twisting spindle.

tortero [tor-tay´-ro], *m.* Knob of spindle for twisting.

torticoli [tor-te-co´-le], *m. (Med.)* Torticollis, the wry neck.

tortilla [tor-teel'-lyah], *f.* 1. Omelet, beaten eggs cooked in a frying pan. 2. *(Mex.)* A pancake made of mashed Indian corn. 3. **Tortilla de huevos**, omelet. **Hacerse tortilla**, to break into small pieces, to cake. **Volverse la tortilla**, *(Met.)* to turn the scale, to take a course contrary to that expected.

tortillera [tor-tel-lyay'-rah], *f.* 1. *(CAm. Mex.)* Tortilla seller. 2. Lesbian (lesbiana).

tortis [tor'-tis]. Used only in the phrase. **Letra de tortis**, a kind of Gothic printing letter.

tortita [tor-tee'-tah], *f. dim.* Small loaf or cake.

tórtola [tor'-to-lah], *f. (Orn.)* Turtle dove.

tortolico [tor-to-lee'-co], *a.* 1. Innocent, candid, inexperienced. 2. *V.* TORTOLILLO.

tortolillo, ito [tor-to-leel'-lyo], *m. dim.* A small cook turtle-dove.

tórtolo [tor'-to-lo], *m.* 1. *(Orn.)* Male turtle-dove. 2. Love-bird (amante).

tortor [tor-tor'], *m. pl. (Naut.)* Fraps.

tortozón [tor-to-thone'], *m.* Kind of large grapes.

tortuga [tor-too'-gah], *f.* Tortoise. **Paso de tortuga**, snail-gallop. **Concha de tortuga**, tortoise-shell. **Tortuga gráfica**, *(Comput.)* Graphics turtle

tortuosamente [tor-too-o'-sah-men-tay], *adv.* Tortuously, circuitously.

tortuosidad [tor-too-o-se-dahd'], *f.* Tortuosity, flexure, tortuousness.

tortuoso, sa [tor-too-o'-so, sah], *a.* Tortuous, winding.

tortura [tor-too'-rah], *f.* 1. Tortuosity, flexure. 2. Rack, torture.

torturar [tor-too-rahr'], *va.* To torture.

torvo [tor'-vo], *va, a.* Fierce, stern, severe, grim.

torzadillo [tor-thah-deel'-lyo], *m.* A kind of twisted cord, less thick than common.

torzal [tor-thahl'], *m.* Cord, twist, twisted or plaited lace, torsel, intertexture.

torzón [tor-thone'], *m. (Vet.) V.* TOROZÓN.

torzonado, da [tor-tho-nah'-do, dah], *a.* Contracted or twisted: applied to animals diseased in the bowels.

torzuelo [tor-thoo-ay'-lo], *a.* **Halcón torzuelo**, the third hawk which leaves the nest.

tos [tos], *f.* Cough. **Tos ferina** or **sofocante**, whooping cough.

tosa [toh'-sah], *f. V.* TOZA.

toscamente [tos'-cah-men-tay], *adv.* Coarsely, rudely, grossly, clownishly, lubbarly, fatly.

toscano, na [tos-cah'-no, nah], *a.* 1. Tuscan: applied to an architectural order. 2. Native of Tuscany.

tosco, ca [tos´-co, cah], *a.* 1. Coarse, rough, unpolished. 2. Ill-bred, uninstructed, clownish, clumsy, crabbed.

tosecilla [to-say-theel'-lyah], *f. dim.* Slight cough.

toser [to-serr'], *vn.* To cough: to feign a cough. -va. 1. *(Fig.)* **No le tose nadie**, nobody can compete with him. 2. **A mí no me tose nadie**, I'll not stand for that.

tosidura [to-see'-doo-rah], *f.* The act of coughing.

tosigar [to-se-gar'], *va. V.* ATOSIGAR.

tósigo [toh'-se-go], *m.* 1. Poison, especially that from the yew-tree. 2. Grief, pain, anguish, vexation.

tosigoso, sa [to-se-go´-so, sah], *a.* 1. Poisonous, venomous. 2. Coughing, having a cough.

tosquedad [tos-kay-dahd'], *f.* Roughness, coarseness; rudeness; clumsiness.

tostada [tos-tah'-dah], *f.* 1. Toast, slice of toasted bread. 2. Disappointment. 3. *(Cono Sur)* Long boring conversation (conversación). **Pegar una tostada a alguno**, *(Coll.)* (1) to play a serious trick upon him; to disappoint him. (2) To put one to the blush.

tostadera [tos-tah-day'-rah], *f.* Toaster, an instrument for toasting.

tostado, da [tos-tah'-do, dah], *a. & pp.* of TOSTAR. 1. Torrid, parched, dried with heat; toasted. 2. Applied to a lively light-brown color.

tostador, ra [tos-tah-dor', rah], *m. & f.* 1. Toaster, one who toasts. 2. Toaster, a toasting instrument.

tostadura [tos-tah-doo'-rah], *f.* Act and effect of toasting.

tostar [tos-tar'], *va.* 1. To toast (pan), to torrefy, to roast. **Tostar café**, to roast coffee. 2. To tan (piel). 3. *(Carib. Cono Sur)* To continue vigorously what one has begun. 4. *(Mex.)* To offend (ofender). -*vr.* To tan.

tostón [tos-tone'], *m.* 1. Soup, made of toasted bread and oil; toasted chick-pea (torrado). 2. Roast sucking pig (cochinillo).

3. Testoon, silver coin (moneda). 4. *(Culin.)* Small cube of toast (cubito). 6. Bore (lata), boring thing. 7. Bad play (comedia).

total [to-tahl'], *m*. 1. Whole (totalidad), total, complement. 2. *(Com.)* Total. **Total debe**, debit total. -*a*. General, universal, total; entire, all-out. **Una revisión total de su teoría**, a complete revision of his theory.

totalitario, ria [to-tah-le-tah'-re-o, ah], *a. & m. & f.* Totalitarian.

totalidad [to-tah-le-dahd'], *f*. Totality, whole quantity. **La totalidad de los obreros**, all the workers. **La totalidad de la población**, the whole population.

totalizar [to-tah-le-thar'], *va*. To total, to add up. -*vn*. To add up to.

totalmente [to-tal-men'-tay], *adv*. Totally, wholly, completely.

totem [to-tem'], *m*. Totem.

totémico, ca [to-tay'-me-co, cah], *a*. Totem. **Poste totémico**, totem pole.

totemismo [to-tay-mees'-mo], *m*. Totemiam.

totilimundi [to-te-le-moon'-de], *m*. Cosmorama. *(Fam.)* Everybody. *V.* MUNDINOVI.

totoloque [to-to-lo'-kay], *m*. A game of the ancient Mexicans.

totoposte [to-to-pos'-tay], *m*. *(Amer.)* Corn-bread of Indian meal.

totora [to-toh'-rah], *f*. *(Amer.)* A cat-tail or reed-mace of Peru and Bolivia.

totovía [to-to-vee'-ah], *f*. *(Orn.)* Woodlark.

totuma, *f.* **totumo,** *m*. [to-too'-mah, mo]. *(Amer.)* 1. A large dish made from a gourd. 2. Chocolate cup, in some parts of America. 3. *(Amer.* and Canary Islands.) A massive head.

toucán [to-oo-cahn'], *m*. *(Orn.)* Toucan.

toxemia [tok-say'-me-ah], *f*. Toxemia, blood poisoning.

toxicar [tok-se-car'], *va*. To poison. *V.* ATOSIGAR.

tóxico, ca [toc'-se-co, cah], *a*. Toxic, poisonous. -*m*. Poison.

toxicohemia [toc-se-co-ay-me-ah], *f*. *(Med.)* Toxicohaemia, toxaemia a poisoned condition of the blood.

toxicología [toc-se-co-lo-hee'-ah], *f*. Toxicology.

toxicológico, ca [toc-se-co-lo'-he-co, cah], *a*. Toxicological, relating to poisons and their effects.

toxicomanía [toc-se-co-mah-nee'-ah], *f*. Drug addiction.

toxicómano [toc-se-coh'-mah-no], *a*. Addicted to drugs. -*m & f*. Drug addict.

toxina [tok-see'-nah], *f*. *(Med.)* Toxin.

toza [to'-thah], *f*. 1. *(Prov.)* Piece of the bark of a tree. 2. *(Amer.)* Log, a bulky piece of wood.

tozo, za [too'-tho, thah], *a*. *(Art.)* Low in stature, dwarf.

tozolada [to-tho-lah'-dah], *f*. **Tozolón**, *m*. Stroke or blow on the neck.

tozudo, da [to-thoo'-do, dah], *a*. Stubborn. *V.* OBSTINADOand TERCO.

tozuelo [to-thoo-ay'-lo], *m*. Fat part of the neck.

traba [trah'-bah], *f*. 1. Ligament, ligature. 2. Hobble (de caballo), cord with which the feet of cattle arc tied. 3. Obstacle, impediment, hindrance; trammel, fetter, shackle; anything which hinders the easy execution of something else. 4. Piece of cloth uniting the two parts of the scapulary of certain monastic habits. **Poner trabas a**, to shackle.

trabacuenta [trah-bah-coo-en'-tah], *f*. 1. Error, mistake. 2. Difference, dispute, controversy.

trabadero [trah-bah-day'-ro], *m*. The small part of animals' feet.

trabado, da [trah-bah'-do, dah], *a. & pp.* of TRABAR. 1. Connected, joined (unido); thickened, inspissated. 2. Robust, strong. 3. Having two white fore feet, or two white feet on one side (caballo).

trabador [trah-bah-dor'], *m*. A carpenter's saw-set.

trabadura [trah-bah-doo'-rah], *f*. Union, junction.

trabajadamente [traaah-bah-hah'-dah-men-tay], *adv. V.* TRABAJOSAMENTE.

trabajado, da [trah-bah-hah'-do, dah], *a. & pp.* of TRABAJAR. 1. Labored. 2. Tired, weary; exhausted with fatigue. 3. Wrought (metales).

trabajador, ra [trah-bah-hah-dor', rah], *m. & f.* 1. Laborer, an assiduous or industrious person, painstaker. 2. A day-laborer.

trabajar [trah-bah-har'], *va.& vn.* 1. To work, to labor, to manufacture, to form by labor. 2. To work, to travail, to toil. 3. To work, to be in action, to be diligent. 4. To work, to act, to execute. 5. To work, to endeavor, to contend for. 6. To solicit, to procure. 7. To support, to sustain: applied to building or machinery. 8. To nourish and produce (tierra). 9. To work the ground, to till the soil. 10. To molest, to vex, to harass. 11. To bear, to produce (árbol, suelo). 12. To trouble (mente). **Trabajar atrozmente**, to work to excess. **Estoy trabajando el latín**, I am working away at Latin. **Trabajar mucho**, to work hard. **Trabajar por horas**, to be paid by the hour. **Trabajar por**, to strive to.

trabajillo [trah-bah-heel', lyo], *m. dim.* Slight work, toil, labor, trouble, or hardship.

trabajo [trah-bah'-ho], *m*. 1. Work, labor, toil, occupation. 2. Obstacle, impediment, hindrance, difficulty. 3. Trouble, hardship, ill-success. 4. Work, a writing on any subject; thing wrought. -*pl*. Poverty, indigence, need, want. **Trabajo de manos**, manual or handiwork. **Trabajo de punto**, knitting, knitting-work. **Día de trabajo**, working-day. **Mucho trabajo para nada**, much ado about nothing. **No hay atajo sin trabajo**, *(Prov.)* no gains without pains. **Trabajo de chinos**, hard slog. **Trabajos forzados**, hard labor. **Tomarse el trabajo de**, to take the trouble to.

trabajosamente [trah-bah-ho'-sah-men-tay], *adv*. Laboriously, with difficulty, painfully.

trabajoso, sa [trah-bah-ho'-so, sah], *a*. 1. Laborious, elaborate. 2. Imperfect, defective. 3. Painful (doloroso), hard. 4. *(Med.)* Pale, sickly. 5. *(And.)* Unhelpful (poco amable); bad-tempered (malhumorado).

trabal [trah-bahl'], *a*. Applied to clash nails.

trabalenguas [trah-bah-len'-goo-ahs], *m*. Tongue twister.

trabamiento [trah-bah-me-en'-to], *m*. Act of joining or uniting.

trabanco [trah-bahn'-co], *m*. Piece of wood attached to a dog's collar, to prevent him from putting down his head.

trabar [trah-bar'], *va*. 1. To join (unir), to unite, to connect. 2. To join, to bring into harmony or concord. 3. To fetter, to shackle (encadenar). 4. To thicken, to inspissate. 5. To dispute, to quarrel, to scuffle. **Trabarse de palabras**, to become angry in a dispute. 6. To set the teeth of a saw. 7. To seize, to take hold of (agarrar). 8. *(CAm. Carib.)* To deceive (engañar). **Trabarse la lengua**, to stammer, to speak with unnatural hesitation. **Trabar conversación**, to enter upon or keep up a long conversation.

trabazón [trah-bah-thone'], *f*. Juncture, union; connection; coalescence.

trabe [trah'-bay], *f*. Beam.

trábea [trah'-bay-ah], *f*. A long gown.

trabilla [trah-beel'-lyah], *f*. 1. *(Dim.)* A small clasp or tie. 2. In knitting a dropped stitch (puntada).

trabón [trah-bone'], *m*. 1. Fetter for a horse's foot. 2. Cross-planks in oil-mills.

trabuca [trah-boo'-cah], *f*. Cracker, a fire-work.

trabucación [trah-boo-cah-the-on'], *f*. Confusion, mistake.

trabucador, ra [trah-boo-cah-dor', rah], *m. & f.* Disturber.

trabucante [trah-boo-cahn'-tay], *pa*. Preponderating; causing mistakes.

trabucar [trah-boo-car'], *va*. 1. To derange, to throw into confusion, to perturbate. 2. To interrupt a conversation, to cut the thread of a discourse. -*vn*. To stumble, to tumble. -*vr*. To equivocate, to mistake.

trabucazo [trah-boo-cah'-tho], *m*. 1. Shot with a blunderbuss. 2. The report of a blunderbuss. 3. *(Coll.)* A sudden fright.

trabuco [trah-boo'-co], *m*. 1. Catapult, ancient battering engine. 2. Blunderbuss.

trabuquete [trah-boo-kay'-tay], *m*. Ancient machine used to throw large stones.

traca

traca [trah'-cah], *f*. 1. *(Naut.)* Strake, the uniform range of the planks of a ship. 2. String of fireworks.

trácala [trah'-cah-lah], *f*. 1. *(Men.)* Artifice scheme, trick. 2. *(And.)* Crowd (gentío). 3. *(Mex.)* Trickster (tramposo).

tracalero, ra [trah-cah-lay'-ro, rah], *a*. *(Mex.)* Tricky, artful.

tracamundana [trah-cah-moon-dah'-nah], *f*. *(Coll.)* 1. A ridiculous exchange of trifles. 2. Commotion, confusion, mess (lío).

tracción [trac-the-on'], *f*. 1. Act and effect of drawing. 2. Traction, pulling a load, as on railways. **Tracción delantera**, front-wheel drive.

tracias [trah'-the-as], *m*. North-north-west wind.

tracio, cia [trah'-the-o, ah], *a*. Thracian, of Thrace.

tracista [trah-thees'-tah], *m*. Projector, schemer, intriguer.

tracoma [trah-co'-mah], *f*. *(Med.)* Trachoma.

tractor [trac-tor'], *m*. Tractor. **Tractor blindado**, armored tractor. **Tractor de oruga**, caterpillar tractor.

tradición [trah-de-the-on'], *f*. 1. Tradition. 2. *(Law.)* V. ENTREGA.

tradicional [trah-de-the-o-nahl'], *a*. Traditional.

tradicionalmente [trah-de-the-o-nahl'-men-tay], *adv*. Traditionally.

traducción [trah-dooc-the-on'], *f*. 1. Translation, version, interpretation. 2. A rhetorical figure, by which a word is used in different senses.

traducir [trah-doo-theer'], *va*. 1. To translate, to interpret in another language, 2. To change, to truck. *(Yo traduzco, traduzca; traduje, tradujera; from Traducir. V. CONDUCIR.)*

traductor, ra [trah-dooc-tor', rah], *m* & *f*. Translator.

traedizo, za [trah-ay-dee'-tho, thah], *a*. That which may be drawn; tractable.

traedor, ra [trah ay dor´, rah], *m*. & *f*. Carrier.

traedura [trah'-ay-doo'-rah], *f*. The act of carrying, bringing, or conducting.

traer [trah-err'], *va*. 1. To fetch, to bring, to carry, to conduct any way. 2. To bring, to carry, to attract (imán), to draw towards oneself. 3. To bring about (causar), to cause, to occasion. 4. To come, to handle, to manage. 5. To assign reasons or authorities to prove a thing (autoridad). 6. To bring to, to oblige, to compel to do something. 7. To bring over, to reduce, to bind, to prevail upon, to persuade. 8. To be engaged in, to carry on, to have. 9. To use, to wear. **Traer medias de seda**, to wear silk stockings. **Traer y llevar cuentos**, to carry tales backwards and forwards. **Traer en bocas** or **lenguas**, to traduce one's reputation, to censure or speak ill of one's actions. **Traer perdido a alguno**, to be deeply in love; to be the ruin of a person. **Traer a consecuencia**, to place a thing in a situation which enhances or diminishes its value; to say something pertinent. **Traer un pleito con alguno**, to be engaged in a lawsuit against someone. **Traer a uno entre ojos**, *(Met.)* to be suspicious of a person. **Traer consigo**, to carry along. **Traer a la mano**, to fetch or carry. **Traer al ojo alguna cosa**, to keep a thing carefully in sight; to impress a thing upon one's mind. **Traer a cuento**, to turn the conversation to a desired point. *-vr*. 1. To be dressed well or poorly. 2. To have a graceful or ungainly deportment. As a reflexive verb used always with the adverbs *bien* or *mal*. **Traerlas**, to be annoying (molestar). **Tiene un padre que se las trae**, she has an excessively severe father.

trafagador [tra-fah-gah-dor'], *m*. Trafficker, dealer.

trafagante [trah-fah-gahn'-tay], *pa*. Trafficking, trading.

trafagar [trah-fah-gar'], *vn*. 1. To traffic, to carry on trade. V. TRAFICAR 2. *(Prov.)* To travel, to journey.

tráfago [trah'-fah-go], *m*. 1. Traffic, commerce, trade. 2. A careful management of affairs.

trafagón, na [trah-fah-gone', nah], *a*. Active, industrious, deeply engaged in trade and commerce.

trafalmejo, ja [trah-fal'-may'-ho, hah], *a*. Bold, intrepid, audacious.

traficación [trah-fe-cah-the-on'], *f*. Traffic, trade, commerce; shopping. V. TRÁFICO.

traficante [trah-fe-cahn'-tay], *pa*. & *m*. Merchant, trader; trading.

traficar [trah-fe-car'], *vn*. 1. To traffic, to carry on trade and commerce, to trade. 2. To travel, to journey.

tráfico [trah'-fe-co], *m*. Commerce, traffic, trade, negotiation. **Tráfico de mercancías**, goods traffic.

trafulla [trah-fool-lyah], *f*. *(Coll.)* Cheating, defrauding, swindling in gaming.

tragacanta [trah-gah-cahn'-tah], *f*. 1. *(Bot.)* Goat's-thorn, milk-vetch. 2. Tragacanth, a gum.

tragacanto [trah-gah-cahn'-to], *a*. Tragacanth: applied to the gum obtained from various species of astragalus.

tragacete [trah-gah-thay'-tay], *m*. Javelin, a Moorish missive weapon.

tragadero [trah-gah-day'-ro], *m*. 1. Esophagus, gullet. 2. Pit, gulf, abyss. **Tragadero de un puerto**, *(Naut.)* mouth of a harbor.

tragadieces [trah-gah-de-eth'-ess], **Tragaveintes** [trah-gah-veyn'-tess], *m*. *(Mex.)* Jukebox.

tragador, ra [trah-gah-dor', rah], *m*. & *f*. Glutton, gobbler.

tragahombres [trah-gah-om´-bres], *m*. *(Coll.)* Bully, hector.

trágala [trah'-gah-lah], *m*. A song of the liberals against the absolutism which began with this word. **Cantarle a uno el trágala**, to crow over one who has to accept what he detested.

tragaldabas [trah-gal-dah'-bas], *m*. *(Coll.)* Glutton.

tragaleguas [trah-gah-lay´-goo-as'], *m*. *(Coll.)* A brisk walker.

tragaluz [trah-gah-looth'], *f*. Skylight.

tragamallas [trah-gah-mahl-lyas], *m*. *(Coll.)* 1. Impostor, cheat, swindler. 2. Glutton, gormandizer.

tragantada [trah-gan-tah'-dah], *f*. A large draught of liquor.

tragantón, na [trah-gan-tone', nah], *m*. & *f*. *(Coll.)* A glutton. *-a*. Gluttonous, voracious.

tragantona [trah-gan-to'-nah], *f*. 1. A plentiful repast. 2. The act of swallowing or forcing down the throat. 3. *(Met.)* Difficulty of believing an extraordinary thing.

tragaperras [trah-gah-payr-rahs], *m*. Slot machine.

tragar [trah-gar'], *va*. 1. To swallow. 2. To devor, to eat voraciously, to glut. 3. To swallow up, to ingulf. 4. To swallow, to receive or believe without examination. **Hacer tragar algo a uno**, to force somebody to listen to something. *-vr*. To dissemble, to play the hypocrite; to pocket an affront. **Tragar el anzuelo**, *(Met.)* to allow oneself to be deceived. **No poder tragar a alguno**, to abhor or dislike one.

tragavirotes [trah-gah-ve-ro'-tess], *m*. *(Coll.)* A man who without cause is rude and puffed with pride.

tragazo [tra-gah'-tho], *m*. *aug*. A large draught.

tragazón [tra-gah-thone'], *f*. Voracity, gluttony.

tragedia [trah-hay'-de-ah], *f*. 1. Tragedy, a dramatic representation which has a mournful end. 2. Tragedy, any mournful event. **Parar en tragedia**, to have a disastrous issue. 3. Among the pagans a song in praise of Bacchus.

tragélafo [trah-hay-lah-fo], *m*. A fabulous animal between a goat and deer.

trágicamente [trah-he-cah-men-tay], *adv*. Tragically.

trágico, ca [trah'-he-co, cah], *a*. 1. Tragic, relating to tragedy. 2. Tragic, calamitous, disastrous.

tragicomedia [trah-he-co-may'-de-ah], *f*. Tragi-comedy.

tragicómico, ca [trah-he-co'-me-co, cah], *a*. Tragi-comical.

trago [trah´-go], *m*. 1. Draught of liquid (cantidad), swallowed at one time; swallow. 2. Calamity, adversity, misfortune (desgracia). **A tragos**, by degrees, slowly, gently. **Echar un trago**, to take a dram. **Un trago de agua**, a drink of water. **No vendría mal un trago de vino**, a drop of wine would not come amiss.

tragón, na [trah-gone, ah], *a*. Gluttonous, voracious, ravenous.

tragón [trah-gone], *m*. Glutton.

tragonazo, za [trah-go-nah´-tho, thah], *a*. *aug*. Applied to a great glutton.

tragonería, tragonía [trah-go-nay-ree´-ah], *f.* Gluttony.

traguillo, ito [trah-geel´-lyo], *m. dim.* of TRAGO.

traición [trah-e-the-on´], *f.* Treason, disloyalty; faithlessness; falsehood. **Matar a uno a traición**, to kill somebody treacherously. **A traición**, treacherously, treasonably.

traicionar [tra-he-the-o-nar´], *va.* To do treason.

traicionero, ra [trah-e-the-o-nay´-ro, rah], *a.* Treasonous, treasonable. *V.* TRAIDOR.

traída [trah-ee´-dah], *f.* Carriage, the act of fetching or carrying from place to place.

traído, da [trah-ee´-do, dah], *a. & pp.* of TRAER. 1. Brought, fetched, carried. 2. Used, worn (usado), second-hand.

traidor, ra [trah-e-dor´, rah], *a.* 1. Treacherous (persona), faithless, disloyal, perfidious, false, traitorous. 2. Insidious, deceitful (animales). *-m.* Traitor, betrayer.

traidora [trah-e-do´-rah], *f.* Traitress.

traidoramente [trah-ee-do-rah-men´-tay], *adv.* Treacherously, treasonably, traitorously, perfidiously.

tráiler [trah-ee-layr], *m.* 1. (Cine) Trailer. 2. *(Aut.)* Caravan.

traílla [trah-eel´-lyah], *f.* 1. Leash, lash (de perro), a cord or leather thong, by which a dog is led. 2. Pack-thread. 3. Instrument for levelling ground; a roadscraper.

traillar [trah-eel-lyar´], *va.* To level ground.

traíña [trah-ee´-nyah], *f.* 1. Net for deep-sea fishing. 2. Jack, a small bowl. *V.* BOLICHE.

trainera [trah-ee-nay-rah], *f.* Small fishing boat.

traja [trah´-hah], *f. (Amer.)* A load which vessels carry on deck.

trajano, na [trah-hah´-no, nah], *a.* Trajan: relating to the Emperor Truman.

traje [trah´-hay], *m.* 1. Suit, dress, habit, guise, apparel, clothes. 2. A complete dress of a woman, wardrobe; attire. 3. Mask, a dress used for disguise. **Traje de etiqueta**, dress suit. **Traje para la nieve**, snowsuit. **Traje para vuelos espaciales**, space suit. **Traje sastre**, tailored suit. **Traje de luces**, bullfighter´s costume. **Traje de novia**, wedding dress.

trajear [trah-hay-ar´], *va.* To dress a person in a manner suited to his or her rank or condition.

traje de etiqueta [trah´-hay day ay-te-kay´-tah], *m.* Dress suit.

trajilla [trah-hee´-lyah], *f.* A harrow without teeth for levelling ground.

trajín [trah-heen´], *m.* 1. Carriage (acarreo). *V.* TRAJINO and TRÁFAGO. 2. Coming and going (ir y venir). 3. **Trajines**, affairs.

trajinante [trah-he-nahn´-tay], *m.* Carrier.

trajinar [tra-he-nar´], *va.* 1. To transport goods from place to place (acarrear). 2. To travel. 3. *(Coll.)* To fidget about. 4. *(Cono Sur)* To swindle (estafar). 5. *(Cono Sur)* To search (registrar). *-vn.* To bustle about (ajetrearse); to travel (viajar).

trajinería [trah-he-nay-ree´-ah], *f.* Carrying trade.

trajinero [trah-he-nay´-ro], *m.* Carrier.

trajino [trah-hee´-no], *m.* Carriage, the act of transporting merchandise.

tralla [trahl´-lyah], *f.* 1. Cord, bassweed rope. 2. Lash, snapper of a whip. 3. *(Mil.)* Pontoons for forming bridges.

trama [trah´-mah], *f.* 1. Weft or proof of cloth. 3. Kind of weaving silk. 3. Deceit, imposition, fraud, plot (complot), machination. 3. *(Comput.)* Raster.

tramador, ra [trah-mah-dor´, rah], *m.* 1. Weaver. 2. Plotter; artful contriver, hatcher.

tramar [trah-mar´], *m.* 1. To weave. 2. To plot, to form crafty designs, to hatch, to scheme. 3. **Está tramando algo**, they´re up to something.

tramilla [trah-meel´-lyah], *f. (Amer.)* Twine.

tramitación [trah-me-ta-the-on´], *f. (For.)* Progressive forwarding of a judicial proceeding according to prescribed procedure.

tramitar [trah-me-tahr], *va.* To transact (despachar); to negotiate (negociar); to proceed with (proseguir).

trámite [trah´-me-tay], *m.* 1. Step (etapa), requirement, each step in a transaction (negocio). 2. *(For.)* Procedure or course

of a judicial process (procedimiento). **Trámites oficiales**, official channels. **Hacer los trámites para un viaje**, to make the arrangements for a journey.

tramo [trah´-mo], *m.* 1. Piece, morsel. 2. Piece of ground separated from another. 3. Flight of stairs (escalera).

tramojo [trah-mo´-ho], *m.* 1. Part of grain, which the reaper holds in his hand. 2. Band for tying the sheaf. 3. Trouble, affliction.

tramón [trah-mone´], *m.* The shortest wool which remains in the comb during the combing.

tramontana [trah-mon-tah´-nah], *f.* 1. The north wind (viento). 2. Vanity (vanidad), pride, haughtiness. **Perder la tramontana**, *(Met.)* to become mad with passion.

tramontano, na [trah-mon-tah´-no, nah], *a.* Transmontane, beyond the mountains.

tramontar [trah-mon-tar´], *vn.* To pass to the other side of the mountains. *-va.* To assist, to relieve. *-vr.* To flee, to escape.

tramoya [trah-mo´-yah], *f.* 1. Machinery used in theaters to represent sudden disappearance, wonderful feats, etc. 2. Craft, artifice.

tramoyista [trah-mo-yees´-tah], *m.* 1. The machinist of a theater. 2. The scene shifter. 3. Impostor, swindler (estafador), deceiver.

trampa [trahm´-pah], *f.* 1. Trapsnare. 2. Trap-door (escotilla). 3. Movable part of a counter fitted with hinges for raising and lowering. **Caer en la trampa**, to fall into the snare, to be deceived by artifice. **Este juego no tiene trampa ni cartón**, this is the real thing. 4. Fraud (estafa), deceit, stratagem, malpractice. **Hacer trampas**, to cheat. 5. Debt fraudulently contracted.

trampal [tram-pahl´], *m.* Quagmire; a dirty or muddy place.

trampantojo [tram-pan-to´-ho], *m.* Trick played before one's eyes in order to deceive (juego de manos).

trampazo [tram-pah´-tho], *m.* The last twist of the cord employed to torture an offender.

trampeador, ra [tran-pay-ah-dor´, rah], *m. & f.* Borrower, swindler, cheat, sharper.

trampear [tram-pay-ar´], *vn. & va.* 1. To stain money on false presences, to swindle one out of his money, to lurch, to shift, to play tricks, to cog. 2. To impose upon, to deceive.

trampilla [tram-peel´-lyah], *f.* 1. Floor peephole (mirilla). 2. Coal bin door. 3. Pants fly (bragueta).

trampista [tram-pees´-tah], *a.* Cheating, deceitful. *-com.* Cheat, swindler.

trampolín [tram-po-leen´], 1. Springboard (de piscina). 2. Diving board. 3. Trampoline. 4. *(Fig.)* Stepping stone, springboard.

tramposo, sa [tram-po´-so, sah], *a.* Deceitful, swindling. *-m.* Cheater, swindler.

tranca [trahn´-cah], *f.* 1. Bar across a door or window, to prevent entrance. 2. *(Naut.)* Cross-bar. 3. Beam (viga). 4. *(Cono Sur)* Safety catch (de escopeta). 5. *(Carib. Aut.)* Traffic jam.

trancada [tran-cah´-dah], *f. V.* TRANCO and TRANCAZO.

trancado [tran-cah´-do], *vn.* A small harpoon for catching eels. *-pp.* of TRANCAR.

trancalilo [tran-cah-ee´-lo], *m.* Knot in thread or ropes.

trancanil [tran-cah-neel´], *m. (Naut.)* Water-way, for carrying off the water from the deck through the scupper holes; stringer plate.

trancar [tran-car´], *va.* 1. To barricade. *V.* ATRANCAR. 2. To bar (ventana).

trancazo [tran-cah-zoh], *m.* 1. Blow (golpe). 2. *(Med.)* Flu.

trance [tranh´-thay], *m.* Blow with a bar; influenza, grippe, moment (momento difícil), hypnotic state (estado hipnótico), drugged condition (estado drogado). **Trance mortal**, last moment of peril. **Estar en el trance de**, to be on the point of.

trancenil [tran-thay-neel´], *m.* A gold or silver husband, garnished with jewels.

tranchete [trahn-chay'-tay], *m*. A broad, curvated knife, used for pruning, etc., shoemaker's heel-knife.

trancho [trahn'-cho], *m*. *(Prov.)* V. ALACHA.

tranco [trahn'-co], *m*. 1. A long step or stride (pasto). 2. Threshold of a door. **A trancos**, in haste, in a trice.

trangallo [tran-gahl'-lyo], *m*. Yoke fixed on shepherds' dogs' necks, during the brooding-time of game.

tranquera [tran-kay'-rah], *f*. 1. Palisade (cercado). 2. *(LAm.)* Cattle gate.

tranquero [tran-kay'-ro], *m*. Jamb or lintel of a door or window, made of stone.

tranquilamente [tran-kee-lah-mehn-tay], *adv*. Quietly, peacefully, tranquilly, composedly.

tranquilidad [tran-kee-lee-dahd], *f*. Tranquility, tranquilness, rest, peace, repose, composure. **Perder la tranquilidad**, to lose patience.

tranquilizante [tran-ke-le-thahn'-tay], *m*. Tranquilizer.

tranquilizar [tran-ke-le-thar'], *va*. To calm, to appease, to tranquillize, to pacify. *-vr*. To calm down.

tranquilo, la [tran-kee'-lo, lah], *a*. Tranquil, calm (mar, mente, estado), quiet, pacific, gentle, contented. **Dejar a uno tranquilo**, to leave somebody along.

tranquilla [tran-keel'-lyah], *f*. 1 *(Dim.)* A small bar. 2. Trap, snare, stratagem.

tranquillón [tran-keel-lyone'], *m*. Mashlin, maslin, mixed grain.

transacción [tran-sac-the-on'], *f*. Composition of a difference, accommodation, adjustment. **Transacción comercial**, business deal.

transalpino, na [tran-al-pee'-no, nah], *a*. Transalpine.

transatlántico or **trasatlántico** [tran-sah-tlan'-te-co, trah-sah-tlan'-te-co], *m*. Transatlantic, ocean liner.

transar, *va*. (Canary Islands and *Amer.*) V. TRANSIGIR. Much used reflexively.

transbordador [trans-bor-dah-dor], *m*. Ferry; shuttle. **Transbordador para coches**, car ferry.

transbordar [trans-bor-dar'], *va*. *(Naut.)* To transship (a través de un río).

transbordo [trans-bor'-do], *m*. 1. Transshipment. 2. Transfer (traslado).

transcendencia [trans-then-den'-the-ah], *f*. V. TRASCENDENCIA.

transcendental [trans-then-den-tahl'], *a*. V. TRACENDENTAL.

transcendente [trans-then-den'-tay], *pa*. V. TRASCENDENTE.

transcender [trans-then-derr'], *va. & vn*. V. TRASCENDER.

transceptor [trans-thep-tor], Transceiver. *(Comput.)*

transcontinental [trans-con-te-nen-tahl'], *a*. Transcontinental, crossing the continent.

transcribir [trans-cre-beer'], *va*. To transcribe.

transcripción [trans-crip-the-on'], *f*. Transcription, the process and result of transcribing.

transcripto, ta, transcrito, ta [trans-creep'-to, tah, cree'-to, tah], *pp. irreg.* of TRANSCRIBIR.

transcurrir [trans-coor-reer'], *vn*. 1. To pass away (tiempo), to elapse. **Han transcurrido 7 años**, 7 years have passed. 2. To be, to turn out (suceso). **La tarde transcurrió aburrida**, the evening was boring.

transcurso [trans-coor'-so], *m*. Course or process of time.

transeúnte [tran-say-oon'-tay], *a*. Transient; transitory. *-com*. 1. Sojourner. 2. Passer-by.

transexual [trans-sayc-soo-ahl], *a*. Transsexual. *-m & f*. Transsexual.

transferencia [trans-fay-ren'-the-ah], *f*. Transfer, transference. **Transferencia bancaria**, banker's order.

transferible [trans-fay-ree'-blay], *a*. Transferable, capable of being transferred.

transferidor, ra [trans-fay-re-dor', rah], *m. & f*. V. TRASFERIDOR.

transferir [trans-fay-reer'], *va*. 1. To move, to remove, to transport. 2. *(LAm.)* To transfer (trasladar), to convey, to make over. 3. To employ a word figuratively.

transfigurable [trans-fe-goo-rah'-blay], *a*. Changeable, that can he transformed.

transfiguración [trans-fe-goo-rah-the-on'], *f*. Transformation, transfiguration.

transfigurar [trans-fe-goo-rar'], *va*. To transfigure, to transform. To be transfigured; to lose form or figure. (Used particularly as a reflexive verb.)

transfijo, ja [trans-fee'-ho, hah], *a*. Transfixed.

transfixión [trans-fik-se-on'], *f*. Transfixion, piercing through.

transflorar [trans-flo-rar'], *va*. To copy a picture or drawing by holding it against the light.

transflorear [trans'-flo-ray-ar'], *va*. To enamel, to inlay, to variegate with colors.

transfojar [trans-fo-har'], *va*. V. TRASHOJAR.

transfollado, da [trans-fol-lyah'-do, dah]. *a*. *(Vet.)* Applied to tumours round a horse's legs.

transformación [trans-for-mah-the-on'], *f*. Transformation, metamorphosis.

transformador, ra [trans-for-mah-dor', rah], *a*. Transforming. *-m. & f*. Transformer, one who transforms. *(Phy. & elec.)* Transformer.

transformamiento [trans-for-mah-me-en'-to], *m*. Transformation.

transformar [trans-for-mar'], *va* 1. To conform, to transmute; to transfigure, to metamorphose. 2. To gain such an ascendency in another's affections, that it almost changes his or her character. *-vr*. To assume different sentiments or manners.

transformativo, va [trans-for-mah-tee'-vo, vah], That possesses power to transform.

transformismo [trans-for-mees-mo], *m*. Evolution, transmutation.

transformista [trans-for-mees-tah], *m & f*. Quick-change artist.

transfregar [trans-fray-gar'], *va*. To rub.

transfretar [trans-fray-tar'], *va*. To cross an arm of the sea.

tránsfuga, tránsfugo [trans'-foo-gah], *m*. Deserter, fugitive.

transfundición [trans-foon-de-the-on'], *f*. V. TRANSFUSIÓN.

transfundir [trans- foon-deer'], *va*. 1. To transfuse (sangre). 2. To communicate (noticia).

transfusión [trans-foo-se-on'], *f*. Transfusion: communication. **Transfusión de sangre**, blood transfusion.

transgangético, ca [trans-gah-hay'-te-co, cah], *a*. Beyond the Ganges.

transgredir [trans-gray-deer'], *va*. To transgress.

transgresión [trans-gray-se-on'], *f*. Transgression, crime, fault, sin.

transgresor, ra [trans-gray-sor', rah], *m. & f*. Transgressor, offender.

transición [tran-se-the-on'], *f*. Transition, change, removal.

transido, da [tran-see'-do, dah], *a*. 1. Worn out with anguish or grief. 2. Avaricious.

transigencia [trans-see-hen-the-ah], *f*. 1. Compromise (acto). 2. Accommodating attitude (actitud).

transigir [tran-se-heer'], *va*. To accommodate differences; to settle dial putts; to compound.

transistor [tran-ses-tor'], *m*. Transistor.

transitable [tran-se-tah'-blay], *a*. That may be passed through; passable (camino), practicable.

transitar [tran-se-tar'], *vn*. To travel, to go on a journey; to pass by a place.

transitivo, va [tran-see-tee'-vo, vah], *a*. Transitive.

tránsito [trahn'-se-to], *m*. 1. Passage, transition. 2. Inn, for travelers. 3. Road, way. 4. Change, removal. 5. Death of holy persons. 6. *(Ast.)* Transit. **Calle de mucho tránsito**, busy street. **Hacer tránsito**, to make a stop.

transitoriamente [trans-see-to-re-ah-men-tay], *adv*. Transitorily.

transitorio, ria [tran-se-to'-re-o, ah], *a*. Transitory (pasajero), perishable.

translación [trans-lah-the-on'], *f*. Translation. V. TRASLACIÓN.

translaticiamente [trans-lah-te-the-ah-men-tay], *adv.* Metaphorically. *V.* TRASLATICIAMENTE.

translaticio, cia [trans-lah-tee'-the-o, ah]. *V.* TRASLATICIO.

translativo, va [trans-lah-tee'-vo, vah], *a. V.* TRASLATIVO.

translimitación [trans-le-me-tah-the-on'], *f.* Sending of troops to the territory of a neighboring state with the purpose of intervening in favor of one of two contending parties.

translimitar [trans-le-me-tar'], *m.* To pass unexpectedly, or by previous authorization, beyond the boundary of a state, for a military operation, without the purpose of violating the territory.

translucidez [trans-loo-the-deth'], *f.* Translucence.

translúcido [trans-loo'-the-do, dah], *a.* Translucent, semi-transparent.

transmarino, na [trans-ma-ree'-no, nah], *a.* Transmarine.

transmigración [trans-me-grah-the-on'], *f.* Transmigration, the removal of families from one country to another.

transmigrar [trans-me-grar'], *vn.* To transmigrate, or pass from one country to another.

transminar [trans-me-nar'], *va.* To undermine.

transmisibilidad [trans-me-se-be-le-dahd'], *f.* Transmissibility.

transmisible [trans-me-see'-blay], *a.* Transmissible, capable of transmission.

transmisión [trans-me-se-on'], *f.* 1. Transmission, transmittal. 2. *(Elec.)* Transmission. **Transmisión en circuito,** hookup. **Transmisión exterior,** outside broadcast. 3. *(Comput.)* **Transmisión de datos en paralelo,** parallel data transmission. **Transmisión de datos en serie,** serial data transmission. **Transmisión asíncrona,** asynchronous transmission. **Transmisión bidireccional alternativa,** half duplex transmission. **Transmisión bidireccional simultánea,** full duplex transmission. **Transmisión en dúplex,** full duplex transmission. **Transmisión en semidúplex,** half-duplex transmission. **Transmisión "simplex",** simplex transmission. **Transmisión síncrona,** synchronous transmission. **Transmisión unidireccional,** symplex transmission.

transmisor, ra [trans-me-sor', rah], *a.* Transmitting. *-m. (Elec.)* Transmitter.

transmitir [trans-me-teer'], *va.* To transfer, to transmit, to make over, to convey.

transmontar [trans-mon-tar'], *va. V.* TRAMONTAR.

transmutable [trans-moo-tah'-blay], *a.* Transmutable, convertible.

transmutación [trans-moo-tah-the-on'], *f.* Transmutation.

transmutar [trans-moo-tar'], *va.* To transmute.

transmutativo, va [trans-moo-tah-tee'-vo, vah], **Transmutatorio, ria** [trans-moo-tah-to'-re-o, ah], *a.* Transmutative, that which transmutes.

transparencia [trans-pa-ren'-the-ah], *f.* Transparency, clearness, diaphaneity.

transparentarse [trans-pa-ren-tar'-say], *vr.* 1. To be transparent (vidrio). 2. To shine through: used sometimes as an active verb. **Se transparentaba su verdadera intención,** his real intention became plain.

transparente [trans-pa-ren-tay], *a.* Transparent, lucid, fine, clear, limpid.

transparante [trans-pah-ren-tay], *m.* 1. Window-shade. 2. A glass window in churches behind the altar.

transpirable [trans-pe-rah'-blay], *a.* Perspirable, transpirable.

transpiración [trans-pe-rah-the-on'], *f.* Transpiration, insensible perspiration.

transpirar [trans-pe-rar'], *vn.* To transpire, to perspire insensibly (sudar). To seep through (líquido).

transpirenaico, ca [trans-pe-ray-nah'-e-co, cah], *a.* Beyond the Pyrenees.

transplantación [trans-plan-tah-the-on'], *f. (Prov.) V.* TRASPLANTE.

transplante [trans-plahn'-tay], *m. V.* TRASPLANTE.

transponedor, ra [trans-po-nay-dor', rah], *m.& f.* Transponer, transplanter.

transponer [trans-po-nerr'], *va.* 1. To remove, to transport, to transpose. 2. To hide, to conceal craftily. 3. To transplant (trasplantar). *-vr.* 1. To be rather drowsy. 2. To set below the horizon. 3. To hide (esconderse). 4. To doze (dormirse).

transportación [trans-por-tah-the-on'], *f.* Transportation, conveyance, carriage.

transportador, ra [trans-por-tah-dor,' rah], *a.* Transporting, conveying. *-m.* Transporter, conveyor, carrier.

transportamiento [trans-por-tah-me-en'-to], *m.* 1. Transportation, carriage. 2. Transport, ecstasy, perturbation which impedes freedom of action.

transportar [trans-por-tar'], *va.* 1. To transport (acarrear), to convey, to remove. 2. *(Mus.)* To change the key. **El avión podrá transportar 400 pasajeros,** the plane will be able to carry 400 passengers. *-vr.* To be in a transport, to be out of one's senses.

transpote [trans-por'-tay], *m.* 1. Transport (acto), transportation, conveyance. **Bajel de transporte***, (Naut.)* transport or transport-ship, to carry stores and soldiers. 2. Transport, fury, fit of passion. 3. To transfer (de diseño).

transportín [trans-por-teen'], *m. V.* TRANSPORTÍN.

transportista [trans-por-tees-tah], *m.* Carrier.

transposición [trans-po-se-the-on'], *f.* Transposition, transposal.

transpositivo, va [trans-po-se-tee'-vo, vah], *a.* Transpositional, transpositive, consisting in transposition.

transterminante [trans-ter-me-nahn'-tay], *pa.* Transgressing the limits.

transterminar [trans-ter-me-nar'], *va.* To pass from the limits of one jurisdiction to another; to trespass.

transtiberino, na [trans-te-bay-ree'-no, nah], *a.* Across the Tiber.

transubstanciación [tran-soobs-tan-the-ah-the-on'], *f.* Transubstantiation.

transubstancial [tran-soobs-tan-the-ahl'], *a.* Converted into another substance.

transubstanciar [tran-soobs-tan-the-ar'], *va.* To transubstantiate.

transversal [trans-verr-sahl'], *a.* Transversal.

transversalmente [trans-ver-sahl-men-tay], *adv.* Transversally, collaterally.

transverso, sa [trans-verr'-so, sah], *a.* Transverse.

tranvía [tran-vee'-ah], *m.* Tram (vehículo), tramcar, streetcar.

tranza [trahn'-thah], *f. (Prov.)* Sale of a debtor's property to satisfy his creditors.

tranzadera [tran-thah-day'-rah], *f.* Knot of plaited cords or ribbons.

tranzar [tran-thar'], *ra.* 1. To plait or weave cords or ribbons; to braid. 2. To cut, to truncate. 3. *V.* REMATAR.

tranzón [tran-thone'], *m.* Part of a forest which has been cut or cleared for fuel.

trapa [trah'-pah], *f.* Noise made by stamping with the feet, or bawling.

trapacear [trah-pa-thay-ar'], *vn.* To deceive by falsehoods and artful contrivances.

trapacería [trah-pah-thay-ree'-ah], *f.* Fraud, deceit, counterfeit. *V.* TRAPAZA.

trapacero, ra [trah-pa-thay'-ro, rah], *f. & m. & f.* Cheating, deceitful. *V.* TRAPACISTA.

trapacete [trah-pa-thay'-tay], *m. (Com.)*

trapacista [trah-pah-thees'-tah], *m. & a.* Impostor, cheat, sharper, swindler; deceiver; fraudulent, false.

trapajo [tah-pah'-ho], *m.* Rag, tatter.

trapajoso, sa [trah-pah-ho'-so, sah], *a.* Ragged, tattered.

trápala [trah'-pah-lah], *f.* 1. A violent noise by stamping with the feet, or bawling. 2. Deceit, cheat by false representations. *-com.* Garrulous, loquacious babbler. *-m.* Garrulity, loquacity, talkativeness.

trapalear [trah-pah-lay-ar'], *vn.* To be loquacious or garrulous; to babble.

trapalón, na [trah-pah-lone', nah], *a. & m. & f.* Loquacious; babbler, prater. Deceitful, bombastic fellow.

trapaza [trah-pah'-thah], /. Fraud, A deceitful trick upon a buyer.

trapazar [trah-pa-thar'], vn. V. TRAPALEAR.

trapazo [trah-pah'-tho], m. A large rag.

trapa [trah'-pay], m. Buckram.

trapeado [trah-pay-ah'-do], m. (Art term) The drapery of a figure.

trapear [trah-pay-ar'], va. (Art.) To drape the figure.

trapecio [trah-pay'-the-o], m. 1. (Goom.) Trapezium. 2. Trapeze for gymnastic exercises.

trapería [trah-pay-ree'-ah], f. 1. Street inhabited by woollen-drapers. 2. Frippery, rag-fair. 3. Woollen draper's shop (tienda).

trapero, ra [trah-pay'-ro, rah], m. & f. & a. Dealing in rags or frippery.

trapezoide [trah-pay-tho'-e-day], m. 1. Trapezoid, a geometrical figure of unequal sides, none parallel. 2. Trapezoid, a bone of the wrist.

trapico [trah-pee'-co], m. dim. Little rag.

trapiche [trah-pee'-chay], m. 1. A sugar-mill (de azúcar), or engine for preparing the sugar-cane. **Trapiche de vapor**, steam sugar-mill. 2. (Cuba) A small sugar plantation. 3. (Mex.) Both the machinery and plantation.

trapichear [trah-pe-chay-ar'], vn. (Coll.) 1. To trade in a small way. 2. (Coll.) To contrive, to seek artifices not always permissible for the attainment of some object. 3. (Cono Sur) To scrape a living by buying and selling (comerciar). -va. To deal in, to trade in.

trapicheo [trah-pe-chay'-o], m. Small trading; a dodge.

trapichero [trah-pe-chay'-ro], m. 1. A worker in a sugar-mill. 2. (And. Carib.) Busybody (entrometido). 3. (Cono Sur) Small-time dealer.

trapiento, ta [trah-pe-en'-to, tah], a. Ragged, tattered.

trapillo [trah-peel'-lyo], m. 1. Courtier of a vulgar woman. 2. Little rag. **Estar, andar** or **salir de trapillo**, to be in an undress, to be in dishabille, to have a loose or negligent dress.

trapío [trah-pee'-o], m. 1. Sprightly manner, graceful gestures, whether respectable or vulgar and loose, which some women have. 2. Liveliness and smartness in a fighting bull.

trapisonda [trah-pe-son'-dah], f. (Coll.) Bustle, noise, confusion, clatter; clatter, deception. (Vul.) Carousing.

trapito [trah-pee'-to], m. dim. V. TRAPICO.

trapo [trah'-po], m. 1. Cloth. 2. Rag (paño), tatter. 3. Sails of a ship. 4. Clothes (vestidos de mujer). **Poner como un trapo**, to reprimand severely. **Trapo de fregar**, dishcloth. **Gasta una barbaridad en trapos**, she spends an awful lot on clothes. **Sacar los trapos a relucir**, to let fly.

traque [trah'-kay], m. Crack, the noise made by a bursting rocket, or the priming of a gun.

tráquea [trah'-kay-ah], f. 1. Windpipe, trachea. 2. Tracheae of insects.

traqueal [trah-kay-ahl'], a. 1. Tracheal, of or pertaining to a trachea. 2. Breathing by means of tracheae.

traquear [trah-kay-ar'], vn. 1. To crack, to make a loud noise. 2. (Carib.) To drink. -va. 1. To frequent, to handle a thing much. 2. To shake, to agitate, to move to and fro.

traqueartería [trah-kay-ar-tay-ree'-ah], f. Traehea, windpipe.

traqueo [trah-kay'-o], m. 1. Noise of artificial fireworks. 2. The act of shaking or moving to and fro.

traqueotomía [trah-kay-o-to-mee'-ah], f. Tracheotomy.

traquescote [trah-kes-co'-tay], (Naut.) Trackscout.

traquetear [trah-kay-tay-ar'], va. To shake (recipiente), to agitate, to move to and fro, to handle too much. -vn. 1. To crackle (cohete), to bang; to rattle (vehículo); to rattle (ametrallador). 2. (Cono Sur, Mex.) To bustle about (apresurarse).

traqueteo [trah-kay-tay'-o], m. Shaking, shake, concussion.

traquiarteria [trah-ke-ar-tay'-re-ah], f. V. TRAQUEARTERIA.

traquido [trah-kee'-do], m. Report of fire-arms.

traquítico, ca [trah-kee'-te-co, cah], a. Trachytic, like trachyte.

traquito [trah-kee'-to], m. Trachyte, a dull grayish volcanic rock of granite-like aspect.

tras [trahs], prep. After, behind (lugar), besides. **Tras una puerta**, behind a door. **Tras de venir tarde**, besides coming late. In composition it is equivalent to trans, as traspasar. Usage authorizes its employment in nearly all cases in place of trans. (Acad.) **Ir or andar tras alguno**, to go in pursuit after one, to seek diligently; to follow after one.

tras [trahs], m. (Coll.) 1. Breech, bottom. V. TRASERO. 2. Blow or stroke attended with noise; crash dash. (Onomatopoetic.) **Tras, tras**, repeated strokes or noise.

trasalcoba [trahs-al-co'-bah], f. Alcove behind the principal recess.

trasalpino, na [trahs-al-pee'-no, nah], a. V. TRANSALPINO.

trasanteayer [trahs-an-tay-ah-yerr'], adv. V. ANTEANTEAYER.

trasañejo, ja [trahs-ah-nyey'-ho, hah], a. Three years old (vino).

trasatlántico, ca [trahs-at-lahn'-te-co, cah], a. V. TRANSATLÁNTICO.

trasbisnieto, ta [trahs-bis-ne-ay'-to, tah], m. & f. V. TATARANIETO.

trasbordar and trasbordo [trans-bor-dahr]. V. sub TRANS.

trasca [trahs'-cah], f. (Prov.) Leather thong.

trascabo [trahs-cah'-bo], m. Trip, a trick by which a wrestler throws his antagonist.

trascantón [trahs-can-tone'], m. Stone placed at the corner of a street; curb-stone. **Dar trascantón or trascantonada**, to hide oneself behind a corner.

trascantonada [trahs-can-to-nah'-dah], f. 1. V. TRASCANTÓN. 2. Action of waiting beside a corner.

trascartarse [trahs-car-tar'-say], vr. To remain behind: applied to a card which, had it come sooner, would have won the game.

trascartón [trahs-car-tone'], m. Drawing of a winning card after the game is lost.

trascendencia [trahs-then-den'-the-ah], f. 1. Transcendence, perspicacity of things. 2. Result, consequence. **Encuentro sin trascendencia**, casual meeting.

trascendental [trahs-then-den-tahl'], a. 1. Transcendental, far-reaching (consecuencias), extending to other things, transcendent. 2. Transcendental, of very high degree, of great importance by reason of its probable consequences (importancia). 3. (Philosophy) Investigating the nature of our faculties, the value of ideas, etc. 4. (Math.) Transcendental, into whose calculation the infinite enters.

transcendentalismo [trahs-then-den-tah-lees'-mo], m. Transcendentalism, every philosophical system transcending observation and experience and rising into abstract investigations.

trascendentalista [trahs-then-den-tah-lees'-tahl], m. & a. Transcendentalism, one who holds the doctrine of transcendentalism.

transcendente [trans-then-den-tay], pa. & a. Transcendent.

trascender [tras-then-derr'], vn. 1 To be transcendent, to extend itself. 2. To emit a good, strong odor; to be pervasive, to penetrate. 3. To penetrate, to perceive quickly and clearly. 4. To transcend, to go beyond (not recognised by the Academy in this sense). 5. To come out (saberse). 6. To spread (propagarse). **En esta novela todo trasciende a romanticismo**, everything in this novel smacks of romanticism. **Por fin ha trascendido la triste noticia**, the sad news had come out at last. (Yo trasciendo, trascienda, from Trascender. V. ENTENDER.)

trascendido, da [trahs-then-dee'-do, dah], a & pp. of TRASCENDER. Acute, endowed with great penetration.

trascocina [trahs-co-thee'-nah], f. Back-kitchen.

trascolar [trahs-co-lar'], va. (Med.) 1. To strain, to percolate. 2. (Coll.) To pass over a mountain. (Yo trascuelo, trascuele, from Trascolar. V. ACORDAR.)

trasconejarse [trahs-co-ne-har'-say], vn. 1. To squat: applied to game pursued by dogs. 2. To sheer off, to escape. 3. (Coll.) To be missing or mislaid: said of papers, documents, or small articles. *(Yo me trascuerdo, trascuerde,* from *Trascordarse.* V. ACORDAR.*)*

trascordarse [trahs-cor-dar'-say], *vr.* To forget.

trascoro [trahs'-co´-ro], *m.* Space in a church at the back of the choir.

trascorral [trahs-cor-rahl´], *m.* 1. Back court or back yard. 2. *(Coll.)* Breech, buttocks.

trascribir [trahs-cre-beer'], *va.* V. TRANSCRIBIR.

trascripción [trahs-crep-the-on], *f.* V. TRANSCRIPCIÓN.

trascuarto [trahs-coo-ar´-to], *m.* Back room.

trascurso [trahs-coor'-so], *m.* Course or process of time. V. TRANSCURSO.

trasdobladura [trahs-do-blah-doo'-rah], *f.* Treble, triple.

trasdoblar [trahs-do-blar'], *m.* To treble, to multiply by three.

trasdoblo [trahs-do'-blo], *m.* Treble, triple. V. TRIPLE.

trasdós [trash-dose'], *m. (Arch.)* Extrados, the back or outer surface of an arch: opposed to soffit.

trasdosear [trahs-do-say-ar'], *m.* To strengthen upon the back.

trasechador [trahs-ay-chah-dor'], *m.* Fighter, contestant.

trasegador [trah-say-gah-dor'], *m.* One who racks wine.

trasegar [trah-say-gar'], *va.* 1. To overset, to turn topsy-turvy. 2. To decant, to rack wine. 3. To mix up (trastornar). *(Yo trasiego, yo trasiegue, trasegué.* from *Trasegar.* V. ACERTAR.)

traseñalador, ra [trah-say-nyah-lah-dor', rah], *m. & f.* One who alters marks.

traseñalar [trah-say-nay-lar'], *m.* To alter or blot out a mark and make a new one.

trasera [trah-say'-rah], *f.* Back or posterior part; croup.

trasero, ra [trah-say'-ro, rah], *a.* Remaining behind, coming after, hinder.

trasero [trah-say-ro]. *m.* 1. Buttock, rump of animals. **Traseros,** in jocular style, our ancestors, or predecessors. 2. *(Anat.)* Bottom.

trasferencia [trans-fay-ren-the-ah], *f.* V. TRANSFERENCIA.

trasferible [trans-fay-re-blay], *a.* V. TRANSFERIBLE.

trasferidor [trahs-fay-re-dor'], *m.* Transferrer. V. TRANSFERIDOR.

trasferir [trahs-fay-reer'], *m.* V. TRANSFERIR.

transfigurable, *a.* **transfiguración** and **trasfigurar** [trans-fe-goo-rah-blay], *va.* V. TRANSFIGURABLE, TRANSFIGURACIÓN, and TRANSFIGURAR.

trasfijo, ja, *a.* and **trasfixión** [trans-fe-ho], *f.* V. TRANSFIJO and TRANSFIXIÓN.

trasflorar and **trasflorear** [trans-flo-rahr], *va.* V. TRANSFLORAR and TRANSFLOREAR.

trasfojar [trahs-fo-har'], *va.* To run over the leaves of a book. V. TRASHOJAR.

trasfollado, da [trahs-fol-lyah'-do, dah], *a.* V. TRANSFOLLADO.

trasformación [trahs-for-mah-the-on'], *f.* Transformation. V. TRANSFORMACIÓN.

trasformador [trahs-for-mah-dor], *m.* V. TRANSFORMADOR.

trasformamiento [trahs-for-ma-me-ayn-to], *m.* V. TRANSFORMACIÓN.

trasformar [trahs-for-mar], *va.* V. TRANSFORMAR.

trasformativo, va [trahs-for-mah-te-vo], *a.* V. TRANSFORMATIVO.

trasfregar [trahs-fray-gar'], *va.* To rub.

trasfretano, na [trash-fray-tah'-no, nah], *a.* Transmarine.

trásfuga, trásfugo [trahs'-foo-gah, trahs'-foo-go], *m.* Deserter, fugitive. V. TRÁNSFUGA.

trasfusión or **transfusión** [trahs-foo-see-on'], *f.* Transfusion. **Trasfusión de sangre,** blood transfusion.

trasgo [trahs'-go], *m.* 1. Goblin (duende), hobgoblin, sprite. V. DUENDE. 2. A lively, restless, noisy boy.

trasgredir [trahs-gray-deer'], *va.* To transgress.

trasgresión [trahs-gray-se-on'], *f.* V. TRANSGRESIÓN.

trasgresor, ra [tahs-gray-sor', rah], *m. & f.* Transgressor. V. TRANSGRESOR.

trasguear [trahs-gray-ar'], *vn.* To play the hobgoblin.

trasguero [trahs-gay'-ro], *m.* One who imitates the tricks of hobgoblins.

trashogar [trahs-o-gar'], *m.* 1. Front of a chimney. 2. V. TRASHOGUERO, 1st def.

trashoguero [trahs-o-gay'-ro], *m.* 1. Iron plate, placed at the back part of a fireplace. 2. Block of wood placed against the wall to keep in the fire.

trashoguero, ra [trahs-o-gay'-ro, rah], *a.* Idling, loitering the whole day near the fire-place.

trashojar [trahes-o-har'], *va.* To run over the leaves of a book.

trashumante [trahs-oo-mahn'-tay], *pa. & a.* Applied to flocks of sheep which pasture in the north of Spain in summer and in the south in winter. **trashumantes,** traveling or merino sheep.

trashumar [trahs-oo-mar'], *va.* To drive sheep to or from the common pasture grounds in spring and autumn.

trasiego [trah-se-ay'-go], *m.* 1. Removal, the act of moving things. 2. The act of decanting liquors.

trasijado, da [trah-se-hah'-do, dah], *a.* Lank, meager: thin-flanked.

trasijar [trah-se-har'], *vn. & vr.* To grow thin or meager.

traslación [trahs-lah-the-on'], *f.* 1. Translation, removal. 2. Translation, version, rendering into another language, and the subject-matter so translated.

trasladante [trahs-lah-dahn'-tay], *pa.* Translating, transcribing.

trasladar [trahs-lah-dar'], *va.* 1. To move (mudar), to remove (quitar), to transport. 2. To translate (pensamiento, sentimiento). 3. To transcribe. **Trasladar su pensamiento al papel,** to put one´s thoughts on paper. *-vr.* To go, to move. **Trasladarse a otro puesto,** to move to a new job.

traslado [trahs-lah'-do], *m.* 1. A copy (copia). 2. Imitation, resemblance, likeness, counterpart. 3. *(Law.)* The reference or act of delivering written judicial proceedings to the other party, in order that on examination of them he may prepare the answer. **Dar traslado a uno de una orden,** to give somebody a copy of an order.

traslapar [trahs-lah-par'], *m.* V. SOLAPAR.

traslaticiamente [trahs'-lah-te-the-ah-men'-tay], *adv.* Metaphorically, figuratively.

traslaticio, cia, traslato, ta [trahs-lah-tee'-the-o, ah], *a.* Metaphorical, figurative.

traslativo, va [trahs-lah-tee'-vo, vah], *a.* Metaphorical, figurative.

traslúcido, da [trahs-loo'-the-do, dah], *a.* Transparent, clear, pellucid.

traslucido, da [trahs-loo-thee'-do, dah], *pp.* of TRASLUCIRSE.

trasluciente [trahs-loo-the-en'-tay], *a.* Translucent, transparent, translucid.

traslucirse [trahs-loo-theer'-say], *vr.* 1. To be transparent (ser transparente); to shine through (ser visible). 2. To conjecture, to infer. 3. *(Fig.)* To leak out (saberse). 4. *(Fig.)* To reveal one´s inmost thoughts (persona).

traslumbramiento [trahs-loom-brah-me-en'-to], *m.* The state of being dazzled by excessive light.

traslumbrarse [trahs-loom-brar'-say], *vr.* 1. To be dazzled with excessive light (ser deslumbrado). 2. To vanish, to disappear.

trasluz [trahs-looth'], *m.* 1. Light which passes through a transparent body. 2. *(Art.)* Transverse light. 3. *(Carib.)* Resemblance (semblanza).

trasmallo [trahs-mahl'-lyo], *m.* 1. Trammel-net, drag-net, a coarse-meshed net, having a smaller one behind it. 2. Iron handle of a hammer.

trasmano [trahs-mah'-no], *m.* Second player at a game of cards.

trasmañana [trahs-mah-nyah'-nah], *f.* The day after tomorrow.

trasmarino, na [trahs-mah-ree'-no, nah], *a.* V. TRANSMARINO.

trasmatar [trahs-mah-tar'], *va. (Coll.)* To persuade oneself of having longer to enjoy life than another; to outlive.

trasmigración [trahs-me-grah-the-on'], *f. V.* TRANSMIGRACIÓN.

trasmigrar [trahs-me-grar'], *va. V.* TRANSMIGRAR.

trasminar [trahs-me-nar'], *va.* To undermine, to excavate, to dig under ground. *-vn.* To emit a strong scent. *-vr.* To pierce, to penetrate.

trasmisible trahs-me-see'-blay], *a. V.* TRANSMISIBLE.

trasmisión [trahs-me-se-on'], *f. V.* TRANSMISIÓN.

trasmisor, ra [trahs-me-sor', rah], *a. V.* TRANSMISOR.

transmitido, da [trahs-me-tee'-do, dah], *a. & pp.* of TRASMITIR. Transmitted, traditive.

trasmitir [trahs-me-teer'], *va. (Law.) V.* TRANSMITIR.

trasmochadero [trahs-mo-chah-day'-ro], *m.* A thicket of fire-wood. *-a.* Serving for fuel.

trasmochar [trahs-mo-char'], *va.* To cut branches of trees for fuel.

trasmontar [trahs-mon-tar'], *va.* To pass to the other side of the mountain. *V.* TRAMONTAR.

trasmota [trahs-mo'-tah], *f. (Prov.)* After wine, made by water poured on the pressed grapes.

trasmudar [trahs-moo-dar'], *va. V.* TRANSMUDAR.

trasmutable [trahs-moo-tah'-blay], *a. V.* TRANSMUTABLE.

trasmutación [trahs-moo-tah-the-on'], *f. V.* TRANSMUTACIÓN.

trasmutar [trahs-moo-tar'], *va.* To alter, to transmute, to convert. *V.* TRANSMUTAR.

trasmutativo, va [trahs-moo-tah-tee'-vo, vah], **Trasmutatorio, ria,** *a. V.* TRANSMUTATIVO.

trasnochada [trahs-no-chah'-dah], *f.* 1. Last night (noche anterior). 2. Watch, the act of watching a whole night (noche sin dormir).

trasnochado, da [trahs-no-chah'-do, dah], *a. & pp.* of TRASNOCHAR. Having watched the whole night; fatigued from night-watching.

trasnochador, ra [trahs-no-chah-dor', rah], *m & f.* Night-watcher.

trasnochar [trahs-no-char'], *vn.* To watch, to sit up a whole night, to have a night out (ir de juerga).

trasnombrar [trahs-nom-brar'], *va.* To change or confound names.

trasnominación [trahs-no-me-nah-the-on'], *f. V.* METONIMIA.

trasoír [trahs-o-eer'], *va.* To mistake, to misunderstand, to hear the wrong thing.

trasojado, da [trahs-o-hah'-do, dah], *a.* Having sunken eyes, emaciated, worn out.

trasoñar [trah-so-nyar'], *vn.* To dream, to fancy erroneously.

traspágina [trash-pah'-he-nah], *f.* Back page.

traspalar [trahs-pah-lar'], *va.* 1. To shovel, to remove with a shovel. 2. To move, to remove. 3. *(Prov.)* To dig under a vine; to clear the ground of grass.

traspapelarse [trahs-pah-pay-lar'-say], *vn.* To be mislaid among other papers (escritura).

trasparencia [trahs-pe-ren'-the-ah], *f.* Transparency. *V.* TRANSPARENCIA.

trasparentarse [trahs-pah-ren-tahr'-say], *vn. V.* TRANSPARENTARSE.

trasparente [trahs-pah-ren'-tay], *a. V.* TRANSPARENTE.

traspasación [trahs-pah-sah-the-on'], *f. (Law.)* Conveyance, transfer. *V.* TRASPASO.

traspasamiento [trahs-pah-sah-me-en'-to], *m.* 1. Transgression, trespass. 2. Transfer, the act of conveying. 3. Grief, anguish.

traspasar [trahs-pah-sar'], *va.* 1. To pass over, to go beyond (límite); to cross (calle). 2. To remove, to transport. 3. To transfix, to transpierce; to introduce with great force. 4. To cross a river. 5. To return, to repass. 6. To transgress, to violate a law. 7. To exceed proper bounds; to trespass. 8. To transfer, to make over. **La bala le traspasó el pulmón**, the bullet pierced his lung. **La escena me traspasó el corazón**, the scene pierced me to the core. *-vn.* To be touched with compasion, to be afflicted.

traspaso [trahs-pah'-so], *m.* 1. Conveyance, transfer (venta). 2. Grief, anguish (pena). 3. Trespass, violation of a law; treachery. 4. Infringement (de ley). 5. Property transferred (propiedad, bienes).

traspeinar [trahs-pay-nar'], *va.* To comb again.

traspellar [trahs-pel-lyar'], *va. V.* CERRAR.

traspié [trahs-pe-ay'], *m.* 1. Slip (tropiezo), stumble. **Dar traspiés,** (1) to stumble without falling. (2) *(Met.)* To stumble, to dip, to commit errors or faults. 2. Trip, a wrestler's trick with his antagonist.

traspilastra [trahs-pe-lahs'-trah], *f. (Arch.) V.* CONTRAPILASTRA.

traspillarse [trahs-peel-lyar'-say], *vr.* To grow thin, to be emaciated.

traspintar [trahs-pin-tar'], *va.* To know from the cards drawn those that are to follow. *-vr.* To be disappointed: to turn out contrary to one's expectation.

traspirable [trahs-pe-rah'-blay], Transpirable. *V.* TRANSPIRABLE.

traspiración [trahs-pe-rah-the-on'], *f. V.* TRANSPIRACIÓN.

traspirar [trahs-pe-rar'], *va. V.* TRANSPIRAR.

trasplantación [trahs-plan-tah-the-on'], *f. (Prov.) V.* TRASPLANTE.

trasplantar [trahs-plan-tar'], *va.* 1. To transplant, to remove plants. 2. To migrate.

trasplante [trash-plahn'-tay], *m.* Transplantation. **Trasplante de corazón**, heart transplant.

trasponedor, ra [trahs-po-nay-dor', rah], *m. & f. V.* TRANSPONEDOR.

trasponer [trahs-po-nerr'], *m. V.* TRANSPONER. *(Yo traspongo, trasponga; traspuse, traspondré, traspusiera; from Trasponer. V.* PONER.*)*

traspontín [trahs-pon-teen'], *m. (Coll.) V.* TRASERO.

trasporarse [trahs-po-rar'-say], *vr. V.* TRANSPORARSE.

trasportación [trahs-por-tah-the-on'], *f.* Transportation. *V.* TRANSPORTACIÓN

trasportador, ra [trahs-por-tah-dor', rah], *V.* TRANSPORTADOR.

trasportamiento [trahs-por-tah-me-en'-to], *m. V.* TRANSPORTAMIENTO.

trasportar [trahs-por-tar'], *va. V.* TRANSPORTAR.

trasporte [trahs-por'-tay], *m. V.* TRANSPORTE.

trasportín [trahs-por-teen'], *m.* A thin and small mattress, put between other mattresses.

trasposición [trahs-po-se-the-on'], *f.* Transposition, transposal. *V.* TRANSPOSICIÓN.

transpositivo, va [trahs-po-se-tee'-vo, vah], *a. V.* TRANSPOSITIVO.

traspuesta [trahs-poo-es'-tah], *f.* 1. Transport, removal. 2. Corner or turning of a mountain, which serves for a lurking-place. 3. Flight (huida), disappearance. 4. Backyard (patio) or court; back door; out offices of a dwelling-house.

traspuesto, ta [trahs-poo-es'-to, tah], *pp. irr.* of TRASPONER. Transported.

traspunte [trahs-poon'-tay], *m.* A prompter in a theater (apuntador). *V.* APUNTADOR.

trasquero [trahs-kay'-ro], *m* Leather cutter, one who cuts out leather thongs.

trasquiladero [trash-ke-lay-day'-ro], *m.* Place where sheep are shorn.

trasquilador [trahs-ke-lah-dor'], *m.* Shearer.

trasquiladura [trahs-ke-lah-doo'-rah], *f* The act of shearing.

trasquilar [trahs-ke-lar'], *va.* 1. To shear sheep (oveja); to cut the bar in an irregular manner (cortar). 2. To clip, to curtail, to diminish.

trasquilimocho, cha [trahs-ke-le-mo'-cho, chah], *a. (Coll.)* Close shorn or cropped.

trasquilón [trahs-ke-lone'], *m.* 1. Cut of the shears: as much wool or hair as is cut off by one snip of the shears. **A trasquilones**, irregularly, rudely 2. *(Coll.)* Part of one's fortune, which has been clipped or lost through the fraud of others.

trastada [trahs-tah'-dah], f. (Coll.) A bad act, or one ill-judged and ill-advised, practical joke (broma pesada), piece of bad behavior (grosería).

trastazo [trahs-tah'-tho], m. (Coll.) A whack, thump, blow.

traste [trahs'-tay], m. 1. Fret, a sort or slender strip of metal fastened at intervals in the neck of a guitar, or like instrument, to determine the intervals of the scale. 2. (Prov.) A small glass or cup, kept in wine-cellars for the use of wine-tasters. 3. (Prov.) V. TRASTO. **Sin trastes**, without head or tail; in a disorderly manner. **Dar al traste con los negocios**, (Coll.) to fail, to be unfortunate in business. **Ir al traste**, to fail.

trasteado [trahs-tay-ah'-do], m. Number of frets upon the neck of a lute or guitar.—**Trasteado, da**, pp. of TRASTEAR.

trasteador, ra [trahs-tay-ah-dor', rah], m. & f. A noisy fellow, who throws everything into disorder and confusion.

trasteante [trahs-tay-ahn'-tay], pa. & a. Applied to a dexterous performer on the guitar.

trastear [trahs-tay-ar'], va. 1. To put frets upon the neck of a guitar. 2. To remove furniture from one part of a house to another (mover). 3. To play well on the guitar. 4. To talk upon a subject in a lively manner (entretener). 5. (Mex.) To feel up (acariciar). -vn. 1. To move things around (mover objetos). 2. (And. CAm.) To move house (mudar de casa). 3. To make bright conversation (conversar).

trastejadura [trahs-tay-hah-doo'-rah], f. V. TRASTEJO.

trastejar [trahs-tay-har'], va. 1. To tile; to cover with tiles. 2. To go over, to examine something in order to repair it.

trastejo [trahs-tay'-ho], m. 1 Tiling, covering houses with tiles. 2. Any uninterrupted and disorderly motion.

trastera [tras-tay'-rah], f. 1. Lumber room (habitación). 2. (Mex.) Cupboard (armarío). 3. (Carib.) Heap of junk.

trastería [trahs-tay-ree'-ah], f. 1. Heap of lumber (trastos). 2. A ridiculous or foolish action.

trasterminante [trahs-ter-me-nahn'-tay], pa. & m. V. TRANSTERMINANTE.

trasterminar [trahs-ter-me-nar'], va. V. TRANSTERMINAR.

trastero [trahs-tay'-ro], m.1. Lumber room (habitación); storage room. 2. (Mex.) Cupboard, closet. 3. (Mex.) Bum (culo). 4. (CAm. Mex.) Dish-rack (para platos).

trastiberino, na [trahs-te-bay-ree'-no], a. V. TRANSTIBERINO.

trastienda [trahs-te-en'-dah], f. 1. Back-room behind a shop (habitación). 2. Prudence, precaution, forecast. 3. (Cono Sur, Mex.) Bum (culo).

trasto [trahs'-to], m. 1. Furniture, movables or goods put in a house or use or ornament; luggage. **Trastos de cocina**, kitchen utensils. 2. Useless person, puppy. 3. Scenery (decorado); stage furniture (accesorios). 4. Gear (avíos). **Tirarse los trastos a la cabeza**, to have a blazing row. **Trastos de pescar**, fishing tackle.

trastornable [trahs-tor-nah'-blay], a. 1. Movable; easily turned, topsy-turvy. 2. Fickle, restless.

trastornadamente [trahs-tor-nah'-dah-men'-tay], adv. Upside down, in confusion.

trastornado, da [trahs-tor-nah'-do, dah], a. 1. Mentally unbalanced (persona). 2. Overthrown, in disorder, in confusion.

trastornador, ra [trahs-tor-nah-dor' rah], m. & f. Disturber, a turbulent person, subverter.

trastornadora [trahs-tor-nah-doo'-rah], f. Overturning, inversion, perversion.

trastornamiento [tras-tor-nah-me-en'-to] m. Overturning, inverting.

trastornar [trahs-tor-nah'], va. 1. To overthrow, to reverse, to overturn (volcar). 2. To confuse (ideas), to perplex the mind (volver loco). 3. To delight (encantar). -vr. 1. To go crazy (persona), to become mentally unbalanced. 2. To fall through (proyecto). **Esa chica le ha trastornado**, that girl has bowled him over.

trastorno [trahs-tor'-no], m. 1. Overthrow, overturn, confusion (perturbación). 2. Calamity, misfortune. 3. Mental disorder.

trastrabado, da [trahs-trah-bah'-do, dah], a. Applied to a horse with the far hind foot and the near fore foot white.

trastrás [trahs-trahs'], m. The last in some children's games.

trastrigo [trahs-tree'-go], m. (Prov.) Wheat of the best quality.

trastrocamiento [trahs-tro-cah-me-en'-to], m. Transposition, inversion.

trastrocar [trahs-tro-car'], va. To invert or change the order of things.

trastrueco, trastrueque [trahs-troo-ay'-co], m. Inversion, transposition.

trastuelo [trahs-too-ay'-lo], m. dim. Little, useless person.

trastumbar [trahs-toom-bar'], va. To throw down, to overturn, to overset.

trasudadamente [trah-soo-dah-dah-men'-tay], adv. With sweat and fatigue.

trasudar [trah-soo-dar'], va. & vn. 1. To sweat, to perspire. 2. To apply oneself to a business with assiduity and care.

trasudor [trah-soo-dor'], m. A gentle sweat; transudation.

trasuntar [trah-soon-tar'], va. 1. To copy (copiar), to transcribe. 2. To abridge.

trasuntivamente [trah-soon-te-vah-men'-tay], adv. Compendiously.

trasunto [trah-soon'-to], m. 1. Copy (copia), transcript. 2. Likeness, close resemblance (semejanza). **Ese chico es un trasunto de su padre**, that boy is the picture of his father.

trasvanarse [trahs-vay-nar'-say], vr. 1. To be forced out of the arteries or veins (sangre). 2. To be spilled.

trasvase [trahs-vah'-say], m. Pouring, decanting; diversion.

trasverberación [trahs-ver-bay-rah-the-on'], f. V. TRANSFIXIÓN.

trasversal [trahs-ver-sahl'], a. Transversal. V. TRANSVERSAL.

trasversalmente [trahs-ver-sahl'-men-tay], adv. V. TRANSVERSALMENTE.

trasverso [trahs-ver'-so], sa, a. Transverse.

trasverter [trahs-ver-tayr'], vn. To overflow, to run over.

trasvinarse [trahs-ve-nar'-say], vr. 1. To leak out (vino). 2. To be guessed, surmised, or supposed.

trasvolar [trahs-vo-lar'], va. To fly across.

trata [trah'-tah], f. The African slavetrade formerly carried on. (Acad.)

tratable [trab-tah'-blay], a. 1. Tractable, ductile, flexible. 2. Tractable, compliant, kindly (amable).

tratadico, illo, ito [trah-tah-dee'-co], m. dim. A brief tract or treatise.

tratadista [trah-tah-dees'-tah], com. Author of treatises.

tratado [trah-tah'-do], m. 1. Treaty, convention, compact, relating to public affairs. 2. Treatise, tractate. **Tratado de paz**, peace treaty. —**Tratado, da**, pp. of TRATAR.

tratador, ra [trah-tah-dor', rah], m. & f Mediator, arbitrator, umpire.

tratamiento [trah-tah-me-en'-to], m. 1. Treatment (de persona, problema), usage. 2. Compellation, style of address, title of courtesy. **Tratamiento de tú**, familiar address.

tratante [trah-tahn'-tay], m. Dealer, merchant. **Tratante en víveres**, dealer in provisions, who buys by wholesale and sells by retail. **Tratante en caballos**, dealer in horses, horses Jockey. -pa. Treating, handling.

tratar [trah tar'], va. 1. To treat on a subject, to discuss: to confer, to consult. 2. To touch, to handle, to manage. 3. To baffle, to trade. 4. To manage to conduct. 5. To use, to treat; (and Med.) to treat, to employ curative measures. 6. (Met.) To study or be careful to attain an object. 7. To have illicit relations with a person (tener relaciones). 8. To give a person the title of courtesy to which he is entitled. -vn. 1. **Tratar de**, to deal with. 2. **Tratar con**, to have to do with. -vr. 1. To entertain a friendly intercourse. 2. To be on terms of intimacy. 3. To live well or ill. **Tratar de hacer alguna cosa**, (Coll.) to be resolved upon doing a thing. **Tener tratada alguna cosa**, to have spoken for or engaged a thing. **La trata muy bien en esa pensión**, they treat her well in that boarding house. **Le trato desde hace 6 meses**, I have known him for

6 months. **No tratamos con traidores**, we don´t treat with traitors. **Se tratan de usted**, they address each other as «usted».

tratillo [trah-teel´-lyo], *m. dim.* A peddling trade.

trato [trah´-to], *m.* 1. Treatment, manner of using; behavior (conducta), conduct. 2. Manner (manera de ser), address. 3. Concernment; pact, agreement. 4. Treat. 5. Trade, traffic, commerce. 6. Friendly intercourse, conversation, communication. 7. Gallantry. Sexual intercourse between man and woman. 8. Treachery, infidelity. 9. Religious meditation, prayer. 10. Compellation, title of courtesy. 11. *(Mex.)* Market stall (puesto). 12. *(Mex.)* Small business (negocio). **Mal trato**, *(Met.)* bad conduct with anyone, ill usage. **Tener buen trato**, *(Coll.)* to be affable and polite. **Tener trato de gentes**, to be accustomed to good society. **Ese no es el trato**, that was not the agreement.

trauma [trah´-oo-mah], *f. (Med.)* Trauma.

traumático, ca [trah-oo-mah´-te-co, cah], *a.* Traumatic, relating to wounds.

traumatismo [trah-oo-mah-tees´-mo], *m.* 1. Traumatism, wound. 2. State in which a grave wound puts the system.

traumatizar [trah-oo-mah-te-thar´], *va.* To traumatize; *(Fig.)* to shock, to affect profoundly.

traumatología [trah-oo-mah-to-lo-he´-ah], *f.* Orthopedic surgery.

traumatólogo, ga [trah-oo-mah-to´-lo-go], *m & f.* Orthopedic surgeon.

travata [trah-vah´-tah], *f.* Tornado, hurricane in the Gulf of Guinea.

traversa [trah-verr´-sah] *f.* 1. *(Naut.)* Back-stay. 2. *(Gil.)* Traverse, a ditch with one or two parapets of planks loaded with earth.

traverso [trah-verr´-so], *m.* A kind of net made of esparto used in tuna fishing.

travertino [trah-ver-tee´-no], *m.* Travertine, a calcareous tufa, which, on exposure, acquires a reddish color.

través [trah-ves´], *m.* 1. Inclination to one side, bias. 2. Misfortune, calamity, adversity. 3. *V.* FLANCO. **De través** or **al través**, across, athwart. *-adv.* 1. Across, crossways. **Mirar de través**, to squint. 2. **Al través**, across, over. **Lo sé a través de un amigo**, I know about it through a friend.

travesaño [trah-vay-sah´-nyo], *m.* 1. Cross-timber; transom. 2. Long holster of a bed. 3. *(CAm. Carib. Mex.)* Sleeper.

travesear [trah-vay-say´-ar´], *m.* 1. To be uneasy, to run to and fro in a restless manner; to be flighty. 2. To jest, to joke. 3. To lead a debauched life: to behave improperly. 4. To talk wittily (hablar). 5. *(Mex.)* To show off one´s horsemanship (jinete).

travesero [trah-vay-say´-ro], *m.* Bolster of a bed; transom.

travesero, ra [trah-vay-say´-ro, rah], *a.* Transverse, across.

travesía [trah-vay-see´-ah], *f.* l. Oblique or transverse position or manner. 2. Distance, road (de pueblo), passage; traject, cross road. **Hacer buena travesía**, *(Naut.)* to have a fine passage. 3. Fortification with traverses. 4. Money won or lost at gambling (en el juego). 5. *(Naut.)* Side wind (viento). 6. *(And. Cono Sur)* Arid plain (desierto).

travesío, ía [trah-vay-see´-o, ah], *a.* 1. Traversing: applied to cattle that traverse the limits of their pasture. 2. Transverse, oblique, or lateral wind.

travesío [trah-vay-see´-o], *m.* Crossing, place where persons or things cross.

travestido, da [trah-ves-tee´-do, dah], *a. (Antiq.)* Disguised.

travestismo [trah-ves-tees´-mo], *m.* Transvestism.

travesura [trah-vay-soo´-rah], *f.* 1. Prank (broma), ludicrous or jocose trick to amuse (gracia). 2. Penetration, lively fancy; sprightly conversation. 3. Mischief, trick, a culpable action, and worthy of reproof or punishment (mala pasada). **Son travesuras de niño**, they´re just childish pranks.

traviesa [trah-ve-ay´-sah], *f.* 1. Oblique petition, passage. *V.* TRAVESÍA. 2. Wager laid by bystanders at card-tables.

travieso, sa [trah-ve-ay´-so, sah], *a.* 1. Transverse, oblique. 2. Restless (inquieto), uneasy, flighty, knavish, turbulent, noisy; mischievous (niños). 3. Subtle, shrewd.

tráxito, ta [trak´-se-to, tah], *a. (Biol.)* Rough.

traxitofito [trak-se-to-fee´-to], *m. (Bot.)* A plant with leaves rough to the touch.

trayecto [trah-yec´-to], *m.* 1. Journey (de persona), run (de vehículo). 2. Trisecting, act of casting over it. 3. Road (camino), route, way; stretch (tramo). **Recorrer un trayecto**, to cover a distance. 4. Trajection, space cast across.

trayectoria [trah-yec-toh´-re-ah], *f.* Trajectory (camino), the curved path described by a projectile.

trayente [trah-yen´-tay], *pa.* Bringing, carrying, conducting.

traza [trah´-thah], *f.* 1. First sketch or draught, trace, outline. 2. Plan, scheme, project, contrivance, a plot, an artifice; manner, means (medio). 3. Appearance, aspect, prospect (aspecto). 4. Skill (habilidad). 5. *(Cono Sur)* Track (huella). **Tiene trazas de ser un pícaro**, he has the looks of a rogue. **Tener traza para hacer algo**, to be skillful at doing something.

trazado, da [trah-thah´-do, dah], *a. & pp.* TRAZAR. Traced, outlined. **Bien or mal trazado**, person of a good or bad disposition or figure.

trazador, ra [trah-thah-dor´, rah], *m. & f.* 1. Planner (persona), sketcher, contriver, inventor, schemer. 2. Tracer. 3. *(Comput.)* Plotter.

trazar [trah-thar´], *va.* 1. To contrive, to devise, to plan out (planificar), to scheme, to project. 2. To trace (en discurso), to mark out. 3. To draw the first sketch or plan. 4. To contrive (medios), to devise.

trazo [trah´-tho], *m.* 1. Sketch (esbozo), plan, design, project. 2. Moulding. *V.* LÍNEA. 3. (Painting) Fold of the drapery. **Trazo de lápiz**, pencil stroke. **Trazo discontinuo**, broken line.

trazumarse [trah-thoo-mar´-say], *vr.* To leak, to ooze. *V.* REZUMARSE.

treballa [tray-bahl´, lyah], *f.* Sauce for goose, consisting of almonds, garlic, bread, eggs, spices, sugar, etc.

trébedes [tray´-bay-des], *f. pl.* Trivet, a tripod used in kitchens.

trebejo [tray-bay´-ho], *m.* 1. Top, play-thing. 2. Fun, jest, joke. *-pl.* 1. The pieces of a chess-board. 2. Implements of an art or trade.

trebeliánica, or **cuarta trebeliánica** [tray-bay-le-ah´-ne-cah], *f.* The fourth part of an estate, to be deducted by the fiduciary heir, who holds it in trust for another.

trébol [tray´-bol], *m. (Bot.)* Trefoil, clover. **Trébol real**, *(Bot.)* Melilot. **Trébol silvestre**, shamrock.

trece [tray´-thay], *a.* 1. Thirteen. **Estarse en sus trece**, to persist, to execute with perseverance. 2. Thirteenth. *V.* DECIMITERCIO. *-m.* The figure 13.

trecemesino, na [tray-thay-may-see´-no, nah], *a.* Of thirteen months.

trecenario [tray-thay-nah´-re-o], *m.* Space of thirteen days.

tracenato, trecenazgo [tray-thay-nah´-to], *m.* Office in the order of Santiago for which thirteen knights are chosen.

treceno, na [tray-thay´-no, nah], *a.* Thirteenth, completing thirteen.

trecésimo, ma [tray-thay´-ee-mo, mah], *a.* Thirtieth, completing thirty.

trechel [tray-chel´], *m. (Bot.)* A somewhat brown variety of wheat.

trecheo [tray-chay´-o], *a.* Passing of ores and soil in basked, which the workmen in a row pass from one to another.

trecho [tray´-cho], *m.* Space, distance of time or place. **A trechos**, by intervals. **De trecho en trecho**, at certain distances.

trecientos, tas [tray-the-en´-tos, tas], *a.* Three hundred.

tredécimo, ma [tray-day´-the-mo, mah], *a.* Thirteenth.

trefe [tray´-fay], *a.* 1. Lean, thin, meagre. 2. Spurious, adulterated.

tregua [tray'-goo-ah], *f.* 1. Truce, cessation of hostilities. 2. Rest, repose. **No dar treguas**, to give no respite.

treílla [tray-eel'-lyah], *f. V.* TRAÍLLA.

treinta [tray'-in-tah], *a. & n.* Thirty, thirtieth.

treintaidoseno, na [trary-in-tah-e-do-say'-no, nah], *a.* 1 Thirty-second. 2. Applied to the cloth the warp of which consists of thirty-two hundreds of threads.

treintanario, treintonario [tray-in-tah-nah'-re-o], *m.* Space of thirty days; thirty masses said for a person deceased; a trental.

treintañal [tray-in-tah-nyahl'], *a.* Containing thirty years.

treintañera [tray-en-tah-nyay'-rah], *f.* Woman of about thirty.

treintena [tray-in-tay'-nah], *f.* 1. Thirty. 2. The thirtieth part.

treinteno, na [tray-in-tay'-no, nah], *a.* Thirtieth.

treja [tray'-hah], *f.* Mode of playing at billiards.

tremadal [tray-mah-dahl'], *m. V.* TREMADAL.

tremebundo, da [tray-may-boon'-do, dah], *a.* Dreadful, frightful, fearful.

tremedal [tray-may-dahl'], *m.* Quagmire, marsh, morass.

tremendo, da [tray-men'-do, dah], *a.* 1. Tremendous, dreadful, terrible (terrible). 2. Awful, grand; worthy of respect. 3. Huge or executive in its line. **Le dio una tremenda paliza**, he gave him a tremendous beating. 4. Inventive, witty, entertaining (persona).

tremente [tray-men'-tay], *pa.* Trembling.

trementina [tray-men-tee'-nah], *f.* Turpentine.

tremer [tray-merr'], *vn.* To tremble.

tremés, tremesino, na [tray-mes'], *a.* Three months old.

tremielga [tray-me-el'-gah], *f. (Zool.)* Electric-ray, cramp-fish, torpedo.

tremís [tray-mees'], *m.* Ancient gold coin.

tremó [tray-mo'], *m.* A pier-glass.

tramolante [tray-mo-lahn'-tay], *pa.* Waving in the air.

tremolar [tray-mo-lar'], *m. dim.* 1. *(Naut.)* To hoist the colors, jacks, or pendants. 2. To wave, to move or scatter through the air.

tremolina [tray-mo-lee'-nah], *f.* 1. Rustling of the wind. 2. Bustle, noise. **Levantar una tremolina**, *(Coll.)* (a) to raise a rumpus, (b) To excite a quarrel.

tremor [tray-mor'], *m.* Trembling, tremor.

trémulamente [tray'-moo-lah-men-tay], *adv.* Tremblingly, tremulously.

tremulante, tremulento, ta [tray-moo-lahn'-tay], *a. V.* TRÉMULO.

trémulo, la [tray'-moo-lo, lah], *a.* Tremulous, quivering, shaking.

tren [trayn], *m.* 1. Traveling equipage, train, retinue. 2. Show, pomp, ostentation. 3. Railroad train. 4. *(Mil.)* Convoy. 5. **Tren de vida**, life style. 6. Speed (velocidad). 7. *(LAm.)* En tren de, in the process of. 8. *(Carib.)* Workshop (taller). 9. *(CAm. Mex.)* Coming and going (trajín). 10. *(Cono Sur, Mex.)* Tram (tranvía). 11. *(Carib.)* Cheeky remark (majadería). **Tren de correo**, mail train. **Tren de recreo**, excursion train. **Tren elevado**, elevated train. **Tren expreso**, fast train. **Cambiar de tren**, to change train. **Tomar un tren**, to catch a train. **Perder el tren**, to miss the train.

trena [tray'-nah], *f.* 1. Scarf, sash. 2. Garland of flowery. 3. *(Coll.)* Prison, jail. 4. Burnt silver.

trenado, da [tray-nah'-do, dah], *a.* Reticulated, formed of network.

trenca [tren'-cah], *f.* Each of two pieces of wood put across in a beehive.

trencellín [tren-thel-lyeen'], *m. V.* TRENCILLO.

trencha [tren'-chah], *f. (Naut.)* A ripping chisel.

trencica, ita [tren-thee'-cah], *f. dim.* o TRENZA.

trencilla [tren-theel'-lyah], *f.* Braid. **Trencilla de oro, de plata, de seda, de algodón**, gold, silver, silk, or cotton braid.

trencillar [tren-theel-lyar'], *va.* To garnish with a band of gold or silver lace and jewels.

trencillo [tren-theel'-lyo], *m.* 1. *(Com.) V.* TRENCILLA. 2. Hat-band of gold or silver, garnished with jewels.

treno [tray'-no], *m.* 1. A kind of sledge. 2. *pl.* Lamentations.

trenque [tren'-kay], *m. (Prov.)* Mole or bank to turn off the current of a river.

trenza [tren'-thah], *f.* 1. Braid of three strands. 2. All a woman's hair though not braided; tress.

trenzadera [tren-thah-day'-rah], *f.* Tape. *V.* TRANZADERA.

trenzado [tren-thah'-do], *m.* 1. Braided hair. 2. A step in dancing.—**Trenzado, da**, *pp.* of TRENZAR.

trenzar [tren-thar'], *va.* To braid the hair. *-vn.* To weave in and out (bailadores). *-vr. (LAm.)* **Trenzarse en una discusión**, to get involved in an argument.

treo [tray'-o], *m. (Naut.)* Square-sail, cross-jack sail.

trepa [tray'-pah], *f.* 1. Climbing (subida). 2. Edging sewed to clothes for ornament. 3. *(Coll.)* Flogging, lashing, beating (paliza). 4. Artful trick; malice; subtlety.

trepado, da [tray-pah'-do, dah], *a.* Strong, robust (animales). *-pp.* of TREPAR.

trepado [tray-pah'-do], *m.* Edging sewed on clothes.

trepador, ra [tray-pah-dor', rah], *a.* Climber, climbing. *-m.* 1. A climbing-place. 2. *(Zool.)* A sea-wolf, wolf-fish. *-f.* 1. *(Bot.)* Climber, a climbing-plant. 2. *pl. (Zool.)* Climbers.

trepanar [tray-pa-nar'], *va.* To Trepan, to trephine.

trépano [tray'-pah-no], *m. (Surg.)* Trepan, trephine, an instrument for perforating the skull.

trepante [tray-pahn'-tay], *pa.* Wily, artful, crafty.

trepar [tray-par'], *vn.* 1. To climb, to clamber, to crawl. 2. To creep upon supports (hiedra). *-va.* To ornament with edging.

trepe [tray'-pay], *m. (Coll.)* Scolding. **Echar un trepe**, to tell off.

trepidación [tray-pe-dah-the-on'], *f.* 1. Tremor, quaking of the earth. 2. An apparent vibration which ancient astronomers attributed to the firmament.

trepidante [tray-pe-dahn'-tay], *a. V.* TEMEROSO and TRÉMULO.

trepidar [tray-pe-dar'], *vn.* 1. To quiver, to tremble. 2. *(Met. Amer.)* To waver, to vacillate.

trépido, da [tray'-pe-do, dah], *a.* Tremulous.

tres [trays], *a. & n.* 1. Three. 2. Third. *V.* TERCERO. 3. The figure. **Capítulo tres**, third chapter. **Tres veces**, Three times. **Ni a la de tres**, on no account.

tresalbo, ba [tray-sahl'-bo, bah], *a.* Having three white feet (caballo).

tresañal [tray-sah-nyahl'], *a. V.* TRESAÑEJO.

tresañejo, ja [tray-sah-nyay'-ho, hah], *a.* Three years old; done three years ago.

tresbolillo (Al) [trays-bo-leel'-lyo], *adv. exp.* Quincunx, a mode of planting trees and grapevines, so that each four form a square with a fifth in the middle, like the five-spot on a die.

trescientos, tas [trays-the-en'-tose, tas], *a. & a.* Three hundred.

tresdoblar [tres-do-blar'], *va.* To triple. *V.* TRIPLICAR.

tresdoble [tres-do'-blay], *m.* The state or quality of being three-fold.

tresillo [tray-seel'-lyo], *m.* Ombre, a game played by three. 2. Three-piece suite (muebles).

tresmesino, na [tres-may-see'-no, nah], *a. V.* TRESMESINO.

tresnal [tres-nahl'], *m. (Prov.)* Collection of triangular plots of ground disposed for irrigation.

trestanto [tres-tahn'-to], *m. V.* TRIPLO.*-adv.* Three times as much.

treta [tray'-tah], *f.* 1. Thrust in fencing. 2. Trick, wile, artifice, craft, finesse.

treudo [tray'-oo-do], *m. (Prov.) V.* CATASTRO.

trezavo, va [tray-thah'-vo, vah], *a.* Thirteenth, any of thirteen equal parts.

treznar [treth-nar'], *va. (Prov.) V.* ATRESNALAR.

tría [tree'-ah], *f.* Frequent entering and going out of bees in a hive.

triaca [tre-ah'-cah], *f.* 1. Theriaca, treacle. 2. An antidote, preservative, or preventive.

triacal [tre-ah-cahl'], *a.* Made of treacle, theriacal.

triache [tre-ah'-chay], *m. (Amer. Cuba)* Coffee of inferior quality.

triangulación [tre-an-goo-lah-the-on'], *f.* Triangulation, laying out triangles on the earth; trigonometrical survey.

triangulado, da [tre-an-goo-lah'-do, dah], *a.* In the shape of a triangle.

triangular [tre-an-goo-lar'], *a.* Triangular.

triangularmente [tre-ahn-goo-lahr-men-tay], *adv.* Triangularly.

triángulo [tre-ahn'-goo-lo], *m.* Triangle. **Triángulo cuadrantal**, spheric triangle having one or more sides quadrants.

trianular [tre-ah-noo-lar'], *a. (Zool.)* Presenting three rings; three-ringed.

triaquera [tre-ah-kay'-rah], *f.* Vessel for theriaca or other medicine.

triar [tre-ar'], *vn.* To go out and in frequently, as bees in a beehive; to work, as bees.

triario [tre-ah'-re-o], *m.* Veteran Roman soldier forming a reserve corps in rear.

tribal [tre-bahl'], *a.* Tribal.

tribón [tre-bon'], *m. V.* TRIGÓN.

tribu [tree'-boo], *f.* Tribe.

tribuir [tre-boo-eer'], *va.* To attribute. *V.* ATRIBUTE.

tribulación [tre-boo-lah-the-on'], *f.* Tribulation, affliction.

tribulante [tre-boo-lahn'-tay], *pa.* Afflicting.

tríbulo [tree'-boo-lo], *m. (Bot.)* Caltrop thistle: generic name of several prickly plants. *V.* ABROJO.

tribuna [tre-boo'-nah], *f.* 1. Rostrum or pulpit among the ancients, tribune (de orador). 2. A raised stand from which to address an assembly. 3. Tribunal, a gallery or raised place in a church where persons of distinction assist at the divine offices. 4. Gallery for spectators in assemblies. **Tribuna del acusado,** dock.

tribunado [tre-boo-nah'-do], *m.* Tribuneship, the office and dignity of tribune.

tribunal [tre-boo-nahl'], *m.* 1. Hall, where judges meet to administer justice. 2. Tribunal, court of justice; judicature. 3. *(Univ.)* Board of examiners (examinadores). 4. *(Fig.)* Tribunal; forum. 5. *(Cono Sur. Mil.)* Court martial. **Tribunal de menores,** juvenile court. **Llevar a uno ante los tribunales,** to take somebody to court.

tribunali (Pro) [tre-boo-nah'-le], *adv.* **Pro tribunali,** 1. Applied to the sentence or decision of a judge, sitting in a court of justice, with the solemnities required by the laws. 2. *(Met.)* In a decisive tone, decisively.

tribunicio, cia [tre-boo-nee'-the-o, ah], *a. V.* TRIBÚNICO.

tribúnico, ca [tre-boo'-ne-co, cah], *a.* Tribunitial.

tribuno [tre-boo'-no], *m.* 1. Tribune, a magistrate of ancient Rome. 2. Tribune, one who defends the rights of the people. 3. An agitator, public haranguer.

tributación [tre-boo-tah-the-on'], *f.* Tribute, contribution. *V.* TRIBUTO.

tributar [tre-boo-tar'], *va.* 1. To pay taxes or contributions. 2. To pay homage and respect.

tributario, ria [tre-boo-tah'-re-o, ah], *a.* Liable to pay taxes or contributions, tributary.

tributo [tre-boo'-to], *m.* 1. Tax, contribution; tribute. 2. Toil, trouble, difficulty.

trica, tricas [tree'-cah], *f. (Prov.)* Quibbles, sophisms.

tricenal [tre-thay-nahl'], *a.* 1. Which is repeated every thirty years. 2. Which lasts thirty years.

tricentésimo, ma [tre-then-tay'-se-mo, mah], *a.* Containing three hundred: three hundredth.

tricésimo, ma [tre-thay'-se-mo, mah], *a.* Thirtieth.

triciclo [tre-thee'-clo], *m.* 1. A three wheeled carriage among the ancients. 2. A tricycle.

tricípete [tre-thee'-pay-tay], *a.* Three headed.

triclinio [tre-clee'-ne-o], *m.* 1. A table with three benches about it. 2. Couch, commonly for three persons, on which the ancient Greeks and Romans reclined to eat. 3. Dining-room of the ancient Romans.

tricolor [tre-co-lor'], *a.* Tri-colored.

tricoma [tre-co'-mah], *f. (Med.)* Plica Polonica, a Polish disease of the hair.

tricordiano, na [tre-cor-de-ah'-no, nah], *a.* Three-stringed, consisting of three cords.

tricorne [tre-cor'-nay], *a.* Three-horned.

tricornio [tre-cor'-ne-o], *a. & n.* 1. Three-horned. 2. A three cornered hat.

tricotar [tre-co-tahr'], *va. vn.* To knit.

tridente [tre-den'-tay], *a.* Trident, having three teeth. -*m.* Trident, Neptune's three-pointed scepter.

tridentífero, ra [tre-den-tee'-fay-ro, rah], *a.* Tridentiferous, bearing a trident.

tridentino, na [tre-den-tee'-no, nah], *a.* Of Trent, in the Tyrol: especially of the church council held there.

tridimensional [tre-de-men-se-o-nahl'], *a.* Tridimensional.

triduano, na [tre-doo-ah'-no, nah], *a.* Tertian.

triduo [tree'-doo-o], *m.* Space of three days.

triedro [tre-ay'-dro], **Ángulo triedro.** The meeting of three plane angles at one point.

trienal [tre-ay-nahl'], *a.* Triennial.

trienio [tre-ay'-ne-o], *m.* Space of three years.

trieñal [tre-ay-nyahl'], *a.* Triennial.

trífido, da [tree'-fe-do, dah], *a. (Poet.)* Trifid, three-cleft.

trifillo, lla [tre-feel'-lyo, lyah], *a. (Bot.)* 1. Three-leaved. 2. Three-lobed, or disposed in three leaflets. 3. *(Zool.)* A beetle.

trifolio [tre-fo'-le-o], *m.* Trefoil. *V.* TRÉBOL.

triforme [tre-for'-may], *a.* Triform.

trifulca [tre-fool'-cah], *f.* 1. *(Coll.)* Quarrel and confusion among various persons. 2. *(Min.)* A combination of levers for moving the bellows.

trifurcar [tre-foor-car'], *va. & vr.* To trifurcate, to divide into three parts, or branches.

trigal [tre-gahl'], *m.* Wheat-field.

trigamia [tre-gah'-mee-ah], *f.* 1. Trigamy, the state of having been married three times. 2. The state of having three husbands or three wives at one time.

trígamo, ma[tree'-gah-mo, mah], *m. & f.* 1. Trigamous, thrice married. 2. *(Bot.)* Applied to plants containing three sorts of flowers on the same flower-head.

trigaza [tre-gah'-thah], *f.* Short straw of wheat.

trigésimo, ma [tre-hay'-se-mo, mah], *a.* Thirtieth.

trigla [tree'-glah], *f. (Zool.)* Red surmullet, garnet.

triglifo [tre-glee'-fo], *m. (Arch.)* Triglyph.

trigo [tree'-go], *m.* Wheat. -*pl.* Crops; grain-fields. **Trigo candeal,** white wheat. **Trigo marzal,** spring wheat. **Trigo mocho,** summer or beardless wheat. **Trigo sarraceno,** buckwheat. **No es trigo limpio,** he's a shady character. **Meterse en trigo ajeno,** to meddle in someone else's affairs.

trigón [tre-gone'], *m.* A triangular musical instrument, having wire strings.

trígono [tree'-go-no], *m.* 1. *(Ast.)* Three celestial signs. 2. *(Geom.)* Triangle.

trigonometría [tre-go-no-may-tree'-ah], *f.* Trigonometry.

trigonométrico, ca [tre-go-no-may'-tre-co, cah], *a.* Trigonometrical.

trigrama [tre-grah'-mah], *m.* A word of three letters: trigram.

trigueño, ña [tri-gay'-nyo, nyah], *a.* Swarthy, brownish.

triguera [tre-gay'-rah], *f.* 1. *(Bot.)* Common wheat-grass. 2. Canary-seed.

triguero, ra [tre-gay'-ro, rah], *a.* Growing among wheat.

triguero [tre-gay'-ro], *m.* 1. Sieve for corn. 2. Corn-merchant, grain-dealer (comerciante).

trilátero, ra [tre-lah'-tay-ro, rah], *a.* Trilateral, having three sides.

trilingüe [tre-leen'-goo-ay], *a.* 1. Trilingual, talking or relating to three languages. 2. Trilingual, recorded in three languages.

trilio [tree'-le-o], *m. (Bot.)* Trillium.

trilítero, ra [tre-lee'-tay-ro, rah], *a.* Triliteral, employing or consisting of three letters. A characteristic of Semitic languages.

trilla [treel'-lyah], *f.* 1. (*Zool.*) Red surmullet, gurnard. 2. A sort of harrow for separating corn from chaff. 3. The act and time of thrashing. 4. (*Carib.*) Short cut (atajo). 5. (*Mex.*) Track (senda).

trilladera [treel-lyah-day'-rah], *f.* A harrow used to separate corn from chaff.

trillado, da [treel-lyah´-do, dah], *a. & pp.* of TRILLAR. 1. Thrashed, beaten (camino). 2. Trite (gastado), stale, hackneyed. **Camino trillado**, beaten track, common routine.

trillador, ra [treel-lyah-dor', rah], *a.* Thrashing, threshing. **Máquina trilladora**, threshing machine. *-m. & f.* Thresher.

trilladura [treel-lyah-doo'-rah], *f.* Act of thrashing.

trillar [treel-lyar'], *va.* 1. To thrash, to separate corn from the chaff, to tread out corn. 2. To beat, to abuse. 3. To frequent, to visit often; to repent.

trillís [treel-lyees'], *m.* A song-bird of Chili, a species of thrush.

trillizos [treel-lyee'-thos], *m. pl.* Triplets.

trillo [treel'-lyo], *m.* 1. A harrow, used in Spain for thrashing, or separating corn from the chaff. 2. (*Amer.*) Foot-path, pathway, trail little used.

trillón [treel-lyone'], *m.* Trillion, a million billions.

trilogía [tree-lo-hee'-ah], *f.* Trilogy.

trimembre [tre-mem'-bray], *a.* Consisting of three members or parts.

trimestral [tre-mes-trahl´], *a.* 1. Trimestrial, belonging to a trimester or period of three months. 2. Lasting three months.

trimestralmente [te-mays-trahl'-men-tay], *adv.* Quarterly, three monthly.

trimestre [tre-mes'-tray], *m.* Space of three months.

trimielga [tre-me-ayl'-gah], *f. V.* TORPEDO, 1st def.

trinacrio, ia [tre-nah'-cre-o, ah], *a.* (*Port.*) Sicilian, Trinacrian.

trinado [tre-nah'-do], *m.* 1. Trill, shake, quiver, tremulous sound. 2. Twittering of birds.

trinar [tre-nar'], *vn.* 1. To trill, to quaver, to shake the voice; to speak in a tremulous voice (enfadarse). 2. (*Met. Coll.*) To get vexed or furious. **Está que trina**, he´s hopping mad.

trinca [treen'-cah], *f.* 1. Assemblage of three things or persons of the same class or description. 2. (*Naut.*) Any cord used for making fast. **A la trinca**, (*Naut.*) close-hauled. 3. (*And. Cono Sur*) Band (pandilla), gang. 4. (*Carib. Mex.*) Drunkenness (embriaguez). 5. (*Cono Sur*) Marbles (canicas).

trincadura [trin-cah-doo'-rah], *f.* A barge of very large size with two masts and leg-of-mutton sails.

trincafía [trin-cah-fee'-ah], *f.* (*Naut.*) Clove-hitch, a kind of turn or knot.

trincafiar [trin-cah-fe-ar'], *va.* (*Naut.*) To marl.

trincar [trin-car'], *va.* 1. To break, to chop, to divide into small pieces. 2. (*Naut.*) To fasten the rope-ends. **Trincar las puertas**, (*Naut.*) to bar in the port-lids. 3. (*Peru. Coll.*) To tie strongly, to secure. 4. *vn.* (*Coll.*) To drink wine or liquor in company with others.

trincha [treen'-chah], *f.* 1. A belt for securing the outer clothes to the body. 2. (*Amer.*) Socket chisel, cutting gouge.

trinchante [trin-chahn'-tay], *m.* 1. Carver at table. 2. Carving-knife (cuchillo).

trinchar [trin-char'], *va.* 1. To carve (cortar), to divide meat. 2. To dispose or decide with an air of authority.

trinchera [trin-chay'-rah], *f.* 1. (*Mil.*) Trench (zanja), entrenchment, ditch to cover the troops from the enemy's fire. 2. Trench coat (prenda). 3. (*Naut.*) Parapet upon the gunwales of the quarter-deck. 4. (*LAm.*) Fence (cercado).

trinchero [trin-chay'-ro], *m.* Any plate on which meat is eaten at table; trencher.

trincherón [trin-chay-rone'], *m. aug.* A large plate or platter.

trinchete [trin-chay'-tay], *m.* Shoemaker's paring-knife; stone cutter's chisel. *V.* TRANCHETE.

trincos [treen'-cose], *m.* (*Orn.*) Kind of stork like a swam.

trineo [tre-nay'-o], *m.* Sledge, sled.

trinidad [tre-ne-dahd'], *f.* The Trinity.

trinitaria [tre-ne-tah'-re-ah], *f.* (*Bot.*) Three-colored violet, pansy, heart's-ease, forget me-not.

trinitario, ria [tre-ne-tah'-re-o, ah], *a. & n.* 1. Trinitarian. 2. (*Mex.*) A member of a society hired to carry the corpse and accompany the funeral procession.

trinitrotolueno [tre-ne-tro-to-loo-ay´-no], *m.* (*Chem.*) Trinitrotoluene, high explosive. It is used more in the abbreviation TNT.

trino, na [tree'-no, nah], *a.* Containing three distinct things; ternary.

trino [tree'-no], *m.* (*Ast.*) 1. Trine, the aspect of two planets when 120° apart. 2. Triune, three in one. *V.* TRINADO.

trinomio [tre-no'-me-o], *m.* (*Alg.*) Trinomial, an algebraic quantity of three terms.

trinquetada [trin-kay-tah'-dah], *f.* (*Naut.*) Sailing under the foresail.

trinquete [trin-kay'-tay], *m.* 1. (*Naut.*) Foremast, foresail. 2. Tennis, a game.

trinquetilla [trin-kay-teel'-lyah], *f.* (*Naut.*) Fore stay-sail.

trinquis [treen'-kis], *m.* (*Coll.*) A draught of wine or liquor. (*Acad.*)

trío [tree'-o], *m.* 1. Working of bees in a hive. 2. (*Mus.*) Trio.

triones [tre-o'-nes], *m.* (*Ast.*) Stars, called Charles's Wain, the Great Dipper.

triorque [tre-or'-kay], *m.* (*Orn.*) Triorchis, a kind of falcon.

tripa [tree'-pah], *f.* 1. Gut, intestine, bowel. **Tripas para longanizas**, hogs' casings for sausages. 2. Belly (vientre), especially of the pregnant woman. 3. Belly or wide part of vessels (vasijas). *-pl.* 1. Core, the inner part of fruit (fruta). 2. The interior of something. **Hacer de tripas corazón**, to hide one's dissatisfaction or disappointment; also to pluck up heart.

tripartido, da [tre-par-tee'-do, dah], *a. & pp.* of TRIPARTIR. Tripartite, divided into three parts.

tripartir [tre-par-teer'], *va.* To divide into three parts.

tripartito, ta [tre-par-tee'-to, tah], *a.* Tripartite.

tripastos [tre-pahs'-tos], *m.* Pulley with three sheaves.

tripe [tree'-pay], *m.* Shag, a kind of woollen cloth.

tripería [tre-pay-ree'-ah], *f.* Shop where tripe is sold; a heap of tripe.

tripero, ra [tre-pay'-ro, rah], *m. & f.* 1. One who sells tripe. 2. Woollen belt to keep the belly warm; cummerbund.

tripétalo, la [tre-pay'-ta'-lo, lah], *a.* (*Bot.*) Tripetalous.

tripilla [tre-peel'-lyah], *f. dim.* A small gut.

tripitrape [tre-pe-trah'-pay], *m.* 1. (*Coll.*) Heap of old furniture and lumber. 2. Confusion of thoughts or ideas.

triple [tree'-play], *a.* Triple, treble. *-m.* Triple. **Es el triple de lo que era**, it is three times what it was. *-adv.* **Esta cuerda es triple gruesa que ésa**, this string is three times thicker than that bit.

tríplica [tree'-ple-cah], *f.* (*Law.*) Rejoinder.

triplicación [tre-ple-cah-the-on'], *f.* Multiplication by three.

triplicado, da [tre-ple-cah'-do, dah], *a. & pp.* of TRIPLICAR. Triplicate.

triplicar [tre-ple-car'], *va.* 1. To treble, to triple. 2. (*Law. Prov.*) To rejoin.

tríplice [tree'-ple-thay], *a.* Treble, triple.

triplicidad [tre-ple-the-dahd'], *f.* Triplicity, trebleness.

triplito [tre-plee'-to], *m.* (*Min.*) Triplite, a ferrous manganese phosphate.

triplo, pla [tree'-plo, plah], *a.* Treble, triplicate, triple: used as a substantive.

trípode [tree'-po-day], *com.* Tripod, trivet.

trípol, trípoli [tree'-pol, tree'-po-le], *m.* Tripoli, rottenstone, tripolite, a polishing powder.

tripón, na [tre-pone', nah], *a.* Pot-bellied, big-bellied.

triptongo [trip-ton´-go], *m.* Triphthong.

tripudio [tre-poo'-de-o], *m.* Dance, ball.

tripudo, da [tre-poo'-do, dah], *a.* Pot-bellied, big-bellied.

tripulación [tre-poo-lah-the-on'], *f.* Crew (de barco, avión).

tripulante [tre-poo-lahn'-tay], *m.* Crew member.

tripular [tre-poo-lar'], *va.* *(Naut.)* To man ships; to fit out, to equip.

triquina [tre-kee'-nah], *f.* Trichina, a worm, parasitic in muscles in the larval stage and in the intestines when mature. The cause of the disease trichinosis.

triquinosis [tre-ke-no'-sis], *f.* Trichinosis, a serious disease produced by trichinosis in the muscles and intestines of the body.

triquiñuela [tre-ke-nyoo-ay'-lah], *f.* *(Coll.)* Cheat, fraud.

triquitraque [tre-ke-trah'-kay], *m.* 1. Crack, clack, clattering, clashing. 2. Fire-cracker, pulling-cracker. 3. Rocket, serpent.

trirreme [trir-ray'-may], *m.* *(Naut.)* Trireme.

tris [trees], *m.* 1. Noise made by the breaking of glass (estallido). 2. Trice, an instant. **Venir en un tris,** to come in an instant. 3. *(LAm.)* Noughts and crosses (juego).

trisa [tree'-sah], *f.* *(Zool.)* Shad. V. SÁBALO.

trisagio [tre-sah'-he-o], *m.* Trisagion, angelic chorus of Holy, holy, holy; any festivity repeated three days.

trisarquía [tre-sar-kee'-ah], *f.* Triumvirate.

trisca [tris'-cah], *f.* 1. Noise made by treading on something which breaks under the feet; any noise. 2. *(Carib.)* Mockery (mofa); private joke (chiste).

triscador, ra [tris-cah-dor', rah], *m.* & *f.* 1. A noisy, rattling person. 2. *m.* *(Tech.)* Saw-set, an instrument for setting the teeth of a saw.

triscar [tris-car'], *vn.* 1. To stamp, to make a noise with the feet. 2. To caper, to frisk about, to frolic. -*va.* Among carpenters to set the teeth of a saw; to bend these alternately to the one side or the other. V. also TRABAR.

trisecar [tre-say-car'], *va.* To divide into three equal parts, to trisect.

trisección [tre-sec-the-on'], *f.* Trisection, division into three parts.

trisílabo, ba [tre-see'-lah-bo, bah], *a.* Trisyllabic, containing three syllables.

tristacho, cho [tris-tah'-cho, chah], *a.* *(Prov.)* Sorrowful, melancholy.

triste [trees'-tay], *a.* 1. Sorrowful, sad (estado), mournful (canción). 2. Gloomy (cuarto), dismal (paisaje), heavy, morose. 3. Abject, mean, low. 4. Dull, gloomy, sombre, murky. 5. *(Fig.)* Sorry, sad. 6. *(LAm.)* Poor (pobre). 7. *(And.)* Shy (tímido). **Poner triste a uno,** to make somebody sad. **Hizo un triste papel,** he cut a sorry figure. **Su padre es un triste vigilante,** his father is just a poor old watchman.

tristecico, ica, illo, illa, ito, ita [ ], *a. dim.* of TRISTE.

tristemente [trees-tay-men'-tay], *adv.* Mournfully, heavily, grievously.

tristeza [tris-tay'-thah], *f.* 1. Grief, sorrow, affliction, melancholy, gloom. 2. Lowness or depression of spirits. **Morirse de tristeza,** *(Met.)* to be broken-hearted; also, to die broken-hearted.

trisulco, ca [tre-sool'-co, cah], *a.* 1. Three pronged, having three points. 2. Of three furrows, or channels.

trísulo [tree'-soo-lo], *m.* *(Chem.)* A salt produced by two neutral salts, both with the same acid, but with different bases.

tritíceo, ea [tre-tee'-thay-o, ah], *a.* Triticean, belonging to wheat, wheaten.

tritón [tre-tone'], *m.* 1. *(Myth.)* Triton. 2. *(Zool.)* Triton, newt.

trítono [tree'-to-no], *m.* *(Mus.)* Tritone, an interval of three tones: the ratio of 45 to 32.

trituración [tre-too-rah-the-on'], *f.* Trituration, pulverization.

triturador, ra [tre-too-rah-dor', rah], *a.* Crushing. -*f.* Crusher, crushing machine.

triturar [tre-too-rar'], *vn.* To triturate, to comminute, to crush.

triunfada [tre-oon-fah'-dah], *f.* Trumping at cards.

triunfador, ra [tre-oon-fah-dor', ah], *m.* & *f.* Conqueror, victor, triumpher.

triunfal [tre-oon-fahl'], *a.* Triumphal.

triunfalmente [tre-oon-fahl'-men-tay], *adv.* Triumphally.

triunfante [tre-oon-fahn'-tay], *a.* & *pa.* Triumphant (ganador), magnificent, conquering.

triunfantemente [tre-oon-fahn'-teh-men-tay], *adv.* Triumphantly.

triunfar [tre-oon-far'], *vn.* 1. To conquer. 2. To triumph, to celebrate a victory (salir victorioso), to exult, to conquer the passions. 3. To make an idle show of grandeur and wealth. 4. To trump at cards. **Triunfar en la vida,** to succeed in life. **Triunfar en un concurso,** to win a competition.

triunfo [tre-oon'-fo], *m.* 1. Triumph, victory (victoria); conquest; exultation. 2. Slap with the back of the band. 3. Trump card. **Ha sido un verdadero triunfo,** it has been a real triumph.

triunviral [tre-oon-ve-rahl'], *a.* Triumviral, pertaining to the triumvirs.

triunvirato [tre-oon-ve-rah'-to], *m.* Triumvirate.

triunviro [tre-oon-vee'-ro], *m.* Triumvir.

trivial [tre-ve-ahl'], *a.* 1. Frequented, beaten (carretera, camino). 2. Trivial, vulgar, common, known by all.

trivialidad [tre-ve-ah-le-dahd'], *f.* Trivialness, triteness; vulgarity; idleness.

trivialmente [tre-ve-ahl'-men-tay], *adv.* Trivially.

trivio [tree'-ve-o], *m.* Crossroad, point where three roads meet.

triza [tree'-thah], *f.* 1. Mite, a small particle. 2. *(Naut.)* Cord, rope. **Hacer algo trizas,** to smash something to bits.

tro [tro], *m.* A musical instrument, after the fashion of a violin, used in Siam.

trocable [tro-cah'-blay], *a.* Changeable.

trocadamente [tro-cah-dah-men-tay], *adv.* Contrarily, false.

trocado [tro-cah'-do], *m.* Change, small coin.

trocado, da [tro-cah'-do, dah], *a.* & *pp.* Of TROCAR. Changeful, permuted.

trocador, ra [tro-cah-dor', rah], *m. dim.* One who exchanges or permutes.

trocaico [tro-cah'-e-co], *a.* Trochaic.

trocar [tro-car'], *va.* 1. To exchange, to barter; to change (cambiar), to commute; to equivocate (confundir). 2. To vomit (comida). 3. *(Cono Sur)* To sell (vender); *(And.)* to buy (comprar). -*vr.* 1. To be changed or reformed. 2. To exchange seats with another. **Trocar la alegría en tristeza,** to change gaiety into sadness.

trocar [tro-car'], *m.* *(Surg.)* Trocar.

trocatinta [tro-cah-teen'-tah], *f.* *(Coll.)* 1. A sad or unintentional mistake, in taking one thing for another 2. A ridiculous barter or exchange.

trocatinte [tro-cah-teen'-tay], *m.* Mixed color, changing color.

trocear [tro-thay-ar'], To divide into pieces.

troceo [tro-thay'-o], *m.* *(Naut.)* Parrel, a thick rope for securing the yards.

trocha [troh'-chah], *f.* 1. A narrow path across a high road. 2. *(LAm.)* Gauge. 3. *(Cono Sur)* Lane. 4. *(And.)* Trot (trote). 5. *(And.)* Portion (porción).

trochemoche (A) [tro-chay-mo'-chay], *adv.* Helter-skelter, pell-mell, in confusion and hurry.

trochoela [tro-choo-ay'-lah], *f. dim.* Little path.

trociscar [tro-thees-car'], *pa.* To make troches or lozenges.

trocisco [tro-thees'-co], *m.* Troche, lozenge, a medicine prepared as a cake.

trocla [tro'-clah], *f.* V. POLEA.

troco [tro'-co], *m.* *(Zool.)* V. RUEDA.

trofeo [tro-fay'-o], *m.* Trophy (objeto), colors, things taken from an enemy; emblem of triumph; victory; pageant. Trophies, military insignia.

trófico, ca [tro'-fe-co, cah], *a.* Trophic, relating to nutrition.

trofología [tro-fo-lo-hee'-ah], *f.* Dietetic regimen, or a treatise concerning it.

trofológico, ca [tro-fo-lo'-he-co, cah], *a.* Dietetic.

troglodita [tro-glo-dee'-tah], *con.* & *a.* 1. Troglodyte, a cave-dweller. 2. Name given by the Greeks to certain barbarous peoples of Africa who lived in caverns. 3. A barbarous, cruel man. 4. A great eater. 5. A chimpanzee. 6. A wren.

troglodítico, ca [tro-glo-dee'-te-co, cah], *a.* Troglodytic.

trogón [tro-gone'], *m.* Trogon. *V.* TROGÓNIDOS.

trogonidos [tro-go'-ne-dose], *m. pl.* Trogons, a family of climbing birds, of warm climates, having brilliant plumage.

troj [troh], *f. V.* TROJE.

trojado, da [tro-hah'-do, dah], *a.* Contained in a knapsack.

troje, troj [tro'-hay], *f.* Granary, mow.

trojero [tro-hay'-ro], *m.* Store-keeper, guard of a granary.

trola [tro-lah], *f.* Fib, lie.

trolebús [tro-lay-boos'], *m.* Trolley bus.

trolero [tro-lay'-ro], *m.* Fibber, liar.

tromba [trom'-bah], *f.* A water-spout.

trombón [trom-bone'], *m.* Trombone, a brass wind-instrument. *V.* SACABUCHE.

trombosis [trom-bo'-sis], *f. (Med.)* Thrombosis.

trompa [trom'-pah], *f.* 1. Trumpet, horn (instrumento). 2. Proboscis or trunk of an elephant. 3. A large top. 4. *(CAm. Mex.)* Shut your trap. 5. *(Anat.)* Tube, duct. 6. Drunkenness (borrachera). -*m.* Trumpeter. **Trompa de Eustaquio,** Eustachian tube connecting the middle ear with the pharynx.

trompada [trom-pah'-dah], *f.* 1. *(Coll.)* Blow with a top. 2. Encounter of two persons face to face. 3. *(Andal. and Amer.)* A blow with a fist.

trompar [trom-par'], *vn.* To whip a top.

trompazo [trom-pah'-tho], *m.* 1. Blow with a top, trumpet, or fist. 2. Misfortune, accident.

trompear [trom-pay-ar'], *vn.* A top, to play at chess.

trompero [trom-pay'-ro], *m.* Top maker. 2. Cheat, impostor.

trompero, ra [trom-pay'-ro, rah], *a.* Deceptive, false, deceiving.

trompeta [trom-pay'-tah], *f.* 1. Trumpet (instrumento). 2. Trumpet-shell. 3. Reefer (droga). 4. *(Cono Sur)* Daffodil. -*m.* Trumpeter.

trompetada [trom-pay-tah'-dah], *f. (Coll.) V.* CLARINADA.

trompetazo [trom-pay-tah'-tho], *m.* 1. Stroke with a trumpet. 2. Trumpet-blast.

trompetear [trom-pay-tay-ar'], *(Coll.)* To sound the trumpet.

trompetería [trom-pay-tay-ree'-ah], *f.* Pipes of an organ.

trompetero [trom-pay-tay'-ro], *m.* Trumpeter (de orquesta), horn-blower; trumpet-maker.

trompetilla [trom-pay-teel'-lyah], *f.* 1. *(Dim.)* A small trumpet. 2. Hearing trumpet. 3. Proboscis, lancet of gnats and other insects. 4. A Philippine cigar of conical shape.

trompetista [trom-pay-tis'-tah], *m & f.* Trumpet player.

trompicar [trom-pe-car'], *vn.* To stumble frequently; to falter. -*va.* 1. *(Coll.)* To appoint one irregularly to an employment which belonged to another. 2. To trip, to make stumble.

trompicón [trom-pe-cone'], *m.* Stumbling. *V.* TROPEZÓN.

trompilla [trom-peel'-lyah], *f. dim.* A small trumpet or horn.

trompillar [trom-pil-lyar'], *vn.* To stumble, to falter. *V.* TROMPICAR.

trompis [trom'-pis], *vn.* In colloquial phrase, **andar a trompis,** to come to fisticuffs.

trompo [trom'-po], *m.* 1. Man at chess. 2. Whipping-top (juguete). 3. *(I Am.)* Clumsy person (desmañado); rotten dancer (bailador). **Ponerse como un trompo,** *(Met.)* to be as full as a top; to cut or drink to satiety.

trompón [trom-pone'], *m.* A big whipping-top. **A trompón** or **de trompón,** in a disorderly manner.

tron [tron], *m. (Coll.)* Report of firearms.

tronada [tro-nah'-dah], *f.* Thunderstorm.

tronado [tro-nah'-do], *a.* 1. Old (viejo), broken-down. 2. **Estar tronado,** to be potty (loco); to be ruined (arruinado). 3. *(LAm.)* To be high (drogas).

tronador, ra [tro-nah-dor', rah], *m. & f.* 1. Thunderer, thundering. 2. Squib, cracker, rocket.

tronar [tro-nar'], *v. imper.* To thunder. -*vn.* 1. To thunder, to make a noise like thunder or the discharge of guns, to fulminate. 2. To break relations with anyone. 3. Among gamblers, to lose all one's money. **Por lo que pueda** or **por**

lo que pudiere tronar, for what may happen. *(Yo trueno, truene,* from *Tronar. V.* ACORDAR.)

troncal [tron-cahl'], *a.* Relating to the trunk or stock.

troncar [tron-car'], *va.* 1. To truncate, to mutilate, to cut off. 2. To interrupt a conversation, to cut the thread of a discourse.

tronchado [tron-chah'-do], *a. (Her.)* Applied to a shield having a diagonal bar. **Tronchado, da,** *pp.* of TRONCHAR.

tronchante [tron-chahn'-tay], *a.* Killingly funny.

tronchar [tron-char'], *va. 1.* To cut by the trunk or root (cortar), to chop down (talar); to break with violence. 2. *(Fig.)* To cut off (vida); to shatter (esperanza). -*vr.* 1. To fall down (árbol). 2. To tire oneself out (cansarse). 3. **Troncharse de risa,** to split one's sides laughing.

tronchazo [tron-chah'-tho], *m.* 1. *(Aug.)* A large stalk. 2. A blow with a stalk or stem.

troncho [tron'-cho], *m. 1.* Sprig, stem, or stalk of garden plants. 2. *(Cono Sur)* Piece (trozo). 3. *(And.)* Knot (enredo).

tronchudo, da [tron-choo'-do, dah], *a.* Having a long stem or stalk.

tronco [tron'-co, *m.* 1. Trunk of a tree; a log of wood. 2. Stock, the origin of a family. 3. Trunk of an animal without the trend and limbs. 4. An illiterate, despicable, useless person. 5. Hind pair of horses in a coach. **Estar hecho un tronco,** to be bereft of feeling and sensation: literally, to be like a log of wood.

troncón [tron-cone'], *m. aug.* A large stalk or trunk; a large log of wood.

tronera [tro-nay'-rah], *f.* 1. *(Mil.)* Embrasure of a battery. 2. *(Naut.)* Loophole. 3. Louver. 4. Dormer, a small sky-light. 5. A harum-scarum fellow, a hare-brained, foolish person (tarambana). 6. Paper cracker; squib. -*pl.* 1. Holes and pockets of truck and billiard-tables. 2. Openings.

tronerar [tro-nay-rar'], *va. V.* ATRONERAR.

tronerilla [tro-nay-reel'-lyah], *f. dim.* of TRONERA.

tronga [tron'-gah], *f.* (Slang or low) Kept mistress, concubine.

tronido [tro-nee'-do], *m.* Thunder. *V.* TRUENO.

tronitoso, sa [tro-ne-to'-so, sah], *a. (Coll.)* Resounding, thundering.

trono [tro'-no], *m.* Throne; royal dignity; seat of the image of a saint. -*pl.* Thrones, seventy choirs of angels. **Heredar el trono,** to inherit the crown.

tronquillo [tron-keel'-lyo], *m.* Ornamental metal-work for applying to the covers of books.

tronquista [tron-kees'-tah], *m.* Coachman that drives a pair of horses.

tronquito [tron-kee'-to], *m. dim.* of TRONCO.

tronzar [tron-thar'], *va.* 1. To shatter, to break into pieces. 2. To plait, to fold. 3. To cut up (cortar). 4. To tire out (persona).

tronzo, za [tron'-tho, thah], *a.* Having one or both ears cut off (caballos).

tropa [tro'-pah], *f. 1.* Troop (multitud), a body of soldiers. 2. Troop, a small body of calvary. 3. A number of people collected together; crowd, multitude; troop, herd. 4. Beat to arms. 5. *(Cono Sur)* Convoy of carts (vehículos). 6. *(Mex.)* Rude person (maleducado). **En tropa,** in crowds, without order. **Tropas de asalto,** storm troops.

tropel [tro-pel'], *m.* 1. Noise made by a quick movement of the feet. 2. Hurry (prisa), bustle, confusion, huddle. 3. Heap of things, confusedly tumbled together; crowd. **De tropel,** tumultuously, in a throng.

tropelía [tro-pay-lee'-ah], *f.* 1. Precipitation, hurry, confusion. 2. Vexation, oppression, injustice, outrage (atropello).

tropellar [tro-pel-lyar'], *va. (Prov.)* To trample.

tropezadero [tro-pay-thah-day'-ro], *m.* Any stumbling or slippery place; a bad, uneven road or path.

tropezado, da [tro-pay-thah'-do, dah], *a. & pp.* of TROPEZAR. Stumbled, obstructed.

tropezador, ra [tro-pay-thah-dor', rah], *m. & f.* Tripper, stumbler.

tropezadura [tro-pay-thah-doo'-rah], *f.* Stumbling, obstructing, entangling.

tropezar [tro-pay-thar'], *vn.* 1. To stumble in walking. 2. To be detained or obstructed. 3. To slip into crimes or blunders. 4. To wrangle, to dispute (reñir). 5. To discover a fault or defect. 6. To meet accidentally (topar). 7. To light on, to happen, to find. 8. To slip up (cometer un error). *-vr.* To stumble, to cut the feet in walking (caballos). **Tropezar con uno,** to turn into somebody. **Tropezar con dificultad,** *(Fig.)* to run into a difficulty. *(Yo tropiezo, tropiece,* from *Tropezar. V.* ACRECENTAR.)

tropezón, na [tro-pay-thone', nah], *a.* Stumbling, tripping frequently. **A tropezones,** with a variety of obstructions.

tropezón [tro-pay-thone'], *m.* 1. *V.* TROPIEZO. 2. Act of tripping.

tropezoncico, illo, ito [tro-pay-thon-thee'-co], *m. dim.* of TROPEZÓN.

tropezoso, sa [tro-pay-tho'-so, sah], *a.* Apt to stumble or trip.

tropical [tro-pe-cahl'], *a.* 1. Tropical, belonging to the tropics. 2. *(Cono Sur)* Rhetorical, melodramatic.

trópico [tro'-pe-co], *m. (Ast.)* Tropic, either of two parallels at a distance from the equator N. and S. of 23° 28' and corresponding to the solstitial points.

trópico, ca [tro'-pe-co, cah], *a.* 1. *(Ast.)* Tropical. 2. *(Rhet.)* Tropical, containing tropes.

tropiezo [tro-pe-ay'-tho], *m.* 1. Stumble, trip. 2. Obstacle (obstáculo), obstruction, impediment. 3. Slip (error), fault, error. 4. Difficulty, embarrassment. 5. Quarrel, dispute (riña).

tropilla [tro-peel'-lyah], *f. dim.* A small bray or detachment of troops.

tropo [tro'-po], *m. (Rhet.)* Trope, figurative sense.

tropología [tro-po-lo-hee'-ah], *f.* 1. Figurative language, allegorical sense, tropology. 2. Mingling of morality and doctrine in a discourse; tropology.

tropológico, ca [tro-po-lo'-he-co, cah], *a.* 1. Topological, expressed by tropes. 2. Doctrinal, moral, relative to reform in customs.

troposfera [tro-pos-fay'-rah], *f.* Troposphere.

troque [tro'-kay], *m.* A kind of bunch formed in cloths when dyeing them.

troquel [tro-kel'], *m.* Die, in which a hollow figure is engraved.

troquillo [tro-keel'-lyo], *m. (Arch.)* Trochilus, concave moulding next the torus.

trotamundos [tro-tah-moon'-dos], *m. & f.* Globetrotter.

trotaconventos [tro-tah-con-ven'-tose], *f. (Vulg.)* Procuress. *V.* ALCAHUETA.

trotador, ra [tro-tah-dor', rah], *m. & f.* Trotter.

trotar [tro-tar'], *vn.* To trot: to move swiftly, to be in haste. *-va.* To make a horse trot.

trote [tro'-tay], *m. 1.* Trot. **Al trote,** in a trot: in haste or hastily. **Tomar al trote,** to run away. 2. Traveling (viajes); bustle (ajetreo). 3. **De mucho trote,** tough (ropa). 4. **Trotes,** shady affair (asunto turbio). 5. **Trotes,** hardships (apuros). **Yo ya no estoy para esos trotes,** I can't go chasing around like that any more.

trotillo [tro-teel'-lyo], *m. dim.* A light trot.

trotón, na [tro-tone', nah], *a.* Trotting, whose ordinary pace is a trot (caballo).

trotón [tro-tone'], *m.* A trotter.

trotonería [tro-to-nay-ree'-ah], *f.* A continual trot.

trovador, ra [tro-vah-dor', rah], *m. & f.* 1. Troubador, versifier, poet. 2. Finder.-*a.* Versifying; parodic.

trovar [tro-var'], *va.* 1. To versify. 2. To imitate a metrical composition by turning it to another subject, to parody. 3. To invert or pervert the sense of a thing.

trovero [tro-vay'-ro], *m.* Trouvère.

trovista [tro-vees'-tah], *m.* Finder; versifier.

Troya [tro'-yah], *f.* Troy. **Aquí fue Troya,** here was Troy applied to the site of a memorable place. **¡Arda Troya!** let happen what will: proceed with the disorder! (ironical).

troyano, na [tro-yah'-no, nah], *a.* Trojan.

troza [tro'-thah], *f.* Trunk of a tree to be sawn into boards.

trozo [tro'-tho], *m.* 1. Piece or part of a thing cut off. 2. *(Naut.)* Junk for making oakum. 3. *(Gil.)* Division of a column, forming the van or rear guard. 4. Throstle, a species of spindle. **Trozo de madera,** a log. **Trozos escogidos,** selections, selected passages.

trucar [troo-car'], *m.* To play the first card.

trucha [troo'-chah], *f.* 1 Trout. 2. Crane. *V.* CABRIA. **Ayunar, o comer trucha,** either to fast or eat trout; the best or nothing.

truchero [troo-chay'-ro], *m.* A fisherman who catches and sells trout.

truchimán, na [troo-che-mahn', nah], *a. (Coll.)* Fond of business, or of making agreements. *-m. & f.* A go-between. *V.* TRUJAMÁN.

truchimanear [troo-che-mah-nay-ar'], *vn.* To act as a go-between.

truchuela [troo-choo-ay'-lah], *f.* Small codfish. *V.* ABADEJO.

truco [troo'-co], *m.* 1. A skillful push at trucks. **Trucos,** trucks, a game resembling billiards. 2. *(And. Cono Sur)* Punch (puñetazo). 3. *(Cono Sur)* Popular card game.

truculento, ta [troo-coo-len'-to, tah], *a.* Truculent, fierce.

trueco [troo-ay'-co], *m.* Exchange, barter. *V.* TRUEQUE. **A trueco,** in exchange.

trueno [troo-ay'-no], *m.* 1. Thunderclap. 2. Report of firearms; a noise like thunder (de cañón). 3. Wild youth (tarambana). 4. *(Carib.)* Binge (juerga). 5. *(And.)* Gun.

trueque [troo-ay'-kay], *m.* Exchange (cambio), truck, barter, commutation. *V.* TRUECO.

trufa [troo'-fah], *f.* 1. Imposition, fraud, deceit. 2. *(Bot.)* Truffle.

trufador, ra [troo-fah-dor', rah], *m. & f.* Fabulist, story-teller, liar.

trufar [troo-far'], *va.* To stuff or cook with truffles. *-vn.* To tell stories, to deceive. *V.* MENTIR.

trufeta [troo-fay'-tah], *f.* A sort of linen.

truhán, na [troo-ahn', nah], *m. & f.* 1. A scoundrel, a knave. 2. Buffoon, jester, juggler, mountebank.

truhanada [troo-ah-nah'-dah], *f. V.* TRUHANERÍA.

truhanamente [troo-ah-nah-men'-tay], *adv.* Jestingly, buffoon-like.

truhanear [troo-ah-nay-ar'], *vn.* 1. To deceive, to swindle. 2. To banter, to jest, to play the buffoon.

truhanería [troo-ah-nay-ree'-ah], *f.* 1. Imposture, swindle. 2. Buffoonery, low jest.

truhanesco, ca [troo-ah-nes'-co, cah], *a.* Belonging to a buffoon.

tuhanillo, illa [troo-ah-neel'-lyo], *m. & f. dim.* A mean, petty buffoon.

truja [troo'-hah], *f. (Prov.)* Place where olives are kept before being pressed in the mill.

trujal [tro-hahl'], *m.* 1. *(Prov.)* Oilmill. 2. Copper, in which the materials for manufacturing soap are prepared. 3. *(Prov.) V.* LAGAR.

trujaleta [troo-hah-lay'-tah], *f. (Prov.)* Vessel in which the juice of olives falls from the mill.

trujamán [troo-hah-mahn'], *m.* 1. Dragoman, interpreter. 2. Broker, factor.

trujamanear [troo-hah-mah-nay-ar'], *vn.* 1. To act as an interpreter. 2. To exchange, to barter, to buy, or sell goods for others; to act as a broker or factor. 3. To play the buffoon.

trujamanía [troo-hah-mah-nee'-ah], *f.* Brokering, brokerage.

trujillano, na [troo-heel-lyah'-no, nah], *a.* Of Trujillo.

trujimán, na [troo-he-mahn', nah], *a. V.* TRUJAMÁN.

trulla [trool'-lyah], *f.* 1. Noise, bustle (bullicio); multitude. 2. Trowel, mason's level.

trullo [trool-lyo], *m.* 1. *(Orn.)* Teal. 2. *(Prov.)* Kind of vat for pressed grapes. 3. Nick, jail.

truncadamente [troon-cah'-dah-men-tay], *adv.* In a truncated manner.

truncado, da [troon-cah'-do, dah], *a. & pp.* of TRUNCAR. Truncate.

truncar [troon-car'], *va.* 1. To truncate (acordar), to maim; to mutilate a discourse. 2. *(Fig.)* To cut short (carrera, vida).

trunco, ca [troon'-co, cah], *a.* V. TRONCHADO, TRUNCADO.

trupial [troo-pe-ahl'], *m. (Orn.)* Troupial. V. TURUPIAL.

truque [troo'-kay], *m.* A game of cards.

truquero [troo-kay'-ro], *m.* Keeper or owner of a truck-table.

truquiflor [troo-ke-floor'], *m.* A game at cards.

trusas [troo'-sas], *f. pl. 1.* Trunk-hose, wide slashed breeches, in Greek fashion, which reached to the middle of the thigh. 2. *(Carib.)* Bathing trunks (bañador). 3. *(And. Mex.)* Panties, knickers (de mujer).

truyada [troo-yah'-dah, troo-jah'-dah in Cuba], *f. (Amer.)* Crowd multitude.

tsar [sahr], *m.* (Russian spelling) Czar, tsar. V. ZAR.

tsetse [tset-say'], *f.* Tsetse fly, a blood-sucking fly of southern Africa; its bite is deadly to cattle and horses, but not harmful to man, to the ass, and the goat.

tú [too], *pron. pers.* Thou: used in the familiar style of friendship. **Hoy por ti y mañana por mí,** *(Coll.)* turn about is fair play.

tu [too]. Possessive pronoun. Thy, thine. Plural *tus.* Apocopated from *tuyo, tuya.*

tuáutem [too-ah'-oo-tem], *m. (Coll.)* Principal person, leader, mover, author; essential point.

tuba [too'-bah], *f.* 1. *(Mus.)* Tuba. 2. Liquor obtained from the Nipa and other palms of the Philippine Islands.

tuberculífero, ra [too-ber-coo-lee'-fay-ro, rah], *a.* Tuberculous, affected by tuberculosis; tubercular, characterized by the presence of tubercles.

tuberculiforme [too-ber-coo-le-for'-may], *a.* Tubercular, tuberculiform.

tuberculina [too-ber-coo-lee'-nah], *f. (Med.)* Tuberculin (used in the diagnosis and treatment of tuberculosis).

tuberculización [too-ber-coo-le-thah-the-on'], *f.* Tuberculosis, tuberculization.

tubérculo [too-berr'-coo-lo], *m.* 1 *(Bot.)* Tuber, a thick underground stem like the potato. 2. *(Med.)* Tubercle in the lungs, etc.

tuberculosis [too-ber-coo-lo'-sees], *f.* Tuberculosis.

tuberculoso, sa [too-ber-coo-lo'-so, sah], *a.* Tuberculous, affected with tuberculosis.

tubería [too-bay-ree'-ah], *f.* Tubing a series of tubes or pipes.

tuberossa [too-bay-ro'-sah], *f. (Bot.)* Tuberose, oriental hyacinth.

tuberosidad [too-bay-ro-se-dahd'], *f.* Tuberosity; swelling.

tuberoso, sa [too-bay-ro'-o, sah], *a.* Tuberous.

tubífero, ra [too-bee'-fay-ro, rah], *a. (Biol.)* Provided with tubes.

tubiforme [too-be-for'-may], *a.* Tubiform, tubular, tube shaped.

tubo [too'-bo], *m.* Tube. V. CAÑÓN. **Tubo de radio,** radio tube. **Tubo lanzatorpedos,** torpedo tube. **Tubo digestivo,** alimentary canal. **Tubo de imagen,** television picture tube. **Tubo de respiración,** breathing-tube.

tubular [too-boo-lar'], *a.* 1. Tubular; tube-shaped. 2. Fitted to receive a tube.

tubuliforme [too-boo-le-for'-may], *a.* Tubuliform, like a tubule.

tubuloso, sa [too-boo-lo'-so, sah], *a.* Tubulose, tubulous; tubular. *-f. (Chem.)* A special arrangement of vessels to which a tube may be adapted, crossing through a cork or plug.

tucán [too-cahn'], *m.* 1. Toucan, a climbing bird of South America, noted for its great and long beak. 2. Constellation near the Antarctic pole.

tucía [too-thee'-ah], *f.* Tutty. V. ATUTÍA.

tuciorista [too-the-o-rees'-tah], *com.* One who follows the safest doctrine.

tudel [too-del'], *m.* A metal pipe with a reed put into a bassoon.

tudesco [too-des'-co], *m.* 1. A kind of wide cloak. V. CAPOTE. 2. German, native of Germany.

tueca, tueco [too-ay'-cah], *f. & m.* Cavity made by wood-lice in timber.

tuera [too-ay'-rah], *f. (Bot.)* Colocynth, bitter apple.

tuerca [too-err'-cah], *f.* Nut or female screw.

tuerce [too-err'-thay], *m.* V. TORCEDURA.

tuero [too-ay'-ro], *m.* 1. Dry wood cut for fuel. 2. *(Bot.)* Spicknel, a European aromatic perennial.

tuerto, ta [too-err'-to, tah], *a. & pp. irr.* of TORCER. One-eyed (mutilado), blind of one eye; squint-eyed. **A tuertas,** contrariwise, on the contrary. **A tuertas o a derechas, a tuerto o a derecho,** right or wrong; inconsiderately.

tuerto [too-err'-to], *m.* Wrong, injury.

tuétano [too-ay'-tah-no], *m.* Marrow; pith of trees. **Hasta los tuétanos,** with all vigor and activity; to the quick.

tufarada [too-fah-rah'-dah], *f.* A strong accent or smell.

tufillo [too-feel'-lyo], *m. (Fig.)* Slight smell.

tufo [too'-fo], *m.* 1. A warm exhalation from the earth or from chimneys or lamps which do not burn well. 2. A strong and offensive smell (olor). 3. Locks of hair which fall over the ear. 4. High notion, lofty idea, vanity. 5. V. TOBA.

tugurio [too-goo'-re-o], *m. (Coll.)* Hut, cottage, hovel (chavola); poky little room (cuartucho); den (cafetucho).

tuición [too-e-the-on'], *f. (Law.)* Tuition; protection.

tuína [too-ee'-nah], *f.* A long, full jacket. (In Peru, *tuín,* masculine.)

tuitivo, va [too-e-tee'-vo, vah], *a. (Law.)* Defensive, that which shelters or protects.

tul [tool], *m.* Tulle, an open-meshed fabric of silk or cotton used for veils, mantillas, etc.

tulipán [too-le-pahn'], *m. (Bot.)* Tulip.

tulipero [too-le-pay'-ro], *m. (Bet.)* Tulip-tree.

tullidura [tool-lyo-doo'-rah], *f.* Dung of birds of prey.

tullimiento [tool-lye-me-en'-to], *m.* Contraction of the tendons.

tullir [tool-lyeer'], *vn.* 1. To void, to omit dung (pájaros). 2. To ill-treat (maltratar). 3. To cripple (listar). *-vr.* To be cripled.

tumba [toom'-bah], *f.* 1. Tomb (sepultura), sepulchral monument, vault. 2. Roof of a coach. 3. Tumble. V. TUMBO. **Llevar a uno a la tumba,** to carry somebody off.

tumbacuartillos [toom-bah-coo-ar-teel'-lyose], *m.* Sot, a vicious frequenter of taverns.

tumbadero, ra [toom-bah-day'-ro, rah], *a.* Tumbler; falling. **Redes tumbaderas,** drop-nets for catching wild animals.

tumbado, da [toom-bah'-do, dah], *a. pp.* of TUMBAR. 1. Tumbled. 2. Vaulted, arched.

tumbaga [toom-bah'-gah], *f.* Pinchbeck; ring or toy of pinchbeck.

tumbagón [toom-bah-gone'], *m. aug.* Any large piece made of pinchbeck; bracelet set with stones.

tumbar [toom-bar'], *va.* 1. To tumble, to throw down. 2. To overwhelm (olor), to deprive of sensation. 3. To knock down (derribar). 4. *(LAm.)* To fell (árboles). *-vn.* 1. To tumble. 2. *(Naut.)* To heel, to lie along, to have a false list. 3. **Un olor que tumba,** a smell which knocks you back. *-vr.* 1. *(Coll.)* To lie down, to sleep (acostarse). 2. To go flat (trigo). 3. *(Fig.)* To give up, to decide, to take it easy.

tumbilla [toom-beel'-lyah], *f.* Horse for airing bed-linen.

tumbo [toom'-bo], *m.* 1. Tumble, fall. 2. A matter of consequence. 3. Book containing the privileges and title deeds of monasteries, etc. **Dando tumbos,** with all sort of difficulties.

tumbón [toom-bone'], *m.* 1. Coach; trunk with an arched roof or lid. *(Coll.)* V. TUNO.

tumbona [toom-bo'-nah], *f.* Easy chair (butaca); deckchair (de playa).

tumbonear [toom-bo-nay-ar'], *vn.* 1. To vault, to make arches. 2. V. TUNAR.

tumefacción [too-may-fac-the-on'], *f.* Tumefaction, swelling.

tumefacerse [too-may-fah-therr'-say], *vr.* To tumefy, to swell.

tumefacto, ta [too-may-fac'-to, tah], *a.* Tumescent.

tumescencia [too-mes-then'-the-ah], f. Tumescence, swelling from a tumor.

tumescente [too-mes-then'-tay], a. Tumescent, slightly swollen.

túmido, da [too'-me-do, dah], m. 1. Swollen, tumid, inflated. 2. Pompous, tumid, elevated (estilo).

tumor [too-more'], m. Tumor, extuberance.

tumorcico, illo, ito [too-mor-thee'-co], m dim. A small tumor.

túmulo [too'-moo-lo], m. Tomb, sepulchral monument; funeral pile.

tumulto [too-mool'-to], m. 1. Tumult, uproar, commotion. 2. Faction, mob.

tumultuar [too-mool-too-ar'], m. To raise a tumult, to stir up disturbances, to mob. -vr. To rise, to make a tumult.

tumultuariamente [too-mool-too-ah'-re-ah-men-tay], adv. Tumultuously, outrageously.

tumultuario, ria [too-mool-too-ah'-re-o, ah], a. Tumultuary, tumultuous.

tumultuosamente [too-mool-too-oh'-sah-men-tay], adv. Tumultuously. V. TUMULTUARIAMENTE.

tumultuoso, sa [too-mool-too-oh'-so, sah], a. Tumultuous, glamorous, mobish.

tuna [too'-nah], m. 1. (Bot.) The prickly pear or fly, the fig of the Cactus opuntia. 2. An idle and licentious life; truantship. **Andar a la tuna**, (Coll.) to play the truant; to wander idly about, to loiter. -f. Student music group.

tunal [too-noahl'], m. (Bot.) The prickly pear cactus.

tunantada [too-nan-tah'-dah], f. Rascality, wickedness, debauchery.

tunante [too-nahn'-tay], pa. Leading a licentious life. -m. Truant, idler, rake, a lazy loiterer.-a. Truant, lacy, loitering, sly, cunning, crafty.

tunantería [too-nan-tay-ree'-ah], f. (Coll.) 1. Debauchery, idleness, vagrancy, libertinism. 2. Truantship.

tunar [too-nar'], vn. To lead a licentious, vagrant life, to loiter.

tunda [toon'-dah], f. 1. The soft of shearing cloth. 2. A severe chastisement.

tundente [toon-den'-tay], a. Doing injury to a part of the body without drawing blood; raising a tumor.

tundición [toon-de-the-on'], f. Shearing of cloth.

tundidor [toon-de-dor'], m. Shearer of cloth.

tundidura [toon-de-doo'-rah], f. The act of shearing.

tundir [toon-deer'], va. 1. To shear cloth (paño). 2. (Coll.) To cudgel, to flog. 3. To beat (pegar).

tundizno [toon-deeth'-no], m. Shearings cut from cloth.

tundra [toon'-drah], f. Tundra, treeless plain of Arctic regions.

túnel [too'-nel], m. Tunnel. **Túnel de lavado**, car wash. **Túnel aerodinámico**, wind-tunnel.

tungstato [toongs-tah'-to], m. (Chem.) Tungstate, a salt of tungstic acid.

tungsteno [toongs-tay-to], m. Tungsten, wolfram, a steel-gray, heavy metallic element.

túngstico, ca [toongs'-te-co, cah], a. Tungstic, an oxide and an acid derived from tungsten; tungstenic.

túnica [too'-ne-cah], f. 1. Tunic, a garment worn by the ancients. 2. Tunic, a woollen shirt worn by religious persons. 3. Tunicle, pollicle, or integument which covers the shell of fruit. 4. Tunic, tunicle, integument of parts of the body. 5. A long wide gown.

tunicela [too-ne-thay'-lah], f. 1. Tunic. 2. Garment worn by bishops; wide gown.

tuno [too'-no], m. Truant, rake, cunning rogue, a lazy loiterer. -a. Truant, lazy, loitering; sly, cunning.

tun tun (al), phrase. (Coll.) At random, heedlessly, come what will, impulsively.

tupa [too'-pah], f. 1. (Coll.) Satiety, repletion. 2. The act of pressing close.

tupé [too-pay'], m. 1. Toupée (peluca), foretop. 2. (Met.) Effrontary, insolence.

tupí [too-pee'], a. & m. Name of the principal race of Indians in Brazil and their language which is in general use in the Amazonian regions.

tupido, da [too-pee'-do, dah], a & pp. Of TUPIR. 1. Dense, thick (denso), close-woven (tela). 2. (Met.) Dense, overgrown, rank. 3. (LAm.) Blocked (obstruido). 4. (Mex.) Common (frecuente).

tupir [too-peer'], va. 1. To press close, to squeeze, closing the pores or interstices. 2. (LAm.) To block (obstruir). -vr. To stuff or glut oneself (comer mucho); to overeat.

turaní [too-rah-nee'], **turaniense** [too-rah-ne-en'-say], a. Turanian, a family of agglutinative languages.

turba [toor'-bah], f. 1. Crowd, confused multitude, heap. 2. Turf, sod, peat, used for fuel.

turbación [toor-bah-the-on'], f. Perturbation (alarma), confusion (confusión), disorder; light headedness; the act of exciting disturbances.

turbadamente [toor-bah-dah-men'-tay], adv. In a disorderly manner.

turbado [toor-bah'-do], a. Disturbed, worried, upset; embarrassed; bewildered.

turbador, ra [toor-bah-dor', rah], f. Disturber, perturbator.

turbal [toor-bahl'], m. Turf-bog, peat-moss; collection of peat or fuel.

turbamulta [toor-bah-mool-tah], f. Crowd, multitude.

turbante [toor-bahn'-tay], m. 1. Turban worn by the Turks (sombrero). 2. Disturber.

turbar [toor-bar'], va. To disturb (orden, paz, razón), to alarm, to surprise, to disturb (persona), to disconcert (desconcertar); to upset (alterar). -vr. To be uneasy, alarmed, discomposed.

turbativo, va [toor-bah-tee'-vo, vah], a. Troublesome, alarming.

turbiamente [toor-be-ha-men'-tay], adv. Obscurely, confusedly.

turbiedad [toor-be-ay-dahd'], f. Muddiness, turbidness; obscurity.

turbina [toor-bee'-nah], f. A turbine water-wheel placed horizontally.

turbinado, da [toor-be-nah'do, dah], a. Turbinated, twisted, spiral-framed.

turbinista [toor-be-nees'-tah], f. (Conch.) Wreath shell, spiral shell. Turbo.

turbino [toor-bee'-no], m. Powder made of the root of turbith.

turbio, bia [toor'-be-o, ah], a. 1. Muddy (agua), turbid, disturbed (vista), troubled. 2. Unhappy, unfortunate. 3. Dark, obscure (idioma).

turbión [toor-be-on'], m. 1. A heavy shower of rain. 2. Hurricane; violent concussion of things.

turbit [toor-beet'], m. (Bot.) Turpeth, turbith, the root of an East Indian plant allied to jalap.

turbohélice [toor-bo-ay'-le-thay], m. Turbo-propeller engine.

turbopropulsor [toor-bo-pro-pool-sor'], m. Turboprop.

turborreactor [toor-bor-ray-ac-tor'], m. (Aer.) Turbojet.

turborretropropulsión [toor-bor-ray-tro-pro-pool-se-on], f. Turbo-jet propulsion.

turbulencia [toor-boo-len'-the-ah], f. 1. Turbidness, muddiness. 2. Turbulence, confusion, disorder.

turbulentamente [toor-boo-len-tah-men-tay], adv. Turbulently.

turbulento, ta [toor-boo-len'-to, tah], a. 1. Turbid, thick, muddy. 2. Turbulent (elementos, río), disorderly, tumultuous.

turca [toor'-cah], f. (Coll.) Tipsiness. **Vestirse una turca** or **coger una turca**, to get drunk.

turco, ca [toor'-co, cah], adj. Turkish. -m. & f. A Turk; a Turkish woman. -m. (Slang.) Wine.

turcomano, na [toor-co-mah'-no, nah], a. Turkoman, a Tartar inhabitant of Turkestan, of Turkish origin.

túrdiga [toor'-de-gah], f. 1. Piece of new leather, of which coarse shoes, called *abarcas* are made. 2. Strip of hide.

turdión [toor-de-on'], m. Ancient Spanish dance.

turgencia [toor-han'-the-ah], f. 1. Swelling, turgescence. 2. Ostentation, vanity, pride.

turgente [toor-hen'-tay], *a.* 1. Turgescent, tumid, protuberant. 2. *(Poet.)* Massive, lofty.

túrgido, da [toor'-he-do, dah], *a.* *(Poet.)* Lofty, bulky.

turicha [too-ree'-chah], *f.* V. TURUPIAL.

turífero, ra [too-ree'-fay-ro, rah], *a.* Incense-producing or bearing.

turismo [too-rees'-mo], *m.* Tourism, touring (excursionismo), traveling. **Hacer turismo,** to go touring. **Ahora se hace más turismo que nunca,** numbers of tourists are greater now than ever.

turista [too-rees'-tah], *m. & f.* Tourist, traveler.

turma [toor'-mah], *f.* Testicle. **Turma de tierra,** *(Bot.)* truffle.

turmalina [toor-mah-lee'-nah], *f.* *(Miner.)* Tourmaline, a translucent mineral of various colors, generally blackish: schorl. It is a complex aluminum-boron silicate: used in polariscopes.

turmera [toor-may'-rah], *f.* *(Bot.)* Ledum-leaved rock-rose.

turmeruela [toor-may-roo-ay'-lah], *f.* *(Bot.)* Umbel-flowered rock-rose.

turnar [toor-nar'], *vn.* To alternate, to go or work by turns.

turnio, nia [toor'-ne-o, ah], *a.* 1. Squint-eyed: in this sense it is used as a substantive. 2. Torvous, of a stern countenance.

turno [toor'-no], *m.* 1. Turn (vez, oportunidad), successive or alternate order (orden); change, vicissitude. 2. *(Naut.)* Time in which sailors are employed in some particular business. **Al turno,** by turns. **Por su turno,** in one turn. **Turno de día,** day shift. **Trabajo de turnos,** shift working. **Estuvo con la querida de turno,** he was with his girlfriend of the moment.

turón [too-rone'], *m.* A kind of fieldmouse.

turpial [toor-pe-ahl'], *m.* Troopial. V. TURUPIAL.

turquesa [toor-kay'-sah], *f.* 1. Turquoise or turkois, a precious stone. 2. Mould for making pellets or balls to be thrown from a crossbow.

turquesado, da [toor-kay-sah'-do, dah], *a.* Of the turquoise color.

turquesco, ca [toor-kes'-co, cah], *a.* Turkish. **A la turquesa,** in the Turkish manner.

turquí, turquino, na [toor-kee'], *a.* Of a deep blue color.

turrar [toor-rar'], *va.* To toast, to roast.

turrón [toor-rone'], *m.* Nougat, paste made of almonds, pine-kernels, nuts, and honey.

turronero [toor -ro-nay'-ro], *m.* One who makes or retails the sweetmeat called *turrón.*

tursión [toor-se-on'], *m.* Fish resembling a dolphin.

turulato, ta [too-roo-lah'-to, tah], *a.* *(Coll.)* Billy, stupefied, confounded, startled.

turulés [too-roo-lays'], *a.* Said of a kind of strong grapes.

turumbón [too-room-bone'], *m.* Contusion on the head.

turupial [too-roo-pe-ahl'], *m.* Troopial, a bird of Venezuela, of the size of a thrush, with black and gold plumage, a great songster and easy to tame. V. TURICHA.

tus [toos], *int.* A word used in calling dogs.

tusa [too'-sah], *f.* *(Amer.)* 1. The corn-cob (mazorca). 2. *(Cuba)* Cigarette covered with the finest husk of the corn. 3. *(Cono Sur)* Horse's name. 4. *(Cono Sur)* Clipping (esquileo). 5. *(And.)* Pockmark (hoyo). 6. *(CAm. Carib.)* Whore (puta).

tusco, ca [toos'-co, cah], *a.* Tuscan, Etruscan.

tusílago [too-see'-lah-go], *m.* *(Bot.)* Coltsfoot.

tuso, sa [too'-so, sah], *m. & f.* *(Coll.)* Name given to dogs.

tusón [too-sone'], *m.* 1. Fleece of a sheep. 2. *(Prov.)* Colt not two years old.

tusona [too-so'-nah], *f.* 1. Strumpet, having her head and eyebrows rather shaved, as a punishment, or lost from disease. 2. *(Andal.)* Filly not two years old.

tute [too'-tay], *m.* A special card game.

tuteamiento [too-tay-ah-me-en'-to], *m.* V. TUTERO.

tutear [too-tay-ar'], *m.* To treat with familiarity. **Tutear a uno,** to address somebody as *tú.*

tutela [too-tay'-lah], *f.* Guardianship, tutelage, tutorage, protection (protección). **Tutela dativa,** *(Law.)* guardianship appointed by a court. **Bajo tutela,** in ward.

tutelar [too-tay-lar'], *a.* Tutelar, tutelary.

tuteo [too-tay'-o], *m.* Addressing persons by the pronoun *Tú* (thou).

tutía [too-tee'-ah], *f.* Tutty. V. ATUTÍA.

tutilimundi [too-te-le-moon'-de], *m.* V. MUNDINOVI.

tutiplén [too-te-plen']. *adv.* Only used in the colloquial phrase, **a tutiplén,** abundantly to satiety.

tutor [too-tor'], *m.* 1. Tutor, instructor. 2. Guardian of the person and estate of a minor. 3. Defender, protector.

tutora [too-to'-rah], *f.* Tutorees, guardian;governess.

tutoría [too-to-ree'-ah], *f.* Tutelage, guardianship. V. TUTELA.

tutriz [too-treeth'], *f.* Tutoress, governess. V. TUTORA.

tuya [too'-yah], *f.* Thuya, white cedar or red cedar. One species yields sandarac.

tuyo, ya [too'-yo, yah], *pron. poss.* Thine, yours. **Ese sombrero es tuyo,** that hat is yours. **Los tuyos,** the friends and relatives of the party addressed.

U

u [oo] is the twenty-second letter in the spanish alphabet and fifth of the vowels; it loses its sound after *q* and *g*, and becomes a liquid, except where it is followed by an *a*, as in *gauarismo,* or when marked with a diaresis, as in *agüero,* when it retains its proper sound. The letters *b, v,* and *u* were formerly used as equivalent to each other in writing or printing.

u [oo]. A disjunctive conjunction used in the place of *o,* to avoid cacophony (before *o* or *ho),* as, *plata u oro,* silver or gold; *víctima u holocausto,* a victim or a holocaust.

ualita [oo-ah-lee' tah], *f.* A mineral substance occurring in the aspect of raw cotton.

ubérrimo, ma [oo-berr'-re-mo, mah], *a.* Very fruitful; extremely abundant.

ubicación [oo-be-cah-the-on'], *f.* Situation in a determined place, position.

ubicar [oo-be-car'], *vn. & vr.* 1. To locate or situate, to be located (edificio). 2. To find (encontrar). 3. To classify (clasificar). 4. *(LAm.)* To get a job (en un puesto); to settle in (establecerse).

ubicuidad [oo-be-coo-e-dahd'], *f.* Ubiquity, presence everywhere at once.

ubicuo, cua [oo-bee'-kwo, kwah], *a.* Ubiquitous, omnipresent.

ubiquidad [oo-be-ke-dahd'], *f.* V. UBICUIDAD.

ubiquitario, ria [oo-be-ke-tah'-re-o, ah], *a. & n.* Ubiquitarian, one of a sect which denies transubstantiation, affirming that the body of Jesus Christ in virtue of his divinity is present in the eucharist.

ubio [oo'-be-o], *m.* *(Prov.)* V. YUGO.

ubre [oo'-bray], *f.* Dug or teat of female animals, udder.

ubrera [oo-bray'-rah], *f.* Thrush, ulcerations in the mouth of sucking children.

ucencia [oo-then'-the-ah], *com.* Your excellency. V. VUECELENCIA.

udómetro [oo-doh'-me-tro], *m.* Udometer, a rain-gauge.

uesnorueste [oo-es-no-roo-es'-tay], *m.* V. OESNORUESTE.

uessudueste [oo-es-soo-doo-es'-tay], *a.* V. OESSUDUESTE.

uesto [oo-es'-tay], *m.* 1. West. 2. Zephyr, west wind.

¡uf! *int.* Exclamation denoting weariness or annoyance.

ufanamente [ ], *adv.* Ostentatiously, boastfully.

ufanarse [oo-fah-nar'-say], *vr.* To boast, to be haughty, or elated.

ufanía

ufanía [oo-fah-nee'-ah], *f*. 1. Pride (orgullo), haughtiness. 2. Joy, gaiety, pleasure, satisfaction.

ufano, na [oo-fah'-no, nah], *a*. 1. Proud (orgulloso), haughty, arrogant. 2. Gay (alegre), cheerful, content; masterly.

ufo (**A**) [oo'-fo], *adv*. In a sponging manner; parasitically.

ujier [oo-he-err'], *m*. Usher, an employee in the king's palace, corresponding to a porter.

úlcera [ool'-thay-rah], *f*. Ulcer. **Úlcera duodenal**, *(Med.)* duodenal ulcer.

ulceración [ool-thay-rah-the-or'], *f*. Ulceration.

ulcerado, da [ool-thay-rah'-do, dah], *a*. & *pp*. of ULCERAR. Ulcered, ulcerated.

ulcerar [ool-thay-rar'], *va*. To ulcerate. *-vr*. To exulcerate.

ulcerativo, va [ool-thay-rah-tee'-vo, vah], *a*. Causing ulcera.

ulceroso, sa [ool-thay-ro'-so, sah], *a*. Ulcerous.

ule [oo'-lay], *m*. The caoutchouc, or rubber-tree. *V*. HULE.

ulema [oo-lay'-mah], *m*. Doctor of the law among the Turks.

ulmáceas [ool-mah'-thay-as], *f. pl*. Ulmaceae, the elm family.

ulmaria [ool-mah´-re-ah], *f*. Meadow sweet, meadow-wort, queen of the meadows.

ulterior [ool-tay-re-or'], *m*. Ulterior, posterior, farther (lugar).

ulteriormente [ool-tay-re-or-men-tay], *adv*. Farther, beyond, any more or longer.

ultimado, da [ool-te-mah'-do, dah], *a*. & *pp*. of ULTIMAR. Ended, finished, ultimate.

últimamente [ool'-te-mah-men-tay], *adv*. Lastly (por último), finally, just now, ultimately.

ultimar [ool-te-mar'], *vn*. 1. To end, to finish (terminar). 2. *(LAm.)* To finish off (rematar a persona); to kill (matar).

ultimato [ool-te-mah-to], *m*. Ultimatum.

ultimátum [ool-te-mah'-toom], *m*. 1. Ultimatum: used in diplomacy. 2. *(Coll.)* A final resolution.

ultimidad [ool-te-me-dahd'], *f*. The last stage.

último, ma [ool'-te-mo, mah], *m*. 1. Last (final), latest (más reciente), hindmost; late, latter. 2. Highly finished, most valuable. 3. Remote; extreme (extremo). 4. Final, conclusive, ultimate. **Estar a lo último**, to understand completely. **Estar a lo último or en las últimas**, to be expiring. **Por último**, lastly, finally. **Último entre todos**, last of all, last among them all. **A últimos de mes, semana, etc.**, at the end of the month, week, etc. **Viven en el último piso**, they live on the top floor. **Vestido a la última**, dressed in the latest style. **Pedirme eso encima ya es lo último**, for him to ask that of me as well really is the limit.

últimas [ool´-te-mas], *f. pl*. Last or end syllables.

ultra [ool'-trah], *adv*. Besides, moreover; beyond.

ultracatólico, ca [ool-trah-cah-to'-le-co, cah], *a*. Ultramontane.

ultracongelado [ool-trah-con-he-lah-do], *a*. *(Esp.)* Deep-frozen.

ultraderecha [ool-trah-day-ray-chah], *f*. Extreme right.

ultrajador, ra [ool-trah-hah-dor', rah], *a* & *f*. One who outrages or insults.

ultrajamiento [ool-trah-hah-me-en'-to], *m*. Outrage, affront, injury.

ultrajar [ool-trah-har'], *va*. 1. To outrage, to offend (ofender), to treat injuriously. 2. To despise, to depreciate; to abuse.

ultraje [ool-trah´-hay], *m*. Outrage, contempt, injurious language, abuse.

ultrajosamente [ool-trah-jo-sah-men-tay], *adv*. Outrageously.

ultrajoso, sa [ool-trah-ho'-so, sah], *a*. Outrageous, overbearing.

ultramar [ool-trah-mar'], *a*. Ultramarine, foreign. *-m*. *(Art.)* V. ULTRAMARINO.

ultramarino, na [ool-trah-mah-ree'-no, nah], *a*. Ultramarine, from overseas. *-m. pl*. Fancy, imported groceries.

ultramarino [ool-trah-mah-ree'-no], *m*. Ultramarine, the finest blue, from the lapis lazuli.

ultramaro [ool-trah-mah'-ro], *m*. Ultramarine blue.

ultramicroscopio [ool-trah-me-cros-co´-pe-o], *m*. Dark-field microscope.

ultramoderno, na [ool-trah-mo-der'-no, nah], *a*. Ultramodern.

ultramontanismo [ool-trah- mon-tah-nees'-mo], *m*. Ultramontenism, the policy of the authority of the Pope over any national church.

ultramontano, na [ool-trah-mon-tah'-no, nah], *a*. Ultramontane, supporting the policy of the widest power of the Pope over all ecclesiastical matters.

ultrasónico, ca [ool-tra-so'-ne-co, cah], *a*. Ultrasonic.

ultrasonido [ool-trah-so-nee'-do], *m*. Ultrasonic, ultrasound.

ultratumba [ool-trah-toom'-bah], *f*. Beyond the grave, other world.

ultravioleta [ool-trah-ve-o-lay'-tah], *a*. Ultraviolet.

úlula [oo'-loo-lah], *f*. *(Orn.)* Owl. *V*. AUTILLO.

ulular [oo-loo-lar'], *vn*. *(Prov.)* To howl (animal, viento); to cry aloud, to ululate.

ululato [oo-loo-lah'-to], *m*. Howl, screech, hue and cry.

umbela [oom-bay´-lah], *f*. Umbel, inflorescence resembling a parasol.

umbelífero, ra [oom-bay-loo'-fay-ro, rah], *a*. Umbelliferous, in the form of a parasol. *-f. pl*. The parsley family.

umbilicado, da [oom-be-le-cah'-do, dah], *m*. Navel-shaped; umbilicated.

umbilical [oom-be-le-cahl'], *a*. Umbilical.

umbla [oom'-blah], *f*. Umber, fish of the salmon family.

umbral [oom-brahl'], *m*. 1. Threshold (de entrada): lintel, architrave. 2. Beginning, commencement, rudiment. 3. **Umbrales**, *(S. Am.)* timber for thresholds. **Estar en los umbrales de**, to be on the threshold of.

umbralar [oom-brah-lar'], *va*. To lay down the ground-timber of a door or gate; to place an architrave.

umbrátil [oom-brah´-teel], *a*. Umbratile; resembling.

umbría [oom-bree'-ah], *f*. Umbrosity, umbrageousness; a shady place.

umbrío, a [oom-bree'-o, ah], *a*. Umbrageous.

umbroso, sa [oom-bro'-so, sah], *a*. Shady.

un [oon], *a*. One, a, used for *uno*, but always before words: it is also used occasionally before verbs, to give force to an expression. **Un hombre**, a man.

una [oo´-nah], *a*. V. UNO. **A una**, with one accord.

unánime [oo-nah'-ne-may], *a*. Unanimous.

unanimemente [oo-nah-ne-mah-men-tay], *adv*. Unanimously.

unanimidad [oo-nah-ne-me-dahd'], *f*. Unanimity.

uncia [oon´-the-ah], *f*. An ancient coin.

uncial [oon-the-ahl'], *a*. Uncial, said of a form of (capital) letters used in a manuscripts from the fourth to the eighth contury.

unciforme [oon-the-for'-may], *a*. Unciform, shaped like a hook. *m*. Unciform, a bone of the wrist.

unción [oon-the-on'], *f*. 1. Unction, anointing. 2. Extreme unction. 3. Unction, anything that excites piety and devotion. *-pl*. Course of salivation, practiced in venereal cases.

uncionario, ria [oon-the-o-nah´-re-o, ah], *a*. Being under salivation. *-m*. Place of salivating.

uncir [oon-theer´], *va*. To yoke oxen or mules for labor.

undante [oon-dahn'-tay], *a*. *(Poet.)* V. UNDOSO.

undecágono [oon-day-cah´-go-no], *m*. *(Math.)* Undecagon, a figure having eleven angles and eleven sides.

undécimo, ma [oon-day'-the-mo, mah], *a*. Eleventh.

undécuplo, pla [oon-day'-coo-plo, plah], *a*. Eleven times as much.

undísono, na [oon-dee'-so, nah], *a*. Billowy, sounding like waves.

undívago, ga [oon-dee'-vah-go, gah], *a*. Wavy, moving like the waves.

undoso, sa [oon-do'-so, sah], *a*. Wavy, undulary, undulatory.

undulación [oon-doo-lah-the-on'], *f*. Undulation.

undular [oon-doo-lar´], *vn*. To rise or play in waves, to undulate.

undulatorio, ria [oon-doo-lah-to'-re-o, ah], *a*. Undulatory.

ungarina [oon-gah-ree´-nah], *f*. V. ANGUARINA.

ungido [oon-hee'-do], *m* . Anointed of the Lord, king, sovereign.—**Ungido, da,** *pp.* of UNGIR.

ungimiento [oon-he-me-en'-to], *m.* Unction, the act of anointing.

ungir [oon-heer'], *va.* To anoint, to consecrate.

ungüentario, ria [oon-goo-en-tah'-re-o, ah], *a.* Preparing sweet-scented ointment or perfumes. *m.* Perfume-box, in which sweet-scented ointments are kept; anointer.

ungüento [oon-goo-en'-to], *m.* 1. Unguent, ointment, liniment. 2. Perfume, balsam.

unguiculado, da [oon-ge-coo-lah'-do, dah], *a. (Zool.)* Unguiculate, having claws.

unguífero, ra [oon-gee'-fay-ro, rah], *a.* Unguiferous, bearing a nail or a claw.

ungüis [oon'-goo-ees], *m.* The lachrymal bone of the nose, thin like a nail.

ungulado, da [un-goo-lah'-do, dah], *a.* Ungulate, having hoofs.

uniarticulado, da [oo-ne-ar-te-coo-lah'-do, dah], *a. (Biol.)* Uniarticulate, single-jointed.

unible [oo-nee'-blay], *a.* That which may be united.

unibus [oo-nee-boos], Unibus *(Comput.)*

únicamente [oo'-ne-cah-men-tay], *adv.* Only, simply.

unicario [oo-ne-cah'-re-o], *m.* A tree of India, the leaves of which the Malays boil and mix with the betel, which they constantly chew.

unicaule [oo-ne-cah´-oo-lay], *a.* Having but one stalk (plantas).

unicelular [oo-ne-the-loo-loor], *a.* Unicellular, single-cell.

unicidad [oo-ne-the-dahd'], *f. (Phil.)* Singularity, distinctive quality.

único, ca [oo´-ne-co, cah], *a.* Singular, alone, that of which there is but one; single; unique, sole; only (solo); rare, unmatched, unparalleled. **La única dificultad es que...,** the only difficulty is that.... **Es lo único que nos hacía falta,** that´s all we needed.

unicoloro, ra [oo-ne-co-lo'-ro, rah], *a.* Unicolor, of one color.

unicornio [oo-necor'-ne-o], *m.* 1. Unicorn. 2. A northern constellation, Monoceros. 3. *(Zool.)* Narwhal. 4. A mineral rock, yellow, ashy, or gray.

unidad [oo-ne-dahd'], *f.* 1. Unity (cualidad). 2. Unit, the root of numbers. 3. *(Arith.)* A number less than ten. 4. Principle of dramatic unity. 5. Conformity, union. **Unidad termal británica,** *(Phv.)* BTU. British thermal unit. **Unidad de lugar,** unity of place. **Unidad de información,** bit of information. **Unidad central de procesamiento,** central processing unit.

unidamente [oo-ne-dah-men'-tay], *adv.* Jointly, unanimously, conjunctively, compactly, unitedly.

unido [oo-nee-do], *a.* 1. Joined (juntado), linked. 2. *(Fig.)* United. **Una familia muy unida,** a very united family.

unifamiliar [oo-nee-fah-me-le-ar], *a.* Single-family.

unificar [oo-ne-fe-car'], *va.* To unite into one.

uniflorígero, ra [oo-ne-flo-hay'-ro, rah], **unifloro, ra** [oo-ne-flo'-ro, rah], *a.* One-flowered, uniflorous.

unifoliado, da [oo-ne-fo-le-ah-do, dah], *a.* Unifoliate, unifoliar', one leaved.

uniformar [oo-ne-for-mar'], *va.* 1. To make uniform (igualar). 2. To put into uniform (persona).

uniforme [oo-ne-for'-may], *a.* Uniform.

uniforme [oo-ne-for-may], *m. (Mil.)* Uniform regimentals.

uniformemente [oo-ne-for-may-men-tay], *adv.* Uniformly.

uniformidad [oo-ne-for-me-dahd'], *f.* Uniformity, resemblance, harmony.

unigénito [oo-ne-hay'-ne-to], *a.* Only-begotten.

unilateral [oo-ne-lah-tay-rahl'], *m. (For.)* Unilateral, binding on one party only.

unión [oo-ne-on´], *f.* 1. Union, conjunction. 2. Conformity, resemblance. 3. Concord, unity (cualidad). 4. Union, marriage. 5. Composition of ingredient. 6. Combination, physical or chemical union. 7. Consolidation of the lips of a wound. 8. Alliance, confederacy. coalition, consociation. 9.

Contiguity; continuity. 10. Incorporation, coherence; sameness, similarity. 11. Hoop, ring. 12. Among jewellers match, likeness in form and size of one pearl with another. **La unión hace la fuerza,** united we stand. **En unión con,** together with.

unípara [oo-nee'-pa-rah], *a.* Uniparous, bringing one at a birth.

unípede [oo-nee'-pe-day], *a.* Uniped, having only one foot.

unipersonal [oo-ne-per-so-nahl´], *a.* Unipersonal, consisting of one person only.

unipolar [oo-ne-po-lar'], *a.* Unipolar, having one pole only.

unipolaridad [oo-ne-po-lah-re-dahd'], *f.* A. State of a unipolar body; unipolarity.

unir [oo-neer'], *va.* 1. To join (objetos, piezas), to unite, to conjoin, to couple, to knit. 2. To join, to mix (líquidos), to incorporate, to combine, to coalesce. 3. To bind, to tie (atar), to consociate; to confederate. 4. To approach, to bring near; to close. 5. To collect, to aggregate. 6. To conform. 7. To consolidate. *-vr.* 1. To join (personas), to unite, to associate, to be united; to adhere, to concur. 2. To be contiguous. 3. To be united; to be married. **Les une una fuerte simpatía,** they are bound by a strong affection. **Unirse en matrimonio,** to marry.

unisexual [oo-ne-sec-soo-ahl'], *a. (Bot.)* Unisexual, having flowers of one sex only.

unison [oo-nee'-son], *vn.* Unison, musical consonance.

unisonancia [oo-ne-so-nahn´-the-ah], *f.* Uniformity of sound, unison; monotony.

unísono [oo-nee'-so-no], *a.* 1. Unison, sounding alone. 2. Having the same sound.

unísono [oo-ne-so-no], *m.* Unison, a single unvaried note.

unitario [oo-ne-tah´-re-o], *m.* Unitarian, one who rejects the doctrine of the Trinity.*-a.* Advocating political centralization.

unitarismo [oo-ne-tah-rees'-mo], *m.* 1. The doctrine of those who deny the Trinity. 2. Political centralization.

unitivo, va [oo-ne-tee'-vo, vah], *a.* Unitive.

univalvo, va [oo-ne-vahl'-vo, vah], *a.* Univalve (conchas).

universal [oo-ne-ver-sahl'], *a.* Universal, world (mundial), general, oecumenical; learned, well-informed. **De fama universal,** known all over the world. **Historia universal,** world history.

universalidad [oo-ne-ver-sah-le-dahd'], *f.* 1. Universality. 2. Generality of information.

universalismo [oo-ne-ver-sah-lees'-mo], *m.* Opinion founded on the authority of universal consent.

universalista [oo-ne-ver-sah-lees'-tah], *com.* One who holds the foregoing opinion.

universalmente [oo-ne-ver-sal-men'-tay], *adv.* Universally, generally.

universidad [oo-ne-ver-se-dahd'], *f.* 1. Universality, generality. 2. University. 3. Corporation, community. 4. The whole circle of nature; the vegetable, animal, or mineral kingdom. **Universidad laboral,** technical college.

universitario [oo-ne-ver-se-tah-re-o], *a.* University; academic. *-m.* **Universitaria,** *f.* University.

universo [oo-ne-verr'-so], *m.* The universe.

universo, sa [oo-ne-verr´-so, sah], *a.* Universal.

univocación [oo-ne-vo-cah-the-on'], *f.* Univocation.

unívocamente [oo-nee'-vo-cah-men tay], *adv.* Univocally, unanimously.

univocarse [oo-ne-vo-car'-say], *vr.* To have the same meaning.

unívoco, ca [oo-nee'-vo-co, cah], *a.* 1. Univocal: used as a substantive. 2. Unanimous; resembling.

uno [oo'-no], *m.* 1. One. 2. One, any individual, intimate friend, another, self. 3. *(Math.)* Radical, or root of a number.

uno, na [oo'-no, nah], *a.* 1. One; closely resembling the same (idéntico); sole, only. 2. It is used relatively or to supply a name, as **Uno dijo,** it was said, or one said. **Uno a otro,** one another, reciprocally. **Todo es uno,** it is all the same; it is foreign to the point. **Uno a uno,** one by one. **Uno por uno,** one and then another: used to mark the distinction more forcibly. **Váyase uno por otro**, let one go for the other. **Una cosa**, a thing undetermined. **Una y no más**, never, no more. **Ser para en una**, to be well matched: applied to a married couple. **Ir a una**, to act of the same accord, or to the same end. **Cada uno a la suyo**, everyone should mind his own business. **Uno nunca sabe qué hacer**, one never knows what to do.

untador, ra [oon-tah-dor', rah], *m. & f.* Anointer, surgeon who administers or performs mercurial frictions.

untadura [oon-tah-doo'-rah], *f.* 1. Unction, the act of anointing (acto). 2. Unction, ointment.

untamiento [oon-tah-me-en'-to], *m.* Unction, the act of anointing.

untar [oon-tar'], *va.* 1. To rub, to anoint, to grease, to oint. 2. To suborn, to bribe. **Untar las manos**, to grease the hands, *y. e.* To bribe. 3. To varnish a piece of painting. **Untar los dedos en tinta**, to smear one´s finger with ink. -*vr.* 1. To be greased with unctuous matter. 2. To embezzle.

untaza [oon-tah'-thah], *f.* Grease. V. ENJUNDIA.

unto [oon'-to], *m.* 1. Grease, fat of animals. 2. Unguent, ointment. **Unto de oso**, bear´s grease. **Unto de puerco**, hog´s lard.

untoso, sa [oon-to'-so, sah], *a. (Prov.)* V. UNTUOSO.

untuosidad [oon-too-o-se-dahd'], *f.* Unctuosity, greasiness.

untuoso, sa [oon-too-o'-so, sah], *a.* Unctuous, greasy.

untura [oon-too'-rah], *f.* 1. Unction, act of anointing. 2. Unction, ointment, matter used in anointing.

uña [oo'-nyah], *f.* 1. Nail of the fingers and toes (de la mano, del pie). 2. Hoof (pezuña), claw, or talon of beasts; fang. 3. Painted hook of instruments. 4. Part of the trunk of a felled tree, which sticks to the root. 5. Crust on sores or wounds. 6. Excrescence or hard tumor on the eyelids. 7. Dexterity in stealing or filching. 8. Curved beak of a scorpion. **Uña de la gran bestia**, elk's hoove. **Uñas de cangrejo**, crab's claws. **Hincar** or **meter la uña**, to overcharge, to sell at an exorbitant price. **Mostrar las uñas**, to be inexorable. **Mostrar la uña**, to show one's teeth, to discover one´s foibles. **Comerse las uñas**, to bite one´s nails. **Uña encarnada**, ingrowing nail. **Estar de uñas con uno**, to be at daggers drawn with somebody.

uñada [oo-nyah'-dah], *f.* Impression made with the nail, scratch, nip.

uñarada [oo-nyah-rah'-dah], *f.* Scratch with the nail.

uñate [oo-nyah'-tay], *m.* 1. *(Coll.)* Pinching with the nail. 2. V. UÑETA.

uñaza [oo-nyah´-thah], *f. aug.* Large nail.

uñero [oo-nyay'-ro], *m.* 1. A callous excrescence at the root of a nail. 2. An in-growing nail.

uñidura [oo-nay-doo'-rah], *f.* The act of yoking oxen or mules for labor.

uñir [oo-nyeer'], *va. (Prov.)* To yoke. V. UNCIR.

uñita [oo-nyee'-tah], *f. dim.* Little nail.

uñoso, sa [oo-nyo'-so, sah], *a.* Having long nails or claws.

¡upa! [oo'-pah], *int.* Up, up: a term used to make children get up from the ground. V. AUPA.

upar [oo-par'], *vn. (Coll.)* To endeavor to get up.

uracho [oo-rah'-cho], *m. (Anat.)* Urachus, a ligamentous cord that terminates in the naval-string.

Urania [oo-rah'-ne-ah], *f. (Myth.)* Urania, the muse of astronomy.

uranio [oo-rah'-ne-o], *m. (Chem.)* Uranium, a rare, heavy metallic element.

uranita [oo-rah-nee'-tah], *f. (Chem.)* Uranite, autunite; phosphate of uranium and calcium.

uranografía [oo-rah-no-grah-fee'-ah], *f.* Uranography, ouranography, description of the heavens.

uranometría [oo-rah-no-may-tree'-ah], *f.* Uranometry, the measurement of the heavens.

uranómetro [oo-rah-no'-may-tro], *m.* An instrument for measuring heavenly bodies and their movements.

uranoscopio [oo-rah-nos-co'-pe-o], *m.* Star-gazor, a fish with eyes on the top of the head.

uraño, ña [oo-rah'-nyo, nyah], *a.* Coy, reserved, timid; wild, untamed. V. HURAÑO.

urari [oo-rah'-re], *m.* Woorare, curare, arrow-poison of South America.

urato [oo-rah'-to], *m.* 1. *(Chem.)* Urate, a salt of uric acid. 2. *(Agr.)* A manure of urine and plaster or earth.

urbanamente [oor-bah-nah-men'-tay], *adv.* Courteously, politely, complacently.

urbanidad [oor-bah-ne-dahd'], *f.* Urbanity, civility, politeness, courteousness, gentleness, complaisance.

urbanismo [oor-bah-nees-mo], *m.* 1. Town planning (planificación). 2. *(Carib.)* Real-estate development.

urbanización [oor-bah-ne-thah-the-on], *f.* City planning.

urbanizar [oor-bah-ne-thar'], *va.* To urbanize (tierra).

urbano, na [or-bahn´-no, nah], *a.* 1. Urban (de la ciudad), peculiar to towns or cities. 2. Urbane, courteous (cortés), polite, well-bred.

urca [oor'-cah], *f.* 1. *(Naut.)* Hooker, dogger; a pink-built and sloop-rigged vessel. 2. *(Naut.)* Storehouse. 3. *(Zool.)* Species of whale. V. ORCA.

urce [oor'-thay], *m. (Bot.)* Heath. V. BREZO.

urceiforme [oor-thay-e-for'-may], *a. (Bot.)* Urceolate, swollen below and contracted at the orifice.

urchilla [oor-cheel-lyah], *f.* Archil or orchil, a violet color, used by dyers.

urdidera [oor-de-day'-rah], *f.* 1. Woman who warps. 2. A warping frame.

urdidor, ra [oor-de-dor', rah], *m. & f.* 1. Warper. 2. *m.* Warping-frame, warping mill.

urdidura [oor-de-doo'-rah], *f.* The act of warping.

urdimbre [oor-deem'-bray], *f.* Chain, warp, as opposed to woof.

urdir [oor-deer'], *va.* 1. To warp (tela), to dispose threads for the loom. 2. To contrive, to scheme.

urea [oo-ray'-ah], *f.* Urea, a crystallizable substance excreted in the urine.

urente [oo-ren'-tay], *a.* Hot, burning, parching. *(Acad.)*

uremia [oo-ray'-me-ah], *f. (Ned.)* Uraemia, a morbid state occasioned by presence of urea in the blood.

urémico, ca [oo-ray'-me-co, cah], *a.* Uremic, relating to or affected by uremia.

urétera [oo-ray'-tay-rah], *f. (Anat.)* V. URETRA.

urétere [oo-ray´-tay-ray], *m. (Anat.)* Ureter, the duct by which the urine passes from the kidney to the bladder or cloaca.

urético, ca [oo-ray'-te-co, cah], *a.* Belonging to the urethra.

uretra [oo-ray'-trah], *f. (Anat.)* Urethra, the canal by which urine is expelled from the bladder.

uretritis [oo-ray-tree'-tis], *f.* 1. Urethritis, inflammation of the urethra. 2. Gonorrhoea.

uretrorrea [oo-ray-tror-ray´-ah], *f. (Med.)* Gleet; flux from the urethra.

uretrótomo [oo-ray-tro´-to-mo], *m.* Urethrotome.

urgencia [oor-hen'-the-ah], *f.* Urgency, exigence; obligation. **En caso de urgencia**, in case of necessity.

urgente [oor-hen'-tay], *a.* Urgent, pressing, cogent. **Carta urgente**, express letter.

urgentemente [oor-hen´-tay-men-tay], *adv.* Urgently.

urgir [oor-heer'], *m.* To be urgent, to require speedy cure or immediate execution; to be actually obliged; to turbo, to press forward. **Me urge la respuesta**, the reply presses. **Me urge terminarlo**, I must finish it as soon as I can.

úrico, ca [oo'-re-co, cah], *a.* Uric, relating to urine. **Ácido úrico**, uric acid.

urinálisis [oo-re-nah'-le-sis], *m.* Urinalysis, urine analysis.

urinario, ria [oo-re-nah'-re-o, ah], *a.* Urinary.

urna [oor'-nah], *f.* 1. Urn, in which the ashes of the dead were formerly put. 2. Glass case (de cristal), in which small statues or images are kept. 3. Urn used by painters and sculpters to represent rivers.

urnición [oor-ne-the-on'], *f. (Naut.)* Top-timbers. V. BARRAGANETE.

uro [oo'-ro], *m.* A kind of wild ox.

urogallo [oo-ro-gahl'-lyo], *m. (Orn.)* Bird like a cock.

urología [oo-ro-lo-he'-ah], *f.* Urology.

urólogo, ga [oo-ro'-lo-go], *m & f.* Urologist.

uromancia [oo-ro-mahn'-the-ah], *f.* Uromancy, pretended divination by the examination of urine.

uroscopia [oo-ros-co'-pe-ah],*f.* Uroscopy, methodical inspection of urine for medical diagnosis.

urraca [oor-rah´-cah],*f.* 1. *(Orn.)* Magpie. 2. Chatterbox (habladora).

ursa [oor'-sah],*f.* She-bear. *V.* OSA.

ursulina [oor-soo-lee´-nah],*f.* Nun of the order of St. Ursula.

urticáceas [oor-te-cah´-thay-as], *f. pl. & a.* Urticaceae, the nettle family, including elms, mulberries, hops, etc; urticaceous.

urticaria [oor-te-cah'-re-ah], *f.* Urticaria, nettlerash, hives; an eruptive skin disease provoking great itching.

uruca [oo-roo'-cah],*f. (Bot.)* Arnotto. *V.* ACHIOTE.

uruguayo, ya [oo-roo-goo-ah'-yo, yah], *a. & n.* Belonging to, or native of Uruguay.

usación [oo-sah-the-on'], *f.* Use the act of using.

usadamente [oo-sah'-dah-men-tay], *adv.* According to custom.

usado, da [oo-sah'-do, dah], *a. & pp.* of USAR. 1. Used (sello), employed. 2. Used, worn out (ropa). 3. Experienced, skillful, fashionably frequent. 4. Second hand articles. **Libros usados**, second hand books. **Ropa usada**, second hand wearing apparel; cast-off clothing.

usagre [oo-sah'-gray], *m.* A breaking out in the faces of teething children, scald-head, infantile eczema.

usaje [oo-sah'-hay],*f.* Usage, custom. *V.* LAO.

usanza [oo-sahn'-thah], *f.* Usage, custom.

usar [oo-sar'], *va.* 1. To use (utilizar), to make use of; to wear. 2. To use, to accustom (soler), to habituate, to practice. 3. To exorcise an employment or office. 4 To enjoy a thing. 5. To communicate, to treat or use familiarly. **Sin usar**, unused. - *vn.* To use, to make use. -*vr.* To use, to be in use or fashion, to be wont. **La chistera ya no se usa**, top hats are not worn nowadays.

usencia [oo-sen´-the-ah], *com.* You reverence, a contraction of *vuestra reverencia*: an appellation of honor among friars.

usía [oo-see'-ah], *com.* Your lordship or your ladyship, a contraction of *vuestra señoría.*

usier [oo-se-err'], *m.* Usher, porter. *V.* UJIER.

usiría [oo-se-ree'-ah], *com. V.* USÍA.

usitado, da [oo-se-tah'-do, dah], *a. (Prov.)* Frequently used.

uso [oo'-so], *m.* 1. Use (empleo), employment, service. 2. Usufruct; enjoyment. 3. Use, custom (costumbre), style, fashion (estilo, moda), mode. 4. *(Com. Law.)* Usance, a time fixed for the payment of bills of exchange. 5. Office, exercise; wearing, wear. 6. Frequent continuation, constant use, experience; assiduousness. 7. Wear; wear and tear. **De uso corriente**, in everyday use. **Estar fuera de uso**, to be out of use. **Hacer uso de**, to make use of. **Es un uso muy antiguo**, it is a very ancient custom.

ustaga [oos-tah´-gah], *f. (Naut.)*Tie.

usted, [oos-ted'], *com.* You (your worship, your honor), a contraction of *vuestra merced (vuesarced, usted)*, a pronoun used in polite style to address all persons of respectability, either orally or by letter. **Usted** and **ustedes** used to be written in abbreviation, thus: *Vm., Vms., Vmd., Vmds.* At present *usted* is represented by *Ud.* or *Vd.*, and *ustedes (pl.)* by *Vds.*, and often printed in full. The loose articulating of the *d* frequently causes it to become inaudible, particularly in Spanish America; so that **usted** sounds as *usté.* **El coche de usted**, your car. **Sin usted**, without you.

ustión [oos-te-on'],*f.* Ustion, the act of making medical preparation by burning; exustion.

ustorio [oos-to´-re-o], *a.* Burning. *V.* ESPEJO USTORIO.

usual [oo-soo-ahl'], *a.* 1. Usual, customary, ordinary, general. 2. Tractable, social. **Año usual**, current year.

usualmente [oo-soo-ahl-men-tay], *adv.* Usually.

usuario, ria [oo-soo-ah'-re-o, a], *a. (Law.)* Having the sole use of a thing.

usucapión [oo-soo-cah-pe-on´], *f. (Law.)* Usucapion or usucaption.

usucapir [oo-soo-cah-peer'], *va. (Law.)* To acquire a right of property in anything, by possession for a specified time.

usufructo [oo-soo-frooc-to], *m.* Usufruct, profit, advantage; enjoyment.

usufructuar [oo-soo-frooc-too-ar'], *va.* 1. To enjoy the usufruct of anything. 2. To render productive or fruitful.

usufructuario, ria [oo-soo-frooc-too-ah'-re-o, ah], *a.* Possessing the usufruct of a thing.

usura [oo-soo'-rah], *f.* 1. Interest, payment for the use of money lent. 2. Gain, profit. 3. Usury.

usurar [oo-soo-rar'], *vn. V.* USUREAR.

usurariamente [oo-soo-rah-re-ah-men-tay], *adv.* Usuriously, interestedly.

usuario, ria [oo-soo-ah'-re-o, ah], *a.* Usurious, practising usury.

usurear [oo-soo-ray-ar´], *vn.* To practise usury, to lend or to borrow money on interest. 2. To reap great benefit or advantage.

usurero, ra [oo-soo-ray´-ro, rah], *m. & f.* Usurer, money-lender, griper.

usurpación [oo-soor-pah-the-on'], *f.* Usurpation.

usurpador, ra [oo-soor-pah-dor', rah], *m. & f.* Usurper.

usurpar [oo-soor-par'], *va.* 1. To usurp (corona, derechos); to assume another's once, dignity, or employment; to grasp. 2. To make use of a word instead of another, or in another sense.

utensilio [oo-ten-see'-le-o], *m.* Utensil; tool, device, contrivance. **Utensilios para escribir**, writing materials. **Utensilios para pescar**, fishing tackle.

uterino, na [oo-tay-ree´-no, nah], *a.* 1. Uterine, belonging to the womb. 2. Uterine, born of the same mother.

útero [oo´-tay-ro], *m.* Uterus, womb.

uteromanía [oo-tay-ro-mah-nee'-ah],*f.* Nymphomania.

útil [oo'-teel], *a.* 1. Useful, profitable; commodious. **Es muy útil tenerlo aquí cerca**, it´s very handy having it here close by.

útil [oo'-teel], *m. V.* UTILIDAD. -*pl.* Utensils.

utilidad [oo-te-le-dahd'],*f.* 1. Usefulness (cualidad de útil), utility. 2. Profit. **utildad neta**, net profit.

utilitario, ria [oo-te-le tah'-re-o, ah], *a.* Utilitarian.

utilitarismo [oo-te-le-tah-rees'-mo], *m.* Utilitarianism.

utilizable [oo-te-le-thah'-blay], *a.* Usable, practicable for use.

utilizar [oo-te-le-thar'], *m.* To be useful. -*va.* To reap benefit or profit: to take advantage of or profit by. -*vr.* To interest oneself in a business.

útilmente [oo'-teel-men-tay], *adv.* Usefully.

utopia [oo-to'-pe-ah],*f. V.* UTOPÍA.

utopía [oo-to-pee'-ah],*f.* 1. Utopia, an imaginary island having a perfect social and political system. 2. Plan or system which is charming in theory, but unrealizable in practice.

utópico, ca [oo-to'-pe-co, cah], *a.* Utopian, chimerically good, ideal.

utopista [oo-to-pees'-tah], *m.* 1. A dreamer. 2. Utopian schemer.

utrero, ra [oo-tray'-ro, rah], *m. & f.* Bull or heifer between two and three years old.

utretro [oo-tray´-tro], *adv.* As above.

uva [oo'-vah],*f.* 1. Grape. 2. Tippler 3. Wart on the eyelid. 4. Fruit of the barberry-bush. 5. Tumor on the epiglottis. **Uva de Corinto**, *(Bot.)* currants. **Uva pasa**, raisin. **Uva espín, espina** or **crespa**, goose-berry. -*pl.* Bunch of grapes. **Estar de mala uva**, to be in a bad mood.

uvada [oo-va'-dah],*f.* 1. Abundance of grapes. 2. *(Prov.)* Kind of land measure.

uval [oo-vahl'], *a.* Belonging to grapes.

uvate [oo-vah'-tay], *m.* Conserve of grapes.

uvayema [oo-vah-yay'-mah], *f.* Species of wild vine.

úvea [oo'-vay-ah],*f.* Uvea, the outermost coat of the eye.

uvero, ra [oo-vay´-ro, rah], *m. & f.* Retailer of grapes.

uviforme [oo-ve-for´-may], *a.* Shaped like a bunch of grapes.

úvula [oo´-voo-lah], *f. (Anat.)* Uvula.

uxoricida

uxoricida [ook-so-re-thee'-dah], *m.* Uxoricide, wife-murderer.

uzas [oo'-thas], *f.* Kind of Brazilian crab.

uyama [oo-yah´-mah], *f.* A species of calabash of Guayana, a province of Venezuela.

V

v [vay], *f.* In the Spanish alphabet *V* is the twenty-third letter in order, and should be pronounced as in English. As the Spaniards press very lightly their lower lips against the upper teeth in pronouncing this letter, it frequently sounds like *b* especially at the start of words. *V.* was very often used in manuscript instead of the capital *U*; as, *Vn día* for **Un día**. *V.,* or *Vd.,* stance as a contraction for **Usted,** *(sing.)* you, and VV., or Vds., for Ustedes, *(pl.)* you (formerly Vm. Vmd., Vms. Vmds.); also for vuestra, vuestras; as **V. M,** vuestra majestad, your majesty; V. S. Usía (vuestra señoría), your lordship or ladyship, etc. V in Roman numerals stands for five, for verb in grammar, for wind (viento) in meteorology, and volume in mathematical calculations.

vaca [vah'-cah], *f.* 1. Cow. **Vaca lechera**, milk-cow. 2. Beef. 3. *(Prov.)* Joint stock of two partners in gambling. 4. Tanned leather, cowhide. **Vaca marina**, sea-cow. *V.* MANATÍ. **Vaca sagrada**, sacred cow. **Pasar las vacas gordas**, to have a grand time of it. 5. *(LAm.)* Enterprise with profits on and pro rata basis.

vacación [vah-cah-the-on´], *f.* Vacation, intermission; recess of courts of law and public boards. *-pl.* Holidays. **Vacaciones,** vacation, holiday. **Estar de vacaciones**, to be on vacation.

vacada [vah-cah'-dah], *f.* Drove of cows.

vacancia [vah-can'-the-ah], *f.* Vacancy.

vacante [vah-cahn'-tay], *a.* Vacant, disengaged. *-f.* 1. Vacancy of a post or employment. 2. Vacation, time unengaged. 3. Rent fallen due during the vacancy of a benefice. **Proveer una vacante**, to fill a post.

vacar [vah-car'], *vn.* 1. To cease, to stop; to be vacant. 2. To devote oneself to a particular thing; to follow a business. *-va.* To vacate an office.

vacarí [vah-cah-ree'], *a.* Leathern: said of a leather shield, etc.

vaciadero [vah-the-ah-day'-ro], *m.* Drain, sink (desaguadero).

vaciadizo, za [vah-the-ah-dee'-tho, thah], *a.* Cast, moulded.

vaciado [vah-the-ah'-do], *m.* 1. Form or image, moulded or cast in plaster of Paris or wax; excavation. 2. *(Arch.)* Cavity in a pedestal below its ornamental mouldings. 3. *(Mex.)* Great (estupendo). 4. Hollowing out (acto). —**Vaciado, da**, *pp.* of VACIAR.

vaciador [vah-the-ah-dor'], *m.* Moulder, one who casts or moulds; one who evacuates, hollows, or makes empty.

vaciamiento [vah-the-ah-me-en'-to], *m.* 1. Casting, moulding; evacuating, hollowing. 2. *V.* VACÍO.

vaciar [vah-the-ar'], *va.* 1. To empty (recipiente, contenido), to evacuate, to exhaust, to clear. 2. To mould, to form, to model. 3. To fail into, to discharge itself (río). 4. *(Arch.)* To excavate. 5. To explain at large. **Vació la leche en un vaso**, he poured the milk into a glass. **Vació los bolsillos en la mesa**, he emptied out his pockets on the table. *-vn.* 1. To fall, to decrease (aguas). 2. Not to make good use of one's time. 3. To fade, to lose color or luster. *-vr.* 1. To be spilt (líquidos). 2. To divulge what should be kept secret. 3. To be empty or vacant.

vaciedad [va-the-ay-dahd'], *f.* 1. Emptiness, vacuity. 2. Emptiness, frothiness. 3. An inconsiderate or arrogant speech; obscene language.

vaciero [vah-the-ay´-ro], *m.* Shepherd whose sheep are all dry or barren.

vacilación [vah-the-lah-the-on'], *f.* 1. Hesitation, vacillation, reeling, staggering. 2. Perplexity, irresolution.

vacilante [vah-the-lahn'-tay], *pa. & a.* Vacillating; irresolute; unstable.

vacilar [vah-the-lar'], *vn.* 1. To vacillate, to waver, to fluctuate; to be perplexed; to wander or be confused; to reel, to stagger (persona). 2. To flicker (luz). 3. To hesitate. **Vacilar entre dos posibilidades**, to hesitate between two possibilities. 4. **Vacilar con uno**, to tease somebody. 5. *(CAm, Carib, Mex.)* To get plastered (emborracharse).

vacile [vah-the-lay], *m.* 1. Hesitation (duda). 2. Teasing (guasa). **Estar de vacile**, to chat.

vacío, cía [vah-thee'-o, ah], *a.* 1. Void, empty, vacuous. 2. Unoccupied, disengaged; idle (charla); fruitless. 3. Concave, hollow. 4. Defective, deficient. 5. Vain (vanidoso), arrogant, presumptuous. 6. Not with young (ganado). 7. Unloaded or empty (caballos, mulas). 8. Uninhabited. 9. Unoccupied by people. **El teatro estaba medio vacío**, the theater was half empty.

vacío [vah-thee'-o], *m.* 1. Void, empty space, vacuum, aperture. 2. Mould for casting metal. 3. Vacancy, place or employment unfilled. 4. Concavity, hollowness. 5. Blank space in a book or writing. 6. *(Com.)* Ullage of a cask or other vessel: wantage. 7. Animal not with young. 8. Vacuity, cavity. 9. Flank of animals. **De vacío**, empty: unemployed. **Se nota ahora en un gran vacío en la familia**, one is conscious now of a big gap in the family. **Tener un vacío en el estómago**, to feel hungry.

vacisco [vah-thees'-co], *m.* Fragment in quicksilver mines.

vaco, ca [vah´-co, cah], *a.* Vacant.

vacuidad [vah-coo-e-dahd'], *f.* Vacuity, emptiness.

vacuista [vah-coo-ees´-tah], *m.* Vacuist, a philosopher that holds a vacuum.

vacuna [vah-coo'-nah], *f.* 1. Vaccine (sustancia). 2. Vaccination (acto), shot. **Vacuna antidiftérica**, diphtheria shot. **Vacuna contra la viruela**, smallpox shot.

vacunación [vah-coo-nah-the-on'], *f.* Vaccination (acto de vacunar).

vacunador [vah-coo-nah-dor´], *m.* Vaccinator.

vacunar [vah-coo-nar'], *va.* 1. To vaccinate. 2. To prepare (preparar), to inure (habituar); to forearm (prevenir).

vacuno, na [vah-coo´-no, nah], *a.* Belonging to cattle, vaccine, bovine.

vacuo, a [vah´-coo-o, ah], *a.* Unoccupied. *V.* VACÍO and VACANTE.

vacuo [vah-coo-o], Vacuum.

vade [vah'-day], *m. V.* VADEMÉCUM.

vadeable [vah-day-ah'-blay], *a.* 1. Fordable. 2. *(Met.)* Conquerable, superable.

vadeador, ra [vah-day-ah-dor', rah], *a.* Wading.

vadeamiento [vah-day-ah-me-en'-to], *m.* Act of fording.

vadear [vah-day-ar'], *va.* 1. To wade, to ford (río). 2. To conquer, to surmount (dificultad). 3. To sound, to try to examine. *-vr.* To conduct oneself.

vademécum [vah'-day-may'-coom], *m.* 1. A book, a case, or other portable and useful thing, which is habitually carried on the person. 2. Portfolio in which school children keep their papers.

vadera [vah-day´-rah], *f.* Ford, a shallow part of a river.

¡vade retro! [vah'-day ray'-tro], *adv. exrpres.* Get away! go away!

vadiano, na [vah-de-ah´-no, nah], *a. & n.* Anthropomorphite, ascribing human attributes to a deity.

vado [vah'-do], *m.* 1. Ford (de río), a broad, shallow, level part of a river. 2. Expedient; resource, way out (salida). **No hallar vado**, to see no way out.

vadoso, sa [vah-do'-so, sah], *a.* Shoaly, shallow.

vafe [vah'-fay], *m. (Prov.)* Bold stroke or undertaking.

vagabundear [vah-gah-boon-day-ar'], *vn. (Coll.)* To rove or loiter about, to act the vagrant.

vagabundo, da [vah-gah-boon'-do, dah], *a. & m. & f.* Vagabond, idle vagrant, loitering about: having no fixed abode.

vagamente [vah-gah-men-tay], *adv.* In a vague, unsettled manner.

vagamundear [vah-gah-moon-day-ar'], *vn. V.* VAGABUNDEAR.

vagamundo, da [vah-gah-moon-do], *a. V.* VAGABUNDO.

vagancia [vah-gahn'-the-ah], *f.* Vagrancy.

vagante [vah-gahn'-tay], *pa.* Vagrant (errante).

vagar [vah-gar'], *vn.* 1. To rove or loiter about (entretenerse); to wander (error), to range. 2. To be at leisure, to be idle (gandulear). 3. To revolve in the mind. 4. To be loose and irregular.

vagar [vah-gar'], *m.* 1. Leisure (tiempo libre). 2. Slowness, indolence.

vagarosamente [vah-gah-ro'-sah-men-tay], *adv.* Vagrantly.

vagaroso, sa [vah-gah-ro'-so, sah], *a.* Errant, vagrant.

vagido [vah-hee-do], *m.* Cry of a child: a convulsive sob.

vagina [vah-hee'-nah], *f. (Anat.)* Vagina.

vaginal [vah-he-nahl'], *a.* Vaginal, relating to the vagina.

vaginante [vah-he-nahn'-tay], *a. (Zool.)* Sheathing, used of the upper wings of coleoptora and orthoptera.

vaginitis [vah-he-nee'-tis], *f.* Vaginitis, inflammation of the vagina.

vago, ga [vah'-go, gah], *a.* 1. Errant, vagrant, 2. Restless, uneasy. 3. Vague, wavering, fluctuating, unsettled; lax, loose. 4. *V.* VACO. **Voz vaga,** a vague report.

vago [vah'-go], *m.* 1. *(Prov.)* Uncultivated plot of ground. 2. Vagabond (vagabundo).

vagón [vah-gone'], *m.* A railway coach or car for passengers or merchandise. (Eng. wagon.) **Vagón-cama,** sleeping-car. **Vagón cisterna,** tanker. **Vagón de mercancías,** goods van.

vagón-comedor [vah-gone'-co-may-dor'], *m.* Dining car (trenes).

vagón-dormitorio [vah-gone'-dor-e-toh'-re-o], *m.* Pullman, sleeping car (trenes).

vagoneta [vah-go-nay'-tah], *f.* A small open car for transportation.

vagón-salón [vah-gone'-sah-lone'], *m.* (r.w.) Parlor car.

vaguada [vah-goo-ah'-dah], *f.* 1. Water way. 2. Line of the channel; a line which marks the course of the water in rivers.

vagueación [vah-gay-ah-the-on'], *f.* Restlessness, levity, unsteadiness; flight of fancy.

vaguedad [vah-gay-dahd'], *f.* Levity, inconstancy.

vaguido [vah-gee'-do], *m.* Giddiness, the state of being giddy.

vahar [vah-ar'], *vn.* To exhale, to emit steam or vapor.

vaharada [vah-ah-rah'-dah], *f.* The act of emitting steam, vapor, or breath.

vaharera [vah-ah-ray'-rah], *f.* 1. *(Med.)* Thrush, a disease of sucking children. 2. *(Brov.)* All unripe melon.

vaharina [vah-ah-ree'-nah], *f. (Coll.)* Steam, vapor, mist.

vahear [vah-ay-ar'], *m.* To exhale, to emit steam or vapor.

vahído [vah-ee'-do], *m.* Vertigo, giddiness,

vaho [vah'-o], *m.* 1. Steam, vapor (vapor). 2. Breath (aliento), whiff (olor). 3. *(Med.)* Inhalation.

vaída [vah-ee'-dah], *f. (Arch.)* Vault or arch, cut into four vertical planes.

vaina [vah'-nah], *f.* 1. Scabbard of a sword. 2. Knife or scissors case. 3. Pod (de guisante), capsule, husk (de nuez), hull, cod. 4. *(Naut.)* Bolt-rope tabling, to which the bolt-rope is fastened. 5. *(And.)* Fluke (chiripa). 6. *(Cono Sur)* Swindle (estafa). **Vaina abierta,** scabbard of a large sword formerly used, which covered only one-third of it, in order to be easily drawn.

vainazas [vah-e-nah'-thas], *m. (Coll.)* A humdrum, dull, or dronish person.

vainero [vah-e-nay'-ro], *m.* Scabbard-maker.

vainica [vah-e-nee'-cah], *f.* 1. *(Dim.)* A small pod or husk. 2. Hemstitch.

vainilla [vah-e-neel'-lyah], *f.* 1. *(Dim.)* A small pod or husk. 2. *(Bot.)* Vanilla. 3. Fruit of this plant. 4. A heliotrope which grows in America.

vaivén [vah-e-ven'], *m.* 1. Fluctuation vibration. *(Mech.)* Alternating movement. 2. Unsteadiness, inconstancy, vacilla-

tion. 3. Giddiness. 4. Risk, danger. 5. *(Naut.)* Line, cord, or rope, of different thickness.

vajilla [vah-heel'-lyah], *f.* Table-service of dishes, plates, etc. **Vajilla de porcelana,** Chinaware. **Lavar la vajilla,** to wash up.

val [vahl], *m.* 1. Vale, dale, valley: a contraction of *valle.* 2. *(Brov.)* Sew or drain, sink. 3. Ancient contraction of *vale,* from *valer.*

valaco, ca [vah-lah'-co, cah], *a.* 1. Wallachian. 2. The language spoken in Wallachia, a Romance tongue.

valais [vah-lah'-ees], *m.* Lumber.

valar [vah-lar'], *a.* Relating to a rampart, inclosure, or hedge.

vale [vah'-lay], *m.* 1. Farewell, adieu; valediction. 2. Bond or promissory note. 3. Note of pardon given to schoolboys by the master. 4. First or single hand at cards. 5. Voucher, coupon (cupón); *(LAm.)* Bill (cuenta). **Vale de correo,** money order.

valedero, ra [vah-lay-day'-ro, rah], *a.* Valid, efficacious, binding.

valedor, ra [vah-lay-dor', rah], *m. & f.* Protector (protector), defender.

valencia [vah-len'-the-ah], *f. (Chem.)* Valence.

valenciano, pa [vah-len-the-ah'-no, nah], *a.* Valencian, of Valencia.

valentacho [vah-len-tah'-cho], *m.* Hector, bully, braggadocio.

valentía [vah-len-tee'-ah], *f.* 1. Valor, courage, gallantry, bravery (valor), manliness. 2. Feat, heroic exploit (acto). 3. Brag, boast (dicho). 4. Fire of imagination. 5. *(Art.)* Uncommon dexterity in imitating nature. 6. An extraordinary or vigorous effort.

valentísimo, ma [vah-len-tee'-se-mo, mah], *a. sup.* Most valiant; perfect in an art or science.

valentón [vah-len-tone'], *m.* Braggadocio, hector.

valentón, na [vah-len-tone', nah], *a.* Arrogant, vainglorious.

valentonada, valentona [vah-len-to-nah'-dah], *f.* Brag (dicho), boast.

valentonazo [vah-len-to-nah'-tho], *m. aug.* Bully, boaster. *V.* VALENTÓN.

valentoncillo, lla [vah-len-ton-theel'-lyo, lyah], *a. dim.* A little vain or presumptuous.

valeo [vah-lay'-o], *m.* 1. Round mat; shaggy mat. 2. Rug or plat of bass.

valer [vah-lerr'], *va.* 1. To protect, to defend, to favor, to patronize. 2. To yield, to produce fruits or rent. 3. To equal (ser igual), to be equivalent to. 4. To amount to (contar). 5. To bear a certain price, to be worth. *-vn.* 1. To be valuable, meritorious, deserving. 2. To prevail, to avail. 3. To serve as an asylum or refuge. 4. To be valid or binding; to be a head or have authority; to have power, to be able; to hold. 5. To have course, to be current; also to be worth (monedas). 6. To be in favor, to have influence or interest. *-vr.* 1. To employ, to make use of. 2. To avail oneself of, to have recourse to. **¡Válgate Dios!,** heaven bless or pardon you! exclamation of surprise or disapprobation, according to circumstances. **¡Válgame Dios!,** good God! Bless me! expression of surprise or disgust. **Más vale** or **más valiera,** it is better, it would be better. **Más vale algo que nada,** something is better than nothing. **Más vale tarde que nunca,** better later than never. **Vale lo que pesa,** he is worth his weight in gold. **Más vale maña que fuerza,** *(Prov.)* wiles often do what force cannot. **No poderse valer con alguno,** not to be able to manage a person. **Vale la pena de,** it is worth while; worth the trouble of. **Hacer valer,** to give authority or support. **No poderse valer,** to be incapable; not to know how to help oneself. **El asunto le valió muchos disgustos,** the affair caused him lots of trouble. **No vale nada,** it´s worthless. **Más vale que vayas tú,** it would be better for you to go. **Es viejo pero todavía vale,** it´s old but it still serves. *(Yo valgo, yo valga, valdré. V.* VALER.)

valer [vah-lerr'], *m.* Value.

valeriana

valeriana [vah-lay-re-ah'-nah], *f. (Bot.)* Valerian. **Valeriana griega,** Jacob's-ladder or Greek valerian.

valerosamente [vah-lay-ro-sah-men'-tay], *adv.* Valiantly, courageously.

valeroso, sa [vah-lay-ro'-so, sah], *a.* I. Valiant, brave, courageous, gallant, heroic. 2. Strong, active; powerful.

valetudinario, ria [vah-lay-too-de-nah'-re-o, ah], *a.* Valetudinarian, valetudinary, infirm of health.

valhala [val-hah'-lah], *f.* Walhalla, the paradise of Odin, in Scandinavian mythology.

valí [va-lee'], *m.* Governor of a Moslem province or territory.

valía [ah-lee'-ah], *f.* Appraisement, valuation. 2. Credit, favor, use. 3. Party, faction. **A las valías,** at the highest price which a commodity fetches in the course of a year.

validable [va-le-dah'-blay], *a.* Justifiable, ratifiable.

validación [va-le-dah-the-on'], *f.* Validity of an act.

válidamente [vah'-le-dah-men'-tay], *adv.* In a solid or binding manner.

validar [vah-le-dar'], *va.* To give validity, to render firm or binding.

validez [va-le-deth'], *f.* Validity, stability.

válido, da [vah'-le-do, dah], *a.* 1. Valid, firm, prevalent, weighty, conclusive. 2. Binding, obligatory.

valido, da [vah-lee'-do, dah], *a. & pp.* Of VALER. 1. Availing of, relying upon, confident of. 2. Favored regarded with peculiar kindness; accepted, esteemed. 3. Universally respected. 4. Strong, powerful.

valido [vah-lee'-o], *m.* A favorite of a sovereign; a court minion.

valiente [vah-le-en'-tay], *a.* 1. Strong, robust, vigorous, powerful. 2. Valiant, spirited, brave (valeroso), courageous, active, strenuous; efficacious, valid. 3. Eminent, excellent. 4. *(Coll.)* Glint, excessive.

valiente [vah-le-en'-tay], *m.* 1. Bully, hector, braggadocio. 2. Gallant.

valientemente [vah-le-ayn'-tay-men-tay], *adv.* 1. Vigorously, strongly. 2. Valiantly, courageously, strenuously, manfully. 3. Superabundantly, excessively. 4. Elegantly, with propriety.

valija [vah-lee'-hah], *f.* 1. Valise (portamantas), grip sack. 2. Mail-bag. 3. The post, mail. 4. Satchel (cartera).

valijero [vah-le-hay'-ro], *m.* Postal clerk who distributes mail to towns along a route.

valimiento [vah-le-me-en'-to], *m.* 1. Use, the act of using or employing. 2. Utility, benefit, advantage. 3. A temporary or gratuitous contribution. 4. Interest, favor, protection, support; good graces.

valioso, sa [vah-le-o'-so, sah], *a.* 1. Very valuable (de valor), highly esteemed, of great influence. 2. Rich, wealthy.

valiza [vah-lee'-thah], *f. (Naut.)* Beacon, buoy, pointing out sandbanks, or shoals. **Valiza terrestre,** land-mark.

valizaje [va-le-thah'-hay], *m.* Duties paid by the shipping in some ports, towards keeping in repair the beacons and buoys.

valla [vahl'-lyah], *f.* 1. Intrenchment; ground surrounded with palisades. 2. Barrier (barrera), barricade. 3. *(And. Carib. Mex.)* Cockpit (de gallos). 4. *(And.)* Ditch (zanja).

valladar [val-lyah-dar'], *m.* 1. *(Prov.)* V. VALLADO. 2. Obstacle.

valladear [val-lyah-day-ar'], *va.* To enclose with stakes, pales, or palisades. *V.* VALLAR.

vallado [val-lyah´-do], *m.* Inclosure with stakes or palisades, paling, fence, lock.—**Vallada, do,** *pp.* of VALLAR.

vallar [val-lyar'], *va.* To fence, to hedge, to inclose with pales or states.

valle [vah'-lyay], *m.* 1. Vale, dale, valley. 2. The whole number of villages, places, and cottages situated within a district or jurisdiction. **Hasta el valle de Josafat,** unto the valley of Jehoshaphat, or until the day of judgment.

vallejo [val-lyay'-ho], *m. dim.* A small valley.

vallejuelo [val-lyay-hoo-ay'-lo], *m. dim.* of VALLEJO.

vallico [val-lyee'-co], *m. (Bot.)* Raygrass.

valón, na [vah-lone', nah], *a.* Walloon, belonging to southern provinces of Belgium.

valones [vah-lo'-nes], *m. pl.* A sort of pants or wide breeches, formerly worn in Spain.

valor [vah-lor'], *m.* 1. Value, price (precio); equivalency. 2. Validity, forge. 3. Activity, power. 4. Valor (valentía), fortitude, courage, manliness. 5. Income, revenue. 6. Surety, firmness of an act. **Este contrato será entonces sin ningún valor ni efecto,** *(Law.)* this agreement will then be void and null. **Relaciones de valores,** account of rates. **Sin valor,** worthless. **Valor añadido,** mark-up. **Valores en cartera,** investments. **Tuvo el valor de pedírmelo,** he had the nerve to ask me for it.

valoración [vah-lo-rah-the-on'], *f. V.* VALUACIÓN.

valorar [vah-lo-rar´], *v.* To value, to evaluate, to appraise. **Valorar poco,** to attach a little value to.

valoría [vah-lo-ree'-ah], *f.* Value, price, worth.

valorización ¶[vah-lo-rah-the-on'], *f.* Valuation; appraisal.

valorizar [vah-lo-re-thar'], *va. (Mex.) V.* VALORAR.

vals [vahls], *m.* Waltz.

valsar [val-sar'], *vn.* To waltz.

valación [vah-loo-ah-the-on'], *f.* Appraisement, valuation.

valuador, ra [vah-loo-ah-dor', rah], *m. & f.* Valuer, appraiser.

valva [vahl'-vah], *f.* 1. *(Zool.)* Valve, shell of mollusks. 2. *(Bot.)* Valve, a portion of the pericarp of plank.

valuar [vah-loo-ar'], *va.* To rate, to value, to appraise.

valvasor [val-vah-sor'], *m.* Gentleman, nobleman, hidalgo.

válvula [vahl'-voo-lah], *f.* 1. Valve, as in the piston of a pump. 2. An aperture, opening. **Válvula de radio,** radio tube. **Válvula de seguridad,** Safety valve.

valvulado, da [val-voo-lah'-do, dah], *a. (Bot.)* Valvate, provided with a valve.

valvular [val-voo-lar'], *a.* Valvular, having many valves.

valvulilla [val-voo-leel'-lyah], *f. dim.* Valvule.

¡vamos! [vah´-mose], *int. (Coll.)* Well, come! Well, go on! come on!

vampiro [vam-pee'-ro], *m.* 1. Ghoul. 2. Vampire bat. 3. Usurer, miser, skinflint.

vanadiato [vah-nah-de-ah'-to], *m. (Chem.)* Vanadate, a salt of vanadic acid.

vanádico, ca [vah-nah'-de-co, cah], *a.* Vanadic, of or derived from vanadium.

vanadio [vah-nah'-de-o], *m.* Vanadium, a white metal, not ductile, soluble in nitric acid, but resisting sulphuric and hydrochloric acids.

vanagloria [vah-nah-glo'-re-ah], *f.* Vaingloriousness, ostentatiousness, boast.

vanagloriarse [vah-nah-glo-re-ar'-say], *vr.* To be vainglorious, to boast of, to flourish.

vanaglorioso, sa [vah-nah-glo-re-o'-so, sah], *a.* Vainglorious, conceited, ostentatious.

vanamente [vah-nah-men'-tay], *adv.* 1. Vainly, uselessly. 2. Superstitiously. 3. Without foundation. 4. Arrogantly, presumptuously, proudly; frivolously, idly.

vandalismo [van-dah-lees'-mo], *m.* Vandalism.

vándalo, la [vahn'-dah-lo, lah], *m. & f.* Vandal.

vandálico, ca [van-dah'-le-co, cah], *a.* Vandalic.

vandola [van-do'-lah], *f. (Naut.)* Jurymast.

vanear [vah-nay-ar'], *vn.* To talk nonsense.

vanesa [vah-nay'-sah], *f.* Vanessa, a genus of butterflies.

vaneta [vah-nay´-tah], *f. (Her.)* Scallop.

vanguardia [van-goo-ar'-de-ah], *f.* Vanguard, clan. **Estar en la vanguardia del progreso,** to be in the van of progress.

vanguardismo [van-goo-ar-dees'-mo], *m.* Ultramodern manner.

vanidad [vah-ne-dahd'], *f.* 1. Vanity. 2. Ostentation, vain parade. 3. Nonsense, unmeaning speech. 4. Inanity (necedad), levity, conceit; foppishness; flirtation. 5. Illusion, phantom. **Hacer vanidad,** to boast of anything.

vanidoso, sa [vah-ne-do'-so, sah], *a.* Vain, showy, foppish, haughty.

vanilocuencia [vah-ne-lo-coo-en'-the-ah], *f.* Verbosity, pomposity.

vanílocuo, cua [vah-nee'-lo-coo-o, ah], *a.* Talking foolishly.

vaniloquio [vah-ne-lo'-ke-o], *m.* Useless talk.

vanistorio [vah-nis-to'-re-o], *m. (Coll.)* Ridiculous or affected vanity.

vano, na [vah'-no, nah], *a.* 1. Vain (inútil), wanting solidity. 2. Inane, empty, fallacious. 3. Useless, frivolous (frívolo). 4. Arrogant, haughty, presumptuous, conceited, foppish. 5. Insubstantial, groundless, futile. **En vano**, in vain, unnecessarily, uselessly, wantonly.

vano [vah'-no], *m. (Arch.)* Vacuum in a troll, as the windows, doors, etc.

vapor [vah-pore'], *m.* 1. Vapor, steam, breath. 2. Exhalation, mat. 3. Vertigo, faintness. 4. A steamboat, steamer. *-pl.* Vapors, a hysterical attack. **Vapor de agua**, water vapor. **Echar vapor**, to give off steam.

vaporable [vah-po-rah'-blay], *a.* Vaporous, fumy, exhalable.

vaporación [vah-po-rah-the-on'], *f.* Evaporation.

vaporar, vaporear, vaporizar [vah-po-rar', ray-r', vah-po-re-thar'], *va. V.* EVAPORAR

vaporización [vah-po-re-thah-the-on'], *f.* Vaporization.

vaporizador [vah-po-re-thah-dor], *m.* Vaporizer, sprayer.

vaporoso, sa [vah-po-ro'-so, sah], *a.* Vaporous (de vapor), fumy, vaporish.

vapolación [vah-poo-lah-the-on'], *f. (Coll.)* Whipping, flogging.

vapulamiento [vah-poo-lah-me-en'-to], *m. V.* VAPULACIÓN.

vapular [vah-poo-lar'], *va. (Coll.)* To whip, to flog.

vapuleo [vah-poo-lay'-o], *m. (Coll.)* Whipping, flogging, beating (paliza).

vaquear [vah-kay-ar'], *f.* To cover cows with the bull.

vaquería [vah-kay-ree'-ah], *f.* 1. Herd or drove of black cattle. 2. A barns for grazing cattle; milk-dairy. 3. *(LAm.)* Cattle farming (cuidado de ganado). 4. *(Carib.)* Hunting with a lasso.

vaqueriles [vah-kay-ree'-les], *m. pl.* Winter pasture for cows

vaquerillo [vah-kay-reel'-lyo], *m. dim.* Boy who attends cows.

vaqueriza [vah-kay-ree'-thah], *f.* Stable for cattle in winter.

vaquerizo, za [vah-kay-ree'-tho, thah], *a.* Relating to cows.

vaquero [vah-kay'-ro], *m.* 1. Cowherd, cowboy, cow-keeper (que cuida ganado). 2. Jacket or loose dress worn by women and children. 3. *(LAm.)* Milkman (lechero). 4. *(And.)* Truant (ausente). **Vaqueros**, jeans (pantalones).

vaquero, ra [vah-kay'-ro, rah], *a.* Belonging to cowherds.

vaqueta [vah-kay'-tah], *f.* Sole-leather, tanned cowhide (cuero).

vaquetear [vah-kay-tay-ar'], *va.* To flog with leather thongs.

vaquetco [vah-kay-tay'-o], *m.* Flogging with leather thongs.

vaquilla, vaquita [vah-keel'-lyah], *f. dim.* A small cow, a young cow, a heifer.

vara [vah'-rah], *f.* 1. Rod (barra), slender twig. 2. Pole, staff. 3. Verge, a rod, a wand, an emblem of authority: a cross is fixed to its upper end, on which oaths are administered. **Vara de alguacil**, the appointment, commission, or office of a constable. 4. Verge: it is commonly taken for the very jurisdiction of which it is an emblem. 5. Yard-stick, for measuring. 6. Yard, a measure of three feet, 33 British inches, or 8.36 decimeters; a yard of sloth, of this length. 7. Herd of forty or fifty head of swine. 8. Chastisement, rigor. 9. Shaft of a carriage. **Vara alta**, sway, high hand. **Vara de pescar**, fishing-rod. **Vara o varilla de cortina**, a curtain-rod. **Dar la vara**, to annoy, to pester.

varada [vah-rah'-dah], *f. (Naut.)* The act of a vessel running aground or stranding (encalladura).

varadera [vah-rah-day'-rah], *f.* Skid, or skeed.

varadero [vah-rah-day'-ro], *m.* A ship yard; a place for repairing vessels.

varadura [vah-rah-doo'-rah], *f.* The grounding of a vessel.

varal [vah-rahl'], *m.* 1. A long pole or perch (palo). 2. *(Coll.)* A tall, slender person (persona).

varapalo [vah-rah-pah'-lo], *m.* 1. A long pole or perch (palo); switch. 2. Blow with a stick or pore (golpe). 3. *(Coll.)* Grief, trouble, vexation.

varar [vah-rar'], *va. (Naut.)* 1. To run aground. 2. To launch a new-built ship. *-vn.* 1. *(Naut.)* To ground, to be stranded. 2. To be stopped.

varaseto [vah-rah-say'-to], *m.* Treillage a contexture of poles used in gardens.

varazo [vah-rah'-tho], *m.* Stroke with a pole or stick.

varbasco [varh'-bahs'-co], *m. V.* VERBASCO.

varchilla [var-cheel'-lyah], *f.* Measure of grain, which contains the third part of a *fanega*.

vardasca [var-das'-cah], *f.* A thin twin.

vardascazo [var-das-cah'-tho], *m.* Stroke with a stick.

vareador [vah-ray-ah-dor'], *vn.* One who beats down with a pole or staff.

vareaje [vah-ray-ah'-hay], *m.* 1. Retail trade, selling by the yard; measuring by the yard. 2. The act of beating down the fruit of trees.

varear [vah-ray-ar'], *va.* 1. To beat down the fruit of trees with a pole or rod. 2. To cudgel, to beat. 3. To wound bulls or oxen with a goad. 4. To measure or sell by the yard. *-vr.* To grow thin or lean.

varejón [vah-ray-hone'], *m.* A thick pole or staff.

varendaje [vah-ren-dah'-hay], *m. (Naut.)* Collection of floor-timbers.

varenga [vah-ren'-gah], *f. (Naut.)* Floor-timber.

vareo [vah-ray'-o], *m.* 1. Measurement, measuring. 2. The set of beating down the fruit of trees.

vareta [vah-ray'-tah], *f.* 1. *(Dim.)* A small rod or twig (ramita). 2. Lime twig for catching birds. 3. Stripe in a stuff different in color from the ground. 4. A piquant expression. 5. A circuitous manner of speech (indirecta).

varetazo [vah-ray-tah'-tho], *m.* A stroke with a stick.

varetear [vah-ray-tay-ar'], *va.* To variegate stuffs with stripes of different colors.

varga [var'-gah], *f.* The steepest part of an eminence.

várgano [var'-gah-no], *m. (Prov.)* Fence of a rural farm.

variable [vah-re-ah'-blay], *a.* Variable, changeable; fickle.

variablemente [vah-re-ah-blay-men-tay], *adv.* Variably, fast and loose.

variación [vah-re-ah-the-on'], *f.* 1. Variation varying. 2. Change, mutation. **Variación de la aguja**, *(Naut.)* variation of the compass.

variado, da [vah-re-ah'-do, dah], *a.* Variegated, colored. *-pp.* of VARIAR.

variamente [vah-re-ah-men'-tay], *adv.* Variously, differently.

variante [vah-re-ahn'-tay], *pa.* Varying, deviating. *-f.* Difference or discrepancy, deviation. *-m. (Esp.)* Pickled vegetables. 2. *(And.)* Path (senda), short cut (atajo).

variar [vah-re-ar'], *va.* 1. To change (cambiar), to alter: to shift; to variegate to diversify. *-vn.* 1. To vary, to differ from. 2. *(Naut.)* To cease a deviation of the magnetic needle. **Variar de opinión**, to change one's mind. **Para variar**, for a change.

várice [vah'-re-thay], *f. (Med.)* Varix, a dilated vein.

varicela [vah-re-thay'-lah], *f. (Med.)* Varicella, chicken-pox, an eruptive disease.

várices [vah'-re-thays], *f. pl.* Varicose veins.

varicocele [vah-re-co-thay'-lah], *m. (Med.)* Varicocele, a swelling formed by dilated veins of the scrotum.

varicoso, sa [vah-re-co'-so, sah], *a. (Surg.)* Varicose.

variedad [vah-re-ay-dahd'], *f.* Variety (diversidad), particular distinction; change, variation.

varilarguero [vah-re-lar-gay'-ro], *m.* In bullfighting, the horseman or *picador* armed with a spear to resist the attack of the bull.

varilla [vah-reel'-lyah], *f.* 1. *(Dim.)* A small rod. 2. A curtain-rod. 3. Spindle, pivot. 4. Switch. 5. Rib or stick of a fan. **Un abanico con varillas de márfil**, a fan with ivory ribs. 6. *(Mex.)* Cheap fares. 7. *(Carib.)* Nuisance (vaina).

varillaje [vah-ril-layah´-hay], *m.* Collection of ribs of a fan, umbrella, or parasol.

vario, ria [vah´-re-o, ah], *a.* 1. Various, divers, different. 2. Inconstant, variable, unsteady. 3. Vague, undetermined. 4. Variegated (color). **Hay varias posibilidades,** there are several possibilities. *-pl.* Some, several.

vario [vah-ree´-o], *m.* Pink, minnow.

varioloide [vah-re-o-lo´-e-day], *f. (Med.)* Varioloid, modified small-pox.

varioloso, sa [vah-re-o-lo'-so, sah], *a.* Variolous, variolar, relating to small-pox.

variopinto [vah-re-o-pin-to], *a.* Many-colored, colorful; of diverse colors.

variz [vah-reeth'], *m. (Surg.) V.* VÁRICE.

varón [vah-ron'], *m.* 1. Man, a human being of the male sex. 2. A male human being, grown to manhood, which is considered from 30 to 45 years (hombre). 3. Man of respectability. 4. *(Cono Sur, Mex.)* Beams (vigas). **Buen varón,** (1) a wise and learned man. (2) *(Iron.)* A plain, artless being. **Hijo varón,** male child. **Tuvo 4 hijos, todos varones,** she had 4 children, all boys.

varonesa [vah-ro-nay´-sah], *f.* A woman.

varonía [vah-ro-nee'-ah], *f.* Male issue; male descendants.

varonil [vah-ro-neel'], *a.* Male, manly (viril), of the male kind; masculine; vigorous (enérgetico), spirited.

varonilmente [vah-ro-neel'-men-tay], *adv.* Manfully, valiantly, courageously.

varraco [var-rah´-co], *m. V.* VERRACO.

vasallaje [vah-say-lyah'-hay], *m.* 1. Vassalage, dependence, servitude. 2. Liege-money, a tax paid by vassals to their lord. 3. Surrender, yielding to another.

vasallo, lla [vas-sahl´-lyo, lyah], *m. & f.* 1. Vassal, subject; one who acknowledges a superior lord. 2. Feudatory.

vasallo, lla [vas-sahl'-lyo, lyah], *a.* Subject relating to a vassal.

vasar [vah-sar'], *m.* Buffet on which glasses or vessels are put.

vasco, ca [vas'-co, cah], *a. V.* VASCONGADO.

vascongado, da [vas-con-gah´-do, dah], *a. & m. & f.* The native of the provinces of Álava, Guipúzcoa, and Biscay, and the things belonging to them.

vascuence [vahs-coo-en'-thay], *m.* 1. Basque, Biscay dialect, which is considered the primitive language of Spain, called also *Lengua Euscara,* or *Euskera.*

vascular [vas-coo-lar'], *a.* Vascular.

vasculoso, sa [vas-coo-lo'-so, sah], *a.* Vascular, vasculiferous.

vase [vah´-say], *vr.* Third person singular of the present indicative of *Ir,* to go. In plays, *Exit.*

vasectomía [vah-sayc-to-mee'-ah], *f.* Vasectomy.

vaselina [vah-say-lee´-nah], *f.* Vaseline, trademark for petroleum jelly.

vasera [vah-say´-rah], *f.* Buffet, a kind of cupboard.

vásico [vah´-se'-co], *m. dim.* A small glass, cup, or vessel.

vasija [vah-se'-hah], *f.* 1. Vessel in which liquors or foodstuffs are kept; any butt, pipe, or cask. 2. Collection of vessels in a cellar for keeping liquors.

vasillo, ito [vah-seel´-lyo], *m. dim.* A small glass or cup.

vaso [vah'-so], *m.* 1. Vessel in which anything, but particularly liquids, is put; vase. 2. Tumbler, glass, drinking vessel of any kind; the quantity of liquid contained in it. 3. Vessel, any vehicle in which men or goods are carried on the water; and the burden or capacity of a vessel. 4. The capacity (cantidad), room, or extent of a thing. 5. *(Ast.)* Crater, a southern constellation. 6. Horse's hoof. 7. Vessel, vein, or artery. 8. Receptacle, capacity of one vessel to contain another. **Vaso de barro,** the human body; an earthen vessel. **Vaso de agua,** glass of water.

vasos sanguíneos [vah'-sos san-gee'-nay-os], *m. pl.* Blood vessels.

vástago [vahs´-tah-go], *m.* 1. Stem, bud, shoot. 2. *(Met.)* Descendant, the offspring of an ancestor (hijo, descendiente). 3. *(CAm. And. Carib.)* Trunk of the banana tree (tronco).

vastamente [vas'-tah-men-tay], *adv.* Vastly, extensively.

vastedad [vas-tay-dahd'], *f.* Vastness, immensity.

vasto, ta [vahs'-to, tah], *a.* Vast, huge, immense.

vate [vah´-tay], *m. (Poet.)* Bard, Druid.

Vaticano [vah-te-cah´-no], *m.* 1. Vatican, a hill of Rome, west of the Tiber, containing the basilica of St. Peter and the Pope's palace. 2. *(Met.)* Papal authority, or the pontifical court.

vaticinador, ra [vah-te-the-nah-dor´, rah], *m. & f.* Prophet, diviner.

vaticinar [vah-te-the-nar'], *va.* To divine, to foretell.

vaticinio [vah-te-thee´-ne-o], *m.* Divination, vaticination.

vatídico, ca [vah-tee'-de-co, cah], *a. (Poet.)* Prophetical.

vatio [vah'-te-o], *m.* Watt, an electrical unit of the rate of work, being the rate when the electro-motive force is one volt and the volume of current one ampere; equal to ten ergs per second.

vaya [vah´-yah], *f.* Scoff, jest.*-int.* Go; go to; come! indeed! certainly!

ve [vay], *f.* Name of the letter V.

véase [vay'-ah-say]. See; a direction of reference.

vecera [vay-thay-rah], *f. (Prov.)* Drove of swine and other animals.

vecería [vay-ther-ree'-ah], *f.* Herd of swine, or animals belonging to a neighborhood.

vecero, ra [vay-thay´-ro, rah], *a. &. m. & f.* 1. One who performs alternately, or by turns. 2. Applied to trees which yield fruit one year every two.

vecinal [vay-the-nahl'], *a.* Belonging to the neighborhood.

vecinamente [vay-the-nah-men'-tay], *adv.* Near, contiguously.

vecindad [vay-theen-dahd'], *f.* 1. Population, inhabitants of a place. 2. Vicinity, contiguity, vicinage (vecindad). 3. Right of an inhabitant, acquired by residence in a town for a time determined by law (habitantes). 4. Affinity, similarity, proximity (proximidad). **Hacer mala vecindad,** to be a troublesome neighbor.

vecindario [vay-theen-dahy´-re-o], *m.* 1. Number of inhabitants of a place. 2. Roll or list of the inhabitants of a place. 3. Neighborhood, vicinity; right acquired by residence.

vecino, na [vay-thee'-no, nah], *a.* 1. Neighboring, living in the neighborhood. 2. Neighbor, near to another, adjoining, next, near (cercano). 3. Like, resembling, coincident. **Las dos fincas son vecinas,** the two estates adjoin.

vecino [vay-thee'-no], *m.* 1. Neighbor, inhabitant, housekeeper. 2. Denizen, citizen, freeman. **Un pueblo de 800 vecinos,** a village of 800 inhabitants.

vectación [vec-tah-the-on'], *f.* Action of carrying in a vehicle; passive exercise.

vector [vec-tor'], *m.* 1. *(Aer.)* Vector. 2. *(Geom.)* Radius vector. Vector interrupción, *(Comput.)* interrupt vector.

vectorizar [vec-to-re-thar'], *va.* To vector.

veda [vay'-dah], *f.* Prohibition, interdiction by law.

vedado [vay-dah'-do], *m.* Warren, park, inclosure for game.— **Vedado, da,** *pp.* Of VEDAR.

vedamiento [vay-dah-me-en'-to], *m.* Prohibition.

vedar [vay-dar'], *va.* 1. To prohibit (prohibir), to forbid. 2. To obstruct, to impede (impedir); to suspend or deprive.

vedas [vay'-das], *m. pl.* The Vedas, four sacred books, collections of hymns, the most ancient Sanscrit literature.

vedegambre [vay-day-gahm'-bray], *m. (Bot.)* Hellebore. **Vedegambre** or **verdegambre blanco,** white hellebore or white veratrum.

vedeja [vay-day'-hah], *f. V.* GUEDEJA.

vedijudo, d [vay-day-hoo'-do, dah], *a. (Prov.) V.* VEDIJUDO.

védico, ca [vay'-de-co, cah], *a. (Neol.)* Vedaic, derived from or pertaining to the Vedas.

vedija [vay-dee'-hah], *f.* 1. Entangled lock of wool (lana); flake. 2. Tuft of entangled hair; matted hair (greña).

vedijero, ra [vay-de-hay'-ro, rah], *m. & f.* Collector of loose locks of wool at shearing.

vedijudo, da [vay-de-hoo'-do, dah], **vedijoso,** of [vay-de-ho'-so, sah], *a.* Having entangled or matted hair.

vedijuela [vay-de-hoo-ay'-lah], *f. dim.* Small lock of wool.

veduño [vay-doo'-nyo], *m*. 1. Quality, variety, strain of vines or grapes. 2. *V*. VIDEÑO.

veedor, ra [vay-ay-dor', rah], *m*. & *f*. 1. Spy, watcher, busybody. 2. Overseer, inspector. 3. Caterer, provider of provisions.

veeduría [vay-ay-doo-ree'-ah], *f*. Place or employment of an overseer or inspector; the inspector's office; controllership.

vega [vay'-gah], *f*. 1. A fertile plain or valley; a tract of level and fruitful ground; a mead or a meadow. 2. *(Cuba)* A tobacco field generally by the bank of a river.

vegetabilidad [vay-hay-tah-be-le-dahd'], *f*. Vegetability.

vegetable [vay-hay-tah'-blay], *a*. & *m*. V. VEGETAL.

vegetación [vay-hay-tah-the-on'], *f*. Vegetation (plantas), growing or growth of plants.

vegetal [vay-hay-tahl'], *a*. & *m*. Vegetable, vegetal, plant.

vegetante [vay-hay-tahn'-tay], *pa*. Vegetating.

vegetar [vay-hay-tar'], *vn*. To vegetate, to shoot out.

vegetariano, na [vay-hay-tah-re-ah'-no, nah], *m*. & *f*. & *a*. Vegetarian.

vegetativo, va [vay-hay-tah-tee'-vo, vah], *a*. Vegetative.

veguero, ra [vay-gay'-ro, rah], *a*. Belonging to an open plain. -*m*. 1. *(Cuba)* The steward who takes care of a *vega*. 2. A cigar rudely made of a single leaf.

vehemencia [vay-ay-men'-the-ah], *f*. 1. Vehemence, violence, impetuosity. 2. Efficacy, force. 3. Fervor, heat.

vehemente [vay-ay-men'-tay], *a*. Vehement (insistente), impetuous; persuasive, vivid; fervent (partido), fiery; keen.

vehementemente [vay-ay-men-tay-men-tay], *adv*. Vehemently, fervently, forcibly, urgently, hotly.

vehículo [vay-ee'-coo-lo], *m*. 1. Vehicle, carriage, means of transporting. 2. Vehicle, conductor as of sound or of electricity.

vehme (La Santa) [vay'-may], *f*. Name of a kind of German inquisition during the middle ages. Charles V. abolished it.

veigelia [vay-e-hay'-le-ah], *f*. *(Bot.)* Weigelia, an ornamental plant from China Diervilla, formerly Weigelia roses.

veintavo [vay in-tah'-vo], *m*. The twentieth part of a thing.

veinte [vay'-in-tay], *a*. & *m*. 1. Twenty. 2. *V* VIGÉSIMO. 3. Number or figure 20.

veintena [vay-in-tay'-nah], *f*. 1. A score. 2. The twentieth part.

veintenar [vay-in-tay-nar'], *m*. V. VEINTENA.

veintenario, ria [vay-in-tay-nah'-re-o, ah], *a*. Containing twenty years.

veinteno, na [vay-in-tay'-no, nah], **Veintésimo, ma**, *a*. *(Ant.)* Twentieth **veinteno**, applied to cloth containing two thousand threads in the warp.

veinteñal [vay-in-tay-nyahl'], *a*. Lasting twenty years.

veinticinco [vay-in-te-theen'-co], *a*. & *m*. Twenty-five.

veinticuatreno, na [vay-in-te-coo-ah-tray'-no, nah], *a*. Twenty-fourth.

veinticuatría [vay-in-te-coo-ah-tree'-ah], *f*. Aldermanry, the office and dignity of a *veinticuatro* (alderman) in some towns of Andalusia, such as Seville.

veinticuatro [vay-in te coo-ah'-tro], *a*. Twenty-four (cardinal). -*m*. 1. Alderman of Seville and other towns of Andalusia, the corporation of which consists of twenty-four members. 2. Twenty-fourmo (24mo), a book or pamphlet containing twenty-four leaves to the sheet. 3. The twenty-fourth (ordinal). 4. The figure 24.

veintidós [vay-in-te-dose'], *a*. & *m*. Twenty-two.

veintidoseno, na [vay-in-te-do-say'-no, nah], **Veintedoseno, na**, *a*. 1. Applied to cloth the warp of which contains 2,200 threads. 2. Twenty-second.

veintinueve [vay-in-te-noo-ay'-vay], *a*. & *m*. Twenty-nine.

veintiocheno, na [vay-in-te-o-chay'-no, nah], *a*. V. VEINTE-OCHENO.

veintiocheno, na [vay-in-te-o-chay'-no, nah], *a*. Applied to a warp of 2,800 threads.

veintiocho [vey-in-te-o'-cho], *a*. & *m*. Twenty-eight.

veintiséis [vay-in-te-sa-ees], *a*. & *m*. Twenty-six.

veintiseiseno, na [vay-in-te-say-e-say'-no, nah], *a*. Twenty-sixth.

veintiseiseno, na [vay-in-te-say-e-say'-no, nah], *a*. Applied to the warp of cloth having 2,600 threads.

veintisiete [vay-in-te-se-ay'-tay], *a*. & *m*. Twenty-seven.

veintitantos, tas [vayn-te-tahn'-tos, tahs], *a*. *pl*. Twenty-odd, over twenty.

veintitrés [vay-in-te-trays'], *a*. & *m*. Twenty-three.

veintiún [vay-in-te-oon'], *a*. Abbrev. of **Veintiuno**. Only before nouns.

veintiuna [vay-in-te-oo'-nah], *f*. The game of twenty-one.

veintiuno, na [vay-in-te-oo'-no, nah], *a*. & *n*. Twenty-one.

vejación [vay-hah-the-on'], *f*. Vexation, molestation, oppression.

vejador, ra [vay-hah-dor', rah], *m*. & *f*. Scoffer, molester, teaser.

vejamen [vay-hah'-men], *m*. Taunt, scurrilous criticism.

vejaminista [vay-hah-me-nees'-tah], *m*. Censor, critic.

vejancón, na [vay-han-cone', nah], *a*. & *n*. aug. *(Coll.)* Decrepit; peevish from old age.

vejar [vay-har'], *va*. 1. To vex (molestar), to molest, to harass (acosar). 2. To scoff, to censure. 3. To tease.

vejarrón, na [vay-har-rone', nah], *a*. & *n*. aug. *(Coll.)* Very old.

vejecito, ta [vay-hay-thee'-to, tah], *a*. & *m*. & *f*. dim. *V*. VIEJECITO.

vejestorio [vay-hes-to'-re-o], *m*. *(Coll.)* Old trumpery; a petulant old man.

vejazo, za vay-hah'-tho, thah], *a*. aug. Of VIEJO. (Also noun.)

vejeta [vay-hay'-tah], *f*. The crested lark. *V*. COGUJADA.

vejete [vay-hay'-tay], *m*. *(Coll.)* 1. A ridiculous old man. 2. Actor who impersonates an old man.

vejez [vay-heth'], *f*. 1. Old age. 2. Decay, the state of being worn out. 3. Imbecility and peevishness of old age. 4. A trite story (cuento).

vejezuela [vay-hay-thoo-ay'-lah], *f*. dim. An old hag.

vejezuelo [vay-hay-thoo-ay'-lo], *m*. dim. A little old man.

vejiga [vay-hee'-gah], *f*. 1. Bladder; urinary bladder, gallbladder. 2. Blister; any slight elevation on a plain surface. -*pl*. 1 Pustules of small-box. 2. Wind-galls in horses. **Vejiga natatoria de los peces**, the swimming bladder of a fish.

vejigación [vay-he-gah-the-on'], *f*. Vesication, blistering.

vejigatorio, ria [vay-he-gah-to'-re-o, ah], *a*. Blistering, raising blisters. -*m*. A blistering plaster, vesicatory.

vejigazo [vay-he-gah'-tho], *m*. Blow with a bladder full of wind.

vejigón [vay-he-gone'], *m*. aug. Large bladder or blister.

vejigüela, or **vejiguica, illa, ita** [vay-he-goo-ay'-lah, vay-he-gee'-cah], *f*. dim. Small bladder.

vejón, na [vay-hone', nah], *m*. & *f*. Very old person.

vela [vay'-lah], *f*. 1. Watch, attendance without sleep, vigil (vigilia). 2. Watchfulness (despierto), vigilance. 3. Watchman, night-guard. 4. Pilgrimage. V. ROMERÍA. 5. Candle (candela). **Velas de molde**, mould candles. **Velas de cera**, wax candles. **Velas de sebo**, tallow candles. 6. Night-work in offices (trabajo nocturno). 7. Awning. 8. Sail (deporte), ship. 9. Erect ear of a horse or other animal. 10. *(Naut.)* Sail, sheet. 11. Wing or arm of a windmill. 12. Devout waiting by order, hours, or turn before the most sacred sacrament. 13. *(CAm. Carib.)* Wake (velorio). 14. *(Cono Sur)* Nuisance (molestia). 15. *(Carib. Mex.)* Telling off (bronca). **Vela mayor**, mainsail. **Vela de gavia**, main-top sail. **Vela de sobremesana**, mizzen-top-sail. **Vela de juanete mayor**, main-top-gallantsail. **Vela de juanete de proa**, fore-top-gallant-sail. **Vela de estay**, stay sail. **Velas de proa**, head-sails. **Velas de popa**, after sails. **Velas mayores**, courses. **Vela de cruz**, a squaresail. **Vela de lustrar**, port-sail. **Caída de una vela**, drop or depth of a sail. **Gratil de una vela**, head of a sail. **Vela cazada**, trimmed sail. **Vela larga** or **desaferrada**, unfurled sail. **Vela cargada arriba** or **sobre las candelizas**, a sail hauled up in the brails. **Vela tendida**, taut or full sail. **Vela que flamea**, sail which shivers in the wind. **Vela cuadrada**, square-sail. **Marear una vela**, to set a sail. **Hacerse a la vela**, to set a sail. **En vela**, vigilantly, without sleep. **Alzar velas**, (a) to raise sail, to make ready to sail; (b) *(Met.)* to disappear carrying off one's effects. **Apocar las velas**, to take in sail, to shorten sail.

velacho [vay-lah´-cho], *m. (Naut.)* Foretop-sail.

velación [vay-lah-the-on´], *f.* Watch act of watching. **Velaciones**, nuptial benedictions.

velada [vay-lah´-dah], *f.* 1. Watch. *V.* VELACIÓN. 2. Evening party, evening gathering. **Velada musical**, musicale.

velado [vay-lah´-do], *m. (Coll.)* Husband, married man.

velador, ra [vay-lah-dor´, rah], *m. & f.* 1. Watchman (vigilante), night-guard. 2. Careful observer, vigilant keeper, spy. 3. A large wooden candlestick (candelero), used by tradesmen to work at night; table or bench on which a night-light is placed. 4. *(Cono Sur)* Night light (lámpara). 5. *(Mex.)* Lampshade (pantalla).

veladura [vay-lah-doo´-rah], *f. (Art.)* A mellow and transparent tint employed to alter the tone of what has been painted.

velaje [vay-lah´-hay], *m. (Naut.)* Sails in general. *V.* VELAMEN.

velamen [vay-lah´-men], *m. (Naut.)* Sails in general; set of sails; trim of sails. **Arreglar el velamen**, *(Naut.)* to trim the sails.

velar [vay-lar´], *vn.* 1. To watch (vigilar), to be watchful, to wake. 2. To watch, to keep guard by night. 3. To watch, to be attentive, to be vigilant. 4. *(Naut.)* To appear above the water, as rocks. 5. To assist by turns before the holy sacrament when it is manifested. *-va.* 1. To guard, to watch, to keep. 2. To throw a piece of white gauze over a married couple, after the nuptial benediction has been given. 3. To observe attentively. 4. *(Poet.)* To cover, to hide. 5. To watch with the sick or deceased at night.

velarte [vay-lar´-tay], *m.* Sort of fine broadcloth.

velatorio [vay-lah-to´-re-o], *m.* Funeral wake.

veleidad [vay-lay-e-dahd´], *f.* 1. Velleity, the lowest degree of desire; feeble will. 2. Levity, inconstancy, fickleness, versatility (cualidad).

veleidoso, sa [vay-lay-e-do´-so, sah], *a.* Fickle, inconstant, feeble-willed, giddy, fast and loose.

velejar [vay-lay-har´], *vn. (Naut.)* To make use of sails.

velería [vay-lay-ree´-ah], *f.* A tallow-chandler's shop.

velero [vay-lay´-ro], *m.* 1. Tallow-chandler. 2. Pilgrim.

velero, ra [vay-lay´-ro, rah], *a.* Swift-sailing (barco).

velesa [vay-lay´-sah], *f. (Bot.)* Lendwort.

veleta [vay-lay´-tah], *f.* 1. Weather cock. 2. The float or cork of a fishing-line (pesca). 3. *(Met.)* A fickle person (persona).

velete [vay-lay´-tay], *m.* A light, thin veil.

velfalla [vel-fahl´-lyah], *f.* A sort of linen.

velicación [vay-le-cah-the-on´], *f. (Med.)* Vellication, stimulation.

velicar [vay-le-car´], *va.* To vellicate, to twitch.

velico, illo, ito [vay-lee´-co, ca, eel´-lyo, ee´-to] *m.* 1. *(Dim.)* A small veil. 2. Embroidered gauze.

velilla, ita [vay-leel´-lyah], *f. dim.* A small candle.

vellecillo [vel-lyay-theel´-lyo], *f. dim.* Very short, soft hair.

vellido, da [vel-lyee´-do, dah], *a.* Downy, villous.

vello [vayl´-lyo], *m.* 1. Down, soft hair on parts of the skin; nap. 2. The downy matter which envelops seeds or fruit, gossamer. 3. Short, downy hair of brutes.

vellón [vel-lyone´], *m.* 1. Fleece, wool of one sheep; lock of wool (lana). 2. Old copper coin.

vellonero [vel-lyo-nay´-ro], *m.* Collector of fleeces at shearing.

vellora [vel-lyo´-rah], *f. (Prov.)* Knot taken from woollen cloth.

vellorita [vel-lyo-ree´-tah], *f. (Bot.)* Cowslip.

vellosa [vel-lyo´-sah], *f. (Prov.)* Coarse cloth or rug worn by mariners.

vellosidad [veyl-lyo-se-dahd´], *f.* Downiness, hirsuteness.

vellosilla [vel-lyo-seel´-lyah], *f. (Bol.)* Creeping mouse-ear, mouse ear hawk-weed.

velloso, sa [vel-lyo´-so, sah], *m.* Downy, hairy, cottony.

velludillo [vel-lyoo-deel´-lyo], *m.* Velveteen.

velludo, da [vel-lyoo´-do, dah], *a.* Downy, hairy, shaggy, woolly.

velludo [vel-lyoo´-do], *m.* Shag, velvet.

vellutero [vel-lyoo-tay´-ro], *m. (Prov.)* Velvet worker.

velo [vay´-lo], *m.* 1. Veil, curtain. 2. Veil, a part of female dress. 3. Veil, a part of the dress of nuns. 4. Piece of white gauze thrown over a couple at marriage. 5. Feast at the profession of a nun or at taking the veil. 6. Veil, cover, disguise. 7. Pretence, pretext (pretexto), cover, mask. 8. Confusion, obscurity, perplexity, of the sight or intellect (falta de claridad). **Correr el velo**, to pull off the mask; to disclose something before unknown. **Tomar el velo**, to become a nun.

velocidad [vay-lo-the-dahd´], *f.* Speed, velocity, rapidity. **Velocidad aérea**, air speed. **Velocidad de crucero**, cruising speed. **A toda velocidad**, at full speed. **Disminuir velocidad**, to slow down.

velocímetro [vay-lo-thee´-may-tro], *m.* Speedometer.

velocípedo [vay-lo-thee´-pay-do], *m.* Velocipede; bicycle or tricycle.

velódromo [vay-lo´-dro-mo], *m.* Velodrome.

velón [vay-lonee´], *m.* 1. Lamp in which oil is burnt (lámpara). 2. *(And. Cono Sur, Mex.)* Thick tallow candle. 3. *(CAm.)* Sponger (parásito). 4. *(And. Carib.)* Person who casts covetous glances.

velonera [vay-lo-nay´-rah], *f.* Wooden lamp-stand or bracket.

velonero [vay-lo-nay´-ro], *m.* Lamp-maker.

veloz [vay-loth´], *a.* Swift, nimble, active, fleet.

velozmente [vay-loth-men-tay], *adv.* Swiftly, fleetly, nimbly.

vena [vay´-nah], *f.* 1. Vein, a blood vessel. 2. Fiber of plants. 3. Hollow, cavity. 4. Vein of metal in a mine. 5. Tendency of mind or genius (talento). **Vena poética**, a poetical vein. 6. Diverse quality or color of earth or stones. 7. Vein or stripe in stones; mineral water found under ground. **Coger** or **hallar a alguno de vena**, to find one in a favorable disposition.

venablo [vay-nah´-blo], *m.* Javelin, formerly used in hunting wild boars. **Echar venablos**, to break out into violent expressions of anger.

venadero [vay-nah-day´-ro], *m.* Place much frequented by deer.

venadico, illo, ito [vay-nah-dee´-co], *m.* A small deer.

venado [vay-nah´-do], *m.* 1. Deer, venison. **Pintar venados**, *(Coll.)* to play hooky. 2. *(Carib.)* Deerskin (piel). 3. *(Carib.)* Whore (puta). 4. *(And.)* Contraband (contrabanda).

venajo [vay-nah´-hay], *m.* Current of a stream.

venal [vay-nahl´], *a.* 1. Venal, relating to the veins. 2. Marketable, salable. 3. Venal, mercenary.

venalidad [vay-nah-le-dahd´], *f.* Venality, mercenariness.

venalogía [vay-nah-lo-hee´-ah], *f.* Treatise on the veins.

venate [vay-nah´-tay], *m.* A small bird.

venático, ca [vay-nah´-te-co, cah], *a.* Rather crazy, a bit mad.

vanatorio, ria [vay-nah-to´-re-o, ah], *a.* Venatic, used in hunting.

vencedor, ra [ven-thay-dor´, rah], *m. & f.* Conqueror, victor.

vencejo [ven-thay´-ho], *m.* 1. String, band. 2. *(Orn.)* Swift, black-martin, martlet, martinet.

vencer [ven-therr´], *va.* 1. To conquer, to subdue, to defeat (derrota), to vanquish, to overpower, to master, to foil. 2. To conquer, to surpass, to excel. 3. To surmount, to overcome (dificultad, obstáculo), to clear. 4. To gain a lawsuit. 5. To bend, to turn down. 6. To prevail upon, to persuade. 7. To suffer, to tolerate or bear with patience. 8. To incline, to twist a thing. *-vn.* 1. To fall due. 2. To conquer, to gain, to succeed. *-vr.* To govern one's passions or desires. **Por fin le venció el sueño**, finally sleep overcame him. **Se venció el plazo**, the time´s up.

vencible [ven-thee´-blay], a. Vincible, conquerable; superable.

vencida [ven-thee'-dah], f. Action of conquering or being conquered.

vencido, da [ven-thee'-do, dah], a. & pp. Of VENCER. 1. Conquered, subdued. 2. Due; payable. **Darse por vencido,** to give up. **Con los intereses vencidos,** with the interest which is due. 3. (LAm.) Out of date (billete, permiso).

vencimiento [ven-the-me-en'-to], m. 1. Victory, conquest. 2. Bent, the act of bending or turning down. 3. **Vencimiento de plazo,** (Com.) maturity of a bill of exchange, period of falling due. **Al vencimiento del plazo,** at the expiration of the time that a bill comes due.

venda [ven'-dah], f. 1. Bandage, roller. 2. (Ant.) Fillet, a band tied round the head or other part; a diadem.

vendaje [ven-dah'-hay], m. 1. Commission or the sale of goods by a factor or agent. 2. Ligature with a fillet, bandage, or roller.

vendar [ven-dar´], va. 1. To tie with a band, inlet, bandage, or roller; to filet. 2. To hoodwink, to darken the understanding. **Vendar los ojos,** to hoodwink.

vendaval [ven-dah-vahl'], m. A strong wind south by west.

vendavalada [ven-dah-vah-lah'-dah], f. A storm of southerly wind.

vendedor, ra [ven-day-dor', rah], m. & f. Seller, trader, retailer, huckster, vender.

vendehúmos [ven-day-oo'-mos], m. A person who claims intimacy with people in power in order to sell favors.

vendeja [ven-day´-hah], f. 1. A public sale (venta). 2. Collection of goods offered for sale (géneros).

vender [ven-derr'], va. 1. To sell, to vend. 2. To expose for sale. 3. To soil, to betray for money, to prostitute, to devote to crimes for a reward. 4. To render dear or difficult. 5. To persuade, to delude with false pretences. **Vender salud.** (Coll.) to be or appear very robust. **Vender por mayor,** to sell in the lump, or by wholesale. **Vender al por menor** or **a destajo,** to sell at retail. -vr. 1. To boast of talents or merits one does not possess. 2. To devote oneself to the service of another. **Venderse caro,** to be of difficult access. **Venderse barato,** to make oneself cheap. **Vender cara la vida,** to fight desperately. **Vender al contado,** to sell for cash. **Vender a plazo,** to sell on credit. **Vender gato por liebre,** to sell a cat for a hare (to deceive in the quality of things sold).

vendible [ven-dee'-blay], a. Salable, marketable.

vendica, illa, ita [ven-dee'-cah], f. dim. Small fillet or bandage; a small diadem.

vendición [ven-de-the-on'], f. Sale, selling, rendition.

vendido, da [ven-dee'-do, dah], a. & pp. of VENDER. Sold. **Estar vendido,** to be duped, to be exposed to great risks.

vendimia [ven-dee'-me-ah], f. 1. Vintage. 2. Large gain or profit. **La vendimia de 1998,** the 1998 vintage.

vendimiado, da [ven-de-me-ah'-do, dah], a. & pp. of VENDIMIAR. Gathered vintage.

vendimiador, ra [ven-de-me-ah-dor', rah], m. & f. Vintager.

vendimiar [ven-de-me-ar'] va. 1. To gather the vintage. 2. To enjoy unlawful perquisites; to reap benefits or profit unjustly. 3. (Coll.) To kill, to murder (matar).

venduta [ven-doo-tah], f. 1. (Amer.) Auction (subasta), vendue. 2. (Carib.) Greengrocer's shop (frutería). 3. (Carib.) Swindle (estafa).

vendutero [ven-doo-tay'-ro], m. 1. Auctioneer. 2. (Carib.) Greengrocer.

veneciano, no [vay-nay-the-ah'-no, nah], a. Venetian, relating to Venice.

veneficiar [vay-nay-fe-the-ar'], va. To bewitch, to injure by witchcraft.

venencia [vay-nen'-the-ah], f. A small vessel, like a piece of reed, at the end of a long rod, which is used in Xerez for testing wines.

venenífero, ra [vay-nay-nee'-fay-ro, rah], a. (Poet.) V. VENENOSO.

veneno [vay-nay'-no], m. 1. Poison, venom, anything injurious to health: venenation. 2. Poisonous mineral, ingredients in paints or dye-stuffs. 3. Wrath, fury, passion. 4. Bad, insipid taste. 5. (Met.) Poison, something pernicious to morals and religion.

venenosamente [vay-nay-no-sah-men´-tay], adv. Venomously.

venenosidad [vay-nay-no-se-dahd'], f. Poisonousness, venomousness.

venenoso, sa [vay-nay-no'-so, sah], a. Venomous, poisonous.

venera [vay-nay'-rah], f. 1. Porcelain shell, or Mediterranean scallop, worn by pilgrims who return from St. Jago or Santiago in Galicia. 2. Badge, jewel, or star worn by the knights of military orders. 3. Vein of metal in a mine; spring of water.

venerable [vay-nay-rah'-blay], a. 1. Venerable. 2. Epithet of respect to ancient ecclesiastics and prelates.

venerablemente [vay-nay-rah-blay-men-tay], adv. Venerably; with respect or veneration.

veneración [vay-nay-rah-the-on'], f. 1 Veneration. 2. Worship; honor.

venerador, ra [vay-nay-rah-dor', rah], m. & f. Venerator, worshipper.

venerando, da [vay-nay-rahn'-do, dah], a. Venerable.

venerante [vay-nay-rahn'-tay], va. Venerating, worshipping.

venerar [vay-nay-rar'], va. To venerate, to respect, to worship, to honor.

venéreo, rea [vay-nay'-ray-o, ah], a. Venereal, sensual.

venero [vay-nay'-ro], m. 1. A vein of metal in a mine. 2. A spring of water. 3. Radius or horary line of sun-dials 4. Origin, root, source.

veneruela [vay-ne-roo-ay'-lah], f. 1. A small porcelain shell. 2. Dim of VENERA.

venezolana [vay-nay-tho-lah'-no, nah], a. Venezuelan, of Venezuela.

vengable [ven-gah'-blay], a. Worthy of revenge, that may be revenged.

vengador, ra [ven-gah-dor', rah], m. & f. Avenger, revenger.

vengancilla [ven-gan-theel'-lyah], f. dim. A slight revenge.

venganza [ven-gahn'-thah], f. Revenge, vengeance. **Tomar venganza de uno,** to take vengeance on somebody.

vengar [ven-gar'], va. To revenge, avenge. -vr. To be revenged.

vengativamente [ven-gah-tee'-vah-men-tay], adv. Revengefully.

vengativo, va [ven-gah-tee'-vo, vah], a. Revengeful, vindictive (espíritu, persona).

venia [vay'-ne-ah], f. 1. Pardon (perdón), forgiveness. 2. Leave, permission (permiso). 3. Royal license to minors to manage their own estates. 4. Bow with the head.

venial [vay-ne-ahl'], a. Venial, pardonable; excusable.

venialidad [vay-ne-ah-le-dahd'], f. Veniality.

venialmente [vay-ne-al-men'-tay], adv. Venially.

venida [vay-nee'-dah], f. 1. Arrival (llegada); return (vuelta), regress, coming. 2. Overflow of a river. 3. Attack in fencing. 4. Impetuosity, rashness.

venidero, ra [vay-ne-day'-ro, rah], a. Future, coming. **En lo venidero,** henceforth. -pl. Posterity, successors.

venido, da [vay-nee'-do, dah], a. & pp. of VENIR. Come, arrived. **Venido del cielo,** come from heaven; expressing the excellence of a thing. **Bienvenido** or **bienvenida,** welcome.

venimécum [vay-ne-may'-coom], m. Vademecum.

venir [vay-neer'], vn. 1. To come, to draw near, to advance towards. 2. To come, to move towards another. **Ven acá,** (Coll.) come hither: used to call the attention and to advise anyone. 3. To come, to happen (suceder), to come to pass. 4. To follow, to succeed. 5. To come, to proceed from, to originate in, to be occasioned by; to be inferred, to be deduced. 6. To appear before a judge; to come into court. 7. To assent, to submit, to yield. 8. To answer, to fit, to suit. **Esta chaqueta no me viene,** that jacket does not fit me. 9. To grow, to shoot up. 10. To make an application, to ask. 11. To occur, to be presented in the memory or attention. 12. To resolve, to determine. 13. To attack, to assault. 14. *(Arith.)* To result. 15. To be of one's party or opinion; to accompany. 16. To fall, to be overset. 17. Used impersonally, come here take this. 18. To succeed finally. **Vino a conseguir la plaza**, he obtained the place. **Venir a cuentas**, to calculate, to count. 19. To change the state or quality. 20. To be transferred, to pass from one to another. 21. To adduce; to produce. 22. To excite, to effect; to attain a degree of excellence or perfection. 23. Used to express politely satisfaction or pleasure at the arrival of anyone; to welcome. **Venir de perilla**, to come in the nick of time; to fit or to answer perfectly well. **Cosas que van y vienen**, things which wax and wane. **No hay mal que por bien no venga**, *(Prov.)* there is no evil which may not be turned to good. **¿A qué viene eso?** to what purpose is that? What does it amount to? **Él se mete en lo que no le va, ni le viene**, he meddles in business that does not concern him. **Venirle a la mano alguna cosa**, to get something without exertion. **Venir muy ancho**, to be in abundance; to be beyond the desert of the receiver. **Venir rodado**, to attain an object accidentally. **Venir a las manos**, to come to blows. **No me vengas con historias**, don´t come telling tales to me. **Se puede ver venir la noche**, one can face the evening ahead. **Viene de**, to come from. **Viene a llenar un gran vacío**, it serves to fill a large gap. **El tapón viene justo a la botella**, the stopper fits the bottle exactly. **Venían andando desde mediodía**, they had been walking since midday. *-vr.* To ferment (vino), to attain perfection by fermentation, as bread or wine. It is often used the same as the neuter verb *venir*. **Venirse a buenas**, to yield, to submit, to comply with things required or enforced. **Venirse a casa**, to come home. **Venirse durmiendo**, to be falling asleep. **Venirse abajo**, to fall, to collapse. **Venirse a los ojos**, to show in one's eyes; to betray by one's glances. **Venirse al suelo**, to fall to the ground. **Venirse a la boca**, to taste unpleasantly. **Venirse el cielo abajo**, to rain very heavily. **Como se viene, se va**, easy come, easy go. (*Yo vengo, yo venga*, from *Venir.* V. VENIR.)

venora [vay-no'-rah], *f. (Prov.)* Range of stones or bricks in a drain or trench.

venoso, sa [vay-no'-so, sah], *a.* 1. Venous, belonging to veins. 2. Veiny, veined, full of veins.

venta [ven'-tah], *f.* 1. Sale, act of selling, market; custom. **Venta confidencial**, a trust sale. 2. A poor inn on roads far from towns or villages (posada). **Estar de venta** or **estar en venta**, to be on sale. *(Coll.)* Applied to a woman who stands much at a window, to see and be seen. 3. *(Met.)* Open place exposed to the weather. 4. *(Carib. Mex.)* Small shop, stall.

ventada [ven-tah'-dah], *f.* A gust of wind.

ventaja [ven-tah'-hah], *f.* 1. Advantage, preference; grain, good; commodity, commodiousness; hand; additional pay. 2. Odds given in a game. **Es un plan que tiene muchas ventajas**, it is a plan that has many advantages. **Dejar buena ventaja**, to bring in a good profit.

ventajosamente, *adv.* Advantageously, gainfully.

ventajoso, sa [ven-tah-ho'-so, sah], *a.* Advantageous, comparatively superior; profitable, lucrative, fruitful, good.

ventalla [ven-tahl'-lyah], *f.* Valve. V. VÁLVULA.

ventalle [ven-tahl'-lya], *m.* Fan. V. ABANICO.

ventana [ven-tah'-nah], *f.* 1. Window. 2. Window-shutter. 3. Nostril. 4. Either of the senses of seeing or hearing. 5. *(And.)* Forest clearing (claro de bosque). **Ventana de guillotina**, sash window. **Tirar algo por la ventana**, to throw something out of the window.

ventanaje [ven-tah-nah'-hay], *m.* Number or series of windows in a building.

ventanazo [ven-tah-nah'-tho], *m.* Slap of a window.

ventanear [ven-tah-nay-ar'], *vn.* To frequent the window, to gaze repeatedly from the window.

ventanera [ven-tah-nay'-rah], *a.* Window-gazer: applied to women who are constantly at the window.

ventanero [ven-tah-nay'-ro], *m.* Window-maker.

ventanica, illa [ven-tah-nee'-cah], *f. dim.* 1. A small window. 2. Window (de sobre, taquilla).

ventanico, illo [ven-tah-nee'-co, neel'-lyo], *m. dim.* A small window-shutter.

ventar [ven-tar'], *va. & vn.* V. VENTEAR.

ventarrón [ven-tar-rone'], *m.* Violent wind.

venteadura [ven-tay-ah-doo'-rah], *f.* Split made in timber by the wind.

ventear [ven-tay-ar'], *vn. & a.* 1. To blow. **Ventea muy fresco del N. O.**, it blows very fresh from the N. W. 2. To smell, to scent. 3. To investigate, to examine. 4. To dry, to expose to the air. 5. *(CAm. Mex.)* To brand (animal). 6. *(Cono Sur)* To get far ahead of (adversario). 7. *(And. Carib.)* To fan (abanicar). *-vr.* 1. To be filled with wind or air. 2. To break wind. 3. *(And. Carib. Cono Sur)* To be outdoors a great deal (estar mucho afuera). 4. *(And. Carib.)* To get conceited (engreírse).

venteo [ven-tay'-o], *m.* Vent-hole in a cask.

venteril [ven-tay-reel'], *a.* Suited to a poor inn.

ventero, ra [ven-tay'-ro, rah], *m. & f.* Keeper of a small inn on roads.

ventilación [ven-te-lah-the-on'], *f.* Ventilation; discussion.

ventilado [ven-te-lah'-do], *a.* Draughty, breezy.

ventilador [ven-te-lah-dor'], *m.* Ventilator.

ventilar [ven-te-lar'], *va.* 1. To ventilate (cuarto); to winnow, to fan. 2. To examine, to discuss. 3. To air (asunto). 4. *(Fig.)* To make public (asunto privado). *-vr.* To move with a current of air (cuarto), to circulate (aire).

ventilla [ven-teel'-lyah], *f.* Pallet, valve-pallet of an organ.

ventisca [ven-tees'-cah], *f.* Storm, attended with a heavy fall of snow.

ventiscar [ven-tis-car'], *vn.* To blow hard, attended with snow, to drift, to be drifted by the wind, as snow.

ventisco [ven-tees'-co], *m.* V. VENTISCA.

ventiscoso, sa [ven-tis-co'-so, sah], *a.* Windy, stormy, tempestuous.

ventisquear [ven-tis-kay-ar'], *v. imp.* To snow hard.

ventisquero [ven-tis-kay'-ro], *m.* 1. Snow-drift (montón); glacier. 2. Mountain height most exposed to snow-storms. 3. Snow-storm (tormenta).

ventola [ven-to'-lah], *f. (Naut.)* Tophamper, resistance of the upper works to the wind.

ventolera [ven-to-lay'-rah], *f.* 1. Gust, a sudden blast of wind (ráfaga). 2. Vanity (vanidad); pride, loftiness; fancy. 3. V. REHILANDERA. 4. Whim (capricho), unexpected and extravagant thought or resolution. 5. *(Mex.)* Fart (pedo).

ventolina [ven-to-lee'-nah], *f. (Naut.)* Light, variable wind; cats-paw.

ventor [ven-tor'], *m.* Pointer, pointerdog; fox-hound.

ventorrillo, ventorro [ven-tor-reel'-lyo, ven-tor'-ro], *m.* A petty inn or tavern near a town.

ventosa [ven-to'-sah], *f.* 1. *(Med.)* Cupping-glass. 2. Vent (agujero), air-hole, spiracle. 3. *(Zool.)* Sucker, a muscular organ of certain aquatic creatures for sucking, catching prey, or clinging to rocks. **Pegar una ventosa**, to swindle one out of his money.

ventosear, ventosearse [ven-to-say-ar', ar'-say], *vn. & vr.* To break wind.

ventosero, ra [ven-to-say'-ro, rah], *a.* Fond of cupping.

ventosidad [ven-to-se-dahd'], *f.* Flatulency, windiness.

ventoso, sa [ven-to'-so, sah], *a.* 1. Windy; flatulent. 2. Pointing. 3. Vain, inflated. 4. Windy, tempestuous.

ventral [ven-trahl'], *a.* Ventral: applied to anything used to encircle the belly.

ventrecha [ven-tray'-chah], *f.* Belly of fishes.

ventregada [ven-tray-gah'-dah], *f.* 1. Brood, litter. 2. Abundance.

ventrera [ven-tray'-rah], *f.* Roller or girdle for the belly; sash, cummerbund.

ventricular [ven-tre-coo-lar'], *a.* Ventricular; belonging to the ventricles of the heart.

ventrículo [ven-tree'-coo-lo], *m.* 1. Ventricle, the stomach. 2. Any of the cavities of the heart or brain.

ventril [ven-treel'], *m.* 1. A piece of wood which serves to counterpoise the movement of the beam in oil-mills. 2. Belly-band of a harness.

ventrílocuo [ven-tree'-lo-coo-o], *m.* Ventriloquist.

ventriloquia [ven-tre-lo'-ke-ah], *f.* Ventriloquism, the art or practice of the ventriloquist.

ventrón [ven-trone'], *m. aug.* of VIENTRE.

ventrosidad [ven-tro-se-dahd'], *f. (Med.)* Excessive development of the belly; ventrosity.

ventroso, sa. [ven-tro'-so, sah], **ventrudo, da** [ven-troo'-do, dah], *a.* Big-bellied.

ventura [ven-too'-rah], *f.* 1. Luck (suerte), fortune. 2. Contingency, casualty, hazard, hap, venture. **Buena ventura,** good fortune told by gipsies and vagrants. **Probar ventura,** to try one's fortune, to venture at, on, or upon. 3. Risk, danger. **A ventura** or **a la ventura,** at a venture, at hazard. **Ir a la aventura,** to live in a disorganized way.

venturero, ra [ven-too-ray'-ro, rah], *a.* 1. Casual, incidental. 2. Lucky, fortunate. 3. Vagrant, idle, adventurous.

venturero [ven-too-ray'-ro], *m.* Fortune-hunter, adventurer, land-loper.

venturilla [ven-too-reel'-lyah], *f.* Good luck.

venturina [ven-too-ree'-nah], *f.* Goldstone, a precious stone of a brown color spotted with gold.

venturo, ra [ven-too'-ro, rah], *a.* Future; that which is to come.

venturón [ven-too-rone'], *m. aug.* Great luck.

venturosamente [ven-too-ro-sah-men-tay], *adv.* Luckily, fortunately.

venturoso, sa [ven-too-ro'-so, sah], *a.* Lucky (afortunado), fortunate, successful, happy, prosperous.

venus [vay'-noos], *f.* 1. Venus, the goddess of beauty and love. 2. A beautiful woman. 3. Venery, sensual pleasure. 4. *(Chem.)* Copper. *m. (Acad.)* Venus; Hesper; the evening star, the planet nearest the earth.

venusio [vay-noo'-se-o], *m.* Copper in the highest grade of perfection, inalterable in the free air, and hence highly useful in the industrial arts.

venustidad [vay-noos-te-dahd'], *f.* Beauty, gracefulness.

venusto, ta [vay-noos'-to, tah], *a.* Beautiful, graceful.

venza [ven'-thah], *f.* Scarf-skin, used by gold-beaters.

ver [verr], *va.* 1. To see, to look into (indagar). 2. To see, to observe, to consider, to reflect. 3. To see, to visit. 4. To foresee, to forecast. 5. To fancy, to imagine; to judge. 6. To see, to find out, to discover; to explore. 7. To be present at the report of a lawsuit. 8. To experience. 9. To examine. 10. To see at a future time. 11. Used with the particle *ya,* it is generally a voice; as, **ya verá,** he shall see. **Ver venir,** to see what one is driving at; to await the resolution or determination of another person. **Es de ver, es para ver** or **es digno de ser visto,** it is worth notice, it is worthy of being observed. **Estar de ver,** to be worth seeing. **Estar por ver,** to be yet to come to pass; to be doubtful. **No poder ver a alguno,** to abhor or detest one, not to suffer or endure him. **Al ver,** on seeing a thing. **¿A ver?** is it not so? let us see (for «*vamos a ver*»). **A ver** or **veamoslo,** let us see it. **A más ver** or **hasta más ver,** *(Coll.)* farewell, until we meet again. **Hacer ver,** to show or to make appear. **Si te vi (ya) no me acuerdo,** out of sight, out of mind. **Ver tierras** or **mundo,** to travel. **Tener que ver una persona con otra,** to have relation or connection; to have carnal communication. **Eso nada tiene que ver con esto,** that has nothing to do with this. **Ojos que no ven, corazón que no siente,** *(Prov.)* out of sight, out of mind. **Ver las orejas del lobo,** to see the ears of the wolf, to be in great danger. **Ver visiones,** to build castles in the air. **Ver el cielo abierto,** to see a great opportunity. *-vr.* To be seen; to be in a place proper to be seen; to be conspicuous. 2. To find oneself in a state or situation. **Verse pobre,** to be reduced to poverty. **Verse negro,** to be in great want or affliction; to be greatly embarrassed. 3. To be obvious or evident. 4. To concur, to agree. 5. To represent the image or likeness, to see oneself in a glass. 6. To know the cards, at play. **Ver si,** to try to, to attempt. **Verse en ello,** to consider, to weigh in the mind. **Ya se ve,** (a)

it is undeniable; it is evident; it is as you say, it is easily to be seen certainly, to be sure. (b) *(Iron.)* Likely, indeed, that such a thing should happen. **Verse** or **irse viendo,** to discover, to view what should be concealed. **Verse y desearse,** to have very great care, anxiety, and fatigue in executing a thing. **No tes verás en ese espejo,** you will not succeed. **Verse las caras** (lit. to see each other face to face), there'll be the mischief to pay. **Hacer ver a uno las estrellas,** to make one feel a quick, lively pain; to make him see stars. *(Yo veo, yo vi, yo vea. V. VER.)*

ver [verr], *m.* 1. Sense of sight, seeing. 2. Light, view, aspect, appearance.

vera [vay'-rah], *f.* 1. *(Prov.)* Edge, border. V. ORILLA. 2. An American tree of very hard wood. **A la vera del camino,** beside the road.

veracidad [vay-rah-the-dahd'], *f.* Veracity, fidelity.

veranada [vay-rah-nah'-dah], *f.* Summer season.

veranadero [vay-rah-nah-day'-ro], *m.* Place where cattle pasture in summer.

veranal [vay-rah-nahl'], *a.* Summer, relating to summer.

veranar, veranear [vay-rah-nar', vay rah-nay-ar'], *vn.* To spend or pass the summer. **Veranean en Miami,** they go to Miami for the summer.

veraneante [vay-rah-nay-ahn'-tay], *m & f.* Holidaymaker, vacationer.

veraneo [vay-rah-nay'-o], *m.* 1. The act of passing the summer, or part of it, in some particular way or place. 2. V. VERANERO. **Lugar de veraneo,** summer resort. **Estar de veraneo,** to be away on one's summer holiday.

veranero [vay-rah-nay'-ro], *m.* Place where cattle graze in summer.

veranico, illo, ito [vay-rah-nee'-co], *m. dim.* of VERANO.

veraniego, ga [vay-rah-ne-ay'-go, gah], *a.* 1. Relating to the summer season. 2. Thin or sickly in summer. 3. Imperfect, defective.

verano [vay-rah'-no], *m.* 1. Summer, summer season. 2. In Ecuador, the dry season (época seca).

veras [vay'-ras], *f. pl.* 1. Reality, truth (verdad). 2. Earnestness, fervor, and activity with which things are done or desired. **De veras,** in truth, really; joking apart. **Lo siento de veras,** I am truly sorry. **Ahora va de veras que lo hago,** now I really am going to do it.

veratrina [vay-ra-tree'-nah], *f.* Veratrine, alkaloid of hellebore.

veratro [vay-rah-tro], *m.* V. ELÉBORO.

veraz [vay-rath'], *a.* Veracious.

verbal [ver-bahl'], *a.* Verbal; oral; nuncupative. **Copia verbal,** a literal copy.

verbalmente [ver-bahl-men-tay], *adv.* Verbally, orally.

verbasco [ver-bahs'-co], *m. (Bot.)* Great mullein.

verbásculo [ver-bahs'-coo-lo], *m. (Bot.)* Mullein.

verbena [ver-bay'-nah], *f.* 1. *(Bot.)* Vervain, verbena. 2. In Madrid, the evening given to diversions, before some celebrated saint's day (de santo).

verbenáceas [ver-bay-nah'-thay-as], *f. pl.* The verbena or vervain family of plants.

verberación [ver-bay-rah-the-on'], *f.* Verberation; the act of the wind or water striking against something

verberar [ver-bay-rar'], *va.* To verberate, to bed, to strike; to dart against (viento, agua).

verbigracia [ver-be-grah'-the-h], *adv.* For example, for instance: in abbreviation. *v. g.* or *v. gr.,* corresponding to *e. g.* in English.

verbo [verr'-bo], *m. (Gram.)* Verb. 2. Word, second person of the holy Trinity. **Verbos,** swearing, angry expressions; abusive language. **Verbo activo o transitivo,** transitive or active verb. **Verbo neutro o intransitivo,** intransitive or neuter verb. **Verbo substantivo,** the verb *ser,* as indicating essence or substance. **Verbo unipersonal o impersonal,** an impersonal verb, one used only in the third person.

verbosidad [ver-bo-se-dahd'], *f.* Verbosity, wordiness.

verboso, sa [ver-bo'-so, sah], *a.* Verbose, prolix.

verdacho [ver-dah'-cho], *m.* A kind of gritty green earth, used by painters.

verdad [ver-dahd'], *f.* 1. Truth, veracity, reality. 2. Truth, verity, clear expression; certain existence of things. 3. A sort of delicate paste. 4. Axiom, maxim, truism. 5. Virtue of veracity or truth. **Verdad es que** or **es verdad que**, it is true that. **Tratar de verdad**, to love truth. **A la verdad** or **de verdad**, truly, in fact, in truth. **Es verdad**, it is true. **Decir cuatro verdades a uno**, to tell somebody a few home truths. **Faltar a la verdad**, to lie. **En verdad**, *V.* VERDADERAMENTE.

verdaderamente [ver-dah-day-rah-men-tay], *adv.* Truly, in fact, verily, indeed, legitimately.

verdadero, ra [ver-dah-day'-ro, rah], *a.* True, real, sincere, ingenuous, good, veritable; truthful.

verdal [ver-dahl'], *a.* 1. **Ciruela verdal**, green gage, a plum. 2. *(Calif.)* **Una verdal, o verdeja**, an early white grape of sweet flavor.

verdasca [ver-dahs'-cah], *f. V.* VARDASCA.

verde [verr'-day], *m.* 1. Green, verdure. 2. Verdigris. 3. Youth. 4. Person in the bloom of age. 5. Green barley or grass, given to horses or mules as a purge (hierba). **Verde limón**, bright green. **Verde botella**, bottle green. **Verde pardo**, brown green. 6. *(And.)* Plantain. 7. *(Carib. Mex.)* Country (campo). 8. *(Carib.)* Policeman (policía). **Sentarse en el verde**, to sit on the grass. *-a.* 1. Green, of the color of plants. 2. Unripe (fruta), immature, not perfectly fresh (legumbres). 3. Young, blooming verdant. **Viejo verde**, a dirty old man. 4. Loose, immodest, smutty, savoring of obscenity. 5. **Poner verde a uno**, to give somebody a dressing-down (regañar).

verdea [ver-day'-ah], *f.* A sort of Florence white wine.

verdear [ver-day-ar'], *vn.* 1. To grow green (volverse verde), to get a greenish color. 2. *(Cono Sur)* To drink maté. 3. *(Cono Sur. Agr.)* To graze. *-va.* To collect grapes and olives to sell.

verdeceledón [ver-day-thay-la-done'], *m.* Sea-green, a color made of light blue and straw color.

verdecer [ver-day-therr'], *vn.* To grow green.

verdecico, ica, ito, ita, [ver-day-thee'-co], *a. dim.* of VERDE.

verdecillo [ver-day-theel'-lyo], *m. (Orn.)* Greenfinch.

verdecillo, illa [ver-day-theel'-lyo], *a. dim.* Greenish.

verdeesmeralda [ver-day-es-may-rahl'-dah], *a.* Emerald green.

verdegay [ver-day-gah'-e], *m. & a.* Verditer: applied to a light bright green.

verdeguear [ver-day-gay-ar'], *m.* To grow green.

verdemar [ver-day-mar'], *m. & a.* Sea-green, used by painters.

verdemontaña [ver-day-mon-tah'-nyah], *f.* Mountain-green, a mineral imported from Hungary, and a green paint prepared from it.

verdeoscuro, ra [ver-day-os-coo'-ro, rah], *a. & m. (Prov.)* Dark green, greenish.

verderol [ver-day-role'], *m.* 1. *(Orn.)* The yellow-hammer. 2. Kind of green shellfish.

verderón [ver-day-ron'], *m.* 1. *(Zone.)* A shellfish about two inches long with deep grooves. 2. *(Prov.)* V. VERDEROL, the bird.

verdete [ver-day'-tay], *m.* Verditer, copper acetate. *V.* CARDENILLO.

verdevejiga [ver-day'-hay-hee'-hah], *f.* Sap-green, deep-colored green.

verdezuelo [ver-day-thoo-ay'-lo], *m. V.* VERDEROL.

verdín [ver-deen'], *m.* 1. *V.* VERDINA. 2. Green scum on still water or damp walls (capa). 3. Oxide of copper. 4. Green stain (en la ropa).

verdina [ver-dee'-nah], *f.* The green color of fruits when not ripe.

verdinegro, gra [ver-de-nay'-gro, grah], *a.* Of a deep green color.

verdino, na [ver-dee'-no, nah], *a.* Of a bright green color.

verdiseco, ca [ver-de-say'-co, cah], *a.* Pale green.

verdolaga [ver-do-lah'-gah], *pl. (Bot.)* Purslane.

verdón [ver-done'], *m. (Orn.)* Greenfinch.

verdor [ver-dor'], *m.* 1. Verdure, herbage, green color of plants. 2. Acerbity or unplesant taste of unripe fruit. 3. Vigor and strength of the animal body.

verdoso, sa [ver-do'-so, sah], *a.* Greenish.

verdoyo [ver-do'-yo], *m.* A green mould growing on walls.

verdugado [ver-doo-gah'-do], *m.* Under petticoat formerly worn.

verdugal [ver-doo-gahl'], *m.* Young shoots growing in wood after outting.

verdugo [ver-doo'-go], *m.* 1. The young shoot of a tree. 2. Rapier, a long, narrow sword. 3. Welt, mark of a lash on the skin (látigo). 4. Hangman, executioner, herdsman. 5. Things which afflict the mind (tormento). 6. Very cruel person. 7. *(Arch.)* Row of bricks in a stone or mud wall. 8. Small rings for the cars, hoop. 9. *(Mil.)* Leathern whip.

verdugón [ver-doo-gone'], *m.* 1. A long shoot of a tree. 2. *(Aug.)* A large mark of a lash.

verduguillo [ver-doo-geel'-lyo], *m.* 1. *(Dim.)* A small shoot of a tree. 2. A small, narrow razor. 3. A long, narrow sword.

verdulera [ver-doo-lay'-rah], *f.* 1. Market woman, who sells vegetables and herbs (comerciante). 2. A mean, low woman; a word of contempt.

verdulería [ver-doo-lay-ree'-ah], *f.* Vegetable stand, vegetable shop.

verdulero [ver-doo-lay'-ro], *m.* Greengrocer.

verdura [ver-doo'-rah], *f.* 1. Verdure. 2. Greens, culinary vegetables, garden stuff. 3. Foliage in landscape and tapestry. 4. Vigor, luxuriance.

verdurita [ver-doo-ree'-tah], *f.* Slight heritage or vegetation.

verdusco, ca [ver-doos'-co, cah], *a.* Greenish, verging upon green.

verecundo, da [vay-ray-coon'-do, dah], *a.* Bashful, diffident. *V.* VERGONZOSO.

vereda [vay-ray'-dah], *f.* 1. Path, footpath. 2. Circular order or notice sent to several towns or places. 3. Route of traveling preachers. 4. *(Peru)* Sidewalk (acera). 5. *(And.)* Village (pueblo), settlement. 6. *(Mex.)* Parting (raya). **Entrar en vereda**, to toe the line. **Ir por la vereda**, to do the right thing.

veredario, ria [vay-ray-dah'-re-o, ah], *a.* Hired, on hire (caballos).

veredero [vay-ray-day'-ro], *m.* Messenger sent with orders or despatches.

veredicto [vay-ray-deec'-to], *m.* 1. *(For.)* Verdict, the decision of a trial. 2. Sentence, degree, opinion.

verga [ver'-gah], *f. (Naut.)* Yard. 2. The organ of generation in male animals, penis. 3. Nerve or cord of the crossbow.

vergajo [ver-gah'-ho], *m.* Cord of the penis of the bull and other quadrupeds, especially when separated from them (pizzle).

vergajón [ver-gah-hone'], *a.* **Hierro vergajón**, round iron.

vergarzoso [ver-gar-tho'-so], *m. (Zool.)* A species of American armadillo.

vergel [ver-hel'], *m.* 1. Fruit and flower garden (jardín). 2. Luxuriant vegetation.

vegeta [ver-hay'-tah], *f.* A small twig.

vergeteado, da [ver-hay-tay-ah'-do, dah], *a. (Her.)* Vergette, paley, having the field divided by several small pales.

vergonzante [ver-gon-thahn'-tay], *a.* Bashful, shamefaced (avergonzado).-**com.** An honest, decent, needy person.

vergonzosamente [ver-gon-tho-sah-men-tay], *adv.* Shamefully, bashfully; confoundedly.

vergonzoso, sa [ver-gon-tho'-so, sah], *a.* 1. Bashful (persona), modest, shamefaced; diffident. 2. Shameful; contumelious. **Partes vergonzosas**, privy parts.

verguear [ver-gay-ar'], *va.* To beat with a rod.

vergüenza [ver-goo-en'-thah], *f.* 1. Shame (sentimiento). 2. Bashfulness (timidez); confusion; modesty; diffidence, honor. 3. A base action. 4. Regard of one's own character; dignity, honor. 5. Disgrace (escándalo). **Perder la vergüen-**

za, to become abandoned. **Tener vergüenza**, to be ashamed. **Es una vergüenza**, it is a shameful thing. **Vergüenzas**, privy parts.

vergueta [ver-gay'-tah], *f.* A small switch or rod.

verguilla [ver-geel'-lyah], *f.* Gold or silver wire without silk.

vericueto [vay-re-coo-ay'-to], *m.* A rough and pathless place. **Vericuetos**, strange or ridiculous ideas.

verídico, ca [vay-ree'-de-co, cah], *a.* Veridical, telling the truth.

verificación [vay-re-fe-cah-the-on'], *f.* Inquiry, examen, verification, by argument or evidence.

verificador, ra [vay-re-fe-cah-dor', rah], *a.* Verifying, checking. *-m. & f.* Checker, tester, verifier.

verificar [vay-re-fe-car'], *va.* 1. To verify (hechos), to prove what was doubted. l. To verify, to confirm, to prove by evidence; to examine the truth of a thing. *-vr.* To be verified, to prove true.

verificativo, va [vay-re-fe-cah-tee'-vo, vah], *a.* Tending to prove; verificative.

verija [vay-ree'-hah], *f.* Region of the genitals.

veril [vay-reel'], *m. (Naut.)* The shore of a bay, of a sound, etc.

verilear [vay-re-lay-ar'], *vn. (Naut.)* To sail along the shore.

verino [vay-ree'-no], *m.* A fine sort of South American tobacco, grown in a locality of the same Caste. *(Prov.)* Pimple, small pustule.

verisímil [vay-re-see'-meel], *a.* Probable, likely, credible.

verisimilitud [vay-re-se-me-le-tood'], *f.* Verisimilitude, probability, likelihood.

verisímilmente [vay-re-see'-meel-men-tay], *adv.* Probably, likely.

verja [ver'-hah], *f.* Grate of a door or window; a grate with cross-bars (reja).

verjel [ver hel'], *m.* 1. Flower-garden; beautiful orchard. 2. Anything pleasing to the sight.

vermes [verr'-mes], *m. pl.* Intestinal worms.

vermicular [ver-me-coo-lar'], *a.* Vermiculous, full of grubs; vermicular.

vermicular [ver-me-coo-lar'], *va. (Arch.)* To vermiculate, to ornament an edifice with worm-like figures.

vermiforme [ver-me-for'-may], *a.* Vermiform, worm-like.

vermífugo [ver-mee'-foo-go], *a. & m. (Med.)* Vermifuge, anthelmintic.

verminoso, sa [ver-me-no'-so, sah], *a.* Full of grubs, verminous.

vermíparo, ra [ver-mee'-pa-ro, rah], *a.* Vermiparous, producing worms.

vermívoro, ra [ver-mee'-vo-ro, rah], *a.* Vermivorous, eating worms or grubs.

vermú [ver-moo'], *m.* Vermouth.

vernáculo, la [ver-nah'-coo-lo, lah], *a.* Vernacular, native, of one's own country. **Lengua vernácula**, vernacular language.

vernal [ver-nahl'], *m.* Vernal, belonging to spring.

vernerita [ver-ne-ree'-tah], *f. (Min.)* Wernerite, a translucent sodium-calcium silicate.

vernier [ver-ne-err'], *m. (Opt.)* Vernier.

vero [vay'-ro], *m. (Her.)* Cup or bellformed vase on a shield.

verónica [vay-ro'-ne-cah], *f.* 1. Image of the face of our Lord Jesus Christ. 2. *(Bot.)* Speedwell.

verosímil [vay-ro-see'-meel], *a.* Verisimilar. *V.* VERISÍMIL.

verosimilitud [vay-ro-se-me-le-tood'], *f.* Verisimility. *V.* VERISIMILITUD.

verraca [ver-rah'-cah], *f. (Naut.)* A tent pitched on shore by sailors for sheltering stores or utensils.

verraco [ver-rah'-co], *m.* Boar, male swine.

verraquear [ver-rah-kay-ar'], vn. 1. To grunt like a boar (gruñir). 2. *(Met. Coll.)* To cry angrily and long (niños).

verriondez [ver-re-on-deth'], f. 1. Rutting-time of boars and other animals. 2. Withering state of herbs.

verriondo, da [ver-re-on'-do, dah], a. 1. Foaming like a boar at rutting-time. 2. Witherlag, flaccid.

verrón [ver-rone'], m. V. VERRACO. *(Acad.)*

verrucaria [ver-roo-cah'-re-ah], f. *(Bot.)* Wartwort.

verruga [ver-roo'-gah], f. Wart, pimple.

verrugoso, sa [ver-roo-go'-so, sah], a. Warty.

verruguera [ver-roo-gay'-rah], f. *(Bot.)* European turnsole.

verruguica, illa, ita [ ], f. dim A small wart or pimple.

verruguiento, ta [ver-roo-gee-en'-to, tah], a. Full of warts, warty.

versado, da [ver-sah'-do, dah], a. & pp. Of VERSAR. Versed, conversant. **Versado en diferentes lenguas**, conversant in different languages.

versal [ver-sahl'], a. *(Print.) V.* MAYÚSCULA.

versalilla, versalita [ver-sah-leel'-lyah, ee'-tah], f. & a. *(Print.)* Small capital letter.

versar [ver-sar'], vn. & vr. 1. To be versed or conversant; to grow skilful in the management of a business. With the preposition *sobre*, to treat of, to write upon, to discuss. 2. *(Carib.)* To versify (versificar). 3. *(Carib.)* To chat (charlar). 4. *(Mex.)* To tease (guasear).

versatil [ver-sah'-teel], a. 1. Versatile, which may be turned readily. 2. Changeable, variable.

versatilidad [ver-sah-te-le-dahd'], f. Variability, inconstancy.

versecillo [ver-say-theel'-lyo], m. dim. V. VERSILLO.

versería [ver-say-ree'-ah], f. A collection of verses; poetry.

versico [ver-see'-co], m. dim. V. VERSILLO.

versícula [ver-see'-coo-lah], f. Place where the choir-books are placed.

versicularío [ver-se-coo-lah'-re-o], m. One who takes care of the choir books.

versículo [ver-see'-coo-lo], m. 1. Versicle, a small part of the responsory which is said in the canonical hours. 2. Verse of a chapter.

versificación [ver-se-fe-cah-the-on'], f. Versification.

versificador, ra [ver-se-fe-cah-dor', rah], m. & f. Versifier, versificator.

versificar [ver-se-fe-car'], va. To versify, to make verses.

versiforme [ver-se-for'-may], a. Subject to change of form.

versillo [ver-seel'-lyo], m. dim. A little verse.

versión [ver-se-on'], f. 1. Translation, version. 2. Version, manner of relation. 3 *(Med.)* Version, turning of a child for facilitating delivery.

versista [ver-sees'-tah], m. *(Coll.)* Versifier, verseman, versificator, one who writes blank verse.

verso [verr'-so], m. 1. Verse, a line consisting of a certain succession of sounds and number of syllables; metre. 2. Culverin of a small bore, now disused. **Verso libre**, free verse. **Teatro en verso**, verse drama. *-pl.* Lines.

vértebra [verr'-tay-brah], f. Vertebra, a joint in the back-bone.

vertebrado, da [ver'-tay-brah'-do, dah], a. Vertebrate, having vertebrae. *-m. pl. (Zool.)* Vertebrate animals.

vertebral [ver-tay-brahl'], a. Vertebral.

vertedera [ver-tay-day'-rah], f. *(Agr.)* The mould-board of a plough.

vertedero [ver-tay-day'-ro], m. Sewer, drain, rubbish dump (de basura).

vertedor, ra [ver-tay-dor', rah], m. & f. 1. Nightman, who empties the common sewer. 2. Conduit, sewer. 3. *(Naut.)* scoop (cuchara), made of wood, for throwing out water (botes, barcos).

vertello [ver-tayl'-lyo], m. *(Naut.)* Track to form the parrels.

verter [ver-terr'], va. 1. To spill (contenido, líquido), to shed. 2. To empty vessels (recipiente). 3. To translate writings. 4. To divulge, to publish, to reveal a secret. 5. To exceed, to abound. *-vn.* To flow (río), to run; to fall (pendiente).

vertibilidad [ver-te-be-le-dahd'], f. Versatility, versatileness.

vertible [ver-tee'-blay], a. Movable, changeable, variable.

vertical [ver-te-cahl'], a. Vertical, perpendicular to the horizon. *-m.* The plane which intersects the horizon in the points of the true east and west.

verticalmente [ver-te-cahl'-men-tay], adv. Vertically.

vértice [ver'-te-thay], *m.* Vertex, zenith; crown of the head.

verticidad [ver-te-the-dahd'], *f.* The power of turning, verticity; rotation.

verticilado, da [ver-te-the-lah'-do, dah], *a. (Bot.)* Verticillate.

verticilo [ver-te-thee'-lo], *m. (Bot.)* Verticil, a whorl.

vertiente [ver-te-en'-tay], *com.* 1. Waterfall, cascade. 2. Spring, source. 3. Slope (declive). 4. Side (lado).

vertiginoso, sa [ver-te-he-no'-so, sah], *a.* Giddy, vertiginous.

vértigo [verr'-te-go], *m.* 1. Giddiness, vertigo. 2. Transient disturbance of the judgment. 3. Sudden frenzy (frenesí). **Puede provocar vértigos,** it may cause giddiness. **Con una velocidad de vértigo,** at a giddy speed.

vertimiento [ver-te-me-ayn'-to], *m.* Effusion, shedding.

vesana [vay-sah'-nah], *f. (Agr.)* A straight furrow.

vesania [vay-sah'-ne-ah], *f.* Incipient insanity, craziness

vesical [vay-se-cahl'], *a.* 1. *(Zool.)* Vesical, relating to the bladder. 2. Forming bubbles on escaping from an orifice.

vesícula [vay-see'-coo-lah], *f.* l. *(Anat.)* Vesicle, a membranous sac like a bladder. 2. *(Bot.)* Vesicle, a little air-sac of some aquatic plant. **Vesícula biliar,** the gall-bladder. **Vesícula elemental** or **orgánica,** elementary mass of bioplasm, cell.

vesicular [vay-se-coo-lar'], *a.* **Vesicular,** like a little bladder or vesicle.

vesiculoso, sa [vay-se-coo-lo'-so, sah], *a.* Vesiculate, full of vesicles.

veso [vay'-so], *m. (Zool.)* Weasel, a carnivorous animal.

véspero [ves'-pay-ro], *m.* Vesper, the evening star.

vespertillo [ves-per-teel'-lyo], *m.* Bat. *V.* MURCIÉLAGO.

vespertina [ves-per-tee'-nah], *f.* Evening discourse in universities.

vespertino, na [ves-per-tee'-no, nah], *a.* Vespertine, happening in the evening.

vespertino [ves-per-tee'-no], *m.* Doctrinal sermon preached in the evening.

vesta [ves'-tah], *f.* 1. Vesta, goddess of the domestic hearth. 2. One of the asteroids.

vestal [ves-tahl'], *f. & a.* Vestal virgin, a priestess of the temple of Vesta.

veste [ves'-tay], *f. (Poet.)* Clothes, garments. *V.* VESTIDO.

vestfaliano, na [vest-fah-le-ah'-no, nah], *a.* Westphalian, of Westphalia.

vestíbulo [ves-tee'-boo-lo], *m.* 1. Vestibule, portal, hall, lobby. 2. Vestibule, a cavity of the internal ear.

vestido [ves-tee'-do], *m.* 1. Dress, wearing apparel, clothes, garments, clothing, garb, habiliments. 2. Ornament, embellishment. 3. *(And. CAm. Cono Sur)* Suit (de hombre). **Vestidos usados,** second-hand clothes. **Vestido de noche,** evening-gown. **Vestido y calzado,** without labor. **Vestido de seda,** silk dress. —**Vestido, da,** *pp.* of VESTIR.

vestidura [ves-te-doo'-rah], *f.* 1. Vesture, robe of distinction. 2. Vestment for divine worship.

vestidurilla, ita [ves-te-doo-ree'-lyah], *f. dim.* of VESTIDURA.

vestigio [ves-tee'-he-o], *m.* 1. Vestige, footstep; ruins, remains of buildings. 2. Memorial, mark, sign, index.

vestimenta [ves-te-men'-tah], *f.* Clothes (ropa), garments. -*pl.* Ecclesiastical robes.

vestir [ves-teer'], *va.* 1. To clothe, to dress (cuerpo, persona), to accoutre. 2. To deck, to adorn. 3. To make clothes for others (sastre). 4. To cloak, to disguise, to palliate. 5. To instruct, to inform, to advise. 6. To rough-cast the walls of a building. 7. To affect a passion or emotion. 8. To give liberally, to make liberal presents. 9. *(Met.)* To embellish a discourse. 10. Used of animals and plants in respect to their coverings. -*vn.* To dress in a special color or fashion. **Vestir de uniforme,** to dress in uniform. -*vr.* 1. To be covered; to be clothed. **La primavera viste los campos,** spring clothes the fields. 2. To dress oneself on rising after sickness. **Le viste un buen sastre,** he has his clothes made at a good tailor's. **Vestir bien,** to dress well. **Le gusta vestirse en París,** he

likes to buy his clothes in Paris. **El que de lo ajeno se viste en la calle lo desnudan,** he who wears borrowed plumes risks public exposure. *(Yo visto, él vistió; yo vista, vistiera*; from *Vestir. V.* PEDIR.)

vestuario [ves-too-ah'-re-o], *m.* 1. Vesture, all the necessaries of dress; clothes; uniform; equipment, habiliment for the troop. 2. Tax for the equipment of the troop. 3. Vestry, place where clergymen dress. 4. Money given to ecclesiastics for dress, and stipends to assistants. 5. Green-room, dressing-room in a theatre; vestiary. **Vestuarios,** deacon and subdeacon who attend the priest at the altar.

vestugo [ves-too'-go], *m.* Stem or bud of an olive.

veta [vay'-tah], *f.* 1. Vein of ore, metal, or coal in mines. 2. Vein in wood or marble, grain. 3. Stripe of a different color in cloth or stuff. **Descubrir la veta,** to discover one's sentiments or designs. 4. *(Ecuador)* Sickness, nausea, and headache from great elevations in the Andes. *Cf.* ZAROCHE.

vetado, da [vay-tah'-do, dah], *a. & pp.* Of VETEAR. *V.* VETEADO.

vetar [vay-tar'], *va.* To veto.

veteado, da [vay-tay-ah'-do, dah], *a.* Striped, veined, streaky, cross-grained.

vetear [vay-tay-ar'], *va.* To variegate, to form veins of different colors, to grain.

veteranía [vay-tay-rah-nee'-ah], *f.* Status of being a veteran; long service (servicio).

veterano, na [vay-tay-rah'-no, nah], *a.* Experienced, veteran, long practiced (soldados). -*m.* Veteran, an old soldier.

veterinaria [vay-tay-re-nah'-re-ah], *f.* Veterinary medicine or surgery.

veterinario, ria [vay-tay-re-nah'-re-o], *m & f.* Veterinary surgeon.

vetica, illa [vay-tee'-cah, eel'-lyah], *f. dim.* A small vein; a narrow stripe.

veto [vay'-to], *m.* Veto, official disapproval of a law.

vetustamente [vay-toos-tah-men'-tay], *adv.* Anciently.

vetustez [vay-toos-teth'], *f.* A venerable antiquity, notable old age.

vetusto, ta [vay-toos'-to, tah], *a.* Very ancient.

vez [veth], *f.* 1. Turn, the alternative of things in successive progression. 2. Time, or the determinate time or occasion on which something is performed. 3. Epoch. 4. Return, act or performance of anything that bears a successive progression. 5. Draught, the quantity of liquor drunk at once. 6. Herd of swine belonging to the inhabitants of a place. 7. United with *cada,* it intimates repetition. **Cada vez,** each time. -*pl.* Power or authority committed to a substitute. **A la vez or por vez,** successively, by turns, by order or series. **Una vez,** once. **Dos veces,** twice. **Tres veces,** thrice or three times. **De una vez,** at once. **Más de una vez,** more than once. **En vez,** instead of. **Tal vez,** perhaps. **Rara vez,** seldom, once in a while. **Llegará mi vez,** my turn will come. **Hacer las veces de otro,** to supply one's place. **A veces,** sometimes, by turns, on some occasions. **Todas las veces que,** whenever, as often as. **Muchas veces,** often. **Pocas veces,** seldom. **Varias veces,** several times. **Habíase una vez una princesa,** once upon a time there was a princess.

veza [vay'-thah], *f. (Bot.)* Vetch.

vezar [vay-thar'], *va.* To accustom, to habituate. *V.* AVEZAR.

vía [vee'-ah], *f.* 1. Way, road (calle), route (ruta). *V.* CAMINO. 2. Carriage track, mark of wheels. 3. Grade, track, permanent way, line, of a railway; also rail. 4. Way, mode, manner, method, procedure, gait. 5. Profession, calling, trade. 6. Post-road. 7. Passage, gut in the animal body. 8. Spiritual life. **Vía férrea,** railroad, railway. **Vía láctea,** *(Ast.)* the Milky Way. **Vía pública,** the streets of a town. **Vía terrestre,** overland route. **Vía ancha,** broad gauge. **Vías respiratorias,** respiratory track. **Un país en vías de desarrollo,** a developing country.

viabilidad [ve-ah-be-le-dahd'], *f. (Med.)* Viability, probability of life of the foetus.

viable [ve-ah'-blay], *a.* Viable, capable of living.

viadera [ve-ah-day'-rah], *f.* Part of a loom near the treadles.

viador [ve-ah-dor'], *m.* Passenger, traveler.

viaducto [ve-ah-dooc'-to], *m.* 1. Viaduct. 2. *(Mex.)* Expressway for rapid transit.

viajador, ra [ve-ah-hah-dor', rah], *m. & f. V.* VIAJERO.

viajante [ve-ah-hahn´-tay], *com. & pa.* 1. Traveler, voyager; traveling. 2. Commercial traveler.

viajar [ve-ah-har'], *vn.* To travel, to perform a journey or voyage, to itinerate. **Viajar en coche**, to go in a car.

viajata [ve-ah-hah'-tah], *f.* A short journey, especially one for a few days of diversion.

viaje [ve-ah'-hay], *m.* 1. Journey, tour (largo), voyage (por mar), travel, drive (coche). 2. Way, road. 3. *(Arch.)* Deviation from a right line. 4. Gait. 5. Excursion; errand. 6. Load carried at once. 7. Quantity of water from the general reservoir, to be divided into particular channels or conduits. 8. *(Carib.)* Time (vez). 9. Trip (viaje corto, excursión). **Hacer un viaje por toda Europa**, to tour Europe. **Viaje en coche**, a drive. **Viaje de recreo**, pleasure trip. **Agencia de viajes,** travel agency. **Viaje de ida**, outward journey. **Viaje de ida y vuelta,** return trip. **Viaje de novios**, honeymoon. **Viajes espaciales**, space travel. **Viaje en barco**, boat trip (corto), voyage (largo).

viajero, ra [ve-ah-hay'-ro, rah], *m. & f.* Traveler, passenger.

vial [ve-ahl'], *a.* Wayfaring; belonging to a journey: used in a mystical sense. *-m.* Avenue, a road formed by two parallel rows of trees or shrubbery. *(Acad.)* **Seguridad vial**, road safety. **Circulación vial**, road traffic.

vianda [ve-ahn'-dah], *f.* 1. Food, viands, meat, victuals, fare. 2. A meal served at table.

viandante [ve-an-dahn'-tay], *m & f.* Traveler (viajero), passenger, especially a tramp.

viandista [ve-an-dees'-tah], *m.* Waiter, who serves viands or puts them on the table.

viaraza [ve-ah-rah'-thah], *f.* Loose, diarrhea (animales).

viático [ve-ah'-te-co], *m.* 1. Viaticum, provision for a journey. 2. Viaticum, the sacrament administered to the sick.

víbora [vee´-bo-rah], *f.* 1. Viper. 2. *(Met.)* Viper, a malicious and perfidious person.

viborera [ve-bo-ray´-rah], *f. (Bot.)* Viper´s bugloss. **Viborera común**, common viper's bugloss.

viborezno, na [ve-bo-reth'-no, nah], *a.* Viperine, viperous. *-m.* Young, small viper.

viborillo, illa [ve-bo-reel'-lyo, lyah], *m. & f. dim. V.* VIBOREZNO.

vibración [ve-brah-the-on'], *f.* Vibration (temblor), oscillation, fluttering.

vibrante [ve-brahn'-tay], *pa.* 1. Vibrating, undulating. 2. Bounding (pulso). 3. Ringing (voz, slogan), exciting (reunión).

vibrar [ve-brar'], *va.* 1. To vibrate, to oscillate, to brandish. 2. To throw, to dart. *-vn.* To vibrate, to play up and down or to and fro.

vibrátil [ve-brah´-teel], *a.* 1. Vibratile, capable of vibration. 2. *(Med.)* Vibratory, used of a pain in which the nerves of the patient vibrate like drawing cords.

vibratilidad [ve-brah-te-le-dahd'], *f.* Faculty of producing vibrations.

vibratorio, ria [ve-brah-to'-re-o, ah], *a.* Vibratory.

vibrión [ve-bre-on'], *m. (Biol.)* Vibrio, a microbe endowed with an oscillating movement.

viburno [ve-boor'-no], *m. (Bot.)* Viburnum.

vicaría [ve-cah-ree'-ah], *f.* Vicarship; vicarage. **Vicaría perpetua**, perpetual curacy.

vicaria [ve-cah'-re-ah], *f.* Vicar, the second superior in a convent of nuns.

vicarial [ve-cah-re-ahl'], *a.* Vicarial, relating to a vicar, held by a vicar.

vicariato [ve-cah-re-ah'-to], *m.* Vicarage; the dignity of a vicar; the district subjected to a vicar; vicarship.

vicario [ve-cah'-re-o], *m.* 1. Vicar, deputy in ecclesiastical affairs.-*a.* Vicar, he who exercises the authority of the superior of a convent in his absence; one who transacts all ecclesiastical affairs as substitute for a bishop or archbishop. **Vicario apostólico**, missionary bishop in non-Catholic countries. **Vicario de coro**, choral-vicar, superintendent of the choir. **Vicario general**, vicar-general, an ecclesiastical judge appointed to exercise jurisdiction over a whole territory, in opposition to a **vicario pedáneo**, who has authority over a district only.

vicario, ria [ve-cah'-re-o, ah], *a.* Vicarial, vicarious; vicariate.

vice [vee'-thay], Vice, used in composition to signify deputy, or one of the second rank.

vicealmiranta [ve-thay-al-me-rahn'-tah], *f.* The galley next in order to the admiral's.

vicealmirantazgo [ve-thay-al-me-ran-tath'-go], *m.* 1. Office or rank of viceadmiral. 2. Vice-admiralty.

vicealmirante [ve-thay-al-me-rahn'-tay], *m.* Vice-admiral.

vicecamarero [ve-thay-cah-ma-ray'-ro], *m.* Vice-chamberlain.

vicecancelario [ve-thay-can-thay-lah'-re-o], *m. V.* VICE-CANCILLER.

vicecanciller [ve-thay-can-theel-lyerr'], *m.* Vice-chancellor.

viceconsiliario [ve-thay-con-se-le-ah'-re-o], *m.* Vice-counsellor.

vicecónsul [ve-thay-con'-sool], *m.* Vice-consul.

viceconsulado [ve-thay-con-soo-lah'-do], *m.* Vice-consulate.

vicegerente [ve-thay-hay-ren´-tay], *a.* Vicegerent.

vicelegado [ve-thay-lay-gah'-do], *m.* Vice-legate.

vicelegatura [ve-thay-lay-gah-too'-rah], *f.* Office and jurisdiction of a vicelegate.

vicemaestro [ve-thay-mah-es´-tro], *m.* Vice-principal.

vicenal [ve-thay-nahl'], *a.* Arrived at the age of twenty years.

vicepatrono [ve-thay-pah-tro´-no], *m.* vice-patron.

vicepresidencia [ve-thay-pray-se-den'-the-ah], *f.* Vice-presidency.

vicepresidente [ve-thay-pray-se-den'-tay], *m.* Vicepresident.

viceprovincial [ve-thay-pro-veen´-the-ahl], *m. & a.* Vice-provincial.

vicerrector, ra [ve-ther-rec'-tor, rah], *m. & f.* Vice-rector.

vicerrectorado, *m.* **vicerrectoría,** *f.* [ve-ther-rec-to-rah'-do]. Vicerectorship.

vicesenescal [ve-thay-say-nes-cah'], *m.* Vice-seneschal or steward.

vicesimario, ria [ve-thay-see-mah´-re-o, ah], *a.* Vicenary, belonging to the number twenty: twentieth.

vicésimo, ma [ve-thay'-se-mo, mah], *a.* Twentieth. *V.* VIGÉSI-MO.

viceversa [ve-thay-ver´-sah], *adv.* On the contrary; to the contrary; vice versa.

viciar [ve-the-ar'], *va.* 1. To vitiate, to mar, to spoil or corrupt (costumbres). 2. To counterfeit, to adulterate (sustancia). 3. To forge, to falsify. 4. To annul, to make void. 5. To deprave, to pervert. 6. To put a false construction on a passage or expression. *-vr.* To deliver oneself up to vices (persona); to become too much attached or addicted to anything.

vicio [vee´-the-o], *m.* 1. Defect, imperfection of body, of soul, or of things; viciousness, faultiness, depravation, folly. 2. Vice, moral corruption, depravity. 3. Artifice, fraud. 4. Excessive appetite, extravagant desire. 5. Deviation from rectitude, defect or excess (defecto). 6. Luxuriant growth. **Los sembrados llenan mucho vicio**, the cornfields are luxuriant. 7. Forwardness or caprice of children. **De vicio**, by habit or custom. 8. Vices of horses or mules. 9. **Estar de vicio**, *(LAm.)* To be idle. **Quejarse de vicio**, to complain without cause, or make ado about trifles. **No le podemos quitar el vicio**, we can´t get him out of the habit.

viciosamente [ve-the-o-sah-men'-tay], *adv.* Viciously; falsely; corruptly.

vicioso, sa [ve-the-o'-so, sah], *a.* 1. Vicious. 2. Luxuriant, overgrown, vigorous. 3. Abundant; provided; delightful. 4. *(Prov.)* Spoiled (niños).

vicisitud [ve-the-se-tood'], *f.* Vicissitude, accident (desgracia), upset, sudden change (cambio).

vicisitudinario, ria [ve-the-se-too-de-nah'-re-o, ah], *a.* Changeable, variable.

víctima [veec'-te-mah], *f.* Victim; sacrifice. **Fue víctima de una estafa**, she was the victim of a swindle. **No hay que lamentar víctimas del accidente**, there were no casualties in the accident.

victimario [vec-te-mah'-re-o], *m.* Servant who attends the sacrificing priest.

víctor, vítor [veec'-tor, vee'-tor], *m.* 1. Shout, cry of acclamation. Long live! 2. Public rejoicing in honor of the achiever of some glorious deed. 3. Tablet containing a eulogy of the hero of a festival.

victorear [vic-to-ray-ar'], *va.* To shout, to acclaim, to cheer, to applaud. *V.* VITOREAR.

victoria [vic-to'-re-ah], *f.* Victory, triumph, conquest, palm. *-int.* Victory. **Cantar victoria**, or *la* **Victoria,** to triumph, to obtain victory or to rejoice for victory.

victorial [vic-to-re-ahl'], *a.* Relating to victory.

victoriosamente [vic-to-re-o'-sah-men-tay], *adv.* Victoriously.

victorioso, sa [vic-to-re-oh'-so, sah], *a.* 1. Victorious, conquering. 2. Title given to warriors.

vicuña [ve-coo'-nyah], *f.* Vicuña or vicugna, a South American wool-bearing quadruped, allied to the *Alpaca*, celebrated for in wool.

vid [veed], *f. (Bot.)* Vine, grapevine.

vida [vee'-dah], *f.* 1. Life. 2. Living, continuance in life. 3. Life, the duration of it. 4. Livelihood (profesión). 5. Life, conducts behavior, deportment; state, condition. 6. Life history of one's actions during life. 7. Aliment necessary to preserve life. 8. *(Met.)* Life, anything animating and agreeable, liveliness (de ojos, mirada). **Vida mía or mi vida**, my life: expression of endearment. 9. State of grace, eternal life. 10. Principle of nutrition, vital motions or functions. 11. *(Law.)* The determined number of ten years. **Buscar la vida**, to earn an honest livelihood; to scrutinize the life of another. **Dar mala vida**, to treat very ill. **Darse buena vida**, to give oneself up to the pleasures of life; to conform oneself to reason and law. **De por vida**, for life, during life. **En mi vida** or **en la vida**, never. **Hacer vida**, to live together as husband and wife. **Personas de mala vida**, profligate libertines. **Pasar la vida**, to live very frugally, on necessaries only. **Saber las vidas ajenas**, to spy into other people's affairs. **Tener siete vidas**, to have escaped many perils. **Un amigo de toda la vida**, a lifelong friend. **Vida perra**, dog´s life. **Escapar con vida**, to escape live. **Vender cara la vida**, to sell one´s life dearly.

vidalita [ve-da-lee'-tah], *f.* A special form of Argentine folk poem.

vida media [vee'-dah may'-de-ah], *f. (Chem.)* Half life.

vide [vee'-day] *(imp.* of Lat. videre). See: a direction, in books, to the reader. Commonly abbreviated to **V.** *V.* VÉASE.

vidente [ve-den'-tay], *pa.* He who sees, seeing.

video [vee'-day-o], *m.* Video; video (aparato). **Película de video**, videofilm.

videocámara [vee'-day-o cah'-mah-rah], *f.* Video camera.

videoclub [vee'-day-o cloob], *m.* Videoclub.

videograbadora [vee'-day-o grah-bah-do'-dah], *f.* Video recorder.

videoteca [vee'-day-o-tay-cah], *f.* Video library.

videojuego [vee'-day-o-hoo-ay'-go], *m.* Video game.

¡vidita! [ve-dee'-tah], *f.* My life. Used in South America as an expression of tenderness.

vidorra [ve-dor'-rah], *f.* Gay life, easy life.

vidriado [ve-dre-ah'-do], *m.* Glazed earthenware, crockery.

vidriado, da [ve-dre-ah'-do, dah], *a.* Fretful, peevish, cross. *-pp.* of VIDRIAR.

vidriar [ve-dre-ar'], *va.* To varnish, to glaze earthenware.

vidriera [ve-dre-ay'-rah], *f.* 1. A glass window. 2. A glass case or cover. 3. *(LAm.)* Shop window (escaparate). 4. *(Carib.)* Tobacco stall.

vidriería [ve-dre-ay-ree'-ah], *f.* Glazier's shop, a shop where glasswares are sold: glasshouse, glass-shop, glass ware.

vidriero [ve-dre-ay'-ro], *m.* Glazier, a dealer in glass, glassmaker.

vidrio [vee'-dre-o], *m.* 1. Glass. **Vidrio colorado** or **teñido de color**, stained glass. **Vidrio plano** or **de vidresera**, Window glass. 2. Vessel or other thing made of glass. 3. Anything very nice and brittle. 4. A very touchy person. 5. *(Poet.)* Water. **Pagar los vidrios rotos**, to receive undeserved punishment, to carry the can. 6. *(Cono Sur)* Bottle of liquor.

vidrioso, sa [ve-dre-o'-so, sah], *a.* 1. Vitreous, brittle (frágil), glassy. 2. Slippery, as from ice or sleet (superficie). 3. Peevish, touchy, irascible. 4. Very delicate (asunto).

vidual [ve-doo-ahl'], *a.* Belonging to widowhood.

viduño, vidueño [ve-doo'-nyo], *m.* Peculiar quality of grapes or vines. *V.* VEDUÑO.

viejarrón, na [ve-ay-har-rone', nah], *m. (Coll.)* An old codger: it implies contempt.

viejazo [ve-ay-hah´-tho], *m. (Coll.)* An old man worn out with age.

viejecito, ita, viejezuelo, ela [ve-ay-hay-thee'-to], *a.* somewhat old.

viejo, ja [ve-ay'-ho, hah], **a.** 1. Old, stricken in years. 2. Ancient, antiquated. 3. Applied to a youth of judgment and knowledge beyond his years. **Cuentos de viejas**, old woman´s stories. **Perro viejo**, *(Coll.)* a keen, clever, experienced person; old dog. **Viejo como el mundo**, as old as the hills. **Hacerse viejo**, to grow old. *-m & f.* 1. Old person. 2. **Mi viejo**, my dad.

vienés, sa [ve-ay-nes', sah], *a.* Viennese of Vienna (Austria).

vientecillo [ve-en-tay-theel'-lyo], *m. dim.* A light wind.

viento [ve-en'-to], *a.* 1. Wind (corriente de aire). 2. The air, and the space it occupies. 3. Wind, its direction from a particular point. 4. Wind, anything insignificant or light as wind; vanity, petty pride. 5. Windage of a gun. 6. Scent of dogs (de perros). 7. Nape-bone of a dog, between the ears. 8. Rope or cord, by which a thing is suspended. 9. Anything that violently agitates the mind. 10. That which contributes to an end. 11. Conceit (vanidad). 12. *(And.)* Strings of a kite (cometa). 13. *(CAm. Carib. Med.)* Rheumatism. **Viento galerno**, a fresh gale. **Viento en popa**, wind right aft. **Viento terral** or **de tierra**, a land breeze. **El viento refresca**, *(Naut.)* the wind freshens. **Hace mucho viento**, it is windy. **Echar a uno con viento fresco**, to chuck somebody out. **Contra viento y marea**, come hell or high water.

vientre [ve-en'-tray], *m.* 1. Belly (estómago), abdomen. 2. Fetus in the womb (matriz); pregnancy. 3. The belly or widest part of vessels (de vasija). 4. The body, or essential part of an instrument or act. 5. Stomach, when speaking of a great eater. **Desde el vientre de su madre**, from his birth. **Vientre flojo**, looseness of the bowels.

vientrecillo [ve-en-tra-theel'-lyo], *m. dim.* Ventricle.

viernes [ve-err'-nes], *m.* 1. Friday. 2. Fast day, when meat is not to be eaten. **Cara de viernes**, a wan, thin face. **Viernes Santo**, Good Friday.

viga [vee'-gah], *f.* Beam, balk (de madera). **Viga trasversal**, crossbeam.

vigente [ve-hen'-tay], *a.* In force (leyes, regulaciones).

vigésimo, ma [ve-hay'-se-mo, mah], *a.* Twentieth.

vigía [ve-hee´-ah], *f.* 1. *(Naut.)* Rock which projects but slightly from the sea. 2. *V.* ATALAYA. 3. Act of watching. 3. Lookout, watch.

vigiar [ve-he-ar'], *vn. (Naut.)* To look out, to watch.

vigilancia [ve-he-lahn'-the-ah], *f.* Vigilance, watchfulness, heedfulness. **Burlar la vigilancia de uno,** to escape somebody´s vigilance.

vigilante [ve-he-lahn'-tay], *a.* Watchful, vigilant, careful. *-m.* 1. Watchman (guardián), guard. 2. *(Cono Sur)* Policeman (policía).

vigilantemente [ve-he-lahn'-tay-men-tay], *adv.* Vigilantly, heedfully.

vigilar [ve-he-lar'], *vn.* To watch over (velar por), to keep guard, to look after (cuidar), to tend (máquina); to guard (frontera). **Vigilar a los niños para que no se hagan daño,** to see that children come to no harm.

vigilativo, va [ve-he-lah-tee'-vo, vah], *a.* That which makes watchful.

vigilia [ve-hee'-le-ah], *f.* 1. The act of being awake (estar sin dormir), or on the watch. 2. Lucubration, nocturnal study (estudio). 3. Vigil, a fast kept before a holiday; service used on the night before a holiday. 4. Watchfulness, want of sleep. 5. Watch, limited time for keeping guard. 6. Office of the dead, to be sung in churches. **Pasar la noche de vigilia,** to spend a night without sleep.

vigor [ve-gor'], *m.* Vigor (fuerza), strength, force, energy, drive (empuje).

vigorar [ve-go-rar'], *va.* To strengthen, to invigorate.

vigorizar [ve-go-re-thar'], *va.* 1. To invigorate. 2. *(Met.)* To animate, to inspirit.

vigorosamente [ve-go-ro'-sah-men-tay], *adv.* Vigorously, lustily.

vigorosidad [ve-go-ro-se-dahd'], *f.* Vigorous, strength.

vigoroso, sa [ve-go-ro´-so, sah], *a.* Vigorous, strong, active; generous.

vigota [ve-go´-tah], *f. (Naut.)* Dead-eye, chain plate.

viguería [ve-gay-ree´-ah], *f. (Naut.)* The timber-work of a vessel.

vigués, sa [ve-gays', sah], *a. & n.* Native of Vigo.

vigueta [ve-gay'-tah], *f. dim.* A small beam.

vihuela [ve-oo-ay'-lah], *f.* Guitar.

vihuelista [ve-oo-ay-lees'-tah], *com.* Guitar-player.

vil [veel'], *a.* 1. Mean, despicable (conducta), sordid, servile. 2. Worthless, infamous, ungrateful, vile. 3. Contemptible, abject, paltry.

vilano [ve-lah'-no], *m.* Burr or down of the thistle.

vileza [ve-lay'-thah], *f.* 1. Meanness, vileness, depravity. 2. Contemptibleness, abjectness. 3. A disgraceful action, an infamous deed; turpitude, paltriness. 4. Rabble, mob.

vilipendiador, ra [ve-le-pen-de-ah-dor', rah], *a. & n.* Reviling; reviler.

vilipendiar [ve-le-pen-de-ar'], *pa.* To contemn, to revile.

vilipendio [ve-le-pen'-de-o], *m.* Contempt (desprecio), disdain.

vilipendioso, sa [vc-le-pen-de-oh'-so, sah], *a.* Contemptible, causing contempt.

villa [veel'-lyah], *f.* 1. Town which enjoys by charter peculiar privileges. 2. Corporation of magistrates of a **villa.**

villadiego [vil-lyah-de-ay'-go], *m.* **Coger** or **tomar las de Villadiego,** to run away, to pack off bag and baggage.

villaje [vil lyah'-hay] *m,* Village; hamlet.

villanaje [vil-lyah-nah'-hay], *m.* Villanage, the middling class in villages; peasantry.

villanamente [vil-lyah'-nah-men-tay], *adv.* Rudely, boorishly.

villancejo, villancete [vil-lyan-thay'-ho], *m. V.* VILLANCICO.

villancico [vil-lyan-thee'-co], *m.* Christmas carol: a metric composition sung in churches on certain festivals.

villanciquero [vil-lan-the-kay'-ro], *m.* One who composes small metric compositions, to be sung in churches.

villanchón, na [vil-lyan-chone´, nah], *a.* Clownish, rustic, rude.

villanería [vil-lyah-nay-ree´-ah], *f.* 1. Lowness of birth, meanness. *V.* VILLANÍA. 2. Middling classes of society. *V.* VILLANAJE.

villanesco, ca [vil-lyah-nes´-co, cah], *a.* Rustic, rude, boorish.

villanía [vil-lyah-nee´-ah], *f.* 1. Lowness of birth, meanness. 2. Villainy (cualidad), villainousness, rusticity: indecorous word or act.

villano, na [vil-lyah´-no, nah], *a.* 1. Belonging to the lowest class of country people. 2. Rustic, clownish. 3. Worthless, unworthy. 4. Villainous, wicked.

villano [vil-lyah´-no], *m.* 1. A kind of Spanish dance. 2. A vicious horse. 3. Villain, a rustic; an unsociable villager.

villanote [vil-lyah-no'-tay], *a. aug.* of VILLANO. Highly rude.

villazgo [vil-lyath´-go], *m.* 1. Charter of a town. 2. Tax laid upon towns.

villeta [vil-lyay'-tah], *f. dim.* A small town or borough.

villica, ita [vil-lyee'-cah], *f. dim.* Small town.

villivina [vil-lye-vee'-nah], *f.* A kind of linen.

villoría [vil-lyo-ree'-ah], *f.* Farm-house.

villorín [vil-lyo-reen´], *m.* A sort of coarse cloth.

villorrio [vil-lyor'-re-o], *m.* A small village; a miserable little place or hamlet.

vilmente [veel-men'-tay], *adv.* Vilely; abjectly, contemptibly, villainously.

vilo [vee'-lo]. *adv.* A word only used adverbially, as, **en vilo,** (1) in the air. (2.) *(Met.)* Insecurely.

vilordo, da [ve-lor'-do, dah], *a.* Slothful, lazy, heavy.

vilorta [ve-lor'-tah], *f.* 1. Ring of twisted willow. 2. A kind of cricket, played in Old Castile.

vilorto [ve-lor'-to], *m.* 1. A certain reed which grows in the north of Spain. 2. Snare of this reed.

vimbre [veem'-bray], *m. (Bot.)* Osier. *V.* MIMBRE.

vimbrera [veem-bray'-rah], *f. V.* MIMBRERA.

vinagre [ve-nah'-gray], *m.* 1. Vinegar. 2. Acidity, sourness. 3. *(Met. Coll.)* A person of a peevish temper.

vinagrera [ve-nah-gray'-rah], *f.* 1. Vinegar cruet. 2. Caster, with both vinegar and oil-cruets. 3. *(Peru and Colombia) V.* ACEDÍA.

vinagrero [ve-nah-gray'-ro], *m.* Vinegar-merchant.

vinagreta [ve-nah-gray-tah], *f. (Culin.)* Vinaigrette (salsa).

vinagrillo [ve-nah-greel'-lyo], *m.* 1. *(Dim.)* Weak vinegar. 2. A cosmetic lotion, used by women. 3. Rose-vinegar; snuff prepared with rose-vinegar.

vinagroso, sa [ve-nah-gro'-so, sah], *a.* 1. flourish, peevish, fretful. 2. *(Coll.)* In bad condition.

vinajera [ve-nah-hay'-rah], *f.* Vessel in which wine and water are served at the altar for the mass.

vinariego [ve-nah-re-ay'-go], *m.* Vintager, one who possesses and cultivates a vineyard.

vinario, ria [ve-nah'-re-o, ah], *a.* Belonging to wine.

vinatería [ve-nah-tay-ree'-ah], *f.* 1. Wine-trade (comercio). 2. Wine-shop (tienda).

vinatero [ve-nah-tay'-ro], *m.* Vintner, wine-merchant.

vinaza [ve-nah'-thah], *f.* Last wine drawn from the lees.

vinazo [ve-nah'-tho], *m.* Very strong wine.

vinculable [vin-coo-lah'-blay], *a.* That may be entailed.

vinculación [vin-coo-lah-the-on´], *f.* Entail, act of entailing.

vincular [vin-coo-lar'], *va.* 1. To entail an estate. 2. To ground or toured upon: to assure. 3. To continue, to perpetuate. 4. To secure with chains. **Vincular su suerte a la de otro,** to make one´s fate depend on somebody else´s.

vínculo [veen'-coo-lo], *m.* 1. Tie, link, chain. 2. Entail, an estate entailed. 3. Charge or encumbrance laid upon a foundation. **Vínculo de parentesco,** family ties.

vindicación [vin-de-cah-the-on'], *f.* 1. Vindication, just vengeance or satisfaction for a grievance (venganza). 2. The act of giving every one his due.

vindicar [vin-de-car'], *va.* 1. To vindicate, to revenge, to avenge (vengar). 2. To vindicate (justificar), to claim, to reclaim, to assert. 3. To vindicate, to justify, to defend, to support.

vindicativo, va [vin-de-cah-tee'-vo, vah], *a.* 1. Vindictive, revengeful. 2. Defensive, vindicatory.

vindicta [vin-deec'-tah], *f.* Vengeance, revenge.

vínico, ca [vee'-ne-co, cah], *a.* Vinic, belonging to wine.

vinícola [ve-nee'-co-lah], *a.* Relating to production of wine, wine-growing. -*m. V.* VINARIEGO.

vinicultor, ra [ve-ne-cool-tor'], *m & f.* Wine grower.

viniente [ve-ne-en'-tay], *pa.* Coming.

vinificación [ve-ne-fe-cah-the-on'], *f.* Vivification, fermentation of must and its conversion into wine.

vinílico, ca [ve-nee'-le-co, cah], *a.* Vinyl.

vinilo [ve-nee'-lo], *m. (Chem.)* Vinyl.

vino [vee'-no], *m.* 1. Wine. **Vino clarete**, claret or pale red wine. **Vino de agujas**, sharp, rough wine. **Vino de cuerpo**, a strong-bodied wine. **Vino dulce**, sweet, clear wine. **Vino tinto**, red wine. **Una buena cosecha de vino**, a good vintage. 2. Preparation of fruit or vegetables by fermentation, called by the general name of *wine.* 3. Anything which intoxicates. **Vino de Jerez**, sherry wine. **Vino de Borgoña**, Burgundy wine. **Vino de Champaña**, Champagne wine. **Vino de Oporto**, Port wine. **Vino de frambuesa**, raspberry wine. **Vino de grosella**, currant wine. **Vino de consagrar**, communion wine. **Ahogar las penas en vino**, to drown one's sorrows. **Bautizar el vino**, to water down the wine.

vinolencia [ve-no-len'-the-ah], *f.* Intoxication, inebriation, excess in drinking wine.

vinolento, ta [ve-no-len'-to, tah], *a.* Intoxicated, inebriated.

vinosidad [ve-no-se-dahd'], *f.* Quality of being vinous, vinosity.

vinoso, sa [ve-no'-so, sah], *a.* 1. Vinous, vinose. 2. Intoxicated, inebriated.

vinote [ve-no'-tay], *m.* The liquid remaining in the boiler after the wine is distilled and the brandy made.

vinterana [vin-tay-rah'-nah], *f. (Bot.)* A tree of South America, the bark of which is known by the name of «white cinnamon» in Ecuador, and used as a substitute for cinnamon.

viña [vee'-nyah], *f.* Vineyard (viñedo). **La viña del Señor**, the church.

viñadero [ve-nyah-day'-ro], *m.* Keeper of a vineyard.

viñador [ve-nyah-dor'], *m.* Cultivator of vines; husbandman.

viñedo [ve-nyay'-do], *m.* Country or district abounding in vineyards.

viñero [ve-nyay'-ro], *m.* Vintager who owns and cultivates vineyards.

viñeta [ve-nyay'-tah], *f.* 1. Vignette, an ornament at the beginning or end of chapters in books. 2. *(Not. Acad.)* Vignette, a photograph, engraving, etc., having a border gradually shaded off.

viñetero [ve-nyay-tay'-ro], *m. (Typ.)* A font-case for ornamental letters and vignettes.

viola [ve-o'-lah], *f.* 1. Viola, a tenor violin or alto. 2. *(Bot.)* Violet. *V.* ALHELÍ.

violáceo, ea [ve-o-lah'-thay-o, ah], *a.* Violaceous, violet-colored.

violación [ve-o-lah-the-on'], *f.* Violation.

violado, da [ve-o-lah'-do, dah], *a. & pp.* of VIOLAR. 1. Having the color of violets; made or confectioned with violets. 2. Violated.

violador, ra [ve-o-lah-dor', rah], *m. & f.* Violator, profaner, raper.

violar [ve-o-lar'], *va.* 1. To violate a law, to offend (ley). 2. To ravish, to rape, to violate a woman. 3. To spoil, to tarnish. 4. To profane or pollute the church.

violencia [ve-o-len'-the-ah], *f.* 1. Violence, impetuousness, compulsion, force. 2. Wrong construction, erroneous interpretation. 3. Rape. 4. Excessiveness, intenseness of cold, etc. **Apelar a la violencia**, to resort to violence. **No violencia**, non-violence.

violentamente, *adv.* 1. Violently, forcibly. 2. Unnaturally. 3. Embarrassingly. 4. Distortedly (interpretación).

violentar [ve-o-len-tar'], *va.* 1. To enforce by violent means, to violate. 2. To put a wrong construction on a passage or writing. 3. *(Met.)* To open or break a thing by force (puerta),

to enter a place against the will of its proprietor. -*vr.* To be violent.

violento, ta [ve-o-len'-to, tah], *a.* 1. Violent, impetuous, boisterous, furious. 2. Violent, forced, unnatural (postura). 3. Strained, absurd, erroneous. 4. Embarrassed, awkward (estado de persona). 5. *(LAm.)* Quick, sudden. **Mostrarse violento**, to turn violent. **Para mí todo esto es un poco violento**, this is all a bit awkward.

violero [ve-o-lay'-ro], *m.* A player upon the viola.

violeta [ve-o-lay'-tah], *f. (Bot.)* Violet.

violeto [ve-o-lay'-to], *m.* A clingstone peach. *V.* PELADILLO.

violín [ve-o-leen'], *m.* 1. Violin (instrumento), fiddle. 2. Fiddler, violinist.

violinete [ve-o-le-nay'-tay], *m.* Kit, a pocket-violin, used by dancing-masters.

violinista [ve-o-le-nees'-tah], *m.* Violinist.

violón [ve-o-lone'], *m.* 1. Bass-viol, double bass (instrumento). 2. Player on the bass-viol.

violoncelo [ve-o-lon-thay'-lo], *m.* Violoncello.

violoncillo [ve-o-lon-theel'-lyo], *m.* Small bass-viol or player on it.

violonchelo [ve-o-lon-chay'-lo], *m. V.* VIOLONCELO.

vipéreo, rea [ve-pay'-ray-o, ah], *a. V.* VIPERINO

viperino, na [ve-pay-ree'-no, nah], *a.* Viperine, viperous.

viquitortes [ve-ke-tor'-tes], *m. pl. (Naut.)* Quarter-gallery knees.

vira [vee'-rah], *f.* 1. A kind of light dart or arrow of ancient warfare. 2. Stuffing between the upper leather and inner sole. 3. Welt of a shoe.

viracocha [ve-rah-co'-chah], *m. (Peru)* Name of the Creator among the Incas, and which the Indians later applied to their white conquerors.

virada [ve-rah'-dah], *f. (Naut.)* Tacking, tack. **Virada de bordo**, tack putting the ship about.

virador [ve-ra-dor'], *m.* 1. *(Naut.)* Top rope; viol. 2. Liquid used in photography to tone.

virar [ve-rar'], *vn* 1. *(Naut.)* To tack, to put about. 2. *(And. Cono Sur)* To turn round (volver); to turn over (invertir). -*va.* To wind, to twist. **Virar el cable**, to heave taut. **Virar de bordo**, to tack or go about.

viratón [ve-rah-tone'], *m.* A kind of large daft or arrow.

virazón [ve-rah-thone'], *f. (Naut.)* Sea-breeze.

víreo [vee'-ray-o], *m. V.* VIRIO.

virgen [veer'-hen], *com.* Virgin, maid. Man who has not had carnal connection with a woman.-*a.* Anything in its pure and primitive state. **Cera virgen**, virgin wax. **Plata virgen**, native silver. -*f.* 1. One of the upright posts, between which the beam of an oil-mill moves. 2. The Holy Virgin Mary; image of the Virgin. 3. A nun. **Vírgenes**, nuns vowed to chastity.

virgiliano, na [veer-he-le-ah'-no, nah], *a.* Virgilian, characteristic of Virgil.

virginal [veer-he-nahl'], *a.* Virginal, maiden, virgin.

virgíneo, nea [veer-hee'-nay-o, ah], *a. V.* VIRGINAL.

virginia, [veer-hee'-ne-ah], *f. (Bot.)* Virginia tobacco.

virginidad [veer-he-ne-dahd'], *f.* Virginity, maidenhood.

virgo [veer'-go], *m.* 1. *(Ast.)* Virgin, a sign of the zodiac. 2. Virginity. 3. *(Anat.)* Hymen.

virguería [veer-gay-ree'-ah], *f.* Silly adornment (adorno), frill; pretty thing (objeto). **Hacer virguerías con algo**, to be clever enough to handle something well.

vírgula [veer'-goo-lah], *f.* 1. A small rod. 2. Slight line.

virgulilla [veer-goo-leel'-lyah], *f.* 1. Comma: it is called *coma* in printing and *tilde* in writing. 2. Any fine stroke or light line.

virgulto [veer-gool'-to], *m.* Shrub, bush, small tree.

viril [ve-reel'], *m.* 1. A clear and transparent glass. 2. A small locket or round case in the center of the monstrance, with two plates of glass, between which the host is placed, to expose it to the congregation in Catholic churches.

viril [ve-reel'], *a.* Virile, manly.

virilidad [ve-re-le-dahd'], *f.* 1. Virility (cualidad), manhood (estado). 2. Vigor, strength.

virilla, ita [ve-ree'-lyah], *f. dim.* of VIRA. **Virilla**, ornament of gold or silver formerly worn in shoes.

virilmente [ve-reel'-men-tay], *adv.* In a manly manner.

virio [vee'-re-o], *m. (Orn.)* Vireo, a green and yellow bird of the United States.

viripotente [ve-re-po-ten'-tay], *a.* Marriageable, nubile (mujeres).

virol [ve-role'], *m. (Her.) V.* PERFIL.

virola [ve-ro'-lah], *f.* Collar, hoop, ferrule, ring put upon canes, pocket-knives, etc.

virolento, ta [ve-ro-len'-to, tah], *a.* Diseased with small-pox, pock-marked.

virología [ve-ro-lo-hee'-ah], *f.* Virology.

virotazo [ve-ro-tah'-tho], *m.* 1. *(Aug.) V.* VIROTÓN. 2. Wound with a dart or arrow.

virote [ve-ro'-tay], *m.* 1. Shaft, dart, arrow. 2. Dude, fop, a showy, vain young man; inflated person. 3. A long iron rod fastened to a collar on the neck of a slave, who showed an intention of running away. 4. *(Prov.)* Vine three years old. 5. A puffed-up man, too serious and erratic. 6. A carnival trick. **Mirar por el virote,** *(Met.)* to be attentive to one's own concerns or convenience.

virotón [ve-ro-tone'], *m. aug.* Large dart or arrow.

virreina [vir-ray'-e-nah], *f.* Lady of a viceroy.

virreinato, virreino [vir-ray-e-nah'-to], *m.* Viceroyship; duration of this office; the district governed by a viceroy.

virrey [vir-ray'-e], *m.* Viceroy.

virtual [veer-too-ahl'], *a.* 1. Virtual (real). 2. Potential (potencial).

virtualidad [veer-too-ah-le-dahd'], *f.* Virtuality, efficacy.

virtualmente [veer-too-ahl'-men-tay], *adv.* Virtually, in effect.

virtud [veer-tood'], *f.* 1. Virtue (capacidad), efficacy (eficacia), power, force. 2. Virtue, acting power. 3. Virtue, efficacy without virtuous action. 4. Virtue, medicinal efficacy. 5. Virtue, moral goodness, integrity, rectitude. 6. Habit, disposition, virtuous life. 7. Vigor, courage. 8. In mechanics, the moving power. 9. In the sacraments, their efficacy and value. **En virtud de,** in virtue of. **Hacer virtud,** to do well.

virtuosamente [veer-too-oh'-sah-men-tay], *adv.* Virtuously.

virtuoso, sa [veer-too-oh'-so, sah], *a.* 1. Virtuous, just. 2. Powerful, vigorous.

viruela [ve-roo-ay'-lah], *f.* 1. Pock, a pustule on the skin. 2. Small-pox. **Picado de viruelas,** pockmarked.

virulencia [ve-roo-len'-the-ah], *f.* 1. Virulence, virus. 2. Virulence, acrimony, malignance.

virulento, ta [ve-roo-len'-to, tah], *a.* 1. Virulent, malignant. 2. Purulent.

virus [vee'-roos], *m. (Med.)* Virus, poison, contagion.

viruta [ve-roo'-tah], *f.* Shaving, a thin slice of wood; chip. *-pl.* Cuttings.

visa [vee'-sah], *f.* Visa.

visado [ve-sah'-do], *m.* Visa; permit. **Visado de tránsito,** transit visa.

visaje [ve-sah'-hay], *m.* Grimace. **Hacer visajes,** to make wry faces.

visar [ve-sar'], *va.* To examine a document, to visé (pasaporte).

víscera [vees'-thay-rah], *f.* Viscus, any organ of the body which has an appropriate use. *-pl.* viscera. **Las víceras,** the viscera.

visceral [vis-thay-rahl'], *a.* Visceral, belonging to the viscera.

viscina [vis-thee'-nah], *f. (Chem.)* Viscin, a principle peculiar to birdlime.

viscosa [vis-co'-sah], *f. (Chem.)* Viscose (for making rayon and other synthetic fabrics).

viscosidad [vis-co-se-dahd'], *f.* Viscosity (cualidad), glutinousness, glutinous or viscous matter.

viscoso, sa [vis-co'-so, sah], *a.* Viscous, viscid, glutinous, mucilaginous.

visera [ve-say'-rah], *f.* 1. Eye protector, eye shade, visor, that part of the head-piece which covers the face. 2. Box with a spy-hole, through which a pigeon-keeper observes the pigeons. 3. *(Cuba)* Blind of a horse's bridle.

visibililad [ve-se-be-le-dahd'], *f.* Visibility. **La visibilidad queda reducida a cero,** visibility is down to nil.

visible [ve-see'-blay], *a.* 1. Visible, perceptible to the eye. 2. Visible, apparent, open, conspicuous.

visiblemente [ve-see'-blay-men-tay], *adv.* Visibly, clearly; evidently.

visicalc [ve-se-calc'], *(Comput.)* Visicalc (visible calculator).

visigodo [ve-se-go'-do], *a.* Visigothic.

visillo [ve-seel'-lyo], *m.* Type of window, blind or curtain.

visión [ve-se-on'], *f.* 1. Sight, vision object of sight. 2. Vision, the act of seeing (vista). 3. *(Coll.)* A frightful, ugly, or ridiculous person. 4. Phamtom, apparition, freak . 5. Spiritual vision, revelation, prophecy; beautifical vision. **Ver visiones,** to be led by fancy, to build castles in the air. **Visión beatífica,** celestial bliss. **Su visión del problema,** his view of the problem.

visionario, ria [ve-se-o-nah'-re-o, ah], *a. & n.* Visionary; not real; fanatical.

visir [ve-seer'], *m.* Vizier, the Turkish prime minister.

visita [ve-see'-tah], *f.* 1. Visit. 2. Visitor (persona), visitant. 3. Visit to a temple to pray. 4. Visit of a doctor to a patient. 5. Visitation, inquisition. 6. Recognition, register, examination. 7. House in which the tribunal of ecclesiastical visitors is held. 8. Body of ministers who form a tribunal to inspect prisons; visit to prisons. **Derecho de visita,** right of search. **Visita de médico,** very short call. **Estar de visita en,** to be on a visit to. *-pl. (Coll.)* Frequent visits; haunts, places of resort.

visitación [ve-se-tah-the-on'], *f.* Visitation, visiting, visit.

visitador, ra [ve-se-tah-dor', rah], *m. & f.* visitor (visitante), visitant. 2. Visitor, an occasional judge, searcher, surveyor.

visitante [ve-se-tahn'-tay], *m. & f.* Visitor, guest.

visitar [ve-se-tar'], *va.* 1. To visit, to pay a visit; to visit a temple or church, to visit a patient as physician. 2. To make a judicial visit, search, or survey; to try weights and measures. 3. To search ships; to examine prisons. 4. To travel, to traverse many countries. 5. To inform oneself personally of anything. 6. To appear, as a celestial spirit. 7. To frequent a place. 8. To visit religious persons and establishments as an ecclesiastical judge. 9. *(Theol.)* To send a special counsel from heaven. 10. *(Law.)* To make an abstract of the charge against a prisoner at visitation. *-vr.* 1. To visit, to keep up the intercourse of ceremonial salutations at the houses of each other. 2. To absent oneself from the choir. **Visitar los altares,** to pray before each altar for some pious purpose.

visiteo [ve-se-tay'-o], *m.* Making or receiving of many visits.

visitero, ra [ve-se-tay'-ro, rah], *a. (Coll.)* Visitor, frequent caller.

visitón [ve-se-tone'], *m. (Aug.* of VISITA) *(Coll.)* A long and tedious visit.

visivo, va [ve-see'-vo, vah], *a.* Visive, having the power of seeing.

vislumbrar [vis-loom-brar'], *va.* 1. To have a glimmering sight of a thing: not to perceive it distinctly (entrever). 2. *(Met.)* To know imperfectly, to conjecture by indications. *-vr.* To glimmer, to appear faintly.

vislumbre [vis-loom'-bray], *f.* 1. A glimmering light. 2. Glimmer, glimmering, faint or imperfect view. 3. Conjecture, surmise. 4. Imperfect knowledge, confused perception. 5. Appearance, slight resemblance. 6. Projecting part of a thing which is scarcely discovered.

viso [vee'-so], *m.* 1. Prospect, an elevated spot, affording an extensive view. 2. Luster, the shining surface of things; brilliant reflection of light. 3. Color, cloak, presence, pretext. 4. Apparent likeness; aspect, appearance (aspecto). 5. Gleam

visón

(metal). **A dos visos**, with a double view or design. **Al viso de**, at the sight of.

visón [ve-son'], *m.* Mink.

visor [ve-sor'], *m.* Viewfinder (camara).

visorio, ria [ve-so'-re-o, ah], *a.* Belonging to the sight, visual.

víspera [ves'-pay-rah], *f.* 1. Evening before the day in question; the last evening before a festival. 2. Fore-runner, prelude. 3. Immediate nearness or succession. *-pl.* 1. vesper, one of the parts into which the Romans divided the day. 2. Vespers, the evening service. **En vísperas de**, at the eve of. **Vísperas Sicilianas**, Sicilian vespers: a threat of general punishment.

vista [vees'-tah], *f.* 1. Sight, vision, the sense of seeing. 2. Sight, the act of seeing, vision, view. 3. Sight, eye, eyesight, organ of sight. 4. Aspect, appearance (aspecto). 5. Prospect, view, landscape, vista. 6. Apparition, appearance. 7. Meeting, interview. 8. Clear knowledge or perception. 9. Relation, respective connection, comparison. 10. Intent, view, purpose (intención). 11. First stage of a suit at law. 12. Opinion, judgment. 13. Foresight (perspicacia). 14. View, scene (panorama). 15. Hearing, trial. *-m.* A surveyor in a customhouse. *-f. pl.* 1. Meeting, conference, interview. 2. Presents to a bride by a bridegroom, the day preceding the nuptials. 3. Lights, windows in a building, balconies, verandas. 4. Prospect, an extensive view. **Vista de un pleito**,or **día de la vista de un proceso**, or **una causa**, *(Law.)* the trial or the day of trial of a civil lawsuit, or a criminal prosecution. **A vista de**, in presence of; inconsideration of. **A la vista**, on sight, immediately: before, near, or in view, carefully observing, seeing, or following. **A primera vista**, at first view. **Aguzar la vista**, to sharpen the sigh or perception. **Dar una vista**, to give a passing glance. **Echar la vista**, to choose mentally. **¡Hasta la vista!** good-bye! **Perderse de vista**, *(Coll. and Met.)* to have great superiority in its line (slang, to be «Out of sight»). **Conocer de vista**, to know by sight. **Echar una vista**, to look after. **Tener vista**, to be showy; to be beautiful. **Hacer la vista gorda**, to wink, to connive. **En vista de**, in consequence of; in consideration of. **Comer y tragar con la vista**, *(Met.)* to have a fierce and terrible aspect. **No tenemos ningún cambio a la vista**, we do not have any change in view. **Con la vista puesta en**, with one´s eyes fixed on. **Bajar la vista**, to look down. **A 5 años vista**, 5 years from then. **Con vistas a una solución del problema**, with a view to solving the problem.

vistazo [vees-tah'-tho], *m.* Glance. **Dar un vistazo**, to glance, to play the eye.

vistillas [vees-teel'-lyas], *f. pl.* Eminence, affording an extensive prospect, views.

visto, ta [vees'-to, tah], *a.* Obvious to the sight, clear. *-pp. irr.* of VER. **El está bien visto** or **mal visto**, he is respected, or not respected. **Eso es bien** or **mal visto**, that is proper, or approved; improper, or disapproved. **Visto bueno** (in manuscript, *V°. B°.*), set after a draft, order, permit, license, account, etc., in public offices, means. The preceding document has been examined and found to be correct; consequently it may signify. Pay the bearer; Let him or the merchandise pass, etc. **Visto es** or **vista está**, it is evident. **No visto**, extraordinary, prodigious. **Visto que**, considering that. **Está muy visto**, it is very common.

vistosamente [vees-to'-sah-men-tay], *adv.* Beautifully, delightfully.

vistoso, sa [vees-to'-so, ash], *a.* Beautiful, delightful, showy (ropa), spectacular (partido).

visual [ve-soo-ahl´], *a.* Visual. **Campo visual**, field of vision.

visualidad [ve-soo-ah-le-dahd'], *f.* Visuality, the agreeable effect which beautiful objects as a whole produce.

visualizar [ve-soo-ah-le-thar'], *va.* 1. *(LAm.)* To see (divisar), to make out. 2. *(Fig.)* To visualize (imaginarse).

visura [ve-soo'-rah], *f.* Minute inspection of anything.

vita [vee'-tah], *f. (Naut.)* Cross-beam on the forecastle, to which cables are fastened.

vital [ve-tahl'], *a.* Vital. **De importancia vital**, of vital importance.

vitalicio, cia [ve-tah-lee'-the-o, ah], *a.* Lasting for life; during life. **Pensión vitalicia**, annuity, life pension. **Empleo vitalicio**, employment or place for life.

vitalicista [ve-tah-le-thees'-tah], *com.* One who enjoys an annuity or income for life.

vitalidad [ve-tah-le-dahd'], *f.* Vitality.

vitalismo [ve-tah-lees'-mo], *m.* Vitalism, a doctrine that the phenomena of the organism are due to so-called vital forces, distinct from the general laws of matter.

vitalista [ve-tah-lees'-tah], *a. & n.* Vitalist, relating to vitalism; one who holds that doctrine.

vitalmente [ve-tahl'-men-tay], *adv.* Vitally.

vitamina [ve-tah-mee'-nah], *f.* Vitamin.

vitando, da [ve-tahn'-do, dah], *a.* 1. That ought to be shunned or avoided. 2. Odious, execrable.

vitela [ve-tay'-lah], *f.* 1. Calf. 2. Vellum, calf-skin.

viteline [ve-tay-lee'-nah], *a.* Of a dark yellow color.

vitícola [ve-tee'-co-lah], *a.* Viticultural, relating to cultivation of the grape. *-m.* Viticulturist, vine-grower.

viticultor, ra [ve-te-cool-tor'], *m & f.* Vine grower (cultivador); proprietor of a vineyard (dueño).

viticultura [ve-te-cool-too'-rah], *f.* Viticulture, culture of the vine.

vitiligo [ve-te-lee´-go], *m.* Vitiligo, a skin disease, characterized by spots showing loss of pigment.

vito [vee'-to], *m.* 1. A lively Andalusian dance. 2. *(Med.)* Chorea. **El baile de San Vito**, St. Vitus' dance.

vitola [ve-to'-lah], *f.* 1. *(Mil.)* Ball caliber, gauge for musket and cannon halls. 2. Measure, size for cigars. 3. *(Amer. Met.)* Appearance, mien, of a person (aspecto).

¡vitor! [vee'-tor], *int.* Shout of joy; Huzza! long live!

vítor [vee'-tor], *m.* 1. Triumphal exclamation; public rejoicing. 2. Tablet containing panegyrical epithets to a hero.

vitorear [ve-to-ray-ar'], *va.* To shout, to lheer, to address with acclamations of joy and praise, to clap.

vitoria [ve-to'-re-ah], *f. V.* VICTORIA.

vitorioso, sa [ve-to-re-oh´-so, sah], *a. V.* VICTORIOSO.

vitre [vee'-tray], *m.* Thin canvas.

vítreo, trea [vee'-tray-o, ah], *a.* Vitreous, glassy, resembling glass.

vitrificable [ve-tre-fe-cah'-blay], *a.* Vitrificable.

vitrificación [ve-tre-fe-cah-the-on'],*f.* Vitrification, vitrifaction.

vitrificar [ve-tre-fe-car'], *va.* To vitrify.

vitrina [ve-tree'-nah], *f.* Glass case (aparador), show case, display-window (escaparate).

vitriolado, da [ve-tre-o-lah'-do, dah], *a.* Vitriolate, vitriolated.

vitriólico, ca [ve-tre-o'-le-co, cah], *a.* Vitriolic.

vitriolo [ve-tre-o´-lo], *m.* Vitriol. **Vitriolo azul**, blue vitriol, copper sulphate. **Vitriolo verde**, green vitriol, ferrous sulphate. **Vitriolo blanco**, white vitriol, zinc sulphate.

vitualla [ve-too-ahl'-lyah], *f.* Victuals, viands, food, provisions: generally used in the plural.

vituallado, da [ve-too-al-lyah'-do, dah], *a.* Victualled, provided with victuals.

vitulino, na [ve-too-lee'-no, nah], *a.* Belonging to a calf.

vituperable [ve-too-pay-rah'-blay], *a.* Vituperable, blameworthy, condemnable.

vituperación [ve-too-pay-rah-the-on'], *f.* Vituperation.

vituperador, ra [ve-too-pay-rah-dor', rah], *m. & f.* A blamer, censurer.

vituperante [ve-too-pay-rahn'-tay], *pa.* Vituperating, censuring, decrying.

vituperar [ve-too-pay-rar'], *va.* To vituperate, to censure, to reproach, to decry, to condemn.

vituperio [ve-too-pay'-re-o], *m*. 1. Vituperation, reproach (reproche), blame, censure. 2. Infamy, disgrace.

vituperiosamente [ve-too-pay-re-o-sah-men'-tay], *adv*. Opprobriously, reproachfully.

vituperosamente [ve-too-pay-ro-sah-men'-tay], *adv*. Reproachfully.

vituperoso, sa [ve-too-pay-ro'-so, sah], *a*. Opprobrious, reproachful.

viuda [ve-oo'-dah], *f*. 1. Widow (persona). **Condesa viuda de**, countess widow of. 2. *(Zool.)* Viuda, a noteworthy bird of South America and Africa; a tyrant fly-catcher. 3. *(Bot.)* Mourning widow or mourning bride; scabious.

viudal [ve-oo-dahl'], *a*. Belonging to a widow or widower.

viudedad [ve-oo-day-dahd'], *f*. 1. Widowhood, viduity. 2. Dowry. 3. Usufruct enjoyed during widowhood of the property of a deceased person.

viudez [ve-oo-deth'], *f*. Widowhood.

viudita [ve-oo-dee'-tah], *f. dim*. 1. A spruce little widow. 2. *(Bot.)* Scabious, mourning bride.

viudo [ve-oo'-do], *m*. Widower. -a. Applied to birds that pair.

¡viva! [vee'-vah], *int*. Long live, hurrah, huzza, a shout of joy, triumph, applause, or encouragement. -*m*. Huzza, a shout, a cry of acclamation.

vivac [ve-vahc'], *m*. Town-guard to keep order at night; bivouac, nightguard, a small guard-house.

vivacidad [ve-vah-the-dahd'], *f*. Vivacity, liveliness (personalidad), brightness (inteligencia), vigor; brilliancy.

vivamente [ve-vah-men'-tay], *adv* Vividly, to the life, with a strong resemblance.

vivandero, ra [ve-van-day'-ro, rah], *m. & f. (Mil.)* Sutler.

vivaque [ve-vah'-kay], *m*. Bivouac, a small guard-house.

vivaquear [ve-vah-kay-ar'], *vn*. To bivouac.

vivar [Ve'-var], *m*. 1. Warren for breeding rabbits or other animals; vivary. 2. Burrow a rabbit. 3. Fishpond (estanque).

vivar [ve-var'], *va. (Peru, etc.)* V. VITOREAR.

vivaracho, cha [ve-vah-rah'-cho, cha], *a*. Lively (persona), smart, sprightly, frisky, superficially (atractivo), bright (ojos).

vivario [ve-vah'-re-o], *m*. Fish-pond.

vivaz [ve-vath'], *a*. 1. Lively (vivo), active, vigorous (vigoroso). 2. Ingenious, acute, witty. 3. As used of plants, perennial, evergreen.

vivencia [ve-vayn'-the-ah], *f*. Experience, knowledge gained from experience.

víveres [vee'-vay-res], *m. pl*. Provision for an army or fortress.

vivero [ve-vay'-ro], *m*. 1. *(Bot.)* The mastic-tree. 3. Warren; fish-pond; vivary (de peces). 4. Seedbed (semillero).

viveza [ve-vay'-thah], *f*. 1. Liveliness, vigor, activity, gaiety. 2. Celerity, briskness. 3. Ardor, energy, vehemence. 4. Acuteness, perspicacity, penetration. 5. Witticism. 6. Strong resemblance. 7. Luster, splendor. 8. Grace and brilliancy in the eyes. 9. Inconsiderate word or act. **La viveza de su inteligencia**, the sharpness of his mind. **Contestar con viveza**, to answer sharply.

vividero, ra [ve-ve-day'-ro, rah], *a*. Habitable.

vividor, ra [ve-ve-dor', rah], *m. & f*. A long liver.

vividor, ra [ve-ve-dor', rah], *a*. Frugal, economical, careful, in mode of life.

vivienda [ve-ve-en'-dah], *f*. 1. Dwelling-house, apartments, lodgings. 2. Dwelling, accomodation. **El problema de la vivienda**, the housing problem.

viviente [ve-ve-en'-tay], *a*. Living. **Todo ser viviente**, every living thing.

vivificación [ve-ve-fe-cah-the-on'], *f*. Vivification, enlivening.

vivificador, ra [ve-ve-fe-cah-dor', rah], *m. & f*. One who vivifies, animates, or enlivens.

vivificante [ve-ve-fe-cahn'-tay], *pa*. Vivifying, life-giving.

vivificar [ve-ve-fe-car'], *va*. 1. To vivify, to vivificate, to animate, to enliven. 2. To comfort, to refresh.

vivificativo, va [ve-ve-fe-cah-tee'-vo, vah], *a*. Vivificative, life-giving, animating, comforting.

vivífico, ca [ve-vee'-fe-co, cah], *a*. Vivific, springing from life.

vivíparo, ra [ve-vee'-pah-ro, rah], *a*. Viviparous; opposed to oviparous.

vivir [ve-veer'], *vn*. 1. To have life, to live; to enjoy life. 2. To live, to continue, to last, to keep. 3. To have the means of supporting life. 4. To live; emphatically, to enjoy happiness. 5. To live, to pass life in a certain manner. 6. To be remembered, to enjoy fame. 7. To be, to exist; to be present in memory. 8. To live, to inhabit, to reside, to lodge. 9. To temporize. 10. To guard life. 11. To have eternal life. **Alegría de vivir**, joy of living. **Como se vive se muere**, as we live so shall we die. **No me deja vivir**, he doesn't leave me alone. **¿Quién vive?** *(Mil.)* who is there? **Vivir para ver**, live and learn (or strange enough). **Ha vivido momentos de verdadera angustia**, she went through moments of real agony. **No dejar vivir a uno**, to give somebody no peace. **Vivir por encima de sus posibilidades**, to live beyond one's means. **Ganar lo justo para vivir**, to earn a bare living. **¡Viva el rey!**, long life to the king!, long live the king! **Y vivieron felices y comieron perdices**, and they lived happily ever after.

vivisección [vee-vee-sec-the-on'], *f*. Vivisection, dissection of a living animal for purpose of scientific inquiry.

vivo, va [vee'-vo, vah], *a*. 1. Living, enjoying life, active. 2. Lively (descripción), efficacious, intense (emoción). 3. Disencumbered, disengaged. 4. Alive, kindled. 5. Acute (dolor), ingenious; vivid, bright (color), smart. 6. Hasty, inconsiderate. 7. Diligent, nimble. 8. Pure, clean. 9. Constant, enduring. 10. Vivid, florid, excellent. 11. Very expressive or persuasive. 12. Blessed. 13. Sharp (listo), clever, lively (animado). 14. *(Cono Sur)* Naughty (travieso). **En vivo**, living. *Viva voz*, by word of mouth. **Cal viva**, quicklime. **Carne viva**, quick flesh in a wound. **Ojos vivos**, very bright, lively eyes.

vivo [veé-vo], *m*. 1. Edging, border of clothing, stone, wood, etc., after dressing and trimming, or polishing. 2. *(Arch.)* Jut, any prominent part of a building which juts out. Mange, the itch or scab in dogs.

vizcacha [veeth-cah'-chah], *f*. A large kind of hare, Peruvian hare.

vizcaíno, na [veeth-cah-ee'-no, nah], *a*. Biscayan, of Biscay.

vizcondado [veeth-con-dah'-do], *m*. Viscountship.

vizconde [veeth-con'-day], *m*. Viscount.

vizcondesa [veeth-con-day'-sah], *f*. Viscountess.

viznaga [veeth-nah'-gah], *f. (Bot.)* Carrot-like ammi.

vizvirindo, da [vith-ve-reen'-do, dah], *a. (Mex.)* V. VIVARACHO.

vocablo [vo-cah'-blo], *m*. Word, term, diction, vocable.

vocabulario [vo-cah-boo-lah'-re-o]. *m*. 1. Vocabulary, dictionary, lexicon. 2. *(Coll.)* Person who announces or interprets the will of another.

vocación [vo-cah-the-on'], *f*. 1. Vocation, calling by the will of God. 2. Trade, employment, calling. 3. V. ADVOCACIÓN and CONVOCACIÓN.

vocal [vo-cahl'], *a*. Vocal, oral. -*f* Vowel. *m*. Voter, in a congregation or assembly.

vocalista [vo-cah-lees'-tah], *m & f*. Vocalist, singer.

vocalización [vo-cah-le-thah-the-on'], *f*. Vocalization.

vocalizar [vo-cah-le-thar'], *vn*. To vocalize, to articulate.

vocalmente [vo-cahl'-men-tay], *adv*. Vocally, articulately.

vocativo [vo-cah-tee'-vo], *m. (Gram.)* Vocative, the fifth case of nouns.

voceador, ra [vo-thay-ah-dor', rah], *m. & f*. Vociferator.

vocear [vo-thay-ar'], *va. & vn*. 1. To cry (mercancías), to cry out, to glamor, to scream, to bawl, to halloo. 2. To cry, to publish, to proclaim; to call to: applied occasionally to inanimate things. 3. To shout, to huzza; to applaud by acclamation; to boast publicly (reivindicar).

vocería [vo-thay-reé-ah], *f.* Clamor (jaleo), outcry, hallooing.

vocero [vo-thay'-ro], *m.* (*LAm.*) Spokesman.

vociferación [vo-the-fay-rah-the-on'], *f.* Vociferation, clamor, outcry, boast.

vociferador, ra [vo-the-fay-rah-dor´, rah], *m.* & *f.* Boaster, bragger.

vociferante [vo-the-fay-rahn'-tay], *pa.* & *n.* Vociferating, caller.

vociferar [vo-the-fay-rar'], *vn.* To vociferate, to bawl, to proclaim, to clamor. *-va.* To boast, to brag loudly or publicly (proclamar).

vocinglería [vo-thin-glay-ree'-ah], *f.* 1. Clamor (griterío), outcry, a confused noise of many voices. 2. Loquacity.

vocinglero, ra [vo-thin-glay'-ro, rah], *a.* Brawling, prattling, chattering, vociferous. *-m.* & *f.* Loud babbler.

vodka [vod-kah], *f.* Vodka.

vodu [vo-doo'] *m.* voodoo.

voladera [vo-lah-day'-rah], *f.* One of the float or pallets of a water-wheel.

voladero, ra [vo-lah-day'-ro, rah], *a.* Volatile, flying, fleeting. *-m.* Precipice, abyss.

voladizo, za [vo-lah-dee´-tho, ah], *a.* Projecting from a wall, jutting out.

voladizo, *m.* Any short cover projecting from a wall; corbel.

volado [vo-lah'-do], *m.* V. AZUCARILLO.

volado, da [vo-lah'-do, dah], *a.* 1. (*Typ.*) Superior. 2. (*Cono Sur*) Proyecting (voladizo); protuberant (abultado). *-m.* 1. (*CAm.*) Fib (mentira). 2. (*Carib. Cono Sur*) Flounce, ruffle. 3. (*Mex.*) Game of heads of tails (juego). 4. (*Mex.*) Adventure (aventura).

volador, ra [vo-lah-dor', rah], *a.* 1. Flying, running fast. 2. Hanging in the air. 3. Blowing up with gunpowder (fuegos artificiales). *-m.* 1. Rocket. 2. Flying-fish. *-f.* Fly-wheel of a steam-engine.

volandas, or **en volandas** [vo-lahn´-das], *adv.*1. In the air, through the air, as if flying 2. (*Coll.*) Rapidly, in an instant.

volandera [vo-lan-day'-rah], *f.* 1. (In oil-mills) Runner, the stone which runs edgewise upon another stone. 2. (*Coll.*) A vague or flying report, lie. 3. Wash of an axle-tree, nave-box of a wheel. 4. (*Print.*) Ledge on a type galley.

volandero, ra [vo-lan-day'-ro, rah], *a.* 1. Suspended in the air, volatile. 2. Fortuitous, casual. 3. Unsettled, fleeting, variable, volatile.

volandillas (En) [en vo-lan-deel'-lyas], *adv.* V. VOLANDAS (EN).

volanta [vo-lahn'-tah], *f.* (*Cuba*) A two-wheel covered vehicle with very long shafts.

volante [vo-lahn'-tay], *pa.* & *a.* 1. Flying (que vuela), volant, fluttering, unsettled. 2. Applied to the pulsation of the arteries. 3. Applied to a kind of meteors. **Papel volante,** short writing or manuscript easily disseminated: it generally contains some satire or libel.

volante [vo-lahn'-tay], *m.* 1. An ornament of light gauze hanging from a woman's headdress. 2. Shuttle-cock. 3. Coiningmill, or that part of it which strikes the die. 4. Balance of a watch. 5. (*Mech.*) Fly-wheel, a heavy governing wheel. 6. Livery servant or foot-boy who runs before his master, or rides behind. 7. Lawn tennis. 8. Flier, a long narrow sheet of paper. 9. (*Cuba*) (1) V. VOLANTA. (2) A linen coat. (*Mex.*) A dress-coat.

volantín [vo-lan-teen'], *m.* 1. A certain apparatus for fishing. 2. (*LAm.*) Kite (cometa). 3. (*And.*) Rocket (cohete).

volantón [vo-lan-tone'], *m.* A fledged bird able to fly.

volapié [vo-lah-pe-ay'], *m.* A lot in bull-fighting which consists in wounding the beast while running, the latter standing. **A volapié,** *adv.* Half running, half flying.

volapuk [vo-lah-pook']. *m.* Volapük, a commercial universal language invented by the Swiss professor J. M. Schleyer.

volar [vo-lar'], *vn.* 1. To fly, as with wings. 2. To fly, to pass through the air. 3. To fly, to move swiftly. 4. To vanish, to disappear all of a sudden. 5. To rise in the air like a steeple or pile. 6. To make rapid progress in studies; to subtilize, to refine sentiments; to move with rapidity or violence. 7. To project, to hang over. 8. To execute with great promptitude and facility; to extend, to publish anything rapidly. *-va.* 1. To rouse the game. 2. To fly, to attack by a bird of prey. 3. To blow up, to spring a mine; to blast rocks or mines. 4. (*Met.*) To irritate (irritar), to exasperate. 5. To ascend high. 6. (*LAm.*) To put to flight (ahuyentar). 7. (*Mex.*) To pinch (robar). 8. (*Mex.*) To swindle (estafar). **Echar a volar,** (*Met.*) to disseminate, to give to the public. **Echarse a volar,** to leave the parental nest. **Voy volando,** I'll go as quickly as I can.

volatería [vo-lah-tay-ree'-ah], *f.* 1. Fowling; sporting with hawks. 2. Fowls, a flock of birds. 3. A vague or desultory speech; idle or groundless ideas.*-adv.* Fortuitously, adventitiously.

volátil [vo-lah´-teel], *a.* 1. Volatile, flying through the air, or capable of flying; wafting. 2. Changeable, inconstant, fugitive. 3. (*Chem.*) Volatile, vaporizing slowly at ordinary temperatures.

volatilidad [vo-lah-te-le´-dadh], *f.* Volatility, quality of flying away by evaporation.

volatilización [vo-lah-te-le-thah-the-on'], *f.* Volatilization.

volatilizar [vo-lah-te-le-thar'], *va.* To volatilize, to vaporize, to transform into the gaseous state *-vr.* To be dissipated in vapor, to be exhaled or vaporized.

volatín [vo-lah-teen'], *m.* Rope-dancer, and each of his exercises (acrobacia).

volatinero [vo-lah-te-nay´-ro], *m.* Rope-walker; acrobat.

volatizar [vo-lah-te-thar´], *va.* (*Chem.*) To volatilize.

volcán [vol-cahn'], *m.* 1. Volcano. 2. Excessive ardor: violent passion. 3. (*And. Cono Sur*) Summer torrent (torrente). 4. (*CAm. Carib.*) Pile, heap (montón). 5. (*Carib.*) deafening noise (estrépito).

volcánico, ca [vol-cah'-ne-co, cah], *a.* Volcanic, relating to a volcano.

volcar [vol-car'], *va.* 1. To overset, to capsize, to turn one side upwards. 2. To make dizzy or giddy (marear). 3. To make one change his opinion. 4. To tire one's patience with buffoonery or scurrilous mirth. 5. (*Fig.*) Irritate (irritar). *-vn.* 1. To overturn, to upset. *-vr.* 1. To be upset (recipiente). 2. (*Fig.*) To go out of one´s way. (*Yo vuelco, yo vuelque,* from *Volcar. V.* ACORDAR.

volear [vo-lay-ar'], *va.* To throw anything up in the air so as to make it fly; particularly to bat a ball or serve it in tennis.

volea [vo-lay'-ah], *f.* 1. Swingle-tree, whipple-tree (carruajes). 2. Volley (en el juego de pelota); lob (en tenis).

voleo [vo-lay'-o], *m.* 1. Blow given to a ball in the air. 2. Step in a Spanish dance. 3. (*Coll.*) Scolding, harsh reproof. **De un voleo** or **del primer voleo**, at one blow; at the first blow; in an instant.

volframio [vol-frah'-me-o]. *m.* Wolfram, tungsten.

volibol [vo-le-bol´], *m.* Volley-ball.

volición [vo-le-the-on'], *f.* Volition, power of willing, act of will.

volitivo, va [vo-li-tee'-vo, vah], *a.* Having power to will.

volquearse [vol-kay-ar´-say], *vr.* To tumble, to wallow. V. REVOLCARSE.

volquete [vol-kay'-tay], *m.* Dumping truck.

voltaísmo [vol-tah-ees'-mo], *m.* Voltaism, electricity produced by the contact of dissimilar substances.

voltaje [vol-tah'-hay], *m.* (*Elec.*) Voltage.

voltamperio [vol-tam-pay´-re-o], *m.* (*Elec.*) Volt-ampere.

voltariedad [vol-tah-re-ay-dahd'], *f.* Fickleness, inconstancy, volatility.

voltario, ria [vol-tah-re-o, ah], *a.* Fickle (cambiable), inconstant, giddy.

volteador [vol-tay-ah-dor´], *m.* Tumbler, one who shows or teaches postures and feats of activity.

voltear [vol-tay-ar'], *va.* 1. To whirl, to revolve. 2. To overturn (recipiente), to over set. 3. To change the order or state of things. 4. To knock down, to throw down violently, to fell.

5. To throw an arch across, to construct it. 6. *(Carib.)* To search all over. *-vn.* To roll over (personas, cosas); to tumble, to exhibit feats of agility.

volteo [vol-tay'-o], *m.* 1. Whirl, whirling. 2. Overturning. 3. Tumbling. 4. Dumping.

voltereta [vol-tay-ray'-tah], *f.* Somersault.

volterianismo [vol-tay-re-ah-nees'-mo], *m.* Voltairianism, cynicism, scepticism.

volteriano, na [vol-tay-re-ah'-no, nah], *a.* Voltairian, of Voltaire.

voltímetro [vol-tee'-may-tro], *m. (Elec.)* Voltmeter.

voltio [vol'-te-o], *m.* Volt.

voltizo, za [vol-tee'-tho, thah], *a.* Inconstant, fickle.

volubilidad [vo-loo-be-le-dahd'], *f.* Volubility; inconstancy, fickleness, glibness, fluency.

voluble [vo-loo'-blay], *a.* 1. Easily moved about. 2. Voluble, inconstant, fickle (inconstante). 3. *(Bot.)* Twining, said of a stem which climbs in spirals.

volublemente [vo-loo'-blay-men-tay], *adv.* Volubly.

volumen [vo-loo'-men], *m.* 1. Volume, size, bulkiness (abultado); corpulence. 2. Volume, bound book. 3. *(Geom.)* Volume, space occupied by a body. **Volumen de ventas**, amount of business done. **Poner la radio a todo volumen**, to turn the radio up full.

voluminoso, sa [vo-loo-me-no'-so, sah], *a.* Voluminous; of large bulk.

voluntad [vo-loon-tahd'], *f.* 1. Will, choice, determination. 2. Divine determination. 3. Goodwill, benevolence, kindness. 4. Desire (deseo), pleasure; free will, volition (volición), election, choice. 5. Disposition, precept; intention (intención), resolution. **De voluntad** or **de buena voluntad**, with pleasure, gratefully. **Última voluntad**, one's last will. **Por causas ajenas a mi voluntad**, for reasons beyond my control. **No tiene voluntad para dejar de beber**, he hasn't the willpower to give up drinking.

voluntariamente [vo-loon-tah'-re-ah-men-tay], *adv.* Spontaneously, voluntarily, fain.

voluntariedad [vo-loon-tah-re-ay-dahd'], *f* Free-will, spontaneousness.

voluntario, ria [vo-loon-tah'-re-o, ah], *a.* Voluntary, spontaneous, willing, gratuitous, free.

voluntario [vo-loon-tah'-re-o], *m.* Volunteer; a soldier who serves of his own accord.

voluntariosamente [vo-loon-tah-re-oh'-sah-men-tay], *adv.* Spontaneously, selfishly.

voluntarioso, sa [vo-loon-tah-re-oh'-so, sah], *a.*1 Selfish, humorous, one who merely follows the dictates of his own will; desirous. 2. Headstrong, wilful, willing, well-intentioned.

voluptuosamente [vo-loop-too-o-sah-men'-tay], *adv.* Voluptuously, sensuously; licentiously.

voloptuosidad [vo-loop-too-o-se-dahd'], *f.* Voluptuousness, licentiousness.

voluptuoso, sa [vo-loop-too-oh'-so, sah], *a.* Voluptuous, sensuous; licentious, sensual, lustful.

voluta [vo-loo'-tah], *f. (Arch.)* Volute, an ornament of the capitals of columns. 2. A mollusk having an oval shell of a short spiral.

volvedor [vol-vay-dor'], *m.* Screw-driver (destornillador), turn-screw.

volver [vol-verr'], *va. & vn.* 1. To turn, to give turns (objeto, viajero). 2. To return, to restore, to repay, to give back (devolver), to give up. 3. To come back (regresar), to return, to come again to the same place. 4. To return to the same state. 5. To turn from a straight line (carreteras). 6. To direct, to aim; to remit; to send back a present. 7. To translate languages. 8. To change the outward appearance (transformar); to invert, to change from one place to another. 9. To vomit, to throw up victuals. 10. To make one change his opinion; to convert, to incline. 11. To return a ball. 12. To reflect a sound. 13. To turn away, to discharge. 14. To regain,

to recover. 15. To repeat, to reiterate: in this sense it is accompanied by *a.* 16. To stand out for a person, or to undertake his defence; to defend: here it is used with **por**. 17. To re-establish, to replace in a former situation. 18. To plough land a second time. 19. To resume the thread of a discourse interrupted. 20. To reiterate, to repeat. **Volver la puerta**, to shut the door. **Hacer volver** or **mandar volver**, to recall. **Volver atrás**, to come back. **Volver a uno loco**, to confound one with arguments, so that he appears stupid. **Volver sobre sí**, to reflect on oneself with purpose of amendment, to make up one's losses; to recover serenity of mind. **Volver en sí**, to recover one's senses. **Volver la cara**, to face about. **Me volvió la espalda**, he turned his back on me. **Vuelve fieras a los hombres**, it turns men into wild beasts. **Han vuelto a pintar la casa**, they have painted the house again. *-vr.* 1. To turn, to grow sour. 2. To turn towards one. 3. To retract an opinion (desdecirse), to change. **Volverse blanco**, to become white. **Volverse loco**, to be deranged, to become a fool. **Volverse atrás**, to flinch, to retract. **La burla se volvió contra él**, the jest rebounded on him. **Volverse la tortilla**, to turn the tables or scales. —**N.B. Volver,** followed by a verb in the infinitive preceded by the preposition *a*, is generally omitted in English, and the verb in the infinitive mood is translated in the corresponding tense and person, with the addition of the adverb *again;* as **Él volvió a hablar**, he spoke again. **Ellos lo volverán a negar**, they will deny it again. **Volver a la carga**, to return to the charge, to insist. **Volver lo de arriba abajo**, to turn upside down; to invert the order of things.

volvible [vol-vee'-blay], *a.* That may be turned.

volvimiento [vol-ve-me-en'-to], *m.* Act of turning.

volvo, vólvulo [vol'-vo, vol'-vo-lo], *m.* Volvulus, iliac passion.

vólvoce [vol'-vo-thay], *m.* Volvox, the so-called globe-animalcule, a minute green globe, of microscopic life, now referred to the vegetable kingdom.

vómer [vó-mer], *m.* Vomer, a bone dividing the nostrils vertically.

vómica [vo'-me cah], *f. (Med.)* Vomica, a sac of pus in the lungs or other viscus.

vómico, ca [vo'-me-co, cah], *a.* Causing vomiting: applied to the nut called vomic, or *nux vomica;* it is not, however, *emetic,* as its name implies.

vomipurgante [vo-me-poor-gahn'-tayl, *a.* Purgative and emetic at once.

vomitado, da [vo-me-tah'-do, dah], *a. & pp.* of VOMITAR. *(Coll.)* Meagre; pale-faced.

vomitador, ra [vo-me-tah-dor', rah], *m. &f.* One who vomits.

vomitar [vo-me-tar'], *va.* 1. To vomit (devolver). 2. To foam, to break out into injurious expressions. 3. *(Coll.)* To reveal a secret (secreto), to discover what was concealed. 4. *(Coll.)* To pay what was unduly retained. *-vn.* 1. To vomit (devolver). 2. **Eso me da ganas de vomitar**, that makes me sick.

vomitivo, va [vo-me-tee'-vo, vah], *a.* Emetic, vomitive. *-m. (Med.)* Emetic.

vómito [vo'-me-to], *m.* 1. The act of vomiting (acto) ? Vomit, matter thrown from the stomach. **Provocar a vómito**, to nauseate, to loathe: used in censuring indecent expressions, or to condemn something. **Vómito negro**, a bilious disease; yellow fever.

vomitón, na [vo-me-tone', nah], *a.* Often throwing milk from the stomach: applied by nurses to a sucking child.

vomitona [vo-me-to'-nah], *f. (Coll.)* Violent vomiting after eating heartily.

vomitorio, ia [vo-me-to'-re-o, ah], *a.* Vomitive, emetic. *-m.* Passage or entrance in Roman theaters.

voracidad [vo-rah-the-dahd'], *f.* 1. Voracity, greediness. 2. *(Met.)* Destructiveness of fire etc.

vorágine [vo-rah'-he-nay], *f.* Vortex, whirlpool.

voraginoso sa [vo-rah-he-no'-so, sah], *a.* Engulfing; full of whirlpools.

voraz [vo-rath'], *a.* 1. Voracious (devorador), greedy to eat, ravenous. 2. Extremely irregular, excessively destructive, fierce.

vorazmente [vo-rath'-men-tay], *adv.* Voraciously, greedily, gluttonously.

vormela [vor-may'-lah], *f.* Kind of spotted weasel.

vórtice [vor'-te-thay], *m.* Whirlpool (agua), whirlwind (viento), hurricane. **Vórtice aéreo**, whirlwind, water-spout.

vorticela [vor-te-thay'-lah], *f.* Vorticella, a typical genus of infusorians.

vortiginoso, sa [vor-te-he-no'-so, sah], *a.* Vortical.

vos [vose], *pron.* You, ye. *V.* VOSOTROS. Used as respectful to persons of dignity.

vosearse [vo-say-ar'-say], *vr. (Prov.)* To address as *vos.*

vosotros, tras [vo-so'-tros, trahs], *pron. Pers. pl.* You.

votación [vo-tah-the-on'], *f.* Voting. **Votación a mano alzada**, show of hands.

votado, da [vo-tah'-do, dah], *a. & pp.* of VOTAR. Devoted.

votador, ra [vo-tah-dor', rah], *m. & f.* 1. One who vows or swears. 2. Voter.

votante [vo-tahn'-tay], *a.* Voter in a corporation or assembly.

votar [vo-tar'], *vn.* 1. To vow. 2. To vote (candidato, partido). 3 To give an opinion. 4. To curse, to utter oaths.

votivo, va [vo-tee'-vo, vah], *a.* Votive, offered by a vow.

voto [vo'-to], *m.* 1. Vow (promesa). 2. Vote, suffrage. 3. Opinion, advice, voice: hence, also, voter. **Voto de calidad** or **decisivo**, casting vote. **A pluralidad de votos**, by a majority of votes. 4. A gift offered to saints by the faithful. 5. Supplication to God. 6. Angry oath or execration (juramento). 7. Wish (deseo), desire. **Voto a Dios**, *(Low.)* A menacing oath. **Voto de amén**, a vote blindly given in obedience to the will of another. **Ser** or **tener voto**, (a) to come to a vote; (b) to understand clearly the matter under consideration, or to be free from bias. **Voto de castidad**, vow of chastity. **Pronunciar sus votos**, to take vows. **Derecho al voto**, the right to vote. **Depositar un voto**, to cast a vote. **Por una mayoría de votos**, by a majority vote. **Voto de censura**, vote of censure. **Voto de gracias**, vote of thanks. **Voto de confianza**, vote of confidence. **Votos emitidos**, votes cast. **Voto solemne**, solemn vow. **No tienes ni voz ni voto**, you have no say in this matter.

voz [voth], *f.* 1. Voice. 2. Any sound made by breath (sonido). 3. Clamor, outcry. **Dar voces**, to cry, to call aloud. 4. Vocable, expression, word (vocablo), term. 5. Power or authority to speak in the name of another. 6. Voice, vote, suffrage: right of suffrage; opinion expressed. 7. Rumor (rumor), public opinion. 8. Motive, pretext. 9. Word, divine inspiration. 10. *(Gram.)* Voice, active or passive. 11. *(Mus.)* Vocal music; treble, tenor; tune corresponding to the voice of a singer. 12. Order, mandate of a superior. 13. *(Law.)* **Voz activa**, right or power of voting. **Tomar voz**, to acquire knowledge, to reason: to confirm or support anything by the opinions of others. **A media voz**, with a slight hint; with a low voice; in a submissive tone. **A voces**, clamorous cry, loud voice. **En voz**, (a) verbally; (b) *(Mus.)* in voice. **Anudarse la voz**, to be unable to speak because of violent excitement. **Dar una voz**, to hail one from a distance. **Dar voces al viento**, to toil in vain. **La voz del pueblo**, the voice of the people. **Levantar la voz**, to raise one's voice. **Canción a cuatro voces**, song for four voices. **Voz común**, hearsay. **Tener voz y voto**, to be present as a full member.

vozarrón [vo-thar-rone'], *m.* A strong, heavy voice.

voznar [voth-nar'], *vn.* To cry like swans, to cackle like geese.

vudú [voo-doo'], *m.* Voodoo.

vuduísmo [voo-doo-ees'-mo], *m.* Voodooism.

vuecelencia, vuecencia [voo-ay-thay-len'-the-ah], *com.* A contraction of *vuestra excelencia,* your excellency.

vuelco [voo-el'-co], *m.* Eversion, overturning, upset. **Mi corazón dio un vuelco**, my heart missed a beat.

vuelo [voo-ay'-lo], *m.* 1. Flight, the act of flying. 2. Wing of a bird. 3. Part of a building which projects beyond the wall. 4. Width or fulness of clothes. 5. Ruffle, flounce, ornament set to the wristband of a shirt; frill. 6. Space flown through at once. 7. Elevation or loftiness in discoursing or working. 8. Leap or bound in pantomimes. **Coger al vuelo**, to catch in flight. **Vuelo en formación**, formation flying. **Vuelo libre**, free flight. **Vuelo sin motor**, gliding, glide. **Vuelo sin parar**, non-stop flight. **Vuelo tripulado** manned flight. **Vuelo en picado**, dive. **Tocar las campanas a vuelo**, to peal the bells. **De altos vuelos**, grandiose. **Cortar los vuelos a uno**, to clip somebody's wings.

vuelta [voo-el'-tah], *f.* 1. Turn, the act of turning, gyration, twirl; turn of an arch; circumvolution; circuit. 2. Requital, recompense; regress. 3. Iteration, rehearsal. 4. Back side, wrong side (tela, papel). 5. Whipping, flogging, lashing on the back-side. 6. Turn-out, deviation from a line or straight road. 7. Return from a spot. 8. Turn, time of execution. 9. Turn, inclination, bent. 10. Ruffle. *V.* VUELO. 11. *(Naut.)* Turn, hitch, lashing. 12. Turn, change of things (cambio). 13. Trip, excursion, short voyage. 14. Reconsideration, recollection. 15. Land once, twice, or thrice labored. 16. Wards in a lock or key. 17. Order of stitches in stockings (de puntos). 18. Roll, envelope. 19. Unexpected sally or witticism. 20. Change, surplus money to be returned in dealing. 21. *(Mus.)* Number of verses repeated. 22. *(Mech.)* Rotation stroke; potter's wheel. 23. Stroll, walk (paseo). 24. Beating (paliza). **A vuelta de**, in the course of, within. **A la vuelta**, at your return; that laid aside; about the time; upon. **La vuelta de**, towards this or that way. **Dar una vuelta**, to make a short excursion; to clean something; to examine a thing properly. **Dar vueltas**, to walk to and fro on a public walk; to seek anything; to discuss repeatedly the same topic. **A vuelta** or **a vueltas**, Very near, almost; also, with another thing otherwise. **No tener vuelta de hoja**, to be unanswerable. **Tener vuelta**, *(Coll.)* an admonition to return a thing lent.-*int.* Return; let him return or go back the same way. **No hay que darle vueltas**, *(Met.)* no quibbling about it, it will prove to be the very thing. **Poner de vuelta y media**, to abuse a person by word or action. **Dar media vuelta**, to face about; to turn half somersault. **A la vuelta de la esquina**, round the corner. **De vuelta iremos a verlos**, we'll go and see them on the way back.

vuelto, ta [voo-el'-to, tah], *pp. irr.* of VOLVER.

vuesa [voo-ay'-sah], *a.* Contracted from *vuestra*, and used before *merced, eminencia*, ete.

vuesamerced [voo-ay-sah-mer-thed'], *f.* You, sir; you, madam; your worship, your honor; a contraction of *vuestra merced*, a title of courtesy to a person who is not entitled to that of *vueseñoría* or *vuestra señoría*, your lordship.

vuesarced [voo-ay-sar-thed'], *f.* Contraction of *vuesamerced.*

vueseñoría [voo-ay-say-nyo-ree'-ah], *f.* Contraction of **vuestra señoría**.

vuestro, tra [voo-es'-tro, trah], *a. pron.* Your, yours. It is used absolutely by subjects to a sovereign, or by a sovereign to a subject. **Muy vuestro**, entirely yours. **Vuestra señoría**, your lordship or ladyship.

vulcanita [vool-cah-nee'-tah], *f.* Vulcanite.

vulcanizar [vool-cah-ne-thar'], *va.* To vulcanize, to mix sulphur with rubber at a high temperature.

vulgacho [vool-gah'-cho], *m.* Mob, populace, dregs of the people.

vulgar [vool-gar'], *a.* 1. Vulgar (lengua), common (término), ordinary; vulgar or vernacular dialect, as opposed to the learned languages; without specific peculiarity. 2. Ordinary (persona), coarse (modales, rasgos).

vulgar [vool-gar'], The vulgar.

vulgaridad [vool-gah-re-dahd'], *f.* Vulgarity (acto); vulgarism, manners or speech of the lowest people; vulgar effusion.

vulgarismo [vool-gah-rees'-mo], *m.* Colloquialism, colloquial expression.

vulgarizar [vool-gah-re-thar´], *va.* 1. To make vulgar or common. 2. To translate from another idiom into the common language of the country. *-vr.* To become vulgar.

vulgarmente [vool-gar´-men-tay], *adv.* Vulgarly, commonly; among the common people.

vulgata [vool-gah´-tah], *f.* Vulgate, the Latin version of the Bible, approved by the Roman Church.

vulgo [vool´-go], *m.* 1. Multitude, populace, mob. 2. Way of thinking of the populace. 3. Universality or generality of people.*-adv. V.* VULGARMENTE.

vulnerable [vool-nay-rah´-blay], *a.* Vulnerable.

vulneración [vool-nay-rah-the-on´], *f.* The act of wounding

vulnerar [vool-nay-rar´], *va.* 1. To wound. *V.* HERIR. 2. To injure the reputation.

vulneraria [vool-nay-rah´-re-ah], *f.* (*Bot.*) Kidney vetch.

vulnerario, ria [vool-nay-rah´-re-o, ahl, *a.* 1. Vulnerary, useful in healing wounds. 2. (*Law.*) Applied to an ecclesiastic who has wounded or killed anyone.

vulnerario [vool-nay-rah´-re-o], *m.* Clergyman guilty of killing or wounding.

vulpécula [vool-pay´-coo-lah], *f. V.* VULPEJA.

vulpeja [vool-pay´-hah], *f.* A bitch fox.

vulpinita [vool-pe-nee´-tah], *f.* Vulpinite.

vulpino, na [vool-pee´-no, nah], *a.* 1. Proper to a fox, foxy, vulpine. 2. (*Met.*) Foxy, crafty, deceitful.

vultúridos [vool-too´-re-dos], *m. pl.* A division of the birds of prey; the vultures.

vulva [vool´-vah], *f.* (*Anat.*) Vulva, the external orifice of the female genitals.

vulvaria [vool-vah´-re-ah], *f.* Vulvaria, the fetid orach, a common European plant.

vulvario, ria [vool-vah´-re-o, ah], *a.* (*Anat.*) Vulvar, pertaining to the vulva.

W

w This letter does not belong to the Spanish alphabet and is only used in terms, chiefly proper names, taken from languages of northern Europe. It is named *V doble* (double v). In chemistry W stands for Wolfram (tungsten).

wáter [vah´-tayr], *m.* Lavatory, water closet.

X

x [ay´-kis], *f.* The twenty-fourth letter of the alphabet. This letter is pronounced like cs or gs in English.

xantósilo [csan-tok´-se-lo], *m.* (*Bot.*) Xanthoxlum, prickly ash. *V.* ZANTÓXILO.

xapurcar [csah-poor-car´], *va.* (*Prov.*) To stir up dirty water.

xara [csah´-rah, properly shah´-rah], *f.* The law of the Moors.

xenofobia [csay-no-pho´-be-ah], *m.* Xenophobia.

xenófobo [csay-noh´-pho-bo], *a.* Xenophobic.

xerofagia [csay-ro-fah´-he-ah], *f.* Xerophagy.

xerófila [csay-ro´-fe-lah], *m.* (*Bot.*) Xerophyte

xi [csee], *f.* Fourteenth letter of the Greek alphabet, corresponding to X.

xifoideo, ea [cse-foi-day´-o, ah], *a.* Xiphoid, relating to the xiphoid cartilage.

xifoides [cse-foi´-days], *a. & m.* (*Zool.*) Xiphoid, sword-shaped; the cartilage ending the sternum below.

xilófago, ga [cse-lo´-fah-go], *a.* Xylophagous, feeding on or boring in wood. *-m.* A dipterous insect living in elms.

xilofón, xilófono [se-lo-fone´, se-lo´-fo-no], *m.* (*Mus.*) Xilophone.

xilografía [cse-lo-grah-fee´-ah], *f.* Xylography, wood-engraving.

xilográfico, ca [cse-lo-grah´-fe-co, cah], *a.* Xylographic, relating to engraving upon wood.

xo [cso],int. Whoa! V. JO and CHO.

Y

y [yay, ee gre-ay´-gah], *f.* The twenty-fifth letter of the Castilian alphabet, stands as a vowel and a consonant. **Y,** when alone, or after a vowel, or followed by a consonant, or at the end of a word, is a vowel, and sounds as *e* or *ee* in English: *Hoy y mañana* (today and tomorrow), *o´-e ee mah-nyah´-nah.***Y,** before a vowel in the same syllable, or between two vowels in the same word, is a consonant, and sounds like the English *y* in the words *yard, yell, you.*

y [ee], *conj.* And. It is frequently used in interrogatives, or by way of a reply; as ¿**Y tú, no haces lo mismo?** and you, do you not do the same? ¿**Y tú, dónde has estado?** and you, where have you been? ¿**Y bien?** and well then? **Alfonso, Fernando y Manuel,** Alphonsus, Ferdinand, and Emmanuel. When the conjunction *y* is followed by a word beginning with *i* or *hi,* the conjunction *e* is used instead; as, **Sabiduría e ignorancia,** wisdom and ignorance. **Padre e hijo,** father and son.

ya [yah], *adv.* 1. Already (pasado). 2. Presently, immediately, now (presente). 3. Finally, ultimately. 4. At another time, on another occasion. **Ya no es lo que ha sido,** it is not now what it has been. **Ya estamos en ello,** we've got it, we understand it. **Ya voy,** I am going, or I am going presently. *-part.* Now. **Ya esto, ya aquello,** now this, now that. **Ya que has venido,** since you are coming, or since you are here. *-int.* Used on being brought to recollect something. ¿**No se acuerda Ud. de tal cosa? Ya, ya,** do you not remember such a thing? Yes, yes: **Ya se ve,** yes, you can see it! it is clear, it is so. **Ya estaba yo en eso,** I was already of that mind.

yaacabó [yah-ah-cah-bo´], *m.* A hawk or falcon of Venezuela, whose note sounds like *ya acabó.* (Imitative.)

yaca [yah´-cah], *f.* (*Bot.*) A large-leaved Indian tree.

yacaré [yah-cah-ray´], *m.* (*Zool. Amer.*) Crocodile.

yacedor [yah-thay-dor´], *m.* A lad who takes horses to graze by night.

yacente [yah-then´-tay], *pa. & a.* Jacent, vacant; lying.

yacer [yah-therr´], *vn.* 1. To lie, to lie down. 2. To lie down in the grave. 3. To be fixed or situated in a place; to exist. 4. To graze by night in the field. (*Yo yazgo* or *yago, yazga* or *yaga.* *V.*YACER.)

yaciente [yah-the-en´-tay], *a.* Extended, stretched.

yacija [yah-thee´-hah], *f.* 1. Bed (cama), couch. 2. Tomb, grave (sepultura). **Ser de mala yacija,** to be a vagrant; to be restless; to have a bad bed.

yacimiento [yah-the-me-ayn´-to], *m.* Bed, deposit; site (arqueológico).

yactura [yac-too´-rah], *f.* Loss, damage.

yáculo [yah´-coo-lo], *m.* 1. A serpent which darts from trees in order to attack. 2. (*Zool.*) Dace.

yacumana [yah-coo-mah´-nah], *f.* Name given to the boa in the Amazonian provinces.

yagre [yah´-gray], *m.* Sugar, extracted from the palm or cocoa tree. *V.* JACRA.

yagua [yah´-goo-ah], *f.* Bark of the royal palm.

yak [yahk], *m.* Yak, a bovine quadruped of central Asia.

yalotecnia [yah-lo-tec´-ne-ah], *f.* The art of working glass.

yámbico, ca [yahm´-be-co, cah], *a.* Iambic: applied to a Latin verse.

yambo [yahm´-bo], *m.* An iambic foot.

yanacona [yah-nah-co´-nah], **Yanacuna** [yah-nah-coo´-nah], *com. (Peru)* The Indian bound to personal service.

yankee [yahn´-kee], *com. & a.* 1. A person born or living in New England. 2. A native of the United States.

yanqui [yahn´-kee], *a.* A native of the United States.

yantar [yahn-tar´], *m.* 1. *(Prov.)* Viands, food. 2. A kind of king's taxes.

yapa [yah´-pah], *f.* A thing or quantity which the seller presents to the buyer. *V.* ÑAPA and CONTRA.

yarda [yar´-dah], *f.* An English yard, equal to 91 centimeters; a *vara,* the Spanish measure of 3 feet, is equivalent to 8.36 decimeters.

yarey [yah-ray´-e], *m. (Cuba)* A species of *guano* (palm-tree).

yaro [yah´-ro], *m. (Bot.)* Arum, an aquatic plant.

yareta [yah-ray´-tah], *f.* A kind of combustible; peat.

yatagán [yah-tah-gahn´], *m.* A kind of a sabre-dagger used by the orientals.

yate [yah´-tay], *m.* Yacht, a pleasure craft, sailing or propelled by steam.

yayero, ra [yah-yay´-ro, rah], *a. (Cuba)* Intermeddling, busybody.

yedra, or **yedra arborácea** [yay´-drah], *f. (Bot.)* Ivy. **yedra terrestre,** ground ivy.

yegua [yay´-goo-ah], *f.* 1. Mare. **Yegua madre,** A dam. 2. *(And. Cono Sur)* Old bag, whore. 3. *(And. CAm.)* Cigar stub.

yeguada, yegüería [yay-goo-ah´-dah, yay-goo-ay-ree´-ah], *f.* 1. Stud (caballeriza), a herd of breeding mares and stallions. 2. *(CAm. Carib.)* Piece of stupidity (estupidez).

yeguar [yay-goo-ar´], *a.* Belonging to mares.

yegüero, yegüerizo [yay-goo-ay´-ro, yay-goo-ay-ree´-tho], *m.* Keeper of breeding mares.

yegüezuela [yay-goo-ay-thoo-ay´-lahl, *f. dim.* Little mare.

yelmo [yel´-mo], *m.* Helmet, helm, a part of ancient armor.

yema [yay´-mah], *f.* 1. Bud, first shoot of trees. 2. Yolk of an egg. 3. Center, middle. **Dar en la yema,** *(Met.)* to hit the nail on the head. 4. The best or best placed in its line. 5. Fleshy tip of the finger. 6. *(Coll.)* Ace of diamonds in cards.

yente [yen´-tay], *pa. irr.* of IR. Going, one that goes.

yerba [yerr´-bah], *f. V.* HIERBA, which is the modern spelling of this word. 1. Herb, a generic name for all the smaller plants. 2. Flaw in the emerald which tarnishes its luster. 3. Grass (see plural). **Pisar buena** or **mala yerba,** to be of a good or bad temper. **Yerba carmín,** Virginian poke. **Yerba de cuajo,** *V.* ALCACHOFA. **Yerba doncella,** periwinkle. **Yerba piojera,** stavesacre. **Yerba de mar or marina,** Sea-weed. **Yerba del Paraguay,** Paraguay tea or maté. *-pl.* 1. Greens, vegetables; all kinds of garden stuff. 2. Grass of pasture land for cattle. 3. Poison given in food; poisonous plant. 4. Time when colts are born.

yerbabuena [yer-bah-boo-ay´-nah], *f.* Mint, peppermint. *V.* HIERBABUENA. Mentha.

yerbatear [yer-bah-tay-ar´], *vn. (Amer. Argen.)* To take *maté,* Paraguay tea.

yerbatero, ra [yer-bah-tay´-ro, rah], *a. & n.* 1. Using arrow-poison. 2. *(Peru)* One who sells or carries grass or fodder for horses.

yerbazal [yer-bah-thahl´], *m. V.* HERBAZAL.

yermar [yer-mar´], *va.* To dispeople, to lay waste.

yermo [yerr´-mo], *m.* Desert, wilderness, waste country.

yermo, ma [yerr´-mo, mah], *a.* Waste, desert, uninhabited; herbless. **Tierra yerma,** uncultivated ground.

yernar [yer-nar´], *va. (Coll. Prov.)* To make one a son-in-law by force.

yerno [yer´-no], *m.* Son-in-law. **Engaña yernos,** baubles, geegaws, trifles.

yero [yay´-ro], *m. (Bot.) V.* YERVO.

yerro [yer´-ro], *m.* Error, mistake, inadvertency, fault.

yerto [yerr´-to, tah], *a.* Stiff, motionless, inflexible; rigid, tight.

yervo [yerr´-vo], *m. (Bot.)* Tare, true bitter vetch. Ervum tetrapernum.

yesal, yesar [yay-sahl´], *m.* Gypsumpit, where gypsum is dug.

yesca [yes´-cah], *f.* 1. Spunk, tinder (materia inflamada). 2. Fuel (pábulo), incentive or aliment of passion. 3. Flint and tinder for making a light. *-pl.* Y*escas,* anything excessively dry or combustible.

yesera [yay-say´-rah], *f.* Kiln, where gypsum is calcined and prepared for use.

yesería [yay-say-ree´-ah], *f.* 1. *V.* YESERA. 2. Building constructed with gypsum.

yesero, ra [yay-say´-ro, rah], *a.* Belonging to gypsum.

yesero [yay-say´-ro], *m.* One that prepares or sells gypsum.

yesgo [yes´-go], *m. (Bot. Prov.)* Dwarf elder.

yeso [yay´-so], *m.* Gypsum, gypse, sulphate of lime. **Yeso mate,** plaster of Paris. **Yeso blanco,** whiting.

yesón [yay-sone´], *m.* Piece of rubbish or fragment of gypsum already used in building.

yesoso, sa [yay -so´-so, sah], *a.* Gypseous.

yesquero [yes-kay´-ro], *m.* Tinderbox.

yeyuno [yay-yoo´-no], *m.* Jejunum, the second portion of the small intestines between the duodenum and the ileum.

yezgo [yeth´-go], *m. (Bot.)* Dwarf elder.

y griega [ee gre-ay-gah], *f.* Name of the letter y. (Greek y, as contrasted to the Latin I.)

yo [yo], *pron. pers.* 1. **Yo mismo,** I myself. **Yo, el rey,** I the king. **Soy yo,** it is I. **Soy yo el que lo dice,** I am the one who says it. **Si yo fuera usted,** if I were you. *-m.* **El yo,** the I, the ego.

yodado (or **ato**) [yo-dah´-do, to], *a.* Iodic, containing iodine.

yodo [yo´-do], *m.* Iodine, a bluish black haloid element used in medicine and in photography.

yoduro [yo-doo´-ro], *m.* Iodid, iodide, a compound of iodine.

ýpsilon [eep´-se-lon], *f.* Twentieth letter of the Greek alphabet, corresponding to y.

yoga [yoh´-gah], *m.* Yoga.

yogur [yoh-goor´], *m.* Yoghurt.

yole [yo´-lay], *m. (Naut.)* Yawl.

yuca [yoo´-cah], *f. (Bot.)* Adam's needle; the root of this plant is farinaceous, and eaten like potatoes. Yucca.

yucateco, ca [yoo-cah-tay´-co, cah], *a.* Of Yucatan.

yugada [yoo-gah´-dah], *f.* Extent of ground which a yoke of oxen can plough in a day: a yoke of land.

yugo [yoo´-go], *m.* 1. Yoke, for draught-oxen. 2. Nuptial tie, with which a new-married couple is veiled; marriage ceremony. 3. Oppressive authority, absolute power. 4. Confinement, prison, yoke. 5. Kind of gallows under which the Romans passed their prisoners of war. 6. *(Naut.)* Transom, a beam across the sternpost. **Sacudir el yugo,** to throw off the yoke.

yuguero [yoo-gay´-ro], *m.* Ploughman, ploughboy.

yugular [yoo-goo-lar´], *a. (Anat.)* Jugular.

yumbo, ba [yoom´-b, bah], *m. & f. & a.* A savage Indian of eastern Ecuador.

yunga [yoo-gah], *f. (Peru, Bol.) a. & m. pl.* Name given in Bolivia to the hot region of the north-east where famous coffee is raised.

yunque [yoon´-kay], *m.* 1. Anvil (herramienta). 2. Constancy, fortitude. 3. *(Anat.)* Incus, a bone of the ear. 4. One of the blades of a cloth-shearer's shears. **Estar al yunque,** to bear up under the frowns of fortune; to bear impertinent or abusive language.

yunta [yoon´-tah], *f.* 1. Couple, pair, yoke. 2. *(Prov.) V.* YUGADA.

yuntería [yoon-tay-ree´-ah], *f.* Place where draught-oxen are fed.

yuntero [yoon-tay´-ro], *m. V.* YUGUERO.

yunto, ta [yoon-to, tah], *a.* Joined, united, close. *V.* JUNTO.

yuruma [yoo-roo´-mah], *f.* Starch obtained from a species of palm along the Orinoco.

yusera [yoo-say-rah], *f.* The horizontal stone in oil-mills which lies under the roller.

yusión [yoo-se-on'], *f.* Precepts, command.

yute [yoo'-tay], *m.* 1. Jute, a textile fiber obtained from an Asiatic herb of the linden family. 2. Jute fabric.

yuxtaponer [yoox-tah-po-nerr'], *va.* To juxtapose, to put side by side.

yuxtaposición [yoox-tah-po-se-the-on'], *f.* Juxtaposition.

yuyuba [yoo-yoo'-bah], *f. V.* AZUFAIFA.

Z

z [thay'-dah, thay'-tah], *f.* The twenty-sixth letter of the Spanish alphabet. Whether at the beginning, middle, or end of words, it sounds in Spanish like the English *th* in *thank, cathedral, tenth. Latin words terminating in x* take *z* in Spanish, as *lux, luz; velox, veloz.* In the plural and in compound words it is superseded by *c*, as *paz* makes *paces, pacífico, apaciguar.*

¡za! [thah], *int.* A word used to frighten dogs or other animals.

zábida, zábila [thah'-be-dah, thah'-be-lah], *f. (Bot.)* Common or yellow-flowered aloe.

zaborda, *f.* **zabordamiento,** *m.* [thah-bor'-dah, thah-bor-dah-me-en'-to], *(Naut.)* Stranting; the act of getting on shore.

zabordar [thah-bor-dar'], *vn. (Naut.)* To touch ground, to get on shore, to be stranded.

zabordo [thah-bor'-do], *m. (Naut.)* Stranding.

zaboyar [thah-bo-yar'], *va. (Prov.)* To join-bricks with mortar.

zabra [thab'-brah], *f. (Naut.)* A small vessel, used on the coast of Biscay.

zabucar [thah-boo-car'], *va.* 1. To revolve something. 2. To shake, to agitate. *V.* BAZUCAR.

zabullida [thah-bool-lyee'-dah], *f.* Dipping, ducking.

zabullidor, ra [thah-bool-lyee-dor', rah], *m. & f.* One who ducks or gets under water.

zabullidura [thah-bool-lyo-doo'-rah], *f.* Submersion, ducking.

zabullimiento [thah-bool-lyee-me-en'-to], *m. V.* ZAMBULLIDA.

zabullir [thah-bool'-lyeer'], *va.* To plunge, to immerse, to put under water, to immerge. -*vr.* 1. To plunge suddenly under water, to sink. 2. To lurk, to lie concealed.

zabuqueo [thah-boo-kay'-o], *m. V.* BAZUQUEO.

zacapela, zacapella [thah-cah-pay'-lah, par'-lyah], *f.* Uproar, yell, noisy bustle. *Cf.* GAZAPELA.

zacate [thah-cah'-tay], *m. (Mex. and Philip. Islands)* 1. Grass, herbage. 2. Hay, forage.

zacateca [thah-cah-tay'-cah], *m. (Cuba)* Undertaker, funeral director, sexton.

zacatín [thah-cah-teen'], *m.* A place where garments are sold.

zádiva [thah'-de-vah], *f. (Bot.)* A plant the leaves of which soften corns.

zafacoca [thah-fah-co'-cah], *com. (Amer. Coll.)* Noisy confusion, squabbling; rioting.

zafada [thah-fah'-dah], *f.* 1. Flight, escape. 2. *(Naut.)* The act of lightening the ship.

zafar [thah-far'], *va.* 1. To adorn, to embellish. 2. To disembarrass. 3. *(Naut.)* To lighten a ship. -*vr.* 1. To escape (huir), to avoid risk, to run away. 2. To avoid, to decline; to excuse, to free oneself from trouble, to get clear off. 3. To slip off the border of a wheel: applied to the belt of machinery.

zafareche [thah-fah-ray'-chay], *m. (Prov.) V.* ESTANQUE.

zafarí [thah-fah-ree'], *m.* A sort of pomegranate, with quadrangular seeds.

zafariche [thah-fah-ree'-chay], *m. (Prov.)* Shelf for holding water vessels or jars.

zafarrancho [thah-far-rahn'-cho], *m.* 1. *(Naut.)* The state of being clear for action. **Hacer zafarrancho,** *(Naut.)* to make

ready for action. 2. *(Coll.)* Ravage, destruction, 3. Scuffle, wrangle, squabble.

zafería [thah-fay-ree'-ah], *f.* A small village, a farm-house.

zafiamente [thah-fe-ah-men'-tay], *adv.* Clownishly, lubberly, clumsily.

zafiedad [thah-fe-ay-dahd'], *f.* Clownishness, rusticity, clumsiness.

zafio, fia [thah'-fe-o, ah], *a.* Clownish, coarse, uncivil, ignorant.

zafío [thah-fee'-o], *m. (Zool.) V.* SAFÍO or CONGRIO.

zafir, zafiro [thah-feer', thah-fee'-ro], *m.* Sapphire, a precious stone.

zafíreo, ea [thah-fee'-ray-o, ah], *a.* Sapphire-colored.

zafirino, na [thah-fe-ree'-no, nah], *a.* Of the color of sapphire.

zafo, fa, [thah'-fo, fah], *a.* 1. Free, disentangled, empty. 2. *(Naut.)* Clear. 3. Free, exempt from danger or risk. 4. *(LAm.)* Free (libre).

zafón [thah-fone'], *m. V.* ZAHÓN.

zafra [thah'-frah], *f.* 1. Drip-jar, a large metal bowl, pierced at the bottom, placed over a jar for draining oil; or a dish in which oil is kept. 2. Crop of sugar-cane and the making of sugar. 3. A broad strap which holds the thills of a cart. 4. *(Min.)* Poor ore mingled with rubbish.

zafre [thah'-fray], *m. (Min.)* Zaffre or saffre, cobalt oxyd roasted with silica, and employed chiefly for giving a blue color to porcelain.

zafreño, ña [thah-fray'-nyo, nyah], *a.* Belonging to the town of Zafra.

zaga [thah'-gah], *f.* 1. Load packed on the back part or a carriage. 2. The extremity behind. 3. *(Mil.) V.* RETAGUARDIA. -*m.* The last player at a game of cards. -*adv. V.* DETRÁS. **A zaga** or **en zaga,** behind. **No ir** or **no quedarse en zaga,** *(Coll.)* not to be less than any other, or inferior to any man.

zagal [thah-gahl'], *m.* 1. A stout, spirited young man. 2. Swain, a young shepherd subordinate to the chief herd; subordinate coachman. 3. Under petticoat.

zagala [thah-gah'-lah], *f.* A shepherdess, lass, girl.

zagalejo, ja [thah-gah-lay'-ho, hah], *m. & f. dim.* A young shepherd or shepherdess.

zagalejo [thah-gah lay'-ho], *m.* An under petticoat of close woven stuff worn over the white petticoat.

zagalico, illo, ito [thah-gah-lee'-co], *m. dim.* A little shepherd.

zagalón, na [thah-gah-lone', nah], *m. & f.* An overgrown lad or girl.

zagú [thah-goo'], *m.* The sago-plant. *V.* SAGÚ.

zagua [thah'-goo-ah], *f.* A shrub yielding barilla which grows in southern Europe and northern Africa.

zaguán [thah-goo-ahn'], *m.* Porch, entrance, hall, vestibule (entrada).

zaguanete [thah-goo-ah-nay'-tay], *m.* 1. *(Dim.)* Small entrance of a house. 2. A small party of the king's lifeguards.

zaguero, ra [thah-gay'-ro, rah], *a.* Going or remaining behind.

zahareño, ña [thah-ah-ray'-nyo, nyah], *a.* 1. Intractable, wild, haggard (pájaros). 2. *(Met.)* Sour, haughty, indocile.

zaharí [thah-ah-ree'], *a. V.* ZAFARÍ.

zahén [thah-ayn'], *a.* **Dobla zahén** or **zahena,** a Moorish gold coin.

zaherible [thah-ay-ree'-blay], *a.* Blamable, censurable, blameworthy.

zaheridor, ra [thah-ay-re-dor', rah], *m. & f.* Censurer, one who blames.

zaherimiento [thah-ay-re-me-en'-to], *m.* Censurer, blame.

zaherir [thah-ay-reer'], *va.* 1. To censure, to blame, to reproach; to upbraid (reprender). 2. To mortify one by criticising him with a bad intention (criticar).

zahina [thah-ee'-nah], *f.* Sorghum, a gruminuceous plant resembling broomcorn, cultivated in Spain for fodder.

zahinar [thah-e-nar'], *m.* Land sown with sorghum, sorghum-field.

zahinas [thah-hee'-nahs], *f. pl.* Light und soft fritters, puff-cakes. **Zahinas de levadura**, froth of barm.

zahón [thah-on'], *m.* 1. A leather apron divided at the lower part and tied behind the thighs and at the waist; worn to protect the clothes. 2. *pl.* A kind of wide breeches, overalls.

zahonado, da [thah-oh-nah'-do, dah], *a.* Of a dark color, brownish.

zahondar [thah-on-dar'], *va.* To dig the ground, to penetrate. *V.* AHONDAR. *-vn.* To sink into the ground (pies).

zahora [thah-o'-rah], *f. (Prov.)* Luncheon among friends, with music.

zahorar [thah-o-rar'], *m.* To have a repast with music.

zahorí [thah-o-ree'], *m.* 1. Clairvoyant, seer (adivino). 2. Water diviner (manantiales). 3. Mind reader (que adivina los pensamientos). 4. Very perceptive person (perspicaz).

zahorra [thah-or'-rah], *f. (Naut.)* Ballast. *V.* LASTRE.

zahumerio [thah-oo-may'-re-o], *m. (Obs.) V.* SAHUMERIO.

zahurda [thah-oor'-dah], *f.* 1. Pigsty, hogsty. 2. A small, dirty, miserable house. 3. An ipterous insect of Europe.

zaida [thah-ee'-dah], *f. (Orn.)* A variety of the African heron.

zaino, na [thah'-e-no, nah], *a.* 1. Of a chestnut color (caballos). 2. Vicious (animales). 3. Treacherous, wicked, vicious.

zalá [thah-lah'], *f.* Religious adoration paid by the Moors to God; prayer with various ceremonies.

zalagarda [thah-lah-gar'-dah], *f.* 1. Ambuscade, ambush (emboscada). 2. Gin, trap, snare. 3. Sudden attack, surprise. *f.* Mockfight: vulgar noise. 5. *(Coll.)* Malicious cunning.

zalama, zalamería [thah-lah'-mah, thah-lah-may-ree'-ah], *f.* Flattery, adulation, wheedling.

zalamelé [thah-lah-may-lay'], *m. V.* ZALAMA.

zalameramente [thah-lah-may'-rah-men-tay], *adv.* Fawningly.

zalamero, ra [thah-lah-may'-ro, rah], *m. & f.* Wheedler, flatterer, Owner.

zalea [thah-lay'-ah], *f.* 1. An undressed sheep-skin. 2. Sheepskin mats.

zalear [thah-lay-ar'], *va.* 1. To move a thing with care. 2. To frighten dogs. *V.* ZACEAR.

zalema [thah-lay'-mah], *f.* Bow, courtesy. *(Arab.)*

zaleo [thah-lay'-o], *m.* 1. Skin of a beast lacerated by the wolf, undressed sheep-skin. 2. The act of shaking or moving to and fro.

zalomar [thah-lo-mar'], *vn. (Naut.)* To sing out. *V.* SALOMAR.

zamacuco [thah-mah-coo'-co], *m. (Coll.)* 1. Dunce, dolt. 2. Intoxication, inebriation.

zamanca [thah-mahn'-cah], *f. (Coll.)* Drubbing, flogging, castigation.

zamarra [thah-mar'-rah], *f.* 1. Dress worn by shepherds, made of undressed sheep-skin (chaqueta). 2. The skin so used.

zamarrear [thah-mar-ray-ar'], *va.* 1. To shake (perro), to drag or pull to and fro. 2. To pin up close in a dispute (en discusión). 3. *(Met.)* To drag, to ill-treat.

zamarreo [thah-mar-ray'-o], *m.* Action of dragging or shaking from side to side.

zamarrico [thah-mar-ree'-co], *m. dim.* of ZAMARRO. A portmanteau or bag of sheepskin, having the wool inside.

zamarrilla [thah-mar-reel'-lyah], *f.* 1. *(Dim.)* A short loose coat of sheepskins. 2. *(Bot.)* Poly, mountain germander, a medicinal plant with yellow flowers which are very bitter.

zamarro [thah-mar'-ro], *m.* 1. A shepherd's coat of sheepskins. 2. Sheep or lamb skin. 3. Dolt, stupid person. *-m. pl. (Amer. Colom.)* Leather leggings.

zamarrón [thah-mar-rone'], *m. aug.* of ZAMARRA and ZAMARRO. A large sheep-skin.

zamarruco [thah-mar-roo'-co], *m. (Orn.)* Titmouse.

zambaigo, ga [tham-bah'-e-go, gah], *a. & m. & f.* Son or daughter of an Indian by a Chinese woman, or of a Chinaman and Indian woman.

zambapalo [tham-bah-pah'-lo], *m.* Ancient dance.

zambarco [tham-bar'-co], *m.* A broad breast-harness for coach-horses and mules.

zámbigo, ga [thahm'-be-go, gah], *a.* Bandy-legged.

zambo, ba [thahm'-bo, bah], *a.* 1. Bandy-legged. 2. Applied to the son of an Indian by a Chinese woman, or of a Chinaman by an Indian woman. *-m.* An American wild monkey, resembling a dog, with the head of a horse.

zamboa [tham-bo'-ah], *f.* 1. *(Bot.)* A sweet kind of quince-tree. 2. Citron-tree. *V.* AZAMBOA.

zambomba [tham-bom'-bah], *f.* A kind of rustic drum (tambor), consisting of a skin stretched over the mouth of a jar, with a reed fastened at the centre. This rubbed up and down with the moistened hand produces a strong, hoarse, monotonous sound. *-int.* Whew! interjection denoting surprise.

zambombo [tham-bom'-bo], *m.* Clown, rustic, ill-bred person.

zamborondón, na, zamborotudo, da [tham-bo-ron-done', nah, tham-bo-ro-too'-do, dah], *a.* Clownish, clumsy, ill-shaped.

zambra [thahm'-brah], *f.* 1. A Moorish festival or feast, attended with dancing and music. 2. Shout, noisy mirth (jaleo). 3. Kind of Moorish boat.

zambucar, zambucarse [tham-boo-car'], *vn. & vr.* To be hidden, to be concealed; to hide oneself.

zambuco [tham-boo'-co], *m.* Squatting, lying close to the ground, withdrawn from sight; hiding, concealing.

zambullida [tham-bool-lyee'-dah], *f.* 1. Dipping, ducking, submersion. 2. Infencing, thrust on the breast.

zambullidura [tham-bool-lyee-doo'-rah], *f.* **Zambullimiento** [tham-boo-lyee-me-en'-to], *m. V.* ZABULLIDURA.

zambullir [tham-bool-lyeer'], *va. & vr.* To plunge into water, to dip, to dive (debajo del agua).

zambullo [tham-bool'-lyo], *m. (Naut.)* A large bucket for the use of the sick.

zamorano, na [tham-mo-rah'-no, nah], *a.* Belonging to Zamora. **Gaita Zamorana**, kind of bagpipe.

zampabodigos, zampabollos [tham-pah-bo-dee'-gos, tham-pah-bol'-lyos], *m. (Coll.)* Glutton (glotón). *V.* ZAMPATORTAS.

zampada [tham-pah'-dah], *f. (Prov.)* Act of concealing or putting one thing within another.

zampadura [tham-pah-doo'-rah], *f. V.* ZAMPAMIENTO.

zampalimosnas [tham-pah-le-mos'-nas], *m.* A sturdy beggar.

zampamiento [tham-pah-me-en'-to], *m.* The act of concealing or reveling over a thing.

zampapalo [tham-pah-pah'-lo], *m. (Coll.) V.* ZAMPATORTAS.

zampar [tham-par'], *va.* 1. To conceal in a clever manner; to thrust one thing into another, so as to be covered by it and withdrawn from light (ocultar). 2. To devour eagerly (devorar). 3. To hurl (arrojar). 4. *(LAm.)* To fetch (golpe). *-vr.* 1. To thrust oneself suddenly into a place. 2. To bump (lanzarse).

zampatortas [tham-pah-tor'-tas], *m. (Coll.)* 1. A glutton. 2. Clown, rustic.

zampear [tham-pay-ar'], *vn.* To drive stakes in a ground to make it solid.

zampeado [tham-pay-ah'-do], *m. (Arch.)* Woodwork and masonry in marshy foundations.

zampoña [tham-po'-nyah], *f.* 1. A rustic instrument, a kind of bagpipe. *V.* PIPITAÑA. 2. A poetical vein, genius or talent for poetry. 3. *(Coll.)* Frivolous saying.

zampoñear [tham-po-nyay-ar'], *vn.* 1. To play the bagpipe. 2. *(Met.)* To be prolix and frivolous in conversation, to prose.

zampuzar [tham-poo-thar'], *va.* 1. To plunge, to dip, to dive. 2. To hide, to conceal.

zampuzo [tham-poo'-tho], *m.* Immersion, submersion, concealment.

zamuro [tham-moo'-ro], *m. (Orn.)* Carrion-vulture, vultur aura.

zanahoria [thah-nah-o'-re-ah], *f.* 1. *(Bot.)* Carrot. 2. *(Cono Sur)* Idiot (imbécil); clumsy oaf (desmañado).

zanahoriate [thah-nah-o-re-ah'-tay], *m. V.* AZANORIATE.

zanca [thahn'-cah], *f.* 1. Shank, purl of the leg of a fowl or bird which extends from the claws to the thigh. 2. A long shank or leg. 3. Large pin. **Zancas de araña**, shifts, evasions, subterfuges. **Zancas largas**, *m.* (Long shanks) woodcock, a European bird of the snipe family.

zancada [than-cah'-dah], *f.* Long stride. **En dos zancadas,** *(Coll.)* expeditiously, speedily.

zancadilla [than-cah-dee'l-lyah], *f.* 1. Trip, a stroke or catch by which a wrestler supplants his antagonist. 2. Trick, deceit, craft; act of supplanting. 3. *(Naut.)* Elbow in the hawse. **Echar la zancadilla a uno,** to trip somebody up.

zancado, da [than-cah-do, dah], *a.* Insipid (salmón).

zancajear [than-cah-hay-ar'], *va.* To run about the streets bespattering the legs with dirt and mud.

zancajera [than-cah-hay'-rah], *f.* Coach step.

zancajiento, ta [than-cah-he-en'-to, tah], *a.* Bandy-legged. *V.* ZANCAJOSO.

zancajo [than-cah'-ho], *m.* 1. Heel-bone of the foot. 2. The part of a shoe or stocking which covers the heel. 3. A short, ill-shaped person. 4. An ignorant, stupid person. **No llegar al zancajo** or **a los zancajos,** not to come up or near one in any line.

zancajoso, sa [than-cah-ho'-so, sah], *a.* 1. Bandy-legged. 2. Wearing dirty stockings with holes at the heels. 3. Clumsy, awkward, unhandy.

zancarrón [than-car-rone'], *m.* 1. The bare heel-bone. 2. Any large bone without flesh. 3. A withered, old, ugly person. 4. An ignorant pretender at any art or science.

zanco [thahn'-co], *m.* 1. Stilt. 2. Dancer or walker on stilts. 3. *(Naut.)* Flag-staff. **Subirse en zancos,** to be haughty and elated with good fortune.

zancudo, da [than-coo'-do, dah], *a.* Long-shanked, having long, thin legs. *-m.* A long-beaked mosquito. *-pl.* *(Zool.)* Wading birds, such as the heron, the flamingo, the jacana, etc.

zandalia [than-dah'-le-ah], *f.* Sandal. *V.* SANDALIA.

zandunga [than-doon'-gah], *f.* *V.* SANDUNGA. *(Coll.)* Gracefulness, elegance; cajoling, wheedling; flattering, allurement, fascination.

zandunguero, ra [than-doon-gay'-ro, rah], *m. & f.* *V.* SANDUNGUERO.

zanefa [thah-nay'-fah], *f.* A printed border. *V.* CENEFA.

zanga [thahn'-gah], *f.* Ombre played by four.

zangada [than-gah'-dah], *f.* Raft or float made of cork.

zangala [than-gah'-lah], *f.* Buckram

zangamanga [than-gah-mahn'-gah], *f.* Falsehood, tending to deceive or defraud person.

zanganada [than-gah-nah'-dah], *f.* 1. Dronish or duggardly act. 2. *(Coll.)* An impertinent saying or act.

zangandongo [than-gan-don'-go], *m.* 1. *(Coll.)* Idler, a lazy person, who affects ignorance and grant of abilities. 2. Dolt, an ignorant, stupid, awkward person.

zangandullo, zangandungo [than-gan-dool'-lyo], *m. (Col.)* *V.* ZANGANDONGO.

zanganear [than-gah-nay-ar'], *vn.* To drone, to live in idleness (gandulear).

zángano [thahn'-gah-no], *m.* 1. Drone, a bee which makes no honey; the male bee (gandul). 2. Sluggard, idler, sponger. 3. *(Coll.)* Sly, omening, or playful cunning person, taking it either in a good or bad meaning, according to the sense of the phrase.

zangarilla [than-gah-reel'-lyah], *f.* A small watermill for grinding wheat, on the banks of rivers in Estremadura.

zangarilleja [than-gah-re-lyay'-hah], *f.* Trollop, a dirty, lazy girl.

zangarrear [than-gar-ray-ar'], *vn.* To scrape a guitar.

zangarriana [than-gar-re-ah'-nah], *f.* 1. An infirmity of the head, incident to sheep. 2. *(Coll.)* Badness, melancholy. 3. *(Coll.)* Any periodical disease.

zangarullón [than-gah-rool-lyone'], *m.* A tall, sluggish, lazy lad.

zangolotear [than-go-lo-tay-ar'], *vn.* 1. To move in a violent yet ridiculous manner (agitar). 2. To slam, to move because the screws or nails which hold certain things are loose. 3. To fidget (persona).

zangoloteo [than-go-lo-tay'-o], *m.* A violent yet ridiculous waddling, a wagging motion or movement.

zangolotino, na [than-go-lo-tee'-no, nah], *a.* Said of the boy whom it is desired to pass for a child; childish.

zangón [than-gone'], *m.* *(Coll.)* *V.* ZANGARULÓN.

zangotear [than-go-tay-ar'], *m.* *V.* ZANGOLOTEAR.

zangoteo [than-go-tay'-o], *m.* *V.* ZANGOLOTEO.

zanguanga [than-goo-ahn'-gah], *f.* *(Coll.)* A feigned disease; a fictitious disorder.

zanguango [than-goo-ahn'-go], *m.* *(Coll.)* l. Lazy fellow who always finds pretexts to avoid work. 2. A fool, a booby.

zanguayo [than-goo-ah'-lyo], *m.* *(Coll.)* Tall idler, that pretends to be ill, silly, or unable to work.

zanja [thahn'-hah], *f.* *1.* Ditch (fosa), trench (foso), drain; a pit dug in the ground (hoyo). 2. *(LAm.)* Gully (barranco). 3. *(And.)* fence (límite).

zanjar [than-har'], *va.* 1. To open ditches or drains, to excavate. 2. To lay a foundation, to ground; to establish. 3. To terminate or settle a business amicably.

zanjica, illa, ita [than-hee'-cah], *f.* *dim.* Small drain; slender foundation.

zanjón [than-hone'], *a. aug.* 1. A deep ditch (zanja profunda); lard drain. 2. *(Carib. Cono Sur)* Cliff (risco).

zanjencillo [than-hen-theel'-lyo], *m. dim.* A small drain or trench.

zanqueador, ra [than-kay-ah-dor', rah], *m. & f.* 1. One who waddles in walking. 2. A great walker.

zanqueamiento [than-kay-ah-me-en'-to], *m.* The act of waddling in walking.

zanquear [than-ker-ar'], *vn.* To waddle (andar mal), to trot or run about; to walk much and fast (rápidamente).

zanquilargo, ga [than-ke-lar'-go, gah], *a.* Long shanked, long-legged.

zanquilla, zanquita [than-keel'-lyah, kee'-tah], *f. dim.* Thin, long shank or leg.

zanquituerto, ta [than-ke-too-err'-to, tah], *a.* Bandy-legged.

zanquivano, na [than-ke-vah'-no, nah], *a.* Spindle shanked.

zantoxíleo, ea [than-tok-see'-lay-o, ah], *a.* Like prickly ash.

zantóxilo [than-tok'-se-lo], *m.* Xanthoxylum, prickly ash.

zapa [thah'-pah], *f.* 1. Spade (pala). 2. A trench for military purposes. 2. Shagreen, a skin made rough in imitation of sealskin. 4. Kind of carving in silver.

zapador [thah-pah-dor'], *m. (Mil.)* Sapper.

zapapico [thah-pah-pee'-co], *m.* Pickaxe.

zapar [thah-par'], *m.* To sap, to mine.

zaparrada [thah-par-rah'-dah], *f.* A violent fall.

zaparrastrar [thah-par-ras-trar'], *vn.* To trail (ropa).

zaparrastroso, sa [thah-par-ras-tro'-so, sah], *a.* 1. Dirty from trailing on the ground. 2. Ill-made, badly done.

zaparrazo [thah-par-rah'-tho], *m.* 1. A violent fall, attended with great noise. 2. *(Coll.)* Sudden calamity, misfortune.

zapata [thah-pah'-tah], *f.* 1. A piece of sole leather put on the hinds of a door to prevent its creaking. 2. A kind of colored half-boots. 3. Bracket of a beam. 4. *(Naut.)* Shoe. **Zapata de la quilla,** *(Naut.)* the false keel.

zapatazo [thah-pah-tah'-tho], *m.* 1. *(Aug.)* Large shoe. 2. Blow with a shoe (golpe con zapato). 3. Fall; the noise attending a fall (caída, ruido). 4. Clapping noise of a horse's foot. **Mandar (a uno) a zapatazos,** to lead one by the nose, to have complete control over one. **Tratar (a uno) a zapatazos,** to treat one badly and with scorn.

zapateado [thah-pah-tay-ah'-do], *m.* A dance consisting of keeping time by beating the feet on the floor. **—Zapateado, da,** *pp.* of ZAPATEAR.

zapateador, ra [thah-pah-tay-ah-dor', rah], *m. & f.* Dancer, who beats time with the sole of his shoe.

zapatear [thah-pah-tay-ar'], *va.* 1. To kick or strike with the shoe (patear). 2. To lead by the nose. 3. To beat time with the sole of the shoe. 4. To hit frequently with the button of the foil. 5. To strike the ground with the feet: used of rabbits when chased. *-vr.* To oppose with spirit; not to give up a contested point; to resist in debating.

zapateo [thah-pah-tay'-o], *m.* Act of keeping time by beating the foot on the floor.

zapatera [thah-pah-tay'-rah], *f.* 1. A shoemaker's wife. 2. Olive spoiled in the pickle.

zapatería [thah-pah-tay-ree'-ah], *f.* 1. Trade of a shoemaker; a shoemaker's shop (tienda). 2. Place or street which contains number of shoemakers' shops. 3. Shoemaking business.

zapateril [thah-pah-tay-reel'], *a.* Belonging to a shoemaker.

zapaterillo, illa [thah-pah-tay-reel'-lyo], *m. & f. dim.* A petty shoemaker.

zapatero [thah-pah-tay'-ro], *m.* Shoe maker. **Zapatero de viejo**, cobbler.

zapateta [thah-pah-tay'-tah], *f.* 1. Slap on the sole of a shoe. 2. Caper, leap, Jump.-*int.* Oh!, an exclamation of admiration.

zapatico, illo, ito [thah-pah-tee'-co], *m. dim.* A nice little shoe.

zapatilla [thah-pah-teel'-lyah], *f.* 1. Slipper (para casa). 2. (*Dim.*) A little shoe. 3. Pump (de baile), any shoe with a thin sole neatly finished. 4. Piece of chamois or buckskin put behind the lock of a gun or pistol. 5. Button at the end of a foil. 6. Exterior hoof of animals.

zapatillero [thah-pah-teel-lyay'-ro], *m.* Shoemaker who makes slippers, pumps, and children's shoes.

zapato [thah-pah'-to], *m.* Shoe. **Zapatos abotinados para señoras**, ladies' gaiters. **Zapato de madera**, a wooden shoe. **Andar con zapatos de fieltro**, to proceed with great caution and silence. **Zapatos de tenis**, tennis shoes.

zapatón [thah-pah-tone'], *m.* 1. (*Aug.*) A large, clumsy shoe. 2. A wooden shoe.

zapatudo, da [thah-pah-too'-do, dah], *m.* 1. Wearing large or strong shoes. 2. Large hoofed or clamored (bestias).

¡zape! [thah'-pay], *int.* 1. Shooo! scat! A word used to frighten cats away. 2. An exclamation of aversion, or of negation at cards. 3. God forbid! far be it from me!

zapear [thah-pay-ar'], *va.* 1. To frighten cats away by crying *zape.* 2. (*And. CAm.*) To spy on (espiar).

zapito [thah-pee'-to], *m.* (*Prov.*) Milk pail.

zapote [thah-po'-tay], *m.* (*Bet.*) Sapota-tree, sapodilla, and its luscious apple-shaped fruit.

zapuzar [thah-poo-thar'], *va.* To duck. V. CHAPUZAR.

zaque [thah'-kay], *va.* 1. Bottle or urine bag made of leather (de vino). 2. (*Coll.*) Tippler, drunkard.

zaquear [thah-kay-ar'], *va.* To rack, to defecate: to draw off liquor from one vessel into another.

zaquizami [thah-ke-thah-mee'], *m.* 1. Garret (buhardilla), cockloft. 2. A small, dirty house.

zar [thar], *m.* Czar, the Emperor of all the Russias.

zara [thah'-rah], *f.* (*Bot.*) Indian corn, maize. V. MAÍZ.

zarabanda [thah-rah-bahn'-dah], *f.* 1. Saraband, a lively dance and tune. 2. Bustle, noise.

zarabandista [thah-rah-ban-dees'-tah], *com.* Dancer.

zarabutero, ra [thah-rah-boo-tay'-ro, rah], *a.* (Leroy.) V. EMBUSTERO.

zaradión, zaradique [thah-rah-de-on'], *m.* Medicine for dogs, especially for curing the mange.

zaragata [thah-rah-gah'-tah], *f.* Turmoil, scuffle, quarrel.

zaragatada [thah-rah-gah-tah'-dah], *f.* A roguish or cunning trick.

zaragate, zarayate, or **saragate** [thah-rah-gah'-tay], *m.* (*Mex.*) Loafer, vagabond, rogue. This word, as well as *zángano*, is often used in an affectionate; jocular style, and answers to the English, little rogue, in the same sense.

zaragatona [thah-rah-gah-toh'-nah], *f.* (*Bot.*) Fleawort.

zaragocí [thah-rah-go-thee'], *m.* Kind of plum.

zaragozano, na [thah-rah-go-thah'-no, nah], *a.* Saragossan, of Saragossa.

zaragüelles [thah-rah-goo-el'-lyes], *m. pl.* 1. A sort of drawers or wide breeches; a large pair of breeches ill made. 2. Overalls, or overall pantaloons.

zaramago [thah-rah-mah'-go], *m.* (*Prov.*) V. JARAMAGO.

zaramagullón [thah-rah-mah-gool-lyone'], *m.* (*Orn.*) Didapper, minute merganser.

zarambeque [thah-ram-bay'-kay], *m.* A kind of merry tune and noisy dance.

zaramullo [tha-rah-mool'-lyo], *m.* Busybody, a vain, meddling person.

zaranda [thah-rahn'-dah], *f.* 1. Screen or frame for sifting earth or sand. 2. Riddle of esparto in oblong shape for screening stems of grapes, etc. 3. (*Carib.*) Spinning top (juguete).

zarandador [thah-ran-dah-dor'], *m.* Sifter of wheat.

zarandajas [thah-ran-dah'-has], *f. pl.* 1. Trifles, worthless soraps or remnants. 2. Odds given at the game of trucks.

zarandajillas [thah-ran-dah-heel'-lyas], *f. pl. dim.* Little trifles.

zarandalí [thah-ran-dah-lee'], *adv.* (*Prov.*) Applied to a black-spotted dove.

zarandar, zarandear [thah-ran-dar', thah-ran-day-ar'], *va.* 1. To winnow corn with a sieve. 2. To stir and move nimbly. 3. To separate the precious from the common. 4. To sift and toss about pins in a vessel (cribar). -*vr.* 1. To be in motion, to move to and fro (ir y venir). 2. (*LAm.*) To strut about (pavonearse).

zarandeo [thah-ran-day'-o], *m.* Act of sifting or winnowing.

zarandero [thah-ran-day'-ro], *m.* V. ZARANDADOR.

zarandija [thah-ran-dee'-hah], *f.* (*Zool.*) An insect which burrows in the ground and devastates gardens: the mole-cricket. (*Cf.* SABANDIJA.) V. GRILLOTALPA.

zarandillo [thah-ran-deel'-lyo], *m.* 1. (*Dim.*) A small sieve or riddle. 2. (*Coll.*) One who frisks nimbly about.

zarapallón [thah-rah-pal-lyone'], *m.* A shabby, dirty fellow.

zarapatel [thah-rah-pah-tel'], *m. & f.* A kind of salmagundi.

zarapeto [thah-rah-pay'-to], *m.* (*Coll.*) Intriguer, crafty person.

zarapito [thah-rah-pee'-to], *m.* (*Orn.*) Whimbrel, curlew-jack.

zaratán [thah-rah-tahn'], *m.* Cancer in the breast. (*Arab.*)

zaraza [thah-rah'-thah], *f.* Chintz, a delicate cotton stuff.

zarcear [thar-thay-ar'], *va.* To clean pipes or conduits with briers. -*vn.* To move to and fro.

zarcero, ra [thar-thay'-ro, rah], *a.* Fit to pursue the game among briers: applied to pointers.

zarceto, ta [thar-thay'-to, tah], *m. & f.* (*Orn.*) Widgeon. V. CERCETA.

zarcillo [thar-theel'-lyo], *m.* 1. Earring (pendiente). 2. Tendril of a vine or other climbing plant. 3. (*Prov.*) Hoop of a butt or barrel.

zarco, ca [thar'-co, cah], *a.* 1. Walleyed, of a light blue color (ojos). 2. Clear and pure (agua).

zarevitz [thah-ray-veeth'], *m.* Czarwitz, the first-born son of the Emperor of Russia, and heir-apparent to the throne. His wife is culled *Zarevna.*

zargatona [thar-gah-to'-nah], *f.* V. ZARAGATONA.

zariano, na [thah-re-ah'-no, nah], *a.* Belonging to the Czar.

zarina [thah-ree'-nah], *f.* Czarina, empress, the wife of the Emperor of Russia.

zarja [thar'-hah], *f.* Reel, for winding silk. V. AZARJA.

zaroche [thah-ro'-chay], *m.* (*Ecuador*) Mountain sickness from too rapid advance into rarefied air. V. TEJA.

zarpa [thar'-pah], *f.* 1. Weighing anchor. 2. Dirt or mud sticking to the skirts of clothes (salpicadura). 3. Superior thickness of foundation walls. 4. Claw of a beast or bird. **Echar la zarpa**, to gripe, to claw.

zarpada [thar-pah'-dah], *f.* Clawing, a strike or dig with claws.

zarpanel [thar-pah-nel'], *a.* (*Arch.*) V. CARPANEL.

zarpar [thar-par'], *va.* (*Naut.*) To weigh anchor. **El ancla está zarpada**, (*Naut.*) the anchor is atrip.

zarpazo [thar-pah'-tho], *m.* Sound of a body falling on the ground.

zarposo, sa [thar-po'-so, sah], *a.* Bespattered with mire or dirt.

zarracatería [thar-rah-cah-tay-ree'-ah], *f.* Deceitful flattery.

zarracatín [thar-rah-cah-teen'], *m.* Haggler. miser.

zarrampla [thar-rahm'-plah], *com. (Coll.)* Blockhead; awkward.

zarramplín [thar-ram-pleen'], *m.* Bungler, botcher; an insignificant fellow.

zarramplinada [thar-ram-ple-nah'-dah], *f.* Work clumsily performed; thing of little moment.

zarrapastra [thar-rah-pahs'-trah], *f.* Dirt or mire sticking to the skirts of clothes.

zarrapastrón, na [thar-rah-pas-trone', nah], *a. & n.* Tatterdemalion, ragged fellow.

zarrapastrosamente [thar-rah-pahs-tro-sah-men-tay], *adv.* Raggedly.

zarrapastroso, sa [thar-rah-pas-tro´-so, sah], *a.* Ragged, dirty, uncleanly.

zarria [thar'-re-ah], *f.* 1. Dirt or mire sticking to clothes (salpicadura). 2. Leather thongs for tying on *abarcas.*

zarriento, ta [thar-re-en-to, tah], *a.* Bespattered with mud or mire.

zarrio [thar'-re-o], *m.* V. CHARRO.

zarza [thar'-thah], *f. (Bot.)* Common bramble, the European blackberry-bush. **Zarzas**, *(Met.)* thorns, difficulties.

zarzagán [thar-thah-gahn'], *m.* A cold north-east wind.

zarzaganete [thar-thah-gah-nay'-tay], *m. dim.* A light northeast wind.

zarzaganillo [thar-thah-gah-neel-lyo], *m.* A violent storm at north-east.

zarzahán [thar-thah-ahn'], *m.* A kind of striped silk.

zarzaidea [thar-thah-e-day'-ah], *f. (Bot.)* Raspberry-bush.

zarzal [thar-thahl'], *m.* Briery, a place where briers grow; place full of briers or brambles.

zarzamora [thar-thah-mo'-rah], *f. (Bot.)* Blackberry, berry of the bramble.

zarzaparrilla [thar-thah-par-reel'-lyah], *f. (Bot.)* Sarsaparilla.

zarzaparrillar [thar-thah-par-reel-lyar'], *m.* Plantation of sarsaparilla.

zarzaperruna [thar-thah-per-roo'-nah], *f. (Bot.)* Dog-rose.

zazarrosa [thar-thar-ro´-sah], *f. (Bot.)* Dog-rose. V. ZARZAPERRUNA.

zarzo [thar'-tho], *m.* Hurdle, a texture of canes, sticks, or twigs.

zarzoso, sa [thar-tho'-so, sah], *a.* Briery, full of brambles or briers.

zarzuela [thar-thoo-ay'-lah], *f.* Spanish operetta or musical comedy.

¡zas! [thahs]. Word used to express the sound of repeated blows: raps at a door.

zascandil [thas-can-deel], *m.* 1. *(Coll.)* A crafty impostor or swindler (poco fiable). 2. An upstart.

zata, zatara [thah'-tah, thah-tah'-rah], *f.* Raft made by laying pieces of timber across each other.

zatico, illo [thah-tee'-co], *m.* A small bit of bread.

zato [thah'-to], *m. (Prov.)* Morsel of bread.

zayar [thah-yar´], *va. (Naut.)* To house, to haul a tackle.

zarahán [thah-thah-ahn´], *m.* Sort of flowered silk.

zazosito, ita [thah-thoo-see´-to, tah], *a. dim.* of ZAZOSO.

zazoso, sa [tha-tho'-so, sah], *a.* Pronouncing a *c* or *z* instead of an *s.* V. CECEOSO.

zea [thay'-ah], *f.* 1. Hip-bone. V. CEA. 2. *(Bot.)* Spelt-corn.

zebra [thay'-brah], *f.* Zebra. V. CEBRA.

zebú [thay-boo'], *m.* Zebu, the Indian ox, having a hump on the shoulder, *(Geog.)* V. Appendix.

zeda [thay´-dah], *f.* Name of the letter *z* in Spanish.

zedilla [thay-deel'-lyah], *f.* Cedilla, the ancient letter which was formed of a *c* and a comma under it, thus, *ç*: and the mark, itself.

zedoaria [thay-do-ah´-re-ah], *f. (Bot.)* Zedoary.

zeé [thay-ay'], *a.* V. ZAHÉN.

zelandés, sa [thay-lan-days', sah], *a.* Zenlandian, of Zealand.

zend [thend], *m.* Zend, the ancient Persian language.

zendaveeta [then-dah-vee'-tah], *m.* The sacred books of the Persians, attributed to Zoroaster.

zenit [thay-neet'], *m.* V. CENIT.

zenzalino, na [then-thah-lee'-no, nah], *a.* Belonging to gnats.

zenzalo [then´-thah-lo], *m.* Gnat, mosquito. V. CÉNZALO.

zeppelín [thay-pay-leen´], *m.* Zeppelin.

zequí [thay'-kee], *m.* Zechin; an Arabic gold coin formerly used in Spain, worth about two dollars. V CEQUÍ.

zequia [thay'-ke-ah], *f.* Canal for irrigating lends. V. ACEQUIA.

zeta [thay'-tah], *f.* 1. Name of the letter *z.* V. ZEDA. 2. Sixth letter of Greek alphabet.

zeugma [thay-oog'-mah], *f.* (Rhetoric) Zeugma, a kind of ellipsis.

zigema [the-hay'-mah], *f. (Zool.)* 1. The hammer-headed shark. 2. Zygaena, a genus of moths typical of the zygenidae stoutbodied moths.

zigofilo [the-go-fee´-lo], *m. (Bot.)* Beancaper.

zigzag [theeg-thahg'], *m.* V. ZISZÁS *(Acad.)*

zilórgano [the-lor'-gah-no], *m.* A kind of musical instrument. V.XILÓRGANO.

zimología [the-mo-lo-hee'-ah], *f.* Zymology, the knowledge or study of the principles of fermentation, or a treatise on this subject.

zimosímetro [the-mo-see'-may-tro], *f.* Kind of thermometer.

zimotecnia [the-mo-tec'-ne-ah], *f. (Chem.)* Treatise on fermentation.

zinc [thinc], *m.* Zinc a metal. V. CINC.

zincografía [theen-co-grah-fee'-ah], *f.* Zincography, the art of preparing relief-plates for printing upon zinc instead of stone.

zinga [theen'-gah], *f. (Naut.)* V. SINGLADURA.

zinnia [thee'-ne-ah], *f. (Bot.)* Zinnia.

zipizape [the-pe-thah'-pay], *m. (Coll.)* A noisy scuffle with blows. **Armar un zipizape**, to cause a rumpus.

zirigaña [the-re-gah'-nyah], *f. (Prov.)* Adulation. V. CHASCO and FRIOLERA.

¡zis, zas! [this, thas]. *(Coll.)* Words expressing the sound of repeated blows or strokes.

ziszás [this-thahs´], *m.* Zigzag.

zizaña [the-thah´-nyah], *f.* 1. *(Bot.)* Darnel. 2. Discord, disagreement; anything injurious. 3. Vice mixed with good actions. **Sembrar zizaña**, to sow discord. This word is now written CIZAÑA.

zizañar [the-thah-nyar´], *va.* To sow discord or vice.

zizañero [the-thah-nyay´-ro], *f.* Makebate a breeder of quarrels, firebrand.

zizigia [the-thee'-he-ah], *f.* Syzygy, a point of opposition or conjunction of the moon. (Also spelt **Cicigia**.)

zoantropía [tho-an-tro-pee'-ah], *f.* Insanity in which the patient believes himself transformed into an animal.

zoca [tho'-cah], *f.* Square. V. PLAZA.

zócalo [tho'-cah-lo], *m.* 1. *(Arch.)* Socle or zocle, a flat, square member under the base of a pedestal. 2. Skirting board (de pared). 3. *(Mex.) (Mil.)* Parade ground; town square (plaza); walk (bulevar).

zocato, ta [tho-cah'-to, tah], *m.* 1. Overripe: applied to cucumbers or eggplants which grow yellow. 2. V. ZURDO.

zoclo [tho'-clo], *m.* V. ZUECO.

zoco, ca [tho'-co, cah], *m. (Coll.)* V. ZURDO. -*m.* 1. A wooden shoe. 2. Plinth.

zocoba [tho-co´-bah], *f.* 1. *(Bot.)* Herb in South America used as an antidote to poison. 2. Tree in New Spain yielding fine yellow wood.

zodiacal [tho-de-ah-cahl'], *a.* Zodiacal, relating to the zodiac.

zodíaco [tho-dee'-ah-co], *m. (Ast.)* The zodiac, an imaginary belt or zone about 8° each side of the ecliptic and parallel to it.

zofra [tho´-frah], *f.* A Moorish carpet.

zoilo [tho´-ee-loh], *m.* Zoilus, a malicious critic or censurer.

zolocho, cha [tho-lo'-cho, chah], *a. (Coll.)* Stupid, silly.

zollipar [thol-lye-par'], *vn.* To sob.

zollipo [thoh-lyee'-po], *m.* Sob, sigh.

zoma [tho´-mah], *f.* A coarse sort of flour. V. SOMA.

zombi

zombi [thom´-bee], *m*. Zombie.

zompo, pa [thom´-po, pah], *a*. Clumsy, awkward. *V*. ZOPO.

zona [tho'-nah], *f*. Zone. **Zona de batalla**, battle zone. **Zona fronteriza**, border area.

zoncería [thon-thay-ree'-ah], *f*. Insipidity, tastelessness.

zonote [tho-no'-tay], *m*. Deep deposit of water. *V*. CENOTE. *(Acad.)*

zonzamente [thon-thah-men-tay], *adv*. Insipidly.

zonzo, za [thon'-tho, thah], *a*. 1. Insipid, tasteless. 2. Stupid, thoughtless.

zonzorrión, na [thon-thor-re-on', nah], *m*. & *f*. A very dull and stupid person.

zoo [tho-o], *m*. Zoo.

zoófago, ga [tho-o'-fah-go, gah], *a*. Zoophagous, feeding upon animal substances.

zoófito [tho-o'-fe-to], *m*. *(Zool.)* Zoophyte, an animal which resembles a plant in form or growth, especially which grows in branching colonies.

zoofórica [thoo-fo'-re-cah], *a*. *(Arch.)* Zoophoric: applied to a column bearing the figure of an animal.

zoogloea [tho-o-glo-ay'-ah], *f*. *(Biol.)* Zoogloea, muciform masses of vibrios or other bacteria.

zoografía [thoo-grah-fee'-ah], *f*. Zoography, descriptive zoology.

zooide [tho-oi´-day], *a*. *(Miner.)* Resembling an animal or a part of one.

zoolatría [tho-o-lah-tree'-ah], *f*. Zoolatry, worship of animals.

zoología [tho-o-lo-hee'-ah], *f*. Zoology, the science or branch of biology which treats of animals.

zoológico, ca [tho-o-lo'-he-co, cah], *a*. Zoological, zoologic, pertaining to zoology.

zoólogo [tho-oh'-lo-go], *m* & *f*. Zoologist, a professor of zoology.

zoonomía [tho-o-no-mee'-ah], *f*. Zoonomia, laws of animal life.

zoonosis [tho-os'-po-ro], *m*. Zoonosis.

zoóporo [tho-os'-po-ro], *m*. *(Biol.)* Zoospore, name given to the spores of certain algae provided with cilia or vibratile fliaments.

zootecnia [tho-o-tec'-ne-ah], *f*. Zootechnics, the science relating to the breeding and domestication of animals.

zootomía [tho-o-to-mee'-ah], *f*. Zootomy, dissection of animals; comparative anatomy.

zootómico [tho-o-to'-me-co], *m*. Zootomist.

zoótropo [tho-oh'-tro-po], *m*. Zootrope, zoetrope, the wheel of life, a philosophical toy.

zopas, zopitas [tho'-pas, tho-pee'-tas], *m*. *(Coll.)* Nickname given to a person pronouncing *z* for *s*.

zopenco, ca [tho-pen'-co, cah], *a*. *(Coll.)* Doltish very dull.

zopenco [tho-pen'-co], *m*. *(Coll.)* Block, dolt, blockhead.

zopilote [tho-pe-lo'-tay], *m*. *(Orn. Mex.)* Buzzard, a species of hawk. N. B. In Mexico this word is generally written and pronounced *sopilote.*

zopisa [tho-pee'-sah], *f*. Pitch scraped from the bottom of ships; pitch mixed with wax.

zopo, pa [tho'-po, pah], *a*. 1. Lame, maimed, injured in hands or feet. 2. Clumsy, awkward.

zopo [tho'-po], *m*. A clumsy, stupid fellow.

zoquete [tho-kay'-tay], *m*. 1. Block, a short piece of timber (de madera). 2. Bit or morsel of bread. 3. A rude, thick, sluggish, ugly little person. 4. A dolt, a blookhead (zopenco). 5. Belfry. 6. A Short, thick stick, used in bending or twisting ropes. 7. *(LAm.)* Body dirt (suciedad). 8. *(Carib. Mex.)* Punch (puñetazo).

zoquetería [thoo-kea-tay-ree´-ah], *f*. Heap of blocks, plankcads, or short pieces of timber.

zoquetero, ra [tho-kay-tay'-ro, rah], *a*. Beggarly, poor, indigent, asking charity.

zoquetico, zoquetillo [tho-kay-tee'-co], *m. dim.* A small morsoel of bread.

zoquetudo, da [tho-kay-too'-do, dah], *a*. Rough, ill-finished.

zorcico [thor-thee´-co], *m*. 1. A musical composition in five-eight (5/8) time, popular in the Basque provinces. 2. Wards or dance set to this music.

zorita [tho-ree'-tah], *f*. *(Orn.)* Stook-dove, wood-pigeon.

zorollo [tho-rol'-lyo], *a*. Reaped while unripe (cereales).

zorongo [tho-ron'-go], *m*. 1. A handkerchief folded like a bandage which some people wear upon the head. 2. A broad flattened chignon which some women wear. 3. A lively Andalusian dance and its music.

zorra [thor'-rah], *f*. 1. Fox (animal). 2. Low strong cart for heavy goods. 3. *(Coll.)* Prostitute, strumpet (mujer). 4. Drunkenness, inebriation. 5. A sly, crafty person. 6. *V*. SORRA.

zorrastrón, na [thor-ras-trone', nah], *m*. & *f*. *(Coll.)* Crafty, gunning, roguish person.

zorrazo [thor'-rah´-tho], *m. aug.* 1. A big fox. 2. A very artful fellow; a great knave.

zorrera [thor-ray'-rah], *f*. 1. Fox-hole (madriguera); kennel. 2. A smoking chimney, a smoky kitchen or room (habitación). 3. Heaviness of the head, drowsiness (modorra).

zorrería [thor-ray-ree'-ah], *f*. 1. Artfulness of a fox. 2. Cunning, craft knavery.

zorrero, ra [thor-ray´-ro, rah], *a*. 1. Slow, tardy, inactive; lagging. 2. *(Naut.)* Sailing heavily (barco). 3. Applied to large shot. 4. Cunning, capricious.

zorrero [thor-ray'-ro], *m*. 1. Terrier, a hunting dog. 2. Keeper of a royal forest.

zorrillo [thor-reel'-lyo], *m*. *(Zool.)* Skunk.

zorrita [thor-ree'-tah], *f. dim.* Little bitch fox.

zorro [thor'-ro], *m*. 1. A male fox. 2. Fox, a knave or cunning fellow. 3. *V*. ZORROCLOCO, 2d def. **Estar hecho un zorro**, to be extremely drowsy or heavy with sleep. *-pl*. Fox-skins; foxtails used in dusting furniture.

zorro, ra [thor'-ro, rah], *a*. *V*. ZORRERO.

zorrocloco [thor-ro-clo'-co], *m*. 1. *(Prov.)* A thin paste rolled up in a cylindric shape. 2. A dronish, humdrum heavy fellow; one who feigns weakness to avoid work. 3. *(Coll.)* Caress, demonstration of love or friendship. *V*. ARRUMACO.

zorronglón, na [thor-ron-glone', nah], *a*. Slow, heavy, lazy.

zorruela [thor-roo-ey'-lah], *f. dim.* A little bitch fox.

zorrullo [thor-rool'-lyo], *m*. A cylindrical piece of timber.

zorruno, na [thor-roo'-no, nah], *a*. Vulpine, foxy, fox-like.

zorzal [thor-thahl'], *m*. 1. *(Orn.)* Thrush. 2. Artful, cunning man (listo). 3. *(Cono Sur)* Simpleton (tonto).

zorzaleña [thor-thah-lay'-nyah], *f*. Applied to a small, round kind of olives.

zorzalico, illo, ito [thor-thah-lee'-co], *m. dim.* of ZORZAR.

zoster [thos-terr'], *f*. *(Med.)* Shingles, an eruptive disease.

zote [tho'-tay], *m*. Ignorant, stupid, lazy person.

zozobra [tho-tho'-brah], *f*. 1. Uneasiness, anguish, anxiety (inquietud). 2. *(Naut.)* A foul or contrary wind. 3. An unlucky cast of the die.

zozobrante [tho-tho-brahn´-tay], *pa*. & *a*. That which is in great danger; sinking.

zozobrar [tho-tho-brar'], *m*. 1. *(Naut.)* To be weather-beaten; to sink, to founder; to upset, to capsize. 2. To be in great danger (peligrar). 3. To grieve, to be in pain; to be afflicted (persona).

zua, zuda [thoo'-ah, thoo'-dah], *f*. Persian wheel. *V*. AZUDA.

zubia [thoo'-be-ah], *f*. Drain, channel for water.

zucarino, na [thoo-cah-ree'-no, nah], *a*. Sugary. *V*. SACARINO.

zúchil [thoo'-cheel], *m*. *(Mex.)* 1. A bouquet. 2. A marigold. N. B. In the U. S. of Mexico this word is pronounced and written *Súchil.*

zueca pella [thoo-ay´-cah payl'-lah]. **(Jugar con alguno a la)** *(Coll.)* To tease, to bore, to vex.

zueco [thoo-ay'-co], *m*. 1. A wooden shoe. 2. A sort of shoe with a wooden or cork sole. 3. Clog, galosh or galoche. 4. *(Bot.)* Lady's clipper. 5. *(Poet.)* A plain, simple style.

zuiza [thoo-ee'-thah], *f.* 1. A tournament. 2. A party of young men at a feast. 3. Quarrel, dispute.

zuizón [thoo-e-thone'], *m.* (*Naut.*) A half pike, used in boarding.

zulacar [thoo-lah-car'], *va.* To anoint or cover with bitumen.

zulaque [thoo-lah'-kay], *m.* 1. Bitumen. V. BETÚN. 2. (*Naut.*) Stuff, a composition of quicklime, fish-oil tar, and other ingredients, with which the bottom of a ship is painted.

zulú [thoo-loo'], *com. & a.* Zulu, a warlike tribe of southern Africa.

zulla [thool-lyah], *f.* 1. (*Bot.*) French honey-suckle. 2. (*Coll.*) Human excrements.

zullarse [thool-lyar'-say], *vr.* (*Coll.*) To go to stool, to break wind (ventosear).

zullenco, ca [thool-lyen'-co, cah]. **Zullón, na** (*Coll.*), *a.* Breaking wind behind; flatulent.

zullón [thool-lyone'], *m.* The act of breaking wind, flatulence.

zullonear [thool-lyo-nay-ar'], *va.* To expel wind.

zumacal, zumacar [thoo-mah-cahl'], *m.* Plantation of sumach.

zumacar [thoo-mah-car'], *va.* To dress or tan with sumach.

zumacaya [thoo-mah-cah'-yah], *f.* V. ZUMAYA.

zumaque [thoo-mah'-kay], *m.* 1. (*Bot.*) Sumach-tree. 2. (*Coll.*) Wine.

zumaya [thoo-mah-yah], *f.* (*Orn.*) The common owl, barn-owl.

zumba [thoom'-bah], *f.* 1. A large bell, used by curriers. 2. Joke, jest; facetious raillery.

zumbador, ra [thoom-bah-dor', rah], *a.* Humming, buzzing. *-m.* Buzzer.

zumbar [thoom-bar'], *vn.* 1. To resound, to emit a harsh sound; to buzz (insecto), to hum (máquina). 2. To be near a certain time or place (quedar cerca). Me zumban los oídos, I have a buzzing in my ears. *-va. & vr.* 1. To jest, to joke. **Hacer zumbar las orejas,** (*Coll.*) to make one feel by a smart reprehension. **Ir zumbando,** to go with great violence and celerity. 2. (*And. Carib.*) To clear off (marcharse). 3. (*Carib.*) To overstep the mark (pasarse).

zumbel [thoom-bel'], *m.* 1. (*Coll.*) Frown, an angry mien or aspect. 2. (*Prov.*) Cord with which boys spin tops.

zumbido, zumbo [thoom-bee'-do, thoom'-bo], *m.* 1. Humming, a continued buzzing sound. 2. (*Coll.*) A blow.

zumbilín [thoom-be-leen'], *m.* A dart, or javelin, used in the Philippine Islands.

zumbón, na [thoom-bone', nah], *a.* 1. Waggish (persona), casting jokes. 2. (*Prov. Andal.*) Applied to a kind of pigeon with a small maw: in this sense it is also used as a substantive.

zumiento, ta [thoo-me-en'-to, tah], *a.* Juicy, succulent.

zumillo [thoo-meel'-lyo], *m.* 1. (*Bot.*) Dragon arum, «Aaron's beard.» 2. Deadly carrot.

zumo [thoo'-mo], *m.* 1. Sap, juice (bebida), liquor, moisture; properly, any expressed juice, in contradistinction to that obtained by boiling, which is called *jugo*. 2. (*Met.*) Profit, utility. **Zumo de naranja,** orange squash.

zumoso, sa [thoo-mo'-so, sah], *a.* Juicy, succulent.

zuncho [thoon'-cho], *m.* Band, hoop, collar, ferrule.

zuño [thoo'-nyo], *m.* Frown, angry mien or countenance. V. CEÑO.

zupia [thoo'-pe-ah], *f.* 1. Wine which is fumed (vino), and has a bad taste and color; any liquor of a bad taste and looks. 2. Refuse, useless remains, lees.

zura, zurana [thoo'-rah, thoo-rah'-nah], *f.* Stock-dove. V. ZORITA.

zurcidera [thoor-the-day'-rah], *f.* Bawd, pimp.

zurcido [thoor-thee'-do], *m.* Stitching, uniting, finedrawing.

zurcidor, ra [thoor-the-dor', rah], *m. & f.* 1. Finedrawer, one whose business is to sew up rents. 2. Pimp, procuress.

zurcidura [thoor-the-doo'-rah], *f.* Fine-drawing, sewing up rents, darning.

zurcir [thoor-theer'], *va.* 1. To darn, to sew up rents, to finedraw. 2. To join, to unite. 3. To hatch lies. **¡Que las zurzan!,** to blazes with them!

zurdear [thoor-day-ar'], *vn.* To be left handed.

zardillo, illa [thoor-deel'-lyo], *a. dim.* Applied to one who is somewhat left-handed.

zurdo, da [thoor'-do, dah], *a.* 1. Left: applied to one of the hands. 2. Belonging to the left hand. 3. Left-handed. **A zurdas,** the wrong way.

zurear [thoo-ray-ar'], *vn.* To bill and coo (paloma).

zureo [thoo-ray'-o], *m.* Billing and cooing.

zurita [thoo-ree'-tah], *f.* (*Orn.*) Stock-dove. V. ZORITA.

zuriza [thoo-ree'-thah], *f.* Quarrel, dispute. V. ZUIZA.

zuro, ra [thoo'-ro, rah], *a.* Belonging to a stock-dove.

zurra [thoor'-rah], *f.* 1. The act of tanning or currying leather. 2. Flogging, drubbing, castigation. 3. Quarrel, dispute (pelea). 4. A severe reprimand. 5. To lash into, to criticize (criticar).

zurra, *int.* A term expressive of displeasure or anger.

zurraco [thoor-rah'-co], *m.* (*Coll.*) Cash.

zurrado, da [thoor-rah'-do, dah], *a. & pp.* of ZURRAR. Curried, dressed. *-m.* (*Coll.*) Glove.

zurrador [thoor-rah-dor'], *m.* 1. Leather-dresser, currier, tanner. 2. One who flogs or chastises.

zurrapa [thoor-rah'-pah], *f.* 1. Lees, sediment, dregs. 2. Anything vile or despicable.

zurrapiento, ta [thoor-rah-pe-en'-to, tah], *a.* V. ZURRAPOSO.

zurrapilla [thoor-rah-peel'-lyah], *f.* Small lees in liquor.

zurraposo, sa [thoor-rah-po'-so, sah], *a.* Full of lees and dregs.

zurrar [thoor-rar'], *va.* 1. To curry, to dress leather. 2. To flog, to chastise with a whip (pegar). 3. To contest, to urge with vehemence. *-vr.* 1. To have a sudden call of nature; to dirty oneself. 2. To be possessed by a great dread or fear.

zurriaga [thoor-re-ah'-gah], *f.* 1. Thong, a long leather strap; a whip for tops. 2. (*Orn. Prov.*) Lark. V. CALANDRIA.

zurriagar [thoor-re-ah-gar'], *va.* To flog, to chastise with a whip.

zurriagazo [thoor-re-ah-gah'-tho], *m.* 1. A severe lash or stroke with a whip (azote). 2. Unexpected ill-treatment; unfortunate calamity.

zurriago [thoor-re-ah'-go], *m.* 1. Whip for inflicting punishment. 2. (*Mex. Vulg.*) A mean, despicable fellow.

zurriar [thoor-re-ar'], *vn.* 1. (*Prov.*) To hum, to buzz. 2. To speak in a harsh and violent tone.

zurribanda [thoor-re-bahn'-dah], *f.* 1. Repeated flogging or chastisement with a whip. 2. A noisy quarrel.

zurriburri [thoor-re-boor'-re], *m.* 1. (*Coll.*) Ragamuffin, despicable person, low fellow (persona). 2. Turmoil (confusión). 3. Gang (pandilla).

zurrido, zurrío [thoor-ree'-do, thoor-ree'-o], *m.* 1. Humming, buzzing. 2. Confused noise or bustle.

zurrir [thoor-reer'], *m.* To hum, to buzz, to sound gratingly or confusedly.

zurrón [thoor-rone'], *m.* 1. Bag or pouch in which shepherds carry their provisions; game-bag. 2. Rind of fruits; chaff, husks of grain. 3. Bag, rack, of cow-hide in which Peruvian bark and other merchandise is brought from America; seroon. 4. (*Anat.*) Placenta.

zurrona [thoor-ro'-nah], *f.* Prostitute who wine her gallants.

zurroncillo [thoor-ron-theel'-lyo], *m. dim.* A small bag.

zurronero [thoor-ro-nay'-ro], *m.* One who makes bags or sacks.

zurruscarse [thoor-roos-car'-say], *vr.* (*Coll.*) To experience a sudden call of nature; to dirty oneself.

zurrusco [thoor-roos'-co], *m.* (*Coll.*) A slice of bread which is overtoasted. V. CHURRUSCO.

zurullo [thoo-rool'-lyo], *m.* 1. (*Coll.*) A piece of something lone and round, as of dough. 2. Rolling-pin 3. Human excrement (hez).

zurumbet [thoo-room-bet'], *m. (Bot.)* A large East Indian tree.

zurupeto [thoo-roo-pay´-to], *m.* An intrusive money-broker.
(Acad.)

zutanico, illo [thoo-tah-nee'-co], *m. dim.* of ZUTANO.

zutano, na [thoo-tah'-no, nah], *m. & f.* A word invented to
supply the name of some one, when the latter is not known
or not desired to be expressed. Such a one. It is used with
fulano or *mengano,* or with both; but neither *mengano* nor
zutano can be used alone. When these three words are combined, the phrase always begins with *fulano.* Thus: *Fulano,
zutano y mengano,* such and such a one.

zuzar [thoo-thar'], *va.* To set on dogs. *V.* AZUZAR.

¡zuzo! [thoo'-tho], *int.* A word used to call or set on a dog. *V.*
¡CHUCHO!

¡zuzón! [thoo-thone'], *m. (Bot.)* Groundsel, ragwort. Senecio;
so-called from the hoary pappus. *V.* HIERBA CANA.

APPENDIX

A Vocabulary of Geographical Terms

WHICH ARE NOT IDENTICAL IN THE ENGLISH AND SPANISH LANGUAGES.

NOTE.—Adjectives derived from proper names, geographical and other, are entered in the body of the dictionary and therefore not repeated here. Thus: Abisinio, a, Abyssinian; Cesariano, na, Caesarian, belonging to Julius Caesar.

A

Abisinia [ah-be-see'-ne-ah], Abyssinia, *V.* ETIOPÍA.
Acaya [ah-cah'-yah], Achaea (district of ancient Greece).
Addis Abeba [ah'-dees ah-bay'-bah], Addis Ababa (Ethiopia).
Adrianápolis [ah-dre-ah-no'-po-lees] or **Andrianópolis** [ahn-dre-ah-no'-po-lees], Adrianople or Edirne (Turkey).
Adriático, Mar [mar ah-dre-ah'-te-co], Adriatic Sea.
África Ecuatorial Francesa [ah'-free-cah ay-coo-ah-to-re-ahl' frahn-thay'-sah], French Equatorial Africa.
Alasca [ah-lahs'-cah], Alaska.
Alejandría [ah-lay-han-dree'-ah], Alexandria (Egypt).
Alemania [ah-lay-mah'-ne-ah], Germany.
Aleutianas, Islas [ees'-lahs ah-lay-oo-te-ah'-nas], Aleutian Islands.
Almirantazgo , Islas del [ees'-lahs del al-me-rahn-tath'-go], Admiralty Islands.
Alpes [ahl'-pays]. Alps (mountains in S. Central Europe).
Alsacia-Lorena [al-sah'-the-ah lo-ray'-nah], Alsace-Lorraine.
Amarillo, Mar [mar ah-mah-ree'-lyo], Yellow Sea or Hwang Hai.
Amarillo, Río [ree'-o ah-mah-ree'-lyo] or **Hoang Ho** [ho-ang'-ho]. Yellow River or Hwang Ho.
Amazonas, Río [ree'-o ah-mah-tho'-nas], Amazon River.
Amberes [am-bay' rayo], Antwerp (Belgium).
América Central, *V.* CENTRO AMÉRICA.
América Ibera [ah-may'-ree-cah e-bay'-rah], Latin America.
Amigos, Islas de los, *V.* TONGA.
Amistad, Islas de la, *V.* TONGA.
Andalucía [an-dah-loo-thee'-ah], Andalusia (Spain).
Antártico, Océano [o-thay'-ah-no ahn-tar'-tee-co], Antarctic Ocean.
Antillas, Mar de las, *V.* MAR CARIBE.
Antillas Mayores [ahn-tee'-lyas mah-yo'-rays], Greater Antilles.
Antillas Menores [ahn-tee'-lyas may-no'-rays], Lesser Antilles.
Antioquía [an-te-o-kee'-ah], Antioch (Turkey).
Apalaches, Montes [mon'-tess ah-pah-lah'-chays], Appalachian Mountains.

Apeninos [ah-pay-nee'-nos], Apennines (mountains of Italy).
Aquisgrán [ah-kees-grahn'], Aachen or Aix-la-Chapelle (Germany).
Arabia Saudita [ah-rah'-bee-ah sah-oo-dee'-tah], Saudi Arabia.
Arábigo, Mar [mar ah-rah'-be-go], Arabian Sea.
Ardenas, Sierra [see-ay'-rrah ar-day'-nahs], Ardennes Mountains.
Argel [ar-hel'], Algiers (Algeria).
Argelia [ar-hay'-le-ah], Algeria.
Ártico, Océano [o-thay'-ah-no ar'-tee-co], Arctic Ocean.
Asiria [ah-see'-re-ah], Assyria.
Asís [ah-sees'], Assisi (Italy).
Atenas [ah-tay'-nas], Athens (Greece).
Ática [ah'-te-cah], Attica (Greece).
Atlántico, Océano [o-thay'-ah-no ah-tlahn'-te-co], Atlantic Ocean.
Austria-Hungría [ah'-oos-tree-ah oon-gree'-ah], Austria-Hungary.
Aviñón [ah-ve-nyone'], Avignon (France).
Azincourt [ah-theen-coor'], Agincourt (France).
Azules, Montañas [mon-tah'-nyahs ah-thoo'-lays], Blue Mountains.

B

Babilonia [bah-be-lo'-ne-ah], Babylon.
Baja California [bah'-hah cah-lee-for'-nee-ah], Lower California (Mexico).
Balcanes [bahl-cah'-nays], Balkans.
Baleares, Islas [ees'-lahs bah-lay-ah'-rays], Balearic Islands.
Báltico, Mar [mar bahl'-te-co], Baltic sea.
Barlovento, Islas de [ees'-lahs day bar-lo-vayn'-to], Windward Islands.
Basilea [bah-say-lay'-ah], Basle or Basel (Switzerland).
Baviera [bah-ve-ay'-rah], Bavaria (Germany).
Bayona [bah-yo'-nah], Bayonne (France).
Beirut [bay-root'], Beirut or Beyrouth (Lebanon).
Belén [bay-layn'], Bethlehem (Jordan).
Bélgica [bel'-he-cah], Belgium.

Belgrado [bel-grah'-do], Belgrade or Beograd (Yugoslavia).
Belice [bay-lee'-thay] or **Honduras Británica** [ohn-doo'-rahs bree-tah'-nee-cah], British Honduras.
Bengala [ben-gah'-lah], Bengal.
Berbería [ber-bay-ree'-ah], Barbary Coast (Africa).
Berna [behr'-nah], Berne or Bern (Switzerland).
Birmania [beer-mah'-nee-ah], Burma.
Bizancio [be-than'-the-o], Byzantium. *V.* ISTAMBUL or CONSTANTINOPLA.
Bolonia [bo-lo'-ne-ah], Bologna (Italy).
Borgoña [bor-go'-nyah], Burgundy.
Bósforo, Estrecho del [es-tray´-cho del bos'-fo-ro], Strait of Bosporus or Bosphorus.
Brasil [brah-seel´], Brazil.
Bretaña, Gran [grahn bray-tah'-nyah], Great Britain.
Británicas, Islas [ees'-lahas bree-tah'-nee-cahs], British Isles.
Brujas [broo'-has], Bruges (Belgium).
Bruselas [broo-say'-lahs], Brussels (Belgium).
Bucarest [boo-cah-rest'], Bucharest (Rumania).
Buena Esperanza, Cabo de [cah'-bo day boo-ay´-nah es-pay-rahn'-thah], Cape of Good Hope.
Burdeos [boor-day'-ose], Bordeaux (France).

C

Cabo Bretón, Isla [ees'-lah cah'-bo bray-tone], Cape Breton Island (Nova Scotia, Canada).
Cabo, Ciudad del [thee-oo-dahd' del cah'-bo], Capetown (Union of South Africa).
Cabo de Hornos [cah'-bo day or'-nos], Cape Horn.
Cachemira [cah-chay-mee'-rah], Cashmere or Kashmir (state of the Himalayas).
Calcuta [cahl-coo'-tah], Calcutta (India).
Camboja [cahm-bo'-hah], Cambodia (Indochina).
Canal de la Mancha [cah-nahl' day lah mahn'-chah], English Channel.
Canal de Panamá, Zona del. *V.* ZONA DEL CANAL DE PANAMÁ.
Canarias, Islas [ees'-lahs cah-nah'-re-ahs], Canary Islands.
Cantábrica, Cordillera [cor-dee-lyay'-rah cahn-tah'-bree-cah], Cantabrian Mountains.
Caribe, Mar [mar cah-ree'-bay], or **Mar de las Antillas** [mar day lahs ahn-tee'-lyahs], Caribbean Sea.
Cárpatos, Montes [mon'-tess car' pah-tosc], Carpathian Mountains.
Cartago [car-tah'-go], Carthage (ancient city of N. Africa. Also a city in Costa Rica, C.A.).
Caspio, Mar [mar cahs'-pe-o], Caspian Sea.
Castilla la Nueva [cas-teel'-lyah lah noo-ay'-vah], New Castile (Spain).
Castilla la Vieja [cas-teel'-lyah lah ve-ay'-hah], Old Castile (Spain).
Cataluña [cah-tah-loo'-nyah], Catalonia (Spain).
Cáucaso [cow'-cah-ao], Caucasus.
Cayena [cah-yay'-nah], Cayenne (French Guiana).
Cayo Hueso [cah'-yo oo-ay'-so], Key West (Florida, U.S.A.).
Ceilán [thay-lahn'], Ceylon.
Centro América [then'-tro ah-may'-ree-cah] or **América Central** [then-trahl'], Central America.
Cercano Oriente, *V.* ORIENTE, CERCANO.
Cerdeña [ther-day'-nyah], Sardinia or Sardegna (Italian island in the Mediterranean).
Champaña [cham-pah'-nyah], Champagne (France).
Checoslovaquia [chay-cohs-lo-vah'-kee-ah], Czechoslovakia.
Chipre [chee'-pray], Cyprus (island in the Mediterranean).
Ciudad del Vaticano [the-oo-dahd' del vah-tee-cah'-no], Vatican City.
Colombia [co-lom'-bee-ah], Colombia.
Colonia [co-lo'-ne-ah], Cologne (Germany).
Congo [cohn'-go], Congolese.

Conastantinopla [conas-tan-te-no'-plah], Constantinople, *V.* ISTAMBUL.
Copenhague [co-pen-ah'-gay], Copenhagen (Denmark).
Córcega[cor'-thay-gah], Corsica (island in the Mediterranean).
Corea [coh-ray'-ah], Korea.
Corinto [co-reen'-to], Corinth (Greece).
Costa de Oro [cos'-tah day o'-ro], Gold Coast (W. Africa).
Cracovia [crah-co'-ve-ah], Cracow (Poland).
Creta [cray'-tah], Crete or Krete (island in the Mediterranean).
Croacia [cro-ah-the-ah], Croatia.

D

Dalmacia [dal-mah'-the-ah], Dalmatia.
Damasco [dah-mahs'-co], Damascus (Syria).
Danubio [dah-noo'-be-o], Danube (river of Europe).
Dardanelos [dar-dah-nay'-los], Dardanelles (formerly Hellespont).
Dinamarca [de-nah-mar'-cah], Denmark.
Dordeña [dor-do'-nyah], Dordogne (a river of France).
Dresde [dres'-day], Dresden (Germany).
Duero [doo-ay'-ro], Douro or Duero (river of the Iberian Peninsula).
Dunquerque [doon-kerr'-kay], Dunkirk (France).

E

Edimburgo [ay-deem-boor'-go], Edinburgh (Scotland).
Éfeso [ay-fay'-so], Ephesus (ancient Greek city in Asia Minor).
Egeo, Mar [mar ay-hay'-o], Aegean Sea.
Egipto [ay-heep'-to], Egypt.
Elba [el'-bah], Elbe (river in Europe).
Epiro [ay-pee'-ro], Epirus (ancient Greece).
Escalda [es-cahl'-dah], Scheldt (river in Belgium).
Escocia [es-co'-thee-ah], Scotland.
Esmirna [es-meer'-nah], Smyrna (Turkey).
Eslovaquia [es-lo-vah-ke-ah], Slovakia.
Eslovenia [es-lo-vay-me-ah], Slovenia.
España [es-pah'-nyah], Spain.
Esparta [ea-par'-tah], Sparta (ancient city of Greece).
Estados Pontificios [es-tah'-doas pon-tee-fee'-the-oas], Papal States or States of the Church.
Estados Unidos de América [es-tah'-dos oo-nee'-dos day ah-may'-re-cah], United States of America.
Estocolmo [es-to-col'-mo], Stockholm (Sweden).
Estrómboli [es-trom'-bo-lee], Stromboli (volcano N. of Sicily).
Etiopía [ay-te-o-pee'-ah], Ethiopia (formerly Abyssinia).
Eufrates [ay-oo-frah'-tays], Euphrates (river in Asia).

F

Falkland or **Malvinas, Islas,** *V.* MALVINAS, ISLAS.
Fenicia [fay-nee'-the-ah], Phoenicia.
Filadelfia [fe-lah-del'-fe-ah], Philadelphia (U.S.A.)
Filipinas [fe-le-pee'-nas], Philippines.
Finlandia [fin-lahn'-de-ah], Finland.
Flandes [flahn'-des], Flanders.
Florencia [flo-ren'-the-ah], Florence (Italy).
Francia [fran'-the-ah], France.
Frisias, Islas [ees´-lahs free'-see-ahs], Frisian Islands.

G

Gales [gah'-less], Wales.
Galia [gah'-le-ah], Gaul.

Galilea [gah-le-lay'-ah], Galilee.
Gante [gahn'-tay], Ghent (Belgium).
Garona [gah-ro´-nah], Garonne (river of France).
Gascuña [gas-coo'-nyah], Gascony (France).
Génova [hay'-no-vah], Genoa (Italy).
Ginebra [he-nay'-brah], Geneva (Switzerland).
Gran Bretaña [grahn bray-tah'-nyah], Great Britain.
Grecia [gray'-thee-ah], Greece.
Groenlandia [gro-enn-lahn'-de-ah], Greenland.
Groninga [gro-neen'-gah], Groningen (Netherlands).
Guayana [goo-ah-yah'-nah] Guyanese.

H

Habana [ah-bah'-nah], Havana (Cuba).
Haitiano, Cabo [cah'-bo ah-te-ah'-no], Cap Haitien.
Haití [ah-ee-tee'] or **Santo Domingo** [sahn'-to do-meen'-go] Haiti Island.
Haití, República de [ray-poo'-blee-cah day ah-ee-tee'], Rep. of Haiti.
Hamburgo [am-boor'-go], Hamburg (Germany).
Hangcheú [ahn-chay-oo´] Hangchow (Chinese seaport).
Hankeú [ahn-kay-oo´], Hankow (Chinese city).
Havre, El [el ah'-vr], Le Havre (port of France).
Hawaii, Islas [ees'-lahs ha-wa'-ee], Hawaiian Islands.
Haya, La [lah ah'-yah], The Hague (Netherlands).
Hébridas, Islas [ees'-lahs ay'-bree-dahs], Hebrides Islands.
Helesponto [ay-les-pone'-to], V. DARDALENOS.
Holanda [o-lahn'-dah] or **Países Bajos** [pah-ee'-ses bah'-hos], Holland or The Netherlands.
Hungría [oon gree'-ah], Hungary.

I

Ibérica, Península [pay-neen'-soo-lah e bay'-re-cah], Iberian Peninsula.
Indias Occidentales [in'-dee-ahs ok-thee-den-tah´-less], West Indies.
Indias Orientales [in'-dee-ahs o-ree-en-tah'-less], East Indies.
Índico, Océano [oh-thay'-ah-no in'-dee-co], Indian Ocean.
Indo [in'-do], Indus (river of India and Pakistan).
Inglaterra [in-glah-tay'-rrah], England.
Irak [e-rak'], Iraq.
Irlanda [eer-lahn'-dah], Ireland.
Islandia [ees-lahn'-de-ah], Iceland.
Istambul [ees-tam-bool´], Istanbul (formerly Constantinople).
Italia [e-tah'-le-ah], Italy.

J

Japón [hah-pone], Japan.
Jerusalén [hay-roo-sah-layn'], Jerusalem.
Jónico, Mar [mar ho'-ne-co], Ionian Sea.
Jordania [hor-dah'-ne-ah], Jordan.
Jutlandia [hoot-lahn'-de-ah], Jutland.

K

Kioto [kee-o'-to], Kyoto (Japan).

L

Lagos, Grandes [grahn'-days lah'-gos], Great Lakes (U.S.A.)
Laponia [lah-po'-ne-ah], Lapland.
Lausana [lah-oo-sah'-nah], Lausanne (Switzerland).
Lejano Oriente, V. ORIENTE, LEJANO.
Leningrado [lay-neen-grah'-do], Leningrad (formerly San Petersburgo and Petrogrado, Russia).
Líbano [lee'-bah-no], Lebanon.
Libia [lee'-bee-ah], Libya.
Lieja [le-ay'-hah], Liege (Belgium).
Lila [lee'-lah], Lille (France).
Liorna [lee-or'-nah], Leghorn (Italy).
Lisboa [lis-bo'-ah], Lisbon (Portugal).
Lituania [lee-too-ah'-nee-ah], Lithuania.
Londres [lon'-dress], London (England).
Lorena [lo-ray'-nah], Lorraine. V. ALSACIA-LORENA.
Lovaina [lo-vah'-e-nah], Louvain (Belgium).
Lucerna [loo-ther'-nah], Lucerne or Luzern (Switzerland).
Luisiana [loo-e-se-ah'-nah], Louisiana (U.S.A.).

M

Magallanes, Estrecho de [es-tray'-cho day mah-gal-lyah'-ness], Strait of Magellan.
Maguncia [mah-goon'-the-ah], Mainz (Germany).
Malaca, Península de [pay-neen'-soo-lah day mah-lah'-cah], Malay Peninsula.
Maldivas, Islas [ees'-lahs mal-dee'-vahs], Maldive Islands.
Malvinas or **Falkland, Islas** [ees'-lahs mal-vee'-nahs, fok'-land], Falkland Islands.
Mallorca [mal lyor'-cah], Majorca or Mallorca (island in the Mediterranean).
Mancha, Canal de la [cah-nahl' day lah mahn'-chah], English Channel.
Marfil, Costa de [cos'-tah day mar-feel], Ivory Coast.
Mármara, Mar de [mar day mar'-mah-rah], Sea of Marmora or Marmara.
Marruecos [mah-roo-ay'-cos], Morocco.
Marsella [mar-say'-lyah], Marseille or Marseilles (France).
Martinica [mar-te-nee'-cah], Martinique.
Mauricio [mah-oo-ree'-the-o], Mauritius or Ile de France (British island in Indian Ocean).
Mediterráneo, Mar [mar may-de-tay-rah'-nay-o], Mediterranean Sea.
Menfis [men'-fees], Memphis (cap. Of ancient Egypt).
Menorca [may-nor'-cah], Minorca or Menorca (island in the Mediterranean).
México or **Méjico** [may'-he-co], Mexico.
Misisipi, Río [ree'-o me-see-see'-pee], Mississippi River (U.S.A.).
Misuri [me-soo'-re], Missouri (river and state of U.S.A.).
Molucas, Islas [ees'-lahs mo-loo'-cahs] or **Islas de las Especias** [day lahs es-pay'-thee-ahs], Moluccas or Spice Islands.
Mosa [mo'-sah], Meuse (river of France and Belgium).
Moscú [mos-coo´], Moscow.
Mosela [mo-say'-lah], Moselle (river of France and Germany).
Muerto, Mar [mar moo-err'-to], Dead Sea.

N

Nápoles [nah´-po-less], Naples (Italy).
Negro, Mar [mar nay'-gro], Black Sea.

Niágara, Cataratas del [cah-tah-rah'-tahs del nee-ah'-gah-rah], Niagara Falls.

Nilo [nee'-lo], Nile (river of Africa).

Nínive [nee'-nee-vay], Nineveh (ancient city of Assyrian Empire).

Nipón [nee-pone'], Nippon. *V.* JAPÓN.

Niza [nee'-thah], Nice (France).

Normandía [nor-man-dee'-ah], Normandy (France).

Norte América [nor'-tay ah-may'-ree-cah] or **América del Norte** [del nor'-tay], North America.

Noruega [no-roo-ay'-gah], Norway.

Nueva Escocia [noo-ay'-vah es-co'-thee-ah], Nova Scotia (Canada).

Nueva Gales del Sur [noo-ay'-vah gah'-lea del soor], New South Wales.

Nueva Orleáns [noo-ay'-vah or-lay-ahns'], New Orleans (U.S.A.).

Nueva York [noo-ay'-vah york], New York (U.S.A.).

Nueva Zelanda [noo-ay'-vah thay-lahn'-dah], New Zealand.

O

Odesa [o-day'-sah], Odessa (Russian seaport on Black Sea).

Olimpo, Monte [mon'-tay o-leem'-po], Mount Olympus.

Oriente, Cercano [ther-cah'-no o-ree-en'-tay] Near East.

Oriente Lejano [lay-hah'-no o-ree-en'-tay], Far East.

Ostende [os-ten'-day], Ostend (Belgium).

P

Pacífico, Océano [o-thay'-ah-no pah-thee'-fee-co], Pacific Ocean.

Países Bajos, *V.* HOLANDA.

Palestina [pah-les-tee'-nah], Palestine.

Parnaso [par-nah'-so], Parnassus.

Peloponeso [pay-lo-po-nay'-so], Peloponnesus (Greece).

Pensilvania [pen-sil-vah'-ne-ah], Pennsylvania (U.S.A.).

Perusa [pay-roo'-sah], Perugia (Italy).

Pirineos [pe-re-nay'-ose], Pyrenees (range of mountains separating Spain and France).

Polaco, Corredor [cor-ray-dor' po-lah'-co], Polish Corridor.

Polonia [po-lo'-ne-ah], Poland.

Polo Norte [po'-lo nor'-tay], North Pole.

Polo Sur [po'-lo soor], South Pole.

Pompeya [pom-pay'-yah], Pompeii (Italy).

Praga [prah'-gah], Prague (Czechoslovakia).

Puerto Príncipe [poo-err'-to preen'-thee-pay], Port-au-Prince (Haiti).

Puerto Said [poo-err'-to sah-eed'], Port Said (Egypt).

R

Rangún [rahn-goon'], Rangoon (Burma).

Reino Unido [ray'-no oo-nee'-do], United Kingdom (Great Britain and N. Ireland).

Rin or **Rhin** [rin], Rhine (river in Europe).

Rocosas, Montañas [mon-tah'-nyahs ro-co'-sahs], Rocky Mountains.

Ródano [ro'-dah-no], Rhone (river of Europe).

Rodas [ro'-dahs], Rhodes (island in the Aegean Sea).

Rojo, Mar [mar ro'-ho], Red Sea.

Ruan [roo-ahn'], Rouen (France).

Rumania [roo-mah-ne-ah], Romania.

Rusia [roo'-see-ah], Russia.

S

Sajonia [sah-ho'-nee-ah], Saxony (old German kingdom).

Salónica [sah-loh'-nee-kah], Salonika or Thessalonike (Greece).

Selva Negra [sell'-vah nay'-grah], Black Forest.

Sena [say'-nah], Seine (river of France).

Siam [see-am], *V.* THAILANDIA.

Sicilia [see-thee'-le-ah], Sicily (island of the Mediterranean).

Siracusa [see-rah-coo'-ash], Syracuse (Italy).

Siria [see'-re-ah], Syria.

Somalia [so-mah'-lee-ah], Somalia.

Sud América [sood ah-may'-ree-cah] or **América del Sur** [del soor] South America.

Suecia [soo-ay'-thee-ah], Sweden.

Suiza [soo-ee'-thah], Switzerland.

Surinam, *V.* GUAYANA

T

Tajo [tah'-ho], Tagus, Tajo or Tejo (river of Spain and Portugal).

Támesis [tah'-may-sis], Thames (river of England).

Tánger [tahn'-her], Tangier (Morocco).

Tauro, Montañas [mon-tah'-nyahs tah'-oo-ro], Taurus Mountains (Turkey).

Tebas [tay'-bas], Thebes (ancient cities of Greece and Egypt).

Teherán [tay-rahn'], Tehran or Teheran (Iran).

Tejas [tay'-has], Texas (U.S.A.)

Termópilas [ter-mo'-pee-lahs], Thermopylae (Greek pass).

Terranova [ter-rah-no'-vah], Newfoundland.

Tesalia [tay-sah'-le-ah], Thessaly (Greece).

Thailandia [tah-ee-lahn'-dee-ah] or **Siam** [see-am], Thailand or Siam.

Tierra Santa [tee-ay'-rrah sahn'-tah], Holy Land.

Tiro [tee'-ro], Tyre (ancient Phoenician port, now a port of Lebanon).

Tirreno, Mar [mar te-rray'-no], Tyrrhenian Sea.

Tokio [to'-kyo], Tokyo (Japan).

Tolón [to-lone'], Toulon (France).

Tolosa [to-lo'-sah], Toulouse (France).

Tonga [tohn'-gah] or **Islas de los Amigos** [ees'-lahs day los ah-mee'-gos] or **Islas de la Amistad** [day lah ah-mees-tahd'], Tonga or Friendly Islands.

Toscana [tos-cah'-nah], Tuscany.

Tracia [trah'-thee-ah], Thrace.

Trento [tren'-to], Trent or Trento (Italy).

Troya [tro'-yah], Troy.

Túnez [too'-neth], Tunis.

Turquía [toor-kee'-ah], Turkey.

U

Ucrania [oo-crah-ne-ah], Ukraine.

Unión de los Emiratos Arabes [oo-ne-on day los ay-me-rah-tos ah-rah-bays], United Arab Emirates.

Unión Sudafricana [oo-ne-on' sood-ah-free-cah'-nah], Union of South Africa.

Urales, Montes [mon'-tess oo-rah'-lees], Ural Mountains.

V

Varsovia [var-so'-ve-ah], Warsaw (Poland).
Vaticano, Ciudad del [thee-oo-dahd' del vah-tee-cah'-no], Vatican City.
Venecia [vay-nah'-the-ah], Venice (Italy).
Versalles [ver-sahl'-lyes], Versailles (France).
Vesubio [vey-soo'-be-o], Vesuvius (mountain and volcano of Italy).
Viena [ve-ay'-nah], Vienna (Austria).
Vírgenes, Islas [ees'-lahs veer'-hay-nays] Virgin Islands.
Vizcaya [veeth-cah'-yah], Biscay (Spain).

Z

Zona del Canal de Panamá [tho'-nah del cah-nahl' day pah-nah-mah´], Panama Canal Zone.

Alphabetical List

of the Most Usual Proper Names in Spanish,

INCLUDING BIBLICAL AND HISTORICAL NAMES,

WHICH ARE WRITTEN DIFFERENTLY IN ENGLISH.

Abrahán [ah-brah-ahn´], Abraham.
Adán [ah-dahn´], Adam.
Adela [ah-day'-lah], Adele.
Adalaida [ah-day-lah'-e-dah], Adelaide.
Adolfo [ah-dol'-fo], Adolphus.
Adrián, Adriano [ah-dre-ahn', ah-dre-ah'-no], Adrian, Hadrian.
Ágata [ah'-gah-tah], Agatha.
Agustín [ah-goos-teen´], Augustin, Austin.
Alberto [al-berr'-to], Albert.
Alejandra or **Alejandrina** [ah-lay-hahn'-drah, ah-lay-hahn-dree'-nah], Alexandra, Alexandrina.
Alejandro [ah-lay-hahn'-dro], Alexander.
Alejo [ah-lay'-ho], Alexis.
Alfonso [al-fon'-so], Alphonsus.
Alfredo [al-fray'-do], Alfred.
Alicia [ah-lee'-the-ah], Alice.
Alonso [ah-lon'-so], Alphonsus.
Amadeo [ah-mah-day'-o], Amadeus.
Ambrosio [am-bro'-se-o], Ambrose, Ambrosius.
Amelia [ah-may'-le-ah], Amelie.
Ana [ah'-nah], Ann, Anne, Hannah; *coll*, Nan or Nancy.
Anabel [ah-nah-bel], Annabel.
Andrés [an-drays], Andrew.
Ángela [ahn-hay-lah], Angela, Angie.
Aníbal [ah-nee'-bal], Hannibal.
Anselmo [an-sel'-mo], Anselm.
Antonio [an-to'-ne-o], Anthony; *coll.* Tony.
Aristóteles [ah-ris-to'-tay-less], Aristotle.
Arnaldo [ar-nahl'-do], Arnold.
Arquímedes [ahr-kee'-may-days], Archimedes.
Arturo [ar-too´-ro], Arthur.
Atanasio [ah-tah-nah'-se-o], Athanasius.
Atila [ah-tee'-lah], Attila.
Augusto [ah-goos'-to], Augustus.
Aureliano, Aurelio [ah-oo-ray-le-ah'-no, ah-oo-ray'-le-o], Aurelius.

Balduino [bahl-doo-ee'-no], Baldwin.
Bárbara [bar'-bah-rah], Barbara.; *coll.* Bab.
Bartolo [bar-toh'-lo], Bartholomew; *coll.* Bart.
Bartolomé [bar-to-lo-may´], Bartholomew.
Basilio [bah-see'-le-o], Basil.
Beatriz [bay-ah-treeth´], Beatrix, Beatrice.

Beltrán [bel-trahn´], Bertram.
Benita [bay-nee'-tah], Benedicta.
Benito [bay-nee'-to], Benedict.
Bernabé [ber-nah-bay´], Barnabas, Barnaby.
Bernardo [ber-nar'-do], Bernard.
Bernardino [ber-nar-dee'-no], Bernardinus.
Berta [berr'-tah], Bertha.
Blas [blahs], Blase.
Bonifacio [bo-ne-fah´-the-o], Boniface.
Brígida [bree'-he-dah], Bridget.
Buenaventura [boo-ay'-nah-ven-too'-rah], Bonaventure. *V.* VENTURA

Camila [cah-mee'-lah], Camilla.
Camilo [cah-mee'-lo], Camillus.
Carlos [car'-los], Charles; *coll.* Charley.
Carlota [car-lo´-tah], Charlotte.
Carolina [cah-ro-lee'-nah], Caroline.
Casandra [cah-sahn'-drah], Cassandra.
Casimiro [cah-se-mee'-ro], Casimir.
Catalina or **Catarina** [cah-tah-lee'-nah, ree'-nah], Catharine; *coll.* Kate, Kitty.
Catón [cah-tone'], Cato.
Cayetano [cah-yay-tah'-no], Cajetan.
Cecilia [thay-thee'-le-ah], Cecile; *coll.* Cis.
Cecilio [thay-thee'-le-o], Cecil.
César [thay'-sar], Caesar.
Cipriano [the-pre-ah'-no], Cyprian.
Ciriaco [the-re-ah´-co], Cyriacus.
Cirilo [the-ree'-lo], Cyrilus.
Claudia, Claudina [clah'-oo-de-ah, clah-oo-dee'-nah], Claudia.
Claudio [clah'-oo-de-o], Claude, Claudius.
Clemente [clay-men'-tay], Clement.
Clotilde [clo-teel'-day], Clotilde.
Conrado [con-rah'-do], Conrad.
Constancia, Constancio [cons-tahn'-the-ah, cons-tahn'-the-o], Constance.
Constantino [cons-tan-tee'-no], Constantine.
Constanza [cons-tahn'-thah], Constance.
Cornelio [cor-nay'-le-o], Cornelius.
Cosme [cos'-may], Cosmas.
Cristián [cris-te-ahn´], Christian.
Cristina [cris-tee'-nah], Christina.

Cristobal [cris-to'-bal], Christopher.
Darío [dah-ree'-o], Darius.
Diego [de-ay'-go], James.
Dionisia [de-o-nee'-se-ah], Dionysia.
Dionisio [de-o-nee'-se-o], Dennis.
Domingo [do-meen'-go], Dominic.
Dori [do-re], Doris.
Dorotea [do-ro-tay'-ah], Dorothy.

Edmundo [ed-moon'-do], Edmund.
Eduardo [ay-doo-ar'-do], Edward; *coll.* Eddy, Ned, Neddy.
Elena [ay-lay'-nah], Ellen.
Eleonor [ay-lay-o-nor], Eleanor, Eleanora; Ellie.
Elisabet [ay-le-sah-bayt], Elizabeth.
Elisa [ay-lee'-sah], Eliza.
Eliseo [ay-le-say'-o], Elisha, Ellis.
Ema [ay'-mah], Emma.
Emilia [ay-mee'-le-ah], Emily.
Emilio [ay-mee'-le-o], Emil, Emile.
Engracia [en-grah'-the-ah], Grace.
Enrique [en-ree'-kay], Henry.
Enriqueta [en-re-kay'-tah], Henrietta, Harriet.
Ernesto [err-nays'-to], Ernest.
Esteban [es-tay'-ban], Stephen.
Estela [ays-tay-lah], Stella.
Ester [es-terr'], Esther, Hester.
Eugenio [ay-oo-hay'-ne-o], Eugene.
Eusebio [ay-say'-be-o], Eusebius.
Eustaquio [ay-oos-tah'-ke-o], Eustace.
Eva [ay'-vah], Eve.
Ezequías [ay-thay-kee'-as], Hezekiah.
Ezaquiel [ay-thay-ke-el'], Ezekiel.

Federico [fay-day-ree'-co], Frederic; *coll.* Fred.
Felipa [fay-lee'-pah], Philippa.
Felipe, Filipo [fay-lee'-pay, fe-lee'-po], Philip; *coll.* Phil.
Felisa, Felicia [fey-lee'-se-ah, fay-lee'-the-ah], Felicia.
Fernando [fer-nahn'-do], Ferdinand.
Filemón [fee-lay-mone'], Philemon.
Florancia, Florencio [flo-ren'-the-ah, flo-ren'-the-o], Florence.
Francisca [fran-thees'-cah], Frances; *coll.* Fan, Fanny.
Francisco [fran-thees'-co], Francis.

Gaspar [gas-par'], Jasper.
Gerardo [hay-rar'-do], Gerard.
Gertrudis [herr-troo'-dees], Gertrude.
Gil [heel], Giles.
Gilberto [heel-berr'-to], Gilbert.
Godofredo [go-do-fray'-do], Godfrey.
Gregorio [gray-go'-re-o], Gregory.
Guillermo [gheel-lyerr'-mo], William.
Gustavo [goos-tah'-vo], Gustavus.

Herbarto, Heriberto [er-ber'-to, ay-ree-ber'-to], Herbert.
Herón [ay-rone'], Hiero or Hieron.
Hilario [e-lah'-re-o], Hilary.
Horacio [o-rah'-the-o], Horace, Horatio.
Hugo [oo'-go], Hugh.
Humberto [oom-berr'-to], Humbert.

Ignacio [ig-nah'-the-o], Ignatius.
Ildefonso [il-day-fon'-so], Alphonsus.
Inés [ee-nes'], Agnes, Inez.
Isabel [e-sah-bel], Elizabeth; *coll.* Bess, Bet, Betsy, Betty.
Isidoro, Isidro [e-se-do'-ro, e-see'-dro], Isidor.

Jacobo, Jaime [hah-co'-bo, hah'-e-may], James; *coll.* Jim or Jimmy.
Javier [ha-vee-er'], Xavier.
Jeremías [hay-ray-mee'-as], Jeremy.
Jerónimo [hay-ro'-ne-mo], Jerome; *coll.* Jerry.
Jesucristo [hay-soo-crees'-to], Jesus Christ.
Jesús [hay-soos'], Jesus.
Joaquín [ho-ah-keen'], Joachim.
Jonás [ho-nahs'], Jonah.
Jorge [hor'-hay], George.
José [ho-say'], Joseph.
Josefa [ho-say'-fah], Josephine.
Josué [ho-soo-ay'], Joshua.
Juan [hoo-ahn], John; *coll.* Jack or Johnny.
Juana [hoo-ah'-nah], Jane, Jennie; Joan, Joanna, *coll.* Jinny.
Judit [hoo-deet'], Judith.
Julio [hoo'-le-o], Julius.

Ladislao [lah-dees-lah'-o], Ladislas.
Lamberto [lam-berr'-to], Lambert.
Lázaro [lah'-thah-ro], Lazarus.
Leandro [lay-ahn'-dro], Leander.
León [lay-on'], Leo, Leon.
Leonardo [lay-o-nar'-do], Leonard.
Leonor [lay-o-nor'], Eleanor.
Leopoldo [lay-o-pole'-do], Leopold.
Leticia [lay-tee'-the-ah], Laetitia, Lettice.
Lidia [le-de-ah], Lydia.
Lisandro [lee-sahn'-dro], Lysander.
Livio [lee'-ve-o], Livy.
Lorenzo [lo-renn'-tho], Lawrence.
Lucas [loo'-cas], Luke.
Lucía [loo-thee'-ah], Lucy.
Lucio [loo'-the-o], Lucius.
Lucrecia [loo-cray' the ah], Lucretia.
Luis [loo-ees'], Lewis, Louis.
Luisa [loo-ee'-sah], Louisa.
Lutero [loo-tay'-ro], Luther.

Magdalena [mag-dah-lay'-nah], Magdalen.
Mahoma [mah-o'-mah], Mahomet or Mohammed.
Malaquías [mah-lah-kee'-as], Malachy.
Manuel [mah-noo-el'], Emanuel.
Manuela [mah-noo-ay'-lah], Emma.
Marcelo [mar-thay'-lo], Marcel.
Marcos [mar'-cos], Mark.
Margarita [mar-gah-ree'-tah], Margaret, Margery; *coll.* Madge, Meg.
María [mah-ree'-ah], Mary, Maria; *coll.* Mol. Molly.
Mariana [mah-re-ah'-nah], Marian.
Marta [mar'-tah], Martha.
Mateo [mah-tay'-o], Matthew; *coll.* Mat.
Matías [mah-tee'-as], Mattias.
Matilde [mah-teel'-day], Matilda.
Mauricio [mah-oo-ree'-the-o], Maurice, Morice.
Maximiliano [mak-se-me-le-ah'-no], Maximilian.
Miguel [mee-ghel'], Michael; *coll.* Mike.
Moisés [moi-says'], Moses.

Natalia [nah-tah-le-ah], Natalie.
Nerón [nay-rone'], Nero.
Néstor [ness'-tore], Nestorius.
Nicolás [ne-co-lahs'], Nicholas; *coll.* Nick.
Noé [no-ay'], Noah.

Octavio [oc-tah'-ve-o], Octavius.
Oliverio [o-le-vay'-reo], Oliver; *coll.* Noll.

Pablo [pah'-blo], Paul.

Patricio [pah-tree'-the-o], Patrick.
Pedro [pay'-dro], Peter.
Pelayo [pay-lah' yo], Pelajo.
Pío [pee'-o], Pius.
Platón [plah-tone'], Plato.
Pompeyo [pom-pay'-yo], Pompey.
Prudencia [proo-den'-the-ah], Prudence.

Quintín [keen-teen'], Quentin.

Rafael [rah-fah-el'], Raphael.
Raimundo, Ramón [rah-e-moon'-do rah-mone'], Raymond.
Raquel [rah-kel'], Rachel.
Rebeca [ray-bay'-cah], Rebecca.
Renato [ray-nah'-to], Rene.
Ricardo [re-car'-do], Richard; *coll.* Dick, Dicky.
Roberto [ro-berr'-to], Robert; *coll.* Bob, Rob.
Rodolfo [ro-dole'-fo], Rodolphus, Ralph, Rolph.
Rodrigo [ro-dree'-go], Roderic.
Roger, Rogerio [ro-herr', ro-hay'-re-o], Roger.
Rómulo [ro'-moo-lo], Romulus.
Ronaldo [ro-nahl-do], Ronald.
Rosa [ro'-sah], Rose.
Rosalia [ro-sah-le-ah], Rosalie.
Rosario [ro-sah'-ree-o], Rosary.
Rubén [roo-bayn'], Reuben.
Ruperto [roo-perr'-to], Rupert.
Rut [root], Ruth.

Salomón [sah-lo-mon'], Solomon.
Salustio [sah-loos'-tee-o], Sallust.
Samuel [sah-moo-el'], Samuel; *coll.* Sam.
Sansón [sahn-son'], Samson.
Santiago [sahn-te-ah'-go], *V.* JACOBO.
Sara [sah'-rah], Sarah; *coll.* Sal, Sally.
Severo [say-vay'-ro], Severus.
Sigismundo [se-his-moon'-do], Sigismund.
Silvano [sil-vah'-no], Silvan.
Silvestre [sil-ves'-tray], Silvester.
Silvia [sil-ve-ah], Sylvia.
Sofía [so-fee'-ah], Sophia.
Susana [soo-sah'-nah], Susan, Susanna.

Teodora, Teodoro [tay-o-do'-rah, do'-ro], Thodora, Theodore.
Teodorico [tay-o-do-ree'-co], Theodorick, Dorick.
Teófilo [tay-o'-fe-lo], Theophilus.
Teresa [tay-ray'-sah], Theresa; *coll.* Tracy.
Timoteo [te-mo-tay'-o], Timothy.
Tito [tee'-to], Titus.
Tobías [to-bee'-as], Toby.
Tomás [to-mahs'], Thomas.

Urbano [oor-bah'-no], Urban.

Valentín [vah-len-teen'], Valentine.
Valeria [vah-lay-re-ah], Valerie.
Ventura [ven-too'-rah], Bonaventure.
Vicente [ve-then'-tay], Vincent.

Zacarías [thah-cah-ree'-as], Zachary.

An Alphabetical List of the Abbreviations

MOST COMMONLY USED IN SPANISH.

á. área
(a) alias.
A. Alteza; aprobado (en examen); amperio.
ACTH. Hormona adrenocorticotropa.
a. de J. C. antes de Jesucristo.
admón. administración.
admor. administrador.
adv. adverbio.
afmo. afectísimo.
agr. agriculture.
a la v/. a la vista (bank draft).
alg. álgebra.
alt. altitud.
a.m. antemeridiano.
amb. ambiguo.
anat. anatomía.
ant. antiguo, anticuado.
arit. aritmética.
arq. arquitecto, arquitectura.
art. artículo.
arz. or **arzbpo.** arzobispo.
astr. astronomía.
atto. atento.

B. Beato; Bueno (en examen).
BCG Bacilo Calmette-Guérin, vacuna antituberculosa.
bot. botánica.
bto. bulto; bruto.
Br. or **br.** bachiller.

C. centígrado.
c. or **cap.** capítulo.
C. A. corriente alterna (elec.).
C/a. cuenta abierta.
Cap. capitán.
C. C. corriente continua (elec.).
C. D. corriente directa (elec.).
cénts. céntimos or centavos.
CEPAL Comisión Económica para América Latina (Naciones Unidas).
C. F. caballos de fuerza.
cg. centigramo, centigramos.
Cía. compañía.
cir. cirugía.
cl. centilitro, centilitros.
cm. centímetro, centímetros.
Cnel. coronel.
col. columna.
Com. comercio.
Const. Constitución.
C. P. T. Contador Público Titulado.
cs. centavos or céntimos.
cta. cuenta.

c/u. cada uno.

D. Don.
D. D. T. dicloro-difenil-tricloro-metil-metano.
der. derecha o derecho.
des. desusado.
dg. decigramo.
dic. diciembre.
dim. diminutivo.
div división.
dl. decalitro.
Dls. or **$** dólares.
dm. decímetro.
D. M. Dios mediante.
dom. domingo.
d/p. días plazo.
Dr. doctor.
Dres. doctores.

E. este, oriente.
econ. economía.
elac. or **elect.** electricidad.
E. M. Edad Media.
ENE. estenordeste.
F. P. D. En paz descanse.
esc. escudo; escultura, escultor.
ESE estesudeste.
etc. or **&** etcétera.
etim. etimología.
E.U.A. Estados Unidos de América.

f. femenino, femenina.
F. Fahrenheit.
FAB. franco a bordo.
fam. familia; familiar.
FAO. Organización de las Naciones Unidas para la Agricultura y la Alimentación.
farm. farmacia.
f, c, or **F. C.** ferrocarril.
Fco. Francisco.
feb. febrero.
fig. figurado.
fil. filosofía.
fis. física.
For. forense.
fotog fotografía.
fr. fences.
fut. futuro.
g. or **gm.** or **gr.** gramo.
gal. galicismo; galón.
geog. geografía.
geom. geometría.
ger. gerundio.

gob. gobernador, gobierno.
Gral. general.

h. hijo.
hect. or **ha.** hectárea.
Hg. or **hg.** hectogramo, hectogramos.
Hl. or **hl.** hectolitro, hectolitros.
Hm. or **hm.** hectómetro, hectómetros.
hna., hno. hermana, hermano.
hol. holandés.
hosp. hospital.

ib. *ibidem.*
Ilmo., Ilma. Ilustrísimo, Ilustrísima.
Impr. imprenta.
Ing. ingeniero, ingeniería.
ingl. inglés.
izq. izquierda.

J. C. Jesucristo.
jue. jueves.

kg. kilogramo.
kgm. kilográmetro.
Kl. kilolitro.
Km. kilómetro.
km². kilómetro cuadrado.
Kms./h. kilómetros por hora.
kv. kilovatio.

l. litro litros.
LAB. libre a bordo.
lb., lbs. libra, libras.
Lic. Licenciado, abogado.
lín. línea.
lit. literatura.
lits./seg. litros por segundo.
lun. lunes.

m. metro; masculino; murió;
meridiano; mediodía; minuto.
m3/seg. metros cúbicos por segundo.
mar. martes.
mat. matemáticas.
mec. mecánica.
med. medicina.
meng. menguante.
m/f. mi favor.
mg. miligramo, miligramos.
mierc. miércoles.
Min. minería.
mit. mitología.
m/L. mi letra (bank draft).
MM. miriámetro, miriámetros.
mm. milímetro, milímetros.
Mons. Monseñor.
m.p.h. millas por hora.
m.s.n.m. metros sobre el nivel del mar.
mús. música.

n. noche.
n/. nuestro.
N. Norte.
nac. nacional.
N. B. *Nota Bene.*
NE. nordeste.
neol. neologismo.
NNE. nornordeste.
NO. Noroeste.
No. or **núm.** número. (1°., primero; 2°., segundo; 3°., tercero,
etc.).
nov. noviembre.

N.U. Naciones Unidas.
núm., núms. número, números.
N. S. Nuestro Señor.
N. S. J. C. Nuestro Señor Jesucristo.

O. Oeste.
OACI. Organización de Aviación Civil International (N.U.).
ob. obpo. obispo.
Oct. octubre.
OIT. Organización Internacional del Trabajo (N.U.).
OMS. Organización Mundial de la Salud (N.U.).
ONO. oestenoroeste.
onz. onza.
OSO. oestesuroeste.
OTAN or **OTAS.** Organización del Atlántico del Norte o Septentrional (NATO).

P. Papa.
p. participio.
p. a. participio activo.
p. A. Por ausencia.
PBAI. Proyectil balístico da alcance intermedio.
PBI. Proyectil balístico intercontinental.
pá., págs. página, páginas.
P. D. or **P. S.** Posdata.
p. ej. por ejemplo.
p. esp. peso específico.
pl. plural.
p. m. pasado meridiano.
P. O. Por orden.
P. P. or **p. p.** porte pagado; por poder.
p. pdo. or **ppdo,** próximo pasado.
P. R. Puerto Rico.
prep. preposición; preparatorio.
pres. presente; presidente.
pret. pretérito.
prof. profesor; profeta.
pron. pronombre.
prov. provincia.
P. S. *post scriptum,* posdata.
ps. or **$** pesos.
S. San or Santo; sur.
S. A. sociedad anónima; Sud América.
sáb. sábado.
S. A. de C. V. sociedad anónima de capital variable.
S. A. R. Su Alteza Real.
s/c. su cuenta.
S. C. or **s. c.** su casa.
S. C. de R. L. sociedad cooperativa de responsabilidad limitada.
s/cta. su cuenta.
S. en C. sociedad en comandita.
SE. sudeste, sureste.
sept. septentrional; septiembre.
s. e. u. o. salvo error u omisión.
s/f. su favor; sin fecha.
sing. singular.
S. M. Su Majestad.
SO. sudoeste, surosate.
spre. siempre.
Sr. señor.
Sra., Sras. señora, señoras.
Sres. señores.
Sria. secretaria.
Sría. secretaría.
ptas. pesetas.
pza. pieza.

q. que, quintal.
Q. B. S. M. or **q. b. s. m.** quebesa su mano.
Q. D. G. que Dios guarde.
q. e g. e. que en gloria esté.

q. e. p. d. que en paz descanse.
qm. quintal métrico.
qq. quintales.
quím. química.

Rep. República.
ret. retórica.
R. P. Reverendo Padre.

r. p. m. revoluciones por minuto.
rs. reales (moneda).
Srio. secretario.
Srta. señorita.
S. S. Su Santidad; seguro servidor.
s. s. or **ss.** seguro servidor.
SSE. sudsudeste, sursureste.
SSO. sudsudoeste, sursuroeste.
S. S. S. Su seguro servidor.
Sta. Santa
Sto. Santo.
subj. subjuntivo.

t. tonelada.
TNT. trinitrotolueno.
Tte. teniente.

Tte. Cnel. teniente coronel.

U. or **Ud.** usted.
UIT. Unión Internacional de Telecomunicaciones (N.U.).
UNESCO. Organización de las Naciones Unidas para la Educación, la Ciencia y la Cultura.
UNICEF. Fondo de las Naciones Unidas para la Infancia.
UPU. Unión Postal Universal.
U. R. S. S. Unión de Repúblicas Socialistas Soviéticas.

V. usted; venerable; véase.
v. verbo.
va. verbo activo.
Vd., Vds. Usted, Ustedes.
V. E. Vuestra Excelencia.
vg. or **v. gr.** verbigracia.
vier. viernes.
V. M. Vuestra Majestad.
vn. verbo neutro.
Vo. Bo. visto bueno.
vol. volumen; voluntad.
vulg. vulgarismo.
VV. Ustedes.

zool. zoología.

Weights and Measures

(Pesas y Medidas)

LINEAR
(Lineales)

Metric Measures (Medidas métricas)		**U. S. Measures** (Medidas de E.U.A.)	
Kilómetro	0.62137 millas.	Milla	1.6093 kms.
Metro	39.37 pulgadas.	Milla marina	1.853 "
Decímetro	3.937 "	Yarda	0.9144 ms.
Centímetro	0.3937 "	Pie	0.3048 ms.
Milímetro	0.03937 "	Pulgada	2.54 cms.

SURFACE
(Superficie)

Kilómetro cuadrado	247.104 acres.	Acre	0.4453 hectáreas.
Hectárea	2.471 acres.	Milla cuadrada	259 "
Metro cuadrado	1550 pulg^2.	Yarda cuadrada	0.8361 m^2.
Decímetro cuadrado	15.50 "	Pie cuadrado	929.03 cms^2.
Centímetro	0.155 "	Pulgada cuadrada	6.4516 "

CUBIC
(Volumen)

Metro cúbico	1.308 yardas^3.	Pulgada cúbica	16.387 cm^3.
Decímetro cúbico	61.023 pulgadas^3.	Pie cúbico	0.0283 m^3.
Centímetro cúbico	0.0610	Yarda cúbica	0.7646 m^3.

CAPACITY
(Capacidad)

Hectolitro	2.838 bushels ó 26.418 galones.	Cuarto de gal. (líq.)	0.9463 litros.
		Cuarto de gal. (áridos)	1.101 "
Litro	0.9081 cuarto de galón (áridos) ó 1.0567 cuarto de galón (liq.).	Galón	3.785 "
		Bushel	35.24 "

WEIGHTS
(Pesas)

Tonelada	2204.6 lb.	Onza (avoirdupois)	28.35 gms.
Kilogramo	2.2046 lb.	Libra "	0.4536 kgs.
Gramo	15.432 granos.	Tonelada larga	1.0161 ton. met.
Centigramo	0.1548 "	Tonelada corta	0.9072 " "
		Grano	0.0648 gms.

Monetary Units

of America and the Iberian peninsula

(Monedas de América y de la Península Ibérica)

Country	Monetary Unit
Argentina	Peso
Bolivia	Boliviano
Brasil	Real
Canada	Dólar canadiense
Chile	Peso
Colombia	Peso
Costa Rica	Colón
Cuba	Peso
Ecuador	Dólar USA
El Salvador	Colón
España	Euro
Estados Unidos de América	Dólar
Guatemala	Quetzal
Haití	Gourde
Honduras	Lempira
México	Peso
Nicaragua	Córdoba
Panamá	Balboa
Paraguay	Guaraní
Perú	Nuevo Sol
Portugal	Euro
Republic Dominicana	Peso
Uruguay	Peso
Venezuela	Bolívar